THE CAMBRIDGE

BIOGRAPHICAL ENCYCLOPEDIA

THE CAMBRIDGE

BIOGRAPHICAL ENCYCLOPEDIA

SECOND EDITION

Edited by
DAVID CRYSTAL

CAMBRIDGE
UNIVERSITY PRESS

PUBLISHED BY THE PRESS SYNDICATE OF THE UNIVERSITY OF CAMBRIDGE
The Pitt Building, Trumpington Street, Cambridge, United Kingdom

CAMBRIDGE UNIVERSITY PRESS
The Edinburgh Building, Cambridge CB2 2RU, UK
40 West 20th Street, New York, NY 10011–4211, USA
10 Stamford Road, Oakleigh, VIC 3166, Australia
Ruiz de Alarcón 13, 28014 Madrid, Spain
Dock House, The Waterfront, Cape Town 8001, South Africa

http://www.cambridge.org

First published 1994
Second Edition 1998

Typeset by Cambridge University Press

Printed in the United Kingdom at the University Press, Cambridge

A catalogue record for this book is available from the British Library

Library of Congress Cataloging in Publication Data
The Cambridge biographical encyclopedia / edited by David Crystal. – 2nd ed.
p.   cm.
Includes bibliographical references and index.
ISBN 0-521-63099-1 (hb)
1. Biography–Encyclopedias.   I. Crystal, David, 1941–
CT103.C26   1998
920′ .003–dc21
[B]
97-34577
CIP

ISBN 0 521 63099 1 hardback

Contents

Editor
David Crystal

Editorial Assistant
Hilary Crystal

Database Compilation
Tony McNicholl
Esther Pritchard
Ann Rowlands
Jan Thomas

Design of Ready Reference
Sally Jeffery

Compilation of Ready Reference
Sukie Hunter
Antony James
Esther Pritchard

Consultants
Sidney Landau (USA)
Ken Greenhall (USA)
Phillipa McGuinness (Australia)
Hugh Laracy (New Zealand)
Benjamin Pogrund (South Africa)
Colin Bundy (South Africa)

Preface to the Second Edition

The genre of the biographical dictionary is now well established. Its wide range includes national reference works of the who's-who type, concise treatments of specific subjects, such as literature and science, and major historical or international compilations, such as dictionaries of national biography. The genre has two chief features, which are also its strengths: entries are listed in alphabetical order, guaranteeing readers ease of access, and the summaries of achievement are self-contained, allowing readers to focus clearly on individuals.

The Cambridge Biographical Encyclopedia, as its name suggests, has been designed to add a more truly encyclopedic dimension to an alphabetic work. It retains the strengths of the traditional approach, presenting an A–Z section of around 16 000 entries, but it adds other kinds of information which will help readers escape from the limited confines of many individual entries.

• The **Ready Reference** section is a 150-page presentation of over 10 000 people in tabular form, enabling the 'families' and sequences of relationships in such domains as history, politics, sport, and the arts to be better appreciated. The emphasis here has been on comprehensiveness of treatment, for example providing *all* Nobel prizewinners or *all* a country's rulers, instead of the selection which space constraints impose in a general encyclopedia.

• A tightly disciplined cross-referencing system is an indispensable part of any encyclopedic enterprise. In the present book, over 22 000 cross-references are given at the ends of A–Z entries, where relevant (preceded by >>), linking individual entries within the A–Z text. A further 1500 refer to parts of the Ready Reference section.

Coverage and treatment

The entries in *The Cambridge Biographical Encyclopedia* derive from a specially compiled database which is used to inform all works in the family of Cambridge encyclopedias. This database was originally the result of a collaboration between the firm of W & R Chambers and Cambridge University Press; for example, the American edition of *Chambers Biographical Dictionary* was until 1993 published in the USA by Cambridge University Press under the title of the *Cambridge Biographical Dictionary*. For the present work, the material in the original database has been thoroughly revised, expanded, and updated, and additional features have been added to the A–Z section, so that *The Cambridge Biographical Encyclopedia* now stands out clearly from the traditional genre. The main distinguishing features of the book are described below.

• In common with other encyclopedias in the Cambridge 'family', a particular effort has been made to ensure internationalism of coverage, especially in relation to the leading English-speaking countries, by using contributors in the USA, Canada, Australia, New Zealand, and South Africa. Several hundred additional entries relate to particular subjects from other parts of the world.

• Compared with other works within the genre, *The Cambridge Biographical Encyclopedia* pays proportionately more attention in its A–Z section to 20th-c personalities. The compact nature of the Ready Reference section has enabled us to deal very briefly with a large number of minor historical and political figures, and this has provided space to devote to contemporary figures in subject areas which biographical dictionaries often neglect, such as television, the cinema, sport, science and popular music.

• An important aim was to make progress in resolving other traditional imbalances in the genre. We have been particularly concerned about the generally poor coverage given by biographical dictionaries to women, African-Americans, Aborigines, Maori, and other minority groups, and have paid special attention to the coverage of leading personalities under such headings.

• Most entries in *The Cambridge Biographical Encyclopedia* are relatively short and succinct: the average length is 70 words. In some 40 cases we have introduced whole-page or longer panels. We have tried not to be judgmental about the information the entries contain, preferring to restrict the accounts to core facts about a person's life.

• A small but essential feature of a biographical work is the provision of a pronunciation guide. This is used in all cases where it is not obvious to a native speaker of English how a name should be pronounced. There are a surprisingly large number of names which fall into this category, and as a consequence over 6000 transcriptions will be found in the A–Z section. This feature is of especial importance for users of this book for whom English is not a native language.

Updating for the Second Edition has been rigorous to the beginning of October 1997, with later events being added to the typeset pages, where space permitted, to give some coverage into 1998. We have added some 500 people whose standing has especially grown since the First Edition was published in 1994. They include recent Nobel prizewinners, senior politicians in a number of countries who came to power in elections between 1995 and 1997, many stars from film and television, and a wide range of sporting and media personalities.

No list could be representative, but the following selection of 50 of these new entries will perhaps convey a little of the character of the middle years of the decade which the Second Edition has tried to capture: Madeleine Albright, Clive Anderson, Kofi Annan, Martin Bell, David Blunkett,

Helena Bonham-Carter, Billy Connolly, Roddy Doyle, David Duchovny, Kaffe Fassett, Colin Firth, Dawn French, Jean-Paul Gaultier, Henryk Gorecki, Kelsey Grammer, Ruud Gullit, William Hague, David Helfgott, Tim Henman, Damien Hirst, Juninho, Larry King, David Koresh, Lisa Kudrow, Alexander Lebed, Joshua Lomu, Shannon Lucid, Mary McAleese, Timothy McVeigh, James Mirrlees, Timothy Mo, Benjamin Netanyahu, Michael Nyman, Oasis, Kenzaburo Oe, Terry Pratchett, Roseanne, David Schwimmer, Nigel Short, the Spice Girls, Howard Stern, Patrick Stewart, Quentin Tarentino, Terry Venables, Jacques Villeneuve, Andrew Wiles, Bruce Willis, Oprah Winfrey, Tiger Woods, Gianfranco Zola.

All first efforts to develop a genre in a particular direction for a particular product suffer from the omnipresent constraints of time and space, and this may have led us to fall short of the standards we have set ourselves. As with other books in the Cambridge family, therefore, I very much welcome feedback from readers which will enable the editorial team to improve its coverage or treatment, and I thank the many readers who have taken the trouble to write in with comments about the entries in the First Edition.

David Crystal
Holyhead, September 1997

How to use The Cambridge Biographical Encyclopedia

Headwords

• The order of entries follows the English alphabet, ignoring capital letters, accents, diacritics, or apostrophes.

• The ordering is letter by letter, ignoring all spaces between the words of compound names, eg **Lebrun, Albert** precedes **Le Brun, Charles**, which precedes **Le Carré, John**, which precedes **Lecky, William**.

• We list rulers chronologically, ordering them by country if their titles are the same, eg **William I** (of England) precedes **William I** (of Germany). Names of non-British rulers, saints, etc are Anglicized, with a cross-reference used in cases where a foreign name is widely known, eg **Wilhelm I >> William I** (of Germany).

• When many people have the same name (eg **John**), we list them in the order rulers, saints, popes, others. Rulers with an identifying country or byname (eg **John of Austria**, **John the Baptist**) appear after single-element names, following the letter-by-letter order of the constituent words (eg **John of Trevisa** precedes **John the Baptist**). People with compound names (eg **John Paul I**) follow all instances of single-element names. The aim of this system is to ensure that all Johns, for example, are grouped together, which means that there are occasional exceptions to the letter-by-letter convention (eg **John the Baptist** precedes **Johnson**).

• Parts of a person's name that are not generally used are enclosed in parentheses, eg **Disney, Walt(er Elias)**, **Wells, H(erbert) G(eorge)** Parenthesized elements are ignored in deciding alphabetical sequence, eg **Smith, (Robert) Harvey** precedes **Smith, Henry**.

Spelling Conventions

• All surnames beginning with **St** are located under the spelling **Saint**.

• All surnames beginning with **Mac, Mc**, or **M'** are listed in order of the next letter, eg **McBey, James** precedes **MacBride, Maud**, which precedes **McBride, Willie John**, which precedes **MacBryde, Robert**.

• We transliterate names in non-Roman alphabets, and add a cross-reference in cases where confusion could arise because more than one transliteration system exists. Letter symbols from other languages which do not appear in the English alphabet (such as Polish ł) are given their nearest English equivalents. Chinese names are given in pin-yin. In the case of Arabic, we have not transliterated the alif and ain symbols. No accent is shown on French capital letters.

Entry conventions

• Birth places are usually cited with reference to the location of the present-day town and country, eg towns formerly in Prussia are now identified in Germany. Exceptions include those locations where there is no clear modern equivalent, such as towns in ancient Greece which no longer exist. In some cases, to avoid ambiguity, both former and present-day locations are given.

• If a birthplace is a capital city, the name of the country is not given (this includes the chief cities of the divisions of the UK: London, Cardiff, Edinburgh, and Belfast). If the birthplace is in the USA, it is followed simply by the name of the state, except in the case of New York City, using the abbreviations listed later. In all other cases, the name of a country always follows the name of a town.

• Bold-face type is used within an entry to identify a spouse, child, or other important relative, or to identify someone of special professional significance, such as a partner or collaborator.

Cross-references

• Cross-references are always to headwords in the encyclopedia, with a distinguishing parenthesis if required, eg **Charles I** (of England). We do not include personal titles (eg Baron) in the cross-reference, and we give a distinguishing first name or initial if there are several entries with the same surname, eg **>> Johnson, Lyndon B**. These cross-references selected are those which provide the most relevant further perspective to an entry. Other people mentioned in the text may also have entries in the encyclopedia.

• All cross-references are preceded by the symbol >>, and listed in alphabetical order. Where cross-references share a common element, they are conflated, being separated by /, eg **Catherine de'/ Cosimo de' / Lorenzo de' Medici.**

• If an entry relates to part of the Ready Reference section, this is shown giving the page number introduced by the abbreviation RR (eg RR1122).

Pronunciation Guide

• We give a pronunciation whenever it is unpredictable from the spelling, or where there is a possibility that a reader might choose the wrong form. In foreign names, we give the foreign pronunciation, unless there is a well-known English version. In a few cases, where both forms are current, we give both. The respelling system we use does not permit a level of fine phonetic accuracy, but is sufficient to guarantee a pronunciation which will allow the name to be recognized.

• Bold type is used to show stressed or strongly accented syllables, eg **Xerxes** [**zerk**seez]. We do not usually show the stress in languages (such as French, Chinese, Japanese) which have a very different rhythmical system to English, and where it would be misleading to identify one of the syllables as most prominent. We make an exception in cases where there is a widely used or predictable English pronunciation, as in French names beginning with **la**, eg [la**toor**].

• No distinctive symbol is given to show an unstressed English vowel, as in the first and last [a] vowels of **Balenciaga** [balenthi**ah**ga].

• The symbol [(r)] is used to mark cases where an *r* in the spelling may or may not be pronounced, depending on the accent, eg **Barbarossa** [bah(r)ba**ro**sa]. Speakers who do not pronounce [r] in these places (such as those using Received Pronunciation in Britain) should ignore this symbol; those who do pronounce [r] (such as most Americans) should pay attention to it. This symbol is not used when the transcription of a sound already contains an [r] symbol, in such cases as [er], [eer], and [air].

SYMBOL	SOUND	SYMBOL	SOUND
a	h**a**t	ng	si**ng**
ah	f**a**ther	o	h**o**t
air	h**air**	oh	s**o**ul
aw	s**aw**	oo	s**oo**n
ay	s**ay**	ow	c**ow**
b	**b**ig	oy	b**oy**
ch	**ch**ip	p	**p**in
d	**d**ig	r	**r**ed
e	s**e**t	s	**s**et
ee	s**ee**	sh	**sh**ip
er	b**ir**d	t	**t**in
f	**f**ish	th	**th**in
g	**g**o	th	**th**is
h	**h**at	u	p**u**t
i	s**i**t	uh	c**u**p
iy	l**ie**	v	**v**an
j	**j**et	w	**w**ill
k	**k**it	y	**y**es
l	**l**ip	z	**z**oo
m	**m**an		
n	**n**ip		

Non-English sounds

ã	French n**an**tes
hl	Welsh **ll**an
ĩ	French S**ain**t
õ	French b**on**
kh	Scots lo**ch**, German i**ch**
oe	French s**oeu**r, German m**ö**glich
ü	French t**u**, German m**ü**de

Abbreviations

This listing contains all the abbreviations used in this book where the meaning is not explained within an individual entry. When a date appears in parentheses, the month is abbreviated to the first three letters, eg (3 Jan 1888).

AAF	Army Air Force	Ger	German
ABC	American Broadcasting Companies	GPO	General Post Office
ABC	Australian Broadcasting Corporation	h	hour
AD	Anno Domini	ha	hectare
AFL	American Federation of Labor	Heb	Hebrew
ATV	Associated Television	HMS	Her/His Majesty's Service/Ship
BAFTA	British Academy of Film and Television Arts	hp	horsepower
		HQ	headquarters
BBC	British Broadcasting Corporation	I	Island
BC	Before Christ	IBM	International Business Machines
c.	circa (used with dates)	ICI	Imperial Chemical Industries
-c	century	IRA	Irish Republican Army
C	central	Is	Islands
C	connections	Ital	Italian
CBS	Columbia Broadcasting System	ITN	Independent Television News
CERN	*Conseil Européen pour la Recherche Nucleaire* (European Council for Nuclear Research)	Jr	Junior
		KC	King's Counsel
		KGB	*Komitet Gossudarstvennoi Bezopasnosti* (Committee of State Security)
Chin	Chinese		
CIA	Central Intelligence Agency	km	kilometre(s)
CIO	Congress of Industrial Organizations	L	Lake
Co	Company	Lat	Latin
Co	County	lb	pound(s)
d.	died	LP	long-playing (record)
Dan	Danish	Ltd	Limited
DNA	deoxyribonucleic acid	m	metre(s)
DOS	Disk Operating System	MCC	Marylebone Cricket Club
DSO	Distinguished Service Order	MD	Doctor of Medicine
E	east(ern)	MEP	Member of the European Parliament
EC	European Community	MGM	Metro-Goldwyn-Mayer
edn	edition	mi	mile(s)
EEC	European Economic Community	MI	Military Intelligence
eg	*exempli gratia* (for example)	min	minute(s)
EMI	Electrical and Musical Industries	MIT	Massachusetts Institute of Technology
ENIAC	Electronic Numerical Integrator and Calculator	Mme	Madame
		MP	Member of Parliament
ENSA	Entertainments National Service Association	MRC	Medical Research Council
		MS	Master of Science
EOKA	National Organization of Cypriot Fighters (translation)	MSS	manuscripts
		Mt	Mount
FA	Football Association	Mts	Mountains
FBI	Federal Bureau of Investigation	N	north(ern)
fl.	flourished	na	not available
Fr	French	NASA	National Aeronautics and Space Administration
FRS	Fellow of the Royal Society		
ft	foot/feet	NATO	North Atlantic Treaty Organization
GEC	General Electric Company	NBA	National Basketball Association

NBC	National Broadcasting Company	States of the USA
NE	northeast(ern)	
No	number	AK Alaska
NSW	New South Wales	AL Alabama
p	page	AR Arkansas
PGA	Professional Golfers Association	AZ Arizona
PhD	Doctor of Philosophy	CA California
PLO	Palestine Liberation Organization	CO Colorado
QC	Queen's Counsel	CT Connecticut
R	River	DC District of Columbia
RADA	Royal Academy of Dramatic Art	DE Delaware
RAF	Royal Air Force	FL Florida
RC	Roman Catholic	GA Georgia
Rev	Reverend	HI Hawaii
RKO	Radio-Keith-Orpheum	IA Iowa
RNA	ribonucleic acid	ID Idaho
RR	Ready Reference	IL Illinois
RSC	Royal Shakespeare Company	IN Indiana
S	south(ern)	KS Kansas
SAS	Special Air Service	KY Kentucky
SE	southeast(ern)	LA Louisiana
SFSR	Soviet Federal Socialist Republic	MA Massachusetts
SI	*Système Internationale* (International	MD Maryland
	System)	ME Maine
Snr	Senior	MI Michigan
SS	(i) Saints, (ii) steamship,	MN Minnesota
	(iii) *Schutzstaffel* (Nazi elite guard)	MO Missouri
St(s)	Saint(s)	MS Mississippi
SW	southwest(ern)	MT Montana
trans	translated/translation	NC North Carolina
TUC	Trades Union Congress	ND North Dakota
TV	television	NE Nebraska
UK	United Kingdom	NH New Hampshire
UN	United Nations	NJ New Jersey
UNESCO	United Nations Educational, Scientific	NM New Mexico
	and Cultural Organization	NV Nevada
UNICEF	United Nations Children's Fund	NY New York
	(formerly, United Nations Inter-	OH Ohio
	national Children's Emergency Fund)	OK Oklahoma
UNIVAC	Universal Automatic Computer	OR Oregon
UNO	United Nations Organization	PA Pennsylvania
US(A)	United States (of America)	RI Rhode Island
USS	United States Ship	SC South Carolina
USSR	Union of Soviet Socialist Republics	SD South Dakota
v.	versus	TN Tennessee
VC	Victoria Cross	TX Texas
vol(s)	volume(s)	UT Utah
W	west(ern)	VA Virginia
WBA	World Boxing Association	VT Vermont
WBC	World Boxing Council	WA Washington
WRAC	Women's Royal Air Corps	WI Wisconsin
YMCA	Young Men's Christian Association	WV West Virginia
ZEEP	Zero Energy Experimental Pile	WY Wyoming

Aakjaer, Jeppe [awkyayr] (1866–1930) Novelist and poet, born in Aakjaer, Denmark. A leader of the 'Jutland movement' in Danish literature, his works include the novel *Vredens Bør* (1904, Children of Wrath) and the poems of *Rugens Sange* (1906, Songs of the Rye). He wrote much in the Jutland dialect, into which he translated some of Burns's poems. >> Burns, Robert

Aalto, (Hugo Henrik) Alvar [awltoh] (1898–1976) Architect and designer, the father of Modernism in Scandinavia, born in Kuortane, Finland. He studied at Helsinki Polytechnic, and evolved a unique architectural style based on irregular and asymmetric forms and the imaginative use of natural materials. He designed numerous public and industrial buildings in Finland, including the Finlandia concert hall in Helsinki. In the 1930s he pioneered the use of factory-made laminated birchwood for a distinctive style of Finnish furniture.

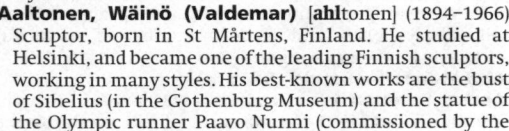

Aaltonen, Wäinö (Valdemar) [ahltonen] (1894–1966) Sculptor, born in St Mårtens, Finland. He studied at Helsinki, and became one of the leading Finnish sculptors, working in many styles. His best-known works are the bust of Sibelius (in the Gothenburg Museum) and the statue of the Olympic runner Paavo Nurmi (commissioned by the Finnish government in 1924).

Aaron [airon] (15th–13th-c BC) Biblical patriarch, the first high priest of the Israelites, and said to be the founder of the priesthood; the elder brother of Moses. He was spokesman for Moses to the Egyptian pharoah in his attempts to lead their people out of Egypt. He later joined rebellious Israelites in making a golden calf for idolatrous worship. He and his sons were ordained as priests after the construction of the Ark of the Covenant and the Tabernacle, and he was confirmed as hereditary high priest by the miracle of his rod blossoming into an almond tree (hence various plants nicknamed 'Aaron's Rod'). >> Moses

Aaron, Hank [airon], popular name of **Henry Lewis Aaron**, nickname **Hammerin' Hank** (1934–) Baseball player, born in Mobile, AL. A right-handed batting outfielder, he set almost every batting record in his 23-season career with Milwaukee Braves, Atlanta Braves, and Milwaukee Brewers: 2297 runs batted in, 1477 extra-base hits, and 755 home runs, still a major league record. >> RR1144

Aasen, Ivar (Andreas) [awsen] (1813–96) Philologist, lexicographer, and writer, born in Sunmøre, Norway. A fervent nationalist, he was the creator of the 'national language' called *Landsmål* (later known as *Nynorsk*, 'New Norwegian'), based on W Norwegian dialects. It eventually achieved recognition alongside the official Dano-Norwegian *Riksmål* ('language of the realm') in 1885.

Abailard >> **Abelard**

Abakanowicz, Magdalena [abakanovich] (1930–) Artist, born in Falenty, near Warsaw. She studied at the Warsaw Academy of Fine Arts (1950–5), and sought to escape from conventional art forms through weaving. In the 1960s she achieved international recognition with her monumental abstract woven fibre installations called 'Abakans'. After 1965 she taught at the State College of Arts, Poznan, becoming professor in 1979.

Abalkin, Leonid Ivanovitch [abalkin] (1930–) Russian economist. He was director of the Institute of Economics of the Academy of Sciences and member of the former Supreme Soviet with special responsibility for economic

affairs. His published works centre on the theoretical problems of political economy under Socialism.

Abarbanel, Isaac ben Jehudah [abah(r)banel] (1437–1508) Jewish writer and philosopher, born in Lisbon. His works comprise commentaries on the Bible and philosophical treatises. His eldest son, **Juda Leon** (known as **Leo Hebraeus** in Latin) (c.1460–1535), a doctor and philosopher, wrote *Dialoghi di Amore* (1535, trans Philosophy of Love).

Abati, Niccolo dell' >> **Abbate, Niccolo dell'**

Abba [aba] Swedish pop group, formed in 1973, with members **Bjorn Ulvaeus** (1945– , guitar, vocals), married to **Agnetha Faltskog** (1950– , vocals), and **Benny Anderson** (1945– , keyboards, vocals), married to **Anni-Frid** (known as **Frida**) **Lyngstad** (1945– , vocals). The group's name is an acronym of their first names. They were especially popular in Europe, always singing in English, with 18 consecutive single releases achieving a place in the top 10 UK singles chart, including eight at number 1. 'Waterloo' won the Eurovision Song Contest in 1974. The group broke up at the end of the decade; Bjorn and Agnetha divorced in 1979, and Benny and Frida in 1981.

Abbado, Claudio [abahdoh] (1933–) Musical conductor, born in Milan, Italy. From a distinguished musical family, he began training in piano, composition, and conducting. He made his British debut in Manchester (1965), was conductor and director at La Scala, Milan (1968–86), and principal conductor of the London Symphony Orchestra (1979–87). Other posts include principal conductor of the Vienna Philharmonic Orchestra (1971), musical director of the Vienna State Opera (1986–91), and principal conductor of the Berlin Philharmonic Orchestra (1989). In 1994 he was artistic director of the Salzburg Easter Festival and triumphed with a spectacular postmodern production of Mussorgsky's *Boris Godunov*.

Abbas I [abas], known as **Abbas the Great** (1571–1629) The fifth Safavid shah of Persia. After his accession (1588), he set about establishing a counterweight to the Turkmen tribal chiefs who had constituted the principal political and military powers in the state. From 1598 he was able to recover Azerbaijan and parts of Armenia from the Ottomans, and Khurasan from the Uzbeks. He transferred his capital from Qazvin to Isfahan, and established diplomatic and economic relations with W Europe.

Abbas (c. 566–c. 652) Ancestor of the Abbasid dynasty of the Islamic empire who ruled as caliphs of Baghdad (750–1258). He was the maternal uncle of the prophet Mohammed. A rich merchant of Mecca, he was at first hostile to his nephew, but ultimately became one of the chief apostles of Islam. >> Mohammed

Abbas, Ferhat [abas] (1899–1985) Algerian nationalist leader, born in Taher, Algeria. He founded a Muslim Students' Association in 1924, then became a chemist. In 1955 he joined the Front de Libération Nationale (FLN), the main Algerian resistance organization, founding in 1958 the 'Provisional Government of the Algerian Republic' in Tunis. After independence in 1962, he was appointed President of the National Constituent Assembly, but fell out of favour and was exiled. He was rehabilitated shortly before his death.

Abbas Hilmi Pasha [abas hilmee] (1874–1943) The last khedive of Egypt (1892–1914). He succeeded his father, Tewfik Pasha, and attempted to rule independently of British influence. At the outbreak of war in 1914 he sided with Turkey, and was deposed when the British made Egypt a protectorate. >> Tewfik Pasha; RR1047

Abbas Pasha [abas **pa**sha] (1813–54) Khedive of Egypt from 1848. A grandson of Mehemet Ali, he took an active part in his grandfather's Syrian war, but later did much to undo the progress made under him, notably by blocking the construction of the Suez Canal. >> Mehemet Ali; RR1047

Abbate, Niccolo dell' [abahtay], also spelled **Abati** (c. 1512–71) Fresco painter, born in Modena, Italy. He died in Paris, having executed frescoes for the palace of Fontainebleau. Few of his frescoes are extant, but the Louvre has a collection of his drawings.

Abbe, Cleveland [ahbuh] (1838–1916) Meteorologist, born in New York City. He wrote on the atmosphere and on climate, and was responsible for the introduction of the US system of Standard Time.

Abbe, Ernst [ahbuh] (1840–1905) Professor of optics, born in Eisenach, Germany. He became professor at the University of Jena in 1870, and in 1878 director of the astronomical and meteorological observatories. He was a partner in the optical works of Carl Zeiss on whose death he became owner in 1888. >> Zeiss

Abbey, Edwin Austin (1852–1911) Painter and illustrator, born in Philadelphia, PA. He settled in England in 1878. He is known for his illustrations of the works of Shakespeare and Robert Herrick, for his panels of *The Quest of the Holy Grail* in Boston Public Library, and for his picture of Edward VII's coronation.

Abbot, C(harles) G(reely) (1872–1973) Astrophysicist, born in Wilton, NH. As director of the Astrophysical Observatory at the Smithsonian Institution (1907–44), he carried out important research on solar radiation. He became the 'grand old man' of US solar physics, devising an apparatus for converting solar energy to power just before his 100th birthday.

Abbot, George (1562–1633) Protestant clergyman, born in Guildford, Surrey, SE England, UK. He studied at Oxford, and rose to be Master of University College (1597), Dean of Winchester (1600), and three times Vice-Chancellor of Oxford University (1600–5). He owed his promotion to the sees of Lichfield (1609), London (1610), and Canterbury (1611) to the Earl of Dunbar. A sincere but narrow-minded Calvinist, he was equally opposed to Catholics and to heretics.

Abbott, Diane (Julie) (1953–) British politician, born in London, England, UK. She studied at Cambridge, and was an administration trainee in the civil service before working for the National Council for Civil Liberties, the Greater London Council, and Lambeth Borough Council. She joined the Labour Party in 1981, and served on the Westminster City Council 1982–6. Elected to parliament as MP for Hackney North and Stoke Newington in 1987, she became the first black woman member of the House of Commons.

Abbott, George (1887–1995) Director, producer, and playwright, born in Forestville, NY. He began his career in 1913 as an actor, but made his name as a writer and Broadway director and producer, establishing himself with *The Fall Guy* (co-written with James Gleason) in 1925. He wrote or co-wrote almost 50 plays and musicals, among them *The Pajama Game* (with Richard Bissell, 1954) and *Damn Yankees* (1955). In addition to an illustrious career as a producer, he directed over 100 theatrical pieces, winning six Tony awards for his work, and was still writing on his 100th birthday.

Abbott, Jacob (1803–79) Clergyman, born in Hallowell, ME, the father of Lyman Abbott. He founded Mount Vernon School for Girls in Boston (1829) and was the author of *The Young Christian* (1832) and many other works. >> Abbott, Lyman

Abbott, Lyman (1835–1922) Congregational clergyman and editor, born in Roxbury, MA. He studied at New York University and joined a law firm before turning to the ministry, becoming ordained in 1860. At the end of the Civil War, he went to New York City where, in addition to a parish, he worked with the American Union Commission for more sympathetic reconstruction policies in the South. He became editor of a new periodical, *The Illustrated Christian Weekly* (1870–6), then joined Henry Ward Beecher at the *Christian Union*, replacing him as editor in 1881. He retired in 1899 to devote his final years to editing, writing, and guest preaching and speaking. He was noted for the intelligence, balance, and tolerance that he combined with traditional Christian teachings. >> Beecher, Henry Ward

Abbott and Costello Comedy film partners: **Bud Abbott**, originally **William A Abbott** (1896–1974), born in Asbury Park, NJ, and **Lou Costello**, originally **Louis Francis Cristillo** (1908–59), born in Paterson, NJ. Both men had theatrical experience before teaming up as a comedy double act, Costello playing the clown and Abbott his straight man. They began performing on radio (1938), appeared on Broadway (1939), and made a number of successful comedy films, beginning with *Buck Privates* (1941).

Abd al-Aziz ibn Saud >> **Saud, al-**

Abd-ar-Rahman I [abderrahman] (731–88) An Umayyad emir who survived the massacre of his family by the Abbasids in 750, and conquered most of Muslim Spain. He founded the emirate of al-Andalus (756), with its capital at Córdoba.

Abd-ar-Rahman III [abderrahman] (891–961) Emir of Córdoba, who ruled from 912 and proclaimed himself caliph in 929. Under him the Umayyad emirate reached the peak of its power, extending its boundaries in successful campaigns against the Fatimids and the kings of Leon and Navarre.

Abd-el-Kader [abdulkader] (1807–83) Algerian nationalist hero, born in Mascara, Algiers. After the French conquest of Algiers, the Arab tribes of Oran elected him as their emir, and with great perseverance he waged a long struggle with the French (1832–47). Eventually crushed by overpowering force, he took refuge in Morocco, and began a crusade against the enemies of Islam, but was defeated at Isly in 1844.

Abd-el-Krim [abdulkrim], nickname **the Wolf of the Rif Mountains** (1882–1963) Berber chief, born in Ajdir, Morocco. He led unsuccessful revolts against Spain and France (1921, 1924–5), formed the Republic of the Rif and served as its president (1921–6), but was brought to surrender by a large Franco-Spanish army under Marshal Pétain. He was exiled to the island of Réunion. Granted amnesty in 1947, he went to Egypt, where he formed the North African Liberation Committee. >> Pétain

Abdias >> **Obadiah**

Abd-ul-Hamid II [abdulhamid], nickname **The Great Assassin** (1842–1918) The last sultan of Turkey (1876–1909). He promulgated the first Ottoman constitution in 1876, but his reign was notable for his cruel suppression of revolts in the Balkans, which led to wars with Russia (1877–8), and especially for the Armenian massacres of 1894–6. A reform movement by the revolutionary Young Turks forced him to summon a parliament in 1908, but he was deposed and exiled in 1909.

Abdul-Jabbar, Kareem [abdul jaber], originally **Lewis Ferdinand Alcindor**, known as **Lew Alcindor** (1947–) Basketball player, born in New York City. A talented player from youth, his exceptional height (7 ft 2 in/2 m 5 cm)

made him a formidable opponent. He studied at the University of California (1965), then joined the National Basketball Association (NBA) Milwaukee Bucks (1969), leading them to victory in the NBA championships (1971). Already converted to Islam, he took an Arabic name (1971). He moved to the L A Lakers in 1984, and went on to establish an individual points record of 38 387. He retired in 1989. >> RR1146

Abdullah (ibn Hussein) [abdula ibn husayn] (1882–1951) First king of Jordan (1946–51), the second son of Hussein ibn Ali and grandfather of King Hussein. Emir of the British mandated territory of Transjordan in 1921, he became king when the mandate ended in 1946, but was assassinated. >> Hussein

Abdullah, Sheikh Mohammed [abdula], nickname **The Lion of Kashmir** (1905–82) Kashmiri statesman, born in Soura, near Srinagar, Kashmir, India. A Muslim, he spearheaded the struggle for constitutional government against the (Hindu) Maharajah of Kashmir during the years between the two World Wars. He was imprisoned in 1931, and on his release formed the All Jammu and Kashmir Moslem Conference (renamed the National Conference in 1938). He agreed to the accession of the state to India, but was imprisoned (1953–68) when he reaffirmed the right of the people of Kashmir 'to decide the future of the State'. He was chief minister from 1975 until his death.

Abd-ul-Medjid [abdulmejid] (1823–61) Sultan of Turkey from 1839. He continued the Westernizing reforms of the previous reign of Mahmut II (1785–1839), reorganizing the court system and education, and granting various rights to citizens, including Christians. In 1854 he secured an alliance with Britain and France to resist Russian demands, thus precipitating the Crimean War (1854–6).

Abdul Rahman (Putra Alhaj), Tunku [abdul rahman] (1903–90) The first prime minister of Malaya (1957–63) and Malaysia (1963–70), born in Alor Star, Kedah, Malaya. The son of the Sultan of Kedah, he trained as a lawyer at Cambridge and joined the civil service in Kedah in 1931. In 1945 he founded the United Malays' National Organization (UMNO), and in 1952 entered Malayan politics, becoming chief minister (1955) and then prime minister. He negotiated the formation of the Federation of Malaysia, remaining as prime minister. He left active politics in 1970, then became the first secretary-general of the Organization of the Islamic Conference. >> RR1073

Abe, Kobo [ahbay] (1924–93) Novelist and playwright, born in Tokyo. He trained as a doctor, but turned to literature after graduating. Recognition in Japan came with the award of the Akutagawa Prize for *The Wall* in 1951. His predominant theme of alienation was explored in a series of works, his novels including *Inter Ice Age Four* (1971), *The Woman in the Dunes* (1965), and *Secret Rendezvous* (1980).

Abegg, Richard [abeg] (1869–1910) Chemist, born in Gdańsk, Poland (formerly Danzig, Germany). At Wrocław (formerly Breslau, Germany), he was one of the first chemists to perceive the chemical significance of the newly-discovered (1897) electron, and his 'rule of eight' (1904) concerning the electric basis of linkages between atoms was an important stage in the development of modern valency theory.

Abel [aybel] Biblical character, the second son of Adam and Eve. He is described as a shepherd, whose offering God accepts; but he was then murdered by his brother, Cain. >> Adam and Eve; Cain

Abel, Sir Frederick (Augustus) [aybel] (1827–1902) Scientist, born in London, England, UK. As chemist to the war department and ordnance committees (1854–88), he applied himself to the science of explosives. He was the inventor (with Sir James Dewar) of cordite, introduced a new method of making gun-cotton, and invented the *Abel tester* for determining the flash-point of petroleum. >> Dewar

Abel, John Jacob [aybel] (1857–1938) Biochemist, born in Cleveland, OH. He studied at Johns Hopkins University, where he became its first professor of pharmacology (1893–1932). In 1914 he showed, by dialysis through cellophane, that blood contains amino acids – a finding which led the way towards dialysis in the treatment of kidney disease. In 1926 he first crystallized insulin and showed it to be a protein.

Abel, Karl Friedrich [ahbel] (1725–87) Musician, born in Köthen, Germany. He was a noted composer of symphonies, and a virtuoso on the viola da gamba. In 1758 he went to England, where he was appointed chamber musician to Queen Charlotte. With Johann Christian Bach he promoted a celebrated series of concerts in London. >> Bach, J C

Abel, Niels Henrik [ahbel] (1802–29) Mathematician, born in Finnøy, Norway. He showed mathematical genius by the age of 15, and in 1823 proved that there was no algebraic formula for the solution of a general polynomial equation of the fifth degree. He developed the concept of elliptic functions independently of Carl Gustav Jacobi, and the theory of Abelian integrals and functions became a central theme of later 19th-c analysis. >> Jacobi; Weierstrass

Abelard, Peter [abelah(r)d] (1079–1142) Theologian, born near Nantes, France. He studied under Roscellinus and Guillaume de Champeaux (c.1070–1171). As lecturer in the cathedral school of Notre Dame in Paris, he became tutor to Héloïse, the 17-year-old niece of the canon Fulbert. They fell passionately in love, but when their affair was discovered, they fled to Brittany, where Héloïse gave birth to a son. After returning to Paris, they were secretly married. Héloïse's relatives took their revenge on Abelard by castrating him. He fled in shame to the abbey of St Denis to become a monk, and Héloïse took the veil at Argenteuil as a nun. In 1121, a synod at Soissons condemned his Nominalistic doctrines on the Trinity as heretical, and Abelard took to a hermit's hut at Nogent-sur-Seine, where his pupils helped him build a monastic school he named the Paraclete. In 1125 he was elected abbot of St Gildas-de-Rhuys in Britanny, and the Paraclete was given to Héloïse and a sisterhood. In his final years he was again accused of numerous heresies and he retired to the monastery of Cluny. After his death, he was buried in the Paraclete at Héloïse's request, and when she died in 1164 she was laid in the same tomb. In 1817 they were buried in one sepulchre at Père Lachaise. >> Roscellinus

Abeles, Sir (Emil Herbert) Peter [ayblz] (1924–) Industrialist, born in Budapest. He studied in Budapest, then went to Sydney in 1949. The following year he founded Alltrans, which in 1967 merged with Thomas Nationwide Transport (TNT). Under his leadership TNT expanded into all forms of road transport, air courier services, and containerized and bulk shipping. In 1979 TNT and Rupert Murdoch's News Limited gained control of Ansett Airlines, and Abeles became joint managing director of the new company, resigning in 1992. Knighted in 1972, he is known for his friendships with prominent politicians, particularly Bob Hawke. >> Hawke, Bob; Murdoch, Rupert

Abell, Kjeld [ahbel] (1901–61) Radical playwright, born in Denmark. He was known for his innovative stage designs and effects. His plays include *Melodien der Blev Vaek* (1935, The Melody That Got Lost), *Anna Sophie Hedvig* (1939), and *Silkeborg* (1946).

3

Abelson, Phillip H(auge) [ayblson] (1913–) Physical chemist, born in Tacoma, WA. He studied at Washington State College and the University of California at Berkeley, and was appointed director of the geophysics laboratory of the Carnegie Institution, WA, in 1953 (president 1971). In 1940 he assisted Edwin Mattison McMillan to bombard uranium with neutrons, which led to the discovery of a new element, neptunium. From 1941 he worked on the Manhattan atomic bomb project, developing diffusion methods for obtaining enriched uranium-235; this was the fuel for the first A-bomb. >> McMillan, Edwin

Abercrombie, Lascelles [aberkrombee] (1881–1938) Poet and critic, born in Ashton-upon-Mersey, Greater Manchester, NW England, UK. He studied at Malvern College and Victoria University, Manchester, became professor of English at Leeds (1922) and London (1929), and reader at Oxford (1935). His works include *The Idea of Great Poetry* (1925) and *Principles of Literary Criticism* (1932).

Abercrombie, Sir (Leslie) Patrick [aberkrombee] (1879–1957) British architect and pioneer of town planning in Britain, the brother of Lascelles Abercrombie. He was professor of town planning at Liverpool (1915–35) and University College, London (1935–46). His major work was the replanning of London, as seen in the *County of London Plan* (1943) and the *Greater London Plan* (1944). >> Abercrombie, Lascelles

Abercromby, Sir Ralph [aberkrombee] (1734–1801) Soldier and hero of the Napoleonic Wars, born in Menstrie, Clackmannanshire, C Scotland, UK. He went to Rugby School, studied law at Edinburgh and Leipzig, served in Europe in the Seven Years' War (1756–63), and was MP for Clackmannanshire (1774–80). He led successful operations against the French in St Lucia and Trinidad (1795–6), and also led the successful amphibious operation of the Anglo-Turkish forces against the French at Aboukir Bay in 1801, but was mortally wounded in the action.

Aberdare, Henry Austin Bruce, Baron [aberdair] (1815–95) British statesman, born in Duffryn, Aberdare, S Wales, UK. He was called to the bar in 1837, and was elected Liberal MP for Merthyr Tydfil (1852–73). Home secretary under Gladstone (1868–73), he then became Lord President of the Council (1873–4). Influential in the movement for the establishment of the University of Wales, he was its first chancellor in 1895. >> Gladstone

Aberdeen, George Hamilton Gordon, 4th Earl of (1784–1860) British statesman and prime minister (1852–5), born in Edinburgh, EC Scotland, UK. He studied at Cambridge, succeeding his grandfather as earl in 1801. He was foreign secretary twice, under the Duke of Wellington (1828–30) and then Sir Robert Peel (1841–6). A confirmed free-trader, he resigned with Peel over the repeal of the corn-laws in 1846. In 1852 he was made prime minister of a coalition government that was immensely popular at first, until he reluctantly committed Britain to an alliance with France and Turkey in the Crimean War in 1854. The gross mismanagement of the war aroused popular discontent, and he was forced to resign. >> Peel, Robert; Wellington; RR1095

Aberhart, William [aberhah(r)t], nickname **Bible Bill** (1878–1943) Canadian politician, born in Huron Co, Ontario, Canada. He studied at Queen's University, Kingston, and in 1915 became principal of Crescent Heights School, Calgary, where he remained until 1935. He then became a member of the Alberta legislature, formed his own Social Credit Party, and became provincial premier (1935–43). He had founded the Calgary Prophetic Bible Institute in 1918, and his evangelical style of public-speaking gave him his byname.

Abernathy, Ralph D(avid) [abernathee] (1926–90) Baptist clergyman and civil rights activist, born in Linden, AL. An early Civil Rights organizer and leading confidante of Martin Luther King, Jr, he was pastor of the West Hunter Street Baptist Church in Atlanta, GA, throughout his civil rights career (1961–90), and became King's chosen successor as head of the Southern Christian Leadership Conference (1968–77). He resigned the leadership to run unsuccessfully for Andrew Young's congressional seat in 1977. Turning away from the Civil Rights movement, he then devoted his attention to the West Hunter Street Baptist Church and the issues of worldwide peace. >> King, Martin Luther; Young, Andrew

Abernethy, John [abernethee] (1764–1831) Surgeon, celebrated for his eccentric lectures and manners, born in London, England, UK. In 1813 he was appointed surgeon to Christ's Hospital, London, in 1814 professor of anatomy and surgery to the College of Surgeons, and in 1815 full surgeon to St Bartholomew's Hospital, a post which he resigned in 1829. His practice increased with his celebrity, which the eccentricity and rudeness of his manners helped to heighten.

Abington, Fanny, *née* **Frances Barton** (1737–1815) Actress, born in London, England, UK. She was flower girl, street singer, milliner, and kitchen-maid before making her first appearance on the stage at the Haymarket in 1755. Extremely versatile, she excelled not only in the parts of Shakespeare's heroines but also in a great variety of comedy roles.

Abney, Sir William (de Wiveleslie) [abnee] (1844–1920) Chemist and educationist, born in Derby, Derbyshire, C England, UK. Assistant secretary (1899) and adviser (1903) to the Board of Education, he was known for his research in photographic chemistry and colour photography, and did important pioneer work in photographing the solar spectrum.

Abrabanel >> **Abarbanel**

Abraham, Abram, or **Ibrahiz** (after 2000 BC–) Revered in the Hebrew Bible as the father of the Hebrew people and of several other nations. According to *Genesis* he came from the Sumerian town of Ur ('Ur of the Chaldees') in modern Iraq, and migrated with his family and flocks to the 'Promised Land' of Canaan, where he settled at Shechem (modern Nablus). He lived to be 175 years old, and was buried with his first wife Sarah in Hebron. By Sarah he was the father of Isaac (whom he was prepared to sacrifice at Moriah at the command of the Lord, as a test of his faith); by Sarah's Egyptian maid, Hagar, he was the father of Ishmael, the ancestor of twelve clans; by his third wife Keturah he had six sons who became the ancestors of the Arab tribes. He is traditionally regarded as the father of Judaism, Christianity, and Islam. (*Gen* 22). >> Hagar; Ishmael

Abraham, Sir Edward (Penley) (1913–) Biochemist, born in Southampton, Hampshire, S England, UK. He studied at Oxford, where he became professor of chemical pathology (1964–80). He had a major role in early studies of the penicillins, and especially of the cephalosporin antibiotics.

Abraham, William, nickname **Mabon** (1842–1922) Trade unionist and politician, born in Cwmavon, Gwent. A leading figure in the miners' union in South Wales, he was a strong advocate of sliding-scale agreements whereby wages were regulated by the selling price of coal, and also a believer in compromise with the coal owners. He was elected MP for the Rhondda (1885–1918) and for the West Rhondda division (1918–20), and devoted himself to mining legislation.

Abrahams, Peter (1919–) Novelist, born in Vrededorp, South Africa. Most of his work was produced in exile. The impoverished township where he was born is vividly recreated in a memoir, *Tell Freedom* (1954). His third novel, *Mine Boy* (1946), won critical notice. His mature work produced novels which dealt mainly with the political struggles of black people, such as *A Wreath for Udomo* (1956), *A Night of their Own* (1965), *This Island Now* (1966), and *The View from Coyaba* (1985).

Abram >> **Abraham**

Abrams, Creighton Williams [aybramz] (1914–74) US army general, born in Springfield, MA. He trained at West Point, commanded a tank battalion in World War 2, and served in the Korean War (1950–3). He commanded US forces in Vietnam (1968–72), and supervised the gradual withdrawal of US troops.

Abravanel >> **Abarbanel**

Absalom [absalom] (11th-c BC) Third and favourite son of King David of Israel in the Old Testament. A handsome, vain young man, he rebelled against his father and drove him from Jerusalem, but in an ensuing battle he was killed by Joab. >> **David**

Absalon or **Axel** [absalon] (1128–1201) Danish clergyman and statesman, the founder of the city of Copenhagen. The foster-brother of **Valdemar I** (1131–82), he was appointed Bishop of Roskilde (1158), and elected Archbishop of Lund (1177). As chief minister to Valdemar he led an army against the Wends in 1169, and extended Danish territories in the Baltic. In 1169 he built a fortress at Havn which became the nucleus of Copenhagen. >> **Saxo Grammaticus**

Abse, Dannie [absee] (1923–) Writer and physician, born in Cardiff, S Wales, UK. He studied at the Welsh National School of Medicine, King's College London, and Westminster Hospital, becoming senior specialist in the chest clinic at the Central Medical Establishment, London, in 1954. His literary output includes several volumes of poetry, two novels, and a number of plays. His autobiographical volumes are *A Poet in the Family* (1974), *A Strong Dose of Myself* (1983), *There was a Young Man from Cardiff* (1991), and the novel *Ash on a Young Man's Sleeve* (1954).

Abu al-Faraj [aboo alfaraj], also known as **Bar-Hebraeus** (1226–86) Syrian historian, born in Armenia. A master of Syriac, Arabic, and Greek, he was equally learned in philosophy, theology, and medicine. At the age of 20, he was made a bishop, and as Bishop of Aleppo rose to the second highest dignity among the Eastern Jacobite (Monophysite) Christians.

Abu al-Faraj al-Isfahani [aboo alfaraj alisfahahnee] (897–967) Arabic scholar and literary historian, born in Baghdad. His greatest work, *Al-Aghani*, is a treasury of Arabic song and poetry.

Abu al-Hassan ibn al Haytham >> **Alhazen**

Abu-Bakr or **Abu-Bekr** [aboo baker] (c. 573–634) The first Muslim caliph, one of the earliest converts to Islam, born in Mecca. He became chief adviser to Mohammed, who married his daughter Aïshah, and on the death of the prophet was elected leader of the Muslim community (632). In his short reign he put down a religious and political revolt, and set in motion the great wave of Arab conquests over Persia, Iraq, and the Middle East. >> **Aïshah; Mohammed**

Abu-Bekr >> **Abu-Bakr**

Abu Mashar >> **Albumazar**

Abu Nasr al-Farabi >> **al-Farabi, Mohammed**

Abu Nuwas [aboo noowas] (c. 760–c. 815) Poet, considered one of the greatest poets of the Abbasid period. He abandoned older, traditional forms for erotic and witty lyrics. He was a favourite at the court in Baghdad, and figures in the *Arabian Nights*. >> **Abbas**

Abu Tammam, Habib ibn Aus [aboo tamam] (807–c. 850) Poet, born near Damascus, Syria. He travelled extensively, and on one of his journeys discovered a private library of desert poetry at Hamadhan. From this he compiled a celebrated anthology of early Arab poetry, the *Hamasu*.

Abzug, Bella [abzug], *née* **Savitzky**, nickname **Battling Bella** (1920–) Feminist, lawyer, and politician, born in New York City. She studied at Hunter College and Columbia University, and practised as a lawyer in New York City. A prominent peace campaigner, she founded Women Strike for Peace (1961) and the National Women's Political Caucus. Winning a seat in Congress (1971), she was a vigorous champion of welfare issues.

Accum, Friedrich [akuhm] (1769–1838) Chemist, born in Buckeburg, Germany. In 1793 he moved to London, where he pioneered the introduction of gas lighting, and did much to arouse public opinion against unclean food and dishonest trading.

Achard, Franz (Karl) [ashah(r)] (1753–1821) Chemist, born in Berlin. He took up Andreas Marggraf's discovery of sugar in beet, and perfected a process for its extraction on a commercial scale, then in 1801 opened the first beet sugar factory, in Silesia. >> **Marggraf**

Achebe, Chinua [achaybay], originally **Albert Chinualumogo** (1930–) Novelist, born in Ogidi, Nigeria. He studied at the University College of Ibadan, and his early career was in broadcasting. He was in Biafran government service during the Nigerian Civil War (1967–70), and then taught at US and Nigerian universities. His first novel, *Things Fall Apart* (1958), presenting an unsentimentalized picture of the Ibo tribe, was heralded as a fresh voice in African literature, and has since been translated into over 40 languages. Writing exclusively in English, his other novels include *Arrow of God* (1964), *Anthills of the Savanna* (1987), which was short-listed for the Booker Prize, and *A Tribute to James Baldwin* (1989). He has also written short stories, poetry, and children's books. His essays include *Beware, Soul Brother* (1971) on his experiences during the War.

Achenbach, Andreas [akhenbakh] (1815–1910) Landscape and marine painter, born in Kassel, Germany. He studied at St Petersburg, then travelled extensively in Holland, Scandinavia, and Italy, where he produced many water-colours. His paintings of the North Sea coasts of Europe had considerable influence in Germany, and he came to be regarded as the father of 19th-c German landscape painting.

Acheson, Dean (Gooderham) [achesn] (1893–1971) US statesman and lawyer, born in Middletown, CT. He studied at Yale and Harvard, and joined the Department of State in 1941, where he was under-secretary (1945–7) and secretary of state in the Truman administration (1949–53). He formulated the Truman Doctrine (1947), helped determine the Marshall Plan (1947), and promoted the formation of NATO (1949). His book *Present at the Creation* (1969) was awarded the Pulitzer Prize. >> **Truman**

Acheson, Edward Goodrich [acheson] (1856–1931) Chemist, born in Washington, PA. In 1891, he developed the manufacture of silicon carbide (carborundum), an extremely useful abrasive, and in 1896 devised a new way of making lubricants based on colloidal graphite.

Acheson, Lila Bell >> **Wallace, DeWitt**

Ackerley, Joseph (Randolf) [akerlee] (1896–1967) Writer, born in Herne Hill, Kent, SE England, UK. In 1956 he published *My Dog Tulip*, and in 1960 his only novel, *We Think the World of You*, in which an Alsatian dog plays a lead role. He was also literary editor of *The Listener* (1935–59).

Ackermann, Rudolph [akerman] (1764–1834) Art publisher, born in Saxony, Germany. In 1795 he opened a print shop in London and published a well-known set of coloured engravings of London. He is said to have introduced lithography as a fine art into England.

Ackroyd, Peter (1949–) Writer, born in London, England, UK. He studied at Cambridge, and spent some time at Yale. He is chiefly known for his biographical studies of Pound, T S Eliot, and Dickens, and also for his fiction, which includes *The Last Days of Oscar Wilde* (1983), *Hawksmoor* (1985, Whitbread), *First Light* (1989), *Dan Leno and the Limehouse Golem* (1994), and *Milton in America* (1996). His other work includes poetry, television criticism, and regular reviews for *The Times* since 1986.

Acland, Sir Richard (Thomas Dyke) [akland] (1906–90) British politician. He studied at Oxford, entered parliament in 1931, but resigned from the Liberals to found, with J B Priestley, the Common Wealth Party (1942). Consistent with its advocacy of public ownership on moral grounds, he gave away his Devon family estate to the National Trust. He became a Labour MP in 1945, but resigned in 1955 in protest against Labour support for Britain's nuclear defence policy. >> Priestley, J B

Acontius, Jacobus >> **Aconzio**

Aconzio, Jacopo [akontsioh], Lat **Jacobus Acontius** (c. 1500–66) Engineer, courtier, and writer, born in Trent, Italy. He went to Basel in 1557, and in 1559 to England, after repudiating Roman Catholicism. His antidogmatic *Stratagemata Satanae* (1565) offers a very early advocacy of toleration.

Acton (of Aldenham), John Emerich Edward Dalberg Acton, Baron (1834–1902) Historian, born in Naples, Italy, grandson of Sir John Acton. He studied at St Mary's College, Oscott, Ireland, and at Munich University. He sat as a Liberal member of parliament (1859–64), and was created a baron in 1869. As a leader of the Liberal Roman Catholics in England, he opposed the doctrine of papal infallibility. In 1895 he was appointed professor of modern history at Cambridge, and was founder editor of the *Cambridge Modern History*. >> Acton, Sir John

Acton, Sir John (Francis Edward) (1736–1811) British naval officer in the service of Tuscany and Naples, and prime minister of Naples under Ferdinand IV (reigned 1759–1806), born in Besançon, France. He became successively admiral and generalissimo of the Neapolitan forces, and then prime minister. He fell from power on the entry of the French into Naples in 1806 and fled to Palermo in Sicily.

Adair, John [adair] (c. 1655–?1722) Scottish surveyor and cartographer, who did notable work in mapping Scotland and its coast and islands. He prepared maps of counties in the central belt of Scotland (1680–6), and in 1703 published *Description of the Sea-Coast and Islands of Scotland* (Part 1).

Adair, John (Eric) [adair] (1934–) British leadership-development consultant and writer. He studied at Cambridge, London, and Oxford universities, and developed his Action-Centred Leadership model while involved with leadership training at Sandhurst (1963–9) and as an associate director of the Industrial Society (1969–73). The model states that a leader has to ensure that needs are met in three related areas – getting the task done, maintaining the team, and establishing the personal requirements of individual members.

Adair, Red [adair], popular name of **Paul Adair** (1915–) Fire-fighting specialist, born in Houston, TX. He is regularly called in as a troubleshooter to deal with major oil fires. In 1984 he and his team put out a major fire on an offshore rig near Rio de Janeiro, and in 1988 they were the first men to board the Piper Alpha oil rig in the North Sea after it was destroyed by an explosion. He was also one of the first called to extinguish the oil fires started in Kuwait

by Saddam Hussein at the end of the Gulf conflict (Operation Desert Storm, 1991). He is the subject of a film, *Hellfighters* (1968), starring John Wayne. >> Hussein, Saddam

Adalbert, St [adalbert] (?–981) Benedictine missionary. In 961 he was sent by Emperor Otto I at the request of St Olga, Princess of Kiev, to convert the Russians. He became the first Bishop of Magdeburg in 968. Feast day 20 June. >> Olga; Otto I

Adalbert, St [adalbert], known as **the Apostle of the Prussians** (956–97) Missionary priest, born in Bohemia. In 982 he was appointed the first native Bishop of Prague, but the hostility of the corrupt clergy obliged him to withdraw to Rome in 990. He then took the Gospel to the Hungarians, the Poles, and finally the Prussians, who murdered him. He was canonized in 999; feast day 23 April.

Adalbert [adalbert] (c. 1000–72) German archbishop, born of a noble Saxon family. In 1043 he was appointed Archbishop of Bremen and Hamburg. As papal legate to the North (1053), he extended his spiritual sway over Scandinavia, and carried Christianity to the Wends.

Adam, Adolphe (Charles) [adã] (1803–56) Composer, born in Paris. The son of the pianist **Louis Adam** (1758–1848), he wrote some successful operas, such as *Le Postillon de Longjumeau* (1835), but is chiefly remembered for the ballet *Giselle* (1841).

Adam, Auguste Villiers de L'Isle >> **Villiers de L'Isle Adam, (Philippe) Auguste**

Adam, James >> **Adam, Robert**

Adam, Juliette [adã], *née* **Lamber** (1836–1936) Writer, born in Verberie, France. During the period of the French empire her salon became renowned for her gatherings of wits, artists, and politicians. She produced stories and books on social and political questions, and in 1879 founded the *Nouvelle Revue*. She later published her *Mémoires* (1895–1905).

Adam, Louis >> **Adam, Adolphe-Charles**

Adam, Paul (Auguste Marie) [adã] (1862–1920) Novelist and essayist, born in Paris. Among his numerous novels are *Chair Molle* (1885) and *La Force* (1899). He was co-founder of *Symboliste* and other French literary periodicals.

Adam, Robert (1728–92) Architect, born in Kirkcaldy, Fife, E Scotland, UK. He studied at Edinburgh and in Italy (1754–8), and became architect of the king's works (1761–9), jointly with Sir William Chambers. He established a practice in London in 1758, and during the next 40 years he and his brother **James Adam** (1730–94), succeeded in transforming the prevailing Palladian fashion in architecture by a series of romantically elegant variations on diverse classical originals. One of their greatest projects was the Adelphi (demolished 1936), off the Strand, London. Good surviving examples of their work are Home House in London's Portland Square, and Register House in Edinburgh. >> Chambers, William; Kauffmann

Adam and Eve Biblical characters described in the Book of Genesis as the first man and woman created by God. Adam was formed from the dust of the ground and God's breath or spirit; Eve was made from Adam's rib. Biblical traditions describe their life in the garden of Eden, their disobedience and banishment, and the birth of their sons Cain, Abel, and Seth. Their fall into sin is portrayed as a temptation by the serpent (the Devil) to disobey God's command not to eat the fruit of the tree of the knowledge of good and evil. Many further traditions emerged in later Jewish and Christian writings. >> Abel; Cain

Adam de la Halle >> **Halle, Adam de la**

Adam of Bremen (?–c. 1085) Ecclesiastical historian. As a canon at Bremen Cathedral from c.1066, he compiled a monumental *Gesta Hammaburgensis ecclesiae pontificum*

(History of the Archbishopric of Hamburg, completed c.1075), the most important source for the history, geography, and politics of N Europe for the 8–11th-c.

Adamic, Louis [adamich] (1899–1951) Writer, born in Blato, Croatia. He emigrated to the USA in 1913, and became a US citizen in 1918. He began writing short stories in the early 1920s, using his personal experiences in his books – for example, as an immigrant in *Laughing in the Jungle* (1932). Other works include *Dinner at the White House* (1946) and *The Eagle and the Root* (1950).

Adamnan, St [adamnan] (c. 625–704) Monk, born in Co Donegal, N Ireland. At 28 he joined the Columbian brotherhood of Iona, and was chosen abbot in 679. He came to support the Roman views on the dating of Easter and the shape of tonsure. His works include the *Vita Sancti Columbae* (Life of St Columba), which reveals much about the Iona community. Feast day 23 September.

Adamov, Arthur [adahmof] (1908–70) Playwright, born in Kislovodsk, Russia. His family lost their fortune in 1917, and moved to France, where he was educated and met Surrealist artists. His early absurdist plays *L'Invasion* (1950, The Invasion) and *Le Professeur Taranne* (1953) present the dislocations and cruelties of a meaningless world. *Ping-Pong* (1955) sees humanity reduced to mechanism. Later plays, such as *Paolo Paoli* (1957) and *La Politique des restes* (1967, trans The Politics of Waste), show a transition to commitment.

Adams, Abigail, *née* **Smith** (1744–1818) Letter writer, born in Weymouth, MA. In 1764 she married John Adams, who worked away from home, which prompted her to become a prolific letter writer. Her correspondence became highly valued as a contemporary source of social history and comment during the early days of the republic. Her husband became second president of the USA (1797–1801), and she was the first lady of the newly built White House. >> Adams, John

Adams, Ansel (Easton) (1902–84) Photographer, born in San Francisco, CA. His work is notable for his broad landscapes of W USA, especially the Yosemite in the 1930s. He was one of the founders with Edward Weston of the f/64 Group (1932), and helped to set up the department of photography at the Museum of Modern Art in New York City (1940). He was a prolific writer and lecturer, always stressing the importance of image quality at every stage of a photographer's work. >> Weston, Edward; White, Minor

Adams, Brooks (1848–1927) Geopolitical historian, born in Quincy, MA, the son of Charles Francis Adams. He studied at Harvard, practised law in Boston, travelled widely, then became a lecturer in Boston University school of law (1904–11). His major work was *The Law of Civilization and Decay* (1896), to which he added a number of other works. He was an impassioned racialist and prophet of American doom, induced by immigrants whom he regarded as nationally corrupting. >> Adams, Charles Francis

Adams, Charles Francis (1807–86) Diplomat and writer, born in Boston, MA, the son of John Quincy Adams. After studying law at Harvard, he was admitted to the bar in 1828. During the Civil War he was minister to Britain (1861–8), and in 1871–2 was one of the US arbitrators on the *Alabama* claims. He published the life and works of his grandfather and father. >> Adams, John; Adams, John Quincy

Adams, Douglas (Noel) (1952–) Writer, born in Cambridge, Cambridgeshire, EC England, UK. He studied at Cambridge, then worked as a writer, producing material for radio and television shows, and also for stage revues. He is known for his humorous science fiction novels, especially *The Hitch Hiker's Guide to the Galaxy* (1979, originally a radio series, 1978, 1980, later televised). Later

works include *The Meaning of Liff* (1984, with John Lloyd), *Mostly Harmless* (1992), and *The Illustrated Hitch Hiker's Guide to the Galaxy* (1994).

Adams, Gerry, popular name of **Gerald Adams** (1948–) Northern Ireland politician, born in Belfast. He joined Sinn Féin, and during the 1970s was interned because of his connections with the IRA. In 1978 he became vice-president of Sinn Féin and later its president. Elected to the Northern Ireland Assembly in 1982, the following year he was also elected to the UK parliament as member for Belfast West, but he declined to take up his seat at Westminster. He achieved national prominence as the chief contact with the IRA during the events relating to the IRA ceasefire (1994–6), and retained his seat in the 1997 general election.

Adams, Harriet S >> **Stratemeyer, Edward L**

Adams, Henry (Brooks) (1838–1918) Historian, born in Boston, MA, the son of Charles Francis Adams. He studied at Harvard, acted as his father's secretary, then worked as a journalist before teaching history at Harvard (1870–7). He wrote several important historical works, including his monumental *History of the United States during the Administrations of Jefferson and Madison* (9 vols, 1870–7), and a classic autobiography, *The Education of Henry Adams* (1907; Pulitzer, 1919). >> Adams, Charles Francis

Adams, Herbert Baxter (1850–1901) Historian and educator, born in Shutesbury, MA. He studied at Amherst College and Heidelberg University, and joined the newly-formed Johns Hopkins University in Baltimore, MD, as professor of history in 1876. His major publication was the *Life and Writings of Jared Sparks* (1893).

Adams, John (1735–1826) US statesman and second president (1797–1801), born in Braintree (now Quincy), MA. The son of a farmer, he distinguished himself at Harvard, and was admitted to the bar in 1758. Of strongly colonial sympathies, he led the protest against the Stamp Act (1765), and in 1774 was sent as a delegate to the first Continental Congress. He proposed the election of Washington as commander-in-chief, and was 'the colossus of the debate' on the Declaration of Independence. He retired from Congress in 1777, only to be sent to France and Holland as commissioner from the new republic, and in 1785–8 was minister to England. In 1789 he became vice-president under Washington. They were re-elected in 1792, and in 1796 Adams was chosen president by the Federalists. Defeated on seeking re-election in 1800, he retired to his home at Quincy. >> Adams, Abigail; Washington, George; RR1097

Adams, John, alias **Alexander Smith** (c. 1760–1829) British seaman, and a ringleader in the mutiny against Captain William Bligh on the *Bounty* in 1789. With other mutineers he founded a colony on Pitcairn I. When the island was visited in 1809 by the US sealer *Topaz*, Adams was the sole European survivor. Revered as the patriarch of the Pitcairn settlement, he received a royal pardon for his part in the mutiny. >> Bligh

Adams, Sir John (1920–84) British nuclear physicist, and founder member of CERN (Centre Européan pour la Recherche Nucléaire) at Geneva. He went from school in London into the Siemens Research Laboratory in Woolwich, then worked on wartime radar development. At Harwell he engineered the world's first major postwar accelerator (the 180 MeV cyclotron) in 1949. At CERN he engineered the 25 GeV proton synchroton (1954), and became director-general there in 1960. In 1961 he established the laboratory at Culham for research on controlled nuclear fusion, and was appointed controller of the new ministry of technology in 1964. He returned to Geneva to mastermind the building of the 450 GeV super-proton-synchroton (1969–76), and was director-general of CERN for a second time (1976–80).

Adams, John Bodkin (1899–1983) British physician. A general practitioner in Eastbourne, SE England, UK, he was tried in March 1957 for the murder of one of his patients, Edith Alice Morrell. Morrell had died in mysterious circumstances, following long courses of heroin and morphine prescribed by Adams, who was a beneficiary of her will. Although found not guilty, he was struck off the Medical Register, but reinstated in 1961. While some believed he had killed patients for personal gain, others have argued that he was practising a form of euthanasia.

Adams, John Couch (1819–92) Astronomer, born in Laneast, Cornwall, SW England, UK. He studied at St John's College, Cambridge, and in 1843 became fellow and mathematical tutor there. In 1845 he deduced mathematically the existence and location of the planet Neptune, his prediction occurring almost simultaneously with that of the French astronomer, Leverrier. Adams was appointed professor of astronomy at Cambridge in 1858, and was director of the Cambridge Observatory from 1861. >> Leverrier

Adams, John Quincy (1767–1848) US statesman and sixth president (1825–9), born in Quincy, MA, the son of John and Abigail Adams. He studied at Harvard, and was admitted to the bar in 1790. Successively minister to The Hague, London, Lisbon, and Berlin, he was elected to the US Senate from Massachusetts (1803–6). In 1809 he became minister to St Petersburg, and from 1815 to 1817 was minister at the court of St James. As secretary of state under President Monroe, he negotiated with Spain the treaty for the acquisition of Florida, and was alleged to be the real author of the Monroe Doctrine. He became president in 1825, but failed to win a second term, and was elected to the House of Representatives, where he became noted as a promoter of anti-slavery views. >> Adams, John; Adams, Louisa; Monroe, James; RR1097

Adams, Louisa (Catherine), *née* **Johnson** (1775–1852) US first lady (1825–9), born in London, England, UK. The daughter of a Maryland merchant and an English mother, she met the young John Quincy Adams in London in 1795 when her father was the first US consul; they were married in 1797. Renowned for her beauty, she stayed by her husband as he pursued his career in Europe and Washington, but often suffered from illness. In 1840 she began a memoir, *The Adventures of a Nobody*, but her many letters provide the most revealing glimpse of her world. >> Adams, John Quincy

Adams, Richard (George) (1920–) Novelist, born in Berkshire, S England, UK. He studied at Oxford, and after wartime service in the army worked as a civil servant in the Department of the Environment (1948–74). He made his name as a writer with the best-selling *Watership Down* (1972), an epic tale of a community of rabbits. Later books include *Shardik* (1974), *The Iron Wolf* (1980), *The Bureaucrats* (1985), *Traveller* (1988), and *Tales from Watership Down* (1996). His autobiography *The Day Gone By* appeared in 1990.

Adams, Roger (1889–1971) Chemist, born in Boston, MA. He studied in Germany, then joined the University of Illinois in 1916. He was influential in changing the emphasis of chemistry education in the USA from pure research towards a meshing of academic and industrial needs, and his university became particularly noted for providing chemists for industry. He is also regarded as one of the founders of the modern field of organic chemistry.

Adams, Samuel (1722–1803) American revolutionary politician, born in Boston, MA, second cousin to President John Adams. He studied at Harvard, became a tax collector, and was elected a member of the Massachusetts legislature (1765–74). He organized opposition to the Stamp Act in 1765, and was the chief agitator at the Boston Tea Party in 1773. A delegate to the first and second Continental Congress (1774–5), he signed the Declaration of Independence in 1776. He was lieutenant-governor of Massachusetts (1789–94), then governor (1794–7). >> Adams, John

Adams, (Llewellyn) Sherman (1899–1986) US politician, born in East Dover, VT. He studied at Dartmouth College, and had a business career before entering New Hampshire politics in 1940. He became a congressman, Governor of New Hampshire, and special assistant to President Eisenhower. He resigned from Eisenhower's service in 1958 following charges of conflict of interest.

Adams, Tony (1966–) Footballer, born in Romford, Essex, SE England, UK. He played for Arsenal's youth team before joining the club as a centre back in 1983, eventually becoming team captain. He was the Professional Footballers' Association Young Player of the Year in 1987. He captained England in 1994, 1995, and during the European Cup in 1996, and by the end of that year had won 46 caps, but he was hampered by injuries in 1997.

Adams, Walter (Sydney) (1876–1956) Astronomer, born in Antioch, Syria, of missionary parents. In 1884 the family returned to the USA, where he studied astronomy at Dartmouth College, NH, and the University of Chicago. He joined the new Mt Wilson Observatory in California when it opened in 1904, and became its director (1923–46). His pioneering work on stellar spectra led to the discovery of a spectroscopic method of measuring the velocities and distances of stars.

Adams, Will(iam) (1564–1620) Navigator, born in Gillingham, Kent, SE England, UK. He took service with the Dutch in 1598, and reached Japan in 1600. The first Englishman to visit Japan, he was cast into prison as a pirate at the instigation of jealous Portuguese traders, but was freed after building two fine ships for Shogun Ieyasu, receiving a pension, the rank of samurai, and 'living like unto a lordship in England' (1600–20). >> Tokugawa

Adams, William (Bridges) (1797–1872) Engineer and inventor, born in Madeley, Staffordshire, C England, UK. He built some of the first steam rail-cars, and in 1847 patented the fish-plate which is universally used for jointing rails.

Adamson, Joy (Friedericke Victoria), *née* **Gessner** (1910–80) Naturalist and writer, born in Austria. Living in Kenya with her third husband, British game warden **George Adamson** (1906–89), she studied and painted wildlife, and made her name with a series of books about the lioness Elsa: *Born Free* (1960), *Elsa* (1961), *Forever Free* (1962), and *Elsa and Her Cubs* (1965). She was murdered in her home by tribesmen.

Adamson, Robert (1821–48) Chemist and pioneer in photography, born in Scotland, UK. In 1843 he helped David Hill apply the calotype process of making photographic prints on silver chloride paper. Working together, they produced some 2500 calotypes, mainly portraits but also landscapes (1843–8). >> Hill, David

Adanson, Michel [adãsõ] (1727–1806) Botanist, born in Aix-en-Provence, France, the first exponent of classification of plants into natural orders, before Linnaeus. His works include *Les Familles naturelles des plantes* (1763, Natural Families of Plants). The baobab genus of African trees, *Adansonia*, is named after him. >> Linnaeus

Adcock, Fleur (1934–) Poet, born in Papakura, New Zealand. She studied at Victoria University, Wellington, taught at the University of Otago, then held various library posts in New Zealand and the UK, where she has lived since 1963. Her poetry is notable for its unsentimental treatment of personal and family relationships, its psychological insights, and its interest in classical themes. She has also edited *The Oxford Book of New Zealand Verse* (1982) and *The Faber Book of Twentieth Century Women's Poetry* (1987), and co-edited *The Oxford Book of Creatures* (1995).

Addams, Charles Samuel (1912–88) Cartoonist, born in Westfield, NJ. He was a regular contributor to *The New Yorker* from 1935 onwards, specializing in macabre humour and a ghoulish group which was immortalized on television in the 1960s as *The Addams Family*.

Addams, Jane (1860–1935) Social reformer and feminist, born in Cedarville, IL. After visiting Toynbee Hall in London she founded in 1899 the social settlement in Hull House, Chicago, which she led for the rest of her life. In 1910 she became the first woman president of the National Conference of Social Work, and in 1911 founded the National Federation of Settlements (president, 1911–35). A committed pacifist and worker for female suffrage, she was president of the Women's International League for Peace and Freedom (1919–35), and shared the Nobel Peace Prize in 1931. >> Kelley, Florence; Lathrop; RR1125

Addams, Vicki >> **Spice Girls, The**

Adderley, Cannonball, popular name of **Julian Edwin Adderley** (1928–75) Jazz saxophonist and composer, born in Tampa, FL. Born into a musical family, he directed the local high school band (1948–56) and US army bands (1950–3), then formed a combo with his brother Nat (1956), which was soon widely acclaimed. His many recordings include the album *Kind of Blue* (1958–9) with the Miles Davis sextet and John Coltrane, and his film work included *Play Misty for Me* (1971). He died at the height of his career following a stroke. >> Coltrane; Davis, Miles

Addington, Henry >> **Sidmouth, 1st Viscount**

Addinsell, Richard [adinsel] (1904–77) Composer, born in Oxford, Oxfordshire, SC England, UK. A student of law at Oxford, he went on to study music in London, Berlin, and Vienna. He composed much film music, including the popular 'Warsaw Concerto' for the film *Dangerous Moonlight* (1941).

Addison, Christopher, 1st Viscount (1869–1951) British statesman, born in Hogsthorpe, Lincolnshire, E England, UK. He qualified in medicine at St Bartholomew's Hospital, London, and became professor of anatomy at Sheffield University. Liberal MP for Hoxton (1910–22), he was parliamentary secretary to the Board of Education (1914), minister of munitions (1916), and Britain's first minister of health (1919). He resigned in 1921 and joined the Labour Party. Elected MP for Swindon, he was made minister of agriculture in 1929. Created a baron in 1937, he assumed leadership of the Labour peers in 1940, becoming Leader of the House of Lords in 1945.

Addison, Joseph (1672–1719) Essayist and politician, born in Milston, Wiltshire, S England, UK. A student at Oxford, he was a distinguished Classical scholar, beginning his literary career in 1693 with a poetical address to Dryden. In 1699 he obtained a pension to train for the diplomatic service, and spent four years abroad. While under-secretary of state (1705–8) he produced his opera *Rosamond* (1706), and in 1708 was elected to parliament for Malmesbury. He became a member of the Kitcat Club, and contributed to the *Tatler*, started by his friend Richard Steele in 1709. In 1711 he and Steele founded the *Spectator*, 274 numbers of which were his own work. In 1716 he became a lord commissioner of trade, and married Charlotte, Countess of Warwick. In the Hanoverian cause, he issued (1715–16) a political newspaper, the *Freeholder*, which cost him many of his old friends, and he was satirized as 'Atticus' by Alexander Pope. In 1717 he was appointed secretary of state under Sunderland, but

resigned his post because of failing health. >> Dryden; Pope, Alexander; Steele, Richard

Addison, Thomas (1793–1860) Physician, born in Longbenton, Northumberland, NE England, UK. He studied medicine at Edinburgh, settled in London, and in 1837 became physician to Guy's Hospital. His chief researches were on pneumonia, tuberculosis, and especially on the disease of the suprarenal capsules now known as *Addison's disease*.

Adela, Princess [adayla] (c. 1062–1137) Princess of England, the youngest daughter of William the Conqueror. In 1080 she married Stephen, Count of Blois, and had nine children, the third of whom came to be King Stephen of England. She had a flair for administration, and was cultured and pious. >> Stephen; William I (of England)

Adelaide, Queen (1792–1849) Consort of King William IV of Great Britain, the eldest daughter of George, Duke of Saxe-Coburg-Meiningen. In 1818 she married William, Duke of Clarence, who succeeded his brother, George IV, to the throne as William IV (1830–7). Their two children, both daughters, died in infancy. >> George IV; William IV

Adelaide, St, Ger **Adelheid** (931–99) Holy Roman Empress, a daughter of Rudolf II of Burgundy. She married Lothair of Italy in 947. After his death in 950 she was imprisoned by his successor, Berengar II, but was rescued by King Otto I of Germany, who married her as his second wife in 951. They were crowned emperor and empress in 962. Their son was **Otto II** (955–83). As queen mother, she exercised considerable influence. She became joint regent for her grandson **Otto III** (980–1002), and then sole regent (991–6). Thereafter she retired to a convent in Alsace. Feast day 16 December. >> Otto I

Adenauer, Konrad [adenower] (1876–1967) German statesman, born in Cologne, Germany. He studied at Freiburg, Munich, and Bonn, before practising law in Cologne, where he became lord mayor in 1917. A member of the Centre Party under the Weimar Republic, he became a member of the Provincial Diet and of the Prussian State Council (president 1920–33). In 1933, he was dismissed from all his offices by the Nazis, and imprisoned in 1934 and again in 1944. In 1945, under Allied occupation, he was again mayor of Cologne, and founded the Christian Democratic Union. As chancellor from 1949 (re-elected 1953 and 1957), his policy was to rebuild West Germany on a basis of partnership with other European nations through NATO and the European Economic Community, with the ultimate aim of bargaining from strength for the reunification of Germany. He retired in 1963.

Ader, Clément [adair] (1841–1926) Engineer and pioneer of aviation, born in Muret, France. In 1890 he built a steam-powered bat-winged aeroplane, the *Eole*, which made the first powered take-off in history, but it could not be steered, and flew for no more than 50 m.

Adie, Kate [aydee], popular name of **Kathryn Adie** (1945–) News reporter and correspondent, born in Sunderland, Tyne and Wear, NE England, UK. She studied at the University of Newcastle upon Tyne, then joined local BBC radio (1969–76), moving to BBC TV South (1977–8). As a reporter for BBC TV News (1979–81), correspondent (1982), and chief correspondent (1989–), she has become a familiar figure presenting reports from the heart of war-torn countries around the world. Among her awards are the Royal Television Society's News Award (1981, 1987), and the BAFTA Richard Dimbleby Award (1989).

Adler, Alfred (1870–1937) Pioneer psychiatrist, born in Vienna. He trained in Vienna, and first practised as an ophthalmologist, but later turned to mental disease and became a prominent member of the psychoanalytical group which formed around Sigmund Freud in 1900. His most widely referenced work, *Studie über Minderwertigkeit von Organen* (1907, trans Study of Organ Inferiority and its Psychical Compensation), aroused great controversy. In 1911 he broke with Freud and investigated the psychology of the individual person considered to be different from others. His main contributions include the concept of the inferiority complex and his special treatment of neurosis as the exploitation of shock. He moved to the USA to teach in 1932. >> Freud, Sigmund

Adler, Dankmar >> **Sullivan, Louis**

Adler, Larry, popular name of **Lawrence Cecil Adler** (1914–) Musician and self-taught virtuoso on the harmonica, born in Baltimore, MD. He studied at Baltimore City College, and began his show business career in New York City at the age of 14. He played as a soloist with some of the world's leading symphony orchestras, and wrote the music for several films, including *Genevieve* (1954). He emigrated to Britain after being blacklisted in the USA for alleged pro-Communist leanings, and there worked as a journalist and restaurant critic, contributing to leading newspapers and magazines. His autobiography *It Ain't Necessarily So* was published in 1985.

Adler, Mortimer J(erome) (1902–) Philosopher and writer, born in New York City. He taught at the University of Chicago (1930–52), where in 1946 he helped design the Great Books programme, and directed the Institute for Philosophical Research from 1952. He popularized the great ideas of Western civilization in such works as *Great Books of the Western World* (54 vols, 1954, revised 1990), *How to Read a Book* (1940, revised 1972), and *Six Great Ideas* (1981).

Adorno, Theodor (Wiesengrund) [aˈdaw(r)noh], originally **Theodor Wiesengrund** (1903–69) Social philosopher and musicologist, born in Frankfurt, Germany. He was a student in Frankfurt and later an associate of the Institute for Social Research, becoming a member of the movement known as the 'Frankfurt School'. In 1934 he emigrated to the USA to teach at the Institute in exile, returning to Frankfurt in 1956. His philosophy is most fully presented in *Negative Dialectics* (1966). His sociological writings on music, mass-culture, and art include *Philosophie der neuen Musik* (1949, Philosophy of Modern Music) and *Mahler* (1960).

Adrian IV, also **Hadrian**, originally **Nicholas Breakspear** (c. 1100–59) The first and only Englishman to become pope (1154–9), born in Abbots Langley, Hertfordshire, SE England, UK. He studied at Merton Priory and Avignon, became a monk in the monastery of St Rufus, near Avignon, and in 1137 was elected its abbot. Complaints about his strictness led to a summons to Rome, where the pope recognized his qualities and appointed him Cardinal-Bishop of Albano in 1146. In 1152 he was sent as papal legate to Scandinavia to reorganize the Church, where he earned fame as the 'Apostle of the North'. One of his early acts as pope is said to have been the issue of a controversial bull granting Ireland to Henry II. In 1155 he crowned Frederick I Barbarossa as Holy Roman Emperor in front of his massed army in a show of strength in support of the papacy, but he later engaged in a bitter struggle with him for supremacy in Europe. >> Frederick I; Henry II (of England)

Adrian VI, originally **Adrian Dedel** (1459–1523) The only Dutch pope (1522–3), born in Utrecht, The Netherlands. He studied in Louvain, became a doctor of theology (1491), and was appointed tutor in 1507 to the seven-year-old Charles, later to be King of Spain (as Charles I) and Holy Roman Emperor (as Charles V). In 1516, Charles made Adrian inquisitor-general of Aragon and co-regent. As pope he tried to attack the sale of indulgences which had prompted Luther's first revolt, and allied with the emperor, England, and Venice against France. >> Charles V (Emperor); Luther

Adrian, Edgar Douglas, 1st Baron Adrian (1889–1977) Neurophysiologist, one of the founders of modern neurophysiology, born in London, England, UK. He became a fellow of Trinity College, Cambridge, where he carried out research on electrical impulses in the nervous system, and later on electrical brain waves. He was appointed professor of physiology at Cambridge (1937–51), Master of Trinity College, Cambridge (1951–6), and Chancellor of the University (1968–75). For his work on the function of neurons, he shared the 1932 Nobel Prize for Physiology or Medicine. >> RR1124

Æ >> **Russell, George William**

Ælfric [alfrik, alfrich], also known as **Ælfric Grammaticus** ('The Grammarian') (c. 955–c. 1020) Anglo-Saxon clergyman and writer, the greatest vernacular prose writer of his time. He became a monk and later abbot at the new monastery of Cerne Abbas in Dorset, S England, and subsequently the first Abbot of Eynsham in Oxfordshire, SC England. He composed two books of 80 *Homilies* in Old English, a paraphrase of the first seven books of the Bible, and a book of *Lives of the Saints*. He also wrote a Latin grammar and Latin–English glossary, accompanied by a Latin *Colloquium* which gives a vivid picture of social conditions in England at the time.

Aelian [eelian], in full **Claudius Aelianus** (c. 170–c. 235) Greek rhetorician, born in Praeneste, near Rome. He taught rhetoric in Rome c.220, and wrote numerous works, including *Varia historia* (Historical Miscellanies) and *De natura animalium* (On the Characteristics of Animals).

Aelred of Rievaulx >> **Ailred of Rievaulx**

Aertsen, Pieter [airtsen] (1508/9–79) Painter, born in Amsterdam. He worked in Antwerp (1535–c.55), the first of a family dynasty of painters. Few of his religious altarpieces survived the turmoils of the Reformation. He is best known for paintings of everyday life and contemporary domestic interiors, but these frequently include some religious reference.

Aeschines [eeskineez] (c. 390 BC–?) Orator, born in Athens. He advocated appeasement of Philip II of Macedon, and was a member of a Greek embassy that negotiated peace with Philip in 346. Demosthenes tried to have him indicted for treason in 343, and in 330 Aeschines tried to prevent Demosthenes from being awarded a golden crown for his services to Athens. Defeated, Aeschines withdrew to Rhodes, where he established a school of eloquence. >> Demosthenes; Philip II (of Macedon)

Aeschylus [eeskilus] (c. 525–c. 456 BC) Playwright, known as 'the father of Greek tragedy', born in Eleusis, near Athens. He served in the Athenian army in the Persian Wars, and was wounded at Marathon (490). The first and gravest of the great dramatists (winning the victory in 485 BC), he increased the number of characters in the action and introduced new staging. He won 13 first prizes in tragic competitions, before being defeated by Sophocles in 468. This may have induced him to leave Athens and go to Sicily. Out of some 60 plays ascribed to him, only seven are extant: *Persians* (472), *Seven against Thebes* (467), *Prometheus Bound*, *Suppliants*, and the trilogy of the *Oresteia* (458), three plays on the fate of Orestes, comprising *Agamemnon* (perhaps the greatest Greek play that has survived), *Choephoroe*, and *Eumenides*. >> Sophocles

Aesop [eesop] (?6th-c BC) Legendary Greek fabulist. The fables attributed to him are in all probability a compilation of tales from many sources. The stories were popularized by the Roman poet Phaedrus in the 1st-c AD, and rewritten in sophisticated verse by La Fontaine in 1668. >> La Fontaine; Phaedrus

Æthel- (Anglo-Saxon name) >> **Athelstan; Ethelbert; Etheldreda; Ethelflaed; Ethelred I; Ethelred II**

Æthelbert >> **Ethelbert**

Æthelflaed >> **Ethelflaed**

Æthelthryth >> **Etheldreda**

Aëtius, Flavius [ayeetius] (c.390–454) Roman general, born in Moesia. In 433 he became patrician, consul, and general-in-chief, and maintained the empire against the barbarians for 20 years. His crowning victory was at Châlons over Attila in 451. Three years later Emperor Valentinian III (reigned 425–55), jealous of his greatness, stabbed him to death. >> Attila; Theodoric I

Afonso I >> **Alfonso I**

Africanus, Sextus Julius [afrikahnus] (c.160–c.240) Traveller and historian, born in Libya. He wrote *Chronologia*, a history of the world from the creation to AD 221. His chronology, which antedates Christ's birth by three years, was accepted by Byzantine Churches.

Aga Khan III [ahga **kahn**], in full **Aga Sultan Sir Mohammed Shah** (1877–1957) Imam of the Ismaili sect of Muslims, born in Karachi, Pakistan. He succeeded to the title in 1885, and in 1910 founded Aligarh University. He worked for the British cause in both World Wars, and in 1937 was president of the League of Nations Assembly. A keen racecourse enthusiast, he owned several Derby winners.

Aga Khan IV, Karim [ahga **kahn**] (1936–) Imam of the Ismaili sect of Muslims, born in Geneva, the grandson of Aga Khan III. He succeeded his grandfather as 49th Imam in 1957. Educated at Le Rosey in Switzerland, he later studied oriental history at Harvard. He married an English woman, **Sarah Croker Poole**, in 1969 (dissolved, 1995), and has two sons and one daughter. He is a leading owner and breeder of race horses in France and Ireland. >> Aga Khan III

Agassiz, Alexander (Emmanuel Rodolphe) [agasee] (1835–1910) Oceanographer, born in Neuchâtel, Switzerland, the son of Louis Agassiz. He moved to the USA in 1849 to join his father, studied engineering and zoology at Harvard, then amassed a fortune in the copper mines of L Superior (1866–9). He became curator (1873–85) of Harvard's Museum of Comparative Zoology, founded by his father, made numerous oceanographic zoological expeditions, and examined thousands of coral reefs to refute Darwin's ideas on atoll formation. >> Agassiz, Louis; Darwin, Charles

Agassiz, Jean Louis Rodolphe [agasee] (1807–73) Naturalist and glaciologist, born in Motier, Switzerland, the father of Alexander Agassiz. In 1832 he was appointed professor of natural history at Neuchâtel. *Etudes sur les glaciers* (1840, Studies of Glaciers), showed that glaciers move, thus indicating the existence of an Ice Age. Professor of natural history at the Lawrence Scientific School, Harvard (1847–73), he founded a Museum of Comparative Zoology (1859), to which he gave all his collections. He published four of ten projected volumes of *Contributions to the Natural History of the United States* (1857–62). In his later years he became a US citizen. >> Agassiz, Alexander

Agate, James (Evershed) [agayt] (1877–1947) Critic and essayist, born in Manchester, Greater Manchester, NW England, UK. He wrote dramatic criticism for several papers and the BBC before becoming drama critic for the *Sunday Times* (from 1923). He was also the author of essays, novels, and a nine-part autobiography in the form of a diary, *Ego*.

Agatha, St (?–251) Christian martyr from Catania, Sicily. According to legend, she rejected the love of the Roman consul, Quintilianus, and suffered a cruel martyrdom in 251. She is the patron saint of Catania, is invoked against fire and lightning, and is also the patron saint of bellfounders. Feast day 5 February.

Agathocles [agathokleez] (361–289 BC) Tyrant of Syracuse, Sicily, from 317 BC. He fought the Carthaginians and invaded Tunisia, styling himself King of Sicily c.304 BC. Under him Sicily achieved her last period of independent power before the Roman conquest.

Agee, James [ayjee] (1909–55) Novelist, poet, film critic, and screen writer, born in Knoxville, TN. He studied at Harvard, and worked for several magazines before being commissioned to rove the Southern states with the photographer Walker Evans, producing *Let Us Now Praise Famous Men* (1941). His film scripts include *The African Queen* (1951) and *The Night of the Hunter* (1955). His only novel, *A Death in the Family* (published 1957), was awarded a posthumous Pulitzer Prize. >> Evans, Walker

Agenbegyan, Abel (1932–) Economist, born in Tbilisi, Georgia. Director of the Institute of Economics and Industrial Engineering, with his colleagues he developed the models for managing the national economy which the Soviet government started to apply in the late 1980s. He was personal adviser to President Gorbachev on economic affairs. >> Gorbachev

Agesilaus [ajeesilayus] (444–360 BC) King of Sparta (399–360 BC). Called on by the Ionians to assist them in 397 BC against Artaxerxes II (reigned 404–358 BC), he launched an ambitious campaign in Asia, but the Corinthian War recalled him to Greece. At Coronea (394 BC) he defeated the Greek allied forces, and peace was eventually concluded in favour of Sparta (387 BC). He precipitated the Battle of Leuctra against Thebes (371 BC), a disaster which signified the end of Spartan ascendancy and the beginning of a decade of Theban supremacy in Greece.

Agnelli, Giovanni [agnelee] (1866–1945) Manufacturer, born in Piedmont, Italy. He studied at a military academy, and became a cavalry officer. In 1899 he founded Fiat (Fabbrica Italiana Automobili Torino). He was appointed a senator in 1923, and mobilized Italian industry in World War 2.

Agnes, St (4th-c) Christian martyr, born in Rome. She is thought to have been killed at Rome c.304 in her 13th year, during the persecutions of Diocletian. She is said to have refused to consider marriage, and consecrated her maidenhood to God. Honoured as the patron saint of virgins, her emblem is a lamb. Feast day 21 January. >> Diocletian

Agnes of Assisi, St (1197–1253) Christian saint, born in Assisi, Italy, the daughter of Count Favorino Scifi and the younger sister of St Clare. In 1211, she joined her sister in a convent, co-founding the order of the Poor Ladies of San Damiano (Poor Clares). In 1219 she became abbess of a newly established community of the order at Monticelli. >> Clare, St

Agnesi, Maria Gaetana [anyayzee] (1718–99) Mathematician and scholar, born in Milan, Italy. The daughter of a professor of mathematics at Bologna, she was a child prodigy, speaking six languages by the age of 11. Her mathematical textbook *Istituzioni analitiche* (1784) became famous throughout Italy. A curve, the *witch of Agnesi*, is named after her.

Agnew, Spiro T(heodore) [agnyoo] (1918–96) US vicepresident, born in Baltimore, MD. After service in World War 2 he graduated in law from Baltimore University (1947). In 1966 he was elected governor of Maryland on a liberal platform, introducing anti-racial-discrimination legislation that year. As a compromise figure acceptable to most shades of Republican opinion, he was Nixon's running mate in 1968 and 1972, and took office as vice-president in 1969. He resigned in 1973, following an investigation into alleged tax violations. >> Nixon

Agnon, Shmuel Yosef, originally **Shmuel Josef Czaczkes** (1888–1970) Novelist, born in Buczacz, Poland. He went to Palestine in 1907, studied in Berlin (1913–24), then settled permanently in Jerusalem and changed his surname to Agnon. He wrote in Hebrew an epic trilogy of novels on Eastern Jewry in the early 20th-c: their translated titles are *Bridal Canopy* (1931), *A Guest for the Night* (1939), and *Days Gone By* (1945). He is also known for several volumes of short stories. In 1966 he became the first Israeli to receive the Nobel Prize for Literature. >> RR1123

Agostini, Giacomo [ago**stee**nee] (1944–) Motor-cyclist, born in Lovere, Italy. He won a record 15 world titles between 1966 and 1975, including the 500 cc title a record eight times (1966–72, 1975); 13 of the titles were on an MV Agusta, the others on a Yamaha. He won 10 Isle of Man TT Races (1966–75), including the Senior TT five times (1968–72). After retirement in 1975, he became manager of the Yamaha racing team. >> RR1164

Agostino (di Duccio) [ago**stee**noh] (1418–81) Sculptor, born in Florence, Italy. His best and most original work is the relief decoration for the Tempio Malatestiano at Rimini, a church designed by Alberti. >> Alberti, Leon Battista

Agoult, Marie de Flavigny, comtesse d' (Countess of) [agoo], pseudonym **Daniel Stern** (1805–76) Writer, born in Frankfurt, Germany, the daughter of the French emigré Comte de Flavigny. She was educated at a convent in Paris. She married Comte d'Agoult in 1827, but in 1834 left him for Franz Liszt, by whom she had three daughters; the youngest, Cosima, married first Hans von Bülow, and later Wagner. A close friend of George Sand, she held a famous salon in Paris, and wrote on numerous subjects. >> Bülow, Hans; Liszt; Sand; Wagner, Richard

Agricola, Georgius [a**grī**kola], Latin name of **Georg Bauer** (1494–1555) Mineralogist and metallurgist, born in Glauchau, Germany. As a practising physician in Chemnitz, his interest in the link between medicine and minerals led him to the study of mining. His *De re metallica* (published 1556, trans 1912), is a valuable record of 16th-c mining and metal working.

Agricola, Gnaeus Julius [a**grī**kola] (40–93) Roman statesman and soldier, born in Fréjus (formerly, Forum Julii). Having served with distinction in Britain, Asia, and Aquitania, he was elected consul in 77, and returned to Britain as governor some time after. In 80 and 81 he extended Roman occupation N into Scotland, and in 84 defeated Calcagus at Mons Graupius. After this campaign, his fleet circumnavigated the coast, for the first time discovering Britain to be an island. The news of Agricola's successes inflamed the jealousy of Domitian, and in 84 he was recalled. >> Domitian

Agricola, Johann [a**grī**kola], originally **Schneider** or **Schnitter**, also called **Magister Islebius** (1492–1566) Protestant reformer, born in Eisleben, Germany. Having studied at Wittenberg and Leipzig, he was sent to Frankfurt by Luther in 1525 to institute Protestant worship there. Appointed in 1536 to a chair at Wittenberg, he resigned in 1540 over his opposition to Luther in the great Antinomian controversy. He later became court preacher in Berlin. >> Luther

Agricola, Rudolphus [a**grī**kola], originally **Roelof Huysmann** (1443–85) Humanist, born near Groningen, The Netherlands. He studied in Italy (1473–80), Heidelberg, and Worms, and his writings had a profound influence on Erasmus. He was the foremost scholar of the Renaissance 'new learning' in Germany. >> Erasmus

Agrippa >> **Herod Agrippa I; Herod Agrippa II**

Agrippa, Marcus Vipsanius [a**grī**pa] (c. 63–12 BC) Roman commander and statesman. His third wife was Julia,

daughter of the emperor Augustus, whom he helped to gain power. He defeated Sextus, the son of Pompey, at Mylae and Naulochus in 36 BC, and Mark Antony at Actium in 31 BC. >> Antonius; Augustus; Julia; Pompey

Agrippa von Nettesheim, Henricus Cornelius [a**grī**pa fon **ne**tes-hiym] (1486–1535) Occultist philosopher, born in Cologne, Germany. He travelled widely and had a varied, if insecure, career as physician, diplomat, teacher, and soldier. His major and influential work, a treatise on magic, *De occulta philosophia*, was completed in 1510 and published in 1533.

Agrippina [agri**pee**na], known as **Agrippina the Elder** (c. 14 BC–AD 33) Roman noblewoman, the daughter of Marcus Vipsanius Agrippa and grand-daughter of Emperor Augustus. She married Germanicus Caesar (15 BC–AD 19), and was the mother of Caligula and Agrippina the Younger. Regarded as a model of heroic womanhood, she accompanied her husband on his campaigns. Her popularity incurred the anger of Emperor Tiberius, who banished her in 29 to the island of Pandateria, where she died of starvation in suspicious circumstances. >> Agrippa, Marcus Vipsanius; Agrippina (the Younger); Augustus; Caligula; Tiberius

Agrippina [agri**pee**na], known as **Agrippina the Younger** (15–59) Roman noblewoman, the daughter of Agrippina (the Elder). She first married Gnaeus Domitius Ahenobarbus, by whom she had a son, the future Emperor Nero. Her third husband was Emperor Claudius, though her own uncle. She persuaded Claudius to adopt Nero as his successor, then proceeded to poison all Nero's rivals and enemies, and finally (allegedly) the emperor himself. Her ascendancy proved intolerable to Nero, who eventually put her to death. >> Agrippina (the Elder); Claudius; Nero

Aguesseau, Henri François d' [agesoh] (1668–1751) Jurist, born in Limoges, France. A steady defender of the rights of the people and of the Gallican Church, he was advocate general and attorney general to the Parlement of Paris, and three times Chancellor of France under Louis XV (1717–18, 1720–22, 1737–50). >> Louis XV

Aguinaldo, Emilio [agwi**nal**doh] (1870–1964) Filipino revolutionary, born near Cavite, Philippines. He led the rising against Spain in the Philippines (1896–8), and then against the USA (1899–1901), but after capture in 1901 took the oath of allegiance to America.

Agutter, Jenny [ag**uh**ter] (1952–) Film and stage actress, born in Taunton, Somerset, SW England, UK. She became known following her role in *The Railway Children* (1970). Her other film credits include *The Snow Goose* (1971, Emmy, Best Supporting Actress), *Equus* (1977, BAFTA), *Child's Play 2* (1991), and *Blue Juice* (1995).

Ahab [**ay**hab] (9th-c BC) King of Israel (c.873–c.852 BC), the son of Omri. He was a warrior king and builder on a heroic scale, extending his capital city of Samaria and refortifying Megiddo and Hazor. He married Jezebel, daughter of the king of Tyre and Sidon, who introduced the worship of the Phoenician god, Baal, and thus aroused the hostility of the prophet Elijah. >> Elijah; Jezebel; RR1064

Ahern, Bertie [a**hern**] (1951–) Irish politician and prime minister (1997–). He studied at Rathmines College of Commerce and University College Dublin, became a hospital accountant and union organizer, and became a member of the Dáil in 1977. After a series of junior posts, he became minister of state at the departments of Taoiseach and Defence (1982), minister for labour (1987–91) and finance (1991–4), and leader of the opposition and President of Fianna Fáil in 1994. He became head of a coalition government after defeating John Bruton in 1997.

Ahidjo, Ahmadou [a-hee**joh**] (1924–89) Cameroonian statesman and president (1960–82), born in Garoua,

Cameroon. He became prime minister in 1958, and led his country to independence in 1960. He was elected the first president of the new Republic of Cameroon, a post which he held until his retirement. He then went into exile in France. >> RR1039

Ahmad Shah Durani [ahmad shah jurahnee] (1724–73) Founder and first monarch of Afghanistan. A chieftain of the Durani clan of the Abdali tribe, and a cavalry general under the Persian emperor Nadir Shah, he was elected king of the Afghan provinces in 1745. He established his capital at Kandahar, and made nine successful invasions of the Punjab. In 1761 he defeated the Marathas decisively at the Battle of Panipat, but was eventually obliged to acknowledge Sikh power in the Punjab. >> RR1031

Ahmed Arabi [ahmed arabee], also known as **Arabi Pasha** (1839–1911) Egyptian soldier and nationalist leader. He was the leader of a rebellion against the khedive, Tewfik Pasha, in 1881 which led to the setting up of a nationalist government. The British intervened to protect their interests in the Suez Canal, and he was defeated at Tel-el-Kebir (1882) and exiled to Ceylon. He was pardoned in 1901. >> Tewfik Pasha

Ahmose I [ahmohs] (16th-c BC) Egyptian pharoah, who founded the 18th dynasty. He freed Egypt from the alien Shepherd Kings (Hyksos), and established control over Nubia. >> RR1046

Ahmose II [ahmohs] (6th-c BC) Egyptian pharoah (ruled 570–26 BC). He cultivated the friendship of the Greeks, and greatly promoted the prosperity of Egypt. A major achievement of his reign was the building of the temple of Isis at Memphis. >> RR1046

Aidan, St [aydn], known as the **Apostle of Northumbria** (?–651) A monk from the Celtic monastery on the island of Iona, born in Ireland. He was summoned in 635 by King Oswald of Northumbria to evangelize the North. He established a church and monastery on the island of Lindisfarne, and was appointed the first bishop there. He later founded several churches throughout Northumbria. Feast day 31 August. >> Oswald, St

Aiken, Conrad (Potter) [ayken] (1889–1973) Poet and novelist, born in Savannah, GA. He studied at Harvard, and made his name with his first collection of verse, *Earth Triumphant* (1914). His *Selected Poems* was awarded the 1930 Pulitzer Prize. He also wrote short stories and novels, including the autobiographical novel *Ushant* (1952). >> Aiken, Joan

Aiken, Howard (Hathaway) [ayken] (1900–73) Mathematician and computer engineer, born in Hoboken, NJ. He studied at Wisconsin and Chicago Universities, then moved to Harvard (1939–61), where he built the Automatic Sequence-Controlled Calculator (ASCC), or Harvard Mark I, the world's first program-controlled calculator (completed in 1943). Mark II was built in 1947.

Aiken, Joan (Delano) [ayken] (1924–) British writer, the daughter of Conrad Aiken. She was educated privately, then worked as a librarian for the UN Information Committee (1943–9) and as features editor for *Argosy* magazine (1955–60). Her many books for children include *All You've Ever Wanted* (1953), *The Kingdom and the Cave* (1960), *Tales of Arabel's Raven* (1974), and *Voices Hippo* (1988). Among her adult novels are *The Silence of Herondale* (1964), *Castle Barebane* (1976), *Mansfield Revisited* (1985), *The Haunting of Lamb House* (1991), and *The Jewel Seed* (1997). >> Aiken, Conrad

Ailey, Alvin [aylee] (1931–89) Dancer and choreographer, born in Rogers, TX. He became a member of Lester Horton's company in 1950, then in New York City trained with Martha Graham and others. He retired from the stage in 1965 to devote himself to the Alvin Ailey American Dance Theater, a hugely popular, multi-racial modern dance ensemble he formed in 1958. His most famous dance is *Revelations* (1960), a celebratory study of religious spirit. >> Graham, Martha

Ailian, Dai (1916–) Dancer and choreographer, born in Trinidad. She studied during the 1930s in Britain, working from 1940 in China, where she was instrumental in introducing the principles and study of Western ballet. In 1959 she co-founded what is now known as the Central Ballet of China, and became the company's artistic adviser.

Ailly, Pierre d' [ayee], Lat **Petrus de Alliaco** (1350–1420) Theologian and nominalist philosopher, born in Compiègne, France. He became Chancellor of the University of Paris and Bishop of Compiègne, and was appointed cardinal (1411) by the anti-pope John XXIII. He was prominent in the election of Pope Martin V in 1417, an event which ended the Great Schism.

Ailred of Rievaulx, St [aylred, reevoh], also **Aelred** or **Ethelred** (1109–66) Chronicler, born in Hexham, Northumberland, NE England, UK. A Cistercian monk at Rievaulx Abbey, he was a friend and adviser to both David I of Scotland and Stephen of England, and wrote a vivid Latin account of the battle between them at Northallerton, Yorkshire (1138). Feast days 12 January, 3 March. >> David I; Stephen

Aimee, Anouk [emay], originally **Françoise Sorya** (1934–) Film actress, born in Paris, France. She studied dance at the Marseilles Opera, and drama under Rene Simon in Paris, and made her film debut in *La Maison Sous la Mer* (1947). Later films include *La Dolce Vita* (1960, The Sweet Life), *Un Homme et Une Femme* (1966, A Man and a Woman), and *Justine* (1969).

Ainsworth, William Harrison [aynzwerth] (1805–82) Historical novelist, born in Manchester, Greater Manchester, NW England, UK. He studied for the law, but began a literary career instead, and is chiefly remembered for popularizing the story of the highwayman Dick Turpin in *Rookwood* (1834) and the legend of Herne the Hunter in *Windsor Castle* (1843). He edited *Ainsworth's Magazine* (1842–54), and wrote nearly 40 popular historical romances.

Ai Qing [iy ching] (1910–96) Poet, born in Jinhua Co, China. He studied painting in France (1928–31), but returned to China and began to write socially and politically conscious poetry. In 1949 he became associate editor of the *People's Literature* journal. He was an active propagandist for Communist-controlled literature, but in 1957 was accused of revisionism. In 1959 he was exiled to Zinjiang for 17 years. He began to publish again in 1978.

Airy, Sir George (Biddell) [airee] (1801–92) Astronomer and geophysicist, born in Alnwick, Northumberland, NE England, UK. He studied at Cambridge, was appointed professor of mathematics there in 1828, and became astronomer royal (1835–81). He reorganized the Greenwich Observatory, and discovered errors in planetary theory in terms of the motion of the Earth and Venus. He determined the mass of the Earth from gravity measurements in mines, and also invented a cylindrical lens for the correction of astigmatism, from which he himself suffered. Greenwich Mean Time, measured using Airy's telescope positioned on the line of zero longitude in his observatory, became Britain's legal time in 1880.

Aïshah or **Ayeshah** [aeesha] (c. 613–78) Third and favourite of the nine wives of the prophet Mohammed, and daughter of Abu-Bakr, the first caliph. When Mohammed died in 632 she resisted the claims to the caliphate of Ali, Mohammed's son-in-law, in favour of her father. She led a revolt against Ali in 656, but was defeated and exiled to Medina. She is known as the 'mother of believers'. >> Abu-Bakr; Ali; Mohammed

Aitken, Sir (John William) Max(well) [ayt ken] (1910–85) Newspaper publisher, born in Montreal, Quebec, Canada, the son of the 1st Lord Beaverbrook. He established a reputation as a socialite before the war, but served with great distinction as a fighter pilot. He became a Conservative MP for Holborn (1945–50), then joined his father in running Beaverbrook Newspapers (the *Daily Express* and the *Sunday Express*). They had frequent disagreements. When Lord Beaverbrook died in 1964, Max renounced his claim to the barony but retained his father's baronetcy. He became a leading ocean-racing skipper, and promoted offshore powerboat racing and motor racing. >> Beaverbrook

Aitken, Robert Grant [ayt ken] (1864–1951) Astronomer, born in Jackson, CA. He was professor of mathematics and astronomy at the University of the Pacific (1891–5), then joined Lick Observatory, CA, where he became director (1930–5). His discovery of more than 3000 double stars gained him the gold medal of the Royal Astronomical Society in 1932.

Akabusi, Kriss (Kezie Uche-Chukwu Duru) [aka boo see] (1958–) Athlete, born in London, England, UK. He joined the army in 1975, and went on to become one of the leading athletes of the 1990s. His achievements include gold medals in the 4 x 100 m relay at the 1986 European Championships and Commonwealth Games (1986), the 400 m hurdles at the 1990 European Championships (also breaking a 22-year world record) and Commonwealth Games, the 4 x 400 m relay at the 1991 World Championships in Tokyo, and the 4 x 400 m relay in the 1993 European Cup. His Olympic medals include silver in the 4 x 100 m relay (1984) and bronze for the same event in 1994. Since 1993 he has become known as a television presenter.

Akahito, Yamabe no [aka hee toh] (8th-c) Japanese poet. A minor official at the imperial court, he seems to have kept his position largely through his poetic ability. He is known as one of the 'twin stars' – Hitomaro being the other – of the great anthology of classical Japanese poetry called the *Manyoshu* (Collection of a Myriad Leaves).

Akbar the Great [ak ber], in full **Jalal ud-Din Muhammad Akbar** (1542–1605) Mughal emperor of India, born in Umarkot, Sind. He succeeded his father, Humayun, in 1556, and assumed power in 1560. The early years of his reign were marred by civil war and rebellion, but after triumphing over his enemies within the empire he turned to foreign conquest, extending his control to the whole of N India. He reformed the tax system, promoted commerce, encouraged science, literature, and the arts, and abolished slavery. Although brought up a Muslim, he pursued a tolerant and eclectic religious policy. >> Jahangir; RR1058

Akeley, Carl (Ethan) (1864–1926) and **Mary Lee Akeley** [ayk lee], *née* **Jobe** (1878–1966) Naturalists and explorers, born in Clarendon, NY and Tappan, OH, respectively. He worked as a taxidermist in Rochester, NY, and then at the Milwaukee Museum. By the time he joined the staff at the Field Museum of Natural History in Chicago (1895), he was perfecting new techniques for making large habitat groups of wild animals – sculpting realistic forms on which real skins, horns, and other bodily parts were placed. He made several trips to Africa (1896, 1905, 1909, 1926), and invented a special motion-picture camera for naturalists to study wildlife (1916). He died in Africa, two years after he married Mary Lee Jobe, his second wife. She had explored in the Canadian Rockies (1913–18), and she continued his African expedition (1926–7). Returning to Africa in 1935 and 1946, she collected further materials for the American Museum of Natural History, New York City. She won international recognition for her work in informing the world of the importance of maintaining primitive and natural life in Africa.

Aken, Jerome van >> **Bosch, Hieronymus**

Akenside, Mark [ay kensiyd] (1721–70) Poet and physician, born in Newcastle upon Tyne, Tyne and Wear, NE England, UK. In 1744 he published his best-known work, the didactic poem *The Pleasures of Imagination*. His haughty and pedantic manner was caricatured in Tobias Smollett's *Adventures of Peregrine Pickle* (1757). In 1761 he was appointed one of the physicians to the queen.

Akhenaton [ake naton], also **Akh(e)naten** or **Amenhotep (Amenophis) IV** [amen hoh tep] (14th-c BC) Egyptian king of the 18th dynasty. He renounced the worship of the old gods, introduced a monotheistic solar cult of the sun-disc (Aton), and changed his name. He built a new capital at Amarna (Akhetaton), where the arts blossomed while the empire weakened. He was married to Nefertiti. >> Nefertiti; Tutankhamen; RR1046

Akhmatova, Anna [akh mah tofa], pseudonym of **Anna Andreyevna Gorenko** (1889–1966) Poet, born in Odessa, Ukraine. She studied in Kiev before moving to St Petersburg. In 1910 she married Nicholas Gumilev, and with him started the Neoclassicist Acmeist movement. After her early collections of lyrical poems, including *Evening* (1912) and *Beads* (1914), she developed an Impressionist technique. Following the publication of *Anno Domini* (1922), she was officially silenced until 1940, when she published *The Willow*. Among her best-known works is *Requiem*, written in the late 1930s, a poetic cycle on the Stalin purges. In 1946 her verse was again banned. She was 'rehabilitated' in the 1950s, and received official tributes on her death. >> Gumilev

Akiba ben Joseph [akee ba ben johzef], also spelled **Akiva** (c.50–135) Rabbi and teacher in Palestine. He founded a rabbinical school at Jaffa, and played a great part in reshaping the Mishnah. He was a supporter of the unsuccessful revolt of bar Kokhba against Hadrian (131–5), and was put to death by the Romans. >> bar Kokhba

Akihito [aki hee toh] (1933–) Emperor of Japan (1989–), born in Tokyo, the son of Hirohito. He studied among commoners at the elite Gakushuin school, and in 1959 married **Michiko Shoda** (1934–), the daughter of a flour company president, who thus became the first non-aristocrat to enter the imperial family. An amateur marine biologist, he is also an accomplished cellist. On becoming emperor in 1989, the new *Heisei* ('the achievement of universal peace') era commenced. >> Showa Tenno; RR1068

Akins, Zöe [ay kinz] (1886–1958) Playwright, born in Humansville, MO. She trained as an actress in New York City, but turned to writing light comedy and film scripts. In 1935 she received the Pulitzer Prize for her dramatization of Edith Wharton's *The Old Maid*. Other plays include *Daddy's Gone A-Hunting* (1921) and *The Greeks Had a Word for It* (1930).

Akiva ben Joseph >> **Akiba ben Joseph**

Aksakov, Sergei Timofeyevitch [ak sah kof] (1791–1859) Novelist, born in Ufa, Russia. He held government posts in St Petersburg and Moscow before a meeting with Gogol in 1832 turned him to literature. His house became the centre of a Gogol cult. He wrote *The Blizzard* (trans, 1834), *Chronicles of a Russian Family* (trans, 1846–56), and *Years of Childhood* (trans, 1858). His writing shows his love of country sports and deep feeling for nature.

Alacoque, St Marguerite Marie [alakok] (1647–90) French nun at Paray-le-Monial, and a member of the Visitation Order. The founder of the devotion to the Sacred Heart, she was canonized in 1920. Feast day 17 October.

Alaia, Azzedine [ali ya] Tunisian fashion designer. He was educated in Tunis, where he studied sculpture, then worked for Dior and other designers before giving his first show in New York City (1982). His designs emphasize the figure, and he is noted for his black leather-studded gauntlets, little black dresses, and use of zippers.

Alain-Fournier, Henri [alī foornyay], pseudonym of **Henri-Alban Fournier** (1886–1914) Writer, born in Sologne, France. He became a literary journalist in Paris, and was killed at St Rémy soon after the outbreak of World War 1. He left a semi-autobiographical fantasy novel, *Le Grand Meaulnes* (1913, trans The Lost Domain), now considered a modern classic.

Alamán, Lucas [alaman] (1792–1853) Mexican statesman and historian, born in Guanajuanto, Mexico. As a deputy to the Spanish Cortes (1820–1), he spoke out for Mexican independence. Mexico's most influential Conservative, and chief minister under Bustamante (1829–32), he founded the National Museum, and died shortly after completing his monumental *Historia de Mexico* (1842–52).

Alanbrooke (of Brookeborough), Alan Francis Brooke, 1st Viscount [alanbruk] (1883–1963) British field marshal, born in Bagnères-de-Bigorre, France. He joined the Royal Field Artillery in 1902, and in World War 1 rose to general staff officer. In World War 2 he commanded the 2nd corps of the British Expeditionary Force (1939–40), covering the evacuation from Dunkirk in France. He became commander-in-chief of home forces (1940–1), Chief of the Imperial General Staff (1941–6), and principal strategic adviser to Winston Churchill. He became a field marshal in 1944, and was created baron in 1945 and viscount in 1946. His war diaries presented a controversial view of Churchill and Eisenhower. >> Churchill, Sir Winston; Eisenhower

Alarcón (y Ariza), Pedro Antonio de [alah(r)hon] (1833–91) Writer, born in Guadix, Spain. He served with distinction in the African campaign of 1859–60, and became a radical journalist. He published a war diary, travel notes, and poems, but is best known for his novels, particularly *Sombrero de tres picos* (1874) on which Manuel de Falla based his ballet *The Three-Cornered Hat*. >> Falla

Alarcón (y Mendoza), Juan Ruiz de [alah(r)hon ee mendohtha] (c. 1580–1639) Playwright, born in Taxco, Mexico. He trained as a lawyer, and in 1626 became a member of the Council of the Indies in Madrid. He was neglected for generations, but is now recognized as a leading playwright of the Golden Age of Spanish drama. Among his character comedies is *La verdad sospechosa* (c.1619, The Suspect Truth), the model for Corneille's *Le Menteur*. >> Corneille, Pierre

Alaric I [alarik] (c. 370–410) King of the Visigoths (395–410), born in Dacia. After his election as king, he invaded Greece (395), but was eventually driven out by Flavius Stilicho. In 401 he invaded Italy until checked by Stilicho at Pollentia (402). He agreed to join the Western emperor, Honorius, in an attack on Arcadius, but when Honorius failed to pay the promised subsidy Alaric laid siege to Rome, and in 410 pillaged the city. Later that year he set off to invade Sicily, but died at Cosenza. >> Honorius, Flavius; Stilicho

Alaric II [alarik] (450–507) King of the Visigoths (485–507), who reigned over Gaul S of the Loire, and over most of Spain. In 506 he issued a code of laws known as the Breviary of Alaric (*Breviarum Alaricianum*). An Arian Christian, he was killed at the Battle of Vouillé, near Poitiers, by the orthodox Clovis, King of the Franks. >> Clovis

Alas (y Ureña), Leopoldo [alas], pseudonym **Clarín** (1852–1901) Writer, born in Zamora, Spain. He was professor of law at Oviedo, but better known as a forceful literary critic (his pseudonym means 'bugle'). He published short stories (*Cuentos morales*, 1896), a drama *Teresa*, and several novels, including *La regenta* (1885, The Regent's Wife).

Alba, Duke of >> **Alva, duque de**

Alban, St [awlbn] (3rd-c) Roman soldier, venerated as the first Christian martyr in Britain. A pagan Romano-Briton living in the town of Verulamium (now St Albans), he was scourged and beheaded AD c.305 for sheltering and changing clothes with a fugitive Christian priest who had converted him. Feast day 17 or 20 June.

Albani, Francesco [albahnee] (1578–1660) Painter of the Bolognese school, born in Bologna, Italy. He studied first under Denis Calvaert (c.1540–1619), and afterwards under Ludovico Carracci. He painted about 45 altarpieces, but most of his work deals with mythological or pastoral subjects. >> Carracci

al-Banna, Hassan [albana] (1906–49) Islamic fundamentalist, born in Mahmudiya, near Cairo. In 1928 he founded in Egypt the Society of Muslim Brothers (better known as the Muslim Brotherhood or Brethren), which preached a return to the purity of early Islam. In 1948 the Egyptian prime minister, Nuqrashi-Pasha, was killed by a Brotherhood member, and in 1949 al-Banna was himself murdered, though he had condemned the assassination. His movement has had considerable influence on contemporary Islamic fundamentalism.

Albany, Louisa Maximilienne Caroline, Countess of [awlbanee] (1752–1824) Wife of Charles Edward Stuart ('Bonnie Prince Charlie'), the daughter of Prince Gustavus Adolphus of Stolberg. In 1772 she married the ageing Prince Charles in Florence. She left him in 1780 and the marriage was dissolved in 1784, whereupon she took up with the Italian playwright, Count Vittorio Alfieri. After his death in 1803 she lived with a French painter, François Fabre. >> Alfieri; Stuart, Charles

Albee, Edward (Franklin) [awlbee, albee] (1928–) Playwright, born near Washington, DC. He studied at Trinity College, CT, and at Columbia University. His major works include *The Zoo Story* (1958), a one-act duologue on the lack of communication in modern society, *The American Dream* (1960), and *Who's Afraid of Virginia Woolf?* (1962, filmed 1966), which won several awards. *A Delicate Balance* (1966), *Seascape* (1975), and *Three Tall Women* (1991) won Pulitzer Prizes. Other plays include *Walking* (1982), *Marriage Play* (1988), and *Fragments* (1993).

Albéniz, Isaac (Manuel Francisco) [albenith] (1860–1909) Composer and pianist, born in Camprodón, Spain. He studied under Liszt, and became a brilliant pianist and composer of picturesque works for piano based on Spanish folk music, notably *Iberia* (1906–9). He also wrote several operas. >> Liszt

Alberoni, Giulio [alberohnee] (1664–1752) Spanish statesman and cardinal, born in Firenzuola, Italy. He became prime minister of Spain and was made a cardinal in 1717. His domestic policies were liberal and wise, but in foreign affairs his decisions were often impetuous and irresponsible. He violated the Treaty of Utrecht by invading Sardinia, and was subsequently confronted by the Quadruple Alliance of England, France, Austria, and Holland, resulting in the destruction of the Spanish fleet. Dismissed in 1719, he returned to Italy. >> RR1088

Albers, Josef (1888–1976) Painter and designer, born in Bottrop, Germany. He trained in Berlin, Essen, and Munich, and from 1920 was involved with the Bauhaus. In 1933 he fled Nazi Germany to the USA, teaching at the experimental Black Mountain College, NC (1933–49) and at Yale (1950–60). He became a US citizen in 1939. As a painter he was interested chiefly in colour relationships, and from 1950 produced a series of wholly abstract canvases, 'Homage to the Square', exploring this theme with great subtlety.

Albert, known as **the Bear** (c. 1100–70) Count of Ballenstëdt from 1123, and founder of the House of Ascania which ruled in Brandenburg for 200 years. In 1134, in return for service in Italy, he was invested by Emperor Lothar III with extensive lands between the Elbe and the Oder.

Albert, known as **Albert the Bold** (1443–1500) Duke of Saxony, the son of Frederick the Gentle. He was joint ruler with his brother Ernest from 1464 until 1485 when, by the Treaty of Leipzig, they divided their inheritance between them. The two branches of the Wettin family then became known as the *Albertine* and *Ernestine* lines.

Albert (1490–1568) Last grand master of the Teutonic Order and first duke of Prussia, the younger son of the Margrave of Ansbach. Elected grand master in 1511, he embraced the Reformation, and declared himself duke following the advice of Martin Luther. >> Luther

Albert, Prince, in full **Francis Albert Augustus Charles Emmanuel, Prince of Saxe-Coburg-Gotha** (1819–61) Prince Consort to Queen Victoria, born at Schloss Rosenau, near Coburg, Germany, the younger son of the Duke of Saxe-Coburg-Gotha and Louisa, daughter of the Duke of Saxe-Coburg-Altenburg. He studied in Brussels and Bonn, and in 1840 married his first cousin, Queen Victoria – a marriage that became a lifelong love match. Ministerial distrust and public misgivings because of his German connections limited his political influence, although his counsel was usually judicious and far-sighted. He planned and managed the Great Exhibition of 1851, whose profits enabled the building of museum sites in South Kensington and the Royal Albert Hall (1871). He died of typhoid in 1861, occasioning a long period of seclusion by his widow. The Albert Memorial in Kensington Gardens was erected to his memory in 1871. >> Victoria

Albert I (1875–1934) King of the Belgians (1909–34), born in Brussels, the younger son of Philip, Count of Flanders. At the outbreak of World War 1 he refused a German demand for the free passage of their troops, and after a heroic resistance led the Belgian army in retreat to Flanders. He commanded the Belgian and French army in the final offensive on the Belgian coast in 1918. After the war he took an active part in the industrial reconstruction of the country. >> RR1035

Albert, Carl (Bert) (1908–) US politician, born in North McAlester, OK. He studied at the universities of Oklahoma and Oxford, then practised as a lawyer in Oklahoma. He became a Democratic member of the US House of Representatives (1947–77), and as majority leader (from 1962) created an alliance between Northern liberals and Southern 'boll weevils' to ensure the passage of President Johnson's Great Society legislation. In 1968, he presided over the disastrous Democratic convention, ruling against the delegates opposed to the war in Vietnam. Speaker of the House in 1971, he finally voted against the war in 1973. He retired in 1977. >> Johnson, Lyndon B

Albert, Eugen (Francis Charles) d' [albair] (1864–1932) Pianist and composer, born in Glasgow, W Scotland, UK. He composed several operas, notably, *Tiefland* (1903), a suite, a symphony, many songs, and much music for the piano.

Albert, Heinrich [albert] (1604–51) Composer, born in Lobenstein, Germany. After studying at Leipzig, he became organist in Königsberg (1631). He did much to develop *Lieder*, and composed many airs, songs, chorales, and hymn tunes.

Alberti, Domenico [albairtee] (c.1710–40) Composer, born in Venice, Italy. His music is almost entirely forgotten, but he is remembered as the inventor of the *Alberti bass*, common in 18th-c keyboard music, in which accompanying chords are split up into figurations based upon each chord's lowest note.

Alberti, Leon Battista [albairtee] (1404–72) Architect,

born in Genoa, Italy. Influenced by Vitruvius Pollio, he wrote *De re aedificatoria* (10 vols, 1485), which stimulated interest in antique Roman architecture. His own designs, which include the churches of S Francesco at Rimini and S Maria Novella at Florence, are among the best examples of the pure Classical style. One of the most brilliant figures of the Renaissance, he was also skilled as a musician, painter, poet, and philosopher. >> Rossellino, Bernardo; Vitruvius

Albertus Magnus, St, Graf von (Count of) **Bollstädt**, known as **Doctor Universalis** ('Universal Doctor') (c. 1200–80) Philosopher, bishop, and doctor of the Church, born in Lauingen, Germany. In 1254 he became provincial of the Dominicans in Germany, and in 1260 was named Bishop of Ratisbon. Of his works the most notable are the *Summa theologiae* and the *Summa de creaturis*. He excelled all his contemporaries in the breadth of his learning, and did more than anyone to bring about that union of theology and Aristotelianism which is the basis of scholasticism. He was canonized in 1931 and named a doctor of the Church by Pope Pius XI. Thomas Aquinas was his most famous pupil. Feast day 15 November. >> Aquinas; Aristotle

Albin, Eleazar (?–1759) English naturalist and watercolourist, who published the first book on British birds with coloured plates. His works include *The History of Insects* (1720), illustrated with his own metal engravings, and *A Natural History of British Birds* (3 vols, 1731–8).

Albinoni, Tomasso (Giovanni) [albinohnee] (1671–1751) Composer, born in Venice, Italy. He wrote 48 operas, and a number of concertos which have been revived in recent times. He was one of the first composers to write concertos for solo violin.

Albinus >> Alcuin

Alboin [alboyn] (?–574) King of the Lombards in Pannonia from 561. He fought against the Ostrogoths, and slew Kunimond, King of the Gepids in 566, marrying his daughter Rosamond. In 568 he invaded Italy, subdued it as far as the Tiber, and made his capital at Pavia.

Albrechtsberger, Johann Georg [albrekhtsberger] (1736–1809) Composer and writer on musical theory, born in Klosterneuburg, Austria. He became court organist at Vienna and chapel master of St Stephen's. Hummel and Beethoven were among his pupils. >> Beethoven; Hummel

Albright, Ivan (Le Lorraine) (1897–1983) Painter, born in North Harvey, IL. He turned to painting after World War 1, in which he served as a medical draughtsman in France. The clinical studies he made then of surgical operations laid the foundations of the meticulous technique he perfected later, as well as promoting an obsession with morbid subject matter. His style has been called 'Magic Realism', and had links with Surrealism, but he remained one of the most idiosyncratic of 20th-c painters.

Albright, Madeleine K(orbel) (1937–) US secretary of state (from 1997), born in Czechoslovakia. Formerly permanent US representative to the UN, in the second Clinton administration she became the first women to head the State Department.

Albright, W(illiam) F(oxwell) (1891–1971) Archaeologist and biblical scholar, born in Coquimbo, Chile, of US missionary parents. He taught at Johns Hopkins University (1929–58), and was also director of the American School of Oriental Research in Jerusalem (1921–9, 1933–6), excavating many notable sites in Palestine, including Gibeah.

Albumazar or **Abu-Mashar** [albumazah(r)] (787–885) Astronomer and astrologer, born in Balkh, Afghanistan. He spent much of his life in Baghdad, where he became the leading astrologer of his day, and his books were widely circulated.

Albuquerque, Affonso d' [albookerkay], known as **Affonso the Great** (1453–1515) Portuguese viceroy of the Indies, born near Lisbon. He landed on the Malabar coast in 1502, conquered Goa (1510), and established the basis of the Portuguese East Indies. He established a reputation for his wisdom and fairness, but was replaced peremptorily by the king in 1515.

Alcaeus [alseeus] (c.620–c.580 BC) One of the greatest Greek lyric poets. He lived at Mytilene on the island of Lesbos, and was a contemporary of Sappho. He was the first exponent of the so-called *Alcaic* four-lined stanza, which was named after him. Of the ten books of odes he is said to have composed, only fragments now remain. >> Sappho

Alcamenes [alkameneez] (5th-c BC) Greek sculptor, the pupil and rival of Phidias. A Roman copy of his 'Aphrodite' is in the Louvre. >> Phidias

Alciatus, Andrea Alciato [alchahtus] (1492–1550) Jurist, born in Milan, Italy. He was one of the leaders of legal humanism, and a correspondent of More and Erasmus. >> Erasmus; More, Thomas

Alcibiades [alsibiyadeez] (c.450–404 BC) Athenian statesman and general, a member of the aristocratic Alcmaeonid family. A ward of Pericles and a pupil of Socrates, he was a leader against Sparta in the Peloponnesian War, and a commander of the Sicilian expedition (415 BC). Recalled from there to stand trial for sacrilege, he fled to Sparta and gave advice which contributed substantially to Athens' defeat in Sicily (413 BC) and her economic discomfiture at home. Falling out with the Spartans in 412 BC, he began to direct Athenian operations in the E Aegean, and won several notable victories; but finding himself unjustly blamed for the Athenian defeat off Notium (406 BC), he went into voluntary exile, where he actively intrigued with the Persians until his assassination in 404 BC. >> Pericles; Socrates; Thrasybulus

Alcindor, Lew >> **Abdul-Jabbar, Kareem**

Alcmaeon [alkmeeon] (6th-c BC) Greek physician and philosopher from Croton, Italy. The first recorded anatomist, he was the true discoverer of the Eustachian tubes, and a pioneer of embryology through anatomical dissection.

Alcman (fl. 620 BC–) Greek lyric poet, probably born in Sardis, Lydia. The first to write erotic poetry, he composed in Doric dialect the *Parthenia* (songs sung by choruses of virgins), bridal hymns, and verses in praise of love and wine.

Alcock, Sir John William (1892–1919) Aviator, born in Manchester, Greater Manchester, NW England, UK. He served as a captain in the Royal Naval Air Service in World War 1, then became a test pilot with Vickers Aircraft. On 14 June 1919, with Arthur Whitten Brown as navigator, he piloted a Vickers-Vimy biplane non-stop from St John's, Newfoundland, to Clifden, Co Galway, Ireland, in a time of 16 h 27 min. Soon afterwards Alcock was killed in an aeroplane accident in France. >> Brown, Arthur

Alcott, (Amos) Bronson [awlkot] (1799–1888) Teacher and philosopher, born near Wolcott, CT, the father of Louisa May Alcott. A member of the New England Transcendentalists, he was highly regarded as an educationist, and in 1859 was appointed superintendent of schools in Concord, MA. >> Alcott, Louisa M

Alcott, Louisa M(ay) (1832–88) Writer, born in Germantown, PA, the daughter of Amos Bronson Alcott. In 1868 she achieved enormous success with the children's classic, *Little Women*, which drew on her own home experiences. A second volume, *Good Wives*, appeared in 1869, followed by *An Old-Fashioned Girl* (1870), *Little Men* (1871), and *Jo's Boys* (1886). >> Alcott, Bronson

Alcuin [alkwin], originally **Ealhwine**, Lat **Albinus** (c. 737–804) Scholar and adviser to the emperor Charlemagne, born in York, North Yorkshire, N England, UK. He studied at the cloister school, of which he became master in 778. In 781, he met Charlemagne at Parma, and joined the court at Aix-la-Chapelle (Aachen). Here he devoted himself first to the education of the royal family, but through his influence the court became a school of culture for the Frankish empire, inspiring the Carolingian Renaissance. His works comprise poems; works on grammar, rhetoric, and dialectics; theological and ethical treatises; lives of several saints; and over 200 letters. >> Charlemagne

Alda, Alan [awlda] (1936–) Actor and director, born in New York City. He made his Broadway debut in *Only in America* (1959), and his film debut in *Gone Are the Days* (1963), but it was his extensive involvement in the television series *M*A*S*H* (1972–83) that earned him his greatest popularity. He won numerous awards for the series (including five Emmies), which provided a showcase for his talents as a socially conscious writer, director, and performer. His acerbic sense of humour has been uppermost in such films as *The Four Seasons* (1981), *Sweet Liberty* (1985), and *A New Life* (1988). Later films include *Crimes and Misdemeanours* (1990), *Canadian Bacon* (1995), and *Everyone Says I Love You* (1997).

Alder, Kurt [alder] (1902–58) Organic chemist, born in Chorzow, Poland (formerly Konigshütte, Germany). With Otto Diels he discovered in 1928 the Diels–Alder diene reaction, valuable in organic synthesis, and they shared the Nobel Prize for Chemistry in 1950. >> Diels

Alderton, John (1940–) Actor, born in Gainsborough, Lincolnshire, EC England, UK. A member of the York Repertory Company, he made his debut in *Emergency Ward 10* (1961), and his West End debut in *Spring and Port Wine* at the Apollo Theatre. From 1969 he has appeared regularly on stage, and become popularly known on television with series such as *Please Sir, My Wife Next Door*, and *Forever Green* (with actress wife Pauline Collins). His films include *Please Sir* (1971), *It Shouldn't Happen to a Vet* (1976), and *Clockwork Mice* (1995).

Aldhelm, St [aldhelm], also spelled **Ealdhelm** (c. 640–709) Anglo-Saxon scholar and clergyman. He studied at Malmesbury and Canterbury, and became the first Abbot of Malmesbury about 675, and the first Bishop of Sherbourne in 705. A great scholar, he wrote Latin treatises, letters, and verses, as well as some English poems that have perished. Feast day 25 May.

Aldington, Richard [awldingtn], originally **Edward Godfree** (1892–1962) Writer, born in Hampshire, S England, UK. He studied at London University, and in 1913 became editor of *The Egoist*, the periodical of the Imagist school. His experiences in World War 1 led to his best-known novel, *Death of a Hero* (1929). He published several volumes of poetry, *Poetry of the English-Speaking World* (1941), and many critical works and biographies. *Wellington* (1946) was awarded the James Tait Black Memorial Prize. He married Hilda Doolittle in 1913 (divorced, 1937). >> Doolittle, Hilda

Aldiss, Brian (Wilson) [awldis] (1925–) Science-fiction writer and novelist, born in Dereham, Norfolk, E England, UK. He studied at Framlingham College, and his first novel, *The Brightfount Diaries*, appeared in 1955. He is best known as a writer of science fiction, such as *Hothouse* (1962) and *The Saliva Tree* (1966). There are two collections of short stories (1988, 1989), and he has produced histories of science fiction such as *Billion Year Spree* (1973) and *Trillion Year Spree* (1986). Among later works are a novel, *Dracula Unbound* (1991), and the poetry collections *At the Caligula Hotel* (1995) and *The Poems of Makhtumkuli* (1996).

Aldred or **Ealdred** [aldred], also found as **Alred** (?–1069) Anglo-Saxon clergyman. He became Abbot of Tavistock (1027), Bishop of Worcester (1044), and Archbishop of York

(1060), and was the first English bishop to visit Jerusalem. He crowned William I, and proved a faithful servant to the Norman king. >> William I (of England)

Aldrich, Nelson W(ilmarth) (1841–1915) US politician, born in Foster, RI. He was elected to Congress (1879–81), after which the Rhode Island legislature chose him for a seat in the US Senate (1881–1911). By the turn of the century he controlled the Senate for the Republicans on domestic issues, ruthlessly defending big business and a high protective tariff.

Aldrich, Thomas Bailey (1836–1907) Writer, born in Portsmouth, NH. He was the author of numerous short stories, novels, and books of poetry. His most successful book, *The Story of a Bad Boy* (1870), was an autobiographical novel about his boyhood.

Aldrin, Buzz [awldrin], popular name of **Edwin Eugene Aldrin** (1930–) Astronaut, born in Montclair, NJ. He trained at West Point, flew combat missions in Korea, and later flew in Germany with the 36th Tactical Wing. In 1966 he set a world record by walking in space for 5 h 37 min during the Gemini 12 mission. He was the second man to set foot on the Moon in the Apollo 11 mission in 1969. >> Armstrong, Neil; Collins, Michael

Aldrovandi, Ulisse [aldrovandee, ooleesay] (1522–1605) Naturalist, born in Bologna, Italy. He studied medicine at the University of Bologna (1553), occupied successively its chairs of botany and natural history, and established its botanical garden in 1567. He published many handsomely illustrated books on birds, fishes, and insects.

Aldus Manutius [aldus manootius], Latin name of **Aldo Manucci** or **Manuzio** (c.1450–1515) Scholar and printer, born in Bassiano, Italy. He was the founder of the Aldine Press, which produced the first printed editions of many Greek and Roman classics. He had beautiful founts of Greek and Latin type made, and was the first to use italics on a large scale. >> Campagnola, Giulio; Francia

Aleardi or Aleardo, conte di (Count of) [aleeah(r)dee] (1812–78) Italian patriot and poet, born in Verona, Italy (then in Austria). He took part in the rising against Austria in 1848, became a deputy in the Italian parliament (1866), and later a senator. He was popular in his time as a writer of patriotic lyrics.

Aleichem, Sholem [alaykhem], also spelled **Sholom** or **Shalom**, pseudonym of **Solomon J Rabinowitz** (1859–1916) Writer, born in Pereyaslev, Ukraine. After working as a rabbi, he devoted himself to writing and Yiddish culture. The pogroms of 1905 drove him to the USA, where he attempted to establish himself as a playwright for the Yiddish theatre in New York City. His short stories and plays portray Jewish life in Russia in the late 19th-c with vividness, humour, and sympathy, and were first widely introduced to a non-Jewish public in 1943 in Maurice Samuel's *The World of Sholom Aleichem*. The popular musical *Fiddler on the Roof* is based on the stories of Aleichem.

Aleixandre, Vicente [alayksahndray] (1898–1984) Poet, born in Seville, Spain. It was the appearance of his collected poems, *Mis poemas mejores* (1937), that established his reputation as a major poet. His later publications include *En un vasto dominio* (1962, In a Vast Domain) and *Antologia total* (1976). He was awarded the Nobel Prize for Literature in 1977.

Alekhine, Alexander Alexandrovich [alekeen] (1892–1946) Chess player, world champion (1927–35, 1937–46), born in Moscow. He became addicted to chess from the age of 11 and gained the title of master at St Petersburg in 1909. After the Russian Revolution, he worked as a magistrate in France, and became a French citizen. He defeated Capablanca in 1927 to win the world championship, and defended it successfully (apart from a

defeat by Euwe in 1935) for nearly 20 years. >> Capablanca; Euwe; RR1149

Alemán, Mateo [aleman] (1547–c. 1614) Novelist, born in Seville, Spain. His great work is a picaresque novel, *Guzmán de Alfarache* (1599, trans The Spanish Rogue), about a boy running away from home. He emigrated to Mexico in 1608.

Alembert, Jean le Rond d' [alābair] (1717–83) Philospher and mathematician, born in Paris. Brought up as a foundling, he was given an annuity from his father and studied law, medicine, and mathematics at the Collège Mazarin. In 1743 he published *Traité de dynamique*, developing the mathematical theory of Newtonian dynamics, including the principle later named after him. Until 1758 he was Denis Diderot's principal collaborator on the *Encyclopédie*, of which he was the scientific editor, and wrote the *Discours préliminaire*, proclaiming the philosophy of the French Enlightenment. >> Diderot

Alessi, Galeazzo [alesee] (1512–72) Architect, born in Perugia, Italy. After studying ancient architecture, he gained a reputation within Europe from his designs for palaces and churches in Genoa and elsewhere. He was a friend of Michelangelo. >> Michelangelo

Alexander I (of Russia) (1777–1825) Tsar of Russia (1801–25), born in St Petersburg, Russia, the grandson of Catherine the Great. The early years of his reign were marked by the promise of liberal constitutional reforms and the pursuit of a vigorous foreign policy. In 1805 Russia joined the coalition against Napoleon, but after a series of military defeats was forced to conclude the Treaty of Tilsit (1807) with France. When Napoleon broke the treaty by invading Russia in 1812, Alexander pursued the French back to Paris. At the Congress of Vienna (1814–15) he laid claim to Poland. During the last years of his reign his increased political reactionism and religious mysticism resulted in the founding of the Holy Alliance. His mysterious death at Taganrog caused a succession crisis which led to the attempted revolutionary coup of the Decembrists. >> Catherine the Great; Napoleon; RR1085

Alexander I (of Scotland) (c. 1077–1124) King of Scots, the fifth son of Malcolm Canmore and Queen Margaret. In 1107 he succeeded his brother, Edgar, but only to that part of the kingdom N of the Forth. He married Sibilla, a natural daughter of Henry I of England. >> Henry I; Margaret (of Scotland) St; RR1095

Alexander I (of Yugoslavia) (1888–1934) King of the Serbs, Croats, and Slovenes (1921–9), then King of Yugoslavia (1929–34), born in Cetinje, Yugoslavia, the second son of Peter I. He tried to build up a strong and unified Yugoslavia, imposing a royal dictatorship in 1929, but was assassinated in Marseilles. >> Peter I (of Serbia); RR1100

Alexander II (of Russia), known as **Alexander the Liberator** (1818–81) Tsar of Russia from 1855, born in St Petersburg, Russia, the son of Nicholas I. He succeeded to the throne during the Crimean War, and signed the Treaty of Paris which ended it in 1856. A determined reformer, the great achievement of his reign was the emancipation of the serfs in 1861 (hence his byname), followed by reform of the legal and administrative systems, and the establishment of elected assemblies in the provinces. Despite his liberal views, his government was severe in repressing peasant unrest and revolutionary movements, and he was assassinated. >> Nicholas I (of Russia); RR1085

Alexander II (of Scotland) (1198–1249) King of Scots, born in Haddington, East Lothian, E Scotland, UK, who succeeded his father, William I, in 1214. He allied with the disaffected English barons and made an incursion as far S as Dover. The accession of Henry III of England allowed a rapprochement, cemented by his marriage in 1221 to Henry's sister, Joan, and the frontier question was settled by the Treaty of York (1237). Her death without children in 1238, and Alexander's marriage to the daughter of a Picardy nobleman, Marie de Coucy, then strained relations with England. His reign is notable for the vigorous assertion of royal authority in the W Highlands and the SW during the years of peace with England. >> RR1095

Alexander III (of Russia) (1845–94) Tsar of Russia (1881–94), born in St Petersburg, Russia, the younger son of Alexander II. He followed a repressive policy in home affairs, especially in the persecution of Jews. Abroad, he consolidated Russia's hold on C Asia to the frontier of Afghanistan, provoking a crisis with Britain (1885). >> Alexander II (of Russia); Nicholas II; RR1085

Alexander III (of Scotland) (1241–86) King of Scots (1249–86), the son of Alexander II. In 1251 he married **Margaret** (1240–75), the eldest daughter of Henry III of England. He completed the consolidation of the W part of the kingdom by annexing the Hebrides and the Isle of Man, after defeating Haakon IV of Norway at Largs in 1263. The period between 1266 and the death of Queen Margaret in 1275 has often been seen as a golden age for Scotland. >> Alexander II (of Scotland); RR1095

Alexander III, originally **Orlando Bandinelli** (c.1105–81) Pope (1159–81), born in Siena, Italy. He was engaged in a struggle with Emperor Frederick I Barbarossa, who refused to recognize him, and set up antipopes until compelled to sign the Treaty of Venice (1177). He was also involved in the quarrel between Henry II of England and Thomas à Becket. >> Becket; Frederick I; Henry II (of England)

Alexander VI, originally **Rodrigo Borgia** (1431–1503) Pope (1492–1503), born in Játiva, Spain, the father of Cesare and Lucretia Borgia. In 1455 he was made a cardinal by his uncle, Calixtus III, and on the death of Innocent VIII was elevated to the papal chair, which he had previously secured by bribery. He endeavoured to break the power of the Italian princes, and to appropriate their possessions for the benefit of his own family, employing the most execrable means to gain this end. During his pontificate, he apportioned the New World between Spain and Portugal, and introduced the censorship of books. >> Borgia, Cesare; Borgia, Lucretia; Savonarola

Alexander, Bill, popular name of **William Alexander** (1948–) Stage director, born in Hunstanton, Norfolk, E England, UK. He worked at the Bristol Old Vic (1971–3), and the Royal Court Theatre, London (1972–8), before joining the Royal Shakespeare Company in 1977, where he became associate director (1984–91), and honorary associate director (1991–). In 1993 he joined the Birmingham Repertory Theatre as artistic director.

Alexander, Cecil Frances, née **Humphreys** (1818–95) Poet and hymn writer, born in Co Wicklow, Ireland. In 1848 she published her immensely popular *Hymns for Little Children*, which included the well-known 'All Things Bright and Beautiful', 'Once in Royal David's City', and 'There is a green hill far away'.

Alexander, Franz (Gabriel) (1891–1964) Psychoanalyst, born in Budapest. He worked at the Institute for Psychoanalysis in Berlin, then settled permanently in the USA in 1932, where he founded the Chicago Institute for Psychoanalysis. His work on psychosomatic disorders was especially influential.

Alexander, Grover (Cleveland) (1887–1950) Baseball player, born in Elba, NE. A right-handed pitcher, he played for the Philadelphia Phillies (1911–17), Chicago Cubs (1918–26), and St Louis Cardinals (1926–9), sharing (with Christy Mathewson) a record of 373 wins. >> Mathewson

Alexander, Jean (1925–) Actress, born in Liverpool, Merseyside, NW England, UK. After several years with repertory companies, she began to appear on television, and eventually joined the cast of the long-running *Coronation Street* (1964–87). Her character of the dowdy, tactless gossip, Hilda Ogden, made her a national institution and won her the Royal Television Society's Best Performance Award in 1984. Her autobiography, *The Other Side of the Street*, was published in 1989.

Alexander, Samuel (1859–1938) Philosopher, born in Sydney, New South Wales, Australia. He studied at Oxford, and in 1893 was appointed to the chair of philosophy at Manchester University. His growing concern for the situation of European Jewry led him to introduce Chaim Weizmann, his colleague at Manchester, to Arthur James Balfour – a meeting which led to the Balfour Declaration, establishing the principle of a Jewish national home. >> Balfour, Arthur; Weizmann

Alexander of Battenberg >> **Battenberg, Alexander of**

Alexander of Hales, known as **Doctor Irrefragabilis** ('Irrefutable Doctor') (c.1170–1245) English theologian and philosopher, born in Hales, Gloucestershire, SWC England, UK. He became a professor of philosophy and theology in Paris, and later entered the Franciscan order. He is known chiefly from the major work ascribed to him, the *Summa theologica*.

Alexander (of Tunis), Sir Harold (Rupert Leofric George) Alexander, 1st Earl (1891–1969) British soldier, born in London, England, UK. He trained at Sandhurst, and in World War 1 commanded a battalion of the Irish Guards on the Western Front. He commanded 1 Corps as rearguard at the Dunkirk evacuation (1940), and was the last man to leave France. In 1942 he commanded in Burma, then became commander-in-chief Middle East (1942–3), his North African campaign being one of the most complete victories in military history. He commanded the invasions of Sicily and Italy (1943), and became supreme allied commander in the Mediterranean. He was later Governor-General of Canada (1946–52) and minister of defence (1952–4) in the Conservative government.

Alexander of Tralles [tra**leez**] (6th-c) Greek physician, born in Tralles. He practised in Rome, where he wrote his *Twelve Books on Medicine*, a major work on pathology which was current for several centuries in Latin, Greek, and Arabic.

Alexander the Great (356–323 BC) see panel on p. 20

Alexander Nevski, St, also spelled **Nevsky** (c.1218–63) Russian hero and saint, prince of Novgorod. In 1240 he defeated the Swedes in a famous battle on the R Neva, near the site of modern Leningrad, and in 1242 he defeated the Teutonic knights on the frozen L Peipus. Although a vassal of the Mongol occupation army, he sought to live with them in peace, and suppressed anti-Mongol revolts. He was canonized by the Russian Orthodox Church in 1547. Feast day 30 August or 23 November.

Alexander Severus [se**verus**] (205–35) Roman emperor (221–35), the cousin and adopted son of Heliogabalus, whom he succeeded. A weak ruler, under the influence of others (especially his mother), he failed to control the military. Though successful against the Sassanid Ardashir I, he was murdered by mutinous troops during a campaign against the Germans. >> Ardashir I; Heliogabalus; RR1084

Alexanderson, Ernst F(rederick) W(erner) (1878–1975) Electrical engineer and inventor, born in Uppsala, Sweden. In 1901 he moved to the USA, and joined the General Electric Company in 1902. He invented the *Alexanderson alternator* for transoceanic communication, antenna structures, and systems for radio reception and transmission. By

ALEXANDER THE GREAT (356–323 BC)

Alexander III, king of the ancient dynasty of Macedonia, was born in Pella. He was the son of Philip II of Macedon, and of Olympias, the daughter of King Neoptolemus of Epirus. From age 13–16, he was tutored by the great philosopher, Aristotle. When Alexander was 16, Philip was planning a crusade to punish the Persians for the invasion of Greece (some 150 years before), and while he marched against Byzantium (340 BC) Alexander acted as regent. At the age of 18, Alexander commanded the left wing of the Macedonian army at the battle of Chaeronea (338 BC). Philip was assassinated two years later, possibly with his son's complicity, and Alexander, having disposed of his rivals, inherited the task of conquering Persia.

He first had to win control of the Greek cities in W Turkey. He crushed the rebellious Illyrians, razed Thebes to the ground (335 BC), crossed the Hellespont (334 BC), and the same year won a major victory over the Persians at Granicus, opening the way to the Greek cities of Asia Minor. Near Issus in Cilica he defeated Darius III, King of Persia (333 BC), occupied Damascus, and after a long, hard siege destroyed Tyre (332 BC). He then marched on to Palestine, liberated Egypt from the Persians, and founded the city of Alexandria (331 BC). Such was his status by this time that, on an expedition through the desert to consult the oracle of Zeus Amon at Siwah, he was hailed as 'son of Amon' – a greeting reserved for a pharaoh. This and other, later incidents contributed to his growing deification as the son of Zeus.

Alexander set out again to meet Darius, and defeated him near Arbela (Gaugamela) in 331 BC. Darius fled, and was eventually murdered. Alexander entered Persepolis, the capital of Persia, in triumph. He then continued to consolidate his empire, dealing with conflicts between Macedonians and Persians, and founding more cities. In 329 BC he overthrew the Scythians, and during 328–327 BC attacked Spitamenes at Sogdiana, where resistance was fierce. Oxyartes' stronghold finally fell to Alexander, and he married his beautiful captive, Princess Roxana (328 BC), who was Oxyartes' daughter.

Meanwhile, Alexander's relations with his followers had become increasingly violent. He murdered many of his colleagues and friends, often for political reasons, sometimes through drunken brawls.

In 327 BC, he made a start on his conquest of India, and at the R Hydaspes (Jhelum) overthrew the ruler Porus in a costly battle. Only a mutiny of his exhausted army at the R Hyphasis (Beas) forced him to abandon plans to go further E, and he began the return march in 326 BC. Two years later, at Babylon, he was taken ill after a long and drunken banquet, and died aged 32. His body was eventually buried in a golden coffin at Alexandria.

The legends that sprang up around Alexander during his lifetime and after his death preclude historians from agreeing on whether he was a far-sighted statesman or a ruthless conqueror. Nevertheless, his conquests were instrumental in spreading the language and culture of the Greeks across the continent to the East.
>> Aristotle; Philip II (of Macedon)

1930 he had perfected a complete television system, and by 1955 a colour television receiver.

Alexandra, Queen (1844–1925) Consort of King Edward VII of Great Britain, the eldest daughter of King Christian IX of Denmark (reigned 1863–1906). She married Edward in 1863 when he was Prince of Wales, and became known for her charity work; in 1902 she founded the Imperial (now Royal) Military Nursing Service, and in 1912 instituted the annual Alexandra Rose Day in aid of hospitals. >> Edward VII; RR1095

Alexandra, Princess, the Hon Lady Ogilvy (1936–) Daughter of George, Duke of Kent, and Princess Marina of Greece. In 1963 she married **Sir Angus James Bruce Ogilvy** (1928–). They have a son, **James Robert Bruce** (1964–) and a daughter, **Marina Victoria Alexandra** (1966–). James married Julia Rawlinson and they have a son, **Alexander Charles** (1996–) and a daughter **Flora Alexandra** (1994–). Marina married Paul Mowatt and they have a daughter, **Zenouska May Mowatt** (1990–), and a son, **Christian Alexander Mowatt** (1993–). >> Kent, George, Duke of

Alexandra Feodorovna [fyodorovna] (1872–1918) German princess, and Empress of Russia as the wife of Nicholas II, born in Darmstadt, Germany, the daughter of Grand Duke Louis of Hesse-Darmstadt and Alice Maud Mary (the daughter of Queen Victoria). She married Nicholas in 1894. Deeply pious and superstitious, she came under the influence of the fanatical Rasputin. During World War 1, while Nicholas was away at the front, she meddled disastrously in politics. When the revolution broke out, she was imprisoned by the Bolsheviks, and shot in a cellar at Yekaterinburg. >> Nicholas II; Rasputin; RR1085

Alexandrov, Pavel Sergeyevich [aleksahndrof] (1896–1982) Mathematician, born in Bogorodsk, Russia.

The leader of the Soviet school of topologists, he developed many of the methods of combinatorial topology. >> Hopf

Alexey I Mihailovitch [aleksay, mihiylovich] (1629–76) Second Romanov tsar of Russia (1645–76), who succeeded his father, Michael Romanov. He waged war against Poland (1654–67), regaining Smolensk and Kiev. His attempts to place the Orthodox Church under secular authority brought him into conflict with the Patriarch, Nikon. By his second wife he was the father of Peter I. >> Peter I (of Russia); Sophia Alexeyevna; RR1085

Alexeyev, Mikhail Vasilevich [aleksayef] (1857–1918) Russian soldier. In World War 1 he was appointed Chief of the Imperial General Staff (1915), and directed the retreat from Warsaw after the crushing German victory. After the Revolution in 1917 he organized the volunteer army against the Bolsheviks.

Alexeyev, Vasiliy [aleksayef] (1942–) Weightlifter, born in Pokrovo-Shishkino, Russia. He set 80 world records (1970–7), more than any other athlete in any sport. Olympic super-heavyweight champion in 1972 and 1976, he won eight world titles and nine European titles. He was made a major in the Russian army, and obtained the title of Master of Sport.

Alexis [aleksis], in full **Alexey Petrovitch** (1690–1718) Prince, born in Moscow, the eldest son of Peter I. Having opposed the tsar's reforms, he was excluded from the succession, and escaped to Vienna, and thence to Naples. Induced to return to Russia, he was condemned to death, then pardoned, but died in prison a few days after. His son became tsar as Peter II (reigned 1727–30). >> Peter I (of Russia)

Alexius I Comnenus [komneenus] (1048–1118) Byzantine emperor (1081–1118), the founder of the Comnenian dynasty, born in Istanbul. He defeated a major invasion mounted by the Normans of Sicily under Robert Guiscard (1081–2) and later under Bohemond I (1083); in alliance with the Cumans he destroyed the Patzinaks at Mount Levounion (1091). He built up a new fleet with the aim of re-establishing Byzantine rule in Asia Minor. This coincided with the arrival of the First Crusade (1096–1100), with which he co-operated to recover Crete, Cyprus, and the W coast of Anatolia. His reign is well known from the *Alexiad*, the biography written by his daughter, Anna Comnena. >> Anna Comnena; Bohemond I; Guiscard; RR1037

al-Farabi, Mohammed [al fa**rah**bee], also known as **Abu Nasr**, **Alfarabius**, and **Avennasar** (c.870–950) Islamic philosopher, born in Farab, Turkmenia. He was much influenced by Plato's *Republic*, and can be regarded as the first Islamic Neoplatonist. He also published a utopian political philosophy of his own, known under the title *The Perfect City*. >> Plato

Al Fayed, Mohamed (1933–) Businessman, born in Egypt. He studied at Alexandria University, and made rapid progress in the international business world, becoming owner of the Ritz Hotel in Paris in 1979, and of Harrods in London in 1985, and one of the world's wealthiest men. One of his children, **Dodi** (1955–97), received worldwide publicity in 1997 when the press discovered his relationship with Princess Diana. A graduate of Sandhurst Military Academy, he became a film producer, renowned for his flamboyant lifestyle. He was killed along with Diana in a car accident in Paris while trying to escape the attentions of paparazzi. >> Diana, Princess of Wales

Alfieri, Vittorio, conte di (Count) [al**fyay**ree] (1749–1803) Poet and playwright, a precursor of the Risorgimento, born in Asti, Italy. He travelled throughout Europe, then turned his hand to writing, achieving great success with his first play *Cleopatra*, in 1775. In Florence (1777) he met the Countess of Albany, the estranged wife of Prince Charles Stuart; after separating from her husband, she became his mistress. He wrote more than a score of tragedies, notably *Saul*, and several other works. >> Albany, Countess of

Alfonsín (Foulkes), Raul [alfon**seen**] (1927–) Argentinian president (1983–9), born in Chascomús, Argentina. He studied at military and law schools, joining the Radical Union Party in 1945. He served in local government (1951–62), but was imprisoned by the Perón government for his political activities in 1953. When constitutional government returned, he was elected president. He ensured that several leading military figures were brought to trial for human rights abuses, and in 1986 was co-recipient of the Council of Europe's human rights prize. >> Perón, Juan

Alfonso I or **Alfonso Henriques**, also spelled **Afonso** (c. 1110–85) Earliest king of Portugal, born in Guimarães, Portugal. He was only two years old at the death of his father, Henry of Burgundy, the conqueror and first Count of Portugal, so that the management of affairs fell to his mother, Theresa of Castile. Wresting power from her in 1128, he defeated the Moors at Ourique (1139), and proclaimed himself king. He took Lisbon (1147), and later all Galicia, Estremadura, and Elvas. >> RR1082

Alfonso III, known as **Alfonso the Great** (?–910) King of León, Asturias, and Galicia (866–910). He fought over 30 campaigns and gained numerous victories over the Moors, occupied Coimbra, and extended his territory as far as Portugal and Old Castile. >> RR1088

Alfonso X, nicknames **Alfonso the Astronomer** or **Alfonso the Wise** (1221–84) King of León and Castile (1252–84), born in Burgos, Spain. He captured Cadiz and Algarve from the Moors, and thus united Murcia with Castile. The founder of a Castilian national literature, he caused the first general history of Spain to be composed in Castilian, as well as a translation of the Old Testament to be made by Toledo Jews. His great code of laws (*Siete Partidas*) and his planetary table were of major importance. In 1282, he lost power following a rising under his son, Sancho IV. >> RR1088

Alfonso XII (1857–85) King of Spain (1874–85), the son of Isabella II. After a period of republican rule following the overthrow of his mother by the army in 1868, he was formally proclaimed king. In 1876 he suppressed the last opposition of the Carlists (supporters of the Spanish pretender Don Carlos de Bourbon and his successors), and drafted a new constitution. In 1879 he married **Maria Christina** (1858–1929), daughter of Archduke Charles Ferdinand of Austria, and was succeeded by his son, Alfonso XIII. >> Alfonso XIII; Carlos, Don; RR1088

Alfonso XIII (1886–1941) King of Spain (1886–1931), the posthumous son of Alfonso XII. In 1906 he married princess Ena, grand-daughter of Queen Victoria. After neutrality during World War 1, the Spanish were defeated by the Moors in Morocco in 1921, and from 1923 he associated himself with the military dictatorship of Primo de Rivera. In 1931 the king agreed to elections, which voted overwhelmingly for a republic. He refused to abdicate, but left Spain, and died in exile. >> Primo de Rivera; RR1088

Alfred, known as **Alfred the Great** (849–99) King of Wessex (871–99), born in Wantage, Berkshire, S England, UK, the fifth son of King Ethelwulf. When he came to the throne, the Danes had already conquered much of Northumbria, parts of Mercia, and East Anglia, and threatened to subdue Wessex itself. He inflicted on them their first major reverse at the Battle of Edington, Wiltshire (878), and began to win back Danish-occupied territory by capturing the former Mercian town of London (886). He stole the military initiative from the Danes by reorganizing his forces into a standing army, building a navy, and establishing a network of burhs (fortified centres). These developments were complemented by his revival of religion and learning, a programme designed to win God's support for victory over the pagan Danes and to consolidate loyalty to himself as a Christian king. He personally translated several edifying Latin works into English. He forged close ties with other English peoples not under Danish rule, and provided his successors with the means to reconquer the Danelaw and secure the unity of England. The famous story of his being scolded by a peasant woman for letting her cakes burn has no contemporary authority, and is first recorded in the 11th-c. >> Orosius; RR1095

Alfvén, Hannes (Olof Gösta) [al**fen**] (1908–95) Theoretical physicist, born in Norrköping, Sweden. He studied at Uppsala, and joined the Royal Institute of Technology, Stockholm, in 1940, moving to the University of California in 1967. He did pioneering work on plasmas and their behaviour in magnetic and electric fields. In 1942 he predicted the existence of waves in plasmas (*Alfvén waves*), which were later observed. He shared the Nobel Prize for Physics in 1970. >> RR1122

Alfvén, Hugo Emil [al**fen**] (1872–1960) Composer and violinist, born in Stockholm. He was a prolific composer in the late Romantic tradition, his works including five symphonies and the ballet *Prodigal Son* (1957). His best-known piece is *Midsommarvaka* (1904, Midsummer Vigil), better known as the *Swedish Rhapsody*.

Algardi, Alessandro [al**gah(r)**dee] (1598–1654) Sculptor, born in Bologna, Italy. His chief work is a colossal relief, in St Peter's, Rome, showing Pope Leo I restraining Attila from marching on the city.

Alger, Horatio [al**jer**] (1832–99) Writer and clergyman, born in Revere, MA. He studied at Harvard, became a Unitarian minister, and wrote highly successful boys' adventure stories on poor-boy-makes-good themes, such as *Ragged Dick* (1867) and *From Canal Boy to President* (1881).

Algren, Nelson (1909–81) Novelist, born in Detroit, MI. He was a leading member of the Chicago School of Realism, producing a series of uncompromising, powerful novels. These include *Somebody in Boots* (1935) and *The Man with the Golden Arm* (1949), a novel about drug addiction, regarded by some as his best work.

Alhazen [alhazen], Arabic **Abu al-Hassan ibn al Haytham** (c. 965–1039) Mathematician and physicist, born in Basra, Iraq. He wrote a work on optics (known in Europe in Latin translation from the 13th-c) giving the first account of atmospheric refraction, reflection from curved surfaces, and the nature of vision.

Ali (?–661) Fourth caliph (656–61), the cousin and son-in-law of Mohammed. He converted to Islam when still a boy, and married the prophet's daughter, Fatima. He withdrew, or was excluded from government during the caliphates of Abu-Bakr and Omar, and disagreed with Uthman in the interpretation of the Koran. Opposition to his caliphate, led by Muawiyah, began a major division within Islam between Sunni and Shiah Muslims. He was murdered in the mosque at Kufa. He is held by Shiah Muslims to be the only true successor to the prophet. >> Abu-Bakr; Fatima; Mohammed; Muawiyah; Omar; Uthman

Ali, (Chaudri) Mohamad (1905–80) Pakistani statesman and prime minister (1955–6), born in Jullundur, India. He studied at Punjab University, and in 1945 was the first Indian to be appointed financial adviser of war and supply. In 1947, on the partition of India, he became the first secretary-general of the Pakistan government, in 1951 finance minister, and in 1955 prime minister. He resigned in 1956 because of lack of support from members of his own party, the Muslim League.

Ali, Muhammad, originally **Cassius (Marcellus) Clay, Jr** (1942–) Boxer, born in Louisville, KY. He was an amateur boxer (1954–60), who then became the Olympic light-heavyweight champion. He won the world heavyweight title in 1964, defeating Sonny Liston when he retired at the end of the sixth round. At that time he joined the Black Muslims and adopted the name Muhammad Ali. In 1967, he refused to be drafted into the army on religious grounds, and was stripped of his title and barred from the ring. He took his case to the Supreme Court and had his boxing licence restored in 1970. In 1971 he was beaten by Joe Frazier, but beat him in 1974, and went on to meet George Foreman later that year, knocking him out in eight rounds to regain his title. He was beaten by Leon Spinks (1953–) in a split decision (Feb 1978), but regained the title the same year – the first man to win the world heavyweight title three times. His flamboyant style has made him a legend, and his slogan 'I am the greatest' became a catch phrase. Ali was President Carter's special envoy to Africa in 1980 (attempting to persuade nations to boycott the Olympics). He has starred in two films, *The Greatest* (1976) and *Freedom Road* (1978), and an Oscar-winning documentary film, *When We Were Kings*, recounting the 1974 Ali v. Foreman fight, appeared in 1996. Ali retired in 1981. >> RR1148

Alia, Ramiz [alia] (1925–) Albanian statesman and president (1985–92), born in Shkoder, Albania. A former president of the youth wing of the ruling Communist Party of Labour of Albania (APL), he was inducted into the Party's central committee in 1954 and made minister of education (1955) and head of agitprop (1958). He entered the APL's secretariat (1960) and Politburo (1961), and on the death of Hoxha (1985) took over as APL leader. Although returned to power in the country's first multi-party elections in 1991, he was defeated in 1992. >> Hoxha; RR1031

Ali Bey [alee bay] (1728–73) Egyptian ruler, a slave from the Caucasus who distinguished himself in the service of Ibrahim Katkhuda and rose to be chief of the Mamluks.

Victorious in the power-struggle that followed the death of Ibrahim in 1754, he had himself declared sultan (1768) and proceeded to establish in Egypt an adminstration independent of Ottoman overlordship. Defeated by Ottoman forces in 1772, he was forced to take refuge in Syria. Under him Egypt briefly achieved independence for the first time in more than 200 years. >> RR1046

Alice Maud Mary, Princess (1843–78) British princess, the second daughter of Queen Victoria. In 1862 she married **Prince Louis of Hesse-Darmstadt** (1837–92). They had four daughters: the eldest became the mother of Louis, Earl Mountbatten; the youngest, Alexandra, married Nicholas II of Russia. >> Alexandra Feodorovna; Mountbatten (of Burma)

Ali Pasha, known as **the Lion of Janina** (1741–1822) Turkish leader. An Albanian brigand and assassin, he became Pasha of Trikala in 1787 and Janina (in Greece) in 1788, and in 1803 became Governor of Rumili. At Janina he maintained a barbarous but cultured court often visited by European travellers, among them Lord Byron. He intrigued with France and Britain, but was deposed in 1820 and put to death. >> RR1093

al-Khwarizmi, (Abu Ja'far Muhammad ibn Musa) [alchwarizmee] (c. 800–c. 850) Arab scholar, who wrote in Baghdad on astronomy, geography, and mathematics. His writings in Latin translation were so influential in mediaeval Europe that the methods of arithmetic based on the Hindu (or so-called Arabic) system of numeration became known in mediaeval Latin, by corruption of his name, as *algorismus*, from which comes the English *algorithm*. The word *algebra* is derived from the word *al-jabr* in the title of his book on the subject.

al-Kindi [alkindee] (c. 800–c. 870) Arab philosopher, born in Kufa, Iraq. Known as 'the philosopher of the Arabs', he was one of the first responsible for spreading Greek thought (particularly that of Aristotle) in the Arab world and synthesizing it with Islamic doctrine. >> Aristotle

Allais, Maurice [alay] (1911–) Economist and engineer, born in Paris. He was professor of economic theory at the Institute of Statistics in Paris (1947–68), and since 1954 has been director of the Centre for Economic Analysis. His primary contributions have been in the reformulation of the theories of general economic equilibrium and maximum efficiency, and in the development of new concepts relating to capital and consumer choice. He received the Nobel Prize for Economics in 1988.

Allan, David (1744–96) Genre and portrait painter, known as the 'Scottish Hogarth', born in Alloa, Clackmannanshire, C Scotland, UK. He studied in Glasgow and in Rome, went to London (1777–80) to paint portraits, and became director of the Edinburgh Academy of Arts in 1786. He illustrated Allan Ramsay's *Gentle Shepherd* and some of Robert Burns' poems. >> Hogarth

Allan, Sir Hugh (1810–82) Shipowner, born in Saltcoats, North Ayrshire, W Scotland, UK. He settled in 1826 in Canada, where his company of shipbuilders prospered, and founded the Allan Line of steamers. His financial support of the 1872 Conservative Party election campaign led to a scandal which brought down the government.

Allan, Sir William (1782–1850) Historical painter, born in Edinburgh, EC Scotland, UK. In 1805 he went to St Petersburg, then spent several years in Russia and Turkey, painting scenes of Russian life. In 1841 he was appointed Queen's Limner (painter) in Scotland. His Scottish historical paintings include scenes from the novels of Sir Walter Scott.

Allbutt, Sir Thomas (Clifford) (1836–1925) Physician, born in Dewsbury, West Yorkshire, N England, UK. He studied at Cambridge, London, and Paris universities, practised medicine at Leeds, and became professor of medicine at

Cambridge in 1892. In 1867 he introduced the short clinical thermometer. He wrote many medical works, especially on the heart and on the history of medicine.

Allcock, Tony, popular name of **Anthony Allcock** (1955–   ) British bowls player. His achievements include world outdoor champion (1980, 1984, 1988), world outdoor singles champion (1992, 1996), world indoor singles champion (1986–7), and world indoor pairs champion with David Bryant (1986–7, 1989–92). His books include *Improve Your Bowls* (1988) and *Bowl to Win* (1994).

Allen, Bryan >> **MacCready, Paul**

Allen, Edgar >> **Doisy, Edward**

Allen, Ethan (1738–89) American soldier, born in Litchfield, CT. He spent his career trying to achieve independence for the Green Mountain area that is now the state of Vermont, commanding (1770–5) an irregular force called the Green Mountain Boys. At the outbreak of the War of Independence (1775–83) he helped take Fort Ticanderoga, in the first colonial victory of the war. On an expedition to Canada he was captured by the British at Montreal and held prisoner (1775–8). He continued the campaign for Vermont's statehood, which was not achieved until just after his death.

Allen, Florence (Ellinwood) (1884–1966) Judge and feminist, born in Salt Lake City, UT. She graduated from New York University Law School in 1913, and was admitted to the Ohio bar in 1914. Working assiduously for women's rights, she became the first woman to sit on a general federal bench and on a court of last resort. She retired in 1959, and in 1965 published the autobiographical *To Do Justly*.

Allen, George (1832–1907) Publisher and engraver, born in Newark, Nottinghamshire, C England, UK. A pupil of Ruskin, whose publisher he subsequently became, he started a business in Bell Yard, Fleet Street, which ultimately merged with others and became the house of Allen and Unwin. >> Ruskin

Allen, Sir George Oswald Browning, known as **Gubby Allen** (1902–89) Cricketer, born in Sydney, New South Wales, Australia. He studied at Cambridge, played for England in 25 Tests, and was captain in the Tests against India in 1936. He is the only player to have taken all ten wickets in an innings at Lord's (10–49 against Lancashire, 1929), and with L E G Ames (1905–90) he holds the all-time Test eighth-wicket record with a partnership of 246 against New Zealand in 1931.

Allen, Sir Harry Brookes (1854–1926) Pathologist, born in Geelong, Victoria, Australia. He studied at Melbourne University, and became its Foundation professor of pathology (1906–24). On a visit to the UK in 1890 he persuaded the General Medical Council in London to recognize medical degrees conferred by Melbourne, pioneering the eventual wider recognition of colonial academic qualifications.

Allen, James Van >> **Van Allen, James**

Allen, Paula Gunn (1939–   ) Poet and novelist, born in Cubero, NM. Of mixed Laguna Pueblo, Sioux, and Chicano parentage, she has been associated with the Native American Studies programme at the University of California, Berkeley. She has written several volumes of poetry and novels, all exploring a bicultural world.

Allen, Ralph, known as **the Man of Bath** (?1694–1764) English philanthropist. A deputy postmaster at Bath, SW England, he made a fortune by improving postal routes in England. He built the mansion of Prior Park, near Bath.

Allen, Red, originally **Henry Allen, Jr** (1908–67) Jazz trumpeter and singer, born in Algiers, LA. As a boy, he marched alongside his father's famous New Orleans Brass Band. In Chicago in 1927, he joined King Oliver's band and travelled with it to New York, where he made his first recordings. He played the Mississippi steamboats (1928–9), then joined Fletcher Henderson's orchestra (1932–4). He recorded prolifically, but when he joined Armstrong's orchestra (1937–40) he was kept in the background. When he finally made it to Europe in 1959, he was lionized, and for the rest of his days he happily played Dixieland either in the raucous band at the Metropole in New York or on European tours. >> Armstrong, Louis; Henderson, Fletcher; Oliver, King

Allen, Steve, originally **Stephen Valentine Patrick William Allen** (1921–   ) Entertainer, born in New York City. Born into a show business family, his early life was spent travelling with their vaudeville act. He later worked in Hollywood for the Columbia Broadcasting System (CBS), and successfully pioneered the first late-evening talk show, *The Tonight Show* (1953). A diversely talented man, he composed many hit songs including 'This Could Be the Start of Something Big' and 'Impossible'.

Allen, Walter (Ernest) (1911–95) Novelist and critic, born in Birmingham, West Midlands, C England, UK. He studied at Birmingham University, then held several university posts in Britain and the USA. His first novel, *Innocence is Drowned*, was published in 1938, and he scored a considerable success with *Dead Man Over All*, in 1950. He wrote several critical works, including *The English Novel: A Short Critical History* (1954).

Allen, William (1532–94) Clergyman, born in Rossall, Lancashire, NW England, UK. He became principal of St Mary's Hall, Oxford, but after the accession of Queen Elizabeth in 1558 he went into exile in Flanders (1561) rather than take the Oath of Supremacy. In 1568 he founded the English college at Douai to train missionary priests for the reconversion of England to Catholicism, and supervised the Reims–Douai translation of the Bible. In 1587 he was created a cardinal. >> Elizabeth I

Allen, William (Hervey) (1889–1949) Writer, born in Pittsburgh, PA. After World War 1, he published his war diary, *Towards the Flame* (1926). His best-known novel is *Anthony Adverse* (1933).

Allen, Woody, originally **Allen Stewart Konigsberg** (1935–   ) Film actor and director, born in Brooklyn, New York City. *What's New, Pussycat?* (1965) saw the start of a prolific film-making career that initially consisted of slapstick lunacy and genre parody in such productions as *Bananas* (1971) and *Love and Death* (1975). *Annie Hall* (1977) marked a shift in style and substance to more concentrated, autobiographical pieces and won him Oscars for writing and direction. Subsequently, he has explored his concerns with mortality, sexual inadequacies, show-business nostalgia, psychoanalysis, and urban living in such films as *Interiors* (1978), *Manhattan* (1979), *Broadway Danny Rose* (1984), and *Hannah and Her Sisters* (1986, Oscar). His books include *Getting Even* (1971) and *Without Feathers* (1976). Later films include *Husbands and Wives* (1992) – whose release ironically coincided with the much-publicized breakdown of his long-term relationship with actress **Mia Farrow** (1945–   ) – *Bullets over Broadway* (1994, Oscar), and *Everyone Says I Love You* (1997). In 1993 his private life received adverse publicity after losing a court battle for custody of three of their children, following the revelation of an affair with Farrow's adopted daughter, Soon-Yi.

Allenby, Edmund Henry Hynman Allenby, 1st Viscount (1861–1936) British soldier, born in Brackenhurst, Nottinghamshire, C England, UK. He trained at Sandhurst, and joined the Inniskilling Dragoons. In World War 1 he commanded the 1st Cavalry Division and then the Third Army in France (1915–17). Thereafter he was appointed commander-in-chief of the Egyptian expeditionary force against the Turks, took Beersheba and Gaza, and entered Jerusalem (1917). In 1918 he routed the Egyptians in the great cavalry battle of Megiddo. He was later high commissioner in Egypt (1919–25).

Allende (Gossens), Salvador [ayenday] (1908–73) Chilean statesman and president (1970–3), born in Valparaíso, Chile. He helped found the Chilean Socialist Party, was elected to the Chamber of Deputies in 1937, served as minister of health for three years, and was a senator (1945–70). He sought, and failed to win, the presidency in 1952, 1958, and 1964, but was narrowly successful in 1970. He tried to build a Socialist society within the framework of a parliamentary democracy, but met widespread opposition from business interests. He was overthrown by a military junta, led by General Augusto Pinochet, and died in the fighting. >> Pinochet

Allende, Isabel [ayenday] (1942–) Novelist, born in Lima, Peru, the niece and god-daughter of Salvador Allende, the former president of Chile. Several months after the overthrow of Chile's coalition government in 1973, she fled Chile, seeking sanctuary in Venezuela. Her first novel, *The House of the Spirits* (1985), which arose directly out of her exile, became a worldwide best-seller and critical success. Her later books include *Of Love and Shadows* (1987) and *The Infinite Plan* (1993). >> Allende, Salvador

Alley, Rewi (1897–1987) Writer and teacher, born in Springfield, Canterbury, New Zealand. After service in World War 1 and a failed farming venture, he went to China in 1927. There he spent the rest of his life promoting the concept of industrial co-operative education. From 1938 he was involved with the *Gung Ho* ('work together') scheme, and from 1945 at Shandan in China he directed a model school to teach peasants how to produce goods for the community by employing low technology methods. He wrote over 70 books, including volumes of travel and poetry. Sympathetic to the Communists, he was one of the few Westerners who remained in China after they came to power there in 1949.

Alleyn, Edward [alen] (1566–1626) Actor, born in London, England, UK, the stepson-in-law of Philip Henslowe. A contemporary of Shakespeare, he was associated with the Admiral's Men, and formed a partnership with Henslowe to run the Bear Garden and build the Fortune Theatre. He founded Dulwich College (1619), and deposited in its library documents relating to his career (including Henslowe's diary), which give a unique insight into the financial aspects of Elizabethan theatre. >> Henslowe; Shakespeare, William

Allgood, Sara (1883–1950) Actress, born in Dublin. At the Abbey Theatre she created the parts of Juno Boyle and Bessie Burgess in Sean O'Casey's *Juno and the Paycock* and *The Plough and the Stars* (1926) respectively. In 1940 she settled in Hollywood, and appeared in over 30 films, including *Jane Eyre* (1943), *The Lodger* (1944), and *Between Two Worlds* (1944).

Alliaco, Petrus de >> **Ailly, Pierre d'**

Allingham, Margery [alinguhm] (1904–66) Detective-story writer, the creator of the fictional detective Albert Campion, born in London, England, UK. She wrote a string of elegant and witty novels, including *Crime at Black Dudley* (1928), *Tiger in the Smoke* (1952), and *The China Governess* (1963).

Allingham, William (1824–89) Poet, born in Ballyshannon, Co Donegal, Ireland. In 1874 he succeeded James Froude as editor of *Fraser's Magazine*. His works include *Day and Night Songs* (1854), illustrated by Rossetti and Millais, and *Irish Songs and Poems* (1887).

Allitt, Beverley [alit] (1969–) British convicted murderer. A nurse by profession, she was convicted in 1993 of the murder of four children in her care and of the attempted murder of three others. Dubbed the UK's first female serial killer, she allegedly suffered from a medical condition termed 'Münchhausen's syndrome by proxy'. >> Münchhausen

Allori, Alessandro [alawree] (1535–1607) Florentine mannerist painter, adopted and trained by Bronzino, whose name he and his son, **Cristofano** (1577–1621), later adopted. They both were portrait painters at the Medici court, and executed religious works for the churches of Florence. >> Bronzino

Allsopp, Samuel [awlsop] (1780–1838) British philanthropist, a member of the brewing firm of Allsopp & Sons, Burton-on-Trent, C England, UK. The youngest of his three sons, **Henry** (1811–87), to whom the development of the firm was largely due, represented Worcestershire in parliament (1874–80), and in 1886 was created Lord Hindlip.

Allston, Washington [awlston] (1779–1843) Artist and writer, born in Waccamaw, SC. The earliest US Romantic painter, he graduated at Harvard, then studied at the Royal Academy in London before going on to Paris and Rome. He eventually settled at Cambridgeport, MA, in 1830. He painted large canvases, particularly of religious scenes, such as 'Belshazzar's Feast', 'The Flood', and 'Elijah in the Desert'.

Almack, William (?–1781) British clubman, of either Yorkshire or Scottish origin (possibly originally **McCall**). He came at an early age to London, opening a gaming club in Pall Mall in 1763, and Almack's Assembly Rooms in King Street, St James's, in 1765. These became centres of London society.

Almagro, Diego de [almagroh] (c. 1475–1538) Conquistador, born in Almagro, Spain. He was on the first exploratory expedition from Peru against the Incas led by Francisco Pizarro (1524–8). In the second expedition (from 1532), he joined Pizarro in 1533 at Cajamarca, and occupied the Inca capital of Cuzco. In 1535–6 he led the conquest of Chile, but came back to Cuzco in 1537 and, after a dispute with Pizarro, occupied it by force, thus beginning a civil war between the Spaniards. Early in 1538 he was defeated by an army led by Pizarro's brother, Hernando, and was captured and executed. >> Pizarro, Francisco

Alma-Tadema, Sir Lawrence [alma tadema] (1836–1912) Painter of Classical-genre paintings, born in Dronrijp, The Netherlands. He studied at the Antwerp Academy of Art, and came to specialize in subjects from Greek, Roman, and Egyptian antiquity. He achieved great popularity with such Classical idyllic scenes as 'Tarquinius Superbus' (1867) and 'The Conversion of Paula' (1898). He was a painstaking technician and spared no expense. For 'The Roses of Heliogabalus' (exhibited Royal Academy, 1896), fresh roses were sent weekly from the S of France so that every petal – and the picture contains thousands – could be depicted accurately. He settled permanently in England in 1873, and was knighted in 1899.

Almeida, Brites de [almayda] (fl.1385–) Legendary Portuguese heroine, born in Aljubarrota, Portugal. She is said to have been a baker; about 1385, during the war between John I and the King of Cadiz, she led her townspeople against the Spanish forces and killed seven of them with her baker's shovel. The incident was celebrated by Camoens in a poem. >> Camoens

Almeida, Francisco de [almayda] (c.1450–1510) Portuguese soldier and first viceroy of the Portuguese Indies (1505–9), until he was superseded by Affonso d'Albuquerque. He was killed in South Africa on his voyage home in a skirmish with natives at Table Bay.

Almeida-Garrett, João Baptista da Silva Leitão [almayda garet] (1799–1854) Writer and politician, born in Oporto, Portugal. A pioneer of the Romantic movement and of modern Portuguese drama, he wrote the historical play *Gil Vicente* (1838), the epic *Camões* (1825), and many ballads.

Almirante, Giorgio [almirantay] (?1915–88) Leader of Italy's neo-Fascist Party, born near Parma, Italy. He helped to found the neo-Fascist movement after the war, becoming national secretary of the Party in 1969. He retired in 1987 because of ill health.

Almodovar, Pedro [almothovar] (1951–) Film director, born in Calzada de Calatrava, Spain. His films are known for their provocative treatment of sexual themes. *Mujeres Al Borde de Un Ataque de Nervous* (1988, Women on the Verge of a Nervous Breakdown) won several prizes, and had an Oscar nomination as Best Foreign Film. Later films include *Atame!* (1990, Tie Me Up! Tie Me Down!) and *High Heels* (1991).

Almquist or **Almqvist, Carl Jonas Love** [almkwist] (1793–1866) Writer, born in Stockholm. He had a bizarrely chequered career as a clergyman and teacher; he was accused of forgery and attempted murder, and fled to the USA. From 1865 he lived in Bremen under an assumed name. His prolific literary output, ranging from Romanticism to (from the late 1830s) Social Realism, encompassed novels, plays, poems, and essays, and was published in a 14-volume series, *Törnrosens Bok* (1832–51, The Book of the Briar Rose).

Alonso, Alicia [alonsoh], originally **Alicia de la Caridad del Cobre Martínez Hoyo** (1921–) Dancer and choreographer, born in Havana. She launched her career in the USA where she studied and performed with the School of American Ballet and George Balanchine. In 1948 she returned to Cuba to form the Alicia Alonso Company, which grew into a national ballet company for Cuba. As a dancer she was famed for several roles, particularly the title role in *Giselle*. >> Balanchine

Alonso, Dámaso [alonsoh] (1898–1990) Poet and philologist, born in Madrid. He travelled widely in Europe and America as teacher and lecturer, then became professor of romance philology at Madrid University, establishing his reputation as an authority on Góngora y Argote. He also published poetry, of which *Hijos de la ira* (1944, Children of Wrath) is the best known. >> Góngora

Aloysius, St >> **Gonzaga, Luigi**

Alp-Arslan (Turk 'hero-lion') (1030–72) Seljuk sultan, who succeeded his uncle Tügrül Beg in 1062. A skilful and courageous commander, he devoted his energies to extending the frontiers of the Seljuk empire. He restored good relations with the Abbasid caliph, and was about to launch a major offensive against its rivals, the Fatimids, when he was recalled to meet a Byzantine offensive in Armenia. At Manzikert in 1071 he defeated a numerically superior army, opening up the interior of Anatolia to penetration by the nomadic Turkmen tribes. >> Fatima; RR1037

Alpher, Ralph (Asher) (1921–) Physicist, born in Washington, DC. After studying at George Washington University, he spent World War 2 as a civilian physicist and afterwards worked at Johns Hopkins University and in industry. Together with Hans Bethe and George Gamow, he proposed in 1948 the 'alpha, beta, gamma' theory, which suggests the possibility of explaining the abundances of chemical elements as the result of thermonuclear processes in the early stages of a hot, evolving universe. These ideas became part of the 'big bang' model of the universe. >> Bethe; Gamow

Alphonso >> **Alfonso**

Alphonsus Liguori, St >> **Liguori, St Alfonso Maria de'**

Alpini, Prospero [alpeenee], Lat **Prosper Alpinus** (1553–1616) Botanist and physician, born in Marostica, Italy. While in Cairo he observed the sexual fertilization of the date palm, in which male and female flowers are on different trees, and described 57 wild or cultivated species in Egypt. In 1594 he became lecturer in botany at Padua, and director of the botanic garden there (1603). His *De medecina Egyptorum* (1591) brought the coffee plant and the banana to European attention.

Alred >> **Aldred**

Alston, Richard [awlston] (1948–) Choreographer, born in Stoughton, West Sussex, S England, UK. He studied at Eton and Croydon College of Art (1965–7), and at the London School of Contemporary Dance (1967–70). He co-founded Strider in 1972 (disbanded 1975), the forerunner of the contemporary dance company Second Stride. He studied in New York with Merce Cunningham (1975–7), then joined Ballet Rambert as resident choreographer (1980–6), and director (1986–92). In 1994 he became artistic director of the Richard Alston Dance Company. >> Cunningham, Merce; Davies, Siobhan; Spink

Altdorfer, Albrecht [altdaw(r)fer] (c. 1480–1538) Painter, engraver, and architect, the leading member of the Danube School of German painting, born in Regensburg, Germany. His most outstanding works are biblical and historical subjects set against highly imaginative and atmospheric landscape backgrounds. He was also a pioneer of copperplate etching.

Alter, David (1807–81) Physicist, born in Westmoreland, PA. He was one of the earliest investigators of the spectrum, and pioneered the use of the spectroscope in determining the chemical constitution of a gas or vaporized solid.

Altgeld, John Peter (1847–1902) US politician and social reformer, born in Nassau, Germany. Brought to the USA in infancy, he served in the Union army during the Civil War. As a judge of the supreme court in Illinois (1886–91), he is remembered chiefly for his pardon of three anarchists convicted of complicity in the 1886 Chicago Haymarket Riots. He was elected the first Democratic Governor of Illinois (1892–6).

Althusser, Louis [alt-hüser] (1918–90) Political philosopher, born in Algiers. He studied in Algiers and in France, was imprisoned in concentration camps during World War 2, and from 1948 taught in Paris. He joined the Communist Party in 1948, and wrote influential works on Marxist theory, including *Pour Marx* (1965, For Marx) and *Lénin et la philosophie* (1969, Lenin and Philosophy). In 1980 he murdered his wife, and was confined in an asylum until his death; self-justifying autobiographical pieces were published in 1992.

Altichiero [altikyayroh] (c. 1330–c. 1395) Painter and possible founder of the Veronese School, born near Verona, Italy. He worked in Verona and also in Padua, where his frescoes in the Basilica of S Antonio (painted 1372–9) and in the Oratory of S Giorgio (1377–84) combine the solid Realism of Giotto with a new Gothic elegance typical of the later 14th-c. In S Giorgio he shared the work with a painter called Avanzo. >> Giotto

Altizer, Thomas J(onathan) J(ackson) [altiyzer] (1927–) Theologian, born in Cambridge, MA. He studied at Chicago University, then taught religion, and later English, at Emory University (1956–68) and the State University of New York (from 1968). As a proponent of one strand of the 1960s 'Death of God' theology, he held that in the Incarnation God became fully human and lost his divine attributes and existence. His writings include *The Gospel of Christian Atheism* (1966) and *The Self-Embodiment of God* (1977).

Altman, Benjamin (1840–1913) Businessman and art collector, born in New York City. Much of his early life is obscure, but it seems he had little formal education. By 1865 he owned a dry-goods store in New York City, and later founded B Altman & Co (1906), which became one of the country's most stylish department stores. He collected paintings and sculptures among other art works during his many visits to Europe, bequeathing his collection to the Metropolitan Museum and a legacy to the National Academy of Design.

Altman, Robert (1925–) Film director, born in Kansas City, MO. After serving in World War 2 as a pilot, he took up writing for radio and magazines, then produced industrial films. His first feature film was *The Delinquents* (1957). He gained instant recognition for *M*A*S*H* (1970), and went on to direct and/or produce a series of highly individualistic films, noted especially for their simultaneous layers of dialogue. Impatient with Hollywood's conservative and commercial approach to film-making, he moved to Europe, although he returned to America to make such films as *Nashville* (1975), *The Player* (1991), and *Kansas City* (1996).

Altman, Sidney (1939–) Biochemist, born in Montreal, Canada. He became affiliated with Yale in 1971, and holds dual citizenship. He showed that the RNA molecule could rearrange itself, thereby altering the material it produces without requiring an enzyme – a breakthrough in our understanding of genetic processes. He shared the Nobel Prize for Chemistry with Thomas Cech in 1989. >> Cech, Thomas

Altounyan, Roger Edward Collingwood [altoonyan] (1922–87) Physician and medical pioneer, born in Syria of Armenian–English extraction. He spent his summer holidays with his four sisters in the Lake District, where they met the author Arthur Mitchell Ransome and became the real-life models of the children in his *Swallows and Amazons* series of adventure books. He qualified as a doctor, later joining a pharmaceutical company, where he developed the drug sodium cromoglycate to combat asthma, from which he was himself a sufferer. A pilot and flying instructor during the war, he developed the Spinhaler device to inhale the drug, based on the aerodynamic principles of aircraft propellors. >> Ransome

Alva or **Alba, Ferdinand Alvarez de Toledo, duque d'** (Duke of) (1507–82) Spanish general and statesman, born in Piedrahita, Spain. A brilliant tactician, he became a general at 26, and a commander-in-chief at 30. After the abdication of Charles V in 1556, he overran the States of the Church, but was obliged by Philip II to conclude a peace and restore all his conquests. On the revolt of the Netherlands, he was sent as lieutenant-general in 1567 to enforce Spanish control there, establishing the 'Bloody Council' which drove thousands of Huguenot artisans to emigrate to England. He defeated William of Orange, and entered Brussels in triumph in 1568. Recalled by his own desire in 1573, he commanded the successful invasion of Portugal in 1581. >> Philip II (of Spain); William I (of the Netherlands)

Alvarado, Pedro de [alvarahthoh] (c.1485–1541) Conquistador, a companion of Cortés during the conquest of Mexico (1519–21), born in Badajoz, Spain. He became Governor of Tenochtitlán, where the harshness of his rule incited an Aztec revolt. He was sent by Cortés on an expedition to Guatemala (1523–7), during which he also conquered parts of El Salvador. He returned to Spain, and in 1529 was appointed Governor of Guatemala. >> Cortés

Alvarez, José [alvareth] (1768–1827) Spanish sculptor of the Classical school. He was imprisoned in Rome for refusing to recognize Joseph Bonaparte as King of Spain, but was later released and employed by Napoleon to decorate the Quirinal Palace. In 1816 he became court sculptor to Ferdinand VII in Madrid. >> Bonaparte, Joseph

Alvarez, Luis W(alter) [alvahrez] (1911–88) Experimental physicist, born in San Francisco, CA. He studied at Chicago University, then joined Ernest Lawrence at the University of California, Berkeley, in 1936, becoming professor of physics in 1945. Before World War 2 he did distinguished work in nuclear physics; during the war he developed radar navigation and landing systems for aircraft. In 1947 he built the first proton linear accelerator. He did much to develop the bubble-chamber, using it to discover new subatomic particles, for which he was awarded the Nobel Prize for Physics in 1968. >> Lawrence, Ernest

Alvarez Quintero [alvareth keentayroh] Playwrights and brothers: **Serafín Alvarez Quintero** (1871–1938) and **Joaquín Alvarez Quintero** (1873–1944), born in Utrera, Spain. They were the joint authors of well over 100 modern Spanish plays, all displaying a characteristic gaiety and sentiment. Some are well known in the translations of Helen and Harley Granville-Barker, such as *Fortunato*, *The Lady from Alfaqueque*, and *A Hundred Years Old* (all produced in 1928), and *Don Abel Writes a Tragedy* (1933). >> Granville-Barker

Alypius [alipius] (fl.c. 360 BC–) Greek writer on music. His surviving work, published in 1652, consists of a list of symbols for the notation of the Greek modes and scales.

Alzheimer, Alois [altshiymer] (1864–1915) Psychiatrist and neuropathologist, born in Marktbreit, Germany. He studied medicine in Würzburg and Berlin universities, and in 1912 became professor of psychiatry and neurology at Breslau University (now Wrocław, Poland). He is remembered for his full clinical and pathological description, in 1906, of pre-senile dementia (*Alzheimer's disease*).

Amadeus >> **Hoffmann, E T W**

Amado, Jorge [amahdoo] (1912–) Novelist, born in Ferradas, Brazil. Brought up on a cacao plantation in NE Brazil, his early writing focused on the poverty and social conditions of the plantation workers. He became a journalist in 1930, was imprisoned for his political beliefs in 1935, and spent several periods in exile. He was elected a Communist deputy of the Brazilian parliament (1946–7). His novels include *Terras do sem-fin* (1944, trans The Violent Land), *Gabriela, cravo e canela* (1958, Gabriela, Clove and Cinnamon), and *Tenda dos milagres* (1969, Tent of Miracles).

Amagatsu, Yushio [amagatsoo] (1948–) Choreographer and dancer, born in Yokosuka, Japan. He became artistic director of the *butoh* dance-theatre troupe Sankai Juku (Studio of the Mountain and Sea). His company, based partly in Paris, was formed in 1975 out of intensive physical and psychological workshops.

Amanullah Khan [amanula kahn] (1892–1960) Ruler of Afghanistan (1919–29), born in Paghman, Afghanistan. After an inconclusive religious war against the British in India (1919–22), independence for Afghanistan was recognized by Britain by the Treaty of Rawalpindi (1922). He assumed the title of king in 1926, but his zeal for Westernizing reforms provoked rebellion in 1928. He abdicated and fled the country in 1929, and went into exile in Rome. >> RR1031

Amarasimha (probably 6th-c) Sanskrit lexicographer. He wrote the *Amara-kosha*, a dictionary of synonyms in verse.

Amati, Andrea [amahtee] (c.1520–80) Violin-maker, the founder member of a famous family of violin-makers from Cremona, Italy. His earliest known label dates from 1564. Other members of the family were his younger brother, **Nicolò** (1530–1600); Andrea's two sons, **Antonio** (1550–1638) and **Geronimo** (1551–1635); and the latter's son, **Nicolò** (1596–1684), the master of Guarnieri and Stradivari. >> Guarnieri; Stradivari

Ambartsumian, Viktor Amazaspovich (1908–96) Astrophysicist, born in Armenia. He studied at the University of Leningrad, was professor of astrophysics there (1934–43) and at Erevan, and founded the Byurakan Astronomical Observatory. He devised and developed theories of young star clusters, and devised a method for computing the mass ejected from nova stars.

Ambedkar, Bhimrao Ramji [ambedker] (1893–1956) Indian politician and champion of the depressed castes, born near Mumbai (Bombay), India. He studied at Bombay, Columbia University in New York City, and the London School of Economics, and practised as a barrister in London. He later became a member of the Bombay Legislative Assembly and leader of 60 million Untouchables. Appointed law minister in 1947, he was the principal author of the Indian Constitution. He resigned in 1951, and with some thousands of his followers he publicly embraced the Buddhist faith not long before his death.

Ambler, Eric (1909–) Novelist and playwright, born in London, England, UK. He studied at Colfe's Grammar School and London University, and worked as an advertising copy-writer before turning to writing thrillers, invariably with an espionage background. He published his first novel, *The Dark Frontier*, in 1936. His best-known books are *Epitaph for a Spy* (1938), *The Mask of Dimitrios* (1939), *Dirty Story* (1967), and *The Intercom Conspiracy* (1970). He has received the Crime Writers' Association Award four times, as well as the Edgar Allan Poe Award (1964). Later books include *Here Lies: An Autobiography* (1985) and *The Story So Far* (1993).

Amboise, Georges d' [ämbwahz] (1460–1510) Clergyman and French statesman, born in Chaumont-sur-Loire, France. Bishop of Montauban (1474) and Archbishop of Rouen (1493), he became cardinal and prime minister under Louis XII in 1498. An able minister, who carried out many important domestic reforms, he effected the Treaty of Blois in 1505 that brought about an alliance between France and Spain. >> Louis XII

Ambrose, St (c. 339–97) Roman clergyman and doctor of the Church, born in Trier, Germany. He practised law in Rome, and in 369 was appointed consular prefect of Upper Italy, whose capital was Milan. When the bishopric fell vacant in 374, he was chosen bishop by universal acclamation, even though he was still only a catechumen undergoing instruction. He was quickly baptized, and consecrated bishop eight days later. He fought for the integrity of the Church at the imperial court, resisting Empress-regent Justina over the introduction of Arian churches. He introduced the use of hymns and made many improvements in the liturgy, notably the *Ambrosian ritual* and *Ambrosian chant*. Feast day 7 December.

Amenhotep II [ahmenhohtep] (15th-c BC) King of Egypt in the 18th Dynasty (1450–1425 BC), the son of Thuthmose III. He fought successful campaigns in Palestine and on the Euphrates. His mummy was found in the Valley of the Tombs of the Kings, Thebes. >> Thuthmose; RR1046

Amenhotep III [amenhohtep] (c. 1411–1379 BC) King of Egypt (1417–1379 BC), the son of Thuthmose IV. He consolidated Egyptian supremacy in Babylonia and Assyria. In a reign of spectacular wealth and magnificence, he built his great capital city, Thebes, and its finest monuments, including the Luxor temple, the great pylon at Karnak, and the colossi of Memnon. >> RR1046

Amenhotep IV >> Akhenaton

Amery, John [aymeree] (1912–45) British pro-Nazi adventurer, the son (later disowned) of L S Amery. Recruited by the Nazis in France, he began pro-Hitler broadcasts from Berlin in 1942. He tried to raise an anti-Bolshevik free corps in the British internee camp at St Denis to fight for the Nazis on the Russian front (1943), and made speeches for Hitler in Norway, France, Belgium, and Yugoslavia (1944). Captured by Italian partisans in 1945, he was tried in London for high treason, and hanged in December 1945. >> Amery, L S

Amery, L(eopold Charles Maurice) S(tennett) (1873–1955) British statesman, born in Gorakpur, India. He studied at Oxford, and became Conservative MP for Sparkbrook, Birmingham, a seat which he held for 34 years. He served as colonial under-secretary, First Lord of the Admiralty, and colonial secretary between 1919 and 1929, then returned to office in Churchill's wartime administration as secretary of state for India and Burma. He became famous for his exhortation to Neville Chamberlain, in May 1940, adapting Cromwell's words, 'In the name of God, go!' >> Chamberlain, Neville

Ames, Joseph [aymz] (1689–1759) Bibliographer and antiquarian, born in Yarmouth, Isle of Wight, S England, UK. He became an ironmonger or ship-chandler in London, and at the suggestion of friends compiled *Typographical Antiquities* (1749), the foundation of English bibliography.

Ames, William [aymz], Lat **Amesius** (1576–1633) Puritan theologian, born in Ipswich, Suffolk, E England, UK. He wrote mostly in Latin, and spent the later half of his life in Holland, where he became a professor of theology. He is celebrated for his exposition of Calvinist doctrine.

Amherst, Jeffrey, 1st Baron Amherst (1717–97) British soldier, born in Sevenoaks, Kent, SE England, UK. Joining the army at the age of 14 he played an important part in the North American phase of the Seven Years' War (1756–63). He was in command of the expedition against the French in Canada, and captured Louisburg (1758). Appointed commander-in-chief of North America in 1759, he captured Montreal in 1760. He was Governor-General of British North America (1760–3), then commander-in-chief of the British army (1772–96).

Amherst (of Arakan), William Pitt, 1st Earl (1773–1857) Colonialist, born in Bath, SW England, UK, the nephew and adopted son of Jeffrey, 1st Baron Amherst. In 1816 he was sent as ambassador to China, but his mission failed when he refused to kow-tow to the emperor. In 1823 he was appointed Governor-General of India, where he weathered the first Burmese War and was rewarded with an earldom (1826). >> Amherst, Jeffrey

Amichai, Yehuda [amichiy] (1924–) Poet, born in Würzburg, Germany. In 1936 he went with his family to what was then Palestine. A dozen volumes of verse since *Now and in Other Days* (1955, trans title) are divided in subject-matter between the idyll of childhood and the struggle of Israel to establish and defend its identity. These include *Now in the Turmoil* (1968, trans title) and *Amen* (1978, trans by Amichai with Ted Hughes).

Amici, Giovanni Battista [ameechee] (1786–1868) Optician, astronomer, and natural philosopher, born in Modena, Italy. He constructed optical instruments, perfecting his own alloy for telescope mirrors, and in 1827 produced the dioptric, achromatic microscope that bears his name. He became director of the Florence observatory in 1835.

Amiel, Henri Frédéric [amyel] (1821–81) Philosopher and writer, born in Geneva. He was professor of aesthetics (1849) and then moral philosophy (1853–81) at the Academy of Geneva. His fame as an intellectual and critic rests on his diaries from 1847 onwards, published posthumously as *Journal in time* (1883).

Amies, Sir (Edwin) Hardy [aymeez] (1909–) Couturier, and dressmaker by appointment to Queen Elizabeth II. He worked as a trainee in Birmingham, C England, UK before becoming a managing designer in London in 1934, where he made his name especially with his tailored suits for women. He founded his own fashion house in 1946, and started designing for men in 1959, receiving the British Fashion Council Hall of Fame Award in 1989. His books include *The Englishman's Suit* (1994). He was knighted in 1989. >> Elizabeth II

Amin (Dada), Idi [ameen] (c.1925–) Ugandan soldier and dictator (1971–9). After a rudimentary education he joined the army, rising from the ranks to become a colonel in 1964. As a friend of prime minister Milton Obote, he was made commander-in-chief of the army and air force, but worsening relations between them resulted in a coup establishing a military dictatorship (1971). He proceeded to expel all Ugandan Asians and many Israelis, seized for-eign-owned businesses and estates, and ordered the killing of thousands of his opponents, making his regime internationally infamous. His decision in 1978 to annex the Kagera area of Tanzania gave President Nyerere the opportunity to send his troops into Uganda. Within six months Amin was defeated. He fled to Libya, and later attempted to make his home in several countries, and eventually settled in exile in Saudi Arabia. >> Museveni; Obote

Amiot, Jacques >> **Amyot, Jacques**

Amis, Sir Kingsley [aymis] (1922–95) Novelist and poet, born in London, England, UK. He studied at Oxford, and became a lecturer in English literature at Swansea (1948–61) and a fellow of Peterhouse, Cambridge (1961–3). He achieved huge success with his first novel, *Lucky Jim* (1954), the story of a comic anti-hero in a provincial uni-versity; Jim appeared again as a small-town librarian in *That Uncertain Feeling* (1956), and as a provincial author abroad in *I Like It Here* (1958). After the death of Ian Fleming, he wrote a James Bond novel, *Colonel Sun* (1968), under the pseudonym of **Robert Markham**, as well as *The James Bond Dossier* (1965). His later novels include *Jake's Thing* (1978), *The Old Devils* (1986, Booker), *The Folks that Live on the Hill* (1990), *The Russian Girl* (1992), and *You Can't Do Both* (1994). He was married (1965–83) to the novelist **Elizabeth Jane Howard** (1923–   ), and was knighted in 1990. >> Amis, Martin

Amis, Martin [aymis] (1949–   ) Novelist and journalist, the son of Kingsley Amis. He studied at Exeter College, Oxford, and wrote his first novel, *The Rachel Papers* (1973), when he was 21. Later works include *Dead Babies* (1975), *Other People* (1981), *Money* (1984), *Time's Arrow* (1991), *The Information* (1995), and *Night Train* (1997). He has also pro-duced a collection of short stories, *Einstein's Monsters* (1986), and a great deal of literary journalism. >> Amis, Kingsley

Amiss, Dennis (Leslie) [aymis] (1943–   ) Cricketer, born in Birmingham, West Midlands, C England, UK. He played with distinction for Warwickshire, and won admiration by the way he endured a battering by West Indian bowlers in 1976, which re-established his place in first-class cricket. He made 50 appearances in Test matches for England, and scored 11 centuries.

Amman, Jakob (c. 1645–c. 1730) Swiss Mennonite bishop whose followers founded the Amish (Ger *Amisch*) sect in the 1690s. Their members still practise an exclusively rural and simple way of life in various parts of the USA and Canada.

Ammanati, Bartolommeo [amanahtee] (1511–92) Architect and sculptor, born in Settignano, Italy. Working in the late Renaissance style he executed the ducal palace at Lucca, part of the Pitti Palace and the Ponte Santa Trinità (destroyed in World War 2) in Florence.

Ammann, Othmar Hermann (1879–1965) Structural engineer, born in Schaffhausen, Switzerland. He emi-grated to the USA in 1904, where he designed some of America's greatest suspension bridges, including the George Washington Bridge (3500 ft) in New York (1931), Golden Gate Bridge (4200 ft) in San Francisco (1937), and Verrazano Narrows Bridge (4260 ft) in New York (1965), each in its day the longest span in the world.

Ammianus Marcellinus [amiahnus mah(r)seleenus] (c.330–90) Roman historian, born of Greek parents in Antioch. He wrote in Latin a history of the Roman Empire from AD 98 in 31 books, of which only the last 18 are extant.

Ammonius [amohnius], known as **Ammonius Saccas** (c. 160–242) Greek philosopher, who received his surname because in his youth he was a sack-carrier in Alexandria. He was the founder of Neoplatonic philosophy, and the teacher of Plotinus, Origen, and Longinus, but left no writings. >> Longinus; Origen; Plotinus

Amontons, Guillaume [amõtõ] (1663–1705) Physicist, born in Paris. He improved the design of various scientific instruments, including the hygrometer, the barometer, and the constant-volume air thermometer. His chief dis-covery (though disregarded at the time) was that equal changes in the temperature of a fixed volume of air result in equal variations in pressure.

Amory, Derick Heathcoat, 1st Viscount Amory [aymoree] (1899–1981) British statesman, born in Tiverton, Devon, SW England, UK. He studied at Oxford, and became a Conservative MP in 1945. He was minister of pensions (1951–3), minister at the board of trade (1953–4), and min-ister of agriculture (1954–8). He became a viscount during his period as Chancellor of the Exchequer (1958–60).

Amory, Thomas [aymoree] (c.1691–1788) English writer and eccentric, of Irish descent. He is best known for his *Life of John Buncle* (2 vols, 1756–66) a combination of autobiog-raphy, fantastic descriptions, deistical theology, and senti-mental rhapsody.

Amos [aymos] (835–765 BC) Old Testament prophet, the ear-liest prophet in the Bible to have a book named after him. A herdsman from the village of Tekoa, near Bethlehem of Judaea, he denounced the iniquities of the N kingdom of Israel.

Ampère, André Marie [ãpair] (1775–1836) Mathematician and physicist, born in Lyon, France. He taught at the Ecole Polytechnique in Paris, the University of Paris, and the Collège de France. He laid the foundations of the science of electrodynamics following Oersted's discovery in 1820 of the magnetic effects of electric currents. His name was given to the basic SI unit of electric current (*ampere, amp*). >> Oersted

Amr ibn al-As [amribnalas] (?–664) Arab soldier. A convert to Islam, he joined the prophet Mohammed in c.629, and took part in the conquest of Palestine in 638. In 639 he undertook the conquest of Egypt, becoming its first Muslim governor (642–44). He helped Muawiyah to seize the caliphate from Ali. >> Mohammed; Muawiyah

Amsberg, Claus-Georg von >> **Beatrix**

Amundsen, Roald (Engelbregt Gravning) [amundsen] (1872–1928) Explorer, born in Borge, Norway. From 1903 to 1906 he sailed the Northwest Passage from E–W, and located the Magnetic North Pole. In 1910 he set sail in the *Fram* in an attempt to reach the North Pole, but hearing that Peary had apparently beaten him to it, he switched to the Antarctic and reached the South Pole in December 1911, one month ahead of Captain Scott. In 1926 he flew the airship *Norge* across the North Pole with Ellsworth and Nobile. In 1928 he disappeared when searching by plane for Nobile and his airship *Italia*, which had gone missing on another flight to the Pole. >> Ellsworth; Nobile; Peary; Scott, R F

Amyot or **Amiot, Jacques** [amyoh] (1513–93) Humanist, born in Melun, France. He translated many Classical texts, the most important being his French version of Plutarch's *Lives*, which was the basis of Sir Thomas North's transla-tion into English, and of some of Shakespeare's history plays. >> North, Thomas; Plutarch

Anacreon [anakreeon] (c. 570–c. 475 BC) Greek lyric poet, from Teos, modern Turkey. He was invited to Samos by Polycrates to tutor his son, and after the tyrant's downfall, was taken to Athens by Hipparchus, son of the tyrant Pisistratus. He was famous for his satires and his elegant love poetry, of which only fragments remain. >> Pisistratus; Polycrates

Anand, Mulk Raj [anand] (1905–) Novelist, critic, and man of letters, born in Peshawar, modern Pakistan. He left India for Britain, where he eventually published his first novel, *Untouchable* (1935), with a preface by E M Forster. His novels, such as *The Coolie* (1936) and *The Village* (1939, the first of a trilogy) promote the underdog in society, depicting life in the poverty-stricken Punjab. He later began an ambitious seven-volume autobiographical work of fiction, *The Seven Ages of Man*.

Ananda [anända] (5th–6th-c BC) The cousin and favourite pupil of the Buddha. Noted for his devotion to the Buddha, and a skilled interpreter of his teachings, he was instrumental in establishing an order for women disciples. >> Buddha

Anastasia [anastahzia], in full **Grand Duchess Anastasia Nikolaievna Romanova** (1901–18?) Youngest daughter of Tsar Nicholas II of Russia, believed to have perished when the Romanov family were executed by the Bolsheviks in 1918. Various people later claimed to be Anastasia, especially Mrs 'Anna Anderson' Manahan, who died in Virginia, USA, in 1984 at the age of 82. For more than 30 years she fought unsuccessfully to establish her identity as Anastasia. Her story inspired two films (*Anastasia*, with Ingrid Bergman; *Is Anna Anderson Anastasia?*, with Lilli Palmer) and several books. >> Nicholas II

Anatoli, Alexander >> **Kuznetsov, Alexander Vasilievich**

Anaxagoras [anaksagoras] (c. 500–428 BC) Greek philosopher, born in Clazomenae. For 30 years he taught in Athens, where he had many illustrious pupils, among them Pericles and Euripides. His scientific speculations led to his prosecution for impiety, and he was banished from Athens. His most celebrated cosmological doctrine was that matter is infinitely divisible into particles, which contain a mixture of all qualities, and that mind (*nous*) is a pervasive formative agency in the creation of material objects. >> Euripides; Pericles

Anaximander [anakzimander] (c.611–547 BC) Greek philosopher, born in Miletus, the successor and perhaps pupil of Thales. He posited that the first principle was not a particular substance like water or air but the *apeiron*, the infinite or indefinite. He is credited with producing the first map, and with many imaginative scientific speculations, for example that the Earth is unsupported and at the centre of the universe. >> Anaximenes; Thales

Anaximenes [anakzimeneez] (?–c.500 BC) Greek philosopher, born in Miletus. He was the third of the three great Milesian thinkers, succeeding Thales and Anaximander. He posited that the first principle and basic form of matter was air, which could be transformed into other substances by a process of condensation and rarefaction. >> Anaximander; Thales

Ancre, Baron de Lussigny, marquis d' [ākruh], originally **Concino Concini** (?–1617) Adventurer, born in Florence, Italy. He entered the French court in 1600, in the train of Marie de' Medici, the wife of Henry IV, and became chief favourite of the queen-regent during the minority of Louis XIII. His prodigality was immense, and he squandered vast sums on the decoration of his palaces. Hated alike by nobility and populace, he was assassinated in the Louvre during a rebellion. >> Marie de' Medicis

Ancus Marcius [angkus mah(r)sius] (7th-c BC) Traditionally, the fourth king of Rome. He is said to have conquered the neighbouring Latin tribes, and settled them on the Aventine.

Anders, Władysław (1892–1970) Polish soldier, born in Blonie, Poland. He served on the staff of the Russian division and Polish Corps in World War 1 (1914–17). At the outbreak of World War 2 he was captured by the Russians (1939–41), but released to command a Polish ex-POW force organized in Russia, which he led through Iran into Iraq. In 1943 he became commander of the 2nd Polish Corps in Italy, capturing Monte Cassino. After the war, deprived of his nationality by the Polish Communist government, he was a leading figure in the Free Polish community in Britain, and inspector-general of the Polish forces-in-exile.

Andersen, Hans Christian (1805–75) Writer, one of the world's great story-tellers, born in Odense, Denmark. After his father's death he worked in a factory, but soon displayed a talent for poetry. He became better known by his *Walk to Amager*, a literary satire in the form of a humorous narrative. In 1830 he published the first collected volume of his *Poems*, and in 1831 a second, under the title of *Fantasies and Sketches*. He wrote many other works, but it is such fairy-tales as 'The Tin Soldier', 'The Tinderbox', and 'The Ugly Duckling' that have gained him lasting fame and delighted children throughout the world.

Anderson, Benny >> **Abba**

Anderson, Carl (David) (1905–91) Physicist, born in New York City. He studied at the California Institute of Technology, and became professor there in 1939. In 1932 he discovered the positron. He did notable work on gamma and cosmic rays, and shared the 1936 Nobel Prize for Physics with Victor Hess. Later he confirmed the existence of intermediate-mass particles called mesons (now muons). >> Dirac; RR1122

Anderson, Clive (Stuart) (1953–) Television presenter and barrister, born in London, England, UK. He studied law at Cambridge, where he was president of Footlights, and was called to the bar in 1976. He wrote scripts for radio and television, began acting as a TV warm-up man, and joined BBC Radio 4 as chairman of the popular *Whose Line Is It Anyway?* (1988). The show later transferred to Channel 4 Television, where he was also given his own chat-show *Clive Anderson Talks Back* (from 1989). Later work includes the BBC documentary series, *Our Man In ...* (1995–), which he also wrote, and he is presenter of *Clive Anderson All Talk* (1996–), and *Hypotheticals* (1997–).

Anderson, Elizabeth Garrett, *née* **Garrett** (1836–1917) Physician, the first English woman doctor, born in London, England, UK. In 1860 she began studying medicine, in the face of opposition to the admission of women, and eventually (1865) qualified as a medical practitioner by passing the Apothecaries' Hall examination. In 1866 she established a dispensary for women in London (later renamed the Elizabeth Garrett Anderson Hospital), where she instituted medical courses for women. In 1870 she was given the degree of MD by the University of Paris. In 1908 she was elected mayor of Aldeburgh, the first woman mayor in England. >> Fawcett, Millicent

Anderson, Gerry (1929–) British creator of puppet-character programmes for television. He entered the British film industry as a trainee with the Colonial Film Unit, later directing several television series. He enjoyed great success with adventure series that combined a range of popular puppet characters with technologically advanced hardware and special effects. Among the best known are *Fireball XL-5* (1961), *Thunderbirds* (1964–6), *Captain Scarlett and the Mysterons* (1967), and *Terrahawks* (1983–4). He also branched out into live action shows with human actors, such as *The Protectors* (1971), *Space 1999* (1973–6), and *Space Precinct* (1993–5).

Anderson, Gillian (1968–) Actor, born in Chicago, IL. Brought up in London, her family returned to the USA, where she became involved in community theatre, and studied at DePaul University. She then found theatre parts in New York City, eventually moving to Los Angeles, where she was offered the part of Dana Scully in the new series *The X-Files* (1993– , Golden Globe, Emmy), which has since become a cult classic. She now lives in Vancouver. >> Duchovny

Anderson, John (1726–96) Scientist, born in Roseneath, Argyll and Bute, W Scotland, UK. He studied at Glasgow, where he became professor of oriental languages, and then of natural philosophy. He also established a bi-weekly class for mechanics, and at his death left all he had to found Anderson's College in Glasgow.

Anderson, John (1893–1962) Philosopher, born in Scotland, UK. He was professor of philosophy at Sydney from 1927, and can be regarded as the founder and main exponent of an Australian school of philosophy, espousing a distinctive blend of realism, empiricism, and materialism.

Anderson, Sir John >> **Waverley, Viscount**

Anderson, Dame Judith, originally **Frances Margaret Anderson** (1898–1992) Actress, born in Adelaide, South Australia. She made her Sydney stage debut in *A Royal Divorce* (1915), and first appeared in New York City in 1918. Her film debut was in 1930, but she preferred the stage, where her reputation as a distinguished classical and contemporary actress grew following such productions as *Mourning Becomes Electra* (1932), *Hamlet* (1936, with John Gielgud), and *Macbeth* (1937). Her rare film appearances include *Rebecca* (1940), *Cat on a Hot Tin Roof* (1958), *A Man Called Horse* (1970), and *Star Trek III* (1984). In 1984 a Broadway theatre was named in her honour. She was made a dame in 1960.

Anderson, Sir Kenneth (Arthur Noel) (1891–1959) British soldier, born in India. He trained at Sandhurst, and was commissioned into the Seaforth Highlanders. In World War 1 he served in France (1914–16), then fought under Allenby in Palestine (1917–18). In World War 2 he fought at Dunkirk (1940), and was commander of the 1st British Army in North Africa (1942–3), capturing Tunis (1943). He later became Governor-General of Gibraltar (1947–52). >> Allenby

Anderson, Lindsay (Gordon) (1923–94) British stage and film director, born in Bangalore, India. He studied at Oxford, made short documentary films during the 1950s, and won an Oscar for *Thursday's Children* (1955). He was a leading proponent of the Free Cinema critical movement, with its focus on working-class themes. He joined the English Stage Company at the Royal Court Theatre, London, in 1957. His first feature film was *This Sporting Life* (1963), followed by *If....* (1968), *O Lucky Man!* (1973), *Britannia Hospital* (1982), and *The Whales of August* (1987). He also acted cameo parts on film.

Anderson, Marian (1902–93) Contralto concert and opera singer, born in Philadelphia, PA. After a Carnegie Hall recital (1929) she toured in Europe and the USSR. She became the first African-American singer at the New York Metropolitan Opera (1955). President Eisenhower made her a delegate to the UN in 1958, and she received many honours and international awards.

Anderson, Maxwell (1888–1959) Historical playwright, born in Atlantic, PA. A verse playwright, he was in vogue in the late 1920s to the early 1940s with numerous plays such as *Elizabeth the Queen* (1930) and *Mary of Scotland* (1933). He also wrote screenplays, most notably that from Remarque's novel *All Quiet on the Western Front* (1930). He was awarded a Pulitzer Prize for *Both Your Houses* in 1933. >> Remarque

Anderson, Philip W(arren) (1923–) Physicist, born in Indianapolis, IN. He studied antenna engineering at the Naval Research Laboratories in World War 2, and at Harvard under John H Van Vleck. He was research scientist at Bell Telephone Laboratories (1949–84), visiting professor of physics at Cambridge (1967–75), and professor of physics at Princeton in 1975. He shared the Nobel Prize for Physics in 1977 for his work on the electronic structure of magnetic and disordered systems. >> Mott, Nevill F; Van Vleck; RR1122

Anderson, Sherwood (1876–1941) Writer, born in Camden, OH. He left his family and his lucrative position as manager of a paint factory to devote his entire time to writing. His first novel was *Windy McPherson's Son* (1916), but his best-known work is the collection of short stories, *Winesburg, Ohio* (1919).

Anderson, Thomas (1819–74) Organic chemist, born in Scotland, UK. He studied at Edinburgh and Stockholm, became professor of chemistry at Glasgow, and is remembered for his discovery of pyridine.

Anderson, Willa >> **Muir, Edwin**

Andersson, Bibi, popular name of **Birgitta Andersson** (1935–) Actress, born in Stockholm. She began her career in 1949 as a film extra, and is best known for her roles in many Ingmar Bergman films, such as *The Seventh Seal* (1956) and *Persona* (1966). As a theatre actress she has been attached to both the Malmö Municipal Theatre and the Royal Dramatic Theatre, Stockholm. Her later stage successes have been at Dramaten, where she also began directing in the early 1990s. She has been the recipient of many awards, including the British Academy Award for Best Foreign Actress (1971) for her part in *The Touch*. >> Bergman, Ingmar

Andersson, Dan(iel) (1888–1920) Poet and novelist, born in Skattlösbergett, Sweden. One of Sweden's foremost writers of his time, he treated religious and metaphysical themes in his novels, such as the autobiographical *De Tre Hemlösa* (1918, Three Homeless Ones). His poems about traditional charcoal-burners in *Kolarhistorier* (1914) and *Kolvakterens Visor* (1915) turned them into national folk-figures.

Andersson, Johan Gunnar (1874–1960) Archaeologist, born in Knista, Sweden. Trained as a geologist, he went to China in 1914 as technical adviser to the government, but became fascinated by fossil remains. He was the first to identify prehistoric pottery in China, at Yang-shao-ts'un, Hunan, in 1921. He also initiated excavations in the limestone caves at Chou-k'ou-tien near Peking (1921–6), finding important fossils of *Homo erectus* (Peking Man).

Anderton, Sir (Cyril) James (1932–) British police officer. Educated in Manchester, NW England, UK, he joined the local police force in 1953, becoming chief inspector in 1967, and chief constable of the Greater Manchester Police Force (1976–91). He was known for his outspoken and sometimes controversial opinions. He was knighted in 1991.

Andrássy, Gyula, Gróf (Count) [ondrahshee] (1823–90) Statesman and prime minister (1867–71), born in Kassa, Hungary (now Košice, Slovak Republic). A supporter of Kossuth, he was prominent in the struggle for independence (1848–9), after which he remained in exile until 1858. When the Dual Monarchy was formed in 1867, he was made prime minister of Hungary (1871–9). >> Kossuth; RR1057

Andre, Carl [ondray] (1935–) Sculptor, born in Massachusetts. Best known for his minimalist sculptures of the 1960s, such as 'Equivalents', his initial experiments with wood-cutting were inspired by Constantine Brancusi. A job on the Pennsylvania Railroad in the 1960s led to experimentation with mass-produced materials. An interest in mathematics and the philosopher Laozi are evident in his work. >> Brancusi; Laozi

André, John [ondray] (1751-80) British soldier, born in London, England, UK, of French-Swiss descent. In 1774 he joined the army in Canada, and became aide-de-camp to Sir Henry Clinton, and adjutant-general. When Benedict Arnold obtained the command of West Point in 1780, André was selected to negotiate with him for its betrayal. While returning to New York he was captured and handed over to the US military authorities. He was tried as a spy, and hanged. >> Arnold, Benedict; Clinton, Henry

Andreä, Johann Valentin [andraye] (1586-1654) Theologian, born near Tübingen, Germany. Long regarded as the founder or restorer of the Rosicrucians, he wrote *Chymische Hochzeit Christiani Rosenkreuz* (1616).

Andrea da Firenza [andraya da firentsa], originally **Andrea Bonaiuti** (fl.c.1343-77) Florentine painter. His most famous work is the monumental fresco cycle in the Spanish Chapel of the Dominican Church of S Maria Novella in Florence, painted c.1366-8. His only other documented work is the 'Life of S Ranieri', frescoes in the Campo Santo in Pisa, completed in 1377.

Andrea del Sarto >> Sarto, Andrea del

Andreev, Leonid Nikolayevich >> Andreyev, Leonid Nikolayevich

Andress, Ursula (1936–) Film actress, born in Bern. She made her international debut in *Dr No* (1963), her later films including *What's New, Pussycat?* (1965), *Casino Royale* (1967), and *The Clash of the Titans* (1981).

Andretti, Mario (Gabriele) [andretee] (1940–) Motor-racing driver, born in Montona, Italy. After moving to the USA in 1955, he became a US citizen in 1959. He started out in midget car racing, then progressed to the US Automobile Club circuit, in which he was champion three times. In a Formula One career stretching from 1968 to 1982, he competed in 128 Grand Prix, winning 16. His most successful year was 1978, when he won the racing drivers' world championship. He was also twice winner, in 1969 and 1981, of the Indianapolis 500. >> RR1164

Andrew (Albert Christian Edward), Duke of York (1960–) British prince, the second son of Queen Elizabeth II. He studied at Gordonstoun School, Moray, NE Scotland, UK, and Lakefield College, Ontario, SE Canada, then trained at the Royal Naval College, Dartmouth, where he was commissioned as a helicopter pilot. He saw service in the Falklands War (1982). In 1986 he married **Sarah (Margaret) Ferguson** (1959–), and was made Duke of York. They have two children, **Princess Beatrice Elizabeth Mary** (1988–) and **Princess Eugenie Victoria Helena** (1990–). The couple separated in 1992, and divorced in 1996. >> Elizabeth II

Andrew, St (d. c.60) One of the 12 apostles, the brother of Simon Peter. A fisherman, he was converted by John the Baptist. Tradition says he preached the Gospel in Asia Minor and Scythia, and was crucified in Achaia (Greece) by order of the Roman governor. He is the patron saint of Scotland and of Russia. Feast day 30 November. >> John the Baptist, St; Peter, St

Andrew, Agnellus (Matthew) (1908-87) Roman Catholic bishop and broadcaster, born near Glasgow, W Scotland, UK. Ordained in 1932, he became assistant to the head of religious broadcasting at the BBC (1955-67), and adviser to the Independent Broadcasting Authority (1968-75). Meanwhile he became known as a TV commentator for many papal and national events, and was founder and director of the National Catholic Radio and TV Centre at Hatch End, Greater London (1955-80). Having been made titular Bishop of Numana, he became from 1980 external head of the Vatican commission for communication.

Andrewes, Lancelot (1555-1626) Anglican clergyman and scholar, born in Barking, Essex, SE England, UK. He studied at Cambridge, took orders in 1580, and rose to become Dean of Westminster in 1601. He attended the Hampton Court Conference, and took part in the translation of the Authorized Version of the Bible (1607). In 1605 he was consecrated Bishop of Chichester; in 1609 he was translated to Ely, and in 1618 to Winchester. A powerful preacher and defender of Anglican doctrines, he is considered one of the most learned theologians of his time.

Andrews, Eamon (1922-87) Broadcaster, born in Dublin, Ireland. He began sports commentating for Radio Eireann in 1939 and subsequently worked on various programmes for BBC Radio, including *Sports Report* (1950-62). On television he hosted the parlour game *What's My Line?* (1951-63) and *This is Your Life* (1955-87). Active as a chat show host and children's programmes presenter, as well as being a keen businessman, he later returned to *What's My Line?* (1984-7).

Andrews, Frank M(axwell) (1884-1943) US air force officer, born in Nashville, TN. He trained at West Point, and between the wars became the first commander of the general-headquarters air force (1935-9). In World War 2 he was head of the US Caribbean Defense Command (1941-2) and the Middle East Command (1942-3), before succeeding Eisenhower as commander of the US forces in Europe. Andrews airforce base in Washington is named after him.

Andrews, Julie, originally **Julia Elizabeth Wells** (1935–) Singer and actress, born in Walton-on-Thames, Surrey, SE England, UK. Radio stage successes led to her selection for the New York City production of *The Boyfriend* (1954), and several long-running Broadway musicals, notably *My Fair Lady* (1956) and *Camelot* (1960). With her film debut in *Mary Poppins* (1964) she won an Oscar, and this was followed by a further nomination for *The Sound of Music* (1965). Voted the world's most popular star, she broadened her range in *S.O.B.* (1981), *Victor/Victoria* (1982), *Duet for One* (1987), and *A Fine Romance* (1992). Since 1970 she has appeared almost exclusively in films directed by her second husband, Blake Edwards (1922–).

Andrews, Roy Chapman (1884-1960) Naturalist and explorer, born in Beloit, WI. He is best known as the discoverer, in Mongolia, of fossil dinosaur eggs, but he made many and valuable contributions to palaeontology, archaeology, botany, zoology, geology, and topography. He made several expeditions to C Asia, sponsored by the American Museum of Natural History, of which he became director (1935-42).

Andrews, Thomas (1813-85) Physical chemist, born in Belfast. He practised as a physician in Belfast, where he became professor of chemistry (1849-79). He is noted for his discovery of the critical temperature of gases, above which they cannot be liquefied, however great the pressure applied.

Andreyev, Leonid Nikolayevich [andrayef], also spelled **Andreev** (1871-1919) Writer and artist, born in Orel, Russia. He suffered much from poverty and ill health as a student, and attempted suicide, before taking to writing and portrait painting. Many of his works have been translated into English, such as *Krasnysmekh* (1905, The Red Laugh) and *Rasskaz o semi poveshennykh* (1908, The Seven That Were Hanged).

Andrianov, Nikolay [andriahnof] (1952–) Gymnast, born in Vladimir, Russia. He won 15 Olympic medals (including seven golds) between 1972 and 1980. In addition, he won 12 world championship medals, including the overall individual title in 1978. >> RR1159

Andrić, Ivo [andrich] (1892-1975) Yugoslav diplomat and writer, born near Travnik, Bosnia and Herzegovina. A member of the diplomatic service, he was minister in Berlin at the outbreak of war in 1939. His chief works (trans titles), *The Bridge on the Drina* (1945) and *Bosnian Story* (1945), earned him the 1961 Nobel Prize for Literature and the nickname 'the Yugoslav Tolstoy'. >> Tolstoy

Andronicus [an**dron**ikus], known as **Cyrrhestes** (1st-c BC) Greek architect, born in Cyrrhus. He constructed the Tower of the Winds at Athens, known in the Middle Ages as the Lantern of Demosthenes.

Andronicus, Livius >> **Livius Andronicus**

Andronicus of Rhodes [an**dron**ikus] (fl.70–50 BC) Greek philosopher. He lived in Rome in Cicero's time, and edited the writings of Aristotle. >> Aristotle; Cicero

Andropov, Yuri Vladimirovich [an**dropof**] (1914–84) Russian politician, born in Nagutskoye, Russia. He began work in the shipyards of the upper Volga at Rybinsk (later called Andropov), where he became politically active. After World War 2 he was brought to Moscow to work for the Communist Party central committee. He was ambassador in Budapest (1954–7), and came to the notice of the strict ideologist, Mikhail Suslov, for his part in crushing the Hungarian uprising of 1956. In 1967 he was appointed KGB chief, and in 1973 became a full member of the Politburo. His firm handling of dissident movements enhanced his reputation, enabling him to be chosen as Brezhnev's successor in 1983, but he died after less than 15 months in office. >> Brezhnev; Suslov

Aneirin or **Aneurin** [a**niy**rin] (fl.6th–7th-c) Welsh court poet. His principal work, the *Gododdin*, celebrates the British heroes who were annihilated by the Saxons in the bloody Battle of Cattraeth (Catterick, North Yorkshire) about the year 600. The poem's language, metrical forms, and general technique suggest a long tradition of praise-poetry in the Brythonic language.

Anfinsen, Christian B(oehmer) (1916–95) Biochemist, born in Monessen, PA. He studied at Harvard, and taught there before moving to the National Institutes of Health in Bethesda, MD (1950–82). His chief work was on the sequence of amino acids which make up the enzyme ribonuclease, for which he shared the Nobel Prize for Chemistry in 1972. >> RR1123

Angas, George Fife (1789–1879) Shipowner, born in Newcastle upon Tyne, Tyne and Wear, NE England. He is regarded as a founder of South Australia. He was appointed commissioner for the formation of the colony in 1834, and emigrated to Adelaide in 1851.

Angeles, Victoria de los [an**jeles**] (1923–) Lyric soprano, born in Barcelona, Spain. Her operatic debut was at Barcelona in 1944. She then performed at the Paris Opera and La Scala, Milan (1949), Covent Garden (1950), the New York Metropolitan (1951), and subsequently at all the great houses and festivals throughout the world. After retiring from the stage in 1969, she continued to give recitals.

Angelico, Fra [an**jel**ikoh], originally **Guido di Pietro**, monastic name **Giovanni da Fiesole** (c. 1400–55) Painter, born in Vicchio, Italy. He entered the Dominican monastery of San Domenico at Fiesole, and in 1436 was transferred to Florence where he worked for Cosimo de' Medici. In 1445 he was summoned by the pope to Rome, where he worked until his death. His most important frescoes are in the Florentine convent of S Marco, which is now a museum. These aids to contemplation are characterized by pale colours, crisp delineation of form, the use of local landscape as background, and an air of mystical piety. In Rome only the frescoes in the chapel of Nicholas V survive. >> Cosimo de' Medici

Angélique, Mère >> **Arnauld, Angélique; Jacqueline-Marie-Angélique**

Angell, Sir Norman [**ayn**jl], originally **Ralph Norman Angell-Lane** (1872–1967) Writer and pacifist, born in Holbeach, Lincolnshire, EC England, UK. He wrote *The Great Illusion* (1910) and *The Great Illusion, 1933* (1933) to prove the economic futility of war even for the winners. He was awarded the Nobel Peace Prize in 1933.

Angelou, Maya [an**jeloo**] (1928–) Writer, singer, dancer, and African-American activist, born in St Louis, MO. She has had a variety of occupations in what she describes as 'a roller-coaster life'. She toured Europe and Africa in the musical *Porgy and Bess*, and in New York City joined the Harlem Writers Guild. In the 1960s she was involved in black struggles, then spent several years in Ghana as editor of *African Review*. Her multi-volume autobiography, commencing with *I Know Why the Caged Bird Sings* (1970), was a critical and popular success. Her later books include *All God's Children Need Travelling Shoes* (1986) and *My Painted House, My Friendly Chicken and Me* (1994). She has published several volumes of verse, including *And Still I Rise* (1987) and *Complete Collected Poems of Maya Angelou* (1995).

Angiolieri, Cecco [anjoh**lyay**ree] (c.1260–c.1312) Poet, born in Siena, Italy. Nothing is known of his life except from his sonnets, the only kind of verse he wrote, which reveal a cynical, sardonic character. He attacked Dante in three poems. >> Dante

Anglesey, Henry William Paget, 1st Marquess of [**angg**lsee] (1768–1854) British soldier, born in London, England, UK. He studied at Oxford, and sat in parliament at intervals between 1790 and 1810. He served in the army with distinction in Flanders (1794), Holland (1799), and the Peninsular War (1808), and for his services as commander of the British cavalry at Waterloo, where he lost a leg, he was made Marquess of Anglesey. In 1828 he was appointed Lord-Lieutenant of Ireland, where he advocated Catholic Emancipation. From 1846 to 1852 he was Master-General of the Ordnance.

Angleton, James (Jesus) (1917–87) Public official, born in Boise, ID. He studied at Yale, and in World War 2 became a member of the Office of Strategic Services. As director of counter-intelligence at the CIA (1954–74), he came to distrust everyone, pursuing Soviet agents within the CIA itself as well as throughout the world. His resignation was demanded in 1974 following the revelation that he had conducted clandestine mail-opening and surveillance searches within the Agency in pursuit of a Soviet 'mole'. The classic image of a paranoid intelligence officer, he was said to relax by reading poetry and cultivating orchids.

Angliss, Sir William Charles (1865–1957) Businessman, born in Dudley, West Midlands, C England, UK. He emigrated to Australia in 1884, eventually opening a butcher's shop in Melbourne. In 1934, when the family company was sold to the Vestey family interests, it had become the largest meat exporter in Australia.

Angoulême, Louis Antoine de Bourbon, duc d' (Duke of) [ă**goolem**] (1775–1844) French soldier and aristocrat, the eldest son of Charles X of France. He fled from France with his father after the revolution of 1789, and in 1799 married his cousin, **Marie Thérèse** (1778–1851), the only daughter of Louis XVI. After the Restoration in 1814 he made a feeble effort to oppose Napoleon on his return from Elba. In 1823 he led the French army of invasion into Spain to restore Ferdinand VII (reigned 1808–33) to his throne. After the July revolution in 1830, he renounced his claim to the throne, and accompanied his father into exile. >> Charles X; Louis XVI; Napoleon

Angry Young Men >> **Amis, Kingsley; Braine, John; Osborne, John; Sillitoe, Alan; Wain, John**

Ångström, Anders (Jonas) [**ang**struhm, **awng**stroem] (1814–74) Physicist, born in Lödgö, Sweden. He was keeper of the observatory at Uppsala (1843), and became professor of physics there in 1858. He wrote on heat, magnetism, and especially optics. The *ångstrom* unit, for measuring wavelengths of light, is named after him.

Animuccia, Giovanni [animoo**chia**] (c.1500–71) Composer, born in Florence, Italy. In 1555 he became choirmaster at St Peter's in the Vatican. He was influenced by St Philip Neri, for whose oratory he composed the *Laudi* – semi-dramatic religious pieces in popular style from which oratorio developed. >> Neri

Aniston, Jennifer (1969–) Actor, born in Sherman Oaks, CA. She trained at the High School for the Performing Arts in New York City, worked off-Broadway, then went to Hollywood, where she eventually achieved success through her role as Rachel Green in the acclaimed television series *Friends* (1994–). Roles in feature films include *Leprechaun* (1993), *She's the One* (1996), and *Til There Was You* (1997).

An Lushan >> Lushan, An

Anna Amalia [amah lia] (1739–1807) Duchess of Saxe-Weimar and notable patron of German literature. Widowed in 1758 after only two years of marriage, she acted as regent for her infant son, Charles Augustus, with great skill and prudence (1758–75). She attracted to the court at Weimar the leading literary figures in Germany, and founded the Weimar Museum.

Anna Comnena [kom**nay**na] (1083–1148) Byzantine princess and historian, the daughter of Alexius I Comnenus. In 1097 she married Nicephorus Bryennius, for whom she tried in vain to gain the imperial crown after her father's death in 1118. She took up literature, and after her husband's death (1137) retired to a convent where she wrote the *Alexiad*, an account of Byzantine history and society for the period 1069–1118. >> Alexius I

Anna Ivanovna [**ivah**novna] (1693–1740) Tsarina of Russia from 1730, the younger daughter of Ivan V and niece of Peter the Great. After the early death of Peter II (1715–30) she was elected to the throne by the Supreme Council in 1730, with conditions that severely limited her authority. She proceeded to abolish the Council, and ruled as an autocrat with her German favourite, **Ernst Johann Biron** (1690–1772), who became the real power behind the throne. >> Peter I (of Russia); RR1085

Annan, Kofi (1938–) UN secretary-general (from 1997), born in Kumasi, Ghana. He studied in the USA and Switzerland, joining the UN in 1962, and held posts in the High Commission for Refugees and the World Health Organization. After joining the UN secretariat, he became (1993) under-secretary-general for peacekeeping operations. He replaced Boutros-Ghali to become the first secretary-general from sub-Saharan Africa. >> Boutros-Ghali

Annas [**an**as] (1st-c) Israel's high priest, appointed in AD 6 and deposed by the Romans in 15, but still described later by this title in the New Testament. He apparently questioned Jesus after his arrest (*John* 18) and Peter after his detention (*Acts* 4). His other activities are described in the works of Flavius Josephus. >> Caiaphas; Jesus Christ; Josephus; Peter, St

Anne (1665–1714) Queen of Great Britain and Ireland (1702–14), born in London, England, UK, the second daughter of James II (then Duke of York) and his first wife, Anne Hyde. In 1672 her father became a Catholic, but Anne was brought up as a staunch Protestant. In 1683 she married Prince George of Denmark (1653–1708), bearing him 17 children. Probably only six were born alive and only one survived infancy – William, Duke of Gloucester, who died in 1700 at the age of 12. For much of her life she was greatly influenced by her close friend and confidante, Sarah Churchill, the future Duchess of Marlborough. In 1688, when her father James II was overthrown, she supported the accession of her sister Mary and her brother-in-law William, and in 1701, after the death of her own son, signed the Act of Settlement designating the Hanoverian descendants of James I as her successors. Her reign saw the union of the parliaments of Scotland and England (1707), and the War of the Spanish Succession (1701–13). She finally broke with the Marlboroughs in 1710–11, when Sarah was supplanted by a new favourite, Sarah's cousin, Mrs Abigail Masham, and the Whigs were replaced by a Tory administration. She was the last Stuart monarch. >> Churchill, Sarah; James II (of England); Mary II; Masham; William III; RR1095

Anne, St (fl.1st-c BC–1st-c AD) Wife of **St Joachim**, and mother of the Virgin Mary, first mentioned in the *Protevangelium* of James, in the 2nd-c. She is the patron saint of carpenters. Feast day 26 July. >> Mary (mother of Jesus)

Anne (Elizabeth Alice Louise), Princess (1950–) British Princess Royal, the only daughter of Queen Elizabeth II and Prince Philip, born in London, England, UK. In 1973 she married Lieutenant (now Captain) Mark Phillips of the Queen's Dragoon Guards, but they were divorced in 1992; their children are: **Peter Mark Andrew** (1977–) and **Zara Anne Elizabeth** (1981–). She married **Timothy Laurence** (1955–) in 1992. An accomplished horsewoman, she has ridden in the British Equestrian Team, and was European cross-country champion (1972). She is a keen supporter of charities and overseas relief work; as president of Save the Children Fund she has travelled widely promoting its activities. >> Edinburgh, Duke of; Elizabeth II; Phillips, Mark

Anne Boleyn >> Boleyn, Anne

Anne of Austria (1601–66) Queen of France, born in Valladolid, Spain, the eldest daughter of Philip III of Spain and wife of Louis XIII of France, whom she married in 1615. The marriage was unhappy, and much of it was spent in virtual separation, due to the influence of the king's chief minister Cardinal Richelieu. In 1638, however, they had their first son, Louis, who succeeded his father in 1643 as Louis XIV. Anne was appointed regent for the boy king (1643–51), and wielded power with Cardinal Mazarin as prime minister. After Mazarin's death in 1661, she retired to a convent. >> Louis XIII; Louis XIV; Mazarin; RR1049

Anne of Bohemia (1366–94) Queen of England, the first wife of Richard II. The daughter of Emperor Charles IV (reigned 1355–78), she married Richard in 1382. >> Richard II; RR1095

Anne of Brittany (1476–1514) Duchess of Brittany and twice queen of France. She struggled to maintain Breton independence, but in 1491 was forced to marry Charles VIII of France (reigned 1483–98), whereby Brittany was united with the French crown. In 1499, a year after his death, she married his successor, Louis XII. >> Louis XII

Anne of Cleves (1515–57) German princess and queen consort of England, the fourth wife of Henry VIII, the daughter of John, Duke of Cleves, a noted champion of Protestantism in Germany. A plain-featured and unattractive girl, she was selected for purely political reasons after the death of Jane Seymour, and was married to Henry in 1540. The marriage was annulled by parliament six months later. >> Henry VIII; Seymour, Jane

Anne of Denmark (1574–1619) Danish princess, and queen of Scotland and England. The daughter of King Frederik II of Denmark (reigned 1559–88), in 1589 she married James VI of Scotland, the future James I of England. She was a lavish patron of the arts and architecture, and appeared in dramatic roles in court masques by Ben Jonson. >> James I (of England); Jonson

Annenberg, Walter (Hubert) (1908–) Publisher and philanthropist, born in Milwaukee, WI. Inheriting a communications empire that included the *Philadelphia Inquirer*, the *Racing Form*, and broadcasting stations, he founded *Seventeen* magazine (1944) and the immensely successful *TV Guide* (1953), besides purchasing *The Philadelphia Daily News* (1957). A prominent Republican, he served as US ambassador to Britain (1969–74). He assembled a large art collection that he donated to the Metropolitan Museum of Art, and used some of his huge fortune to endow a graduate school of communications at the University of Pennsylvania.

Annigoni, Pietro [anigohnee] (1910–88) Painter, born in Milan, Italy. He was one of the few 20th-c artists to put into practice the technical methods of the old masters. His most usual medium was tempera, although there are frescoes by him in the Convent of S Marco at Florence (executed in 1937). His Renaissance manner is shown at its best in his portraits, such as those of Queen Elizabeth II (1955, 1970) and President Kennedy (1961).

Anno, Mitsumasu [anoh] (1926–) Children's writer and illustrator, born in Tsuwano, Japan. Renowned for his visual puzzles, his best work can be seen in *Topsy-Turvies: Pictures to Stretch the Imagination* (1970) and *Anno's Alphabet: an Adventure in Imagination* (1975).

Annunzio, Gabriele d' >> d'Annunzio, Gabriele

Anouilh, Jean (Marie Lucien Pierre) [onwee] (1910–87) Playwright, born in Bordeaux, France, of French and Basque parentage. His first play, *L'Hermine* (1931), was not a success; but his steady output soon earned him recognition as one of the leading playwrights of the contemporary theatre. He was influenced by the Neoclassical fashion inspired by Giraudoux. His many plays include *Le Voyageur sans bagage* (1938, trans Traveller Without Luggage), *Le Bal des voleurs* (1938, Thieves' Carnival), *La Sauvage* (1938), *L'Invitation au château* (1948) (adapted by Christopher Fry as *Ring Round the Moon*, 1950), *L'Alouette* (1953, The Lark), and *Becket* (1959). >> Giraudoux

Anquetil, Jacques [ãketeel] (1934–87) Racing cyclist, born in Normandy, France. He won the Tour de France five times, including four successive wins between 1961 and 1964. He retired in 1969. >> RR1152

Anschütz, Ottomar [anshüts] (1846–1907) Photographer, born in Yugoslavia. He was a pioneer of instantaneous photography, and was one of the first to make a series of pictures of moving animals and people.

Anselm, St (1033–1109) Scholastic philosopher and clergyman, born in Aosta, Italy. He left Italy in 1056 and settled at the Benedictine abbey of Bec in Normandy. He moved to England to succeed Lanfranc as Archbishop of Canterbury in 1093. His strong principles brought him into conflict both with William II and Henry I, and he was temporarily exiled by each of them. Much influenced by Augustine he sought 'necessary reasons' for religious beliefs, notably the famous ontological argument for the existence of God. He may have been canonized as early as 1163; feast day 21 April. >> Lanfranc; William II (of England)

Ansermet, Ernest (Alexandre) [ansermay] (1883–1969) Conductor and musical theorist, born in Vevey, Switzerland. He studied at Lausanne, and gave up teaching mathematics in 1910 to devote his time to music. He was conductor of the Montreux Kursaal in 1912 and of Diaghilev's Russian Ballet (1915–23). In 1918 he founded the Orchestre de la Suisse Romande, whose conductor he remained till 1967. His compositions include a symphonic poem, piano pieces, and songs. >> Diaghilev

Ansett, Sir Reginald (Myles) (1909–81) Pioneer of passenger flight, born in Inglewood, Victoria, Australia. He opened a regular air service to Melbourne in 1936, and by 1957 had formed the largest private transport system in the S hemisphere, with a country-wide network of air and coach services. In 1979 Ansett's group was taken over by a consortium of Rupert Murdoch's News Ltd and Sir Peter Abeles' TNT. >> Abeles

Ansgar or **Anskar, St**, Ger **St Scharies**, known as **the Apostle of the North** (801–65) Frankish clergyman and missionary to Scandinavia, born in Picardy, France. He became a Benedictine monk, and in 826 he was sent to preach the Gospel in Denmark. In 829 he was allowed to build the first church in Sweden. Consecrated archbishop of the newly founded archdiocese of Hamburg in 831 he was named as papal legate to all the Northern peoples. He is the patron saint of Scandinavia. Feast day 3 February.

Anson, George Anson, Baron (1697–1762) English naval commander, born at Shugborough Park, Staffordshire, C England, UK. He entered the navy in 1712, and was made a captain in 1724. In 1739 he received the command of a Pacific squadron, and sailed from England (1740), circumnavigating the globe in three years and nine months. In 1761 he was appointed Admiral of the Fleet. He wrote *Voyage Round the World* (1748), the story of his travels.

Anstey, Christopher [anstee] (1724–1805) Writer, born in Brinkley, Cambridgeshire, EC England, UK. He studied at King's College, Cambridge, where he became a fellow (1745–54). In 1766 he wrote the *New Bath Guide*, an epistolary novel in verse, which achieved great popularity.

Anstey, F [anstee], pseudonym of **Thomas Anstey Guthrie** (1856–1934) Writer, born in London, England, UK. He studied at Trinity Hall, Cambridge, and in 1880 was called to the bar. A whimsical humorist, he wrote *Vice Versa* (1882), *The Brass Bottle* (1900), and many other novels and dialogues. He also joined the staff of *Punch* (1887–1930).

Antar, in full **l'Antarah Ibn Shaddād Al-Absi** (6th-c) Arab poet and warrior, born of a Bedouin chieftain and a black slave near Medina, Saudi Arabia. The author of one of the seven Golden Odes of Arabic literature, and the subject of the 10th-c *Romance of Antar*, he is regarded as the model of Bedouin heroism and chivalry.

Antenor [antaynaw(r)] (6th-c BC) Athenian sculptor, known to have executed bronze statues of 'Harmodius' and 'Aristogiton', and a statue of a kore (a freestanding figure of a maiden) in the Acropolis.

Antheil, George [antiyl] (1900–59) Composer, born in Trenton, NJ. He studied in New York City under Ernest Bloch, spending some years in Europe as a professional pianist before becoming known as the composer of the *Jazz Symphony* (1925), the *Ballet Mécanique* (1926), and the opera *Transatlantic* (1930). The sensation caused by the ballet, written for 10 pianos and a variety of eccentric percussion instruments, overshadowed his more traditional later works, which include five symphonies, concertos, operas, and chamber music. >> Bloch, Ernest

Anthony, St >> Antony, St; Antony of Padua

Anthony, C L >> Smith, Dodie

Anthony, Susan B(rownell) (1820–1906) Social reformer and women's suffrage leader, born in Adams, MA. Early active in temperance and anti-slavery movements, she became the champion of women's rights in 1854. In 1869 with Elizabeth Cady Stanton she founded the National American Woman Suffrage Association. She also organized the International Council of Women (1888) and the International Woman Suffrage Alliance in Berlin (1904). >> Stanton

Antigonus I [antigonus], known as **Cyclops** or **Monophthalmos** (Gr 'One-eyed') (382–301 BC) Macedonian soldier, one of the generals of Alexander the Great. After Alexander's death, he received the provinces of Phrygia Major, Lycia, and Pamphylia. On Antipater's death in 319 BC, he aspired to the sovereignty of Asia, and waged incessant wars against the other generals, making himself master of all Asia Minor and Syria. In 306 BC he assumed the title of king, together with his son Demetrius Poliorcetes, but was defeated and slain at Ipsus in Phrygia. >> Alexander the Great; Cassander; Lysimachus; Seleucus; Antipater (of Macedon)

Antigonus II [antigonus], known as **Gonatas** (c. 319–239 BC) King of Macedon. He did not mount his throne until 276 BC, seven years after the death of his father, Demetrius Poliorcetes. Pyrrhus of Epirus overran Macedonia in 274 BC, but Antigonus soon recovered his kingdom, and consolidated it despite incessant wars. >> Pyrrhus; RR1055

Antill, John Henry (1904–86) Composer, born in Ashfield, New South Wales, Australia. Entering the New South Wales Conservatory at 21, he studied composition with Alfred Hill, becoming a member of the Conservatory orchestra and later of the ABC (now Sydney) Symphony Orchestra. His major work, the ballet *Corroboree* (1944), blends Aboriginal and western themes. Other compositions include operas and choral works, ballet suites, and a symphony. >> Hill, Alfred

Antiochus I [antiohkus], known as **Antiochus Soter** (Gr 'Saviour') (324–261 BC) Seleucid king of Syria. He was the son of Seleucus I, one of Alexander's generals, whose murder in 280 gave him the whole Syrian empire, but left him too weak to assert his right to Macedonia. He gained his surname for a victory over the Gauls, but fell in battle with them. >> Seleucus I

Antiochus II [antiyokus], known as **Antiochus Theos** ('God') (286–247 BC) Seleucid king of Syria, the son and successor of Antiochus I. He married Berenice, the daughter of Ptolemy II, exiling his first wife, Laodice, and her children. On his death there followed a struggle between the rival queens. Berenice and her son were murdered, and the succession went to Laodice's son, Seleucus II (reigned 246–226 BC). >> Antiochus I; Ptolemy II

Antiochus III [antiohkus], known as **Antiochus the Great** (c.242–187 BC) Seleucid king of Syria, the grandson of Antiochus II, who succeeded his brother, Seleucus III, in 223 BC. He waged war with success against Ptolemy IV Philopator, and though defeated at Raphia near Gaza (217 BC), he obtained entire possession of Palestine and Coele Syria (198 BC). He later became involved in war with the Romans, who had conquered Macedonia. He crossed over into Greece, but was defeated in 191 BC at Thermopylae, and in 190 or 189 BC by Scipio at Magnesia. To raise tribute money, he attacked a rich temple in Elymais, but the people rose against him and killed him. >> Antiochus II; Scipio Africanus

Antiochus IV [antiyokus], known as **Antiochus Epiphanes** (c. 215–163 BC) Seleucid king of Syria, the son of Antiochus III. He succeeded his brother in 175 BC, then fought against Egypt and conquered a great part of it. He twice took Jerusalem, provoking the Jews to a successful insurrection under Mattathias and his sons, the Maccabees. >> Antiochus III

Antipater [antipater] (of Macedon) (398–319 BC) Macedonian general. He was highly trusted by Philip II of Macedonia and Alexander the Great, and was left by the latter as regent in Macedonia (334 BC). He discharged his duties with great ability, both before and after the death of Alexander. >> Alexander the Great; Philip II (of Macedon)

Antipater [antipater] (of Idumaea) (?–43 BC) The father of Herod the Great, appointed by Julius Caesar procurator of Judaea in 47 BC. He died by poisoning. >> Caesar; Herod

Antipater [antipater] (?–4 BC) Judaean prince, the son of Herod the Great by his first wife. He conspired against his half-brothers and had them executed, then plotted against his father, and was himself executed five days before Herod died. >> Herod

Antiphon [antifon] (5th-c BC) Greek philosopher and Sophist. Nothing is known of his life, but he is generally distinguished from Antiphon the orator. He is important as the author of two works, *On Truth* and *On Concord*, which survive in fragmentary form.

Antiphon [antifon] (c. 480–411 BC) The earliest of the ten Attic orators. He belonged to the oligarchical party, and was influential in establishing the government of the Four Hundred (411BC). On its fall he was condemned to death, in spite of a noble defence.

Antisthenes [antistheneez] (c. 445–c. 365 BC) Greek philosopher, thought to be co-founder, with his pupil Diogenes, of the Cynic school. He was a rhetorician and a disciple of Gorgias, and later became a close friend of Socrates. Only fragments of his many works survive. >> Diogenes of Sinope; Gorgias; Socrates

Antoine, André [ātwahn] (1858–1943) Actor-manager, born in Limoges, France. He founded the Théâtre Libre (1887), and was director of the Odéon (from 1906).

Antonelli, Giacomo [antonelee] (1806–76) Clergyman, born in Sonnino, Italy. In 1819, he went to Rome, and entered the Grand Seminary, where he gained the favour of Pope Gregory XVI (1831–46). In 1847 he was made cardinal-deacon by Pius IX, and in 1848 was premier and minister of foreign affairs. He accompanied the pope in his flight to Gaeta in 1848, and returned with him to Rome, becoming foreign secretary (1850), and supporting the policy of absolute papal administrative power. >> Pius IX

Antonello da Messina [antoneloh da meseena] (c. 1430–79) Painter, born in Messina, Italy. He was the only major 15th-c Italian artist to come from Sicily. An accomplished master of oil painting, he helped popularize the medium, his style being a delicate synthesis of the northern and Italian styles. In 1475 he was working in Venice where his work influenced Giovanni Bellini's portraits. His first dated work, the 'Salvator Mundi' (1465), and a self-portrait are in the London National Gallery. >> Bellini, Giovanni

Antonescu, Ion [antoneskoo] (1882–1946) Romanian general and dictator for the Nazis in World War 2, born in Pitesti, Romania. He served as military attaché in Rome and London, and became chief-of-staff and minister of defence in 1937. In September 1940 he assumed dictatorial powers and forced the abdication of Carol II. He headed a Fascist government allied to Nazi Germany until 1944, when he was overthrown and executed for war crimes. >> Carol II; Michael; RR1084

Antoninus, M Aurelius >> **Aurelius**

Antoninus Pius [antoniynus piyus], originally **Titus Aurelius Fulvus** (AD 86–161) Roman emperor, born in Lanuvium. He inherited great wealth, and in 120 was made consul. Sent as proconsul into Asia by Emperor Hadrian, in 138 he was adopted by him, and the same year came to the throne. His reign was proverbially peaceful and happy. In public affairs he acted as the father of his people, and the persecution of Christians was partly stayed by his mild measures. In his reign the empire was extended, and the Antonine Wall, named after him, built between the Forth and Clyde rivers. He was called *Pius* for his defence of Hadrian's memory. Marcus Aurelius was his adopted son and successor. >> Aurelius; Hadrian; RR1084

Antonioni, Michelangelo [antoniohnee] (1912–) Film director, born in Ferrara, Italy. After studying political economy at Bologna University, he began as a film critic before becoming an assistant director in 1942. He made several documentaries (1945–50) before turning to feature films, often scripted by himself, and notable for their preoccupation with character study rather than plot. He gained an international reputation with *L'avventura* (1959), followed by other outstanding works, such as *La* *notte* (1961, The Night), *Blow-up* (1966), *Zabriskie Point* (1969), *Professione: Reporter* (1975, The Passenger), and *Il mistero di Oberwald* (1979, The Oberwald Mystery). He lost the power of speech after a stroke in 1985, but managed to make a further film, *Beyond the Clouds* (1995). He received an Academy lifetime achievement award in 1995.

Antonius, Marcus [an**toh**nius] or **Mark Antony** (c. 83–30 BC) Roman triumvir, related on his mother's side to Julius Caesar. After assisting Caesar in Gaul (53–50 BC), he went to Rome to become tribune of the plebians (49 BC). Caesar left him in charge in Italy, and at Pharsalia (48 BC) Antony led the left wing of Caesar's army against Pompey. In 44 BC he was made consul together with Caesar, and on Caesar's assassination, the flight of the conspirators left him with almost absolute power. Besieged and defeated at Mutina by Octavian Augustus (43 BC), he fled beyond the Alps; but in Gaul he visited the camp of Lepidus, and gained the favour of the army, with which he returned to Rome. Augustus, Antony, and Lepidus then established themselves as triumvirs to share the whole Roman world, defeating Brutus and Cassius at Philippi (42 BC). After meeting Cleopatra in Asia, he followed her to Egypt (41–40 BC), until called back by news of a quarrel in Italy between his kinsmen and Augustus. A new division of the Roman world was now arranged, Antony taking the East, and Augustus the West, while Lepidus had to be content with Africa; Antony also married Augustus's sister Octavia (40 BC). Differences grew up between Antony and Augustus, and in 37 BC Antony separated from Octavia and rejoined Cleopatra. His position in the East, his relations with Cleopatra, and his unsuccessful campaigns against the Parthians (36 and 34 BC), were seized upon by Augustus, and in the naval engagement of Actium (31 BC) Antony and Cleopatra were defeated. Antony went back to Egypt, where, deceived by a false report of Cleopatra's suicide, he committed suicide. >> Brutus; Caesar; Cassius; Cleopatra; Lepidus; Octavia; Pompey

Antonov, Oleg Konstantinovich [antonof] (1906–84) Soviet aircraft designer, born in Troitskoe, Russia. He studied at the Leningrad Polytechnic Institute, became head of the experimental design department in 1946, and designer in general for the aircraft industry in 1962. He received the Lenin Prize in 1962 and the Order of Lenin twice. After World War 2 he became senior designer with the ministry of aviation (until 1963). The author of over 50 books on glider and aircraft design, his name is perpetuated in the AN-225 six-engined super heavylift aircraft which carried the Soviet shuttle orbiter *Buran* above its fuselage, shown at the Paris Airshow in 1989.

Antony or **Anthony, St**, known as **Antony the Great**, also called **Antony of Egypt** (c. 251–356) Religious hermit, the father of Christian monasticism, born in Koman, Upper Egypt. He sold his possessions for the poor at the age of 20 and withdrew into the wilderness. He spent 20 years in the most rigorous seclusion, during which he withstood a series of temptations by the devil which became famous in Christian theology and art. In 305 he left his retreat to found a monastery, at first only a group of separate and scattered cells near Memphis and Arsinoë – one of the earliest attempts to instruct people in the monastic way of life. Feast day 17 January.

Antony or **Anthony of Padua, St** (1195–1231) Monk, born in Lisbon. At first an Augustinian monk, in 1220 he entered the Franciscan order, and became one of its most active propagators. He was canonized by Gregory IX (c.1170–1241) the year after his death. According to legend, he preached to the fishes when people refused to listen to him; hence he is the patron of the lower animals, and is often shown accompanied by an ass. Feast day 13 June.

Anville, Jean Baptiste Bourguignon d' [āveel] (1697–1782) Geographer and map-maker, born in Paris. He greatly improved the standards of ancient and mediaeval mapmaking, and became the first geographer to the King of France.

Anzengruber, Ludwig [an**tsengruber]** (1839–89) Playwright and novelist, born in Vienna. He was a bookshop assistant, a touring actor, and a police clerk before the success of his play, *Der Pfarrer von Kirchfeld* (1870, The Pastor of Kirchfeld), enabled him to devote the rest of his life to writing. He was the author of several novels, of which the best is *Der Sternsteinhof* (1885, The Sternstein Farm), and about 20 plays, mostly about Austrian peasant life.

Anzilotti, Dionisio [antsi**lo**tee] (1867–1950) Jurist, born in Pistoia, Italy. Professor at Rome (1911–37), he was a founder of the positive school of international law, which derived law from the practice of nations rather than from theorizing. Later he became a judge of the Permanent Court of International Justice (1921–30), and its president (1928–30).

Aouita, Said [a**wee**ta] (1960–   ) Athlete, born in Rabat, Morocco. A middle- and long-distance track athlete, he set world records at 1500 m and 5000 m in 1985 to become the first man for 30 years to hold both records. He has since broken world records at 2 mi and 2000 m. The 1986 overall Grand Prix winner, he was the 1984 Olympic and 1987 World 5000 m champion. >> RR1133

Apelles [a**pe**leez] (4th-c BC) Greek painter, probably born in Colophon, Asia Minor. He visited Macedon, where he became the friend of Alexander the Great, and is said to have accompanied him on his expedition to Asia. None of his work has survived, but his fame lives in ancient writings. >> Alexander the Great

Apgar, Virginia (1909–1974) Physician and anesthesiologist, born in Westfield, NJ. Best known for pioneering work in anesthesia relating to childbirth, in 1952 she developed the *Apgar Score* to evaluate newborns. She also created the first department of anesthesiology at Columbia–Presbyterian Medical Center (1938–49) where she was the first woman both to head a department and to hold a full professorship in anesthesiology (1949). A deepening interest in maternal and child health eventually led in 1959 to an executive position with the National Foundation–March of Dimes, where she spent the rest of her life fostering public support for birth defect research.

Apollinaire, Guillaume [apoli**nair**, gi**yom**], pseudonym of **Wilhelm Apollinaris de Kostrowitzki** (1880–1918) Poet and art critic, born in Rome, Italy. He settled in Paris in 1900, and became a leader of the movement rejecting poetic traditions in outlook, rhythm, and language. His work, bizarre, Symbolist and fantastic, is expressed chiefly in *L'Enchanteur pourissant* (1909, The Decaying Enchanter), *Le Bestiaire* (1911, The Bestiary), *Les Alcools* (1913, The Spirits) and *Calligrammes* (1918). Wounded in World War 1, during his convalescence he wrote the play *Les Mamelles de Tirésias* (1918, The Breasts of Tiresias), for which he coined the term *surrealist*.

Apollinaris the Younger [apoli**nah**ris] (c.310–c.390) Syrian clergyman, the son of Apollinaris the Elder, presbyter of Laodicea. One of the sternest opponents of Arianism, he became Bishop of Laodicea from 360. He upheld a doctrine (*Apollinarianism*) condemned by the Council of Constantinople (381) as denying the true human nature of Christ.

Apollodoros or **Apollodorus** [apo**lo**dorus] (5th-c BC) Athenian painter. He is said to have introduced the technique of *chiaroscuro* (light and shade).

Apollodoros or **Apollodorus** [apo**lo**doros] (2nd-c BC) Athenian scholar. He was the author of a work on mythology and one on etymology, and is best known for his verse *Chronicle* of Greek history from the fall of Troy.

Apollodoros or **Apollodorus** [apolodoros] (2nd-c) Greek architect, who designed Trajan's column in Rome. He was executed in AD 129 for his fearless criticism of Emperor Hadrian's design for a temple.

Apollonius [apo**loh**nius], known as **Dyskolos** ('Bad-tempered') (2nd-c) Greek grammarian, the first to reduce Greek syntax to a system. He wrote a treatise *On Syntax* and shorter works on pronouns, conjunctions, and adverbs.

Apollonius of Perga [apo**loh**nius], known as **the Great Geometer** (280–210 BC) Greek mathematician, born in Perga, Anatolia. He was the author of the definitive ancient work on conic sections which laid the foundations of later teaching on the subject.

Apollonius of Tyana [apo**loh**nius] (c.3–c.97) Greek philosopher and seer, born in Tyana, Cappadocia. A zealous neo-Pythagorean teacher, he was hailed as a sage and a worker of miracles. He was worshipped after his death, and a century later Philostratus wrote a largely apocryphal history presenting him as a sort of heathen rival to Christ. >> Philostratus

Apollonius [apo**loh**nius], known as **Apollonius Rhodius** (3rd-c BC) Greek scholar, born in Alexandria, Egypt, but long resident in Rhodes. He wrote many works on grammar, and an epic poem about the quest for the Golden Fleece, the *Argonautica*, which was greatly admired by the Romans.

Appel, Karel Christian (1921–) Painter, born in Amsterdam. He studied at the Royal College of Art in Amsterdam, and became one of an influential group of Dutch, Belgian, and Danish Expressionists known as 'Cobra'. His work, featuring swirls of brilliant colour and aggressively contorted figures, has many affinities with American abstract Expressionism. He settled in New York City in the 1960s.

Appert, Nicolas François [apair] (1752–1841) Chef and inventor, born in Châlons-sur-Marne, France. In 1795 he began experiments aimed at preserving food in hermetically sealed containers. His success, which earned him a French government prize in 1810, was due to his use of an autoclave for sterilization. He opened the world's first commercial preserved food factory in 1812, initially using glass jars and bottles, changing to tin-plated metal cans in 1822. >> Donkin

Appia, Adolphe [ap**i**a] (1862–1928) Scene designer and theatrical producer, born in Geneva, Switzerland. He was one of the first to introduce simple planes instead of rich stage settings, and pioneered the symbolic use of lighting, particularly in the presentation of opera.

Appian of Alexandria [apian], Gr **Appianos** (2nd-c) Roman historian and lawyer, a native of Alexandria, Egypt. He compiled 24 books of Roman conquests down to Vespasian, written in Greek, of which nine survive complete. >> Vespasian

Appleton, Sir Edward (Victor) (1892–1965) Physicist, born in Bradford, West Yorkshire, N England, UK. He studied at Cambridge, and worked at the Cavendish Laboratory from 1920, becoming professor of physics at London University in 1924. In 1936 he returned to Cambridge as professor of natural philosophy, and became secretary of the Department of Scientific and Industrial Research (1939). In 1949 he was appointed Vice-Chancellor of Edinburgh University. In 1947 he won the Nobel Prize for Physics for his contribution towards exploring the ionosphere. His work revealed the existence of a layer of electrically charged particles in the upper atmosphere (the *Appleton layer*) which plays an essential

part in making radio communication possible between distant stations.

Apponyi, Albert Georg, Gróf (Count) [o**pon**yuh] (1846–1933) Hungarian statesman, born in Vienna. He entered the Hungarian Diet in 1872, and was leader of the moderate Opposition which became the National Party in 1891. In 1899 he and his supporters went over to the Liberal Government Party, and he became President of the Diet (1901–3). He frequently represented his country at the League of Nations.

Apraxin, Fyodor Matveyevich, Graf (Count) [a**prak**sin] (1671–1728) Russian naval commander, known as the 'father of the Russian navy'. In the service of Peter the Great from 1682, he was appointed admiral in 1707 and built up the navy into a powerful fighting force. In the Great Northern War (1700–21) he routed the Swedish fleet in 1713, thus taking control of the Baltic. >> Peter I (of Russia)

Apuleius, Lucius [apu**lay**us] (2nd-c) Roman writer, satirist, and rhetorician, born in Madaura, Numidia. He studied at Carthage and Athens, travelled widely, and was initiated into numerous religious mysteries. Having married a wealthy widow, Aemilia Pudentilla, he was charged by her relations with having employed magic to gain her affections. His *Apologia* was an eloquent vindication. He settled in Carthage, where he devoted himself to literature and the teaching of philosophy and rhetoric. His romance, *Metamorphoses* or *The Golden Ass*, is a satire on the vices of the age, especially those of the priesthood and of quacks.

Aquaviva, Claudius [akwa**vee**va] (1543–1615) Clergyman, born in Naples, Italy. He entered the Society of Jesus in 1567, and was appointed fifth general of the Jesuit order in 1581. He was a great educator and organizer; his book, *Ratio atque institutio studiorum* (1586, The Reason and Establishment of Studies), laid the basis for later Jesuit education.

Aquila [akwila], known as **Ponticus** ('from Pontus') (2nd-c) Translator of the Old Testament into Greek, a native of Sinope. He is said to have been first a pagan, then a Christian, and finally a Jew.

Aquinas, St Thomas [a**kwiy**nas], known as **Doctor Angelicus** ('angelic doctor') (1225–74) Scholastic philosopher and theologian, born in the castle of Roccasecca, near Aquino, Italy. He studied with the Benedictines of Monte Cassino, and at the University of Naples; and, against the bitter opposition of his family, entered the Dominican order of mendicant friars (1244). His brothers kidnapped him and kept him a prisoner in the paternal castle for over a year; in the end he made his way to Cologne to become a pupil of Albertus Magnus. In 1252 he went to Paris, and taught there, until in 1258 he was summoned by the pope to teach successively in Anagni, Orvieto, Rome, and Viterbo. He died at Fossanuova on his way to defend the papal cause at the Council of Lyon, and was canonized in 1323. His prolific writings display great intellectual power, and he came to exercise enormous intellectual authority throughout the Church. In his philosophical writings he tried to combine and reconcile Aristotle's scientific rationalism with Christian doctrines of faith and revelation. His best-known works are two huge encyclopedic syntheses. The *Summa contra Gentiles* (1259–64) deals chiefly with the principles of natural religion. His incomplete *Summa theologiae* (1266–73) contains his mature thought in systematic form, and includes the famous 'five ways' or proofs of the existence of God. *Thomism* now represents the general teaching of the Catholic Church. Feast day 7 March. >> Albertus Magnus, St

Aquino, Cory [a**kee**noh], popular name of **(Maria) Corazon Aquino**, *née* **Cojuangco** (1933–) Philippines politician and president (1986–92), born in Tarlac province. She studied at

Mount St Vincent College, New York, before marrying a young politician, **Benigno S Aquino** (1932–83), in 1956, who became the chief political opponent to Ferdinand Marcos. Imprisoned on charges of murder and subversion (1972–80), he was assassinated by a military guard at Manila airport in 1983 on his return from three years of exile in the USA. Corazon was drafted by the Opposition to contest the 1986 presidential election, and claimed victory over Marcos, accusing the government of ballot-rigging. She took up her husband's cause, leading a non-violent 'people's power' campaign which succeeded in overthrowing Marcos. She survived several coup attempts during her presidency, but did not stand for re-election in 1992. >> Marcos; RR1081

Arabi Pasha >> **Ahmed Arabi**

Arafat, Yasser [arafat], originally **Mohammed Abed Ar'ouf Arafat** (1929–   ) Palestinian leader, born in Jerusalem. He studied at Cairo University (1952–6), and co-founded the Fatah resistance group in 1959. This group gained control of the Palestine Liberation Organization, founded in 1964, and he became the chairman of its executive committee. In the 1980s the growth of factions within the PLO reduced his power, and in 1983 the Israeli invasion forced him to leave Beirut, and to relocate the PLO executive in Tunis. In 1988, King Hussein of Jordan surrendered his right to administer the West Bank, indicating that the PLO might take over the responsibility. Arafat, to the surprise of many Western politicians, persuaded most of his colleagues to formally acknowledge the right of Israel to co-exist with an independent state of Palestine. Elected president of the PLO Central Committee in 1988, his support for Saddam Hussein in the 1990 Gulf Crisis hurt his international standing, but his reputation was largely restored following his support of Palestinian participation in the Madrid peace talks of 1991. He continues to be criticized by Palestinian hardliners for his role in the negotiations which led to the recognition of a Palestinian state in 1993. He shared the Nobel Peace Prize in 1994. >> Hussein (ibn Talal); Hussein, Saddam

Arago, (Dominique) François (Jean) [aragoh] (1786–1853) Scientist and statesman, born in Estagel, France. At 17 he entered the Polytechnic, in 1804 became secretary to the Observatory, and in 1830 its chief director. He took a prominent part in the July Revolution (1830), and in 1848 was a member of the provisional government. His scientific achievements were mainly in the fields of astronomy, magnetism, and optics.

Aragon, Louis [aragõ] (1897–1982) Political activist and writer, born in Paris. One of the most brilliant of the Surrealist group, he co-founded the journal *Littérature* with André Breton in 1919. He published two volumes of poetry, *Feu de joie* (1920) and *Le Mouvement perpétuel* (1925), and a Surrealist novel, *Le Paysan de Paris* (1926). After a visit to the Soviet Union in 1930 he became a convert to Communism, later writing a series of social-realistic novels entitled *Le Réel* (1933–51). >> Breton, André

Araki, Sadao [arakee] (1877–1966) Japanese soldier and politician. An ultra-nationalist, he was a leader of the right-wing *Kodaha* ('Imperial Way') faction of the army. After World War 2 he was convicted as a war criminal and sentenced to life imprisonment, but released in 1965.

Aram, Eugene (1704–59) Scholar and murderer, born in Ramsgill, North Yorkshire, N England, UK. Though self-taught, he became a schoolmaster, amassed considerable materials for a comparative lexicon, and postulated the relationship between Celtic and Indo-European tongues. In 1745 he was tried for the murder of a wealthy shoe-maker, but acquitted for want of evidence. In 1759, on fresh evidence coming to light about the murder charge,

he was tried at York, and hanged. His story was the subject of a romance by Edward George Lytton and a ballad by Thomas Hood.

Aranda, Pedro Pablo Abarca y Bolea, conde de (Count of) (1718–99) Spanish statesman and general, born in Siétamo, Spain. He was made ambassador to Poland in 1760, but in 1766 was recalled to Madrid and made prime minister, with the task of restoring order after risings. He became prime minister again in 1792, but antagonized Godoy, and died in Aragon in enforced retirement. >> Godoy; RR1088

Arany, János [awrony] (1817–82) Poet, born in Nagy-Szalonta, Hungary. With **Sandor Petőfi** (1823–49) he was a leader of the popular national school, and is regarded as one of the greatest of Hungarian poets. His chief work is the *Toldi* trilogy (1847–54), the story of the adventures of a young peasant in the 14th-c Hungarian court.

Arason, Jón [arason] (c. 1484–1550) Icelandic national hero and clergyman, the last Roman Catholic bishop in Iceland, born in Eyjafjörður, Iceland. He was a turbulent, charismatic figure, and a poet of both religious and satirical verse. In 1524 he was consecrated Bishop of Hólar. He fiercely resisted the imposition of Lutheranism from Denmark by the crown, and was declared an outlaw. Eventually he and two of his sons were captured in an ambush, and summarily beheaded.

Arbarbanel >> **Abarbanel, Isaac ben Jehudah**

Arber, Agnes [ah(r)ber], *née* **Robertson** (1879–1960) Botanist and philosopher, born in London, England, UK. Her works include *Herbals, Their Origin and Evolution* (1912), *Water Plants* (1920), and several later philosophical books, such as *The Manifold and the One* (1957).

Arber, Werner [ah(r)ber] (1929–   ) Microbiologist, born in Gränichen, Switzerland. He studied at Geneva University and the University of Southern California, becoming professor of molecular biology at Basel from 1970. In the 1960s he proposed that when bacteria defend themselves against attack by viruses, they use selective enzymes which cut the DNA chain of the infecting virus. He shared the Nobel Prize for Physiology or Medicine in 1978. >> RR1124

Arblay, Madame d' >> **Burney, Fanny**

Arbus, Diane [ah(r)buhs], *née* **Nemerov** (1923–71) Photographer, born in New York City. She sought to portray people 'without their masks', achieving fame in the 1960s with her ironic studies of social poses and the deprived classes. She married fellow photographer **Allan Arbus** in 1941, but they divorced in 1969, and she later took her own life.

Arbuthnot, John [ah(r)buhthnot] (1667–1735) Physician and writer, born in Inverbervie, Aberdeenshire, NE Scotland, UK. A close friend of Jonathan Swift and all the literary celebrities of the day, he was also a distinguished doctor and writer of medical works, and a physician in ordinary to Queen Anne (1705). In 1712 he published five satirical pamphlets against the Duke of Marlborough, called *The History of John Bull*, which was the origin of the popular image of John Bull as the typical Englishman. He helped to found the Scriblerus Club, and was the chief contributor to the *Memoirs of Martinus Scriblerus* (1741). >> Anne; Marlborough

Arc, Joan of >> **Joan of Arc, St**

Arcadius [ah(r)kaydius] (377–408) Emperor of the Eastern Roman Empire, born in Spain. After the death of his father, Emperor Theodosius (395), he received the E half of the Roman Empire, the W half falling to his brother Honorius. An ineffectual ruler, he was dominated by his ministers and by his wife (married 395), Empress **Eudoxia** (?–404). >> Honorius, Flavius; Theodosius; Theophilus

Arcaro, Eddie [ah(r)karoh], popular name of **George Edward Arcaro** (1916–   ) Jockey, born in Cincinnati, OH.

He was winner of the Kentucky Derby on five occasions, and was six times the leading money-winner in the USA. In 1941 and 1948 he won the horse-racing triple crown (the Kentucky Derby, Preakness Stakes, and Belmont Stakes). >> RR1161

Arcesilaus [ah(r)sesi**lay**us] (c. 316–c. 241 BC) Greek philosopher, born in Pitane, Aeolia. He became the sixth head of the Academy founded by Plato; he modelled his philosophy on the critical dialectic of Plato's earlier dialogues but gave it a sharply sceptical turn, directed particularly against Stoic doctrines. >> Plato

Arch, Joseph (1826–1919) Preacher and reformer, born in Barford, Warwickshire, C England. While still a farm labourer he became a Primitive Methodist preacher. In 1872 he founded the National Agricultural Labourers' Union, and later was MP for NW Norfolk.

Archelaus [ah(r)ke**lay**us] (5th-c BC) Greek philosopher and cosmologist. He is reputed to have been the pupil of Anaxagoras and the teacher of Socrates. >> Anaxagoras; Socrates

Archelaus [ah(r)ke**lay**us] (1st-c) Ethnarch of Judaea, the son of Herod the Great, who succeeded his father in AD 1. His heirship being disputed by his brother Herod Antipas, Archelaus went to Rome, where his authority was confirmed by Octavianus Augustus. After a nine-year reign, he was deposed by Augustus for his tyranny, and banished. >> Augustus; Herod; Herod Antipas

Archer, Fred(erick) (1857–86) Champion jockey, born in Cheltenham, Gloucestershire, SWC England, UK. He rode his first race in 1870, and during his career rode 2748 winners, including the Derby five times. His record of 246 winners in one season remained intact until it was beaten by Gordon Richards in 1933. >> Richards, Gordon

Archer (of Weston-Super-Mare), Jeffrey (Howard) Archer, Baron (1940–) Writer and former parliamentarian. He became Conservative MP for Louth (1969–74), but resigned after a financial disaster that led to bankruptcy. In order to pay his debts he turned to writing fiction. His first book, *Not a Penny More, Not a Penny Less* (1975), was an instant best-seller. Later books include *Shall We Tell the President?* (1977), *Kane and Abel* (1979), *First Among Equals* (1984), *As the Crow Flies* (1991), *The Fourth Estate* (1996), and the plays *Beyond Reasonable Doubt* (1987) and *Exclusive* (1990). Several of his books have been dramatized on television. He was created a life peer in 1992.

Archer, Robyn (1948–) Singer and actress, born in Adelaide, South Australia. She studied at Adelaide University and became a teacher of English until 1974, when she took up a singing career. In 1975 she played Jenny in Weill's *Threepenny Opera*, since when her name has been linked particularly with the German cabaret songs of Weill, Eisler, and Dessau. Her one-woman cabaret *A Star is Torn* (1979) and her 1981 show *The Pack of Women* both became successful books and recordings, the latter also being produced for television in 1986. In 1989 she was commissioned to write a new opera, *Mambo*, for the Nexus Opera, London. She is artistic director of the 1998 and 2000 Adelaide Festivals.

Archer, Thomas (1668–1743) Baroque architect, born in Tanworth, Warwickshire, C England, UK. He studied at Oxford, then travelled abroad. His works include the churches of St John, Westminster (1714) and St Paul, Deptford (1712), and Roehampton House in Surrey.

Archilochus of Paros [ah(r)**kil**okus] (760–670 BC) Greek poet from the island of Paros, regarded as the first of the lyric poets. Much of his renown is for vituperative satire. Only fragments of his work have survived.

Archimedes [ah(r)ki**mee**deez] (c. 287–212 BC) Greek mathematician, born in Syracuse. He probably visited Egypt and studied at Alexandria. In popular tradition he is remembered

for the construction of siege-engines against the Romans, the *Archimedes' screw* still used for raising water, and his cry of *eureka* ('I have found it') when he discovered the principle of the upthrust on a floating body. His real importance in mathematics, however, lies in his discovery of formulae for the areas and volumes of spheres, cylinders, parabolas, and other plane and solid figures. He founded the science of hydrostatics, but his astronomical work is lost. He was killed at the siege of Syracuse by a Roman soldier whose challenge he ignored while immersed in a mathematical problem.

Archipenko, Alexander Porfirievich [ah(r)chi**peng**koh] (1887–1964) Sculptor, born in Kiev, Ukraine. He studied at the Kiev School of Art (1902–5) and in Paris (1908–21), where he was influenced by Cubism, and became famous for his combinations of sculpture and painting, as in 'Medrano II' (1914). After 1923 he settled in New York City, and taught at many institutions, including the New Bauhaus at Chicago (1937–9).

Arcimboldo, Giuseppe [ah(r)chim**bohl**doh], also spelled **Arcimboldi** (c. 1530–93) Painter, born in Milan, Italy. He became a designer of stained-glass windows for Milan cathedral. He later moved to Prague, where he was court painter to the Habsburgs, executing the work for which he is best known – fantastic heads composed of fragmented landscape, animals, vegetables, flowers, and other non-human objects, brightly coloured and with a great attention to detail.

Ardashir I [ah(r)da**sheer**] or **Artaxerxes** (c. 211–42) Founder of the new Persian dynasty of the Sassanids. He overthrew Ardavan (Artabanus V), the last of the Parthian kings in AD c.226. He murdered Darius III, but was defeated by Alexander Severus in 233.

Arden, Elizabeth, originally **Florence Nightingale Graham** (1878–1966) Beautician and businesswoman, born in Woodbridge, Ontario, Canada. A nurse by training, she went to New York City in 1907 and opened a beauty salon on Fifth Avenue in 1910, adopting the personal and business name of 'Elizabeth Arden'. She produced cosmetics on a large scale, and developed a worldwide chain of salons. With her rival, Helena Rubinstein, she made make-up acceptable to 'respectable' American women, to whom Arden introduced eyeshadow, mascara, and lipstick tinted to match their outfits. As Elizabeth N Graham she operated Maine Chance Stables in Kentucky, where the 1947 Kentucky Derby winner was bred. >> Lauder, Estée; Rubinstein, Helena

Arden, John (1930–) Playwright, born in Barnsley, South Yorkshire, N England, UK. He studied at King's College, Cambridge, and the Edinburgh College of Art. His first play, the romantic comedy *All Fall Down*, was produced in 1955. His aggressive awareness of N England is particularly evident in *The Workhouse Donkey* (1963), a caricature of northern local politics, and in *Sergeant Musgrave's Dance* (1959), following the tradition of Brecht in its staging. He has continually experimented with dramatic form and theatrical technique. His wife, **Margaretta D'Arcy**, has collaborated with him in many plays, such as *The Happy Haven* (1960), *The Island of the Mighty* (1972), and *Whose is the Kingdom?* (1988). He has also written television and radio scripts, essays, such as *Awkward Corners* (1988, with his wife), and the novels *Silence Among the Weapons* (1982), *Books of Bale* (1988), and *Jack Juggler and the Emperor's Whore* (1995).

Arendt, Hannah [arent] (1906–75) Philosopher and political theorist, born in Hanover, Germany. She moved to the USA in 1940 as a refugee from the Nazis, becoming a US citizen in 1951. She held several academic posts, notably at the University of Chicago (1963–7) and the New School for Social Research, New York City (from 1967). An active worker in various Jewish organizations, her books include *Origins of Totalitarianism* (1951), *Eichmann in Jerusalem* (1963), and *The Life of the Mind* (1978).

Arensky, Anton Stepanovich [arenskee] (1861–1906) Composer, born in Novgorod, Russia. He studied under Rimsky-Korsakov, and from 1895 conducted the court choir at St Petersburg. His compositions include five operas, two symphonies, and vocal and instrumental pieces. >> Rimsky-Korsakov

Aretaeus [areteeus] (2nd-c) Greek physician of Cappadocia, considered to rank next to Hippocrates. The first four books of his great work on medicine, preserved nearly complete, treat of the causes and symptoms of diseases; the other four, of the cures. >> Hippocrates

Aretino, Pietro [areteenoh] (1492–1557) Poet, born in Arezzo, Italy. In Rome (1517–27) he distinguished himself by his wit, impudence, and talents, and secured the favour of Pope Leo X, which he subsequently lost by writing his 16 salacious *Sonetti lussuriosi* (1524, Lewd Sonnets). A few years later he settled in Venice, there also acquiring powerful friends. His poetical works include five witty comedies and a tragedy. >> Leo X

Argand, Aimé [ah(r)gã] (1755–1803) Physicist and chemist, born in Geneva, Switzerland. He lived for a time in England, where in 1784 he invented the *Argand burner*, the first scientifically designed oil lamp, which came to be used in lighthouses.

Argand, Jean-Robert [ah(r)gã] (1768–1822) Mathematician, born in Geneva, Switzerland. After him is named the *Argand diagram*, in which complex numbers are represented by points in the plane.

Argelander, Friedrich Wilhelm August [ah(r)gelander] (1799–1875) Astronomer, born in Memel, Germany. Between 1852 and 1861 he plotted the position of all stars of the N hemisphere above the ninth magnitude.

Argensola [ah(r)khensohla] Poets and brothers: **Bartolomé Leonardo de Argensola** (1562–1631) and **Lupercio de Argensola** (1559–1613), born in Barbastro, Spain. Both studied at Huesca University, and entered the service of Maria of Austria. Their poems led them to be styled the 'Spanish Horaces', but they were also official historians of Aragon. >> Horace

Argenson, René Louis, marquis d' [ah(r)zhãsõ] (1694–1757) French statesman, born in Paris. He became councillor to the Parlement of Paris in 1716, and foreign minister under Louis XV (1744–7). His journal is an important source of information about the period.

Argentina, La, popular name of **Antonia Mercé** (1890–1936) Dancer, born in Buenos Aires. She moved to Spain with her parents, both Spanish dancers, when she was two, becoming a dancer with Madrid Opera at 11. She later devoted herself to Spanish dance, for which she became internationally renowned.

Argyll, Archibald Campbell, 5th Earl of [ah(r)giyl] (1530–73) Scottish Protestant, a follower of Mary, Queen of Scots, and one of those involved in the assassination of Darnley. He later supported James VI and I and became Lord High Chancellor of Scotland (1572). >> Darnley; James I (of England); Mary, Queen of Scots

Argyll, Archibald Campbell, Marquess and 8th Earl of [ah(r)giyl] (1607–61) Scottish political leader during the English Civil War. He became a member of Charles I's privy council in 1626, but in 1638 joined the Covenanters in support of Scottish Presbyterianism. In the English Civil War he joined the parliamentary side, and formed a Scottish government under Cromwell's patronage. After the execution of the king he repudiated Cromwell, accepting the proclamation of Charles II as king in Scotland (1649), but following the defeat of the Scottish army at Worcester he

submitted to Cromwell again. At the Restoration of Charles II in 1660 he was executed. >> Charles I (of England); Charles II (of England); Cromwell, Oliver

Argyll, Archibald Campbell, 9th Earl of [ah(r)giyl] (1629–85) Scottish royalist, born in Dalkeith, Midlothian, EC Scotland, UK. He was imprisoned by Cromwell for a suspected royalist plot (1657–60), but his titles were restored after the Restoration. In 1681 he opposed the Test Act, and was sentenced to death for treason, but escaped to Holland. In 1685, he conspired with Monmouth to overthrow the king; he landed in Scotland, but failed to rouse the Covenanters to his cause, and was executed. >> Cromwell, Oliver; Monmouth

Argyll, John Campbell, 2nd Duke of [ah(r)giyl] (1678–1743) Scottish Unionist, one of the strongest supporters of the Act of Union of 1707, born in Petersham, SW Greater London, England, UK. An outstanding soldier, he took part in the War of the Spanish Succession (1701–14). At the time of the Jacobite rising in Scotland (1715–16) he commanded the Hanoverian forces that dispersed the Jacobite troops without a battle.

Aribau, Bonaventura Carles [aribahoo] (1798–1862) Economist and writer, born in Barcelona, Spain. He became a banker in Madrid, and was appointed director of the Mint and of the Spanish Treasury (1847). He was the author of *Oda a la Patria* (1832, Ode to the Fatherland), a poem which had a tremendous influence on contemporary Catalan writers.

Ariosto, Ludovico [ariostoh] (1474–1533) Poet, born in Reggio nell'Emilia, Italy. He intended to take up law, but abandoned it for poetry. In 1503 he was introduced to the court of the Cardinal Ippolito d'Este at Ferrara, where he produced his great poem, *Orlando furioso* (1516), the Roland epic that forms a continuation of Boiardo's *Orlando innamorato*. When the cardinal left Italy (1518), the duke, his brother, invited the poet to his service. He then composed his comedies, and gave the finishing touch to his *Orlando*. Besides his great work, he wrote comedies, satires, sonnets, and a number of Latin poems. >> Boiardo; Roland

Aristarchus of Samos [aristah(r)kos], also spelled **Aristarchos** (c.310–230 BC) Alexandrian astronomer who seems to have anticipated Copernicus, maintaining that the Earth moves round the Sun. Only one of his works has survived. >> Copernicus

Aristarchus of Samothrace [aristah(r)kos] (c.215–145 BC) Alexandrian grammarian and critic, best known for his edition of Homer. He wrote many commentaries and treatises, edited several authors, and was the founder of a school of philologists.

Aristides [aristiydeez], known as **Aristides the Just** (c.530–c.468 BC) Athenian soldier and statesman. He became chief archon (489–488 BC), but about 483 BC his opposition to Themistocles' naval policy led to his ostracization. When the Persians invaded in 480 BC Aristides returned from banishment to serve at the Battle of Salamis, and was the Athenian general at Plataea (479 BC). Through him, Athens, not Sparta, became the ruling state of the Delian League. >> Themistocles

Aristides [aristiydeez] (2nd-c) Greek Christian apologist. He wrote an early *Apology for the Christian Faith*, mentioned by Eusebius and Jerome, which came to light late in the 19th-c. >> Eusebius of Caesarea; Jerome, St

Aristippus [aristipus] (4th-c BC) Greek philosopher, a native of Cyrene in Africa, hence the name of his followers, the *Cyrenaics*, who became an influential school. Their main doctrines were hedonism and the primacy of one's own immediate feelings. He became a pupil of Socrates at Athens, and taught philosophy both at Athens and Aegina. >> Socrates

Aristogeiton >> **Harmodius**

Aristophanes [aristofaneez] (c. 448–c. 388 BC) Greek playwright. He is said to have written 54 plays, but only 11 are extant. His writings fall into three periods. To the first period, ending in 425 BC, belong *The Acharnians*, *The Knights*, *The Clouds*, and *The Wasps*, the poet's four masterpieces, named from their respective choruses, and *Peace*, in all of which full rein is given to political satire. To the second, ending in 406 BC, belong *The Birds*, *Lysistrata*, *Thesmophoriazusae*, and *Frogs*. To the third, ending c.388 BC, belong *The Ecclesiazusae* and *The Plutus*, comedies in which the role of the chorus, which was the distinctive characteristic of the Old Comedy, and political allusions disappear.

Aristotle [aristotl] (384–322 BC) see panel

Arius [ahrius] (Gr **Areios**) (c. 250–336) Founder of Arianism, born in Libya. He trained in Antioch, and became a presbyter in Alexandria. He claimed (c.319) that, in the doctrine of the Trinity, the Son was not co-equal or co-eternal with the Father, but only the first and highest of all finite beings, created out of nothing by an act of God's free will. He won some support, but was deposed and excommunicated in 321 by a synod of bishops at Alexandria. The subsequent controversy was fierce, so the Council of Nicaea (Nice) was called in 325 to settle the issue. Out of this came the definition of the absolute unity of the divine essence, and the equality of the three persons of the Trinity. Arius was banished, but recalled in 334, and died in Constantinople.

Arkwright, Sir Richard (1732–92) Inventor of mechanical cotton-spinning, born in Preston, Lancashire, NW England, UK. He became a barber in Bolton, later (with John Kay) devoting himself to inventions in cotton-spinning. In 1768 he set up his celebrated spinning-frame in Preston – the first machine that could produce cotton thread of sufficient strength to be used as warp. He introduced several mechanical processes into his factories, and many of his rivals copied his designs. Popular opinion went against him on the grounds that his inventions reduced the need for labour, and in 1779 his large mill near Chorley was destroyed by a mob. He was knighted in 1786. >> Kay; Paul, Lewis

Arlen, Michael [ah(r)len], originally **Dikran Kouyoumdjian** (1895–1956) Novelist, born in Ruschuk, Bulgaria. He studied in England and was naturalized in 1922. He made his

---

ARISTOTLE (384–322 BC)

Aristotle was born in Stagira, on the peninsula of Chalcidice in Macedon, N Greece (hence his nickname 'the Stagirite'). His father was Nicomachus, court physician to Amyntas III of Macedonia (the father of Philip II of Macedon and grandfather of Alexander the Great), and he was no doubt introduced to Greek medicine and biology at an early age. In 367 BC, after his father's death he was sent to Athens, and became first a pupil then a teacher at Plato's Academy. He remained there for 20 years, until Plato's death in 347 BC, and gained a particular reputation in rhetoric.

Plato was succeeded as head of the Academy by his nephew Speusippus. Perhaps in pique, but more probably because of the rise of anti-Macedonian feeling in Athens, Aristotle left Athens to travel for some 12 years with other colleagues and friends from the Academy, notably Theophrastus (his own pupil and eventual successor at the Lyceum). He went first to the new town of Assus in Asia Minor, where Hermeias of Atarneus had invited him to help set up a new school, and where he worked particularly on political theory. He there married Hermeias' niece, **Pythias**, and after her early death either married **Herpyllis** or took her as his mistress. In addition to Pythias' daughter (also called **Pythias**), he and Herpyllis had a son, **Nicomachus** (named after his father). His will attests to his happy family life.

After three years at the Assus Academy, Aristotle then moved to join a new philosophical circle at Mytilene on Lesbos, where he developed his interest in and study of biology. In c.343BC he was invited by Philip II of Macedon to educate his son, the future Alexander the Great. He was tutor to Alexander for three years, but his influence seems to have been negligible.

After a brief spell on his father's property at Stagira, Aristotle returned to Athens in 335 BC to found his own school, the Lyceum (near the temple of Apollo Lyceius), where he taught for the next 12 years. His followers became known as *peripatetics*, supposedly from his practice of walking up and down the *peripatos* ('covered walkway') of the gymnasium during his lectures. He made the Lyceum into a major research centre, specializing in history, biology, and zoology, thus complementing the mathematical emphasis of the Platonists at the Academy.

Alexander the Great died in 323 BC, and there was a strong anti-Macedonian reaction in Athens. Aristotle, of course, had long-standing Macedonian connections, and took refuge in Chalcis in Euboea, reportedly saying that he was saving the Athenians from sinning twice against philosophy (Socrates being their first victim). He died the following year.

Aristotle's work represents an enormous encyclopedic output over virtually every field of knowledge: logic, metaphysics, ethics, politics, rhetoric, poetry, biology, zoology, physics, and psychology. Indeed, he established many of the areas of enquiry which are today recognizable as separate subjects; and in several cases gave them their names and special terminology. Particular themes which run through his work are the emphasis on teleological explanations, and his analyses of such fundamental dichotomies as matter and form, potentiality and actuality, substance and accident, and particulars and universals.

His popular published writings are all lost, and the bulk of the work that survives consists of unpublished material in the form of lecture notes or students' textbooks which were edited and published by Andronicus of Rhodes in the middle of the 1st-c BC. But even this incomplete corpus is extraordinary for its range, originality, systematization, and sophistication. It exerted an enormous influence on mediaeval philosophy (especially through Aquinas), on Islamic philosophy (especially through Averroës), and indeed on the whole Western intellectual and scientific tradition. During the Renaissance he was dubbed 'the Master of those that know', or simply 'the Philosopher'. Aristotle's most widely read books today include the *Organon* (treatises on logic), *Metaphysics* (the book written after the *Physics*), *Nicomachean Ethics*, *Politics*, *Poetics*, and *De Anima*.
>> Alexander the Great; Aquinas; Averroës; Plato

---

reputation with *Piracy* (1922), *The Green Hat* (1924), and his short story collections, *The Romantic Lady* (1921) and *These Charming People* (1923).

Arlington, Henry Bennet, 1st Earl of (1618–85) English statesman, born in Arlington, N Greater London, England, UK. He studied at Oxford, becoming secretary of state under Charles II and one of the king's Cabal ministry. In 1674 he was unsuccessfully impeached for popery and self-aggrandizement. After serving as Lord Chamberlain he retired to Suffolk. >> Charles II (of England)

Arliss, George, originally **Augustus George Andrews** (1868–1946) Actor, born in London, England, UK. His reputation as an actor was made in the USA, where he lived for 22 years from 1901. He is remembered for his successful film representations of famous historical characters, and won an Oscar for *Disraeli* (1929).

Arlott, (Leslie Thomas) John (1914–91) Writer, journalist, and broadcaster, born in Basingstoke, Hampshire, S England, UK. Educated there, he worked as a police detective (1934–45) before joining the BBC, where as a cricket commentator on radio and television he became one of the country's most recognizable broadcasting voices. He wrote numerous books about cricket and cricketers, including *How to Watch Cricket* (1949, 1983) and *Arlott on Cricket* (1984). He won the Sports Journalist of the Year Award in 1979, and was Sports Presenter of the Year in 1980.

Armani, Giorgio [ah(r)**mah**nee] (1935–) Fashion designer, born in Piacenza, Italy. He studied medicine in Milan, and after military service worked in a department store until he became a designer for Nino Cerruti (1930–) in 1961. He set up his own company in 1975, designing first for men, then women, including loose-fitting blazers and jackets.

Armfelt, Gustaf Mauritz (1757–1814) Swedish soldier and statesman, born near Turku, Finland. In the service of Gustav III, he fought in the war against Russia (1788–90) and negotiated the peace. He became Gustav IV's ambassador to Vienna (1802–4) and his army commander in Pomerania against Napoleon (1805–7). After the deposition of Gustav in 1809 he was expelled from Sweden, and entered the service of Tsar Alexander I. >> Gustav III; Gustav IV; Napoleon

Arminius [ah(r)**min**ius] (?–19) Chief of the German Cherusci, who served as an officer in the Roman army and acquired Roman citizenship. However, in AD 9 he allied with other German tribes against the Romans, and annihilated an entire Roman army of three legions commanded by Publius Quintilius Varus. He was later murdered by some of his own kinsmen. >> Varus

Arminius, Jacobus [ah(r)**min**ius], Lat name of **Jakob Hermandszoon** (1560–1609) Theologian, born in Oudewater, The Netherlands. He studied at Utrecht, Leyden, Geneva, and Basel, and was ordained in 1588. Despite early opposition to the strict Calvinistic doctrine of predestination he was made professor of theology at Leyden in 1603. In 1604 his colleague Gomarus attacked his doctrines, and from this time on he was engaged in a series of bitter controversies. In 1608 Arminius asked the States of Holland to convoke a synod to settle the controversy, but he died before it was held. >> Gomarus

Armitage, Edward (1817–96) Painter, born in London, England, UK. He studied under Delaroche, and became professor at the Royal Academy schools in 1875. He produced chiefly historical and biblical subject-paintings. >> Delaroche

Armitage, Karole (1954–) Dancer and choreographer, born in Madison, WI. Trained in classical ballet, she moved from the Ballets de Genève, Switzerland (1972–4) to the Merce Cunningham Dance Company in New York (1976–81).

She then began a choreographic career which took her to Paris, where she created pieces for Paris Opéra Ballet. >> Cunningham, Merce

Armitage, Kenneth (1916–) Sculptor, born in Leeds, West Yorkshire, N England, UK. He studied at the Royal College of Art and the Slade School of Art, London (1937–9), and exhibited at the Venice Biennale in 1952 with other British sculptors. His bronzes are usually of semi-abstract figures, united into a group by stylized clothing.

Armour, Jean >> **Burns, Robert**

Armour, Tommy, popular name of **Thomas Dickson Armour** (1895–1968) Golfer, born in Edinburgh, EC Scotland, UK. He emigrated to the USA in 1925, where he became a successful golfer, winning the US Open (1927) and the British Open (1931). After retiring from competition he became a teaching professional. >> RR1157

Armstead, Henry Hugh (1828–1905) Sculptor, born in London, England, UK. His best-known works are reliefs and bronze statues for the Albert Memorial, the fountain at King's College, Cambridge, and the reredos at Westminster Abbey.

Armstrong, Edwin H(oward) (1890–1954) Electrical engineer and inventor, born in New York City. He studied at Columbia University, and during World War 1 became interested in methods of detecting aircraft. In the course of his research he devised the superheterodyne radio receiver, and by 1939, as professor at Columbia University (1935–54), he had perfected the frequency-modulation system of radio transmission which virtually eliminated the problem of interference from static.

Armstrong, Gillian (May) (1952–) Film director, born in Melbourne, Victoria, Australia. A student of theatre design and later of film, she won a scholarship to the Film and Television School in Sydney. Early works include the drama *The Singer and the Dancer* (1976), which won the Australian Film Institute (AFI) Award for Best Short. Several of her films focus attention on the difficulties facing independent women, such as *My Brilliant Career* (1979), *High Tide* (1987), *The Last Days of Chez Nous* (1991), and *Little Women* (1996). She has won many AFI awards, including Best Film and Best Director.

Armstrong, Henry, originally **Henry Jackson**, nickname **Hammerin' Hank** (1912–88) Boxer, born in Columbus, MS. He is the only man to have held three world titles at different weights simultaneously. His first title was at featherweight, which he won in 1937, and the following year he added both the welterweight and lightweight crowns. He lost the featherweight and lightweight titles in 1939, but he successfully defended his welterweight title a record 20 times. >> RR1148

Armstrong, Henry Edward (1848–1937) Chemist, born in London, England, UK. He studied chemistry in London and Leipzig, and became professor of chemistry (1871–1913) in the London institutions which later formed Imperial College. His major contribution was in chemical education, where he pioneered the heuristic method, and he was a forceful advocate for environmental concern.

Armstrong, Johnnie (?–1529/30) Celebrated Scottish Border freebooter and cattle-rustler ('reiver'), and hero of many Border ballads. He was either John Armstrong of Gilnockie, near Langholm, Dumfries and Galloway, who was hanged in 1529, or John Armstrong ('Black Jock') of Mangerton, who was executed in 1530.

Armstrong, Louis, nickname **Satchmo** (1898/1900–71) Jazz trumpeter and singer, born in New Orleans, LA. Having learned to play the cornet in a waifs' home, he moved to Chicago in 1922 to join King Oliver's band. His melodic inventiveness, expressed with uninhibited tone and range on the trumpet, established the central role of the improvising soloist in jazz, especially in a series of recordings known as the 'Hot Fives' and 'Hot Sevens' (1925–8). Thereafter, every jazz musician emulated Armstrong's melodic style and rhythmic sense. He was also a popular singer (hit recordings include 'When It's Sleepy Time Down South', 'Mack the Knife', 'Hello Dolly!') and entertainer, in such films as *Pennies from Heaven* (1936), *Cabin in the Sky* (1943), and *High Society* (1956), but he remained primarily a jazz musician, touring the world with his New Orleans-style sextet. >> Oliver

Armstrong, Neil (Alden) (1930–) Astronaut, born in Wapakoneta, OH. He studied at Purdue University, then became a fighter pilot in Korea and later a civilian test pilot. In 1962 he was chosen as an astronaut and commanded Gemini 8 in 1966. In 1969 with Buzz Aldrin and Michael Collins he set out in Apollo 11 on a successful Moon-landing expedition. On 20 July 1969 Armstrong and Aldrin became in that order the first men to set foot on the Moon. Armstrong later taught aerospace engineering at Cincinnati University (1971–9). He published *First on the Moon* in 1970. >> Aldrin; Collins, Michael

Armstrong (of Ilminster), Robert, Baron (1927–) British civil servant. He studied at Oxford, and entered the civil service in 1950, becoming deputy head of the Home Office and the Treasury. In 1970 he became principal private secretary to the prime minister, Edward Heath, and under Margaret Thatcher was secretary to the cabinet and head of the home civil service. He achieved unwanted notoriety when he gave evidence in the 'Spycatcher' case in Australia (1987), and admitted that he had sometimes been 'economical with the truth'. He retired from the civil service in 1988, and was made a life peer. >> Heath; Thatcher

Armstrong, William (16th-c) 'Kinmont Willie' of the Border ballad of that name, a Dumfriesshire moss-trooper. He was rescued in 1596 by Walter Scott, 1st Lord Scott of Buccleuch (1565–1611), from Carlisle Castle.

Armstrong, William George, Baron (1810–1900) Inventor and industrialist, born in Newcastle upon Tyne, Tyne and Wear, NE England, UK. In 1840 he produced a much improved hydraulic engine, in 1842 an apparatus for producing electricity from steam, and in 1845 the hydraulic crane. His factory later became famous for its ordnance, especially the Armstrong breech-loading gun. His house at Cragside, Northumbria, was the first to be be lit by incandescent electric light bulbs developed by Swan. >> Swan

Armstrong-Jones, Antony >> **Snowdon, 1st Earl of**
Armstrong-Jones, Lady Sarah >> **Margaret, Princess**

Arnarson, Ingólfur (late 9th-c) Viking from Hördaland, Norway. He was honoured as the first settler of Iceland in AD 874, and his descendants held the hereditary post of supreme chieftain of the Icelandic parliament (*Althing*) after its foundation in 930.

Arnason, Jón, known as **the Grimm of Iceland** (1819–88) Collector of folk-tales, born in Iceland. He collected and published a huge collection of Icelandic folk-tales and fairy-tales (1862–4), translated as *Legends of Iceland* by Eiríkur Magnússon (1864–6). >> Grimm

Arnaud, Arsène >> **Claretie, Jules**

Arnaud, Yvonne (Germaine) [ah(r)noh] (1892–1958) Actress, born in Bordeaux, France. She studied in Paris, and trained as a concert pianist, before taking up acting. She enjoyed a long career on the British stage, appearing in many musicals and farces. She made her film debut in *Desire* and appeared in several cinema adaptations of her stage successes, such as *The Ghosts of Berkeley Square* (1947) and *Mon Oncle* (1958). Resident for many years near Guildford, Surrey, a theatre there was opened in her honour in 1965.

Arnauld, Angélique [ah(r)noh], known as **Mère Angélique de Saint Jean** (1624–84) French Jansenist religious, the niece of Antoine Arnauld. She entered the convent of Port-Royal des Champs in Paris, where she became sub-prioress then abbess (1678). During the persecution of the Port-Royalists she was known for her heroic courage. >> Arnauld, Antoine

Arnauld, Antoine [ah(r)noh], known as **the Great Arnauld** (1612–94) French philosopher, lawyer, mathematician, and priest, associated with the Jansenist movement and community at Port Royal, Paris. He was a controversialist, and his activities as head of the Jansenists led to his expulsion from the Sorbonne, persecution, and ultimately refuge in Belgium. While at Port Royal he collaborated with Pascal and **Pierre Nicole** (1625–95) on the work known as the *Port Royal Logic* (1662). >> Pascal

Arnauld, Jacqueline-Marie-Angélique [ah(r)noh], known as **Mère Angélique** (1591–1661) French Jansenist, the sister of Antoine Arnauld. She was made abbess of Port-Royal in 1602 at the age of 11, and ultimately reformed the convent by the severity of her discipline. >> Arnauld, Antoine

Arndt, Ernst Moritz [ah(r)nt] (1769–1860) Poet and German patriot, born in the island of Rügen (then Swedish). He studied at Stralsund, Greifswald, and Jena, and in 1805 became professor of history at Greifswald. In his *Geist der Zeit* (1806, Spirit of the Times) he attacked Napoleon with such boldness that he had to take refuge in Stockholm (1806–9). In 1818 he became professor of history in the new University of Bonn; but, aiming steadily at constitutional reforms, he was suspended in 1819 and not restored till 1840. His other works include political addresses, reminiscences, letters, and poems.

Arne, Thomas (Augustine) (1710–78) Composer, born in London, England, UK. He studied at Eton, became skilful as a violinist, then turned to composing with his first opera *Rosamond* (1733). He was appointed composer to Drury Lane Theatre, for which he composed famous settings of Shakespearean songs. 'Rule, Britannia' (originally written for *The Masque of Alfred*) is his, as well as two oratorios and two operas.

Arnheim, Rudolf [ah(r)nhiym] (1904–) Art theorist and psychologist, born in Berlin. He studied at the University of Berlin, worked in Rome with the International Institute of Educational Films (1933–8), then taught at both the New School for Social Research and Sarah Lawrence College (1943–68), Harvard University (1968–74), and the University of Michigan (from 1974). He taught film history, but is most noted as a pioneering theorist of the psychology of the arts. Among his influential books are *Art as Visual Perception* (1954, 1974), *Toward a Psychology of Art* (1966), and *Entropy and Art* (1971).

Arnim, Achim von, originally **Karl Joachim Friedrich Ludwig von Arnim** (1781–1831) Writer of fantastic but original romances, born in Berlin. He stirred up a warm sympathy for old popular poetry, and published over 20 volumes, mainly tales and novels, including (with Clemens von Brentano) the folk-song collection *Des Knaben Wunderhorn*. His wife, **Bettina** (1785–1859), Brentano's sister, was as a girl infatuated with Goethe, and afterwards published a (largely fictitious) *Correspondence* with him, as well as 10 volumes of tales and essays. >> Brentano, Clemens

Arnim, Jürgen, Freiherr (Baron) **von** (1891–1971) German soldier, born of an old Silesian military family. He served at first in the infantry in World War 1, then became a tank expert. In World War 2 he took over the 5th Panzer Army in Tunisia in 1943, and succeeded Rommel in command of Army Group Africa. In May 1943 he surrendered his troops to the Allies, and was interned in Britain and later in the USA. >> Rommel

Arno, Peter, originally **Curtis Arnoux Peters** (1904–68) Cartoonist, born in New York City. He was one of the first contributors to the *New Yorker* magazine, from 1925, with satirical drawings of New York cafe society. He also wrote musical revues, including *Here Comes the Bride* (1931).

Arnobius the Elder [ah(r)**noh**bius] (?–330) A teacher of rhetoric in Sicca, Numidia (Africa). He became a Christian c.300, and wrote a vigorous defence of Christianity (*Adversus nationes*).

Arnold, Aberhard (1883–1935) Founder of the Bruderhof movement in Nazi Germany, born in Wrocław, Poland (formerly Breslau, Germany). He studied theology at Halle, but disqualified himself from the degree through his insistence on being baptised on profession of faith. A convinced pacifist associated with the Student Christian Movement, he linked spiritual authenticity with an awareness of economic injustice. A selection of his writings and addresses, *God's Revolution*, was published in 1984.

Arnold, Benedict (1741–1801) American soldier and turncoat, born in Norwich, CT. On the outbreak of the War of Independence (1775–83) he joined the colonial forces, assisted Ethan Allen in the capture of Fort Ticonderoga (1775), and took part in the unsuccessful siege of Quebec in 1775, for which he was made a brigadier-general. He fought with distinction at L Champlain, Ridgefield, and Saratoga. Though greatly admired by Washington, he had influential enemies, and in 1777 five of his inferiors in rank were promoted over his head. In 1780 he obtained the command of West Point, which, through a conspiracy with John André, he agreed to betray. On the capture of André, he fled to the British lines, and was given a command in the royal army. He went to England in 1781, living in London until his death. >> Allen, Ethan; André, John

Arnold, Sir Edwin (1832–1904) Poet and journalist, born in Gravesend, Kent, SE England, UK. He taught at King Edward's School, Birmingham, and in 1856 became principal of Deccan College, Poona. Returning in 1861, he became editor of the *Daily Telegraph* in 1863. He is best known for *The Light of Asia* (1879), on Buddhism.

Arnold, Henry Harley, popular name **Hap Arnold** (1886–1950) US air force officer, born in Gladwyne, PA. He trained at West Point, and learned to fly with the Wright brothers. He became commanding general of the US Army Air Corps (1938), chief of US Army Air Forces (1941), and the first general of the independent US Air Force in 1947. >> Wright brothers

Arnold, Joseph (1782–1818) Botanist, born in Beccles, Suffolk, E England, UK. He studied medicine at Edinburgh, and accompanied Sir Thomas Stamford Raffles as naturalist to Sumatra, where he died. He discovered the largest flower known, *Rafflesia arnoldi*. >> Raffles

Arnold, Sir Malcolm (Henry) (1921–) Composer, born in Northampton, Northamptonshire, C England, UK. He studied at the Royal College of Music (1938–40) and was principal trumpet player with the London Philharmonic Orchestra until 1948. Of his film scores, *Bridge over the River Kwai* received an Oscar (1957). His works include nine symphonies, the overture *Tam O'Shanter*, 18 concertos, five ballets, two one-act operas, and a great deal of vocal, choral, and chamber music. He was knighted in 1993.

Arnold, Mary Augusta >> **Ward, Mary Augusta**

Arnold, Matthew (1822–88) Poet and critic, born in Laleham, Surrey, SE England, UK, the eldest son of Dr Thomas Arnold of Rugby. He studied at Oxford, and became one of the lay inspectors of schools in 1851, an office from which he retired in 1886. He made his mark with *Poems: A New Edition* (1853–4), which contained 'The

Scholar Gipsy' and 'Sohrab and Rustum', and confirmed his standing as a poet with *New Poems* (1867), which contained 'Dover Beach' and 'Thyrsis'. Appointed professor of poetry at Oxford in 1857, he published several critical works, including *Essays in Criticism* (1865, 1888) and *Culture and Anarchy* (1869), and books on religious themes such as *Literature and Dogma* (1872) and *Last Essays on Church and Religion* (1877). >> Arnold, Thomas; Ward, Mary Augusta

Arnold, Samuel (1740–1802) Composer, born in London, England, UK. He became organist to the Chapels Royal (1783) and to Westminster Abbey (1793). He is best remembered for his valuable collection of cathedral music (1790) and his 36-volume edition of Handel (1786–97).

Arnold, Thomas (1795–1842) Educationist, scholar, and headmaster of Rugby School, born in East Cowes, Isle of Wight, S England, UK the father of Matthew Arnold and Mary Augusta Ward. He studied at Oxford, took deacon's orders in 1818, and in 1828 was appointed headmaster of Rugby. He reformed the school system (especially by introducing sports and ending bullying). The style of teaching he introduced was graphically described in Thomas Hughes's *Tom Brown's Schooldays* (1857). In 1841 he was appointed professor of modern history at Oxford. >> Arnold, Matthew; Hughes, Thomas; Ward, Mary Augusta

Arnold of Brescia [bre**shia**] (c.1100–55) Clergyman and politician, born in Brescia, Italy. He adopted the monastic life, but his criticism of the Church's wealth and temporal power led to his banishment from Italy (1139). In France he met with bitter hostility from St Bernard of Clairvaux, and took refuge for five years in Zürich. An insurrection against the papal government in Rome drew him there (1143), and for 10 years he struggled to found a republic on ancient Roman lines. On the arrival of Emperor Frederick I in 1155, he was executed. >> Bernard of Clairvaux, St

Arnolfo di Cambio [ah(r)**nol**foh dee **kam**bioh] (c.1245–1302) Italian sculptor and architect, the designer of Florence Cathedral. A pupil of Nicola Pisano, he worked on his master's shrine of S Dominic, Bologna, and the pulpit at Siena before going to Rome in 1277. His tomb of Cardinal de Braye at Orvieto set the style for wall-tombs for more than a century. The remains of his sculptural decoration for Florence Cathedral are in the cathedral museum. >> Pisano, Nicola

Arnon, Daniel I(srael) (1910–) Plant physiologist, born in Warsaw. Raised in the USA, he spent his career at the University of California, Berkeley (1936–78). He demonstrated that water (hydroponic) culture of tomatoes, using mineral supplements, produces similar yields as soil crops, but is economically feasible only if available soil is incapable of supporting growth (1939). His pioneering investigations of photosynthesis began in the late 1940s, when he and colleagues isolated chloroplasts from spinach cells, and in 1954 published results of the first photosynthetic process outside the living cell.

Arp, Jean or **Hans** (1887–1966) Sculptor, born in Strasbourg, France. He was one of the founders of the Dada movement in Zürich in 1916. During the 1920s he produced many abstract reliefs in wood, but after 1928 he worked increasingly in three dimensions, becoming a major influence on organic abstract sculpture, based on natural forms. In 1921 he married the artist, **Sophie Tauber** (1889–1943). After World War 2, he wrote several poems and essays.

Arpád [ah(r)pad] (?–907) The national hero of Hungary. A Magyar chieftain in the Caucusus, he led the Magyars from the Black Sea into the Valley of the Danube (c.896) and occupied modern Hungary. He founded the Arpád royal dynasty of Hungary, from St Stephen (997) to 1301.

Arrabal, Fernando [ara**bal**] (1932–) Playwright and novelist, born in Melilla, Spanish Morocco. He studied law in

Madrid and drama in Paris, then settled permanently in France. His first play, *Pique-nique en campagne* (1958, trans Picnic on the Battlefield), established him in the tradition of the Theatre of the Absurd. He coined the term *panic theatre*, intended to shock the senses, employing sadism and blasphemy to accomplish its aims. Other plays include *Le Cimetière des voitures* (1958, The Car Cemetery) and *Et ils passèrent des menottes aux fleurs* (1969, And They Put Handcuffs on the Flowers) – a work based on conversations with Spanish political prisoners, which was eventually banned in France and Sweden while becoming his first major success in America in 1971. He writes in Spanish, his work being translated into French by his wife.

Arrau, Claudio [arow] (1903–91) Pianist, born in Chillán, Chile. He studied at the Stern Conservatory, Berlin (1912–18), and taught there (1924–40). He is renowned as an interpreter of Bach, Beethoven, Chopin, Schumann, Liszt, and Brahms. His musical thoughts were collected in *Conversations with Arrau* by Joseph Horowitz (1982).

Arrhenius, Svante (August) [araynius] (1859–1927) Scientist, born near Uppsala, Sweden. He became professor of physics at Stockholm in 1895, and a director of the Nobel Institute in 1905. He did valuable work in connection with the dissociation theory of electrolysis, and was awarded the Nobel Prize for Chemistry in 1903.

Arriaga, Juan Crisóstomo [ariahga] (1806–26) Composer, born in Bilbao, Spain. A child prodigy, his first opera, *Los esclavos felices* (The Happy Slaves), was produced in 1820. He became assistant professor at the Paris Conservatoire in 1824. Although he died at the age of 19, his compositions show remarkable maturity, and include three string quartets and a symphony.

Arrian [arian], Lat **Flavius Arrianus** (c. 95–180) Greek historian, a native of Nicomedia in Bithynia. An officer in the Roman army, in 136 he was appointed prefect of Cappadocia (legate in 131–7). His chief work is the *Anabasis Alexandrou*, or history of the campaigns of Alexander the Great, which has survived almost entire. His accounts of the people of India, and of a voyage round the Euxine, are valuable for studies of ancient geography.

Arrol, Sir William (1839–1913) Engineer, born in Houston, Renfrewshire, W Scotland, UK. He studied at night school, and started his own engineering business at the age of 29. His firm constructed the second Tay Railway Bridge (1882–7), the Forth Railway Bridge (1883–90), and Tower Bridge in London (1886–94). He was also an MP (1892–1906).

Arrow, Kenneth J(oseph) (1921–) Economist, born in New York City. He studied at Columbia University, and became professor at Stanford (1949–68) and Harvard (1968–79). His primary field was the study of collective choice based on uncertainty and risk. He shared the 1972 Nobel Prize for Economics. >> RR1125

Arrowsmith, Aaron (1750–1823) Cartographer, born in Winston, Durham, NE England, UK. In about 1770 he moved to London, and by 1790 had established a great map-making business. His nephew, **John Arrowsmith** (1790–1873), was also an eminent cartographer.

Arsinoë [ah(r)sinohee] (316–270 BC) Macedonian princess, the daughter of Ptolemy I, and one of the most conspicuous of Hellenistic queens. She married first (c.300 BC) the aged Lysimachus, King of Thrace, secondly (and briefly) Ptolemy Ceraunus, and finally (c.276 BC) her own brother, Ptolemy II Philadelphus. Several cities were named after her. >> Lysimachus; Ptolemy I; Ptolemy II

Arsonval, (Jacques-)Arsène d' [ah(r)sõval] (1851–1940) Physicist, born in Borie, France. He was director of the laboratory of biological physics at the Collège de France from 1882, and professor from 1894. He invented the reflecting

galvanometer named after him, and experimented with high-frequency oscillating current for electromedical purposes.

Artaud, Antonin [ah(r)toh] (1896–1948) Playwright, actor, director, and theorist, born in Marseille, France. A Surrealist in the 1920s, in 1927 he co-founded the Théâtre Alfred Jarry. He propounded a theatre that dispensed with narrative and psychological realism, dealing instead with the dreams and interior obsessions of the mind. His main theoretical work is the book, *Le Théâtre et son double* (1938, The Theatre and its Double). As the creator of what has been termed the Theatre of Cruelty, his influence on postwar theatre was profound. A manic depressive, his last years were spent in a mental institution.

Artaxerxes >> **Ardashir**

Artaxerxes I [ah(r)tazerkseez], known as **Longimanus** ('long-handed') (5th-c BC) King of Persia (464–425 BC), the second son of Xerxes I. In a long and peaceful reign, he sanctioned the Jewish religion in Jerusalem, and appointed Nehemiah as Governor of Judea in 445. >> Nehemiah; Xerxes I; RR1063

Artedi, Peter [ah(r)taydee] (1705–35) Swedish ichthyologist and botanist, known as 'the father of ichthyology'. He wrote *Ichthyologia*, a systematic study of fishes, edited by Linnaeus, his closest friend, and published in 1738. The classification of animals and plants in his work inspired Linnaeus. >> Linnaeus

Artemisia I [ah(r)temizia] (5th-c BC) Ruler of Halicarnassus and the neighbouring islands. She accompanied Xerxes in his expedition against Greece, and distinguished herself at Salamis (480 BC). >> Xerxes

Artemisia II [ah(r)temizia] (?–c. 350 BC) Sister and wife of Mausolus, ruler of Caria. She succeeded him on his death (c.353–352 BC), and erected a magnificent mausoleum at Halicarnassus to his memory, which was one of the seven wonders of the ancient world. Also known as a botanist, *Artemisia* (wormwood) is named after her.

Artevelde, Jacob van [ah(r)tevelduh] (c.1295–1345) Flemish statesman, born in Ghent, Belgium. He organized an alliance of Flemish towns in the conflict between France and England at the outbreak of the Hundred Years' War (1337–1453). Elected Captain of Ghent in 1338, he ruled like an autocrat. When Edward III of England declared himself King of France in 1340, he insisted on Ghent making a treaty that accepted Edward's sovereignty. In 1345 he proposed that Edward the Black Prince should be made Count of Flanders, but was assassinated in an ensuing riot. >> Edward III

Arthur (?6th-c) Semi-legendary king of the Britons. He may originally have been a Romano-British war leader in W England called **Arturus**; but he is represented as having united the British tribes against the invading Saxons, and as having been the champion of Christendom as well. He is said to have fought against the invaders in a series of momentous battles, starting with a victory at 'Mount Baden' (?516) and ending with defeat and death at 'Camlan' (537), after which he was buried at Glastonbury. The *Anglo-Saxon Chronicle* makes no mention of him, however; he first appears in Welsh chronicles long after the event. The story of Arthur blossomed into a huge literature, interwoven with legends of the Holy Grail and courtly ideas of the Round Table of knights at Camelot, in such writers as Geoffrey of Monmouth, Chrétien de Troyes, Layamon, and Sir Thomas Malory. >> Geoffrey; Malory; Troyes

Arthur, Chester A(lan) (1830–86) US statesman, lawyer, and 21st president (1881–5), born in Fairfield, VT. He became the head of an eminent law firm and leader of the Republican Party in New York State. He was made vice-president of the USA when Garfield became president in 1881, and president after Garfield's assassination. >> Garfield; RR1097

Arthur, Sir George (1784–1854) British diplomat, born near Plymouth, Devonshire, SW England, UK. He was Governor of British Honduras (1814–22), Van Diemen's Land (1823–36), Upper Canada (1837–41), and Bombay (1842–6).

Arthur, Prince (1187–?1203) Duke of Brittany, and claimant to the throne of England as the grandson of Henry II. He was the posthumous son of Geoffrey, Duke of Brittany, Henry's fourth son, and on the death of his uncle, Richard I (1199) he became a claimant to the throne. The French king, Philip II, upheld Arthur's claim until Richard's brother, John, came to terms with Philip. Arthur was soon in his uncle's hands and was imprisoned, first at Calais and then at Rouen, where he died. It was popularly believed that King John was responsible for his death. >> Henry II (of England); John

Arthur, Prince (1486–1502) The eldest son of Henry VII, born in Winchester, Hampshire, S England, UK. When still under two years old a marriage was arranged between him and Catherine of Aragon in order to provide an alliance between England and Spain. The wedding took place in 1501, but Arthur, a sickly youth, died soon after. >> Catherine of Aragon; Henry VII

Arthurs, Paul >> **Oasis**

Artigas, José Gervasio [ah(r)teegas] (1764–1850) National hero of Uruguay, born in Montevideo. He became the most important local patriot leader in the wars of independence against Spain, and also resisted the centralizing pretensions of Buenos Aires. He spent the last 30 years of his life in exile in Paraguay.

Artin, Emil (1898–1962) Mathematician, born in Vienna. He studied in Leipzig, and taught at Göttingen and Hamburg before emigrating to the USA in 1937, where he held posts at Indiana and Princeton before returning to Hamburg in 1958. His work was mainly in algebraic number theory and class field theory. >> Waerden

Artzybashev, Boris [ah(r)tsibahshef] (1899–1965) Illustrator and writer, born in Kharkov province, Ukraine, the son of Mikhail Artzybashev. He studied in St Petersburg before emigrating to the USA in 1919, where he became a book illustrator and writer of children's stories.

Artzybashev, Mikhail Petrovich [ah(r)tsibahshef] (1878–1927) Writer, born in Kharkov province, Ukraine. His liberalist novel *Sanin* (1907) had an international reputation at the turn of the century.

Arundel, Thomas [aruhndl] (1353–1414) English clergyman and statesman, the third son of Robert FitzAlan, Earl of Arundel. Chancellor of England (1386–96), he became Archbishop of York in 1388 and Archbishop of Canterbury in 1396. Banished by Richard II in 1397, he returned from exile with Henry IV and crowned him in 1399. He then became Chancellor again, and was a bitter opponent of the Lollards. >> Henry IV (of England); Richard II

Arup, Sir Ove (Nyquist) [aruhp] (1895–1988) Civil engineer, born of Danish parents in Newcastle upon Tyne, Tyne and Wear, NE England, UK. He studied philosophy and engineering in Denmark before moving to London in 1923. He became increasingly concerned with the solution of structural problems in Modernist architecture, and was responsible for the structural design of Coventry Cathedral and St Catherine's College, Oxford. He later evolved the structural design which permitted the realization of the Sydney Opera House (1956–73).

Asad, Hafez al- [asad] (1928–) Syrian general and president (1971–), born in Qardaha, Syria. A member of the minority Alawi sect of Islam, he rose to high government office through the military and the Arab nationalist Ba'ath Party. He was minister of defence and commander of the air force (1966–70), instigated a coup in 1970, and became prime minister and then president. After the 1973 Arab–Israeli War, he negotiated a partial withdrawal of Israeli troops from Syria. In 1976 he sent Syrian troops into Lebanon, and did so again in early 1987, by 1989 imposing Syrian control over the greater part of Lebanon. A contender for leadership in the Arab world, he was one of the few Arab leaders to support Iran in its war with rival Iraq. He also supports the Palestinian radicals against Arafat's mainstream PLO. Having long enjoyed Soviet support, he was isolated in the early 1990s by the end of the Cold War and the growth of Russian–American co-operation in the Middle East. >> Arafat; RR1092

Asam Architects and decorators: **Cosmas Damian Asam** (1686–1739) and **Egid Quirin Asam** (1692–1750), born in Bavaria, sons of the fresco painter Hans Georg Asam (1649–1711). They worked together, the former as a fresco painter and the latter as a sculptor, combining architecture, sculpture, painting, and lighting effects in church interiors to produce highly emotional decoration and melodramatic high altars, such as that of the Abbey Church at Weltenburg.

Asbjörnsen, Peter Christian [asbyoe(r)nsen] (1812–85) Folklorist, born in Oslo (formerly, Christiania). He studied at the university there, then for four years was a tutor in the country. In long journeys on foot he collected a rich store of popular poetry and folklore, and, with his lifelong friend **Jörgen Moe** (1813–82), Bishop of Christiansand, published the famous collection of Norwegian folk tales, *Norske Folkeeventyr* (1841–4).

Asbury, Francis (1745–1816) Clergyman, born in Handsworth, Staffordshire, C England, UK. In 1771 he was sent as a Methodist missionary to America. He founded the Methodist Episcopal Church, and in 1785 was the first to assume the title of bishop.

Asch, Sholem (1880–1957) Writer, born in Kutno, Poland. He emigrated to America in 1914 and became a US citizen in 1920. His prolific output of novels and short stories, most of them originally in Yiddish, includes *The Mother* (1930), *The War Goes On* (1936), *The Nazarene* (1939), and *Moses* (1951).

Ascham, Roger [asham] (1515–68) Humanist, born in Kirby Wiske, North Yorkshire, N England, UK. He studied at Cambridge, where he became reader in Greek (c.1538). In defence of archery he published *Toxophilus* (1545), which ranks among English classics on account of its style. He was tutor to the Princess Elizabeth (1548–50), and later became Latin secretary to Queen Mary I. His principal work was *The Scholemaster*, a treatise on Classical education, published in 1570.

Asclepiades [asklepiyadeez] (1st-c BC) Greek physician, born in Pruss, Bithynia. He seems to have been a peripatetic teacher of rhetoric before settling in Rome as a physician, where his introduction of Greek medical ideas proved influential.

Ascoli, Graziadio Isaia [askohlee] (1829–1907) Philologist, born in Görz (Gorizia), Italy. He was appointed professor of philology in Milan in 1860, and is known mainly for his work on Italian dialectology. He founded and edited *Archivio glottologico italiano* in 1873.

Ashari, al- [ashahree] (873/4–935/6) Islamic theologian and philosopher, born in Basra, Iraq. In 915 he moved to Baghdad, where he formed his own school of followers. His major work is *Maqalat*, which defends the idea of God's omnipotence and reaffirms traditional interpretations of religious authority within Islam.

Ashbee, Charles Robert (1863–1942) Designer, architect, and writer, born in Isleworth, W Greater London, England,

UK. He studied at Cambridge, and was founder and director of the Guild of Handicraft (1888–1908) in London's East End (later in Gloucestershire), employing over 100 craftworkers, the largest-scale attempt to put into practice the ideals of the Arts and Crafts movement. As an architect he specialized in church restoration, and he was also a noted silversmith. >> Mairet; Scott, MacKay Hugh Baillie

Ashbery, John (Lawrence) (1927–) Poet and critic, born in New York City. He studied at Harvard, Columbia, and New York universities, then spent some years as an art critic in Europe. He became associated with the New York School of poetry, publishing his first volume in 1953. *Some Trees* (1956) attracted considerable critical attention, and his 12th collection, *Self-Portrait in a Convex Mirror* (1975) received several prizes, including the Pulitzer Prize. Later volumes include *Ice Storm* (1987), *Flow Chart* (1991), and *Hotel Lautreamont* (1992).

Ashburton, Baron >> Dunning, John

Ashby (of Brandon), Eric, Baron (1904–92) Botanist and educator, born in London, England, UK. He studied at London and Chicago universities, and was appointed professor of botany at Sydney University in 1938. He held the chair of botany at Manchester (1947–50), then became President and Vice-Chancellor of Queen's University, Belfast (1950–9) and Vice-Chancellor of Cambridge University (1967–9). He chaired the Royal Commission on Environmental Pollution (1970–3). Knighted in 1956, he was created a life peer in 1973.

Ashcroft, Dame Peggy, originally **Edith Margaret Emily Ashcroft** (1907–91) Actress, born in London, England, UK. She first appeared on the stage with the Birmingham Repertory Company in 1926, and scored a great success in London in *Jew Süss* in 1929. She acted leading parts at the Old Vic in the season of 1932–3. Her famous roles included Juliet in Sir John Gielgud's production of *Romeo and Juliet* (1935). Her films include *The Thirty-nine Steps* (1935) and *A Passage to India* (1984), for which she won an Oscar as best supporting actress. She was created a dame in 1956, and a new London theatre was named after her in 1962.

Ashdown, Paddy, popular name of **Jeremy John Durham Ashdown** (1941–) British politician, born in India. After a childhood and youth spent in India and Ulster, he joined the Royal Marines, serving in the special boat squadron. He then studied Mandarin at Hong Kong University, and spent five years in the diplomatic service. He overturned a large Conservative majority in his constituency of Yeovil and entered the House of Commons as a Liberal in 1983. In 1988 he won the leadership election for the new Liberal and Social Democratic Party.

Ashe, Arthur (Robert) (1943–93) Tennis player, born in Richmond, VA. After studying at the University of California at Los Angeles on a tennis scholarship, he was selected for the US Davis Cup side in 1963, and won the US national singles and open championships in 1968. He turned professional in 1969, winning Wimbledon in 1975 when he defeated Jimmy Connors. He retired in 1980, the first male African-American tennis player to have achieved world ranking. >> Connors; RR1173

Asher, Jane (1946–) Actress and cake designer, born in London, England, UK. She studied at North Bridge House and Miss Lambert's Parents' National Educational Union. From 1957 she performed regularly in the theatre and on television, her films including *Alfie* (1966), *Henry VIII and His Six Wives* (1970), and *Paris By Night* (1988). Among her many books on baking are *Calendar of Cakes* (1989) and *Jane Asher's Complete Book of Cake Decorating Ideas* (1993), and she is proprietor of Jane Asher's Party Cakes Shop and Tea Room in Chelsea, London. She is married to the cartoonist Gerald Scarfe >> Scarfe, Gerald

Ashkenazy, Vladimir [ashke**nah**zee] (1937–) Pianist and conductor, born in Nizhni Novgorod (formerly Gorky), Russia. He graduated from Moscow Conservatory (1960) and in 1962 was joint winner (with John Ogdon) of the Tchaikovsky Piano Competition, Moscow. He left the Soviet Union in 1963 and made his London debut that year. He settled in Iceland in 1973 with his wife, an Icelandic pianist, and became musical director of the Royal Philharmonic Orchestra, London (1987–5) and the Radio Symphony Orchestra, Berlin (1989–). >> Ogdon

Ashley, Lord >> Shaftesbury, Earl of

Ashley, Laura, *née* **Mountney** (1925–85) Fashion designer, born in Merthyr Tydfil, S Wales, UK. She married Bernard Ashley in 1949, and they started a business manufacturing furnishing materials and wallpapers with patterns based upon document sources mainly from the 19th-c. When she gave up work to have a baby, she experimented with designing and making clothes, and this transformed the business into an international chain of boutiques selling clothes, furnishing fabrics, and wallpapers. Her work was characterized by a romantic style and the use of natural fabrics, especially cotton.

Ashmole, Elias (1617–92) Antiquary, born in Lichfield, Staffordshire, C England, UK. He qualified as a lawyer in 1638 and subsequently combined work for the royalist cause with the study of mathematics, natural philosophy, astronomy, astrology, and alchemy, entering Brasenose College, Oxford. In 1652 he issued his *Theatrum chymicum*, and in 1672 his major work, a *History of the Order of the Garter*. In 1677 he presented to the University of Oxford a fine collection of rarities, thus founding the *Ashmolean Museum* (built in 1682).

Ashmun, Jehudi (1794–1828) Philanthropist, born in Champlain, NY. He was the founder in 1822 of the colony of Liberia for liberated slaves on the W coast of Africa.

Ashton, Sir Frederick (William Mallandaine) (1906–88) British choreographer, born in Guayaquil, Ecuador. Following education at an English public school, he studied under Léonide Massine and Marie Rambert, who commissioned his first piece, *A Tragedy of Fashion* (1926). After a year in America, he returned to Britain to help found the Ballet Club, which later became Ballet Rambert (now the Rambert Dance Company). He joined the Vic Wells Ballet in 1935 as dancer/choreographer, and remained there as the company developed into the Royal Ballet. In 1963 he succeeded Ninette de Valois as director of the company, a post he held for seven years. He was knighted in 1962. >> Massine; Rambert; Valois

Ashton, Sir John William, known as **Will Ashton** (1881–1963) Landscape painter, born in York, North Yorkshire, N England, UK. His family moved to Adelaide, South Australia, when he was three. In 1899 he returned to England and studied in the artists' colony at St Ives, Cornwall. He quickly established a reputation as a landscape artist, especially for his bridges of the Seine and other French and Mediterranean subjects, and was a leading opponent of modern trends in painting.

Ashton, Julian (Rossi) (1851–1942) Painter and teacher, born in Alderstone, Surrey, SE England, UK. In 1878 he emigrated to Australia and, while working as an illustrator for the Melbourne newspaper *The Age*, covered the capture of the Ned Kelly gang. He later moved to Sydney, and in 1896 founded the Sydney Art School. He organized the Grafton Gallery (London) exhibition of Australian art in 1898, and worked strenuously for the recognition of Australian artists.

Ashton, Winifred >> Dane, Clemence

Ashurbanipal >> Assurbanipal; Sardanapalus

Asimov, Isaac [**az**imov] (1920–92) Novelist, critic, and popular scientist, born in Petrovichi, Russia. He was brought to the USA when he was three, studied chemistry at Columbia University, and developed a career both as an academic biochemist and as a science fiction writer. Among his leading titles are the 'Foundation' novels – *Foundation* (1951), *Foundation and Empire* (1952), and *Second Foundation* (1953); the so-called Robot novels – *The Caves of Steel* (1954) and *The Naked Sun* (1957); and the short stories which form the collection *I, Robot* (1950). Increasingly regarded as a scientific seer, he added the term *robotics* to the language. He wrote two volumes of autobiography (1979 and 1980), and later novels include *The Disappearing Man and other stories* (1985) and *Nightfall* (1990).

Asinius >> **Pollio**

Aske, Robert (?–1537) English rebel leader, a Yorkshire attorney at Gray's Inn, who headed the Catholic rising known as the Pilgrimage of Grace in protest at Henry VIII's dissolution of the monasteries. He was hanged in York for treason.

Askew, Anne (1521–46) Protestant martyr, born near Grimsby, North East Lincolnshire, EC England, UK. Early embracing the Reformed doctrines, in 1545 she was arrested on a charge of heresy. After examination and torture on the rack, she was burned at Smithfield.

Askey, Arthur, nickname **Big-hearted Arthur** (1900–82) Comedian, born in Liverpool, Merseyside, NW England, UK. He made his professional debut in 1924, and became a leading comedian in summer seasons at British seaside resorts, achieving national recognition on radio with *Band Wagon* (from 1938). He used his smallness of stature (1.6 m/5 ft 2 in) in his humour, and cultivated a cheery manner. His twangy pronunciation of 'I thank you!' became a catchphrase.

Aśoka or **Ashoka** [aʃohka] (3rd-c BC) King of India (c.264–238 BC), the last ruler of the Mauryan dynasty. After his invasion of the Kaliṅga country, he renounced armed conquest and became a convert to Buddhism, which subsequently spread throughout India and beyond. He adopted a policy called *dharma* (principles of right life), advocating toleration, honesty, and kindness, and had his teachings engraved on rocks and pillars at certain sites. With his death the Mauryan empire declined and his work was discontinued. >> RR1058

Aspasia [aspayzha] (5th-c BC) Mistress of Pericles, born in Miletus, Anatolia. Intellectual and vivacious, she was lampooned in Greek satire, but was held in high regard by Socrates and his followers, and was a great inspiration to Pericles, who successfully defended her against a charge of impiety. >> Pericles; Socrates

Aspdin, Joseph (1779–1855) Bricklayer and inventor, born in Leeds, West Yorkshire, N England, UK. A stonemason by trade, in 1824 he patented what he called *Portland cement*, manufactured from clay and limestone.

Aspel, Michael (Terence) (1933–) British broadcaster and writer. Following national service, he became a radio actor (1954) and a television announcer (1957), but came to public prominence as a television newsreader (1960–8). In 1968 he became a freelance broadcaster, known for his genial interviewing style in *Aspel and Company* (1984–93) and as presenter of *This is Your Life* (from 1988). He writes regularly for magazines, and his books include one for children (*Hang On!*, 1982) and an autobiography (*Polly Wants a Zebra*, 1974).

Aspinall, Sir John (Audley Frederick) [aspinawl] (1851–1937) Mechanical engineer, born in Liverpool, Merseyside, NW England, UK. He rose from locomotive fireman to be chief mechanical engineer and general manager of the Lancashire and Yorkshire Railway (1899–1919). He designed many types of locomotives and completed one of the first main-line railway electrification schemes in Britain, from Liverpool to Southport, in 1904.

Asplund, Erik Gunnar (1885–1940) Architect, born in Stockholm. He designed the Stockholm City Library (1924–7), and was responsible for most of the buildings in the Stockholm Exhibition of 1930. Their design was acclaimed for the imagination with which the architect used simple modern forms and methods, such as the cantilever and glass walls.

Asquith, Herbert Henry Asquith, 1st Earl of Oxford (1852–1928) British statesman and prime minister (1908–16), born in Morley, West Yorkshire, N England, UK. He studied at Oxford, was called to the bar in 1876, and was Liberal member for East Fife (1886–1918). He became home secretary (1892–5), Chancellor of the Exchequer (1905–8), and succeeded Campbell-Bannerman as prime minister. He introduced the Parliament Act of 1911, limiting the power of the House of Lords. He was also confronted by the suffragette movement, the threat of civil war over Home Rule for Ireland, and the international crises which led to World War 1. In 1915 he headed a war coalition, but was ousted in 1916 by supporters of Lloyd George and others who thought his conduct of the war was not sufficiently vigorous. He lost his East Fife seat in 1918, then returned to the Commons as MP for Paisley in 1920. His disagreements with Lloyd George weakened the Liberal Party, though he was later recognized as leader again (1923–6). He was created an earl in 1925. >> Campbell-Bannerman; Lloyd-George, David; RR1095

Assad, Hafez al- >> **Asad, Hafez al-**

Assassin, The Great >> **Abd-ul-Hamid II**

Asselyn, Jan [aslin] (1610–52) Painter, born in Amsterdam. He travelled to Italy, and became a successful painter of Italianate landscapes which depict imaginary Arcadian vistas inspired by the Roman countryside.

Asser [aser] (850–?909) Welsh scholar, bishop, and counsellor to Alfred the Great. He spent his youth in the monastic community at St David's. Gaining a reputation for scholarship, he was enlisted into the royal service by Alfred, and made Bishop of Sherborne sometime before 900. He is best known for his unfinished Latin biography of King Alfred. >> Alfred

Asser, Tobias (Michael Carel) [aser] (1838–1913) Jurist, born in Amsterdam. A professor of international law at Amsterdam (1862–93), he was a founder of the Institute of International Law in 1873. In 1911 he shared the Nobel Peace Prize with Austrian pacifist **Alfred Fried** (1864–1921) for his work in creating the Permanent Court of Arbitration at the Hague Peace Conference of 1899.

Assisi, Francis of, St >> **Francis of Assisi, St**

Assurbanipal or **Ashurbanipal** [asoorbanipal] (7th-c BC) King of Assyria (668–627 BC), the last of the great Assyrian kings, the son of Esarhaddon and grandson of Sennacherib. A patron of the arts, he founded at Nineveh the first systematically gathered and organized library in the Middle East, containing a vast number of texts on numerous subjects copied from temple libraries throughout his empire. >> Esarhaddon; Sardanapalus; Sennacherib; RR1032

Astaire, Fred [astair], originally **Frederick Austerlitz** (1899–1987) Dancer, singer, and actor, born in Omaha, NE. He was teamed with his elder sister **Adele** (1897–1981) as a touring vaudeville act, rising to stardom with her in the 1920s on Broadway in specially written shows such as *Lady Be Good* and *Funny Face*. In Hollywood, with new partner Ginger Rogers, he revolutionized the film musical with a succession of original dance-tap routines in such films as *Top Hat* (1935) and *Swing Time* (1936). He announced his retirement in 1946, but returned to create further classic musicals, such as *Easter Parade* (1948), then turned to straight acting, winning an Oscar nomination for *The*

Towering Inferno (1974) and an Emmy for *A Family Upside Down* (1978). He received a special Academy Award in 1949 for his contributions to the musical. >> Rogers, Ginger

Astbury, John, known as **Astbury of Shelton** (1688–1743) Potter, probably born in Staffordshire, C England, UK. In the early 18th-c he established a factory in Shelton, Staffordshire, where he developed a distinctive type of earthenware pottery known as *Astbury ware*. His style was continued by his son **Thomas Astbury** from c.1725.

Astbury, William Thomas (1889–1961) X-ray crystallographer, born in Longton, Staffordshire, C England, UK. He studied at Cambridge and London, and from 1945 held the new chair of biomolecular structure at Leeds. Using X-ray diffraction photographs, his pioneering studies on protein fibres laid the basis for much later work. He probably coined the phase *molecular biology*; and with Florence Bell in 1938 offered the first hypothetical structure for the key genetic material DNA.

Astley, Philip (1742–1814) Theatrical manager and equestrian, born in Newcastle-under-Lyme, Staffordshire, C England, UK. In 1770 he started a circus at Lambeth, and built Astley's Amphitheatre (1798), once one of the sights of London. He also established amphitheatres in Paris and several other venues in Europe.

Astley, Thea (1925–) Novelist and short-story writer, born in Brisbane, Queensland, Australia. Educated in Queensland, she was brought up a Roman Catholic, and much of her writing has been influenced by her Catholicism and the environment of N Queensland. She has won the prestigious Miles Franklin Award three times, for novels including *The Slow Natives* (1965) and *The Acolyte* (1972). An acute observer of contemporary Australia, and a skilled satirist, her novels often focus on misfits, and attack the narrow-mindedness of middle-class life. In 1979 she published a collection of related short stories, *Hunting the Wild Pineapple*, and in 1980 retired from Macquarie University to write full time, her works since then including *Reaching Tin River* (1990) and *Vanishing Points* (1992). In 1996 she won the Age Book of the Year award for *The Multiple Effects of Rainshadow*.

Aston, Francis (William) (1877–1945) Physicist, born in Birmingham, West Midlands, C England, UK. He studied at Birmingham and Cambridge, and was noted for his work on isotopes. He invented the mass spectrograph in 1919, for which he was awarded the Nobel Prize for Chemistry in 1922. The *Aston dark space* in electronic discharges is named after him.

Astor, (Roberta) Brooke, *née* **Russell** (?1902–) Socialite, philanthropist, and writer, born in Portsmouth, NH. Largely self-educated, she was a magazine journalist and the author of four books. She married three times (once divorced, twice widowed). Her third husband, **Vincent Astor**, left her with a fortune that allowed her to become a philanthropist of major proportions. She awarded an average of 100 grants a year ($9 million a year) to civic projects, social projects, and cultural institutions in New York City. The New York Public Library, where she served as a trustee, was one of her major beneficiaries.

Astor, John Jacob (1763–1848) Fur trader and financier, founder of the America Fur Company and the Astor family, born in Waldorf, Germany. In 1784 he sailed to the USA and invested his small capital in a fur business in New York City. He founded the settlement of *Astoria* in 1811. He became one of the most powerful financiers in the USA, and at his death left a legacy to found a public library in New York City.

Astor, John Jacob (1864–1912) US financier, a great-grandson of John Jacob Astor, the fur trader. He served in the Spanish-American War, and built part of the Waldorf Astoria hotel in New York. He was drowned in the *Titanic* disaster.

Astor (of Hever), John Jacob Astor, Baron (1886–1971) Newspaper proprietor, born in New York City, New York, USA, the son of William Waldorf Astor, 1st Viscount. He studied at Oxford, was aide-de-camp to the viceroy of India (1911–14), and was elected MP for Dover in 1922. He became chairman of the Times Publishing Company after the death of Lord Northcliffe, resigning his directorship in 1962. >> Astor, 1st Viscount

Astor, Mary, originally **Lucille Langhanke** (1906–87) Film actress, born in Quincy, IL. She made her film debut in *The Beggar Maid* (1921) and was soon established as a beautiful innocent in such historical dramas as *Beau Brummell* (1924) and *Don Juan* (1926). She won an Oscar for *The Great Lie* (1941, with Bette Davis). Later roles included *Meet Me in St Louis* (1944) and *Return to Peyton Place* (1961), and she was also active on stage and television.

Astor, Nancy (Witcher) Astor, Viscountess, *née* **Langhorne** (1879–1964) British politician, born in Danville, VA, USA. Wife of Waldorf Astor, she succeeded her husband as Conservative MP for Plymouth in 1919, and was the first woman to take a seat in the House of Commons. She was known for her interest in social problems, especially temperance and women's rights. >> Astor, Waldorf

Astor, William Waldorf Astor, 1st Viscount (1848–1919) Newspaper proprietor, born in New York City, a great-grandson of John Jacob Astor, the fur trader. Defeated in the election for governor of New York State (1881), he was US minister to Italy (1882–5). He emigrated to Britain in 1892 and bought the *Pall Mall Gazette* and *Pall Mall Magazine*. He became a British citizen in 1899, bought *The Observer* in 1911, and was made a viscount in 1917.

Astor, (William) Waldorf Astor, 2nd Viscount (1879–1952) British politician, born in New York City, New York, USA, the son of William Waldorf Astor, 1st Viscount. He studied at Oxford, and was elected MP for Plymouth in 1910. On passing to the House of Lords in 1919 he became parliamentary secretary to the local government board (later the Ministry of Health) and his wife, Nancy Astor, succeeded him in the lower house. He was proprietor of *The Observer*. >> Astor, Nancy

Astorga, Emanuele, Baron d' [aˈstaw(r)ga] (c. 1680–1757) Composer, born in Agosta, Italy. He composed numerous chamber cantatas and some operas, but is best known for his *Stabat Mater* (1707).

Astruc, Jean [asˈtrük] (1684–1766) Physician and biblical scholar, medical consultant to Louis XV, born in Sauve, France. His work on Moses laid the foundations for modern criticism of the Pentateuch. He also wrote on the diseases of women and on venereal disease.

Asturias, Miguel Angel [asˈtoorias] (1899–1974) Novelist and poet, born in Guatemala City. A law graduate from the National University, he spent many years in exile, particularly in Paris, where he studied anthropology. His novels, many of which reflect Mayan Indian influences, include *El señor presidente* (1946, The President), *Hombres de maíz* (1949, Men of Maize), and a trilogy on the foreign exploitation of the banana trade. In the Guatemalan civil service from 1946, he was ambassador to France, 1966–70. He was awarded the Lenin Peace Prize in 1966 and the Nobel Prize for Literature in 1967.

Atahualpa [ataˈwalpa] (?–1533) Last Inca ruler of Peru. On the death of his father, he received the N half of the Inca empire, and in 1532 overthrew his brother, Huascar, who ruled the S half. A year later he was captured by invading Spaniards under Francisco Pizarro. Although his subjects paid a vast ransom to secure his release, Atahualpa was executed. >> Pizarro, Francisco

Atanasoff, John (Vincent) [atanasof] (1903–95) Physicist and computer pioneer, born in Hamilton, NY. He studied at the University of Florida, Iowa State College, and the University of Wisconsin. In 1942, with the help of Clifford Berry (1918–63), he built an electronic calculating machine – the ABC (Atanasoff-Berry Computer) – one of the first calculating devices using vacuum tubes.

Atatürk [ataterk], originally **Mustafa Kemal** (1881–1938) Turkish army officer, politican, and president (1923–38), born in Salonika, Greece. He raised a nationalist rebellion in Anatolia in protest against the post-war division of Turkey, and in 1921 established a provisional government in Ankara. In 1922 the Ottoman Sultanate was formally abolished, and in 1923 Turkey was declared a secular republic, with Kemal as president. He became a virtual dictator, and launched a social and political revolution introducing Western fashions, the emancipation of women, educational reform, the replacement of Arabic script with the Latin alphabet, and the discouragement of traditional Islamic loyalties in favour of a strictly Turkish nationalism. In 1935 he assumed the surname Atatürk ('Father of the Turks'). >> RR1093

Athanaric [athanarik] (?–381) Prince of the W Goths, who fought three campaigns against the Roman Emperor Valens (ruled 364–78). He was finally defeated in 369, and driven out by the Huns from the N of the Danube.

Athanasius, St [athanayzius] (c. 296–373) Christian theologian and prelate, born in Alexandria. A distinguished participant at the Council of Nicaea (325), he was chosen Patriarch of Alexandria and Primate of Egypt. As a result of his stand against the heretic Arius, he was dismissed from his see on several occasions by emperors sympathetic to the Arian cause. However, his teaching was supported after his death at the Council of Constantinople (381). His writings include works on the Trinity, the Incarnation, and the divinity of the Holy Spirit. The *Athanasian Creed* (representing his beliefs) was little heard of until the 7th-c. Feast day 2 May. >> Arius

Atheling >> **Edgar the Ætheling**

Athelstan or **Æthelstan** [athelstan] (c.895–939) Anglo-Saxon king, the grandson of Alfred the Great, and the son of Edward the Elder, whom he succeeded as King of Wessex and Mercia in 924. A warrior king of outstanding ability, he extended his rule over parts of Cornwall and Wales, and kept Norse-held Northumbria under control. In 937 he defeated a confederation of Scots, Welsh, and Vikings from Ireland in a major battle (Brunanburh), and his fame spread far afield. At home, he improved the laws, built monasteries, and promoted commerce. >> Alfred; Edward (the Elder); Skallagrímsson; RR1095

Athenaeus [atheneeus] (2nd-c) Greek writer, born in Naucratis, Egypt. He lived first in Alexandria and later in Rome. He wrote *Deipnosophistae* (Banquet of the Learned), a collection of anecdotes and excerpts from ancient authors reproduced as dinner-table conversations.

Athenais >> **Eudocia**

Atherton, David (1944–) Conductor, born in Blackpool, Lancashire, NW England, UK. He studied at Cambridge, and was founder and musical director of the London Sinfonietta (1967–73). In 1968 he became the youngest ever conductor of the Henry Wood Promenade Concerts, later joining the Royal Liverpool Philharmonic Orchestra as principal conductor and artistic adviser (1980–3) and principal guest conductor (1983–6). He was principal guest conductor of the BBC Symphony Orchestra (1985–9), and has been musical director and principal conductor with the Hong Kong Philharmonic Orchestra since 1989.

Atherton, Gertrude (Franklin), *née* **Horn** (1857–1948) Novelist, born in San Francisco, CA. Left a widow in 1887, she travelled extensively, living in Europe most of her life and using the places she visited as backgrounds for her novels. The most popular of her books are *The Conqueror* (1902), a fictional biography of Alexander Hamilton, and *Black Oxen* (1923).

Atherton, Mike, popular name of **Michael Andrew Atherton** (1968–) Cricketer, born in Manchester, Greater Manchester, NW England, UK. He studied at Cambridge and made his first-class debut for the University v Essex in 1987, his debut for Lancashire the same year, and his first-team debut for England in 1989 against Australia. A leading batsman, he was appointed England captain (1993–), touring the West Indies (1993–4), Australia (1994–5), South Africa (1995–6), and Zimbabwe and New Zealand (1996–7). His captaincy has experienced mixed fortunes, and England's failure to regain the Ashes at home in 1997 led to speculation about his future role. Awards include Cricket Writer's Young Cricketer of the Year (1990) and the Cornhill Player of the Year (1994).

Atholl, Katherine Marjory Murray, Duchess of [athol], *née* **Russell** (1874–1960) Conservative politician, born in Banff, Aberdeenshire, NE Scotland, UK. She studied at the Royal College of Music, and was an accomplished pianist and composer. In 1899 she married the future 8th Duke of Atholl, **John George Murray** (1871–1942), becoming Duchess of Atholl in 1917. She became MP for Kinross and Perthshire in 1923, and was the first Conservative woman minister as parliamentary secretary to the Board of Education (1924–9). She was responsible for translating an unexpurgated edition of *Mein Kampf* to warn of Hitler's intentions, and published the best-selling *Searchlight on Spain* in 1938. After losing her parliamentary seat in 1939, she worked to aid refugees from totalitarianism.

Atiyah, Sir Michael (Francis) [ateeah] (1929–) Mathematician, born in London, England, UK. He studied at Trinity College, Cambridge (1952), lectured at Cambridge and Oxford, became professor of mathematics at Oxford (1963–9), and was appointed Master of Trinity College, Cambridge, in 1990. He has worked on algebraic geometry, algebraic topology, index theory of differential operators, and the mathematics of quantum field theory, where he has been particularly concerned with bridging the gap between mathematicians and physicists. In 1966 he was awarded the Fields Medal.

Atkin (of Aberdovey), James Richard Atkin, Baron (1867–1944) Judge, born in Brisbane, Queensland, Australia. He studied at Oxford, and became a lawyer specializing in commercial cases. In the Court of Appeal (1919–28) and the House of Lords (1928–44) he delivered notable opinions in many leading cases, and made important contributions to legal education.

Atkinson, Thomas (Wittlam) (1799–1861) Architect and travel-writer, born in Cawthorne, South Yorkshire, N England, UK. He became successively a quarryman, stonemason, and architect. Between 1848 and 1853 he travelled some 40 000 miles in Asiatic Russia with his wife **Lucy**, painting and keeping journals which formed the basis of several works on that part of the world.

Atkinson, Rowan (Sebastian) (1955–) British comic actor and writer, born in Newcastle upon Tyne, Tyne and Wear, NE England, UK. He studied electrical engineering at the universities of Newcastle upon Tyne and Oxford, first appeared in Oxford University revues at the Edinburgh Festival Fringe, and in 1981 became the youngest performer to have had a one-man show in the West End. Subsequent appearances include *The Nerd* (1984), *The New Revue* (1986), and *The Sneeze* (1988). Television roles include *Not the Nine O'Clock News* (1979–82), *Blackadder* (1983–9), *The Thin Blue Line* (1995–6), and *Mr Bean* (from 1990–4, 1996 in the USA). Film credits include *Four Weddings and a Funeral* (1994), *The Lion King* (voiceover, 1994), and *Bean: the Ultimate Disaster Movie* (1997).

Atlas, Charles, originally **Angelo Siciliano** (1893–1972) Body-builder, born in Acri, Italy. At the age of 10 he emigrated to the USA with his parents. Dissatisfied with his poor physique, he took up body-building, and became popularly known as 'America's Most Perfectly Developed Man'. Together with businessman Charles P Roman, he successfully marketed a mail-order body-building course.

Attenborough, Sir David (Frederick) [atenbruh] (1926–) Naturalist and broadcaster, born in London, England, UK, the brother of Richard Attenborough. After service in the Royal Navy (1947–9) and three years in an educational publishing house, he joined the BBC in 1952 as a trainee producer. The series *Zoo Quest* (1954–64) allowed him to undertake expeditions to remote parts of the globe to capture intimate footage of rare wildlife in its natural habitat. He was the controller of BBC 2 (1965–8) and director of programmes (1969–72) before returning to documentary-making with such series as *Life on Earth* (1979), *The Living Planet* (1984), *The First Eden* (1987), and *The Private Life of Plants* (1995). He was knighted in 1985 and made a Companion of Honour in 1996. >> Attenborough, Richard

Attenborough, Sir Richard (Samuel), Baron [atenbruh] (1923–) Actor and film director, born in Cambridge, Cambridgeshire, EC England, UK, the brother of David Attenborough. He trained at the Royal Academy of Dramatic Art, London, before making his film debut in *In Which We Serve* (1942). Initially typecast as weak and cowardly youths, he was seen to chilling effect as Pinkie in *Brighton Rock*, on stage in 1943 and on film in 1947. He won British Academy Awards as the kidnapper in *Seance on a Wet Afternoon* (1964) and the bombastic sergeant major in *Guns at Batasi* (1964). He became a producer in partnership with Bryan Forbes, and directed such large-scale epics as *A Bridge Too Far* (1977). A 20-year crusade to film the life of Mahatma Gandhi led to an Oscar for *Gandhi* (1982). In 1987 he made *Cry Freedom*, a biography of the black activist Steve Biko, and in 1992 a biography of Charles Chaplin. The following year he directed *Shadowlands*, the story of C S Lewis's marriage, and in 1996 appeared *In Love and War*. He married actress Sheila Sim (1922–) in 1944, was knighted in 1976, and became a baron in 1993. >> Attenborough, David; Forbes, Bryan

Atterbury, Francis (1663–1732) Anglican clergyman and controversialist, born in Milton, Buckinghamshire, SC England, UK. He studied at Oxford, took holy orders, and became Dean of Carlisle (1704), Prolocutor of Convocation (1710), Dean of Christ Church (1712), and Bishop of Rochester and Dean of Westminster (1713). In 1715 he refused to sign the bishops' declaration of fidelity, and in 1722 was committed to the Tower for complicity in an attempt to restore the Stuarts. He was deprived of all his offices, and exiled.

Atticus, Titus Pomponius [atikus] (109–32 BC) Intellectual, businessman, and writer, born in Rome. He acquired the surname Atticus because of his long sojourn in Athens (85–65) to avoid the Civil War. He was a wealthy and highly cultivated man who espoused the Epicurean philosophy and combined his literary activities with a successful business career. Cicero's *Letters to Atticus* form a famous and prolific correspondence. >> Cicero

Attila [atila], known as **the Scourge of God** (c. 406–53) King of the Huns (434–53). He ruled with his elder brother until 445, his dominion extending over Germany and Scythia from the Rhine to the frontiers of China. In 447 he devastated all the countries between the Black Sea and the Mediterranean, defeating Emperor Theodosius II (ruled 408–50). In 451 he invaded Gaul, but was routed by Aëtius, the Roman commander, and Theodoric I, King of the Visigoths, on the Catalaunian Plain. He retreated to Hungary, but then made an incursion into Italy, devastating several cities, Rome itself being saved only by the personal mediation of Pope Leo I. The Hunnish empire decayed after his death. >> Aëtius; Leo I; Theodoric I

Attlee, Clem, popular name of **Clement Richard Attlee, 1st Earl Attlee** (1883–1967) British statesman and prime minister (1945–51), born in London, England, UK. He studied at Oxford, and was called to the bar in 1905. He became a Labour MP in 1922, Ramsay MacDonald's parliamentary secretary (1922–4), under-secretary of state for war (1924), and postmaster-general (1931). He succeeded Lansbury as Leader of the Opposition in 1935. In Churchill's war cabinet, he was dominions secretary (1942–3) and deputy prime minister (1942–5). As Leader of the Opposition he accompanied Eden to the San Francisco and Potsdam conferences (1945), and after the Labour victory returned to Potsdam as prime minister. He carried through a vigorous programme of reform, nationalizing several industries, and introducing the National Health Service. Independence was granted to India (1947) and Burma (1948). He was again Leader of the Opposition (1951–5), then resigned and accepted an earldom. >> RR1095

Attwell, Mabel Lucie (1879–1964) Artist and writer, born in London, England, UK. She studied at Heatherley's and other art schools, and married cartoonist **Harold Earnshaw**. She was noted for her child studies, both humorous and serious, with which she illustrated her own and other stories for children. Her immensely popular 'cherubic' style was continued in annuals and children's books by her daughter, working under her mother's name.

Atwood, Margaret (Eleanor) (1939–) Novelist, short-story writer, poet, and critic, born in Ottawa, Ontario, Canada. She studied at the University of Toronto and Radcliffe College, becoming a lecturer in English literature. Her first published work, a collection of poems entitled *The Circle Game* (1966), won the Governor-General's Award. Since then she has published many volumes of poetry and short stories, but is best known as a novelist. Her controversial *The Edible Woman* (1969) is one of several novels focusing on women's issues. Her futuristic novel, *The Handmaid's Tale* (1985, filmed with a script by Pinter, 1990), was short-listed for the Booker Prize, as was *Cat's Eye* in 1989. Later books include *The Robber Bride* (1994) and *Alias Grace* (1996). >> Pinter

Auber, Daniel-François-Esprit [ohbair] (1782–1871) Composer of operas, born in Caen, France. His best-known works are *La Muette de Portici*, usually entitled *Masaniello* (1828), and *Fra Diavolo* (1830).

Aubert, Marie Henriette Suzanne [ohbair], known as **Mother Aubert** (1835–1926) Catholic nun and religious founder, born in Lyon, France. She moved to New Zealand in 1860 to do missionary work among the mainly rural Maori people, arriving in Wellington in 1899 to work with the urban poor. She undertook commercial production of Maori herbal remedies and published books in the Maori language. In 1892 she founded a religious order to extend and continue her charitable work, the Daughters of Our Lady of Compassion.

Aubert, Pierre [ohbair] (1927–) Swiss statesman, born in La Chaux-de-Fonds, Switzerland. A member of the local assembly (1960–8), in annual elections he became vice-president of Switzerland (1982) then president (1983, 1987). >> RR1091

Aublet, Jean Baptiste (Christophe Fusée) [ohblay] (1720–78) Botanist and humanist, born in Salon, France.

He spent over 10 years in Mauritius and the French West Indies, where he established gardens of medicinal plants, and made extensive collections in French Guiana, founding forest botany in tropical America. He was also the first secular slavery abolitionist.

Aubrey, John [awbree] (1626–97) Antiquary and folklorist, born in Easton Percy, Wiltshire, S England, UK. He studied at Oxford and London, training as a lawyer, but was never called to the bar. Only his quaint, credulous *Miscellanies* (1696) of folklore and ghost-stories was printed in his lifetime, but he left a large mass of unpublished materials. He also collected biographical and anecdotal material on celebrities of his time, which appeared in *Letters by Eminent Persons* (1813), better known as *Brief Lives*.

Aubusson, Pierre d' [ohbüsõ] (1423–1503) French soldier and clergyman, and Grand Master of the Knights Hospitallers from 1476, born in Monteil-au-Vicomte, France. His outstanding achievement was his defence of Rhodes in 1480 against a besieging army of Turks under Sultan Mohammed II. In 1481 he made a treaty with the Turks under Sultan Bayezit II by agreeing to imprison the sultan's rebellious brother, Djem; and in 1489 was created cardinal for handing Djem over to Pope Innocent VIII.

Auchinleck, Sir Claude John Eyre [okhinlek] (1884–1981) British soldier. He studied at Wellington College, and joined the 62nd Punjabis in 1904. In 1941 he became commander-in-chief in India, then succeeded Wavell in N Africa. He made a successful advance into Cyrenaica, but was later thrown back by Rommel. His regrouping of the 8th Army on El Alamein paved the way for ultimate victory, but at the time he was made a scapegoat for the retreat, and was replaced by General Alexander in 1942. In 1943 he returned to India, and was created field-marshal in 1946.

Auchinloss, Louis Stanton, pseudonym **Andrew Lee** (1917–) Novelist, short-story writer, and critic, born in Lawrence, NY. He trained as a lawyer and was admitted to the New York bar in 1941. His first novel, *The Indifferent Children* (1947), appeared under his pseudonym, but later books carried his own name, such as *Pursuit of the Prodigal* (1960) and *The Embezzler* (1966). Later works include *The Country Cousin* (1978), *Diary of a Yuppie* (1987), and *Lady of Situations* (1991).

Auden, W(ystan) H(ugh) [awden] (1907–73) Poet and essayist, born in York, North Yorkshire, N England, UK. He studied at Oxford, and in the 1930s wrote passionately on social problems from a far-left standpoint, especially in his collection of poems *Look, Stranger!* (1936). He went to Spain as a civilian in support of the Republican side, and reported on it in *Spain* (1937), followed by a verse commentary (with prose reports by Christopher Isherwood) on the Sino-Japanese war in *Journey to a War* (1939). He also collaborated with Isherwood in three plays in the 1930s: *The Dog Beneath the Skin* (1935), *The Ascent of F6* (1936), and *On the Frontier* (1938). He emigrated to New York early in 1939, and became a US citizen in 1946. There he became converted to Anglicanism, tracing his conversion in *The Sea and the Mirror* (1944) and *For the Time Being* (1944). Later works include *Homage to Clio* (1960) and *City Without Walls* (1969). He was also professor of poetry at Oxford (1956–61). >> Isherwood; Macneice

Audley (of Walden), Thomas Audley, Baron [awdlee] (1488–1544) English nobleman, born in Earls Colne, Essex, SE England, UK. He studied law, and became attorney for the Duchy of Lancaster (1530) and king's serjeant (1531). Active in furthering Henry VIII's designs, he profited abundantly by ecclesiastical confiscations. In 1529 he was appointed Speaker of the House of Commons and in 1532 became Lord Chancellor. He was created a baron in 1538.

Audouin, Jean Victor [ohdwĩ] (1797–1841) Entomologist and naturalist, born in Paris. Trained as a doctor, he became professor of entomology at the Jardin des Plantes in Paris. He was co-author of the *Dictionnaire classique d'histoire naturelle* (1822), and compiled the ornithological section of the compendious *Description de l'Égypte* (1826). *Audouin's gull* was named after him.

Audrey, St >> **Etheldreda, St**

Audubon, John James [awduhbon] (1785–1851) Ornithologist and bird artist, born in Les Cayes, Haiti. He was sent to the USA in 1804 to look after his father's property near Philadelphia, and married Lucy Bakewell, the daughter of an English settler. He spent several years seeking out every species of bird in America in order to catalogue them. In 1826 he took his work to Europe, where he cultivated a rugged backwoodsman image that went down well with fashionable society. In 1827 he published the first of the 87 portfolios of his massive *Birds of America* (1827–38). Between 1840 and 1844 he produced a 'miniature' edition in 7 volumes, which became a best-seller. The National Audubon Society, dedicated to the conservation of birds in the USA, was founded in his honour in 1866.

Auenbrugger, Leopold [owenbruger] (1722–1809) Physician, born in Graz, Austria. He was the first to use percussion (tapping parts of the body and using the sound to aid diagnosis) in medical practice. He also wrote the libretto for one of Salieri's operas. >> Salieri

Auer, Carl, Freiherr (Baron) **von Welsbach** [ower] (1858–1929) Chemist, born in Vienna. He invented the incandescent gas mantle and the osmium lamp. He also discovered the cerium–iron alloy known as *Auer metal* or mischmetal, now used as flints in petrol lighters.

Auerbach, Berthold [owerbakh], originally **Moses Baruch Auerbacher** (1812–82) Novelist, born in Nordstetten, Germany. He studied at the universities of Tübingen, Munich, and Heidelberg, and developed a special interest in Spinoza, on whose life he based a novel (1837), and whose works he translated (1841). In his *Schwarzwälder Dorfgeschichten* (1843, Black Forest Village Stories), on which his fame chiefly rests, he gives charming pictures of Black Forest life. >> Spinoza

Auerbach, Frank [owerbak] (1931–) Artist, born in Germany. He moved to Britain in 1939, and studied at St Martin's School of Art (1948–52) and the Royal College of Art (1952–5). He works with oil paint of predominantly earth colours. His subject matter is figurative, portraits of a few close friends, and familiar views of Primrose Hill and Camden Town in London.

Auerbach, Red [owerbak], popular name of **Arnold Jacob Auerbach** (1917–) Basketball coach, born in New York City. During his career as coach of the Boston Celtics (1950–66), his teams won nine National Basketball Association championships, eight of them consecutively (1959–66). Famous for lighting a cigar after each victory, he retired from coaching in 1966 to become the team's general manager.

Augereau, Pierre François Charles, duc de (Duke of) **Castiglione** [ohzheroh] (1757–1816) French soldier, born in Paris. He achieved rapid promotion under Napoleon in Italy, where he fought with distinction at Lodi and Castiglione (1796). He opposed Napoleon's assumption of power as first consul in 1799, but was reconciled and promoted marshal in 1804 and created Duke of Castiglione in 1808. >> Napoleon

Augier, (Guillaume Victor) Emile [ohzhiay] (1820–89) Playwright, born in Valence, France. His *Théâtre complet* (1890) fills seven volumes, and includes several social comedies, such as *Le Gendre de M Poirier* (1854, with Jules Sandeau) and *Les Fourchambault* (1878).

August, Bille [owgust] (1948–) Film director and photographer, born in Denmark. He studied in Stockholm and Copenhagen, and since 1979 has directed several feature films and TV films. *Pelle Erobreren* (1987, Pelle the Conqueror) was awarded the Golden Palm in Cannes in 1988, and in 1989 won an Oscar in the Best Foreign Language Film category. Later films include *Jerusalem* (1996).

Augustine, St [awguhstin], also known as **Augustine of Canterbury** (?–604) Clergyman, the first Archbishop of Canterbury, born probably in Rome. He was prior of the Benedictine monastery of St Andrew in Rome, when in 596 he was sent, with 40 other monks, by Pope Gregory I to convert the Anglo-Saxons to Christianity. Landing in Thanet, the missionaries were kindly received by Æthelbert, King of Kent, whose wife was already a Christian. A residence was assigned to them at Canterbury, where they devoted themselves to monastic exercises and preaching. The conversion and baptism of the king contributed greatly to the success of their efforts. In 597 Augustine went to Arles, and there was consecrated Bishop of the English. Feast day 26/27 May. >> Gregory I; Mellitus

Augustine, St [awguhstin], originally **Aurelius Augustinus**, also known as **Augustine of Hippo** (354–430) The greatest of the Latin Fathers of the Church, born in Tagaste, Numidia (modern Algeria). His father was a pagan, but he was brought up a Christian by his devout mother, Monica. He went to Carthage to study, and had a son (Adeonatus) by a mistress there. He became deeply involved in Manicheanism, which seemed to offer a solution to the problem of evil, a theme which was to preoccupy him throughout his life. In 383 he moved to teach at Rome, then at Milan, and became influenced by Scepticism and then by Neoplatonism. After the dramatic spiritual crises described in his autobiography, he finally became converted to Christianity and was baptized (together with his son) by St Ambrose in 386. He returned to N Africa and became Bishop of Hippo in 396, where he was a relentless antagonist of the heretical schools of Donatists, Pelagians, and Manicheans. The *Confessions* (400) is a classic of world literature and a spiritual autobiography, as well as an original work of philosophy. *The City of God* (412–27) is a work of 22 books presenting human history in terms of the conflict between the spiritual and the temporal. Feast day 28 August.

Augustulus, Romulus [awgustyulus], nickname of **Flavius Momyllus Romulus Augustus** (5th-c) Last emperor of the W half of the old Roman Empire (ruled 475–476). His father, Orestes, had risen to high rank under Emperor Julius Neppos, on whose flight he conferred the vacant throne on Augustus (he received his nickname, a diminutive form of Augustulus, because he was still a child at the time), retaining power in his own hands. After Orestes was killed by the barbarians, Augustulus was forced to retire to a villa near Naples. >> RR1084

Augustus, (Gaius Julius Caesar Octavianus) (63 BC–AD 14) Founder of the Roman Empire, the son of Gaius Octavius, senator and praetor, and great nephew (through his mother, Atia) of Julius Caesar. On Caesar's assassination (44 BC), he abandoned student life in Illyricum and returned to Italy where, using Caesar's money and name (he had acquired both under his will), he raised an army, defeated Antony, and extorted a wholly unconstitutional consulship from the Senate (43 BC). When Antony returned in force from Gaul later that year with Lepidus, Octavian made a deal with his former enemies, joining the so-called Second Triumvirate with them, and taking Africa, Sardinia, and Sicily as his province. A later redivision of power gave him the entire western half of the Roman world, and Antony the eastern. While Antony was distracted there by his military

schemes against Parthia, and his liaison with Cleopatra, Octavian consistently undermined him at home. Matters came to a head in 31 BC, and the Battle of Actium followed, Octavian emerging victorious as the sole ruler of the Roman world. Though taking the inoffensive title *princeps* ('first citizen'), he was in all but name an absolute monarch. His new name, Augustus ('exalted'), had historical and religious overtones, and was deliberately chosen to enhance his prestige. His long reign (27 BC–AD 14) was a time of peace and reconstruction at home, sound administration and steady conquest abroad. In gratitude the Romans awarded him the title *Pater Patriae* ('Father of his Country') in 2 BC, and on his death made him a god (*divus Augustus*). >> Antonius; Caesar; Herod; Herod Agrippa I; Julia; Lepidus; Livia; Maecenas; RR1084

Augustus II, known as **Augustus the Strong** (1670–1733) King of Poland and elector of Saxony, born in Dresden, Germany (formerly Saxony). He succeeded to the electorship as Frederick Augustus I in 1694, and became a Roman Catholic in order to secure his election to the Polish throne as Augustus II in 1697. In alliance with Peter the Great of Russia and Frederik IV of Denmark, he planned the partition of Sweden, invading Livonia in 1699. Defeated by Charles XII of Sweden, he was deposed in 1706 and replaced by Stanislaus Leszczynski. After the defeat of the Swedes by Peter the Great at Poltava (1709), he recovered the Polish throne. >> Charles XII; Saxe; RR1082

Augustus I (1526–86) Elector of Saxony, born in Freiberg, modern Germany, who succeeded his brother Maurice as leader of the German Protestant princes. He first favoured the Calvinistic doctrine of the sacraments, and then, becoming Lutheran, persecuted the Calvinists (from 1574). He gave a great impetus to the arts, education, and commerce, reorganizing Saxony into a model state. The Dresden library and most galleries owe their origin to him.

Aulén, Gustaf Emmanuel Hildebrand [owlen] (1879–1977) Lutheran theologian and church music composer, born in Ljungby, Sweden. Professor of systematic theology at Lund (1913–33) and Bishop of Strängnaumäs (1933–52), he was a leading representative of the Scandinavian school of theology. His most famous study, *Christus victor* (1931), presented the death of Christ as a triumph over the powers of evil. He was also president of the Royal Swedish Academy of Music (1944–50).

Aumale, Henri-Eugène-Philippe-Louis d'Orléans, duc d' (Duke of) [ohmal] (1822–97) French soldier, born in Paris, the fourth son of Louis-Philippe. After an army career, at the revolution of 1848 he retired to England, where he wrote *Histoire des princes de Condé* (1869–97) and other works. Elected to the Assembly in 1871, in 1886 he bequeathed his magnificent château of Chantilly to the nation. >> Louis-Philippe

Aungerville or **de Bury, Richard** [awnggervil] (1287–1345) Clergyman, born in Bury St Edmunds, Suffolk, E England, UK. He studied at Oxford, became a Benedictine monk at Durham, and tutored Edward III. He was made successively dean of Wells and Bishop of Durham, besides acting for a time as High Chancellor. His principal work, *Philobyblon*, describes the state of learning in England and France.

Aung San Suu Kyi, Daw [owng san soo kyee] (1945–) Political leader, born in Yangon, Myanmar (formerly Rangoon, Burma), the daughter of the assassinated General Aung San, who was hailed as the father of Burmese independence. She studied in India and at Oxford, and came to be committed to the cause of democracy in her country. Social unrest forced dictator General Ne Win (1911–) to resign in 1988, and the military took power. In response, she co-founded the National League for Democracy (NLD), but was later arrested along with many NLD members (1989). The NLD won a resounding victory in the ensuing elections, but she was to remain under house arrest. Awarded the Nobel Peace Prize in 1991, she was released in July 1995.

Aurangzeb or **Aurungzib** [awrangzeb] ('ornament of the throne'), kingly title **Alamgir** (1618–1707) Last of the Mughal emperors of India, the third son of Emperor Shah Jahan. When Shah Jahan became seriously ill in 1657, Aurangzeb defeated his brothers and confined his father, beginning his rule without formal coronation in 1658. During his long reign, the empire remained outwardly prosperous and extended its boundaries, but his puritanical and narrow outlook alienated the various communities, particularly the Hindus, whom he treated with great harshness. Opposed by his own rebellious sons and by the Mahratta empire in the S, he died a fugitive at Ahmadnagar. >> Shah Jahan; RR1058

Aurelian [awreelian], in full **Lucius Domitius Aurelianus** (c.215–75) Roman emperor, born of humble origins in Dacia or Pannonia. Enlisting early as a common soldier he rose rapidly to the highest military offices. On the death of Claudius II (270), he was elected emperor by the army. By restoring good discipline in the army, order in domestic affairs, and political unity to the Roman dominions, he merited the title awarded him by the Senate, *Restitutor Orbis* ('Restorer of the World'). He was assassinated by his own officers during a campaign against the Persians. >> Zenobia; RR1084

Aurelius [awreelius], in full **Caesar Marcus Aurelius Antoninus Augustus**, originally **Marcus Annius Verus** (121–80) One of the most respected emperors in Roman history, born in Rome. When only 17, he was adopted by Antoninus Pius, who had succeeded Hadrian and whose daughter Faustina was selected for his wife. From 140, when he was made consul, till the death of Antoninus in 161, he discharged his public duties with great conscientiousness, at the same time devoting himself to the study of law and philosophy, especially Stoicism. Peaceful by temperament, his reign suffered from constant wars, and though in Asia, Britain, and on the Rhine the barbarians were checked, permanent peace was never secured. His death was felt to be a national calamity, and he was retrospectively idealized as the model of the perfect emperor. >> Antoninus Pius; RR1084

Auric, Georges [ohrik] (1899–1983) Composer, born in Lodève, France. He studied under Vincent d'Indy, and became one of *Les Six*. His compositions range widely from full orchestral pieces and ballets to songs and film scores, such as *Passport to Pimlico* (1949) and *Moulin Rouge* (1952). In 1962 he was appointed director of the Paris Opéra and Opéra-Comique, but in 1968 resigned most of his official positions in order to compose. >> Cocteau; d'Indy, Vincent; Durey; Honegger; Milhaud; Poulenc; Tailleferre

Auriol, Jacqueline [ohreeol] (1917–) French aviator, the daughter-in-law of Vincent Auriol. She broke the women's jet speed record in 1955 by flying at 715 mph (1150 kph) in a French *Mystère*. She published *I Live To Fly* in 1970. >> Auriol, Vincent

Auriol, Vincent [ohreeol] (1884–1966) French statesman, born in Revel, France. He studied law at Toulouse, and entered politics in 1914. A socialist politician, he became president of the two constituent assemblies of 1946, and the first president of the Fourth Republic (1947–54). >> RR1049

Aurobindo, Sri [owrobindoh gohsay], originally **Aurobindo Ghose** (1872–1950) Philosopher, poet, and mystic, born in

Calcutta, India. He studied at Cambridge, and became a professor in Baroda and Calcutta. Renouncing nationalism and politics for yoga and Hindu philosophy, he founded an ashram at Pondicherry in 1910. His writings include *The Life Divine* (1940) and *Aurobindo on Himself* (1953).

Aurungzeb(e) >> **Aurangzeb**

Ausonius, Decimus Magnus [awsohnius] (c.309–92) Latin poet, born in Burdigala (Bordeaux, France). He taught rhetoric there for 30 years, and was then appointed by Emperor Valentinian I to be tutor to his son Gratian. He later held the offices of quaestor, prefect of Latium and consul of Gaul. His works include epigrams, poems on his deceased relatives and on his colleagues, epistles in verse and prose, and idylls.

Austen, Jane (1775–1817) Novelist, born in Steventon, Hampshire, S England, UK, where her father was rector. She spent the first 25 years of her life there, and later lived in Bath, Southampton, Chawton, and Winchester. The fifth of a family of seven, she began writing for family amusement as a child. *Love and Friendship* (published 1922) dates from this period. Her early published work satirized the sensational fiction of her time, and applied common sense to apparently melodramatic situations – a technique she later developed in evaluating ordinary human behaviour. Of her six great novels, four were published anonymously during her lifetime and two under her signature posthumously. *Sense and Sensibility*, published in 1811, was begun in 1797; *Pride and Prejudice* appeared in 1813; *Mansfield Park*, begun in 1811, appeared in 1814; *Emma* in 1815. Her posthumous novels were both published in 1818; *Persuasion* had been written in 1815, and *Northanger Abbey*, begun in 1797, had been sold in 1803 to a publisher, who neglected it, and reclaimed it in 1816.

Austen, Winifred (1876–1964) Wildlife artist, born in Ramsgate, Kent, SE England, UK. She illustrated Patrick Chalmers' *Birds Ashore and Aforeshore* (1935), and painted postcards under the signature 'Spink'.

Auster, Paul [awster] (1947–) Novelist, born in Newark, New Jersey, USA. He studied at Columbia University, then lived in France for four years. Since 1974 he has published poems, essays, novels and translations. His use of detective-story techniques to explore modern urban identity is evident in *The New York Trilogy* (1985–6). Later books include *The Music of Chance* (1990) and *Leviathan* (1992).

Austerlitz, Frederick >> **Astaire, Fred**

Austin, Alfred (1835–1913) Poet, born in Leeds, West Yorkshire, N England, UK. He studied at the University of London, and was called to the bar in 1857, but then abandoned law for literature. His works include *The Season: a Satire* (1861), *The Human Tragedy* (1862), and an autobiography (1911). He became Poet Laureate in 1896.

Austin (of Longbridge), Herbert Austin, Baron (1866–1941) Car manufacturer, born in Little Missenden, Buckinghamshire, SC England, UK. He studied at Brampton College, went to Australia in 1884, and worked in engineering shops there. He returned to England in 1893, and in 1895, with the Wolseley Company, produced his first three-wheeled car. In 1905 he opened his own works near Birmingham, its enormous output including the popular 'Baby' Austin 7 (1921). He was also Conservative MP for King's Norton (1918–24).

Austin, John (1790–1859) Jurist, born in Creeting Mill, Suffolk, E England, UK. In 1818 he was called to the bar, and in 1826 was appointed professor of jurisprudence in the University of London. His *Province of Jurisprudence Determined*, defining the sphere of ethics and law, came to revolutionize English views on the subject.

Austin, J(ohn) L(angshaw) (1911–60) Philosopher, born in Lancaster, Lancashire, NW England, UK. He studied at

Oxford, where he was a leading figure in the Oxford Philosophy movement, and became professor there in 1952. His distinctive contribution was the meticulous examination of ordinary linguistic usage to resolve philosophical perplexities, pioneering the analysis of speech acts. His best-known works are *Philosophical Papers* (1961), *Sense and Sensibilia* (1962), and *How to Do Things with Words* (1962).

Austin, Robert Sargent (1895–1973) British etcher. He studied at the Royal College of Art, and became an artist and teacher, with a great knowledge of all techniques of printmaking. His mature work from the decade 1930–40 includes some of the finest prints of the period. Most of his life was spent refining the traditional art of line engraving.

Austin, Stephen Fuller (1793–1836) Founder of the state of Texas, born in Austinville, VA. He served in the Missouri legislature, then moved to Texas, where his father had obtained a grant of land from the Mexican government. In 1822 he founded a colony on the Brazos R, and became leader of the movement for Texan independence.

Austral, Florence [awstral], originally **Florence Wilson** (1894–1968) Soprano, born in Richmond, Victoria, Australia. She adopted the name of her country as a stage name prior to her debut in 1922 at Covent Garden, London. She appeared in the complete cycles of *The Ring* at Covent Garden and at the Berlin State Opera, which she joined as principal in 1930. She returned to Australia after World War 2, where she taught until her retirement in 1959.

Avedon, Richard [avedon] (1923–) Photographer, born in New York City. Educated at a public school, he was a fashion photographer for *Harper's Bazaar* (1945–65). Known for his stark portraits of people in unusual poses, he published his first book of celebrity portraits, *Observations*, in 1959. In 1963 he left his studio to photograph aspects of the Civil Rights and Anti-War movements. He worked for *Vogue*, and won a national award for visual excellence in 1976.

Avennasar >> **al-Farabi, Mohammed**

Aventinus [aventiynus], Latin name of **Johannes Thurmayr** (1477–1534) Humanist scholar and historian, born in Abensberg (Latin *Aventinum*), Bavaria, Germany. Known as the 'Bavarian Herodotos', he taught Greek and mathematics at Cracow, and wrote a history of Bavaria. >> Herodotos

Avenzoar [avenzoher], Arabic **Ibn Zohr** (c. 1072–1162) Arab physician, born in Seville. Considered the greatest clinician in the western caliphate, he published influential medical works describing such conditions as kidney stones and pericarditis.

Averroës [averoheez], Latin form of **Ibn Rushd** (1126–98) The most famous of the mediaeval Islamic philosophers, born in Córdoba, Spain. He was a judge successively at Córdoba, Seville, and in Morocco, and wrote on jurisprudence and medicine. In 1182 he became court physician to Caliph Abu Yusuf, but in 1185 was banished in disgrace (for reasons now unknown) by the caliph's son and successor. Many of his works were burnt, but after a brief period of exile he was restored to grace and lived in retirement at Marrakesh until his death. The most important of his works were the *Commentaries on Aristotle*, many of them known only through their Latin (or Hebrew) translations, which greatly influenced later Jewish and Christian writers and offered a partial synthesis of Greek and Arabic philosophical traditions.

Avery, Milton (Clark) [ayveree] (1893–1965) Painter, born in Altmar, NY. Largely self-taught, he was a figurative rather than an abstract artist, exploring simplified areas of flat colour, applied thinly. He also painted seascapes in a rather more Expressionist style, in 1933 began to make drypoints, and in 1950 launched a series of monotypes.

Avery, Oswald (Theodore) [ayveree] (1877–1955) Bacteriologist, born in Halifax, Nova Scotia, Canada. He studied medicine at Colgate University, then spent his career at the Rockefeller Institute Hospital, New York City (1913–48). His work on pneumococci was a key step in the genesis of molecular biology.

Avery, Sewell (Lee) [ayveree] (1874–1960) Corporate executive, born in Saginaw, MI. He joined the United States Gypsum Co in 1901, which as president (1905–37) and chairman (until 1951) he developed into a major international building materials manufacturer, despite the Depression of the 1930s. His effective but autocratic tenure as chief executive officer and chairman of Montgomery Ward (1931–55) was marked by fights with executives, stockholders, and directors. In a highly publicized episode in 1944, federal soldiers literally carried him from his office for noncompliance with a War Labor Board order.

Avery, Tex [ayveree], originally **Frederick Bean** (1908–80) Film cartoon director, born in Texas. He joined the Walter Lantz animation studio in 1929, then moved to Warner Brothers, where he was noticed for his zany comedy, creating Daffy Duck, and developing Bugs Bunny in *A Wild Hare* (1940). With MGM his creations included Droopy (1943) and Screwy Squirrel (1944). In 1955 he moved into television commercials, and later joined Hanna–Barbera for the television series *The Flintstones* (1979).

Avicebron [avisebron], Arabic **Solomon ibn Gabirol** (c.1020–c.1070) Poet and philosopher of the Jewish 'Golden Age', born in Málaga, Spain. Most of his prose work is lost: an ethical treatise in Arabic survives, as does a Latin translation of his most famous work, *Fons Vitae*, a dialogue on the nature of matter and the soul, which was influential among later Christian scholastics. His poetry became part of the mystical tradition of the Kabbalah.

Avicenna [avisena], Arabic **Ibn Sina** (980–1037) Philosopher and physician, born near Bokhara, Kazakastan. Renowned for his learning, he became physician to several sultans, and for some time vizier in Hamadan, Persia. He was one of the main interpreters of Aristotle to the Islamic world, and the author of some 200 works on science, religion, and philosophy. His medical textbook, *Canon of Medicine*, long remained a standard work.

Avison, Charles [ayvison] (c.1709–70) Composer, born in Newcastle upon Tyne, Tyne and Wear, NE England, UK. Also known as a critic, he wrote an *Essay on Musical Expression* (1752).

Avogadro, Amedeo [avohgadroh] (1776–1856) Scientist, born in Turin, Italy. In 1811 he formulated the hypothesis, known as *Avogadro's law*, that equal volumes of gases contain equal numbers of molecules, when at the same temperature and pressure. The principle did not come to be accepted until the work of Cannizzaro in the 1850s. Avogadro became professor of physics at Turin (1834–59). >> Cannizzaro

Avon, 1st Earl of >> **Eden, Sir Anthony**

Axel >> **Absalon**

Axelrod, Julius [akselrod] (1912–) Pharmacologist, born in New York City. As chief of the pharmacology section of the National Institute of Mental Health from 1955, he discovered the substance which inhibits neural impulses, laying the basis for significant advances in neurophysiology. He shared the Nobel Prize for Physiology or Medicine in 1970. >> RR1124

Ayckbourn, Sir Alan [aykbaw(r)n] (1939–) Playwright, born in London, England, UK. He began his theatrical career as an acting stage manager in repertory before joining Stephen Joseph's Theatre-in-the-Round company at Scarborough. After his first success, *Relatively Speaking* (1967), he was quickly established as a master of farce. He has made considerable experiments with staging and dramatic structure: *The Norman Conquests* (1974) is a trilogy in which each play takes place at the same time in a different part of the setting, and *Way Upstream* (1982) is set on and around a boat and necessitates the flooding of the stage. Among his most successful farces are *Absurd Person Singular* (1973) and *Joking Apart* (1979). He has also collaborated in musicals, notably *Jeeves* (with Andrew Lloyd Webber, 1975), and is recognized as a theatre director. His later plays include *Woman in Mind* (1986), *Man of the Moment* (1990), *Invisible Friends* (1991), and *Communicating Doors* (1995). He was knighted in 1997.

Ayer, Sir A(lfred) J(ules) [air] (1910–89) Philosopher, born in London, England, UK. He studied at Oxford, where he was a pupil of Gilbert Ryle. He became professor at University College London, then at Oxford (1947–59). His first and best book was *Language, Truth and Logic* (1936), a concise and forceful account of the antimetaphysical doctrines of the Vienna Circle of philosophers he had become acquainted with in the 1930s. His later publications include *The Problem of Knowledge* (1956) and *The Central Questions of Philosophy* (1972). He was knighted in 1970. >> Ryle, Gilbert; Schlick

Ayers, Sir Henry [airz] (1821–97) Politician, born in Portsea, Hampshire, S England, UK. He emigrated to South Australia in 1841 and took up a post with the South Australia Mining Association, with which he was associated for 50 years. Elected in 1863 to the first Legislative Council for the state under responsible government, he was a member of the Council for 36 years, and premier on several occasions. *Ayers Rock* was named after him in 1873. >> Gosse, William Christie

Ayeshah >> **Aïshah**

Aykroyd, Dan (1952–) Actor, born in Ottawa, Canada. He studied at Carleton University, Ottawa, joined the Second City Comedy improvization group in Toronto, made a name for himself as a stand-up comedian, then joined the cast of the anarchic television show *Saturday Night Live* (1975–9). He wrote the screenplay for and starred in *The Blues Brothers* (1980), and earned a Best Supporting Actor Oscar nomination for his first dramatic role in *Driving Miss Daisy* (1989). Later films include *Exit to Eden* (1994), *Feeling Minnesota* (1996), and *Grosse Pointe Blank* (1997).

Aylmer, Sir Felix (Edward) [aylmer], originally **Aylmer-Jones** (1889–1979) British actor. He studied at Oxford, and made his first stage appearance in 1911, after which he went to Birmingham Repertory, developing into a character actor with a remarkable range. He served as president of British Actors' Equity (1949–69), the British professional actors' union, and was also an enthusiastic Dickens scholar.

Aylmer, John [aylmer] (1521–94) Clergyman, born in Norfolk, E England, UK. In 1541 he graduated from Cambridge and became tutor to Lady Jane Grey. He fled to the European mainland to escape persecution during the reign of Mary I, then returned to become Archdeacon of Lincoln (1562) and Bishop of London (1577). He showed equal rigor to Catholics and Puritans, and was pilloried as 'Morrell', the 'proude and ambitious pastoure', in Spenser's *Shepherd's Calendar*. >> Grey, Lady Jane; Mary I

Aylward, Gladys [aylwerd] (1902–70) Missionary in China, born in London, England, UK. In 1930, she spent her entire savings on a railway ticket to Tientsin in N China. With a Scottish missionary, Mrs Jeannie Lawson, the pair founded an inn, the famous Inn of the Sixth Happiness, in an outpost at Yangcheng. From there, in 1938, she trekked across the mountains leading over 100 children to safety when the war with Japan brought fighting to the area. She returned to England in 1948, preached for five years, then in 1953 settled in Taiwan as head of an orphanage.

Ayrton, Michael [airton] (1920–75) Painter, sculptor, book illustrator, and art critic, born in London, England, UK. His early painting falls into the wartime English neo-Romantic movement. In 1954 he took up sculpture and began treating subjects from Classical mythology. His fascination with the legend of the minotaur led to his building of a maze in brick and stone in the Catskill Mountains, NY.

Ayton, Sir Robert [ayton] (1570–1638) Poet and courtier, born in Kinaldie, near St Andrews, Fife, E Scotland, UK. He studied at St Andrews University and in Paris, and became a courtier of James I in London. He wrote lyrics in English and Latin, and is credited with the prototype of the song 'Auld Lang Syne'. >> James I (of England)

Aytoun, William Edmonstoune [aytoon] (1818–65) Poet and humorist, born in Edinburgh, EC Scotland, UK. He studied at Edinburgh University, and was called to the Scottish bar in 1840. In 1836 he began a lifelong connection with *Blackwood's Magazine*, to which he contributed parodies and burlesque reviews. In 1845 he was appointed professor of rhetoric and belles lettres at Edinburgh. His works include *Lays of the Scottish Cavaliers* (1848) and the *Bon Gaultier Ballads* (1855).

Ayub Khan, Mohammad [ayub kahn] (1907–74) Pakistani soldier and president (1958–69), born in Hazara, India. He studied at Aligarh Moslem University, trained at Sandhurst, and became commander-in-chief of Pakistan's army (1951) and a field marshal (1959). He became president after a bloodless army coup, and established a stable economy and political autocracy. In 1969, after widespread civil disorder, he relinquished power and martial law was re-established. >> RR1080

Azaña (y Díaz), Manuel [athanya] (1880–1940) Spanish statesman and president (1936–9), born in Alcalá de Henares, Spain. A barrister, author, and lecturer in Madrid University, he became war minister in 1931, then prime minister (1931–3), and leader of the Republican Left (1936). He was elected president of the Second Republic, but was forced into exile by General Franco. >> Franco; RR1088

Azariah, Vedanayakam Samuel (1874–1945) Clergyman and first Indian bishop of the Anglican Church of India, Burma, and Ceylon, born in Vellalanvillai, Madras, India. A firm believer in co-operation between foreign and Indian church workers, and in the development of indigenous leadership in a united Indian Church, he was appointed Bishop of Dornakal, Andhra Pradesh, in 1912. He was chairman of the National Christian Council of India, Burma, and Ceylon from 1929.

Azeglio, Massimo Taparelli, marchese d' (Marquess of) [azelyoh] (1798–1866) Italian statesman, painter, and writer, born in Turin, Italy. A son-in-law of Manzoni, he studied painting in Rome, and wrote political novels. He took a leading part in the Risorgimento and the 1848 revolution, and became Prime Minister of Sardinia (1848–52). >> Manzoni

Azikiwe, Nnamdi [azeekeeway] (1904–96) Nigerian statesman and president (1963–6), born in Zungeri, Nigeria. He studied at US universities, and in 1937 began to take a leading part in the Nigerian nationalist movement, becoming president of the National Council of Nigeria and the Cameroons. He became prime minister of the E region (1954–9), Governor-General of Nigeria (1960–3), and was elected the first president of the Nigerian republic. While in Britain during the military uprising of 1966 his office was suspended, although he returned privately to Nigeria. >> RR1079

Azorín [athorin], pseudonym of **José Martínez Ruiz** (1874–1967) Novelist and critic, born in Monóvar, Spain. He studied law, then became a writer, his novels including *Don Juan* (1922) and *Dona Inés* (1925). He was also one of the leading literary critics of his time.

Baade, (Wilhelm Heinrich) Walter [bahduh] (1893–1960) Astronomer, born in Schröttinghausen, Germany. He studied at Münster and Göttingen, and worked at the Hamburg Observatory (1919–31). He moved to the USA in 1931, and spent the rest of his career at the Mt Wilson (1931–58) and Palomar (1948–58) Observatories. His work gave new estimates for the age and size of the universe.

Baader, Andreas [bahder] (1943–77) Anarchist and terrorist, born in Munich, Germany. He became associated with the student protest movement of the later 1960s and was imprisoned in 1968. Critical of Germany's post-war materialism and military dominance by the USA, he formed with Ulrike Meinhof the Rote Armee Fraktion (Red Army Faction), a band of underground urban guerrillas. The Faction helped Baader escape from prison in 1970 and carried out a series of terrorist outrages. He was captured and sentenced to life imprisonment in 1977. An attempt was made by the Faction to secure his release by holding a Lufthansa airliner hostage at Mogadishu, Somalia, and when this was thwarted he committed suicide. >> Meinhof

Baader, Franz Xaver von [bahder] (1765–1841) Roman Catholic theologian and mystical philosopher, born in Munich, Germany. A follower of Böhme, he regarded Hume's philosophy as atheistic, and opposed Kant by maintaining that the true ethical end is not obedience to a moral law, but a realization of the divine life. >> Böhme; Hume, David; Kant

Baal-Shem-Tov, originally **Israel ben Eliezer**, also known by his acronym, **Besht** (c.1699–1760) Jewish teacher and healer in Poland, born in Ukraine. He founded the Jewish spiritual movement of Hasidism c.1750.

Babangida, Ibrahim [babanggeeda] (1941–) Nigerian soldier, politician, and president (1985–93), born in Minna, Nigeria. He studied at military schools in Nigeria, and carried out further training in the UK and USA. He took part in the overthrow of the government of Shehu Shagari in 1983, and was made commander-in-chief of the army. In 1985 he led a coup against President Buhari and assumed the presidency himself. He stood down in August 1993, following a period of controversy over election results, leaving the military regime in power. >> RR1079

Babar or **Babur**, (Arabic 'tiger'), originally **Zahir-ud-din Muhammad** (1483–1530) First Mughal Emperor of India, born in Ferghana, Kyrgyzstan. After failing to establish himself in Samarkand, he invaded India, defeating Ibrahim Lodi decisively at the Battle of Paniput in 1526, and laying the foundation for the Mughal Empire. The following year he defeated the Hindu Rajput confederacy. A soldier of genius, he was also a cultured man with interests in architecture, music, and literature. Himself a Muslim, he initiated a policy of toleration towards his non-Muslim subjects. >> RR1058

Babbage, Charles (1791–1871) Mathematician and inventor, born in London, England, UK. He studied at Cambridge, where he became professor of mathematics (1828–39), and spent most of his life attempting to build two calculating machines. His 'difference engine' was intended for the calculation of tables of logarithms and similar functions by repeated addition performed by trains of gear wheels. An unfinished portion of the machine is now in the Science Museum, London. His 'analytical engine' was designed to perform many different computations, using punched cards. The idea was too ambitious to be realized by the mechanical devices available at the time, but can now be seen to be the essential germ of the electronic computer of today, and Babbage is thus regarded as the pioneer of modern computers. >> Lovelace, Augusta Ada

Babbitt, Bruce (Edward) (1938–) US statesman, born in Flagstaff, Arizona, USA. He trained as a lawyer, served as Arizona's attorney-general (1975–8), and became state governor (1978–87). An unsuccessful candidate for the Democratic presidential nomination in 1988, he was appointed secretary of the interior in 1993, and was reappointed in the 1997 administration.

Babbitt, Irving (1865–1933) Critic and writer, born in Dayton, OH. He studied at Harvard and at the Sorbonne, becoming professor of French at Harvard (1894–1933). He was a leader of the 'new selective humanism' which flourished in America in the 1920s. His books include *Literature and the American College* (1908), *The New Laokoön* (1910), and *On Being Creative* (1932).

Babbitt, Isaac (1799–1862) Goldsmith, born in Taunton, MA. In 1824 he manufactured the first Britannia metal tableware, using an alloy of copper, tin, and antimony. In 1839, he invented a journal box lined with a soft, silver-white alloy now called *Babbitt metal*, which is still used in some metal bearings to reduce friction.

Babbitt, Milton (1916–) Composer and theorist, born in Philadelphia, PA. He studied at New York University and then Princeton, where he later taught (1938). He was a leading proponent of total serialism, and composed many works for the electronic synthesizer. In recognition, The Columbia-Princeton Music Center made him a director.

Babcock, Harold (Delos) (1882–1968) Physicist, born in Edgerton, WI. He was on the staff of the Mount Wilson Observatory, CA (1909) when he measured the magnetic field of the star 78 Virginis, which provided a link between electromagnetic and relativity theories. With his son, **Horace Welcome Babcock** (1912–), he invented the solar magnetograph (1951).

Babcock, Stephen (Moulton) (1843–1931) Agricultural chemist and originator of scientific dairying, born near Bridgewater, NY. He studied at Tufts College, Cornell, and Göttingen, and taught agricultural chemistry at Wisconsin University (1887–1913). He devised the *Babcock test* for measuring fat in milk, which much improved the quality of dairy produce.

Bab-ed-Din [babuhdin], (Arabic 'gateway of righteousness'), popular name of **Mirza Ali Mohammed** (1819–50) Religious leader, born in Iran. In 1844 he declared himself the Bab ('Gateway') to the prophesied 12th Imam, then claimed to be the Imam himself. He was imprisoned in 1847, and later executed at Tabriz. The religion he founded (*Babism*) was the forerunner of the Baha'i faith. >> Baha-Allah

Babel, Isaac (Emmanuilovich) [babel] (1894–?1941) Short-story writer, a protégé of Maxim Gorky, born in the Jewish ghetto of Odessa, Ukraine. He worked as a journalist in St Petersburg, then served in the tsar's army and in various Bolshevik campaigns. He wrote stories of the Jews in Odessa in *Odesskie rasskazy* (1916, Odessa Tales), and stories of war in *Konarmiya* (1926, Red Cavalry). He was exiled to Siberia in the mid-1930s, and died in a concentration camp.

Babeuf, François-Noël [baboef], originally **Gracchus Babeuf** (1760–97) Political agitator in revolutionary France, born in St Quentin, France. During the Revolution, he helped organize a conspiracy aiming to destroy the Directory and establish an extreme democratic and communistic system. When this was discovered, he was guillotined.

Babilée, Jean [babeelay], originally **Jean Gutman** (1923–) Dancer and choreographer, born in Paris. He studied at the Paris Opéra Ballet School, and enjoyed some of his greatest successes as a member of the Ballets de Champs-Elysées and Ballets de Paris. In the 1950s he was a guest of the Paris Opéra Ballet and American Ballet Theatre, before forming his own company.

Babinet, Jacques [babeenay] (1794–1872) Physicist, born in Lusignan, France. He standardized light measurement by using the red cadmium line's wavelength as the standard for the angstrom unit. *Babinet's principle*, that similar diffraction patterns are produced by two complementary screens, is named after him.

Babington, Antony (1561–86) Conspirator, born in Dethick, Derbyshire, C England, UK. In 1586 he was induced by Ballard and other Catholic emissaries to put himself at the head of a conspiracy aiming to murder Queen Elizabeth I and release Mary, Queen of Scots. Cipher messages were apparently intercepted by Walsingham in which Mary was implicated by her approval of the plot, and these were later used against her. Babington fled, was captured at Harrow, and executed with the others. >> Elizabeth I; Throckmorton; Walsingham, Francis

Babinski, Joseph (François Felix) [babinskee] (1857–1932) Neurologist, born in Paris. He is known for his description of a foot reflex which is symptomatic of upper motor neurone disease. Independently of **Alfred Fröhlich** (1871–1953), a Viennese pharmacologist, he investigated an endocrinal disorder, adiposogenital dystrophy, or *Babinski–Fröhlich disease*.

Babits, Mihály [bahbeech] (1883–1941) Poet of the 20th-c literary renaissance, born in Szekszárd, Hungary. He studied at Budapest University and became a teacher, before turning to literature. He was also a novelist, and a translator of Dante, Shakespeare, and the Greek classics.

Babrius [babrius] (2nd-c) Greek writer of fables. Little is known of him except that he collected Aesopic fables, which he turned into popular verse. These had almost all been lost, until 123 of them were discovered at Mt Athos, Greece, in 1841. >> Aesop

Babson, Roger (Ward) (1875–1967) Statistician, business forecaster, and writer, born in Gloucester, MA. An indifferent student, he was pushed by his father to study bookkeeping and engineering. He set up the Business Statistical Organization Inc (1904) and published the *Composite Circular* and the *Babsonchart*, which advised his clients on when to buy and sell their stocks, bonds, and commodities. He established the Babson Institute (later Babson College) in 1919, and in 1927 he founded Webber College (FL) to train women for business. His statistical compilations were of great importance to a generation of businessmen during the pre-computer era. He published some 40 books, mostly on statistical and financial matters.

Babur >> **Babar**

Baby Doc >> **Duvalier, Jean-Claude**

Bacall, Lauren [bakawl], originally **Betty Joan Perske** (1924–) Actress, born in New York City. A student at the American Academy of Dramatic Arts, she made her stage debut in 1942. She married her co-star Humphrey Bogart in 1945, appearing with him in such thrillers as *The Big Sleep* (1946) and *Key Largo* (1948). After Bogart's death in 1957, she turned to the stage, her Broadway successes including the musical *Applause!* (1970–2), for which she received a Tony award. Later films include *Murder on the Orient Express* (1974), *The Shootist* (1976, BAFTA), *Mr North* (1988), and *Appointment with Death* (1988), and she received an Oscar nomination for her supporting role in *The Mirror Has Two Faces* (1996). She was also married (1961–9) to the actor **Jason Robards Jr**. Her autobiography, *By Myself* (1979), was an international best-seller. >> Bogart; Robards

Bacchylides [bakilideez] (5th-c BC) Greek lyric poet, the nephew of Simonides of Ceos, and a contemporary of Pindar in Hiero's court at Syracuse. Fragments of his Epinician Odes (written to celebrate victories in the great athletic festivals) were discovered in 1896. >> Pindar; Simonides of Ceos

Bacciochi, Maria Anna Elisa [bakiokee], *née* **Bonaparte** (1777–1820) Eldest of the sisters of Napoleon, born in Ajaccio, Corsica. She married Felice Bacciochi, and was created a princess by her brother in 1805, and made Grand Duchess of Tuscany in 1809.

Baccio della Porta >> **Bartolommeo, Fra**

Bach, C(arl) P(hilipp) E(manuel), known as **the Berlin Bach** or **the Hamburg Bach** (1714–88) Composer, born in Weimar, Germany, the second surviving son of J S Bach. He studied at the Thomasschule, Leipzig, where his father was cantor, and at Frankfurt University. In 1740 he became cembalist to the future Frederick II, and later became *Kapellmeister* at Hamburg (1767). He was famous for his playing of the organ and clavier, for which his best pieces were composed. He published *The True Art of Clavier Playing* (1753), the first methodical treatment of the subject, introduced the sonata form, and wrote numerous concertos, keyboard sonatas, church music, and chamber music. >> Bach, J S; Frederick II (of Prussia)

Bach, Edward (1880–1936) British medical microbiologist. He theorized that the dew condensing on a plant would, when exposed to sunlight, absorb the energy of the plant into the water molecules. From this premise he developed a system of herbal remedies prepared from 38 different species of flower. He believed that every disorder arises as a result of an imbalance of inner energy, and that nature has a cure for all illness in the form of healing plants. *Bach flower remedies* are especially used for disharmonies of the personality and emotional state.

Bach, J(ohann) C(hristian), known as **the London Bach** or **the English Bach** (1735–82) Composer, born in Leipzig, Germany, the 11th son of J S Bach. He studied under his brother C P E Bach in Berlin, and from 1754 worked in Italy. After becoming a Catholic, he was appointed organist at Milan in 1760, and for a time composed only ecclesiastical music, including two Masses, a requiem, and a 'Te Deum', but later he began to compose opera. In 1762 he was appointed composer to the London Italian opera, and became musician to Queen Charlotte. >> Bach, C P E; Bach, J S

Bach, J(ohann) C(hristoph) F(riedrich), known as **the Bückeburg Bach** (1732–95) Composer, born in Leipzig, Germany, the ninth son of J S Bach. He studied there at the Thomasschule and at Leipzig University, and became in 1750 *Kapellmeister* at Bückeburg. He was an industrious but undistinguished church composer. >> Bach, J S

Bach, Johann Sebastian (1685–1750) see panel on p. 59

Bach, W(ilhelm) F(riedemann), known as **the Halle Bach** (1710–84) Composer, born in Weimar, Germany, the eldest and most gifted son of J S Bach. He studied at the Thomasschule and Leipzig University, and in 1733 became organist at Dresden and in 1747 at Halle. His way of life became increasingly dissolute, and from 1764 he lived without fixed occupation at Brunswick, Göttingen, and Berlin, where he died. He was the greatest organ player of

JOHANN SEBASTIAN BACH (1685–1750)

Bach was born at Eisenach, Germany, the 11th son and youngest child of **Johann Ambrosius Bach** (1645–95) and Elisabeth Lämmerhirt, the least distinguished members of a remarkable musical family. By the time he was 10, his parents had died, and he was brought up by his older brother **Johann Christoph Bach** (1671–1721), who was the organist at Ohrdruf and taught him the organ and clavier. At 15 he won a place as a chorister at Michaelskirche, a boarding school for poor boys in Lüneburg, where his family were already appreciated.

His musical experience thus far had developed from the string-playing tradition of his immediate family to composing and performing keyboard and sacred music. From 1703–7 he was organist at Neukirche Arnstadt, where he had keenly followed the building of the new organ. However, he began to neglect his duties as choirmaster, preferring to immerse himself in keyboard music. He also angered the authorities with his innovative chorale accompaniments, and by his failure to produce cantatas. To make matters worse, after two years service at Arnstadt, in October 1705 when he was 19, he walked 370 km/230 mi to hear Dietrich Buxtehude, the Danish composer and organ player at St Mary's church in Lübeck, and returned to his post three months later than expected, in January 1706. In June 1707 he left Arnstadt and became organist at St Blasius, Mülhausen, where the pastor was a strict priest who objected to any but the simplest music in church. That October he married his cousin **Maria Barbara Bach** (1684–1720).

Bach transferred to the ducal court at Weimar as *Konzertmeister* in 1708 and, after being passed over for the job of *Kapellmeister* there, became *Kapellmeister* to Prince Leopold of Anhalt-Cöthen in 1717, in whose service he became known as an outstanding organist. The prince was a Calvinist, so music played only a small part in his worship, and Bach was at liberty to compose and perform many secular works. He gave recitals, and wrote the Toccata and Fugue in D Minor, the Fantasia and Fugue in G Minor, the Prelude and Fugue in C, as well as other instrumental music, including the Brandenburg Concertos (1721), and the first book of *Das wohltemperiete Klavier* (1722, The Well-Tempered Clavier).

Widowed suddenly in 1720, and left with four children (he had six by Maria, but only four survived), in 1721 he married **Anna Magdalena Wilcken** (1701–60), an accomplished singer, harpsichordist, and copyist, for whom he wrote a collection of keyboard pieces. Of their 13 children, six survived, and for them he wrote his *Clavierbüchlein* (1720, Little Book for the Keyboard). Six sonatas for the solo violin, also written then, were forgotten and not found until the next century.

A devout Lutheran, Bach's desire to get back into church music became strong and, after much deliberation, he accepted a lower position as cantor of the Thomasschule in Leipzig in 1723, where he remained for the rest of his life, despite disagreements with his colleagues and the authorities. In an attempt to strengthen his position there, he solicited the title of Court Composer to the Elector of Saxony, presenting the *Goldberg Variations* (1722), a harpsichord work named after one of his pupils. But his main task at Leipzig was to supply cantatas for the city churches each Sunday, and he wrote about 300 of these, of which 200 remain. He composed much of his best work in this period, including the *St Matthew Passion* (1727 and/or 1729). From 1729–1741 he was also director of the Collegium Musicum (the local music society), giving weekly concerts, and his family home became a centre of musical pilgrimage. Many eminent musicians, who included several relations, became his pupils.

A visit in 1747 to his son Carl Philip Emmanuel, who was court harpsichordist, resulted in an invitation from Frederick the Great of Prussia to try his latest Silbermann pianofortes and improvise a fugue. As a result Bach subsequently offered the king his collection, *Das musikalisches Opfer* (1747, Musical Offering), which included a trio for flute, violin, and clavier. At about the same time (1748–9) he completed the full Mass in B Minor, which he never performed. A conscientious copyist, his eyes had long been failing him, and despite an operation he became almost totally blind. He died of a stroke at Leipzig while engaged on a series of fugues for the keyboard – the monumental work *Die Kunst der Fuge* (The Art of Fugue).

Bach is celebrated as one of the world's greatest musicians, the most outstanding member of the celebrated Bach family. His main achievement was his development of polyphony (especially in counterpoint and fugue), but ironically, because of his success as an organist, his genius as a composer was not fully recognized until the following century. He had a profound influence on the works of Haydn, Mozart, and Beethoven.
>> Bach, C P E / J C / J C F / W F; Beethoven; Buxtehude; Haydn; Mozart

his time, but very few of his compositions were published, as he rarely bothered to write them down. >> Bach, J S

Bachelard, Gaston [bashuhlah(r)] (1884–1962) Philosopher, born in Bar-sur-Aube, France. He had an unusual range of interests and influence in the history of science, psychoanalysis, and literary criticism, which were connected in such works as *La Psychoanalyse du feu* (1937) and *La Flamme d'une chandelle* (1961).

Bacher, Ali [bakher] (1942–) Cricketer and sports administrator, born in Roodepoort, South Africa. His career was deeply intertwined with South Africa's exclusion from and subsequent return to international sport. He cap-tained Transvaal and South Africa with great success, but his Test career was cut short by international sports boy-cotts of South African teams. He was a leading figure in organizing the 'rebel' tours to South Africa in the 1980s, but rapidly adjusted to political change, and emerged as a key figure in the new non-racial administrative structures by the end of that decade. In 1990 he received the Jack Cheetham Memorial Award for his efforts to normalize sport in South Africa. >> D'Oliveira; Gooch

Bachman, John [bakman] (1790–1874) Clergyman and naturalist, born in Rhinebeck, NY. From 1815 he was Lutheran pastor in Charleston, SC. He was co-author with John

James Audubon of *The Viviparous Quadrupeds of North America* (1845–9). >> Audubon

Bachofen, Johann Jakob [bahkhohfen] (1815–87) Jurist and historian, born in Basel, Switzerland. Professor of Roman law at Basel from 1841, he is known for his work on the theory of matriarchy, *Das Mutterrecht* (1841).

Baciccia [bacheechia], popular name of **Giovanni Battista Gaulli** (1639–1709) Painter, born in Genoa, Italy. He is best known for his ambitious and spectacular Baroque illusionistic ceiling frescoes, such as the ceiling of the Jesuit Church of the Gusí in Rome. He also painted portraits of the papal court which are of a quieter mood.

Back, Sir George (1796–1878) Arctic explorer, born in Stockport, Greater Manchester, NW England, UK. He sailed with Sir John Franklin on Polar expeditions (1818–22, 1825–7), and in 1833–5 went in search of explorer Sir John Ross, discovering Artillery Lake and the Great Fish River (now *Back's River*), which he traced to the Frozen Ocean. In 1836–7 he further explored the Arctic shores. He was knighted in 1839, and made admiral in 1857. >> Franklin, John; Ross, John

Backhuysen or **Bakhuizen, Ludolf** [bakhoysen] (1631–1708) Dutch marine painter, born in Emden, Germany. He is best known for his 'Rough Sea at the Mouth of the Maas' (Louvre) and several seascapes in London, Amsterdam, and The Hague.

Bacon, Francis, Viscount St Albans (1561–1626) Philosopher and statesman, born in London, England, UK, the younger son of Sir Nicholas Bacon. He studied at Cambridge and Gray's Inn (1576), and was called to the bar in 1582. Becoming an MP in 1584, he was knighted by James I in 1603. He was in turn solicitor general (1607), attorney general (1613), privy counsellor (1616), Lord Keeper (1617), and Lord Chancellor (1618). He became Baron Verulam in 1618, and was made viscount in 1621. However, complaints were made that he accepted bribes from suitors in his court, and he was publicly accused before his fellow peers, fined, imprisoned, and banished from parliament and the court. Although soon released, and later pardoned, he never returned to public office, and he died in London, deeply in debt. His philosophy is best studied in *The Advancement of Learning* (1605) and *Novum Organum* (1620). His stress on inductive methods gave a strong impetus to subsequent scientific investigation. >> Bacon, Nicholas

Bacon, Francis (1909–92) Artist, born in Dublin, Republic of Ireland. He settled permanently in England in 1928. After working as an interior designer he began painting in c.1930 without any formal training, making a major impact in 1945 with his 'Three Figures at the Base of a Crucifixion'. Although the initial inspiration for his work was Surrealism, he made frequent use of imagery annexed from old masters, usually translated into blurred and gory figures imprisoned in unspecific, architectural settings. A technical perfectionist, Bacon destroyed a great deal of his prolific output. He is widely regarded as Britain's most important post-war artist.

Bacon, Francis Thomas (1904–92) British engineer, the designer of a practical fuel cell. He studied at Cambridge, then worked for Sir Charles Parsons as an engineer (1925–40). He proposed the use of hydrogen-oxygen fuel cells in submarines, and carried out research at the Anti-Submarine Establishment (1941–6) and at Cambridge University (1946–56). He was principal consultant to the National Research and Development Council (1956–62) and the Atomic Energy Authority (1971–3). His designs were first put to practical use in space to provide power, heat, and clean drinking water on board US spacecraft. He was elected a fellow of the Royal Society (1973), and

awarded the first Grove Medal (1991). >> Grove, William Robert; Parsons, Charles

Bacon, Henry (1866–1924) Architect, born in New York City. He studied briefly at the University of Illinois (1884), then trained as a draughtsman. He is best remembered for his last work, the Lincoln Memorial in Washington, DC.

Bacon, John >> **Baconthorpe, John**

Bacon, John (1740–99) Sculptor, born in London, England, UK. He became one of the first students of the Royal Academy Schools, and is responsible for the monuments to William Pitt the Elder in Westminster Abbey and the Guildhall, the statue of Dr Johnson in St Paul's, and others.

Bacon, Nathaniel (c. 1642–76) American colonial leader, born in Suffolk, E England, UK. He emigrated to Virginia in 1673, and made himself prominent by his raids against the Indians. His activities prompted the English governor to declare him a rebel in 1676, whereupon Bacon captured and burned Jamestown. For a time he controlled most of Virginia, but died suddenly, and the rebellion ended.

Bacon, Sir Nicholas (1510–79) English statesman, born in Drinkstone, Suffolk, E England, UK. He attained high legal offices which, as a Protestant, he lost under Mary I. Following the accession of Elizabeth I (1558), he was made Lord Keeper of the Great Seal, and along with Cecil was given the management of Church affairs. A staunch anti-Catholic, he was an implacable enemy of Mary, Queen of Scots. His son was Francis Bacon. >> Bacon, Francis; Cecil, William; Elizabeth I; Mary, Queen of

Bacon, Roger, known as **Doctor Mirabilis** ('Wonderful Doctor') (c.1220–92) Philosopher and scientist, probably born in Ilchester, Somerset, SW England, UK. He studied at Oxford and Paris, and gained a reputation for diverse and unconventional learning in philosophy, magic, and alchemy. He seems to have returned to Oxford in 1247 to develop his interests in experimental science and, more surprisingly, to become a Franciscan. But he suffered censorship and eventually imprisonment from the Order for the heresy of his 'suspected novelties', and he died in Oxford soon after his eventual release from prison. He has been associated with scientific inventions such as the magnifying glass and gunpowder, and with speculations about lighter-than-air flying machines, microscopes, and telescopes. His views on experimentalism have often seemed strikingly modern, and despite surveillance and censorship from the Franciscans he published many works on mathematics, philosophy, and logic whose importance was recognized only in later centuries.

Baconthorpe or **Bacon, John,** known as **Doctor Resolutus** ('Resolute Doctor') (c.1290–c. 1346) Philosopher and theologian, born in Baconsthorpe, Norfolk, E England, UK, the grandnephew of Roger Bacon. A Carmelite by training, he taught at Cambridge, and wrote commentaries on the Arab philosopher Averroës. He anticipated Wycliffe's teaching that priests should be subordinate to kings. >> Averroës; Bacon, Roger; Wycliffe

Badarayana The name applied to an unknown Indian philosopher, the reputed author of the *Vedanta* (or *Brahama*) *Sutra*, sometimes identified with the 5th-c sage Vyasa, who is traditionally credited with compiling the *Mahabharata*. Nothing is known of Badarayana apart from his connection with the *Vedanta Sutra*, which cannot be dated with certainty. He may simply be a personification of an anonymous process of editing.

Baden-Powell, Robert Stephenson Smyth Baden-Powell, Baron [baydn powel] (1857–1941) British general and founder of the Boy Scout movement, born in London, England, UK. He studied at Charterhouse, joined the army in 1876, served in India and Afghanistan, and won fame during the Boer War as the defender of Mafeking (1899–1900). He is best known as the founder in 1908 of the Boy Scouts and in 1910, with his sister **Agnes** (1858–1945), of the Girl Guides. He published *Scouting for Boys* in 1908, founded the Wolf Cubs in 1916, and was acclaimed world chief scout in 1920.

Bader, Sir Douglas (Robert Stuart) [**bah**der] (1910–82) Wartime aviator, born in London, England, UK. Commissioned from Cranwell in 1930, he lost both legs in a flying accident in 1931 and was invalided out, but overcame his disability and returned to the RAF in 1939. He commanded the first RAF Canadian Fighter Squadron, evolving tactics that contributed to victory in the Battle of Britain, but was captured in August 1941 after a collision with an enemy aircraft over Béthune. A great pilot and leader of what Churchill called 'the Few', he set an example of fortitude and heroism that became a legend. He was knighted in 1976.

Badoglio, Pietro [bah**dol**yoh] (1871–1956) Italian soldier and prime minister (1943–4), born in Grazzano Monferrato, Italy. He served in World War 1, and was promoted field-marshal in 1926. He was Governor-General of Libya (1928–33) and directed the conquest of Abyssinia, now Ethiopia (1935–6). On Italy's entry into World War 2 in 1940 he was made commander-in-chief, but resigned during the Greek humiliation of Italian arms in Albania. Following Mussolini's downfall (1943) he formed a non-Fascist government, negotiated an armistice with the Allies, declared war on Germany, and held power till 1944. >> Mussolini

Baeck, Leo [bek] (1873–1956) Jewish religious leader, born in Lissa, Germany. He was rabbi (1912–42) in Berlin, and was the political leader of German Jewry when the Nazis came to power. He was imprisoned in the Theresienstadt concentration camp (1942–5), and after the war became a lecturer in Britain.

Baedeker, Karl [**bay**deker] (1801–59) Publisher, born in Essen, Germany. He started his own publishing business at Koblenz in 1827, and is best known for the authoritative guidebooks which still bear his name.

Baekeland, Leo (Hendrik) [**bayk**land] (1863–1944) Chemist, born in Ghent, Belgium. He studied and taught at the University of Ghent until 1889, when he emigrated to the USA. He invented photographic printing paper usable with artificial light, discovered the first synthetic phenolic resin (*Bakelite*), and was a founder of the plastics industry. >> Swinburne, James

Baer, Karl Ernst von [bair] (1792–1876) Naturalist, and pioneer in embryology, born in Piep, Estonia. After studying at Dorpat and Würzburg universities, he became professor at Königsberg (1817–34) and then at St Petersburg. He discovered the mammalian egg (ovum) in the ovary, and the notochord (embryo backbone), and formulated the 'biogenetic law' that in embryonic development general characters appear before special ones. >> Pander

Baeyer, Johann (Friedrich Wilhelm Adolf) von [**bay**er] (1835–1917) Organic chemist, born in Berlin. He studied at Heidelberg, and became professor of chemistry at Strasbourg (1872) and Munich (1875–1915). His researches covered many aspects of chemistry, notably the synthesis of the dye indigo and the elucidation of its structure, the mechanism of photosynthesis, the condensation of phenols and aldehydes, the polyacetylenes, the stability of polymethylene rings, the terpenes, and the basicity of organic oxygen compounds. He was awarded the 1905 Nobel Prize for Chemistry.

Baez, Joan [biy**ez**] (1941–) Folksinger, born in Staten Island, New York City. During the revival of traditional folk music in the 1960s she became popular with young audiences for her songs and political views. She gave free concerts supporting civil rights, UNESCO, and anti-

Vietnam war rallies, and was imprisoned briefly (1967) for refusing to pay tax towards war expenses. In 1968 she published an autobiography, *Daybreak*, and a further volume *And A Voice To Sing With* appeared in 1987. A legendary protest figure for over three decades, she continues to perform at fund-raising events around the world.

Baffin, William (c. 1584–1622) Navigator, probably born in London, England, UK. From 1612 to 1616 he was pilot on several expeditions in search of the Northwest Passage. The most significant of these were the voyages under the command of Robert Bylot in the *Discovery*, during which they visited Hudson Strait (1615), and were the first Europeans to find Baffin Bay (1615) and Lancaster, Smith, and Jones Sounds (1616). He was possibly the first person to determine a degree of longitude at sea by lunar observation. Thereafter he carried out extensive surveys of the Red Sea (1616–21), and was killed at the siege of Ormuz.

Bagehot, Walter [**ba**juht] (1826–77) Economist and journalist, born in Langport, Somerset, SW England, UK. He graduated in mathematics at University College, London, was called to the bar in 1852, and succeeded his father-in-law, James Wilson (1805–60), as editor of the *Economist* in 1860. His *English Constitution* (1867) is still a standard work. He advocated many constitutional reforms, including the introduction of life peers.

Bagford, John (1650–1716) Antiquary, born in London, England, UK. Originally a shoemaker, he made a scrap-book collection of English broadside ditties and verses in 64 volumes for Robert Harley, Earl of Oxford, known as *The Bagford Ballads*. >> Harley

Bagley, Sarah (fl.1835–47) Labour leader, of whose early life nothing is known. She was active during the 1830s and 1840s in the mills of Lowell, MA, where she led 'turn-outs' (strikes) and organized the Female Labor Reform Association. She played a major role in the successful campaign for a 10-hour working day in Massachusetts.

Baha-Allah [bahhah**ula**], (Arabic 'glory of God'), originally **Mirza Huseyn Ali** (1817–92) Religious leader, born in Teheran, the founder of the Islamic Baha'i sect. He became a follower of Bab-ed-Din, the founder of the Persian Babi sect. Persecuted and imprisoned in 1852, he was exiled to Baghdad, Constantinople, and Acre. In 1863 he proclaimed himself as the prophet that Bab-ed-Din had foretold, and became the leader of the new Baha'i faith. >> Bab-ed-Din

Bahr, Hermann (1863–1934) Playwright, novelist, and critic, born in Linz, Austria. He studied in Vienna and Berlin, and took a leading part in the Naturalism and Expressionism of the Habsburg empire period. He published social novels and comedies, and was appointed manager of the Deutsches Theater, Berlin (1903), and of the Burgtheater, Vienna (1918).

Baïf, Jean Antoine de [bah**eef**] (1532–89) French poet, born in Venice, Italy. He was a member of the *Pléiade*, author of *Les amours de Méline* (1552), and other works. He attempted to introduce blank verse into French poetry, and experimented with combinations of poetry and music.

Baikie, William Balfour [**bay**kee] (1825–64) Explorer, naturalist, and linguist, born in Kirkwall, Orkney Is, NE Scotland, UK. He studied medicine at Edinburgh, and in 1848 became a naval surgeon. On the Niger expedition of 1854, he succeeded through the captain's death to the command of the *Pleiad*, and penetrated 400 km/250 mi farther than any previous traveller. On a second expedition in 1857 he founded a settlement at Lukoja. Within five years he had opened the navigation of the Niger, translated parts of the Bible and prayer book into Hausa, and founded a city state.

Bailey, David (Royston) (1938–) Photographer, born in London, England, UK. Originally specializing in fashion photography as a freelance from 1959, his creative approach soon extended to portraits expressing the spirit of the 1960s and to some outstanding studies of the nude. He writes extensively on all aspects of his craft and has been a director of televison commercials and documentaries since the 1970s. His publications include *Nudes 1981–84* (1984) and *The Lady is a Tramp* (1995).

Bailey, Sir Donald (Coleman) (1901–85) Engineer, born in Rotherham, South Yorkshire, N England, UK. He studied at Sheffield, and joined the Ministry of Supply. During World War 2 he designed the prefabricated, mobile, rapidly-erected *Bailey bridge*. He was knighted in 1946.

Bailey, Francis Lee (1933–) US criminal lawyer. A graduate of Harvard Law School, he founded a detective agency there to conduct his own case research. As a defence attorney, he defended the Boston Strangler, Albert Desalvo, and the kidnapped heiress, Patty Hearst, convicted of bank robbery with her left-wing terrorist abductors. >> Desalvo; Hearst, Patty

Bailey, James Anthony >> Barnum, P T

Bailey, Liberty Hyde (1858–1954) Horticulturalist and botanist, born in South Haven, MI. He was a botanical assistant at Harvard, becoming professor of horticulture at Michigan State (1885) and Cornell (1888) universities. In 1920 he founded the Bailey Hortorium of New York State College. He edited various works, such as the *Standard Cyclopedia of Horticulture* (1914–17), and coined the term *cultivar*.

Bailey, Nathan or **Nathaniel** (?–1742) English lexicographer. He was the compiler of *An Universal Etymological English Dictionary* (1721, supplement 1727), used by Dr Johnson as the basis of his own dictionary. All that is known about Bailey is that he was a Seventh-day Adventist, and kept a boarding-school in Stepney, London. >> Johnson, Samuel

Bailey, Trevor, nickname **Barnacle Bailey** (1923–) Cricketer, writer, and sports broadcaster, born in Westcliff-on-Sea, Essex, SE England, UK. An all-rounder, he played in 61 Test matches, where his adhesive batting earned him his nickname. He made over 2200 runs in Test cricket, and took 132 Test wickets. He played for Essex for 20 years. On retirement he established a reputation as a radio commentator.

Baillie, Lady Grizel [baylee], *née* **Hume** (1665–1746) Poet, born in Borders, Scotland, SE Scotland, UK, the daughter of the Scottish Covenanter, **Sir Patrick Hume** (1641–1724). In 1684 she supplied him with food during his concealment in the vault beneath Polwarth Church near Duns, Scottish Borders, and helped shelter the Covenanting scholar, Robert Baillie of Jerviswood, whose son she married in 1692. She is remembered for her songs. >> Baillie, Robert

Baillie, Dame Isobel [baylee] (1895–1983) Soprano, born in Hawick, Scottish Borders, SE Scotland, UK. She worked as an assistant in a music shop, then as a clerk in Manchester Town Hall, and made her debut with the Hallé Orchestra in 1921. After studies in Milan, she won immediate success in her opening season in London in 1923. Regarded as one of this century's greatest oratorio singers, she gave over 1000 performances of the *Messiah*.

Baillie, John [baylee] (1886–1960) Theologian, born in Gairloch, Highland, N Scotland, UK. He studied at Inverness Academy and Edinburgh, and trained for the ministry at New College, Edinburgh, Marburg, and Jena. After World War 1 he went to the USA, where he taught at Auburn Theological Seminary (1920–7) and Union Seminary (1930–5), both in New York, before returning to Scotland. He was a key contributor to mid-century religious, social, and intellectual life in Scotland.

Baillie, Matthew [baylee] (1761–1823) Physician and anatomist, born in Shotts, North Lanarkshire, C Scotland, UK. After seven years at Glasgow and Oxford (1773–80), he studied anatomy under his uncle William Hunter, and in 1783 took over Hunter's anatomy school in London. He was the author of the first treatise in English on morbid anatomy (1793). >> Hunter, William

Baillie (of Jerviswood), Robert [baylee] (1634–84) Presbyterian conspirator, a native of Lanarkshire, C Scotland, UK, who joined Monmouth's supporters in London. On the discovery of the alleged Rye House Plot (1683) to murder Charles II of England and James, Duke of York, he was arrested and sent to Scotland. He was tried at Edinburgh, condemned to death on flimsy evidence, and hanged. >> Monmouth

Baillieu, William Lawrence [baylyoo] (1859–1936) Businessman, born in Queenscliff, Victoria, Australia. He gained an interest in the London Bank of Australia, and invested in lead and zinc extraction at Broken Hill, New South Wales. A member of the Legislative Council of Victoria (1901–22), he was involved in most significant business developments of the period and was a founder of the Melbourne newspaper *The Herald*. His son, **Clive Latham Baillieu** (1889–1967), became 1st Baron Baillieu of Sefton in 1953.

Bailly, Jean Sylvain [bahyee] (1736–93) Astronomer and politician, born in Paris. He studied Halley's comet and the satellites of Jupiter, later writing his great *Histoire de l'astronomie* (1775–87). As president of the National Assembly and Mayor of Paris during the Revolution in 1789, he conducted himself with great integrity, but lost his popularity by allowing the National Guard to fire on anti-royalist crowds. He withdrew from public affairs but was guillotined.

Baily, Edward Hodges (1788–1867) Sculptor, born in Bristol, SW England, UK. He executed many of the well-known London statues, including that of Lord Nelson in Trafalgar Square.

Baily, Francis (1774–1844) Astronomer, born in Newbury, Berkshire, S England, UK. He made a large fortune as a stockbroker, and on his retirement in 1825 devoted himself to astronomy. He detected the phenomenon known as *Baily's beads* during an eclipse of the Sun in 1836, and calculated the mean density of the Earth.

Bain, Alexander [bayn] (1818–1903) Empirical philosopher and psychologist, born in Aberdeen, Aberdeenshire, NE Scotland, UK. He became professor of logic at Aberdeen University (1860–81), and founded the journal *Mind* in 1876. His psychology was firmly based on physiology, and he sought to explain mind through a physical theory of the association of ideas.

Bainbridge, Beryl (1934–) British writer, born in Liverpool, Merseyside. She began writing in the 1960s, and became known for her terse, black comedies, such as *The Dressmaker* (1973, filmed 1979), *Filthy Lucre* (1986) and *An Awfully Big Adventure* (1989, filmed 1995). Several novels tackle historical subjects, notably *Young Adolf* (1978), *Watson's Apology* (1984), and *The Birthday Boys* (1991). She has also written several plays, both for theatre and television. Later works include collections of her journalistic essays (1993) and stories (1994), and the novel *Every Man for Himself* (1996).

Bainton, Edgar Leslie (1880–1956) Composer, teacher, and conductor, born in London, England, UK. He studied at the Royal College of Music, London, before being appointed professor, and later principal, of the Conservatory of Music, Newcastle upon Tyne. In 1938 he was appointed director of the Conservatory in Sydney, New South Wales, and from that time played a key role in the music life of his adopted city, conducting the State Symphony Orchestra and later the Sydney Symphony Orchestra. A prolific composer, he wrote three operas, chamber music, song settings, and piano pieces.

Bainton, Roland (1894–1984) Congregational minister and Reformation scholar, born in Ilkeston, Derbyshire, C England, UK. Taken to Canada by his father in 1898, he was educated at Whitman College and Yale University. He taught Church history at Yale Divinity School (1920–62), and became a leading scholar of the Protestant Reformation in America.

Baird, John Logie (1888–1946) Electrical engineer and television pioneer, born in Helensburgh, Argyll and Bute, W Scotland, UK. He studied electrical engineering at Glasgow University, later settling in Hastings (1922), where he began research into the possibilities of television. In 1926 he gave the first demonstration of a television image. His 30-line mechanically scanned system was adopted by the BBC in 1929, being superseded in 1936 by his 240-line system. In the following year the BBC chose a rival 405-line system with electronic scanning made by Marconi-EMI. Other lines of research initiated by Baird in the 1920s included radar and infra-red television (*Noctovision*); he also succeeded in producing three-dimensional and coloured images (1944), as well as projection onto a screen and stereophonic sound.

Baird, Spencer Fullerton (1823–87) Naturalist, born in Reading, PA. He studied at Dickinson College, Carlisle, and in 1846 was appointed professor of natural history at Dickinson College, where he built up a vast collection of North American fauna. He published *Catalogue of North American Mammals* (1857) and *Catalogue of North American Birds* (1858), and was co-author of *A History of North American Birds* (1874–84). *Baird's sandpiper* and *Baird's sparrow* are named in his honour.

Baire, René >> **Lebesgue, Henri**

Bairnsfather, (Charles) Bruce (1888–1959) Cartoonist, born in Murree, India. He served in France during World War 1, and became famous for his war cartoons featuring the character 'Old Bill'. During World War 2, he was an official war cartoonist attached to the US army in Europe.

Bajazet >> **Bayezit I**

Ba Jin, pseudonym of **Li Feigan** (1904–) Writer, born in Chengdu, Sichuan, China. He studied in Shanghai and Nanjing, and also in France (1927–9), and became an enthusiastic anarchist. His major trilogy (*Family*, 1931, *Spring*, 1938, and *Autumn*, 1940) attacked the traditional family system, and was immensely popular with the younger generation. During the Cultural Revolution (1966–76) he was purged and punished, and compelled to do manual work. He re-emerged in 1977, and published a collection of essays about his experience entitled *Random Thoughts* (1979).

Baker, Sir Benjamin (1840–1907) Civil engineer, born in Keyford, Somerset, SW England, UK. In 1861 he entered into a long association with John Fowler as consulting engineer. They together designed the London Metropolitan Railway, Victoria Station, and many bridges, including the Forth Rail Bridge (1883–90). Baker was also consulting engineer for the Aswan Dam in Egypt (1902) and the Hudson River Tunnel in New York (1888–91). >> Fowler, John

Baker, Chet, popular name of **Chesney H Baker** (1929–88) Jazz trumpeter and singer, born in Yale, OK. He played in US army bands (1946–52), then joined the Gerry Mulligan Quartet, and his brilliant interplay with Mulligan brought critical and popular success. As a leader, his signature tune became 'My Funny Valentine', which epitomized his image as a lonely, searching wanderer. His boyish good looks led to minor movie roles in the 1950s, but his erratic personal life made him a perpetual outsider. A full-length

documentary film, *Let's Get Lost* (1987), shadowed him on his incessant round of European jazz clubs, with juxtaposed clips of his bright-eyed youth. He died in Amsterdam, purportedly by leaping from his hotel window, but suspicions remain that he was pushed.

Baker, George, known as **Father Divine** (?1877–1965) Evangelist, born near Savannah, GA. He began preaching to poor blacks in the rural South, migrated N, and eventually established himself in New York City, where he launched the Peace Mission movement in 1919. Calling himself Father Divine, he established a large following among African-Americans in New York and Philadelphia. He preached communal living and racial equality, and prohibited tobacco, liquor, and cosmetics. Although more than 170 Peace Mission settlements were established, the movement did not long survive the death of its founder.

Baker, Sir Herbert (1862–1946) Architect, born in Kent, SE England, UK. He designed Groote Schuur, near Cape Town, for Cecil Rhodes, the Union government buildings at Pretoria, and (with Edwin Lutyens) New Delhi in India. Other well-known buildings of his include the new Bank of England and South Africa House in London. >> Lutyens

Baker, James A(ddison), III (1930–) US secretary of state (1989–92), born in Houston, TX. He studied at Princeton and the University of Texas Law School, saw service in the US Marines, and became a successful corporate lawyer. He was appointed under-secretary of commerce (1975–6) in the Gerald Ford administration, and managed Ford's 1976 presidential and George Bush's 1979 Republican Party nomination campaigns. President Reagan appointed him White House chief-of-staff in 1981 and treasury secretary in 1985. After directing Bush's victorious presidential campaign in 1988, he became secretary of state in 1989, and in 1992 returned to the White House as chief-of-staff, to run Bush's re-election campaign. >> Bush, George; Ford, Gerald; Reagan

Baker, Dame Janet (Abbott) (1933–) Mezzo-soprano, born in Hatfield, South Yorkshire, N England, UK. She studied music in London in 1953, making her debut in 1956 at Glyndebourne. She has enjoyed an extensive operatic career, especially in early Italian opera and the works of Benjamin Britten. As a concert performer, she is noted for her interpretations of Mahler and Elgar. She became a Companion of Honour in 1994.

Baker, Josephine, originally **Freda Josephine McDonald** (1906–75) Dancer and entertainer, born in St Louis, MO. An amateur singer and dancer, she made her Broadway debut in *Shuffle Along* (1921). In 1925 she went to Paris with a show called *La Revue Nègre*, but the show failed, and she and many cast members were stranded there. Hired to appear in an all-black act at the Folies Bergère, she became an instant success with her scanty costume, lively dancing, and scat singing. As the epitome of *le jazz hot*, 'Josephine' remained the toast of France for five decades, gaining an international status. She never accepted the second-class status assigned to most US blacks, and long boycotted the USA, becoming a French citizen in 1937. In the 1950s she took up the cause of racial equality in America, and was among those who addressed the crowds before the Lincoln Memorial at the end of the 1963 March on Washington. Her plans for a 'world village' at her estate in France collapsed under financial debt, and in order to raise money she made a comeback in 1973–5.

Baker, Kenneth (Wilfred) (1934–) British statesman. He studied at Oxford, and in 1960 entered local politics as a Conservative councillor in Twickenham. In 1968 he was elected an MP, representing Acton and later Mole Valley. After holding junior posts (1970–4) he became parliamentary private secretary to Edward Heath when he was

Leader of the Opposition. In the Margaret Thatcher administration he rose from minister of state in the Department of Trade to become secretary of state for the environment (1985–6) and for education (1986–9), responsible for introducing a controversial education reform bill: in-service training days for teachers then came to be known as *Baker days*. He was later appointed chairman of the Conservative Party (1989–90) and home secretary (1990–2). He was made a Companion of Honour in 1992.

Baker, Norma Jean >> **Monroe, Marilyn**

Baker, Richard (Douglas James) (1925–) Broadcaster and author, born in London, England, UK. He studied in Cambridge, worked as an actor and teacher, and joined the BBC as an announcer in 1950. He became known as a television newsreader (1954–82), and as a commentator on major state occasions. He also introduced the television productions of BBC Promenade Concerts (1960–95), and has presented many radio series, such as *Start the Week with Richard Baker* (1970–87). He was BBC radio personality of the year in 1984. His books include *The Magic of Music* (1975), *London, a theme with variations* (1989), and *Richard Baker's Companion to Music* (1993).

Baker, Sir Samuel (White) (1821–93) Explorer, born in London, England, UK. In 1860 he undertook the exploration of the Nile sources, meeting Speke and Grant at Gondokoro in 1863. In 1864 Baker reached the inland sea into which the Nile flows, and named it Albert Nyanza (now L Mobutu Sese Seko). He was knighted in 1866. >> Grant, James Augustus; Speke

Baker, Snowy, popular name of **Reginald Leslie Baker** (1884–1953) Athlete, born in Sydney, New South Wales, Australia. A swimming champion at 13, two years later he played rugby union for his state. At the age of 18 he won the Australian middleweight and heavyweight boxing titles in one night. At Sydney University he gained blues for cricket, rugby, rowing, and athletics. It was claimed that in his career he played at least 26 sports. He later moved to Hollywood, where he starred in a number of movies, and taught horsemanship to film stars.

Bakewell, Joan (Dawson) (1933–) Broadcaster and writer, born in Stockport, Greater Manchester, NW England, UK. She studied at Cambridge, and became known for her regular contributions and series on BBC television, such as *Late Night Line Up* (1965–72), *Holiday* (1974–8), and *Heart of the Matter* (1988–). Her ITV work included four series of *Reports Action* (1976–8), and she also did a great deal of radio broadcasting, such as *PM* (1979–81). Television critic of *The Times* (1976–81), she was a *Sunday Times* columnist (1988–90), and writes regularly for magazines. Her books include *A Fine and Private Place* (1977, with John Drummond), *The Complete Traveller* (1977), and *The Heart of the Heart of the Matter* (1996). She won the Richard Dimbleby Award in 1994.

Bakewell, Robert (1725–95) Agriculturist, born in Dishley, Leicestershire, C England, UK. By selection and inbreeding he improved the standard and methods of management of sheep, cattle, and draught horses. He established the Leicester breed of sheep and Dishley breed of longhorn cattle, and aroused a wide interest in breeding methods.

Bakhuizen >> **Backhuysen, Ludolf**

Bakst, Léon [bahkst], originally **Lev Samoilovich Rosenberg** (1866–1924) Painter, born in St Petersburg, Russia. He painted religious and genre works in Moscow, and then turned to scenery design at the Hermitage Court Theatre in St Petersburg. In 1908 he went to Paris, where he was associated with Diaghilev from the beginnings of the Russian ballet, designing the decor and costumes for numerous productions (1909–21). >> Diaghilev

Bakunin, Mikhail Aleksandrovich [bakoonin] (1814–76)

Anarchist, born near Moscow. He took part in the German revolutionary movement (1848–9) and was condemned to death. Sent to Siberia in 1855, he escaped to Japan, and arrived in England in 1861. In September 1870 he attempted an abortive rising at Lyon. As leader of anarchism, he was the opponent of Karl Marx in the Communist International, and at the Hague Congress in 1872 was outvoted and expelled. >> Marx

Balaguer, Joaquín (Vidella) [balagair] (1907–) Dominican Republic president (1960–2, 1966–78, 1986–95), born in Villa Bisonó, Dominican Republic. Professor of law at Santo Domingo University from 1938, he served in the dictatorial regime of Rafael Trujillo (president, 1930–60), after whose assassination he fled to the USA in 1962. He returned in 1965 to win the presidency as leader of the Christian Social Reform Party. He returned to power in 1986, at the age of 79. >> RR1045

Balakirev, Mili Alekseyevich [balakiryef] (1837–1910) Composer, born in Nizhni Novgorod, Russia. He turned to composing after an early career as a concert pianist, and became the leader of the national Russian school of music. He founded the Petersburg Free School of Music (1862), and was director of the Imperial Capella (1883). His compositions include two symphonies, a symphonic poem *Tamara*, and the oriental fantasy for piano, *Islamey*.

Balanchine, George [baluhncheen], originally **Georgi Melitonovich Balanchivadze** (1904–83) Ballet dancer and choreographer, born in St Petersburg, Russia. He studied at the ballet school of the Imperial Theatres, then formed his own small company. In 1924 he defected with a group of dancers during a European tour, and after performing in London as the Soviet State Dancers, Diaghilev took them into his Russian Ballet in Paris, and he changed his name to Balanchine. In 1925 he succeeded Nijinska as choreographer and ballet-master. He helped to found Les Ballets Russes de Monte Carlo in 1932, and Les Ballets the following year, then opened the School of American Ballet in New York City in 1934. After the war he directed a private company, the Ballet Society, which in 1948 emerged as the New York City Ballet. With that company he created over 90 works of enormous variety. He was also a successful musical comedy and film choreographer. >> Diaghilev; Kirstein; Nijinska

Balard, Antoine Jérôme [balah(r)] (1802–76) Chemist, born in Montpelier, France. Professor at the Sorbonne and Collège de France, he discovered bromine (1826), hypochlorous acid, and chlorine monoxide.

Balassa or **Balassi, Bálint** [bawlawshaw] (1554–94) Hungarian knight, adventurer, and lyric poet, born in Kékkö. His poetry was inspired by military heroism, love, and religion, and he also experimented in drama. He died fighting the Turkish invaders.

Balbo, Cesare, conte (Count) [balboh] (1789–1853) Italian statesman and writer, born in Turin, Italy. He was a prime minister in the first Piedmontese constitutional ministry. He published a biography of Dante in 1839, and a historical essay demonstrating his view that Italy had only prospered when free from foreign domination.

Balbo, Italo [balboh] (1896–1940) Italian politician and aviator, born in Ferrara, Italy. One of the leaders of the March on Rome, he was the first minister of aviation in Italy, and led mass flights to Brazil (1929) and the USA (1933). In 1933 he became Governor of Libya. In 1940 he was killed when his plane was brought down at Tobruk.

Balboa, Vasco Núñez de [balboha] (1475–1519) Explorer, born in Jerez de los Caballeros, Spain. In 1511 he joined an expedition to Darién as a stowaway. Taking advantage of an insurrection, he took command, founded a colony at Darién, and extended Spanish influence into neighbouring areas. On one of these expeditions he climbed a peak and sighted the Pacific Ocean, the first European to do so, and took possession for Spain. The governorship was granted in 1514 to Pedro Arias Dávila (?1440–1531), for whom Balboa undertook many successful expeditions, but after a disagreement in 1519 Balboa was beheaded.

Balbuena, Bernardo de [balbwayna] (1568–1627) Poet and clergyman, born in Valdepeñas, Spain. He spent his working life in Central America, where all his poetry was written, and became Bishop of Puerto Rico in 1620. His main work was an epic on the national hero, Bernardo del Capio (1624).

Balch, Emily Greene (1867–1961) Social reformer and pacifist, born in Jamaica Plain, MA. She studied at Bryn Mawr College and the Sorbonne, then taught economics at Wellesley College, MA (1896–1918). An active pacifist, she helped establish the Women's International League for Peace and Freedom (1919), and proved an indefatigable administrator, writer, and promoter for peace. She shared the Nobel Peace Prize in 1946. >> RR1125

Balchen, Bernt (1899–1973) Aviator and Arctic explorer, born in Tveit Topdal, Norway. In 1924 he was commissioned in the Royal Norwegian Naval Air Force, and flew rescue missions over the Arctic. He was chief pilot to Byrd's first Antarctic expedition (1928–30) and to Ellsworth's Antarctic expedition (1932–5). He became a US citizen in 1931, and in 1935 returned to Norway as manager of DNL (Norwegian Air Lines). He returned to active US duty in 1948, commanding an Arctic Rescue Unit, and as adviser to the Pentagon. >> Byrd, Richard; Ellsworth

Balchin, Nigel (Marlin) [bawlchin] (1908–70) Novelist, born in Wiltshire, S England, UK. He studied at Cambridge, after which he combined writing with his work as an industrial psychologist. During World War 2 he was scientific adviser to the Army Council, from which experience he wrote his best-known novel, *The Small Back Room* (1943). Later novels explore the problems of psychologically and physically disabled men, as in *A Sort of Traitors* (1949) and *The Fall of a Sparrow* (1955).

Balcon, Sir Michael (Elias) (1896–1977) Film producer, born in Birmingham, West Midlands, C England, UK. He entered the film industry in 1921, and founded Gainsborough Pictures in 1928. In 1931 he took charge of production at Gaumont–British Pictures, where he made *The Thirty-Nine Steps* (1935). After a brief period working for MGM in Hollywood, he became executive producer for Ealing Films (1938–59), and is remembered for a string of successful comedies and thrillers, including *Whisky Galore* (1948), *The Blue Lamp* (1949), and *The Lavender Hill Mob* (1951). He was knighted in 1948.

Baldinucci, Filippo [baldinoochee] (1624–96) Art historian, born in Florence, Italy. He was entrusted by Cardinal Leopoldo Medici with the arrangement of the Medici collection.

Baldovinetti, Alesso [baldovinetee] (c. 1425–99) Painter, born in Florence, Italy. His frescoes, noted for their landscape backgrounds, are mostly poorly preserved as a result of his experiments in technique, but he also executed mosaics of great beauty and worked on stained glass.

Baldung or **Grien, Hans** (c.1476–1545) Painter and engraver, born in Weiersheim, Germany. He may have been a pupil of Dürer. His mature works display deliberate exaggeration of late Gothic styles to obtain often morbid quasi-Expressionist effects in the manner of Grünewald, as in 'Die Frau und den Tod' (Basel, Death and the Maiden) and 'Die Eitelkeit' (Vienna, Vanity). >> Dürer

Baldwin I (1172–c. 1205) Emperor of Constantinople, born in Valenciennes, France. He succeeded his father as Count of Hainault and Flanders in 1195. In 1202 he joined the fourth Crusade, and in 1204 was chosen the first Latin emperor of Constantinople. The Greeks, invoking the aid of the Bulgarians, rose and took Adrianople. Baldwin laid siege to the town, but was defeated in 1205 and died in captivity. >> RR1037

Baldwin (?–1190) Clergyman, born in Exeter, Devon, SW England, UK, in poor circumstances. He became Bishop of Worcester in 1180, and Archbishop of Canterbury in 1184. He crowned Richard I, made a tour of Wales preaching in favour of the Crusades, and himself died on a Crusade.

Baldwin, James (Arthur) (1924–87) Writer, born in Harlem, New York City. After a variety of jobs he moved to Europe, where he lived (mainly in Paris) from 1948 to 1957, before returning to the USA as a civil rights activist. His novels, in which autobiographical elements appear, include *Go Tell it on the Mountain* (1954), *Giovanni's Room* (1957), and *Just Above My Head* (1979). Other works include collections of essays and plays – *The Amen Corner* (1955), *Blues for Mr Charlie* (1964), and *The Women at the Well* (1972).

Baldwin, James (Mark) (1861–1934) Psychologist, born in Columbia, SC. A specialist in child psychology and social psychology, he was professor at Toronto (1889), Princeton (1893), Johns Hopkins (1903), and the University of Mexico (1909), settling in Paris in 1913. He was the founder-editor of the *Psychological Review* (1894–1909), and editor of the *Dictionary of Philosophy and Psychology* (1901–6).

Baldwin, Mark (Phillip) (1954–) Choreographer and dancer, born in New Zealand. He studied at the University of Auckland, New Zealand, and became a dancer with the New Zealand Ballet and Australian Dance Theatre before joining the Rambert Dance Company in London (1982–92), also as choreographer (1992–4). He became resident choreographer with Sadlers Wells (1994–5) and with the Scottish Ballet (1996–). In 1996 he received the Time Out Dance Award and the Grand Prix International Special Judges' Prize for his dance film video *Danse 8*.

Baldwin, Matthias (William) (1795–1866) Locomotive engineer and industrialist, born in Elizabethtown, NJ. A jeweller up to the age of 30, he began to make hydraulic presses and printing machinery, and by 1827 was manufacturing steam engines. His first locomotive, *Old Ironsides*, was completed in 1832 and remained in service for 20 years. The Baldwin Locomotive Works built over 1000 engines by 1861, and remained for many years the world's largest manufacturer.

Baldwin, Robert (1804–58) Canadian statesman, born in Toronto (formerly York), Ontario, Canada. He was called to the bar in 1825, and became a member of the Legislative Assembly of Upper Canada in 1829. He condemned the Rebellion of 1837 and supported the Union of Upper and Lower Canada. With **Louis Hippolyte Lafontaine** (1807–64) he was joint prime minister of the united province of Canada (1842–3, 1848–51).

Baldwin (of Bewdley), Stanley Baldwin, 1st Earl (1867–1947) British statesman and prime minister (1923–4, 1924–29, 1935–37), born in Bewdley, Hereford and Worcester, WC England, UK. He studied at Cambridge, and became vice-chairman of the family iron and steel business. A Conservative MP in 1908, he became President of the Board of Trade (1921), and unexpectedly succeeded Bonar Law as premier. His period of office included the General Strike (1926) and was interrupted by the Ramsay MacDonald coalition (1931–5), in which he served as Lord President of the Council. He skilfully avoided a party split by his India Act (1935), but the Hoare-Laval pact and the policy of non-intervention in Spain (1936) came to be regarded as betrayals of the League of Nations. He displayed considerable resolution during the constitutional crisis culminating in Edward VIII's abdication (1937). He had the party politician's sure touch in domestic matters, but was criticized for his apparent failure to recognize the threat from Nazi Germany. He resigned and was made an earl in 1937. >> RR1095

Bale, John (1495–1563) Clergyman and playwright, born in Cove, Suffolk, E England, UK. A Carmelite by training, he became a Protestant in 1533, and was later made Bishop of Ossory in Leinster. He became so obnoxious to Catholics with his polemical writings that his house was attacked and five servants killed. On Queen Elizabeth I's accession he was made a prebendary of Canterbury. His drama, *King John*, is considered the first English historical play.

Balenciaga, Cristóbal [balenthiahga] (1895–1972) Fashion designer, born in Guetaria, Spain. He trained as a tailor, and in 1915 opened dressmaking and tailoring shops of his own in Madrid and Barcelona. He left Spain for Paris in 1937 because of the Spanish Civil War, and became a fashion designer. He retired in 1968.

Balewa, Sir Abubakar Tafawa [balaywa] (1912–66) Nigerian statesman and first federal prime minister (1957–66), born in Bauchi, Nigeria. A member of the Northern People's Congress, he entered the Federal Assembly in 1947, was minister of works (1952–3) and of transport (1953–7), then became premier. He was knighted when Nigeria became independent in 1960, and was assassinated in the military uprising of 1966. >> RR1079

Balfe, Michael William [balf] (1808–70) Composer, born in Dublin, Republic of Ireland. In 1823 he moved to London, and in 1825–6 studied in Italy under Rossini, which inspired him to sing in opera with considerable success. In 1833 he returned to England, and in 1846 was appointed conductor of the London Italian Opera. Of his numerous operas, operettas, and other compositions, the most enduring success was *The Bohemian Girl* (1843). >> Rossini

Balfour, Arthur James Balfour, 1st Earl [balfer] (1848–1930) British statesman and philosopher, born in Whittinghame, East Lothian, E Scotland, UK. He studied at Cambridge, and entered parliament in 1874 as a Conservative MP for Hertford. He was returned for East Manchester (1885), was secretary for Scotland (1886), chief secretary for Ireland (1887), and First Lord of the Treasury and Leader of the House of Commons (1892–3). His premiership saw the end of the Boer War (1902), the Education Act (1905), and the establishment of the Committee of Imperial Defence. In 1911 he resigned the leadership of the House owing to the constitutional crisis. He followed Churchill to the Admiralty (1915) and served under Lloyd George as foreign secretary (1916–19). He was responsible for the famous *Balfour declaration* (1917) which promised Zionists a national home in Palestine, and as Lord President of the Council (1921) was responsible for the controversial note cancelling Allied war debts to America.

Balfour, Francis (Maitland) (1851–82) Embryologist, born in Edinburgh, EC Scotland, UK, the brother of Arthur Balfour. He studied at Cambridge, where he became the first professor of animal morphology in 1882 after publishing his *Treatise on Comparative Embryology* (1880). >> Balfour, Arthur James

Balfour, George (1872–1941) Electrical engineer and pioneering contractor, the founder of the construction firm of Balfour Beatty Ltd, born in Portsmouth, Hampshire, S England, UK. He served an apprenticeship in a foundry in Dundee, and qualified as a journeyman engineer. After working for a New York company specializing in electric tramways and power plants, he founded his own company in 1909 with an accountant, Andrew Beatty. They built and operated the tramway systems for many towns, and the first major hydro-electric schemes in Scotland, as well as pioneering the National Grid in the 1930s. He was Unionist MP for Hampstead (London) from 1918 until his death.

Bálint >> **Balassa**

Ball, C(harles) Olin (1893–1970) Food technologist, born in Abilene, KS. While in graduate school at George Washington University (1919–22) he researched the sterilization of canned foods for the National Canners Association. He then worked for the American Can Co in Illinois and New York (1922–41), where he generated some of his 29 patents, including the basic heat–cool–fill canning method (1936), the method and apparatus for open-can sterilization (1937), and processes for canning milk (1938–9). He later taught food science at Rutgers University (1949–63).

Ball, John (?–1381) English rebel. An excommunicated priest, he was executed as one of the leaders in the Peasants' Revolt of 1381, led by Wat Tyler. >> Tyler, Wat

Ball, John (1818–89) Botanist and alpinist, born in Dublin. He was the first president of the Alpine Club (1857) and author of the *Alpine Guide* (1863–8). Liberal MP for Carlow, Ireland, he was colonial under-secretary (1855–7), and wrote on the botany of Morocco and South America.

Ball, Lucille (Désirée) (1911–89) Comedienne, born in Celaron, NY. An amateur performer as a child, she was a model and chorus girl before moving to Hollywood. An effervescent redhead with a rasping voice and impeccable timing, she began working in television in 1951 and became one of its best-loved characters, starring in such domestic comedies as *I Love Lucy* (1951–5), *The Lucy Show* (1962–8), and *Here's Lucy* (1968–73). She purchased her own studio with first husband **Desi Arnaz**, and also became a successful production executive, occasionally returning to the cinema for such popular comedies as *The Facts of Life* (1960) and *Yours, Mine and Ours* (1968).

Ball, Michael (Ashley) (1962–) Actor and singer, born in the West Midlands, C England, UK. He studied at the Guildford School of Acting (1981–4), then made his professional debut. His first starring role was in *The Pirates of Penzance* (1985, Manchester Opera House), and he made his West End debut in *Les Miserables* later that year. Other major productions include *Phantom of the Opera* (1987), *Aspects of Love* (1989, Broadway debut 1990), and *Passion* (1996). Television work includes his own series (1993, 1994) and he has made many recordings. The Variety Club of Great Britain voted him Most Promising Artiste in 1989.

Ball, Murray Hone (1939–) Cartoonist, born in Fielding, New Zealand. He is known for the wry social comment of his widely syndicated comic strips: *Bruce the Barbarian*, *Stanley the Palaeolithic Hero*, and *Footrot Flats*.

Balla, Giacomo (1871–1958) Artist, born in Turin, Italy. After a visit to Paris in 1900 he was strongly influenced by Impressionism and Divisionism. He was one of the founders of Futurism and a signatory to the 1910 Futurist Manifesto. Primarily concerned with conveying movement and speed in painterly terms, he achieved this by imitating time-lapse photography. By 1930, he was painting in a more conventional style. >> Boccioni; Marinetti; Severini

Ballantyne Printers and brothers: **James Ballantyne** (1772–1833) and **John Ballantyne** (1774–1821), born in Kelso, Scottish Borders, SE Scotland, UK. They studied at Kelso Grammar School (1783) with Sir Walter Scott. James studied for the law, but in 1797 started the Tory *Kelso Mail*. In 1802, having already printed some ballads for Scott, he produced the first two volumes of the *Border Minstrelsy*.

After moving the firm to Edinburgh, Scott became a secret partner in the business, which in 1808 expanded into the printing, publishing, and bookselling firm of John Ballantyne & Co, but by 1826 the firm was bankrupt. >> Scott, Walter

Ballantyne, John >> **Bellenden, John**

Ballantyne, R(obert) M(ichael) (1825–94) Writer of boys' books, born in Edinburgh, EC Scotland, UK, a nephew of James and John Ballantyne. He studied at the Edinburgh Academy, joined the Hudson's Bay Company in 1841, and worked as a clerk at the Red River Settlement in the backwoods of N Canada until 1847, before returning to Edinburgh in 1848. He wrote his first stories on his experiences in Canada, with books such as *The Young Fur Traders* (1856). *The Coral Island* (1858) is his most famous work. >> Ballantyne, James

Ballard, J(ames) G(raham) (1930–) Writer, born in Shanghai, China. He studied at Cambridge, and became a science fiction writer, fashioning a series of novels at once inventive, experimental, and often bizarre. His early novels, including his first, *The Drowned World* (1962), offer a view of the world beset by elemental catastrophe. He has been admired chiefly for his short stories, particularly those included in such collections as *The Terminal Beach* (1964), *The Disaster Area* (1967), and *Vermilion Sands* (1973). His 1973 novel *Crash* was made into a controversial film by David Cronenberg in 1996. *Empire of the Sun* (1984; filmed by Spielberg, 1987), a mainstream novel which is portentously autobiographical, was short-listed for the Booker Prize. A sequel, *The Kindness of Women*, appeared in 1991. Later works include *Rushing to Paradise* (1994) and *A User's Guide to the Millennium* (1996). >> Spielberg

Ballesteros, Sevvy [ba-ye**stair**os], popular name of **Severiano Ballesteros** (1957–) Golfer, born in Pedrena, Spain. A highly combative, adventurous player, he has continually set records. When he won the (British) Open in 1979 he was the youngest player to do so in the 20th-c, and he took the title again in 1984 and 1988. Other wins include the US Masters (1980, 1983) and the World Matchplay (1981–2, 1984–5, 1991). The leading money winner in Europe in the years 1976–8, 1986, and 1988, he is the first man to win 50 European golf tournaments. His brothers Manuel, Baldomero, and Vicente are also all top golfers. >> RR1157

Ballou, Hosea [ba**loo**] (1771–1852) Clergyman, born in Richmond, NH. Originally a Baptist minister, he was the chief founder of the Universalist Church, from 1817 working as a pastor in Boston.

Balmain, Pierre (Alexandre Claudius) [balmĩ] (1914–1982) Fashion designer, born in St Jean-de-Maurienne, France. He started studying architecture in Paris, but turned to dress designing, working for Edward Molyneux and Lucien Lelong, and in 1945 opened his own house. Famous for elegant simplicity, his designs included evening dresses, tailored suits, sportswear, and stoles. He also designed for the theatre and cinema. >> Mortensen

Balmer, Johann Jakob [bal**mer**] (1825–98) Physicist, born in Lausanne, Switzerland. He derived a formula for frequencies of hydrogen lines in the visible spectrum. The *Balmer series* is the atomic spectrum of hydrogen in the visible and near ultraviolet regions of the spectrum.

Balmont, Konstantin Dmitryevitch (1867–1943) Poet, translator, and essayist, born in Gumische, Russia. A leading Russian Symbolist, his work was coloured by the wide travelling he did during his periodic exiles, which added a vein of exoticism to his work.

Balnaves, Henry [bal**na**vis] (c. 1512–79) Reformer, born in Kirkcaldy, Fife, E Scotland, UK. In 1543 he was appointed secretary of state by the regent, James Hamilton. Shortly after, however, he was imprisoned with John Knox in Blackness Castle for his Protestantism. When the castle was captured by the French (1547), Balnaves, with Knox and others, was sent to Rouen. While in prison there, he wrote a treatise on justification, published in 1584 as *The Confession of Faith*. In 1566 he was allowed to return to Scotland, and took an active part on the side of the Lords of the Congregation. >> Knox, John

Balthasar, Hans Urs von [bal**tazah(r)**] (1905–88) Catholic theologian, born in Lucerne, Switzerland. The author of some 60 books on theology, philosophy, and spirituality, he drew considerable inspiration for his theology from the religious experiences of the mystic **Adrienne von Speyr** (1902–67), with whom he formed a secular institute after leaving the Jesuits. His chief work is *Herrlichkeit* (1961–9, trans The Glory of the Lord: a Theological Aesthetic).

Balthus, in full **Count Balthasar Klossowski de Rola** (1908–) Painter, born in Paris. He had no formal training, but received early encouragement from Bonnard and Derain. He held his first one-man exhibition at the Galerie Pierre, Paris, in 1934, and later became director of the French School in Rome. His work includes landscapes and portraits, but he is chiefly known for his interiors with adolescent girls, painted in a highly distinctive naturalistic style with a hint of Surrealism. He has grown in fame and popularity in recent years, despite the fact that he has lived for many years as a virtual recluse. >> Bonnard, Pierre; Derain

Baltimore, David (1938–) Microbiologist, born in New York City. He studied chemistry at Swarthmore, the Massachusetts Institute of Technology, and Rockefeller University, then conducted research into virology at the Salk Institute (1965–8), became professor of biology at MIT (1972), and was later director of the Whitehead Institute at Cambridge, MA. In 1970 he discovered the reverse transcriptase enzyme which can transcribe DNA into RNA. For his research into the connection between viruses and cancer he shared the 1975 Nobel Prize for Physiology or Medicine. >> RR1124

Baltimore, George Calvert, Baron (c. 1580–1632) English statesman and colonialist, born in Kiplin, North Yorkshire, N England, UK. He entered parliament in 1609, was knighted in 1617, and became secretary of state (1619–25). In 1625 he declared himself a Catholic, resigned his office, was created Baron Baltimore in the Irish peerage, and retired to his Irish estates. He then made plans to found a province in America, and after failing in Newfoundland and Virginia, applied for a charter further S, in what is now Maryland. He died before the grant was made final, and the patent passed to his son, **Cecil Baltimore** (c.1605–75).

Balzac, Honoré de (1799–1850) Novelist, born in Tours, France. He studied at the Collège de Vendôme and the Sorbonne. From 1819 to 1830 he led a life of frequent privation and incessant industry, incurring a heavy burden of debt which harassed him to the end of his career. His first success was *Les Chouans* (1829, The Chouans). After writing several other novels, he formed the idea of presenting in *La Comédie humaine* (The Human Comedy) a complete picture of modern civilization. Among the masterpieces which form part of his vast scheme are *Le Père Goriot* (Father Goriot), *Les Illusions perdues* (Lost Illusions), *Les Paysans* (The Peasants), *La Femme de trente ans* (The Thirty-Year-Old Woman), and *Eugénie Grandet*, in which detailed observation and imagination are the main features. His industry was phenomenal, writing 85 novels in 20 years, but his work did not bring him wealth. During his later years he lived principally in his villa at Sèvres. In 1849, when his health had broken down, he travelled to Poland to visit Eveline Hanska, a rich Polish lady, with whom he had corresponded for more than 15 years. In 1850 she became his wife, and three months later, Balzac died.

Bambaataa (1958–) Record producer, arranger, and disc jockey, born in New York City. He worked in high schools and public parks during the 1970s, and developed the style of music known as 'rap'. His record *Planet Rock* (1982) was a major influence on dance records on both sides of the Atlantic.

Bampton, Deborah (Ellen) (1961–) British football player and manager. She joined Arsenal Ladies' Football Club as player-manager (1992–3), where her honours included the Women's Football Association Cup, League Cup, and National League (1992–3). She is a member, and former captain, of the England Women's Football Team (82 caps), and player-manager of Croydon Women's Football Club.

Banach, Stefan [**bah**nahkh] (1892–1945) Mathematician, born in Krakow, Poland. He studied at Lvov, where he became lecturer in 1919, and professor in 1927. He is regarded as one of the founders of functional analysis, and he founded an important school of Polish mathematicians.

Ban Chao [ban chow], also spelled **Pan Ch'ao** (32–102) Chinese military leader and administrator, who first established Chinese control over Turkestan. Deputy commander of an army which crushed an opposing force of 70 000, he later (AD 91) became protector of the Western Regions and conquered the whole of W Turkestan up to the Caspian for the Han dynasty. After his death his younger brother **Ban Yong** tightened Chinese control of Turkestan. >> Ban Gu; Ganying

Bancroft, Anne, originally **Anna Maria Italiano** (1931–) Actress, born in New York City, USA. She made her professional debut on television in an adaptation of Turgenev's *Torrents of Spring*. For her performance in the stage production of *The Miracle Worker* in 1959, she won a Tony Best Actress award, and an Oscar for the film version in 1962. Later films include *The Slender Thread* (1965), *The Graduate* (1968), *The Elephant Man* (1980), *84 Charing Cross Road* (1986), and *Torch Song Trilogy* (1988).

Bancroft, Edward (1744–1821) Secret agent and inventor, born in Westfield, MA. He moved to England, and was a double agent – working for both Benjamin Franklin and the British government simultaneously – during the American Revolution. He then remained in England and made discoveries in textile dyes manufacturing. >> Franklin, Benjamin

Bancroft, George (1800–91) Historian and statesman, born in Worcester, MA. He studied divinity at Harvard, and history at Göttingen. His major work was a monumental *History of the United States* (10 vols, 1834–40, 1852–74). A Democrat, he was secretary to the navy (1845–6) and established the Naval Academy at Annapolis. He was also US minister to Britain (1846–9), Prussia (1867–71), and the German empire (1871–4).

Bancroft, Hubert Howe (1832–1918) Historian, born in Granville, OH. He settled in San Francisco in 1852, started a bookshop, and amassed a fortune. In 1905 he collected and transferred to the University of California 60 000 volumes, mainly on American history and ethnography. His main work was the 39-volume *History of the Pacific States of America* (1875–90).

Bancroft, Richard (1544–1610) Anglican clergyman, born in Farnworth, Lancashire, NW England, UK. He graduated from Cambridge in 1567, and after a series of preferments was consecrated Bishop of London in 1597. He attended Queen Elizabeth I during her last illness, and took the lead at the Hampton Court Conference. He succeeded Whitgift as Archbishop of Canterbury in 1604, and assisted in re-establishing episcopacy in Scotland. >> Whitgift

Bancroft, Sir Squire (1841–1926) Actor-manager, born in London, England, UK. He made his debut at Birmingham (1861), and in 1867 married **Marie Wilton** (1840–1921), a distinguished actress. From 1865 to 1880 the Prince of Wales's Theatre witnessed their triumphs in a wide range of comedies, and until 1885 they were successful lessees of the Haymarket.

Banda, Hastings (Kamuzu) (c.1906–97) Malawi statesman, prime minister (1963–6) and first president (1966–94), born in Kasungu, Malawi. He studied medicine in the USA and in Britain. His opposition to the Central African Federation caused him to give up his successful London practice (1955) and return via Ghana to Nyasaland (1958). Leader of the Malawi African Congress, he was jailed in 1959, became minister of national resources (1961), then prime minister and president of the Malawi (formerly, Nyasaland) republic. Made life president in 1971, he established a strong, one-party control of Malawi, but following growing opposition he was defeated in a referendum for multi-party democracy in 1993, and was defeated in the 1994 elections. >> RR1073

Bandaranaike, Sirimavo (Ratwatte Dias) [banda-ra**niy**kuh], *née* **Ratwatte** (1916–) Sri Lankan (Ceylonese) prime minister (1960–5, 1970–7, 1994–), born in Ratnapura, Sri Lanka. Following the assassination of her husband, S W R D Bandaranaike, in 1959, she became leader of the Sri Lanka Freedom Party, won the Ceylon general election (1960), and became the world's first woman prime minister. She held the position for a second time following independence, and again in 1994. >> Bandaranaike, S W R D; RR1090

Bandaranaike, S(olomon) W(est) R(idgeway) D(ias) [banda**raniy**kuh] (1899–1959) Sri Lankan (Ceylonese) statesman and prime minister (1956–9), born in Colombo. He studied at Oxford, and was called to the bar in 1925. He became president of the Ceylon National Congress, then helped to found the United National Party, which formed the government of Ceylon in 1948–56. In 1951 he resigned from the government and organized the Sri Lanka Freedom Party, which returned him to parliament as Leader of the Opposition, and in 1956 he became prime minister on a policy of nationalization and neutralism. He was assassinated by a Buddhist monk. >> Bandaranaike, Sirimavo; RR1090

Bandeira (Filho), Manuel (Carneiro de Sousa) [ban**dair**a] (1886–1968) Poet, born in Recife, Brazil. His first books of poetry, *A Cinza das Horas* (1917, Destruction of the Hours) and *Carnaval* (1919, Carnival), identified him with the contemporary Modernist movement. His works were highly influential among aspiring Brazilian writers, and he became a much respected national figure.

Bandelier, Adolph (Francis Alphonse) [bande**leer**] (1840–1914) Archaeologist and anthropologist, born in Bern. He pioneered the study of the pre-Columbian Indian cultures of SW USA, Peru, and Bolivia. From 1880 he worked principally on the pueblos of Arizona and New Mexico, using a mixture of documentary research, ethnography, and archaeological survey, then spent a decade in Peru and Bolivia (1892–1903). Bandelier National Monument, a rugged gorge near Santa Fe, New Mexico, was established in his memory in 1916.

Bandello, Matteo [ban**del**oh] (c.1485–1561) Clergyman and writer of *novelle* or tales, born in Castelnuovo, Italy. For a while a Dominican, he was driven from Milan by the Spaniards after the Battle of Pavia (1525), and settling in France was made Bishop of Agen (1550). His 214 tales (1554–73) were used as source material by Shakespeare and others.

Bandiera Revolutionaries and brothers: **Attilio Bandiera** (1810–44) and **Emilio Bandiera** (1819–44) [band**yair**a], born in Venice, Italy. As lieutenants in the Austrian navy, where their father, Baron Francesco Bandiera (1785–1847) was an admiral, they attempted a rising in Naples against Austrian rule in favour of Italian independence, but were betrayed and shot at Cosenza.

Bandinelli, Baccio [bandinelee] (c.1493–1560) Sculptor, born in Florence, Italy. A rival of Michelangelo, he executed the statues of 'Hercules and Cacus' outside the Palazzo Vecchio, and 'Adam and Eve' (National Museum, Florence). His best works are the bas-reliefs in the Florence Cathedral. >> Michelangelo

Banerjea, Sir Surendranath [banerjee] (1848–1925) Indian politician and journalist, born in Calcutta, India. A fervent nationalist, he founded the Calcutta Indian Association in 1876 and was editor of The Bengali newspaper (1879–1921). He was one of the initiators of the Indian National Congress, but subsequently broke with Congress because of its extremism.

Banerjee, Satyendranath [banerjee] (1897–) Artist, born in West Bengal, India. He became a protégé of Rabindranath Tagore, and a teacher at the Calcutta College of Arts. Examples of his work are hung in art galleries throughout India and in private collections. >> Tagore

Bang, Bernhard (Lauritz Frederik) (1848–1932) Veterinary surgeon, born in Sorø, Denmark. He studied medicine but later became interested in the healing of animals, and in 1880 was appointed professor of veterinary surgery at Copenhagen, where he investigated bacillary diseases, mainly of cattle. He is known particularly for his work on bovine brucellosis, known as Bang's disease.

Ban Gu [ban goo], also spelled **Pan Ku** (AD 32–92) Chinese historian, the brother of Ban Chao. His History of the Former Han (Han Shu) was, like Sima Qian's earlier work, based on official documentation, other histories and oral traditions, but with wider social, scientific, and artistic coverage. Started by AD 54, and completed by Ban Gu's sister **Ban Zhao**, it is a major source on the earlier Han dynasty. Equivalent to 800 000 English words, it established the format for the great series of standard histories on all succeeding dynasties. >> Ban Chao; Sima Qian

Banim Novelists and brothers: **John Banim** (1798–1842) and **Michael Banim** (1796–1874), born in Kilkenny, Ireland. John studied art at Dublin and became a miniature painter; Michael became a postmaster. They collaborated in such novels as the Tales of the O'Hara Family (1826), a faithful portrayal of humble Irish folk.

Bani-Sadr, Abolhassan [banee sadr] (1935–) Iranian politician, and first president of the Islamic Republic of Iran (1980–1), associated with Ayatollah Khomeini from 1966. He studied economics and sociology at the Sorbonne in Paris, having fled there in 1963 after a brief imprisonment in Iran. An important figure in the Iranian Revolution of 1978–9, he was soon criticized by the fundamentalists and dismissed. He fled to France where he was granted asylum. >> Khomeini; RR1063

Bankhead, Tallulah (1903–68) Actress, born in Huntsville, AL. She was brought up in New York City and Washington, and made her stage debut in 1918. She won Critic awards for her two most famous stage roles, Regina in The Little Foxes (1939) and Sabina in The Skin of Our Teeth (1942). Her most outstanding film portrayal was in Lifeboat (1944).

Banks, Don (1923–80) Composer, born in Melbourne, Victoria, Australia. He attended the Melbourne Conservatory (1947–9), then studied in London, Salzburg, and Florence. Having settled in England, he became music director of Goldsmith's College (1969–71). He returned to Australia in 1973, became head of Composition and Electronic Music Studies at Canberra School of Music in 1974, and head of the School of Composition Music

Studies at the Sydney Conservatory in 1978. His work was particularly influenced by Milton Babbitt and by jazz. His compositions include a horn concerto, a violin concerto, a trilogy for orchestra, An Australian Entertainment (1979), and many film and TV scores. >> Babbitt, Milton

Banks, Gordon (1937–) Footballer, born in Sheffield, South Yorkshire, N England, UK. An outstanding goalkeeper, he started his career with Chesterfield and Leicester City but was transferred to Stoke City. His performances in the 1966 and 1970 World Cups were outstanding. A serious eye injury sustained in a car crash in 1972 ended his playing career.

Banks, Iain (1954–) Novelist, born in Fife, E Scotland, UK. He worked as a testing technician in Scotland and as a solicitor's clerk in England before attracting equal measures of fame and notoriety with his first novel, a gruesome Gothic fantasy, The Wasp Factory (1984). Later books include The Bridge (1986) and Whit (1995).

Banks, Sir Joseph (1743–1820) Botanist, born in London, England, UK. He studied at Oxford, and in 1766 made a voyage to Newfoundland collecting plants. He then accompanied James Cook's expedition round the world in the Endeavour (1768–71). In 1778 he was elected president of the Royal Society, an office he held for 41 years. An important patron of science, he founded the African Association, and the colony of New South Wales owed its origin mainly to him. Through him the bread-fruit was transferred from Tahiti to the West Indies, and the mango was introduced from Bengal, along with many fruits of Ceylon and Persia. >> Thompson, Benjamin

Banks, Lynne (Reid) (1929–) British writer and actress. She studied in Canada, and in London at the Italia Conti Stage School and the Royal Academy of Dramatic Art. After a brief career as an actress (1949–54), she joined ITN as a reporter (1955–62), taught English in Israel (1963–71), and became a full-time lecturer from 1971. Her best-known novel is The L-Shaped Room (1960, filmed 1962), and she has also written plays and biographical novels. Her many books for children include The Adventures of King Midas (1977), The Indian in the Cupboard (1980, filmed 1995), The Mystery of the Cupboard (1993), and Angela and Diabola (1997).

Banks, Nathaniel P(rentiss) (1816–94) US politician and soldier, born in Waltham, MA. A factory worker, he studied law, and became successively a member of the state and national legislatures. He was Speaker of the House of Representatives in 1856, and in 1857, 1859, and 1861 was elected Governor of Massachusetts. In the Civil War he commanded on the Potomac, and received the thanks of Congress for the capture of Fort Hudson (1863).

Banna, al- >> **al-Banna, Hassan**

Bannatyne, George (1545–1608) Antiquary and collector of poems, born in Edinburgh, EC Scotland, UK. He became a wealthy merchant in Edinburgh, but his claim to fame was his 800-page manuscript of early Scottish poetry of the 15th and 16th-c (the Bannatyne Manuscript). The Bannatyne Club was founded in his honour in 1823 to encourage the study of Scottish history and literature.

Banneker, Benjamin [baneker] (1731–1806) Astronomer and mathematician, born near Baltimore, MD, the grandson of an Englishwoman and a freed black slave, but son of a slave father and freed black mother. He was allowed to attend a local elementary school, where he showed a talent for mathematics and science. Although his main occupation was as a farmer, he devoted his spare time to applied sciences, publishing an almanac (1792–1802) that used his astronomical and tide calculations and his weather predictions, along with proverbs, poems, and essays contributed by himself and others; this almanac was often cited by opponents of slavery as evidence of

African-Americans' abilities. Thomas Jefferson had him hired in 1791 to assist the surveyors laying out the new capital and the District of Columbia. He in turn did not shrink from urging Jefferson to abolish slavery and to adopt more progressive policies for black Americans, of whom he was probably the best known in his day and for some decades after. >> Jefferson, Thomas

Bannerman, Helen Brodie, *née* **Boog Watson** (1826–1946) Children's writer and illustrator, born in Edinburgh, EC Scotland, UK. Her husband was a doctor in the Indian Medical Service and she spent much of her life in India, where she produced the children's classic, *The Story of Little Black Sambo* (1899), and several other illustrated books for children.

Bannister, Edward (Mitchell) (1828–1901) Painter, born in St Andrews, New Brunswick, Canada. A prominent black painter in his day, he moved to Boston (c.1848), studied at the Lowell Institute under William Rimmer (1855), and settled in Providence, RI (c.1870). His recently rediscovered landscapes, such as 'Fishing' (1881), were painted in the naturalistic Barbizon style, a French approach (c.1830–70) popular in America.

Bannister, Sir Roger (Gilbert) (1929–) Athlete and neurologist, born in Harrow, NW Greater London, England, UK. He studied at Oxford, and completed his medical training at St Mary's Hospital, London, in 1954. At an athletics meeting at Iffley Road, Oxford, on 6 May 1954, he became the first man to run the mile in under 4 minutes (3 min 59·4 s), with the help of pacemakers. He was knighted in 1975, and appointed Master of Pembroke College, Oxford, 1985–93. >> Chataway

Banting, Sir Frederick Grant (1891–1941) Physiologist, the discoverer of insulin, born in Alliston, Ontario, Canada. He studied medicine at Toronto University and later became professor there (1923). Working under J J R Macleod, in 1922 he discovered (with his assistant Charles H Best) the hormone insulin, used in the control of diabetes. For this discovery he was jointly awarded, with Macleod, the Nobel Prize for Physiology or Medicine in 1923, voluntarily sharing his own part of the award with Best. He established the Banting Research Foundation in 1924 and the Banting Institute at Toronto in 1930. He was knighted in 1934. >> Best, Charles H; Macleod, J J R

Banville, (Etienne Claude Jean Baptiste) Théodore (Faullain) de [bãveel] (1823–91) Poet and playwright, born in Moulins, France. He was given the title *roi des rimes* (King of Rhymes) for his ingenuity in handling the most difficult forms of verse – the mediaeval ballades and rondels. His *Gringoire* (1866) holds an established place in French repertory.

Bao Dai [bow diy], (Vietnamese 'keeper of greatness'), originally **Nguyen Vinh Thuy** (1913–97) Indo-Chinese ruler, born in Hué, Vietnam, the son of Emperor Khai Dai. He ruled as Emperor of Annam (1932–45), then in 1949, having renounced his hereditary title, returned to Saigon as chief of the State of Vietnam within the French Union. In 1955 he was deposed and South Vietnam became a republic. >> RR1099

Baptist, John the >> John the Baptist, St

Bär, Karl Ernst von >> Baer, Karl Ernst von

Bara, Theda, *née* **Theodosia Goodman**, nickname **the Vamp** (1890–1955) Film actress, born in Cincinnati, OH. She acted briefly in stock companies and then in Hollywood as an extra. Following the creation of the Hollywood studio machine, she was assigned her new name, billed as the daughter of an Eastern potentate, and turned into an overnight star in *A Fool There Was* (1915). She received her nickname because of her screen portrayal of exotic 'man-hungry' women, her famous line 'Kiss me, my fool!', and the

offscreen image she cultivated (such as giving interviews while stroking a snake). She made some 40 movies, mostly by 1919, when she went to New York to become a Broadway actress. Handicapped by her reputation, she was forced to return to Hollywood, where she found tastes had changed. After a few unsuccessful movies, she retired in 1926.

Barabbas [barabas] (1st-c) Political rebel and murderer (as described in *Mark* 15, *Luke* 23), who was arrested but apparently released by popular acclaim in preference to Pilate's offer to release Jesus of Nazareth. He was possibly also called 'Jesus Barabbas' (in some manuscripts of *Matt* 27.16-17). >> Jesus Christ

Baraka, Imamu Amiri, originally **Le Roi Jones** (1934–) Writer and political activist, born in Newark, NJ. He studied at Howard University, travelled widely, and taught at many institutions, notably the State University of New York, Long Island (from 1980). He published a number of works as Le Roi Jones, then became a Muslim and changed his name (1967). Based in Newark, NJ, he has worked as a publisher (1958), and founded a repertory theatre (1965) and a community centre (1966). In addition to his poetry, such as *Reggae or Not!* (1982), he has written plays, short stories, essays, and nonfiction.

Bárány, Robert [baranyuh] (1876–1936) Physician and otologist, born in Vienna. He headed the ear, nose, and throat unit at Uppsala University in Sweden from 1917, and pioneered the study of the balancing apparatus of the inner ear, for which he was awarded the 1914 Nobel Prize for Physiology or Medicine.

Barba, Eugenio (1936–) Italian theatre director and founder of Odin Teatret, an experimental theatre company and centre for collective research in performance. In 1979 he established the International School of Theatre Anthropology. His theoretical writings include *The Floating Islands* (1984), *Beyond the Floating Islands* (1986), and *The Paper Canoe* (1994).

Barbara, St (?–c.200) Christian virgin martyr, the patron saint of artillerymen. According to legend, which seems to have no foundation in historic fact, she was a maiden of great beauty whose father immured her in a tower to discourage suitors. On discovering that she had become a Christian, her father beheaded her, and was instantly struck by lightning. Her emblem is a tower. Feast day 4 December.

Barbarelli, Giorgio >> Giorgione

Barbari, Jacopo de' (c. 1475–c. 1516) Venetian painter and engraver. He worked from 1500 in Germany (where he was known as **Jakob Walch**) and the Netherlands. From 1510 he was court painter at Brussels. He is chiefly noted for his engravings, mainly of mythological figures, which were influential in the development of N European graphic art.

Barbarossa, Frederick I >> Frederick I

Barbarossa [bah(r)barosa], ('Redbeard'), nickname of **Khair-ed-Din** (?–1546) Barbary pirate, born in Mitilini, Greece. With his brothers he became a Turkish corsair, attacking shipping in the Mediterranean. After the execution of his brother Horuk (1518), he captured Algiers (1529) and was made admiral of the Ottoman fleet (1533), conquering Tunisia, and defeating the Holy Roman Emperor (Charles V) at Preveza (1538). >> Charles V (Emperor)

Barbauld, Anna Letitia [bah(r)bawld], *née* **Aikin** (1743–1825) Writer, born in Kibworth-Harcourt, Leicestershire, C England, UK. She married a dissenting minister, Rochemont Barbauld, in 1774, and during the next 10 years published her best work, including *Early Lessons for Children* and *Hymns in Prose for Children*. With her brother she began the well-known series *Evenings at Home* in 1792.

Barber, Chris (1930–) Jazz musician, born in Welwyn Garden City, Hertfordshire, SE England, UK. A trombonist and vocalist, he joined the Ken Colyer band, taking it over in 1954. By the end of the decade the Chris Barber Jazz Band was well established, and had made several hit singles, notably 'Petite Fleur', with soloist Monty Sunshine (1928–). Several successful albums followed, including *Chris Barber Bandbox* and *Best of Chris Barber* (both 1960).

Barber, Samuel (1910–81) Composer, born in West Chester, PA. He studied at the Curtis Institute, Philadelphia, and won the American *Prix de Rome*. His early music includes the overture to *The School for Scandal* (1931) and the popular *Adagio for Strings*, and is in traditional neo-Romantic vein. His later works lay more emphasis on chromaticism and dissonance, and include the *Capricorn Concerto* (1944) and the ballet *Medea* (1946). His first full-length opera *Vanessa* was performed at the Salzburg Festival (1958, Pulitzer), followed by *Antony and Cleopatra* (1966).

Barbera >> **Hanna-Barbera**

Barbie, Klaus, known as **the Butcher of Lyon** (1913–91) Nazi leader, born in Bad Godesberg, Germany. He joined the Hitler Youth in 1931, graduating to the SS, and worked for the Gestapo in the Netherlands, Russia, and finally Lyon, where he sent thousands of people to Auschwitz. After the War, he fled to South America with his family under an assumed name, but was traced by Nazi hunters, and extradited from Bolivia in 1983. He was tried in France on 177 crimes against humanity, found guilty, and sentenced to life imprisonment.

Barbirolli, Sir John (Giovanni Battista) [bah(r)birolee] (1899–1970) Conductor and cellist, born in London, England, UK of French and Italian parents. He served in World War 1, played in several leading string quartets (1920–4), succeeded Toscanini as conductor of the New York Philharmonic (1937), and returned to England as permanent conductor (1943–58) of the Hallé Orchestra in Manchester. In 1939 he married oboist **Evelyn Rothwell** (1911–). He was created a knight in 1949, and awarded the Gold Medal of the Royal Philharmonic Society in 1950. >> Toscanini

Barbo, Praise-God >> **Barebone, Praise-God**

Barbour, John [bah(r)ber] (c.1320–95) Poet, clergyman, and scholar, probably born in Aberdeen, NE Scotland, UK, known as 'the father of Scottish poetry and history'. He was Archdeacon of Aberdeen from 1357, or earlier, till his death. His national epic, *The Brus*, written in the 1370s, is a narrative poem on the life and deeds of King Robert I, the Bruce, preserving many oral traditions. >> Bruce, Robert

Barbusse, Henri [bah(r)büs] (1873–1935) Novelist, born in Asnières, France. A volunteer, he fought in World War 1, which inspired his masterpiece, *Le Feu* (1916, trans Under Fire). Other works include *Le Couteau entre les dents* (1921, The Knife between the Teeth) and *Le Judas de Jésus* (1927). A noted pacifist, he later settled in the Soviet Union.

Barca, Pedro Calderón de la >> **Calderón de la Barca, Pedro**

Barclay, Alexander (c. 1475–1552) Poet and writer, probably born in Scotland, UK. In 1508 he was chaplain of Ottery St Mary, Devon, and perhaps c.1511 became a monk at Ely. His famous poem, *The Shyp of Folys of the Worlde* (1509), is partly a translation and partly an imitation of the German *Das Narrenschiff* (1494, The Ship of Fools) by Sebastian Brant. >> Brant, Sebastian

Barclay, John (1582–1621) Satirical writer, born in Pont-à-Mousson, France. He lived in London and Rome and wrote, mostly in Latin, politico-satirical novels directed against the Jesuits, such as *Euphormio* (1603), and *Argenis* (1621) on allegorical romance.

Barclay, Robert (1648–90) Quaker, born in Gordonstoun, Moray, NE Scotland, UK. He studied at the Scots College in Paris, returning to Scotland (1664), where he became a

Quaker in 1667. He published many tracts in defence of Quakerism, especially *Apology for the True Christian Divinity* (1678). He became one of the proprietors of East New Jersey in 1682, and was appointed its nominal nonresident governor.

Barclay, Robert (1843–1913) British banker, under whom in 1896 the merger of 20 banks took place to form Barclay & Co Ltd. In 1917 the name was changed to Barclay's Bank Ltd.

Barclay, William (1907–78) Theologian, religious writer, and broadcaster, born in Wick, Highland, N Scotland, UK. He studied at the universities of Glasgow and Marburg, and was ordained in the Church of Scotland in 1933. In 1963 he was appointed to the chair of divinity and biblical criticism at Glasgow, from which he retired in 1974. He is remembered for his many popular writings and broadcasts, such as *A New Testament Wordbook* (1955). His *Daily Study Bible* won international acclaim, and in 1968 he published his own translation of the New Testament.

Barclay-Allardice, Robert, known as **Captain Barclay** (1779–1854) Scottish soldier and sportsman, celebrated for walking 1000 mi in 1000 consecutive hours. He succeeded to the estate of Urie in 1797, and joined the army in 1805, before retiring to take up management of his estates. His remarkable walking feat was performed at Newmarket from June to July 1809.

Barclay de Tolly, Mikhail Bogdanovich, Knaz (Prince) [bah(r)kliy duh tolyuh] (1761–1818) Russian soldier of Scottish descent, born in Luhda-Grosshof, Livonia (modern Estonia and Latvia). He entered a Russian regiment in 1786 and gained rapid promotion. In the war against Finland he defeated the Swedes, and forced a surrender by crossing the frozen Gulf of Bothnia in strength (1808). Tsar Alexander I appointed him minister of war in 1810. Forced to give battle to Napoleon at Smolensk (1812), he was defeated and was superseded by Kutuzov. He fought at Borodino (1812), was again promoted commander-in-chief after the Battle of Bautzen (1813), served at Dresden and Leipzig (1813), and took part in the capture of Paris (1814). In 1815 he was made a prince.

Bar-Daisan >> **Bardesanes**

Bardeen, John [bah(r)deen] (1908–91) Physicist, born in Madison, WI. He studied electrical engineering at Wisconsin University, and mathematical physics at Princeton (1936). After World War 2, he joined a new solid-state physics group at Bell Telephone Laboratories, where with Walter Brattain and William Shockley he developed the point-contact transistor (1947), for which they shared the Nobel Prize for Physics in 1956. Professor at Illinois University (1951–75), with Leon Cooper and John Schrieffer he received the Nobel Prize for Physics again in 1972 for the first satisfactory theory of superconductivity (the *Bardeen–Cooper–Schrieffer* or *BCS theory*), thereby becoming the first person to receive the Nobel Prize for Physics twice. >> Brattain; Cooper; Schrieffer; Shockley

Bardesanes [bah(r)desahneez], also called **Bar-Daisan** (154–222) Syrian Christian theologian and poet, born in Urfa, Turkey (formerly Edessa). Known as 'the last of the Gnostics', he wrote numerous hymns, and was the author of *Dialogue of Destiny*, written in Syriac.

Bardot, Brigitte [bah(r)doh], originally **Camille Javal** (1934–) Film actress, born in Paris. A ballet student and model, her appearance on the cover of *Elle* led to her film debut in Jean Boyer's *Le Trou Normand* (1952, Crazy for Love). *Et Dieu créa la femme* (1956, And God Created Woman) established her reputation as a sex kitten. Her roles exploited an image of petulant sexuality that was reinforced by a much publicized off-camera love life. Her many screen credits include *La Verité* (1960, The Truth), *Le Mépris*

(1963, *Contempt*) and *Viva Maria* (1965). She retired from the screen in 1973 and has devoted herself to campaigning for animal rights. >> Vadim

Barebone or **Barbon, Praise-God** (c. 1596–1679) Leather merchant and controversial Anabaptist preacher, born in London. He was nominated by Oliver Cromwell to sit in the Short Parliament of 1653, which was nicknamed after him the Barebone's Parliament. His fiery preaching attracted huge crowds and often occasioned riots. Fiercely opposed to the restoration of Charles II, he was imprisoned in the Tower in 1661–2.

Barenboim, Daniel [ba̱renboym] (1942–) Pianist and conductor, born in Buenos Aires. Educated at Santa Cecilia Academy in Rome, he studied with his father, then with Nadia Boulanger and others. He made his debut with the Israel Philharmonic Orchestra in 1953. A noted exponent of Mozart and Beethoven, he gained his reputation as pianist/conductor with the English Chamber Orchestra. He was musical director of the Orchestre de Paris (1975–87), and musical director-designate of the new Paris Opéra at the Place de la Bastille in 1987. He became musical director of the Chicago Symphony Orchestra in 1991. In 1967 he married the cellist **Jacqueline du Pré** (d.1987). >> Boulanger, Nadia; du Pré

Barents, Willem [ba̱ruhnts], also spelled **Barentz** (?–1597) Dutch navigator. He was pilot to several Dutch expeditions in search of the Northeast Passage, and died off Novaya Zemlya. His winter quarters were found undisturbed in 1871, and in 1875 part of his journal was recovered by another expedition. The *Barents Sea* was named after him.

Barère (de Vieuzac), Bertrand [barair] (1755–1841) Revolutionary and regicide, born in Tarbes, France. He was originally a moderate in the National Convention, but later helped form the Committee of Public Safety, which he defended with great eloquence. After the fall of Robespierre (1794) he was imprisoned, but escaped. He served under Napoleon, was later exiled at the Restoration, but returned to Paris under an amnesty in 1830. >> Robespierre

Barham, Richard (Harris), pseudonym **Thomas Ingoldsby** (1788–1845) Humorist, born in Canterbury, Kent, SE England, UK. He studied at Oxford, was ordained (1813), and in 1821 received a minor canonry of St Paul's Cathedral. In 1837 he began his series of burlesque metrical tales under his pseudonym which, collected under the title of *The Ingoldsby Legends* (3 vols, 1840–7), became popular for their droll humour, irony, and esoteric learning.

Bar-Hebraeus >> **Abu al-Faraj**

Barke, James (1905–58) Novelist, born in Torwoodlee, Scottish Borders, SE Scotland, UK. His novels include *The World his Pillow* (1933) and *The Land of the Leal* (1939), but he is chiefly remarkable for his devoted research on the life of Robert Burns, resulting in a five-volume cycle of novels (1946–54), an edition of *Poems and Songs of Robert Burns* (1955), and the posthumous *Bonnie Jean*, about Burns and Jean Armour. >> Burns, Robert

Barker, Sir Ernest (1874–1960) Political scientist, born in Cheshire, NWC England, UK. He studied at Oxford, and was fellow of several Oxford Colleges before becoming principal of King's College, London (1920–7), and professor of political science and fellow of Peterhouse, Cambridge (1928–39). His works include *Reflections on Government* (1942) and *Principles of Social and Political Theory* (1951).

Barker, George Granville (1913–91) Poet, born in Loughton, Essex, SE England, UK. He lived abroad, teaching at universities in the USA and Japan, but has lived mainly by his writing. He published his first book of poetry in 1933, his early career suffering by comparison with his contemporary Dylan Thomas. He wrote prolifically in the following decades, a major work being *The True Confession of George Barker* (1950). He also published essays, plays, scripts, and novels, and his *Collected Poems* appeared in 1987. >> Thomas, Dylan

Barker, Harley Granville >> **Granville-Barker, Harley**

Barker, Howard (1946–) Playwright, born in London, England, UK. He studied history at the University of Sussex. His first play, *Cheek*, was produced at the Royal Court Theatre in London in 1970. He has since written over 20 plays, including *Stripwell* (1975), *Victory* (1983), *The Power of the Dog* (1984), and *The Possibilities* (1988). Later works include *A Hard Heart* (1992) and *The Europeans* (1993).

Barker, Ronnie, popular name of **Ronald William George Barker** (1929–) Comic actor, born in Bedford, Bedfordshire, SC England, UK. An amateur performer, he made his professional debut at Aylesbury Repertory Theatre in *Quality Street* (1948). An affable figure, adept at precisely detailed characterizations, tongue-twisting comic lyrics, and saucy humour, his many radio and television appearances include *The Frost Report* (1966–7), the widely popular *Porridge* (1974–7), *Open All Hours* (1976, 1981–5) and, in partnership with Ronnie Corbett, the long-running *The Two Ronnies* (1971–87). His film roles include *Wonderful Things* (1958), *Robin and Marian* (1976), and *Porridge* (1979). He retired in 1987 and his autobiography, *Dancing in the Moonlight*, appeared in 1993. >> Corbett, Ronnie

Barkhausen, Heinrich Georg [bah(r)khowzen] (1881–1956) Physicist, born in Bremen, Germany. In 1911 he was appointed professor of low current technology in the Technische Hochschule, Dresden, and in 1928 was awarded the Heinrich Herz Medal. In 1919 he discovered that the magnetization of iron proceeds in discrete steps and devised a loudspeaker system to render this discontinuity audible (the *Barkhausen effect*).

Barkla, Charles Glover [bah(r)kla] (1877–1944) Physicist, born in Widnes, Lancashire, NW England, UK. He became professor of physics at London (1909–13) and of natural philosophy at Edinburgh (1913–44). He conducted notable research into X-rays and other short-wave emissions, and was awarded the 1917 Nobel Prize for Physics.

Barkley, Alben W(illiam) [bah(r)klee] (1877–1956) US vice-president (1949–53) and legislator, born in Lowes, KY. As a representative and senator, he backed the wartime administrations of Woodrow Wilson and Franklin Roosevelt. In 1949, under Harry Truman, he was the oldest vice-president to take office, and as 'the Veep' became something of a humorous figure. >> Truman

bar Kokhba, Simon [kokhba], also spelled **bar Kochba** (?–135) Jewish leader in Palestine. With the rabbi Akiba ben Joseph, he led a rebellion of Jews in Judaea from 132 in response to the founding of a Roman colony (Aelia Capitolina) in Jerusalem. It was suppressed by Hadrian with ruthless severity, and he was killed at the Battle of Bethar. >> Akiba ben Joseph; Hadrian

Barlach, Ernst [bah(r)lak] (1870–1938) Expressionist sculptor, playwright, and poet, born in Wedel, Germany. He was identified with the German Expressionist school of both art and drama. While he was best known as a sculptor in wood, his greatest achievement was his war memorial at Güstrow Cathedral, a great bronze 'Angel of Death', which was removed by Hitler as 'degenerate'. Barlach's plays include *Der tote Tag* (1912, The Dead Day) and *Der Findling* (1922, The Foundling).

Barlow, Joel (1754–1812) Poet and politician, born in Redding, CT. He served as military chaplain during the War of Independence, and became US consul at Algiers and ambassador to France in 1811. His *Columbiad* (1807) is a historical review of events from the time of Columbus to the French Revolution. His best-known work is the mock-heroic poem, 'Hasty Pudding' (1796).

Barlow, Peter (1776–1862) Physicist, born in Norwich, Norfolk, E England, UK. His *New Mathematical Tables* (1814) were reprinted as late as 1947 as *Barlow's Tables*. He also worked on the strength of ship's timbers, on tidal engineering, and on ship's magnetism and its correction. The *Barlow lens* is an achromatic lens used as an astronomical eyepiece and in photography.

Barna, Victor, originally **Győző Braun** (1911–72) Table tennis player, born in Budapest. He won a record 20 English titles between 1931 and 1953, including five singles titles (1933–5, 1937–8), and also won 15 world titles, including five singles (1930, 1932–5). One of the game's greatest players, he emigrated to France before becoming a British citizen in 1938. After retirement, he played exhibitions and formed the Swaythling Club, a social club for ex-table tennis internationals.

Barnabas [**bah**nuhbuhs] (1st-c) Christian missionary, originally a Levite from Cyprus called Joseph (*Acts* 4.36). He was a companion and supporter of Paul during Paul's early ministry to the Gentiles, but later separated from him after a dispute over John Mark (*Acts* 15.36) and went to Cyprus. The so-called *Letter of Barnabas* is a spurious 2nd-c work.

Barnard, Christiaan (Neethling) (1922–) Surgeon, born in Beaufort West, South Africa. He graduated from Cape Town medical school, and after research in America returned to Cape Town in 1958 to work on open-heart surgery and organ transplantation. In December 1967 at Groote Schuur Hospital he performed the first successful human heart transplant. The recipient, Louis Washkansky, died of pneumonia 18 days later, drugs given to prevent tissue rejection having heightened the risk of infection. A second patient, Philip Blaiberg, operated on in January 1968, survived for 594 days. Barnard retired in 1983.

Barnard, Edward (Emerson) (1857–1923) Astronomer, born in Nashville, TN. He made a systematic photographic survey of the sky and correctly concluded that those areas apparently devoid of stars, which he called 'black nebulae', were in fact clouds of obscuring matter. He discovered the fifth satellite of Jupiter in 1892. In 1916 he discovered the star which has the greatest known motion relative to other stars (*Barnard's star*). >> Wolf, Max

Barnard, Marjorie Faith, pseudonym **M Barnard Eldershaw** (1897–1987) Novelist, historian, and biographer, born in Sydney, New South Wales, Australia. She studied at Sydney University and became librarian at the Commonwealth Scientific and Industrial Research Organization. She wrote many books in conjunction with **Flora Sydney Patricia Eldershaw** (1897–1956) under their joint pseudonym. Best known are *A House is Built* (1929) and the anti-Utopian novel *Tomorrow and Tomorrow* (1947, eventually published in unexpurgated form in 1983). Her substantial *A History of Australia* (1962) was also a popular work.

Barnardo, Thomas John [bah(r)**nah**(**r**)doh] (1845–1905) Physician and philanthropist, the founder of homes for destitute children, born in Dublin. A clerk by profession, he was converted to Christianity in 1862 and, after a period spent preaching in the Dublin slums, moved to London in 1866 to study medicine with the aim of becoming a medical missionary. Instead he founded in 1867, while still a student, the East End Mission for destitute children in Stepney and a number of homes in Greater London, which came to be known as the *Dr Barnardo's Homes*.

Barnato, Barney [bah(r)**nah**toh], originally **Barnett Isaacs** (1852–97) Financier and speculator, born in London, England, UK. He went out to Kimberley, South Africa, with a small circus in 1873, made a fortune in diamonds there, and engineered the Kaffir boom in mining stocks (1895).

Barnave, Antoine (Pierre Joseph Marie) [bah(r)nahv] (1761–93) French revolutionary, born in Grenoble, France. He brought back the royal family from their abortive flight to Varennes (1791), but subsequently developed royalist sympathies, advocated a constitutional monarchy, and was guillotined.

Barnes, Djuna (1892–1982) Writer and illustrator, born in Cornwall-on-Hudson, NY. She began her career as a reporter and illustrator for magazines, then became a writer of one-act plays and short stories, published in a variety of magazines and anthologies. Her works include the novel *Nightwood* (1936) and a blank-verse tragedy *The Antiphon* (1958).

Barnes, Ernest William (1874–1953) Anglican clergyman, born in Birmingham, West Midlands, C England, UK. He studied at Cambridge where, as one of the most outstanding mathematical scholars of his time, he became a lecturer in 1902. He was ordained in 1908, became Master of the Temple in 1915, and Bishop of Birmingham in 1924. His strongly-held modernist and pacifist views involved him in continued controversy within the Church of England.

Barnes, John (Charles Bryan) (1963–) Footballer, born in Kingston, Jamaica. He played for Watford, moving to Liverpool in 1988, and to Newcastle in 1997. By early 1997 he had won 79 caps playing for England

Barnes, Julian (1946–) Novelist, born in Leicester, Leicestershire, C England, UK. He began as a contributor to *New Review*, for which he wrote the infamous 'Edward Pygge' gossip column. Several of his books show the influence of Flaubert. His novels include *Metroland* (1981), *Flaubert's Parrot* (1984), *A History of the World in 10½ Chapters* (1989), and *The Porcupine* (1992).

Barnes, Peter (1931–) Playwright and writer of screenplays, born in London, England, UK. His only major commercial success has been *The Ruling Class* (1968). Later plays, which include *The Bewitched* (1974), *Laughter* (1978), *Red Noses* (1985), and *Sunset and Glories* (1990), show him to be a master of non-naturalistic techniques drawn from Elizabethan theatre, mediaeval and 19th-c farce, German Expressionist drama, and the *commedia dell'arte*. Other plays include *Lunar Park Eclipsis* (1995) and *Corpsing* (1996).

Barnes, Thomas (1785–1841) Editor and journalist, born in London, England, UK. He studied at Cambridge, became dramatic critic of *The Times* in 1809, and editor in 1817, a post which he held for 24 years. During his editorship *The Times* became known as 'the Thunderer'.

Barnes, William (1801–86) Pastoral poet, born in Sturminster Newton, Dorset, S England, UK. He taught in a school at Dorchester, then went to Cambridge and took holy orders. He became curate of Whitcombe in 1847, and rector of Winterborne Came, Dorset, in 1862. His three volumes of poetry were collected in 1879 as *Poems of Rural Life in the Dorset Dialect*. He also wrote several philological works.

Barnett, Samuel A(ugustus) (1844–1913) Anglican clergyman and social reformer, born in Bristol, SW England, UK. He studied at Oxford, and in 1873 went to a Whitechapel parish where his sympathy with the poor of London was aroused. In 1884 he founded Toynbee Hall in Whitechapel, and went on to advocate other educational reforms, poor relief measures, and universal pensions. In 1894 he became Canon of Bristol, and from 1906 was Canon of Westminster. >> Toynbee

Barneveldt, Jan van Olden [bah(r)nevelt] (1547–1619) Dutch statesman and lawyer, born in Amersfoort, The Netherlands. As adviser to Prince Maurice, he opposed his warlike schemes and in 1609 concluded a truce with Spain. This caused a political rift which eventually resulted in his being represented as a secret friend of Spain. He was illegally arrested, condemned as a traitor, and executed. >> Maurice (Prince of Orange)

Barney, Natalie (Clifford) (1876–1972) Socialite and writer, born in Dayton, OH. Born into a wealthy family, she was educated in France and New York City (1894), before settling in Paris (1898), where she established an international salon at her home. She wrote poetry, plays, and novels, and became notorious for her love affairs with women. Her memoirs include *Souvenirs indiscrets* (1960, Indiscreet Memories) and *Traits et portraits* (1963).

Barnum, P(hineas) T(aylor) (1810–91) Showman, born in Bethel, CT. He ran a museum in New York City, introducing freak shows, and in 1842 sponsored the famous dwarf 'General Tom Thumb' (Charles Stratton), using flamboyant publicity. He managed the US tour of Jenny Lind in 1847, and in 1881 joined with his rival **James Anthony Bailey** (1847–1906) to found the famous Barnum and Bailey circus. >> Lind, Jenny; Stratton

Barocci or **Baroccio, Federigo** [barochee] (c. 1528–1612) Painter, born in Urbino, Italy. In 1548 he went to Rome and fell under the influence of Correggio. He later developed a very personal colour scheme of vivid reds and yellows, and his fluent pictorial style had considerable influence on Rubens and his school. His 'Madonna del Popolo' is in the Uffizi Gallery, Florence. >> Correggio; Rubens

Baroja (y Nessi), Pío [baroha] (1872–1956) Writer, born in San Sebastián, Spain. He wrote more than 70 volumes of novels and essays, distinguished by quiet humour and a vivid style derived from the 19th-c Russian and French masters. His best novels are those with a Basque setting.

Baronius, Caesar [baronius], originally **Cesare Baronio** (1538–1607) Church historian, born in Sora, Italy. He was one of the first pupils of St Philip Neri, and attached himself to his Congregation of the Oratory, becoming its superior in 1593. He wrote the first critical Church history, the *Annales Ecclesiastici* (1588–1607). He became a cardinal in 1596, and was made Vatican librarian. >> Neri

Barr, Alfred H (1902–81) US museum director. He became director of the Museum of Modern Art in New York City (1929–43). Under his leadership the museum staged a number of controversial exhibitions in the 1930s and 1940s, which provided openings for such designers as Philip Johnson, Eliot Noyes, Charles Eames, and Eero Saarinen. >> Eames; Johnson, Philip; Noyes, Eliot; Saarinen, Eero

Barras, Paul François Jean Nicolas, comte de (Count of) [bara] (1755–1829) French revolutionary, born in Foxemphoux, France. An original member of the Jacobin Club, he voted for the king's execution. He conducted the siege of Toulon, and suppressed the revolt in the S of France. Hated by Robespierre, he played the chief part in the tyrant's overthrow, and was appointed virtual dictator by the terrified Convention. In 1795, faced with a royalist rising, he called his young friend Napoleon to his aid, who assured his own future with the historical 'whiff of grapeshot'. The Directory being appointed, Barras was nominated one of the five members. Once more dictator in 1797, he guided the state almost alone, until his covetousness had rendered him so unpopular that Napoleon overthrew him easily in the coup of 18 Brumaire (9 Nov) 1799. >> Napoleon; Robespierre; Tallien

Barrault, Jean-Louis [baroh] (1910–94) Actor and producer, born in Le Vesinet, France. He was a member of the Comédie Française (1940–6), then with his actress wife,

Madeleine Renaud (1903–), founded his own company, le Troupe Marigny, which became celebrated for its performances of Molière, Claudel, and the Gide translation of *Hamlet*. He became director of the Théâtre de France (1959–68), the Théâtre des Nations (1965–7, 1972–4), and first director of the Théâtre d'Orsay (1974). His films include *La Symphonie fantastique* (1942), *Les Enfants du paradis* (1945, The Children of Paradise), *La Ronde* (1950), and *The Longest Day* (1962). His theories of dramatic art are expressed in his autobiographical *Réflexions sur le théâtre* (1949, Reflections on the Theatre).

Barre, Raymond (1924–) French statesman and prime minister (1976–81), born in St Denis, Réunion. He made his reputation as an influential neo-liberal economist at the Sorbonne and as vice-president of the European Commission (1967–72). He was minister of foreign trade under President Giscard d'Estaing, and was appointed prime minister after the resignation of Jacques Chirac. During the 1980s he built up a firm political base in the Lyon region, representing the centre–right Union for French Democracy. He contested the 1988 presidential election, but was eliminated in the first ballot. >> Chirac; Giscard d'Estaing; RR1049

Barré, (Mohammed) Siad [baray] (1919–95) Somali soldier and president (1969–91). Educated at a military academy in Italy, he served as a police officer in the British and Italian trust administrations (1941–50). He joined the Somali army as a colonel in 1960, and became president after a military coup. Towards the end of his rule, the country broke up into warring factions, and he was deposed, leaving behind civil war, famine, and an international crisis in which many aid agencies, the UN, and the USA became involved. >> RR1088

Barrès, (Auguste) Maurice [bares] (1862–1923) Politician and novelist, born in Charmes-sur-Moselle, France. A member of the Chamber of Deputies (1889–93), he was an apostle of nationalism, individualism, provincial patriotism, and national energy. He wrote a trilogy on his own self-analysis (*Le Culte du Moi*, 1888–91), a nationalistic trilogy that included *L'Appel du Soldat* (1906), and many other works, including *Colette Baudoche* (1909).

Barrie, Sir J(ames) M(atthew) (1860–1937) Novelist and playwright, born in Kirriemuir, Angus, E Scotland, UK. He studied at Edinburgh University, then wrote a series of autobiographical novels, and from 1890 wrote for the theatre, beginning with the successful *Walker, London* (1893), *Quality Street* (1902), *The Admirable Crichton* (1902), and *What Every Woman Knows* (1908), which established his reputation. It is, however, as the creator of *Peter Pan* (1904) that he will be chiefly remembered. An unfailing romantic, he continued his excursions into fairyland in such later plays as *Dear Brutus* (1917) and *Mary Rose* (1920).

Barrington, George, originally **George Waldron** (1755–1804) Writer and adventurer, born in Maynooth, Co Kildare, Ireland. In London he turned pickpocket, and was transported to Botany Bay (1790). Set free in 1792, he rose to the position of high constable of Parramatta, New South Wales, and published historical works on Australia.

Barrington, Sir Jonah (1760–1834) Judge, politician, and memorialist, born in Abbeyleix, Co Laois, Ireland. He studied at Trinity College, Dublin, was called to the Irish bar in 1788, and became MP for various constituencies. He became involved in intricate political manoeuvres and was gradually overwhelmed by debts, resulting in his disgrace and dismissal in 1830. After settling in France, he wrote *The Rise and Fall of the Irish Nation* (1833) and *Personal Sketches of his own Time* (3 vols, 1827–32).

Barrington, Ken(neth Frank) (1930–81) Cricketer, born in Reading, Berkshire, S England, UK. First capped in 1955, he did not return to Test cricket until 1959, when he became a permanency, playing in 82 Tests, and making a total of 6806 runs for an average of 58·67. He scored 20 Test centuries, including 256 against Australia at Old Trafford in 1964. He retired early from top-class cricket because of ill health, and died in Barbados during the England tour of the West Indies while acting as assistant manager. >> RR1150

Barron, James (1768–1851) Naval officer, probably born in Norfolk, VA. After youthful service in the Revolution, he became a lieutenant in the US navy (1798). Commanding the USS *Chesapeake* in its disastrous fight with the British *Leopold* (1807), he was court-martialled and found guilty of negligence. After five years with the French navy, he returned to the US navy. Convinced that Stephen Decatur was leading an effort to block his career, he challenged and killed Decatur in a duel (1820). Despised by most in the navy, he remained on inactive status until his death. >> Decatur

Barros, João de (1496–1570) Historian, born in Viseu, Portugal. Governor of Portuguese Guinea, he is known for his monumental *Decades* (1552–1615), the history of the Portuguese in the East Indies, which earned him the title of the 'Portuguese Livy'.

Barrow, Clyde >> **Bonnie and Clyde**

Barrow, Errol Walton (1920–87) Barbadian politician and prime minister (1961–76, 1986–7), born in Barbados. He flew in the Royal Air Force (1940–7), then studied at London University and Lincoln's Inn. Returning to Barbados he was elected to the House of Assembly in 1951, co-founding the Democratic Labour Party (DLP). In the elections following independence (1961) the DLP was victorious, and he became the first prime minister. >> RR1035

Barrow, Isaac (1630–77) Mathematician and theologian, born in London, England, UK. He studied at Trinity College, Cambridge, where he became a fellow in 1649. He was professor of geometry at Gresham College, London (1662), and the first Lucasian professor of mathematics at Cambridge (1663), but resigned in 1669 to make way for Isaac Newton. He founded the library of Trinity College, Cambridge, where he became Master in 1673. >> Newton, Isaac

Barrow, Sir John (1764–1848) Naval administrator and traveller, born in Dragley Beck, Lancashire, NW England, UK. He worked on a whaler in Greenland waters, taught mathematics at a school in Greenwich, and in 1792 was appointed private secretary to Lord Macartney, the British envoy to China. As second secretary to the Admiralty (1804–45), he promoted Arctic expeditions by Sir John Ross, Sir James Clark Ross, and Sir John Franklin. *Barrow Strait* and *Point Barrow* in the Arctic, and *Cape Barrow* in the Antarctic, were named in his honour, as was the northern duck, *Barrow's goldeneye*. >> Franklin, John; Ross, James Clark; Ross, John

Barr Smith, Robert (1824–1915) Pastoralist and wool-broking pioneer, born in Lochwinnoch, Renfrewshire, W Scotland, UK. He studied at Glasgow University, then settled in South Australia in 1854, where he joined the company established by a fellow Scot, Thomas Elder. The two men went into partnership under the style of Elder, Smith & Co to become one of the world's largest wool-brokers, with extensive pastoral holdings. Closely involved for many years with Adelaide University, he established the library there which bears his name. >> Elder, Thomas

Barry, comtesse du >> **du Barry, comtesse**

Barry, Sir Charles (1795–1860) Architect, born in London, England, UK. He was apprenticed to a firm of surveyors before going to Italy (1817–20). On his return, he designed the Travellers' Club (1831), the Manchester Athenaeum (1836), the Reform Club (1837), and the new Palace of Westminster (Houses of Parliament, 1840–70), completed after his death by his son **Edward Middleton Barry** (1830–80). His work showed the influence of the Italian Renaissance. His fifth son, **Sir John Wolfe-Barry** (1836–1918), was engineer of the Tower Bridge and Barry Docks.

Barry, James (1741–1806) Historical painter, born in Cork, Co Cork, Ireland. He studied in Italy (1766–70), and in 1782 was appointed professor of painting at the Royal Academy, from which his irritable temper brought about his expulsion (1799). His most celebrated paintings are 'Adam and Eve' (1771) and 'Venus Rising from the Waves' (1772).

Barry, John (1745–1803) US naval officer, born in Co Wexford, Ireland. He went to sea early and settled in Philadelphia by 1760. An ardent patriot, he became a Continental Navy captain, and commanded the USS *Lexington* and *Effingham* (1776–8). He took the Marquis de Lafayette back to France after the victory at Yorktown (1781), and captured numerous British vessels in 1782. After the Revolution, he worked in the merchant trade before being recalled to the naval service in 1794, becoming the senior captain in the navy, and commanding all US ships in the West Indies (1798–9). He returned to Philadelphia in 1801, and remained the senior naval officer until his death.

Barrymore, Ethel, originally **Ethel Blythe** (1879–1959) Actress, born in Philadelphia, PA, the sister of Lionel and John Barrymore. In 1897–8 she scored a great success in London with Sir Henry Irving in *The Bells*, and continued to make noteworthy appearances for over 40 years. She also acted in films, notably *None But the Lonely Heart* (1944, Oscar), as well as in radio and television. >> Barrymore, John/Lionel

Barrymore, John, originally **John Blythe**, known as **the Great Profile** (1882–1942) Actor, born in Philadelphia, PA, the younger brother of Ethel and Lionel Barrymore. He made his name in Shakespearean roles, his *Hamlet* being particularly famous, but he was also known for his turbulent personal life. His classical nose and distinguished features won him his nickname, which was the title of the last film in which he appeared (1940). >> Barrymore, Ethel/Lionel

Barrymore, Lionel, originally **Lionel Blythe** (1878–1954) Actor, born in Philadelphia, PA, the elder brother of Ethel and John Barrymore. He made a name for himself in *Peter Ibbetson* (1917) and *The Copperhead* (1918), thereafter taking many roles in films and radio plays, notably *Free Soul* (1931, Oscar), *Grand Hotel*, *Captains Courageous* (1937), and *Duel in the Sun* (1947). In the USA he played Scrooge annually for many years on radio. After twice accidentally breaking a hip he was confined to a wheelchair, but undeterred he scored a great success as Dr Gillespie in the original *Dr Kildare* film series. >> Barrymore, Ethel/John

Barstow, Dame Josephine (Clare) (1940–) Soprano, born in Sheffield, South Yorkshire, N England, UK. She studied at Birmingham University and the London Opera Centre (1965–66), making her debut with Opera for All (1964). Resident principal with Sadlers Wells (1967–8) and the Welsh National Opera (1968–70), she made her Covent Garden debut in 1969 and her US debut in 1977. She continues to perform with major opera houses around the world, and was made a dame in 1995.

Barstow, Stan(ley) (1928–) Novelist, born in Horbury, West Yorkshire, N England, UK. Raised in a working-class environment, he began work in the engineering industry. He achieved immediate success with his first novel, *A Kind of Loving* (1960), which was later adapted for film and stage. He was among a number of contemporary writers who depicted the realities of working-class life during the l950s and 1960s. Later novels include *A Brother's Tale* (1980), *Just you Wait and See* (1986), *Next of Kin* (1991), and *In My Own Good Time* (1996).

Bart, Jean >> **Barth, Jean**

Bart, Lionel (1930–) Composer and lyricist, born in London, England, UK. In 1959, *Lock Up Your Daughters* ended the US domination of the musical theatre in London. He followed it with *Fings Ain't Wot They Used T'be* (1959), *Oliver* (1960, adapted from Dickens's *Oliver Twist*), and *Blitz!* (1962), a cavalcade of East End life during the Second World War. *Maggie May*, a between-the-wars story of a Liverpool prostitute, followed in 1964, but his Robin Hood musical, *Twang!* (1965), was a flop, as was *La Strada* (1969).

Barth, Heinrich [bah(r)t] (1821–65) Explorer, born in Hamburg, Germany. After studying archaeology at Berlin, in 1849 he was appointed by the British government to a mission to C Africa to supress slavery. He continued his explorations on his own, travelling nearly 12 000 mi. Afterwards he was appointed professor of geography at Berlin University.

Barth, John (Simmons) (1930–) Novelist and short-story writer, born in Cambridge, MD. He studied at Johns Hopkins University, and was a professional drummer before turning to literature and teaching. Much admired by academic critics, his novels include *The Floating Opera* (1956), *Giles Goat-Boy* (1966), *Tidewater Tales* (1987), and *The Last Voyage of Somebody the Sailor* (1991).

Barth or **Bart, Jean** [bah(r)t] (1650–1702) Privateer, born in Dunkirk, France. He served first in the Dutch navy, but on the outbreak of war with Holland joined the French service. In 1691, in command of a small squadron in the North Sea, he destroyed many English vessels. In 1694, after a desperate struggle with a superior Dutch fleet, he recaptured a convoy of 96 ships and brought them to Dunkirk. Soon after he was taken prisoner and carried to Plymouth, but escaped in a fishing-boat to France. King Louis XIV received him with distinction at Versailles, and in 1697 appointed him to the command of a squadron.

Barth, Karl [bah(r)t] (1886–1968) Theologian, born in Basel, Switzerland. He studied at Bern, Berlin, Tübingen, and Marburg. While pastor at Safenwil, Aargau, he wrote a commentary on St Paul's Epistle to the Romans (1919) which established his theological reputation. He became professor at Göttingen (1921), Münster (1925), and Bonn (1930), refused to take an unconditional oath to Hitler, was dismissed, and so became professor at Basel (1935–62). His theology emphasized the finiteness of man, and God's unquestionable authority and 'otherness'. His many works include the monumental *Kirchliche Dogmatik* (4 vols, 1932–67, Church Dogmatics, incomplete).

Barthélemy Saint-Hilaire, Jules [bah(r)taylemee sãtilair] (1805–95) French statesman and scholar, born in Paris. He was co-founder of the journal *Le Bons Sens* (1830), became professor at the Collège de France, and produced a massive 35-volume translation of Aristotle (1833–95). He became a member of the Chamber of Deputies in 1848, and was foreign minister (1880–1).

Barthelme, Donald (1931–89) Novelist and short-story writer, born in Philadelphia, PA. He worked as a journalist and magazine editor before turning to fiction. Associated with the avant-garde movement of the 1960s, he was an experimentalist who rejected the traditions of the conventional novel form, as seen in *Snow White* (1967), *The Dead Father* (1975), and *Paradise* (1986). He also published many short stories.

Barthes, Roland (Gérard) [bah(r)t] (1915–80) Writer, critic, and teacher, born in Cherbourg, France. After researching and teaching he began to write, and his collection of essays entitled *Le Degré zéro de l'écriture* (1953, trans Writing Degree Zero) immediately established him as France's leading critic of Modernist literature. His literary criticism avoided the traditional value judgments and investigation of the author's intentions, addressing itself instead to analysis of the text as a system of signs whose underlying structure forms the 'meaning' of the work as a whole. For 16 years he was a member of the faculty of the Ecole Pratique des Hautes Etudes in Paris, and from 1976 was professor of literary semiology at the Collège de France, gaining international recognition as a developer of semiology and structuralism.

Bartholdi, (Frédéric) Auguste [bah(r)**thol**dee], Fr [bah(r)-toldee] (1834–1904) Sculptor, born in Colmar, France. He specialized in enormous monuments, such as the 'Lion of Belfort', and created the colossal bronze Statue of Liberty, 'Liberty Enlightening the World', in New York harbour, unveiled in 1886.

Bartholin, Thomas >> **Rudbeck, Olof**

Bartholomé, Paul Albert [bah(r)tolomay] (1848–1928) Sculptor, born in Thiverval, France. He is best known for the group of statuary inspired by his wife's death, 'Aux morts' (1895), and for the monument to Rousseau in the Panthéon.

Bartholomew, John George (1860–1920) Cartographer, born in Edinburgh, EC Scotland, UK. He studied at Edinburgh, then entered his father's firm. His works include the *Survey Atlas of Scotland* (1895–1912) and a *Physical Atlas of the World* (2 vols, 1889–1911). He is best known for his system of layer colouring of contours.

Bartlett, Sir Frederic (Charles) (1886–1969) Psychologist, born in Stow-on-the-Wold, Gloucestershire, SWC England, UK. Professor of experimental psychology at Cambridge (1931–52), he wrote on practical (ergonomic) problems in applied psychology, but is best-known for his pioneering cognitive approach to understanding human memory.

Bartlett, John (1820–1905) Publisher and bookseller, born in Plymouth, MA. He was for many years owner of the University Book Store at Harvard (1849–63). He is best known as the compiler of *Bartlett's Familiar Quotations* (1855).

Bartlett, Josiah (1729–95) Physician and US governor, born in Amesbury, MA. A self-taught physician in Kingston, NH (1750–79), he reformed medical diagnosis and treatment. A member of the Continental Congress (1775–6, 1778–9), he signed the Declaration of Independence, afterwards serving as common pleas judge. Chief justice of the state superior court (1788–90), he was New Hampshire's first governor (1790–4).

Bartók, Béla [**bah(r)**tok] (1881–1945) Composer, born in Nagyszentmiklós, Hungary. He studied in Pressburg and at the Budapest Academy of Music, then toured widely as a pianist. He first collected folksongs in 1904, discovering a treasury of national material, which he recorded and classified. From 1907 he was professor of piano at the Budapest Academy, a post relinquished only in 1934 in order to devote more time to ethnomusicological research. He left Hungary in 1939, and settled in the USA. His works include the opera *Duke Bluebeard's Castle*, the ballets *The Wooden Prince* and *The Miraculous Mandarin*, two violin and three piano concertos, orchestral music including the *Concerto for Orchestra*, chamber music including six string quartets, works for violin and piano, songs, choruses, and folksong arrangements.

Bartolommeo, Fra [bah(r)tolo**may**oh], originally **Baccio della Porta** (1472–1517) Painter, leading artist of the High Renaissance, born near Florence, Italy. Under the influence of Savonarola he publicly burnt many of his paintings and in 1500 became a Dominican novice, but Raphael's visit to

Florence in 1504 encouraged him to take up painting again. He worked in Venice (1507), then in Florence (c.1509–12), before going to Rome. His work is distinguished by controlled composition, delicate drawing, and the use of colour. >> Raphael; Savonarola

Bartolozzi, Francesco [bah(r)tolotsee] (1727–1815) Engraver, born in Florence, Italy. He settled in London to become engraver to George III, and in 1802 was superintendent of the Royal Academy of Engravers in Lisbon. His prints, said to be more numerous than those of any engraver, include line engravings and stippled works, printed in brown and red, called *Bartolozzi red*.

Bartolus [bah(r)tohlus], Latin name of **Bartolo di Sassoferrato** (c.1314–57) Jurist and judge, born in Venatura, Italy. Professor at Pisa and Perugia, he was the leader of the school of commentators on Roman law who sought to derive principles of general application which could be used to solve contemporary problems. He was also a founder of international private law.

Barton, Clara, popular name of **Clarissa Harlowe Barton** (1821–1912) Founder of the American Red Cross, born in Oxford, MA. She worked as a schoolteacher (1836–54), and during the Civil War (1861–5) helped to obtain supplies and comforts for the wounded. In Europe, she worked for the International Red Cross in the Franco-Prussian War (1870–1), and established the US branch of the Red Cross in 1881, becoming its first president (1881–1904). As a result of her campaigning, the USA signed the Geneva Convention in 1882.

Barton, Sir Derek (Harold Richard) (1918–) Organic chemist, born in Gravesend, Kent, SE England, UK. He studied at Imperial College, London, and was professor there for over 20 years, before moving in 1985 to Texas A & M University. He introduced conformational analysis as a method for studying the shape of organic molecules and the effect of shape on reactivity, and shared the Nobel Prize for Chemistry in 1969. >> RR1123

Barton, Sir Edmund (1849–1920) Australian statesman and jurist, the first prime minister of the Australian Commonwealth (1901–3), born in Sydney, New South Wales, Australia. He was leader of the Federation movement from 1896, headed the committee that drafted the Commonwealth constitution bill, and led the delegation that presented it to the British parliament in 1900. >> RR1033

Barton, Elizabeth, known as **the Maid of Kent** or **the Nun of Kent** (?1506–34) Prophet, born in Kent, SE England, UK. A domestic servant in Aldington, she began to go into trances and make prophetic utterances against the authorities after an illness in 1525. She denounced Henry VIII's divorce and marriage to Anne Boleyn, was charged with treason, and hanged at Tyburn. >> Henry VIII

Barton, Frances >> **Abington, Fanny**

Barton, Gordon Page (1929–) Transport entrepreneur and Australian politician, born in Surabaya, Java. He studied at Sydney University, and purchased the Interstate Parcel Express Company which formed the base for the international Ipec and Skypac freight and courier network, becoming managing director in 1962. An interest in progressive politics led to his forming the Liberal Reform Group, which later became the Australia Party.

Barton, John (1928–) Stage director, born in London, England, UK. He studied at King's College, Cambridge, where he was a fellow (1954–60), and joined the Royal Shakespeare Company at Stratford-upon-Avon in 1960, where he became associate director (1964–91). He wrote and directed *The Hollow Crown* (1961), an anthology about English monarchs, and is the author of *Playing Shakespeare* (1984), based on the television series he made in 1982.

Bartram, John (1699–1777) Botanist, born near Darby, PA. Self-taught, he built up an unrivalled collection of North American plants in a garden near Philadelphia, and was called by Linnaeus 'the greatest natural botanist in the world'. His son, **William** (1739–1823), was also a naturalist. >> Linnaeus

Baruch [barukh] (7th–6th-c BC) Biblical character, described as the companion and secretary of the prophet Jeremiah (*Jer* 36), possibly of a wealthy family. His name became attached to several Jewish works of much later date, known as: 1 Baruch (the Book of Baruch); 2 (the Syriac Apocalypse of) Baruch; and 3 (the Greek Apocalypse of) Baruch. There is also a Christian Apocalypse of Baruch in Ethiopic.

Baruch, Bernard (Mannes) (1870–1965) Financier and US statesman, born in Camden, SC. Educated in New York City, he began life as an office boy, but made a fortune by speculation. He became a powerful political influence – 'the adviser of presidents' and of Churchill in World War 2. >> Churchill, Sir Winston

Bary, Heinrich Anton de >> **de Bary, Heinrich Anton**

Baryshnikov, Mikhail Nikolaievich [barishnikof] (1948–) Dancer, born in Riga, Latvia. He trained at the Riga Choreography School, then with the Kirov Ballet in St Petersburg. In 1974 he defected to the West while on tour in Canada, joining the American Theater Ballet, and later the New York City Ballet, where he worked with George Balanchine. He returned to American Theater Ballet, taking over as artistic director (1980–9), and in 1990 formed the White Oak Dance Project with Mark Morris. He has taken part in several Hollywood films, including *The Turning Point* (1977). >> Balanchine; Kirkland

Basaldella, Mirko [basaldela] (1910–1969) Sculptor and painter, born in Udine, Italy. He studied in Venice, Florence, and Milan, and first exhibited in Rome in 1936. He is best known for the bronze memorial doors he designed for the Ardeatine caves near Rome.

Baselitz, Georg [baselitz] (1938–) Avant-garde artist, born in Deutschbaselitz, Germany. He studied art in East Berlin (1956–7), before emigrating to the West in 1957. He had his first one-man show in Berlin in 1961. His violent subject-matter and his 'wild Expressionist' style have affinities with Munch and Kokoschka. His forte is painting figures, animals, trees, and other objects upside down. >> Kokoschka; Munch

Basevi, George [basayvee] (1794–1845) Architect, born in London, England, UK. A pupil of Sir John Soane, he travelled in Greece and Italy (1816–19), designed in Neoclassical style the Fitzwilliam Museum in Cambridge, laid out part of London's Belgravia, and designed country mansions and Gothic churches. >> Soane

Basho, Matsuo (1644–94) Poet, born in Ueno (Iga), Japan. He was raised in an atmosphere of poetry. Becoming master of the haiku, he started his own school, but later retired to a hermitage. Influenced by Zen Buddhism, he then journeyed extensively, and composed his celebrated book of travels *The Narrow Road to the Deep North* (1689) in a mixture of poetic prose and haiku.

Basie, Count [baysee], popular name of **William Basie** (1904–84) Jazz pianist, organist, and bandleader, born in Red Bank, NJ. After several years touring the vaudeville circuit as a soloist and accompanist to blues singers, he reached Kansas City, where he became pianist and co-arranger with the Bennie Moten band. He formed his own band in 1935, which became established in New York City as the Count Basie Orchestra until 1950, when big bands appeared to be no longer viable. But after two years of leading an octet, he re-formed a 16-piece orchestra and continued to lead it until his death. Over nearly 50 years as a bandleader, he remained true to music rooted in the

Kansas City style, recognized for his highly distinctive piano playing. Among his most popular compositions are 'One O'Clock Jump' and 'Jumpin' at the Woodside'. >> Young, Lester

Basil, Wassili de >> **de Basil, Colonel Wassili**

Basil, St, known as **Basil the Great** (c. 329–79) One of the greatest of the Greek fathers, born in Caesarea, Cappadocia, the brother of Gregory of Nyssa. He studied at Byzantium and Athens, lived for a time with hermits in the desert, and in 370 succeeded Eusebius of Caesarea as bishop of his native city. A fierce opponent of Arianism, he improved monastic standards and wrote many seminal works. Feast day 1 Jan (E), 2 Jan (W). >> Gregory of Nyssa

Basil I, known as **Basil the Macedonian** (c.812–886) Byzantine emperor. He rose in the imperial service from obscure origins to become co-ruler in 867 with Michael III, whom he murdered in the same year. The dynasty he founded ruled Constantinople until 1056. >> RR1037

Basilides [basilideez] (2nd-c) Gnostic philosopher, who founded a sect in Alexandria. His esoteric doctrines seem to have blended Christian thought with elements from Zoroaster, Indian philosophy, and magic. His disciples (*Basilidians*) were active in Egypt, Syria, Italy, and even Gaul into the 4th-c.

Basil II, known as **Basil Bulgaroctonus** ('slayer of the Bulgars') (c.958–1025) Byzantine emperor, who came to the throne as sole ruler in 976. A palace revolution was crushed by his alliance with Vladimir I the Great, Prince of Kiev. Vladimir's troops became the core of the future Varangian Guard, the elite unit of the Byzantine army. Basil's 15-year war against the Bulgarians culminated in the victory in the Belasica Mountains which earned him his surname. Bulgaria was annexed to the empire by 1018, while the E frontier was extended to L Van in Armenia. >> Vladimir I; RR1037

Basilius, John >> **Bessarion, John**

Basinger, Kim [baysinjer] (1953–) Film actress, born in Athens, Georgia. She appeared in television commercials and was a top model before making her feature film début in *Hard Country* (1981). Other films include *The Real McCoy* (1993), *The Getaway* (1994), and *LA Confidential* (1997).

Baskerville, John (1706–75) Printer, born in Wolverley, Hereford and Worcester, WC England, UK. He became a writing master in Birmingham, and from 1740 carried on a successful japanning (varnishing) business there. In about 1750 he began to make experiments in letter founding, and produced the types named after him. In 1758 he became printer to Cambridge University.

Baskin, Leonard (1922–) Graphic artist and sculptor, born in New Brunswick, NJ. He studied at New York University and Yale, and later in France and Italy. His sculptures, begun in the 1950s, show his dedication to social humanism, as seen in the wood, bronze, and stone series 'Dead Men', 'Birdmen', and 'Oppressed Men'. His etchings, woodblocks, and graphics exhibit his elegiac and technically sophisticated approach, as seen in 'Man of Peace' (1952) and 'Angel of Death' (1959). He taught at Smith College, Northampton, MA (1953–74). In 1990 he undertook his major work, the long-delayed Franklin D Roosevelt Memorial for Washington, DC.

Basov, Nikolai Gennadiyevich [basof] (1922–) Physicist, the inventor of masers and lasers, born in St Petersburg, Russia. At the Lebedev Physics Institute in Moscow (deputy director 1958–73, director from 1973), his work provided the theoretical basis for the development of the maser in 1955, for which he shared the 1964 Nobel Prize for Physics. In 1958 he invented the laser. >> Prokhorov; RR1122

Bass, George [bas] (1771–1803) Naval surgeon, born in Aswarby, Lincolnshire, EC England, UK. With Matthew Flinders he explored (1795–1800) the strait between

Tasmania and Australia that bears his name. He died while mining in South America. >> Flinders

Bass, Michael Thomas [bas] (1799–1884) Brewer, born in Burton-on-Trent, Staffordshire, C England, UK. He entered the family business (founded by his grandfather, William Bass, in 1777), which he expanded considerably. He helped to improve the lot of working people both as employer and as Liberal MP (1848–83). His son, **Michael Arthur Bass** (1837–1909), became Baron Burton in 1886.

Bassani, Giorgio [basahnee] (1916–) Novelist and poet, born in Bologna, Italy. He lived until 1943 in Ferrara, where much of his fiction is set. His first major success was *Cinque storie ferraresi* (1956, Five Stories of Ferrara), most of them composed in the aftermath of World War 2. A sensitive chronicler of Italian Jews and their suffering under Fascism, other major works include *Il giardino dei Finzi-Contini* (1962, The Garden of the Finzi-Continis, filmed in 1971) and *L'airone* (1968, The Heron, Campiello Prize).

Bassano, Jacopo da [basahnoh], also known as **Giacomo da Ponte** (c. 1510–92) Founder of genre painting in Europe, born in Bassano, Venice, Italy. His best paintings are of peasant life and biblical scenes, and include the altarpiece of the Nativity at Bassano, 'Calvary' (c.1538, Cambridge), and 'Pastoral' (c.1565–70, Lugano). His four sons were also painters.

Bassi, Agostino Maria [basee] (1773–1856) Biologist and pioneer bacteriologist, born in Lodi, Italy. He studied at Pavia, and his work on animal diseases partly anticipated that of Louis Pasteur and Robert Koch. As early as 1835 he showed that a disease of silkworms (muscardine) was fungal in origin and contagious, and proposed that many other diseases are transmitted by micro-organisms.

Bassompierre, François de [basõpyair] (1579–1646) French soldier and statesman, born in Harouel, France. Promoted to the rank of Marshal of France in 1622, he later served as ambassador to Switzerland, Spain, and England, but he was implicated in an unsuccessful plot to overthrow Cardinal Richelieu, and was imprisoned in the Bastille (1631–43). His *Memoirs*, written in the Bastille, are an important source for contemporary history.

Bastian, Adolf [bastian] (1826–1905) Ethnologist, born in Bremen, Germany. He studied at Berlin, Heidelberg, Prague, Jena, and Würzburg, and travelled widely, collecting material for his ethnological studies in most continents. He is best known for his theory that variations in folk cultures could be traced back to the effects of local geographical conditions on a basic set of elementary ideas (*Elementargedanken*) common to mankind.

Bastian, Henry (Charlton) (1837–1915) Biologist and physician, born in Truro, Cornwall, SW England, UK. He studied at University College, London, where he became professor of pathological anatomy (1867), hospital physician (1871), and professor of clinical medicine (1887–95). He championed the doctrine of spontaneous generation, and became one of the founders of British neurology through his work on aphasia.

Bastien-Lepage, Jules [bastyī luhpahzh] (1848–84) Painter, born in Damvillers, France. His pictures are mostly of genre rustic scenes, such as 'The Hayfield' (1878, Musée d'Orsay), but he also produced portraits, such as those of Sarah Bernhardt and the Prince of Wales (later Edward VII).

Bastos, Augustos Roa (1917–) Paraguayan novelist, living in exile since 1947. The author of several works of fiction, he has been a journalist, screenwriter, and teacher, and until his retirement in 1985 was a professor at the University of Toulouse. *I the Supreme* (1947, trans title) is his masterpiece.

Bata, Tomas (1876–1932) Industrialist, born in Zlin, Czech Republic. From a small shoemaking business, he built up the largest leather factory in Europe, in 1928 producing 75 000 pairs of shoes a day.

Batchelor, Joy (1914–91) Animated-cartoon producer, born in Watford, Hertfordshire, SE England, UK. A fashion artist for *Harper's Bazaar*, she tried her hand at animation with *Robin Hood* (1935), and in 1941 married fellow-producer John Halas, to form the Halas–Batchelor animation unit. They made the first British feature-length cartoon, *Handling Ships*, in 1945, and the *Charley* series (1947). Other films included Orwell's *Animal Farm* (1954) and the television series *Tales of Hoffnung* (1965). >> Halas, John

Bateman, H(enry) M(ayo) (1887–1970) Cartoonist, born in Sutton Forest, New South Wales, Australia. He lived in England from infancy. From 1906, he developed a purely visual style of comic strip for *Punch* and other periodicals. He is best known for a series of humorous drawings depicting embarrassing 'The Man Who...' situations such as *The Guardsman Who Dropped His Rifle*. >> Caran d'Ache

Bates, Alan, originally **Arthur Bates** (1934–) Actor, born in Allestree, Derbyshire, C England, UK. He trained at the Royal Academy of Dramatic Art, London, and made his stage debut in 1955. His film debut was in *The Entertainer* (1960), and he was then seen in some of the most popular British films of the decade, including *A Kind of Loving* (1962), *Georgy Girl* (1966), and *Women in Love* (1969). Later films include *The Go-Between* (1971), *We Think the World of You* (1988), *Hamlet* (1990), *Secret Friends* (1991), and *Gentlemen Don't Eat Poets* (1997). Television work includes the series *The Mayor of Casterbridge* (1978), *An Englishman Abroad* (1982, BAFTA), *Pack of Lies* (1987), and *Oliver's Travels* (1995).

Bates, Daisy May, *née* **O'Dwyer** (1863–1951) Anthropologist, born in Tipperary, Ireland. She was commissioned by *The Times* to investigate the condition of Aborigines, and from 1899 spent most of her life in the N and W of Australia. She made detailed notes of Aboriginal life and customs, and worked for Aboriginal welfare, setting up camps for the aged. >> Morant; Sutherland, Margaret Ada

Bates, H(erbert) E(rnest) (1905–74) Novelist, playwright, and short-story writer, born in Rushden, Northamptonshire, C England, UK. He began his working life as a solicitor's clerk, provincial journalist, and warehouse clerk. His first play, *The Last Bread*, and his first novel, *The Two Sisters*, appeared in 1926. He is one of the greatest exponents of the short-story form. His best-known works are *Fair Stood the Wind for France* (1944), *The Jacaranda Tree* (1949), and *The Darling Buds of May* (1958), which became a popular television series in the UK.

Bates, H(enry) W(alter) (1825–92) Naturalist and traveller, born in Leicester, Leicestershire, C England, UK. He explored the valley of the Amazon (1848–59), accompanied by his friend Alfred Russel Wallace for the first four years, returning with 8000 species of hitherto unknown insects. In 1861 he published his distinctive contribution to the theory of natural selection in a paper explaining the phenomenon of mimicry. >> Wallace, Alfred Russel

Bates, (Michael) Jeremy (1962–) Tennis player, born in Solihull, West Midlands. He was educated at Strodes Grammar School and Solihull Sixth Form College, and after winning national tennis titles at junior level turned professional in 1980. A member of the Davis Cup team (1984–95), his achievements include the Wimbledon mixed doubles title (1987), the mixed doubles champion Australian Open (1991), and the singles title Korean Open (1994). A former British number one, he retired in 1996.

Bates, William (1860–1931) US ophthalmologist. His book, *Better Eyesight Without Glasses* (1919), explained poor sight as a disturbance of normal mind–body co-ordination which results from mental, emotional, or other disturbances. He developed a series of exercises to achieve healthy eyesight which emphasize relaxation, memory, imagination, and perception to improve the communication between the eyes and the brain.

Bateson, Gregory (1904–80) Anthropologist, born in Grantchester, Cambridgeshire, EC England, UK, the son of biologist William Bateson. He studied physical anthropology at Cambridge, but made his career in the USA. With Margaret Mead he was involved with the culture-and-personality movement, publishing *Balinese Character* in 1942. Influenced by cybernetics, he went on to study problems of communication and learning among aquatic mammals and human schizophrenics. Later works include *Mind and Nature* (1978). >> Bateson, William; Mead, Margaret

Bateson, William (1861–1926) Geneticist, born in Whitby, North Yorkshire, N England, UK. He studied at Rugby School and Cambridge, became Britain's first professor of genetics at Cambridge (1908–10) and director of the new John Innes Horticultural Institution there (1910–26), as well as professor of physiology at the Royal Institution (1912–26). He produced the first translation of the heredity studies of Gregor Mendel (1900), and played a dominant part in establishing Mendelian ideas. He is known as 'the father of genetics', a term he himself coined. >> Mendel

Bath, Henry Frederick Thynne, 6th Marquess of (1905–92) Stately home operator, born in Longleat House, Wiltshire, S England, UK. He inherited the family Elizabethan manor house, containing a fine art collection and library but in a poor state of repair. Faced with crippling death duties, he caused a sensation by opening the house to the paying public as a tourist attraction in 1949. He introduced lions and other wild animals to the estate grounds in the 1960s, creating the first safari park.

Batista (y Zaldívar), Fulgencio [bateesta] (1901–73) Cuban soldier and dictator, born in Oriente province. A labourer's son, he rose from sergeant-major to colonel in the army coup against President Machado (1931–3) and was later elected president (1940–4), fostering a major programme of social and economic reform. He stepped down in 1944, and travelled abroad, but returned to power following another army revolt in 1952, overthrowing President Prio. This regime was marked by oppression and corruption, and he was overthrown by Fidel Castro in 1959. He then found refuge in the Dominican Republic. >> Castro; RR1043

Batoni or **Battoni, Pompeo Girolamo** [batohnee] (1708–87) Painter, born in Lucca, Italy. He trained and settled in Rome. From 1735 he received many important commissions for religious, mythological, and historical paintings, but it is for his portraits, particularly of distinguished foreign visitors, that he is most famous.

Batten, Jean (1909–82) Pioneer aviator, born in Rotorua, New Zealand. In 1934, in a Gypsy Moth, she broke Amy Johnson's record for the flight from England to Australia by nearly five days. She became the first woman to complete the return journey, and in 1935 flew over the S Atlantic to Argentina. >> Johnson, Amy

Battenberg, Prince Alexander of (1820–93) First prince of Bulgaria, and uncle of Earl Mountbatten, born in Verona, Italy. An officer in the Hessian army, he was elected prince of the new principality of Bulgaria in 1879. In 1885 he annexed E Romania after an uprising there, thereby provoking the hostility of Serbia. In 1886 he was overpowered by pro-Russian army conspirators in his palace in Sofia, and forced to abdicate. >> Mountbatten, Prince Louis Alexander

Battenberg, Prince Louis Alexander of >> **Mountbatten, Prince Louis Alexander**

Battling Bella >> **Abzug, Bella**

Batuta, ibn >> **Ibn Battutah**

Baudelaire, Charles (Pierre) [bohduhlair] (1821–67) Symbolist poet, born in Paris. He was sent on a voyage to India, but stopped off at Mauritius. On his return to Paris in 1842, he met Jeanne Duval, a half-caste, who became his mistress and inspiration. He spent much of his time in the studios of Delacroix, Manet, and Daumier. His masterpiece is a collection of poems, *Les Fleurs du mal* (1857), for which author, printer, and publisher were prosecuted for impropriety in 1864, but which earned the praise of critics and was to exert an influence far into the 20th-c. Later works include *Les Paradis artificiels* (1860) and *Petits Poèmes en prose* (1869). His preoccupation with the macabre, the perverted, and the horrid was an essential feature of his work. >> Daumier; Delacroix; Manet

Baudouin I [bohdwï] (1930–93) King of the Belgians (1951–93), born at Stuyvenberg Castle, near Brussels, the elder son of Leopold III and his first wife, Queen Astrid. He succeeded to the throne in July 1951 on the abdication of his father over the controversy of the latter's conduct during World War 2. In 1960 he married the Spanish **Doña Fabiola de Mora y Aragón**. A Roman Catholic, in 1990 he resigned his throne for a day to overcome a constitutional crisis caused by his refusal to sign a law legalizing abortion. >> Leopold III; RR1035

Baudry, Paul Jacques Aimé [bohdree] (1828–86) Painter, born in La Roche-sur-Yon, France. He is chiefly known for the 30 large panels, illustrative of music and dancing, executed for the foyer of the Paris Opera (1866–76).

Bauer, Georg >> **Agricola, Georgius**

Bauhin, Caspar or **Gaspard** (1560–1624) Botanist and physician, born in Basel, Switzerland. He was professor of anatomy and botany at Basel, and compiled an influential medical textbook, *Theatrum anatomicum* (1605, trans Microcosmographia, A Description of the Body of Man). He was also the author of *Pinax theatri botanici* (1623, Illustrated Exposition of Plants), which introduced a system of binomial nomenclature by genus and species. It was much used by Linnaeus and still important as a compendium of all plants known in the early 17th-c. >> Linnaeus

Baum, Vicki [bowm], originally **Vicki Hedvig** (1888–1960) Novelist, born in Vienna. After writing several novels and short stories in German, she made her name with *Grand Hotel* (1930), which became a best-seller and a popular film. She emigrated to the USA in 1931, where her later novels included *Falling Star* (1934), *Headless Angel* (1948), and *The Mustard Seed* (1953).

Baumé, Antoine [bohmay] (1728–1804) Chemist, born in Senlis, France. He invented the hydrometer named after him, and the *Baumé scale* of measurement for use with a hydrometer, and many dyeing processes.

Baumeister, Willi [bowmiyster] (1889–1955) Painter, born in Stuttgart, Germany. For some years he was a professor at the Frankfurt School of Art, but the Hitler regime prohibited him from teaching and he turned to scientific research on colour and to prehistoric archaeology. These interests are reflected in his work such as 'African Histories', a series of paintings depicting strange organic forms, and his illustrations for the Bible stories and the 'Epic of Gilgamesh' (1942–53).

Baumer, Gertrude [bowmer] (1873–1954) Leader of the German feminist movement, born in Hohenlimburg, Germany. She studied at Berlin University, and became president of the League of German Women's Associations (1910–19). She also edited the newspaper *Die Frau* (1893–1944). A member of the Reichstag (1920–33), she lost this position on the advent of Nazi power. After World War 2 she founded the Christian Social Union.

Baumgarten, Alexander Gottlieb [bowmgah(r)tn] (1714–62) Philosopher of the school of Christian von Wolff, born in Berlin. In 1740 he became professor of philosophy at Frankfurt-an-der-Oder. His main works were *Metaphysica* (1739) and *Aesthetica* (1750–58), a long unfinished treatise which pioneered this field and helped establish the modern term *aesthetics*. >> Wolff, Christian

Baur, Ferdinand Christian [bowr] (1792–1860) Theologian and New Testament critic, born in Schmiden, Germany. He held the Tübingen chair of theology from 1826, and founded the 'Tübingen School' of theology, the first to use strict historical research methods in the study of early Christianity.

Bausch, Pina [bowsh], popular name of **Philippine Bausch** (1940–) Choreographer and dancer, born in Solingen, Germany. She trained first at the Essen Folkwangschule and then in New York City. After a season with the Metropolitan Opera Ballet Company and another with US choreographer Paul Taylor, she returned to Essen, where she staged several operas for the Wuppertal Theatre. Her success led to an invitation to found her own company, and she began to produce her own work in the 1970s, including *Rite of Spring* (1975), *Café Muller* (1978), and *1980* (1980). Her choreography and particularly her unusual stagings mark a turning point in contemporary dance, and remain a powerful influence. In 1996 her company performed at the Edinburgh International Festival's 50th anniversary celebrations.

Bawden, Sir Frederick >> **Pirie, Norman Wingate**

Bawden, Nina (Mary) (1925–) Writer, born in London, England, UK. She studied at Oxford, and worked in town and country planning (1946–7). She has written several novels for adults, including *Who Calls the Tune* (1953), *Under the Skin* (1964), *Walking Naked* (1981), *Circles of Deceit* (1987, televised 1990), *Family Money* (1991), and *Nice Change* (1997). She is also well known as a writer of adventure stories for children, such as *The Witch's Daughter* (1966), and her most successful work, *Carrie's War* (1973), based on her own childhood experiences. Later stories include *Keeping Henry* (1988) and *Granny the Pag* (1995).

Bax, Sir Arnold (Edward Trevor), pseudonym **Dermot O'Byrne** (1883–1953) Composer, born in London, England, UK. He studied piano at the Royal Academy of Music, London. His love of all things Celtic was expressed early in Irish short stories, which he wrote under his pseudonym, and musically in orchestral pieces (1912–13), songs set to the words of revival poets, the choral *St Patrick's Breastplate* (1923–4), and *An Irish Elegy* (1917), for English horn, harp, and strings. Between 1921 and 1939 he wrote his seven symphonies. Other works include tone poems, such as *In the Faery Hills* (1909) and *Tintagel* (1917), chamber music, and piano concertos. In 1942 he was made Master of the King's (from 1952 Queen's) Musick.

Baxendale, Leo (1930–) Strip cartoonist, born in Lancashire, NW England, UK. He first worked as a label designer, and later joined the *Lancashire Evening Post* (1950). He began to freelance strips to the *Beano* comic, beginning with *Little Plum* (1953), followed by *Minnie the Minx* (1953) and *The Bash Street Kids*. He designed the new weekly comic *Wham* (1964), and despite leaving the field in 1974 remains the most imitated artist in British comics.

Baxter, George (1804–67) Engraver and print maker, born in Lewes, East Sussex, SE England, UK, the son of John Baxter. He developed a method of printing in oil colours, using copper or steel plates for his outlines, with neutral tones on the same plate obtained by aquatint or stipple. His process was patented in 1835. >> Baxter, John

Baxter, James Keir (1926–72) Poet, playwright, and critic, born near Dunedin, New Zealand. He worked as a labourer, journalist, and teacher and led a bohemian life until he was converted to Roman Catholicism. He later founded a religious community on the Wanganui R. He published more than 30 books of poetry, notably *In Fires of No Return* (1958), *Howrah Bridge* (1961), and *Autumn Testament* (1972).

Baxter, John (1781–1858) Printer, the first to use an ink-roller, born in Surrey, SE England, UK. He settled in Lewes and published the illustrated *Baxter's Bible* and the first book of cricket rules. >> Baxter, George

Baxter, Richard (1615–91) Nonconformist clergyman, born in Rowton, Shropshire, WC England, UK. He adopted Nonconformist views as minister at Kidderminster (1640–60). During the Civil War, his sympathies were almost wholly with the Puritans, and after Naseby he acted as army chaplain. At the Restoration he was appointed a royal chaplain, but in 1662 the Act of Uniformity drove him out of the Church of England. Frequently persecuted for his views, he was imprisoned for 18 months in 1685 for alleged sedition.

Bayard, Pierre du Terrail, chevalier de [bayah(r)] (c. 1476–1524) French soldier, known as 'the knight without fear and without reproach', born in the Château Bayard, near Grenoble, France. In the service of Louis XII he fought with legendary bravery at Milan (1501) and Barletta (1502), and campaigned in Spain and against the Genoese and Venetians, taking Brescia by storm in 1512. At Marignano he gained a brilliant victory for Francis I, and defended Mézières in 1521. He was mortally wounded while defending the passage of the R Sesia in Italy. >> Francis I; Louis XII

Bayazid I >> **Bayezit I**

Bayer, Johann (1572–1625) Astronomer, born in Rhain, Germany. His *Uranometria* (1603) depicts the positions of nearly a thousand stars in addition to those given by Tycho Brahe. His designations by the letters of the Greek alphabet in preference to the Arabic proper names are still used for the brighter stars. >> Brahe

Bayes, Thomas (1702–61) Mathematician, born in London, England, UK. He was one of the first six Nonconformist ministers to be publicly ordained in England. He is principally remembered for his posthumously published *Essay Towards Solving a Problem in the Doctrine of Chances* (1763), in which he was the first to study the idea of statistical inference, and to estimate the probability of an event from the frequency of its previous occurrences.

Bayezit I [bajazet], also spelled **Bajazet** or **Bayazid**, nickname **Yildirim** ('Thunderbolt') (c. 1354–1403) Sultan of the Ottoman empire. He succeeded his father (1389), and conquered Bulgaria, with parts of Serbia, Macedonia, and Thessaly, and most of Asia Minor. His rapid conquests earned him his nickname. For 10 years he blockaded Constantinople, defeating a large army of crusaders under Sigismund of Hungary (1396). He would have entirely destroyed the Greek empire if he had not been defeated by Timur near Ankara (1402). >> Sigismund; Timur; RR1093

Bayle, Pierre (1647–1706) Protestant philosopher and critic, born in Carlat, France. In 1675 he took the chair of philosophy at Sedan until forced into exile at the University of Rotterdam in 1681, where he published a strong defence of liberalism and religious toleration. He was dismissed from the university in 1693 following the accusation that he was an agent of France and an enemy of Protestantism. In 1696 he completed his major work, the *Dictionnaire historique et critique*, a sceptical analysis of philosophical and theological arguments, which came to be influential in the 18th-c Enlightenment.

Baylis, Lilian Mary (1874–1937) Theatrical manager, born in London, England, UK. In 1890 the family emigrated to South Africa, where she became a music teacher in Johannesburg. Returning to England in 1898, she helped with the management of the Royal Victoria Hall (afterwards the Old Vic), becoming manager in 1912; under her the theatre became a joint home of Shakespeare and opera. In 1931 she acquired Sadler's Wells Theatre for the exclusive presentation of opera and ballet.

Bayliss, Sir William Maddock (1860–1924) Physiologist, born in Wolverhampton, West Midlands, C England, UK. He studied science at University College, London, and taught physiology there (1888–1924). Much of his experimental work was done with his colleague Ernest Henry Starling, including work on the cardiovascular system and the discovery of secretin, the first known hormone (which word they coined). His best-known work is *Principles of General Physiology* (1915). He was knighted in 1922. >> Starling

Baylor, Elgin (Gay) (1934–) Basketball player, born in Washington, DC. He spent his playing career with the Minneapolis (later Los Angeles) Lakers (1958–72), and went on to coach with the New Orleans Jazz before returning to Los Angeles as an executive with the Clippers.

Bazaine, Achille (François) [bazen] (1811–88) French soldier, born in Versailles, France. In the war with Austria of 1859 he captured Solferino in Italy, and in the Mexican expedition was placed in command of the army (1862). He was promoted Marshal of France in 1864. In the Franco-Prussian War of 1870–1, he was trapped by the Prussians at Metz, and surrendered after a siege of 54 days. For this he was court-martialled and imprisoned in 1873, but a year later escaped to Spain.

Bazaine, Jean René [bazen] (1904–75) Painter, born in Paris. His style developed through Cubism to abstract art. He produced a number of very successful tapestry designs as well as stained glass and mosaics.

Bazalgette, Sir Joseph William [bazaljet] (1819–91) Engineer, born in Enfield, N Greater London, England, UK. He constructed London's drainage system and the Thames embankment, and was a notable pioneer of public health engineering. He was knighted in 1874.

Bazin, René [bazí] (1853–1932) Novelist, born in Angers, France. He depicted with charm and colour the life of peasant folk in the various French provinces, and in some of his novels, such as *Les Oberlé* (1901), dealt with the social problems of his time.

Baziotes, William [baziohteez] (1912–63) Painter, born in Pittsburgh, PA. He studied at the National Academy of Design in New York City (1933–6). His early work was influenced by Picasso, but in the 1940s he was one of a number of American painters whose art developed from European Surrealism. His dream-like images often contain suggestions of animal forms. >> Picasso

Beach, Amy (Marcy), *née* **Cheney** (1867–1944) Composer and pianist, born in Henniker, NH. She made her professional debut as a pianist in Boston in 1884, the next year appearing with the Boston Symphony. Also in 1884 she married **Dr Henry H A Beach** (d.1910), who encouraged her shift to composing, even though she had little formal instruction in it. Her *Gaelic Symphony*, premiered by the Boston Symphony in 1896, was the first such work by an American woman, as was the piano concerto the orchestra premiered four years later (with the composer as soloist). She later lived in Europe (1910–14), where she again gave piano concerts, usually of her own work. She composed over 150 works – many of them settings of well-known poems – and gained some prominence both in Europe and the USA, but she was continually hampered by the era's resistance to woman composers, reflected in the fact that she went through most of her public career known as 'Mrs H H A Beach'.

Beach, Sylvia Woodbridge (1887–1962) Bookseller and publisher, born in Baltimore, MD. In 1919 she established the Shakespeare and Company bookstore in Paris, which became an avant-garde publishing house and mecca for US expatriates. In 1922 she published the first edition of James Joyce's *Ulysses*, which had been rejected by other publishers as pornographic. In 1941 she closed her bookstore in defiance of the German occupation, and later was interned for seven months. She never re-opened the store, but she was widely honoured for her support of Joyce and other authors.

Beach Boys, The US singing/instrumental group, formed in California in 1961, consisting orginally of brothers **Brian Wilson** (1942– , vocalist, bass guitar, keyboards, songwriter), **Carl Wilson** (1946– , vocalist, guitar) and **Dennis Wilson** (1944–83, vocalist, drums), with cousin **Mike Love** (1941– , vocalist) and **Al(an) Jardine** (1942– , vocalist, bass guitar, guitar); later also **Bruce Johnston** (1944–) and others. They found fame in the 1960s with Brian's cheerful songs of teenage West Coast life, surfing, fast cars and motorcycles, and all-American girls, including 'I Get Around', 'California Girls', and 'Good Vibrations'. In 1966, with the technically innovative album *Pet Sounds*, an increasingly reclusive Brian Wilson emulated the Beatles' imaginative use of recording techniques in a 'concept album'. Later, more pensive hit singles included 'I Can Hear Music' and 'Darling'.

Beachcomber >> **Morton, John Cameron**

Beaconsfield, Earl of >> **Disraeli, Benjamin**

Beadle, George (Wells) (1903–89) Biochemical geneticist, born in Wahoo, NE. He taught at Stanford University (1937–46) and California Institute of Technology (1946–61), and was president of Chicago University (1961–8). He studied the genetics of maize, the fruit fly (*Drosophila*), and the bread mould (*Neurospora*). In association with Edward Laurie Tatum, he developed the idea that specific genes control the production of specific enzymes. Beadle and Tatum shared the Nobel Prize for Physiology or Medicine in 1958 with Joshua Lederberg. >> Lederberg; Tatum, Edward L

Beaglehole, John Cawte (1901–71) Writer and historian, born in Wellington, New Zealand. He graduated from Victoria University College, to which he returned in 1936 as lecturer in history, remaining there as professor of British Commonwealth history (1963–6). His life's work was the masterly Hakluyt Society edition of *The Journals of Captain James Cook on his Voyages of Discovery* (1955–67), associated with which was his *The Endeavour Journal of Sir Joseph Banks* (1962). He was awarded the Order of Merit in 1970.

Beale, Dorothea (1831–1906) Pioneer of women's education, born in London, England, UK. She was principal of Cheltenham Ladies' College (1858–1906), and in 1885 founded St Hilda's College, Cheltenham, as the first English training college for women teachers. She sponsored St Hilda's Hall in Oxford for women teachers in 1894. >> Buss

Beale, Mary, *née* **Cradock** (1632–99) Painter, born in Barrow, Suffolk, E England, UK. She became a portrait painter and a devoted follower of the most celebrated portraitist of her day, Sir Peter Lely. Very little is known of her work before c.1670, but several of her husband's diaries record her painting commissions, which include several portraits of clerics. >> Lely

Beamon, Bob, popular name of **Robert Beamon** (1946–) Athlete, born in New York City. A long jumper who was not considered a great stylist, he smashed the world record at the 1968 Olympic Games in Mexico City with a jump of 8·9 m/29 ft 2 in – 55 cm/21 in further than the previous record.

Bean, Alan L(aVern) (1932–) Astronaut, born in Wheeler, TX. He studied at the University of Texas, then served as a naval test pilot (1955) before joining the crewed spaceflight program (1963). He was a crew member of the historic Apollo 12 Moon-walk mission, and commander of the second crew to occupy the orbiting Skylab 3. Following retirement in 1975, he continued to work for NASA as an adviser.

Bean, Charles Edwin Woodrow (1879–1968) Journalist and war historian, born in Bathurst, New South Wales, Australia. He studied at Oxford University, and became offical correspondent to the Australian Imperial Force (AIF). He landed with the AIF at Gallipoli in 1915, then accompanied the troops to France where he served until the end of the war. His major work was the 12-volume *Official History of Australia in the War of 1914–18* (1921–39), writing six of the volumes himself, and editing the others.

Beard, Charles A(ustin) (1874–1948) Historian, born in Knightstown, IN. He studied at DePauw University, Oxford, and Columbia, where he taught from 1907, resigning in 1917 on an issue of academic freedom in wartime. After work on European history he produced his best-known book, *An Economic Interpretation of the Constitution of the United States* (1913). His wife, **Mary Ritter Beard**, was a collaborator in many of his works. >> Beard, Mary Ritter

Beard, Dan(iel Carter), nickname **Uncle Dan** (1850–1941) Illustrator and youth leader, born in Cincinnati, OH. He was a surveyor (1874–8) before he became an illustrator. He wrote *What to Do and How to Do It: The American Boy's Handy Book* (1882), the first of his 16 books on handicrafts, and was praised by Mark Twain for his illustrations in *A Connecticut Yankee in King Arthur's Court* (1889). To promote magazines that he edited, he organized the Sons of Daniel Boone (1905) and the Boy Pioneers of America (1909), precursors of the Boy Scouts. When the Boy Scouts of America were formed (1910), he designed the Scout hat, neckerchief, and shirt. As National Scout Commissioner (1910–41), he argued for voluntary leadership within the Scouts, and became known as 'Uncle Dan' to a generation of American boys.

Beard, Mary Ritter (1876–1958) Feminist and historian, born in Indianapolis, IN. She studied at DePauw University, and became involved in women's suffrage, both in England and the USA. In 1910 she became a member of the Woman Suffrage movement, then worked for the Congressional Union under Alice Paul's leadership (1913–17). Her best-known publication is *Women as a Force in History* (1946). With her husband, **Charles Austin Beard**, she wrote several influential works on American history. >> Beard, Charles Austin; Paul, Alice

Beardsley, Aubrey (Vincent) [beerdzlee] (1872–98) Illustrator, born in Brighton, East Sussex, SE England, UK. He became famous through his fantastic posters and illustrations for *Morte d'Arthur*, *Salomé*, *The Rape of the Lock*, and other works, as well as for the *Yellow Book* magazine (1894–96) and his own *Book of Fifty Drawings*, mostly executed in black and white, in a highly individualistic asymmetrical style. With Wilde he is regarded as leader of the 'Decadents' of the 1890s. >> Wilde, Oscar

Beatles, The (1960–70) see panel on p. 83

Beaton, Sir Cecil (Walter Hardy) (1904–80) Photographer and designer, born in London, England, UK. He studied at Cambridge, and became an outstanding photographer of fashion and high-society celebrities, including royalty. He also designed scenery and costumes for many ballet, operatic, theatrical, and film productions, including *My Fair Lady* and *Gigi*. His publications include *My Royal Past* (1939), *The Glass of Fashion* (1959), and *The Magic Image* (1975), and he also wrote several volumes of autobiography (1961–78).

Beaton or **Bethune, David** (1494–1546) Scottish statesman

THE BEATLES (1960–70)

The Beatles pop group was formed in 1960 by two songwriters and performers: **John (Winston) Lennon** (1940–80), rhythm guitar, keyboards, vocals; and **(James) Paul McCartney** (1942–), bass guitar, vocals. Together with **George Harrison** (1943–), lead guitar, sitar, vocals; and **Pete Best** (1941–), drums, they learned their trade in Liverpool's Cavern Club, and at venues in Hamburg. In 1962 Brian Epstein signed them up for a 5-year management contract, at which point **Ringo Starr**, originally **Richard Starkey** (1940–), was invited to join the group in place of Pete Best on drums, and their simple beat record 'Love Me Do' was released. This was followed in 1963 by 'She Loves You', which became Britian's best-selling single ever, with 1.6 million copies sold in the UK alone.

The youth of Britain and the Western world were just asserting an identity of their own, and the Beatles, with their 'Beatlecut' hairstyles, and laid-back, somewhat cynical attitudes, slotted easily into the role of champions of the swinging sixties. When the group topped the bill on the TV show 'Sunday Night at the London Palladium' in 1963, their fans congregated outside the Palladium amid so much hysteria that the term *Beatlemania* was coined by the press. 'She Loves You' was released in the USA soon afterwards. An appearance on the *Ed Sullivan Show*, together with the overwhelming success of a concert tour of American stadia, and the release of further hit records such as 'I want to Hold Your Hand', 'Can't Buy Me Love', and 'A Hard Day's Night' spread Beatlemania around the world. The group quickly surpassed all previous figures for concert attendances and record sales, and the Beatles were mobbed by thousands of screaming fans wherever they appeared.

Although their early songs were simple, they won acclaim from serious musicians; *The Times* music critic, William Mann, hailed Lennon and McCartney as the outstanding English composers of 1963. Their songwriting skills matured rapidly in the period 1962–6. Their enormous output assimilated a wide range of styles, including such lyrically beautiful ballads as 'Yesterday', songs of rhythmical complexity such as 'Paperback Writer', and social cameos such as 'Eleanor Rigby'.

Their first world tour began at Copenhagen in 1964, and in Melbourne the largest collection of Australians ever assembled in one place was recorded to have been waiting for the group's arrival. In 1965 the Beatles were each awarded an MBE by the Queen, giving rise to indignant protests from other medal holders.

Their image was sustained with the making of several critically acclaimed films for cinema and television, including *A Hard Day's Night* (1964), *Help!* (1965), and *The Magical Mystery Tour* (1967). The group stopped performing in public in 1966. In 1967, encouraged by their highly publicized experimentation with hallucinogenic drugs, they recorded 'Sgt Pepper's Lonely Hearts Club Band', a compelling album exploring the problems of adolescence and alienation. It included titles such as 'She's Leaving Home', 'A Day in the Life', and 'Lucy in the Sky with Diamonds'. Held together by thematically-linked lyrics and effects, it was to become the most influential and prestigious work in the history of pop music. It was unprecedented in that it relied heavily on studio effects, taking 700 hours of studio time, and could not be performed on stage. Just after the release of 'Sgt Pepper' in the UK, the recording of 'All You Need is Love' at the Abbey Road studios was transmitted worldwide as part of the first global television link-up, 'Our World'.

The death of Brian Epstein from an alleged drug overdose in August 1967 heralded the beginning of the end. The Beatles announced they would manage their own affairs, and formed Apple Publishing Ltd shortly afterwards. But 1968 saw the gradual build-up of pressures within the group. They flew to India to seek relief in the study of meditation. On their return John Lennon was sued for divorce by his first wife Cynthia, and married Yoko Ono in 1969. Almost simultaneously, Paul McCartney's much publicized relationship with Jane Asher ended, and he married Linda Eastman.

The group played together for the last time to cut the Album *Abbey Road* in August 1969, and finally dissolved with some acrimony early in 1970. However, following Lennon's death, the other three members of the group sang together again in 1994 to record his 'Free as a Bird', and were all involved in the issue of the Beatles anthology in 1995.
>> Harrison, George; Lennon; McCartney; Starr, Ringo

---

and Roman Catholic clergyman, born in Balfour, Fife, E Scotland, UK. He studied at the universities of St Andrews, Glasgow, and Paris, and was at the French court (1519) as Scottish 'resident' and twice later as ambassador to negotiate James V's marriages. In 1525 he took his seat in the Scots Parliament as Abbot of Arbroath and was appointed Privy Seal. Made a cardinal in 1538, he became Archbishop of St Andrews. On James's death, he produced a forged will, appointing himself and three other regents of the kingdom during the minority of Mary, Queen of Scots. The nobility, however, elected the Protestant Earl of Arran regent. Beaton was arrested, but soon regained favour and was made chancellor (1543). He was assassinated by a band of conspirators in his castle of St Andrews. >> Mary, Queen of Scots; Wishart

Beaton or **Bethune, James** (1470–1539) Scottish clergyman and statesman, the uncle of Cardinal David Beaton. He graduated from St Andrews in 1493, and rose rapidly to be Archbishop of Glasgow (1509) and of St Andrews (1522). A zealous supporter of France and an opponent of the Reformation, he initiated the persecution of Protestants. >> Beaton, David; Hamilton, Patrick

Beatrix, in full **Beatrix Wilhelmina Armgard** (1938–) Queen of The Netherlands (1980–), born in Soestdijk, The Netherlands, the eldest daughter of Queen Juliana and Prince Bernhard Leopold. In 1966 she married West German diplomat **Claus-Georg Wilhelm Otto Friedrich Gerd von Amsberg** (1926–); their son, **Prince Willem-Alexander Claus George Ferdinand** (1967–) is the first male heir to the Dutch throne in over a century. There are two other sons, **Johan Friso Bernhard Christiaan David** (1968–) and **Constantijn Christof Frederik Aschwin** (1969–). She acceded to the throne on her mother's abdication in 1980. >> Bernhard Leopold; Juliana; RR1077

Beats >> **Burroughs, William S; Corso; Ferlinghetti; Ginsberg; Kerouac; Snyder**

Beattie, James (1735–1803) Poet and essayist, born in Laurencekirk, Aberdeenshire, NE Scotland, UK. After some years as a schoolmaster in Fordoun he became a master at Aberdeen Grammar School, and in 1760 professor of moral philosophy at Aberdeen. He is chiefly remembered for his long poem, *The Minstrel* (1771–74), a forerunner of Romanticism.

Beatty, David Beatty, 1st Earl (1871–1936) Naval commander, born in Nantwich, Cheshire, NWC England, UK. He entered the navy in 1884, and by 1912 had been appointed to command the 1st Battle Cruiser Squadron. At the outbreak of World War 1 he steamed into Heligoland Bight and destroyed three German cruisers. In 1915 he pursued German battle cruisers near the Dogger Bank, sinking the *Blücher*, and in 1916 fought in the Battle of Jutland. He succeeded Lord Jellicoe as commander-in-chief of the Grand Fleet in 1916, and became First Sea Lord in 1919. >> Jellicoe

Beatty, Warren [baytee], originally **Henry Warren Beaty** (1937–) Actor and film-maker, born in Richmond, VA, the younger brother of actress Shirley MacLaine. He made his film debut in *Splendor in the Grass* (1961). A broodingly handsome leading man, his enduring Casanova image has done a disservice to his many political interests and consistent efforts to expand the scope of his talents. At the same time as acting, he produced *Bonnie and Clyde* (1967), co-wrote *Shampoo* (1975), and co-directed *Heaven Can Wait* (1978). He was the producer, co-writer and star of *Reds* (1981), which won him an Oscar as Best Director. Later films include *Dick Tracy* (1990), *Bugsy* (1991), and *Love Affair* (1994). >> MacLaine

Beauchamp, Pierre [bohshã] (1636–1705) Dancer, choreographer, and ballet master, born in Versailles, France. He became superintendent of the Court Ballets of Louis XIV, and in 1671 was appointed director of the Académie Royale de Danse. Some credit him with the invention of classical ballet's five positions. He also created his own notation system.

Beaufort, Sir Francis [bohfert] (1774–1857) Naval officer, born in Navan, Co Meath, Ireland. He was hydrographer to the British navy (1829–55), devising the *Beaufort scale* of wind force and a tabulated system of weather registration. He was promoted to rear-admiral in 1846.

Beaufort, Henry [bohfert] (1377–1447) English clergyman, the second illegitimate son of John of Gaunt and his mistress Catherine Swynford, and half-brother of Henry IV. He was chancellor three times (1403–4, 1413–17, and 1424–6), and in 1426 was made a cardinal. In 1431 he conducted the young King Henry VI to Paris, to be crowned as King of France and England, and for several years was the dominant figure in his government. >> Henry VI; John of Gaunt

Beaufort, Lady Margaret, Countess of Richmond [bohfert] (1443–1509) Daughter of John Beaufort, 1st Duke of Somerset, and mother of King Henry VII. In 1455 she married Edmund Tudor, Earl of Richmond. The Lancastrian claim to the English crown was transferred to her with the extinction of the male line, and it was in the right of his mother's descent from John of Gaunt that Henry VII ascended the throne after the defeat of Richard III in 1485. >> Henry VII

Beauharnais, Alexandre, vicomte de (Viscount of) [bohah(r)nay] (1760–94) French soldier, son of the governor of Martinique, where he was born. In 1779 he married Joséphine de Tascher de la Pagerie who later became the wife of Napoleon. He became president of the Constituent Assembly in Paris in June 1791, and was given command of the army of the Rhine in 1793. During the Reign of Terror he was arrested as an aristocratic 'suspect' and guillotined. >> Joséphine; Napoleon

Beauharnais, Eugène Rose de [bohah(r)nay] (1781–1824) French soldier, the son of Alexandre de Beauharnais and Joséphine. In 1805 he was made a prince of France and Viceroy of Italy. In 1806 he married Princess Amelia Augusta of Bavaria, and was formally adopted by Napoleon and made heir apparent to the throne of Italy. After Napoleon's abdication in 1814 he retired to Bavaria, and was created Duke of Leuchtenberg. >> Beauharnais, Alexandre de; Joséphine; Napoleon

Beauharnais, Hortense Eugénie Cécile [bohah(r)nay] (1783–1837) Queen of Holland, born in Paris, the daughter of Alexandre, Vicomte de Beauharnais. As a child she was a great favourite of her stepfather, Napoleon, and in 1802 married her brother Louis, King of Holland; the youngest of their three children became Napoleon III. >> Beauharnais, Alexandre de; Napoleon III; RR1077

Beaumarchais, Pierre Augustin Caron de [bohmah(r)shay], originally **Pierre Augustin Caron** (1732–99) Comic playwright, born in Paris. He married the wealthy widow of a court official, whereupon he assumed the title by which he was known thereafter. He is best known for his two satirical comedies, *Le Barbier de Séville* (1775, The Barber of Seville) and *La Folle Journée ou le mariage de Figaro* (1784, The Marriage of Figaro). Both are still popular plays in France, but in England are chiefly known through Mozart's and Rossini's operatic adaptations. The Revolution cost Beaumarchais his fortune, and, suspected of an attempt to sell arms to the *émigrés*, he had to take refuge in Holland and England (1793).

Beaumont, Francis [bohmont] (c. 1584–1616) Playwright, born in Gracedieu, Leicestershire, C England, UK. He studied at Oxford, and entered the Inner Temple in 1600. He became a friend of Ben Jonson, and worked closely with John Fletcher, with whom he wrote several plays. Modern research finds Beaumont's hand in only about 10 plays, but these include the masterpieces. *The Woman Hater* (1607) is attributed solely to Beaumont, and he had the major share in *The Knight of the Burning Pestle* (1609). *Philaster*, *The Maid's Tragedy*, and *A King and No King* established their joint popularity. >> Fletcher, John

Beaumont, William [bohmont] (1795–1853) Army surgeon, born in Lebanon, CT. He is remembered for his treatment in 1822 of a young Canadian patient, Alexis St Martin, who had received a gunshot wound that had left a permanent opening in his stomach. For several years following the accident Beaumont was able to make unprecedented direct observations of the activities of the stomach, and in 1833 wrote a pioneering study on the nature of gastric juice and the physiology of digestion.

Beauregard, P(ierre) G(ustave) T(outant) [bohregah(r)d] (1818–93) Confederate soldier, born near New Orleans, LA. He trained at West Point, and was appointed to the command at Charleston, SC. He was virtually in command at the first Battle of Bull Run (1861). In the spring of 1862 he was defeated at Shiloh, and in 1864 commanded the military division of the West, defeating Butler at Drewry's Bluff. >> Butler, Benjamin F

Beaurepaire, Sir Francis Joseph Edmund [bohrepair] (1891–1956) Freestyle swimmer, born in Melbourne, Victoria, Australia. A prominent figure in the Olympics of 1908, 1912, 1920, and 1924, his most prestigious year was 1910, when he set four world records. He was active in local politics, and became Lord Mayor of Melbourne (1940–2).

Beauvoir, Simone de >> **de Beauvoir, Simone**

Beaverbrook (of Beaverbrook and of Cherkley), (William) Max(well) Aitken, Baron (1879–1964) Politician and newspaper magnate, born in Maple, Ontario, Canada. He moved to Britain in 1910, entered parliament

(1911–16), and became private secretary to Bonar Law. When Lloyd-George became premier, he was made minister of information (1918). In 1919 he took over the *Daily Express*, which he made into the most widely-read daily newspaper in the world. He founded the *Sunday Express* (1921) and bought the *Evening Standard* (1929). In World War 2 Churchill successfully harnessed Beaverbrook's dynamic administrative powers to the production of much-needed aircraft. He was made minister of supply (1941–2), Lord Privy Seal, and lend-lease administrator in the USA. >> Churchill, Sir Winston; Lloyd-George, David

Beazley, Kim (Christian) (1948–) Politician, born in Perth, Western Australia, Australia. He was educated at the University of Western Australia and Oxford University as a Rhodes Scholar, returning to take up an academic post at Murdoch University. In 1980 he was elected as an MP for the West Australian seat of Swan, but transferred to the seat of Brand in 1996. He held a number of portfolios, including defence, employment, education, and training, during the Australian Labor Party's 13 years in power, and became deputy Prime Minister (1995–6). Since 1996 he has been leader of the Australian Labor Party Opposition.

Bebel, Ferdinand August [**bay**bel] (1840–1913) Socialist, born in Cologne, Germany. He became a leader of the German Social Democrat movement, and its chief spokesman in the Reichstag. He wrote widely on Socialism, on the Peasants' War, and on the status of women.

Beccafumi, Domenico [beka**foo**mee], originally **Domenico di Pace** (c.1486–1551) Painter, born in Siena, Italy. His paintings are characterized by unusual perspective, complicated figure poses, and complex colour effects, and the result is individual enough to be usually regarded as an early manifestation of the post-Renaissance style known as Mannerism. Much of his best work remains in the Pinacoteca, Siena.

Beccaria, Cesare, marchese de (Marquess of) [be**kah**ria] (1738–94) Jurist and philosopher, born in Milan, Italy. In 1764 he published anonymously *Dei delitti e delle pene* (On Crimes and Punishments), denouncing capital punishment and torture, and advocating the prevention of crime by education. The work had a widespread influence on the punishment and prevention of crime. In 1768 he was made professor of political philosophy at Milan.

Becher, Johann Joachim [**bekh**er] (1635–82) Chemist, born in Speyer, Germany. He worked on minerals, and his *Physica subterranea* (1669) was the first attempt to bring physics and chemistry into close relation.

Bechet, Sidney [be**shay**, be**shay**] (1897–1959) Jazz musician, born in New Orleans, LA. He took up the soprano saxophone in 1919, his forceful style making him the first significant saxophone voice in jazz. He re-emerged in 1940 as a figurehead of the traditional jazz revival. The warmth of his reception during many tours in Europe led him to make his permanent home in Paris.

Bechstein, Karl [**bek**stiyn], Ger [**bekh**shtiyn] (1826–1900) Piano manufacturer, born in Gotha, Germany. He founded his famous factory in Berlin in 1856.

Beck, Aaron T(emkin) (1921–) Psychiatrist, born in Rhode Island. He became professor of psychiatry and director of the Center for Cognitive Therapy at the University of Pennsylvania. He introduced cognitive therapy as a treatment approach for neurotic disorders, particularly depression. His books include *Depression: Causes and Treatment* (1972) and *Love is Never Enough* (1988).

Beck, Julian (1925–85) Actor, producer, and director, born in New York City. With **Judith Malina** (1926–) he was cofounder of the Living Theater. Known for his experimental and improvisatory approach, among his publications is *The Life of the Theater* (1972).

Beckenbauer, Franz [**bek**enbower], nickname **the Kaiser** (1945–) Footballer, born in Munich, Germany. As player, coach, manager, and administrator, he became a dynamic force in German football during the 1970s. He captained the West German national side to European Nations Cup success in 1972 and to the World Cup triumph of 1974. In 1972 he was European Footballer of the Year. He became manager of Germany in 1986, and is currently president of Bayern Munich.

Becker, Boris [**bek**er] (1967–) Tennis player, born in Leimen, Germany. He first came to prominence in 1984 when he finished runner-up in the US Open. In 1985 he became the youngest ever winner of the men's singles at Wimbledon, as well as the first unseeded winner. He successfully defended his title in 1986, and won it for a third time in 1989. He won the US Open in 1989, the Australian Open in 1991 and 1996, and the Association of Tennis Professionals world title in 1992. >> RR1173

Becker, Carl (Lotus) [**bek**er] (1873–1945) Historian, born near Waterloo, IA. He studied at Wisconsin University, and became professor of European history at Cornell University (1917–41). He combined his learning with a popular style, and made himself master of 18th-c thought on both sides of the Atlantic. *The Heavenly City of the Eighteenth Century Philosophers* (1932) was the best presentation of Enlightenment ideas in his day.

Becker, Gary (Stanley) (1930–) Economist, born in Pottstown, PA. Except for a period at Columbia University (1957–69), he has worked at the University of Chicago as an active participant in the 'Chicago school' of economics. Since the mid-1960s, he has concentrated on his 'new economics of the family', his controversial ideas challenging the singular consumptive nature of the family, viewing it instead as a multi-person unit which produces 'joint utility' from the skills and knowledge of different family members. He was awarded the Nobel Prize for Economics in 1992.

Becket, St Thomas à (1118–70) Saint and martyr, Archbishop of Canterbury, born in London, England, the son of a wealthy Norman merchant. He studied in London and Paris, then took up canon law at Bologna and Auxerre. In 1155, he became Chancellor, the first Englishman since the Conquest to hold high office. A skilled diplomat and brilliant courtly figure, he changed dramatically when created Archbishop of Canterbury (1162), resigning the chancellorship, and becoming a zealous ascetic, serving the Church as vigorously as he had the king. He thus came into conflict with Henry II's aims to keep the clergy in subordination to the state. He unwillingly consented to the Constitutions of Clarendon (1164) defining the powers of Church and state, but remained in disfavour. He fled the country after having his goods confiscated and the revenues of his sees sequestered. After two years in France, he pleaded personally to the pope, and was reinstated in his see. In 1170 he was reconciled with Henry, and returned to Canterbury, amid great public rejoicing. New quarrels soon broke out, however, and Henry's rashly-voiced wish to be rid of 'this turbulent priest' led to Becket's murder in Canterbury cathedral (29 Dec 1170) by four of the king's knights. He was canonized in 1173, and Henry did public penance at his tomb in 1174. In 1220 his bones were transferred to the Trinity Chapel, for many years a popular place of pilgrimage, as described by Chaucer in the prologue to *The Canterbury Tales*. Feast day 29 December. >> Henry II; Theobald

Beckett, Sir Edmund >> Grimthorpe, Edward Beckett
Beckett, Margaret (Mary) (1943–) British stateswoman. She studied at Manchester College of Science and

Technology, became a metallurgist, then became a research assistant for the Labour party (1970–4). Elected an MP in 1974, she went on to hold a number of political posts, eventually becoming deputy leader of the Labour Party (1992–4, including a short term as leader in 1994). She held shadow ministerial posts in social security (1984–9), the Treasury (1989–92), health (1994–5), and trade and industry (1995–7), and became president of the Board of Trade and secretary of state for trade and industry in 1997.

Beckett, Samuel (Barclay) (1906–89) Writer and playwright, born in Dublin. He became a lecturer in English at the Ecole Normale Supérieure in Paris and later in French at Trinity College, Dublin. From 1932 he lived mostly in France and was, for a time, an associate of James Joyce. His early poetry and first two novels, *Murphy* (1938) and *Watt* (c.1943, published 1953), were written in English, but not the trilogy *Molloy* (1951), *Malone Meurt* (1951, Malone Dies), and *L'Innommable* (1953, The Unnamable), or the plays *En attendant Godot* (1954, Waiting for Godot), which took London by storm, and *Fin de partie* (1956, End Game), all of which first appeared in French. His later works include *Happy Days* (1961), *Not I* (1973), and *Ill Seen Ill Said* (1981). He was awarded the 1969 Nobel Prize for Literature. Although there were one or two increasingly short pieces in later years, he wrote very infrequently towards the end. >> Joyce, James; Whitelaw, Billie

Beckett, Walter >> **Boyd, Martin**

Beckford, William Thomas (1760–1844) Writer and art collector, born in Fonthill, Wiltshire, S England, UK. From 1777 he spent much time on the European mainland, meeting Voltaire in 1778, and later making a grand tour in Flanders, Germany, and Italy. He is best known for his Gothic novel, *Vathek*, which was published in France in 1787. He returned to England in 1796, and proceeded to erect a Gothic palace, Fonthill Abbey, designed by James Wyatt, where he lived in seclusion until 1822. >> Voltaire; Wyatt, James

Beckmann, Ernst Otto (1853–1923) Organic chemist, born in Solingen, Germany. Professor at Erlangen and Leipzig, he discovered the molecular transformation of the oximes of ketones into acid amides, invented apparatus for the determination of freezing and boiling points, and devised the sensitive *Beckmann thermometer*.

Beckmann, Max (1884–1950) Expressionist painter, draughtsman, and printmaker, born in Leipzig, Germany. He trained at Weimar, and in 1904 moved to Berlin where he began painting large-scale, dramatic works. The suffering he experienced as a hospital orderly in World War 1 led him to develop a highly individual style influenced by Gothic art, which he used to give voice to the disillusionment he saw around him in post-war Germany. When he learnt that his work was to be included in an exhibition of Degenerate Art to be mounted by the Nazis in 1937, he fled to Holland, where he lived until emigrating to the USA in 1947.

Becquerel, (Antoine) Henri [bekerel] (1852–1908) Physicist, born in Paris. An expert on fluorescence, he discovered the *Becquerel rays*, emitted from the uranium salts in pitchblende, which led to the isolation of radium and to the beginnings of modern nuclear physics. For his discovery of radioactivity he shared the 1903 Nobel Prize for Physics with the Curies. >> Curie, Marie

Beddoes, Thomas (1760–1808) Physician and writer, born in Shifnal, Shropshire, WC England, UK. He studied medicine and became reader in chemistry at Oxford, but his sympathies with the French Revolution led to his resignation (1792). From 1798 to 1801 he developed at Clifton (Bristol) a 'pneumatic institute' for the cure of diseases by the inhalation of gases, with Humphry Davy his assistant. >> Davy, Humphry

Beddoes, Thomas Lovell (1803–49) Poet, born in Clifton, Bristol, SW England, UK, the eldest son of Thomas Beddoes. He studied at Oxford, and in 1822 published *The Bride's Tragedy*, a sombre murder drama. From 1825 he was engaged in the composition of a Gothic-Romantic drama, *Death's Jest-book*, which appeared in 1850, a year after his suicide. >> Beddoes, Thomas

Bede or **Baeda, St**, known as **the Venerable Bede** (c. 673–735) Anglo-Saxon scholar, theologian, and historian, born near Monkwearmouth, Durham, NE England. At the age of seven he was placed in the care of Benedict Biscop at the monastery of Wearmouth, and in 682 moved to the new monastery of Jarrow in Durham, where he was ordained priest in 703 and remained a monk for the rest of his life, studying and teaching. His devotion to Church discipline was exemplary and his industry enormous. He wrote homilies, lives of saints, lives of abbots, hymns, epigrams, works on chronology, grammar and physical science, and commentaries on the Old and New Testaments; and he translated the Gospel of St John into Anglo-Saxon just before his death. His greatest work was his Latin *Historia ecclesiastica gentis anglorum* (Ecclesiastical History of the English People), which he finished in 731, and which is the single most valuable source for early English history. He was canonized in 1899; feast day 25 May. >> Benedict Biscop

Bedford, David (1949–) Distance athlete, born in London, England, UK. An athlete of great stamina, he set the 10 000 m world record in 1972 (27:30·8). His only major championship victory was the international cross-country title in 1971. After retiring from competition he stayed in athletics as a promoter.

Bedford, John of Lancaster, Duke of (1389–1435) English prince, the third son of Henry IV. In 1414 his brother, Henry V, created him Duke of Bedford, and during the war with France he was appointed Lieutenant of the Kingdom. After Henry's death (1422), Bedford became Guardian of England, and Regent of France during the minority of his nephew, Henry VI. He defeated the French in several battles, but in 1428 failed to capture Orléans. In 1431 he had Joan of Arc burned at the stake in Rouen, and crowned Henry VI King of France in Paris; but in 1435 a treaty was negotiated between Charles VII and the Duke of Burgundy, which ruined English interests in France. >> Henry VI; Joan of Arc

Bedford, 13th Duke of >> **Russell, John Robert**

Bédier, (Charles Marie) Joseph [baydyay] (1864–1938) Scholar and mediaevalist, born in Paris. In 1893 he was appointed professor of mediaeval French language and literature at the Collège de France. His *Roman de Tristan et Iseult* in 1900 gained him a European reputation, and *Les Légendes épiques* (1908–13) developed his theory of the origin of the great cycles of romance.

Bednorz, (Johannes) Georg [bednaw(r)ts] (1950–) Physicist, born in Germany. He studied at Münster and Zürich universities, then joined Karl Müller at the IBM Zürich Research Laboratory at Rüschlikon (1982). Their work was chiefly directed to finding novel superconductors which would show superconductivity at higher temperatures than the near-absolute zero level previously observed. Following the success of this project in 1986–7, they shared the 1987 Nobel Prize for Physics. >> Müller, Karl

Bedser, Sir Alec (Victor) (1918–) Cricketer, born in Reading, Berkshire, S England, UK. With his twin brother, **Eric** (1918–), he was in the Surrey side which won seven consecutive county championships in the 1950s. He was the leading English bowler in the eight years after World War 2, and took 236 wickets in 51 Tests. Against Australia at Trent Bridge in 1953 he took 14 wickets for 99 runs, and in all first-class cricket he took 1924 wickets. He later managed MCC (Marylebone Cricket Club) teams abroad, and for a time was chairman of the selection committee. He was knighted in 1997. >> RR1150

Bee or **Bega, St** (7th-c) Irish princess, who took the veil from St Aidan. She founded the nunnery of St Bees in Cumberland. >> Aidan, St

Beebe, (Charles) William (1877–1962) Naturalist and explorer, born in Brooklyn, New York City. From 1899 he was curator of ornithology for the New York Zoological Society. He wrote many widely read books, including *Galapagos* (1923) and *The Arcturus Adventure* (1925), and explored ocean depths down to almost 1000 m in a bathysphere (1934).

Beecham, Sir Thomas (1879–1961) Conductor and impresario, born in St Helens, Merseyside, NW England, UK. He studied at Oxford, travelled extensively, and began his career as conductor with the New Symphony Orchestra in 1906. He soon branched out as a producer of opera, introducing British audiences to Diaghilev's Russian ballet. He was principal conductor (1932) and artistic director (1933) of Covent Garden, and in 1943 was conductor at the Metropolitan Opera, New York. In 1944 he returned to Britain, having married **Betty Humby** (d.1958), the pianist. In 1947 he founded the Royal Philharmonic Orchestra and conducted at Glyndebourne (1948–9). He did much to foster the works of Delius, Sibelius, and Richard Strauss, and was noted for his candid pronouncements on musical matters, his 'Lollipop' encores, and his after-concert speeches. >> Diaghilev

Beecher, Catharine Esther (1800–78) Educator and writer, born in East Hampton, NY, the daughter of Lyman Beecher. She was educated at home and private school (1810–16), then founded the Hartford Female Seminary, launching a life-long campaign as a lecturer, author, and advocate for women's education. In 1852, to promote female education in the W states, she founded the American Women's Education Association. Among her publications was *Treatise of Domestic Economy* (1841), and in 1869 she and her sister Harriet Beecher Stowe collaborated on a new edition, retitled *The American Woman's Home*, which became an influential guide for generations of US houswives. Although she was in the forefront on many social issues of her day, she did not believe that women should be involved in political affairs, and she opposed women's suffrage. >> Beecher, Lyman; Stowe, Harriet Beecher

Beecher, Henry Ward (1813–87) Congregationalist clergyman, orator, and writer, born in Litchfield, CT, the son of Lyman Beecher. He studied at Amherst College, MA, and in 1847 became the first pastor of Plymouth Congregational Church, New York City, where in his preaching he contended for temperance and denounced slavery. On the outbreak of the Civil War in 1861 his Church raised and equipped a volunteer regiment, and in 1865 he became an earnest advocate of reconciliation. For many years he wrote for *The Independent*, and after 1870 edited *The Christian Union* (later *Outlook*). >> Beecher, Lyman

Beecher, Lyman (1775–1863) Presbyterian minister and revivalist, born in New Haven, CT. He studied at Yale, and was ordained in 1799. He preached at East Hampton, Long Island, NY (1799–1810), then at Litchfield, CN (1810–26), his brand of Calvinism calling for constant church services and strong opposition to drinking. He then worked in Boston, and in 1832 went to Cincinnati as head of the newly founded Lane Theological Seminary, and to serve as pastor of the Second Presbyterian Church. His evangelical zeal and arrogance led to years of strife with more conservative Presbyterians, but he stayed until 1859, when he retired to the Brooklyn home of his son Henry. >> Beecher, Catharine/Henry Ward; Stowe, Harriet Beecher

Beecher Stowe, Harriet >> **Stowe, Harriet (Elizabeth) Beecher**

Beeching, Richard, Baron (1913–85) Engineer and administrator, born in Maidstone, Kent, SE England, UK. He studied at Imperial College, London, became chairman of the British Railways Board (1963–5), and deputy chairman of ICI (1966–8). He is best known for the scheme devised and approved under his chairmanship (the *Beeching Plan*) for the substantial contraction of the rail network of the UK. He was created a life peer in 1965.

Beene, Geoffrey (1927–) Fashion designer, born in Haynesville, LA. He studied fashion in New York City and Paris, in 1949 beginning a design career noteworthy for unconventional designs even before he started his own New York company (1962). His high-quality, ready-to-wear clothing for women and men, subtly coloured and distinctively simple, brought him eight Coty Awards.

Beer, Gavin de >> **de Beer, Sir Gavin**

Beerbohm, Sir (Henry) Max(imilian) [beerbohm], nickname **the Incomparable Max** (1872–1956) Writer and caricaturist, born in London, England, UK, the half-brother of Sir Herbert Beerbohm Tree. He studied at Oxford, and published his first volume of essays under the title *The Works of Max Beerbohm* (1896). In 1910 he married US actress Florence Kahn (d.1951), and went to live, except during the two World Wars, in Rapallo, Italy. His caricatures were collected in various volumes beginning with *Twenty-five Gentlemen* (1896) and *Poet's Corner* (1904). His best-known work was his only novel, *Zuleika Dobson* (1911), a parody of Oxford undergraduate life. >> Tree, Herbert Beerbohm

Beerbohm Tree, Herbert >> **Tree, Sir Herbert (Draper) Beerbohm**

Beethoven, Ludwig van [baytohvn] (1770–1827) see panel on p. 88

Beeton, Isabella Mary, *née* **Mayson**, known as **Mrs Beeton** (1836–65) British writer on cookery. She studied in Heidelberg and became an accomplished pianist. In 1856 she married **Samuel Orchard Beeton**, a publisher. She became a household name after the publication of her *Book of Household Management*, first published in parts (1859–60) in a women's magazine founded by her husband, and covering cookery and other branches of domestic science.

Bega, St >> **Bee, St**

Beggarstaff, J and **W** >> **Nicholson, William Newzam Prior**

Begin, Menachem (Wolfovitch) [baygin] (1913–92) Israeli statesman and prime minister (1977–83), born in Brest-Litovsk, Belarus. He studied law at Warsaw University, and as an active Zionist became head of the Betar Zionist movement in Poland in 1931. At the invasion of Poland in 1939 he fled to Lithuania, where he was arrested by the Russians. Released in 1941, he enlisted in the Free Polish Army, and was sent to British-mandated Palestine in 1942. Discharged from the army the following year, he became commander-in-chief of the Irgun Zvai Leumi resistance group. In 1948 he founded the right-wing Herut Freedom Movement, becoming chairman of the Herut Party, and in 1973 led the Likud front, a right-of-centre nationalist party, forming a coalition government in 1977. In the late 1970s he sought a peaceful settlement with the Egyptians, and attended peace conferences in Jerusalem (1977), and at Camp David at the invitation of President Carter (1978). He shared the 1978 Nobel Peace Prize with President Sadat of Egypt. >> Sadat; RR1064

LUDWIG VAN BEETHOVEN (1770–1827)

Beethoven was born in Bonn, the son of Johann van Beethoven, tenor in the choir of the archbishop-elector of Cologne, and his wife, Maria Magdalena. His first music lessons were from his father, an unstable yet ambitious man whose rough temper, excessive drinking, and anxiety to mould a second Mozart did not destroy Beethoven's talent or his love for music. He studied and performed successfully, despite becoming the main breadwinner of the family by the time he was 18. His father's increasingly serious alcoholism and the earlier death of his grandfather (1773) had plunged the family into deepening poverty.

Despite his father's hopes, Beethoven made little impact on the musical world until he was 11, when he left school and became assistant organist to Christian Gottlob Neefe at the court of Bonn, receiving instruction from him and other musicians. In 1783 he became the continuo player for Bonn opera, and accompanied their rehearsals on the keyboard. In 1787 he was sent to Vienna to receive further instruction, and took some lessons from Mozart. However, he returned in two months, called back by the death of his mother.

In 1790 he met Haydn, who agreed to teach him in Vienna, and Beethoven moved to Vienna permanently. There he also studied with Albrechtsberger and, possibly, Salieri. He was befriended by Prince Karl Lichnowsky (to whom he dedicated his Piano Sonata in C Minor, the *Pathétique*). Lichnowsky was the first of many friends to give him financial support throughout his working life. In 1795 he performed in public in Vienna for the first time, and published his Op.1 trios and Op.2 piano sonatas.

Beethoven's creative life is traditionally divided into three periods. In the first (1792–1802), the individuality of his style gradually developed, and he composed mainly for the piano. Among these works were his Symphony no.1 in C (1800) and Symphony no.2 in D (1802), his first six quartets, and the *Pathétique* (1799). The Moonlight Sonata in C Sharp Minor (1801) heralded the begining of the second period.

In 1802 Beethoven suffered seriously from depression, brought about by a realization that his hearing problems, first noticed in 1796, were becoming critical and would lead to incurable deafness. Deafness did not effect his ability to compose, but it curtailed his ability to perform and teach (as all communication with him had to be through written notes). In his despair he wrote a will-like document to his two brothers, known as the 'Heliegenstadt Testament', in which he confessed his misery and indicated that he felt close to death. He recovered, however, and the works of this middle period, known as his 'heroic period', show him determined to strive creatively in the face of despair.

His third symphony (twice the then normal length for a symphony) was originally dedicated to Napoleon Bonaparte, whom he saw as a revolutionary hero and liberator. But when Beethoven heard Napoleon had proclaimed himself emperor, he defaced the title page in disillusionment and called the work *Eroica* (1803). Other works during this period include the Kreuzer Sonata (1803), symphonies 3–7, the Violin Concerto in D Major (1806), the Razumovsky Quartets (1806), the Emperor Concerto (1809), and the Archduke Trio Op.97 (1811).

In his only opera, *Fidelio* (written 1805, revised 1806 and 1814), the dominating themes are fidelity, personal liberation, and a symbolic passage from darkness into light. That married infidelity is central to the opera probably reflects Beethoven's desire to marry. At the time of the composition he was deeply in love with a socially unattainable pupil, Josephine von Brunsvik. In 1801 he had wanted to marry Countess Giulietta Guicciardi, also a pupil, to whom he had dedicated the Moonlight Sonata, but she eventually married someone else in 1803. Beethoven always regretted not marrying, but even his love for Therese Malfatti in 1810 ended without marriage. On his death a letter, written in 1812, was found among his belongings. It was addressed to his 'Immortal Beloved', and various suppositions have been made about the identity of the recipient (if, indeed, it had ever been sent).

From 1813 (the beginning of his third period, also known as the 'silent period') he composed less, and his domestic life became increasingly chaotic. He lived in squalor and dressed negligently, although he was always a prolific bather, and theories about the cause of his deafness stemming from rheumatic inflammation centre around his habit of pouring cold water over his head while composing, to refresh himself, and then not drying his plentiful hair, but impatiently working or walking with it wet in all weather.

He became increasingly argumentative and irascible as he became more and more tormented by his deafness. In 1812, Goethe described him as 'an utterly untamed personality', whose aggressive attitude to life was perhaps understandable but not easy to live with. However, despite his difficult personality and anti-social eccentricities, the poet Franz Grillparzer, who wrote a funeral address for Beethoven, summed up the feelings of Beethoven's friends with these words: 'despite all these absurdities, there was something so touching and ennobling about him that one could not help admiring him and feeling drawn to him'.

Beethoven gave his last public performance on the piano in 1814, but continued to be respected as an important composer by Viennese society, despite his unkemptness and arrogance. His achievements in the last decade of his life include the *Diabelli Variations* (1820–3), the last piano sonatas, the last six string quartets, the Mass in D Major, *Missa solemnis* (1823), and the Choral Symphony, no. 9 (1824) – in which he set *An die Freude* (Ode to Joy) by Friedrich von Schiller in the final movement. (Beethoven greatly admired the work of Schiller and Goethe; the emotion of *Sturm und Drang* (Storm and Stress) found a musical voice in many of his compositions.)

In his later years he became preoccupied with the prolonged litigation to obtain custody of his dead brother's son, Karl, who did not fare well under Beethoven's erratic guidance, growing up to be an unhappy and wild young man. In 1826, Karl attempted suicide. After much discussion it was decided he should join the army, and together they spent a few final weeks with Beethoven's surviving brother in the country before Karl was to leave. On his return journey in December 1826, Beethoven was taken ill with peritonitis, which developed into dropsy. He died during a thunderstorm after a long and painful illness. His last action was to raise a clenched fist.

>> Albrechtsberger; Goethe; Grillparzer; Haydn; Mozart; Napoleon; Salieri; Schiller

Behaim, Martin [bayhiym] (1449–1507) Navigator and geographer, born in Nuremberg, Germany. He settled in Portugal about 1484 and was associated with the later Portuguese discoveries along the coast of Africa. He revisited Nuremberg in 1490, and there constructed the oldest extant terrestrial globe. A crater on the near side of the Moon is named after him.

Beham, Hans Sebald [bayham] (1500–50) Painter and engraver, born in Nuremberg, Germany. He was one of Albrecht Dürer's seven followers known as the 'Little Masters'. Working in Frankfurt, he produced hundreds of woodcuts and copper engravings as illustrations for books. >> Dürer

Behan, Brendan (Francis) [beean] (1923–64) Writer, born in Dublin. He left school at 14 to become a house painter, and soon joined the IRA. In 1939 he was sentenced to three years in Borstal for attempting to blow up a Liverpool shipyard, and soon after his release given 14 years by a Dublin military court for the attempted murder of two detectives, but was released by a general amnesty (1946). He was in prison again in Manchester (1947), and deported in 1952. His first play, *The Quare Fellow* (1956; filmed 1962), starkly dramatised the prison atmosphere prior to a hanging. His exuberant Irish wit, spiced with balladry and bawdry and a talent for fantastic caricature, found rein in his next play *The Hostage* (1958, first produced in Irish as *An Giall*). It is also evident in the autobiographical novel, *Borstal Boy* (1958), and in *Brendan Behan's Island* (1963). >> Behan, Domenic

Behan, Dominic [beean] (1928–89) Novelist and folklorist, born in Dublin, Ireland, the brother of Brendan Behan. He adapted old airs and poems into contemporary Irish Republican material, notably in *The Patriot Game*. Resentfully overshadowed for much of his life by the legend of his brother, he lived largely outside Ireland from 1947 as a journalist and singer. He ultimately settled in Scotland, where he won acceptance as a writer and nationalist. His only novel, *The Public Life of Parable Jones*, was published just before his death. >> Behan, Brendan

Behn, Aphra [ben], *née* **Amis** (1640–89) Writer and adventurer, born in Wye, Kent, SE England, UK. She was brought up in Suriname, where she made the acquaintance of the enslaved negro prince Oroonoko, the subject afterwards of one of her novels, in which she anticipated Rousseau's 'noble savage'. She returned to England in 1663, then became a professional spy in Antwerp, sending back political and naval information. She turned to writing, as perhaps the first professional woman author in England, and wrote many coarse but popular Restoration plays, such as *The Rover* (1678), and later published *Oroonoko* (1688).

Behrens, Peter [bairenz] (1868–1940) Architect and designer, born in Hamburg, Germany. Trained as a painter, he was appointed director of the Dusseldorf Art and Craft School (1903–7). In 1907 he became artistic adviser to Walther Rathenau at the AEG electrical company in Berlin, for whom he designed a turbine assembly works (1909) of glass and steel, a landmark in industrial architectural style. He was professor at Dusseldorf and Vienna, and trained several notable modern architects, including Le Corbusier, Ludwig Mies van der Rohe, and Walter Gropius. >> Rathenau

Behring, Emil (Adolf) von [bayring] (1854–1917) Bacteriologist and pioneer in immunology, born in Hansdorf, Germany. He was professor of hygiene at Halle (1894–5) and Marburg (from 1895), and discovered antitoxins for diphtheria and tetanus. He was awarded the first Nobel Prize for Physiology or Medicine (1901).

Behrman, S(amuel) N(athaniel) [bairman] (1893–1973) Playwright, screenwriter, and journalist, born in Worcester, MA. The production of a sophisticated comedy, *The Second Man* (1927), made him famous, and he was tagged the 'American Noel Coward'. >> Coward

Beiderbecke, Bix [biyderbek], popular name of **Leon Bismarck Beiderbecke** (1903–31) Cornettist, born in Davenport, IA. He was largely self-taught on piano and cornet, playing in local bands as a teenager. When expelled from a military academy, he began the short career that made him one of the most celebrated jazz performers of the 1920s. His bell-like tone and lyrical solo improvisations were heard to best effect in various small groups. His later career ravaged by alcoholism, he succumbed to pneumonia at the age of 28. >> Whiteman, Paul

Beilby, Sir George Thomas [beelbee] (1850–1924) Industrial chemist, born in Edinburgh, EC Scotland, UK. He improved the method of shale oil distillation, and invented a manufacturing process for synthesizing alkaline cyanides. He was knighted in 1916.

Beilstein, Friedrich Konrad [bilstiyn] (1838–1906) Encyclopedist of organic chemistry, born in St Petersburg, Russia. He studied chemistry in Germany, and was lecturer at Göttingen and later professor at St Petersburg from 1866. His name is synonymous with his *Handbook of Organic Chemistry* (1881), which formed a substantially complete catalogue of organic compounds.

Béjart, Maurice [bayzhah(r)], originally **Maurice Jean Berger** (1927–) Choreographer, born in Marseille, France. He trained at the Marseilles Opéra Ballet and then in Paris and London. He moved to the Royal Swedish Ballet, and in 1954 founded his own company in Brussels, where he worked as choreographer and director, returning to France in 1979. He became director of Béjart Ballet Lausanne (1987–92) and Rudra Béjart Ballet Lausanne (1992–).

Beke, Charles Tilstone (1800–74) Explorer and biblical critic, born in London, England, UK. A scholar of ancient history, philology, and ethnography, he wrote *Origines Biblicae, or Researches in Primeval History* (1834). He explored Abyssinia (1840–3), where he studied the course of the Blue Nile, mapped 70 000 sq mi, and collected 14 vocabularies. In 1874 he explored the region at the head of the Red Sea in search of Mt Sinai.

Békésy, Georg von [baykezee] (1899–1972) Aural physiologist, born in Budapest. He studied physics there, then worked as a telephone research engineer in Hungary (1924–46). His research, first in Stockholm (1946–7), then at Harvard (1947–66), led to a study of the human ear and how it analyses and transmits sounds to the brain. He was awarded the Nobel Prize for Physiology or Medicine in 1961.

Bekhterev, Vladimir Mikhailovich [byekterof] (1857–1927) Neuropathologist, born in Viatka province, Russia. As professor at Kazan he studied neural electricity, and founded the Psychoneurological Institute in St Petersburg (Leningrad). He developed a theory of conditioned reflexes, independently of Pavlov. >> Pavlov

Bel, Joseph Achille Le >> **Le Bel, Joseph Achille**

Belasco, David [belaskoh] (1853–1931) Producer and playwright, born in San Francisco, CA. He began as a child actor, then worked in several San Francisco theatres (1873–9). He moved to New York City (1880) to manage the Madison Square theatre and the Lyceum, before building his own theatre (1906). As a producer he experimented with visual effects, which had an important influence on standards of theatrical production.

Belcher, Sir Edward (1799–1877) British naval commander, born in Halifax, Nova Scotia, Canada. He entered the navy in 1812, and explored the W coast of America (1836–42). In 1852 he commanded a fruitless expedition sent out to search for Sir John Franklin. He was knighted in 1867. >> Franklin, John

Bel Geddes, Norman [bel gedis] (1893–1958) Industrial and theatrical designer, born in Adrian, MI. He studied at the Art Institute of Chicago, and in 1918 became stage designer at New York's Metropolitan Opera. From 1920 to 1937 his designs for Broadway plays, notably *The Miracle* (1923), and film sets marked him as an innovator in modern stage lighting. A vigorous self-promoter and a visionary, he pioneered industrial design with the 1927 establishment of a firm to create streamlined versions of household appliances, cars, ships, and aeroplanes.

Belidor, Bernard Forest de [belidaw(r)] (1698–1761) Engineer, born in Catalonia, Spain. As professor of artillery at La Fère military academy, he wrote some of the best-known and most comprehensive engineering handbooks in pre-revolutionary France, covering military engineering (ballistics and fortifications) and civil engineering. His works influenced engineering practice for a century after their publication.

Belisarius [belisairius] (505–65) Byzantine general under Emperor Justinian, born in Germania, Illyria. He defeated the Persians (530), suppressed an insurrection in Constantinople (532), and defeated the Vandals in Africa (533–4) and the Ostrogoths in Italy (535–40). He later again drove back the Persians (542), and repelled an assault of the Huns on Constantinople (559). Falsely accused of conspiracy against the emperor, he was imprisoned (562), but was restored to favour soon after. >> Justinian

Bell, Acton >> Brontë, Anne

Bell, Alexander Graham (1847–1922) Educationist and inventor, born in Edinburgh, EC Scotland, UK, the son of Alexander Melville Bell. He studied at Edinburgh and London, and worked as assistant to his father in teaching elocution (1868–70). In 1870 he went to Canada, and in 1871 moved to the USA and became professor of vocal physiology at Boston (1873), devoting himself to the teaching of deaf-mutes and to spreading his father's system of 'visible speech'. After experimenting with various acoustical devices he produced the first intelligible telephonic transmission with a message to his assistant on 5 June 1875, and patented the telephone in 1876. He defended the patent against Elisha Gray, and formed the Bell Telephone Company in 1877. In 1880 he established the Volta Laboratory, and invented the photophone (1880) and the graphophone (1887). After 1897 his principal interest was in aeronautics. >> Bell, Alexander Melville; Curtiss, Glenn; Gray, Elisha

Bell, Alexander Melville (1819–1905) Educationist, born in Edinburgh, EC Scotland, UK, the father of Alexander Graham Bell. A teacher of elocution at Edinburgh University and University College, London, he moved to Canada in 1870, then settled in Washington, DC. In 1867 he published *Visible Speech*, a system showing the position of the vocal organs for each sound. >> Bell, Alexander Graham

Bell, Andrew (1753–1832) Educationist, founder of the 'Madras System' of education, born in St Andrews, Fife, E Scotland, UK. After taking Episcopal orders he went to India (1787), and in 1789 became superintendent of the Madras military orphanage. Finding it impossible to obtain teaching staff, he taught with the aid of the pupils themselves by introducing the monitorial system. His pamphlet entitled *An Experiment in Education* (1797) attracted little attention in Britain until in 1803 Joseph Lancaster also published a tract recommending the monitorial system. In 1811 he became superintendent of the National Society for the Education of the Poor, whose schools soon numbered 12 000. >> Lancaster, Joseph

Bell, Sir Charles (1774–1842) Anatomist and surgeon, famous for his neurological discoveries, born in Edinburgh,

EC Scotland, UK. He lectured in anatomy and surgery in London, was appointed surgeon to the Middlesex Hospital in 1812, and became professor of surgery at Edinburgh from 1836. He distinguished between the sensory and motor nerves in the brain, studied gunshot wounds, and worked on the functions of the spinal nerves. The type of facial paralysis known as *Bell's palsy* is named after him.

Bell, Currer >> Brontë, Charlotte

Bell, Ellis >> Brontë, Emily (Jane)

Bell, George Kennedy Allen (1883–1958) Clergyman and ecumenist, born on Hayling I, Hampshire, S England, UK. He studied at Oxford, was ordained in 1907, and became Dean of Canterbury (1924–9), and Bishop of Chichester (1929–58). A strong supporter of the ecumenical movement, he risked misunderstanding during World War 2 by his efforts towards peace with Germany and his condemnation of the policy of saturation bombing.

Bell, Gertrude (Margaret Lowthian) (1868–1926) Archaeologist and traveller, born at Washington Hall, Durham, NE England, UK. She studied at Oxford, and travelled much in the Middle East. During World War 1 she was seconded to the Mesopotamia Expeditionary Force in Basra and Baghdad, subsequently becoming oriental secretary to the British High Commission in Iraq, and first director of antiquities there.

Bell, Henry (1767–1830) Engineer and pioneer of steam navigation, born in Linlithgow, West Lothian, EC Scotland, UK. In 1812 he successfully launched the 30-ton *Comet* on the Clyde. Plying regularly between Greenock and Glasgow, it was the first passenger-carrying steam-boat in European waters.

Bell, John (1811–1895) Sculptor, born in Hopton, Suffolk, E England, UK. He produced the Guards' Memorial (1858) in Waterloo Place, and the American group in the Hyde Park Albert Memorial (1873). He popularized carved wooden breadknives and trenchers.

Bell, John Stewart (1928–90) Physicist, born in Belfast. He studied at Belfast University, and worked at the UK Atomic Energy Research Establishment before joining the staff at CERN in Geneva (1960). Here he developed the equations known as *Bell's inequalities*, which predicted how measurements on one proton would affect measurements made on another. Subsequent experimental results have validated his predictions, confirming him as one of the leading theoretical physicists of his generation.

Bell, Lawrence (Dale) (1894–1956) Aircraft designer and constructor, born in Mentone, IN. In 1935 he formed the Bell Aircraft Corporation, and among its more notable productions was the P-59 Airacomet, the first US jet-propelled aircraft (1942). From 1941 he produced a famous line of helicopters, and in 1947 the first rocket-propelled aeroplane, the Bell X-1, the first manned aircraft to exceed the speed of sound.

Bell, Martin (1938–) Television journalist, born in Cambridge, Cambridgeshire, EC England, UK. He studied at Cambridge and joined the BBC in 1962, becoming overseas reporter (1964–76), diplomatic correspondent (1976–7), chief North American correspondent (1977–89), Berlin correspondent (1989–93), Vienna correspondent (1993–4), and foreign affairs correspondent (1994–6). Awards include the Royal Television Society's Reporter of the Year (1976, 1992) and the Radio and Television Industries Club Newscaster of the Year (1995). He fought an 'anti-sleaze' campaign in the 1997 general election, and was returned – much to his own surprise, describing himself as an 'accidental MP' in his maiden speech – as Independent MP for Tatton.

Bell, Patrick (1799–1869) Clergyman and inventor, born in Auchterhouse, Angus, E Scotland, UK. He worked on the development of a mechanical reaper, the prototype of which earned a £50 premium from the Highland and Agricultural Society in 1827. Its adoption by British farmers was very slow, however, and when four of his reapers were sent to the USA they enabled Cyrus McCormick and others to realize their full potential. >> McCormick

Bell, Robert Anning (1863–1933) Painter, designer, illustrator, and decorator, born in London, England, UK. He studied painting from 1881 at the Royal Academy Schools, Westminster School of Art and in Paris. He executed mosaics in the Houses of Parliament and Westminster Cathedral, and held successive posts at Liverpool University (from 1894), Glasgow School of Art (1911), and the Royal College of Art, London, where he was professor of design (1918–24).

Bell, Thomas (1792–1800) Naturalist, born in Poole, Dorset, S England, UK. A dental surgeon at Guy's Hospital (1817–61), he lectured in and became professor of zoology at King's College, London, in 1836. His *British Stalk-eyed Crustacea* (1853) remains a standard work on British crabs and lobsters.

Bell, Vanessa, née **Stephen** (1879–1961) Painter and decorative designer, a leading member of the Bloomsbury Group, born in London, England, UK, the elder sister of Virginia Woolf. She studied at the Royal Academy Schools (1901–4), and in 1907 married the critic **Clive Bell** (1881–1964), but in 1916 left him to live at Firle, East Sussex, with Duncan Grant, a fellow-contributor to Roger Fry's Omega Workshops (1913–19). Elected to the London Group in 1919, she exhibited with them regularly from 1920. >> Fry, Roger; Grant, Duncan; Stephen, Leslie; Woolf, Virginia

Bella, Stefano della (1610–64) Engraver, born in Florence, Italy. He worked for Cardinal Richelieu and for the Grand Duke of Tuscany. His engravings were in the manner of Jacques Callot, and his enormous output consisted of battle-pieces, landscapes, and animal and masque designs. >> Callot

Bellamy, David (James) (1933–) British botanist, writer, and broadcaster. He studied at London University, taught at Durham (1960–80), and became a professor at Nottingham in 1987. He established the Conservation Foundation in 1988. The writer of numerous conservation-oriented books, he is best known for his eccentric manner in TV programmes designed to create a greater awareness and understanding of the natural environment. Working as both presenter and scriptwriter, his many programmes include *Life in Our Sea* (1970), *Bellamy's Britain* (1975), *Bellamy's Birds' Eye View* (1988), and *Bellamy's Border Raids: The Peak District* (1994).

Bellamy, Edward (1850–98) Novelist, born in Chicopee Falls, MA. He was admitted to the bar in 1871, then turned to journalism. He achieved immense popularity with his Utopian romance *Looking Backward* (1888), a work which predicted a new social order and influenced economic thinking in the USA and Europe.

Bellany, John (1942–) Painter and etcher, born in Port Seton, East Lothian, E Scotland, UK. He studied at Edinburgh College of Art (1960–5) and at the Royal College of Art (1965–8). He is one of the generation of Scots who, in the 1970s, adopted an expressive form of Realism inspired by Leger and by German art. >> Leger

Bellarmine, St Robert [belermin], originally **Roberto Francesco Romolo Bellarmino** (1542–1621) Jesuit theologian, born in Montepulciano, Italy. He entered the order of Jesuits at Rome in 1560, and studied theology at Padua and Louvain. In 1570 he was appointed to the chair of theology at Louvain, but returned to Rome in 1576 to lecture at the Roman College. In 1592 he became rector there, was made a cardinal in 1599 against his own inclination, and in 1602

Archbishop of Capua. After the death of Clement VIII, he evaded the papal chair, but was induced by Paul V to hold an important place in the Vatican from 1605 until his death. He was canonized in 1930, and was the chief defender of the Church in the 16th-c. In the 17th-c, stone beer jugs with a caricature of his likeness, called *bellarmines*, were produced by Flemish Protestants to ridicule him. Feast day 17 May.

Bellay, Joachim du [belay] (1522–60) Poet and prose writer, born in Lire, France. After his friend and fellow-student, Ronsard, he was the most important member of the *Pléiade*. His *Défense et illustration de la langue Française* (1549, The Defence and Illustration of the French Language), the manifesto of the *Pléiade*, advocating the rejection of mediaeval linguistic traditions and a return to Classical and Italian models, had a considerable influence at the time. >> Ronsard

Bell Burnell, Susan Jocelyn, née **Bell** (1943–) Radio astronomer, born in York, North Yorkshire, N England, UK. She studied at Glasgow and Cambridge, and later joined the staff of the Royal Observatory, Edinburgh. In 1967 she was a research student at Cambridge working with Antony Hewish when she noticed an unusually regular signal, shown to be bursts of radio energy at a constant interval of just over a second – the first pulsar. >> Gold; Hewish

Belleau, Rémy [beloh] (1528–77) Poet, born in Nogent le Rotrou, France. He was a member of the *Pléiade*, and published in 1556 a translation of Anacreon that was at first believed to be an original imitation. *Bergerie* (1565) is a medley of delicately descriptive prose and verse, of which 'Avril' still appears in anthologies. >> Anacreon

Belle-Isle, Charles Louis Fouquet, duc de (Duke of) [bel eel] (1684–1761) French statesman and soldier, born in Villefranche, France. After serving in many wars, he became a Marshal of France in 1741. In the War of the Austrian Succession (1740–8) he stormed Prague in 1742, then led the skilful retreat to Eger. He raised the siege of Genoa (1747), and drove the Austrians into Lombardy before the war ended. During the Seven Years' War he was minister for war (1758–60).

Bellenden or **Ballantyne, John** (?–1587) Scottish writer and clergyman. He studied at St Andrews and the Sorbonne. His translations in 1533 of Boece's *Historia Gentis Scotorum*, and of the first five books of Livy, are interesting as vigorous specimens of early Scottish prose. He enjoyed great favour at the court of James V, and became Archdeacon of Moray and Canon of Ross. Becoming involved in ecclesiastical controversy, he went into exile in Rome.

Bellingham, John >> Perceval, Spencer

Bellingshausen, Fabian Gottlieb Benjamin von [bellings-howzn] (1778–1852) Explorer, born in Ösel, Estonia. In 1819–21 he led an expedition around the world which made several discoveries in the Pacific, and sailed to 70°S, probably discovering the Antarctic continent. The *Bellingshausen Sea* was named after him.

Bellini, Gentile [beleenee] (c. 1429–1507) Painter, born in Venice, Italy, the son of Jacopo Bellini and brother of Giovanni Bellini. He worked in his father's studio, and was chosen to paint the portrait of Sultan Muhammad II in Constantinople (c.1480, National Gallery, London). He is also known for his scenes of Venice. >> Bellini, Giovanni/Jacopo

Bellini, Giovanni [beleenee] (c. 1430–1516) Painter, born in Venice, Italy, the son of Jacopo Bellini and brother of Gentile Bellini. One of his chief contributions to Italian art was his successful integration of figures with landscape background. Another is his naturalistic treatment of light.

Almost all his pictures are religious, although he painted the occasional pagan allegory. He is perhaps best known for a long series of Madonnas to which he brought a humanistic sensibility usually absent in Raphael's more austere renderings of the subject. All the most talented younger painters of his day – Giorgione and Titian among them – came to his studio, and through them his innovations were perpetuated. >> Bellini, Gentile/Jacopo; Giorgione; Titian

Bellini, Jacopo [be**lee**nee] (c. 1400–70) Painter, born in Venice, Italy, the father of Gentile Bellini and Giovanni Bellini. He studied under Gentile da Fabriano, and painted a wide range of subjects; but only a few Madonnas in Italy and drawings in the Louvre and the British Museum remain, which show his interest in architectural and landscape setting. >> Bellini, Gentile/Giovanni; Fabriano

Bellini, Vincenzo [be**lee**nee] (1801–35) Operatic composer, born in Catania, Italy. An organist's son, he was sent by a Sicilian nobleman to the Conservatorio of Naples. Il Pirata (1827) carried the composer's name beyond Italy, but he is now best known for La Sonnambula (1831) and Norma (1832). He influenced several later operatic composers, including Wagner. >> Wagner, Richard

Bellman, Carl Michael (1740–95) Poet and writer of popular songs, born in Stockholm. His most important collections of songs are the Fredmans Epistlar (1790, Epistles of Fredman), with their overtones of biblical parody and burlesque, and the Fredmans sånger (1791, Songs of Fredman). The songs combine broad humour and rococo charm, and are still popular throughout Scandinavia.

Bello, Andrés [**bay**oh] (1781–1865) Venezuelan writer and polymath, born in Caracas. He studied in Caracas, then lived in London (1810–29), before finally settling in Chile, where he became a senior public servant, senator, and first rector of the University (1843). The most remarkable Latin American intellectual of the 19th-c, his writings embrace language, law, education, history, philosophy, poetry, drama, and science.

Belloc, (Joseph) Hilaire (Pierre) [be**l**ok] (1870–1953) Writer, born in St Cloud near Paris, France, the son of a French barrister and his English wife. The family moved to England during the Franco-Prussian war, and he studied at the Oratory School, Birmingham, under Newman, and at Oxford. He became a naturalized British subject in 1902, and a Liberal MP in 1906, but, disillusioned with politics, did not seek re-election in 1910. He was a close friend of G K Chesterton, who illustrated many of his books. He is best known for his nonsensical verse for children: The Bad Child's Book of Beasts (1896) and the Cautionary Tales (1907). He also wrote many travel books, including Path to Rome (1902) and The Old Road (1910), reconstructing the Pilgrim's Way; several historical studies such as Robespierre (1901) and Napoleon (1932); and religious works, including Europe and the Faith (1920) and The Great Heresies (1938). He was an energetic Roman Catholic apologist. >> Chesterton; Newman, John Henry

Bellotto, Bernardo [be**l**otoh] (1720–80) Painter, born in Venice, Italy, the nephew of Antonio Canaletto. He attained high excellence as a painter, and also as an engraver on copper. He is known for his detailed views of many European cities, renowned for their accuracy and realism. His paintings of Warsaw were used after World War 2 in the restoration of the historic areas of the city. >> Canaletto

Bellow, Saul (1915–) Writer, born in Lachine, Quebec, Canada. In 1924 his family moved to Chicago, and he attended university there and at Northwestern University. He abandoned his postgraduate studies at Wisconsin University to become a writer, and his first novel, The Dangling Man, appeared in 1944. Other works include The Victim (1947), Henderson the Rain-King (1959), Herzog (1964), Humboldt's Gift (1975; Pulitzer, 1976); both A Theft and The Bellarosa Connection appeared in 1989. Later works include a collection of essays It All Adds Up (1994). He was awarded the Nobel Prize for Literature in 1976.

Bellows, George (Wesley) (1882–1925) Painter and lithographer, born in Columbus, OH. He was a leading figure in the movement known as The Eight, which sought to break away from Postimpressionism into the vivid harshness of social realism. He delighted in prize fights, festivals, and the teeming life of the cities. Probably his most famous work is 'Dempsey and Firpo' (1924, Museum of Modern Art, New York City). >> Henri, Robert; Sloan, John

Belmondo, Jean-Paul [bel**mon**doh] (1933–) Actor, born in Neuilly-sur-Seine, France. He studied at the Paris Conservatoire, took part in provincial tours, and appeared in several films, but it was the film A Bout de Souffle (1959, Breathless) which made him famous. Later films include Le Voleur (1967, The Thief) and Hold Up (1985).

Belmont, Alva (Erskine Smith Vanderbilt), née **Smith** (1853–1933) Social reformer, born in Mobile, AL. A committed socialite, she worked her way into the New York social elite as the wife (1875, divorced 1895) of **William Kissam Vanderbilt** (1849–1920), and married her daughter to the Duke of Marlborough. After the death of her second husband, **Oliver Belmont** (1908), she developed an interest in women's rights, became involved with militant feminism, and being a wealthy widow made large donations to the suffrage movement. She later became president of the National Woman's Party (1921–33).

Belo, Carlos (Felipe Ximenes) (1948–) Roman Catholic bishop, born in East Timor, Indonesia. Ordained bishop in 1983, he became an outspoken critic of the Indonesian regime's actions in East Timor, and shared the Nobel Prize for Peace in 1996. >> Ramos-Horta

Belon, Pierre [bel**ō**] (1517–64) Naturalist, born near Le Mans, France. He travelled in Asia Minor, Egypt, and Arabia, and wrote valuable treatises on trees, herbs, birds, and fishes. He was one of the first to establish the homologies between the skeletons of different vertebrates.

Belshazzar [bel**sha**zer], Gr **Balt(h)asar** (?–539 BC) Son of Nabonidus, king of Babylon (556-539 BC), and ruler after his father was exiled in 550 BC. In the Book of Daniel, mysterious writing appears on the wall of his palace, which Daniel interprets as predicting the fall of the empire to the Persians and Medes. He died during the capture of Babylon. >> RR1034

Bely, Andrey [be**lee**], pseudonym of **Boris Nikolayevich Bugayev** (1880–1934) Novelist, poet, and critic, born in Moscow. A leading Symbolist writer, he early met Vladimir Soloviev, the religious philosopher, and fell under his influence. While at Moscow University he wrote Decadent poetry which he published in Severnaya simfoniya (1902, The Northern Symphony). Serebryany golub (1910, The Silver Dove) was his first and most accessible novel, and was followed by his masterpiece Peterburg (1913–14, St Petersburg). The autobiographical Kotik Letayev (1922) is his most original work, a stream-of-consciousness attempt to show how children become aware of what is going on in the world. His later novels are more overtly satirical of the pre-revolutionary Russian scene but are still highly experimental. He is regarded as one of the most important Russian writers of the 1920s. >> Soloviev

Belzoni, Giovanni Battista [belt**zoh**nee] (1778–1823) Explorer and antiquity-hunter, born in Padua, Italy. In 1815 he went to Egypt, and there was commissioned by Mehemet Ali to construct hydraulic machinery for irrigation purposes. He devoted himself thereafter to tomb robbing and the exploration of Egyptian antiquities, including the removal from Thebes of the colossal bust of Rameses II, which he sent to the British Museum. >> Mehemet Ali

Bembo, Pietro [**bem**boh] (1470–1547) Poet and scholar, born in Venice, Italy. In 1513 he was made secretary to Pope Leo X, and in 1539 a cardinal by Paul III, who appointed him to the dioceses of Gubbio and Bergamo. Bembo was the restorer of good style in both Latin and Italian literature, especially with his treatise on Italian prose (*Prose della volgar lingua*, 1525), which marked an era in Italian grammar.

Bemelmans, Ludwig [**bem**elmanz] (1898–1962) Writer and illustrator, born in Merano, Italy (formerly, Meran, Austria). He studied in Bavaria, emigrated to New York City (1914), worked at various occupations, then began writing for periodicals. He became famous for his children's books, such as *Madeline* (1939), which he also illustrated.

Benacerraf, Baruj (1920–) Immunologist, born in Caracas. He was research director at the National Centre for Scientific Research in Paris (1950–6) and professor at New York University (1957–68) and Harvard (from 1970). His research led to the discovery of immune-response genes that regulate immunology in organ transplants, for which he shared the 1980 Nobel Prize for Physiology or Medicine. >> RR1124

Benaud, Richie [**ben**oh], popular name of **Richard Benaud** (1930–) Cricketer, broadcaster, and international sports consultant, born in Penrith, New South Wales, Australia. He played in 63 Test matches for Australia (captain in 28), including three successful tours of England (1953, 1956, 1961). An all-rounder, he scored 2201 Test runs, including three centuries, and took 248 wickets with subtle leg-spin bowling. He is now a well-known cricket commentator.

Benavente y Martínez, Jacinto [bena**ven**tay ee mah(r)**tee**neth] (1866–1954) Playwright, born in Madrid. He intended to enter the legal profession, but turned to literature. After publishing some poems and short stories he won recognition as a playwright, writing over 150 plays, including several brilliantly satirical society comedies. His masterpiece is *Los intereses creados* (1907, trans The Bonds of Interest), an allegorical play in the *commedia dell'arte* style.

Ben Bella, (Mohammed) Ahmed [ben **be**la] (1918–) A key figure in the Algerian War of Independence against France, and Algeria's first prime minister (1962–3) and president (1963–5), born in Maghnia, Algeria. He fought with the Free French in World War 2, and in 1949 became head of the Organisation Spéciale, the paramilitary wing of the Algerian nationalist Parti du Peuple Algérien. In 1952 he escaped from a French-Algerian prison to Cairo, where he became a key member of the Front de Libération Nationale (FLN). Captured by the French in 1956, he spent the remainder of the war in a French prison. Following independence (1962) he became president, but was deposed in 1965. After 15 years of imprisonment, he went into voluntary exile in 1980, returning to Algeria in 1990.

Benbow, John (1653–1702) English naval commander, born in Shrewsbury, Shropshire, WC England, UK. He was master of the fleet at Beachy Head (1690), and at Barfleur and La Hague (1692). He commanded squadrons off Dunkirk (1693–5), and as a rear-admiral was commander-in-chief West Indies from 1698. In 1702, he came up against a superior French force off Santa Marta. For four days he kept up a running fight, almost deserted by the rest of his squadron, until his right leg was smashed by a chain shot and he was forced to return to Jamaica, where he died.

Bench, Johnny (Lee) (1947–) Baseball player, born in Oklahoma City, OK. Playing in the National League with the Cincinnati Reds, he was the outstanding catcher of the 1970s. He hit over 200 home runs, and led the league three times in seven years for runs batted in. He was the National League's Most Valuable Player on several occasions. >> RR1144

Benchley, Robert (Charles) (1889–1945) Humorist, critic, and parodist, born in Worcester, MA. He worked first at *Vanity Fair*, and then as a drama critic for *Life* (1920–9) and *The New Yorker* (1929–40). He was at his most brilliant writing sketches, which surfaced in several collections including *From Bed to Worse* (1934) and *My Ten Years in a Quandary, and How They Grew* (1936). His humour derives from the predicament of the 'little man', beset on all sides by the complexity of existence in the modern world. He also appeared in cameo roles in many films.

Bender, Charles Albert, known as **Chief Bender** (1884–1954) Baseball player, born in Crow Wing Co, MN. A Chippewa Indian, he won 210 games during his 16-year career as a right-handed pitcher (1903–25), mostly with the Philadelphia Athletics. He was elected to the Baseball Hall of Fame in 1953.

Bendix, Vincent (1882–1945) Inventor, born in Moline, IL. At 16 he ran away to New York City, and studied engineering at night school. He founded the Bendix Co of Chicago (1907), mass-producing automobiles, and pioneering the starter drive (1913). The Bendix Corporation was formed in 1924, which eventually produced a wide range of technical equipment. His interest in aviation prompted the Bendix Transcontinental Air Race (1931), and he later formed Bendix Helicopters.

Benedek, Ludwig von (1804–81) Austrian soldier, born in Oedenburg, Hungary. He distinguished himself in Galicia (1846), Italy (1847), and Hungary (1849), and in 1859 drove back the Piedmontese at Solferino. In 1866 he commanded the northern Austrian army in the war with Prussia; but after the defeat of Sadowa in 1866 he was superseded.

Beneden, Eduard van [**ben**eden] (1846–1910) Cytologist, born in Liège, Belgium. In 1887 he demonstrated the constancy of the number of chromosomes in the cells of an organism, decreasing during maturation and restored at fertilization.

Benedict of Nursia, St (c.480–c.547) The founder of Western monasticism, born in Nursia near Spoleto, Italy. He studied at Rome, and became convinced that the only way of escaping the evil in the world was in seclusion and religious exercise; so as a boy of 14 he withdrew to a cavern or grotto near Subiaco, where he lived for three years. The fame of his piety led to his being appointed the abbot of a neighbouring monastery at Vicovaro, but he soon left it, as the morals of the monks were not strict enough. Multitudes still sought his guidance; and from the most devoted he founded 12 small monastic communities. He ultimately established a monastery on Monte Cassino, near Naples, afterwards one of the richest and most famous in Italy. In 515 he is said to have composed his *Regula monachorum*, which became the common rule of all Western monasticism. He was declared the patron saint of all Europe by Pope Paul VI in 1964. Feast day 11 July.

Benedict XV, originally **Giacomo della Chiesa** (1854–1922) Pope (1914–22), born in Pegli, Sardinia, Italy. He studied at the University of Genoa, and the Collegia Capranica in Rome, and was ordained in 1878. He became secretary to the Papal Embassy, Spain, in 1883, then secretary to Cardinal Rampolla, bishop (1900), Archbishop of Bologna (1907), and cardinal (May, 1914). Although a junior cardinal, he was elected to succeed Pius X in September 1914, soon after the outbreak of World War 1. He made repeated efforts to end the war, and organized war relief on a munificent scale.

Benedict, Ruth, *née* **Fulton** (1887–1948) Anthropologist, born in New York City. She studied philosophy and English literature at Vassar College, NY, before going on to study anthropology under Franz Boas at Columbia University. She became a leading member of the culture-and-personality movement in American anthropology of the 1930s and 1940s. Her most important contribution lay in her 'configurational' approach to entire cultures, according to which each culture tends to predispose its individual members to adopt an ideal type of personality. Her best-known work is *Patterns of Culture* (1934). >> Boas

Benedict Biscop, St [bishop] (c. 628–c. 689) Anglo-Saxon clergyman. He became a monk in 653, journeyed to Rome five times, and in 669–671 was Abbot of St Peter's, Canterbury. In 674 he founded a monastery at Wearmouth, endowing it richly with books, and in 682 founded a second monastery at Jarrow. He is said to have introduced stone edifices and glass windows to England. One of his pupils was the Venerable Bede. Feast day 12 January. >> Bede

Benediktsson, Einar (1864–1940) Poet and entrepreneur, born near Reykjavík. He studied law at Copenhagen and became a country magistrate in Iceland. A fervent nationalist, he became convinced that only foreign investment could bring prosperity to Iceland. He devoted many years to touring Europe seeking capital (unsuccessfully) for his ambitious industrial schemes to exploit Iceland's natural resources of hydro power and fishing. He published five volumes of ornate poetry that harked back to the skaldic tradition.

Beneš, Edvard [benesh] (1884–1948) Czech statesman and president (1935–8, 1941–5 in exile, 1945–8), born in Kožlany, Czech Republic. He studied law and became professor of sociology at Prague. As a refugee during World War 1 he worked in Paris with Tomeš Masaryk for Czechoslovak nationalism, and was foreign minister of the new state (1918–35) and also premier (1921–2). He succeeded Masaryk as president in 1935, but resigned in 1938 and left the country, resuming office in 1941 on the setting up of a government in exile in England. He returned to his country in 1945, and was re-elected president, but resigned after the Communist coup of 1948. >> Masaryk, Tomeš; RR1043

Benesh, Rudolph (1916–75) and **Benesh, Joan** (1920–) [benesh], *née* **Rothwell** Dance notators, husband and wife, born in London, England and Liverpool, Merseyside, NW England, UK, respectively. Rudolph was a painter and Joan a former member of the Sadler's Wells Ballet. Together they copyrighted (1955) a dance notation system, called Choreology, that has been included in the syllabus of London's Royal Academy of Dancing and is used to document all important Royal Ballet productions. They opened their own institute in 1962, and have been a major influence on many notators and educators.

Benét, Stephen (Vincent) [binay] (1898–1943) Writer, born in Bethlehem, PA, the brother of William Benét. He published a number of novels, short stories, and volumes of poetry, his first book appearing at the age of 17. His long narrative poem on the Civil War, 'John Brown's Body', was awarded the Pulitzer Prize in 1929. >> Benét, William

Benét, William (Rose) [binay] (1886–1950) Poet, editor, novelist, and playwright, born in Fort Hamilton, NY, the brother of Stephen Benét. His main claim to fame is as a poet, his collections including *Merchants from Cathay* (1913), *Moons of Grandeur* (1920), and *The Stairway of Surprise* (1947). >> Benét, Stephen; Wylie, Elinor

Benfey, Theodor [benfiy] (1809–81) Philologist, born near Göttingen, Germany. His early work was in the fields of

classical and Hebrew philology, the *Lexicon of Greek Roots* (1839–42). Having learned Sanskrit in a few weeks to win a bet, he later turned his attention to Sanskrit philology. He was professor at Göttingen from 1848. His best-known work is the *Sanskrit–English Dictionary* (1866).

Ben-Gurion, David [ben gurion], originally **David Gruen** (1886–1973) Israeli statesman and prime minister (1948–53, 1955–63), born in Plonsk, Poland. Attracted to the Zionist Socialist movement, he emigrated to Palestine in 1906, working as a farm labourer and forming the first Jewish trade union in 1915. Expelled by the Ottomans for pro-Allied sympathies, he helped to raise the Jewish Legion in America and served in it in the Palestine campaign against Turkey in World War 1. He was general secretary of the General Federation of Jewish Labour (1921–33), and in 1930 became leader of the Mapai (Labour) Party, which became the ruling party in the state of Israel, whose birth he announced in May 1948. After his retirement from political life, he came to symbolize the Israeli state. >> RR1064

Benjamin, Judah P(hilip) (1811–84) Lawyer, born in St Thomas, Virgin Is. He was admitted to the Louisiana bar in 1832, and practised in New Orleans. He sat in the US Senate (1852–60), and joined Jefferson Davis's cabinet as attorney general at the opening of the Civil War (1861). He was for a few months secretary of war, and then secretary of state until Davis's capture in 1865, when he escaped to England. Called to the English bar in 1866, he became a QC in 1872 and wrote a legal classic, *The Sale of Personal Property* (1868). >> Davis, Jefferson

Benjamin of Tudela (?–1173) Rabbi, born in Navarre, Spain. From 1159 to 1173 he made a journey from Saragossa through Italy and Greece to Palestine, Persia, and the borders of China, returning via Egypt and Sicily. He was the first European traveller to describe the Far East.

Benn, Anthony (Neil) Wedgwood, known as **Tony Benn** (1925–) British statesman, born in London, England, UK, the son of Viscount Stansgate. He studied at Oxford, and became a Labour MP (1950–60). He was debarred from the House of Commons on succeeding to his father's title, but was able to renounce it in 1963, and was re-elected to parliament the same year. He was postmaster-general (1964–6), minister of technology (1966–70), and assumed responsibility for the ministry of aviation (1967) and ministry of power (1969). He was Opposition spokesman on trade and industry (1970–4), and on Labour's return to government became secretary of state for industry, minister for posts and telecommunications, and secretary of state for energy. Representing the left wing of Labour opinion, he unsuccessfully stood for the deputy leadership of the party in 1981. He lost his seat in the general election of 1983, but returned to represent Chesterfield from 1984. He unsuccessfully challenged Neil Kinnock for the party leadership in 1988. Among his many publications on politics is *The Benn Diaries 1940–90* (1995). >> Kinnock; Stansgate

Benn, Gottfried (1886–1956) Poet and physician, born in Mansfeld, Germany. He embraced the philosophy of Nihilism as a young man, and later became one of the few intellectuals to favour Nazi doctrines. Trained in medicine as a venereologist, he began writing Expressionist verse dealing with the uglier aspects of his profession, such as *Morgue* (1912). After 1945 his poetry became more versatile though still pessimistic, and he became recognized as a leading poet of the century.

Bennet, Henry >> **Arlington, Earl of**

Bennett, Alan (1934–) Playwright, actor, and director, born in Leeds, West Yorkshire, N England, UK. He came to prominence as a writer and performer in *Beyond the Fringe*, a revue performed at the Edinburgh Festival in 1960, and wrote a television series, *On the Margin* (1966), before his first stage play, *Forty Years On* (1968). Despite his own self-effacing qualities, he has remained in the public eye. A great deal of his writing is political comedy, a number of plays displaying a preoccupation with British institutions. There is an ambitious treatment of monarchy in *The Madness of George III* (1991). Other plays include *Enjoy* (1980), *Kafka's Dick* (1986), *Single Spies* (1988), and *Getting On* (1995). He has also written much for television, including *An Englishman Abroad* (1983), *The Insurance Man* (1986), *Talking Heads* (1987), a series of six monologues related to his northern, working-class roots, and the documentary *Portrait or Bust* (1994). The autobiographical *Writing Home* appeared in 1994.

Bennett, (Enoch) Arnold (1867–1931) Novelist, born near Hanley, Staffordshire, C England, UK. He studied locally and at London University, and was a solicitor's clerk in London, but quickly transferred to journalism, and in 1893 became assistant editor (editor in 1896) of the journal *Woman*. He published his first novel, *The Man from the North*, in 1898. In 1902 he moved to Paris for 10 years and from then on was engaged exclusively in writing. His claims to recognition as a novelist rest mainly on the early *Anna of the Five Towns* (1902), the more celebrated *The Old Wives' Tale* (1908), and the *Clayhanger* series – *Clayhanger* (1910), *Hilda Lessways* (1911), *These Twain* (1916), subsequently issued (1925) as *The Clayhanger Family* – all of which feature the 'Five Towns', centres of the pottery industry. He was an influential critic, and as **Jacob Tonson** on *The New Age* he was a discerning reviewer. His *Journals* were published posthumously.

Bennett, Brian >> **Shadows, The**

Bennett, Floyd (1890–1928) Aviator, born near Warrensburg, NY. A naval pilot during World War 1, he accompanied Richard Byrd on the Macmillan expedition to Greenland (1925). In May 1926 he piloted Byrd on the first aeroplane flight over the North Pole, and received the Congressional Medal of Honour. >> Byrd, Richard

Bennett, James Gordon (1795–1872) Journalist, born in Keith, Moray, NE Scotland, UK, the father of James Gordon Bennett. He emigrated to America in 1819, and became a journalist in New York City in 1826. In 1835 he started the *New York Herald*, which he edited until 1867, pioneering many journalistic innovations. >> Bennett, James Gordon (1841–1918)

Bennett, James Gordon (1841–1918) Journalist, born in New York City, the son and successor of James Gordon Bennett. He sent Henry Morton Stanley in 1870 to find David Livingstone, and with the *Daily Telegraph* financed Livingstone's Congo journey (1874–8). He also promoted polar exploration, storm warnings, motoring, and yachting. >> Bennett, James Gordon (1795–1872)

Bennett, Michael, originally **Michael Bennet Difiglia** (1943–87) Dancer, choreographer, director, and producer, born in Buffalo, NY. He began his career as a chorus boy before turning to Broadway show choreography. His first hit, *Promises, Promises* (1968), was followed by *Coco* (1970), *Company* (1970), *Follies* (co-director, 1971), *Seesaw* (1973), and the popular masterpiece *A Chorus Line* (1975).

Bennett, Richard Bedford Bennett, 1st Viscount (1870–1947) Canadian statesman and prime minister (1930–5), born in New Brunswick, Canada. A lawyer by training, he was elected to parliament in 1911, and became Conservative leader from 1927. As prime minister, he convened the Empire Economic Conference in Ottawa in 1932, out of which came a system of empire trade preference known as the Ottawa Agreements. He retired to Britain in 1939. >> RR1039

Bennett, Sir Richard Rodney (1936–) Composer, born in Broadstairs, Kent, SE England, UK. He studied at the Royal Academy of Music, London, and in Paris under Pierre Boulez. Well known for his music for films, he has also composed operas, orchestral works, chamber music, and experimental works for one and two pianos. Some of his music uses the 12-tone scale, and his interest in jazz has prompted such works as *Jazz Calendar* (1963) and *Jazz Pastoral* (1969). His more recent work shows a growing emphasis on internal rhythmic structure. Among his other works are the two operas commissioned by Sadler's Wells, *The Mines of Sulphur* (1965) and *A Penny for a Song* (1968), the opera commissioned by Covent Garden, *Victory* (1970), and the choral work, *Spells* (1975). He was appointed Professor of Composition at the Royal Academy of Music in 1995. He was knighted in 1998. >> Boulez

Bennett, Willard Harrison (1903–87) Physicist and inventor, born in Findlay, OH. He studied at the University of Michigan, and in 1930 joined the faculty of Ohio State University. In the 1950s, he invented a device that produced a model of the Van Allen radiation belt. His radio frequency mass spectrometer, a device that measured the mass of atoms, first went into space in 1957 aboard the Russian satellite Sputnik.

Bennett, William J(ohn) (1943–) US Federal official, born in Brooklyn, NY. Outspoken and controversial, as chairman of the National Endowment for the Humanities (1981–5) he reversed Liberal policies. He became secretary of education (1985–8) promoting a conservative agenda, cutting federal student aid, and urging schools to become a force for moral education. As President Bush's 'drug tzar' (1989–91) he co-ordinated the campaign against drugs, but resigned in frustration.

Bennett, Sir William Sterndale (1816–75) Pianist and composer, born in Sheffield, South Yorkshire, N England, UK. He studied at the Royal Academy, London, and at Leipzig, became professor of music at Cambridge (1856), and in 1868 was appointed principal of the Royal Academy of Music. His compositions include piano pieces, songs, and the cantatas *The May Queen* (1858) and *The Women of Samaria* (1867).

Benny, Jack, originally **Benjamin Kubelsky** (1894–1974) Comedian, born in Waukegan, IL. A child prodigy violinist, he performed as part of a vaudeville double-act. After navy service during World War 1, he returned to the stage, making his film debut in the short *Bright Moments* (1928). Following his Broadway success in *The Earl Carroll Vanities* (1930) and his radio debut in *The Ed Sullivan Show* (1932), he earned his own radio series which, combined with its subsequent television incarnation, *The Jack Benny Show* (1950–65), won him the loyalty and warm affection of a mass audience. A gentle, bemused, self-effacing figure, his humour lacked malice, relying for its effect on his mastery of timing and an act based on his ineptitude as a fiddler, his claiming of perennial youth, and an unfounded reputation as the world's cheapest man.

Benoît de Sainte-Maure [benwah] (12th-c) Poet, born in either Sainte-Maure near Poitiers, or Sainte-More near Tours, France. His vast romance *Le Roman de Troie* (The Romance of Troy) was a source book to many later writers, notably Boccaccio, who in turn inspired Chaucer and Shakespeare to use Benoît's episode of Troilus and Cressida. >> Boccaccio

Benozzo di Lese >> **Gozzoli, Benozzo**

Benson, Sir Frank (Robert) (1858–1939) Actor-manager, born in Alresford, Hampshire, S England, UK. He first appeared in Henry Irving's production of *Romeo and Juliet* in 1882 at the Lyceum, and was knighted by King George V on the stage of Drury Lane during a Shakespeare tercentenary matinee (1916). The company he formed was the forerunner of the Royal Shakespeare Company. >> Irving

Benson, Frank (Weston) (1862–1951) Artist, born in Salem, MA. He studied in Paris, and became a teacher at the Museum of Fine Arts in Boston. He painted women and children, created sensitive etchings and wash drawings of wild fowl, and produced a series of murals for the Library of Congress.

Bentham, George (1800–84) Botanist, born in Stoke, Devon, SW England, UK, the son of Samuel Bentham. Abandoning law for botany, he was secretary of the Horticultural Society of London (1829–40), and compiled, with Sir Joseph Hooker, the great *Genera Plantarum* (3 vols, 1862–83), among many other important botanical works. >> Bentham, Samuel; Hooker, Joseph

Bentham, Jeremy (1748–1832) Philosopher, jurist, and social reformer, born in London, England, UK. He entered Oxford at the age of 12, and was admitted to Lincoln's Inn at 19. He is best known as a proponent of utilitarianism in his pioneering works *A Fragment on Government* (1776) and *Introduction to the Principles of Morals and Legislation* (1789), which argued that the proper objective of all conduct and legislation is 'the greatest happiness of the greatest number', and developed a 'hedonic calculus' to estimate the effects of different actions. He was made an honorary citizen of the French Republic in 1792, and published copiously on penal and social reform, economics, and politics. He also founded University College, London, where his clothed skeleton is preserved on public view. >> Bentham, Samuel; Helvétius

Bentham, Sir Samuel (1757–1831) Inventor and naval architect, born in London, England, UK, the brother of Jeremy Bentham and father of George Bentham. For nearly 20 years he devoted his energies to building up Britain's naval strength during the critical period of the Napoleonic Wars. His campaign against corruption and maladministration in the Admiralty dockyards aroused such bitterness that in 1812 he was forced to resign, though not before many of his reforms had been put into effect. >> Bentham, George; Bentham. Jeremy

Bentinck, Lord (William) George (Frederick Cavendish) (1802–48) British politician, born at Welbeck Abbey, Nottinghamshire, C England, UK. He entered parliament in 1828, supported Catholic Emancipation and the Reform Bill, but left the Whigs in 1834 to form a separate Conservative parliamentary group with Lord Stanley. On Peel's third betrayal of his party in introducing free trade measures, Bentinck led the Tory Opposition to Peel. A great lover of racing and field sports, he stamped out many dishonest turf practices. >> Derby, 14th Earl; Peel

Bentinck, William, 1st Earl of Portland (1649–1709) English soldier and courtier, born in Holland. A friend from boyhood of William III, he was entrusted with the secrets of his foreign policy, and after the revolution was created an English peer, and given large estates. >> William III

Bentinck, William Henry Cavendish, 3rd Duke of Portland (1738–1809) British statesman and prime minister (1783, 1807–9), born in Bulstrode, Buckinghamshire, SC England, UK. He entered Lord Rockingham's cabinet in 1765, and succeeded him as leader of the Whig Party. He was twice prime mininster, but his best work was done as home secretary under Pitt, when he was given charge of Irish affairs (1794–1801). >> Pitt (the Younger); Rockingham; RR1095

Bentinck, Lord William (Henry Cavendish) (1774–1839) British statesman and Governor-General of India (1828–35), born in Bulstrode, Buckinghamshire. He became Governor of Madras (1803–7), but was recalled when his prohibition of sepoy beards and turbans caused the massacre at Vellore (1806). He served in the Peninsular War (1808–14), in 1827 became Governor-General of Bengal, and in 1828 first Governor-General of India. His administration resulted in better internal communications, brought about many educational reforms with the help of Thomas Macaulay, and prohibited *suttee*. >> Macaulay

Bentine, Michael [ben teen] (1921–96) Comedy performer, born in Watford, Hertfordshire, SE England, UK. He made his stage debut in 1941 and, after wartime service in the RAF, worked at the Windmill Theatre (1946) and in the show *Starlight Roof* (1947). One of the early members of The Goons (1950–2), he left the popular radio series to pursue a solo career, and appeared on television in *After Hours* (1959–60) and *It's a Square World* (1960–4), which allowed him to indulge his eccentric penchant for zany, surreal humour. Later television series, often for children, included *The Golden Silents* (1965), *Potty Time* (1973–80), and *Mad About It* (1981). He wrote novels and autobiographies, including *The Long Banana Skin* (1975) and *A Shy Person's Guide to Life* (1984).

Bentley, E(dmund) C(lerihew) (1875–1956) Journalist and novelist, born in London, England, UK. He is chiefly remembered as the author of *Trent's Last Case* (1913), which is regarded as a milestone in the development of the detective novel. A close friend of G K Chesterton, he originated and gave his name to the type of humorous verse-form known as the *clerihew*. >> Chesterton

Bentley, Richard (1662–1742) Classical scholar, born in Oulton, West Yorkshire, N England, UK. He studied at Cambridge, and became archdeacon of Ely and keeper of the Royal Libraries (1694). He established an international reputation with his dispute with Charles Boyle, 4th Earl of Orrery (1697–9), in which he proved that the so-called *Epistles of Phalaris* were spurious. He was appointed Master of Trinity College, Cambridge, in 1700, where he was involved in an unbroken series of quarrels and litigations. He published critical texts of many Classical works, including the Greek New Testament.

Bentley, Thomas >> **Wedgwood, Josiah**

Benton, Thomas Hart, known as **Old Bullion** (1782–1858) US statesman, born near Hillsborough, NC. He became senator for Missouri (1820–51), and the chief Democratic spokesman in the US Senate. He received his byname from his opposition to paper currency, and he also made himself unpopular by opposing slavery in the territories.

Benton, Thomas Hart (1889–1975) Painter of large historical murals on American themes and realistic genre scenes, born in Neosho, MO. He admired the Cubists in Paris (1909–11), but after returning to the USA he reacted against European modernism, and in the late 1920s set about creating a populist American art based on ordinary Middle-Western experience: cowboys, gamblers, oil wells, and native Americans (eg 'Independence and the Opening of The West', 1959–62, Truman Library, Independence, MO).

Bentsen, Lloyd Millard, Jr (1921–) US statesman, born in Mission, TX. He studied law at Texas University, Austin, and served as a combat pilot during World War 2. He was a member of the US House of Representatives (1948–54), then built up a substantial fortune as president of the Lincoln Consolidated insurance company in Houston. He returned to Congress as a senator for Texas in 1971, and was vice-presidential running-mate to Michael Dukakis in the Democrats' 1988 presidential challenge. In Bill Clinton's administration he served as secretary to the treasury (1993–4). >> Clinton, Bill; Dukakis

Bentzon, Niels Viggo (1919–) Danish composer and pianist. He studied at the Royal Danish Academy of Music, and has been a reader there since 1960. His compositions include opera, symphonies, ballets, piano concertos, and chamber music.

Benvenuto Tisi >> **Garofalo, Benvenuto do**

Benz, Karl (Friedrich) (1844–1929) Engineer and car manufacturer, born in Karlsruhe, Germany. He developed a two-stroke engine (1877–9) and founded a factory for its manufacture, leaving in 1883 when his backers refused to finance a mobile engine. He then founded a second company, Benz & Co, Rheinisch Gasmotorenfabrik, at Mannheim. His first car – one of the earliest petrol-driven vehicles – was completed in 1885 and sold to a French manufacturer. In 1926 the firm was merged with the Daimler-Motoren-Gesellschaft to form Daimler-Benz & Co.

Benzer, Seymour (1921–) Geneticist, born in New York City. He studied physics at Purdue University, and taught biophysics there until 1965, when he moved to the California Institute of Technology. He first showed that genes can be split and then recombined, and he did much to relate genes as chemical entities to their observed behaviour in biological systems.

Ben-Zvi, Itzhak [ben **tsvee**] (1884–1963) Israeli statesman and president (1952–63), born in Poltava, Ukraine. Having migrated to Palestine in 1907 he became a prominent Zionist, and was a founder of the Jewish Labour Party. He was elected president of Israel on the death of Weizmann in 1952. A prominent scholar and archaeologist, he wrote on the history of the Middle East. >> Weizmann; RR1064

Bérain, Jean (the Elder) [bayrí] (c. 1637–1711) Artist, born in Lorraine, France. He was the leading designer of stage scenery, costumes, fêtes, and displays at the court of Louis XIV. His arabesques, grotesques, and *singeries* (monkey designs), often combined with Chinese motifs, herald the lighter Rococo style of the early 18th-c.

Béranger, Pierre Jean de [bayrãzhay] (1780–1857) Poet, born in Paris. After a scanty education he left regular employment as a clerk at the University of Paris for an impecunious literary life in 1798. His lyrics, coloured by his politics – a curious compound of republicanism and Bonapartism – led to spells of imprisonment in 1821 and 1828, but their vivacity, satire, and wit endeared him to the masses.

Bérard, Christian [bayrah(r)] (1902–49) French painter and designer. His attitude to his own work was curiously over-sensitive. He was always a reluctant exhibitor, and disliked having his paintings reproduced. His fame rests mainly on his stage decor, especially for the productions of Molière by Barrault. >> Barrault

Berberian, Cathy >> **Berio, Luciano**

Berceo, Gonzalo de [berthayoh] (c. 1180–c. 1246) The earliest known Castilian poet, born in Berceo, Spain. He became a deacon and wrote more than 13 000 verses on devotional subjects, of which the best is a Life of St Oria. His poems were not discovered and published until the late 18th-c.

Berchem, Claes Pietersz(oon) [berkhem], also called **Nicolaes Pieterszoon Berghem** (1620–83) Dutch landscape painter, born in Haarlem, The Netherlands. Also known for his pastoral scenes, his work is represented in most European collections.

Berchet, Giovanni [berket] (1783–1851) Poet, born in Milan, Italy. In 1816 he published a pamphlet, *Lettera semiseria di Grisostomo*, which became a manifesto of the Romantic movement in Italy. He left Italy to avoid arrest (1821), and lived in exile, mainly in England, until the abortive Revolution of 1848. His best-known works are *I Profughi di Parga* (1821), *Il romito del Cenisio*, and *Il trovatore*.

Berdyayev, Nikolai Alexandrovich [berdyayef] (1874–1948) Religious philosopher, born in Kiev, Ukraine.

An aristocrat by birth, he developed strong revolutionary sympathies as a student, and supported the 1917 Revolution. He secured a professorship at Moscow, but his unorthodox spiritual and libertarian ideals led to his dismissal (1922). He moved to Berlin to found an Academy of the Philosophy of Religion, which he later transferred to Clamart, near Paris. He described himself as a 'believing freethinker', and his fierce commitment to freedom and individualism brought him into conflict with both ecclesiastical and political powers.

Berengar of Tours [berãgah(r), toor] (c. 999–1088) Scholastic theologian, born probably in Tours, France. In 1031 he was appointed preceptor of the cathedral school in Tours, and about 1040 archdeacon of Angers. An opponent of the doctrine of transubstantiation, he was excommunicated by Pope Leo IX in 1050. He spent his last years in a cell on an island in the Loire.

Berenice [berenees] (1st-c) The daughter of Herod Agrippa I. Four times married, she then became the mistress of Flavius Titus, son of Emperor Vespasian, during the Jewish rebellion (AD 70), and followed him to Rome. She is the heroine of Racine's tragedy. She is known as the 'Jewish Berenice', to distinguish her from several other women of that name from the house of Ptolemy. >> Herod Agrippa I; Vespasian

Berenson, Bernard or **Bernhard** [berenson] (1865–1959) Art critic, born in Vilnius, Lithuania. He moved to the USA in 1875, studied at Harvard, and became a leading authority on Italian Renaissance art. He became a US citizen, but in 1900 went to live in Italy, producing a vast amount of critical literature. He bequeathed his villa and art collection to Harvard University, which turned it into the Center for Italian Renaissance Culture.

Beresford, Bruce (1940–) Film director, born in Sydney, New South Wales, Australia. He studied in Sydney and worked at the British Film Institute (1966–71) before directing his first feature, *The Adventures of Barry McKenzie* (1972). He was a key figure in the revival of the Australian film industry, and won the Australian Film Institute's Best Director award for *Don's Party* (1976) and *Breaker Morant* (1979). He has since received international recognition for *Tender Mercies* (1982), *Driving Miss Daisy* (1989, Oscar), and *Black Robe* (1991), an Australian–Canadian co-production. Later films include *Silent Fall* (1994), *Last Dance* (1995), and *Paradise Road* (1997). In 1991 he directed *Elektra* for the South Australian State Opera.

Beresford, Charles William de la Poer Beresford, Baron (1846–1919) Naval commander, born in Philipstown, Co Offally, Ireland. He entered the British navy in 1859, and was promoted captain in 1882 for his services at the bombardment of Alexandria. He was a Lord of the Admiralty (1886–8), sat in parliament as a Conservative, and commanded the Mediterranean Fleet (1905–7) and Channel Fleet (1907–9).

Beresford, Jack (1899–1977) British oarsman. He competed for Great Britain at five Olympics (1920–36) as sculler and oarsman, winning three gold and two silver medals, and received the Olympic Diploma of Merit in 1949. He won the Diamond Sculls at Henley four times, and was elected president of the Thames Rowing Club in 1971.

Beresford, William Carr Beresford, 1st Viscount (1768–1854) British soldier, the illegitimate son of the first Marquess of Waterford. He entered the army in 1785, took the command (1809) of the Portuguese army in the Peninsular War (1808–14), and defeated Soult at Albuera (1811). He was present at the capture of Badajoz (1812), and at Salamanca was severely wounded. In the Wellington administration (1828–30), he was Master-General of the Ordnance. >> Soult

Berg, Alban (1885–1935) Composer, born in Vienna. He studied under Schoenberg (1904–10), and after World War 1 taught privately in Vienna. With the last of his *Four Songs* (1909–10) he displays a free harmonic language tempered wih Romantic tonal elements which remained his characteristic style. He is best known for his opera *Wozzeck* (1925), his violin concerto, and the *Lyric Suite* for string quartet. His unfinished opera, *Lulu*, was posthumously produced. >> Schoenberg

Berg, Patty, popular name of **Patricia Jane Berg** (1918–) Golfer, born in Minneapolis, MN. She won 57 tournaments during her career, including 15 majors. On three occasions she won two majors in a single year (1948, 1955, 1957). >> RR1159

Berg, Paul (1926–) Molecular biologist, born in New York City. He studied at Pennsylvania State and Western Reserve universities, and became professor of biochemistry at Washington University, St Louis, and from 1959 at Stanford University. He devised a method for introducing 'foreign' genes into bacteria, so causing the bacteria to produce proteins determined by the new gene; this method of genetic engineering proved of great value in giving biochemical syntheses of insulin and interferon. He shared the 1980 Nobel Prize for Chemistry. >> RR1123

Berganza, Teresa [berganza] (1935–) Mezzo-soprano, born in Madrid. She made her debut in 1955, and became specially noted for Mozart and Rossini roles. She first sang in England at Glyndebourne (1958), then at Covent Garden (1959), and subsequently in concert and opera all over the world. In 1994 she became the first woman elected to the Spanish Royal Academy of Arts.

Bergen, Candice >> **Malle, Louis**

Berger, Hans (1873–1941) Psychiatrist, born in Neuses bei Coburg, Germany. He studied medicine at Jena University, where he stayed for the rest of his career, becoming professor of psychiatry in 1919. He is known for his invention of the electroencephalograph (1929).

Berger, John (Peter) (1926–) Novelist, playwright, and art critic, born in London, England, UK. After studying at the Central and Chelsea Schools of Art he began to work as a painter and a drawing teacher, but soon turned to writing. His Marxism and artistic background are ever present in his novels, which include *A Painter of Our Time* (1958), *The Foot of Clive* (1962), and *Corker's Freedom* (1964). *G* (1972), a story of migrant workers in Europe, won the Booker Prize. In later years he has been living in a peasant farming community in the French Jura, where he worked on a projected trilogy, *Into Their Labours*, about modern peasant life, completed in 1991. Later novels include *Photocopies* (1996).

Berger, Samuel R, known as **Sandy Berger** (1945–) US public official and lawyer. Educated at Cornell and Harvard, he practised law with a Washington firm (1973–7, 1981–92), and also served as the State Department's deputy director of policy and planning (1977–80). Formerly the Deputy Assistant to the President for National Security Affairs (1993–6), he was appointed Assistant in Clinton's second administration. He is the author of *Dollar Harvest* (1971) on American rural politics.

Bergerac, Savinien Cyrano de >> **Cyrano de Bergerac, Savinien**

Berggrav, Eivind (1884–1959) Lutheran bishop, born in Stavanger, Norway. After some years as a teacher, pastor, and prison chaplain, he became Bishop of Tromsø and then Bishop of Oslo and Primate of the Norwegian Church (1937–50). He led the Church's opposition to the Quisling government, and was imprisoned (1941–5). He was a strong supporter of the ecumenical movement, becoming a president of the World Council of Churches (1950–4).

Berghem, Nicolaes Pieterszoon >> **Berchem, Claes Pietersz**

Bergius, Friedrich [bergius] (1884–1949) Organic chemist, born in Goldschmieden, Germany. He researched into coal hydrogenation for the production of motor fuels under high pressure, and the hydrolysis of wood to sugar, for which he shared the 1931 Nobel Prize for Chemistry. After World War 2 he left Germany for Argentina. >> RR1123

Bergman, Hjalmar (Fredrik Elgérus) (1883–1931) Novelist, poet, and playwright, born in Örebro, Sweden. His plays include *Maria, Jesu Moder* (1905) and the comedy *Swedenhielms* (The Swedenhielm Family, 1925). His novels, including the broadly comical *Murkurells i Wadköping* (1919, trans God's Orchid), were often popular satires on his native Örebro.

Bergman, (Ernst) Ingmar (1918–) Film and stage director, born in Uppsala, Sweden. A trainee director in the Stockholm theatre, he began his film career in 1943, making his film debut with *Kris* (1945, Crisis). His explorations of personal torment won many international prizes for such films as *Det Sjunde Inseglet* (1957, The Seventh Seal), *Smultronstallet* (1957, trans Wild Strawberries), *Jungfrukallan* (1960, The Virgin Spring, Oscar), and *Sasom i en Spegel* (1961, Through a Glass Darkly, Oscar), which are outstanding for their photographic artistry, haunting imagery, and subtle exploration of facial characteristics. Preoccupied with guilt, anguish, emotional repression, and death, he created a succession of bleak masterpieces including *Vis Kingar och Rop* (1972, Cries and Whispers) and *Hostsonaten* (1978, Autumn Sonata). His later film, *Fanny och Alexander* (1982, Fanny and Alexander, Oscar), was an unexpectedly life-affirming evocation of autobiographical elements from his own Dickensian childhood. He then largely retired from the film-making scene, but later work includes the script for *Private Confessions* (1996). Publications include his autobiography *Laterna Magica* (1987, The Magic Lantern) and *Images: My Life in Film* (1994). >> Sydow; Ullmann

Bergman, Ingrid (1915–82) Film and stage actress, born in Stockholm. After studying at the Royal Dramatic Theatre, she made her film debut in *Munkbrogreven* (1934). Unaffected and vivacious, she became an immensely popular romantic star in such films as *Casablanca* (1942), *Spellbound* (1945), and *Notorious* (1946). In 1950 she gave birth to the illegitimate child of director Roberto Rossellini. The ensuing scandal led to her ostracization from the US film industry. She continued her career in Europe, and was welcomed back by Hollywood on her return in 1956. Nominated seven times for an Academy Award, she won Oscars for *Gaslight* (1944), *Anastasia* (1956), and *Murder on the Orient Express* (1974). >> Rossellini, Isabella; Rossellini, Roberto

Bergson, Henri (Louis) [bergsõ] (1859–1941) Philosopher, born in Paris. He became professor at the Collège de France (1900–21), a highly original thinker who became something of a cult figure. He contrasted the fundamental reality of the dynamic flux of consciousness with the inert physical world of discrete objects, which was a convenient fiction for the mechanistic descriptions of science. The *élan vital*, or 'creative impulse', not a deterministic natural selection, is at the heart of evolution; and intuition, not analysis, reveals the real world of process and change. His own writings are literary, suggestive, and analogical rather than philosophical in the modern sense. His most important works are *Essai sur les données immédiates de la conscience* (1889, trans Time and Free Will), *Matière et mémoire* (1896, Matter and Memory), and *L'Evolution créatrice* (1907, Creative Evolution). He was awarded the Nobel Prize for Literature in 1927.

Bergström, Sune Karl [bairgstroem] (1916–) Biochemist, born in Stockholm. He studied medicine and chemistry at the Karolinska Institute in Stockholm, and taught chemistry at Lund (1948–58) before becoming professor at the Institute (1958–81). He isolated and purified prostaglandins, for which he shared the 1982 Nobel Prize for Physiology or Medicine. >> RR1124

Beria, Lavrenti Pavlovich [beria] (1899–1953) Soviet secret police chief, born in Mercheuli, Georgia. He served as a member of the OGPU (the forerunner of the KGB) in the Caucasus (1921–31), before becoming first secretary of the Georgian Communist Party. He was appointed minister for internal affairs (1938) by his patron, Stalin, and served as vice-president of the State Committee for Defence during World War 2, being accorded the title of marshal in 1945. On Stalin's death in March 1953, he attempted to seize power, but was foiled by fearful military and party leaders. Following his arrest he was tried for treason, and was executed in December 1953. He was a plotter of ruthless ambition, and a notoriously skilled organizer of forced labour, terror, and espionage. >> Stalin; Yezhov

Berigan, Bunny, originally **Roland Bernhart** (1908–42) Swing trumpeter and crooner, born in Hilbert, WI. He epitomized the Jazz Era, starring in dance bands at the University of Wisconsin as an undergraduate – tall, dark, and handsome playing love songs in a raccoon coat. He won featured billing with several orchestras including Benny Goodman (1935–6, where he had his first hits 'Sometimes I'm Happy' and 'King Porter Stomp'), and twice with Tommy Dorsey (1937 with a hit song 'Marie', and 1940). Before and after the stints with Dorsey, he led his own band, but in spite of a huge hit playing and singing 'I Can't Get Started With You', his business sense was hopeless, even when he was sober. His health disintegrated, and he died at 34. >> Dorsey, Tommy; Goodman, Benny

Bering, Vitus (Jonassen) [bayring], also spelled **Behring** (1681–1741) Navigator, born in Horsens, Denmark. He led an expedition in the Sea of Kamchatka (1728) to determine whether the continents of Asia and America were joined. In 1733 he was given command of the 600-strong Great Northern Expedition to explore the Siberian coast and Kuril Is, and in 1741 sailed from Ohkotsk towards the American continent. He was wrecked on the island of Avatcha (now *Bering I*), where he died. *Bering Sea* and *Bering Strait* are named after him. >> Steller

Berio, Luciano [berioh] (1925–) Composer and teacher of music, born in Oneglia, Italy. He studied at the Music Academy in Milan, and founded an electronic studio. He moved to the USA in 1962, taught composition at the Juilliard School, New York City, and returned to Italy in 1972. In 1950 he married the US soprano **Cathy Berberian** (1925–83), for whom he wrote several works; the marriage was dissolved in 1966. He is particularly interested in the combining of live and pre-recorded sound, and the use of tapes and electronic music, as in his compositions *Mutazioni* (1955, Mutations) and *Omaggio a James Joyce* (1958, Homage to James Joyce). His *Sequenza* series for solo instruments (1958 onwards) are striking virtuoso pieces. Other works include *Passaggio* (1963), *Laborintus II* (1965), *Opera* (1969–70), and *Continuo* (1991). >> Nono

Berkeley, Busby [berklee], originally **William Berkeley Enos** (1895–1976) Choreographer and director, born in Los Angeles, CA. He worked as an actor, stage manager, and dance director, directing his first Broadway show, *A Night in Venice*, in 1928. He became one of the cinema's most innovative choreographers, noted for his mobile camerawork and dazzling kaleidoscopic routines involving spectacular multitudes of chorus girls. His work enhanced such films as *Forty Second Street* (1933), *Gold Diggers of 1933* (1934), and *Dames* (1934). In later years, ill health restricted his opportunities, but he enjoyed a Broadway triumph as the supervising producer of the 1971 revival of *No, No, Nanette*.

Berkeley, George [bah(r)klee] (1685–1753) Anglican bishop and philosopher, born at Dysert Castle, Kilkenny, Ireland. He studied at Trinity College, Dublin, where he remained, as fellow and tutor, until 1713. His most important books were published in these early years: *Essay towards a New Theory of Vision* (1709), *A Treatise concerning the Principles of Human Knowledge* (1710), and *Three Dialogues between Hylas and Philonous* (1713). In these works he developed his celebrated claim that 'to be is to be perceived' – that the contents of the material world are 'ideas' that only exist when they are perceived by a mind. He became dean of Londonderry (1724), but became obsessed with a romantic scheme to found a college in the Bermudas to promote 'the propagation of the Gospel among the American savages'. After years of intensive lobbying in London for support he sailed for America with his newly married wife (1728) and made a temporary home in Rhode Island. He waited there nearly three years: the grants did not materialize, and the college was never founded. He returned first to London and then in 1734 became Bishop of Cloyne. His remaining literary work was divided between questions of social reform and of religious reflection.

Berkeley, Sir Lennox (Randall Francis) [bah(r)klee] (1903–89) Composer, born in Boars Hill, Oxfordshire, SC England, UK. A pupil of Nadia Boulanger, his early compositions, the largest of which is the oratorio *Jonah* (1935), show the influence of his French training. Later works, notably the 'Stabat Mater' (1947), the operas *Nelson* (1953) and *Ruth* (1956), and the orchestral *Windsor Variations* (1969) and *Voices of the Night* (1973), have won him wide recognition for their combination of technical refinement with lyrically emotional appeal. He was knighted in 1974. >> Berkeley, Michael; Boulanger, Nadia

Berkeley, Michael (Fitzhardinge) [bah(r)klee] (1948–) British composer, the son of Lennox Berkeley. He studied at the Royal Academy of Music, London, and with Richard Rodney Bennett. He has composed concertos, orchestral, chamber, and choral works, including a powerful plea for peace in a nuclear age, the oratorio *Or Shall We Die?* (1983, text by Ian McEwan). He is well known for his introductions to music on radio and television. >> Bennett, Richard Rodney; Berkeley, Lennox

Berkoff, Steven [berkof] (1937–) Playwright, actor, and director, born in London, England, UK. After studying at the Ecole Jacques Lecoq in Paris, he founded the London Theatre Group, for whom he directed his own adaptations from the classics, including Kafka's *Metamorphosis* (1969). His own plays include *Greek* (1979, a variant of the Oedipal myth transferred to contemporary London), *West* (1983, an adaptation of the Beowulf legend), *Kvetch* (1987), and *Acapulco* (1992). Other plays and adaptations include *Agamemnon* (1963), *The Trial* (1970), and *The Fall of the House of Usher* (1974). An autobiography, *Free Association*, appeared in 1996.

Berkowitz, David [berkohvits] (c.1953–) Convicted US murderer, who dubbed himself 'Son of Sam' in a note to the New York Police Department. He terrorized the city for a year (1976–7), preying on courting couples and lone women. He was finally caught because of a parking ticket: he watched as it was stuck on his car, and then went and tore it to pieces. A woman witnessed this, noticed a strange smile on his face, and reported him to the police. Berkowitz's car was traced and he was arrested. In pursuit of a plea of insanity he claimed at his trial that Satanic voices told him to kill. Deemed sane, he received a prison sentence of 365 years in 1977.

Berlage, Hendrick Petrus [**ber**laguh] (1856–1934) Architect and town planner, born in Amsterdam. He designed the Amsterdam Bourse (1903) in a neo-Romanesque style, but was later influenced by Frank Lloyd Wright, and was largely responsible for the spread of his theories in The Netherlands. His other buildings include Holland House, London (1914), and the Gemeente Museum in The Hague (1934). >> Wright, Frank Lloyd

Berle, A(dolf) A(ugustus) [berl] (1895–1971) Lawyer, economist, and public official, born in Boston, MA. He studied at Harvard, and practised law in Boston and New York City before becoming a professor of corporate law at Columbia in 1927. He joined Franklin D Roosevelt's 'brains trust' for the 1932 presidential campaign, and served as an assistant secretary of state (1938–44) and ambassador to Brazil (1945–6). He published several important works on business organization and on Latin America. He retired from Columbia in 1963, but continued teaching as a professor emeritus until his death. >> Roosevelt, Franklin D

Berle, Milton [berl], originally **Milton Berlinger**, nickname **Mr Television** (1908–) Entertainer, born in New York City. From childhood he appeared in vaudeville and silent films, but his later attempts to gain a radio audience (in the 1940s) were unsuccessful. His comic style was better suited to the screen, and he was nationally popular on US television (1940–66).

Berlichingen, Götz von >> **Götz von Berlichingen**

Berlin, Irving [ber**lin**], originally **Israel Baline** (1888–1989) Composer who helped to launch 20th-c American popular music, born in Temun, Russia. Taken to the USA as a child, he worked for a time as a singing waiter in a Bowery beer hall, introducing some of his own songs, such as 'Alexander's Ragtime Band'. The 1940s saw him at the peak of his career, with the hit musicals *Annie Get Your Gun* (1946) and *Call Me Madam* (1950). 'God Bless America' (1939) and 'White Christmas' (1942) achieved worldwide popularity. In 1954 he received a special presidential citation as a composer of patriotic songs, and in all he wrote the words and music for over 900 songs. He retired in 1962, and lived as a recluse in Manhattan.

Berlin, Sir Isaiah (1909–97) Philosopher and historian of ideas, born in Riga, Latvia. Most of his academic career was at Oxford, where he became a fellow of All Souls (1932), professor of social and political theory (1957), and Master of Wolfson College (1966). His philosophical works include *Karl Marx* (1939), *Historical Inevitability* (1954), *Two Concepts of Liberty* (1959), and *Vico and Herder* (1976). Later works include *The Crooked Timber of Humanity* (1990) and *The Magus of the North* (1993). He was widely recognized as one of the leading intellectual voices of his generation.

Berliner, Emile [ber**liner**] (1851–1929) Inventor, born in Hanover, Germany. He worked as an apprentice printer until he emigrated to the USA in 1870, and later became chief inspector for the Bell Telephone Company. In the years after 1876 he patented several improvements to Alexander Graham Bell's telephone, demonstrated the flat disc gramophone record, and developed a method of making several copies of a record in shellac from a single master disc. In 1915 he invented the first acoustic tiles. >> Bell, Alexander Graham

Berlinguer, Enrico [**bair**linggair] (1922–84) Italian politician, born in Sussari, Sardinia. From his early 20s he devoted himself to making the Italian Communist Party a major force in Italian politics, and became secretary-general (1972). In 1976, under his leadership, it won more than a third of the Chamber of Deputies' seats, prompting him to propose the 'historic compromise': an alliance of the Catholics with the Communists. His proposal was rejected, but his vision of 'Eurocommunism' had a lasting impact.

Berlioz, (Louis-)Hector [ber**liohz**] (1803–69) Composer, born in La Côte-Saint-André, France. He entered the Paris Conservatoire in 1826, where he fell in love with the actress **Harriet Smithson**, whom he subsequently married (1833, d.1854); the *Symphonie Fantastique* expresses his devotion to her. Gaining the Prix de Rome in 1830, he spent two years in Italy. After 1842 he won a brilliant reputation in Germany, Russia, and England, but on his return to France he failed to gain a hearing for his major works. The deaths of his second wife (**Maria Recio**, 1862) and his son, ill health, and his fruitless struggle to win a regular place in French music, clouded his later years. His compositions include the *Grande messe des morts* (1837), the dramatic symphony *Roméo et Juliette* (1839), the overture *Le Carnival romain* (1843), the cantata *La Damnation de Faust* (1846), and his comic opera *Béatrice et Bénédict* (1860–2). One of the founders of 19th-c programme music, his books include a treatise on orchestration and an autobiography.

Berlitz, Charles (Frambach) (1914–) Languages educationist, the vice-president of Berlitz Schools of Languages and of Berlitz Publications, born in New York City. He is the grandson of **Maximilian Delphinus Berlitz**, who founded the Berlitz School in 1878 as a German emigré to the USA.

Bernadette of Lourdes, St, originally **Marie Bernarde Soubirous** (1844–79) Visionary, born in Lourdes, France, the daughter of François Soubirous, a miller. She claimed in 1858 to have received 18 apparitions of the Blessed Virgin at the Massabielle Rock in 1858, which has since become a notable place of pilgrimage. She became a nun with the Sisters of Charity at Nevers, and was canonized in 1933. Feast day 18 February or 16 April.

Bernadotte, Folke, Greve (Count) [berna**dot**] (1895–1948) Humanitarian and diplomat, born in Stockholm. The nephew of King Gustav V of Sweden, he acted as mediator during both world wars. Appointed by the UN to mediate in Palestine, he produced a partition plan, but was assassinated by Jewish terrorists in Jerusalem. >> Gustav V

Bernadottte, Jean >> **Charles XIV** (of Sweden)

Bernal, John Desmond [ber**nal**] (1901–71) Crystallographer, born in Nenagh, Co Tipperary, Ireland. He studied at Cambridge, and became professor of physics and then of crystallography at Birkbeck College, London (1937–68). He developed modern crystallography and was a founder of molecular biology, pioneering work on the structure of water. A Communist from his student days, he was active in international peace activity during the Cold War.

Bernanos, Georges [bairnanos] (1888–1948) Writer, born in Paris. He did not begin to write seriously until he was 37 and had taken degrees in law and letters. A Catholic polemicist, he attacked indifference and was preoccupied with problems of sin and grace. His most memorable novels are *Sous le soleil de Satan* (1926, trans The Star of Satan) and *Le Journal d'un curé de campagne* (1936, The Diary of a Country Priest).

Bernard, Claude [bairnah(r)] (1813–78) Physiologist, born near Villefranche, France. He studied medicine at Paris, and became assistant at the Collège de France to Magendie (1841), succeeding him as professor of experimental physiology (1855). He made several discoveries on the role of the pancreas and liver, changes in temperature of the blood, and the sympathetic nerves. His *Introduction to the Study of Experimental Medicine* (1865) is a scientific classic. >> Magendie

Bernard, Emile [bairnah(r)] (1868–1941) Painter and writer, born in Lille, France. A fellow student with Van

Gogh and Toulouse-Lautrec at the Académie of Fernand Cormon, he later worked with Gauguin. In Paris he joined the Group Synthétiste (1889), and launched a magazine, *La Rénovation esthétique* (1890). He is credited with founding the so-called Cloisonnist style. >> Gauguin

Bernard of Clairvaux, St [klairvoh], known as **the Mellifluous Doctor** (1090–1153) Theologian and reformer, born in Fontaines, France. He entered the Cistercian monastery of Cîteaux (1113), and became the first abbot of the newly-founded monastery of Clairvaux, in Champagne (1115). His studious, ascetic life and stirring eloquence made him the oracle of Christendom; he founded more than 70 monasteries; and he is regarded by the Catholic Church as the last of the Fathers. His writings comprise more than 400 epistles, 340 sermons, a Life of St Malachy, and distinct theological treatises. He was canonized in 1174. The monks of his reformed branch of the Cistercians are often called *Bernardines*. Feast day 20 August.

Bernard of Menthon, St [mãtõ], known as **the Apostle of the Alps** (923–1008) Clergyman, born in Savoy, Italy. As archdeacon of Aosta he founded the hospices in the two Alpine passes that bear his name. *St Bernard dogs* are named after him. He was canonized in 1115; feast day 28 May or 15 June.

Bernard of Morval or **Morlaix** (12th-c) Benedictine monk of Cluny in Burgundy, France, said to have been born of English parents in Morval. He is the author of the Latin poem, *De contemptu mundi*, in 3000 long hexameters, some of which were translated by John Mason Neale into hymns, among them 'Jerusalem the Golden' and 'The World is Very Evil'. >> Neale

Bernardino >> Pinturicchio

Bernardino of Siena, St [bernah(r)deenoh, syayna] (1380–1444) Franciscan monk, born in Massa di Carrara, Italy. He entered the order in 1404, was appointed its vicar-general for Italy (1438), and made himself famous by his rigid restoration of the rule. He was canonized in 1450; feast day 20 May.

Bernays, Edward L [bernayz] (1891–1995) Public relations executive, born in Vienna, the nephew of Sigmund Freud. He was brought to the USA in 1892. After creating US World War 1 propaganda, he founded the country's first public relations firm (1919), for which he and his future wife, **Doris E Fleischman**, coined the term 'counsel on public relations'. He was still counselling industrial and government clients after his 100th birthday. Known as the father of public relations, he pioneered public relations based on social science and market research. He wrote numerous books and articles, including the first book on public relations, *Crystallizing Public Opinion* (1923). >> Freud, Sigmund

Berners, Gerald Hugh Tyrwhitt-Wilson, 14th Baron (1883–1950) Composer, born in Bridgnorth, Shropshire, WC England, UK. His early works appeared under the name of Gerald Tyrwhitt. His total output was small, but includes an orchestral fugue and several ballets, of which the best known are *The Triumph of Neptune* and *Wedding Bouquet*.

Berners, John Bourchier, 2nd Baron (c.1467–1533) Writer and soldier, born probably in Oxford, Oxfordshire, SC England, UK. A notable figure in the reigns of Henry VII and Henry VIII, he became captain deputy of Calais in 1520, where he translated the works of Froissart and others.

Bernhard, Duke of Weimar [bernhah(r)t] (1604–39) Protestant general, born in Weimar, Germany. In the Thirty Years' War he distinguished himself at the Battle of Wimpfen (1622). He supported Gustav II Adolf of Sweden (1631), commanded the left wing at Lützen (1632), and after Gustav's death had the chief command. He lost at Nördlingen (1634), and was abandoned by the Swedes, but in alliance with Richelieu won victories at Rheinfelden and Breisach (1638). >> Gustav II

Bernhard Leopold [bernhah(r)t] (1911–) Prince of The Netherlands, born in Jena, Germany, the son of Prince Bernhard Casimir of Lippe. In 1937 he married Juliana, the only daughter of Wilhelmina, Queen of The Netherlands; they have four daughters. During World War 2, he commanded the Netherlands Forces of the Interior (1944–5). In 1976 he was involved in a bribery scandal, in which he was found to have received money for promoting the Dutch purchase of aircraft from the Lockheed Aircraft Corporation. >> Juliana

Bernhardt, Sarah [bernhah(r)t], originally **Henriette Rosine Bernard** (1844–1923) Actress, born in Paris. She entered the Paris Conservatoire in 1859, and in 1867 won fame as Zanetto in Coppée's *Le Passant* (1869), and as the Queen of Spain in *Ruy Blas* (1872). After 1876 she made frequent appearances in London, the USA, and Europe. In 1882 she married **Jacques Daria** or **Damala** (d.1889), a Greek actor, from whom she was divorced shortly afterwards. She founded the Théâtre Sarah Bernhardt in 1899. In 1915 she had a leg amputated, but did not abandon the stage.

Berni or **Bernia, Francesco** [bairnee] (c. 1497–1535) Poet, born in Lamporecchio, Tuscany. His recast or *rifacimento* of Boiardo's *Orlando innamorato* (1542) is still read in Italy in preference to the original. He played a large part in establishing Italian as a literary language. >> Boiardo

Bernini, Gian Lorenzo [berneenee] (1598–1680) Baroque sculptor, architect, and painter, born in Naples, Italy, the son of a sculptor, **Pietro Bernini** (1562–1629). He went to Rome at an early age and was introduced to the papal court. He completed the bronze baldacchino in St Peter's (1633), and the fountain of the four river gods in the Piazza Navona (1647). In 1656 he decorated the apse of St Peter's with the so-called Cathedra Petri, designed the colonnade in front of the cathedral, and in 1663 the grand staircase to the Vatican.

Bernoulli, Daniel [bernoolee] (1700–82) Mathematician, born in Groningen, The Netherlands, the son of Johann Bernoulli. He studied medicine and mathematics, and became professor of mathematics at St Petersburg in 1725. In 1732 he returned to Basel to become professor of anatomy, then botany, and finally physics. He worked on trigonometric series, mechanics, vibrating systems, and hydrodynamics (anticipating the kinetic theory of gases), and solved a differential equation proposed by Jacopo Riccati, now known as *Bernoulli's equation*. >> Bernoulli, Johann; Venturi, Giovanni Battista

Bernoulli, Jakob or **Jacques** [bernoolee] (1655–1705) Mathematician, born in Basel, Switzerland, the brother of Johann Bernoulli. He became professor of mathematics at Basel in 1687. He investigated infinite series, the cycloid, transcendental curves, the logarithmic spiral, and the catenary. In 1690 he applied Gottfried Leibniz's newly discovered differential calculus to a problem in geometry, first using the term *integral*. His *Ars conjectandi* (1713) was an important contribution to probability theory. >> Bernoulli, Johann; Leibniz

Bernoulli, Johann or **Jean** [bernoolee] (1667–1748) Mathematician, born in Basel, Switzerland, the brother of Jakob Bernoulli. He did mathematical and chemical research, and became professor at Groningen (1695) and Basel (1705). He wrote on differential equations, finding the length and area of curves, isochronous curves, and curves of quickest descent. He founded a dynasty of mathematicians which continued for two generations. >> Bernoulli, Daniel; Bernoulli, Jakob

Bernstein, Carl [**bern**stiyn] (1944–) Journalist and writer, born in Washington, DC. With Bob Woodward (1943–) he was responsible for unmasking the Watergate cover-up, which resulted in a constitutional crisis and the resignation of President Richard Nixon. For their coverage of the acknowledged investigative story of the century, Bernstein and Woodward won for the *Washington Post* the 1973 Pulitzer Prize for public service. Together they wrote the best seller, *All the President's Men* (1974), which became a successful film, and *The Final Days* (1976), an almost hour-by-hour account of President Nixon's last months in office. >> Nixon

Bernstein, Eduard [**bern**shtiyn] (1850–1932) Socialist leader, born in Berlin. He lived in England from 1888 to 1901. An associate of Engels, he was an advocate of revisionism, an evolutionary parliamentary form of Marxism, and was periodically a member of the Reichstag from 1902 to 1928. >> Engels

Bernstein, Leonard [**bern**stiyn] (1918–90) Conductor, pianist, and composer, born in Lawrence, MA. He studied at Harvard and the Curtis Institute of Music, and achieved fame suddenly in 1943 by conducting the New York Philharmonic as a substitute for Bruno Walter. His compositions include three symphonies – *Jeremiah* (1942), *The Age of Anxiety* (1949), and *Kaddish* (1961–63) – a television opera, *Trouble in Tahiti*, and the musicals *On the Town* (1944) and *West Side Story* (1957). Later works include a Mass commissioned for the opening of the John F Kennedy Center of the Performing Arts (1971), the ballet *The Dybbuk* (1974), *Songfest* (1977), *Halil* (1981), and a revision of his operetta *Candide* (1956/88). >> Sondheim

Berosus or **Berossus** [be**roh**sus] (fl.c. 260 BC) A priest of Babylon, who wrote in Greek three books of Babylonian–Chaldean history, in which he made use of the archives in the temple of Bel at Babylon. Only a few fragments have been preserved by Josephus, Eusebius, and Syncellus.

Berra, Yogi, popular name of **Lawrence Peter Berra** (1925–) Baseball player and coach, born in St Louis, MO. He played with the New York Yankees (1946–63), including 14 World Series (a record). He also set the record for most home runs by a catcher in the American League (313). He went on to manage and coach the Yankees, then did the same for their arch rivals, the New York Mets. In 1986 he went on to coach the Houston Astros. His most famous quotation was 'It ain't over 'til it's over'. >> RR1144

Berri, Nabih (1939–) Lebanese soldier and statesman, born in Freetown, Sierra Leone. He studied law at Beirut University, and in 1978 became leader of Amal ('Hope'), a branch of the Shiite nationalist movement founded by Iman Musa Sadr. Backed by Syria, it became the main Shiite military force in West Beirut and Southern Lebanon during the country's civil wars, until its defeat in 1988. He joined the Lebanese government in 1984 as minister of justice.

Berrigan, Daniel J(oseph) (1921–) Catholic radical, born in Virginia, MN, the brother of Philip Berrigan. Ordained a Jesuit in 1952, he then studied in France, where he was influenced by the worker-priest movement. As a high-school teacher and theology professor at Le Moyne College, Syracuse, NY (1957–63) he encouraged students in social work and political activism; he also won recognition as a poet. Later, while holding other posts, he was increasingly involved in anti-war protest. In 1968 he was convicted, with eight others, of destroying draft records in Catonsville, MD, for which he served 18 months in prison. His protest activities and experiences inspired many of his writings. >> Berrigan, Philip; Clark, Ramsey

Berrigan, Philip F(rancis) (1923–) Catholic priest and activist, born in Two Harbors, MN, the brother of Daniel Berrigan. He served in three European campaigns in the US Army (1943–6), was ordained in 1955, and held a series of pastoral and teaching posts. From 1962 he made the peace movement the focus of his life's work, coming to national attention along with his brother in 1968 for destroying draft registration files in Catonsville, MD. He was sentenced to six years in prison, but went underground, and was subsequently captured by federal authorities in a Manhattan church (1970). He married **Elizabeth McAlister** in 1969, but did not formally leave the priesthood. In 1973, he and his wife founded Jonah House – a community committed to a nonviolent approach to fighting the arms race. His community staged at least 120 actions at weapons factories and nuclear facilities in the USA, Europe, and Australia, and he was indicted some 100 times, serving over six years in prison between 1970 and 1992. He has also written several books. >> Berrigan, Daniel; Clark, Ramsey

Berruguete, Alonso [be**rooget**] (c. 1489–1561) Painter and sculptor, born near Valladolid, Spain, the son of Pedro Berruguete. He became the major Spanish sculptor of the 16th-c, and an important figure in the introduction of the Italian Mannerist style into Spain. He was appointed court painter to Charles V, and later ennobled. He is best known for the wood and alabaster carvings for the choir of Toledo Cathedral. >> Berruguete, Pedro

Berruguete, Pedro [be**rooget**] (c. 1450–1504) Painter, born near Valladolid, Spain, the father of Alonso Berruguete. He became court painter to Ferdinand and Isabella, and visited Italy (c.1447), where he helped to decorate the palace library at Urbino. The new, Venetian-inspired feeling for light and colour, and the interest in perspective which he acquired in Italy, made him the first truly Renaissance painter in Spain. His later work can be seen in the cathedrals of Toledo and Avila. >> Berruguete, Alonso

Berry, Charles Ferdinand, duc de (Duke of) (1778–1820) Aristocrat, born in Versailles, France, the second son of Charles X. During the Revolution and empire (1789–1815) he lived in exile, and in 1814 returned to France. In 1815 he was appointed commander of the troops in and around Paris, and in 1816 married **Caroline Ferdinande Louise** (1798–1870), the eldest daughter of Francis, afterwards King of the Two Sicilies. He was assassinated by the Bonapartist fanatic Pierre Louis Louvel in front of the Opéra. >> Charles X

Berry, Chuck, popular name of **Charles Edward Anderson Berry** (1926–) Rock singer, born in St Louis, MO. The biggest influence on pre-Beatles rock, he learnt to play the guitar at high school. He served three years in a reform school for armed robbery (1944–7), then worked in a factory and trained as a hairdresser before moving to Chicago in 1955 and launching his professional career. His successes include 'Maybellene' (1955), 'Rock And Roll Music' (1957), and 'Johnny B Goode' (1958). In 1959 he was charged with transporting a minor over state lines for immoral purposes and was jailed for two years in 1962. After his release his creativity never fully recovered, although 'My Ding A Ling' (1972) was one of the most successful singles of his career.

Berry, James Gomer >> **Kemsley, James Gomer Berry**

Berryman, John (1914–72) Poet, biographer, novelist, and academic, born in McAlester, OK. He studied at Columbia and Cambridge (UK) universities, and taught at several universities before becoming professor of humanities at the University of Minnesota (1955–72). Often pigeon-holed as a confessional poet, he disparaged the label. *Homage to Mistress Bradstreet* (1956), established his reputation. His major work is *Dream Songs*, which he began in 1955; *77 Dream Songs* (1964) won the Pulitzer Prize in 1965. He became a severely disturbed alcoholic, and committed suicide in Minneapolis.

Bert, Paul [bair] (1833–86) Physiologist and French republican statesman, born in Auxerre, France. A professor at the Sorbonne (1869), he did pioneering work in studying blood gases, the toxic effects of oxygen at high pressure, and anaesthetics.

Berthelot, (Pierre Eugène) Marcellin [bairteloh] (1827–1907) Chemist and French statesman, born in Paris. He became the first professor of organic chemistry at the Collège de France (1865), and was foreign minister (1895–6). He helped to found the study of thermochemistry, introducing a standard method for determining the latent heat of steam. His syntheses of many fundamental organic compounds helped to destroy the classical division between organic and inorganic compounds.

Berthelot, Sabin [bairtuhloh] (1794–1880) Naturalist, born in Marseilles, France. In 1820 he went to the Canaries, where he became an expert botanist, and was later appointed French consul there (1847). *Berthelot's pipit* was named in his honour.

Berthier, Louis Alexandre [bairtyay] (1753–1815) French general, the first marshal of the French empire, born in Versailles, France. In the French Revolution he rose to be chief-of-staff in the Army of Italy (1795), and in 1798 proclaimed the republic in Rome. He became chief-of-staff to Napoleon, who made him Prince of Neuchâtel and Wagram. After Napoleon's fall he had to surrender the principality of Neuchâtel, but was allowed to keep his rank as peer and marshal. >> Napoleon I; Pius VI

Berthollet, Claude Louis, comte (Count) [bairtolay] (1748–1822) Chemist, born in Talloires, France. He studied at Turin, moving to Paris in 1772. He aided Antoine Lavoisier in his research into gunpowder and in forming the new chemical nomenclature. In 1785 he showed the value of chlorine for bleaching, and showed ammonia to be a compound of hydrogen and nitrogen. He was made a senator and a count by Napoleon, yet voted for his deposition in 1814, and on the Bourbon restoration was created a peer. >> Lavoisier

Bertillon, Alphonse [berteeyō] (1853–1914) Police officer, born in Paris. As chief of the identification bureau in Paris, in 1882 he devised a system of identifying criminals by anthropometric measurements (later superseded by fingerprints).

Bertoia, Harry [bairtoya], originally **Enrico Bertoia** (1915–78) Sculptor and designer, born in San Lorenzo, Italy. He emigrated to the USA in 1930, where he studied and taught painting and metal crafts at the Cranbrook Academy of Art, Bloomfield Hills, MI. He worked for the Evans Products Co, Venice, CA (1943–6), then established his own workshop in Bally, PA. Although he regarded himself primarily as a sculptor, he was known for his early Cubist-influenced silver coffee and tea services and for his furniture, most especially the *Bertoia chair* (1952), with its slender metal legs and frame, and mesh-like seat.

Bertolucci, Bernardo [bertohloochee] (1940–) Film director, born in Parma, Italy. He became an assistant to Pier Paolo Pasolini on *Accatone* (1961). His collection of poetry, *In cerca del mistero* (1962, In Search of Mystery), won the Premio Viareggio Prize, and he made his directorial debut the same year with *La commare seca* (The Grim Reaper). The success of *Il conformista* (1970, The Conformist) and *Ultimo tango a Parigi* (1972, Last Tango in Paris) allowed him to make the Marxist epic *Novecento* (1976, 1900). After a number of unrealized projects during the 1980s, *The Last Emperor* (1987) won nine Oscars. Later films include *Stealing Beauty* (1996). >> Pasolini

Bertrand, Henri Gratien, comte (Count) [bairtrã] (1773–1844) French soldier and military engineer, one of Napoleon's generals, born in Châteauroux, France. Aide-de-camp to the emperor from 1804, he shared the emperor's banishment to both Elba and St Helena. After Napoleon's death he returned to France, where he was appointed commandant of the Polytechnic School (1830). >> Napoleon

Bérulle, Pierre de [bayrül] (1575–1629) Clergyman and French statesman, born near Troyes, France. A leader of the Catholic reaction against Calvinism, he founded the French Congregation of the Oratory (1611) and introduced the Carmelite Order into France. He was minister of state until dismissed by Richelieu, and was made a cardinal in 1627. >> Richelieu

Berwald, Franz (Adolf) [bairvalt] (1796–1868) Composer, born in Stockholm. His reputation rests largely on the four symphonies he composed during the 1840s, the *Sérieuse* and *Capricieuse* (1842) and the *Singulière* and *Eb* in 1845. Other works include the opera *Estrella de Soria* (1841), and many operetta and chamber music pieces. He was the outstanding Swedish composer of the 19th-c.

Berwick, James Fitzjames, 1st Duke of (1670–1734) Marshal of France, born in Moulins, France, the illegitimate son of James VII (of Scotland) and II (of England) (by Arabella Churchill). Educated in France as a Catholic, he was created Duke of Berwick (1687). At the 'Glorious Revolution' of 1688 he fled from England, but supported his father's attempts to regain the throne. He was created a marshal of France (1706), and in the War of the Spanish Succession (1701–14) established the throne of Philip V by the decisive victory over the English at Almansa (1707). >> Churchill, Arabella; James II (of England); Philip V

Berzelius, Jöns Jakob, Baron [berzaylius] (1779–1848) Chemist, born near Linköping, Sweden. He studied at Uppsala and taught at Stockholm. His accurate determination of atomic weights established the laws of combination and John Dalton's atomic theory. He introduced modern symbols, an electrochemical theory, discovered the elements selenium, thorium, and cerium, and first isolated others. He was made a baron in 1835. >> Dalton, John; Wöhler

Besant, Annie [beznt], *née* **Wood** (1847–1933) Theosophist, born in London, England, UK, the sister-in-law of Sir Walter Besant. After her separation in 1873 from her husband, the Rev Frank Besant, she became vice-president of the National Secular Society (1874). A close associate of Charles Bradlaugh, she was an ardent proponent of birth control and Socialism. In 1889, after meeting Madame Blavatsky, she developed an interest in theosophy, and went out to India, where she became involved in the independence movement. >> Besant, Walter; Blavatsky; Bradlaugh; Krishnamurti; Stopes

Besant, Sir Walter [beznt] (1836–1901) Novelist and social reformer, born in Portsmouth, Hampshire, S England, UK, the brother-in-law of Annie Besant. He studied at King's College, London, and at Cambridge. After a few years as a professor in Mauritius, he devoted himself to literature. In 1871 he entered into a literary partnership with James Rice (1843–82), writing several novels. His *All Sorts and Conditions of Men* (1882) and *Children of Gideon* (1886), describing conditions in the slums of the east end of London, and other novels advocating social reform, resulted in the establishment of the People's Palace (1887) for popular recreation. He was knighted in 1895. >> Besant, Annie

Besht >> **Baal-Shem-Tov**

Bessarion or **Basilius, John** [besarion] (1403–72) Byzantine theologian, born in Trebizond, Turkey. He was one of the earliest scholars to transplant Greek literature and philosophy into the West. As Archbishop of Nicaea, he accompanied the Greek emperor, John Palaeologus, to Italy in 1438

to effect a union between the Greek and the Roman churches. Soon afterwards he joined the Roman Church, and was made cardinal by Pope Eugenius IV.

Bessel, Friedrich Wilhelm (1784–1846) Mathematician and astronomer, born in Minden, Germany. In 1810 he was appointed director of the observatory and professor at Königsberg. He catalogued stars, predicted a planet beyond Uranus as well as the existence of dark stars, investigated Johann Kepler's problem of heliocentricity, and systematized the mathematical functions involved, which now bear his name. >> Kepler

Bessemer, Sir Henry [besemer] (1813–98) Inventor and engineer, born in Charlton, Hertfordshire, SE England, UK. A self-taught man, he learned metallurgy in his father's type foundry, and made numerous inventions. In 1855–6, in response to the need for guns in the Crimean War (1853–6), he took out a series of patents covering an economical process in which molten pig-iron can be turned directly into steel by blowing air through it in a tilting converter (the *Bessemer process*). He established a steelworks at Sheffield in 1859, specializing in guns and, later, steel rails. >> Kelly, William; Mushet, David

Besser, Joe >> Stooges, The Three

Bessmertnova, Natalia [besmairtnova] (1941–) Ballerina, born in Moscow. She trained at the Bolshoi Ballet School (1952–61), joining the company upon graduation. She has figured significantly in ballets devised by her husband Yuri Grigorovich, particularly *Ivan the Terrible* (1975). >> Grigorovich

Besson, Jacques [besõ] (c.1535–c.1575) Mathematician, engineer and inventor, born in Grenoble, France. He is remembered for his *Théâtre des Instruments Mathématiques et Méchaniques* (1578), which included designs for a wide range of instruments and machines.

Besson, Luc [besõ] (1959–) Film director, born in Paris, France. He worked his way up in film, television, and promotional video before making his first feature film, *Le Dernier combat* (1983), filmed in monochrome, and virtually dispensing with dialogue. He followed this with *Subway* (1985), a thriller set largely in the labyrinthine tunnels of the Paris Métro. Later films include *The Big Blue* (1988) and *Nikita* (1990).

Best, Charles H(erbert) (1899–1978) Physiologist, born in West Pembroke, ME. As a research student at Toronto University he helped Sir Frederick Banting to isolate the hormone insulin (1922), used in the control of diabetes. He was head of the department of physiology at Toronto from 1929 and director of medical research from 1941. He discovered choline (a vitamin that prevents liver damage) and histaminase (the enzyme that breaks down histamine), and introduced the use of the anti-coagulant, heparin. >> Banting

Best, George (1946–) Footballer, born in Belfast. He was the leading scorer for Manchester United in the Football League First Division (1967–8), and won a European Cup Medal and the title of European Footballer of the Year (1968). Becoming increasingly unable to cope with the pressure of top-class football, his career was virtually finished by the time he was 25 years old. Attempted comebacks with smaller clubs in England, the USA, and Scotland were unsuccessful. >> RR1156

Bethe, Hans (Albrecht) [baytuh] (1906–) Physicist, born in Strasbourg, France (formerly Germany). He studied at the universities of Frankfurt and Munich, and taught in Germany until 1933. He moved first to England, then to the USA, where he held the chair of physics at Cornell University until his retirement (1937–75). During World War 2 he was director of theoretical physics for the atomic bomb project based at Los Alamos. In 1939 he proposed the first detailed theory for the generation of energy by stars through a series of nuclear reactions. He also contributed with Ralph Alpher and George Gamow to the 'alpha, beta, gamma' theory of the origin of the chemical elements during the early development of the universe. He was awarded the 1967 Nobel Prize for Physics. >> Alpher; Gamow

Bethlen, Gábor, Ger **Gabriel Bethlen** (1580–1629) King of Hungary (1620–1). Born into a Hungarian Protestant family, he was elected Prince of Transylvania in 1613. In 1619 he invaded Hungary and had himself elected king in 1620. Although he had to come to terms with the Holy Roman Emperor Ferdinand II (ruled 1619–37) the following year, relinquishing his claims to the Hungarian throne, Ferdinand was obliged to grant religious freedom to Hungarian Protestants. >> RR1057

Bethmann-Hollweg, Theobald (Theodor Friedrich Alfred) von [baytman holvayk] (1856–1921) German statesman, born in Hohenfinow, Germany. He studied law, and rose in the service of Brandenburg, Prussia, and the empire, till he became imperial chancellor (1909). He described the Belgian neutrality treaty as 'a scrap of paper', and played an important role before and after the outbreak of war in 1914. He was dismissed in 1917.

Bethune, David >> Beaton, David

Bethune, Norman (1899–1939) Surgeon, born in Gravenhurst, Ontario, Canada. He studied at Toronto University, and became a specialist in chest surgery, especially the treatment of tuberculosis. He worked as a surgeon in the Spanish Civil War (1936–7), and was in China during the Japanese war (1938–9), where he became a national hero.

Betjeman, Sir John [bechuhman] (1906–84) Poet, broadcaster, and writer on architecture, born in London, England, UK. He studied at Magdalen College, Oxford, but left university without a degree. He began to write for the *Architectural Review* and became general editor of the *Shell Guides* (1934). His first collection of verse was *Mount Zion; or In Touch with the Infinite* (1933). Other collections include *New Bats in Old Belfries* (1945), *A Few Late Chrysanthemums* (1954), and *Collected Poems* (1958). Nostalgic and wary of change, he preferred the countryside to the city, and was impassioned in his abhorrence of modern architecture. He was knighted (1969), and succeeded Cecil Day-Lewis as Poet Laureate in 1972. >> Day-Lewis

Bettelheim, Bruno [betlhiym] (1903–90) Psychologist, born in Vienna. He studied at the University of Vienna, and began working with emotionally disturbed children. When the Nazis annexed Austria in 1938 he was placed in concentration camps. Released in 1939, he emigrated to the USA, and taught at the University of Chicago, where he was appointed director of the Sonia Shankman Orthogenic School in 1944, becoming internationally renowned for his work with autistic children. His many works include *Love Is Not Enough* (1950), *Truants from Life* (1954), and *A Good Enough Parent* (1987).

Betti, Ugo (1892–1953) Playwright and poet, born in Camerino, Italy. He studied law and became a judge in Rome (1930–44), and librarian of the ministry of justice (1944–53). He is best known for his 26 plays, notably *La padrona* (1929, The Landlady). Collections of verse include *Il re pensieroso* (1922, The Thoughtful King), and he also wrote three books of short stories.

Beust, Friedrich Ferdinand, Graf von (Count of) [boyst] (1809–86) Austrian statesman, born in Dresden, Germany. He was imperial chancellor (1867–71), and ambassador to London (1871–8) and Paris (1878–82). His chief achievement was the reconciliation of Hungary to Austria.

Beuys, Joseph [boys] (1921–86) Avant-garde artist, born in Krefeld, Germany. He studied art at Düsseldorf Academy, where he later became professor of sculpture (1961–71). His sculpture consisted mainly of 'assemblages' of bits and pieces of rubbish; for one typical exhibit he smeared frankfurters with brown shoe polish. He also staged multimedia 'happenings'. He was much admired and imitated by the younger avant-garde from the 1960s onwards. A prominent political activist, he was one of the founders of the Green Party in Germany.

Bevan, Aneurin, known as **Nye Bevan** (1897–1960) British statesman, born in Tredegar, Blaenau Gwent, SE Wales, UK. One of 13 children of a miner, he began work in the pits at 13. Active in trade unionism in the South Wales coalfield, he led the Welsh miners in the 1926 General Strike. He joined the Labour Party (1931), establishing a reputation as an irreverent and often tempestuous orator. In 1934 he married **Jennie Lee**. Appointed minister of health in the 1945 Labour government, he introduced the revolutionary National Health Service (1948). He became minister of labour in 1951, but resigned the same year over the National Health charges proposed in the Budget. From this period dated *Bevanism*, the left-wing movement to make the Labour Party more socialist and less 'reformist', which made him the centre of prolonged disputes with his party leaders. He ceased to be a *Bevanite* at the 1957 Brighton party conference, when he opposed a one-sided renunciation of the hydrogen bomb by Britain. >> Lee, Jennie

Bevan, Brian, nickname **the Galloping Ghost** (1924–91) Rugby league player, born in Sydney, New South Wales, Australia. A wing-threequarter, he scored a record 796 tries in 18 seasons (1945–64). He played for Blackpool Borough and Warrington, and was one of the inaugural members of the Rugby League Hall of Fame in 1988. >> RR1167

Bevan, Edward (John) (1856–1921) Industrial chemist, born in Birkenhead, Merseyside, NW England, UK. After a private education he studied chemistry at Owens College, Manchester, and became a consulting chemist. In 1892, with Charles Cross, he patented the viscose process of rayon manufacture. >> Cross, Charles

Beveridge, William Henry Beveridge, Baron (1879–1963) Economist, born in Rangpur, India. He studied at Oxford, and became a leading authority on unemployment insurance. He entered the Board of Trade (1908) and became director of labour exchanges (1909–16). He was director of the London School of Economics (1919–37) and Master of University College, Oxford (1937–45). He chaired the inter-departmental committee which produced the *Beveridge Report* on social insurance (1942), which formed the basis of much social legislation. He was elected to parliament as a Liberal (1944), but was defeated in 1945, and became a peer in 1946.

Bevin, Ernest (1881–1951) British statesman, born in Winsford, Somerset, SW England, UK. Orphaned at seven, and self-taught, he early came under the influence of trade unionism and the Baptists, and was for a time a lay preacher. A paid official of the dockers' union, he gained a national reputation in 1920 when he won most of his union's claims against an eminent barrister, earning the title of 'the dockers' KC'. He built up the National Transport and General Workers' Union, and became its general secretary (1921–40). In 1940 he became a Labour MP, minister of labour and national service in Churchill's coalition government, and in the Labour government was foreign secretary (1945–51). >> Churchill, Sir Winston

Bewick, Thomas [byooik] (1753–1828) Wood engraver, born in Ovingham, Northumberland, NE England, UK. Among his best works are the woodcuts for *The Chillingham Bull* (1789) and for the *History of British Birds* (1797–1804).

Bewick's swan was named in his honour shortly after his death.

Beyle, Marie-Henri >> **Stendhal**

Beza, Theodore [bayza], Fr **Bèze, Théodore de** (1519–1605) Religious reformer, born in Vézelay, France. He studied Greek and law at Orléans. He became known as a writer of witty (but indecent) verses in *Juvenilia* (1548), but after an illness he took a serious view of life, and went to Geneva to join Calvin. He was Greek professor at Lausanne (1549–54), and with Calvin founded the academy at Geneva (1559), and became professor of theology and first rector there. On Calvin's death (1564), he became leader of the Genevese Church. >> Calvin, John

Bhartrihari [bah(r)trihahree] (7th-c) Hindu poet and philosopher. He was the author of three *satakas* ('centuries') of stanzas on practical conduct, love, and renunciation of the world, and an influential Sanskrit grammar.

Bhasa [bahsa] (3rd-c) Earliest known Sanskrit playwright. He was the author of plays on religious and legendary themes, some of which were discovered only in 1912.

Bhave, Vinoba [bahvay] (1895–1982) Land reformer, born in Gagode, Gujarat, India. Mahatma Gandhi took him under his care as a young scholar, an event which changed his life. Distressed in 1951 by the land hunger riots in Telengana, Hyderabad, he began a walking mission throughout India to persuade landlords to give land to the peasants. He was claimed to be the most notable spiritual figure in India after the death of Gandhi. >> Gandhi

Bhindranwale, Sant Jarnail Singh [bindranwahlay] (1947–84) Indian politician and former Sikh extremist leader. He trained at the orthodox Damdani Taksal Sikh missionary school, becoming its head priest in 1971. His campaign broadened into a demand for a separate state of 'Khalistan' during the early 1980s, precipitating a bloody Hindu-Sikh conflict in Punjab. After taking refuge in the Golden Temple complex at Amritsar with about 500 devoted followers, he was killed by the Indian Security Forces.

Bhumibol Adulyadej [poomeepol adoolyahday] (1927–   ) King of Thailand, born in Cambridge, MA. He studied in Bangkok and Switzerland and became monarch as King Rama VI in 1946 after the assassination of his elder brother. He married **Queen Sirikit** in 1950 and has one son, **Crown Prince Vajiralongkorn** (1952–   ), and three daughters. The longest reigning monarch in Thailand's history, he is a highly respected figure, viewed in some quarters as semi-divine. >> RR1093

Bhutto, Benazir [bootoh] (1953–   ) Pakistani stateswoman and prime minister (1988–91, 1993–6), born in Karachi, the daughter of the former prime minister, Zulfikar Ali Bhutto. She studied at Oxford, returned to Pakistan, and was placed under house arrest (1977–84) after the military coup led by General Zia ul-Haq. She moved to England (1984–6), becoming the joint leader in exile of the Opposition Pakistan People's Party, then returned to Pakistan to launch a nationwide campaign for 'open elections'. She married a wealthy landowner, **Asif Ali Zardari**, in 1987 and was elected prime minister barely three months after giving birth to her first child. She was defeated in the 1991 election, and found herself in court defending herself against several charges of misconduct while in office. She continued to be a prominent focus of Opposition discontent, and won a further election in 1993, but was replaced in 1996. >> Bhutto, Zulfikar Ali; Zia ul-Haq; RR1080

Bhutto, Zulfikar Ali [bootoh] (1928–79) Pakistani statesman, president (1971–3), and prime minister (1973–7), born in Larkana, Sind, India. He graduated from the universities of California and Oxford, and lectured in law at

Southampton (1952–3) and in Pakistan. He became minister of commerce (1958), and foreign minister (1963), then founded the Pakistan People's Party (1967), which won the army-supervised elections in West Pakistan (1971). As president and prime minister he did much to rebuild national morale, introducing constitutional, social, and economic reforms. Opposition to his government strengthened among right-wing Islamic parties, and he was ousted by the army (1977). The military leader, General Zia ul-Haq, instituted proceedings against corruption, under which Bhutto was convicted of conspiring to murder and was sentenced to death in 1978. In spite of worldwide protest and appeals for clemency, the sentence was carried out. >> Bhutto, Benazir; Zia ul-Haq; RR1080

Biandrata, Giorgio >> **Blandrata, Giorgio**

Bias [**biy**as] (6th-c BC) Native of Priene in Ionia, famous for his pithy sayings. He was one of the 'Seven Wise Men' of Greece.

Bible Bill >> **Aberhart, William**

Bichat, (Marie-François) Xavier [beesha] (1771–1802) Physician, born in Thoirette, France. He studied at Lyon and Paris, and in 1801 was appointed physician to the Hôtel-Dieu. He was the first to simplify anatomy and physiology by reducing the complex structures of the organs to their elementary tissues.

Bickerdyke, Mary Ann, *née* **Ball,** known as **Mother Bickerdyke** (1817–1901) Nurse and humanitarian, born in Knox Co, OH. A farmer's daughter with little formal education, at age 42 she was left a widow with three children. She supported herself by practising 'Botanic' medicine, and when the Civil War broke out she volunteered to work in the hospitals at the Union army base at Cairo, IL. From then until the surrender at Appomattox, she worked as a nurse and caregiver both in battle and behind the lines, taking time out only to give speeches and gain support for the Sanitary Commission. After the war, she worked for various social service causes. Receiving a special pension from Congress in 1886, she retired to Kansas in 1887.

Bickford, William (1774–1834) Inventor, born near Camborne, Cornwall, SW England, UK. A leatherseller by trade, he was distressed by the frequent accidents caused by premature detonation of explosive charges in mines. After several attempts he was successful in combining gunpowder and flax yarn into a reliable slow-burning fuse, which he patented in 1831.

Bidault, Georges (Augustin) [beedoh] (1899–1983) French statesman and prime minister (1946, 1949–50, 1958), born in Paris. He became a professor of history and edited the Catholic newspaper *L'Aube*. He was leader of the MRP (Movement Républicaine Populaire), and in addition to becoming prime minister, also served as deputy prime minister (1950, 1951) and foreign minister (1944, 1947, 1953–54). He opposed de Gaulle over the Algerian War, and was charged with plotting against the security of the state. He went into exile in 1962, returning in 1968. >> de Gaulle; RR1049

Bidder, George Parker, nickname **The Calculating Boy** (1806–78) Engineer and precocious mathematician, born in Moretonhampstead, Devon, SW England, UK. He studied at Camberwell and Edinburgh, and became a civil engineer, inventing the railway swing bridge and designing the Royal Victoria Docks, which were opened in 1856.

Biddle, John (1615–62) Preacher, the founder of English Unitarianism, born in Wotton-under-Edge, Gloucestershire, SWC England, UK. He entered Magdalen Hall, Oxford (1634), and was elected master of the Gloucester Free School (1641). In 1645 he was imprisoned for rejecting in his preaching the deity of the Holy Ghost, and during the Commonwealth was banished to the Scilly Is (1655–8). In

1662 he was again apprehended and fined £100. He could not pay it, so was sent to jail, where he died.

Biddle, Nicholas (1750–78) US naval officer, born in Philadelphia, PA. One of the first five captains commissioned by Congress (1775), he participated in the capture of New Providence I, Bahamas (1776), and captured several British ships. He was killed when his ship, the USS *Randolph*, exploded.

Biela, Wilhelm von [**bay**la] (1782–1856) Austrian army officer and astronomer. In 1826 he observed the periodic comet named after him, although it had already been seen in 1772.

Bienville, Jean Baptiste le Moyne, sieur de (Lord of) [byanveel] (1680–1768) Explorer and governor, born in Montreal, Quebec, Canada. He entered the French navy at 12 and spent most of his life in the king's service as an explorer and colonial administrator. He founded Mobile, AL (1710) and New Orleans, LA (1718), and was the Governor of French Louisiana (1701–13, 1717–14, 1733–43). Worn out from Indian wars, he resigned and went to Paris.

Bierce, Ambrose (Gwinett) [beers] (1842–?1914) Journalist and writer, born in Meigs Co, OH. He fought in the Civil War, then became a journalist, working in both the USA and England. He was the author of such collections of sardonically humorous tales as *The Fiend's Delight* (1872), *In the Midst of Life* (1898), and *The Devil's Dictionary* (1906). A misanthrope, he disappeared in Mexico.

Bierstadt, Albert [**beer**shtat] (1830–1902) Painter, born near Düsseldorf, Germany. He studied art at Düsseldorf (1853–7), then settled in New York City. He became associated with the Hudson River School, painting Romantic panoramic landscapes in which truth to topographical detail was secondary to dramatic and awe-inspiring effect. His paintings of the Rocky Mts gained him great popularity.

Biffen, (William) John (1930–) British politician. He studied at Cambridge (1953), and went into industry, later moving to the Economist Intelligence Unit. He entered the House of Commons in 1971, and following the 1979 general election was made chief secretary to the Treasury. A monetarist in economic policy, he favoured a more pragmatic approach in social matters than the prime minister, Margaret Thatcher, and, although he became a successful Leader of the Commons, was removed from the cabinet after the 1987 general election.

Biffen, Sir Rowland Harry (1874–1949) Botanist and geneticist, born in Cheltenham, Gloucestershire, SWC England, UK. He studied at Cambridge, and became the first professor of agricultural botany there (1908). Using Mendelian genetic principles, he pioneered the breeding of hybrid rust-resistant strains of wheat. >> Mendel

Bigelow, Erastus (Brigham) [**bi**geloh] (1814–79) Inventor, born in West Boylston, MA. He invented looms for various kinds of material, a carpet loom, and a machine for making knotted counterpanes. He was founder of the Massachusetts Institute of Technology in 1861.

Biggers, Earl (Derr) (1884–1933) Novelist, born in Warren, OH. He studied at Harvard, and created the famous character Charlie Chan in his series of detective novels, starting with *The House without a Key* (1925).

Biggs, Ronald (1929–) Convicted thief and member of the gang who perpetrated the Great Train Robbery (1963). He was among the first five to be arrested for the theft, having been traced by fingerprints left at the gang's farm hideout. Convicted and sentenced to 25 years for conspiracy and 30 years (to run concurrently) for armed robbery, he escaped from Wandsworth Prison in 1965 and fled to Australia. Pursued by the police, he eventually settled in Brazil. There, he was saved from extradition because his girlfriend was pregnant (under Brazilian law, fathers of Brazilian children cannot be extradited). He still lives in Brazil. The question of his extradition arose again in 1997, after his son came of age, but he was allowed to stay.

Bigi, Francesco di Cristofano >> Franciabigio

Bihzad, Ustad Kamal al-Din [beezad] (c. 1440–?) Painter and calligrapher, born in Herat, Afghanistan. The most famous Persian painter of the end of the 15th-c, he was called 'the Marvel of the Age'. Only a few of his works remain.

Bikila, Abebe [bikeela] (1932–73) Ethiopian marathon runner. Virtually unknown, and running in bare feet, he won the marathon at the 1960 Olympics in Rome, setting a new world record and becoming the first black African to win a gold medal.

Biko, Stephen (Bantu) [beekoh], known as **Steve Biko** (1946–77) South African political activist, founder and leader of the Black Consciousness Movement, born in King William's Town, Cape Province. He became involved in politics while studying medicine at Natal University, and was one of the founders (and first president) of the all-black South African Students Organization (1969). In 1972 he became honorary president of the Black People's Convention, a coalition of over 70 black organizations. The following year he was served with a banning order severely restricting his movements and freedom of speech and association, and in 1975 the restrictions were increased. He was detained four times in the last few years of his life, and died in police custody, allegedly as a result of beatings received. He was the subject of a film made by Richard Attenborough (*Cry Freedom*, 1987). >> Kentridge

Bilk, Acker, popular name of **Bernard Stanley Bilk** (1929–) Jazz musician, composer, and band leader, born in Somerset, SW England, UK. He took up the clarinet while doing National Service, later joining Ken Colyer's Band as clarinettist, and forming the Bristol Paramount Jazz Band in 1951. Hit singles include 'Somerset' (1960), 'Stranger on the Shore' (1961, first number one simultaneously in UK and USA), and 'Aria' (1976). Still performing and recording into the 1990s, his later albums include *That's My Home* (1994) and *Three in the Morning* (1995).

Bill, Max (1908–94) Swiss politician, artist and teacher, born in Winterthur, Switzerland. He trained at the Zürich School of Arts and Crafts (1924–7) and at the Bauhaus in Dessau (1927–9), later becoming director of the Institute for Design, Ulm (1951–6) and professor of enivonmental design at the Institute for Fine Arts, Hamburg (1967–74). Working as an architect as well as a painter, sculptor, and product designer, he developed the essential Bauhaus principles of co-operative design along purely functionalist lines. He was a delegate to the Swiss parliament (1967–71).

Billinger, Richard (1893–1965) Poet, born in St Marien-kirchen, Austria. He was the author of collections of lyrics, as well as novels coloured by peasant life in Upper Austria.

Billings, Josh, originally **Henry Wheeler Shaw** (1818–85) Humorous writer, born in Lanesboro, MA. A land agent in Poughkeepsie, NY, he began writing in his 40s, publishing facetious almanacs and collections of witticisms. He relied heavily on deliberate misspelling, as in the 'Essa on the Muel' (Essay on the Mule), which launched his writing career.

Billings, William (1746–1800) Composer, born in Boston, MA. He studied music on his own and became one of the earliest professional musicians in the Colonies. After publishing his first collection of church music, the *New England Psalm Singer* (1770), he pursued in Boston a career of composing, reforming church music, and starting

musical ensembles. He founded the continent's first singing class in Stoughton, MA (1774) and the first church choir. His 'Chester', with its text 'Let tyrants shake their iron rod ... New England's God forever reigns', became a favourite of Revolutionary troops, and remains his best-known work. Despite his prominence, he was never able to make an adequate living, and died in poverty.

Billroth, (Christian Albert) Theodor [bilroht] (1829–94) Surgeon, born in Bergen, Austria. He became professor of surgery at Zürich (1860–7) and Vienna (1867–94). A pioneer of modern abdominal surgery, he performed the first successful excision of the larynx (1874) and the first resection of the intestine (1881). A brilliant musician, he was a friend of Brahms. >> Brahms

Billy the Kid >> Bonney, William H, Jr

Binchy, Maeve [binshee, mayv] (1940–) Writer, born in Dublin, Ireland. She studied history at University College Dublin, then became a teacher, travel writer, and columnist, joining the *Irish Times* in 1969. She has written plays for television and the stage, but is most widely known as a romantic novelist. Her books include *Light a Penny Candle* (1982), *Circle of Friends* (1990), and *The Glass Lake* (1994), and she has also written several volumes of short stories.

Bindoff, Stanley Thomas, known as **Tom Bindoff** (1908–80) Historian, born in Brighton, West Sussex, S England, UK. He studied at London University, where he taught throughout his life, and was professor at Queen Mary College (1951–75). He wrote several important works on British and W European diplomatic history, particularly *Tudor England* (1950), which (under the 'Pelican' imprint) launched the first academic paperback history series.

Binet, Alfred [beenay] (1857–1911) Psychologist, the founder of intelligence tests, born in Nice, France. Director of physiological psychology at the Sorbonne from 1892, his first tests were used on his children; later, with Théodore Simon, he expanded the tests (1905) to encompass the measurement of relative intelligence amongst deprived children (the *Binet–Simon* tests).

Binford, Lewis (Roberts) (1930–) US archaeologist, pioneer of the anthropologically-oriented 'processual' school of archaeology ('New Archaeology'). He studied at Michigan University and taught at Ann Arbor, Chicago, Santa Barbara, and Los Angeles before becoming professor of anthropology at the University of New Mexico, Albuquerque. His original manifesto *New Perspectives in Archaeology* (1968, with Sally R Binford) has subsequently been elaborated in such works as *Bones* (1981) and *In Pursuit of the Past* (1983).

Bing, Sir Rudolf (1902–97) Opera administrator, born in Vienna. He worked in Berlin and Darmstadt (1928–33) before managing the opera at Glyndebourne (1935–49). He was co-founder and director (1947–9) of the Edinburgh Festival, and general manager of the Metropolitan Opera, New York City (1950–72). He took British nationality in 1946, and was knighted in 1971.

Bingham, Hiram [bingham] (1875–1956) Explorer and senator, born in Honolulu, Hawaii, the son of an American missionary. He studied South American history, then taught at Yale (1907–24). He explored Latin America during the early 1920s, and is noted for discovering the Inca ruins of Machu Picchu (1911). He was chief of the Air Personnel Division of the Air Service in Washington during World War 1, serving in the same position for the Allied Expeditionary Forces in France. He became the Republican Senator for Connecticut (1924–32) and president of the National Aeronautic Association (1928–34). Becoming ever more conservative over the years, he headed the Civil Service Commission's Loyalty Review Board (1951–3) and forced the dismissal of many government employees.

Bingham, Millicent [bingham], *née* **Todd** (1880–1968) Geographer and litterateur, born in Washington, DC. She studied at Harvard, and travelled widely, publishing *Peru, Land of Contrasts* in 1914. Her interest in urban geography later led to her translation of Vidal de la Blanche's *Principles of Human Geography* (1926). After her marriage in 1920 to the psychologist **Walter Van Dyke Bingham**, she spent summers on a family-owned island in Maine where, in 1936, they allowed the Audubon Society to establish the first camp for adult conservation leaders. From the 1930s, following the lead of her mother, Mabel Loomis Todd (1856–1932), who had published the poetry and letters of Emily Dickinson, she became an authority on this author, and wrote *Ancestors' Brocades: the Literary Debut of Emily Dickinson* (1945).

Bintley, David (Julian) (1957–) British choreographer and dancer. He studied at the Royal Ballet School, then joined Sadlers Wells Royal Ballet (1976–86), becoming resident choreographer and principal dancer (1983–6). From 1986–93 he was resident choreographer and principal dancer with the Royal Ballet before joining the Birmingham Royal Ballet as artistic director (1995–).

Binyon, (Robert) Laurence (1869–1943) Poet and art critic, born in Lancaster, Lancashire, NW England, UK. On leaving Oxford, he joined the British Museum, and became keeper of Oriental prints and paintings (1913–33). His poetic works include *Lyric Poems* (1894), *Odes* (1901), and *Collected Poems* (1931). He also wrote plays, and translated Dante into *terza rima*. He was professor of poetry at Harvard (1933–4). Extracts from his poem 'For the Fallen' (set to music by Elgar) adorn war memorials throughout the British Commonwealth.

Biondi, Matt(hew) [byondee] (1965–) Swimmer, born in Morego, CA. At the 1986 world championships he won a record seven medals, including three golds, and at the 1988 Olympics won seven medals, including five golds. He set the 100 m freestyle world record of 48·24 s in Austin, TX, in 1988.

Biot, Jean Baptiste [beeoh] (1774–1862) Physicist and astronomer, born in Paris. Professor of physics at the Collège de France, he made a balloon ascent with Joseph Louis Gay-Lussac to study magnetism at high altitudes in 1804. He invented a polariscope and established the fundamental laws of the rotation of the plane of polarization of light by optically active substances. In 1820 he collaborated with Félix Savart to demonstrate the relationship between an electric current and the magnetic field it produces (the *Biot–Savart law*). >> Gay-Lussac; Savart

Birch, A(rthur) J(ohn) (1915–) Chemist, born in Sydney, New South Wales, Australia. He studied at the universities of Sydney and Oxford. At Oxford, in collaboration with Sir Robert Robinson, he was instrumental in the development of the oral contraceptive pill. In 1948 he made the first synthetic male sex hormone, which led to the production of norethisterone, an analogue of progesterone. He was Smithson Fellow of the Royal Society, Cambridge (1949–52), professor of organic chemistry at the University of Sydney (1952–5) and the University of Manchester (1955–67), then joined the Australian National University as dean of the research school of chemistry (1967–70) and foundation professor of organic chemistry (1967–80, emeritus 1982). He has also worked as a consultant to UNESCO and to industry. >> Robinson, Robert

Birch, (Louis) Charles (1918–) Biologist, eco-philosopher, and radical theologian, born in Melbourne, Victoria, Australia. He studied at the universities of Melbourne and Adelaide, then taught at Sydney, where he became professor of biology (1960–84, then emeritus). A member of the Club of Rome since 1974, in 1990 he won the Templeton Prize for Progress in Religion. His books include *Genetics and the Quality of Life* (1975), *The Liberation of Life* (1981), *On Purpose* (1990), and *Regaining Compassion* (1993). Much of his work shows his concern for the philosophical and theological implications of science.

Bird, Dickie, popular name of **Harold Dennis Bird** (1933–) Cricket umpire, born in Barnsley, South Yorkshire, N England, UK. He played county cricket for Yorkshire (1956–9) and Leicestershire (1960–4) before establishing himself as a popular and respected umpire. During his career he umpired many major events, including 68 test matches, 92 one-day internationals (a world record), 159 international matches (a world record), and a record three World Cup Finals (1975, 1979, 1983), retiring as a test umpire in 1996. His books include *From The Pavilion End* (1988).

Bird, Robert Montgomery (1806–54) Writer, born in Newcastle, DE. He gave up a career in medicine to become a writer, producing the popular tragedy *The Gladiator* in 1831. His novels include *Calavar, a Mexican Romance* (1834) and *Nick of the Woods* (1837).

Bird, Vere Cornwall (1910–) Antiguan statesman and prime minister (1981–94). In the pre-independence period he was elected to the Legislative Council and became chief minister (1960–7) and premier (1967–71, 1976–81). When full independence, as Antigua and Barbuda, was achieved in 1981 he became prime minister, and he and his party were re-elected in 1984 and 1989. >> RR1032

Birdseye, Clarence (1886–1956) Businessman and inventor, born in New York City. He is best known for developing a process for freezing food in small packages suitable for retailing. He founded the General Seafoods Company in 1924, later becoming president of Birdseye Frosted Foods (1930–4) and of Birdseye Electric Company (1935–8). Some 300 patents are credited to him; among his other inventions were infrared heat lamps, the recoilless harpoon gun, and a method of removing water from food.

Birdwood, William Riddell (1865–1951) Australian military leader, born in Kirkee, India, where his father was an official of the government of Bombay. He trained at Sandhurst, and in 1914 was put in command of the Australian and New Zealand contingents then arriving in Egypt for the Dardanelles offensive. He planned the landing at Gallipoli and, upon evacuation from the Peninsula, took his troops to the Western Front. After the war he returned to India to command the Northern Army, becoming commander-in-chief in 1925.

Birendra, Bir Bikram Shah Dev [birendra] (1945–) King of Nepal from 1972, the son of King Mahendra, born in Kathmandu. He studied at St Joseph's College, Darjeeling, Eton, and Tokyo and Harvard universities. He married **Queen Aishwarya Rajya Laxmi Devi Rana** in 1970, and has two sons and one daughter. During his reign, there has been gradual progress towards political reform, but Nepal remained essentially an absolute monarchy until 1990, when Birendra was forced to concede much of his power. >> RR1077

Birgitta, St >> **Bridget, Brigit**, or **Birgitta** (of Sweden), **St**

Biringuccio, Vannoccio (Vincenzio Agustino Luca) [biringgoochio] (1480–1539) Metallurgical engineer, born in Siena, Italy. His *De la pirotechnia* (1540) was the earliest printed work covering the whole of mining and metallurgy as well as other important industrial processes.

Birkbeck, George (1776–1841) Physician and educationist, born in Settle, North Yorkshire, N England, UK. As professor of natural philosophy at Anderson's College, Glasgow, he delivered his first free lectures to the working classes (1799). In 1804 he became a physician in London. He was the founder and first president of the London Mechanics' or Birkbeck Institute (1824), the first in the UK, which developed into Birkbeck College, a constituent college of London University.

Birkeland, Kristian [beerkuhlahnd] (1867–1917) Physicist, born in Oslo. Professor of physics at the university there, he demonstrated the electromagnetic nature of the aurora borealis, and in 1903 developed a method for obtaining nitrogen from the air.

Birkenhead, Frederick Edwin Smith, 1st Earl of (1872–1930) Lawyer and statesman, born in Birkenhead, Merseyside, NW England, UK. He studied at Oxford (becoming a fellow of Merton in 1896), and was called to the bar in 1899. He entered parliament in 1906 and established himself as a brilliant orator and wit. He was attorney general in 1915, and Lord Chancellor in 1919. He played a major part in the Irish settlement of 1921 and was created earl. He was also secretary of state for India (1924–8). His greatest achievement as a lawyer was the preparation of the series of Acts reforming land law.

Birkett (of Ulverston), (William) Norman Birkett, Baron (1883–1962) Lawyer and politician, born in Ulverston, Cumbria, NW England, UK. He studied at Cambridge, was called to the bar (1913), and earned a brilliant reputation as counsel in notable murder trials. He was a Liberal MP (1923–4, 1929–31). A judge of the King's Bench Division (1941-50), he figured prominently in the summing up of the Nuremberg Trials (1945–6). A lord justice of appeal (1950–7), he was raised to the peerage in 1958.

Birkhoff, George (David) [berkof] (1884–1944) Mathematician, born in Overisel, MI. He studied at Harvard and Chicago universities, and was professor at Wisconsin (1902–9), Princeton (1909–12), and Harvard (1912–39). His main research was in the theory of dynamical systems, where he extended the work of Poincaré, and in the development of ergodic theory.

Birley, Eric (1906–) Historian and archaeologist, born in Manchester, Greater Manchester, NW England, UK. He studied at Oxford, and became a lecturer at Durham University in 1931. He was later appointed professor of Romano-British history and archaeology at Durham (1956–71).

Birney, (Alfred) Earle (1904–95) Poet, playwright, novelist, and teacher, born in Calgary, Alberta, Canada. He was best known as a poet, having produced over 20 books of verse. His first collection, *David and Other Poems* (1942) and *Now is Time* (1945) both won the Governor-General's Award. His novel *Turvey* (1949) won the Stephen Leacock Medal, and in 1953 he received the Lorne Pierce Medal for Literature. He also founded the first creative writing department in the country, at the University of British Columbia.

Birney, James (Gillespie) (1792–1857) Anti-slavery leader, born in Dernville, KY. He published the *Philanthropist* (1836), and stood as the anti-slavery presidential candidate in 1840 and 1844 (on behalf of the Liberty Party).

Biró, Ladislao José [biro] (1899–1985) Hungarian inventor. Working with a magazine, he realized the advantage of quick-drying ink, and in 1940 went to Argentina with his ideas for developing a ballpoint pen, which eventually became a great success (the *biro*). He was responsible for several other inventions, including a lock, a heat-proof tile, and a device for recording blood pressure.

Biron, Ernst Johann >> **Anna Ivanovna**

Birrell, Augustine (1850–1933) British statesman and writer, born near Liverpool, Merseyside, NW England, UK. He studied at Cambridge, was called to the bar in 1875, and was Liberal MP for West Fife (1889–1900) and Bristol North (1906–18). He became president of the board of education (1905–7), and chief secretary for Ireland (1907–16), resigning after the Easter Rising of 1916. He was the author of *Obiter Dicta* (1884–87), volumes of essays whose charm inspired the verb *to birrell* meaning to comment on life gently and allusively, spicing good nature with irony.

Birt, John (1944–) Broadcasting executive, born in Liverpool, Merseyside, NW England, UK. He studied engineering at Oxford, joined Granada Television (1968), and worked on the public affairs programme *World in Action* before moving to London Weekend Television (1971) as producer of *The Frost Programme*. Directly responsible for the political programme *Weekend World*, he became noted for his rigorous professionalism. British television was undergoing a critical period of change when the BBC's director general, Michael Checkland, appointed him deputy director (1987). He became director-general in 1993, and initiated a radical and controversial programme of reforms. He received an Emmy in 1995.

Birtwistle, Sir Harrison (1934–) Composer, born in Accrington, Lancashire, NW England, UK. He studied at the Royal Manchester College of Music and the Royal Academy of Music in London. While in Manchester he formed with other young musicians the New Manchester Group for the performance of modern music. In 1967 he formed the Pierrot Players with Peter Maxwell Davies; much of his work being written for them and for the English Opera Group. In 1975 he was appointed musical director of the National Theatre, and in 1993 became composer in residence to the London Philharmonic Orchestra at the South Bank Centre. Two works of 1965, the instrumental *Tragoedia* and vocal/instrumental *Ring a Dumb Carillon*, established him as a leading composer. Among his later works are the operas *Punch and Judy* (1966–7), *The Masque of Orpheus* (1973–84), *Gawain* (1990), and *The Second Mrs Kong* (1994). Other works include *The Fields of Sorrow* (1971), *Pulse Sampler* (1981), *Panic* (1995), and *Slow Frieze* (1996). He was knighted in 1988. >> Davies, Peter Maxwell

Biscoe, John >> **Enderby, Samuel**

Biscop, Benedict >> **Benedict Biscop, St**

Bishop, Elizabeth (1911–79) Poet, born in Worcester, MA. A graduate of Vassar College, she received a Pulitzer Prize for her first two collections, *North and South* (1946) and *A Cold Spring* (1955). She lived for some time in Brazil (1952–67), and taught at Harvard from 1970.

Bishop, Sir Henry Rowley (1786–1855) Composer, born in London, England, UK. He exercised considerable influence in his lifetime with his glees and 88 operas, few of which have survived, though some songs from them have remained popular, including 'Home, Sweet Home'. He was musical director at Covent Garden (1810–24), and received the first knighthood conferred upon a musician (1842). He held professorships at Edinburgh and Oxford.

Bishop, J(ohn) Michael (1936–) Virologist, born in York, PA. After working at Massachusetts General Hospital, Boston (1962–4), he performed virology research at the National Institutes of Health (1964–8). He joined the University of California, San Francisco, in 1968, and became director of the G W Hooper Research Foundation in 1981. He and colleague **Harold E Varmus** (1939–) received the 1989 Nobel Prize for Physiology or Medicine for their work which demonstrated that external agents, such as viruses or mutagens, may transform a cell's normal genes into cancer-generating oncogenes.

Bishop, John Peale (1892–1944) Poet, fiction writer, and essayist, born in Charles Town, WV. He was managing editor of *Vanity Fair* after World War 1, but joined the exodus of US literati to Paris in 1922. *Collected Poems* was published in 1948.

Bishop, William Avery (1894–1956) Airman, born in Owen Sound, Ontario, Canada. A member of the Canadian Expeditionary Force (1914), he joined the Royal Flying Corps (1915), and became the most successful Allied 'ace' of World War 1, officially credited with the destruction of 72 enemy aircraft. In 1917 he was awarded the VC for single-handedly downing seven German planes. He was appointed the first Canadian air marshal in 1939, and was director of the Royal Canadian Air Force throughout World War 2.

Bismarck, Otto Eduard Leopold, Fürst von (Prince of) (1815–98) see panel

Bissell, Melville (Reuben) (1843–89) Inventor, born in Hartwick, NY. After first working in his father's grocery store, he opened a crockery business at Grand Rapids. He amassed a fortune through industry and real estate, and went on to develop and successfully market the carpet sweeper (1876) on a worldwide scale.

Bissell, Richard >> **Abbott, George**

Biya, Paul [beeya] (1933–) Cameroonian president (1982–) and prime minister (1975–82), born in Muomeka'a, Cameroon. He completed his studies at Paris University and from 1962 held a number of ministerial posts under President Adhidjo before being appointed prime minister.

He was nominated as president-designate and there was a smooth transfer of power in 1982. Despite an attempt to overthrow him, he was re-elected in 1988 with more than 98% of the popular vote. >> RR1039

Bizet, Georges [beezay], originally **Alexandre César Léopold Bizet** (1838–75) Composer, born in Paris. He studied at the Paris Conservatoire under Halévy, whose daughter he married in 1869, and in Italy. Although he won the Prix de Rome in 1857 with *Le Docteur miracle*, his efforts to achieve a reputation as an operatic composer were largely unsuccessful. His incidental music to Daudet's play *L'Arlésienne* (1872) was remarkably popular and survives in the form of two orchestral suites. His masterpiece was the four-act opera *Carmen*, completed just before his untimely death from heart disease. A symphony in C was first performed in 1935. >> Daudet, Alphonse; Halévy, Fromental

Bjelke-Petersen, Sir Joh(annes) [byelk] (1911–) Australian statesman, born in Dannevirk, New Zealand, of Danish parents. He entered state politics in 1947 as a Country Party (now National Party) member of the Legislative Assembly, becoming a minister in 1963. In 1968, he was made police minister, then deputy leader and, following the sudden death of Jack Pizzey, premier of

---

OTTO EDUARD LEOPOLD BISMARCK, FÜRST VON (PRINCE OF) (1815–98)

Bismarck was born at Schönhausen, Brandenburg, the son of Ferdinand von Bismarck-Schönhausen, a member of the landed aristocracy, and Wilhelmine Mencken. He studied law and agriculture at Göttingen (Berlin) and Greifswald, then he entered Prussian service as a judicial administrator. In 1847, he married **Johanna von Puttkamer**, after an earlier and unsuccessful pursuit of an English woman. He became known in the new Prussian parliament (1847) as an ultra-royalist, opposing equally the constitutional demands of 1848 and the scheme of a German empire proposed by the Frankfurt parliament of 1849.

In 1851, as Prussian member of the resuscitated German Diet of Frankfurt, he opposed the predominance of Austria, and demanded equal rights for Prussia. In 1859 he was sent as minister to St Petersburg, and in 1862 to Paris. Recalled the same year to take the foreign portfolio, he was appointed prime minister under the new king, William (Wilhelm) I of Prussia (ruled 1861–88). Not being able to pass the military reorganization bill and the budget, he closed the chambers, announcing that the government would be obliged to do without them. For four years the army reorganization went on, until the death of the King of Denmark (1863) reopened the question of who should rule the duchies of Schleswig and Holstein, and excited a fever of German national feeling. Prussia defeated Denmark, with Austria's support (1863–4), annexing the duchies. However, in 1866 a quarrel with Austria (The Seven Weeks' War) ended in the humiliation of Austria at the battle of Königgratz (1866), and the reorganization of Germany under the leadership of Prussia. During the war Bismarck was recognized as the guiding spirit and, from being universally disliked, he became highly popular. He was created a count in 1866.

To encourage unification, Bismarck was instrumental in encouraging Prince Leopold of Hohenzollern to take the throne of Spain in 1869. The French government demanded

his withdrawal, giving Bismarck the opportunity of harnessing into action the intensified feeling of unity amongst Germans. The Franco-Prussian War (1870–1), which he deliberately provoked, resulted in the defeat of Napoleon III of France. Bismarck was then made a prince, and chancellor of the new German empire.

After the peace of Frankfurt, the sole aim of his policy, domestic and foreign, was to consolidate the young empire and secure it, through political combinations, against outside attack. To counteract Russia and France, he formed in 1879 the Austro–German Treaty of Alliance (published in 1888), which Italy joined in 1886; and he presided over the Berlin Congress in 1878. However, his long and bitter cultural conflict (*Kulturkampf*) with the Vatican – inspired by his suspicion of the Catholics' extra-German loyalties, and involving discriminatory legalization against the Church in Prussia – was a failure. Apart from this, his domestic policy was marked by universal suffrage; reformed coinage; codification of the law; nationalization of the Prussian railways; repeated augmentation of the army; a protective tariff; and various attempts to combat socialism and to establish government monopolies.

The famous phrase 'man of blood and iron' was used by Bismarck (who became known as the 'Iron Chancellor') in a speech in 1862, and two attempts were made on his life: in 1866 and 1874. Finally, disapproving of the policies of the new emperor William (Wilhelm) II (ruled 1888–1918), he resigned the chancellorship in 1890. In the same year he was made Duke of Lauenburg, a title which he refused to use. He was finally reconciled to William II in 1894, but his tombstone names him as a servant of William I.

Bismarck spent the last years of his life writing his memoirs, a greatly exaggerated literary work, part of which was suppressed for a time because of its damaging reflections on William II. However, a published volume of letters to his wife gives a picture of a warm and affectionate family life, quite different from his cold political image. >> Napoleon III; William I (Emperor); William II (Emperor)

Queensland. A vocal supporter of states' rights as against federal intervention, he controlled a strongly right-wing government opposed to Aboriginal land rights and trade unions. He was knighted in 1982, but forced to resign the premiership in 1987 after a badly-judged attempt to enter federal politics. He and many of his colleagues faced corruption charges, and he himself was tried on a perjury charge which was later dropped. His wife, **Flo(rence) Bjelke-Petersen** (1920–) was elected to the federal Senate in 1981, became deputy leader of the National Party in the Senate in 1985, and retired in 1993.

Bjerknes, Jakob (Aall Bonnevie) [byerknes] (1897–1975) Meteorologist, born in Stockholm, the son of Norwegian physicist Vilhelm Bjerknes. Professor at the Geophysical Institute, Bergen, with his father he formulated the theory of cyclones on which modern weather-forecasting is based. He moved to the USA in 1939, and in 1940 was appointed the first professor of meteorology at the University of California, Los Angeles. He became a US citizen in 1946. >> Bjerknes, Vilhelm

Bjerknes, Vilhelm F(riman) K(oren) [byerknes] (1862–1951) Physicist and meteorologist, born in Kristiania (now Oslo, Norway). He was professor at Stockholm (1895–1907), Kristiania (1907–12), Leipzig (1912–17), and Oslo (1926–51). A pioneer of weather-forecasting, he studied the large-scale dynamics of air masses, and with his son Jacob and others developed the theory of fronts. >> Bjerknes, Jacob; Shaw, Napier

Björling, Jussi [byerling], originally **Johan Jonaton Björling** (1911–60) Tenor, born in Stora Tuna, Sweden. From 1928 he studied at the Stockholm Conservatory, making his debut as principal with the Royal Swedish Opera in 1930. Although his repertoire was mainly Italian he sang rarely in Italy, but became a favourite in the USA, especially at the Metropolitan Opera, New York City, and made numerous recordings.

Bjørnson, Bjørnstjerne (Martinius) [byernsn] (1832–1910) Writer and Norwegian statesman, born in Kvikne, Norway. He studied at Molde, Kristiania (now Oslo) and Copenhagen, was a playwright and novelist of wide-ranging interests, and a lifelong champion of liberal causes. An ardent patriot, he sought to free the Norwegian theatre from Danish influence and revive Norwegian as a literary language. He was named Norway's national poet, and his poem, 'Ja, Vi Elsker Dette Landet' (1870, trans Yes, We Love This Land of Ours) became the national anthem. His other major works include the novel *Fiskerjenten* (1868, The Fisher Girl), the epic poem *Arnljot Gelline* (1870), and his greatest plays, *Over Aevne I og II* (1883, 1895, trans Beyond Our Power, Beyond Human Might). He was awarded the 1903 Nobel Prize for Literature.

Bjornson, Maria [byaw(r)nsn] (1949–) Stage designer, born in Paris. She has designed sets and costumes for straight drama and opera in many British theatres, with several productions for the Royal Shakespeare Company, including *A Midsummer Night's Dream* (1981), *The Tempest* (1982), and *Hamlet* (1984). In 1986 she designed Hal Prince's production of Andrew Lloyd Webber's *The Phantom of the Opera* and in 1989 Trevor Nunn's production of Lloyd Webber's *Aspects of Love*.

Bjørnsson, Sveinn [byernsn] (1881–1952) Icelandic diplomat and statesman, the first president of the Republic of Iceland (1944–52), born in Copenhagen. He studied law at Copenhagen, became a member of parliament (1914–16, 1920), and ambassador to Denmark (1920–4, 1926–41). During the German occupation of Denmark he was elected Regent of Iceland, and when the republic was declared in 1944 he became president. >> RR1058

Blache, Paul Vidal de la >> **Vidal de la Blache, Paul**

Black, Conrad Moffat (1944–) London-based financier, born in Montreal, Canada. He studied at Carleton, Laval, and McGill universities, and became a businessman. He achieved control of Argus Corporation, a holding company controlling a large number of Canadian corporations, becoming chairman in 1979 and chief executive in 1985. He repositioned himself in the newspaper business, buying London's *Daily Telegraph* (1985), Quebec's *Le Soleil*, Ottawa's *Le Droit*, and over 40 small newspapers in the USA. He has also earned some attention as a commentator on economic and political affairs.

Black, Eugene Robert (1898–1992) Banker, and president of the World Bank (1949–62), born in Atlanta, GA. He studied at the University of Georgia and became a banker on Wall Street. He joined the World Bank in 1947 as executive director, becoming president in 1949. He was instrumental in altering the emphasis of the Bank from post-World War 2 reconstruction to providing loans for economic development, particularly to the Third World.

Black, Hugo (La Fayette) (1886–1971) Judge, born in Clay Co, AL. He practised law in Alabama and became a police court judge. In 1926 he entered the US Senate, and was appointed to the Supreme Court in 1937. He held that the Fourteenth Amendment made the Bill of Rights generally applicable to the states, and that the First Amendment's guarantees of freedoms were absolute.

Black, Sir James (1924–) Pharmacologist, born in Uddingston, South Lanarkshire, WC Scotland, UK. He studied medicine at St Andrews, Scotland, then taught at various universities, in 1984 becoming professor of analytical pharmacology at King's College, London. His reasoning on how the heart's workload could be reduced led to the discovery of beta-blockers in 1964, and his deductions in 1972 on acid secretion in the stomach resulted in the introduction of cimetidine in the treatment of stomach ulcers. He shared the Nobel Prize for Physiology or Medicine in 1988. >> RR1124

Black, Joseph (1728–99) Chemist, born in Bordeaux, France. He studied at Belfast, Glasgow, and Edinburgh, and in 1756 showed that the causticity of lime and alkalis is due to the absence of the 'fixed air' (carbon dioxide) present in limestone and the carbonates of the alkalis. He evolved the theory of 'latent heat', on which his scientific fame chiefly rests, and founded the theory of specific heats. In 1766 he became professor of medicine and chemistry at Edinburgh.

Black, Sir Misha (1910–77) British designer and writer on design, born in Baku, Russia. Trained as an architect, his early work was mainly in commercial exhibition design. He designed the famous pre-World War 2 cafes for Kardomah, becoming a consultant for the firm (1936–50). His outstanding post-war design work was for British Rail, London Transport, and P & O. He later became professor of industrial design at the Royal College of Art, London (1959–75). >> Gray, Milner Connorton

Black, Shirley Temple >> **Temple, Shirley**

Blackburn, Helen (1842–1903) Social reformer, born in Knightstown, Co Kerry, Ireland. She moved with her family to London (1859), where she became secretary of the National Society for Women's Suffrage (1874–95). Her many publications include *Women's Suffrage: a Record of the Movement in the British Isles* (1902).

Blackburn, Robert (1885–1955) Aircraft designer, born in Leeds, West Yorkshire, N England, UK. He designed his first plane in 1910, and founded the Blackburn Aircraft Company in 1914 under contract to build military biplanes.

Blacket, Edmund Thomas (1817–83) Architect, born in London, England, UK. He arrived in Sydney in 1842, and was appointed chief architect for the diocese. He became government architect for New South Wales (1849), returning to private practice in 1854 to design the new University of New South Wales. His academic and ecclesiastical work, including cathedrals in Sydney and Perth, was Victorian Gothic in style, but in commercial designs he adopted classical forms.

Blackett, Patrick M(aynard) S(tuart) Blackett, Baron (1897-1974) Physicist, born in London, England, UK. He studied at Cambridge University and at the Cavendish Laboratory, Cambridge. He was the first to photograph nuclear collisions involving transmutation (1925), and in 1932, independently of Carl Anderson, he discovered the positron. He pioneered research on cosmic radiation, for which he was awarded the Nobel Prize for Physics in 1948. He was professor at London (1933-7), Manchester (1937-53), and the Imperial College of Science and Technology (1953-74). >> Anderson, Carl

Black Hawk (1767-1838) Chief of the Sauk and Fox Indians, born in Virginia Colony. He was an ally of the British in the War of 1812 and, opposing the removal west of his tribe, fought against the USA (1831-2). He was defeated at Bad Axe River in Wisconsin.

Blackman, Frederick Frost (1866-1947) Botanist, born in London, England, UK. He studied science at Cambridge, and worked at the Cambridge Botany School (1891-1936). He is renowned for his fundamental research on the respiration of plants, and on the limiting factors affecting their growth.

Blackmore, R(ichard) D(oddridge) (1825-1900) Novelist, born in Longworth, Berkshire, S England, UK. He studied at Oxford, and was called to the bar in 1852, but poor health made him take to market gardening and literature in Teddington. *Clara Vaughan* (1864) was the first of 15 novels, mostly with a Devonshire background, of which *Lorna Doone* (1869) is his masterpiece and an accepted classic of the West Country.

Blackmun, Harry (Andrew) (1908-) Jurist, born in Nashville, IL. He studied mathematics and law at Harvard, and was called to the Minnesota bar in 1932. He was judge of the eighth circuit of the US Court of Appeals (1959-70), and in 1970 was nominated to the Supreme Court, where he was an effective influence in moderating the views of his more conservative colleagues. He retired in 1994.

Black Prince >> **Edward the Black Prince**

Blackstone, Harry, originally **Harry Boughton** (1885-1965) Magician, born in Chicago, IL. In a career that began in vaudeville in 1904 and continued in television in the 1960s, he enjoyed his greatest success touring with a full evening magic show (1920-50). Although he featured elaborate 'effects' magic – a floating lightball, a vanishing birdcage – he was also adept at sleight-of hand and card tricks, all abetted by his distinguished looks and bearing.

Blackstone, Sir William (1723-80) Jurist, born in London, England, UK. He studied at Oxford, and in 1746 was called to the bar. He became the first holder of the Vinerian chair of English law at Oxford (1758). MP for Hindon, Wiltshire (1761-70), and Principal of New Inn Hall, Oxford, he was made solicitor general to the queen (1763) and a judge of the court of common pleas (1770-80). From 1765 to 1769 he published his celebrated *Commentaries on the Laws of England*, which became the most influential exposition of English law.

Blackwell, Sir Basil (Henry) (1889-1984) Publisher and bookseller, born in Oxford, Oxfordshire, SC England, UK. He studied at Oxford, and joined the family bookselling business in 1913, but also published independently, founding the Shakespeare Head Press (1921). He succeeded to the chairmanship in 1924, and from that time joined the family bookselling interest with that of publishing.

Blackwell, Elizabeth (1821-1910) The first woman doctor in the USA, born in Bristol, SW England, UK, the sister of

Emily Blackwell. Her family emigrated to the USA in 1832. After fruitless applications for admission to various medical schools, she entered that of Geneva, NY, and graduated in 1849. She next visited Europe and, after much difficulty, was admitted into La Maternité in Paris, and St Bartholomew's Hospital in London. In 1851 she returned to New York City, where she established a successful practice. From 1869 she lived in England, founding the London School of Medicine for Women. >> Blackwell, Emily; Jex-Blake

Blackwell, Emily (1826-1910) Physician, born in Bristol, the sister of Elizabeth Blackwell. The first woman doctor to undertake major surgery on a considerable scale, she was educated at Cleveland (Western Reserve) University, followed by work in Europe, where she was assistant to Sir James Simpson. In 1856 she helped open her sister's dispensary in New York City, and became dean and professor of obstetrics and diseases of women at the Women's Medical College (1869-99). >> Blackwell, Elizabeth; Simpson, James

Blackwood, Algernon Henry (1869-1951) Writer, born in Shooters Hill, Kent, SE England, UK. He studied at Edinburgh University before working his way through Canada and the USA, as related in his *Episodes before Thirty* (1923). His best-known novels are *The Centaur* and *Julius Le Vallon*. His works reflect his taste for the supernatural and the occult, seen especially in his books of short stories, such as *John Silence* (1908), *Tongues of Fire* (1924), and *Tales of the Uncanny and Supernatural* (1949).

Blackwood, William (1776-1834) Publisher, born in Edinburgh, EC Scotland, UK. He established himself as a bookseller in Edinburgh in 1804, and in 1817 started *Blackwood's Magazine*. His sons **Alexander Blackwood** (1806-45) and **Robert Blackwood** (1808-52) took over the firm between 1834 and 1852, followed by **John Blackwood** (1818-79), who published all but one of George Eliot's novels.

Blaine, James G(illespie) (1830-93) Journalist and statesman, born in West Brownsville, PA. He was a newspaper editor (1854-60), then a member of the US House of Representatives (1863-76), becoming speaker (1869-75). He was defeated in the Republican nominations for the presidency in 1876, 1880, 1884, and 1892.

Blainey, Geoffrey Norman (1930-) Social historian, born in Melbourne, Victoria, Australia. He studied at Melbourne University, where he became professor of economic history (emeritus since 1988). In 1966 *The Tyranny of Distance* showed how geographical isolation had shaped the history and the people of Australia. *Triumph of the Nomads* (1975) and *A Land Half Won* (1980) completed his trilogy, *A Vision of Australian History*. He reached a wide popular audience through his books, as well as a television programme *The Blainey View*, and became well known in the 1980s for his controversial views on immigration to Australia.

Blair, Eric Arthur >> **Orwell, George**

Blair, Harold (1924-76) Tenor, born near Cherbourg, Queensland, Australia, of an Aboriginal mother and an Italian father. After winning a talent competition on radio, he was accepted by the Melbourne Conservatory. He became the first Aborigine to gain a Diploma in Music (1949), and left to tour the USA. Returning to Australia in 1951, he joined the ABC Jubilee Tour to all capital cities. His latent interest in politics led to his standing, unsuccessfully, for the Victorian State parliament (1963), after which he worked for the South Australian Department of Aboriginal Affairs before returning to Victoria to teach music.

Blair, Robert (1699-1746) Poet and preacher, born in Edinburgh, EC Scotland, UK. He studied at Edinburgh

University, and in 1731 was ordained minister of Athelstaneford, East Lothian. He is best known as the author of *The Grave* (1743), a blank-verse poem which heralded the 'churchyard school' of poetry.

Blair, Tony, popular name of **Anthony Charles Lynton Blair** (1953–) British politician and prime minister (1997–), born in Edinburgh, EC Scotland, UK. Educated in Edinburgh, he studied law at Oxford, and was called to the bar in 1976. He was elected Labour MP for Sedgefield in 1983, becoming his party's spokesperson on Treasury affairs (1985–7) and trade and industry (1987–8). He joined the shadow cabinet in 1988, becoming responsible for energy (1988), employment (1989), and home affairs (1992). He was elected leader of the Labour Party in 1994 and led it to power in a landslide victory in 1997. His wife, **Cherie Blair**, is also a barrister.

Blaise or **Blasius, St** (?–c.316) Armenian clergyman and martyr, born in Sebastia, Cappadocia. Made Bishop of Sebastia, he is said to have suffered martyrdom during a period of persecution. Woolcombers claim him as their patron, and he is invoked in case of throat trouble and cattle disease. Feast day 3 February.

Blake, Eugene (Carson) (1906–85) Presbyterian clergyman and ecumenist, born in St Louis, MO. He studied at Princeton, and served pastorates in New York and California before becoming Stated Clerk of the Presbyterian Church, USA. In 1967 he was appointed general secretary of the World Council of Churches, a demanding post he held for five years.

Blake, Nicholas >> **Day-Lewis, Cecil**

Blake, Peter (1932–) Artist, born in Dartford, Kent, SE England, UK. From the mid-1950s, while still a student at the Royal College of Art, he became a pioneer of the Pop Art movement in Britain, using media imagery from sources such as comics, advertisements, and popular magazines. His most widely known work is the cover design for the Beatles' LP *Sergeant Pepper's Lonely Hearts Club Band* (1967).

Blake, Quentin (Saxby) (1932–) Children's writer and illustrator, born in London, England, UK. He read English at Cambridge, and became a freelance illustrator, producing cartoons for *Punch* and other periodicals. Acclaimed for his illustrations in the books of Russell Hoban, Roald Dahl, and other children's authors, he also produced books of his own, such as *Mister Magnolia* (Kate Greenaway Medal), and *The Quentin Blake Book of Nonsense Verse* and *... Nonsense Stories* (both 1996). He was head of the Department of Illustration at the Royal College of Art (1978–86), and became a visiting professor there in 1989. >> Dahl; Hoban

Blake, Robert (1599–1657) English naval commander, born in Bridgwater, Somerset, SW England, UK. He studied at Oxford, and led the life of a quiet country gentleman until he was 40. Returned for Bridgwater in 1640 to the Short Parliament, he cast in his lot with the parliamentarians. In the Civil War his defence of Taunton (1644–5) against overwhelming odds proved a turning point in the war. Appointed admiral in 1649, he destroyed Prince Rupert's fleet and captured the Scilly Is and Jersey. In the first Dutch War (1652–4) he defeated Tromp at the Battle of Portland (1653) and shattered Dutch supremacy at sea. He destroyed the Barbary Coast pirate fleet off Tunis (1655), and destroyed a Spanish treasure fleet at Santa Cruz off Tenerife (1657). >> Rupert; Sandwich, 1st Earl of; Tromp, Maarten

Blake, William (1757–1827) Poet, painter, engraver, and mystic, born in London, England, UK. After studying at the Royal Academy School he began to produce watercolour figure subjects and to engrave illustrations for magazines. His first book of poems, *Poetical Sketches* (1783), was followed by *Songs of Innocence* (1789) and *Songs of Experience* (1794), which contain some of his best-known lines (such as 'Tyger! Tyger! burning bright') and express his ardent belief in the freedom of the imagination and his hatred of rationalism and materialism. His mystical and prophetical works include the *Book of Thel* (1789), *The Marriage of Heaven and Hell* (1791), and *The Song of Los* (1795), which mostly have imaginative designs interwoven with their text, printed from copper treated by a peculiar process, and coloured by his own hand or that of his wife, **Catherine Boucher**. Among his designs of poetic and imaginative figure subjects are a series of 537 coloured illustrations to Edward Young's *Night Thoughts* (1797). His finest artistic work is to be found in the 21 *Illustrations to the Book of Job* (1826), completed when he was almost 70. >> Varley

Blakemore, Colin (Brian) (1944–) British physiologist. He studied at Cambridge, California, and Oxford universities, then worked at Cambridge (1968–79), and has been professor of physiology at Oxford since 1979. He also holds posts in Oxford as director of the Centre for Cognitive Neuroscience (1989) and associate director of the Centre in Brain and Behaviour (1991). He gave the BBC Reith lectures in 1976, and was the presenter of the BBC TV series *The Mind Machine* in 1988. He received the Royal Society's Michael Faraday Award in 1989.

Blakeslee, Albert (Francis) (1874–1954) Botanist and geneticist, born in Geneseo, NY. He studied at Harvard, then became professor of botany at Connecticut Agricultural College, and (from 1915) plant geneticist at the Carnegie Institute laboratories on Long Island, NY (director, 1936). He became world-famous for his genetic research into plants.

Blakey, Art [blaykee], popular name of **Arthur Blakey**, also known as **Abdulla Ibn Buhaina** (1919–90) Jazz drummer and bandleader, born in Pittsburgh, PA. He emerged from big band work in the 1930s to become a leading exponent of the attacking 'hard bop' style from the 1950s. From 1954 he led the Jazz Messengers, a sextet or septet which he constantly renewed with outstanding young players.

Blalock, Alfred [blaylok] (1899–1964) Surgeon, born in Culloden, GA. He studied at Johns Hopkins University and Vanderbilt University Hospital, and joined the staff at Vanderbilt (1925–41) and Johns Hopkins (1941–64), where he pioneered the surgical treatment of various congenital defects of the heart. He performed the first 'blue baby' operation with the paediatrician Helen Taussig. >> Taussig

Blamey, Sir Thomas Albert [blaymee] (1884–1951) Australian field marshal, born in Wagga Wagga, New South Wales, Australia. He joined the regular army in 1906, attended Staff College at Quetta, and became chief-of-staff of the Australian Corps in 1918. At the outbreak of World War 2 he was given command of the Australian Imperial Forces in the Middle East. On the establishment of the SW Pacific Command he led Allied land forces in Australia (1942), and received the Japanese surrender in 1945.

Blampied, Edmund (1886–1966) Artist, born in Jersey, Channel Is. He is best known for his etchings which depict everyday farming life, in particular horses and peasants. During the German occupation he designed the Jersey occupation stamps, and later the Channel Islands 'victory' issue.

Blanc, (Jean Joseph Charles) Louis [blã] (1811–82) French statesman and historian, born in Madrid. His chief work on socialism, the *Organisation du travail* (1840, The Organisation of Labour), denounces the principle of competitive industry and proposes the establishment of co-operative workshops, subsidized by the state. After the revolution of 1848, he was appointed a member of the provisional government, but was forced to flee to England. On the fall of the empire, he returned to France, and was elected in 1871 to the National Assembly, and in 1876 to the Chamber of Deputies.

Blanchard, Jean Pierre François [blăshah(r)] (1753–1809) Balloonist, and inventor of the parachute, born in Les Andelys, France. With John Jeffries he was the first to cross the English Channel by balloon, from Dover to Calais, in 1785. He was killed during practice parachute jumps from a balloon. >> Jeffries, John

Blanchflower, Danny, popular name of **Robert Dennio Blanchflower** (1926–93) Footballer, born in Belfast. Studious, cultured and articulate when off-field, he was a powerful influence in the Northern Ireland side which reached the World Cup quarter finals in 1958. Transferring from Aston Villa to Tottenham Hotspur, he masterminded the London club's double success in the League and the FA Cup (1960–1).

Blanda, (George) Frederick (1927–) Player of American football, born in Youngwood, PA. He studied at the University of Kentucky before joining the National Football League Chicago Bears (1949). He moved to the American Football League Houston Oilers (1960), and was traded to the Oakland Raiders (1967) before retiring (1976). During his career he established records in all areas of the game, and was elected to the Football Hall of Fame (1981).

Blandrata or **Biandrata, Giorgio** [blandrahta] (c.1515–88) Physician and theologian, born in Saluzzo, Italy, the founder of Unitarianism in Poland and Transylvania. The freedom of his religious opinions compelled him to flee to Geneva in 1556, where he became a member of a Calvinist congregation, but in 1558 Calvin's displeasure at his anti-Trinitarianism drove him to Poland. In 1563 he became physician to John Sigismund, Unitarian Prince of Transylvania. >> Calvin, John

Blankers-Koen, Fanny [kern], popular name of **Francina Blankers-Koen** (1918–) Athlete, born in Amsterdam. She dominated women's events in the London Olympics of 1948, winning four gold medals: the 100 m and 200 m, the 80 m hurdles, and the 4 × 100 m relay.

Blanqui, (Louis) Auguste [blăkee] (1805–81) Revolutionary, born in Puget-Théniers, France. An extremist, he worked from 1830 at building up a network of secret societies committed to violent revolution. He spent 33 years in prison, and was in prison in 1871 when he was elected president of the revolutionary Commune of Paris. In 1881 his followers, known as *Blanquists*, joined the Marxists.

Blasco Ibáñez, Vicente [blaskoh eevahnyeth] (1867–1928) Novelist, born in Valencia, Spain. He dealt in realistic fashion with provincial life and social revolution. Notable works are *Sangre y arena* (1909, Blood and Sand), and *Los cuatro jinetes del Apocalipsis* (1916, The Four Horsemen of the Apocalypse), which vividly portrays World War 1 and earned him world fame.

Blashford-Snell, Colonel John (1936–) Explorer and youth leader, born in Hereford, Hereford and Worcester, WC England, UK. He trained at Sandhurst, and was commissioned into the Royal Engineers (1957). He participated in over 40 expeditions, and led the Blue Nile (1968), British Trans-Americas (1972), and Zaire River (1975/84) expeditions under the aegis of the Scientific Exploration Society. He then went on to lead two major youth projects: Operation Drake (1978–80) and Operation Raleigh, which involved over 4000 young people in adventurous scientific and community projects in over 73 countries (1984–8).

Blasis, Carlo [blasees] (1797–1878) Dancer, choreographer, and teacher, born in Naples, Italy. He danced in France, Italy, London, and Russia, and became director of the Dance Academy in Milan in 1837. He was the author of noted treatises on the codification of ballet technique (1820, 1840, 1857), and is regarded as the most important ballet teacher of the 19th-c.

Blasius, St >> **Blaise, St**

Blass, Bill, popular name of **William Ralph Blass** (1922–) Fashion designer, born in Fort Wayne, IN. He began his New York fashion career in 1946, joining Maurice Rentner Ltd in 1959 (it became Bill Blass Ltd after 1970). The winner of eight Coty Awards, he created high-priced, beautifully cut and tailored women's wear notable for its inventive combinations of patterns and textures.

Blatch, Harriet (Eaton Stanton), *née* **Stanton** (1856–1940) Suffrage leader, born in Seneca Falls, NY. She studied mathematics at Vassar College, and went on to found the Equality League of Self-Supporting Women (1907), becoming a staunch activist in support of women's rights. In 1908 she founded the Women's Political Union.

Blaue Reiter, Der (Ger 'blue rider') >> **Campendonck; Kandinsky; Klee; Macke; Marc**

Blavatsky, Helena Petrovna [blavatskee], *née* **Hahn**, known as **Madame Blavatsky** (1831–91) Theosophist, born in Yekaterinoslav, Ukraine. She had a brief marriage in her teens to a Russian general, but left him and travelled widely in the East. She moved to the USA in 1873, and in 1875, with Henry Steel Olcott, founded the Theosophical Society in New York City, later carrying on her work in India. Her psychic powers were widely acclaimed, but did not survive investigation by the Society for Psychical Research. However, this did not deter her large following, which included Annie Besant. >> Besant, Annie; Olcott

Bleasdale, Alan [bleezdayl] (1946–) Playwright, born in Liverpool, Merseyside, NW England, UK. He was a schoolteacher before he turned to writing. He became known through the popular TV series, *The Boys from the Blackstuff* (1982), about a group of unemployed Liverpudlians, which won several awards. *The Monocled Mutineer*, a television series set during World War 1, followed in 1986, another series, *GBH*, in 1991, and *Melissa* in 1997. He has written several stage plays, including *Are You Lonesome Tonight?* (1985), a respectful musical about Elvis Presley.

Blériot, Louis [blayryoh] (1872–1936) Airman, born in Cambrai, France. He made the first flight across the English Channel from Baraques to Dover on 25 July 1909 in a small 24-hp monoplane.

Blessington, Marguerite Gardiner, Countess of (1789–1849) Writer and socialite, born near Clonmel, Co Tipperary, Ireland. After her husband's death (1829), she held a salon at her Kensington mansion, Gore House, where she wrote many sketches of London life, and formed a relationship with the Comte d'Orsay (1801–57). Her best-known work was *Conversations with Lord Byron* (1834). Her lavish tastes left her deep in debt, and with d'Orsay she fled to Paris (1849), where she died two months later.

Bleuler, Eugen [bloyler] (1857–1939) Psychiatrist, born in Zollikon, Switzerland. Professor at Zürich (1898–1927), he carried out research on epilepsy, then turned to psychiatry, and in 1911 published a study on what he called *schizophrenia* or 'splitting of the mind'. Jung was one of his pupils. >> Jung

Blicher, Steen Steensen [bleeker] (1782–1848) Poet and novelist, born near Viborg, Denmark. His home province of Jutland forms the background of much of his work. He became a teacher and clergyman, and took a great interest in the social and spiritual problems of his day. His major works include a collection of poetry, *Traekfuglene* (1838, The Migratory Birds), and his books of short stories, often in dialect, such as *E Bindstouw*.

Bligh, William [bliy] (c. 1754–c. 1817) British Naval officer, born in Plymouth, Devon, SW England, UK. He went to sea at the age of 15, and in 1787 was chosen by Sir Joseph Banks to command HMS *Bounty* on a voyage to Tahiti to collect plants of the bread-fruit tree. During a six-month stay on the island the men became demoralized, and on 28 April 1789 the first mate, Fletcher Christian, led a mutiny; Bligh and 18 of his men were cast adrift in an open boat with a small stock of provisions and no chart. They reached Timor, in the East Indies, on 14 June, having travelled nearly 4000 mi. In 1805 he was appointed Governor of New South Wales, and was imprisoned by mutinous soldiers during the so-called 'Rum Rebellion' (1808–10). Exonerated of all blame, he was promoted admiral on his retirement in 1811. >> Christian, Fletcher; Macarthur, John

Bliss, Sir Arthur (Edward Drummond) (1891–1975) Composer, born in London, England, UK. He studied at the Royal College of Music, and in 1921 became professor of composition there, but resigned his post after a year to devote himself to composing. He was music director of the BBC (1942–4), and on the death of Bax in 1953 became Master of the Queen's Musick. His compositions include the ballets *Checkmate* (1937) and *Miracle in the Gorbals* (1944), the opera *The Olympians* (1949), chamber music, and piano and violin works. >> Bax

Blitzstein, Marc [blitstiyn] (1905–64) Composer, born in Philadelphia, PA. A pianist and composer as a youth, he enrolled in 1924 in the newly established Curtis Institute to study composition. He went on to study with Boulanger in Paris and Schoenberg in Berlin, where he encountered the socially conscious works of Brecht and Weill. In the 1930s he began to write pieces with explicit social themes for the musical theatre, notably *The Cradle Will Rock* (1937), and he became a member of the Communist Party (1938–49). After serving in the US Air Force in World War 2, which inspired his *Airborne Symphony* (1946), he returned to writing works for the musical stage; the most ambitious of these was *Regina* (1949), but none of them achieved the success of his adaptation of the Brecht/Weill *Threepenny Opera* (1954). >> Boulanger, Nadia; Brecht; Schoenberg; Weill

Blixen, Karen, Baroness, pseudonym **Isak Dinesen**, *née* **Karen Christence Dinesen** (1885–1962) Writer and story teller, born in Rungsted, Denmark. She studied in Denmark, England, Switzerland, Italy, and France, and in 1914 married her cousin, **Baron Bror Blixen Finecke**, and went with him to Kenya. They were divorced in 1921, and in 1931 she returned to Denmark. She wrote *Seven Gothic Tales* (1934), which she later translated into Danish. Other works include *Out of Africa* (1937) and *Last Tales* (1957).

Bloch, Ernest [blokh] (1880–1959) Composer, born in Geneva, Switzerland. He studied in Brussels, Frankfurt, and Munich, eventually teaching at the Geneva Conservatory (1911–15). In 1916 he went to America, where he held several teaching posts, and became a US citizen (1924). His compositions include the *Israel* symphony (1912–16), *Trois Poèmes juifs* (1913), the 'epic rhapsody' *America* (1926), and the Hebrew *Sacred Service* (1930–3).

Bloch, Felix [blokh] (1905–83) Physicist, born in Zürich, Switzerland. He studied at Leipzig, left Germany for the USA in 1933, and became professor of theoretical physics at Stanford University (1934–71). During World War 2 he worked on radar, and shared the 1952 Nobel Prize for Physics for work on magnetic resonance imaging. The **Bloch bands** are sets of discrete but closely adjacent energy levels arising from quantum states when a nondegenerate gas condenses to a solid. >> RR1122

Bloch, Konrad (Emil) [blokh] (1912–) Biochemist, born in Neisse, Germany. He studied at the Technische Hochschule, Munich, and Columbia University, and emigrated to the USA in 1936. In 1954 he was appointed the first professor of biochemistry at Harvard University. He shared the 1964 Nobel Prize for Physiology or Medicine for work on the mechanism of cholesterol and fatty acid metabolism. >> RR1124

Bloch, Marc [blokh] (1886–1944) Historian, born in Lyon, France. He studied in Paris, Leipzig, and Berlin, became professor of mediaeval history at Strasbourg from 1919, and professor of economic history at the Sorbonne (1936). He rejoined the army in 1939, joined the Resistance in 1943, and was captured and shot by the Germans. His work has been extensively translated since his death.

Bloch, Martin [blokh] (1883–1954) Expressionist painter, born in Neisse, Germany. After studying in Berlin and Munich, he was forced to leave Germany in 1934, went to Denmark, and later to England, where he opened a school of painting with Roy de Maistre. He became a British citizen in 1947.

Block, Alexander >> Blok, Alexander Alexandrovich

Bloembergen, Nicolas [bloombergen] (1920–) Physicist, born in Dordrecht, The Netherlands. He studied at the universities of Utrecht and Leyden, and in 1946 moved to the USA where he joined the staff of Harvard. He introduced a modification to Charles Townes's early design of the maser, enabling it to work continuously rather than intermittently. He shared the 1981 Nobel Prize for Physics. >> RR1122

Blok, Alexander Alexandrovich (1880–1921) Poet, born in St Petersburg, Russia. In 1903 he married the daughter of Mendeleyev. His first book of poems, *Songs about the Lady Fair* (1904), was influenced by the mysticism of Soloviev. He welcomed the 1917 Revolution and in 1918 wrote two poems, 'Dvenadtsat' (trans The Twelve), a symbolic sequence of revolutionary themes, and 'Skify' (The Scythians), an ode, inciting Europe to follow Russia. >> Soloviev

Blomdahl, Karl-Birger (1916–68) Composer, born in Stockholm. He was professor of composition in Stockholm (1960–64) and head of music of Radio Sweden from 1965. Much inspired by Hindemith, he composed symphonies, concertos, operas, chamber, and electronic music. >> Hindemith

Blondel or **Blondel de Nesle** [blôdel] (12th-c) French minstrel. According to legend he accompanied Richard I to Palestine on the Crusades, and located him when imprisoned in the Austrian castle of Dürrenstein (1193) by means of the song they had jointly composed. >> Richard I

Blondie US new wave group, formed in 1974 with members **Deborah 'Debbie' Harry** (1945– , vocals) and **Chris Stein** (1950– , guitar), later joined by **Jimmy Destri** (1954– , keyboards), **Gary Valentine** (bass), and **Clem Burke** (1955 –, drums). Their 1978 album *Parallel Lines* included the hit single 'Heart Of Glass', which reached number 1 in both the UK and US music charts. Much of the visual appeal of the group was focused on Debbie Harry, and the group lost impetus in the early 1980s once she began to branch out into films and television. Acting in films from 1978, she made an impact in *Videodrome* (1983), her later films including *Satisfaction* (1988), *Hairspray* (1988), *Body Bags* (1993), and *Heavy* (1995).

Blondin, Charles [blôdï], originally **Jean François Gravelet** (1824–97) Acrobat and tightrope-walker, born in Hesdin, France. In 1859 he crossed Niagara Falls on a tightrope, and later did the same with variations (eg blindfolded, with a wheelbarrow, with a man on his back, on stilts). He was still performing in his early 70s.

Blood, Thomas, known as **Captain Blood** (c. 1618–80) Irish adventurer. A parliamentarian during the English Civil

War, he was deprived of his estate at the Restoration. He put himself (1663) at the head of a plot to seize Dublin Castle, but the plot was discovered and his chief accomplices executed. In 1671, with three accomplices he entered the Tower and stole the crown, while one of his associates took the orb. They were pursued and captured; but Blood was pardoned by King Charles, who took him to court and restored his estate. >> Charles II (of England)

Bloom, Claire (1931–) Actress, born in London, England, UK. She was educated in Bristol and made her debut at the Oxford Repertory Theatre (1946). A distinguished Shakespearean actress on stage and television, she has acted major roles in other classic and modern plays, including *A Street Car Named Desire* (1974) and *The Cherry Orchard* (1981). Her numerous films include *Limelight* (1952), *Look Back in Anger* (1959), *The Spy Who Came in From the Cold* (1966), *Sammy and Rosie Get Laid* (1987), and *Crimes and Misdemeanours* (1990). She has had many roles in television drama, including *Brideshead Revisited* (1981), *Shadowlands* (1985, BAFTA), *Shadow on the Sun* (1988), and *Family Money* (1997). >> Roth, Philip

Bloom, Harold (1930–) Literary critic, born in New York City. He studied at Cornell and Yale, then taught English at Yale (1955–77), becoming professor of humanities there. His books include *The Anxiety of Influence* (1973), *The Book of J* (1990), and *The Western Canon* (1994) – a controversial recommended short-list of 26 great authors whom everyone should have read (plus 850 others considered worthwhile). *Omens of Millennium: The Gnosis of Angels, Dreams, and Resurrection* appeared in 1996.

Bloom, Ursula, pseudonym of **Mrs Gower Robinson** (1892–1984) Novelist and playwright, born in Chelmsford, Essex, SE England, UK. Her novels, which include *Pavilion* (1951) and *The First Elizabeth* (1953), are mainly historical romances. Most of her plays were written for radio production.

Bloomer, Amelia, *née* **Jenks** (1818–94) Champion of women's rights and dress reform, born in Homer, NY. She founded and edited the feminist paper *The Lily* (1849–55). In her pursuit of dress equality she wore her own version of trousers for women, which came to be called *bloomers*.

Bloomfield, Leonard (1887–1949) Linguist, born in Chicago, IL. He studied at Harvard, Wisconsin, and Chicago universities. After holding several university posts, he was appointed professor of German and linguistics at Ohio State University (1921), becoming professor of Germanic philology at Chicago University in 1927, and professor of linguistics at Yale in 1940. He played a major part in making linguistics an independent scientific discipline, developing a behaviourist approach in his major work *Language* (1933), and motivating a *Bloomfieldian* school of linguistics which was influential until the 1950s.

Bloomfield, Robert (1766–1823) Poet, born in Honington, Suffolk, E England, UK. A shoemaker's apprentice, he wrote *The Farmer's Boy* in a garret. Published in 1800, it proved very popular. He subsequently published *Rural Tales* (1802) and *Wild Flowers* (1806).

Bloor, Ella, *née* **Reeve**, known as **Mother Bloor** (1862–1951) Radical and feminist, born on Staten Island, New York City. Married at the age of 19, she became interested in women's rights, her political interests leading to her divorce in 1896. Following a second unsuccessful marriage she moved into politics as an activist. In 1901 she joined the Socialist Party, and in 1919 was one of the founders of the American Communist Party.

Blount, Charles, 8th Lord Mountjoy, Earl of Devonshire [bluhnt] (1563–1606) English soldier, and conqueror of Ireland. In 1600 he accepted the Irish command against the rebellion of Hugh O'Neill, Earl of Tyrone, winning a decisive victory at Kinsale (1601). He became Lord Lieutenant of Ireland, then returned to England where he was given an earldom by James I. >> O'Neill, Hugh

Blow, John (c.1649–1708) Composer, born in Newark, Nottinghamshire, C England, UK. He became organist at Westminster Abbey (1668), Master of the Children at the Chapel Royal (1674), and Master of the Children at St Paul's (1687). He is known for his vast output of anthems and church services, and also for his masque, *Venus and Adonis* (1687), which was performed before Charles II.

Blow, Susan Elizabeth (1843–1916) Educationist, born in St Louis, MO. Religious from childhood, she became intensely interested in the philosophy of the German Idealists. After studying the works of Freidrich Froebel, she opened the first US public kindergarten in St Louis (1873) and a training school for kindergarten teachers (1874). The movement grew rapidly, leading to the formation of the New York Kindergarten Association and an International Union. >> Froebel

Blücher, Gebhard Leberecht von, Fürst von (Prince of) **Wahlstadt** [bloocher, blooker], nickname **Marshal Forward** (1742–1819) Prussian field marshal, born in Rostock, Germany. He fought against the French in 1793 and 1806, and in 1813 took chief command in Silesia, defeating Napoleon at Leipzig, and entering Paris (1814). In 1815 he assumed the general command, suffered a severe defeat at Ligny, but completed Wellington's victory at Waterloo by his timely appearance on the field. >> Napoleon; Wellington

Blue, Lionel (1930–) British rabbi and broadcaster. He studied at Oxford and London universities, was ordained a rabbi in 1960, and joined Leo Baeck College in London in 1967. He was convener of the ecclesiastical court of the Reform Synagogues of Great Britain (1971–88). He is well known for his humorous and off-beat comments on life, both on radio (notably his weekly contribution to the *Today* programme on BBC Radio 4) and in such books as *A Taste of Heaven* (1977), *Bolts from the Blue* (1986), *Blue Horizons* (1989), and *Tales of Body and Soul* (1994).

Blum, Léon [blum] (1872–1950) French statesman and prime minister (1936–7, 1938, 1946–7), born in Paris. A lawyer, he was elected to the chamber in 1919, becoming one of the leaders of the Socialist Party. During World War 2 he was interned in Germany. He remained the leader of the Socialists on his return, and in 1946 was elected prime minister of the six-week caretaker government. >> RR1049

Blum, René [blum] (1878–1942) Impresario and critic, born in Paris. He took over the administration of the Ballet Russes after Diaghilev's death in 1929, renaming it the Ballet Russes de Monte Carlo. He was arrested in France while the company was on tour in the USA, and died in Auschwitz. >> Diaghilev

Blumberg, Baruch S(amuel) (1925–) Biochemist, born in New York City. He studied at Columbia and Oxford, and became professor of biochemistry at the University of Pennsylvania in 1964. He discovered the 'Australia antigen' that led to the development of a vaccine against hepatitis B, and shared the Nobel Prize for Physiology or Medicine in 1976. >> RR1124

Blume, Judy [bloom] (1938–) Writer of teenage fiction, born in New Jersey. A controversial writer, her third book, *Are You There, God? It's Me, Margaret* (1970), brought her acclaim for her candid approach to the onset of puberty and for her natural style, but attempts were made to restrict its circulation. Later books include *Deenie* (1973), *Blubber* (1974), *Forever* (1975), and *Subterfuge* (1980).

Blume, Peter [bloom] (1906–) Painter, born in Smorgon, Belarus. He emigrated in 1911 and, after various occupations, became an artist who used bizarre imagery in a

Surrealistic manner. He worked in Italy as an intermittent artist in residence at the American Academy of Rome (1956–73). Based in Sherman, CT, since then, his most famous work is 'The Eternal City' (1934–7), a denunciation of Fascism in Italy.

Blumenbach, Johann Friedrich [**bloo**menbahkh] (1752–1840) Anthropologist, born in Gotha, Germany. He studied at Jena and Göttingen, where he became professor of medicine in 1776. By his study of comparative skull measurements, he established a quantitative basis for racial classification.

Blunden, Edmund (Charles) (1896–1974) Poet and critic, born in Yalding, Kent, SE England, UK. He studied at Oxford, was professor of English literature at Tokyo (1924–7), and fellow of Merton College, Oxford (from 1931). He joined the staff of *The Times Literary Supplement* (1943), and from 1953 lectured at the University of Hong Kong. He later became professor of poetry at Oxford (1966–8). A lover of the English countryside, he is essentially a nature poet, as is evident in *Pastorals* (1916) and *The Waggoner and Other Poems* (1920), but his prose work *Undertones of War* (1928) is widely considered his best. >> Owen, Wilfred

Blunkett, David (1947–) British statesman. He studied at Sheffield University, and lectured in industrial relations and politics at Barnsley College of Technology (1973–81). A member of Sheffield City Council (1970–88), he became an MP in 1987. He was opposition spokesman for the environment (1988–92), joined the shadow cabinet (1992), and was spokesman on health (1992–4), education (1994–5), education and employment (1995–7), and chairman of the Labour Party (1993–4). He became secretary-of-state for education in the 1997 Labour government.

Blunt, (Sir) Anthony (Frederick) (1907–83) Art historian and Soviet spy, born in Bournemouth, Dorset, S England, UK. In 1926 he went to Trinity College, Cambridge, and became a fellow there in 1932. Influenced by Guy Burgess, he acted as a 'talent-spotter', supplying to him the names of likely recruits to the Communist cause, and during his war service in British Intelligence was in a position to pass on information to the Soviet government. In 1964, after the defection of Philby, a confession was obtained from Blunt in return for immunity from prosecution, and he continued as surveyor of the Queen's pictures, a post he held from 1945 to 1972. His full involvement in espionage was made public only in 1979. A distinguished art historian, he had been director of the Courtauld Institute of Art (1947–74). His knighthood (1956) was annulled in 1979. >> Burgess, Guy; Philby

Blunt, Wilfrid Scawen (1840–1922) Poet and traveller, born in Petworth, West Sussex, S England, UK. He studied at Stonyhurst and Oscott, and served in the diplomatic service (1859–70). He travelled in the Near and Middle East, espoused the cause of Arabi Pasha and Egyptian nationalism (1882), stood for parliament and was imprisoned in 1888 for activity in the Irish Land League. He wrote political verse and love poems, and bred Arab horses.

Bly, Nellie, pseudonym of **Elizabeth Seaman**, *née* **Cochrane** (c. 1865–1922) Journalist, born in Cochrane Mills, PA. As a reporter for the *New York World* she won renown for such stories as her exposé of conditions in an insane asylum on New York City's Blackwell's Island, where she posed as an inmate. In 1889–90 she made a round-the-world trip in 72 days, bettering the 80-day record of Jules Verne's fictional Phineas Fogg. A pioneering woman journalist, she took her pseudonym from a Stephen Foster song about a social reformer.

Bly, Robert (1926–) Poet, critic, translator, and editor, born in Madison, MN. His first collection was *Silence in the Snowy Fields* (1962), followed by *The Shadow-Mothers* (1970), *Sleepers Joining Hands* (1972), and *Talking All Morning* (1980).

Blyth, Chay, popular name of **Charles Blyth** (1940–) British yachtsman, the first to sail single-handed 'the hard way' round the world (1970–1). Educated at Hawick, he joined the Parachute Regiment of the Royal Army (1958–67). He rowed the Atlantic from W to E with John Ridgeway (1966), before making his epic voyage westward around the globe. With a crew of paratroopers he won the Whitbread Round the World Yacht Race (1973–4), travelling eastwards. He has set further ocean-sailing records, and was a key figure in the organization of the British Steel Challenge, Round World Yacht Race (1992–3), retracing his original westward voyage. >> Ridgeway, John

Blyth, Edward (1810–73) Naturalist and zoologist, born in London, England, UK. A druggist in London, he spent so much time on ornithology that his business failed. He was curator of the museum of the Asiatic Society in Bengal (1841–62). Several birds are named after him, including *Blyth's kingfisher*, *Blyth's pipit*, and *Blyth's warbler*.

Blythe, Ethel / John / Lionel >> **Barrymore, Ethel / John / Lionel**

Blyton, Enid (Mary) (1897–1968) Children's writer, born in London, England, UK. She trained as a Froebel kindergarten teacher, then became a journalist. In 1922 she published her first book, *Child Whispers*, a collection of verse, but it was in the late 1930s that she began writing her many children's stories featuring such characters as Noddy, the Famous Five, and the Secret Seven. She identified closely with children, and always considered her stories highly educational and moral in tone, but in the 1980s her work was criticized in some quarters for racism, sexism, and snobbishness. She published over 600 books, and is one of the most translated British authors.

Boadicea >> **Boudicca**

Boal, Augusto [**boh**al] (1931–) Brazilian theatre director, playwright, and theorist. His revolutionary models of political theatre-making have gained an international reputation, especially through his book *Teatro do Oprimido* (1975, Theatre of the Oppressed).

Boas, Franz [**boh**as] (1858–1942) Anthropologist, born in Minden, Germany. Having studied geography at Kiel, his expeditions to the Arctic and to British Columbia shifted his interest to the tribes there, and motivated his emigration to the USA in 1886. Professor at Columbia from 1899, he became the dominant figure in establishing modern anthropology in the USA. He and his pupils established new and less simple concepts of culture and of race, as outlined in his collection of papers, *Race, Language and Culture* (1940). >> Mead, Margaret

Bobrowski, Johannes [bob**rof**skee] (1917–65) Poet, born in Tilsit, Germany. His early poems appeared in *Das Innere Reich*, the Nazi journal. He served on the E front in World War 2, and was taken prisoner. He returned to East Germany in 1949, when his poems began to appear in the communist magazine *Sinn und Form*. He published only two volumes: *Sarmatische Zeit* (1961, Sarmatian Times) and *Schattenland Strome* (1962, Shadowland Rivers), but his generous historical vision has ensured a growing reputation.

Bocage, Manoel Barbosa du [boo**kah**zhuh] (1765–1805) Lyric poet, born in Setúbal, Portugal. He sailed in 1786 to India and China, returning to Lisbon in 1790, where, recognized as a poet, he joined the literary coterie *Nova Arcadia*. He was essentially a Romantic, but his sonnets are Classical in form.

Boccaccio, Giovanni [bo**kah**chioh] (1313–75) Poet and scholar, born in Tuscany or Paris. He abandoned a career in commerce, and at Naples (1328) turned to story-writing in verse and prose. He mingled in courtly society, and fell in love with the noble lady whom he made famous under the name of Fiammetta. Until 1350 he lived alternately in Florence and Naples, producing prose tales, pastorals, and poems. The *Teseide* was partly translated by Chaucer in the *Knight's Tale*. The *Filostrato*, dealing with the loves of Troilus and Cressida, was also in great part translated by Chaucer. After 1350 he became a diplomat entrusted with important public affairs, and a scholar devoted to the cause of the new learning. In 1358 he completed his great collection of tales, the *Decameron*, begun some 10 years before. During his last years he lived principally in retirement at Certaldo, and would have entered into holy orders, moved by repentance for the follies of his youth, had he not been dissuaded by Petrarch. >> Petrarch

Boccherini, Luigi (Rodolfo) [bokereenee] (1743-1805) Composer, born in Lucca, Italy. He was a cellist and prolific composer at the courts of the Infante Don Luis in Madrid and Frederick II of Prussia. He is best known for his chamber music, and for his cello concertos and sonatas.

Boccioni, Umberto [bochohnee] (1882-1916) Artist and sculptor, born in Reggio di Calabria, Italy. He was the most original artist of the Futurist school, and its principal theorist. An important bronze sculpture, 'Unique Forms of Continuity in Space' (1913), is in the Museum of Modern Art, New York City. >> Marinetti; Severini

Bock, Fedor von (1880-1945) German soldier, born in Kostrzyn, Poland. He studied at Potsdam Military School, served as a staff officer in World War 1, and commanded the German armies which invaded Austria (1938), Poland (1939), and the Lower Somme, France (1940). Promoted to field marshal in 1940, he participated in the invasion of Russia with remarkable success (1941), but was dismissed by Hitler for failing to capture Moscow (1942). He was killed in an air-raid.

Böcklin, Arnold [boeklī] (1827-1901) Painter, born in Basel, Switzerland. His work, mainly of mythological subjects, combined Classical themes of nymphs and satyrs with dark Romantic landscapes, rocks, and castles, characteristic of 19th-c German painting.

Bode, Johann Elert [bohduh] (1747-1826) Astronomer, born in Hamburg, Germany. He became director of the Berlin Observatory. The arithmetical relation he observed between the distances of the planets from the Sun is called *Bode's law*.

Bodenheim, Maxwell [bohdenhiym], originally **Bodenheimer** (1893-1954) Writer, born in Hemanville, MS. He lived in Chicago from 1902 and, after being expelled from high school (1908), mixed with the literary figures of Chicago before moving to New York City (1915). He published *Minna and Myself* (1918), the first of his 11 volumes of poetry; he also published novels, including *Replenishing Jessica* (1925), which were considered cynical and indecent. As the editor of *Others*, a poetry magazine, he is credited with discovering Hart Crane. Having lived most of his life as a bohemian and alcoholic, he and his third wife were murdered in Greenwich Village. >> Crane, Hart

Bodenstein, Andreas Rudolf >> **Carlstadt**

Bodhidharma [bodhidah(r)ma] (6th-c) Monk and founder of the Ch'an (or Zen) sect of Buddhism, born near Madras, India. He travelled to China in 520, where he had a famous audience with the Emperor. He argued that merit applying to salvation could not be accumulated through good deeds, and taught meditation as the means of return to Buddha's spiritual precepts.

Bodichon, Barbara, *née* **Leigh Smith** (1827-90) Advocate of women's rights, born in London, England, UK. She studied at Bedford College, London, and in 1852 opened a primary school in London. She wrote *Women at Work* (1857) and was a founder of the feminist magazine *The Englishwoman's*

Journal (1858). She was one of the founders of the college for women that became Girton College, Cambridge.

Bodin, Jean [bohdī] (1530-96) Political philosopher, born in Angers, France. He had a successful legal career and was also active politically. His major work was *Six livres de la République* (1576, The Six Bookes of a Commonweale, 1606), on the definition and limits of sovereignty, which argued for a limited form of monarchy.

Bodley, Sir Thomas (1545-1613) Scholar and diplomat, born in Exeter, Devon, SW England, UK. He studied languages and divinity at Geneva, where his Protestant family had been forced to take refuge during the persecutions of Mary I, but in 1558 went to Magdalen College, Oxford, and was appointed Greek lecturer at Merton College (1564). In the service of Queen Elizabeth I he was ambassador to Denmark, France, and Holland. In 1587 he married a wealthy widow, then spent huge sums on the extension of the university library, which was renamed the Bodleian and opened in 1602. He was knighted in 1604. >> Savile

Bodmer, Johann Georg (1786-1864) Inventor, born in Zürich, Switzerland. He was a mechanical engineering genius whose many inventions reflected the wide range of his interests in textile machinery, machine tools, screw propellers, armaments, steam engines, furnaces, boilers, and locomotives.

Bodoni, Giambattista [bodohnee] (1740-1813) Printer, born in Saluzzo, Italy. He designed (1790) a modern typeface still widely used today. His press in Parma published editions of the classics widely admired for their elegance.

Boë, Franz de la >> **Sylvius, Franciscus**

Boece or **Boethius, Hector** [boys], also spelled **Boyis** (c.1465-c.1536) Historian, born in Dundee, E Scotland, UK. He studied at Montaigu College, Paris, where he was a regent or professor of philosophy (c.1492-98), and then became principal of the newly founded university of Aberdeen. He is best known for his *Scotorum historiae a prima gentis origine* (1526, trans The History and Chronicles of Scotland), which, though largely based on legendary sources, was very well received at the time.

Boehm or **Böhm, Theobald** [boem] (1794-1881) Flautist and inventor, born in Munich, Germany. In 1828 he opened a flute factory in Munich, and determined to make a flute which would be acoustically perfect. As this involved making holes in places where they could not be fingered, he devised a key mechanism to overcome the problem, and in 1847 produced the model on which the modern flute is based. Certain features of his system have also been applied to the clarinet.

Boehme, Jakob >> **Böhme, Jakob**

Boeing, William E(dward) [bohing] (1881-1956) Aircraft manufacturer, born in Detroit, MI. He formed the Pacific Aero Products Co in 1916 to build seaplanes he had designed with Conrad Westerfelt. Renamed as the Boeing Airplane Company in 1917, it eventually became the largest manufacturer of military and civilian aircraft in the world.

Boerhaave, Hermann [boorhahvuh] (1668-1738) Physician and botanist, born in Voorhout, The Netherlands. He studied at Leyden, where he became professor of medicine and botany (1709). The two works on which his fame chiefly rests, *Institutiones medicae* (1708, Medical Principles) and *Aphorismi de cognoscendis et curandis morbis* (1709, Aphorisms on the Recognition and Treatment of Diseases), were translated into various European languages. In 1724 he also became professor of chemistry, and his *Elementa chemiae* (1724, Elements of Chemistry) is a classic.

Boesak, Allan (Aubrey) [busak] (1945-) Clergyman, born in Kakamas, South Africa. Lecturer and student chaplain at Western Cape University, president of the alliance of Black Reformed Christians in South Africa (1981), and president of the World Alliance of Reformed Churches (1982–), he sees the Christian Gospel in terms of liberation of the oppressed. An outspoken opponent of apartheid, he is leader of the coloured (mixed-race) community in South Africa.

Boesky, Ivan [beskee] (1937–) Financier, born in Detroit, MI. The son of a Russian immigrant, he studied law and worked as a tax accountant before moving into securities analysis, forming his own firm in 1975. Credited with (or blamed for) pioneering the junk-bond market, later a symbol of the excesses of the 1980s, he had become one of Wall Street's most successful arbitragers when he admitted to insider trading charges in 1986. Fined $100 million, he served time in prison before being given parole for good behaviour in 1990.

Boethius, Anicius Manlius Severinus [boheethius] (c.AD 480–524) Roman philosopher and statesman, born of a patrician Roman family. He studied at Athens, and there gained the knowledge which later enabled him to produce the translations of Aristotle and Porphyry that became the standard textbooks on logic in mediaeval Europe. He became consul in 510 during the Gothic occupation of Rome, and later chief minister to the ruler Theodoric; but in 523 he was accused of treason and after a year in prison at Pavia was executed. It was during his imprisonment that he wrote the famous *De consolatione philosophiae* (Consolation of Philosophy), in which the personification of Philosophy solaces the author by explaining the mutability of all earthly fortune. The *Consolation* was for the next millennium probably the most widely read book after the Bible.

Boethius, Hector >> Boece, Hector

Boëx, Joseph and **Séraphin** >> Rosny

Boff, Leonardo (1938–) Franciscan liberation theologian, born in Concordia, Brazil. He was ordained in Brazil in 1964, studied at Würzburg, Louvain, Oxford, and Munich, and became professor of systematic theology in Petrópolis, Rio. His best-known work, *Jesus-Christ Liberator* (1972), offers hope and justice for the oppressed rather than religious support of the *status quo* in Church and society. He has written several books on reforming Church structures from grass-roots 'basic communities', including *Church: Charism and Power* (1984), which provoked official ecclesiastical censure.

Bogan, Louise [bohgan] (1897–1970) Poet and writer, born in Livermore Falls, MA. She studied at Boston University (1915–16), moved to New York City, and served as poetry editor of *The New Yorker* (1931–69). She was an influential critic, as in *Achievement in American Poetry 1900–1950* (1951), and a noted lyrical poet, as in *The Blue Estuaries* (1968).

Bogarde, Sir Dirk [bohgah(r)d], originally **Derek Niven van den Bogaerde** (1921–) Actor and novelist, born in London, England, UK. He began acting in repertory theatre and made his film debut as an extra in *Come On George* (1940). After war service, he was signed to a long-term contract with Rank Films, spending many years playing smalltime crooks, military heroes, and breezy comic leads (notably in the 'Doctor in the House' series) until he was voted Britain's top box-office star (1955, 1957). His major films include *A Tale of Two Cities* (1958), *Victim* (1961), *The Servant* (1963), *Death in Venice* (1971), and *Providence* (1977). He has published several volumes of autobiography, and his novels include *A Gentle Occupation* (1980) and *A Period of Adjustment* (1994). He was knighted in 1992.

Bogardus, James (1800–74) Inventor, born in Catskill, NY. His inventions include the dry gas meter, a pyrometer, a deep-sea sounding machine, a dynamometer, and in 1839 a method of engraving postage stamps, which was adopted by the British government. He also erected the first cast-iron building in the USA.

Bogart, Humphrey (DeForest) [bohgah(r)t] (1899–1957) Film actor, born in New York City. He made his film debut in *Broadway's Like That* (1930). Alternating between stage and screen, he was frequently cast as a vicious hoodlum, most memorably in *The Petrified Forest* (1936), but eventually attained stardom with his roles in *High Sierra* (1941), *The Maltese Falcon* (1941), and *Casablanca* (1942, with Ingrid Bergman). *To Have and Have Not* (1944) also marked the debut of **Lauren Bacall**, who became his fourth wife in 1945. Over the next 15 years he created an enduring screen persona of the lone wolf, as in *The Big Sleep* (1946). Later films include *The African Queen* (1951, Oscar) and *The Caine Mutiny* (1954). >> Bacall; Bergman, Ingrid

Bogdanov, Michael [bogdahnov] (1938–) Stage director, born in London, England, UK. He studied at the universities of Dublin, Munich, and the Sorbonne, and went on to direct several major productions for the Royal Shakespeare Company and the National Theatre. In 1986 he became co-founder and artistic director of the touring English Shakespeare Company. >> Pennington, Michael

Bogdanovich, Peter [bogdanovich] (1939–) Film director, born in Kingston, NY. His particular interest was in reviving the film genre of the 1930s and 1940s. His second film, *The Last Picture Show* (1971), depicting social change in a 1950s Texas town, received critical acclaim, though the sequel, *Texasville* (1990), was less successful. Later films include *Noises Off* (1992) and *The Thing Called Love* (1993).

Bogorad, Lawrence [bogorad] (1921–) Plant physiologist, born in Tashkent, Uzbekistan. Brought to the USA in 1923, he taught at the University of Chicago, moving to Harvard in 1967. A pioneer in the study of chloroplasts, his early studies of chlorophyll synthesis in green algae contributed to research into the biosynthesis of compounds with similar structure, such as haemoglobin and the cytochromes. In the 1960s he worked on accessory plant pigments and the genetics of chloroplast formation.

Bohemond I [bohimond] (c. 1056–1111) Prince of Antioch, the eldest son of Robert Guiscard. He led his father's army against Alexius I Comnenus in Thessaly in 1083 but was defeated. He joined the First Crusade (1096), and took a prominent part in the capture of Antioch (1098). While the other crusaders advanced to storm Jerusalem, Bohemond established himself as prince in Antioch. He was taken prisoner by the Turks (1100–3), then returned to Europe to marry Constance, the daughter of Philip I of France (1106). He then collected troops to wage war against Alexius, who agreed to hand over lands to Bohemond in return for peace in 1107. >> Alexius; Guiscard

Böhm, Karl [boem] (1894–1981) Conductor, born in Graz, Austria. He studied in Vienna and held permanent posts as an opera conductor in Dresden (1934–43), Vienna (1943–5, 1954–6), and elsewhere, and also appeared frequently in London, New York City, and Bayreuth. Remembered chiefly for his Mozart performances, he also conducted premieres of operas by Richard Strauss, a personal friend. >> Strauss, Richard

Böhm, Theobald >> Boehm, Theobald

Böhme or **Boehme, Jakob** [boemuh] (1575–1624) Theosophist and mystic, born in Altseidenberg, Germany. He became a shoemaker, but in 1600 had a mystical experience which led him towards meditation on divine things. *Aurora* (1612) contains revelations upon God, humanity, and nature, and shows considerable knowledge of Scripture and of the writings of alchemists. It was condemned by the ecclesiastical authorities of Gürlitz, and he was cruelly persecuted, but in 1623 he published *The Great*

Mystery and *On the Election of Grace*, and his influence spread beyond Germany to Holland and England.

Bohr, Aage (Niels) [baw(r)] (1922–) Physicist, born in Copenhagen, the son of Niels Bohr. He studied at the universities of Copenhagen and London, and worked in his father's Institute of Theoretical Physics in Copenhagen from 1946, becoming professor of physics at Copenhagen (1956). He was director of the Institute (1963–70), and from 1975 to 1981 director of Nordita (Nordic Institute for Theoretical Atomic Physics). With Ben Mottelson, he secured experimental evidence for the support of Leo James Rainwater's collective model of the atomic nucleus, and shared the Nobel Prize for Physics with them in 1975. >> Bohr, Niels; Mottelson; Rainwater

Bohr, Niels (Henrik David) [baw(r)] (1885–1962) Physicist, born in Copenhagen. He studied at Copenhagen University, and went to England to work at Cambridge and Manchester, later becoming Director of the Institute of Theoretical Physics at Copenhagen from 1920 until his death. He greatly extended the theory of atomic structure when he explained the spectrum of hydrogen by means of an atomic model and the quantum theory (1913). During World War 2 he assisted atomic bomb research in America, returning to Copenhagen in 1945. He was founder and director of the Institute of Theoretical Physics at Copenhagen (1920–2), and was awarded the Nobel Prize for Physics in 1922. >> Bohr, Aage; Wheeler, John Archibald

Boiardo, Matteo Maria, conte di (Count of) **Scandiano** [boyah(r)doh] (c. 1441–94) Poet, born in Scandiano, Italy. He studied at Ferrara, and in 1462 married the daughter of the Count of Norellara. He lived at the court of Ferrara where he was employed on diplomatic missions, and was appointed governor in 1481 of Modena, and in 1487 of Reggio. His fame rests on the unfinished *Orlando Innamorato* (1486), a long narrative poem in which the Charlemagne romances are recast into *ottava rima*. >> Roland

Boieldieu, François Adrien [bwaeldyoe] (1775–1834) Composer, born in Rouen, France. His opera *Le Calife de Bagdad* (1800, The Caliph of Baghdad), which was performed in Paris, brought him acclaim. He conducted at St Petersburg (1803–10) and on his return produced his two masterpieces, *Jean de Paris* (1812) and *La Dame blanche* (1825, The White Lady).

Boileau(-Despréaux), Nicolas [bwahloh] (1636–1711) Poet and critic, born in Paris. He studied law and theology at Beauvais, but, as a man of means, devoted himself to literature. In 1677 the king appointed him, with Racine, official royal historian. *L'Art poétique* (Poetic Art), imitated by Pope in the *Essay on Criticism*, was published in 1674, along with the first part of the serio-comic *Lutrin*. His influence as a critic has been profound. He set up good sense, sobriety, elegance, and dignity of style as the cardinal literary virtues. >> Racine

Bois, Guy Péne du >> **du Bois, Guy Péne**

Bois W E B Du >> **Du Bois, W E B**

Boisbaudran, Paul Emile Lecoq de [bwahbohdrā] (1838–1912) Physical chemist, born in Cognac, France. A founder of spectroscopy, he discovered gallium, samarium, and dysprosium.

Bois-Reymond, Emil du [bwah raymō] (1818–96) Physiologist, the discoverer of neuroelectricity, born in Berlin. He became professor of physiology at Berlin in 1855, where he investigated the physiology of muscles and nerves, and demonstrated electricity in animals.

Boito, Arrigo [boeeto] (1842–1918) Composer and poet, born in Padua, Italy. He studied at the Milan Conservatory. His first important work was the opera *Mefistofele* (1868), which survived its initial failure and later grew in popularity. He wrote his own and other libretti, including those for Verdi's *Otello* and *Falstaff*.

Bo Juyi [boe jooyee], also spelled **Po Chü-i** (772–846) Poet, government official, and governor of Hangzhou, born in Hsingcheng, Shensi Province, China. He was known in his lifetime even in Japan and Korea, and was probably the first poet to be printed (c.810). His 3840 pieces of vernacular poetry and prose afford valuable insight into the daily life of Tang period scholar-gentry. *Song of Unending Sorrow*, on the Xuanzong and Yang Guifei love-tragedy, is one of the world's finest tragic poems. >> Xuanzong

Bok, Edward (William) (1863–1930) Editor, born in Den Helder, The Netherlands. Emigrating to the USA at the age of six, he later worked as a stenographer, and became editor of the *Brooklyn Magazine* at 19. He ran the Bok Syndicate Press (1886–91) and was editor-in-chief of *The Ladies' Home Journal* (1889–1919). He published several books in celebration of the American gospel of business success, and a highly influential autobiography, *The Americanization of Edward Bok* (1920, Pulitzer).

Bokassa, Eddine Ahmed [bohkasa], originally **Jean Bédel Bokassa** (1921–96) Central African Republic soldier, president (1966–79), and emperor (1977–9), born in Bobangui, Central African Republic. He joined the French army in 1939 and in 1963, after independence, was made army commander-in-chief. He led a coup which overthrew President David Dacko (1965), made himself life-president, and in 1977 was crowned emperor as Bokassa I. He became increasingly dictatorial and was held responsible for the deaths of numerous people. In 1979 he was himself ousted and went into exile, but in 1988 was returned for trial and found guilty of murder and other crimes. His death sentence was eventually commuted.

Bol, Ferdinand (c. 1616–1680) Dutch painter who studied under Rembrandt in the 1630s and was one of his most talented followers. Working in Amsterdam, for many years he painted in a style so close to his master's that some of his portraits have been mistaken for Rembrandt's. >> Rembrandt

Bolden, Buddy, popular name of **Charles Joseph Bolden** (1877–1931) Jazz cornetist, born in New Orleans, LA. He is the putative founder of jazz, a figure of mythic significance. He reputedly played his trumpet so powerfully that he could be heard for 10 miles in all directions. No recorded evidence survives, though scholars spent decades searching for an Edison cylinder said to have been made at the turn of the century. In 1907, his uncontrollable fits of violence led to his incarceration for life, and he died in a fire at an asylum.

Boldrewood, Rolf, pseudonym of **Thomas Alexander Browne** (1826–1915) Novelist, born in London, England, UK. His family emigrated to Australia in 1830. He was educated in Sydney, then became a squatter in Victoria and later an inspector of goldfields. His novels depict life at the cattle stations and diggings, and include *Robbery under Arms* (1888) and *Babes in the Bush* (1900).

Bolet, Jorge [bohlay] (1914–90) Pianist, born in Havana. He studied at the Curtis Institute of Music, Philadelphia, from the age of 12, where he became head of piano studies. He is renowned for his interpretation of Liszt, and of the German, Spanish, and Russian Romantics. He became a US citizen in 1944.

Boleyn, Anne [bolin], also spelled **Bullen** (c.1507–36) English queen, the second wife of **Henry VIII** from 1533–6. Daughter of Sir Thomas Boleyn by Elizabeth Howard, she secretly married Henry (Jan 1533), and was soon declared his legal wife (May); but within three months his passion for her had cooled. It was not revived by the birth (Sep 1533) of a princess (later Elizabeth I), still less by that of a stillborn son (Jan 1536). She was arrested and brought to the Tower, charged with treason, and beheaded (19 May). Henry married Jane Seymour 11 days later. >> Elizabeth I; Henry VIII; Seymour, Jane

Bolger, James Brendan [bol jer] (1935–) New Zealand prime minister (1990–), born in Opunake, New Zealand. A farmer, he entered parliament in 1972 for the National Party as the member for King Country, and became Leader of the Opposition in 1986, and then prime minister.

Bolingbroke >> **Henry IV** (of England)

Bolingbroke, Henry St John, 1st Viscount (1678–1751) English statesman and writer, born in London, England, UK. He studied at Eton, and may have gone to Oxford. After travelling in Europe, he entered parliament (1701), becoming secretary for war (1704), foreign secretary (1710), and joint leader of the Tory Party. He was made a peer in 1712. On the death of Queen Anne (1714), his Jacobite sympathies forced him to flee to France, where he wrote *Reflections on Exile*. He returned for a while to England (1725–35), but unable to attain political office he went back to France (1735–42). His last years were spent in London, where his works included the influential *Idea of a Patriot King* (1749).

Bolívar, Simón [bol*lee*vah(r), **bo**livah(r)], known as **the Liberator** (1783–1830) The national hero of Venezuela, Colombia, Ecuador, Peru, and Bolivia, born in Caracas. Having travelled in Europe, he played the most prominent part in the wars of independence in N South America. In 1819, he proclaimed and became president of the vast Republic of Colombia (modern Colombia, Venezuela, and Ecuador), which was finally liberated in 1822. He then took charge of the last campaigns of independence in Peru (1824). In 1826 he returned N to face growing political dissension. He resigned office (1830), and died on his way into exile. >> San Martin

Bolkiah, Hassanal [bolkia] (1946–) Sultan of Brunei, the son of Sultan Sir Omar Ali Saifuddin. He was educated in Malaysia, and at Sandhurst Royal Military Academy. Appointed crown prince in 1961, he became sultan in 1967 on his father's abdication. On independence (1984) he also became prime minister and defence minister. As head of an oil- and gas-rich microstate, he is reputed to be the richest individual in the world, with an estimated wealth of $25 billion. A moderate Muslim, he has two wives, **Princess Saleha** (m.1965), and **Mariam Bell** (m.1981), a former air stewardess. >> RR1036

Böll, Heinrich (Theodor) [boel] (1917–85) Writer, born in Cologne, Germany. A trilogy, *Und sagte kein einziges Worte* (1953, trans Acquainted with the Night), *Haus ohne Hüter* (1954, The Unguarded House), and *Das Brot der frühen Jahre* (1955, The Bread of our Early Years), depicting life in Germany during and after the Nazi regime, gained him a worldwide reputation. His later novels, characteristically satirizing modern German society, included *Die verlorene Ehre der Katharina Blum* (1974, The Lost Honour of Katharina Blum). He was awarded the 1972 Nobel Prize for Literature.

Bolm, Adolph (1884–1951) Dancer, choreographer, and teacher, born in St Petersburg, Russia. He danced in Anna Pavlova's first tours (1908–9), also joining Sergey Diaghilev's Ballets Russes. From 1911 he travelled the world with the company, remaining in the USA after the 1916 tour. He was closely associated with the Chicago Civic Opera and the companies now known as American Ballet Theatre and San Francisco Ballet. >> Diaghilev; Pavlova

Bologna, Giovanni da [bolonya], also called **Giambologna** (1529–1608) Sculptor and architect, born in Douai, France. He went to Italy in 1551 and executed much sculptural work in Florence for the Medici, including the 'Flying Mercury' (1564) and various fountains in the Boboli gardens, the 'Rape of the Sabines' (1580), and 'Hercules and

the Centaur' (1599). His bronzes can be seen in the Wallace Collection and elsewhere.

Bolt, Robert (1924–95) Playwright, born in Sale, Greater Manchester, NW England, UK. He studied at Manchester University, served in the RAF and worked as a teacher before achieving success with *A Man for All Seasons* (1960). Other plays included *The Tiger and the Horse* (1960) and *State of Revolution* (1977). He had also written screenplays, including *Lawrence of Arabia* (1962), *Dr Zhivago* (1965), *Ryan's Daughter* (1970), and *The Mission* (1986). He was an antinuclear activist in the 1960s, joining the 'Committee of 100', and was jailed for a month in 1961. He continued writing, despite being partly paralysed and left with speech difficulties, following a stroke in 1979.

Boltwood, Bertram (Borden) (1870–1927) Radiochemist, born in Amherst, MA. He studied at Yale, Munich, and Leipzig, became professor at Yale (1897–1900, 1910–27), and from 1904 concentrated on research into radio-chemistry, becoming the leading US figure in this field. He discovered the radioactive element ionium, and introduced lead:uranium ratios as a method for dating rocks (1907).

Boltzmann, Ludwig (Eduard) [bolts man] (1844–1906) Physicist, born in Vienna. He studied at Vienna, where he became professor in 1895. He did important work on the kinetic theory of gases and established the principle of the equipartition of energy (*Boltzmann's law*). He laid the foundations of statistical mechanics by applying the laws of mechanics and the theory of probability to the motion of atoms, and his name was given to the *Boltzmann constant*, a fundamental constant of physics.

Bolyai, János (1802–60) Mathematician, born in Cluj, Romania. After attempting to prove Euclid's parallel postulate, he realized that it was possible to have a consistent system of geometry in which this postulate did not hold, and so became one of the founders of non-Euclidean geometry. >> Euclid; Lobachevsky

Bolzano, Bernhard [bolzahnoh] (1781–1848) Catholic theologian, philosopher, and mathematician, born in Prague. He became a priest in 1804 and professor of the philosophy of religion in 1805, but was deprived of his chair in 1819 for nonconformity. He was a pioneer in giving a rigorous foundation to the theory of functions of a real variable, and investigating the mathematical concept of the infinite.

Bombard, Alain Louis [bombah(r)] (1924–) Physician and marine biologist, born in Paris. In 1952, after preliminary trials in the Mediterranean, he set out across the Atlantic alone in his rubber dinghy *L'Hérétique* without food or water to prove his claim that shipwreck castaways could sustain life on nothing more than fish, plankton, rain water and controlled drinking of small amounts of sea water. He landed at Barbados 62 days later. He started a marine laboratory at Saint-Malo for the study of the physiopathology of the sea.

Bomberg, David (1890–1957) Painter, born in Birmingham, West Midlands, C England, UK. He trained as a lithographer before studying painting in London, and was a founder member of the London Group (1913). In Paris he met avant-garde artists including Modigliani, Derain, and Picasso, and their influence is clear in such large compositions as 'The Mud Bath' and 'In the Hold' (1913–14), which combine abstract and Vorticist influences.

Bombois, Camille [bobwah] (1883–1970) Primitive painter, born in Venarey-les-Laumes, France. He worked in a travelling circus, and as a labourer, painting as a hobby. By 1923 he had been discovered by collectors and was able to devote all his time to painting his very personal landscapes, and pictures of wrestlers and acrobats.

Bonaparte >> Napoleon I / III

Bonaparte, (Maria Annunciata) Caroline [bohnapah(r)t] (1782–1839) Queen of Naples (1808–15), born in Ajaccio, Corsica, the youngest sister of Napoleon I. She married **Joachim Murat** in 1800, and brought a brilliant court life to the Neapolitan palaces of Caserta and Portici. After her husband's execution she lived in Austria (1815–24) and Trieste (1824–31) before settling in Florence. >> Murat; Napoleon I; RR1067

Bonaparte, Charles Joseph [bohnapah(r)t] (1851–1921) Lawyer and reformer, born in Baltimore, MD, the great-nephew of Napoleon I. He practised law in Baltimore, where he fought the corruption rampant both in the city and state government, and in 1881 founded the Civil Service Reform Association of Maryland and the National Civil Service Reform League. His activities led to a friendship with Theodore Roosevelt who, as president, appointed him secretary of the navy (1905) and attorney general (1906–9). Although he led Roosevelt's anti-trust campaign, he was himself essentially a conservative who had no great faith in the masses. After leaving the Department of Justice, he returned to practise law in Baltimore, and founded the National Municipal League. >> Roosevelt, Theodore

Bonaparte, Charles Louis Napoleon >> Napoleon III

Bonaparte, (Marie-Anne) Elisa [bohnapah(r)t] (1777–1820) Grand Duchess of Tuscany, born in Ajaccio, Corsica, the eldest surviving sister of Napoleon. She married **Félix Baciochi** in 1797. As Duchess of Lucca from 1805, she managed the economy of her small state so profitably that in 1809 Napoleon assigned her to Tuscany, where she revived the court glories of the Pitti Palace. >> Napoleon I

Bonaparte, François Charles Joseph >> Napoleon II

Bonaparte, Jérôme [bohnapah(r)t] (1784–1860) King of Westphalia (1807–13), born in Ajaccio, Corsica, the youngest brother of Napoleon. He served in the navy (1800–2) and lived in New York (1803–5), marrying **Elizabeth Patterson** (1785–1879) in Baltimore in 1803, a marriage which Napoleon declared null and void. Jérôme was given a high military command by Napoleon in the Prussian campaign of 1806, led an army corps at Wagram in 1809, incurred his brother's displeasure during the invasion of Russia in 1812, but fought with tenacity at Waterloo. After accepting exile in Rome, Florence, and Switzerland, he returned to Paris in 1847. His nephew Napoleon III appointed him governor of the Invalides, and created him a marshal of France. >> Napoleon I; Napoleon III

Bonaparte, Joseph [bohnapah(r)t] (1768–1844) King of Naples and Sicily (1806–8) and of Spain (1808–13), born in Corte, Corsica, the eldest surviving brother of Napoleon I. He served Napoleon on diplomatic missions and was a humane sovereign in S Italy, but faced continuous rebellion as a nominated ruler in Spain, where his army was decisively defeated by Wellington at Vitoria (1813). He spent much of his life in exile in New Jersey, but settled in Florence for the last years of his life. >> Napoleon I; RR1067

Bonaparte, Louis [bohnapah(r)t] (1778–1846) King of Holland (1806–10), born in Ajaccio, Corsica, the third surviving brother of Napoleon I. He was a soldier, who married Napoleon's step-daughter, **Hortense Beauharnais**, in 1802. He ruled Holland as King Lodewijk I, but abdicated because Napoleon complained that he was too attached to the interests of the Dutch. He became Count of Saint-Leu, and settled in Austria and Switzerland, later living in Florence. He was the father of Napoleon III. >> Beauharnais, Hortense; Napoleon III; RR1077

Bonaparte, Lucien [bohnapah(r)t] (1775–1840) Prince of Canino, born in Ajaccio, Corsica, the second surviving brother of Napoleon I. In 1798 he was made a member of the Council of Five Hundred, and just before the 18th Brumaire was elected its president. He was successful as minister of the interior, and as ambassador to Madrid (1800) undermined British influence. He had never wholly shaken off his early strong republicanism, and having denounced the arrogant policy of his brother towards the court of Rome, he was 'advised' to leave Roman territory. In 1810, on his way to America, he was captured by the English and kept a prisoner until 1814, after which he returned to Italy. >> Napoleon I

Bonaparte, Napoleon Joseph Charles Paul [bohnapah(r)t] (1822–91) French politican, born in Trieste, Italy, the son of Jérôme Bonaparte and nephew of Napoleon I. He entered military service in Württemberg in 1837, and was expelled from France in 1845 for republicanism. In 1848, having taken the name Jérôme on his elder brother's death, he was elected to the National Assembly. In 1851 he was named as the successor to Napoleon III. In 1859 he married the **Princess Clotilda**, daughter of Victor Emmanuel II of Sardinia. After the fall of the empire he took up residence in England, but returned to France in 1872 and sat in the Chamber of Deputies. In 1886, as pretender to the throne, he was exiled from France. >> Bonaparte, Jérôme

Bonaparte, (Marie-) Pauline [bohnapah(r)t] (1780–1825) Princess Borghese, born in Ajaccio, Corsica, the favourite sister of Napoleon I. She married **General Leclerc** in 1797 and accompanied him on the expedition to Haiti (1802), during which he died. In 1803 she married **Prince Camillo Borghese**, her private life soon shocking the patrician family into which she married. She loyally supported Napoleon in his exile on Elba. >> Napoleon I

Bonaventura or **Bonaventure, St** [bonavencher], known as **Doctor Seraphicus** ('Seraphic Doctor'), originally **Giovanni di Fidanza** (c. 1221–74) Theologian, born near Orvieto, Italy. He became a Franciscan (1243), a professor of theology at Paris (1253), general of his order (1257), and Cardinal Bishop of Albano (1273). He was canonized by Sixtus IV (1482), and in 1587 was declared by Pope Sixtus V the sixth of the great Doctors of the Church. Feast day 15 July.

Bond, Alan (1938–) Businessman, born in London, England, UK. He emigrated to Fremantle, Western Australia, in 1951, and formed a company dealing in insurance, property, and resources. The Bond Corporation developed extensive interests in Australian newspapers and television, brewing, oil and gas, and gold mining. In 1983 his syndicate's yacht *Australia II* was the first since 1870 to challenge the USA successfully for the America's Cup. With the ending of the economic boom in 1987, his empire began to fall: receivers were appointed to Bond Brewing in 1989, and in 1992 he was declared bankrupt and convicted on a charge of dishonesty in business dealings with a merchant bank. He was acquitted after spending six months in jail, but in 1996 he was sentenced to three years' imprisonment for failing to declare assets, and in 1997 received an additional 4-year sentence on charges of fraud.

Bond, Edward (1934–) Playwright and director, born in London, England, UK. His first play, *The Pope's Wedding*, was given a Sunday night reading at the Royal Court Theatre, London, in 1962 and aroused great controversy. *Saved* (1965) achieved notoriety through a scene in which a baby in a pram is stoned to death. Later plays such as *Narrow Road to the Deep North* (1968) use historical themes to look at broad contemporary issues. Other plays include a reworking of Shakespeare's play *Lear* (1971), a trilogy *The War Plays* (1985), and *At the Inland Sea* (1996), sub-titled 'a play for young people'.

Bond, (Thomas) Michael (1926–) Writer of children's stories, born in Berkshire, S England, UK. Educated in

Reading, he was a television cameraman (1947–66) before becoming a full-time writer. He created the much-loved character Paddington Bear in *A Bear Called Paddington* (1958), who has since featured in many books, as well as in a long-running television short cartoon. In 1983 he began a series of novels for adults relating the adventures of Monsieur Pamplemousse, such as *Monsieur Pamplemousse takes the Train* (1993).

Bondfield, Margaret Grace (1873–1953) Trade unionist and British stateswoman, born in Chard, Somerset, SW England, UK. She became chairman of the TUC in 1923 and as Labour minister of labour (1929–31) was the first woman to be a British cabinet minister.

Bondi, Sir Hermann (1919–) Mathematical physicist and astronomer, born in Vienna. He studied at Cambridge, where he held academic posts (1945–54) after working for the British Admiralty during World War 2. He was appointed professor of mathematics at King's College, London (1954), director-general of the European Space Research Organisation (1967–71), chief scientific adviser, Ministry of Defence (1971–7), chief scientist, Department of Energy (1977–80), chairman of the Natural Environment Research Council (1980–4), and Master of Churchill College, Cambridge (1983–90). He is best known as one of the originators of the steady-state theory of the universe. >> Gold; Hoyle, Fred

Bone, Henry (1755–1834) Enamel painter, born in Truro, Cornwall, SW England, UK. In London he enamelled watches and fans, and made enamel portraits, brooches, and other ornaments. In 1801 he became enamel painter to George III.

Bone, Sir Muirhead (1876–1953) Artist, born in Glasgow, W Scotland, UK. Although he studied architecture, he was self-taught as an artist. His work, which has been likened technically to that of Piranesi, combines meticulous realism with a strong sense of composition, and his subject matters range from the architectural to portraiture and landscape. During his long career he made over 500 etchings, drypoints, and lithographs, besides many thousands of drawings and watercolours. >> Piranesi

Boner, Ulrich [bo-ner] (c. 1300–49) Swiss writer of fables. A Dominican friar in Bern from 1324, his *Edelstein*, a collection of fables and jokes, was one of the first German books printed, in 1461.

Bong, Richard (Ira) (1920–45) Aviator, born in Superior, WI. The greatest US fighter ace of World War 2, he shot down 40 Japanese aircraft in three combat tours in the Southwest Pacific (1942–4). He was killed in the crash of an experimental P-80 jet near Los Angeles.

Bongo, Omar, originally **Albert-Bernard Bongo** (1935–) Gabonese president (1967–), born in Lewai, Gabon. In 1960 he joined the civil service, then moved into the political arena and succeeded President M'ba in 1967. The following year he created a one-party state based on the Gabonese Democratic Party, and in 1973 announced his conversion to Islam, adopting the name Omar. In 1986 he was re-elected for the third time. >> RR1051

Bonham-Carter, Helena [bonam] (1966–) Actress, born in London, England, UK. Noted for playing quintessential English heroines, she made her cinematic debut as Lady Jane Grey in *Lady Jane* (1985). Later film credits include *Hamlet* (1990), *Howard's End* (1992), *Mary Shelly's Frankenstein* (1994), *Mighty Aphrodite* (1995), *Twelfth Night* (1996), and *Portraits Chinois* (1997).

Bonham-Carter (of Yarnbury), Mark Raymond Bonham-Carter, Baron [bonam] (1922–94) Administrator, the son of Lady Violet Bonham-Carter. He studied at Oxford and Chicago universities, contested several seats as a Liberal candidate, and represented Torrington as MP

(1958–9). He was director of the Royal Opera House (1958–82), a governor and vice-chairman of the BBC (1975–81), a governor of the Royal Ballet (1960–85), then chairman of the governors. He was the first chairman of the Race Relations Board (1966–70) and chairman of the Community Relations Commission (1971–7). He was created a life peer in 1986. >> Bonham-Carter, Lady Violet

Bonham-Carter, Lady Violet, Baroness Asquith of Yarnbury [bonam] (1887–1969) English Liberal politician and publicist, the daughter of H H Asquith by his first marriage. In 1915 she married **Sir Maurice Bonham-Carter** (d.1960), a scientist and civil servant. She was created a life peeress in 1964. Jo Grimond was her son-in-law. >> Asquith; Bonham-Carter, Mark; Grimond

Bonhoeffer, Dietrich [bon-hoefer] (1906–45) Lutheran pastor and theologian, and opponent of Nazism, born in Wrocław, Poland (formerly Breslau, Germany. He studied at Tübingen and Berlin, and left Germany in 1933 in protest against the Nazi enforcement of anti-Jewish legislation. He worked in London until 1935, then returned to Germany to combat anti-Semitism, becoming head of a pastoral seminary of the German Confessing Church until its closure by the Nazis in 1937. He became deeply involved in the German resistance movement and in 1943 was imprisoned until 1945, when he was hanged at Flossenbürg. His writings include *Widerstand und Ergebung* (1951, trans Letters and Papers from Prison) on the place of Christian belief in the modern world.

Boniface, St [bonifas], originally **Wynfrith**, known as **the Apostle of Germany** (c.680–c.754) Anglo-Saxon missionary, born in Wessex, England. A Benedictine monk, he taught in the monastery of Nursling near Romsey. He set out in 718 to preach the Gospel to all the tribes of Germany, assisting Willibrord (719–22), and was consecrated Bishop (723), Archbishop, and Primate of Germany (732). He was killed at Dokkum by heathens. Feast day 5 June. >> Walburga; Willibald; Willibrord

Boniface, St >> Bruno, St

Boniface VIII [bonifas], originally **Benedetto Caetani** (c.1235–1303) Pope (1294–1303), born in Anagni, Italy. He was made cardinal priest in 1291. As pope he tried to reassert papal superiority over temporal powers, particularly Edward I of England and Philip IV of France. In 1303 he was briefly kidnapped by the French at Anagni, and died in Rome shortly after being released. His brief captivity led to the papacy taking up residence at Avignon. >> Edward I (of England)

Bonington, Sir Chris(tian John Storey) (1934–) Mountaineer and photo-journalist, born in London, England, UK. He trained at the Royal Military Academy, Sandhurst. His first mountaineering ascents include Annapurna II (1960), Nuptse (1961), and the first British ascents of the North Wall of the Eiger (1962) and Mt Vinson in Antarctica (1983). He led or co-led many successful expeditions, including Annapurna South Face (1970) and Everest (1972, 1975 SW face), and reached the summit of Everest himself in 1985. He was knighted in 1996.

Bonington, Richard Parkes (1802–28) Painter, born near Nottingham, Nottinghamshire, C England, UK. About 1817 his family moved to Calais, and there and at Paris he studied art, and became a friend of Delacroix. His first works were exhibited in the Salon in 1822, mostly sketches of Le Havre and Lillebonne. He excelled in light effects achieved by the use of a large expanse of sky, broad areas of pure colour, and the silhouetting of dark and light masses, as well as his rich colouring of heavy draperies and brocades. >> Delacroix

Bonino, Emma [bo-neenoh] (1949–) Politician, born near Turin, Italy. Born into a poor farming family, at the age of

28 she became pregnant and chose to have an abortion, then illegal in Italy. To draw attention to the squalid conditions of underground abortions, she made hers public, was sent to jail, went on hunger strike, and helped to change the law. She then joined the small Radical Party and campaigned successfully for the introduction of a divorce law. In 1995 she was chosen European Commissioner for fisheries, consumer affairs, and humanitarian aid, with responsibility for the controversial Common Fisheries Policy.

Bonnard, Abel [bonah(r)] (1883–1968) Poet, novelist, and essayist, born in Poitiers, France. He won the national poetry prize with his first collection of poems, *Les Familiers* (1906), and took up the psychological novel with *La Vie et l'amour* (1913, Life and Love). He was minister of education in the Vichy government (1942–4), fled to Spain and was sentenced to death in his absence (1945). He returned to France (1958) and was banished (1960).

Bonnard, Pierre [bonah(r)] (1867–1947) Painter and lithographer, born in Paris. He trained at the Académie Julien, then joined the group called *Les Nabis*, which included Denis and Vuillard, with whom he formed the Intimist group. Ignoring the movement towards abstraction, he continued to paint interiors and landscapes, in which everything is subordinated to the subtlest rendering of light and colour effects. >> Vuillard

Bonner, Edmund (c.1500–69) English clergyman and bishop. The reputation he gained at Oxford recommended him to Wolsey, who made him his chaplain. His zeal in King Henry VIII's service after Wolsey's fall earned him due promotion, and in 1540 he was made Bishop of London, but was imprisoned (1549–53) for refusing to recognize royal supremacy during the minority of Edward VI. He was restored to office under Mary I. Following Elizabeth I's accession (1558), he refused the oath of supremacy, and died in prison. >> Elizabeth I; Henry VIII; Wolsey

Bonner, James (Frederick) (1910–) Molecular biologist, born in Ansley, NE. He was a National Research Council fellow in Switzerland (1934–5), then joined the California Institute of Technology (1936–81). His early research on ribosomes led to his major contributions to studies of messenger RNA. Using dormant potato buds, he demonstrated that repressed genes can be 'derepressed' by removing their chromosomes' histone protein covering.

Bonner, Neville Thomas (1922–) Australian politician, born in Tweed Heads, New South Wales, Australia. He had little formal education, but was president of the One People of Australia League (1967–73). He filled a casual Senate vacancy in 1971, becoming the first Aboriginal member of the Australian parliament. The following year, standing for the Liberal Party, he was elected as a representative for Queensland. He stood unsuccessfully as an independent member in 1983.

Bonner, Yelena (1923–) Civil rights campaigner, born in Moscow. After the arrest of her parents in Stalin's 'great purge' of 1937, she was brought up in Leningrad by her grandmother. She joined the Soviet Communist Party in 1965, but became disillusioned after the invasion of Czechoslovakia (1968) and drifted into dissident activities. She married **Andrei Sakharov** in 1971 and resigned from the party a year later. During the next 14 years she and her husband led the Soviet dissident movement. Following a KGB crackdown, Sakharov was banished to internal exile in Gorky in 1980, and Bonner suffered a similar fate in 1984. The couple were finally released in 1986 by the Gorbachev administration, and remained prominent campaigners for greater democratization. >> Sakharov

Bonnet, Charles (Etienne) [bonay] (1720–93) Naturalist and philosopher, born in Geneva, Switzerland. He is known for his discovery of parthenogenesis, and he also developed the 'catastrophic' theory of evolution.

Bonney, William H, Jr, known as **Billy the Kid**, originally (?) **Henry McCarty** (1859–81) Bandit and gunfighter, born in New York City. His family moved West, eventually to New Mexico. A killer from the age of 12, he achieved legendary notoriety for his hold-ups and robberies in the SW. He was captured by Sheriff Pat Garrett in 1880, and sentenced to hang, but escaped from jail, to be tracked down and shot by Garrett some months later. >> Garrett, Pat

Bonnie and Clyde Notorious robbery partners: **Clyde Barrow** (1909–34), born in Telico, TX, and **Bonnie Parker** (1911–34), born in Rowena, TX. Despite the popular romantic image of the duo, they and their gang were also responsible for a number of murders. The pair met in 1932. When Barrow first visited Parker's house, he was arrested on seven accounts of burglary and car theft, convicted, and sentenced to two years in jail. Parker smuggled a gun to him and he escaped. With their gang, which included Barrow's brother and wife, they continued to rob and murder until they were shot dead at a police roadblock in Louisiana.

Bonnie Prince Charlie >> Stuart, Charles
Bono, Edward de >> de Bono, Edward
Bono, Emilio de >> de Bono, Emilio

Bononcini or **Buononcini, Giovanni (Maria)** [bononcheenee] (1642–78) Composer, born near Modena, Italy. In 1671 he became a violinist in the court orchestra, and subsequently chapel master of the cathedral. Between 1666 and his death he published a great quantity of chamber and vocal music, together with a treatise, the *Musico prattico*, which was influential in its day. His sons **Giovanni Battista Bononcini** (1670–1755) and **Marc Antonio Bononcini** (1675–1726) were notable composers, the former especially remembered for his rivalry with Handel. >> Handel

Bonpland, Aimé >> Humboldt, Alexander von
Bony, Jean [bonee] (1908–) Architectural historian, born in Le Mans, France. A scholar of French and English Gothic architecture, he joined the faculty of the University of California, Berkeley, in 1962. His publications include *The English Decorated Style* (1979) and *French Gothic Architecture of the 12th and 13th Centuries* (1983).

Bonynge, Richard >> Sutherland, Joan

Boole, George (1815–64) Mathematician and logician, born in Lincoln, Lincolnshire, EC England, UK. He was largely self-taught, and though without a degree was appointed professor of mathematics at Cork in 1849. He did important work on finite differences and differential equations, but is primarily known for his *Mathematical Analysis of Logic* (1847) and *Laws of Thought* (1854), pioneering works in modern symbolic logic. >> Venn, John (1834–1923)

Boone, Daniel (c. 1734–1820) Pioneer, born in Berks Co, PA. His family moved to North Carolina, and from there he went to Kentucky. From 1769 he lived in the forest, exploring much of the country with his brother, and helping to open up a trail through the Cumberland Gap in the Appalachian Mts. He was twice captured by Indians, and (1775–8) repeatedly repelled Indian attacks on a stockade fort which he had erected, now Boonesboro. He was a legend even in his lifetime.

Boorman, John (1933–) Film director, born in Shepperton, Surrey, SE England, UK. He worked for Southern Television, and became head of the BBC documentary unit (1962). He made his first feature film *Catch Us if You Can* (1965), and followed this with the stylish American thriller *Point Blank* (1967). Later films include *Deliverance* (1972), *Excalibur* (1981), *Hope and Glory* (1987), *Where the Heart Is* (1990), and *Beyond Rangoon* (1995).

Boorstin, Daniel J(oseph) (1914–) Writer, academic, and librarian, born in Atlanta, GA. He studied at Harvard, won a Rhodes scholarship to Oxford, and was admitted to the English bar (1937). He became professor of American history at the University of Chicago (1944–69) and director of the National Museum of History and Technology (1969–73). His major works include *The Americans* trilogy (1958, 1965, 1973) and *The Discoverers* (1983).

Boot, Harry >> **Randall, John**

Boot, Sir Jesse, Baron Trent (1850–1931) Drug manufacturer, born in Nottingham, Nottinghamshire, C England, UK. At 13 he inherited his father's herbalist shop, and in 1877 opened his first chemist's shop in Nottingham. He began large-scale drug manufacture (1892), and soon after the turn of the century was controlling the largest pharmaceutical retail trade in the world, with over a thousand branches by 1931.

Booth, Charles (1840–1916) Shipowner, statistician, and social reformer, born in Liverpool, Merseyside, NW England, UK. He joined his brother Alfred in founding the Booth Steamship Co. An ardent radical in his youth, he settled in London in 1875 and devoted 18 years to the preparation of his great *Life and Labour of the People in London* (17 vols, 1902), the prototype of the modern social survey.

Booth, Edwin (Thomas) (1833–93) Actor, born in Harford County, MD, the brother of John Wilkes Booth. He played Tressel at the age of 16 to his father's Richard III, and rose to the top of his profession, touring abroad on several occasions. In 1864 he produced *Hamlet* in New York City for a record run. >> Booth, John Wilkes

Booth, Hubert Cecil (1871–1955) British engineer. In 1900 he demonstrated the principle of extracting dust from carpets by suction, and in 1901 patented an electrically powered machine which he called a 'vacuum cleaner'. The machine was mounted on a horse-drawn wagon, and was equipped with a long tube for access into buildings. His Vacuum Cleaning Co provided the first mechanical cleaning service. >> Hoover, William

Booth, John Wilkes (1839–65) Assassin, born near Bel Air, MD, the brother of Edwin Thomas Booth. He became an actor, and though less well-known than his brother, was popular in the South during the early 1860s. A strong supporter of the Southern cause, in 1865 he entered into a conspiracy to avenge the defeat of the Confederates, and shot President Lincoln at Ford's Theatre, Washington, DC, on 14 April. He managed to escape to Virginia, but was tracked down and shot. >> Booth, Edwin; Lincoln

Booth, William (1829–1912) Religous leader, founder and general of the Salvation Army, born in Nottingham, Nottinghamshire, C England, UK. In 1844 he was converted and became a Methodist New Connexion minister on Tyneside. He began 'The Christian Mission' in London's East End (1865), which in 1878 developed into the Salvation Army. The Army spread throughout the world, with a whole new network of social and regenerative agencies. His book, *In Darkest England and the Way Out* (1890), tells of his philosophy and motivation. His eldest son, **William Branwell Booth** (1856–1929), was chief-of-staff from 1880 and succeeded his father as general (1912). His second son, **Ballington Booth** (1857–1940), was commander of the army in Australia (1883–5) and the USA (1887–96), but resigned after disagreement with his father, and founded a similar organization, Volunteers of America. One of his daughters, **Evangeline Cora Booth** (1865–1950), became a US citizen and was elected general in 1934. A grand-daughter, **Catherine Branwell Booth** (1884–1987), was a commissioner in the Army. >> Smith, Rodney

Boothby (of Buchan and Rattray Head), Sir Robert (John Graham) Boothby, Baron (1900–86) Politician, born in Edinburgh, EC Scotland, UK. He studied at Oxford, and in 1924 was elected Conservative MP for East Aberdeenshire, the seat he held until 1958. He was parliamentary private secretary to Winston Churchill (1926–9), and parliamentary secretary to the ministry of food (1940–1). He became an original member of the Council of United Europe (1948) and was a British delegate to its consultative assembly (1949–54). Well-known as a commentator on public affairs on radio and TV, he was raised to the peerage in 1958.

Boothe, Clare >> **Luce, Clare Boothe**

Bopp, Franz (1791–1867) Philologist, born in Mainz, Germany. After four years' study in Paris, he produced a major study of Indo-European grammar (1816). In 1821 he was appointed to the chair of Sanskrit and comparative grammar in Berlin. His greatest work (written originally in German) is *A Comparative Grammar of Sanskrit, Zend, Greek, Latin, Lithuanian, Old Slavonic, Gothic and German* (6 vols, 1833–52).

Bór, General >> **Komorowski, Tadeusz**

Bora, Katherine von (1499–1552) German nun. Having adopted Lutheran doctrines, she ran away from the Cistercian convent of Nimptschen, near Grimma, in 1523, and married **Martin Luther** in 1525. >> Luther

Borah, William E(dgar) (1865–1940) US politician, born in Fairfield, IL. Elected Republican senator for Idaho in 1906, he advocated disarmament, and was instrumental in blocking the United States' entry into the League of Nations.

Bordeaux, Henri [baw(r)doh] (1870–1963) Writer, born in Thonon, France. He studied law before he took to writing novels concerned with the defence of family life, often with a Savoy background, such as *La Peur de vivre* (1902), *Les Roquevillard* (1906), and *La Maison* (1913).

Borden, Lizzie (Andrew) (1860–1927) Alleged murderess, born in Fall River, MA. In one of the most sensational murder trials in US history, she was accused of murdering her wealthy father and hated step-mother with an axe in 1892. She claimed to have been outside in the barn at the time of the murder, and despite a wealth of circumstantial evidence she was acquitted. She lived out her life in Fall River, and was buried alongside her father and step-mother. The case is immortalized in the rhyme *Lizzie Borden took an axe...*

Borden, Sir Robert (Laird) (1854–1937) Canadian statesman and prime minister (1911–20), born in Grand Pré, Nova Scotia, Canada. He practised as a barrister, became leader of the Conservative Party (1901), overthrew Laurier's Liberal government over the issue of reciprocity with the USA (1911), and became prime minister. He organized Canada for war, and was influential in arranging a separate Canadian membership in the League of Nations. >> RR1039

Border, Allan (Robert) (1955–) Cricketer, born in Sydney, New South Wales, Australia. Educated in Sydney, he became a professional cricketer in 1977, made his Test debut against England in 1978–9, and became captain in 1984–5. The Australian team was most successful under his leadership, regaining the Ashes in 1989 and retaining them in 1990–1 and 1993. A left-hander, he was Australia's most prolific batsman, and on his retirement in 1994 held Test records for the most catches (156), the most Test appearances (156), and having captained Australia in more Tests than any other captain (93). His most outstanding achievement is as the highest run-scorer in the history of Test cricket: in 1993 he beat Sunil Gavaskar's record with 10 123 runs, and he increased this record to a final 11 174 runs. He was Australian of the Year in 1990. >> Gavaskar

Bordet, Jules (Jean Baptiste Vincent) [baw(r)day] (1870–1961) Physiologist, born in Soignies, Belgium. He became director of the Pasteur Institute, Brabant (1901), professor at Brussels (1907), and recognized the immunity factors in blood serum. He discovered alexine and (1906) the microbe of whooping cough (Bordetella). He was awarded the 1919 Nobel Prize for Physiology or Medicine.

Bordone, Paris [baw(r)**doh**nay] (1500–71) Painter of the Venetian school, born in Treviso, Italy. He worked there and in Vicenza, Venice, and Paris. He was strongly influenced by his greater contemporary, Titian, his most celebrated work being 'Fisherman presenting the Ring of St Mark to the Doge' (1540, Venice Academia). >> Titian

Borel, (Félix Edouard Justin) Emile [borel] (1871–1956) Mathematician and French statesman, born in Saint Affrique, France. He studied then taught at the Ecole Normale Supérieure, and became professor at the Sorbonne in 1909. In addition to his mathematical work, he was active in politics, scientific popularization, and journalism; he was a member of the Chamber of Deputies (1924–36) and minister for the navy (1925–40). His mathematical work was mainly in analysis, measure theory, and probability. >> Lebesgue

Boreman, Arthur I(ngram) (1823–96) US governor and senator, born in Waynesburg, PA. A Virginia lawyer opposed to secession, he led the Wheeling Convention (1861) to establish a pro-union government in West Virginia, becoming the first governor (Republican, 1863–9) of the new state. In the US Senate (1869–75), he chaired the committee on the territories, returning to the law afterwards.

Borg, Björn (Rune) (1956–) Tennis player, born in Södertälje, Sweden. He left school at 14 to concentrate on tennis, and at 15 was selected for the Swedish Davis Cup team. He was Wimbledon Junior Champion at 16. In 1976 he won the first of his record five consecutive Wimbledon singles titles (1976–80). He also won the Italian championship twice and the French Open six times between 1974 and 1981. His Wimbledon reign ended in 1981 when he lost in the final to John McEnroe. He retired in 1983, having written his autobiography, *My Life and Games* (1980). >> McEnroe; RR1173

Borge, Victor [baw(r)guh] (1909–) Entertainer and pianist, born in Denmark. He studied at the Royal Danish Academy of Music, Copenhagen, and in Vienna and Berlin. He made his debut as a pianist in 1926, and as a revue actor in 1933. Since 1940 he has worked in the USA for radio, television, and theatre, and has performed with leading symphony orchestras on worldwide tours since 1956. He is best known for his comedy sketches combining music and narrative.

Borges, Jorge Luis [baw(r)khes] (1899–1986) Writer, born in Buenos Aires. He studied there and at Geneva and Cambridge. From 1918 he was in Spain, where he was a member of the avant-garde Ultraist literary group, returning to Argentina in 1921. His first book of poems, *Fervor de Buenos Aires*, was published in 1923, and in 1941 appeared the first collection of the intricate and fantasy-woven short stories for which he is famous. Later collections include *Ficciónes* (1944, 1946, Fictions), *El Aleph* (1949), and *El Hacedor* (1960, trans Dreamtigers).

Borgia, Cesare [baw(r)ja] (c.1476–1507) Italian soldier, born probably in Rome, the illegitimate son of Cardinal Rodrigo Borgia (later Pope Alexander VI), and brother of Lucrezia Borgia. He was appointed Archbishop of Valencia (1492) and a cardinal (1493) after his father's election to the papacy. In 1499 he succeeded his elder brother **Juan** (whom he was suspected of murdering) as captain-general of the papal army. In two campaigns, he made himself master of Romagna, Perugia, Siena, Piombini, and Urbino, and planned a kingdom of central Italy. After the death of Alexander (1502), his enemies rallied. He surrendered at Naples in 1504, was imprisoned, escaped in 1506, but soon after died while fighting for the King of Navarre. Though he remains a monster in the public perception, he was praised by Machiavelli as a model prince. He also encouraged art, and was the protector of Leonardo da Vinci. >> Alexander VI; Borgia, Lucrezia; Leonardo da Vinci; Machiavelli

Borgia, Lucrezia [baw(r)ja] (1480–1519) Noblewoman, born in Rome, the illegitimate daughter of Cardinal Rodrigo Borgia (later Pope Alexander VI), and the sister of Cesare Borgia. She was three times married to further her father's political ambitions. The third of these was in 1501, to **Alfonso** (1486–1534), son of the Duke of Este, who inherited the Duchy of Ferrara, where she established a brilliant court of artists and men of letters, and devoted herself to the patronage of art and education. Her reputation for wantonness and crime is more legend than fact. >> Alexander VI; Borgia, Cesare

Borgia, Rodrigo >> **Alexander VI**

Borglum, (John) Gutzon (de la Mothe) [baw(r)gluhm] (1867–1941) Sculptor, born in St Charles, ID. He won renown for works of colossal proportions, such as the famous Mt Rushmore National Memorial, hewn out of the mountainside (completed in 1939). Other huge works include the head of Lincoln in the US Capitol Rotunda.

Bork, Robert H(eron) (1927–) Legal scholar and judge, born in Pittsburgh, PA. After briefly practising law (1954–62), he joined the faculty of Yale Law School (1962–81), where he became known for his expertise in constitutional and anti-trust law. He was US solicitor general (1971–7) and acting attorney general (1973–4), and was appointed to the federal court of appeals for the District of Columbia (1982–8). President Reagan nominated him to the Supreme Court in 1987, but his conservative views led to his being rejected by a controversial US Senate vote. He stepped down from the bench in 1988 to write and lecture on judicial and public policy for the American Enterprise Institute.

Borlaug, Norman (Ernest) [baw(r)log] (1914–) Agricultural scientist, born in Cresco, IA. He studied at the University of Minnesota, and was research scientist at the Rockefeller Foundation's Co-operative Agriculture Program in Mexico (1944–60). During this period he developed strains of grain that greatly increased crop production, notably the tripling of Mexico's wheat yields. Dedicated to the alleviation of world hunger, he was director of both the Inter-America Food Crop Program (1960–3) and the International Maize and Wheat Improvement Center (1964–79). He received the Nobel Peace Prize in 1970.

Borman, Frank (1928–) Astronaut, born in Gary, IN. He trained at West Point, and became an air force pilot (1951–6). He studied aeronautical engineering at the California Institute of Technology, then taught at West Point and the Aerospace Research Pilots School. In 1962 NASA selected him for astronaut training. He was crew member of two historic missions: the Gemini 7 space endurance flight (1965) and the first manned flight around the Moon in Apollo 8 (1968). He worked for NASA until 1970, when he joined Eastern Airlines, becoming chairman of the board of directors in 1976.

Bormann, Martin (1900–?45) Nazi politician, born in Halberstadt, Germany. He participated in the abortive Munich putsch of 1923 and became one of Hitler's closest advisers. He was made *Reichsminister* (party chancellor) in 1941, and was with Hitler to the last. His own fate is uncertain, but he was possibly killed by Russian snipers in the mass breakout by Hitler's staff from the Chancellery (1945). A skeleton accidentally uncovered by an excavator in Berlin in 1972 has been officially recognized as his by forensic experts. >> Hitler

Born, Max (1882–1970) Physicist, born in Wrocław, Poland (formerly Breslau, Germany). He became professor of theoretical physics at Göttingen (1921–33), lecturer at Cambridge (1933–6), and professor of natural philosophy at Edinburgh (1936–53). In 1954 he shared the Nobel Prize for Physics with Walter Bothe for work in the field of quantum physics. >> Bothe; RR1122

Borodin, Alexander Porfiryevich [boro**deen**] (1833–87) Composer and scientist, born in St Petersburg, Russia. He showed a precocious aptitude for music, but was trained for medicine and distinguished himself as a chemist. His first systematic musical studies were undertaken in 1862, under Balakirev, who conducted his first symphony in 1869. His compositions include the unfinished opera, *Prince Igor* (edited and published by Rimsky-Korsakov), three symphonies, and the symphonic sketch *In the Steppes of Central Asia*. >> Balakirev; Rimsky-Korsakov

Borotra, Jean, nickname **the Bounding Basque** (1898–1994) Tennis player, born in Arbonne, near Biarritz, France. He won the men's singles title at Wimbledon in 1924, and his extraordinary fitness enabled him to compete in veterans' events at that same venue when he was almost 80. He also won the French and Australian championships, as well as several Davis Cup medals between 1927 and 1932. >> RR1173

Borovansky, Edouard [boro**van**skee] (1902–59) Dancer, choreographer, and ballet director, born in Přerov, Czech Republic. He studied at Prague's National Theatre and School, prior to dancing with Anna Pavlova's company. A soloist in the Ballet Russe de Monte Carlo (1932–9), he stayed on in Melbourne during an Australian tour, opening a ballet school with his wife **Xenia Nikolaeva** in 1940. Out of this grew the Borovansky Ballet (1942), which proved to be a major influence on the Australian Ballet when it was formed 20 years later. >> Pavlova

Borromeo, St Charles [boro**may**oh] (1538–84) Cardinal and archbishop, born in Arona, Italy. In 1560, at the age of 22, he was appointed Cardinal of Milan by his uncle, Pope Pius IV. He did much to bring the Council of Trent (1545–63) to a successful conclusion, and had the principal part in drawing up the famous *Catechismus romanus* (1566). He was renowned for his determined efforts to maintain ecclesiastical discipline and for his poor relief during the famine of 1570 and the plague of 1576. He also introduced the confessional box. In 1578 he founded the community later known as the Oblates of St Ambrose. He was canonized in 1610; feast day 4 November. >> Pius IV

Borromini, Francesco [boro**mee**nee], originally **Francesco Castello** (1599–1667) Baroque architect and sculptor, born in Bissone, Italy. He spent all his working life in Rome, where he was associated with his great rival Bernini in the Palazzo Berberini (1620–31) and the baldacchino in St Peter's (1631–3). His own chief buildings include the S Carlo alle Quattro Fontane (1641) and the oratorio of S Philippo Neri (1650). Although now considered one of the great Baroque architects, his influence was felt only after his death, and then more in N Italy and C Europe than in Rome. >> Bernini

Borrow, George (Henry) (1803–81) Writer and traveller, born in East Dereham, Norfolk, E England, UK. He was educated at Norwich, began to train as a solicitor, then worked for a publisher in London. From 1825 to 1832 he wandered in England, sometimes in gypsy company, as described in *Lavengro* (1851) and *The Romany Rye* (1857). As agent of the Bible Society he visited St Petersburg (1833–5),

Portugal, Spain, and Morocco (1835–9), and later visited SE Europe (1844) and Wales (1854).

Boru >> **Brian**

Borzov, Valeri [**baw(r)**zof] (1949–) Athlete, born in Sambor, Ukraine. At the 1972 Olympic Games in Munich he won both the 100 m and 200 m sprints, beating the Americans in what had become their monopoly events. >> RR1134

Bosch, Carl [bosh] (1874–1940) Chemist, born in Cologne, Germany, the brother-in-law of Fritz Haber. He became president of I G Farbenindustrie in 1925. He shared the Nobel Prize for Chemistry in 1931 for his part in the invention and development of chemical high-pressure methods, notably the *Haber–Bosch process*, by which hydrogen is obtained from water gas and superheated steam. >> Haber; RR1123

Bosch, Hieronymus, originally **Jerome van Aken** (c.1450–1516) Painter, named after the town in which he was born, 's Hertogenbosch in N Brabant, and in which he seems to have spent the whole of his life. He is noted for his allegorical pictures displaying macabre devils, freaks, and monsters. Among his best-known works are 'The Garden of Earthly Delights' (Prado) and 'The Temptation of St Anthony' (Lisbon). He had considerable influence on the Surrealists.

Bose, Sir Jagadis Chandra [bohs] (1858–1937) Physicist and botanist, born in Mymensingh, India. He became professor of physical science at Calcutta (1885–1915), then founded the Bose Research Institute there (1917–37). He was known for his study of electric waves, their polarization and reflection, and for his experiments demonstrating the sensitivity and growth of plants.

Bose, Subhas Chandra [bohs], known as **Netaji** ('Respected Leader') (c.1897–?1945) Indian Nationalist leader, who called for complete Indian independence, born in Cuttack, Orissa, India. Frequently imprisoned, he became president of the All-India Congress (1938–9). He supported the Axis in the war and became commander-in-chief of the Japanese-sponsored Indian National Army. He was reported killed in Formosa.

Bosman, Herman Charles (1905–51) Short-story writer, essayist, and novelist, born in Kuils River, near Cape Town, South Africa. His literary reputation has been largely posthumous. He taught in a remote country district near Groot Marico, in the Transvaal. This provided the setting for his short stories about rural Afrikaners – affectionate, sardonic, wry, and moving tales. He also wrote a memorable prison memoir, *Cold Stone Jug* (1949), and two novels.

Bossuet, Jacques Bénigne [bosway] (1627–1704) Catholic churchman, and pulpit orator, born in Dijon, France. He studied at Dijon and Paris, received a canonry at Metz (1652), and in 1661 preached before Louis XIV. His reputation as an orator spread over France, and he became tutor to the Dauphin. As Bishop of Meaux (1681) he took a leading part in the Gallican controversy, asserting the king's independence from the Roman Catholic Church in secular matters.

Boston, Ralph (1939–) Athlete, born in Laurel, MS. A leading long-jumper of the 1960s, he established an unusual treble by winning the gold medal at the 1960 Rome Olympics, a silver at Tokyo in 1964, and a bronze at Mexico City in 1968. He was the first man to jump over 27 ft/8·2 m.

Boston Strangler >> **Desalvo, Albert**

Boswell, James (1740–95) Man of letters and biographer of Dr Johnson, born in Edinburgh, EC Scotland, UK. He studied at Edinburgh High School and University, then studied civil law at Glasgow, but his ambition was literary fame. At 18 he began his often scandalous journal (only published in the 20th-c), and in 1760 ran away to London, where he led a debauched life. He first met Johnson in 1763, and took him on the memorable journey to the Hebrides. His *Journal of a Tour to the Hebrides* (1785) appeared after Johnson's death. Its success led him to plan his masterpiece, the *Life of Samuel Johnson* (1791). >> Johnson, Samuel

Bosworth, Joseph (1789–1876) Philologist, born in Derbyshire, C England, UK. Professor of Anglo-Saxon at Oxford from 1858, he compiled *An Anglo-Saxon Dictionary* (1838), and in 1867 gave £10 000 to endow a chair of Anglo-Saxon at Cambridge.

Both, Andries (c. 1612–41) Painter, born in Utrecht, The Netherlands, the brother of Jan Both. Traditionally he was thought to have collaborated with his brother by painting the figures in Jan's landscapes, but is now recognized as the author of paintings and drawings of genre scenes more akin to the work of Brouwer. >> Both, Jan; Brouwer

Both, Jan [bot] (c. 1618–52) Painter, born in Utrecht, The Netherlands, the brother of Andries Both, and a leading exponent of 'Italianate' landscape. He lived in Italy (1638–41) and there perfected his style of painting views of the Roman countryside bathed in a golden light and populated by picturesque peasants. >> Both, Andries

Botha, Louis [bohta] (1862–1919) South African soldier, statesman, and prime minister (1910–19), born in Greytown, Natal, South Africa. He succeeded Joubert (1900) as commander-in-chief of the Boer forces during the war, and in 1907 became prime minister of the Transvaal colony under the new constitution. In 1907 and 1911 he attended imperial conferences in London, and in 1910 became the first premier of the Union of South Africa. >> Joubert; RR1088

Botha, P(ieter) W(illem) [bohta] (1916–) South African statesman, prime minister (1978–84), and first state president (1984–9), born in Paul Roux, Orange Free State, South Africa. The longest-serving member of the South African Assembly (which he first entered in 1948), in his 14 years as minister of defence (1966–80) he presided over the controversial military intervention in Angola. He attempted to introduce constitutional reforms, but his plans led to wide international condemnation. In 1989 he suffered a stroke which compelled him to cede the state presidency to his party successor, F W de Klerk. >> de Klerk; RR1088

Botha, Roelof Frederik [bohta], known as **Pik Botha** (1932–) South African politician. After a career in the diplomatic service (1953–70), he entered politics and was elected to parliament. He became South Africa's permanent representative at the UN, then ambassador to the USA. He returned to domestic politics in 1977, becoming foreign minister in the government of P W Botha and that of F W de Klerk. In 1994–6 he served as minister for minerals and energy in Nelson Mandela's first cabinet. >> Botha, P W; de Klerk; Mandela, Nelson

Botham, Ian (Terence) [bohtham] (1955–) Cricketer, born in Heswall, Cheshire, NW England, UK. An all-rounder, he appeared in 102 Test matches for England, 65 of them consecutively, and including 12 as captain (1980–1). He held the record number of Test wickets (383 wickets at an average of 28·40 runs) until overtaken by Richard Hadlee, and has four times taken 10 wickets in a match. He scored 5200 runs in Tests (average 33·54), including 14 centuries. Off-the-field brushes with authority alternated with successful charity fund-raising campaigns such as his walk from John o' Groats to Land's End and his re-enactment of Hannibal's crossing of the Alps. He first played for Somerset in 1974, joined Worcester in 1987, and moved to Durham in 1992. He retired from first-class cricket in 1993. >> RR1149

Bothe, Walther (Wilhelm Georg) [bohtuh] (1891–1957) Physicist, born in Oranienburg, Germany. From 1934 he was head of the Max Planck Institute for Medical Research at Heidelberg. His work on the development of coincidence technique in counting processes brought him a share of the Nobel Prize for Physics in 1954. >> RR1122

Bothwell, James Hepburn, 4th Earl of (c.1535–78) Third husband of **Mary, Queen of Scots**. One of the greatest nobles in Scotland, he was held responsible for the abduction and murder of Mary's second husband, Lord Darnley (1567). He was made Duke of Orkney, then married Mary, but faced opposition from the nobles. He fled to Denmark after Mary's surrender to rebel forces at Carberry Hill, and was imprisoned in Dragsholm, where he died insane. >> Darnley; Mary, Queen of Scots

Botolph, St (?–c.680) Saxon abbot. He founded a monastery in 654 in Icanhoe (Ox Island), usually identified as Boston ('Botolph's Stone') in Lincolnshire, EC England. Feast day 17 June.

Bottesini, Giovanni [boteseenee] (1821–89) Musician, a master of the double bass, born in Crema, Italy. He was also successful as a conductor and composer, and his works include symphonies, overtures, and several operas, including *Cristoforo Colombo* (1847) and *Ali Babà* (1871).

Botticelli, Sandro [botichelee], originally **Alessandro Filipepi** (1445–1510) Painter, born in Florence, Italy. He trained, probably, under Filippo Lippi. By 1480 he had his own workshop, and was responsible for frescoes which form part of the 1482 scheme of decoration of the Sistine Chapel. He produced mostly religious works, but is best known for his treatments of mythological subjects, notably 'Primavera' (c.1477, Spring) and the 'Birth of Venus' (c.1485), both in the Uffizi. His work also includes portraits, and the illustrations for Dante's *Divina commedia*, which he executed in pen and ink and silverpoint. >> Lippi, Fra Filippo

Bottomley, Gordon (1874–1948) Poet and playwright, born in Keighley, West Yorkshire, N England, UK. He is best remembered for his *Poems of Thirty Years* (1925) and his collections of plays, including *King Lear's Wife and Other Plays* (1920). His poetry anticipated Imagism.

Botvinnik, Mikhail Moiseyevich [botveenik] (1911–95) Chess player, world champion (1948–57, 1958–60, 1961–3), born in St Petersburg, Russia. An electrical engineer by training, he won the 1948 tournament following the death of Alexander Alekhine. After regaining his title twice, from Vasily Smyslov and Mikhail Tal, he lost in 1963 to Tigran Petrosian, and devoted most of his remaining career to training Soviet players and to the development of chess computers. >> Petrosian; Smyslov; Tal; RR1149

Boucher, François [booshay] (1703–70) Painter, born in Paris. He worked on a range of material from stage design to tapestry, and from 1755 was director of the Gobelins factory. He is recognized as a leading Rococo painter at the court of Louis XV, where he produced several portraits of Madame de Pompadour. His work is usually considered, along with that of his pupil, Fragonard, as being wholly representative of the frivolous spirit of his age. >> Fragonard

Boucher (de Crèvecoeur) de Perthes, Jacques [booshay duh pairt] (1788–1868) Archaeologist, born in Rethel, France. From 1837 at Moulin-Quignon in the Somme valley he discovered flint hand axes in association with the bones of extinct animals, from which he drew conclusions about the great antiquity of the human race. His views were at first greeted with incredulity, but came to be upheld 20 years later.

Boucicault, Dion [booseekolt, -koh], originally **Dionysius Lardner Boursiquot** (1820–90) Playwright, actor, and theatre manager, born in Dublin. A versatile theatrical personality, he wrote or adapted some 130 plays, including *London Assurance* (1841) and *The Poor of New York* (1857), becoming one of the most popular playwrights of his era. Most of his plays are now forgotten, but *The Octoroon* (1860) is notable for its condemnation of slavery. He moved to America in 1853, where, along with George Henry Boker (1823–90) and others, he worked to pass the first American Copyright Law of 1856. He was later based in London (1862–72), then returned to the USA.

Boudicca [boodika, boodīka], also known as **Boadicea** (1st-c) British warrior-queen, wife of **Prasutagus**, king of the Iceni, a tribe inhabiting what is now Norfolk and Suffolk, E England. On her husband's death (60), the Romans seized her territory and treated the inhabitants brutally. She gathered a large army, destroyed the Roman colony of Camulodunum, took Londinium and Verulamium, and put to death as many as 70 000 Romans. Defeated in battle by Suetonius Paulinus, she took poison.

Boudin, (Louis) Eugène [boodī] (1824–98) Painter, born in Honfleur, France. A precursor of Impressionism, he is noted for his seascapes, which include 'On the Beach of Deauville' (1869, Louvre).

Bougainville, Louis Antoine, comte de (Count of) [booganveel] (1729–1811) Navigator, mathematician, and French soldier, born in Paris. He studied law and then mathematics, publishing an important treatise on integral calculus. Entering the French navy in 1763, he was responsible for colonizing the Falkland Is for France, and for their transfer to Spain. In command of the ships *La Boudeuse* and *L'Etoile*, he accomplished the first French circumnavigation of the world (1766–9), which he described in his *Voyage autour du monde* (1771, A Voyage round the World). The largest of the Solomon Is is named after him, as is the plant *bougainvillaea*. After the outbreak of the Revolution he devoted himself solely to scientific pursuits. Napoleon I made him a senator, count of the empire, and member of the Légion d'Honneur.

Boughton, Rutland (1878–1960) Composer, born in Aylesbury, Buckinghamshire, SC England, UK. Strongly influenced by Wagner's principles of music drama, and also by Socialist ideas, his aim was to develop an English style, with a strong choral element, his subjects based on British legend, and he founded the Glastonbury Festival (1914–26). His works include the opera *The Immortal Hour* (1913), a choral drama *Bethlehem* (1915), *The Queen of Cornwall* (1924), five music dramas (1908–45) intended to form an Arthurian cycle (never performed complete), and other stage, choral, and instrumental works.

Bouguer, Pierre [boohgair] (1698–1758) Physicist, born in Le Croisie, France. In 1735 he was sent with others to Peru to measure a degree of the meridian at the equator. His views on the intensity of light laid the foundation of photometry. In 1748 he invented the heliometer.

Bouillon, Godfrey of >> **Godfrey of Bouillon**

Boulanger, Georges (Ernest Jean Marie) [boolazhay] (1837–91) French soldier and statesman, born in Rennes, France. In 1886, as the protégé of Clemenceau, he was appointed minister of war. He introduced many reforms in soldiers' pay and living conditions and became a popular national figure. When he lost office in 1887, 'Boulanger fever' increased. Deprived of his command in 1888, he was elected deputy for Dordogne and Nord, and demanded a revision of the constitution. Fearing a coup, the government prosecuted Boulanger, who lost courage and fled the country.

Boulanger, Nadia [boolazhay] (1887–1979) Composer, born in Paris. She studied at the Conservatoire (1897–1904), where she won several prizes, and went on to write many

vocal and instrumental works, winning second prize at the Grand Prix de Rome in 1908 for her cantata, *La Sirène* (The Siren). After 1918 she devoted herself to teaching, first at home, and later at the Conservatoire and the Ecole Normale de Musique, where she had international influence. She was also a noted organist and conductor. Her sister, **(Marie-Juliette Olga) Lili Boulanger** (1893–1918), was also a composer.

Boule, (Pierre) Marcellin [bool] (1861–1942) Palaeontologist, born in Montsalvy, France. Professor at the Musée National d'Histoire Naturelle, he worked on the geology of the mountains of C France, and on human fossils. He made the first complete reconstruction of a Neanderthal skeleton.

Boulez, Pierre [boolez] (1925–) Conductor and composer, born in Montbrison, France. He studied at the Paris Conservatoire (1943–5), and became musical director of Barrault's Théâtre Marigny (1948), where he established his reputation as an interpreter of contemporary music. During the 1970s he devoted himself mainly to his work as conductor of the BBC Symphony Orchestra (1971–5) and of the New York Philharmonic (1971–7), before becoming director of the Institut de Recherche et de Co-ordination Acoustique Musique at the Pompidou Centre in Paris (1976–91). His early work as a composer rebelled against what he saw as the conservatism of such composers as Stravinsky and Schoenberg. Of his later works, *Le Marteau sans maître* (1955, The Hammer Without a Master) gained him a worldwide reputation, confirmed by *Pli selon pli* (Fold according to Fold) and his third piano sonata.

Boulle, André Charles >> **Buhl, André Charles**

Boullée, Etienne-Louis [boolay] (1728–99) Architect, born in Paris. He was elected to the Académie in 1762, and became architect to the King of Prussia. He was an important figure in the development of Neoclassicism in France, notable also for his visionary designs for ambitious projects of an austerely formal and geometric nature, such as the design (1784) for a colossal spherical monument to Isaac Newton.

Boult, Sir Adrian (Cedric) [bohlt] (1889–1983) Conductor, born in Chester, Cheshire, NW England, UK. After studying at Oxford and Leipzig, he conducted the City of Birmingham Orchestra (1924–30), and was then appointed musical director of the BBC and conductor of the newly formed BBC Symphony Orchestra. After his retirement from broadcasting in 1950, he was conductor-in-chief of the London Philharmonic Orchestra until 1957, and continued to conduct regularly until 1981. He was knighted in 1937.

Boulton, Matthew [bohltn] (1728–1809) Engineer, born in Birmingham, West Midlands, C England, UK. He entered into partnership with James Watt, and in 1774 they established a firm manufacturing steam engines, which proved remunerative only after 18 years. They also improved coining machinery. >> Watt, James

Boumédienne, Houari [boomaydyen], originally **Mohammed Boukharrouba** (1927–78) Algerian soldier, statesman, and president (1965–78), born in Guelma, Algeria. He studied at El Azhar University in Cairo, and became a teacher. In 1954 he joined the FLN (Algerian National Liberation Front) for whom he conducted guerrilla operations against the French, serving as chief-of-staff (1960–2) with the rank of colonel. When Algeria gained independence in 1962, he became minister of national defence. In 1965 he led a military coup against President Ben Bella and established an Islamic Socialist government. Shortly before his death, he was seeking to establish a North African Socialist federation. >> Ben Bella; RR1031

'Bourbaki, Nicolas' [boorbakee] (20th-c) The pseudonym of a group of mostly French mathematicians from the

Ecole Normale Supérieure, including Henri Cartan, Claude Chevalley, Jean Dieudonné, and André Weil. In the 1930s they conceived the plan of writing a treatise on pure mathematics which would set out the subject in a strictly logical development from its basic principles. Publication of *Eléments de mathématiques* by 'Nicolas Bourbaki' started in 1939, and continued until the 1980s, with books on several areas of mathematics, many of them highly influential. >> Cartan; Dieudonné; Weil, André

Bourbon, Charles de [boorbõ], known as **Constable de Bourbon** (1490–1527) French soldier, born in Montpensier, France. As son of the Count of Montpensier and of the only daughter of the Duke of Bourbon, he united the estates of both these branches of the Bourbon family. For his bravery at the Battle of Marignano (1515) he was made Constable of France; but losing the favour of Francis I he concluded a private alliance with the Emperor Charles V and Henry VIII of England. He invaded France in 1524, and was chief imperial commander at Pavia, in which Francis I was taken prisoner. He was made Duke of Milan, and commanded in N Italy, but was killed while attacking Rome in 1527. >> Francis I

Bourchier, Thomas [boorshyay] (c.1404–1486) English statesman and clergyman, an important figure during the Wars of the Roses. He became Bishop of Worcester (1434), of Ely (1444), Archbishop of Canterbury (1454), and a cardinal (1473). He was Lord Chancellor (1455–6), and crowned Edward IV (1461), Richard III (1483), and Henry VII (1485).

Bourdelle, (Emile) Antoine [boordel] (1861–1929) Sculptor, painter, and teacher, born in Montauban, France. He studied at the Ecole des Beaux-Arts, Paris, and under Rodin. He found inspiration in Greek art, relating its style to his own time. He illustrated a number of books, and his teaching had considerable influence. >> Rodin

Bourdon, Eugène [boordõ] (1808–84) Inventor and industrialist, born in Paris. In 1835 he founded a machine shop in Paris to manufacture model steam-engines for educational and demonstration purposes. In 1849 he patented a simple but ingenious device which is still in widespread use today for measuring the pressure of steam and many other fluids, the *Bourdon gauge*.

Bourgeois, Jeanne >> **Mistinguett**

Bourget, Paul (Charles Joseph) [boorzhay] (1852–1935) Writer, born in Amiens, France. He began as a poet and essayist, writing his first novel, *L'Irréparable* in 1884. Later works include *Le Disciple* (1889), *L'Etape* (1902), and *Un Divorce* (1904). In later years he became better known for his critical works.

Bourguiba, Habib (ibn Ali) [boorgeeba] (1903–) Tunisian politician, prime minister (1956–7), and president (1957–87), born in Monastir, Tunisia. He studied law in Paris and became a radical Tunisian nationalist in 1934. Over the next 20 years he served three prison sentences imposed by the French authorities. In 1956, however, his moderation led to his being accepted as Tunisia's first prime minister, becoming president in 1957. His authority was threatened by riots instigated by Islamic fundamentalists in 1983 and 1984, and subsequently he exercised little influence on policy. In 1987 he was deposed by his prime minister, General Ben Ali. >> RR1093

Bourignon, Antoinette [booreenyõ] (1616–80) Religious mystic, born in Lille, France. Believing herself called to restore the pure spirit of the Gospel, she fled from home and entered a convent. In Amsterdam (1667) she gathered followers and printed enthusiastic works, but was driven out. *Bourignonism* so prevailed in Scotland in c.1720 that until 1889 a solemn renunciation was demanded from every entrant into the ministry.

Bourke-White, Margaret [berk], originally **Margaret White** (1906–71) Photo-journalist, born in New York City. She studied at Columbia University, and started as an industrial and architectural photographer. She became a staff photographer and associate editor on *Life* magazine when it started publication in 1936. She covered World War 2 for *Life*, and was the first woman photographer to be attached to the US armed forces, producing reports of the siege of Moscow (1941) and the opening of the concentration camps in 1944. She was also an official UN war correspondent during the Korean War.

Bourne, Francis Alphonsus [baw(r)n] (1861–1935) Archbishop and cardinal, born in London, England, UK. He studied at St Sulpice, Paris, and Louvain University, and was ordained a priest (1884). He became Bishop of Southwark (1897), succeeded Vaughan as Archbishop of Westminster (1903), and was created a cardinal in 1911. He is remembered for his zeal for education, and his organization of the International Eucharistic Congress in 1908. >> Vaughan, Herbert

Bourne, Hugh [baw(r)n] (1772–1852) Founder of the Primitive Methodists, born in Fordhays, Staffordshire, C England, UK. His zeal as a Wesleyan preacher for large open-air meetings received no approval from the leaders of the denomination, and in 1808 he was cut off from the Wesleyan connection. He gathered round him many devoted followers, and formed a new group, adopting the title of Primitive Methodists in 1810; colloquially, they were sometimes also called Ranters. >> Clowes, William (1780–1851)

Bournonville, August [boornõveel] (1805–79) Dancer and choreographer, born in Copenhagen. After training with the Royal Danish Ballet, he moved to Paris (1926) to study at the Paris Opera. He spent the rest of his career (from 1828) with the Royal Danish Ballet, first as a dancer and (from 1830) as director. >> Vestris, Auguste

Boussingault, Jean-Baptiste (Joseph) [boosīgoh] (1802–87) Agricultural chemist, born in Paris. He studied at the School of Mines and at St Etienne, and became professor of chemistry at Lyon. He demonstrated that plants absorb nitrogen from the soil, and that carbon is assimilated by plants from the carbon dioxide of the atmosphere.

Boutros Ghali, Boutros [galee] (1922–) Egyptian diplomat, who took office as the sixth secretary-general of the United Nations (1992–7). The former deputy prime minister of Egypt, he was the first to hold the post from the Continent of Africa. He became head of La Francophonie in 1997.

Bouts, Dierick [bowts], also spelled **Dirk**, or **Thierry** (c.1415–75) Painter, born in Haarlem, The Netherlands. He is usually placed with the Flemish school. He worked at Louvain and Brussels, coming under the influence of Rogier van der Weyden, and produced austere religious paintings, with rich and gem-like colour. >> Weyden

Boveri, Theodor Heinrich [boveree] (1862–1915) Biologist and pioneer of cytology, born in Bamberg, Germany. He studied at Munich, and from 1893 taught zoology and anatomy at Würzburg. His studies of cell-division in the roundworm *Ascaris* and in sea-urchin eggs showed that normal development requires an appropriate number of chromosomes for the species, and that chromosome deficiency leads to abnormality.

Bovet, Daniel [bohvay] (1907–92) Pharmacologist, born in Neuchâtel, Switzerland. He studied chemistry at Geneva, and conducted research at the Pasteur Institute in Paris (1929–47), where he developed the first antihistamine drug and the first synthetic muscle-relaxants, for which he was awarded the 1957 Nobel Prize for Physiology or Medicine. In 1947 he emigrated to Italy, where later he was appointed professor of psychology at the University of Rome (1971–82).

Bow, Clara [boh] (1905-65) Film actress, born in New York City. After winning a beauty contest at 17, she went on to Hollywood stardom. She was chosen by Elinor Glyn to star in *It* (1927), the film adaptation of her novel, and Bow became popularly known as 'the It Girl'. Her films were box-office hits (1927-30), but her strong Brooklyn accent prevented her successful transition to sound, and she subsequently retired (1933).

Bowditch, Henry (Pickering) (1840-1911) Physiologist, born in Boston, MA. He interrupted his studies in Boston to fight in the American Civil War (1861-5). He then trained as a doctor at Harvard, and spent three years in Europe studying experimental physiology and microscopy. He produced important experimental work on cardiac contraction, on the innervation of the heart, and on the reflexes.

Bowditch, Nathaniel (1773-1838) Astronomer and mathematician, born in Salem, MA. Self-taught after age 10, he worked in a ship's chandlery, and by 15 had compiled an astronomical almanac. He went to sea (1795-1803), serving as master on his last voyage. He began by correcting errors in the writings of others, especially John Hamilton Moore's *Practical Navigator*; his contributions were so extensive that by 1802 the book became the *New American Practical Navigator* and was credited to him; it has remained to this day the 'seaman's bible'. He chose to pursue research on his own, while working as an insurance actuary. His publications include a translation of four volumes of Laplace's *Mécanique céleste*, which appeared with his commentary and updating as *Celestial Mechanics* (1829-39). He was also president of the American Academy of Arts and Sciences (1829-38). >> Laplace

Bowdler, Thomas [bowdler] (1754-1825) Doctor and man of letters, born in Ashley, Somerset, SW England, UK. He retired from medical practice and settled in the Isle of Wight to devote himself to literary pursuits. He is immortalized as the editor of *The Family Shakespeare* (10 vols, 1818), in which 'those words and expressions are omitted which cannot with propriety be read aloud in a family'. *Bowdlerizing* has since become a synonym for prudish expurgation.

Bowen, Elizabeth (Dorothea Cole) (1899-1973) Novelist and short-story writer, born in Dublin. She moved to England when she was seven, and later lived in London and Italy. In 1923 she published her first collection of short stories, *Encounters*. Her best-known novels are *The Death of the Heart* (1938) and *The Heat of the Day* (1949).

Bowen, Norman L(evi) (1887-1956) Geologist, born in Kingston, Ontario, Canada. He studied at Queen's University, Ontario, and became professor there (1919-21) and at Chicago (1937-47). He was a pioneer in the field of experimental petrology, particularly the study of silicates and igneous rocks.

Bowes-Lyon, Elizabeth >> **Elizabeth** (Queen Mother)

Bowie, David [bowee], originally **David Robert Jones** (1947-) Rock singer, born in London, England, UK. He changed his name in 1966 ('Bowie', a Western knife) to avoid confusion with another pop singer (David Jones of the Monkees). His early career was undistinguished and he came close to becoming a Buddhist monk before the success of 'Space Oddity' (1969) – a song based on the Kubrick film *2001: a Space Odyssey*. His career blossomed throughout the 1970s as he adopted a range of extreme stage images to suit a variety of musical styles. His albums have included *Hunky Dory* (1971), *The Rise and Fall of Ziggy Stardust and the Spiders from Mars* (1972), and *Heroes* (1977). He has also acted in films, including *The Man Who Fell to Earth* (1976), *Merry Christmas, Mr Lawrence* (1983), had a leading role in the animated film *Labyrinth* (1986), and starred in a long

Broadway run of *The Elephant Man*. Later films include *Basquiat* (1996).

Bowie, Jim [booee, bohee], popular name of **James Bowie** (c. 1796-1836) US pioneer, born in Logan Co, KY. After settling in Texas, he became a naturalized Mexican citizen. As a colonel in the Texan army, he was killed at the Battle of the Alamo. He may have been the inventor of the curved dagger or sheath-knife, that was later named after him.

Bowlby, (Edward) John (Mostyn) [bohlbee] (1907-90) British psychiatrist, the son of an eminent surgeon. He studied at Cambridge, and became staff psychologist at the London Child Guidance Clinic (1937-40). After World War 2 he moved to the Tavistock Clinic (1946-72), to become chairman of the department for children and parents (1946-68). His early research concerned crime and juvenile delinquency, but he is best known for his work on the effects of maternal deprivation upon the mental health and emotional development of children.

Bowles, Erskine [bowlz] (1945-) US public official. Educated at the University of North Carolina and Columbia University, he became an investment banker (1975-93) and administrator of the US Small Business Administration (1993-4). He joined the White House as deputy chief-of-staff (1994-5), and after returning to his business career (1995-6) became chief-of-staff in Clinton's second administration. >> Clinton, Bill

Bowles, Paul (Frederick) [bohlz] (1910-) Novelist, composer, poet, travel writer, and translator, born in New York City. After studying at the University of Virginia, he studied music in Paris, and became a composer and music critic. His first novel, *The Sheltering Sky*, appeared in 1949 and was acclaimed as being among the best post-war books. He became a resident of Tangier in 1952, and wrote three other novels, *Let It Come Down* (1952), *The Spider's House* (1955), and *Up Above the World* (1966). *Without Stopping* (1972) is an autobiography, and *Two Years beside the Strait* (1990) a journal of the years 1987-9.

Bowles, William Lisle [bohlz] (1762-1850) Clergyman and poet, born in King's Sutton, Northamptonshire, C England, UK. He studied at Oxford, became vicar of Bremhill in Yorkshire, and later was chaplain to the prince regent (1818). In his poetry he was a forerunner of the Romantic movement in English poetry. His *Fourteen Sonnets, Written Chiefly on Picturesque Spots During a Journey* (1789), published anonymously, was widely admired.

Bowman, Isaiah (1878-1950) Geographer, born in Waterloo, Ontario, Canada. He studied at Harvard and Yale, and became assistant professor at Yale (1909-15), during which time he joined three important expeditions to the Andes. He became director of the American Geographical Society (1915-35), and was appointed chief territorial specialist at the Versailles Peace Conference. He was also president of Johns Hopkins University (1935-48).

Bowman, Sir William (1816-92) Physician and ophthalmic surgeon, born in Nantwich, Cheshire, NWC England, UK. With **Richard B Todd** (1809-60) he published *Physiological Anatomy and Physiology of Man* (1845-56). He gained a high reputation for his work on the mechanism of kidney function, and also for his *Lectures on Operations on the Eye* (1849), describing the ciliary muscle.

Bowyer, William (1699-1777) Printer and Classical scholar. He studied at Cambridge, and in 1722 went into partnership with his father, **William Bowyer** (1663-1737). In 1767 he was nominated printer to the Houses of Parliament. His chief production was a Greek New Testament.

Boyce, William (1710-79) Composer, born in London, England, UK. In 1736 he was appointed composer to the Chapel Royal and, in 1758, organist. He held a high rank as a composer of choral and orchestral music, and his works include the song 'Hearts of Oak', the serenata of *Solomon* (1743), and a valuable collection of *Cathedral Music* (1760).

Boycott, Charles Cunningham (1832–97) British army captain and estate manager, born in Burgh St Peter, Norfolk, E England, UK. He was the agent for Lord Erne in Co Mayo, Ireland, when bad harvests in 1879 made famine likely, and the Land League under Parnell requested lower rents to ease the tenants' burden. When Boycott tried to evict tenants in 1880, Parnell suggested they avoid any form of contact or communication with Boycott. His name thus became the source of the verb *to boycott*.

Boycott, Geoffrey (1940–) Cricketer and broadcaster, born in Fitzwilliam, West Yorkshire, N England, UK. He gained his county cap for Yorkshire in 1963, and was capped for England the following year. He played 108 times for England (1964–82), scoring 8114 runs (average 47·72), in 1981 overtaking Gary Sobers' world record of 8032 Test runs. Total runs in his career were 48 426 (average 56·83). Captain of Yorkshire (1971–8), he was a controversial batsman, and the county was divided about the value of his contribution to the club. Since retiring from first-class cricket in 1986, he has become known as a cricket commentator. Among his books is *Boycott on Cricket* (1990). >> Sobers; RR1149

Boyd, Anne (1946–) Composer and flautist, born in Sydney, New South Wales, Australia. She studied composition there and at York University, UK. After some years teaching in England and Australia, she became founding head of the department of music at Hong Kong University (1981). Her interest in ethno-musicology, in Australian aboriginal music, and the ethnic music of Japan and Java, is reflected in such compositions as *As I Crossed the Bridge of Dreams* and her children's opera, *The Little Mermaid*.

Boyd, Arthur Merric (1862–1940) Painter, born in Opoho, New Zealand. He arrived in Australia in 1886, and became particularly known for his watercolours. >> Boyd, Martin; Boyd, Merric

Boyd, Arthur Merric Bloomfield (1920–) Painter, sculptor, and potter, born in Murrumbeena, Victoria, Australia, the younger son of Merric Boyd. He studied at the National Gallery of Victoria Art School and at Rosebud, Victoria. After the war he exhibited with the Contemporary Arts Society in Melbourne, then returned to Murrumbeena and the pottery established by his father, where he worked with his brother-in-law John Perceval. He moved to London in 1959, and took up a fellowship in creative arts at the Australian National University, Canberra, in 1972. In 1993 he gave his 1000 ha property 'Bundanon' as a gift to Australia. >> Boyd, Guy Martin; Boyd, Merric; Perceval, John

Boyd, Benjamin (c. 1796–1851) Australian colonist, born at Merton Hall, near Newton Stewart, Dumfries and Galloway, SW Scotland, UK. He arrived in Hobson's Bay in 1842, and became one of the largest and most powerful squatters in SE New South Wales. He spent a fortune trying to found 'Boyd Town' as a commercial port. When the enterprise failed, he sailed off in 1849 to join the Gold Rush in California.

Boyd, Guy Martin (à Beckett) (1923–) Sculptor, born in Murrumbeena, Victoria, Australia, the elder son of Merric Boyd. Starting as a potter, he moved on to sculpture in 1964. His commissions include mural reliefs for Tullamarine (Melbourne) and Kingsford Smith (Sydney) airports. >> Boyd, Arthur Merric Bloomfield; Boyd, Merric

Boyd, Martin (à Beckett), pseudonyms **Martin Mills** and **Walter Beckett** (1893–1972) Writer and poet, born in Lucerne, Switzerland, the younger son of Arthur Merric

Boyd. Brought up in Melbourne, he lived for much of his life in Britain. His first novels, such as *The Montforts* (1928), appeared under pseudonyms. His best work is now referred to as the Langton tetralogy: *The Cardboard Crown* (1952), *A Difficult Young Man* (1955), *Outbreak of Love* (1957), and *When Blackbirds Sing* (1962). >> Boyd, Arthur Merric; Boyd, Merric

Boyd, (William) Merric (1888–1959) Ceramic artist, born in St Kilda, Victoria, Australia, the elder son of Arthur Merric Boyd. He studied at the pioneering porcelain works at Yarraville, Victoria, and then served with the Royal Flying Corps in World War 1 at Wedgwood, Stoke-on-Trent. He returned to Australia in the early 1920s, founding a famous studio at Murrumbeena, outside Melbourne, and experimenting with new ceramic techniques. >> Boyd, Arthur Merric; Boyd, Arthur Merric Bloomfield; Boyd, Guy

Boyd, Robin Gerard Penleigh (1919–71) Architect, critic, and writer, born in Melbourne, Victoria, Australia. He reached a wide audience with his books *Australia's Home* (1952), *The Australian Ugliness* (1960), and *The Great Australian Dream* (1972). His critical work shaped the direction of Australian architecture and was acknowledged with several awards.

Boyd, William (Andrew Murray) (1952–) Novelist, born in Accra, Ghana. His early years were spent in Ghana and Nigeria, and he then attended Gordonstoun school, Scotland. He taught English at Oxford until 1982. His novels, which often have an African setting, include *A Good Man in Africa* (1981, filmed 1994), *Brazzaville Beach* (1990, James Tait Black), *The Blue Afternoon* (1993), and *The Destiny of Nathalie 'X'* (1995). His writing also includes short stories and the screenplays *Good and Bad at Games* (1985), *Scoop* (1987), and *Chaplin* (1992).

Boyd, William (Clouser) (1903–) Biochemist, born in Dearborn, MS. He studied at Harvard, and from 1948 taught at the Boston medical school as professor of immunochemistry. He examined racial groups by systematically classifying blood samples on a worldwide basis. By 1950, in his book *Genetics and the Races of Man*, he was able to present evidence for the existence of 13 human races, distinguishable by blood type.

Boyd Orr (of Brechin Mearns), John Boyd Orr, Baron (1880–1971) Biologist, born in Kilmaurs, East Ayrshire, SW Scotland, UK. He studied at Glasgow University, became director of the Rowett Research Institute and professor of agriculture at Aberdeen (1942–5), and was the first director of the UN Food and Agriculture Organization (1945–8). His pessimistic reports on the world food situation got him a reputation as an apostle of gloom, but his great services in improving that situation brought him the Nobel Peace Prize in 1949, in which year he was made a peer.

Boye, Karin (Maria) (1900–41) Poet and novelist, born in Göteborg, Sweden. She studied at Uppsala and Stockholm, and became a leader of the Socialist *Clarté* movement. She was the founder editor of the poetry magazine *Spektrum* (1931), to which she contributed much of her own poetry and translations. Her poetry collections include *Moln* (1922, Cloud), and *De Sju Dödsynderna* (1941, The Seven Deadly Sins), and she wrote several novels, including *Kris* (1934, Crisis) and *Kallocain* (1940).

Boyer, Charles [boyay] (1899–1978) Actor, born in Figeac, France. He studied at the Sorbonne and the Paris Conservatoire. Having become established as a star of the French stage and cinema, he settled in Hollywood in 1934, and was known as the screen's 'great lover' from such romantic roles as *Mayerling* (1936), *The Garden of Allah* (1936), and *Algiers* (1938). His later appearances included *Barefoot in the Park* (1967) and *Stavisky* (1974). In 1943 he received a special Academy Award for his work in promoting Franco-American cultural relations.

Boyer, Herbert (Wayne) [boyer] (1936–) Biochemist, born in Pittsburgh, PA. He studied at Pittsburgh, and from 1966 worked at the University of California, San Francisco. In collaboration with **Stanley Cohen** (1935–) of Stanford University, he successfully spliced a gene from a plasmid of one organism into the plasmid of another (1973). The technique they developed became the foundation of genetic engineering.

Boyer, Jean Pierre [boyay] (1776–1850) Haitian politician, mulatto-born in Port-au-Prince. Sent early to France, in 1792 he entered the army. He distinguished himself against the British during their invasion of Haiti, and established an independent republic in the W part of the island. After the death of Christophe, he united the negro district with the mulatto in 1820. He governed Haiti well for 15 years, but his partiality towards the mulattos made the pure negroes rise in 1843. He fled, and died in Paris. >> Christophe

Boyer, Sir Richard (James Fildes) [boyer] (1891–1961) Broadcasting administrator, born in Taree, New South Wales, Australia. He was a member of the Australian delegation to the League of Nations in 1939, and was appointed to the Australian Broadcasting Commission in 1940. After Prime Minister Curtin affirmed the independence of the Australian Broadcasting Company, Boyer accepted the chairmanship in 1945. The ABC Lectures were renamed the *Boyer Lectures* in his honour after his death.

Boyis, Hector >> **Boece, Hector**

Boyle (of Handsworth), Sir Edward (Charles Gurney) Boyle, Baron (1923–81) British statesman and educational administrator. He studied at Oxford, and was Conservative MP for the Handsworth Division of Birmingham (1950–70), parliamentary secretary at the Ministry of Education (1957–59) and minister of education (1962–4). He was also Vice-Chancellor of Leeds University (1970–81).

Boyle, Jimmy, popular name of **James Boyle** (1944–) Convicted murderer, born in the Gorbals, Glasgow, W Scotland, UK. A member of a powerful gang in Glasgow, he was twice charged with murder and cleared, and was eventually imprisoned for serious assault. His reputation as 'Scotland's Most Violent Man' appeared to be confirmed when he was convicted for the murder of Babs Rooney and given a life sentence. In 1973 he was one of the first offenders to participate in Barlinnie Prison Special Unit's rehabilitation programme. He went on to produce many sculptures, and to write his autobiography, *A Sense of Freedom* (1977). After his release, he worked with young offenders and has become Scotland's most celebrated reformed criminal.

Boyle, Kay (1902–92) Novelist, short story writer, poet, and essayist, born in St Paul, MN. She was educated in the USA, studying music and architecture, then lived in Europe for 30 years as part of the literary fraternity of Paris's Left Bank, and as a correspondent for *The New Yorker* (1946–53). Her novels include *Plagued by the Nightingale* (1931) and *Generation Without Farewell* (1960), but she is particularly known for her several volumes of short stories, such as *The Smoking Mountain* (1951). She was accused of being a Communist in the McCarthy witch-hunts in the 1950s, and was outspoken against US involvement in Vietnam. >> McCarthy, Joseph

Boyle, Robert (1627–91) Chemist and natural philosopher, born at Lismore Castle, Co Waterford, Ireland. He studied at Eton, went to the European mainland for six years, then devoted himself to science. Settling at Oxford in 1654, with Robert Hooke as his assistant, he carried out experiments on air, vacuum, combustion, and respiration. In 1661 he published his *Sceptical Chymist*, in which he criticized the current theories of matter, and defined the chemical element as the practical limit of chemical analysis. In 1662 he arrived at *Boyle's law*, which states that the pressure and volume of gas are inversely proportional. He also researched into calcination of metals, properties of acids and alkalis, specific gravity, crystallography, and refraction, and first prepared phosphorus. As a director of the East India Company (for which he had procured the Charter) he worked for the propagation of Christianity in the East, circulated at his own expense translations of the Scriptures, and by bequest founded the *Boyle Lectures* in defence of Christianity. >> Hooke; Mariotte; van der Waals

Boys, Sir Charles Vernon (1855–1944) Physicist, born in Wing, Leicestershire, C England, UK. His many inventions include an improved torsion balance, the radiomicrometer, a calorimeter, and a camera with moving lens, with which he photographed lightning flashes.

Brabazon (of Tara), John Theodore Cuthbert Moore-Brabazon, Baron (1884–1964) British statesman and aviator, the first holder of a flying licence. He studied at Cambridge, and during World War 1 served with the Royal Flying Corps. He was responsible for several innovations in aerial photography. In 1918 he entered parliament and became private parliamentary secretary to Churchill at the War Office. Between 1923 and 1927 he served two periods of office as parliamentary secretary to the ministry of transport. He became minister of transport (1940) and of aircraft production (1941), but resigned because of public displeasure at his outspoken criticism of Britain's ally, the USSR.

Brabham, Jack [brabuhm], popular name of **Sir John Arthur Brabham** (1926–) Motor-racing driver, born in Sydney, New South Wales, Australia. He served with the Royal Australian Air Force, and started his racing career in 1947. After winning the Australian Grand Prix in 1955, he went to the UK, where he joined the successful Cooper team. He won his first Formula 1 World Drivers' Championship at Sebring, FL, in 1959 by pushing his car over the finishing-line, and won the title again the following year. In 1966 he won his third world title, and also the Constructor's Championship, with a car of his own design, the Repco-Brabham. He retired from the circuits in 1970, and was knighted in 1979. >> RR1164

Brace, Charles Loring (1826–90) Philanthropist and social reformer, born in Litchfield, CT. He founded the Children's Aid Society in 1853, and pioneered philanthropic methods based on self-help.

Bracegirdle, Anne (c. 1663–1748) English actress. She was renowned for her beauty, and for her performances (1688–1707) in the plays of Congreve at Drury Lane under Betterton (c.1635–1710). She is believed to have been married to **William Congreve**, and was buried in Westminster Abbey. >> Congreve, William

Bracken, Thomas (1843–98) Poet and journalist, born in Co Monaghan, Ireland. He settled in Dunedin, New Zealand, in 1869, and came to be regarded as the local equivalent of Tennyson and Longfellow. His reputation declined in the 1930s, but he is remembered as the author of the national anthem, 'God Defend New Zealand!'. >> Longfellow; Tennyson

Bracton, Henry de (?–1268) English jurist, a 'justice itinerant', who in 1264 became archdeacon of Barnstaple and chancellor of Exeter Cathedral. His *De legibus et consuetudinibus Angliae* (On the Laws and Customs of England) is the earliest attempt at a systematic treatment of the body of English law.

Bradbury, Malcolm (1932–) Writer and critic, born in Sheffield, West Yorkshire, N England, UK. He studied at Leicester, and taught there at the university, before becoming professor of American studies at the University of East Anglia in 1970. The travels and travails of an academic have provided material for several of his novels, such as *Eating People is Wrong* (1959), *Stepping Westward* (1965), *The History Man* (1975, also a television series), and *Rates of Exchange* (1982). His work for television inspired the novella *Cuts* (1987); these worlds collide in *Dr Criminale* (1992). In his critical writing, he has sponsored Modernist and post-Modernist ideas, and his books include monographs on Evelyn Waugh (1962) and Saul Bellow (1982), and *The Modern American Novel* (1983). Later works include the comic fiction anthology *Present Laughter* (1994) and *The Atlas of Literature* (1996).

Bradbury, Ray(mond Douglas) (1920–) Writer of science fiction, born in Waukegan, IL. An avid reader of sensational fiction and comics, he began early to contribute to magazines and short-story anthologies. While he has written notable novels – *Fahrenheit 451* (1953), *Dandelion Wine* (1957), and *Death is a Lonely Business* (1985) – he is primarily a short-story writer, and has created some of the finest examples in the genre. Well-known stories include *The Day It Rained Forever*, *R is for Rocket*, and those collected as *The Martian Chronicles* (1950, filmed 1966). Later novels include *A Graveyard for Lunatics* (1990), *White Whale* (1992), and *Quicker than the Eye* (1996).

Braddock, Edward (1695–1755) British general, born in Perth and Kinross, E Scotland, UK. After service in France and The Netherlands, he was appointed commander of all British troops in North America (1754). He was sent in 1755 to expel the French from Fort Duquesne (now Pittsburgh), but was defeated by the French and their Indian allies, and was mortally wounded in the battle. The remnants of his force were led away by George Washington. >> Dinwiddie; Washington, George

Braddock, James J(oseph), nickname **the Cinderella Man** (1905–74) World heavyweight champion boxer, born in New York City. He was defeated in a light-heavyweight contest in 1929 and seemed destined for oblivion, especially after breaking both hands in a fight in 1933. But he fought his way back, and shocked the boxing world when he defeated Max Baer (1909–59) on points for the world heavyweight title in 1935 – a comeback that earned him his nickname. He lost the title in 1937 to Joe Louis. >> Louis, Joe; RR1148

Braddon, Russell Reading (1921–) Writer, playwright, and film and television script-writer, born in Sydney, New South Wales, Australia. He studied at Sydney University, and during World War 2 was a prisoner of the Japanese for four years, and worked on the Burma Railway. His experiences were published as *The Naked Island* (1952) and *End of a Hate* (1958). A string of popular novels followed, but he is perhaps best known for his biographies, such as *Cheshire VC* (1954), *Nancy Wake* (1956), and *Joan Sutherland* (1962).

Braden, Bernard (1916–93) Radio and television presenter, born in Canada. Educated in Vancouver, he became an engineer, announcer, and radio actor in local radio (1937–43), and also for the Canadian Broadcasting Corporation (1940–9). In England from 1949, he acted in various plays, including *A Street Car Named Desire*. Joining the BBC, he presented radio shows such as *Breakfast with Braden*, often co-presenting with his wife, **Barbara Kelly** (married 1942), and became a popular host of several TV series, such as *The Brains Trust*, *On the Braden Beat*, and *All Our Yesterdays*.

Bradfield, John Job Crew (1867–1943) Civil engineer and designer, born in Sandgate, Queensland, Australia. He studied at Sydney University, and designed the bridge across Sydney Harbour, eventually opened in 1932. He also planned an underground electric railway system for Sydney, and designed many other bridges, dams, and highways.

Bradford, Barbara Taylor (1933–) Journalist and novelist, born in Leeds, West Yorkshire, N England, UK. She joined the *Yorkshire Evening Post* as reporter (1949–51) and women's editor (1951–3), became fashion editor of *Woman's Own* (1953–4), a columnist on *The London Evening News* (1955–7), and executive editor of *The London American* (1959–62). Moving to the USA, she worked as a columnist for leading newspapers, including the Chicago Tribune/New York Daily News Syndicate (1970–5) and the Los Angeles Times Syndicate (1975–81). She gained success with her first novel, *Woman of Substance* (1980), and later books include *Hold the Dream* (1985), *The Women in his Life* (1990), and *Her Own Rules* (1996).

Bradford, William (1590–1657) Colonist and religious leader, born in Austerfield, South Yorkshire, N England, UK. A Nonconformist from boyhood, he joined a separatist group in 1606 and went with them to Holland in 1609. One of the moving spirits in the Pilgrim Fathers' expedition to the New World in 1620, he sailed on the *Mayflower*, and in 1621 took over from John Carver as elected governor of Plymouth Colony. >> Carver, John

Bradlaugh, Charles [**brad**law] (1833–91) Social reformer and free-thinker, born in London, England, UK. He became a busy secularist lecturer and pamphleteer under the name of 'Iconoclast'. In 1880 he was elected MP for Northampton but, as an unbeliever, he refused to take the oath, and was expelled and re-elected regularly until 1886, when he took the oath and his seat. In 1886 he was prosecuted, with Annie Besant, for republishing a pamphlet advocating birth control (*The Fruits of Philosophy*); the conviction was subsequently quashed on appeal. >> Besant, Annie; Stopes

Bradlee, Benjamin (Crowninshield) (1921–) Journalist and writer, born in Boston, MA. A founder of the *New Hampshire Sunday News*, he subsequently joined the *Washington Post* and worked for *Newsweek*. His book *Conversations with Kennedy* appeared in 1975. In 1965 he became managing editor of the *Washington Post*, and encouraged the investigative journalism which reached its high point in the Watergate scandal. >> Nixon

Bradley, A(ndrew) C(ecil) (1851–1935) Critic, born in Cheltenham, Gloucestershire, SWC England, UK, the brother of Francis Herbert Bradley. He studied at Balliol College, Oxford, where he became a fellow in 1874. He was professor of literature and history at Liverpool (1882), of English language and literature at Glasgow (1890), and of poetry at Oxford (1901–6). He made his name with his magisterial *Shakespearean Tragedy* (1904). >> Bradley, F H

Bradley, F(rancis) H(erbert) (1846–1924) Philosopher, born in Clapham, Surrey, SE England, UK, the brother of Andrew Cecil Bradley. He became a fellow of Merton College, Oxford (1870), but a kidney disease caused him to live as a semi-invalid most of his life. He was probably the most important figure in the British idealist movement of this period, and was much influenced by Kant and Hegel. His most important works are *Ethical Studies* (1876), *Principles of Logic* (1883), and the highly original and influential *Appearance and Reality* (1893). >> Bradley, A C

Bradley, Henry (1845–1923) British philologist and lexicographer. In 1886 he became joint editor of the *Oxford English Dictionary* with Sir James Murray, and senior editor in 1915. He wrote *The Making of English* (1904) and *English Place-Names* (1910). >> Murray, James

Bradley, James (1693–1762) Astronomer, born in Sherborne, Gloucestershire, SWC England, UK. He studied at Oxford, and became professor of astronomy there in 1721. In 1742 he succeeded Edmond Halley as professor of astronomy at Greenwich. He published his discovery of the aberration of light (1729), providing the first observational proof of the Copernican hypothesis. In 1748 he discovered that the inclination of the Earth's axis to the ecliptic is not constant. >> Halley

Bradley, Omar N(elson) (1893–1981) US general, born in Clark, MO. He trained at West Point, and entered the army in 1915. A brigadier in 1941, he commanded II Corps in Tunisia and Sicily (1943). In 1944 he commanded the US forces at the Normandy invasion, and later the US 12th Army Group through France. He became the first permanent chairman of the US joint chiefs-of-staff (1949–53), and in 1950 was promoted to five-star general.

Bradman, Sir Don(ald George) (1908–) Cricketer, born in Cootamundra, New South Wales, Australia. One of the greatest batsmen in the history of the game, he played for Australia from 1928 to 1948 (captain, 1936–48). He made the highest aggregate and largest number of centuries in Tests against England, and holds the record for the highest Australian Test score against England (334 at Leeds in 1930). His batting average in Test matches was 99·94 runs per innings. The first Australian cricketer to be knighted (1949), he was chairman of the Australian Cricket Board (1960–3, 1969–72). >> RR1149

Bradshaw, George (1801–53) Printer and Quaker, born in Salford, Greater Manchester, NW England, UK. He became a Manchester mapmaker, but is best known for the series of railway guides (*Bradshaws*) which he originated in 1839.

Bradshaw, John (1602–59) Judge, born near Stockport, Greater Manchester, NW England, UK. Called to the bar in 1627, he held various appointments before being made president in 1649 at the trial of Charles I. He was made permanent president of the Council of State and Chancellor of the Duchy of Lancaster. However, his 'stiff republicanism' estranged him from Cromwell. >> Cromwell, Oliver

Bradstreet, Anne, *née* **Dudley** (1612–72) Puritan poet, born probably in Northampton, Northamptonshire, C England, UK. In 1628 she married a Nonconformist minister, **Simon Bradstreet** (1603–97), who later became Governor of Massachusetts. In 1630 they emigrated to New England with the Winthrops. Her first volume of poems, *The Tenth Muse Lately Sprung Up in America*, was published by her brother-in-law in London in 1650 without her knowledge. She is considered the first English poet in America. >> Winthrop, John (1588–1649)

Brady, Ian (1938–) Convicted murderer, born in Glasgow, W Scotland, UK. He was found guilty of the murder of two children, John Kilbride (12) and Lesley Ann Downey (10), and a 17-year-old boy, Edward Evans, in 1966. In a case which horrified the public, it was revealed that Brady, with his lover **Myra Hindley** (1942–), from Gorton, lured young children into their home in Manchester and subjected them to torture before killing them. The lovers were described as the 'Moors Murderers' because they buried most of their victims on Saddleworth Moor in the Pennines. Hindley confessed to two other murders in 1986.

Brady, James Buchanan, nickname **Diamond Jim Brady** (1856–1917) Financier, born in New York City. He worked for the New York Central Railroad, became a salesman of railroad equipment (1879), and in 1888 was the only agent in the USA for the Fox Pressed Steel Car Truck Company of England. Known for living in high style as one of the great Broadway 'sports', he wore diamond jewellery estimated at $2 million in value. But he remained a serious businessman, accumulating a large fortune, much of which he gave for urological studies at Johns Hopkins University and New York City Hospital.

Brady, Matthew (1799–1826) Bushranger, born in Manchester, Greater Manchester, NW England, UK. In 1820, for stealing a basket of groceries, he was transported for seven years to New South Wales. From there he was sent in 1823 to the penal colony of Macquarie Harbour in Van Diemen's Land (now Tasmania), a penal station for desperate criminals. He escaped with a small group in the following year, and with his gang terrorized the island. He was eventually captured, and hanged in Hobart.

Brady, Matthew (1823–96) Photographer, born near Lake George, NY. He operated a portrait studio in New York City using daguerreotype from 1844, but gave it up to take on a major project to record the American Civil War with the Union armies. Although widely acclaimed, this effort ruined him financially and, despite a belated government grant, he died in poverty in a New York City almshouse.

Brady, Nicholas >> **Tate, Nahum**

Bragg, Braxton (1817–76) US general, born in Warrenton, NC. A Confederate commander, he fought in several great battles of the Civil War, but though successful at Chickamauga, his tenure of command was ultimately disappointing. After the war he became a civil engineer.

Bragg, Sir (William) Lawrence (1890–1971) Physicist, born in Adelaide, South Australia, the son of Sir William Henry Bragg. Father and son shared the 1915 Nobel Prize for Physics for their work on X-ray crystallography. He was professor of physics at Victoria University, Manchester (1919–37) and headed the Cavendish Laboratory in Cambridge (1938–53), where he supported Crick and Watson in their work, using X-ray crystal studies to deduce the helical structure of DNA. He was knighted in 1941, and was also director of the Royal Institution (1954–65). >> Bragg, William Henry; Crick; Watson, James

Bragg, Mabel Caroline, pseudonym **Watty Piper** (1870–1945) Writer and educator, born in Milford, MA. She taught at the Rhode Island State Normal School (1889–1909), worked in publishing, and embarked on a career in education in Newton, MA (1916–30) and Boston University (1930–40). She is also known for her children's books, notably *The Little Engine That Could* (1945).

Bragg, Melvyn (1939–) Novelist and broadcaster, born in Wigton, Cumbria, NW England, UK. He studied at Oxford, and joined the BBC as a producer in 1961, publishing his first novel, *For Want of a Nail*, in 1965. Later novels include *The Hired Man* (1969), *The Silken Net* (1974), *Love and Glory* (1983), *A Time to Dance* (1990), *Crystal Rooms* (1992), and *Credo* (1996). His other writing includes screenplays and musicals. He has been presenter and editor of ITV's *The South Bank Show* since 1978, and presenter of BBC Radio 4's *Start the Week* since 1988. He was head of arts (later, controller) at London Weekend Television (1982–90), and became chairman of Border Television in 1990.

Bragg, Sir William (Henry) (1862–1942) Physicist, born in Wigton, Cumbria, NW England, UK. With his son, William Lawrence Bragg, he founded X-ray crystallography. After studying at Cambridge, he became professor of mathematics at Adelaide, Australia (1886), and professor at Leeds in 1909, where from 1912 he worked in conjunction with his son. They were awarded a joint Nobel Prize for Physics in 1915, the only father–son partnership to share this honour. Bragg moved to University College, London the same year, and became director of the Royal Institution in 1923. >> Bragg, Lawrence

Brahe, Tycho [**brah**hoe, **tiy**koh] (1546–1601) Astronomer, born in Knudstrup, Sweden. In 1573 he discovered serious errors in the astronomical tables, and commenced work to rectify this by observing the stars and planets with unprecedented positional accuracy. He rejected the Copernican theory, but it fell to Kepler to show this model to be essentially correct, using Brahe's data. >> Copernicus; Kepler

Brahms, Johannes (1833–97) see panel below

Braid, James (?1795–1860) Surgeon and hypnotist, born in Rylawhouse, Fife, E Scotland, UK. He studied at Edinburgh University, and spent most of his life practising surgery in Manchester. In 1841 he attended a popular demonstration of 'Mesmerism' and devoted much of the rest of his working life to investigating the phenomena associated with what he himself first called *neurohypnotism*, later shortened to *hypnotism*.

Braid, James (1870–1950) Golfer, born in Earlsferry, Fife, E Scotland, UK. He trained as a joiner, and went to work in St Andrews, the home of golf, where he became an outstanding player. He won the Open championship five times (1901–10), four *News of the World* matchplay championships (1903–11), and the French Championship (1910). With Harry Vardon and John Henry Taylor he formed what was known as the 'Great Triumvirate' of British golf in the Edwardian era. >> Taylor, John Henry; Vardon; RR1157

Braille, Louis [brayl] (1809–52) Educationist, born in Coupvray, France. Blind from the age of three, at 10 he entered the Institution des Jeunes Aveugles in Paris. He studied organ playing, and became professor of the Institute in 1826. In 1829 he devised a system of raised-point writing which the blind could both read and write. >> Moon

Brailsford, Henry Noel (1873–1958) Socialist writer and political journalist, born in Yorkshire, N England, UK. He studied at Glasgow University, and became assistant professor of logic there, leaving to join the Greek Foreign Legion in the war with Turkey (1897). His Socialism was pre-eminently international in outlook and was the key to everything he did (see *The War of Steel and Gold*, 1914). He joined the Independent Labour Party in 1907 and edited its weekly publication, *The New Leader* (1922–6).

JOHANNES BRAHMS (1833–97)

Brahms was born in Hamburg, the son of Jakob Brahms, who played the horn and double-bass in the Hamburg Stadttheatre. His family life is believed to have been happy, but little is heard of his mother except that she was 17 years his father's senior. Jakob Brahms was not an outstanding musician and he was very poor, but young Johannes was a particularly gifted pianist, so from the age of 14 he supplemented the family income by playing to audiences of sailors in the rough dockland inns. He managed to do some composition work, and gave a few recitals (his first in 1848, aged 15), but he had little time then to concentrate on composition.

In 1850 he met and gave concerts with Eduard Reményi (1830–98), the Hungarian violinist whose national music influenced much of Brahms's later work. Away on a concert tour with Reményi in 1853, he met the violinist **Joseph Joachim** (1831–1907), who was much impressed with his talent, and who introduced him to the older composer Robert Schumann and his wife, Clara. At that time he wrote his first substantial work, the Piano Sonata in C Major, Op.1 (1852–3), and Schumann wrote an article praising Brahms's genius in the journal *Neue Zeitschrift für Musik*, which quickly established his reputation in musical circles. Joachim and the Schumanns were to become Brahms's confidantes and friends, and in 1854, on hearing of Schumann's mental breakdown and attempted suicide, he journeyed to be near him, and developed a close attachment to Clara.

Two years later, Schumann died, and although Brahms supported Clara and her children, and remained devoted to her for the rest of her life, they never married. Brahms remained a bachelor, and there has been much speculation over the nature of their relationship. There is, however, no doubt that she was an enormous support to him, moderating his intense self-criticism, and inspiring much of his work. (Brahms was always ready to take advice and re-work his music.)

During this period Brahms composed works principally for the piano, including three sonatas and some songs. Between 1857–60 he spent a few months each year at the court in Detmold, where he held a part-time post as director of music to the prince of Lippe-Detmold. For the orchestra there he composed two serenades and the first version of his Piano Quartet in G Minor, Op.25. He also began the task of composing a symphony but, finding that prospect a little too ambitious, he gave up and used the music instead for his Piano Concerto in D Minor.

In 1859, still based in Hamburg, he founded and became the conductor of a ladies' choir, and published a good deal of music. He hoped to be offered the conductorship of the Hamburg Philharmonic Orchestra, but he was passed over, and so accepted a post as director of the Singakademie in Vienna for one season in 1863. Apart from conducting the Vienna Philharmonic Society between 1872 and 1875, he took no further formal posts, preferring to remain independent.

Brahms settled in Vienna in 1863, travelling to Austria and Germany for occasional public appearances, where he played his own work. In the late 1860s, after his mother died (1865), he finished *Ein deutsches Requiem* (1857–68, The German Requiem), which he had begun at the time of the turmoil surrounding Schumann's death. From 1869 it was performed with success all over Germany. It is still considered one of the best examples of 19th-c choral music, and Brahms's most important work. There followed in 1873 the highly acclaimed orchestral version of his *Variations on a Theme by Haydn* (1861). By the late 1870s he must have been more satisfied with his abilities, finding the confidence to complete his Symphony No 1 in C Minor (1876), which he had discussed with Clara years before. His second, third, and fourth symphonies followed in 1877, 1883, and 1885 respectively. In 1891 Brahms heard clarinettist Richard Mühlfeld (1856–1907) play at Meiningen, and was inspired to write four works for him; otherwise his last years were spent almost exclusively in composing piano music.

The *Vier ernste Gesänge* (1896, Four Serious Songs) were Brahms's last composition (he wrote 214 solo songs in all). During his early 60s, he developed cancer of the liver. A journey to Bonn to attend Clara Schumann's burial in 1896 further weakened him, and he died the next spring. One of the foremost German composers of the era, prolific in almost every field, Brahms had had universal recognition accorded to him, including being offered the freedom of Hamburg. He was no revolutionary, but his classical principles and the truly Romantic spirit which informed his music had a profound influence on later composers. >> Schumann, Clara / Robert

Brain, Dennis (1921–57) Horn player, born in London, England, UK. He studied under his father **Aubrey Brain** (1893–1955) at the Royal Academy of Music, also becoming an organist, then worked with the Royal Philharmonic and Philharmonia Orchestras as chief horn player. Amongst the composers who wrote works especially for him were Britten, Hindemith, and Malcolm Arnold.

Braine, John (Gerard) (1922–86) Writer, born in Bradford, West Yorkshire, N England, UK. The success of his first book, *Room at the Top* (1957), enabled him to become a full-time novelist. The theme of aggressive ambition and determination to break through social barriers identified him with the 'Angry Young Men' of the 1950s. His novels deal mostly with the north of England and northerners, and include *The Vodi* (1959), *Life at the Top* (1962), and *One and Last Love* (1981). Many of his writings have been adapted for television.

Brainerd, David (1718–47) Presbyterian missionary, born in Haddam, CT. He studied for three years at Yale College, where his opinions caused doctrinal disputes and his expulsion. He worked successfully among the American Indians from 1742, and his devotion found expression in his *Journal*, published posthumously in 1749.

Braithwaite, Edward Kamau (1930–) Poet and academic historian, born in Bridgetown, Barbados. His major achievement is contained in *The Arrivants: a New World Trilogy* (1973), which comprises his first three volumes: *Rights of Passage* (1967), *Masks* (1968), and *Islands* (1969). Later works include *Mother Poem* (1972) and *Sun Poem* (1982). His historical writing includes *The Folk Culture of the Slaves of Jamaica* (1970).

Braithwaite, R(ichard) B(evin) (1900–90) Philosopher, born in Banbury, Oxfordshire, SC England, UK. He studied physics and mathematics at Cambridge, but switched to philosophy. He became a fellow at Cambridge (1924), lecturer in moral science (1928–53), and professor of moral philosophy (1953–67). He is best known for his theories in the philosophy of science, and the study of moral and religious philosophy, particularly the application of mathematical game theory. Notable works include *Scientific Explanation* (1953) and *Theory of Games as a Tool for the Moral Philosopher* (1955).

Bramah, Joseph [brama] (1748–1814) Inventor, born in Stainborough, South Yorkshire, N England, UK. He made numerous inventions, including a beer machine used at the bar of public-houses, a safety lock, a hydraulic press (1795), and a machine for printing bank-notes (1806). He was one of the first to propose the application of the screw-propeller.

Bramante, Donato [bramantay], originally **Donato di Pascuccio d'Antonio** (c.1444–1514) High Renaissance architect, born near Urbino, Italy. He started as a painter, and worked in Milan (1477–99), where he executed his first building projects, such as Sta Maria delle Grazie. He was employed in Rome from 1499 by Popes Alexander VI and Julius II. He designed the new Basilica of St Peter's (begun in 1506), as well as the Belvedere courtyard, the Tempietto di Sta Pietro in Montorio (1502), the Palazzo dei Tribunale (1508), and the Palazzo Caprini (1514).

Branagh, Kenneth (Charles) [brana] (1960–) Actor and director, born in Belfast. He studied at the Royal Academy of Dramatic Art, London, and joined the Royal Shakespeare Company in 1984. In 1987 he co-founded and became co-director of the Renaissance Theatre Company, starring in successful tours in 1988 and 1989. He has appeared in television drama and in several films, including the remake of *Henry V* (1989), which he also directed, *Much Ado About Nothing* (1993) and *In the Bleak Midwinter* (1995). He directed and starred in a 4-hour film production of *Hamlet* in 1997. He married actress Emma Thompson in 1989

(separated, 1995), and was European Actor of the Year in 1990. >> Thompson, Emma

Brancusi, Constantin [brankoozee] (1876–1957) Sculptor, born in Pestisani, Romania. He won a scholarship to the Bucharest Academy and arrived in Paris in 1904. 'The Kiss' (1908) was his most abstract sculpture of the period, representing two block-like figures. His 'Sleeping Muse' (1910) shows Rodin's influence, but is the first of his many characteristic, highly polished egg-shaped carvings. Other works include several versions of 'Mademoiselle Pogany' (1913–31), 'Bird in Space' (1925), and 'The Sea Lions' (1943). >> Rodin

Brand, Stewart (1938–) Editor and writer, born in Rockford, IL. He studied at Stanford, and became associated with the Merry Pranksters, a west-coast group of bohemian writers and intellectuals. He then became the founding editor of the counterculture *The Whole Earth Catalogue* series (1968–71), and later editor-in-chief of *The Whole Earth Software Catalogue* (1983–5). He became a research scientist at the Media Lab of the Massachusetts Institute of Technology in 1986, and published an account of its work the following year.

Brandauer, Klaus Maria von [brandower] (1944–) Actor, born in Alt Aussee, Austria. He worked for many years in theatre in Germany and in Vienna, where he has long been associated with the Burgtheater. He made his film début in 1972, and became internationally known after his role in *Mephisto* (1980), which won an Oscar for Best Foreign Film. He received an Oscar nomination for his role as Baron Blixen in *Out of Africa* (1985). Later films include *Hanussen* (1988) and *The Russia House* (1990).

Brandeis, Louis (Dembitz) [brandiys] (1856–1941) Judge, born in Louisville, KY. He studied at Louisville, Dresden, and Harvard, and practised in Boston. He conducted many labour arbitrations, and was frequently involved in cases challenging the power of monopolies and cartels. He formulated the economic doctrine of the New Freedom adopted by Woodrow Wilson for his 1912 presidential campaign, and was appointed to the US Supreme Court in 1916. Brandeis University in Waltham, MA, is named after him. >> Wilson, Woodrow

Brando, Marlon (1924–) Film and stage actor, born in Omaha, NE. A product of the New York Actors' Studio, he made his debut in 1943, and appeared in several plays before achieving fame in *A Streetcar Named Desire* (1947). His many films include *The Wild One* (1953), *Julius Caesar* (1953), *One-Eyed Jacks* (which he also directed, 1961), *Mutiny on the Bounty* (1962), and *Last Tango in Paris* (1972). An Oscar winner for *On the Waterfront* (1954) and *The Godfather* (1972), he refused the latter honour in protest at the film industry's treatment of American Indians, and has been a prominent campaigner for the Civil Rights movement. He ended a period of absence from the screen with the anti-apartheid drama *A Dry White Season* (1988), the comedy *The Freshman* (1990), and *Don Juan de Marco* (1995). >> Strasberg

Brandreth, Gyles (Daubeney) (1948–) British writer, broadcaster, and politician. He studied at Oxford, where he became president of the Oxford Union, and editor of *Isis*. He worked as a freelance journalist from 1968, and as a columnist for several magazines, including the *TV Times*. He founded the National Scrabble Championships in 1971, and has on three occasions held the world record for length of after-dinner speech. Long interested in word games, and the quirks and eccentricities of language, his books include *I Scream for Ice Cream* (1974), *The Book of Mistaikes* (1982), and many more on puzzles and entertainment. Other writing includes novels, such as *Who is Nick Saint?* (1996), and many books for children. He is best known for his television series, such as *Chatterbox* (1977–8) and *Catchword* (1986), and he presented for TV-AM (1983–90). He became an MP in 1992.

Brandt, Bill [brant], popular name of **William Brandt** (1904–83) Photographer, born in London, England, UK. He studied with Man Ray in Paris in 1929 and returned to London in 1931. Later in the 1930s he made a series of striking social records, contrasting the lives of the rich and the poor, and during World War 2 he worked for the ministry of information recording conditions in London in the Blitz. His greatest creative work was his treatment of the nude, in which his essays in pure form, as published in *Perspective of Nudes* (1961) and *Shadows of Light* (1966), approached the surreal. >> Ray, Man

Brandt, Willy [brant], originally **Karl Herbert Frahm** (1913–92) West German statesman and chancellor (1969–74), born in Lübeck, Germany. He joined the Social Democrats at 17 and, as a fervent anti-Nazi, fled to Norway (1933), where he changed his name. In 1940 he went to Sweden, working as a journalist in support of the German and Norwegian resistance movements. In 1945 he returned to Germany, and was a member of the Bundestag (1949–57). A pro-Western, anti-Communist leader, he became mayor of West Berlin (1957–66), achieving international renown during the Berlin Wall crisis (1961). In 1966 he led his party into a coalition government with the Christian Democrats under Kiesinger's chancellorship and, as foreign minister, instituted a policy of reconciliation between East and West Europe (*Ostpolitik*). He was elected chancellor in 1969, and was awarded the Nobel Prize for Peace in 1971, but was forced to resign the chancellorship following the discovery that a close aide had been an East German spy. He headed an influential international commission (the *Brandt Commission*) on economic development (1977–83). >> Kiesinger

Brangwyn, Sir Frank (1867–1956) Artist, born in Bruges, Belgium. He was apprenticed to William Morris for four years, and then went to sea and travelled widely. Although he excelled in many media, particularly in etching, he was most famous for his vigorously coloured murals, such as his 'British Empire Panels' (1925, Swansea Guildhall). In 1936 a Brangwyn Museum was opened in Bruges. >> Morris, William

Branner, H(ans) C(hristian) (1903–66) Novelist, short-story writer, and playwright, born in Ordrup, Denmark. A former actor and publisher, he wrote several psychological novels, including *Legetøj* (1936, Toys) and *Ingen Kender Natten* (1955, Nobody Knows the Night). His plays include *Rytteren* (1949, trans The Riding Master) and *Söskende* (1952, Brethren).

Branson, Richard (Charles Nicholas) (1950–) Businessman, born in Sharnley Green, Surrey, SE England, UK. He launched a mail-order business in discount records in 1969, opening his first shop in London in 1971, under the name Virgin. This was followed by a series of highly successful business enterprises, including a recording company, various retailing operations, the travel company Voyager Group (1980), the airline Virgin Atlantic (1984), Virgin Radio (1993), Virgin Direct (1995), and V2 Music (1996). He is also known for his sporting achievements, notably the record-breaking Atlantic crossing in *Virgin Atlantic Challenger II* in 1986, and the first crossing by hot-air balloon of the Atlantic (1987) and Pacific (1991).

Brant, Joseph, Mohawk name **Thayendanegea** (1742–1807) Mohawk Indian chief, and brother-in-law of the Irish fur trader, Sir William Johnson. He served the British in the French and Indian War, and in Pontiac's War (1763–6), and in the American War of Independence (1775–83) commanded the Mohawks on the British side. In 1785 he went to England to persuade the British government to indemnify the Indians for their losses in the war, and in London was received at court and lionized by society. In later years an earnest Christian, he founded the first Episcopal Church in Upper Canada. >> Johnson, William

Brant, Sebastian (1458–1521) Poet and humanist, born in Strassburg, Germany. He studied and lectured at Basel. He is best known for his allegory *Das Narrenschiff* (1494), a satire on the follies and vices of his times, the most famous German literary work of his century. It was translated into English as *The Shyp of Folys* by Alexander Barclay and Henry Watson in 1509.

Branting, Karl Hjalmar (1860–1925) Swedish statesman and prime minister (1920, 1921–3, 1924–5), born in Stockholm. He was co-founder of the Social Democratic Party in 1889, becoming leader of the party from 1907. In 1921 he shared the Nobel Peace Prize for his work in international diplomacy. >> RR1090

Brantôme, Pierre de Bourdeille, seigneur de (Lord of) (c. 1530–1614) French soldier and writer, born in Périgord, France. He studied at Paris and at Poitiers. In 1561 he accompanied Mary, Queen of Scots, to Scotland, and joined the expedition sent to Malta to assist the Knights of St John against the sultan (1565); he also served in Italy, Africa, and Hungary. He was made chamberlain to Charles IX and Henry III (of France), and fought against the Huguenots. From c.1594 he began to write his memoirs, and lived in retirement. >> Charles IX; Henry III (of France); Mary, Queen of Scots

Braque, Georges [brak] (1882–1963) Painter, born in Argenteuil, France. He was one of the founders of classical Cubism, and worked with Picasso (1908–14). After World War 1 he developed a personal nongeometric, semi-abstract style. His paintings are mainly of still-life, the subject being transformed into a two-dimensional pattern, and they are among the outstanding decorative achievements of our time, with a pervasive influence on other painters. Two of his paintings are 'The Port of La Ciotat' (1907, John Hay Whitney Collection, New York) and 'The Black Birds' (1957, Aimé Maeght Collection). >> Picasso

Brasher, Chris(topher William) [braysher] (1928–) British writer, broadcaster, and athlete. He studied at Cambridge, where he was president of both the mountaineering and athletics clubs. He represented Britain in the Olympics of 1952, and won the gold medal for the 3000 m steeplechase in the 1956 Games. He became a reporter for the BBC *Tonight* programme (1961–5), and head of BBC general features (1969–72). He was the race director for the London Marathon (1980–91), an event he founded after running in the New York City Marathon in 1979. >> Lebow

Brassaï [brasaee], professional name of **Gyula Halasz** (1899–1984) Painter and photographer, born in Brasso, Hungary. Coming to Paris in 1923, he worked as a journalist, and from 1930 used photography to record the underworld and night-life of 1930s Paris. His first collection, *Paris de nuit* (1933, Paris by Night), caused a sensation. He became a French citizen in 1948. >> Kertész

Brassey, Thomas (1805–70) Engineer, born in Buerton, Cheshire, NWC England, UK. He was articled to a land surveyor, and in 1836 settled in London as a railway contractor. His operations soon extended to all parts of the world; for his contract of the Great Northern Railway (1847–51) he employed between 5000 and 6000 men.

Bratby, John (1928–92) Artist and writer, born in London, England, UK. He studied at Kingston Art School and the Royal College of Art. A leading protagonist of English 'New Realism', in the mid-1950s he was associated with the 'kitchen sink' school because of his preoccupation with working-class domestic interiors, as in 'Baby in Pram' (Liverpool). He represented Britain at the 1956 Vienna

Biennale, but after that his reputation declined. He also wrote several novels, including *Breakdown* (1960), with his own illustrations.

Brattain, Walter H(ouser) (1902–87) US physicist, born in Amoy, China, where his father was a teacher. He grew up on a cattle ranch in the State of Washington, and studied at the universities of Oregon and Minnesota. In 1929 he joined Bell Telephone Laboratories, where he worked as a research physicist on the surface properties of semiconductors. With Bardeen and Shockley he developed the point-contact transistor, using a thin germanium crystal. He shared the Nobel Prize for Physics in 1956. >> Bardeen; Shockley; RR1122

Braudel, Fernand [brohdel] (1902–85) Historian, born in Lorraine, France. He studied at the Sorbonne, and taught in Algerian schools (1923–32), in Paris (1932–5), and at Saõ Paulo University (1935–8). He wrote, from memory, his great work *La Mediterranée et le monde mediterranéen à l'époque de Philippe II* (The Mediterranean and the Mediterranean World at the Time of Philip II) in a German prison camp in Lübeck throughout World War 2, after which it was published (1949). He then became professor at the Collège de France (1949–72).

Brauer, Adrian >> Brouwer, Adriaen

Braun, Eva [brown] (1910–45) Mistress of Adolf Hitler, born in Munich, Germany. She was secretary to Hitler's staff photographer, became Hitler's mistress in the 1930s, and is said to have married him before they committed suicide together in the air-raid shelter (the bunker) of the Chancellery during the fall of Berlin. >> Hitler

Braun, (Karl) Ferdinand [brown] (1850–1918) Physicist, born in Fulda, Germany. In 1909 he shared the Nobel Prize for Physics for his work on wireless telegraphy and cathode rays. >> RR1122

Braun, Wernher von [brown] (1912–77) Rocket pioneer, born in Wirsitz, Germany. He studied engineering at Berlin and Zürich, and founded in 1930 a society for space travel which maintained a rocket-launching site near Berlin. By 1936 he was director of a rocket research station at Peenemünde. Hitler personally released him when he was imprisoned on espionage charges for refusing to co-operate with Himmler over the V-2 project. He never approved of the military use of the rocket, and surrendered willingly to US troops in 1945. He became a US citizen in 1955 and a director of the US army's Ballistic Missile Agency at Huntsville, AL, where in 1958 he was chiefly responsible for the launching of the first US artificial Earth satellite, Explorer 1. He was also director of the Marshall Space Flight Center (1960–70), where he developed the Saturn rocket for the Apollo 8 Moon landing (1969).

Brazil, Angela (1868–1947) Writer of girls' school stories, born in Preston, Lancashire, NW England, UK. She was a governess for some years before beginning to write tales notable for their healthy realism. Her first success was *The Fortunes of Philippa* (1906), and this was followed by over 50 school novels. Her last book was *The School of the Loch* (1946).

Brazza, Pierre Savorgnan de (1852–1905) Explorer, born in Rio de Janeiro, Brazil. He became a French citizen in 1874, and entered the French navy, serving in Gabon, where he explored the Ogowe (1876–8). In 1878 he explored the country N of the Congo, where he secured vast grants of land for France, and founded stations, including that of Brazzaville.

Breakspear, Nicholas >> Adrian IV

Bréal, Michel [brayal] (1832–1915) Comparative philologist and mythologist, born in Rhenish Bavaria. In 1858 he settled in Paris, and in 1866 became professor of comparative grammar at the Collège de France. He founded the science of semantics with his *Essai de sémantique* (1897).

Bream, Julian (Alexander) [breem] (1933–) Guitarist and lutenist, born in London, England, UK. A protégé of Andrés Segovia, he made his debut in London in 1950. He has edited much music for guitar and lute, and among the composers who have written for him are Britten, Henze, Tippett, and Walton. He formed the Julian Bream Consort in 1961, specializing in early ensemble music. In 1990 he performed at his 40th anniversary concert at the Wigmore Hall, London. >> Segovia

Breasley, Scobie, popular name of **Arthur Edward Breasley** (1914–) Jockey and trainer, born in Wagga Wagga, New South Wales, Australia. A successful rider for over 20 years before coming to Britain in 1950, he was retained to ride for the stable of Sir Gordon Richards in 1956. He was champion jockey in 1957, 1961, 1962, and 1963. He retired in 1968, and became a trainer. >> Richards, Gordon; RR1161

Breasted, James Henry [brestid] (1865–1935) Archaeologist and historian, the founder of American Egyptology, born in Rockford, IL. He studied at Yale and Berlin before joining the faculty at Chicago in 1894. His five-volume *Ancient Records of Egypt* (1906) transcribed every hieroglyphic inscription then known. In 1919, with funding from John D Rockefeller, he set up his own Oriental Institute in Chicago to promote research on ancient Egypt and W Asia.

Brecht, (Eugene) Bertolt (Friedrich) [brekht] (1898–1956) Poet, playwright, and theatre director, born in Augsburg, Germany. His early plays won him success, controversy, and the Kleist Prize in 1922. Popularity came with *Die Dreigroschenoper* (1928, The Threepenny Opera), and from then until 1933 his work was particularly concerned with encouraging audiences to think rather than identify, and with experimentation in epic theatre and alienation effects. Hitler's rise to power forced him to leave Germany, and he lived in exile for 15 years, chiefly in the USA. During this period, he wrote some of his greatest plays, including *Mutter Courage und ihre Kinder* (1938, Mother Courage and her Children) and *Der Kaukasische Kreidekreis* (1945, The Caucasian Chalk Circle). After his return to East Berlin in 1948, his directorial work on these and other plays with the Berliner Ensemble firmly established his influence as a major figure in 20th-c theatre. In 1955 he received the Stalin Peace Prize. >> Weigel, Helene; Weill

Breckenridge, Sophonisba Preston (1866–1948) Social worker and educator, born in Lexington, KY. Reared in a prominent Southern family, she graduated from Wellesley College (1888), became the first woman lawyer in Kentucky (1895), and earned a doctorate from the University of Chicago (1901). In 1907 she went to live at Chicago's Hull House. Soon known for her studies exposing slum conditions, she was also instrumental in professionalizing social work as an administrator and teacher at the University of Chicago (1920–42), and as a founder (1927) of the *Social Service Review*, which she edited until her death.

Breckinridge, John C(abell) (1821–75) Vice-president of the USA (1857–61), born near Lexington, KY. He practised law there until 1847, when he was chosen major of a volunteer regiment for the Mexican War. He sat in Congress (1851–5), and in 1856 was elected vice-president under Buchanan. In 1860 he was the pro-slavery candidate for the presidency, but was defeated by Lincoln. He was appointed a Confederate major-general in 1862, and secretary of war in Jefferson Davis's cabinet. At the end of the Civil War he fled to Europe, returning in 1868. >> Buchanan, James; Davis, Jefferson

Breitmann, Hans >> **Leland, Charles**

Bremner, Rory (Keith Ogilvy) (1961–) British satirical impressionist, writer, and performer. He studied at King's College, London, and began performing in tours and one-man shows in 1985. He made several series for BBC television (1986–92) and *Rory Bremner – Who Else?* for Channel 4 (1992–), as well as a number of videos. Awards include the Top Male Comedy Performer BAFTA (1994, 1995, 1996) and the Royal Television Society's Award (1995).

Brenan, Gerald (1894–1987) Travel writer and novelist, born in Malta. He went to Spain and settled in Yegen, an isolated village which became the focus of his classic *South from Granada* (1957). This was preceded by his best-known book, *The Spanish Labyrinth* (1943), still regarded as one of the most perceptive studies of modern Spain.

Brendan, St, known as **the Navigator** (484–577) Abbot and traveller, traditionally the founder of the monastery of Clonfert in Co Galway (561), and other monasteries in Ireland and Scotland. The Latin *Navigation of St Brendan* (c.1050) recounts his legendary voyage to a land of saints far to the W and N, possibly the Hebrides and the Northern Isles, or even Iceland. Feast day 16 May.

Brendel, Alfred (1931–) Pianist, born in Wiesenberg, Czech Republic. He made his debut in Graz (1948), and has since performed widely throughout Austria, where he lives. He is known for his interpretations of Mozart, Beethoven, Schubert, Liszt, and Schoenberg. He tours internationally, and has written many essays on music.

Brennan, Christopher (John) (1870–1932) Poet and critic, born in Sydney, New South Wales, Australia. He studied Classics and philosophy at Sydney University. While reading philosophy at Berlin University (1892), he became interested in French Symbolist poetry, which influenced his future writing. He published only a select number of volumes of verse, the best of which (such as *XXI Poems: Towards the Source*, 1897) were written before 1900.

Brennan, William J(oseph), Jr (1906–97) Judge, born in Newark, NJ. He studied at Harvard, joined a Newark law firm, and specialized in labour law. He was appointed to the New Jersey Superior Court (1949) and the state Supreme Court (1952), and President Eisenhower appointed him to the US Supreme Court in 1956. During a distinguished career he is remembered for judgments which reflected his concern to balance individual rights with the interests of the community as a whole. He retired in 1990.

Brenner, Sydney (1927–) Molecular biologist, born in Germiston, South Africa. He studied at Witwatersrand University and Oxford, and joined the MRC Molecular Biology Laboratory in Cambridge (1957), becoming its director in 1980. He did notable work on the information code of DNA, and in the 1970s moved to basic studies designed to relate, in detail, an animal's nervous system to its genetic make-up.

Brentano, Clemens von [brentahnoh] (1778–1842) Poet, born in Ehrenbreitstein, Germany, the uncle of Franz and Lujo Brentano. He became a Roman Catholic in 1818 and withdrew to the monastery of Dülmen, near Münster (1818–24), where he recorded the revelations of the nun Anna Katharina Emmerich. One of the founders of the Heidelberg Romantic school, he was mostly successful in his novellas, particularly in the *Geschichte vom braven Kasperl und dem schönen Annerl* (1817, The Story of Just Caspar and Fair Annie), and with his brother-in-law Ludwig Achim von Arnim he edited *Des Knaben Wunderhorn* (1805–8), a collection of folk songs. >> Arnim, Achim von; Brentano, Franz; Brentano, Lujo

Brentano, Franz [brentahnoh] (1838–1917) Psychologist and philosopher, born in Marienberg, Germany, the brother of Lujo Brentano. He became a Catholic priest (1864), and taught philosophy at Würzburg until 1873. He then abandoned the priesthood, and moved to teach at Vienna until his retirement (1895). In his most important work, *Psychologie vom empirischen Standpunkt* (1874, Psychology from an Empirical Standpoint), he developed the doctrine of 'intentionality', characterizing mental events as involving the 'direction of the mind to an object'. >> Brentano, Lujo

Brentano, Heinrich von [brentahnoh] (1904–64) German statesman, born in Offenbach, Germany. A successful lawyer, he was one of the founders of the Christian Democratic Party. He went into politics in Hesse (1945), and was elected to the Federal Diet at Bonn (1949), where he played a prominent part in drafting the Constitution. He became foreign minister in 1955, but resigned in 1961.

Brentano, Lujo [brentahnoh], popular name of **Ludwig Josef Brentano** (1844–1931) Political economist, born in Aschaffenburg, Germany, the brother of Franz Brentano. In 1868 he went to England to study the condition of the working-classes, and especially trades associations and unions. He became professor of political theory at several universities in Europe (1871–1931). A prominent pacifist, he was awarded the Nobel Peace Prize in 1927. >> Brentano, Franz

Brent-Dyer, Elinor Mary (1894–1969) Writer of the 'Chalet School' girls' stories, born in South Shields, Tyne and Wear, NE England UK. She studied at Leeds University, and became a teacher, and was later head of the Margaret Roper Girls' School in Hereford. Her first schoolgirl novel, *Gerry Goes to School*, appeared in 1922, inaugurating her 98 titles. Her fourth book, *The School at the Chalet* (1925), established her famous series, whose final book, *Prefects of the Chalet School*, was published posthumously in 1970.

Brenton, Howard (1942–) Playwright, born in Portsmouth, Hampshire, S England, UK. He studied at Cambridge, wrote for fringe theatre companies during the late 1960s, and was resident playwright at the Royal Court Theatre, London (1972–3). His plays include *Weapons of Happiness* (1976), *The Romans in Britain* (1980), *The Genius* (1983), *Moscow Gold* (1990, with Tariq Ali), and *Berlin Bertie* (1992). He has also collaborated with David Hare on a number of projects, notably *Pravda* (1985), and has written a political thriller, *Diving for Pearls* (1989). >> Hare, David

Brenz, Johann [brents] (1499–1570) Lutheran reformer, born in Weil, Germany. He was co-author of the Württemberg Confession of Faith, and his Catechism (1551) stands next to Luther's in Protestant Germany.

Bresson, Robert [bresõ] (1907–) Film director, born in Bromont-Lamothe, France. At first a painter and photographer, he started serious work in the cinema with *Les Anges du péché* (1943, The Angels of Sin), but it was his next production *Le Journal d'un curé de campagne* (1951, Diary of a Country Priest) which brought international acclaim, subsequently repeated with *Un Condamné à mort s'est echappé* (1956, trans A Man Escaped) and *Le Procès de Jeanne d'Arc* (1962, The Trial of Joan of Arc). Later productions are *Lancelot du lac* (1974), *Le Diable, probablement* (1977, The Devil, Probably), and *L'Argent* (1983, Money).

Breton, André [bruhtõ] (1896–1966) Poet, essayist, and critic, born in Tinchebray, France. In 1916 he joined the Dadaist group, and in 1922 turned to Surrealism. He published his first Surrealist manifesto in 1924, and became editor of *La Révolution surréaliste*. His major novel, *Nadja*, was published in 1928, and his collected poems in 1948.

Breton, Nicholas [bretn] (c.1545–c.1626) Poet, born in London, England, UK. He studied at Oxford and became a prolific writer of all kinds of verse, prose, and pamphlets. His best-known poem is 'The Passionate Shepheard' (1604). His prose *Wits Trenchmour* (1597) is a fishing idyll on which

Izaak Walton drew for *The Compleat Angler*. >> Walton, Izaak

Breuer, Marcel (Lajos) [broyer] (1902–81) Architect and designer, born in Pécs, Hungary. A student at the Bauhaus in Germany from 1920, he took charge of the furniture workshop by 1924, and designed probably the first modern tubular steel chair. In 1937 he joined Walter Gropius in the USA as associate professor of architecture at Harvard (1937–46) and in architectural practice. Working independently after 1947, he designed the majority of his architectural projects, including the UNESCO building in Paris (with Bernard Zehrfuss and Pier Luigi Nervi). A significant figure in the 'Modern Movement', his classic furniture designs, in particular, represented major developments in materials and techniques. >> Gropius; Nervi

Breughel >> **Brueghel**

Breuil, Henri (Edouard Prosper) [broey] (1877–1961) Archaeologist, born in Mortain, France. He trained as a priest, became interested in cave art in 1900, and was responsible for the discovery of the decorated caves at Combarelles and Font-de-Gaume in the Dordogne the following year. Professor at the Collège de France (1929–47), his work marked the beginning of the study of palaeolithic art.

Brewer, Ebenezer Cobham (1810–97) Clergyman and writer, born in London, England, UK. He studied law at Trinity Hall, Cambridge (1835), one year after receiving orders. He then became a London schoolmaster. His most enduring work is his *Dictionary of Phrase and Fable* (1870).

Brewster, Sir David (1781–1868) Physicist, born in Jedburgh, Scottish Borders, SE Scotland, UK. He studied for the Church, became editor of the *Edinburgh Magazine* (1802), and of the *Edinburgh Encyclopaedia* (1808). He had previously been interested in the study of optics, and in 1816 he invented the kaleidoscope. In 1818 he was awarded the Rumford gold and silver medals for his discoveries on the polarization of light. He was Principal of Edinburgh University from 1859. >> Thompson, Benjamin

Breytenbach, Breyten [braytinbokh] (1939–) Painter, poet, and essayist, born in Bonnievale, South Africa. He left South Africa in 1960, and settled in Paris, where he exhibited as a painter. The first of over a dozen volumes of poetry was *Ysterkoei Moet Sweet* (1964, The Iron Cow Must Sweat). In 1975 he returned to South Africa in disguise, was arrested, and sentenced to nine years imprisonment for 'terrorism'. He wrote of his prison years in *True Confessions of an Albino Terrorist* (1984). Since the early 1980s, he has written mainly in English. Much of his poetry, prose, and memoirs defy conventional categories.

Brezhnev, Leonid Ilich [brezhnyef] (1906–82) Russian statesman, general secretary of the Soviet Communist Party (1964–82), and president of the Supreme Soviet (1977–82), born in Kamenskoye, Ukraine. He trained as a metallurgist, and became a political commissar in the Red Army in World War 2. After the war, he was a party official in the Ukraine and Moldavia, becoming a member (1952–7) and then chairman (1960–4) of the Presidium of the Supreme Soviet. He was general secretary of the Party Central Committee after Khrushchev, and gradually emerged as the most powerful figure in the Soviet Union, the first to hold simultaneously the position of general secretary and president.

Brian [breean], known as **Brian Boroimhe** or **Boru** ('Brian of the Tribute') (c. 926–1014) King of Ireland (1002–14). In 976 he became chief of Dál Cais, and after much fighting made himself King of Leinster (984). After further campaigns in all parts of the country, his rule was acknowledged over the whole of Ireland. He was killed after defeating the Vikings at Clontarf. >> RR1064

Brian, (William) Havergal (1876–1972) Composer, and writer on music, born in Dresden, Staffordshire, C England, UK. Championed by such figures as Beecham and Wood, his success seemed secure, but he suffered a long period of neglect after World War 1. A revival of interest in his music occurred in the last decade or so of his life. He wrote 32 symphonies, a huge setting of Shelley's *Prometheus Unbound*, a violin concerto, and five operas, including *The Tigers* (1916–19) and *Faust* (1955–6).

Briand, Aristide [breeã] (1862–1932) French statesman and prime minister (1909–11, 1913, 1915–17, 1921–2, 1925–6, 1929), born in Nantes, France. He was founder (with Jean Jaurés) of *L'Humanité*, and framer of the law for the separation of Church and state (1905). A socialist, he was 11 times elected French premier, and also served as foreign minister (1925–32), helping to conclude the *Kellogg–Briand Pact* (1928), outlawing war as a means of solving disputes. He shared the Nobel Prize for Peace in 1926, and advocated a United States of Europe. >> Kellogg, Frank B; Jaurés; RR1049

Brickhill, Paul (Chester Jerome) (1916–91) Writer, born in Sydney, New South Wales, Australia. He studied at Sydney University, and worked in journalism before serving with the Royal Australian Air Force during World War 2. Shot down in North Africa, he was for two years a prisoner-of-war in Stalag Luft III, Germany; he described his escape from the camp in *The Great Escape* (1951). He became the most successful non-fiction writer of the post-war period, with *The Dam Busters* (1951), *Escape or Die* (1952), and *Reach for the Sky* (1954).

Bride, St >> **Bridget, Brigid,** or **Bride, St**

Bridger, James (1804–81) Fur trader, scout and 'mountain man', born in Richmond, VA. Working with fur companies in the Northwest (1822–42), he was the first white man to see the Great Salt Lake (1824). He established Fort Bridger in Wyoming (1843) and found Bridger's Pass (1849). After being driven out by Mormons (1853), he guided a military force in its campaign against the Mormons (1857–8). He served as a guide to several major expeditions in the West (1859–66), then retired to his farm near Kansas City, MO.

Bridges, Jeff (1949–) Film actor, born in Los Angeles, California, the son of actor Lloyd Bridges. He appeared in the television series *Sea Hunt* as a child, and after military academy and the coastguards he became a professional actor, receiving Oscar nominations for *The Last Picture Show* (1971), *Starman* (1984), and *Tucker* (1988). Later films include *The Fisher King* (1991), *Fearless* (1993), *Wild Bill* (1995), and *The Mirror Has Two Faces* (1996).

Bridges, Robert (Seymour) (1844–1930) Poet, born in Walmer, Kent, SE England, UK. He studied at Oxford, qualified in medicine, and practised in London. He published three volumes of graceful lyrics (1873, 1879, 1880), wrote several plays, the narrative poem *Eros and Psyche* (1885), and other works, including a great deal of literary criticism. He was also an advocate of spelling reform. From 1907 he lived in seclusion at Oxford, publishing comparatively little; then in 1929, on his 85th birthday, he issued his most ambitious poem, *The Testament of Beauty*. He became poet laureate in 1913. >> Hopkins, Gerard Manley

Bridges, (Henry) Styles (1898–1961) US state governor, born in West Pembroke, ME. A magazine editor and investment banker, he served on the New Hampshire Public Service Commission (1930–4). As Republican governor of New Hampshire (1935–7), he spent state money carefully, funding relief aid for mothers and dependent children, and appointing the first woman state judge. In the US Senate (1937–61), he came to chair the appropriations committee, and used it as the base to promote his ultra-conservative views.

Bridget, Brigid, or **Bride, St** (453–523) Abbess, said to be the daughter of an Ulster prince. She entered a convent at Meath in her 14th year, and founded four monasteries for women, the chief at Kildare, where she was buried. She was regarded as one of the three great saints of Ireland, the others being St Patrick and St Columba, and was held in great reverence in Scotland (as St Bride). Feast day 1 February.

Bridget, Brigit, or **Birgitta** (of Sweden)**, St** (c.1302–73) Visionary, born in Finsta, Sweden. At the age of 13 she was married to a young nobleman, **Ulf Gudmarsson,** by whom she had eight children. After his death in 1344, she founded the monastery of Vadstena, which became the cradle of the new order of *Bridgettines* as a branch of the Augustinian order. In 1349 she travelled to Rome where she founded a Swedish hospice. She made a pilgrimage to Palestine and Cyprus in 1372 and died in Rome on her return. She was canonized in 1391; feast day 23 July or 8 October. Her daughter, **St Katarina of Sweden** (1335–81), was canonized in 1489; feast day 22 March.

Bridgman, Laura (Dewey) (1829–89) Blind deaf-mute, born in Hanover, NH. At the age of two a violent fever destroyed her sight, hearing, smell, and in some degree taste. Dr Samuel Howe educated her at the Perkins institution, where she later became a skilful teacher of blind deaf-mutes. >> Howe, Samuel

Bridgman, P(ercy) W(illiams) (1882–1961) Physicist, born in Cambridge, MA. He studied at Harvard, and became professor of physics and mathematics there in 1919. He obtained under high pressure a new form of phosphorus, proved experimentally that viscosity increases with high pressure, and was awarded the Nobel Prize for Physics in 1946 for his work on high-pressure physics and thermodynamics.

Bridie, James, pseudonym of **Osborne Henry Mavor** (1888–1951) Playwright, born in Glasgow, W Scotland, UK. He qualified as a doctor at Glasgow University and became a successful consultant. Always interested in the theatre, he seized his chance when the Scottish National Players produced his *Sunlight Sonata* in 1928, written under the pseudonym of Mary Henderson. After that, he wrote a stream of plays, among them *The Anatomist* (1931), *Mr Bolfry* (1943), and *Dr Angelus* (1947). He played a leading part in the foundation of the Glasgow Citizen's Theatre.

Bridport, Lord >> **Hood, Alexander**

Brierley, Sir Ronald (Alfred) [briyerlee] (1937–) Businessman, born in Wellington, New Zealand. Educated in Wellington, in 1961 he founded Brierley Investments Ltd, becoming its chairman (1961–89) and president (1989–). This was an entrepreneurial enterprise designed to acquire control of already substantial companies and to improve their commercial performance. Following a programme of often audacious but generally well-planned takeovers and mergers, and rejecting the pejorative label of 'corporate raider', he built his firm into a multi-billion-dollar operation. By the time he resigned as chairman, BIL had extensive interests in Australia, Britain, and the USA as well as New Zealand. He became chairman of Tozer Kemsley & Millbourn (Holdings) in 1986, and was knighted in 1988.

Briers, Richard (David) (1934–) Actor, born in Croydon, S Greater London, England, UK. He studied at the Royal Academy of Dramatic Art, London, and made his London debut in *Guilt and Gingerbread* (1959). He has since played many major parts, but is probably better known for his television series *Brothers-in-Law*, *Marriage Lines*, *The Good Life*, and *Ever Decreasing Circles*. Among his books is *A Taste of the Good Life* (1995). >> Kendal

Briggs, Barry (1934–) Speedway rider, born in Christ-church, New Zealand. He appeared in a record 17 consecutive world championship finals (1954–70), during which he scored a record 201 points and took part in 87 races, winning the title in 1957–8, 1964, and 1966. He won the British League Riders' championship six times (1965–70). His career started with Wimbledon (1952), and he also rode for New Cross, Southampton, Swindon, and Hull. After retiring (1976), he ran a motorcycle business in Southampton, and was a co-promoter of the 1982 world championships in Los Angeles. >> RR1164

Briggs, Henry (1561–1630) Mathematician, born in Warley Wood, West Yorkshire, N England, UK. He studied at St John's College, Cambridge, and became a fellow in 1588. In 1596 he was the first professor of geometry at Gresham College, London, and in 1619 was professor of geometry at Oxford. He proposed the use of the base 10 for logarithms instead of that (e'='2..717) used by John Napier, and published logarithmic and trigonometric tables to 14 decimal places. >> Napier, John

Briggs, Raymond (Redvers) (1934–) Children's illustrator and writer, born in London, England, UK. He studied at Wimbledon School of Art and the Slade School of Art, London. He became a freelance illustrator in 1957. In 1966 his *Mother Goose Treasury* appeared with over 900 pictures, winning him the Kate Greenaway Medal. *Father Christmas* (1973), using the comic-strip format, won a second Greenaway Medal. *The Snowman* (1978, animated film, 1982) enchanted adults and children alike. His anxiety for the future well-being of the planet is expressed in *When the Wind Blows* (1982), which has also appeared as a play (1983) and an animated film (1987). Later books include *Unlucky Wally* (1987) and *The Bear* (1994).

Brigham Young >> **Young, Brigham**

Bright, John (1811–89) Radical British statesman and orator, born in Rochdale, Greater Manchester, NW England, UK. When the Anti Corn-Law League was formed in 1839 he was a leading member, and engaged in free trade agitation throughout the country. In 1843 he became MP for Durham, and strongly opposed the corn laws until they were repealed. Elected in 1857 for Birmingham, his name was closely associated with the Reform Act of 1867. He accepted office as President of the Board of Trade (1868), but retired through illness in 1870, returning in 1881 as Chancellor of the Duchy of Lancaster. He was regarded as one of the most eloquent speakers of his time.

Bright, Richard (1789–1858) Physician, born in Bristol, SW England, UK. He studied at Edinburgh, London, Berlin, and Vienna, and from 1820 was connected with Guy's Hospital. *Bright's disease* of the kidneys is named after him.

Brigid, St >> **Bridget, Brigid,** or **Bride, St**

Brigit, St >> **Bridget, Brigit,** or **Birgitta** (of Sweden)**, St**

Brillat-Savarin, (Jean) Anthelme [breeyah savarî] (1755–1826) French politician, gastronome, and writer, born in Belley, France. He was a deputy in 1789, and Mayor of Belley in 1793. During the French Revolution he took refuge in Switzerland, and afterwards in America. His *Physiologie du goût* (1825, The Physiology of Taste), an elegant and witty compendium of the art of dining, has been repeatedly republished and translated; an English form is *A Handbook of Gastronomy*, with 52 etchings by Lalauze (1884).

Brindley, James (1716–72) Engineer and canal builder, born in Thornsett, Derbyshire, C England, UK. Apprenticed to a millwright, he became an engineer, and contrived a water engine for draining a coalmine (1752). Francis Egerton, 3rd Duke of Bridgewater, employed him to build the canal between Worsley and Manchester (1759), a difficult enterprise completed in 1772. He also commenced the Grand Trunk Canal, and completed the Birmingham,

Chesterfield, and other canals. He was illiterate, solving most of his problems without writings or drawings. >> Egerton

Brinell, Johan August [brinel] (1849–1925) Engineer and metallurgist, born in Bringetofta, Sweden. He invented the *Brinell machine* for measuring the hardness of alloys and metals.

Brink, André (1935–) Novelist, short-story writer, playwright, critic, and translator, born in Vrede, South Africa. An Afrikaner dissident, he emerged as a writer in the 1950s, but it was not until his seventh novel – which he later translated into English as *Looking on Darkness* (1974) – was banned by the South African authorities that he began to attract international attention. Later books include *Rumours of Rain* (1978), *Chain of Voices* (1982), *States of Emergency* (1988), and *Imaginings of Sand* (1996). He received the Martin Luther King Memorial Prize and the French Prix Medicis Etranger in 1980, and has twice been runner-up for the Booker Prize.

Brisbane, Albert (1809–90) Social reformer, born in Batavia, NY. The son of a wealthy landowner, he had little formal schooling, but in 1828 went off to Europe where he studied at various universities. He adopted the social philosophy of Charles Fourier – essentially a Socialism that called for establishing small co-operative communities – and after his return to the USA (1834) embarked on a phase of promoting 'Fourierism' (which he tended to rename 'associationism' through his writing and editing). He did little to introduce Fourierist communities, however, and by 1851 he had effectively withdrawn from social activism. He then concentrated on managing his family's business and on publishing his various ideas, including his major work, *General Introduction to Social Theory* (1876). >> Fourier, Charles

Brisbane, Sir Thomas Makdougall (1773–1860) British soldier and astronomer, born in Largs, North Ayrshire, W Scotland, UK. At 16 he entered the army, and served with distinction in Flanders, the West Indies, Spain, and North America, being promoted major-general in 1813. He was Governor of New South Wales (1821–5). He catalogued 7385 stars, and received the Copley Medal from the Royal Society. Brisbane, the capital of Queensland, was named after him.

Brissot (de Warville), Jacques Pierre [breesoh] (1754–93) French revolutionary politician, born near Chartres, France. After completing his studies in Paris he abandoned the legal profession for that of journalism. He was imprisoned for four months in the Bastille on the false charge of having written a brochure against the queen. In 1789 he was present at the storming of the Bastille, and was elected representative for Paris in the National Assembly. He exercised a predominant influence over all the early movements of the revolution, and was recognized as the head of the Girondins or Brissotins. In the Convention his moderation made him suspect, and with 20 other Girondins he was guillotined.

Bristow, Eric, nickname **the Crafty Cockney** (1957–) Darts player, born in London, England, UK. World professional champion a record five times (1980–81, 1984–6), he was also the beaten finalist twice. His other major championships include the World Masters (1977, 1979, 1981, 1983–4), the World Cup individual (1983, 1985), and the *News of the World* Championship (1983–4). >> RR1152

Britannicus, in full **Claudius Tiberius Britannicus Caesar** (41–55 AD) The son of the emperor Claudius and Messalina, surnamed in honour of his father's triumph in Britain (43). Claudius's fourth wife, Agrippina the Younger, caused her husband to adopt her son Nero, and treat Britannicus as an imbecile; and Nero, after his accession, had his step-

brother poisoned. >> Agrippina (the Younger); Claudius; Messalina; Nero

Brittain, Vera (Mary) [britn] (1893–1970) Writer, born in Newcastle-under-Lyme, Staffordshire, C England, UK. After studying at Oxford she served as a nurse in World War 1, recording her experiences with war-found idealism in *Testament of Youth* (1933). She later wrote *Testament of Friendship* (1940) and *Testament of Experience* (1957). In 1925 she married **George Catlin** (1896–1979), professor of politics at Cornell. Her daughter is the politician, Shirley Williams. >> Williams, Shirley

Brittan, Sir Leon (1939–) British statesman, born in London, England, UK. He studied at Cambridge and Harvard, and qualified as a barrister. He became a Conservative MP in 1974, and from 1979 held ministerial posts under Margaret Thatcher, including Treasury chief secretary (1981–3), home secretary (1983–5), and trade and industry secretary (1985–6). He resigned from the cabinet in 1986 because of his involvement in a political dispute over the sale of the Westland Helicopter Co. In 1989 he was nominated as a vice-president of the European Commission with special responsibility for competition policy. >> Thatcher

Britten (of Aldeburgh), (Edward) Benjamin Britten, Baron (1913–76) Composer, born in Lowestoft, Suffolk, E England, UK. During the 1930s he wrote incidental music for plays and documentary films. He then moved to the USA (1939–42), where he wrote his violin concerto and the *Sinfonia da Requiem*. Back in the UK, his works were largely vocal and choral – exceptions include the famous *Variations and Fugue on a Theme of Purcell* (also known as *The Young Person's Guide to the Orchestra*). He then wrote three operas: *Peter Grimes* (1945), *Billy Budd* (1951), and *Gloriana* (1953), as well as several chamber operas and children's operas. His later operas include *A Midsummer Night's Dream* (1960) and *Death in Venice* (1973). He was also an accomplished pianist, often accompanying Peter Pears. He helped to found the annual Aldeburgh Festival in 1948, and became a life peer in 1976. >> Forster, E M; Pears

Broad, Charlie Dunbar (1887–1971) Philosopher, born in London, England, UK. He became professor of moral philosophy in Cambridge (1933–53), but also had a strong interest in parapsychology, and was president of the Society for Psychical Research.

Broadbent, Donald (Eric) (1926–93) British psychologist. He joined the scientific staff of the Medical Research Council's Applied Psychology Research Unit in Cambridge after World War 2 (director, 1949–58). A major figure in postwar experimental psychology, he was the most influential British psychologist in the movement to import ideas from communication theory and cybernetics into cognitive psychology. In 1974 he became a member of the external staff of the Medical Research Council, based in Oxford.

Broadwood, John (1732–1812) Piano manufacturer, born in Cockburnspath, Scottish Borders, SE Scotland, UK. He walked to London to become a cabinet maker, married the daughter of the Swiss-born harpsichord-maker, Burkhardt Tschudi (1702–73), and founded with him the great London pianoforte house (1770). His grandson, **Henry Fowler Broadwood** (1811–93), was also a great improver of the piano.

Broca, Paul (Pierre) [brohka] (1824–80) Surgeon and anthropologist, born in Sainte-Foy-le-Grande, France. He was the first to locate the motor speech centre in the brain, and was also a major influence on the development of physical anthropology in France.

Broch, Hermann [brokh] (1886–1951) Novelist and essayist, born in Vienna. He spent his early adult life working in his father's textile business, and was over 40 when he began to study philosophy and mathematics at Vienna University. When the Nazis invaded Austria in 1938 he was imprisoned, but influential friends obtained his release and facilitated his emigration to America in 1940. Major works include *Der Tod des Virgil* (1945, The Death of Virgil) and *Die Schlafwandler* (3 vols, 1931–2, The Sleepwalkers).

Brockhaus, Friedrich Arnold [brokhows] (1772–1823) Publisher, born in Dortmund, Germany. He founded the firm of Brockhaus in Leipzig and published the famous dictionary, *Konversations-Lexikon*, begun by R G Lömbel in 1796 and completed in 1811. The business was carried on by his descendants.

Brockhouse, Bertram N (1915–) Physicist, born in Lethbridge, Alberta, Canada. He studied at the University of Toronto, joined Chalk River Nuclear Laboratories, moving to McMaster University in 1962. He shared the Nobel Prize for Physics in 1994 for his work in developing the field of neutron spectroscopy. >> Shull

Brockhurst, Gerald Leslie (1891–1979) Artist and etcher, born in Birmingham, West Midlands, C England, UK. He studied at the Birmingham School of Art, and at the age of 22 won the Royal Academy's Gold Medal and Scholarship which took him to France and Italy. His etchings and lithographs are almost entirely concerned with the themes of young womanhood and portraiture. Influenced by the early Italian Renaissance painters, his acknowledged masterpiece, 'Adolescence', was exhibited at the Royal Academy in 1933.

Brockway, (Archibald) Fenner, Baron (1888–1988) British politician and pacifist, a founder of the Campaign for Nuclear Disarmament, born in Calcutta into a missionary family. He went into journalism, joined the Independent Labour Party, became a militant pacifist, and was imprisoned during World War 1. Elected to parliament for the first time in 1929–31, and again in 1950–64, he was made a life peer in 1964.

Brod, Max (1884–1968) Writer, born in Prague. He became a Zionist and emigrated to Palestine in 1939. Although he is known in the English-speaking world as the long-time friend, editor, and biographer of Franz Kafka, he was a versatile and prolific writer in his own right. His works include the historical novel *Tycho Brahes Weg zu Gott* (1916, trans The Redemption of Tycho Brahe) and a novel about Jesus Christ, *Der Meister* (1951, The Master). >> Kafka

Broderick, Matthew (1963–) Actor, born in New York City. He starred as the computer hacker who nearly starts World War 3 in *War Games* (1983), and gained commercial success in *Ferris Bueller's Day Off* (1986). He earned a Tony award for the Broadway production of the Neil Simon comedy hit *Brighton Beach Memoirs* (1982 –3), and another for the musical *How to Succeed in Business Without Really Trying* (1995). He made his directorial debut with *Infinity* (1996).

Brodsky, Joseph (1940–96) Poet, born in St Petersburg, Russia, of Jewish parents. Convicted as a 'social parasite', he was exiled, moved to the USA, and was naturalized in 1977. He wrote in both Russian and English. Collections include *Ostanovka v pustynie* (1970, A Halt in the Wilderness), *Chast rechi* (1977, A Part of Speech), and *Uraniia* (1984, To Urania). He was awarded the Nobel Prize for Literature in 1987, and later published essays and a prose meditation on Venice, *Watermark* (1992).

Brogan, Sir Denis (William) (1900–74) Historian, born in Rutherglen, Glasgow, W Scotland, UK. He studied at Glasgow, Oxford, and Harvard, and became a fellow of Corpus Christi College, Oxford (1934), and professor of political science at Cambridge (1939). He is chiefly known for his work on historical and modern America.

Broglie, Louis (Victor Pierre Raymond), 7ᵉ duc de (7th Duke of) [broy, broglee] (1892–1987) Physicist, born in Dieppe, France. He studied at the Sorbonne, where he later became professor of theoretical physics (1928). In 1929 he was awarded the Nobel Prize for Physics for his pioneer work on the wave nature of the electron (*de Broglie waves*).

Broglie, (Louis César Victor) Maurice, 6ᵉ duc de (6th Duke of) [broy, broglee] (1875–1960) Physicist, born in Paris. He founded a laboratory at Paris, where he made many contributions to the study of X-ray spectra, and was professor at the Collège de France (1942–6).

Brome, Richard [broom] (?–c.1652) Jacobean playwright, of whom little is known except that he had been in his earlier days servant to Ben Jonson. He wrote as many as 24 popular plays, notably *The Northern Lass* and *The Jovial Crew*. >> Jonson

Bromfield, Louis (1896–1956) Writer, born in Mansfield, OH. He studied at Cornell Agricultural College and Columbia University, joined the French army in 1914, then returned to journalism in the USA. He moved to France in 1923, where he wrote his most highly acclaimed novels, such as *Early Autumn* (1926, Pulitzer) and *A Good Woman* (1927). Later works include *Until the Day Break* (1942) and *Mr Smith* (1951).

Bron, Eleanor (1938–) Actress and writer, born in Stanmore, N Greater London, England, UK. She studied at Cambridge, and from the early 1960s has made regular stage appearances, including a one-woman show, *Desdemona – If You Had Only Spoken* (1991). On television she became known in *Not So Much a Programme, More a Way of Life* (1964) and her films include *Alfie* (1966), *Black Beauty* (1994), and *A Little Princess* (1995). She has written several series for television (with John Fortune), and her books include *The Pillow Book of Eleanor Bron* (1985) and a novel, *Double Take* (1996).

Brongniart, Alexandre [brongniah(r)] (1770–1847) Naturalist and geologist, born in Paris. From 1808 professor at the Sorbonne and Museum of Natural History, he was also director of the porcelain manufactory at Sèvres from 1800. He introduced the term *Jurassic* for the limestones and clays of the Cotswolds. His son **Adolphe Théodore Brongniart** (1801–76) was a noted botanist.

Bronhill, June, originally **June Gough** (1927–) Soprano, born in Broken Hill, New South Wales, Australia, from which she adapted her stage name. After winning the Sydney *Sun* aria competition in 1950, she went to London for further study. She made an immediate success at Sadler's Wells in musicals and operetta (1954), and later took the lead in *Lucia di Lammermoor* at Covent Garden (1959). She has continued to sing, mainly in Australia, in operas, operettas, and musical comedies, and also works as a stage actress.

Bronson, Charles, originally **Charles Buchinski** (1920–) Film actor, born in Ehrenfield, PA. He made his name with roles in *The Magnificent Seven* (1960) and *The Great Escape* (1963), becoming known for his 'tough-guy' characters in such violent thrillers as *The Mechanic* (1972), and *Death Wish* (1974). Other films include *The Dirty Dozen* (1967), *Ten to Midnight* (1983), and *The President's Assassin* (1987).

Brønsted, Johannes Nicolaus [breonsted] (1879–1947) Physical chemist, born in Varde, Denmark. He studied engineering and chemistry at the Polytechnic Institute, Copenhagen, and became professor of chemistry there (1908). He is known for a novel definition of acids and bases, the *Brønsted–Lowry definition* (independently introduced in 1923 by British chemist **Thomas Martin Lowry**), which defines an acid as a substance with a tendency to lose a proton, and a base as a substance that tends to gain a proton.

Bronstein, Lev Davidovich >> **Trotsky, Leon**

Brontë [brontee], originally **Brunty** or **Prunty** Three literary sisters, **Anne** (1820–49), **Charlotte** (1816–55), and **Emily** (1818–48), born in Thornton, West Yorkshire, N England, UK. They were the daughters of **Patrick Brontë** (1777–1861), a clergyman of Irish descent, and his Cornish wife, **Maria Branwell** (1783–1821), and sisters of **Maria Brontë** and **Elizabeth Brontë**, who both died in childhood, and **Branwell Brontë** (1817–48), a brother who squandered his many talents and drank to excess. The family moved to Haworth, now part of Keighley, when their father became rector there (1820). Their childhood was spent in the sole companionship of one another on the wild Yorkshire moors. They constructed two fantasy worlds of their own, *Gondal* and *Angria*, described by the children in verse and prose in rival collections of notebooks. They also collaborated in a joint publication, under a pseudonym, of a collection of *Poems by Currer, Ellis and Acton Bell* (1846). Branwell's debts caused them to leave home and find employment, but they always returned to Haworth. Emily, Branwell, and Anne all died of tuberculosis within a year of each other. >> Brontë, Anne/Charlotte/ Emily

Brontë, Anne [brontee], pseudonym **Acton Bell** (1820–49) She went as governess to the Inghams at Blake Hall in 1839 and to the Robinsons at Thorpe Green (1841–5), a post she had to leave because of her brother's Branwell's unfortunate love for Mrs Robinson. Her two novels, *Agnes Grey* (1845) and *The Tenant of Wildfell Hall* (1848), were unsuccessful at the time. >> Brontë (above)

Brontë, Charlotte [brontee], pseudonym **Currer Bell** (1816–55) She returned in 1835 as a teacher to her old school, Roe Head, but gave up this post and two others, both as governess. Back at Haworth, the three sisters planned to start a school of their own and, to augment their qualifications, Charlotte and Emily attended the Pensionnat Héger in Brussels (1842). Their plans foundered, however, and Charlotte returned to Brussels as an English teacher (1843–4). Her first novel *The Professor*, did not achieve publication until after her death. Her masterpiece, *Jane Eyre* (1847), was followed by *Shirley* (1849), and *Villette* (1853). She married her father's curate, Arthur Bell Nicholls, in 1854, and died during pregnancy in the following year, leaving the fragment of another novel, *Emma*. Two stories, *The Secret* and *Lily Hart*, were published for the first time in 1978. >> Brontë (above)

Brontë, Emily (Jane) [brontee], pseudonym **Ellis Bell** (1818–48) In 1837 she became a governess in Halifax, then attended the Pensionnat Héger in Brussels with Charlotte, and in 1845 embarked upon a joint publication of poems after the discovery by the latter of her Gondal verse. She is known for her single novel, *Wuthering Heights* (1847). >> Brontë (above)

Bronzino, Il [bronzeenoh], originally **Agnolo di Cosimo di Mariano** (1503–72) Mannerist painter, born in Monticelli, Italy. He was a pupil of Raffaello del Garbo and of Pontormo, who adopted him. He decorated the chapel of the Palazzo Vecchio in Florence, and painted the 'Christ in Limbo' in the Uffizi (1552). His 'Venus, Folly, Cupid and Time' is in the National Gallery, and his portraits include most of the Medici family, as well as Dante, Boccaccio, and Petrarch. His nephew, Alessandro Allori, and his nephew's son, both Florentine painters, adopted his name. >> Pontormo

Brook, Peter (Stephen Paul) (1925–) Theatre and film director, born in London, England, UK. He studied at Oxford, and his involvement in the theatre began while at university. He directed many classical plays at the Birmingham Repertory Theatre, went to Stratford in 1947, and was also director of productions at the Royal Opera House, Covent Garden (1947–50). During the 1950s he worked on many productions in Britain, Europe, and the USA, and in 1962 returned to Stratford to join the newly established Royal Shakespeare Company for which he directed, among other productions, *King Lear* (1962), *Marat/Sade* (1964), *US* (1966), and *A Midsummer Night's Dream* (1970). Most of his work in the 1970s was done with the Paris-based Centre for Theatre Research, with which he travelled widely in Africa and Asia. Among his films are *The Beggar's Opera* (1952), *Lord of the Flies* (1962), and *King Lear* (1969). Later Paris productions include an adaptation of *The Mahabharata* (televised in 1989) and *The Tempest* (1990).

Brooke, Sir Basil Stanlake >> **Brookeborough, Basil Stanlake Brooke**

Brooke, (Bernard) Jocelyn (1908–66) Writer, poet, and amateur botanist, born in Kent, SE England, UK. He tried various occupations before joining the family wine firm. During World War 2 he enlisted in the Royal Army Medical Corps, and re-enlisted after the war; but following the critical success of *The Military Orchid* (1948) he bought himself out and thereafter devoted himself to writing. He followed this with the second and third parts of what became an autobiographical trilogy (known subsequently as *The Orchid Trilogy*), *A Mine of Serpents* (1949) and *The Goose Cathedral* (1950).

Brooke, Lord >> **Greville, Fulke**

Brooke, Rupert (Chawner) (1887–1915) Poet, born in Rugby, Warwickshire, C England, UK. He studied at Cambridge, travelled in Germany, and visited the USA and Tahiti. He died a commissioned officer on Skyros on his way to the Dardanelles, and was buried there. His *Poems* appeared in 1911, and *1914 and Other Poems* in 1915, after his death. His handsome appearance and untimely death made him a favourite poet among young people in the interwar period.

Brookeborough, Basil Stanlake Brooke, 1st Viscount (1888–1973) Northern Ireland statesman and prime minister (1943–63), born in Fermanagh. Elected to the Northern Ireland parliament in 1929, he became minister of agriculture (1933), of commerce (1941), and prime minister of the province, resigning in 1963. He was a staunch supporter of Unionist policy, determined to preserve the ties between Northern Ireland and the UK.

Brookes, Sir Norman (Everard) (1877–1968) Tennis player, born in Melbourne, Victoria, Australia. He went to Wimbledon in 1905, winning the all-comers' singles title, and returned the following year to win the singles, doubles, and mixed doubles titles. He won again at Wimbledon in 1914, and played Davis Cup tennis until 1921, captaining six winning teams. He was knighted in 1939. >> RR1173

Brookner, Anita (1928–) Writer and art historian, born in London, England, UK. An authority on 18th-c painting, she was the first woman Slade professor at Cambridge University (1967–8), and has been a reader at the Courtauld Institute of Art since 1977. As a novelist she was a late starter, but in eight years (1981–8) she published as many novels, winning the Booker Prize with *Hôtel du Lac* (1984). Other titles include *Family and Friends* (1985), *A Friend from England* (1987), *Incidents in the Rue Laugier* (1995), and *Visitors* (1997).

Brooks, Gwendolyn (Elizabeth) (1917–) Poet, born in Topeka, KS. Based in Chicago, she graduated from Wilson Junior College there (1936) and was publicity director for the National Association for the Advancement of Colored People in Chicago (1930s). She taught at many institutions, and succeeded Carl Sandburg as poet laureate of Illinois (1968). Her verse narrative, *Annie Allen* (1949), won the first Pulitzer Prize awarded to an African-American woman (1950). Later volumes include *Riot* (1970), *To Disembark* (1981), and *Blacks* (1991). >> Sandburg

Brooks, Mel, originally **Melvin Kaminsky** (1926–) Film actor and director, born in New York City. After some years as a gag-writer and comic, he turned to film-making with *The Producers* (1967), following this with a number of zany comedies satirizing established movie styles, among them *Blazing Saddles* (1974) and *Silent Movie* (1976). He usually writes the script, and acts in his productions, as well as directing them. Other films include *High Anxiety* (1977) and *History of the World Part One* (1980), and he co-produced *The Fly* (1986) and *84 Charing Cross Road* (1986). Later films include *Spaceballs* (1987), *Robin Hood: Men in Tights* (1993), and *Dracula: Dead and Loving It* (1995). He married actress **Anne Bancroft** (1931–) in 1964.

Broom, Robert (1866–1951) Palaeontologist, born in Paisley, Renfrewshire, W Scotland, UK. He studied medicine at Glasgow, and practised in Australia before moving to South Africa in 1897. He was appointed professor of zoology and geology at Victoria College (1903–10), and in 1934 became palaeontologist at the Transvaal Museum, Pretoria. In 1947 he found a partial skeleton of the hominid *Australopithecus*, including the pelvis, which proved that it had walked upright about 1–2 million years ago. His studies on human ancestry are given in his book *Finding the Missing Link* (1950).

Broome, David (1940–) Show jumper, born in Cardiff, S Wales, UK. He won the World Championship on *Beethoven* in 1970, was three times European champion, on *Sunsalve* (1961) and *Mister Softee* (1967, 1969), and was the individual bronze medallist at the 1960 and 1968 Olympics. He returned to the British Olympic team in 1988 after a 20-year absence. >> RR1153

Broonzy, Big Bill, popular name of **William Lee Conley Broonzy** (1893–1958) Blues singer, composer, and musician, born in Scott, MS. He began musical life as a fiddler, but switched to guitar when he moved to Chicago in 1920. He was one of the most eclectic stylists among the great blues performers, encompassing American folk-song and jazz as well as rural and urban blues. In the 1950s the folk-music revival brought him a wider audience, and he toured extensively, performing in Europe, Africa, and South America.

Brophy, Brigid (Antonia) (1929–95) Writer and critic, born in London, England, UK. She studied at Oxford, and married **Sir Michael Levey** in 1954. Her novels included *Hackenfeller's Ape* (1953), *Flesh* (1962), *In Transit* (1970), and *Palace Without Chairs* (1978). Among her non-fiction titles are *Black Ship to Hell* (1962) and *Black and White: a Portrait of Aubrey Beardsley* (1968), and she co-wrote the controversial *Fifty Works of English and American Literature We Could Do Without* (1967, with Michael Levey and Charles Osborne). She was vice-president of the Anti-Vivisection League of Great Britain, and active in the Public Lending Right campaign in the UK.

Brosnan, Pierce [broznan] (1952–) Actor, born in Co Meath, Ireland. After an unsettled childhood, he moved to London, where he joined an experimental theatre group and studied at the Drama Centre. After several stage roles in London, he moved to Los Angeles, where he was offered the lead in the detective series *Remington Steele* (1982–7). Although early singled out as a possible James Bond, it was not until 1995 that he finally played the role, in *Goldeneye*. His other film credits begin with *The Long Good Friday* (1980), and include *Mrs Doubtfire* (1993), *Mars Attacks!* (1996), and *Dante's Peak* (1997).

Brosse, Salomon de (1565–1626) Architect to Marie de Médicis, born in Verneuil, France. He designed the Luxembourg Palace in Paris (1615–20), and Louis XIII's hunting lodge (1624–6), the nucleus of Versailles. >> Marie de Médicis

Brothers, Richard (1757–1824) British religious fanatic and ex-naval officer, born in Newfoundland, Canada. He announced himself in 1793 as the 'nephew of the Almighty', apostle of a new religion, the Anglo-Israelites. In 1795, for prophesying the destruction of the monarchy, he was sent to Newgate and subsequently to an asylum.

Brougham, Henry Peter, Baron Brougham and Vaux [broom] (1778–1868) Jurist and politician, born in Edinburgh, EC Scotland, UK. He studied at Edinburgh University, helped to found the *Edinburgh Review* (1802), was called to the English bar in 1808, and entered parliament in 1810. His eloquence and boldness made him a popular hero for some time (1820–30). He accepted a peerage and the chancellorship (1830), assisted materially in carrying the Reform Bill, and introduced several law reforms. He designed the *brougham* (carriage), which is named after him.

Broughton, William Grant [brawtn] (1788–1853) First Anglican bishop of Sydney, born in London, England, UK. He studied at Cambridge, and was ordained in 1818, ministering in Hampshire before accepting an invitation from the Duke of Wellington to become the second archdeacon of New South Wales. He arrived in Sydney in 1829, and became Bishop of Australia in 1836. With the division into more manageable dioceses (1847), he was restyled Bishop of Sydney and Metropolitan of Australia.

Brouwer or **Brauer, Adriaen** [brower] (c. 1605–38) Painter, born in Oudenaarde, Belgium. He studied at Haarlem under Frans Hals, and settled at Antwerp (c.1630). His favourite subjects were scenes from tavern life, country merrymakings, card players, smoking and drinking groups, and roisterers generally. >> Hals

Brouwer, Luitzen Egbertus Jan [brower] (1881–1966) Mathematician, born in Overschie, The Netherlands. He studied at Amsterdam University at the age of 16, where he was professor (1912–51). He founded the intuitionist or constructivist school of mathematical logic, which does not accept the law of the excluded middle, and in which the existence of a mathematical object can only be proved by giving an explicit method for its construction. He also made fundamental advances in topology, proving the invariance of dimension, and the fixed point theorem named after him.

Browder, Earl (Russell) (1891–1973) Writer and communist leader, born in Wichita, KA. After an elementary schooling he entered trade-union and socialist politics. He was general secretary of the US Communist Party (1930–44) but was expelled in 1946 for his views supporting the peaceful coexistence of socialism and capitalism. He served several prison sentences for his beliefs and activities.

Brower, David (Ross) [brower] (1912–) Conservationist, born in Berkeley, CA. He worked for the National Park Service in Yosemite National Park before joining the University of California Press as an editor in 1941. In 1952 he became executive director of the Sierra Club, and soon developed a reputation as a militant environmentalist. Under his leadership, the Sierra Club blocked billions of dollars worth of construction projects in wilderness areas. Sierra Club conservatives forced him from the post in 1969, and he then formed the John Muir Institute and Friends of the Earth, which initiated the first Earth Day (22 Apr 1969). >> Leopold; Muir, John

Brown, Sir Arthur Whitten (1886–1948) Aviator, born in Glasgow, W Scotland, UK. As navigator with Sir John William Alcock he made the first non-stop crossing of the Atlantic in a Vickers-Vimy biplane on 14 June 1919, and shared a £10 000 prize given by the London *Daily Mail*. Both men were knighted after the flight. >> Alcock

Brown, Capability >> **Brown, Lancelot**

Brown, Charles Brockden (1771–1810) Novelist, born in Philadelphia, PA. He was the first professional American writer, and is often called 'the father of the American novel'. *Wieland* (1798), *Ormund* (1799), and *Jane Talbot* (1804) are among his Gothic Romances.

Brown, Edmund G(erald), known as **Pat Brown** (1905–96) US state governor, born in San Francisco, CA. He studied law, then opened a practice in San Francisco (1927–43), serving as district attorney there (1943–50) and as California's Democratic attorney general (1950–8). Becoming governor (1959–67), he expanded the state university system and initiated a statewide water project. His most public moment came in 1960, when he decided that California law did not allow him to commute the execution of Caryl Chessman. He retired to his law practice in San Francisco. >> Chessman

Brown, Ford Madox (1821–93) British historical painter, born in Calais, France. He studied art at Bruges, Ghent, and Antwerp. In Paris he produced his 'Manfred on the Jungfrau' (1841), a work intensely dramatic in feeling, but sombre in colouring. A visit to Italy (1845) led him to seek a greater richness of colouring, as in 'Chaucer Reciting his Poetry' (1851). He was a close associate of William Morris, and in 1861 was a founder member of Morris, Marshall, Faulkner & Co, for which he produced designs for furniture and stained glass. He completed 12 frescoes for Manchester Town Hall just before his death. >> Morris, William

Brown, George (Alfred) >> **George-Brown, Baron**

Brown, George Douglas, pseudonym **George Douglas** (1869–1902) Writer, born in Ochiltree, East Ayrshire, SW Scotland, UK. He studied at Glasgow and Oxford universities, then settled in London as a journalist. He is best known for *The House with the Green Shutters* (1901), written under his pseudonym.

Brown, (James) Gordon (1951–) Scottish politician, born in Glasgow, W Scotland, UK. He studied history at Edinburgh University, and while still a student there was elected rector (1972–5). He lectured at Glasgow College of Technology, and entered the House of Commons in 1983 as Labour member for Dunfermline East. Despite losing the sight of one eye in a sporting accident, he rose swiftly within the Labour Party, becoming Opposition chief secretary to the Treasury (1987–9), Opposition trade and industry secretary (1989–92), Shadow Chancellor (1992–7) under the leadership of John Smith, then Tony Blair, and Chancellor of the Exchequer (1997–) in the Labour government.

Brown, Herbert (Charles), originally **Herbert Brovarnik** (1912–) Chemist, born in London, England, UK. His Ukrainian family moved to Chicago when he was two. He studied at Chicago University, and later became professor at Purdue. He shared the Nobel Prize for Chemistry in 1979 for his work in introducing boron compounds as important reagents in synthesis. >> Wittig; RR1123

Brown, James (1928–) Pop singer, songwriter, and producer, born in Barnwell, SC. He began his professional career backed by a former Gospel group, The Famous Flames, with whom he recorded his first 'cry' ballads, 'Please, Please, Please' and 'Try Me' (1958). Mixing Gospel and blues roots with his own aggressive energy, he put together a band and roadshow which by 1962 had made him America's leading rhythm and blues star, and earned him the nickname 'Soul Brother Number One'. 'Out Of Sight' (1964) brought him his first international success. Later recordings in the 1960s include 'America Is My

Home' and 'Say It Loud, I'm Black and I'm Proud'. In 1988 he was jailed for six years on charges that included aggravated assault. His sentence was commuted (1990) to a prison-based work programme until 1991.

Brown, Jim, popular name of **James Nathaniel Brown** (1936–) Player of American football, born in St Simon Island, GA. An All-American halfback at Syracuse University (1956), he had nine outstanding years with the Cleveland Browns in the National League (1957–66), during which he led the league eight times in rushing. Later he had a successful film career in Hollywood.

Brown, John (c.1735–88) Physician, founder of the Brunonian system of medicine, born in Bunkle parish, Scottish Borders, SE Scotland, UK. He taught at Duns and Edinburgh, and after studying medicine became assistant to Professor William Cullen. His system of medicine divided all diseases into the sthenic, depending on an excess of excitement, and the asthenic; the former to be removed by debilitating medicines, and the latter by stimulants. >> Cullen, William

Brown, John (1800–59) Militant abolitionist, born in Torrington, CT. He supported himself with many different jobs while wandering through the country advocating antislavery. He was twice married, and had 20 children. In 1859 he led a raid on the US Armory at Harper's Ferry in Virginia, with the intention of launching a slave insurrection. The raid failed, and after being convicted of treason against Virginia, he was hanged at Charlestown. The song 'John Brown's Body' commemorates the Harper's Ferry raid, and was popular with Northern soldiers in the Civil War. >> Smith, Gerrit

Brown, Lancelot, known as **Capability Brown** (1715–83) Landscape gardener, born in Kirkharle, Northumberland, NE England, UK. He established a purely English style of garden lay-out, using simple artifices to produce natural effects, as in the laid-out gardens at Blenheim, Kew, Stowe, Warwick Castle, and others. He acquired his nickname from telling clients that their gardens had excellent 'capabilities'.

Brown, Melanie >> **Spice Girls, The**

Brown, Michael (Stuart) (1941–) Molecular geneticist, born in New York City. He studied medicine at Pennsylvania, and became professor at the Southwestern Medical School at Texas University in 1971. He conducted research into cholesterol metabolism with Joseph Goldstein at Texas, leading to the discovery of low-density or LDL receptors, for which they were awarded the Nobel Prize for Physiology or Medicine in 1985. >> Goldstein, Joseph

Brown, Robert (1773–1858) Botanist, born in Montrose, Angus, E Scotland, UK. He studied at Aberdeen and Edinburgh, and in 1798 visited London, where his ability so impressed Sir Joseph Banks that he was appointed naturalist to Matthew Flinders's coastal survey of Australia (1801–5). He brought back nearly 4000 species of plants for classification. In 1810 he received charge of Banks' library and collections, and when they were transferred to the British Museum in 1827 he became botanical keeper. He was the first to note that, in general, living cells contain a nucleus, and to name it. In 1827 he first observed the *Brownian movement* of fine particles in a liquid. >> Banks, Joseph; Flinders

Brown, Trisha (1936–) Choreographer, born in Aberdeen, WA. In New York City she helped to found the experimental Judson Dance Company in 1962. Throughout the 1960s and 1970s she created a series of original 'equipment pieces', where dancers were rigged in block and tackle harness to allow them to walk on walls or down the trunks of trees. She also ran an improvisational group, Grand Union

(1970–6), and in the late 1970s began to work in traditional theatres, adding design and music to her pieces for the first time.

Browne, Charles Farrar, pseudonym **Artemus Ward** (1834–67) Humorist, born in Waterford, ME. In 1858 he wrote for the *Cleveland Plain Dealer* a description of an imaginary travelling menagerie, followed by letters in which grotesque spelling and a mixture of business platitudes and sermonizing served to convey sound sense and shrewd satire. In 1861, as Artemus Ward, he became a lecturer, giving performances whose artistic wretchedness gave rise to countless jokes. In 1866 he travelled to London, where he contributed to *Punch*, and became popular as 'the genial showman'.

Browne, Hablot Knight, pseudonym **Phiz** (1815–82) Illustrator, born in London, England, UK. He was apprenticed to a line engraver, but soon took to etching and watercolour painting, and gained a medal from the Society of Arts for an etching of 'John Gilpin' (1833). In 1836 he became illustrator of *The Pickwick Papers*, and maintained his reputation by his designs for other works by Dickens. >> Dickens

Browne, Robert (c. 1550–1633) Clergyman, founder of the *Brownists*, born in Tolethorpe, Leicestershire, C England, UK. After graduating from Cambridge (1572), he became a schoolmaster in London, and an open-air preacher. In 1580 he began to attack the established Church, and soon after formed a distinct Church on congregational principles at Norwich. Reconciling himself to the Anglican Church, he became master of Stamford grammar school (1586), and rector of Achurch, Northamptonshire (1591). Of a very violent temper, he was sent to Northampton jail at the age of 80 for an assault on a constable, and died there.

Browne, Sir Thomas (1605–82) Writer and physician, born in London, England, UK. He studied at Oxford, then travelled in Ireland, France, and Italy, and settled in Norwich (1637). His greatest work is his earliest, the *Religio medici*, written about 1635 – a confession of faith, revealing a deep insight into the mysteries of the spiritual life. His other works include *Pseudodoxia epidemica* (1646), *Hydriotaphia*; *Urn Burial* (1658), and the *Garden of Cyrus* (1658). He was knighted in 1671.

Browne, Thomas Alexander >> **Boldrewood, Rolf**

Browne, Tom (1870–1910) Strip cartoonist, illustrator, and painter, born in Nottingham, Nottinghamshire, C England, UK. With his creation of *Weary Willie and Tired Tim*, he became known as 'the father of British comic style'. Moving to London, he quickly became a popular cartoonist for magazines, posters, and picture postcards. When *Comic Cuts* was launched (1890), his bold linear style proved perfect for cheap reproduction, and he was soon drawing front pages for several comics a week.

Browning, Elizabeth Barrett, *née* **Barrett** (1806–61) Poet, born in Durham, Co Durham, NE England, UK, the wife of Robert Browning. She seriously injured her spine (c.1821), and was long an invalid. Her first poems were published at 19, and other volumes appeared in 1838 and 1844. In 1845 she met **Robert Browning**, with whom she eloped in 1846. Her best-known work is *Sonnets from the Portuguese* (1850), 'Portuguese' being Browning's pet name for her. In her later years she developed an interest in spiritualism, and also in Italian politics. >> Browning, Robert

Browning, John Moses (1855–1926) Gunsmith and inventor, born in Ogden, UT. He produced his first gun from scrap metal at the age of 13. He patented a breech-loading single-shot rifle in 1879, and the Browning automatic pistol in 1911. The Browning machine gun (1917) and the Browning automatic rifle (1918) became standard army weapons for many years.

Browning, Robert (1812–89) Poet, born in London, England, UK, the husband of **Elizabeth Barrett**. The son of a clerk, he received scant formal education. His early work attracted little attention until the publication of *Paracelsus* (1835). *Bells and Pomegranates* (1841–6) included several of his best-known dramatic lyrics, such as 'How they Brought the Good News from Ghent to Aix'. In 1846 he married Elizabeth Barrett, and with her settled in Florence, where he wrote *Men and Women* (1855) and began *Dramatis Personae* (1864). Their son, **Robert Barrett Browning** (1849–1912), the sculptor, was born there. After the death of his wife (1861) he settled in London, where he wrote his masterpiece, *The Ring and the Book* (1869). >> Browning, Elizabeth

Brownlee, John (1900–69) Operatic baritone, born in Geelong, Victoria, Australia. He studied at Melbourne and Paris, where he made his debut in 1926. Nellie Melba then engaged him to sing opposite her in *La Bohème* at Covent Garden, thus beginning his distinguished international career. He was a regular soloist with the Paris Opéra until 1936, and a founding soloist with the Glyndebourne Festival Opera. He made his first appearance with the Metropolitan Opera, New York City, in 1937, and appeared there regularly until 1958. He then became director of the Manhattan School of Music. >> Melba

Brownson, Orestes (Augustus) (1803–76) Clergyman and writer, born in Stockbridge, VT. He was successively a Presbyterian, a Universalist, a Unitarian pastor and, from 1844, a Roman Catholic. He founded and edited *Brownson's Quarterly Review* (1844–65, and 1872 onwards), and wrote many books, including *The Convert* (1857) and *The American Republic* (1865).

Broz, Josip >> **Tito**

Brubeck, Dave, popular name of **David Warren Brubeck** (1920–) Pianist, composer, and bandleader, born in Concord, CA. He studied music at the College of the Pacific, CA, leading a 12-piece jazz band and at the same time studying composition under Darius Milhaud. Towards the end of World War 2 he was stationed in Europe, leading a service band, but in 1946 he began to make his reputation as an experimental musician with his Jazz Workshop Ensemble. He reached a wider public with the Dave Brubeck Quartet, formed in 1951. He has also composed larger works such as ballets, a Mass, and pieces for jazz group and orchestra, and continued to tour and record with small groups through the 1980s. >> Milhaud

Bruce, Christopher (1945–) Dancer and choreographer, born in Leicester, Leicestershire, C England, UK. He studied tap, acrobatics, and ballet, and on graduating from the Ballet Rambert School (1963) immediately joined the company. In 1967 he established his reputation in Glen Tetley's *Pierrot lunaire*. His work is a fusion of classical and modern dance idioms, with a strong undercurrent of social consciousness. He became associate choreographer of English National Ballet (formerly London Festival Ballet) (1986–91), resident choreographer at Houston Ballet (1989–), and artistic director at Rambert Dance Company (1994–).

Bruce, Sir David (1855–1931) Microbiologist and physician, born in Australia. As an officer in the Royal Army Medical Corps (1883–1919), he identified in Malta the bacterium that causes the cattle disease *brucellosis*, and undulant fever in humans, named *Brucella* (1887).

Bruce, David K(irkpatrick) E(ste) (1898–1977) US statesman and diplomat, born in Baltimore, MD. He served in World War 1 and was admitted to the Maryland bar in 1921. After a period with the foreign service (1925–7), he turned his attention to business and farming (1928–40). As director of the economic co-operation mission (1948–9) he administered the Marshall Plan in France. He was ambassador to France (1949–52), West Germany (1957–9), and Britain (1961–9), and a representative to the Vietnam Peace Talks in Paris (1970–1), liaison officer to Communist China (1973–4), and ambassador to NATO (1974–6). >> Marshall, George C

Bruce, James, nickname **the Abyssinian** (1730–94) Explorer, born in Larbert, Falkirk, C Scotland, UK. He became consul-general in Algiers (1763–5), and in 1768 journeyed to Abyssinia by the Nile, Aswan, the Red Sea, and Massowah. In 1770 he reached the source of the Abbai, or headstream of the Blue Nile. His *Travels to Discover the Sources of the Nile* was published in 1790.

Bruce, Lenny, originally **Leonard Alfred Schneider** (1925–66) Satirical comedian, born in New York City. He first appeared as a night-club performer in Baltimore. The satire and 'black' humour of his largely improvised act often overstepped the bounds of what was considered respectable; in 1961 he was imprisoned for obscenity, and in 1963 was refused permission to enter Britain. In 1963 he was found guilty of illegal possession of drugs, and it was his use of these which contributed to his death three years later.

Bruce, Robert, 4th Lord of Annandale (?–1245) Scottish nobleman. He married Isabel, the second daughter of David, Earl of Huntingdon and Chester, brother of King William the Lion, and thus founded the royal house of Bruce.

Bruce, Robert (1274–1329) King of Scots (1306–29) as Robert I, and hero of the Scottish War of Independence. As Earl of Carrick, in 1296 he swore fealty to Edward I of England, but soon joined the Scottish revolt under Wallace. In 1306 he quarrelled with John Comyn, his political rival, stabbing him to death; then assembled his vassals and was crowned king at Scone. He was forced to flee to Ireland, but returned in 1307 and defeated the English at Loudoun Hill. After Edward's death (1307), the English were forced from the country, and all the great castles were recovered except Berwick and Stirling. This led to the Battle of Bannockburn (1314), when the English were routed. Sporadic war with England continued until the Treaty of Northampton (1328), which recognized the independence of Scotland, and Bruce's right to the throne. He was succeeded by David II, the son of his second wife.

Bruce (of Melbourne), Stanley Melbourne Bruce, 1st Viscount (1883–1967) Australian statesman and prime minister (1923–9), born in Melbourne, Victoria, Australia. He entered parliament in 1918, and represented Australia in the League of Nations Assembly. After serving as prime minister, he was high commissioner in London (1933–45), and represented Australia at meetings of Churchill's war Cabinet. He settled in England for the last 20 years of his life. >> Churchill, Sir Winston; RR1033

Bruch, Max [brukh] (1838–1920) Composer, born in Cologne, Germany. He became musical director at Coblenz in 1865, and conducted the Liverpool Philharmonic Society (1880–3), introducing many of his choral works. He is best known for his violin concerto in G minor, the *Kol Nidrei* variations in which he employs the idioms of Hebrew and Celtic traditional melodies, and the *Konzertstück*.

Brücke, die (Ger 'bridge') >> **Kirchner; Nolde; Pechstein; Schmidt-Rottluff**

Bruckner, Anton [brukner] (1824–96) Composer and organist, born in Ansfelden, Austria. He held several posts as organist, and became professor of composition at the Vienna Conservatory (1868–91). His fame chiefly rests on his nine symphonies (the last unfinished), but he also wrote four impressive Masses, several smaller sacred works and many choral works. His music, which shows the influence of Wagner and Schubert, was given a mixed reception during his lifetime.

Brudenell, James Thomas >> **Cardigan, James Thomas Brudenell**

Brueghel, Pieter [broygl], also spelled **Bruegel** or **Breughel**, known as **the Elder** (c.1520–69) The most original of all 16th-c Flemish painters, probably born in the village of Brueghel, near Breda. He studied under Pieter Coecke van Aelst (1502–50), and was much influenced by Bosch. In about 1551 he began to travel through France and Italy, later settling in Brussels, where he painted his major works. His genre pictures of peasant life reach their finest expression in 'The Blind Leading the Blind', (1568, Naples), the 'Peasant Wedding', and the 'Peasant Dance' (c.1568, Vienna). His eldest son, **Pieter Brueghel the Younger** (c.1564–1637), is known as 'Hell' Brueghel, because of his paintings of devils, hags, and robbers. His younger son, **Jan Brueghel** (1568–1625), known as 'Velvet' Brueghel, painted still-life, flowers, landscapes, and religious subjects on a small scale. >> Bosch

Brugmann, Karl (1849–1919) Philologist, born in Wiesbaden, Germany. Professor of Sanskrit at Freiburg (1884) and Leipzig (1887), he wrote a *Comparative Grammar of the Indo-Germanic Languages* (1886–3, trans title). He was a leading exponent of the Neogrammarian school, stressing the fixity of sound laws.

Brugsch, Heinrich Karl (1827–94) Egyptologist, born in Berlin. He was director of the School of Egyptology in Cairo (1870–90), helped to decipher demotic script, and published a hieroglyphic–demotic dictionary (1867–82).

Bruhn, Erik [broon], originally **Belton Evers** (1928–86) Dancer and ballet director, born in Copenhagen. He trained at the Royal Danish Ballet School, joining the company in 1947. An unrivalled exponent of the Bournonville style, he toured the world as guest performer with many companies. He was the director of the Royal Swedish Ballet (1967–72) and artistic director of the National Ballet of Canada (1983–6).

Brumby, Colin James (1933–) Composer and teacher, born in Melbourne, Victoria, Australia. He studied at the Conservatory in Melbourne, then in Europe, returning to become senior lecturer at the University of Queensland, Brisbane. His output includes two operas, nine operettas for younger audiences, a symphony (1982), nine concertos, choral works, film scores, and chamber music.

Brumel, Valeri Nikolayevich (1942–) Athlete, born in Razvedki, Russia. He won the Olympic gold medal in the high jump at Tokyo in 1964, and between 1960 and 1963 raised the world record to 2·28 m.

Brummell, George Bryan, known as **Beau Brummell** (1778–1840) Dandy, born in London, England, UK. At Eton, and during a brief sojourn at Oxford, he was less distinguished for studiousness than for the exquisiteness of his dress and manners; and after four years in the army, having come into a fortune, he entered on his true vocation as arbiter of elegancies. A close friend and protégé of the prince regent (the future George IV), they quarrelled in 1813, and gambling debts forced Brummell to flee to France (1816). He died in the lunatic asylum in Caen.

Brun, Charles Le >> **Le Brun, Charles**

Bruna, Dick [broona] (1927–) Dutch artist and writer. The creator of a highly successful series of picture books for young children, he started in the book-trade but gave this up to concentrate on graphic art. His first book was *The Apple*, published in England in 1966, 13 years after it appeared in Holland. His books include such characters as Miffy the rabbit, and the small dog Snuffy.

Brundage, Avery (1887–1975) International athletics administrator, born in Detroit, MI. He was a member of the US decathlon team in the 1912 Olympic Games at Stockholm, but was far more influential in his long spell as president of the US Olympic Association (1929–53), and in his 20 years as president of the International Olympic Committee (1952–72).

Brundtland, Gro Harlem [bruntland] (1939–) Norwegian stateswoman and first woman prime minister of Norway (1981, 1986–9, 1990–6), born in Oslo. She studied medicine at Oslo and Harvard, qualifying as a physician. In 1960 she married a leader of the Opposition Conservative Party, **Arne Olav**, and they have four children. She joined the Labour Party and entered politics (1969), after working in public medicine services in Oslo. She was appointed environment minister (1974–9) and, as leader of the Labour Party group, became prime minister for the first time. In 1987 she chaired the World Commission on Environment and Development which produced the report *Our Common Future*. In 1988 she was awarded the Third World Foundation Prize for leadership in environmental issues. >> RR1079

Brunel, Isambard Kingdom [broonel] (1806–59) Engineer, born in Portsmouth, Hampshire, S England, UK, the son of **Marc Brunel**. He worked in his father's office, and helped to plan the Thames Tunnel. He himself planned the Clifton Suspension Bridge (1829–31, completed 1864), and the Hungerford Suspension Bridge (1841–5) over the Thames. He designed the *Great Western* (1837), the first steamship built to cross the Atlantic, the *Great Britain* (1843), the first ocean screw-steamer, and the *Great Eastern* (1853–8), then the largest vessel ever built. He was also engineer to the Great Western Railway, and constructed many docks. >> Brunel, Marc

Brunel, Sir Marc Isambard [broonel] (1769–1849) Engineer and inventor, born in Hacqueville, France. He fled from the French Revolution in 1793, going first to the USA, where he was architect and chief engineer in New York. He settled in England in 1799, constructed many public works, and solved many of the problems of underwater tunnelling. His main achievement was the 460 m/503 yd Thames Tunnel from Rotherhithe to Wapping (1825–43). He was knighted in 1841. >> Brunel, Isambard Kingdom

Brunelleschi, Filippo [brooneleskee] (1377–1446) Architect, goldsmith, and sculptor, born in Florence, Italy. One of the figures responsible for the development of the Renaissance style in Florence, his chief work is the dome of the cathedral there. Erected between 1420 and 1461, it is (measured diametrically) the largest in the world, and served as the model for Michelangelo's design for St Peter's in Rome. Other well-known buildings by him in Florence are the Church of San Lorenzo (1418–29) and the Ospedale degli Innocenti (1419–44). He is also noted for his innovations in the use of perspective.

Bruner, Jerome (Seymour) [brooner] (1915–) Psychologist, born in New York City. He studied at Duke University and Harvard, and was professor of psychology at Harvard (1952–72), Oxford (1972–80), and the New School for Social Research, New York City. In a number of works published in the 1960s he stressed the centrality of teaching for underlying cognitive structure, and the usefulness of the 'spiral curriculum'. His humanities programme 'Man: a Course of Study', described in *Toward a Theory of Instruction* (1966), has been held to be a landmark in curriculum development. He has pioneered techniques for investigating infant perception, and is a leading advocate of the value of the phenomenological tradition in psychology.

Brüning, Heinrich (1885–1970) German statesman, born in Münster, Germany. He studied at Bonn and the London School of Economics, and was leader of the Catholic

Centre Party from 1929, and chancellor (1930–2), when he was forced to resign by the Nazis. He left Germany in 1934, and became professor of government at Harvard (1939–52), and professor of political science at Cologne (1951–5).

Brunne, Robert of >> **Mannyng, Robert**

Brunner, (Heinrich) Emil (1889–1966) Reformed theologian, born in Winterthur, Switzerland. Following service as a pastor (1916–24), he became professor of systematic and practical theology at Zürich (1924–55). The author of nearly 400 books and articles, his reputation outside the European mainland was established by the translations of *The Mediator* (1927) and *The Divine Imperative* (1932).

Bruno, St (925–65) Clergyman, born in Cologne, Germany. The brother of Otto I, the Great, he was imperial chancellor in 940, and in 953 crushed a rebellion against Otto. He became Archbishop of Cologne in 953, and Duke of Lorraine in 954. He was distinguished both for piety and learning. Feast day 11 October. >> Otto I

Bruno, St, also known as **Boniface** (970–1009) Missionary, born in Querfurt, Germany. Educated at Magdeburg Cathedral School, he entered the monastery in Ravenna in 997, and worked as a missionary bishop in Poland, Hungary, and the Ukraine. He reached Prussia but met fierce opposition, and was put to death with his companions. Feast day 19 June.

Bruno, Giordano, originally **Filippo Bruno**, nickname **Il Nolano** (1548–1600) Philosopher and scientist, born in Nola, Italy. He became a Dominican friar but was too unorthodox to stay in the order. He travelled widely in France, Germany, England, and Italy, propounding an extreme pantheistic philosophy. His enthusiastic championship of Copernicus brought him into conflict with the Inquisition. He was arrested in 1593 in Venice, and after a 7-year trial was burned at the stake in Rome. >> Copernicus

Bruno of Cologne, St (c.1030–1101) Clergyman, the founder of the Carthusian order, born in Cologne, Germany. He became rector of the cathedral school at Reims, but withdrew in 1084 to the wild mountains of Chartreuse, near Grenoble. Here with six friends he founded the austere Carthusian order on the site of the present Grande Chartreuse. In 1091, at the invitation of Pope Urban II, he established a second Carthusian monastery at Della Torre in Calabria. Feast day 6 October.

Brunoff, Jean de (1899–1937) and **Laurent de Brunoff** (1925–) [broonof] Illustrators, father and son, creators of Babar the Elephant, hero of a series of picture books. Drawn originally by Jean, he first appeared in 1931 in *L'Histoire de Babar, le petit éléphant* (The Story of Babar, the Little Elephant).

Brusilov, Alexey [brusilof] (1856–1926) Soldier, born in Tbilisi, Georgia. In World War 1 he led the invasion of Galicia (1914) and in the Carpathians. From 1916 he distinguished himself on the Eastern Front, notably in the successful *Brusilov Offensive* against the Austrians in 1916. He became chief-of-staff in 1917. After the revolution he commanded forces in the war against Poland (1920).

Brustein, Robert [broostiyn] (1927–) Drama critic, teacher, and director, born in New York City. In 1966, as dean of the School of Drama at Yale, he founded the Yale Repertory Theater. He is also director of the American Repertory Theater, which took up residence at Harvard in 1980.

Brutus, Lucius Junius [brootus] (fl.500 BC–) Legendary Roman hero who established Republican government at Rome. He was the son of a rich Roman, on whose death Lucius Tarquinius Superbus seized the property and killed an elder brother. He escaped by feigning idiocy, from which he got his name (*brutus* means 'stupid'). When popular indignation was roused at the rape of Lucretia by Sextus, he drove the royal family from Rome. He was elected one of the first two consuls (509 BC). >> Lucretia

Brutus, Marcus Junius [brootus] (c. 85–42 BC) Roman politician. He sided with Pompey when the civil war broke out, but submitted to Caesar, and was appointed Governor of Cisalpine Gaul. He divorced his wife to marry **Portia**, the daughter of his master, Cato. Cassius persuaded him to join the conspiracy against Caesar (44 BC); but, defeated by Mark Antony and Octavian at Philippi, he killed himself. >> Caesar; Cassius

Bruyère, Jean de la >> **La Bruyère, Jean de**

Bryan, William (Jennings) (1860–1925) Lawyer and US politician, born in Salem, IL. He graduated from Illinois College in 1881, studied law at Chicago, and practised at Jacksonville and in Nebraska. Elected to Congress in 1890, as Democratic candidate for the presidency he was crushingly defeated by McKinley in 1896 and 1900, and by Taft in 1908. A great populist stump-orator, and founder editor of *The Commoner*, he was appointed secretary of state by Woodrow Wilson (1913), but as an ardent pacifist resigned in 1915. >> McKinley; Taft, William Howard; Wilson, Woodrow

Bryant, Bear, popular name of **Paul William Bryant** (1913–83) Coach of American football, born in Kingsland, AR. As a player with the University of Alabama football team, he won the 1935 Rose Bowl game. He started coaching in 1945 at Maryland, and from 1958 was coach at Alabama. He broke the all-time career victories record in 1981 with 315 victories (not broken until 1985), and retired with 323. At the university a hall and stadium are both named after him.

Bryant, William Cullen (1794–1878) Poet and journalist, born in Cummington, MA. He graduated in law, and from 1816 practised in Great Barrington, MA, but in 1817 achieved fame as a poet following the publication of 'Thanatopsis'. He continued to practise at the bar until 1825, but more and more turned to newspaper contributions in prose and verse, becoming co-owner and editor of the New York *Evening Post* in 1829.

Bryden, Bill, popular name of **William Bryden** (1942–) Stage director and playwright, born in Greenock, Inverclyde, WC Scotland, UK. He became assistant director at the Belgrade Theatre, Coventry (1965–7), and associate director of the Royal Lyceum Theatre, Edinburgh (1971–4), where his productions included two of his own plays, *Willie Rough* (1972) and *Benny Lynch* (1974). He was an associate of the National Theatre (1975–85), where he was director of the Cottesloe Theatre (1978–80), and later became head of drama for BBC Television Scotland (1984–93).

Bryson, Bill (1951–) Writer, born in Des Moines, IA. In 1977 he moved to England and settled in North Yorkshire. His travel books include the best-sellers *The Lost Continent* and *Neither Here Nor There* (1991), and among his books on the English language are *Mother Tongue* (1990) and *Made in America* (1994). *Notes From A Small Island* (1995) recounts his final trip around Britain before returning to America.

Bryussov, Valery Yakovlevich [bryusof] (1873–1924) Poet, critic, and translator, born in Moscow. He was one of the leaders of the Russian Symbolist movement which looked to France for its inspiration, and he translated many of the major Modernist writers in Europe. He became an enthusiastic Bolshevik in 1917.

Brzezinski, Zbigniew [bzhezin**skee] (1928–) Academic and politician, born in Poland. He settled in the USA and became a US citizen in 1958. He taught at Harvard's Russian Research Center during the 1950s and then, as professor of public law and government, at Columbia University. A member of the state department's policy planning council during the Johnson administration, he became national security adviser to President Carter (1977–80) and was the chief architect of a tough human rights policy, directed against the Soviet Union. From 1981 he resumed his position at Columbia, and also taught at Georgetown University. >> Carter, Jimmy; Johnson, Lyndon B

Buber, Martin [boober] (1878–1965) Jewish theologian and philosopher, born in Vienna. He studied philosophy at Vienna, Berlin, and Zürich, then became attracted to Hasidism, founding and editing a monthly journal *Der Jude* (1916–24). He taught comparative religion at Frankfurt (1923–33), and directed a Jewish adult education programme until 1938, when he fled to Palestine to escape the Nazis. He became professor of social philosophy at Jerusalem, where he wrote on social and ethical problems. He is best known for his religious philosophy, expounded most famously in *Ich und Du* (1923, I and Thou), contrasting personal relationships of mutuality and reciprocity with utilitarian or objective relationships.

Bucer or **Butzer, Martin [but**ser] (1491–1551) Protestant reformer, born in Schlettstadt, Germany. He entered the Dominican order, and studied theology at Heidelberg. In 1521 he left the order, married a former nun, and settled in Strasbourg (1523). In the disputes between Luther and Zwingli he adopted a middle course. At the Diet of Augsburg he declined to subscribe to the proposed Confession of Faith, and afterwards drew up the *Confessio tetrapolitana* (1530). He became professor of theology at Cambridge in 1549. His chief work was a translation and exposition of the Psalms (1529). >> Luther; Zwingli

Buchan, Alexander [buhkn] (1829–1907) Meteorologist, born in Kinnesswood, Perth and Kinross, E Scotland, UK. He postulated the *Buchan spells* theory, based on earlier statistics, that the British climate is subject to successive warm and cold spells falling approximately between certain dates each year.

Buchan, Elspeth [buhkn], *née* **Simpson** (1738–91) Scottish religious, the wife of a potter. In 1784 she founded a fanatical sect in Irvine, the *Buchanites*, announcing herself to her 46 followers as the Woman of Revelations xii.

Buchan, John, Baron Tweedsmuir [buhkn] (1875–1940) Writer and statesman, born in Perth, Perth and Kinross, E Scotland, UK. He studied at Glasgow and Oxford, and in 1901 was called to the bar. During World War 1 he served on HQ staff (1916–17), when he became director of information. He was MP for the Scottish Universities (1927–35), was made a baron, and became Governor-General of Canada until 1940. In 1937 he was made a privy councillor and Chancellor of Edinburgh University. Despite his busy public life, he wrote over 50 books, especially fast-moving adventure stories, such as *Prester John* (1910) and *The Thirty-nine Steps* (1915). His biographical works include *Montrose* (1928) and *Sir Walter Scott* (1932).

Buchanan, George [byookan**an] (c. 1506–82) Scholar and humanist, born near Killearn, Stirling, C Scotland, UK. He studied at the universities of Paris and St Andrews, then taught at the College of Sainte Barbe in Paris (1528–37). Charged with heresy at St Andrews after writing a satirical poem about friars, *Franciscanus*, he fled to France, where he taught at Bordeaux (1539–42). In 1547 he went to teach in Coimbra, Portugal, where he was confined by the Inquisition as a suspected heretic (1547–53). He returned to Scotland in 1561 and was appointed Classical tutor to Mary, Queen of Scots, but abandoned the queen's cause after the murder of Lord Darnley (1567). He later became tutor to the four-year-old King James VI of Scotland (1570–8). His main works were *De juri regni apud Scotos* (1579, an attack on the divine right of monarchs and a justification for the deposition of Mary), and a monumental but unreliable history of Scotland, *Rerum scoticarum historia* (20 vols). >> James I (of England)

Buchanan, James [byoo**kan**an] (1791–1868) Fifteenth president of the USA (1857–61), born in Stony Batter, PA. He studied at Dickinson College, and in 1812 was admitted to the bar. He became secretary of state in 1845, and succeeded in settling the Oregon boundary question. Receiving the nomination of the Democratic Party, he was elected president in 1856, and during his administration the slavery question came to a head. He was strongly in favour of the maintenance of slavery, and he freely supported the attempt to establish Kansas as a slave state. After his retirement in 1861, he took no part in public affairs. >> RR1097

Buchanan, James M(cGill) [byoo**kan**an] (1919–) Economist, born in Murfreesboro, TN. He studied at universities in Tennessee and in Chicago, and taught at the University of Virginia from 1956. He became director of the Center for Public Choice in 1969, and joined George Mason University in 1983. He was awarded the Nobel Prize for Economics in 1986 for his work on the theories of public choice.

Buchanan, Ken(neth) [byoo**kan**an] (1945–) Boxer, born in Edinburgh, EC Scotland, UK. For almost 10 years he was one of the world's leading lightweight boxers, being British champion (1968–71, 1973–4), European champion (1974–5), and World Boxing Association lightweight champion (1970–2). On retiring from the ring he entered the hotel business in Edinburgh, and later was associated with a boxing school for young fighters.

Buchman, Frank (Nathan Daniel) [**buhk**man] (1878–1961) Evangelist, founder of the 'Group' and 'Moral Rearmament' movements, born in Pennsburg, PA. He was a Lutheran minister in charge of a hospice for under-privileged boys in Philadelphia (1902–7), travelled extensively in the East, and in 1921, believing that there was an imminent danger of the collapse of civilization, founded at Oxford the 'Group Movement'. It was labelled the 'Oxford Group' until 1938, when it rallied under the slogan 'Moral Rearmament'. After World War 2 the movement emerged in a more political guise as an alternative to capitalism and communism.

Büchner, Eduard [**bükh**ner] (1860–1917) Chemist, born in Munich, Germany, the brother of Hans Büchner. He was awarded the Nobel Prize for Chemistry in 1907 for demonstrating that alcoholic fermentation is due not to physiological but to chemical processes in the yeast. >> Büchner, Hans

Büchner, Georg [**bükh**ner] (1813–37) Playwright and pioneer of Expressionist theatre, born in Goddelau, Germany. He studied medicine and science, became involved in revolutionary politics, and to escape arrest fled to Zürich, where he died of typhoid at the age of 24. His best-known works are the poetical dramas *Dantons Tod* (1835, The Death of Danton) and *Woyzeck* (1837), used by Alban Berg as the basis for his opera *Wozzeck*.

Büchner, Hans [**bükh**ner] (1850–1902) Bacteriologist, born in Munich, Germany, the brother of Eduard Büchner. Professor at Munich (1880–1902) and director of the Hygienisches Institut from 1894, he discovered that blood serum contains protective substances against infection. >> Büchner, Eduard

Buck, Frank (1884–1950) Big-game hunter and collector, born in Gainesville, TX. From 1911 he led several expeditions all over the world to capture wild animals for zoos and circuses. He was popular as a lecturer, and wrote many books, including *Bring 'Em Back Alive* (1930), *Wild Cargo* (1931), and *Fang and Claw* (1935), which were turned into movies starring Buck himself.

Buck, Pearl S(ydenstricker), pseudonym **John Sedges** (1892–1973) Novelist, born in Hillsboro, WV. She lived in China from infancy, and her earliest novels are coloured by her experiences there. *The Good Earth* (1931) earned her the 1938 Nobel Prize for Literature. In 1935 she returned to the USA and wrote many novels about the contemporary American scene, such as *The Patriot* (1939) and *Dragon Seed* (1942). Five novels were written under her pseudonym. >> Lo Guangzhong

Buck, Sir Peter (Henry), originally **Te Rangi Hiroa** (1879–1951) Maori scholar and writer, born in Urenui, New Zealand. He practised medicine, was an MP (1909–14), served in World War 1, then became an anthropologist. In 1927 he joined the Bishop Museum in Honolulu, Hawaii, and was director there from 1936 until his death. He was knighted in 1946.

Buckingham, George Villiers, 1st Duke of [**buhk**ingam] (1592–1628) English statesman and court favourite, born in Brooksby, Leicestershire, C England, UK. He was knighted by James I, and raised to the peerage as Viscount Villiers (1616), Earl of Buckingham (1617), Marquess (1618), and Duke (1623). In 1623 he failed to negotiate the marriage of Prince Charles to the daughter of the Spanish king, but later arranged the marriage to Henrietta Maria of France. The abortive expedition against Cadiz (1625) exposed him to impeachment by the Commons, and only a dissolution rescued him. An expedition against France failed (1627), and while planning a second attack he was assassinated at Portsmouth by John Felton, a discontented subaltern. >> Charles I (of England); Eliot, John

Buckingham, George Villiers, 2nd Duke of [**buhk**ingam] (1628–87) English statesman, born in London, England, UK. After his father's assassination, he was brought up with Charles I's children, and went into exile after the Royalist defeat in the Civil War. His estates were recovered at the Restoration, and he became a member of the Cabal of Charles II. He was instrumental in Clarendon's downfall (1667), but lost power to Arlington, and was dismissed in 1674 for alleged Catholic sympathies. >> Arlington, 1st Earl of; Charles II (of England); Clarendon, 1st Earl of

Buckle, George Earle (1854–1935) Journalist, born in Bath, SW England, UK. He was editor of *The Times* from 1884 to 1912. He completed Monypenny's *Life of Disraeli* (1914–20), and edited six volumes of Queen Victoria's *Letters* (1926–32).

Buckley, William, nickname **the Wild White Man** (1780–1856) Convict, born near Macclesfield, Cheshire, NWC England, UK. He was a bricklayer, then joined the army, but was transported to Australia in 1802 for stealing. He escaped the following year from a new convict settlement at Port Phillip, near Melbourne, was adopted by a native tribe, and lived with them for 32 years before being found by an expedition. He became a bodyguard to the colonel in command of the new colony, then moved to Van Diemen's Land (Tasmania), where he died.

Buckley, William F(rank), Jr (1925–) Writer, born in New York City. After briefly attending the University of Mexico, he served in the US army during World War 2. He entered journalism, and founded the conservative journal *National Review* (1955), a platform for his influential political views. He worked for the Information Agency Advisory 1 Commission (1969–72), and was delegate to the UN General Assembly (1973). His books dealt with contemporary politics, and in the 1970s he turned to writing spy novels.

Buckminster Fuller, Richard >> Fuller, Buckminster

Buckner, Simon B(olivar), Jr (1886–1945) US general, born in Munfordville, KY. He trained at West Point, commanded the Alaska Defense Force (1940), and took part in operations for the recapture of the Aleutian Is (1942–3). He commanded the 10th army in the Central Pacific command, and in April 1945 led the invasion of Okinawa, where he was killed in action.

Budaeus, Guglielmus [bu**day**us], Latin name of **Guillaume Budé** (1467–1540) Scholar, born in Paris. He studied in Paris and Orléans, and held several diplomatic posts under Louis XII and Francis I. At his suggestion Francis founded the Collège de France. As royal librarian he founded the collection which later became the Bibliothèque Nationale. Of his works on philology, philosophy, and jurisprudence, the two best known are on ancient coins (1514) and the *Commentarii linguae Graecae* (1519, Commentaries on the Greek Language).

Budd, Zola, married name **Pieterse** (1966–) Athlete, born in Bloemfontein, South Africa. Dogged by controversy, she set a world record time of 15 min 1·83 sec for the 5000 m while still a South African citizen. In 1984 she was accorded British citizenship on the strength of her parental background, and became eligible to participate in the 1984 Olympic Games. Her presence was not universally welcomed, and her disappointing performance was best remembered for the incident in which she accidentally tripped the American Mary Decker during the 3000 m. She set further world records for the 5000 m (1984, 1985), then dropped out of international running until South Africa was re-admitted to international sports in 1992.

Buddha ('the enlightened one') (c. 563–c. 483 BC) The title of Prince **Gautama Siddhartha**, the founder of Buddhism, born the son of the rajah of the Sakya tribe ruling in Kapilavastu, Nepal. When about 30 years old he left the luxuries of the court, his beautiful wife, and all earthly ambitions for the life of an ascetic; after six years of austerity and mortification he saw in the contemplative life the perfect way to self-enlightenment. According to tradition, he achieved enlightenment when sitting beneath a banyan tree near Buddh Gaya, Bihar. For the next 40 years he taught, gaining many disciples and followers, and died at the age of about 80 in Kusinagara, Oudh. His teaching is summarized in the *Four Noble Truths*, the last of which affirms the existence of a path leading to deliverance from the universal human experience of suffering. The goal is *Nirvana*, which means 'the blowing out' of the fires of all desires, and the absorption of the self into the infinite.

Buddhaghosa [buda**goh**sa] (5th-c) Buddhist scholar, born near Buddh Gaya, or Ghosa, India. He studied the Buddhist texts in Ceylon, and is best known for the *Visuddhimagga* (The Path of Purity), a compendium of Buddhist doctrines. >> Buddha

Budé, Guillaume >> **Budaeus, Guglielmus**

Budenny, Simeon Mikhailovich [boo**de**nee] (1883–1973) Russian soldier, born in Kozyurin, Russia. He fought as a Cossack private in the Russo-Japanese War (1904–5). After the revolution he became a Bolshevik, raised a Cossack unit to fight the White forces on the Don, and defeated the Whites in the Battles of Tsaritsyn (1918–19). He served in the war against Poland (1920), and was made a marshal in 1935. In 1941 he commanded the SW sector against the German invasion, but was relieved by Timoshenko after a disaster at Kiev. >> Timoshenko

Budge, (John) Don(ald) (1915–) Tennis player, born in Oakland, CA. In 1938 he became the first player to win all four Grand Slam events in the same year. He was at his peak in 1937–8: in both years he won the Wimbledon singles, the men's doubles (with his compatriot Gene Mako) and, with fellow-American Alice Marble (1913–90), the mixed doubles. He then turned professional. >> RR1173

Bueno, Maria (Ester Audion) [**bway**noh] (1939–) Tennis player, born in São Paulo, Brazil. She won Wimbledon in 1959, 1960, and 1964, and was US champion on four occasions. With the American Darlene Hard (1936–), she won the Wimbledon doubles title five times and the US doubles four times. Ill health brought her retirement from top-class tennis at the relatively early age of 29. >> RR1173

Buffalo Bill >> **Cody, William F**

Buffet, Bernard [bu**fay**] (1928–) Painter, born in Paris. He made his name in the early 1950s with murky still-lifes, and interiors with skinny, miserable figures painted in a sharp linear style and a neutral, almost monochromatic palette which seemed to catch the mood ('existential alienation') of postwar Paris. He has exhibited regularly in Paris and occasionally in London. In 1973 a Buffet Museum was established in Japan.

Buffon, Georges-Louis Leclerc, comte de (Count of) [bu**fõ**] (1707–88) Naturalist, born in Montbard, France. He studied at Dijon, then devoted himself to science. In 1739 he was made director of the Jardin du Roi, and formed the design of his *Histoire naturelle* (1749–67, Natural History). His wide-ranging ideas led to fresh interest in natural science, and foreshadowed the theory of evolution. He was made a count in 1773.

Bugatti, Ettore (Arco Isidoro) [boo**ga**tee] (1881–1947) Car manufacturer, born in Milan, Italy. He began designing cars in 1899, and set up his works in Strasbourg (1907). In World War 1 he moved to Italy and later to France, where his racing cars won international fame in the 1930s.

Buhl or **Boulle, André Charles** [bool] (1642–1732) Cabinetmaker, born in Paris. In the service of Louis XIV he introduced *boullework*, a style of decorating furniture by inlaying metals, shells, and pearls on ebony – a technique which was carried on by his sons, **Jean**, **Pierre**, **André**, and **Charles Buhl**. The spelling *Buhl* is a 19th-c distortion.

Bujones, Fernando [boo**hoh**nes] (1955–) Dancer, born in Miami, FL. He studied with Alicia Alonso in Havana and at the School of American Ballet in New York City. In 1972 he joined American Ballet Theater, rising to the status of principal in 1974, the same year that he won the gold medal in Varna, Yugoslavia. >> Alonso, Alicia

Bukharin, Nikolay Ivanovich [boo**kha**rin] (1888–1938) Russian Marxist revolutionary and political theorist, born in Moscow. Called by Lenin 'the darling of the Party', he was active in the Bolshevik underground (1905–17), and after the Febuary Revolution returned to Russia, playing a leading role in the organization of the October Revolution in Moscow. As a member of the Politburo (1924–9) he was a firm supporter of Lenin's New Economic Policy, and opposed Stalin's collectivization campaign. In 1937 he was arrested in Stalin's Great Purge, expelled from the Party, tried on trumped-up charges, and shot. In 1987 he was officially rehabilitated by a board of judical inquiry, and posthumously readmitted to the Party in 1988. >> Lenin; Stalin

Bukowski, Charles [boo**kof**skee] (1920–94) Poet, short-story writer, and novelist, born in Andernach, Germany. He moved with his parents to the USA in 1922. An underground writer, his works include four novels, several collections of short stories, and many volumes of verse. A cult figure who did not achieve popular success, he had a sardonic sense of humour which is reflected in some of his titles, such as *Play the Piano Drunk Like a Percussion Instrument until the Fingers Begin to Bleed a Bit* (1979).

Bulfinch, Charles (1763–1844) Architect, born in Boston, MA. America's first native-born architect, he graduated from Harvard and was inspired by Neoclassical buildings on a European tour (1785–7). He sought to make Boston a US model of Classical elegance through town planning and the development of the Federal Style, his buildings include the Massachusetts State House (1795-7), India Wharf (1803-7), and Massachusetts General Hospital (1818-23). Succeeding Latrobe as architect of the US Capitol (1817-30), he completed the W portico, original dome, and landscaping before retiring to Boston. His domed capitol buildings influenced the design of state capitals across the country throughout the 19th-c. >> Latrobe

Bulgakov, Mikhail Afanasievich [bulgakof] (1891-1940) Writer, born in Kiev, Ukraine. He studied medicine, but in 1920 worked as a journalist in Moscow, where he wrote several plays, novels, and short stories. His major novels include *Belaya gvardiya* (1925, The White Guard, rewritten as a play, 1926) and *Master i Margerita* (1938, The Master and Margarita). Several of his works were considered too outspoken, were withdrawn, and re-emerged only in the 1960s.

Bulgakov, Sergey Nikolayevich [bulgakof] (1871-1944) Philosopher, economist, and Orthodox theologian, born in Livny, Russia. A professor of political economy at Kiev (1901-6) and then Moscow (1906-18), he became disillusioned with Socialism after 1906, and became a priest in 1918. Expelled from Russia (1923), he was appointed dean and professor of the Orthodox Theological Academy in Paris (1925-44), where he expounded Sophiology, the view that *sophia* (the Divine Wisdom) mediates between God and the world.

Bulganin, Nikolay Alexandrovich [bulgahnin] (1895-1975) Soviet statesman and prime minister (1955-8), born in Nizhni Novgorod (formerly, Gorky), Russia. An early member of the Communist Party, he was Mayor of Moscow (1933-7), a member of the Military Council in World War 2, and minister of defence in 1946. After Stalin's death he became vice-premier in Malenkov's government, and was made premier after Malenkov resigned (1955), with Khrushchev wielding real power. 'B and K' travelled extensively abroad, conducting propaganda through lengthy letters to Western statesmen. He was dismissed in 1958, and retired into obscurity. >> Khrushchev; Malenkov; RR1085

Bull, John (c.1562-1628) Musician, born in Somerset, SW England, UK. He was appointed organist in the Queen's Chapel (1586), first music lecturer at Gresham College (1597), and organist to James I (1607). A Catholic, he fled abroad to escape persecution in 1613, and in 1617 became organist of Antwerp Cathedral. A virtuoso player, he was one of the founders of contrapuntal keyboard music. He has been credited with composing the air 'God Save the King'.

Bullard, Sir Edward (Crisp) (1907-80) Geophysicist, born in Norwich, Norfolk, E England, UK. He studied in Cambridge, was professor at Toronto (1946-9), director of the National Physical Laboratory (1950-5), and director of the department of geodesy and geophysics at Cambridge (1964-74). He made the first satisfactory measurements of geothermal heat-flow through the oceanic crust, and helped to develop the theory of continental drift. He was knighted in 1953.

Bullen, Anne >> Boleyn, Anne

Buller, Sir Redvers (Henry) (1839-1908) British soldier, born in Crediton, Devon, SW England, UK. He saw active service in the war with China (1860), the Red River expedition (1870), the Ashanti War (1874), the Kaffir War (1878), and the Zulu War (1879), where his rescue of fellow-soldiers in action at Inhlobane won him the VC. He was chief-of-staff in the 1st Boer War (1881), and was commander-in-chief in the 2nd Boer War (1899-1900), when he raised the siege of Ladysmith (1900).

Bullinger, Heinrich [bulingger] (1504-75) Religious reformer, born in Bremgarten, Switzerland. In 1529 he married a former nun, and became a disciple of Zwingli, whom he succeeded in 1531 as leader of the reformed party in Switzerland. He drew up the Helvetic Confessions of 1536 and 1566. >> Zwingli

Bullock, Alan (Louis Charles) Bullock, Baron (1914-) British historian. He studied at Oxford, was appointed censor of St Catherine's Society, Oxford (1952-62), and became Vice-Chancellor of Oxford University (1969-73), and Master of St Catherine's College, Oxford (1960-80). He was chairman of the Schools Council (1966-9), and also of the Committee on Reading and Other Uses of the English Language (1972-4), the 'Bullock Report' being published as *A Language for Life* in 1975. He is also the author of numerous works on 20th-c Europe, including studies of Hitler, Bevin, and Stalin, and co-edited (with Oliver Stallybrass) the Fontana *Dictionary of Modern Thought* (1977). He was made a peer in 1976.

Bülow, Bernhard (Heinrich Martin Karl), Fürst von (Prince of) [büloh] (1849-1929) German statesman and chancellor (1900-9), born in Flottbeck, Germany. He was foreign secretary (1897) before becoming chancellor, and was made a count (1899) and a prince (1905). He was identified with an aggressive foreign policy in the years before World War 1.

Bülow, Hans (Guido), Freiherr von (Baron) [büloh] (1830-94) Pianist and conductor, born in Dresden, Germany. He studied law, but under the influence of Wagner made himself the musico-political spokesman of the new German School. In 1851 he took pianoforte lessons from Liszt, married Liszt's daughter, **Cosima** (1857), and became an outstanding conductor. In 1864 he became court pianist and director of the music school at Munich, but resigned when his wife deserted him for Wagner in 1869, and thereafter became an opponent of Wagner and his School. >> Liszt; Wagner, Richard

Bultmann, Rudolf (Karl) (1884-1976) Lutheran theologian, Hellenist, and New Testament scholar, born in Wiefelstede, Germany. He studied at Tübingen, taught at Marburg, Wrocław, (formerly Breslau, Germany), and Giessen, then became professor of New Testament at Marburg (1921). An early exponent of form criticism (*History of the Synoptic Tradition*, 1921) he is best known for his highly influential programme (1941) to 'demythologize' the New Testament and interpret it existentially, employing the categories of the earlier work of Heidegger. >> Heidegger; Moltmann

Bulwer-Lytton, Edward George Earle >> Lytton, Edward George Earle Bulwer-Lytton

Bulwer-Lytton, Robert >> Lytton, Robert Bulwer-Lytton

Bunau-Varilla, Philippe Jean [bünoh vareeya] (1859-1940) Engineer, born in Paris. The chief organizer of the Panama Canal project, he was instrumental in getting the waterway routed through Panama instead of Nicaragua. He was made Panamanian minister to the USA and negotiated the *Hay-Bunau-Varilla Treaty* (1903), giving the USA control of the Canal Zone.

Bunche, Ralph (Johnson) [buhnch] (1904-71) US diplomat, born in Detroit, MI. He studied at Harvard and the University of California in Los Angeles, then taught political science at Howard University, Washington (1928-50). He directed the UN Trusteeship department (1947-54), and became UN mediator in Palestine, where he arranged for a ceasefire. Awarded the Nobel Peace Prize (1950), he became an under-secretary for Special Political Affairs (1954-67), and later under-secretary-general (1968-71).

Buncho, Tani (1773-1840) Painter, born in Edo (modern Tokyo). The son of a poet, he was familiar with the styles of various schools and Chinese works, and attempted a synthesis of these with European techniques. An illustrator of books and a prolific painter of a variety of subjects, he excelled in landscapes. He also introduced the Nanga style of painting to Edo.

Bundy, McGeorge (1919–96) US government administrator, born in Boston, MA. He studied at Yale, and became a junior fellow at Harvard (1941). After working in intelligence during World War 2, he joined Harvard as dean of arts and sciences (1953). He is remembered for his major role in foreign policy decisions during the Kennedy and Johnson administrations, notably in the Vietnam War. After resigning (1966), he became president of the Ford Foundation, and was later appointed history professor at New York University. >> Johnson, Lyndon B; Kennedy, John F

Bundy, Ted (1954–89) US convicted murderer. He was a law student who is believed to have killed at least 36 females, both adults and children, over a number of years. Convicted in 1979 on several charges, including the murder of a 12-year-old girl, he was sentenced to death. He was executed in Florida in 1989 after a string of unsuccessful appeals.

Bunin, Ivan Alexeyevich [boonin] (1870–1953) Writer, born in Voronezh, Russia. He worked as a journalist and clerk, writing lyrics and novels of the decay of the Russian nobility and of peasant life. His best-known work is *Gospodin iz San-Francisco* (1922, The Gentleman from San Francisco). He was the first Russian to receive the Nobel Prize for Literature (1933). After the Revolution, he lived in Paris.

Bunny, Rupert (Charles Wulsten) (1864–1947) Artist, born in St Kilda, Victoria, Australia. He studied in Melbourne and then in London, later moving to Paris. His work was not influenced by the prevailing Impressionist school, but more by Classical mythology. He later turned to large decorative and exotic scenes.

Bunsen, Robert Wilhelm (1811–99) Chemist and physicist, born in Göttingen, Germany. After studying at Göttingen, Paris, Berlin, and Vienna, he became professor of chemistry at Heidelberg (1852). He shared with Gustav Robert Kirchhoff the discovery of spectrum analysis (1859), which facilitated the discovery of new elements, including caesium and rubidium. He invented the *Bunsen burner*, the grease-spot photometer, a galvanic battery, an ice calorimeter and, with Sir Henry Roscoe, the actinometer. >> Kirchhoff

Bunting, Basil (1900–85) Poet, born in Scotswood, Northumberland, NE England, UK. He worked as a journalist in Paris, was much influenced by Pound and the American Modernists, and published his early poetry abroad. After some years in Paris, where he worked on translation, he returned to Britain and established his reputation with *Briggflatts* (1966), a semi-autobiographical poem deeply rooted in the North East. >> Pound, Ezra

Bunton, Emma >> Spice Girls, The

Buñuel, Luis [buhnwel] (1900–83) Film director, born in Calanda, Spain. He studied at Madrid University, and his first films (made with Salvador Dali) were a sensation with their Surrealistic, macabre approach: *Un Chien andalou* (1928, An Andalusian Dog) and *L'Age d'or* (1930, The Golden Age). His career then went into eclipse until he settled in Mexico (1947), where he directed such major films as *Los olvidados* (1950, trans The Young and the Damned), *Viridiana* (1961), *The Discreet Charm of the Bourgeoisie* (1972), and *That Obscure Object of Desire* (1977). His work is characterized by a poetic, often erotic, use of imagery, a black humour, and a hatred of Catholicism, often expressed in blasphemy. >> Dali

Bunyan, John (1628–88) Writer, born in Elstow, Bedfordshire,

SC England, UK. He worked as a tinker, and fought in the parliamentary army during the English Civil War (1644–5). In 1653 he joined a Christian fellowship, preaching around Bedford. In 1660 he was arrested and spent 12 years in Bedford county gaol, where he wrote prolifically, including *Grace Abounding* (1666). Briefly released after the Declaration of Indulgence (1672), he was reimprisoned for six months in the town gaol, and there wrote the first part of the *The Pilgrim's Progress*, a vision of life told allegorically as if it were a journey. Returning to his career, he acted as pastor in Bedford for 16 years, where he wrote the second part of *The Pilgrim's Progress* (1684).

Buonaparte >> Bonaparte

Buonarroti >> Michelangelo

Buoninsegna, Duccio di >> Duccio di Buoninsegna

Buononcini, Giovanni >> Bononcini, Giovanni

Burbage, Richard [berbij] (c. 1569–1619) Actor, born in London, England, UK. He was the leading performer with Shakespeare's company from 1594 until his death, and was the first creator on stage of many of Shakespeare's greatest roles, including Hamlet, Othello, and Lear. >> Shakespeare, William

Burbank, Luther (1849–1926) Horticulturalist, born in Lancaster, MA. He developed the *Burbank potato* on a farm near Lunenberg, MA, and in 1875 moved to Santa Rosa, CA, where he bred over 800 new strains of fruits and flowers.

Burchfield, Charles (Ephraim) (1893–1967) Painter, born in Ashtabula Harbor, OH. Although he attended Cleveland School of Art and briefly lived in New York City (1916), he spent most of his life in small towns in Ohio and upstate New York, and it was not until c.1929 that he could escape the factory jobs to devote himself to art. Known primarily for his watercolours, several of his works are drawn from nature, such as 'February Thaw' (1920), or offer a vision of urban America, as in 'Black Iron' (1935). His paintings of railroads and mines, commissioned by *Fortune* magazine in the late 1930s, brought his work to a wider public.

Burchfield, Robert (William) (1923–) Scholar and lexicographer, born in Wanganui, New Zealand. He studied at Victoria University College, Wellington, and at Oxford, where he became a lecturer in English language (1952–63), then a tutorial fellow (1963–79) and senior research fellow at St Peter's College (1979–90, now emeritus fellow). In 1957 he was appointed editor of a new *Supplement to the Oxford English Dictionary* which appeared in four volumes between 1972 and 1986. He has also written several books on the English language, and was co-author of a report (1979) on the quality of spoken English on BBC radio. >> Onions

Burchleigh, Baron >> Cecil, William

Burckhardt, Jacob (Christopher) [berkhah(r)t] (1818–97) Historian, born in Basel, Switzerland. He studied theology and later art history in Berlin and Bonn, became editor of the *Basler Zeitung* (1844–5), and was professor of history at Basel University (1858–93). He is known for his works on the Italian Renaissance and on Greek civilization.

Burdett-Coutts, Angela Georgina Burdett-Coutts, Baroness [berdet koots] (1814–1906) Philanthropist, born in London, England, UK, the daughter of **Sir Francis Burdett** (1770–1844) and grand-daughter of Thomas Coutts. She inherited her grandfather's fortune in 1837, and used it to mitigate suffering. She established a shelter for fallen women, built model homes, and endowed churches and colonial bishoprics. In 1871 she received a peerage, and in 1872 she became the first woman to be given the freedom of the City of London. >> Coutts, Thomas

Buren, Martin Van >> Van Buren, Martin

Burford, Eleanor >> Hibbert

Bürger, Gottfried August (1747–94) Lyric poet and writer of ballads, born in Molmerswende, Germany. In 1764 he began to study theology, but migrated to Göttingen (1768) and entered on a course of jurisprudence. In Göttingen he was associated with a group of poets (the *Göttinger Hain*) who worked with folk songs and ballads. He wrote many ballads, including *Lenore* (1773), which was translated by Sir Walter Scott, and which had a major effect on the development of Romanticism in Europe.

Burger, Warren E(arl) (1907–95) Judge, born in St Paul, MN. He studied at the University of Minnesota, then taught and practised law in St Paul from 1931 before becoming assistant attorney general of the USA (1953), and in 1955 judge of the US Court of Appeals for the District of Columbia. He was appointed chief justice of the US Supreme Court in 1969.

Burges, William [berjiz] (1827–81) Architect and designer, born in London, England, UK. Much influenced by Pugin and Viollet-le-Duc, he employed a strong mediaeval element in both his architecture and his furniture. Castell Coch (1876–81), near Cardiff, a reconstruction on 13th-c foundations, was designed as a hunting lodge for the 3rd Marquess of Bute. His other project for the marquess, Cardiff Castle (1868–81), is a more eclectic mixture of mediaeval and exotic styles again applied to the remains of a fortress. >> Pugin; Viollett-le-Duc

Burgess, Anthony, pseudonym of **John Anthony Burgess Wilson** (1917–93) Writer and critic, born in Manchester, Greater Manchester, NW England, UK. He studied at Xaverian College and Manchester University, lectured at Birmingham University (1946–50), worked for the Ministry of Education, and taught at Banbury Grammar School (1950–4). He then became an education officer in Malaya and Brunei (1954–9), where his experiences inspired his *Malayan Trilogy* (1965). His many novels include *A Clockwork Orange* (1962), *1985* (1978), *Earthly Powers* (1980), and *Any Old Iron* (1989). He wrote several critical studies and film scripts, including *Jesus of Nazareth* (1977). His musical compositions include symphonies, a ballet, and an opera. He also wrote under the name of **Joseph Kell** as well as under his original name. In his later years he lived in Monaco.

Burgess, (Frank) Gelett (1866–1951) Writer and humorist, born in Boston, MA. He attended Massachusetts Institute of Technology, then moved to San Francisco, where he worked as a draftsman for the Southern Pacific Railroad (1888–91). From 1897 he worked as an editor in New York City, then married an actress, and lived a bohemian life in France (1914–18). He is known for publishing *The Lark* (1895–7), a humorous magazine, which carried his famous quatrain, 'The Purple Cow'. He continued to write, but with little success, and in 1949 retired to California.

Burgess, Guy (Francis de Moncy) (1910–63) British traitor, born in Devonport, Devon, SW England, UK. He studied at Eton, Dartmouth, and Cambridge, where he became a communist. Recruited as a Soviet agent in the 1930s, he worked with the BBC (1936–9), wrote war propaganda (1939–41), and again joined the BBC (1941–4) while working for MI5. Thereafter, he was a member of the Foreign Office, and second secretary under Philby in Washington in 1950. Recalled in 1951 for 'serious misconduct', he and Maclean disappeared, re-emerging in the Soviet Union in 1956. He died in Moscow. >> Maclean, Donald; Philby

Burgh, Hubert de [ber] (?–1243) English statesman. He was the patriotic justiciar of England (1215–32), and virtual ruler for the last four years of this period, but now is chiefly remembered as the jailer of Prince Arthur. He was created Earl of Kent in 1227. >> Arthur, Prince

Burghley or **Burghleigh, Lord** >> **Cecil, William**

Burgoyne, John, nickname **Gentleman Johnnie** (1722–92) British general and playwright, born in Sutton, Bedfordshire, SC England, UK. He entered the army in 1740, and gave distinguished service in the Seven Years' War (1756–63). He then sat in parliament as a Tory, and in 1777 was sent to America, where he led an expedition from Canada into New York State, taking Ticonderoga, but being forced to surrender at Saratoga. He later joined the Whigs, and commanded in Ireland (1782–3). His best-known work was his comedy, *The Heiress* (1786).

Buridan, Jean [booreedã] (c.1300–c.1358) Scholastic philosopher, probably born in Béthune, France. He studied under William of Ockham and taught in Paris, publishing works on mechanics, optics, and logic. He gave his name to the famous problem of decision-making called *Buridan's ass*, where an ass faced with two equidistant and equally desirable bales of hay starves to death because there are no grounds for preferring to go to one bale rather than the other. >> William of Ockham

Burke, Clem >> **Blondie**

Burke, Edmund (1729–97) British statesman and political philosopher, born in Dublin. Educated at a Quaker boarding-school and at Trinity College, Dublin, he began studying law (1750), but then took up literary work. His early writing includes his *Philosophical Inquiry into the Origin of Our Ideas of the Sublime and Beautiful* (1756). He became secretary for Ireland, and entered parliament in 1765. His main speeches and writings belong to the period when his party was opposed to Lord North's American policy (1770–82). His *Reflections on the French Revolution* (1790) was read all over Europe.

Burke, John (1787–1848) Genealogist, born in Co Tipperary, Ireland. He was the compiler of *Burke's Peerage* – the first dictionary of baronets and peers in alphabetical order, published in 1826.

Burke, Martha Jane >> **Calamity Jane**

Burke, Robert O'Hara (1820–61) Traveller and explorer of Australia, born in St Clerans, Co Galway, Ireland. He studied in Belgium, served in the Austrian army (1840), joined the Irish constabulary (1848), and emigrated to Australia in 1853. As leader of the Burke and Wills expedition (1860), he was one of the first white men to cross the Australian continent from S to N. Both Burke and Wills died of starvation on the return journey. >> King, John; Leichhardt; Wills, William John

Burke, Thomas (1886–1945) Writer, born in London, England, UK. He is best known for his *Limehouse Nights* (1916), but he was the author of about 30 books, including *Nights in Town* (1915), *The Streets of London* (1941), and *The English Inn* (1930).

Burke, Thomas Henry (1829–82) British politician. Permanent Irish under-secretary from 1868, he was murdered with Lord Frederick Cavendish in Phoenix Park, Dublin. >> Cavendish, Spencer Compton

Burke, William (1792–1829) Murderer, born in Orrery, Ireland. With his partner, **William Hare** (c.1790–c.1860), born in Londonderry, he carried out a series of infamous murders in Edinburgh in the 1820s, with the aim of supplying dissection subjects to Dr Robert Knox, the anatomist. Hare, the more villainous of the two, turned king's evidence, and died a beggar in London in the 1860s; Burke was hanged, to the general satisfaction of the crowd.

Burleigh, Henry Thacker [berlee] (1866–1949) Baritone, composer, and arranger, born in Erie, PA. He learned African-American songs from his maternal grandfather, born a slave, and his voice gained him entry to the National Conservatory of Music in New York (1892–6), where he studied under Dvořák. He was soloist at St George's Church in New York City (1894–1946), gave concerts in America and Europe, and also worked as a music editor (1911–49). He composed many songs and ballads, but made his greatest mark through his arrangements of black spirituals such as 'Deep River' (1916). >> Dvořák

Burleigh, Lord >> **Cecil, William**

Burlington, Richard Boyle, 3rd Earl of (1694–1753) Architect and patron of the arts, born in London, England, UK. A great admirer of Palladio, he was himself an enthusiastic architect. He refashioned the Burlington House in Piccadilly of his great-grandfather, the 1st earl, and by his influence over a group of young architects was responsible for fostering the Palladian precept which was to govern English building for half a century. >> Palladio

Burne-Jones, Sir Edward Coley (1833–98) Painter and designer, born in Birmingham, West Midlands, C England, UK. He studied at Oxford, where he met William Morris, and through the encouragement of Rossetti, relinquished the Church for art. His later oils, inspired by the early Italian Renaissance, are characterized by a Romantic and contrived Mannerism. His subjects, drawn from the Arthurian romances and Greek myths, include 'The Days of Creation', 'The Beguiling of Merlin', and 'The Mirror of Venus', exhibited in 1877. He also designed stained glass and tapestries, and illustrated several books for William Morris, notably Chaucer. He was made a baronet in 1894. >> Morris, William; Rossetti, Dante Gabriel

Burnet, Alastair [ber**net**], popular name of **Sir James William Alexander Burnet** (1928–) British journalist and television news presenter. He studied at Worcester College, Oxford, then became editor of The Economist (1965–74) and The Daily Express (1974–6). He became a nationally known personality when he joined ITN as a news presenter (1976–91), and he later became associate editor for News at Ten (1982–91). He was knighted in 1984.

Burnet, Sir (Frank) Macfarlane [ber**net**] (1899–1985) Physician and virologist, born in Traralgon, Victoria, Australia. Director of the Institute for Medical Research, Melbourne, he became a world authority on viral diseases, perfecting the technique of cultivating viruses in living chick embryos. He shared the 1960 Nobel Prize for Physiology or Medicine for researches on immunological intolerance in relation to skin and organ grafting. >> RR1124

Burnett, Frances (Eliza), née **Hodgson** (1849–1924) Writer, born in Manchester, Greater Manchester, NW England, UK. In 1865 her family emigrated to Tennessee, where she married (1873, divorced 1898), and had her first literary success with That Lass o' Lowrie's (1877). She wrote several plays and over 40 novels, notably Little Lord Fauntleroy (1886) and The Secret Garden (1909).

Burnett, Ivy Compton >> **Compton-Burnett, Ivy**

Burnett, James >> **Monboddo, Lord**

Burney, Charles (1726–1814) Musicologist, born in Shrewsbury, Shropshire, WC England, UK, the father of **Fanny Burney**. After composing three pieces, Alfred, Robin Hood, and Queen Mab, for Drury Lane (1745–50), he went as organist to King's Lynn, Norfolk (1751–60). He travelled in France, Italy, Germany, and Austria (1770–2) to collect material for his General History of Music (1776–89), long considered a standard work. In 1783 he became organist to Chelsea Hospital. >> Burney, Fanny

Burney, Fanny, popular name of **Frances Burney**, married name **Madame d'Arblay** (1752–1840) Writer and diarist, born in King's Lynn, Norfolk, E England, UK. She educated herself by reading English and French literature and observing the distinguished people who visited her father. Her first and best novel, Evelina, was published anonymously in 1778, and influenced Jane Austen. She was given a court appointment in 1786, but her health declined; she retired on a pension and married a French emigré, **General d'Arblay**, in 1793. Her Letters and Diaries (1846) show her skill in reporting events of her time.

Burnham, Daniel H(udson) [ber**nuhm**] (1846–1912) Architect and leader of the Chicago School, born in Henderson, NY. He first worked in partnership with **John Wellborn Root** (1850–91). His pioneering designs into urban planning in Chicago were widely influential, and include the Reliance Building (1890–5) and the Monadnock Building (1890–1). He also designed the Selfridge Building in London (1908).

Burnham, (Linden) Forbes (Sampson) [ber**nuhm**] (1923–85) Guyanese statesman and prime minister (1964–80), born in Kitty, Guyana. He studied law in London, and was co-founder of the Marxist–Leninist People's Progressive Party in 1949. In 1955 he broke away, and was co-founder in 1957 of the more moderate, Socialist People's National Congress. As prime minister he led his country to independence in 1966. In 1980 a new constitution was adopted, and he became executive president until his death in office. >> RR1056

Burnham, Harry Webster Lawson, 1st Viscount [ber**nuhm**] (1862–1933) British politician, born in London, England, UK. He studied at Oxford, became a Liberal and later Unionist MP, and succeeded his father as director of The Daily Telegraph in 1903. He is chiefly known as chairman of the committees which inquired into the salaries of teachers and which recommended the Burnham Scales.

Burns, Arthur F(rank) (1904–87) Economist, born in Stanislau, Austria. He moved to the USA at the age of 10, studied at Columbia University, then taught there (1933–62). He was a leading expert on business cycles, and co-authored Measuring Business Cycles (1946) with W C Mitchell. He served as an economic adviser to presidents Eisenhower and Nixon before holding the influential position of chairman of the Federal Reserve (1970–8). He also served as the US ambassador to the Federal Republic of Germany (1981–5). >> Eisenhower; Nixon

Burns, George, originally **Nathan Birnbaum** (1896–1996) Comedian and actor, born in New York City, NY. He made his debut at the age of 13 as a singer, later performing as a dancer, skater, and comic. In 1923 he teamed up with **Gracie Allen** (1905–64) and they became a husband and wife comedy duo popular in the United States for more than three decades in vaudeville, radio, films, and television. He later co-starred in the film The Sunshine Boys (1975), for which he received an Oscar. Well known for his omnipresent cigar, dry wit, and comic timing, other films included Oh God (1977), Going in Style (1979), and Oh God! You Devil (1984).

Burns, Robert (1759–96) Scotland's national poet, born in Alloway, South Ayrshire, SW Scotland, UK. The son of a poor farmer, his education was thoroughly literary, and he studied the technique of writing, influenced also by the popular tales and songs of Betty Davidson, an old woman who lived with his family. On his father's death (1784) he was left in charge of the farm. At the same time his entanglement with **Jean Armour** (1767–1834) began, and as the farm went to ruin, his poverty, passion, and despair produced in 1785 an extraordinary output of poetry, including 'The Jolly Beggars'. Looking for money to emigrate to Jamaica, he published the famous Kilmarnock edition of his poems (1786), which brought such acclaim that he was persuaded to stay in Scotland. Going to Edinburgh, where he was feted, he began the epistolary flirtations with 'Clarinda' (Agnes Maclehose). In 1788 he married Jean Armour and leased a farm near Dumfries, in 1789 being made an excise officer. By 1790, when he wrote 'Tam o' Shanter', the farm was failing. He left for Dumfries, briefly adopting Radical views, but turning patriot again in 1795. >> Maclehose

Burns, Tex >> **L'Amour, Louis**

Burnside, Ambrose Everett (1824–81) Union general in the US Civil War, born in Liberty, IN. He trained at West Point, and in the Civil War commanded a brigade at the first Battle of Bull Run, capturing Roanoke I. He was repulsed at Fredericksburg (1862), but held Knoxville (1863), and led a corps under Grant through the Battles of the Wilderness and Cold Harbor (1864). After the war he became Governor of Rhode Island, and a US senator in 1875. He lent his name to a style of side whiskers, later known as *sideburns*.

Burnside, William (1852–1927) Mathematician, born in London, England, UK. He entered St John's College, Cambridge, in 1871, became a fellow of Pembroke until 1886, and was professor of mathematics at the Royal Naval College, Greenwich (1885–1919). He worked in mathematical physics, complex function theory, differential geometry, and probability theory, but his lasting work was in group theory. His *Theory of Groups* (1897) was the first English textbook on the subject.

Burr, Aaron (1756–1836) US statesman, born in Newark, NJ. He studied at Princeton, was called to the bar in 1782, and became attorney general (1789–91), US senator (1791–7), and Republican vice-president (1800–4). In 1804 he killed his political rival, Alexander Hamilton, in a duel, and fled to South Carolina. He then prepared to raise a force to conquer Texas, and establish a republic. He was tried for treason (1807), acquitted, spent some wretched years in Europe, and in 1812 resumed his law practice in New York City. >> Hamilton, Alexander; Randolph, Thomas

Burra, Edward (1905–76) Artist, born in London, England, UK. He studied at the Chelsea School of Art and the Royal College of Art, and travelled widely in Europe and the USA. Well known as a colourist, his Surrealist paintings of figures against exotic (often Spanish) backgrounds are invariably in watercolour, as in 'Soldiers' (1942, Tate, London). He also designed for the ballet.

Burrell, Sir William (1861–1958) Ship-owner and art collector, born in Glasgow, W Scotland, UK. He entered his father's business at the age of 15, and gradually accumulated a collection of 8000 works of art from all over the world, which he gave in 1944 to the city of Glasgow, with provision for a gallery. The *Burrell Collection* was finally opened to the public in 1983.

Burritt, Elihu, nickname **the Learned Blacksmith** (1810–79) Pacifist, born in New Britain, CT. He worked as a blacksmith in his native town and at Worcester, MA, but devoted all his leisure to mathematics and languages. Through his published works and through his travels in the USA and Europe he became known as an 'apostle of peace'.

Burroughs, Edgar Rice [buhrohz] (1875–1950) Writer, born in Chicago, IL. He had many unsuccessful jobs before making his name with the 'Tarzan' stories, beginning with 'Tarzan of the Apes' (1914). In later years he became a war correspondent.

Burroughs, John [buhrohz] (1837–1921) Naturalist and writer, born near Roxbury, NY. A teacher and later a tax inspector, he settled down in 1874 on a farm near Aesopus, NY, where he built himself a secluded cabin for his studies. His books, such as *Wake-Robin* (1871), mostly deal with country life, but he also wrote the first biography of Walt Whitman (1867). The John Burroughs Memorial Association was established in his memory, to encourage writing in natural history. >> Whitman

Burroughs, William Seward [buhrohz] (1855–98) Inventor, born in Auburn, NY. He worked in his father's shop at St Louis, MO, developing a mechanical calculating machine in 1885, and a commercially successful adding machine in 1892. His grandson was William S Burroughs. >> Burroughs, William S

Burroughs, William S(eward) [buhrohz] (1914–97) Writer, born in St Louis, MO. He studied at Harvard, and became a heroin addict while doing odd jobs in New York City. In 1953 he published *Junkie*, an account of his experiences, and his novels *Naked Lunch* (1959) and *The Soft Machine* (1961) established him as a spokesman of the Beat movement of the late 1950s. His later work, much concerned with innovations in the novel form, includes *Nova Express* (1964), *The Wild Boys* (1971), *Cities of the Red Night* (1981), and *The Western Lands* (1987). >> Ginsberg; Kerouac

Burrows, William (Ward) (1758–1805) American marine officer, born in Charleston, SC. A Revolutionary War veteran, he practised law in Philadelphia during the 1790s, returning to service in 1798 when President Adams named him first commandant of the newly formed Marine Corps. After overseeing the early development of the service, he retired in 1804. >> Adams, John

Burt, Sir Cyril (Lodowic) (1883–1971) Psychologist, born in London, England, UK. He studied at Oxford and Würzburg, becoming professor of education (1924–31) and psychology (1931–50) at University College, London. He was largely responsible for the theory and practice of intelligence and aptitude tests, ranging from the psychology of education to the problems of juvenile delinquency. He was knighted in 1946. In the 1980s, the validity of some of his findings was called into question.

Burton, Decimus (1800–81) Architect, born in London, England, UK. At the age of 23 he planned the Regent's Park colosseum, an exhibition hall with a dome larger than that of St Paul's, and in 1825 designed the new layout of Hyde Park and the triumphal arch at Hyde Park Corner. He designed the Palm House at Kew Gardens (1844–8) with engineer Richard Turner.

Burton, Michael Arthur, Lord >> **Bass, Michael Thomas**

Burton, Richard, originally **Richard Walter Jenkins** (1925–84) Stage and film actor, born in Pontrhydfen, Neath and Port Talbot, SC Wales, UK. The 12th child of a coalminer, Richard Jenkins, he was brought up in his sister's house after his mother's death. He was befriended by his English teacher, Philip H Burton, who encouraged his acting and study of English, and eventually adopted him. He went to Oxford, and in 1943 changed his name to Burton. He acted in Liverpool and Oxford, served in the RAF, and returned to the stage in 1948, when he made his film debut. He made his stage reputation in Fry's *The Lady's Not for Burning* (1949), and had a triumphant season at Stratford (1951). His early Hollywood films include *My Cousin Rachel* (1952) and *The Robe* (1953) for which he received one of his six Oscar nominations. In 1954 he was the narrator in the famous radio production of Dylan Thomas's *Under Milk Wood*. His romance with Elizabeth Taylor during the making of *Cleopatra* (1962) and their eventual marriage (1964–74) projected them both into the 'superstar' category. Among his later films were *Beckett* (1964), *Equus* (1977), and *1984* (released after his death). In his later years, interest in his social life grew, especially after his second marriage to Elizabeth Taylor (1975–6). >> Taylor, Elizabeth (Rosemond)

Burton, Sir Richard (Francis) (1821–90) Explorer, born in Torquay, Devon, SW England, UK. He studied in Europe and Oxford, where he was expelled in 1842. In 1856 he set out with Speke on the journey which led to the discovery of L Tanganyika (1858), and afterwards travelled in North

America, holding consular posts in Fernando Pó, Santos, Damascus, and Trieste. He wrote many books on his travels, and translated several Eastern works. He was knighted in 1886. **Lady Burton**, *née* **Isabel Arundell** (1831–96), who shared in much of his travelling and writing, burned her husband's journals after his death. >> Speke

Burton, Robert (1577–1640) Writer, born in Lindley, Leicestershire, C England, UK. He studied at Oxford, then taught there, taking orders in 1614. His great work was the *Anatomy of Melancholy* (1621), a learned miscellany on the ideas of his time, which influenced many subsequent authors.

Bury, J(ohn) B(agnell) [beree] (1861–1927) Historian and Classical scholar, born in Co Monaghan, Ireland. He studied at Trinity College, Dublin, became professor of modern history (1893–1902) and Greek (1899–1902) at Dublin, and thereafter professor of modern history at Cambridge. He wrote a monumental *History of the Later Roman Empire* (1889) at the age of 28, and other major histories of Greece and Rome.

Busby, Sir Matt(hew) (1909–94) Footballer and football manager, born in Bellshill, North Lanarkshire, C Scotland, UK. After a comparatively undistinguished playing career with Manchester City and Liverpool, he became manager of Manchester United in 1945. Almost immediately the club won the FA Cup in 1948 and the League shortly afterwards. Rebuilding the team, he seemed likely to bring the European Cup to Britain for the first time in 1958, but his young side was largely wiped out in an air crash at Munich airport. He himself was severely injured, but patiently reconstructed the team until European Cup success eventually came in 1968.

Busch, Adolf (1891–1952) Violinist, born in Siegan, Germany. In 1919 he formed the Busch Quartet and Busch Trio, with his brother **Hermann** (1897–1975) as cellist and his son-in-law Rudolf Serkin as pianist. He emigrated to America in 1939. Another brother, **Fritz** (1890–1951), was an eminent conductor and noted Mozartian. >> Serkin

Busch, Wilhelm (1832–1908) Cartoonist and writer, born near Hanover, Germany. He worked as an illustrator for the *Fliegende Blätter* (1859–71), and wrote satirical verse-stories with his own illustrations, such as *Max und Moritz* (1865, the prototypes for Rudolph Dirks' *Katzenjammer Kids*) and *Herr und Frau Knopp* (1876).

Bush, Alan (Dudley) (1900–) Composer and pianist, born in London, England, UK. He studied at the Royal Academy of Music (1918–22), where he was a notable composition teacher (1925–78), and also at Berlin University (1929–31). In 1924 he became active in the British working-class movement and founded the Workers' Music Association (1936), becoming its president in 1941. His works include four operas, four symphonies, concertos for violin and piano, choral works, chamber works, and songs.

Bush, George (Herbert Walker) (1924–) US statesman and 41st president (1989–93), born in Milton, MA. He joined the US navy in 1942, as its youngest pilot. After the war he studied economics at Yale and went into business in the Texas oilfields. In 1966 he devoted himself to politics, and was elected to the US House of Representatives. Unsuccessful for the US Senate in 1970, he became US permanent representative to the UN. During the Watergate scandal he was chairman of the Republican National Committee. Under President Ford he headed the US Mission to Beijing, then became director of the CIA. In 1980 he campaigned for the Republican nomination, but lost to Reagan, later becoming his vice-president. In 1988 he won the Republican nomination for the presidency, and defeated Governor Michael Dukakis of Massachusetts in the general election. He lost to Bill Clinton in the 1992 election. >> Clinton; Ford, Gerald R; Reagan; RR1097

Bush, Vannevar (1890–1974) Electrical engineer and inventor, born in Everett, MA. He studied at Tufts College and the Massachusetts Institute of Technology. He devoted most of his considerable research effort from 1925 to the development of mechanical, electro-mechanical, and electronic calculating machines or analogue computers, which led directly to the digital computers universally used today. He was instrumental in setting up the 'Manhattan Project' in 1942 which led to the US atomic bomb. >> Terman, Fred

Bushnell, David (?1742–1824) Inventor and physician, born in Saybrook, CT. He studied at Yale, then built the first US submarine, *Bushnell's turtle*, which was tried unsuccessfully against British ships. He was a continental army engineer (1779–83), then spent several years in France, returning to the USA in 1795 to teach and practise medicine in Georgia. >> Holland, John

Bushnell, Horace (1802–76) Congregational minister and theologian, born in Bantam, CT. He studied at Yale (1827), and was reading for the bar when he felt called to the ministry, becoming ordained in 1833. After a visit to Europe in 1845–6, he returned to publish one of his most influential works, *Christian Nurture* (1847). In 1849 he experienced a mystical vision of God and the Gospel; when he revealed this, he was attacked by the more traditional congregationalists, but he continued to preach and write. Poor health led him to move to California in 1856, where he helped to establish the first University of California at Berkeley. He returned to Connecticut in 1858, and continued to write, becoming influential among US Protestant theologians with his emphasis on bringing religion into harmony with human experience and nature.

Bushnell, Nolan (1943–) Inventor of the video game, born in Clearfield, UT. An engineering student with a part-time job in an amusement arcade, he determined to make available an arcade version of a computer game then only available on the college mainframe computer. When the first microprocessor chip became available (1971), he set up his own company, Atari, devised and built a simple tennis game, 'Pong' (1973), which could be linked to a TV set, and started the video game explosion. >> Hoff, Ted

Busoni, Ferruccio (Benvenuto) [busohnee] (1866–1924) Pianist and composer, born in Empoli, Italy. An infant prodigy, in 1889 he became professor of the pianoforte at Helsinki, and later taught and played in Moscow, Boston, and Berlin. The influence of Liszt is apparent in his great piano concerto. Of his four operas *Doktor Faust*, completed posthumously by a pupil in 1925, is his greatest work.

Buss, Frances Mary (1827–94) British pioneer in women's education. At the age of 23 she founded the North London Collegiate School for Ladies, and became its head (1850–94) – the first woman to call herself a headmistress. She was immortalized in verse with Dorothea Beale of Cheltenham Ladies' College ('Miss Buss and Miss Beale, Cupid's darts do not feel'). >> Beale, Dorothea

Bussell, Darcey (Andrea) (1969–) Ballerina, born in London, England, UK. She studied at the Arts Educational School and the Royal Ballet School, joining Sadler's Wells Royal Ballet (now Birmingham Royal Ballet) in 1987. The following year she moved to the Royal Ballet as soloist, becoming first soloist (1989), then principal (1989), and is currently the company's youngest principal dancer. She has made guest appearances internationally for various companies, and danced leading roles in works by MacMillan and Ashton. In 1990 she was voted Most Promising Artiste by the Variety Club of Great Britain.

Bustamente, Sir (William) Alexander [bustamentay],

originally **William Alexander Clarke** (1884–1977) Jamaican politician and prime minister (1962–7), born near Kingston. He was adopted at the age of 15 by a Spanish seaman, and spent an adventurous youth abroad before returning to become a trade union leader (1932). In 1943 he founded the Jamaica Labour Party (JLP) as the political wing of his union, and in 1962, when Jamaica achieved independence, became its first prime minister. He was knighted in 1955. >> RR1068

Butcher, Rosemary (1947–) Choreographer, born in Bristol, SW England, UK. The first dance graduate of Dartington College in Devon, she went to New York City, and began choreographing her own work in 1976. Her work is minimal and often made in conjunction with other artists. An example is the fast-moving *Flying Lines* (1985), which incorporates music by Michael Nyman (1944–) and an installation by Peter Noble.

Bute, John Stuart, 3rd Earl of (1713–92) British statesman and prime minister (1762–3), born in Edinburgh, EC Scotland. UK. After early court appointments, he became a favourite of George III, who made him one of the principal secretaries of state (1761). As prime minister, his government was highly unpopular. Its principal objective was the supremacy of the royal prerogative, and he was soon forced to resign. From 1768 his life was chiefly spent in the country, where he engaged in scientific study. >> George III; RR1095

Butenandt, Adolf Friedrich Johann [bootuhnant] (1903–95) Biochemist, born in Bremerhaven-Lehe, Germany. He studied at Marburg and Göttingen, and went on to carry out research into sex hormones. He isolated oestrone from pregnancy urine (1929), and in 1931 isolated the male hormone androsterone, also investigating the chemical structure of progestin. He shared the 1939 Nobel Prize for Chemistry, but was forbidden to accept it by the Nazi regime. >> RR1123

Buthelezi, Mangosuthu Gatsha [bootuhlayzee], known as **Chief Buthelezi** (1928–) South African Zulu leader and politician, born in KwaZulu Natal, South Africa. Installed as chief of the Buthelezi tribe in 1953, he was assistant to the Zulu king Cyprian (1953–68) before being elected leader of Zululand in 1970. He became chief minister of KwaZulu, the black South African homeland, in 1976. He is founder-president of Inkatha, a politico-cultural body which has the aim of achieving a non-racist democratic political system, and which in the 1980s developed paramilitary tendencies. In 1994 he was appointed minister for home affairs in Nelson Mandela's first cabinet. >> Mandela, Nelson

Butler, Alban (1710–73) Hagiographer and Roman Catholic priest, born in Appletree, Northamptonshire, C England, UK. He studied at Douai in France, became professor there, and was for some time chaplain to the Duke of Norfolk. He later became head of the English College at St Omer. His great work, the *Lives of the Saints* (1756–59), makes no distinction between fact and fiction.

Butler, Benjamin F(ranklin) (1818–93) Lawyer, general, and congressman, born in Deerfield, NH. He studied at Waterville College, ME, and was admitted to the bar in 1840, becoming noted as a criminal lawyer, a champion of the working-classes, and an ardent Democrat. In 1861 he was appointed major-general of volunteers, took possession of New Orleans (1862), and made an expedition against Fort Fisher (1864). Elected to Congress in 1866, he was prominent in the Republican efforts for the reconstruction of the Southern states and the impeachment of President Andrew Johnson. >> Johnson, Andrew

Butler, Lady Eleanor (1745–1829) Recluse, born in Dublin. In 1779 she and her friend Sarah Ponsonby (1755–1831) resolved to live in seclusion, and settled in a cottage in Plasnewydd, in the vale of Llangollen, accompanied by a maidservant. They became famous throughout Europe as the 'Maids of Llangollen' or 'Ladies of the Vale'.

Butler, Joseph (1692–1752) Moral philosopher and theologian, born in Wantage, Berkshire, S England, UK. He studied at Oxford, took orders, and was appointed preacher at the Rolls Chapel, London (1718). While holding various church appointments, he wrote his major work, *The Analogy of Religion* (1736), in which he argued that objections against revealed religion may also be levelled against the whole constitution of nature. He was made Bishop of Bristol (1738), Dean of St Paul's (1740), and Bishop of Durham (1750).

Butler, Josephine Elizabeth, *née* **Gray** (1828–1906) Social reformer, born in Milfield, Northumberland, NE England, UK. She promoted women's education and successfully crusaded against licensed brothels and the white-slave traffic. She wrote *Personal Reminiscences of a Great Crusade* (1896).

Butler, Nicholas (Murray) (1862–1947) Educationist, born in Elizabeth, NJ. He became professor of philosophy and education at Columbia University in 1890, and president (1901–45). He helped to found and organize what is now Teachers' College at Columbia. He was the author of many books on public questions, president of the Carnegie Endowment for International Peace (1925–45), and shared the Nobel Peace Prize in 1931. >> RR1125

Butler, Reg(inald Cotterell) (1913–81) Sculptor, born in Buntingford, Hertfordshire, SE England, UK. He studied architecture, taught at the Architectural Association School in London (1937–9), then practised as an engineer (1939–50). He turned to sculpture in 1951, and soon became recognized as one of the leading exponents of 'linear' constructions in wrought iron, but in his later years turned to a more realistic style.

Butler, R(ichard) A(usten), Baron Butler, known as **Rab Butler** (1902–82) British statesman, born in Attock Serai, India. He studied at Cambridge, and became Conservative MP for Saffron Walden in 1929. After a series of junior ministerial appointments, he became minister of education (1941–5), introducing the forward-looking Education Act of 1944, and then minister of labour (1945). He became Chancellor of the Exchequer (1951), Lord Privy Seal (1955), Leader of the House of Commons (1955), home secretary (1957), first secretary of state and deputy prime minister (1962). He narrowly lost the premiership to Douglas-Home in 1963, and acted as foreign secretary (1963–4) in his administration. He then became Master of Trinity College, Cambridge (1965–78), and was made a life peer. >> Home

Butler, Samuel (1612–80) Satirist, baptized at Strensham, Hereford and Worcester, WC England, UK. He was educated at Worcester grammar school, and perhaps Oxford or Cambridge. He held several secretarial posts before becoming steward of Ludlow Castle (1661) and in later years was secretary to the Duke of Buckingham. His great poetic work, *Hudibras*, appeared in three parts (1663, 1664, 1678). A burlesque satire on Puritanism, it secured immediate popularity, and was a special favourite of Charles II.

Butler, Samuel (1835–1902) Writer, painter, and musician, born at Langar Rectory, Nottinghamshire, C England, UK. He studied at Cambridge, and became a sheep farmer in New Zealand (1859–64). On returning to England, he worked on his Utopian satire, *Erewhon* (1872) – the word is an inversion of 'nowhere' – in which many conventional practices and customs are reversed. Its supplement, *Erewhon Revisited* (1901), dealt with the origin of religious belief. His musical compositions include two oratorios, gavottes, minuets, fugues, and a cantata. He is best known for his autobiographical novel *The Way of All Flesh*, published posthumously in 1903.

Butlerov, Alexander Mikhailovich [butlayrof] (1828–86) Organic chemist, born in Chistopol, Russia. He studied at the University of Kazan, and became professor of chemistry there in 1849. In 1864 he correctly predicted the existence of tertiary alcohols, based on his grasp of structure theory, and was the first to introduce the idea of isomeric molecules existing in chemical equilibrium (tautomerism).

Butlin, Billy, popular name of **Sir William (Edmund) Butlin** (1899–1980) Holiday camp promoter, born in South Africa. He moved with his parents to Canada, and after serving in World War 1, worked his passage to England with only £5 capital. After a short period in a fun fair he went into business on his own. In 1936 he opened his first camp at Skegness, followed by others at Clacton and Filey. During World War 2 he served as director-general of hostels to the ministry of supply. After the War more camps and hotels were opened, both at home and abroad. He was knighted in 1964.

Butor, Michel (Marie François) [bütaw(r)] (1926–) Writer and critic, born in Lille, France. He studied at the Sorbonne, and taught at Manchester (1951–3), Thessaloniki (1954–5), and Geneva (1956–7). One of the popular writers of the *roman nouveau* ('new novel'), his works include *L'Emploi du temps* (1959, Passing Time), *Degrés* (1960, Degrees), and the non-fiction *Mobile* (1962). He has also written several volumes of poetry, his collection *A la frontière* appearing in 1996.

Butt, Dame Clara (1872–1936) Contralto singer, born in Southwick, West Sussex, S England, UK. She made her debut in 1892, and became known for her performances in oratorios. She was made a dame in 1920. Elgar's *Sea Pictures* were especially composed for her.

Butterfield, Sir Herbert (1900–79) Historian, born in Yorkshire, N England, UK. He studied at Peterhouse, Cambridge, where he later became fellow (1923–55) and master (1955–68), as well as lecturer (1930–44), professor of modern history (1944–63), and Regius professor (1963–8). He won initial recognition as a diplomatic historian with *The Peace-Tactics of Napoleon 1806–8* (1929). His *The Origins of Modern Science* (1949) inaugurated the worldwide development of the history of science.

Butterfield, William (1814–1900) Architect, born in London, England, UK. Associated with the Oxford Movement, he was a leading exponent of the Gothic Revival. His designs include Keble College, Oxford; St Augustine's College, Canterbury; the chapel and quadrangle of Rugby School; All Saints', Margaret Street, London; and St Albans, Holborn.

Butterley, Nigel Henry (1935–) Composer and pianist, born in Sydney, New South Wales, Australia. He studied at the New South Wales Conservatory, and later in London. He worked as a producer and planner for the music department of the Australian Broadcasting Commission from 1955, and in 1966 won the prestigious Italia Prize with *In the Head the Fire*, a musical work for radio commissioned by the ABC. Other compositions include a violin concerto, *Explorations for Piano and Orchestra*, and a two-act opera, *Lawrence Hargrave Flying Alone* (1987). *From Sorrowing Earth*, his first major orchestral work in more than a decade, was considered the best work from an Australian composer by the Australian Music Centre in 1992.

Button, Dick, popular name of **Richard Button** (1929–) Ice skater, born in Englewood, NJ. He was five times world champion (1948–52), and gold medal winner in the 1948 and 1952 Olympics. As an innovative competitor and as a commentator for ABC television he was instrumental in popularizing the sport in the USA.

Buttrose, Ita (Clare) (1942–) Journalist, publisher, and broadcaster, born in Sydney, New South Wales, Australia. She was educated in Sydney, and joined Australian Consolidated Press at age 15 as a copy girl, going on to become editor of the *Australian Women's Weekly*, Australia's leading women's magazine. In 1981 she moved to News Limited as editor-in-chief of the *Sunday Telegraph*, becoming the first woman in Australia to edit either a daily or a Sunday paper. In 1988 she became editor of that paper's opposition, *The Sun Herald*, and by 1989 had started her own magazine, called *Ita*. She is chairman of the National Advisory Committee on AIDS, and one of the best-known women in Australia.

Butzer, Martin >> **Bucer, Martin**

Buxtehude, Diderik or **Dietrich** [bukstehooduh] (1637–1707) Organist and composer, born in Oldesloe or Helsingborg, Sweden (formerly in Denmark). In 1668 he was appointed organist at the Marienkirche, Lübeck, where he began the famous *Abendmusiken* – Advent evening concerts of his own sacred music and organ works. In 1705 Bach walked c.200 mi across Germany, and Handel travelled from Hamburg, to attend his concerts. >> Bach, J S; Handel

Buys Ballot, Christoph H(endrick) D(iederick) [biyz balot] (1817–90) Meteorologist, born in Kloetinge, The Netherlands. He studied and taught at the University of Utrecht, and founded the Royal Netherlands Meteorological Institute in 1854. He was the inventor of the aeroklinoscope and of a system of weather signals. He stated the law of wind direction in relation to atmospheric pressure in 1857 (*Buys Ballot's law*).

BV >> **Thomson, James** (1834–82)

Byars, Betsy (Cromer) [biyerz] (1928–) Children's novelist, born in Charlotte, NC. She began to write in the 1960s, but had no great impact until *The Summer of the Swans* (1970) was awarded the Newbery Medal. Specializing in kitchen sink drama – contemporary realism – she produced a number of popular novels, including *The Eighteenth Emergency* (1973) and *Goodbye, Chicken Little* (1979).

Byatt, A(ntonia) S(usan), *née* **Drabble** (1936–) Writer and critic, the sister of Margaret Drabble. She studied at Cambridge, and became a lecturer in English at University College, London. Her novels include *Virgin in the Garden* (1978) and *Still-Life* (1985), the first two parts of a projected sequence tracing English life from the mid-1950s to the present day, and *Possession* (1990, Booker). Later works include *Angels and Insects* (1992), *The Djinn in the Nightingale's Eye* (1994), and *Babel Tower* (1996). She has also written short stories, and several critical works, including a monograph on Iris Murdoch. >> Drabble

Bygraves, Max (Walter) (1922–) Entertainer, born in Rotherhithe, SE Greater London, England, UK. Educated there, he worked for an advertising agency before joining the RAF (1940–5), where he became involved in entertainment for the troops. A professional entertainer since 1946, he has performed all over the world, and is among the best-selling recording artists. His catchphrase, 'I wanna tell you a story', is also the title of his autobiography (1976).

Byng, George, 1st Viscount Torrington (1663–1733) English sailor, born in Wrotham, Kent, SE England, UK. He joined the navy at 15, and gained rapid promotion as a supporter of William of Orange. Made rear-admiral in 1703, he captured Gibraltar, and was knighted for his gallant conduct at Málaga. In 1708 he defeated the French fleet of James Stuart, the Pretender, and in 1718 destroyed the Spanish fleet off Messina. He was created viscount in 1721. >> Stuart, Prince James

Byng (of Vimy), Julian Hedworth George Byng, 1st Viscount (1862–1935) British general, born in Wrotham Park, Hertfordshire, SE England, UK. He commanded the 9th Army Corps in Gallipoli (1915), the Canadian Army Corps (1916–17), and the 3rd Army (1917–18). After World War 1 he became Governor-General of Canada (1921–6) and Commissioner of the Metropolitan Police (1928–31), and was made a viscount in 1928 and a field marshal in 1932.

Byrd, Harry (Flood) (1887–1966) US politician, born in West Virginia, the brother of Richard Evelyn Byrd. He took up farming from 1906, and was president of the Shenandoah Valley Turnpike Company (1908–18). Elected to the state Senate (1915–25), he became Democratic State Committee chairman in 1922, and was successfully nominated for governor (1926–30). Appointed US senator for Virginia (1933–65), he became chairman of the US Senate Finance Committee, and was noted for his extreme conservatism and support for segregation. >> Byrd, Richard E

Byrd, Richard E(velyn) (1888–1957) Aviator, explorer, and rear-admiral, born in Winchester, VA, the brother of Harry Byrd. He was navigator on the first aeroplane flight over the North Pole (9 May 1926), and was awarded the Congressional Medal of Honour. He organized the largest and best-equipped expedition to date to explore Antarctica, and flew as navigator over the South Pole (28–29 Nov 1929). He carried out further Antarctic explorations in 1933–4 and 1939–41, using aircraft, radio, and modern technology to support, rather than replace, traditional methods of exploring on foot with dogs and sledges. >> Balchen; Bennett, Floyd; Byrd, Harry

Byrd, William (1543–1623) Composer, probably born in Lincoln, Lincolnshire, EC England, UK. His early life is obscure, but it is likely that he was one of the Children of the Chapel Royal, under Tallis. He was organist of Lincoln Cathedral until 1572, when he was made joint organist with Tallis of the Chapel Royal. In 1575 Byrd and Tallis were given an exclusive licence for the printing and sale of music. A firm Catholic, Byrd was several times prosecuted as a recusant, but he wrote music of great power and beauty for both the Catholic and the Anglican services, as well as madrigals, songs, keyboard pieces, and music for strings. >> Tallis

Byrd, William (1674–1744) Tobacco planter, colonial official, and diarist, born in Virginia Colony. During two periods in London (1697–1705, 1715–26) as a student of law and a colonial agent, he showed himself an elegant socialite and man of learning. In 1737 he founded the town of Richmond, VA, and in 1743 became president of the Council of State, of which he had been a member since 1709.

Byrne, Donn, pseudonym of **Brian Oswald Donn-Byrne** (1889–1928) Novelist and short-story writer, born in New York City. He studied at Dublin, the Sorbonne, and Leipzig universities. A cowpuncher in South America and garage-hand in New York City, his works include *Messer Marco Polo* (1921) and *Hangman's House* (1926).

Byrne, John (1940–) Playwright and stage designer, born in Paisley, Renfrewshire, W Scotland, UK. His first play, *Writer's Cramp*, was produced at the Edinburgh Festival Fringe (1977). *The Slab Boys* (1978), concerning the lives of employees at a carpet factory, grew into a trilogy with *Cuttin' A Rug* (1980), and *Still Life* (1983). He also wrote the highly acclaimed *Tutti Frutti* (1987), a BBC Scotland television series about an ageing rock group.

Byrnes, James F(rancis) (1879–1972) US secretary of state, public official, and Supreme Court justice, born in Charleston, SC. He served as a Democratic member for South Carolina in the US House of Representatives (1910–25) and the US Senate (1930–41), where he promoted the passage of landmark legislation such as the Neutrality Act (1935) and the Lend–Lease Act (1941). Appointed by President Franklin D Roosevelt to the Supreme Court in 1941, he stepped down after one year to head the Office of Economic Stabilization (1942) and the Office of War Mobilization (1943). The title of 'assistant president' was bestowed on him by Roosevelt, and he was considered as a running mate both in 1940 and 1944. He accompanied Roosevelt to Yalta (1945), and served as secretary of state under Truman (1945–7). As Governor of South Carolina (1950–5), despite his belief in segregation, he worked to suppress Ku Klux Klan activities and to improve the education of African-Americans. >> Roosevelt, Franklin D

Byrns, Joseph (Wellington) (1869–1936) US state representative, born in Cedar Hill, TN. His family moved to Nashville from their farm to provide him, the eldest of six children, with an education. A lawyer in Nashville in 1891, he served in the Tennessee House and Senate before becoming a Democratic member of the US House of Representatives (1909–36). As a member of the Committee on Appropriations he championed governmental economy and tariff reductions, though he secured the massive wartime appropriations requested by President Wilson. In 1933 he became majority leader, successfully shepherding 'New Deal' legislation through the House, setting aside his fiscal conservatism to support his party. Elected speaker of the House (1935–6), he managed the Democratic majority through persuasion, using a team of deputy whips to poll congressmen before critical votes. >> Roosevelt, Franklin D; Wilson, Woodrow

Byron (of Rochdale), George (Gordon) Byron, 6th Baron, known as **Lord Byron** (1788–1824) Poet, born in London, England, UK. His first 10 years were spent in poor surroundings in Aberdeen, but then he inherited the title of his great-uncle, and went on to Dulwich, Harrow, and Cambridge, where he led a dissipated life. An early collection of poems, *Hours of Idleness* (1807) was badly reviewed, and after replying in satirical vein, he set out on his grand tour, visiting Spain, Malta, Albania, Greece, and the Aegean. He then published the popular *Childe Harold's Pilgrimage* (1812), and several other works, becoming the darling of London society, and giving to Europe the concept of the 'Byronic hero'. He married **Anne Isabella (Annabella) Milbanke** (1792–1860) in 1815, but was suspected of a more than brotherly love for his half-sister, **Augusta Leigh** and was ostracized. He left for Europe, where he met Shelley, and spent two years in Venice. Some of his best works belong to this period, including *Don Juan* (1819–24). He gave active help to the Italian revolutionaries, and in 1823 joined the Greek insurgents who had risen against the Turks. He died of malaria at Missolonghi. >> Lovelace, Augusta Ada; Shelley, Percy

Byron, Robert (1905–41) Writer on travel and architecture, Byzantinist, and aesthete, born in Wiltshire, S England, UK. He studied at Oxford, where he collected Victoriana. He is best remembered for his travelogues, which include *First Russia, Then Tibet* (1933) and *The Road to Oxiana* (1937), which won the *Sunday Times* Literary Award. He died during World War 2 when his ship was torpedoed.

Caballé, Montserrat [kabayay] (1933–) Soprano, born in Barcelona, Spain, where she studied at the Liceo. She made her operatic debut in Basel (1956), and soon earned an international reputation, especially in operas by Donizetti and Verdi. In 1964 she married the tenor **Bernabé Marti**.

Cabell, James (Branch) [kabl] (1879–1958) Writer and critic, born in Richmond, VA. He made his name with his novel *Jurgen* (1919), the best known of a sequence of 18 novels, collectively called *Biography of Michael*. They are set in the imaginary mediaeval kingdom of Poictesme and written in an elaborate, sophisticated style showing the author's fondness for archaisms.

Cabet, Etienne [kabay] (1788–1856) Reformer and communist, born in Dijon, France. After the revolution of 1830 he was elected as deputy (1831), but was exiled for his radical pamphleteering (1834). He set out his social doctrine in a book, *Voyage en Icarie* (1840), a 'philosophical and social romance', describing a communistic utopia. In 1849 he led a group to Texas to found a utopian settlement called Icaria on the Red R, and later moved to Nauvoo, IL.

Cable, George W(ashington) (1844–1925) Writer, born in New Orleans, LA. He earned a precarious living in New Orleans before taking up a literary career in 1879. In 1884 he went to New England. His Creole sketches in *Scribner's Magazine* made his reputation. Among his books are *Old Creole Days* (1879), *The Grandissimes* (1880), and *Lovers of Louisiana* (1918).

Cabot, John [kabot], Ital **Giovanni Caboto** (1425–c.1500) Navigator, born possibly in Genoa, who discovered the mainland of North America. Little is known about his life. About 1490 he settled in Bristol, and set sail in 1497 with two ships, accompanied by his three sons, sighting Cape Breton I and Nova Scotia on 24 June. He set out on another voyage in 1498, and died at sea. >> Cabot, Sebastian

Cabot, John M(oors) [kabot] (1901–81) US diplomat, born in Cambridge, MA. He studied at Oxford, entered the diplomatic service in 1927, then specialized in Eastern Europe and Latin America, becoming assistant secretary of state for Inter-American Affairs (1953–4). He wrote *The Racial Conflict in Transylvania* (1926) and *Towards Our Common American Destiny* (1955).

Cabot, Sebastian [kabot] (1474–1557) Explorer and navigator, the son of John Cabot, born in Venice, Italy, or Bristol. He accompanied his father to the American coast, then entered the service of Ferdinand V of Spain as a cartographer (1512). In 1526 he explored the coast of South America for Emperor Charles V, but failed to colonize the area, and was imprisoned and banished to Africa. He returned to Spain in 1533, and later to England, where he was made inspector of the navy by Edward VI. >> Cabot, John

Cabral or **Cabrera, Pedro Alvarez** [kabral] (c.1467–c.1520) Explorer, born in Belmonte, Portugal. In 1500 he sailed from Lisbon bound for the East Indies, but was carried to the unknown coast of Brazil, which he claimed on behalf of Portugal. He then made for India, but was forced to land at Mozambique and provided the first description of that country. He made the first commercial treaty between Portugal and India, and returned to Lisbon in 1501. He was given no further missions, and remained for the rest of his life at Santarém.

Cabrera, Pedro Alarez >> **Cabral, Pedro Alvarez**

Cabrera Infante, Guillermo [kabraira infantay] (1929–) Writer, born in Gibara, Cuba. He studied at Havana University, and emigrated to England, UK in 1966. Film critic, journalist, and translator of Joyce's *Dubliners* (1972), he is known chiefly for his fiction, particularly *Tres tristes tigres* (1967, Three Sad Tigers) and *La Habana para un infante defunto* (1979, trans Infante's Inferno).

Cabrini, St Francesca Xavier [kabreenee] (1850–1917) Nun, born near Lodi, Italy. She founded the Missionary Sisters of the Sacred Heart (1886), emigrated to the USA in 1889, and became renowned for her social and charitable work. Canonized in 1946, she was the first US saint. Feast day 13 November.

Caccini, Giulio [kacheenee] (c. 1550–1618) Composer and singer, born in Rome. With Jacopo Peri he paved the way for opera by setting to music the drama *Euridice* (1602). Particularly significant was his *Nuove musiche* (1602), a collection of canzonets and madrigals. >> Peri

Cadbury, George (1839–1922) Businessman, born in Birmingham, West Midlands, C England, UK, the son of **John Cadbury**. In partnership with his brother **Richard Cadbury** (1835–99), he expanded his father's cocoa and chocolate business, and established for the workers the model village of Bournville (1879), a prototype for modern methods of housing and town planning. He also became proprietor of the *Daily News* (1902), and was an ardent Quaker.

Cadbury, Henry (Joel) (1883–1974) Quaker scholar, born in Philadelphia, PA. He studied at Haverford College and at Harvard, then taught biblical studies at Haverford, Bryn Mawr, and Harvard, where he subsequently held a chair in divinity (1934–54). He was active in the work of the American Friends Service Committee.

Cadbury, John (1801–89) Quaker businessman, the son of **Richard Tapper Cadbury**, who had settled in Birmingham, West Midlands, C England, UK in 1794. He founded the cocoa and chocolate business of Cadburys. >> Cadbury, George

Cade, Jack [kayd] (?–1450) Irish leader of the insurrection of 1450 against Henry VI. After an unsettled early career he lived in Sussex, possibly as a physician. Assuming the name of Mortimer, and the title of Captain of Kent, he marched on London with a great number of followers, and entered the city. A promise of pardon sowed dissension among the insurgents; they dispersed, and a price was set upon Cade's head. He attempted to reach the coast, but was killed near Heathfield, East Sussex. >> Henry VI; William of Waynflete

Cadell, Francis (Campbell Boileau) [kadl] (1883–1937) Painter, born in Edinburgh, EC Scotland, UK. He studied in Paris (1899–1903), visited Munich in 1907, and returned to Edinburgh in 1909. In 1912 he founded the Society of Eight. One of the 'Scottish Colourists', he painted landscapes, interiors, and still-life, in broad patches of brilliant, high-keyed colour.

Cadillac, Antoine Laumet de la Mothe, sieur de (Lord of) [kadlak], Fr [kadayak] (1658–1730) French soldier and colonialist, born in Gascony, France. He went to America with the French army in 1683, and founded the settlement of Fort-Pontehartrain du Détroit (1701), which became the city of Detroit. In 1711 he was appointed Governor of Louisiana, but returned to France in 1716.

Cadmus, Paul [kadmuhs] (1904–) Painter, born in New York City. Based in Weston, CT, he is a provocative artist who combines wit and social protest. His most famous (and notorious) paintings are 'The Fleet's In' (1934), and 'Fantasia on a Theme by Dr S' (1946).

Cadwaladr [kad**wo**lader] (?–1172) Prince of Gwynedd, NW Wales. He conquered large parts of Wales with his older brother **Owain** until he was expelled by him (1143). He went to Ireland to seek help, where he was blinded by pirates. Reconciled to Owain, he eventually fled to England, where Henry II restored him to his lands after the conquest of Wales (1158). >> Henry II (of England)

Cadwallon [kad**wa**lon] (?–634) Pagan king of Gwynedd, NW Wales (from c.625). With Penda, the Mercian king, he invaded the Christian kingdom of Northumbria in 633 and slew King Edwin at the Battle of Heathfield (Hatfield Chase), near Doncaster. He ravaged the kingdom, according to the Venerable Bede, but was himself defeated and killed by King Oswald at the Battle of Heavenfield near Hexham. >> Bede; Edwin; Oswald, St

Caedmon [**kad**mon] (?–c. 680) The first English poet of known name. Bede reports that, unlearned till mature in years, Caedmon became aware in a semi-miraculous way that he was called to exercise the gift of religious poetry. He became a monk at Whitby, and spent the rest of his life composing poems on the Bible histories and on religious subjects. >> Bede

Caesalpinus >> **Cesalpino, Andrea**

Caesar, in full **Gaius Julius Caesar** see panel on p. 165

Cage, John (1912–92) Composer, born in Los Angeles, CA. A pupil of Schoenberg, he was associated with ultra-Modernism. He variously exploited the 'prepared piano' (distorting the sound of the instrument with objects placed inside); unorthodox musical notation in the form of pictures or graphics; indeterminacy in music, or 'aleatory' (chance-dependent) music, in which (following one method) a dice would be thrown to determine the elements of a composition; and silence as an art form. He wrote copiously about music, and was also an authority on mushrooms. >> Schoenberg

Cage, Nicholas, originally **Nicholas Coppola** (1964–) Film actor, born in Long Beach, CA. He made his film debut in a small role in *Fast Times at Ridgemont High* (1982), and became well known after his appearances in *The Cotton Club* (1984) and *Peggy Sue Got Married* (1986). He won critical acclaim for his performance as a suicidal alcoholic in *Leaving Las Vegas* (1995, Oscar). Later films include *The Rock* (1996), *Con Air* (1997), and *Face/Off* (1997).

Cagliostro, Alessandro, conte di (Count of) [kal**yoh**stroh], originally **Giuseppe Balsamo** (1743–95) Adventurer and charlatan, born in Palermo, Italy. He learned some chemistry and medicine at a monastery, married the beautiful **Lorenza Feliciani**, and from 1771 they visited many centres in Europe as Count and Countess Cagliostro. Successful as physician, philosopher, alchemist, and necromancer, he carried on a lively business in his 'elixir of immortal youth', and founded lodges of 'Egyptian freemasons'. In 1789 he was imprisoned for life in San Leo, near Urbino.

Cagney, James (1899–1986) Film actor, born in New York City. He studied at Columbia, and after 10 years as an actor and dancer in vaudeville, his film performance as the gangster in *The Public Enemy* (1931) brought him stardom. His ebullient energy and aggressive personality kept him in demand for the next 30 years, including such varied productions as *A Midsummer Night's Dream* (1935), *Angels with Dirty Faces* (1938), and *Yankee Doodle Dandy* (1942), for which he was awarded an Oscar. He retired to his farm in New York State in 1961, but returned for a brief appearance in *Ragtime* (1981).

Caiaphas [**ky**afas] (1st-c) Son-in-law of Annas, eventually appointed by the Romans to be his successor as high priest of Israel (c.18–36). In the New Testament he interrogated Jesus after his arrest (*Matt* 26; *John* 18) and Peter after his detention in Jerusalem (*Acts* 4). >> Annas; Jesus Christ

Caiger-Smith, Alan [**kay**ger] (1930–) British potter. He studied at Camberwell School of Arts and Crafts and at Cambridge, prior to training in pottery at the Central School of Art and Design in 1954. He established the Aldermaston Pottery (1955), producing tin-glazed earthenware with free hand brushwork and, occasionally, rich lustres.

Caillaux, Joseph (Marie Auguste) [kiyoh] (1863–1944) French statesman, financier, and prime minister of France (1911–12), born in Le Mans, France. He trained as a lawyer, was elected to the Chamber of Deputies in 1898, and became finance minister in several governments. His brief term as prime minister ended when he was overthrown for showing too conciliatory an attitude towards Germany. In 1914, his second wife shot Gaston Calmette, editor of *Figaro*, who had launched a campaign against him and published a number of their private letters; after a famous trial, she was acquitted. He stayed in politics until France fell in 1940, when he retired. >> RR1049

Cailletet, Louis Paul [kiytay] (1832–1913) Ironmaster, born in Châtillon-sur-Seine, France. While engaged in research on the liquefaction of gases (1877), he liquefied hydrogen, nitrogen, oxygen, and air for the first time by compression, cooling, and sudden expansion. This was also done by Swiss physicist Raoul Pictet (1846–1929) at about the same time.

Cain [kayn] Biblical character, the eldest son of Adam and Eve, brother of Abel and Seth. He is portrayed (*Gen* 4) as a farmer whose offering to God was rejected, in contrast to that of his herdsman brother Abel. This led to his murder of Abel, and Cain's punishment of being banished to a nomadic life. >> Abel; Adam and Eve

Cain, James M(allahan) [kayn] (1892–1977) Writer, born in Annapolis, MD. His earliest ambition was to become a professional singer, and music forms the background of some of his stories. He was a reporter for many years, and also taught journalism. His novels include *The Postman Always Rings Twice* (1934), *Double Indemnity* (1943), and *The Butterfly* (1947). Several of his stories were filmed.

Caine, Michael [kayn], originally **Maurice Micklewhite** (1933–) Film actor, born in London, England, UK. He spent many years as a struggling small-part actor in a variety of media, before winning attention for his performance as an aristocratic officer in *Zulu* (1963). His stardom was consolidated with roles such as down-at-heel spy Harry Palmer in *The Ipcress File* (1965) and its two sequels, and as the Cockney Romeo in *Alfie* (1966). Later films include *Sleuth* (1972), *California Suite* (1978), and *Educating Rita* (1983). Nominated four times for the Academy Award, he won an Oscar for *Hannah and Her Sisters* (1986). Later films include *Dirty Rotten Scoundrels* (1988), *Noises Off* (1992), and *Blood and Wine* (1996).

Cairns, Sir Hugh William Bell (1896–1952) Surgeon, born in Port Pirie, South Australia. He studied at Adelaide University, Oxford, and London, and was made Nuffield professor of surgery at Oxford (1937). During World War 2 he became adviser on head injuries to the Ministry of Health, and neurosurgeon to the army.

Cairoli, Charlie [kiy**roh**lee] (1910–80) Circus clown, born in France. The son of a juggler, he made his debut as a circus performer at the age of five. He moved to Britain in 1938, and was for 39 years a star attraction of the Blackpool Tower Circus, until ill health forced his retirement a year before his death.

Caitanya [kiy**tahn**ya] (c. 1486–1533) Hindu mystic, born in Nadia, Bengal. A Sanskrit teacher before becoming an itinerant holy man, following conversion in 1510, he spent the latter part of his life in Puri, inspiring disciples in both Bengal and Orissa with his emphasis on joy and love of Krishna, and the place of singing and dancing in worship.

(GAIUS) JULIUS CAESAR (c. 101–44 B C)

Caesar belonged to the Julii, an ancient but not particularly distinguished aristocratic Roman family. When he was 16, his father, Gaius Caesar, died, and he was encouraged and influenced by his mother, Aurelia. In 84 BC he married **Cornelia**, the daughter of the radical Lucius Cornelius Cinna, and thus incurred the hostility of Lucius Cornelius Sulla, the ruthless politican who was involved in a bitter revolutionary feud with Marius, the husband of Caesar's aunt.

When Sulla returned to Italy from the East in 83 BC, he ordered Caesar to divorce Cornelia. Risking his life, Caesar refused, making a timely departure to do military service in Asia and Cilicia. He returned to Rome after Sulla's death in 78 BC to prepare for a political career. On his way to Rhodes to study oratory, he was captured by pirates (75–74 BC), but he escaped by raising a ransom, and retaliated by crucifying his captors.

Elected *pontifex* (member of the council of priests) in Rome in 73 BC, he supported the legal attack on Sulla's legislation, and was elected *quaestor* (a low-ranking magistrate in the treasury) in 68 or 69 BC. This was his first real political position, serving his office in Farther Spain (*Hispania Ulterior*). Cornelia died the same year, and Caesar went on to marry **Pompeia**, who was distantly related to Gnaeus Pompeius (Pompey). However, he divorced her in 62 BC over a fertility rite scandal in which she had been involved. In 65 BC, as one of the *curule aediles* (judicial magistrates) of Rome, he spent lavishly on games and public buildings. He was elected *pontifex maximus* in 63 BC, and was accused of conspiracy in the suppression of Catiline. Elected *praetor* (magistrate) for 62 BC he became governor of Farther Spain (61–60 BC), by which time he had emerged as a highly controversial political figure. He was elected *consul* (chief magistrate and effective head of state) in 59 BC.

Caesar reconciled Pompey and Marcus Licinius Crassus and, to protect his interests in the state, established with them the informal alliance known as the First Triumvirate, sealing the agreement by giving Pompey his only child, Julia, in marriage (59 BC). The same year Caesar married Calpurnia, the daughter of consul Lucius Piso. He then obtained the provinces of Gallia Cisalpina, Gallia Transalpina, and Illyricum, and for nine years (58–50 BC) conducted campaigns (the Gallic Wars) which extended Roman power in the West.

In the first campaign he defeated the Helvetii and Ariovistus, in 57 BC the Belgic confederacy and the Nervii, and in 56 BC the Veneti and other peoples of Brittany and Normandy. In 55 BC he invaded Britain, and on a second invasion in 54 BC crossed the R Thames and enforced at least the nominal submission of the SE of the island.

On his return to Gaul, he was defeated by the rebellious Eburones, but exacted a terrible vengeance from their leaders. Visiting N Italy, he had to return to quell a general rebellion headed by Vercingetorix. The struggle was severe, and at Gergovia, the capital of the Arverni, Caesar was defeated; but in 52 BC, with the capture of Alesia, he crushed the united armies of the Gauls.

In the meantime Crassus had been defeated and killed in Asia (53 BC), and Pompey was becoming more distant from Caesar. After the death of Julia in 54 BC, the link was all but broken. The Senate called upon Caesar, at the time in Cisalpine Gaul, to resign his command and disband his army, and entrusted Pompey with extensive powers. Pompey's forces outnumbered Caesar's legions, but were scattered over the empire. Supported by his victorious troops, Caesar moved S (49 BC), crossed the R Rubicon into Italy from Cisalpine Gaul (the river formed the border), and entered into a civil war with Pompey. He pursued Pompey to Brundisium, and moved from there to Greece.

Within three months Caesar was master of all Italy, and after subduing Pompey's legates in Spain he was appointed dictator. Pompey had meanwhile gathered a powerful army in Egypt, Greece, and the East, while his fleet controlled the sea. Caesar, crossing the Adriatic, was driven back from Dyrrhachium with heavy losses. However, in a second battle, at Pharsalia (48 BC), the senatorial army was routed, and Pompey fled to Egypt, where he was murdered by an officer of King Ptolemy.

Caesar was appointed dictator for a year and consul for five years, but he did not return to Rome. Instead he went to Egypt, where he engaged in the Alexandrine War on behalf of Queen Cleopatra in 47 BC, and risked what he had won by his public dalliance with her. On his return he overthrew Pharnaces, a son of Mithradates in Pontus, and after a short stay in Rome routed the Pompeian generals, Scipio and Marcus Porcius Cato, at Thapsus in Africa (46 BC). After his victories in Gaul, Egypt, Pontus, and Africa, he put down an insurrection in Farther Spain by Pompey's sons (45 BC).

Hailed as 'Father of his Country', Caesar was made dictator for life, and consul for 10 years in 45 BC. His person was declared sacred, his statue placed in temples, his portrait struck on coins, and the month Quintilis renamed Julius in his honour. Ambitious plans were ascribed to him. He proposed to make a digest of the whole of Roman law, to found libraries, to drain the Pontine Marshes, to enlarge the harbour at Ostia, to dig a canal through the Isthmus, and to launch a war against the Dacians in C Europe, and the Parthians in the East.

In the midst of these vast designs he was assassinated in March 44 BC. The conspirators, mostly aristocrats led by Brutus and Cassius, believed that they were striking a blow for the restoration of republican freedom, which they felt Caesar's autocracy was negating. However, the result of their action was to plunge the Roman world into a fresh round of civil wars, in which the Republic was finally destroyed.

Caesar was one of the great generals of history; his name became synonymous with leadership, hence the titles *Kaiser*, and *Tsar*. He was second only to Cicero as an orator. His historical writings, among them the *Commentarii de bello Gallico* (The Gallic Wars) and *Commentarii de bello civile* (The Civil Wars), are simple and direct. Yet, for all his genius, he failed to find a solution to the political problems of the late Republic, an achievement which was left to his adopted son Octavianus (63 BC–AD 14), the future emperor Augustus.

>> Augustus; Brutus, Marcus Junius; Cassius; Cinna; Cleopatra VII; Crassus, Marcus Licinius; Marius, Gaius; Pompey the Great; Sulla

Caius, John [keez] (1510–73) Physician and scholar, born in Norwich, Norfolk, E England, UK. He became a student at Gonville Hall, Cambridge (1529), and a fellow in 1533. He studied medicine at Padua, then lectured on anatomy in London (1544–64). President of the College of Physicians nine times, he was physician to Edward VI, Mary I, and Queen Elizabeth I. In 1559 he became the first Master of Gonville and Caius College, Cambridge.

Cajetan [kajetan], Ital **Gaetano**, originally **Thomas de Vio** (c. 1469–1534) Clergyman and theologian, born in Gaeta, Italy. He became General of the Dominicans (1508), cardinal (1517), Bishop of Gaeta (1519), and legate to Hungary (1523). In 1518 he sought to induce Luther to recant at Augsburg. >> Luther

Calamity Jane, popular name of **Martha Jane Burke**, *née* **Cannary** (c.1852–1903) Frontierswoman, born in Princeton, MO. She became a living legend for her skill at riding and shooting, particularly in the Gold Rush days in the Black Hills of Dakota. She teamed up with the renowned US marshal, **Wild Bill Hickock** (1847–76), at Deadwood, SD, before he was murdered. She is said to have threatened 'calamity' for any man who tried to court her, but in 1885 she married.

Calas, Jean [kalahs] (1698–1762) Huguenot merchant, born in Lacabarède, France. In 1761 he was accused, on the flimsiest evidence, of murdering his eldest son (a suicide) in order to prevent him becoming a Roman Catholic. He was found guilty, and executed by being broken on the wheel. Voltaire led a campaign which resulted in a revision of the trial, and the parliament at Paris in 1765 declared Calas and all his family innocent. >> Voltaire

Caldara, Antonio [kaldahra] (1670–1736) Composer, born in Venice, Italy. He became deputy *Kapellmeister* in Vienna, and amongst his choral works are some outstanding examples of the polyphonic style. He also wrote many operas and oratorios, and some trio-sonatas in the style of Corelli. >> Corelli, Arcangelo

Caldecott, Randolph [kawldikot] (1846–86) Artist and illustrator, born in Chester, Cheshire, NWC England, UK. He began as a bank-clerk in Whitstable and Manchester, and moved to London to follow an artistic career. He illustrated Washington Irving's *Old Christmas* (1876) and numerous children's books, such as *The House that Jack Built* (1878) and *Aesop's Fables* (1883). The *Caldecott Medal* has been awarded annually since 1938 to the best US artist-illustrator of children's books.

Calder, Alexander (Stirling) [kawlder] (1898–1976) Artist and pioneer of kinetic art, born in Philadelphia, PA. He trained as an engineer (1915–19) before studying art at the School of the Art Students' League in New York City (1923). He specialized in abstract hanging wire constructions, some of which were connected to motors (Marcel Duchamp christened them 'mobiles' in 1932). His best-known works, however, were unpowered, relying upon air currents to set them rotating and casting intricate shadows. >> Duchamp

Calder, (Peter) Ritchie, Baron Ritchie-Calder of Balmashannar [kawlder] (1906–82) Journalist and educationist, born in Forfar, Angus, E Scotland, UK. Specializing in the spread of scientific knowledge to lay readers, he wrote numerous books including *Men Against the Desert* (1951), *Men Against the Jungle* (1954), *Living with the Atom* (1962), and *The Evolution of the Machine* (1968). He was made a life peer in 1966.

Calderón de la Barca, Pedro [kolduhron duh la bah(r)ka] (1600–81) Playwright, born in Madrid. He studied law and philosophy at Salamanca, and in 1635 was appointed to the court of Philip IV, where he began to write plays. He served in the army in Catalonia (1640–2), and in 1651 entered the priesthood. Recalled to court, he became chaplain of honour to Philip and continued to write plays, masques, and operas for the court, the Church, and the public theatres until his death. He wrote over 100 plays on secular themes, such as *El príncipe constante* (1629, The Constant Prince) and *El alcalde de Zalamea* (1640, The Mayor of Zalamea). In addition he wrote many religious plays, including over 70 outdoor dramas for the festival of Corpus Christi.

Caldwell, Erskine [kawldwel] (1903–87) Writer, born in White Oak, GA. He worked amongst the 'poor whites' in the Southern states, where he absorbed the background for his best-known work, *Tobacco Road* (1932). Other books include *God's Little Acre* (1933), *Love and Money* (1954), and *Close to Home* (1962).

Caldwell, Sarah [kawldwel] (1924–) Opera director and conductor, born in Maryville, MO. She studied violin, and while affiliated to Boston University formed her own opera company in Boston (1958). Overseeing every detail of the productions, staging, and music, she was notorious for just meeting last-minute deadlines and averting financial crises, but she made her opera company one of the most distinguished and innovative in the USA, especially noted for its productions of modern works such as Schoenberg's *Moses and Aaron*. In the 1970s she began to appear as a guest conductor of major orchestras.

Caletti-Bruni, Francesco >> **Cavalli, Francesco**

Calgacus [kalgakus] (1st-c) Caledonian chieftain in N Britain, leader of the tribes defeated by Agricola at the Battle of Mons Graupius. Agricola's biographer, Tacitus, attributes to him a heroic speech on the eve of the battle, with a ringing denunciation of Roman imperialism. >> Agricola

Calhoun, John C(aldwell) [kalhoon] (1782–1850) US statesman, born in Abbeville County, SC. He studied at Yale, and became a successful lawyer. In Congress he supported the measures which led to the war of 1812–15 with Great Britain, and promoted the protective tariff. In 1817 he joined Monroe's cabinet as secretary of war, and was vice-president under John Quincy Adams (1825–9), and then under Jackson. In 1832 he entered the US Senate, becoming a leader of the states-rights movement, and a champion of the interests of the slave-holding states. In 1844, as secretary of state, he signed a treaty annexing Texas; but, once more in the Senate, he strenuously opposed the war of 1846–7 with Mexico. >> Adams, John Quincy; Jackson, Andrew; Monroe, James

Caliari, Paolo >> **Veronese**

Caligula [kaligyula], nickname of **Gaius Julius Caesar Germanicus** (12–41) Roman emperor (37–41), the youngest son of Germanicus and Agrippina, born in Antium. Brought up in an army camp, he was nicknamed Caligula from his little soldier's boots (*caligae*). His official name, once emperor, was Gaius. Extravagant, autocratic, vicious, and mentally unstable, he wreaked havoc with the finances of the state, and terrorized those around him, until he was assassinated. Under him, Hellenistic court practices, such as ritual obeisance, made their first (though not last) appearance in Rome. >> Agrippina (the Elder); Germanicus; RR1084

Calisher, Hortense (1911–) Novelist and short-story writer, born in New York City. Her milieu is New York, and her characters are usually drawn from the upper middle-class. Her novels include *The New Yorkers* (1969), *Queenie* (1971), and *The Bobby-Soxer* (1986).

Calixtus [kalikstus], originally **Callisen Georg** (1586–1656) Lutheran theologian, born in Medelbye, Germany. From 1603 he studied at Helmstedt, where he became professor of theology. Although acknowledged by learned Romanists to be one of their ablest opponents, he was declared guilty of heresy for statements which seemed favourable to Catholic dogmas, and for others which approached too near to the Calvinistic standpoint. He nonetheless retained his chair till his death.

Calkins, (Earnest) Elmo (1868–1964) Advertising executive and writer, born in Geneseo, IL. A talented copywriter, first in Illinois and then in New York, he was founding president of Calkins and Holden, New York City (1902–31), regarded as the prototypal modern agency for producing integrated advertising campaigns incorporating high-quality copy and art. He co-authored with Ralph Holden the first advertising textbook, *Modern Advertising* (1905). In his later years he was an essayist and author. Severely hearing-impaired since his youth, he often wrote on the problems of the deaf.

Callaghan (of Cardiff), (Leonard) James Callaghan, Baron [kalahan], known as **Jim Callaghan** (1912–) British statesman and prime minister (1976–9), born in Portsmouth, Hampshire, S England, UK. He joined the Civil Service (1929), and in 1945 was elected Labour MP for South Cardiff. As Chancellor of the Exchequer under Harold Wilson (1964–7), he introduced the controversial corporation and selective employment taxes. He was home secretary (1967–70) and foreign secretary (1974–6), and became prime minister on Wilson's resignation. He resigned as Leader of the Opposition in 1980, and became a life peer in 1987. His autobiography, *Time and Chance*, was published in 1987. >> Wilson, Harold; RR1095

Callaghan, Morley (Edward) [kalahan] (1903–) Novelist, short-story writer, and memoirist, born in Toronto, Ontario, Canada. He studied at Toronto University, and was befriended by Hemingway. He was called to the bar in 1928, but while in Paris Hemingway encouraged him to give up law for literature, and helped him get some of his stories published in expatriate literary magazines. His first novel was *Strange Fugitive* (1928) and his first collection of stories *A Native Argosy* (1930). He returned to Toronto in 1929. Later novels include *The Loved and the Lost* (1951), *The Many Colored Coat* (1960), and *A Time for Judas* (1983). >> Hemingway

Callas, Maria (Meneghini) [kalas], originally **Maria Kalogeropoulos** (1923–77) Operatic soprano, born in New York City of Greek parents. She studied at Athens Conservatory, and in 1947 appeared at Verona in *La Gioconda*, winning immediate recognition. She sang with great authority in all the most exacting soprano roles, excelling in the intricate *bel canto* style of pre-Verdian Italian opera. >> Onassis

Callendar, Hugh Longbourne (1863–1930) Physicist, born in Hatherop, Gloucestershire, SWC England, UK. He studied at Cambridge, and was professor of physics at McGill University, Montreal (1893), University College London (1898), and the Imperial College of Science (1902). He devised a constant-pressure air thermometer which could measure up to 450°C, and also an accurate platinum resistance thermometer.

Calles, Plutarco Elias [kayes] (1877–1945) Mexican political leader and president of Mexico (1924–8), born in Guaymas, Mexico. A former schoolmaster and tradesman, he took part in the revolt against Porfirio Diaz (1910), and became secretary of the interior (1920–4), then president. In 1929 he founded the National Revolutionary Party. He was defeated by Lázaro Cárdenas, and from 1936 to 1941 was exiled to the USA. >> Cárdenas; Diaz, Porfirio

Callicrates >> Ictinos

Callimachus [kalimakus] (5th-c BC) Greek sculptor, working in Athens in the late 5th-c BC. Vitruvius says he invented the architectural Corinthian capital. Several statues have

been identified as his, including the 'Draped Venus' in the Boston Museum of Fine Arts. >> Vitruvius

Callimachus [kalimakus] (299–210 BC) Greek poet, grammarian, and critic, born in Cyrene, Libya. He became head of the Alexandrian Library, and prepared a catalogue of it, in 120 volumes. He wrote numerous prose works which have not survived, a number of *Hymns* and *Epigrams*, and a long elegiac poem, *Aitia*, among others.

Callistratus [kalistratus] (4th-c BC) Athenian orator and statesman, whose eloquence is said to have fired the imagination of the youthful Demosthenes. In 366 BC he allowed the Thebans to occupy Oropus, and was prosecuted, but defended himself successfully in a brilliant speech. He was prosecuted again in 361 for his Spartan sympathies and was condemned to death, but went into exile before sentence was pronounced. He returned from exile in Macedonia, hoping to win public support, but was executed. >> Demosthenes

Callot, Jacques [kayoh] (c.1592–1635) Etcher and engraver, born in Nancy, France. In 1612 he went to Rome to study, then moved to Florence where he earned a reputation for his spirited etchings. For Louis XIII, who invited him to Paris, he executed etchings of the siege of La Rochelle, but refused to commemorate the capture of his native town. His 1600 realistic engravings cast vivid light on the events and manners of the 17th-c.

Callow, Simon (1949–) Actor, director, and writer, born in London, England, UK. He made his London debut in *The Plumber's Progress* (1975), and joined Joint Stock in 1977, later playing major roles at the Bristol Old Vic and the National Theatre. He has also appeared in several films, notably *A Room With a View* (1986), *Postcards from the Edge* (1990), *Four Weddings and a Funeral* (1994), and *Jefferson in Paris* (1995). He has directed several new plays in fringe theatres, and the film *The Ballad of the Sad Café* (1990). He published an autobiography, *Being An Actor* (1984).

Calloway, Cab(ell) (1907–94) Jazz musician, born in Rochester, NY. A versatile song and dance man, he led a succession of outstanding big bands (1928–53). He was featured in the 1979 movie *The Blues Brothers*. >> Tharpe

Calman, Mel (1931–94) British cartoonist and writer. He studied at Goldsmith's College, London, then worked as a regular and freelance cartoonist for several British national newspapers from 1957, joining *The Times* in 1979. His many publications include *Bed-Sit* (1963), *This Pestered Isle* (1973), *How About A Little Quarrel Before Bed?* (1981), and *Calman at the Royal Opera House* (1990).

Calmette, (Léon Charles) Albert [kalmet] (1863–1933) Bacteriologist, born in Nice, France. A pupil of Pasteur and founder of the Pasteur Institute at Saigon, he was the discoverer of an anti-snakebite serum there. In 1895 he founded the Pasteur Institute at Lille (director, 1895–1919). He is best known for the vaccine BCG (*Bacille Calmette–Guérin*), for inoculation against tuberculosis, which he jointly developed with **Dr Camille Guérin** (1872–1961). He was the brother of newspaper editor Gaston Calmette. >> Caillaux; Pasteur

Calvert, Frederick Crace (1819–73) Chemist, born in London, England, UK. A consulting chemist in Manchester, he was largely instrumental in introducing carbolic acid as a disinfectant.

Calvert, George >> **Baltimore, George Calvert**

Calvi, Robert [kalvee], originally **Gian Roberto Calvini** (1920–82) Banker and financier, born in Milan, Italy. Working his way up through Banco Ambrosiano, he became its chairman in 1975, and continued to build a vast financial empire. In 1978, a report by the Bank of Italy on Ambrosiano concluded that several billion lire had been illegally exported. In May 1981, he was arrested, found guilty, and sentenced to four years' imprisonment, but released pending an appeal. By 1982, his bank, on the verge of financial collapse, was temporarily saved by patronage letters from the Vatican's bank which, under the leadership of Paul Marcinckus, had jointly perpetrated with Ambrosiano several dubious business deals. Calvi's body was found hanging from scaffolding under Blackfriars Bridge in London. A verdict of suicide was recorded, which was overturned in 1983, when an inquest delivered an open verdict on the death. The ramifications of the collapse of Banco Ambrosiano, and of the involvement of the Vatican and possibly the Mafia continued well after his death.

Calvin, John (1509–64) Protestant reformer, born in Noyon, France. He studied Latin at Paris, then law at Orléans, where he developed his interest in theology. In Bourges and other centres he began to preach the reformed doctrines, but was forced to flee from France to escape persecution. At Basel he issued his influential *Christianae religionis institutio* (1536, Institutes of the Christian Religion), and at Geneva was persuaded by Guillaume Farel to help with the reformation. The reformers proclaimed a Protestant Confession of Faith, under which moral severity took the place of licence. When a rebellious party, the Libertines, rose against this, Calvin and Farel were expelled from the city (1538). Calvin withdrew to Strasbourg, where he worked on New Testament criticism, and married **Idelette de Bure** (1540). In 1541 the Genevans recalled him, and he founded a theocracy which controlled almost all the city's affairs. By 1555 his authority was confirmed into an absolute supremacy. The father-figure of Reformed theology, he left a double legacy to Protestantism by systematizing its doctrine and organizing its ecclesiastical discipline. His commentaries, which embrace most of the Old and New Testaments, were collected and published in 1617. >> Farel

Calvin, Melvin (1911–) Chemist, born in St Paul, MN. He studied at the universities of Minnesota and Manchester (UK), then became professor of chemistry at the University of California, Berkeley (1947–71) and head of the Lawrence Radiation Laboratory there (1963–80). He is best known for his research into the role of chlorophyll in photosynthesis, for which he received the Nobel Prize for Chemistry in 1961.

Calvino, Italo [kalveenoh] (1923–85) Writer, essayist, and journalist, born in Santiago de las Vegas, Cuba, of Italian parents. He spent his early years in San Remo, and studied at Turin, where he worked as a publisher. His first novel, *Il sentiero dei nidi di ragno* (1947, The Path to the Nest of Spiders), described resistance against Fascism in a highly naturalistic manner. In later works, such as *I nostri antenati* (1960, Our Ancestors), he adopted a more condensed style of story-telling, hovering between allegory and pure fantasy, while *Se una notte d'inverno un viaggiatore* (1979, If On a Winter's Night a Traveller) tests the limits of experiment in fiction.

Cam or **Cão** (15th-c) Portuguese explorer. In 1482 he discovered the mouth of the Congo, near whose bank an inscribed stone erected by him as a memorial was found in 1887. His voyages southwards along the West African coast later enabled Bartholomew Diaz to find the sea route to the Indian Ocean around the Cape. >> Diaz, Bartholomew

Camara, Helder (Pessoa) [kamara] (1909–) Roman Catholic theologian and clergyman, born in Fortaleza, Brazil. Archbishop of Olinda and Recife (1964–84), he has been a champion of the poor and of non-violent social change in Brazil, and also in the Catholic Church at large through his influence at Vatican Council II. He received

international recognition with the award of the Martin Luther King, Jr, Peace Prize (1970) and the People's Prize (1973).

Camargo, Maria Anna de [kamah(r)goh] (1710–70) Dancer, born in Brussels. She won European fame for her performances at the Paris Opera, where she made her debut in 1726, and is said to have been responsible for the shortening of the traditional ballet skirt which allowed more complicated steps to be seen. She was also one of the first celebrities to lend her name to merchandizing shoes and wigs.

Cambacérès, Jean Jacques Régis de [kābasayres] (1753–1824) Lawyer, born in Montpellier, France. He became arch-chancellor of the French Empire (1804) and Duke of Parma (1808). As Napoleon's chief legal adviser, his civil code formed the basis of the *Code Napoléon*. >> Napoleon

Cambio, Arnolfo di >> **Arnolfo di Cambio**

Cambon, Joseph [kābō] (1756–1820) Financier and revolutionary, born in Montpellier, France. During the Revolution he was a member of the Legislative Assembly and the Convention (1792), and although a moderate, he voted for the king's death. As head of the committee on finance (1793–95), he produced the 'Great Book of the Public Debt' in an attempt to stabilize the finances. He was banished as a regicide in 1815. >> Louis XVI

Cambrensis, Giraldus >> **Giraldus Cambrensis**

Cambridge, Ada (1844–1926) Writer and poet, born in St Germains, Norfolk, E England, UK. By the time she married **George Cross** at the age of 26, she had published short stories, poems, and a book of hymns. They left almost immediately for Australia, where her husband was to be a missionary priest, and settled eventually in Melbourne. A woman with a strong sense of class, her writing called attention to women's social position and encouraged them to think for themselves. She wrote 18 novels, including *A Marked Man* (1890), *Fidelis* (1895), and *Materfamilias* (1898).

Cambyses II [kambiyseez], Persian **Kambujiya** (?–522 BC) King of the Medes and Persians, who succeeded his father, Cyrus II, in 529 BC. He put his brother Smerdis to death, and in 527 or 525 BC invaded and conquered Egypt. When news came, in 522 BC, that Gaumáta, a Magian, had assumed Smerdis's character, and usurped the Persian throne, Cambyses marched against him from Egypt, but died in Syria. >> Cyrus II; RR1063

Camden, William (1551–1623) Antiquarian and historian, born in London, England, UK. He studied at Oxford, and became second master of Westminster School (1575), then headmaster (1593). A dedicated scholar, he compiled a pioneering topographical survey of the British Isles in Latin, *Britannia* (1586, English trans, 1610). The *Camden Society* (founded 1838), which promoted historical publications, was named after him.

Camerarius, Joachim [kamerairius] (1500–74) Classical scholar and Lutheran theologian, born in Bamberg, Germany. A friend of Melanchthon, he embraced the Reformation at Wittenberg in 1521, and helped to formulate the Augsburg Confession of 1530. He was professor of Greek and Latin at Tübingen (1535) and Leipzig (from 1541). >> Melanchthon

Camerarius, Rudolf Jakob [kamerairius] (1665–1721) Botanist, born in Tübingen, Germany. He followed his father in becoming professor of medicine at Tübingen. He showed by experiment in 1694 that plants can reproduce sexually, and identified the stamens and carpels as the male and female sexual apparatus, respectively. He also described pollination.

Cameron, James (Mark) (1911–85) Journalist, born in London, England, UK. His career began as an office boy for the *Weekly News* (1935), and progressed to Fleet Street in 1940, working for *The Daily Express*, *Picture Post*, and the *New Chronicle* (1952–60). He became known as a roving reporter on war, poverty, and injustice, renowned for his integrity, dry wit, and concise summaries. He was also a writer and presenter of many television programmes, including *Men of Our Time* (1963), the intermittent *Cameron Country*, and the autobiographical *Once Upon a Time* (1984).

Cameron, Julia Margaret, *née* **Pattle** (1815–79) British photographer, born in Calcutta, India. In 1838 she married an Indian jurist, **Charles Hay Cameron** (1795–1880), and moved to England in 1848. At the age of 48 she was given a camera, and went on to become an outstanding amateur photographer in the 1860s. Her close-up portraits of such Victorian celebrities as Tennyson, Darwin, Carlyle, and Newman received permanent acclaim.

Cameron, Verney Lovett (1844–94) Explorer, born in Radipole, Dorset, S England, UK. He entered the navy in 1857, and in 1872 was appointed to command an African E coast expedition to relieve David Livingstone. Starting from Bagamoyo in 1873, he met Livingstone's followers bearing his remains to the coast. He made a survey of L Tanganyika, then continued to Benguela, the first European to cross Africa from coast to coast. In 1878 he travelled overland to India, to satisfy himself of the feasibility of a Constantinople–Baghdad railway. >> Livingstone

Camillus, Marcus Furius [kamilus] (447–365 BC) Roman patrician who first appears as censor in 403 BC. He was five times made dictator, and carried out several military victories. In 390 BC, according to legend, he is said to have driven the Gauls from Rome. He routed the Aequi, Volsci, and Etrusci, and in 367 BC defeated the Gauls near Alba.

Camm, Sir Sydney (1893–1966) Aircraft designer, born in Windsor, Berkshire, S England, UK. He joined Hawker Engineering Company (later Hawker Siddeley Aviation) in 1923, and became their chief designer. He had a unique design record of highly successful single-engined military aircraft, notably the Fury, Hart, and Demon biplanes, and his first monoplane, the Hurricane. He also designed the piston-engined Tornado, Typhoon, and Tempest; the jet-engined Sea Hawk and Hunter; and the jump-jet Harrier.

Camoens or **Camões, Luís de** [kamohenz] (1524–80) The greatest Portuguese poet, born in Lisbon. He studied for the Church at Coimbra, but declined to take orders. He became a soldier, and during service at Ceuta lost his right eye. He went to India (1553) and Macao (1556), and was shipwrecked while returning to Goa (1558), losing everything except his major poem, *Os Lusiados* (The Lusiads, or Lusitanians). After returning to Portugal in 1570, he lived in poverty and obscurity. *The Lusiads* was published in 1572, and was an immediate success, but did little for his fortunes, and he died in a public hospital. The work has since come to be regarded as the Portuguese national epic.

Camp, Walter (Chauncy) (1859–1925) Player of American football, born in New Britain, CT, the 'father of American football'. At Yale University (1888–92) he helped to shape American football rules, introducing the 11-man side (as against 15), the concept of 'downs' and 'yards gained', and the creation of a new points-scoring system.

Campagnola, Domenico [kampanyohla] (c. 1490–c. 1564) Painter, born in Padua, Italy. A pupil of Giulio Campagnola and assistant of Titian, he is known for his religious frescoes in Padua, as well as for his masterly engravings and line drawings in the manner of Titian.

Campagnola, Giulio [kampanyohla] (1482–c.1515) Engraver, born in Padua, Italy. He designed type for Aldus Manutius, and produced fine engravings after Mantegna, Bellini, and Giorgione. >> Aldus Manutius

Campanella, Tommaso [kampanela] (1568–1639) Philosopher, born in Stilo, Italy. Entering the Dominican order in 1583, he taught at Rome and Naples. He evolved an empirical, anti-Scholastic philosophy, for which he was imprisoned by the Inquisition. He was arrested again in 1599 for heresy and conspiracy against Spanish rule, and was not finally released until 1626. From prison he wrote his famous utopian work, *La Città del Sole* (c.1602, City of the Sun). He eventually fled to Paris in 1634, as a protégé of Richelieu. >> Richelieu

Campbell, Alexander (1788–1866) Leader of the 'Disciples of Christ', otherwise known as *Campbellites*, born near Ballymena, Antrim. He emigrated to the USA with his father in 1809, in 1813 succeeding him as pastor of an independent Church at Brush Run, PA. He advocated a return to the simple Church of New Testament times, and in 1826 published a translation of the New Testament. In 1841 he founded Bethany College in West Virginia.

Campbell, Sir Colin, Baron Clyde (1792–1863) British field marshal, born in Glasgow, W Scotland, UK. He fought in the Peninsular War against Napoleon, where he was twice badly wounded, and after 30 years of duty in various garrisons fought in China (1842) and in the second Sikh war (1848–9). In the Crimean War he commanded the Highland Brigade in a campaign which included the renowned repulse of the Russians by the 'thin red line' at Balaclava. During the Indian Mutiny he commanded the forces in India, and effected the final relief of Lucknow. He was created baron in 1858.

Campbell, Donald (Malcolm) (1921–67) Land and water speed-record contestant, born in Horley, Surrey, SE England, UK, the son of Sir Malcolm Campbell. An engineer by training, he sought to emulate his father's achievements. He set new world speed records several times on both land and water, culminating in 1964 with a water-speed record of 276·33 mph on L Dumbleyung in Australia, and a land-speed record of 403·1 mph at L Eyre salt flats in Australia. In an attempt to become the first man to break 300 mph on water, he was killed when his *Bluebird* turbo-jet hydroplane crashed on Coniston Water in England. >> Campbell, Malcolm

Campbell, John W(ood), Jr, pseudonym **Don A Stuart** (1910–71) Science-fiction writer, born in Newark, NJ. His first published novel, *When the Atoms Failed* (1930), was one of the earliest to make reference to computers. He developed in his stories the new idea that machines could dominate humans, notably in *Twilight* (1934). His works were highly influential, and he has come to be regarded as the father of modern science-fiction.

Campbell, Kim (Avril Phaedra Douglas) (1947–) Canadian stateswoman, and Canada's first woman prime minister (1993), born in British Columbia, Canada. Her first public office was as school trustee with the Vancouver School Board (1980). She later ran unsuccessfully as a Social Credit candidate in the British Columbia provincial election, then was elected for the province in 1988 as a federal conservative. She served as minister of justice and defence in Brian Mulroney's cabinet, before becoming leader of the party and prime minister in spring 1993, but disastrously lost the general election some months later. >> Mulroney, Brian

Campbell, Sir Malcolm (1885–1948) Land and water speed-record contestant, born in Chislehurst, Kent, SE England, UK. He held both speed records from 1927 onwards. In 1935 he became the first man to break 300 mph on land with 301·1292 mph at Bonneville Salt Flats, UT. In 1939 he achieved his fastest speed on water with 141·74 mph. He called all his cars and boats *Bluebird*, after the symbol of unattainability in the play of that name by Maurice Maeterlinck. >> Campbell, Donald

Campbell, Mrs Patrick, *née* **Beatrice Stella Tanner** (1865–1940) Actress, born in London, England, UK. She married in 1884, and went on the stage in 1888. Though her mercurial temperament made her the terror of managers, she possessed outstanding charm and talent, and leapt to fame in *The Second Mrs Tanqueray* (1893). She played Eliza in Shaw's *Pygmalion* (1914), and formed a long friendship with the author. >> Shaw, George Bernard

Campbell, Reginald John (1867–1956) Clergyman, born in London, England, UK. He entered the Congregational ministry in 1895, and was pastor of the City Temple, London (1903–15). In 1907 he startled the evangelical world by his exposition of an 'advanced' *New Theology*. He became an Anglican in 1916.

Campbell, (Ignatius) Roy (Dunnachie) (1901–57) Poet and journalist, born in Durban, South Africa. He became an ardent admirer of all things Spanish, and fought with Franco's armies during the Civil War. His books of poetry include *The Flaming Terrapin* (1924), *The Wayzgoose* (1928), and *Flowering Rifle* (1939). A collected edition of his poems appeared in 1949. >> Plomer

Campbell, William Wallace (1862–1938) Astronomer, born in Hancock Co, OH. He joined the Lick Observatory in California in 1891, became its director (1901–30), and was also president of the University of California (1923–30). He is best known for his work on the radial velocity of stars.

Campbell-Bannerman, Sir Henry (1836–1908) British statesman and prime minister (1905–8), born in Glasgow, W Scotland, UK. He studied at Glasgow and Cambridge, became a Liberal MP (1868), was chief secretary for Ireland (1884), war secretary (1886, 1892–5), Liberal leader (1899), and prime minister. A 'pro-Boer', he granted the ex-republics responsible government, and his popularity united the Liberal Party. He supported the Lib–Lab pact of 1903, which played a part in the Liberal landslide of 1906. >> RR1095

Campen, Jacob van [kampen] (1595–1657) Architect and painter, born in Haarlem, The Netherlands. Greatly influenced by Italian style, he built the first completely Classical building in Holland. His masterpiece was the Mauritshuis, The Hague (1633), for Prince Johan Maurits von Nassau; the interior was destroyed in 1704. Other works include Amsterdam Theatre (1637) and Town Hall (1647–55, now the royal palace).

Campendonck, Heinrich [kampendongk] (1889–1957) Expressionist painter, born in Krefeld, Germany. He was a member of the *Blaue Reiter* group founded by Marc and Kandinsky. >> Kandinsky; Marc

Campese, David (Ian) [kampeezee], nickname **Campo** (1962–) Rugby union player, born near Queanbeyan, New South Wales, Australia. One of the fastest wingers in international rugby, his powerful sprinting meant that by the end of 1990 he had 46 tries to his credit, a record for international rugby. A flamboyant player, he was the star of Australia's 1991 World Cup victory. He spends the winter playing in Sydney's club competition and the off season playing in Italy. >> RR1167

Campi, Bernardino [kampee] (1522–c.1592) Italian artist, the son of a goldsmith, and possibly a kinsman of the painter and architect **Antonio Campi** (1536–c.1591). He imitated Titian with such success that it has been difficult to distinguish the copies from the originals. His works may be seen in Mantua and Cremona. >> Titian

Campi, Giulio [kampee] (c.1502–72) Architect and painter, born in Cremona, Italy. He was influenced by Giulio Romano, and founded the Cremonese school of painting, to which his brothers **Vincenzo Campi** (1539–91) and **Antonio Campi** (1536–c.1591) also belonged. His work includes a fine altarpiece at Cremona. >> Giulio Romano

Campin, Robert [kampin] (c. 1378–1444) Artist, born in Tournai, France. He was called **the Master of Flémalle** from his paintings of Flémelle Abbey near Liège. About 1400 he settled in Tournai, where Rogier van der Weyden was one of his pupils. >> Leyden

Campion, Edmund, St (1540–81) The first of the English Jesuit martyrs, born in London, England, UK. He studied at Oxford, and although made a deacon in the Church of England (1569) he leaned towards Roman Catholicism. Fearing arrest, he escaped to Douai, and in 1573 joined the Jesuits in Bohemia. In 1580 he was recalled from Prague, where he was professor of rhetoric, for a Jesuit mission to England. He circulated his *Decem rationes* (Ten Reasons) against Anglicanism in 1581, and was arrested, tortured, tried on a charge of conspiracy, and hanged in London. He was beatified in 1886, and canonized in 1970; feast day 1 December. >> Parsons, Robert

Campion, Jane (1954–) Film director, born in Waikanae, New Zealand. She studied at art school in Wellington and at the Australian Film, Television, and Radio School in Sydney, the city where she is now based. Her films include *Peel* (1984), which won the 1986 Cannes Palme d'Or for best short film, her highly original first feature *Sweetie* (1989), and *An Angel at My Table* (1990), based on Janet Frame's autobiographies. *The Piano* (1993), a love story set in colonial New Zealand, which she wrote as well as directed, shared the Palme d'Or at the 1993 Cannes Film Festival, the first such award for an Australian production and the first for a woman director. Later films include *The Portrait of a Lady* (1996). >> Frame

Campion, Thomas (1567–1620) Physician, poet, and composer, born in Witham, Essex, SE England, UK. He studied at Cambridge and abroad, and set his own lyrics to music. As well as poetry in Latin and English he left several books of 'ayres' for voice and lute.

Campoli, Alfredo [kampohlee] (1906–91) Violinist, born in Rome. He went to London in 1911, and quickly won a reputation as a soloist. During the lean years of the 1930s he became better known for his salon orchestra. This was disbanded at the outbreak of World War 2, after which he emerged as one of the outstanding violinists of his time.

Camus, Albert [kahmü] (1913–1960) French existentialist writer, born in Mondovi, Algeria. He studied philosophy at Algiers, and worked as an actor, teacher, playwright, and journalist there and in Paris. Active in the French resistance during World War 2, he became co-editor with Sartre of the left-wing newspaper *Combat* after the liberation until 1948. He earned an international reputation with his nihilistic novel, *L'Etranger* (1942, The Outsider). Later novels include *La Peste* (1947, The Plague) and *La Chute* (1956, The Fall), and he also wrote plays and several political works. He received the Nobel Prize for Literature in 1957. >> Sartre

Canaletto [kanaletoh], originally **Giovanni Antonio Canal** (1697–1768) Painter, born in Venice, Italy. He studied at Rome, then painted a renowned series of views in Venice, many as souvenirs for foreign visitors. He spent most of the years 1746–56 in England, where his views of London and elsewhere proved extremely popular. He later returned to Venice and was elected to the Venice Academy in 1763.

Canaris, Wilhelm [kanahris] (1887–1945) Naval commander, born in Aplerbeck, Germany. He entered the imperial German Navy in 1905, and served in World War 1. Though disapproving of aspects of the Nazi regime, he rose under Hitler to become admiral of the German navy and chief of the *Abwehr*, the military intelligence service of the high command of the armed forces. Associated with the 1944 bomb plot against Hitler, he was arrested, imprisoned, and hanged. >> Hitler

Candela, (Outeriño) Felix [kandela] (1910–) Architect and engineer, born in Madrid. He fled to Mexico in 1939 as a republican refugee from the Spanish civil war. He worked as a construction foreman, builder, architect, and structural engineer to become one of the world's foremost designers of slender reinforced concrete hyperbolic paraboloid shell roofs. His creations have included the Sports Palace for the Olympic Games in Mexico City (1968). He emigrated to the USA in 1971.

Candolle, Augustin Pyrame de [kādol] (1778–1841) Botanist, born in Geneva, Switzerland. He studied medicine in Geneva, and from 1798 botany in Paris, and by 1813 had developed a general scheme of plant taxonomy which was to dominate plant classification for 50 years. He used the scheme in a major series of volumes on botany, completed by his son **Alphonse de Candolle** (1806–93). He also did much to establish plant geography and to relate vegetation to soil type, a study supported by his extensive expeditions.

Canetti, Elias [kanetee] (1905–94) Writer, born in Rustschuck, Bulgaria. He was educated at schools in England, Austria, Switzerland, and Germany, and lived in England from 1938, though continued to write in German. His interest in crowd psychology produced two important works: the novel *Die Blendung* (1936, trans as both Auto da Fé and The Tower of Babel) and the study *Masse und Macht* (1960, Crowds and Power). He was awarded the Nobel Prize for Literature in 1981.

Cange, seigneur du >> **du Cange, Charles du Fresne**

Caniff, Milt(on Arthur) (1907–88) Strip cartoonist, born in Hillsboro, OH. He created his first daily strip, *Dickie Dare*, in 1933, then joined the *New York Daily News* to create a similar serial, *Terry and the Pirates* (1934). Suddenly abandoning *Terry*, he created a new series about an ex-pilot, *Steve Canyon* (1947), which continued until the artist's death.

Canmore, Malcolm >> **Malcolm III**

Canning, George (1770–1827) British statesman, born in London, England, UK. He studied at Oxford and Lincoln's Inn, and entered parliament for Newport, Isle of Wight (1794) as a supporter of Pitt. He became under-secretary of state (1796), treasurer of the navy (1804–6), and minister for foreign affairs (1807). His disapproval of the Walcheren expedition led to a misunderstanding with Castlereagh, which resulted in a duel. He became MP for Liverpool (1812), ambassador to Lisbon (1814), President of the Board of Control (1816), and MP for Harwich (1822). Nominated Governor-General of India (1822), he was on the eve of departure when Castlereagh's suicide saw him installed as foreign secretary. In this post he gave a new impetus to commerce by advocating tariff reductions. He was the first to recognize the free states of Spanish America; promoted the union of Britain, France, and Russia in the cause of Greece (1827); protected Portugal from Spanish invasion; contended earnestly for Catholic Emancipation; and prepared the way for a repeal of the Corn Laws. In 1827 he formed an administration with the aid of the Whigs, but died the same year. >> Pitt, William (the Younger); Stratford

Cannizzaro, Stanislao [kaneedzahroh] (1826–1910) Chemist, born in Palermo, Italy. He was professor of chemistry at Genoa, Palermo, and Rome. In 1860, while at Genoa, he marched with Garibaldi's Thousand. He was the first to appreciate the importance of Amedeo Avogadro's work in connection with atomic weights. He co-ordinated organic and inorganic chemistry, and discovered the reaction named after him. >> Avogadro; Garibaldi

Cannon, Annie Jump (1863–1941) Astronomer, born in Dover, DE. She became deaf through contracting scarlet fever, entered Radcliffe College to study astronomy, and was appointed to the staff of the Harvard College Observatory in 1896. She reorganized the classification of stars in terms of surface temperature, and developed great skill in cataloguing them. Her classification of over 225 000 stars brighter than 9th or 10th magnitude was a major contribution.

Cannon, W(alter) B(radford) (1871–1945) Physiologist, born in Prairie du Chien, WI. He studied medicine at Harvard, where he taught (1899–1942), becoming renowned for his use of X-rays in the study of the alimentary tract, and for his work on the effects of haemorrhage and shock. He went on to study hormones and nerve transmission, and developed the concept of a constant internal physiological environment, which he named *homoeostasis*.

Cano, Alonso [kahnoh] (1601–67) Painter, sculptor, and architect, born in Granada, Spain. He studied in Seville, and in 1639 was appointed court painter and architect. He designed the facade of Coranada Cathedral (c.1664).

Cano, Juan Sebastian del [kahnoh] (?–1526) The first man to circumnavigate the globe, born in Guetaria on the Bay of Biscay. In 1519 he sailed with Magellan in command of the *Concepción*. After Magellan's death in the Philippines, he safely navigated the *Victoria* home to Spain, arriving in 1522. >> Magellan

Canova, Antonio [kanohva] (1757–1822) Sculptor, born in Possagno, Italy. He studied at Venice and Rome, and came to be regarded as the founder of a new Neoclassicist school. His best-known works are the tombs of popes Clement XIII (1787–92) and XIV (1783–7), several statues of Napoleon, and one of his sister Princess Borghese reclining as Venus Victrix (1805–7). In 1802 he was appointed by Pius VII curator of works of art.

Cantelupe, St Thomas de or **St Thomas of Hereford** [kanteloop] (c.1218–1282) Clergyman, born in Hambleden, Buckinghamshire, SC England, UK. He studied at Oxford, Paris, and Orléans, and was made Chancellor of Oxford University (1262). He supported the barons against Henry III, and was appointed Chancellor of England (1264–5) by Simon de Montfort. In 1275 he became Bishop of Hereford. Excommunicated by his archbishop over a dispute about jurisdiction (1282), he took his case to Rome, but died on the way there. His relics were brought to Hereford, where his shrine became almost as revered as that of Becket at Canterbury. He was canonized in 1320; feast day 3 October. >> Montfort, Simon de (c.1208–65)

Canth, Minna, *née* **Ulrika Vilhelmina Johnsson** (1844–97) Playwright and feminist, born in Tampere, Finland. A powerful exponent of the Realist school, her best-known plays are *Työmiehen Vaimo* (1885, A Working-class Wife) and *Kovan Onnen Lapsia* (1888, Children of Misfortune). Later she turned to Tolstoyan psychological dramas about women, as in *Anna Liisa* (1895). >> Tolstoy

Canton, John (1718–72) Physicist, born in Stroud, Gloucestershire, SWC England, UK. A schoolmaster in London, he was elected a fellow of the Royal Society in 1749. He invented an electroscope and an electrometer, originated experiments in induction, was the first to make powerful artificial magnets, and in 1762 demonstrated the compressibility of water.

Cantona, Eric [kantona] (1966–) Footballer, born in Paris, France. Brought up in Marseille, he made his professional debut for Auxerre in 1983, and won his first French International cap in 1987. He moved to Leeds United in 1991 and to Manchester United in 1993, becoming the first foreigner to win the Professional Footballers' Association Player of the year award in 1994. An aggressive and tempestuous player, his career was interrupted by a series of suspensions, and his temperament became a focus of public debate when he was sentenced to 120 hours community service after kicking out at a Crystal Palace fan who had been insulting him. A football idol for a generation of fans, he announced his retirement in 1997.

Cantor, Eddie, originally **Edward Israel Iskowitz** (1892–1964) Entertainer, born in New York City. A natural clown, he became a touring vaudeville artiste and starred in Broadway reviews, notably *Kid Boots* (1923–6). His highly successful radio show, *The Chase and Sanborn Hour* (1931), ran for 18 years. He then moved successfully into television, hosting *The Eddie Cantor Variety Theater* show (1955).

Cantor, Georg (Ferdinand Ludwig Philipp) (1845–1918) Mathematician, born in St Petersburg, Russia. He studied at Berlin and Göttingen, and in 1877 became professor of mathematics at Halle. He worked out a highly original arithmetic of the infinite which resulted in a theory of infinite sets of different sizes, adding a new and important branch to mathematics. He suffered a nervous breakdown in 1884, and died in an asylum. >> Zermelo

Canute or **Cnut**, sometimes known as **the Great** (c. 995–1035) King of England (from 1016), Denmark (from 1019), and Norway (from 1028), the younger son of Sweyn Forkbeard. He first campaigned in England in 1013, and after his father's death (1014) successively challenged Ethelred the Unready and Edmund Ironside for the English throne. He defeated Edmund in 1016 at the Battle of Assandun (possibly Ashdon, Essex), secured Mercia and Northumbria, and became King of all England after Edmund's death. In 1017 he married **Emma of Normandy**, the widow of Ethelred. He ruled England according to the accepted traditions of English kingship, and maintained the peace throughout his reign. The story of his failure to make the tide recede was invented by the 12th-c historian, Henry of Huntingdon, to demonstrate the frailty of earthly power compared to the might of God. >> Edmund II; Ethelred II; Sweyn; RR1095

Cao Xuequin [chow shwechin], also spelled **Ts'ao Hsüeh-ch'in** (1715–63) Writer, born into a family who had grown rich as directors of the Nanjing Imperial Textile Works. The family wealth was later squandered, and he was reduced to straightened circumstances as a teacher and poet in Beijing. His memories are re-enacted in his great book, *Dream of the Red Chamber*, or *A Dream of Splendour* (also translated as *Story of the Stone*), the most famous of all Chinese traditional novels. He probably wrote over 80 chapters in 1760, then left the work unfinished; 40 chapters were added by Gao Ngo and the book was published in 1791. It is important for its realistic detail of upper-class family life in the early 18th-c, and is now recognized as the finest literary achievement of the early Qing period. It has been serialized on Chinese television in recent years.

Cao Yu [chow yoo], pseudonym of **Wan Jiabao** (1910–96) Playwright, born in Tianjin, China. The most significant 20th-c playwright in China, he studied Western literature at Qinghua University (1930–4). His best-known work, *Thunderstorm*, was staged in 1935; other major plays included *Metamorphosis* (1940) and *Family* (1941). After the foundation of the People's Republic in 1949 he was appointed to numerous official posts. In 1979 he wrote the play *The Consort of Peace*.

Capa, Robert, originally **Andrei Friedmann** (1913–54) Photojournalist, born in Budapest. He recorded the Spanish Civil War (1935–7), covered China under the Japanese attacks of 1938, and reported World War 2 in Europe from the Normandy invasion onwards. He was killed by a landmine in the Indo-China fighting which preceded the war in Vietnam.

Capablanca, José Raúl [kapablangka] (1888–1942) Chess player, born in Havana. At the age of four he learned chess by watching his father's games, and within nine years had defeated the Cuban champion, Corzo. He studied engineering at Columbia University, playing chess at the Manhattan Club, New York City, where he achieved a sensational win in a match against US champion Marshall (1909). In 1921 he won the world championship, defeating Lasker without losing a game. His defeat by Alekhine in 1927 was a major surprise, and despite further tournament successes he never regained his title. >> Alekhine; Lasker, Emanuel; RR1149

Čapek, Josef [chapek] (1887–1945) Writer and painter, born in Schwadonitz, Czech Republic, the elder brother of Karel Čapek. His early literary works, written in collaboration with his brother, include the allegorical *Ze Života hmyzu* (1921, The Insect Play). From such anxious visions of the future he progressed to a philosophy of sceptical humanism which found expression in his one novel, *Stín Kapradiny* (1930), and in his essays. >> Čapek, Karel

Čapek, Karel [chapek] (1890–1938) Writer, born in Schwadonitz, Czech Republic, the brother of Josef Čapek. He is remembered above all for his play *R.U.R.* (Rossum's Universal Robots), produced in 1921, showing mechanization rampant. With his brother he wrote the comic fantasy *Ze Života hmyzu* (1921, The Insect Play), one of several pieces foreshadowing totalitarianism, as well as short stories on crime and mystery, prophetic science-fiction, and travelbooks. >> Čapek, Josef

Capell, Edward (1713–81) Scholar, born near Bury St Edmunds, Suffolk, E England, UK. He published an edition of Shakespeare (10 vols, 1768) based on the Folio and Quarto texts, and a full commentary, *Notes and Various Readings to Shakespeare* (3 vols, 1783).

Capella, Martianus Mineus Felix [kapela] (fl.480) North African scholar and writer. His *Satiricon*, a kind of encyclopaedia, highly esteemed during the Middle Ages, is a medley of prose and verse, full of curious learning.

Capet, Hugo or **Hugh** [kapet] (c. 938–96) King of France, founder of the third Frankish royal dynasty (the Capetians), which ruled France until 1328. Son of Hugh the Great, whom he succeeded as Duke of the Franks in 956, he was elected king and crowned at Noyon (987). His 40 years in power were marked by constant political intrigue and struggle, both among the feudal aristocracy and with his Carolingian rivals, but his position was invariably saved by the disunity of his enemies. >> RR1049

Capgrave, John (1393–1464) Chronicler, theologian, and provincial of the Augustine Friars in England, born in Lynn, Norfolk, E England, UK. He was ordained priest c.1418, having already entered his order in Lynn. His works include Bible commentaries, sermons, a life of St Catherine in verse, and *A Chronicle of England from the Creation to 1417*.

Capito or **Köpfel, Wolfgang Fabricius** [kapeetoh] (1478–1541) Religious reformer, born in Hagenau, Alsace. He entered the Benedictine order, and in 1515 became professor of theology at Basel. He approved of Luther's action, but in 1519 entered the service of Archishop Albert of Mainz. He did not declare for the Reformation until later, when he became a Protestant leader in Strasbourg. >> Luther

Capone, Al [kapohn], popular name of **Alphonse Capone** (1899–1947) Gangster, born in New York City. He achieved worldwide notoriety as a racketeer during the prohibition era in Chicago. Such was his power that no evidence sufficient to support a charge against him was forthcoming until 1931, when he was sentenced to 10 years' imprisonment for tax evasion. Released on health grounds in 1939, he retired to his estate in Florida.

Capote, Truman [kapohtee], pseudonym of **Truman Streckfus Persons** (1924–84) Writer, born in New Orleans, LA. He won several early literary prizes, and his first novel, *Other Voices, Other Rooms*, was published in 1948. Other works are *The Grass Harp* (1951), *Breakfast at Tiffany's* (1958), which was highly successful as a film, and *In Cold Blood* (1966), described as a 'nonfiction novel' because of the way he tells of actual events in novelistic form.

Capp, Al, originally **Alfred Gerald Caplin** (1909–79) Strip cartoonist, born in New Haven, CT. He studied at Designers Art School, Boston (1929), and entered strips as assistant to Bud Fisher on *Mutt and Jeff* (1930). Joining Associated Press, he took on a daily joke, *Mr Gilfeather* (1932), then became assistant to Ham Fisher on *Joe Palooka* (1933), introducing hill-billy characters, and developed *L'il Abner* (1934). Capp's chunky artwork coupled with hilarious hill-billy dialogue soon made the strip a success, inspiring two films, a stage musical, and an animated series. >> Fisher, Bud

Capra, Frank (1897–1991) Film director, born in Palermo, Italy. When he was six, his family emigrated to California, where he studied at the Institute of Technology. He began in film work in 1921, and had several box-office hits. Among his best-known films are *Mr Deeds Goes to Town* (1936) and *You Can't Take It with You* (1938), which won Oscars, *Lost Horizon* (1937), *Arsenic and Old Lace* (1942), and *State of the Union* (1948). He retired for some years before his later films, *A Hole in the Head* (1959) and *A Pocketful of Miracles* (1961).

Caprivi, Georg Leo, Graf von (Count of) [ka**pree**vee] (1831–99) German soldier and political leader, chancellor of Prussia (1890–4), born in Berlin. Entering the Prussian army in 1849, he fought in the Franco-Prussian war (1870–1), and as head of the Admiralty (1883–8) reorganized the navy. On Bismarck's fall in 1890, he became imperial chancellor and Prussian prime minister. His principal measures were the army bills of 1892–3 and the commercial treaty with Russia in 1894.

Caracalla or **Caracallus** [kara**ka**la], popular name of **Marcus Aurelius Severus Antoninus Augustus**, originally **Septimius Bassianus** (188–217) Roman emperor, born in Lugdunum (Lyon, modern France), the son of the emperor Septimius Severus. He ascended the throne in 211 as joint emperor with his brother **Publius Septimius Antoninus Geta**, whom he soon murdered. His open reliance on the army alienated the senatorial class and earned him an unfavourable reputation in the historical tradition. He campaigned extensively abroad, in Germany, on the Danube, and in the East, and was assassinated while preparing for war against the Parthians. His chief title to fame was the edict of 212, which granted Roman citizenship to all free members of the empire. >> Severus; RR1084

Caractacus [ka**rak**takus], **Caratacus**, or **Caradoc** (1st-c) A chief of the Catuvellauni, the son of Cunobelinus. He mounted a gallant but unsuccessful guerrilla operation in Wales against the Romans in the years following the Claudian conquest (43). Betrayed by the Brigantian queen, Cartimandua, he was taken to Rome (51), where he was exhibited in triumph, and pardoned by Claudius. >> Cartimandua; Claudius; Cymbeline

Caran d'Ache [karä dash], pseudonym of **Emmanuel Poiré** (1858–1909) Caricaturist, born in Moscow. He studied in Moscow, then came to Paris, where he became a contributor to many periodicals. He was a pioneer in the development of the *bande dessinée* (French comic strip), and a major influence on H M Bateman. His pseudonym came from the Russian word for 'pencil'. >> Bateman

Caratacus >> **Caractacus**

Carausius, Marcus Aurelius [ka**row**sius] (c.245–293) Army officer, born in Menapia (modern Belgium). He set himself up in Britain as emperor (c.287), and ruled there until his murder by one of his officers, Allectus. Originally a Batavian pilot, he was put in command of the Roman fleet in the Channel to ward off pirates.

Caravaggio [kara**va**jioh], originally **Michelangelo Merisi** (1573–1610) Baroque painter, born in Caravaggio, Italy, whence his nickname. He studied in Milan and Venice, and went to Rome, where Cardinal del Monte became his chief patron. His works include several altarpieces and religious paintings, using dramatic contrasts of light and shade, notably several paintings of St Matthew (1599–1603) and 'Christ at Emmaus' (c.1602–3, National Gallery, London). In 1606, his temper led him to kill a man, and he fled to Naples and Malta.

Caravaggio, Polidoro Caldara da [kara**va**jioh] (c.1492–1543) Painter, born in Caravaggio, Italy. He aided Raphael in his Vatican frescoes. His 'Christ Bearing the Cross' is in Naples. >> Raphael

Cardan, Jerome [**kah(r)**dan, kah(r)**dah**noh], Ital **Geronimo Cardano**, Lat **Hieronymus Cardanus** (1501–76) Mathematician and physician, born in Pavia, Italy. He became professor of mathematics at Padua, and of medicine at Pavia and Bologna. He wrote over 100 treatises on physics, mathematics, astronomy, astrology, rhetoric, history, ethics, dialectics, natural history, music, and medicine. His *Ars magna* (1545, Great Art) was influential in the development of algebra, giving the first published algebraic solution of cubic and quartic equations.

Cardano, Girolamo >> **Cardan, Jerome**

Carden, Joan Maralyn (1937–) Operatic and concert soprano, born in Melbourne, Victoria, Australia. A principal artist with the Australian Opera since 1971, she made her debut at Covent Garden, London, in 1974. One of her most celebrated performances is of the four heroines in *The Tales of Hoffmann*, and she is renowned for her performances of Mozart. She won the Dame Joan Hammond Award for Outstanding Service to Opera in Australia in 1987.

Cárdenas, Lázaro [**kah(r)**thenas] (1895–1970) Mexican soldier and political leader, president of the Mexican Republic (1934–40), born in Jiquilpan, Mexico. He joined the revolutionary army in 1913, was a general by 1923, and Governor of Michoacán (1928–32). He rose from relative obscurity through the patronage of former president Plutarco Calles. Cárdenas wrested control of the government from Calles and instituted a broad programme of social and economic reforms. Often wrongly accused of being a Communist, he carried out the long overdue promises of the 1910 revolution, ensuring Mexico's stability. >> Calles; RR1075

Cardew, Michael (1901–82) British potter. After studying under Bernard Leach at St Ives (1923–6), he set up his own studio at Winchcombe in the Cotswolds, moving in 1939 to Wenford Bridge in Cornwall. In 1942 he took over the Achimota College on the Gold Coast (now Ghana), and started his own stoneware pottery at Vumé on the Volta.

Cardigan, James Thomas Brudenell, 7th Earl of (1797–1868) British general, born in Hambleden, Buckinghamshire, SC England, UK. He studied at Oxford, entered the army in 1824, and purchased his promotion, commanding the 15th Hussars (until 1833), then the 11th Hussars (1836–47). He commanded a cavalry brigade in the Crimea, and led the fatal charge of the Light Brigade at Balaclava (25 Oct 1854). He then became inspector-general of cavalry (1855–60). The woollen jacket known as a *cardigan* is named after him.

Cardin, Pierre [kah(r)dĩ] (1922–) French fashion designer, born in Venice, Italy. After working during World War 2 for a tailor in Vichy, he went to Paris in 1944. He worked in fashion houses and on costume design, notably for Cocteau's film *Beauty and the Beast* (1947). He opened his own house in 1953, and has since been prominent in fashion for both women and men. >> Cocteau

Cardozo, Benjamin (Nathan) [kah(r)**doh**zoh] (1870–1938) Judge, born in New York City. He sat on the bench of the New York Court of Appeals (1913–32) and in the US Supreme Court (1932–8), in which he handed down important opinions on congressional power, control of interstate commerce, and the relationship of the Bill of Rights to states' rights. He was generally liberal, and favoured greater involvement of courts in public policy.

Carew, Thomas [ka**roo**] (1595–1639) Poet, born in West Wickham, Kent, SE England, UK. He studied at Oxford and the Middle Temple, and became a diplomat. A friend of Jonson and Donne, he wrote polished lyrics in the Cavalier tradition, and a masque *Coelum britannicum* (1634) which was performed at court. >> Donne; Jonson

Carey, George Leonard [**kair**ee] (1935–) Anglican clergyman, born in London, England, UK. After service in the RAF, he studied divinity at King's College, London. He held Church posts in London and Durham, then became Principal of Trinity Theological College, Bristol (1982–7). He was appointed Bishop of Bath and Wells in 1987 and Archbishop of Canterbury in 1991.

Carey, Henry C(harles) [**kair**ee] (1793–1879) Political economist, born in Philadelphia, PA. He became a partner in his father's bookselling business, retiring in 1835 to devote himself to economics. Originally a zealous freetrader, he came to regard free trade as an ideal, but impossible in the existing state of US industry: a period of protection was indispensable.

Carey, Peter [**kair**ee] (1943–) Writer, born in Bacchus Marsh, Victoria, Australia. He attended Geelong Grammar School before beginning a career as an advertising copywriter. His first book, *The Fat Man in History* (1974), was a collection of short stories, and he was quickly regarded as an innovative force in Australian writing. Later books include *Bliss* (1981), *Illywhacker* (1985), *Oscar and Lucinda* (1988, Booker), *The Tax Inspector* (1991), *The Unusual Life of Tristan Smith* (1994), and *Jack Maggs* (1997). He co-wrote the screenplays for *Bliss* (1985) and *Until the End of the World* (1990).

Carey, William [**kair**ee] (1761–1834) Missionary and orientalist, born in Paulerspury, Northamptonshire, C England, UK. He joined the Baptists in 1783, and three years later became a minister. In 1793 he and John Thomas were chosen as the first Baptist missionaries to India, where he founded the Serampur mission (1799). From 1801 to 1830 he was Oriental professor at Fort William College, Calcutta.

Carissimi, Giacomo [ka**ree**simee] (1605–74) Composer, born in Marino, Italy. Organist in Tivoli, Assisi, and from 1628 in Rome, he did much to develop the sacred cantata. His works include the oratorio *Jephte* (1650, Jephthah).

Carl XVI Gustaf (1946–) King of Sweden since 1973, born in Stockholm, the grandson of King Gustav VI. His father died in an air accident (1947), and he became crown prince from his grandfather's accession (1950). A new constitution restricting monarchical powers was approved by the Swedish parliament just before his accession. In 1976 he married **Silvia Sommerlath**, the daughter of a West German businessman. They have three children: **Victoria** (1977–), **Carl Philip** (1979–), and **Madeleine** (1982–). He is a keen all-round sportsman, proficient in yachting, skiing, and shooting. >> Silvia; RR1090

Carle, Eric (1929–) Picture book artist, born in Germany. Using a distinctive collage technique he has written and illustrated several children's books. He is best-known for *The Very Hungry Caterpillar* (1970), in which the voracious creature burrows through the pages of the book in search of delicacies.

Carleton, Guy, Baron Dorchester (1724–1808) British soldier, born in Strabane, Northern Ireland. Governor of Quebec (1775–7), he successfully defended the city against the Americans under Benedict Arnold, whom he subsequently defeated again on L Champlain in 1776. He was British commander-in-chief in America (1782–3). As Governor of Quebec (1786–9, 1793–6), and Governor of Lower Canada (1791–6), he did much to save Canada for Britain. >> Arnold, Benedict

Carlile, Richard (1790–1843) Journalist and radical reformer, born in Ashburton, Devon, SW England, UK. A disciple of Thomas Paine, he sold the prohibited radical weekly *Black Dwarf* throughout London in 1817. He was imprisoned several times for his publications, which included his *Political Litany*, Paine's works, and a journal, *The Republican* (1819–26). >> Paine

Carlile, Wilson (1847–1942) Anglican clergyman, born in London, England, UK. In 1882 he founded the Church Army, and was made a prebendary of St Paul's in 1906.

Carling, Will, popular name of **William David Charles Carling** (1965–) Player of rugby union football, born in Bradford-on-Avon, Wiltshire, S England, UK. He studied at Durham University, where he played for the university, and later for Harlequins, then joined the army, but resigned his commission to devote more time to rugby. In 1988 at the age of 22 he made his England debut against France, was appointed captain (1988–96), and played a major role in the Grand Slam victories of 1991, 1992, and 1995. He is the most capped English rugby captain of all time (58), and holds the world record for victories as captain (43 matches). He received national publicity in 1995 when the media focused on rumours of a possible relationship with Princess Diana. >> Diana, Princess of Wales

Carlisle, Anthony >> Nicholson, William

Carlos, Don (1788–1855) Spanish pretender to the throne, the second son of Charles (Carlos) IV of Spain, born in Madrid. On the accession of his niece **Isabella II** (1830–1904) in 1833, he asserted his claim to the throne – a claim reasserted by his son, **Don Carlos, Count de Montemolin** (1818–61), and by the latter's nephew, **Don Carlos** (1848–1909). *Carlist* risings, whose strength lay in the Basque provinces, occurred in 1834–9 and 1872–6.

Carlson, Carolyn (1943–) Dancer and choreographer, born in California. She studied at San Francisco Ballet School and with Alwin Nikolais, and was invited to create a piece for the Paris Opera Ballet in 1973. Her solo was so well-received that a special post, *Danseuse étoile choreographique*, was invented for her. From 1980 she directed her own troupe at Venice's Teatro Fenice, but later returned to Paris. >> Nikolais

Carlson, Chester (Floyd) (1906–68) Physicist, born in Seattle, WA. He graduated in physics at the California Institute of Technology, and worked in electronics, later specializing also in patent work. By 1938 he had devised a basic system of electrostatic copying on plain paper, which after 12 years' work by assistants gave the xerographic method which is now widely used.

Carlsson, Ingvar (Costa) (1934–) Swedish statesman and prime minister (1986–91). He studied at Lund and North Western (USA) universities, and was secretary in the prime minister's office (1958–60) before entering active party politics. He became president of the youth league of the Social Democratic Labour Party in 1961, and in 1964 was elected to the Riksdag (parliament). He became deputy to Olof Palme (1982), and succeeded him as prime minister after Palme's assassination in 1986. >> Palme; RR1090

Carlstadt or **Karlstadt** [**kah**(r)**l**shtat], originally **Andreas Rudolf Bodenstein** (?–1541) German reformer, born prior to 1483 in Carlstadt, Bavaria. In 1517 he joined Luther, who in 1521 rebuked his iconoclastic zeal, and whom he afterwards opposed on the question of the Eucharist.

Accused of participation in the Peasants' War, he fled to Switzerland, and became professor of theology at Basel. >> Luther

Carlucci, Frank (Charles) [kah(r)**loo**chee] (1930–) US statesman, born in Scranton, PA. He studied at Princeton and Harvard, worked in the Nixon administration (1969–74), then served under presidents Ford (1974–6) and Carter (1977–81) as US ambassador to Portugal, and later as deputy director of the CIA. He found himself out of step with the 'hawks' in the Reagan administration (1981–9), and left to work at Sears World Trade after barely a year as deputy secretary of defence. In 1986 he became National Security Adviser, and served as defence secretary from 1987, supporting Soviet–US arms reduction initiatives. >> Carter, Jimmy; Ford, Gerald R; Nixon

Carluccio, Antonio (Mario Gaetano) [kah(r)**loo**chioh] (1937–) Restaurateur, born in Vietri Sul Mare, Italy. He studied at the Roland Matura Schule, Vienna, and became a wine merchant in England (1975–81). He joined the Neal Street Restaurant in London as restaurateur (1981–), became proprietor (1989–), and joint proprietor (with his wife) of Carluccio's food retailers (1992–). His numerous television appearances include BBC's *Food and Drink* (1986–), *Hot Chefs* (1991), and the series *Antonio Carluccio's Italian Feasts* (1996) with accompanying book. Among other books are *An Invitation to Italian Cooking* (1986) and *A Passion for Pasta* (1993).

Carlyle, Jane Baillie, *née* **Welsh** (1801–66) Diarist, born in Haddington, East Lothian, E Scotland, UK, the wife of Thomas Carlyle. She was tutored by the revivalist minister Edward Irving, and he introduced her in 1821 to his friend Carlyle, whom she married in 1826. Forthright and quick-witted, she declined to become a writer, despite Carlyle's promptings. She supported Carlyle loyally through his depressions and chronic ill health, and after her death he retired from public life, writing an anguished memoir of her in his *Reminiscences* (1881). He also edited her letters and diaries, which are full of vivid insights and quality writing, and show her to have been one of the most accomplished women of her time. >> Carlyle, Thomas; Irving, Edward

Carlyle, Thomas (1795–1881) Man of letters, born in Ecclefechan, Dumfries and Galloway, SW Scotland, UK. He studied at Edinburgh University, and taught for several years before beginning to write articles for the *Edinburgh Encyclopaedia*, and becoming absorbed in German literature, notably Goethe. In 1826 he married **Jane Baillie Welsh**. His best-known work is *Sartor Resartus* (1833–4). He then moved to London, where he wrote his other major works on the French Revolution (3 vols, 1837) and Frederick the Great (1858–65). After his wife's death, he retired from public life, and wrote little. >> Carlyle, Jane Baillie

Carmen Sylva, pseudonym of **Elizabeth, Queen of Romania** (1843–1916) The daughter of Prince Hermann of Wied Neuwied, who married **King** (then Prince) **Carol I** of Romania in 1869. Her only child, a daughter, died in 1874, and out of her sorrow arose her literary activity. Two poems, printed privately at Leipzig in 1880 under the name 'Carmen Sylva', were followed by *Stürme* (1881), *Leidens Erdengang* (1882, trans Pilgrim Sorrow), and several other works. >> Carol I

Carmichael, Hoagy, popular name of **Howard Hoagland Carmichael** (1899–1981) Jazz pianist and composer, born in Bloomington, IN. While at Indiana University he met and was influenced by jazz musicians, notably Bix Beiderbecke, to whom Carmichael dedicated his first composition, 'Riverboat Shuffle' (1924). During the 1930s he wrote many compositions, several of which became classics. He later worked in Hollywood, and won an Oscar for 'In the Cool Cool Cool of the Evening' (1951). Arguably, his most successful composition was 'Stardust' (1927). >> Beiderbecke, Bix

Carmichael, Stokely (1941–) Radical activist, born in Trinidad. He emigrated to the USA in 1952, and was shocked by the racism he encountered. Involved in Civil Rights while attending Howard University (1960–4), he was elected leader of the Student Nonviolent Co-ordinating Committee, and changed the group's focus from integration to black liberation. He popularized the phrase 'black power', and as a Black Panther came to symbolize black violence to many whites. He later favoured forging alliances with radical whites, which led to his resignation from the Panthers in 1968. He and his wife, **Miriam Makeba**, moved to Guinea in 1969, where he supported Pan-Africanism. He eventually returned to the USA, but did not continue with Civil Rights activities. >> Makeba

Carnap, Rudolf (1891–1970) Philosopher, born in Wuppertal, Germany. He studied at Freiburg and Jena, becoming lecturer at Vienna (1926–31), and professor of philosophy at Prague (1931–5), Chicago (1936–52), and California, Los Angeles (1954–70). He was one of the leaders of the 'Vienna Circle' of logical positivists. His writings include *Der logische Aufbau der Welt* (1928, The Logical Construction of the World), *Logische Syntax der Sprache* (1934, Logical Syntax of Language), and *Meaning and Necessity* (1947), as well as semantic studies of induction and probability. >> Neurath, Otto; Reichenbach, Hans; Schlick; von Wright

Carnarvon, George Edward Stanhope Molyneux Herbert, 5th Earl of [kah(r)**nah(r)**von] (1866–1923) Amateur Egyptologist, born at Highclere Castle, Berkshire, S England, UK. From 1907 he sponsored Howard Carter's excavations of royal tombs at Thebes. He died shortly after the spectacular discovery of Tutankhamen's tomb in the Valley of the Kings in 1922. >> Carter, Howard; Tutankhamen

Carné, Marcel [kah(r)**nay**] (1909–96) Film director, born in Paris. He trained as a film technician, later working as an assistant to René Clair. From 1931 his collaboration as director with the poet and scriptwriter Jacques Prévert resulted in a series of outstanding productions, including *Quai des brumes* (1938, trans Port of Shadows), *Le Jour se lève* (1939, Daybreak) and *Les Enfants du paradis* (1944, Children of Paradise). After the break-up of the partnership in 1949, his late work was irregular and less distinguished. >> Clair; Prévert

Carneades [kah(r)**nee**adeez] (c. 214–129 BC) Greek philosopher, born in Cyrene. He became head of the Academy, which under his very different, sceptical direction became known as the 'New Academy'. He had the reputation of a virtuoso dialectician, who could argue equally persuasively for quite opposing points of view.

Carnegie, Andrew [kah(r)**nay**gee, or **kar**negee] (1835–1919) Industrialist and philanthropist, born in Dunfermline, Fife, E Scotland, UK. His family emigrated to Pittsburgh in 1848, and after several jobs he invested in the business which grew into the largest iron and steel works in the USA. He retired in 1901, a multimillionaire, to Skibo Castle in Sutherland. He gave millions of dollars to libraries and public institutions in the UK and USA, and several buildings are named after him.

Carnegie, Dale [kah(r)**nay**gee, or **kar**negee], originally **Dale Carnegey** (1888–1955) Lecturer on public speaking, born in Maryville, MO. After holding various jobs, he began lecturing on public speaking and self-esteem. His theories caught the public imagination, and were published in highly successful books, notably *How to Win Friends and Influence People* (1936).

Carnot, Lazare (Nicolas Marguerite) [kah(r)noh] (1753–1823) French statesman, known as 'the organizer of victory' during the Revolutionary Wars, born in Nolay, France. He entered the army as an engineer, and became a member of the Legislative Assembly (1791). He survived the Terror, and became one of the Directors (1795), but in 1797, suspected of Royalist sympathies, he escaped to Germany. Back in Paris, he became minister of war (1800), and helped to organize the Italian and Rhenish campaigns. He commanded at Antwerp in 1814, and during the Hundred Days was minister of the interior.

Carnot, (Nicholas Léonard) Sadi [kah(r)noh] (1796–1832) Scientist, born in Paris. He became a captain of engineers in the army, and spent much of his life investigating the design of steam engines. His findings were the foundation of the science of thermodynamics.

Caro, Sir Anthony [kahroh] (1924–) Sculptor, born in London, England, UK. He studied engineering at Cambridge but turned to sculpture after World War 2, attending the Regent Street Polytechnic (1946) and the Royal Academy Schools (1947–52). His work is abstract, typically large pieces of metal welded together and painted in primary colours.

Carol I (1839–1914) The first king of Romania, born in Hohenzollern-Sigmaringen. He was elected Prince of Romania in 1866 and became king in 1881. He promoted economic development and military expansion, and brutally crushed a peasant rebellion in 1907. He married **Princess Elizabeth of Wied** (1869), a prolific writer under the pseudonym Carmen Sylva. At the outset of World War 1, he declared Romanian neutrality, but his successor (his nephew King Ferdinand I) declared for the Allies in 1916. >> Carmen Sylva; RR1084

Carol II (1893–1953) King of Romania (1930–40), born in Sinaia, Romania. He renounced his right of succession (1925) as a result of a love affair (he divorced his second wife, **Princess Helen of Greece** (1928), mother of his son **Michael**, to live with **Magda Lypescu**) and went into exile in Paris. He returned through a coup in 1930, proclaiming a dictatorship in 1938. He was forced to abdicate in 1940 in favour of his son, and left Romania. >> Michael; RR1084

Caroline of Ansbach, Wilhelmina (1683–1737) Queen of George II of Great Britain, born in Ansbach, Germany, the daughter of a German prince. She exercised a strong influence over her husband, and was a leading supporter of his chief minister, Robert Walpole. >> Walpole, Robert

Caroline of Brunswick, Amelia Elizabeth (1768–1821) Wife of George IV of the Great Britain, born in Brunswick, Germany, the daughter of George III's sister, Augusta. She married the Prince of Wales in 1795, but the marriage was disagreeable to him, and although she bore him a daughter, **Princess Charlotte**, they lived apart. When George became king (1820), she was offered an annuity to renounce the title of queen and live abroad; when she refused, the king persuaded the government to introduce a Divorce Bill. Although this failed, she was not allowed into Westminster Abbey at the coronation (1821). >> Charlotte, Princess; George IV

Carossa, Hans [karosa] (1878–1956) Writer and physician, born in Tölz, Germany. A doctor in Bavaria, he became prominent with his autobiographical *Eine Kindheit* (1922, A Childhood). Other writings include a diary of his observations during World War 1, and numerous novels.

Carothers, Wallace (Hume) [karuhtherz] (1896–1937) Industrial chemist, born in Burlington, IA. He taught at various universities before concentrating on research. Working for the Du Pont Company at Wilmington, he produced the first successful synthetic rubber, neoprene, and followed this with nylon.

Carpaccio, Vittore [kah(r)pachioh] (c. 1460–c. 1525) Painter, born in Venice, Italy. His most characteristic work is seen in the nine subjects from the life of St Ursula (1490–5). In 1510 he executed for San Giobbe his masterpiece, 'The Presentation in the Temple', now in the Accademia.

Carpenter, Karen >> **Carpenters, The**

Carpenter, Mary (1807–77) Educationist and reformer, born in Exeter, Devon, SW England, UK, the sister of William Carpenter. Trained as a teacher, she opened a girls' school in Bristol in 1829, and took an active part in the movement for the reformation of neglected children. In 1846 she founded a ragged school in Bristol, and several reformatories for girls. >> Carpenter, William

Carpenter, Richard >> **Carpenters, The**

Carpenter, William Benjamin (1813–85) Biologist, born in Exeter, Devon, SW England, UK, the brother of Mary Carpenter. He studied medicine at Bristol, London, and Edinburgh, and in 1844 was appointed professor of physiology at the Royal Institution, London, and professor of forensic medicine at University College (1849). He took part in a deep sea exploration expedition (1868–71), and did valuable research on the Foraminifera (a type of unicellular animal). >> Carpenter, Mary

Carpenters, The Brother and sister vocal duo, both born in New Haven, CN. **Karen Carpenter** (1950–83, vocals, drums) and **Richard Carpenter** (1946– , vocals, keyboards). They began working together in the mid -1960s, and their second album, *Close To You*, reached US number 1 in 1970. During the 1970s, they appealed to fans of all ages. The partnership ended following the breakdown of Karen's health in 1974; she died of a cardiac arrest, which was linked to her anorexia.

Carpentier, Alejo (1904–80) Writer, born in Havana. For many years he lived in France and Venezuela, but returned to Cuba after the revolution and served in several official government posts. One of the major Latin American writers of this century, his numerous books include *El siglo de las luces* (1962, trans Explosion in the Cathedral), *El reino de este mundo* (1949, The Kingdom of this World), and *Los pasos perdidos* (1953, The Lost Steps).

Carpini, John of Plano [kah(r)peenee], Ital **Giovanni da Pian del Carpini** (c.1182–c.1253) Franciscan monk and traveller, born in Umbria, Italy. A disciple of Francis of Assisi, he was head of the mission sent by Pope Innocent IV to the Emperor of the Mongols. He started from Lyon in April 1245, crossed the Volga in April 1246, and in July reached the Karakoram Mts. The latter part of the journey across C Asia was a ride of nearly 3000 mi in 100 days, a feat of endurance for a man over 60 years of age. He returned in 1247, and wrote an account of his travels and a profile of the Mongol peoples *Historia Mongalorum*. He was later appointed Archbishop of Autivari.

Carpocrates of Alexandria [kah(r)pokrateez] (2nd-c) Greek religious leader. He founded the gnostic sect of *Carpocratians*, who sought through contemplation the union, or return, of the individual soul to God.

Carr, Emily (1871–1945) Painter and writer, raised in Victoria, British Columbia, Canada. She studied art at the California School of Design in San Francisco, and by 1913 had produced a large body of work on native themes. Her mature and original work began at age 57, when she travelled E to meet members of the Group of Seven. Nature themes replaced native themes after 1932, and her work became less designed and more freely expressive of natural rhythms. Her book *Klee Wyck* won the Governor-General's Award in 1941, and her other works include *The Book of Small* (1942).

Carr, Emma Perry (1880–1972) Chemist and educator, born in Holmesville, OH. She was assistant professor and then professor of chemistry at Mount Holyoke College (1919–46), where she was not only an inspiring teacher but also an innovator in research programmes. Over several decades she made significant contributions to both empirical and theoretical problems of analysing organic molecules with ultraviolet absorption spectroscopy. Her laboratory inspired numerous young women to take up scientific careers.

Carr, Philippa >> **Hibbert**

Carrà, Carlo [kara] (1881–1966) Painter, born in Quargnento, Italy. Largely self-taught, he adopted a Futurist style, then in 1917 met Giorgio di Chirico and for some years was influenced by his 'metaphysical painting' movement. His best-known work is 'Le canal' (Zürich). >> Chirico; Severini

Carracci [karahchee] A family of painters, born in Bologna, Italy. The most famous was **Annibale Carracci** (1560–1609), whose style was much influenced by Correggio and Raphael. With his brother, **Agostino Carracci** (1557–1602), he painted the gallery of the Farnese Palace, Rome. Together with their cousin, **Ludovico Carracci** (1555–1619), they founded an influential academy of painting in Bologna (1582). >> Correggio; Raphael

Carranza, Venustiano >> **Villa, Pancho**

Carr-Boyd, Ann Kirsten (1938–) Composer, teacher, and music historian, born in Sydney, New South Wales, Australia. She studied at Sydney University, and became a leading authority on Aboriginal and early Australian music. Her many orchestral, chamber, and instrumental compositions include *Symphony in Three Movements* (1964), *Australian Baroque* (1984), and *Suite Veronese* (1985).

Carré, John Le >> **Le Carré, John**

Carrel, Alexis (1873–1944) Biologist, born in Ste Foy-lès-Lyon, France. He studied at Lyon University, and moved to the Rockefeller Institute for Medical Research in New York City in 1906. He discovered a method of suturing blood-vessels which made it possible to replace arteries, and was awarded the 1912 Nobel Prize for Physiology or Medicine. He did much research on the prolongation of the life of tissues, and helped Henry Dakin develop 'Dakin's solution' for sterilizing deep wounds. >> Dakin

Carreño de Miranda, Juan [karenyoh day miranda] (1614–85) Painter, born in Avilés, Spain. Assistant and successor of Velasquez at the Spanish court, he painted religious pictures and frescoes, as well as portraits. >> Velasquez

Carreras, José Maria [karairas] (1946–) Lyric tenor, born in Barcelona, Spain. He made his debut at Covent Garden and at the Metropolitan Opera (1974), La Scala (1975), and Salzburg (1976). After severe illness in the mid-1980s, he returned to the stage.

Carrére, John Merven >> **Hastings, Thomas**

Carrier, Jean Baptiste [karay] (1756–94) French revolutionary, born in Yolet, France. In the National Convention he helped to form the Revolutionary Tribunal, voted for the death of the king, and assisted in the overthrow of the Girondists. At Nantes in 1793 he massacred in four months 16 000 Vendéan and other prisoners, chiefly by drowning them in the R Loire (the *noyades*, 'drownings'). After the fall of Robespierre he was tried and guillotined. >> Robespierre

Carrier, Willis (Haviland) (1876–1950) Engineer and inventor, born in Angola, NY. He designed his first machine to control humidity for a New York City printing plant in 1902. He formed the Carrier Engineering Corporation in 1915, and in 1939 invented a practical air-conditioning system for skyscrapers.

Carriera, Rosalba [karyaira] (1675–1757) Painter, born in Venice, Italy. She was famed for her flattering portraits and miniatures, some of them in pastel, especially on ivory. She moved to Paris (1720), where she received many famous commissions, including one of Louis XV as a child.

Carrière, Eugène [karyair] (1849–1906) Artist, born in Gournay-sur-Marne, France. He lived and worked in Paris, specializing in domestic groups and portraits. His soft tonalities inspired Edmond de Goncourt to call him 'the modern Madonna painter'. >> Goncourt

Carrington, Peter (Alexander Rupert) Carrington, 6th Baron (1919–) British statesman, born in London, England, UK. He trained at Sandhurst, winning the Military Cross in World War 2, and held several junior posts in government (1951–6), before becoming high commissioner to Australia (1956–9). He then served as First Lord of the Admiralty (1959–63) and Leader of the House of Lords (1963–4). He was secretary of state for defence (1970–4) and briefly for energy (1974), and also chairman of the Conservative Party (1972–4). Upon the Conservative return to office he was foreign secretary (1979–82), until he and his ministerial team resigned over the Argentinian invasion of the Falkland Is. He later became secretary-general of NATO (1984–8) and Chancellor of the University of Reading.

Carroll, Charles (1737–1832) US statesman, born in Annapolis, MD, the cousin of John Carroll. He studied in St Omer and Paris, served on several committees of correspondence and in the Continental Congress (1776–8), and was the first senator from Maryland to the US Senate (1789–92). He was the last survivor of the signatories of the Declaration of Independence. >> Carroll, John

Carroll, James (1854–1907) Physician, born in Woolwich, E Greater London, England, UK. He emigrated in childhood to Canada and the USA. Serving as a surgeon in the US army, and in association with Walter Reed, he did valuable research on yellow fever, deliberately infecting himself with the disease in the process (1900). In 1902 he became professor of bacteriology and pathology at Columbia and the Army Medical School. >> Reed, Walter

Carroll, John (1735–1815) First US Roman Catholic bishop, born in Upper Marlboro, MD, the cousin of Charles Carroll. He studied in Europe, where he entered the Jesuit order (1753) and was ordained (1769). In 1774 he returned to Maryland to do pastoral work, and in 1776 joined in an unsuccessful mission to obtain a promise of Canadian neutrality in the Revolution. He became Bishop of Baltimore in 1790, and was made archbishop in 1808. As the Church's leader during a crucial early period, he brought in European missionaries, started three seminaries, and cofounded (1789) a college that became Georgetown University. >> Carroll, Charles

Carroll, Lewis, pseudonym of **Charles Lutwidge Dodgson** (1832–98) Writer, born in Daresbury, Cheshire, NWC England, UK. He studied at Oxford, took orders in 1861, and became a lecturer in mathematics (1855–81). His nursery tale, *Alice's Adventures in Wonderland* (1865), and its sequel, *Through the Looking-Glass* (1872), quickly became classics. 'Alice', to whom the story was originally related during boating excursions, was the second daughter (who died in 1934) of Henry George Liddell, the head of his Oxford college. He wrote a great deal of humorous verse, such as 'The Hunting of the Snark' (1876), as well as several mathematical works. He lived much of his life in the N of England. 'The Walrus and the Carpenter' was written on Whitburn Sands, Sunderland, and most of 'Jabberwocky' was also composed in Whitburn, where there is a statue in his memory. >> Liddell, Henry George

Carruthers, Jimmy [karuhtherz] (1929–90) Boxer, born in Paddington, New South Wales, Australia. In the course of a very short professional boxing career – only 19 bouts, all of which were won – he established himself as the greatest of

Australian boxers. He became world bantamweight champion by knocking out Vic Toweel in the first round in 1952. He retired while not yet 25 to become a boxing referee and pub owner.

Carson, Johnny, popular name of **John William Carson** (1925–) Television personality and businessman, born in Corning, IA. He studied journalism at Nebraska University, then worked in local radio and television from 1950. He hosted *Carson's Cellar* (1951) and wrote and performed on *The Red Skelton Show* (1954). Following *The Johnny Carson Show* (1955–6) and a stage appearance in *Tunnel of Love* (1958), he was engaged as an occasional host of *The Tonight Show*, a position that was made permanent in 1962. Consistently top of the ratings, his breezy, relaxed manner, comic monologue, and selection of guests made him an American institution. He retired from the show in 1992.

Carson, Kit, popular name of **Christopher Carson** (1809–68) Frontiersman, born in Madison Co, KY. A Missouri trapper and hunter, his knowledge of Indian habits and languages led to his becoming guide in John Frémont's explorations (1842). He was Indian agent in New Mexico (1853), and fought for the Union in the Civil War. Several places are named after him. >> Frémont

Carson, Rachel (Louise) (1907–64) Naturalist and publicist, born in Springdale, PA. She studied at Johns Hopkins University, and worked in marine biology in the US Fish and Wildlife Service (1936–49). She was an effective writer, and during the 1940s her books on marine ecology became influential. In 1962 her *Silent Spring* directed much public attention to the problems caused by agricultural pesticides, and she became a pioneer in the conservationist movement of the 1960s.

Carson, Willie, popular name of **William Fisher Hunter Carson** (1942–) Jockey, born in Stirling, C Scotland, UK. In 1972 he became the first Scotsman to be champion jockey, and recorded his first Classic success, on *High Top*, in the 2000 Guineas. He had to wait until 1979 for his first Derby winner, *Troy*, but immediately won again on *Henbit* in 1980; he was champion jockey five times, in 1972, 1973, 1978, 1980 and 1983. He rode 3828 winners in his career, including 18 Classics, before retiring in 1997. >> RR1161

Carstairs, John Paddy, originally **John Keys** (1914–70) Novelist, film director, filmscript writer, and artist. He studied art at the Slade School of Art, London, painting light-hearted landscapes in various media. His best-known novel is *Love and Ella Rafferty* (1947), and he also wrote the autobiographical *Honest Injun* (1943).

Carstens, Asmus Jakob (1754–98) Painter, born near Schleswig, Denmark. He studied art at Copenhagen, and from 1783–8 barely supported himself by portrait painting in Lübeck and Berlin before his 'Fall of the Angels' gained him a professorship in the Academy of Art in Berlin (1790). He lived in Rome from 1792, working on Classical themes.

Cartan, Elie (Joseph) [kah(r)tã] (1869–1951) Mathematician, born in Dolomieu, France. He held posts at Montpellier, Lyon, and (1912–40) the Sorbonne, becoming one of the most original mathematicians of his time. He worked on Lie groups and differential geometry, and founded the subject of analysis on differentiable manifolds, which is essential to modern fundamental physical theories. Among his discoveries are the theory of spinors, the method of moving frames and the exterior differential calculus. His son, **Henri-(Paul) Cartan** (1904–) also became a mathematician, known for his work in the theory of analytic functions. >> Lie, Sophus

Carte, Richard D'Oyly >> **D'Oyly Carte, Richard**

Carter, Angela (1940–92) Writer, born in Eastbourne, East Sussex, SE England, UK. She studied at Bristol University,

and her first novel, *Shadow Dance*, was published in 1966. She then wrote novels and short stories characterized by feminist themes and fantasy narratives, including *The Magic Toyshop* (1967, screenplay 1986), *The Infernal Desire Machines of Dr Hoffman* (1972), *Nights at the Circus* (1984), and *Wise Children* (1991).

Carter, Benny, popular name of **Bennet Lester Carter** (1907–) Alto saxophonist, born in New York City. Although also a trumpeter and clarinetist, it was the warm tone of the alto saxophone that set the swing era style. He was among the outstanding early writers of big band arrangements, composing for the Fletcher Henderson and Benny Goodman orchestras, among others. He led big bands of his own, though none gained particular recognition. A spell in London in 1936 as musical director of the Henry Hall Orchestra had significant influence on the development of British jazz. He was composer-in-residence to the first Glasgow Jazz Festival in 1987. >> Goodman, Benny; Henderson, Fletcher; Wilson, Teddy

Carter, Elliott Cook, Jr (1908–) Composer, born in New York City. He studied at Harvard University, and with Nadia Boulanger in Paris. Prizes and fellowships enabled him to alternate further periods of study with teaching at St John's College, Annapolis (1940–2), Peabody Conservatory (1946–8), Columbia University (1948–50), Queens College, New York City (1955–6), and Yale (1960–2). His second string quartet won a Pulitzer Prize in 1960. His other works, often of great complexity, include two symphonies, four concertos, and several sonatas. >> Boulanger, Nadia

Carter, Howard (1874–1939) Archaeologist, born in Swaffham, Norfolk, E England, UK. He joined Flinders Petrie's archaeological survey of Egypt as an artist in 1891, from 1907 conducting his own research under the patronage of George Herbert. His discoveries included the tombs of Hatshepsut (1907), Thutmose IV and, most notably, Tutankhamen (1922), a find on which he worked for the remainder of his life. >> Carnarvon; Hatshepsut; Petrie; Tutankhamen

Carter, Jimmy, popular name of **James (Earl) Carter** (1924–) US statesman and 39th president (1977–81), born in Plains, GA. He trained at the US Naval Academy, and served in the US navy until 1953, when he took over the family peanut business and other enterprises. As Governor of Georgia (1970–4) he expressed an enlightened policy towards the rights of African-Americans and women. In 1976 he won the Democratic presidential nomination, and went on to win a narrow victory over Gerald Ford. He arranged the peace treaty between Egypt and Israel (1979), and was much concerned with human rights at home and abroad. His administration ended in difficulties over the taking of US hostages in Iran and the Soviet invasion of Afghanistan, and he was defeated by Ronald Reagan in the 1980 election. He has been much involved in international diplomacy in several parts of the world, notably in relation to the crisis in Haiti in 1994. >> Ford, Gerald R; Mondale; Reagan; RR1097

Carteret, John, 1st Earl Granville [kah(r)tuhret] (1690–1763) British statesman and chief minister (1742–4), born in London, England, UK. He entered the House of Lords in 1711, and became ambassador to Sweden (1719), secretary of state (1721), and Lord-Lieutenant of Ireland (1724–9). As Earl Granville, he was driven from power by the Pelhams (1744) because of his pro-Hanoverian policies, though from 1751 was president of the Council under Henry Pelham, and twice refused the premiership. >> Pelham, Henry

Carteret, Philip [kah(r)tuhret] (?–1796) English navigator, who sailed as lieutenant in John Byron's voyage round the world (1764–6), and commanded the *Swallow* in Samuel

Wallis's expedition round the world (1766). Separated from Wallis while clearing the Strait of Magellan, he discovered Pitcairn I and other small islands (one of the Solomons bears his name) and returned round the Cape of Good Hope to England in 1769. >> Wallis, Samuel

Cartier, Sir Georges Etienne [kah(r)tyay] (1814–73) Canadian statesman and prime minister (1858–62), born in Antoine, Quebec, Canada. A lawyer by profession, he became attorney general for Lower Canada in 1856, and was joint prime minister with Sir John A Macdonald. He worked for Canadian confederation and expansion in the West. >> Macdonald, John A; RR1039

Cartier, Jacques [ka(r)tyay] (1491–1557) Navigator, born in St-Malo, France. He made three voyages of exploration to North America (1534–42), surveying the coast of Canada and the St Lawrence R, and providing the basis for later French claims in the area.

Cartier-Bresson, Henri [ka(r)tyay bresõ] (1908–) Photographer, born in Paris. He studied painting and literature before taking up photography after a trip to Africa (1930). His first pictures were published in 1933. In the later 1930s he worked as assistant to the film director Jean Renoir, and after the war was a co-founder of the independent photographic agency, Magnum Photos. He works only in black-and-white, concerned exclusively with the capturing of visual moments illustrating contemporary life. His books include *The World of Henri Cartier-Bresson* (1968). In the mid-1970s he gave up photography, and returned to his earlier interests of painting and drawing. >> Kertész; Renoir, Jean

Cartimandua [kah(r)timandyooa] (1st-c) Pro-Roman queen of the Yorkshire Brigantes. She protected the N borders of the Roman province of Britain after the conquest (43), until her overthrow by her ex-husband, the anti-Roman Venutius, in 68–9. >> Caractacus

Cartland, (Mary) Barbara (Hamilton) (1901–) Popular romantic novelist, born in Edgbaston, West Midlands, C England, UK. She published her first novel, *Jigsaw*, in 1923, and has since produced over 600 books, mostly novels of chaste romantic love designed for women readers, but also including biographies, books on food, health, and beauty, and several volumes of autobiography. She earned a place in the *Guinness Book of Records* for writing 26 books in 1983. She married first, in 1927, **Alexander George McCorquodale** (d.1964), whom she divorced in 1933; then in 1936 his cousin, **Hugh McCorquodale** (d.1963). By her first marriage she is the mother of **Raine, Dowager Countess Spencer**, step-mother of the Princess of Wales. She is an ardent advocate of health foods, and fitness for the elderly. >> Diana, Princess of Wales

Cartwright, Edmund (1743–1823) Inventor of the power loom, born in Marnham, Nottinghamshire, C England, UK. He studied at Oxford, became a clergyman (1779), and after visiting Arkwright's cotton-spinning mills devised his power loom (1785–90), and also a wool-combing machine (1790). Attempts to use the loom at Doncaster and Manchester met with fierce opposition, and it was not until the 19th-c that it came into practical use. In 1809 the government awarded him a grant of £10 000 for his achievements. >> Arkwright; Cartwright, John

Cartwright, John (1740–1824) Political reformer, born in Marnham, Nottinghamshire, C England, UK, the elder brother of Edmund Cartwright. He served in the navy (1758–70), and in 1775 became major to the Nottinghamshire militia. He then began to write on politics, advocating annual parliaments, the ballot, and manhood suffrage, afterwards taking up reform in farming, abolition of slavery, the national defences, and the liberties of Spain and Greece. >> Cartwright, Edmund

Cartwright, Peter (1785–1872) Methodist preacher of the US frontier, born in Amherst Co, VA. He was ordained in Kentucky in 1806, and in 1823 moved to Illinois. He wrote his autobiography (1856) and *The Backwoods Preacher* (1869).

Caruso, Enrico [karoozoh] (1873–1921) Operatic tenor, born in Naples, Italy. He made his debut in Naples in 1894, later making his first appearance in London (1902) and in New York City (1903). The extraordinary power of his voice, combined with his acting ability, won him worldwide recognition.

Carver, George Washington (c.1864–1943) Scientist, born near Diamond Grove, MO. He was born into an African-American slave family, and received little formal education in his early years. He finally graduated from Iowa State Agricultural College in 1894, and became renowned for his research into agricultural problems and synthetic products, especially from peanuts, sweet potatoes, and soybeans. For much of his life he worked to make Tuskegee Institute, AL, a means of education for the disadvantaged black farmers of the South, and became famous as a teacher and humanitarian.

Carver, John (c. 1575–1621) Colonist in America, born in Nottinghamshire or Derbyshire, C England, UK. After emigrating to Holland in 1609, he joined the Pilgrim Fathers and became their agent for the expedition to the New World. He chartered the *Mayflower*, sailing in June 1620, and was elected first governor of the colony at New Plymouth, MA. He died within five months of their landing.

Carver, Raymond (1939–88) Poet and short-story writer, born in Clatskanie, OR. He taught at the universities of Iowa, Texas, and California. His collections include *Will You Please Be Quiet, Please?* (1976), and *Cathedral* (1983). *In a Marine Light: Selected Poems* appeared in the year he died.

Carver, Richard Michael Power Carver, Baron (1915–) British soldier, born in Surrey, SE England, UK. He studied at Winchester College, and was commissioned into the Royal Tank Corps in 1935. In World War 2 he served with distinction in North Africa (1941–3), in Italy (1943) and Normandy (1944), and commanded the 4th Independent Armoured Brigade in North West Europe (1944–5). He later became chief of the general staff (1971–3) and of the defence staff (1973–6).

Carver, Robert (c.1490–c.1567) Composer, canon of Scone, who was attached to the Chapel Royal of Scotland. Five of his Masses have survived, each displaying a florid style with free use of counterpoint; one is the only early 16th-c British example based on the *cantus firmus*, 'L'Homme armé'.

Cary, John [kairee] (c.1754–1835) English cartographer. He began as an engraver in London, England, UK, and became a publisher and land surveyor (c.1783). His *New and Correct English Atlas* appeared in 1787, followed by county atlases, and the *New Universal Atlas* of 1808. In 1794 he undertook a road survey of England and Wales, published as *Cary's New Itinerary* (1798).

Cary, (Arthur) Joyce (Lunel) [kairee] (1888–1957) Writer, born in Londonderry, Co Londonderry. He studied art in Edinburgh and Paris, then law at Oxford, and fought in West Africa in World War 1. Injuries and ill health dictated his early retirement to Oxford, where he took up writing. Out of his African experience came several novels, such as *Mister Johnson* (1939). His best-known work is his trilogy, *Herself Surprised* (1940), *To be a Pilgrim* (1942), and *The Horse's Mouth* (1944). >> Cary, Tristram

Cary, Tristram [kairee] (1925–) Composer and teacher, born in Oxford, Oxfordshire, SC England, UK, the son of Joyce Cary. He studied at Trinity College of Music, and pioneered the development of electronic music, establishing his own studio in 1952. He became a director of the celebrated Electronic Music Studios in London, and was professor of electronic music at the Royal College of Music, London (1967–74). In 1979 he joined Adelaide University, South Australia. He has written much music for films, theatre, radio, and television. >> Cary, Joyce

Casals, Pablo [kaˈsals], Catalan **Pau** (1876–1973) Cellist, conductor, and composer, born in Vendrell, Spain. He studied at the Royal Conservatory, Madrid, became professor of cello at Barcelona, and in 1899 began to appear as a soloist. In 1919 he founded the Barcelona Orchestra, which he conducted until he left Spain at the outbreak of the Civil War (1936). In 1950 he founded an annual festival of classical chamber music in Prades, France. His own compositions consist of choral and chamber works. During his later years, he conducted master classes. >> Cortot; Thibaud

Casanova (de Seingalt), Giacomo Girolomo [kasaˈnohva] (1725–98) Adventurer, born in Venice, Italy. By 1750 he had worked as a clergyman, secretary, soldier, and violinist in various countries, and in 1755 was imprisoned for being a magician. He escaped in 1756, and for nearly 20 years wandered through Europe, visiting most of its capitals, and meeting the greatest men and women of the day. Alchemist, cabalist, and spy, he was everywhere introduced to the best society, and had always to 'vanish' after a brief period of felicity. In 1785 he established himself as librarian with the Count of Waldstein, in Bohemia, where he died. His main work is his autobiography, first published in complete form in 1960. His seductions are the first things many think of in connection with his name.

Casas, Las Bartolomé de >> **Las Casas, Bartolomé de**

Casella, Alfredo [kaˈsela] (1883–1947) Composer and musician, born in Turin, Italy. He studied piano at the Paris Conservatoire and first came to notice as a composer in 1908. His work was varied but mainly Neoclassical in character, and includes three operas, two symphonies, and concertos for cello, violin, and organ, as well as chamber music, many piano pieces, and songs. He also produced some noteworthy editions of classical composers.

Casement, (Sir) Roger (David) [ˈkaysment] (1864–1916) British consular official, born in Dun Laoghaire (formerly Kingstown), Co Dublin, Ireland. He acted as consul in various parts of Africa (1895–1904) and Brazil (1906–11), where he denounced the Congo and Putumayo rubber atrocities. Knighted in 1911, ill health caused him to retire to Ireland in 1912. An ardent Irish nationalist, he tried to obtain German help for the cause. In 1916 he was arrested on landing in Ireland from a German submarine to head the Sinn Féin rebellion, and hanged for high treason in London. His controversial 'Black Diaries', revealing, among other things, homosexual practices, were long suppressed by the government, but ultimately published in 1959.

Casey, Richard Gardiner Casey, Baron (1890–1976) Australian statesman, born in Melbourne, Victoria, Australia. He was elected to the House of Representatives in 1931. He became first Australian minister to the USA in 1940, minister of state in the Middle East (a war cabinet rank) in 1942, and minister for external affairs in 1951. A life peerage was conferred on him in 1960.

Casey, William J(oseph) (1913–87) Lawyer and government official, born in New York City. During World War 2 he supervised spy missions in Europe. After the War, he worked in corporate law, focusing on his stock investments, then served as a tough chairman of the Securities and Exchange Commission (1971–3). As President Reagan's director of the Central Intelligence Agency (1981–7), he was known for extremely aggressive and sometimes questionable policies when it came to pursuing Communists. He allegedly supported illegal aid to the Nicaraguan Contras, but died before giving formal testimony. >> North, Oliver

Cash, Johnny, nickname **the Man in Black** (1932–) Country music singer, songwriter, and guitarist, born in Kingsland, AR. He worked in a car factory and spent four years in the US air force, before moving to Memphis and signing for Sun Records in 1955. Early songs included 'Cry, Cry, Cry' and 'I Walk The Line'. An interest in expressing counterculture ideas in the language of country music was reflected in his association with Bob Dylan in the late 1960s. His nickname came from a 1971 hit of that name. >> Dylan

Cash, Martin (1810–77) Bushranger, born in Enniscorthy, Co Wexford, Ireland. He was transported to Australia for theft and attempted murder (1827), escaped from a prison at Port Arthur (1837), and took up a career of bushranging throughout Tasmania. After shooting a constable he was sentenced to death (1843), later commuted to life imprisonment on the penal settlement of Norfolk I, where he became a model prisoner. He married a fellow-prisoner, received a pardon in 1853, returned to Hobart where he was appointed a constable, and was for some years caretaker of the Botanic Gardens there.

Casimir, Hendrik [ˈkazimeer] (1909–) Physicist, born in The Hague, The Netherlands. He studied physics at Leyden, Copenhagen, and Zürich, and was director of the Philips Research Laboratories from 1946. In 1934 he helped to devise a general theory of superconductivity which explained many of the phenomena; the later theory by Bardeen and others both includes and extends Casimir's earlier idea. >> Bardeen

Čáslavská, Vera [ˈkaslavska] (1942–) Gymnast, born in Prague. She switched from ice skating to gymnastics as a 15 year-old, and went on to win 22 Olympic, world, and European titles. She won three Olympic gold medals in 1964, and four in 1968. She donated her medals one each to the four Czech leaders (Dubcek, Svoboda, Cernik, Smrkorsky) deposed following the Russian invasion. She married Josef Odložil, the Olympic 1500 m silver medalist in the Mexico City Olympics (1968). >> RR1160

Caslon, William [ˈkazlon] (1692–1766) Type-founder, born in Cradley, Hereford and Worcester, WC England, UK. He set up in business as a gun engraver and toolmaker in London in 1716, but soon began cutting type for printers. His 'old face' *Caslon types* were extensively used in Europe and the USA until the end of the 18th-c, and were later revived.

Casorati, Felice [kazoˈrahtee] (1886–1963) Painter, born in Novara, Italy. He was one of the exponents of Italian Neoclassicism, and is noted for his series of portraits of women.

Cass, Lewis (1782–1866) US statesman, born in Exeter, NH. He was called to the Ohio bar in 1803, but rose to be general in the War of 1812. He was then for 18 years civil governor of Michigan. He became secretary of war (1831–6), minister at Paris (1836–42), a member of the US Senate, and secretary of state (1857–60). He twice failed in a bid for the presidency. >> Schoolcraft

Cassander [kaˈsander] (c.358–297 BC) Ruler of Macedon after the death of his father Antipater in 319 BC, and its king from 305 BC. An active figure in the power struggle after Alexander's death (323 BC), he murdered Alexander's mother, widow, and son, and contributed to the defeat of Antigonus I Monophthalmos at Ipsus in 301 BC. >> Antigonus I; Antipater (of Macedon); Olympias; RR1055

Cassatt, Mary [kaˈsat] (1844–1926) Impressionist painter, born in Allegheny, PA. She studied in Spain, Italy, and Holland, but worked mainly in France, where she was a pupil and close follower of Degas. She was renowned for her etching and drypoint studies of domestic scenes. >> Degas

Cassavetes, John [kasa**vee**teez] (1929–89) Actor and director, born in New York City, USA. Trained in New York as an actor, he had several roles in film and television before directing *Shadows* in 1959. He received a Best Supporting Actor nomination for his role in *The Dirty Dozen* (1967). Other acting credits include *Rosemary's Baby* (1969), *Two Minute Warning* (1976), and *The Third Day Comes* (1986); other directing credits *Husbands* (1970), *Love Streams* (1984), and *Big Trouble* (1985).

Cassel, (Karl) Gustav (1866–1945) Economist, born in Stockholm. Professor at Stockholm from 1904, he became known as a world authority on monetary problems.

Cassell, John (1817–65) British publisher. After apprenticeship as a carpenter, he moved to London as a temperance advocate (1836). In 1847 he started as a tea and coffee merchant, and in 1850 turned to writing and publishing educational books and magazines for the working classes (*Cassell's Magazine*, 1852).

Cassian, St John (?360–c. 435) Monk and theologian, born in Dobruja, Romania. He spent some years as an ascetic in the Egyptian deserts, before being ordained in 403. He instituted several monasteries in the S of France, including the Abbey of St Victor at Massilia (Marseilles), which served as a model for many in Gaul and Spain. He was the author of *Collationes* (on the Desert Fathers) and a book on monasticism. Feast day 23 July.

Cassidy, Butch, originally **Robert LeRoy Parker** (1866–?1909) Outlaw, born in Beaver, UT. As a youth he learned cattle rustling and gunfighting. After serving time in Wyoming State Prison (1894–6) he joined the infamous Wild Bunch and was partner with the Sundance Kid. Together they roamed America, robbing banks, trains, and mine stations with the law in constant pursuit. From 1901 they lived mainly in South America, where (according to one theory) they were trapped and killed. >> Sundance Kid

Cassin, René [kasĩ] (1887–1976) Jurist and French statesman, born in Bayonne, France. He studied at Aix and Paris universities, and was professor of international law at Lille (1920–9) and at Paris (1929–60). During World War 2 he joined Charles de Gaulle in London. He was principal legal adviser in negotiations with the British government, and held important posts in the French government in exile in London and Algiers, and subsequently in the Council of State (of which he was president, 1944–60) in liberated France. After the war he was increasingly concerned with the safeguarding of human rights, and played a leading part in the establishment of UNESCO. In 1968 he was awarded the Nobel Peace Prize. >> de Gaulle

Cassini, Giovanni Domenico [ka**see**nee], also known as **Jean Dominique Cassini** (1625–1712) Astronomer, born in Perinaldo, Italy. In 1650 he became professor of astronomy at Bologna, and in 1669 the first director of the observatory at Paris. He greatly extended knowledge of the Sun's parallax, the periods of Jupiter, Mars, and Venus, and was the first to record observations of zodiacal light. *Cassini's division* (the gap between two of Saturn's rings) is named after him. *Cassini's laws*, describing the rotation of the Moon, were formulated in 1693. He was succeeded as director at Paris by a dynasty of Cassinis.

Cassini, Oleg [ka**see**nee] (1913–) Fashion designer, born in Paris. The son of an emigré Russian countess, he moved to the USA in 1936. He began by designing costumes for Hollywood movies before establishing his own New York City firm in 1950. His trademarks included provocative sheaths, cocktail dresses, and, in the early 1960s, his

widely copied 'Jackie Kennedy' look. His dashing good looks, urbane manner, and associations with glamorous women made him as much a fixture of the society and gossip columns as in the fashion section of the media.

Cassiodorus (Flavius Magnus Aurelius) [kasioh**daw**rus] (c. 490–c. 580) Roman writer and monk, born in Scylaceum (Squillace), Calabria. He was secretary to the Ostrogothic king, Theodoric, quaestor and praetorian prefect, sole consul in 514, and after Theodoric's death (526) chief minister to Queen Amalasontha. His *Institutiones* is an encyclopedic course of study for the monks of the Vivarium, which he founded and to which he retired. >> Theodoric

Cassirer, Ernst [ka**see**rer] (1874–1945) Philosopher, born in Wrocław, Poland. He studied at Berlin, Leipzig, Heidelberg, and Marburg, where he was attracted to neo-Kantianism. He worked as a tutor and civil servant, then became professor of philosophy at Hamburg (1919), and rector (1930), but he resigned when Hitler came to power, and taught at Oxford (1933–5), Göteborg (1935–41), Yale (1941–4) and Columbia (from 1944 until his death). His best-known work, *Die Philosophie der symbolischen Formen* (1923–9, The Philosophy of Symbolic Forms), analyses the symbolic functions underlying all human thought, language, and culture.

Cassius [**ka**sius], in full **Gaius Cassius Longinus** (?–42 BC) Roman soldier and politician. An opponent of Caesar during the civil war with Pompey, he was pardoned by him after Pharsalus (48 BC). Despite gaining polical advancement through Caesar and the promise of the post of Governor of Syria, he later turned against him again, and played a leading part in the conspiracy to murder him (44 BC). He raised an army in Syria, defeated Dolabella, and marched against the Triumverate, but was defeated by Caesar's avengers at Philippi (42 BC), and committed suicide. >> Antonius; Caesar; Dolabella

Cassius, Dio(n) >> **Dio Cassius**

Cassivellaunus [kasive**law**nus] (1st-c BC) British chief of the Catavellauni, a British tribe living in the area of modern Hertfordshire, SE England, UK. He led the British resistance to Julius Caesar on his second invasion, 54 BC. >> Caesar

Casson, Sir Hugh (Maxwell) [**ka**sn] (1910–) British architect. He studied at Cambridge, and was professor of interior design at the Royal College of Art (1953–75). He directed the architecture of the Festival of Britain (1948), and was president of the Royal Academy (1976–84). He was knighted in 1952.

Casson, Sir Lewis [**ka**sn] (1875–1969) Actor-manager and producer, born in Birkenhead, Merseyside, NW England, UK. He is known especially for his productions of Shakespeare and Shaw. He married **Sybil Thorndike** in 1908. >> Horniman; Thorndike, Sybil

Castagno, Andrea del [kas**tan**yoh], originally **Andrea di Bartolo de Simone** (c. 1421–57) Painter, born in Castagno, Italy. After early privations he attracted the attention of Bernardetto de' Medici, who sent him to study in Florence. In c.1440 he painted some effigies of men hanged by their heels, which established his reputation as a painter of violent scenes. His celebrated 'Last Supper', painted for S Apollonia, is now in the Castagno Museum, as are his series of 'Famous Men and Women', painted for a villa after Legnaia. In his own time he was praised as a draughtsman.

Castelnau, Noel Marie Joseph Edouard, vicomte de (Viscount of) **Curières de** [kastel**noh**] (1851–1944) French soldier, born in Aveyron, France. He studied at St Cyr, and served in the Franco–Prussian War (1870–1). He was a member of the Conseil de Guerre in 1913 and took command of the Army of Lorraine in 1914. As commander of all French armies in France, he directed the Champagne offensive (1915), and became Joffre's chief-of-staff. >> Joffre

Castelnuovo-Tedesco, Mario [kastel**nwoh**voh te**des**koh] (1895–1968) Composer, born in Florence, Italy. He studied under Pizzetti, began composing as a boy, and in 1926 brought out his opera *La Mandragola*, based on Machiavelli's book. In addition to two other operas, he produced orchestral and instrumental works, but is probably best known for his songs, especially his complete series of the lyrics from Shakespeare's plays. >> Pizzetti

Castelo Branco, Camilo, visconde de (Viscount of) **Correia Botelho** [ka**ste**loo **brang**koo] (1825–90) Writer, born in Lisbon. He studied medicine, then began training for the priesthood, but took to writing. His works include such Gothic romances as *Mysterios de Lisboa* (1854, The Mysteries of Lisbon), *Vingança* (1858, Revenge), and his best-known book, *Amor de Perdição* (1862, Fatal Love). In 1885 he was created viscount for his services to literature.

Castigliano, (Carlo) Alberto [kasteel**yah**noh] (1847–84) Civil engineer, born in Asti, Italy. He studied at the Polytechnic in Turin and worked as a railway engineer in N Italy. He is noted for the introduction of strain energy methods of structural analysis in his two theorems of 1873 and 1875, the second of which also states the principle of least work. These theorems represented a great advance on the methods of classical theory of structures, especially in their application to statically indeterminate systems.

Castiglione, Baldassare, conte di (Count of) **Novilara** [kasteel**yoh**nay] (1478–1529) Writer and diplomat, born near Mantua, Italy. He studied at Milan, began a career at court, and in 1505 was sent by the Duke of Urbino as envoy to Henry VII of England, who made him a knight. His chief work, *Il cortegiano* (1528, The Courtier), is a manual for courtiers. He also wrote Italian and Latin poems, and many letters illustrating political and literary history.

Castilho, Antonio Feliciano, Viscount [kas**teel**yoh] (1800–75) Poet, blind from childhood, born in Lisbon. His volumes, *Cartas de Echo e Narciso* (1821, Letters from Echo and Narcissus) and *Amor e melancholia* (1828, Love and Melancholy), inaugurated the Portuguese Romantic movement. He also translated Virgil, Ovid, Shakespeare, and Goethe.

Castle (of Blackburn), Barbara (Anne) Castle, Baroness, *née* **Betts** (1911–   ) British stateswoman, born in Bradford, West Yorkshire, N England, UK. She studied at Oxford, in 1944 married a journalist, **Edward Cyril Castle**, later Baron Castle (1907–79), and became Labour MP for Blackburn in 1945. She was chairman of the Labour Party (1958–9), minister of overseas development (1964–5), and a controversial minister of transport (1965–8), introducing a 70 mph speed limit, and the 'breathalyser' test for drunken drivers. She became secretary of state for employment and productivity (1968–70) and for social services (1974–6). She then returned to the back benches, but was later elected to the European Parliament, where she became vice-chair of the Socialist group (1979–86). She became a life peer in 1990. Her writing includes *The Castle Diaries* (1980, 1984), *Sylvia and Christabel Pankhurst* (1987), and a volume of autobiography, *Fighting All the Way* (1993).

Castle, Roy (1932–94) Entertainer, born in Scholes, West Yorkshire, N England, UK. A talented musician, dancer, and actor, he starred in cabaret, theatre, film, and television, becoming known for such programmes as BBC television's *Record Breakers*. Following his death from lung cancer, the Roy Castle Cause for Hope Foundation, a research centre into the disease, was launched in Liverpool in 1994, with a scheduled completion in 1997.

Castle, Vernon (1887–1918) and **Irene Castle** (1893–1969) English champion ballroom dancers, husband and wife. He was originally **Vernon Blythe**, born in Norwich, Norfolk, E England, UK. She was **Irene Foote**, from New Rochelle, New York, USA. They married in 1911 and became the leading exhibition ballroom dancers and teachers of the period. He devised such famous dances as the One-step, the Maxixe, the Turkey-trot, the Castle Walk, and the Hesitation Waltz. She retired from dancing after his death as an airman in the Royal Flying Corps.

Castle, William (Ernest) (1867–1962) Biologist, born in Ohio. He studied at Harvard, became professor of geology there (1897) and later of genetics (1908–36). His research was in the field of heredity and natural selection.

Castlereagh, Robert Stewart, Viscount [**ka**slray] (1769–1822) British statesman, born in Dublin, Ireland. He studied at Cambridge, and became Whig MP for Co Down (1790), turning Tory in 1795. He was created Viscount Castlereagh in 1796, and became Irish secretary (1797), President of the Board of Control (1802), and minister of war (1805–6, 1807–9). His major achievements date from 1812, when, as foreign secretary under Lord Liverpool, he was at the heart of the coalition against Napoleon (1813–14). He represented England at Chaumont and Vienna (1814–15), Paris (1815), and Aix-la-Chapelle (1818). He advocated 'Congress diplomacy' among the great powers, to avoid further warfare. Believing that he was being blackmailed for homosexuality, he committed suicide at Foots Cray, his Kentish seat. >> Liverpool, Earl of; Thistlewood

Castner, Hamilton (Young) (1859–99) Analytical chemist, born in New York City. He studied at Columbia University, moved to Britain in 1886, and invented a new process for the isolation of sodium from brine by electrolysis.

Castriota, George >> **Skanderbeg**

Castro (Ruz), Fidel (1927–   ) Cuban revolutionary, prime minister (1959–   ), and president (1976–   ), born near Birán, Cuba. He studied law in Havana. In 1953 he imprisoned after an unsuccessful rising against Batista, but released under an amnesty. He fled to the USA and Mexico, then in 1956 landed in Cuba with a small band of insurgents. In 1958 he mounted a full-scale attack and Batista was forced to flee. As prime minister he proclaimed a 'Marxist–Leninist programme', and set about far-reaching reforms. His overthrow of US economic dominance, and the routing of the US-connived emigré invasion at the Bay of Pigs (1961), was balanced by his dependence on Russian aid. >> Batista; RR1043

Catchpole, Margaret (1762–1819) Australian pioneer, born near Ipswich, Suffolk, E England, UK. She was servant to the Cobbold family of brewers in Ipswich. Twice sentenced to death, for stealing a horse and for escaping from Ipswich jail, she was transported to New South Wales in 1801. She later managed a farm, ran a store, acted as midwife, and led a useful life in the community. Her letters home, and to the Cobbold family, formed the basis of Richard Cobbold's book about her (1845), and provide a valuable account of early 19th-c life in the new colony. >> Cobbold

Catesby, Robert [**kayts**bee] (1573–1605) Chief conspirator involved in the Gunpowder Plot, born in Lapworth, Warwickshire, C England, UK. A Catholic of wealth and lineage, he had suffered much as a recusant both by fines and imprisonment. He was named as an accomplice in the Rye Plot (1603) against James I, and was shot dead while resisting arrest after the failure of the Gunpowder Plot (1605). >> Fawkes; James I (of England).

Cather, Willa (Sibert) [**ka**ther] (1876–1947) Novelist, poet, and journalist, born near Winchester, VA. Her formative years were spent in Nebraska, and she went to university there (1891–5). After her first novel, *Alexander's Bridge* (1912), she wrote a trilogy dealing with immigrants to the USA, the third of which, *My Antonia* (1918), is generally regarded as her best book. Other novels include *Death Comes for the Archbishop* (1927) and *One of Ours* (1922, Pulitzer).

Catherine I (1684–1727) Tsarina of Russia (1725–7), who succeeded her husband Peter I, the Great. She was of lowly birth, and was baptized a Roman Catholic with the name of Martha. In 1705 she became mistress to Peter, changing her name to Catherine, and converting to Orthodoxy in 1708. The tsar married her in 1712, and in 1722 passed a law allowing him to nominate a successor. He chose Catherine, having her crowned empress (tsaritsa) in 1724, and after his death, Prince Menshikov (c.1660–1729) ensured her succession to the throne. She was succeeded by Peter's grandson, Peter II. >> Peter I (of Russia); RR1085

Catherine II, known as **Catherine the Great** see panel below

Catherine, St (?–307) Traditionally, a virgin of royal descent in Alexandria. She publicly confessed the Gospel at a sacrificial feast appointed by Emperor Maximinus, and was beheaded, after being tortured on a spiked wheel (later known as a *catherine wheel*). Her remains were miraculously spirited to Mt Sinai, where her shrine is on display in St Catherine's monastery. Feast day 25 November.

Catherine de' Medici [**may**deechee] (1519–89) Queen of France, the wife of Henry II, and regent (1560–74), born in Florence, Italy, the daughter of Lorenzo de' Medici, Duke of Urbino. Married at 14, she was slighted at the French court, but during the minority of her sons, Francis II (1559–60) and Charles IX (1560–3), she assumed political influence which she retained as queen mother until 1588. She tried to pursue moderation and toleration, to give unity to a state increasingly torn by religious division and aristocratic faction, but she nursed dynastic ambitions, and was drawn into political and religious intrigues, conniving in the infamous Massacre of St Bartholomew (1572). >> RR1049

Catherine of Aragon [**a**ragon] (1485–1536) Queen of England, the first wife of Henry VIII (1509–33), born in

---

CATHERINE II, THE GREAT (1729–96)

Catherine was born Princess Sophie Friederike Auguste von Anhalt-Zerbst in Stettin, Prussia (now Poland). She was the daughter of a minor German prince, Christian August von Anhalt-Zerbst, but her mother was related to the dukes of Holstein. In 1744 she was given the title Grand Duchess Catherine Alekseyevna, and the next year, at 15, was married to her cousin Karl Ulrich, Duke of Holstein-Gottorp, heir to the Russian throne as Peter III.

The liaison was not a happy one. Catherine was much humiliated by her neurotic husband, and soon became notorious for her love affairs. She is said to have placed her favourites in high offices, regardless of their capabilities, though Grigoiy Potemkin, who had a brilliant military and political career, was a notable exception.

After her husband's accession in 1761, Catherine was further humiliated by him when he banished her to a separate household. However, Peter III's manner, and his open hatred of all things Russian, quickly made him unpopular. Through a conspiracy co-ordinated by her lover, Grigoiy Orlov, Catherine gained the support of the army, and Peter was dethroned. A few days afterwards he was murdered by Orlov and others, possibly at her instigation. In 1762 Catherine had herself crowned empress in Moscow, and began a reign which was to last 34 years, despite the fact that she had no real claim to the Russian throne.

Bankruptcy, plague, and a war with Turkey (1768–74) all added to the problems of ruling a vast and underdeveloped country. These came to a head with the revolution of 1773–5, incited by Yemelyan Pugachev. Catherine's army finally defeated him and his Cossack troops at the battle of Tsaritsyn (1775). After the revolt Catherine recognized her reliance on the nobles in order to be able to control the country. They became the people she needed to placate and cultivate, so she reversed any thoughts she had had to emancipate their serfs, and instigated instead a series of provisional reforms (beginning in 1775) giving the nobles greater rights of serf ownership. The 1785 Charter to the Nobility finally completed the establishment of the nobility as a separate estate within Russian society, and assured their extensive and exclusive privileges. Catherine disregarded her earlier attention to the plight of the peasants, who suffered a steady decline in their rights and status. In fact, forced labour paid for many of her reforms and improvements. The French Revolution in 1789 put an end to any remaining sympathies she may have harboured for the peasants.

Catherine actively encouraged trade and industry, and aimed to maximize all the resources of her adopted country in order to increase its wealth and power. She hoped also to create a national culture, equal to that of France. Her government was carried out with great energy and ability, and the dominions and power of Russia rapidly increased. In foreign affairs, her reign marked a turning point for Russia. On her accession she withdrew Russian support from the Prussian ruler Frederick II, the Great, but did not renew hostilities against him. Common Russian and Prussian interest in Poland led eventually to the three partitions with Austria of Poland in 1772, 1793, and 1795, and established a long tradition of Russian–Prussian co-operation. The extinction of Poland as a nation state in 1795 ended a centuries-old conflict. The triumphs of her reign were completed by the two Turkish wars of 1768–74 and 1787–91, and these, together with the annexation of the Crimea in 1783 (masterminded by Potemkin), finally removed the Tatar threat to Russian security, and irreversibly established Russian control over the N coast of the Black Sea.

Catherine was one of 18th-c Russia's most successful rulers, and her long reign covered an important period in Russian history. She combined political acumen with social reform and a high regard for Russian culture. She corresponded with Voltaire and others, and saw herself as a patron of literature and the arts. Despite her early attempts to be an enlightened despot, influenced by Rousseau, Locke, and other European philosophers, her later autocratic pragmatism ensured that, on her death, there was scarcely a free peasant left in Russia. The death of Louis XVI of France (1793) had frightened all Europe's monarchy into greater conservatism.

She disliked her son Paul, the legitimate heir, who was unbalanced, like his (presumed) father, and did everything she could to keep him under her shadow. She died from a stroke at the age of 67, and was succeeded by Paul, who was deposed by her favourite grandson, Alexander, five years later.

>> Frederick II (of Prussia); Paul; Potemkin; Pugachev

Alcalá de Henares, Spain, the fourth daughter of Ferdinand and Isabella of Spain. She was first married in 1501 to Arthur (1486–1502), the son of Henry VII, and following his early death was betrothed to her brother-in-law Henry, then a boy of 11. She married him in 1509, and bore him five children, but only the Princess Mary survived. In 1527 Henry began a procedure for divorce, which he obtained in 1533, thereby breaking with the pope, and starting the English Reformation. Catherine then retired to lead an austere religious life until her death. >> Henry VIII

Catherine of Braganza [bra**gan**za] (1638–1705) Wife of Charles II of England, born in Vila Viçosa, Portugal, the daughter of King John IV of Portugal. She was married to Charles in 1662 as part of an alliance between England and Portugal, but failed to produce an heir. She helped to convert him to Catholicism just before his death, after which she returned to Portugal (1692). >> Charles II (of England).

Catherine of Siena, St [**syay**na], originally **Caterina Benincasa** (1347–80) Nun and mystic, born in Siena, Italy. She became a Dominican, and gained a great reputation for holiness, writing many devotional pieces, letters, and poems. She prevailed on Pope Gregory XI to return the papacy from Avignon to Rome. Christ's stigmata were said to have been imprinted on her body. She was canonized in 1461, and is the patron saint of Italy. Feast day 29 April.

Catherine of Valois [valwah] (1401–37) Queen of England, the wife of Henry V, and the youngest daughter of Charles VI ('the Foolish') of France. After a stormy courtship, when England and France went to war over Henry's dowry demands, she married Henry at Troyes in 1420. In 1421 she gave birth to a son, the future Henry VI. After Henry's death in France in 1422, she secretly married **Owen Tudor**, a Welsh squire, despite parliamentary opposition; their eldest son, Edmund, Earl of Richmond, was the father of Henry VII. >> Henry V

Catherwood, Frederick >> **Stephens, John Lloyd**

Catiline [**kat**ilyn], in full **Lucius Sergius Catilina** (c. 108–62 BC) An impoverished Roman politician of patrician extraction who tried to exploit the economic unrest of Rome and Italy in the 60s BC for his own political ends. His conspiracy against the state was foiled by Cicero late in 63 BC, and he fell in battle early in 62 BC. >> Cicero

Catlin, George (1796–1872) Artist and writer, born in Wilkes-Barre, PA. He studied law, but soon turned to drawing and painting. During 1832–40 he was studying the Indians of the Far West, painting portraits and pictures, illustrative of life and manners, which are now in the National Museum at Washington. He spent eight years in Europe with a Far West show, travelled (1852–7) in South and Central America, and again lived in Europe until 1871.

Cato, Marcus Porcius [**kay**toh], known as **Cato the Elder** or **Cato the Censor** (234–149 BC) Roman statesman, orator, and man of letters, born in Tusculum, Latium. Deeply conservative, and strongly opposed to the contemporary fashion of all things Greek, when made censor (184 BC) he conducted such a vigorous campaign that he was thereafter known by this name. Sent on a mission to Carthage (175 BC), he was so impressed by the power of the Carthaginians that afterwards he ended every speech in the Senate with the words: 'Carthage must be destroyed'. His treatise on agriculture is the oldest extant literary prose work in Latin.

Cato, Marcus Porcius [**kay**toh], known as **Cato the Younger** or **Cato Uticensis** (95–46 BC) Roman statesman, the great-grandson of Cato the Censor. A man of uncompromising principles and deep conservatism, his career was marked by an unswerving opposition to Caesar. A supporter of Pompey in the Civil War, after Pharsalus (48 BC) he escaped to Africa. On hearing of Caesar's overwhelming victory at Thapsus (46 BC), he killed himself. >> Cato (the Elder); Pompey

Catroux, Georges [katroo] (1877–1969) French general and diplomat, born in Limoges, France. He served in World War 1, was Governor-General of Indo-China (1939–40), commanded the Free French forces in Syria and the Near East (1940–1), and became Governor-General of Algeria in 1943. He was also ambassador to the Soviet Union (1945–8).

Catt, Carrie Chapman, *née* **Lane** (1859–1947) Reformer and pacifist, born in Ripon, WI. She studied at Iowa State College, joined the staff of the National American Woman Suffrage Association in 1890, and later became its president (1900–4, 1915–47), effecting dramatic changes in the organization, and helping to bring about the 19th Amendment (1920), thus securing the vote for women. She helped establish the League of Women Voters (1919), and spent the later years of her life campaigning for world peace.

Cattell, Raymond B(ernard) [ka**tel**] (1905–) Psychologist, born in Staffordshire, C England, UK. He studied at London University, taught at Harvard, Clarke, and Duke universities before World War 2, and after the war became director of the Laboratory of Personality Assessment at Illinois University. He later moved to the University of Hawaii. He is best known for his application of the statistical techniques of factor analysis to the study of personality differences.

Cattermole, George (1800–68) Watercolour painter and book illustrator, born in Dickleborough, Norfolk, E England, UK. He was known for his antiquarian and architectural paintings, and for his illustrations of Sir Walter Scott's 'Waverley Novels'.

Catullus, Gaius Valerius [ka**tuh**lus] (c. 84–c. 54 BC) Lyric poet, born in Verona, Italy. He settled in Rome (c.62 BC), where he met 'Lesbia' whom he addressed in his verses. He entered as an aristocrat into the contest of parties, and several of his poems attack Caesar and other political enemies. His extant works comprise 116 pieces, many of them extremely brief, while the longest contains only some 400 lines.

Cauchy, Augustin Louis, Baron [kohshee] (1789–1857) Mathematician, born in Paris. He studied to become an engineer, but ill health forced him to retire and teach mathematics at the Ecole Polytechnique. He did important work on partial differential equations, the wave theory of light, and the mathematical theory of elasticity, but is primarily remembered as the founder of the theory of functions of a complex variable. In algebra he gave a definitive account of the theory of determinants, and developed the ideas of group theory.

Causley, Charles [**kawz**lee] (1917–) Poet, born in Launceston, Cornwall, SW England, UK. He left school at 15, joined the Navy, and trained as a teacher after World War 2. He wrote his first poetry while in the Navy, publishing his first collection, *Hands to Dance*, in 1951. He became known as a poet of the sea, and also as a children's poet. Later volumes include *Union Street* (1957), *Figgie Hobbin* (1970), and *Early in the Morning* (1988), and his *Collected Poems 1951–1997* were published in 1997.

Cavaco Silva, Anibal [ka**va**soh **seel**va] (1939–) Portuguese politician and prime minister (1985–95), born in Loulé, Portugal. He studied economics in Britain and the USA, became a university teacher, and then a research director in the Bank of Portugal. With the re-establishment of constitutional government after 1976, he entered politics and became minister of finance (1980–1), and in 1985 leader of the Social Democratic Party and prime minister. Under his leadership Portugal joined the European Community in 1985 and the Western European Union in 1988. >> RR1082

Cavafy, Constantine [kavafee], pseudonym of **Konstantine Petrou Kavafis** (1863–1933) Poet, born in Alexandria, Egypt, of a Greek family. After his father's death in 1872 he was taken to England for five years, and apart from three years in Istanbul (1882–5) he spent the rest of his life in Alexandria, where he worked as a civil servant, making it the setting of much of his poetry. His first book was privately published when he was 41, and reissued five years later with an additional seven poems. He published no further work during his lifetime, but in recent years he has come to be regarded as a major modern Greek poet.

Cavalcanti, Alberto [kavalkantee], originally **Alberto de Almeida-Cavalcanti** (1897–1982) Film director and producer, born in Rio de Janeiro, Brazil. He began his career in Britain during the 1930s, making documentaries for the General Post Office, and later produced some notable films for Ealing Studios, including *Champagne Charlie* (1944), and *Nicholas Nickleby* (1947). In the early 1950s he returned to Brazil, and became a leading figure in the revival of Brazilian cinema. After 1954 he worked in Europe, eventually settling in France.

Cavalcanti, Guido [kavalkantee] (c. 1230–1300) Poet, born in Florence, Italy. He was a friend of Dante, and wrote about 50 poems in the 'new style' of the period. A member of the Papal Party (the Guelphs), he married the daughter of Farinata degli Uberti, the leader of the rival, Imperial Party (the Ghibellines), and was banished.

Cavalieri, (Francesco) Bonaventura [kavalyayree] (1598–1647) Mathematician, born in Milan, Italy. Professor at Bologna University, his 'method of indivisibles' began a new era in geometry and paved the way for the introduction of integral calculus.

Cavalieri, Emilio de' [kavalyayree] (c. 1550–1602) Composer, born in Rome. He lived mainly at the Florentine court of the Medici, where he was inspector general of arts. His dramatic works were forerunners of opera and oratorio.

Cavalli, (Pier) Francesco [kavalee], originally **Francesco Caletti-Bruni** (1602–76) Composer, who assumed the name of his patron, born in Crema, Italy. A pupil of Monteverdi, he was organist and *maestro di capella* of St Mark's in Venice. As an opera and church composer he prepared the way for Alessandro Scarlatti. >> Monteverdi; Scarlatti, Alessandro

Cavallini, Pietro [kavaleenee] (c. 1250–c. 1330) Painter and artist in mosaic, born in Rome. A contemporary of Giotto, whom he influenced, his best-known work is the series of mosaics in the Church of Santa Maria at Trastevere, Rome. >> Giotto

Cavell, Edith [kavel] (1865–1915) Nurse, born in Swardeston, Norfolk, E England, UK. She became a nurse in 1895, and matron of the Berkendael Medical Institute, Brussels, in 1907. She tended friend and foe alike in 1914–15, yet was executed by the Germans for helping Belgian and Allied fugitives to escape capture.

Cavendish >> **Jones, Henry**

Cavendish, Henry (1731–1810) Physicist and chemist, born in Nice, France. He studied at Cambridge, but left to devote himself to science after being bequeathed a fortune. In 1760 he studied the 'inflammable air', now known as hydrogen gas, and later ascertained that water resulted from the union of two gases. The *Cavendish experiment* was an ingenious means of estimating the density of the Earth.

Cavendish, Spencer Compton, 8th Duke of Devonshire (1833–1908), known as the **Marquess of Hartington** (1858–91) British statesman, born in Lower Holker, Lancashire, NW England, UK. He studied at Cambridge, entered parliament (1857), and between 1863 and 1874 was a Lord of the Admiralty, under-secretary for war, war secretary, postmaster-general, and chief secretary for Ireland. In 1875 he became Leader of the Liberal Opposition during Gladstone's temporary abdication, later serving under him as secretary of state for India (1880–2) and as war secretary (1882–5). He disapproved of Irish Home Rule, and having led the breakaway from the Liberal Party became head of the Liberal Unionists from 1886, serving in the Unionist government as Lord President of the Council (1895–1903). His younger brother, **Lord Frederick Cavendish** (1836–82), also a Liberal MP from 1865, was appointed chief secretary for Ireland, but immediately after his arrival in Dublin was murdered by 'Irish Invincibles' in Phoenix Park. >> Gladstone, W E

Cavendish, Sir Thomas (c. 1555–c. 1592) Navigator, and circumnavigator of the globe, born near Ipswich, Suffolk, E England, UK. He shared in Sir Richard Grenville's expedition to Virginia (1585). In 1586 he sailed with three ships for the Pacific, returning by the Cape of Good Hope to England in 1588, and was knighted. A second expedition (1591) ended in disaster, and he died off Ascension. >> Grenville, Richard

Cavendish, William, 4th Duke of Newcastle (1592–1676) English soldier and patron of the arts. He studied at Cambridge, was created Knight of the Bath (1610), Viscount Mansfield in 1620, and Earl (1628), Marquess (1643), and Duke (1665) of Newcastle. He gave strong support to Charles I in the Civil War, and was general of all forces north of the Trent. After Marston Moor (1644) he lived on the European mainland, at times in great poverty, until the Restoration. A noted patron of poets and playwrights, he was himself the author of several plays, and of two works on horsemanship. >> Charles I (of England)

Caventou, Joseph (Bienaimé) [kavatoo] (1795–1877) Chemist, born in St Omer, France. He became professor at the Ecole de Pharmacie, Paris. In 1817, in collaboration with Pierre Joseph Pelletier, he introduced the term *chlorophyll*. They also discovered quinine (1820), strychnine, brucine, and cinchonine. >> Pelletier

Cavour, Camillo Benso, conte di (Count of) [kavoor] (1810–61) Piedmontese statesman and premier (1852–9), who brought about the unification of Italy (1861), born in Turin, Italy. As premier, he greatly improved economic conditions, and brought the Italian question before the Congress of Paris. He resigned over the Peace of Villafranca (which left Venetia Austrian), but returned in 1860, and secretly encouraged the expedition of Garibaldi, which gained Sicily and S Italy. >> Victor Emmanuel II

Cawley, Yvonne (Fay), *née* **Goolagong** (1951–) Tennis player, born in Barellan, New South Wales, Australia, of Aboriginal descent. A popular and relaxed player, she won the Wimbledon singles championship in 1971, and made a comeback to win it again in 1981. She won the Australian Open four times, and many other championships during her career, including the Italian Open and the South African Open.

Caxton, William (c. 1422–c. 1491) The first English printer, born possibly in Tenterden, in the Weald of Kent, SE England, UK. He was trained in London as a cloth merchant, and lived in Bruges (1441–70). In Cologne he probably learned the art of printing (1471–2), and soon after printed the first book in English, *The Recuyell of the Historyes of Troye* (1473–4). About the end of 1476 he set up his wooden press at Westminster, and produced the *Dictes or Sayengis of the Philosophres* (1477), the first book printed in England. Of about 100 books printed by him, including the *Canterbury Tales*, over a third survive only in unique copies or fragments. >> Worde

Cayley, Arthur [kaylee] (1821–95) Mathematician, born in Richmond, SW Greater London, England, UK. He studied languages and mathematics at London and Cambridge, graduated with distinction, but on failing to find a position in mathematics, took up law and was called to the bar in 1849. In 1863 he became professor of pure mathematics at Cambridge. He originated the theory of invariants and covariants, and worked on the theories of matrices and analytical geometry, and on theoretical astronomy.

Cayley, Sir George [**kay**lee] (1771–1857) Pioneer of aviation, born in Scarborough, North Yorkshire, N England, UK. In 1808 he constructed and flew a glider, probably the first heavier-than-air machine, and made the first successful man-carrying glider (1853). He also interested himself in railway engineering, allotment agriculture, and land reclamation methods, and invented a new type of telescope, artificial limbs, the caterpillar tractor, and the tension wheel. He helped to found the Regent Street Polytechnic, London (1839).

Cazaly, Roy [ka**zay**lee] (1893–1963) Legendary Australian Rules footballer, born in Melbourne, Victoria, Australia. Leaping master of the high mark (jumping high in the air above other players to catch the ball), the call 'Up there Cazaly' was chanted by South Melbourne crowds and became a rallying cry for Australian troops in World War 2. A star player for St Kilda (1913–20), he was named Champion of the State in 1920, and transferred to South Melbourne in 1921 before moving to Tasmania.

Ceadda, St >> **Chad, St**

Ceauşescu, Nicolae [chow**shes**koo] (1918–1989) Romanian statesman and president (1967–89), born in Scornicești, Romania. He studied at Bucharest, joined the Communist Party at 15, and held several junior political posts before becoming President of the State Council (1967) and general secretary of the Romanian Communist Party (1969). Under his leadership, Romania became increasingly independent of the USSR, and for many years was the only Warsaw Pact country to have cordial relations with China. He became the first president of the Republic in 1974, and established a strong personality cult. His policy of replacing traditional villages by collectives of concrete apartments caused much controversy in the late 1980s. In 1989 he was deposed when the army joined a popular revolt against his repressive government. Following a trial by military tribunal, he and his wife, **Elena**, were shot. >> RR1084

Cecchetti, Enrico [che**ke**tee] (1850–1928) Dancer, teacher, and choreographer, born in Milan, Italy. After performing in Italy, London, and the USA, he settled in Russia (1887), first as dancer with the Imperial Ballet in St Petersburg (Leningrad), then as teacher. He was ballet master of Diaghilev's Ballet Russes for 15 years. Though he choreographed several works, he is remembered for the influential ballet technique he developed, which is still highly regarded today. >> Diaghilev

Cech, Thomas R [chek] (1947–) Biochemist, born in Chicago, IL. At the University of Colorado (1977–) he showed that RNA could have an independent catalytic function aiding a chemical reaction without being consumed or changed. This had major implications for genetic engineering, as well as for understanding how life arose. He and Sidney Altman shared the 1989 Nobel Prize for Chemistry. >> Altman

Cecil, Lord (Edward Christian) David (Gascoyne) [**se**sil] (1902–86) Literary critic, born in London, England, UK. He was professor of English literature at Oxford (1948–70), and is known chiefly as a literary biographer, in such works as *Sir Walter Scott* (1933), *Jane Austen* (1935), and *Thomas Hardy* (1943).

Cecil (of Chelwood), Robert Cecil, 1st Viscount [**se**sil] (1864–1958) Conservative statesman, born in London, England, UK, the son of Robert Cecil (3rd Marquess of

Salisbury). He studied at Oxford, was called to the bar (1887), and entered parliament in 1903. He was minister of blockade (1916–18), and president of the League of Nations Union (1923–45). He was awarded the Nobel Peace Prize in 1937. >> Cecil, Robert, 3rd Marquess of Salisbury

Cecil, Robert (Arthur Talbot Gascoyne), 3rd Marquess of Salisbury [**se**sil] (1830–1903) British statesman and prime minister (1885–6, 1886–92, 1895–1902), born in Hatfield, Hertfordshire, SE England, UK. He studied at Oxford, and became a Conservative MP in 1853. In 1865 he was made Viscount Cranborne, and in 1868 Marquess of Salisbury. He was twice Indian secretary (1866, 1874), became foreign secretary (1878), and on Disraeli's death (1881) was Leader of the Opposition. He was prime minister on three occasions, much of the time serving as his own foreign secretary. He resigned as foreign secretary in 1900, but remained as head of government during the Boer War (1899–1902). He retired in 1902. >> Cecil, Robert, 1st Viscount; Disraeli; RR1095

Cecil, Robert (Arthur James Gascoyne), 5th Marquess of Salisbury [**se**sil] (1893–1972) British statesman, born in Hatfield, Hertfordshire, SE England, UK. He studied at Oxford, and became Conservative MP for South Dorset in 1929, and in 1935 foreign under-secretary. In the Churchill government of 1940 he was paymaster general, and dominions secretary until 1941, when he was called to the Lords. He was colonial secretary and Lord Privy Seal, and in the Churchill government of 1951 became secretary of state for commonwealth relations and Lord President of the Council. From 1951 to 1957 he was Leader of the House of Lords. In 1957 he resigned the lord presidency in protest against the government's action in releasing Archbishop Makarios of Cyprus from his exile. >> Churchill, Sir Winston; Makarios III

Cecil, William, 1st Baron Burghley or **Burghleigh** [**se**sil] (1520–98) English statesmen, born in Bourn, Lincolnshire, EC England, UK. He studied at Cambridge and Gray's Inn, London, served under Somerset and Northumberland, became secretary of state (1550), and was knighted (1551). During Mary I's reign he conformed to Catholicism. In 1558 Elizabeth appointed him chief secretary of state, and for the next 40 years he was the chief architect of Elizabethan greatness, influencing her pro-Protestant foreign policy, securing the execution of Mary, Queen of Scots, and preparing for the Spanish Armada. He used an army of spies to ensure security at home. In 1571 he was created Baron Burghley, and in 1572 became Lord High Treasurer – an office he held until his death. >> Elizabeth I; Mary, Queen of Scots

Cecilia, St (2nd-c or 3rd-c) Christian martyr, and patron saint of music. According to tradition, she was a Roman maiden of patrician birth compelled to marry a young pagan, Valerian, despite a vow of celibacy. She succeeded in persuading him to respect her vow, and converted him to Christianity. They were both put to death for their faith. Later tradition made her a singer, hence her association with music-making. Feast day 22 November.

Cela, Camilo José [**the**la] (1916–) Writer, born in La Coruña, Spain. He studied at Madrid University, and served in Franco's forces during the Civil War. His first novel, *La familia de Pascual Duarte* (1942, The Family of Pascual Duarte), was banned for its seemingly gratuitous violence. The range of his work is vast and varied, but he is best known for *La Colmena* (1951, The Hive), which recreates daily life in Madrid in the aftermath of the Spanish Civil War. In 1989 he was awarded the Nobel Prize for Literature.

Celestine V, St, originally **Pietro di Morrone** (c. 1215–96) Pope, born in S Italy. After a long life of ascetic severities, he reluctantly accepted election as pope in 1294. He resigned his office after five months – the first pope to abdicate – for which Dante places him at the entrance of hell, and was imprisoned by his successor, Boniface VIII. He founded the *Celestines*, and was canonized in 1313; feast day 19 May. >> Boniface VIII

Céline, Louis-Ferdinand [sayleen], pseudonym of **Louis-Ferdinand Destouches** (1894–1961) Writer, born in Paris. He was invalided out of the army early in World War 1, travelled widely during the war years, then practised medicine. His reputation is based on the two autobiographical novels he wrote during the 1930s: *Voyage au bout de la nuit* (1932, Journey to the End of the Night) and *Mort à crédit* (1936, trans Death by Instalments). During World War 2 he collaborated with the Vichy government and, a declared anti-semite, fled to Germany and Denmark in 1944. He later returned to Paris.

Cellini, Benvenuto [cheleenee] (1500–71) Goldsmith, sculptor, engraver, and writer, born in Florence, Italy. He is particularly known for his autobiography (1558–62). By his own account, it seems he had no scruples about murdering or maiming his rivals, and at the siege of Rome (1527) he killed the Constable of Bourbon. He was several times imprisoned. His best work includes the gold saltcellar made for Francis I of France, and his bronze 'Perseus'. He lived at times in Rome, Mantua, Naples, and Florence. >> Bourbon; Leoni

Celsius, Anders [selsius] (1701–44) Astronomer, born in Uppsala, Sweden. He became professor at Uppsala (1730), and devised the centigrade scale (*Celsius scale*) of temperature in 1742. He advocated the introduction of the Gregorian calendar, and made observations of the aurora borealis. In 1740 he became director of the observatory at Uppsala that had been built in his honour.

Celsus, Aulus Cornelius [selsus] (1st-c) Roman writer. He compiled an encyclopedia on medicine, rhetoric, history, philosophy, war, and agriculture. The only extant portion of the work is the *De Medicina*, one of the first medical works to be printed (1478).

Cenci, Beatrice [chenchee] (1577–99) Noblewoman, born in Rome. Her story became the subject of many literary works, including a tragedy by Shelley (1819, *The Cenci*). She was the youngest daughter of a wealthy Roman nobleman, Count Francesco Cenci, who conceived an incestuous passion for her. With her stepmother and her brother, Giacomo, she plotted his murder in 1598. The Cenci family were arrested and tortured, and all three were beheaded, by order of Pope Clement VIII.

Cendrars, Blaise [sãdrah(r)], pseudonym of **Frédéric Louis Sauser** (1887–1961) Writer, poet, and traveller, born in Chaux-de-Fonds, Switzerland. When he was 15 he ran away from home to work for a jewel merchant with whom he travelled through Russia, Persia, and China. He wrote his first long poem in America, *Pâques à New York* (1912, Easter in New York). His novels include *La Confession de Dan Yack* (1927–29, trans Antarctic Fugue), and *L'Or* (1925, trans Sutter's Gold).

Cenni di Peppi >> **Cimabue**

Centlivre, Susannah [sentleever], *née* **Freeman** (c.1667–c.1723) Playwright, probably born in Holbeach, Lincolnshire, EC England, UK. She was first married at 16 and twice widowed. In 1700 she produced a tragedy, *The Perjured Husband*, and subsequently appeared on the stage in Bath in her own comedy, *Love at a Venture* (1706). In 1706 she married her third husband, **Joseph Centlivre**, head cook to Queen Anne at Windsor. Her 18 plays include *The Gamester* (1705) and *A Bold Stroke for a Wife* (1717).

Centlivres, Albert van de Sandt [sentleever] (1887–1966) Judge, born in Cape Town, South Africa. He studied at the South African College, and was a Rhodes Scholar at Oxford. He became a judge of the Cape provincial division of the Supreme Court of South Africa (1935), a judge of appeal (1939), and chief justice (1950–7). He played a substantial part in restoring Roman–Dutch law in South Africa.

Cerdic [chairdik] (?–534) Saxon leader who invaded Britain, landing in Hampshire with his son **Cynric** in 495. By 500 he had created the kingdom of Wessex for himself, and founded the West Saxon royal dynasty.

Čerenkov, Pavel Alekseyevich >> **Cherenkov, Pavel Alexeyevich**

Cerinthus [serinthus] (c. 100) Jewish Gnostic heretic, born in Alexandria. He is said to have lived in Ephesus contemporaneously with the aged apostle John. >> John, St

Cernan, Eugene (Andrew) [sernan] (1934–) Astronaut, born in Chicago, IL. A US navy officer (1956), he became a test pilot and went on to study aeronautical engineering at the Naval Postgraduate School, Monterey. He undertook astronaut training (1963) and was a crew member of several historic missions: Gemini 9 (1966), Apollo 10 (1969), and Apollo 17 (1972). He was involved in the Apollo–Soyuz Test Project (1975), later resigning from the navy to enter private business.

Cerrito, Fanny >> **Saint-Léon, Arthur**

Cerutty, Percy Wells [seruhtee] (1895–1975) Athletics coach and trainer, born in Prahan, Victoria, Australia. A childhood respiratory disease severely restricted his own athletic career, although in his middle 50s he became a noted distance runner. He was in charge of the Australian team at the 1952 Olympic Games in Helsinki. He coached John Landy (1930–), who recorded the second ever sub-four-minute mile (1954), and Herb Elliott, and pioneered such concepts as training over sand dunes and the idea of the 'pain barrier'. >> Elliott, Herb

Cervantes (Saavedra), Miguel de [servanteez], Span [thairvantes] (1547–1616) Writer of *Don Quixote*, born in Alcalá de Henares, Spain. His first major work was the *Galatea*, a pastoral romance (1585), and he wrote many plays, only two of which have survived. He became a tax collector in Granada (1594), but was imprisoned for failing to make up the sum due to the treasury. Tradition maintains that he wrote *Don Quixote* in prison at Argamasilla in La Mancha. When the book came out (1605), it was hugely popular. He wrote the second part in 1615, after several years of writing plays and short novels.

Césaire, Aimé (Fernand) [sayzair] (1913–) Poet, novelist, and Martinique politician, born in Basse-Pointe, Martinique. He studied there and in Paris, returning to Martinique as a teacher. The influential *Cahier d'un retour au pays natal* (1947, Notebook of a Return to my Native Land) records his conscious adoption of an African identity. This theme is returned to in later poems and plays, such as *Une saison au Congo* (1967, A Season in the Congo) and an African version of Shakespeare's *The Tempest* (1969). He has represented the progressive element in the politics of Martinique since 1945.

Cesalpino, Andrea [chezalpeenoh], Latin **Caesalpinus** (1519–1603) Botanist, anatomist, physician, and physiologist, born in Arezzo, Italy. He was professor of medicine and director of the botanic garden in Pisa (1553–92), then became physician to Pope Clement VIII. He propounded a theory of the circulation of the blood that pre-dated the work of Harvey, and initiated scientific plant classification based on methods suggested by Theophrastus. He was the author of *De plantis* (1583), the first textbook establishing botany as a scientific subject. >> Harvey, William; Theophrastus

Cesari, Giuseppe [chayzaree], known as **Il Cavaliere d'Arpino** (the Cavalier of Arpino) (c. 1568–c. 1640) Painter, born in

Arpino, Italy. Honoured by five popes, he is best known for the frescoes in the Capitol at Rome.

Céspedes, Pablo de [**thays**pethayz] (1538–1608) Painter, born in Córdoba, Spain. He studied at Rome under Michelangelo and Raphael. In 1577 he became a canon at Córdoba, where he established a school of art, and was also active as an architect and writer. He painted the 'Last Supper' in Córdoba cathedral. >> Michelangelo; Raphael

Cessna, Clyde (Vernon) [**ses**na] (1879–1954) Aviator, born in Hawthorne, LA. After developing a simply designed monoplane with the innovatory cantilever wing (1917), he partnered businessman Victor Roos and produced Cessna–Roos aircraft. Cessna became sole owner (1927) and founded the successful Cessna Aircraft Company, mass-producing modern, multi-purpose planes.

Cetewayo or **Cetshwayo** [kete**way**oh] (c. 1826–84) Ruler of Zululand from 1873, born near Eshowe, South Africa. In 1879 he defeated the British at Isandhlwana, but was himself defeated at Ulundi. He presented his case in London, and in 1883 was restored to part of his kingdom, but soon after was driven out by an anti-royalist faction.

Cetti, Francesco [**che**tee] (1726–78) Jesuit and naturalist, born in Mannheim, Germany. He was educated in Lombardy and at the Jesuit College in Monza, and in 1766 was appointed professor of mathematics at the university of Sassari. He was a distinguished naturalist as well as a theologian and philosopher. The bird *Cetti's warbler* (*Cettia cetti*) was named after him.

Ceulen, Ludolph van [**koe**len] (1540–1610) Mathematician, born in Hildesheim, Germany. He devoted himself to finding the value of π and finally worked it out to 35 decimal places (*Ludolph's number*). It was inscribed on his tombstone at Leyden.

Ceva, Giovanni [**chay**va] (?1647–1734) Geometer, born in Milan, Italy. He gave his name to a theorem on concurrent lines through the vertices of a triangle.

Cézanne, Paul [**sayzan**] (1839–1906) Postimpressionist painter, born in Aix-en-Provence, France. He studied law at Aix, then was persuaded by his friend Emile Zola to go to Paris (1862), where he began to paint. He was influenced by Pissarro, with whom he worked at Auvers and Pontoise (1872–3). He abandoned his early sombre Expressionism for the study of nature, and began to use his characteristic glowing colours. In his later period (after 1886), he emphasized the underlying forms of nature – 'the cylinder, the sphere, the cone' – by constructing his pictures from a rhythmic series of coloured planes, thus becoming the forerunner of Cubism. He obtained recognition only in the last years of his life. Among his best-known paintings are 'L'Estaque' (c.1888, Musée d'Orsay, Paris), 'The Card Players' (1890–2, Musée d'Orsay, Paris), and 'The Gardener' (1906, Tate, London). Picasso called him 'the father of us all'. >> Pissarro; Zola

Chaban-Delmas, Jacques (-Pierre-Michel) [shabã delmas], originally **Jacques Delmas** (1915–) French statesman and prime minister (1969–72), born in Paris. He studied political science and law, and worked as a journalist before joining the army (1938). An active member of the Resistance, he began work as liaison officer for the Free French government (1943), being promoted to general in 1944. He later added his Resistance code-name *Chaban* to his surname. With the establishment of the Gaullist Party (1947) he became a leading left-wing figure, and held a series of Cabinet posts before becoming President of the National Assembly (1958–69). He was appointed premier under President Pompidou, after which he was made inspector-general of finances (1973), and served again as President of the National Assembly (1978–81 and 1986–8). >> Pompidou; RR1049

Chabaneau, François [shabanoh] (1754–1842) Chemist, born in Nontron, France. Professor of mathematics at Passy when only 17, he turned to the study of physics and chemistry. Later he became professor of mineralogy, physics, and chemistry at Madrid, where he carried out the research on platinum which resulted in an ingot of malleable platinum (1783).

Chabrier, (Alexis) Emmanuel [shabreeyay] (1841–94) Composer, born in Ambert, France. He studied law in Paris, and devoted himself to music in 1879 after hearing Wagner's *Tristan und Isolde*. He wrote operas, piano works, and songs, but his best-known pieces were inspired by the folk music of Spain, notably his orchestral rhapsody *España* (1883). >> Wagner, Richard

Chabrol, Claude [shabrol] (1930–) Film critic and director, born in Paris. He financed his own first production *Le Beau Serge* (1958, Handsome Serge), and with *Les Cousins* (1959) became identified with the French *Nouvelle Vague*, a style which had become more publicly acceptable when he produced *Les Biches* (1968, The Does). His most widely-known films are dramas of abnormality in the provincial bourgeoisie, notably *Le Boucher* (1970, The Butcher), *Les Noces rouges* (1973, Red Wedding), and *Inspector Lavardin* (1986). Later films include *L'Enfer* (1993, Torment).

Chad, St, Old English **Ceadda** (?–672) Anglo-Saxon clergyman, born in Northumberland, NE England, UK. A pupil of St Aidan in Lindisfarne, he spent part of his youth in Ireland, became Abbot of Lastingham (664), and Bishop of York (666). Doubt having been cast on the validity of his consecration, he withdrew in 669, but was immediately made Bishop of Mercia, fixing the see at Lichfield. Feast day 2 March. >> Aidan

Chadli, Benjedid [**chad**lee] (1929–) Algerian soldier and president (1978–92), born in Sebaa, Algeria. In 1955 he joined the guerrillas who were fighting for independence as part of the National Liberation Front (FLN). Under Houari Boumédienne, defence minister in Ben Bella's government, he was military commander of Algiers, and when Boumédienne overthrew Ben Bella in 1965 he joined the Revolutionary Council. He succeeded Boumédienne as secretary-general of the FLN and president, but was forced to resign by the army in 1992. >> Ben Bella; Boumédienne; RR1031

Chadwick, Sir James (1891–1974) Physicist, born in Manchester, Greater Manchester, NW England, UK. He studied at Cambridge, and in Berlin under Geiger. He then worked at the Cavendish Laboratory with Rutherford, investigating the structure of the atom, and discovered the neutron, for which he received the Nobel Prize for Physics in 1935. He led the UK's work on the atomic bomb in World War 2, and was knighted in 1945. >> Geiger; Rutherford, Ernest

Chadwick, Lynn (Russell) (1914–) Sculptor, born in London, England, UK. He studied architecture, but after war service began making mobiles (c.1946), then rough-finished solid metal sculptures. In 1956 he won the International Sculpture Prize at the Venice Biennale.

Chadwick, Roy (1893–1947) Aeronautical engineer, born in Farnworth, Greater Manchester, NW England, UK. He studied at the Manchester College of Technology, and joined the AVRO company in 1911, designing and manufacturing aeroplanes. During World War 1 he designed many famous types, including the Avro 504 trainer, and in World War 2 produced the Manchester and Lancaster heavy bombers. Following the war he designed the jetpropelled Tudor and Ashton. He was killed in a test flight of the Tudor II prototype.

Chagall, Marc [sha**gal**] (1887–1985) Artist, born in Vitebsk, Belarus. He studied at St Petersburg and Paris, left Russia in 1922, and settled near Paris. During World War 2 he moved to the USA, where he began to design ballet sets and costumes. He illustrated several books, but is best known for his paintings of animals, objects, and people from his life, dreams, and Russian folklore. The word *Surrealist* is said to have been coined by Apollinaire to describe the work of Chagall. >> Apollinaire

Chagas, Carlos Ribeiro Justiniano [**shah**gas] (1879–1934) Physician and microbiologist, born in Oliveira, Brazil. He studied at the Medical School of Rio de Janeiro, where he was introduced to the concepts and techniques of bacteriology and scientific medicine. He joined the Instituto Oswaldo Cruz, working on malaria prevention. During one of his field missions, he first described a disease caused by a trypanosome, since named after him (*Chagas' disease*).

Chaikin, Joseph [**chiy**kin] (1935–) Actor and theatre director, born in New York City. His early work as an actor was with the Living Theater, notably in *The Connection* (1960) and *Man is Man* (1962). In 1963 he founded The Open Theater, which for a decade produced some of the most original work in the US theatre, such as *America Hurrah* (1965), *Terminal* (1969), and *Nightwalk* (1973). He suffered a stroke in 1984 but went on to co-write *The War in Heaven* (1991) with Sam Shepard.

Chain, Sir Ernst Boris [chayn] (1906–79) Biochemist, born in Berlin. After studying physiology and chemistry in Berlin, he fled from Nazi Germany to Britain, where he taught at Cambridge (1933–5) and Oxford (1935–48). With Sir Howard Florey at Oxford he was a key figure in the successful isolation of penicillin (discovered earlier by Sir Alexander Fleming), and all three shared the 1945 Nobel Prize for Physiology or Medicine. He was director of the International Research Centre for Chemical Microbiology in Rome (1948–61), and professor of biochemistry at Imperial College, London (1961–73). He was knighted in 1970. >> Fleming, Alexander; Florey

Chaliapin >> **Shalyapin, Fyodor Ivanovich**

Challender, Stuart (1947–91) Conductor, born in Hobart, Tasmania, Australia. He studied at the Melbourne Conservatory, and became music director of the Victoria Opera in 1968. In 1977 he went to Europe, conducting a wide range of operatic repertoire in Basel, Nuremberg, and Zürich. In 1980 he returned to Australia to become resident conductor of the Australian Opera, and in 1987 became chief conductor and artistic director of the Sydney Symphony Orchestra. He appeared as guest conductor for various orchestras, including the Chicago Symphony and the English National Opera. In 1991 he publicly announced that he had AIDS, but worked to the end of his life, conducting masterful performances of Strauss's *Der Rosenkavalier*.

Challoner, Richard [**cha**loner] (1691–1781) Roman Catholic clergyman and writer, born in Lewes, East Sussex, SE England, UK. He studied at Douai (1704) and was ordained in 1716, remaining there as a professor until 1730. He then served as a missionary priest in London, becoming Bishop of Debra (1741) and Vicar Apostolic of the London district (1758). His best-known works are the prayer book, *The Garden of the Soul* (1740), and his revision of the Douai version of the Bible (5 vols, 1750).

Chalmers, James (1782–1853) Bookseller and inventor, born in Arbroath, Angus, E Scotland, UK. A bookseller and newspaper publisher in Dundee, he advocated faster mail services in 1825, and is one of several candidates cited as the inventor of adhesive postage stamps.

Chalmers, Judith (1937–) British television presenter. She studied in Manchester and the London Academy of Music and Dramatic Art, then began broadcasting with BBC Manchester, moving to BBC London in 1960. In 1972 she joined Thames Television, where she presented the long-running holiday programme *Wish You Were Here...?* (1973–). She hosted her own daily programme for Radio 2 (1990), and has been commentator for many royal and state occasions.

Chalmers, Thomas (1780–1847) Theologian and reformer, born in Anstruther, Fife, E Scotland, UK. He studied at St Andrews, was ordained in 1803, and became a minister in Glasgow (1815), where his oratory took the city by storm. He became professor of moral philosophy at St Andrews (1823), and of theology at Edinburgh (1827). In the Disruption of 1843 he led 470 ministers out of the Established Church of Scotland to found the Free Church of Scotland.

Chamberlain, Sir (Joseph) Austen (1863–1937) British statesman, born in Birmingham, West Midlands, C England, UK, the eldest son of Joseph Chamberlain. He studied at Cambridge, was elected a Liberal Unionist MP (1892), and sat as a Conservative MP until his death. He was Chancellor of the Exchequer (1903–6, 1919–21), secretary for India (1915–17), Unionist leader (1921–2), foreign secretary (1924–9), and First Lord of the Admiralty (1931). He shared the 1925 Nobel Peace Prize for negotiating the Locarno Pact. >> Chamberlain, Joseph; RR1125

Chamberlain, Joseph (1836–1914) British statesman, born in London, England, UK. He entered the family business at 16, became Mayor of Birmingham (1873–5), and a Liberal MP (1876). He became President of the Board of Trade (1880), but resigned over Gladstone's Home Rule Bill (1886), which split the Liberal Party. From 1889 he was leader of the Liberal Unionists, and in the coalition government of 1895 took office as secretary for the Colonies. In 1903 he resigned office to be free to advocate his ideas on tariff reform, and in 1906 withdrew from public life after a stroke. >> Chamberlain, Austen; Chamberlain, Neville; Gladstone, W E

Chamberlain, Lindy (Alice Lynne) (1948–) Mother of the 'dingo baby', born in Whakatane, New Zealand. The disappearance of her nine-week-old daughter, Azaria, at Uluru (Ayers Rock), in 1980, made her the subject of national obsession in Australia. Married to pastor **Michael Chamberlain** (who was tried with her, and whom she has since divorced), she claimed the baby was taken by a dingo. She was found guilty of murder, and gaoled, but released in 1986 when a baby's jacket was found at the base of the rock. A judicial inquiry found that forensic evidence used in the 1982 trial was unreliable, and that the dingo story was probably correct. In 1988 the Northern Territory Court of Criminal Appeal quashed all convictions against the couple, and they received A$1 million in compensation. The saga is recounted in John Bryson's *Evil Angels* (1985), and was later filmed, and her autobiography *Through My Eyes* appeared in 1990.

Chamberlain, (Arthur) Neville (1869–1940) British statesman and prime minister (1937–40), born in Birmingham, West Midlands, C England, UK, the son of Joseph Chamberlain by his second marriage. He studied at Rugby and Birmingham, was Mayor of Birmingham (1915–16), a Conservative MP from 1918, Chancellor of the Exchequer (1923–4, 1931–7), and three times minister for health (1923, 1924–9, 1931). He played a leading part in the formation of the National Government (1931). As prime minister, he advocated 'appeasement' of Italy and Germany, returning from Munich with his claim to have found 'peace for our time' (1938). Criticism of his war leadership and initial military reverses led to his resignation as prime minister (1940), and his appointment as Lord President of the Council. >> Chamberlain, Joseph; Runciman; RR1095

Chamberlain, Owen (1920–) Physicist, born in San Francisco, CA. He worked on the Manhattan atomic bomb project (1942–6) and at the Argonne National Laboratory, then became a professor at the University of California, Berkeley. In 1959 he was awarded the Nobel Prize for Physics jointly with his colleague Emilio Segrè for research on the antiproton. >> Segrè

Chamberlain, Wilt(on) Norman, nickname **Wilt the Stilt** (1936–) Basketball player, born in Philadelphia, PA. He studied at Kansas University. Height 1·85 m/7 ft 1 in, he played for the Philadelphia 76ers against the New York Knickerbockers in 1962, and scored 100 points in one game, a National Basketball Association (NBA) record. He scored a record 4029 points that season, and was seven times the NBA leading scorer (1960–6). During his career (1960–73) he scored 31 419 points at an average of 30·1 per game. He had a brief spell playing for the Harlem Globetrotters. >> RR1146

Chamberlin, Edward Hastings (1899–1967) Economist, born in La Couner, WA. He studied at Harvard, and taught there until his death. His *Theory of Monopolistic Competition* (1933), a market analysis that incorporates such factors as advertising, product differentiation, style and brand preference, and locational advantages, is regarded as one of the most influential books of 20th-c economics. A collection of his other papers, *Towards a More General Theory of Value*, was published in 1957.

Chamberlin, Thomas (Chrowder) (1843–1928) Geologist, born in Mattoon, IL. He studied at Beloit College, where he became professor of geology (1872–82), He was chief geologist of the Wisconsin Geological Survey and later professor of geology at Chicago (1892–1918). His best-known work was in connection with the fundamental geology of the Solar System.

Chambers, Sir E(dmund) K(erchever) (1866–1954) Scholar and literary critic, born in Berkshire, S England, UK. He studied at Oxford, and was a civil servant with the Board of Education (1892–1926). His books include *The Elizabethan Stage* (1923) and *William Shakespeare* (1930).

Chambers, Ephraim (c. 1680–1740) Encyclopedist, born in Kendal, Cumbria, NW England, UK. While apprenticed to a globemaker in London he conceived the idea of a *Cyclopaedia, or Universal Dictionary of Arts and Sciences* (2 folio vols, 1728). A French translation inspired Diderot's *Encyclopédie*. >> Diderot

Chambers, John Graham (1843–83) Sportsman and journalist, born in Llanelli, Carmarthenshire, SW Wales, UK. A champion walker and oarsman, he founded the Amateur Athletic Club in 1866, and drew up the rules for amateur athletic competitions. In 1867 he drew up the rules for boxing, promulgated under the aegis of the 8th Marquess of Queensberry. >> Queensberry

Chambers, R(aymond) W(ilson) (1874–1942) British scholar and literary critic. He studied at University College, London, where he became professor of English language and literature (1922–41). His works include studies of *Widsith* and *Beowulf*, and an influential essay on *The Continuity of English Prose* (1932).

Chambers, Robert (1802–71) Publisher and writer, born in Peebles, Scottish Borders, SE Scotland, UK, the brother of William Chambers. He began as a bookseller in Edinburgh (1818), and gave his leisure to literary composition, writing many books on Scottish history, people, and institutions, and contributing regularly to *Chambers's Edinburgh Journal*. His son **Robert Chambers** (1832–88) became head of the firm in 1883, and conducted the *Journal* until his death. >> Chambers, William

Chambers, Whittaker, originally **Jay Vivian Chambers** (1910–61) Journalist, writer, and Soviet agent, born in Philadelphia, PA. He studied at Columbia University, gained a modest reputation as a writer, and later translated several works, notably *Bambi*, into English. He was an active US Communist (1925–9, 1931–8), writing for the *Daily Worker* and editing the *New Masses*. Along the way he became an actual agent of Soviet intelligence, and passed classified government information to Moscow. Disillusioned by Stalin's purges, he became a virulent anti-Communist and edited *Time* magazine's foreign affairs section. In 1948, he testified that many executive branch officials were Communist sympathizers, and said that Alger Hiss had given him classified materials; this brought about a libel suit by Hiss, who was found guilty. The Hiss–Chambers trial remains a symbol of the whole era that extended from the idealism of communism in the 1930s to the disillusionment of the late 1940s. >> Hiss, Alger

Chambers, Sir William (1726–96) Architect, born of Scottish ancestry in Göteborg, Sweden. He studied in Italy and France and practised in England, becoming a leading architect in the Palladian style. His works include Somerset House (1776) and the pagoda in Kew Gardens. He was knighted in 1770.

Chambers, William (1800–83) Publisher and writer, born in Peebles, Scottish Borders, SE Scotland, UK. He was apprenticed to a bookseller in Edinburgh (1814), and in 1819 went into business for himself. In 1832 he started *Chambers's Edinburgh Journal*, and soon after united with his brother Robert Chambers in founding the printing and publishing firm of W & R Chambers. As Lord Provost of Edinburgh (1865–9), he promoted a successful scheme for improving the older part of the city. Shortly before his death he received the offer of a baronetcy. >> Chambers, Robert

Chamfort, Sébastien Roch Nicolas [shãfaw(r)] (c.1741–94) Writer, born in Clermont, France. He made an entrance into the literary circles of Paris, and lived for years by his wit, writing tales, dramas, and maxims, many of which were widely circulated at the time. He joined the Jacobins at the outbreak of the French Revolution (1789), but his remarks on the Terror brought him into disfavour. Threatened with arrest, he tried to commit suicide, and died after several days' suffering.

Chamisso, Adelbert von [shameesoh], originally **Louis Charles Adelaide Chamisso de Boncourt** (1781–1838) Poet and biologist, born in Champagne, France. The French Revolution drove his parents to Prussia, and he served in the Prussian army (1798–1807). In Geneva he joined the literary circle of Madame de Staël and later studied at Berlin. He accompanied a Russian exploring expedition round the world as naturalist (1815–18), and on his return was appointed keeper of the Botanical Garden of Berlin. In 1819 he was the first to discover in certain animals what he called 'alternation of generations'. He is best known for his fairy tale *Peter Schlemihl* (1813), the story of the man who lost his shadow. >> Staël

Champaigne, Philippe de [shãpen] (1602–74) Painter of portraits and religious subjects, born in Brussels. After moving to Paris in 1621 he assisted with decorations for the Luxembourg palace with Nicholas Poussin, and in 1628 was appointed painter to Marie de Médicis. His works include many portraits, notably his triple portrait of Cardinal Richelieu. After 1647 he began to associate with the Jansenists, after which his work becomes more austere. >> Marie de Médicis; Poussin

Champlain, Samuel de [shãplĩ] (1567–1635) Governor of Canada, born in Brouage, France. In a series of voyages he travelled to Canada (1603), exploring the E coast (1604–7), and founding Quebec (1608). He was appointed Lieutenant of Canada (1612), and established alliances with several

Indian nations. When Quebec fell briefly to the British, he was taken prisoner (1629–32). From 1633 he was Governor of Quebec. L Champlain is named after him.

Champollion, Jean François [shăpolyŏ] (1790–1832) Founder of Egyptology, born in Figeac, France. He studied at Grenoble, and went to Paris (1807), subsequently becoming professor of history at Grenoble (1809–16). Best known for his use of the Rosetta Stone to decipher Egyptian hieroglyphics (1822–4), he was the first to place the study of early Egyptian history and culture on a firm footing. In 1831 a chair of Egyptology was founded for him at the Collège de France.

Chance, Britton (1913–) Biophysicist and biochemist, born in Wilkes-Barre, PA. He studied at Pennsylvania University and became professor of biophysics there in 1949. He invented many automatic control systems, precision-timing circuits, and optical instruments used for radar and shipping in World War 2. His best-known work is his demonstration in 1943 of the existence of the complex formed between an enzyme and its substrate. He did valuable work on problems of energy generation in biological cells.

Chancellor, Richard (?–1556) English seaman, chosen in 1553 as 'pilot-general' of Sir Hugh Willoughby's expedition in search of a Northeast Passage to India. The ships were parted in a storm, and Chancellor proceeded alone into the White Sea, travelling overland to Moscow, where he concluded a treaty giving freedom of trade to English ships. In 1555 he made a second voyage to Moscow, but was lost at sea on the way home.

Chandler, Happy, popular name of **Albert Benjamin Chandler** (1898–1991) Public official and baseball commissioner, born in Corydon, KY. He served as Governor of Kentucky (1935–9) and a Democratic US senator (1939–45) before being named as baseball's second commissioner (1945–51). He presided over the game during the breaking of baseball's colour line by Jackie Robinson in 1947. He was known as a 'players' commissioner' because he took an interest in all aspects of the game. He served a second term as Governor of Kentucky (1955–9), and in 1982 was elected to baseball's Hall of Fame. >> Robinson, Jackie

Chandler, Raymond (Thornton) (1888–1959) Writer, born in Chicago, IL. He studied in England, France, and Germany, then worked as a freelance writer in London. In World War 1 he served in the Canadian army in France and in the Royal Flying Corps. During the Depression he began to write short stories and novelettes for the detective-story pulp magazines of the day, later turning to 'private-eye' novels, such as *The Big Sleep* (1939) and *Farewell, My Lovely* (1940), several of which were filmed. He is the creator of the cynical but honest detective antihero, Philip Marlowe.

Chandos, Oliver Lyttelton Chandos, 1st Viscount [chandos] (1893–1972) British statesman and industrialist. He studied at Cambridge, and by 1928 was managing director of the British Metal Corporation. In 1940 he became MP for Aldershot, and President of the Board of Trade. When the Conservatives were returned to office in 1951 he went to the colonial office until his resignation from politics to return to business in 1954, when he was raised to the peerage. He played a leading part in drawing up plans of constitutional reform for many of the African colonial territories.

Chandragupta II [chandragupta], also known as **Vikramaditya** (Sanskrit 'sun of valour') (4th-c) Indian emperor (c.380–c.415), the third of the imperial Guptas of N India. He extended control over his neighbours by both military and peaceful means. A devout Hindu, he tolerated Buddhism and Jainism, and patronized learning.

During his reign, art, architecture, and sculpture flourished, and the cultural development of ancient India reached its climax. >> RR1058

Chandrasekhar, Subrahmanyan [chandrasayker] (1910–95) Astrophysicist, born in Lahore, Pakistan (formerly, India). He studied at the Presidency College, Madras, before going to Cambridge University. In 1936 he went to America and worked at the University of Chicago and the Yerkes Observatory, becoming a US citizen in 1953. He studied the final stages of stellar evolution, showing that the final fate of a star (as a supernova or as a white dwarf), depends on its mass. Massive stars will be unable to evolve into white dwarfs, and this limiting stellar mass (about 1·4 solar masses) is called the *Chandrasekhar limit*. He was awarded the Nobel Prize for Physics in 1983.

Chanel, Coco [shanel], popular name of **Gabrielle Chanel** (?1883–1971) Fashion designer, born in Saumur, France. She worked as a milliner until 1912, and after World War 1 opened a couture house in Paris. She revolutionized women's fashions during the 1920s, her designs including the 'chemise' dress and the collarless cardigan jacket. Many of the features she introduced, such as the vogue for costume jewellery and the evening scarf, still retain their popularity. She retired in 1938, but made a surprisingly successful come-back in 1954.

Chaney, Lon [chaynee], originally **Alonso Chaney** (1883–1930) Film actor, born in Colorado Springs, CO. He was famous for spine-chilling deformed villains and other horrific parts, as in *The Hunchback of Notre Dame* (1923) and *The Phantom of the Opera* (1925), and came to be called 'the man of a thousand faces'. His son, **Lon Chaney, Jr** (1907–73), was also an actor in horror films, and starred in a film version of Steinbeck's *Of Mice and Men* (1939).

Chang, M(in)-C(hueh) (1909–91) Reproductive biologist, born in Taiyuan, China. He emigrated to England to study animal husbandry at Cambridge and Edinburgh, and worked on artificial insemination. In 1945 he joined the staff of the Worcester Foundation for Experimental Biology in Worcester, MA, collaborating with Gregory Pincus and John Rock on the creation of an oral contraceptive for women. The birth control pill was ready for human testing by 1956, and was marketed as Enovid in 1960. He is also credited with being the discoverer of *in vitro* fertilization from work conducted in the 1950s, as well as a process known as the capacitation of sperm. >> Pincus

Chang Kuo-t'ao >> **Zhang Guotao**

Channing, William (Ellery) (1780–1842) Clergyman and writer, born in Newport, RI. He studied at Harvard, and in 1803 was ordained to the Congregational Federal Street Church in Boston. He ultimately became the leader of the Unitarians, and was widely known for his essays.

Chaplin, Charlie, popular name of **Sir Charles Spencer Chaplin** (1889–1977) Film actor and director, born in London, England, UK. His skill in comedy developed under Fred Karno, with whom he went to Hollywood in 1914. In his early comedies he adopted the bowler hat, out-turned feet, moustache, and walking-cane which became his hallmark, as in *The Kid*, *The Gold Rush*, and many others. His art was essentially suited to the silent film, and when sound arrived he experimented with new forms, as in *City Lights* (1931), with music only, and *Modern Times* (1936), part speech and part mime. His first sound film was *The Great Dictator* (1940). In *Limelight* (1952) he acted, directed, and composed the music and dances. His left-wing sympathies caused him to leave the USA for Switzerland in 1952. He was married four times, was awarded an Oscar in 1972, and was knighted in 1975.

Chapman, George (c.1559–1634) Poet and playwright, born near Hitchin, Hertfordshire, SE England, UK. He studied at Oxford, then worked in London. He is best known for his translations of Homer's *Iliad* (1598–1611) and *Odyssey* (1616), followed by the minor works (c.1624). He joined Jonson and Marston in the composition of *Eastward Ho* (1605), and in 1607 *Bussy d'Ambois* appeared, which had a sequel in 1613. >> Jonson; Marston

Chapman, Mark (David) (c. 1955–) US convicted murderer. A security guard from Hawaii, he shot and killed former Beatles member John Lennon outside Lennon's apartment in Manhattan (8 Dec 1980). Much attention was paid at Chapman's trial to his psychiatric state, as his lawyer initially entered a plea of insanity which Chapman later overturned with a plea of guilty. He was found guilty of murder, sentenced to life imprisonment, and ordered to receive psychiatric treatment. >> Lennon

Chapman, Sydney (1888–1970) Applied mathematician and geophysicist, born in Eccles, Lancashire, NW England, UK. He studied engineering at Manchester, and mathematics at Cambridge, and was professor at Manchester (1919–24), Imperial College, London (1924–46), and Oxford (1946–53). From 1954 he worked at the High Altitude Observatory at Boulder, CO, and the Geophysical Institute in Alaska. He made a major contribution to the kinetic theory of gases, and developed the theory of thermal diffusion. He also developed theories on geomagnetism, atmospheric tides, and geomagnetic storms.

Chappe, Claude [shap] (1763–1805) Engineer and inventor, born in Brulon, France. He was studying for a career in the Church, but his plans were altered with the French Revolution, and he decided instead to develop his interest in telegraphy. In 1793 he developed a hand-operated semaphore system, operating in towers built on high ground, equipped with two movable signal-arms, and telescopes. The system was soon copied throughout Europe.

Chappell, Greg(ory Stephen) (1948–) Cricketer, born in Unley, South Australia, the brother of Ian Chappell. He played 88 times for his country (1970–84), 48 as captain, and scored 24 Test centuries. He also played in England for Somerset for two years. >> Chappell, Ian; RR1149

Chappell, Ian (Michael) (1943–) Cricketer, born in Unley, South Australia, the brother of Greg Chappell. He played 75 times for Australia (1976–80), scoring over 5000 runs and 14 Test centuries. His pugnacious, driving style of captaincy made Australia a side universally respected in the 1970s. He is now a well-known sports commentator. >> Chappell, Greg

Chappell, William (1809–88) British antiquary, a member of a great London music publishing house. His *Collection of National English Airs* (2 vols, 1838–40) grew into *Popular Music of the Olden Time* (2 vols, 1855–9). He took a principal part in the foundation of the Musical Antiquarian Society (1840), the Percy Society, and the Ballad Society (1868).

Charcot, Jean Baptiste (Etienne Auguste) [shah(r)koh] (1867–1936) Explorer, born in Neuilly, France, the son of Jean Martin Charcot. A doctor, he commanded two Antarctic expeditions in the *Français* (1903–5) and *Pourquoi Pas?* (1908–1910), and after World War 1 carried out hydrographic surveys off Greenland. He later went down with the *Pourquoi Pas?* off Iceland. >> Charcot, Jean

Charcot, Jean Martin [shah(r)koh] (1825–93) Pathologist, one of the founders of neurology, born in Paris. He worked at the Salpêtrière, and had Freud among his pupils. He contributed much to the knowledge of chronic and nervous diseases, and made hypnotism a scientific study. The way joints deteriorate in some types of nervous disease was named after him (*Charcot's joint*). >> Freud, Sigmund

Chardin, Jean Baptiste Siméon [shah(r)dĩ] (1699–1779) Painter, born in Paris. He was selected to assist in the restoration of the royal paintings at Fontainebleau, and later attracted attention as a signpainter. He emerged as a genre painter, and produced many pictures of peasant life and domestic scenes, notably 'Bénédicité' (1740, Louvre, The Grace).

Chardin, Pierre Teilhard de >> **Teilhard de Chardin, Pierre**

Chardonne, Jacques [shah(r)don], pseudonym of **Jacques Boutelleau** (1884–1968) Writer, born in Barbezieux, France. He wrote domestic novels mainly set in his native Charente, among them *Claire* (1931) and *Romanesques* (1937). He also wrote essays and a chronicle of the French collapse in 1940.

Chardonnet, (Louis Marie) Hilaire Berignaud, comte de (Count of) [shah(r)donay] (1839–1924) Chemist, born in Besançon, France. He trained as a civil engineer, and by 1878 was working on artificial fibres. He became a pioneer of the artificial-silk (rayon) industry.

Chargaff, Erwin [chah(r)gaf] (1905–) Biochemist, born in Czernowitz, Czech Republic. He studied at Vienna, Yale, Berlin, and Paris, and worked at Columbia University, New York City, from 1935. His pioneer work on nucleic acids showed that the DNA of an organism has a composition characteristic of the organism; and his work on the ratio of bases present in DNA (the *Chargaff rules*) provided a fundamental contribution to the double helix structure for DNA advanced in 1953.

Charlemagne or **Charles the Great** [shah(r)luhmayn] (742–814) King of the Franks (771–814), and emperor of the West (800–14), the eldest son of Pepin the Short. He defeated the Saxons (772–804) and the Lombards (773–4), fought the Arabs in Spain, and took control of most of Christian W Europe. In 800 he was crowned emperor by Pope Leo III. In his later years he consolidated his vast empire, building palaces and churches, and promoting Christianity, education, agriculture, the arts, manufacture, and commerce, so much so that the period has become known as the *Carolingian Renaissance*. His reign was an attempt to consolidate order and Christian culture among the nations of the West, but his empire did not long survive his death, for his sons lacked both his vision and authority. >> Louis I; Pepin III; RR1049

Charles I, (of Austria–Hungary) (1887–1922) Emperor of Austria (1916–18, as **Karl I**) and king of Hungary (1916–19, as **Károly IV**), born at Persenbeug Castle, Austria. The last of the Habsburg emperors, he succeeded his grand-uncle, Francis Joseph, in 1916, and became heir presumptive on the assassination at Sarajevo (1914) of his uncle, Archduke Francis Ferdinand. In 1919 he was deposed by the Austrian parliament and exiled to Switzerland. Two attempts to regain his Hungarian throne in 1921 failed. >> RR1033

Charles I (of England) (1600–49) King of Britain and Ireland (1625–49), born in Dunfermline, Fife, E Scotland, UK, the second son of **James I**. He failed in his bid to marry the infanta Maria of Spain (1623), marrying instead the French princess, **Henrietta Maria**, and thus disturbing the nation, for the marriage articles permitted her the free exercise of the Catholic religion. Three parliaments were summoned and dissolved in the first four years of his reign; then for 11 years he ruled without one, using instead judges and prerogative courts. He warred with France (1627–9), and in 1630 made peace with Spain, but his continuing zeal for money led to unpopular economic policies. His attempt to anglicize the Scottish Church brought active resistance (1639), and he then called a parliament (1640). In 1642, having alienated much of the realm, he entered into the Civil War, which saw the annihilation of his cause at Naseby (14 Jun 1645), and his surrender to the Scots at Newark (1646). After many negotiations, during which his attempts at duplicity exasperated opponents, and a second Civil War (1646-8), he came to trial at Westminster, where his dignified refusal to plead was interpreted as a confession of guilt. He was beheaded at Whitehall (30 Jan 1649). >> Cromwell, Oliver; Fairfax; Hampden; Harrison, Thomas; Haselrig; Henrietta Maria; Holles; Laud; Montrose; Rupert, Prince; Strafford; RR1095

Charles II (of England) (1630-85) King of Britain and Ireland (1660-85), born in London, England, UK, the son of Charles I. As Prince of Wales, he sided with his father in the Civil War, and was then forced into exile. On his father's execution (1649), he assumed the title of king, and was crowned at Scone, Scotland (1651). Leading poorly organized forces into England, he met disastrous defeat at Worcester (1651). The next nine years were spent in exile until an impoverished England, in dread of a revival of military despotism, summoned him back as king (1660). In 1662 he married the Portuguese princess, **Catherine of Braganza**. It was a childless marriage, though Charles was the father of many illegitimate children. His war with Holland (1665-7) was unpopular, and led to the dismissal of his adviser, Lord Clarendon (1667), who was replaced by a group of ministers (the Cabal). He negotiated skilfully between conflicting political and religious pressures, including the trumped-up 'Popish Plot', and refused to deny the succession of his brother James. For the last four years of his life, he ruled without parliament. >> Catherine of Braganza; Charles I (of England); Clarendon, Edward Hyde; Gwyn; Monk, George; Shaftesbury, 1st Earl of; Walter, Lucy; RR1095

Charles II (of Spain) (1661-1700) King of Spain (1665-1700), the last ruler of the Spanish Habsburg dynasty, born in Madrid. The congenitally handicapped son of Philip IV (reigned 1621-65), he presided over the final decline of Spanish hegemony. Under him Spain joined the League of Augsburg (1686) and the ensuing hostilities against France. To prevent the dismemberment of his patrimony, he bequeathed the entire Spanish Habsburg inheritance to Louis XIV's younger grandson, Philip of Anjou, in 1700, although his intentions were subsequently thwarted by the War of the Spanish Succession and the territorial settlement of Utrecht (1713). >> Philip V; RR1088

Charles III (of Spain) (1716-88) King of Naples and Sicily (1734-59) before becoming King of Spain (1759-88), born in Madrid. Generally regarded as an archetypal enlightened despot, he was driven by the belief that the Spanish monarchy and the colonial empire were in need of political, economic, and cultural reform. He encouraged commercial reforms in the colonies, and encouraged an ambitious building programme at home, undertook agricultural improvements, and brought the Roman Catholic Church under state control. In the Seven Years' War (1756-63) he sided with France and against Great Britain, receiving Louisiana from his ally while conceding Florida to Britain in return for Havana and Manila (1763). Later, however, by joining the anti-British coalition in support of the Americans, he regained Florida by the Treaty of Paris (1783).

Charles IV (of Spain) (1748-1819) King of Spain (1788-1808), born in Portici, Italy, the son of Charles III (reigned 1759-88). His government was largely in the hands of his wife, **Maria Luisa** (1751-1819) and her favourite, Manuel de Godoy. Nelson destroyed his fleet at Trafalgar, and in 1808 he abdicated under pressure from Napoleon. He spent the rest of his life in exile. >> Godoy; Napoleon; Nelson; RR1088

Charles V (of France), known as **Charles the Wise** (1338-80) King of France, born in Vincennes, France. He came to the throne in 1364, and in a series of victories regained most of the territory lost to the English in the Hundred Years' War. >> RR1049

Charles V (Emperor) (1500-58) Holy Roman Emperor (1519-56), born in Ghent, Belgium, the son of Philip of Burgundy and Joanna of Spain. He was made joint ruler of Spain (as **Charles I**) with his mother (1517), and was elected to the Holy Roman Empire (1519). His rivalry with Francis I of France dominated west European affairs, and there was almost constant warfare between them. In 1525 the defeat of Francis led to the formation of the Holy League against Charles by Pope Clement VII, Henry VIII, Francis, and the Venetians. In 1527 Rome was sacked and the pope imprisoned, and although Charles disclaimed any part of it, the Peace of Cambrai (1529) left him master of Italy. At the Diet of Augsburg (1530) he confirmed the 1521 Edict of Worms, which had condemned Luther, and the Protestants formed the League of Schmalkald. After further battles, in 1538 the pope, Francis, and Charles agreed at Nice to a 10 years' truce. Charles's league with the pope drove the Protestants to rebellion. They were crushed at Mühlberg (1547); but in 1552 Charles was defeated by Maurice of Saxony, and Protestantism received legal recognition. In 1555 he divided the empire between his son (Philip II of Spain) and his brother (Emperor Ferdinand I), retiring to the monastery of Yuste in Spain. >> Clement VII; Francis I; Philip II (of Spain); RR1057

Charles VI (of France), known as **Charles the Foolish** (1368-1422) King of France, born in Paris, who came to the throne as a young boy in 1380. He was defeated by Henry V at the Battle of Agincourt (1415). From 1392, he suffered from fits of madness. >> Henry V; RR1049

Charles VII (of France), known as **Charles the Victorious** (1403-61) King of France (1422-61), born in Paris. At his accession, the N of the country was in English hands, with Henry VI proclaimed King of France, but after Joan of Arc roused the fervour of both nobles and people, the siege of Orléans was raised (1429), and the English gradually lost nearly all they had gained in France. Under his rule France recovered in some measure from her calamities. >> Henry VI; Joan of Arc; RR1049

Charles IX (of France) (1550-74) King of France (1560-74), born in St Germain-en-Laye, France. The second son of Henry II and Catherine de' Medici, he succeeded his brother Francis II. His reign coincided with the Wars of Religion. He was completely subject to his mother, whose counsels drove him to authorize the massacre of Huguenots on St Bartholomew's Day (1572), the memory of which haunted him until his death. >> Henry II (of France); RR1049

Charles X (of France) (1757-1836) The last Bourbon king of France (1824-30), born at Versailles, France. The grandson of Louis XV, he received the title of Comte d'Artois, and in 1773 married Maria Theresa of Savoy. He lived in England during the French Revolution, returning to France in 1814 as lieutenant-general of the kingdom. He succeeded his brother Louis XVIII, but his repressive rule led to revolution, and his eventual abdication and exile. >> Louis XVIII; RR1049

Charles XII (of Sweden) (1682-1718) King of Sweden (1697-1718), born in Stockholm, the son of Charles XI. Following an alliance against him by Denmark, Poland, and Russia, he attacked Denmark (1699), and compelled the Danes to sue for peace. He then defeated the Russians at Narva (1700), and dethroned Augustus II of Poland (1704). He invaded Russia again in 1707, and was at first victorious, but when Cossack help failed to arrive, he was defeated at Poltava (1709). He escaped to Turkey, where he stayed until 1714. He then formed another army and attacked Norway, but was killed at the siege of Halden. After his death, Sweden, exhausted by his wars, ceased to be numbered among the great powers. >> Augustus II; RR1090

Charles XIV (of Sweden), originally **Jean Baptiste Jules Bernadotte** (1763–1844) King of Sweden (1818–44), born a lawyer's son in Pau, France. He joined the French army in 1780, and fought his way up to become marshal (1804). In 1799 he was minister of war, and for his conduct at Austerlitz was named Prince of Pontecorvo (1805). He fought in several Napoleonic campaigns (1805–9), then was elected heir to the throne of Sweden (1810), turning Protestant, and changing his name to Charles John. He refused to comply with Napoleon's demands, and was soon involved in war with him, taking part in the final struggle at Leipzig (1813). In 1814 he was rewarded with the Kingdom of Norway, recreating the union of the two countries. Thereafter he had a peaceful reign, though his conservative rule led to opposition at home in the 1830s. >> Napoleon; RR1090

Charles (Philip Arthur George), Prince of Wales (1948–) Eldest son of Queen Elizabeth II and Prince Philip, Duke of Edinburgh, and heir apparent to the throne, born at Buckingham Palace, London, England, UK. Duke of Cornwall as the eldest son of the monarch, he was given the title of Prince of Wales in 1958, and invested at Caernarfon (1969). He studied at Cheam and Gordonstoun, and entered Trinity College, Cambridge, in 1967. He served in the RAF and Royal Navy, (1971–6), and in 1981 married **Lady Diana Frances**, younger daughter of the 8th Earl Spencer. They had two sons: **Prince William Arthur Philip Louis** (1982–) and **Prince Henry Charles Albert David** (1984–). The couple separated in 1992, and divorced in 1996. During this period he was, along with Princess Diana, the focus of continual media interest, attracting unprecedented attention from biographers. >> Diana, Princess of Wales; Edinburgh; Elizabeth II; RR1108

Charles, (Mary) Eugenia (1919–) Dominican politician and prime minister (1980–95), born in Pointe Michel, Dominica. After qualifying as a barrister in London, she returned to the West Indies to practise. She entered politics in 1968, two years later became co-founder and first leader of the centrist Dominica Freedom Party (DFP), and became an MP in 1975. Two years after independence, the DFP won the 1980 general election and she became the Caribbean's first female prime minister. She was re-elected in 1985. >> RR1045

Charles, Ezzard >> Louis, Joe

Charles, Jacques Alexandre César [shah(r)l] (1746–1823) Physicist, born in Beaugency, France. A clerk with an interest in science, which led eventually to a chair in physics at Paris, he became famous by making the first manned ascent by hydrogen balloon, reaching 3000 m/9800 ft in 1783. His interest in gases subsequently led him to formulate *Charles's law*, which relates the volume of a gas at constant pressure to its temperature.

Charles, Ray, originally **Ray Charles Robinson** (1930–) Entertainer, born in Albany, GA. Blind from the age of seven, he attended a special school and studied music. Influenced by jazz and blues, he became a versatile performer, developing an original blend of music identified as 'soul'. He made many hit records, 'What'd I say' (1959) being his first million-seller. He has received eight Grammy Awards, and co-wrote an autobiography *Brother Ray: Ray Charles' Own Story* (1978).

Charles, Robert (1936–) Golfer, born in Carterton, New Zealand. In 1963 he became the only left-handed golfer to win the British Open championship, and 30 years later he was still performing creditably in the same competition. In 1963 he also won five US Tour events. >> RR1157

Charles d'Orléans >> Orléans, Charles

Charles Edward Stuart >> Stuart, Charles Edward

Charles Martel [mah(r)tel] (Old French, 'the hammer') (c.688–741) Mayor of the palace for the last Merovingian kings of the Franks, the illegitimate son of Pepin of Herstal, and the undisputed head of the Carolingian family by 723. He conducted many campaigns against the Frisians and Saxons, as well as in Aquitaine, Bavaria, and Burgundy. He halted Muslim expansion in W Europe at the Battle of Poitiers (732). Established as effective ruler of much of Gaul, but never crowned king, he left the kingdom to his sons, Carloman and Pepin, and in 751 Pepin was anointed as the first Carolingian king of the Franks. >> Pepin III

Charles the Great >> Charlemagne

Charlevoix, Pierre François Xavier de [shah(r)lvwah] (1682–1761) Jesuit explorer of North America, born in St Quentin, France. In 1720 he was sent by the French regent to find a route to W Canada. He travelled by canoe up the St Lawrence River across the Great Lakes and down the Mississippi to New Orleans, and was finally shipwrecked in the Gulf of Mexico. He became the only traveller of that time to describe the interior of North America.

Charlotte (Augusta), Princess (1796–1817) Princess of Great Britain and Ireland, the only daughter of George IV and Caroline of Brunswick, who separated immediately after her birth. The heir to the British throne, she was brought up in strict seclusion. In 1816 she married Prince Leopold of Saxe-Coburg (later to be King Leopold I of the Belgians), but died in childbirth the following year. >> George IV; Leopold I (of Belgium)

Charlotte Sophia of Mecklenburg-Strelitz (1744–1818) Queen of Great Britain and Ireland, the wife of George III. She married George shortly after his accession to the throne, in 1761, and bore him 15 children. Their eldest son was the future George IV, born in 1762. >> George III; George IV

Charlton, Bobby, popular name of **Sir Robert Charlton** (1937–) Footballer, born in Ashington, Northumberland, NE England, UK, the brother of Jack Charlton. He was with the one club, Manchester United, throughout his career (1954–73), winning five League Championship medals, an FA Cup-winner's medal (1963), and a European Cup-winner's medal (1968). He won 106 caps for England, scored 49 goals for the national team (an English record), and was a member of the World Cup-winning side of 1966. He is now a director of Manchester United, and was knighted in 1994. >> Charlton, Jack; RR1155

Charlton, Jack(ie), popular name of **John Charlton** (1935–) Footballer, born in Ashington, Northumberland, NE England, UK, the brother of Bobby Charlton. He was a part of the great Leeds United side of 1965–75 under Don Revie's management. He was almost 30 before he was capped for England, but then retained his place for five years. He later became manager of Middlesborough (1973), Sheffield Wednesday (1977), and Newcastle United (1984). He became manager of the Republic of Ireland team (1986–95), taking them to the last stages of the World Cup in 1990 and 1994. >> Charlton, Bobby; RR1156

Charney, Jule Gregory (1917–81) Meteorologist, born in San Francisco, CA. The son of Russian immigrants, he studied with Rossby before travelling to the University of Oslo in Norway as a National Research Fellow. At the Institute for Advanced Study in Princeton, (1948–56), he and others pioneered the first computer-generated weather forecast, and he then established a Joint Numerical Weather Prediction Unit in Maryland, which generated daily predictions of gross climate and weather patterns. At the Massachusetts Institute of Technology (1956–81) he chaired the Committee on International Meteorological Co-operation and helped organize the Global Atmospheric Research Program. >> Rossby

Charnley, Sir John (1911–82) Orthopaedic surgeon, born in Bury, Lancashire, NW England, UK. He studied at

Manchester University, becoming a consultant at the Manchester Royal Infirmary, and later at Wrightington Hospital. In the 1950s and 1960s he played a key role in both the technology and the surgical techniques of hip replacements.

Charonton, Enguerrand >> **Quarton, Enguerrand**

Charpentier, Gustave [shah(r)pãtyay] (1860–1956) Composer, born in Dieuze, France. He studied at the Lille Conservatory, and the Paris Conservatoire under Massenet. He founded a free school of music for the poor, the Conservatoire Populaire de Mimi Pinson, wrote dramatic and choral works, and composed both the music and libretti for the operas *Louise* (1900) and *Julien* (1913). >> Massenet

Charrenton, Enguerrand >> **Quarton, Enguerrand**

Charteris, Leslie [chah(r)teris], originally **Leslie Charles Bowyer Yin** (1907–93) Crime-story writer, born in Singapore. He studied at Cambridge, then worked in a wide variety of jobs, changed his name in 1928, and settled in the USA (1932), working as a Hollywood screenwriter. He became a US citizen in 1941. He is especially known as the creator of Simon Templar, 'the Saint'.

Chartier, Alain [shah(r)tyay] (c. 1385–c. 1435) Writer, born in Bayeux, France. His preoccupation with the plight of France in the Hundred Years' War formed the background to his two best works, the *Livre des quatre dames* (1415–16, Book of the Four Ladies) and the *Quadrilogue invectif* (1422), a four-part debate on the ills of France. He also wrote the allegorical poem, *La Belle Dame sans merci* (1424).

Chase, James Hadley, pseudonym of **René Raymond** (1906–85) Novelist, born in London, England, UK. He started the vogue for tough realism in gangster stories in the UK with his *No Orchids for Miss Blandish* (1939), the first of a number in similar vein. >> Chandler, Raymond; Hammett

Chase, Mary Ellen (1887–1973) Writer, born in Blue Hill, ME. She studied at Maine and Minnesota universities, becoming a professor at Minnesota (1922–6) and at Smith College, Northampton, MA (1926–55). Her autobiographies and novels revealed a passion for her native Maine and its seafaring inhabitants, notably *Mary Peters* (1934) and *Silas Crockett* (1935).

Chase, Salmon P(ortland) (1808–73) Jurist and statesman, born in Cornish, NH. In 1830 he settled as a lawyer in Cincinnati, where he acted as counsel for the defence of fugitive slaves. He was twice Governor of Ohio (1855–9), and became secretary of the Treasury (1861–4). In 1864 Abraham Lincoln appointed him Chief Justice of the USA; as such he presided at the trial of President Andrew Johnson (1868). >> Johnson, Andrew

Chase, Samuel (1741–1811) Jurist, born in Princess Anne, MD. He was a delegate to the Continental Congresses from 1774, and signed the Declaration of Independence. He opposed the new Constitution, but supported the Washington administration in 1795, and won nomination to the Supreme Court in 1796. He delivered many distinguished opinions, stressing the supremacy of national treaties over state laws, and the inherent limitations on legislative powers. He was impeached in 1804 at the instance of President Jefferson for his partisan hostility to political offenders, but was acquitted in 1805. >> Jefferson, Thomas

Chase, William Merritt (1849–1916) Painter of landscapes, portraits, and still-lifes, born in Franklin, IN. He studied in Munich, then returned to the USA, where he gained a great reputation as a teacher.

Chasles, Michel [shahl] (1793–1880) Mathematician, born in Epernon, France. He entered the Ecole Polytechnique in 1812, and became a military engineer, but resigned to devote himself to mathematics, becoming professor of geometry at the Sorbonne in 1846. He greatly developed synthetic projective geometry by means of cross-ratio and homographies without the use of co-ordinates.

Chataway, Sir Chris(topher John) (1931–) Athlete and statesman, born in London, England, UK. He studied at Oxford, and was one of Britain's finest middle-distance runners in the 1950s. A member of the Olympic team (1952, 1956), he helped Roger Bannister break the four-minute mile in 1954, and achieved a new world record time in the 5000 m. In 1959 he entered parliament as a Conservative MP, and was minister of posts and telecommunications (1970–2) and minister for industrial development (1972–4) before taking up a career in the City. He was knighted in 1995. >> Bannister, Roger

Chateaubriand, François Auguste René, vicomte de (Viscount of) [shatohbreeã] (1768–1848) French politician and writer, born in St Malo, France. *Atala* (1801) established his literary reputation, and *Le Génie du christianisme* (1802, The Genius of Christianity) made him prominent among men of letters. He held various political and diplomatic posts after the Restoration, but was disappointed in his hope of becoming prime minister. In his later years, he wrote his celebrated autobiography, *Mémoires d'outre-tombe* (Memoirs from Beyond the Tomb), not published as a whole until 1902. >> Récamier

Châtelet-Lomont, Gabrielle Emilie le Tonnelier de Breteuil, Marquise du (Marchioness of) [shatlay lohmõ] (1706–49) Scholar and writer, born in Paris. After her marriage to the **comte du Châtelet-Lomont** (1725), she studied mathematics and the physical sciences. In 1733 she met Voltaire, who came to live with her at her husband's estate at Cirey. Her chief work was her translation into French of Newton's *Principia mathematica*, posthumously published in 1759. >> Voltaire

Chatelier, Henry le [shatlyay] (1850–1936) Chemist, born in Paris. In 1888 he discovered the law of reaction governing the effect of pressure and temperature on equilibrium. He devised a railway water-brake, an optical pyrometer, and made contributions to metallurgy and ceramics.

Chatham, 1st Earl of >> **Pitt, William, 1st Earl of Chatham**

Chatterjee, Bankim Chandra (1838–94) Writer, born in Katalpura, Bengal. One of the most influential figures in 19th-c Indian literature, his novels included *Durges Nandini* (1864) and *Anandamath* (1882), a novel of the Sannyasi rebellion of 1772 from which the Nationalist song *Bande Mataram* ('Hail to thee, Mother') was taken.

Chatterton, Thomas (1752–70) Poet, born in Bristol, SW England, UK. In 1768 he hoaxed the whole city with a description, 'from an old manuscript', of the opening of Bristol Bridge in 1248. His poems, purporting to be by Thomas Rowley, a 15th-c monk, were sent to Horace Walpole, but (though Walpole was taken in) were soon denounced as forgeries. He then went to London, where he wrote many successful stories, essays, and other works. When his patron, Lord Mayor Beckford, died, his publishers ceased to support him. Starving and penniless, he took poison. The debate over the authenticity of the Rowley poems waged for 80 years, and he received posthumous tributes from many poets including Byron, Keats, and Shelley. >> Walpole, Horace

Chatwin, Bruce (1940–89) Writer and traveller, born in Sheffield, South Yorkshire, N England, UK. He worked at Sotheby's as an expert on modern art for eight years until he temporarily went blind. To recuperate, he went to Africa, where he was converted to a life of nomadic asceticism, and began writing books which combine fiction, anthropology, philosophy, and travel. They include *In Patagonia* (1977, Hawthornden Prize), *The Viceroy of Ouidah* (1980), *On The Black Hill* (1982, Whitbread), and *Utz* (1988), a novella which was short-listed for the Booker Prize.

Chaucer, Geoffrey (c. 1343–1400) see panel below

Chauliac, Guy de [shohliak] (c. 1300–68) Surgeon, born in Chauliac, France. The most famous surgeon of the Middle Ages, he wrote *Chirurgia magna* (1363), which was translated into French over a century later and used as a manual by generations of doctors.

Chaussée, Pierre Claude Nivelle de La >> **La Chaussée, Pierre Claude Nivelle de**

Chavannes, Puvis de >> **Puvis de Chavannes, Pierre**

Chávez, Carlos [**chah**vays] (1899–1978) Composer, born in Mexico City. He formed the Mexican Symphony Orchestra in 1928, becoming director of the National Conservatory. As an official in the Ministry of Fine Arts, his influence on every aspect of Mexican music was enormous. His works, little known outside his own country, are influenced by Mexican folk music, and include ballets, symphonies, and concertos and an unusual *Toccata for Percussion* (1942).

Chavez, Cesar (Estrada) [sha**vez**, **shah**vez] (1927–93) Labour leader, born in Yuma, AZ. A migrant farmworker in his youth (he attended 65 elementary schools, and never graduated from high school), he became a community and labour organizer of agricultural workers in the 1950s. In 1962 he started the National Farm Workers Association, based in the SW among the mainly Chicano and Filipino farmworkers; in 1966 this union was chartered by the AFL–CIO as the United Farm Workers of America, and he remained its president until his death. He became widely known for organizing a series of national grape boycotts that helped the union to gain improved wages and working conditions for its members.

Chayefsky, Paddy [chiye**f**skee], originally **Sidney Chayefsky** (1923–81) Stage and television playwright, born in New York City, NY. He studied at the City College of New York, and after army service in World War 2 began writing for radio and television. Best known for *Marty* (1953) and *The Bachelor Party* (1954), he received three Oscars for his film writing.

GEOFFREY CHAUCER (c. 1343–1400)

Chaucer was born in London, the son of John Chaucer, a prosperous wine merchant and deputy to the king's butler, and his wife Agnes. Little is known of his early education, but his work shows that he was well-read, fluent in French, and competent in Latin and Italian. In 1357 he entered the service of Elizabeth, Countess of Ulster, the wife of Prince Lionel – later Duke of Clarence. He went to France with Edward III's army in 1359, was taken prisoner in the Ardennes during the siege of Reims, then ransomed and returned to England after the Treaty of Brétigny in 1360.

Nothing more is certain of his life until c.1366, when he married **Philippa Roet** or **Pan**, the sister of John of Gaunt's future wife, and one of Queen Philippa's ladies. They had two sons, Lewis and Thomas. He became an esquire of King Edward III's household, with a regular pension, in 1367, and is described as 'our beloved yeoman' and as 'one of the yeomen of the king's chamber'. He is first recorded as a poet in 1369–70 with the reading of his 'Book of the Duchesse', a poem written as an elegy on the death by plague of John of Gaunt's first wife, Blanche, Duchess of Lancaster, in 1369.

With the king's army he journeyed to France again in 1369; as well as to Flanders, France, and Milan in the 1370s on a variety of diplomatic and commercial missions, for which he received generous financial reward, on top of being offered, rent-free, the gatehouse of Aldgate from the city of London. He was appointed Comptroller of the Customs and Subsidy of Wools, Skins, and Tanned Hides in the port of London in 1374. At this time John of Gaunt also conferred on him a pension for life, and in 1386 he was elected a knight of the shire for Kent.

Between 1369–87 he wrote 'The Parlement of Foules', 'The Hous of Fame', 'The Legend of Good Women', and also what ultimately appeared as the tales of the Clerk, Man of Law, Prioress, Second Nun, and Knight gathered together in the *Canterbury Tales*. However, the crowning work of the middle period of his life is 'Troilus and Criseyde' (1385–7), in which his immense power of human observation, his sense of humour, and his dramatic skill are lavishly displayed. 'The Legend of Good Women' has an admirable prologue, but was never finished.

Chaucer's earlier writings show the influence of Ovid and French literature. (French was also the language of the court.) He translated part of the long French poem by three authors, the 'Roman de la Rose' (c.1240–80, Romance of the Rose) which was based in part on Ovid's *Ars amatoria* (c.1 BC, Art of Love). However, the most important literary influence acting upon him during this middle period of his life was Italian. Much of his subject-matter he derived from his great Italian contemporaries, especially Dante, Petrarch, and Boccaccio, whose works he would have become familiar with during his diplomatic travels in Italy. It was the spirit not the letter of these masters which he imitated, though a great deal of 'Troilus and Criseyde' is quite close to Boccaccio in style.

About the end of 1386 Chaucer lost his offices, possibly owing to a change in the political climate after the death of Edward III and the regency usurpation of young Richard II by Thomas Woodstock, Duke of Gloucester; no friend to Gaunt or his associates. He fell upon still harder times after the death of his wife (who was independently wealthy) in 1387, selling his pension for a lump sum in 1388. These problems perhaps prevented him accepting an invitation to Calais for protection: several of his friends were executed in the Merciless Parliament and he was in some danger. In 1389 Richard regained control, and Chaucer was appointed Clerk of the King's Works (1389–91). In 1394 Richard granted him a pension for life; but the advances of payment Chaucer applied for, and the issue of letters of protection from arrest for debt, indicate his distressed condition. On the accession, in 1399, of Henry IV, his fortunes took an upward turn, and he was granted a large pension which enabled him to spend his few remaining months in comfort.

It was during the 1390s that he wrote his most famous work, the unfinished *Canterbury Tales*: 24 stories supposedly told by the Canterbury Pilgrims on their journey to the shrine of the martyr, Thomas à Becket. The work is unique for its variety, humour, grace and realism, and it remains one of the classics of narrative poetry in English.

After his death Chaucer's body was laid in that part of Westminster Abbey which afterwards came to be called Poet's Corner. The first great poet of the English nation, his work was a major factor in establishing the S English dialect as the literary language of England.

>> Boccaccio; Dante; John of Gaunt; Ovid; Petrarch; Richard II

Chebyshev, Pafnuty Lvovich [chebishof] (1821–94) Mathematician, born in Okatovo, Russia. A graduate of Moscow University, he became an assistant at St Petersburg in 1847 and later professor (1860–82). In number theory he made important contributions to the theory of the distribution of prime numbers, and in probability theory he proved fundamental limit theorems. His theory of approximation to functions by polynomials has become important in modern computing. The mathematical school that he founded at St Petersburg influenced Russian mathematics for the rest of the century.

Cheever, John (1912–82) Short-story writer and novelist, born in Quincy, MA. By the time he was 22 the *New Yorker* was accepting his work, and for years he contributed a dozen stories a year to it. After World War 2 he taught composition and wrote scripts for television, but in 1951 a Guggenheim Fellowship allowed him to devote his attention to writing. His books include *The Wapshot Chronicle* (1957, National Book Award) and its sequel, *The Wapshot Scandal* (1964, Howell's Medal for Fiction), and *The Stories of John Cheever* (1979, Pulitzer).

Che Guevara >> **Guevara, Che**

Cheke, Sir John [cheek] (1514–57) Humanist and scholar, born in Cambridge, Cambridgeshire, EC England, UK. Fellow of St John's College, Cambridge from 1529, he adopted the doctrines of the Reformation, and was appointed the first Regius professor of Greek at Cambridge (1540). In 1554 he was appointed tutor to the Prince of Wales (later Edward VI), whose accession secured him a seat in parliament (1547) and a knighthood (1552). After the accession of Mary I he was imprisoned (1553–4), then went abroad to teach. In 1556 he was brought back to the Tower, where he was forced to recant his Protestantism publicly.

Chekhov, Anton (Pavlovitch) [chekof] (1860–1904) Playwright and master of the short story, born in Taganrog, Russia. He studied medicine at Moscow, and began to write while a student. His first book of stories (1886) was successful, and gradually he adopted writing as a profession. His early full-length plays were failures, but when *Chayka* (1896, The Seagull) was revived in 1898 by Stanislavsky at the Moscow Art Theatre, it was a great success. He then wrote his masterpieces: *Dyadya Vanya* (1900, Uncle Vanya), *Tri sestry* (1901, The Three Sisters), and *Vishnyovy sad* (1904, The Cherry Orchard). Meanwhile he continued to write many short stories, the best of which have continued to be highly acclaimed. In 1897 he fell ill with tuberculosis and lived thereafter either abroad or in the Crimea. In 1901 he married the actress **Olga Knipper** (1870–1959), who remained for many years the admired exponent of female roles in his plays.

Chelcicky, Petz [chelchitskee] (c. 1390–1460) Reformer and theologian, probably born in Chelčice, Bohemia. A radical follower of the Hussites, he abjured towns and commerce, and founded the sect which became the Moravian Brothers. The Christian doctrine of his *The Net of True Faith* (1450) was later promulgated by Tolstoy. >> Tolstoy

Chelmsford, Frederick John Napier Thesiger, 1st Viscount and 3rd Baron (1868–1933) Colonial administrator, born in London, England, UK. He was Governor of Queensland (1905–9) and of New South Wales (1909–13), and Viceroy of India (1916–21) where he helped increase the number of Indians taking part in government, but was also noted for his severity against the nationalists. He became First Lord of the Admiralty (1924).

Chemnitz, Martin [kemnits] (1522–86) Lutheran theologian, born in Treuenbrietzen, Germany. He studied at Wittenberg under Melanchthon, became librarian at Königsberg in 1549, and continued his theological studies. He entered the Lutheran ministry in 1553 as pastor, and in 1567 became superintendant of Braunschweig. He worked to unite the Lutheran Church (split after Luther's death), and was primarily responsible for the Formula of Concord (1577). >> Luther; Melanchthon

Chen Duxiu [chen dooshoo], also spelled **Ch'en Tu-hsiu** (1879–1942) One of the founders of the Chinese Communist Party (CCP). As dean of the Faculty of Letters at Beijing University, he founded the journal *New Youth* (1915), which first published both Hu Shi and Lu Xun, and influenced the young Mao Zedong. He saw Marxism as a vehicle for modernization, met a Comintern agent in 1920, and established Communist cells in several cities, six of which founded the CCP in 1921. His repeated criticisms of the policy of entryism into the Guomindang led to expulsion from the CCP in 1930. Imprisoned from 1932–7, he left politics and concentrated on writing. He believed in the rejuvenation of China by destroying Confucian traditions and social patterns, and emulating Western political and scientific thought. >> Hu Shi; Li Dazhao; Lu Xun; Mao Zedong

Chen Ning Yang >> **Yang, Chen Ning**

Chen Yi (1901–72) Chinese Communist leader, born in Lochih, Szechwan. He studied in France, and joined the Communist Party on his return. He supported Mao Zedong in the struggle with the Kuomintang and the Japanese (1934). He formed the 4th Route Army in Kiangsi (1940), and commanded the East China Liberation Army (1946), restyled the 3rd (East China) Army (1948). Created Marshal of the People's Republic in 1955, he became foreign minister in 1958. He was dropped from the Politburo during the Cultural Revolution in 1969. >> Mao Zedong

Chénier, André (Marie) de [shaynyay] (1762–94) Poet, born in Istanbul, the third son of the French consul-general. At three he was sent to France, and at 12 placed at the Collège de Navarre, Paris. His poems include the idylls 'Le Mendiant', 'L'Aveugle', and 'Hermès', the last being an imitation of Lucretius. In 1787 he went to England as secretary to the French ambassador, but returned to Paris (1790) to find himself in the ferment of the Revolution, which at first he supported; but alarmed by its excesses he offended Robespierre by pamphlets, and was guillotined. Little of his work was published until 25 years after his death, when he was acclaimed as a major figure of the Romantic movement. >> Robespierre

Chennault, Claire (Lee) [shenawlt] (1890–1958) Aviator, born in Commerce, TX. A schoolteacher, he obtained an infantry commission in 1917, then transferred to the signal corps and became a pilot. Forced out of the service in 1937 because of deafness, he went to work for the Chinese Nationalists, recruiting some 50 US pilots and equipping them with P-40 aircraft for operations against the Japanese. In a brief career of seven months in 1941–2, his 'Flying Tigers' became the most publicized flying unit of World War 2. He went on to hold senior US commands in China, retiring in 1945, but continued to serve the Nationalists as an air consultant until his death.

Cheops [keeops], Greek form of **Khufu** (26th-c BC) King of Memphis in Egypt, second ruler of the fourth dynasty. He is famous as the builder of the Great Pyramid. The *Ship of Cheops* is a funeral ship found dismantled at Giza in 1954 in one of five boat pits around the pyramid. >> RR1046

Cherenkov, Pavel (Alexeyevich) [cherengkof] (1904–90) Physicist, born in Novaya Chigla, Russia. He studied at Voronezh, and worked at the Academy of Sciences. In 1934 he noted the emission of blue light from water and other transparent media when atomic particles, moving at a speed greater than light in that medium, are passed through it. Subsequent researches by Tamm and Frank led to a definite explanation of this *Cherenkov effect*, for which all three shared the Nobel Prize for Physics in 1958. >> Frank, Ilya Mikhailovich; Tamm; RR1122

Cherkassky, Shura (Alexander Isaakovich) [cherkaskee] (1911–95) Pianist, born in Odessa, Ukraine. He settled in America in 1922 and studied at the Curtis Institute, Philadelphia. He excelled in the Romantic repertoire, and toured and recorded widely.

Chermayeff, Serge [chermiyef] (1900–96) Architect and designer, born in the Caucasus. Educated in England, he took up journalism, then became a director of Waring & Gillow (1928), for which he established a 'Modern Art Studio'. His early design work was for interiors, including studios for Broadcasting House, London (1931). In 1940 he emigrated to the USA where, in addition to his architectural work, he taught design and architecture. He held professorships at Harvard (1952–62) and Yale (1962–9).

Chernenko, Konstantin Ustinovich [chernyengko] (1911–85) Soviet statesman and president (1984–5), born in Bolshaya Tes, Russia. He joined the Communist Party in 1931, and held several local posts. An associate of Brezhnev for many years, he became a member of the Politburo in 1978, and the Party's chief ideologist after the death of Suslov. Regarded as a conservative, Chernenko was a rival of Andropov in the Party leadership contest of 1982, and became Party general secretary and head of state after Andropov's death in 1984. He suffered from ill health, and died soon after, to be succeeded by Gorbachev. >> Andropov; Brezhnev; Gorbachev; Suslov; RR1085

Cherubini, (Maria) Luigi (Carlo Zenobio Salvatore) [kerubeenee] (1760–1842) Composer, born in Florence, Italy. He studied at Bologna and Milan, and wrote a succession of operas, at first in Neapolitan, later (having moved to Paris) in French style. His best-known opera is *Les Deux Journées* (1880, The Two Days, or The Water-Carrier). His later work was mainly ecclesiastical. In 1822 he became director of the Paris Conservatoire.

Cherwell, Frederick Alexander Lindemann, 1st Viscount [chah(r)wel] (1886–1957) Scientist, born in Baden-Baden, Germany. He was brought up in England, but went to university at Berlin and the Sorbonne. In 1914 he became director of the Experimental Physics Station at Farnborough, where he evolved the mathematical theory of aircraft spin, and tested it in a daring flight. In 1919 he became professor of experimental philosophy at Oxford, and later director of the Clarendon Laboratory. A close friend of Churchill, he became his scientific adviser in 1940. He was created a baron in 1941, and was paymaster-general on two occasions (1942–5, 1951–3). >> Churchill, Sir Winston

Cheshire (of Woodhall), (Geoffrey) Leonard Cheshire, Baron (1917–92) British bomber pilot and philanthropist. He studied at Oxford, and was repeatedly decorated (including the VC, 1944) for his leadership and bravery during World War 2. He was one of the official British observers of the destruction caused by the atomic bomb over Nagasaki (1945). This experience, together with his new-found faith, Catholicism, made him determine to establish co-operative communities for ex-servicemen dedicated to living in peace. His initial venture failed, but he found himself looking after a homeless, cancer-stricken ex-serviceman who urged him to welcome others in a similar situation, and from this grew the Cheshire Homes for the Disabled. In 1959 he married **Sue Ryder**, and he was created a life peer in 1991. >> Ryder, Sue

Chesney, Francis Rawdon [cheznee] (1789–1872) Soldier and explorer of the Euphrates, born in Annalong, Co Down. In 1829 he surveyed the Isthmus of Suez, providing data later used in the construction of the Suez Canal. After 1831 he four times explored a route to India by rail and sea

via Syria and the Euphrates. He transported two steamers overland from the Mediterranean to the Euphrates, and one successfully reached the Gulf in 1836, but the British government ignored his results.

Chesnius >> Duchesne, André

Chesnut, Mary, Boykin, *née* **Miller** (1823–86) Diarist, born near Camden, SC. She married **James Chesnut**, a wealthy planter, defender of slavery, and staunch secessionist. He joined the US Senate as a Democrat in 1859, but resigned in 1860 to help form the Confederacy. He then served with the Confederate army, leaving his wife to write her journal of life on the Southern home-front, especially in Richmond and South Carolina. First published in 1905 as *A Diary from Dixie*, it is recognized as a lively and compelling contribution to the literature of the Civil War.

Chesnutt, Charles W(addell) (1858–1932) Writer, born in Cleveland, OH. Working first as a school principal, he studied to become an attorney, and established a legal stenography firm. The son of emancipated blacks, he wrote works on the theme of social injustice. He made a subtle attack on plantation owners in *The Goophered Grapevine* (1887), which was the first published work by a black novelist. His writing explored contemporary humanitarian issues, and was an important influence on the work of some later writers.

Chessman, Caryl (Whittier), nickname **The Red Light Bandit** (1921–60) Convict and writer, born in St Joseph, MI. He was sentenced to death in 1948 on 17 charges of kidnapping, robbery, and rape, but was granted eight stays of execution by the Governor of California amounting to a record period of 12 years under sentence of death, without a reprieve. During this period he conducted a brilliant legal battle from prison, learned four languages, and wrote bestselling books against capital punishment, such as *Cell 2455 Death Row* (1956). His execution provoked worldwide criticism of US judicial methods. >> Brown, Edmund G

Chesterfield, Philip Dormer Stanhope, 4th Earl of (1694–1773) English statesman, orator, and man of letters, born in London, England, UK. He studied at Cambridge, travelled in Europe, and became an MP (1715). In 1726 he succeeded his father as earl and became ambassador to Holland. He returned to England and parliament as a bitter antagonist of Robert Walpole, joined the Pelham ministry (1744), and became Irish lord-lieutenant (1745), and one of the principal secretaries of state (1746–8). Intimate with Swift, Pope, and other contemporary authors, his own best-known work was his guide to manners and success, *Letters to his Son* (1774). >> Pelham, Thomas; Walpole, Robert

Chesterton, G(ilbert) K(eith) (1874–1936) Critic, novelist, and poet, born in London, England, UK. He studied art at the Slade School of Art, London, then turned to writing. Much of his best work took the form of articles for periodicals, including his own *G.K.'s Weekly*. He wrote a great deal of poetry, as well as literary critical studies and works of social criticism. The amiable detective-priest who brought him popularity with a wider public first appeared in *The Innocence of Father Brown* (1911). Chesterton became a Catholic in 1922, and thereafter wrote mainly on religious topics, including lives of Francis of Assisi and Thomas Aquinas.

Chetham, Humphrey [chetm] (1580–1653) Merchant and philanthropist, born in Manchester, Greater Manchester, NW England, UK. He became a cloth manufacturer in Manchester, and was the founder of Chetham Hospital and a public library in the city.

Chettle, Henry [chetl] (?–c. 1607) Playwright and pamphleteer, born in London, England, UK. A printer by trade, he turned to writing when his printing-house failed. He wrote a picaresque romance, *Piers Plainnes Seven Yeres Prentiship* (1595), and from 1598 wrote plays for Philip Henslowe's Rose Theatre in Bankside, especially *The Tragedy of Hoffman* (1602), collaborating on many others. >> Henslowe

Chevalier, Albert [shevalyey] (1861–1923) Entertainer, born in London, England, UK. He appeared as an actor at the old Prince of Wales' Theatre in 1877, and in 1891 became a music-hall singer. Writing, composing, and singing costermonger ballads, he immortalized such songs as 'My Old Dutch' and 'Knocked 'em in the Old Kent Road'.

Chevalier, Maurice [shevalyay] (1888–1972) Film and vaudeville actor, born in Paris. He began as a child singer and dancer in small cafes, then danced at the Folies Bergères (1909–13). His first Hollywood film was *The Innocents of Paris* (1929), and 30 years later his individual, strawhatted, *bon-viveur* personality, with his distinctive French accent, was still much acclaimed, as in the musical *Gigi* (1958). He received a special Academy Award in 1958. >> Mistinguett

Chevallier, Gabriel [shevalyay] (1895–1969) Novelist, born in Lyon, France. He won wide acclaim with his *Clochemerle* (1934), an earthy satire on petty bureaucracy, after a series of less successful psychological novels. Other books include *Clarisse Vernon* (1933), *Le Petit Général* (1951, The Little General), and *Clochemerle Babylone* (1954).

Chevreul, Michel Eugène [shevroei] (1786–1889) Chemist, born in Angers, France. He studied chemistry at the Collège de France in Paris, then lectured at the Collège Charlemagne, and became a director of the Gobelins tapestry works. In 1830 he became professor and then director (1864–79) of the Museum of Natural History. His best-known work is on animal fats, soap-making, candle-making, waxes, and natural dyes. Between 1828 and 1864 he studied the psychology of colour, and (when he was over 90) the psychological effects of ageing.

Chevrolet, Louis [shevrohlay] (1878–1941) Automobile designer and racing driver, born in La Chaux de Fonds, Switzerland. He emigrated to the USA in 1900, and became a motor-racing driver, setting records on every important racing circuit in the USA. In 1911 with William Crapo Durant (1861–1947) he founded the Chevrolet Motor Co, but had little confidence in it, and sold his interest to Durant in 1915, who then incorporated it with General Motors in 1916. He was also involved in motor-boat racing and aircraft production.

Ch'i Pai-shih [chee piyshee], also known as **Ch'i Huang** (1863–1957) Artist, born in Hsiang T'an, China. In his youth he was a carpenter and wood-carver, and took up the study of painting only at 27. He also mastered calligraphy, poetry, and seal-carving. Sometimes called 'China's Picasso', his art is deeply rooted in folk tradition. He painted birds, flowers, fruit, landscapes, and many other subjects with a theme from daily life previously considered to be inappropriate subjects for art. >> Picasso

Chiang Ch'ing >> **Jiang Qing**

Chiang Ching-kuo >> **Jiang Jingguo**

Chiang Kai-shek >> **Jiang Jieshi**

Chiarelli, Luigi [kyarelee] (1884–1947) Playwright, born in Trani, Italy. A journalist who took to the stage, he had his first play, *Vita intima*, performed in 1909. His great success was *La Maschera e il volta* (1916, The Mask and the Face), a farcical comedy translated into nearly every European language.

Chichele, Henry [chichlay] (c. 1362–c. 1443) English clergyman and diplomat. Envoy to the Vatican in 1405 and 1407, in 1408 he became Bishop of St David's, and in 1414 Archbishop of Canterbury. He was the founder of two colleges at Oxford in 1437: St John's and All Souls.

Chichester, Sir Francis (Charles) [chichester] (1901–72) Pioneer air navigator, adventurer, and yachtsman, born in Barnstaple, Devon, SW England, UK. He studied at Marlborough, and emigrated to New Zealand in 1919, where he made a fortune as a land agent. He became interested in flying, and made several pioneer flights, but was badly injured by a crash in Japan (1931) while attempting a solo flying circumnavigation. He served in Britain as an air-navigation expert during World War 2. In 1953 he took up ocean sailing, winning the first solo transatlantic yacht race (1960) in *Gipsy Moth III*, sailing from Plymouth to New York City in 40 days; he repeated the success in 1962 in 33 days. He made a successful solo circumnavigation of the world (1966–7) in *Gipsy Moth IV*, sailing from Plymouth to Sydney in 107 days, and from there back to Plymouth, via Cape Horn, in 119 days. He was knighted in 1967.

Chifley, Joseph Benedict (1885–1951) Australian statesman and prime minister (1945–9), born in Bathurst, New South Wales, Australia. In early life an engine driver, he entered parliament in 1928, and became defence minister in 1929. As Labor prime minister, he expanded social services and reformed the banking system. He continued as leader of the Labor Party until his death. >> RR1033

Chikatilo, Andrei [chikateeloh] (1938–94) Russian convicted murderer. He was convicted and sentenced to death in Russia in 1992 for the murders of 52 adults and children committed over a 12-year period. It is believed to be the world's worst serial-killing case. He was executed in 1994.

Child, Charles M(anning) (1869–1954) Developmental biologist, born in Ypsilanti, MI. He taught and performed research at the University of Chicago (1895–1934), spending summers at various institutions for marine biology. After his retirement, he moved to Stanford University (1939–54), where he remained active in both education and scientific publishing. He made major contributions to studies of the origin and development of the invertebrate nervous system, and is best known for his 'gradient theory' of regeneration (1911), which states that the dominant section of the regenerating part is developed first. He founded the journal *Physiological Zoology* in 1928.

Child, Francis James (1825–96) Philologist, born in Boston, MA. He studied at Harvard, where with the exception of two years' study in Germany he remained on the faculty until his death, teaching rhetoric, oratory, and English literature. His most important scholarly contributions include his five-volume edition of Spenser's *Poetical Works* (1855), for many years the authoritative text, and seminal papers on the language and versification of Chaucer (1863) and Gower (1873). Working from variant manuscript sources, he pioneered a comparative approach to folklore in *English and Scottish Popular Ballads* (10 vols, 1883–98). Known as the *Child Ballads*, this collection provided the basis for ballad studies, and remains the most complete work of its kind.

Childe, (Vere) Gordon [chyld] (1892–1957) Archaeologist, born in Sydney, New South Wales, Australia. He studied at Sydney and Oxford universities, and his early books, notably *The Dawn of European Civilisation* (1925), and *The Most Ancient Near East* (1928), established him as the most influential archaeological theorist of his generation. He was professor of archaeology at Edinburgh (1927–46) and director of the University of London Institute of Archaeology (1946–56). He returned to Australia on retirement, where he committed suicide.

Childers, (Robert) Erskine [childerz] (1870–1922) Irish nationalist and writer, born in London, England, UK. He studied at Cambridge, fought in the South African and First World Wars, and wrote a popular spy story, *The Riddle of the Sands* (1903), and several works of nonfiction. After the establishment of the Irish Free State, he joined the Irish Republican Army, and was active in the Civil War. He was captured and executed. His son **Erskine Hamilton Childers** (1905–74) was president of Ireland (1973–4).

Childs, Lucinda (1940–) Dancer and choreographer, born in New York City. She trained with Merce Cunningham, and as a founder member of the experimental Judson Dance Theatre (1962–4) developed a minimalist style of choreography, often incorporating dialogue. In 1976 she performed her own solo material in the Robert Wilson/Philip Glass opera *Einstein on the Beach*. Since the late 1970s she has embraced the work of other artists in her choreography. >> Cunningham, Merce; Glass, Philip; Wilson, Robert

Chiluba, Frederick >> **Kaunda, Kenneth**

Chinualumogo, Albert >> **Achebe, Chinua**

Chipp, Don(ald) Leslie (1925–) Australian politician, born in Melbourne, Victoria, Australia. He studied at the University of Melbourne, and entered the federal parliament as the Liberal member for Higinbotham, Victoria, in 1960. He remained in the House of Representatives until he became a senator for Victoria in 1977. He founded the Australian Democrats in 1977, a party which aimed to be a centre group that would 'keep the bastards honest'. He was the Democrats' parliamentary leader from 1978 until 1986, when he retired.

Chippendale, Thomas (1718–79) Furniture-maker and designer, baptised at Otley, West Yorkshire, N England, UK. He set up a workshop in St Martin's Lane, London, England, UK, in 1754, in partnership with a merchant, James Rannie (d.1766). He soon became famous for his graceful Neoclassical furniture, especially chairs, which he made mostly from mahogany in the Rococo, chinoiserie, and Gothic Revival styles. *The Gentleman and Cabinetmaker's Director*, which he published in 1754, was the first comprehensive trade catalogue of its kind. He was succeeded by his second partner, Thomas Haig, and his son **Thomas** (c.1749–1822).

Chirac, Jacques (René) [shirak] (1932–) French prime minister (1974–6, 1986–8) and president (1995–). Educated in Paris, he became a civil servant, and was first elected to the National Assembly in 1967. He gained extensive governmental experience before being appointed prime minister by Giscard d'Estaing. He resigned over differences with d'Estaing and broke away to lead the Gaullist Party. Mayor of Paris since 1977, he was an unsuccessful candidate in the 1981 and 1988 presidential elections, but won in 1995. >> Giscard d'Estaing; RR1049

Chirico, Giorgio de [kireekoh] (1888–1978) Artist, born in Volo, Greece. He studied at Athens and Munich, working later in Paris, and with Carrà in Italy. About 1910 he began to produce a series of dreamlike pictures of deserted squares, which had considerable influence on the Surrealists. His whole style after 1915 is often called 'metaphysical painting', including semi-abstract geometric figures and stylized horses. In the 1930s he reverted to an academic style. >> Carrà

Chisholm, Caroline [chizm] (1808–77) Social worker and philanthropist, born near Northampton, Northamptonshire, C England, UK. She married an officer in the army of the East India Company, and in 1838 they settled in Windsor, New South Wales. Concerned at the plight of impoverished immigrant women in the colony, she established an office to provide shelter for the new arrivals, then set about finding them work. She persuaded the British government to grant free passage to families of convicts already transported, and established the Family Colonization Loan Society. In 1866 she returned to England.

Chisholm, Erik [chizm] (1904–65) Composer, born in Glasgow,

W Scotland, UK. He studied under Tovey, and from 1930, as conductor of the Glasgow Grand Opera Society, produced many rarely heard works. In 1945 he was appointed professor of music at Cape Town. His works include two symphonies, concertos for piano and violin, other orchestral music, and operas. >> Tovey, Donald Francis

Chisholm, Melanie >> **Spice Girls, The**

Chissano, Joaquim (Alberto) [chisahnoh] (1939–) Mozambique statesman, prime minister (1974–75), and president (1986–), born in Chibuto, Mozambique. During the campaign for independence in the early 1960s he joined the National Front for the Liberation of Mozambique (Frelimo) and became secretary to its leader, Samora Machel. When internal self-government was granted in 1974 he was appointed prime minister. He then served under Machel as foreign minister, and on Machel's death in 1986 succeeded him as president. >> Machel; RR1076

Chisum, John Simpson [chizm] (1824–84) Cattleman, born in Hardeman Co, TN. He moved to Texas in 1837, and entered the cattle business in 1854. By 1866 he had begun to move his ranching operations to New Mexico, where he settled in 1873 and took the lead in imposing law and order. At his peak, 'The Cattle King of America' owned 60 000–90 000 head of cattle. His role in the Lincoln County War (1878–9) is a subject of dispute.

Chittenden, Russell H(enry) (1856–1943) Biochemist and educator, born in New Haven, CT. He created at Yale the first American course in physiological chemistry (later known as biochemistry), remaining there until 1922, and bringing Yale's Sheffield Scientific School into prominence as its director (1898–1922). He made pioneering studies in the enzymatic digestion of proteins and starch, isolated glycogen ('animal starch') in 1875, and advocated a low-protein diet for humans. He also investigated the toxicology of human alcohol and chemical addiction.

Chladni, Ernst (Florens Friedrich) [kladnee] (1756–1827) Physicist, born in Wittenberg, Germany. The founder of the science of acoustics, he invented the euphonium. His study of the vibration of solid bodies resulted in the patterns known as *Chladni figures*.

Chlodovech or **Chlodwig** >> **Clovis I**

Choiseul(-Amboise), Etienne François, duc de (Duke of) [shwazoei] (1719–85) French statesman and minister of Louis XV, born in Lorraine, France. He served with credit in the Austrian Wars of Succession, and became Duc de Choiseul and foreign minister in 1758. He arranged the alliance between France and Austria against Frederick the Great (1756), and obtained good terms for France at the end of the Seven Years' War (1763). He improved the army and navy, and developed trade and industry. Madame du Barry alienated Louis from his able minister, who retired in 1770. >> du Barry; Louis XV

Chomsky, (Avram) Noam (1928–) Linguist and political activist, born in Philadelphia, PA. He studied at Pennsylvania and Harvard universities, and became professor of linguistics at the Massachusetts Institute of Technology, where he wrote *Syntactic Structures* (1957), introducing a new theory of language called transformational generative grammar. His opposition to the Vietnam War involved him in the radical movement, and in 1969 he published *American Power and the New Mandarins*, attacking politically liberal intellectuals who force their ideology on other nations. He has since continued to publish major works in both linguistics and politics.

Chopin, Frédéric (François) [shohpi] (1810–49) Composer and pianist, born in Zelazowa Wola, Poland, where his French father had settled. He played in public at the age of eight, and published his first work at 15. He studied at the Warsaw Conservatory under Elsner (1826–9), then visited

Vienna and Paris, becoming the idol of the *Salons*. He lived with the novelist George Sand (Madame Dudevant) from 1838 until 1847, when they became estranged. Chopin wrote mainly for the piano, including 50 mazurkas, 27 études, 25 préludes, 19 nocturnes, 13 waltzes, 12 polonaises, four ballades, three impromptus, three sonatas, two piano concertos, and a funeral march. >> **Sand**

Chopin, Kate [shohpin], *née* **Katherine O'Flaherty** (1851–1904) Novelist, short-story writer, and poet, born in St Louis, MO. Educated in St Louis, she married **Oscar Chopin**, a Creole cotton trader from Louisiana, by whom she had six children. After her husband died of swamp fever (1882), she returned with her children to St Louis, where she began to compose sketches of her life, collected in *Bayou Folk* (1894) and *A Night in Acidie* (1897). This work gives no indication of the furore she aroused with the publication of a realistic novel of sexual passion, *The Awakening* (1899), which was harshly condemned by the public. Interest in her work was revived largely by Edmund Wilson, and she has since been embraced by feminists because of her concerns about the freedom of women. >> **Wilson, Edmund**

Chorley, Richard John (1927–) Geomorphologist, born in Minehead, Somerset, SW England, UK. He studied at Oxford, and became professor of geography at Cambridge in 1974. He is a leader in the group which challenged traditional geography and led to the British phase of the so-called 'quantitative revolution'. He used general system theory in the study of landforms, advocated geography as human ecology, and developed the use of models in explanation.

Chou En-lai >> **Zhou Enlai**

Chrétien, (Joseph Jacques) Jean [kraytyen] (1934–) Canadian statesman and prime minister (1993–), born in Shawinigan, Quebec, Canada. He studied at Laval University, was called to the bar, and elected to the House of Commons as a Liberal in 1963. He has occupied a range of portfolios, including minister of state and minister of national revenue in Lester B Pearson's cabinet, and minister of finance, justice, and others in Pierre Trudeau's cabinet. Known as 'the little guy from Shawinigan', and making use of a folksy and engaging style, he has been a popular politician. In 1990 he became leader of the Liberal Party, and prime minister when his party won the 1993 general election. >> **Pearson, Lester B; Trudeau**

Chrétien de Troyes [kraytyî duh trwah] (?–c.1183) Mediaeval poet, born in Troyes, France. He enjoyed the patronage of Marie de Champagne, the daughter of Louis VII. His best-known works are the great metrical Arthurian romances, such as *Lancelot* and *Perceval*, which introduce all the fantastic ingredients of Celtic legend, and add the theme of the Holy Grail. *Erec et Enide* (c.1160) is the earliest known Arthurian romance.

Christaller, Walter [kristaler] (1893–1969) Geographer, born in Berneck, Germany. He studied at Erlangen and Freiburg, and was the originator of 'central place theory' (1933), which has found practical application as a planning tool in North America and, after World War 2, in the NE polders of The Netherlands.

Christensen, Willam [kristensen], originally **William Farr Christensen** (1904–89) Dancer, choreographer, and founder of the San Francisco Ballet, born in Brigham City, UT. He trained with Michel Fokine, danced in vaudeville, and in 1932 opened a ballet school in Portland, OR, from which emerged the Portland Ballet. With his brothers, **Harold** (1904–89) and **Lew** (1909–84), he founded the San Francisco Ballet Company in 1937, the same year that he joined the San Francisco Opera Ballet as ballet master and choreographer. In 1952 he established the Utah Ballet, which since 1968 has been called Ballet West. >> **Fokine**

Christian X (1870–1947) King of Denmark (1912–47), born in Charlottenlund, Denmark. During his reign, Denmark's link with Iceland was severed (1918, 1944), but North Sleswig was recovered from Germany (1920). During the German occupation (1940–5), he attracted great acclaim by remaining in Denmark, seeking with some success to save the country, without undue collaboration, from the harshest effects of occupation. >> **RR1044**

Christian, Charlie, popular name of **Charles Christian** (1916–42) Jazz guitarist, born in Dallas, TX. He was hired by bandleader Benny Goodman in 1939, playing mainly with the Goodman sextet rather than the big band. Christian pioneered the use of the amplified guitar as a solo instrument, freeing the guitar from a purely rhythmic role. He was one of the musicians whose after-hours sessions at Minton's Playhouse in New York City laid the basis of the bebop revolution. >> **Goodman, Benny**

Christian, Fletcher (18th-c) Seaman and ringleader of the mutiny against Captain William Bligh on the *Bounty* in 1789, born in Cockermouth, Cumbria, NW England, UK. Educated at Cockermouth Grammar School, he declined to go to university, and joined the navy instead at the age of 18. He served with Bligh on various ships, and was selected by him as midshipman on the *Britannia* sailing to the West Indies in 1787. A close friendship developed, and Bligh appointed him as first mate on the *Bounty*. After the mutiny, Christian and eight other mutineers took refuge on Pitcairn I, where they founded a settlement. In all probability, he was killed by the Tahitians. >> **Bligh**

Christie, Dame Agatha (Mary Clarissa), *née* **Miller** (1890–1976) Writer, born in Torquay, Devon, SE England, UK. Under the surname of her first husband (**Colonel Archibald Christie**, divorced 1928), she wrote more than 70 detective novels, featuring the Belgian detective, Hercule Poirot, or the enquiring village lady, Miss Marple. In 1930 she married archaeology professor **Max Mallowan**, with whom she travelled on several expeditions. Her play *The Mousetrap* opened in 1952, and holds the record for the longest unbroken run in a London theatre. Several of her stories have become popular films, such as *Murder on the Orient Express* (1974) and *Death on the Nile* (1978). She was made a dame in 1971. >> **Mallowan**

Christie, James (1730–1803) Auctioneer, born in London, England, UK. He founded the well-known London auctioneering firm in 1766. Two of his sons were **James** (1773–1831), antiquary and auctioneer, and **Samuel Hunter** (1784–1865), student of magnetism and professor of mathematics at Woolwich (1806–50). Samuel's son, **Sir William Henry Mahoney** (1845–1922), was astronomer royal (1881–1910).

Christie, John (1882–1962) Opera patron, born in Eggesford, Devon, SW England, UK. In the 1930s he built a small theatre on his country estate in East Sussex, which is now internationally known as Glyndebourne Opera. It has developed a reputation especially for its productions of Mozart.

Christie, John Reginald Halliday (1898–1953) Murderer, born in Yorkshire, N England, UK. He was hanged at London for the murder of his wife, and confessed to the murder of six other women, including the wife of **Timothy John Evans**, who lived in the same house. Evans had been convicted and hanged for the murder of his infant daughter in 1950, and also charged with his wife's murder. After a special inquiry, Evans was granted a free pardon in 1966. The trial of Christie thus played an important part in altering British legislation affecting the death penalty.

Christie, Julie (1940–) British actress, born in Chukua, Assam. She studied at the Central School of Music and Drama, London, and worked in repertory, becoming known through her role in *Billy Liar* (1963). In 1965 she won an Oscar for *Darling*. She consolidated her career with *Dr Zhivago* (1965), *Far From the Madding Crowd* (1967), and *The Go-Between* (1971). Subsequent films have highlighted her involvement with a variety of political issues, although she returned to more mainstream productions with *Heat and Dust* (1982), *Power* (1985), *Fools of Fortune* (1990), and *Hamlet* (1996).

Christie, Linford (1960–) Sprinter, born in Jamaica, now living in Britain. In 1993 he held the World, Olympic, Commonwealth, and European Cup titles for the 100 m, achieving 9·87 seconds at the world championships in Stuttgart, Germany (a European record, and 0·01 seconds outside the world record). He retired in 1997.

Christie, Sir William Henry Mahoney (1845–1922) British astronomer, the grandson of **James Christie**. He was astronomer royal (1881–1910).

Christina (1626–89) Queen of Sweden (1632–54), born in Stockholm, the daughter and successor of Gustav II Adolf. She was educated as a prince on her father's orders during her minority, when the affairs of the kingdom were ably managed by Axel Oxenstierna. When she came of age (1644) she negotiated the Peace of Westphalia, bringing to an end the Thirty Years War (1648). She patronized the arts and attracted some of the best minds in Europe, such as Hugh Grotius, Salamatius, and Descartes, to her court. In 1654 she suddenly abdicated and proclaimed Charles X Gustav her successor. She was received into the Catholic Church (proscribed in Sweden) and went to Rome. She aspired to the throne of Poland vacated by her cousin, John Casimir (1667), but failed. For the rest of her life she lived in Rome as a pensioner of the pope, and was a generous and discerning patron of the arts. She founded the Accademia dell'Arcadia for philosophy and literature, and sponsored the sculptor Bernini and the composers Corelli and Scarlatti. >> Gustav II; Oxenstierna; RR1090

Christine de Pisan [peezan] (c. 1363–c. 1431) Poet, born in Venice, Italy. Brought up in Paris, in 1378 she married **Etienne Castel**, who became the king's secretary, but who died in 1389. Left with three children and no money, she was obliged to call upon her literary talents, and between 1399 and 1415 produced a number of works in both prose and verse, including *Cité des dames* (1405, The City of Ladies) and *Livres des trois vertus*, an educational and social compendium for women. She withdrew to a nunnery in c.1418.

Christo, originally **Christo Javacheff** (1935–) Avant-garde artist, born in Gabrovo, Bulgaria. He studied art first in Sophia (1951–6), then briefly in Vienna (1957), before moving to Paris in 1958. In 1964 he moved permanently to New York City. His huge outdoor sculptures, which include wrapping objects (trees, cars, buildings) in canvas or plastic sheeting, and creating 'assemblages' of stacked oil drums, have continued to arouse controversy, especially among environmentalists.

Christoff, Boris (1914–93) Bass-baritone, born in Plovdiv, Bulgaria. He studied law in Sofia, then studied singing in Rome and Salzburg. His debut recital was in Rome (1946). He sang at La Scala in Milan in 1947, at Covent Garden in 1949, and from 1956 in the USA.

Christophe, Henry [kristof] (1767–1829) Haitian revolutionary, born a slave on the island of Grenada. He joined the black insurgents on Haiti against the French (1790), and became one of their leaders, under Toussaint L'Ouverture. He was appointed resident in 1807, and despite civil war was proclaimed king in the N part of the island as Henry I in 1811. He ruled with vigour, but his avarice and cruelty led to an insurrection, and he shot himself. >> Toussaint L'Ouverture

Christopher, St (3rd-c) Syrian Christian martyr. According to tradition, he was a man of gigantic stature. His name in

Greek (*Christophoros*) means 'Christ-bearing', which gave rise to the legend that he had carried the Christ-child across a river. He is said to have suffered martyrdom under Emperor Decius (reigned 249–251). He is the patron saint of wayfarers, and now motorists. Feast day 25 July.

Christopher, Warren M(inor) (1925–) Lawyer and government official, born in Scranton, ND. In 1950, he joined the Los Angeles law firm O'Melveny & Myers, and in the 1960s analyzed race riots and aided international textile negotiations. Deputy attorney general (1967–9) and deputy secretary of state (1977–81), in 1989–91 he led successful US negotiations for the release of 52 hostages held in Iran. He remained a respected voice in the Democratic Party in the following years, and President Clinton appointed him secretary of state in 1993. He resigned at the 1996 election. >> Clinton, Bill

Christophersen, Henning [kristofersen] (1939–) Danish statesman, born in Copenhagen. A member of the Danish parliament (1971–84), he became leader of the Danish Liberal Party in 1978. He was minister of foreign affairs (1978–9) and minister of finance and deputy prime minister (1982–4). He has been a member of the EC Commission since 1984, and was a vice-president in charge of economic and monetary co-operation during 1985–95.

Christus, Petrus [kristus] (c. 1420–c. 1473) Painter, born in Baerle, Brabant, who became a master in Bruges in 1444. He is often said to have been the pupil or assistant of Jan van Eyck. He may have visited Italy, and it is thought that he was an important source for the transmission of the Eyckian technique to Italian painters, in particular Antonello da Messina. >> Antonello da Messina; Eyck, Jan van

Christy, Edwin P(earce) [kristee] (1815–62) Entertainer, born in Philadelphia, PA, the originator of the Christy Minstrels show. He was singing with two assistants at a public house in Buffalo in 1842, but steadily increased the success of his 'black-face' minstrelsy, taking his show to New York City and London. Many of his songs were commissioned from Stephen Foster. He retired in 1855, and committed suicide during a fit of insanity. >> Foster, Stephen

Chrysander, Friedrich [krisander] (1826–1901) Musical historian, the biographer and editor of Handel, born in Lübtheen, Germany. He founded the Handel Society in 1856. >> Handel

Chrysippus [kriysipus] (c. 280–c. 206 BC) Stoic philosopher, born in Soli, Cilicia. He went to Athens as a youth, and studied under Cleanthes to become the third and greatest head of the Stoa. He wrote over 700 works, of which only fragments remain. >> Cleanthes

Chrysler, Walter (Percy) [kriyzler] (1875–1940) Automobile manufacturer, born in Wamego, KS. He started his working life as an apprentice in a Union Pacific Railroad machine shop, and by 1912 was works manager of the Buick Motor Co. By 1916 he had become company president, resigning to become a director of Willys-Overland and Maxwell Motor Co (from 1925, the Chrysler Corporation). He introduced the 'Plymouth' motor car and designed the first high compression engine.

Chrysostom, St John [krisostom] (c.347–407) Church Father, born in Antioch. His name comes from the Greek, 'golden-mouthed', on account of his eloquence. He spent six years as a monk in the mountains, but returned in 381 to Antioch, where he was ordained, and gained a reputation as the greatest orator of the Church. In 398 he was made Archbishop of Constantinople, where he carried out many reforms, but his reproof of vices moved the Empress Eudoxia (ruled 395–404) to have him deposed and banished (403). His body was brought to Constantinople and reburied with honour in 438. Feast day 13 September.

Chu, Steven (1948–) Physicist, born in St Louis, MO. He was a member of the technical staff at Bell Telephone Laboratories (1976–8) and head of the quantum electronics and research department of AT & T Bell Laboratories (1983–7) before becoming a physics professor at Stanford. He has made major contributions to laser spectroscopy, the analysis of positronium atoms, and studies of gaseous sodium at temperatures approaching absolute zero.

Chubb, Charles (1772–1846) British locksmith. He patented improvements in 'detector' locks, originally (1818) patented by his brother, **Jeremiah Chubb**, of Portsea. He was in the hardware business in Winchester and Portsea, before settling in London.

Chulalongkorn, Phra Paramindr Maha (1853–1910) King of Siam (1868–1910, as **Rama V**), born in Bangkok. His father, **Mongkut (Rama IV)**, was the model for the oscar-winning film *The King and I* (1956), drawn from the reminiscences of Chulalongkorn's governess, Anna Leonowens (1834–1914). He was educated by English teachers, acquiring Western linguistic and cultural skills, after which he went to a Buddhist monastery until he was 20. He completed the reforms Mongkut had begun to modernize Siam. He abolished slavery, proclaimed liberty of conscience, and introduced modern buildings, transport systems, and communications. He sent his crown prince to study in Britain, and ultimately paid for his Westernization by being forced to accept treaties with France and with Britain. >> RR1093

Chun Doo-Hwan (1931–) South Korean soldier and president (1980–8), born in Taegu, South Korea. He trained at the Korean military academy and joined the South Korean army in 1955. After President Park Chung Hee's assassination in 1979, he took charge of the Korean Central Intelligence Agency (KCIA) and led the investigation into Park's murder. He assumed control of the army and the government following a coup in 1979. After becoming president he retired from the army to head the newly formed Democratic Justice Party. Under his rule, the country's 'economic miracle' continued, but popular opposition to the authoritarian nature of the regime mounted, forcing his retirement. He was found guilty of treason and corruption in 1996, and sentenced to death (commuted to life imprisonment), but released in 1997. >> RR1070

Chung, Kyung-Wha (1948–) Violinist, born in Seoul. She moved to New York City in 1960 and studied at the Juilliard School, New York City, until 1967, when she made her debut with the New York Philharmonic. Her sister **Myung-Wha Chung** (1944–) is a distinguished cellist, and her brother **Myung-Whung Chung** (1953–) a pianist and conductor who in 1989 was appointed music director of the new Bastille Opera, Paris.

Church, Frederick (Edwin) (1826–1900) Painter, born in Hartford, CT. Considered a member of the Hudson River School, he studied with Thomas Cole, and travelled in Europe and South America. By 1870 he began construction of his exotic mansion, Olana, on the Hudson R. His panoramic scenes reveal his dramatic use of lighting and naturalistic details, as seen in his 'Niagara' (1857) and 'The Heart of the Andes' (1859). >> Cole, Thomas

Church, Sir Richard (1785–1873) Soldier, born in Cork, Co Cork, Ireland. He ran away from school to join the British army, and was commissioned in the 13th Foot (later Somerset Light Infantry) in 1800. He took part in the Greek War of Independence (1821–32), and was appointed generalissimo of the Greek insurgent forces (1827). He led the revolution in Greece in 1843, and was promoted general (1854), having earned the nickname of 'Liberator of Greece'. He was knighted in 1822.

Church, Richard Thomas (1893–1972) Writer, born in London, England, UK. He made his name first as a poet, but he is known also for his novels, literary criticism, travel books, and stories for children, especially *A Squirrel called Rufus*. His novel *The Porch* (1937) won the Femina Vie-Heureuse Prize.

Churcher, Betty, popular name of **Elizabeth Ann Churcher** (1931–) Arts administrator, born in Brisbane, Queensland, Australia. She studied in London at the Courtauld Institute and the Royal College of Art. She held a range of academic positions in Australia, wrote the award-winning book *Understanding Art* (1974), and was chairman of Australia Council's Visual Arts Board (1983–7) and director of the Art Gallery of Western Australia (1987–9). She was director of the Australian National Gallery (1990–7), during which time the Gallery received critical praise, broke attendance records, and mounted such acclaimed exhibitions as 'The Age of Angkor', from the National Museum of Phnom Penh.

Churchill, Arabella (1648–1730) English aristocrat, the elder sister of John Churchill, 1st Duke of Marlborough. In 1665 she entered the service of the Duchess of York, wife of the future James II, and became his mistress. With James she had two daughters, and two sons: **James Fitzjames (Duke of Berwick)**, and **Henry Fitzjames (Duke of Albemarle)**. >> Berwick; James II (of England); Marlborough

Churchill, Caryl Lesley (1938–) Playwright, born in London, England, UK. She began writing while a student at Oxford. Her first play was *Light Shining in Buckinghamshire* (1976), about the Levellers. Her greatest commercial success has been *Serious Money* (1987), satirizing the world of City financial brokers. Other plays include *Cloud Nine* (1979), *Top Girls* (1982), *Fen* (1983), *Softcops* (1984), *Mad Forest* (1990), and *Skriker* (1994).

Churchill, Charles (1731–64) Satirical poet, born in London, England, UK. He studied at Cambridge, but ruined his academic career with a clandestine marriage at the age of 17. With his father's help he was ordained priest in 1756, but gave up the Church in 1763. He achieved fame with his *Rosciad* (1761), a fierce attack on contemporary actors. Other works include *The Apology* (1761), *The Prophecy of Famine* (1763), and *The Candidate* (1764).

Churchill, John >> Marlborough, John Churchill

Churchill, Randolph (Frederick Edward Spencer) (1911–68) Journalist, born in London, England, UK, the son of Sir Winston Churchill. He studied at Oxford, and served in World War 2 as an intelligence officer on the general staff. He was Conservative MP for Preston (1940–5). A forthright commentator on current affairs, he wrote *The Rise and Fall of Sir Anthony Eden* (1959), and published two volumes of a full-length biography of his father (1966, 1967). >> Churchill, Sir Winston

Churchill, Lord Randolph (Henry Spencer) (1849–95) British statesman, born in Blenheim Palace, Oxfordshire, SC England, UK, the third son of the 7th Duke of Marlborough, and the father of Winston Churchill. He studied at Oxford, entered parliament in 1874, and became conspicuous in 1880 as the leader of a guerrilla band of Conservatives known as the 'Fourth Party'. He was secretary for India (1885–6), and for a short while Chancellor of the Exchequer and Leader of the House of Commons. He resigned after his first budget proved unacceptable, and thereafter devoted little time to politics. >> Churchill, Sir Winston

Churchill, Sarah, *née* **Jennings** (1660–1744) English aristocrat, the wife of John Churchill, 1st Duke of Marlborough. In 1673 she entered the service of the Duke of York (the future James II), and became a close friend of his younger daughter, Princess Anne (the future Queen Anne): in their private correspondence, Anne was called 'Mrs Morley' and Sarah was 'Mrs Freeman'. After Anne became queen, Sarah dominated her household and the Whig ministry. Anne finally broke with the Marlboroughs in 1711, when Sarah was supplanted by a new favourite, her cousin Mrs Abigail Masham. >> Anne; Marlborough; Masham

Churchill, Winston (1871–1947) Historical novelist, born in St Louis, MO. He trained at the US Naval Academy, then turned to writing. His works include *Richard Carvel* (1899), *The Crisis* (1901), and *The Crossing* (1904). He lived most of his life in New Hampshire.

Churchill, Sir Winston (Leonard Spencer) (1874–1965) see panel below

Churchward, George Jackson (1857–1933) Locomotive engineer, born in Stoke Gabriel, Devon, SW England, UK.

SIR WINSTON (LEONARD SPENCER) CHURCHILL (1874–1965)

Churchill was born at Blenheim Palace, Woodstock, Oxfordshire, a direct descendant of John Churchill, 1st Duke of Marlborough (1650–1722). The eldest son of Lord Randolph Churchill, Conservative statesman, and Jennie Jerome, daughter of a New York financier, the often lonely boy was brought up by his affectionate nurse, Mrs Everest. He was educated at Harrow, where he was an academically undistinguished student. He went on to Sandhurst, after sitting the exam three times, and entered the Fourth Hussars in 1895, the year his father died.

His early army career was punctuated by well-received journalistic writings and a self-inflicted course of reading, launching him on a literary career which he pursued throughout his life. He served with the Malakand field force in 1897, and with the 1898 Nile expeditionary force, when he fought hand-to-hand against the Dervishes at Omdurman. During the Boer War he was captured in an ambush, but successfully escaped. However, routine army life bored him, and in 1899 he resigned his commission to concentrate on a literary and political career, becoming Conservative MP for Oldham the next year.

Following his opposition to Chamberlain's tariff-reform policy, he joined the Liberals in 1904, becoming colonial under-secretary (1905), and as President of the Board of Trade (1908–10) introduced legislation for the establishment of labour exchanges. In 1908 he married **Clementine Ogilvy Hozier**, a relationship which was to provide much happiness and security throughout his lifetime. In 1910 he became home secretary, and in 1911, when the Germans provocatively sent a gunboat to Agadir against the French, he transferred to the Admiralty, where he worked to bring the navy to readiness for the war he foresaw.

In 1915 Churchill was excluded from the coalition government of World War 1 because of the controversy arising from the failed attempt to open the Dardanelles Straits, and the disastrous Gallipoli campaign– responsibility for which was given to him. He resigned and joined the army in France, but was soon returned to parliament as a private member, becoming Lloyd George's minister of munitions in 1917. This gave him the opportunity of concentrating on the task of tank production, which he had instigated while at the Admiralty. From 1919 to 1921 he was secretary of state for war, with responsibility also for the Royal Air Force.

In 1924 he was returned for Epping as a 'Constitutionalist' supporter of the Conservatives, unexpectedly becoming Chancellor of the Exchequer (1924–9), under Baldwin. In this capacity, he brought about Britain's return to the gold standard and played a leading role in the defeat of the General Strike of 1926. Disagreements with Chamberlain over rearmamament, appeasement, and the Government of India bill led to his exclusion from office in 1929. For a decade he agonised over the government's inaction in the face of the growing threat of Hitler's Germany. During this period he wrote his biography of Marlborough, and built a private intelligence centre at Chartwell, his home.

When Britain declared war on Germany (3 Sept 1939), Chamberlain brought Churchill back to his post as First Lord of the Admiralty. Following Chamberlain's resignation, when Germany invaded the low countries, Churchill became the obvious choice to lead the nation with a coalition government (May 1940). This heralded the beginning of his 'walk with destiny' for which he considered all his earlier life a preparation. He offered the British people nothing but 'blood, toil, tears and sweat', leading Britain against Germany and Italy, and incomparably expressing the national spirit of resistance. During World War 2 he worked round the clock, travelled 150 000 mi, and was called upon constantly to make vital decisions. He shaped the Atlantic Charter in 1941, devised the strategy of El Alamein in 1942, gave the highest priority to the battle against the U-boats, repelled the Luftwaffe assault on Britain, and inspired Europe's resistance to Germany with his voice. He was on close personal terms with President Franklin D Roosevelt, while sustaining the often difficult alliance with the Soviet Union. It was Churchill who announced the unconditional surrender of Germany (8 May 1945). Shortly afterwards the parliamentary coalition was dissolved and he formed a caretaker government.

The general election of July 1945 came at the height of his wartime fame, and Labour's victory left Churchill, shocked and defeated, as Leader of the Opposition. In his international speeches he warned about the tyranny behind the 'Iron Curtain' (his phrase) and fostered the conception of European and Atlantic unity, later to bear fruit in NATO and other supranational organizations. He defeated Labour in 1951 with a narrow majority, and remained in office until his resignation in 1955. This was a period of personal honours– he was awarded the Nobel Prize for Literature in 1953, most especially for *The Second World War* (6 vols, 1948–53), and he was knighted in the same year.

After his resignation, Churchill remained on the back benches, and in his last years was often described as 'the greatest living Englishman'. He achieved a world reputation not only as a gifted strategist and inspiring war leader, but as a great orator, a talented painter, and a stylish writer with a profound sense of history. In 1963 he was accorded the unique distinction of honorary US citizenship by an Act of Congress. His death in London after declining ill-health was followed by a state funeral at which dignitaries from all over the world paid their respects.
>> Baldwin, Stanley; Chamberlain, Neville; Churchill, Lord Randolph / Randolph; Lloyd-George, David; Roosevelt, Franklin D

He was chief mechanical engineer of the Great Western Railway (1902–21). Although not a great innovator, he showed rare judgment in combining the best features of British and foreign locomotive practice in his designs, such as the 4-6-0 'Star' series introduced in 1906, which was the outstanding British express locomotive for the next 20 years.

Churriguera, Don José [chureegayra] (1650–1725) Architect, born in Salamanca, Spain. He was royal architect to Charles II, and developed the extravagant style which is known as *Churrigueresque*. He designed Salamanca Cathedral. His brothers **Joaquin** (1674–1720) and **Alberto** (1676–1750) were also architects.

Chu-ta >> Zhu Da

Chu-teh >> Zhu De

Chuter-Ede, Baron >> Ede, James Chuter

Ciano, Galeazzo, conte di (Count) **Cortellazzo** [chyahnoh] (1903–44) Italian politician, born in Livorno, Italy, the son-in-law of Mussolini. A leading Fascist, he became minister of propaganda (1935) and of foreign affairs (1936–43), supporting his father-in-law's expansionist and war policy. He was nevertheless unenthusiastic about Mussolini's alliance with Germany, and from 1942 openly opposed it. Having participated in Mussolini's deposition (Jul 1943), in 1944 he was put on trial by Mussolini's supporters, and shot. >> Mussolini

Cibber, Colley [siber] (1671–1757) Actor and playwright, born in London, England, UK. He spent most of his career at the Theatre Royal in Drury Lane. In 1696, his first comedy, *Love's Last Shift*, established his fame both as a dramatist and actor. As a manager and playwright, he greatly improved the decency of the theatre. From 1730 he was Poet Laureate.

Cibber, Mrs [siber], *née* **Susannah Maria Arne** (1714–66) Actress and singer, born in London, England, UK, the sister of the composer Thomas Arne. A fine contralto, she made her stage debut in her brother's *Rosamund* (1733), and the following year married **Theophilus Cibber** (1703–58, the son of Colley Cibber); from then on she was known as 'Mrs Cibber'. Handel wrote parts for her in his *Messiah* and *Samson*. Thereafter she turned to drama, and played opposite David Garrick at Drury Lane with enormous success. >> Arne; Cibber, Colley; Garrick

Ciccone, Madonna Louise >> Madonna

Cicero, Marcus Tullius [siseroh], also known in English as **Tully** (106–43 BC) Roman orator, statesman, and man of letters, born in Arpinum, Latium. At Rome he studied law, oratory, philosophy, and literature, and embarked upon a political career, attaining the consulship in 63 BC. He foiled Catiline's revolutionary plot, survived an attempt on his life, and persuaded the Senate to execute Catiline. He spoke against Clodius in 61 BC, and was exiled when Clodius became tribune in 58 BC. In 57 BC he was recalled by the people, but lost the esteem of both Caesar's and Pompey's factions by vacillating between the two. Living in retirement (46–44 BC), he wrote most of his chief works on rhetoric and philosophy. In 43 BC he delivered his famous speeches against Antony, the so-called 'Philippics', urging the Senate to declare war on Antony. He was murdered near Caieta by Antony's soldiers as he tried to escape after the triumverate of Antony, Lepidus, and Octavian was formed. >> Antonius; Roscius; Tiro; Verres

Cid, El [sid], Span [theed], popular name of **Rodrigo** or **Ruy Díaz de Vivar** (c. 1043–99) Spanish hero, born in Burgos, Spain. A soldier of fortune in the service of both Christian and Muslim kings, he soon became known as the *Cid* (from the Moorish *Sidi*, 'lord'); *Campeador* ('warrior') is often added. He was constantly fighting from 1065, his great achievement being the capture of Valencia in 1094.

Cidenas [sidaynas] (4th-c BC) Babylonian astronomer, the head of an astronomical school at Sippra. He discovered the precession of the equinoxes.

Cierva, Juan de la [thyairva] (1895–1936) Aeronautical engineer, born in Murcia, Spain. He trained as a civil engineer but became interested in flying, and designed and built a number of gliders and aircraft (1912–19). Following the crash of one of his planes, he developed the autogiro, an aircraft with a freely rotating rotor which provides lift, achieving the first successful flight in 1923.

Cilea, Francesco [cheelia] (1866–1950) Operatic composer, born in Palmi, Italy. He was director of the Naples Conservatory from 1916 to 1936. He wrote several operas, of which the best known is *Adriana Lecouvreur* (1902).

Cilento, Lady Phyllis Dorothy [silentoh], *née* **McGlew** (1894–1987) Medical practitioner, writer, and broadcaster, born in Sydney, New South Wales, Australia. She studied at Adelaide University, and became lecturer in mothercraft and obstetrical physiotherapy at the University of Queensland. Her life's work was devoted to family planning, childbirth education, and nutrition. She married **Raphael West Cilento** in 1920. >> Cilento, Raphael West

Cilento, Sir Raphael West [silentoh] (1893–1985) Medical administrator, born in Jamestown, South Australia. He studied at Adelaide University, became director of the Australian Institute of Tropical Medicine at Townsville, Queensland, from 1922, director of public health and quarantine in New Guinea (1924–8), and director-general of health and medical services for Queensland (1934–45). Knighted in 1935, after World War 2 he served in Germany and New York, and worked with the UN (1946–51). >> Cilento, Phyllis Dorothy

Cimabue [cheemabooay], originally **Cenni di Peppi** (c.1240–c.1302) Painter, born in Florence, Italy. He adopted traditional Byzantine forms at first, but soon turned to nature, and led the way to the naturalism of his great pupil, Giotto. He executed several important frescoes in the Church of St Francis at Assisi. >> Giotto

Cimarosa, Domenico [cheemarohsa] (1749–1801) Composer of operas, born in Aversa, Italy. He studied music at Naples, and produced his first opera there in 1772. He was court musician at St Petersburg (1787) and *Kapellmeister* at Vienna (1791) succeeding Salieri, where his comic opera *Il Matrimonio segreto* (1792, The Secret Marriage) was a great success, then in 1793 he returned to Naples. He wrote many other works, including church and chamber music. >> Salieri

Cimon [siymon] (?–449 BC) Athenian commander, the son of Miltiades, particularly prominent in the 470s and 460s BC. Active in the mopping-up operations in the Aegean after the Persian Wars, his greatest exploit was the defeat, on the same day, of the Persian land and naval forces at the R Eurymedon (c.469 BC). In politics, he was less successful. His opposition to democracy at home and support for Sparta abroad brought him into conflict with Pericles, and he was ostracized in 461 BC. >> Miltiades; Pericles

Cincinnatus, Lucius Quinctius [sinsinahtus] (5th-c BC) Roman statesman, farmer, and folk hero. Called from the plough and given absolute power to rescue the Roman army of the consul Minucius, which had been trapped by the Aequi (458 BC), he voluntarily gave up this power and returned to his farm, as soon as the crisis was over.

Cineas [sinias] (?–270 BC) Greek politician from Thessaly. The friend and minister of Pyrrhus, the King of Epirus, he was said to be the most eloquent man of his time. >> Pyrrhus

Cinna, Lucius Cornelius [sina] (?–84 BC) Prominent Roman politician of the turbulent 80s BC. Driven from Rome and illegally deposed while consul in 87 BC, he recaptured the city with the help of Marius amid much bloodshed,

and was all-powerful there until his murder in 84 BC.
>> Marius, Gaius

Cipriani, Giambattista [chipriahnee] (1727–85) Historical painter, born in Florence, Italy. In 1755 he accompanied Sir William Chambers to London, where his graceful drawings, engraved by Bartolozzi, gained great popularity. He was a member of the St Martin's Lane Academy, and in 1768 was elected a foundation member of the Royal Academy. >> Bartolozzi

Cisneros, Henry (Gabriel) [siznairohs, seesnayrohs] (1947–) Mayor and cabinet official, born in San Antonio, TX. As mayor of his native city (1982–90) he gained a national reptutation for being a progressive. He wrote several books, including *Target '90: Goals and Decisions for San Antonio's Future*. In 1992, President Clinton named him secretary of housing and urban affairs. >> Clinton

Citrine (of Wembley), Walter McLennan Citrine, Baron [sitreen] (1887–1983) Trade union leader, born in Liverpool, Merseyside, NW England, UK. An electrician by trade, he became general secretary of the Trades Union Congress (1926–46), and president of the International Federation of Trades Unions (1928–45). Knighted in 1935 and created a peer in 1946, he became chairman of the Central Electricity Authority in 1947.

Citroën, André Gustave [sitrohen] (1878–1935) Engineer and motor manufacturer, born in Paris. He was responsible for the mass production of armaments during World War 1. After the war he applied these techniques to the manufacture of low-priced small cars. In 1934 he became bankrupt and lost control of the company which still bears his name.

Civitali, Matteo [chivitahlee] (1435–1501) Architect and sculptor, born in Lucca, Italy. His best work is seen in the cathedral at Lucca.

Ci-Xi or **Tz'u-hsi** [tsoe shee], **Xiaogin** or **Hsiao-ch'en**, family name **Yehonala**, known as **the Empress Dowager** (1835–1908) Chinese consort of the Xianfeng emperor (1851–62), born in Beijing, who rose to dominate China by manipulating the succession to the throne. She bore the Xianfeng emperor his only son, who succeeded at the age of five as the T'ung Chih emperor, but kept control even after his majority in 1873. After his death (1875), she flouted the succession laws of the imperial clan to ensure the succession of another minor, aged three, as the Guangxu emperor, and continued to assert control even when the new emperor reached maturity. In 1900 she took China into war against the combined treaty powers in support of the Boxer movement. Only after her death was it possible to begin reforms. >> Zai Tian

Cixous, Hélène [seeshoo] (1937–) Academic and feminist, born in Algiers. She studied at the Lycée Bugeaud in Algiers, moving to France in 1955, where she began to teach. In 1965 she became an assistant lecturer at the Sorbonne, and took an active part in the student uprisings of 1968. Later, as professor at Vincennes, she established experimental literature courses. Her work is mostly concerned with the relationship between psychoanalysis and language, especially in its significance for women.

Claiborne, Craig [klaybaw(r)n] (1920–) Chef and writer, born in Sunflower, MS. A lover of food, accomplished cook, and trained journalist, he became food editor of the *New York Times* in 1957, and his stylish but impartial restaurant reviews set a new standard for food reporting. His cookbooks include the best-selling *New York Times Cook Book* (1961) and *Craig Claiborne's Southern Cooking* (1987).

Clair, René, pseudonym of **René Chomette** (1898–1981) Film producer, born in Paris. He was a soldier, journalist, critic, and actor, before he wrote and directed his first film in 1923. He produced both silent and talking films, in

France and the USA, which were noted for a light touch and whimsical irony. His major works include *Sous les toits de Paris* (1930, Under the Roofs of Paris), *The Ghost Goes West* (1935), and *It Happened Tomorrow* (1944). He returned to France in 1946, and continued to make films for nearly 20 years.

Claparède, Edouard [klapared] (1873–1940) Psychologist and educationist, born in Geneva, Switzerland. After studies at Geneva, Leipzig, and Paris, he founded the journal *Archives de psychologie* (1901). As professor at Geneva, he was director of the experimental psychology laboratory, and in 1912 founded the J J Rousseau Institute for the study of educational science. An exponent of functionalism, he pioneered studies in problem-solving and sleep.

Clapeyron, Bénoit Paul Emile [klapayrõ] (1799–1864) Civil engineer, born in Paris. He studied at the Ecole Polytechnique and the Ecole des Mines. He was principally engaged in the construction of railways and bridges, including the design of locomotives, where he was the first to make use of the expansive action of steam in the cylinder. For the analysis of beams resting on more than two supports he developed the 'theorem of three moments', and in 1834 published an exposition of Carnot's paper on the power and efficiency of various types of heat engine. >> Carnot, Sadi

Clapperton, Hugh (1788–1827) Explorer, born in Annan, Dumfries and Galloway, SW Scotland, UK. At sea with the Royal Navy from the age of 13, he attained the rank of captain. He was sent in 1821 with Dixon Denham to discover the source of the Niger. They travelled S across the Sahara to L Chad in 1823; from there he pushed on alone to Sokoto, returning to England in 1825, the first European to have entered N Nigeria. He started again from the Bight of Benin in December 1825, travelling N in company with Richard Lander and others, but died near Sokoto. >> Denham, Dixon; Lander, Richard

Clapton, Eric (1945–) Rock guitarist and singer, born in Ripley, Surrey, SE England, UK. In the 1960s he was in British rhythm-and-blues bands The Yardbirds and John Mayall's Bluesbreakers, then 'supergroups' Cream and Blind Faith. He has since played and recorded with most of the great names of rock music. 'Layla', recorded in 1970 with Duane Allman and others under the name of Derek and the Dominoes, is considered a rock classic by many, as are 'I Shot the Sheriff', 'Lay Down Sally', and 'Wonderful Tonight'. His album *Eric Clapton: Unplugged* reached number 3 in the UK charts in 1992, and he was voted Variety Club Best Recording Artist the same year.

Clare of Assisi, St (1194–1253) Abbess, born of a noble family in Assisi, Italy. She gave up her possessions and joined a Benedictine convent (1212), and in 1215 founded with St Francis the order of Franciscan nuns, known as the Poor Clares. She was canonized in 1255. In 1958 she was designated patron saint of television, on the grounds that at Christmas 1252, while in her cell at the Convent of San Damiano, she both saw and heard the Mass in the Church of St Francis in Assisi. Feast day 11 August.

Clare, Anthony (Ward) (1942–) British psychiatrist and broadcaster. He studied at University College, Dublin, and London University, became registrar at St Patrick's Hospital, Dublin (1967–9), then was appointed professor in the Department of Psychological Medicine at St Bartholomew's Hospital Medical College (1982–8), London, and professor of clinical psychiatry, Trinity College, Dublin (1985–95). His many broadcasts include BBC's *In the Psychiatrist's Chair* (1982–), and among his books are *Let's Talk About Me* (1981), *Depression and How to Survive It* (1993, with Spike Milligan), and *In the Psychiatrist's Chair II* (1995). >> Milligan

Clare, John (1793–1864) Poet, born in Helpston, Cambridgeshire, EC England, UK. Though almost without schooling, he began to cultivate verse writing, and his *Poems Descriptive of Rural Life* (1820) had a good reception. Despite some patronage, he was forced to live in poverty, and spent the last 23 years of his life in an asylum at Northampton, where he wrote some of his best poetry.

Clarence, George, Duke of (1449–78) The third son of Richard, Duke of York, and brother of Edward IV and Richard III, born in Dublin. According to tradition, he was put to death in the Tower of London by drowning 'in a butt of Malmsey'. Created Duke of Clarence on Edward's accession in 1461, in 1469 he married **Isabella**, the elder daughter of Richard Neville, Earl of Warwick, against Edward's wishes. He supported Warwick against his brother in the brief restoration of Henry VI in 1470, but deserted to his brother's side in 1471. He quarrelled with his other brother, Richard, Duke of Gloucester, over Richard's marriage to his sister-in-law Anne Neville in 1472, but was later reconciled. In 1478 he was impeached by his brothers for treason, and secretly executed. >> Edward IV; Richard III; Warwick, Richard Neville; York

Clarence, William, Duke of >> **William IV**

Clarendon, Edward Hyde, 1st Earl of (1609–74) English statesman and historian, born near Salisbury, Wiltshire, S England, UK. He trained as a lawyer, and in 1640 became a member of the Short Parliament. At first he supported the popular party, but in 1641 became a close adviser of Charles, and headed the Royalist Opposition in the Commons until 1642. He was knighted in 1643, and made Chancellor of the Exchequer. He became High Chancellor (1658), and at the Restoration was created Baron Hyde (1660) and Earl of Clarendon (1661). In 1660 his daughter **Anne** (1638–71) secretly married the king's brother, James (later James II). Unpopular as a statesman, Clarendon irritated Cavaliers and Puritans alike, and in 1667 he fell victim to a court cabal. Impeached for high treason, he left the country for France. His major work is the *History of the Rebellion in England* (3 vols, 1704–7). >> Charles I (of England); James II (of England).

Clarendon, George William Frederick Villiers, 4th Earl of (1800–70) British statesman, born in London, England, UK. He studied at Cambridge, entered the diplomatic service, and was appointed ambassador at Madrid (1833). In 1838 he succeeded his uncle as 4th Earl, and in 1840 was made Lord Privy Seal under Melbourne. Under Russell he became President of the Board of Trade (1846), and Irish viceroy (1847–52). As secretary of state for foreign affairs (1853), he incurred the responsibility for the Crimean War, and Roebuck's resolution in 1855 cost him his office, which he resumed at Palmerston's desire. He was foreign secretary again under Lord John Russell (1865–6) and William Gladstone (1868–70). >> Gladstone, W E; Palmerston; Russell, John; Villiers

Claretie, Jules [klaruhtee], originally **Arsène Arnaud** (1840–1913) Novelist, born in Limoges, France. While a schoolboy in Paris he published a novel, and soon became a leading critic, political writer, and popular novelist. He first made a hit on the stage with his Revolution plays, *Les Muscadins* (1874), *Le Régiment de Champagne* (1877) and *Les Mirabeau* (1878). In 1885 he became director of the Comédie Française.

Clarín >> **Alas, Leopoldo**

Clark, Charles Manning Hope (1915–91) Historian and writer, born in Burwood, New South Wales, Australia. He studied at Melbourne and Oxford universities, and in 1949 became the first professor of Australian history at the Australian National University, Canberra (emeritus in 1977). His six-volume *History of Australia* (1962–88), along with his *Short History of Australia* (1963), did much to popularize the study of Australian history in schools and colleges.

Clark, George Rogers (1752–1818) Surveyor and soldier, born near Charlottesville, VA. A surveyor by profession, he explored the Ohio R region. At the outset of the Revolution, he was commander of the Kentucky militia. Taking the offensive with a small force, he conducted an epic campaign involving intensive overland marches and the capture of several British outposts, and ending in the 'Night of the Long Knives' at Fort Sackville, Vincennes, IN (1779). He continued to fight the British and their Indian allies, and by the end of the Revolution had secured the old Northwest (Michigan, Indiana, Illinois) for the new United States – a military reality the politicians recognized in the Treaty of Paris (1783). After 1803 he was engaged mainly in supervising land allotments in the new territory.

Clark, (John) Grahame Douglas (1907–95) Archaeologist, born in Shortlands, Kent, SE England, UK. He studied at Cambridge, where he taught from 1935, serving as professor of archaeology (1952–74), and was Master of Peterhouse (1973–80). His *Archaeology and Society* (1939) and *World Prehistory* (1961, 1977) pioneered the use of the archaeological record to document the economic and social life of prehistoric communities.

Clark, Jim, popular name of **James Clark** (1936–68) Motor-racing driver, born in Kilmany, Fife, E Scotland, UK. He won his first race in 1956, becoming Scottish National Speed Champion (1958–9). After joining the Lotus team in 1960, he went on to become World Champion Racing Driver (1963, 1965), and respected by all in the industry as a gentleman. He won in all 25 Grands Prix. He was killed during a Formula Two race in Hockenheim, Germany. >> RR1164

Clark, Joe, popular name of **(Charles) Joseph Clark** (1939–) Canadian statesman and prime minister (1979–80), born in High River, Alberta, Canada. At first a journalist, then professor of political science, he was elected to the Federal parliament in 1972, becoming leader of the Progressive Conservative Party (1976) and of the Opposition. In 1979 he became Canada's youngest ever prime minister. His minority government lost the general election the following year, and he was deposed as Party Leader in 1983. After 1984 he was Canada's minister for external affairs, and retired from politics to take up a post with the UN in 1993. >> RR1039

Clark, Josiah Latimer (1822–98) Electrical engineer, born in Great Marlow, Buckinghamshire, SC England, UK. In 1854 he patented a pneumatic delivery tube, and made important inventions in connection with submarine cables. He also invented a single-lens stereo-camera.

Clark, Kenneth (Mackenzie) Clark, Baron (1903–83) Art historian, born in London, England, UK. He studied at Oxford, became keeper of the Department of Fine Art in the Ashmolean Museum (1931–3), director of the National Gallery (1934–45), and professor of fine art at Oxford (1946–50). He was also chairman of the Independent Television Authority (1954–7). In addition to his acclaimed scholarly work on Leonardo da Vinci, he wrote many popular books on his subject, and became widely known through his television series *Civilisation* (1969). He was given a life peerage in 1969. >> Leonardo da Vinci

Clark, Mark (Wayne) (1896–1984) US general, born in Maddison Barracks, NY, of a military family. He trained at West Point, and served abroad in World War 1. Designated as commander II Corps under Eisenhower for the invasion of North Africa, he subsequently became his deputy. He commanded the 5th Army at the Salerno landing (1943) and the capture of Rome (1944), and was much criticized for choosing the latter instead of encircling the German forces. He commanded the US 6th Army in the Far East (1947–9), and relieved Ridgway in command of UN forces in Korea (1952–3). >> Eisenhower; Ridgway, Mathew B

Clark, Michael (1962–) Dancer and choreographer, born in Aberdeen, NE Scotland, UK. He trained at the Royal Ballet School, and went on to dance with the Royal Ballet and Ballet Rambert. After studying with Merce Cunningham in New York for a short time, he began to choreograph. While developing his own style he worked as a dancer with Karole Armitage in Paris, starting his own company in 1984. >> Armitage, Karole; Cunningham, Merce

Clark, Ramsey (William) (1927–) Attorney general and political activist, born in Dallas, TX. He was named attorney general (1967–9) during the anti-Vietnam War years. Although he prosecuted activists such as the Berrigan brothers, he was known to be a reasonable liberal who moved to the left in his beliefs and causes after returning to private practice. Twice an unsuccessful candidate for the US Senate from New York in the 1970s, he later returned to public prominence as an outspoken critic of two Republican administrations. He himself was roundly criticized for his support of extremist politicians such as Saddam Hussein. >> Berrigan, Daniel J; Berrigan, Philip F; Hussein, Saddam

Clark, Robert Sterling (1877–1956) and **Francine Clary Clark** (1876–1960) Art collectors, husband and wife, born in New York City and in France, respectively. An heir to the Singer sewing machine fortune, he was the grandson of Edward Clark, the business partner of Isaac Singer. Robert studied at Yale, served in the army until 1905, and led a scientific expedition to China (1908–9). In 1911 he settled in Paris as an art collector, marrying Francine in 1919. Little is known of Francine's early life. The Clarks moved to New York City in 1949, settling in Williamstown, MA, where they built up a collection of Old Master and 19th-c American paintings. In 1955 they established the Sterling and Francine Clark Art Institute in Williamstown, and both are buried beneath the front steps of the original marble building. >> Singer, Isaac (Merritt)

Clark, Sir Wilfrid (Edward Le Gros) (1895–1971) Anatomist, born in Hemel Hempstead, Hertfordshire, SE England, UK. He qualified in medicine in London (1916), and served as medical officer in Borneo before returning to teach anatomy at London and Oxford (1934–62). Distinguished for his work on the anatomy of primates and especially the brain, he helped expose in the 1950s the 'Piltdown Man' hoax. >> Dawson, Charles

Clark, William (1770–1838) Explorer, born in Caroline Co, VA. He joined the army in 1789, and became joint leader with Meriwether Lewis of the successful transcontinental expedition to the Pacific coast and back (1804–6). He later became superintendent of Indian affairs in Louisiana Territory, and the Governor of Missouri Territory. >> Lewis, Meriwether

Clarke, Sir Arthur C(harles) (1917–) Writer of science fiction, born in Minehead, Somerset, SW England, UK. He studied at King's College, London, and worked in scientific research before turning to fiction. He was a radar instructor in World War 2, and originated the idea of satellite communication in a scientific article in 1945. A prolific writer, his themes are exploration – in both the near and distant future – and the position of humanity in the hierarchy of the universe. His first book was *Prelude to Space* (1951), and while he is credited with some of the genre's best examples – *Rendezvous with Rama* (1973), *The Fountains of Paradise* (1979) – his name will always be associated first with *2001: a Space Odyssey* (1968) which, under the direction of Stanley Kubrick, became a highly successful film. Later

works include the sequels to *2001, 2010: Space Odyssey II* (1982, film 1984), *2062: Odyssey III* (1988), and *3001: the Final Odyssey* (1997). Other books include *The Garden of Rama* (1991) and *The Snows of Olympus* (1994). Nonfiction publications include *Arthur C Clarke's Mysterious World* (1980, also a TV series) and *Arthur C Clarke's Chronicles of the Strange and Mysterious* (1987). He emigrated to Sri Lanka in the 1950s, and was knighted in 1998. >> Kubrick

Clarke, Austin (1896–1974) Poet and playwright, born in Dublin. He studied at University College, Dublin, and spent 15 years in England as a journalist before returning to Dublin in 1937. *The Vengeance of Fionn*, the first of 18 books of verse, was published in 1917. His *Collected Poems* were published in 1974. He was also a noted playwright and an adherent of verse drama, promoted through the Dublin Verse-Speaking Society which he formed in 1941. His first novel, *The Bright Temptation* (1932), was banned in Ireland until 1954.

Clarke, Charles Cowden (1787–1877) Shakespearean scholar, born in Enfield, N Greater London, England, UK. He became a bookseller in London (1820), and a music publisher in partnership with Alfred Novello, whose sister **Mary Victoria Novello** (1809–98) he married in 1828. He gave public lectures on Shakespeare and other literary figures, and with his wife published an annotated edition of Shakespeare (1869) and *The Shakespeare Key* (1879). >> Novello

Clarke, David Leonard (1937–76) Archaeologist, born in Kent, SE England, UK. He studied at Peterhouse, Cambridge, where he became a fellow (1966–76). His teaching and writing, particularly in *Analytical Archaeology* (1967), transformed European archaeology in the 1970s. It demonstrated the importance of systems theory, quantification, and scientific reasoning in archaeology, and drew ecology, geography, and comparative anthropology firmly within the ambit of the subject.

Clarke, Edith (1883–1959) Electrical engineer, born in Howard Co, MD. Using her inheritance to attend Vassar, she went on to study engineering at the University of Wisconsin, worked for American Telephone and Telegraph (1912–18), and became the first woman to receive an MS in electrical engineering from the Massachusetts Institute of Technology (1919). She then worked at General Electric (1922–45), focusing on large electrical power systems, and developed a calculating device that predicted the electrical behaviour of these systems. She postponed her retirement to a farm in Maryland by teaching at the University of Texas at Austin (1947–56).

Clarke, Frank (Wigglesworth) (1847–1931) Geologist, born in Boston, MA. He was professor of physics at Howard University and at Cincinnati (1874–83), chief chemist to the US Geological Survey (1883–1925), and did much work on the recalculation of atomic weights. He was the first to calculate the chemical composition of the Earth's crust.

Clarke, Sir Fred(erick) (1880–1952) Educationist, born in Witney, Oxfordshire, SC England, UK. He studied modern history at Oxford, and became professor of education at Southampton (1906–11), Cape Town (1911–29), and McGill University, Montreal (1929), and director of the Institute of Education, London (1936–45). His most influential work was *Education and Social Change* (1940).

Clarke, Gillian (1937–) Poet, born in Cardiff, S Wales, UK. She studied at University College, Cardiff, and went on to publish several collections of poetry, such as *Letting in the Rumour* (1989) and *The King of Britain's Daughter* (1993). She was editor of *The Anglo-Welsh Review* (1976–84), and became chair of the Welsh Academy in 1987.

Clarke, James Freeman (1810–88) Minister and theologian, born in Hanover, NH. He studied at Harvard, became a Unitarian pastor, and in 1841 founded the Unitarian Church of the Disciples at Boston. He held a chair of natural theology at Harvard (1867–71).

Clarke, Jeremiah (c. 1674–1707) Composer, probably born in London, England, UK. He studied under John Blow at the Chapel Royal, and became organist of Winchester College in 1692, and of St Paul's Cathedral three years later, following his master at the Chapel Royal in 1704. The real composer of the Trumpet Voluntary long attributed to Purcell, Clarke wrote operas, theatre music, religious and secular choral works, and music for harpsichord. He committed suicide as the result of an unhappy love affair. >> Blow, John

Clarke, Kenneth (Harry) (1940–) British statesman. He studied at Cambridge, was called to the bar in 1963, and became a Conservative MP in 1970, representing Rushcliffe, Nottinghamshire. After junior posts in the Heath administration (1971–4), he entered Margaret Thatcher's government in 1979, in 1988 was appointed secretary of state for health, became home secretary under John Major in 1992, and Chancellor of the Exchequer (1993–7). >> Heath, Edward; Major; Thatcher

Clarke, Marcus (Andrew Hislop) (1846–81) Novelist, born in London, England, UK. He emigrated to Australia at the age of 18, where he became a journalist. His best-known work is a story of the convict settlements, *For the Term of his Natural Life* (1874).

Clarke, Martha (1944–) Dancer and choreographer, born in Maryland. She trained at the American Dance Festival in Connecticut and at the Juilliard School, New York City. She spent a few seasons in Anna Sokolow's company before moving to Europe. On her return to the USA she became (1972) one of the first female members of Pilobolus, a collectively-run dance-theatre ensemble, and later helped to form the trio Crowsnest. >> Sokolow

Clarke, Ron(ald William) (1937–) Athlete, born in Melbourne, Victoria, Australia. As a youth he was selected to carry the Olympic torch at the Melbourne Games of 1956, but he first concentrated on his career as an accountant. At one time he held the world records at such varied distances as 3 mi, 5 mi, 10 mi, 3000 m, 5000 m, and 10 000 m, but despite holding six world records simultaneously he only came sixth in the 10 000 m in the Mexico City Olympics in 1968, being badly affected by the altitude. He retired after the 1970 Commonwealth Games.

Clarke, Samuel (1675–1729) Philosopher and theologian, born in Norwich, Norfolk, E England, UK. He studied at Cambridge, where he became a friend and disciple of Newton. He was chaplain to the Bishop of Norwich (from 1698), and to Queen Anne (from 1706), and became rector of St James's, Westminster, in 1709. His Boyle Lectures of 1704–5 contained his 'Demonstration of the Being and Attributes of God' and expounded a 'mathematical' proof of God's existence. >> Newton

Clarke, Thomas James (1858–1916) Irish nationalist and revolutionary, born in Hurst Castle, Isle of Wight, S England, UK. At 21 he emigrated to the USA, where he became involved in Clan-na-Gael, the clandestine US wing of the Irish Republican Brotherhood, promoting anti-British action. Sent to England in 1883, he was arrested for participation in the dynamite campaign against London civilians and was sentenced to penal servitude for life. Released in 1898, he spent some years in the USA, returning to Ireland in 1907. At his urging, the Irish Republican Brotherhood set up a military council, which brought about the Easter Rising of 1916. After the surrender he was court-martialled and shot.

Clarkson, Jeremy (Charles Robert) (1960–) British journalist and television presenter. A junior reporter on the Rotherham Advertiser (1978–83), he founded the Motoring Press Agency (1983), then joined the BBC as presenter on *Top Gear* (1989–) and *Jeremy Clarkson's Motorworld* (1995–). He is a regular columnist for leading newspapers and for *Top Gear* magazine, which he founded in 1993.

Claude, Albert [klohd, klawd] (1898–1983) Cell biologist, born in Longlier, Belgium. He studied medicine at Liège University and joined the Rockefeller Institute for Medical Research in New York City (1929–72), later concurrently holding posts in Brussels (1948–72). He became a US citizen in 1941, but also retained his Belgium citizenship. He is considered the founder of modern cell biology. He introduced the use of the centrifuge to separate the components of cells for analysis, and in 1942 was the first to use an electron microscope in biological research. He shared the Nobel Prize for Physiology or Medicine in 1974. >> Palade; RR1124

Claude, Georges [klohd] (1870–1960) Chemist and physicist, born in Paris. He is noted for his work on gases, and is credited with the invention of neon lighting for signs (1910). He supported the Vichy government in World War 2, and was imprisoned as a collaborator (1945–9).

Claudel, Camille [klohd] (1864–1943) Sculptor, born in La Fère-en-Tardenois, France, the sister of the poet Paul Claudel. She became the student, model, and mistress of August Rodin, producing works which, while close to his, nonetheless show great individuality. After a fiery relationship, Claudel and Rodin parted company in 1898, but she continued to sculpt and achieved great renown around the turn of the century. However, the break with Rodin affected her mental stability, and from 1913 until her death she was confined to various institutions. >> Claudel, Paul; Rodin

Claudel, Paul [klohdel] (1868–1955) Catholic poet, essayist, and playwright, born in Villeneuve-sur-Fère, France. A convert at the age of 18, he joined the diplomatic service, and held posts in many parts of the world. His plays, such as *L'Annonce fait à Marie* (1912, The Annunciation to Mary) and his poetry, such as *Cinq grandes odes* (1910, Five Great Odes), are remarkable for their spiritual intensity. >> Claudel, Camille

Claude Lorrain [klohd], originally **Claude Gellée** (1600–82) Landscape painter, born in Champagne, France. He studied with various Italian painters, then settled in Rome (1627). He painted about 400 landscapes, including several with biblical or Classical themes, such as 'The Sermon on the Mount' (1656, Frick Collection, New York City). His compositions, if rather formal, are always graceful and well considered, and his colour is singularly mellow and harmonious. He also produced many drawing and etchings.

Claudianus, Claudius [klawdius] (340–410) The last of the great Latin poets, born in Alexandria, Egypt. He went to Rome in AD 395, and obtained patrician dignity by favour of Stilicho. He wrote first in Greek, then in Latin. Several of his works have survived, notably his epic poem *De raptu Proserpinae* (The Rape of Proserpine), the work for which he was famed in the Middle Ages. >> Stilicho

Claudius [klawdius], in full **Tiberius Claudius Caesar Augustus Germanicus** (10 BC–AD 54) Roman emperor (41–54), the grandson of the Empress Livia, the brother of Germanicus, and the nephew of the Emperor Tiberius. Kept in the background because of his physical disabilities, he devoted himself to historical studies, and thus survived the vicious in-fighting of the imperial house. Becoming emperor largely by accident in the chaos after Caligula's murder, he proved to be an able and progressive ruler, despite his gross and sometimes ridiculous indulgence of his wives and freedmen. Through his lavish public works and administrative reforms, he made a lasting contribution to the government of Rome and the empire, and through the annexation of Britain, Mauretania, and Thrace, a significant extension of its size. He died poisoned, it was widely believed, by his fourth wife **Agrippina**. >> Agrippina (the Younger); Caligula; Messalina; RR1084

Claudius, Appius [**kloh**dius], nickname **Caecus** ('the blind') (4th–3rd-c BC) Aristocratic Roman statesman, general, and law-giver, the first clear-cut figure in Roman history. His fame rests primarily on his great reforming censorship (c.312–307 BC), during which he opened up the political process to the lower orders, and inaugurated a number of life-enhancing public projects at Rome, such as the building of the city's first aqueduct, the Aqua Appia, and Rome's first trunk road, the Appian Way. A fervent expansionist, he fought in many of Rome's early wars. He was regarded by the Romans as the father of Latin prose and oratory. He became blind in his old age, hence his byname.

Clausewitz, Karl (Philip Gottlieb) von [**klow**zevits] (1780–1831) General, born in Burg, Germany. He served with distinction in the Prussian and Russian armies, and ultimately became director of the Prussian army school, and Gneisenau's chief-of-staff. His posthumously published *Vom Kriege* (1833, On War), advocating a policy of total war, revolutionized military theory, and was extremely influential in Germany and beyond. >> Gneisenau

Clausius, Rudolf (Julius Emanuel) [**klow**zius] (1822–88) Physicist, born in Köslin, Germany. He studied at Berlin, and in 1869 became professor of natural philosophy at Bonn. He worked on optics and electricity, formulated the second law of thermodynamics, and was influential in establishing thermodynamics as a science.

Claussen, Sophus (Niels Christen) [**klow**sen] (1865–1931) Poet, born in Heletoft, Denmark. He is generally regarded as the greatest Symbolist poet of his country. He lived for many years in France, where he was influenced by the French Symbolists, but brought a personal eroticism to nearly everything he wrote. He published several volumes of verse, and some plays, and his collected works were published in seven volumes in 1910.

Clavell, James (du Maresq) [kla**vel**] (1924–94) Novelist, cinema scenarist, director, and producer, born in Sydney, New South Wales, Australia. He has worked mainly in the USA. Though his screen credits include *The Fly* (1958), *The Great Escape* (1963), and *To Sir With Love* (1967), he is known primarily as the author of a series of best-selling novels with an Oriental setting. *King Rat* was published in 1962, and was followed by *Tai-Pan* (1966), *Shogun* (1975), *Noble House* (1981), and *Gai-Jin* (1993).

Claverhouse, John Graham of >> **Dundee, Viscount**

Clay, Cassius >> **Ali, Muhammad**

Clay, Cassius Marcellus (1810–1903) Abolitionist, born in Madison Co, KY, the cousin of Henry Clay. He was the son of a wealthy slaveholding planter but, while at Yale, heard William Lloyd Garrison speak, and was converted to abolitionism. Returning to Kentucky, he studied law, then served in the state legislature. He freed his own slaves in 1844 and, in the next year, founded a newspaper, *The True American* (later the *Examiner*), to combat slavery. He was appointed ambassador to Russia in 1861, but delayed his departure to help strengthen the defences of Washington, DC. He returned in 1862 when named a major-general in the Union army, then went back to take up his diplomatic post in Russia (1863–9) and participated in the purchase of Alaska. On his return he was active in Republican politics, but he became increasingly reclusive, and was judged insane in his final months. >> Clay, Henry; Garrison, William Lloyd

Clay, Henry (1777–1852) US statesman and orator, born in Hanover Co, VA. The son of a Baptist preacher, he became a lawyer (1797), entered the US House of Representatives in 1811, and was chosen its speaker, a post he held for many years. He was active in bringing on the War of 1812 with Britain, and was one of the commissioners who arranged the Treaty of Ghent which ended it. In 1824, 1831, and 1844 he was an unsuccessful candidate for the presidency, and he served in the US Senate (1831–42). He made several attempts to hold the Union together in the face of the issue of slavery, for which he earned the title of 'the great pacificator'. >> Clay, Cassius Marcellus

Clay, Lucius (DuBignon) (1897–1978) US soldier, born in Marietta, GA. He trained at West Point, and served in a succession of engineering posts, many involving water and hydroelectric projects. As a deputy chief-of-staff (1942–4), he oversaw the army's vast production and procurement programmes. In 1944 he went overseas to command the Normandy base and the port of Cherbourg, which supplied the Allied forces. He helped establish a military government in the US zone of occupation, served as military governor there (1947–9), and organized the Berlin airlift (1948). He retired in 1949, and began a second career as a business executive and Republican Party activist. President Kennedy chose him to be his personal representative in Berlin during the 1961 Berlin Crisis. He later became chairman of Radio Free Europe (1965–74).

Clayton, John (fl.c. 1650–) English scientist. Educated as a theologian, he first discovered that gas could be distilled from crude coal and stored, but did not realize the commercial importance of his discovery. He also did work on stained glass.

Clayton, John (Middleton) (1796–1856) US statesman, born in Dagsboro, DE. He studied at Yale, and practised as a lawyer. In 1829 he became a US senator, and while secretary of state (1849–50) negotiated the Clayton–Bulwer Treaty with Britain.

Clayton, Lisa (1959–) Yachtswoman, born in Birmingham, West Midlands, C England, UK. In 1995 she became the first British woman to circumnavigate the globe, in a single, unaided, continuous journey. Her voyage, in a 39 ft sloop, *Spirit of Birmingham*, took 285 days.

Cleanthes [klee**an**theez] (c. 331–232 BC) Greek Stoic philosopher, born in Assos, Troas. He studied under Zeno of Citium in Athens for 19 years and succeeded him as head of the Stoa in 262. His own contributions to Stoicism were especially in the areas of theology and cosmology, and his principal extant writing is the *Hymn to Zeus*. >> Zeno of Citium

Cledwyn (of Penrhos), Cledwyn Hughes, Baron [**kled**win] (1916–) British statesman, born in Holyhead, Anglesey, NW Wales, UK. He studied at the University College of Wales, Aberystwyth, and became a solicitor in 1940. Elected Labour MP for Anglesey (1951–79), he became minister of state for the Commonwealth (1964–6), secretary of state for Wales (1966–8), and minister of agriculture, fisheries and food (1968–70). He later served as leader of the Opposition in the Lords (1982–92) and Opposition spokesman on the Civil Service, foreign affairs, and Welsh affairs (1983–92). He was made a Companion of Honour in 1977, and a life peer in 1979.

Cleese, John (Marwood) [kleez] (1939–) Comic actor and writer, born in Weston-super-Mare, Somerset, SW England, UK. As a student at Cambridge he joined the Footlights Revue (1963). He appeared in the Broadway production of *Half a Sixpence* (1965) and returned to Britain to write and perform in such television series as *The Frost Report* (1966). He joined *Monty Python's Flying Circus* (1969–74), an anarchic series that changed the face of British television humour with its inspired lunacy, surreal comedy, and animated graphics. The troupe subsequently collaborated on such films as *The Life of Brian* (1979), and *The Meaning of Life* (1983). Tall and angular, he has specialized in explosive, manic eccentricity and physical humour. He enjoyed spectacular success as the writer and star of the series *Fawlty Towers* (1975, 1979) and the film *A Fish Called Wanda* (1988). Later films include *Splitting Heirs* (1993) and *Fierce Creatures* (1997), the not-quite-sequel to *Wanda*. He also founded Video Arts Ltd, producing industrial training films, and, with **Robin Skynner** (1922–), wrote the best-seller *Families and How to Survive Them* (1983). He married the actress **Connie Booth** in 1968 (dissolved, 1978). >> Palin; Scales

Clegg, Samuel (1781–1861) Inventor, born in Manchester, Greater Manchester, NW England, UK. He was taught some science by John Dalton, and then became an apprentice at Boulton and Watt's engineering works, where he saw William Murdock's early experiments with coal gas lighting. He left the firm in 1805 and continued to work on improved methods of producing coal gas, leading to his appointment in 1813 as chief engineer of the Chartered Gas Co, for whom he successfully illuminated an entire district of London by gas (1814). >> Dalton, John; Murdock, William

Cleisthenes [**kliys**theneez] (6th-c BC) Prominent Athenian politician of the Alcmaeonid family, and founder of Athenian democracy. His constitutional reforms (c.508 BC) paved the way for the radical democracy established by Ephialtes and Pericles (c.461 BC).

Cleland, John [**klay**land] (1709–89) Novelist, born in London, England, UK. He studied at Westminster School, and after working and travelling abroad, published *Fanny Hill, or the Memoirs of a Woman of Pleasure* (1750). A best-seller in its time, it achieved a second *succès de scandale* on its revival and prosecution under the Obscene Publications Act in 1963. He also practised journalism and playwriting, excelling at neither, and dabbled in Celtic philology.

Clemenceau, Georges [**klemã**soh] (1841–1929) French statesman and prime minister (1906–9, 1917–20), born in Mouilleron-en-Pareds, France. He trained as a doctor, worked as a teacher in the USA (1865–9), then returned to France, where he became a member of the National Assembly, and in 1876 a leader of the extreme left in the Chamber of Deputies. The destroyer of many ministries, he was himself twice premier. Known as 'the tiger', he presided at the Peace Conference in 1919, showing an intransigent hatred of Germany. A brilliant journalist, he founded *L'Aurore*, and other papers. >> RR1049

Clemens, Samuel Langhorne >> Twain, Mark

Clement I, St, known as **Clemens Romanus** or **Clement of Rome** (late 1st-c) One of the apostolic Fathers of the Church, reckoned variously as the second or third successor of St Peter at Rome, possibly 88–97 or 92–101. He may have been a freedman of Jewish parentage belonging to Caesar's household. The first of two epistles attributed to him is generally accepted as his (written c.96); it is written to the Corinthian Church, and treats of social dissensions, the nature of early Christian ministry, and the resurrection. He was probably martyred. Later, several spurious works were circulated in his name, such as the *Clementine Homilies*. Feast day 23 November. >> Peter, St

Clement V, originally **Raymond Bertrand de Got** (c.1260–1314) Bishop and pope (1305–14), born in Bordelais, France. He became Archbishop of Bordeaux in 1299. As pope, he suppressed the Templars, and removed the seat of the papacy to Avignon (1309), a movement disastrous to Italy.

Clement VII, originally **Giulio de' Medici** (1478–1534) Pope (1523–34), born in Florence, Italy. He allied himself with Francis I of France against the Holy Roman Emperor Charles V, was besieged by the Constable de Bourbon, and for a while became his prisoner. His indecisiveness, along with his refusal to sanction Henry VIII's divorce from Catherine of Aragon, hastened the Reformation. He was also a patron of artists and scholars. >> Bourbon

Clement of Alexandria, St, Lat **Clemens Alexandrinus** (c. 150–c. 215) Theologian and Father of the early Church, probably born in Athens. He first studied philosophy, then became head of the celebrated Catechetical school in Alexandria, where he related Greek philosophical thought to Christian belief. In 203 the persecution under Severus compelled him to flee to Palestine. His most distinguished pupil was Origen. Feast day 5 December. >> Origen

Clemente, Bob [kle**men**tay], popular name of **Roberto (Walker) Clemente** (1934–1972) Baseball player, born in Carolina, Puerto Rico. An outstanding outfielder, he played for the Pittsburgh Pirates for 17 years (1955–72), making more than 3000 hits and 240 home runs. He led the National League in batting four times, and was in the World Series in 1971. He was killed in an air-crash while flying on a relief mission to the victims of the earthquake at Managua in Nicaragua, and in 1973 was immediately elected to the National Baseball Hall of Fame without the usual five-year wait. >> RR1144

Clementi, Muzio [kle**men**tee] (1752–1832) Composer and pianist, born in Rome. In 1766 he was brought to England, where he conducted the Italian Opera in London (1777–80), toured as a virtuoso pianist (1781), and went into the piano-manufacturing business. He wrote the *Gradus ad Parnassum* (1817–26), on which subsequent piano methods have been based. He composed mainly piano and chamber music.

Clementis, Vladimir [kle**men**tees] (1902–52) Czech statesman, born in Tesovec, Slovakia. He studied at Prague, became a Czech Communist MP (1935), and in 1945 was vice-minister of foreign affairs in the first Czech postwar government. A chief organizer of the 1948 coup, he succeeded Masaryk as foreign minister, but was forced to resign in 1950 as a 'deviationist'. Following a political purge, he was hanged. >> Masaryk, Jan

Clements, Sir John Selby (1911–88) British actor and director. He studied at Cambridge, and first appeared on stage at the Lyric, Hammersmith (1930). His first marriage, to **Inga Maria Ahlgren**, was dissolved in 1946. In that year he married the actress **Kay Hammond** (d.1980), and they became one of Britain's most famous theatrical partnerships. From 1966 to 1973 he was director of Chichester Festival Theatre.

Cleon [**klee**on] (?–422 BC) The first Athenian of rich, bourgeois stock to play a prominent role in 5th-c BC politics. Routinely dismissed as an upstart, demagogue, and warmonger, it was his capture of the Spartans on the island of Sphacteria (425 BC) that gave Athens her trump card in the peace negotiations of the late 420s BC.

Cleopatra VII (69–30 BC) Queen of Egypt (51–48 BC, 47–30 BC), the daughter of Ptolemy Auletes. A woman of great intelligence, she made the most of her physical charms to strengthen her own position within Egypt, and to save the country from annexation by Rome. Thus, Julius Caesar, to whom she bore a son **Caesarion**, supported her claim to the throne against her brother (47 BC), while Antony, by whom she had three children, restored to her several portions of the old Ptolemaic empire, and even gave to their joint offspring substantial areas of the Roman East (34 BC). Defeated along with Antony at Actium (31 BC), she preferred suicide to being captured and exhibited at Rome in Octavian's victory parade. The asp, which she used to cause her death, was an Egyptian symbol of royalty. >> Antonius; Caesar; RR1046

Clerc, Jacques-Philippe Le >> **Le Clerc, Jacques-Philippe**

Clerk, Sir Dugald [klah(r)k] (1854–1932) Engineer, born in Glasgow, W Scotland, UK. He studied at Anderson's College, Glasgow, and in Leeds. Having investigated the properties of petroleum oils, from 1877 he devoted himself to research on the theory and design of gas engines. In 1881 he patented a gas engine working on the two-stroke principle which became known as the *Clerk cycle*, extensively used for large gas engines and later for small petrol engines. He was knighted in 1917.

Clerk Maxwell, James >> **Maxwell, James**

Cleve, Cornelis [klayvuh] (1520–67) Painter, born in Antwerp, Belgium, the son of Joos van Cleve. He specialized in portraits of the rich Flemish bourgeoisie. In 1554 he went to England, hoping for the patronage of Philip II of Spain, who was there for his marriage to Mary I (Mary Tudor), but his arrival coincided with that of a collection of pictures by Titian and others from Italy, which ousted the Flemish school from royal favour. The disappointment mentally deranged Cornelis, who never entirely recovered, being known thereafter as *Sotte* ('mad') *Cleve*. >> Cleve, Joos van der Beke; Titian

Cleve, Joos van der Beke (c. 1480–1540) Painter, born in Antwerp, Belgium. Most of his work was done there, though he also worked in Cologne, and was invited to Paris to paint portraits of Francis I and his family. He is best known for his religious pictures, and is sometimes called 'the Master of the Death of the Virgin' from two triptychs of that subject at Munich and Cologne. >> Cleve, Cornelis

Cleveland, (Stephen) Grover (1837–1908) US statesman and the 22nd and 24th president (1885–9, 1893–7), born in Caldwell, NJ. He became a lawyer, Mayor of Buffalo, and in 1882 Democratic Governor of New York. In his first term as president, he strongly advised a readjustment of the tariff on various imports. In 1895 he evoked intense excitement throughout the world by applying the Monroe Doctrine to Britain's dispute with Venezuela over the frontier question with what is now Guyana. >> RR1097

Cleveland, John (1613–58) Cavalier poet, born in Loughborough, Leicestershire, C England, UK. He studied at Christ's College, Cambridge, and also at St John's, where he was elected to a fellowship in 1634. He joined the Royalist army, and was appointed judge advocate at Newark, but was obliged to surrender with the garrison. He was extremely popular as a poet in his day, being known for his elegies and satires.

Clewlow, Warren (Alexander Morten) (1936–) Businessman, born in KwaZulu Natal, South Africa. He studied at Natal University, Durban, and became a chartered accountant. Executive chairman of the Barlow Rand Group of Companies, South Africa's largest industrial corporation, he is also chairman of the State President's Economic Advisory Council, and president of the South Africa Foundation. He was named 'Marketing Man of the Year' in 1988.

Cliburn, Van [klaybern], popular name of **Harvey Lavan Cliburn, Jr** (1934–) Pianist, born in Shreveport, LA. He soloed with orchestras as a teenager before being catapulted to fame as the first American to win Moscow's Tchaikovsky Prize (1958). He embarked on an international solo career, specializing in the 19th-c standard repertoire, but in 1978 largely ceased performing for personal reasons. The piano competition he began at Fort Worth, TX, in 1962 became an important international event.

Cliff, Clarice (1899–1972) Ceramic designer, born in Tunstall, Staffordshire, C England, UK. She attended local art schools at Tunstall and Burslem, and set up a design studio at Wilkinson's Newport showroom, where she developed a style using bold designs painted with stylized trees and abstract patterns in vivid colours with bold brushwork. By 1929 the Newport pottery was given over entirely to the decoration of her work, which was marketed under the name 'Bizarre'.

Clifford, John (1836–1923) Clergyman, born in Sawley, Derbyshire, C England, UK. He studied at the Baptist College in Nottingham, and at University College London, and from 1858 to 1915 was pastor of Praed Street Baptist Church in Paddington. A leading passive resister to the Education Act of 1902 and a strong Nonconformist Liberal, he was created first president of the Baptist World Alliance (1905–11).

Clifford, William (Kingdon) (1845–79) Mathematician, born in Exeter, Devon, SW England, UK. He entered King's College, London, at the age of 15, and then Trinity College, Cambridge, in 1863. In 1871 he became professor of applied mathematics at University College, London. He wrote on projective and non-Euclidean geometry, and on the philosophy of science, and is especially known for his development of the theory of biquaternions.

Clift, (Edward) Montgomery (1920–66) Film and stage actor, born in Omaha, NE. A stage performer in New York City for 10 years, he appeared in *Red River* (1946), and was briefly considered the most promising of post-war actors. His performances in *The Search* (1948), *A Place in The Sun* (1951), and *From Here to Eternity* (1953) earned him Oscar nominations. A car accident in 1957 left him permanently scarred.

Cline, Howard Francis [kliyn] (1915–71) Historian, born in Detroit, MI. He studied at Harvard, and went on to direct the Hispanic Foundation at the Library of Congress (1952–71). A pioneer ethnohistorian, he studied social and ethnic history, particularly of Mexico, and this was the subject of two of his major works: *The United States and Mexico* (1953) and *Mexico: Evolution to Revolution* (1962).

Clinton, Bill, popular name of **William Jefferson Clinton** (1946–) US statesman and 42nd president (1993–), born in Hope, AR. He studied at Georgetown University, Oxford, and Yale Law School, entered Arkansas politics as state attorney general, and became Democratic governor (1979–81, 1983–92). He defeated George Bush for the presidency in 1992, and was elected to a second term in 1996. >> Bush; Clinton, Hillary; RR1097

Clinton, De Witt [duh wit] (1769–1828) US politician, born in Little Britain, NY. He became a lawyer in 1788, sat in the New York state legislature (1797) and US Senate (1798–1802), was appointed Mayor of New York City (1802), but was defeated by Madison in the presidential contest of 1812. He planned the Erie Canal scheme ('Clinton's ditch'), which he opened in 1825. >> Madison, James

Clinton, George (1739–1812) US soldier and politician, born in Little Britain, NY. He was a member of the New York Provincial Assembly (1768–75), and in 1775 attended the second Continental Congress. In the American War of Independence (1775–83) he was a brigadier of militia, and in 1777 was chosen first Governor of New York, a post he held for six successive terms (1777–95). In 1804 and 1808 he was elected vice-president of the USA. >> Clinton, James

Clinton, Sir Henry (c.1738–95) Soldier, born in Newfoundland, Canada, the son of the Newfoundland governor. He served with distinction in the Seven Years' War (1756–63), and was promoted major-general in 1772. Sent to America in 1775, he fought at Bunker Hill, and in 1776 was repulsed in an attack on Charleston. After Burgoyne's surrender in 1778, Clinton succeeded Howe as commander-in-chief. In 1780 he captured Charleston and the entire

Southern army, but after Cornwallis' capitulation at Yorktown in 1781 he resigned his command and returned to England. >> Burgoyne; Cornwallis; Howe, William; Lincoln, Benjamin

Clinton, Hillary (Rodham) (1947–) Lawyer and US first lady (1993–), born in Chicago, IL. She studied at Wellesley College, MA, and at Yale Law School, where she met and married (1975) future US president, Bill Clinton. The couple moved to Little Rock, AR, in 1976, where she became a partner in a law firm and served as head of the Rural Health Advisory Committee, concerned with providing health care to isolated areas. She led the drive for statewide school reforms, and was twice named one of the nation's top 100 lawyers. In 1993 President Clinton unveiled her proposals for the first national health-care programme in the United States. >> Clinton, Bill

Clinton, James (1736–1812) American soldier, born in Little Britain, NY, the brother of George Clinton. He fought with distinction in the French and Indian War (1755–63) and as a brigadier-general during the War of Independence (1775–83). >> Clinton, George

Clitherow, St Margaret [klithroh], *née* **Middleton** (c.1556–86) One of the '40 martyrs' of England and Wales, born in York, North Yorkshire, N England, UK. The wife of a York butcher, she was converted to Catholicism in 1574. She harboured priests in her home, for which she was tried and condemned to death. She was executed by being crushed to death under a large weight. She was canonized in 1970; feast day 25 March.

Clive (of Plassey), Robert Clive, Baron (1725–74) Soldier, and administrator in India, born in Styche, Shropshire, WC England, UK. In 1743 he joined the East India Company, and took part in the campaigns against the French. In 1755 he was called to avenge the so-called Black Hole of Calcutta, and at Plassey (1757) defeated a large Indian–French force. For three years he was sole ruler of Bengal in all but name. In 1760, he returned to England, entered parliament, and was made a baron (1762). He returned to Calcutta (1765), effectively reformed the civil service, and re-established military discipline. His measures were seen as drastic, and he became the subject of a select committee enquiry upon his return to England in 1767. >> Siraj ad Daula

Clodion [klodyő], pseudonym of **Claude Michel** (1738–1814) Sculptor, born in Nancy, France. He was trained in Paris and Rome, where he stayed from 1762 to 1771. One of the most brilliant Rococo sculptors, he specialized in small terracottas and low reliefs of dancing nymphs and satyrs, unmistakably erotic.

Clooney, Rosemary (1928–) Singer, born in Kentucky. She joined Tony Pastor's orchestra in 1945, singing duets with her younger sister, Betty. In 1950, she recorded a dialect song, 'Come On-a My House' and became a pop star, following it with a string of hits including 'Hey There' (1951) and 'This Ole House' (1952). In 1954 she co-starred in the movie *White Christmas*. Personal problems in the aftermath of divorce from actor Jose Ferrer silenced her for almost 20 years, but she began appearing in nostalgia shows in the 1970s, and to record regularly for the Concord label.

Clopinel, Jean >> **Jean de Meung**

Clopton, Sir Hugh (?–1497) Silk merchant and philanthropist, born in Stratford-upon-Avon, Warwickshire, C England, UK. A mercer in London, he became sheriff (1486) and mayor (1492). At Stratford he built a stone bridge over the river, and New Place (c.1483), which was Shakespeare's home (1597–1616). >> Shakespeare, William

Close, Chuck (1940–) Artist, born in Menroe, WA. He studied painting at Yale (1962–4), and since 1967 has lived in New York City. In 1967–8 he began copying portrait photographs, painstakingly reproducing every detail, and has since continued with this 'Super-Realist' method. In the 1980s, he adopted the techniques of finger-painting and collage to achieve the same results.

Close, Glenn (1947–) Actress, born in Greenwich, CT. A student of anthropology and acting, she made her Broadway debut in *Love for Love* (1974). Her subsequent theatre work includes *The Singular Life of Albert Nobbs* (1982, Obie), *The Real Thing* (1984–5, Tony), and *Sunset Boulevard* (1995, Tony). She received an Emmy nomination for *Something About Amelia* (1984). Her role as the psychotic mistress in *Fatal Attraction* (1987) brought her international fame, which was consolidated with the success of *Dangerous Liaisons* (1988). Later films include *Reversal of Fortune* (1990), *Once Upon a Forest* (1993), *101 Dalmatians* and *Mars Attacks!* (both 1996), and *Paradise Road* (1997).

Clotilde or **Clotilda, St** [klohtilduh] (474–545) Queen consort of Clovis I, king of the Franks, and daughter of Chilperic, king of Burgundy. She married in 493, and after Clovis's death lived a life of austerity and good works at the Abbey of St Martin at Tours. Feast day 3 June. >> Clovis

Clouet, François [klooay] (c. 1516–1572) Portrait painter, probably born in Tours, France, the son of Jean Clouet. He succeeded his father as court painter to Francis I, and continued in that office under Henry II, Francis II, and Charles IX. His masterpiece is the Louvre portrait of Elizabeth of Austria; that of Mary, Queen of Scots, in the Wallace Collection is attributed to him. >> Clouet, Jean

Clouet, Jean [klooay], also found as **Jehan** or **Janet** (c.1485–1540/41) Portrait painter, probably the son of **Jehan Clouet** (c.1420–c.1480), a Flemish painter who moved to France as court painter to the Duke of Burgundy. He became court painter to Francis I, whose portrait in the Louvre is supposed to be by him. >> Clouet, François

Clough, Anne Jemima [kluhf] (1820–92) Educationist, born in Liverpool, Merseyside, NW England, UK, the sister of Arthur Hugh Clough. A vigorous proponent of higher education for women, she secured the admission of women to Manchester and Newcastle colleges. In 1871 she became the first principal of the first hall for women students at Cambridge: Newnham Hall, later called Newnham College. >> Clough, Arthur Hugh

Clough, Arthur Hugh [kluhf] (1819–61) Poet, born in Liverpool, Merseyside, NW England, UK. He studied at Rugby and Oxford, travelled in Europe, and espoused progressive social views. Experimental techniques in his long poem *The Bothie* (1848), and the ironic narrative *Amours de Voyage* (1849), have influenced modern poets. His best-known poem, beginning 'Say not the struggle nought availeth', was published posthumously in 1862. >> Clough, Ann Jemima

Clough, Brian [kluhf] (1935–) Footballer and manager, born in Middlesbrough, NE England, UK. When injury terminated his playing career, he became a manager at an early age. He took Derby County and Nottingham Forest to League championship wins and, in the case of Nottingham Forest, two European Cup successes.

Clovis I [klohvis], Ger **Chlodwig** or **Chlodovech** (c. 465–511) Merovingian king, who succeeded his father, Childeric (481), as king of the Franks. He overthrew the Gallo-Romans, and took possession of the whole country between the Somme and the Loire by 496. In 493 he married (St) **Clotilde**, and was converted to Christianity along with several thousand warriors after routing the Alemanni. In 507, he defeated the Visigoth, Alaric II, captured Bordeaux and Toulouse, but was checked at Arles by the Ostrogoth, Theodoric. He then took up residence in Paris. >> Alaric II; Clotilde, St; Remy; Theodoric

Clowes, William [klohz] (1779–1847) Printer, born in Chichester, West Sussex, S England, UK. In 1803 he started a London printing business carried on by his son, **William** (1807–83), and was the first printer to use steam-driven machines.

Clowes, William [klohz] (1780–1851) Nonconformist, born in Burslem, Staffordshire, C England, UK. He became a potter, and in the course of a dissolute youth achieved an ephemeral reputation as a champion dancer. In 1805 he was converted to Methodism, becoming a co-founder with Hugh Bourne of the Primitive Methodists (1810). >> Bourne, Hugh

Clune, Frank [kloon], popular name of **Francis Patrick Clune** (1893–1971) Writer of biography, history, and travel, born in Sydney, New South Wales, Australia. His early life was one of travel and adventure at sea. He served with the Australian Imperial Forces in World War 1, and was wounded at Gallipoli. At the age of 40 he decided to write the story of his early years, published as *Try Anything Once* (1933). He wrote over 60 books, often in collaboration with P R ('Inky') Stephensen, and was one of Australia's best-selling writers. Stories such as *Ben Hall the Bushranger* (1947), and *Wild Colonial Boys* (1948) aroused interest in Australian history.

Clunies Ross, Sir Ian [klooneez] (1899–1959) Veterinary scientist, born in Bathurst, New South Wales, Australia. He joined the newly formed [Australian] Council for Scientific and Industrial Research in 1926, but resigned upon being appointed Australian representative on the International Wool Secretariat (1937), where he served as chairman until 1940. That year he became professor of veterinary science at Sydney University. When the CSIR became the [Australian] Commonwealth Scientific and Industrial Research Organization in 1949, he was its first chairman.

Clurman, Harold (Edgar) [kloorman] (1901–80) Theatre director and critic, born in New York City. He was playreader for the Theater Guild (1929–31), co-founder of the Group Theater (1931–40), and one of its directors. His book *The Fervent Years* (1946) is a history of the Group. He later worked as a director in Hollywood and on Broadway. An influential drama critic, his writings include *Lies Like Truths* (1958) and *The Divine Pastime* (1974).

Cluverius or **Clüver, Phillip** [klooveerius, klüver] (1580–1622) Geographer and antiquarian, born in Gdańsk, Poland (formerly, Danzig of Germany). He studied law at Leyden, and visited many countries, including Norway, England, Scotland, France, and Italy. He wrote *Introductio in universam geographium* (1624, Introduction to Universal Geography), and is regarded as the founder of historical geography.

Clyde, Lord >> **Campbell, Sir Colin**

Clynes, Joseph Robert [kliynz] (1869–1949) Trade unionist and British statesman, born in Oldham, Lancashire, NW England, UK. He worked in a cotton mill from the age of 10 and educated himself. Organizer of the Lancashire Gasworkers' Union (1891), he was president (1892) and secretary (1894–1912) of Oldham's Trade Council. He entered parliament (1910) for the Labour Party, and became food controller (1918), vice-chairman (1922), and Lord Privy Seal in Britain's first Labour cabinet (1924).

Cnut >> **Canute**

Coanda, Henri [kawanda] (1885–1972) Aeronautical engineer, born in Romania. He built the first jet-propelled aeroplane, using a ducted fan, not a turbojet, and, because of a phenomenon not then understood, the hot exhaust gases set fire to the structure. He later investigated this effect, and the entrainment of a free jet alongside a curved surface now bears his name. He subsequently became an aircraft designer with the British & Colonial Aeroplane Co (later the Bristol Aircraft Co).

Coase, Ronald (Harry) [kohs] (1910–   ) Economist, born in London, England, UK. Educated in England, he worked as a statistician in the British War Cabinet before emigrating to the USA in 1951. He taught at the universities of Virginia (1958–64) and Chicago (1964–79). Two journal articles in particular are the basis of his widespread influence: 'The Nature of the Firm' (1937), which analyzed the economics of 'transaction costs', and 'The Problem of Social Cost' (1960), which led to the development of the economics of property rights and the economics of law. He was awarded the Nobel Prize for Economics in 1991.

Coates, Eric (1886–1957) Composer, born in Hucknall, Nottinghamshire, C England, UK. He studied in Nottingham and at the Royal Academy of Music, London, working as a violinist. Sir Henry Wood performed several of his early works at Promenade Concerts. Success as a composer of attractive light music enabled him to devote himself to composition after 1918. Among his best-known compositions are the *London Suite* (1933), *The Three Elizabeths* (1944), and a number of popular waltzes and marches. >> Wood, Henry

Coates, Wells Wintemute (1895–1958) Canadian architect, born in Tokyo. He practised as an architect from 1929, studying in Canada and London, and in 1933 formed the MARS group of architects. He was responsible for the design of the BBC studios, the EKCO laboratories, and many other buildings in Great Britain and in Canada, and he also played an important part in the development of industrial design. He was one of the principal figures of the modern movement in architecture.

Cobb, Ty(rus Raymond), nickname **the Georgia Peach** (1886–1961) Baseball player, born in Narrows, GA. An outstanding base runner and batter, in a 23-year career with Detroit and Philadelphia he had over 4000 base hits, a record which survived 57 years until broken in 1985. His career batting average was an all-time record at ·367, and he led the American League 12 times in batting. >> RR1144

Cobbe, Frances Power [kob] (1822–1904) Social worker and feminist, born in Newbridge, near Dublin. She travelled in Italy and the East, and wrote *Cities of the Past* (1864) and *Italics* (1864). A strong theist, a supporter of women's rights, and a prominent anti-vivisectionist, she was associated with Mary Carpenter in the founding of ragged schools. >> Carpenter, Mary

Cobbett, William (1763–1835) Journalist and reformer, born in Farnham, Surrey, SE England, UK. He moved on impulse to London (1783), spent a year reading widely, and joined the army, serving in New Brunswick (1785–91). In 1792 he married and went to the USA, where he wrote fierce pieces against democratic government under the name 'Peter Porcupine'. Returning to England in 1800, he was welcomed by the Tories, and started his famous *Weekly Political Register* (1802), which continued until his death, changing in 1804 from its original Toryism to an uncompromising Radicalism. In 1810 he was imprisoned for two years for criticizing the flogging of militiamen by German mercenaries, and in 1817 he went again to the USA, fearing a second imprisonment. Returning in 1819 he travelled widely in Britain, and finally became an MP (1832). His works include a *History of the Protestant Reformation* (1824–7) and *Rural Rides* (1830).

Cobbold, Richard (1797–1877) Writer, born in Ipswich, Suffolk, E England, UK. He wrote *Margaret Catchpole* (1845) and other works, and for 50 years was rector of Wortham, near Diss. >> Catchpole

Cobden, Richard (1804–65) Economist and politican, 'the apostle of free trade', born in Heyshott, West Sussex, S

England, UK. He worked as a clerk and commercial traveller in London, then went into the calico business, settling in Manchester. In 1835 he visited the USA, and the Levant (1836–7), after which he published two pamphlets preaching free trade, nonintervention, and speaking against 'Russophobia'. In 1838 he helped to found the Anti-Corn-Law League, becoming its most prominent member. He became an MP in 1841. His lectures and parliamentary speeches focused opinion on the Corn Laws, which were repealed in 1846.

Cobden-Sanderson, Thomas James (1840–1922) Printer and bookbinder, born in Alnwick, Northumberland, NE England, UK. A lawyer by training, he became a leader of the 19th-c revival of artistic typography, working with William Morris. In 1900 he founded the Doves Press at Hammersmith, London, whose masterpiece was the beautiful *Doves Bible* (1903). After the press closed in 1916, he threw the type into the Thames. >> Morris, William

Cobham, Lord >> **Oldcastle, John**

Coborn, Charles [**koh**baw(r)n], pseudonym of **Colin Whitton McCallum** (1852–1945) Cockney comedian of Scottish descent. He spent his childhood in London's East End, went on the stage in 1875, and immortalized the songs 'Two Lovely Black Eyes' (1886) and 'The Man who Broke the Bank at Monte Carlo' (1890). In 1928 he published the autobiographical *The Man who Broke the Bank*.

Coburn, John [**koh**bern] (1925–) Artist and tapestry designer, born in Ingham, Queensland, Australia. During war service in the Far East he studied the arts of India, Burma, and China, which influenced his subsequent work using formalized leaf designs to make two-dimensional patterns of shape and colour. In Aubusson, France, he worked from 1969 to 1972 on his best-known commissions, the *Curtain of the Sun* and *Curtain of the Moon* for the prosceniums of the new Sydney Opera House.

Coch(e)ba, Simon bar >> **bar Kokhba, Simon**

Cochise [**koh**chees] (?1812–74) Chiricahua Apache chief, born in present-day Arizona or New Mexico. Initially friendly towards whites, he embarked on a campaign against them in 1861 after he had been imprisoned on the false charge of kidnapping a white child. With the murder of his father-in-law, Mangas Coloradas, in 1863, he became the main war chief of the Apaches. For many years he engaged in a series of violent actions against white settlers and the US army, but he was gradually restricted to a small mountainous range. After winning assurances from the US government that he and his band could remain in the Chiricahua Mts, he surrendered in 1872. >> Crook

Cochlaeus [**koh**layus], originally **Johann Dobneck** (1479–1552) Theologian and humanist, born in Wendelstein, Germany. He studied at the University of Cologne, became a teacher, and was ordained a priest c.1518. After initial sympathy with Luther, he became his most active critic at numerous confrontations, including the Diet of Worms (1521). Of his numerous works the best known is *Acts and Writings of Luther* (1549). >> Luther

Cochran, Sir Charles Blake [**kok**ran] (1872–1951) Theatrical producer, born in Lindfield, West Sussex, S England, UK. He began his career as an actor, then turned impresario. His spectacular presentation of *The Miracle* (1911) won him renown as a producer. His most successful production was *Bless the Bride* by Herbert and Ellis (1947), which ran for 886 performances. He was knighted in 1948.

Cochran, Jacqueline [**kok**ran] (1910–80) Aviator, born in Pensacola, FL. She received her pilot's licence in 1932, became the first woman to fly in the Bendix transcontinental air race in 1935, and in 1938 secured the transcontinental record. The International League of Aviators named her the world's outstanding woman pilot (1937–50, 1953). She

became director of Women Auxiliary Service Pilots in the US air force in 1943. In 1953 she became the first woman to fly faster than sound (in an F-86 Sabre fighter), and in 1964 flew faster than twice the speed of sound.

Cockcroft, Sir John Douglas (1897–1967) Nuclear physicist, born in Todmorden, West Yorkshire, N England, UK. He studied at Manchester and Cambridge, and became professor of physics at Cambridge (1939–46). With Walton he succeeded in disintegrating lithium by proton bombardment (the first artificial transmutation) in 1932, pioneering the use of particle accelerators, and they shared the Nobel Prize for Physics (1951). During World War 2 he was director of Air Defence Research (1941–4). He became the first director of Britain's Atomic Energy Establishment at Harwell in 1946. He was knighted in 1948, and in 1959 appointed the first Master of Churchill College, Cambridge. >> Walton, E T S

Cocker, Edward (1631–75) English engraver, who also taught penmanship and arithmetic. He was reputedly the author of *Cocker's Arithmetic* (1678), which went through 112 editions. Its reputation for accuracy gave rise to the expression 'according to Cocker', but it has been exposed as a poor and inaccurate forgery made by his editor and publisher.

Cockerell, Charles Robert (1788–1863) British architect, the son of Samuel Pepys Cockerell. He travelled in the Levant and Italy (1810–17), was professor of architecture in the Royal Academy (1840–57), and designed the Taylorian Institute at Oxford and the Fitzwilliam Museum at Cambridge. >> Cockerell, Samuel Pepys

Cockerell, Sir Christopher (Sydney) (1910–) Engineer, born in Cambridge, Cambridgeshire, EC England, UK. He studied at Cambridge and worked on radio and radar, before turning to hydrodynamics. In the early 1950s, experimenting with air as a lubricant between a boat's hull and the water, he invented the amphibious hovercraft. The first full-scale machine was built in 1958. He was knighted in 1969.

Cockerell, Samuel Pepys (1754–1827) British architect. He laid out Brunswick and Mecklenburg Squares in London, and designed the tower of St Anne's, Soho. >> Cockerell, Charles Robert

Cocteau, Jean [kok**toh**] (1889–1963) Poet, playwright, and film director, born in Maisons-Lafitte, France. He had early success with his poems, which he fully exploited, and figured as the sponsor of Picasso, Stravinsky, Giorgio de Chirico, and the musical group known as *Les Six*. He was an actor, director, scenario writer, novelist, critic, and artist, all of his work being marked by vivacity and a pyrotechnic brilliance. His best-known works include his novel *Les Enfants terribles* (1929, Children of the Game), his play *Orphée* (1926, Orpheus), and his films *Le Sang du poète* (1932, The Blood of the Poet) and *La Belle et la bête* (1945, Beauty and the Beast). >> Auric; Chirico; Durey; Honegger; Milhaud; Picasso; Poulenc; Stravinsky; Taillefaire

Cody, Samuel Franklin [**koh**dee] (1862–1913) Aviator, born in Texas. He moved to England in 1896 and acquired British nationality. He experimented with man-lifting kites, participated in the planning and construction of the first British dirigible, and built an early aeroplane in 1908. He was killed in a flying accident.

Cody, William F(rederick) [**koh**dee], known as **Buffalo Bill** (1846–1917) Showman, born in Scott Co, IA. He received his nickname after killing nearly 5000 buffalo in eight months for a contract to supply workers on the Kansas Pacific Railway with meat. He served as a scout in the Sioux Wars, but from 1883 toured with his Wild West Show. The town of Cody in Wyoming stands on part of his former ranch.

Coe, Kelvin (1946–92) Ballet dancer, born in Melbourne, Victoria, Australia. He joined the Australian Ballet for its inaugural season in 1969, and went on to dance virtually every lead role in its repertoire. He appeared as a guest with the Sydney Dance Company, American Ballet Theatre, Bolshoi Ballet, and London Festival Ballet. He retired as the Australian Ballet's principal dancer in 1981, but continued dancing on a more restricted basis. A popular performer in classical and contemporary pieces, he is widely considered to have been Australia's best male dancer.

Coe, Sebastian [koh] (1956–) Athlete, born in London, England, UK, the world's most outstanding middle-distance runner of the 1980s. He studied at Loughborough College, won the bronze medal in the 800 m at the 1978 European Championships, and the following year broke his first world records (800 m and 1 mi). Altogether he broke eight world records including the mile three times. At the 1980 Olympics he won the gold medal in the 1500 m and the silver in the 800 m, repeating the achievement four years later. Fitness problems followed, and he was omitted from the British team that went to the 1988 Olympics. He retired from running after the 1990 Commonwealth Games to pursue a career in politics, becoming a Conservative MP in 1992, but lost his seat in the 1997 general election. >> RR1135

Coetzee, John Michael [kohtzee] (1940–) Writer and critic, born in Cape Town. The political situation in his native country provides him with the base from which to launch his allegories and fables, attacking colonialism and demythologizing historical and contemporary myths of imperialism. His first work of fiction was *Dusklands* (1974), followed by *In the Heart of the Country* (1977), *Waiting for the Barbarians* (1980), *Life and Times of Michael K* (1983, Booker), *Foe* (1986), *Age of Iron* (1990), and *The Master of Petersburg* (1994). His critical work includes *White Writing* (1988) and *Giving Offense: Essays on Censorship* (1996).

Coffin, Henry Sloane (1877–1954) Protestant clergyman and educator, born in New York City. He graduated from Yale in 1897, and studied abroad for two years before taking a divinity degree at Union Theological Seminary in 1900. An evangelical liberal, he held a number of Presbyterian pastorates, and as president of the union seminary (1926–45) promoted open inquiry into theological issues. He retired in 1945, but remained active as a lecturer and preacher. His *Religion Yesterday and Today* appeared in 1940.

Coggan (of Canterbury and of Sissinghurst), (Frederick) Donald Coggan, Baron (1909–) Clergyman, born in London, England, UK. He studied at Cambridge, was a lecturer in Semitic languages at Manchester (1931–4), professor of the New Testament at Wycliffe College, Toronto (1937–44), Principal of London College of Divinity (1944–56), Bishop of Bradford (1956–61), Archbishop of York (1961–74), and finally Archbishop of Canterbury (1974–80), when he was made a life peer. He is the author of several theological works, including *Sure Foundation* (1981) and *A New Way for Preaching* (1996).

Coggeshall, Ralph de [kogshawl] (?–c. 1227) Chronicler, a native of Cambridgeshire, EC England, UK. He was abbot of the Cistercian abbey of Coggeshall, Essex (1207–18), and continued the Latin Chronicle (*Chronicon Anglicanum*) kept at the Abbey, covering the period 1187–1224.

Cohan, George Michael (Keohane) (1878–1942) Actor, dramatist, and director, born in Providence, RI. He began in vaudeville as a child in his family's act, the Four Cohans, and was writing for the act by the age of 15. As an actor he is remembered in such roles as the father in O'Neill's *Ah, Wilderness!* (1933), and as a writer of such songs as 'Yankee Doodle Dandy', which featured in his musical *Little Johnny*

Jones (1904), and which gave the title of the film made of his life in 1942.

Cohan, Robert [kohhan] (1925–) Dancer, choreographer, teacher, and director, born in New York City, New York, USA. He trained with Martha Graham and danced with her company, becoming co-director in 1966. He moved to London as artistic director of the new London Contemporary Dance Theatre in 1967, choreographing works with a wide range of subject matter. He then started the London Contemporary Dance School, and developed a British version of Graham's expressive dance technique, before retiring in 1988. >> Graham, Martha

Cohen, Hermann (1842–1912) Philosopher, born in Coswig, Germany. Professor of philosophy at Marburg (1876–1912), he founded the Marburg School of neo-Kantianism, which applied Kantian methods to the presuppositions of science. He later taught at the Rabbinic seminary in Berlin, and propounded a synthesis of Judaism and idealism which had a deep influence on such early 20th-c Jewish thinkers as Martin Buber and Franz Rosenzweig. >> Buber; Rosenzweig

Cohen, Leonard (1934–) Poet, novelist, songwriter, and singer, born in Montreal, Quebec, Canada. He published his first book of poetry *Let us Compare Mythologies* (1956), soon after graduating from McGill University. A highly popular poet and songwriter, he is also the author of several novels, notably *Beautiful Losers* (1966). The first of his many song albums was *Songs of Leonard Cohen* (1967). In 1983 he completed an opera with composer Louis Furey.

Cohen, Seymour (Stanley) (1917–) Biochemist, born in New York City. He did valuable early work in the 1940s using radioactive labelling of bacteriophage, which suggested that DNA plays a key part in heredity.

Cohen, Stanley (1922–) Cell biologist, born in New York City. He taught at the universities of Michigan (1946–8) and Colorado (1948–52) before joining Rita Levi-Montalcini's laboratory at Washington University, St Louis (1953–9). He discovered the epidermal growth factor from mouse tissue extract, which accelerated the maturation of newborn mice. He continued his studies of this substance at Vanderbilt University (1959–86), determining its amino acid sequence and action on cells and wound healing. In 1986, he and Levi-Montalcini received the Nobel Prize for Physiology or Medicine for their fundamental contributions to cell and organ development. >> Levi-Montalcini

Cohen, Stanley (1935–) >> **Boyer, Herbert**

Cohen, William S (1940–) US statesman. He became Republican senator for Maine in 1973, serving three terms before retiring in 1996. He was a leading critic of the administration in the Watergate and Iran-Contra scandals. He was made secretary of defense in the 1997 administration, following Clinton's election promise to appoint a Republican to his cabinet. >> Clinton, Bill

Cohl, Emile, originally **Emile Courtet** (1857–1938) Cartoonist, and inventor of the animated cartoon film, born in Paris. A pupil of the caricaturist, **André Gill** (1840–85), his first cartoons were published in *Le Rire* (1880). He became comedy film writer/director at the Gaumont Studio, where he used simple stick figures to produce the first frame-by-frame animated cartoon film, *Fantasmagorie* (1908). Sent to New York City by Eclair Films, he adapted the George McManus strip, *The Newlyweds and Their Baby*, into the first animated series (1912).

Cohn, Ferdinand (Julius) (1828–98) Botanist and bacteriologist, born in Wrocław, Poland (formerly Breslau, Prussia). He received his doctorate from Berlin at the age of 19. Professor of botany at Breslau (1859) and founder of the Institute of Plant Physiology, he is regarded as the father of bacteriology, in that he was the first to account it a separate science. He did important research in plant pathology, and worked with Robert Koch on anthrax. >> Koch, Robert

Cohn, Roy M(arcus) (1927–86) Lawyer, born in New York City. Admitted to the bar at the age of 21, he became assistant attorney for subversive activities and soon special assistant to the US attorney general. As chief counsel to McCarthy's Communist-hunting subcommittee (1953–4), he was an often celebrated, often denigrated national figure. From 1954 to 1986 he became a political power broker and much-sought legal talent with Saxe, Bacon & Bolan (and predecessor firms) in New York City. Known as a loyal advocate, he gave lavish annual parties for his famous, fashionable clients and friends at his estate in Greenwich, CN. Three times tried and acquitted on federal charges of conspiracy, bribery, and fraud, he was disbarred two months before his death. >> McCarthy, Joseph

Cohnheim, Julius Friedrich [kohnhiym] (1839–84) Pathologist, born in Demmin, Poland. He held chairs in Kiel, Wrocław (formerly Breslau, Germany), and Leipzig, working on many problems, including infectious diseases and cancer. He first elucidated completely the microscopical events of inflammation, and provided the first proof that tuberculosis was an infectious disease.

Coke, Sir Edward [kook] (1552–1634) Jurist, born in Mileham, Norfolk, E England, UK. He studied at Norwich and Cambridge, was called to the bar in 1578, and rose to become speaker of the House of Commons (1593), attorney general (1594), Chief Justice of the Common Pleas (1606), Chief Justice of the King's Bench (1613), and privy councillor. He brutally prosecuted for treason Essex, Raleigh, and the Gunpowder conspirators, but after 1606 stands out as a vindicator of national liberties against the royal prerogative. He was dismissed in 1617, and from 1620 led the popular party in parliament, serving nine months in prison. The Petition of Right (1628) was largely his doing. Most of his epoch-making Law Reports were published during his lifetime (1600–15). >> Essex, 2nd Earl of; Fawkes; Raleigh (1552–1618)

Coke, Thomas (1747–1814) Methodist clergyman, born in Brecon, Powys, E Wales, UK. He studied at Oxford (1768), and became an Anglican curate in Somerset, but in 1777 joined the Methodists, and was attached to the London circuit. In 1784 he was appointed by John Wesley as the superintendent of the Methodist Church in America. He visited the USA nine times, and assumed the title of bishop in 1787. He died in the Indian Ocean on a missionary voyage to Ceylon (now Sri Lanka). >> Wesley, John

Coke, Thomas William >> **Leicester of Holkham, Thomas, William Coke**

Colbert, Claudette [kolbair], originally **Lily Claudette Chauchoin** (1903–96) Film actress, born in Paris. She went to the USA as a child, and started in films with spirited comedy roles, becoming a star with *It Happened One Night* (1934), which won her an Oscar. This was followed by 10 years of romantic comedy successes, including *Tovarich* (1937) and *The Palm Beach Story* (1942), and varied character parts up to the 1960s, such as in *Parrish* (1960). On the stage her career continued into the 1980s.

Colbert, Jean Baptiste [kolbair] (1619–83) French statesman, born in Reims, France. In 1651 he entered the service of Mazarin, and became the chief financial minister of Louis XIV (1661). He found the finances in a ruinous condition, and introduced a series of successful reforms, doubling the revenue in 10 years. He reorganized the colonies, provided a strong fleet, improved the civil code, and introduced a marine code. The Academies of Inscriptions, Science, and Architecture were founded by him, and he

became a patron of industry, commerce, art, science, and literature. However, his successes were undone by wars and court extravagance, and he died bitterly disappointed. >> Louis XIV; Mazarin

Coldstream, Sir William (1908–87) Painter, and teacher of art, born in Belford, Northumberland, NE England, UK. He studied at the Slade School of Art, London, (1926–9), joined the London Group in 1933, and helped to found the Euston Road School (1937). From 1949 he was professor of fine art at University College, London. A highly skilled administrator, he helped reshape British art education, especially through his work on the national advisory committee (1958–71) which produced the two *Coldstream Reports*.

Cole, George (1925–) Actor, born in London, England, UK. Educated in Morden, Greater London, he joined the cast of *White Horse Inn* (1939). He has had many parts on stage, screen, and television, in serious works such as *The Three Sisters* (1967) as well as comedy. His many films include the *St Trinian's* series and other comedies, but he is probably best known in the UK as Arthur Daly from the long-running television series, *Minder*. Other television work includes *The Bounder*, *Blott on the Landscape*, *My Good Friend* (1995–6), and *An Independent Man* (1996).

Cole, George Douglas Howard (1889–1958) Economist, historian, and detective-story writer, born in London, England, UK. He studied at Oxford, where he became reader in economics (1925) and professor of social and political theory (1944). Historian, chairman (1939–46, 1948–50), and president from 1952 of the Fabian Society, he wrote numerous books on socialism. He often wrote in collaboration with his wife, **Margaret Isobel Cole**, and her brother, Raymond Postgate.

Cole, Sir Henry, pseudonym **Felix Summerley** (1808–82) Designer, writer, and civil servant, born in Bath, SW England, UK. He introduced the penny postage system and is one of several candidates cited as the inventor of the adhesive stamp. Under his pseudonym he set up a firm for 'art manufacture', published illustrated children's books, and published the first Christmas card. He planned and largely organized the Great Exhibition of 1851 under the patronage of Prince Albert. He also set up a national system of art education, and was director of the South Kensington Museum (1853–73), which became the Victoria and Albert Museum. He was knighted in 1875.

Cole, Nat King, originally **Nathaniel Adams Cole**, family name formerly **Coles** (1919–65) Entertainer, born in Montgomery, AL. During the 1930s he became popular as a jazz pianist and singer, forming his own instrumental trio of piano, guitar, and double bass in 1937 which set the pattern for many later jazz trios. Among many hit records were 'Route 66' and 'Walking My Baby Back Home', but probably his best-known song is 'Unforgettable', which enjoyed a recent revival in a posthumous electronically arranged duet with his daughter, **Natalie Cole** (1950–).

Cole, Thomas (1801–48) Painter, born in Bolton, Lancashire, NW England, UK. He emigrated with his family to America in 1819, settling in Catskill, NY, and became founder of the Hudson River school of landscape painters. In 1830 two of his pictures appeared in the Royal Academy, and he afterwards made sketching tours through England, France, and Italy; but all his best landscapes were American, especially the 'Voyage of Life' series (from 1839). >> Kensett

Coleman, Ornette (1930–) Alto saxophonist, multi-instrumentalist, and composer, born in Fort Worth, TX. His experiments in free-form jazz and atonality from the mid-1950s attracted equal measures of praise and scepticism. Following early recordings with Don Cherry (1936–), he persevered through a discouraging climate for avant-garde jazz, becoming more generally accepted in the 1960s as a major innovator. A writer of jazz works in unconventional forms, he has also composed several classical pieces.

Colenso, John William [ko̱lensoh] (1814–83) Clergyman, born in St Austell, Cornwall, SW England, UK. He studied at Cambridge, and was appointed the first Bishop of Natal in 1853. He mastered the Zulu language, prepared a grammar and dictionary, and translated the Prayer Book and part of the Bible. *The Pentateuch and the Book of Joshua Critically Examined* (1862–79), which cast doubts upon biblical accuracy, was regarded as heretical, and he was eventually deposed in 1869.

Colepeper or **Culpeper, John, Baron** [ku̱hlpeper] (1600–60) English royalist statesman, a native of Sussex. He served abroad, and was returned for Kent in 1640 to the Long Parliament. There he opposed the Grand Remonstrance, but supported episcopacy. In 1642 he was created Chancellor of the Exchequer, and in 1643 Master of the Rolls. He was an influential counsellor of both Charles I and Charles II. >> Charles I (of England); Charles II (of England)

Coleridge, (David) Hartley (1796–1849) Man of letters, born in Clevedon, Somerset, SW England, UK, the eldest son of Samuel Taylor Coleridge. He was brought up by Robert Southey at Greta Hall, and studied at Merton College, Oxford, but forfeited an Oriel College fellowship by intemperance. He spent two years in London, tried taking pupils at Ambleside, occasionally writing for *Blackwood's Magazine*, lived for some time in Grasmere, then moved to Leeds, where he wrote biographies. He later returned to Grasmere, where he continued to write poetry. >> ; Coleridge, Samuel Taylor; Southey

Coleridge, Samuel Taylor (1772–1834) Poet, born in Ottery St Mary, Devon, SE England, UK. He studied at Cambridge, imbibed revolutionary ideas, and left to enlist in the Dragoons. His plans to found a communist society in the USA with Robert Southey came to nothing, and he turned instead to teaching and journalism in Bristol. Marrying **Sara Fricker** (Southey's sister-in-law), he went with her to Nether Stowey, where they made close friends with William and Dorothy Wordsworth. From this connection a new poetry emerged, in reaction against Neoclassic artificiality. *Lyrical Ballads* (1798) opens with his magical 'Rime of the Ancient Mariner'. After visiting Germany (1798–9), he developed an interest in German philosophy. In 1800 he went to the Lake District, but his career prospects were blighted by his moral collapse, partly due to opium. He rejected Wordsworth's animistic views of nature, and relations between them became strained. He began a weekly paper, *The Friend* (1809), and settled in London, writing and lecturing. In 1816 he published 'Christabel' and the fragment, 'Kubla Khan', both written in his earlier period of inspiration. His small output of poetry proves his gift, but he is known also for his critical writing, and for his theological and politico-sociological works. >> Coleridge, Hartley/Sara; Southey; Wordsworth

Coleridge, Sara (1802–52) Scholar, born in Keswick, Cumbria, NW England, UK, the daughter of Samuel Taylor Coleridge. She was brought up in Robert Southey's household, married her cousin, **Henry Nelson Coleridge** in 1829, and helped to edit her father's writings. Her own works were *Pretty Lessons for Good Children* (1834) and *Phantasmion* (1837), a fairy tale. >> Coleridge, Samuel Taylor; Southey

Coleridge-Taylor, Samuel (1875–1912) Composer, born in London, England, UK. He studied at the Royal College of Music, and became a music teacher and conductor. He composed a trilogy on the theme of *Hiawatha* (1898–1900), and other popular cantatas and orchestral works.

Colet, John [ko̱let] (c.1467–1519) Theologian and Tudor humanist, born in London, England, UK. He studied at Oxford, travelled in Italy, then returned to England where he became a priest. While lecturing at Oxford, he worked with Thomas More and Erasmus. In 1505 he became dean of St Paul's, where he continued to deliver controversial lectures on the interpretation of Scripture, and founded St Paul's School (1509–12). >> Erasmus; More, Thomas

Colette, Sidonie Gabrielle [ko̱let] (1873–1954) Novelist, born in Saint-Sauveur-en-Puisaye, France. Her early books were written in collaboration with her first husband, **Henri Gauthier-Villars** (pseudonym **Willy**); after their divorce in 1906 she appeared in music-halls in dance and mime, then settled as a writer. Her novels include the 'Claudine' series (1900–3), *Chéri* (1920), and *Gigi* (1945). In 1912 she married **Henry de Jouvenel**, and in 1935, **Maurice Goudeket**. She won many awards for her work, and became a legendary figure in Paris.

Coligny, Gaspard II de, seigneur de (Lord of) **Châtillon** [koleenyee] (1519–72) Huguenot leader, born in Châtillon-sur-Loing, France. He fought in the wars of Francis I and Henry II, and in 1552 was made Admiral of France. In 1557 he became a Protestant, and commanded the Huguenots during the second and third Wars of Religion. Catherine de' Medici made him one of the first victims in the St Bartholomew's Day massacre in Paris. >> Catherine de' Medici; Francis I; Henry II (of France)

Collett, (Jacobine) Camilla, *née* **Wergeland** (1813–95) Novelist, born in Kristiansand, Norway, the sister of Hendrik Arnold Wergeland. A champion of women's rights and social justice, she brought realism to Norwegian fiction in such books as *Amtmandens Døttre* (1855, The Magistrate's Daughter) and *I den Lange Neeter* (1862, In the Long Nights). >> Wergeland

Collier, Jeremy (1650–1726) Clergyman and nonjuror, born in Stow cum Quy, Cambridgeshire, EC England, UK. He studied at Cambridge, afterwards becoming rector of Ampton near Bury St Edmunds, and lecturer at Gray's Inn. He refused to take the oath of allegiance to William III and Mary in 1689, waged war on the crown with incisive pamphlets, and was arrested in 1692 on suspicion of being involved in a Jacobite plot. In 1697 he published his *Short View of the Immorality and Profaneness of the English Stage*, which fell like a thunderbolt among the wits. He continued to preach to a congregation of nonjurors, and was consecrated a nonjuring bishop in 1713. >> William III

Collings, Jesse (1831–1920) British politician, born in Littleham-cum-Exmouth, Devon, SW England, UK. Elected Radical MP for Ipswich in 1880, he sat for Bordesley as a Unionist (1886–1918), and was specially identified with the Agricultural Labourers' Union and measures for promoting allotments and smallholdings ('three acres and a cow'). He was also under-secretary for the Home Office (1895–1902).

Collingwood, Cuthbert, Baron (1750–1810) British admiral, born in Newcastle upon Tyne, Tyne and Wear, NE England, UK. He joined the navy at 11, and from 1778 his career was closely connected with that of Nelson. He fought at Brest (1794), Cape St Vincent (1797), and Trafalgar (1805), where he succeeded Nelson as commander. He was created baron after Trafalgar, and is buried beside Nelson in St Paul's Cathedral. >> Nelson

Collingwood, R(obin) G(eorge) (1889–1943) Philosopher, historian, and archaeologist, born in Coniston, Cumbria, NW England, UK. He studied at Oxford, where he became professor of philosophy (1934–41). He was an authority on the archaeology of Roman Britain, and much of his philosophical work was concerned with the relationship between history and philosophy.

Collingwood, William (Gershom) (1854–1932) Artist and archaeologist, born in Liverpool, Merseyside, NW England, UK. He studied philosophy and aesthetics at Oxford, then trained as an artist in London under Alphonse Legros. He moved to Coniston in the Lake District to be private secretary and collaborator to John Ruskin, and was for a time a professor at Reading University. He is best known for his archaeological studies on Viking remains. >> Legros; Ruskin

Collins, Joan (Henrietta) (1933–) Actress, born in London, England, UK. She made her film debut in *Lady Godiva Rides Again* (1951) and used her sultry appeal and headline-catching private life to build a career as an international celebrity. By the 1970s she was appearing in low-budget horror films and softcore pornography, but her fortunes were revitalized with a leading role in the universally popular television soap opera *Dynasty* (1981–9). Married four times, she has written one volume of autobiography, *Past Imperfect* (1978), and her novels include *Prime Time* (1988), *My Secrets* (1994), and *Second Act* (1996). Her sister is the best-selling novelist **Jackie Collins**.

Collins, Michael (1890–1922) Irish politician and Sinn Féin leader, born near Clonakilty, County Cork. He became an MP (1918–22), and with Arthur Griffith was largely responsible for the negotiation of the treaty with Great Britain in 1921. He was killed in an ambush between Bandon and Macroom. >> Griffith, Arthur

Collins, Michael (1930–) Astronaut, born in Rome. He trained at West Point, became a test pilot, and joined the space programme in 1963. He was one of the members of the Gemini 10 project, and remained in the command module during the successful Apollo 11 Moon-landing expedition. He became under-secretary of the Smithsonian Institution in 1978. >> Aldrin; Armstrong, Neil

Collins, Phil(ip David Charles) (1951–) Singer and drummer, born in London, England, UK. He began as a child actor, went on to play drums with several groups, including Genesis, Eric Clapton, and Led Zeppelin, and became known in the early 1980s as a singer, 'You Can't Hurry Love' reaching No 1 in the UK (1982) and 'Sussudio' No 1 in the USA (1985). He also starred in the film *Buster* (1988).

Collins, (William) Wilkie (1824–89) Novelist, born in London, England, UK. He spent four years in business, then entered Lincoln's Inn, but gradually took to literature, becoming a master of the mystery story. His best-known works are *The Woman in White* (1860) and *The Moonstone* (1868).

Collins, William (1721–59) Poet, born in Chichester, West Sussex, S England, UK. He studied at Oxford, then went to London to make a living by literature. Dr Johnson once rescued him from the bailiffs by obtaining an advance from a bookseller on the promise of Collins to translate the *Poetics* of Aristotle. It was during this period that he wrote his *Odes*, upon which his fame rests. He later retired to Chichester, where his poems include 'Ode on the Superstitions of the Highlands' – a work in which, says Lowell, 'the whole Romantic School is foreshadowed'. >> Johnson, Samuel; Lowell, Robert

Collins, William (1789–1853) Publisher, born in Eastwood, East Renfrewshire, W Scotland, UK. A weaver by trade, he opened a private school for the poor in Glasgow in 1813. He set up business in Glasgow as a bookseller and publisher, specializing in church history and school textbooks.

Collot d'Herbois, Jean Marie [koloh dairbwah] (1751–96) French revolutionary, born in Paris. Originally a provincial actor, he was attracted by the revolution back to Paris, and joined the Jacobin Club in 1791. In 1793 he became president of the National Convention and a member of the Committee of Public Safety. Sent by Robespierre to Lyon, he took revenge by guillotine and grapeshot on the inhabitants for having once hissed him off the stage. He joined in the successful plot against Robespierre (1794), but was himself expelled from the Convention, and banished to Cayenne (1795). >> Robespierre

Colm, St >> Columba, St

Colman, St (?–676) Irish monk of Iona, W Scotland, UK. In 661 he became Bishop of Lindisfarne, but in 664 withdrew to Iona on the defeat of the Celtic party over the dating of Easter at the Council of Whitby. Feast day 18 February/8 August in some parts of Ireland. >> Columba, St

Colman, George, known as **the Elder** (1732–94) Playwright and manager, born in Florence, Italy, the son of the English envoy. He studied at Oxford, and was called to the bar in 1755. In 1760 his first piece, *Polly Honeycombe*, was produced at Drury Lane with great success. Next year came *The Jealous Wife*, and in 1766 *The Clandestine Marriage*, written in conjunction with Garrick. In 1767 he purchased, with three others, Covent Garden Theatre, and held the office of manager for seven years, until he sold his share. He then purchased the Haymarket Theatre. >> Colman, George (the Younger); Garrick

Colman, George, known as **the Younger** (1762–1836) Theatre manager and playwright, born in London, England, UK, the son of George Colman (the Elder). He studied at Oxford and Aberdeen, followed his father as manager of the Haymarket, and became Examiner of Plays in 1824. He was the author of many popular comedies, such as *The Heir at Law* (1797) and *John Bull* (1803). >> Colman, George (the Elder)

Colman, Ronald (1891–1958) Film and stage actor, born in Richmond, SW Greater London, England, UK. His dashing good looks, mellifluous voice, and gentlemanly manner made him a popular romantic leading man for three decades, and he was one of the few major Hollywood stars to survive the transition to the sound era. He made his screen debut in 1919 in *The Live Wire*, and starred in heroic parts in *A Tale of Two Cities* (1935), *The Prisoner of Zenda* (1937), and *Random Harvest* (1942).

Colombo, Joe Cesare [kolomboh] (1930–71) Designer, born in Milan, Italy. One of the most versatile Italian designers of the 1960s, his interests included lighting, glass, furniture and, in particular, multi-function storage furniture. A logical extension of this led him to design compact 'core' units containing all the requirements necessary for the living environment. The best example was his 'Total Furnishing Unit' (1971) at the Museum of Modern Art, New York City.

Colquhoun, Robert [kohoon] (1914–62) Artist, born in Kilmarnock, East Ayrshire, W Scotland, UK. He studied at the Glasgow School of Art, and in Italy, France, Holland, and Belgium. His enigmatic, dreamlike figures (such as 'Girl with a Circus Goat') are usually presented in a characteristic colour scheme of reds and browns.

Colt, Samuel (1814–62) Inventor, born in Hartford, CT. He ran away to sea in 1827, and c.1832 travelled throughout the USA, lecturing on chemistry. In 1835 he took out his first patent for a revolver, which after the Mexican War was adopted by the US army, founding the fortunes of his company, Colt's Patent Fire-Arms.

Colton, Frank Benjamin (1923–) Chemist and inventor, born in Bialystok, Poland. He emigrated to the USA in 1934, studied at Northwestern University and the University of Chicago and, as a researcher at the Mayo Foundation, helped develop an improved synthesis of cortisone. His pioneering work in steroid chemistry led in 1960 to the development of Enovid, the first oral contraceptive, for which he was patentee. He worked for G D Searle & Co from 1951 until his retirement in 1986.

Coltrane, John (William) (1926-67) Saxophonist and composer, born in Hamlet, NC. He emerged in the 1950s as one of the most influential jazz performers of the post-bebop era. After working with the Dizzy Gillespie Big Band and with such modernists as pianist Bud Powell, he began to shape his distinctive style when he joined the influential Miles Davis Quintet (1955). The intensity of his attack and dense flow of notes influenced a generation of future saxophone players, as did his adoption of the soprano saxophone as a second instrument to the tenor. He led his own small groups after 1960, remaining a controversial avant-garde figure. >> Davis, Miles; Gillespie; Powell, Bud

Colum, Padraic (1881-1972) Poet and playwright, born in Co Longford, Ireland. He studied at Trinity College, Dublin, and was a leader of the Irish literary revival. He wrote several plays for the Abbey Theatre, and helped to found the *Irish Review* (1911). From 1914 he lived in the USA, and published two studies on Hawaiian folklore (1924, 1926). He wrote several volumes of poetry, and also children's stories.

Columba, St, also **Columcille** or **Colm** (521-97) Missionary and abbot, born in Gartan, Co Donegal, Ireland. He founded monasteries at Derry (546), and Durrow (553), and then at Iona, in the Inner Hebrides (c.563), from where he and his followers brought Christianity to Scotland. In his system, bishops were subordinate to abbots, and Easter was kept on a different day from the Roman churches. He is said to have copied 300 books with his own hand. Feast day 9 June.

Columban or **Columbanus, St** (c.543-615) Missionary and abbot, 'the younger Columba', born in Leinster, Ireland. About 585 he went to Gaul and founded the monasteries of Anegray, Luxeuil, and Fontaine in the Vosges. His adherence to the Celtic Easter involved him in controversy, and the courage with which he rebuked the vices of the Burgundian court led to his expulsion. He later went to Lombardy, and in 612 founded the monastery of Bobbio, in the Appenines. Feast day 23 November.

Columbus, Christopher see panel on p. 221

Columcille, St >> **Columba, St**

Colville, Alexander (1920-) Painter, born in Toronto, Ontario, Canada. He moved to Amherst, Nova Scotia in 1929, and has lived and painted in Wolfville, Nova Scotia, since 1971. The subject matter of his paintings, produced in a range of mediums, is usually taken from the immediate environment, but they are highly representational, always with both beautiful and disturbing elements. The Hewitt Gallery in New York gave him his first commercial exhibitions (1952 and 1955), and Dalhousie Art Gallery (Halifax) presented his first retrospective in 1984.

Comaneci, Nadia [komaneech] (1961-) Gymnast, born in Onesti, Moldova. Representing Romania, she was the star of the 1976 Olympic Games, when at the age of 14 (coached by Bela Karolyi) she won gold medals in the beam, vault, and floor disciplines. She retained the beam and floor exercise gold medals in 1980. In 1976 she became the first gymnast to obtain a perfect score of 10 for her performance on the parallel bars and beam. Later she became an international judge, and coach to the Romanian national team. In 1989 she defected to the USA via Hungary, amid much publicity, and began a career as a model. >> RR1160

Combe, William [koom] (1741-1823) Writer and adventurer, born in Bristol, SW England, UK. He inherited a fortune in 1762, led the life of an adventurer, and spent much time in debtors' jails. He studied at Oxford, and wrote metrical satires such as *The Diaboliad* (1776), but made his name with his three verse satires on popular travel-books, introducing the character of Dr Syntax. >> Gilpin, William

Comenius, John Amos [komeenius], Czech **Komenský, Jan Ámos** (1592-1670) Educational reformer, born in Moravia, Czech Republic. He studied at Herborn and Heidelberg, became rector of the Moravian school of Prerau (1614-16) and minister at Fulnek, but fled to Poland at the beginning of the Thirty Years' War. Settling at Lissa (1628), he worked out his new theory of education, and was chosen Bishop of the Moravian Brethren in 1632. He visited England and Sweden, and in 1650 went to Hungary, where he composed his *Orbis sensualium pictus* (1658, The Visible World in Pictures), the first picture book for children. He then settled in Amsterdam.

Comfort, Alex(ander) (1920-) British physician, writer, and poet. He studied at Cambridge University and the London Hospital. His working life, on both sides of the Atlantic, has been devoted to the study and treatment of the physical and mental problems of growing old. As well as numerous academic texts, he has published books of poems (such as *Haste to the Wedding*, 1961), plays, and novels, including *Tetrarch* (trilogy, 1980) and *The Philosophers* (1989).

Comgall, St (c. 516-601) Abbot, born in Ulster. He founded the great abbey of Bangor in Co Down (c.558). He is said to have lived on the Hebridean island of Tiree for a time, and accompanied St Columba on his journey to the N of Scotland. Feast day 10 May. >> Columba

Comines, Philippe de [komeen], also spelled **Commynes** (1445-1511) French statesman and historian, born in the castle of Comines, near Courtrai, France. In 1463 he entered the court of Burgundy, but in 1472 passed over to the service of Louis XI of France. He was rewarded with the rich fief of Talmont, married the heiress of Argenton, and became one of Louis's most trusted advisers. He accompanied Charles VIII (1470-98) on his Italian expedition (1494), and was present at the Battle of Fornovo. His *Mémoires* (1524) are the earliest French example of history as distinguished from chronicle. >> Louis XI

Commodus, Lucius Aurelius [komodus] (161-92) Roman emperor from 180, the son of Marcus Aurelius and Faustina. His reign was one of the worst chapters of Roman imperial despotism. After the discovery of his sister Lucilla's plot against his life in 183, he gave uncontrolled vent to his savagery. At length his mistress, Marcia, had him strangled by Narcissus, a famous athlete. His death brought to an end the dynasty of the Antonine emperors. >> Aurelius; RR1084

Commynes, Philippe de >> **Comines, Philippe de**

Compton, Arthur (Holly) (1892-1962) Physicist, born in Wooster, OH. He studied at Princeton University, and became professor of physics at Chicago (1923). He was a leading authority on nuclear physics, X-rays, and quantity production of plutonium. He observed and explained the **Compton effect**, the increase in wavelength of X-rays scattered by collisions with electrons, for which he shared the Nobel Prize for Physics in 1927. He became Chancellor of Washington University in 1945, and also professor of natural history there (1953-61). >> RR1122

Compton, Denis (Charles Scott) (1918-97) Cricketer, born in London, England, UK. He played cricket for England 78 times, and scored 5807 runs at an average of 50·06. His county team was Middlesex. In the 1947 season he scored a record 3816 runs, including a record 18 centuries. During his career (1936-57) he made 38 942 runs and took 622 wickets. A winger at soccer, he won an England cap during the war years. His career was spent with Arsenal, and along with his brother, **Leslie Compton** (1912-84), he won a Football Association Cup-winner's Medal in 1950. He became a journalist and broadcaster when he retired from active sport. >> RR1150

CHRISTOPHER COLUMBUS (1451–1506)

Columbus was born Cristóbal Colón (Sp) or Cristoforo Colombo (It), in the Italian port city of Genoa, the son of Domenico Colombo, a weaver, and Suzanna Fontanarossa. There is no real evidence that he was Italian, and it is thought that his family might have been Spanish Jews; his writings are in Spanish, including his private notes. Little is recorded of his early life, but it seems that he went to sea at the age of 14, as a pirate, later visiting the Greek Island of Chios. In 1476, while fighting against Genoa with the Portuguese off Cape St Vincent, the ship he was aboard caught fire, and he swam to the shore of Portugal with the help of a wooden oar. Lisbon was then a busy commercial centre, at the westernmost edge of the known world, and congregated there were seafarers, astronomers, geographers, and scientists, all keenly debating the possibility of the existence and discovery of a 'new world', or of reaching the East by sailing west.

Soon after coming ashore, he sailed to Iceland and back. However, the imaginative young Columbus was obsessed with the idea that his landing near Lisbon had been by divine intervention. Encouraged by a Florentine astronomer, Paolo Toscanelli, he dreamed of a much greater journey, beyond the W horizons to reach India; a feat he hoped would bring him glory as well as financial reward. His ambition was much aided by the wife he took in 1478. She was **Felipa Perestrello e Moniz**, and her father was a sea captain from one of Portugal's most influential families. Columbus settled for a while on Porto Santo in the Madeira Is with his new family, and gained considerable sailing experience in the South Atlantic, where his imagination was further roused by sightings of flotsam from other lands.

He began to seek a patron for his intended expedition. His plans were vague, and his proposal to John II of Portugal in 1484 was rejected, so he turned to Spain. After years of alternately being encouraged and repulsed, his voyage was patronized by King Ferdinand and Queen Isabella of Castile in April 1492. On Friday 3 August, he set sail from the Spanish port of Palos in command of the *Santa María* – a decked ship 36 m long, with 50 men, and attended by two little caravels, the *Pinta* and the *Niña*, captained by Martin Alonso Pinzón and his brothers. The whole squadron comprised only 120 adventurers.

He first reached the Canary Is; and though he found it hard to keep up the courage of his crews, San Salvador in the Bahamas was sighted on Friday 12 October 1492. The expedition went ashore and planted the royal banner, taking possession of the land in the name of Spain. Columbus then visited Cuba and Hispaniola (Haiti), leaving 38 men there among the natives with supplies and munitions for a year. By this time his flagship had been wrecked, and he set sail on 4 January 1493 with his two caravels on the return journey to Spain. The voyage was tormented by animosity between Columbus and Pinzón, who disapproved of leaving the men behind, and by appalling storms. However they reached Palos on 15 March 1493, and Columbus was received with the highest honours by the court.

Columbus' second voyage was altogether a more ambitious one, with a fleet of three carracks and 17 small caravels sailing from Cádiz (25 Sep 1493). After calling at the Canary Is for supplies, they sighted Dominica in the West Indies (3 Nov 1493), going on to Guadeloupe and Puerto Rico. En route, they found that the colony left on Hispaniola had been massacred.

The expedition went on to found the city of Isabella. But after a succession of wretched quarrels with his associates, and a long illness in Hispaniola, Columbus returned to Spain much dejected in 1496.

On his third voyage (1498–1500) he discovered the South American mainland, but was sent home in irons by a newly appointed royal governor after a revolt against his despotic command. The King and Queen repudiated this action, and restored Columbus to favour. His last great voyage (1502–4) along the S side of the Gulf of Mexico was accomplished against royal orders, and in great hardship. Columbus had failed to find the straits he believed would lead him to India; the coveted prize of Indian trade went to the Portugese, when Vasco da Gama reached it travelling east in 1498.

Columbus spent his last years more or less forgotten, trying to regain his lost grandeur – unaware, as was everyone else at that time, that he had reached America. He died, sick in body and mind, at Valladolid, in Spain, and was buried in a monastery near Seville. In 1536 his remains were taken to Santa Domingo in Hispaniola, but in 1899 they were brought back to Spain and buried in Seville Cathedral in 1902.

Undoubtedly one of the greatest mariners of all time, his tyrannical administration lost him not only the governorship of the lands he discovered, but the distinction and prosperity he had so craved.
>> Ferdinand the Catholic; Isabella I; Pinzón

Compton, Fay (1894–1978) Actress, born in London, England, UK, the daughter of the actor **Edward Compton** (1854–1918), and the sister of Sir Compton Mackenzie. She first appeared on the stage in 1911, and won acclaim in London in *Peter Pan* (1918). She later played many famous parts, especially in plays by Barrie. >> Barrie; Mackenzie, Compton

Compton, Henry (1632–1713) Anglican bishop, born in Compton Wynyates, Warwickshire, C England, UK. He entered the Church in 1662, and became Bishop of Oxford (1674) and of London (1675). He cordially welcomed William of Orange, and crowned him William III, with his wife Mary. >> William III

Compton, John George Melvin (1926–) St Lucian politician and prime minister (1979, 1982–96), born in Canouan, St Vincent and the Grenadines. He graduated at the London School of Economics and was called to the English bar. In 1951 he established a law practice in St Lucia, and joined the St Lucia Labour Party, leaving in 1961 to form the United Workers' Party. At independence in 1979 he was St Lucia's first prime minister. He was defeated in the same year by the Labour Party, but was returned in 1982, and narrowly re-elected in 1987. >> RR1086

Compton-Burnett, Dame Ivy [berˈnet] (1884–1969) Novelist, born in Pinner, NW Greater London, England, UK. She studied classics at London, and became a prolific writer. Her rather stylized novels have many features in common, being set in upper-class Victorian or Edwardian society; the characters usually belong to a large family, spanning several generations. Her first novel was *Pastors and Masters* (1925), later works including *Brothers and Sisters* (1929) and *Mother and Son* (1955, James Tait Black). She was made a dame in 1967.

Comrie, Leslie John [komree] (1893–1950) Astronomer, and pioneer in mechanical computation, born in Pukekohe, New Zealand. He studied at Auckland University College and Cambridge. After teaching in the USA, he joined HM Nautical Alamanac Office in 1926, becoming superintendent (1930–6). Regarded as the foremost computer and table-maker of his day, in 1936 he founded the Scientific Computing Service Ltd.

Comstock, Henry (Tompkins Paige) (1820–70) Prospector, born in Trent, Ontario, Canada. He went to Nevada in 1856 and claimed the ground where he found (1859) the silver lode that was given his name. He sold his right for a small sum, and turned to prospecting and road-building elsewhere.

Comte, Auguste [kõt] (1798–1857) Philosopher and sociologist, the founder of Positivism, born in Montpellier, France. He studied for a while at Paris, and was for some years a disciple of Saint-Simon. He published his lectures on positivist philosophy in six volumes (1830–42). He taught mathematics privately, and in his later years was supported by his friends. His *Système de politique positive* (4 vols, 1851–4, System of Positive Polity), shows the influence of his brief relationship with Clothilde de Vaux. In his philosophy, all sciences are regarded as having passed through a theological and then a metaphysical stage into a positive or experiential stage; the sociological development is from militarism to industrialism. In positive religion, the object of reverence is humanity, and the aim the well-being and progress of the race. >> Littré; Saint-Simon, Claude-Henri de Rouvroy

Conan Doyle >> **Doyle, Arthur Conan**

Conant, James Bryant (1893–1978) Chemist, diplomat, and educator, born in Dorchester, MA. He studied organic chemistry at Harvard, and became noted for his work on chlorophyll and haemoglobin. He then taught at Harvard (1916–33), becoming president there (1933–53). He chaired the national Defense Research Committee (1941–6), which developed the atomic bomb, and was instrumental in the targeting of Hiroshima. His diplomatic career in the 1950s included four years as high commissioner and ambassador to West Germany. He later conducted an extensive Carnegie Corporation study of US high schools which resulted in *The American High School Today* (1959).

Condamine, Charles Marie de la >> **Lacondamine, Charles Marie de**

Condé, Louis I de Bourbon, Prince de [kõday] (1530–69) Leader of the Huguenots during the French Wars of Religion, born in Vendôme, France, the younger brother of **Antony of Bourbon** (1518–61), king of Navarre. He fought in the wars between Henry II and Spain (1551–7), and joined the Huguenots on the accession of Francis II (1559). He was defeated at Dreux during the first civil war (1562); and in the second war (1567–9) was defeated at Jarnac, taken prisoner, and shot.

Condé, Louis II de Bourbon, Prince de [kõday], known as **the Great Condé** (1621–86) French military leader, born in Paris. During the Thirty Years' War he defeated the Spaniards (1643, 1648) and Bavarians (1645–6). The court party came to terms with the Fronde by his help; but his arrogance led to his imprisonment, and when he was released he joined the rebels. Defeated at the Battle of the Dunes, near Dunkirk (1658), he was then pardoned, and

became one of Louis XIV's greatest generals, defeating the Spanish in Franche-Comté (1668) and William of Orange at Seneffe (1674). Ill health led to his retirement to Chantilly. >> Louis XIV; Turenne

Conder, Charles Edward (1868–1909) Painter and lithographer, born in London, England, UK. He arrived in Sydney in 1884, worked as a lithographer, and contributed to the *Sydney Illustrated News*. In 1888 he joined Tom Roberts, Arthur Streeton, and Frederick McCubbin in their camp at Box Hill, Victoria. He went to Paris (1890), and later to London, where he was influenced by Whistler and the 'Japonais' cult. From then until his death he worked in delicate water-colours on silk, and he is especially noted for his fan designs. >> McCubbin; Roberts, Tom; Streeton; Whistler, James

Condillac, Etienne Bonnot de [kõdeeyak] (1715–80) Philosopher, born in Grenoble, France. He was ordained a Catholic priest in 1740, and became a tutor to the Duke of Parma, and Abbé de Mureaux. He based all knowledge on the senses, his works including *Essai sur l'origine des connaissances humaines* (1746, Essay on the Origin of Human Knowledge), and *Traité des sensations* (1754, Treatise on Sensations).

Condon, Edward U(hler) (1902–74) Theoretical physicist, born in Alamogordo, NM. He studied at the universities of California and Göttingen, and his posts included chairs in physics at Washington, Minnesota, and Colorado. He was distinguished for his research in atomic spectroscopy. In World War 2 he did notable work on the Manhattan atomic bomb project, as associate director with Oppenheimer, and was afterwards director of a US Army Air Force study of Unidentified Flying Objects (1945–51). >> Oppenheimer, J Robert

Condorcet, Marie Jean Antoine Nicolas de Caritat, marquis de (Marquess of) [kõdaw(r)say] (1743–94) French statesman, philosopher, and mathematician, born in Ribemont, France. He studied at Paris, and his work in mathematics became highly regarded in the 1760s. At the Revolution he made eloquent speeches and wrote famous pamphlets on the popular side, was sent to the Legislative Assembly (1791), and became its president, siding usually with the Girondists. Accused and condemned by the extreme party, he was captured, and found dead in prison. In his philosophy, he proclaimed the ideal of progress, and the indefinite perfectibility of the human race.

Cone, Claribel (1864–1929) and **Etta Cone** (1870–1949) Art collectors and sisters, both born in Jonesboro, TN. Their family moved to Baltimore, MD (c.1870), and their brothers founded the Cone Mills, a textile business. The sisters studied locally, and Claribel attended the Woman's Medical College of Baltimore, then worked in the pathology laboratory (1894–1903) of the Johns Hopkins Medical School. They established an artistic salon and began collecting antiques, textiles, and modern paintings. They amassed an impressive collection of modern and contemporary art during their trips abroad. After both sisters died, funds and their collection were bequeathed to the Baltimore Museum of Art.

Cone, James Hal (1938–) Chief advocate of black theology in the USA, born in Arkansas. A professor of systematic theology at Union Theological Seminary, New York City, his many writings include *A Black Theology of Liberation* (1970), *God of the Oppressed* (1975), and the autobiographical *My Soul Looks Back* (1987).

Confucius [konfyooshuhs], Lat name of **Kongfuzi** or **K'ung Fu-tse** (Chin 'Venerated Master Kong') (551–479 BC) Chinese philosopher, born in the state of Lu (modern Shantung). Largely self-educated, he married at 19, became a local administrator, and in 531 BC began his career as a teacher. In 501 BC he was appointed Governor of Chung-tu, then minister of works, and later minister of justice. His ideas for social reform made him the idol of the people; but his enemies caused him to leave Lu, and he travelled widely, followed by many disciples. He later edited the ancient writings, and the *Confucian Analects*, memorabilia compiled soon after his death, are a collection of his sayings and doings. His moral teaching stressed the importance of the traditional relations of filial piety and brotherly respect.

Congreve, William [konggreev] (1670–1729) Playwright and poet, born in Bardsey, West Yorkshire, N England, UK. He studied at Trinity College, Dublin, and became a lawyer in London, but then took up a career in literature. His first comedy, *The Old Bachelor*, was produced under Dryden's auspices in 1693, and was highly successful, as were *The Double Dealer* (1693), *Love for Love* (1695), and *The Way of the World* (1700). His one tragedy, *The Mourning Bride* (1697), was much admired by his contemporaries. He largely ceased writing after 1700. >> Dryden

Congreve, Sir William [konggreev] (1772–1828) Artillery officer and scientist, born in London, England, UK. He studied at Woolwich Academy, and in 1808 invented the *Congreve rocket*, first used in the Napoleonic wars. He became comptroller of the Royal Laboratory of Woolwich Arsenal in 1818, and served as MP for Gatton, Devon, from 1818 until his death. >> Walker, John (1781–1859).

Conkling, Roscoe (1829–88) US politician, born in Albany, NY. The son of a prominent judge and himself a lawyer, he served as a Republican in the US House of Representatives (1859–63, 1865–7) and the US Senate (1867–81). Famed for his florid oratory, he was one of the most influential politicians of his day, leader of the powerful New York Republican machine, and an open foe of civil service reform. Nominated and confirmed for a Supreme Court seat after his resignation from the Senate in 1881, he declined, and instead became a corporate lawyer.

Connally, Thomas Terry, known as **Tom Connally** (1877–1963) US politician and lawyer, born near Waco, TX. He served in the US House of Representatives (1917–29) and the US Senate (1929–53). He was a conservative on domestic policy, supporting Southern business interests and opposing anti-lynching legislation; but he was an influential internationalist on foreign policy issues, supporting US participation in the UN and NATO.

Connaught, Prince Arthur, Duke of [konawt] (1850–1942) British prince and soldier, born in London, England, UK, the third son of Queen Victoria. After training at the Royal Military Academy, Woolwich, he served in Canada, Gibraltar, Egypt, and India (1869–90). Thereafter he was commander-in-chief in Ireland (1900–4) and in the Mediterranean (1907–9), and Governor-General of Canada (1911–16). He was created Duke of Connaught and Strathearn in 1874. In 1879 he married **Princess Louise Margaret of Prussia** (1860–1917). Of their children, **Margaret** (1882–1920) married the future King Gustav VI Adolf of Sweden in 1905. >> Gustav IV; Victoria

Connelly, Marc(us Cook) (1890–1980) Playwright, born in McKeesport, PA. As a journalist who took to the theatre, he achieved several outstanding successes in collaboration with George S Kaufman, including *Dulcy* (1921), *To the Ladies* (1922), the amusing 'Expressionist' *Beggar on Horseback* (1924), and *Hunter's Moon* (1958). His greatest individual success was *Green Pastures* (1930, Pulitzer). >> Kaufman, George S

Connery, Sean, originally **Thomas Connery** (1930–) Film actor, born in Edinburgh, EC Scotland, UK. After a succession of jobs, his powerful physique won him a role in the chorus line of the London stage production of *South Pacific* (1951). Sporadic film work followed, although there were more significant opportunities in television drama, particularly

Requiem for a Heavyweight (1956). In 1963 he was cast in *Dr No* as Ian Fleming's secret agent James Bond, a part he subsequently played on seven occasions. The film's unexpected success established him as an international box-office attraction. Later films include *The Man Who Would Be King* (1975), *Highlander* (1986), *The Name of the Rose* (1987), *Indiana Jones and the Last Crusade* (1989), *The Russia House* (1991), *Just Cause* (1995), and *The Rock* (1996). He won an Oscar as an aging Irish cop with true grit in *The Untouchables* (1987). >> Moore, Roger

Connolly, Billy (1942–) Comedian, actor, and television presenter, born in Glasgow, W Scotland, UK. After leaving school, he worked as an apprentice welder in Glasgow, then entered show business, becoming well known during the 1980s for his one-man theatre comedy performances. Television appearances increased during the 1990s, including several documentary series, such as his tours of Scotland (1994) and Australia (1996). His film credits date from 1979, with *Absolution*, and include *The Big Man* (1989), *Pocahontas* (1995), the Muppet's *Treasure Island* (1996), (for BBC TV) *Deacon Brodie* (1996), and *Mrs Brown* (1997).

Connolly, Cyril (Vernon) (1903–74) Writer and journalist, born in Coventry, West Midlands, C England, UK. He studied at Oxford, contributed to the *New Statesman* and other periodicals, and wrote regularly for the *Sunday Times*. He was founder/editor of *Horizon* (1939–50), and briefly literary editor of the *Observer*. His only novel was *The Rock Pool* (1936). Among his works are *Enemies of Promise* (1938), *The Unquiet Grave* (1944), miscellaneous aphorisms and reflections, and various collections of essays.

Connolly, James (1868–1916) Irish political leader and insurgent, born in Edinburgh, EC Scotland, UK. He joined the British army at the age of 14, and was stationed in the Curragh and Dublin, but deserted to get married to an Irish girl in Scotland. Returning to Ireland in 1896, he organized the Irish Socialist Republican Party and founded *The Workers' Republic*, the first Irish Socialist paper. He toured the USA as a lecturer (1902–10), and helped found the Industrial Workers of the World ('Wobblies'). Back in Ireland, he organized Socialist 'citizen armies', and after taking part in the Easter rebellion (1916) he was arrested and executed.

Connolly, Maureen (Catherine), nickname **Little Mo** (1934–69) Tennis player, born in San Diego, CA. She won the US championship in 1951 at the age of 16, and thereafter lost only four matches in her career. She won the Wimbledon singles title (1952–4), the US title (1951–3), the French Open (1953–4), and the Australian title (1953), thus becoming the first woman to win all four major titles in the same year (1953). She married **Norman Brinker** in 1954, broke her leg in a riding accident the same year, and was forced to retire. She died of cancer. >> RR1173

Connors, Jimmy, popular name of **James Scott Connors**, nickname **Jimbo** (1952–) Tennis player, born in Belleville, IL. The All-American and National Intercollegiate champion from the University of California in 1971, he went on to become Wimbledon champion in 1974 (against Ken Rosewall) and 1982 (against John McEnroe). He won the US Open in 1974, 1976, 1978, and 1982–3. A left-handed player, he was one of the first to use the two-handed backhand. >> McEnroe; Rosewall; RR1173

Conrad II (c. 990–1039) King of Germany from 1024 and Holy Roman Emperor from 1027, the son of the Duke of Franconia and the founder of the Salian dynasty. In 1026 he crossed the Alps, crushed a rebellion in Italy, was crowned at Milan, and was anointed Holy Roman Emperor by the pope in 1027. He was soon recalled to Germany to put down four revolts, which he achieved by 1033, and in the same year was crowned King of Burgundy. >> RR1057

Conrad III (1093–1152) King of Germany, and the first Hohenstaufen king of the Germans, the son of Frederick of Swabia. In 1125 he unsuccessfully contested the crown of Italy with Emperor Lothair III; when the emperor died, the princes of Germany offered Conrad the throne, and he was crowned at Aachen (1138). When St Bernard of Clairvaux preached a new crusade, Conrad travelled to Palestine with a large army (1148). He designated his nephew, Frederick I Barbarossa, as his successor. >> Bernard of Clairvaux; Frederick I; RR1057

Conrad, Joseph, originally **Józef Teodor Konrad Korzeniowski** (1857–1924) Novelist, born in Berdichev, Ukraine. He joined the British merchant navy, and became a British national in 1886. He sailed to many parts of the world, married in 1896, and settled in Ashford, Kent. His first novel was *Almayer's Folly* (1894). His best-known works are *The Nigger of the Narcissus* (1897), *Lord Jim* (1900), *Nostromo* (1904), *The Secret Agent* (1907), *Under Western Eyes* (1911), and *Chance* (1914). He also wrote many short stories; and the short novel *Heart of Darkness* (1902) anticipates many 20th-c themes and effects. His fiction has been a favourite subject for film and television adaptation.

Conran, Jasper (1959–) Fashion designer, born in London, England, UK, the son of Sir Terence Conran. He trained at the Parsons School of Art and Design in New York City, leaving in 1977, when he joined Fiorucci briefly as a designer. In 1978 he founded his own company in London, producing his first collection of easy-to-wear, quality clothes. Awards include the British Fashion Council Designer of the Year (1986–7) and the British Fashion Collections Award (1991). >> Conran, Terence

Conran, Sir Terence (Orby) (1931–) Designer and businessman, born in Esher, Surrey, SE England, UK. He founded and ran the Habitat Company (1971), based on his own success as a furniture designer and the virtues of good design and marketing. He has since been involved in the management of several related businesses and has won many design awards. His many books include *The Soft Furnishings Book* (1986) and *Terence Conran on Design* (1996). He was knighted in 1983. >> Conran, Jasper; Hamlyn

Conscience, Hendrik (1812–83) Novelist, born in Antwerp, Belgium. From 1866 he was director of the Wiertz Museum. His *Phantazy* (1837), a collection of tales, and his most popular romance, *De leeuw van Vlaanderen* (1838, The Lion of Flanders), earned him a place as 'the father of the Flemish novel'. His series of pictures of Flemish life carried his name over Europe.

Constable, Archibald (1774–1827) Publisher, born in Carnbee, Fife, E Scotland, UK. He began as a bookseller in Edinburgh, then drifted into publishing, and was chosen as publisher of the *Edinburgh Review* (1802). He published for all the leading writers of the time, and his early appreciation of Scott became the envy of the book trade. In 1812 he purchased the copyright of the *Encyclopaedia Britannica*; but in 1826 came the financial crash which ruined Constable and plunged Scott heavily into debt. >> Scott, Walter

Constable, John (1776–1837) Landscape painter, born in East Bergholt, Suffolk, E England, UK. He trained at the Royal Academy (1799). In 1816 he married **Maria Bicknell**; and in 1828 received an inheritance which enabled him to continue as a painter. Among his best-received works were 'Haywain' (1821, National Gallery, London) and 'The White Horse' (1819, Frick Collection, New York City), which both gained gold medals in France. Although his work was not especially popular in Britain, he continued to exhibit regularly at the Royal Academy, becoming a member in 1829. His later years were saddened by the death of his wife, and by ill health. He is today considered, along with Turner, as the leading painter of the English countryside. >> Turner, J M

Constant (de Rebeque), (Henri) Benjamin [kõstã duh rebek] (1767–1830) French politician and novelist, born in Lausanne, Switzerland. He studied at Oxford, Erlangen, and Edinburgh, and settled in Paris as a publicist (1795). He supported the Revolution, but was banished in 1802 for his opposition to Napoleon. He returned in 1814, and became Leader of the Liberal Opposition. His best-known work is the novel *Adolphe* (1816), based on his relationship with Mme de Staël. >> Staël

Constantine I (Emperor), known as **the Great**, originally **Flavius Valerius Constantinus** (c. 274–337) Roman emperor, born in Naissus, Moesia, the eldest son of Constantius Chlorus. Though proclaimed emperor by the army at York on his father's death in 306, it was not until his defeat of Maxentius at the Milvian Bridge in Rome (312) that he became emperor of the West; and only with his victory over Licinius, the emperor of the East, that he became sole emperor (324). Believing that his victory in 312 was the work of the Christian God, he became the first emperor to promote Christianity, from which came the byname 'Great'. His Edict of Milan (313), issued jointly with Licinius, brought toleration to Christians throughout the empire, and his new capital at Constantinople, founded on the strategically important site of Byzantium (324), was from the outset a Christian city. >> RR1084

Constantine I (of Greece) (1868–1923) King of Greece (1913–17, 1920–2), born in Athens. He played a leading part in Greece's victories in the Balkan Wars (1912–13), and succeeded his father, George I, as king. During World War 1, his policy of neutrality led to bitter conflict with interventionist forces led by liberal politician Venizelos, culminating (1916–17) in virtual civil war, Anglo–French intervention, and his abdication. Restored after the War, he abdicated once again (1922) following Greece's defeat by Turkey and an internal military revolt. >> George I (of Greece); Venizelos; RR1054

Constantine II (of Greece) (1940–) King of Greece (1964–73), born near Athens, who succeeded his father Paul I. In 1964 he married **Princess Anne-Marie of Denmark** (1946–), and has two sons and a daughter. He fled to Rome in 1967 after an abortive coup against the military government which had seized power, and was deposed in 1973. The monarchy was abolished by a national referendum in 1974. >> Paul I; RR1054

Constantine, Learie (Nicholas) Constantine, Baron (1901–71) West Indian cricketer and statesman, born in Trinidad. In 1928 he became the first West Indian player in England to reach 1000 runs and 100 wickets in one season. During World War 2 he was appointed to look after the interests of the West Indians who had been sent to Britain to help in the war effort. He took a law degree and became known as an opponent of racial discrimination. Knighted in 1962, he was awarded a life peerage in 1969.

Constantius Chlorus [konstantius klawrus] (c. 250–306) Roman emperor, the nephew of Claudius II Gothicus and the father of Constantine the Great. He took the title of Caesar in 292, had Britain, Gaul, and Spain as his government, and, after re-establishing Roman power in Britain and defeating the Alemanni, took the additional title of Augustus in 305. >> Constantine I; RR1084

Conte, Lamsana [kontay] (c. 1945–) Guinean politician and soldier. Formerly military commander of the Boke Region of West Guinea, on the death of President Seke Toure in 1984 he led a bloodless coup and set up a Military Committee for National Recovery, with himself as president. He did much to restore Guinea's international standing, and thousands of exiles returned. In 1985 an attempt to overthrow him was thwarted by loyal troops.

Conti, Tom [kontee], popular name of **Thomas A Conti** (1941–) Actor and director, born in Paisley, Renfrewshire, W Scotland, UK. He studied at the Royal Scottish Academy of Music, made his acting debut in 1960, and has since performed and directed regularly in London theatres. Television appearances include *The Norman Conquests* and *Glittering Prizes*, and among his films are *Galileo* (1974), *Merry Christmas, Mr Lawrence* (1982), *Shirley Valentine* (1989), and *Someone Else's America* (1994). He was voted Best Stage Actor by the Variety Club of Great Britain in 1978, and he received a Tony Award for Best Actor in 1979.

Converse, Harriet (Arnot) Maxwell (1836–1903) Writer and defender of Indian rights, born in Elmira, NY. She lived in New York City after 1866, writing essays and romantic verse. Devoting herself after 1881 to studying and preserving Iroquois culture, she published works which are no longer highly regarded, but, more lastingly, she collected Indian artifacts for major museums, and successfully defended Native Americans' property rights in several lawsuits.

Conway, Moncure Daniel (1832–1907) Clergyman and abolitionist, born in Stafford Co, VA. A Methodist turned Unitarian preacher, he lectured in England on the Civil War, and became a pastor in London (1864–97). He was active in the cause to abolish slavery, and in 1862 became co-editor of an anti-slavery newspaper, *Commonwealth*.

Conwell, Russell (Herman) (1843–1925) Lawyer, Baptist minister, and lecturer, born in South Worthington, MA. Raised on his family farm, a station on the Underground Railroad, he was an impassioned orator on the rights of all men and women. He volunteered for the Union army and was commissioned as 'the Boy Captain' at age 19. Severely wounded at the Battle of Kenesaw Mountain (1864), he was left for dead, and later credited the experience with converting him to Christianity. He was admitted to the bar in 1865 and moved to Minneapolis, where he established a law practice and founded a daily newspaper. Returning to Massachusetts, he became pastor of a moribund Baptist Church in Lexington, and in 1882 took charge of the Grace Baptist Church in Philadelphia. In 1888 the night school he founded under the Church auspices became Temple College.

Conyngham, Barry Ernest (1944–) Composer, lecturer, and performer, born in Sydney, New South Wales, Australia. He studied at Sydney University and at the State Conservatory. Influenced by jazz in his early years, he has used computer-generated sound, and Japanese influences are also strong in his work. Much of his varied output is for film or theatre, including the operas *Edward John Eyre* and *Ned*. Other works include a cello concerto, and a concerto for contrabass and orchestra, *Shadows of Noh* (1989).

Coogan, Jackie, popular name of **John Leslie Coogan** (1914–84) Actor, born in Los Angeles, CA. A child of show-business parents, he appeared in silent films from an early age. He featured in *The Kid* (1921) and became Hollywood's first major child star, earning international fame and fortune. However, his parents squandered his money, and the ensuing legal case (1938) led ultimately to the Child Actors Bill, which established a code of practice. In later years he is remembered for his role in the television series *The Addams Family* (1964–6).

Cook, Arthur James (1883–1931) Miners' leader, born in Wookey, Somerset, SW England, UK. A coal miner in the Rhondda and a leading figure in the South Wales branch of the union, he became general secretary of the national union in 1924 and was one of the miners' leaders during the General Strike of 1926. A powerful orator, he fought successfully to hold the union together after the strike.

Cook, Eliza (1818–89) Poet, born in London, England, UK. She contributed to magazines from an early age, and issued volumes of poetry in 1838, 1864, and 1865. She wrote *Eliza Cook's Journal* (1849–54), much of it republished as *Jottings from my Journal* (1860).

Cook, Frederick (Albert) (1865–1940) Explorer and physician, born in Calicoon Depot, NY. He studied medicine at the universities of Columbia and New York, before being invited in 1891 to join an Arctic expedition as surgeon to Greenland, led by Robert E Peary. In 1906 he claimed to have made the first ascent of Mt McKinley, Alaska, reported in *To the Top of the Continent* (1908), and in 1908 claimed to be the first man to reach the North Pole. His claim to the Pole was questioned by Peary, who said his own visit in 1909 was the first. An investigative committee set up by Copenhagen University discredited both of Cook's claims, but he denied this vehemently in *My Attainment of the Pole* (1911). His imprisonment for fraud in 1923 brought his character into further question, and although he was pardoned shortly before his death the controversy continues to the present day. >> Peary

Cook, James (1728–79) Navigator, born in Marton, North Yorkshire, N England, UK. He spent several years as a seaman in North Sea vessels, then joined the navy (1755), becoming master in 1759. He surveyed the area around the St Lawrence River, Quebec, then in the *Endeavour* carried the Royal Society expedition to Tahiti to observe the transit of Venus across the Sun (1768–71). He circumnavigated New Zealand and charted parts of Australia. In his second voyage he sailed round Antarctica (1772–5), and discovered several Pacific island groups. Thanks to his dietary precautions, there was only one death among the crew. His third voyage (1776–9) aimed to find a passage round the N coast of America from the Pacific; but he was forced to turn back, and on his return voyage was killed by natives on Hawaii. >> Förster, Johann Reinhold; Vancouver

Cook, Peter (Edward) (1937–95) Comedian and actor, born in Torquay, Devon, SW England, UK. He studied at Cambridge and first achieved prominence as one of the writers and performers of *Beyond the Fringe* (1959–64), and a sequel *Behind the Fridge* (1971–2). He invented the stage character E L Wisty, a forlorn figure perplexed by the complexities of life. From 1965 to 1971 he collaborated with Dudley Moore in the irreverent television programme, *Not Only... But Also*. He made regular film appearances, notably in *The Bed-Sitting Room* (1970), and was long associated with the satirical magazine, *Private Eye*. >> Miller, Jonathan; Moore, Dudley

Cook, Robin, popular name of **Robert Finlayson Cook** (1946–) British statesman, born in Bellshill, North Lanarkshire, C Scotland, UK. He studied at Edinburgh University, trained as a teacher, then became an MP in 1974. He was opposition spokesman for the Treasury and economic affairs (1980–3), then held various posts in the shadow cabinet, including spokesman on health and social security (1987–92). He managed the leadership campaigns of Neil Kinnock (1983) and John Smith (1992). Chief opposition spokesman on trade and industry (1992–4) and foreign affairs (1994–7), and chair of the Labour Party (1996–), he became foreign secretary in the Blair government in 1997. >> Blair, Tony; Kinnock; Smith, John

Cook, Stanley Arthur (1873–1949) Bible scholar, born in King's Lynn, Norfolk, E England, UK. He was professor of Hebrew at Cambridge (1932–8), wrote on Old Testament history, and was joint editor of the *Cambridge Ancient History*.

Cook, Sue, popular name of **Susan Lorraine Cook** (1949–) British broadcaster. She studied at Leicester University, then joined Capital Radio as a producer and presenter (1974–6). She moved to the BBC, working on a wide range of radio documentaries and topical features, then took up a role as a reporter and presenter on BBC television's *Nationwide* (1979–83). She became well known for her later television work, including *Breakfast Time*, *Holiday*, and *Crimewatch UK*, while also working with several charities to do with children, animals, and the elderly.

Cook, Thomas (1808–92) Railway excursion and tourist pioneer, born in Melbourne, Derbyshire, C England, UK. He became a Baptist missionary in 1828. In 1841 he arranged an excursion railway trip between Leicester and Loughborough to attend a temperance meeting, and this later became a regular event. In the 1860s he became an agent for the sale of travel tickets, and built up the business of Thomas Cook & Son.

Cooke, (Alfred) Alistair (1908–) Journalist and broadcaster, born in Manchester, Greater Manchester, NW England, UK. He studied at Cambridge, and won a scholarship to study at Yale and Harvard. He returned to England, working as a film critic for the BBC, and as London correspondent for a US broadcasting company (NBC). He returned to the USA in 1937, and became a US citizen in 1941. A sympathetic and urbane commentator on current affairs and popular culture in the USA, he has reported for several British newspapers, written numerous books, including *One Man's America* (1952), and edited *The Vintage Mencken* (1954). His 'Letter from America', first broadcast by the BBC in 1946, is the longest-running solo radio feature programme. He is also well-known for his BBC TV series *America* (1972–3), which produced a best-selling book.

Cooke, Deryck Victor (1919–76) Writer and broadcaster on music, born in Leicester, Leicestershire, C England, UK. A distinguished Mahler scholar, he published a book on the composer (1960), and completed a realization of Mahler's Tenth Symphony (premiered 1964). He also wrote on Bruckner and Wagner (notably a posthumously published study of *The Ring*, 'I Saw the World End', 1979). >> Mahler

Cooke, George >> Maskelyne, John Nevil

Cooke, Morris (Llewellyn) (1872–1960) Mechanical engineer, born in Carlisle, PA. He studied at Lehigh University (1895), then worked as a machinist in Philadelphia. He developed an interest in scientific management, and became director of the Department of Public Works of Philadelphia (1911–16). His pamphlet 'Snapping Cords', helped force a reduction in electricity rates charged by Philadelphia Electric to rural users, seen as a landmark in the movement for cheap power. He became chairman of the Mississippi Valley Committee in 1932, administered the Rural Electrification Administration (1935–7), and was made chairman of the Water Resources Policy Commission in 1950.

Cooke, Sam, originally **Sam Cook** (1935–64) Soul singer, born in Chicago, IL. He started his career as a Gospel singer, but from 1956 onwards recorded many rhythm-and-blues and soul classics, much covered by other artists, including 'You Send Me', 'Cupid', and 'Twistin' the Night Away'. He was shot dead in a motel room in 1964.

Cooke, Sir William Fothergill (1806–79) Inventor, born in London, England, UK. He studied medicine, took up telegraphy, and in 1837 became Sir Charles Wheatstone's partner. In 1845 they patented the single needle apparatus. He received the Albert Gold Medal (1867), and was knighted in 1869. >> Wheatstone

Cookson, Dame Catherine (Ann) (1906–) Novelist, born in East Jarrow, Tyne and Wear, NE England, UK. She did not begin to write until her 40s, publishing her first novel, *Kate Hannigan*, in 1950. Most of her novels are set in the NE of England, several of them belonging to a series tracing the fortunes of a single character or family, such as *Tilly Trotter* (1981). Other novels include *Rooney* (1957), *The Round Tower* (1968), *The Moth* (1986), and *Branded Man* (1997). A national survey showed that in 1988 a third of all fiction borrowed from public libraries in the UK was by this author. She was made a dame in 1993.

Cookworthy, William (1705–80) Porcelain manufacturer, born in Kingsbridge, Devon, SW England, UK. A Plymouth pharmacist and a Quaker, he was the discoverer of kaolin near St Austell (1756), and established a china factory near Plymouth.

Cooley, Denton A(rthur) (1920–) Cardiac surgeon, born in Houston, TX. He studied at Johns Hopkins University, and in 1954 joined the Baylor University College of Medicine, where he was professor of surgery (1962–9). He was also the founder (1962) and chief of the surgical division of the Texas Heart Institute in Houston. With Michael DeBakey and others, he pioneered open-heart surgery as well as the surgical treatment of diseases of the arteries. >> DeBakey

Coolidge, (John) Calvin (1872–1933) US statesman and 30th president (1923–29), born in Plymouth, VT. He became a lawyer, was Governor of Massachusetts (1919–20), vice-president (1921–3), then president on Harding's death. A strong supporter of US business interests, he was triumphantly re-elected by the Republicans in 1924, but refused to be renominated in 1928. His economic policies led to a major stock market crash during his term of office. >> Harding, Warren G; RR1097

Coolidge, William D(avid) (1873–1975) Physical chemist, born in Hudson, MA. He studied at Massachusetts Institute of Technology and Leipzig, spent much of his career with the General Electric Co at Schenectady, NY, and worked on the Manhattan atomic bomb project in World War 2. He is best known as the developer of the modern vacuum X-ray tube.

Coombs, Herbert Cole, nickname **Nugget Coombs** (1906–) Australian public servant, born in Perth, Western Australia. He studied at the London School of Economics, and joined the [Australian] Commonwealth Bank as an assistant economist, moving to the Treasury in 1939. He became governor of the bank in 1949, and in 1959 the inaugural governor of the Reserve Bank of Australia, a position he held until he retired in 1968. He became Pro-Chancellor of the Australian National University (ANU) in 1959, and Chancellor in 1968. Since his 'retirement' he has worked with Aboriginal people in C Australia and the Kimberley region of Western Australia, and has written extensively on resource allocation and the environment. The personal adviser to seven Australian prime ministers, he is widely acknowledged as one of the most influential figures in his country since World War 2.

Coon, Carleton (Stevens) (1904–81) Anthropologist, born in Wakefield, MA. He studied at Harvard, and was professor there (1934–48) and at Pennsylvania (1948–63). His many archaeological expeditions led him to discover the remains of Aterian fossil man (N Africa, 1939), Hotu man (Iran, 1951) and Jebel Ighoud man No 2 (Sierra Leone, 1965).

Cooney, Ray(mond) (1932–) Playwright, director, and producer, born in London, England, UK. He appeared in several stage comedies and farces in the 1950s and 1960s. Best known as an author and director, his own first play, a farce, *One for the Pot*, appeared in 1961, and was followed by many others, including *Run for Your Wife* (1983), *Wife Begins at Forty* (1986), and *Funny Money* (1996). In 1983 he created the Theatre of Comedy, based at the Shaftesbury Theatre, London.

Cooper, Ashley >> **Shaftesbury, Anthony Ashley Cooper**

Cooper, Sir Astley (1768–1841) Surgeon, born in Brooke, Norfolk, E England, UK. After studying in London and Edinburgh, he lectured on anatomy at St Thomas's Hospital (1789) and at the College of Surgeons (1793). In 1800 he became surgeon to Guy's Hospital, and in 1813 professor of comparative anatomy in the College of Surgeons. He raised surgery from its primitive state to a science, and was the first man to tie the abdominal aorta in treating an aneurysm. In 1820 he removed a tumour from the head of King George IV, and was made a baronet, and in 1828 was appointed sergeant-surgeon to the king. >> George IV

Cooper, Gary (Frank) (1901–61) Film actor, born in Helena, MT. A newspaper cartoonist in Los Angeles before working as an extra in silent films, his first leading role came in *The Winning of Barbara Worth* (1926). With the coming of sound, he continued as a star for more than 30 years, not only as the archetypal hero of Westerns, notably in *High Noon* (1952), and in the Hemingway epics *A Farewell to Arms* (1932) and *For Whom the Bell Tolls* (1943), but also representing the best of American small-town virtues in *Mr Deeds Goes to Town* (1936) and *Meet John Doe* (1941). In addition to two Oscars for Best Actor, he received a special Academy Award in 1960 for his many memorable performances.

Cooper, Dame Gladys (1888–1971) Actress, born in London, England, UK. She made her debut in 1905, and leapt to fame as Paula in *The Second Mrs Tanqueray* (1922). She achieved success in films as well as on the stage, receiving Oscar nominations as best supporting actress on three occasions. She was made a dame in 1967.

Cooper, Henry (1934–) Boxer, born in Bellingham, Kent, SE England, UK, the only man to win the Lonsdale Belt outright on three occasions. He beat Brian London to win his first British heavyweight title in 1959, and won his first Lonsdale Belt in 1961 when he beat Joe Erskine. After flooring Cassius Clay at Wembley in 1963, he had his only world title fight at Highbury Stadium in 1966, when a bad cut against Muhammad Ali (formerly, Cassius Clay) forced his early retirement. He lost his British heavyweight title in a disputed contest against Joe Bugner in 1971, and announced his retirement. He does much work for charity, and is a popular television personality. >> Ali, Muhammad

Cooper, James Fenimore (1789–1851) Novelist, born in Burlington, NJ. Expelled from Yale, he joined the navy in 1806, but in 1811 resigned his commission, married, and began to write novels. He is best known for his frontier adventures such as *The Last of the Mohicans* (1826, filmed 1936 and 1992) and *The Pathfinder* (1840). He also wrote novels and historical studies about the sea. After visiting England and France, he was US consul at Lyon (1826–9). His later years were much disturbed by literary and newspaper controversies and actions for libel.

Cooper, Jilly, née **Sallitt** (1937–) Writer and journalist, born in Yorkshire, N England, UK. She was educated in Salisbury, became a reporter on a local paper (1957–9), and tried many other occupations before becoming a writer. She produced a regular column for the *Sunday Times* (1969–82) and *The Mail on Sunday* (1982–7), and has written a number of general interest works, including *How To Stay Married* (1969), *Jolly Marsupial* (1982), and *Angels Rush In* (1990). Her novels, always among the best sellers, include *Bella* (1976), *Riders* (1978), *Polo* (1991), *Araminta's Wedding* (1993), and *Appassionata* (1996).

Cooper, Leon Neil (1930–) Physicist, born in New York City. He studied at Columbia University, and taught at Ohio State and (from 1958) Brown University, RI. His theory of the behaviour of electron pairs (*Cooper pairs*) in certain materials at low temperatures was a major contribution to the theory of superconductivity, which he helped to develop. He shared the Nobel Prize for Physics in 1972. >> RR1122

Cooper, Peter (1791–1883) Manufacturer, inventor, and philanthropist, born in New York City. He erected the Canton Iron Works in Baltimore in 1828, and in 1830 built there *Tom Thumb*, the first locomotive engine ever made in America. He afterwards built an iron-wire factory in New York, blast-furnaces in Pennsylvania, and invented a washing machine and many other devices. To provide the working classes with educational advantages, he erected and endowed the Cooper Union (1854–9) in New York City.

Cooper, Susie, popular name of **Susan Vera Cooper** (1902–95) Ceramic designer and manufacturer, born in Burslem, Staffordshire, C England, UK. After designing for A E Gray (1922–9), she founded a decorating studio at Tunstall, known as Susie Cooper Pottery. In 1931 she moved to Burslem and used earthenware supplied mainly by Wood & Sons. She became famous for functional shapes with simple hand-painted patterns, and in 1940 was appointed a Royal Designer for Industry. In 1950 she acquired a bone-china factory, renamed Susie Cooper China Ltd, which became part of the Wedgwood group in 1966 and closed in 1980.

Cooper, Thomas (1759–1839) Social agitator, scientist, and educator, born in London, England, UK. Trained as a lawyer and doctor, and with a smattering of chemistry and philosophy, he espoused radical ideas which closed off advancement in England, so in 1794 he emigrated to the USA with Joseph Priestley. He practised both law and medicine in Pennsylvania, but also became a pamphleteer in support of Thomas Jefferson. After serving as a Pennsylvania state judge (1804–11), he turned to teaching chemistry, first at Carlisle (now Dickinson) College (1811–15), then at the University of Pennsylvania (1815–19). He became president of South Carolina College, teaching the sciences and political economy, and helped open the first medical school and insane asylum in the state. His libertarianism led him to become a defender of states' rights, and he promoted the Southern view on the tariff, nullification, and even slavery; following his own logic, he was one of the first to argue for secession. >> Jefferson, Thomas; Priestley, Joseph

Cooper, Tommy (1922–84) Comic and magician, born in Caerphilly, S Wales, UK. A member of the Horse Guards (1939–46), he began performing with the Combined Services Entertainment in the Middle East, where he acquired his trademark headgear of a red fez. In 1947 he appeared at the Windmill Theatre, then achieved television renown in numerous variety shows and his own 1950s series *It's Magic*. His act thrived on his apparently inexpert ability to misperform elaborate tricks. He died during the transmission of the television show *Live From Her Majesty's*.

Cooper, Dame Whina (1895–1994) Maori leader, born in Hokianga, New Zealand. After experience as a local community organizer and businesswoman, from the 1930s she became nationally known for her efforts to help her people recover from the problems caused by European settlement. In 1951 she became the founding president of the Maori Women's Welfare League, and in 1975 led a historic march to publicize Maori land claims. She was made a dame in 1981.

Coote, Sir Eyre (1726–83) British soldier, born in Ash Hill, Co Limerick, Ireland. He entered the army early, saw service in Scotland, then served in India (1756–62). In 1760 he defeated the Comte de Lally at Wandiwash, and his capture of Pondicherry in 1761 completed the downfall of the

French in India. In 1777 he became commander-in-chief in India, and in 1781 his rout of Haidar Ali at Porto Novo saved the presidency for a second time. >> Haidar Ali

Cope, Edward Drinker (1840–97) Naturalist and palaeontologist, born in Philadelphia, PA. Professor at the university of Pennsylvania from 1889, he was a noted hunter of vertebrate fossils, and contributed materially to the discussion of evolution. He was a supporter of Lamarck's theories. >> Lamarck; Marsh, O C

Copeland, William Taylor (1797–1868) China manufacturer, probably born in Stoke-on-Trent, Staffordshire, C England, UK. He managed the Spode concerns in Stoke and London (1827–33), became the partner of Spode in 1833, and from 1846 produced Parian (imitation marble) groups and statuettes, and bone china. He also invented a filter press for working clay, was one of the founders of the North Staffordshire Railway, and became MP for Stoke (1837–52, 1857–65). >> Spode

Coper, Hans [kohper] (1920–81) Studio potter, born in Chemnitz, Germany. He went to live in England in 1939, joined the Studio of Lucie Rie in 1947, and established his own workshop in 1958. Originally a painter and sculptor, his thrown vases are more sculptural than domestic, and he is remembered as one of the most influential of British studio potters. >> Rie

Copernicus, Nicolas [kopernikus], Polish **Mikolaj Kopernik** (1473–1543) The founder of modern astronomy, born in Toruń, Poland. He studied mathematics and optics at Kraców, then canon law at Bologna, before becoming canon of Frombork. His 400-page treatise, *De revolutionibus orbium coelestium* (On the Revolutions of the Celestial Spheres, completed 1530) in which he put forward the theory of the Earth rotating daily about its own axis and annually about the Sun, had a hostile reception when it was published (1543), as it challenged the ancient teaching of the Earth as the centre of the universe. >> Rheticus

Copland, Aaron [kohpland] (1900–90) Composer, born in New York City. He studied under Rubin Goldmark, and in France under Nadia Boulanger, returning to the USA in 1924. A series of early works influenced by Stravinsky, Neoclassical in outlook and employing jazz idioms, was followed by compositions in which he tapped a deeper vein of US tradition and folk music, as in the ballets *Billy the Kid* (1938) and *Appalachian Spring* (1944). He also composed film scores, two operas, and three symphonies. >> Boulanger, Nadia; Stravinsky

Copleston, Frederick (Charles) [kohplston] (1907–94) Jesuit philosopher, born near Taunton, Somerset, SW England, UK. He studied at Oxford, was ordained in 1937, and became professor of the history of philosophy at Heythrop College (1939) and of metaphysics at the Gregorian University, Rome (1952). He wrote several books on individual philosophers and movements, as well as an eight-volume *History of Philosophy* (1946–66).

Copley, Sir Godfrey [kohplee] (?–1709) Philanthropist, born in Yorkshire, N England, UK. He left a fund in trust to the Royal Society which has been applied since 1736 to the provision of the annual *Copley Medal* for philosophical research.

Copley, John Michael Harold [koplee] (1933–) Theatrical producer, born in Birmingham, West Midlands, C England, UK. He became stage manager at Sadler's Wells in 1953, and in 1960 joined the Covent Garden Opera Company as deputy stage manager, becoming resident producer in 1972. He has produced for many opera houses and festivals in Europe, the USA, and Canada, and has had a long and successful connection with the Australian Opera.

Copley, John Singleton [koplee] (1738–1815) Portrait and historical painter, born in Boston, MA. In 1774 he left for England, where he was commissioned to paint the king and queen for Governor Wentworth. He studied in Italy, and returned to London at the end of 1776. His paintings include the 'Death of Major Peirson' (1783, Tate, London), and a group of the royal princesses in Buckingham Palace.

Coppard, A(lfred) E(dgar) (1878–1957) Short-story writer and poet, born in Folkestone, Kent, SE England, UK. He became a professional writer in 1919, published *Adam and Eve and Pinch Me* (1921), and soon became celebrated for his tales of country life and character. His *Collected Poems* appeared in 1928, and his autobiography *It's Me, O Lord!* in 1957.

Coppin, Fanny (Marion Jackson) (1837–1913) Educator and missionary, born in Washington, DC. Purchased out of slavery as a girl, she went on to graduate from college, and as head principal of the Institute for Colored Youth, Philadelphia (1869–1902), pioneered training for urban blacks. Active in the missionary movement, she spent nearly 10 years after 1902 in South Africa.

Coppola, Francis Ford [kopohla] (1939–) Film director and screenwriter, born in Detroit, MI. He studied the theatre in New York City, and film-making in Los Angeles. His first feature as director was *Dementia 13* (1963), and this was followed by the musical *Finian's Rainbow* (1967). Among his outstanding productions were *The Godfather* (1972; *Part II*, 1974; *Part III*, 1990) and his controversial study of the Vietnam War, *Apocalypse Now* (1979). Later films include *The Cotton Club* (1984), *Peggy Sue Got Married* (1987), *Tucker, the Man and the Dream* (1988), and *Bram Stoker's Dracula* (1992).

Coram, Thomas [kawram] (c. 1668–1751) Philanthropist, born in Lyme Regis, Dorset, S England, UK. A shipwright by trade, he went to America in 1693 and settled in Taunton, Massachusetts (1694–1704). There he strengthened the Anglican Church, and promoted settlement schemes in Georgia and Nova Scotia. Back in London (c.1720) he planned and founded the Foundling Hospital (1741), of which Hogarth was a patron. >> Hogarth

Corbet, Christian Cardell (na) Painter and art historian, born in Southern Ontario, Canada. He studied at the University of Guelph, was appointed artist to Elizabeth the Queen Mother in 1966, and received international recognition for 'Elizabeth Holding her Ribbon' (1995). An authority on Canadian women in the fine arts, he is the author of several works on Canadian women artists, and founder of the Corbet Collection of Canadian Women Artists (1993). The first president of the Canadian Portrait Society (1996), he is also noted for his abstract works representing botanical-fragmented studies.

Corbett, James John, nickname **Gentleman Jim** (1866–1933) Heavyweight boxing champion, born in San Francisco, CA. He won the world heavyweight championship in 1892 by knocking out John L Sullivan in the 21st round, and lost it in 1897 to Robert Fitzsimmons in the 4th round. He failed to regain his title in two fights with his former sparring partner, James J Jeffries, in 1900 and 1903. He also made several appearances on stage and in films. >> Fitzsimmons; Jeffries, James J; Sullivan, John L

Corbett, Ronnie, popular name of **Ronald Balfour Corbett** (1930–) Comedian, born in Edinburgh, EC Scotland, UK. After national service in the Royal Air Force, and 18 months as a civil servant, he entered showbusiness. Spotted in Danny La Rue's nightclub by David Frost, he appeared on television in *The Frost Report* (1966–7) and *Frost on Sunday* (1968–9). His diminutive stature, impish sense of fun, and comic monologues soon gained him national popularity. His television series have included *Sorry!* (1981–8), *Small Talk* (1994–6), and a fruitful partnership with Ronnie Barker led to the long-running *The Two Ronnies*

(1971–87). Film appearances comprise *Casino Royale* (1967) and *No Sex Please, We're British* (1972). A keen amateur golfer, he has written *Armchair Golf* (1986). >> Barker, Ronnie; Frost, David

Corbin, Arthur (Linton) (1874–1967) Legal scholar, born in Linn Co, KS. He studied at the University of Kansas and at Yale, where he taught for many years, transforming the educational system. His major interest was contract law, a field in which he was the national leader.

Corbin, Margaret, *née* **Cochran** (1751–c. 1800) Revolutionary heroine, born in Franklin Co, PA. When she was five, her father was killed in an Indian raid in which her mother was taken captive, and she was raised by an uncle. Her husband, **John Corbin**, enlisted in the Revolution, and she accompanied him as cook, laundress, and nurse for the troops. During the Battle of Harlem Heights in 1776, Corbin was mortally wounded; she took over his battle station and was wounded, suffering the permanent loss of the use of one arm. After the battle, she was accorded some of the benefits accorded to veterans, thereby becoming the first woman pensioner of the USA. She apparently remarried, but vanished from view c.1783.

Corbusier, Le >> **Le Corbusier**

Corday (d'Armont), (Marie) Charlotte [kaw(r)day] (1768–93) Noblewoman, born in St Saturnin, France. She sympathized with the aims of the Revolution, but was horrified by the acts of the Jacobins. She managed to obtain an audience with the revolutionary leader, Jean Paul Marat, while he was in his bath, and stabbed him. She was guillotined four days later. >> Marat

Cordobés, El [kaw(r)**doh**bez], nickname of **Manuel Benitez Pérez** (c.1936–) Matador, born in Palma del Rio, Spain. The idol of the crowds in the 1960s, his athleticism and vulgarity in the ring shocked purists, who saw him as more of an acrobat than a torero, but his theatrical style and disregard of danger made him the highest paid matador in history. He retired in 1972.

Corelli, Arcangelo [ko**rel**ee] (1653–1713) Composer, born in Fusignano, Italy. From c.1675 he lived in Rome, where he was in great demand as a violinist, spending the last 22 years of his life in the service of Cardinal Ottoboni. His *Concerti grossi*, and his solo and trio sonatas for violin, mark an epoch in chamber music, and greatly influenced a whole generation of composers.

Corelli, Marie [ko**rel**ee], pseudonym of **Mary Mackay** (1855–1924) Novelist, born in London, England, UK. She trained for a musical career, but then became a writer of romantic melodramas which proved to be extremely popular, such as *A Romance of Two Worlds* (1886), *Barabbas* (1893), and *The Sorrows of Satan* (1895).

Coren, Alan [ko**ren**] (1938–) British writer and journalist. He studied at Oxford, Yale, and California universities, before joining *Punch* as an assistant editor in 1963. He became editor of *Punch* (1978–87), editor of *The Listener* (1988–9), and continues to contribute to other papers. He has published several humorous books, including *The Bulletins of Idi Amin* (1974), *Present Laughter* (1982), *Bin Ends* (1987), *More Like Old Times* (1990), and *A Bit on the Side* (1995). In 1996 appeared *The Alan Coren Omnibus*.

Corey, Elias J(ames) [**kaw**ree] (1928–) Molecular chemist, born in Methuen, MA. He joined the University of Illinois (1951–9), then moved to Harvard. He is known for the technique of retrosynthetic analysis, used in synthesizing complex pharmaceuticals, in which a chemist plans the molecule to be synthesized and studies its theoretical structure. He was awarded the Nobel Prize for Chemistry in 1990.

Cori, Carl F(erdinand) (1896–1984) and **Gerty T(heresa) Cori** (1896–1957) [**ko**ree], *née* **Radnitz** Biochemists, husband and wife, born in Prague. They studied medicine at Prague University, marrying when they graduated, and at Trieste. In 1922 they emigrated to the USA, worked at the State Institute for the Study of Malignant Disease in Buffalo, NY, then in the Medical School at Washington University, St Louis. Their research was into glucose–glycogen metabolism and the enzymes of animal tissue, and they shared the Nobel Prize for Physiology or Medicine in 1947. >> RR1124

Corinth, Lovis [**ko**rint] (1858–1925) Painter, born in Tapiau, Germany. He studied at Königsberg, Munich, and in Paris. From conventional nude, landscape painting, and especially portraiture, his style became markedly Impressionistic, while later work verged on Expressionism. From 1900 he lived in Berlin, and with Marx Liebermann and Slevogt led the secession movement against the Berlin academic school, becoming its president in 1915. >> Liebermann; Slevogt

Coriolanus, Gaius or **Gnaeus Marcius** [korio**lay**nus] (5th-c BC) Roman folk hero, so named from his capture of the Volscian town of Corioli. Banished by the Romans for tyrannical behaviour (491 BC), he took refuge with the Volscians, and proceeded to lead them against his native city. After entreaties from his mother and wife, he spared Rome, and was executed by the Volscians.

Coriolis, Gustave-Gaspard [korio**h**lis] (1792–1843) Mathematician and engineer, born in Paris. He was assistant professor of analysis and mechanics at the Ecole Polytechnique, Paris (1816–38). In his first major book, *Du calcul de l'effet des machines* (1829, On the Calculation of Mechanical Action), he attempted to adapt theoretical principles to applied mechanics. He was the first to describe the inertial force known as the *Coriolis force*, of major significance in the study of meteorology, ballistics, and oceanography.

Corkery, Daniel (1878–1964) Irish cultural leader, born in Cork, Co Cork, Ireland. He studied at University College, Cork, and was professor of English there (1931–47). He published a collection of short stories, *A Munster Twilight* (1917), and a novel, *The Threshold of Quiet* (1917). He profoundly influenced new Irish writers, and his love of the Irish language was the basis of his literary evangelism, as revealed in *The Fortunes of the Irish Language* (1954). He was elected to the Irish Senate in 1951.

Corliss, George Henry (1817–88) Engineer and inventor, born in Easton, NY. Of his many improvements to the steam engine the most important were the *Corliss valve* with separate inlet and exhaust ports, and his use of springs to assist in closing valves more quickly. In 1856 he founded the Corliss Engine Co.

Cormack, Allan Macleod (1924–) Physicist, born in Johannesburg, South Africa. He worked at the Groote Schuur Hospital after graduating in physics at Cape Town University. There he developed a technique for computer-assisted X-ray imaging (*CAT scanning*) which has proved valuable in diagnostic medicine. He shared the Nobel Prize for Physiology or Medicine in 1979. >> RR1122

Corneille, Guillaume [kaw(r)nay], originally **Cornélis van Beverloo** (1922–) Painter, born in Liège, Belgium. A leading European exponent of action painting, his works include 'Drawing in Colour', belonging to the 'and the country loses itself in infinity' series (1955), and 'Summer Flowers' (1958).

Corneille, Pierre [kaw(r)**nay**] (1606–84) Playwright, born in Rouen, France. He trained as a lawyer, but in 1629 went to Paris, where his comedy *Mélite* was highly successful, and he became a favourite of Cardinal Richelieu. Other comedies followed, then in 1636 *Le Cid*, a classical tragedy, took Paris by storm. Other major tragedies were *Horace* (1639), *Cinna* (1639), and *Polyeucte* (1640). *Le Menteur* (1642, The Liar) entitles him to be called the father of French comedy as well as of French tragedy. A master of the alexandrine verse form, he wrote many other plays, and in 1671 he joined Molière and Quinault in writing the opera *Psyché*. After his marriage in 1640 he lived in Rouen until 1662, then settled in Paris. >> Corneille, Thomas; Molière; Richelieu

Corneille, Thomas [kaw(r)nay] (1625–1709) Playwright, born in Rouen, France, the brother of Pierre Corneille. He was a playwright of merit, his tragedies – *Timocrate* (1656), *Ariane* (1672), and others – being in general superior to his comedies. He also wrote a verse translation of Ovid's *Metamorphoses*. >> Corneille, Pierre

Cornelius, Peter [kaw(r)**nee**lius] (1824–74) Composer, born in Mainz, Germany, the nephew of Peter von Cornelius. Going to Weimar in 1852, he became devoted to Liszt, Wagner, and the New German school, and produced his famous comic opera, *Der Barbier von Bagdad* (1858, The Barber of Baghdad), and his grand opera, *Der Cid* (1865). >> Cornelius, Peter von

Cornelius, Peter von [kaw(r)**nee**lius] (1783–1867) Painter who influenced the revival of fresco painting in 19th-c Germany, born in Düsseldorf, Germany. In 1811 he joined a group of painters (the Nazarenes) in Rome, and helped in the decoration of the Casa Bartoldi. He went to Munich in 1819, where he executed the large frescoes of Greek mythology in the Glyptothek and the New Testament frescoes in the Ludwigskirche. In 1841 he became director of the Academy in Berlin. >> Cornelius, Peter

Cornelius Nepos >> **Nepos, Cornelius**

Cornell, Ezra [kaw(r)**nel**] (1807–74) Industrialist and philanthropist, born in Westchester Landing, NY. He began as a carpenter and millwright, and in association with Samuel Morse devised insulation for telegraph wires on poles. He founded several telegraph companies, including the Western Union Telegraph in 1855. In 1865, in association with **Andrew Dickson White** (1832–1918), he founded and endowed Cornell University, which opened in Ithaca, NY, in 1868. >> Morse

Cornell, Joseph [kaw(r)**nel**] (1903–72) Artist, born in Nyack, NY. A self-taught artist, he was one of the first exponents of a form of sculpture called 'assemblage', in which unrelated objects are brought together to create new forms and sometimes suprising juxtapositions. His first one-man exhibition was in New York City in 1932, and his work has been included in many subsequent exhibitions of Surrealist art.

Cornell, Katharine [kaw(r)**nel**] (1893–1974) Actress, producer, and manager, born in Berlin of US parents. She was educated in New York City, and made her first stage appearance in 1916. She appeared in many stage productions before embarking on a career as a producer, presenting a number of Shakespearean and Shavian classics.

Cornforth, Sir John Warcup (1917–) Organic chemist, born in Sydney, New South Wales, Australia. He studied at the universities of Sydney and Oxford, and joined the staff of the Medical Research Council in 1946. He served as the director of the Milstead Laboratory of Chemical Enzymology from 1962, and in 1975 became the Royal Society research professor at Sussex University. He showed how cholesterol is synthesized in the living cell, and followed this by notable work on the stereochemistry of enzyme-catalyzed reactions, for which he shared the 1975 Nobel Prize for Chemistry. >> RR1123

Cornwallis, Charles Cornwallis, 1st Marquess [kaw(r)n**wo**lis] (1738–1805) British general and statesman, born in London, England, UK. He studied at the Military Academy of Turin, and served in the Seven Years' War. Though personally opposed to taxing the American

colonists, he accepted a command in the war, and defeated Gates at Camden (1780), but was forced to surrender at Yorktown (1781). In 1786 he became Governor-General of India, where he defeated Tippoo Sahib, and introduced the series of reforms known as the *Cornwallis Code*. He returned in 1793, to be made marquess. He was Lord-Lieutenant of Ireland (1798–1801), and negotiated the Peace of Amiens (1802). He was re-appointed Governor-General of India in 1804. >> Gates; Tarleton; Tippoo Sahib

Cornwell, David John Moore >> **Le Carré, John**

Cornwell, Patricia (Daniels) (1957–) Novelist, born in Miami, Florida, USA. After an unsettled childhood, she studied at Davidson College, North Carolina. Working as a police reporter, and (from 1984) in the Virginia medical examiner's office, she gained a wide range of experience which she put to use in her novels. In the 1990s she became one of the world's best-selling women novelists, producing a book each year, and known especially for the character of medical examiner Dr Kay Scarpetta introduced in her first novel *Postmortem* (1990). Later books include *Body of Evidence* (1991), *Cause of Death* (1996), and the first non-Scarpetta mystery, *Hornet's Nest* (1997). Her very first book was *A Time for Remembering* (1983), a biography of Ruth Bell Graham (wife of Billy Graham), with whom she was in close contact as a child. >> Graham, Billy

Cornyshe, William [kaw(r)nish] (c. 1465–1523) Composer at the courts of Henry VII and Henry VIII, where he was employed as musician, actor, and producer of entertainments. In 1509 he became master of the Children of the Chapel Royal, and was in charge of the music at the Field of Cloth of Gold, 1520. He composed religious and secular choral works.

Coronado, Francisco Vázquez de [koro**nah**thoh] (1510–54) Conquistador and explorer of Mexico, born in Salamanca, Spain. In 1540 he commanded an expedition which penetrated into what is now the SW of the USA, and discovered the Grand Canyon of Colorado.

Corot, (Jean Baptiste) Camille [koroh] (1796–1875) Landscape painter, born in Paris. He studied at Rouen, took up art in 1822, and after visiting Italy, settled in Paris (1827). His main sketching ground was at Barbizon, in the Forest of Fontainebleau; but he made two other visits to Italy in 1835 and 1843. Several of his masterpieces, such as 'La Danse des nymphes' (1850) are in the Louvre.

Correggio [ko**re**jioh], originally **Antonio Allegri** (c.1494–1534) Renaissance painter, born in Correggio, Italy. In 1518 he began his great series of mythological frescoes for the convent of San Paolo at Parma, and between 1521 and 1524 was engaged upon 'The Ascension' in the cupola of San Giovanni. The decoration of the cathedral of Parma was commissioned in 1522. He also painted many easel pictures on religious themes, such as 'The Adoration of the Shepherds', known as 'The Night' (c.1530, Dresden). He returned to Correggio in 1530.

Correns, Karl (Franz Joseph) Erich (1864–1933) Botanist, born in Munich, Germany. He taught at Tübingen (1892–1902), Leipzig (1902–9), and Münster (1909–14) universities, and from 1914 was director of the Kaiser Wilhelm Biological Institute at Berlin. He rediscovered the neglected results reported in Mendel's paper on the principles of heredity, and confirmed them by his research on the garden pea. >> Mendel

Corrigan-Maguire, Mairead (1944–) and **Williams, Betty** (1943–) Roman Catholic women who founded the movement for peace in Northern Ireland known as the 'Peace People' (1976). The movement involved people from both the Catholic and Protestant communities who wished to see an end to the sectarian violence plaguing the province. They shared the Nobel Peace Prize in 1976.

Corso, Gregory (Nunzio) [kaw(r)soh] (1930–) Poet, born in New York City. He spent three years in prison as a juvenile, then worked as a manual labourer, reporter, and merchant seaman (1950–3). Based in New York City, he was a central member of the Beat poetry movement (1960s), as seen in *The Happy Birthday of Death* (1960). Important volumes include *Elegiac Feelings American* (1970), dedicated to Jack Kerouac, and among later works are *Writings from Ox* (1981) and *Mindfield: New and Selected Poems* (1989). He also taught at the State University, Buffalo, NY.

Corson, Juliet (1841–97) Cookery educator, born in Roxbury (now Boston), MA. She largely educated herself by reading at home, until at 16 she took a job in a library in New York City. She began to contribute articles and poems to newspapers, and by 1873 was secretary for the Women's Educational and Industrial Society of New York. In 1876 she opened the New York Cooking School in her home, and within a few years was enjoying wide success as a pioneer advocate of better foods and cooking for poor families. She became internationally recognized as an expert on dietetics and food education, her numerous publications including *Juliet Corson's New Family Cookbook* (1885) and *Family Living on $500 a Year* (1887).

Cort, Henry (1740–1800) Ironmaster, born in Lancaster, Lancashire, NW England, UK. He became a navy agent in London, then in 1775 bought an ironworks near Plymouth, inventing the 'puddling' process for converting pig iron into wrought iron, as well as a system of grooved rollers for the production of iron bars. Ruined by a prosecution for debt, he was ultimately pensioned.

Cortazar, Julio [kaw(r)tazah(r)], pseudonym **Julio Denis** (1914–84) Writer, born in Brussels. He grew up in Argentina where he was educated, and from 1935 to 1945 taught in secondary schools in several towns. He worked as a translator for publishers (1945–51), then moved to Paris, where he lived until his death, writing and freelancing for Unesco. He is one of the most widely recognized Spanish-American writers outside the Spanish-speaking world, owing this particularly to the filming of *Rayuela* (1963, Hopscotch), and of a short story, 'Blow-Up' (from *Blow-Up and Other Stories*, 1968), by the Italian director Antonioni. >> Antonioni

Cortés, Hernán [kaw(r)tez], also spelled **Cortéz** (1485–1547) The conqueror of Mexico, born in Medellín, Spain. He studied at Salamanca, then accompanied Velázquez in his expedition to Cuba (1511). In 1519 he commanded an expedition against Mexico, fighting his first battle at Tabasco. He founded Vera Cruz, marched to Tlaxcala, and made allies of the natives. He then marched on the Aztec capital, capturing the king, Montezuma; but the Mexicans rose, and Cortés was forced to flee. He then launched a successful siege of the capital, which fell in 1521. He was formally appointed governor and captain-general of New Spain in 1522, but his authority was later superseded. He spent the years 1530–40 in Mexico, then returned to Spain. >> Montezuma; Velázquez de Cuellar

Cortona, Pietro (Berrettini) da [kaw(r)tohna] (1596–1669) Painter and architect, born in Cortona, Italy. With Bernini he ranks as one of the great figures of the Baroque in Rome. With Lanfranco and Guercino he was the founder of the Roman High Baroque style in painting. He specialized in highly illusionistic ceiling painting in which paint is combined with stucco and gilt, notably in his 'Allegory of Divine Providence' and 'Barberini Power' (1633–39) in the Palazzo Barberini in Rome. >> Bernini; Guercino, Il; Lanfranco

Cortot, Alfred [kaw(r)toh] (1877–1962) Pianist and conductor, born in Nyon, Switzerland, of French parents. After winning the first prize for piano-playing at the Paris

Conservatoire in 1896, he became known in France as an outstanding player of Beethoven's concertos. In 1905, with Jacques Thibaud and Pablo Casals, he founded a trio whose chamber music performances won great renown. He was professor of the pianoforte at the Paris Conservatoire (1917–20), and author of several books on musical appreciation, interpretation, and piano technique. >> Casals; Thibaud

Corvinus, Matthew >> **Matthias I**

Corvo, Baron >> **Rolfe, Frederick William**

Cory, Charles (Barney) [kawree] (1857–1921) Naturalist and traveller, born in Boston, MA. He developed an early interest in ornithology, and travelled widely in the E USA and the Caribbean. He became curator of zoology at the Chicago Field Museum, and published his monumental *Birds of the Americas* (4 vols, 1918–19). *Cory's shearwater* was named in his honour.

Coryate, Thomas [kawreeit] (c. 1577–1617) Traveller, born in Odcombe, Somerset, SW England, UK. He entered Gloucester Hall, Oxford (1596), but left without a degree, and after the accession of King James I in 1603 became a court jester. In 1608 he set out on a journey on foot of 1975 miles through Paris, Lyon, Turin, Venice, Zürich, and Strasbourg, and in 1611 published *Coryat's Crudities*. A further journey to the Middle East and India was published in 1616.

Cosby, Bill [kozbee], popular name of **William Henry Cosby** (1937–) Comedian, born in Philadelphia, PA. After service in the US navy (1956–60), he began performing as a nightclub comic, abandoning his studies to pursue this career full time. An appearance on *The Tonight Show* in 1965 led to him being cast in the television series *I Spy* (1965–8), where his role won him three consecutive Emmy Awards. He made his film debut in *Hickey and Boggs* (1971), and has appeared in *Uptown Saturday Night* (1974), *California Suite* (1978), and *Leonard: Part VI* (1987). His TV series *The Cosby Show* (1984–92) has consistently topped the ratings, and he returned with a further series *Cosby* in 1996. He has recorded more than 20 albums and won eight Grammy Awards, and his book *Fatherhood* (1986) was a best seller.

Cosgrave, Liam [kozgrayv] (1920–) Irish statesman and prime minister (1973–7) born in Templeogue, Co Dublin, the son of William Cosgrave. Educated at St Vincent's College, Dublin, he was called to the bar in 1943, and became a member of the Dail (1943–81). He was minister for external affairs (1954–7) before becoming leader of the Fine Gael Party (1965–77). >> Cosgrave, William; RR1064

Cosgrave, William Thomas [kozgrayv] (1880–1965) Irish statesman and first president of the Irish Free State (1922–32), born in Dublin. He joined the Sinn Féin movement at an early age, and took part in the Easter Rising (1916). He was elected a Sinn Féin MP (1918–22), and after his years as president became Leader of the Opposition (1932–44). >> Cosgrave, Liam; RR1064

Cosimo, Agnolo di >> **Bronzino, Il**

Cosimo, Piero di >> **Piero di Cosimo**

Cosimo de' Medici [kozeemoh day maydichee] (1389–1464) Financier, statesman, and philanthropist, born in Florence, Italy. Known posthumously as 'father of his country', he began the glorious epoch of the Medici family. As ruler of Florence he procured for Florence (nominally still republican) security abroad and peace from civil dissensions. He employed his wealth in encouraging art and literature, building the Medici library, the first public library in Europe, as well as many other magnificent buildings, and made the city the centre of the new learning. >> Guicciardini; Medici

Cosmas [kozmas], known as **Indicopleustes** ('Indian Traveller') (6th-c) A merchant of Alexandria, who travelled widely in Ethiopia and Asia. He returned to Egypt c.550, and in monastic retirement wrote a Greek work on Christian topography to prove the authenticity of the biblical account of the world.

Cosmas and **Damian, Saints** (3rd-c) Arabian twin brothers, said to have been physicians at Aegaea, Cilicia, who were cast into the sea as Christians, but rescued by an angel. Thereafter, burning and stoning having proved ineffectual, they were beheaded by Diocletian. They are the patron saints of physicians. Feast day 26 September (W), 1 July/1 November (E). >> Diocletian

Cossington-Smith, Grace (1892–1984) Painter, born in Neutral Bay, Sydney, New South Wales, Australia. She studied at Dattilo Rubbo's Art School in Sydney, and in England and Germany. A pioneer of Modernist painting in Australia, she was instrumental in introducing Postimpressionism to Australia. Her 1915 painting, 'The Sock Knitter', is seen as a key work in the Australian Modernist movement. Her painting is characterized by individual, square brush strokes and radiant colours. Her many paintings of Sydney landscapes, still-lifes, and interiors include 'Kuringai Avenue' (1943), 'Fruit in the Window' (1957), and, arguably her most famous painting, 'The Lacquer Room' (1935). She received acclaim rather late in her career, and in 1973 a major retrospective exhibition of her work toured Australia.

Costa, Lucio (1902–) Architect, born in Toulouse, France, of Franco-Brazilian parents. He is considered the father of modern Brazilian architecture. He studied in Rio de Janeiro, and in 1956 his plan for the city of Brasilia was chosen by an international jury for its clarity and ability to integrate monumentality and daily life. He later devoted much of his time to the Brazilian Society for Historical Preservation, and became an authority on the colonial architecture of Brazil.

Costa, Manuel Pinto da (1937–) First president of the equatorial islands of São Tomé and Príncipe (1975–90), born in Aguada Grande, Venezuela. In 1972 he founded the Movement for the Liberation of São Tomé and Príncipe (MLSTP) in Gabon, and in 1974, taking advantage of a military coup in Portugal, returned and persuaded the new government in Lisbon to recognize the MLSTP as the sole representative of the people and to grant independence a year later. He became president in 1975, and set his country on a politically non-aligned course. He retired following the defeat of his party in the first multi-party elections. >> RR1086

Costello, Elvis, originally **Declan Patrick McManus** (1955–) Singer and songwriter, born in London, England, UK. The son of big-band singer **Ross McManus**, he started his own career with the unrecorded band Flip City and as a solo folk club singer. Signed to Stiff Records in 1977, his debut album *My Aim Is True* established his reputation. For his second album, *This Year's Model* (1978), he was joined by The Attractions – a three-piece group consisting of Steve Nieve, Pete Thomas, and Bruce Thomas, who worked with Costello on most of his albums over the next eight years. Later albums include *Goodbye Cruel World* (1984) and *King of America* (1986).

Costello, John (Aloysius) (1891–1976) Irish politician and prime minister (1948–51, 1954–7), born in Dublin. He studied at University College, Dublin, and was called to the bar in 1914. He became attorney general (1926–32), and in 1948 was prime minister of a government of several parties, his own Fine Gael Party being the chief member. One of his first acts was to repeal the External Relations Act, which paved the way that year for the formal change from the State of Eire to the Republic of Ireland. >> RR1064

Costello, Lou >> **Abbott and Costello**
Coster, Dirk >> **Hevesy, George Charles de**
Coster, Laurens >> **Janszoon, Laurens**

Costner, Kevin (1955–) Motion-picture actor and director, born in Compton, CA. He studied at California State University (1978), became an actor, and established a reputation in the critically acclaimed films *Bull Durham* (1988) and *Field of Dreams* (1989). He directed and starred in the epic film *Dances With Wolves* (1990), a major triumph which won seven Oscars. Further successes followed with starring roles in *Robin Hood: Prince of Thieves* (1991), *JFK* (1991), *The Bodyguard* (1992), *Waterworld* (1995), and *Tin Cup* (1996).

Cosway, Richard (1742–1821) Miniaturist, born in Tiverton, Devon, SW England, UK. He studied with **Thomas Hudson** (1701–79) in London, and became a fashionable painter of portraits, patronized by the Prince of Wales. The use of watercolour on ivory is a notable feature of his work. In 1781 he married the artist **Maria Hadfield** (1759–1838), also a miniaturist.

Cotes, Roger [kohts] (1682–1716) Mathematician, born in Burbage, Leicestershire, C England, UK. He studied at Trinity College, Cambridge, where he became a fellow in 1705, and professor of astronomy and natural philosophy in 1706. In 1713 he took holy orders. He collaborated with Isaac Newton in revising the second edition of Newton's *Principia*, and contributed a preface defending Newton's methodology. >> Newton

Cotman, John Sell (1782–1842) Watercolourist, born in Norwich, Norfolk, E England, UK. He studied art in London, and returned to Norwich in 1806, where he became a leading member of the Norwich School. At Yarmouth (1811–23) he executed some fine oil paintings and etchings, but lack of success made him sell his pictures and possessions and return to London (1834), where he became drawing master of King's College. His best work shows a masterly arrangement of masses of light and shade, with a minimum of modelling, as in 'Greta Bridge' (c.1805). His two sons were also landscape painters.

Cottee, Kay (1954–) Yachting record holder, born in Sydney, New South Wales, Australia. She was the first woman to complete a solo, nonstop, unassisted circumnavigation of the world, arriving in Sydney harbour in June, 1988. She sailed 25 000 nautical miles in her 12-m Cavalier 37 sloop *First Lady* in 189 days, a record time for a woman. She was named Australian of the Year in 1989.

Cotten, Joseph (1905–94) Film actor, born in Los Angeles, CA. A member of Orson Welles Mercury Theater radio ensemble from 1937, he appeared in the Broadway production of *The Philadelphia Story* (1939–40), before starring in *Citizen Kane* (1941), *The Magnificent Ambersons* (1942), and *Journey into Fear* (1942). His many later films include *Gaslight* (1944), *The Third Man* (1949), and *Heaven's Gate* (1980).

Cotton, Charles (1630–87) Writer, born at Beresford Hall, Staffordshire, C England, UK. In 1664 he issued anonymously his burlesque poem, *Scarronides, or the First Book of Virgil Travestie*. Later works include a treatise on fly-fishing contributed in 1676 to the fifth edition of Walton's *Compleat Angler*, and a translation of Montaigne's *Essays* (1685).

Cotton, Sir (Thomas) Henry (1907–87) Golfer, born in Holmes Chapel, Cheshire, NW England, UK. Educated at Alleyn's School, he became a professional golfer, and won the British Open Championship (1934, 1937, and 1948). He played in the Ryder Cup against America four times between 1929 and 1953. In his latter years he ran a golf complex in Portugal, and was much in demand as a teacher and consultant. >> RR1157

Cotton, John (1585–1652) Puritan clergyman, born in Derby, Derbyshire, C England, UK. He was a tutor at Cambridge, and from c.1612 held a post at Boston, Lincolnshire. Cited for his Puritan views before Laud, in 1633 he emigrated to Boston, MA, where he became the head of Congregationalism in the USA. >> Laud

Cotton, Sir Robert Bruce (1571–1631) Antiquary, born in Denton, Northamptonshire, C England, UK. He studied at Cambridge, and at Cotton House in Westminster accumulated books, manuscripts, and coins dispersed by the dissolution of the monasteries. James I created him a baronet in 1611, and frequently consulted him. He was returned to parliament in 1604, and from c.1620 identified himself with the constitutional opposition to the crown, writing several critical political tracts. In 1629 he was imprisoned and had his library impounded, but was released on the occasion of the birth of an heir to the throne (1630). His son, **Sir Thomas Cotton** (1594–1662), had the books restored to him and greatly increased the library; and his great-grandson, **Sir John Cotton** (1679–1731), bestowed them on the nation in 1700.

Coty, François [kohtee] (1874–1934) Industrialist and newspaper proprietor, born in Ajaccio, Corsica. He built up the famous perfumery firm which bears his name, obtained control of *Figaro* in 1924, and founded the *Ami du Peuple* in 1928. He was a member of the Corsican Senate.

Coty, René [kohtee] (1882–1962) French statesman, the last president of the French Fourth Republic (1953–9), born in Le Havre, France. A barrister, he was elected a Left Republican deputy in 1923, entered the Senate in 1935, and was minister of reconstruction in 1947. After the constitutional crisis precipitated by the generals in Algeria in May 1958, he assisted the return to power of General de Gaulle and the birth of the Fifth Republic in 1959. >> de Gaulle; RR1049

Coubertin, Pierre de [koobairtĩ] (1863–1937) Educator, born in Paris. One of the first French advocates of physical education, he toured the USA and Europe to study educational methods, and visited Greece, where excavators were uncovering the ancient Olympic site. The visit inspired his proposal to revive the Olympic Games, and in 1894 the delegates at an international athletics conference in Paris voted to hold an Olympic competition at Athens in 1896. He became the first president (1896–1925) of the International Olympic Committee.

Couch, Arthur Quiller >> **Quiller-Couch, Arthur**

Coué, Emile [kooay] (1857–1926) Pharmacist, hypnotist, and pioneer of 'auto-suggestion', born in Troyes, France. A pharmacist in Troyes from 1882, he became a psychotherapist, and in 1910 opened a free clinic in Nancy. His system became world-famous as *Couéism*, expressed in the famous formula 'Every day, in every way, I am becoming better and better'.

Coughlin, Charles E(dward) [coglin] (1891–1979) Activist Catholic priest, born in Ontario, Canada. Pastor of the Shrine of the Little Flower in Michigan (1926–66), he won a huge audience in the 1930s for his radio broadcasts. At first a supporter of President Franklin D Roosevelt, he later adopted ultraconservative views and anti-Semitic rhetoric, and opposed US entrance into World War 2. In 1942 the Catholic hierarchy ordered him to stop broadcasting, and his inflammatory magazine, *Social Justice*, was barred from the mails as violating the Federal Espionage Act. >> Roosevelt, Franklin D

Coulomb, Charles (Augustin de) [koolõ] (1736–1806) Physicist, born in Angoulême, France. After serving as a military engineer for nine years, he retired to a small estate and devoted himself to scientific research. He experimented on friction, and invented the torsion balance for measuring the force of magnetic and electrical attraction. The *coulomb*, the unit of quantity in measuring current electricity, is named after him.

Coulton, George Gordon [koolton] (1858–1947) Historian, born in King's Lynn, Norfolk, E England, UK. He became a lecturer at Cambridge, Oxford, Toronto, and Edinburgh.

His many works include *Life in the Middle Ages* (1928–29) and *Mediaeval Thought* (1939). He wrote an autobiography, *Fourscore Years* (1943).

Couper, Archibald Scott [kooper] (1831–92) Organic chemist, born in Kirkintilloch, East Dunbartonshire, WC Scotland, UK. He studied classics at Glasgow and philosophy at Edinburgh, then turned to chemistry, and studied in Paris under **Charles Adolphe Wurtz** (1817–84). In 1858 he asked Wurtz to present to the French Academy a paper in which he argued that carbon had a valence of two or four; and that its atoms could self-link to form chains. Wurtz procrastinated in his presentation, and Friedrich August Kekulé von Stradonitz published first. Couper returned to Edinburgh ignored as a chemist, and suffered a permanent depressive illness. His work was later discovered by Kekulé's successor at Bonn, and given belated recognition. >> Kekulé von Stradonitz

Couperin, François [kooperĩ] (1668–1733) Composer, born in Paris. He was taught by his father, whom he eventually followed as organist of Saint-Gervais (1685). In 1693 he also became organist to Louis XIV, and in 1717 composer-in-ordinary of chamber music to the king. Known mainly as a harpsichord composer (whose influence on Bach was profound), he also composed chamber concertos and church music. >> Bach, Johann Sebastian

Courant, Richard (1888–1972) Mathematician, born in Lublinitz, Germany. He studied at Wrocław, Poland (formerly Breslau, Germany), Zürich, and (as a pupil of David Hilbert) Göttingen universities, where he became professor in 1920, founding the Mathematics Institute in 1929. In 1933 he was forced by the Nazis to retire, and after a year at Cambridge he went to the USA, where he became professor at New York University (1934–58), and director of the Institute of Mathematical Sciences (later the Courant Research Institute) (1953–8). He worked in applied analysis, particularly in partial differential equations and the Dirichlet problem. >> Dirichlet; Hilbert

Courbet, Gustave [koorbay] (1819–77) Painter, born in Ornans, France. He was sent to Paris to study law, but turned to painting. The founder of Realism, in 1844 he began exhibiting pictures in which everyday scenes were portrayed with complete sincerity and absence of idealism, such as 'Burial at Ornans' (1849, Musée d'Orsay, Paris). His best-known work is the large 'Studio of the Painter: an Allegory of Realism' (1855, (Musée d'Orsay, Paris). Republican in sympathies, he joined the Commune in 1871, and on its suppression was imprisoned. Released in 1873, he fled to Switzerland.

Cournand, André F(rédéric) [koornã] (1895–1988) Physician, born in Paris. He studied at the Sorbonne, emigrated to the USA in 1930, and joined the staff of Columbia University/Bellevue Hospital (1930–64). He became a US citizen in 1941. A specialist in heart surgery, he shared the 1956 Nobel Prize for Physiology or Medicine for developing cardiac catheterization. In 1960 he became professor of clinical physiology at Columbia University, where he expanded his work to include research on the lungs. >> Forssmann; Richards, Dickinson

Courrèges, André [koorezh] (1923–) Fashion designer, born in Pau, France. He studied civil engineering, but later turned to fashion in Paris, where he was trained by Balenciaga, and opened his own house in 1961. Famous for stark, futuristic, 'Space Age' designs, he has featured trouser suits, white boots, and short skirts. He produces ready-to-wear as well as couture clothes. >> Balenciaga

Court, Margaret (Jean) [kaw(r)t], *née* **Smith** (1942–) Tennis player, born in Albury, New South Wales, Australia. She was the winner of more Grand Slam events (66) than any other player: 10 Wimbledon (including the singles in

1963, 1965, 1970), 22 US, 13 French, and 21 Australian titles. In 1970 she became the second woman (after Maureen Connolly) to win all four major titles in one year. She retired in 1977. >> Connolly, Maureen; RR1173

Courtauld, Samuel [kaw(r)tohld] (1876–1947) British industrialist, a descendant of Samuel Courtauld (1793–1881), the founder of the silk manufacturing company in 1816. As chairman of Courtaulds Ltd he promoted the British rayon and nylon industry, and was a patron of art and music. He built the Courtauld Institute of Art in Portman Square, London, and donated it along with his art collection to London University.

Courteney, Tom [kaw(r)tnee], popular name of **Thomas Daniel Courteney** (1937–) Actor, born in Hull, NE England, UK. He trained at the Royal Academy of Dramatic Art, London, and made his professional debut in 1960 with the Old Vic company in Edinburgh. He played Hamlet at the 1968 Edinburgh Festival, and won acclaim for his performance as Norman in the Ayckbourn comedy trilogy, *The Norman Conquests* (1974). Other stage appearances include *The Dresser* (1980), the title role in the musical, *Andy Capp* (1982), *Dealing with Clair* (1988), and *Art* (1996). His first film appearance was in *The Loneliness of the Long-Distance Runner* (1962). Subsequent films include *Billy Liar* (1963), *King Rat* (1965), *Doctor Zhivago* (1965), *One Day in the Life of Ivan Denisovitch* (1971), and *The Dresser* (1983).

Courtneidge, Dame Cicely (Esmerelda) [koortnij] (1883–1980) Actress, born in Sydney, New South Wales, Australia. She began acting at the age of eight, and made her London debut at 14 in a musical version of *Tom Jones*. She later became widely known in musicals, pantomimes, and revues, having a great success in *By-the-Way* (1935), which also starred her husband, **Jack Hulbert** (1892–1978). She also appeared in several straight comedies, including her final West End stage appearance in *Move Over, Mrs Markham* (1971). She was made a dame in 1972.

Cousin, Jean [koozī], known as **Jean Cousin the Elder** (c. 1490–c. 1560) Engraver, glass-stainer, and painter, born in Soucy, France. He was probably responsible for two stained glass windows in Sens Cathedral, and a picture of a nude woman ('Eva Prima Pandora') in the Louvre. His son, **Jean Cousin (the Younger)** (c.1522–c.1594), was also a versatile artist, who continued many aspects of his father's work.

Cousin, Victor [koozī] (1792–1867) Philosopher, born in Paris. After the 1830 revolution, he became a member of the Council of Public Instruction, and in 1832 a peer of France and director of the Ecole Normale. In 1848 he aided the government of Cavaignac, but after 1849 left public life. His eclectic philosophy can be seen in his *Fragments philosophiques* (1826) and *Du vrai, du beau, et du bien* (1854, On the True, the Beautiful, and the Good).

Cousins, Frank [kuhzinz] (1904–86) Trade-union leader, born in Nottingham, C England, UK. He worked in the pits at 14, turned lorry driver, and by 1938 was a full-time union organizer. In 1955 he became general secretary of the Transport and General Worker's Union. He was minister of technology (1964–6) until he resigned over the prices and incomes policy, MP for Nuneaton (1965–6), and chairman of the Community Relations Commission (1968–70).

Cousins, Robin (1957–) Ice skater, born in Bristol, SW England, UK. He trained at the Bristol Ice Dance and Figure Skating Club (1968–80), and in 1980 became only the second British male to win an Olympic figure-skating gold medal. Other achievements include the European Championship gold (1980) and World Championship silver medals (1979, 1980), and he was World freeskating champion for three successive years (1978–80). He turned professional in 1980, and has been artistic director of the

Ice Castle International Training Center in California since 1989.

Cousteau, Jacques (Yves) [koostoh] (1910–97) Naval officer and underwater explorer, born in Saint-André, France. He invented the aqualung diving apparatus (1943) and a process of underwater television. In 1945 he founded the French Navy's Undersea Research Group, and commanded the research ship *Calypso* in 1950. He became director of the Oceanographic Museum of Monaco in 1957. He wrote widely on his subject, and his films included the Oscar-winning *The Golden Fish* (1960).

Cousy, Bob [koozee], popular name of **Robert Joseph Cousy** (1928–) Basketball player, born in New York City. He played professionally with the Boston Celtics (1950–63), then went on to coach with the Cincinatti Royals and the Kansas City–Omaha Kings. He became a sports commentator, and was elected to basketball's Hall of Fame in 1971. He has been the author of several books on the sport, including *Basketball In My Life* (1956) and *The Killer Instinct* (1976).

Couthon, Georges [kootō] (1756–94) French revolutionary, born in Orcet, France. An advocate at the outbreak of the Revolution, he was sent by Puy de Dôme to the National Convention, and in 1793 became a member of the Committee of Public Safety. He crushed the insurrection in Lyon with merciless severity (1793), and helped to usher in the Terror. Robespierre's fall also brought down Couthon, and he was executed. >> Robespierre

Coutts, Morton (1904–) Brewer, born in Taihape, New Zealand. He entered the family trade of brewing in 1919. Although working at a traditional craft he was also extremely inventive. In 1926 he built the third short-wave transmitter in the world, and established the first radio link between New Zealand and England. In 1956 he revolutionized the industry by patenting the first major innovation in brewing since the 16th-c, the continuous fermentation process. In the same year he became the first brewer outside the USA to win the Schwarz Award of the American Master Brewers, and in 1992 Kiwi Lager – a beer based on his research and recipes – was proclaimed Best Beer in the World at the international awards in England.

Coutts, Thomas [koots] (1735–1822) Banker, born in Edinburgh, EC Scotland, UK. He founded the London banking-house of Coutts & Co with his brother **James Coutts**, on whose death in 1778 he became sole manager. >> Burdett-Coutts

Couve de Murville, (Jacques) Maurice [koov duh mürveel] (1907–) French statesman and prime minister (1968–9), born in Reims, France. He studied law, literature, and political science before joining the Ministry of Finance (1940). He later worked in the foreign ministry, and played a diplomatic role in the European postwar settlement. During the 1950s he served as ambassador to various countries. President de Gaulle appointed him foreign minister (1958–68), finance minister (1968), then premier. He held numerous important posts throughout his distinguished career, gaining a reputation for his cool professionalism. >> RR1049

Coverdale, Miles (1488–1568) Bible scholar, born in York, North Yorkshire, N England, UK. He studied at Cambridge, was ordained priest in 1514, and joined the Augustinian Friars at Cambridge, but was converted to Protestantism. His own translation of the Bible appeared in 1535 (the first complete one in English), and he then superintended the work which led to the 'Great Bible' (1539). He also edited the work known as 'Cranmer's Bible' (1540). Forced to live abroad for several years, he returned to England in 1548 and became Bishop of Exeter in 1551. On Queen Mary's accession he went abroad again, but returned in 1559 to live in London.

Coward, Sir Noel (Pierce) (1899–1973) Actor, playwright, and composer, born in London, England, UK. An actor from the age of 12, his first play, written with Esme Wynne, was produced in 1917. Among his many successes were *The Vortex* (1924), *Hay Fever* (1925), *Private Lives* (1930), and *Blithe Spirit* (1941), all showing his strong satirical humour, and his gift for witty dialogue. He wrote the music as well as the lyrics for most of his works, including the musical *Bitter Sweet* (1929), the play *Cavalcade* (1931), and the revue *Words and Music* (1932), with its 'Mad Dogs and Englishmen'. He was also an accomplished singer, produced several films based on his own scripts, and published two volumes of autobiography, *Present Indicative* (1937) and *Future Indefinite* (1954).

Cowdrey, Sir (Michael) Colin [kowdree] (1932–) Cricketer, born in India. He studied at Oxford, and was captain of the Oxford XI in 1954 when he was already a Kent player. He played in 114 Tests for England (23 as captain), scoring 7624 runs (average 44·06), and made six tours of Australia. In his long first-class career (1951–75) he was captain of Kent (1957–71), and scored 107 centuries, of which 22 were in Test matches. He became chairman of the International Cricket Council (1989–93), and was knighted in 1992. His son, **Chris Cowdrey** (1957–), has also captained Kent and England. >> May, Peter; Ramadhin; RR1149

Cowell, Henry (Dixon) [kowel] (1897–1965) Composer, born in Menlo Park, CA. He studied in New York City and Berlin, and earned his living as a pianist, lecturer, and writer. As a composer he was noted for his experimental techniques, including note-clusters produced on the piano by using the fist or forearm. He founded *The New Musical Quarterly* in 1927. His works include two ballets, an unfinished opera, and 20 symphonies.

Cowen, Sir Frederic (Hymen) [kowen] (1852–1935) Composer, born in Kingston, Jamaica. He was brought to England as a child, and became conductor of the Philharmonic (1888–92, 1900–7), and of the Scottish Orchestra (1900–10). He composed operas, cantatas, oratorios, symphonies, overtures, pianoforte pieces, and some 300 songs.

Cowen, Sir Zelman [kowen] (1919–) Jurist, administrator, and writer, born in St Kilda, Victoria, Australia. After serving in World War 2 with the Royal Australian Navy, he studied law at Oxford University, and became a fellow of Oriel College in 1947. From 1951 he was professor of public law at Melbourne University, and in 1967 was appointed emeritus professor. He was Vice-Chancellor of the University of New England, New South Wales (1967–70) and of Queensland University (1970–7). Knighted in 1976, he succeeded Sir John Kerr as Governor-General of Australia (1977–82). He then became Provost of Oriel College, Oxford (1982–90) and Pro-Vice-Chancellor of Oxford (1988–90), and also served as chairman of the UK Press Council (1983–8). >> Kerr, Sir John

Cowley, Abraham (1618–67) Poet, born in London, England, UK. He studied at Cambridge, and was publishing poetry at the age of 15. During the Civil War he went with the queen to Paris, was sent on Royalist missions, and carried on her correspondence in cipher with the king. After the Restoration (1660), he retired to Chertsey. His main works were the influential *Pindarique Odes* (1656), and his unfinished epic on King David, *Davideis* (1656).

Cowley, Malcolm (1898–1989) Critic and editor, born in Belsano, PA. He studied at Harvard, then struggled to make a living as a writer in New York City and Paris. His books include *Exile's Return* (1934), about the illustrious group of US writers who convened in Paris after World War 1, and *The Dream of the Golden Mountains* (1980). Long

associated with *The New Republic* as literary editor (1929–44), he is credited with resuscitating the career of William Faulkner by editing a Viking Portable selection of his work (1949). >> Faulkner

Cowper, William [kooper] (1666–1709) Surgeon and anatomist, born in Petersfield, Hampshire, S England, UK. He settled as a surgeon in London, wrote *The Anatomy of Human Bodies* (1698), and discovered *Cowper's glands*.

Cowper, William [kooper] (1731–1800) Poet, born in Berkhamsted, Hertfordshire, SE England, UK. He studied at Westminster School, and was called to the bar in 1754. He suffered frequently from mental instability, and attempted suicide several times. While living in Olney, he collaborated with the clergyman John Newton to write the *Olney Hymns* (1779). His ballad of John Gilpin (1783) was highly successful, as was his long poem about rural ease, *The Task* (1785).

Cox, (Charles) Brian (1928–) British academic. He studied at Cambridge, taught English at Hull University (1954–66), then became professor at Manchester and pro-Vice-Chancellor (1987). A member of the Kingman Committee on the English Language, he became chairman of the National Curriculum English Working Group (1988–9). As well as a series of *Black Papers on Education* (1969–77), his publications include *The Free Spirit* (1963) and *Joseph Conrad: the Modern Imagination* (1974). He has also written books of poetry, *Collected Poems* appearing in 1993. His name is most widely known in UK English circles as the author of the report produced on the teaching of English in the National Curriculum (the *Cox Report*). >> Kingman

Cox, Brian (1946–) British actor, director, and writer. He studied at the London Academy of Music and Dramatic Art, and made his debut with the Dundee Repertory in 1961. An experienced actor, he has played many Shakespearean leading roles, including *Titus Adronicus* (1987) and *King Lear* (1990–1). Among his films are *Hidden Agenda* (1990) and *Rob Roy* (1994), and television appearances include *Acting in Tragedy* in the BBC Masterclass series (1990) and *Food for Ravens* (1997).

Cox, Courtenay (1964–) Actor, born in Birmingham, AL. She studied architecture for a year at Mount Vernon College, became a model in New York City, then took a range of parts in films and television, and became well known through her role as Monica Geller in the acclaimed television series *Friends* (1994–). Roles in feature films began with *Down Twisted* (1986), and include *Ace Ventura: Pet Detective* (1994), *Scream* (1996), and *Commandments* (1997).

Cox, David (1783–1859) Landscape painter, born near Birmingham, West Midlands, C England, UK. He taught as a drawing-master in Hereford (1814–26), publishing *A Treatise on Landscape Painting*. In 1839 he turned his attention seriously to oil-painting, and executed about a hundred works in oil, mainly inspired by the scenery of North Wales. His son, **David Cox** (1809–85), was a noted watercolourist.

Cox, Phillip Sutton (1939–) Architect, born in Sydney, New South Wales, Australia. He studied at the University of Sydney, began designing mainly institutional and domestic buildings, and in the 1980s entered the commercial world with well-known structures such as the Yulara Tourist Resort, Ayers Rock (1983), the Sydney Football Stadium (1988), and the National Maritime Museum, Darling Harbour, Sydney (1990). These buildings exploit the tensile properties of steel cables and clean white surfaces to dramatic effect. He has a strong interest in regional history, and is author of *The Australian Homestead* (1972) and *Australian Colonial Architecture* (1978). He has been professor of architecture at the University of New South Wales since 1989.

Cox, Richard (1500–81) Clergyman and Protestant reformer, born in Whaddon, Buckinghamshire, SC England, UK. He studied at Cambridge, and became headmaster of Eton, and Vice-Chancellor of Oxford (1547–52). On the accession of Mary I he was imprisoned, and went into exile in Frankfurt, where he was a bitter opponent of John Knox and his Calvinist doctrines. Back in England, he was appointed Bishop of Ely (1559–80). >> Knox, John

Cox, William (1764–1837) Pioneer Australian road builder, born in Wimbourne Minster, Dorset, S England, UK. He arrived in Australia in 1800 as a lieutenant in the New South Wales Corps, and purchased land which he farmed. In 1814 Governor Lachlan Macquarie made him superintendent of works for a new road over the Blue Mountains, which he completed in just six months. He then returned to farming, and established a flock of sheep famous for the quality of its wool. >> Macquarie

Coxie, Michiel, also spelled **Coxcie** or **Coxius** (1499–1592) Painter, born in Mechelen, The Netherlands. He introduced the Italian Classical style into Flanders. Frescoes in S Maria dell' Anima at Rome are his work. He was court painter to Philip II of Spain.

Coysevox, Antoine [kwazuhvoks] (1640–1720) Sculptor, born in Lyon, France. He became court sculptor to Louis XIV in 1666 and was responsible for much of the Baroque decoration at the Palace of Versailles, most notably the Galérie des Glaces and the Salon de la Guerre. He also sculpted portrait busts of many important figures of the time.

Cozens, Alexander [kuhznz] (?–1786) Watercolour painter, born in St Petersburg, Russia, the son of the English shipbuilder to the Tsar. After studying in Italy, he moved to England in 1746. In 1785 he published a treatise describing his method of using accidental ink-blots as the basis for landscape compositions. >> Cozens, John Robert

Cozens, John Robert [kuhznz] (1752–c. 1797) Watercolour landscape painter, born in London, England, UK, the son of Alexander Cozens. In 1776 he travelled through Switzerland to Rome, painting what he saw on his way, and in 1782–3 made a second visit to Italy. Turner and Girtin copied his drawings, and John Constable pronounced that he was 'the greatest genius that ever touched landscape'. >> Constable, John; Cozens, Alexander; Girtin; Turner, J M W

Cozzens, James Gould [kuhznz] (1903–78) Novelist, born in Chicago, IL. He published his first novel, *Confusion*, at the age of 19, fought in the US Army Corps in World War 2, then wrote *Guard of Honour* (1948, Pulitzer). His most popular success was *By Love Possessed* (1958, filmed 1961), but his appeal has waned since his death.

Crabbe, George (1754–1832) Poet, born in Aldeburgh, Suffolk, E England, UK. He trained as a surgeon, but turned to literature. He was ordained in 1782, and held livings in Suffolk and Wiltshire. His best-known work from this early period is *The Village* (1783), a realistic portrait of rural life. He then wrote nothing for over 20 years. His later narrative poems include *The Parish Register* (1807), *The Borough* (1810), and other volumes of *Tales*.

Craddock, Charles Egbert, pseudonym of **Mary Noailles Murfree** (1850–1922) Writer, born in Murfreesboro, TN. She wrote short stories in the *Atlantic Monthly* from 1878, published as *In the Tennessee Mountains* (1884), and thereafter became a prolific novelist of mountain backwoods life.

Cradock, Fanny, née **Phyllis Primrose-Pechey** (1909–94) British writer and television cook. From 1955 she became known for her 'bon viveur' television cookery programmes, dressed in a ball gown, and presented with her monocled husband, Johnny. Her writing included cookery books, children's books, several novels (under the pen name **Frances Dale**), and columns on cookery and restaurants in the daily press, which became notorious for their social pretension and outspoken opinions.

Crafts, James Mason >> **Friedel, Charles**

Craig, Edward (Henry) Gordon (1872–1966) Stage designer, actor, director, and theorist, born in Stevenage, Hertfordshire, SE England, UK. He worked for nine years as an actor in Irving's company, but left the Lyceum in 1897 to be both a director and a designer. He settled in Italy in 1906, where he published the theatre journal, *The Mask* (1908–29), which together with his scene designs and his books, *On the Art of the Theatre* (1911) and *The Theatre Advancing* (1921), had a profound influence on modern theatre practice. >> Irving, Henry

Craig, James, 1st Viscount Craigavon (1871–1940) Politician, born in Belfast. A Unionist MP in the British parliament (1906–21), he was resolutely opposed to Home Rule for Ireland. When the Stormont parliament was established in 1921, he became the first prime minister of Northern Ireland (1921–40).

Craig, Sir James (Henry) (1748–1812) British soldier, born in Gibraltar. He joined the army at 15 and served with distinction in America, where he was wounded at Bunker Hill and helped capture Ticonderoga (1777). In 1795, as major-general, he took Cape Colony and served as its governor until 1797. He later became Governor-General of Canada (1807–11).

Craigie, Sir William Alexander [kraygee] (1867–1957) Scholar, born in Dundee, E Scotland, UK. He studied at St Andrews, and became professor of Anglo-Saxon at Oxford (1916–25), and of English at Chicago (1925–35). He was joint editor of the *New English Dictionary* (1901–33), and also editor of dictionaries on Scots and on American English.

Craik, Kenneth (1914–45) British experimental psychologist. He studied at Edinburgh and Cambridge, and spent much of World War 2 on applied military research on topics which included servo-mechanisms and 'human factors' in design. In 1944 he was appointed director of the new Unit for Research in Applied Psychology at Cambridge. He pioneered the psychological school of thought in which the mind is considered as a complex example of an information-processing system. He died tragically young following a cycling accident.

Cram, Donald (1919–) Chemist, born in Chester, VT. He taught at the University of California, Los Angeles, from 1947. He elucidated mechanisms of molecular recognition, working mostly on the properties of crown ether molecules, for which he shared the Nobel Prize for Chemistry in 1987. >> RR1123

Cram, Steve, popular name of **Stephen Cram** (1960–) Athlete, born in Gateshead, Tyne and Wear, NE England, UK. The European junior champion at 3000 m in 1979, he won senior titles at 1500 m in 1982 and 1986. He won the World Championship gold medal at 1500 m in 1983, and the Commonwealth Games gold medals at 1500 m (1982, 1986) and 800 m (1986). In 1985 he set three world records in 20 days at 1500 m, 1 mi, and 2000 m. His time for the mile was 3 min 46·32 s. >> RR1135

Crampton, Thomas Russell (1816–88) Engineer, born in Broadstairs, Kent, SE England, UK. He was a pioneer of locomotive construction, and was responsible for the first successful cross-channel submarine cable, between Dover and Calais, in 1851. He built the Berlin waterworks (1855), and many railway systems.

Cranach, Lucas [krahnakh], known as **Lucas Cranach the Elder** (1472–1553) Painter, born in Kronach, Germany, from where he took his name. In 1504 he became court painter at Wittenberg to the Elector Frederick. His paintings include sacred and a few classical subjects, hunting scenes, and portraits. He was closely associated with the German Reformers, many of whom (including Luther and Melanchthon) were portrayed by himself and his pupils. A 'Crucifixion' in the Stadkirche, Weimar, is his masterpiece. Of three sons, all painters, the second, **Lucas Cranach the Younger** (1515–86), painted so like his father that their works are difficult to distinguish.

Crandall, Prudence, married name **Philleo** (1803–90) Educator and abolitionist, born in Hopkinton, RI. Her short-lived attempt to train young black women as teachers in her Canterbury, CN, boarding school (1833–4) provoked the passage of a local 'black law', and harassment ranging from arrest to violent attacks. She worked for women's rights and temperance throughout her life.

Crane, (Harold) Hart (1899–1932) Poet, born in Garrettsville, OH. After an unhappy childhood, he settled in New York City as a writer in 1923. His work is contained in *The White Buildings* (1926), a collection on New York life, and *The Bridge* (1930), an epic using Brooklyn Bridge as its focal point. He drowned himself while returning from a visit to Mexico.

Crane, Stephen (1871–1900) Writer and war correspondent, born in Newark, NJ. He began as a journalist in New York City, and became known as a novelist through *Maggie: A Girl of the Streets* (1893) and *The Red Badge of Courage* (1895), a vivid story of the Civil War. He also wrote poems and short stories, and worked as a war correspondent in Greece and Cuba.

Crane, Walter (1845–1915) Painter and illustrator, born in Liverpool, Merseyside, NW England, UK. He came under the influence of the pre-Raphaelites, and became a leader with William Morris in the Arts and Crafts movement, and in early Socialism. He was particularly celebrated as an illustrator of children's books. He was director of Manchester School of Art (1893–6), Reading College (1896–8), and principal of the Royal College of Art (1898–9). >> Morris, William

Cranko, John [krangkoh] (1927–73) Dancer, choreographer, and director, born in Rustenburg, South Africa. He studied at the Cape Town University ballet school, and at Sadler's Wells School in London. He choreographed for both Sadler's Wells and the Royal Ballet companies, and in 1961 became ballet director of the Stuttgart Ballet. He is known chiefly for his full-length dramatic works, such as *Romeo and Juliet* (1962) and *Onegin* (1965). >> Haydee

Cranmer, Thomas (1489–1556) Archbishop of Canterbury, born in Aslockton, Nottinghamshire, C England, UK. He studied at Cambridge, took orders in 1523, and became a divinity tutor. His suggestion that Henry VIII appeal for his divorce to the universities of Christendom won him the king's favour and he was appointed a royal chaplain. He was made Archbishop of Canterbury in 1533, making allegiance to the pope 'for form's sake'. He later annulled Henry's marriages to Catherine of Aragon and to Anne Boleyn (1536), and divorced him from Anne of Cleves (1540). He was largely responsible for the Book of Common Prayer (1549, 1552). On Henry's death, Cranmer rushed Protestant changes through. He had little to do with affairs of state, but agreed to the plan to divert the succession from Mary to Lady Jane Grey (1553), for which he was arraigned for treason. Accused later of heresy, and sentenced to death, he retracted the seven recantations he had been forced to sign, before being burned alive. >> Grey, Lady Jane; Henry VIII; Mary I; Ridley, Nicholas (c.1500–55)

Crashaw, Richard [krayshaw] (c. 1613–49) Religious poet, born in London, England, UK. He studied at Cambridge, went to Paris, became a Catholic (1644), and in 1649 was given a Church post in Loretto, Italy. He is best known for his volume of Latin poems, *Epigrammatum sacrorum liber*

(1634, A Book of Sacred Epigrams), and *Steps to the Temple* (1646).

Crassus, Lucius Licinius (140–91 BC) Roman orator. In 95 he was elected consul, along with Quintus Scaevola. During their consulship a rigorous law was enacted banishing from Rome all who had not the full rights of citizens, which was one of the chief causes of the Social War (90–88). Crassus is the chief speaker in Cicero's *De oratore*, and represents the writer's own opinions. >> Cicero

Crassus, Marcus Licinius, nickname **Dives** (Lat 'wealthy') (c.115–53 BC) Roman politician. As praetor he defeated Spartacus at the Battle of Lucania (71 BC), and in 70 BC was made consul with Pompey. The richest of Roman citizens, he became a friend of Caesar, and formed the first triumvirate with him and Pompey (60 BC). In 53 BC, as Governor of Syria, he attacked the Parthians, but was routed and killed at the Battle of Carrhae. >> Caesar; Pompey; Spartacus

Crates of Chalkis [krahteez, kalkis] (fl.335–325 BC) Greek engineer, one of several who carried out notable works for Alexander the Great, including the building of the new city and port of Alexandria in the Nile delta. Other projects included works of drainage, irrigation, and water supply.

Cratinus [kratiynus] (c. 519–423 BC) Greek comic poet. Next to Aristophanes, he best represents the Old Attic comedy. He limited the number of actors to three, and was the first to add to comedy the interest of biting personal attack. Of his 21 comedies, only some fragments are extant. A younger **Cratinus**, a contemporary of Plato, belonged to the Middle Comedy. >> Aristophanes

Craven, Dan(iel Hartman), known as **Danie** (1911–93) Rugby union player and administrator, born in Lindley, South Africa. He was captain of South Africa against the visiting Lions side in 1938. He became chairman of the South African Rugby Board in 1956, and over the next 30 years worked to keep South Africa within the Rugby Union fold and, later, to have it reinstated.

Crawford, Joan, originally **Lucille Fay Le Sueur** (1904–77) Film actress, born in San Antonio, TX. At first a nightclub dancer, she started in silent films in 1925, taking the lead in *Our Dancing Daughters* (1928). She became an established star in the 1930s and 1940s, winning an Oscar for *Mildred Pierce* (1945); her last great role was in *Whatever Happened to Baby Jane?* (1962), in which she co-starred with her long-standing rival, Bette Davis. After her death, a very critical biography, *Mommie Dearest*, by her adopted daughter Christine, was filmed in 1981. >> Davis, Bette

Crawford, Sir John (Grenfell) (1910–85) Economist and administrator, born in Sydney, New South Wales, Australia. He studied at Sydney University, and held various senior positions in agricultural and rural economics, including director of the [Australian] Commonwealth Bureau of Agricultural Economics (1945–50). He held the chair of economics at the Australian National University, Canberra (1960–7), was Vice-Chancellor there (1968–73), and Chancellor of the University of Papua New Guinea (1972–5).

Crawford, Michael (1942–) British actor. His performance in *No Sex Please, We're British* (1971) established him as a comedy actor. In the 1970s the television series *Some Mothers Do 'Ave 'Em*, in which he played the accident-prone misfit Frank Spencer, made him a household name in Britain. He went on to star in such musicals as *Billy* (1974), *Flowers for Algernon* (1979), *Barnum* (1981), and *The Phantom of the Opera* (1986, Tony). His films include *The Knack* (1964), *How I Won the War* (1966), *Hello Dolly* (1968), and *The Condorman* (1980). >> Torvill and Dean

Crawford, Osbert Guy Stanhope (1886–1957) British archaeologist and pioneer aerial photographer, born in

Mumbai (Bombay), India. He studied at Oxford, served with the Royal Flying Corps in World War 1, and identified the potential of aerial photography in archaeology, producing *Wessex from the Air* (1928). He served as the first archaeology officer of the Ordnance Survey (1920–40), and did much to develop the cartographic recording of archaeology. In 1927 he founded the journal *Antiquity*, which he edited until his death.

Crawford, Thomas (1814–57) Sculptor, born in New York City. He studied in Rome. His works include the Washington monument at Richmond, and the bronze figure of Liberty surmounting the dome of the capitol at Washington.

Craxi, Bettino [krak see] (1934–   ) Italian statesman and prime minister (1983–7), born in Milan, Italy. He was active in the Socialist Youth Movement, and joined the Central Committee of the Italian Socialist Party in 1957. A member of the National Executive in 1965, he became deputy secretary (1970–6), general secretary (1976), and Italy's first Socialist prime minister. >> RR1065

Cray, Seymour R (1925–96) Computer designer, born in Chippewa Falls, WI. He studied at Wisconsin University, and established himself at the forefront of large-scale computer design through his work at Engineering Research Associates, Remington Rand, UNIVAC, and Control Data Corporation. In 1972 he organized Cray Research Inc in Chippewa Falls to develop and market the most powerful computer systems available.

Crayon, Geoffrey >> **Irving, Washington**

Crazy Horse, Sioux name **Tashunka Witco** (c.1842–77) Oglala Sioux chief, born near the Black Hills, SD. He participated in all the major Sioux actions to protect the Black Hills against white intrusion, believing himself immune from battle injury. In 1876 he was named supreme war and peace chief of the Oglalas, uniting most of the Sioux still free. He led the Sioux and Cheyenne to victory at the Battle of Rosebud, and defeated Custer's forces at Little Bighorn (1876). Pursued by US forces, with his band of some 1000 facing starvation, he surrendered the following year. He died at the hands of a US soldier, allegedly while resisting being forced into a jail cell. He is regarded as a symbol of Sioux resistance and as their greatest leader, and a gigantic figure of Crazy Horse has been sculpted (by Korczak Ziolkowski) out of a mountain in the Black Hills of South Dakota. >> **Custer, George Armstrong; Sitting Bull**

Creed, Frederick George (1871–1957) Inventor, born in Nova Scotia, Canada. He moved to Glasgow, Scotland, in 1897, and there perfected the *Creed teleprinter*, used in news offices all over the world.

Creeley, Robert (White) (1926–   ) Poet and novelist, born in Arlington, MA. He studied for a while at Harvard, then worked at a variety of jobs until he began to write. Influenced by the Black Mountain school, he developed a spare, minimalist style evident in *For Love: Poems 1950–60* (1960). His manner becomes even more fragmentary in later volumes, notably *Words* (1965), *Pieces* (1969), *Hello: A Journal* (1978), and *Memory Gardens* (1986).

Creevey, Thomas (1768–1838) British politician and diarist, born in Liverpool, Merseyside, NW England, UK. He was a Whig MP for Thetford (1802), and later for Appleby, and became treasurer of ordnance (1830) and treasurer of Greenwich Hospital. He is chiefly remembered for the *Creevey Papers*, a journal important as a source of Georgian social history.

Cremer, Sir (William) Randal [kree mer] (1838–1908) Pacifist, born in Fareham, Hampshire, S England, UK. An active trade unionist, he was a strong advocate of British neutrality in the Franco-Prussian war, and founded the Workmen's Peace Association, the germ of the International Arbitration

League. A radical MP from 1885, he edited the peace journal *Arbitor* from 1889. He was awarded the Nobel Peace Prize in 1903.

Crémieux, Benjamin [kraymyoe] (1888–1944) Writer and critic, born in Narbonne, France. He is known for his works on modern European literature, including *XX siècle* (1924) and for his translation of the plays of Pirandello. He died in Buchenwald concentration camp.

Cremin, Lawrence (Arthur) [cremin] (1925–90) Historian and educator, born in New York City. He taught at Teachers' College, Columbia (1948–90), becoming president there (1974–84), and then president of the Spencer Foundation (1985–90). His major published works include a Pulitzer Prize-winning three-volume history of American education (1970–80) and *Popular Education and its Discontents* (1990).

Crerar, Henry Duncan Graham [kreerer] (1888–1965) Canadian soldier, born in Hamilton, Ontario, Canada. He studied at Upper Canada College and the Royal Military College, Kingston, and worked as a civil engineer while holding a commission in the militia. In World War 2 he was chief of Canadian army staff (1940–1), commanded the 2nd Canadian Division (1942) and the Canadian Corps in Italy (1942–4), and succeeded Andrew McNaughton in command of the Canadian Land Forces in Europe (1944).

Cresson, Edith [kresō], *née* **Campion** (1934–   ) French stateswoman and prime minister (1991–2), born in Boulogne-Billancourt, France. She studied at the School of Higher Commercial Studies, joined the Socialist Party (1965), was mayor of Thure (1977), and was appointed the first female agriculture minister (1981). She subsequently held a number of government posts before achieving the distinction of becoming France's first woman prime minister, under the presidency of Mitterrand. Always an outspoken figure, she lost public support and resigned. In 1995 she became a member of the European Commission. >> **Mitterrand; RR1049**

Cretzschmar, Philipp Jakob [krech mah(r)] (1786–1845) Naturalist and physician, born in Sulzbach, Germany. He studied medicine at Würzburg and Halle, and after army service settled in Frankfurt, where he practised as a doctor and taught zoology. *Cretzschmar's bunting* was named in his honour.

Cribb, Tom (1781–1848) Prizefighter and bare-knuckles champion of the world, born in Bitton, South Gloucestershire, SWC England, UK. He twice defeated Jem Belcher for the bare-knuckles championship (1807, 1809), and also defeated the US black pugilist Tom Molineaux (1810, 1811). He retired with an unbeaten record, and became a publican in London.

Crichton, James [kriytn], known as **the Admirable Crichton** (1560–c.1582) Leading figure of the Scottish Enlightenment, born in Clunie, Perth and Kinross, E Scotland, UK. He studied at St Andrews, and earned a tremendous reputation as a scholar, poet, linguist, and swordsman on the European mainland. While in Mantua in the service of the duke, he was killed in a nocturnal brawl by the duke's son. His popular reputation rests on the fantastic account of his exploits written by Sir Thomas Urquhart in his panegyric on the Scots nation, *The Discoverie of a Most Exquisite Jewel* (1652). 'Admirable Crichton' became synonymous with all-round talents, the ideal man; the phrase was used by J M Barrie for his play about a perfect butler, *The Admirable Crichton* (1902). >> **Urquhart**

Crick, Francis (Harry Compton) (1916–   ) Biophysicist, born in Northampton, Northamptonshire, C England, UK. He studied at London and Cambridge, and from 1949 carried on research in molecular biology at the Cavendish Laboratory. In 1953, with the help of X-ray diffraction photographs taken by Maurice Wilkins and Rosalind Franklin, he and J D Watson constructed a molecular model of the genetic material DNA. In 1958 he proposed that the DNA determines the sequence of amino acids in a polypeptide through a triplet code. He shared the 1962 Nobel Prize for Physiology or Medicine with Watson and Wilkins. >> Franklin, Rosalind; Levene; Watson, James; Wilkins, Maurice

Crile, George Washington [kriyl] (1864–1943) Surgeon and physiologist, born in Chili, OH. He spent much of his working life in Cleveland, OH, where he was founder and first director of the Cleveland Clinic Foundation (1921–40). He did important experimental work on the causes and prevention of surgical shock, and devised a method (which he called 'anoci-association') of combining drugs and anaesthetics which relaxed the patient and made surgical complications easier to control.

Crippen, Hawley Harvey, known as **Dr Crippen** (1862–1910) Murderer, born in Michigan. He studied medicine and dentistry, eventually settling in London, England, UK (1900) with his second wife, Cora Turner. Having transferred his affections to his secretary, Ethel le Neve, he poisoned his wife, dissected the body, and interred the remains in the cellar. He and his mistress attempted to escape to Canada on board the *SS Montrose* as Mr and Master Robinson. The suspicious captain contacted Scotland Yard by radiotelegraphy (the first use of radio for a murder case). They were arrested, and Crippen was hanged in London.

Cripps, Sir (Richard) Stafford (1889–1952) British statesman, born in London, England, UK. He studied at London University, was called to the bar in 1913, and made a fortune in patent and compensation cases. In 1930 he was appointed solicitor general in the second Labour government, and became an MP in 1931. During the 1930s he was associated with several extreme left-wing movements, and was expelled from the Labour Party in 1939 for his 'popular front' opposing Chamberlain's policy of appeasement. He sat as an independent MP during World War 2, was ambassador to the Soviet Union (1940–2), and in 1942 became Lord Privy Seal, and later minister of aircraft production. In the 1945 Labour government, he was readmitted to the Party and appointed President of the Board of Trade. In 1947 he became minister of economic affairs and then Chancellor of the Exchequer, introducing a successful austerity policy. In 1950 he resigned due to illness. >> Chamberlain, Neville

Crispi, Francesco [kreespee] (1819–1901) Italian statesman and prime minister (1887–90, 1893–6), born in Ribera, Sicily. He was called to the bar but, joining the revolutionary movement of 1848, had to flee to France. He organized the successful movement of 1859–60, and re-entered Sicily with Garibaldi. In the restored Kingdom of Italy he became deputy, president of the chamber, minister, and premier. >> Garibaldi; RR1065

Crispin, St (?–c. 287) Christian martyr. According to legend, under the reign of Diocletian he fled from Rome, with his brother **St Crispinian**, and worked as a shoemaker in Soissons, while striving to spread Christianity. He and his brother were martyred by being thrown into molten lead. They are the patron saints of shoemakers. Feast day 25 October. >> Diocletian

Cristofori, Bartolomeo [kristoforee] (1655–1731) Harpsichord-maker, born in Padua, Italy. He is usually credited with the invention of the pianoforte in c.1710.

Critias (c. 460–403 BC) Athenian orator and politician, a pupil of Socrates. In 411 BC he took part in the oligarchical revolution that set up the government of Four Hundred. Exiled in 406 BC, he returned two years later, and as a strong supporter of Sparta became one of the Thirty Tyrants set up by the Spartans after their defeat of Athens at the end of the Peloponnesian War (431–404 BC). He had a high reputation as an orator, and wrote poetry and tragedies. >> Socrates

Crivelli, Carlo [krivelee] (c.1430–c.1495) Painter of the Venetian school, born in Venice, Italy. Trained probably by the Vivarini family in Venice, where he was imprisoned for adultery, he spent most of his time working elsewhere in the Marches of Italy. His style is a highly individual combination of old-fashioned International Gothic opulence with the new Renaissance passion for setting figures in architectural frameworks and against landscapes. >> Vivarini

Croce, Benedetto [krohchay] (1866–1952) Philosopher, historian, and critic, born in Pescasseroli, Italy. He studied at Rome, and in Naples devoted himself at first to literature and antiquarian studies, founding the review, *La Critica* (1903), and making major contributions to idealistic aesthetics in his *Estetica* (1902, Aesthetic) and *La Poesia* (1936, Poetry). In 1910 he became senator, and was minister of education (1920–1) when, with the rise of Mussolini, he had to resign his professorship at Naples. He was opposed to totalitarianism, and with the fall of Mussolini (1943) helped to resurrect Liberal institutions in Italy. >> Mussolini

Crocker, Chester A(rthur) (1941–) US statesman, born in New York City. He studied at Ohio State and Johns Hopkins universities, and worked as a journalist, then as a lecturer at the American University (1969–70). During the Nixon administration, he served on the National Security Council (1970–2), then returned to academic life at Georgetown University, becoming its director of African studies in 1976. An expert on southern African politics, he joined the Reagan administration (1981–9) as assistant secretary of state for African affairs, helping to plan the peace settlement for Namibia. >> Nixon; Reagan

Crockett, Davy, popular name of **David Crockett** (1786–1836) Backwoodsman, born in Green Co, TN. He distinguished himself against the Creek Indians in Jackson's campaign of 1814, and was elected to the Tennessee state legislature (1821) and to the Congress (1826). He died fighting for Texas at the Battle of the Alamo. Highly embellished stories of his exploits have assumed mythological proportions. >> Jackson, Andrew

Crockett, Samuel Rutherford (1860–1914) Popular novelist, born in Little Duchrae, Dumfries and Galloway, SW Scotland, UK. He studied at Edinburgh University and New College, Edinburgh, and became a Free Church minister in Penicuik. He wrote sardonic congregational sketches, of which 24, collected as *The Stickit Minister* (1893), brought immediate fame. Resigning the ministry for full-time writing in 1895, he wrote a variety of books, including tales of mediaeval Scotland, European historical romances, and (often sensational) stories of mining, industrialism, and Edinburgh slums.

Crockford, William (1775–1844) British founder of a famous gaming club in London (1827). He was previously a fishmonger, but his successes at gambling led to a change in his fortunes. He is reputed to have won over £1 million at the game of hazard.

Croesus [kreesuhs] (?–c.546 BC) The last king of Lydia (c.560–546 BC), who succeeded his father, Alyattes. He made the Greeks of Asia Minor his tributaries, and extended his kingdom E from the Aegean to the Halys. His conquests and mines made his wealth proverbial. Cyrus II defeated and imprisoned him (546 BC), but his death is a mystery. >> Cyrus II

Croft, William (1678–1727) Organist and composer, born in Nether Ettington, Warwickshire, C England, UK. In 1700

he became a chorister in the Chapel Royal, and in 1707 sole organist. In 1708 he succeeded his teacher, John Blow, as organist of Westminster Abbey and choirmaster of the Chapel Royal. Thirty of his anthems for state ceremonies were printed in 1724. >> Blow, John

Croke, Thomas William (1824–1902) Clergyman, born in Ballyclough, Co Cork, Ireland. He studied at Paris and Rome, and is said to have fought at the barricades during the 1848 Revolution. A close friend of Cardinal Manning, he became Roman Catholic Bishop of Auckland, New Zealand (1870). In 1875 he was promoted Archbishop of Cashel and Emly. A strong nationalist, he backed the Gaelic League and the Land League. Croke Park in Dublin is named after him. >> Manning, Henry Edward

Croker, Richard, known as **Boss Croker** (1841–1922) US politician, born in Co Cork, Ireland. His family emigrated to New York when he was a child. He entered New York City politics in 1862, secured control of the Tammany Hall machine in 1886, and dominated Democratic Party politics for the next 16 years, surviving a major corruption scandal in 1894. After the election of the reforming idealist Seth Low (1850–1916) as mayor in 1901, he left the USA (1903), and spent the rest of his life on a large estate in Ireland.

Croker, Thomas Crofton (1798–1854) Antiquary and folklorist, born in Cork, Co Cork, Ireland. He worked as a clerk at the Admiralty (1818–59). In 1825 he published his *Fairy Legends and Traditions of the South of Ireland* anonymously, a work which charmed Sir Walter Scott and was translated into German by the brothers Grimm (1826). A second series followed in 1827. >> Grimm brothers; Scott, Walter

Crome, John, known as **Old Crome** (1768–1821) Landscape painter, chief of the Norwich School, born in Norwich, Norfolk, E England, UK. He was apprenticed to a house painter (1783), then became a drawing master, and founded the Norwich Society of Artists (1803). His subjects derived from the scenery of Norfolk, such as 'Poringland Oak' and 'Mousehold Heath' (Tate, London).

Cromer, Evelyn Baring, 1st Earl of [krohmer] (1841–1917) Colonial administrator, born in Cromer, Norfolk, E England, UK. He became British controller-general of Egyptian finance (1879–80), finance minister of India (1880–3), and agent and consul-general in Egypt (1883–1907). He reformed Egyptian administration and agricultural policies, and put its finances on a sound footing.

Crompton, Richmal, pseudonym of **Richmal Samuel Lamburn** (1890–1969) Writer of children's books, born in Bury, Greater Manchester, NW England, UK. She studied at London, and taught Classics at Bromley High School until she contracted poliomyelitis in 1923. She wrote the first of the 'William' books (*Just William*) in 1922, and had written 40 of them before her death.

Crompton, Rookes Evelyn Bell (1845–1940) Engineer, born near Thirsk, North Yorkshire, N England, UK. After army service in India, he became involved in the generation and distribution of electricity for lighting, on which he became an international authority. He strongly supported standardization in industry, and was involved in the establishment of the National Physical Laboratory and in what is now the British Standards Institution.

Crompton, Samuel (1753–1827) Inventor of the spinning-mule, born in Firwood, Greater Manchester, NW England, UK. In 1779 he devised a machine which produced yarn of such astonishing fineness that the house was beset by persons eager to know the secret. He had no funds to obtain a patent, so he was forced to sell his idea to a Bolton manufacturer for very little return. The mule was such a great success that he was awarded a national grant of £5000 in 1812. His later ventures, in bleaching and cotton, were failures.

Cromwell, Oliver see panel on p. 241

Cromwell, Richard (1626–1712) English statesman, the third son of Oliver Cromwell. He served in the parliamentary army, sat in parliament (1654, 1656), and was a member of the Council of State (1657). In 1658 he succeeded his father as Lord Protector (his two elder brothers having died); but he soon fell out with parliament, which he dissolved in 1659. He recalled the Rump Parliament of 1653, but found the task of ruling beyond him, and was forced to abdicate in 1659. After the Restoration (1660) he lived in France and Geneva, under the alias 'John Clarke', but returned to England in 1680, and spent the rest of his life in Cheshunt, SE England, UK. >> Cromwell, Oliver; Monk, George

Cromwell, Thomas, Earl of Essex (c. 1485–1540) English statesman, born in London, England, UK, known as *malleus monachorum*, 'the hammer of the monks'. He served as a soldier on the European mainland (1504–12), then entered Wolsey's service in 1514, and became his agent and secretary. He arranged Henry VIII's divorce from Catherine of Aragon, and put into effect the Act of Supremacy (1534) and the dissolution of the monasteries (1536–9). He became privy councillor (1531), Chancellor of the Exchequer (1533), secretary of state and Master of the Rolls (1534), vicar-general (1535), Lord Privy Seal and Baron Cromwell of Oakham (1536), Knight of the Garter and dean of Wells (1537), Lord Great Chamberlain (1539), and finally Earl of Essex (1540). In each of his offices, he proved himself a highly efficient administrator and adviser to the king; but Henry's aversion to Anne of Cleves, consort of Cromwell's choosing, led to his ruin. He was sent to the Tower and beheaded. >> Catherine of Aragon; Henry VIII; Wolsey

Cronenberg, David (1943–) Film director and screenplay writer, born in Toronto, Ontario, Canada. He studied at the University of Toronto, and went on to become one of the most prolific and acclaimed exponents of the horror film genre to have emerged in recent years. His work is often stylish and experimental, with plots typically concerning the aftermath of some disastrous biological mishap, as in the highly successful *The Dead Zone* (1983) and *The Fly* (1986), which gave him cult status. Other films include *Rabid* (1977), *Scanners* (1981), *Dead Ringers* (1988), and the controversial *Crash* (1996).

Cronin, A(rchibald) J(oseph) [krohnin] (1896–1981) Novelist, born in Cardross, Argyll and Bute, W Scotland, UK. He studied medicine at Glasgow (1919), but in 1930 took up literature, and at once was successful with *Hatter's Castle* (1931). Subsequent works include *The Citadel* (1937) and *The Keys of the Kingdom* (1942). Several of his books were filmed, and the television series *Dr Finlay's Casebook* was based on his stories.

Cronin, James Watson [krohnin] (1931–) Physicist, born in Chicago, IL. He studied at Southern Methodist and Chicago universities, then worked at Brookhaven National Laboratory, NY. He taught at Princeton (1958–71), then became professor at Chicago University. In 1964 with Val Fitch he demonstrated the non-conservation of parity and charge conjugation in certain atomic particle reactions. This surprising result is of fundamental interest in particle physics, and they shared the Nobel Prize for Physics in 1980. >> Fitch, Val

Cronje, Piet [kronyay] (1835–1911) Boer general, born in Colesberg, South Africa. He was a leader in the Boer Wars (1881, 1899–1900), defeated Methuen at Magersfontein, but surrendered to Lord Roberts at Paardeberg (1900). >> Roberts, Frederick Sleigh

Cronkite, Walter (Leland), Jr [krongkiyt] (1916–) Journalist and broadcaster, born in St Joseph, MO. A student at

OLIVER CROMWELL (1599–1658)

Oliver Cromwell was born in Huntingdon, Cambridgeshire, to a strongly Protestant family. He was the younger son of Henry Cromwell of Hinchinbrook, who became a member of one of Queen Elizabeth's parliaments, and his wife, Elizabeth Steward, the daughter of Sir Thomas Steward of Ely. His first cousin was the great parliamentarian, John Hampden. Cromwell's education was strongly Calvinist and anti-Catholic. He went to study at Cambridge, but left there at 18 to take care of his mother after his father's death. He then briefly studied law at Lincoln's Inn. In 1620 he married Elizabeth Bourchier, the daughter of a prosperous London merchant, with whom he had four daughters and five sons.

Cromwell sat as MP for Huntingdon in the stormy parliament of 1628–9, during which he became a convinced critic of King Charles I. After the dissolution of parliament by the King, he farmed on his small estate at Huntingdon, then at St Ives and later at Ely, where he had been left property by an uncle (1638). He sat for Cambridge during the Short Parliament of 1640, and during the Long Parliament was a vehement supporter of Puritanism.

When war broke out (1642) between the King's forces and the parliamentarians, he fought for the latter at Edgehill. He formed his unconquerable Ironsides force, combining rigid discipline with strict morality, and it was his cavalry that secured the victory at Marston Moor (1644). He also led the New Model Army to decisive success at Naseby (1645) under Fairfax. Then he marched on London to coerce the Presbyterians in parliament, and was probably responsible for abducting the King from Holmby (1647). He failed to persuade Charles I to accept constitutional limitations, and the King fled from captivity at Hampton Court Palace to the Isle of Wight to negotiate with the Scots his return to the throne. The Royalists took up arms again, and the second Civil War broke out. Cromwell quelled the Welsh insurrection in support of Charles I, and defeated the invading army of

Hamilton. He then brought the King to trial, and was one of the signatories of his death warrant (1649).

After Charles' execution, the monarchy was abolished and the Commonwealth established, with Cromwell as chairman of the Council of State. As army commander and Lord-Lieutenant of Ireland, he ruthlessly concluded the ongoing fighting there by storming Drogheda and Wexford and massacring their garrisons (1649). In 1650 he turned his attention to Scotland, where Charles II had been acclaimed King, finally subduing the Scots at Dunbar (1650) and Worcester (1651). The latter battle effectively ended the Civil War, and united the three kingdoms of England, Scotland, and Ireland.

In 1653 he dissolved the Rump of the Long Parliament and, after the failure of his Puritan Convention (Barebone's Parliament), established a Protectorate (1653). He refused the offer of the crown in 1657. At home he reorganized the national Church and established Puritanism, but permitted religious toleration: he readmitted Jews into Britain, allowed private use of the Book of Common Prayer, and did not make things much worse for the English Catholics than they had been before; the fiery zeal of his youth gave way to a more tolerant pragmitism. He also provided judicial administration in Scotland (which prospered under his rule), and gave Ireland parliamentary representation. Under him the Commonwealth became the head and champion of Protestant Europe. In his foreign policy he ended the war with Portugal (1653) and Holland (1654); made treaties with France against Spain (1655, 1657); defeated the Spanish at the Battle of the Dunes (1658), and took Dunkirk.

Cromwell died in London, and was buried in the tomb of the kings at Westminster Abbey. After the restoration in 1660 he was convicted of treason; his body was disinterred and hung from the gallows at Tyburn. He was succeeded by his son Richard, who was forced into exile in France in 1659. >> Charles I / II (of England); Cromwell, Richard; Hampden

---

Texas University (1933–5), he became a radio news and sports reporter in Kansas City. Employed by the United Press (1939–48), he provided vivid eye-witness accounts of the war in Europe. At CBS from 1950, he hosted a number of shows and narrated *You Are There* (1953–6), but became a national institution as the anchorman of the *CBS Evening News* (1962–81), where his studious impartiality and straightforward reporting earned him a reputation for honesty and trust.

Cronstedt, Axel Fredrik, Baron [kronstet] (1722–65) Metallurgist, born in Turinge, Sweden. He first isolated nickel (1751) and noted its magnetic properties. He made a useful chemical classification of minerals, and also discovered a zeolite (a water-softening silicate).

Crook, George (1829–90) US soldier, born in Ohio. He fought on the Federal side in the Civil War (1861–5), commanding the army of West Virginia in 1864. In the Indian Wars he captured Cochise and pacified the Apaches (1871), fought in the Sioux War (1876), and fought the Apaches again under Geronimo (1882–6). >> Cochise; Geronimo

Crookes, Sir William (1832–1919) Chemist and physicist, born in London, England, UK. He studied at London, then superintended the meteorological department of the Radcliffe Observatory, Oxford, and from 1855 lectured on

chemistry at Chester. In 1859 he founded the *Chemical News*, and edited it until 1906. He was an authority on sanitation, discovered the metal thallium (1861), improved vacuum tubes and promoted electric lighting, and invented the radiometer (1873–6). He was knighted in 1897.

Cropsey, Jasper (Francis) (1823–1900) Painter, born in Staten Island, NY. He studied architecture, but after travelling in Europe (1847, 1856), he settled in Hastings-on-Hudson, NY (1864), and concentrated on landscape painting. Considered a member of the Hudson River school, his theatrical and naturalistic canvases, such as 'View of the Kaaterskill House' (1855) and 'Autumn on the Hudson River' (1860), reveal his Romantic approach to nature. >> Kensett

Crosby, Bing, popular name of **Harry Lillis Crosby** (1904–77) Singer and film star, born in Tacoma, WA. He began his career while still at school, playing the drums in the evenings, and later became one of the trio known as Paul Whiteman's Rhythm Boys. He began to make films, specializing in light comedy roles, and his distinctive style of crooning made him one of the best-known names in the entertainment world. His recordings of 'White Christmas' and 'Silent Night' were the hits of the century. He starred in many films, notably the *Road* films with Bob Hope and Dorothy Lamour (1914–96), and he won an Oscar for *Going My Way* (1944). Later films include *The Bells of St Mary's* (1945), *White Christmas* (1954), and *High Society* (1956). A keen golfer, he continued to perform and give concerts until his death on a golf course in Spain. >> Hope, Bob

Crosby, Fanny popular name of **Frances Jane Crosby**, later **Mrs Van Alstyne** (1820–1915) Hymn writer, born in Southeast, NY. Blind from infancy, she was pupil and teacher in New York City's Institute for the Blind. She composed about 6000 popular hymns, including 'Safe in the Arms of Jesus' (played at President Grant's funeral) and 'Pass Me Not, O Gentle Saviour' (reportedly a favourite of Queen Victoria). Moody and Sankey acknowledged a great debt to her. >> Moody

Crosland, Tony, popular name of **(Charles) Anthony Raven Crosland** (1918–77) British statesman, born in St Leonards, East Sussex, SE England, UK. He studied at Oxford, where he also taught after serving in World War 2. He was elected a Labour MP in 1950 and became secretary for education and science (1965–7), President of the Board of Trade (1967–9), secretary for local government and regional planning (1969–70), environment secretary (1974–6), and foreign secretary (1976–7). A strong supporter of Hugh Gaitskell, he was a key member of the revisionist wing of the Labour Party, and wrote one of its seminal texts, *The Future of Socialism* (1956). >> Gaitskell

Cross, Charles (Frederick) (1855–1935) British chemist. With Edward Bevan he invented the modern method of producing artificial silk. >> Bevan, Edward

Crossley, Sir Francis (1817–72) Carpet manufacturer and philanthropist, born in Halifax, West Yorkshire, N England, UK. He was Liberal MP for Halifax (1852–9), then for the West Riding, and presented a public park (1857), almshouses, and an orphanage to Halifax.

Crossman, Richard (Howard Stafford) (1907–74) British statesman, born in Cropredy, Oxfordshire, SC England, UK. He studied at Oxford, where he became a philosophy tutor, and was leader of the Labour group on Oxford City Council (1934–40). In 1938 he joined the staff of the *New Statesman*. In 1945 he became a Labour MP, and under Wilson was minister of housing and local government (1964–6), then secretary of state for social services and head of the Department of Health (1968–70). He was editor of the *New Statesman* (1970–2). His best-known work is his series of political diaries, begun in 1952, keeping a detailed record of the day-to-day workings of government. They were published in four volumes (1975–81), despite attempts to suppress them. >> Wilson, Harold

Crothers, Rachel (1878–1958) Playwright, born in Bloomington, IL. Following a university education at Illinois State (1892), she studied dramatic art in Boston and New York City. Her first play, *The Three of Us* (1906), was the first of many successful works in which she wrote sensitively and good-humouredly about the position of women in contemporary US society.

Crowley, Aleister, originally **Edward Alexander Crowley** (1875–1947) British writer and 'magician'. He became interested in the occult while an undergraduate at Cambridge, and later founded the order known as the Silver Star. He travelled widely, settling for some years in Sicily with a group of disciples at the Abbey of Thelema, near Cefalù. Rumours of drugs, orgies, and magical ceremonies led to his expulsion from Italy. He liked to be known as 'the great beast' and 'the wickedest man alive' – and certainly many who associated with him died tragically.

Crowley, Bob, popular name of **Robert Crowley** (1954–) British stage designer. He has worked at the Bristol Old Vic, the Royal Exchange, Manchester, Greenwich Theatre,

and the National Theatre, where he designed Bill Bryden's revival of *A Midsummer Night's Dream* (1982) and Howard Davies's production of Ibsen's *Hedda Gabler* (1989). He has also worked extensively at the Royal Shakespeare Company.

Crowther, Geoffrey Crowther, Baron [krowther] (1907–72) Economist, born in Claymont, DE. He studied at Cambridge, Yale, and Columbia universities. He was on the staff of *The Economist* from 1932, becoming its editor (1938–56). The *Crowther Report* (1959), produced during his period as chairman of the Central Advisory Council for Education (1956–60), recommended the raising of the school-leaving age to 16, and was the first British education report to consider the implications of economic and social change for the education of young people.

Crowther, Samuel (Adjai) [krowther] (c.1809–91) Missionary, born in Ochugu, West Africa. He was carried off as a slave in 1819, and sold more than once, but rescued by a British man-of-war and landed at Sierra Leone in 1822. He was baptized in 1825, and accompanied the Niger expeditions of 1841 and 1854. He was the first African to be ordained by the Church Missionary Society (1842), and was consecrated bishop of the Niger territory in 1864.

Cruden, Alexander [krooden] (1701–70) Scholar and bookseller, born in Aberdeen, NE Scotland, UK. He worked as a tutor, then started as a bookseller in London. In 1737 appeared his *Concordance of the Holy Scriptures*. He suffered from bouts of insanity and, assuming the title of 'Alexander the Corrector', from 1755 went through the country reproving Sabbath-breaking and profanity.

Cruft, Charles (1852–1939) British showman who organized the first dog show in London, England, UK in 1886. He was for many years general manager of James Spratt. The annual shows have since become world-famous, and have helped to improve standards of dog-breeding.

Cruickshank, Andrew [krukshangk] (1907–88) Actor, born in Aberdeen, NE Scotland, UK. Educated at Aberdeen Grammar School, he was intended for a career in civil engineering, but found his way into provincial repertory theatres instead. He reached the London stage in 1935, where he took part in several long-running plays. He became known worldwide for his portrayal of Dr Cameron in the BBC television series *Dr Finlay's Casebook*.

Cruikshank, George [krookshangk] (1792–1878) Caricaturist and illustrator, born in London, England, UK. He often contributed to topical magazines, and illustrated several children's books. His best-known work includes Grimm's *German Popular Stories* (1824–6) and Dickens's *Oliver Twist* (1837–9). In his later years he used his etchings and oil paintings in a vigorous protest against drunkenness, as in the series for 'The Bottle' (1847).

Cruise, Tom [krooz] (1962–) Film actor, born in Syracuse, NY. After an itinerant childhood, his plans for a professional wrestling career were abandoned through injury. He tried his hand at acting, struggling through night classes and auditions, and went on to make many successful films including *Top Gun* (1985), *Rain Man* (1988), *Days of Thunder* (1990), *A Few Good Men* (1992), *The Firm* (1993), and *Interview with the Vampire* (1995). He received Golden Globe Awards and Oscar nominations for best actor for both *Born on the Fourth of July* (1989) and *Jerry Maguire* (1996).

Crutzen, Paul (1933–) Chemist, born in Amsterdam. He studied at Stockholm University, then joined the Max Planck Institute for Chemistry in Mainz, Germany. In 1970 he was among the first to draw attention to the vulnerability of the ozone layer, and demonstrated that the presence of nitrogen oxides increase the rate of ozone's decomposition. He shared the 1995 Nobel Prize for Chemistry with Mario Molina and Sherwood Rowland. >> Molina, Mario; Rowland, Sherwood

Cruveilhier, Jean [krüvaylyay] (1791–1874) Anatomist, born in Limoges, France. A pioneer of the descriptive method, he was the first to describe multiple sclerosis and progressive muscular atrophy (*Cruveilhier's paralyses*). He became professor of pathology at Montpellier in 1824, and of pathological anatomy in Paris in 1836.

Cruyff, Johann [kriyf] (1947–) Footballer, born in Amsterdam. He joined his first club, Ajax, at the age of 10, and at 19 made his debut in the Dutch League. He won 11 Dutch League and Cup medals with Ajax, and helped them to three consecutive European Cup successes (1971–3). In 1973 he joined Barcelona (Spain) and won Spanish League and Cup medals with them. He captained Holland in the 1974 World Cup final (beaten by West Germany). He returned to Holland as a player in 1983, joining Feyenoord in 1984, but moved back to Barcelona as manager in 1988, guiding the Spanish champions to the European Cup for the first time in 1992. >> RR1156

Crystal, Billy (1947–) Film actor, born in Long Beach, NY. A successful stand-up comic, he played television's first openly gay character in the comedy series *Soap*, before becoming established as a feature film actor in films such as *Throw Momma From The Train* (1987), and *When Harry Met Sally* (1989). Later films include *City Slickers* and its sequel (1991, 1994), *Forget Paris* (1995), which he also directed, and *Fathers' Day* (1997).

Ctesias [tesias] (5th-c BC) Greek historian and physician. He was physician to Artaxerxes II Mnemon of Persia, and accompanied him in the expedition against his rebellious brother Cyrus (401 BC). He wrote a history of Persia in 23 books, *Persika*, of which only fragments remain. >> Cyrus (the Younger)

Ctesibius [tesibius] (2nd-c BC) Alexandrian Greek, the inventor of the force-pump and water organ, and improver of the clepsydra or water-clock. He was the teacher of Hero of Alexandria. >> Hero of Alexandria

Cuauhtémoc [kwowtaymok] (c. 1495–1525) The last Aztec ruler, successor to Montezuma, who resisted the Spaniards under Cortés at the siege of Tenochitlán (now Mexico City) in 1521. He was later executed while on an expedition with Cortés to Honduras. >> Cortés; Montezuma; RR1075

Cubitt, Thomas (1788–1855) Builder, born in Buxton, Derbyshire, C England, UK. He revolutionized trade practices in the building industry, and with his brother **Lewis Cubitt** (1799–1883) was responsible for many large London projects, including Belgravia and the E front of Buckingham Palace.

Cubitt, Sir William (1785–1861) Civil engineer, born in Dilham, Norfolk, E England, UK. He was a miller, a cabinetmaker, and a millwright until 1812, and then chief engineer in Robert Ransome's Orwell Works at Ipswich, in which he was a partner (1821–6). He moved to London in 1823. His constructions include the Bute Docks at Cardiff, the Southeastern Railway, and the Berlin waterworks. Lord Mayor of London (1860–1), Cubitt Town on the Isle of Dogs is named after him.

Cudworth, Ralph (1617–88) Philosopher and theologian, born in Aller, Somerset, SW England, UK. He studied at Cambridge, where he became a tutor, and leader of the 'Cambridge Platonists'. He was professor of Hebrew (1645), rector of North Cadbury, Somerset (1650), and Master of Christ's College (1654). His best-known work, *The True Intellectual System of the Universe* (1678), aimed to establish the reality of a supreme divine intelligence against materialism. >> More, Henry; Whichcote

Cuellar, Javier Pérez de >> **Pérez de Cuellar, Javier**

Cueva, Juan de la [kwayva] (c. 1550–c. 1607) Poet and playwright, born in Seville, Spain. He is known especially for his use of new metrical forms and his introduction of historical material into drama.

Cugnot, Nicolas Joseph [koonyoh] (1725–1804) Military engineer, born in Poid, France. About 1770 he invented a three-wheeled steamdriven artillery carriage with a speed of 2–3 mph. Lack of support prevented further development.

Cui, César Antonovich [kwee] (1835–1918) Composer, born in Vilna, Lithuania. An expert on fortification, he became lieutenant-general of engineers. Practically a self-taught musician, he composed *William Ratcliff* (1861) and other operas, as well as songs and piano music. He was associated with Borodin and others as one of 'The Five' in Russian music.

Cukor, George D(ewey) [kooker] (1899–1983) Film director, born in New York City. He worked first on Broadway, but went to Hollywood in 1929, starting a career of 50 years directing with *Girls About Town* (1931) and *Little Women* (1933). He was particularly successful with the great actresses of the star system – Garbo, Crawford, Hepburn – but his range was wide, including *Gaslight* (1944), *A Star is Born* (1954), and *My Fair Lady* (1964, Oscar). His last film was *Rich and Famous* (1981).

Culbertson, Ely (1891–1955) Contract bridge authority, born in Romania. He developed contract bridge's first successful bidding system, and established himself as the world's best player in a 1931–2 win. A revolutionary as a youth, he devised a peace plan in 1940, including ideas later adopted by the UN.

Cullberg, Birgit Ragnhild (1908–) Dancer, choreographer, and ballet director, born in Nyköping, Sweden. She studied in England with Kurt Jooss, and later in New York with Martha Graham. In the mid-1940s she toured the European mainland with Svenska Dansteatern, a group she co-founded with Ivo Cramér (1921–44). She was resident choreographer of the Royal Swedish Ballet (1952–7), and formed the Cullberg Ballet at the Swedish National Theatre in 1967. >> Graham, Martha; Jooss

Cullen, Countée (Porter) (1903–46) Poet, born in New York City. A leader of the Harlem Renaissance, he began his literary career with *Color* (1925). He published several other volumes of verse, a novel *One Way to Heaven* (1932), and collaborated with Arna Bontemps (1902–73) in the play *St Louis Woman* (1946).

Cullen, Paul (1803–78) Roman Catholic clergyman, born in Prospect, Co Kildare, Ireland. He studied in Rome, was ordained in 1829, and was successively vice-rector and rector of the Irish College in Rome, and rector of the College of Propaganda. Consecrated Archbishop of Armagh and Primate of Ireland (1850), he helped to found the Catholic University in 1854, and Clonliffe College (the Dublin diocesan seminary) in 1859. He was created a cardinal priest in 1866, the first Irishman to attain that dignity.

Cullen, William (1710–90) Physician, born in Hamilton, South Lanarkshire, WC Scotland, UK. He studied at Edinburgh, and in 1740 set up as a physician in Glasgow, where he was appointed to the chair of medicine (1751). In 1755 he moved to Edinburgh, occupying a series of chairs in chemistry and medicine. He is largely responsible for the recognition of the important part played by the nervous system in health and disease.

Cullman, Oscar (1902–) Biblical scholar and theologian, born in Strasbourg, France. As professor at Basel (from 1938) and Paris (from 1948), he was the chief representative in New Testament studies of the 'biblical theology' movement in the 1950s and 1960s. An exponent within the German school of the concept of salvation-history (*Heilsgeschichte*), he maintained that biblical thinking is essentially historical: God reveals Himself in historical events, not the isolated personal challenges of Bultmann's existential demythologizing approach. >> Bultmann

Culmann, Karl (1821–81) Engineer, born in Bergzabern, Germany. He studied at the Polytechnikum in Karlsruhe, and from 1855 taught at the polytechnic institute in Zürich. His principal work was in graphical statics, which he systematized and elevated into a major method of structural analysis, introducing the use of force and funicular polygons and the method of sections.

Culpeper, John >> **Colepeper, John**

Culpeper, Nicholas (1616–54) Astrologer, born in London, England, UK. He studied at Cambridge, and in 1640 began to practise astrology in Spitalfields. In 1649 he published an English translation of the College of Physicians' Pharmacopoeia, *A Physical Directory*, and in 1653 appeared *The English Physician Enlarged, or the Herbal*. Both books had an enormous sale.

Cumberland, Richard (1631–1718) Philosopher and theologian, born in London, England, UK. He studied at Cambridge, and was successively rector of Brampton, Northamptonshire (1658), vicar of All Saints, Stamford (1667), and Bishop of Peterborough (1691). He is associated with the Cambridge Platonists. His *De legibus naturae* (1672, On the Laws of Nature) was written as a direct response to Hobbes, and in some respects anticipated utilitarianism in espousing a principle of universal benevolence. >> Hobbes

Cumberland, Richard (1732–1811) Playwright, born in Cambridge, Cambridgeshire, EC England, UK. He went to Trinity College, Cambridge, and was a fellow at 20. Becoming private secretary to Lord Halifax in 1761, he became secretary to the Board of Trade (1776–82). Thereafter he retired to Tunbridge Wells, where he wrote farces, tragedies, comedies, pamphlets, essays and two novels, *Arundel* and *Henry*. His plays include *The Brothers* (1769), *The Jew* (1794), and *The Wheel of Fortune (1795)*. He was caricatured by Sheridan in *The Critic* as Sir Fretful Plagiary.

Cumberland, William Augustus, Duke of (1721–65) British general, born in London, England, UK, the second son of George II. He adopted a military career and, in the War of the Austrian Succession (1740–8), was wounded at Dettingen (1743) and defeated at Fontenoy (1745). He crushed the Young Pretender's rebellion at Culloden (1746), and by his harsh policies afterwards earned the lasting title of 'Butcher'. In the Seven Years' War (1756–63), he surrendered to the French (1757), and thereafter retired. >> George II; Stuart, Charles

Cummings, E(dward) E(stlin) (1894–1962) Writer and painter, born in Cambridge, MA. He studied at Harvard, served in World War 1 in France, then studied art at Paris. His writings attracted more interest than his paintings (though a collection of his work was published in 1931). His several successful collections of poetry, starting with *Tulips and Chimneys* (1923), are striking for their unorthodox typography and linguistic style. *Complete Poems* appeared in 1968. He also wrote a travel diary, a morality play, *Santa Claus* (1946), and a collection of six 'non-lectures' delivered at Harvard entitled *i* (1953). His best-known prose work, *The Enormous Room* (1922), describes his wartime internment in France.

Cunard, Sir Samuel [kyoo**nah(r)d**] (1787–1865) Shipowner, born in Halifax, Nova Scotia, Canada. He succeeded early as a merchant and shipowner, and emigrated to Britain in 1838. For the new steam rail service between Britain and America, he joined with George Burns in Glasgow and David McIver in Liverpool to found (1839) the British and North American Royal Mail Steam Packet Company, later known as the Cunard Line.

Cunliffe, Barry, popular name of **Barrington Windsor**

Cunliffe (1939–) Archaeologist, born in Portsmouth, Hampshire, S England, UK. He studied at Cambridge, taught at Bristol and Southampton, and in 1972 became professor of European archaeology at Oxford. He established a reputation in his 20s with excavations at the Roman palace of Fishbourne near Chichester (1961–7). He has since worked to notable effect in Roman Bath and at various sites in Wessex. Among his general books are *The Celtic World* (1979), *Greeks, Romans and Barbarians* (1988), and *Iron Age Britain* (1995).

Cunningham, Sir Alan Gordon (1887–1983) British soldier, born in Dublin, the brother of Andrew Browne Cunningham. He trained at the Royal Military Academy, and served with distinction in World War 2. From Kenya in 1941 he struck through Italian Somaliland, and freed Abyssinia and British Somaliland from the Italians. He later served as high commissioner for Palestine (1945–8). >> Cunningham, Andrew Browne

Cunningham, Allan (1791–1839) Botanist and explorer, born in London, England, UK. He became clerk to the curator of Kew Gardens, and plant collector for Sir Joseph Banks, first in Brazil, then in New South Wales (1816), where he worked for 15 years. His writings and most of his collections are preserved at Kew, and many indigenous Australian trees now bear his name. >> Banks, Joseph

Cunningham (of Hyndhope), Andrew Browne Cunningham, 1st Viscount (1883–1963) British naval commander, the brother of Sir Alan Cunningham. He trained at Dartmouth, and entered the navy in 1898. In World War 2 he was admiral commander-in-chief of British naval forces in the Mediterranean (1939–43), and commanded Allied naval forces for the invasion of North Africa (1942) and Italy (1942). He was promoted Admiral of the Fleet in 1943, and was First Sea Lord (1943–6). >> Cunningham, Alan

Cunningham, Imogen (1883–1976) Photographer, born in Portland, OR. After working with Edward Curtis, she opened her own portrait studio in Seattle in 1910, but her personal style was pictorial Romanticism, particularly in still-life flower studies. In 1932 she met Edward Weston and was converted to his 'straight photography' purists, Group f/64, which insisted on sharply-defined images and precise tonal gradation. After the break-up of the Group she continued with her portrait gallery for almost another 40 years, and in her 90s was still teaching at the Art Institute in San Francisco. >> Curtis, Edward; Weston

Cunningham, John (1917–) Military and civil aircraft pilot, born in Croydon, S Greater London, England, UK. He attended the Whitgift School and was apprenticed to the De Havilland Aircraft Company at Hatfield (1935–8). He became a group captain in 1944, specializing in night defence against German bombers, earning the title 'Cat's Eyes Cunningham' during this period. After World War 2 he became chief test pilot of the De Havilland Aircraft Company (1946–78) and then the chairman of the De Havilland Flying Foundation.

Cunningham, Merce (1919–) Dancer, choreographer, teacher, and director, born in Centralia, WA. He experienced a range of dance forms before attending the Bennington School of Dance to study modern dance. He danced with the Martha Graham Company (1939–45), and started his own company in 1952. He is one of the major figures in the development of a concern with form and abstraction in modern dance and has received many awards.

Cunninghame Graham, Robert Bontine (1852–1936) Writer and politician, born in London, England, UK. He studied at Harrow, and from 1869 was chiefly engaged in ranching in the Argentine, until he succeeded to the family estates in Scotland in 1883. He was Liberal MP for North-West

Lanarkshire (1886–92), and the first president of the Scottish Labour Party in 1888. He wrote a great number of travel books, but is best known for his essays and short stories. He was elected the first president of the National Party of Scotland in 1928, and of the Scottish National Party in 1934. He died in Argentina, where he was known as 'Don Roberto'.

Cunobelinus >> **Cymbeline**

Cuomo, Mario [**kwoh**moh] (1932–) US politician, born in New York City. He studied at St John's University, NY, and became Governor of New York State (1983–94). He was often mentioned as a possible presidential candidate in 1984, 1988, and 1992.

Cupitt, Don (1934–) Anglican clergyman and theologian. He studied at Cambridge, and was a curate in Salford (1959–62) before returning to Cambridge, where he became dean of Emmanuel College (1966–91). His publications include *Crisis of Moral Authority* (1972), *The Sea of Faith* (1984) to accompany the television series of the same name, *The New Christian Ethics* (1988), and *Solar Ethics* (1995).

Curie, Marie [**kyoo**ree], *née* **Manya Sklodowska** (1867–1934) Physicist, born in Warsaw, who worked in Paris with her French husband **Pierre Curie** (1859–1906) on magnetism and radioactivity, and discovered radium. She emigrated to France in 1891, and studied at the Sorbonne. Her husband, who also studied at the Sorbonne, became professor of physics there in 1901. Pierre and his brother, **Jacques Curie**, discovered piezoelectricity. For her thesis she studied the 'rays' earlier discovered by Becquerel. Pierre and Marie Curie shared the 1903 Nobel Prize for Physics with Becquerel for the discovery of radioactivity. After her husband's death in a road accident (1906), Mme Curie succeeded to his chair, isolated polonium and radium in 1910, and was awarded the Nobel Prize for Chemistry in 1911. She died of leukaemia, probably caused by long exposure to radiation. >> Becquerel; Joliot-Curie

Curl, Robert, Jr (1933–) Chemist, born in Alice, TX. He studied at the University of California, Berkeley, moving to Rice University, Houston, in 1958. He shared the Nobel Prize for Chemistry in 1996 for his contribution to the discovery of fullerenes (1985). >> Kroto; Smalley

Curlewis, Sir Adrian Herbert [ker**loo**is] (1901–85) Judge, surf life-saver, and administrator, born in Sydney, New South Wales, Australia. He studied law at Sydney University, and became a judge of the New South Wales district court (1948–71). He was president of the Surf Life-Saving Association of Australia (1933–74), and president of the International Council of Surf Life-Saving (1956–73).

Curley, James Michael (1874–1958) US representative and mayor, born in Boston, MA. He left high school, continuing his education in the public library, and became a powerful orator, campaigning against Democratic political bosses. He served in the US House of Representatives as a Democrat (1911–14), then left to run for Mayor of Boston, defeating 'Honey Fitz' Fitzgerald. As mayor (1914–18, 1922–6, 1930–4), he funded massive public works projects, and as Governor of Massachusetts championed social welfare legislation while bribery charges against him were investigated. Convicted in 1937, he received contributions from Bostonians to pay his fine. Indicted for influence peddling while back in the US House of Representatives (1943–5), he left to become Mayor of Boston again (1945–9), serving five months in jail midterm, until pardoned by President Truman. His political career finished, he wrote *I'd Do It Again* (1957), and inspired Edwin O'Connor's novel, *The Last Hurrah* (1956). >> Fitzgerald, John Francis

Curnonsky [koorn**ö**skee], pseudonym of **Maurice Edmond Saillant** (1872–1956) French gourmet and journalist. One of the first to write about 'good food' and where to find it, he published *La France gastronomique* (28 vols, 1921–8) and

Le Trésorier gastronomique de France (1933). In 1940 he founded the journal *Cuisine et vins de France*, and in 1953 published a book of the same name.

Curran, John Philpot (1750–1817) Lawyer and orator, born in Newmarket, Co Cork, Ireland. He studied at Trinity College, Dublin, and Middle Temple, London, and was called to the Irish bar in 1775, where he earned a considerable reputation for his wit and powers of advocacy. He entered the Irish parliament in 1783, and strongly opposed the Union, which he described as 'the annihilation of Ireland'. He later became Master of the Rolls in Ireland (1806–14).

Curry, John (Anthony) (1949–94) Ice skater, born in Birmingham, West Midlands, C England, UK. He began skating when a child, was British junior figure-skating champion (1967), and British national champion (1970). He competed in various world-class competitions, set a new standard for artistic interpretation by introducing ballet-like movements into the free-skating routine, and won the gold medal for men's figure skating in his second winter Olympic Games (1976). He later turned professional and formed the John Curry Theatre of Skating and the School of Skating (1978). >> RR1162

Curry, John (Steuart) (1897–1946) Painter, born in Jefferson Co, KS. He studied at the Art Institute of Chicago (1916–18), made drawings for the Ringling Brothers Circus in 1932, and later became artist in residence at the University of Wisconsin (1936–46). 'Tornado Over Kansas' (1933) is a fine example of his populist subject matter, and 'The Mississipi' (1935) demonstrates his sensitivity to social issues.

Curthose, Robert >> **Robert Curthose**

Curtice, Harlowe H(erbert) (1893–1962) Automobile industry executive, born in Petrieville, MI. In a 44-year career at General Motors he began as a bookkeeper, headed the AC Spark Plug and Buick divisions, and became president of the company, the largest US corporation, during the post-World-War-2 boom years (1953–58). He was known for his single-minded focus on sales, and national advocacy of corporate issues.

Curtin, John (Joseph) (1885–1945) Australian statesman and prime minister (1941–5), born in Creswick, Victoria, Australia. He was active in trade union work, and edited a Perth newspaper. In 1928 he entered parliament, became leader of the Labor Party (1934), and was prime minister during most of World War 2. He organized national mobilization during the Japanese war, and died in office. >> RR1033

Curtis, Charles (Gordon) (1860–1953) Inventor, born in Boston, MA. He studied civil engineering at Columbia University, then law at the New York Law School. He is best known for his invention of the *Curtis impulse steam turbine* in 1896, 12 years after the reaction turbine had been patented by Sir Charles Parsons. >> Parsons, Charles

Curtis, Edward (Sheriff) (1868–1952) Photographer and writer, born in Madison, WI. Brought up in Seattle, WA, he devoted almost the whole of his career from 1896 to recording the North American Indian tribes and their way of life, stressing their peaceful arts and culture. He published the first of 20 volumes in 1907, the last appearing in 1930.

Curtis, Tony, originally **Bernard Schwarz** (1925–) Actor, born in New York City, USA. After many small film parts early in his career, he proved he could play light comedy roles as in *Some Like It Hot* (1959) while also displaying his dramatic ability in *The Boston Strangler* (1968). Other films include *The Vikings* (1958), *Spartacus* (1960), and *The Great Imposter* (1961).

Curtiss, Glenn (Hammond) (1878–1930) Air pioneer and inventor, born in Hammondsport, NY. Originally a bicycle mechanic, he established a motorcycle factory in Hammondsport in 1902, and in 1905 set a world speed record of 137 mph on a motor-cycle of his own design. He also designed motors for airships, and with Alexander Graham Bell formed the Aerial Experiment Association (1907). In 1908 he achieved the first public one-kilometre flight in the USA. In 1911 he invented the aileron, and also flew the first practical seaplane (hydroplane), as well as the flying boat. During World War 1 he produced military aircraft such as the JN-4 (Jenny), the Navy-Curtiss flying boat, speedboats, and Liberty engines. >> Bell, Alexander Graham

Curtius, Ernst (1814–96) Classical archaeologist, born in Lübeck, Germany, the brother of Georg Curtius. He studied at Bonn, Göttingen, and Berlin, and became professor at Göttingen (from 1856) and Berlin (from 1868). His most notable excavations were at Olympia in Greece (1875–80). >> Curtius, Georg

Curtius, Georg (1820–85) Philologist, born in Lübeck, Germany, the brother of Ernst Curtius. One of the greatest of Greek scholars, he was professor of classical philology at Prague (1849), Kiel (1854), and Leipzig (1862–5). >> Curtius, Ernst

Curtiz, Michael, originally **Mihaly Kertész** (1888–1962) Film director, born in Budapest. He was a stage actor from 1906, then became a film actor and director in 1912. By the time he moved to Hollywood (1926), he had directed some 60 films in Europe. Working in every film genre he made some 125 Hollywood films, winning an Oscar for *Casablanca* (1943). Known for his fractured English and regarded as a production-line director, he later gained from re-appraisals of his best work.

Curwen, John (1816–80) Music educationist, born in Heckmondwike, West Yorkshire, N England, UK. He became a Nonconformist minister in 1838, but devoted himself to promoting the tonic sol-fa musical system. His method came to be widely used, and in 1864 he left his ministry, having established a publishing house for music.

Curzon, Sir Clifford (1907–82) Pianist, born in London, England, UK. He studied at the Royal Academy of Music in London, and in Berlin (1928–30). He taught for some years at the Royal Academy, but resigned in 1932 to devote himself to concert work, specializing in Mozart and other Viennese classics. He was knighted in 1971.

Curzon (of Kedleston), George Nathaniel Curzon, Marquess (1859–1925) British statesman, born in Kedleston Hall, Derbyshire, C England, UK. He studied at Oxford, became an MP in 1886, and travelled widely in Eastern countries. He became under-secretary for India (1891–2), and for foreign affairs (1895), and in 1898 was made Viceroy of India and given an Irish barony. He introduced many social and political reforms, established the North West Frontier Province, and partitioned Bengal. He resigned after a disagreement with Lord Kitchener (1905), returning to politics in 1915 as Lord Privy Seal. He became foreign secretary (1919–24), and was created a marquess (1921). >> Kitchener

Cusack, Cyril [kyoosak] (1910–93) Actor, director, and playwright, born in Durban, South Africa. In 1932 he joined the Abbey Theatre, Dublin, remaining there for 13 years and appearing in over 65 plays. In 1945 he left the Abbey to form his own company, touring Ireland with a repertory of Irish and European plays, and making several visits abroad. He has also made a name with telling cameo parts in films.

Cusack, (Ellen) Dymphna [kyoosak] (1902–81) Writer, born in Wyalong, New South Wales, Australia. She studied at Sydney University, and trained as a teacher. The first of her 12 novels, *Jungfrau*, was published in 1936. Other novels include *Pioneers on Parade* (1939), written with Miles Franklin, and *Come In Spinner* (1951), written with Florence James. She also wrote several plays, illustrating her preoccupation with social and political disadvantage. >> Franklin, Miles

Cushing, Caleb (1800–79) Lawyer and public official, born in Salisbury, MA. After serving in the Massachusetts legislature and the US House of Representatives as a Whig (1835–41) and Democrat (1841–3), he was appointed commissioner to China. He became attorney general (1853–7), and spoke out on many issues beyond the law. Opposed to slavery and secession, when Lincoln won the election of 1860 he became a Republican, and served as a legal consultant to him and his cabinet. Under President Grant, he carried through several notable diplomatic-legal negotiations, and in 1873 Grant nominated him to be chief justice of the Supreme Court, but partisan attacks led Cushing to withdraw his name. He then served as US ambassador to Spain (1873–7). An accomplished orator and linguist, he was also extremely well read – Emerson called him the most eminent scholar of his day. >> Emerson; Grant, Ulysses; Lincoln, Abraham

Cushing, Harvey Williams (1869–1939) Neurosurgeon and physiologist, born in Cleveland, OH. He studied at Johns Hopkins, Yale, and Harvard universities, graduating in medicine in 1895, then taught at Harvard (1912–32) and Yale (from 1933). His main research field was the brain and the pituitary gland, describing the symptoms of the pituitary malfunction now called *Cushing's disease*.

Cushing, Peter (1913–94) Actor, born in Kenley, Greater London, England, UK. He studied at the Guildhall School of Music and Drama, making his stage debut in 1935. A trip to the USA resulted in his Hollywood film debut in *The Man in the Iron Mask* (1939). After the war he established himself as a classical actor with the Old Vic Company (1948–9). He was chiefly known for his long association with the Gothic horror films produced by Hammer Studios, such as *The Curse of Frankenstein* (1956), *Dracula* (1958), and *The Mummy* (1959). His numerous other films include *Hamlet* (1948), *Dr Who and the Daleks* (1965), and *Star Wars* (1977). He also enjoyed a long screen association with the character of Sherlock Holmes. His writing includes *An Autobiography* (1986) and *Past Forgetting* (1988).

Cushing, Richard J(ames) (1895–1970) Roman Catholic cardinal, born in Boston, MA. Ordained in 1921, he worked for the Society for the Propagation of the Faith, and was auxiliary Bishop of Boston (from 1939) before becoming Boston's archbishop (1944). He established numerous schools and charitable institutions, including the Missionary Society of St James the Apostle, which sends priests as missionaries to South America. He was made a cardinal in 1958. Blunt-spoken, making no claim to be a conventional scholar-priest, he was also known for his close ties with the Kennedy family. >> Kennedy, Joseph P

Cushman, Charlotte (Saunders) (1816–76) Actress, born in Boston, MA. One of the first major native-born US actresses, she began as an opera singer but turned to acting after she overstrained her voice; the vocal damage left her with a husky, veiled quality that she used to great advantage, often playing male roles (including Romeo and Hamlet). By 1842 she was managing as well as starring at the Walnut Street Theatre in Philadelphia. After moving to England in 1845, she became the toast of the London stage. She spent the next 25 years living in England or Rome, then returned to the USA, where she made a triumphal farewell tour in 1874–5.

Custer, George Armstrong (1839–76) US soldier, born in New Rumley, OH. He trained at West Point (1861), and after a brilliant career as a cavalry commander in the Civil War served in the campaigns against the Indian tribes of the Great Plains. His actions were controversial, but his gift for self-publicity made him a symbol of the cavalry. He led his 7th US Cavalry to a massive defeat by a combined Sioux–Cheyenne force at the Little Bighorn, MT (25 Jun 1876), with no survivors from his immediate command. 'Custer's Last Stand' shocked the nation, but did no lasting good to the Indians' cause. Although a lieutenant-colonel in the cavalry, he is often referred to by his Civil War rank of general. >> Crazy Horse; Sitting Bull

Cuthbert, St (c. 635–87) Missionary, born in Ireland or Northumbria. He became a monk (651), prior of Melrose (661), and prior of Lindisfarne (664). In 676 he left to become a hermit, but in 684 was persuaded to take the bishopric of Hexham, then of Lindisfarne. After two years he returned to his cell, on the island of Farne, where he died. His body was moved to many places, and finally buried at Durham in 999. Feast day 20 March.

Cuthbert, Betty, known as **The Golden Girl** (1938–) Sprinter, born in Ermington, New South Wales, Australia. Possibly Australia's greatest woman sprinter, she won gold medals for the 100 m, 200 m, and 4 × 100 m relay at the Melbourne Olympics in 1956, and won the 400 m at the 1964 Tokyo Olympics. She was awarded the prestigious Helms Award in 1964. Diagnosed as having multiple sclerosis, in recent years she has campaigned to raise awareness of the disease.

Cutner, Solomon >> **Solomon** (music)

Cuvier, Georges (Léopold Chrétien Frédéric Dagobert), Baron [küvyay] (1769–1832) Anatomist, born in Montbéliard, France. In 1795, he was appointed assistant professor of comparative anatomy in the Jardin des Plantes in Paris, and in 1798 professor of natural history at the Collège de France. After the Restoration he was made Chancellor of the University of Paris, admitted into the cabinet by Louis XVIII, and under Louis-Philippe was made a peer of France (1831). He originated the natural system of animal classification, and through his studies of animal and fish fossils he established the sciences of palaeontology and comparative anatomy.

Cuyp or **Cuijp, Albert** [kiyp] (1620–91) Painter, born in Dordrecht, The Netherlands. He excelled in the painting of landscapes, often suffused with golden sunlight, and containing cattle and other figures, such as 'Herdsmen with Cows by a River' (National Gallery, London). His father **Jacob Gerritsz Cuyp** (1594–1651) was primarily a portrait painter.

Cymbeline [simbeleen], also known as **Cunobelinus** (?–c. 43) Pro-Roman king of the Catuvellauni, who from his capital at Camulodunum (Colchester) ruled most of SE Britain. Shakespeare's character was based on Holinshed's half-historical Cunobelinus.

Cynewulf [kinewulf] (8th-c) Anglo-Saxon poet, identified by some with Cynewulf, Bishop of Lindisfarne (737–80). Four poems, 'Juliana', 'Christ', 'Elene', and 'The Fates of the Apostles', have his name worked into the text in runes.

Cynthius >> **Giraldi, Giambattista**

Cyprian, St [siprian], originally **Thascius Caecilius Cyprianus** (c. 200–58) One of the great Fathers of the Church, probably born in Carthage. He became a Christian c.245, and was made Bishop of Carthage in 248, when his zealous efforts to restore strict discipline brought him a host of enemies. He was forced to flee from Roman persecution, and eventually suffered martyrdom under Valerian (reigned 253–60). At a synod in Carthage in 256 he argued for a notion of Church unity as expressed through the consensus of bishops. His writings remained influential. Feast day 16 September. >> Valerian

Cypselus [sipselus] (c. 655–625 BC) Tyrant of Corinth, and one of the earliest in a series of self-made rulers who arose in many Greek cities in the 7th-c and 6th-c BC. He seized

power against the narrow and exclusive oligarchy of the Bacchiads who had ruled Corinth since the 8th-c BC, and founded the *Cypselid* dynasty. >> Periander

Cyrankiewicz, Jozef [sirangkyayvits] (1911–89) Polish politician and prime minister (1947–52, 1954–70), born in Tarnow, Poland. He studied in Cracow, where he became secretary of the Socialist Party in 1935. He was taken prisoner by the Germans in 1939, escaped, and organized resistance, but was recaptured and sent to Auschwitz in 1941. He became secretary-general of the Socialist Party in 1945, prime minister on two occasions, and chairman of the Council of State (1970–2).

Cyrano de Bergerac, Savinien [siranoh duh berzherak] (1619–55) Satirist and playwright, born in Paris. In his youth he fought more than a thousand duels, mostly on account of his extremely large nose. His works include satirical accounts of visits to the Moon and Sun, *Histoire comique des états et empires de la lune* and ... *du soleil*, published posthumously in 1656 and 1662, which suggested 'Gulliver' to Swift. His life was the subject of the play by Edmond Rostand (1897). >> Rostand; Swift, Jonathan

Cyril, St (c.827–69) and **Methodius, St** (c.825–85), Brothers, born in Thessalonica, Greece, who became missionaries to the Slavs. Cyril first worked among the Tartar Khazars, and Methodius among the Bulgarians of Thrace and Moesia. Together they went to Moravia, where they prepared a Slavonic translation of the Scriptures and the chief liturgical books. Cyril died in Rome, leaving Methodius to complete the evangelization of the Slavs as Bishop of Moravia. Called to Rome in 879 to justify his celebration of the Mass in the native tongue, he gained the approval of Pope John VIII. The Cyrillic alphabet, modified out of the Greek by Cyril, superseded a more ancient Slavonic alphabet. Feast day 14 February (W), 11 May (E).

Cyril of Alexandria, St (376–444) Theologian, one of the Fathers of the Church, born in Alexandria, Egypt. He became Patriarch of Alexandria in 412, and vigorously implemented orthodox Christian teaching. He expelled the Jews from the city (415), and relentlessly persecuted Nestorius, whose doctrine was condemned at the Council of Ephesus (431). Feast day 9 June (E) or 27 June (W). >> Nestorius

Cyril of Jerusalem, St (c. 315–86) Theologian, and Bishop of Jerusalem, who took a leading part in the doctrinal controversies concerning Arianism. Twice expelled from his see, he regained it and spoke for the Orthodox churchmen at the Council of Constantinople (381). Feast day 18 March. >> Arius

Cyrrhestes >> **Andronicus**

Cyrus II [siyrus], known as **the Great** (?–529 BC) The founder of the Achaemenid Persian empire, the son of Cambyses I. He defeated the Medes (549 BC), became King of Persia (548 BC), and took Lydia (c.546 BC) and Babylon (539 BC). His empire eventually ran from the Mediterranean to the Hindu Kush. He had a policy of religious conciliation: the nations which had been carried into captivity in Babylon along with the Jews were restored to their native countries, and allowed to take their gods with them. >> RR1063

Cyrus [siyrus], known as **Cyrus the Younger** (424–401 BC) The second son of Darius II of Persia (reigned 423–404 BC). He was accused of conspiring against his brother, Artaxerxes II, and sentenced to death (404 BC), but was afterwards pardoned and restored as satrap of Asia Minor. In 401 BC he led an army of Greek mercenaries against his brother, but was killed at Cunaxa. >> Xenophon

Czerny, Karl [chernee] (1791–1857) Pianist and composer, born in Vienna. He studied under Beethoven and Clementi, and himself taught Liszt, Thelberg, and Döhler. His piano exercises and studies were widely used. >> Beethoven; Clementi; Liszt

Daché, Lilly [da**shay**] (1892–1989) Fashion designer, born in Béigles, France. Apprenticed to her milliner aunt at age 12, she emigrated to the USA as a teenager. In the 1920s she funded the House of Daché in New York City, where her thousands of hat designs came to identify her indelibly with hats, particularly her signature turbans, half-hats, and snoods.

Dadd, Richard (1819–87) Painter, born in Chatham, Kent, SE England, UK. He studied at the Royal Academy Schools, travelled extensively in Europe and the Middle East, and was considered a promising young artist. However, in 1843 he suffered a mental breakdown, murdered his father, and spent the rest of his life in asylums. He is best known for the fantastically detailed fairy paintings which made up the bulk of his output after his incarceration.

Dafoe, Willem [da**foh**] (1955–) Film actor, born in Appleton, WI. He joined an avante-garde theatre group and toured extensively with them for two years in the USA and Europe, then became a founding member of the Wooster Group. He made his film debut with a small part in *Heaven's Gate* (1980), and went on to the Oscar-nominated role of Sergeant Elias in *Platoon* (1986) and the controversial title role in *The Last Temptation of Christ* (1988). Later films include *Tom and Viv* (1994), *The English Patient* (1996), *Speed 2* (1997), and *Foolish Heart* (1998).

Dafydd ap Gruffydd [**da**vith ap **gri**fith] (?–1283) Prince of Gwynedd in North Wales, the brother of Llywelyn ap Gruffydd. He opposed his brother's accession, but eventually supported him in his battles with the English. He succeeded his brother in 1282, but was betrayed and executed the following year – the last native prince of Wales.

Dafydd ap Gwilym [**da**vith ap **gwil**im] (c.1320–c.1380) Poet, born probably in Brogynin, Cardiganshire, W Wales, UK. He wrote love songs, satirical poems, and nature poems in the complex *cywydd* metre which he perfected, much extending the range of such poetry. His work may be compared with that of the troubadours. >> Llywelyn

da Gama, Vasco >> Gama, Vasco da

Daguerre, Louis Jacques Mandé [dagair] (1789–1851) Photographic pioneer, born in Cormeilles, France. He had been a scene painter in Paris, when, from 1826 onwards, and partly in conjunction with Nicéphore Niepce, he perfected the photographic process named after him. >> Niepce

Dahl, Roald (1916–90) Writer, born in Llandaff, Cardiff, S Wales, UK, of Norwegian parents. Educated at Repton School, he worked for the Shell Oil Co in London and Africa, then served as a fighter pilot in the RAF during World War 2. He specialized in writing short stories of unexpected horror and macabre surprise, such as in *Someone Like You* (1953) and *Kiss, Kiss* (1960). His children's books display a similar taste for the grotesque, such as *James and the Giant Peach* (1961), *Charlie and the Chocolate Factory* (1964), and *BFG* (1982); several have been made into successful films.

Dahlgren, John (Adolphus Bernard) (1809–70) US naval commander, born in Philadelphia, PA. He joined the navy in 1826, and did much to advance the science of naval gunnery by founding an ordnance workshop at Washington, where he designed a new type of naval gun (1850). He commanded the South Atlantic blockade squadron in the Civil War.

Dahmer, Jeffrey (1960–94) US convicted murderer. He confessed to 17 killings, committed in the USA over several years, and was found guilty in 1992 of 15 of these murders. His insanity plea having been rejected by the jury, he was sentenced to life imprisonment. He was killed in prison by a fellow prisoner.

Dahrendorf, Ralf (Gustav) Dahrendorf, Baron [**dah**rendaw(r)f] (1929–) Sociologist, born in Hamburg, Germany. He studied at Hamburg University and the London School of Economics, and held a succession of academic posts in Germany and the USA in the 1950s and 1960s. He was a member of the European Community Commission (1970–4), then moved to Britain to become Director of the London School of Economics (1974–84). In 1987 he was appointed Warden of St Antony's College, Oxford. He was knighted in 1982, and became a life peer in 1993.

Daiches, David [**day**chiz] (1912–) British academic. He studied at Edinburgh and Oxford universities, and taught at Edinburgh before moving to the USA as professor of English at Chicago (1939–43) and Cornell (1946–51), then returning to Cambridge (1951–6). He has published numerous works on English literature, including *Literature and Society* (1938) and *Critical Approaches to Literature* (1956), as well as several books about Scotland, such as *Robert Burns and his World* (1971) and *Scotland and the Union* (1977). Later works include *A Weekly Scotsman and Other Poems* (1994).

Daimler, Gottlieb (Wilhelm) [**daym**ler] (1834–1900) Engineer, born in Schorndorf, Germany. He worked from 1872 on improving the gas engine, and in 1885 patented a high-speed internal combustion engine. With Maybach he converted a horse-drawn carriage into a petrol-engined vehicle (1886), and designed one of the earliest roadworthy motor cars (1889). In 1890, he founded the Daimler Automobile Co in Cannstatt, near Stuttgart. >> Maybach

Dakin, Henry Drysdale [**day**kin] (1880–1952) Chemist, born in London, England, UK. Noted for his researches on enzymes and his work on antiseptics, he developed *Dakin's* or the *Carrel–Dakin solution* (a 0.5% solution of sodium hypochlorite), widely used for treating wounds in World War 1. >> Carrel

Daladier, Edouard [daladyay] (1884–1970) French statesman and prime minister (1933, 1934, 1938–40), born in Carpentras, France. In 1927 he became leader of the Radical Socialists, and in 1933 minister of war, and prime minister of a short-lived government, a pattern which was repeated in 1934. In 1936 he was minister of war in the Popular Front Cabinet, and as premier (1938) supported appeasement policies and signed the Munich Pact. In 1940 he resigned, became successively war and foreign minister, and on the fall of France was arrested and interned until 1945. After the war he continued in politics until 1958. >> RR1049

Dalai Lama [**da**liy **lah**ma], (Mongolian, 'ocean-like guru') Spiritual and temporal head of Tibet, currently **Tenzin Gyatso** (1935–), born in Taktser, China, into a peasant family. He was designated the 14th Dalai Lama in 1937, but his rights were exercised by a regency until 1950. He fled to Chumbi in S Tibet after an abortive anti-Chinese uprising in 1950, but negotiated an autonomy agreement with the People's Republic the following year, and for the next eight years served as nominal ruler of Tibet. After China's suppression of the Tibetan national uprising of 1959, he was forced into permanent exile, settling at Dharamsala in Punjab, India, where he established a democratically-based alternative government. He was awarded the 1989 Nobel Prize for Peace in recognition of his commitment to the nonviolent liberation of his homeland.

Dalcroze, Emile Jaques >> **Jaques-Dalcroze, Emile**

Dale, Sir Henry (Hallett) (1875–1968) Physiologist, born in London, England, UK. He studied at Cambridge and London, and became director of the National Institute for Medical Research, London, in 1928. He discovered acetylcholine and histamine, and in 1936 shared the Nobel Prize for Physiology or Medicine for work on the chemical transmission of nerve impulses. >> RR1124

Dale, Richard (1756–1826) US naval officer, born in Norfolk Co, VA. After an adventurous career at sea, including two imprisonments by the British, he served as first lieutenant under John Paul Jones on the *Bonhomme Richard* in the battle with the *Serapis* (1779). After 1783 he alternated between merchant ships and the US navy, commanding the squadron that blockaded Tripoli (1801–2), then retired to a quiet life in Philadelphia. >> Jones, John Paul

Dalén, (Nils) Gustav [daˈlayn] (1869–1937) Engineer and inventor, born in Stenstorp, Sweden. He studied at Göteborg and Zürich, and invented automatic acetylene lighting for unmanned lighthouses and railway signals, for which he was awarded the Nobel Prize for Physics in 1912. He was blinded a year later by an explosion in a chemical experiment, but continued to work until his death.

Daley, Richard J(oseph) (1902–76) Administrator, born in Chicago, IL. He was admitted to the Illinois bar (1933), and served as a senator and state representative (1936–46), state director of revenue (1948–50), and clerk of Cook Co (1950–5). He was elected Mayor of Chicago in 1955, a position he held until his death.

Dalgarno, George [dalˈgah(r)noh] (c. 1626–87) Educationist, born in Old Aberdeen, NE Scotland, UK. He studied at Marischal College, and kept a school for 30 years in Oxford. He published a book on philosophy using letters of the alphabet for ideas, *Ars signorum, vulgo character universalis* (1661), and a deaf sign language, *Didascalocophus, or the Deaf and Dumb Man's Tutor* (1680).

Dalglish, Kenny [dalˈgleesh], popular name of **Kenneth Mathieson Dalglish** (1951–) Footballer and manager, born in Glasgow, W Scotland, UK. He joined Glasgow Celtic in 1967, transferring to Liverpool in 1977 for a then record fee between two British clubs of £440 000. He won 102 caps for Scotland, in addition to three European Cups. Unexpectedly invited to manage Liverpool while still a player, he confounded the pundits by being an instant success. In his first season, Liverpool won both Cup and League. He is the only player to have scored 100 goals in both English and Scottish football. He joined Newcastle United as manager in 1997. >> RR1157

Dalhousie, James Andrew Broun Ramsay, 1st Marquess of [dalˈhowzee] (1812–60) British Governor-General of India (1847–56), born at Dalhousie Castle, Midlothian, EC Scotland, UK. He studied at Oxford, and became an MP (1837), Earl of Dalhousie (1838), and President of the Board of Trade (1845). In India (1847) he encouraged the development of railways and irrigation works. He annexed Satara (1847) and Punjab (1849), but the annexation of Oudh (1856) caused resentment which fuelled the 1857 rebellion. He was made a marquess in 1849, and retired through ill health in 1856.

Dali, Salvador (Felipe Jacinto) [dahˈlee], Span **Dali** (1904–89) Artist, born in Figueras, Spain. After studying at the Academy of Fine Arts, Madrid, he moved to Paris and joined the Surrealists (1928), becoming one of the principal figures of the movement. His study of abnormal psychology and dream symbolism led him to represent 'paranoiac' objects in landscapes remembered from his Spanish boyhood. In 1940 he settled in the USA, became a Catholic, and devoted his art to symbolic religious paintings. He wrote *The Secret Life of Salvador Dali* (1942), and collaborated with Luis Buñuel in the Surrealist films *Un Chien andalou* (1928, An Andalusian Dog), and *L'Age d'or* (1930, The Golden Age). One of his best-known paintings is 'The Persistence of Memory' (known as 'The Limp Watches', 1931, Museum of Modern Art, New York City). >> Buñuel

Dalin, Olof von (1708–63) Writer and historian, born in Vinberg, Sweden. He was the most influential literary figure of the Swedish Enlightenment. He published anonymously Sweden's first moralizing periodical, *Then Svänska Argus* (1732–4, The Swedish Argus), which is regarded as the foundation stone of modern Swedish prose, and compiled a monumental history of Sweden (1747–62). Among his many varied works were a verse tragedy, *Brynilda* (1738), and his prose allegorical masterpiece, *Sagan om Hästen* (1740, The Story of the Horse).

Dallapiccola, Luigi [dalaˈpeekohla] (1904–75) Composer, born in Pisino, Italy. He studied at Florence, becoming a pianist and music teacher. After World War 2 he taught composition in the USA for several years. His compositions make wide use of 12-note technique, and include songs, a piano concerto, three operas, a ballet, and choral works such as *Canti di prigionia* (1938–41, Songs of Prison).

Dallas, George Mifflin (1792–1864) Lawyer and statesman, born in Philadelphia, PA. He studied at Princeton College, was admitted to the bar, and entered the diplomatic service. In 1831 he was sent to the US Senate by Pennsylvania. He was US minister to Russia (1837–9), and in 1844 was elected vice-president of the USA under Polk. Dallas in Texas and in Oregon are both named after him. >> Polk, James K

Dalou, (Aimé) Jules [daloo] (1838–1902) Sculptor, born in Paris. After being the curator of the Louvre during the Commune, he fled to England in 1871, and taught at the Royal College of Art. His realistic modelling influenced many English sculptors of the time. His monument, 'Triumph of the Republic', is at the Place de la Nation, Paris.

Dalton, (Edward) Hugh (John Neale) Dalton, Baron (1887–1962) British statesman, born in Neath, SC Wales, UK. He studied at Cambridge and the London School of Economics, and was a Labour MP (1924–31, and from 1935). He became minister for economic warfare (1940) and President of the Board of Trade (1942) in Churchill's wartime coalition. As Labour Chancellor of the Exchequer (1945–7), he nationalized the Bank of England (1946), but resigned as a result of 'budget leakages' to a journalist. He was made a life peer in 1960. >> Churchill, Sir Winston

Dalton, John [dawltn] (1766–1844) Chemist, born in Eaglesfield, Cumbria, NW England, UK. After 1781 he became assistant in a boarding-school kept by a cousin in Kendal, where in 1787 he commenced a meteorological journal, continued all his life, recording 200 000 observations. In 1793 he was appointed teacher of mathematics and science in New College, Manchester. He first described colour blindness (*Daltonism*) in 1794, exemplified in his own case and that of his brother. His chief physical researches were on mixed gases, the force of steam, the elasticity of vapours, and the expansion of gases by heat, his law of partial pressures being also known as *Dalton's law*. In chemistry he worked on the absorption of gases, and his atomic theory was able to interpret the laws of chemical combination and the conservation of mass, and gave a new basis for all quantitative chemistry. One of the leading early scientists, he remained a man of quiet demeanour and simple habits, reflecting his Quaker beliefs. He 'never found time' to marry. >> Proust, Joseph Louis

Daly, (John) Augustin (1838–99) Playwright and manager, born in Plymouth, NC. After a career as a drama critic, he went into management, opening the Fifth Avenue Theatre, New York City, in 1869, and his own theatre, Daly's, in 1879. In 1893 he opened the London Daly's. He wrote and adapted nearly 100 plays, and was chosen by Tennyson to adapt *The Foresters* for the stage in 1891. >> Tennyson

Daly, Mary (1928–) Feminist and theological writer, born in Schenectady, NY. She studied theology at St Mary's College, Indiana, and Fribourg University, Switzerland, and taught at Fribourg (1959–66) and Boston College (from 1969). Having analyzed the effects of male bias in *The Church and the Second Sex* (1968), she abandoned her attempts to reform official Roman Catholic attitudes and became a post-Christian radical feminist in *Beyond God the Father* (1973). Later books include *Pure Lust: Elemental Feminist Philosophy* (1984).

Dam, Carl Peter Henrik (1895–1976) Biochemist, born in Copenhagen. He was professor at Copenhagen (1923–40), and in 1940 went to the USA where he taught at the University of Rochester (1942–5) and became a member of the Rockefeller Institute for Medical Research (1945). He was also on the staff of the Polytechnic Institute, Copenhagen (1941–65). For his discovery of the coagulant agent vitamin K (1934) he shared the Nobel Prize for Physiology or Medicine in 1943. >> RR1124

Damadian, Raymond (Vahan) [damadian] (1936–) Biophysicist and inventor, born in Forest Hills, NY. He studied violin and mathematics before taking a medical degree and doing postgraduate work in biophysics at Harvard. He also served in the US air force. His invention of the magnetic resonance imaging (MRI) scanner revolutionized the field of diagnostic medicine. His Fonar Corporation manufactures the device for distribution worldwide.

Damasus I, St [damasus] (c. 304–384) Pope (366–84), possibly of Spanish descent. A Roman deacon, his election was violently contested, but confirmed by Valentinian I. He opposed Arianism, and condemned Apollinaris the Younger at the Council of Constantinople in 381. In 382 he proclaimed the primacy of the see of Rome. He commissioned St Jerome, his secretary, to undertake the Vulgate version of the Bible. Feast day 11 December. >> Apollinaris; Arius; Jerome, St

D'Amboise, Jacques [dambwahz] (1934–) Ballet dancer and choreographer, born in Dedham, MA. After training with the School of American Ballet, he joined the New York City Ballet in 1949. For more than 30 years he performed leading roles in such Balanchine classics as *Apollo*. He began choreographing works in 1963. In 1977 he formed the National Dance Institute to teach dance to children in inner-city schools. >> Balanchine

Damian or **Damianus, St** >> **Cosmas** and **Damian, Saints**

Damiani, Pietro, St [damiahnee], also known as **St Peter Damian** (1007–72) Ecclesiastic, born in Ravenna, Italy. He herded swine in boyhood, but joined the hermitage at Fonte Avellana in 1035 and rose to be cardinal and Bishop of Ostia (1057) and one of the Doctors of the Church. Feast day 21 February.

Damien, Father Joseph [damyi], originally **Joseph de Veuster** (1840–89) Missionary, born in Tremelo, Belgium. He was renowned for his great work among the lepers of the Hawaiian island of Molokai, where he lived from 1873 until his death from the disease. He became internationally known after Robert Louis Stevenson published a passionate defence of his character and work. He was beatified in 1995. >> Stevenson, Robert Louis

Damocles [damokleez] (4th-c BC) Legendary courtier of the elder Dionysius, tyrant of Syracuse (405–367 BC). He extolled the happiness of royalty, but the tyrant showed him the precarious nature of fortune in a singular manner. While seated at a richly-spread table, Damocles looked up to see a keen-edged sword suspended over his head by a single horse-hair.

Damon and **Pythias** [daymon, pithias], also found as **Phintias** (4th-c BC) Two Pythagoreans of Syracuse, remembered as the models of faithful friendship. Condemned to death by the elder Dionysius, tyrant of Syracuse (405–367 BC), Pythias begged to be allowed to go home to arrange his affairs, and Damon pledged his own life for his friend's. Pythias returned just in time to save Damon from death. Struck by so noble an example, the tyrant pardoned Pythias, and desired to be admitted into their sacred fellowship.

Dampier, William [dampeer] (1652–1715) Navigator and buccaneer, born in East Coker, Somerset, SW England, UK. He journeyed to Newfoundland and the West Indies, then joined a band of buccaneers along the Pacific coast of South America (1679). In 1683 he sailed across the Pacific, visiting the Philippines, China, and Australia. On his return to England, he published his *New Voyage round the World* (1697). He then led a voyage of discovery to the South Seas (1699), exploring the NW coast of Australia, and giving his name to the *Dampier Archipelago* and *Strait*. He made further journeys there in 1703 and 1708.

Damrosch, Leopold [damrosh] (1832–85) Conductor and composer, born in Posen, Germany. He was leader (1857–9) of the Weimar court orchestra under Liszt, and conductor at Wrocław, Poland (formerly Breslau, Germany) (1859–60, 1862–71)), before emigrating to New York City. He ultimately became conductor at the Metropolitan Opera House, and did much to popularize Wagner in the USA. >> Damrosch, Walter; Wagner, Richard

Damrosch, Walter (Johannes) [damrosh] (1862–1950) Conductor, composer, and educator, born in Wrocław, Poland (formerly Breslau, Germany), the son of Leopold Damrosch. He moved to the USA with his family in 1871, and was largely trained in music by his father. When his father died, he took over his post as conductor of the New York Symphony Society (1885–1903), and began an assistantship at the Metropolitan Opera (1885–91). He began his own company, the Damrosch Opera Company (1895–9), mainly to promote Wagner's operas; he also produced his own opera, *The Scarlet Letter* (1896). He then became director of a reorganized New York Symphony Society (1903–27), turning away from opera to orchestral works. He retired in 1927 to become music adviser to NBC radio. Among his achievements was the Music Appreciation Hour for young people, which he narrated and conducted after opening each session with, 'Good morning, my dear children'. He retains a special place in America's musical life for introducing generations to the world of classical music. >> Damrosch, Leopold

Dana, Charles A(nderson) [dayna] (1819–97) Newspaper editor, born in Hinsdale, NH. He spent two years at Harvard, and was a member of the Brook Farm community (1841–6) with George Ripley. He edited the New York *Tribune* (1848–62), which opposed the extension of slavery to new territories. From 1863 to the close of the Civil War he was assistant-secretary of war. In 1867 he purchased the New York *Sun*, and successfully managed it on democratic lines. With George Ripley he edited the *New American Cyclopaedia* (1857–63) and the *American Cyclopaedia* (1873–6). >> Ripley, George

Dana, James D(wight) [dayna] (1813–95) Mineralogist and geologist, born in Utica, NY. He studied at Yale, and was a scientific observer on the US exploring expedition under Charles Wilkes (1838–42), visiting the Antarctic and Pacific. With his father-in-law, **Benjamin Silliman** (1779–1864), he edited the *American Journal of Science* from 1840, and became professor of natural history (1849–64) and geology (1864–90) at Yale. >> Wilkes, Charles

Dana, Richard (Henry) [dayna] (1815–82) Writer and lawyer, born in Cambridge, MA. While a student at Harvard, he shipped as a common sailor, and made a voyage round Cape Horn to California and back, which he described in *Two Years before the Mast* (1840). After graduating in 1837 he was admitted to the Massachusetts bar in 1840, and was especially distinguished in maritime law. Among his works are *The Seaman's Friend* (1841) and *To Cuba and Back* (1859).

Danby, Lord >> **Leeds, Thomas Osborne**

Dance, George, known as **George Dance the Elder** (1695–1768) Architect, born in London, England, UK. He designed the Mansion House (1739) and many other London buildings, and was surveyor to the City of London (1735–68). His son, **George Dance, the Younger** (1741–1825), was also an architect, and succeeded his father as surveyor. An exponent of Neoclassicism, deriving from his studies in Italy, his best-known building was Newgate Prison (1770–83). He was one of the original Royal Academicians.

Dandolo, Enrico [dandoloh] (c. 1110–1205) Italian statesman, born in Venice, Italy. In 1173 he was ambassador to Constantinople, and in 1192 became Doge of Venice. In 1202 he marched at the head of the Fourth Crusade, subduing Trieste and Zara, the coasts of Albania, the Ionian Is, and (1205) Constantinople, where he established the empire of the Latins.

Dandy, Walter (Edward) (1886–1946) Neurosurgeon, born in Sedalia, MO. He studied at Johns Hopkins University, and remained on the staff there until his death. He did important work on the pathophysiology and surgical treatment of hydrocephalus, and developed a number of fundamental diagnostic and neurosurgical techniques. He also demonstrated the significance of ruptured vertebral discs in cases of low back pain, and pioneered spinal surgery.

Dane, Clemence, pseudonym of **Winifred Ashton** (c.1891–1965) Novelist and playwright, born in London, England, UK. Her novels include *Regiment of Women* (1917), *Legend* (1919), and *The Flower Girls* (1954). Many of her plays achieved long runs, notably *A Bill of Divorcement* (1921), and the ingenious reconstruction of the poet's life in *Will Shakespeare* (1921).

Dane, Nathan (1752–1835) Lawyer and statesman, born in Ipswich, MA. A delegate to the Continental Congress in 1785, and later a commissioner to revise the statutes of Massachusetts, he published a nine-volume *General Abridgement and Digest of American Law*, the first comprehensive work on US law (1823–9). He arranged that the income from this work be used to establish a chair in the Harvard Law School, provided that Joseph Story was the first holder. >> Story

Dangerfield, Thomas (1650–85) Conspirator, born in Waltham, Essex, SE England, UK. A thief, vagabond, and soldier, in 1679 he accused the Presbyterians of plotting to destroy the government. Imprisoned when this was shown to be a lie, he claimed he had been deceived by Catholics plotting against the life of Charles II. Convicted of libel, he was whipped and pilloried, and on returning from Tyburn was killed by a blow from a bystander.

D'Angers, David >> **David, Pierre Jean**

Dang Xianzu [dang shantsoo], also spelled **Tang Hsien-tsu** (1550–1616) Chinese playwright and minor official. He wrote a play-cycle, *The Four Dreams*, in which a character takes up monasticism due to the futility of his future life seen in a dream. His most famous work, *The Peony Pavilion*, deals (in 55 scenes) with a love of such intensity that it can raise the dead.

Daniel, Arnaut [danyel] (late 12th-c) Provençal poet, born at the Castle of Rebeyrac, Périgord, France. He became a member of the court of Richard Coeur de Lion and was esteemed one of the best of the troubadours, particularly for his treatment of the theme of love. He introduced the sestina, the pattern of which was later adapted by Dante and Petrarch. >> Dante; Petrarch; Richard I

Daniel, Glyn (Edmund) (1914–86) Archaeologist, born in Barry, Vale of Glamorgan, S Wales, UK. He studied at Cardiff and at Cambridge, where he lectured (1945–74) and became professor of archaeology (1974–81). His career was devoted less to excavation and research than to stimulating popular interest in archaeology through writing, editing, and broadcasting. He was a pioneer historian of archaeology and an energetic editor, both of the journal *Antiquity* (1958–86) and of the book series *Ancient Peoples and Places* published from 1955. On television he achieved particular popularity in the 1950s as chairman of the archaeological panel game, *Animal, Vegetable, Mineral*.

Daniel, Samuel (1562–1619) Poet, born near Taunton, Somerset, SW England, UK. He entered Oxford in 1597, but left it without a degree. In 1607 he became one of the queen's grooms of the privy chamber, and had charge of a company of young players at Bristol. His works include sonnets, epistles, masques, and dramas; but his chief production was a poem in eight books, *A History of the Civil Wars between York and Lancaster*.

Daniell, John Frederic (1790–1845) Chemist and meteorologist, born in London, England, UK. Professor of chemistry at King's College, London, from 1831, he wrote an *Introduction to Chemical Philosophy* (1839). He invented a hygrometer (1820), a pyrometer (1830), and the *Daniell electric cell* (1836).

Danilova, Alexandra Dionysievna [danilohva] (1904–97) Dancer and teacher, born in Peterhof, Russia. She studied at the Imperial and State Ballet Schools in St Petersburg, and in 1924 toured Europe, joining Diaghilev until his death. She danced as prima ballerina with the Ballet Russe de Monte Carlo (1938–52), and created leading parts in the works of Balanchine and Massine. She then taught at the School of American Ballet. >> Balanchine; Diaghilev; Massine

Dankworth, John (Philip William) (1927–) Jazz musician, composer, and arranger, born in London, England, UK. He trained at the Royal Academy of Music, London, and has been a leading figure in the British popular music and jazz scene since the 1950s. An accomplished saxophonist, and bandleader since 1953, he has also composed works for combined jazz and symphonic ensembles, such as *The Diamond and the Goose* (1981) for choir and orchestra, and film scores including *Saturday Night and Sunday Morning* (1960). With his wife, the singer **Dame Cleo Laine** (1927–), he has recorded many acclaimed musical albums. Cleo Laine was made a dame in 1997.

d'Annunzio, Gabriele [danuntseeoh] (1863–1938) Writer, born in Pescara, Italy. He studied at Rome, and during the 1890s wrote several novels, influenced by the philosophy of Nietzsche, notably *Il trionfo della morte* (1894, The Triumph of Death). His best-known poetic work is *Laudi del cielo del mare della terra e degli eroi* (1899, In Praise of Sky, Sea, Earth, and Heroes), and his major plays include *La figlia di Iorio* (1904, The Daughter of Jorio) and the tragedy *La* *gioconda* (1899), which he wrote for the actress Eleonora Duse. Their tempestuous relationship was exposed in his erotic novel, *Il fuoco* (1900, trans The Flame of Life). An enthusiastic patriot, he urged Italian entry into World War 1, and served as a soldier, sailor, and finally airman. In 1919 he seized and held Fiume, despite the Allies, and ruled as dictator until he was removed by the Italian government (1920). He became a strong supporter of the Fascist Party under Mussolini. >> Duse; Mussolini; Nietzsche

Dante (Alighieri) see panel below

Danton, Georges (Jacques) [dãtõ] (1759–94) French revolutionary politician, born in Arcis-sur-Aube, France. He became a lawyer, and was practising in Paris at the outbreak of the Revolution. In 1790 he formed the Cordelier's Club, a rallying point for revolutionary extremists, and in 1792 became minister of justice. He voted for the death of the king (1793), and was one of the original members of the Committee of Public Safety. He tried to abate the pitiless severity of his own Revolutionary Tribunal, but lost the leadership to Robespierre. He was arrested, brought before the Tribunal, and charged with conspiracy. Despite a heroic and eloquent defence, he was guillotined. >> Robespierre; Saint-Just

Dantzig, Rudi von (1933–) Dancer, choreographer, and ballet director, born in Amsterdam. He studied with **Sonia Gaskell** (1904–74), making his debut in 1952 in her Ballet Recital Group, later known as the Netherlands Ballet and then as the Dutch National Ballet. He became her choreographer, co-director and, eventually, the company's sole director. He was one of the founding members of Netherlands Dance Theatre, a group that broke away from the Netherlands Ballet in 1959.

Da Ponte, Giacomo >> **Bassano, Jacopo da**

Da Ponte, Lorenzo [da **pon**tay], originally **Emanuele Conegliano** (1749–1838) Poet, born in Ceneda, Italy. He was professor of rhetoric at Treviso until political and domestic troubles drove him to Vienna, where as a poet to the Court Opera he wrote the libretti for Mozart's operas *The Marriage of Figaro* (1786), *Don Giovanni* (1787), and *Così fan*

DANTE ALIGHIERI (1265–1321)

Dante was born in Florence, of a bourgeois family of noble descent, the son of Alighiero di Bellincione d'Alighiero, a moneylender, and his first wife Bella. He was baptized **Durante**, later contracted into Dante.

He first saw his lifelong love, **Beatrice Portinari** (c.1265–90), when they were both nine in 1274. There is no evidence that she returned his passion, and only one further meeting between the two, nine years later, is recorded. She was married at an early age to one Simone de' Bardi, but neither this nor the poet's own subsequent marriage interfered with his pure and platonic devotion to her. Dante married **Gemma Donati** c.1285, to whom he had been betrothed since 1277. She was the daughter of a powerful Guelph family. Nothing of his wife appears in his writings, but his feelings for Beatrice intensified after her early death in 1290. After this, Dante embarked upon a dedicated period of study of the Classics, religion, and philosophy. The story of his boyish but unquenchable passion is subsequently told in *La Vita nuova* (c.1293, The New Life), a collection of lyric poems in the form of an autobiographical novel.

In 1289 he fought as a cavalryman at Campaldino, where Florence defeated the Ghibellines, and at Caprona. He entered public life in 1295 by joining the Guild of Physicians and Apothecaries, and from there moved to public office. He is recorded in the guild register as 'Dante d'Alighieri, Poeta'. In c.1300 he became politically active in Florence during the struggles of Guelphs with Ghibellines, further complicated by the struggles between the powerful anti-papal Colonna family and Pope Boniface VIII.

After filling minor public offices and going on some embassies abroad, Dante briefly became one of the six priors of Florence (1300). He was then recorded as being the leader of a large group of Guelphs, and he procured the banishment of the heads and leaders of the rival factions, showing characteristic sternness and impartiality to Guelph and Ghibelline alike. In 1301, following the threatened interference of Charles of Valois against the Guelphs, he was sent on an embassy to Pope Boniface VIII in Rome. Political machinations and deception meant he never again

set foot in his native city. He was banished from Florence in 1309, accused of opposing the Pope and Charles of Valois, and he was sentenced to death in his absence. From then on he was a wanderer, almost having to beg his way through life. He eventually settled in Ravenna (1318), where he remained for most of the rest of his life.

During his exile he was politically active, and he also completed his most celebrated work, the epic poem *Divinia commedia* (Divine Comedy), begun c.1307. It is his spiritual testament, narrating a journey through Hell (*Inferno*) and Purgatory (*Purgatoria*), guided by Virgil, and finally to Paradise (*Paradiso*), guided by Beatrice. It gives an insight into the highest culture and knowledge of the age in poetic form. The Divine Comedy elevated the vernacular Italian language from daily use into art. This was a breakthrough, and Dante had hesitated to employ Italian on such a theme; he is said to have begun his poem in Latin. However, he became a champion of the use of vernacular as a vehicle for great art, writing persuasively in its favour in the unfinished *De vulgari eloquentia* (c.1304–7, Concerning Vernacular Eloquence).

Another important work is the fragment called the *Convivio* (c.1304–7, Banquet), which takes the form of a commentary on some of the author's *canzoni*, or short poems, of which there are only three. The work, if completed, would have contained 14. *De monarchia* (c.1313, On Monarchy), in Latin, expounded Dante's theory that the pope should not have temporal authority over a nation's monarch. *Canzoniere* is a collection of short poems, *canzoni*, sonnets, etc, and there are a dozen epistles addressed mainly to leading statesmen or rulers. Dante was a political thinker in the mediaeval tradition, a rhetorician, and a philosopher, the chief poet of the Italians, and one of the world's greatest writers. He had seven children: six sons and a daughter named **Antonia** who, after her father's death, became a nun, taking the name of Sister Beatrice. He died from malaria shortly after he had finished the *Paradiso*, and was buried with much pomp at Ravenna, where his body still lies, restored in 1865 to the original sarcophagus.

>> Boniface VIII

tutte (1790). In 1805 he moved to New York City, where he became professor of Italian literature at Columbia College in 1825. >> Moore, Clement; Mozart

D'Arblay, Madame >> **Burney, Fanny**

Darby, Abraham (c.1678–1717) Iron-master, born near Dudley, West Midlands, C England, UK. He founded the Bristol Iron Company (1708), and is generally acknowledged to be the first man, in 1709, to use coke successfully in the smelting of iron. His works at Coalbrookdale produced the finest iron then made. Under his son, **Abraham Darby** (1711–63), the foundry manufactured large numbers of cast-iron cylinders for Newcomen's atmospheric steam engines, and later the first high-pressure steam boiler for Trevithick. His grandson, **Abraham Darby** (1750–91), made the world's first cast-iron bridge, of 100-ft span, erected over the R Severn in 1779. >> Newcomen; Trevithick; Wilkinson, John

Darby, Sir (Henry) Clifford (1909–92) Geographer, born in Resolven, Neath and Port Talbot, SC Wales, UK. He studied at Cambridge, where he lectured (1931–45) and became a fellow of King's College (1932–45, 1966–81). He was the first professor of geography at Liverpool (1945–9), and was later professor at University College, London (1949–66), and at Cambridge (1966–76). A leader in promoting the relationships between geography and other subjects, he was general editor of *The Domesday Geography of England* (7 vols, 1952–77), and was knighted in 1988.

Darby, John Nelson (1800–82) Clergyman, born in London, England, UK. He studied at Westminster School and Trinity College, Dublin, and was for a year or two an Anglican clergyman. In 1830 he was the principal founder of the Plymouth Brethren, and in 1840 an exclusive sect of it known as *Darbyites*.

D'Arcy, Margaretta >> **Arden, John**

Dare, Virginia (1587–?) The first English child born in North America, born in Roanoke, NC. Her parents were Ananias Dare and Elinor White. She disappeared along with the 117 Roanoke colonists in 1588.

Dargomizhsky, Alexander Sergeyevitch [dah(r)go-**mish**skee](1813–69) Composer, born in Tula, Russia. At the age of 22 he retired from government service to devote himself to music, and composed his first opera, *Esmeralda*. Later, under the influence of the Russian nationalist composers, his setting of Pushkin's *The Stone Guest* (completed by Rimsky-Korsakov) anticipated the work of Moussorgsky in its dramatic power and naturalistic treatment of words. >> Moussorgsky; Pushkin; Rimsky-Korsakov

Darío, Rubén [da**ree**oh], pseudonym of **Félix Rubén García Sarmiento** (1867–1916) Poet, born in Metapa, Nicaragua. He lived a wandering life of journalism, amours, and diplomatic appointments. His *Azul* (1888, Blue) and *Prosas Profanas* (1896, Profane Hymns) gave new vitality to Spanish poetic modernism. After 1898 he worked mainly in Europe, where he wrote *Cantos de vida y esperanza* (1905, Songs of Life and Hope).

Darius I [**dah**rius], known as **the Great** (548–486 BC) King of Persia (521–486 BC), one of the greatest of the Achaemenids. He is noteworthy for his administrative reforms, military conquests, and religious toleration. His division of the empire into provinces called *satrapies* outlasted the Achaemenids. His conquests, especially in the East and Europe (Thrace and Macedonia) consolidated the frontiers of the empire. Patriotic Greek writers made much of the failure of his two punitive expeditions against Athens, the first miscarrying through the wreck of his fleet off Mt Athos (492 BC), the second coming to grief at Marathon (490 BC); but in Persian eyes they were probably not very important. Although a worshipper himself of Ahura Mazda, who turned Zoroastrianism into a state religion, he showed an unusual respect for the religions of his subjects. >> Miltiades; Xerxes I; RR1063

Dark, Eleanor, *née* **O'Reilly**, pseudonym **Patricia O'Rane** or **P O'R** (1901–85) Writer, born in Sydney, New South Wales, Australia. Employed briefly as a stenographer, she married a general practitioner in 1922, and a year later moved to Katoomba in the Blue Mountains. From 1921 she wrote short stories and verse for various magazines, mostly under her pen name. Her novels include *Slow Dawning* (1932), *The Little Company* (1945), and the historical trilogy, *The Timeless Land* (1941), *Storm of Time* (1948), and *No Barrier* (1953). She was awarded the Australian Literature Society's gold medal in 1934 and 1936, and in 1978 received the Australian Society of Women Writers' Alice Award.

Darlan, (Jean Louis Xavier) François [dah(r)lã](1881–1942) French politican and naval officer, born in Nérac, France. He passed through the Ecole Navale in 1899, attaining flag rank in 1929. He became in turn minister of the navy and mercantile marine, vice-president of the Council of Ministers, and secretary of state for foreign affairs and the navy. During the Vichy regime he was admiral of the fleet, vice-premier, foreign minister, and minister for national defence. He was assassinated in Algiers, after he had concluded an armistice with the Allies, by an anti-Vichy agent.

Darling, Grace (1815–42) Heroine, born in Bamburgh, Northumberland, NE England, UK. She lived with her father, **William** (1795–1860), the lighthouse keeper on one of the Farne Islands. On 7 September 1838, she braved raging seas in an open rowing boat to rescue the survivors of the *Forfarshire*, which was stranded on one of the other islands in the group.

Darling, Jay Norwood, known as **Ding Darling** (1876–1962) Cartoonist, born in Norwood, MI. As a staff cartoonist on the Des Moines *Register* (1906–49) and the New York *Tribune* (later *Herald Tribune*) (1917–49), he won the Pulitzer Prize in 1923 and 1943. An active wildlife conservationist, he was chief of the US Biological Survey (1934–5) and president of the National Wildlife Federation (1936).

Darlington, William (1782–1863) Botanist, born in Birmingham, PA. The California pitcher plant (*Darlingtonia*) is named after him.

Darnley, Henry Stewart, Lord (1545–67) Nobleman, the second husband of Mary, Queen of Scots and father of James I of England, born at Temple Newsom, Yorkshire, N England, UK. He married **Mary** (his cousin) in 1565, and was made Earl of Ross and Duke of Albany. His debauchery and arrogance made him unpopular, and his part in the murder (1566) of the Queen's secretary, David Rizzio, caused his downfall. He became estranged from the Queen, and during an illness was killed at Edinburgh when Kirk O'Field, the house in which he was sleeping, was destroyed by gunpowder – the result of a plot probably organized by the Earl of Bothwell, perhaps with Mary's knowledge. >> Bothwell; James I (of England); Mary, Queen of Scots; Rizzio

Darrow, Charles (1889–1967) The inventor of the board game *Monopoly*, born in the UK. He offered the game to Parker Bros (the present owners) in the early 1930s, was turned down, and began producing the game himself. By 1935 his game was becoming popular, and Parker Bros reconsidered, purchasing the copyright in exchange for a royalty. Over 100 million sets in 23 languages had been sold worldwide by 1992.

Darrow, Clarence (Seward) (1857–1938) Lawyer, born in Kinsman, OH. He was admitted to the bar in 1878, and practised in Ohio and Illinois. When 37, he became counsel for Chicago and North Western Railways, but left this post when a strike of the American Railway Union occurred, and defended Eugene Debs who had called it. He took on further labour cases, and after World War 1 was involved in several notable defences, including the murder case against Nathan Leopold and Richard Loeb (1924), and the trial of John T Scopes (1925) for the teaching of Darwinian evolution in school. He was noted for his liberal views on segregation. >> Debs

Dart, Raymond (Arthur) (1893–1988) Palaeoanthropologist, born in Brisbane, Queensland, Australia. He studied at the universities of Queensland and Sydney, and taught at University College, London (1919–22), before becoming professor of anatomy at Johannesburg (1923–58). His discovery in a quarry at Taung, near the Kalahari Desert, of *Australopithecus africanus* in 1924 substantiated Darwin's view of Africa as the cradle of the human species. >> Darwin, Charles

Dart, Thurston (1921–71) Keyboard player, conductor, and musical scholar, born in London, England, UK. He studied at the Royal College of Music and London University, became professor of music at Cambridge (1962) and at London (1964), and was also director of the Philomusica of London (1955–9). A specialist in early music, he edited several editions of 16th-c and 17th-c English works.

Daru, Pierre Antoine (Noel Mattieu Bruno), comte (Count) [darü] (1767–1829) Military administrator and historian, born in Montpellier, France. He entered the army at 16, was imprisoned during the Terror, but was appointed secretary of the war industry in 1800 and intendant-general in Austria and Prussia. He was minister of war from 1811, and later was ennobled by Louis XVIII. He wrote histories of Venice and of Britain.

Darusmont, Frances >> **Wright, Fanny**

Darwin, Charles (Robert) see panel on p. 255

Darwin, Erasmus (1731–1802) Physician, born in Elton, Nottinghamshire, C England, UK, the grandfather of Charles Darwin. He studied at Cambridge and Edinburgh universities, and at Lichfield became a popular physician and prominent figure, known for his freethinking opinions, poetry, large botanical garden, mechanical inventions, and position in the Lunar Society. Many of his ideas on evolution anticipated later theories. His chief prose work is *Zoonomia, or the Laws of Organic Life* (1794–6). After his second marriage (1781), he settled in Derby. >> Darwin, Charles

Dashkova, Ekaterina Romanovna [dashkohva] (1743–1810) Russian princess and writer, born in St Petersburg. In 1759 she married **Prince Mikhail Ivanovich Dashkov** (?–1762). She was a leading supporter of the Empress Catherine II in the conspiracy that deposed her husband, Peter III, in 1762. She travelled widely in Europe, and was director of the Academy of Arts and Sciences in St Petersburg (1783–96). She wrote several plays, and was the first president of the Russian Academy (1783). >> Catherine II (the Great)

Dashwood, Edmée Elizabeth Monica >> **Delafield, E M**

Dassanowsky, Elfriede von [dasanofskee] (1924–) Operatic singer, pianist, and music educator, born in Vienna. At age 15, she was then the youngest female student admitted to the Vienna Academy of Music and Art. Her anti-fascist stance during the late 1930s halted her career, and she did not make her debut until 1946, when she became known as a pianist and a mezzo-soprano operatic singer. To promote the rebuilding of democratic cultural institutions in postwar Austria and Germany, she directed and performed in concerts for the Allied High Command (1947–9), founded new musical theatre ensembles in Vienna, and was instrumental in the revival of German-language cinema, founding Belvedere Film Productions in 1946. She moved to the USA in 1955, where she was a vocal coach in the film world of the 1960s,

and became a US citizen in 1962. She has since come to be recognized as a leading figure of postwar European culture.

Dassault, Marcel [dasoh], originally **Marcel Bloch** (1892–1986) Aviation pioneer, industrialist, and politician, born in Paris. He studied aeronautical design and electrical engineering at the Ecole Nationale Supérieure de L'Aéronautique (1913), and joined Henri Potez in building aircraft during World War 1. During World War 2 he was imprisoned in Buchenwald, and later converted from Judaism to Roman Catholicism. Following the war he adopted the name Dassault (his brother's code name in the French Resistance), and founded his own company, building a series of highly successful aircraft in the 1950s, such as the Mystère and Mirage, guided weapons, and specialized equipment. He was deputy in the National Assembly (1951–5), and for the Oise (1957–8), and was elected to the National Assembly in 1986.

Daswanth, also found as **Daswarth** or **Dasvanth** (16th-c) Painter at the court of the emperor Akbar the Great. Akbar was interested in the development of an Indian school of painting, and established an academy in which Hindu artists worked under the guidance of Persian painters. Daswanth was one of its three leading artists. Most of the surviving paintings of the 'Hamzanama', the adventures of Amir Hamza, the uncle of the prophet leader, were painted at the academy during Akbar's reign. >> Akbar

Daubigny, Charles François [dohbeenyee] (1817–78) Artist, born in Paris. He studied for a while in Italy (1835–6), but worked mainly in Paris. He was a member of the Barbizon School, painting landscapes, especially moonlight and river scenes, such as 'The Banks of the Oise' (1872, Reims). >> Rousseau, Théodore; Troyon

Daubrée, Gabriel Auguste [dohbray] (1814–96) Geologist and mineralogist, born in Metz, France. Professor of mineralogy and director of the Ecole des Mines at Paris, he was a pioneer of experimental geology. The mineral *daubreelite* is named after him.

Daudet, Alphonse [dohday] (1840–97) Writer, born in Nîmes, France. He moved to Paris in 1857, where he devoted himself to literature. He wrote a book of poems and several theatrical pieces, including *L'Arlésienne*, for which Bizet composed incidental music. Some of his best work appears in the journals, notably his sketches of Provençal subjects, collected as *Lettres de mon moulin* (1869, Letters from My Mill), and the extravaganza *Tartarin de Tarascon* (1872), with its two sequels. >> Bizet; Daudet, Léon

Daudet, (Alphonse Marie) Léon [dohday] (1867–1942) Writer and political activist, born in Paris, the son of Alphonse Daudet. He studied medicine but turned to journalism, and in 1899 helped to found the right-wing royalist newspaper *Action française*, of which he became editor in 1908. He sat in the Chamber of Deputies (1919–24), and spent some time in Belgium as a political exile. He is best remembered for his memoirs and critical works, especially *Le Stupide XIXe Siècle* (1922, The Stupid Nineteenth Century). >> Daudet, Alphonse

d'Aumale, duc >> **Aumale, duc d'**

Daumier, Honoré (Victorin) [dohmyay] (1808–79) Painter and caricaturist, born in Marseille, France. He won contemporary fame for satirical cartoons about government corruption, and was imprisoned for caricaturing the king. An opponent of artificial Classicism, he painted strongly realistic subject pictures, such as *The Third Class Carriage* (c.1862, New York City).

Daurat or **Dorat, Jean** [dohra] (c. 1510–1588) Scholar and poet, born in Limoges, France. As president of the Collège de Coqueret he superintended the studies of Ronsard,

CHARLES (ROBERT) DARWIN (1809–82)

Darwin was born in Shrewsbury, Shropshire. He was the son of Robert Waring Darwin and his wife Susannah; and the grandson of the scientist Erasmus Darwin, and of the potter Josiah Wedgwood. His mother died when he was eight years old, and he was brought up by his sister. He was taught Classics at Shrewsbury, then sent to Edinburgh to study medicine, which he hated, and a final attempt at educating him was made by sending him to Christ's College, Cambridge, to study theology (1827). During that period he loved to collect plants, insects, and geological specimens, guided by his cousin William Darwin Fox, an entomologist. His scientific inclinations were encouraged by his botany professor, John Stevens Henslow, who was instrumental, despite heavy paternal opposition, in securing a place for Darwin as a naturalist on the surveying expedition of HMS *Beagle* to Patagonia (1831–6).

Under Captain Robert Fitzroy, he visited Tenerife, the Cape Verde Is, Brazil, Montevideo, Tierra del Fuego, Buenos Aires, Valparaiso, Chile, the Galapagos, Tahiti, New Zealand, and Tasmania. In the Keeling Is he devised his theory of coral reefs. During this five-year expedition he obtained intimate knowledge of the fauna, flora, and geology of many lands, which equipped him for his later investigations. By 1846 he had published several works on the geological and zoological discoveries of his voyage – works that placed him at once in the front rank of scientists. He developed a friendship with Sir Charles Lyell, became secretary of the Geological Society (1838–41), and in 1839 married his cousin **Emma Wedgwood** (1808–96).

From 1842 he lived at Down House, Downe, Kent, a country gentleman among his gardens, conservatories, pigeons, and fowls. The practical knowledge he gained there, especially in variation and interbreeding, proved invaluable. Private means enabled him to devote himself to science, in spite of continuous ill-health; it was not realized until after his death that he had suffered from Chagas's disease, which he had contracted from an insect bite while in South America.

At Down House he addressed himself to the great work of his life – the problem of the origin of species. After five years collecting the evidence, he began to speculate on the subject. In 1842 he drew up his observations in some short notes, expanded in 1844 into a sketch of conclusions for his own use. These embodied the principle of natural selection, the germ of the Darwinian Theory, but with typical caution he delayed publication of his hypothesis.

However, in 1858 Alfred Russel Wallace sent him a memoir of the Malay Archipelago, which, to Darwin's surprise, contained in essence the main idea of his own theory of natural selection. Lyell and Joseph Hooker persuaded him to submit a paper of his own, based on his 1844 sketch, which was read simultaneously with Wallace's before the Linnean Society in 1858. Neither Darwin nor Wallace was present at that historic occasion.

Darwin then set to work to condense his vast mass of notes, and put into shape his great work, *On the Origin of Species by Means of Natural Selection*, published in 1859. This epoch-making work, received throughout Europe with the deepest interest, was violently attacked because it did not agree with the account of creation given in the Book of Genesis. But eventually it succeeded in obtaining recognition from almost all biologists.

Darwin continued to work at a series of supplemental treatises: *The Fertilisation of Orchids* (1862), *The Variation of Plants and Animals under Domestication* (1867), and *The Descent of Man and Selection in Relation to Sex* (1871), which postulated that the human race derived from a hairy animal belonging to the great anthropoid group, and was related to the progenitors of the orang-utan, chimpanzee, and gorilla. In his 1871 work he also developed his important supplementary theory of sexual selection. Later works include *The Expression of Emotions in Man and Animals* (1872), *Insectivorous Plants* (1875), *The Effects of Cross and Self Fertilisation in the Vegetable Kingdom* (1876), *Different Forms of Flowers in Plants of the Same Species* (1877), and *The Formation of Vegetable Mould through the Action of Worms* (1881).

Darwin died after a long illness, leaving eight children, several of whom achieved great distinction. Though not the sole originator of the evolution hypothesis, nor even the first to apply the conception of descent to plants and animals, he was the first thinker to gain for that theory a wide acceptance among biological experts. By adding to the crude evolutionism of Erasmus Darwin, Lamarck, and others, his own specific idea of natural selection, Darwin supplied a sufficient cause, which raised it from a hypothesis to a verifiable theory.

>> Darwin, Erasmus; Fitzroy, Robert; Hooker, Joseph Dalton; Lamarck; Lyell, Charles; Wallace, Alfred Russel

---

Joachim du Bellay, Baif, and Belleau. These poets, with whom he was united in the *Pléiade*, he trained for the task of reforming the vernacular and ennobling French literature by imitation of Greek and Latin models. He was appointed court poet by Charles IX. >> Baif; Bellay; Belleau; Ronsard

Dausset, Jean [dohsay] (1916–   ) Immunologist, born in Toulouse, France. After studying medicine in Paris, service in World War 2 in a blood transfusion unit developed his interest in haematology and in the immune response to transfusion. His work in this field led to 'tissue typing', which has since helped to reduce rejection risks in organ transplant surgery. He shared the Nobel Prize for Physiology or Medicine in 1980. >> RR1124

Davenant or **d'Avenant, Sir William** [dav enant] (1606–68)

Poet and playwright, born in Oxford, Oxfordshire, SC England, UK. His father kept the Crown at Oxford, at which Shakespeare used to stop between London and Stratford – hence the rumour that he was Shakespeare's illegitimate son. In 1628 he took to writing for the stage, his most successful work being *The Wits* (1636). In 1638, he became Poet Laureate, and was later manager of the Drury Lane Theatre. He was knighted in 1643 for services to the Crown during the Civil War. In 1656, he helped to revive drama, banned under Cromwell, and brought to the stage the first public opera in England. >> Cromwell, Oliver; Shakespeare, William

David (?–c. 962 BC) Second king of Israel, and the first of the dynasty that governed Judah and Israel until the exile, the youngest son of Jesse of Bethlehem. According to Jewish tradition he is the author of several of the Psalms, and according to some Christian traditions he is the ancestor of Jesus. He was a warrior under King Saul (and his son-in-law), but his successes against the Philistines (including the killing of Goliath) caused the king's jealousy, and he was forced to become an outlaw. After Saul's death, he became king over Judah in Hebron, and later was chosen king of all Israel. He made Jerusalem the political and religious centre of his kingdom, building a palace for himself on its highest hill, Zion (the 'city of David'), and placing the Ark of the Covenant there under a tent. He united the many tribes of Israel, and extended his territory from Egypt to the Euphrates. The later part of his reign was troubled by the revolts of his sons **Absalom** and **Adonijah**. He was succeeded by Solomon, his son by Bathsheba. >> Saul; Solomon; RR1064

David I (c. 1085–1153) King of Scots (1124–53), the youngest son of Malcolm Canmore and Queen (later St) Margaret. Educated at the court of Henry I of England, he became Earl of Huntingdon through his marriage to **Maud de Senlis** (c.1113). Once king, he emphasized his independence, systematically strengthened royal power, and firmly secured the foundations of the mediaeval Kingdom of Scotland. In 1136, as a nominal supporter of the claims of his niece, Empress Matilda, to the English crown, he embarked on wars of territorial conquest against Stephen. He was defeated in 1138 at the Battle of the Standard, near Northallerton, but from 1141 occupied the whole of N England to the Ribble and the Tees. >> Henry I (of England); Malcolm III; Margaret of Scotland; Matilda; Stephen; RR1095

David II (1324–71) King of Scots (1329–71), the only surviving son of Robert Bruce, born in Dunfermline, Fife, E Scotland, UK. He became king at the age of five. In 1334, after the victory of Edward III of England at Halidon Hill (1333) he fled to France. He returned in 1341, and later invaded England, but was defeated and captured at Neville's Cross (1346), and was kept prisoner for 11 years. After his death he was succeeded by his sister's son, Robert II. >> Bruce, Robert (1274–1329); Edward III; Robert II; RR1095

David or **Dewi, St** (?–601) Patron saint of Wales, born near St Bride's Bay, Pembrokeshire, SW Wales, UK. He was Bishop of Moni Judeorum, or Menevia (afterwards St David's), presided over two Welsh Synods, at Brefi and Caerleon, and founded many churches in S Wales. He died at Menevia, which became a shrine in his honour. Feast day 1 March.

David, Elizabeth, *née* **Gwynne** (1913–92) British writer of cookery books. She studied at the Sorbonne, Paris, returned to England with a love of French cuisine, travelled to the Mediterranean, and spent the war years in Egypt. Returning to Britain (1946), she published *A Book of Mediterranean Food* (1950), quickly followed by *French Country Cooking* (1951) and *Italian Food* (1954). She ran a kitchen shop in London (1965–73) which became a model for such shops throughout Britain and the USA, and continued writing, publishing *Spices, Salt and Aromatics in the English Kitchen* (1970). Her books, together with her articles in magazines and national newapapers, are credited with reviving (if not originating) current British interest in spices and exotic fruits.

David, Gerard [daveed] (c.1460–1523) Painter, born in Oudewater, The Netherlands. In 1484 he entered the Painters' Guild of Bruges, of which he became dean in 1501. Among his best works are the two altarpiece panels, 'The Judgment of Camlyses' (1498, Bruges).

David, Jacques Louis [dahveed] (1748–1825) Painter, born in Paris. He won the Prix de Rome in 1774, and studied in Italy until 1780. Returning to France, he became known for his paintings of classical themes and historical events, such as 'The Oath of the Horatii' (1784, Louvre). He entered with enthusiasm into the Revolution, and painted several of its leaders. After Robespierre's death he was twice imprisoned, and narrowly escaped with his life. Released in 1795, he produced his masterpiece, 'Les Sabines' (1799, commonly known as 'The Rape of the Sabines', Louvre), and in 1804 was appointed court painter by Napoleon. After the Bourbon restoration, he was banished in 1816 as a regicide, and died in Brussels. >> Robespierre

David, Pierre Jean [daveed], known as **David d'Angers** (1789–1856) Sculptor, born in Angers, France. He studied under Jacques Louis David in Paris, and then in Rome, where he was influenced by Ingres and Canova. He executed the pediment of the Pantheon, in Paris (1835–7), his most prestigious commission; he was also a prolific sculptor of portrait busts and medallions. In the Angers museum 200 of his works are preserved, as well as 400 of his medallions, and many drawings. >> Canova; David, Jacques Louis; Ingres

David-Neel, Alexandra (1868–1969) Oriental scholar and traveller in Tibet, born in Paris. She studied Sanskrit in Sri Lanka and India, then toured internationally as an opera singer. She continued to travel in Europe until 1911, when she returned to India, visiting the Dalai Lama in exile at Darjeeling and studying Tibetan Buddhism. Expelled from India in 1916, she went to Burma, Japan, and Korea, arriving in Beijing in 1917. She returned to Tibet in 1934, but was forced to leave by the Japanese advance of 1944, and retired to Digne in France. >> Dalai Lama

Davidson, Donald (1917–) Philosopher, born in Springfield, MA. He became professor at the University of California, Berkeley, and an influential analytical philosopher, with contributions to the philosophy of language, mind, and action.

Davidson, Jo (1883–1952) Sculptor, born in New York City. He studied at the Art Student League (C.1899) and Yale Art School (c.1890), then worked for some years in New York City. From 1907 he lived primarily in Paris, retiring to the USA in 1940. He is known for his sculptured portraits, which include Woodrow Wilson (1916), Gertrude Stein (1920), and Allied war leaders (1918–19).

Davidson (of Lambeth), Randall Thomas Davidson, Baron (1848–1930) Anglican clergyman, born in Edinburgh, EC Scotland, UK. He studied at Oxford, was chaplain to Archbishop Tait (his father-in-law) and to Queen Victoria, Dean of Windsor, Bishop of Rochester (1891) and of Winchester (1895), and Archbishop of Canterbury (1903–28). >> Tait, Archibald Campbell

Davie, Alan (1920–) Painter, born in Grangemouth, Falkirk, C Scotland, UK. He studied at Edinburgh College of Art (1937–40). His paintings in the subsequent decade had much in common with contemporary American Abstract Expressionism. His imaginative use of pictographic images suggestive of myth and magic, increasingly bold and colourful since the early 1970s, reflects his preoccupation with Zen and oriental mysticism.

Davies, Christian, known as **Mother Ross** (1667-1739) Soldier, born in Dublin. She went to Flanders in search of her husband, **Richard Welsh**, who had been pressed into Marlborough's army. There she enlisted as a private under the name of **Christopher Welsh**, and fought in the Battle of Blenheim (1704) and other battles, eventually being reunited with her husband in 1706. When he was killed at the Battle of Malplaquet (1709), she married a grenadier, **Hugh Jones**, who was killed the following year. She returned to Dublin, where she married another soldier, called Davies. She died in Chelsea Pensioners' Hospital for old soldiers.

Davies, Clement (Edward) (1884–1962) British politician, leader of the Liberal Party (1945–56), born in Llanfyllin, Powys, E Wales, UK. He studied at Cambridge, and was called to the bar in 1909. Elected MP for Montgomeryshire in 1929, he held his seat until his death. Although offered a post as education secretary in Churchill's 1951–5 government, he declined, and saved the Liberal Party from being subsumed in the Conservative Party (as had the National Liberals). In doing this, he lost his only chance of holding office, but put Party above career. >> Churchill, Sir Winston

Davies, David Davies, Baron (1880–1944) Philanthropist, born in Llandinam, Powys, E Wales, UK. He was a major benefactor of the University College of Wales, Aberystwyth, and the National Library of Wales. A Liberal MP for Montgomeryshire (1906–29) and close associate of Lloyd-George, after World War 1 he turned his attention to support for the League of Nations. In 1933 he founded the New Commonwealth Society. >> Lloyd-George, David

Davies, Sir Henry Walford (1869–1941) Composer, organist, and broadcaster, born in Oswestry, Shropshire, WC England, UK. He became professor of music at Aberystwyth (1919–26), organist of St George's Chapel, Windsor (1927–32), and Master of the King's Music (1934–41). He was a prolific composer of religious music, and an influential educationist through his radio talks on music.

Davies, Howard (1945–) Stage director, born in Reading, Berkshire, S England, UK. After taking a director's course at Bristol University, he became associate director of Bristol Old Vic, and joined the Royal Shakespeare Company (RSC) in 1975. He became an associate director to establish and run the Warehouse, the RSC's London studio theatre (1977–82), and a National Theatre associate director in 1988.

Davies, (Edward) Hunter (1936–) Writer, journalist, and broadcaster, born in Renfrew, Renfrewshire, W Scotland, UK. He studied at Durham University, joined the *Sunday Times* as a reporter (1960), and became chief feature writer (1967) and editor of the *Sunday Times Magazine* (1975–7). He is well known for his 'Father's Day' column in *Punch* (1979–89, televised 1983), and as presenter of the radio programme *Bookshelf* (1983–6). He has written several novels, including *A Very Loving Couple* (1971) and *Saturday Night* (1989), as well as a great deal of non-fiction, such as *The Joy of Stamps* (1983), *The Good Guide to the Lakes* (1984), and *Living on the Lottery* (1996). >> Forster, Margaret

Davies, Paul (Charles William) (1946–) Physicist and popularizer of science, born in London. He studied at University College London, and became professor of theoretical physics at Newcastle (1980–90), then professor of mathematical physics at Adelaide, Australia (professor of natural philosophy since 1993). His numerous popular books on science, such as *God and the New Physics* (1983), reflect his research interests in particle physics and quantum gravity. The connections between science and religion are explored in several works, notably *The Mind of God* (1992), and he received the Templeton Prize for Progress in Religion in 1995.

Davies, Sir Peter Maxwell (1934–) Composer, born in Manchester, Greater Manchester, NW England, UK. He studied at Manchester, Rome, and Princeton, and was composer-in-residence at the University of Adelaide in 1966. He founded and co-directed the Pierrot Players (1967–70) and was founder/artistic director of The Fires of London (1971–87). A prolific composer, his works include *Taverner* (1972) and three other operas, *Eight Songs for a Mad King* (1969), symphonies, concertos, works for individual instruments and instrumental ensembles, songs, and a considerable amount of chamber music (for which he received the Cobbett Medal in 1989). Since 1970 he has worked mainly in Orkney, frequently using Orcadian or Scottish subject matter for music. He became associate composer/conductor with the Scottish chamber Orchestra in 1985, and was made composer laureate in 1994. He was knighted in 1987.

Davies, (William) Robertson (1913–95) Writer, playwright, essayist, and critic, born in Thamesville, Ontario, Canada. He studied in Canada and at Oxford, worked as a teacher, actor, and journalist, was editor of the Peterborough *Examiner* (1942–63), and became professor of English at the University of Toronto (1960–81). He was best known for 'The Deptford Trilogy': *Fifth Business* (1970), *The Manticore* (1972), and *World of Wonders* (1975). *What's Bred in the Bone* (1985) was shortlisted for the Booker Prize.

Davies, Sarah Emily (1830–1921) Feminist and educational reformer, born in Southampton, Hampshire, S England, UK. A vigorous campaigner for higher education for women, in 1869 she founded a small college for women students at Hitchin, which was transferred to Cambridge as Girton College in 1873. She was Mistress of Girton (1873–5), and honorary secretary (1882–1904).

Davies, Siobhan [shuh**vawn**], originally **Susan Davies** (1950–) Dancer and choreographer, born in London, England, UK. She studied art and then modern dance at the London Contemporary Dance School, and joined the company in 1969, later becoming joint director and resident choreographer. She started her own company in 1981, joined with Ian Spink to found Second Stride, and launched her own company again in 1988. Her works include *Relay* (1972), *Plainsong* (1981), and *Wyoming* (1988). She has twice received the Laurence Olivier Award for outstanding achievement in dance (1993, 1996). >> Alston; Spink

Davies, W(illiam) H(enry) (1871–1940) Poet, born in Newport, SE Wales, UK. Emigrating to the USA in 1893, he lived as a tramp and casual workman until the loss of a leg while 'jumping' a train caused him to return to England, where he began to write. He lived a wandering life to raise enough money to have his poems printed (1905). Once known, he wrote several books of poetry, essays, and a well-known prose work, *The Autobiography of a Super-tramp* (1908).

da Vinci, Leonardo >> **Leonardo da Vinci**

Daviot, Gordon >> **Mackintosh, Elizabeth**

Davis, (Daisie) Adelle (1904–74) Nutritionist and writer, born in Lizton, IN. She studied at the University of California and at hospitals in New York City, then settled in California to work as a consulting nutritionist, planning diets for people suffering from various diseases and ailments. In 1954 she published *Let's Eat Right to Keep Fit*, which quickly gained a devoted following for her emphasis on a proper diet as prerequisite for emotional and physical well-being. What particularly distinguished her approach was her claim that diet (especially one rich in vitamins and minerals) could actually prevent or cure diseases. For this she was often criticized by the medical establishment, and she died before her broad views began to be accepted by many in the field of health.

Davis, Andrew (Frank) (1944–) British conductor. He studied at the Royal College of Music in London, King's College, Cambridge, and with Franco Ferrara in Rome. He made his debut in 1970 conducting the BBC Symphony Orchestra, became assistant conductor of the Philharmonia Orchestra (1973–7), principal guest conductor of Royal Liverpool Philharmonic (1974–7), and musical director of the Toronto Symphony Orchestra (1975–88, conductor laureate from 1988). In 1988 he was appointed music director of the Glyndebourne Festival Opera, and has been chief conductor of the BBC Symphony Orchestra since 1989.

Davis, Arthur Vining (1867–1962) Industrialist and philanthropist, born in Sharon, MA. Working with Charles Hall at the Pittsburgh Reduction Co, he poured the first commercial aluminum in 1888. By 1907, as director of the company, he converted it into the Aluminum Company of America (Alcoa), which he served as general manager, president, and chairman of the board until retiring in 1958. As the nation's premier manufacturer of aluminum, he often had to fend off antitrust suits from the government. He gave most of his $400 million estate to the Davis Foundation, which supports educational, scientific, and cultural institutions. >> Hall, Charles

Davis, Bette, popular name of **Ruth Elizabeth Davis** (1908–89) Film actress, born in Lowell, MA. After a short stage career she went to Hollywood in 1930, and had her first success in *The Man who Played God* (1932). Numerous leading roles followed, among them *Of Human Bondage* (1934), *Dangerous* (1935, Oscar), and *Jezebel* (1938, Oscar), which established her as a major star for the next three decades. She was outstanding in *Whatever Happened to Baby Jane?* (1962), in which she co-starred with her long-term rival, Joan Crawford. Later appearances included *Death on the Nile* (1979), *The Whales of August* (1987) opposite Lillian Gish, and many television productions. >> Crawford, Joan

Davis, Carl (1936–) Composer and conductor, born in New York City. He studied in New York and Copenhagen, and in 1958 became assistant conductor of New York City Opera. A prolific composer, among his works for ballet are *Liaison Amoureuses* (1988, Northern Ballet Theatre), *The Savoy Suite* (1993, English National Ballet), and *Alice in Wonderland* (1995, English National Ballet). His music for television includes *The World at War* (1972, Emmy), *The Accountant* (1989, BAFTA), and *Pride and Prejudice* (1995), and for film *The French Lieutenant's Woman* (1981, BAFTA), *Scandal* (1988), and *Waterloo* (1995). He has also written for the theatre, as well as concert works. >> McCartney

Davis, Sir Colin (Rex) (1927–) Conductor, born in Weybridge, Surrey, SE England, UK. He studied at Christ's Hospital and the Royal College of Music, and became assistant conductor of the BBC Scottish Orchestra (1957–9), then moved to Sadler's Wells as a conductor and (1961–5) musical director. He was chief conductor of the BBC Symphony Orchestra (1967–71) and musical director at Covent Garden (1971–86). At Covent Garden he gained his reputation as a Wagner conductor of international standing with a new production of the *The Ring*. He became chief conductor of the Bavarian Radio Symphony Orchestra (1983–92) and was appointed principal conductor of the London Symphony Orchestra in 1995. He was knighted in 1980.

Davis, Dwight F(illey) (1879–1945) Public official, born in St Louis, MO. In 1900 he donated an international challenge cup for lawn tennis, competed for annually. The *Davis Cup* signifies the world team championship.

Davis, Fred >> **Davis, Joe**

Davis, Geena (1957–) Film actress, born in Wareham, MA. She studied at Boston University and was a model before she made her film debut with a small role in *Tootsie* (1982). She won an Oscar for Best Supporting Actress for *The Accidental Tourist* (1988), and critical acclaim for her role as Thelma in the controversial film *Thelma and Louise* (1991). Other films include *Beetlejuice* (1989), *Angie* (1994), and *The Long Kiss Goodnight* (1996).

Davis, Jack (1917–) Writer and actor, born in Perth, Western Australia. He is a prominent Aboriginal writer who draws much from the traditions of his own people, the Nyoongarah of the SW of Western Australia. Director of the Aboriginal Centre (1967–71), he began to publish relatively late in his life. His poetry includes *The Firstborn* (1970), *Jagardoo* (1978), and *Black Life: Poems* (1992). His plays include *Kullark* (1979, Home), *The Dreamers* (1982), *No Sugar* (1986), and *Wahngin Country* (1992).

Davis, Jefferson (1808–89) US statesman, president of the Confederate States during the Civil War (1861–5), born in Christian Co, KY. After training at West Point, he served in several frontier campaigns. He entered Congress for Mississippi (1845), fought in the Mexican War (1846–7), and became secretary of war (1853–7). In the US Senate he led the extreme States' Rights Party, and supported slavery, in 1861 being chosen president of the Confederacy. At the close of the Civil War he was imprisoned for two years, then released on bail. Though indicted for treason, he was never brought to trial, and was included in the amnesty of 1868. >> Miles, Nelson

Davis, Joe, popular name of **Joseph Davis** (1901–78) Billiards and snooker champion, born in Whitwell, Derbyshire, C England, UK. The first great snooker player, he popularized the game in the 1920s. Responsible for inaugurating the World Championship in 1927, he won every title between then and 1946, when he retired from world championship play. He retired from all competitive play in 1964. In 1955 at the Leicester Square Hall he became the first man to compile an officially recognized maximum snooker break of 147. His brother, **Fred Davis** (1913–), followed the same career, winning the first of his 10 world titles in 1948. >> RR1168

Davis, John (c. 1550–1605) Navigator, born in Sandridge, Devon, SW England, UK. In 1585–7 he undertook three Arctic voyages in search of a Northwest Passage, in the last of which he reached 73°N, and discovered the Strait later named after him. He discovered the Falkland Is in 1592. On a journey to the East Indies he was killed by Japanese pirates at Bintang, near Singapore.

Davis, Judy (1956–) Actress, born in Perth, Western Australia. Originally a singer in jazz and pop groups, she studied at the National Institute of Dramatic Arts in Sydney (1974–7), made her film debut in *High Rolling* (1976), then worked with the Adelaide State Theatre Company, appearing in such plays as *Visions* (1978). Her performance as the strong-willed, 19th-c heroine of the film *My Brilliant Career* (1979) earned her international attention. Later films include *Heatwave* (1981), *High Tide* (1987), *Barton Fink* (1991), *The Ref* (1994), and *Children of the Revolution* (1996). Her work in *A Passage to India* (1984) brought her an Oscar nomination, as did her role in Woody Allen's *Husbands and Wives* (1992).

Davis, Miles (Dewey) (1926–91) Trumpeter, composer, and bandleader, born in Alton, IL. He became the most influential stylist and most admired instrumentalist of the postwar era, from 1948 leading a nonet that introduced the style known as 'cool jazz'. He displayed a wistful, introverted, expressive lyricism (as in 'Round About Midnight', 1955), introduced new modal structures ('Milestones', 1958), soloed in elegant orchestrations ('Porgy and Bess', 1958), and fused jazz harmonies with rock instrumentation and rhythms (*In a Silent Way*, 1969). After retiring for six years due to ill health, he resumed performing at the 1981 Kool Jazz Festival, New York City.

Davis, Sammy, Jr (1925–90) Singer, actor, and dancer, born in New York City. He began his career tap-dancing in vaudeville with his father, and went on to solo performing and recording success in the 1950s and 1960s. In 1956 he starred on Broadway in *Mr Wonderful*, and in 1964 in *Golden Boy*. His films include *Porgy and Bess* (1959), *Robin and the Seven Hoods* with fellow 'rat-pack' members Frank Sinatra and Dean Martin (1964), *Sweet Charity* (1968), and *Taps*

(1980). He continued to entertain and record until the early 1980s.

Davis, Steve (1957–) Snooker player, born in London, England, UK. He dominated snooker in the 1980s, winning the world championship six times: 1981, 1983–4, and 1987–9. His first major honour was the Coral UK Championship in Preston (1980), thereafter winning every major honour the game had to offer. In Oldham, during the Lada Classic (1982), he became the first man to compile a televised maximum 147 break. In the late 1980s, he topped the rankings every year. >> RR1168

Davis, Stuart (1894–1964) Painter and graphic artist, born in Philadelphia, PA. He studied art with Robert Henri in New York City (1910–13), and worked with John Sloan as an illustrator for the left-wing journal, *The Masses* (1913–16). The Armory Show in 1913 converted him to avant-garde French art, especially Cubism. His imitation collages such as 'Lucky Strike' (1921, Museum of Modern Art, New York) anticipated Pop Art by 35 years. >> Henri; Sloan, John

Davis, William Morris (1850–1934) Geomorphologist, born in Philadelphia, PA. He studied at Harvard, where he became an instructor in physical geography (1878), assistant professor (1885), and professor of geology (1899–1912) until his retirement. He was responsible for introducing professional geography into the USA, and formulated the cycle of erosion.

Davison, Emily (1872–1913) Suffragette, born in London, England, UK. She studied at London University and Oxford, and in 1906 became a militant member of the Women's Social and Political Union. Frequently imprisoned, she often resorted to hunger-striking. In the 1913 Derby, wearing a WSPU banner, she tried to catch the reins of the king's horse and was trampled underfoot, dying several days later.

Davisson, Clinton J(oseph) [dayvison] (1881–1958) Physicist, born in Bloomington, IL. He studied at Chicago and Princeton, where he was instructor in physics before taking up industrial research at the Bell Telephone Laboratories. In 1927, with Lester Halbert Germer, he discovered the diffraction of electrons by crystals, thus confirming Louis Victor de Broglie's theory of the wave properties of electrons. In 1937 he shared the Nobel Prize for Physics. >> Germer; Broglie, Louis Victor

Davitt, Michael [davit] (1846–1906) Founder of the Irish Land League, born in Straid, Co Mayo, Ireland. Before becoming a journalist, he worked in a cotton mill, where he lost an arm in an accident. In 1866 he joined the Fenian Movement, and was arrested in 1870 for sending guns to Ireland from the USA, and sentenced to 15 years penal servitude. Released in 1877, he began an anti-landlord crusade which culminated in the Land League (1879). During a further period of imprisonment, he was elected an MP (1882), but disqualifed from taking his seat. A strong Home Ruler and opponent of Parnell, he was twice more an MP (1892–3, 1895–9). >> Parnell

Davout, Louis Nicolas [davoo] (1770–1823) French soldier, born in Annoux, France. He was educated with Napoleon at the military school of Brienne. As general, he accompanied Napoleon to the East, and mainly secured the victory at Aboukir (1799). A marshal of the empire (1804), he fought at Austerlitz (1805), Auerstädt (1806), Eckmühl (1809), Wagram (1809), and in the Russian campaign (1812–13), and was created Duke of Auerstädt (1808) and Prince of Eckmühl (1811). On Napoleon's return from Elba in 1815, he was appointed war minister; and after Waterloo he received the command of the remnant of the French army under the walls of Paris. In 1819 he was made a peer of France. >> Kutuzov; Napoleon

Davy, Edward (1806–85) Physician and scientist, born in Ottery St Mary, Devon, SW England, UK. He studied medicine, and commenced business in London as a chemist, but at about 30 began experimenting with telegraphy. He emigrated to Adelaide, South Australia, in 1838, where he involved himself in civic affairs, and continued his experiments on subjects including starch production and the smelting of copper. As inventor of the electromagnetic repeater, he stands alongside Wheatstone and Cooke as one of the founders of wireless telegraphy. >> Cooke, William Fothergill; Wheatstone

Davy, Sir Humphry (1778–1829) Chemist, born in Penzance, Cornwall, SW England, UK. In 1795 he was apprenticed to a Penzance surgeon, and in 1797 took up chemistry. He investigated the respiration of gases, and discovered the anaesthetic effect of laughing gas. In 1801 he became a lecturer at the Royal Institution. His fame chiefly rests on his discovery that chemical compounds could be decomposed into their elements using electricity. In this way he discovered potassium, sodium, barium, strontium, calcium, and magnesium. In 1815 he invented the miner's safety lamp. In 1812 he was knighted, made a baronet in 1818, and in 1820 became president of the Royal Society.

Dawes, Charles G(ates) (1865–1951) US statesman and financier, born in Marietta, OH. He was head of the Commission which drew up the *Dawes Plan* (1924) for German reparation payments to Europe after World War 1, for which he shared the Nobel Peace Prize in 1925. He was Republican vice-president of the USA under Coolidge (1925–9). >> Coolidge, Calvin; RR1097

Dawes, Sophie, baronne de (Baroness of) **Feuchères** (1790–1840) Adventuress, born in St Helens, Isle of Wight, S England, UK. She grew up in a workhouse, found work as a servant in London, and became the mistress of the Duc de Bourbon (1756–1830). He arranged for her education and for her marriage to the **Baron de Feuchères** (1818), and presented her at the court of Louis XVIII. Bequeathed a fortune in the duke's will she was suspected of his murder (1830), but was not prosecuted due to lack of evidence.

Dawkins, (Clinton) Richard (1941–) British zoologist, born in Nairobi, Kenya. His family returned to England in 1949, where he studied zoology at Oxford. He taught at the University of California, Berkeley (1967–70) then returned to Oxford. His work on animal behaviour and genetics emphasizes that apparently selfish behaviour is designed to ensure survival of the gene, apparently above that of the carrier (*The Selfish Gene*, 1976), and this and wider views on behaviour and evolution have been developed in *The Blind Watchmaker* (1986), *River out of Eden* (1995), *Climbing Mount Improbable* (1996), and other works. He introduced the concept of a cultural analogue of the gene, the *meme*, to capture the notion that some ideas seem to take on a life of their own within society, even affecting the course of evolution. One of the most successful popularizers of his subject, he became Charles Simonyi professor of public understanding of science at Oxford in 1995. He remains a controversial media figure, known as much for his aggressive atheism as for his scientific views on evolution.

Dawson, Charles (1864–1916) Solicitor and antiquarian, born at Fulkeith Hall, Lancashire. An amateur geologist, he was the victim (or perpetrator?) of the celebrated 'Piltdown Man' hoax, when cranial fragments, found by him at Piltdown from 1908 to 1912, together with parts of a jawbone unearthed later, were accepted by anthropologists as the 'Missing Link' in Darwin's theory of evolution, and named after him *Eoanthropus dawsoni* ('Dawson's Dawn Man'). It was not until 1953 that the skull was formally denounced as a fake. >> Clark, Wilfred; Darwin, Charles

Dawson, George Mercer (1849–1901) Geologist, born in Pictou, Nova Scotia, Canada. He studied at McGill University, and did much pioneer geological work in British Columbia and the Yukon, where Dawson City was named after him.

Dawson, Peter (1882–1961) Bass-baritone, born in Adelaide, South Australia. He won a solo competition at Ballarat, Victoria, in 1901 and the following year left for London, where he studied for three years. He made his debut at Covent Garden in 1909, and appeared regularly in oratorios, but he was best known for his ballad singing. He was a prolific recording artist, using a variety of pseudonyms, including **Will Danby**, **Hector Grant**, and **Will Strong**. Many of the ballads he sang were written by Dawson himself, under the name **J P McColl**.

Day, Doris, originally **Doris Kappelhoff** (1924–) Singer and film actress, born in Cincinnati, OH. A vocalist with several big bands, and a radio favourite in the 1940s, she made her film debut in *Romance on the High Seas* (1948). Her sunny personality, singing talent, and girl-next-door image made her an asset to many standard Warner Brothers musicals of the 1950s. Her films include *Calamity Jane* (1953), *Young at Heart* (1954), and *The Pajama Game* (1957). The popularity of the comedy *Pillow Talk* (1959) earned her an Oscar nomination. She retired from the screen after *With Six You Get Egg Roll* (1968), but appeared occasionally on television and also in *The Doris Day Show* (1968–73).

Day, Dorothy (1897–1980) Writer and radical social reformer, born in New York City. A life-long Socialist, she worked in the New York City slums as a probationary nurse. Converted to Catholicism in 1927, she co-founded the monthly *Catholic Worker* in 1933. Under the influence of the French itinerant priest **Peter Maurin** (1877–1949), she founded the Catholic Worker Movement, which established 'houses of hospitality' and farm communities for people hit by the Depression. A pacifist and a fervent supporter of farm-worker unionization in the 1960s, she helped turn her Church's attention to peace and justice issues.

Day, Sir (Judson) Graham (1933–) Business executive, born in Halifax, Nova Scotia, Canada. He studied in Canada, and spent eight years in private practice as a lawyer before joining Canadian Pacific in 1964. In 1975 he went to British Shipbuilders as deputy chairman and chief executive designate, but left in 1977 to take a chair at Dalhousie University. In 1983 he returned to British Shipbuilders as chairman and chief executive, later becoming chairman of the Rover Group (1986–91), Cadbury Schweppes (1989–93), and Power Gen (1990–3). He was knighted in 1989.

Day, John (1522–84) Printer, born in Dunwich, Suffolk, E England, UK. One of the first English music printers, he produced the earliest church service book with musical notation (1560), and in the same year Archbishop Matthew Parker's English version of the psalms, with music by Tallis and others. His most celebrated publication was John Foxe's *Actes and Monuments* (1563), better known as the *Book of Martyrs*. >> Foxe, John; Parker, Matthew; Tallis

Day, Sir Robin (1923–) Journalist and broadcaster, born in London, England, UK. After service in the Royal Artillery (1943–7), he studied law at Oxford (1947–51) and was called to the bar in 1952. He became a freelance broadcaster in 1954, working first at ITN (1955–9), then joining the BBC's *Panorama*, which he presented from 1967 to 1972. He brought an acerbic freshness to interviewing techniques, and has proved a formidable inquisitor of political figures. His radio work includes *It's Your Line* (1970–6) and *The World at One* (1979–87), while his television credits include *Question Time* (1979–89). Among his publications is *...But With Respect – Memorable Interviews* (1993). He was knighted in 1981.

Dayan, Moshe [diyan] (1915–81) Israeli general and statesman, born in Deganya, Palestine. During the 1930s he joined the illegal Jewish defence organization, Haganah,

and was imprisoned by the British (1939–41), then released to fight with the Allies in World War 2 (when he lost his left eye, thereafter wearing his distinctive black eye patch). He became chief-of-staff (1953–8), joined the Knesset as a Labour member in 1959, but left the Labour Party in 1966 to set up the Rafi Party with Ben-Gurion. He won international acclaim as defence minister in 1967 when his heavily outnumbered forces triumphed over Egypt, Jordan, and Syria in the Six Day War, and he himself became a symbol of Israeli dash and courage. As foreign minister, he helped to secure the historic peace treaty with Egypt (1977). He resigned from the Begin government in 1979, and launched a new centre party in 1981. >> Begin; Ben-Gurion

Day-Lewis, C(ecil) (1904–72) Poet, born in Ballintubber, Co Kildare, Ireland. He studied at Oxford, and became a teacher. During the 1930s he was known as a leading left-wing writer, but in 1939 he broke away from Communism. He was professor of poetry at Oxford (1951–6), and wrote detective stories under the pseudonym of **Nicholas Blake**. His *Collected Poems* appeared in 1954, and his autobiographical *The Buried Day* in 1960. He was created Poet Laureate in 1968. >> Day-Lewis, Daniel

Day-Lewis, Daniel (1958–) Film actor, born in London, England, UK, the son of C Day-Lewis. He trained at the Bristol Old Vic, and became well known for *My Beautiful Launderette* (1985) and *Room With A View* (1985). He won several awards for his portrayal of handicapped Irish writer Christy Brown in *My Left Foot* (1989, Oscar). Later films include *The Last of the Mohicans* (1992), *Age of Innocence* (1992), *In the Name of the Father* (1993), and *The Crucible* (1996). Major theatre performances include *Romeo and Juliet* (1983) and *Hamlet* (1989). >> Day-Lewis, C

Deák, Francis [dayak] (1803–76) Hungarian statesman, born in Zala (formerly Söjtör), Hungary. He practised as an advocate, entered the National Diet in 1832, and played the part of a moderate, becoming in 1848 minister of justice. Hailed in 1861 as leader in the Diet, by his efforts Hungary's constitution was restored in 1867 and the dual monarchy of Austria–Hungary established.

Deakin, Alfred (1856–1919) Australian statesman and prime minister (1903–4, 1905–8, 1909–10), born in Melbourne, Victoria, Australia. He became minister of public works and water supply, and solicitor general of Victoria; then, under the Commonwealth, attorney general (1901) and prime minister. One of the architects of federation, he established the industrial arbitration system and the first protective tariff, outlined defence policies, advocated the White Australia policy, and introduced the Commonwealth Literary Fund. >> RR1033

Deakin, Arthur (1890–1955) Trade union leader, born in Sutton Coldfield, West Midlands, C England, UK. A full-time trade union official from 1919, in 1935 he became assistant to Ernest Bevin, general secretary of the Transport and General Workers Union. In 1945 he himself became general secretary of the union, and president of the World Federation of Trade Unions (1945–9). He was also one of the founders of the International Confederation of Free Trade Unions. >> Bevin

Dean, Christopher >> **Torvill and Dean**

Dean, Dixie, popular name of **William Ralph Dean** (1907–80) Footballer and record goal-scorer, born in Birkenhead, Merseyside, NW England, UK. He turned professional with Tranmere Rovers at the age of 16, then joined Everton in 1925, and scored 349 goals in 399 games. In 1938 he played for Notts County for one season before injury ended his career. He still holds the remarkable scoring record of 60 League goals in one season.

Dean, James (Byron) (1931–55) Film actor, born in Marion, IN. He started acting at the University of California, Los

Angeles, in 1952 moving to New York City, where he eventually obtained a part in *See the Jaguar* on Broadway. He gained overnight success in the film *East of Eden* (1955). He made only two more films, *Rebel Without a Cause* (1955) and *Giant* (1956), before his death in a car crash. In just over a year he became the personification of contemporary American youth, and a cult figure, and for many years after his death he remained a symbol of youthful rebellion and self-assertion.

Dean, Laura (1945–) Dancer, choreographer, and teacher, born in New York City. She studied at Manhattan's High School of Performing Arts and School of American Ballet, danced in Paul Taylor's company (1965–6), and worked with Meredith Monk, Kenneth King, and Robert Wilson. She began choreographing in 1967, and in 1976 formed Laura Dean Dancers and Musicians, mainly featuring her own scores and those of composer Steve Reich. >> Monk, Meredith; Reich, Steve; Taylor, Paul; Wilson, Robert

Deane, Silas (1737–89) Diplomat and legislator, born in Groton, CT. He was the first diplomat sent abroad by the united colonies. In France in 1776, he persuaded the French government to send military supplies to the colonies under the guise of a holding company, and in concert with Arthur Lee (1740–1792) and Benjamin Franklin negotiated two treaties with France (1778). He was recalled to America following insinuations made against him of disloyalty and embezzlement, and although the accusations were never proved, they ended his career. He returned to Europe as a private citizen to prove his innocence, advocating reconciliation with the British. After the American Revolution he lived as an impoverished exile in Belgium and then London. In 1842, Congress re-examined the evidence in his case, and made restitution of $37 000 to his heirs. >> Franklin, Benjamin

Deane, Sir William (Patrick) (1931–) Governor-general of Australia, born in St Kilda, Victoria, Australia. He studied arts and law at the University of Sydney, Trinity College Dublin, and the Hague Academy of International Law. On his return to Australia, he entered the Sydney bar, became a QC, and was made a judge in the Supreme Court of New South Wales (1977), the Federal Court Bench (1977), and the Australian High Court (1982). He replaced Bill Hayden as governor-general in 1995. While he was expected to be a non-activist figurehead, he has in fact been outspoken on a number of issues, including the issue of reconciliation with Australian's indigenous population. >> Hayden

Dearie, Blossom (1926–) Singer, pianist, and songwriter, born in East Durham, NY. She sang with Woody Herman and other swing bands, and in 1958 became a nightclub singer accompanying herself on piano. Early recordings on Verve emphasized ballads, but on her own label, Daffodil, since 1974 she has added satirical songs such as 'I'm Hip' and 'Bruce', and a lengthening list of her own songs, including 'Inside a Silent Tear' and 'I Like You, You're Nice'. Her memorable nightclub performances are, at her insistence, early evening soirées in front of silent, non-smoking, non-eating audiences, with a single spotlight on her at the piano.

Déat, Marcel [dayah] (1894–1955) French statesman, born in Guerigny, France. He was the founder of the Socialist Party of France (1933), which was Fascist in outlook. His pro-Nazi sympathies procured him the post of minister of labour in the Vichy government, and achieved notoriety by his ruthless deportation of French workers to Germany. He fled to Germany in 1945, and was sentenced to death in absentia, but evaded arrest until his death in Turin.

Deayton, (Gordon) Angus [dayton] (1956–) Writer and broadcaster, born in Caterham, Surrey, S England, UK. Educated at Oxford, he contributed widely to revues and radio shows as a writer and performer, joining Rowan Atkinson in his stage show (1986–90), and becoming well known for his role as Victor Meldrew's long-suffering neighbour in BBC television's *One Foot in the Grave* (from 1989), receiving the Newcomer of the Year TV Comedy Award in 1991. He is best known on television as the host of *Have I Got News for You* (from 1990) and as writer/presenter of *In Search of Happiness* (1995). His books include *The Uncyclopaedia of Rock* (1987) and *In Search of Happiness* (1995).

DeBakey, Michael (Ellis) [debaykee] (1908–) Cardiovascular surgeon, born in Lake Charles, LA. He received his medical training at Tulane University, where he subsequently taught surgery until 1948, when he moved to Baylor University College of Medicine in Houston, TX. There, with Denton Cooley and others, he developed a centre of international reputation in the field of cardiovascular surgery. Among his many publications are *The Living Heart Guide to Eating Out* (1993) and *The New Living Heart Diet* (1996). >> Cooley

de Bary, Heinrich Anton [duh baree] (1831–88) Botanist, born in Frankfurt, Germany. Successively professor of botany at Freiburg and Halle, he then moved to Strasbourg, where he was also the first rector of the reorganized university. He studied the morphology and physiology of the fungi and the Myxomycetae, and is recognized as the founder of modern mycology.

de Basil, Colonel Wassili [duh bazil, vasilee], originally **Vasily Grigorievich Voskresensky** (1881–1951) Ballet impresario, personality, and publicist, born in Kaunas, Lithuania. Originally an army officer, he began his theatrical career in Paris as assistant to Prince Zeretelli, director of an itinerant Russian opera company. In 1932 he and René Blum co-founded the Ballet Russe de Monte Carlo, heir to Diaghilev's Ballets Russes. The company gained considerable international acclaim with its high calibre dancers. >> Blum, René; Diaghilev

Debayle, Anastasio / Luis >> **Somoza, Anastasio**

de Beauvoir, Simone [duh bohvwah(r)] (1908–86) Existentialist writer and novelist, born in Paris. She studied philosophy with Sartre at the Sorbonne, where she became professor (1941–3). Closely associated with his literary activities after World War 2, she remained his companion until his death (1980). Her own works provide existentialism with an essentially feminine sensibility, notably *Le Deuxième sexe* (1949, The Second Sex) and her masterpiece *Les Mandarins* (1954, Prix Goncourt). With Sartre she founded *Les Temps modernes* in 1945. >> Sartre

de Beer, Sir Gavin (Rylands) [duh beer] (1899–1972) Zoologist, born in London, England, UK. He served in both world wars and between them graduated from Oxford, then taught there (1923–38). After World War 2 he was professor of embryology in London, and from 1950 to 1960 director of the British Museum (Natural History). His work refuted some early theories in embryology, and he went on to contribute to theories of animal evolution, as well as to historical problems such as the origin of the Etruscans.

de Bono, Edward (Francis Charles Publius) [duh bohnoh] (1933–) Psychologist and writer, born in Malta. He studied medicine at the Royal University of Malta, then went as a Rhodes Scholar to Oxford, where he read psychology, physiology, and medicine. He was a lecturer in medicine at Cambridge (1976–83), and is now involved with a number of organizations to promote the skills of thinking which break out of the trammels of the traditional (*lateral thinking*). These include the Cognitive Research Trust, Cambridge (director since 1971), and the Supranational Independent Thinking Organization (secretary-general since 1983). His books include *The Use of Lateral Thinking* (1967), *Teaching Thinking* (1976), *I Am Right, You Are Wrong* (1990), and *Edward de Bono's Textbook of Wisdom* (1996).

de Bono, Emilio [duh **boh**noh] (1866–1944) Fascist politician and general, born in Cassano d'Adda, Italy. He was a quadrumvir in Mussolini's March on Rome (1922), Governor of Tripolitania (1925), and colonial secretary (1939), and commanded the Italian forces invading Abyssinia (1935). He voted against Mussolini in the Fascist Supreme Council (1943), and was summarily tried and executed as a traitor by neo-Fascists in Verona. >> Mussolini

Debray, Regis [duhbray] (1941–) French Marxist theorist. He studied at the Ecole Normale Supérieure, gained international fame through his association with the Marxist revolutionary Che Guevara in Latin America during the 1960s, and was sentenced to 30 years' imprisonment in Bolivia (1967). He was released from jail in 1970, and was appointed a specialist adviser to President Mitterrand on Third World affairs (1981). His most influential writings have been *Strategy for Revolution* (1970) and *The Power of the Intellectual in France* (1979). >> Guevara; Mitterrand

Debrett, John [duh**bret**] (c. 1750–1822) British publisher. He took over a publishing house in London, England, UK, in 1781, and compiled his *Peerage of England, Scotland and Ireland*, which first appeared in 1802. He was also the first to publish the major accounts of the discovery of Australia.

Debreu, Gerard [debroe] (1921–) Economist, born in Calais, France. He studied at the University of Paris, went to the USA in 1950 as a researcher with the Cowles Foundation at Chicago University, and was a professor at Yale (1955–61), then professor of mathematics and economics at the University of California, Berkeley (from 1962). He became a US citizen in 1975. His work on the equilibrium between prices, production, and consumer demand in a free-market economy was recognized by the award of the Nobel Prize for Economics in 1983.

de Broglie >> Broglie, duc de

Debs, Eugene V(ictor) (1855–1926) US politician, born in Terre Haute, IN. He worked as a locomotive fireman, and in 1893 became president of the American Railroad Union, in 1894 leading a successful national strike for higher wages. He helped to establish the Socialist Party of America, was imprisoned for labour agitation, and between 1900 and 1920 stood five times as socialist candidate for president. His pacifism brought him imprisonment (1918–21).

Deburau, Jean-Gaspard [debüroh], originally **Jan Kaspar Dvorak** (1796–1846) Mime artist, born in Kolín, Czech Republic, into a family of acrobats. He joined the Théâtre des Funambules in Paris (1816), and developed the character of Pierrot into a pale-faced hero, to the delight of audiences.

Debussy, Claude (Achille) [debüsee] (1862–1918) Composer, born in St Germain-en-Laye, France. Educated at the Paris Conservatoire (1873–84), he studied piano under Antoine-François Marmontel, and in 1884 won the Prix de Rome. His early successes were the *Prélude à l'après-midi d'un faune* (1894, Prelude to the Afternoon of a Faun), and his piano pieces, *Images* and *Préludes*, in which he experimented with novel techniques and effects, producing the pictures in sound which led to his work being described as 'musical Impressionism'. He extended this new idiom to orchestral music in *La Mer* (1905, The Sea) and other pieces.

Debye, Peter (Joseph Wilhelm) [duh**biy**] (1884–1966) Physicist and chemist, born in Maastricht, The Netherlands. He studied at Munich (where he later lectured), and was professor successively at Zürich, Utrecht, Göttingen, and Leipzig, and director of the Kaiser Wilhelm Institute for Physics, Berlin (1935–40). In 1936 he was awarded the Nobel Prize for Chemistry. In 1940 he went to the USA as professor of chemistry at Cornell. He was specially noted for his work on molecular structure, and also for his method of X-ray diffraction analysis using powdered crystals.

Decamps, Alexandre Gabriel [duhkã] (1803–60) Painter, born in Paris. A pioneer of the Romantic school, he was a great colourist, specializing in Oriental scenes and biblical subjects. One of his best pictures, 'The Watering Place', is in the Wallace collection in London.

Decatur, Stephen [dee**kay**ter] (1779–1820) US naval commander, born in Sinepuxent, MD. He became a midshipman (1798), and joined the Tripoli Squadron as a first lieutenant in 1801. He led a daring raid into the harbour of Tripoli and burned the captured USS *Philadelphia* (1804). He held various commands in home waters (1805–12) and served on the court martial that suspended Captain James Barron (1808). He led the USS *United States* to victory over HMS *Macedonian* (1812). In 1815 he surrendered the *President* after fighting against a much larger British naval force. He commanded the squadron that ended corsair raids from Algiers, Tunis, and Tripoli (1815) and returned home to give a famous toast, 'Our country! In her intercourse with foreign nations may she always be in the right; but our country, right or wrong'. He was killed in a duel with Barron. >> Barron

Decius [**dee**shus], in full **Caius Messius Quintus Trajanus Decius** (c.200–251) Roman emperor, born in Lower Pannonia. He was sent by Emperor Philip the Arab (ruled 244–9) to reduce the rebellious army of Moesia (249). The soldiers proclaimed him emperor against his will, and he defeated and killed Philip near Verona. Decius' brief reign was one of warring with the Goths, and he was killed near Abricium in 251. Under him the Christians were persecuted with great severity. >> RR1084

Decroux, Etienne-Marcel [duh**kroo**] (1898–1991) French actor. He was responsible for the renaissance of mime in the 20th-c by developing and teaching a system of physical expression he termed *mime corporel*. In 1940 he opened a school in Paris, and from 1941 onwards toured extensively, both teaching and performing. >> Marceau

Dedekind, (Julius Wilhelm) Richard [**day**dekind] (1831–1916) Mathematician, born in Braunschweig, Germany. He studied at Göttingen, where he wrote his doctoral thesis under Carl Friedrich Gauss in 1852. He taught at Göttingen (1854–8), then in Zürich, and returned to Braunschweig in 1862 as professor at the Polytechnic. He gave one of the first precise definitions of the real number system, did important work in number theory, and introduced many concepts which have become fundamental in modern algebra, in particular that of an 'ideal', building on the work of Ernst Kummer. >> Gauss; Kummer

de Duve, Christian (René) [duh **düv**] (1917–) Biochemist, born in Thames Ditton, Surrey, SE England, UK. He graduated in medicine at Louvain in 1941, held a chair of biochemistry there from 1951, and held a similar post concurrently at Rockefeller University, New York City, from 1962. He had a major part in discovering the lysosomes which contain the enzymes within animal and plant cells, and afterwards in studying their activity and the diseases linked with their disfunction. He shared the Nobel Prize for Physiology or Medicine in 1974. >> RR1124

Dee, John (1527–1608) Alchemist, geographer, and mathematician, born in London, England, UK. He studied at Cambridge and on the European mainland, where he travelled widely. He brought back many astronomical instruments, earned the reputation of a sorcerer, and was astrologer to the court of Elizabeth I. He gave advice to those seeking routes to the New World and Far East, and helped write the first English translation of Euclid's works. >> Euclid

Deeping, (George) Warwick (1877–1950) Novelist, born in Southend, Essex, SE England, UK. He trained as a doctor, but after a year gave up his practice to devote himself to writing. His early novels were mainly historical, and it was not until after World War 1 that he gained recognition with his best-seller, *Sorrell and Son* (1925).

Deere, John (1804–86) Inventor and manufacturer, born in Rutland, VT. He worked as a blacksmith until 1837, when he moved to Illinois. With a partner he designed a series of new ploughs, which sold modestly during the 1840s. He then designed on his own the first cast steel plough, a major advance that made it substantially easier for farmers to break and turn the heavy soil of the Great Plains. By 1855 his factory was selling more than 10 000 units a year. He continued to manage Deere and Co, manufacturers of agricultural implements, until his last illness.

Defoe, Daniel [de**foh**] (1660–1731) Writer, born in London, England, UK. He was educated at a dissenting academy, travelled widely in Europe, and set up in the hosiery trade. In 1688 he joined William III's army, and strenuously supported the King's party. In 1702 his satire *The Shortest Way with the Dissenters* raised much anger with Dissenters and High-Churchmen alike, and he was imprisoned at Newgate for seditious libel, where he continued his pamphleteering. On his release in 1704 he started *The Review*, writing it single-handed, three times a week, until 1713. During this time, his political conduct became highly equivocal; he supported, rejected, then supported again the Tory minister, Harley. After the accession of George I (1714) he returned to the writing of fiction, and achieved lasting fame with *Robinson Crusoe* (1719–20). His other major works include *A Journal of the Plague Year*, *Moll Flanders* (both 1722), and *Roxana* (1724). >> Harley; William III

De Forest, Lee [di **fo**rist] (1873–1961) Inventor, born in Council Bluffs, IA. He studied at Yale and Chicago universities, and became a pioneer of radio, introducing the grid into the thermionic valve, by which feeble radio signals could be amplified. He invented the Audion and the idea of cascading valves to obtain greater amplification, essential for successful radio transmission and reception. He also did much early work on sound reproduction for films. He was widely honoured as 'the father of radio' and 'the grandfather of television'.

Degas, (Hilaire Germain) Edgar [popularly **day**gah, Fr duh**gah**] (1834–1917) Artist, born in Paris. After studying at the Ecole des Beaux-Arts, he went to Italy, where he was influenced by the Renaissance painters. On his return to Paris he associated with the Impressionists and took part in most of their exhibitions from 1874 to 1886. He was also influenced by Japanese woodcuts and by photography. Among his best-known works are 'Dancer Lacing her Shoe' (c.1878, Paris) and 'Jockeys in the Rain' (1879, Glasgow). Later, because of failing sight, he concentrated on sculpture.

de Gasperi, Alcide >> **Gasperi, Alcide de**

de Gaulle, Charles (André Joseph Marie) [duh gohl] (1890–1970) French general and first president of the Fifth Republic (1958–69), born in Lille, France. He fought in World War 1, and became a strong advocate of mechanized warfare, but his efforts to modernize the French Army made little progress. With the fall of France (Jun 1940), he fled to England to raise the standard of the 'Free French', and entered Paris at the head of one of the earliest liberation forces (Aug 1944). He became head of the provisional government, then withdrew to the political sidelines. Following the troubles in North Africa he became prime minister (1958), and emerged as the one man able to inspire confidence after the postwar procession of indecisive leaders. In late 1958 he became president, and practised a high-handed yet extremely successful foreign policy, repeatedly surviving political crises by the lavish use of the referendum. Independence was granted to all French African

colonies (1959–60), and Algeria became independent (1962). He developed an independent French nuclear deterrent, signed a historic reconciliation treaty with West Germany, and blocked Britain's entry into the European Economic Community. He had an overwhelming victory in the 1968 election, after the 'student revolution', but in 1969 resigned after the defeat of his referendum proposals for Senate and regional reforms. He then retired to Colombey-les-Deux-Eglises. >> Soustelle; RR1049

de Havilland, Sir Geoffrey [duh **ha**viland] (1882–1965) Aircraft designer, born in Haslemere, Surrey, SE England, UK. He built his first plane in 1908 and became director of the firm bearing his name, producing many famous aircraft during and between the two world wars, including the Tiger Moth, the Mosquito, and the Vampire jet. He established a height record for light aircraft in 1928, won the King's Cup air race at the age of 51, and was knighted in 1944.

De Havilland, Olivia (Mary) (1916–) Actress, born in Tokyo. Brought up in the USA, she made her stage debut in 1933, and joined Warner Brothers (1935–42). She received Best Supporting Actress nominations for her performances in *Gone With The Wind* (1939) and *Hold Back The Dawn* (1941). She won Oscars for *To Each His Own* (1946) and *The Heiress* (1949). She later played many television roles, and published an autobiography, *Every Frenchman Has One* (1963).

Dehmel, Richard [**day**mel] (1863–1920) Poet, born in Brandenburg, Germany. He wrote intellectual verse showing the influence of Nietzsche. His works include *Weib und Welt* (1896, Woman and World) and *Schöne wilde Welt* (1913, Beautiful, Wild World). >> Nietzsche

Dehmelt, Hans G(eorg) [duh**melt**] (1922–) Physicist, born in Goerlitz, Germany. He moved to the USA to perform research at Duke University (1952–5), then went to the University of Washington. A pioneer in the field of particle physics, he shared the 1989 Nobel Prize for Physics for his work on trapping and separating ions and subatomic particles. >> RR1122

Deighton, Len [**day**tn], popular name of **Leonard Cyril Deighton** (1929–) Thriller writer, born in London, England, UK. He became, variously, an art student, a railway platemaker, and an air-steward. His first novel, *The Ipcress File* (1962), was written when he was 33, and became a best seller, as have almost all his books. A leading author of spy novels, notable titles are *Funeral in Berlin* (1964), *Only When I Larf* (1968) and the trilogy *Berlin Game* (1984), *Mexico Set* (1985), and *London Match* (1986). Later works include *City of Gold* (1992) and *Hope* (1995).

Déjazet, Virginie >> **Sardou, Victorien**

Dekker, Thomas (c.1570–c.1641) Playwright, born in London, England, UK. He was a prolific writer, but only a few of his plays were printed. His best-known works are the comedy, *The Shoemaker's Holiday* (1600), and *The Honest Whore* (1604; part II, 1630). He wrote several plays in collaboration with other Elizabethan playwrights, and was also well known as a writer of prose pamphlets giving a lively account of London life. During the 1630s he dropped out of notice, and nothing is known of his last years. >> Middleton; Webster, John

de Klerk, F(rederick) W(illem) [duh **klairk**] (1936–) South African statesman and president (1989–94), born in Johannesburg, South Africa. He studied at Potchestroom University, and established a legal practice in Vereeniging. He served in the National Party cabinets under Vorster and P W Botha, and in 1989, when he was minister of education, succeeded Botha as leader in a 'palace coup', becoming president when Botha resigned. He won a general election, though with a reduced number of seats, and set about the dismantling of apartheid.

Nelson Mandela was released in February 1990; the state of emergency was lifted; the principal apartheid laws were repealed; constitutional talks were instituted; and victory in a whites-only referendum enabled de Klerk to press on with his reforms. International sanctions were lifted, and the world resumed sporting links with South Africa. However communal violence continued, particularly between the African National Congress and the Zulu Inkatha Freedom Party; and the Goldstone Commission, appointed by de Klerk, discovered that whites in the police and armed forces were responsible for fomenting some of this inter-black violence. The culmination of the process was the signing of a new constitutional agreement with Mandela in late 1993, and in the same year he and Mandela were jointly awarded the Nobel Peace Prize. De Klerk later served as vice-president (1994–6) in the Mandela administration, and announced his retirement from politics in August 1997. >> Botha P W; Buthelezi; Mandela; Vorster; RR1088

de Kooning, Willem or **William** [duh **koo**ning] (1904–97) Painter, born in Rotterdam, The Netherlands. He studied at Rotterdam, and emigrated to the USA in 1926. By the 1950s he had emerged as a leader of the Abstract Expressionist movement, especially as seen in action painting. Among his best-known works is his controversial series 'Woman I–VI' (1952–3, New York City), with its violent, aggressive images. In his later years, he worked increasingly with clay sculptures. >> Gottlieb; Mitchell, Joan; Motherwell; Tworkov

Delacroix, (Ferdinand Victor) Eugène [duhla**krwah**] (1798–1863) Painter, and leader of the Romantic movement, born in Charenton, France. He exhibited his 'Dante and Virgil in Hell' at the Paris Institute in 1822, following this with 'The Massacre at Chios' (1823, Louvre). These pictures, with their loose drawing and vivid colouring, aroused a storm of criticism. In his later work he moved even further away from traditional treatment in his canvases of historical and dramatic scenes, often violent or macabre in subject, such as 'Liberty Guiding the People' (1831, Louvre). >> Guérin

Delafield, E M, pseudonym of **Edmée Elizabeth Monica Dashwood**, *née* **de la Pasture** (1890–1943) Novelist, born in Llandogo, Monmouthshire, SE Wales, UK. She was the author of several novels, and a series beginning with *Diary of a Provincial Lady* (1931).

de la Mare, Walter (John) [mair] (1873–1956) Writer, born in Charlton, Kent, SE England, UK. He studied at London, worked for an oil company (1890–1908), then devoted himself to writing. His first work, *Songs of Childhood* (1902), was under the pseudonym of **Walter Ramal**. He wrote several volumes of poetry, novels, and short stories, including the prose romance *Henry Brocken* (1904), the poetic collection *The Listeners* (1912), and his fantastic novel *Memoirs of a Midget* (1921).

Delaney, Shelagh [de**lay**nee] (1939–) Playwright, born in Salford, Greater Manchester, NW England, UK. She left school at 16 and began writing her first and best known play, *A Taste of Honey* (1958) a year later. Later works failed to achieve equal acclaim, though she has produced notable screenplays for *Charlie Bubbles* (1968) and *Dance with a Stranger* (1985).

de la Renta, Oscar (1932–) Fashion designer, born in Santo Domingo, Dominican Republic. After studying art in Santo Domingo and Madrid, he worked at Balenciaga's couture house in Madrid. He joined the house of Lanvin-Castille in Paris in 1961, but after two years went to Elizabeth Arden in New York City. In 1965 he started his own company. He has a reputation for opulent, ornately trimmed clothes, particularly evening dresses, but he also designs day wear and accessories. >> Arden, Elizabeth; Balenciaga

de la Roche, Mazo [rosh] (1885–1961) Novelist, born in Newmarket, Ontario, Canada. She wrote *Jalna* (1927), the first of a series of novels about the Whiteoak family. *Whiteoaks* (1929) was dramatized with considerable success. She also wrote children's stories and travel books.

Delaroche, (Hippolyte) Paul [duhlarosh] (1797–1856) Painter, born in Paris. He studied under Gros, from whom he absorbed the technique of the large historical subject painting, as seen in his 'Death of Queen Elizabeth' (1828), and 'Execution of Lady Jane Grey' (1834, National Gallery, London). His major work was the series of murals for the Ecole des Beaux-Arts, where he became professor of painting (1833). >> Gros

de la Rue, Warren [duh la **roo**] (1815–89) Astronomer and physicist, born in Guernsey. He studied at Paris, and early entered his father's business – the manufacture of paperwares – for which he devised many new processes, including an envelope-making machine. He invented the silver chloride battery and did research on the discharge of electricity in gases. A pioneer of celestial photography, he invented the photoheliograph.

De La Salle, Jean Baptiste >> **La Salle, St Jean Baptiste de**

de la Tour, Georges >> **La Tour, Georges de**

de la Tour, Maurice Quentin >> **La Tour, Maurice Quentin de**

Delaunay, Robert [duhloh**nay**] (1885–1941) Painter, born in Paris. At first a stage designer, he turned to painting in 1905. He was associated with *Der Blaue Reiter* (1911–12), but is principally known as the co-founder of Orphism. He painted many pictures of Paris (particularly of the Eiffel Tower), and his research into colour orchestration as applied to abstract art was influential. >> Delaunay, Sonia; Macke

Delaunay, Sonia (Terk) [duhlohnay], *née* **Stern** (1885–1979) Painter and textile designer, born in Ukraine. Brought up in St Petersburg, she studied art at Karlsruhe and in Paris where, in 1905, she attended the Académie de la Palette. In 1909 she made a marriage of convenience with the art critic **Wilhelm Uhde**, but that ended shortly, and in 1910 she married the French painter **Robert Delaunay** and together they founded the movement known as Orphism. In 1918 they designed sets and costumes for Diaghilev. She was a textile designer of international importance, and her work was included in the Exposition des Arts Décoratifs in 1925. >> Delaunay, Robert; Diaghilev

de la Warr, Thomas West, 12th Baron [waw(r)] (1577–1618) English soldier and colonist. After serving under the Earl of Essex, and suffering a brief imprisonment for involvement in Essex's revolt, he became a member of the Virginia Company; he was appointed the first governor of Virginia in 1610. Returning to England in 1611, he wrote the *Relation* about Virginia. He died on a return voyage to Virginia. The state of Delaware is named after him. >> Essex, (2nd Earl of)

Delbrück, Max [delbrük] (1906–81) Biophysicist, born in Berlin. He studied physics at Göttingen, and worked with Bohr at Copenhagen before turning to chemistry at the Kaiser Wilhelm Institute in Berlin, and to biology from 1937 (at the California Institute of Technology). He did much to create bacterial and bacteriophage genetics, and to inspire early work in biophysics and molecular biology. He exchanged research information with Alfred Day Hershey and Salvador Luria, and with them shared the Nobel Prize for Physiology or Medicine in 1969. He became a US citizen in 1945. >> Bohr, Niels; Hershey; Luria, Salvador

Delcassé, Théophile [delkasay] (1852–1923) French statesman and foreign minister (1898–1905, 1914–15), born in

Pamiers, France. He promoted the *entente cordiale* with Britain, which was the basis of the Allied coalition in World War 1.

de Leon, Daniel [duh **lee**on] (1852–1914) Radical socialist, born in Curaçao, Netherlands Antilles. He studied in Hildesheim, Germany, and in Amsterdam, emigrating to the USA in 1874. He studied law at Columbia University, practised in Texas, then lectured in Latin American diplomacy at Columbia (1883–9). He supported the Socialist Labor Party from 1890, and founded the Socialist Trade and Labor Alliance in 1895; but a split developed in protest against his authoritarianism, and the seceders of 1899 ultimately became the Socialist Party of America. He assisted in the formation of the Industrial Workers of the World (1905), merging it with his Alliance, but broke away from them and founded a rival body, the Workers' International Industrial Union.

Delescluze, (Louis) Charles [duhlayklüz] (1809–71) French radical Republican and journalist, born in Dreux, France. His revolutionary politics drove him from France to journalism in Belgium (1835), but the February Revolution (1848) brought him back to Paris. His writing made him popular, but brought him imprisonment (1849–53), and he was transported until 1859. He played a prominent part in the Paris Commune, and died on the last barricade.

Delfont (of Stepney), Bernard >> **Grade, Lew**

Delibes, (Clément Philibert) Léo [duhleeb] (1836–91) Composer, born in St Germain du Val, France. He became second director at the Opéra, Paris (1864) and a Conservatoire professor (1881). He wrote light operas, of which *Lakmé* had the greatest success, but he is chiefly remembered for the ballet *Coppélia* (1870). >> Hoffmann, E T W

Delille, Jacques [duhleel] (1738–1813) Poet, born near Aigues-Perse, France. After holding a canonry at Moissac, he was presented by the Comte d'Artois with the abbacy of Saint-Séverin. His verse translations include Virgil's *Georgics* (1769) and Milton's *Paradise Lost* (1805). *Les Jardins* (1782), a didactic poem, was generally accepted as his masterpiece. During his life he was regarded by his countrymen as the greatest French poet of the day, but his fame was short-lived.

DeLillo, Don (1936–) Novelist, born in New York City, USA. His novels, recognized as leading examples of American postmodernism, are highly self-aware evocations of contemporary society which defines itself through the pseudo-rituals of its subcultures, such as American football in *End Zone* (1972). Other books include *Americana* (1971), *White Noise* (1986), and *Mao II* (1991).

de Lisle, Leconte >> **Leconte de Lisle, Charles Marie René**

de Lisle, Rouget >> **Rouget de Lisle, Claude Joseph**

Delius, Frederick [**dee**lius] (1862–1934) Composer, born in Bradford, West Yorkshire, N England, UK, of German–Scandinavian descent. He followed a commercial career until he was 20, when he went to Florida as an orange planter, studying music in his spare time. He entered Leipzig Conservatory in 1886, and became a friend of Grieg. After 1890 he lived almost entirely in France, composing prolifically. He wrote six operas, including *A Village Romeo and Juliet* (1901), and a variety of choral and orchestral works, such as *Appalachia* (1902) and *On Hearing the First Cuckoo in Spring* (1912). In 1924 he became paralysed and blind, but with the assistance of **Eric Fenby** (1906–97), his amanuensis from 1928, he continued to compose. >> Grieg, Edvard

Dell, Floyd (James) (1887–1969) Writer, editor, and social critic, born in Barry, IL. He joined the Socialist Party at 16, and worked as a reporter and editor in Iowa and Chicago (1905–13). His Chicago studio was a gathering place for

many of the literary figures who contributed to the 'Chicago Renaissance'. Moving in 1913 to New York City's Greenwich village, he edited *Masses* (1914–17), wrote plays for various left-wing clubs, and earned a reputation as a bohemian after an affair with Edna St Vincent Millay. When the government suspended *Masses* because of its opposition to America's role in World War 1, he was indicted under the Espionage Act (1918), but never convicted. He became an editor of the *Liberator* (1918–24) and *New Masses* (1924–9), and wrote a series of novels. From 1935 to 1947 he worked in Washington, DC, for various government agencies, then disappeared from public view. >> Millay

della Casa, Lisa [dela **kah**za] (1919–) Soprano, born in Burgdorf, Switzerland. She studied in Zürich, and first appeared at Solothurn-Biel in 1943, subsequently joining the company at the Stadttheater, Zürich. Her appearance at the Salzburg Festival of 1947 led to her engagement with the Vienna State Opera Company. A specialist in the operas of Richard Strauss, she sang all three soprano roles in *Der Rosenkavalier*.

della Robbia, Luca >> **Robbia, Luca della**

Deller, Alfred (George) (1912–79) Countertenor, born in Margate, Kent, SE England, UK. A church chorister from the age of 11, he began a full-time musical career in 1947. He made many recordings of early English songs, notably those of Dowland and Purcell, and in 1950 formed the *Deller Consort*, devoted to the authentic performance of early music. In 1963 he founded the Stour Music Festival. >> Dowland; Purcell, Henry

Del Mar, Norman (René) (1919–94) Conductor and horn player, born in London. He studied at the Royal College of Music, and became assistant conductor of the Royal Philharmonic Orchestra (1947–8), principal conductor of the English Opera Group (1948–56), and conductor of the BBC Scottish Symphony Orchestra (1960–5). His son, **Jonathan Del Mar** (1951–), also became a conductor.

Delon, Alain [delõ] (1935–) Film actor, born in Paris. He became known following his success as one of the lead roles in a thriller adapted from a Patricia Highsmith novel, *Purple Moon* (1960). Later films include *Rocco and His Brothers* (1960), *The Leopard* (1962), *The Assassination of Trotsky* (1972), and *Swann in Love* (1984).

De Long, George Washington (1844–81) Arctic explorer, born in New York City. In 1879 he commanded the *Jeanette* in an attempt to reach the North Pole via the Bering Strait. Having abandoned his ship in the pack ice in 1881, he travelled 300 mi by sledge and boat to the Siberian coast, but only two of his crew reached safety.

Delorme, Marion [duh**law(r)m**] (1613–50) Courtesan, born in Paris, where at an early period of her life her beauty and wit gathered a group of high-born lovers round her – among them the 1st Duke of Buckingham, Saint-Evremond, the Duc de Brissac and the Duc de Gramont. Even Richelieu was not insensible to her charms, and caused her to be separated from the Marquis de Cinq-Mars, whose mistress she was until he was executed in 1642. During the early days of the Fronde uprising (1648–53) her house was the rallying-point of its chiefs, and Mazarin was about to imprison her when she suddenly died. >> Mazarin; Richelieu; Buckingham, 1st Duke of

Delorme, Philibert [duh**law(r)m**] (c.1510–70) Architect, born in Lyon, France. Royal architect to Henry II (of France), he built the Tuileries for Catherine de' Medici, as well as several chateaux. >> Catherine de' Medici

de Lorris, Guillaume >> **Guillaume de Lorris**

Delors, Jacques [duh**law(r)**] (1925–) French and European statesman, born in Paris. He served as social affairs adviser to Jacques Chaban-Delmas (1969–72). He joined the Socialist Party in 1973, represented it in the European

Parliament from 1979, and served as minister of economy and finance in the administration of President Mitterrand (1981–4). He became President of the European Commission in 1985, and was elected to a second 4-year term in 1988, extended until 1995 despite difficulties ratifying the Maastricht Treaty. He oversaw significant budgetary reforms and the move towards a free Community market in 1992, with increased powers residing in Brussels. >> Chaban-Delmas; Mitterrand

de los Angeles, Victoria >> **Angeles, Victoria de los**

Delvaux, Paul [delvoh] (1897–1994) Surrealist painter, born in Antheit, Belgium. He lived mainly in Brussels, where he studied. Influenced by Chirico and Magritte, he produced a series of paintings depicting nude and semi-nude girls in dreamlike settings, such as 'The Call of the Night'. He was professor of painting at Brussels (1950–62). >> Chirico; Magritte

Demades [demadeez] (c. 380–319 BC) Athenian orator and politician. A bitter enemy to Demosthenes, he supported Philip II of Macedon, and after the Battle of Chaeronea (338 BC) secured an honourable peace. In 332 BC, after Antipater had crushed a revolt against Macedonian rule, Demades procured the death of Demosthenes and his followers, but was himself executed by Cassander, the son of Antipater. >> Antipater (of Macedon); Demosthenes (c.383–322 BC); Philip II (of Macedon)

de Man, Paul [man] (1919–83) Cultural theorist, born in Belgium. Controversy has surrounded his writings for collaborationist journals during World War 2. After the war he emigrated to the USA, and taught at several universities, including Yale, where he became a leading exponent of the critical method known as *deconstruction*. His most important essays were published in *Blindness and Insight* (1971) and *Allegories of Reading* (1979).

Demarco, Richard [demah(r)koh] (1930–) Artist, broadcaster, and teacher, born in Edinburgh, EC Scotland, UK. He studied at the College of Art (1949–53), and became a leading promoter of modern art in Scotland, especially at the Edinburgh Festival since 1967, and has presented annual programmes of theatre, music, and dance. He was co-founder of the Traverse Theatre Club, and director (1966–92) of the Richard Demarco Gallery.

de Mestral, Georges [duh mestral] (1907–90) Swiss engineer who invented Velcro fastening. After a shooting trip in 1948 his clothes had picked up a number of burrs, which he later studied under a microscope. He saw the possibility of making a fastener based on the same principle of hundreds of tiny hooks, and eventually succeeded, producing the now familiar strips of nylon in 1956.

Demetrius (Russian prince) >> **Dmitri**

De Mille, Agnes [duh mil] (1905–93) Dancer, choreographer, and writer, born in New York City, the niece of film director Cecil B De Mille. She studied at the University of California, went to London, and danced with Marie Rambert's company. *Three Virgins and a Devil* (1941) marked her breakthrough into choreography, and she went on to choreograph for musicals such as *Oklahoma!* (1943) and *Carousel* (1945). She is also known for her wit and eloquent public speaking, and her contribution to television and film. Her publications include the autobiographical *Dance to the Piper* (1952) and *Martha* (1991), her tribute to Martha Graham. >> De Mille, Cecil B; Graham, Martha; Rambert

De Mille, Cecil B(lount) [duh mil] (1881–1959) Film producer and director, born in Ashfield, MA. He was an actor and writer before making the first US feature film in Hollywood, *The Squaw Man* (1913). He made a reputation for box-office spectacles with such films as *The Ten Commandments* (1923, remade in Cinema-Scope, 1957), *The Plainsman* (1937), and *The Greatest Show on Earth* (1952). He

also organized the first commercial passenger airline service in the USA (1917). >> De Mille, Agnes

Demirel, Süleyman [demirel] (1924–) Turkish prime minister (1965–71, 1974–7, 1979–80, 1991–3), and president (1993–), born in Islam Kömy, Turkey. He qualified as an engineer at Istanbul Technical University, and worked on hydro-electric schemes in the USA and Turkey before entering politics. In 1964 he became president of the centrist Justice Party, now subsumed in the True Path Party. He served three terms as prime minister, until a military coup in 1980 resulted in a three-year ban on political activity. He was placed in detention, but released in 1983. >> RR1093

de Mita, (Luigi) Ciriaco [duh meeta] (1928–) Italian statesman and prime minister (1988–9), born in Fusco, Italy. He joined the Christian Democratic Party, and in 1963 was elected to the Chamber of Deputies. He held a number of ministerial posts in the 1970s, and in 1982 became secretary-general of the Party. >> RR1065

Demme, Jonathan (1944–) Film director, born in Long Island, NY. He has directed pop videos, documentaries, and television episodes, making his cinematic directorial debut with *Caged Heat* (1974). He won a Best Director Oscar for the psychological thriller *Silence of the Lambs* (1991). Later films include *Cousin Bobby* (1992), *Philadelphia* (1993), and *Beloved* (1998).

Democritus [demokritus] (c.460–370 BC) Greek philosopher, born in Abdera, Thrace. He travelled in the East, and was by far the most learned thinker of his time. He wrote many physical, mathematical, ethical, and musical works, but only fragments survive. His *atomic system* assumes an infinite multitude of everlasting atoms, from whose random combinations springs an infinite number of successive world-orders in which there is law but not design. This system, derived from Leucippus, was developed by Epicurus and Lucretius. >> Epicurus; Leucippus; Lucretius

de Moivre, Abraham [duh mwahvruh] (1667–1754) Mathematician, born in Vitry, France. A Protestant, he moved to England in c.1686, and supported himself by teaching. His principal work is *The Doctrine of Chances* (1718) on probability theory, but he is best remembered for the fundamental formula on complex numbers known as *de Moivre's theorem*.

De Morgan, Augustus (1806–71) Mathematician, born in Madura, India. He studied at Cambridge, and became the first professor of mathematics at University College, London (1828). He helped to develop the notion of different kinds of algebra, and collaborated with Boole in the development of symbolic logic. >> Boole

De Morgan, William (Frend) (1839–1917) Pre-Raphaelite ceramic artist and novelist, born in London, England, UK, the son of Augustus De Morgan. He studied art at the Academy Schools, began as a designer of tiles and stained glass, but became interested in pottery, and in 1871 established a kiln in Chelsea. In 1905 he abandoned pottery and at the age of 65 began writing novels in a whimsical Dickensian manner, such as *Joseph Vance* (1906) and *Somehow Good* (1908). >> De Morgan, Augustus; Hunt, William Holman

Demosthenes [demostheneez] (?–413 BC) Athenian soldier. During the Peloponnesian Wars (431–404 BC) he captured Anacterium (425 BC) and helped Cleon to reduce Sphacteria, but failed to conquer Boeotia the next year. In 413 BC, having been sent to Sicily to the relief of Nicias, he was captured by the Syracusans and put to death. >> Cleon; Nicias

Demosthenes [demostheneez] (c. 383–322 BC) The greatest of the Greek orators, the son of a rich Athenian arms manufacturer. After studying rhetoric and legal procedure, he took up the law as a profession, becoming first a speechwriter, then an assistant to prosecutors in public (state)

trials. In c.354 BC he entered politics, but did not gain prominence until 351 BC, when he delivered the first of a long series of passionate speeches (the 'First Philippic') advocating all-out resistance to Philip of Macedon. Swayed by his oratory, the Athenians did eventually go to war (340 BC), only to be thoroughly defeated at Chaeronea (338 BC). Put on trial by the peace party of Aeschines, he fully vindicated himself in his oratorical masterpiece, *On the Crown*. He was exiled for embezzlement in 325 BC, and committed suicide after the failure of the Athenian revolt from Macedon following Alexander's death. >> Aeschines; Demades; Philip II (of Macedon)

Dempsey, Jack, popular name of **William Harrison Dempsey**, nickname **the Manassa Mauler** (1895–1983) World heavyweight champion boxer, born in Manassa, CO. He worked in copper mines before taking to the ring as 'Kid Blackie' in 1914. In 1919 he defeated Jess Willard to win the world heavyweight title, which he lost to Gene Tunney in 1926. After several years fighting exhibitions, Dempsey retired from the ring in 1940, and became a successful restaurateur on Broadway in New York City. >> Tunney; RR1148

Demuth, Charles [de**mooth**] (1883–1935) Painter and book illustrator, born in Lancaster, PA. He studied at the Pennsylvania Academy of the Fine Arts, then went to Paris (1912–14), where he saw the work of the early Cubists and took back their ideas to America. From 1919 he was a major exponent of 'Precisionism', with its hard outlines and semi-abstract treatment of industrial or urban scenery, as seen in 'My Egypt' (1927), a view of grain elevators.

Dench, Judi, popular name of **Dame Judith Olivia Dench** (1934–) Actress, born in York, North Yorkshire, N England, UK. She studied at the Central School of Dramatic Art in London, and made her stage debut as Ophelia in *Hamlet* (1957) in Liverpool. A member of the Old Vic Company (1957–61), she became one of Britain's most distinguished classical actresses. Her television credits include many individual plays, and the popular situation comedy *A Fine Romance* (1981–4), in which she co-starred with **Michael Williams** (1935–), her husband since 1971. Her films include *The Third Secret* (1964), *A Handful of Dust* (1987), *Henry V* (1989), and *Mrs Brown* (1997). She was created a dame in 1988, and made her directorial debut in the same year with a production of *Much Ado About Nothing*. In 1997 she appeared in David Hare's *Amy's View* at the National Theatre.

Denck, Hans (c. 1495–c. 1527) Anabaptist theologian, born in Habach, Germany. He became rector of the Sebaldusschule in Nuremberg in 1523. From 1524 he preached a doctrine resembling Evangelical Quakerism in various parts of Germany, was expelled from the school (1525), and became a leader of the Anabaptists in Augsburg.

Deneuve, Catherine [duh**noev**], originally **Catherine Dorléac** (1943–) Actress, born in Paris. She made her film debut in *Les Collégiennes* (1956), and became well known through the unexpected popularity of the musical *Les Parapluies de Cherbourg* (1964, The Umbrellas of Cherbourg). Her major films include *Repulsion* (1965), *Belle de Jour* (1967), *Le Sauvage* (1975), *Le Dernier Métro* (1980, The Last Metro), *Indochine* (1992), and *Ma Saison préférée* (1994). She was married to the photographer David Bailey (1965–70), and had a child by director Roger Vadim (1963), and another by actor Marcello Mastroianni (1972). >> Bailey, David; Mastroianni; Vadim

Deng Xiaoping [duhng syowping] or **Teng Hsiao-p'ing** (1904– 97) Leader of the Chinese Communist Party, after 1978 the dominant figure in Chinese politics, born in Sichuan province, China. He studied in France, where he joined the Communist Party, and in the Soviet Union, and became associated with Mao Zedong during the period of the Jiangxi Soviet (1928–34). In 1954 he became secretary-general of the Chinese Communist Party, but reacted strongly against the excesses of the Great Leap Forward (1958–9). When Mao launched the Cultural Revolution (1966), Deng was criticized and purged along with Liu Shaoqi, but retained the confidence of Premier Zhou Enlai and was restored to power in 1974. Again dismissed in 1976, after the death of Mao he was restored once more to power, and from 1978 had taken China through a rapid course of pragmatic reforms. >> Liu Shaoqi; Mao Zedong; Zhou Enlai; RR1040

Denham, Dixon [**den**am] (1786–1828) British soldier, and African traveller, born in London, England, UK. Educated at Merchant Taylor's School, he served with distinction in the Napoleonic wars. He was sent as expedition leader to join Hugh Clapperton and Walter Oudney on an expedition to discover the source of the Niger. They reached L Chad in 1823, and he explored the shores of the lake while Clapperton and Oudney pushed further W; he returned to England in 1825. He was appointed Governor of Sierra Leone in 1828, but died of fever soon after taking up the post. *Denham's bustard* was named after him. >> Clapperton

Denham, Sir John [**den**am] (1615–69) Poet, born in Dublin, Republic of Ireland. He studied at London and Oxford, succeeded to his father's estate, and at the outbreak of the Civil War was high sheriff of Surrey. His best-known works were the tragedy, *The Sophy* (1641), and his descriptive poem, *Cooper's Hill* (1642). At the Restoration he was appointed surveyor-general of works, and in 1661 created a Knight of the Bath.

Denikin, Anton Ivanovich [**den**ikin] (1872–1947) Russian soldier, born near Warsaw, Poland. He entered the army at the age of 15, and rose to be lieutenant-general in World War 1. After the Revolution of 1917 he led the White Army in the S against the Bolsheviks (1918–20). He won the Ukraine, but was defeated by the Red Army at Orel (1919), and in 1920 resigned his command and escaped to Constantinople. Thereafter he lived in exile in France (1926–45) and the USA (1945–7).

De Niro, Robert [duh **nee**roh] (1943–) Actor and director, born in New York City. A student of acting with Stella Adler (1902–) and Lee Strasberg, he worked off-Broadway, making his film debut in 1965. He received Oscars for his supporting role in *The Godfather, Part II* (1974), and for his portrayal of boxer Jake La Motta in *Raging Bull* (1980). His many films include *Taxi Driver* (1976), *The Deerhunter* (1978), *Midnight Run* (1988), *Awakenings* (1990), *Mary Shelley's Frankenstein* (1994), *Casino* (1995), and *Sleepers* (1996). He made his directorial debut with *A Bronx Tale* (1993), in which he also starred. >> Strasberg

Denis or **Denys, St** [**den**is], Fr [duhnee] (3rd-c) Traditional apostle of France, and the first Bishop of Paris, born possibly in Rome. He was sent from Rome c.250 to preach the Gospel to the Gauls. He was martyred at Paris under the Roman Emperor Valerian (reigned 253–60). Feast day 9 October.

Denis, Julio >> **Cortazar, Julio**

Denis, Maurice [duh**nee**] (1870–1943) Artist and art theorist, born in Grandville, France. One of the original group of Symbolist painters, *Les Nabis*, he wrote several influential critical works, and in 1919 helped to found the Studios of Sacred Art, devoted to the revival of religious painting. Perhaps his most famous picture is 'Hommage à Cézanne' (1900, Paris). >> Bonnard, Pierre; Roussel, Ker Xavier; Vallotton; Vuillard

Denness, Mike [de**nes**], popular name of **Michael Denness** (1940–) Cricketer, born in Bellshill, North Lanarkshire, C Scotland, UK. He captained Kent and England, and in his first-class career made over 25 000 runs and hit four Test centuries.

Denning (of Whitchurch), Alfred Thompson Denning, Baron (1899–) British judge, born in Whitchurch, Hampshire, S England, UK. He studied at Oxford, was called to the bar in 1923, became a KC in 1938, and a judge of the High Court of Justice in 1944. In 1963 he led the inquiry into the circumstances of John Profumo's resignation as secretary of state for war. As Master of the Rolls (1962–82) he was responsible for many often controversial decisions. He was knighted in 1944, and made a life peer in 1957. Among his books are *The Road to Justice* (1955) and *What Next in the Law* (1982). >> Profumo

Dennis, John (1657–1734) Critic and playwright, born in London, England, UK. He studied at Cambridge, toured France and Italy, took his place among the men of fashion, and produced biting criticism to support the Whigs. He wrote nine plays, but had little success with them. Pope's *Essay on Criticism* (1711) contained a contemptuous allusion to one of his plays, which began a long feud.

Denny-Brown, Derek (Ernest) (1901–81) Neurologist, born in Christchurch, New Zealand. He trained at the University of New Zealand and at Oxford, where he worked with Charles Sherrington. After clinical work in London, he went to Harvard in 1941, where he remained. He was particularly interested in the diseases of the basal ganglia and of the muscles. >> Sherrington, Charles

Dent, Edward Joseph (1876–1957) Musicologist, born in Yorkshire, N England, UK. Professor of music at Cambridge (1926–41), he made translations of many libretti, wrote an opera, and published lives of Scarlatti, Busoni, and Handel. In 1923 he helped to found the International Society for Contemporary Music.

Dent, J(oseph) M(alaby) (1849–1926) Publisher, born in Darlington, Durham, NE England, UK. He worked as a bookbinder in London before opening his own bookbinding business in 1892. In 1888 he founded the publishing house of J M Dent & Sons, which brought out the pocket-sized *Temple Classics* (from 1893) and *Everyman's Library* (from 1904).

Deodoro da Fonseca, Manuel [dayodooroo da fonsayka] (1827–92) Brazilian general and president (1889–91), born in Alagoas province, Brazil. He served in the War of the Triple Alliance, headed the revolt that overthrew Emperor Pedro II, and instituted the republic. He was forced out of office in 1891. >> RR1036

De Palma, Brian (1940–) Film director, born in Newark, NJ. He won a number of prizes directing short films before making his feature-length debut with *The Wedding Party* (1966). He enjoyed commercial success with *Carrie* (1976) and *The Untouchables* (1987), later films including *Bonfire of the Vanities* (1990), *Carlito's Way* (1993), and *Mission Impossible* (1996).

Depardieu, Gérard [daypah(r)dyoe] (1948–) Actor, born in Châteauroux, France. An unruly child, he was encouraged to enter dramatics as a therapy and made his film debut in *Le Beatnik et le minet* (1965). He continued in occasional film roles while appearing on stage and television, including the series *L'Inconnu* (1974). His films include *Le Dernier Métro* (1980), *Danton* (1982), and *Jean de Florette* (1986). Among later films are *Cyrano de Bergerac* (1990), *Green Card* (1990), *Germinal* (1992), and *Unhook the Stars* (1997). He also directed himself in *Le Tartuffe* (1984).

Depew, Chauncey Mitchell [duhpyoo] (1834–1928) Lawyer, businessman, and public official, born in Peekskill, NY. He studied at Yale, then worked as a lawyer, and participated in Republican Party affairs. He was the first US ambassador to Japan (1866). Rising through the Vanderbilt industrial–financial empire, he became president of the New York Central Railroad in 1885. He served in the US Senate (1899–1911), and became known as an orator and after-dinner wit. 'I get my exercise acting as pallbearer to my friends who exercise', he once quipped, explaining his good health and long life.

De Priest, Oscar Stanton [duh preest] (1871–1951) US representative, born in Florence, AL. The son of freed slaves, he moved north as a boy after a neighbour was lynched. Working as a painter in Chicago at 17, he had his own decorating firm by 1905. A Republican realtor, he became the first black member of the City Council (1915–17), resigning because of alleged mob connections. A shrewd politician, he fought against Jim Crow laws in the US House of Representatives (1929–35), then returned to Chicago politics and real estate.

de Quincey, Thomas [duh kwinsee] (1785–1859) Writer, born in Manchester, Greater Manchester, NW England, UK. Educated at Manchester Grammar School, he ran away, and wandered in Wales and London. He then spent a short time at Oxford, where he became addicted to opium. On a visit to Bath, he met Coleridge, and through him Southey and Wordsworth; and in 1809 went to live near them in Grasmere. There he set up as an author, largely writing magazine articles. His *Confessions of an Opium-Eater* appeared as a serial in 1821, and brought him instant fame. In 1828 he moved to Edinburgh, and for 20 years wrote for various magazines. >> Coleridge, Samuel Taylor; Southey; Wordsworth

Derain, André [duhrĩ] (1880–1954) Artist, born in Chatou, France. He is most famous for his Fauvist pictures (1904–8), when he was associated with Vlaminck and Matisse. Later landscape pictures show a Romantic Realism influenced by Cézanne. He also designed for the theatre (notably the Diaghilev ballet) and illustrated several books. >> Cézanne; Diaghilev; Matisse; Vlaminck

Derby, Edward Geoffrey Smith Stanley, 14th Earl of [dah(r)bee] (1799–1869) British statesman and prime minister (1852, 1858-9, 1866-8), born at Knowsley Hall, Lancashire, NW England, UK. He studied at Oxford, entered parliament as a Whig in 1828, and became chief-secretary for Ireland (1830), and colonial secretary (1833), when he carried the Act for the emancipation of West Indian slaves. In 1834 he withdrew from the Party, and soon after joined the Conservatives (subsequently party leader, 1846–68). He entered the House of Lords as a baronet in 1844, retired from the Cabinet in 1845, when Peel decided to repeal the Corn Laws, and in 1846 headed the Protectionists in the Lords. In 1851 he succeeded his father as Earl of Derby. Premier on three occasions, his third administration passed the Reform Bill (1867). >> Peel; RR1095

Derby, James Stanley, 7th Earl of [dah(r)bee], known as **the Great Earl of Derby** (1606–51) English soldier, born in Knowsley, Merseyside, NW England, UK. He fought on the Royalist side throughout the Civil War. After the Battle of Worcester in 1651, he helped Charles II to make his escape, but was himself captured by the Parliamentary forces and beheaded at Bolton. >> Charles II (of England)

Deringer, Henry [derinjer] (1786–1868) Manufacturer of small arms, born in Philadelphia, PA. He supplied rifles to the US army, and in 1852 invented the pocket pistol known as a *deringer*, later spelled *derringer*.

De Rita, Joe >> Stooges, The Three

Dernesch, Helga [dernesh] (1939–) Operatic soprano, born in Vienna. She studied at the Vienna Conservatory, made her debut in Bern (1961), and sang at Covent Garden in 1970. She has sung throughout Europe and the USA, and is specially noted for her portrayals of Wagner, Strauss, and the modern German repertory. Since 1979 she has sung mezzo-soprano roles.

Derrida, Jacques [derida] (1930–) French philosopher-linguist, born in Algeria. He studied in Paris, and teaches at the

Ecole Normale Supérieure there. His critique of the referentiality of language and the objectivity of structures founded the school of criticism called *deconstruction*. Among his highly influential works are *De la Grammatologie* (1967, Of Grammatology), *L'écriture et la différence* (1967, Writing and Difference), and *La dissémination* (1972, Dissemination). His essay *Apories* appeared in 1996. The award of an honorary degree by Cambridge University in 1992 was publicly contested, prompting attacks on and defences of his work.

Dershowitz, Alan M(orton) [**der**shovitz] (1938–) Lawyer and writer, born in New York City. He studied at Yale, then served as a clerk to US Supreme Court justice Arthur Goldberg, and became Harvard Law School's youngest ever tenured law professor at age 28. He became one of the nation's leading defence and appeal lawyers, taking on cases having to do primarily with issues of civil liberties or constitutional rights, including Dr Benjamin Spock in his antiwar actions, and the radical lawyer William Kunstler. His most celebrated case was the successful appeal and acquittal of Claus von Bulow, published as *Reversal of Fortune* (1986), and later made into a film (in which he played a bit part). An outspoken critic of what he sees as flaws in the legal system, he has written in defence of his aggressive tactics in *The Best Defense* (1982). He has also written a widely syndicated newpaper column on the law, and been a frequent guest on television programmes involving legal matters. >> Kunstler; Spock

de Ruyter, Michiel Adriaanszoon >> **Ruyter, Michiel Adriaanszoon de**

Derzhavin, Gavril Romanovich [dairz**h**avin] (1743–1816) Poet, born in Kazan, Russia. In 1762 he entered the army as a private. He became secretary of state (1791), imperial treasurer (1800), and minister of justice (1802). He published much lyric poetry, and is considered one of Russia's greatest poets.

Desaguliers, John Theophilus [dayzagülyay] (1683–1744) Scientist and inventor, born in La Rochelle, France. He studied at Oxford, became experimental assistant to Sir Isaac Newton, and later popularized Newtonian theories and their practical applications. He proposed a scheme for heating vessels such as salt-boilers by steam instead of fire, and improved the design of Thomas Savery's steam engine by adding a safety valve, and using an internal water jet to condense the steam in the displacement chambers. >> Newton; Savery

Desai, Anita [de**si**y], *née* **Mazumdar** (1937–) Novelist, born in Mussoorie, India. She studied at Delhi University, and her works include novels for adults and children and short stories. *Clear Light of Day* (1980) and *In Custody* (1980) were both short-listed for the Booker Prize, and *The Village by the Sea* won the Guardian Award for children's fiction in 1982. Later novels include *Baumgartner's Bombay* (1988) and *Journey to Ithaca* (1995).

Desai, Morarji (Ranchhodji) [day**si**y] (1896–1995) Indian statesman and prime minister (1977–9), born in Gujarat, India. He studied at Bombay University, became a civil servant, and entered politics in 1930. After various ministerial posts, he was a candidate for the premiership in 1964 and 1966, but was defeated by Indira Gandhi. He became deputy prime minister in 1969 to lead the Opposition Congress Party. Detained during the state of emergency (1975–7), he was then appointed leader of the newly-formed Janata Party, and elected premier. The Janata government was, however, characterized by internal strife, and he was forced to resign. >> Gandhi, Indira; RR1065

Desalvo, Albert [de**sal**voh] (?–1973) Convicted US sex offender. After his arrest in late 1964 for sex attacks on women in their homes, he confessed to a psychiatrist that he was the Boston Strangler who had murdered 13 women between 1962 and 1964 in Boston, MA. He was never tried for the murders, because under Massachusetts law a doctor who receives information from a suspect cannot use it as evidence. Sentenced to life imprisonment for his other crimes, he was found stabbed to death in his cell in Walpole Prison, MA.

Desani, Govindas (Vishnoodas) [de**sah**nee] (1909–) Novelist, born in Nairobi, Kenya. He moved to Britain in 1926, and from 1928 became a press correspondent, lecturer, and broadcaster. His best-known work is *All About H Hatterr* (1948), which has been resurrected as a modern classic. He became a US citizen in 1979.

Desargues, Girard [dayzah(r)g] (1591–1661) Mathematician, born in Lyon, France. By 1626 he was in Paris, and took part as an engineer in the siege of La Rochelle in 1628. He founded the use of projective methods in geometry, inspired by the theory of perspective in art, and introduced the notion that parallel lines 'meet at a point at infinity'. His work on the sections of a cone greatly influenced Pascal. From 1645 he began a new career as an architect in Paris and Lyons. >> Pascal

Descartes, René [daykah(r)t], Lat **Renatius Cartesius** (1596–1650) Rationalist philosopher and mathematician, born in La Haye, France. Trained at the Jesuit College at La Flèche, he remained a Catholic throughout his life, but soon became dissatisfied with scholasticism. While serving in the Bavarian army in 1619, he conceived it to be his task to refound human knowledge on a basis secure from scepticism. He expounded the major features of his project in his most famous work, the *Meditationes de prima philosophia* (1641, Meditations on First Philosophy). He began his enquiry by claiming that one can doubt all one's sense experiences, even the deliverances of reason, but that one cannot doubt one's own existence as a thinking being: *cogito, ergo sum* ('I think, therefore I am'). From this basis he argued that God must exist and cannot be a deceiver; therefore, his beliefs based on ordinary sense experience are correct. He also argued that mind and body are distinct substances, believing that this dualism made possible human freedom and immortality. His *Discours de la méthode pour bien conduire sa raison, et chercher la vérité dans les sciences* (1637, Discourse on the Method for Rightly Conducting One's Reason and Searching for Truth in the Sciences) contained appendices in which he virtually founded co-ordinate or analytic geometry, and made major contributions to optics. In 1649 he moved to Stockholm to teach Queen Christina of Sweden. >> Christina; Ryle, Gilbert

Deschamps, Eustache [daysh**ā**], known as **Morel** (c. 1345–c. 1406) Poet, born in Vertus, France. He was brought up by Machaut, who may have been his uncle and who probably taught him his craft. He held important posts in Champagne, but after his patron, Charles V, died, his possessions were ravaged by the English. He composed many lyrics, besides *Le Miroir de mariage*, a long poem satirizing women, and the first treatise on French versification. >> Guillaume de Machaut

de Sica, Vittorio [**see**ka] (1901–74) Actor and film director, born in Sora, Italy. He studied in Naples and Rome, established himself as a romantic star of Italian stage and screen in the 1930s, and became a director in 1940. He achieved international success in the neo-Realist style with *Sciuscià* (1946, Shoeshine), *Ladri di biciclette* (1948, Bicycle Thieves), and *Miracolo a Milano* (1951, Miracle in Milan). His subsequent work was more smoothly sophisticated, but *Il giardino dei Finzi-Contis* (1970, The Garden of the Finzi-Contis) provided a late triumph.

Desiderio da Settignano [dezi**der**yoh da seti**nyah**noh] (c. 1428–61) Sculptor, born in Settignano, Italy. He worked in the early Renaissance style, influenced by Donatello and Della Robbia, producing many notable portrait busts of women and children. >> Donatello; Robbia

Desmarets, Jean, Sieur de (Lord of) **Saint-Sorlin** [daymaray] (1595–1676) Writer, born in Paris. He was the author of many volumes of poetry and critical works, notably *Comparison of the French Language and Poetry with That of Greek and Latin* (1670, trans title). He was the first chancellor and co-founder of the Académie Française, and a protagonist in the 'ancients versus moderns' controversy.

Desmond, Paul, originally **Paul Breitenfeld** (1924–77) Jazz alto saxophonist, born in San Francisco, CA. As soon as he joined Dave Brubeck's quartet in 1951, that band became one of the greatest international successes in jazz history. Two styles have seldom been so diametrically opposed and yet so complementary. Brubeck, the sober, dedicated organizer, played rollicking, noisy piano, and Desmond, the carefree, free-living bachelor, superimposed spindly, delicate melodies. Renowned for his wit, he published one humorous piece, 'How Many of You Are There in the Quartet?' (*Punch*, 1973), and no more. His tune 'Take Five' (recorded with Brubeck in 1959) is one of the great popular and critical successes of modern jazz. He left Brubeck in 1967, with occasional reunions, and kept as busy as he wished as a freelancer. >> Brubeck

Desmond, Gerald Fitzgerald, 15th Earl of (c. 1538–83) Irish Catholic nobleman, who (1579–80) rebelled against Queen Elizabeth I, sacked Youghal by night, and was proclaimed a traitor. He was eventually killed in a cabin in the Kerry mountains.

Desmoulins, (Lucie Simplice) Camille (Benoist) [daymoolī] (1760–94) French revolutionary and journalist, born in Guise, France. He studied law in Paris, but owing to a stutter never practised. He nonetheless was an effective crowd orator, and played a dramatic part in the storming of the Bastille. He was also an influential pamphleteer. A member of the Cordeliers' Club from its foundation, he was elected to the National Convention and voted for the death of the king. He actively attacked the Girondists, but by the end of 1793 argued for moderation, thus incurring the hostility of Robespierre. He was arrested and guillotined. >> Robespierre

de Soto, Hernando or **Fernando** [duh **soh**toh] (c. 1496–1542) Spanish explorer, born in Jerez de los Caballeros, Spain. In 1539 he entered Florida and crossed the Mississippi (1541), but died of a fever on its banks.

Despard, Charlotte, *née* **French** (1844–1939) Social reformer, a sister of John French. She was an advocate of women's rights and Irish self-determination. Her politics seriously embarrassed her brother during his viceroyalty of Ireland. >> French, John

Despenser, Hugh [de**spen**ser] (1262–1326) English baron. He became chief adviser to Edward I, but was banished with his son, **Hugh**, in 1321. Recalled the next year by Edward II, he was created Earl of Winchester. After Queen Isabella's landing in England (1326), he was captured by the queen's party and hanged at Bristol, as was his son at Hereford. >> Edward II; Isabella of France

Despiau, Charles [despyoh] (1874–1946) Sculptor, born in Mont-de-Marsan, France. He was discovered by Rodin, who took him as a pupil. He is noted for his severely Neoclassical portrait busts. >> Rodin

des Prés / Prez, Josquin >> **Josquin des Prez**

Dessalines, Jean Jacques [desa**leen**] (c.1758–1806) Emperor of Haiti (1804–6), born a slave probably in Grande Rivière du Nord, Saint Domingue (Haiti). In the slave insurrection of 1791 he was second only to Toussaint L'Ouverture. After compelling the French to leave Haiti (1803), he was created governor and crowned emperor as Jacques I; but his cruelty and debauchery alienated his adherents, and he was assassinated. >> Toussaint L'Ouverture; RR1056

Dessau, Paul [de**sow**] (1894–1979) Composer and conductor, born in Hamburg, Germany. After studies in Berlin, he conducted opera at Cologne from 1919, Mainz from 1923, and the Berlin State Opera from 1925. During the Nazi era he moved to Paris (1933) and the USA (1939). From 1942 he collaborated with Brecht, writing incidental music for *Mutter Courage* and other plays. Like Brecht, he settled in East Berlin in 1948, and produced the operas *Die Verurteilung des Lukullus* (text by Brecht), *Puntila* (text after Brecht), *Lanzelot*, and *Einstein*. >> Brecht

Destri, Jimmy >> **Blondie**

Dettori, Frankie [de**to**ree], popular name of **Lanfranco Dettori** (1970–) British flat race jockey, born in Italy. A champion apprentice in 1990, his later achievements include the Queen Elizabeth II Stakes (1990), French Derby (1992), Irish Derby (1994), Prix de l'Arc de Triomphe (1995), and the English Classic races The Oaks (1994, 1995), St Leger (1995, 1996), and Two Thousand Guineas (1996). He was champion jockey for two successive seasons (1994–5), and in 1996 was winner of all seven races on one card at Ascot.

Deutscher, Isaac [**doy**cher] (1907–67) Marxist historian of Russia, born in Cracow, Poland. A journalist, he joined the Communist Party in 1926 and edited Communist periodicals until his expulsion in 1932 for leading an anti-Stalinist opposition. He went to London in 1939, and worked on the editorial staff of *The Economist* (1942–9) and *The Observer* (1942–7). His great biography of Trotsky appeared in three volumes: *The Prophet Armed* (1954), *The Prophet Unarmed* (1959), and *The Prophet Outcast* (1963). A visiting professor at many US universities in the 1960s, he was prominent in the 'Teach-In' movement against the US's undeclared war in Vietnam. >> Trotsky

de Valera, Eamon [deva**lay**ra] (1882–1975) Irish statesman, prime minister (1932–48, 1951–4, 1957–9), and president (1959–73), born in New York City. Brought up on a farm in Co Limerick, he became a teacher in Dublin, and was active in various Republican movements. A commandant in the 1916 rising, he was arrested and narrowly escaped the firing squad. He became an MP in 1917, and leader of Sinn Féin (1917–26). He was elected president of Dáil Eireann, and in 1926 became leader of Fianna Fáil, his newly-formed Republican opposition party, which won the 1932 elections. In spite of his colourful early career, his leadership was moderate, and he opposed extremism and religious intolerance. >> Pearse, Patrick; RR1064

Devant, David >> **Maskelyne, John Nevil**

Devereux, Robert >> **Essex, Robert Devereux, 2nd / 3rd Earl of**

Devi, Phoolan [de**vee**], known as **Dasyu Sundari** ('Beautiful Bandit') (1957–) Bandit and folk hero, born to a low-caste family in India. After a childhood of abuse and humiliation, she was kidnapped by bandits in Uttar Pradesh, then joined the gang, becoming the mistress of one of its leaders. Following a period of capture and further abuse, she escaped to become one of India's most notorious criminals, wanted for many robberies and for the revenge shooting in 1981 of over 20 high-caste village men who had abused her. At the same time she was attracting a national reputation among oppressed people. After negotiating with the authorities, she surrendered in 1983 in a much publicized ceremony. Released from prison in 1994, she became a Buddhist convert, and in 1995 launched a new political party in support of the lower castes. Mala Sen's story of her life, *India's Bandit Queen* (1991) was the basis of the acclaimed film *Bandit Queen* (1995).

Devine, George (Alexander Cassidy) (1910–65) Actor and theatre director, born in Hendon, NW Greater

London, England, UK. With Michel Saint-Denis and others he founded the London Theatre Studio (1936–9) in an attempt to reform British theatre training. After the War, he continued this work at the Old Vic Centre (1947–52), and directed the Young Vic touring company. In 1956 he became artistic director of the newly formed English Stage Company at the Royal Court Theatre, and for the rest of his career was instrumental in the development and success of this 'writer's theatre'. The *George Devine Award*, inaugurated in 1966, gives encouragement to young theatre practitioners. >> Saint-Denis

Devlin, Bernadette >> **McAliskey, Bernadette**

Devlin, Frank >> **Hashman, Judy**

Devlin, Joseph (1872–1934) Irish nationalist, born in Belfast. An Ulster Catholic constitutional nationalist politician and machine boss, he became Nationalist MP for Kilkenny North (1902–6), but then captured and retained West Belfast. After the Northern Ireland settlement of 1920, he became a member in the Stormont parliament at various times for Armagh, Tyrone, Fermanagh, and Catholic Belfast.

Devlin (of West Wick), Patrick Arthur Devlin, Baron (1905–92) British judge. He studied at Cambridge, was called to the bar in 1929, became a KC in 1945, and a High Court judge in 1948. An eminent barrister, he was knighted in 1948 and created a life peer in 1961. He was made a Lord Justice of Appeal in 1960 and a Lord of Appeal in Ordinary in 1961, before retiring in 1964. Following the publication of the Wolfenden Report in 1957, he participated in a lengthy philosophical debate over whether the law could or should enforce moral principles upon society in general. Among his many publications are *Trial by Jury* (1956) and *The Judge* (1979). >> Wolfenden

DeVoto, Bernard (Augustine) [de**voh**toh] (1897–1955) Writer, critic, and historian, born in Ogden, UT. He taught marksmanship in the army during World War 1, then graduated from Harvard in 1920. He held an instructorship at Northwestern University and published three novels before joining the Harvard faculty in 1929. His critical study, *Mark Twain's America*, appeared in 1932. He then left Harvard to become editor of *The Saturday Review of Literature* (1936–8). He later published three surveys of the exploration and settlement of the American West, and produced an edition of the journals of Lewis and Clark (1953). >> Clark, William; Lewis, Meriwether

Devoy, John [de**voy**] (1842–1928) Journalist and nationalist, born in Kill, Co Kildare, Ireland. He served in the French Foreign Legion and the British army, where he became an agent for the 'Fenian' secret society. Sentenced in 1866 to 15 years' imprisonment for organizing cells, he was amnestied on condition of exile from the UK. He settled in the USA as a journalist on the New York *Herald*, and helped organize Clan-na-Gael. Through Thomas James Clarke he helped tie the Easter Rising of 1916 to alliance with Germany in World War 1, and subsequently roused US support for the victims of its repression. >> Clarke, Thomas James

Devoy, Susan (Elizabeth Anne) [de**voy**] (1964–   ) Sportswoman, born in Rotorua, New Zealand. She first played in the World Squash Championships in Canada in 1981, and won her first New Zealand national title in 1983. For the rest of the decade she dominated women's squash. In 1984 she won the Swedish, Swiss, Irish, French, and Finnish Opens, and was the youngest ever winner (at 20) of the British Open. Ranked first in the world (1984–91), she held the British Open title (1984–90) and was four times World Open champion between 1985 and 1992. She retired from professional play in 1992.

de Vries, Hugo (Marie) [vrees] (1848–1935) Botanist, born in Haarlem, The Netherlands. He was professor at Amsterdam (1878–1918), where he carried out research into the nature of mutation in plant-breeding. His conclusions paralleled those of Mendel, whose work he discovered in 1900. >> Mendel

De Vries, Peter [vrees] (1910–93) Novelist and short-story writer, born in Chicago, IL. He studied at Calvin College and Northwestern University, and in 1943 became a regular staff contributor to the *New Yorker*, where he developed the comic manner later displayed in such novels as *The Tunnel of Love* (1954) and *The Mackerel Plaza* (1958). His upbringing in the Dutch Reformed Calvinist faith provided the background for his later, serious novel about a child's terminal illness, *The Blood of the Lamb* (1961).

Dewar, Sir James [d**yoo**er] (1842–1923) Chemist and physicist, born in Kincardine, Fife, E Scotland, UK. He studied chemistry at Edinburgh, and in 1875 became professor at Cambridge. Two years later he also became professor at the Royal Institution, London, where he lived, lectured, and pursued a wide range of experimental research; he visited Cambridge rarely. In the 1870s he invented the *Dewar flask* (or thermos flask), using it in his studies of low temperatures and gas liquefaction. With Frederick Abel he invented cordite, for long the British standard military propellant. >> Abel, Frederick

de Wet, Christiaan (Rudolf) [wet] (1854–1922) Afrikaner statesman and general, born in Smithfield district, Orange Free State, South Africa. He became conspicuous in the Transvaal War of 1880–1, and in the war of 1899–1902 was the most audacious of all the Boer commanders. In 1907 he became minister of agriculture of the Orange River Colony, and in 1914 joined the South African insurrection, but was captured. Sentenced to six years' imprisonment, he was released in 1915.

Dewey, George (1837–1917) US naval commander, born in Montpelier, VT. He graduated from the naval academy, and during the Civil War (1861–5) served with Admiral Farragut. As commander of the US Asiatic squadron (1897–9) he was in Hong Kong when war was declared with Spain in 1898. He set sail directly for the Philippines and destroyed the Spanish fleet in Manila Bay. >> Farragut

Dewey, John (1859–1952) Philosopher and educator, born in Burlington, VT. He studied at Vermont and Johns Hopkins universities, taught at Michigan (1884) and Chicago (1894), and became professor of philosophy at Columbia University in 1904. He was a leading exponent of pragmatism. His philosophy of education, which stressed development of the person, understanding of the environment, and learning through experience, was extremely influential. His writings include (on philosophy) *The Quest for Certainty* (1929) and (on education) *The Child and the Curriculum* (1902).

Dewey, Melvil (1851–1931) Librarian, born in Adams Centre, NY. He designed the *Dewey system* of book classification by decimals for the Amherst College Library in 1876. He became chief librarian and professor of library economy at Columbia University (1883–8) and director of the New York State Library (1889–1906).

Dewey, Thomas E(dmund) (1902–71) US politician, born in Owosso, MI. After studying law at the universities of Michigan and Columbia, he became district attorney for New York County in 1937, and Governor of New York State in 1942, being re-elected to this office in 1946 and 1950. He was Republican nominee for president in 1944 and 1948 when, by virtue of his campaign organization (the *Dewey machine*), he appeared to be a much stronger candidate than President Truman. >> Truman, Harry S

Dewi, St >> **David, St**

de Witt, Jan [wit] (1625–72) Dutch statesman, the grand pensionary (chief minister) of the United Provinces of the Netherlands (1653–72), born in Dordrecht, The Netherlands. As leader of the Republican Party, he sought to abolish the office of stadholder, and to limit the power of the House of Orange. However, when France invaded the Netherlands in 1672, William of Orange was made stadholder and commander of the Dutch forces. De Witt's brother, Cornelius, was accused of conspiracy and imprisoned. De Witt went to see him in prison at The Hague, where they were killed by an infuriated mob. >> William III

De Wolfe, Elsie (1865–1950) US interior designer. Her design for the Trellis Room of the Colony Club (1906) established her reputation, and her book *The House in Good Taste* (1915) reinforced it. She introduced the term *good taste* into the language.

Dexter, John (1925–90) British stage director. He began as an actor in repertory and television, before becoming a director in 1957. During the next 20 years, he directed plays for the Royal Court Theatre, London, and became an associate of the National Theatre (1963–6). In New York City his direction of *Equus* won him a Tony award in 1974. He was director of the Metropolitan Opera, New York (1974–81), and also directed opera in London, Paris, and Hamburg. He co-founded the New Theatre Company in 1986.

Dexter, Ted, popular name of **Edward Ralph Dexter** (1935–) Cricketer and sports commentator, born in Milan, Italy. He studied at Cambridge, became a cricketer in 1958, and captained Sussex (1960–65) and England (1962–5). He scored 4502 runs, including eight Test centuries. He excelled in most sports, notably golf. In 1964 he stood unsuccessfully for parliament as a Conservative against James Callaghan. After retiring from first-class cricket in 1965, he became a freelance journalist (1965–88) and a sports promotion consultant. He was appointed chairman of the Test Selection board in 1989, resigning in 1993 after a series of defeats against Australia. >> Callaghan, James

d'Hérelle, Felix [dayrel] (1873–1949) Bacteriologist, born in Montreal, Quebec, Canada. He studied there and worked in Central America, Europe, and Egypt before holding a chair at Yale (1926–33). In 1915 he discovered the bacteriophage, a type of virus which infects bacteria, and this finding later proved to be of great value to research in molecular biology.

Diaghilev, Sergei Pavlovich [deeagilef] (1872–1929) Ballet impresario, born in Novgorod, Russia. He obtained a law degree, but was preoccupied with the arts. In 1898 he became editor of *Mir Iskousstva* (World of Art), and during the next few years arranged exhibitions and concerts of Russian art and music. His permanent company was founded in 1911, and remained perilously in existence for 20 years, triumphantly touring Europe. Many of the great dancers, composers, and painters of his period contributed to the success of his Ballets Russes. He also encouraged several major choreographers (eg Fokine, Nijinsky, Balanchine), and gave them opportunities for artistic collaboration. >> Balanchine; Fokine; Nijinsky; Stravinsky

Diamond, Neil (1941–) Singer and songwriter, born in New York City. He began writing songs while studying at New York University. He wrote the hits 'I'm A Believer' (1966) and 'A Little Bit Me, A Little Bit You' (1967) for the Monkees, and had his first No 1 hit with 'Cracklin' Rosie' (1970). His albums include *Touching You, Touching Me* (1970), *Jonathon Livingston Seagull* (1974), and *Headed for the Future* (1986). His songs have been taken up by many recording artists, including The Hollies, Elvis Presley, and UB40.

Diana, Princess of Wales, formerly **Lady Diana (Frances) Spencer** (1961–97) Former wife of Charles, Prince of Wales, and youngest daughter of the 8th Earl Spencer, born at Sandringham, Norfolk, E England, UK. She was educated in Norfolk, and at West Heath School, Sevenoaks, Kent. She

became Lady Diana Spencer when her father succeeded to the earldom in 1975, and worked as a kindergarten teacher in Pimlico before marrying the Prince of Wales to great popular acclaim in 1981. They had two sons, **Prince William (Arthur Philip Louis)** (1982–) and **Prince Henry (Charles Albert David)** (1984–), known as **Prince Harry**. Seriously interested in social concerns, she became a popular public figure in her own right, and was honorary president of many charities. The royal couple were legally separated in 1992, and divorced in 1996. She continued to travel and work with a range of good causes, both in Britain and abroad, while receiving unprecedented worldwide media attention, with newspapers competing to report on her family situation and on her (real or imaginary) personal relationships; and it was while trying to escape the pursuit of paparazzi in Paris that she died in a car accident in August 1997. >> Al Fayed; Charles, Prince of Wales

Diane de France [deean duh frãs] (1538–1619) Duchess of Angoulême, born in Paris, a natural daughter of Henry II of France and a Piedmontese (according to others, of Diane de Poitiers). Formally legitimized, she married **Orazio Farnese** (1553) but was widowed the same year; she married **François de Montmorency** in 1559. Widowed again 1579, she became a favourite of Henry III who gave her the estate of Angoulême. She enjoyed great influence at court under Henry IV, and superintended the education of the future Louis XIII. >> Diane de Poitiers; Henry II (of France); Henry III (of France)

Diane de Poitiers [deean duh pwatyay] (1499–1566) Mistress of Henry II of France. She was married at 13, and left a widow at 32. She then won the affections of the boy dauphin, already wedded to Catherine de' Medici. On his accession (1547) Diane enjoyed great influence, and was made Duchess of Valentinois. After his death (1559) she retired to her Château d'Anet. >> Henry II (of France)

Diaz or **Dias, Bartolomeu** [deeaz] (c. 1450–1500) Navigator and explorer, probably born in Portugal. In 1487 John II gave him two vessels to follow up the discoveries already made on the W coast of Africa. Driven by a violent storm, he sailed round the Cape of Good Hope, and discovered Algoa Bay. The discontent of his crew compelled him to return (1488). He also travelled with Vasco da Gama in 1497, and with Cabral in 1500, during whose expedition he was lost in a storm. >> Cabral; Gama

Díaz, (José de la Cruz) Porfirio [deeaz] (1830–1915) President of Mexico (1876–80, 1884–1911), born in Oaxaca, Mexico. He fought against the French occupation of Mexico (1862–7). Defeated in the presidential election of 1875, he seized power, and served as president for 30 years, until the revolution of Francisco Madero forced him to resign (1911) and flee into exile. His regime did much to stimulate material progress in Mexico. >> Madero; RR1075

Diaz de Vivar, Rodrigo / Ruy >> Cid, El

Dibdin, Charles (1745–1814) Composer, writer, and theatre manager, born in Southampton, Hampshire, S England, UK. He early attracted notice by his singing, and began a stage career in 1762. In 1789 he started his popular series of one-man musical entertainments. He wrote over 1000 songs (such as 'Poor Jack' and 'Tom Bowling') and many stage works, musical pieces, and novels.

Dibdin, Michael (John) (1947–) Novelist, born in Chichester, West Sussex. He studied at the universities of Sussex and Alberta, launching his career as an author with *The Last Sherlock Holmes Story* (1978). In 1988 he won the Crime Writer's Award, the Gold Dagger, for *Ratking*. Later books include *Dirty Tricks* (1991), *Dark Spectre* (1995), and *Cosi Fan Tutti* (1996).

Dibelius, Karl Friedrich Otto [dibaylius] (1880–1967) Lutheran clergyman and ecumenical leader, born in

Berlin. Suspended from church duties following a 1933 sermon to Nazi leaders, he continued to support the Confessing Church, despite being forbidden to speak or publish. As Bishop of Berlin (1945–61), Chairman of the Council of the Evangelical Church in Germany (1949–61), and President of the World Council of Churches (1954–61), he defended religious freedom in East Berlin and encouraged ecumenism. His theologian cousin, **Martin Dibelius** (1883–1947), pioneered the use of form criticism in New Testament studies.

Dick, Philip (Kendred) (1928–) Writer of science fiction, born in Chicago, IL. Educated at Berkeley High School, he worked as a record store manager and as a radio announcer. He is known both for his short stories and his novels, such as *Do Androids Dream of Electric Sheep?* (1968) and *Galactic Pot-Healer* (1969). He was given the Hugo Award in 1963. Later works include *A Scanner Darkly* (1977) and *The Transmigration of Timothy Archer* (1982).

Dicke, Robert H(enry) (1916–) Physicist, born in St Louis, MO. He studied physics at Princeton and Rochester universities, and spent his career at Princeton from 1946. He deduced in 1964 that a 'big bang' origin of the universe should have left an observable remnant of microwave radiation; and this was detected by Penzias and Wilson. In the 1960s he carried out important work on gravitation, including the proposal that the gravitational constant (G) slowly decreases with time (the *Brans–Dicke theory*, 1961). >> Penzias; Wilson, Robert Woodrow

Dickens, Charles (John Huffam) (1812–70) Novelist, born in Landport, Hampshire, S England, UK, the son of a clerk in the navy pay office. In 1814 he moved to London, then to Chatham, where he received some schooling. He found a menial post with a solicitor, then took up journalism, becoming a reporter at Doctors' Commons, and at 22 joined a London newspaper. He published various papers in the *Monthly Magazine*, following this up with sketches and papers for the *Evening Chronicle*. In 1836 his *Sketches by Boz* and *Pickwick Papers* were published; and that year he married Catherine, the daughter of his friend George Hogarth. They had 10 children, but were separated in 1858. Dickens worked relentlessly, producing several successful novels which created a Shakespearean gallery of characters and also campaigned against many of the social evils of his time. The novels first appeared in monthly instalments, notably *Oliver Twist* (1837–9), *Nicholas Nickleby* (1838–9), and *The Old Curiosity Shop* (1840–1). Thereafter a great part of his life was spent abroad. His later novels include *David Copperfield* (1849–50), *Bleak House* (1852–3), *A Tale of Two Cities* (1859), *Great Expectations* (1860–1), and the unfinished *The Mystery of Edwin Drood* (1870). In addition, he gave talks and readings, and wrote many pamphlets, plays, and letters. His novels have provided the basis for many successful adaptations in the theatre, in the cinema, on radio, and on television.

Dickey, James (Lafayette) (1923–97) Poet and writer, born in Atlanta, GA. He served in World War 2 before entering Vanderbilt University (1949–50). *The Stone* (1960) was his first published book of poems. He travelled widely and taught at a succession of universities, later becoming poetry consultant to the Library of Congress (1966–8). In addition to his poetic works, he is known for his novel *Deliverance* (1970), for which he also wrote the film (1972) screenplay.

Dickinson, Emily (Elizabeth) (1830–86) Poet, born in Amherst, MA. At the age of 23 she withdrew from all social contacts, and lived a secluded life at Amherst, writing in secret over 1000 poems. Hardly any of her work was published until after her death, when her sister Lavinia brought out three volumes (1891–6). Her writing, intensely personal and often spiritual, shows great originality both in thought and in form, and has had considerable influence on modern poetry, especially in the USA. >> Higginson

Dick-Read, Grantly (1890–1959) British gynaecologist. He studied at Cambridge and at the London Hospital. His unorthodox work, *Natural Childbirth* (1933), with its rejection of anaesthetics during childbirth and its advocacy of prenatal relaxation exercises, caused controversy, but later found common acceptance. In 1948 he emigrated to South Africa, where in 1954 he conducted a tour of African tribes investigating childbirth.

Dickson, Leonard (Eugene) (1874–1954) Mathematician, born in Independence, IA. He studied at the University of Texas, and taught at Chicago for most of his life. He did important work in group theory, finite fields, and linear associative algebras, and his encyclopedic *History of the Theory of Numbers* (1919–23) is the definitive work on the subject.

Dic Penderyn >> **Lewis, Richard**

Diddley, Bo, originally **Ellas McDaniel** (1928–) Singer, composer, and guitarist, born in McComb, MS. He moved to Chicago in 1934, where he taught himself guitar, and went on to become one of the most influential rhythm-and-blues artists of the mid-50's, beginning with his double-sided hit single, 'Bo Diddley/I'm a Man' (1955). Later hits included 'Say Man' (1959) and 'Road Runner' (1960), and he produced several albums during the 1960s.

Diderot, Denis [deederoh] (1713–84) Writer and philosopher, born in Langres, France. Trained by the Jesuits, he became a tutor and bookseller's hack (1733–44), before beginning as a writer. Always controversial, his *Pensées philosophiques* (1746, Philosophical Thoughts) was burned by the Parliament of Paris for its anti-Christian ideas, and he was imprisoned for his *Lettre sur les aveugles* (1749, trans Essay on Blindness). For 20 years he worked tirelessly as editor of an expanded French version of Chambers's *Cyclopaedia* (1751–76), known as the *Encyclopédie*, a major work of the age of the Enlightenment. A prolific and versatile writer, he published novels, plays, satires, essays, and letters.

Didi [deedee], popular name of **Valdir Pereira** (1928–) Footballer, born in Campos, Brazil, and always known by the affectionate diminutive. Despite a slightly crippled right leg, he was the master strategist of the Brazil side which won the 1958 World Cup in Sweden. A spell with Real Madrid was unsuccessful, but he later managed the Peruvian national side which reached the quarter-finals of the World Cup in Mexico (1970).

Didion, Joan (1934–) Writer, born in Sacramento, CA. She studied at the University of California, Berkeley (1952–6) and married the writer **John Gregory Dunne** in 1964. She became associate feature editor of *Vogue* in New York City (1956–63), and also worked and wrote for the *Saturday Evening Post*, *Esquire*, and *National Review*. Her novels portray contemporary social tensions in a laconic style that has aroused much admiration. Her books include *Run River* (1963), *A Book of Common Prayer* (1977), *Democracy* (1984), and *The Last Thing He Wanted* (1996).

Didius Julianus, Marcus [didius juliahnus] (c. 135–193) Roman soldier and emperor. A former governor of Gaul, he purchased power on 28 March 193 by bribing the praetorian guard in a famous 'auction of the empire' held after the murder of Pertinax (who ruled for three months in 193). He did not hold power for long, as the Senate soon declared for his rival Lucius Septimius Severus and deposed him, and he was murdered in his palace. >> Severus, Lucius Septimius

Didot, Firmin [deedoh] (1764–1836) Printer, born in Paris. As a printer, and especially as an engraver and founder, he raised the family name to the highest eminence. He revived and developed the stereotyping process, and produced fine editions of many classical, French, and English works.

Didrikson, Babe, nickname of **Mildred Ella Zaharias**, *née* **Didrikson** (1914–56) Golfer and athlete, born in Port Arthur, TX. A great all-round athlete, she was in the All-American basketball team (1930–2), then turned to athletics and won two gold medals at the 1932 Olympics; she also broke the world record in the high jump, but was disqualified for using the new Western Roll technique. Excelling also in swimming, tennis, and rifle-shooting, she turned to golf, and won the US National Women's Amateur Championship (1946), then 17 championships including the British Ladies' Amateur Championship (1947). In 1948 she turned professional, and won the US Women's Open three times (1948, 1950, 1954). She married George Zaharias, a noted wrestler.

Diebenkorn, Richard [deebenkaw(r)n] (1922–93) Painter, born in Portland, OR. In 1946 he enrolled at the California School of Fine Arts, San Francisco, where he also taught (1947–50). During the 1950s he developed a style close to Abstract Expressionism while retaining suggestions of the Californian landscape and of city motifs; his two major series of paintings, developed over many years, focus on Berkeley and Ocean Park.

Diefenbaker, John G(eorge) [deefenbayker] (1895–1979) Canadian statesman and prime minister (1957–63), born in Neustadt, Ontario, Canada. He studied at the Univesity of Saskatchewan, and was called to the bar in 1919. In 1940 he entered the Canadian Federal House of Commons, becoming leader of the Progressive Conservatives (1956), and was elected prime minister after 22 years of Liberal rule. His government introduced important agricultural reforms, and extended the federal franchise to Canada's native peoples. He remained active in national politics until his death. >> RR1039

Diels, Otto [deelz] (1876–1954) Chemist, born in Hamburg, Germany. He studied at Berlin and became professor of chemistry at Kiel University (1916–48). With his pupil Kurt Alder he demonstrated in 1928 the 'diene synthesis' (*Diels–Alder reaction*), which is of far-reaching importance, especially in the plastics and petrochemicals industry. They shared the Nobel Prize for Chemistry in 1950. >> Alder

Diemen, Antony Van >> **Tasman, Abel Janszoon**

Dies, Martin, Jr [diyz] (1900–72) US representative, born in Colorado, TX. He was a lawyer and rancher in Jasper, TX (1920–31) before serving as a Democrat in the US House of Representatives (1931–45). He chaired the notorious Special Committee to Investigate Un-American Activities. After a further period in the House (1953–9), he retired to Jasper.

Diesel, Rudolph (Christian Carl) [deezl] (1858–1913) Engineer, born in Paris. He studied at the Munich Polytechnic, and joined the refrigeration firm Linde in Paris in 1880. He moved to the Berlin branch in 1890, and continued his search for an efficient internal combustion engine. He patented a design in 1892 and, subsidized by Krupps, constructed a 'rational heat motor', demonstrating the first compression-ignition engine in 1897. He spent most of his life at his factory at Augsburg. He was lost overboard from the steamer *Dresden* while on his way to London.

Dietrich, Marlene [deetrikh], originally **Maria Magdalene von Losch** (1904–92) Film actress, born in Berlin. She became famous in a German film *Der blaue Engel* (1930, The Blue Angel), and developed a glamorous and sensual film personality in such Hollywood films as *Morocco* (1930) and *Blond Venus* (1932). During World War 2, she often appeared in shows for Allied troops, and continued to make films after the War, such as *Judgment at Nuremberg* (1961). She also became an international cabaret star.

Increasingly reclusive, she refused to be photographed for the 1984 documentary *Marlene*, but contributed a pugnacious vocal commentary. >> Sternberg

Dieudonné, Jean Alexandre [djoedonay] (1906–) Mathematician, born in Lille, France. He studied at the Ecole Normale Supérieure, and held chairs in Rennes, Nancy, Chicago, the Institut des Hautes Etudes Scientifiques, and Nice. The leading French mathematician of his generation, and a founder of the Bourbaki group, his *Eléments d'analyse* (1960–82) in nine volumes carries on the French tradition of the definitive treatise on analysis. >> Bourbaki

Digby, Sir Kenelm (1603–65) Diplomat, scientist, and writer, born in Gayhurst, Buckinghamshire, SC England, UK. He was brought up a Catholic, studied at Oxford, but left to travel abroad. In Madrid he met Prince Charles (1623), and on returning to England was knighted and entered his service. During the Civil War he was imprisoned by the parliament (1642–3), and had his estates confiscated. After the Restoration, he was chancellor to Queen Henrietta Maria until 1664. >> Charles I (of England); Henrietta Maria

Digges, Leonard (1520–c. 1559) English applied mathematician, known for his valuable work in surveying, navigation, and ballistics. He was probably self-educated, but his books on surveying and navigation went through many editions in the 16th-c. He took part in Thomas Wyatt's rebellion in 1554, was condemned to death, but later pardoned and fined. >> Wyatt, Thomas (the Younger)

Dilke, Sir Charles Wentworth [dilk] (1843–1911) Radical politician, born in London, England, UK. He studied at Cambridge, and was called to the bar. He was returned to parliament for Chelsea in 1868, held office as under-secretary for foreign affairs, and was president of the local government board under Gladstone. In 1885 he married **Emilia Frances Pattison** (*née* **Strong**), but his connection with a Mrs Crawford, and a divorce case, led to defeat in 1886 and temporary retirement. He returned to public life in 1892 as MP for the Forest of Dean. >> Gladstone, W E

Dill, Sir John Greer (1881–1944) British soldier, born in Lurgan, Co Armagh. He trained at Sandhurst, and served in the 2nd Boer War (1899–1902) and World War 1, in which he was promoted brigadier-general. In World War 2 he commanded I Corps in France, became Chief of the Imperial General Staff (1940–1), and was head of the British Service Mission in Washington from 1941.

Dillenius, Johann Jacob [dileenius] (1687–1747) Botanist and botanical artist, born in Darmstadt, Germany. He moved to England in 1721, and from 1734 was first Sherardian professor of botany at Oxford. His work was of fundamental importance in the study of mosses.

Dillinger, John (Herbert) [dilinjer] (1903–34) Gangster, born in Indianapolis, IN. He specialized in armed bank robberies, terrorizing Indiana and neighbouring states (1933–4). After escaping from Crown Point county jail, where he was held on a murder charge, he was shot dead by FBI agents in Chicago.

Dillon, John (1851–1927) Irish nationalist politician, born in Blackrock, Co Dublin. He studied at the Catholic University medical school in Dublin, and qualified as a surgeon, but turned to politics. He became a supporter of Parnell in the Land League, and in 1880 was returned for Tipperary. From 1885 to 1918 he sat for East Mayo. After the divorce case involving Parnell in 1890, he became leader of the Anti-Parnellite group (1896–9), and in 1918 led the remnant of the Irish Nationalist Party, but he was defeated in the election of 1919 by de Valera, and retired from politics. >> de Valera; Parnell

Dillon, Matt (1964–) Film actor, born in Larchmont, NY. At the age of 15 he was cast in *Over The Edge* (1979), but his first major film role was in Francis Ford Coppola's *The Outsiders* (1983). Later films include *Kansas* (1988), *Beautiful Girls* (1996), and *Wild Things* (1998).

Dilthey, Wilhelm [diltiy] (1833–1911) Philosopher, born in Biebrich, Germany. He studied at Heidelberg and Berlin, then taught at Basel, Kiel, Wrocław, Poland (formerly Breslau, Germany), and finally Berlin (1882), where he was professor of philosophy. Using some of Hegel's writings as a point of departure, he argued that human knowledge can only be understood as involving the knower's life lived in a historically conditioned culture. His ideas exerted considerable influence on Heidegger. >> Hegel; Heidegger

DiMaggio, Joe [dimajioh], popular name of **Joseph (Paul) DiMaggio**, nicknames **Joltin' Joe** and **the Yankee Clipper** (1914–) Baseball player, born in Martinez, CA. He spent his entire career with the New York Yankees (1936–51). An outstanding fielder, he also holds the record for hitting safely in 56 consecutive games (1941). His second wife was the film star, Marilyn Monroe. >> Monroe, Marilyn; RR1144

Dimbleby, David (1938–) Broadcaster, born in London, England, UK, the son of Richard Dimbleby. He studied at Oxford, joined the BBC as a reporter (1960–1), and became a leading presenter and interviewer on BBC television current-affairs programmes, such as *Panorama* (1974–77, 1980–2, 1989–) and *Election and Results* (1979, 1983, 1987, 1992, 1997). He is also chairman of the BBC's *Question Time* (1994–) >> Dimbleby, Jonathan/Richard

Dimbleby, Jonathan (1944–) Broadcaster, writer, and journalist, the son of Richard Dimbleby, born in London, England, UK. He studied at University College, London, and became a reporter for the BBC (1969–71). Well known as a presenter of television current-affairs documentaries (1972–88), he hosted *On the Record* for BBC-TV (1988–93), and regularly fronts programmes on major national events, such as the general election. In 1997 he presented the BBC television series *The Last Governor* about Chris Patten's governorship of Hong Kong. His controversial 'official' biography of the Prince of Wales appeared in 1994. >> Dimbleby, David/Richard; Patten

Dimbleby, Richard (Frederick) (1913–65) Broadcaster, born in Richmond on Thames, SW Greater London, England, UK. He was educated at Mill Hill School, near London, and worked on the editorial staff of various newpapers before joining the BBC in 1931. He became the Corporation's first foreign correspondent, its first war correspondent, and was the first radio man to go into Berlin and Belsen at the end of World War 2. In the postwar era he established himself as a magisterial TV anchorman on *Panorama* and a commentator on major events, especially royal occasions and major funerals (such as President Kennedy and Winston Churchill). >> Dimbleby, David/Jonathan

Dimitrov, Georgi Mikhailovich [dimeetrof] (1882–1949) Communist politician and premier (1946–9), born in Pernik, Bulgaria. A printer by trade, he began his political career as a union activist, and helped to form the Bulgarian Communist Party in 1919. After leading an unsuccessful uprising in 1923, he was forced to flee to the Soviet Union, and became active in the Communist International. He was accused of complicity in the burning of the Reichstag in 1933; acquitted, he was deported to Moscow, where he became secretary-general of the Comintern (1935–43) and directed Bulgarian resistance to Nazi occupation (1944–5). He returned to Bulgaria in 1945 as head of the transitional government, and became premier. >> RR1037

d'Indy, (Paul Marie Théodore) Vincent [dãdee] (1851–1931) Composer, born in Paris. He studied law there from a sense of family duty, but at the same time developed an interest in musical composition under the guidance of César Franck. He helped to found the Schola Cantorum in

1894, and taught there and at the Conservatoire until his death. His works include several operas and orchestral pieces, notably *Symphonie sur un chant montagnard français* (1886, Symphony on a French Mountaineering Song). >> Franck, César

Dine, Jim [diyn] (1935–) Artist, born in Cincinatti, OH. He studied at Ohio University and the Boston Museum of Fine Arts School. In 1959 he exhibited his first series of objects as images, alongside Claes Oldenburg, with whom he has since occasionally collaborated on artistic projects. One of the foremost US Pop artists, he later turned to more traditional representational painting. >> Oldenburg

Dinesen, Isak >> **Blixen, Karen**

Ding Ling, also spelled **Ting Ling**, pseudonym of **Jiang Bingzhi** (1904–86) Novelist and short-story writer, born in Linli Co, China. A radical feminist, she studied at Beijing University, joined the League of Left-Wing Writers in 1930, and became editor of its official journal. She joined the Communist Party in 1932, but her outspoken comments on male chauvinism and discrimination led to her being disciplined by the Party leaders, until her novel, *The Sun Shines Over the Sanggan River* (1948), about land-reform, restored her to favour. In 1958, however, she was 'purged', and sent to raise chickens in the Heilongjiang reclamation area. She was imprisoned (1970–5) during the Cultural Revolution, but rehabilitated by the Party in 1979.

Dinkins, David (1927–) US politician, born in Trenton, NJ. He attended Howard University and Brooklyn Law School (1953). After election to the New York state assembly (1965), he served as city clerk (1975–85). In his bid to become mayor of the city, he first won the Democratic Party primary. His policy of racial harmony was popular among black and white voters, and he was elected New York's first black mayor in 1989, but in 1993 lost his bid for re-election to Rudolph Giuliani, the first Republican to be elected mayor of New York City since 1965.

Dinwiddie, Robert [dinwidee] (1693–1770) Colonial administrator, born in Germiston, near Glasgow, W Scotland, UK. He was appointed collector of customs for Bermuda (1727) and surveyor-general for southern America (1738). Appointed lieutenant-governor of Virginia in 1751, he tried to prevent French occupation of the Ohio district in 1753. In 1755 General Edward Braddock was defeated near Fort Duquesne in Ohio, thus precipitating the French and Indian War (1755–63). Dinwiddie was recalled in 1758. >> Braddock, Edward

Dio Cassius [diyoh kasius], also found as **Dion Cassius** and **Cassius Dio Cocceianus** (c. 150–c. 235) Roman senator and prominent man of affairs, from Bithynia in Asia Minor, who wrote a comprehensive history of Rome in Greek, extending from the foundation of the city down to his own day (229). Large parts still survive, either in full or an abbreviated form, and are an invaluable source, particularly for historians of the early Roman empire.

Dio Chrysostomus >> **Dion Chrysostom**

Diocletian [diyokleeshn], in full **Gaius Aurelius Valerius Diocletianus** (245–316) Roman emperor (284–305), a Dalmatian of humble birth, born in Diocles. He rose through the ranks of the army to become the greatest of the soldier emperors of the 3rd-c. He saw the answer to the empire's problems in a division of power at the top and a re-organization of the provincial structure below. In 286 the empire was split in two, with Diocletian retaining the East, and Maximian, a loyal friend, taking the West. Further refinement followed in 293 when, under the famous tetrarchy, the empire was divided into four. Towards the end of his reign he initiated a fierce persecution of Christians throughout the empire. He abdicated in 305. >> RR1084

Diodorus Siculus [diyohdawrus sikyulus] (1st-c BC) Greek historian, born in Agyrium, Sicily. He travelled in Asia and Europe, and lived in Rome, collecting for 30 years the materials for his immense *Bibliothēkē Historikē*, a history of the world in 40 books. The first five books are extant entire; the next five are lost; the next 10 are complete; and there are only fragments of the remainder.

Diogenes Laërtius [diyojeneez lairtius] (3rd-c) Greek writer, born in Laërte, Cilicia. He is remembered for his *Lives, Teachings and Sayings of the Great Philosophers*, in 10 books, a compilation of excerpts.

Diogenes of Apollonia [diyojeneez, apolohnia] (5th-c BC) Greek philosopher who continued the pre-Socratic tradition of speculation about the primary constituent of the world, which he identified as air, operating as an active and intelligent life-force. He was caricatured along with Socrates in Aristophanes' comedy *The Clouds* in 423 BC. >> Aristophanes

Diogenes of Sinope [diyojeneez] (c. 410–c. 320 BC) Cynic philosopher, born in Sinope, Pontus. He moved to Athens, was fascinated by the teaching of Antisthenes, and became an austere ascetic. His unconventional behaviour, which became legendary in antiquity (eg looking with a lantern in daylight for an honest man), was intended to portray the ideal of a life lived according to nature. >> Antisthenes

Dion Cassius >> Dio Cassius

Dion Chrysostom [diyon krisostom], also found as **Dio Chrysostomus** (c. 40–c. 112) Greek rhetorician and philosopher, born in Prusa, Bithynia. He went to Rome under Vespasian, but was banished by Domitian. He then visited, in the disguise of a beggar, Thrace, Mysia, and Scythia. On Nerva's accession (96) he returned to Rome, and lived in great honour under him and Trajan. About 80 orations or treatises on politics and philosophy are extant. >> Domitian; Nerva; Trajan; Vespasian

Dionne, Cécile, Yvonne, Annette, Emilie, and **Marie** [deeon] (1934–) Quintuplets, born near Callander, Ontario, Canada. They were the first documented set of quintuplets to survive beyond a few days. During their childhood they became international celebrities appearing in feature films and advertising. Two have since died: Emilie (1954) and Marie (1970).

Dionysius Exiguus [diyohnisius eksigyoous], also known as **Dennis the Little** (?–556) Scythian Christian scholar, abbot of a monastery in Rome. One of the most learned men of his time, he fixed the dating of the Christian era in his *Cyclus Paschalis* (525).

Dionysius of Alexandria, St [diyohnisius], also known as **Dionysius the Great** (c. 200–264) Greek theologian, born in Alexandria. A pupil of Origen, he succeeded him as head of the catechical school in Alexandria in 231. He became Bishop of Alexandria in 247. In the persecutions under Decius he escaped to a refuge in the Libyan desert, but was restored at the death of Decius in 251. He was banished again in 257, under Valerian, but returned in 261. Only fragments of his writings have survived. Feast day 17 November. >> Decius; Origen; Valerian

Dionysius of Halicarnassus [diyoniysius] (1st-c BC) Influential Greek critic, historian, and rhetorician, from Halicarnassus in Asia Minor, who lived and worked in Rome at the time of Augustus. Much of his writing survives, including about half of his masterpiece, *Early Roman History*. Extending from earliest times to the outbreak of the First Punic War (264 BC), it is a mine of information about early Roman society.

Dionysius the Areopagite [diyoniysius, ariopagiyt] (1st-c) Greek Church leader, one of the few Athenians converted by the apostle Paul (*Acts* 17.34). Tradition makes him the first Bishop of Athens and a martyr. The Greek writings bearing his name were probably written by an Alexandrian. They are first mentioned in 533, from which time they were generally accepted as genuine, and had a great influence on the development of theology. >> Paul, St

Dionysius the Elder [diyoniysius] (c. 431–367 BC) Tyrant of Syracuse (405–367 BC) and ruler of half of Sicily, whose influence extended over most of S Italy. His reign was dominated by intermittent warfare with the Carthaginians, his chief rivals for power in Sicily. A patron of the arts, he invited Plato to his court, and even won a prize himself for tragedy at one of the great Athenian dramatic festivals. >> Dionysius (the Younger); Plato

Dionysius the Younger [diyoniysius] (c. 397–? BC) Tyrant of Syracuse (367–357/6 BC), the son and successor of Dionysius the Elder. Groomed by Plato as a potential philosopher-king, he turned out to be a rake and an oppressor. Twice overthrown, he ended his days in exile at Corinth. >> Dionysius the Elder; Plato; Timoleon

Dionysius Thrax [diyoniysius thrayks] (1st–2nd-c) Greek grammarian, a native of Alexandria, who taught at Rhodes and at Rome. His *Technē grammatikē* is the basis of all European works on grammar.

Diophantus [diyofantus] (c. 200–299) Greek mathematician, who lived in Alexandria c.275. Of his three known works, only six books of *Arithmetica*, the earliest extant treatise on algebra, have survived. His name was later given to that part of algebra which treats of the finding of particular rational values for general expressions under a surd form (*Diophantine analysis*).

Dior, Christian [deeaw(r)] (1905–57) Fashion designer, born in Granville, France. He was the founder of the international fashion house of that name, and first began to design clothes in 1935. After working for Piguet and Lelong in Paris, he founded his own Paris house in 1945, and achieved worldwide fame with his long-skirted 'New Look' (1947). His later designs included the 'H' line and the 'A' line.

Dioscorides, Pedanius [diyoskorideez] (fl. 1st-c) Greek physician, born in Anazarbus, Cilicia. He wrote *De materia medica*, the standard work on the medical properties of plants and minerals for many centuries.

Diouf, Abdou (1935–) Senegalese politician and president (1981–), born in Louga, Senegal. After studying at Paris University he returned to work as a civil servant before entering politics, becoming prime minister in 1970, then president. In 1982 he became president of the loose Confederation of Senegambia, and was re-elected president of Senegal (1983, 1988). >> RR1087

Dippel, Johann Konrad (1673–1734) Theologian and alchemist, born in Burg Frankenstein, Germany. As a chemist in Berlin, he invented a panacea known as *Dippel's animal oil*, a distillation of animal bone and offal. He also discovered Prussian blue.

Dirac, Paul A(drien) M(aurice) [dirak] (1902–84) Physicist, born in Bristol, SW England, UK. He studied engineering at Bristol and physics at Cambridge, where he became professor of mathematics (1932–69). His main research was in the field of quantum mechanics, in which he applied relativity theory, and developed the theory of the spinning electron. His proposal of the existence 'anti-matter'- atomic particles of opposite charge to that normally found – was confirmed by Anderson in 1932. He shared the Nobel Prize for Physics in 1933. He moved to the USA in 1968, and in 1971 became professor of physics at Florida State University, Tallahassee. >> Anderson, Carl; RR1122

Dirichlet, Peter Gustav Lejeune [diriklay] (1805–59) Mathematician, born in Düren, Germany. He entered the Collége de France in Paris (1822), became extraordinary professor at Berlin (1828), and professor at Göttingen (1855). His main work was in number theory, Fourier series, and the boundary value problems in mathematical physics which now carry his name.

Dirks, Rudolph (1877–1968) Strip cartoonist, born in Heinde, Germany. His family moved to Chicago when he was seven. He started selling joke cartoons to *Life* magazine in 1894, then joined the *New York Journal* where he created the long-running strip, *The Katzenjammer Kids* (1897). He later retitled his characters as *The Captain and the Kids* (1914), while the original *Katzenjammer Kids* continued in parallel for decades. He retired in 1958, and his strip was continued by his son, **John**.

Dirksen, Everett (McKinley) (1896–1969) US representative and senator, born in Pekin, IL. After serving in the army, he engaged in family businesses before entering local politics in 1926. As a Republican member of the US House of Representatives (1933–51), he supported the 'New Deal' domestic programme while championing isolationist foreign policy. A political pragmatist, he drafted the Legislative Reorganization Act of 1946. In the US Senate (1951–69) he was a conservative McCarthyite until 1956, when he became an Eisenhower loyalist and moderate, chosen as Republican whip in 1957 and Republican leader in 1959. Ironically the high point of his career came during the Kennedy and Johnson presidencies, when he delivered key Republican support for the Test Ban Treaty of 1963 and the Civil Rights acts of 1964, 1965, and 1968. >> Eisenhower; Johnson, Lyndon B; Kennedy, John F; McCarthy, Joseph R

Disney, Walt(er Elias) (1901–66) Artist and film producer, born in Chicago, IL. After World War 1, he worked as a commercial artist before setting up a small studio in which he produced animated cartoons, his most famous character being Mickey Mouse (1928, with Disney providing the original voice). Among his early successes were the *Silly Symphonies* (from 1929) and the first full-length coloured cartoon film, *Snow White and the Seven Dwarfs* (1937). This was followed by *Pinocchio* (1940), *Dumbo* (1941), and *Fantasia* (1940), the first successful attempt to realize music in images. In 1948 he began his series of coloured nature films, including *The Living Desert* (1953). He also produced several swashbuckling colour films for young people, such as *Treasure Island* (1950) and *Robin Hood* (1952), and family films such as *Mary Poppins* (1964). He opened Disneyland, the first of several family amusement parks, in California in 1955, and others followed in Florida (1971), Tokyo (1983), and Paris (1992). His studios are still highly active, making feature films for cinema and television.

Disraeli, Benjamin, 1st Earl of Beaconsfield [dizraylee, bekuhnsfeeld] (1804–81) British statesman and twice prime minister (1868, 1874–80), born in London, England, UK, the eldest son of an Anglicized Jew, baptized in 1817. He made his early reputation as a novelist, publishing his first novel, *Vivian Grey*, in 1826. He is better known for his two political novels, *Coningsby* (1844) and *Sybil* (1846), which date from his period as a Romantic Tory, critical of industrial developments. He became leader of the 'Young England' movement which espoused these values, and came to prominence as a critic of Peel's free trade policies, especially the repeal of the Corn Laws (1845–6). Leader in the Commons of the Conservatives, after the Peelites left the Party, he was Chancellor of the Exchequer in Derby's minority governments of 1852 and 1858–9. While chancellor in the government of 1866–8, he piloted the 1867 Reform Bill through the Commons. He became prime minister on Derby's resignation in 1868, but was defeated soon afterwards in the general election. His second administration was notable both for diplomacy and social reform, though much of the latter only consolidated legislation begun under Gladstone. During his administration, Britain became half-owner of the Suez Canal (1875), and

the queen assumed the title Empress of India (1876). His skilful diplomacy at the Congress of Berlin (1878) contributed to the preservation of European peace after conflict between the Russians and the Turks in the Balkans. Defeated in 1880 by Gladstone and the Liberals, he then effectively retired. >> Derby, 14th Earl; Gladstone; Peel; Victoria; RR1095

Dittersdorf, Karl Ditters von (1739–99) Composer and violinist, born in Vienna. A friend of Haydn, he also played in Viennese string quartets with Mozart. The composer of 13 Italian operas, and much orchestral and piano music, he is chiefly remembered for his contribution to the development of the German comic operatic tradition (*Singspiel*). >> Haydn, Franz Joseph; Mozart

Divine, Father >> **Baker, George**

Dix, Dorothea (Lynde) (1802–87) Reformer and nurse, born in Hampden, ME. She became a teacher, and in 1821 established her own school in Boston, running it successfully until 1834, when a tubercular illness forced her to give it up. She then dedicated herself to the study of conditions in insane asylums, prisons, and almshouses, travelling over 10 000 mi on her investigations (1842–5), and initiating several reforms. In 1861 she became superintendent of women nurses for the federal government, overseeing the recruitment, training, and placement of some 2000 women who cared for the Union war-wounded. After the war she resumed her work among the insane, and travelled widely in Europe and Japan.

Dix, Otto (1891–1969) Realist painter, born in Gera-Unternhaus, Germany. He is best known for his etchings and paintings of World War 1 casualties, portrayed with biting realism, and of Berlin prostitutes in the decadent post-war period. A brilliant and savage portraitist and social commentator, his work was regarded as unwholesome by the Nazis, who included it in the famous exhibition of Degenerate Art. After World War 2 he painted mostly religious subjects.

Dixon, Jeremiah >> **Mason, Charles**

Djilas, Milovan [jeelas] (1911–95) Yugoslav politician and writer, born in Montenegro. Originally a friend of Tito, he rose in the government as a result of his wartime exploits as a partisan. He was later discredited and imprisoned as a result of outspoken criticism of the Communist system as practised in Yugoslavia, but was released from prison under amnesty at the end of 1966. His books include *The New Class* (1957) and *Conversations with Stalin* (1962), as well as a number of novels, short stories, and political memoirs. >> Tito

Dmitri [duhmeetree], also known as **Demetrius** (1583–91) Russian prince, the youngest son of Tsar Ivan the Terrible. He was murdered by the regent Boris Godunov, but about 1603 was impersonated by a runaway Moscow monk, Grigoriy Otrepieff, the 'false Dmitri', who was crowned tsar by the army in 1605 but killed in 1606 in a rebellion. A second and a third 'false Dmitri' arose within the next few years, but their fate was no better. >> Godunov, Boris; Ivan IV

Dobbie, Sir William George Sheddon (1879–1964) British soldier, born in Madras, India. He trained at the Royal Military Academy, Woolwich, joined the Royal Engineers, and served in South Africa in the 2nd Boer War (1899–1902). He commanded in Malaya (1935–9), and was Governor of Malta (1940–2) during its resolute resistance to German and Italian air attack.

Dobell, Sir William [dohbel] (1899–1970) Portrait painter, born in Newcastle, New South Wales, Australia. He studied at the Julian Ashton Art School in Sydney, and at the Slade School of Art, London. Returning to Sydney, he worked during World War 2 in a camouflage unit with other artists. Dobell's controversial portrait of Joshua Smith won the

Archibald Prize in 1944. Later work included a portrait of the then prime minister of Australia, Sir Robert Menzies. He left all his estate to establish the art foundation which bears his name.

Döbereiner, Johann Wolfgang [doeberiyner] (1780–1849) Chemist, born in Bug bei Hof, Germany. Professor at Jena from 1810, he is remembered as the inventor of *Döbereiner's lamp*, in which hydrogen, produced in the lamp by the action of sulphuric acid on zinc, burns on contact with a platinum sponge.

Dobrée, Bonamy [dobray] (1891–1974) British literary scholar. He was professor of English literature at Leeds (1936–55), and wrote on Restoration comedy (1924) and tragedy (1929), as well as on many individual authors.

Dobrynin, Anataoly Fedorovich [dobreenin] (1919–) Soviet diplomat and statesman, born in Krasnoya Gorka, near Moscow. Educated as an engineer, he joined the diplomatic service in 1941, and became Soviet ambassador to Washington (1962–86) and secretary for foreign affairs (1986–8).

Dobson, Frank (1888–1963) Sculptor, born in London, England, UK. He was associated with the London Group for many years, and was professor of sculpture at the Royal College of Art until 1953. His individual style, with simplified contours and heavy limbs, is shown at its best in his female nudes.

Dobzhansky, Theodosius [dobzhanskee] (1900–75) Geneticist, born in Nemirov, Ukraine. He studied zoology at Kiev and taught genetics in Leningrad before going to the USA in 1927, where he joined Thomas Hunt Morgan at Columbia University to work on the genetics of the fruit fly *Drosophila*. He taught thereafter at the California Institute of Technology (1929–40), Columbia (1940–62), and Rockefeller University (1962–71). His work gave the experimental evidence which linked Darwinian evolutionary theory with Mendel's laws of heredity; and he applied his ideas to the concept of race in human beings, defining races as Mendelian populations differing in gene frequencies. >> Mendel; Morgan, Thomas Hunt

Docherty, Tommy [dokertee], popular name of **Thomas Henderson Docherty** (1928–) Footballer and manager, born in Glasgow, W Scotland, UK. He played 25 times for Scotland, and managed 10 clubs including Aston Villa, Manchester United, Derby County, and Queen's Park Rangers. From September 1971 he managed the Scotland side for just over a year. On leaving football he built a successful career as an after-dinner speaker.

Doctorow, Edgar (Lawrence) [doktoroh] (1931–) Novelist, born in New York City. He studied at Columbia University, and held teaching posts in several colleges and universities. His first novel was *Welcome to Hard Times* (1961), and his best-known work, *Ragtime* (1975), was filmed in 1981. Later books include *Loon Lake* (1980), *The World's Fair* (1985), and *The Waterworks* (1994).

Dodd, Charles Harold (1884–1973) Biblical scholar and Congregational pastor, born in Wrexham, NE Wales, UK. He lectured at Oxford, held a theological chair at Manchester, then was elected to the Norris–Hulse chair of divinity at Cambridge (1936–49) – the first Nonconformist incumbent for nearly three centuries. In 1949 he became general director for the New English Bible translation.

Dodd, Ken(neth) (1929–) Stand-up comedian, singer, and actor, born in Liverpool, Merseyside, NW England, UK. He made his debut at the Empire Theatre, Nottingham (1954), and played summer seasons all round Britain for the next 10 years. He has appeared regularly on stage in variety and pantomime, on radio, and occasionally on television. He has also had hits with songs, such as 'Tears' and 'Happiness'.

Dodge, Grenville (Mellen) (1831–1916) Soldier and engineer, born in Danvers, MA. He fought in the Civil War, and was promoted to major-general in 1864. After the War, as chief engineer of the Union Pacific Railway from 1866, he was responsible for the construction of some of the most famous American railroads.

Dodge, Henry (1782–1867) US politician and pioneer, born in Vincennes, IN. He served in the War of 1812 and the Black Hawk War of 1832, and became famous as a frontiersman. In 1836 he was appointed Governor of the Territory of Wisconsin, and became a member of the US House of Representatives in 1841. He was also US senator for Wisconsin (1848–57).

Dodge, Mary (Elizabeth), *née* **Mapes** (1831–1905) Writer, born in New York City. She married William Dodge, a lawyer, in 1851, and after his death in 1858 turned to writing books for children, especially *Hans Brinker; or, The Silver Skates* (1865), which became a children's classic.

Dodgson, Charles Lutwidge >> **Carroll, Lewis**

Dodsley, Robert (1704–64) Playwright and publisher, born in Mansfield, Nottinghamshire, C England, UK. In 1735 his *Toy Shop* was performed at Covent Garden, through Pope's influence, with great success. He set up as a bookseller, but still continued to write plays, such as *Rex et Pontifex* (1745), and *Cleone* (1758). He published work by Dr Johnson, Pope, and others, and founded the *Annual Register* with Edmund Burke in 1759. He is chiefly remembered for his *Select Collection of Old Plays* (12 vols, 1744–45) and his *Poems by Several Hands* (3 vols, 1748; 6 vols, 1758). >> Burke, Edmund; Pope, Alexander

Doe, Samuel (1951–90) Liberian soldier and president (1985–90), born in Tuzin, Grand Gedeh Co, Liberia. He joined the army in 1969 and became a sergeant in 1975. In 1980 he led an assault on the presidential palace in which President William Tolbert was killed, thus ending the rule of the Americo-Liberians who had been in office since the 19th-c. Other members and associates of the deposed government were publicly executed. He became commander-in-chief of the armed forces, head of state as chairman of the military Peoples Redemption Council (1981), and was narrowly elected president in 1985 in a promised return to civilian government. Following the outbreak of civil war in 1990, he was captured, tortured, and murdered. >> RR1072

Doenitz or **Dönitz, Karl** [doenits] (1891–1980) German naval commander, born in Grünau, Germany. He entered the submarine service of the German Navy in 1916, and became a staunch advocate of U-boat warfare. He planned Hitler's U-boat fleet, was made its commander in 1936, and in 1943 became commander-in-chief of the German navy. Becoming führer on the death of Hitler, he was responsible for the final surrender to the Allies, and in 1946 was sentenced to 10 years' imprisonment for war crimes. >> Hitler

Doesburg, Theo van [doozberg], originally **Christian Emil Marie Küpper** (1883–1931) Painter, architect, and writer, born in Utrecht, The Netherlands. He began as a poet, but took up painting and exhibited at The Hague in 1908. With Piet Mondrian he founded the avant-garde magazine *De Stijl* (1917–31), and devoted himself to propagating the new aesthetic ideas of this movement, based on a severe form of geometrical abstraction known as neo-Plasticism. He later became increasingly involved in architectural projects. >> Mondrian

Doherty, Peter (Charles) [dokertee] (1940–) Immunologist, born in Brisbane, Queensland, Australia. He studied veterinary science at the universities of Queensland and Edinburgh, and with Zinkernagel carried out research into the immune system, using laboratory mice, at the

John Curtin School of Medical Research at the Australian National University, Canberra, in the 1970s. In 1988 he moved to the St Jude Children's Research Hospital at the University of Tennessee. He shared the Nobel Prize for Physiology or Medicine in 1996 for his contribution to the discovery of how the immune system recognizes virus-inflected cells – research which was first reported in 1974. He also shared the Paul Erlich Prize (1983) and the Albert Lasker Medical Research Award (1995) for this research. >> Zinkernagel

Dohnányi, Ernst von [dohnanyee], Hung **Ernö** (1877–1960) Composer and pianist, born in Pozsony, Hungary (now Bratislava, Slovak Republic). He studied at Budapest, travelled widely as a pianist, and taught at Berlin (1908–15). He had some success with his opera *The Tower of Voivod* (1922), but is best known for his piano compositions, especially *Variations on a Nursery Song* (1913), for piano and orchestra. He was musical director of Hungarian radio (1931), and in 1948 left Hungary as an exile, living in Argentina and (from 1949) the USA, where he was composer in residence at Florida State University.

Doisy, Edward (Adelbert) [doyzee] (1893–1987) Biochemist, born in Hume, IL. He studied at Harvard, and was director of the department of biochemistry at St Mary's Hospital, St Louis (1924–65). In collaboration with US embryologist **Edgar Allen** (1892–1943) he conducted research on reproduction and hormones. In 1939 he isolated two forms of the coagulant agent vitamin K, and shared the Nobel Prize for Physiology or Medicine in 1943. >> RR1123

Dolabella, Publius Cornelius [dolabela] (c.70–43 BC) Roman politician and Cicero's profligate son-in-law. Having obtained the tribuneship (47 BC), he brought forward a bill cancelling all debts, which led to bloody struggles in Rome. On Caesar's murder (44 BC) he usurped the consulate, and obtained the province of Syria. He proceeded to wring money from the towns of Asia with a recklessness that brought about his outlawry. Laodicea, in which he had shut himself up, was taken by Cassius, and Dolabella commanded one of his own soldiers to kill him. >> Cassius; Cicero

Dolci, Danilo [dohlchee] (1925–97) Social worker, 'the Gandhi of Sicily', born in Trieste, Italy. He qualified as an architect, but decided to fight poverty in Sicily, building schools and community centres in the poorest areas, helped by social workers from many European countries. Opposition to his work led to his imprisonment on two occasions. Although not a Communist, he was awarded the Lenin Peace Prize in 1956. >> Gandhi, Mahatma

Dole, Bob, popular name of **Robert Joseph Dole** (1923–) US Republican politician, born in Russell, Kansas. A senator for Kansas, and for several years the minority leader in the Senate, he sought the Republican nomination for the presidency in 1980 and 1988. He became majority leader in the Senate in 1994, following Republican gains in the 1994 elections, resigning in 1996 to campaign for the presidency. He was defeated by Bill Clinton in the presidential election. He is married to **Elizabeth Dole** (1936–), born in Salisbury, NC, who became Secretary of Transportation in the Reagan administration in 1983, and Secretary of Labor under Bush (1989–90).

Dolenz, Micky >> **Monkees, The**

Dolet, Etienne [dolay] (1509–46) Printer and humanist, born in Orléans, France. He is often called 'the first martyr of the Renaissance'. He studied at Paris, Padua, and Venice, then settled in Lyon (1534), where he set up a printing press on which he printed translations of the classics, as well as Erasmus and Rabelais. He was arrested more than once for publishing heretical books, and in 1544 was found guilty of heresy, and burned in Paris.

Dolin, Anton [dohlin], professional name of **Patrick Healey-Kay** (1904–83) Dancer and choreographer, born in Slinfold, West Sussex, S England, UK. He was a principal with Diaghilev's Ballet Russes from 1924, and a principal with the Vic-Wells Ballet during the 1930s. He co-founded the Markova–Dolin Ballet, which became known particularly for its interpretations of *Giselle*. From 1950 to 1961 he served as London Festival Ballet's first artistic director, choreographing for the company. He was knighted in 1981. >> Diaghilev; Markova

D'Oliveira, Basil (Lewis) [dolivaira] (1934–) Cricketer, born in Cape Town, South Africa. As a Cape Coloured he had no prospects of first-class cricket within South Africa, but moved to England in 1960 to play league cricket in Lancashire, and eventually joined Worcester. Selected for England in 1966, he played 44 times as an aggressive middle-order batsman and useful change bowler, and scored five Test centuries. He was chosen for the 1968–9 England tour of South Africa, and the refusal of the South African government to admit him led to the cancellation of the tour and the subsequent exclusion of South Africa from international cricket.

Dollfuss, Engelbert [dolfoos] (1892–1934) Austrian statesman and chancellor (1932–4), born in Texing, Austria. He studied at Vienna and Berlin, and became leader of the Christian Socialist Party. As chancellor, he suspended parliamentary government, drove the Socialists into revolt, and militarily crushed them (Feb 1934). In July 1934, an attempted Nazi putsch in Vienna culminated in his assassination.

Döllinger, Johann Joseph Ignaz von [doelingger] (1799–1890) Roman Catholic theologian, born in Bamberg, Germany. He was professor of ecclesiastical history and law at Munich almost continuously from 1826 to 1871, when he was elected rector. Following the decree of papal infallibility, in 1871 he issued a letter withholding his submission. Excommunicated, he took a leading part in the summoning of the congress in Munich out of which arose the Old Catholics.

Dollo, Louis (Antoine Marie Joseph) [doloh] (1857–1931) Palaeontologist, born in Lille, France. After studying in Lille, in 1882 he became assistant keeper (and in 1891, keeper) of mammals in the Royal Museum of Natural History in Brussels. In 1893 he enunciated *Dollo's law* of irreversibility in evolution.

Dollond, John (1706–61) Optician, born in London, England, UK. A silk weaver by trade, in 1752 he turned to the study of optics, and devoted himself with the help of his son **Peter** (1738–1820) to the invention of an achromatic telescope.

Dolmetsch, (Eugène) Arnold (1858–1940) Musician, born in Le Mans, France. He is known for the revival of interest in early music and musical instruments, especially the recorder. He established workshops at his home in Haslemere, Surrey, and promoted festivals on early music there from 1925. He became a British citizen in 1931. After his death, his family continued and expanded the Haslemere musical tradition, under the direction of his youngest son, Carl. >> Dolmetsch, Carl

Dolmetsch, Carl (1911–97) Musician, born in Fontenay-sous-Bois, France, the son of Arnold Dolmetsch. He became an expert in early instruments, like his father, studying the violin, and playing all the instruments in the viol family. He proved to be a recorder virtuoso, for nearly 60 years working in partnership with his accompanist, **Joseph Saxby** (who also died in 1997), and became musical director of the Society of Recorder Players (1937–97). He took over the direction of the Haslemere Festival on his father's death in 1940, introduced workshops for children in 1948, and began an international summer school in 1970. >> Dolmetsch, Arnold

Dolomieu, Déodat Guy Gratet de [dolomyoe] (1750–1801) Geologist and mineralogist, born in Dolomieu, France. Renowned for his researches on volcanic rocks, he gave his name to *dolomite*.

Dolphy, Eric (Allan) (1928-64) Musician and composer, born in Los Angeles, CA. He played the flute, alto saxophone, clarinet, and bass clarinet, from 1958 working with Chico Hamilton, Charles Mingus, John Coltrane, and other leading musicians of the period, as well as with his own quintet. Despite his early death (related to diabetes), he proved to be one of the most influential musicians of the decade.

Domagk, Gerhard (Johannes Paul) [dohmak] (1895–1964) Biochemist, born in Lagow, Germany. He studied at Kiel, and taught at Greifswald and Münster, before becoming director of the I G Farbenindustrie Laboratory for Experimental Pathology and Bacteriology in 1927. He discovered the chemotherapeutic properties of sulphanilamide, and thus ushered in a new age in chemotherapy. In 1939, on instruction from the German government, he refused the Nobel Prize for Physiology or Medicine.

Domar, Evsey D(avid) [dohmah(r)] (1914–) Economist, born in Lodz, Poland (formerly, Russia). Initially educated in China, he completed his studies in the USA. He taught at several universities, moving to the Massachusetts Institute of Technology in 1958. He is the co-inventor of the *Harrod–Domar model* of dynamic equilibrium in economic growth. >> Harrod

Domenichino [domenikeenoh], originally **Domenico Zampieri** (1581–1641) Painter, born in Bologna, Italy. He trained under Ludovico Carracci, and joined the Bolognese artists in Rome. His masterpiece is 'The Last Communion of St Jerome' (1614) in the Vatican. >> Carracci

Domenico Veneziano [domeneekoh venetsiahnoh] (c. 1400–61) Italian painter. He is especially known for his altarpiece in the Uffizi at Florence.

Domingo, Plácido [dominggoh] (1941–) Tenor, born in Madrid. He moved to Mexico with his family, and studied piano and conducting at the National Conservatory of Music, Mexico City. In 1959 he made his debut as a baritone, took his first tenor role in 1960, and became a member of the Israeli National Opera (1962–5). He first sang in New York City in 1966, at La Scala in 1969, and at Covent Garden in 1971. His vocal technique and acting ability have made him one of the world's leading lyric-dramatic tenors, notably in works by Puccini and Verdi. He has made numerous recordings and film versions of operas.

Dominic, St (c. 1170–1221) Founder of the Order of Friars Preachers, born in Calaruega, Old Castile. He studied at Palencia, where he acquired such a name for piety and learning that he was made a canon in 1193. He led a life of rigorous asceticism, and devoted himself to missionary work, notably among the Albigenses of S France. His preaching order was approved by Pope Honorius III in 1216. By the time of his death, his order occupied 60 houses, and had spread as far as England, where from their dress the friars were called Black Friars. He was canonized in 1234 by Gregory IX. Feast day 8 August.

Domino, Fats, originally **Antoine Domino** (1928–) Singer, pianist, and composer, born in New Orleans, LA. His cheerful boogie-woogie piano style, with strong backbeat and a bluesy feel, helped popularize rock-and-roll in the 1950s and early 1960s. His songs include 'Blueberry Hill', 'Ain't That a Shame', 'Blue Monday', and 'I'm Walkin'.

Domitian [domishn], in full **Titus Flavius Domitianus** (51–96) Roman emperor (81–96), the younger son of Vespasian, and the last of the Flavian emperors. An able but autocratic ruler, he thoroughly alienated the ruling class by his rapacity and tyrannical ways. Becoming paranoid about opposition after the armed revolt of Saturninus, the Governor of Upper Germany (89), he unleashed a reign of terror in Rome which lasted until his own assassination. >> Vespasian; RR1084

Donaldson (of Lymington), John Francis Donaldson, Baron (1920–) British judge. He studied at Cambridge, and was called to the bar in 1946, practising mainly in commercial cases. He became a judge in 1966, a Lord Justice of Appeal (1979–82), and Master of the Rolls in 1982. He was knighted in 1986.

Donat, Aelius >> **Donatus, Aelius**

Donat, Robert [dohnat] (1905-58) Actor, born in Manchester, Greater Manchester, NW England, UK. He worked on the stage in the 1920s, and had many leading film roles over the next 20 years, including *The Thirty-nine Steps* (1935), *Good-bye, Mr Chips* (1939, Oscar), *The Young Mr Pitt* (1942), and *The Winslow Boy* (1948). Ill health limited his later career, and his final appearance was in *The Inn of the Sixth Happiness* (1958), shortly before his death.

Donatello [donateloh], originally **Donato di Betto Bardi** (c. 1386-1466) The greatest of the early Tuscan sculptors, born in Florence, Italy. He may be regarded as the founder of modern sculpture, as the first producer since classical times of statues complete and independent in themselves, and not mere adjuncts of their architectural surroundings. Among his works are the marble statues of saints Mark and George for the exterior of Or San Michele; and the tomb of Pope John XXIII in the Baptistery.

Donati, Giambattista [donahtee] (1826–73) Astronomer, born in Pisa, Italy. Director of the observatory at Florence, he discovered the brilliant comet (*Donati's comet*) of 1858. Noted for his researches on stellar spectra, he was the first to observe the spectrum of a comet.

Donatus, Aelius [donaytus] (c. 300–c. 399) Latin grammarian and rhetorician, who taught in Rome AD c.360. His treatises on Latin grammar were in the Middle Ages the only textbooks used in schools, so that *Donat* in W Europe came to mean a 'grammar book'. He also wrote commentaries on Terence and Virgil.

Donatus Magnus [donaytus magnus] (?–c. 355) Bishop of Carthage. He was a leader of the *Donatists*, a 4th-c puritan Christian sect in N Africa. The schism arose in 311, following the controversial appointment of Caecilian as Bishop of Carthage. Donatus's opposition was overruled by Emperor Constantine in 316, and when the new movement grew in strength, he was exiled to Gaul (347).

Don Carlos >> **Carlos, Don**

Donegan, Lonnie, originally **Anthony Donegan** (1931–) Singer and guitarist, born in Glasgow, W Scotland, UK. While playing in traditional jazz bands he introduced 'skiffle' sessions between jazz sets, playing American folk music with a strong rhythm section. He had success both in Britain and the USA with such songs as 'Rock Island Line' (which launched a skiffle craze), 'Gamblin' Man', and 'Cumberland Gap', as well as such comic novelties as 'My Old Man's a Dustman'. He was a widely acknowledged influence on later British guitar-based rock and pop music from the Beatles onwards.

Dönitz, Karl >> **Doenitz, Karl**

Donizetti, (Domenico) Gaetano (Maria) [donizetee] (1797–1848) Composer, born in Bergamo, Italy. He studied music at Bergamo and Bologna, and produced his first opera in 1818 at Venice. The work which carried his fame beyond Italy was *Anna Bolena* (1830), and he had several other successes, notably *Lucia di Lammermoor* (1835). Stricken by paralysis, he became mentally ill.

Donkin, Bryan (1768–1855) Engineer and inventor, born in Sandhoe, Northumberland, NE England, UK. He was apprenticed to a paper-maker, and assisted Fourdrinier to perfect an automatic paper-making machine (1804). With Richard Bacon he patented one of the first rotary printing machines (1813), and although the machine was not successful, the composition roller he had invented to ink the machine became the industry standard. He also improved on the food-preserving invention of Appert by using sealed tins instead of glass jars, opening a canning factory in 1812. >> Appert; Fourdrinier

Donleavy, J(ames) P(atrick) (1926–) Writer, born in New York City. He served in the US Navy during World War 2, then studied microbiology at Dublin, and became a friend of Brendan Behan. His first novel, *The Ginger Man* (1955) was hailed as a comic masterpiece. Among his other works are *A Singular Man* (1963), *The Beastly Beatitudes of Balthazar B* (1968), *The Onion Eaters* (1971), *Leila* (1983), *Are you Listening, Rabbi Low?* (1987), and *That Darcy, That Dancer, That Gentleman* (1990). Later novels include *The Lady Who Liked Clean Rest Rooms* (1996) and *Wrong Information is Being Given Out at Princeton* (1997). He has been an Irish citizen since 1967, and published *J P Donleavy's Ireland* in 1986. >> Behan, Brendan

Donn-Byrne, Brian Oswald >> **Byrne, Donn**

Donne, John [duhn] (?1572–1631) Poet, born in London, England, UK. Educated at Oxford and Cambridge, he studied law in London, and in 1598 became secretary to Thomas Egerton (1540–1617), keeper of the Great Seal. His career prospects were excellent, but his secret marriage to the Lord Keeper's niece had him dismissed and cast into prison. Originally a Catholic, he then joined the established Church, eventually taking Orders. He was made dean of St Paul's, where his sermons were extremely popular. His creative years fall into three periods. The first (1590–1601) was a time of passion and cynicism, as seen in his *Elegies* and *Songs and Sonnets*. The second, from his marriage to his ordination, was a period of anguished meditation and flattery of the great, as seen in his *Anniversaries* and funeral poems. His third period includes sonnets and hymns, and shows that in transferring his allegiance from the world to God he retained his earlier passion.

Donnelly, Ignatius [donelee] (1831–1901) Politician and writer, born in Philadelphia, PA. After qualifying for the bar in 1852, he moved to Minnesota in 1856, becoming lieutenant-governor and governor (1859–63) and later radical Republican congressman (1863–9). As a prophet of reform his most enduring legacy is a novel, *Caesar's Column* (1891), predicting tyranny and oppression. *The Great Cryptogram* (1888) sought to prove Bacon had written the plays usually attributed to Shakespeare, and had hidden ciphered messages in the plays declaring his authorship.

Donoghue, Steve [donuhyoo], popular name of **Stephen Donoghue** (1884–1945) Jockey, born in Warrington, Cheshire, NWC England, UK. He won the Derby six times, including a record three consecutive wins (1921–3). Champion jockey in 10 successive years (1914–23), he won a total of 14 classics.

Donoso, (Yanez) José [donosoh] (1928–96) Novelist, born in Santiago, Chile. He studied at the University of Chile and at Princeton (1949–51), and became a longshoreman, teacher, editor, and journalist. His first collection of short stories won Chile's Municipal Prize in 1951, and in 1962 he received the William Faulkner Foundation Prize for Chile, for his novel *Coronation* (1957).

Donovan, Terence (1936–96) Photographer, born in London. After leaving secondary school at the age of 11, he took a course at the London School of Engraving and Lithography before joining the photographic studio of John French. In 1959 he set up on his own, and became well known for his monochrome, documentary-style, street-fashion photographs characterizing the London of the swinging '60s.

Donovan, William (Joseph), nickname **Wild Bill Donovan** (1883–1959) US soldier and public official, born in Buffalo, NY. A much-decorated World War 1 veteran, he was an assistant to the US attorney general (1925–9), and served as an unofficial observer for the government in Italy, Spain, and the Balkans (1935–41). Assigned to head the US Office of Strategic Services (1942–5), he had responsibility for espionage, counter-espionage, and clandestine military operations during World War 2. He was later appointed ambassador to Thailand (1953–4).

Doohan, Michael [dooan] (1965–) Motor-cyclist, born in Brisbane, Queensland, Australia. He first raced in 1984, and won his first Grand Prix in 1990, achieving a total of 44 Grand Prix wins by mid-1997. Despite a serious crash in 1992, riding for Honda in 1997 he became only the third rider (following Hailwood and Agostini) to win four successive 500cc world championships, and in September of that year reached Agostini's long-standing record for the number of wins in a season (11). >> Agostini; Hailwood

Dooley, Mr >> **Dunne, Finley Peter**

Doolittle, Hilda, pseudonym **H D** (1886–1961) Poet, born in Bethlehem, PA. She lived in London from 1911, and became an exponent of Imagism. She wrote several books of poetry, beginning with *Sea Garden* (1916) and *Hymen* (1921), and also several prose works and translations. In 1913 she married **Richard Aldington**, and after their divorce (1937) settled near L Geneva. >> Aldington

Doolittle, James H(arold) (1896–1993) US air force officer, born in Alameda, CA. He commanded 16 B-25 bombers which raided Tokyo in 1942, with decisive effects on Japanese naval strategy. He later commanded the 12th Army Air Force (AAF) in North Africa, the 15th AAF in Italy (1943), and the 8th AAF in Britain for operations in North West Europe (1944). After the war he was vice-president and director of Shell Oil (1945–59).

Doppler, Christian Johann (1803–53) Physicist, born in Salzburg, Austria. He studied at Vienna, where he became professor of physics (1851), and is best known for his explanation of the perceived frequency variation of sound and light waves because of the relative motion of the source and the detector (the *Doppler effect*).

Dora, Sister >> **Pattison, Dorothy**

Dorat, Jean >> **Daurat, Jean**

Dorati, Sir Antal [dorahtee] (1906–) Conductor, born in Budapest. He studied at the Liszt Academy and Vienna University, after which he worked with the Budapest Royal Opera, where he made his conducting debut (1924). He worked with the Dresden Opera (1928), and the Münster State Opera (1929–32), after which he spent several years touring. Following his US debut (1937), he became musical director of the new American Ballet Theater. He established an international career, and was appointed senior conductor of the London Royal Philharmonic (1975–9). His autobiography, *Notes of Seven Decades* was published in 1979, and he was knighted in 1984.

Doré, (Paul) Gustave [doray] (1832–83) Painter and book illustrator, born in Strasbourg, France. He first made his mark by his illustrations to books by Rabelais (1854) and Balzac, notably the latter's *Contes drolatiques* (1865). These were followed by illustrated editions of Dante, the Bible, Milton, and other works.

Doren, Carl / Mark Van >> **Van Doren, Carl / Mark**

Doria, Andrea [dawria] (c. 1466–1560) Genoese commander and statesman, born in Oneglia, Italy. In 1513 he received command of the Genoese fleet, and defeated the Turkish corsairs off Pianosa (1519). The imperial faction were restored to power in Genoa (1522), and Doria transferred his allegiance to Francis I of France. In command of the French fleet, he defeated the Emperor Charles V, blockaded

Genoa, and proclaimed the independence of the republic in 1527. In 1529, fearing the predominance of Francis, he transferred his allegiance to Charles V and established an aristocratic government which lasted to the end of the republic in 1797. >> Charles V (Emperor); Fieschi, Giovanni Luigi de; Francis I

Dorn, Friedrich Ernst (1848–1916) Chemist, born in Guttstadt, Germany. He studied at Königsberg, and is known for his discovery of radon.

Dorn, Marion (1900–64) US textile designer. She specialized in fabric and carpet design, and moved to England in the 1920s. After establishing her reputation with private patrons, she became design consultant with the Wilton Royal Carpet factory in the 1930s. Among her commissions were carpet designs for Claridges (1932) and the SS *Orion* (1935).

Dornberger, Walter (Robert) (1895–1980) Rocket engineer, born in Giessen, Germany. An engineer and officer in the German army, he set up an experimental rocket station at Kummersdorf which successfully fired a 650 lb-thrust motor in 1932. In World War 2 the work was transferred to Peenemünde, where he directed the development of the V-2 rockets. After spending three years as a prisoner-of-war in England (1945–7), he went to the USA as a consultant to the air force. In 1950 he joined the Bell Aircraft Corporation, and worked on the Rascal air-to-surface missile and the Dyna-Soar manned Space Glider programme.

Dornier, Claude [daw(r)nyer] (1884–1969) Aircraft engineer, born in Kempten, Germany. He studied at Munich Technical College, and began work (1910) at the Zeppelin factory at Friedrichshafen. In 1911 he designed the first all-metal plane, and with the backing of Zeppelin opened an aircraft division at Friedrichshafen and Altenrhein, where he made seaplanes and flying-boats, including the famous 12-engined Do X (1929). The Dornier 17 twin-engined bomber was a standard Luftwaffe type in World War 2. >> Zeppelin

Dörpfeld, Wilhelm [doepfelt] (1853–1940) Archaeologist, born in Barmen, Germany. He was Schliemann's collaborator and successor at Troy, and professor at Jena (1923). The chronology of Troy set out in his *Troja und Ilion* (1902) served to date European prehistory for the first decades of the 20th-c. >> Schliemann

Dors, Diana, originally **Diana Fluck** (1931–84) Actress, born in Swindon, Wiltshire, S England, UK. A student at the Royal Academy of Dramatic Art, she made her film debut in *The Shop at Sly Corner* (1946). Promoted as a sex symbol, she was cast in various low-budget comedies, and despite an effective dramatic performance in *Yield to the Night* (1956) was usually seen in blowsy supporting assignments. Her accomplished stage work in *Three Months Gone* (1970) brought her a selection of good character parts, as in *The Amazing Mr. Blunden* (1972). She retained her personal popularity, performing in cabaret and as a television agony aunt. She returned to the screen in *Steaming* (1984) immediately prior to her death.

Dorsey, Jimmy >> Dorsey, Tommy

Dorsey, Tommy [daw(r)see], popular name of **Thomas Dorsey** (1905–56) Trombonist and bandleader, born in Shenandoah, PA. Renowned for his sweet-toned instrumental style, his work hovered between jazz and dance music. His big bands were sometimes co-led by his brother **Jimmy Dorsey** (1904–57, alto saxophone, clarinet). The Dorsey Brothers Orchestra existed from 1932 to 1935, reforming again in 1953 until Tommy's death. Both brothers were in great demand as session musicians in the late 1920s, with the expansion of radio in the USA, and their fame was revived through a regular television show in the 1950s.

Doshi, Balkrishna Vithaldas [doshee] (1927–) Architect, born in Poona, India. He studied in Poona and Bombay, and worked as senior designer with Le Corbusier at Chandigarh and Ahmedabad (1951–7). His architectural works include the City Hall, Toronto (1958), the Indian Institute of Management (1962–74, with Kahn), in Ahmedabad, and Vidyadhar Nagar New Town, Jaipur. >> Le Corbusier

Dos Passos, John (Roderigo) (1896–1970) Novelist and war correspondent, born in Chicago, IL. He studied at Harvard, and was an ambulance driver in the later years of World War 1, out of which came his antiwar novel, *Three Soldiers* (1921). He then worked in Europe and elsewhere as a newspaper correspondent. His best-known work is the trilogy on US life, *U.S.A.* (1930–6).

Dos Santos, Jose Eduardo (1942–) Angolan politician and president (1979–), born in Luanda. He joined the People's Movement for the Liberation of Angola (MPLA) in 1961 and was forced into exile in what later became Zaire, during the civil war between the MPLA and the National Union for the Total Independence of Angola (UNITA). He returned to Angola in 1970, and held key positions under President Agostinho Neto, succeeding him in 1979. By 1989 he had negotiated the withdrawal of South African and Cuban forces, and a ceasefire between MPLA and UNITA. A formal peace agreement was signed in 1991 and general elections held in September 1992 at which Dos Santos received just less than the full 50% needed to avoid a second round of voting. UNITA claimed the election was rigged (denied by UN observers), and the civil war recommenced before the second round could be held. >> Savimbi; RR1032

Dosso Dossi, originally **Giovanno di Nicolò Lutero** (c.1479–1542) Religious painter, born near Mantua, Italy. He was the leader of the Ferrarese school in the early 16th-c.

Dostoevsky or **Dostoyevsky, Fyodor (Mikhailovich)** [dostoyefskee] (1821–81) Novelist, born in Moscow. He became a military engineer, but turned to literature, publishing *Bednye lyudi* (Poor Folk) in 1846. Joining revolutionary circles in St Petersburg, he was condemned to death (1849), reprieved at the last moment, and sent to hard labour in Siberia. In 1859 he returned to St Petersburg, where he wrote his masterpiece, *Prestupleniye i nakazaniye* (1866, Crime and Punishment), one of the most powerful realistic works of fiction. Other important books are *Idiot* (1868–9, The Idiot) and *Bratya Karamazovy* (1879–80, The Brothers Karamazov). Domestic trials, financial troubles (caused by gambling debts), and ill health (epilepsy) clouded his later life. He lived for a time in W Europe (1867–71), then returned to work as a journalist in St Petersburg.

Dou or **Douw, Gerard** [dow] (1613–75) Painter, born in Leyden, The Netherlands. He studied under Rembrandt (1628–31), and at first mainly occupied himself with portraiture, but soon turned to genre painting. His 200 works include his own portrait, his wife's, and his celebrated 'Dropsical Woman' (1663), in the Louvre. >> Rembrandt

Douanier, Le >> Rousseau, Henri

Doubleday, Abner (1819–93) US soldier, born in Ballston Spa, NY. He trained at West Point, and fought in the Mexican War and against the Seminoles in Florida. He commanded the Federal troops that fired the first shot in defence of Fort Sumter as the Civil War commenced, and then distinguished himself at the Battle of Gettysburg. He retired from the army in 1873, and wrote many newspaper and magazine articles as well as two accounts of his war experiences (drawing on his 67 volumes of diaries). In nothing he wrote does he ever mention baseball, nor does his *New York Times* obituary; but in 1908 a commission eager to establish the American origins of baseball credited him with being its inventor on the basis of a dubious letter from one Abner Graves, who claimed to have been present in Cooperstown, NY, on the day in 1839 Doubleday laid out the field and rules. Although the claim has long since been recognized as popular folklore – even by the Baseball Hall of Fame in Cooperstown – Doubleday remains synonymous with baseball to most Americans.

Doubleday, Frank (Nelson) (1862–1943) Publisher, born in New York City. He left school to work for the publisher Charles Scribner's, becoming manager of the new *Scribner's Magazine* (1886). He went on to co-found the Doubleday & McClure Co (1900), then expanded his interests, establishing the Country Life Press and opening a chain of bookshops. His company eventually became Doubleday & Co.

Douglas, Lord Alfred (Bruce) (1870–1945) British poet, the son of the 8th Marquess of Queensberry. He wrote a number of sonnets, collected in *In Excelsis* (1924) and *Sonnets and Lyrics* (1935). He is remembered for his association with Oscar Wilde, to which his father objected, thereby provoking Wilde to bring the ill-advised libel action which led to his own arrest and imprisonment. >> Queensberry; Wilde, Oscar

Douglas, David (1798–1834) Botanist, born in Scone, Perth and Kinross, E Scotland, UK. He travelled in North America as a collector for the Horticultural Society of London, and discovered many trees, shrubs, and herbaceous plants which he introduced to Britain. The Oregon Pine (*Pseudotsuga menziesii*) was renamed the *Douglas fir* after him, and his name was also given to the *Douglas squirrel*.

Douglas, Donald (Wills) (1892–1981) Aircraft designer and manufacturer, born in New York City. He attended the US Naval Academy and Massachusetts Institute of Technology. Chief engineer to the Glenn L Martin Aircraft Company in 1915, in 1920 he set up his own company (Davis–Douglas Co) in California. His Douglas World Cruisers made a historic round-the-world flight in 1924. The prototype for the DC series of commercial transport planes was flown in 1933, and during World War 2 he produced the B-19 bomber and other craft. He was chairman of his company, Douglas Aircraft, until it merged with McDonnell Aircraft as the McDonnell Douglas Corporation in 1967. >> Martin, Glenn L; McDonnell

Douglas, Gawain or **Gavin** (c.1474–1522) Poet and bishop, born in Tantallon Castle, East Lothian, E Scotland, UK. He studied at St Andrews for the priesthood, became dean of St Giles, Edinburgh (1501), and Bishop of Dunkeld (1515). His works include *The Palace of Honour* (c.1501) and a translation of the *Aeneid* (finished c.1513), the first to be published in English. After the death of James IV of Scotland at Flodden, he became involved in political intrigues, and in 1521 was forced to flee to London.

Douglas, George >> **Brown, George Douglas**

Douglas, Kirk, originally **Issur Danielovitch Demsky** (1916–) Film actor, born in Amsterdam, NY. He made his Broadway debut in 1941, served in the US Navy, and embarked on a screen career in 1946. His films include *Champion* (1949), *The Bad and the Beautiful* (1952), *Lust for Life* (1956), and *Spartacus* (1960), and from the 1970s he also worked as a director. His son, Michael Douglas, also became an actor. >> Douglas, Michael

Douglas, Mary, née **Tew** (1921–) Social anthropologist, born in Italy. She studied at Oxford, carried out fieldwork among the Lele of the Belgian Congo (now Democratic Republic of Congo), and became professor of social anthropology at University College, London (1970–8). She then moved to the USA, becoming Avalon Foundation professor in the humanities at Northwestern University (1981–5), and then emeritus professor. She is especially known for her studies of systems of cultural classification and beliefs about purity and pollution, and has contributed to economic anthropology, and to the study of moral accountability.

Douglas, Michael (Kirk) (1944–) US film actor and producer, born in New Brunswick, NJ, the son of Kirk Douglas. He studied at the University of California, and achieved recognition in the television police series *The Streets of San Francisco* (1972–5), but left to co-produce *One Flew Over the Cuckoo's Nest* (1975), which won five Academy Awards, including one for Best Picture. He starred in and produced *Romancing the Stone* (1984), and won a Best Actor Oscar for his performance in *Wall Street* (1987). Other acting roles include *Fatal Attraction* (1987), *The American President* (1995), and *The Ghost and the Darkness* (1996). >> Douglas, Kirk

Douglas, Stephen A(rnold) (1813–61) US lawyer and statesman, born in Brandon, VT. He became attorney-general of Illinois in 1834, a member of the legislature in 1835, secretary of state in 1840, and judge of the Supreme Court in 1841. He was returned to Congress in 1843, and to the US Senate in 1847. His policy was to 'make the United States an ocean-bound republic'. In the question of slavery he maintained that each territory should decide whether it should be a free or a slave state. In 1860 he was nominated for the presidency, but was defeated by Lincoln. >> Lincoln, Abraham

Douglas, Tommy, popular name of **Thomas Clement Douglas** (1904–86) Baptist minister and Canadian politician. As premier of Saskatchewan (1944–61), he led the first Socialist government elected in Canada, and was later leader of the federal New Democratic Party for 10 years. He helped establish Democratic Socialism in the mainstream of Canadian politics, and with the introduction of medicare in Saskatchewan is recognized as the Canadian 'father of socialized medicine'.

Douglas, William O(rville) (1898–1980) Judge, born in Maine, MN. He studied at Whitman College and Columbia University, and was a law professor at Yale, then a member (1934) and chairman (1937–9) of the Securities and Exchange Commission. A strong supporter of the 'New Deal', he was appointed to the Supreme Court in 1939. He strongly supported civil rights and liberties, and guarantees of freedom of speech and freedom of the press.

Douglas (of Kirtleside), William Sholto Douglas, Baron (1893–1969) British air force officer. He studied at Oxford, served in World War 1 as a fighter pilot, and at the outbreak of World War 2 was assistant chief of air staff. He became head of Fighter Command (1940–2), Middle East Air Command (1943–4), and Coastal Command (1944–5), and directed the successful anti-submarine campaign in the later stages of the War. He then commanded the British Air Force of Occupation in Germany (1945–6), and was military governor of the British zone of occupation (1946–8). After leaving the air force he became chairman of British European Airways (1949–64).

Douglas-Hamilton, Iain (1944–) British zoologist. He studied at Oxford, and was appointed to make a study of elephants in the wild in L Manyara National Park, Tanzania (1966). The methods he developed became the basis of all future elephant studies, and his book recounting his experiences, *Among the Elephants* (1972), was a best seller. He returned to Africa (1976) to extend his elephant study across the continent, and drew the world's attention to the devasting effect of ivory-poaching, leading eventually to the international ban on the sale of ivory (1989).

Douglas-Home, Sir Alec >> **Home of the Hirsel**

Douglas-Home, William [duhglas hyoom] (1912–92) Playwright, born in Edinburgh, EC Scotland, UK, the brother of Sir Alec Douglas-Home. He studied at Oxford and the Royal

Academy of Dramatic Art, appeared on the West End stage, and published his first play in 1937. He became known for his comedies of upper middle-class and political life, notably *The Chiltern Hundreds* (1947), *The Reluctant Debutante* (1955), *The Reluctant Peer* (1964), *Lloyd George Knew my Father* (1972), and *Her Mother Came Too* (1982). >> Home of the Hirsel

Douglass, Andrew (Ellicott) (1867–1962) Astronomer, born in Windsor, VT. After research work at the Lowell Observatory at Flagstaff, AZ, he became professor of physics and astronomy at Arizona University (1906) and later director of the Stewart Observatory (1918–38). He investigated the relationship between sunspots and climate by measuring the annual growth-rings of long-lived Arizona pines and sequoias, and provided a time-sequence for dating purposes. He coined the term *dendrochronology* ('tree-dating').

Douglass, Frederick (c. 1817–95) Abolitionist and journalist, born in slavery at Tuckahoe, MD. He escaped in 1838, and in 1841 emerged as a major anti-slavery force. He stayed in England for a time, where friends bought his freedom. He also supported the cause of women's rights, and became US minister to Haiti.

Douhet, Giulio [dooay] (1869–1930) Italian general, born in Caserta, Italy. In 1909 he foresaw the importance of air supremacy, and became commander of Italy's first military aviation unit (1912–15). He was head of the Italian Army Aviation Service in 1918, and promoted to general in 1921. His writings on strategic bombing and the future devastation of major cities by mass bomber raids influenced attitudes to civil defence prior to World War 2.

Doulton, Sir Henry [dohltn] (1820–97) Pottery manufacturer, born in London, England, UK. He entered his father's pottery there, and in 1846 introduced stoneware drain pipes instead of flat-bottomed brick drains. In 1848 he started works near Dudley, later the largest in the world, and introduced fine porcelain ware in the 1880s, for which the company is better known.

Douw, Gerard >> Dou, Gerard

Dove, Arthur (Garfield) (1880–1946) Painter, born in Canadaigua, NY. From 1903 he earned his living as a commercial illustrator. In 1910 he began a series of abstract paintings, and in the 1920s experimented with collage incorporating mirrors, sand, and metal. His later abstract work is suggestive of natural organic forms.

Dow, Gerard >> Dou, Gerard

Dow, Henry (Herbert) [dow] (1866–1930) Chemist, inventor, and industrialist, born in Belleville, Ontario, Canada. He moved to the USA with his family as an infant. He began experimenting with brines while a student at Case School of Applied Science, Cleveland, and ultimately built a great chemical empire upon them. He invented a simple electrolytic method for extracting bromine from brine, and his use of a direct current generator in the process is regarded as the foundation of the electrochemical industry in the USA. He established the Dow Chemical Co in 1897. He later introduced the first process for making synthetic indigo, and was the first to extract iodine from brine.

Dowding, Hugh (Caswell Tremenheere) Dowding, Baron (1882–1970) British air chief marshal of World War 2, born in Moffat, Dumfries and Galloway, SW Scotland, UK. He served in the Royal Artillery and the Royal Flying Corps in World War 1. As commander-in-chief of Fighter Command (1936–40), he organized the air defence of Britain, which resulted in the victorious Battle of Britain (1940). He retired in 1942, and was created a peer in 1943.

Dowell, Sir Anthony (1943–) Dancer and director, born in London, England, UK. He studied at the Sadler's Wells

and Royal Ballet Schools, and joined the Royal Ballet company in 1961, becoming one of the premier male ballet dancers of the period, noted for his lightness and elegance in classical roles. He was principal dancer of the American Ballet Theatre (1978–80), and became artistic director of the Royal Ballet in 1986. He was knighted in 1995. >> Sibley, Antoinette

Dowie, John Alexander (1847–1907) Religious leader, born in Edinburgh, EC Scotland, UK. He emigrated to Australia in 1860 and became a Congregational pastor in Sydney. In 1888 he emigrated to the USA, where he organized the Christian Catholic Church in Zion (1896). He became a faith healer, and proclaimed himself 'Elijah the Restorer', in 1901 founding near Chicago the prosperous industrial and banking community called 'Zion City'. He was deposed from his autocratic rule there in 1906.

Dowland, John (1563–1626) Composer, lutenist, and songwriter, born possibly in Westminster, London, England, UK. He studied at Oxford, and having failed to become a court musician to Queen Elizabeth I, entered the service of the Duke of Brunswick (1594), and subsequently went to Italy. He returned to England in 1596, where he wrote his first book of 'ayres'. In 1598 he became lutenist to Christian IV of Denmark, producing further collections of music. In London he composed *Lachrimae* (1605), which contains some of the finest instrumental consort music of the period.

Dowling, Stephen (1904–86) Strip cartoonist, born in Liverpool, Merseyside, NW England, UK. After art studies and advertising agency work he teamed with his brother, copywriter Frank Dowling, to create newspaper strips, starting with *Tich* (1931) in the *Daily Mirror*, followed by *Ruggles* (1935–60), a family soap opera, and *Belinda Blue-Eyes* (1936–42), before the enormously successful fantasy super-hero *Garth* (1942).

Downes, Terry (1936–) Boxer, born in London, England, UK. He was British middleweight champion (1958–9, 1959–62), and held the world championship (1961–2). During his career he won 35 out of 44 professional bouts.

Downing, Sir George (1684–1749) Landowner, and founder of Downing College, Cambridge, born in Cambridgeshire, EC England, UK. Being childless, he stipulated that his estates should pass to each of four cousins in turn, and if they died without issue the money should be used to found a college named after him. Even when the last cousin died childless in 1764, the widow refused to give up the estates, and Downing College did not receive its charter until 1800.

Downpatrick, Edward Lord >> Kent, Edward, Duke of

Dowson, Ernest Christopher (1867–1900) Poet of the 'decadent' school, born in Lee, SEC Greater London, England, UK. He studied at Oxford, became part of the Rhymers' Club group, and was a friend of Arthur Symons and W B Yeats. He spent the rest of his life in France, where he died of alcoholism. >> Symons, Arthur; Yeats, W B

Doyle, Sir Arthur Conan (1859–1930) Writer, the creator of Sherlock Holmes, born in Edinburgh, EC Scotland, UK. He studied medicine at Edinburgh, but poverty as a medical practitioner made him turn to writing. His first book, *A Study in Scarlet* (1887), introduced the super-observant, deductive Sherlock Holmes, his good-natured question-raising friend, Dr Watson, and the whole apparatus of detection mythology associated with Baker Street, Holmes's fictitious home. After *The Adventures of Sherlock Holmes* was serialized in the *Strand Magazine* (1891–3), the author tired of his popular creation, and tried to kill off his hero, but was compelled in 1903 to revive him. Conan Doyle himself set greater stock by his historical romances, such as *The White Company* (1890). He served as a physician in the Boer War (1899–1902), and his pamphlet, *The War in South Africa* (1902), earned him a knighthood (1902). He also wrote on spiritualism, to which he became a convert in later life.

Doyle, Richard (1824–83) Caricaturist, book illustrator, and watercolour painter, born in London, England, UK. He became a contributor to *Punch* in 1843, designed the famous cover that was used from 1849 to 1956, furnished the well-known 'Ye Manners and Customs of ye Englyshe' and the first of the famous 'Brown, Jones, and Robinson' travel and other adventures. In 1850 he left, resenting the journal's anti-Catholic position, and devoted himself to painting and book illustration.

Doyle, Roddy (1958–) Novelist, born in Dublin, Republic of Ireland. He studied at University College, Dublin, then taught English and geography at a local school, and began writing in his spare time. His first success came with *The Commitments* (1987), the first of the internationally acclaimed Barrytown trilogy, which he completed with *The Snapper* (1990) and *The Van* (1991). Later novels include *Paddy Clarke Ha Ha Ha* (1993, Booker Prize) and *The Woman Who Walked into Doors* (1996).

D'Oyly Carte, Richard [doylee kah(r)t] (1844–1901) Theatrical impresario, born in London, England, UK. After working in his father's musical instrument-making business he became a concert agent, and from 1875 produced the first operettas by 'Gilbert and Sullivan', with whom he formed a partnership. In 1881 he built the Savoy Theatre in London, the first to be lit by electricity. Another theatre building, a Royal English Opera House (1891), failed. After his death the D'Oyly Carte company continued to perform Gilbert and Sullivan in traditional style for many years. >> Gilbert, W S; Sullivan, Arthur

Drabble, Margaret (1939–) Novelist and critic, born in Sheffield, South Yorkshire, N England, UK. She studied at Cambridge. She has written biographies of Arnold Bennett (1974) and Angus Wilson (1994). Her novels include *A Summer Bird-Cage* (1962), *The Ice Age* (1977), *The Radiant Way* (1987), *The Gates of Ivory* (1991), and *The Witch of Exmoor* (1996). She was the editor of the 5th edition of the *Oxford Companion to English Literature* (1985). Her elder sister is the novelist A S Byatt. She married her second husband, biographer Michael Holroyd, in 1982. >> Byatt; Holroyd

Draco [draykoh] (7th-c BC) Athenian law-giver. Archon at Athens in 621 BC, he revised the laws of Athens with admirable impartiality; but the severity of his penalty – death for almost every offence – made the strict execution of his code (since proverbial for its rigour) unpopular, and it was superseded by that of Solon. >> Solon

Drake, Sir Francis (c. 1540–96) Elizabethan seaman, born in Crowndale, Devon, SW England, UK. In 1567 he commanded the *Judith* in his kinsman John Hawkyns's ill-fated expedition to the West Indies, and returned there several times to recover the losses sustained from the Spaniards, his exploits gaining him great popularity in England. In 1577 he set out with five ships for the Pacific, through the Straits of Magellan, but after his fleet was battered by storm and fire, he alone continued in the *Golden Hind*. He then struck out across the Pacific, reached the Pelew Is, and returned to England via the Cape of Good Hope in 1580. The following year, the queen visited his ship and knighted him. In 1585 he sailed with 25 ships against the Spanish Indies, bringing home tobacco, potatoes, and the dispirited Virginian colonists. In the battle against the Spanish Armada, which raged for a week in the Channel (1588), his seamanship and courage brought him further distinction. In 1595 he sailed again to the West Indies, but died of dysentery off Porto Bello. >> Hawkyns; Howard, Charles; Medina-Sidonia

Draper, Henry (1837–82) Pioneer of astronomical photography, born in Prince Edward Co, VA. He taught natural science and later physiology at the City of New York University (1860–82), but retired in order to devote himself to astronomical research. With a 71 cm (28 in) reflecting telescope he showed photographic methods to be an important means of studying the heavens. An important catalogue of stellar spectra is named after him.

Draper, John William (1811–82) Chemist, born in St Helens, Merseyside, NW England, UK. In 1832 he emigrated to Virginia, where he became a pioneer in photography. He was the second American to make a photographic portrait (1839); that of his sister (1840) may be the oldest extant portrait. In 1850, he took the first microphotographs. He made major contributions to the study of the chemical effects of radiant energy. He was affiliated with New York University (1839–82), and at its School of Medicine he granted some of the first PhDs in the USA (1867–72).

Draper, Ruth (1884–1956) Monologue performer, born in New York City. She made her stage debut in 1915. Following successful solo appearances for the US troops in France in 1918, she toured extensively, appearing in 1926 before George V at Windsor. Her repertoire comprised monologues of her own devising, and embraced 57 characters.

Drayton, Michael (1563–1631) Poet, born in Hartshill, Warwickshire, C England, UK. His earliest work was *The Harmony of the Church* (1591), a metrical rendering of scriptural passages, which gave offence to the authorities, and was condemned to be destroyed. His best-known works are *England's Heroical Epistles* (1597), *Poly-Olbion* (1612–22), an ambitious description of the English countryside, and the celebrated sonnet 'Since there's no help, come let us kiss and part', from the sequence *Idea* (1619).

Drazha >> **Mihailović, Dragoljub**

Drebbel, Cornelis (Jacobszoon) (c. 1572–1633) Inventor, born in Alkmaar, The Netherlands. He prepared a map of Alkmaar, and designed a water-supply system for the town, then moved to England (1604), where he spent most of the rest of his life. Among his inventions were a clock driven by changes in atmospheric pressure, a new method for the manufacture of sulphuric acid, and a rudimentary submarine (1620) which was successfully tested in the R Thames.

Drees, Willem (1886–1988) Dutch statesman and prime minister (1948–58), born in Amsterdam. He became a government stenographer, then entered politics, joining the Socialist Democratic Workers' Party and becoming its chairman in 1911. He sat in the Second Chamber from 1933 until the German invasion of 1940, after which he played an important part in the resistance movement. In 1947, as minister of social affairs, he introduced the state pension. A special stamp was issued to commemorate his 100th birthday. >> RR1077

Dreiser, Theodore (Herman Albert) [driyzer] (1871–1945) Writer, born in Terre Haute, IN. He became a journalist in Chicago, St Louis, and New York City. His first novel *Sister Carrie* (1900), starkly realistic, was criticized for obscenity, and he did not write another until 1911, when *Jennie Gerhardt* won acclaim. *An American Tragedy* (1925), based on a famous murder case, brought him success. In 1939 he moved to Hollywood.

Dresser, Christopher (1834–1904) Designer and writer, born in Glasgow, W Scotland, UK. His first area of study was botany, from which he developed the stylized plant motifs which became the basis for his interest in decorative design. He designed glass, ceramics, and cast-iron furniture for a number of manufacturers, but his outstanding works were well-researched items of functional metalwork such as teapots and soup tureens.

Dressler, Marie, originally **Leila Koerber** (1869–1934) Stage and film actress, born in Coburg, Canada. This versatile comic actress began her career at 14 with a touring theatrical company, and for many years performed in vaudeville, plays, and musical productions, enjoying her greatest success with the song, 'Heaven will protect the working girl'. In 1910, she began a film career that went from Mack Sennett comedies – including *Tillie's Punctured Romance* (1914) with Chaplin – to *Anna Christie* (1930) and *Min and Bill* (1931), for which she won an Oscar.

Drew, Richard (1899–1980) US inventor of masking tape. A salesman for a manufacturer of sandpaper, he recognized the need in the motor trade for an adhesive tape that could be removed without damaging the paint of the vehicle to which it was applied. With the backing of his employers, 3M, he developed masking tape by 1925, and Scotch Cellulose Tape by 1930, transforming the fortunes of the previously struggling company.

Dreyer, Carl Theodor [drayer] (1889–1968) Film-maker, born in Copenhagen. His early career as a journalist and critic led to his writing scripts in 1912. He made his debut as a director with *Praesidenten* (1919, The President). Later works included *La Passion de Jeanne d'Arc* (1928) and *Vampyr* (1932). He returned to journalism in the 1930s and subsequently concentrated on documentaries. His last film was *Gertrud* (1964).

Dreyer, John (Louis Emil) [drayer] (1852–1926) Astronomer, born in Copenhagen. He worked at Birr Castle, Ireland, then became director of Armagh Observatory. He produced the standard catalogue on star clusters, nebulas, and galaxies, the *New General Catalogue* (NGC), which is still in use today.

Dreyfus, Alfred [drayfuhs] (1859–1935) French Jewish army officer, born in Mulhouse, France. An artillery captain on the General Staff, he was falsely charged with delivering defence secrets to the Germans (1894). He was court-martialled and transported to Devil's I, French Guiana. The efforts of his wife and friends to prove him innocent provoked a vigorous response from militarists and anti-Semites, and deeply divided the French intellectual and political world. After the case was tried again (1899), he was found guilty but pardoned, and in 1906 the verdict was reversed. Proof of his innocence came when German military documents were uncovered in 1930. >> Zola

Dreyfuss, Henry [drayfus] (1904–72) Designer and writer on design, born in New York City. After an early career in stage design, in 1928 he opened his own design office. An important aspect of his work was his pioneering research into anthropometry, as seen in *Designing for People* (1955) and *The Measure of Man* (1959). Among the products which he designed were telephones, vacuum cleaners, televisions, agricultural machinery, and airliner interiors.

Dreyfuss, Richard [drayfus] (1947–) US film actor, born in New York City. After working on Broadway and in repertory, he gained attention with his roles in *Dillinger* (1973) and *American Graffiti* (1973). He became well known following his performances in *Jaws* (1975), *Close Encounters of the Third Kind* (1977), and *The Goodbye Girl* (1977, Oscar). Later films include *Down and Out in Beverly Hills* (1986), *Tin Men* (1987), *Stakeout* (1987), *Always* (1989), *Postcards from the Edge* (1990), *The American President* (1995), and *Night Falls on Manhattan* (1997).

Driesch, Hans (Adolf Eduard) [dreesh] (1867–1941) Zoologist and philosopher, born in Bad Kreuznach, Germany. He studied at Jena and other universities, becoming professor of philosophy at Heidelberg (1912), Cologne (1919), and Leipzig (1921). He did valuable work in embryology and parapsychology, and became an exponent of vitalism. He was forced to retire early by the Nazis.

Drinkwater, John (1882–1937) Poet, playwright, and critic, born in London, England, UK. He was an insurance clerk who achieved an immediate success with his play *Abraham Lincoln* (1918), following this with *Mary Stuart* (1921) and other historical dramas. His first volume of poems appeared in 1923, and he also wrote several critical studies. He was one of the founders of the Pilgrim Players, and became manager of the Birmingham Repertory Theatre.

Drobny, Jaroslav (1921–) Tennis player, and all-round sportsman, born in Prague. He was a member of the Czech ice-hockey side which won an Olympic silver medal in 1948. In the same year he was rendered homeless by the Communist takeover of Czechoslovakia, and he competed in tennis first of all as a stateless player, then under the banner of Egypt. He lost two Wimbledon finals, to Ted Schroeder (1949) and Frank Sedgman (1951), before taking the title in 1954 against Ken Rosewall of Australia. >> Rosewall; Sedgman; RR1173

Droste-Hülshoff, Annette Elisabeth, Freiin (Baroness) **von** [drostuh hülshohf] (1797–1848) Poet, born near Münster, Germany. Commonly regarded as Germany's greatest woman writer, she led a retired life on her family estate. Her poetry is mainly on religious themes and on the Westphalian countryside. She also wrote a novella, *Die Judenbuche* (1842, The Jew's Beech). Her works were published posthumously in 1851.

Drucker, Peter F(erdinand) (1909–) Management consultant, born in Vienna. Educated in Austria and England, he became an economist with a London international bank before going to live in the USA in 1937, becoming a US citizen. He was professor of philosophy and politics at Bennington College (1942–50), professor of management at the Graduate School of Business, New York University (1950–72), and was appointed professor of social sciences at the Claremont Graduate School in California in 1972. Among his many publications are *Managing for the Future* (1992) and *Managing at a Time of Great Change* (1995).

Drummond, Dugald (1840–1912) Locomotive engineer, born in Ardrossan, North Ayrshire, SW Scotland, UK. The chief mechanical engineer of the London & South Western Railway from 1905, he made his reputation in Scotland in 1876–8 with the 4-4-0 'Abbotsford' class, examples of which were still running in the 1960s.

Drummond, George (1687–1766) Entrepreneur and philanthropist, born in Perth and Kinross, E Scotland, UK and known as the founder of the New Town in Edinburgh. He was appointed accountant-general of excise, and was six times Lord Provost of Edinburgh between 1725 and 1764. He was the driving force behind the building of the Royal Infirmary (1738) and the Royal Exchange (1760, now the City Chambers), the expansion of Edinburgh University, and the proposal to create a New Town to the N of Princes Street.

Drummond, Henry (1786–1860) Banker, politician, and religious leader, born near Alresford, Hampshire, S England, UK. He was MP for Plumpton Earls (1810–13) and West Surrey (1847–60). He founded a chair of economics at Oxford (1825), and became the founder and chief prophet of the Catholic Apostolic (or Irvingite) Church, based on the messianic creed of Edward Irving. >> Irving, Edward

Drummond, James Eric, 16th Earl of Perth (1876–1951) British statesman, born in Fulford, North Yorkshire, N England, UK. He was first secretary-general of the League of Nations (1919–32), and ambassador in Rome (1933–9).

Drummond, Thomas (1797–1840) Engineer and statesman, born in Edinburgh, EC Scotland, UK. He entered the Royal Engineers in 1815, and in 1820 joined the ordnance survey, whose work was immensely facilitated by his improved heliostat and lime-light (the *Drummond light*). He became head of the boundary commission under the Reform Bill, and under-secretary for Ireland (practically its governor) in 1835.

Drummond (of Hawthornden), William (1585–1649) Poet, born at Hawthornden, near Edinburgh, EC Scotland, UK. He studied law at Bourges and Paris, then became laird of Hawthornden, where he devoted his life to poetry, writing many for Mary Cunningham of Barns, who died on the eve of their marriage (1615), and mechanical experiments. He was the first Scottish poet to write in a form of English not from Scotland. His chief collection, *Poems*, appeared in 1616. His prose works include several royalist pamphlets.

Drury, Alfred (1857–1944) Sculptor, born in London, England, UK. Among his works are 'St Agnes' (1896, Chantrey Collection), 'Edward VII' (1903), 'Sir Joshua Reynolds' (1931, Burlington House quadrangle), and the 'London Troops' war memorial at the Royal Exchange.

Drusus Germanicus, Nero Claudius [drootsus jermanikus], also known as **Drusus Senior** (39–9 BC) Roman soldier, the son of Livia Drusilla, stepson of the emperor Augustus, and younger brother of Emperor Tiberius. His campaign against the Rhaeti and other Alpine tribes (15 BC) was celebrated by Horace in his *Odes*. Until his death he was engaged chiefly in establishing Roman supremacy in Germany, and received the title Germanicus; the celebrated **Germanicus Caesar** was his son. >> Caesar; Germanicus; Livia; Tiberius

Druten, John van [drootn] (1901–57) Playwright, born in London, England, UK. He became famous with the production of his play *Young Woodley* in 1928. After several years and considerable success in the USA, he became a US citizen in 1944. *The Voice of the Turtle*, his most successful play with an American setting, was produced in 1943.

Dryden, John (1631–1700) Poet, born in Aldwinkle, Northamptonshire, C England, UK. He studied at Cambridge, and went to London in 1657, where he wrote several plays and satires for the court. His first successful play, written in heroic couplets, was *The Indian Emperor* (1665). After 1676, he began to write in blank verse, producing his best play, *All for Love* (1678). In 1668 he became Poet Laureate and in 1670 historiographer royal. Called to defend the king's party, he wrote a series of satires, notably *Absalom and Achitophel* (1681), which did much to turn the tide against the Whigs. To this era also belong the didactic poem *Religio laici* (1682), which argues the case for Anglicanism, and *The Hind and the Panther* (1687), marking his conversion to Catholicism. His political reward was a place in the customs; but he lost his laureateship on the accession of William III (1688). He also wrote a number of important critical works, many in his late years. >> Lee, Nathaniel; Shadwell

Drygalski, Erich Dagobert von [drigalskee] (1865–1949) Geophysicist and explorer, born in Königsberg, Germany. He headed expeditions to Greenland (1891–3), and in the *Gauss* to the Antarctic (1902–3), where he discovered and named the Gaussberg volcano.

Drysdale, Russell (1912–81) Painter, born in Bognor Regis, West Sussex, S England, UK. His family settled in Melbourne in 1923, and he studied at the George Bell Art School, Melbourne, in London, and in Paris, where he was influenced by Surrealism. His powerful scenes of the outback were a major contribution to modern art in Australia. He was knighted in 1969, and became a Companion of the Order of Australia in 1980.

du Barry, Marie Jeanne Gomard de Vaubernier, comtesse (Countess), *née* Bécu (c. 1743–93) The favourite mistress of Louis XV, born in Vaucouleurs, France. Brought up in a Paris convent, she won the notice of Louis XV (1768), and married **Comte Guillaume du Barry** before

becoming official royal mistress. Her influence reigned supreme until the death of Louis in 1774, when she was dismissed from court. She lived on her estates until the Revolution when, accused of being a counter-revolutionary, she was tried by the Tribunal of Paris and guillotined. >> Louis XV

Dubček, Alexander [dubchek] (1921–92) Czechoslovakian statesman, born in Uhrovek, Slovak Republic. He joined the Communist Party in 1939, fought as a Slovak patriot against the Nazis (1944–5), and rose to become first secretary in the Party (1968). He introduced a series of far-reaching economic and political reforms, including abolition of censorship and increased freedom of speech (the 'Prague Spring'). His liberalization policy led to the occupation of Czechoslovakia by Soviet forces (Aug 1968), and in 1969 he was replaced by Husak. He became president of the Federal Assembly, but was then expelled from the Presidium, and deprived of Party membership in 1970. In 1989, following a popular uprising, and the resignation of the Communist government, he was elected chairman of the Czechoslovak parliament. >> Husak

Dubinsky, David, originally **David Dobnievski** (1892–1982) Labour leader, born in Brest-Litovsk, Belarus. Beginning his labour activism in Russia, for which he was exiled to Siberia, he escaped and emigrated to the USA in 1911. He joined the International Ladies' Garment Workers' Union (ILGWU) in New York City as a cloak-cutter, and was elected its president (1932–66). Under his leadership the ILGWU became one of the most successful unions in America. An early supporter of the Congress of Industrial Organizations (CIO), he led the ILGWU back into the American Federation of Labor (AFL) in 1940. When the AFL and the CIO merged (1955) he became a member of the new executive council and then a vice-president of the AFL–CIO. He also took an active role in areas outside unions, helping to form the American Labor Party (1936), the Liberal Party (1944), and Americans for Democratic Action (1947).

Dubois, (Marie) Eugène (François Thomas) [dübwah] (1858–1940) Palaeontologist, born in Eijsden, The Netherlands. He studied medicine in Amsterdam and taught there from 1899. His interest in the 'missing link' between the apes and man took him to Java in 1887, where in the 1890s he found the humanoid remains named as *Pithecanthropus erectus* (Java Man), which he claimed to be the missing link. His view was contested and ridiculed, but in the 1920s it eventually became widely accepted.

Dubois, Guillaume [dübwah] (1656–1723) French statesman, cardinal, and prime minister (1722), born in Brives-la-Gaillarde, France. He was first tutor and then secretary to the Duc de Chartres (1674–1723); and when the latter (as Duke of Orléans) became regent in 1715, Dubois was virtually all powerful. He was appointed foreign minister, Archbishop of Cambrai (both in 1720), and a cardinal (1721), before becoming prime minister. >> RR1049

du Bois, Guy Péne [doo bwah] (1884–1958) Painter, born in Brooklyn, NY. He studied with William Chase (1904–1916) and Robert Henri in New York City (1905), and became a member of the Ash Can school of painting, which stressed social realism. He later changed his style, developing an elegant and satirical approach which may be seen in 'The Opera Box' (1926). >> Henri

Du Bois, W(illiam) E(dward) B(urghardt) [doo boyz] (1868–1963) Historian, sociologist, and equal rights campaigner, born in Great Barrington, MA. He studied at Fisk, Harvard, and Berlin universities, and in his writings explored the history and lives of African-Americans. In politics he campaigned for full equality, opposing the tactics of Booker T Washington. He helped found the

National Association for the Advancement of Colored People, and in his old age lived in Ghana, where he died. >> Washington, Booker T

Dubos, René (Jules) [dü boh] (1901–82) Bacteriologist, born in Saint-Brice, France. He studied in Paris, emigrated to the USA in 1924, and completed his studies at Rutgers University. He worked at Rockefeller University in New York City from 1927, becoming professor in 1957. He became a US citizen in 1938. In 1939 he discovered tyrothricin, the first commercially produced antibiotic. He later became more interested in the environment, and published several works on the subject, including *So Human an Animal* (1968, Pulitzer).

Dubuffet, Jean [dübüfay] (1901–85) Artist, born in Le Havre, France. He studied at the Académie Julian in Paris, and invented the concept of Art Brut, pioneering the use of rubbish (eg discarded newspapers, broken glass, rough plaster daubed and scratched like an old wall) to create images. He is regarded as a forerunner of the Pop Art and Dada-like fashions of the 1960s.

du Cange, Charles du Fresne, seigneur (Lord) [dü kâzh] (1610–88) Scholar, born in Amiens, France. He became a parliamentary advocate, and a prolific writer and editor. He is best known for his glossaries of the Middle Ages, published in 1678 and 1688.

Duccio di Buoninsegna [doochioh dee bwoninsenya] (c. 1260–c. 1320) Painter, founder of the Sienese school, born in Siena, Italy. In his work the Gothic tradition in Italian art is seen in its most highly developed state. His masterpiece is the 'Maestà' for the altar of Siena cathedral (1311), from which came the 'Annunciation' and 'Transfiguration' in the National Gallery, London.

Duce, Il >> Mussolini, Benito

Duchamp, Marcel [düshâ] (1887–1968) Painter, born in Blainville, France. He was associated with several modern movements, including Cubism and Futurism, and shocked his generation with such works as 'Nude Descending a Staircase' (1912, Philadelphia). He was one of the pioneers of Dadaism. In 1915 he left Paris for New York City, where he laboured eight years on an abstract glass construction bizarrely entitled 'The Bride Stripped Bare by Her Bachelors, Even' (1915–23, Philadelphia). He became a US citizen in 1955. >> Duchamp-Villon; Ray, Man; Villon, Jacques

Duchamp-Villon, Raymond [düshâ veeyô] (1876–1918) Sculptor, born in Damville, France, the brother of Jacques Villon and half-brother of Marcel Duchamp. He began as a medical student, turning to sculpture in 1898, and by 1914 was one of the leading Cubist sculptors in Paris. His most striking work is the bronze 'Horse' (1914, Paris). >> Duchamp; Villon, Jacques

Duchenne, Guillaume Benjamin Amand [düshen] (1806–75) Physician, born in Boulogne, France. He studied at Douai and Paris, became a pioneer in electrophysiology, and was the founder of electrotherapeutics. He was the first to describe locomotor ataxia, in 1858.

Duchesne, André [düshen], Lat **Chesnius** or **Quercetanus** (1584–1640) Historian, born in Ile-Bouchard, France. He was royal historiographer, and is known as 'The father of French history'. He wrote histories of England, Scotland, and Ireland, of the popes down to Paul V, and of the House of Burgundy. He also made collections of the early Norman and French histories.

Duchesne, Père >> Hébert, Jacques René

Duchovny, David (1960–) Actor, born in New York City. He studied at Princeton and Yale, became an actor, and took a range of parts in low-budget films, becoming known in his role as Jake, the narrator in the *Red Shoe Diaries* (1992–). He achieved star success when he was given the role of Fox Mulder in the new series *The X-Files* (1993– , Golden Globe Best Actor), which has since become a cult classic. His feature film credits began with *Working Girl* (1988), and include *Beethoven* (1992) and *Kalifornia* (1993). >> Anderson, Gillian

Duclos du Hauron, Louis [dükloh dü ohrô] (1837–1920) Scientist and inventor, born in Langon, France. Interested in photography from 1859, his publication *Les Couleurs en photographie* (1869, Colour in Photography) outlined for the first time the principles of additive and subtractive colour reproduction. In 1878 he published *Photographie en couleur* (Photography in Colour), describing practical methods which he patented, and in 1891 proposed the anaglyph method of viewing stereoscopic images.

Duddell, William du Bois (1872–1917) British engineer. He worked on radiotelegraphy, and in 1897 invented an improved version of the oscillograph. He also designed a high-frequency generator. The Physical Society instituted the *Duddell Medal* in his honour.

Dudevant, Madame >> Sand, George

Dudley, Lord Guildford (?–1554) The fourth son of the Lord Protector John Dudley, Earl of Warwick, and briefly husband of **Lady Jane Grey**. His father married him to the unwilling Jane Grey in 1553 as Edward VI lay dying, and then proclaimed her queen. After the accession of Mary I (Edward's sister), Dudley and his wife were imprisoned and beheaded on Tower Hill. >> Edward VI; Grey, Lady Jane; Mary I; Warwick, John Dudley

Dudley, Sir Robert >> Leicester, Robert Dudley, Earl of

Dudley, William (Stuart) (1947–) Stage designer, born in London, England, UK. He studied at St Martin's and the Slade School of Art, London, and designed his first stage set at the Nottingham Playhouse in 1970. He subsequently designed many productions for the Royal Court, and has worked extensively at the National Theatre (associate designer since 1981) and the Royal Court. He has also worked in opera, his designs including Peter Hall's production of *The Ring* at Bayreuth in 1983. He was designer of the year (Lawrence Olivier Awards) in 1986.

Dudok, Willem Marinus [doodok] (1884–1974) Architect, born in Amsterdam. Trained as an army engineer, he became city architect of Hilversum in 1915. Mixing modern and traditional elements, his fully developed style is characterized by dramatic massing of asymmetrical plain brick blocks, deep-set windows, and vertical elements. His masterwork was the Hilversum Town Hall (1928–30).

Dufay, Guillaume [düfay] (c. 1400–74) Composer, probably born in Cambrai, France. By 1420 he was in Italy and sang in the papal choir (1428–33, 1435–7). He was later a canon at Cambrai (1439–50, 1458–74), and also employed for lengthy periods at the courts of Ferrara and Savoy. During a year spent in Florence he wrote one of his most famous motets *Nuper rosarum flores*, for the dedication of the dome of Florence Cathedral (1436). He also wrote Masses and a large number of secular songs.

Duffy, Sir Charles Gavan (1816–1903) Irish nationalist, and prime minister of Victoria State, Australia, born in Co Monaghan, Ireland. He helped to start the *Nation* (1842), the Young Ireland organ, and for 12 years engaged in agitation, being tried for sedition and treason. On the break-up of the Independent Irish Party, he emigrated in 1856 to Australia, where after the establishment of the Victorian constitution, he became minister of public works in 1857, minister of lands in 1858 and 1862, and prime minister in 1871. He returned to Europe in 1880, becoming known as a writer.

Du Fresne, Charles >> Du Cange, Charles Du Fresne
Du Fu [doo foo], also spelled **Tu Fu** (712–70) Poet, friend, and

admirer of Li Bo. Born into a noble family near Changan (Xian) he became a minor official at the Tang court of Xuanzong despite failing the imperial examinations. Like Li Bo, he wrote lyrical poems on friendship and wine, but his Confucianism also inspired poems of human feeling, social criticism, political comment, and hostility to war. A prolific writer, his best work includes 'Autumn Day', 'Ballad of Lovely Ladies', 'Journey from the Capital', and 'The War Chariot'. No contemporary European source can rival his poems for social and historical detail. >> Li Bo; Xuanzong

Dufy, Raoul [düfee] (1877–1953) Artist and designer, born in Le Havre, France. He studied at the Ecole des Beaux-Arts, and was much influenced by Fauvism, which he later abandoned. From 1907 to 1918 he produced many fabric designs and engraved book illustrations, and in 1919 went to the Riviera, where he began a long series of swift calligraphic sketches of seascapes, regattas, and racecourse scenes.

Dughet, Gaspard [doogay], also called **Gaspard Poussin** and known as **Le Guaspre** (1615–75) Painter, born in Rome. His sister married Nicholas Poussin, and he called himself after his more famous brother-in-law. He specialized in landscapes which, while modelled on the Roman countryside, combine the classical manner of Poussin and the more lyrical style of Claude Lorrain. His works were often taken as models for landscaped gardens and parks. >> Claude Lorrain; Poussin

Duhamel, Georges [dooamel] (1884–1966) Novelist, poet, and man of letters, born in Paris. He studied medicine and became an army surgeon, which provided the background for such works as *Civilisation* (1918, Prix Goncourt). His best-known works are his novel cycles *Salavin* (1920–32) and *Chronique des Pasquier* (1933–44, The Pasquier Chronicles).

Duhamel du Monceau, Henri-Louis [dooamel dü môsoh] (1700–82) Technologist, born in Paris. He proved the distinction between potassium and sodium salts, showed that soda can be made from rock-salt, and improved the making of starch, soap, and brass. He also reviewed agricultural practice and introduced Tull's methods into France. >> Tull

Dühem, Pierre (Maurice Marie) [düem] (1861–1916) Philosopher of science and physicist, born in Paris. He studied at the Ecole Normale Supérieure, held teaching positions at Lille, and Rennes, and became professor of physics at Bordeaux (1895). His early scientific work was in thermodynamics, and many of his ideas were well in advance of their time. He made important contributions to the history of science, in particular reviving an interest in mediaeval science.

Dukakis, Michael [dookakis] (1933–) US politician, born in Boston, MA. He studied at Swarthmore College and Harvard, then entered Massachusetts politics, and became governor of the state (1975–9, 1983–91). In 1988 he was Democratic nominee for the presidency.

Dukas, Paul (Abraham) [dükah] (1865–1935) Composer, born in Paris. Some of his music is classical in approach, but he tended mainly towards Impressionism. His best-known work is the symphonic poem *L'Apprenti sorcier* (1897, The Sorcerer's Apprentice). He also wrote several orchestral and piano pieces, and was professor of composition at the Paris Conservatoire from 1927 until his death.

Dulbecco, Renato [dulbekoh] (1914–) Molecular biologist, born in Catanzaro, Italy. He studied medicine at Turin, in 1947 moved to the USA to Indiana University, and worked at the Salk Institute, La Jolla, CA, from 1963. He used a simple model system to show how certain viruses can transform some cells into a cancerous state, for which he shared the 1975 Nobel Prize for Physiology or Medicine with his former students, David Baltimore and Howard Temin. >> Baltimore, David; Temin

Dulles, Allen W(elsh) [duhles] (1893–1969) Intelligence officer, born in Washington, DC, the brother of John Foster Dulles. He studied at Princeton, and entered the US diplomatic service, serving in Vienna, Bern, Paris, Berlin, and Istanbul. He was chief of Division of Near Eastern Affairs, Department of State (1922–6), worked for a law firm (1926–42), then served in Europe with the US Office of Strategic Services (1942–5). Upon the formation of the Central Intelligence Agency, he was made deputy director (1951), then director (1953). The 1961 disaster at the Bay of Pigs in the attempt to overthrow Fidel Castro brought recrimination on the head of the Kennedy administration, which responded by making a scapegoat of the CIA, and he was forced to resign. >> Castro; Dulles, John Foster

Dulles, John Foster [duhlez] (1888–1959) US Republican secretary of state (1953–9), born in Washington, DC. He studied at Princeton and the Sorbonne, and became a lawyer. During World War 2 he advocated a world governmental organization, and in 1945 advised at the Charter Conference of the UN, thereafter becoming US delegate to the General Assembly. As US secretary of state he opened a vigorous diplomacy of personal conferences with statesmen in other countries. He resigned in 1959, and was awarded the Medal of Freedom shortly before his death. Dulles airport, in Washington, is named after him. >> Dulles, Allen W

Dulong, Pierre Louis [dülô] (1785–1838) Chemist, born in Rouen, France. He trained in medicine and science at Paris, and later became director of its Ecole Polytechnique. His name is now most linked with the *Dulong–Petit law* (1819), which relates the specific heat capacity of a solid element to its relative atomic mass, and which for over a century was a valuable route for finding approximate atomic weights. >> Petit, Alexis (Thérèse)

Dumas, Alexandre [dümah], known as **Dumas père** ('father') (1802–70) Novelist and playwright, born in Villers-Cotterêts, France. He moved to Paris in 1823, where he obtained a clerkship, and began to write. At 27 he became famous with his play *Henri III* (1829). After several other plays, some in collaboration, he turned to travelogues and historical novels. He gained enduring success as a storyteller, his purpose being to put the history of France into novels. Among his best-known works are *Le Comte de Monte Cristo* (1844–5, The Count of Monte Cristo), *Les Trois Mousquetaires* (1845, The Three Musketeers), and *La Tulipe noire* (1850, The Black Tulip). He spent two years in exile in Brussels (1855–7), and helped Garibaldi in Italy (1860–4). >> Dumas, Alexandre (fils); Garibaldi

Dumas, Alexandre [dümah], known as **Dumas fils** ('son') (1824–95) Writer, born in Paris, the illegitimate son of Alexandre Dumas. He studied at the Institution Goubaux and the Collège Bourbon, then left school for the world of letters. His novels include *La Dame aux camélias* (1848, The Lady of the Camellias), which he later adapted into the play *Camille* (1852) that inspired Verdi to write *La Traviata* (1853), and *L'Affaire Clémenceau* (1864). He also wrote essays, letters, speeches, and prefaces, but is best known for his plays, such as *Le Demi-monde* (1855, The Half-World), *Le Fils naturel* (1856, The Natural Son), and *Monsieur Alphonse* (1873). >> Dumas, Alexandre (père)

Dumas, Jean Baptiste André [dümah] (1800–84) Organic chemist, born in Alais, France. He studied at Geneva, then went to Paris (1821), where he lectured at the Ecole Polytechnique. By propounding new ideas on the theories of relations between organic compounds, he laid the foundations for Kekulé's later work. He later became professor of chemistry at the Athenée, the Ecole Centrale (which he founded), and the Sorbonne. In 1848 he moved into politics, becoming Master of the Mint in 1868. >> Kekulé

du Maurier, Dame Daphne [dü **moh**ryay] (1907–89) Novelist, born in London, England, UK, the grand-daughter of George du Maurier. She wrote several successful period romances and adventure stories, including *Jamaica Inn* (1936), *Rebecca* (1938), and *The Flight of the Falcon* (1965). She also published plays, short stories, and literary reminiscences. She was made a dame in 1969. >> du Maurier, George; du Maurier, Gerald

du Maurier, George (Louis Palmella Busson) [dü mohryay] (1834–96) Artist and illustrator, born in Paris, France. He studied chemistry in London (1851), but on returning to Paris adopted art as a profession. In 1860 he went back to London, where he gained a reputation as a designer and book illustrator. Finally he joined the staff of *Punch*, and became widely known as a gentle, graceful satirist of fashionable life. He wrote and illustrated three novels, notably *Trilby* (1894). >> du Maurier, Daphne; du Maurier, Gerald

du Maurier, Sir Gerald [dü **moh**ryay] (1873–1934) Actor-manager, born in London, England, UK, the younger son of George du Maurier. He studied at Harrow, and left a business career for the stage, making his reputation in criminal roles, beginning with *Raffles* (1906). He became joint manager of Wyndham's Theatre (1910–25), and was knighted in 1922 for his services to the stage. He was manager of the St James's Theatre from 1926 until his death. >> du Maurier, Daphne; du Maurier, George

Du Mont, Allen B(alcom) [doo**mont**] (1901–65) Electronics engineer, born in New York City. Working in the laboratories of the Westinghouse Lamp Company he developed methods for the mass production of radio valves. He established his own company in 1931, improved the cathode-ray tube and used it in the oscilloscope he developed, and in 1937 began production of the first fully electronic TV receivers using cathode-ray tubes.

Dumont D'Urville, Jules Sébastien César [dümō dürveey] (1790–1842) Navigator, born in Condé-sur-Noireau, France. He entered the navy in 1807, and commanded expeditions to survey the South Pacific (1826–9) and the Antarctic (1837–40), discovering Joinville I and Adélie Land. A French Antarctic station is named after him.

Dumouriez, Charles François (du Périer) [dümooryay] (1739–1823) French general, born in Cambrai, France. In 1792 he defeated the Prussians at Valmy and the Austrians at Jemappes, but in 1793 lost to the Austrians at Neerwinden. His leanings towards the monarchy caused him to be denounced by the revolutionaries, and to save his head he went over to the Austrians. He later settled in England.

Dunant, (Jean) Henri [dünā] (1828–1910) Philanthropist, born in Geneva, Switzerland. He inspired the foundation of the International Red Cross after seeing the plight of the wounded on the battlefield of Solferino. His efforts helped to bring about the conference at Geneva (1863) from which came the Geneva Convention (1864), and in 1901 he shared the first Nobel Peace Prize. >> RR0000

Dunaway, Faye (1941–) Film actress, born in Bascom, FL. She made her Broadway debut in *A Man for All Seasons* (1962), but it was an off-Broadway success in the play *Hogan's Goat* (1965) which led her to a television debut, a personal contract with Otto Preminger, and a film debut in *The Happening* (1966). Her first starring role was in *Bonnie and Clyde* (1967). Later films include *Chinatown* (1974, Oscar nomination), *Don Juan DeMarco* (1995), *Network* (1976, Oscar), the television production of *Rebecca* (1997), and *Fanny Hill* (1998).

Dunbar, Paul (Lawrence) [duhn**bah**(r)] (1872–1906) Poet, born in Dayton, OH, the son of escaped Negro slaves. He gained a reputation with *Lyrics of Lowly Life* (1896), many of which were in dialect. He published several other volumes of verse, and four novels. His *Complete Poems* appeared in 1913.

Dunbar, William [duhn**bah**(r)] (c. 1460–c. 1520) Poet, probably born in East Lothian, E Scotland, UK. He studied at St Andrews, became a Franciscan novice, and travelled widely, before leaving the order and entering the diplomatic service. He was a courtier of James IV, who gave him a pension in 1500. His poems include *The Thrissil and the Rois* and *Lament for the Makaris*, and several satires, such as *The Dance of the Sevin Deadly Synnis*. His name disappears from the records after 1513.

Dunbar, William [duhn**bah**(r)] (1749–1810) Planter and scientist, born near Elgin, Moray, NE Scotland, UK. He moved to West Florida in 1773, and built a plantation near Natchez, MI. A correspondent of Thomas Jefferson, and the first surveyor-general of his area, he undertook explorations of the Quachita and Red R areas in present-day Texas, Arkansas, and Louisiana (1804–5).

Duncan I >> **Macbeth**

Duncan, Andrew (1744–1828) Physician, born near St Andrews, Fife, E Scotland, UK. He studied medicine at Edinburgh, and in 1773 started the publication 'Medical and Philosophical Commentaries', which was the only journal of its kind in Britain at that time. In 1792 he prompted the Royal College of Physicians in Edinburgh to establish a lunatic asylum, which came to fruition in 1807.

Duncan, Isadora, originally **Angela Duncan** (1877–1927) Dancer and choreographer, born in San Francisco, CA. She travelled widely in Europe, performing her own choreography, and founding schools in several cities, such as Berlin, Salzburg, and Vienna. She was one of the pioneers of modern dance, basing her work on Greek-derived notions of beauty and harmony, but using everday movements of running, skipping, and walking. Her unconventional views on marriage and women's liberation gave rise to scandal. She was killed in a car accident in Nice. >> Yesenin

Duncan, Robert (Edward), originally **Edward Howard Duncan**, adopted name **Robert Edward Symmes** (1919–88) Poet, born in Oakland, CA. Adopted when young, he assumed his new name in 1941. He studied at University of California, Berkeley (1936–8, 1948–50), taught at Black Mountain College (1956–7), and became associated with the San Francisco Bay area group of poets, as seen in *The Opening of the Field* (1960). He was also an editor, playwright, and artist.

Duncan-Sandys, Duncan Edwin Sandys, Baron [duhngkn **sandz**] (1908–87) British statesman and founder of the Civic Trust (1956). He studied at Oxford, worked for the diplomatic service (1930–3), and became Conservative MP for Norwood, London (1935–45), and for Streatham, (1950–74). He was minister of supply in the Churchill government (1951), minister of housing and local government (1954), minister of defence (1957–9), minister of aviation (1959–60), and secretary of state for commonwealth relations (1960–4), and for the colonies (1962–4). In 1935 he married **Diana Churchill**, the daughter of Winston Churchill (divorced 1960). He was made a life peer in 1974. >> Churchill, Sir Winston

Dundee, John Graham of Claverhouse, 1st Viscount, known as **Bloody Claverse** or **Bonnie Dundee** (c. 1649–89) Scottish soldier, born of a noble family. In 1672 he entered the Prince of Orange's horse-guards, and at the Battle of Seneff saved William's life. He returned to Scotland in 1677, and defeated the Covenanters at Bothwell Brig

(1679). He was made a privy councillor in 1683, and became Viscount Dundee (1688). Joined by the Jacobite clans, he raised the standard for James II against William and Mary, but died from a musket wound after his successful battle against Mackay at the Pass of Killiecrankie. >> James II (of England)

Dunér, Nils Christofer [du̇nair] (1839–1914) Astronomer, born in Billeberga, Sweden. He studied at Lund, and was senior astronomer there before he became professor of astronomy and director of the observatory at Uppsala (1888–1909). He made a study of variable and double stars, was an expert on stellar spectroscopy, and made important observations of the Sun's rotational period.

Dunham, Katherine [duhnham] (1910–) Dancer, choreographer, and teacher, born in Chicago, IL. She studied anthropology at Chicago University, and researched dance in the West Indies and Caribbean before her 1938 appointment as dance director of the Federal Theater Project. She later worked on Broadway and in Hollywood. Her Dunham School of Dance (1945–55) exerted considerable influence on the direction of African-American dance. She choreographed for opera, toured extensively with her own company, and wrote several books about her field.

Dunhill, Thomas Frederick [duhnhil] (1877–1946) Composer and teacher, born in London, England, UK. He studied under Charles Stanford and taught at the Royal College of Music. He made his name with chamber works, songs, and the light opera *Tantivy Towers* (1931) to words by A P Herbert. >> Herbert, A P; Stanford, Charles

Dunlop, (Ernest) Edward, nickname **Weary** (1907–93) Army surgeon, born in Wangaratta, Victoria, Australia. An accomplished sportsman, he graduated from Melbourne University, enlisted in the Australian Army Medical Corps in 1939, and in 1942, as a prisoner-of-war, was forced by the Japanese to work on the Burma–Siam Railway. Revered by his fellow prisoners, he ministered to the sick under appalling conditions, and was hailed as the 'Christ of the Burma Road'. After the war he continued his work as a surgeon, and fostered Australian–Asian relations. Named Australian of the Year in 1977, by the time he died he was a national hero, and his ashes were scattered over the Burma railway by prime minister Paul Keating in 1994. >> Keating

Dunlop, Frank (1927–) Stage director and administrator, born in Leeds, West Yorkshire, N England, UK. He studied at University College, London. After founding and directing Piccolo Theatre, Manchester (1954), he became an associate director of the Bristol Old Vic (1956), director of Nottingham Playhouse (1961–4), associate director at the National Theatre (1967–71), and administrator (1968–71). He founded the Young Vic in 1970, became the company's director (1978, 1980–3), and was director of the Edinburgh Festival (1983–91).

Dunlop, Joey, popular name of **(William) Joseph Dunlop** (1952–) Motor-cyclist, an outstanding rider at Isle of Man TT races, born in Ballymoney, Northern Ireland. Between 1977 and 1988 he won 13 races (one short of the all-time record of Mike Hailwood), including the Senior Tourist Trophy (TT) in 1985 and 1987–8. He won the Formula One TT for the sixth successive season in 1988, and was Formula One world champion 1982–6. >> Hailwood; RR1164

Dunlop, John Boyd (1840–1921) Inventor, born in Dreghorn, North Ayrshire, W Scotland, UK. He was a flourishing veterinary surgeon near Belfast, when (c.1887) he invented the pneumatic tyre, at first for bicycles. His company, formed in 1889, became known as the Dunlop Rubber Co in 1900.

Dunlop, Ronald (Ossary) (1894–1973) Painter, born in Dublin. He studied at the Manchester and Wimbledon Schools of Art. A member of the London Group, he is best known for his palette-knife painting with rich impasto and glowing colour. His writings on art include *Landscape Painting* (1954) and the autobiographical *Struggling with Paint* (1956).

Dunmore, Helen (1952–) British poet and novelist. She studied at the University of York and began writing poetry, her collections including *The Apple Fall* (1983), *The Raw Garden* (1988), and *Secrets* (1994). Her children's novels include *Going to Egypt* (1992) and *Fatal Error* (1996), and among her books for adults are *Zennor in Darkness* (1993) and *Talking to the Dead* (1996). In 1996 she won the inaugural Orange Prize for women fiction writers for her novel *A Spell of Winter* (1995).

Dunn, Douglas (1942–) Post-modern dancer and choreographer, born in Palo Alto, CA. While at Princeton he studied dance, moving to New York City and the Merce Cunningham studio. While working for the Cunningham company (1969–73) he met Yvonne Rainer. As well as performing in her work, he joined her as one of the founders of the experimental dance group Grand Union, with which he was associated for six years until 1976. In 1977 he founded his own company. >> Cunningham, Merce; Rainer

Dunn, Douglas (Eaglesham) (1942–) Poet, born in Renfrewshire, W Scotland, UK. His early work, including *Terry Street* (1969) and *Love or Nothing* (1974), was noted for its registration of urban experience. Later volumes, such as *Barbarians* (1979), *Elegies* (1985), and *Northlight* (1988) have more emotional and more intellectual appeal. His short story collections include *Secret Villages* (1985) and *Boyfriends and Girlfriends* (1995).

Dunne, Finley Peter (1867–1936) Journalist and humorist, born in Chicago, IL. As **Mr Dooley**, he became widely known from 1900 as the exponent of American-Irish humorous satire on current personages and events. Many of his essays were republished in book form, such as *Mr Dooley in Peace and War* (1898).

Dunne, J(ohn) W(illiam) (1875–1949) British inventor and philosopher. He designed the first British military aeroplane (1906–7), and wrote the best-selling speculative works *An Experiment with Time* (1927), *The Serial Universe* (1934), *The New Immortality* (1938), and *Nothing Dies* (1940).

Dunning, John, 1st Baron Ashburton (1731–83) British statesman and lawyer, born in Ashburton, Devon, SW England, UK. He studied for the bar, and became an MP in 1768. A critic of the administration of Lord North, he is best remembered for passing the 1780 resolution – in reality against North rather than George III – that 'the influence of the crown has increased, is increasing, and ought to be diminished'. He entered the Cabinet as Chancellor of the Duchy of Lancaster in Rockingham's administration (1782), and was created a baronet in the same year. >> Rockingham

Dunning, William A(rchibald) (1857–1922) Historian and educator, born in Plainfield, NJ. He studied and taught at Columbia University, New York City, until his death. His major work was a three-volume *History of Political Theories* (1916), but his chief significance lies in his direction of doctoral research on US history. In particular the *Dunning school* produced detailed studies of individual states under Reconstruction.

Dunois, Jean d'Orléans, comte (Count) [dünwah], known as **the Bastard of Orléans** (1403–68) French general in the Hundred Years' War, born in Paris, the natural son of Louis, Duke of Orléans (1372–1407). He defeated the English at Montargis (1427), defended Orléans with a small force until its relief by Joan of Arc (1429), then inflicted further defeats on the English, forcing them out of Paris, and by 1453 from Normandy and Guyenne. >> Joan of Arc

Duns Scotus, Johannes [duhnz skohtus], known as **Doctor Subtilis** (Lat 'the Subtle Doctor') (c.1265–1308) Mediaeval philosopher and theologian, probably born in Maxton, Scottish Borders, SE Scotland, UK. He became a Franciscan, studied at Oxford, and lectured there. His works are chiefly commentaries on the Bible, Aristotle, and the *Sentences* of Peter Lombard. A critic of preceding scholasticism, his dialectical skill gained him his nickname; but his defence of the papacy led to his ideas being ridiculed at the Reformation (hence the word *dunce*). >> Lombard, Peter

Dunstable, John [duhnstabl] (?–1453) The most important English composer of the 15th-c, whose influence on his continental contemporaries was considerable. He wrote motets, Masses, and secular songs, including the three-part 'O rosa bella'. He was also skilled in mathematics and astronomy.

Dunstan, St (c. 909–88) Abbot, born near Glastonbury, Somerset, SW England, UK. Educated at the abbey of Glastonbury, he became a monk there, and was appointed abbot in 945. He began a great work of reformation, making the abbey a centre of religious teaching. An adviser to King Edmund, he later became Bishop of Worcester (957) and of London (959), then (under King Edgar) Archbishop of Canterbury (960). Feast day 19 May. >> Edgar

Duparc, (Marie Eugène) Henri (Fouques-) [düpah(r)k] (1848–1933) Composer, born in Paris. He studied under César Franck, and is remembered for his songs which, though only 15 in number, rank among the world's greatest. His self-criticism led him to destroy much of his writing and correspondence, and he wrote little after 1890. >> Franck, César

Duplessis, Maurice LeNoblet [düplesee] (1890–1959) Liberal premier and attorney general of Quebec (1936–9, 1944–59). First a successful lawyer in Trois-Rivières, he built a powerful political machine in the province, and was known throughout most of his long career in the Quebec legislature as **'le chef'**. He asserted the authority of the state over the Church, undertook enormous public works projects, and in several infamous episodes dealt harshly with striking unions and other opposition.

Dupond, Patrick [düpô] (1959–) Dancer, born in Paris. He was the youngest dancer ever accepted into the Paris Opera Ballet (at the age of 15), and at 17 won top honours at the Varna international competition. In 1980 he reached the rank of *étoile*, and he has since been a guest performer with various companies around the world. In 1988 he became artistic director of Ballet de Nancy.

Du Pont, Pierre Samuel [doo pont] (1870–1954) Businessman and management innovator, born in Wilmington, DE. A graduate of Massachusetts Institute of Technology, he joined the family gunpowder company. As president (1915–20) he introduced and developed many new industrial management techniques, including a systematic approach to strategic planning, control systems, and the pioneering of modern industrial accounting methods. He became president of General Motors in 1920 after the Du Pont company had rescued it from near bankruptcy. >> Sloan, Alfred P

Dupont, Samuel Francis [doopont] (1803–65) US naval officer, born in Bergen Point, NJ. He entered the navy in 1815. In the Civil War he organized the blockade of the South Atlantic area by Federal naval forces, and captured the ports of South Carolina and Georgia. He was unjustly blamed for the failure of the Federal attack on Charleston in 1863, and relieved of his command.

du Pré, Jacqueline [doo **pray**] (1945–87) Cellist, born in Oxford, Oxfordshire, SC England, UK. She made her debut at the age of 16 and quickly established an international reputation. In 1967 she married the pianist **Daniel Barenboim**, with whom she gave many recitals. Her career as a player ended in 1973, when she developed multiple sclerosis, but thereafter she continued as a teacher. >> Barenboim

Dupré, Jules [düpray] (1811–89) Landscape painter, born in Nantes, France. He studied in England with Constable, and was a leader of the Barbizon school. >> Constable, John

Dupré, Marcel [düpray] (1886–1971) Organist, born in Rouen, France. He won the Prix de Rome for composition in 1914, and became renowned throughout Europe for his organ recitals. The composer of many chorales and an organ concerto, he also wrote on improvisation, and directed the Conservatoires at Fontainebleau (1947–54) and Paris (1954–6).

Dupuytren, Guillaume, Baron [düpweetrĩ] (1777–1835) Surgeon, born in Pierre Buffière, France. From 1812 he was professor of clinical surgery in Paris, and surgeon to Louis XVIII and Charles X. He invented many surgical instruments, and devised surgical techniques for many conditions, including *Dupuytren's contracture* (a flexion deformity of the hand).

Duquesne, Abraham, Marquis [düken] (1610–88) French naval officer, born in Dieppe, France. In the Swedish service (1644–7) he rose to vice-admiral and won victories over a Danish–Dutch naval alliance. Returning to France, in 1650 he brought Bordeaux, which had declared for the Fronde, under control. He defeated Ruyter and Tromp several times in 1672–3, and the united fleets of Spain and Holland off Sicily in 1676. >> Ruyter; Tromp

Durand, Asher B(rown) [duhrand] (1796–1886) Painter, engraver, and illustrator, born in Jefferson Village, NJ. He served an engraving apprenticeship from 1812, and painted portraits of eminent Americans (1835–40). After a visit to Europe in 1840 he was associated with the Hudson River School, painting Romantic and dramatic landscapes. His graphic work strongly influenced the design of US paper currency.

Durand, J(ean) N(icolas) L(ouis) [dürã] (1760–1834) Architect, theorist, and educator, born in Paris. He studied architecture at Paris, built little, but had a great influence on contemporary Neoclassical architecture through his teaching at the Ecole Polytechnique (1795–1830) and his *Recueil et parallèle des édifices en tout genre* (1800, Collection and Comparison of Buildings of All Types).

Durante, Francesco [durantay] (1684–1755) Composer, born in Naples, Italy. Head of the Conservatorio di Santa Maria di Loreto in Naples (1742–5), he wrote a wide variery of church and chamber music.

Durante, Jimmy [durantee], popular name of **James Francis Durante**, nickname **Schnoz** or **Schnozzle Durante** (1893–1980) Comedian, born in New York City. He began his career as a saloon pianist in Coney Island before partnering two vaudevillians in a club act. They opened the Club Durant in New York City in 1923. He had a large nose which he used to comic advantage, hence his nickname. He became a popular and versatile entertainer on Broadway and radio, and in later years appeared in the films *Jumbo* (1962) and *It's a Mad, Mad, Mad, Mad World* (1963).

Duras, Marguerite [dürã], pseudonym of **Marguerite Donnadieu** (1914–96) Novelist, born in Gia Dinh, Vietnam. She was educated in Indo-China, and went to France in 1932. Her reputation was made by the novels she wrote in the 1950s, such as *Un Barrage contre le Pacifique* (1950, trans The Sea Wall), *Le Marin de Gibraltar* (1952, The Sailor from

Gibraltar), and *Le Square* (1955). She achieved a wider celebrity with the screenplay for Alain Resnais' film *Hiroshima Mon Amour* (1959, Hiroshima, My Love). Her autobiographical novel *L'Amant* (1984, The Lover) was made into a successful film (1992). >> Resnais

Durbin, Deanna, originally **Edna Mae Durbin** (1921–) Entertainer, born in Winnipeg, Manitoba, Canada. When the family moved to California, her singing voice attracted the attention of talent scouts and she appeared in the short film *Every Sunday* (1936), becoming a star with the release of *Three Smart Girls* (1936). Her adult work included *It Started With Eve* (1941), *Christmas Holiday* (1944), and *Lady on a Train* (1945). She made her last film in 1948 and retired to Paris.

Dürer, Albrecht [dyoorer], Ger [dürer] (1471–1528) Painter and engraver, born in Nuremberg, Germany. He studied under Michael Wolgemut (1434–1519), travelled widely (1490–4), and in 1497 set up his own studio, producing many paintings. In 1498 he published his first great series of designs on wood, the illustrations of the Apocalypse. He was much employed by Emperor Maximilian I, in whose honour he drew the 'Triumphal Car' and (with others) the 'Triumphal Arch', the largest known woodcut (9 sq m/100 sq ft).

Durey, Louis [düree] (1888–1979) Composer, born in Paris. In 1916, under the influence of Erik Satie, he became one of the group of young French composers known as Les Six, but broke with them in 1921. He wrote large orchestral and choral works, but is chiefly known for his songs and chamber music. >> Auric; Cocteau; Honegger; Milhaud; Poulenc; Satie; Tailleferre

D'Urfey, Thomas [derfay] (1653–1723) Playwright and songwriter, born in Exeter, Devon, SW England, UK. He was a prolific author, his comedies especially being popular. Among these were *The Fond Husband* (1676), *Madame Fickle* (1677), and *Sir Burnaby Whig* (1681). In 1683 he published his *New Collection of Songs and Poems*, which was followed by a long series of songs, (6 vols, 1719–20).

Durham, John George Lambton, Earl of [duhram], known as **Radical Jack** (1792–1840) British statesman, born in London, England, UK. He studied at Eton, served for two years in the dragoons, and in 1813 was returned as a Whig. He was a strong Liberal, his nickname stemming from his reformist views, and in 1821 brought forward a scheme for parliamentary reform much more advanced than that of 1832. In the administration of his father-in-law, Lord Grey (1830), he was Lord Privy Seal, and one of the four persons who drew up the Reform Bill. In 1838 he was appointed Governor-General of Canada, and submitted an influential report on the union of Canada and imperial government. >> Grey, Charles

Durkheim, Emile [derkhiym] (1858–1917) Sociologist, born in Epinal, France, generally regarded as one of the founders of sociology. He studied at Paris, and became a teacher, then taught at the University of Bordeaux (1887) and at the Sorbonne. His writings include *Les Règles de la méthode sociologique* (1894, The Rules of Sociological Method) and a definitive study of suicide (1897). He is perhaps best known for his concept of 'collective representations', the social power of ideas stemming from their development through the interaction of many minds.

Durrell, Gerald (Malcolm) [duhrel] (1925–95) British zoologist, traveller, writer, and broadcaster, born in Jamshedpur, India, the brother of Lawrence Durrell. He was a student keeper at Whipsnade Zoo (1945–6), then went on several animal collecting expeditions to Cameroon, Guyana, and other countries. His popular animal stories and reminiscences include *My Family and Other Animals* (1956), *A Zoo in My Luggage* (1960), *Birds, Beasts and Relatives*

(1969), *Catch me a Colobus* (1972), *The Mockery Bird* (1981), *Marrying Off Mother* (1991), and *The Aye-Aye and I* (1992). His television work includes *The Amateur Naturalist* (1983) and *Ourselves and Other Animals* (1987). He founded the Jersey Zoological Park in 1958, and was founder chairman of Wildlife Preservation Trust International in 1972. >> Durrell, Lawrence

Durrell, Lawrence (George) [duhrel] (1912–90) British novelist and poet, born in Darjeeling, India. He studied at Canterbury, and eloped with his future wife to Paris, where he began to write novels. He taught English in Athens, then served in the Foreign Office in Cairo, Athens, and Belgrade, settling in Cyprus (1953). He first made his name with *Prospero's Cell* (1945), followed by the cosmopolitan multi-love story comprising the 'Alexandria Quartet' (1957–60): *Justine, Balthazar, Mountolive*, and *Clea*. A series of five novels commenced in 1974 with *Monsieur*, followed by *Livia* (1978), *Constance* (1982), *Sebastian* (1983), and *Quinx* (1985). He also wrote several books of poems, short stories, and travel books. >> Durrell, Gerald

Dürrenmatt or **Duerrenmatt, Friedrich** [dürenmat] (1921–90) Writer, born in Konolfingen, Switzerland. He studied at Bern and Zürich, and turned from painting to writing. His plays include *Die Ehe des Herrn Mississippi* (1952, The Marriage of Mr Mississippi), which established his international reputation, *Die Physiker* (1962, The Physicists), and *Die Frist* (1977, The Appointed Time). He also wrote novels, short stories, critical essays, and works for radio.

Duse, Eleonora [doozay] (1859–1924) Actress, born near Venice, Italy. She rose to fame in Italy, then triumphed throughout the European capitals (1892–3), mainly acting in plays by contemporary French playwrights, Ibsen, and the works of her lover, Gabriele d'Annunzio. Her histrionic genius ranks 'The Duse' as one of the world's greatest actresses. She retired through ill health in 1909, but returned to the stage in 1921, and died during a US tour. >> d'Annunzio

Dussek, Jan Ladislav (1760–1812) Composer and pianist, born in Czaslau, Czech Republic. In Amsterdam he produced his earliest works for the piano, and he was very popular in London (1788–1800). He was instructor to Prince Louis Ferdinand of Prussia (1803–6), and in 1808 entered Talleyrand's service. He composed over 30 sonatas. >> Talleyrand

Dutrochet, René Joachim Henri [dütrohshay] (1776–1847) Physiologist, born in Néon, France. He qualified in medicine at Paris, and became physician to Joseph Bonaparte of Spain. He was the first to study and to name osmosis. >> Bonaparte, Joseph

Duun, Olav [doon] (1876–1939) Novelist, born in Namsdal, Norway. He worked as a teacher from 1904 to 1926. An important representative of new Norwegian writing in *Landsmål* ('national language') between the two World Wars, he made his reputation with a major series of saga-like novels about four generations of peasant landholders in Namsdal in *Juvikfolke* (6 vols, 1918–23, The People of Juvik).

Duval, Claude [düval] (1643–70) Highwayman, born in Domfront, France. He moved to England at the Restoration (1660) in the train of the Duke of Richmond. Taking soon to the road, he pursued a successful career, gaining a popular reputation, especially for his gallantry towards women. He was captured drunk, and hanged at Tyburn, London.

Duvalier, François [doovalyay], known as **Papa Doc** (1907–71) Haitian politician and president (1957–71), born in Port-au-Prince. He trained as a doctor (which gave him his byname) at the University of Hawaii, where he worked until 1943. He became director of the National Public Health Service (1946) and minister of health and labour (1948). He organized opposition to the military government of Paul Magloire (1950–6), promoted black nationalism, and was elected president. He held power from 1957 until his death, ruling in an increasingly arbitrary fashion. His regime saw the creation of the dreaded civilian militia known as the Tonton Macoute, and the exile of many people. He became president for life in 1964, and was succeeded in this post by his son, Jean-Claude. >> Duvalier, Jean-Claude; RR1056

Duvalier, Jean-Claude [doovalyay], known as **Baby Doc** (1951–) Haitian politician and president (1971–86), born in Port-au-Prince, the son of François ('Papa Doc') Duvalier. After studying law at the university of Haiti he followed his father into politics, becoming known as 'Baby Doc'. At the age of 20 he became president-for-life, ruling, as had his father, through a private army. In 1986 he was deposed in a military coup led by General Henri Namphrey, and went into exile in Grasse, France. >> Duvalier, François; RR1056

Duve, Christian de >> de Duve, Christian

Duveen (of Millbank), Joseph Duveen, Baron (1869–1939) Art dealer, born in Hull, E England, UK. Starting in his father's antique shop, he developed a business in the USA specializing in Old Masters. He established significant collections in the USA and Europe, was a benefactor of the National Gallery, and gifted a gallery in the British Museum to house the Elgin marbles.

Du Vigneaud, Vincent [doo **veen**yoh] (1901–78) Biochemist, born in Chicago, IL. He studied at Illinois, Rochester, Johns Hopkins, and Edinburgh universities, and became professor of biochemistry at Cornell (1938). He researched sulphur-containing vitamins, isolated Vitamin H, and deduced the structure of biotin (1942), before turning his attention to the pituitary hormones, oxytocin and vasopressin. He determined their structure, and in 1953 succeeded in synthesizing oxytocin, for which he was awarded the 1955 Nobel Prize for Chemistry.

Dvořák, Antonín (Leopold) [dvaw(r)zhak] (1841–1904) Composer, born near Prague. He was sent to the organ school in Prague in 1857, and began to earn his living from the viola. In 1877 Brahms introduced his music to Vienna, and was a great influence on him. His work, basically classical in structure, but with colourful Slavonic motifs, won increasing recognition, culminating in European acclaim for his *Stabat mater* (1880). By then he had written six symphonies and much chamber and piano music, and in 1891 he was offered the directorship of the New York Conservatory. In the USA he wrote his ninth symphony, the ever-popular 'From the New World'. In 1895 he returned to Prague. >> Brahms

Dwight, John (c. 1637–1703) Potter, born in Oxfordshire, SC England, UK. He studied at Oxford, SC England, UK, and became a registrar at Chester. At his pottery in Fulham (1671–98), he patented a 'transparent earthenware' resembling porcelain, thus pioneering the English pottery industry.

Dworkin, Ronald (Myles) (1931–) Legal scholar, born in Wooster, MA. A leading theorist of jurisprudence, his work challenges strict adherence to the letter of the law in favour of individual liberties and moral principles, in books such as *Taking Rights Seriously* (1977), *A Matter of Principle* (1985), and *Law's Empire* (1986). He taught at Yale (1962–9), then at Oxford, concurrently at New York University from 1975.

Dyce, William (1806–64) Historical and religious painter, born in Aberdeen, NE Scotland, UK. In 1825 he went to Rome, where he developed sympathies with the Nazarenes, and transmitted these to the Pre-Raphaelites. From 1844 he was professor of fine arts at King's College, London. He executed frescoes in several London locations, including the new House of Lords. Aberdeen's Dyce airport is named after him.

Dyck, Anthony van >> van Dyck, Anthony

Dyer, Anson [diyer], originally **Ernest Anson-Dyer** (1876–1962) Animator, born in Brighton, West Sussex, S England, UK. Hailed as 'Britain's answer to Walt Disney', he studied at Brighton Art School, and designed stained glass windows before trying animation with a series of *Dicky Dee's Cartoons* (1915). For the Cartoon Film Company he produced the bimonthly *John Bull's Animated Sketchbook* (1916), followed by 10 *Kine Komedy Kartoons* (1917). In 1935 he began a series of colour cartoons based on the Stanley Holloway character, *Old Sam*, his biggest popular success. >> Disney; Holloway

Dyke, Dick Van >> Van Dyke, Dick

Dylan, Bob [dilan], pseudonym of **Robert Zimmerman** (1941–) Folk-singer and songwriter, born in Duluth, MN. Taking his professional name from the poet Dylan Thomas, he rose to fame in the 1960s, following the folk tradition of Woody Guthrie but introducing a fresh social and political awareness. His lyrics made his songs the dominant influence in the popular music and culture of the period. Opposition to war, the nuclear bomb, and racial and social injustice are the themes of some of his most famous songs, such as 'Blowin' in the Wind' and 'The Times They are a-Changin''. In the late 1960s he changed from specific protest to more general and personal themes, and to a more traditional Country and Western style of music, as in *Nashville Skyline* (1969). In 1979 he became a convert to Christianity, which led to religious albums such as *Saved*. In the 1980s he returned to Judaism, and remains one of the seminal influences on popular songwriting. >> Guthrie, Woody; Thomas, Dylan

Dympna, St [dimpna] (9th-c) Irish princess, said to have been slain by her father at Gheel in Belgium for resistance to his incestuous passion. She is the patron of the insane. Feast day 15 May.

Dyson, Sir Frank (Watson) (1868–1939) Astronomer, born in Measham, Leicestershire, C England, UK. Astronomer-royal for Scotland (1905–10) and England (1910–33), he is known for his observations in 1919 which supported Einstein's hypothesis that light could be deflected by a gravitational field, and for his work on the distribution of stars and on solar eclipses. He was knighted in 1915.

Dyson, Freeman John (1923–) Physicist, born in Crowthorne, Berkshire, S England, UK. He studied at Cambridge, and became professor of physics at Cornell University (1951–3), then at the Institute of Advanced Study, Princeton (1953–94). He is well known for his research in quantum theory, especially quantum electrodynamics and the stability of matter, and for contributions to public debate on scientific issues.

Dzerzhinsky, Felix Edmundovich [jerzhinskee] (1877–1926) Russian revolutionary, born in Vilna. In 1897 he was exiled to Siberia for political agitation, fought in the 1905 revolution, and in 1917 became chairman of the secret police and a member of the Bolshevik central committee. After 1921 he reorganized the railway system, and was chairman of the supreme economic council (1924–6).

Eadgar >> **Edgar**

Eadmer or **Edmer** (c.1060–c.1128) Monk and historian, born in Canterbury, Kent, SE England, UK. He was secretary and chaplain to Archbishop Anselm. His major works were the six-volume *Historia novorum in Anglia* (c.1115), and *Vita Anselmi* (c.1124). >> **Anselm**

Eads, James B(uchanan) [eedz] (1820–87) Engineer and inventor, born in Lawrenceburg, IN. He invented a diving bell, and founded a salvage company that made a fortune from sunken river steamboats. In 1861 he built in 100 days eight ironclad Mississippi steamers for the government, followed by other ironclads and mortar-boats. He is best remembered for the steel triple-arched Eads Bridge (1867–74) across the Mississippi at St Louis, with a central span of 158 m/520 ft.

Eagles, John >> **Eccles, John**

Eakins, Thomas [eekinz] (1844–1916) Painter, born in Philadelphia, PA. He studied in Paris under Gérôme, and became known for his portraits and genre pictures, especially of sporting scenes. His best-known work is his realistic depiction of a surgical operation, 'The Gross Clinic' (1875, Philadelphia), which was controversially received on account of its detail. He was also an accomplished photographer, and exercised considerable influence through his teaching. >> **Gérôme**

Ealdhelm, St >> **Aldhelm, St**

Ealdred >> **Aldred**

Eames, Charles [eemz] (1907–78) Designer, born in St Louis, MO. A student of architecture, he taught at Cranbrook Academy of Art from 1936. With Eero Saarinen he won a design competition at the New York Museum of Modern Art (1940), and staged the first ever one-man design show there (1946). In 1949 he designed his own house in Santa Monica, CA, constructed entirely from standardized components, and this became a prototype of worldwide interest. He is best known for his furniture, including the celebrated 'Lounge Chair' (1956). He also did original work in graphics and exhibition design, and in the films he produced for IBM and the US government. >> **Barr; Saarinen, Eero**

Eardley, Joan [eerdlee] (1921–63) Painter, born in Warnham, West Sussex, S England, UK. She studied at Goldsmith's College of Art, London, and the School of Art, Glasgow. She worked in Glasgow, then (from 1950) in Catterline on the E coast of Scotland. She is best known for her studies of poor children from the Glasgow tenements, and for her Scottish landscapes and seascapes.

Earhart, Amelia [ay(r)hah(r)t] (1897–1937) Aviator, born in Atchison, KS. She was the first woman to fly the Atlantic, as a passenger, and followed this by a solo flight in 1932. In 1935 she flew solo from Hawaii to California. In 1937 she set out to fly round the world, but her plane was lost over the Pacific.

Early, Jubal A(nderson) (1816–94) US soldier, born in Franklin County, VA. He trained at West Point, and during the American Civil War commanded a Confederate brigade at Bull Run, and a division at Fredericksburg and Gettysburg (1863). In 1864 he was relieved of his command after a rout at Waynesboro. He fled to Canada, but returned in 1869 to his former profession as a lawyer in Virginia.

Earp, Wyatt (Berry Stapp) [erp] (1848–1929) Gambler, gunfighter, and lawman, born in Monmouth, IL. He drifted through the West working at a variety of jobs from confidence trickster to assistant marshal. During his stay in Tombstone, AZ, he befriended Doc Holliday, who joined with the Earp brothers against the Clanton gang in the famous gunfight at the OK Corral (1881). Earp collaborated in the writing of his biography *Wyatt Earp, Frontier Marshal* (1931), published after his death. The book portrayed him as a heroic frontiersman of the Wild West. >> **Holliday**

East, Sir Alfred (1849–1913) Painter and etcher, born in Kettering, Northamptonshire, C England, UK. He studied at the Glasgow School of Art, and is best known for his landscapes of Japan. From 1902 he produced a large number of etchings, and in 1906 wrote *The Art of Landscape Painting in Oil Colour*. A gallery devoted to his work has been opened in Kettering.

East, Michael (c.1580–1648) Composer and organist. He probably spent several years in the service of the Lord Chancellor, and was subsequently organist of Lichfield Cathedral. His works include church music and madrigals, and he was a contributor to *The Triumphes of Oriana*, the madrigal collection dedicated to Queen Elizabeth I in 1603.

Eastlake, Sir Charles Lock (1793–1865) Historical painter, born in Plymouth, Devon, SW England, UK. He made his name with two full-length portraits of Napoleon sketched while a prisoner on HMS *Bellerophon* in Portsmouth harbour (1815). He produced many Italianate genre paintings, and became a director of the National Gallery from 1855.

Eastlake, Charles Lock (1836–1906) Architect, furniture designer, and writer, born in Plymouth, Devon, SW England, UK, the nephew of the painter Sir Charles Lock Eastlake. He is best known for his writing. His book *Hints on Household Taste in Furniture, Upholstery and Other Details* (1868) was especially influential in the USA, where it gave rise to the *Eastlake* style. He later became a keeper at the National Gallery in London (1878–98). >> **Eastlake, Sir Charles Lock**

Eastman, George (1854–1932) Inventor and philanthropist, born in Waterville, NY. He turned from banking to photography, producing a successful roll-film (1884), and the 'Kodak' box camera (1888). In 1889 he manufactured the transparent celluloid film used by Edison and others in experiments which made possible the moving-picture industry. >> **Edison**

Eastwick, Edward Backhouse (1814–43) Orientalist, born in Warfield, Berkshire, S England, UK. After service with the East India Company he was appointed (1845) professor of Hindustani at Haileybury College, and assistant political secretary in the India Office (1859). He was secretary of the legation in Persia (1860–3), and produced many translations from Persian. He later became MP for Penryn and Falmouth (1868–74).

Eastwood, Clint (1930–) Film actor and director, born in San Francisco, CA. He began acting in television Westerns, especially the *Rawhide* series (1959–65), and became an international star with three Italian-made 'spaghetti' Westerns, beginning with a *A Fistful of Dollars* (1964). In the USA his box-office status was confirmed with several violent crime thrillers, such as *Dirty Harry* (1971), and from that time he began to combine acting performances with directing, beginning with *Play Misty for Me* (1971) and continuing with *Bronco Billy* (1980), *Heartbreak Ridge* (1986), and *Bird* (1987), among many others. In 1992 he directed the highly successful film *Unforgiven* which received two Oscars (best picture, best director). Later films include *A Perfect World* (1994), *Bridges of Madison County* (1995), and *Absolute Power* (1997), which he also directed. He was elected mayor of Carmel-by-the-Sea, CA (1986–8).

Eban, Abba (Solomon) [eeban], originally **Aubrey Solomon** (1915–) Israeli diplomat and statesman, born in Cape Town, South Africa. He studied in England, taught at Cambridge, and worked in the Middle East Arab Centre in Jerusalem (1944). He was Israeli UN representative in New York City (1948), and ambassador in Washington, DC (1950–9). He then returned to Israel, where he won a seat in the Knesset, and until 1974 served under several prime ministers, most notably as foreign minister (1966–74).

Ebbinghaus, Hermann [aybinghows] (1850–1909) Experimental psychologist, born in Barmen, Germany. He taught at Berlin, and became professor at Wrocław, Poland (formerly Breslau, Germany) (1894–1905), then at Halle. He is best remembered for *Über das Gedächtnis* (1885, On Memory), which first applied experimental methods to memory research, and which introduced the nonsense syllable as a standard stimulus for such work.

Eberhart, Richard (Ghormley) [ayberhah(r)t] (1904–) Poet and teacher, born in Austin, MN. He studied at the universities of Minnesota, Dartmouth, Cambridge, England and Harvard, then worked as a teacher (1933–41) and, after service in World War 2, for a family business (1946–52). He taught at Dartmouth (1956–70), and was a consultant in poetry to the Library of Congress (1959–61). His books of poetry include *Undercliff* (1953), *Selected Poems, 1930–1965* (1965, Pulitzer), and *Shifts of Being* (1968). Later works include *Fields of Grace* (1972), *Throwing Yourself Away* (1984), and *New and Collected Poems* (1990), and he also published *Collected Verse Plays* (1962).

Ebert, Friedrich [aybert] (1871–1925) German statesman, the first president of the German Republic (1919–25), born in Heidelberg, Germany. A saddler at Heidelberg, he became a Social Democrat journalist and a Reichstag member (1912). Chairman of his party (1913), he was a Socialist leader in the revolution of 1918. >> RR1051

Eccles or **Eagles, John** (c. 1650–1735) Composer, born in London, England, UK. He became master of the King's Band of Musick in 1700, composed the music for the coronation of Queen Anne, and published many volumes of theatre music, songs, and masques. Two other brothers, **Henry** (c.1652–1742) and **Thomas** (after 1652–after 1735), were violinists. The former achieved success in Paris, but little is known of the latter, except that he played in London taverns. >> Anne

Eccles, Sir John (Carew) (1903–) Physiologist, born in Melbourne, Victoria, Australia. He studied at Melbourne and Oxford, became director of the Kanematsu Institute of Pathology at Sydney (1937), and was professor of physiology at Otago University (1944–51), then at Canberra (1951–66). In 1968 he moved to the State University of New York at Buffalo. A specialist in neurophysiology, he was knighted in 1958, and shared the 1963 Nobel Prize for Physiology or Medicine for work on the functioning of nervous impulses. >> RR1124

Ecevit, Bülent [ejevit] (1925–) Turkish statesman and prime minister (1974, 1977, 1978–9), born in Istanbul. He worked as a government official and journalist, and developed a reputation as a writer and translator. He became an MP for the centre-left Republican People's Party in 1957, minister of labour (1961–5), secretary-general of his Party (1966), and subsequently chairman (1972). He headed a coalition government in 1974, during which he ordered the invasion of Cyprus. In 1978 he imposed martial law on Turkey. After the military coup of 1980, he was imprisoned twice for criticizing the military regime. He retired from politics in 1987. >> RR1093

Ecgberht / Ecgbryht >> Egbert

Echegaray y Eizaguirre, José [aychaygahree ee ayeethageeray] (1832–1916) Spanish statesman, mathematician, and playwright, born in Madrid. He taught mathematics, held portfolios in various ministries (1868–74), then won literary fame from his many plays in prose and verse, sharing the 1904 Nobel Prize for Literature. He returned to politics as minister of finance (1905), and to science as professor of physics at Madrid University (1905). His masterpiece was *Elgran Galeoto* (1881, trans The World and his Wife). >> RR1123

Eck, Johann Mayer von (1486–1543) Roman Catholic theologian, born in Egg, Switzerland. He became professor of theology at Ingolstadt (1510), and was the ruling spirit of that university until his death. After his Leipzig disputation with Luther, he wrote on papal authority, and went to Rome in 1520, returning with the bull which declared Luther a heretic. >> Luther

Eckart / Eckehart, Johannes >> Eckhart, Johannes

Eckener, Hugo [ekener] (1868–1954) Aeronautical engineer, born in Flensburg, Germany. He helped develop the rigid airship, and became a director of the Zeppelin firm (1911). He piloted the ZR3 on the first Trans-Atlantic airship flight (1924), and commanded the *Graf Zeppelin* on the first airship flight around the world (1929). >> Zeppelin

Eckerman, Johann Peter [ekerman] (1792–1854) Writer, born in Winsen, Germany. He studied at Göttingen. The publication of a critical appreciation of Goethe led to his move to Weimar, where he assisted Goethe in preparing the final edition of his works. He achieved fame with his *Gespräche mit Goethe* (3 vols, 1836–48, Conversations with Goethe). >> Goethe

Eckert, J(ohn) Presper, Jr (1919–95) Engineer and inventor, born in Philadelphia, PA. He studied at the University of Pennsylvania, and took up a career in electrical engineering, obtaining over 85 patents for his electronic inventions. He is best known for his work, with John W Mauchly, on the Electronic Numerical Integrator And Calculator (ENIAC), one of the first modern computers. >> Mauchly

Eckhart, Johannes [ekhah(r)t], also spelled **Eckart** or **Eckehart**, known as **Meister Eckhart** ('Master Eckhart') (c. 1260–c. 1327) Theologian and mystic, born in Hocheim, Germany. He entered the Dominican order, studied and taught in Paris, and became Dominican provincial in Saxony (1303–11). From 1312 he preached at Strasbourg, Frankfurt, and Cologne. His teaching was a mystic pantheism, influential on later religious mysticism and speculative philosophy. In 1325 he was arraigned for heresy by the Archbishop of Cologne, and two years after his death his writings were condemned by Pope John XXII.

Eckstine, Billy [ekstiyn], popular name of **William Clarence Eckstein** (1914–93) Singer, born in Pittsburgh, PA. He left Howard University after winning a talent contest, and began singing in nightclubs. He appeared with Earl Hines's dance band (1939–43), and went on to form his own in 1944. His band promoted the new bebop style of popular music, and featured many newcomers who later established themselves as successful performers. Among his hit records he was probably best known for 'That Old Black Magic'. >> Hines

Eco, Umberto [aykoh] (1929–) Novelist and critic, born in Alessandria, Italy. He studied at Turin University, has taught semiotics at the University of Bologne for many years, and published several important works on the subject. His novel *Il nome della rosa* (1980, The Name of the Rose), an intellectual detective story, achieved instant fame, and attracted much critical attention; it was filmed in 1986. Later novels are *Foucault's Pendulum* (trans, 1988) and *L'isola del giorno prima* (1994, The Island of the Day Before).

Eddery, Pat(rick James John) (1952–) Jockey, born in Newbridge, Ireland. He was champion jockey (1974–7), and won the Derby in 1975 and 1982. He won the Oaks twice, as well as the St Leger. He also had a particularly good record in France, winning the Prix de l'Arc de Triomphe in 1980, 1985, and 1986. >> RR1160

Eddington, Sir Arthur S(tanley) (1882–1944) Astronomer, born in Kendal, Cumbria, NW England, UK. He studied at Manchester and Cambridge, where he became professor of astronomy (1913) and director of the Cambridge Observatories, working mainly on the internal structure of stars. In 1919 his observations of star positions during a total solar eclipse gave the first direct confirmation of Einstein's general theory of relativity. He became a renowned popularizer of science, notably in *The Nature of the Physical World* (1928). He was knighted in 1930. >> Einstein

Eddy, Mary Baker, married name **Glover** (1821–1910) Founder of the Christian Science Church, born in Bow, NH. Brought up a Congregationalist, she had little formal education, because of ill health. In 1866 she received severe injuries after a fall, but read about the palsied man in Matthew's Gospel, and claimed to have risen from her bed similarly healed. Thereafter she devoted herself to developing her spiritual discovery. She set out her beliefs in *Science and Health with Key to the Scriptures* (1875), founded the Christian Science Association in 1876, organized the Church of Christ, Scientist, at Boston in 1879, and founded the *Christian Science Monitor* in 1908.

Ede, James Chuter, Baron Chuter-Ede of Epsom [eed] (1882–1965) British statesman, born in Epsom, Surrey, SE England, UK. He studied at Cambridge, and became a teacher (1905–14) and local councillor (1920–7), before entering parliament briefly in 1923. He became home secretary in the 1945 Labour government, and Leader of the House of Commons in 1951. A humanitarian reformer, he was responsible for the Criminal Justice Act of 1948. He became a life peer in 1964.

Edel, (Joseph) Leon [edl] (1907–97) Biographer, born in Pittsburgh, PA. He taught at New York University (1953–73), devoting his scholarly career to Henry James, writing a magisterial five-volume biography of James (1953–85), and publishing numerous editions of his letters and other writings. >> James, Henry

Edelman, Gerald (Maurice) [aydlman] (1929–) Biochemist, born in New York City. He studied at Pennsylvania and Rockefeller universities, and became professor of biochemistry at Rockefeller in 1966. His special interest was in the chemical structure and mode of action of the antibodies which form part of a vertebrate animal's defence against infection. He shared the Nobel Prize for Physiology or Medicine in 1972. >> Mountcastle; RR1124

Eden, Sir (Robert) Anthony, 1st Earl of Avon [eedn] (1897–1977) British statesman and prime minister (1955–7), born at Windlestone Hall, Durham, NE England, UK. He studied at Oxford, and served in World War 1 (MC, 1917). He became a Conservative MP in 1923, and was foreign under-secretary (1931), Lord Privy Seal (1933) and foreign secretary (1935), resigning in 1938 over differences with Chamberlain. In World War 2 he was first dominions secretary, then secretary of state for war, and foreign secretary (1940–5). Again foreign secretary (1951–5), he was involved with the negotiations in Korea and Indo-China, and the 1954 Geneva Summit Conference. He succeeded

Churchill as prime minister, and in 1956 ordered British forces (in collaboration with the French and Israelis) to occupy the Suez Canal Zone. His action was condemned by the UN and caused a bitter controversy in Britain which did not subside when he ordered a withdrawal. In failing health, he abruptly resigned in 1957. He was created an earl in 1961. >> Chamberlain, Neville; Churchill, Sir Winston; Mollet; Selwyn-Lloyd; RR1095

Ederle, Gertrude (Caroline) [ayderlee] (1906–) The first woman to swim the English channel, born in New York City. She won a gold medal at the 1924 Olympic Games as a member of the US 400 m relay team, and two bronze medals. On 6 August 1926 she swam the Channel from Cap Gris Nez to Kingsdown in 14 h 31 min, very nearly two hours faster than the existing men's record.

Edgar or **Eadgar** (943–75) King of all England (from 959), the younger son of Edmund I (reigned 939–46). He was chosen as King of Mercia and Northumbria when his brother Eadwig (?–959) was deposed there in 957, and King of all England after the death of Eadwig, who still controlled Wessex and Kent. He encouraged the English monastic revival, and c.973 introduced a uniform currency based on new silver pennies. >> RR1095

Edgar, David (Burman) (1948–) Playwright and teacher, born in Birmingham, West Midlands, C England, UK. He studied drama at Manchester University, and was a journalist before writing for the stage full-time. He has written many plays, beginning with *The National Interest* (1971), and including *Saigon Rose* (1976), an eight-hour adaptation of *Nicholas Nickleby* for the Royal Shakespeare Company (1980), *The Shape of the Table* (1990), and *Pentecost* (1995). He also writes for television and radio. He has taught at Birmingham University since 1989.

Edgar the Ætheling ('Prince') [athuhling] (c. 1050–1125) Anglo-Saxon prince, the son of Edward the Ætheling and grandson of Edmund Ironside. Though chosen as king by some influential Englishmen after the battle of Hastings, he was never crowned. He submitted to William the Conqueror (1066), but then rebelled and fled to Scotland (1068). He was finally reconciled with William in 1074. He joined Robert Curthose, to fight against Henry I for the English crown, but was taken prisoner at the Battle of Tinchebrai (1106), and lived in obscurity after his release. >> Edward the Ætheling; Henry I; Robert Curthose; William I (of England)

Edger, Kate Millington (1857–1935) New Zealand teacher and suffragist, born in England, UK. She studied in Auckland, and in 1877 became the first woman university graduate in New Zealand, and the first woman in the British Empire to earn a BA. In 1877 she joined the staff of Christchurch Girls High School, and became the founding principal of Nelson College for Girls (1882–93). For the next 30 years she was prominent in women's organizations.

Edgerton, Harold E(ugene) [ejerton] (1903–90) Engineer, born in Fremont, NE. He studied at the Massachusetts Institute of Technology, where in 1934 he became professor of electrical engineering. A specialist in stroboscopes and high-speed photography, he produced a krypton-xenon gas arc which was employed in photographing the capillaries in the white of the eye without hurting the patient.

Edgeworth, Maria (1767–1849) Writer, born in Blackbourton, Oxfordshire, SC England, UK. Her work influenced Walter Scott, whom she visited on several occasions. She is best known for her children's stories, and her novels of Irish life, such as *Castle Rackrent* (1800) and *The Absentee* (1812). >> Scott, Walter

Edinburgh, Prince Philip, Duke of [edinbruh] (1921–   )
The husband of Queen Elizabeth II of the United Kingdom,
the son of Prince Andrew of Greece and Princess Alice of
Battenberg, born in Corfu, Greece. He studied at Cheam,
Gordonstoun, and Dartmouth, and entered the Royal
Navy in 1939 as Lieutenant Philip Mountbatten. He
became a naturalized British subject in 1947, when he
was married to the **Princess Elizabeth** (20 Nov). Seriously
interested in science and the technology of industry, as
well as in youth adventure training, he is also a keen
sportsman, yachtsman, qualified airman, and conservationist. In 1956 he began the Duke of Edinburgh Award
scheme to foster the leisure activities of young people.
>> Elizabeth II

Edison, Thomas (Alva) (1847–1931) Inventor and physicist, born in Milan, OH. He began as a railroad newsboy,
and after purchasing some old type published the *Grand
Trunk Herald*, the first newspaper printed in a train. He
became a telegraph operator and developed the Edison
Universal Stock Printer, which enabled him to set up as a
manufacturer of printing telegraphs (1871). He quit manufacturing for research in 1876 and invented the phonograph (1877), the carbon-filament light bulb (1879), and
motion picture equipment. He discovered thermionic
emission (1883), which became the basis for the electronic
valve. Altogether he held patents for over 1000 inventions.
>> Sprague; Swan; Thomson, Elihu

Edmer >> **Eadmer**

Edmund I (921–46) King of the English (939–46), the half-
brother of Athelstan. On Edmund's accession, Scandinavian
forces from Northumbria, reinforced by levies from Ireland,
quickly overran the E Midlands. He re-established his control over the S Danelaw (942) and Northumbria (944) and,
until his murder by an exile, ruled a reunited England.
>> Athelstan; RR1095

Edmund II, known as **Edmund Ironside** (c. 980–1016) King
of the English for a few months in 1016, the son of Ethelred
the Unready. He was chosen king by Londoners on his
father's death (Apr 1016), while Canute was elected at
Southampton by the Witan. Edmund hastily levied an
army, defeated Canute, and attempted to raise the siege of
London, but was routed at Ashingdon, or possibly Ashdon,
Essex (Oct 1016). He agreed to a partition of the country,
but died a few weeks later, leaving Canute as sole ruler.
>> Canute; Ethelred II; RR1095

Edmund, St, known as **St Edmund the Martyr** (c. 841–70)
King of East Anglia, the adopted heir of Offa of Mercia. He
fought against the Danish invasion at Hoxne in Suffolk
(870), and was defeated. Tradition claims that he was
taken captive, and when he refused to abjure his Christian
faith he was shot to death with arrows by the pagan Danes.
A miracle cult quickly sprang up, and in 903 his remains
were moved from Hoxne to Bury St Edmunds. Feast day 20
November. >> Offa

Edmund, St, originally **Edmund Rich** (1170–1240) Clergyman, born in Abingdon, Oxfordshire, SC England, UK. He
studied and taught at Oxford and Paris, became famous as
a preacher, and was commissioned by the pope to preach
the Sixth Crusade throughout England (c.1227). As
Archbishop of Canterbury (1234), he became the spokesman of the national party against Henry III, defending
Church rights and speaking out against the king's continental policies. Revered for his gentleness, austerity, and
purity, he was canonized in 1247; feast day 16 November.
>> Henry III (of England)

Edrich, (William) John (1916–86) Cricketer, born in
Norfolk, E England, UK. He played in 39 Tests, and in 1938
became one of a handful of players to have scored 1000
runs before the end of May. With Compton he shared a
record third-wicket Test partnership of 370 against South
Africa at Lord's in 1947. >> Compton, Denis; RR1150

Edward I (1239–1307) King of England (1272–1307), the
elder son of Henry III and Eleanor of Provence, born in
London, England, UK. He married **Eleanor of Castile** (1254)
and later **Margaret of France**, the sister of Philip IV (1299).
In the Baron's War (1264–7), he at first supported Simon de
Montfort, but rejoined his father, and defeated de
Montfort at Evesham (1265). He then won renown as a crusader to the Holy Land, and did not return to England until
1274, two years after his father's death. In two devastating
campaigns (1276–7, 1282–3) he annexed N and W Wales,
and ensured the permanence of his conquests by building
magnificent castles. He re-asserted English claims to the
overlordship of Scotland when the line of succession
failed, and decided in favour of John Balliol (c.1250–1315)
as king (1292). But Edward's insistence on full rights of
suzerainty provoked the Scottish magnates to force Balliol
to repudiate Edward and ally with France (1295), thus
beginning the Scottish Wars of Independence. Despite
prolonged campaigning and victories such as Falkirk
(1298), he could not subdue Scotland as he had done
Wales. He died while leading his army against Robert
Bruce. >> Bruce, Robert (1274–1329); Eleanor of Castile;
Henry III; Montfort, Simon de; Wallace, Sir William;
RR1095

Edward II (1284–1327) King of England from 1307, the
fourth son of Edward I and Eleanor of Castile, born in
Caernarfon, Gwynedd, NW Wales, UK. In 1301 he was created Prince of Wales, the first English heir-apparent to bear
that title, and in 1308 married **Isabella**, the daughter of
Philip IV of France. Throughout his reign, Edward misman-
aged the barons, who sought to rid the country of royal
favourites (such as **Piers de Gaveston**) and restore their
rightful place in government. The Ordinances of 1311
restricted the royal prerogative in matters such as appointments to the king's household. Edward was humiliated by
reverses in Scotland, where he was decisively defeated by
Robert Bruce in the Battle of Bannockburn (1314). The
Ordinances were formally annulled (1322), but the king's
new favourites, the Despensers, were acquisitive and
unpopular, and earned the particular enmity of Queen
Isabella. With her lover, Roger Mortimer Earl of March
(c.1287–1330), she toppled the Despensers (1326) and
imprisoned Edward in Kenilworth Castle. He renounced
the throne in favour of his eldest son (1327), who succeeded
as Edward III, and was then murdered in Berkeley Castle,
near Gloucester. >> Bruce, Robert (1274–1329); Despenser;
Edward I; Edward III; Isabella of France; RR1095

Edward III, known as **Edward of Windsor** (1312–77) King of
England from 1327, born in Windsor, Berkshire, S England,
UK, the elder son of Edward II and Isabella of France. He
married Philippa of Hainault in 1328, and their eldest child
Edward, later called the Black Prince, was born in 1330. By
banishing Queen Isabella from court, and executing her
lover, Roger Mortimer Earl of March (c.1287–1330), he
assumed full control of the government (1330), and began
to restore the monarchy's authority and prestige. He supported the attempts of Edward Balliol (c.1250–1315) to
wrest the Scots throne from David II, and his victory at
Halidon Hill (1333) forced David to seek refuge in France
until 1341. In 1337, after Philip VI had declared Guyenne
forfeit, he revived his hereditary claim to the French crown
through Isabella, the daughter of Philip IV, thus beginning
the Hundred Years' War. Renowned for his valour and military skill, he destroyed the French navy at the Battle of
Sluys (1340), and won another major victory at Crécy
(1346). >> David II; Edward II; Edward the Black Prince;
Philip VI; Philippa of Hainault; RR1095

Edward IV (1442–83) King of England (1461–70, 1471–83), the eldest son of Richard, Duke of York, born in Rouen, France. His father claimed the throne as the lineal descendant of Edward III's third and fifth sons (respectively Lionel, Duke of Clarence, and Edmund, Duke of York), against the Lancastrian King Henry VI (the lineal descendant of Edward III's fourth son, John of Gaunt). Richard was killed at the Battle of Wakefield (1460), but Edward entered London in 1461, was recognized as king on Henry VI's deposition, and with the support of his cousin, Richard Neville, Earl of Warwick, decisively defeated the Lancastrians at Towton. He threw off his dependence on Warwick, and secretly married **Elizabeth Woodville** (1464). Warwick forced him into exile in Holland (Oct 1470), and Henry VI regained the throne. Edward returned to England (Mar 1471), was restored to kingship (11 Apr), then defeated and killed Warwick at the Battle of Barnet (14 Apr), and destroyed the remaining Lancastrian forces at Tewkesbury (4 May). Henry VI was murdered soon afterwards, and Edward remained secure for the rest of his reign. >> Henry VI; Warwick, Richard Neville; Woodville; York, Richard, 3rd Duke; RR1095

Edward V (1470–83) King of England (Apr–Jun 1483), born in London, England, UK, the son of Edward IV and Elizabeth Woodville. Shortly after his accession, he and his younger brother, Richard, Duke of York, were imprisoned in the Tower by their uncle Richard, Duke of Gloucester, who usurped the throne as Richard III. The two princes were never heard of again, and were most probably murdered (Aug 1483) on their uncle's orders. In 1674 a wooden chest containing the bones of two children was discovered in the Tower, and these were interred in Westminster Abbey as their presumed remains. >> Edward IV; Richard III; Simnel; Warbeck; RR1095

Edward VI (1537–53) King of England (1547–53), born in London, England, UK, the son of Henry VIII by his third queen, Jane Seymour. During his reign, power was first in the hands of his uncle, the Duke of Somerset, and after his execution in 1552, of John Dudley, Duke of Northumberland. Edward became a devout Protestant, and under the Protectors the English Reformation flourished. He died of tuberculosis in London, having agreed to the succession of Lady Jane Grey (overthrown after nine days by Mary I). >> Grey, Lady Jane; Henry VIII; Seymour, Jane; Simnel; Somerset, Edward Seymour; Warwick, John Dudley; RR1095

Edward VII (1841–1910) King of the United Kingdom (1901–10), born in London, England, UK, the eldest son of Queen Victoria. Educated privately, and at Edinburgh, Oxford, and Cambridge, in 1863 he married **Alexandra**, the eldest daughter of Christian IX of Denmark. They had three sons and three daughters: **Albert Victor** (1864–92), Duke of Clarence; **George** (1865–1936); **Louise** (1867–1931), Princess Royal; **Victoria** (1868–1935); **Maud** (1869–1938), who married Haaken VII of Norway; and **Alexander** (born and died 1871). As Prince of Wales, his behaviour led him into several social scandals, and the queen excluded him from affairs of state. As king, he carried out several visits to Continental capitals which strove to allay international animosities. >> Alexandra, Queen; Victoria; RR1095

Edward VIII (1894–1972) King of the United Kingdom (Jan–Dec 1936), born in Richmond, SW Greater London, England, UK, the eldest son of George V. He studied at Osborne, Dartmouth, and Oxford, joined the navy and (in World War 1) the army, travelled much, and achieved considerable popularity. He succeeded his father in 1936, but abdicated (11 Dec) in the face of opposition to his proposed marriage to **Wallis Simpson**, a commoner who had been twice divorced. He was then given the title of Duke of Windsor, and the marriage took place in France in 1937. They lived in Paris, apart from a period in the Bahamas (1940–5), where Edward was governor. He died in Paris and was buried at Windsor Castle. >> George V; Windsor, Duchess of; RR1095

Edward (Antony Richard Louis), Prince (1964–) Prince of the United Kingdom, the third son of Queen Elizabeth II. He studied at Gordonstoun School, Scotland, then spent several months as a house tutor in New Zealand at Wanganui School. After graduating from Cambridge with a degree in history, he joined the Royal Marines in 1986, but left the following year and began a career in the theatre, beginning as a production assistant with Andrew Lloyd Webber's Really Useful Theatre Company. >> Elizabeth II

Edward the Ætheling (Prince) [athuhling] (?–1057) English nobleman, the son of Edmund Ironside, and the nephew of Edward the Confessor. After Edmund's death in 1016, he was taken for safe keeping to Hungary, and married a lady of the royal house, by whom he had a son, Edgar. When it became apparent that the ascetic Edward the Confessor would never have an heir, Edward the Ætheling was recognized as the proper heir to his throne. An embassy was sent to the European mainland in 1054 to bring him back to England; but he died shortly after landing in England in 1057. >> Edmund II; Edward the Confessor; St; Margaret (of Scotland), St

Edward the Black Prince (1330–76) Prince of England, born in Woodstock, Oxfordshire, SC England, UK, the eldest son of Edward III. He was created Earl of Chester (1333), Duke of Cornwall (1337), and Prince of Wales (1343). In 1346, though still a boy, he fought at Crécy, and is said to have won his popular title (first cited in a 16th-c work) from his black armour. He won several victories in the Hundred Years' War, including Poitiers (1356). He had two sons: **Edward** (1356–70) and **Richard**, the future Richard II. In 1362 he was created Prince of Acquitane, and lived there until a revolt forced him to return to England (1371). A great soldier, he was a failure as an administrator. >> Edward III; Richard II

Edward the Confessor, St (c. 1003–66) King of England (1042–66), the elder son of Ethelred the Unready and Emma of Normandy, and the last Anglo-Saxon king before the Conquest. After living in exile in Normandy, he joined the household of his half-brother Hardicanute in 1041, then succeeded him on the throne. He married **Edith**, the only daughter of the powerful Earl Godwinson of Wessex in 1045. Until 1052 he maintained his position against the Godwin family by building up Norman favourites, and in 1051 very probably recognized Duke William of Normandy (later William I) as his heir. But the Godwins regained their ascendancy, and on his deathbed in London, Edward (who remained childless) named Harold Godwinson (Harold II) to succeed. The Norman Conquest followed soon after. Edward's reputation for holiness began in his lifetime, and he rebuilt Westminster Abbey in the Romanesque style. His cult grew in popularity, and he was canonized in 1161; feast day 13 October. >> Ethelred II; Godwin; Hardicanute; Harold II; William I (of England); RR1095

Edward the Elder (c. 870–924) King of Wessex (from 899), the elder son of Alfred the Great. He built on his father's successes and established himself as the strongest ruler in Britain. By one of the most decisive military campaigns of the whole Anglo-Saxon period, he conquered and annexed to Wessex the S Danelaw (910–18). He also assumed control of Mercia (918). Although he exercised no direct power in the North, all the chief rulers beyond the R Humber, including the King of the Scots, formally recognized his overlordship in 920. >> Alfred; RR1095

Edward the Martyr, St (c. 963–78) King of England (975–8). During his reign there was a reaction against the policies in support of monasticism espoused by his father, Edgar. He was murdered by supporters of his stepmother, Elfrida, and canonized in 1001; feast day 18 March. >> Edgar; RR1095

Edwardes, George >> **Monckton, Lionel**

Edwardes, Sir Michael (Owen) (1930–) British business executive, born in South Africa. He studied at Rhodes University, and joined the Chloride Group of companies in Africa in 1951. He first worked in Britain in 1966, as commercial director then as general manager of Chloride's smallest subsidiary, Alkaline Batteries. He developed a reputation for rescuing ailing companies, and in 1977 was challenged to rescue British Leyland from commercial collapse, which he succeeded in doing over the next five years. He was knighted in 1979.

Edwards, Eli >> **McKay, Claude**

Edwards, Gareth (Owen) (1949–) Rugby player, born in Gwaun-cae-Gurwen, Neath and Port Talbot, SC Wales, UK. With Barry John he formed a wonderful half-back partnership, but he also played full-back or centre. He was first capped for Wales while in his teens, and was appointed captain before he was 21. He won 63 caps, including 10 'B' internationals. >> John, Barry; RR1167

Edwards, Sir George (Robert) (1908–) Designer of aircraft, born in Higham's Park, E Greater London, England, UK. He studied engineering at London University, then joined the design staff of Vickers-Armstrong at Weybridge, where he was experimental manager in World War 2, becoming chief designer in 1945. Responsible for Viking, Valiant, Viscount, and Vanguard aircraft, he was managing director and later chairman of the British Aircraft Corporation. He received the US Guggenheim Award and the Royal Aeronautical Society Gold Medal.

Edwards, Jonathan (1703–58) Theologian and metaphysician, born in East Windsor, CT. He studied at Yale, was ordained in 1727, and ministered at the Congregationalist Church in Northampton, MA. He was successful for many years, but his extreme Calvinistic orthodoxy led to controversy, and he was dismissed in 1750. He then worked as a missionary with the Housatonnuck Indians until 1757, when he became president of the University College of New Jersey (later, Princeton), but died soon after his installation. His works, which include *Freedom of the Will* (1754), led to the religious revival known as the 'Great Awakening'. >> Edwards, Jonathan (1745–1801)

Edwards, Jonathan (1745–1801) Theologian, born in Northampton, MA, the son of Jonathan Edwards. He graduated from New Jersey, and became pastor at White Haven, CT (1769), Colebrook, CT (1796), and president of the new college at Schenectady, NY (1799). His works include *A Dissertation concerning Liberty and Necessity* (1797) and *On the Necessity of the Atonement* (1785). >> Edwards, Jonathan (1703–58)

Edwards, Robert >> **Steptoe, Patrick**

Edwin, St (584–633) King of Northumbria from 616, brought up in North Wales. Under him, Northumbria became united. He pushed his power W as far as Anglesey and Man, obtained the overlordship of East Anglia, and (by a victory over the West Saxons) that of all England, save Kent. He was converted to Christianity, and baptized with his nobles in 627. He fell in battle with the Mercians and Welsh at Hatfield Chase, and was afterwards canonized; feast day 12 October. >> Cadwallon; Paulinus; Penda

Egalité, Philippe >> **Orléans, Louis Philippe Joseph**

Egan, Sir John Leopold [eegn] (1939–) Industrial executive, born in Coventry, West Midlands, C England, UK. He studied at Imperial College, London, and the London Business School. In 1968 he entered the motor industry, first with General Motors, then with British Leyland and Massey Ferguson. In 1980 he became chairman and chief executive of the then ailing Jaguar company, and restored the company's high reputation in Britain and abroad. He was knighted in 1986.

Egas Moniz, António (Caetano de Abreu Freire) (1874–1955) Neurosurgeon and diplomat, born in Avença, Portugal. Professor of neurology at Coimbra (1902) and Lisbon (1911–44), he was also a deputy in the Portuguese parliament (1903–17) and foreign minister (1918), and led the Portuguese delegation to the Paris Peace Conference (1918). He is best remembered as the founder of modern psychosurgery, and he shared the 1949 Nobel Prize for Physiology or Medicine for the development of prefrontal lobotomy as a radical treatment for some mental disorders. >> RR1124

Egbert, in Anglo-Saxon **Ecgberht** or **Ecgbryht** (?–839) King of Wessex (802–39). After his victory in 825 over the Mercians at Ellendun (now Wroughton) in Wiltshire, S England, UK, the areas of Essex, Kent, Surrey, and Sussex submitted to him; but his conquest of Mercia itself (829) was soon reversed. He extended his control over Cornwall, defeating an alliance between the Vikings and Britons at Hingston Down (838). These successes gave him mastery over S England from Kent to Land's End, and established Wessex as the strongest Anglo-Saxon kingdom. >> RR1095

Egede, Hans [aygeduh], known as **the Apostle of Greenland** (1686–1758) Missionary, born in Norway. He was a pastor in the Lofoten Is (1707–17), and in 1721 founded the first mission in Greenland. He then returned to Copenhagen, where he founded a seminary for training missionaries to Greenland and was appointed bishop (1740). He published the first book written in the Eskimo language (1742).

Egerton, Francis, 3rd Duke of Bridgewater [ejuh(r)tn] (1736–1803) British canal builder, known as 'the father of British inland navigation'. Faced with the problem of transporting the Manchester coal mined on his estate at Worsley, a distance of 16 km/10 ml, he engaged James Brindley to construct (1759–61) a canal which proved to be highly successful. In 1776 he extended it to reach Liverpool, a total distance of 64 km/40 mi. The earliest canal in England, it became known as the Bridgewater Canal. >> Brindley

Ehrenberg, Christian Gottfried [airenberg] (1795–1876) Naturalist, born in Delitzsch, Germany. Professor at Berlin from 1839, he travelled in Egypt, Syria, Arabia, and C Asia. His works on microscopic organisms founded a new branch of science, and he discovered that phosphorescence in the sea is caused by living organisms.

Ehrenburg, Ilya Grigoryevich [airenberg] (1891–1967) Writer, born in Kiev, Ukraine. He worked for many years in Paris as a journalist, returning at intervals to the USSR. He wrote poetry, short stories, travel books, essays, and several novels, notably *Padeniye Parizha* (1941, The Fall of Paris) and *Burya* (1948, The Storm), both of which won Stalin Prizes.

Ehrenreich, Barbara [airenriyk] (1941–) Sociologist and writer, born in Butte, MT. An independent writer, she became known for her outspoken feminist–socialist analyses of contemporary issues, particularly health and the politics of sex and class. Her books include *For Her Own Good* (co-authored, 1978) and *The Worst Years of Our Lives* (1990). In 1983 she became co-chair of the Democratic Socialists of America.

Ehrlich, Paul [airleekh] (1854–1915) Bacteriologist, born of Jewish family in Strzelin, Poland. After studying at Leipzig, he carried out research at Berlin, becoming a pioneer in haematology, immunology, and chemotherapy. He discovered a cure for syphilis (Salvarsan), and propounded the side-chain theory in immunology. He shared the 1908 Nobel Prize for Physiology or Medicine. >> RR1124

Ehrlich, Paul Ralph [airlik] (1932–) Entomologist and ecologist, born in Philadelphia, PA. An entomologist at the University of Kansas (1953–9), he made major contributions to field research on Arctic insects and parasitic mites, then in 1959 moved to Stanford, where he performed extensive studies of butterflies. He became a crusader for the human conservation of natural resources following a 1966 trip to India, which made him aware of the ecological effects of poverty and overpopulation. His best-selling book, *The Population Bomb* (1968), predicted worldwide famine and advocated the concept of zero population growth. He became professor of population studies at Stanford in 1976, won Sweden's Crafoord Prize in 1990, and became a MacArthur Fellow for his work in population biology and the conservation of biological diversity. His wife, **Anne** (1933–), contributes to his work, and is a director of Friends of the Earth.

Eichmann, (Karl) Adolf [iykhman] (1906–62) Nazi war criminal, born in Solingen, Germany. He became a member of the SS in 1932, and organizer of anti-Semitic activities. Captured by US forces in 1945, he escaped from prison some months later, having kept his identity hidden, and in 1950 reached Argentina. He was traced by Israeli agents, taken to Israel in 1960, condemned, and executed. >> Wiesenthal

Eiffel, (Alexandre) Gustave [efel] (1832–1923) Civil engineer, born in Dijon, France. He designed several notable bridges and viaducts, before working on his most famous project, the *Eiffel Tower*. He also designed the steel framework of the Statue of Liberty, NY, and built the first aerodynamics laboratory, near Paris.

Eigen, Manfred [iygen] (1927–) Physical chemist, born in Bochum, Germany. He studied in Göttingen, and directed the Max Planck Institute for Physical Chemistry there from 1964. He developed methods for the study of very fast chemical reactions, and for this work shared the 1967 Nobel Prize for Chemistry. >> RR1123

Eijkman, Christiaan [iykman] (1858–1930) Physician and pathologist, born in Nijkerk, The Netherlands. He studied at Amsterdam, and became professor of public health and forensic medicine at Utrecht (1898–1928). Investigating the disease beriberi in Java, his observations of dietary deficiency led to the discovery of vitamins. He shared the 1929 Nobel Prize for Physiology or Medicine. >> RR1124

Einem, Gottfried von [iynem] (1917– 96) Composer, born in Bern. His most successful works have been for the stage, including several ballets and the operas *Dantons Tod* (1947, Danton's Death) and *Der Besuch der alten Dame* (1971, The Visit of the Old Woman). He also wrote orchestral, choral and chamber music, concertos, and many songs.

Einstein, Albert see panel on p. 302

Einstein, Alfred [iynstiyn] (1880–1952) Musicologist, born in Munich, Germany. In 1933 he fled the Nazi régime and went to live in Florence and London. He collaborated in several well-known musical reference books, including *Eaglefield's Dictionary of Modern Music*, but is perhaps best remembered for his work on Mozart, especially the revision of Köchel's catalogue. He was a cousin of the physicist Albert Einstein. His posthumous *Essays on Music* were published in 1958. >> Einstein, Albert; Köchel

Einthoven, Willem [aynthohfn] (1860–1927) Dutch physiologist, born in Semarang, Indonesia. He studied at Utrecht, and became professor of physiology at Leyden in 1886. He invented the string galvanometer for measuring the electrical rhythms of the heart, and introduced the term *electrocardiogram*. He was awarded the Nobel Prize for Physiology or Medicine in 1924.

Eisenhower, Dwight D(avid) [iyznhower], nickname **Ike** (1890–1969) US general and 34th president (1953–61), born in Denison, TX. He trained at West Point, and by 1939 had become chief military assistant to General MacArthur in the Philippines. In 1942 he commanded Allied forces for the amphibious descent on French N Africa. His greatest contribution to the war effort was his talent for the smooth co-ordination of Allied staff, and this led to his selection as Supreme Commander for the 1944 cross-channel invasion of the continental mainland, which he resolutely launched despite capricious weather conditions. In 1950 he was made the Supreme Commander of the Combined Land Forces in Nato, and in 1952 the popularity which he had gained in Europe swept him to victory in the presidential elections, standing as a Republican, and he was re-elected in 1956. During his presidency the US government was preoccupied with foreign policy, and pursued a campaign against Communism, but was also actively involved in the civil rights movement. >> RR1097

Eisenstaedt, Alfred [iyznstat] (1898–95) Photojournalist, born in Dirschau, Germany (now Tczew, Poland). He started freelancing as a photojournalist in the 1920s, and emigrated to the USA in 1935, where he became one of the original photographers working on *Life* (1936–72). Voted Photographer of the Year in 1951, his worldwide assignments and telling photo essays made him one of the outstanding practitioners of the century. His publications include *Witness to Our Time* (1966), *The Eye of Eisenstaedt* (1969), and *Photojournalism* (1971).

Eisenstein, Sergey (Mikhaylovich) [iyznstiyn] (1898–1948) Film director, born in Riga, Latvia. He launched into films from theatrical scene painting, and became a major influence on the development of the cinema. His films are noticeable for the substitution of the group or crowd for the traditional hero, and for his skilful cutting and recutting to achieve mounting Impressionistic effects, as in the Odessa steps sequence of *Potemkin* (1925). Later films included *Alexander Nevski* (1938) and *Ivan the Terrible*, parts I (1945), II (1946), and III (1947).

Eisler, Hanns [iysler] (1898–1962) Composer, born in Leipzig, Germany. He studied under Schoenberg at the Vienna Conservatory (1919–23). A committed Marxist, he wrote political songs, choruses, and theatre music, often in collaboration with Brecht. From 1933 he worked in Paris, London, and Copenhagen, and moved to Hollywood in 1938, teaching and writing film music. Denounced in the McCarthy anti-Communist trials, he returned to Europe in 1948. He settled in East Germany in 1952, composing popular songs and organizing workers' choirs. He wrote about 600 songs and choruses, and music for over 40 films and for nearly 40 plays. >> Brecht; McCarthy, Joseph R; Schoenberg

Eisner, Will, popular name of **William Erwin Eisner** (1917–) Comic-book artist and writer, born in New York City. After studying at the Art Students League, he became staff artist on the *New York American*. In 1937 he set up the first 'shop' for mass-producing strips for *Wags*, in which he developed *The Flame* into the long-running weekly serial *Hawks of the Seas*. In 1940 he produced the first comic-book insert for Sunday newspapers, starring his own character, *The Spirit*.

Ekelöf, (Bengt) Gunnar [ekeloef] (1907–68) Poet, born in Stockholm. He was considered one of the most significant Swedish poets of this century. Much influenced by the French Symbolists, he published his first book of poetry, *Sent på Jorden* (trans Late Arrival on Earth), in 1932. *En Mölna-elegi* (1960, A Mölna Elegy) was translated into

ALBERT ENSTEIN (1879–1955)

Einstein was born into a Jewish family at Ulm, Germany. He was moved to Munich the following year, where his father Hermann and his uncle Jakob opened a small electrical and engineering works. His mother, Paulina Koch, encouraged him to study music during his youth, and he became an accomplished violinist, but it was Jakob who inspired his fascination for mathematics. Initially an unremarkable student, he was educated at Munich and Aarau, eventually going on to graduate in physics and mathematics from the Federal Polytechnic University in Zürich in 1900. He became a Swiss citizen in 1905, and was appointed examiner at the Swiss Patent Office (1902–9).

He married fellow-student **Mileva Marić** in 1903, and they had two sons, Hans Albert and Edward (who later had a mental breakdown). However, the outbreak of World War 1 caused him to be separated from his family – he was in Berlin while they were in Switzerland. They were divorced in 1919. A gifted physicist in her own right, Mileva and Albert would work together on the mathematics of his theoretical thinking. In recognition of this he later gave her the money that came with his Nobel Prize. She gave up physics to look after their son Edward. A second marriage, to **Elsa**, his first cousin (d.1936), took place in 1919.

From 1905 Einstein published papers on theoretical physics in the prestigious monthly *Annalen der Physik*, including his special theory of relativity, which in its embryonic form was an essay he had written aged 16. Entitled 'Zur Elektrodynamik bewegter Körper' (On the Electrodynamics of Moving Bodies), the theory showed that in the case of rapid relative motion involving velocities approaching the speed of light, puzzling phenomena such as decreased size and mass are to be expected. This provided a new system of mechanics which accommodated James Clerk Maxwell's electromagnetic-field theory, as well as the hitherto inexplicable results of the Michelson–Morley experiments (1881, 1887) on the speed of light. He was professor at the universities of Zürich (1909), and Prague (1911), at Zürich Polytechnic (1912), then worked in Berlin, where he was director of the Kaiser Wilhelm Physical Institute (1914–33). On accepting the post in Berlin, he reassumed his German citizenship, relinquishing it again in 1933.

'Die Grundlagen der allgemeinen Relativitätstheorie' (The Foundation of the General Theory of Relativity) was published in 1916. This theory accounted for the slow rotation of the elliptical path of the planet Mercury, which Newtonian gravitational theory failed to do. Fame and recognition came suddenly in 1919, when the Royal Society of London photographed the solar eclipse and publicly verified Einstein's general theory of relativity. In 1921 he was awarded the Nobel Prize for Physics for his photoelectric law and work in the field of theoretical physics, but such was the controversy still aroused by his theories on relativity that these were not specified in the text of the award.

Einstein was regarded suspiciously in Berlin for his outspoken pacifism and socialism, and also for his Jewish background. He was a supporter of Zionism, publishing *About Zionism* (Uber Zionismus) in 1931. After Hitler's rise to power, he was deprived of his post at Berlin and his home at Caputh. He left Germany, and from 1934 lectured at the Institute of Advanced Study, Princeton, NJ, took US citizenship, and became professor at Princeton in 1940.

From the 1930s he was increasingly outspoken in support of world peace. In 1933 he joined with Sigmund Freud to write *Warum Krieg* (Why War?). However, when it was brought to his attention by German chemists that the splitting of uranium atoms could result in a mammoth explosion, he carried out experiments at Princeton verifying this possibility, and was persuaded in September 1939 to write to President Roosevelt warning him of the possibility that Germany would try to make an atomic bomb. Despite his pacifism, Einstein felt that force should be used to prevent this happening, and in this way he helped to initiate the Manhattan Project (research work led by Robert Oppenheimer into the creation of the atomic bombs dropped on Hiroshima and Nagasaki), although he was not directly involved in it himself.

After the war, Einstein urged international control of atomic weapons, and protested against the proceedings of the un-American Activities Senate Subcommittee, which had arraigned many scientists. In 1952 he was offered the presidency of Israel, but declined. He spent the rest of his life trying, by means of his unified field theory (1950), to establish a merger between quantum theory and his general theory of relativity, thus bringing subatomic phenomena and large-scale physical phenomena under one set of determinate laws. His attempt was not successful. After many years of struggle with deteriorating health, he died in his sleep in hospital at Princeton.

Einstein ranks with Galileo and Newton as one of the great conceptual revisors of our understanding of the universe. He was the originator of completely new ways of looking at space, time, and gravitational forces, as well as being a champion of pacifism and liberalism, and the 'grand old man' of world peace.

>> Freud, Sigmund; Maxwell, James Clerk; Newton, Isaac

English, as were his *Selected poems* (1966) and *Guide to the Underworld* (1967).

Ekman, Vagn Walfrid (1874–1954) Oceanographer, born in Stockholm. He began making contributions to oceanography while still a student at Uppsala University, with a report (1902) explaining why drift ice movement diverged from wind direction. After working at the International Laboratory for Oceanographic Research in Oslo (1902–8), he was appointed professor of mathematical physics at Lund (1910–39). He designed several instruments for investigating ocean currents, and his name is remembered in the common oceanographic terms *Ekman layer* and *Ekman spiral*.

El Cid >> **Cid, El**

Elder, Sir Thomas (1818–97) Entrepreneur, born in Kirkcaldy, Fife, E Scotland, UK. He emigrated to Adelaide, South Australia, in 1854. With his brother he financed copper mines in South Australia, then in partnership with Robert Barr Smith founded the firm of Elder, Smith & Co in 1863. This grew into one of the world's largest woolbroking firms, building up extensive pastoral holdings to maintain the supply of wool, stretching into Western Australia and Queensland. He brought in camels to provide efficient transport in the outback, which proved invaluable for some of the early expeditions into the 'centre' made by Warburton, Ross, Giles, and Lewis, all of whose expeditions were financed by Elder. The company he helped establish is perpetuated in the international brewing and resources group, Elders IXL. >> Barr Smith; Giles, William; Warburton

Eldershaw, Flora M Barnard >> **Barnard, Marjorie Faith**

Eldridge, Roy (David), nickname **Little Jazz** (1911–89) Trumpet player, born in Pittsburgh, PA. A passionate improviser, able to play with ease in the ultra-high register, he was in demand as a featured soloist with top bands of the 1930s, such as McKinney's Cotton Pickers and the Teddy Hill and Fletcher Henderson Orchestras. He continued to perform until suffering a stroke in 1980. >> Henderson, Fletcher

Eleanor of Aquitaine (c. 1122–1204) Queen consort of Louis VII of France (1137–52) and, after the annulment of this marriage, of Henry II of England (1154–89). She was imprisoned (1174–89) for supporting the rebellion of her sons, two of whom became kings as Richard I (in 1189) and John (1199). >> Henry II (of England)

Eleanor of Castile [kasteel] (1246–90) Queen consort of Edward I of England (1254–90), the daughter of Ferdinand III. She accompanied Edward to the Crusades, and is said to have saved his life by sucking the poison from a wound. She died at Harby, Nottinghamshire, and the *Eleanor Crosses* at Northampton, Geddington, and Waltham Cross are the survivors of the 12 erected by Edward at the halting places of her cortège. The last stopping place was Charing Cross, London, where a replica now stands. >> Edward I

Eleanor of Provence [provãs] (1223–91) Queen consort of Henry III of England (1236–72), the daughter of Raymond Berengar IV, Count of Provence. In the Barons' War of 1264 she raised an army of mercenaries in France to support her husband, but her invasion fleet was wrecked. After the accession of her son, Edward I, in 1272 she retired to a convent. >> Edward I; Henry III

Eleonora of Arborea [elionawra, ah(r)bawria] (c. 1350–1404) Sardinian ruler, regarded as the national heroine of Sardinia, the daughter of a district chieftain (*giudice*). In 1383 she defeated an incursion from Aragon, and became regent of Arborea for her infant son, **Frederick**. In 1395 she introduced a humanitarian code of laws, *Carta di logu*, which was far ahead of its time. Her statue stands in the Piazza Eleonora in Oristano. She gave special protection to hawks and falcons, and *Eleonora's falcon* is named after her.

Elgar, Sir Edward (1857–1934) Composer, born in Broad Heath, Hereford and Worcester, WC England, UK. He was largely self-taught, and in his youth worked as a violinist before becoming conductor of the Worcester Glee Club and the County Asylum Band, and organist of St George's Roman Catholic Church, Worcester. After his marriage to **Caroline Alice Roberts** (1889) he went to London, but in 1891 settled in Malvern, devoting himself to composition. The *Enigma Variations* (1899) and the oratorio *The Dream of Gerontius* (1900) made him the leading figure in English music. After the Elgar Festival (London, 1904) he was knighted. His further works included oratorios, symphonies, concertos, and incidental music. From 1924 he was Master of the King's Musick.

Elgin, Thomas Bruce, 7th Earl of Elgin and 11th Earl of Kincardine [elgin] (1766–1841) British diplomat and art connoisseur. While ambassador to the Ottoman sultan (1799–1803) he became interested in the decorated sculptures on the ruined Parthenon at Athens, and, because they were in danger of wilful damage and destruction, arranged for some of them to be transported to England. This action brought criticism and accusation of vandalism, but the earl was vindicated by a government committee, and the *Elgin Marbles* were purchased for the nation in 1816 and ultimately placed in the British Museum.

Elia >> **Lamb, Charles**

Eliade, Mirca [elyad] (1907–86) Historian and philosopher of comparative religion, born in Bucharest, Romania. He was a student of Indian philosophy and Sanskrit at Calcutta University (1928–31) before becoming a lecturer in the history of religion and metaphysics at Bucharest (1933–9). He served in the diplomatic service during World War 2, and later taught at the Sorbonne (1946–8) and Chicago University (1957–85). A pioneer in the systematic study of world religions, he published numerous books and papers.

Elijah [eliyja] (9th-c BC) (9th-c BC) Hebrew prophet, whose activities are portrayed in four Bible stories (1 *Kings* 17-19, 21; 2 *Kings* 1-2). He was prominent in opposing the worship of Baal in Israel under King Ahab and Jezebel, and by virtue of his loyalty to God was depicted as ascending directly into heaven. >> Ahab; Jezebel

Elion, Gertrude (Belle) (1918–   ) Chemist, born in New York City. She graduated from Hunter College, New York (1937) and New York University (1941), then joined the Burroughs Wellcome laboratory (1944). In 1951, working with George Hitchings, she made and tested 6-mercaptopurine (6MP) which proved useful in cancer treatment, especially childhood leukaemia. Other work included drugs for the treatment of malaria, gout, viral herpes, and auto-immune disorders. In 1988 they shared, with James Black, the Nobel Prize for Physiology or Medicine, and in 1991 she was awarded the US National Medal of Science. >> Black, James; Hitchings

Eliot, Charles William (1834–1926) Educationist, born in Boston, MA. Trained as a mathematician and chemist at Harvard and in Europe, he taught at Harvard and the Massachusetts Institute of Technology before assuming the presidency of Harvard (1869–1909). Having signalled his progressivism in *The New Education* (1869), he presided over a period of intense growth and reform at Harvard, which included the admission of women (1879) and the establishment of Radcliffe College (1894). His landmark report (1892) on secondary schools led to the standardization of public school curricula and the formation in 1901 of the Board of College Entrance Examinations. In later years he became widely known as the editor of the Harvard Classics, a set of significant books that were said to provide a complete education in 'a five-foot shelf'.

Eliot, George, pseudonym of **Mary Ann Evans** or **Marian Evans** (1819–80) Novelist, born at Arbury Farm, Astley, Warwickshire, C England, UK. She took charge of the family household when her mother died (1836), and was taught at home. After the death of her father (1849) she travelled abroad, then settled in London, and began to write for the *Westminster Review*. She became assistant editor, and the centre of a literary circle, one of whose members was G H Lewes, with whom she lived until his death. Her first story appeared in 1857. Her major novels were *Adam Bede* (1859), *The Mill on the Floss* (1860), *Silas Marner* (1861), *Middlemarch* (1871–2), and *Daniel Deronda* (1876). After Lewes's death (1878), she married an old friend, **John Cross**, in 1880, but died soon after. >> Lewes

Eliot, Sir John (1592–1632) English statesman, born in Port Eliot, Cornwall, SW England, UK. He entered parliament in 1614, was knighted in 1618, and appointed vice-admiral of Devon in 1619. Formerly a follower of Buckingham, he broke with him in 1625, and was largely instrumental in securing his impeachment. In 1628 Eliot denounced arbitrary taxation and helped to force the Petition of Right from Charles I. After further protests against the king, he was sent with eight others to the Tower, where he was kept in confinement until his death, from consumption. >> Buckingham; Charles I (of England)

Eliot, John, known as **the Apostle to the Indians** (1604–90) Missionary, born in Widford, Hertfordshire, SE England, UK. He studied at Cambridge, took orders, left England on religious grounds and settled in Roxbury, MA, where he served as pastor. In 1646 he began to preach to the Indians at Nonantum nearby, and translated the Bible into their language (1661–3) – the first Bible printed in America. His book *The Christian Commonwealth* (1659) was suppressed for its republican sentiments.

Eliot, Sir Thomas >> **Elyot, Thomas**

Eliot, T(homas) S(tearns) (1888–1965) Poet, critic, and playwright, born in St Louis, MO. He studied at Harvard and Paris, then obtained a travelling scholarship to Oxford, and was persuaded to stay in England by Ezra Pound, to whom he had shown his poems. His marriage (1915) to **Vivian Haigh Wood** settled him in England. He worked as a teacher and in a bank before becoming a director of Faber publishers. The enthusiastic support of Pound led to his first book of poetry, *Prufrock and Other Observations* (1917), and he was introduced by Bertrand Russell into the Bloomsbury Circle. He then published *The Waste Land* (1922) and *The Hollow Men* (1925), and edited the quarterly review, *The Criterion*, from its beginning to its demise (1922–39). In 1927 he became a British subject, and was baptized and confirmed, adhering to the Anglo-Catholic movement within the Church of England. There followed several other works, including his major poetic achievement, *Four Quartets* (1944), and a series of plays, notably *Murder in the Cathedral* (1935) and *The Cocktail Party* (1950). His first wife died in 1947 after a long mental illness, and in 1957 he married **Valerie Fletcher**. He also wrote much literary and social criticism, dealing with individual authors as well as general themes, wherein he could be highly provocative. In 1948 he was awarded the Nobel Prize for Literature. >> Moore G E; Pound, Ezra; Russell, Bertrand

Elisha [eliysha] (second half of 9th-c BC) Hebrew prophet in succession to Elijah; his activities are portrayed in 1 *Kings* 19 and 2 *Kings* 2. He was active in Israel under several kings from Ahab to Jehoash, was credited with miraculous signs, counselled kings, and attempted to guide the nation against her external enemies, especially the Syrians.

Elizabeth I, known as **the Virgin Queen** and later **Good Queen Bess** see panel on p. 305

Elizabeth II (1926–) Queen of the United Kingdom (1952–) and head of the Commonwealth, born in London, England, UK, the daughter of George VI. Formerly Princess Elizabeth Alexandra Mary, she was proclaimed queen on 6 February 1952, and crowned on 2 June 1953. Her husband was created Duke of Edinburgh on the eve of their wedding (20 Nov 1947), and styled Prince Philip in 1957. They have three sons, **Charles Philip Arthur George** (14 Nov 1948), **Andrew Albert Christian Edward** (19 Feb 1960), and **Edward Anthony Richard Louis** (10 Mar 1964), and a daughter **Anne Elizabeth Alice Louise** (15 Aug 1950). >> Andrew, Duke of York; Anne, Princess; Charles, Prince; Edinburgh, Duke of; Edward, Prince; George VI; RR1095

Elizabeth (of Bohemia) (1596–1662) Queen of Bohemia, the eldest daughter of James I (of England) and Anne of Denmark. She married **Frederick V**, Elector Palatine, in 1613. Driven from Prague and deprived of the Palatinate by Maximilian of Bavaria, the couple lived in exile in The Hague with their numerous children, continually beset by financial difficulties. Frederick died in 1632, but Elizabeth

outlived him by 30 years. Her son, **Charles Louis**, was restored to the Palatinate in 1648, but his mother remained in Holland. She died in London in 1662 while on a visit to her nephew, the newly-restored Charles II of England. >> James I (of England)

Elizabeth (Queen Mother), originally **Lady Elizabeth Bowes-Lyon** (1900–) Queen-consort of Great Britain, born in St Paul's Walden Bury, Hertfordshire, SE England, UK. Her father became 14th Earl of Strathmore in 1904. Much of her childhood was spent at Glamis Castle in Scotland, where she helped the nursing staff in World War 1. In 1920 she met the **Duke of York**, the second son of George V; they were married in April 1923. **Princess Elizabeth** (later Queen Elizabeth II) was born in 1926 and **Princess Margaret** in 1930. After her husband came to the throne as King George VI in 1936, she scored striking personal success in royal visits to Paris (1938) and to Canada and the USA (1939). She was with the king when Buckingham Palace was bombed in 1940, travelling with him to visit heavily damaged towns throughout the war. After George VI's death (1952), the Queen Mother continued to undertake public duties, flying thousands of miles each year and becoming a widely loved figure. In 1978 she became Lord Warden of the Cinque Ports, the first woman to hold the office. >> Elizabeth II; George VI; Margaret, Princess

Elizabeth, St (1207–31) Hungarian princess, born in Presburg, Hungary, the daughter of Andreas II. At the age of four she was betrothed to **Louis IV, Landgrave of Thuringia**, whom she married in 1221. Louis died on his way to the Sixth Crusade in 1227, whereupon Elizabeth was deprived of her regency by her husband's brother. She renounced wealth, and devoted the rest of her life to the service of the poor, building a hospice at Marburg. She was canonized by Pope Gregory IX in 1235; feast day 17 November.

Elizabeth (of Romania) >> **Carmen Sylva**

Elizabeth (of York) >> **Henry VII**

Elizabeth Petrovna [petrovna] (1709–62) Empress (tsaritsa) of Russia (1741–62), the daughter of Peter the Great and Catherine I, born in Kolomenskoye, near Moscow. She was passed over for the succession in 1727, 1730, and 1740, but finally became empress on the deposition of Ivan VI. She was guided by favourites throughout her reign. A war with Sweden was brought to a successful conclusion, and her animosity towards Frederick the Great led her to take part in the War of the Austrian Succession and in the Seven Years' War. >> Frederick II; Peter I (of Russia); RR1085

Elkin, Stanley (Lawrence) (1930–95) Writer and academic, born in New York City. He studied at the University of Illinois. He is pre-eminently a novelist, though he has also written short stories and novellas. *Boswell* (1964) marked his debut, with later works including *The Living End* (1979), *George Mills* (1982), and *The Magic Kingdom* (1985).

Elkington, George Richards (1801–65) British inventor and manufacturer. Based in Birmingham from 1832, he introduced electroplating, in association with his cousin, **Henry Elkington** (1810–52).

Ellery, William (1727–1820) US statesman, born in Newport, RI. He sat in the Congress of 1776, and was a signatory of the Declaration of Independence.

Ellet, Charles, known as **the Brunel of America** (1810–62) Civil engineer, born in Penn's Manor, PA. He studied bridge engineering in Paris, returning in 1832 to the USA. He built the first wire suspension bridges in America, including one over the Schuylkill R at Fairmount (1842) and another over the Ohio R at Wheeling (1849). He also constructed the James River and Kanawha Canal. During the Civil War he advocated and demonstrated the use of

ELIZABETH I (1533–1603)

Queen of England and Ireland (1558–1603), Elizabeth was born at Greenwich Palace, the daughter of Henry VIII and his second wife Anne Boleyn, who was later beheaded. When her father married his third wife, Jane Seymour, in 1536, Elizabeth and her elder half-sister Mary Tudor (the future Mary I) were declared illegitimate by parliament in favour of Jane Seymour's son, the future Edward VI. Elizabeth's childhood was precarious – she suffered her mother's execution, and her father's dislike – but she was well-educated and, unlike her sister, was brought up in the Protestant faith. During the reign of Edward VI (1547–53) when she was 16, Thomas Seymour, Lord High Admiral of England, plotted to marry her and overthrow the government, but Elizabeth evaded his advances and he was subsequently executed for treason. During the reign of Mary I (1553–8), her identification with Protestantism aroused the suspicions of her Catholic sister, and she was imprisoned in the Tower of London.

Her accession to the throne in 1558 on Mary's death was greeted with general approval, in the hope of religious tolerance after the persecutions of the preceding reigns. Under the able guidance of Sir William Cecil (later Lord Burghley) as secretary of state, Mary's Catholic legislation was repealed, and the Church of England fully established (1559–63). Cecil also gave support to the Reformation in Scotland, where Mary, Queen of Scots, had returned in 1561 to face conflict with the Calvinist reformers led by John Knox.

Imprisoned and forced to abdicate in 1567, Mary, Queen of Scots, escaped to England, where she was placed in confinement and soon became a focus for Catholic resistance to Elizabeth. In 1570 the papal bull, *Regnans in excelsis*, pronounced Elizabeth's excommunication and absolved her Catholic subjects from allegiance to her. Government retribution against English Catholics, at first restrained, became more repressive in the 1580s. Several plots against the queen were exposed, and the connivance of Mary in yet another plot in 1586 (the Babington conspiracy) led to her execution at Fotheringay Castle in 1587. The harsher policy against Roman Catholics, England's support for the Dutch rebellion against Spain, and the licensed piracy of such men as John Hawkyns and

Francis Drake against Spanish possessions in the New World, all combined to provoke an attempted Spanish invasion in 1588. The Great Armada launched by Philip II of Spain, reached the English Channel, only to be dispersed by storms and English harassment, and limped back to Spain after suffering considerable losses.

For the remainder of her reign, Elizabeth continued her policy of strengthening Protestant allies and dividing her enemies. She allowed marriage negotiations with various foreign suitors, but with no real intention of getting married or of settling the line of succession. With the death of Mary, Queen of Scots, she was content to know that the heir apparent, James VI of Scotland, was a Protestant. She indulged in romances with such court favourites as Robert Dudley, Earl of Leicester, and later with Robert Devereux, Earl of Essex, until his rebelliousness led to his execution in 1601.

Elizabeth's fiscal policies caused growing resentment, with escalating taxation to meet the costs of foreign military expeditions. Famine in the 1590s brought severe economic depression and social unrest, only partly alleviated by the Poor Law of 1597, which charged parishes with providing for the needy. England's vaunted sea-power stimulated voyages of discovery, with Drake circumnavigating the known world in 1577, and Sir Walter Raleigh mounting a number of expeditions to the North American coast in the 1580s. But England's only real Elizabethan colony was Ireland, where opportunities for English settlers to enrich themselves at the expense of the native Irish were now exploited more ruthlessly than ever before, and provoked a serious rebellion under Hugh O'Neill, Earl of Tyrone, in 1597.

At Elizabeth's death in March 1603, the Tudor dynasty came to an end, and the throne passed peacefully to the Stuart king, James VI of Scotland as James I of England. Her long reign had coincided with the emergence of England as a world power and the flowering of the English Renaissance. The legend of the 'Virgin Queen,' assiduously promoted by the queen herself and her court poets and playwrights, outlived her to play a crucial part in shaping the English national consciousness.

>> Cecil, William; Drake; Essex, 2nd Earl of; Hawkyns; Leicester, Earl of; Mary I, Tudor; Mary, Queen of Scots; Philip II (of Spain); Raleigh; Seymour, Thomas

---

ram-boats, built and commanded a fleet of them on the Mississippi, and captured Memphis (1862), but was killed in action.

Ellicott, Charles John (1819–1905) British clergyman and scholar. He was professor of divinity at King's College, London, (1858), Cambridge (1860), Bishop of Gloucester and Bristol (1863–97), Bishop of Gloucester alone from 1897, and chairman for 11 years of the New Testament Revision Committee.

Ellington, Duke, popular name of **Edward Kennedy Ellington** (1899–1974) Composer, arranger, bandleader, and pianist, born in Washington, DC. He was an itinerant piano player in dance bands in Washington and New York City until 1924, when he became leader of the house band at the Kentucky Club and then (1927–32) at the Cotton Club. He developed a unique sound for his musicians by blending instruments ingeniously into startling har-

monies. Among his early successes were 'Black and Tan Fantasy' (1927), 'Creole Love Call' (1927), and 'Mood Indigo' (1930). After a European tour in 1933, he worked on extended concert pieces, beginning with 'Reminiscing in Tempo' (1935), and initiated a series of annual concerts at Carnegie Hall (1943–50). His creative peak is generally said to be 1939–42, with such recordings as 'Warm Valley', 'Cotton Tail', and 'Take the A Train'. Later works included suites such as 'Such Sweet Thunder' (1957) and 'Gutelas Suite' (1971), film scores, ballets, and a series of 'sacred concerts' (1968–74) performed in cathedrals around the world. >> Hodges

Elliott, Denholm (1922–92) Actor, born in London, England, UK. He studied at the Royal Academy of Dramatic Art, London, prior to service in the RAF during World War 2, when he spent three years in a prisoner-of-war camp. A prolific performer in all media, and an inveterate scene-stealer, he won awards for both stage and screen, including British Film Awards for *Trading Places* (1983), *A Private Function* (1984), and *Defence of the Realm* (1985), and an Oscar nomination for *A Room with a View* (1986).

Elliott, Herb, popular name of **Herbert James Elliott** (1938–) Athlete, born in Perth, Western Australia. Winner of the gold medal in the 1500 m at the 1960 Olympics in Rome, his time of 3 min 35·6 s for that event was unbeaten for seven years. He was never beaten on level terms over a mile or 1500 m, and he ran the sub-4-minute mile 17 times. He was noted for the rigour and severity of his training schedule. >> Cerutty

Elliott, John Dorman (1941–) Businessman, born in Melbourne, Victoria, Australia. He studied at Melbourne University, and in 1972 formed a consortium to acquire Henry Jones (IXL) Ltd. A series of mergers and takeovers followed, first with Elder, Smith & Co, then with Carlton and United Brewers, to form Elders IXL, later Foster's Brewing Group. He was managing director from 1981, then chairman and chief executive (1985–90) and deputy chairman (1990–2). He was president of the Liberal Party of Australia (1987–90), and rumours of his entry into politics have been constant. He became known as 'the last of the beer barons' when he was faced with bankruptcy proceedings in 1992.

Ellis, Sir Albert (1869–1951) Businessman, born in Roma, Queensland, Australia. In 1900 he discovered immense quantities of high-grade phosphate rock on the Pacific islands of Nauru and Banaba (Ocean I). His subsequent career was concerned with the mining of these resources. In the 1970s (Banaba) and 1980s (Nauru), indigenous demands for rehabilitation of the devasted islands led to major legal actions. He was knighted in 1938.

Ellis, Alexander John, original surname **Sharpe** (1814–90) British philologist. He studied at Cambridge, wrote much on mathematical, musical, and philological questions, and did more than any other scholar to advance the scientific study of phonetics, of early English pronunciation, and of existing English dialects. His major work was *Early English Pronunciation* (1869–89).

Ellis, Alice Thomas, originally **Anna Margaret Haycraft**, née **Lindholm** (1932–) Novelist, born in Liverpool, Merseyside, NW England, UK. She studied at the Liverpool College of Art. A writer of cookery books under her original name, it was *The Sin Eater* (1977), which established her reputation as a novelist. *The 27th Kingdom* (1982) is often considered her most successful novel. Other books include *Pillars of Gold* (1992), *Cat Among the Pigeons* (1994), *Fairy Tale* (1996), and an autobiography, *A Welsh Childhood* (1990).

Ellis, (Henry) Havelock (1859–1939) Physician and writer on sex, born in Croydon, S Greater London, England, UK. He travelled widely in Australia and South America before studying medicine in London. His interest in human biology and his personal experiences led him to compile the seven-volume *Studies in the Psychology of Sex* (1897–1928), the first detached treatment of the subject, which was highly controversial at the time.

Ellis, Ruth (1926–55) Convicted murderer, born in Rhyl, Denbighshire, NE Wales, UK. A night-club hostess, in a jealous rage she repeatedly shot her former lover, David Blakely, a motor-racing driver, outside a Hampstead pub (10 Apr 1955). The case achieved notoriety as a 'crime passionnel' – Blakely was trying to extricate himself from their tempestuous, often violent, relationship at the time of his murder. Ellis was the last woman to receive the death penalty in Britain, and was hanged on 13 July 1955.

Ellis, William Webb (1805–72) British sportsman, and reputedly the inventor of rugby football. According to a rather doubtful tradition, he was a pupil at Rugby School in 1823 when he broke the rules by picking up and running

with the ball during a game of association football, thus inspiring the new game of rugby. >> RR1167

Ellison, Ralph (Waldo) (1914–94) Writer, born in Oklahoma City, OK. He studied as a musician at the Tuskegee Institute, AL, then joined the Federal Writers' Project in New York City. His major work was the novel *Invisible Man* (1952), a semi-autobiographical account of a young black intellectual's search for identity and authentic consciousness, set mainly in the New York City slums. He also published two volumes of essays, *Shadow and Act* (1964) and *Going to the Territory* (1986). His last work, the short story *Flying Home*, was published posthumously in 1996.

Ellmann, Richard (1918–87) Biographer and academic, born in Detroit, MI. He studied at Yale University, then taught at Northwestern University (1951–68), Yale (1968–70), and Oxford (1970–1987). He is best known for his biographies of Yeats, Oscar Wilde, and James Joyce.

Ellsworth, Lincoln (1880–1951) Explorer, born in Chicago, IL. He helped survey the route for the Canadian transcontinental railway (1902), and led a surveying expedition across the Andes (1924). He made the first trans-Arctic crossing in the airship *Norge* with Umberto Nobile, and in 1935 the first flight across Antarctica. He claimed for the USA some of the territory he flew over, *Ellsworth Mountains* and *American Highland*, an area of almost a million square kilometres. >> Nobile

Ellsworth, Oliver (1745–1807) Public official and jurist, born in Windsor, CT. A lawyer prominent in Connecticut politics, he served in the Continental Congress (1777–83) and was a major figure at the Constitutional Convention in 1787, contributing to the Connecticut Compromise, under which the Senate represents states and the House represents population. As one of Connecticut's first two senators (1789–96), he played a major role in proposing the Bill of Rights and other fundamentals of the US government. President Washington appointed him Chief Justice of the US Supreme Court (1796–1800); while serving (1799), he went to Paris to negotiate a treaty that averted a war with France. Poor health forced him to resign in 1800.

Elman, Mischa (1891–1967) Violinist, born in Talnoy, Ukraine. He made his public debut at age five, studied at the St Petersburg Conservatory, and made his professional debut in Berlin at 13. In 1908 he made his first appearance in the USA in New York City, and settled there in 1911. He pursued an international career, especially admired for his treatment of the Romantic repertoire.

Elms, Lauris Margaret (1931–) Opera and Lieder singer, born in Melbourne, Victoria, Australia. She studied in Paris, made her debut in 1957 at Covent Garden in Verdi's *Un ballo in maschera*, and became principal resident artist there. She has appeared with all leading Australian companies, and is renowned for her Azucena in Verdi's *Il Trovatore*. She has made a number of acclaimed recordings, including *Peter Grimes* under the composer Benjamin Britten. >> Britten

Elmslie, George Grant (1871–1952) Scottish architect and designer. His most notable works were designed during his partnership with William Gray Purcell (1912–20), such as the Edison Building, Chicago (1912), and the Woodbury County Courthouse, Sioux City, Iowa (1915–17). He also designed furniture, metalwork, and stained glass.

Elsheimer, Adam [els*hymer*] (1578–1610) Painter, born in Frankfurt, Germany. He worked in Venice after 1598, and in Rome after 1600. Basing his style on a close study of Tintoretto and other Italian masters, he excelled in the portrayal of atmosphere and effects of light, and exerted a profound influence on the development of German landscape painting. >> Tintoretto

Elster, Julius (1854–1920) German physicist. He collaborated with the German physicist **Hans Friedrich Geitel** (1855–1923) in producing the first photoelectric cell and photometer, and a Tesla transformer. Among other achievements, they determined in 1899 the charge on raindrops from thunderclouds, and established that radioactive substances producing ionization cause the conductivity of the atmosphere. >> Tesla

Elton, Charles Sutherland (1900–91) Ecologist, born in Liverpool, Merseyside, NW England, UK. He studied at Liverpool College, and New College, Oxford, where he spent most of his career (1936–67). He was one of the first to carry out scientific studies of animals in their natural environment, and his book *Animal Ecology* (1927) is considered to have established the basic principles of modern animal ecology. He is recognized as having done more than anyone else to explain the complex inter-relationships of different animal communities, and their effect on their habitat.

Eluard, Paul [elwah(r)], pseudonym of **Eugène Grindal** (1895–1952) Poet, born in Saint-Denis, France. He was one of the founders of the Surrealist movement in literature. His first collection of poetry was *Capitale de la douleur* (1926, Capital of Sorrow). Many of his works reflect the major events of the century, such as the World Wars, the Resistance, and the aspirations of the Communist Party, which he joined in 1942.

Elvehjem, Conrad (Arnold) [elvayjem] (1901–62) Biochemist, born in McFarland, WI. He studied and spent his entire career at Wisconsin University, ultimately as president (1958–62). In 1937 he showed that nicotinic acid cured two related deficiency diseases, canine blacktongue and human pellagra; it is now known as vitamin B_6. He also showed that certain elements are essential in animal nutrition at trace levels, including copper, cobalt, and zinc.

Elvström, Paul [elvstroem] (1928–) Yachtsman, born in Gentofte, Copenhagen. He is the only yachtsman to win four individual Olympic gold medals: in the Firefly class in 1948, and in the Finn class in 1952, 1956, and 1960. He was also the first to win the same event at four consecutive Olympics. He came fourth in the Tornado class at the 1984 Olympics, his seventh Games, with his daughter, **Trine** (1962–).

Elyot, Sir Thomas, also spelled **Eliot** (c. 1490–1546) Writer and diplomat, born in Wiltshire, S England, UK. In 1523 he became clerk of the king's council, and was ambassador to Emperor Charles V in 1531–2. His chief work, *The Boke Named the Gouernour* (1531), is the earliest English treatise on moral philosophy. He was a strong supporter of the use of English (as opposed to Latin) in scholarly work.

Elytis, Odysseus [eleetis], pseudonym of **Odysseus Alepoudhelis** (1911–96) Poet, born in Heraklion, Crete, Greece. He studied at Athens University and at the Sorbonne, Paris, and worked in broadcasting and as a critic of art and literature. His pseudonym is said to combine the three most prevalent themes in his work: Greece, hope, and freedom. Deeply influenced by the Surrealists, he began publishing verse in the 1930s. His best-known work is *To axion esti* (1959, The Axion Esti). In 1979 he was awarded the Nobel Prize for Literature.

Emanuel or **Manuel I**, known as **the Great** or **the Fortunate** (1469–1521) King of Portugal (1495–1521), born in Alcochete, Portugal. He consolidated royal power, and his reign, marred only by persecution of the Jews, was the Golden Age of Portugal. He prepared the code of laws which bears his name, and made his court a centre of chivalry, art, and science. He sponsored the voyages of Vasco da Gama, and others, which helped to make Portugal the first naval power of Europe and a world centre of commerce. >> Gama; RR1082

Emecheta, (Florence Onye) Buchi (1944–) Novelist, born in Lagos, Nigeria. She moved to England with her student husband, and studied at London University. Her novels are powerful social documents, graphic in their depiction of man's inhumanity to woman. Relevant titles are *In the Ditch* (1972), *Second-Class Citizen* (1974), *The Bride Price* (1976), *The Slave Girl* (1977), and *The Joys of Motherhood* (1979). Later works include *The Rape of Shavi* (1983) and *Gwendolen* (1989).

Emerson, Ralph Waldo (1803–82) Poet and essayist, born in Boston, MA. He studied at Harvard, and became a teacher, then (1829) pastor of a Unitarian Church in Boston, but his controversial views caused his resignation. In 1833 he travelled to Europe, and visited Thomas Carlyle, thereafter corresponding with him for 38 years. In 1834 he moved to Concorde, MA, where he wrote his prose rhapsody, *Nature* (1836), and many poems and essays, notably *The Conduct of Life* (1860). He was a transcendentalist in philosophy, a rationalist in religion, and a bold advocate of spiritual individualism. >> Carlyle, Thomas; Thoreau

Emett, Rowland (1906–90) Cartoonist and designer of eccentric mechanical displays, born in London, England, UK. He studied at Birmingham College, and after his earliest joke drawings for *Punch* (1939), evolved a unique and fantastic style depicting a quaint, Victorian world. Many of his cartoons have been turned into working models.

Emin Pasha, originally **Eduard Schnitzer** (1840–92) Doctor and explorer, born in Neisse, Germany. He studied medicine at Wrocław, Poland (formerly Breslau, Germany), and Berlin, and became a medical officer in the Turkish army in 1865. In 1876 General Gordon appointed him chief medical officer of the Equatorial Province, and governor in 1878. A skilful linguist, he added enormously to the knowledge of African languages, made important surveys and wrote valuable geographical papers, and sent to Europe rich collections of plants and animals. He brought an end to slavery in the region. Isolated by enemies, he was 'rescued' by H M Stanley's expedition in 1889, accompanied Stanley to Zanzibar, but immediately returned to extend the German sphere of influence about L Victoria. While on a journey to the West African coast, he was murdered by Arab slave-traders. >> Gordon, Charles George; Stanley, Henry Morton

Emmerich, Anna Katharina [emereekh], known as **the Nun of Dülmen** (1774–1824) Visionary and nun, born near Coesfeld, Germany. She entered the Augustinian order in 1802, and from 1812 bore the stigmata of Christ's passion. Her revelations were recorded by the poet Clemens von Brentano. >> Brentano, Clemens von

Emmet, Robert (1778–1803) Irish patriot, born in Dublin. He left Trinity College, Dublin, to join the United Irishmen, and travelled on the European mainland for the Irish cause, at one point meeting Napoleon. In 1803 he plotted an insurrection against the English, but it proved a failure. He was captured and hanged in Dublin.

Empedocles [empedokleez] (c.490–c.430 BC) Greek philosopher and poet, born in Acragas, Sicily. In *On Nature* he agreed with Parmenides that there could be no absolute coming to exist or ceasing to exist; all change in the world is the result of two contrary cosmic forces, Love and Strife, mixing and separating four everlasting elements, Earth, Water, Air, and Fire. The doctrine of four elements became central to Western thought for 2000 years through its adoption by Aristotle. >> Aristotle

Empson, Sir William (1906–84) Poet and critic, born in Howden, near Hull, NE England, UK. He studied at Cambridge, and became professor of English literature at Tokyo (1931–4) and Peking (1937–9, 1947–53), working in the interim with the BBC's Far Eastern Service. In 1953 he became professor of English literature at Sheffield

University. He wrote several major critical works, notably *Seven Types of Ambiguity* (1930), and his *Collected Poems* were published in 1955. He was knighted in 1979.

Encke, Johann Franz [engkuh] (1791–1865) Astronomer, born in Hamburg, Germany. He studied at the University of Göttingen, was director of the Seeberg Observatory near Gotha, Germany (1822–5), and subsequently became director of the Observatory at Berlin University. He determined the period of the comet which now bears his name (1819), and accurately calculated the distance from the Earth to the Sun.

Endecott, John [endikot], also spelled **Endicott** (c. 1588–1665) Colonist, born in Dorchester, Dorset, S England, UK. In 1628 he landed in America and became manager of a plantation near Salem. He was local governor in 1630, and on four more occasions between 1644 and 1664. Under his leadership the colony of Massachusetts made rapid progress.

Ender, Kornelia (1958–) Swimmer, born in Bitterfeld, Germany. Representing East Germany, she won three Olympic silver medals in 1972, aged 13, and between 1973 and 1976 broke 23 world records (the most by a woman under modern conditions). At the 1973 and 1975 World Championships she won 10 medals, including a record eight golds. In 1976 she became the first woman to win four gold medals at one Olympic Games: the 100 m and 200 m freestyle, the 100 m butterfly, and the 4 × 100 m medley relay.

Enderby, Samuel (fl.1830–9) Entrepreneur, General Gordon's grandfather, one of a firm of London merchants who fitted out three Antarctic expeditions (1830–9). The name *Enderby Land* was given in 1831 to a tract of Antarctica by its discoverer, John Biscoe, a navigator employed by the company. >> Gordon, Charles George

Enders, John (Franklin) (1897–1985) Microbiologist, born in West Hartford, CT. He studied literature at Harvard, but then switched to bacteriology. He researched problems of tuberculosis and pneumococcal infections before studying viral diseases, and in 1946 helped set up a laboratory for poliomyelitis research at Boston. He shared with Frederick Robbins and Thomas Weller the 1954 Nobel Prize for Physiology or Medicine for the cultivation of polio viruses in human tissue cells, thus greatly advancing virology and making possible the development of a polio vaccine by Salk. In 1962 he developed an effective vaccine against measles. >> Robbins, Frederick; Salk; Weller

Endlicher, Stephen (Ladislaus) [endlikher] (1804–49) Botanist, born in Pressburg (now Bratislava, Slovak Republic). He studied at Budapest and Vienna, and formulated a system of plant classification (later known to be erroneous) which was widely used for over half a century. His great work was *Genera plantarum* (1836–40).

Endo, Shusaku (1923–96) Novelist and short story writer, born in Toyko. He graduated in French literature from Keio University, then studied for several years in Lyon. Widely regarded as the leading writer in Japan, he was elected to the Nihon Geijutsuin, the Japanese Arts Academy, in 1981. His books include (trans titles) *Silence* (1966), *The Sea and Poison* (1972), *Wonderful Fool* (1974), *Volcano* (1978), *When I Whistle* (1979), and *Stained Glass Elegies* (1984).

Enesco, Georges [eneskoh], originally **Georges Enescu** (1881–1955) Composer, born in Dorohoiu, Romania. He studied in Vienna, and under Massenet and Fauré in Paris. Successful as a virtuoso and teacher of the violin (his pupils included Yehudi Menuhin), he was also active as a composer. His works include music in Romanian national style, an opera, *Oedipus*, three symphonies, and orchestral and chamber music. >> Fauré; Massenet; Menuhin

Enfield, Harry (1961–) British comedian, actor, and writer. He studied at the University of York, where he began acting, then toured a fringe show, and after appearing on Channel 4's *Saturday Night Live* became known for his character-based comedy shows. *Sir Norbert Smith – a Life?* (1989) won the Silver Rose at Montreux, as did *The End of an Era* (1994). He achieved national recognition after his own BBC television series in 1991–2, following this with *Harry Enfield and Chums* (1994, 1996).

Engels, Friedrich (1820–95) Socialist philosopher, collaborator with Marx, and founder of 'scientific socialism', born in Barmen, Germany. From 1842 he lived mostly in England. He first met Marx at Brussels in 1844 and collaborated with him on the *Communist Manifesto* (1848). He spent his later years editing and translating Marx's writings. >> Feuerbach; Marx, Karl

Engler, (Gustav Heinrich) Adolf (1844–1930) Botanist, born in Sagan, Germany. He studied at Breslau University, and worked at universities in Munich, Kiel, and Wrocław, Poland (formerly Breslau, Germany), before becoming professor and director of the botanical gardens at Berlin (1889–1921). He proposed a major system of plant classification that is still widely used.

Ennin or **Jikaku Daishi** [diyshee] (9th-c) Japanese Tendai Buddhist, the abbot of Mt Hiei monastery. He travelled widely in Tang China as a pilgrim and member of an official embassy, keeping an accurate diary which recorded impressions of careful bureaucracy, strong government, advanced social development, prosperity, and a resplendent aristocracy and court. The diary is a major source on Tang China, and superior to Marco Polo's later portrait of the Yuan period. >> Marco Polo

Ennius, Quintus [enius] (c. 239–169 BC) Latin epic poet and playwright, born in Rudiae, Italy. He is said to have served in the Punic Wars, and returned to Rome with Cato the Elder, where he taught Greek, and attained the rank of Roman citizen. He introduced the hexameter into Latin; but only fragments of his many writings survive. >> Cato (the Elder)

Enoch [eenok] Biblical character, the son of Jared, and the father of Methuselah. He was depicted as extraordinarily devout, and therefore as translated directly into heaven without dying (*Gen* 5.24). In the Graeco-Roman era his name became attached to Jewish apocalyptic writings allegedly describing his visions and journeys through the heavens (1, 2, and 3 *Enoch*).

Enright, D(ennis) J(oseph) (1920–) Writer, born in Leamington, Warwickshire, C England, UK. He studied at Cambridge and at Alexandria, Egypt. Many years teaching in universities abroad are recalled in *Memoirs of a Mendicant Professor* (1969). He has written five novels, and much criticism, but is best known for his poetry. A dozen volumes since 1953, including *Some Men Are Brothers* (1960), *Unlawful Assembly* (1968), and *A Faust Book* (1979) are represented in his *Collected Poems* (1987). Later collections include *Old Men and Comets* (1993).

Ensor, James (Sydney) Ensor, Baron (1860–1949) Painter, born in Ostend, Belgium. He became known for his bizarre and fantastic images, using masks, skeletons, and other ghostly effects as symbols of the evils of society. His paintings aroused much controversy when they were first shown, as in his best-known work, 'Entry of Christ into Brussels' (1888, Brussels). He was made a baron in 1929.

Enver Pasha (1881–1922) Turkish soldier and politician, born in Istanbul. A leader in the revolution of Young Turks in 1908, he later became minister of war (1914). He fled to Russia in 1918 after the Turkish surrender, and was killed in an insurrection in Turkestan.

Epaminondas [epaminondas] (c. 418–362 BC) Theban general and statesman, whose victory at Leuctra (371 BC) broke the military power of Sparta and made Thebes the most powerful state in Greece. His death at the Battle of Mantinea abruptly brought this supremacy to an end.

Epée, Charles Michel, Abbé de l' [epay] (1712–89) Educationist, born in Versailles, France. In 1765 he began to educate two deaf and dumb sisters, and invented a language of signs. He also pioneered the use of 'spatial aids' to assist the memorizing of vocabulary by associating words with particular locations in space. His attempts succeeding, at his own expense he founded a deaf and dumb institute, which was converted into a public institution two years after his death.

Ephraem Syrus, St [efrayim **siy**rus], known as **the Harp of the Holy Spirit** (c. 306–378) Theologian, born in Nisibis, Syria. He devoted himself to prayer, fasting, and the study of the Scriptures. He was a prolific writer, mostly in verse, and had a great influence on Syriac and Greek hymnography. Much of his works are still available, part of them in Syriac, part in Greek, Latin, and Armenian translations. Feast day 28 Jan (E), 9 Jun (W).

Epictetus [epik**tay**tus] (c. 50–c. 130) Stoic philosopher, born in Hierapolis. At first a Roman slave, on being freed he devoted himself to philosophy. He was banished by Emperor Domitian, and settled at Nikopolis in Epirus. He wrote no works; the *Enchiridion* is a collection of maxims dictated to a disciple. >> Domitian

Epicurus [epi**kyoo**rus] (c. 341–270 BC) Greek philosopher, born in Samos. He visited Athens when he was 18, then opened a school at Mitylene (310 BC), and taught there and at Lampsacus. In 305 BC he returned to Athens, where he established a successful school of philosophy, leading a life of great temperance and simplicity. He divided philosophy into three parts: logic; physics, where he developed the atomistic ideas of Democritus; and ethics, where he held that pleasure is the chief good, by which he meant freedom from pain and anxiety, not (as the term *epicurean* has since come to mean) one who indulges sensual pleasures without stint. He is said to have written 300 volumes on many subjects, but only a few letters and other fragments have survived. >> Democritus

Epiphanius, St [epi**fa**nius] (c. 315–403) Bishop of Salamis, (367–403), born in Bezanduca, Palestine. He devoted most of his life to defending orthodox belief against heresy. His major work *Panarion* (374–77, Refutation of all Heresies) lacks moderation, but is a valuable source of the history of theology. Feast day 12 May.

Epstein, Sir Jacob [**ep**stiyn] (1880–1959) Sculptor, born in New York City, New York, USA. He studied at the Ecole des Beaux-Arts in Paris, moving to London, England in 1905, and becoming a British subject. Several of his symbolic sculptures, such as 'Ecce homo' (1934), resulted in accusations of indecency and blasphemy. He was an outstanding modeller of bronze portrait heads of celebrities and children. In the 1950s, his last two large works, 'Christ in Majesty' (in aluminium; Llandaff Cathedral) and 'St Michael and the Devil' (in bronze; Coventry Cathedral), won more immediate acclaim. He was knighted in 1954.

Erard, Sébastien [ayrah(r)] (1752–1831) Piano and harp maker, born in Strasbourg, France. At his Paris workshop he was the inventor of the harp with double pedals, the mechanical harpsichord, and the piano with double escapement.

Erasistratus [era**si**stratus] (of Ceos) (c. 250 BC) Greek physician, born in Ceos. He founded a school of anatomy at Alexandria, and is considered one of the pioneers of modern medicine. He is said to have been the first to trace arteries and veins to the heart, and to have named the tricuspid valve in the heart.

Erasmus, Desiderius [e**raz**mus], originally **Gerrit Gerrits-**

zoon (1466–1536) Humanist, born in Rotterdam, The Netherlands. After six years in an Augustinian monastery, he became private secretary to the Bishop of Cambrai, and a priest (1492). He went to Paris, where he lived as a teacher, then moved to England in 1498, and became professor of divinity and of Greek at Cambridge. Here he wrote his satire, *Encomium moriae* (1509, The Praise of Folly). After 1514 he lived alternately in Basel and England, then in Louvain (1517–21). His masterpiece, *Colloquia*, appeared in 1519, an audacious handling of Church abuses. He also made the first translation of the Greek New Testament into English (1516) and edited the works of St Jerome (1519). In 1521 he left Louvain, and lived mainly in Basel, where he was engaged in continual controversy, but enjoyed great fame and respect in his later years. >> Jerome, St

Erastus, Thomas [e**ras**tus], originally **Thomas Liebler**, also spelled **Lieber** or **Lüber** (1524–83) Theologian and physician, born in Basel, Switzerland. He studied theology at Basel, and philosophy and medicine in Italy, and was appointed physician to the counts of Henneberg. He was professor of medicine at Heidelberg, physician to the Elector Palatine (1558), and professor of ethics at Basel from 1580. In theology he was a follower of Zwingli, was opposed to Calvin's system of Church government, and argued against the practice of excommunication. His name is preserved in *Erastianism*, a doctrine (which he himself neither maintained nor denied) giving the state authority over Church matters. >> Calvin, John; Zwingli

Eratosthenes [era**tos**theneez] (c. 276–c. 194 BC) Greek astronomer and scholar, born in Cyrene. He became chief librarian at Alexandria, and is remembered for the first scientific calculation of the Earth's circumference, which was correct to within 80 km/50 mi.

Ercilla y Zúñiga, Alonso de [er**thee**lya ee **thoo**nyiga] (1533–c. 1595) Poet, born in Madrid. After a literary education, he joined the expedition against the Araucanians in Chile, whose heroism inspired his monumental epic poem, *La Araucana* (1569–89). An unfounded suspicion of his complicity in an insurrection nearly led to his execution. Fearing for his life, he returned to Spain, made a tour through Europe, and for some time was chamberlain to Emperor Rudolf II (ruled 1576–1612). In 1580 he returned to Madrid, where he lived in poverty till his death.

Ercker, Lazarus (c. 1530–c. 1593) Metallurgist, born in Annberg, Germany. He studied at the University of Wittenberg, and was appointed control tester of coins in Prague in 1567. He is best known for his book *Description of Leading Ore Processing and Mining Methods* (1574, trans title), considered to be the first manual of analytical and metallurgical chemistry. The book was translated and published until the mid-18th-c.

Erhard, Ludwig [**air**hah(r)t] (1897–1977) German statesman, economist, and Christian Democratic chancellor (1963–6), born in Furth, Germany. Professor of economics at Munich, in 1949 he was elected to the Federal Parliament at Bonn, and made Chancellor of the Exchequer in the Adenauer administration. He was the pioneer of the West German 'economic miracle' of recovery from wartime devastation. He succeeded Adenauer as chancellor, but economic difficulties forced his resignation. >> Adenauer

Erickson, Arthur Charles (1924–) Architect, born in Vancouver, British Columbia, Canada. He studied at British Columbia and McGill universities, and established Arthur Erickson Architects after various partnerships. He received international recognition for the design of the Simon Fraser University buildings, British Columbia (1963), confirmed by his avant-garde design of Lethbridge University, Alberta (1971).

Ericsson, John (1803–89) Inventor, born in Långbanshyttan,

Sweden. He was a Swedish army engineer before he moved to England (1826), where he invented the first successful screw-propeller (1836). In 1839 he went to the USA, becoming a US citizen in 1848. He designed the warship *Princeton*, the first steamer with engines and boilers entirely below the water-line, and in 1861 built the ironclad *Monitor* and other vessels. His inventions revolutionized the construction of warships. He is also known to have investigated solar-power as an energy source. >> Nobel

Erigena, John Scotus [erijena], also known as **John the Scot** (c. 810–c. 877) Philosopher and theologian, born in Scotia (now Ireland), who stands outside the mainstream of mediaeval thought. He taught at the Court of Charles I, the Bald in France, then supported Hincmar in the predestination controversy with his *De praedestinatione* (851, On Predestination), which the Council of Valence condemned as *pultes Scotorum* ('Irishman's porridge'). He also translated into Latin and provided commentaries on the Greek writings of the theologians of the Eastern Church. His major work, *De divisione naturae* (c.865, On the Division of Nature), tried to fuse Christian and Neoplatonic doctrines, but his work was later condemned for its pantheistic tendencies. >> Hincmar

Erik the Red, originally **Erik Thorvaldsson** (10th-c) Norwegian sailor who explored the Greenland coast and founded the Norse colonies there (985). His son **Leif Eriksson** landed in 'Vinland', often identified as America (1000). Both men are the subject of Icelandic sagas.

Erik the Saint (12th-c) Patron saint of Sweden. He became king of Sweden c.1155, and is said to have led a Christian crusade for the conversion of Finland. He is thought to have been murdered at Mass in Uppsala by a Danish pretender to his throne. He was married to **Kristina**, and became father of **King Knut Eriksson** (died c.1195).

Erixson, Sven, nickname **X-et** (1899–1970) Artist, born in Tumba, Sweden. He spent much time in the Mediterranean countries and took his motifs from there as well as from Sweden. His enormously colourful paintings gave him great popularity, and made him much in demand for large-scale public commissions, such as his tapestry *Melodies on the Square* (1937–9) in the Concert Hall in Gothenburg. He was also active as a scenic artist in the theatre.

Erlanger, Joseph [erlanger] (1874–1965) Physiologist, born in San Francisco, CA. Professor of physiology successively at Johns Hopkins, Wisconsin, and Washington (St Louis) universities, he shared with his former student Herbert Gasser the 1944 Nobel Prize for Physiology or Medicine for their collaborative work on nerve fibres and nerve impulse transmission. >> Gasser

Ernst, Max(imillian) (1891–1976) Painter, born in Brühl, Germany. After studying philosophy at Bonn, he turned to painting. In 1919 he founded at Cologne the German Dada group, and later became part of the Surrealist movement in Paris. He settled in the USA in 1941, but returned to France in 1953. His use of the subconscious as inspiration can be seen in 'Oedipus Rex' (1921) and 'Polish Rider' (1954).

Ershad, Hussain Muhammad [airshad] (1929–) Bangladeshi soldier, chief martial law administrator, and president (1983–90). Appointed army chief-of-staff by President Ziaur Rahman in 1978, he repeatedly demanded that the armed forces should be involved in the country's administration. In 1982 he led a bloodless military coup, becoming president the following year. He resigned at the end of 1990, was arrested on charges of plundering the nation, and sentenced to 10 years' imprisonment in 1991. He was released in 1997. >> RR1034

Erskine, John (1879–1951) Educator, novelist, and musician, born in New York City. As a youth he showed serious talent as a pianist, but after studying at Columbia University (1903) he became a professor of English. Most of

his academic career was at Columbia (1909–37), where his emphasis on studying the classic texts gave rise to the 'great books' programmes adopted by many educational institutions. As a literary scholar, his editions (1915–22) introduced Lafcadio Hearn's writings to the West and he co-edited the *Cambridge History of American Literature* (1917–21). Another reputation was launched with *The Private Life of Helen of Troy* (1925), the first of his satirical novels treating legendary individuals in modern settings. He kept up his interest in music, giving occasional public concerts, and he was active in the new Juilliard School, New York City, serving as its president (1928–37). >> Hearn

Erskine, Thomas Erskine, Baron (1750–1823) Lawyer, born in Edinburgh, EC Scotland, UK. In 1764 he was sent to sea, in 1768 he bought a commission in the army, then took up law. His success was immediate with a brilliant defence (1778) of Captain Baillie, Lieutenant-Governor of Greenwich Hospital, who was threatened with a criminal prosecution for libel, and in 1781 he secured the acquittal of Lord George Gordon. In 1783 he became a KC, and an MP for Portsmouth. His sympathy with the French Revolution led him to join the 'Friends of the People', and to undertake the defence in many political prosecutions of 1793–4. In 1802 he was appointed chancellor to the Prince of Wales, an ancient office revived in his favour. In 1806 he was appointed Lord Chancellor, but resigned the following year and gradually retired into private life. >> Gordon, Lord George

Erté [ertay], originally **Romain de Tirtoff** (1892-1990) Fashion designer, born in St Petersburg, Russia. He went to Paris, where he became a dress and theatrical-costume designer. He worked for the *Folies-Bergère* (1919–30), and designed the costumes for the American musical revues *The Ziegfeld Follies* and *George White's Scandals*. In the 1960s he produced lithographs and sheet-metal sculptures. His autobiography, *Things I Remember*, was published in 1976.

Ervine, St John (Greer) [ervin] (1883–1971) Playwright and critic, born in Belfast. He was manager of the Abbey Theatre, Dublin (1915–16), where his first plays were produced. After World War 1, in which he lost a leg, he won a high reputation as a drama critic, working on *The Observer* and *The Morning Post*, and for the BBC (1932). His plays include *Anthony and Anna* (1926), *The First Mrs Fraser* (1929), and *Robert's Wife* (1937), and he also wrote seven novels and several biographies.

Erzberger, Matthias [airtsberger] (1875–1921) German statesman, born in Buttenhausen, Germany. He became controversial when, as German propaganda minister, he began to advocate peace without annexations as early as 1917 and again in 1918–19. As a member of the armistice delegation, he advocated acceptance, despite fierce German opposition, of the terms of the Versailles Treaty, and was a strong supporter of the idea of the League of Nations. Finance minister and vice-premier in 1919, he drastically reformed the tax system, and nationalized the German railways. Unsuccessful in a libel action against an unscrupulous political opponent, he resigned in 1921 and was assassinated by members of an extremist group.

Esaki, Leo [esahkee], originally **Esaki Reiona** (1925–) Physicist, born in Osaka, Japan. He studied physics at Tokyo, and in 1957, working for the Sony Corporation, developed the *Esaki diode* (or tunnel diode), a semiconductor device with widespread electronic uses in computers and microwave systems. In 1960 he moved to the IBM Research Center in New York City, and shared the Nobel Prize for Physics in 1973. >> RR1122

Esarhaddon [eesah(r)hadn] (?–669 BC) King of Assyria (680–669 BC), the son of Sennacherib and father of Assurbanipal. He is best known for his conquest of Egypt (671 BC). >> Assurbanipal; Sennacherib; RR1032

Esau [eesaw] Biblical character, the elder son of Isaac. He was depicted as his father's favourite son, but was deprived of Isaac's blessing and his birthright by his cunning brother Jacob (*Gen* 27). The story was used to explain why Esau's descendants, the Edomites, were thereafter hostile to Jacob's descendants, the Israelites. >> Isaac; Jacob

Eschenbach, Wolfram von >> **Wolfram von Eschenbach**

Escoffier, (Georges) Auguste [eskofyay] (c. 1847–1935) Chef, born in Villeneuve-Loubet, France. He became *chef de cuisine* to the general staff of the Rhine army in the Franco-Prussian war (1871) and of the Grand Hotel, Monte Carlo, before coming to the Savoy, London, and finally to the Carlton. The inventor of *Pêche Melba* and *tournedos Rossini* for the singer and composer respectively, and other dishes, he wrote several books on culinary art. >> Melba; Rossini

Esdras >> **Ezra the Scribe**

Esop >> **Aesop**

Espert, Nuria (1935–) Actress and stage director, born in Barcelona, Spain. She began her professional career at 12, and at 24 she co-founded the Nuria Espert Theatre Company. She has played the title role in *Hamlet*, and both Prospero and Ariel in the same production of *The Tempest*. Other productions include Brecht's *The Good Person of Setzuan* and Wilde's *Salomé*. Appearing as an actress in productions all over the world, she also directed a revival of Lorca's *The House of Bernarda Alba* in London (1986), and Puccini's *Madame Butterfly* for Scottish Opera. In 1992 she returned to Barcelona to direct Euripides' *Medea*.

Espronceda (y Delgado), José de [espronthetha] (1808–42) Poet and revolutionary, born in Almendro de los Barros, Spain. He was imprisoned several times for revolutionary activities in France and Spain. He wrote Romantic poems in the Byronic manner, and is often called 'the Spanish Lord Byron'. He also wrote novels, plays, and political works. >> Byron, George

Espy, James (Pollard) [espee] (1785–1860) Meteorologist, born in Pennsylvania. He served as meteorologist to the US Navy and the US War Department, and from 1852 worked at the Smithsonian Institution, Washington. He was one of the first to use the telegraph to collect meteorological data, and gave the first correct explanation of cloud formation.

Essex, Robert Devereux, 2nd Earl of (1566–1601) English soldier and courtier to Elizabeth I, born in Netherwood, Hereford and Worcester, WC England, UK. He served in The Netherlands (1585–6), and distinguished himself at Zutphen. At court, he quickly rose in the favour of Elizabeth, despite his clandestine marriage in 1590 with Sir Philip Sidney's widow. In 1591 he commanded the forces sent to help Henry IV of France, and took part in the sacking of Cadiz (1595). He became a privy councillor (1593) and earl marshal (1597). However, he alienated the Queen's advisers, and there were constant quarrels with Elizabeth (notably the occasion when he turned his back on her, and she boxed his ears). His six months' lord-lieutenancy of Ireland (1599) proved a failure, and he was imprisoned and deprived of his dignities. He attempted to raise the City of London, was found guilty of high treason, and was beheaded in the Tower. >> Elizabeth I; Wotton

Essex, Robert Devereux, 3rd Earl of (1591–1646) English parliamentary soldier, born in London, England, UK, the eldest son of Robert, 2nd Earl of Essex. In 1604 the earldom was restored to him after his father's execution for treason in 1601, and in 1642 he received the command of the Parliamentary army. He was brave, but a poor general. The drawn Battle of Edgehill, the capture of Reading, and the relief of Gloucester were followed by a blundering march into Cornwall, from where he fled by sea. >> Essex, 2nd Earl of

Estes, Richard [esteez] (1932–) Painter, born in Keewane, IL. He studied at the Art Institute of Chicago (1952–6), and in 1959 moved to New York City. For several years he worked in the illustration and advertising industry before becoming a full-time painter in 1966. In the late 1960s he began painting precise copies of photographs, particularly of New York street-scenes. His meticulously detailed 'Super-Realist' works can easily be confused with photographs.

Esther (5th-c BC) Biblical queen, a foster-daughter of the Jew, Mordecai. According to the Book of Esther she was chosen by the Persian King Ahasuerus (possibly Xerxes I) as his wife in place of the disgraced Queen Vashti, and brought about the deliverance of her people. >> Mordecai

Estigarribia, José Félix [esteegareebia] (1888–1940) Paraguayan general and war hero, born in Caraguatay, Paraguay. He won fame as a brilliant commander in the Chaco War, on the strength of which he became president (1939–40). He died in a plane crash near Asunción.

Ethelbert or **Æthelbert** [ethelbert] (c. 552–616) King of Kent (c.560–616), the first English king to adopt Christianity. During his long reign, Kent achieved hegemony over England S of the Humber. He received with kindness the Christian mission from Rome led by St Augustine, which landed in Thanet in 596, and allowed them to settle at Canterbury, and he himself was baptized with his court. He was also responsible for the first written code of English laws. >> Augustine, St (of Canterbury)

Etheldreda or **Æthelthryth, St** [etheldreeda], also known as **St Audrey** (c. 630–679) Anglo-Saxon nun, the founder of a monastery at Ely, and revered as a virgin saint, although twice married. The daughter of King Anna of East Anglia, she was widowed after three years of her first marriage, which was said never to have been consummated. In 660 she married **Ecgfrith**, future king of Northumbria, but refused to consummate it. Instead she took the veil and withdrew to the double monastery at Coldingham founded by her aunt, Æbbe, and in 673 founded a double monastery herself on the Isle of Ely, of which she was appointed abbess. Feast day 23 June.

Ethelflaed or **Æthelflaed** [ethelflad] (?–918) Anglo-Saxon ruler of Mercia, the daughter of Alfred the Great. She married **Ethelred**, the ealdorman of Mercia (c.888), and fought alongside him to repel the Danish invaders, their battle culminating in a decisive victory near Tettenhall in 911. After Ethelred's death in that year, she was recognized as 'Lady of the Mercians'. She built fortified strongholds throughout Mercia, and led counter-attacks on the Danes. >> Alfred

Ethelred I [ethelred], also spelled **Æthelred** (c. 830–71) King of Wessex (865–71), the elder brother of Alfred the Great. During his reign, the Danes launched their main invasion of England. He died soon after his victory over the invaders at Ashdown, Berkshire. >> Alfred; RR1095

Ethelred II [ethelred], known as **Ethelred the Unready**, also spelled **Æthelred** (c. 968–1016) King of England (978–1016), the son of Edgar. He was aged about 10 when the murder of his half-brother, Edward the Martyr, placed him on the throne. In 1002 he confirmed an alliance with Normandy by marrying as his second wife Duke Richard's daughter **Emma** – the first dynastic link between the two countries. Renewed attacks by the Vikings on England began as raids in the 980s, and in 1013 Sweyn Forkbeard secured mastery over the whole country, forcing Ethelred into exile in Normandy. After Sweyn's death (1014), he returned to oppose Canute, but the unity of English resistance was broken when his son, Edmund Ironside, rebelled. He died in London. 'Unready' is a mistranslation of *Unraed*, not recorded as his nickname until after the Norman Conquest; it means 'ill-advised' and is a pun on his given name, Ethelred (literally, 'good counsel'). >> Canute; Edgar; Edmund II; Edward the Martyr; Sweyn; RR1095

Ethelred, St >> **Ailred of Rievaulx, St**

Ethelred the Unready >> **Ethelred II**

Etherege, Sir George [etherij] (1635–92) Restoration playwright, probably born in Maidenhead, S England, UK. His three plays, *The Comical Revenge; or, Love in a Tub* (1664); *She Would if She Could* (1668); and *The Man of Mode; or, Sir Fopling Flutter* (1676), were highly popular in their day, and introduced the comedy of manners to the English theatre.

Etty, William (1787–1849) Painter, born in York, N Yorkshire, UK. He studied at the Royal Academy Schools, then with Lawrence, and in 1822–3 went to Italy, where he was deeply influenced by the Venetian masters. He depicted Classical and historical subjects, and became renowned for his nudes. >> Lawrence, Thomas

Etzioni, Amitai (Werner) [etziohnee] (1929–) Sociologist, born in Cologne, Germany. Raised in Palestine, he emigrated to the USA in 1957. He taught at Columbia (1958–80), then at George Washington University, and wrote prolifically for both scholarly and popular audiences, often on organizational analysis. His books include *A Comparative Analysis of Complex Organizations* (1961) and *The Moral Dimension* (1988).

Eucken, Rudolf Christoph [oyken] (1846–1926) Philosopher, born in Aurich, Germany. He studied at the University of Göttingen, then became professor of philosophy at Basel (1871–4) and at Jena (1874–1920). He propounded a distinctive philosophy of ethical activism, and sought to identify and vindicate the spiritual significance of history and life. In his writings he strongly criticized naturalist philosophy, and *Der Sozialismus und seine Lebensgestaltung* (1920, Socialism: an Analysis) is an attack on socialism. He was awarded the Nobel Prize for Literature in 1908.

Eucleides of Megara [yookleedeez, megara] (c. 435–c. 365 BC) Greek philosopher, a disciple of Socrates, mentioned by Plato as one of those present during Socrates' last hours. He founded a school of *Megarians*, who were evidently influenced by Parmenides as well as by Socrates, and who are associated with various developments in logic. None of their writings have survived. >> Parmenides; Socrates

Euclid [yooklid], Gr **Eucleides** (4th–3rd-c BC) Greek mathematician who taught in Alexandria c.300 BC, and who was probably the founder of its mathematical school. His chief extant work is the 13-volume *Elements*, which became the most widely known mathematical book of Classical antiquity, and is still much used in geometry. The approach which obeys his axioms became known as *Euclidean geometry*. >> Theaetetus

Eudocia [yoodohsha], originally **Athenais** (401–65) Byzantine princess, born in Athens, the wife of the Eastern Roman emperor Theodosius II (ruled 408–50). She was baptized a Christian and changed her name before her marriage in 421. After a quarrel with her sister-in-law, Pulcheria, she retired to Jerusalem in 443, where she supervised the building of several churches. She wrote a panegyric on Theodosius's victories over the Persians (422), paraphrases of Scripture, hymns, and poetry.

Eudoxos of Cnidus [yoodoksus] (c. 408 BC–c. 353 BC) Greek geometer and astronomer, born in Cnidus, Asia Minor. In geometry he established principles that laid the foundation for Euclid, then applied the subject to the study of the Moon and planets. He introduced an ingenious system of 27 nested spheres in an attempt to explain planetary motion. >> Euclid

Eugene of Savoy, Prince, in full **François Eugène de Savoie Carignan** (1663–1736) Austrian general, born in Paris. He was refused a commission by Louis XIV of France,

and entered the service of the Emperor Leopold against the Turks. Made field marshal in 1693, he defeated the Turks on several occasions, putting an end to their power in Hungary (1699–1718). He fought against France in two wars between 1689 and 1714, and while in command of the imperial army he helped Marlborough at Blenheim (1704), Oudenaarde (1708), and Malplaquet (1709). Crippled by the withdrawal of Holland and England, he was defeated by Villars (1712). He later won several further victories against the Turks, capturing Belgrade in 1718. >> Leopold I; Marlborough; Villars

Eugénie, Empress >> **Napoleon III**

Euhemerus [yooheemerus] (fl.300 BC) Greek philosopher and mythographer, probably from Messene, Sicily, the author of *Sacred History*. He was the first to try to link mythical beings and events with historical fact, explaining the gods as distorted representations of ancient warriors and heroes. His name lives on in the term *Euhemerism*.

Euler, Leonhard [oyler] (1707–83) Mathematician, born in Basel, Switzerland. He studied mathematics there under Jean Bernoulli, and became professor of physics (1731) and then of mathematics (1733) at the St Petersburg Academy of Sciences. In 1738 he lost the sight of one eye. In 1741 he moved to Berlin as director of mathematics and physics in the Berlin Academy, but returned to St Petersburg in 1766, soon afterwards losing the sight of his other eye. He was a giant figure in 18th-c mathematics, publishing over 800 different books and papers, on every aspect of pure and applied mathematics, physics and astronomy. His *Introductio in analysin infinitorum* (1748) and later treatises on differential and integral calculus and algebra remained standard textbooks for a century and his notations, such as e and π have been used ever since. For the princess of Anhalt-Dessau he wrote *Lettres à une princesse d'Allemagne* (1768–72), giving a clear non-technical outline of the main physical theories of the time. He had a prodigious memory, which enabled him to continue mathematical work and to compute complex calculations in his head when he was totally blind. He is without equal in the use of algorithms to solve problems. >> Bernoulli, Jean; Venturi

Euler-Chelpin, Hans Karl August Simon von [oyler kelpin] (1873–1964) Biochemist, born in Augsburg, Germany. He studied at Berlin, Göttingen and Paris, became lecturer in physical chemistry at Stockholm (1900), and afterwards professor of chemistry and director of the Stockholm Biochemical Institute (1929). He shared the Nobel Prize for Chemistry in 1929 for research into enzymes and fermentation. >> RR1123

Eunomius [yoonohmius] (c. 335–c. 394) Clergyman, born in Cappadocia, Turkey. He was Bishop of Cyzicus c.360, but was deposed for his Arian views. He became the leader of an extreme sect of Arians, known as the *Anomoeans* or *Eunomians*. >> Arius

Euphranor [yoofranaw(r)] (4th-c BC) Greek painter and sculptor from Corinth, famed for his decoration of the Stoa Basileios at Athens.

Euphronios [yoofronios] (c. 520–470 BC) Greek potter and vase painter. His name is inscribed, as either painter or potter, on 15 vessels which constitute some of the finest surviving examples of vessels painted in the so-called 'red figure' style.

Euripides [yuripideez] (c. 480–406 BC) Greek tragic playwright, born in Athens. He abandoned painting for literature, writing about 80 dramas, of which 19 survive, such as *Alcestis, Medea, Orestes*, and *Electra*. *The Bacchae* and *Iphigenia in Aulis* were put on the Athenian stage only after the author's death, when his work became very popular. He died at the court of Archelaus, King of Macedonia.

Eusden, Laurence [yoosden] (1688–1730) Poet, born in Spofforth, North Yorkshire, N England, UK. He became poet laureate in 1718, not on merit but by patronage. He was lampooned by Pope, and died rector of Coningsby, Lincolnshire. >> Pope, Alexander

Eusebio [yoo**say**bioh], in full **Eusebio Ferreira da Silva**, nickname **the Black Pearl** (1942–   ) Footballer, born in Lourenço Marques, Mozambique. He was largely responsible for Portugal's rise in international football in the 1960s. He made his international debut in 1961, and played for his country 77 times. At club level he played for Benfica, winning 15 Portuguese League and Cup-winner's medals. He appeared in four European Cup finals, winning just once, in 1962. He retired in 1978 after a brief spell playing in the USA, and was later appointed coach to Benfica. >> RR1156

Eusebius of Caesarea [yoo**see**bius] (c. 264–340) Historian of the early Church, probably born in Palestine. He became Bishop of Caesarea c.313, and in the Council of Nicaea held a moderate position between the views of Arius and Athanasius. His great work, the *Ecclesiastical History*, is a record of the chief events in the Christian Church until 324. >> Arius; Athanasius

Eusebius of Nicomedia [yoo**say**bius, nikoh**mee**dia] (?–c.342) Syrian clergyman. He was bishop first of Beryus (Beirut) in Syria, then of Nicomedia. He defended Arius at the Council of Nicaea (325), and afterwards became the leader of an Arian group known as the *Eusebians*. Exiled to Gaul for his views, he returned in 328 and influenced Emperor Constantine to move towards Arianism, and baptized him in 337, just before his death. He had also been responsible for the deposition of Athanasius in 335. In 339 he was appointed Patriarch of Constantinople, and enjoyed the favours of Emperor Constantius. >> Arius; Athanasius; Constantine I (Emperor); Ulfilas

Eustachio, Bartolommeo [yoo**stak**yoh] (1520–74) Anatomist and pioneer of modern anatomy. He discovered the *Eustachian tube* in the ear and the *Eustachian valve* of the heart. Professor of anatomy at Rome, he wrote *Opuscula anatomica* (1564) and *Tabulae anatomicae* (1714).

Euthymides [yoo**thi**mideez] (6th-c–5th-c BC) Greek vase painter of the so-called 'red figure' style. He was a contemporary of Euphronios, and seemingly a rival, as amongst the six surviving signed vessels one is inscribed with the words: 'Euphronios never did anything like it'. His painted figures are amongst the earliest to show foreshortened limbs. >> Euphronios

Eutyches [yoo**tikeez**] (c. 375–c. 454) Archimandrite (monastic superior) at Constantinople. He was the founder of *Eutychianism*, holding that, after the incarnation, the human nature became merged in the divine, and that Jesus Christ had therefore but one nature. He was condemned by a synod at Constantinople in 448, but the Council of Ephesus (449) decided in his favour and restored him, deposing his opponents. The Council of Chalcedon (451) annulled this decision, and Eutyches died in banishment. His sect was put down by penal laws. >> Jesus Christ

Euwe, Max (Machgielis) [**ü**vuh] (1901–81) Chess player, born in Watergrafsmeer, The Netherlands. He was a professor of mathematics and mechanics, and after his academic retirement served as president of FIDE (Fédération Internationale des Echecs), 1970–8, arbitrating over the turbulent Fischer–Spassky world championship match in Reykjavík, Iceland, in 1972. A prolific annotator, he contributed more to the literature of chess than any other great master. He was the only amateur to win the world championship in the history of chess, by defeating Alekhine (1935–7). >> Alekhine; Fischer, Bobby; Spassky; RR1149

Evans, Sir Arthur (John) (1851–1941) Archaeologist, born in Nash Mills, Hertfordshire, SE England, UK. He was curator of the Ashmolean Museum, Oxford (1884–1908), where he developed an interest in the ancient coins and seals of Crete. Between 1899 and 1935 he excavated the city of Knossos, discovering the remains of the civilization which in 1904 he named *Minoan* after Minos, the Cretan king of Greek legend. He was knighted in 1911. >> Ventris

Evans, Bill, popular name of **William Evans** (1929–80) Jazz pianist, born in Plainfield, NJ. He studied music at Southeastern Louisiana College and at Mannes School of Music, New York City, playing when he could. Musicians admired his intricate, ruminative style, but he made no impression on fans until he joined Miles Davis's great sextet in 1958. He stayed only six months but played on some brilliant recordings, including the classic 'Kind of Blue' (1959). In 1960, he led a trio at the Village Vanguard, and found critical and popular success. For the rest of his career, he recorded prolifically, partly to support a heroin habit, but nevertheless with great acclaim, winning three Grammy Awards and numerous prizes. Among his best works are *At the Village Vanguard* (1961), *Know What I Mean* (1961), *Intermodulation* (1966), and *Alone Again* (1977). In the period covered by these records, he was the dominant stylist in jazz, and a major influence. >> Davis, Miles

Evans, Caradoc, pseudonym of **David Evans** (1878–1945) Short-story writer and novelist, born in Llanfihangel-ar-Arth, Carmarthenshire, SW Wales, UK. He became a journalist in London in 1906, and published his first collection of short stories, *My People*, in 1915. His stories were bitter satires of the Welsh people, depicting them as hypocrites, greedy, and lustful. His play *Taffy* (1923) added to his self-defined reputation as 'the best-hated man in Wales'. He returned to Wales in 1940 and changed his style, writing more positively about the Welsh, and leaving later critics with mixed views about his role in Anglo-Welsh literature.

Evans, Dame Edith (Mary) (1888–1976) Actress, born in London, England, UK. She earned a great reputation for her versatility, with many notable appearances in the plays of Shakespeare and Shaw. Her most famous role was as Lady Bracknell in Wilde's *The Importance of Being Earnest*. During World War 2 she entertained the troops at home and abroad, and in 1946 was created a dame. In 1948, she made her first film appearance in *The Queen of Spades*, and she continued to be active on both stage and screen into her eighties.

Evans, Frederick Henry (1853–1943) British photographer. Retiring from his profession as a bookseller in 1898, he devoted himself to architectural photography, especially of the cathedrals of England and France, emphasizing their structural rhythms and repetitions. He found similar order and pattern in his studies of trees and in photomicrographs, as well as in his austerely-formed landscapes. His best work was done in the early years of the 20th-c, but he remained unsympathetic to the modern activism then emerging.

Evans, Gareth (John) (1944–   ) Australian statesman, born in Melbourne, Victoria, Australia. He studied at the universities of Melbourne and Oxford, taught law at Melbourne University (1971–6), and was a commissioner for the Australian Law Reform Commission, before becoming Labor Party senator for Victoria in 1978. He was attorney general (1983–4), then served in a range of portfolios, including transport and communications, and became minister for foreign affairs and trade in 1988. His co-authored books include *Australia's Constitution: Time for Change?* (1983) and *Australia's Foreign Relations* (1991). He was one of the chief architects of the Cambodian peace plan which culminated with general elections in 1993. In 1996 he became deputy leader of the opposition and shadow treasurer.

Evans, Sir Geraint (Llewellyn) (1922–92) Baritone, born in Pontypridd, Rhondda Cynon Taff, S Wales, UK. He studied in London and on the European mainland, making his operatic debut at Covent Garden in 1948. He soon earned international fame, particularly in comic roles such as Mozart's Leporello, Verdi's Falstaff, and Wagner's Beckmesser. He was knighted in 1971, and retired from the operatic stage in 1984.

Evans, Gil, popular name of **Ian Ernest Gilmore Green** (1912–88) Jazz pianist, composer, and arranger, born in Toronto, Ontario, Canada. He was principal arranger for the Claude Thornhill Orchestra (1944–8), which led to a collaboration with trumpeter Miles Davis that lasted until 1960. He was one of the first modern jazz arrangers to use electronics and rock influences successfully in combination with the swing and bebop idioms. >> Davis, Miles

Evans, (Thomas) Godfrey (1920–) Cricketer, born in Finchley, NW Greater London, England, UK. He studied at Kent College, Canterbury, and joined the Kent county staff at the age of 16. First capped as wicket-keeper for England in 1946, he played in 91 Test matches, made many new records in his time, and still holds the record for the longest time (97 min) for a batsman to score his first run in an innings, set in a Test match against Australia in 1947. >> RR1150

Evans, Harold (1928–) Journalist, born in Manchester, Greater Manchester, NW England, UK. He studied at the universities of Durham and Chicago. He was an assistant editor on the *Manchester Evening News* and editor of *Northern Echo*, before becoming editor of *The Sunday Times* (1967–83). He was a pioneer of investigative journalism, successfully appealing to the European Court of Human Rights against the suppression by the House of Lords of articles exposing the thalidomide scandal.

Evans, Marian / Mary Ann >> Eliot, George

Evans, Maurice (1901–89) Stage, cinema, and TV actor, born in Dorchester, Dorset, S England, UK. After his professional stage debut in London in 1926, he enjoyed his first success with *Journey's End* (1929). He went on to the Old Vic, then made his Broadway debut in *Romeo and Juliet* (1936) with Katharine Cornell. Therafter he settled in the USA, playing mainly in Shakespeare, Shaw, and other classic plays, but also making several films and appearing on television, most regularly in *Bewitched*. During World War 2 he was in charge of the US army's Entertainment Section in the Central Pacific, and performed a famous modern-dress version of Hamlet for the troops. >> Cornell, Katharine

Evans, Merlyn (1910–73) Painter, born in Cardiff, S Wales, UK. He studied at the Glasgow School of Art. His paintings are mainly Surrealist in character, with semi-abstract figures. In 1966 he won the Gold Medal for Fine Art at the National Eisteddfod of Wales.

Evans, Oliver (1755–1819) Inventor, born in Newport, DE. He improved flour mills, introducing the first automated continuous production line (1784), and invented the first high-pressure steam engine (1790). His amphibious steam dredging machine (1804) is considered the first US steam land carriage.

Evans, Timothy John >> Christie, John

Evans, Walker (1903–75) Photographer, born in St Louis, MI. In 1933 he started as an architectural photographer, but from 1935 began to record social deprivation in the Southern states for the US government Farm Security Administration, the two themes being combined in his *American Photographs* (1938). He was associate editor of *Fortune* (1945–65), and professor of graphic design at Yale (1965–74). His work with the writer James Agee to document the lives of the share-croppers of the Deep South,

eventually published as *Let Us Now Praise Famous Men* (1941), is considered to be one of the best writer–photographer collaborations. >> Agee

Evans-Pritchard, Sir Edward Evan (1902–73) Social anthropologist, born in Crowborough, East Sussex, SE England, UK. He studied at Oxford, where he later became professor of anthropology (1946–70). He is best known for two books, *Witchcraft, Oracles and Magic among the Azande* (1937) and *The Nuer* (1940), resulting from field studies of these peoples of the Sudan. >> Seligman

Evarts, William Maxwell (1818–1901) Lawyer and statesman, born in Boston, MA. He studied at Yale and Harvard. He was defence counsel for President Andrew Johnson in the impeachment proceedings of 1868, and US counsel before the *Alabama* Tribunal in Geneva in 1872. He became US attorney general (1868–9), secretary of state (1877–81), and a member of the US Senate (1885–91). >> Johnson, Andrew

Evatt, Elizabeth (Andreas) (1933–) Reformist lawyer, born in Sydney, New South Wales, Australia. She studied at Sydney and Harvard universities, and was the youngest law student ever accepted to the Sydney University Law School, and the first woman to win the university law medal. She became deputy president of the Australian Conciliation and Arbitration Commission (1973–89), chaired the Royal Commission on Human Relationships (1974–7), was first Chief Judge of the Family Court of Australia (1976–88), and is currently president of the Law Reform Commission and Chancellor of the University of Newcastle. She was a member of the UN Committee on the Elimination of Discrimination Against Women (1984–92), and in 1992 was elected to the UN Human Rights Committee.

Evatt, Herbert Vere, nickname **Doc Evatt** (1894–1965) Australian statesman and jurist, born in East Maitland, New South Wales, Australia. He studied at Sydney University, served in the New South Wales State Assembly, was called to the bar in 1929, and became justice of the High Court of Australia (1930–40). He entered the federal parliament as a Labor member in 1940. As minister of external affairs (1941–9), he was a frequent visitor to Britain, a delegate at international conferences, and responsible for developing an Australian foreign policy independent to Britain's. He represented Australia in Churchill's War Cabinet, and was president of the UN General Assembly (1948–9). He was Leader of the Opposition in the federal parliament (1951–60), after which he became Chief Justice of New South Wales.

Evelyn, John [evelin, eevlin] (1620–1706) Diarist and writer, born in Wotton, Surrey, SE England, UK. He studied at Oxford and London, and travelled abroad during the Civil War. He was much at court after the Restoration, acted on public committees, and became one of the Commissioners of the Privy Seal (1685–7) and treasurer of Greenwich Hospital (1695–1703). His main literary work is his *Diary*, a detailed sourcebook on life in 17th-c England.

Everdingen, Allart van [everdingen] (1621–75) Landscape painter and etcher, born in Alkmaar, The Netherlands. He is best known for his Scandinavian landscapes, and for the etchings of animals he made to illustrate *Reynard the Fox* by Hendrick van Alcmar.

Everest, Sir George (1790–1866) Military engineer, born in Gwernvale, Powys, E Wales, UK. He worked on the trigonometrical survey of India (1818–43), being appointed surveyor general in 1830. He was elected a Fellow of the Royal Society in 1827, and knighted in 1861. Mt Everest was renamed in his honour in 1865.

Everett, Edward (1794–1865) Statesman and scholar, born in Dorchester, MA. He studied at Harvard, and was elected professor of Greek there (1815), and president (1846–9). He was Governor of Massachusetts (1835–9), US minister at the court of St James's, UK (1841–5), and briefly secretary of state at the end of 1852. He is remembered as an outstanding lecturer and orator.

Everly Brothers, The [eve(r)lee] American duo **Don Everly** (1937– , guitar, vocals), and **Phil Everly** (1939– , guitar, vocals). They had their first major hit with 'Bye Bye Love' (1957), and the style – close harmonies over acoustic guitars and a rock n' roll beat – became their trademark. Other hit records include 'Wake Up Little Susie' (1957), 'Cathy's Clown' (1960), and 'That'll Be The Day' (1965). Their unique sound had a profound influence on The Beatles, and Simon and Garfunkel, as well as the *California sound* rock groups. They split up in 1973 because of personal problems, but after ten years of estrangement they reformed in 1983 with a sell-out concert in the Royal Albert Hall, London.

Evert (Lloyd), Chris(tine Marie) [evert] (1954–) Tennis player, born in Fort Lauderdale, FL. She won her first Wimbledon title in 1974 at age 19, and later won in 1976 and 1981. She also won the US singles title in 1975–80 and 1982, the French Open in 1974–5, 1979–80, and 1984, and the Australian Open in 1982 and 1984. She married British tennis player **John Lloyd** (marriage dissolved, 1987), and in 1988 US skier **Andy Mill**. She retired from professional tennis in 1989. >> RR1173

Evita >> **Perón, Eva**

Evoe >> **Knox, Edmund George Valpy**

Evremond, Saint >> **Saint-Evremond**

Ewald, Johannes [ivahl] (1743–81) Poet and playwright, born in Copenhagen. After serving as a soldier, he devoted himself to poetry. He is best known for his prose tragedy, *Rolf Krage* (1770) and his mythological play *Balders Död* (1773, The Death of Baldur). The national song of Denmark comes from his operetta, *Fiskerne* (1779, The Fishermen).

Ewart, James Cossar [yooert] (1851–1933) Zoologist, born in Penicuik, Midlothian, EC Scotland, UK. Professor of natural history at Aberdeen (1879–82) and Edinburgh (1882–1927), he carried out notable experiments in animal breeding and hybridization, and disproved the theory of telegony (the supposed influence of a previous sire on the progeny of the same mother born to other sires).

Ewart, William [yooert] (1798–1869) Politician and reformer, born in Liverpool, Merseyside, NW England, UK. He studied at Oxford. As an MP (1828–68) he played a leading part in humanitarian reforms, including the abolition of capital punishment for minor offences and of hanging the corpses of executed criminals in chains. He carried a free libraries bill in 1850.

Ewell, Richard Stoddart [yooel] (1817–72) US soldier, born in Washington, DC. He served in Mexico and against the Apaches, but in the Civil War he resigned from the US army to join the Confederates (1861), serving under Jackson and Lee. He fought at Gettysburg and the Wilderness, and commanded the defences of Richmond. He was eventually captured with his entire force at Sailor's Creek in 1865. >> Jackson, Thomas Jonathan; Lee, Robert E

Ewing, Sir (James) Alfred [yooing] (1855–1935) Engineer and physicist, born in Dundee, E Scotland, UK. He was professor of engineering at Tokyo (1878–83) and Dundee (1883–90), of mechanism and applied mechanics at Cambridge (1890–1903), director of naval education (1903–16), and Principal of Edinburgh University (1916–29). He discovered and explained magnetic hysteresis (1890).

Ewing, Juliana (Horatia) [yooing], *née* **Gatty** (1841–85) Writer of children's literature, born in Ecclesfield, South Yorkshire, N England, UK. She was first published at 20, and suggested to her mother the starting of *Aunt Judy's Magazine* (1866), which she later edited, publishing in it many of her charming stories, such as *Jackanapes*. Her numerous books included *A Flat Iron for a Farthing* (1870), *Lab-lie-by-the-Fire* (1873), and *Daddy Darwin's Dovecot* (1881).

Ewing, Maria (Louise) (1950–) Mezzo-soprano, born in Detroit, MI. She studied at the Cleveland Institute of Music, giving her first public performance in Meadowbrook in *Rigoletto* (1968). In 1976 she made debuts at the Metropolitan Opera House, New York, and La Scala, Milan. Her major roles include *Carmen*, *Lady Macbeth*, *Salomé*, and *La Périchole*.

Ewing, (William) Maurice [yooing] (1906–) Marine geologist, born in Lockney, TX. He studied at the Rice Institute, TX, became director of the Lamont-Doherty Geological Observatory, NY, from 1949, and professor of geology at Columbia University in 1959. He pioneered marine seismic techniques, made the first measurements of the thickness of the oceanic crust, determined the global extent of mid-ocean ridges, and in 1957 discovered a deep central rift in them. His work was an important contribution to the understanding of the ocean floor, and to the theory of plate tectonics. >> Heezen

Eworth, Hans (c. 1520–after 1573) Flemish painter. He was recorded in the Antwerp Guild in 1540, but was active chiefly in England, being based in London from c.1545 for about 20 years. His surviving paintings are mainly portraits (signed with the monogram HE), though he is known also to have undertaken work for masques and pageants.

Exekias or **Execias** [ekseekias] (c. 550–525 BC) Greek potter and vase painter who worked in the so-called 'black figure' style. The most famous of his vessels, on which is inscribed 'Exekias made and decorated me', is in the Vatican Museum, and depicts Achilles and Ajax playing dice.

Eyadema, (Etienne) Gnassingbe [ayadayma] (1937–) Togolese politician and soldier, born in Pya, Togoland. He joined the French army in 1953 and experienced extensive foreign service, attaining the rank of sergeant. Returning to Togoland in 1962 he became army commander-in-chief (1965). Two years later he led a bloodless coup to oust President Nicolas Grunitzky. He banned all political activity until he had founded a new organization, the Assembly of the Togolese People, as the only legal party. Although there were several attempts to overthrow him, he began to introduce a degree of democracy into the political system.

Eyck, Jan van [iyk] (c. 1389–1441) Painter, born near Maastricht, The Netherlands. The greatest Flemish artist of the 15th-c, he was successively in the service of John of Bavaria, Count of Holland, and Philip 'the Good' of Burgundy, for whom he undertook diplomatic missions in Spain and Portugal. From 1431 he lived in Bruges. All the works which can be definitely attributed to him date from the last 10 years of his life. His most famous work is the altarpiece 'The Adoration of the Holy Lamb' in the Church of St Bavon at Ghent.

Eyre, Edward John [air] (1815–1901) Explorer and colonist, born in Hornsea, East Riding of Yorkshire, NE England, UK. He emigrated to Australia at 17, settled on the Lower Murray as a sheep farmer, and was appointed a magistrate. In 1840–1 he explored the region between South and Western Australia, and discovered *L Eyre*. In 1847 he became Governor of New Zealand, in 1854 of St Vincent, and in 1862 of Jamaica. In 1865 he suppressed a native rebellion at Morant Bay with the utmost severity, carrying out many executions. Eyre was recalled to England and prosecuted amidst great public controversy, but was cleared.

Eyre, Sir Richard (Charles Hastings) [air] (1943–) Theatre, film, and television director, born in Barnstaple, Devon, SW England, UK. He studied at Cambridge, and became associate director of the Lyceum Theatre, Edinburgh (1967–70), then director of productions (1970–2). He was artistic director of the Nottingham Playhouse (1973–8), then producer of the BBC Television *Play for Today* series (1978–81). Associate director of the National Theatre, London (1981–8), he became artistic director (1988–97). He was knighted in 1997.

Eysenck, Hans (Jurgen) [īysingk] (1916–97) Psychologist, born in Berlin. He studied in France and at London University, and was professor of psychology at London University (1955–83). Much of his work was psychometric research into the normal variations of human personality and intelligence, and he was an outspoken critic of claims made without adequate empirical evidence. He frequently championed the view that genetic factors play a large part in determining the psychological differences between people, and often held controversial views, particularly with his study of racial differences in intelligence.

Ezekiel [eezeekiel] (early 6th-c BC) Biblical prophet. A priest of Jerusalem, he was taken captive to Babylon by Nebuchadnezzar in 597 BC. He is the author of a book of Old Testament prophecies which looked forward to a new Jerusalem after the destruction of the old. >> Nebuchadnezzar II

Ezra the Scribe [ezra] (5th–4th-c BC) Religious leader who lived in Babylon during the reign of King Ataxerxes (I or II). He reorganized the Jewish community in Jerusalem, and renovated its religious cult. He may have brought part of the Mosaic law with him. An Old Testament book bears his name, as well as the apocryphal works of 1 and 2 Esdras (the Greek equivalent of *Ezra*).

Faber, Frederick William [**fay**ber] (1814–63) Priest and hymn writer, born in Calverley, West Yorkshire, N England, UK. He studied at Oxford, and took Anglican orders, but under the influence of Newman became a Roman Catholic and founded a lay community of converts (the *Wilfridians*) in 1845. He was ordained priest in 1847, and in 1849 became head of the Oratory which moved to Brompton Road in 1854. He wrote many theological works, but is remembered for his *Hymns* (1861), which include 'My God, How Wonderful Thou Art' and 'Sweet Saviour, bless us ere we go'. >> Newman, John Henry

Fabergé, Peter Carl [**fa**berzhay], originally **Karl Gustavovich Fabergé** (1846–1920) Goldsmith and jeweller, born in St Petersburg, Russia. Educated in several countries, in 1870 he inherited his father's establishment in St Petersburg, moving from the design and manufacture of conventional jewellery to the creation of more elaborate and fantastic objects, most famous of which are probably the celebrated imperial Easter eggs, first commissioned by Alexander III for his tsarina in 1884. He died in exile in Lausanne, after his business had been destroyed by the events of the Russian revolution.

Fabius, Laurent [fabyoos] (1946–   ) French statesman and prime minister (1984–6), born in Paris. He studied at the Ecole Normale Supérieure and the Ecole Nationale d'Administration, joined the Council of State as an auditor in 1973, and became economic adviser to the Socialist Party (PS) leader, François Mitterrand, in 1976. Elected to the National Assembly in 1978, he was appointed budget minister when the PS gained power in 1981, minister for research and industry in 1983, and prime minister at the age of 37. He introduced a liberal, 'free-market' economic programme, which had some success, but he resigned following his party's electoral defeat in March 1986. >> Mitterrand; RR1049

Fabius Maximus, Quintus [**fay**bius **mak**simus], known as **Fabius Cunctator** (Lat 'the delayer') (c. 260–203 BC) Roman general, statesman, and hero of the Second Punic War, whose refusal to engage Hannibal in set battle earned him his nickname. Originally a term of abuse, it became an honorific title after 216 BC, when Rome's massive and unnecessary defeat at the Battle of Cannae proved that his cautious tactics had been right.

Fabre, Ferdinand [**fah**bruh] (1830–98) Novelist, born in Bédarieux, France. He wrote *L'Abbé Tigrane* (1873) and other stories of rustic life in Cévennes.

Fabriano, Gentile da [fabri**ah**noh] (c.1370–c.1427) Painter, born in Fabriano, Italy. He worked chiefly in Venice and Brescia until 1419, and thereafter in Rome, Florence, and Siena. He painted religious subjects, notably 'The Adoration of the Magi' (1423, Florence), but few of his paintings have survived.

Fabricius, David [fa**bree**syoos] (1564–1617) Astronomer and clergyman, born in Esens, Germany. In 1586 he discovered the first variable star (Mira, in the constellation Cetus). He was pastor at Resterhaave and Osteel in East Friedland, where he was murdered. His son, **Johannes Fabricius** (1587–1615), discovered the Sun's spots and its revolution.

Fabricius, Hieronymus [fa**bree**tsius], also known as **Girolamo Fabrici** (1537–1619) Anatomist, born in Acquapendente, Italy. He studied under Fallopius at Padua, becoming his successor as professor of anatomy

there in 1562. He made the first detailed description of the valves of the veins, the placenta, and the larynx. William Harvey was one of his pupils. >> Fallopius; Harvey, William

Fabricius, Johann Christian [fa**bree**tsius] (1745–1808) Entomologist, born in Tøndern, Denmark. He studied at Copenhagen, and Uppsala, Sweden, and became professor of natural history at Kiel (1775). One of the founders of entomological taxonomy, his classification of insects was based on the structure of the mouth.

Fabritius, Carel [fa**bree**tsius] (c.1624–54) Painter, born in Beemster, The Netherlands. He studied under Rembrandt, and from c.1650 lived mainly in Delft, where he was killed in an explosion. Vermeer was much influenced by Fabritius's sensitive experiments in composition and the painting of light as in the tiny 'View of Delft' (1652, National Gallery, London). >> Rembrandt; Vermeer

Fabry, Marie Paul Auguste Charles [fabree] (1867–1945) Physicist, born in Marseilles, France. He became professor at Marseilles (1904) and the Sorbonne (1920). Co-inventor of the Fabry–Pérot interferometer with Alfred Pérot, he is also known for his research into light in connection with astronomical phenomena, and as the discoverer of the ozone layer in the upper atmosphere.

Fadeyev, Aleksandr Aleksandrovich [fa**day**ef] (1901–56) Novelist, born in Kimry, near Kalinin, Russia. He became a Communist in 1918, and fought in Siberia. Deeply influenced by Tolstoy, his works include *Molodaya gvardiya* (1946, The Young Guard). As general secretary of the Soviet Writers' Union (1946–55) he mercilessly exposed any literary 'deviationism' from the Party line, but after becoming a target himself he committed suicide in Moscow.

Fahd (ibn Abd al-Aziz) (1923–   ) Ruler of Saudi Arabia (1982–   ), born in Riyadh. Effectively ruler since the assassination of his older half-brother **Faisal** in 1975, he became king on the death of his other half-brother, **Khaled**. >> Faisal (ibn Abd al-Aziz); RR1086

Fahrenheit, Gabriel (Daniel) [**fa**renhiyt] (1686–1736) Physicist, born in Gdańsk, Poland (formerly Danzig, Germany). He invented the alcohol thermometer in 1709, following this with a mercury thermometer in 1714. He spent most of his life in The Netherlands.

Faidherbe, Louis Léon César [faydairb] (1818–89) French soldier and scholar, born in Lille, France. Appointed Governor of Senegal in 1854, he greatly extended the frontiers of his province (1858–61). In the Franco-Prussian War, commanding the Army of the North, he was defeated near St Quentin in 1871. After the peace he was dispatched by the French government to Egypt to study the monuments. He wrote on Numidian and Phoenician inscriptions (1870–4), the anthropology of Algiers and the French Sudan (1874–84), and treatises on the Fula and Berber languages (1875–7).

Fairbairn, Sir William [**fair**bairn] (1789–1874) Engineer, born in Kelso, Scottish Borders, SE Scotland, UK. He worked as a millwright in Manchester before opening a shipbuilding yard in London, pioneering the use of wrought iron for hulls. For Stephenson's bridges over the Menai Strait and at Conway, he designed the rectangular tubes ultimately adopted, and hydraulic rivetting machines that were partly used for their construction. He aided Joule and Lord Kelvin in 1851 in their investigations, and guided the experiments of the government committee

(1861–5) on the use of iron for defensive purposes. >> Joule; Kelvin; Stephenson, Robert

Fairbank, John K(ing) (1907–91) Historian, born in Huron, SD. He studied at Harvard, then spent six years travelling in China, teaching himself Chinese in order to read the country's 19th-c archives. He taught at Harvard (1936–77), where he developed a pioneering modern East Asian history programme with his colleague Edwin O Reischauer and directed the East Asian Research Center (1955–73). A target of Senator McCarthy's anti-Communist hearings in the 1950s, he went on to become a leading advocate of normalizing relations with Communist China in the 1960s. The creator of the field of modern Chinese history, his books include *The United States and China* (1948) and *China: a New History* (1992). >> McCarthy, Joseph R; Reischauer, Edwin O

Fairbanks, Douglas, (Elton), Snr, originally **Douglas Elton Ulman** (1883–1939) Film actor, born in Denver, CO. He first appeared in stage plays in 1901, but in 1915 went into films and made a speciality of swashbuckling hero parts, as in *The Three Musketeers* (1921), *Robin Hood* (1922), and *The Thief of Baghdad* (1924), in which he did all his own stunts. He was a founder of United Pictures. In 1920 he married **Mary Pickford** (divorced, 1935). >> Fairbanks, Douglas, Jr; Pickford

Fairbanks, Douglas (Elton), Jr (1909–) Film actor, writer, producer, and businessman, born in New York City, the son of Douglas Fairbanks, Snr. In his youth he made Hollywood movies in the style of his father, such as *Sinbad the Sailor* (1947), and also gained a reputation as a producer. He later became interested in international affairs, and made a name for himself as a diplomat. He was appointed to the boards of many companies, and received many international honours. An autobiography, *The Salad Days*, appeared in 1988. >> Fairbanks, Douglas, Snr

Fairchild, Sherman (1896–1971) Inventor and businessman, born in Oneonta, NY. In 1916 he invented a flash camera, as well as an aerial camera for the US War Department. He started his own company in 1920 to manufacture the aerial camera, founded an aerial survey company, and became known as 'the father of aerial mapping photography'. He also started an aircraft factory, and developed the first US planes to have enclosed cockpits. Other inventions included a radio compass, wing flaps, hydraulic brakes, and retractable landing gear. Eventually his companies were grouped under Fairchild Industries, and he remained chairman until his death.

Fairey, Sir (Charles) Richard (1887–1956) Aeronautical engineer and industrialist, born in Hendon, NW Greater London, England, UK. He studied at Finsbury Technical College, became chief engineer to aircraft manufacturers Short Brothers in 1913, and formed Fairey Aviation Company in 1915, starting by building Short designs. Over 100 different types were produced during his 40 years as head of the firm, and by 1925 half the aircraft in the RAF were of Fairey origin. After World War 2, the company worked on guided weapons and helicopters, and the Fairey 'Delta' was the first aircraft to fly at over 1000 mph (1132 mph) in 1956.

Fairfax, John (1804–77) Australian newspaper proprietor, born in England, UK. He ran a newspaper in Warwickshire, but went to Sydney in 1838 after being bankrupted by a defamation writ. In 1841, with Charles Kemp, he bought the *Sydney Herald*, changing its name in 1842 to *The Sydney Morning Herald*. In 1853, after Kemp's retirement, John Fairfax & Sons became responsible for the newspaper, and it became an influential, widely read journal. The dynasty he founded continued until one of his descendants, **Warwick Geoffrey Oswald Fairfax** (1960–), privatized the company in 1987, and took out loans which eventually sent it into receivership. John Fairfax Ltd was sold in 1991 to the Tourang consortium.

Fairfax (of Cameron), Thomas Fairfax, 3rd Baron (1612–71) English parliamentary general, born in Denton, North Yorkshire, N England, UK. In the Civil War, he distinguished himself at Marston Moor (1644), and in 1645 was given command of the New Model Army, defeating Charles I at Naseby. Cromwell replaced him in 1650 for refusing to march against the Scots, who had proclaimed Charles II king, and he then withdrew into private life. In 1660 he was head of the commission sent to The Hague to arrange for the king's return. >> Charles I (of England); Charles II (of England); Cromwell, Oliver

Fairfield, Cicily Isabel >> **West, Dame Rebecca**

Fairweather, Ian (1891–1974) Painter, born in Bridge of Allan, Stirling, C Scotland, UK. He trained at the Slade School of Art, London. From 1924 he travelled extensively, living and working in, amongst other places, Germany, Canada, China, Japan, India, as well as Australia. In 1940 he served as a captain in the British army in India until, invalided out in 1943, he returned to Australia. In 1952 he attempted to sail from Darwin to Indonesia in a homemade raft. Although he eventually landed, he had been presumed lost at sea, and an obituary had already appeared in the Australian press. He returned to Australia in 1953.

Faisal I [fiyzl], also spelled **Faysal** (1885–1933) King of Iraq (1921–33), born in Ta'if, Iraq, son of Hussein ibn Ali, king of the Hejaz. He played a major role in the Arab revolt of 1916, and was for a short while King of Syria after World War 1. Installed as King of Iraq by the British, he became a leader of Arab nationalism. >> Hussein ibn Ali; RR1063

Faisal II [fiysl], also spelled **Faysal** (1935–58) King of Iraq (1939–58), born in Baghdad, the great-grandson of Hussein ibn Ali. He succeeded his father, King Ghazi, who was killed in an accident, and after an education at Harrow, England, was installed as king. In February 1958 he concluded with his cousin King Hussein of Jordan a federation of the two countries in opposition to the United Arab Republic of Egypt and Syria. In July that year, he and his entire household were assassinated during a military coup, and Iraq became a republic. >> Hussein; Kassem; RR1063

Faisal (ibn Abd al-Aziz) [fiyzl], also spelled **Faysal** (1904–75) King of Saudi Arabia (1964–75), born in Riyadh. Appointed Viceroy of Hejaz in 1926, he became minister for foreign affairs in 1930, crown prince in 1953, and succeeded his half-brother Saud as king. He was assassinated in the royal palace in Riyadh by his nephew Faisal ibn Musaid. >> Fahd; Ibn Saud; RR1086

Faithfull, Emily (1835–95) Publisher and feminist, born in Headley, Surrey, SE England, UK. In 1860 she founded a printing house with women compositors, and was appointed printer and publisher-in-ordinary to Queen Victoria. In 1863 she started the *Victoria Magazine*, advocating the claims of women to remunerative employment.

Fajans, Kasimir [fahyans] (1887–1975) Physical chemist, born in Warsaw. He studied at Heidelberg and Munich, and moved to the USA in 1936, teaching at the University of Michigan thereafter. He became a US citizen in 1942. His early work was on radioactive elements, but he is now best known for *Fajans' rules*, dealing with the types of bond between atoms in compounds.

Falco, Louis [falkoh] (1942–93) Modern dancer and choreographer, born in New York City. After studying with José Limón, Martha Graham, and Charles Weidman, he joined the Limón company in 1960. In 1967 he formed his own company and began to choreograph, his works being adopted by many of the world's major contemporary dance companies. His film work includes the dance element of the successful theatre school story, *Fame* (1980). >> Graham, Martha; Limón; Weidman

Falcone, Giovanni [fal**koh**nay] (1939–92) Judge, born in Palermo, Sicily. In 1978 he was appointed to Palermo where he began a campaign against the Mafia, leading to the successful prosecution of 338 top members in 1987. He became director-general of the criminal affairs division in the Justice Ministry in Rome, and several attempts were made on his life. He was killed when a one-ton bomb exploded under his car.

Falconet, Etienne Maurice [falkohnay] (1716–91) Sculptor, born in Paris. A pupil of **François Le Moyne** (1688–1737), he was director of sculpture at the Sèvres Porcelain Factory (1757–66). His figures of Venus, bathers, and similar subjects epitomize the Rococo style of the period of Louis XV. He was invited to Russia in 1766 by Catherine II to execute what is his most impressive work, an equestrian monument to Peter I in St Petersburg. After suffering a stroke in 1783, he turned to writing art theory, nine volumes of which had been published by 1787.

Faldo, Nick [fal**doh**], popular name of **Nicholas Alexander Faldo** (1959–) Golfer, born in Welwyn Garden City, Hertfordshire, SE England, UK. He had early successes in winning the Professional Golfing Association championships in 1978, 1980, and 1981, and in 1987 won the Open Championship at Muirfield, UK, in appalling conditions, winning again in 1990 and 1992. In 1989 he won the US Masters, successfully defended his title in 1990, and won it again in 1996. >> RR1157

Falguière, Jean Alexandre Joseph [falgyair] (1831–1900) Sculptor and painter, born in Toulouse, France. He is celebrated for his portrait statues rather than for his larger compositions. Several sculptures and paintings are in the Luxembourg in Paris; his statue of Lafayette stands in Washington, DC.

Falk, Johann Daniel [falk] (1768–1826) Writer and philanthropist, born in Gdańsk, Poland. He founded the 'company of friends in need' for helping destitute children, and established the Falk Institute at Weimar. Of his writings the best known are his satirical works, such as *Der Mensch* (1795), and a study on Goethe.

Falkender, Marcia Matilda Falkender, Baroness [folkender] (1932–) British political worker. She studied at Queen Mary College, London, then worked at Labour Party headquarters before becoming private and political secretary to Prime Minister Harold Wilson (1956–73). Her background influence during the 1964–70 Labour government is chronicled in her book *Inside No. 10* (1972). She was given a life peerage in 1974. >> Wilson, Harold

Falkenhayn, Erich (Georg Anton Sebastian) von [**fal**kenhiyn] (1861–1922) German soldier, born near Grudziadz, Poland. He served as an adviser with the Chinese army, and with the international force in the Boxer Rebellion (1900). He was Prussian war minister in 1913 and succeeded Moltke as chief of general staff in September 1914, but was dismissed after the failure of his offensive strategy in 1916. He commanded in the invasion of Romania (1916–17), and was then transferred to Palestine. His last command was in Lithuania in 1918. >> Moltke, Helmuth (Karl Bernhard)

Falla, Manuel de [fal**ya**] (1876–1946) Composer, born in Cadiz, Spain. He won prizes in 1905 as a pianist and for his first opera, then moved to Paris (1907–14), where he published his first piano compositions. On returning to Madrid, his works became known for their colourful national Spanish idiom. He is best known for his ballet, *The Three-Cornered Hat* (1919). With the outbreak of the Spanish Civil War, he settled in Argentina. >> Verdaguer

Fallon, Martin >> **Higgins, Jack**

Fallopius, Gabriel [fal**oh**pius], Ital **Gabriello Fallopio** (1523–62) Anatomist, born in Modena, Italy. He studied at Ferrara, then became professor of anatomy at Pisa (1548) and Padua (1551). He made several discoveries relating to bones and to the organs of reproduction. The *Fallopian tubes* connecting the ovary with the uterus are named after him.

Falstaff >> **Fastolf; Oldcastle**

Faltskog, Agnetha >> **Abba**

Falwell, Jerry L [**faw**lwel] (1933–) Religious leader, born in Lynchburg, VA. After studying at Baptist Bible College, MO, he was ordained a minister. In 1956, he founded Thomas Road Baptist Church, Lynchburg, which became the basis of an extensive evangelical campaign. He was also responsible for founding The Moral Majority, Inc, and Liberty University. He has published widely, and broadcasts regularly to large audiences.

Faneuil, Peter [**fan**l] (1700–43) Merchant and philanthropist, born in New Rochelle, NY. He made a fortune in Boston, MA, where in 1742 he built the Faneuil Hall (known as 'the cradle of American liberty'), presenting it to the town.

Fanfani, Amintore [fan**fah**nee] (1908–) Italian statesman and prime minister (1954, 1958–9, 1960–3, 1982–3), born in Pieve Santo Stefano, Italy. A former professor of political economics, he was prime minister on five occasions. Nominated a life senator in 1972, he became president of the Italian Senate in 1968–73 and 1976–82. He is a member (and former secretary and chairman) of the Christian Democratic Party. >> RR1065

Fangio, Juan Manuel [**fan**jioh] (1911–95) Motor-racing driver, born in Balcarce, Argentina, of Italian descent. He served his apprenticeship to road racing first as a mechanic, then in South American events with a car he built himself. He first took part in European Grand Prix racing in 1949, and by 1957 had won the World Championship a record five times (1951, 1954–7). He won 24 Grands Prix. After his retirement (1958) he joined Mercedes-Benz in Argentina. He was once held hostage by Castro's revolutionaries in Cuba. >> Castro; RR1164

Fantin-Latour, (Ignace) Henri (Jean Théodore) [fātī latoor] (1836–1904) Painter, pastellist, and lithographer, born in Grenoble, France. He studied at Paris, and stayed for a while in England. He is best known for his flower studies and portrait groups, such as 'Hommage à Manet' (1870, Louvre). In his later years he specialized in lithography.

Farabi, al- >> **al-Farabi, Abu Nasr**

Faraday, Michael (1791–1867) Chemist, experimental physicist, and natural philosopher, born in Newington Butts, Surrey, SE England, UK. Apprenticed to a bookbinder, he devoted his leisure to science. In 1813 he was engaged by Davy as his assistant at the Royal Institution, and in 1827 he succeeded to Davy's chair of chemistry. His research contributed to an extremely broad area of physical science, such as the condensation of gases, the conservation of force, and studies on benzene and steel. His major work is the series of *Experimental Researches on Electricity* (1839–55), in which he reports a wide range of discoveries about the nature of electricity, notably electrolysis, and the relationship between electricity and magnetism. >> Davy; Maxwell, James C

Farel, Guillaume [farel] (1489–1565) Protestant reformer, born in Gap, France. He studied at Paris, where he became a convert to Protestantism, and was forced to flee to Switzerland (1524). After being twice compelled to leave Geneva, he returned there in 1534, the town council soon after proclaiming the Reformation. He was responsible for making Calvin stay in Geneva, but the severity of the ecclesiastical discipline which Calvin imposed caused their expulsion from the city (1538). He later returned with Calvin to Geneva, and then went to Neuchâtel (1543), where he died. >> Calvin, John

Farge, John La >> **La Farge, John**

Fargo, William (George) (1818–81) Pioneer expressman, born in Pompey, NY. He worked as an agent for Livingstone, Wells, and Pomeroy's Express before joining with Henry Wells and Daniel Dunning to found Wells & Co, the first express company to operate W of Buffalo, NY. The two companies merged (1850) to form the American Express Co, of which Fargo was secretary and Wells president. The two men later founded Wells, Fargo & Co (1852). Fargo became president of the American Express Co in 1868, and served two terms as Mayor of Buffalo (1862–6). >> Wells, Henry

Farigoule, Louis >> **Romains, Jules**

Farina, Battista [fareena], nickname **Pinin** (1893–1966) Automobile designer, born in Turin, Italy. He established his car bodywork design business in Turin in 1930, producing many classic designs for prestigious Italian car makers. He also designed car bodies for mass production. His nickname was adopted in the company name (Pininfarina) in 1961, and by his son **Sergio Pininfarina** (1926–) who took charge in 1959.

Farinacci, Roberto [farinahchee] (1892–1945) Italian statesman, born in Isernia, Italy. He became Fascist party secretary (1924–6), a member of the Fascist grand council (1935), and a minister of state (1938). An ardent racialist and anti-Semite, notorious for his extremism and pro-Nazi tendencies, he edited the *Regime Fascista*, the Party organ. He was ultimately captured and shot, on the same day and by the same band of partisans as Mussolini, while attempting to flee to Switzerland. >> Mussolini

Farjeon, Eleanor [fah(r)jn] (1881–1965) Writer, born in London, England, UK. She wrote fantasies and children's stories, and collaborated with her brother **Herbert** in *Kings and Queens* (1932). There is a *Farjeon Award* for outstanding work in children's books.

Farman, Henri [fah(r)mã] (1874–1958) Pioneer aviator and aircraft manufacturer, born in Paris. With his brother **Maurice Farman** (1878–1964) he became involved with aircraft in 1908, winning a prize for a circular flight of 1 km. In 1912 they established a factory at Boulogne-sur-Seine to manufacture the *Farman biplane*, and built the first long-distance passenger plane, the *Goliath*, in 1917. They were the first to use ailerons, which are now standard fittings on all aircraft.

Farnaby, Giles [fah(r)nabee] (c. 1560–1640) Composer, probably born in Truro, Cornwall, SW England, UK. He was a joiner by trade, but graduated in music at Oxford, and lived for a time near Lincoln. By 1614 he seems to have moved to London. His works include madrigals and settings of the psalms, but he is best remembered for his keyboard music.

Farnese, Alessandro [fah(r)nayzay] (1545–92) Italian general, born in Rome. He fought in the service of Philip II of Spain, who was his uncle, and distinguished himself against the Turks at Lepanto (1571). As Governor-General of the Spanish Netherlands (1578–92), he captured Antwerp (1585), and compelled Henry IV of France to raise the siege of Paris (1590). >> Henry IV (of France); Philip II (of Spain)

Farouk I [farook] (1920–65) Last reigning king of Egypt (1936–52), born in Cairo, the son of Fuad I. He was educated in England, and studied at the Royal Military Academy, Woolwich. After World War 2 he turned increasingly to a life of pleasure. The defeat of Egypt by Israel (1948) and continuing British occupation led to increasing unrest, and General Neguib's coup (1952) forced his abdication and exile, and in 1959 he became a citizen of Monaco. He was succeeded by his infant son as **Fuad II**, but the establishment of a Regency Council was forestalled by the formation of a republic some months later. >> Fuad I; RR1046

Farquhar, George [fah(r)ker] (c. 1677–1707) Playwright, born in Londonderry, Co Londonderry. He studied at Dublin, and became an actor in a Dublin theatre, but soon left the stage and joined the army. His first comedy, *Love and a Bottle* (1698), proved a success, as were several other plays, notably *The Recruiting Officer* (1706). His best work, *The Beaux' Stratagem* (1707), was written during his last illness.

Farragut, David (Glasgow) [faraguht] (1801–70) US naval commander, born near Knoxville, TN. Entering the navy in 1810, he saw service against the British in 1812, and against pirates in 1820. In the Civil War he led the Union forces that captured New Orleans (1862), and took part in the siege and capture of Vicksburg (1863) and Mobile Bay (1864). He was made an admiral in 1866, but his health prevented him from continuing in active service.

Farrakhan, Louis [farakan], originally **Louis Eugene Walcott** (1933–) Black Muslim leader, born in New York City. He grew up in Roxbury, MA, and was converted to the Nation of Islam by Malcolm X. Following Malcolm X's defection (1963–4) he became the national representative for Elijah Muhammad; but when Muhammad's son allowed whites to join the movement (after 1975), Farrakhan split away and formed a revitalized movement, Final Call to the Nation of Islam. An eloquent speaker, he continued to work for black separatism and economic power. He often employed an abrasive rhetoric that alienated white and Semitic groups, but in the early 1990s he began to soften his image, including playing the violin in classical concerts to show that he was not totally opposed to whites and their culture. He was the chief organizer of the 'million man march' of black men on Capitol Hill, Washington, in 1996. >> Malcolm X; Muhammad, Elijah

Farrar, Frederic William (1831–1903) British clergyman and writer, born in Mumbai (Bombay), India. He was ordained in 1854, taught at Harrow, became headmaster of Marlborough (1871–6), honorary chaplain to Queen Victoria (1869–73), and later a chaplain-in-ordinary. He was made a canon of Westminster and rector of St Margaret's in 1876, archdeacon of Westminster in 1883, chaplain to the House of Commons in 1890, and dean of Canterbury in 1895. His theological writings were many, but he is chiefly remembered for the best seller, *Eric, or Little by Little* (1858), one of several school stories.

Farrar, Geraldine (1882–1967) Soprano, born in Melrose, MA. She began vocal studies in Boston, and went to Europe for further training at 17. After a successful debut in 1901 at the Berlin Opera, she appeared with Caruso in *La Bohéme* at Monte Carlo in 1903. Her US debut came three years later at the Metropolitan in New York City; she remained there for 16 seasons, her famous roles including the lead in *Madame Butterfly*. A vivacious personality with a cult following, she also appeared in a number of silent films, beginning with *Carmen* (1915). She retired from opera in 1922, and from recitals in 1931.

Farrell, James T(homas) (1904–79) Writer of starkly realist novels of American life, born in Chicago, IL. His best-known work is the *Studs Lonigan* trilogy (1932–5, filmed 1960), set in the slums of Chicago.

Farrell, M J >> **Keane, Molly**

Farrell, Suzanne (1945–) Ballerina, born in Cincinnati, OH. She trained at the School of American Ballet, became a soloist at the New York City Ballet (1963), and joined Maurice Béjart's Ballet of the 20th Century (1970). Balanchine persuaded her to return to the NYCB in 1975, and created several new works for her, including *Union Jack* (1976). >> Balanchine; Béjart

Farren-Price, Ronald William (1930–) Pianist, born in Brisbane, Queensland, Australia. He studied at Melbourne University, and under Claudio Arrau in London. Since 1967 he has toured extensively in the USA and Europe, performed as a soloist with many major orchestras, and recorded widely. In 1955 he became reader in music at Melbourne University. >> Arrau

Farrer, William James (1845–1906) Plant breeder, born in Docker, Cumbria, NW England, UK. He studied medicine at Cambridge, but tuberculosis forced him to give up and emigrate to Australia in 1870. He found work as a surveyor, but in 1886 he settled on his own property near Tharwa, New South Wales, where an early interest in grasses led him to systematic experiments with different strains of wheat. He pioneered scientific wheat-breeding, and his work was almost solely responsible for the growth and success of the Australian wheat industry.

Farr-Jones, Nick, popular name of **Nicholas Campbell Farr-Jones** (1962–) Rugby union player, born in Sydney, New South Wales, Australia. A fierce cover defender, he was captain of the Australian team (1988–90), and celebrated his 50th Test during the 1991 World Cup. He works as a solicitor in Sydney.

Farrow, Mia (1945–) Film actress, born in Los Angeles, CA. She made her stage debut off-Broadway in 1963, and had a 2-year role (as Alison Mackenzie) in the TV soap *Peyton Place*. Her film roles include *Rosemary's Baby* (1968), *The Great Gatsby* (1973), and several Woody Allen films, notably *The Purple Rose of Cairo* (1985), *Hannah and Her Sisters* (1986), and *Husbands and Wives* (1992). Later films include *Widow's Peak* (1994), *Reckless* (1995), and *Miracle at Midnight* (1997). Earlier married to Frank Sinatra (1966–8), her relationship with Woody Allen (with whom she had nine children, five of them adopted) broke up in acrimony in 1992, following her discovery of Allen's affair with their adopted teenage daughter.

Farson, James (Negley) (1890–1960) Writer, born in Plainfield, NJ. He trained as a civil engineer, then travelled to England and to Russia, where he had an export business and where he witnessed the 1917 revolution. From then on he led an adventurous life as airman, sailor, and journalist, which is reflected in his varied works. These include *Sailing Across Europe* (1926), *Bomber's Moon* (1941), and *A Mirror for Narcissus* (1957).

Fasch, Johann Friedrich (1688–1758) Organist and composer, born in Buttelstedt, Germany. Educated at the Thomasschule, Leipzig, he was appointed *Kapellmeister* at Zerbst in 1722. He composed numerous works, including church music, orchestral works, and chamber music, many of which were greatly admired by J S Bach. >> Bach, Johann Sebastian

Fassbinder, Rainer Werner [fasbinder] (1946–82) Film director, born in Bad Wöshofen, Germany. He began his career as an actor in fringe theatre in Munich, founding his own 'anti-theatre' company. His work in cinema began in 1969, and was much influenced by Jean-Luc Godard. He completed over 40 full-length films, largely politically committed criticisms of contemporary Germany, notably *Die bitteren Tränen der Petra von Kant* (1972, The Bitter Tears of Petra von Kant) and *Die Ehe der Maria Braun* (1979, The Marriage of Maria Braun), which won first prize at the 1979 Berlin Film Festival. The most prolific writer-director-actor of the New German Cinema of the 1970s, he died at 36 as a result of alcohol and drug abuse. >> Godard

Fassett, Kaffe [kayf] (1937–) Fashion designer, born in San Francisco, CA. He studied painting at the Museum of Fine Arts in Boston before migrating to England in 1964. Discovering the potential of hand knitting and needlepoint, he formed a design company producing knitting kits for Rowan, needlepoint for Ehrman, and fabrics for the Designers Guild. His television broadcasts and books, such as *Glorious Interiors* (1995), have made his colourful designs popular in Europe and the USA.

Fastolf, Sir John (1378–1459) English soldier, born in Caister, Norfolk, E England, UK. He distinguished himself at Agincourt (1415), and still more at the 'Battle of the Herrings' (1429), so called because he formed a *laager* of herring barrels, and beat off a whole French army. He was accused of cowardice at Patay (1429), but later cleared of the charge. His Norfolk life is mirrored faithfully in the *Paston Letters*. His identification with 'Sir John Falstaff' is at least incomplete, for Oldcastle was almost certainly Shakespeare's prototype. >> Oldcastle

Fateh Singh, Sant [fate sing] (1911–72) Sikh religious leader and campaigner for Sikh rights, born in the Punjab. He was involved in religious and educational activity in Rajasthan, founding many schools and colleges there. In 1942 he joined the Quit India Movement, and was imprisoned for his political activities. During the 1950s he agitated for a Punjabi-speaking autonomous state, which was achieved with the creation of the Indian state of Punjab in 1966.

Fatima (c. 605–33) The youngest daughter of the Prophet Mohammed, and wife of the fourth Muslim caliph, Ali; from them descended the *Fatimids*, the dynasty of Shiite caliphs, who ruled over Egypt and N Africa (909–1171), and later over Syria and Palestine. >> Ali; Mohammed

Faulkner or **Falkner, William (Harrison)** [fawkner] (1897–1962) Writer, born in New Albany, MS. He served with the RAF in World War 1, and began his literary career with *Soldier's Pay* (1926), a novel on the aftermath of war. With *The Sound and the Fury* (1929) he began to experiment in literary form and style. *Sartoris* (1929) was the first in a series dealing with the social and racial problems of an imaginary Southern county, Yoknapatawpha. Other major novels include *As I Lay Dying* (1930), *Absalom, Absalom!* (1936), *Intruder in the Dust* (1948), and *The Reivers* (1962). He was awarded the Nobel Prize for Literature in 1949.

Faure, Edgar (Jean) [fohr], pseudonym of **Edgar Sanday** (1908–88) French writer, statesman, and prime minister (1952, 1955–6) born in Béziers, France. He trained as a lawyer in Paris, entering politics as a Radical-Socialist. He was minister of finance and economic affairs several times in the 1950s, becoming premier for two short periods. He was later minister of agriculture (1966), education (1968), and social affairs (1969), president of the National Assembly (1973–8), and a member of the European Parliament from 1979. He wrote several detective novels under his pseudonym. >> RR1049

Fauré, Gabriel (Urbain) [fohray] (1845–1924) Composer, born in Pamiers, France. He became organist (1896) at La Madeleine, Paris, and director of the Conservatoire (1905–20). Though chiefly remembered for his songs, including the evergreen *Après un rêve* (c.1865), he also wrote operas and orchestral pieces, such as *Masques et bergamasques* (1919), and a much-performed *Requiem* (1887–90).

Fauves >> **Marquet; Matisse; Rouault; Vlaminck**

Favart, Charles Simon [favah(r)] (1710–92) Playwright, born in Paris. He began writing libretti for comic opera while working as a pastry cook, and success led him to become stage manager (1743) and director (1758) of the

Opéra-Comique. With his wife, **Marie-Justine-Benoiste Duranceray** (1727–71), he pioneered a new realism in costume. Among his best out of more than 100 comic operas are *Les Amours de Bastien et Bastienne* and *Les Trois Sultanes*.

Favre, Brett [fahvr] (1969–) Player of American football, born in Pass Christian, MS. He set six school passing records while at Southern Mississippi, and was selected by the National Football League Atlanta Falcons in 1991. He later joined the Green Bay Packers as quarterback, and in 1997 became only the second player to win the NFL's Most Valuable Player Award in consecutive years (1995–6). >> Montana, Joe

Fawcett, Dame Millicent, *née* **Garrett** (1847–1929) Women's rights campaigner, born in Aldeburgh, Suffolk, E England, UK, the sister of Elizabeth Garrett Anderson. Keenly interested in the higher education of women and the extension of the franchise to her sex, she was made president of the National Union of Women's Suffrage Societies (1897–1919). >> Anderson, Elizabeth

Fawcett, Percy (Harrison) (1867–1925) Explorer, born in Torquay, Devon, SW England, UK. He entered the army at 19, rose to become lieutenant-colonel, and after service in Ceylon, Hong Kong, and elsewhere was in 1906 given a border delimitation assignment on behalf of the Bolivian government. This led to several hazardous expeditions in the Mato Grosso area in search of traces of ancient civilizations. In 1925 he disappeared with his eldest son near the Xingú R.

Fawkes, Guy (1570–1606) Conspirator, born in York, North Yorkshire, N England, UK, of Protestant parentage. He became a Catholic at an early age, and served in the Spanish army in The Netherlands (1593–1604). He crossed to England at Catesby's invitation, and became a member of the Gunpowder Plot. Caught red-handed, he was tried and hanged. >> Catesby

Fawkner, John Pascoe (1792–1869) Pioneer and founder of Melbourne, born in London, England, UK. He travelled to Australia with his father, who had been sentenced to transportation. When the colony of Port Phillip was abandoned, the family were shipped to Tasmania. After being involved in various enterprises, John engaged a ship to explore Western Port and Port Phillip Bay on the mainland of Australia, and established a settlement at the mouth of the Yarra R, the site of the future city of Melbourne. The settlement developed into a town, and Fawkner became a member of its council. Later, when the new colony was separated from New South Wales, he was a member of the first legislative council for Victoria.

Faxian [fahshyan], also spelled **Fa-hsien** (AD c. 360–c. 430) Buddhist pilgrim, explorer, and diarist. Inspired by the visit of Kumarajiva to China (386) he made a momentous journey through Turkestan, India, and SE Asia (399–414) looking for Buddhist Scriptures. In India he visited every region except the Deccan, learned Sanskrit, and translated the earliest *Life* of Buddha into Chinese. He later wrote his memoirs (AD 416) in Nanjing: *Account of Buddhist Countries* is the oldest known travel book in Chinese literature, and an important source on contemporary C Asia and India. His trip inspired many later visits to India, including that of Xuanzang in the 7th-c. >> Xuanzang

Faye, Hervé Auguste Etienne (1814–1902) Astronomer, born in Benoît-du-Sault, France. He became professor of astronomy at the Ecole Polytechnique in 1873, and director of the Paris Observatory in 1878. In 1843 he discovered *Faye's comet*.

Feather, Vic, popular name of **Victor (Grayson Hardie) Feather, Baron Feather (of the City of Bradford)** (1908–76) Trade union leader, born in Gainsborough, Lincolnshire, EC England, UK. Educated at Hanson Grammar School,

Bradford, he began work at 14, and joined the Shopworkers' Union. Shop steward at 15, and chairman of his branch committee at 21, he was a stirring speaker, and in 1937 joined the staff of the Trade Union Council, becoming assistant secretary (1947–60), assistant general secretary (1960–9), and general secretary (1969–73). He fought the Conservative government's anti-union Industrial Relations bill (1972), and helped to form an independent advisory organization to settle labour disputes. He was president of the European Trade Union Conference (1973–4).

Febronius, Justinus >> **Hontheim, Johann von**

Fechner, Gustav (Theodor) [fekhner] (1801–87) Physicist, philosopher, anthropologist, and psychologist, born in Gross Särchen, Germany. His interest in mind-body relationships led to his book *Elemente der Psychophysik* (1860, Elements of Psychophysics), in which he developed the ideas of Ernst Heinrich Weber on the measurement of sensory thresholds, and laid the foundations for psychophysics. He was also the founder of experimental aesthetics, and his methods were influential in the development of experimental psychology. >> Weber, Ernst Heinrich

Fedden, Sir (Albert Hubert) Roy (1885–1973) Aeroengine designer, born in Bristol, SW England, UK. He established the engine building department of the Bristol Aeroplane Co in 1920, where he was chief engineer until 1942. Initiating a famous range of piston engines, including the Pegasus and Hercules, he was also notable for his unique development of the sleeve-valve engine. He held a variety of governmental and international posts until 1960, and was president of the Royal Aeronautical Society in 1938, 1939, and 1945.

Fehling, Hermann von [fayling] (1812–85) Chemist, born in Lübeck, Germany. Professor of chemistry at Stuttgart, he introduced the solution, an important oxidizing agent, which bears his name.

Feiffer, Jules [fiyfer] (1929–) Cartoonist and writer, born in New York City. He studied at the Art Students League of New York and at Pratt Institute, later gaining recognition for his cartoon work in the Greenwich Village newspaper *Village Voice* (1956). His first collection of cartoons was called *Sick, Sick, Sick* (1958). *Passionella, and Other Stories* followed (1959), and featured the popular character 'Munro'. He produced many collections during the 1960s, becoming famous for *Feiffer*, a satirical cartoon strip. He also wrote revues, plays, screenplays, and novels.

Feigenbaum, Mitchell [fiygenbowm] (1945–) Mathematician, born in Philadelphia, PA. He is one of a small group of scientists who in the 1970s were growing more concerned about the inability of science to explain irregular occurrences in everyday life, such as the shape of clouds, the irregular flow from a dripping tap, and many other events that could be described as chaotic. He developed the mathematics of what is now called Chaos Theory, used in fields such as meteorology, aerodynamics, and ecology. >> Lorenz; May, Robert

Feininger, Lyonel (Charles Adrian) [fiyninger] (1871–1956) Painter, born in New York City. He worked as a political cartoonist, then devoted himself to painting (1907). After World War 1 he taught at the Bauhaus in Weimar and Dessau, and adopted a style reminiscent of Cubism. After the Nazi rise, he returned to the USA, where he helped to found the New Bauhaus in Chicago.

Feld, Eliot (1942–) Dancer, choreographer, and artistic director, born in New York City. He trained at the School of American Ballet, and appeared in both Broadway and Hollywood versions of *West Side Story* before joining American Ballet Theatre (ABT) in 1963, where he began to choreograph. He left ABT to found the short-lived

American Ballet Company (1969–71), rejoined ABT for a few seasons, and formed Eliot Feld Ballet in 1974. In 1978 he started the New Ballet School, an organization that offers inner-city children the chance to become dance professionals.

Fell, John (1625–86) Anglican priest, born in Longworth, Oxfordshire, SC England, UK. He maintained the Church of England services during the rule of Cromwell, despite opposition. After the Restoration he was made dean of Christ Church, Oxford, and royal chaplain. He governed the college strictly, restored its buildings, and installed the press. In 1676 he became Bishop of Oxford. He rebuilt the episcopal palace at Cuddesdon. The verse 'I do not like thee, Doctor Fell' is ascribed to Tom Brown (1663–1704), one of his students.

Feller, William (1906–70) Mathematician, born in Zagreb, Croatia. He studied at Zürich and Göttingen, and after teaching at Kiel, left Germany in 1933 for Stockholm. In 1939 he emigrated to the USA, holding chairs at Brown (1939–45), Cornell (1945–50), and Princeton (1950–70) universities. He is best known for his work in probability theory.

Fellini, Federico [feleenee] (1920–93) Film director, born in Rimini, Italy. He studied at Bologna, and was a cartoonist, journalist, and scriptwriter before becoming an assistant film director in 1942. His highly individual films, always from his own scripts, include *La strada* (1954, The Road, Oscar), *Le notte di Cabiria* (1956, Nights of Cabiria, Oscar), *Fellini's Roma* (1972), *Amarcord* (1973, I Remember, Oscar), *Otto e mezzo* (1963, 8½), and, his most famous and controversial work, *La dolce vita* (1960, The Sweet Life; Cannes Festival prizewinner), a *succès de scandale* for its cynical evocation of modern Roman high life. In 1943 he married the actress **Giulietta Masina** (1920–   ), star of several of his films. Among his later productions are *Città della donna* (1980, City of Women) and *Ginger e Fred* (1986, Ginger and Fred), and *La voca della luna* (1990, Voices of the Moon). He was presented with an Honorary Academy Award in 1993.

Fenby, Eric >> **Delius, Fredrick**

Fénelon, François de Salignac de la Mothe [faynelõ] (1651–1715) Roman Catholic theologian, born in Fénelon, France. Ordained in 1675, in 1689 Louis XIV made him tutor to his grandson, and in this position he wrote several works, notably *Les Aventures de Télémaque* (1699, The Adventures of Telemachus), which deserved the king's censure for its political undertones. He became Archbishop of Cambrai in 1695. In 1697 he wrote *Explanation of the Sayings of the Saints on the Interior Life* (trans title). The book was condemned by the pope, a decision which Fénelon accepted, and he retired to Cambrai.

Fenley, Molissa (1954–   ) Dancer and choreographer, born in Las Vegas, NV. Raised in Nigeria, she studied dance at Mills College, CA, before moving to New York City, where she made her choreographic debut in 1978. Her reputation rests on physically demanding, high-energy solos such as *Eureka* (1982) and *State of Darkness* (1988).

Fenning, Frederick William (1919–88) British nuclear physicist and pioneer of nuclear reactor technology. He studied at Cambridge University, and in 1940 joined the Cavendish Laboratory, researching neutron diffusion problems associated with the development of an atomic bomb. Later in the war he was sent to Canada, where he played a major role in starting up the ZEEP reactor at Chalk River. After the war at Harwell he worked on reactor design, and, as chief physicist then director of reactor technology at Risley, he was particularly associated with work on the Advanced Gas-Cooled Reactor (AGR) which led to the operation of the Windscale (now Sellafield) AGR. He

returned to Harwell as deputy director in 1966, later becoming deputy director of the Atomic Energy Research Establishment (1979–84).

Fenton, Roger (1819–69) Photographer, born in Heywood, Lancashire, NW England, UK. He was a founder and the first honorary secretary of the Photographic Society in 1853. In 1855 he went to the Crimea as the world's first accredited war-photographer, using the large cameras and wet-plates of the period to record the serving officers and men and the conditions of the campaign. It is for this work that he is best known, although little action could be depicted, and he ignored the painful side of warfare.

Ferber, Edna (1887–1968) Writer, born in Kalamazoo, MI. She began as a reporter in Wisconsin, and wrote numerous novels and short stories, including *Dawn O'Hara* (1911), *So Big* (1924, Pulitzer), *Cimarron* (1929), and *Saratoga Trunk* (1941). She is probably best remembered as the writer of *Show Boat* (1926), which inspired the musical of that name.

Ferdinand I (of Bulgaria), in full **Ferdinand Karl Leopold Maria** (1861–1948) King of Bulgaria, born in Vienna. The youngest son of Prince Augustus of Saxe-Coburg and Princess Clementine of Orléans, he served in the Austrian army. On the abdication of Prince Alexander of Bulgaria, Ferdinand was offered, and accepted, the crown in 1887. In 1908 he proclaimed Bulgaria independent, and took the title of king or tsar. Allying himself with the Central Powers, he invaded Serbia in 1915. His armies were routed, and he abdicated in 1918, his son **Boris III** (1894–1943) succeeding him.

Ferdinand I (of the Two Sicilies) (1751–1825) King of Naples, as Ferdinand IV (1759–99, 1799–1806) and of the Two Sicilies (1816–25), born in Naples, Italy. He joined England and Austria against France in 1793, and suppressed the French-supported Roman Republic (1799), but in 1801 was forced to make a treaty with Napoleon. In 1806 he took refuge in Sicily, under English protection, being reinstated by the Congress of Vienna (1815). In 1816 he united his two states into the Kingdom of the Two Sicilies and, despite demands for constitutional government, retained a harsh absolutism. >> Napoleon

Ferdinand, known as **the Catholic** (1452–1516) King of Castile as Ferdinand V (from 1474), of Aragon and Sicily as Ferdinand II (from 1479), and of Naples as Ferdinand III (from 1503), born in Sos, Aragon, Spain. In 1469 he married **Isabella**, sister of Henry IV of Castile, and ruled jointly with her until her death. He introduced the Inquisition (1478–80), and in 1492, after the defeat of the Moors, expelled the Jews. Under him, Spain gained supremacy following the discovery of America, and in 1503 he took Naples from the French, with the help of the Holy League. After Isabella's death (1504) he was regent of Castile for his insane daughter **Juana**, and in 1512 gained Navarre, thus becoming monarch of all Spain. To him and Isabella, Spain owed her unity and greatness as a nation and the foundation of her imperial influence. >> Isabella I

Ferdusi >> **Firdausi**

Ferguson, Adam (1723–1816) Philosopher and historian, born in Logierait, Perth and Kinross, E Scotland, UK. He became professor first of natural philosophy (1759) then of moral philosophy (1764) at Edinburgh, and was a member of the Scottish 'common sense' school of philosophy along with Thomas Reid and Dugald Stewart. He travelled to Philadelphia as secretary to the commission sent out by Lord North to negotiate with the American colonists in 1778–9. His works include an *Essay on the History of Civil Society* (1767), *The History of the Progress and Termination of the Roman Republic* (1783), and *Principles of Moral and Political Science* (1792). >> North, Frederick; Reid, Thomas; Stewart, Dugald

Ferguson, Alex(ander Chapman) (1941–) Football player and manager, born in Glasgow, W Scotland, UK. He began playing with Queens Park Rangers (1958–68) before joining a number of Scottish clubs. As a manager (from 1974), he had success with Aberdeen (1978–86), including the European Cup Winners' Cup (1983), the Super Cup (1983), the Scottish FA Cup four times, and the League Cup (1985). He then took over at Manchester United (1986–) where his successes include the FA Cup (1990), the European Cup Winners' Cup (1991), the Super Cup (1991), and the Rumbelows Cup (1992). His team also won the inaugural FA Premier League Championship (1992–3), became record twice winners of the League and Cup double (1994, 1996), and clinched the Premier League title (1996–7).

Ferguson, Harry George (1884–1960) Engineer and inventor, born in Hillsborough, Co Down. He started his own garage business in Belfast at the age of 16, and built his own aeroplane, which made the first flight from Irish soil in 1909. Over many years he developed the Ferguson farm tractor, with a hydraulic linkage which controlled the depth of ploughing, and made the tractor itself more stable and efficient. These machines played a large part in the mechanization of British agriculture during and after World War 2.

Ferguson, Patrick (1744–80) British soldier and inventor, born in Pitfour, Aberdeenshire, NE Scotland, UK. He served in the army in Germany and Tobago. In 1776 he invented a breech-loading rifle, firing seven shots a minute, and sighted for ranges of 100–500 yd. With it he armed a corps of loyalists, who helped to defeat the Americans at the Battle of Brandywine (1777). He was killed at the Battle of King's Mountain, SC.

Ferguson, Robert, known as **the Plotter** (c.1637–1714) Conspirator, born near Alford, Aberdeenshire, NE Scotland, UK. In 1662 he was ousted as a Presbyterian from the vicarage of Godmersham in Kent. For 10 years he played a leading part in every treasonable scheme against the last two Stuart kings, and twice had to flee the kingdom; but after the Revolution of 1688, of which he published a history (1706), he conspired as busily for the Jacobite cause. He was arrested for treason in 1704, but not tried.

Ferguson, Sarah >> **Andrew, Duke of York**

Fergusson, John Duncan (1874–1961) Painter, born in Perth and Kinross, E Scotland, UK. He took up painting after a medical training. He is best known for his series of World War 1 paintings of naval dockyards and his portraits of the female nude, which reveal an understanding of Cézanne, Cubism, and Fauve colour, as well as an interest in new ideas about dance, movement, and rhythm. >> Cézanne; Fauves

Ferlinghetti, Lawrence (Monsanto) [ferlinggetee], originally **Lawrence Ferling** (1919–) Poet, born in New York City. He studied at the universities of North Carolina, Columbia, and the Sorbonne (1948–51), then settled in San Fransisco. He taught French (1951–3), and was a founder of City Lights (1952), a bookstore and publishing house. Regarded as a founder of the Beat poetry movement, as seen in *A Coney Island of the Mind* (1958), he was also a playwright and novelist. Later books of poetry include *Open Eye, Open Heart* (1973) and *The Populist Manifestos* (1981).

Fermat, Pierre de [fermah] (1601–65) Mathematician, born in Beaumont-de-Lomagne, France. He studied law at Toulouse, where he became a councillor of parliament. His passion was mathematics, most of his work being communicated in letters to friends containing results without proof. His correspondence with Pascal marks the foundation of probability theory. He studied maximum and minimum values of functions in advance of the differential calculus, but is best known for his work in number theory, the proofs of many of his discoveries being first published by Leonhard Euler a hundred years later. His 'last theorem' was the most famous unsolved problem in mathematics: it states that there are no integers positive x, y, and z with $x^n+y^n=z^n$ if n is greater than 2; a proof was announced by British mathematician Andrew Wiles in 1993. In optics, *Fermat's principle* was the first statement of a variational principle in physics: the path taken by a ray of light between two given points is the one in which the light takes the least time compared with any other possible path. >> Euler, Leonhard; Kummer; Pascal; Wiles

Fermi, Enrico [fermee] (1901–54) Nuclear physicist, born in Rome. He studied at Pisa, Göttingen, and Leyden, and became professor of theoretical physics at Rome in 1927. In 1934 he and his colleagues split a number of nuclei by bombardment with neutrons, for which he was awarded the 1938 Nobel Prize for Physics. He did not return to Italy from his Nobel Prize presentation in Stockholm because the Italian anti-Semitic Laws affected his Jewish wife, but became professor at Columbia University (1939). He played a prominent part in developing atomic energy, and constructed the first US nuclear reactor (1942). >> Teller

Fermor, Patrick (Michael) Leigh (1915–) English travel writer. He was involved in resistance operations in the Balkans during World War 2. He is best known for two books, *A Time of Gifts* (1977), and *Between the Woods and the Water* (1986), recounting a leisurely walk from Rotterdam to Constantinople, begun in 1933 after expulsion from King's School, Canterbury. Despite the 40-year delay in publishing them, they are regarded as an accurate account of the mood of pre-war Europe. Later works include *Three Letters from the Andes* (1991).

Fernandel [fernǎdel], stage name of **Fernand Joseph Désiré Contandin** (1903–71) Film comedian, born in Marseille, France. He worked in a bank and soap factory before his debut on the stage in 1922, and from 1930 appeared in over a hundred films, interrupted only temporarily by military service and Nazi occupation. He established himself internationally with his moving portrayal of the naive country priest of *The Little World of Don Camillo* (1953), and with his versatile handling of six separate roles in *The Sheep has Five Legs* (1953), which gave full rein to his extraordinary facial mobility.

Fernandez, Juan [fernandez], Span [fernandeth] (c.1536–1604) Navigator, in the service of Spain. In 1563 he discovered the Pacific island now named after him, and lived there with a grant for animal stock from the Spanish government. He also discovered San Felix and San Ambrosio Is.

Ferrabosco, Alfonso [feraboskoh] (c. 1543–88) Composer, born in Bologna, Italy. He moved to England before 1562, and was for some time in the service of Queen Elizabeth I. He left England in 1578 and entered the service of the Duke of Savoy. His son, also called **Alfonso** (1575–1628), was born in Greenwich, and served as composer for James I and Charles I.

Ferranti, Sebastian Ziani de [ferantee] (1864–1930) Electrical engineer and inventor, born in Liverpool, Merseyside, NW England, UK. He studied at University College London. From his early experiments with dynamos and alternators he conceived the idea of the large-scale generation and distribution of electricity at high voltages. In 1887 he was appointed chief electrician to the London Electric Supply Corporation, and designed a power station at Deptford to supply power to all of London N of the Thames. This scheme was temporarily frustrated by the Electricity Lighting Act of 1888, but it nevertheless contained all the elements of the national electricity grid system which came into being some 40 years later. From 1882 to 1927 he took out 176 patents, and the firm of Ferranti Ltd which he founded in 1905 is still in the forefront of electrical and electronic engineering.

Ferrar, Nicholas (1592–1637) Anglican clergyman and spiritual mystic, born in London, England, UK. After studying medicine, and a brief period in politics, he became a deacon in the Church of England (1626). At Little Gidding in Huntingdonshire he founded a small religious community which engaged in constant services and perpetual prayer, while carrying out a range of crafts, such as bookbinding. It was broken up by the Puritans in 1647.

Ferrari, Enzo [feˈrahree] (1898–1988) Racing-car designer, born in Modena, Italy. He became a racing driver in 1920 (with Alfa-Romeo), founded the company which bears his name (1929), and was its president until 1977. In 1940 he began designing his own cars. Since 1951, the marque has won nearly 100 of over 400 Grand Prix races in which they have competed.

Ferraro, Geraldine A(nne) [feˈrahroh], married name **Zacarro** (1935–) US politician, born in Newburgh, NY. She studied at Marymount College, Fordham University, and New York Law School, establishing a successful law practice (1961–74). She was assistant district attorney for the Queens district of New York (1974–8), then worked at the Supreme Court, heading a special bureau for victims of violent crime. She was elected to the US House of Representatives in 1981, where she gained a reputation as an effective, liberal-minded politician. She was selected in 1984 by Walter Mondale to be the first female vice-presidential candidate of a major party. In 1992 she ran in the New York senatorial primary, but lost the nomination despite much popular support. >> Mondale

Ferrel, William (1817–91) Meteorologist, born in Fulton Co, PA. He studied the effects of the earth's rotation on wind and marine currents, and invented a tide-predicting machine. His name is preserved in the meteorological term *Ferrel cell*, identifying a segment of the wind circulation model of the Earth.

Ferrer, José (Vincente) (1912–92) Actor, director, and producer, born in Santurce, Puerto Rico. He studied at Princeton, made his Broadway debut in 1935, and played the leading role in *Charley's Aunt* (1940). The star of many other plays and films, he produced and played the leading role in *Cyrano de Bergerac* on stage (1946), and won an Oscar for the film version (1950).

Ferrier, Kathleen (1912–53) Contralto singer, born in Higher Walton, Lancashire, NW England, UK. A singing prize at a local music festival led her to undertake serious studies in 1940, and she rapidly won a great reputation. One of her greatest successes was in Mahler's *Das Lied von der Erde* (The Song of the Earth) at the first Edinburgh Festival (1947).

Ferris, George (Washington Gale) (1859–96) Engineer, born in Galesburg, IL. He was an engineer on a number of bridge projects during the 1880s. His huge revolving observation wheel for the 1892 World's Columbian Exposition in Chicago was the original *Ferris wheel*.

Fessenden, Reginald Aubrey (1866–1932) Radio engineer and inventor, born in East Bolton, Quebec, Canada. He studied at Bishop's University, Quebec, moving to New York City, where he met Thomas Edison. After a varied career in industry and academic life as teacher, chemist, and electrical engineer, he became interested in adapting wireless telegraphy for voice transmission. He developed the principle of amplitude modulation (AM) and made a broadcast of speech and music on 24 Dec 1906 from Brant Rock, MA, which was heard over 500 mi away. His work was of great importance for the growth of commercial broadcasting. >> Edison

Fessenden, William Pitt (1806–69) US politician, born in Boscawen, NH. He studied at Bowdoin College, and was admitted to the Maine bar in 1827. He served in the US House of Representatives as a Whig (1841–3), and was elected senator for Maine in 1854. He was opposed to slavery, and with fellow sympathizers helped to form the Republican Party. Chairman of the US Senate Finance Committee during the Civil War, he was appointed secretary of the Treasury in 1864. He returned to the Senate in 1865, and chaired the Joint Committee on Reconstruction.

Festinger, Leon (1919–) Psychologist, born in New York City. He studied at the State University of Iowa, then taught at several universities, moving in 1968 to the New School for Social Research in New York City. His work centred on the introduction and development of the concept of 'cognitive dissonance'. According to the theory, people are unable to tolerate conflicting cognitions (beliefs, thoughts, perceptions) for any length of time, and have to resolve such internal conflicts by rejecting or devaluing one or more of the cognitions. The theory has proved useful in the understanding of a variety of psychological phenomena.

Fettes, Sir William [feˈtiz] (1750–1836) Scottish merchant and philanthropist. He made a fortune from tea and wine, was twice Lord Provost of Edinburgh and left £166 000 to found Fettes College (1870), designed by David Bryce (1803–76).

Feuchtwanger, Lion [ˈfoykhtvanger] (1884–1958) Writer, born in Munich, Germany. He studied in Berlin and Munich, and won a European reputation with the 18th-c historical novel *Jud Süss* (1925), as well as the 14th-c tale *Die hässliche Herzogin* (1923), which as *The Ugly Duchess* (1927) was a great success in Britain. His thinly disguised satire on Hitler's Munich putsch, *Erfolg* (1930, Success), earned him the hatred of the Nazis. In 1933 he fled to France, where in 1940 he was interned by the German army, but escaped to the USA. He also wrote numerous dramas, and collaborated with Brecht in a translation of Marlowe's *Edward II*. His later works included detailed part-biographies of Goya (1952) and Rousseau (1954). >> Brecht

Feuerbach, Ludwig (Andreas) [ˈfoyerbakh] (1804–72) Philosopher, born in Landshut, Germany. He studied theology at Heidelberg and Berlin, then philosophy at Erlangen. His most famous work, *Das Wesen des Christentums* (1841, The Essence of Christianity), claims that religion rises from one's alienation from oneself, and the projection of ideal human qualities onto a fictitious supreme 'other'. His naturalistic materialism had a strong influence on Marx and Engels. >> Engels; Marx, Karl

Feydeau, Georges Léon Jules Marie [faydoh] (1862–1921) Playwright, born in Paris. His name is synonymous with French bedroom farce. He wrote his first of almost 40 plays, *La Tailleur pour dames* (Ladies' Tailor), in 1886. His plays are still performed in France and elsewhere, such as *Une Puce à l'oreille* (1907), produced as *A Flea in Her Ear* at the National Theatre, London, in 1965.

Feynman, Richard (Phillips) [ˈfiynman] (1918–88) Physicist, born in New York City. He worked on the US atomic bomb in World War 2, then became a professor of theoretical physics at Cornell (1945) and the California Institute of Technology (1951). He shared the Nobel Prize for Physics in 1965 for his work on quantum electrodynamics, and is also known for his visual representation of the behaviour of interacting particles, known as *Feynman diagrams*. >> Wheeler, John Archibald; RR1122

Fiacre, St [feeˈakruh], also found as **Fiachrach** (?–670) Irish hermit, who founded a monastery in France, on the site of the village of Saint-Fiacre-en-Brie, near Paris. In 1640 Nicholas Sauvage who lived at the Hôtel St Fiacre, Paris, introduced a carriage-hire service, the carriages coming to be known as *fiacres*.

Fibich, Zdenko (Zdeněk) [feebeekh] (1850–1900) Composer, born in Šebořic, Czech Republic. He wrote operas, symphonies, and works for solo piano and was *Kapellmeister* in Prague from 1878. One of his melodies, *Poéme*, has remained a popular favourite.

Fibonacci, Leonardo [fibonahchee], also known as **Leonardo Pisano** (c. 1170–c. 1250) Mathematician, born in Pisa, Italy. Arguably the most outstanding mathematician of the Middle Ages, he popularized the modern decimal system of numerals, and in his greatest work, the *Liber quadratorum* (1225, The Book of Square Numbers), made an advanced contribution to number theory. He also discovered the *Fibonacci sequence* of integers in which each number is equal to the sum of the preceding two (0,1,1,2,3,5,8...).

Fichte, Johann Gottlieb [fikhtuh] (1762–1814) Philosopher, born in Rammenau, Germany. He studied theology and then philosophy at Jena, becoming an ardent disciple of Kant. As professor of philosophy at Jena (1794) he modified the Kantian system by substituting for the 'thing-in-itself' as the absolute reality, the more subjective *Ego*, the primitive act of consciousness. In 1805 he became professor at Erlangen, where he published the more popular versions of his philosophy. His historical importance is as the author of *Reden an die deutsche Nation* (1807–8, Addresses to the German Nation), in which he invoked a metaphysical German nationalism to resistance against Napoleon. In 1810 the University of Berlin was opened, and Fichte, who had drawn up its constitution, became its first rector. >> Kant

Ficino, Marsilio [ficheenoh] (1433–99) Philosopher, born in Figline, Italy. A Latin and Greek scholar, he became head of the Platonic Academy in Florence in 1462. He devoted most of his life to translating the works of Plato and his successors into Latin from the original Greek, and trying to reconcile Platonism with Christianity.

Fick, Adolph Eugen (1829–1901) German physiologist, professor at Zürich and Würzburg. A law of diffusion in liquids was named after him, when he discovered that the mass of solute diffusing through unit area per second is proportional to the concentration gradient.

Fick, August (1833–1916) Philologist, born in Petershagen, Germany. Professor at Göttingen (1876) and Wrocław, Poland (formerly Breslau, Germany) (1887)), he pioneered the comparative study of Indo-European vocabulary with his Indo-Germanic dictionary (1870). He also wrote works on Greek personal names and the original language of the *Iliad*.

Fiedler, Arthur [feedler] (1894–1979) Conductor, born in Boston, MA. Trained as a violinist in Boston and Berlin, he joined the Boston Symphony (1915–30), first playing violin, then viola. Determined to conduct, he founded his own chamber orchestra, the Boston Sinfonietta, in 1924. In 1929 he launched the Esplanade summer series, free concerts by the Boston Symphony along the Charles R. In 1930 he took over the Boston Pops Orchestra, and for almost a half century was the best-known conductor of light classical music in the USA.

Field, Cyrus W(est) (1819–92) Financier, born in Stockbridge, MA. After a career as a paper manufacturer, he helped to finance the first telegraph cable across the Atlantic (1866), achieved after several attempts. He also organized the New York, Newfoundland, and London Telegraph Co (1854), and the Atlantic Telegraph Co (1856), but suffered heavy financial losses. >> Field, David Dudley

Field, David Dudley (1805–94) Jurist, born in Haddam, CT, the brother of Cyrus W Field. He studied at Williams College, MA, and was admitted to the New York bar in 1828, where he worked to reform the judiciary system. A great advocate of codification, in 1857 he was appointed by the state to prepare penal, political, and civil codes. The resulting *Field codes* have been adopted by many States, and by other countries as well. >> Field, Cyrus W

Field, Eugene (1850–95) Writer, born in St Louis, MO. He became a journalist at 23, and from 1883 was a columnist with the *Chicago Morning News*, achieving a reputation as humorist and poet with his column 'Sharps and Flats'. He wrote the well-known nursery lullaby 'Little Boy Blue', and published several books of children's verse.

Field, John (1782–1837) Composer and pianist, born in Dublin. An infant prodigy, he was apprenticed to Clementi, who used him to demonstrate the capabilities of his pianos. In 1804 he settled in Russia as a music teacher, in 1821 moving to Moscow. He wrote mainly for the piano (including seven concertos), and is credited with originating the nocturne. His music influenced Chopin. >> Chopin, Frédéric; Clementi

Field, Joshua >> **Maudslay, Henry**

Field, Marshall (1834–1906) Merchant, born in Conway, MA. He started as a clerk in Pittsfield, MA, moving to Chicago in 1856. He founded the Chicago department store known from 1881 as Marshall Field & Co, one of the world's largest and most progressive emporia.

Field, Nathan (1587–?1619) Actor and playwright, born in London, England, UK. He was educated at St Paul's school, and in 1600 became one of the children of the Queen's Chapel. He was one of the comedians of the Queen's Revels (1604–13) and various other troupes. As a playwright he collaborated with Beaumont and Fletcher and with Massinger in the latter's *The Fatal Dowry* (1632), and wrote two comedies, *A Woman is a Weathercocke* (1612) and *Amends for Ladies* (1618). >> Beaumont, Francis; Fletcher, John; Massinger

Fielding, Henry (1707–54) Playwright and novelist, born at Sharpham Park, Glastonbury, Somerset, SW England, UK. He studied at Leyden, and began to write theatrical comedies, becoming author/manager of the Little Theatre in the Haymarket (1736). However, the sharpness of his burlesques led to the Licensing Act (1737), which closed his theatre. In search of an alternative career, he was called to the bar (1740), but his interests lay in journalism and fiction. On Richardson's publication of *Pamela* (1740), he wrote his famous parody, *Joseph Andrews* (1742). Several other works followed, notably *The History of Tom Jones, A Foundling* (1749), which established his reputation as a founder of the English novel. As a reward for his government journalism, he was made justice of the peace to Westminster, where he helped to form the Bow Street Runners within the police force. >> Richardson, Samuel

Fields, Dame Gracie, originally **Grace Stansfield** (1898–1979) Singer and variety star, born in Rochdale, Greater Manchester, NW England, UK. She first appeared on stage at the age of 10, made her London debut in 1915, and by 1928 was firmly established in variety. With her sentimental songs and broad Lancashire humour, she won a unique place in the affections of British audiences. Her theme tune, 'Sally', she first sang in 1931. She was created a dame in 1978.

Fields, W C, originally **William Claude Dukenfield** (1879–1946) Actor, born in Philadelphia, PA. He ran away from home and became a vaudeville actor and juggler in the early 1900s, touring widely in England, then around the world, including Australia and Hawaii. He appeared in the Ziegfeld Follies, but established his comic persona in silent films such as *Sally of the Sawdust* (1925). His distinctive voice found its full scope with the coming of sound in the cinema, and he was in regular demand during the 1930s.

Fiennes, Sir Ranulph (Twisleton-Wykeham-) [fiynz] (1944–) Explorer and expedition leader, born in Windsor, Berkshire, S England, UK. Educated at Eton, he served with the Royal Scots Greys and the SAS. He was the leader of several expeditions, from hovercraft on the White Nile (1969) to the Transglobe (1979–82), tracing the Greenwich Meridian across both Poles. He made several attempts to reach the North Pole unsupported. With Michael Stroud he completed the first unsupported crossing on foot of the Antarctic in 1993, covering 1350 mi in 95 days. He has published several books recounting his adventures.

Fieschi, Giovanni Luigi, Conte de' (Count of) [fieskee] (c. 1522–1547) Italian nobleman, whose family had a feud with that of the famous admiral, Andrea Doria. During an attempt to overthrow Doria, Fieschi was drowned, and Doria wreaked vengeance on the Fieschi estates. The feud has been the subject of much literary attention. >> Doria

Fieschi, Giuseppe Maria [fieskee] (1790–1836) Republican conspirator, born in Murato, Corsica. A member of a French republican group, he helped to construct 'an infernal machine' of 25 guns firing simultaneously at King Louis-Philippe in 1835. Eighteen people were killed, but the king escaped almost unhurt, and Fieschi was executed after trial. >> Louis-Philippe

Fiesole, Giovanni da >> **Angelico, Fra**

Figg, James (c. 1695–1734) Fencer and pugilist, born in Thame, Oxfordshire, SC England, UK. He gave displays of quarterstaff, fencing, and boxing in Marylebone, and ran a booth at Southwark. He is regarded as one of the greatest of 18th-c sporting figures, and is portrayed in Hogarth's *Rake's Progress* and *Southwark Fair*.

Figueroa, Leonardo de [figeroha] (c. 1650–1730) Architect, born in Seville, Spain. He was the designer of several major buildings in Seville, distinctive for their surface complexity.

Filarete, Antonio [filaraytay], originally **Antonio di Pietro Averlino** (c. 1400–c.1469) Sculptor, architect, and theorist, possibly born in Florence. He is thought to have trained with Ghiberti. The bronze doors of St Peter's, Rome, are his earliest surviving work. In 1450 he settled in Milan, where he worked for Francesco Sforza, Duke of Milan, from 1451 to 1465, and where he adopted the name *Filarete* ('lover of virtue'). His major project there was the Ospedale Maggiore (begun 1457), a vast enterprise never completed to his design, He is best known for his remarkable *Trattato d'architettura* (1460–64) which includes a scheme for an ideal city built to a symmetrical plan. >> Ghiberti

Filchner, Wilhelm [filkhner] (1877–1957) Geographer and explorer, born in Munich, Germany. He studied at Munich University, joined the Trigonometrical Division in Prussia, and later worked with the Berlin Earth-Magnetic Institute and the Potsdam Astrophysics Institute. He led expeditions across the Pamirs in C Asia (1900) and to Tibet (1903, 1926, 1934) with his wife and Albert Tafel, and led the Second German Antarctic Expedition (1911–12), during which his ship, the *Deutschland* became frozen in the ice for nine months. With Erich Przybyllok, his companion on earlier trips, he undertook a magnetic survey of Nepal (1939–40) and established magnetic stations in China and Tibet. He lived in India during World War 2, as his anti-Nazi feelings were well known, then returned to Zürich to write.

Fillmore, Millard (1800–74) US statesman and 13th president (1850–3), born in Summer Hill, NY. He educated himself, and became a lawyer. A member of the State Assembly in 1829, he was elected to Congress in 1833, and became comptroller of New York State in 1847. He was vice-president to Zachary Taylor in 1848, becoming president on his death. On the slavery question he was a supporter of 'compromise'. >> Taylor, Zachary; RR1097

Finch, Peter, originally **George Frederick Ingle-Finch** (1912–77) Actor, born in London, England, UK. He worked in Australia in vaudeville, radio, and film during the Depression but later returned to Britain, portraying a wide variety of film roles, as in *The Nun's Story* (1959), *Sunday, Bloody Sunday* (1971), and *Network* (1976), for which he received the first-ever posthumous Oscar.

Fine, Larry >> **Stooges, The Three**

Finger, Bill >> **Kane, Bob**

Fink, Albert (1827–97) Structural engineer, born in Darmstadt, Germany. He studied engineering and architecture at Darmstadt, and emigrated to the USA in 1849. He invented in 1852 the *Fink truss*, which became widely used on US and other railway bridges, and to support the roofs of buildings. He also carried out pioneering studies of transportation costs, which inaugurated the science of railway economics.

Finlay, Ian Hamilton (1925–) Poet and artist, born in Nassau and brought up in Scotland. He became widely known as the leading British exponent of concrete poetry in the 1960s. In 1969 he began his work with landscape gardening and inscriptions, extending his theme of words and images.

Finley, James (1762–1828) Civil engineer, born in Pennsylvania. He was one of the first to build a suspension bridge using masonry towers and wrought iron chains, completing one of 21 m/70 ft span in 1801. In 1810 a similar bridge of 74 m/244 ft span was built at Newburyport on the Merrimack R.

Finnbogadóttir, Vigdís [finbohgadoteer] (1930–) President of Iceland (1980–96), born in Reykjavík, the first woman in world history to be elected head of state. She studied French language and literature at the University of Grenoble and the Sorbonne (1949–53), then returned to Iceland to work for the National Theatre and to teach. From 1972 to 1980 she was the director of the Reykjavík City Theatre. In 1980 she stood for the non-political office of President of Iceland, winning a narrow victory against three male candidates; she was returned unopposed in 1984, re-elected in 1988, and returned again for a fourth term in 1992. >> RR1058

Finney, Albert (1936–) Actor, born in Salford, Greater Manchester, NW England, UK. He studied at the Royal Academy of Dramatic Art, London, and has performed a wide variety of roles, from Shakespearean characters to modern working-class individuals, on both stage and screen. It was his definitive portrayal of the working-class rebel in *Saturday Night and Sunday Morning* (1960) that established him as a star. He directed the film *Charlie Bubbles* (1967), and was associate artistic director of the Royal Court Theatre (1972–5). He has received Oscar nominations for *Tom Jones* (1963), *Murder on the Orient Express* (1974), *The Dresser* (1983), and *Under the Volcano* (1984). Later films include *Miller's Crossing* (1990), *The Playboys* (1992), *The Browning Version* (1994), and *The Run of the Country* (1995).

Finney, Tom, popular name of **Sir Thomas Finney** (1929–) Footballer, born in Preston, Lancashire, NW England, UK. He played for Preston North End all his footballing life. He also played for England 76 times, and is considered to have been one of the best wingers in the game. He was knighted in 1998. >> RR1155

Finnian, St (c. 495–579) Irish clergyman, and chief patron of Ulster. He established a monastery at Moville, after a pilgrimage to Rome. He should not be confused with **St Finnian of Clonnard** (c.522), who is said to have taught 3000 pupils at the monastery of Clonard. Feast day 10 September.

Finsch, Friedrich Hermann Otto (1839–1917) Naturalist and traveller, born in Silesia. He became assistant curator at the Dutch National Museum in Leyden, before becoming curator of the Bremen Museum (1864–78). He travelled all over the world, and published accounts of the birds he saw, particularly in East Africa and Polynesia, but is best remembered as an expert on parrots. From 1905 he was head of the ethnographical department of the Municipal Museum in Brunswick. *Finsch's wheatear* was named in his honour.

Finsen, Niels Ryberg (1860–1904) Physician and scientist, born in the Faroe Is, Denmark. He studied at the University of Copenhagen, and taught anatomy there. He discovered the curative power of different colours of light, and founded phototherapy. He was awarded the Nobel Prize for Physiology or Medicine in 1903.

Finzi, Gerald Raphael [finzee] (1901–56) Composer, born in London, England, UK. He taught at the Royal Academy of Music (1930–3), his compositions including orchestral pieces as well as church music. A lover of literature, he is best known for his settings for voice and piano of poems by Hardy, Milton, and Wordsworth.

Fiorelli, Giuseppe [fyorelee] (1823–96) Archaeologist, born in Naples, Italy. His excavations at Pompeii helped preserve the ancient city. As professor of archaeology at Naples University and director of excavations (1860–75), he established the meticulous method of studying archaeological sites layer by layer. He founded a training school where foreigners as well as Italians could learn archaeological technique, and made a particular study of the materials and building methods used in Pompeii. Director of the National Museum at Naples from 1863, he was director general of Italian Antiquities and Fine Arts (1875–96).

Firbank, (Arthur Annesley) Ronald (1886–1926) Novelist, born in London, England, UK. He studied at Cambridge, where he became a Roman Catholic, but left without taking a degree, and travelled in Europe. His novels (written on piles of blue postcards) are slight but innovative, and anticipate Evelyn Waugh, Anthony Powell, and Ivy Compton-Burnett. His last complete work before his premature death from a disease of the lungs, *Concerning the Eccentricities of Cardinal Pirelli* (1926), is quintessential Firbank, the dialogue witty and inconsequential, the hero meeting his end while in ardent pursuit of a choir boy. >> Compton-Burnett; Powell; Waugh, Evelyn

Firdausi or **Ferd(a)usi** [firdowsee], pseudonym of **Abú al-Qásim Mansúr** (940–c. 1020) The greatest of Persian poets, born near Tús, Khorassan. His major work was the epic poem, *Shah Náma* (1010, The Book of Kings), based on actual events from the annals of Persia. He also wrote a number of shorter pieces.

Firestone, Harvey S(amuel) (1868–1938) Industrialist, born in Columbiana, OH. He started by selling solid rubber carriage tyres in Chicago, and in 1900 founded the Firestone Tire and Rubber Co in Akron, OH. He pioneered the pneumatic tyre for the Ford Model T, non-skid treads, and tyres for farm tractors and motor trucks. To break the monopolistic power of rubber growers in SE Asia, he started rubber plantations in Liberia in 1924.

First, Ruth (1925–82) Radical opponent of apartheid, as activist, journalist, writer, and academic, born in Johannesburg, South Africa. She joined the Communist Party as a student, and worked for various left-wing newspapers and magazines (1946–60). In 1949 she married **Joe Slovo**; both were arrested and charged with treason in 1956. In 1964 she left South Africa, and subsequently taught at universities in England and Mozambique. In 1982 she was assassinated by a parcel bomb in her office at Maputo, Mozambique. >> Slovo

Firth, Colin (1960–) Actor, born in Grayshott, Hampshire, UK. He studied drama in London, worked in the West End, and went on to play a series of acclaimed character parts in film and television. He received a BAFTA nomination for his role in the television production of *Tumbledown* (1989), and another for *Pride and Prejudice* (1995), where his brooding performance as the handsome Mr Darcy attracted unprecedented public interest. Later films include the television production of *Nostromo* (1996), *The English Patient* (1996), and *Fever Pitch* (1997).

Firth, J(ohn) R(upert) (1890–1960) Linguist, born in Keighley, West Yorkshire, N England, UK. He studied at the University of Leeds, became professor of English at the University of the Punjab, Lahore (1919–28), senior lecturer in phonetics at University College, London (1928–38), senior lecturer in the School of Oriental and African Studies in 1938, and head of the department of phonetics and linguistics in the School in 1941. In 1944 he was appointed professor of general linguistics at London University, the first such chair in Great Britain. He is particularly remembered for his development of prosodic phonology and the contextual theory of meaning. >> Halliday, M A K

Firth, Mark (1819–80) Industrialist and philanthropist, born in Sheffield, South Yorkshire, N England, UK. In 1849 with his father and brother he established there the great Norfolk steelworks. He was a munificent benefactor to Sheffield, his gifts including almshouses, a park, and the Firth College (1879), now part of the university.

Firth, Sir Raymond (William) (1901–) Social anthropologist, born in Auckland, New Zealand. He studied there and under Bronislaw Malinowski at the London School of Economics, and carried out fieldwork (1928–9) on the island of Tikopia in the Solomon Is. He spent two years at Sydney University before returning to the London School of Economics (1932–68), becoming professor of anthropology in 1944. His major contributions have been in the fields of economic anthropology, social change, and anthropological theory, especially social organization. He was knighted in 1973. >> Malinowski

Fischer, Bobby, popular name of **Robert (James) Fischer** (1943–) Chess player, born in Chicago, IL. He was world champion in 1972–5, taking the title from Boris Spassky (USSR) in a much-publicized match. He has a ranking of 2785 (on the Elo grading system), the highest ever, making him the greatest of all Grand Masters. He resigned his title shortly before a defence against Anatoly Karpov in 1975, and did not then compete at a major international level until 1992, when he defeated Spassky in a match which generated unprecedented levels of publicity for a chess match. >> Karpov; Spassky; RR1149

Fischer, Bram, popular name of **Abram Louis Fischer** (1908–75) Lawyer, born into a prominent Afrikaans family. He studied law in South Africa and as a Rhodes Scholar at Oxford. He became an active member of the Communist Party, while also reaching the heights of the legal profession. He defended those charged in the prolonged Treason Trial of the 1950s, and led the defence team at the 1964 Rivonia trial. In 1964, he was arrested and charged with membership of the then underground Communist Party, and in 1966 was sentenced to life imprisonment.

Fischer, Carl (1849–1923) Music publisher, born in Buttstadt, Germany. He trained as a musician and emigrated to the USA in 1872, opening a music store in New York City. He sold instruments and other firms' scores, but soon found a market for reproducing music; by 1880 he was moving to larger quarters, and his firm went on to become one of the major US publishers of a wide spectrum of music. The firm also published *The Metronome* (1885) for bandleaders and *Musical Observer* (later *Musical Courier*).

Fischer, Emil (Hermann) (1852–1919) Organic chemist, born near Cologne, Germany. He had a dissolute youth, but went on to hold chairs in Würzburg and Berlin. His extensive work included elucidating the chemistry of carbohydrates and the founding of protein chemistry, and he was awarded the Nobel Prize for Chemistry in 1902. He is widely seen as the leading figure in the field of organic chemistry.

Fischer, Ernst Otto (1918–) Inorganic chemist, born in Munich, Germany. He studied at the Munich Technical University, and spent his career there, becoming director of the Inorganic Chemistry Institute in 1964. Working independently, he shared the Nobel Prize for Chemistry in 1973 for explaining how certain metals and organic substances can merge to form organometallic sandwich compounds. >> RR1123

Fischer, Hans (1881–1945) Chemist, born in Höchst, Germany. He studied at Marburg and at Munich, where he became professor of chemistry (1921). He investigated the biological pigments that occur in animal and vegetable life, discovered the stucture of haemin, the red non-protein part of haemoglobin, and synthesized it in 1929. His studies of chlorophylls showed that they are porphyrins related in structure to haemin. He later discovered the structure of bilirubin, and synthesized it in 1944. For his work on porphyrins he was awarded the 1930 Nobel Prize for Physics.

Fischer-Dieskau, Dietrich [**fish**er **dees**kow] (1925–) Baritone, born in Berlin. He made his professional debut at Freiburg in 1947, and joined the Berlin Municipal Opera as a principal baritone. He became one of the foremost interpreters of German *Lieder*, particularly the song-cycles of Schubert, and has also appeared in a wide range of operatic roles. He performed in the premier of Britten's *A War Requiem* in 1962, as well as in the *Songs and Proverbs of William Blake* (1965) which Britten had composed for him. He has also written several books on music. >> Britten; Legge; Schubert

Fischer von Erlach, Johann Bernard [**fi**sher fon **air**lakh] (1656–1723) Architect, born in Graz, Austria. He studied in Rome, perhaps under Bernini or his pupil Carlo Fontana, then moved to Vienna, where he became the court architect (1704) and a leading exponent of the Baroque style. He designed many churches and palaces, notably the Karlskirche at Vienna, and the University church at Salzburg. He also wrote a major work on architectural history (1721). >> Bernini; Fontana

Fish, Hamilton (1808–93) Politician, born in New York City. As secretary of state under Grant (1869–77) he signed the Washington Treaty of 1871, and acted as arbitrator between the USA and Great Britain during the 'Alabama' crisis, helping to bring about a satisfactory settlement. >> Grant, Ulysses S

Fishbein, Morris (1889–1976) Physician, writer, and journal editor, born in St Louis, MO. He studied at Rush Medical College in Chicago, joined the staff of the *Journal of the American Medical Association*, becoming editor (1924–49), and gradually acquired enormous influence in US medical politics. For decades he was known as the 'voice of the AMA', campaigning against government involvement in medical practice. He sought to increase health consciousness among lay people through his syndicated newspaper column, his *Modern Home Medical Adviser* (1935), and many other popular books.

Fisher, John, St (1469–1535) Clergyman and humanist, born in Beverley, East Riding of Yorkshire, NE England, UK. He studied at Cambridge, where he became professor of divinity (1503). He zealously promoted the New Learning, and resisted the Lutheran schism. In 1527 he pronounced against the divorce of Henry VIII, refused the oath of succession, and was sent with More to the Tower. In 1535 he was made a cardinal, and soon after was tried and beheaded on Tower Hill. He was canonized in 1935; feast day 22 June. >> More, Thomas

Fisher, Alva John (1862–1947) US inventor of the domestic electric washing machine. A Chicago engineer, in 1910 he patented a washing machine powered by a small electric motor and fitted with a self-reversing gearbox to ensure the clothes were not compacted into a solid mass. It was marketed as the 'Thor' by the Hurley Machine Co of Chicago, and was the forerunner of the modern washing machine.

Fisher, Andrew (1862–1928) Australian politician and prime minister (1908–9, 1910–13, 1914–15), born in Crosshouse, East Ayrshire, SW Scotland, UK. A coal-miner from the age of 12, he emigrated to Queensland in 1885. From mining, he gradually moved into trade union activity and politics, entering the Queensland state assembly in 1893 and the first federal parliament in 1901. He was Australian Labor Party leader in 1907, then prime minister. At the start of World War 1 he made the dramatic promise to support the war effort 'to the last man and the last shilling'. He later became Australian high commissioner in London (1916–21). >> RR1033

Fisher, Bud, popular name of **Harry C(onway) Fisher** (1885–1954) Cartoonist, born in Chicago, IL. He studied at Chicago University. then became staff cartoonist of the *San Francisco Chronicle* (1905), where he introduced a regular strip, *A Mutt*, illustrating the racing tips of a gambler named Mr A Mutt and involving Mutt's family, cat included (1907). He later moved to the *San Francisco Examiner*, where Jeff, Mutt's partner, was introduced in 1908, but the title did not change to *Mutt and Jeff* until 1915. In the 1920s he was the highest-paid cartoonist in the world.

Fisher, Dorothy Canfield, *née* **Dorothea Frances Canfield** (1879–1958) Writer, born in Lawrence, KS. She studied Romance languages at Columbia University, then became a writer, publishing her early fiction and later non-fiction under her maiden and married names respectively. Among other contributions to education she popularized the Montessori teaching method in the USA in the 1910s. She was also a founding member of the Book-of-the-Month Club editorial board (1926–50).

Fisher (of Lambeth), Geoffrey Fisher, Baron (1887–1972) Archbishop of Canterbury (1945–61), born in Higham-on-the-Hill, Warwickshire, C England, UK. He studied at Oxford, was ordained in 1912, and became headmaster of Repton School (1914–32). He was 45 when he took up his first ecclesiastical appointment, as Bishop of Chester (1932). In 1939 he became Bishop of London, and as archbishop crowned Queen Elizabeth II in Westminster Abbey (1953). He was created a life peer in 1961.

Fisher (of Kilverstone), John Arbuthnot, Baron (1841–1920) British naval commander, born in Ceylon (now Sri Lanka). He entered the navy in 1854, and saw service in the China Wars (1859–60) and the Egyptian War (1882). A Lord of the Admiralty from 1892–7, he was commander-in-chief on the North American and West Indies station (1897–9). From 1904, appointed First Sea Lord, he effected great improvements in naval training, dockyard organization, and armaments, and introduced 'Dreadnought' battleships and 'Invincible' battle cruisers in preparation for war against Germany. He resigned in 1915 in protest against the Dardanelles expedition.

Fisher, Sir R(onald) A(ylmer) (1890–1962) Statistician and geneticist, born in East Finchley, N Greater London, England, UK. He studied at Cambridge, and became statistician at the

Rothamsted agricultural research institute (1919). There he developed his techniques for the design and analysis of experiments where it is not possible to control every element that could affect the outcome. His analysis of variance has become standard practice in medical, biological, and agricultural research. He also worked on genetics and evolution, and studied the genetics of human blood groups, elucidating the Rhesus factor. He became professor of eugenics at University College, London (1933–43), and of genetics at Cambridge (1943–57). After his retirement, he moved to Australia.

Fisk, Sir Ernest Thomas (1886–1965) Pioneer of radio, born in Sunbury-on-Thames, Surrey, SE England, UK. Trained by the Marconi company as a ship's radio operator, he arrived in Australia in 1910 to demonstrate the company's equipment, and became resident engineer in the following year. In 1918 he successfully received in Sydney a morse signal from Marconi's transmitter at Caernarfon, North Wales, the first direct radio signal between the two countries. In 1924 he made the first human voice contact between Australia and England when he spoke to Marconi in England. He had already established the Amalgamated Wireless (Australasia) Co (AWA), becoming its managing director in 1916 and chairman in 1932. He was knighted in 1937. In 1944 he resigned from AWA to return to England as managing director of EMI, but moved back to Sydney on his retirement in 1951. >> Marconi

Fitch, James Marston (1909–) Architectural preservationist and historian, born in Washington, DC. Trained as an architect at Tulane, he moved to New York City, where he worked as an architectural editor (1936–53). He embraced Modernism, but developed an interest in the social concerns of architecture. His early support of 'progressive' urban renewal gave way in the late 1940s to a commitment to historical preservation. He then taught at Columbia University (1954–77), where in 1964 he founded the nation's first historic preservation programme. His books include *American Building: The Environmental Forces that Shape It* (1947) and *Architecture and the Aesthetics of Plenty* (1961). After retiring from Columbia he became (1979) director of historic preservation at the architectural firm of Beyer Blinder Belle in New York City.

Fitch, John (1743–98) Inventor and pioneer of steampower, born in Windsor, CT. In 1787 he successfully demonstrated a prototype steam boat on the Delaware R, before building and operating a larger paddle-wheeled ferry between Philadelphia and Burlington, NJ. Despite the reliability of his vessels, and holding US and French patents for steamboats (1791), he was not successful commercially. >> Fulton, Robert

Fitch, Val (Logsdon) (1923–) Nuclear physicist, born in Merriman, NE. He became interested in physics when, as a US army serviceman, he was sent to work on the atomic bomb project at Los Alamos, NM, in the early 1940s. He studied at McGill and Columbia universities, then joined Princeton University, where he did important work in particle physics. He shared the Nobel Prize for Physics with James Cronin in 1980. >> Cronin, James

Fitt, Gerry, popular name of **Gerard, Baron Fitt (of Bell's Hill)** (1926–) Northern Ireland politician, born in Belfast. He was a merchant seaman (1941–53) before entering local politics (1958–81), becoming a Republican Labour MP (1966). He founded and led the Social Democratic and Labour Party (1970–9), until he resigned the leadership to sit as an Independent Socialist. He lost his Westminster seat in 1983 when he received his peerage. He had earlier been a member of the Northern Ireland

Executive (1973–5), and was its deputy chief executive in 1974.

Fittig, Rudolf [fitig] (1835–1910) Scientist, born in Hamburg, Germany. He studied at Göttingen, and became professor of organic chemistry at Tübingen (1869) and at Strasbourg (1876). He is best known for his work on organic compounds, in particular their reaction with sodium.

Fitton, Mary (c. 1578–1647) English courtier, maid of honour to Elizabeth I. She was the mistress of William Herbert, Earl of Pembroke, and Sir Richard Leveson, and has been identified by some commentators as the 'dark lady' of Shakespeare's sonnets 127–157. >> Herbert, William; Shakespeare, William

Fitzgerald, Barry, pseudonym of **William Joseph Shields** (1888–1961) Actor, born in Dublin. Educated at Merchant Taylor's (Protestant) school, he worked in the Irish civil service and took part in amateur dramatics until 1929, when he took up full-time acting, and went to the USA, arriving in Hollywood in 1937. He starred in over 40 films, including *Naked City* (1948) and *The Quiet Man* (1952), and returned to Ireland in 1959.

Fitzgerald, Lord Edward (1763–98) Irish rebel, born at Carton House, Co Kildare, Ireland. He served in the British army in the American War of Independence (1775–83), and was elected MP for Athy in the Irish parliament (1783). He joined the United Irishmen in 1796, and tried to arrange for a French invasion of Ireland. The plot was betrayed; Fitzgerald was seized in Dublin, and later died of wounds received in the ensuing scuffle.

Fitzgerald, Edward (1809–83) Scholar and poet, born near Woodbridge, Suffolk, E England, UK. He studied at Cambridge, where he developed close literary friendships with Thackeray, Carlisle, and Tennyson (who dedicated his poem *Tiresias* to him). He published several works anonymously, including translations of six plays by Calderón in 1853. He is best known for his free poetic translation of quatrains from the *Rubáiyát of Omar Khayyám* (1859).

Fitzgerald, Ella (1918–96) Singer, born in Newport News, VA. Discovered in 1934 singing in an amateur contest in Harlem, she joined Chick Webb's band and recorded several hits, notably 'A-tisket A-tasket' (1938). Her lucid intonation and broad range made her a top jazz singer. Her series of recordings for Verve (1955–9) in multi-volume 'songbooks' are among the treasures of American popular song. After 1971 her concert schedule was occasionally interrupted because of diabetes, and she had both legs amputated in 1994.

Fitzgerald, F(rancis) Scott (Key) (1896–1940) Novelist, born in St Paul, MN. He captured the spirit of the 1920s ('the jazz age') in *The Great Gatsby* (1925), his best-known book. In 1920 he married **Zelda Sayre** (1900–47), moving in 1924 to the French Riviera, where her subsequent mental breakdown and his alcoholism attracted wide publicity. His other novels include *The Beautiful and the Damned* (1922) and *Tender is the Night* (1934). In 1937 he returned to Hollywood.

Fitzgerald, Garrett (Michael) (1926–) Irish statesman and prime minister (1981–2, 1982–7), born in Dublin. He studied at Dublin, where he became a barrister and a lecturer in political economy (1959–73). In 1969 he was elected Fine Gael member of the Irish parliament for Dublin SE, and became minister for foreign affairs (1973–7), and leader of the Fine Gael Party (1977–87). >> RR1064

Fitzgerald, George Francis (1851–1901) Physicist, born in Dublin. He was professor of natural philosophy at Dublin (1881–1901). Independently of Lorentz, he concluded that a body becomes shorter as its velocity increases (the *Lorentz–Fitzgerald contraction*), a notion used by Einstein as part of his theory of special relativity. >> Einstein; Lorentz

Fitzgerald, John Francis, nickname **Honey Fitz** (1863–1950) Businessman and mayor, born in Boston, MA. After serving as a Democratic state senator and representative (1895–1901), and running a newspaper, he became the colourful, popular Mayor of Boston (1906–8, 1910–14). His administrations were plagued by charges of corruption and political patronage, and a subsequent attempt to be elected as governor and senator failed. He was the grandfather of John, Robert, and Edward Kennedy. >> Kennedy, Edward M/ John F/Robert F

Fitzgerald, Penelope (Mary), *née Knox* (1916–) Novelist and biographer, born in Lincoln, EC England, UK. She studied at Somerville College, Oxford. Her first publication was a biography of Edward Burne-Jones (1975), followed by a portrait of her father, Edmund Knox, editor of *Punch*, and his three brothers, entitled *The Knox Brothers* (1977). Her fiction includes *Offshore* (1979, Booker Prize), *Innocence* (1986), and *The Gate of Angels* (1990).

Fitz-Gibbon, Bernice Bowles, nickname **Fitz** (?1895–1982) Advertising executive, born in Waunakee, WI. She developed a speciality in retail advertising at Macy's (1923–35), John Wanamaker (1936–40), and Gimbels, New York City (1940–54), where as publicity director she was one of the highest-paid women in advertising. She wrote such famous slogans as 'Nobody, but nobody, undersells Gimbels'. She later headed her own advertising consultancy (1954–76).

Fitzherbert, Mrs Maria Anne, *née Smythe* (1756–1857) Wife of George IV, probably born in Brambridge, Hampshire, S England, UK. A Roman Catholic widow, she secretly married **George** (then Prince of Wales) in 1785. This marriage, contracted without the king's consent, was invalid under the Royal Marriages Act of 1772; the prince afterwards denied that there had been a marriage at all. On his marriage to Princess Caroline of Brunswick in 1795 the connection was interrupted, resumed with the pope's consent, and finally broken off in 1803. >> George IV

FitzRoy, Sir Charles Augustus (1796–1858) Administrator, born at Shipley Hall, Derbyshire, C England, UK. He became Lieutenant-Governor of Prince Edward I (1837) and Lieutenant-Governor of the Leeward Is (1841–5), and in 1846 was appointed Governor-in-Chief of New South Wales. He recommended to the British parliament that some superior post should be established in Australia to which inter-colony disputes could be referred, and in 1851 he was commissioned 'Governor-General of All Her Majesty's Australian Possessions', thus paving the way for the federation of Australian colonies 50 years later.

Fitzroy, Robert (1805–65) Naval officer and meteorologist, born near Bury St Edmunds, Suffolk, E England, UK. In command of the *Beagle* he surveyed the coasts of Patagonia and Tierra del Fuego (1828–30). In 1831, accompanied by Charles Darwin as scientific observer, he circumnavigated the globe in the *Beagle*, and collaborated with Darwin in publishing in 1839 a *Narrative of the Surveying Voyages of HMS Adventure and Beagle*. Appointed Governor of New Zealand in 1843, he was recalled in 1845 because he maintained that the Maoris had as much right to claim land as the settlers. In 1854 he was attached to the meteorological department of the board of trade. He invented the *Fitzroy barometer*, and instituted the storm warnings that developed into daily weather forecasts. >> Darwin, Charles

Fitzsimmons, Bob, popular name of **Robert Prometheus Fitzsimmons** (1863–1917) Boxer, born in Helston, Cornwall, SW England, UK. He was brought up in New Zealand, and moved to the USA in 1890, where he won the world middleweight (1891), heavyweight (1897), and light heavy-

weight championships (1903). He continued fighting until the age of 52. His career record was 40 victories (32 knockouts) and 11 losses.

Fitzwilliam, Richard, 7th Viscount Fitzwilliam of Meryon (1745–1816) Irish peer, founder by bequest of the Fitzwilliam Museum in Cambridge. The original building was completed in 1875, and later extended.

Fizeau, Armand Hippolyte Louis [feezoh] (1819–96) Physicist, born in Paris. In 1849 he was the first to measure the velocity of light by an experiment confined to the Earth's surface, and later collaborated with Léon Foucault. Fizeau also demonstrated the use of the Doppler principle in determining star velocity in the line of sight. >> Foucault, Léon

Flagg, James Montgomery (1877–1960) Illustrator, born in Pelham Manor, NY. Based in New York City, he studied at the Art Students League (1893), and in England and France. Working in pen and ink, watercolour, and oils, he was a prolific illustrator for periodicals. He is known for his World War 1 posters, including the 'I Want You' portrait of Uncle Sam, and for his popular images of young women of the time, commonly called 'Flagg Girls'.

Flagstad, Kirsten (1895–1962) Soprano, born in Hamar, Norway. She studied in Stockholm and Oslo, where she made her operatic debut in 1913. She excelled in Wagnerian roles, and was acclaimed in most of the world's major opera houses. In 1958 she was made director of the Norwegian State Opera.

Flaherty, Robert (Joseph) (1884–1951) Pioneer documentary film-maker, born in Iron Mountain, MI. Trained as a mining prospector, he took a movie camera on his expeditions to Hudson Bay in 1913, returning many times to make the silent *Nanook of the North* (1922). He then made further productions in the South Seas: *Moana* (1924) and *Tabu* (1930). For the commercial cinema his films included *Elephant Boy* (1937) and *The Louisiana Story* (1948).

Flaminius, Gaius [flaminius] (?–217 BC) Roman general and statesman, of plebeian origin. Consul in 223 BC, he distributed the Ager Gallicus tribal lands left uninhabited since 283 BC. He was the first Roman commander to cross the R Po when he defeated the Insubres at the Addua (223 BC). He extended his road, the *Flaminian Way*, from Rome to Ariminum (Rimini) in 220 BC, and built the *Circus Flaminius*. Consul again in 217 BC, he tried to stem Hannibal's invasion of Etruria, but was defeated and killed at L Trasimeno. >> Hannibal

Flamsteed, John (1646–1719) The first Astronomer Royal of England (1675–1719), born in Denby, Derbyshire, C England, UK. He studied at Cambridge, and in 1676 instituted reliable observations at Greenwich, near London, providing data from which Newton was later able to verify the gravitational theory. >> Newton

Flanagan, Barry (1941–) Sculptor, born in Prestatyn, Denbighshire, NE Wales, UK. He studied at Birmingham College of Arts and Crafts (1957–8), and under Sir Anthony Caro in 1961, then taught art in London (1967–71). His early sculptures were made of cloth or hessian filled with shavings or foam. Since 1973 he has returned to more traditional materials such as stone and bronze, as in his bronze Leaping Hare sculptures (1990, Osaka). >> Caro

Flanders, Michael (1922–75) Variety performer, born in London, England, UK. He contributed lyrics for such London revues as *Air on a Shoestring* (1953), and translated Stravinsky's *A Soldier's Tale* for the Edinburgh Festival (1954). He is best rembered for *At The Drop of a Hat* (1956) and songs, such as the 'Hippopotamus Song', created and performed with Donald Swann. >> Swann

Flaubert, Gustave [flohbair] (1821–80) Novelist, born in Rouen, France. He studied law at Paris, then turned to writing. His masterpiece was *Madame Bovary* (1857), which was condemned as immoral and its author (unsuccessfully) prosecuted. His other works include *Salammbô* (1862), and *La Tentation de St Antoine* (1874, The Temptation of St Anthony). *Trois contes* (1877, Three Tales) reveals his mastery of the short story, while his genius as a letter writer is apparent in the volumes of his *Correspondance* (1926–33). >> Maupassant

Flavin, Dan [flayvin] (1933–96) Artist, born in New York City. He attended the US Air Force Meteorological Technician Training School, Maryland University, and the New York School of Social Research, but had no art education. He was known for his 'electric light icons', constructed from fluorescent tubes, sometimes referred to as 'Luminism'.

Flavius Arrianus >> **Arrian**

Flaxman, John (1755–1826) Sculptor and illustrator, born in York, North Yorkshire, N England, UK. He studied at the Royal Academy, and thereafter was constantly engaged upon sculpture, but his chief source of income was the Wedgwood house, which he furnished with renowned pottery designs. He also studied at Rome (1787–94), where he began his illustrations to the *Iliad* and *Odyssey* (1793), and other works. In 1810 he became professor of sculpture at the Royal Academy.

Fleck, Sir Alexander Fleck, Baron (1889–1968) Industrial chemist, born in Glasgow, W Scotland, UK. He studied at Glasgow University, and lectured there for two years, before working as a physical chemist on radium and later on the manufacture of sodium. He became chairman of ICI in 1953, and was chairman of the committee which investigated the nationalized coal industry.

Flecker, James Elroy (1884–1915) Poet, born in London, England, UK. He studied Oriental languages at Cambridge, and entered the consular service. His best-known works are the drama *Hassan* (staged, 1923) and *The Golden Journey to Samarkand* (1913).

Fleischer, Max [fliysher] (1883–1972) Cartoonist, inventor, and animated film producer, born in Vienna. He was taken to New York City at the age of four. He developed the rotoscope (1917), a device still used for transferring live action film into animated cartoon via tracing. With his brother **Dave** (1894–1979) he produced many *Out Of The Inkwell* films, which combined live action with animation. The brothers also created the 'bouncing-ball' sing along cartoons, silent but synchronized to the cinema orchestras. Having made the first experimental sound-on-film cartoons in the mid-1920s, Max went on to produce the *Betty Boop Talkartoons* (1930) and his best-remembered series, *Popeye the Sailor* (1933) from the strips by E C Segar, followed by the feature-length cartoons, *Gulliver's Travels* (1939) and *Mr Bug Goes to Town* (1941). >> Segar

Flémalle, Master of >> **Campin, Robert**

Fleming, Sir Alexander (1881–1955) Bacteriologist, born near Darvel, East Ayrshire, SW Scotland, UK. He studied at St Mary's Hospital, London, where he became professor (1919) after serving in the army during World War 1. He was the first to use antityphoid vaccines on human beings, pioneered the use of Salvarsan against syphilis, and discovered the antiseptic powers of lysozyme. In 1928 he discovered penicillin, for which he shared the Nobel Prize for Physiology or Medicine in 1945. He was elected to the Royal Society in 1943, and was knighted in 1944. >> Ehrlich, Paul; Wright, Edward; RR1124

Fleming, Ian (Lancaster) (1908–64) Writer and journalist, born in London, England, UK. He studied languages at Munich and Geneva universities, worked with Reuters in Moscow (1929–33), then became a banker and stockbroker (1933–9). He served with British Naval Intelligence during World War 2, and was foreign manager of the *Sunday Times* (1945–59). He achieved worldwide fame and fortune as the creator of a series of spy novels, starting with *Casino Royale* (1953), built round the exploits of his amoral hero James Bond, and providing the basis for a series of highly successful films. >> Fleming, Peter; Stephenson, William

Fleming, John A(dam) (1877–1956) Geophysicist, born in Cincinnati, OH. He joined the Department of Terrestrial Magnetism of the Carnegie Institution of Washington, DC (1904), became its director (1910–46), and continued to serve as an advisor in international scientific relations after his retirement. During his directorship, he designed geomagnetic observatories in Huancayo, Peru, Watheroo, Australia, and Kensington, MD. He took charge of the Institution's World War 2 contracts dealing with radio communications, ordnance devices, magnetic instruments, and ionospheric research. He expanded the field of geomagnetism by inventing or modifying geomagnetic instruments, designing isomagnetic world charts, and contributing to research in solar and lunar physics.

Fleming, Sir John Ambrose (1849–1945) Physicist, born in Lancaster, Lancashire, NW England, UK. He studied at London and Cambridge, and became professor of electrical engineering at University College, London (1885–1926). He invented the thermionic valve, and was a pioneer in the application of electricity to lighting and heating on a large scale. He was knighted in 1929.

Fleming, Peggy (Gale) (1948–) Ice skater, born in San Jose, CA. A skater from age nine, she won the world championship three times (1966–8), and an Olympic gold medal in 1968 in Mexico City, where her elegant style won her worldwide acclaim. After skating in professional revues, she served as a commentator for ABC television.

Fleming, (Robert) Peter (1907–71) Travel writer and journalist, born in London, England, UK, the brother of Ian Fleming. He studied at Oxford, and became assistant literary editor of the *Spectator*. In 1932 he joined an expedition to Central Brazil following Colonel Percy Fawcett who had disappeared without trace in 1925. It provided the colourful copy which surfaced in *Brazilian Adventure* (1933), a landmark in travel literature and an immediate best seller. In a similar vein are *One's Company* (1934) and *News From Tartary* (1936). >> Fawcett, Percy; Fleming, Ian

Fleming, Sir Sandford (1827–1915) Civil engineer and scientist, born in Kirkcaldy, Fife, E Scotland, UK. He went to Canada in 1845, and became chief engineer of the Intercolonial Railway (1867–76) and of the Canadian Pacific Railway (1872–80). He surveyed several famous routes, including Yellowhead and Kicking Horse passes. After retiring from the railways he developed a scheme for a telegraph communication system for the British empire, the first link being a cable under the Pacific from Canada to Australia.

Fleming, Tom (1929–) Actor, director, and poet, born in Edinburgh, EC Scotland, UK. After co-founding the Gateway Theatre, Edinburgh (1953–62), where he worked as actor and director, he joined the Royal Shakespeare Company. In 1965 he was appointed the first director of the Edinburgh Civic Theatre Trust, and founded a new company at the Royal Lyceum Theatre in the city. He has subsequently appeared as an actor and director in many Scottish theatres. His books of poetry include *So That Was Spring* (1954) and *Sax Roses for a Luve Frae Hame* (1961). He has also been a radio and television commentator since 1952, specializing in state and royal events.

Flemming, Walther (1843–1905) Biologist, born in Sachsenberg, Germany. He studied medicine at five German universities, and in 1876 became professor of anatomy at Kiel. In 1882 he gave the first modern account of cytology, including the process of cell division, which he named *mitosis*.

Fletcher, John (1579–1625) Playwright, born in Rye, East Sussex, SE England, UK. He came of a literary family, and studied at Cambridge, but little else is known about him apart from his theatrical work. It is difficult to disentangle his own plays from those in which he collaborated with Beaumont, Massinger, Rowley, and Shakespeare. He is best known for his collaboration with Beaumont in such works as *Philaster* (1610), *A King and No King* (1611), and *The Maid's Tragedy* (1611). Collaboration with Shakespeare probably resulted in *Two Noble Kinsmen* and *Henry VIII*. >> Beaumont, Francis; Massinger; Rowley, William; Shakespeare, William

Fletcher, John Gould (1886–1950) Poet and essayist, born in Little Rock, AR. He followed the Imagists while living in London and Paris (1908–33), but later turned to American subjects. He won the Pulitzer Prize in 1939 for his *Selected Poems*. He published the autobiographical *Life Is My Song* in 1937.

Fleury, André-Hercule de [floeree] (1653–1743) French clergyman and statesman, born in Lodève, France. As a young priest he entered court service (1679), became almoner to Louis XIV (1683), Bishop of Fréjus (1698), and in 1715 tutor to the future Louis XV. Replacing the Duc de Bourbon as chief minister (1726), he was made cardinal, and effectively controlled the government of Louis XV until 1743. Through skilful diplomacy he limited French involvement in the War of the Polish Succession (1733–8), restoring the country's prestige as a mediator. His moderation gave France the tranquillity her tangled finances demanded, and he carried out legal and economic reforms which stimulated trade. >> Louis XV

Flexner, Abraham (1866–1959) Educational reformer, born in Louisville, KY. After a 19-year career in secondary school teaching, he graduated in psychology at Harvard (1906). His Carnegie Foundation report on medical education in the USA and Canada (1910), exposed the abuses of a profit-driven system lacking standards for students, curricula, or facilities, and sparked a revolution in American medical education. He also campaigned for improvements to secondary education, and championed the German University model of intellectualism and research against the American vocationalism. He was the founder and first director (1930–9) of the Institute for Advanced Study, Princeton.

Flexner, Simon (1863–1946) Microbiologist and medical administrator, born in Louisville, KY. He taught at Johns Hopkins (1895–9) and Pennsylvania universities (1899–1903), then became director of laboratories at the newly established Rockefeller Institute for Medical Research (1903–35). His research was in bacteriology, virology, and immunology. He isolated the dysentery bacillus (1900), developed a serum for cerebrospinal meningitis (1907), and led the team that determined the cause of poliomyelitis.

Flinders, Matthew (1774–1814) Explorer, born in Donington, Lincolnshire, EC England, UK. He joined the navy in 1789, and became a navigator. In 1795 he sailed to Australia, where he explored the SE coast, and later (1801–3) circumnavigated the country. On his way home he was wrecked off the Great Barrier Reef, then kept prisoner by the French Governor of Mauritius until 1810. The *Flinders R* in Queensland, and the *Flinders Range* in South Australia are named after him.

Flood, Henry (1723–91) Irish statesman. He studied at Dublin and Oxford, and was leader of the Popular Party in the Irish parliament after his election in 1759. In 1775 he became vice-treasurer of Ireland, but was removed in 1781 as a strong nationalist. In 1783 he was returned for Winchester, and in 1785 for Seaford, but he failed to make a great mark at Westminster.

Florence of Worcester (?–1118) Monk and chronicler. He wrote *Chronicon ex chronicis* which supplements and extends the *Chronicon* written by Marianus Scotus, and is a valuable source for Anglo-Saxon history. >> Marianus Scotus

Florey (of Adelaide), Sir Howard Walter Florey, Baron [**flaw**ree] (1898–1968) Pathologist, born in Adelaide, South Australia. He studied medicine at Adelaide and Oxford, taught at Cambridge and Sheffield, then became professor of pathology at Oxford (1935–62), where he worked with Chain on penicillin, and shared the Nobel Prize for Physiology or Medicine (1945). He was appointed Provost of Queen's College, Oxford (1962) and Chancellor of the Australian National University, Canberra (1965). Knighted in 1944, he became a life peer in 1965. >> Chain

Florio, John [**flaw**rioh], also called **Giovanni Florio** (c. 1533–1625) Lexicographer and translator, born in London, England, UK. About 1576 he was a tutor in foreign languages at Oxford, and in 1578 published his *First Fruits*, accompanied by *A Perfect Induction to the Italian and English Tongues*. His next work was *Second Fruits*, with 6000 Italian proverbs (1591). His Italian and English dictionary, entitled *A World of Words*, was published in 1598. In 1603 he was appointed reader in Italian to Queen Anne, and in 1604 groom of the privy-chamber. His famous translation of Montaigne (1603) has appeared in several modern editions. >> Anne

Floris, originally **Cornelis de Vriendt** (c. 1514–75) Sculptor, ornamentalist, and architect, born in Antwerp, Belgium, the brother of artist **Frans** (1560–70). He studied sculpture under Giovanni da Bologna, visiting Rome c.1538. Most remarkable among his works are the Town Hall, Antwerp (1561–66) and the marble reredos at Tournai Cathedral (1572). >> Bologna

Flory, Paul J(ohn) (1910–85) Chemist, born in Sterling, IL. He studied at Ohio State University, and afterwards worked on the development of commercially successful polymers such as nylon and synthetic rubber, both in industry and at Stanford University (from 1961). For his major contributions to theory and experiment in the chemistry of polymers, he received the Nobel Prize for Chemistry in 1974.

Flotow, Friedrich, Freiherr von (Baron) [**floh**toh] (1812–83) Composer, born in Teutendorf, Germany. He studied music in Paris, and made his reputation with *Le Naufrage de la Méduse* (1839, The Wreck of the Medusa), *Stradella* (1844), and especially *Martha* (1847). From 1856 to 1863 he was director of the theatre at Schwerin.

Fluck, Diana >> Dors, Diana

Fludd, Robert, Lat **Robertus de Fluctibus** (1574–1637) Physician, mystic, and pantheistic theosophist, born in Bearstead, Kent, SE England, UK. He studied at Oxford. Influenced by Paracelsus, he recognized three cosmic elements – God (*archetypus*), world (*macrocosmos*) and man (*microcosmos*). He wrote a treatise in defence of Rosicrucians, *Apologia compendiaria fraternitatem de Rosea Croce* (1616). >> Paracelsus

Flynn, Elizabeth Gurley (1890–1964) Labour leader and social reformer, born in Concord, NH. The daughter of Irish nationalists, she showed an early talent for public speaking on social issues. Dropping out of school by 1907, she became an organizer for the Industrial Workers of the World, and was involved in many famous strikes. She also worked for women's suffrage, peace, and other progressive causes, and was one of the founders of the American Civil Liberties Union (1920). She worked for such causes as the release of civilians imprisoned during World War 1 on war-related charges, and then to free Sacco and Vanzetti. A heart ailment kept her out of action for a decade, but in 1936 she joined the Communist Party and became one of its outspoken leaders in the USA; she served two years in prison (1955–7) under the Smith Act, charged with advocating the overthrow of the US government. She later served as chair of the Communist Party of America (1961–4), and died in Moscow, where she had gone to work on her autobiography. >> Sacco; Vanzetti

Flynn, Errol (Leslie Thomson) (1909–59) Actor, born in Hobart, Tasmania. He moved to England to gain acting experience, joined the Northampton Repertory Company, and after a part in a film was offered a Hollywood contract. His first US film, *Captain Blood* (1935), established him as a hero of historical adventure films, and his good looks and athleticism confirmed him as the greatest Hollywood swashbuckler, in such films as *The Adventures of Robin Hood* (1938) and *The Sea Hawk* (1940). During the 1940s his off-screen reputation for drinking, drug-taking, and womanizing became legendary, and eventually affected his career, which was briefly revived by his acclaimed performance as a drunken wastrel in *The Sun Also Rises* (1957). His autobiography was called *My Wicked, Wicked Ways* (1959).

Fo, Dario [foh] (1926–) Playwright, designer, and actor, born in San Giano, Italy. After working in radio and TV he founded, along with his wife, **Franca Rame**, a radical theatre company in 1959. His populist plays use the comic traditions of farce and slapstick, as well as surreal effects; best known are *Morte accidentale di un anarchico* (1970, Accidental Death of an Anarchist), *Non si paga, non si paga* (1974, Can't Pay, Won't Pay), and *Female Parts* (1981), one-woman plays written with his wife. Later works include *Il Papa e la strega* (1989, The Pope and the Witch) and *Johan Padan a la descoverta de la Americhe* (1992, Johan Padan and the Discovery of America). He won the Nobel Prize for Literature in 1997.

Foch, Ferdinand [fosh] (1851–1929) French marshal, born in Tarbes, France. He taught at the Ecole de Guerre, proved himself a great strategist at the Marne (1914), Ypres, and other battles, and commanded the Allied Armies in 1918.

Fogerty, Elsie [fohgertee] (1865–1945) Teacher of elocution, born in London, England, UK. She trained at the Paris Conservatoire, then taught at the Crystal Palace School of Art and Literature (1889) and Sir Frank Benson's London School of Acting. She was founder and director of the Central School of Speech Training and Dramatic Art in London (1906), and trained such notable actors as Laurence Olivier and John Gielgud. She was also a pioneer in the field of speech therapy. >> Gielgud, John; Olivier

Foix, Gaston [fwah], nickname **the Thunderbolt of Italy** (1489–1512) French nobleman and soldier, the nephew of Louis XII of France. He became Duke of Nemours in 1505, and earned his nickname by the genius and bravery he displayed in the Italian wars. He twice overthrew the Swiss, at Como and Milan (1511), chased the papal troops from Bologna, seized Brescia from the Venetians (1512), and defeated the Spaniards at Ravenna, where he was killed. >> Louis XII

Fokine, Michel [fokeen], originally **Mikhail Mikhaylovich Fokine** (1880–1942) Dancer and choreographer, born in St Petersburg, Russia. He worked with Diaghilev's Ballets Russes in Paris from 1909, and in 1923 went to New York City, becoming a US citizen in 1932. He is credited with the creation of modern ballet from the artificial, stylized mode prevalent at the turn of the century. His works include *Les Sylphides* (1907) and *Petrouchka* (1911). >> Diaghilev

Fokker, Anthony Herman Gerard (1890–1939) Aircraft engineer, born in Kediri, Java. He built his first plane in 1911, and in 1913 founded the Fokker aircraft factory at Schwerin, Germany, which made warplanes for the German air force in World War 1. After the war he set up a factory in The Netherlands, and later operated also in Britain and the USA, where he became a US citizen.

Foley, John Henry (1818–74) Sculptor, born in Dublin. He went to London in 1834, and executed many statues of public figures, including that of Prince Albert for the Albert Memorial. Other major commissions were statues of Edmund Burke and Goldsmith at Trinity College, Dublin, and Henry Grattan on College Green, Dublin. He also designed for the O'Connell Monument in Dublin.

Folger, Emily Clara, *née* **Emily Jordan** (1858–1936) Scholar and book collector, born in Ironton, OH. Married in 1885 to **Henry Clay Folger**, she undertook Shakespeare studies, and collaborated with her husband in forming and cataloguing a famous Shakespeare library. After his death in 1930 she supervised its installation in Washington, DC. >> Folger, Henry Clay

Folger, Henry Clay (1857–1930) Lawyer and businessman, born in New York City. He attended Amherst College and studied law at Columbia University (1881). He became director of the Standard Oil Company of New York (1908), then its president (1911) and chairman (1923). His lifelong interest in Shakespeare culminated in plans to build a Shakespearean library, situated on Capitol Hill, Washington, DC. The completed building (1923) was named after Folger, who bequeathed his collection of Shakespearean materials to the library, together with sufficient funds for its upkeep and expansion. >> Folger, Emily Clara; Shakespeare, William

Folkers, Karl August (1906–) Biochemist, born in Decatur, IL. He studied at Illinois, Wisconsin, and Yale universities, then directed research at Merck & Co, NJ. He became president of the Stanford Research Institute (1963–8), and director of the Institute for Biomedical Research at Texas University. His work on antibiotics and vitamins included, notably, the first isolation of the anti-pernicious anaemia factor, cyanocobalamin (Vitamin B_{12}), by a Merck team in 1948, and the discovery of mevalonic acid, important for the production of many other biochemical compounds.

Follette, Robert M La >> **La Follette, Robert M**

Fonda, Henry (Jaynes) (1905–82) Actor, born in Grand Island, NE. He studied at the University of Minnesota, and after some success on the Broadway stage, went to Hollywood in 1935. His performances in the *Young Mr Lincoln* (1939), *The Grapes of Wrath* (1940), and *The Oxbow Incident* (1943), established him in the role of the American folk hero, the common man of integrity, and he played many such parts over the next 30 years. His last major appearance was in *On Golden Pond* (1981), for which he was awarded an Oscar. >> Fonda, Jane

Fonda, Jane (1937–) Actress, born in New York City, the daughter of Henry Fonda. After appearances on Broadway and in films in the early 1960s, she married (1965–73) director Roger Vadim, with whom she made *La Ronde* (1964) and *Barbarella* (1968). Later roles widened her dramatic scope: *Klute* (1971, Oscar), *Coming Home* (1978, Oscar), *The China Syndrome* (1979), *On Golden Pond* (1981), *The Morning After* (1986), and *Old Gringo* (1989). She is politically active in anti-nuclear and feminist peace movements, often reflected in her films, and in the 1980s she became involved with women's health and fitness activities. >> Fonda, Henry; Vadim

Fonseca, Manuel Deodoro da >> **Deodoro da Fonseca, Manuel**

Fontaine, Hippolyte [fõten] (1833–1917) Engineer, born in Dijon, France. He studied at the Ecole Nationale

Supérieure des Arts et Métiers at Châlons-sur-Marne, after which he worked in a factory as chief of industrial design (1857). He is noted for his discovery that a dynamo can be operated in reverse as an electric motor. Based on this principle, he constructed an electric motor and used it in the first transmission of electricity at Vienne (1873). >> Gramme

Fontaine, Jean de La >> **La Fontaine, Jean de**

Fontaine, Just [fõten] (1933–) Footballer and manager, born in Morocco. He established an enduring record when, playing for France in the final stages of the 1958 World Cup in Sweden, he scored 13 goals, including four against West Germany in the play-off match to determine third place.

Fontana, Carlo [fontahna] (1634/8–1714) Architect, born in Bruciato, near Como, Italy. A pupil of Bernini, he worked as a papal architect in Rome, where he designed many major works including the fountain in the Piazza di San Pietro, and the tombs of Pope Clement XI, Pope Innocent XII, and Queen Christina of Sweden, in St Peter's. He also designed Loyola College in Spain and the Palazzo Durazzo at Genoa. >> Bernini

Fontana, Domenico [fontahna] (1543–1607) Architect, born in Melide, Italy. He was papal architect in Rome, employed on the Lateran Palace, the Vatican Library, and St Peter's dome. He was afterwards royal architect in Naples.

Fontana, Lucio [fontahna] (1899–1968) Artist, born in Rosario, Argentina. He was brought up in Milan, studied at the Accademia di Brera (1928–30), and in 1935 signed the First Manifesto of Italian Abstract Artists. He made his name as the inventor of *Spazialismo* (Spatialism) and as a pioneer of 'environmental art'. He is best known for his bare or monochrome canvases, holed or slashed to create what he called *attese*. These in turn looked forward to the 'gesture' or 'performance' art of the 1960s.

Fontane, Theodor [foontahnuh] (1819–98) Poet and novelist, born in Neuruppin, Germany. He worked in the family chemist's business until he took to literature in Berlin (1849). Periods of residence in Britain (1855–9) as a newspaper correspondent led to ballads such as 'Archibald Douglas', and other British-based pieces. His later realistic novels influenced Thomas Mann; the first of them, *Vor dem Sturm* (1878, Before the Storm), an account of Prussian nobility, was followed by *L'Adultera* (1882) and *Effi Briest* (1898). >> Mann, Thomas

Fontane, Lynne >> **Lunt, Alfred**

Fontenelle, Bernard le Bovier, sieur de (Lord of) [fõtuhnel] (1657–1757) Scientist and man of letters, born in Rouen, France. He was educated at the Jesuit college at Rouen, and in 1697 became secretary to the Académie des Sciences, and later its president. He won a great literary reputation in Paris, producing a wide range of literary genres, including idylls, satires, dialogues, critical essays, histories, and tragedies. His *Entretiens sur la pluralité des mondes* (1868, A Plurality of Worlds), and *Histoire des oracles* (1867, History of the Oracles), are considered his best works.

Fonteyn, Margot [fontayn], in full **Dame Margot Fonteyn de Arias**, originally **Margaret Hookham** (1919–91) Ballerina, born in Reigate, Surrey, SE England, UK. She joined the Sadler's Wells Ballet (later the Royal Ballet) in 1934, where she made her first solo appearance in *The Haunted Ballroom*, and became one of the greatest ballerinas of the 20th-c, both in classic roles and in creating new roles for Ashton. A new partnership with Nureyev in the 1960s extended her performing career. She married **Roberto Emilio Arias** (1918–), then Panamanian ambassador to the Court of St James, in 1955, and was created a dame in 1956. >> Ashton, Frederick; Nureyev

Foot, Sir Dingle (Mackintosh) (1905–78) British politician and lawyer, the brother of Hugh and Michael Foot. He studied at Oxford, where he was president of the Liberal club (1927) and of the Union (1928). He was Liberal MP for Dundee (1931–45), joined the Labour Party in 1956, and became MP for Ipswich (1957–70), and solicitor general (1964–7). He became a QC in 1954, and was knighted in 1964. >> Foot, Hugh/Michael

Foot, Hugh (Mackintosh), Baron Caradon (1907–90) British administrator, the brother of Dingle and Michael Foot. He studied at Cambridge, where he was president of the Union in 1929. He held many government administrative posts abroad, and became a UN permanent representative (1964–70) and a consultant to the UN development programme. He was awarded a life peerage in 1964, and the same year published *A Start in Freedom*. >> Foot, Dingle/Michael

Foot, Michael (Mackintosh) (1913–) British statesman, born in Plymouth, Devon, SW England, UK, the brother of Dingle and Hugh Foot. He studied at Oxford, and joined the staff of the *Tribune* in 1937, becoming editor (1948–52, 1955–60). He was also acting editor of the *Evening Standard* (1942–4) and a political columnist on the *Daily Herald* (1944–64). He became a Labour MP in 1945, and was secretary of state for employment (1974–6), and deputy leader (1976–80) then leader (1980–3) of the Labour Party, resigning after his party's heavy defeat in the general election. He retired from the Commons in 1992. A pacifist, he was a strong supporter of the Campaign for Nuclear Disarmament. A prolific writer, his best-known work is his biography of Aneurin Bevan. >> Foot, Dingle/Hugh

Foote, Andrew (Hull) (1806–63) US naval officer, born in New Haven, CT. He entered the navy in 1822, and was promoted captain in 1849. In 1856 he stormed four Chinese forts at Canton, which had fired on him. In the Civil War he organized the western flotilla, and in February 1862 stormed Fort Henry. Shortly afterwards he was wounded, and was forced to resign as rear admiral.

Foote, Arthur (William) (1853–1937) Composer, born in Salem, MA. A noted organist, he taught at the New York Conservatory (1920–37). He wrote church and chamber music, as well as books on harmony and keyboard technique.

Forbes, Bryan (1926–) Actor, script-writer, and director, born in London, England, UK. He studied at the Royal Academy of Dramatic Art, London, and made his debut in 1942. He acted on stage and in films in Britain and the USA (1948–60), and formed Beaver Films with Sir Richard Attenborough in 1959. He wrote and produced many films, including *The Slipper and the Rose* (1976) and *International Velvet* (1978). Included in the plays he has directed are *Macbeth* (1980) and *The Living Room* (1987), and his television productions include *The Endless Game* (1989, Channel 4). Later publications include *A Divided Life* (1992) and *Quicksand* (1996). >> Attenborough, Richard; Newman, Nanette

Forbes, Edward (1815–54) Naturalist, born in Douglas, Isle of Man. He studied medicine at Edinburgh, but from 1836 devoted himself to the natural sciences. He became professor of botany at King's College, London (1843), and professor of natural history at the School of Mines (1851) and Edinburgh (1853). He did much to advance and systematize several disciplines in natural history, made formative observations in oceanography, and was one of the founders of the science of biogeography.

Forbes, George (1849–1936) Electrical engineer, born in Edinburgh, EC Scotland, UK. He was the inventor of the carbon brush for dynamos. He also made improvements in the method of measuring the velocity of light (with **James**

Young, 1811–83), and in the field of range-finding. In 1880 he forecast the existence of the planet Pluto.

Forbes, Malcolm (Stevenson) (1919–90) Publisher, born in New York City. In 1957 he became editor and publisher of *Forbes*, a struggling business magazine, and greatly boosted its circulation and profits, making him a millionaire. He had a passionate interest in ballooning as well as Fabergé eggs, of which he had one of the world's foremost collections. >> Fabergé

Forbes, (Joan) Rosita (1893–1967) Writer and traveller, born in Swinderby, Lincolnshire, EC England, UK. Having visited a wide range of countries, and particularly Arabia and N Africa, she used her experiences as the raw material for exciting travel books, including *The Secret of the Sahara-Kufara* (1922), *From Red Sea to Blue Nile* (1928), *The Prodigious Caribbean* (1940), *Appointment in the Sun* (1949), and *Islands in the Sun* (1950).

Forbes-Robertson, Sir Johnston (1853–1937) Actor, born in London, England, UK. Educated at Charterhouse, he made his debut in 1874, and soon established himself as a West End favourite. In 1895, he became actor-manager of the London Lyceum, crowning his productions there with *Hamlet* in 1897. His later years were marked by success in *The Passing of the Third Floor Back* (1913). In 1900 he married **Gertrude Elliot** (1874–1950), a US actress who often partnered him. A daughter, **Jean** (1905–62), carried on the tradition, and became actress-manager in *The Lady of the Camellias* in 1934.

Ford, Anna (1943–) British broadcaster. She studied at Manchester University, then worked in further education as a lecturer and tutor. She joined Granada TV as a presenter and reporter (1974- -6), then moved to the BBC, where her programmes included *Man Alive* (1976–7) and *Tomorrow's World* (1977-8). She became an ITN newscaster (1978–80), helped to present *TV am* (1980–2), then worked as a freelance broadcaster and writer, and (from 1989) with BBC news and current affairs.

Ford, Brian (John) (1939–) Biologist, writer, and broadcaster, born in Corsham, Wiltshire, S England, UK. He studied at Cardiff University, and became a research biologist, his contributions including studies of the development of life from prebiotic molecules in outer space, plant physiology, hemostatic mechanisms, microbial ecology, and the history of science. A pioneer of holism in science, his publications include *Microbiology and Food* (1970), *Cult of the Expert* (1982), *Leeuwenhoek Legacy* (1990), and *First Encyclopedia of Science* (1993). He was founding editor of *Science Diary* (1967), and *Biology History* (1988), and he created several programmes for radio and television, such as *Science Now* and *Food for Thought*.

Ford, Elbur >> Hibbert

Ford, Ford Madox, originally **Ford Hermann Hueffer** (1873–1939) Writer, born in Merton, Surrey, SE England, UK. He collaborated with Conrad on *The Inheritors* (1901) and *Romance* (1903), wrote *The Good Soldier* (1915) and several other works, and founded the *English Review* (1908). After World War 1, he changed his name to Ford, and exiled himself to France and the USA, where he edited *The Transatlantic Review* (1924), wrote poetry, a series of war novels, and the tetralogy *Parade's End* (1920s). >> Conrad, Joseph

Ford, Gerald R(udolph) (1913–) US statesman and 38th president (1974–6), born in Omaha, NE. He studied at Michigan and Yale universities, and served in the US navy during World War 2. He became a Republican member of the US House of Representatives (1949–73), and on the resignation of Spiro Agnew in 1973 was appointed vice-president. He became president in 1974 when Nixon resigned because of the Watergate scandal. The full pardon he granted to Nixon the same year made him unpopular, and this, along with the economic recession of the time, led to his defeat in the 1976 presidential election by Jimmy Carter. >> Agnew; Carter, Jimmy; Nixon; RR1097

Ford, Harrison (1942–) Actor, born in Chicago, IL. He served a long apprenticeship in film and television, interspersed with employment as a carpenter, before achieving stardom in *Star Wars* (1977) and its two sequels. Cast as a resourceful, swashbuckling hero, he found great popularity as the archaeologist adventurer 'Indiana Jones' in a series of films beginning with *Raiders of the Lost Ark* (1981). He enhanced his reputation with testing characterizations in *Witness* (1985, Oscar nomination), *The Mosquito Coast* (1986), *Presumed Innocent* (1990), and *The Fugitive* (1993). Later films include *Clear and Present Danger* (1994) and *The Devil's Own* (1997).

Ford, Henry (1863–1947) Automobile engineer and manufacturer, born in Dearborn, MI. He produced his first petrol-driven motor car in 1893, and in 1899 founded a company in Detroit, designing his own cars. In 1903 he started the Ford Motor Company, pioneering the modern 'assembly line' mass-production techniques for his famous Model T (1908–9), 15 million of which were produced up to 1928. He also branched out into aircraft and tractor manufacture. In 1919 he was succeeded by his son **Edsel Bryant Ford** (1893–1943), and in 1945 by his grandson **Henry Ford II** (1917–87), who revitalized the company when it was in difficulties.

Ford, John (c. 1586–c. 1640) Playwright, born in Ilsington, Devon, SW England, UK. He studied for a while at Oxford and entered the Middle Temple in 1602. He often collaborated with Dekker, Rowley, and Webster. His own plays were greatly influenced by Robert Burton's *Anatomy of Melancholy* (1621), which led him into the stage presentation of the melancholic, the unnatural, and the horrible in such works as *The Lover's Melancholy* (1629) and *'Tis Pity She's a Whore* (1633). >> Burton, Robert

Ford, John, originally **Sean Aloysius O'Fearna** (1894–1973) Film director, born in Cape Elizabeth, ME. He went to Hollywood in 1913, where he worked as stunt man, actor, and assistant director. His skilful portrayal of US pioneering history reached a peak with *Stagecoach* (1935), *The Informer* (1935, Oscar), and *The Grapes of Wrath* (1940, Oscar). After World War 2 his films included *How Green Was My Valley* (1941, Oscar), *My Darling Clementine* (1946), and *The Quiet Man* (1952, Oscar). He made his last feature film, *Seven Women*, in 1965, and received the first American Film Institute Life Achievement Award in 1973.

Forde, (Cyril) Daryll (1902–73) Anthropologist, born in London, England, UK. He studied at University College London, and taught there (1923–8) and at the University of Wales (1930–45), before returning to London as professor of anthropology (1945–69). He carried out anthropological fieldwork in Arizona and New Mexico (1928–9), reported in *Habitat, Economy and Society* (1934), which won him wide acclaim. He made extensive contributions to the anthropology of Africa, and was director of the African Institute (1945–73).

Forel, Auguste Henri [forel] (1848–1931) Psychiatrist and entomologist, born near Morges, Switzerland. He studied at the universities of Zürich and Vienna, was professor of psychiatry at Zürich (1879–98), and made notable contributions in the fields of the anatomy of the brain and nerves, hypnotism, and forensic psychiatry. He also worked for social reform to prevent sexually transmitted diseases and alcoholism. After retiring he continued to work for social reform, and also studied the psychology of ants.

Foreman, George (1948–) Boxer, born in Marshall, TX. Reared in the black ghetto of Houston, he learned to box in a Job Corps camp in Oregon. In the Mexico City Olympic Games (1968) he won the gold medal in the heavyweight class. He turned professional in 1969, and became the world heavyweight champion in 1973, knocking out Joe Frazier, but lost the title to Muhammad Ali in 1974. He later won the US heavyweight championship, defeating Ron Lyle, and successfully defended the title against Joe Frazier in 1976. Foreman retired in 1977, but made a surprise return to the ring as a contender for the world title against Evander Holyfield in 1991, losing on points. He regained his title in 1994, at the age of 45. >> Ali, Muhammad; Frazier; RR1148

Forest, Lee de >> De Forest, Lee

Forester, C(ecil) S(cott) (1899–1966) Writer, born in Cairo. Chiefly a novelist, he also wrote biographical and travel books. He is known especially for his creation of Horatio Hornblower. He won the James Tait Black Memorial Prize for Literature in 1938 with *Ship of the Line*, and several of his works have been filmed, notably *The African Queen* (1935).

Forman, Miloš (1932–) Film director, born in Caslav, Czech Republic. Two feature films, *Lásky jedné plavovlásky* (1965, Loves of a Blonde) and *Hoří, má panenko* (1967, The Firemen's Ball), made in Prague, brought him international recognition. Being abroad at the time of the 1968 Russian repression, he went to the USA, where he became a US citizen. His tragi-comedy of insanity, *One Flew Over the Cuckoo's Nest* (1975), won five Oscar awards, and was successfully followed by his interpretations of stage presentations, *Hair* (1979), *Ragtime* (1980), and *Amadeus* (1983, Oscar). In 1996 he received an Oscar nomination for *The People vs. Larry Flynt*.

Formby, George (1904–61) Entertainer, born in Wigan, Greater Manchester, NW England, UK. He developed an act in music halls throughout England that was subsequently transferred to film. In a series of low-budget, slapstick comedies he portrayed a shy young man with an irrepressible grin and ever-ready ukelele to accompany his risqué songs. From *Boots Boots* (1934) to *George in Civvy Street* (1946) he was one of Britain's most popular film stars.

Forrest, Edwin (1806–72) Actor, born in Philadelphia, PA. He made his debut in Philadelphia in 1820. He had successful seasons in London (1836–7), but in 1845 his Macbeth was hissed by the audience, and a resentment which prompted him to hiss Macready in Edinburgh destroyed his reputation in Britain. The hissing of Macready's Macbeth by Forrest's sympathizers in New York City in 1849 led to a riot which cost 22 lives. >> Macready

Forrest (of Bunbury), John Forrest, Baron (1847–1918) Explorer and politician, born in Bunbury, Western Australia. From 1864 he worked in Western Australia's survey department, and led expeditions from Perth to Adelaide along the coast of the Great Australian Bight (1870) and into the interior (1874). He was state surveyor-general (1883–90), and the first premier of Western Australia (1890–1901). He was elected to the first federal parliament in 1901, serving as minister for defence (1901–3) and as treasurer (1905–14). In 1918 he became the first Australian to be granted a British peerage. >> Gosse, William Christie

Forrest, Nathan Bedford (1821–77) US soldier, born in Bedford Co, TN. With little formal education, he became a wealthy livestock dealer, planter, and slave trader. When the Civil War commenced, he enlisted as a private in the Confederate army, but by 1861 was a lieutenant-colonel in command of his own troop of cavalry. He participated in many of the early battles, including Shiloh, then began to operate on his own, using his cavalry as a 'strike force'. His

motto was the phrase attributed to him: 'Git there fustest with the mostest'. He struck often at Union lines (1862–4), and troops under his command carried out an infamous massacre of black Union troops at Fort Pillow, TN. After the war, he had to rebuild his fortune through planting and railroading. He served as Grand Wizard of the newly organized Ku Klux Klan (1867–9), but resigned in protest at some of its tactics.

Forrestal, James (1892–1949) US statesman, born in Beacon, NY. After World War 1 naval air service and a business career, he entered US government service in 1940. He was secretary of the navy (1944–7), then appointed to the newly created post of secretary of defence. He resigned in 1949, shortly before committing suicide.

Forrester, Jay (Wright) (1918–) Computer engineer, born in Anselmo, NE. He studied at Nebraska University and at Massachusetts Institute of Technology, where (1944–51) he supervised the building of the Whirlwind computer, and devised the first random-access magnetic core store (memory) for an electronic digital computer. He also studied the application of computers to management problems, developing methods for computer simulation.

Forrester, Maureen (1930–) Contralto, born in Montreal, Quebec, Canada. She studied in Berlin, and made her debut in Montreal in 1953. She undertook a recital tour of Europe in 1955, and at the invitation of Bruno Walter sang in Mahler's *2nd Symphony* in New York in 1956. She has since become a noted interpreter of Mahler's work. >> Mahler; Walter, Bruno

Forssmann, Werner (1904–79) Physician, born in Berlin. He studied at Berlin University, was an army doctor until 1945, then practised at various places, becoming chief of surgery at Dresden-Friedrichstadt, and at Dusseldorf in 1958. He became known for his development of new techniques in heart surgery, including cardiac catheterization, in which he carried out dangerous experiments on himself. He shared the 1956 Nobel Prize for Physiology or Medicine. >> RR1124

Forster, E(dward) M(organ) (1879–1970) Writer, born in London, England, UK. He studied at Cambridge, and was a member of the Bloomsbury group. His works include *Where Angels Fear to Tread* (1905), *The Longest Journey* (1907), *A Room with a View* (1908), *Howards End* (1910), and his masterpiece, *A Passage to India* (1924). He also wrote several volumes of essays and short stories. In 1951 he collaborated with Eric Crozier (1914–) on the libretto of Britten's opera, *Billy Budd*. His novel *Maurice* (written 1913–14), on the theme of homosexuality, was published posthumously in 1971. >> Britten; Moore G E

Förster, Johann Reinhold [foe(r)ster] (1729–98) Naturalist and clergyman, born in Dirschau, Germany. He studied theology at Halle, and undertook a survey of new German colonies on the Volga, in SW Russia. He taught at the Dissenter's Academy in Warrington, Cheshire. (1766–9), and accompanied Cook as naturalist on his second world voyage on the *Resolution* (1772–5). A pioneer ornithologist of Antarctica, New Zealand, and the Pacific, he wrote *Observations Made During a Voyage Around the World* (1778). In 1780 he was appointed professor of natural history at Halle. *Förster's tern* is named after him. >> Cook, James

Forster, Margaret (1938–) Writer, born in Carlisle, Cumbria, NW England, UK. She studied at Oxford, and taught in a London school (1961–3) before becoming a writer. She has written several biographical works, such as *Elizabeth Barrett Browning* (1988), and many novels, including *Georgy Girl* (1965, filmed 1966), *Fenella Phizackerley* (1970), *The Battle for Christabel* (1991), *Mothers' Boys* (1994), and *Shadow Baby* (1996). She was a member of the BBC

Advisory Committee on Social Effects of Television (1975–7) and of the Arts Coucil Literary Panel (1978–81). She married Hunter Davies in 1960. >> Davies, Hunter

Forster, William Edward (1818–86) British statesman, born in Bradpole, Dorset, S England, UK. During the Irish famine of 1845 he visited the distressed districts as almoner of a Quaker relief fund. He entered Parliament as a Liberal MP in 1861, rose to cabinet rank and in 1870 carried the Elementary Education Act. Under the Gladstone administration of 1880 he was chief secretary for Ireland. He was a severe critic of Parnell and, determined to re-establish law and order, had him and other Irish leaders arrested. When in 1882 a majority of the cabinet determined to release the 'suspects', he resigned. >> Gladstone, W E; Parnell

Forsyth, Bill [faw(r)siyth], popular name of **William David Forsyth** (1947–) Film-maker, born near Glasgow, W Scotland, UK. He entered the film industry in 1963, making his own documentaries, and was one of the original intake at the National Film School in 1971. *That Sinking Feeling*, a comedy using actors from the Glasgow Youth Theatre, was warmly received at the 1979 Edinburgh Festival. He has made several successful comedies, notably *Gregory's Girl* (1981) and *Local Hero* (1983), as well as productions for television. He moved to Hollywood in the mid-1980s, directing *Housekeeping* (1987), *Breaking In* (1989), and *Being Human* (1993).

Forsyth, Bruce [faw(r)siyth], popular name of **Bruce Joseph Forsyth-Johnson** (1928–) Entertainer, born in Edmonton, N Greater London, England, UK. He trained as a dancer, but is best known as the compère or host on many UK television shows, such as *Sunday Night at the London Palladium* (1958–60) and *The Generation Game* (1971–8, 1992–4). In 1995 he received the Lifetime Achievement Award for Variety.

Forsyth, Frederick [faw(r)siyth] (1938–) Writer of suspense thrillers, born in Ashford, Kent, SE England, UK. Educated at Tonbridge School, Kent, he served in the Royal Air Force and later became a journalist. His reputation rests on three taut thrillers, *The Day of the Jackal* (1971), *The Odessa File* (1972), and *The Dogs of War* (1974). Later novels include *The Fourth Protocol* (1984), *The Fist of God* (1993), and *Icon* (1996).

Forsyth, Gordon Mitchell [faw(r)siyth] (1879–1953) Ceramic designer and teacher, born in Fraserburgh, Aberdeenshire, NE Scotland, UK. He studied in Aberdeen and at the Royal College of Art, and worked in industry before his appointment as superintendent of art instruction at the Stoke-on-Trent School of Art. His influence on the period was enormous, and among his many pupils were Clarice Cliff and Susie Cooper. >> Cliff; Cooper, Susie

Forsythe, William [faw(r)siyth] (1949–) Dancer, choreographer, and artistic director, born in New York City. He trained at the Joffrey Ballet School, and became resident choreographer of the Stutgart Ballet (1976), and artistic director of Frankfurt Ballet (1984). His controversial, rule-bending works, including *Say Bye Bye* (1980) and *Impressing the Czar* (1988), frequently use spoken text and stage mechanics to enhance the steps. He is known for his challenge to, and remodelling of, the ballet vocabulary for contemporary purposes, making explicit the power and athleticism of the modern dancer.

Fort, Paul [faw(r)] (1872–1960) Poet, born in Reims, France. He founded the Théâtre des Arts (1890–3) for presenting a wide range of European drama and recitals of symbolist poetry. He is best known for his popular *Ballades françaises* (1st vol 1897), in which he brought poetry closer to the rhythms of everyday speech. He wrote several plays, and founded and edited the literary magazine *Vers et Prose* (1905–14).

Fortas, Abe [faw(r)tas] (1910–82) Jurist, born in Memphis, TN. After teaching at Yale Law School (1933–7), he served in government agencies (1937–45) before becoming an adviser to the US delegation at the organizational meeting of the UN (1945). He began to practise law privately in Washington, DC, combining a corporate practice with cases in defence of civil liberties. He became an unofficial adviser to Lyndon Johnson, who in 1965 appointed him to the US Supreme Court and nominated him for Chief Justice in 1968, but conservatives who opposed him during the US Senate confirmation proceedings forced him to withdraw. In 1969 it was revealed that he had been accepting money from a foundation set up by a man convicted of stock manipulation, and he became the first man ever forced to resign from the Supreme Court. He then returned to private practice. >> Johnson, Lyndon B

Fosbury, Dick, popular name of **Richard Fosbury** (1947–) Athlete, born in Portland, OR. He pioneered a new technique in high jumping which revolutionized this event after he won the Olympic gold medal at Mexico City in 1968 with a jump of 2·24 m (7 ft 4 in), using what came to be known as the *Fosbury Flop*, where the bar is jumped head-first and backwards.

Foscolo, Ugo [foskoloh] (1778–1827) Writer, born in Zákinthos, Greece. He studied at Spalato and Venice, and his disappointment when Napoleon ceded Venice to Austria found vent in the *Ultime lettere di Jacopo Ortis* (1802, Last Letters of Jacopo Ortis). After a period in the French army, he returned to Milan, and published his best poem, *Dei sepolcri* (1807, Of the Sepulchres). After 1814 he sought refuge in London, where he supported himself by teaching and writing, but his last years were embittered by poverty and neglect.

Fosdick, Harry (Emerson) (1878–1969) Minister, born in Buffalo, NY. Ordained into the Baptist Church, 1903, he became a professor at Union Theological Seminary, New York City (from 1915), and pastor of the interdenominational Riverside Church (1926–46). An outstanding preacher, he was a leading modernist in the controversy on fundamentalism in the 1920s.

Foss, Lukas, originally **Lukas Fuchs** (1922–) Composer, born in Berlin. He studied in Berlin and Paris, and moved to the USA in 1937. He first attracted attention with his cantata, *The Prairie* (1941), and has since written two symphonies, concertos, chamber music, and operas. He was appointed professor of music at the University of California in 1953, and in 1981 became director of the Milwaukee Symphony Orchestra.

Fosse, Bob, popular name of **Robert Louis Fosse** (1927–87) Choreographer and director, born in Chicago, IL. He started performing on stage at the age of 13. In 1950 he made his Broadway debut in the revue *Dance Me a Song*. His choreographic career started with *The Pajama Game* (1954), and with *Redhead* (1959) he began directing as well. Among his Broadway successes was *Sweet Charity* (1966). Moving into film, he was both director and choreographer of *Cabaret* (1972), and for *All That Jazz* (1979) he added the role of screenwriter.

Foster, Jodie, originally **Alicia Christian Foster** (1962–) Film actress and director, born in New York City. After a career in television commercials, she became known for her child roles in *Alice Doesn't Live Here Anymore* (1974), *Bugsy Malone* (1976), and *Taxi Driver* (1976). She studied in Los Angeles and at Yale, and then established herself as an adult actress, receiving Best Actress Oscars for her roles in *The Accused* (1988) and *The Silence of the Lambs* (1991). She made her directorial debut with *Little Man Tate* (1991). Later films include *Somersby* (1992), *Nell* (1994), and *Home for the Holidays* (1995), which she also directed.

Foster, Sir Norman (Robert) (1935–) Architect, born in Manchester, Greater Manchester, NW England, UK. He studied at Manchester and Yale universities, and became a leading exponent of the technological approach to architecture, founding Foster Associates in 1967. He is responsible for many major buildings worldwide, including the Willis Faber & Dumas Building, Ipswich (1979), the Sainsbury Centre for the Visual Arts, University of East Anglia (1977), the Hong Kong and Shanghai Bank, Hong Kong (1979–85), the Third London Airport Terminal (1980), the Terminal Zone at Stansted Airport (1991), and the Century Tower, Tokyo (1991). Later projects include the University of Cambridge Faculty of Law (1996). He was knighted in 1990. >> Rogers, Richard

Foster, Stephen (Collins) (1826–64) Songwriter, born in Pittsburgh, PA. His first songs, such as 'Open the Lattice, Love' (1844), were conventional concert songs of the day. When he began writing 'minstrel songs', influenced by itinerant black singers, his melodies and rhythms brightened. Songs such as 'Oh! Susanna' (1848), 'Old Folks at Home' (1851), and 'Beautiful Dreamer' (1864) sold thousands of song-sheets, and became seminal works of the US songwriting tradition.

Foster, William Z(ebulon) (1881–1961) Writer and communist leader, born in Taunton, MA. Informally educated, he joined the Communist Party in 1921 and was its chairman until 1957. He wrote a number of books and pamphlets on US and world history and politics.

Foucauld, Charles Eugéne, vicomte de (Viscount of) [fookoh], also known as **Brother Charles of Jesus** (1858–1916) Soldier, explorer, missionary-monk, and mystic, born in Strasbourg, France. He led an exploration of Morocco (1883–4), but is better known for his life as an ascetic. He became a Trappist monk in France and Syria, a hermit in Nazareth, a garrison priest at Beni-Abbès, Algeria, and a nomadic hermit among the Tuareg around Tamanrasset, where he was eventually murdered. He felt called to imitate Christ by a life of personal poverty in small contemplative communities financed solely by their own manual labour. His ideals survived in the foundation of the Little Brothers (1933) and Little Sisters (1939) of Jesus, now active worldwide.

Foucault, (Jean Bernard) Léon [fookoh] (1819–68) Physicist, born in Paris. He began by studying medicine, but turned to physics. He determined the velocity of light, and showed that light travels more slowly in water than in air (1850). He invented the gyroscope (1852), and improved the mirrors of reflecting telescopes (1858). In 1851 he demonstrated the rotation of the Earth by using a 67 m/220 ft pendulum hung in the dome of the Panthéon, Paris.

Foucault, Michel [fookoh] (1926–84) Philosopher, born in Poitiers, France. At Paris he studied philosophy, psychology, and psychopathology, then taught at Uppsala, Clermont-Ferrand, and Paris, becoming professor of the history of systems of thought at the Collège de France (1970). He sought consistently to test cultural assumptions in given historical contexts. His most important writings include *Histoire de la folie* (1961, trans Madness and Civilization), *Les mots et les choses* (1966, trans The Order of Things), and the unfinished *Histoire de la sexualité* (1976–84, The History of Sexuality).

Fouché, Joseph, duc d'Otrante (Duke of Otranto) [fooshay] (1763–1829) French statesman, born in Nantes, France. He was elected to the National Convention in 1792 as a Jacobin, and in 1799 became minister of police, a post which he held successfully until 1815. A consummate intriguer, he was banished after the Bourbon restoration, and died in exile in Trieste. >> Tallien

Foulds, John [fowldz] (1880–1939) Composer, born in Manchester, Greater Manchester, NW England, UK. Largely self-taught, he played cello in the Halle Orchestra under Richter, who premiered his *Cello Concerto* (1911). From 1915 he became fascinated with oriental, especially Indian, music, and absorbed Eastern and Western styles in a remarkable fusion. In 1935 he emigrated to India, where he died from cholera. His major works include *A World Requiem* (1921), a tone poem *April-England* (1926–32), *Mantras* for orchestra (1930), and other chamber, orchestral, vocal, and piano pieces.

Fouqué, Friedrich Heinrich Karl, Baron de la Motte [fookay] (1777–1843) Romantic writer, born in Brandenburg, Germany. He served as a Prussian cavalry officer, devoting himself between campaigns to literary pursuits. He published a long series of romances based on Norse legend and old French poetry, his masterpiece being *Undine* (1811).

Fouquet, Jean [fookay] (c. 1420–c. 1480) Painter, born in Tours, France. He opened a prosperous workshop at Tours, and in 1475 received the official title of king's painter. His most notable illuminations are found in the *Antiquities of the Jews* of Josephus and the *Hours of Etienne Chevalier* at Chantilly.

Fouquet, Nicolas, vicomte de (Viscount of) **Melun et de Vaux, Marquis de Belle-Isle** [fookay] (1615–80) French statesman, born in Paris. Mazarin made him *procureur-général* to the parliament of Paris (1650) and superintendent of finance (1653). He became extremely rich, and was ambitious to succeed Mazarin, but Louis XIV himself took up the reins of power on Mazarin's death, and Fouquet was arrested for embezzlement (1661). He was sentenced to life imprisonment in the fortress of Pignerol. >> Louis XIV; Mazarin

Fourdrinier, Henry [foordrinier] (1766–1854) British papermaker and inventor. With his brother **Sealy** (d.1847) and the assistance of Bryan Donkin he patented in 1806 an improved design of a paper-making machine capable of producing a continuous sheet of paper. The same basic type of machine, with further improvements, is still in use today. >> Donkin

Fourier, (François Marie) Charles [fooryay] (1772–1837) Social theorist, born in Besançon, France. He worked as a clerk before publishing his first work *The Social Destiny of Man, or, Theory of the Four Movements* (1808, trans title). After inheriting his mother's estate in 1812, he was able to develop his ideas in such works as *The New Industrial World* (1829, trans title). He advocated a reorganization of society into self-sufficient units (*phalanstères*) which would be scientifically planned to offer a maximum of both co-operation and self-fulfilment to their members (*Fourierism*). Several experimental 'phalanxes' were founded in France and the USA, and though these failed, his ideas attracted great popular interest and many adherents.

Fourier, (Jean Baptiste) Joseph, Baron [fooryay] (1768–1830) Mathematician, born in Auxerre, France. He accompanied Napoleon to Egypt (1798), and on his return (1802) was made prefect of the department of Grenoble, and created baron (1808). He then took up his first interest, applied mathematics, and while working on the flow of heat discovered the equation for it which now bears his name. To solve it, he showed that many functions of a single variable can be expanded in a series of sines of multiples of the variable (the *Fourier series*). >> Lebesgue

Fourneyron, Benoît [foornayrō] (1802–67) Hydraulic engineer, born in St Etienne, France. In 1832 he patented the general design of his hydraulic turbine installations, and eventually built more than 100 of these in different parts of the world.

Fournier, Henri-Alban >> **Alain-Fournier, Henri**

Fou Ts'ong [foo tsong] (1934–) Concert pianist, born in Shanghai, China. Internationally acclaimed as an interpreter of Mozart and Chopin, he studied under the Italian pianist and founder of the Shanghai Symphony Orchestra, Mario Paci. He won third prize in the International Chopin Competition in Warsaw (1955). Since 1958 he has made his base in London and performed extensively on the international circuit.

Fowke, Francis (1823–65) Engineer and architect, born in Belfast, N Ireland, UK. He obtained a commission in the Royal Engineers on the strength of his drawing, and in 1856 was appointed architect and engineer to the government department of science and art. He planned the Albert Hall in London, produced the original designs for the Victoria and Albert Museum in London (completed by Sir Aston Webb), and planned the Royal Scottish Museum in Edinburgh. >> Webb, Aston

Fowler, H(enry) W(atson) (1858–1933) Lexicographer, born in Tonbridge, Kent, SE England, UK. He studied at Oxford, became a schoolmaster at Sedbergh (1882–99), then went to London as a freelance journalist. In 1903 he joined his tomato-growing brother **F(rank) G(eorge) Fowler** (1871–1918) in Guernsey, and their literary partnership began. Their joint reputation rests on *The King's English* (1906) and the *Concise Oxford Dictionary* (1911). Henry later wrote the *Dictionary of Modern English Usage* (1926), a household work for all who attempt to write good English, even though it is sometimes as mannered as the mannerisms he set out to eradicate.

Fowler, Sir John (1817–98) Civil engineer, born in Sheffield, South Yorkshire, N England, UK. From an early age he engaged in railway construction, including the London Metropolitan Railway and the original Underground in London, and Victoria Station. River improvement and dock construction also occupied his attention. He was consulting engineer to Ismail Pasha, Khedive of Egypt (1871–9). He designed the Pimlico Railway Bridge (1860) and, with Sir Benjamin Baker, the Forth Railway Bridge (1882–90). >> Baker, Benjamin; Ismail Pasha

Fowler, Katherine >> Philips, Katherine

Fowler, Robbie (1975–) Footballer, born in Liverpool, Merseyside. He joined Liverpool Football Club in 1990 when aged 16, and made his debut in 1993, scoring the winning goal for his team. His honours include the Coca-Cola (League) Cup (1995) and he has twice been voted the Professional Football Association's Young Player of the Year (1995, 1996). He made his full international debut for England in 1996, and was a member of the Euro 96 squad.

Fowler, William A(lfred) (1911–95) Astrophysicist, born in Pittsburgh, PA. He studied at Ohio State University and the California Institute of Technology. He established a research group working on the application of nuclear physics to all aspects of astronomy, and is one of the founders of the theory of nucleosynthesis, developed in collaboration with Sir Fred Hoyle and others. He shared the Nobel Prize for Physics in 1983. >> Hoyle, Fred; RR1122

Fowles, John (Robert) (1926–) Writer, born in Leigh-on-Sea, Essex, SE England, UK. He studied at Oxford, served in the Royal Marines (1945–6), became a teacher, and published his first novel, *The Collector*, in 1963. His writings combine a topographical interest in Devon, a respect for the Victorian novel of social life and personal relationships, and an interest in contemporary developments in the French novel. His books include *The Magus* (1966), *The French Lieutenant's Woman* (1969, filmed with a script by Pinter, 1981), *The Ebony Tower* (1974, televised 1984), *A Maggot* (1985), and *Tessera* (1993). The autobiographical *Daniel Martin* appeared in 1977. >> Pinter

Fox, Charles James (1749–1806) British statesman and foreign secretary (1782, 1783, 1806), born in London, England, UK. He studied at Oxford, became a Liberal MP at 19, and two years later was a junior lord of the Admiralty. He supported Lord North, but in 1772 resigned over American policy. He became secretary of state after North's downfall, and in 1783 formed a coalition with him, which held office for a short period in 1783. He supported the French Revolution, and strongly opposed the war with France. After Pitt's death (1806) he was recalled to office, but died soon afterwards. >> North, Frederick

Fox, George (1624–91) Founder of the Religious Society of Friends (Quakers), born in Fenny Drayton, Leicestershire. Apprenticed to a Nottingham shoemaker, he felt at 19 a divine call to leave his friends, and Bible in hand he wandered about the country, on a small income. The 'inner light' was the central idea of his teaching, and he argued against the formalism of the established Church, and all social conventions. His life is a record of insults, persecutions, imprisonments, and missionary travel to several parts of the world. As a writer he is remembered by his *Journal* (posthumously published), which records the birth of the Quaker movement.

Fox, Henry Richard >> Holland, 3rd Baron

Foxe, John (1516–87) Preacher and writer, born in Boston, Lincolnshire, EC England, UK. He studied at Oxford and was a fellow of Magdalen College (1538–45) until his strong Protestant views forced his resignation. He lived on the European mainland during the reign of Mary I and returned to England on the accession of Elizabeth I. He wrote numerous controversial sermons, but is best remembered for his book *Actes and Monuments of These Latter and Perillous Dayes* (1563), which quickly became known as the *Book of Martyrs*, giving a vivid account of those who suffered in England for the Protestant cause.

Foxe, Richard, also spelled **Fox** (c. 1448–1528) Clergyman, born in Ropsley, Lincolnshire, EC England, UK. He studied at Oxford, Cambridge, and Paris, and became bishop successively of Exeter, Bath and Wells, Durham, and Winchester. In 1517 he founded Corpus Christi College, Oxford.

Fox Talbot, William Henry >> Talbot, William Henry Fox

Foy, Maximilien Sébastien [fwah] (1775–1825) French soldier, born in Ham, France. He entered the army in 1791, by 1808 was a brigadier general, and retired after the defeat of Napoleon (1815). He was elected to the Chamber of Deputies (1819) where he led the Liberal Opposition, and was a constant advocate of constitutional liberty.

Foyt, A(nthony) J(oseph) (1935–) Motor-racing driver, born in Houston, TX. He was one of the most successful drivers in the Indianapolis 500 (the 500-mi, 200-lap race in the USA, started in 1911), racing in every race from 1958 to 1990, and winning it four times (1961, 1964, 1967, 1977). He has also been successful in sports car and stock car racing. >> RR1165

Fra Angelico >> Angelico, Fra

Fra Bartolommeo >> Bartolommeo, Fra

Fracastoro, Girolamo [frakastawroh] (c.1478–1553) Scholar and physician, born in Verona, Italy. In 1502 he became professor of philosophy at Padua, but also practised successfully as a physician at Verona. He excelled as geographer, astronomer, and mathematician, and wrote on the theory of music. His works *De contagione et contagiosis morbis* (1564, On Contagion and Contagious Diseases) contained the first scientifically correct germ theory of disease, predating Pasteur by 300 years. >> Pasteur

Fra Diavolo [frah dyahvoloh] ('Brother Devil'), popular name of **Michele Pezza** (1760–1806) Brigand and guerrilla leader, born in Itri, Italy. For years he headed a band of desperados in the Calabrian Mts and evaded capture by skilful guerrilla warfare, earning his nickname for his fierce ways. In 1806 he attempted to excite Calabria against France, but was taken prisoner and executed at Naples.

Fraenkel-Conrat, Heinz L(udwig) [frengkl konrat] (1910–) Biochemist, born in Wrocław, Poland (formerly Breslau, Germany). He studied medicine there and biochemistry in Edinburgh before moving to the USA in 1936, becoming a US citizen in 1941, and joining the University of California at Berkeley in 1951. His work with viruses showed by 1955 that some could be split reversibly into a protein component and a nucleic acid, and that the latter alone was an infective agent; it was a 'living chemical', and a basic unit in the new science of molecular biology.

Fragonard, Jean Honoré [fragonah(r)] (1732–1806) Painter and engraver, born in Grasse, France. He studied under Boucher and Chardin in Paris, and gained the 'Prix de Rome' in 1752. A brilliant technician, he painted, with a loose touch and luscious colouring, genre pictures of contemporary life, the amours of the French court (notably *The Progress of Love* for Madame du Barry), and landscapes foreshadowing Impressionism. Several of his works, such as *The Sleeping Bacchante*, are in the Louvre.

Frame, Janet Paterson (1924–) Novelist and short-story writer, born in Dunedin, New Zealand. She studied at Otago University, and trained as a teacher. Her first book was a collection of short stories, *The Lagoon: Stories* (1952), which she followed five years later with a novel, *Owls Do Cry*. Her novels reflect the time she spent in psychiatric hospitals after severe mental breakdowns. Honoured in her homeland, but only belatedly receiving international recognition, key books are *Scented Gardens for the Blind* (1963), *A State of Siege* (1966), *Intensive Care* (1970), *Living in the Maniototo* (1979), and *The Carpathians* (1988). Between 1983 and 1985 she published a three-volume autobiography which was later filmed as *An Angel at my Table*. >> Campion, Jane

Frampton, Sir George James (1860–1928) Sculptor, born in London, England, UK. He studied in London and Paris. Among his works are 'Peter Pan' in Kensington Gardens, London, and the Lions at the British Museum. He was knighted in 1908.

France, Anatole [frãs], pseudonym of **Jacques Anatole François Thibault** (1844–1924) Writer, born in Paris. He worked as a publisher's reader, and in 1879 published his first volume of stories. He wrote several graceful, lively novels, which contrast with his later, satirical, sceptical works. The Dreyfus case (1896) stirred him into politics as a champion of internationalism. Among his later novels are *L'Ile des pingouins* (1908, Penguin Island) and *Les Dieux ont soif* (1912, The Gods are Athirst). He was awarded the Nobel Prize for Literature in 1921. >> Dreyfus

France, Celia (1921–) Dancer, born in London, England, UK. She trained under Marie Rambert, Antony Tudor, and Vera Volkova (1905–75), and performed with Ballet Rambert (1937–40) and Sadler's Wells Royal Ballet (1941–50). She was invited to start a new ballet company for Canada, and in 1951 the National Ballet of Canada was founded under her directorship (1951–74). >> Rambert; Tudor, Antony

Francesca, Piero della >> **Piero della Francesca**

Francesca da Rimini [francheska da reeminee] (?–1285) Daughter of Guido da Polenta, Lord of Ravenna, whose tragic love story has often been recounted in literary and artistic works. She was married to **Gianciotto the Lame**, son of Malatesta, Lord of Rimini; but she already loved Paolo, Gianciotto's brother. Gianciotto, surprising the lovers together, killed them both. The story is woven into Dante's *Inferno*. >> Dante

Francesco di Cristofano >> **Franciabigio**

Francesco di Giorgio [francheskoh di jaw(r)jioh], in full **Francesco Maurizio di Giorgio Martini** or **di Martino** (1439–1502) Painter, sculptor, and architect, born in Siena, Italy. Most of his paintings were executed in his early career, and he is now best known as an architect and architectural theorist, and author of *Trattato di architettura civile e militare*, a discussion of city planning. By 1477 he was working in Urbino where, as a military engineer, he designed the city's fortifications and, it is generally accepted, exploded the first land-mine in 1495 at a siege of Naples.

Francesco di Paola >> **Francis of Paola, St**

Franchet d'Esperey, Louis Félix Marie François [frãshay desperay] (1856–1942) French soldier, born in Mostaganem, Algeria. He trained at St Cyr, and served in the cavalry in Algeria, Tunis, Indo-China, Morocco, and Peking after the Boxer Rising. He was made commanding general of the French Fifth Army in 1914, gaining success at the Marne, but failed in 1918 to check the German offensive in N France. He was appointed commander-in-chief of allied armies in Macedonia, where from Salonika he overthrew Bulgaria and advanced as far as Budapest. He was made a marshal of France in 1921 and elected to the Académie Française in 1934.

Francheville or **Franqueville, Pierre** [frãshveel] (1548–1616) Sculptor, painter, and architect, born in Cambrai, France. He studied in Italy under Bologna. He executed the two colossal statues of Jupiter and Janus in the courtyard of the Grimaldi palace, Genoa, and five statues in the Nicolini Chapel in Florence. Recalled to France by Henry IV in 1604, he made the marble statue of David in the Louvre, Paris, and 'Saturn carrying off Cybele' in the Tuileries Gardens. >> Bologna

Francia [franchia], originally **Francesco di Marco di Giacomo Raibolini** (1450–1517) Goldsmith and painter, born in Bologna, Italy. He achieved fame as a craftsman in metal, in niello, and designed the first italic type for Aldus Manutius. As a painter in oils or in fresco he is particularly noted for his madonnas. His sons, **Giacomo** (c.1486–1557) and **Giulio** (1487–1543), were also painters. >> Aldus Manutius

Francia, José Gaspar Rodriguez [fransya] (1766–1840) Dictator of Paraguay, born near Asunción. He studied theology, then took up law, which he practised for 30 years with a high reputation. He helped to free Paraguay from Spanish rule, and in 1811 became secretary of the national junta, in 1813 one of the two consuls, and in 1814 dictator – first for three years, then for life. Under his firm rule, which excluded all foreign contact, Paraguay rapidly improved. He was an unscrupulous despot, and yet he improved agriculture, promoted education, repressed superstition, and enforced strict justice in his law-courts, however little he regarded it himself.

Franciabigio [franchabeejoh], also called **Francesco di Cristofano Bigi** (1482–1525) Painter, born in Florence, Italy. He worked in collaboration with Andrea del Sarto on the Church of the Annunziata and the Chiostro dello Scalzo, and was much influenced by him and by Raphael. His 'Madonna del Pozzo' was long thought to be by Raphael. >> Raphael; Sarto

Francis I (1494–1547) King of France (1515–47), born in Cognac, France. He was Count of Angoulême and Duke of Valois before succeeding Louis XII as king and marrying his daughter, **Claude**. He combined many of the attributes of mediaeval chivalry and the Renaissance prince, the dominant feature of his reign being his rivalry with the Emperor Charles V, which led to a series of wars (1521–6, 1528–9, 1536–8, 1542–4). After establishing his military reputation against the Swiss at Marignano (1515) in his first Italian campaign, he later suffered a number of reverses, including his capture at Pavia (1525) and imprisonment in Madrid. Though he avoided religious fanaticism, he became increasingly hostile to Protestantism after 1534. >> Bourbon; Charles V (Emperor); Louis XII; Margaret of Angoulême; RR1049

Francis II (Emperor) (1768–1835) Last Holy Roman Emperor (1792–1806), the first emperor of Austria (Francis I, 1804–35), and king of Hungary (1792–1830) and Bohemia (1792–1836), born in Florence, Italy. Defeated on several occasions by Napoleon (1797, 1801, 1805, 1809), he made a short-lived alliance with him, sealed by the marriage of his daughter, **Marie Louise**, to the French emperor. Later he joined with Russia and Prussia to win the Battle of Leipzig (1813). By the Treaty of Vienna (1815), thanks to Metternich, he recovered several territories (eg Lombardy–Venetia). >> Marie Louise; Metternich; Napoleon; RR1057

Francis of Assisi, St [aseezee], originally **Giovanni Bernardone** (?1181–1226) Founder of the Franciscan Order, born in Assisi, Italy. In 1205 he left his worldly life, devoting himself to the care of the poor and the sick, and living as a hermit. By 1210 he had a brotherhood of 11 for which he drew up a rule which became the *Franciscan* way of life, in which all property is repudiated. By 1219 the order had 5000 members. He preached widely in Europe and the Holy Land, and on returning to Italy he is said to have received on his body the marks (*stigmata*) of the wounds of Christ (1224). He was canonized in 1228. He is often represented in art among animals and birds, which he called his sisters and brothers. Feast day 4 October. >> Clare, St

Francis of Paola, St [powla], Ital **Francesco di Paola** (1416–1507) Franciscan monk, the founder of the Minim friars, born in Paola, Italy. After spending a year with the Franciscan community in San Marco, he decided in 1431 on a life of austerity, and became a hermit, living in a cave. His reputation spread through Italy and France, and he was joined by others. Louis XI of France summoned him to his death-bed, and Charles VIII and Louis XII built him convents at Plessis-les-Tours and Amboise. Feast day 2 April.

Francis of Sales, St [saylz], Fr [sahl] (1567–1622) Roman Catholic bishop and writer, born in Sales, France. He studied at Paris and Padua, and became a distinguished preacher, successfully converting the Calvinistic population of Chablais. He became Bishop of Nicopolis (1599) and Bishop of Geneva (1602), where he helped to found a congregation of nuns of the Visitation. He was canonized in 1665; feast day 24 January.

Francis, Dick, popular name of **Richard Stanley Francis** (1920–) Jockey and novelist, born in Surrey, SE England, UK. Starting as an amateur National Hunt jockey he turned professional late, at the age of 28. As a rider, he is probably best remembered for the occasion, during the Grand National (1956), when he was riding the Queen Mother's horse *Devon Loch* and winning until the horse collapsed 50 yd from the post. He retired the following year, became a racing correspondent with the *Daily Express*, and began writing popular thrillers with a racing background. An early autobiography, *Sport of Queens*, was published in 1957, and his award-winning novels include *Forfeit* (1969), *Whip Hand* (1980), and *Reflex* (1981). Later titles include *Proof* (1984), *Straight* (1989), *Comeback* (1991), *Come to Grief* (1995, Edgar Allan Poe Award), and *To the Hilt* (1996).

Francis, James (Bicheno) (1815–92) Engineer and inventor, born in South Leigh, Devon, SW England, UK. He emigrated to the USA in 1833, working first on railroad construction. By 1837 he had been appointed chief engineer to the Proprietors of the Locks and Canals on the

Merrimack River, and when they decided in 1845 to develop the river's power potential he began to work on the design of the turbine that now bears his name. He is also remembered by the *Francis formula* for the flow of water over weirs.

Francis, Sir Philip (1740–1818) Civil servant, born in Dublin. He was educated at St Paul's School, London, and after serving in minor government posts became in 1773 a member of the Council of Bengal. In 1780 he fought a duel with Warren Hastings, with whom he was always disagreeing, and was seriously wounded. He returned to England in 1781 and entered parliament in 1784. He continued his vendetta against Hastings by publishing a number of defamatory pamphlets. He is the probable author of the anonymous 'Junius Letters' – a series of political letters published in the *Public Advertiser* (1769–72). >> Hastings, Warren

Francis, Sam (1923–) Abstract painter, born in San Mateo, CA. He began as a medical student, but turned to painting in 1945, studying at the California School of Fine Arts, San Francisco. He had his first one-man show in Paris in 1955.

Francisco el Viejo >> **Herrera, Francisco**

Francis Ferdinand, Ger **Franz Ferdinand** (1863–1914) Archduke of Austria, the nephew and heir-apparent (from 1896) to the Emperor Francis Joseph. On a visit to Sarajevo, Bosnia, in June 1914 he and his wife Sophie were assassinated by a group of young Serbian nationalists led by Gavrilo Princip. Austria used the incident as a pretext for attacking Serbia, which precipitated World War 1. >> Francis Joseph; Princip; William II (of Germany)

Francis Joseph I, Ger **Franz Josef I** (1830–1916) Emperor of Austria (1848–1916) and king of Hungary (1867–1916), born near Vienna, the grandson of Emperor Francis I. During his reign the aspirations of the various nationalities of the empire were rigorously suppressed. He was defeated by the Prussians in 1866, and established the Dual Monarchy of Austria–Hungary in 1867. His annexation of Bosnia-Herzegovina in 1908 agitated Europe; and his attack on Serbia in 1914 precipitated World War 1. >> Francis Ferdinand; Maximilian, Ferdinand Joseph; RR1033

Francis Xavier, St [zayvier], Span **San Francisco Javier**, known as **the Apostle of the Indies** (1506–52) Roman Catholic missionary who brought Christianity to India and the Far East, born in Navarre, Spain. He studied in Paris, where he became one of the first seven members of the Jesuit order (1534). He began his missionary work in Goa, India (1542), later travelling to the Malay Is (1545) and Japan (1549). He died of a fever while trying to enter China. He was canonized in 1622, and named patron saint of all missionary work in 1927. Feast day 3 December. >> Loyola

Franck, César (Auguste) [frãk, sayzah(r)] (1822–90) Composer, born in Liège, Belgium. He studied at the Liège Conservatoire and at Paris, where he acquired French nationality, and settled as a teacher and organist, composing in his leisure hours. His reputation rests on a few masterpieces all written after the age of 50, the best known being a violin sonata, a string quartet, a symphony, and the *Variations symphoniques* for piano and orchestra.

Franck, James (1882–1964) Physicist, born in Hamburg, Germany. Professor of physics at Göttingen (1920), he worked with Gustav Hertz on the laws governing the transfer of energy between molecules, for which they were jointly awarded the Nobel Prize for Physics in 1925. He emigrated to the USA in 1935, became professor of physical chemistry at Chicago (1938–49), and worked on the development of the atomic bomb in World War 2. He headed the *Franck Committee* of scientists who urged that the bomb should not be used, but could be detonated in an unpopulated area to demonstrate its power. >> Hertz, Gustav

Franco (Bahamonde), Francisco [frangkoh], popular name **el Caudillo** ('the leader') (1892–1975) Spanish general and dictator (1936–75), born in El Ferrol, Galicia. He graduated from Toledo military academy in 1910, acquired extensive combat experience in Morocco, and by 1926 was Spain's youngest general. During the Second Republic (1931–6), he led the repression of the Asturias miners' revolt (1934), and in 1935 served as chief-of-staff. In 1936 he belatedly joined the conspiracy against the Popular Front government (elected Feb 1936) which on 17–18 July launched the rebellion from which the Spanish Civil War (1936–9) resulted. Franco's leadership of the vital Army of Africa, and his close relations with the rebels' Italian and German allies, led to his becoming (Sep 1936) *generalísimo* of the rebel forces and chief of the Nationalist state. Between October 1936 and April 1939 he led the Nationalists to victory, and presided over the construction of an authoritarian regime that endured until his death. During World War 2, he initially stood close to Germany and Italy, opting (1940) for nonbelligerency rather than neutrality. He nevertheless kept Spain out of the war, and from 1943 shrewdly distanced himself from the Axis. During the 1950s, his anti-Communism made possible a rapprochement with the Western powers. In 1969 he announced that upon his death the monarchy would return in the person of Juan Carlos, grandson of Spain's last ruling king. Within two years of Franco's death, almost every vestige of his dictatorship had disappeared. >> Juan Carlos I; RR1088

Francome, John [frangkuhm] (1952–) Jockey and trainer, born in Swindon, Wiltshire, S England, UK. In 1970–85 he rode a record 1138 winners over fences. He won the 1978 Cheltenham Gold Cup, the 1981 Champion Hurdle, and twice won the King George VI Chase (1982, 1984). Only the second man to surpass 1000 winners, he was seven times National Hunt champion jockey (1976, 1979, 1981–5). He retired in 1985, and became a trainer and novelist.

Frank, Anne (1929–45) Jewish diarist and concentration camp victim, born in Frankfurt, Germany. Her family fled from the Nazis to The Netherlands in 1933, and after the Nazi occupation of The Netherlands she hid with her family and four others in a sealed-off office flat in Amsterdam from 1942 until they were betrayed in 1944. She died in Belsen concentration camp. The lively, moving diary she kept during her concealment was published by her father, the only Frank survivor, in 1947, dramatized, and filmed, and she became a symbol of past suffering under the Nazis.

Frank, Hans (1900–46) Nazi politician, born in Karlsruhe, Germany. He studied at Munich, Vienna, and Kiel universities, was minister of justice in Bavaria (1933), president of the German Law Academy (1934), and in 1939 became Governor-General of Poland, where he established concentration camps and conducted a policy of persecution and extermination. He was condemned as a war criminal and hanged.

Frank, Ilya Mikhailovich (1908–90) Physicist, born in St Petersburg, Russia. He studied at Moscow State University, and was appointed professor of physics there (1944), after working for four years at the State Optical Institute. By 1937, working with P A Cherenkov and I Y Tamm, they were able to explain the 'Cherenkov effect' – an effect which is dramatically visible in the blue glow in a uranium reactor core containing heavy water. Cherenkov, Frank, and Tamm shared the Nobel Prize for Physics in 1958. >> Cherenkov; Tamm

Frank, Robert (1924–) Photographer and film maker, born in Zürich, Switzerland. A freelance photographer in Zürich (1943–7), he emigrated to New York City, where he did fashion and advertising photography for *Harper's* and the *New York Times* among others. The first European to receive a Guggenheim Award in 1955, he spent the next two years travelling across America to capture images of daily life, publishing *The Americans* in 1959. In 1958 he collaborated with the painter Alfred Leslie and author Jack Kerouac to film the free-swinging *Pull My Daisy*. One of the founders of the New American Cinema Group, he spent most of his time making films until 1966, when he virtually gave up photography. Since 1969 he has lived in Cape Breton, Nova Scotia. >> Kerouac

Frankau, Gilbert [frangkow] (1884–1953) Novelist, born in London, England, UK. His early works were great successes, and he continued to write best sellers, for he had a flair for anticipating popular taste. His books include *One of Us* (1912), *Peter Jackson, Cigar Merchant* (1919), *Men, Maids and Mustard-Pots* (1923), and *World Without End* (1943).

Frankau, Pamela [frangkow], pseudonym **Eliot Naylor** (1908–67) British novelist. Her early novels, such as *The Marriage of Harlequin*, epitomized the era of the 'bright young things'. Her later novels were more serious in intent. Typical are *The Willow Cabin* (1949) and *A Wreath for the Enemy* (1954). *The Offshore Light* (1952) was written under her pseudonym.

Frankenthaler, Helen [frangkentahler] (1928–) Abstract painter, born in New York City. She studied under the Mexican painter Rufino Tamayo and at Bennington College, Vermont. She developed a technique of applying very thin paint to unprimed canvas, allowing it to soak in and create atmospheric stains and blots on the surface. Her best-known picture is 'Mountains and Sea' (1952). >> Motherwell; Tamayo

Frankfurter, Felix (1882–1965) Law teacher and judge, born in Vienna. He studied at the College of the City of New York and at Harvard, taught at Harvard Law School (1914–39), and served as an associate justice of the US Supreme Court (1939–62). He founded the American Civil Liberties Union, though he advocated judicial restraint in opposing legislative and executive policy.

Frankland, Sir Edward (1825–99) Organic chemist, born in Churchtown, Lancashire, NW England, UK. He was introduced to chemistry as an apprentice to a druggist in Lancaster, eventually taking his PhD at the University of Marburg. He became professor at the Royal Institution, London, in 1863. He propounded the theory of valency (1852–60), and with Lockyer discovered helium in the Sun's atmosphere in 1868. He made major contributions to applied chemistry, particularly in the areas of water and sewage purification. He was knighted in 1897. >> Lockyer

Franklin, Aretha [areetha], nicknames **Lady Soul** and **The Queen of Soul** (1942–) Soul singer and pianist, born in Memphis, TN. She had established her name on the Gospel circuit with her father before she signed a recording contract with Columbia Records in 1960, but it was only after moving to Atlantic Records in 1967 that her full potential was realized. Her hit singles include 'Baby, I Love You' and 'Respect', and her albums *Lady Soul* (1968), *Amazing Grace* (1972), and *Aretha* (1986).

Franklin, Benjamin (1706–90) US statesman, writer, and scientist, born in Boston, MA. He set up a printing house in Philadelphia, bought the *Pennsylvania Gazette* (1729), and built a reputation as a journalist. In 1736 he became clerk of the Assembly, in 1737 postmaster of Philadelphia, and in 1754 deputy postmaster-general for the colonies, and was sent on various diplomatic missions to England. In

1746 he began his research into electricity, proving that lightning and electricity are identical, and suggesting that buildings be protected by lightning conductors. In 1776 he was actively involved in framing the Declaration of Independence. A skilled negotiator, he successfully won Britain's recognition of US independence (1783). He was US minister in Paris till 1785, then three times President of the Pennsylvania Executive Council. He played a major part in the Federal Constitutional Convention (1787), then retired from public life. His *Autobiography* was begun in 1771, but never completed. >> Deane, Silas

Franklin, Frederic (1914–) Dancer, ballet director, and teacher, born in Liverpool, Merseyside, NW England, UK. He worked with the Markova–Dolin Ballet (1935–7) and the Ballets Russes de Monte Carlo (1938–49, 1954–6), becoming company ballet master in 1944. Later he worked with various companies including his own *Slavenska–Franklin* Ballet (founded 1951), the National Ballet of Washington (artistic director, 1962–74), Pittsburgh Ballet Theatre (co-director), and Chicago Ballet.

Franklin, Sir John (1786–1847) Arctic explorer, born in Spilsby, Lincolnshire, EC England, UK. He joined the navy at 14, and was present at the Battles of Copenhagen (1801) and Trafalgar (1805). Knighted in 1829, he became Governor of Van Diemen's Land (Tasmania) (1834–45). He then commanded an expedition to discover the Northwest Passage, but his ships were beleaguered by thick ice in the Victoria Strait, and he and his crew died. Their remains, and a record of the expedition, were found several years later. He is credited with the discovery of the Passage, because his ships came within a few miles of known American waters. >> Belcher; Grinnell, Henry; Hall, Charles Francis; Hayes, Isaac Israel; Kane, Elisha; McClure; Peabody; Rae; Ross, John

Franklin, John Hope (1915–) Historian, born in Rentiesville, OK. He studied at Fisk and Harvard universities, then taught at several African-American institutions, joining Howard University in 1947. In 1956 he became chairman of the department of history at Brooklyn College, and professor of American history at Chicago University in 1964. He was the first African-American president of the American Historical Association (1978–9), and has published several books viewing American history from an African-American standpoint.

Franklin, (Stella Maria Sarah) Miles, pseudonym **Brent of Bin Bin** (1879–1954) Novelist, born in Talbingo, New South Wales, Australia. A freelance writer in Sydney and Melbourne, she emigrated in 1906 to the USA, and remained abroad, living in England and America, until 1927. Her best-known novel, *My Brilliant Career* (1901), was described as 'the very first Australian novel' on account of its original and distinctive Australian character. Its sequel, *My Career Goes Bung*, written soon afterwards, was not published until 1946. Other novels include *Some Everyday Folk – and Dawn* (1909), *Bring the Monkey* (1933), and *All That Swagger* (1936). The annual *Miles Franklin Awards* are now among Australia's most prestigious literary prizes.

Franklin, Rosalind (Elsie) (1920–58) X-ray crystallographer, born in London, England, UK. She studied chemistry at Cambridge, and worked in research associations in Britain and in Paris (1947–50) before joining a research group at King's College, London (1951–3). There she extended the X-ray diffraction studies by Maurice Wilkins on DNA, and obtained exceptionally good diffraction photographs using a hydrated form of DNA; these were of great value to James Dewey Watson and Francis Crick in their deduction of the full structure of DNA, which effectively created modern molecular biology in 1953. Her death prevented her being awarded a share of the Nobel

Prize; it is not awarded posthumously. >> Crick; Watson, James; Wilkins, Maurice

Franqueville, Pierre >> **Francheville, Pierre**

Franz (rulers) >> **Francis**

Frasch, Hermann (1851–1914) Industrial chemist, born in Gailsdorf, Germany. He emigrated to the USA in 1868, and worked there and in Canada as a chemist in the petroleum industry. He is best known for the *Frasch process* of extracting sulphur from deep underground deposits by the use of superheated steam.

Fraser, Lady Antonia, *née* **Pakenham** (1932–) British writer. She studied at Oxford, and as a writer became active in several arts and literary associations, chairing the Society of Authors (1974–5). She is best known for her books about important historical figures, such as *Mary Queen of Scots* (1969, James Tait Black), *Kings and Queens of England* (1975, 1988), and *The Six Wives of Henry VIII* (1992). Other books include *Your Royal Hostage* (1987) and *Political Death* (1994). She married Harold Pinter in 1980. >> Pinter, Harold

Fraser (of North Cape), Bruce Austin Fraser, Baron (1888–1981) British naval officer, born in Acton, W Greater London, England, UK. Educated at Bradfield College, he entered the Royal Navy in 1902 and became a gunnery specialist. He served at sea in World War 1 and was chief of staff Mediterranean Fleet (1938–9). In World War 2 he was controller of the navy (1939–42), and commander-in-chief Home Fleet (1943–4), Eastern Fleet (1944), and British Pacific Fleet (1945–6). He was a British signatory at the Tokyo Bay Peace Ceremony (1945). He was made a peer in 1946, and later became First Sea Lord (1948–51).

Fraser, Dawn (1937–) Swimmer, born in Balmain, near Sydney, New South Wales, Australia. She is the only swimmer to take the same individual title at three consecutive Olympics, winning the 100 m freestyle in 1956, 1960, and 1964. She also won a gold medal in the 4 × 100 m freestyle relay in 1956. She took six Commonwealth Games gold medals, and set 27 world records. In 1962 she became the first woman to break the one-minute barrier for the 100 m. In 1964 she was banned by the Australian association for 10 years (later reduced to four) following an overexuberant party in Tokyo after winning her third Olympic title. She was however named as 1964 Australian of the Year, and in 1988 was selected as Australia's greatest female athlete. She was elected as an Independent member of the New South Wales Legislative Assembly (1988–91), representing Balmain.

Fraser, (John) Malcolm (1930–) Australian statesman and prime minister (1975–83), born in Melbourne, Victoria, Australia. He studied at Melbourne and Oxford, and in 1955 became the youngest MP in the House of Representatives. He was minister for the army (1966–8), defence (1969–71), and education and science (1968–9, 1971–2), and became leader of the Liberal Party in 1975, and prime minister in a Liberal–National coalition. His government was defeated in the 1983 elections, and soon after he resigned his parliamentary seat, becoming a farmer in Nareen, W Victoria. He has also become involved in international affairs, particularly as a member of the Commonwealth Group of Eminent Persons which worked to replace apartheid in South Africa. >> Kerr, Sir John; RR1033

Fraser, Simon (1776–1862) Fur trader, born in Bennington, VT. He moved to Canada in 1784. He worked as a clerk in the North-West Co, was promoted to partner in 1801, and was sent in 1805 to establish the first trading posts in the Rocky Mountains. Following Mackenzie's route, he opened up a vast area which he called New Caledonia between the plains and the Pacific, and in 1808 followed the *Fraser R*, named after him, to its mouth. He headed the Red River Department of the North-West Co during conflict with settlers of the rival Hudson's Bay Co, before his retirement in 1818. *Simon Fraser University*, in British Columbia, is named after him.

Fraunhofer, Joseph von [frownhohfer] (1787–1826) Physicist, born in Straubing, Germany. In 1807 he founded an optical institute at Munich, where he improved prisms and telescopes, enabling him to discover the dark lines in the Sun's spectrum which have been named after him. He also pioneered the use of diffraction gratings to examine spectra. In 1823 he became professor and academician at Munich.

Frayn, Michael (1933–) Playwright, novelist, and journalist, born in London, England, UK. He studied at Cambridge, and first established his reputation with witty, gently satirical columns in *The Manchester Guardian* and *The Observer*, and a series of novels in the same vein, including *The Russian Interpreter* (1966). He wrote many plays, notably three successful comedies of the 1970s: *Alphabetical Order* (1975), *Donkey's Years* (1976), and *Clouds* (1976). His greatest commercial success was *Noises Off* (1982). *Benefactors* (1984) received the Lawrence Olivier Award for Play of the Year. Later work includes the script for the film *Clockwise* (1986), the novel *The Trick of It* (1989), and the plays *Look, Look* (1990) and *Now You Know* (1995). He has also translated and adapted work by Chekov and Tolstoy for the National Theatre.

Frazer, Sir James George (1854–1941) Social anthropologist, classicist, and folklorist, born in Glasgow, W Scotland, UK. He studied at Glasgow and at Cambridge, where he spent most of his adult life as a fellow of Trinity College. His major work was *The Golden Bough* (1890; rewritten in 12 vols, 1911–15). He became professor of social anthropology at Liverpool in 1907, and was knighted in 1914.

Frazier, Joe, popular name of **Joseph Frazier** (1944–) Boxer, born in Beaufort, SC. At the Tokyo Olympic Games (1964) he won the gold medal in the heavyweight class and later turned professional (1965). He went on to become the world heavyweight champion (1970), defeating Jimmy Ellis in New York City, but lost the title to George Foreman (1973) at Kingston, Jamaica. This was the only defeat of his professional career. He retired in 1976, and staged an unsuccessful comeback fight in 1981. >> Foreman; RR1148

Frederick I (Emperor), known as **Frederick Barbarossa** ('Redbeard') (c. 1123–90) Holy Roman Emperor, born of the Hohenstaufen family. He succeeded his uncle, Conrad III, in 1152. His reign was a continuous struggle against unruly vassals at home, the city republics of Lombardy, and the papacy. He went on several campaigns in Italy, and though severely defeated at Legnano (1176), he quelled Henry the Lion of Bavaria, and asserted his feudal superiority over Poland, Hungary, Denmark, and Burgundy. He led the Third Crusade against Saladin (1189), and was victorious at Philomelium and Iconium. >> Henry the Lion; Saladin; RR1057

Frederick I (of Prussia) (1657–1713) King of Prussia (1701–13), born in Königsberg, Germany. He succeeded to the electorate of Brandenburg in 1688 (as Frederick III) and was made the first King of Prussia for his loyalty to Emperor Leopold against the French. He maintained a large court, established a standing army, and was a great patron of the arts and learning.

Frederick II (Emperor) (1194–1250) Holy Roman Emperor, born in Jesi, near Ancona, the grandson of Frederick I. He succeeded Henry VI in 1220, and was the last emperor of the Hohenstaufen line. He was also King of Sicily (1198) and of Germany (1212). He keenly desired to consolidate imperial power in Italy at the expense of the papacy, and devoted himself to organizing his Italian territories, but his plans were frustrated by the Lombard cities and by the popes. Embarking on the Sixth Crusade in 1228, he took possession of Jerusalem, and crowned himself king there (1229). Returning to Italy, he continued his struggles with the papacy until his death. >> RR1057

Frederick II (of Prussia), known as **the Great** (1712–86) King of Prussia (1740–86), the son of Frederick William I, born in Berlin. His childhood was spent in rigorous military training and education. In 1733 he married, and lived at Rheinsberg, where he studied music and French literature, and himself wrote and composed. As king, he fought to oppose Austrian ambitions, and earned a great reputation as a military commander in the War of the Austrian Succession (1740–8). He seized Silesia, and defeated the Austrians at Mollwitz (1741) and Chotusitz (1742). The second Silesian War (1744–5) left him with further territories which, by good luck and great effort, he retained after fighting the Seven Years' War (1756–63). In 1772 he shared in the first partition of Poland. Under him, Prussia became a leading European power. When he died, he had doubled the area of his country, and given it a strong economic foundation. >> Quantz; RR1051

Frederick IX (of Denmark) (1899–1972) King of Denmark (1947–72), born near Copenhagen, the son of Christian X. He married **Ingrid**, the daughter of King Gustav VI Adolf of Sweden, in 1935, and they had three daughters, **Margrethe** (later Queen Margrethe II), **Benedikte**, and **Anne-Marie**, who married the former King Constantine II of Greece. During World War 2, Frederick encouraged the Danish resistance movement, and was imprisoned by the Germans (1943–5). >> Christian X; RR1044

Frederick (Augustus), Duke of York (1763–1827) Second son of King George III of Britain. A soldier by profession, he was unsuccessful both in the field in The Netherlands (1793–99) and as British commander-in-chief (1798–1809), and earned the description of the 'grand old Duke of York' in the nursery rhyme. However, his painstaking reform of the army proved of lasting benefit, especially to Wellington. He founded the Duke of York's School in London, and is commemorated by the Duke of York's column in Waterloo Place, London. >> George III; Wellington

Frederick William, known as **the Great Elector** (1620–88) Elector of Brandenburg (1640–88), born near Berlin. On his accession, he found the state exhausted by the Thirty Years' War. He therefore made a treaty of neutrality with the Swedes, regulated the finances, sought to re-people the deserted towns, and reorganized the army and administrative system of the Hohenzollern state. He recovered some territory and gained East Pomerania by the Treaty of Westphalia (1648), retrieving the sovereignty of Prussia from Poland (1657). His reforms laid the foundation of future Prussian greatness.

Frederick William III (1770–1840) King of Prussia (1797–1840), the son of Frederick William II (1744–97), born in Potsdam, Germany. At first cautiously neutral towards Napoleon's conquests, he eventually declared war (1806) and was severely defeated at Jena and Auerstadt, with the loss of all territory W of the Elbe. To further Prussia's recovery, he sanctioned the reforms of Hardenburg and Stein, and the military reorganization of Scharnhorst and Gneisenau, sharing in the decisive victory of Leipzig with Alexander I (1813). By the Treaty of Vienna (1815) he recovered his possessions, and thereafter tended to support the forces of conservatism. >> Alexander I (of Russia); Gneisenau; Napoleon; Scharnhorst; Stein, Karl; William I (of Germany); RR1051

Frederick William IV (1795–1861) King of Prussia, born in Cölln, Germany. He succeeded his father, Frederick William III, in 1840, and began his reign by granting minor reforms and promising radical changes, but always evaded the fulfilment of these pledges. He survived the revolution of 1848, and refused the imperial crown offered him by the Liberal Frankfurt Diet in 1849. In 1857, after suffering a stroke, he resigned the administration to his brother, who from 1858 acted as regent till his accession, as William I, on Frederick William's death. >> Frederick William III; William I (of Germany); RR1051

Fredriksson, Gert (1919–) Swedish canoeist. During 1948–60 he won eight Olympic medals, including six golds, and 13 world titles, all at either kayak singles or pairs. His winning margin of 6·7 sec in the 1948 Olympic singles final was the biggest for any kayak race other than the 10 000 m. When he won his last Olympic gold in 1960, he was aged 40 years 292 days – the oldest canoeing gold medallist.

Freedman, Barnet (1901–58) Painter and lithographer, born in London, England, UK. He trained at the Royal College of Art. A pioneer in the revival of colour lithography, he designed posters, book illustrations, and book covers. He was visiting instructor at the Royal College of Art from 1928, and at the Ruskin School, Oxford. He worked for London Transport, Shell-Mex, BP Ltd, the BBC, and the General Post Office. In 1935 his design was selected for the George V jubilee stamp, and in 1940 he was appointed official war artist to the Admiralty.

Freeman, Sir Ralph (1880–1950) Civil engineer, born in London, England, UK. He studied at the City and Guilds of London Institute, and joined (1901) the firm of consulting engineers which in 1938 became Freeman, Fox & Partners, specializing in the design of steel bridges. His first notable design was for Sydney Harbour Bridge, a construction of 500 m/1670 ft span (1932). He was later involved with his partner Sir Gilbert Roberts in the design of the long-span suspension bridges over the estuaries of the Forth, Severn, and Humber rivers, though he did not live to see any of them built. >> Roberts, Gilbert

Freer, Charles Lang (1856–1919) Art collector and businessman, born in Kingston, NY. He worked for various railroads, then moved to Detroit in 1879, and was a founder of the American Car & Foundry Co (1899). He became a collector of oriental art, pottery, and paintings, most notably the work of James Whistler. He donated funds and his collection to the Smithsonian Institution for the construction of the Freer Gallery (1906). >> Whistler, James

Frege, (Friedrich Ludwig) Gottlob [frayguh] (1848–1925) Mathematician and logician, born in Wismar, Germany. He studied at Jena and Göttingen, and became professor of mathematics at Jena (1896). His *Begriffsschrift* (1879, Concept-script) outlined the first complete system of symbolic logic. The technical difficulties involved gave rise to his distinctive philosophical doctrines, forcefully set out in his *Grundlagen der Arithmetik* (1884, The Foundations of Arithmetic). His *Grundgesetze der Arithmetik* (1893–1903, Basic Laws of Arithmetic) contained a postscript acknowledging that Russell had spotted a contradiction in his thinking. Depressed by the poor reception of his ideas, he wrote little after 1903. >> Russell, Bertrand

Frei (Montalva), Eduardo [fray] (1911–82) Chilean statesman and president (1964–70), born in Santiago. He studied in Chile, and became one of the leaders of the Social-Christian Falange Party in the late 1930s, and of the new Christian Democratic Party after 1957. His presidency saw an ambitious programme of social reform. >> RR1039

Freleng, Fritz (Isadore) (1906–95) Animated cartoon director and producer, born in Kansas City, KS. After winning a cartoon contest, he joined Disney, then moved to Hollywood to animate *Oswald the Rabbit*. He made a trial sound cartoon, *Bosko the Talk-Ink Kid* (1929), then made *Looney Tunes*, starting with *Sinkin' in the Bathtub* (1930). He is best known for Sylvester the lisping cat in *Tweety Pie* (1946), for which he won his first Oscar, and the Mexican mouse, *Speedy Gonzalez* (1955).

Frelinghuysen, Theodorus Jacobus [freelinghiyzn] (1691–1748) Protestant clergyman, born in Lingen, Germany. He received a classical education and was ordained in the Dutch Reformed Church in 1717. Sent to America in 1719 as a missionary, he established several churches in the Raritan Valley of New Jersey, and is considered a leading force in the establishment of the Dutch Reformed faith in the New World. All five of his sons became ministers.

Frémont, John C(harles) [freemont] (1813–90) Explorer, mapmaker, and politician, born in Savannah, GA. He began surveying in 1838, and over the next few years mapped much of the territory between the Mississippi and the West coast. Settling in California in 1848, he became the first senator from there in 1850. In 1856 he was the Republican and anti-slavery candidate for the presidency, but was defeated by James Buchanan; nominated again in 1864, he withdrew in favour of Abraham Lincoln. Appointed an officer in the Union army in 1861, he resigned in 1862. He was then involved in railway development in the West, and became Governor of Arizona (1878–82). >> Buchanan, James; Lincoln, Abraham

French, Daniel (Chester) (1850–1931) Sculptor, born in Exeter, NH. He studied sculpture in New York City, and in 1873–4 produced 'The Minute Man' for the town of Concorde, MA. Following a period in Florence, he studied at the Ecole des Beaux Arts in Paris (1886–8). He produced an 18 m/60 ft high 'Statue of The Republic' for the 1893 Chicago World's Fair, and the seated figure of Abraham Lincoln for the Washington Lincoln Memorial (1918–22).

French, Dawn (1957–) Comedy writer and actress, born in Holyhead, Anglesey, NW Wales, UK. After leaving school she won a debating scholarship to study in New York City, then attended the Central School of Speech and Drama in London, where she met Jennifer Saunders. They formed a comedy partnership, moving from clubs to theatre and into television, becoming widely known with *Girls On Top* (1985–6) and *French and Saunders* (from 1987). The series *Murder Most Horrid* was created especially for her, and she has also starred in BBC's *The Vicar of Dibley* . She is married to comedy performer Lenny Henry. >> Henry, Lenny; Saunders, Jennifer

French, John (Denton Pinkstone), Earl of Ypres (1852–1925) British field marshal (1913), born in Ripple, Kent, SE England, UK. He joined the navy (1866), then the army (1874), and distinguished himself in the Sudan (1884–5) and South Africa (1899–1901). Chief of the Imperial General Staff (1911–14), he held supreme command of the British Expeditionary Force in France (1914–15), but was criticized for indecision, and resigned. He was made a viscount (1915) and earl (1921), and was Lord-Lieutenant of Ireland (1918–21). >> Despard, Charlotte

French, Marilyn (1929–) Novelist, born in New York City. She studied at Hofstra College, then lectured there and at Harvard. She is best known for her first novel, *The Woman's Room* (1977), hailed as a pioneering feminist text for its angry study of the continuing subjection of women. Later books include *Her Mother's Daughter* (1992) and *Our Father* (1994).

Freneau, Philip (Morin) [frenoh] (1752–1832) Sailor and poet, born in New York City. He studied at the College of New Jersey (later Princeton University), commanded a privateer in the American War of Independence, was captured by the British, and wrote *The British Prison Ship* (1781). He wrote many patriotic poems, publishing them in the *National Gazette* (1791–3), which he founded and edited. He is considered the leading US poet of the 18th-c.

Freni, Mirella [**fre**nee] (1936–) Soprano, born in Modena, Italy. She made her debut as Micaëla in *Carmen* at Modena in 1955, and went on to sing with the Netherlands Opera (1959–60), and at Glyndebourne (1960). She has since performed at many other venues, including Milan, Vienna, and Salzburg.

Frescobaldi, Girolamo [freskoh**bal**dee] (1583–1643) Composer, born in Rome. He studied the organ at Ferrara Cathedral, became organist at S Maria in Trastevere, Rome, and travelled much in the Low Countries. From 1608 until his death he was organist at St Peter's in Rome. He composed chiefly organ works and madrigals.

Fresnel, Augustin Jean [fray**nel**] (1788–1827) Physicist, born in Broglie, France. He studied engineering at the Ecole des Ponts et Chaussées. He began his investigations of interference fringes in light in 1814, and did much to substantiate the wave theory of light. He also developed a more effective lighthouse lens, adapting an idea originated by Buffon (1748). The *Fresnel lens* is still used in lighthouses, and in many other fields. >> Buffon

Freud, Anna [froyd] (1895–1982) Psychoanalyst, born in Vienna, the daughter of Sigmund Freud. She chaired the Vienna Psychoanalytic Society, and emigrated with her father to London in 1938, where she organized (1940–5) a residential war nursery for homeless children. She was a founder of child psychoanalysis. >> Freud, Sigmund; Klein, Melanie

Freud, Sir Clement (Raphael) [froyd] (1924–) British politician, writer, broadcaster, and caterer. His training in London as a chef was interrupted by World War 2, and he was a liaison officer at the Nuremberg war crimes trials (1946) before completing his training in Cannes. He was the proprietor of the Royal Court Theatre Club (1952–62) and a columnist for various national newspapers before becoming a Liberal MP (1972–87). He is a long-serving member of the BBC Radio 4 *Just a Minute* team (from 1968), and has published a number of books about food, including *The Gourmet's Tour of Great Britain and Ireland* (1989). He was knighted in 1987.

Freud, Lucian [froyd] (1922–) Painter, born in Berlin, the grandson of Sigmund Freud. He moved to Britain in 1933, and studied at the Central School of Arts and Crafts in London (1938–9) and the East Anglian School of Painting and Drawing, Dedham. In his early years he was one of the neo-Romantic group of English painters along with Minton, Craxton, Sutherland, and Piper, but since the 1950s he has developed a realistic style. >> Freud, Sigmund; Minton, John; Piper, John; Sutherland, Graham

Freud, Sigmund see panel on p. 348

Freyberg, Bernard Freyberg, Baron (1889–1963) New Zealand soldier, born in London, England, UK. He travelled to New Zealand with his parents in 1891, and was educated at Wellington College there. In World War 1 he served with the Royal Naval Division in Gallipoli and France, winning the VC at Beaumont Hamel. In World War 2 he commanded New Zealand forces in the Middle East, Commonwealth forces in ill-fated operations (1941) in Greece, Crete, and later the Sahara Desert, and commanded the New Zealand Corps in Italy (1944–5). He was Governor-General of New Zealand (1946–52), created a baron in 1951, and made Lieutenant-Governor of Windsor Castle (1956–63).

Freyssinet, Marie Eugène Léon [frayseenay] (1879–1962) Civil engineer, born in Objat, France. He studied at the Ecole Polytechnique and the Ecole des Ponts et Chaussées in Paris. He developed pre-stressed concrete, and from 1930 was one of the leading exponents of this virtually new structural material, employing it to full advantage in bridges, foundations, a dam in Algeria, the airport runway at Orly, and a water tower at Orléans.

Frey-Wyssling, Albert Friedrich [fray **vis**ling] (1900–) Botanist, born in Küsnacht, Switzerland. He studied in Zürich, Jena, and Paris, and became professor of botany in Zürich in 1938. He did much to establish submicroscopic studies of plant cells by the use of polarization microscopy, in the period before c.1940. Thereafter, X-ray diffraction and electron microscopy techniques became available to confirm and extend his results by these more direct methods. He is considered the founder of molecular biology.

Frick, Ford (Christopher) (1894–1978) Baseball executive, born in Wawaka, IN. A New York sports writer for many years (1922–34), he also made radio sports broadcasts (1930–4). He served as National League president (1934–51) and commissioner (1951–65), and was elected to the Baseball Hall of Fame in 1969.

Frick, Henry (Clay) (1849–1919) Industrialist, born in West Overton, PA. He had little education, but grasped at post-Civil-War expansion by forming a company to supply the Pittsburgh steel mills with coke, and was a millionaire at 30. He became chairman of the Carnegie Steel Co in 1889, reorganizing it to become the largest steel manufacturer in the world. A hard and ruthless employer, he was shot and stabbed during the steel strike at Homestead, PA, in 1892, but recovered. He broke with Carnegie in 1900, and became director of United States Steel (1901). He built up the distinguished Frick Collection of fine art, which he bequeathed to New York City, and also endowed hospitals, schools, and a large park in Pittsburgh.

Frick, Wilhelm (1877–1946) Nazi politician, born in Alsenz, Germany. He participated in Hitler's Munich putsch (1923), led the Nazi faction in the Reichstag from 1924, and as minister of the interior from 1933 banned trade unionism and freedom of the press, and encouraged anti-Semitism. Ousted by Himmler in 1943, he became 'Protector' of Bohemia and Moravia. He was found guilty of war crimes at Nuremberg and executed. >> Himmler; Hitler

Fricker, Peter (Racine) (1920–90) Composer, born in London, England, UK. He studied at the Royal College of Music, and became musical director of Morley College, London (1952–64), professor of music at the University of California, Santa Barbara (1964–5), then resident composer there. Influenced by Bartók and Schoenberg, he wrote several symphonies, the oratorio *The Vision of Judgement* (1957–8), and other chamber, choral, and keyboard works. >> Bartók; Schoenberg

Fried, Alfred >> Asser, Tobias

Friedan, Betty (Naomi) [free**dan**], *née* **Goldstein** (1921–) Feminist leader and writer, born in Peoria, IL. She studied at Smith College, and became known in 1963 with the publication of her book *The Feminine Mystique*. She was the founder and first president of the National Association for Women in 1966. In *The Second Stage* (1981), she emphasized the importance of both the new and traditional female roles.

Friedel, Charles [**free**del] (1832–99) Chemist, born in Strasbourg, France. A student of Pasteur, he became curator at the Ecole des Mines, then professor of mineralogy there (1876–84), and professor of organic chemistry at the Sorbonne. His early work was on the production of artificial minerals (diamonds). Later he moved to organic chemistry, where he collaborated with the US chemist **James Mason Crafts** (1839–1917) developing the *Friedel–Crafts reaction* for the synthesis of benzene homologues. >> Pasteur

SIGMUND FREUD (1856–1939)

Freud was born to a Jewish family in Freiberg, Moravia (now Príbor, Czech Republic), the son of Jakob Freud, a wool merchant, and his wife Amalie Nathansohn. Intensely intellectual as a child, at the age of 17 he began to study medicine at the University of Vienna. After graduating, in 1882, he joined the staff of the Vienna General Hospital, specializing in neurology, and collaborating with the Austrian neurologist Josef Breuer in the treatment of hysteria by the recall of painful experiences under hypnosis. He then studied in Paris (1883–5) under Jean Martin Charcot, and it was there that he changed from neurology to psychopathology, the branch of psychology that deals with the abnormal workings of the mind. Returning to Vienna, in 1886 he married Martha Bernys, to whom he had been engaged, but whom he had not seen for two years. They had six children, and she remained a constant support throughout his often turbulent and controversial career.

In private practice Freud began to develop the technique of conversational 'free association', finding hypnosis inadequate. He refined psychoanalysis as a method of treatment, interpreting the data of childhood and dream recollection, and allowing the patient to express thoughts in a state of relaxed consciousness. In 1893 he published a paper with Breuer which was expanded in 1895 to Studien über Hysterie (Studies in Hysteria), marking the beginnings of psychoanalysis. Recalling significant events from his own childhood (triggered by the death of his father in 1896) and from those of his patients, he became convinced, despite his own puritan sensibilities, of the certainty of infantile sexuality. This gave rise to the concept of the 'Oedipus complex', the name he gave to the erotic feelings of a son for his mother, and its associated sense of competition with the father. Such a view isolated Freud from Breuer and from the medical profession in general, who looked on his theory with incredulity and hostility.

One of the means he used to analyse himself was to decode his dreams in terms of their organization and meaning or purpose. His major work, Die Traumdeutung (1900, The Interpretation of Dreams), argued that dreams are disguised wish-fulfilment – manifestations of repressed sexual desires and energy. In 1902 he was appointed to a chair of neuropathology in Vienna, despite widespread academic anti-Semitism, and began to gather disciples. He started a weekly seminar (the original 'Psychological Wednesday Society') in his home with such kindred minds as Alfred Adler, and produced further crucial works: Zur Psychopathologie des Alltagslebens (1904, The Psychopathology of Everyday Life), and Drei Abhandlungen zur Sexualtheorie (1905, Three Essays on the Theory of Sexuality), which met with intense and uncomprehending opposition.

In 1908 the group that attended his weekly seminars called themselves the Vienna Psychoanalytical Society, and in 1910 the International Psychoanalytical Association, with Carl Jung as the first president. Both Adler and Jung broke with Freud to develop their own theories in 1911 and 1913 respectively.

Undeterred, Freud produced Totem und Tabu (1913, Totem and Taboo), Jenseits des Lustprinzips (1920, Beyond the Pleasure Principle), and Das Ich und das Es (1923, The Ego and the Id), elaborating his theories of the division of the unconscious mind into the 'id', the 'ego', and the 'super-ego'. In 1927 he published a controversial view of religion, Die Zukunft einer Illusion (The Future of an Illusion), and in 1930 was awarded the prestigious Goethe Prize. It was not until then that his work ceased to arouse active opposition from public bodies.

In collaboration with Albert Einstein, he published Warum Krieg? (Why War?) in 1933. At the same time Hitler effectively banned psychoanalysis, and after Austria had been overrun, Freud and his family were extricated from the hands of the Gestapo and allowed to emigrate. He settled in Hampstead, London, where he died a year later as a result of cancer of the jaw and cheek, for which he had undergone more than 30 operations since its diagnosis in 1923. His daughter, Anna, went on to become the founder of child psychoanalysis.

Although many psychiatrists and psychologists now disagree with some of Freud's ideas, his insight has had strong and useful influences in many fields: his research into unconscious drives has had a significant impact on criminology, sociology, and anthropology. His work changed the way many people think about personality and motivation, and caused a re-evaluation of the importance which attaches to early family relationships and their effect on the developing personality. But his most important influence was to inspire modern psychiatry by his examination of mental illness. However, although he inspired fields of scientific study, often his methods were not very scientific. In fact, he described himself to his friend Wilhelm Fleiss not as a scientist but as an 'adventurer', and his methods were often fearlessly unscientific, partly because of the new and controversial nature of his study. The main weakness of Freudian analysis is that, in order to explore the abnormal, he had to establish what 'normal' was. To do this he looked to himself, and extrapolated from his own experiences into a general theory. This established male sexuality as the norm, and made for a phallocentric theory in which woman could only be accomodated by his theory of penis envy.

However, despite the obvious problems with Freud's work, his great success was to put sexuality on the scientific agenda, liberating its study from the social taboos that had bedevilled his work and made him such a controversial figure. His use in analysis of mythologies, literature, and art also established the role of culture in the development of personality, and vice versa. This partially accounted for the broad base of interest his work inspired in the artists (especially the Surrealists) and writers who followed him. His influence extended so broadly into modern life that, in 1945, the Oscar-winning film Spellbound presented as popular entertainment a plot which was a psychological thriller solved through psychoanalytic detective work and dream analysis against sets designed by the great Surrealist, Salvador Dali.

>> Adler; Charcot, Jean Martin; Dali; Einstein; Freud, Anna; Jung

Friedman, Herbert [freedman] (1916–) Astrophysicist, born in New York City. He studied at Brooklyn College and Johns Hopkins University, and spent his career at the US Naval Research Laboratory in Washington. He did pioneering work in the use of rockets in astronomy, using them from the 1940s onwards to carry detectors to study the Sun's X-rays. Following Rossi's discovery in 1962 of the first non-solar X-ray source, Friedman showed in 1964 that one such source coincided with the Crab nebula, a remnant of a supernova. >> Rossi, Bruno

Friedman, Milton [freedman] (1912–) Economist, born in New York City. He studied at Chicago and New York universities, and after eight years at the National Bureau of Economic Research (1937–45) became professor of economics at Chicago (1946–83). A leading monetarist, his work includes the permanent income theory of consumption, and the role of money in determining events, particularly the US Great Depression. His ideas have been influential with a number of right-wing governments. He was awarded the Nobel Prize for Economics in 1976.

Friedrich, Carl J(oachim) [freedrikh] (1901–84) Political scientist, born in Leipzig, Germany. Educated in Germany, he emigrated to the USA in 1922 and began a long teaching career at Harvard (1926–71). He also served as a government adviser to Germany (1946–9), and to Puerto Rico in the 1950s. A prolific writer on comparative political thought, his analyses of totalitarianism and communism were particularly controversial. His book, *An Introduction to Political Theory* (1967), concluded that people favour a minimum rather than a maximum of freedoms.

Friedrich, Caspar David [freedrikh] (1774–1840) Painter, born in Greifswald, Germany. He studied at the Academy of Copenhagen (1794–8), then settled in Dresden. His work portrays landscapes as vast and desolate expanses in which people, often seen as solitary figures, are depicted as melancholy spectators of Nature's power. He taught at the Dresden Academy from 1816, and became a professor in 1824.

Friel, Brian [freel] (1929–) Playwright, born in Killyclogher, Co Tyrone, Ireland. He was a teacher in Derry, writing short stories and radio plays, before turning to the live theatre with *This Doubtful Paradise* (staged in Belfast in 1959). He gained recognition with *Philadelphia, Here I Come!* (1964), the first of numerous plays – including *The Freedom of the City* (1974), *Faith Healer* (1979), *Translations* (1980), *Dancing at Lughnasa* (1990), *Wonderful Tennessee* (1993), and *Molly Sweeney* (1995) – which have made him internationally the best known of contemporary playwrights in Ireland.

Friends >> **Aniston, Jennifer; Cox, Courtenay; Kudrow, Lisa; LeBlanc, Matt; Perry, Matthew; Schwimmer, David**

Fries, Elias Magnus [frees] (1794–1878) Botanist, born in Femsjö, Sweden. He studied at the University of Lund, then became professor at Uppsala, and keeper of the botanic garden there. He wrote on fungi, lichens, and the flora of Scandinavia, and introduced a classificatory system for fungi which, apart from a few minor exceptions, is still valid. The genus *Freesia* is named after him.

Friese-Greene, William [freez green], originally **William Edward Green** (1855–1921) Photographer and inventor, born in Bristol, SW England, UK. In the 1880s he designed a camera to expose a sequence of photographs for projection by lantern slides as a moving image, and is thus claimed by some as the English inventor of cinematography; but he did not in fact propose perforated strips of film for either photography or projection. His first successful picture, using celluloid film, was shown in public in 1890.

Friesz, (Emile) Othon [frees] (1879–1949) Painter, born in Le Havre, France. He attended the Ecole des Beaux Arts, where his teachers included Dufy. At first an enthusiastic Impressionist, he was later influenced by Cézanne. >> Cézanne; Dufy

Frietschie or **Fritchie, Barbara** [fritchee], *née* **Haver** (1766–1862) US heroine, born in Lancaster, PA. She married **John Casper Frietschie**, a glove-maker, in 1806. According to legend, on 6 September 1862, at the age of 95, she boldly displayed the Union flag as Confederate soldiers passed by her home in Frederick, MD. In tribute to her bravery, she was not harmed. When an account of the incident reached John Greenleaf Whittier, he immortalized it in his poem with the lines: 'Shoot, if you must, this old gray head but spare your country's flag', she said'. A replica of her house was built in 1926. >> Whittier

Friml, (Charles) Rudolf [friml] (1879–1972) Composer, born in Prague. He studied at the Prague Conservatory, and settled in the USA in 1906, where he made his name as a composer of light operas, including *Rose Marie* (1924) and *The Vagabond King* (1925). He became a US citizen in 1925.

Frisch, Karl von (1886–1982) Ethologist, born in Vienna. He studied at Munich and Trieste, then taught zoology at several universities, much of his career being spent at Munich, where he founded the Zoological Institute (1932). He was a key figure in developing ethology using field observation of animals combined with ingenious experiments. His 40-year study of the honey bee showed that forager bees communicate information (on the location of food sources) in part by use of coded dances. In 1973 he shared the Nobel Prize for Physiology or Medicine. >> RR1124

Frisch, Max (Rudolf) (1911–91) Playwright and novelist, born in Zürich, Switzerland. He became a newspaper correspondent and a student of architecture, while developing his literary career. His novels include *Stiller* (1954), a satire on the Swiss way of life, *Homo Faber* (1957), and *Bluebeard* (1983). His plays, modern morality pieces, include *Nun singen sie wieder* (1945, Now They Sing Again), *Andorra* (1962), and *Triptych* (1981).

Frisch, Otto Robert (1904–79) Physicist, born in Vienna. He studied at Vienna, and in 1945 became head of the nuclear physics division at Harwell. He and Meitner (his aunt) first described 'nuclear fission' in 1939 to explain Hahn's results with uranium and neutrons. He moved to Birmingham in 1939, and worked with Peierls on uranium fission and associated neutron emission, then became involved in atomic research at Los Alamos, USA. In 1947 he became professor of natural philosophy at Cambridge, UK, and directed the nuclear physics department of the Cavendish Laboratory. >> Hahn, Otto; Meitner; Peierls

Frisch, Ragnar (Anton Kittil) (1895–1973) Economist, born in Oslo, Norway. A pioneer of econometrics, he created national economic planning decision models, and advised developing countries. In 1969 he shared the first Nobel Prize for Economics. >> RR1125

Frith, Francis (1822–98) Topographical photographer, born in Chesterfield, Derbyshire, C England, UK. He travelled extensively in Egypt and the Near East (1856–9), using the large 40 x 50 cm cameras and complicated wet-plate process of the period to produce the first photographic traveller's records to be seen in Britain. From 1864 he toured throughout Britain and established a nationwide service of photographs of local scenes as prints and postcards, a business which by the end of his life had extended into Europe and survived commercially until 1971.

Frith, William Powell (1819–1909) Painter, born in Aldfield, North Yorkshire, N England, UK. He is best known for his huge canvases of Victorian scenes, such as *Ramsgate Sands* (1854, bought by Queen Victoria for Buckingham Palace), *Derby Day* (1858, Tate, London) and *The Railway Station* (1862, Holloway College, London).

Fritsch, Elizabeth (1940–) Potter, born in Shropshire, WC England, UK. She studied at the Royal Academy of Music prior to attending the Royal College of Art (1968–71). Her work, sometimes inspired by music, uses coiling spires and geometric patterns in coloured slips with a matt texture akin to ivory frescoes. She established a workshop in London in 1985.

Frobenius, Ferdinand Georg [froh**been**ius] (1849–1917) Mathematician, born in Berlin. He studied at Göttingen and Berlin, where he took his doctorate in 1870, then taught at Zürich (1875–92), before returning to Berlin as professor. He founded the theory of group representations, which was later to become essential in quantum mechanics, and a major theme of 20th-c mathematics.

Froberger, Johann Jakob [**froh**berger] (1616–67) Composer, born in Stuttgart, Germany. A pupil of Frescobaldi, he was court organist at Vienna (1637–57), and made concert tours to Italy, Paris, London, and Brussels. Of his many compositions, the best remembered are his suites for harpsichord. >> Frescobaldi

Frobisher, Sir Martin [**froh**bisher] (c. 1535–94) Navigator, born in Altofts, West Yorkshire, N England, UK. He made several attempts to find the Northwest Passage to Cathay (1576–8), reaching Labrador and Hudson Bay. *Frobisher Bay* is named after him. In 1585 he commanded a vessel in Drake's expedition to the West Indies, and in 1588 he was knighted for his services against the Armada. He was mortally wounded at the siege of Crozon, near Brest. >> Drake

Fröding, Gustaf [**froe**ding] (1860–1911) Poet, born near Karlstad, Sweden. He studied at Uppsala, became a schoolmaster and journalist, and suffered several periods of mental illness. Perhaps the greatest Swedish lyric poet, he is often compared with Burns. His use of dialect and folksong rhythm in the portrayal of local characters can be seen in his first collection, *Guitarr och Dragharmonika* (1891, Guitar and Concertina). >> Burns

Froebel, Friedrich (Wilhelm August) [**froe**bl] (1782–1852) Educationist, born in Oberweissbach, Germany. He studied at Jena, Göttingen, and Berlin, and in 1805 began teaching at Franfurt. In 1816 he put into practice his educational system, whose aim, to help the child's mind grow naturally and spontaneously, he expounded in *Die Menschenerziehung* (1826, The Education of Man). In 1836 he opened his first kindergarten school at Blankenburg, and spent the rest of his life organizing other such schools, as well as providing educational materials (eg geometrical shapes) for young children, to encourage learning through play.

Fröhlich, Alfred >> **Babinski, Joseph**

Froissart, Jean [frwasah(r)] (c. 1333–c. 1404) Historian and poet, born in Valenciennes, France. He served Philippa of Hainault, the wife of Edward III of England (1361–9), and also travelled widely in Scotland, France, and Italy. Returning to Hainault, he began to compile his *Chronicles*, wrote poems for noble patrons, and became private chaplain to Guy of Châtillon. His *Chronicles*, covering European history from 1325 to 1400, deal in particular with the Hundred Years' War, and were heavily influenced by his devotion to chivalric principles. >> Philippa of Hainault

Froment, Nicolas [fromã] (fl.1450–90) Painter, born in Uzes, France. He left some fine examples of the late Gothic style, containing features surprisingly Flemish in appearance. He was court painter to King René of Anjou, whose portrait is incorporated in his masterpiece, a triptych in the cathedral of Aix-en-Provence, having as its centrepiece Moses and the burning bush.

Fromm, Erich (1900–80) Psychoanalyst and social philosopher, born in Frankfurt, Germany. He studied at the universities of Frankfurt, Heidelberg, Munich, and the Berlin Institute of Psychoanalysis, and held various university appointments before becoming professor of psychiatry at New York University in 1962. A neo-Freudian, he is known for his investigations into motivation. His works include *Escape from Freedom* (1941) and *The Sane Society* (1955).

Frontenac, Louis de Buade, comte de (Count of) [frôtenak] (1620–98) French-Canadian statesman, born in St Germain-en-Laye, France. He served in the army, and in 1672 was appointed governor of the French possessions in North America. He was recalled for misgovernment in 1682, but was sent out again in 1689. He extended the boundaries of New France down the Mississippi, launched attacks on New England villages, repulsed the British siege of Quebec, and broke the power of the Iroquois.

Frost, Sir David (Paradine) (1939–) Broadcaster and businessman, born in Tenterden, Kent, SE England, UK. He studied at Cambridge, participated in the Footlights revues, and edited *Granta* before moving into television in 1961. He presented *That Was the Week That Was* (BBC, 1962–3), an innovative, satirical, and irreverant late-night revue show, and has since hosted many programmes in Britain and America, such as *The Frost Report* (1966–7), *The David Frost Show* (1969–72), *The Guinness Book of World Records* (from 1981), *The Spitting Image Movie Awards* (1987), and a range of *Frost Over …* programmes, dealing with America, Australia, and several other countries. He has interviewed world leaders in such programmes as *The Nixon Interviews* (1976–7) and *The Shah Speaks* (1980). A co-founder of London Weekend Television, in 1983 he was a co-founder, director, and presenter of Britain's TV–AM. His many international honours include the Golden Rose of Montreux (1967) and two Emmy Awards (1970, 1971). His publications include *How to Live Under Labour* (1964), *I Gave Them a Sword* (1978), and *The World's Shortest Books* (1987). He was knighted in 1993. >> Hamlyn

Frost, John (1784–1877) Chartist leader, born in Newport, SE Wales, UK. A prosperous tailor and draper, he became Mayor of Newport (1836–7). On 4 November 1839 he led a Chartist insurrection designed to seize control of Newport, which was repulsed by troops with heavy loss of Chartist lives. He was sentenced to death, but the sentence was commuted to transportation for life to Tasmania. In 1856, given an unconditional pardon, he returned to a triumphant welcome in Newport.

Frost, Robert (Lee) (1874–1963) Poet, born in San Francisco, CA. He studied at Harvard, and became a teacher, cobbler, and New Hampshire farmer before going to Britain (1912–15), where he published *A Boy's Will* (1913) and *North of Boston* (1914), which gave him an international reputation. Back in the USA, he taught at Amherst and Michigan universities. *New Hampshire* (1923) won the Pulitzer Prize, as did his first *Collected Poems* in 1930 and *A Further Range* (1936). A last collection, *In the Clearing*, appeared in 1962. At the time of his death, he was regarded as the unofficial laureate of the USA.

Frost, Terry, popular name of **Terence Frost** (1915–) Painter, born in Leamington Spa, Warwickshire, C England, UK. After World War 2 he attended evening classes at Birmingham Art College, then moved to St Ives, Cornwall. His first abstract paintings date from 1949. He held various teaching posts, and became professor of painting at Reading University (1977–81), then emeritus professor there.

Froude, James Anthony [frood] (1818–94) Writer and historian, born in Dartington, Devon, SW England, UK. He studied at Oxford, where he became part of the Oxford Movement. His early novels were controversial, notably *The Nemesis of Faith* (1848), and he was forced to resign his post. He then worked as an essayist and editor, and wrote his *History of England* (12 vols, 1856–69). He became Rector of St Andrews in 1869, and professor of modern history at Oxford in 1892. >> Froude, William

Froude, William [frood] (1810–79) Engineer and applied mathematician, born in Dartington, Devon, SW England, UK, the brother of James Anthony Froude. He studied at Oxford and worked as a railway engineer until 1846, then devoted himself to hydrodynamics and developed a method by which data derived from scale model ships could be applied to the full-size ship. His name is preserved in the *Froude dynamometer*, a device he designed for measuring the power output of large engines. >> Froude, James Anthony

Frumentius, St [fru**men**shius] (c. 300–c. 380) The apostle of Ethiopia, born in Phoenicia. He was captured by Ethiopians while on a voyage, became the king's secretary, and gradually secured the introduction of Christianity. He was consecrated Bishop of Axum by Athanasius in Alexandria (c.346). According to the historian Rufinus (345–410), he was accorded the title 'Abuna' (Our Father), which is still used for the Patriarch of the Ethiopian Orthodox Church. Feast day 30 November and 18 December. >> Athanasius, St

Fry, Charles Burgess (1872–1956) Sportsman, born in Croydon, S Greater London, England, UK. An outstanding all-rounder, he gained his Blue at Oxford for athletics, cricket, and soccer, and later represented his country in all three. Best remembered as a cricketer, he played 26 Tests for England. With Don Bradman he holds the record of six consecutive centuries in first-class cricket. He acted as India's delegate to the League of Nations, after World War 1, and was at one point offered the throne of Albania, but declined. >> Bradman

Fry, Christopher, pseudonym of **Christopher Harris** (1907–) Playwright, born in Bristol, SW England, UK. Educated at Bedford, he was a teacher and actor before becoming director of Tunbridge Wells Repertory Players (1932–6) and of the Playhouse at Oxford (1940). After service in World War 2 he began a series of major plays in free verse, often with undertones of religion and mysticism, including *A Phoenix Too Frequent* (1946) and *The Lady's Not For Burning* (1949). His later works include *Curtmantle* (1962) and *A Yard of Sun* (1970). He has also produced highly successful translations of Anouilh and Giraudoux.

Fry, Elizabeth (1780–1845) Quaker prison reformer, born in Norwich, Norfolk, E England, UK. In 1810 she became a preacher in the Society of Friends. After seeing the terrible conditions for women in Newgate prison, she devoted her life to prison reform at home and abroad. She also founded hostels for the homeless, and charitable societies.

Fry, Joseph (1728–87) Quaker businessman and type-founder, born in Sutton Benger, Wiltshire, S England, UK. He settled in Bristol as a doctor, but went into a pottery enterprise. He founded the well-known chocolate business (later taken over by Cadburys), and from 1764 onwards became eminent as a typefounder.

Fry, Roger (Eliot) (1866–1934) Art critic, aesthetic philosopher, and painter, born in London, England, UK. He studied at Cambridge, and is mainly remembered for his support of the Postimpressionist movement in England. He propounded an extreme formal theory of aesthetics, seeing the aesthetic quality of a work of art solely in terms of its formal characteristics. He was director of the Museum of Art in New York City (1905–10). When he returned to London he organized a young artists' collective named the Omega Workshops (1913–19). He became professor of fine art at Cambridge in 1933. >> Bell, Vanessa; Grant, Duncan

Frye, (Herman) Northrop (1912–91) Literary critic and editor, born in Sherbrooke, Quebec, Canada. A professor of English at Victoria College, University of Toronto, from 1939, he achieved international recognition for his literary theories, expounded in his study of William Blake, *Fearful Symmetry* (1947), also seen in his grammar of mythic form, *Anatomy of Criticism* (1957), and his study of the Bible's symbolism, *The Great Code* (1982). One of the century's leading literary theorists, he tried to establish an objective and universally accepted terminology for literature studies.

Fuad I [foo**ahd**] (1868–1936) King of Egypt (1922–36), the son of Khedive Ismail Pasha, born in Cairo. He was Sultan of Egypt from 1917, and became king when the British protectorate was ended. In an attempt to control the ultra-nationalist Wafd Party, he suspended the constitution in 1931, but was forced to restore it in 1935. He was succeeded by his son Farouk I. >> Farouk I; Ismail Pasha; RR1046

Fuchs, Klaus (Emil Julius) [fookhs] (1912–88) Physicist and atom spy, born in Rüsselsheim, Germany. He studied at Kiel and Leipzig, and escaped from Nazi persecution to Britain in 1933. Interned on the outbreak of World War 2, he was released and naturalized in 1942. From 1943 he worked in the USA on the atom bomb, and in 1946 became head of the theoretical physics division at Harwell, UK. In 1950 he was sentenced to 14 years' imprisonment for disclosing nuclear secrets to the Russians. On his release in 1959 he worked at East Germany's nuclear research centre until his retirement in 1979. >> Shawcross; Rosenberg, Julius

Fuchs, Leonhard [fookhs] (1501–66) Physician and botanist, born in Wemding, Germany. He was professor of medicine at Tübingen. Interested in the medicinal properties of plants, he wrote *Historia stirpium* (1542), the first organized and illustrated account of plants intended as a guide for plant collection. The genus *Fuchsia* was named after him.

Fuchs, Sir Vivian Ernest [fookhs] (1908–) Antarctic explorer and geologist, born in the Isle of Wight, S England, UK. He studied at Brighton College and Cambridge. After four geological expeditions in East Africa (1929–38), he served in West Africa and Germany during World War 2, then became director of the Falkland Islands Dependencies Survey (1947–50) and later of the British Antarctic Survey (1958–73). He is best known as the leader of the Commonwealth Trans-Antarctic Expedition (1955–8) which completed the first land crossing of Antarctica, taking 99 days for the journey of 2000 mi. He was knighted in 1958.

Fuentes, Carlos [fwen**tez**] (1928–) Novelist and playwright, born in Mexico City. He studied at the University of Mexico and the Institut des Hautes Etudes Internationales in Geneva. He became cultural attaché to the Mexican Embassy in Geneva (1950–2), press secretary to the UN Information Centre, Mexico City, and served as the Mexican ambassador to France (1975–7). His first collection of short-stories was *Los dias enmascarados* (1954, The Masked Days), and his novel *La muerte de Artemio Cruz* (1962, The Death of Artemio Cruz) established him as a major international writer. Other titles include *Terra nostra* (1975), *The Hydra Head* (1979), and selected essays, *Myself with Others* (1988). A further collection of short-stories, *La frontera de cristal*, appeared in 1995. He became professor of Latin American Studies at Harvard in 1987.

Fugard, Athol (Harold Lanigan) [foo**gah**(r)d] (1932–) Playwright, theatre director, and actor, born in Middleburg, Cape Province, South Africa. He studied at Port Elizabeth Technical College and Cape Town University, became director of the Serpent Players in Port Elizabeth (1965), and co-founded the Space Experimental Theatre, Cape Town (1972). His plays, set in contemporary South Africa, met with official opposition, notably *Blood Knot* (1960) and *Boesman and Lena* (1969). Later works include *Road to Mecca*

(1985), *A Place with the Pigs* (1988), *My Children, My Africa!* (1989), and *Playland* (1992). He has also written several film scripts, and a novel *Tsotsi* (1980).

Fukui, Kenichi [fookwee] (1918–) Chemist, born in Nara, Japan. He studied at Kyoto University, becoming professor of physical chemistry there (1951–82), and director of the Institute for Fundamental Chemistry in 1988. He worked on the theory of chemical reactions, and developed the frontier orbital method for predicting the path of pericyclic organic reactions. He shared the Nobel Prize for Chemistry in 1981. >> RR1123

Fulbright, J(ames) William (1905–95) Politician, lawyer, and writer, born in Sumner, MO. He studied at Arkansas, Oxford, and George Washington universities, then taught law in Washington and Arkansas. He entered the US House of Representatives as a Democrat in 1943, and the US Senate in 1945. As chairman of the US Senate Committee on Foreign Relations, he became a major critic of the Vietnam War. He lost his Senate seat in 1974. He was also known for introducing the international exchange programme for scholars (*Fulbright scholarships*).

Fuller, (Richard) Buckminster (1895–1983) Inventor, designer, poet, and philosopher, born in Milton, MA. He studied at Harvard, then served in the US Navy (1917–19). He developed the Dymaxion ('dynamic and maximum efficiency') House in 1927, and the Dymaxion streamlined, omnidirectional car in 1932. He also developed the geodesic dome. An enthusiastic educationist, he held a chair at Southern Illinois University (1959–75), and in 1962 became professor of poetry at Harvard. His many books include *Nine Chains to the Moon* (1938) and *Critical Path* (1981).

Fuller, J(ohn) F(rederick) C(harles) (1878–1966) British general and military thinker, born in Chichester, West Sussex, S England, UK. He served in South Africa, and in World War 1 as a staff officer with the Tank Corps. He planned the breakthrough tank battle of Cambrai in 1917, and proposed the unfulfilled 'Plan 1919', advocating an all-mechanized army. His ideas were discounted, and he retired in 1933 to continue his prophetic if controversial military writings.

Fuller, Loie, popular name of **Marie Louise Fuller** (1862–1928) Dancer, choreographer, and producer, born in Fullersburg, IL. She began her career in vaudeville and as a circus artist (1865–91). In 1891 her exotic solo skirt-dance, using multi-directional coloured lights on the yards of swirling silk she wore, created a sensation, especially in Europe. She founded a school in 1908, and was a model for Toulouse-Lautrec, Auguste Rodin, and many other prominent artists.

Fuller, (Sarah) Margaret (1810–50) Writer, feminist, and revolutionary, born in Cambridgeport, MA. She entered the Transcendentalist circle that centred on Emerson, and despite a lack of higher education became known as one of its brightest stars. Her *Woman in the Nineteenth Century* (1845) is the earliest major piece of US feminist writing. She died in a shipwreck after taking part in the abortive Italian revolution of 1848. >> Emerson

Fuller, Roy (Broadbent) (1912–91) Poet and novelist, born in Oldham, Lancashire, NW England, UK. He trained as a solicitor, and served in the Royal Navy during World War 2. His first collection, *Poems*, appeared in 1939, and his war-time experiences prompted *The Middle of a War* (1942) and *A Lost Season* (1944). His later poetic works include *Brutus's Orchard* (1957) and *Retreads* (1979). His novels include *Second Curtain* (1953) and *Image of a Society* (1956). He was professor of poetry at Oxford (1968–73). *New and Collected Poems, 1934–84* were published in 1985, and two volumes of memoirs in 1989 and 1991.

Fuller, Thomas (1608–61) Clergyman and antiquary, born in Aldwinkle St Peter's, Northamptonshire, C England, UK. He studied at Cambridge, was appointed preacher to the Chapel Royal at the Savoy, London (1641–3), and during the Civil War was chaplain to the royalist commander, Ralph Hopton (1598–1652). With the restoration of the monarchy (1660) he was appointed chaplain-extraordinary to Charles II. He published many works noted for their wittiness, anecdotes, epigrams, and puns, such as *The Holy State, The Profane State* (1642). His most famous work, *History of the Worthies of Britain*, was published by his son the year after his death.

Fulton, Robert (1765–1815) Engineer, born in Lancaster Co, PA. He became a painter of miniature portraits and landscapes, then went to London (1786) and studied mechanical engineering. His inventions include a machine for spinning flax, a dredging machine, and the torpedo, but he is best known for his commercially successful development of the paddle-wheel steamboat which he first demonstrated on the Hudson R in 1807. >> Fitch, John

Funk, Casimir (1884–1967) Biochemist, born in Warsaw, Poland. He studied in Berlin and Bern, and became head of the biochemical department at the Cancer Hospital Research Institute, London (1913–15). He emigrated to the USA in 1915, and later headed a research institute in Warsaw (1923–7) and Paris (1928–39). He was best known for his work on vitamins, which he identified and named *vitamines* in 1912.

Funk, Walther (1890–1960) Nazi politician, born in Trakehnen, Germany. He studied at Berlin and Leipzig, was one of Hitler's chief advisers, and succeeded Schacht as minister of economics and president of the Reichsbank. He played a leading part in planning the economic aspects of the attack on Russia, and in the exploitation of occupied territories. Captured in 1945, he was sentenced to life imprisonment as a war criminal, but was released in 1957 because of illness. >> Hitler; Schacht

Furetière, Antoine [fürtyair] (1619–88) Scholar and lexicographer, born in Paris. He took holy orders to obtain a living while pursuing a literary career. A writer of comic verse and fables, he compiled a massive *Dictionnaire universel*, only to be expelled from the Académie, which was preparing its own. Furetière's was eventually published in Rotterdam in 1690.

Furman, Bess (1894–1969) Journalist, born in Danbury, NB. As a Washington correspondent for the Associated Press in the 1930s she covered Eleanor Roosevelt, and became one of the best-known woman journalists of the day. She later reported from Washington for the *New York Times* (1943–61). >> Roosevelt, Eleanor

Furness, Christopher Furness, Baron (1852–1912) Shipowner, born in West Hartlepool, Co Durham, NE England, UK. He became a shipbroker in 1876 and soon afterwards established the Furness Line. He went into partnership with Edward Withy in 1885, which marked the beginning of a huge shipbuilding and engineering business. A Liberal MP, he was one of the first to start a co-partnership scheme among his employees. He was knighted in 1895, and created baron in 1910.

Furness, Frank (1839–1912) Architect, born in Philadelphia, PA. He trained with Richard Morris Hunt, then fought in the Union cavalry in the Civil War. Returning to Philadelphia, he practised first with John Fraser and George W Hewitt, and after 1881 with Allen Evans. He was an outstanding exponent of the picturesque eclectic style, which blended colours, textures, and ornamental details from foreign styles of every period. Among his nearly 400 public and institutional buildings are the Pennsylvania

Academy of the Fine Arts (1871–6) and the building regarded as his masterpiece, the Library (now the *Furness Building*), University of Pennsylvania (1888–91). He was reduced to obscurity in his later years, a victim of fashionable Neoclassicism, but his reputation revived in the 1960s, when post-Modernists found inspiration in the decorative richness of his style. >> Hunt, Richard; Morris

Furnivall, Frederick James [fernival] (1825–1910) Philologist, born in Egham, Surrey, SE England, UK. He studied at London and Cambridge universities, and won fame as an oarsman and racing-boat designer. He was called to the bar and, influenced by Maurice and Christian Socialism, helped to found the Working Men's College in London. He achieved fame as a philologist and editor of English texts, giving a great impulse to Early English scholarship. He founded the Early English Text Society, and edited some score of texts, including Chaucer, besides writing the introduction to the 'Leopold' Shakespeare. He also edited the Philological Society's dictionary (from 1861) that became the *Oxford English Dictionary*. >> Maurice, Frederick Denison

Furphy, Joseph, pseudonym **Tom Collins** (1843–1912) Novelist, born near Melbourne, Victoria, Australia. He worked as a farmer and a bullock-driver before moving to Shepparton, Victoria, in 1883, where he worked at the iron-foundry established by his elder brother. He contributed a series of articles to the *Bulletin* magazine under his pseudonym, and wrote a lengthy novel, *Such is Life*, which was revised, shortened, and published in 1903. His reputation rests on this one major work, which encapsulated his hard-working philosophy and marked a move away from literature's Romantic concept of Australia's pioneering days.

Furth, Harold P(aul) (1930–) Physicist, born in Vienna. He moved to the USA in 1941, where he carried out research in nuclear radiation at the University of California, Berkeley (1955–67), before moving to Princeton (1967–). A world leader in the fields of plasma physics and controlled thermonuclear fusion, he became widely known for his refutation of the claim that fusion can be achieved at room temperature in a glass of water.

Furtwängler, (Gustav Heinrich Ernst Martin) Wilhelm [foortvengler] (1886–1954) Conductor, born in Berlin. He studied in Munich, and in 1922 became conductor of the Gewandhaus concerts in Leipzig and of the Berlin Philharmonic. International tours established his reputation, though his highly subjective interpretations of the German masters aroused controversy. His ambivalent attitude to the Hitler regime cost him some popularity outside Germany, but after the War he quickly re-established himself.

Fuseli, Henry [fyoozelee], originally **Johann Heinrich Füssli** (1741–1825) Painter and art critic, born in Zürich, Switzerland. He went to England in 1763, where he worked as a translator, then studied painting in Italy (1770–8). His 200 paintings include 'The Nightmare' (1781, Detroit) and two series to illustrate Shakespeare's and Milton's works, by which he is chiefly known. He became professor of painting at the Royal Academy in 1799.

Fust, Johann (c. 1400–1466) Printer and goldsmith, born in Mainz, Germany. In 1450 and 1452 he made loans to the printer Gutenberg, to help complete the printing of his Bible. When the loans were not repaid he sued for the debt, receiving, in lieu of payment, Gutenberg's printing plant, with which he started his own business, taking Peter Schöffer, his son-in-law, as partner. They published the Gutenberg Bible in 1456. >> Gutenberg, Johannes; Schöffer

Fysh, Sir (Wilmot) Hudson (1895–1974) Civil aviation pioneer, born in Launceston, Tasmania, Australia. He served with the Australian Flying Corps in World War 1. He established the Queensland and Northern Territory Aerial Services Limited in 1920, now known as QANTAS. In 1931 he was involved in the pioneering Australia–England airmail flights, which led to the formation of Qantas Empire Airways as a joint venture with Imperial Airways of the UK. In 1947 Qantas was acquired by the Australian government. Fysh became managing director, was knighted in 1953, and retired as chairman in 1966. He was a notable aviation historian, and wrote a number of books on the early days of civil aviation.

Gabarek, Jan [gabarek] (1947–) Jazz musician, born in Mysen, Norway. He taught himself to play the saxophone, principally tenor and soprano, and in 1962, a year after taking up the instrument, he won a competition for amateur players. He played and recorded with the George Russell orchestra and quartet, and during the 1980s his collaborations with bassist Eberhard Weber and Brazilian percussionist Nana Vasconcelos were among several highly acclaimed performances.

Gabelentz, Hans Conon von der [gabelents] (1807–74) Linguist, born in Altenburg, Germany. He knew 80 languages, and spoke 30 of them fluently. He is remembered for his great work on the Melanesian languages (1860–73).

Gabelsberger, Franz Xaver [gahbelsberger] (1789–1848) Bureaucrat and inventor, born in Munich, Germany. He devised the chief German system of shorthand, having in 1809 entered the Bavarian civil service.

Gabin, Jean [gabĩ], originally **Jean-Alexis Moncorgé** (1904–76) Actor, born in Paris. He started his stage career as a music hall singer and dancer, and played light juvenile leads in films from 1930, but a series of dramatic roles brought him greater depth and international recognition, especially in *Pépé le moko* (1936), *Quai des brumes* (1938, trans Port of Shadows) and *Le Jour se lève* (1939, trans Daybreak). After World War 2 he continued to appear frequently in tough character roles until shortly before his death.

Gabirol, Ibn >> Avicebrón

Gable, Christopher (1940–) Dancer and choreographer, born in London, England, UK. He studied at the Royal Ballet School, and was soon dancing solo roles as a principal and partner to Lynn Seymour. He retired as a dancer in 1967, having created roles in Kenneth MacMillan's *Images of Love* (1964) and Frederick Ashton's *The Two Pigeons* (1961). He became founder and artistic director of the Central School of Ballet in London in 1982 and artistic director of the Manchester-based Northern Ballet Theatre in 1986. In 1987 he choreographed *A Simple Man*, based on the life of the artist L S Lowry, for television. >> Lowry; Seymour, Lynn

Gable, (William) Clark (1901–60) Actor, born in Cadiz, OH. He had various industrial jobs before joining a small theatrical stock company. His first leading film role was in *The Painted Desert* (1931). Growing popularity in tough but sympathetic parts soon labelled him 'the King of Hollywood', reaching its peak with his portrayal of Rhett Butler in *Gone With the Wind* (1939). In 1942, after the death of his third wife (Carole Lombard) in an air crash, he joined the US 8th Air Force, and was decorated for bomber combat missions. His final film was *The Misfits* (1961). >> Lombard, Carole

Gabo, Naum [gahboh], originally **Naum Neemia Pevsner** (1890–1977) Constructivist sculptor, born in Bryansk, Russia. He studied at Munich University, and in 1920 helped to form the group of Russian Constructivists, who had considerable influence on 20th-c architecture and design. Forced into exile, he lived in Berlin, Paris, and England, moving to the USA in 1946. Several examples of his geometrical 'constructions in space', mainly made in transparent plastics, are in the Museum of Modern Art, New York City. >> Pevsner, Antoine

Gabor, Dennis [gabaw(r)] (1900–79) Physicist, born in Budapest. After obtaining a doctorate in engineering in Berlin (1927) he worked as a research engineer, but left Germany in 1933. In 1948 he joined Imperial College, London, and was appointed professor of applied electron physics (1958–67). He is credited with the invention in 1947 of the technique of holography, a method of photographically recording and reproducing three-dimensional images, for which he was awarded the Nobel Prize for Physics in 1971.

Gaboriau, Emile [gabawryoh] (c.1835–73) Writer of detective fiction, born in Saujon, France. He had already contributed to some of the smaller Parisian papers, when he leapt to fame with *L'Affaire Lerouge* (1866, trans The Widow Lerouge) featuring his detective Lecoq. It was followed by *Le Dossier 113* (1867), *Monsieur Lecoq* (1869), *Les Esclaves de Paris* (1869, The Slaves of Paris), and several others.

Gabriel, Jacques Ange [gabryel] (1698–1782) Architect, born in Paris. As court architect to Louis XV he planned a number of additions to Versailles and other palaces, and designed the Petit Trianon (1768). He also laid out the Place de la Concorde (1753).

Gabriel, Peter (1950–) Singer and songwriter, born in Surrey, SE England, UK. He co-founded and starred in the rock group Genesis, but left to pursue a solo career in 1975. His LP *Peter Gabriel* (1977), the first of four similarly named albums, was a number 7 hit in the UK. Renowned for the visual effects which accompany his videos, a collection of video hits was released as *CV* (1988), topping the UK music video chart. In 1982 he inaugurated the 'World of Music, Arts and Dance' (WOMAD) festival; and he later wrote the score for the controversial film *The Last Temptation of Christ* (1988).

Gabrieli, Andrea [gabrielee] (c. 1533–86) Composer, born in Venice, Italy. After studying under Lassus he became organist of St Mark's Church. He wrote Masses and other choral works. Several of his organ pieces foreshadow the fugue. >> Gabrieli, Giovanni; Lassus

Gabrieli, Giovanni [gabrielee] (c. 1555–1612) Composer, nephew, and pupil of Andrea Gabrieli, born in Venice, Italy. He composed choral and instrumental works in which he exploited the acoustics of St Mark's in Venice with brilliant antiphonal and echo effects, using double choirs, double ensembles of wind instruments, and other devices, as in his well-known *Sonata pian' e forte*. He published much of his uncle's music, and became a renowned teacher. >> Gabrieli, Andrea

Gadamer, Hans-Georg [gahdamer] (1900–) Philosopher, born in Marburg, Germany. A pupil of Heidegger at Frieberg, he became rector at Leipzig and held chairs at Frankfurt (1947) and Heidelberg (1949–68). His major work is *Wahrheit und Methode* (1960, trans Truth and Method). He is known particularly for his theory of hermeneutics, on the nature of understanding and interpretation.

Gaddafi or **Qaddafi, Colonel Muammar** [gadafee] (1942–) Libyan political and military leader, born into a nomadic family. He abandoned university studies to attend military academy in 1963, and formed the Free Officers Movement which overthrew King Idris in 1969. He became chairman of the Revolutionary Command Council, promoted himself to colonel (the highest rank in the revolutionary army) and became commander-in-chief of the Libyan armed forces. As *de facto* head of state, he set about eradicating colonialism by expelling foreigners and closing down British and US bases. He also encouraged a religious revival and return to the fundamental principles of Islam. A somewhat unpredictable figure, he openly supported violent revolutionaries in other parts of the world while ruthlessly pursuing Libyan dissidents both at home and abroad. He waged a war in Chad, threatened other neighbours, and in the 1980s saw his territory bombed and his aircraft shot down by the Americans. He also protected the alleged perpetrators of the bombing of the American PanAm flight which crashed on Lockerbie, Scotland (1988).

Gaddi, Agnolo [gadee] (c. 1350–1396) Painter and architect, born in Florence, Italy, the son of Taddeo Gaddi. He painted the frescoes of 'The Discovery of the Cross' in S Croce at Florence, and of the 'Legends of the Holy Girdle' in the cathedral at Prato. His work shows the influence of Giotto. >> Gaddi, Taddeo; Giotto

Gaddi, Gaddo [gadee] (c. 1260–1332) Florentine painter, the founder of the Gaddi family. He worked in mosaic at Rome and Florence. >> Gaddi, Agnolo/Taddeo

Gaddi, Taddeo [gadee] (c. 1300–66) Painter, born in Florence, Italy, the son of Gaddo Gaddi. He was Giotto's best pupil and also his godson. His finest work is seen in the frescoes of 'The Life of the Virgin' in the Baroncelli chapel of S Croce. Though the best-known of Giotto's followers, his style deviated from that of his master, whom he does not match in figure painting, but whom he excels in architectural perspective. >> Gaddi, Agnolo/Gaddo; Giotto

Gaddis, William (1922–) Novelist, born in New York City. He studied at Harvard, then worked as a freelance speech and scriptwriter before making his mark with the novel *The Recognitions* (1955), a complex story using experimental language, which drew acclaim from some quarters and incomprehension from others. A radical satirist, he is one of America's most prominent contemporary novelists; his other works include *JR* (1976), *Carpenter's Gothic* (1985), and *A Frolic of His Own (1993)*.

Gade, Niels (Wilhelm) [gaduh] (1817–90) Composer, born in Copenhagen. He began as violinist, but on a royal grant studied at Leipzig, and became a friend of Schumann and Mendelssohn. He composed eight symphonies, a violin concerto, several choral works, and a number of smaller pieces. The Scandinavian element in his music distinguishes him from the Leipzig school. >> Mendelssohn, Felix; Schumann, Robert

Gadolin, Johan [gadolin] (1760–1852) Chemist, born in Turku, Finland. He became professor of chemistry there, and isolated the oxide of the rare element, *gadolinium*, named after him.

Gadsden, Christopher (1724–1805) American revolutionary leader, born in Charleston, SC. He was a member of the first Continental Congress (1774), became a brigadier-general in the Continental army during the Revolution, and was Lieutenant-Governor of South Carolina.

Gadsden, James (1788–1858) US soldier and diplomat, born in Charleston, SC. He studied at Yale College, then served in the War of 1812 and against the Seminoles. In 1853 he was appointed US minister to Mexico, and negotiated the purchase (the *Gadsden Purchase*) of part of Arizona and New Mexico for railway construction.

Gagarin, Yuri (Alekseyevich) [gagahrin] (1934–68) Russian cosmonaut, born in Gagarin (formerly, Gzhatsk), Russia. He joined the Soviet air force in 1957, and in 1961 became the first man to travel in space, completing a circuit of the Earth in the *Vostok* spaceship satellite. A Hero of the Soviet Union, he shared the Galabert astronautical Prize with John Glenn in 1963. He was killed in a plane accident while training. >> Glenn, John

Gage, Thomas (1721–87) British soldier, whose actions helped precipitate the American Revolution, born in Firle, East Sussex. He accompanied Braddock's ill-fated expedition in Pennsylvania (1754), and the successful campaign in Quebec (1759), and became Military Governor of Montreal in 1760. He was commander-in-chief of the British forces in America (1763–72), and in 1774 Governor of Massachusetts. In April 1775 he sent a force to seize arms from the colonists at Concord, and next day the skirmish at Lexington took place which began the American Revolution. After the Battle of Bunker Hill (Jun 1775) he was relieved by Howe. >> Howe, William

Gahn, Johan Gottlieb (1745–1818) Chemist and mineralogist, born in Voxna, Sweden. He worked at the University of Uppsala, and discovered manganese in 1774. He shared the discovery of phosphoric acid in bones with Carl Wilhelm Scheele in 1770. The mineral *gahnite* is named after him. >> Scheele

Gaillard, Slim (1916–91) Singer, songwriter, and musician, born in Detroit, MI. As part of the duo **Slim & Slam** (with Slam Stewart on bass), he had several hits, the biggest of which was the novelty song 'Flat Foot Floogie' (1938). A light, humorous performer, he claimed to have invented his own 'scat' singing language, which he called *Vout*.

Gainsborough, Thomas [gaynzbruh] (1727–88) Landscape and portrait painter, born in Sudbury, Suffolk, E England, UK. In his youth he copied Dutch landscapes, and at 14 was sent to London, where he learnt the art of Rococo decoration. He moved to Bath in 1759, where he established himself with his portrait of Earl Nugent (1760). His best-known paintings include 'The Blue Boy' (c. 1770, San Marino), 'The Harvest Wagon' (1767, Birmingham) and 'The Watering Place' (1777, Tate, London). He moved to London in 1774, painting futher portraits and landscapes, notably 'George III' and 'Queen Charlotte' (1781, Windsor), and 'Cottage Door' (1780, Pasadena).

Gaiseric or **Genseric** [giyserik] (c. 390–477) King of the Vandals and Alans (428–77), who led the Vandals in their invasion of Gaul. He crossed from Spain to Numidia (429), captured and sacked Hippo (430), seized Carthage (439), and made it the capital of his new dominions. He built up a large maritime power, and his fleets carried the terror of his name as far as the Peloponnese. He sacked Rome in 455, and defeated fleets sent against him.

Gaisford, Thomas [gaysfuh(r)d] (1780–1855) English Greek scholar. He became professor of Greek at Oxford in 1812, and in 1831 Dean of Christ Church. He produced editions of Herodotos, Hephaestion, Stobaeus, and Suidas. The Gaisford Prizes were founded in his memory.

Gaitskell, Hugh (Todd Naylor) (1906–63) British statesman, born in London, England, UK. He studied at Oxford, and became a Socialist during the 1926 General Strike. An MP in 1945, he was minister of fuel and power (1947) and of economic affairs (1950), and Chancellor of the Exchequer (1950–1). In 1955 he was elected Leader of the Opposition by a large majority over Bevan. He bitterly opposed Eden's Suez action (1956), and refused to accept a narrow conference vote for unilateral disarmament (1960). This caused a crisis of leadership in which he was challenged by Harold Wilson (1960), but he retained the loyalty of most Labour MPs. >> Bevan, Aneurin; Eden; Wilson, Harold

Gaius [gayus] (fl.130–180) Roman jurist, of whom little is known except as author of *Institutiones* (c.161, Institutes), four books of Roman law, referred to by Emperor Valentian III in the *Law of Citations* (426). They are the only substantial texts of classical Roman law that have survived. They were lost until the German historian Barthold Niebuhr discovered a manuscript at Verona in 1816.

Gajdusek, D(aniel) Carleton (1923–) Virologist, born in Yonkers, NY. He studied at the University of Rochester and at Harvard. He spent much time in Papua New Guinea, studying the origin and dissemination of infectious diseases amongst the Fore people, especially a slowly developing lethal viral disease called *kuru*. He shared the Nobel Prize for Physiology or Medicine (1976) for his work in degenerative neurological disorders. >> RR1124

Gál, Hans (1890–1987) Composer and writer on music, born in Brunn, Austria. He studied at Vienna University, subsequently teaching there (1919–29) and in Mainz (1929–38). The Anschluss drove him out, and he settled in Edinburgh, where he became a university lecturer (1945–56), remaining in Scotland for the rest of his life. His music, in a late Romantic style, included five operas, four symphonies, and many other works.

Galba, Servius Sulpicius (3 BC–AD 69) Roman emperor (68–9). He became consul in 33, and administered Aquitania, Germany, Africa, and Hispania Tarraconensis with competence and integrity. In 68 the Gallic legions rose against Nero, and in June proclaimed Galba emperor. But he soon made himself unpopular by favouritism, ill-timed severity, and avarice, and was assassinated by the praetorians in Rome. >> Nero; Otho; RR1084

Galbraith, J(ohn) Kenneth [golbrayth] (1908–) Economist and diplomat, born in Iona Station, Ontario, Canada. He studied at the universities of Toronto, California, and Cambridge, and became professor of economics at Harvard (1945–75, then emeritus), where he spent his career, except for a short period at Princeton, wartime service in Washington, and two years (1961–3) as US ambassador to India. He was an advisor to Presidents Kennedy and Johnson, and is one of the major intellectual forces in American liberalism. His books include *American Capitalism: the Concept of Countervailing Power* (1952), *The Affluent Society* (1958), *The New Industrial State* (1967), *The Age of Uncertainty* (1977, also TV series), *A History of Economics* (1987), and *A Journey through Economic Time* (1994).

Galdós, Benito Pérez >> **Pérez Galdós, Benito**

Galen [gaylen], in full **Claudius Galenus** (c. 130–201) Greek physician, born in Pergamum, Mysia. He studied medicine at Pergamum, Smyrna, Corinth, and Alexandria, and later lived in Rome. He was a voluminous writer on medical and philosophical subjects, and gathered up all the medical knowledge of his time, thus becoming the authority used by subsequent Greek and Roman medical writers.

Galerius [galeerius], in full **Gaius Galerius Valerius Maximus** (c. 250–311) Roman emperor (305–11), born near Serdica, Dacia. He was a Roman soldier of humble extraction who rose from the ranks to become deputy ruler of the E half of the empire under Diocletian (293), and chief ruler after Diocletians's abdication in 305. He was a notorious persecutor of the Christians (303–11) until near the end of his reign, when after an illness he granted them some toleration. >> Diocletian; RR1084

Galignani, John Anthony [galinyahnee] (1796–1873) Parisian publisher, born in London, England, UK. With his brother **William** (1798–1882) he greatly improved *Galignani's Messenger*, started in Paris by their father in 1814, and made it a medium for advocating cordiality between England and France. The brothers founded at Corbeil a hospital for Englishmen; and in 1889 the *Galignani Home* for aged printers and booksellers was opened at Neuilly.

Galileo [galilayoh], in full **Galileo Galilei** (1564–1642) Astronomer and mathematician, born in Pisa, Italy. He entered Pisa University as a medical student in 1581, and became professor of mathematics at Padua (1592–1610), where he improved the refracting telescope (1610), and was the first to use it for astronomy. His bold advocacy of the Copernican theory brought severe ecclesiastical censure. He was forced to retract before the Inquisition, and was sentenced to indefinite imprisonment – though the sentence was commuted by the pope, at the request of the Duke of Tuscany. Under house arrest in Florence, he continued his research, though by 1637 he had become totally blind. Among his other discoveries were the law of uniformly accelerated motion towards the Earth, the parabolic path of projectiles, and the law that all bodies have weight. The validity of his scientific work was formally recognized by the Roman Catholic Church in 1993. >> Marius, Simon

Gall, Franz Joseph [gal] (1758–1828) Anatomist, born in Tiefenbrunn, Germany. As a physician in Vienna (1785), he evolved a theory in which a person's talents and qualities were traced to particular areas of the brain. His lectures on phrenology were popular, but suppressed in 1802 as being subversive of religion.

Gall, St (c. 550–645) Irish monk, one of the 12 who followed St Columban to the European mainland in c.585. In 614 he fixed his cell at a point on the Steinach R in Switzerland, around which grew up a great Benedictine abbey and the town of St Gall. Feast day 16 October. >> Columban

Gallagher, Liam >> **Oasis**

Gallagher, Noel >> **Oasis**

Gallant, Mavis, *née* **Young** (1922–) Short-story writer and novelist, born in Montreal, Quebec, Canada. Educated bilingually, she has lived mainly in Paris since 1950, contributing regularly to *The New Yorker*. Now recognized as one of Canada's foremost short-story writers, she was not widely read in Canada until publication of *From the Fifteenth District* (1979). Among later works are *Home Truths* (1981), *Overhead in a Balloon* (1985), and *In Transit* (1988). Her novels include *Green Water, Green Sky* (1959) and *A Fairly Good Time* (1970).

Gallatin, (Abraham Alphonse) Albert [galatī] (1761–1849) Financier and statesman, born in Geneva, Switzerland. He studied at Geneva in 1779, then went to the USA (1780), settling in Pennsylvania. He was elected to the US House of Representatives (1795), where he set up the House Committee on Finance (later the Ways and Means Committee), and became secretary of the Treasury (1801–13). He played an important part in the peace negotiations with Britain in 1814, and signed the Treaty of Ghent, later becoming minister at Paris (1815–23) and at London (1826–7). A student of Indian tribes, in 1842 he founded the American Ethnological Society of New York.

Gallaudet, Thomas (Hopkins) [galuhdet] (1787–1851) Educationist, born in Philadelphia, PA. He studied at Yale University, and became interested in the education of the deaf. He learned sign language in Europe, and went on to establish the American Asylum for Deaf-mutes in Hartford, CT (1816). Following retirement (1830), New York University appointed him its first professor for the philosophy of education.

Gallé, Emile [galay] (1846–1904) Designer and glass maker, born in Nancy, France. His study of botany influenced much of his work, including the decoration of his father's ceramics. His own interests turned towards glass. By 1874 he was settled in Nancy running a glass workshop, which grew to employ 300 workers, as well as managing what had been his father's pottery. His distinctive designs for glass became internationally known after the Paris Exposition (1889). With Victor Prouvé (1858–1943) and Louis Majorelle (1859–1926) he formed the Ecole de Nancy in 1901.

Galle, Johann Gottfried [gahluh] (1812–1910) Astronomer, born in Pabsthaus, Germany. In 1846, at Berlin

Observatory, he discovered the planet Neptune, whose existence had been postulated in the calculations of Leverrier. >> Leverrier

Galliano, John (Charles) [galiahnoh] (1960–) Fashion designer, born in Gibraltar. His family moved to London when he was six, and he studied at East London College and St Martin's School of Art. He then set up a studio in London, and quickly established himself, receiving the British Fashion Council Designer of the Year Award in 1987. After setting up a studio in Paris in 1994, he again won the British Designer Award (1994, 1995), and after a period with Givenchy became designer-in-chief at Christian Dior in 1996. >> Dior; Givenchy

Galli-Curci, Amelita [galee koorchee] (1882–1963) Soprano, born in Milan, Italy. She studied piano at the Milan Conservatory, but as a singer was self-taught. She first appeared in opera in 1909, toured Europe, and in 1916 joined the Chicago Opera Company. From 1919 onwards, she worked principally at the Metropolitan Opera, New York City, becoming a US citizen in 1921. She was forced to retire early, following a throat injury.

Galliéni, Joseph Simon [galyaynee] (1849–1916) French soldier, born in St Béat, France. He served in the war of 1870–1, in West Africa and Tonkin, was Governor of Upper Senegal from 1886, then Governor-General of Madagascar (1897–1905). As minister for war, and military governor in Paris from 1914, he saw to the city fortifications, and contributed to the victory of the Marne (1914) by his foresight and planning. He was posthumously created Marshal of France in 1921.

Gallienne, Eva / Richard Le >> Le Gallienne, Eva / Richard

Gallienus, Publius Licinius Egnatius [galiaynus] (c.218–68) Roman emperor, from 253 colleague and from 260 successor to his father, Valerian. His authority was limited to Italy, for in the provinces the legions frequently revolted, and proclaimed their commanders Caesars. In 268, while besieging one of his rivals in Milan, he was murdered by some of his officers. A hostile tradition perhaps misrepresents his achievements. >> Valerian; Zenobia; RR1084

Gallitzin, Demetrius Augustine [galitzin], known as **the Apostle of the Alleghenies** (1770–1840) Priest, born in The Hague, The Netherlands. He became a Roman Catholic in 1787, emigrated to the USA in 1792, and was ordained a priest in 1795. Sent as a missionary to Cambria County, PA, he founded the town of Loretto (1799). He was vicar-general for W Pennsylvania, and wrote several tracts defending his faith against Protestant attack.

Gallo, Ernest (1910–) Vintner, born near Modesto, CA. The son of an immigrant Italian grape grower, in 1933 he and his brother **Julio Gallo** (1911–93) took over the family's Modesto vineyards, and learned to make wine. E and J Gallo Winery became the world's largest winery, gradually upscaling its image as its Thunderbird fortified wine of the 1950s gave way to Bartles and James wine coolers in the 1980s, and its 'jug wines' were supplemented by vintage varietal wines. The firm is generally credited with improving the quality of American table wine.

Gallo, Robert >> Montagnier, Luc

Gallup, George (Horace) (1901–84) Public opinion expert, born in Jefferson, IA. He was professor of journalism at Drake and Northwestern universities until 1932, and, after a period directing research for an advertising agency, became professor at the Pulitzer School of Journalism, Columbia University. In 1935 he founded the American Institute of Public Opinion, and evolved the *Gallup polls* for testing the state of public opinion.

Gallus, Gaius Cornelius [galus] (c. 70–26 BC) Poet, born in Forum Julii (now Fréjus) in Gaul. He lived in Rome in intimate friendship with Virgil and Ovid, and was appointed prefect of Egypt by Augustus, but he fell into disfavour, and after being banished he committed suicide. From his four books of elegies upon his mistress 'Lycoris' (the actress Cyntheris), he is considered the founder of Roman elegy. Only a few fragments of his work are extant. >> Ovid; Virgil

Galois, Evariste [galwah] (1811–32) Mathematician, born in Bourg-la-Reine, France. He was educated privately and at the Collège Royal de Louis-le-Grand. Despite mathematical ability he failed the entrance for the Ecole Polytechnique to study maths, and settled for the Ecole Normale Supérieure in 1829 to train as a teacher, but was expelled in 1830 for republican sympathies. He engaged in political agitation, was imprisoned twice, and was killed in a duel aged 21. His mathematical reputation rests on fewer than 100 pages of posthumously published work of original genius in the branch of higher algebra known as group theory. >> Jordan, Camille

Galsworthy, John [golzwerthee] (1867–1933) Novelist and playwright, born in Kingston Hill, Surrey, SE England, UK. He studied at Oxford, and was called to the bar in 1890, but chose to travel and set up as a writer. From the start he was a moralist and humanitarian, but his novels were also to be documentaries of their time. The six linked novels comprising *The Forsyte Saga* (1906–28), recording the life of the affluent British middle-class before 1914, began a new vogue for 'serial' novels. His plays (31 in all) illustrate his reforming zeal and his interest in social and ethical problems; they include *Strife* (1909), *Justice* (1910), and *The Skin Game* (1920). He was awarded the Nobel Prize for Literature in 1932.

Galt, Sir Alexander Tilloch [gawlt] (1817–93) Canadian statesman, born in London, England, UK. He emigrated to Canada in 1835, and entered the Canadian parliament in 1849. He served as finance minister (1858–62, 1864–6) and as high commissioner in Britain (1880–3).

Galt, John [gawlt] (1779–1839) Novelist and essayist, born in Irvine, North Ayrshire, W Scotland, UK. Educated at Greenock Grammar School, he went to London at 25 as a merchant, writing in his spare time. His business failed (1808) and he travelled to the European mainland, where he met Byron, and produced a poorly received biography. He gained recognition when his work was published in *Blackwood's Magazine* in 1820. His memorable novels include *The Ayrshire Legatees* (1820), *The Provost* (1822), and *The Entail* (1823). >> Byron, George

Galtieri, Leopoldo (Fortunato) [galtyairee] (1926–) Argentinian soldier and junta president (1981–2), born in Caseras, Buenos Aires. Trained at the National Military College, he progressed to the rank of lieutenant-general (1979), when he joined the ruling junta, becoming its president. To deflect attention from a worsening national economy he ordered the invasion of the long-disputed Malvinas (Falkland) Is in 1982. Their recovery by Britain, after a brief and humiliating war, brought about his downfall. He was court-martialled in 1983 and sentenced to 12 years' imprisonment for negligence in starting and losing the Falklands War. >> Moore, Jeremy; RR1032

Galton, Sir Francis [gawltn] (1822–1911) Scientist and explorer, born in Birmingham, West Midlands, C England, UK. He studied at Birmingham, London, and Cambridge, but left the study of medicine to travel in N and S Africa. He is best known for his studies of heredity and intelligence, such as *Hereditary Genius* (1869), which led to the field he called *eugenics*. Several of his ideas are referred to in the work of his cousin, Charles Darwin. Galton was knighted in 1909. >> Darwin, Charles

Galuppi, Baldassare [galoopee] (1706-85) Light operatic composer, born in the island of Burano, near Venice, Italy. He was educated in Venice, where he lived most of his life, apart from visits to London (1741-3) and St Petersburg (1765-8). His comic operas were extremely popular, and he also composed sacred and instrumental music. He is the subject of a well-known poem by Browning, 'A Toccata of Galuppi's'. >> Browning, Robert

Galvani, Luigi [galvahnee] (1737-98) Physiologist, born in Bologna, Italy. He studied at Bologna, where he became professor of anatomy (1762). Investigating the effects of electrostatic stimuli applied to the muscle fibre of frogs, he discovered he could also make the muscle twitch by touching the nerve with various metals without a source of electrostatic charge, and greater reaction was obtained when two disimilar metals were used. He attributed the effect to 'animal electricity'. His work inspired his friend Volta, leading to the production of the electrical battery, and also initiated research into electrophysiology. The *galvanometer* is named after him. >> Volta

Galway, James [gawlway] (1939-) Flautist, born in Belfast. He studied in London and Paris, and played in various orchestras in London and in the Berlin Philharmonic (1969-75). He became a soloist in 1975, and has since followed a highly successful solo career, playing on a solid gold flute of remarkable tonal range. He published an autobiography in 1978, and was involved in a TV series, *James Galway's Music in Time*, in 1983.

Gama, Vasco da [gahma] (c. 1469-1525) Navigator, born in Sines, Alentejo, Portugal. He led the expedition which discovered the route to India round the Cape of Good Hope (1497-9), and in 1502-3 led a squadron of ships to Calicut to avenge the murder of a group of Portuguese explorers left there by Cabral. In 1524 he was sent as viceroy to India, but he soon fell ill, and died at Cochin. His body was brought home to Portugal. >> Cabral

Gamage, Albert Walter [gamij] (1855-1930) Merchant, born in Hereford, Hereford and Worcester, WC England, UK. He became a draper's apprentice in London, and in 1878 founded the famous store in Holborn which bore his name.

Gamaliel [gamalyel] (?-c. 50) Palestinian rabbi, the teacher of St Paul, mentioned in the New Testament (*Acts* 22:3). A prominent Pharisee, he taught 'the law' early in the 1st-c. Tolerant and peaceful, he seems to have placed Christianity on a par with other sects, and encouraged long-suffering on all sides. >> Paul, St

Gambetta, Leon (Michel) [gābeta] (1838-82) French Republican statesman and prime minister (1881-2), born in Cahors, France. He was called to the bar in 1859, and elected deputy in 1869. After the surrender of Napoleon III he helped to proclaim the Republic (1870), became minister of the interior in the Government of National Defence, made a spectacular escape from the siege of Paris in a balloon, and for five months was dictator of France. He led the resistance to MacMahon (1877), became president of the Chamber (1879) and briefly prime minister, but fell from office before implementing a programme of radical reform. >> MacMahon; Napoleon III; RR1049

Gambier, James Gambier, Baron [gambeer] (1756-1833) British naval commander, born in the Bahamas. He fought with distinction in Howes' action off Ushant (1794), was promoted rear-admiral (1795), and served as Lord Commissioner of the Admiralty (1795-1801, 1804-6). He was also Governor of Newfoundland (1802-4). As admiral he commanded the British fleet at the bombardment of Copenhagen in 1807. At the Battle of Aix Roads in 1809 he disregarded signals from the naval commander, but was acquitted by a court martial. >> Howe, Richard

Gamble, Josias Christopher (1776-1848) Industrialist, born in Enniskillen, Co Fermanagh. He was a founder with **James Muspratt** (1793-1886) of the British chemical industry based in the St Helens area near Liverpool. A graduate in theology from Glasgow, he spent a period as a cleric before manufacturing chemicals in Dublin and Glasgow, and most profitably in partnership with Muspratt in St Helens, making bleaching powder, soda ash, and sulphuric acid.

Gambon, Sir Michael (John) (1940-) Actor, born in Dublin. He joined the National Theatre for its inaugural season in 1963, returning to it in 1978 after appearances in repertory at Birmingham and elsewhere. He played for the Royal Shakespeare Company (1982-3), and has made several television appearances, notably in the title role of Dennis Potter's play *The Singing Detective* (1986, BAFTA). His films include *Paris by Night* (1989), *A Dry White Season* (1990), *Mobsters* (1992), and *Nothing Personal* (1997). He was knighted in 1998.

Gamelin, Maurice Gustave [gamlī] (1872-1958) French soldier, born in Paris. Trained at the Military Academy of St Cyr, he attained lieutenant-colonel's rank in 1914, but no divisional command until 1925. In 1935 seniority brought him the post of chief-of-staff of the army and president of the Supreme War Council, but his unfitness for overall command was exposed in his pronouncement that 'to attack is to lose'. In 1940, blind to the lessons of the 1939 Polish campaign, he refused to rethink his outmoded defensive strategy of 'solid fronts', which crumbled under the German *Blitzkrieg*. He was hurriedly replaced by General Weygand, tried, and imprisoned (1943-5). >> Weygand

Gamow, George [gamov], originally **Georgy Antonovich Gamov** (1904-68) Physicist, born in Odessa, Ukraine. He studied at Leningrad University, where later he was professor of physics (1931-4). He did research at Göttingen, developing a quantum theory for radioactivity, then moved to the USA as professor of physics at George Washington University (1934-55) and at Colorado (1956-68). In 1948, with Ralph Alpher and Hans Bethe, he developed the 'big bang' theory of the origin of the universe. In molecular biology he hypothesized that patterns within DNA chains formed a genetic code, a proposal shown by the mid-1950s to be correct. He was also a writer, and received acclaim as a popularizer of science, beginning with *Mr Tomkins in Wonderland* (1936). >> Alpher; Bethe; Lemaître

Gandar, Laurence (Owen Vine) (1915-) Journalist, born in Durban, South Africa. He studied at Natal University, Pietermaritzburg, and served with South African forces in World War 2. He entered journalism in 1936, and became editor of *The Rand Daily Mail*, Johannesburg, in 1957. His challenges to apartheid, through campaigning journalism and his own articles, transformed the newspaper and set new standards for South African journalism as a whole. Prosecution for publishing reports on jail conditions led to the newspaper's owners sidelining him as editor in 1966. He stayed on as editor-in-chief until 1969, when he became the founding director of the Minority Rights Group in Britain, returning to South Africa in 1972.

Gandhi see panel on p. 359

Gandhi, Indira (Priyadarshini) [gandee] (1917-84) Indian stateswoman and prime minister (1966-77, 1980-4), born in Allahabad, India, the daughter of Jawaharlal Nehru. She studied at Visva-Bharati University (Bengal) and Oxford, and in 1942 married **Feroze Gandhi** (d.1960). She became president of the Indian Congress Party (1959-60), minister of information (1964), and prime minister following the death of Shastri. After her conviction for election malpractices, she declared a state of emergency (1975-7), and was premier again in 1980. She achieved a considerable reputation through her work as a leader of the developing nations, but was unable to stem sectarian violence at home. She was assassinated in New Delhi by Sikh extremist members of her bodyguard. >> Gandhi, Rajiv; Nehru, Jawaharlal; Shastri; RR1058

Gandhi, Rajiv [gandee] (1944–91) Indian statesman and prime minister (1984–9), born in Mumbai (Bombay), India, the eldest son of Indira Gandhi and the grandson of Nehru. He studied at Cambridge University, and became a pilot with Indian Airlines (1968). Following the death of his brother **Sanjay Gandhi** (1946–80) in an air crash, he was elected to his brother's Amethi parliamentary seat (1981) and appointed a general secretary of the Congress Party (1983). After the assassination of Indira Gandhi (1984), he became prime minister, and secured a record majority in the parliamentary elections later that year. He attempted to cleanse and rejuvenate the Congress, inducting new technocrats, and introducing a freer market economic programme. He was forced to resign as premier after his party was defeated in the general election of November 1989, and was assassinated 18 months later while campaigning for the Congress Party. >> Gandhi, Indira; Nehru, Jawaharlal; RR1058

Gangeśa [ganggesha] (c.1200) Indian philosopher, and founder of the *Navya-nyaya* or new *Nyaya* school of Hindu philosophy, in Mithila, Bihar. His approach, emphasizing philosophical logic, rather than the knowledge of the external world claimed in the *Nyaya* philosophy stemming from Gautama, was continued by his son **Vardhamana**. >> Gautama

Ganying, also spelled **Kan-ying** (1st-c) Emissary sent by Chinese general Ban Chao from the Caspian to Rome. He traversed Persia and Mesopotamia, but never reached Rome. >> Ban Chao

Gao Gang or **Kao Kang** [gow gahng] (c. 1902–55) One of the leaders of the Chinese Communist Party, born in Shensi province, China. In the mid-1930s he was in charge of a

---

GANDHI (1869–1948)

Mohandas Karamchand Gandhi was born in Poorbandar, in W India, the son of Karamchand Gandhi, the chief minister of Poorbandar, and his fourth wife, Putlibai, a deeply religious Hindu. From her he formed a deep moral belief in non-violence, and in fasting as a means of spiritual cleansing. An undistinguished student, he was married at the age of 13, and at 19 his family sent him to London to study law at the Inner Temple.

On his return to India in 1891 he was unable to find a suitable post as a barrister, so he accepted a year's contract in Natal, South Africa, from 1893. Having suffered the humiliation of racial prejudice there for the first time in his life, he was persuaded to remain in South Africa to oppose the forthcoming bill which would deprive Indians of the right to vote. His mission was not entirely successful, but he was instrumental in bringing the plight of the Indians in South Africa to the attention of the world; and in so doing launched himself as a tenacious political campaigner. He remained in South Africa for 20 years, opposing further discriminatory legislation by means of non-violent defiance. His law practice funded his civil activities and, with the support of his wife, he threw his home open to political colleagues. During the Boer War (1899–1902) he aided the British by raising an Ambulance Corps of more than 1000 Indians, for which he was awarded the War Medal.

Gandhi returned to India in 1914 and, while supporting the British in World War 1, took an increasing interest in Home Rule for India. He became a dominant influence in the National Congress Movement (which had been formed in 1885), re-shaping it, and becoming an international political figure of his generation. His policies remained unchanged: non-violent, non-cooperation to achieve independence. However, following his civil disobedience campaign, during which British soldiers killed nearly 400 people at the massacre of Amritsar (1919), he was jailed for conspiracy for 2 years. On his release, the Hindu and Muslim factions of the Congress Party were warring. Reasoning with them proved pointless and, in an attempt to restore the non-violent campaign, Gandhi undertook a much-publicized personal fast for three weeks. By 1928 he was back at the head of the Congress Party, and in 1930 launched his spectacular attack on the punitive salt taxes, leading a 320 km/200 mi march to the sea to collect salt, in symbolic defiance of the government monopoly. More than 60 000 were imprisoned and he was rearrested.

On his release in 1931, he negotiated a truce between Congress and the government, and travelled to London to attend the Round Table Conference on Indian constitutional reform. Back in India, he renewed the civil disobedience campaign and was arrested again – the pattern, along with his 'fasts unto death', of his political activity for the next six years. He assisted in the adoption of the constitutional compromise of 1937, under which Congress ministers accepted office in the new provincial legislatures. At the outbreak of World War 2, convinced that only a free India could give Britain effective moral support, he urged complete independence more and more strongly. He described the Cripps proposal in 1942 for a constituent assembly with the promise of a new Constitution after the war as 'a post-dated cheque on a crashing bank'. In August 1942 he was arrested for concurring in civil disobedience action to obstruct the war effort, and not released until May 1944.

Two years later Gandhi negotiated with the British Cabinet Mission which recommended the new constitutional structure, culminating in the formation of the new dominions of India and Pakistan. Although disappointed that India was not united in its freedom, he hailed Britain's decision to grant India independence as 'the noblest act of the British nation'. His last months were darkened by communal strife between Hindu and Muslim; but his fasts to shame the instigators helped to avert deeper national tragedy. However, he was assassinated in Delhi by a Hindu fanatic, Nathuram Godse, on 30 January 1948.

In his lifetime, Mahatma ('the great soul') Gandhi was venerated as a moral teacher, a reformer who sought an India as free from caste as from materialism, and a dedicated patriot who gave the Home Rule movement a new quality. In Asia particularly he has been regarded as a great influence for peace, whose teachings held a message not only for India, but for the world.
>> Cripps; Nehru

small independent Communist area at Baoan, Shanxi, where the Long March led by Mao Zedong ended. A close political ally of Mao, he later became chief Party secretary of Manchuria (1949). He set the national pace in economic development, but in 1955 was accused of attempting to set up a 'separate kingdom'. He apparently committed suicide. >> Mao Zedong

Gaozu [gow tsoo], also spelled **Kao-tsu**, originally **Liu Bang** (247–195 BC) First Han dynasty emperor of China. A bandit leader and former prison guard from eastern peasant stock, he seized the throne from the Qin by conquest (202 BC, but he backdated it to 206). He consolidated Qin achievements, building a new capital at Chang-an (modern Xian), re-established suzerainty over the S, and reorganized the empire into 13 provinces. One of only two commoners in Chinese history to found a major dynasty, he showed contempt for the scholar-aristocracy by urinating in their hats. Dying of septicaemia because he despised doctors, he was succeeded by his widow, Empress Lü. >> Lü; Wendi

Gaozu [gow tsoo], also spelled **Kao-tsu**, originally **Li Yuan** (c. 618–26) First emperor of the Tang dynasty in China (618–907). An official related to the Sui emperors (590–618) and the Turks, he captured Chang-an (Xian) in 617, encouraged by his son Li Shimin. He suppressed 11 other claimants, each with an army ruling part of China, then abdicated in favour of Li Shimin (Emperor Taizong). >> Taizong

Garavani, Valentino >> **Valentino**

Garbarek, Jan (1947–) Saxophonist and composer, born in Mysen, Norway. In 1967 he joined the Scandinavian orchestra led by US avant-garde composer George Russell, and in 1970 worked in the USA for a while under such leaders as Keith Jarrett (1945–) and Don Cherry (1936–). Since returning to Europe he has formed successive small bands which have explored influences from India, South America, and Scandinavian folk roots, often using electronics. He is one of the few European jazz musicians whose work has influenced his American contemporaries.

Garbett, Cyril Foster (1875–1955) Anglican clergyman, born in Tongham, Surrey, SE England, UK. He studied at Keble College and Cuddesdon College, Oxford, and became Bishop of Southwark (1919–32), Bishop of Winchester (1932–42), then Archbishop of York. He was one of the most outspoken leaders of the Church, greatly concerned for the welfare of the impoverished dwellers in inner-city areas. Publications include *The Church and Social Problems* (1939) and a trilogy on Church and State (1947–52).

Garbo, Greta, originally **Greta Lovisa Gustafsson** (1905–90) Film actress, born in Stockholm. A shop-girl who won a bathing beauty competition at 16, she won a scholarship to the Royal Theatre Dramatic School in Stockholm, and starred in Mauritz Stiller's *Gösta Berling's Saga* (1924); he gave his star the name Garbo, chosen before he met her. She went to the USA in 1925, and her greatest successes, following *Anna Christie* (1930) – her first talking picture – were *Queen Christina* (1933), *Anna Karenina* (1935), *Camille* (1936), and *Ninotchka* (1939). She retired from films in 1941, after the failure of *Two-Faced Woman*. She became a US citizen in 1951, but remained a total recluse for the rest of her life. >> Stiller

Garborg, Arne Evenson (1851–1924) Writer, born in Jaeren, Norway. He was an advocate for social reform, and a leader in the movement to establish a new Norwegian literary language called *Nynorsk* (New Norwegian). He wrote a cycle of lyric poems, *Haugtussa* (1895, The Hill Innocent), and a series of realistic novels, such as *Trette Men* (1891, Tired Men). He also wrote a drama on religious problems, *Laereren* (1896, The Teacher), and later attacked Lutheran theology in two controversial works.

García Gutiérrez, Antonio [gah(r)**thee**a goo**tyair**eth] (1813–84) Playwright, born in Chiclana, Spain. He worked in the consular service from 1864, and was director of the Archaeological Museum in Madrid from 1872. An exponent of 19th-c Romanticism, he is best known for his play *El trovador* (1836, The Troubadour), on which Verdi based his opera, *Il trovatore*.

García Lorca, Federico >> **Lorca, Federico García**

García Márquez, Gabriel >> **Márquez, Gabriel García**

García Perez, Alan [gah(r)**see**a pe**rez**] (1949–) Peruvian statesman and president (1985–90), born in Lima. He studied at the Catholic University, Lima, and in Guatemala, Spain, and France. He was elected to the National Congress (1978) as a member of the moderate, left-wing party, becoming party secretary-general in 1982. He was the first civilian to win the presidential post in democratic elections. >> RR1081

García Robles, Alfonso [gah(r)**see**a rob**lez**] (1911–91) Mexican diplomat, born in Zamora, Mexico. After studying law in Mexico, Paris, and The Netherlands, he became a member of the Mexican foreign service. He was undersecretary for foreign affairs (1964–71), and was instrumental in forming the Treaty of Tlateloco (1967), which aimed to abolish nuclear weapons in Latin America. In 1977 he became Mexican delegate on the UN Disarmament Committee. He shared the Nobel Peace Prize in 1982. >> RR1125

Gard, Roger Martin du >> **Martin du Gard, Roger**

Gardel, Carlos [gah(r)**del**] (1890–1935) Popular singer, born in Toulouse, France. He was brought up in Buenos Aires, and made his name as a tango singer and later as a film star. Probably the best-known Latin American singer of the 20th-c, he died in an aircraft accident in Medellín, Colombia.

Garden, Mary (1874–1967) Soprano, born in Aberdeen, NE Scotland, UK. Taken to America as a child, she studied singing in Chicago, then in Paris. Her career began sensationally when she took over in mid-performance the title role in Charpentier's new opera *Louise* at the Opéra-Comique in 1900, when the singer was taken ill. Debussy chose her for Mélisande in *Pelléas et Mélisande* (1902), and Massenet and Erlanger also wrote leading roles for her. She sang at Covent Garden (1902–3), her US debut was in 1907, and in 1910 she began a 20-year association with Chicago Grand Opera, which she also briefly directed (1921–2). She returned to Scotland in 1939.

Gardiner, Samuel Rawson (1829–1902) Historian, born in Ropley, Hampshire, S England, UK. He studied at Oxford, taught at King's College, London (1871–85), and became a fellow of All Souls' College, Oxford (1884). The first instalment of his great *History of England from the Accession of James I to the Restoration* appeared in 1863, and at his death he had brought the work down to 1656. His other works include *The Thirty Years' War* (1874) and *The Student's History of England* (1890–2).

Gardiner, Stephen (c. 1483–1555) Clergyman, born in Bury St Edmunds, Suffolk, E England, UK. Master of Trinity Hall, Cambridge, he became Wolsey's secretary in 1525. Between 1527 and 1533 he was sent to Rome to further Henry VIII's divorce from Catherine of Aragon, and was made Bishop of Winchester in 1531. He supported the royal supremacy in his *De vera obedientia* (1535), helped to encompass Thomas Cromwell's downfall, and was involved in framing the Six Articles. He was appointed Chancellor of Cambridge in 1540. He opposed doctrinal reformation, and for this he was imprisoned and deprived of his offices on Edward VI's accession. Released and restored by Mary I in 1553, he became an arch-persecutor of Protestants. >> Cromwell, Thomas; Henry VIII; Wolsey

Gardner, Ava (Lavinnia), originally **Lucy Johnson** (1922–90) Film actress, born in Smithfield, NC. Signed by MGM as a teenager, she emerged from the ranks of decorative starlets with her portrayal of a ravishing femme fatale in *The Killers* (1946). A green-eyed brunette, once voted the world's most beautiful woman, she remained a leading lady for two decades, her films including *Mogambo* (1953), *The Barefoot Contessa* (1954), and *Night of the Iguana* (1964). In later years she continued to work as a character actress in films and on television. She was married to **Mickey Rooney** (1920–), **Artie Shaw**, and **Frank Sinatra**. Her autobiography, *Ava: My Story* (1990), was published posthumously. >> Shaw, Artie; Sinatra

Gardner, Erle Stanley (1889–1970) Crime novelist, born in Malden, MA. After travelling a great deal while young, he settled in California, studied in law offices, and was admitted to the bar, where he became an ingenious lawyer for the defence (1922–38). In the 1940s he set up The Court of Last Resort, an organization to help those unjustly imprisoned. He is best known as the writer of the 'Perry Mason' books, beginning with *The Case of the Velvet Claws* (1933). His books enjoyed enhanced popularity when they were made into a long-running television series. He also wrote a series of detective novels featuring the District Attorney Doug Selby (*The DA...*).

Garfield, James A(bram) (1831–81) US statesman and 20th president (Mar–Sep 1881), born in Orange, OH. He was a farmworker, teacher, lay preacher, and lawyer, before being elected to the Ohio State Senate in 1859. He fought in the Civil War until 1863, when he entered Congress and became leader of the Republican Party. After his election as president, he identified himself with the cause of civil service reform, thereby irritating many in his own Party. He was shot at Elberon, NJ, by a disappointed office-seeker, Charles Guiteau, and died two months later. >> RR1097

Garfinkel, Harold [gah(r)fingkel] (1917–) Sociologist, born in Newark, NJ. He studied at Harvard University, then joined the department of sociology at the University of California (1954), where he remained until he retired in 1988. He is the founder of the sociological tradition of ethnomethodology, an approach to social science which focuses on the practical reasoning processes that ordinary people use in order to understand and act within the social world.

Garfunkel, Art (1942–) Singer and actor, born in Forest Hills, NY. He teamed up with Paul Simon as a teenager, forming a duo called Tom and Gerry, and (as Simon and Garfunkel) issuing their first album, *Wednesday Morning 3 am* in 1964. 'The Sound Of Silence' (1965) brought them their first major success as a duo, followed in 1968 by the soundtrack for the film *The Graduate* and the album *Bridge Over Troubled Water* (1970), which won a record six Grammies and topped both the UK and US charts. The duo split up following Garfunkel's decision to go into acting. He made his debut in *Catch 22* (1970), and later films included *Carnal Knowledge* (1971), *Bad Timing* (1979), *Good to Go* (1986), and *Boxing Helena* (1993). He continued to record as a soloist, beginning with the album, *Angel Clare* (1973), and achieved a UK number 1 with 'Bright Eyes' (1979), the theme song from the film *Watership Down*. There have been occasional reunion concerts with Simon. >> Simon, Paul

Garibaldi, Giuseppe [garibawldee] (1807–82) Italian patriot, born in Nice, France. In 1834 he joined Mazzini's 'Young Italy' movement, and was condemned to death for participating in the attempt to seize Genoa, but escaped to South America. Returning to Europe, in 1849 he joined the revolutionary government of Rome, but was again forced to leave Italy. After working in New York, he returned to Italy in 1854 and took up the life of a farmer on the island of Caprera. With the outbreak in 1859 of Italy's war of liberation, he returned to action; with his 'thousand' volunteers he sailed from Genoa (May 1860) and arrived in Sicily, where he assisted Mazzinian rebels to free Sicily from Neapolitan control. Crossing with his army to the mainland, he swiftly overran much of S Italy, and drove King Francis of Naples from his capital (Sep 1860). Thereafter he allowed the conquest of S Italy to be completed by the Sardinians under Victor Emmanuel II. With the Kingdom of Italy a reality, and refusing all personal reward, he retired into private life on Caprera. >> Mazzini; Victor Emmanuel II

Garioch, Robert [gariokh], pseudonym of **Robert Garioch Sutherland** (1909–81) Poet and translator, born in Edinburgh, EC Scotland, UK. He studied at Edinburgh University, spent most of his professional career as a teacher in Scotland and England, and became writer-in-residence at Edinburgh University (1971–3). He wrote in the Scots language, and translated into Scots a wide variety of works. His prose works included *Two Men and a Blanket* (1975), an account of his experience in prisoner-of-war camps during World War 2. >> MacLean, Sorley

Garland, (Hannibal) Hamlin (1860–1940) Writer, born in West Salem, WI. Leaving his farming family, he went to Boston to teach, and joined the literary set there. In his short stories, poetry, and novels, he vividly described the farm life of the Midwest. He is best-remembered for his 'Middle Border' autobiographical novels, starting with *A Son of the Middle Border* (1917). Its sequel, *A Daughter of the Middle Border* (1921), won the Pulitzer Prize.

Garland, Judy, originally **Frances Gumm** (1922–69) Actress and singer, born in Grand Rapids, MN. She made her first stage appearances in vaudeville with her parents, and became a juvenile film star in *Broadway Melody of 1938*, followed by *The Wizard of Oz* (1939) and *Meet Me in St Louis* (1944), directed by Vincente Minnelli, whom she later married. A demanding series of musical leads coupled with drug problems exhausted her by 1950, and she spent the next four years in variety performances, returning to films with the 1954 remake of *A Star is Born*. Concerts and occasional films continued with public success, but her private life was full of overwhelming difficulties, and she died in London, apparently from an overdose of sleeping pills. >> Minnelli, Liza; Minnelli, Vincente

Garner, Errol (Louis) (1923–77) Jazz musician, born in Pittsburgh, PA. He was an exhilarating pianist who emerged in 1946 and developed an international following as a concert performer. One of his best-known compositions is 'Misty'.

Garner, John Nance (1868–1967) US vice-president and businessman, born near Detroit, TX. During his two terms (1933–41) as vice-president under Franklin D Roosevelt, he became alarmed at the increase in the executive powers, and unsuccessfully opposed Roosevelt's renomination in 1940. >> Roosevelt, Franklin D

Garnerin, André Jacques [gah(r)neri] (1769–1823) Aeronaut, born in Paris. A former balloon inspector in the French army, he gave the first public demonstration of a descent by parachute from a free-flying balloon at Paris in 1797, and thereafter made exhibition jumps in many countries including one of 8000 ft in England in 1802. He was assisted in making improvements to the design of his parachutes by his brother, **Jean Baptiste Olivier** (1766–1849).

Garnett, David (1892–1981) Novelist, born in Brighton, East Sussex, SE England, UK. He studied botany at the Royal College of Science, and after World War 1 started a bookshop in Soho, and became associated with the

Bloomsbury Group. His first book, *Lady into Fox* (1922), was highly acclaimed, and followed by *A Man in the Zoo* (1924), *The Grasshoppers Come* (1931), and *Aspects of Love* (1955), which was adapted as a musical after his death by Andrew Lloyd Webber. >> Moore G E

Garnett, Tony (1936–) Television and film producer, born in Birmingham, West Midlands, C England, UK. After studying psychology at London University he became an actor, then joined the BBC Drama Department in 1964 as a script editor, working on the 'Wednesday Play' series. As a producer he has tackled a variety of political topics and social ills, and enjoyed a long association with director Kenneth Loach on such influential television and film work as *Cathy Come Home* (1966) and *Kes* (1969). He made his directorial debut with *Prostitute* (1980). Now resident in Los Angeles, he has directed *Handgun* (1982), and returned to production on Roland Joffé's *Fat Man and Little Boy* (1989). >> Loach

Garnier, Francis [gah(r)nyay], originally **Marie Joseph François Garnier** (1839–73) Explorer, born in St Etienne, France. As a naval officer, he fought in the Chinese war (1860–2). Appointed to a post in Cochin-China (S Vietnam), he was second-in-command of the Mekong R Expedition (1866–8) during which he mapped 3100 mi of unknown territory in Cambodia and Yunnan. He aided in the defence of Paris (1870–1), and in the Tonkin War (1873) took Hanoi, but was killed in a further battle to retain it.

Garnier, Robert [gah(r)nyay] (c. 1545–90) Poet and playwright, born in La Ferté Bernard, France. He studied law at Toulouse and practised at the Paris bar before returning to his home region. He was the most distinguished of the predecessors of Corneille. His *Oeuvres complètes* (2 vols) include eight acclaimed tragedies, of which perhaps the best are *Antigone* (1580) and *Les Juives* (1583). >> Corneille

Garnier, Tony [gah(r)nyay], popular name of **Antoine Garnier** (1869–1948) Architect, born in Lyon, France. He studied at the Ecole des Beaux Arts in Paris. As architect of Lyon he made a major contribution to the forming of 20th-c architectural and urban planning through his utopian ideal, *Une Cité Industrielle*, exhibited in 1904 and published in 1917. He pioneered sophisticated reinforced concrete buildings at Lyon, including the Grange Blanche hospital (1911–27) and the Stadium (1913–18).

Garofalo, Benvenuto do [garofaloh], also called **Benvenuto Tisi** or **Tisio** (1481–1559) Painter, the last and foremost artist of the Ferrarese school, born in Ferrara, Italy. He worked chiefly in the churches and palaces of his native city, in Bologna, and in Rome. The church of San Lorenzo, Ferrara, contains his 'Adoration of the Magi', and his 'Sacrifice to Ceres' is in the National Gallery, London.

Garrett, Elizabeth >> **Anderson, Elizabeth Garrett**
Garrett, João >> **Almeida-Garrett, João**
Garrett, Pat, popular name of **Patrick Floyd Garrett** (1850–1908) Lawman, born in Chambers Co, AL. From the age of 17 he led the life of a cowboy and buffalo hunter, eventually settling in Lincoln Co, NM. He became sheriff of the town, and is remembered for tracking down and killing the escaped murderer, Billy the Kid. >> Bonney

Garrett, Peter (Robert) (1953–) Popular singer and political activist, born in Sydney, New South Wales, Australia. He studied at the Australian National University and the University of New South Wales, and became a lawyer. Since 1977 he has been lead singer with the band Midnight Oil, which has achieved considerable fame in Australia and abroad, many of their songs dealing with issues such as Aboriginal land rights, conservation, and prison reform. He became widely known in 1985 when he stood for parliament, narrowly missing out on becoming a senator for the Nuclear Disarmament Party. He was also president of the

Australian Conservation Foundation (1989–93), a job he combined with that of a rock-and-roll star.

Garrick, David (1717–79) Actor, theatre manager, and playwright, born in Hereford, Hereford and Worcester, WC England, UK. His first play was performed at Drury Lane in 1740, and the following year he won acting fame as Richard III. For 30 years he dominated the English stage, in a wide range of parts. As joint manager of Drury Lane (1747–76) he encouraged innovations in scenery and lighting design. >> Colman, George (the Elder); Loutherbourg; More, Hannah

Garrison, William Lloyd (1805–79) Abolitionist, born in Newburyport, MA. Educated informally, he emerged in 1830 as the foremost anti-slavery voice in the USA. His newspaper *The Liberator* argued the case for immediate abolition, and his American Anti-Slavery Society mobilized the energies of thousands of people in the cause. >> Grimke sisters

Garrod, Sir Archibald (Edward) (1857–1936) Physician, born in London, England, UK. He studied at Oxford, where he went on to hold a chair of medicine (1920–7). His classical study of four inherited human metabolic diseases, described in his *Inborn Errors of Metabolism* (1909), was far ahead of its time: he both showed that Mendelian genetics applied to humans, and correctly proposed a connection between an altered gene (a mutation) and a blocked metabolic pathway causing a specific disease. This concept, basic to biochemical genetics, was strangely neglected for 30 years.

Garrod, Dorothy (Annie Elizabeth) (1892–1968) Archaeologist, born in London, England, UK. She studied at Cambridge, directed expeditions to Kurdistan (1928) and Palestine (1929–34), and took part in the excavations in the Lebanon (1958–64). An expert on the Palaeolithic or Old Stone Age, she became the first woman to hold a professorial chair at Cambridge in 1939.

Garstin, Sir William Edmund (1849–1925) Engineer, born in India. He studied at King's College, London, and became an official in the Indian Public Works Department (1872). Transferred to Egypt in 1885, he was responsible for the plans and building of the Aswan Dam and the barrages of Asyut and Esna. He compiled two valuable reports on the hydrography of the Upper Nile, initiated the geological survey of Egypt (1896), and erected the new buildings of the National Museum of Egyptian Antiquities (1902).

Gascoigne, George [gaskoyn] (c. 1525–77) Poet and playwright, born in Cardington, Bedfordshire, SC England, UK. He studied at Cambridge, entered Gray's Inn, wrote poems, and sat in parliament (1557–9), but was disinherited for his extravagance. He served in Holland (1573–5) under the Prince of Orange, but was taken prisoner and detained for four months. He then settled in Walthamstow, where he collected and published his poems, and translated from Greek, Latin, and Italian. He wrote *Certayne Notes of Instruction on Making of Verse* (1575), which is the first English essay on the subject.

Gascoigne, Paul [gaskoyn], nickname **Gazza** (1967–) Footballer, born in Gateshead, Tyne and Wear, NE England, UK. He was an apprentice footballer with Newcastle United before turning professional in 1985. After Tottenham Hotspur signed him in 1988, he established himself as an outstanding player and a flamboyant personality, becoming a member of the England team, and had won 48 caps by the end of 1996. His goal scoring success helped Tottenham reach the 1991 FA Cup Final against Nottingham Forest. During the game he sustained a serious knee injury which seemed to threaten his agreed transfer deal to a top Italian club, Lazio, for a record £5 million fee. After a long recovery he moved to Lazio in time for the 1992–3 season, where he continued to be a controversial figure on and off the field. He received a further serious leg injury in 1994, and moved to Rangers from Lazio in 1995. >> RR1157

Gaskell, Mrs Elizabeth (Cleghorn), *née* **Stevenson** (1810–65) Writer, born in London, England, UK. In 1832 she married **William Gaskell** (1805–84), a Unitarian minister in Manchester. She did not begin to write until middle age, when she published *Mary Barton* (1848). Her other works include *Cranford* (1853), *Ruth* (1853), *North and South* (1854–5), *Wives and Daughters* (1865), and a biography of Charlotte Brontë.

Gasperi, Alcide de [gas**pay**ree] (1881–1954) Italian statesman and prime minister (1945–53), born in Trentino, Italy. He studied at Innsbruck and Vienna, entered parliament in 1911, and was imprisoned by Mussolini as an anti-facist (1927). From 1929 he worked in the Vatican library until he became prime minister of the new republic, heading a succession of coalition cabinets. A founder of the Christian Democratic Party, he was also a strong believer in a United Europe. >> Mussolini; RR1065

Gass, William H(oward) (1924–) Novelist, born in Fargo, ND. After studying at Ohio, Wesleyan, Delaware, and Cornell universities, he became a philosopher and literary critic, as well as a novelist. A stylistic experimenter, he was criticized for neglecting characterization, punctuation, and plot, but nevertheless won acclaim for his first novel *Omensetter's Luck* (1966), his novella *Willie Masters' Lonesome Wife* (1968), and his collection of short stories *In the Heart of the Heart of the Country* (1968). The collected essays, *Finding a Form*, appeared in 1996.

Gassendi, Pierre [gasādee] (1592–1655) Philosopher and scientist, born in Champtercier, France. Ordained priest (1616), he became professor of philosophy at Aix (1617) and professor of mathematics at the Collège Royal in Paris (1645). He was a strong advocate of the experimental approach to science, and tried to reconcile an atomic theory of matter (based on the Epicurean model) with Christian doctrine. He is best known for his *Objections* (1642) to Descartes' *Meditations*, but he also wrote on others, including Copernicus. His works include *Institutio astronomica* (1647) and the *Syntagma philosophicum* (Philosophical Treatise), published posthumously in 1658. >> Copernicus; Descartes

Gasser, Herbert (Spencer) (1888–1963) Physiologist, born in Platteville, WI. He became professor of pharmacology at Washington University, St Louis, in 1916, and of physiology at Cornell in 1931. From 1935 he was Director of the Rockefeller Institute for Medical Research. With Joseph Erlanger he made possible the electronic measurement of nerve impulses, and they shared the 1944 Nobel Prize for Physiology or Medicine for their joint work on nerve fibres and nerve impulse transmission. >> Erlanger

Gassette, José Ortega y >> **Ortega y Gassett, José**

Gates, Bill, popular name of **William Henry Gates** (1955–) Computer engineer and entrepreneur, born in Seattle, WA. At age 15 he constructed a device to control traffic patterns in Seattle, and in 1975 co-wrote a compiler for BASIC and interested the MITS company in it. He dropped out of Harvard in 1975 to spend his time writing programmes. In 1977, he co-founded Microsoft to develop and produce DOS, his basic operating system for computers. When in 1981 International Business Machines (IBM) adopted DOS for its line of personal computers, his company took a giant step forward; by 1983 he had licensed DOS to more than 100 vendors, making it the dominant operating system. By age 35 he had become one of the wealthiest men in America.

Gates, Horatio (1728–1806) US general, born in Maldon, Essex, SE England, UK. He joined the British army, served in America in the Seven Years War (1756–63), and then settled there. In the War of Independence he sided with his adoptive country, and in 1777 took command of the Northern department, compelling the surrender of the British army at Saratoga, NY. In 1780, he commanded the Army of the South, but was routed by Cornwallis near Camden, SC, and was superseded. He retired to Virginia until 1790, emancipated his slaves, and settled in New York City. >> Cornwallis; Tarleton

Gatling, Richard Jordan (1818–1903) Inventor, born in Maney's Neck, NC. He assisted his father in the construction of cotton-sowing machines, then studied medicine, but never practised. During the American Civil War he turned to the development of firearms, and is best remembered for his invention of the rapid-fire *Gatling gun* (1861–2), a crank-operated revolving multibarrel machine gun. His weapon came to public notice again in 1991, when it was used as the principal weapon platform on US A10 aircraft during the Gulf War.

Gatting, Michael William, known as **Mike Gatting** (1957–) Cricketer, born in Kingsbury, NW Greater London, England, UK. He made his mark as a forceful batsman with Middlesex, becoming captain in 1983. As England captain (1986–8), he was involved in a dispute with a Pakistan umpire during the 1987–8 tour, and lost the captaincy in 1988. He led a 'rebel' tour in South Africa in 1989–90, for which he received a 3-year Test ban, but returned to Test cricket in 1992. By 1997 he had played in 79 Tests, scoring 4409 runs.

Gatty, Harold (Charles) (1903–57) Aviator and writer, born in Campbell Town, Tasmania, Australia. He trained for a naval career but went to California in 1927. His interest in navigation led him to open a laboratory which made and repaired instruments, and prepared maps. He devised a ground-speed-and-drift indicator which still forms the basis of the automatic pilots used in modern aircraft. He flew as navigator on several record-breaking flights (1929–31), served with the US and Australian forces in the Pacific during World War 2, and published *The Raft Book* (1943) on star navigation, which became standard equipment in all US army and air force life-rafts. After the war he settled in Fiji and founded Fiji Airways. His best-selling book *Nature is your Guide* was published shortly after his death.

Gatty, Margaret >> **Ewing, Juliana Horatia**

Gaudí (I Cornet), Antonio [gow**dee**] (1852–1926) Architect, born in Riudoms, Spain. He studied at the School of Architecture in Barcelona, and became the most famous exponent of Catalan 'modernisme', one of the branches of the Art Nouveau movement. He is best known for the extravagant and ornate church of the Holy Family in Barcelona, which occupied him from 1884 until his death.

Gaudier-Brzeska, Henri [**gohd**yay **bres**ka] (1891–1915) Sculptor, born in St Jean de Braye, France. He lived in London from 1911, and exhibited with the London Group in 1914 before joining the French army. He was killed in action at Neuville-Saint-Vaast. A pioneering Modernist who drew upon African tribal art, he rapidly developed a highly personal abstract style exemplified in carvings and drawings.

Gaudron, Mary [**god**ron] (1943–) Judge, born in Moree, New South Wales, Australia. She studied at St Ursula's College, Armidale, and Sydney University, and became a lawyer. In 1974 she was the youngest ever federal judge when appointed deputy-president of the Arbitration Commission, and in 1981 was the youngest ever NSW solicitor general. Seen as a progressive, in 1987 she became the first woman to be appointed to the High Court of Australia.

Gauguin, (Eugène Henri) Paul [gohgï] (1848–1903) Post-impressionist painter, born in Paris. He went to sea at 17, settled in Paris in 1871, married, and became a successful stockbroker who painted as a hobby. By 1876 he had begun to exhibit his own work. He left his family, visited Martinque (1887), and became the leader of a group of painters at Pont Aven, Brittany (1888). From 1891 he lived mainly in Tahiti and the Marquesas Is, using local people as his subjects. He gradually evolved his own style, *Synthétisme*, reflecting his hatred of civilization and the inspiration he found in primitive peoples. Among his best-known works are 'The Vision After the Sermon' (1888, Edinburgh), and the major allegorical work 'D'où venons-nous? Que sommes-nous? Où allons-nous?' (1897–8, Where Do We Come From? What Are We? Where Are We Going?, Boston). He also excelled in wood carvings of pagan idols.

Gaulle, Charles de >> **de Gaulle, Charles**

Gaultier, Jean-Paul [gohtyay] (1952–   ) Fashion designer, born in Paris. At the age of eighteen he was designing for the Pierre Cardin fashion house, then joined the couture houses of Jacques Esterel and Jean Patou before producing his own independent collection in 1976. Among his well-known designs were the pointed corsets worn by Madonna during her 1990 Blonde Ambition World Tour. He reached a new audience as co-host of the magazine show *Eurotrash* on British television. >> **Madonna**

Gaumont, Léon Ernest [gohmõ], Eng [**goh**mont] (1864–1946) Cinema inventor, manufacturer, and producer, born in Paris. He synchronized a projected film with a phonograph in 1901, and was responsible for the first talking pictures, demonstrated at Paris in 1910. He also introduced an early form of coloured cinematography in 1912.

Gaunt, John of >> **John of Gaunt**

Gauss, (Johann) Carl Friedrich [gows] (1777–1855) Mathematician, born in Brunswick, Germany. A prodigy in mental calculation, he conceived most of his mathematical theories by the age of 17, and was sent to study at Brunswick and Göttingen. He wrote the first modern book on number theory, in which he proved the law of quadratic reciprocity, and discovered the intrinsic differential geometry of surfaces. He also discovered, but did not publish, a theory of elliptic and complex functions, and pioneered the application of mathematics to such areas as gravitation, magnetism, and electricity. In 1807 he became professor of mathematics and director of the observatory at Göttingen, and in 1821 was appointed to conduct the trigonometrical survey of Hanover, for which he invented a heliograph. The unit of magnetic induction has been named after him. >> **Weber, Wilhelm Eduard**

Gautama or **Gotoma** [goh̄tama] (c. 563–c. 483 BC) Philosopher, born in Bihar, India. The founder of *Nyaya*, one of the six classical systems of Hindu philosophy, his *Nyaya Sutras* are principally concerned with ways of knowing and of reaching valid logical conclusions. Their claim that one can obtain real knowledge of the external world was disputed by Sriharsha and the *Navya-nyaya* school founded by Gangesa. >> **Gangesa**

Gautier, Théophile [gohtyay] (1811–72) Writer and critic, born in Tarbes, France. From painting he turned to literature, and became an extreme Romantic. In 1830 he published his first long poem, 'Albertus', and his celebrated novel *Mademoiselle de Maupin* appeared in 1835. His most important collection was *Emaux et camées* (1852, Enamels and Cameos).

Gavaskar, Sunil (Manohar) [ga̱vaskah(r)] (1949–   ) Cricketer, born in Mumbai (Bombay), India. He played 125 Test matches for India, scoring a record 10 122 runs, and between 1974–5 and 1986–7 played in a record 106 consecutive Test matches. He scored 25 834 runs in first-class cricket at an average of 51·46 per innings. His highest innings was 236 not out against the West Indies in Madras in 1983–4, the highest score made by an Indian batsman in Test cricket. >> RR1149

Gaveston, Piers de >> **Edward II**

Gay, John (1685–1732) Poet and playwright, born in Barnstaple, Devon, SW England, UK. He was apprenticed to a London silk mercer, but turned to literature, writing poems, pamphlets, and in 1727 the first series of his popular satirical *Fables*. His greatest success was *The Beggar's Opera* (1728), which achieved an unprecedented theatrical run of 62 performances. He was a friend of Pope and Swift. >> **Pepusch; Pope, Alexander; Swift, Jonathan**

Gaye, Marvin (1939–84) Soul singer, born in Washington, DC. He started singing and playing the organ in church, and at 15 joined The Rainbows, signing a recording contract with the Tamla/Motown company in 1961. Most of his early recordings were in the beat ballad idiom. The classic 'I Heard It Through the Grapevine' (1968) was his last Motown recording, and he then adopted a more independent attitude, notably with 'What's Going On' (1971). Later albums include *Here My Dear* (1979), *In Our Lifetime* (1981), and *Midnight Love* (1982). He was killed by a gunshot during a quarrel with his father.

Gay-Lussac, Joseph Louis [gay luh sak] (1778–1850) Chemist and physicist, born in St Léonard, France. He studied at the Ecole Polytechnique in Paris, and became assistant to Berthollet (1801). He began a series of investigations into gases, temperature, and the behaviour of vapours. He made hydrogen-filled-balloon ascents to 7000 m/23 000 ft (1804) to study the laws of terrestrial magnetism and to collect samples of air for analysis, which led to his major discovery, the law of combining volumes of gases named after him (1808). In 1809 he became professor of chemistry at the Polytechnique in Paris, and from 1832 at the Jardin des Plantes. >> **Berthollet; Thénard**

Gazza >> **Gascoigne, Paul**

Geber [jayber] (14th-c) Spanish alchemist, who took the name of **Geber** (Latin for **Jabir**) to trade on the reputation of **Jabir ibn Hayyan**, a celebrated Arabic alchemist. Geber's principal writings are the clearest exposition of alchemical theory and of laboratory procedures produced before the 16th-c, and were widely read. They include *Liber fornacum* (1678, Book of Furnaces).

Gedda, Nicolai (1925–   ) Tenor, born in Stockholm. He studied at the Stockholm Academy, and made his operatic debut in *Le Postillon de Longjuneau* (1952) in Stockholm, which led to appearances in Paris and London. He sang most leading lyrical tenor roles in opera repertory, specializing in works by Lehár.

Geddes, Jenny [gedis] (c. 1600–c. 1660) Scottish vegetable-seller, traditionally reputed to have started the riots in St Giles' church, Edinburgh, when Laud's prayer book was introduced on Sunday, 23 July 1637. Her story appears in full detail in Phillips's continuation of Baker's *Chronicle* (1660). >> **Laud**

Geddes, Sir Patrick [gedis] (1854–1932) Biologist, sociologist, and pioneer of town planning, born in Perth, Perth and Kinross, E Scotland, UK. He studied at University College, London. A disciple of Darwin, he wrote *The Evolution of Sex* (1889) while he was professor of botany at Dundee (1889–1914). He became more interested in sociology and the development of human communities, and wrote *City Development* (1904) and *Cities in Evolution* (1915). >> **Darwin, Charles**

Geertgen Tot Sint Jans [geer chen] (c.1460–c.1490) Painter, born in Leyden, The Netherlands. Little is known about his life; his name means 'little Gerard of the Brethren of

St John', and he worked for this religious Order in Haarlem, The Netherlands. Only about 15 paintings are now attributed to him. These works, mostly fragments of larger altarpieces, and all religious in subject, are characterized by strong colours, convincing landscape and, perhaps most notably, very individual figures.

Geertz, Clifford (James) (1923–) Cultural anthropologist, born in San Francisco, CA. He studied at Antioch College and Harvard, taught at the universities of California (1958–60) and Chicago (1960–70), then became professor of social science at Princeton's Institute of Advanced Study in 1970. His fieldwork led to such publications as *The Religion of Java* (1960) and *Islam Observed* (1968). His essays, collected in *The Interpretation of Cultures* (1973) and *Local Knowledge* (1983), were particularly influential.

Gehrig, (Henry) Lou(is) [gerig], nickname **the Iron Horse** (1903–41) Baseball player, born in New York City. He played a record 2130 consecutive games for the New York Yankees (1925–39). An outstanding first-baseman, he ended his career with a batting average of ·340 and hit 493 home runs. His career was cut short by illness – amyotrophic lateral sclerosis, widely known as 'Lou Gehrig's disease' in the USA. >> RR1144

Geiger, Hans Wilhelm [giyger] (1882–1945) Physicist, born in Neustadt-an-der-Haardt, Germany. He studied at Erlangen, worked under Ernest Rutherford at Manchester (1906–12), investigated beta-ray radioactivity and, with Walther Müller, devised a counter to measure it. He was professor at Kiel (1925) and at Tübingen (1929), and later worked in Berlin. >> Müller; Rutherford, Ernest

Geisel, Ernesto [giyzl] (1908–96) Brazilian general and president (1974–9), born in Rio Grande do Sul, Brazil. His military presidency was notable for its policy of 'decompression', the gradual relaxation of political repression, with a promised return to democracy. However, after continuing economic difficulties and further repressive political measures, he did not stand for re-election in 1979. >> RR1036

Geisel, Theodor Seuss >> **Seuss, Dr**

Geissler, Heinrich [giysler] (1814–79) Inventor, born in Igelshieb, Germany. He became a glass-blower and settled in Bonn in 1854, making scientific instruments. The *Geissler tube*, by which the passage of electricity through rarefied gases can be seen, and the *Geissler mercury pump*, are among his inventions.

Geitel, Hans Friedrich >> **Elster, Julius**

Gelasius I, St [jelayshius] (?–496) Pope (492–6), African by birth. He was one of the earliest bishops of Rome to assert the supremacy of the papal chair. He repressed Pelagianism, renewed the ban against the oriental patriarch, drove out the Manichaeans from Rome, and wrote against the Eutychians and Nestorians. Feast day 21 November. >> Eutyches; Manichaeus; Nestorius; Pelagius

Geldof, Bob [geldof], popular name of **Robert Frederick Xenon Geldof** (1954–) Rock musician and philanthropist, born in Dublin. He studied at Black Rock College, worked in Canada as a pop journalist, then returned home in 1975 to form the successful rock group, the Boomtown Rats (1975–86). Moved by television pictures of widespread suffering in famine-stricken Ethiopia, he established the pop charity 'Band Aid' trust in 1984, which raised £8 million for Africa famine relief through the release of the record 'Do they know it's Christmas?'. In 1985, simultaneous 'Live Aid' charity concerts were held in London and Philadelphia which, transmitted by satellite throughout the world, raised a further £48 million. He was awarded an honorary knighthood in 1986.

Gelée >> **Claude Lorrain**

Gelfand, Izrail M(oiseyevich) (1913–) Mathematician,

born in Krasnye Okny, Moldova. He studied in Moscow, where he became professor in 1943. The leader of an important school of Soviet mathematicians, he has worked mainly in Banach algebras, the representation theory of Lie groups, which is important in quantum mechanics, and in generalized functions, used in solving the differential equations that arise in mathematical physics. >> Banach; Lie, Sophus

Gell-Mann, Murray [gelman] (1929–) Theoretical physicist, born in New York City. He studied at Yale and the Massachussets Institute of Technology, becoming professor of theoretical physics at the California Institute of Technology in 1956. At 24 he made a major contribution by introducing the concept of *strangeness* into the theory of elemental particles. This allowed new classifications and predictions, outlined by Gell-Mann and Ne'eman in their book *The Eightfold Way* (1964). He proposed the existence of sub-atomic particles, which he named *quarks*, and subsequent research brought widespread acceptance of his hypothesis. In 1994 he published *The Quark and the Jaguar*. He was awarded the Nobel Prize for Physics in 1969.

Gemayel, Amin [gemiyel] (1942–) Lebanese statesman and president (1982–8). Trained as a lawyer, he supported his brother, Bashir Gemayel, in the 1975–6 civil war, and was his successor to the presidency. Politically more moderate, his policies intially proved no more successful in determining a peaceful settlement of the problems of Lebanese government. >> Gemayel, Bashir/Pierre; RR1071

Gemayel, Bashir [gemiyel] (1947–82) Lebanese army officer and statesman, the brother of Amin Gamayel. He joined the militia of his father's Phalangist Party, and came to be the Party's political director in the Ashrefieh sector of E Beirut, where he was an active leader of the Christian militia in the civil war of 1975–6. By the systematic elimination of rivals he came to command the military forces of E Beirut. He distanced his party from Israeli support, and aimed to expel all foreign influence from Lebanese affairs. Having twice escaped assassination, he was killed in a bomb explosion while still president-elect. >> Gemayel, Amin/Pierre

Gemayel, Sheikh Pierre [gemiyel] (1905–84) Lebanese politician, a member of the Maronite Christian community of Lebanon, the father of Amin and Bashir Gamayel. He studied at Beirut and Paris, and trained as a pharmacist. In 1936 he founded the Kataeb or Phalangist Party, modelled on the Spanish and German Fascist organizations, and in 1937 became its leader. He was twice imprisoned (1937, 1943), held various ministerial posts (1960–7), and led the Phalangist militia in the 1975–6 civil war. >> Gemayel, Amin/Bashir

Gems, Pam, popular name of **Iris Pamela Gems** (1925–) Playwright, born in England, UK. After bringing up four children she turned to playwriting, and was involved with the Women's Theatre Season at the Almost Free (1975). Her first West End success came with a feminist study of four girls in a London flat: *Dusa, Fish, Stas and Vi* (1977). She is best known for her work with the Royal Shakespeare Company (RSC), most notably the musical biography of *Piaf*, starring Jane Lapotaire, which moved to the West End and New York City (1980–1). Other productions with the RSC include *Camille* (1984) and *The Danton Affair* (1986). Among later plays are *Deborah's Daughter* (1994) and *Stanley* (1995).

Geneen, Harold (Sydney) [geneen] (1910–) Accountant and industrialist, born in Bournemouth, Dorset, S England, UK. He worked as a clerk for a firm of Wall St stockbrokers (1926–32) while studying at night to obtain a degree from New York University. He became a director of International Telephone and Telegraph (ITT) in 1959, taking on the role of chairman in 1964. He stepped down as chief executive in 1977, and published his views on management in his book *Managing* (1984).

Genet, Jean [zhuhnay] (1910–86) Writer, born in Paris. In his youth he spent many years in reformatories and prisons, and began to write in 1942 while serving a life sentence for theft. His first novel, *Notre-Dame des fleurs* (1944, Our Lady of the Flowers) created a sensation for its portrayal of the criminal world. He later turned from novels to plays, such as *Les Bonnes* (1947, The Maids) and *Les Paravents* (1961, The Screens). In 1948 he was granted a pardon by the president after a petition by French intellectuals. Sartre's book *Saint Genet* (1952) widened his fame among the French intelligentsia. He wrote little in his later years. >> Sartre

Geneviève, St [zhenuhvyev] (c. 422–512) Patron saint of Paris, born in Nanterre, France. After taking the veil, she acquired an extraordinary reputation for sanctity, increased by her assurance that Attila and his Huns would not touch Paris in 451, and by her expedition for the relief of the starving city during Childeric's Frankish invasion. In 460 she built a church over the tomb of St Denis, where she herself was buried. Feast day 3 January. >> Attila

Genghis Khan [jengis kahn], also spelled **Jingis** or **Chingis Khan** ('Very Mighty Ruler'), originally **Temujin** (1162/7–1227) Mongol conqueror, born in Temujin on the R Onon. He succeeded his father at 13, and struggled for many years against hostile tribes, subjugating the Naimans, conquering Tangut, and receiving the submission of the Turkish Uigurs. In 1206 he changed his name to the one by which he is now known, and from 1211, in several campaigns, he overran the empire of N China, the Kara-Chitai empire, the empire of Kharezm, and other territories. By his death the Mongol empire stretched from the Black Sea to the Pacific.

Gennaro, San >> **Januarius, St**

Gennep, Charles-Arnold Kurr van [genep] (1873–1957) Ethnographer and folklorist, born in Württemberg, Germany, but raised in France. He worked for the French government in various cultural organizations (1903–10, 1919–21), and held brief academic appointments at Neuchâtel, Oxford, and Cambridge. He became an energetic collector and publisher of folklore materials, including the *Manuel de folklore français contemporaine* (1937–58). However he is principally known for his earlier work, *Les Rites de passage* (1909), a comparative study of rituals marking transitions of social status.

Genscher, Hans-Dietrich [gensher] (1927–) German statesman, born in Reideburg, Germany. He trained as a lawyer, studying at Leipzig before coming to the West in 1952. He became secretary-general of the Free Democratic Party (FDP) in 1959, and was minister of the interior for five years before becoming in 1974 vice-chancellor and foreign minister in Schmidt's coalition government. In the same year, he became Chairman of the FDP, a post to which he was re-elected in 1982. He retained his Cabinet post after 1982 in the coalition between the FDP and the Christian Democrats. >> Schmidt, Helmut

Genseric >> **Gaiseric**

Genth, Frederick Augustus (1820–93) Mineralogist, born in Wächtersbach, Germany. He studied at Giessen and Marburg universities, went to the USA in 1848, and became professor of chemistry and mineralogy at Pennsylvania (1872). He investigated the cobalt-ammonium compounds, and discovered 24 new minerals, one of which is named *genthite*.

Gentile, Giovanni [jenteelay] (1875–1944) Philosopher, born in Castelvetrano, Italy. He was professor of philosophy at Palmero, Pisa, and Rome, and became with Croce the leading exponent of 20th-c Italian idealism. He quarrelled with Croce's complex distinctions between the theoretical and practical categories of mind, arguing that nothing is real except the pure act of thought. He became a philosophical mouthpiece for Mussolini, and was minister of education (1922–4). He was assassinated by an anti-Fascist Communist in Florence in 1944. >> Croce; Mussolini

Gentile da Fabriano >> **Fabriano, Gentile da**

Gentileschi, Artemisia [jentileskee] (1597–c.1651) Painter, born in Rome, the daughter of Orazio Gentileschi. She lived in Naples, but visited England (1638–9) and left a self-portrait at Hampton Court. Her chief work is 'Judith and Holofernes' in the Uffizi, Florence. >> Gentileschi, Orazio

Gentileschi, Orazio [jentileskee] (1562–1647) Painter, born in Pisa, Italy. He settled in England in 1626, the first Italian painter called to England by Charles I, having been patronized by the Vatican and the Medicis in Genoa. He was responsible for the decoration of the Queen's House at Greenwich (partly transferred to Marlborough House), and painted 'The Discovery of Moses' in Madrid, 'The Flight into Egypt' in the Louvre, and 'Joseph and Potiphar's Wife' at Hampton Court. >> Gentileschi, Artemisia

Gentz, Friedrich von (1764–1832) German political writer, born in Wrocław, Poland (formerly Breslau, Germany). In 1786 he entered the public service of Prussia, but in 1802 exchanged into that of Austria. He wrote bitterly against Napoleon, became a friend and adviser to Metternich, and was secretary-general of the Congress of Vienna (1814), and of subsequent European conferences. He was the theorist and practical exponent of 'Balance of Power' in Europe. >> Metternich

Gény, François [zhaynee] (1861–1959) Legal theorist, born in Baccarat, France. He was professor of law at Nancy (1901–25). He contended that lawyers must supplement the norms derived from the codes, case-law, and doctrine by objective factors such as social data, history, and reason, so as to arrive at a decision which takes account of surrounding circumstances. His approach influenced legal thinking in many countries.

Geoffrey of Monmouth (c. 1100–54) Welsh chronicler, consecrated Bishop of St Asaph in 1152. His *Historia regum Britanniae* (History of the Kings of Britain), composed before 1147, profoundly influenced English literature, introducing the stories of King Lear and Cymbeline, the prophecies of Merlin, and the legend of Arthur in the form known today. The stories have little basis in historical fact. >> Cymbeline

Geoffroy Saint-Hilaire, Etienne [zhofrwah sīt eelair] (1772–1844) Zoologist, born in Etampes, France. He studied law, medicine, and science, became professor of zoology in the Museum of Natural History at Paris (1793), and began the great zoological collection. He was one of the scientific commission that accompanied Napoleon to Egypt (1798–1801). In 1809 he was appointed professor of zoology in the University of Paris. He endeavoured to establish the unity of plan in organic structure, and he raised teratology to a science, principally in his *Philosophie anatomique* (1818–20). >> Napoleon

George I (of Great Britain) (1660–1727) King of Great Britain and Ireland (1714–27), born in Osnabrück, Germany, the great-grandson of James I of England, and proclaimed king on the death of Queen Anne. Elector of Hanover since 1698, he had commanded the imperial forces in the Marlborough wars. He divorced his wife and cousin, the Princess Dorothea of Zell, imprisoning her in the castle of Ahlde, where she died (1726). He took relatively little part in the government of the country. His affections remained with Hanover, and he lived there as much as possible. >> Anne; Marlborough, Duke of; RR1095

George I (of Greece) (1845–1913) King of Greece (1863–1913), born in Copenhagen, the second son of King Christian IX of Denmark (reigned 1863–1906). He served in the Danish Navy. On the deposition of Otto (King of Greece, 1832–62) he was elected king in 1863 by the Greek National Assembly, and married in 1867 the Grand Duchess Olga, niece of Tsar Alexander II of Russia. His reign saw the consolidation of Greek territory in Thessaly and Epirus, and the suppression of a Cretan insurrection (1896–7). Involved in the Balkan War (1912–13), he was assassinated at Salonika, and was succeeded by his son Constantine I. >> Constantine I (of Greece); RR1054

George II (1683–1760) King of Great Britain and Ireland (1727–60), and Elector of Hanover, born at Herrenhausen, Hanover, the son of George I. In 1705 he married Caroline of Anspach (1683–1737). Though he involved himself more in the government of the country than his father had, the policy pursued during the first half of the reign was that of Walpole. In the War of the Austrian Succession, he was present at the Battle of Dettingen (1743), the last occasion on which a British sovereign commanded an army in the field. His reign also saw the crushing of Jacobite hopes at the Battle of Culloden (1746), the foundation of British India after the Battle of Plassey (1757), the beginning of the Seven Years' War, and the capture of Quebec (1759). >> George I (of Great Britain); Stuart, Charles; Walpole, Robert; RR1095

George II (of Greece) (1890–1947) King of Greece (1922–4, 1935–47), born near Athens. He first came to the throne after the second deposition of his father, Constantine I. He was himself driven out in 1924, but was restored in late 1935 after a plebiscite. When Greece was overrun by the Germans, he withdrew to Crete, then to Egypt and Britain. After a plebiscite in 1946 in favour of the monarchy, he re-ascended the Greek throne, and died in Athens. >> Constantine I (of Greece); RR1054

George III (1738–1820) King of Great Britain and Ireland (1760–1820), elector (1760–1815) and king (from 1815) of Hanover, born in London, England, UK, the eldest son of Frederick Louis, Prince of Wales (1707–51). His father predeceased him, and he thus succeeded his grandfather, George II. Eager to govern as well as reign, he caused considerable friction. With Lord North he shared in the blame for the loss of the American colonies, and popular feeling ran high against him for a time in the 1770s. In 1783 he called Pitt (the Younger) to office, which brought an end to the supremacy of the old Whig families. In 1810 he suffered a recurrence of a mental derangement, and the Prince of Wales was made regent. >> George II; North, Frederick; Pitt, William (the Younger); RR1095

George IV (1762–1830) King of Great Britain and Hanover (1820–30), born in London, England, UK, the eldest son of George III. He became prince regent in 1810, because of his father's insanity. Rebelling against a strict upbringing, he went through a marriage ceremony with Mrs Fitzherbert, a Roman Catholic, which was not recognized in English law. The marriage was later declared invalid, and 1795 he married Princess Caroline of Brunswick, whom he tried to divorce when he was king. Her death in 1821 ended a scandal in which the people sympathized with the queen. >> Caroline of Brunswick; Cooper, Astley; Fitzherbert; George III; William IV; RR1095

George V (1865–1936) King of the United Kingdom (1910–36), born in London, England, UK, the second son of Edward VII. He served in the navy, travelled in many parts of the empire, and was created Prince of Wales in 1901. He married Mary of Teck in 1893. His reign saw the Union of South Africa (1910), World War 1, the Irish Free State settlement (1922), and the General Strike (1926). >> Edward VII; Mary of Teck; RR1095

George VI (1895–1952) King of the United Kingdom (1936–52), born at Sandringham, Norfolk, E England, UK, the second son of George V. He studied at Dartmouth Naval College and Trinity College, Cambridge, and served in the Grand Fleet at the Battle of Jutland (1916). In 1920 he was created Duke of York, and married Lady Elizabeth Bowes-Lyon in 1923. An outstanding tennis player, he played at Wimbledon in the All-England championships in 1926. He ascended the throne in 1936 on the abdication of his elder brother, Edward VIII. During World War 2 he set a personal example coping with wartime restrictions, continued to reside in bomb-damaged Buckingham Palace, visited all theatres of war and delivered many broadcasts, for which he overcame a speech impediment. In 1947 he toured South Africa and substituted the title of Head of the Commonwealth for that of Emperor of India, when that subcontinent was granted independence by the Labour government. Unnoticed by the public, his health was rapidly declining, yet he persevered with his duties, his last great public occasion being the opening of the Festival of Britain in 1951. >> Edward VIII; Elizabeth (Queen Mother); George V; RR1095

George, St (early 4th-c) Patron of chivalry, and guardian saint of England and Portugal. He may have been tortured and put to death by Diocletian at Nicomedia, or he may have suffered (c.250) at Lydda in Palestine, where his alleged tomb is exhibited. His name was early obscured by fable, such as the story of his fight with a dragon to rescue a maiden. Feast day 23 April. >> Diocletian

George, Henry (1839–97) Social reformer and economist, born in Philadelphia, PA. He was probably the most influential 19th-c US social analyst, renowned for his fervent writing and magnetic speaking style. Primarily self-taught, his formal schooling ended at age 14, and he worked as a sailor, journalist, and printer before embarking on *Progress and Poverty* (1879), which he wrote while working as a state gas-meter inspector in California. His theory called for a 'single-tax' on land, exclusive of improvements, that would be sufficient to finance all government expenses. His popularity led him to run, though unsuccessfully, for Mayor of New York City in 1886.

George, Stefan [gayorguh] (1868–1933) Poet, born in Büdesheim, Germany. He studied in Paris, Munich, and Berlin, and travelled widely. In Germany he founded a literary group, and edited its journal. His poems show the influence of the French Symbolists, dispensing with punctuation and capitals, and conveying an impression rather than a simple meaning. In *Das neue Reich* (1928, The New Reich) he advocated a new German culture, not in accord with that of the Nazis. He exiled himself in 1933, and died in Switzerland.

George-Brown, Baron, originally **George (Alfred) Brown** (1914–85) British statesman, born in London, England, UK. He was an official of the Transport and General Workers' Union before becoming an MP in 1945 and minister of works (1951). As Opposition spokesman on defence (1958–61), he supported Gaitskell in opposing unilateral disarmament. Vice-chairman and deputy Leader of the Labour Party (1960–70), he unsuccessfully contested Wilson for Party leadership in 1963. As secretary of state for economic affairs (1964–6), he instigated a prices and incomes policy, and later became foreign secretary (1966–8). Having lost his seat in the 1970 election, he was created a life peer. >> Gaitskell; Wilson, Harold

Georgescu-Roegen, Nicholas [zhaw(r)zheskoo roegen] (1906–) Economist, born in Constanza, Romania. He studied at universities in Bucharest and Paris, and emigrated to the USA in 1947. He taught at Harvard for two years, then moved to Vanderbilt University, where he remained until his retirement in 1976. His early achievements were based on highly technical mathematical economics, largely in utility theory and input–output analysis, and he also wrote on production theory, the nature of expectations, agrarian economies, and the Marxist prediction of capitalist breakdown. He later explored the area of growth modelling, and formulated the principles of bioeconomics.

Gephardt, Richard Andrew [**gep**hah(r)t] (1941–) US representative, born in St Louis, MO. A lawyer and Democratic alderman in St Louis, he went to the US House of Representatives in 1977. He ran for the Democratic nomination as president in 1986, losing to Michael Dukakis, and became house majority leader in 1989. >> Dukakis

Gérard, François (Pascal Simon), Baron [zhayrah(r)] (1770–1837) Painter, born in Rome. He was brought up in Paris, and became a member of the Revolutionary Tribunal in 1793. His portrait of Isabey the miniaturist (1796) and his 'Cupid and Psyche' (1798), both in the Louvre, established his reputation. He later painted several historical subjects, such as the 'Battle of Austerlitz' (1808, Versailles). He was made court painter and baron by Louis XVIII.

Gerard, John [**je**rah(r)d] (1545–1612) Herbalist and barber-surgeon, born in Nantwich, Cheshire, NWC England, UK. His London garden became famous for its rare plants, and for 20 years (1577–98) he was superintendent of Lord Burghley's gardens. He wrote *The Herball, or General Histoire of Plantes* (1597). Containing over 1000 species, it was the first plant catalogue. >> Cecil, William

Gerardus Magnus >> **Groote, Geert de**

Gerber, (Daniel) Frank (1873–1952) Baby-food manufacturer, born in Douglas, MI. After high school he joined the family tannery at age 16, and rose to partner and manager until 1905, when the business closed. In 1901 he helped found the Fremont Canning Co to market local produce, becoming its president in 1917. The company started manufacturing baby foods in 1927 at the behest of his son, **Daniel (Frank) Gerber**, who was assistant general manager of the company and himself a new father. The Gerbers tested batches of babyfood on Daniel's daughter, Sally, and other babies. By 1941 the baby food line was outselling adult food products, and in 1943 the Gerber Products Co dropped its adult foods.

Gere, Richard [geer] (1949–) Actor, born in Philadelphia, PA. He studied at the University of Massachusetts, became a pop musician, and went on to gain extensive experience in the theatre, which included the London production of *Grease* (1972). He received acclaim for an off-Broadway appearance in *Killer's Head* (1975), then made his screen debut with a small role in *Report to the Commissioner* (1975). His major films include *Yanks* (1979), *American Gigolo* (1980), *An Officer and A Gentleman* (1982), *Pretty Woman* (1990), *First Knight* (1995), and *Primal Fear* (1996).

Gerhard, Roberto [**gair**hah(r)t] (1896–1970) Composer, born in Valls, Spain. He studied piano with Granados (1915–6), and composition with Felipe Pedrell (1916–22) and Schoenberg (1923–8). He left Barcelona to settle in England in 1939, becoming a British subject (1960). There he wrote most of his music, which was characterized by virtuosic orchestral, rhythmic, and melodic inventiveness. He composed ballets, an opera *The Duenna* (1945–7), five symphonies, concertos for violin and piano, chamber music, incidental music, and some electronic music. >> Granados; Schoenberg

Gerhardie, William Alexander [gair**hah(r)**dee] (1895–1977) Novelist, born of English parents in St Petersburg, Russia.

He was educated in St Petersburg, served in the British embassy in Petrograd (1917–18), and later with the military mission in Siberia, before going to Worcester College, Oxford. He is best-remembered for his novel *The Polyglots* (1925). Other works include his autobiography *Memoirs of a Polyglot* (1931), a biographical history of *The Romanoffs* (1940), and *God's Fifth Column, a Biography of the Age (1890–1940)*, edited, after his death, in 1981.

Gerhardt, Charles (Frédéric) [**gair**hah(r)t] (1816–56) Chemist, born in Strasbourg, France. He studied at Leipzig and Giessen, and became professor at the universities of Montpellier (1844) and Strasbourg (1855). Between 1849 and 1855 he published his views of homologous and heterologous series and the theory of types with which his name is associated, and researched into anhydrous acids and oxides.

Gerhardt, Wolfgang >> **Mengele, Josef**

Géricault, (Jean Louis André) Théodore [zhayreekoh] (1791–1824) Painter, born in Rouen, France. A pupil of Guérin, he was a great admirer of the 17th-c Flemish schools. He painted many unorthodox and realistic scenes, notably 'The Raft of the Medusa' (1819, Louvre), based on a shipwreck which had caused a sensation in France. It was harshly criticized, and he withdrew to England, where he painted racing scenes and landscapes. >> Guérin

Gerlach, Walter >> **Stern, Otto**

German, Sir Edward, originally **Edward German Jones** (1862–1936) Composer, born in Whitchurch, Shropshire, WC England, UK. He studied at the Royal Academy of Music, was made musical director of the Globe Theatre, London (1888), and became known for his incidental music to Shakespeare. He emerged as a light opera composer when he completed Sullivan's *Emerald Isle* (1901) after the composer's death. His own works include *Merrie England* (1902), *Tom Jones* (1907), several symphonies, suites, chamber music, and songs. He was knighted in 1928. >> Sullivan, Arthur

Germanicus [jer**man**ikus], in full **Gaius Germanicus Caesar** (15 BC–AD 19) The son, father, and brother of Roman emperors (Tiberius, Caligula, and Claudius respectively), and heir apparent himself from AD 14. A man of great charm but mediocre ability, his sudden and suspicious death in Antioch marked a turning point in Tiberius's reign. It crystallized the growing disenchantment with the emperor, and sent his reign on its downward spiral. >> Caligula; Claudius; Tiberius

Germanus, St [jer**mah**nus] (c. 378–448) Bishop of Auxerre. He was invited to Britain to combat Pelagianism in 429. Under him the Christian Britons won the bloodless 'Alleluia Victory' over the Picts and Saxons at Maes Garmon (*Germanus' field*) in Flintshire. Feast day 31 July. >> Pelagius

Germer, Lester (Halbert) [**ger**mer] (1896–1971) Physicist, born in Chicago, IL. He studied at Columbia University, then joined the research staff of the Western Electric Co (1917–53). He worked with Clinton Davisson on experiments that demonstrated the diffraction of electrons by crystals (1927), confirming the theories of Louis-Victor de Broglie. >> Broglie, Louis Victor; Davisson

Gérome, Jean Léon [zhayrohm] (1824–1904) Historical genre painter, born in Vesoul, France. He began to exhibit in 1847, and in 1863 became professor of painting in the Ecole des Beaux-Arts, where he taught Redon and Eakins. His 'Polytechnic Student' is in the Tate, London. A first-rate draughtsman, he achieved distinction as a sculptor and a decorative painter of anecdotal and erotic subjects. >> Eakins; Redon

Geronimo [je**ro**nimoh], Indian name **Goyathlay** (1829–1909) Chiricahua Apache Indian, born in Mexico. The best known of all Apache leaders, he forcibly resisted the internment of 4000 of his people on a reservation at San Carlos (1874), subsequently surrendering then escaping from white control on several occasions. In 1886 the local US commander promised him exile in Florida and a return to Arizona if he surrendered. The promise was not kept, and he and his followers were put to hard labour. In his old age, he became a Christian and a public figure. He dictated his autobiography, *Geronimo: His Own Story*, shortly before his death. >> Miles, Nelson

Gerry, Elbridge (1744–1814) US statesman, born in Marble-head, MA. He attended the first National Congress. Elected Governor of Massachusetts in 1810, he rearranged the electoral districts so as to secure the advantage to the Republican Party. Because the shape of one of the states resembled a salamander, his name gave rise to the term *gerrymander*. He later became vice-president of the USA (1813–14).

Gershwin, George, originally **Jacob Gershvin** (1898–1937) Composer, born in New York City. He published his first song in 1914, and had his first hit, 'Swanee', in 1919. In 1924 he began collaborating with his brother Ira as lyri-cist, producing numerous classic songs, such as 'Lady Be Good' (1924) and 'I Got Rhythm' (1930). He also composed extended concert works including *Rhapsody in Blue* (1924), *An American in Paris* (1928), and *Girl Crazy* (1930), importing jazz, blues, and pop-song devices into classical contexts. His masterpiece is generally considered to be the jazz-opera *Porgy and Bess* (1935), with such hit songs as 'Summertime' and 'It Ain't Necessarily So'. >> Gershwin, Ira

Gershwin, Ira, originally **Israel Gershvin**, pseudonym **Arthur Francis Gershwin** (1896–1983) Songwriter, born in New York City. His precocious younger brother George was the toast of Broadway, so Ira started writing lyrics under a pseudonym. In 1921, he wrote a hit show *Two Little Girls in Blue* with Vincent Youmans (1898–1946), and by 1924 his successes gave him enough confidence not only to drop the pseudonym but to work with his brother. Among their hits were 'I Got Rhythm' (1930), 'I Got Plenty o' Nothin'' (1935), and 'They Can't Take That Away From Me' (1938). His lyrics were sometimes ostentatious, as when he strung together *'s wonderful ... 's marvelous ... 's what I likes* in ''S Wonderful' (1927), but usually nicely colloquial. After his brother's death, he kept on working, and had such hits as 'My Ship' (1941 with Kurt Weill) and 'Long Ago and Far Away' (1944 with Jerome Kern). >> Gershwin, George; Kern; Weill

Gerson, Jean de [zhayrsõ], originally **Jean Charlier** (1363–1429) Theologian and mystic, born in Gerson, France. He was educated in Paris. As Chancellor of the University of Paris from 1395, he supported the proposal for putting an end to the Great Schism between Rome and Avignon by the resignation of both the contending pon-tiffs. His fortunes were marred by the animosity of the Duke of Burgundy after denouncing the murder of the Duke of Orléans. Gerson prudently retired to Germany, returning to France only after the Duke's death in 1419.

Gerstäcker, Friedrich [gersteker] (1816–72) Writer and traveller, born in Hamburg, Germany. He worked his way through the USA, South America, Polynesia, and Australia, and wrote colourful adventure stories, including *Mississippi River Pirates* (1848).

Gertrude, St (626–59) Frankish religious. The daughter of Pepin the Elder, she became abbess of the monastery at Nivelles, Brabant, on the death of her mother, and after refusing to marry Dagobert I. Feast day 17 March.

Gertrude of Helfta, known as **the Great** (1256–1302) German mystic. She entered the convent of Helfta near Eisleben at the age of five, and when 25 began to have visions which she described in Latin treatises. She was never formally canonized.

Gesell, Arnold (Lucius) [guhzel] (1880–1961) Psychologist, born in Alma, WI, the brother of Gerhard Gesell. He stud-ied at Clark and Yale universities, became Director of the Clinic of Child Development at Yale in 1911, and also taught at Yale School of Medicine (1915–48). He later acted as research consultant to the Gesell Institute of Child Development (1950–8). He devised standard scales for measuring the progress of infant development, supplement-ing his writing with extensive use of film. His books include *An Atlas of Infant Behavior* (1934) and *Child Development* (1949). >> Gesell, Gerhard

Gesell, Gerhard (Alden) [guhzel] (1910–93) Jurist, born in Los Angeles, CA, the brother of Arnold Gesell. He studied at Yale, then worked for several years as a government lawyer before joining a private Washington firm. He had been in private practice for 25 years when President Johnson appointed him a US district judge for Washington (1968). In 1971 he ruled that the *Washington Post* had a First Amendment right to publish the leaked government doc-uments known as the 'Pentagon Papers'. (In that famous case, first the *New York Times* and later *The Post* published documents that disclosed official misinformation regard-ing US policy in Vietnam.) His judgment was eventually upheld by the Supreme Court. >> Gesell, Arnold; Johnson, Lyndon B

Gesner, Conrad von (1516–65) Naturalist and physician, born in Zürich, Switzerland. He studied in Bourges, Paris, and Basel, becoming professor of Greek at Lausanne (1537) and of philosophy then of natural history at Zürich (1541). His *Bibliotheca universalis* (1545–9) contained the titles of all the books then known in Hebrew, Greek and Latin, with criticisms and summaries of each. His *Historia animalium* (1551–8) attempted to bring together all that was known in his time of every animal. He also collected over 500 plants undescribed by the ancients.

Gessner, Salomon (1730–88) Pastoral poet, who also painted and engraved landscapes, born in Zürich, Switzerland. He ran a publishing house in Zürich, publishing books he had written and illustrated himself. His *Tod Abels* (1758, Death of Abel), a type of idyllic heroic prose poem, had the greatest success. His landscape paintings are all in the conventional classic style, but his engravings are of real merit.

Gesualdo, Don Carlo, Prince of Venosa [jezualdoh] (c. 1560–1613) Composer and lutenist, born in Naples, Italy. He achieved notoriety for ordering the murder of his unfaithful wife and her lover in 1590. He wrote many sacred vocal works and published six books of madrigals, remarkable for bold homophonic progressions and telling use of dissonance.

Getty, J(ean) Paul (1892–1976) Oil billionaire and art col-lector, born in Minneapolis, MN. He studied at the University of California, Berkeley, and at Oxford, entered the oil business in his early twenties, and made a quarter of a million dollars in his first two years. His father (also a successful oil man) died in 1930, leaving him $15 million. He merged his father's interests with his own, and went on to acquire and control more than 100 companies, becom-ing one of the world's richest men. His personal wealth was estimated in 1968 at over one billion dollars, and he acquired a huge and extremely valuable art collection. Known for his eccentricity, he was married and divorced five times, and developed a legendary reputation for miserliness, installing a pay-telephone for guests in his English mansion.

Getz, Stan(ley) (1927–91) Jazz saxophonist, born in Phila-delphia, PA. He studied for a year at the Juilliard School,

New York City, then quit to concentrate on jazz. He worked under Stan Kenton, Benny Goodman, and Woody Herman before setting up his own groups, and developing a distinctive 'cool' sound. He lived in Scandinavia for several years, then returned to the USA, where in the 1960s he popularized a bossa-nova style. >> Goodman, Benny; Herman; Kenton

Geulincx or **Geulingx, Arnold** [goelingks], pseudonym **Philaretus** (1624–69) Philosopher, born in Antwerp, Belgium. He taught at the Catholic University of Louvain, but was expelled for his anti-scholasticism in 1658. He then converted to Calvinism, and became professor of philosophy at Leyden in 1665. He was a leading exponent of Descartes' philosophy, and is best known for his doctrine of 'Occasionalism': God himself 'occasions' every mental or physical process, while body and mind operate separately, without causal interaction, like two clocks which are perfectly synchronized. His main works are *Quaestiones quodlibeticae* (1653, Miscellaneous Questions), re-edited by him as *Saturnalia* (1665), *Logica restituta* (1662), and *De virtute* (1665). >> Descartes

Geyl, Pieter [gayl] (1887–1966) Historian and patriot, born in Dordrecht, The Netherlands. He studied at The Hague, at Leyden, and in Italy, then served as London correspondent of the *Nieuwe Rotterdamsche Courant* (1913–19). He was appointed the first professor of Dutch studies at London University (1919–36) and professor of modern history at Utrecht (1936–58). During World War 2, he was imprisoned in Buchenwald (1940–1), then interned in The Netherlands until 1944. His works include *Geschiedenis van der Nederlandse Stam* (1930–37, History of the Dutch People).

Ghazali, Abu Hamid Mohammed al- [gazahlee] (1058–1111) Islamic philosopher, theologian, and jurist, born in Tus, Iran (near modern Meshed). He was appointed professor of philosophy at Nizamiyah College, Baghdad (1091–5), where he exercised great academic and political influence, but later suffered a spiritual crisis which caused him to abandon his position for the ascetic life of a mendicant *sufi* (mystic), spending his time in meditation and spiritual exercises. After a brief return to teaching he retired to Tus to found a monastic community. He was a prolific author, best known for the monumental *The Revival of the Religious Sciences* (trans title).

Gheorgiu-Dej, Gheorghe [gyaw(r)gyoo dezh] (1901–65) Romanian prime minister (1952–5) and president (1961–5), born in Bîrlad, Romania. He joined the Romanian Communist Party (RCP) in 1930, and was imprisoned in 1933 for his role in the Grivita railway strike. On his release in 1944 he became secretary-general of the RCP and minister of communications (1944–6), and was instrumental in establishing a Communist regime. He then served in a variety of economic posts (1946–52) and as prime minister, before becoming state president. Although retaining the support of Moscow, he adopted increasingly independent policies during the 1960s.

Ghiberti, Lorenzo [geebairtee] (1378–1455) Goldsmith, bronze-caster, and sculptor, born in Florence, Italy. In 1401 he won the competition to make a pair of bronze gates for the Baptistry of Florence Cathedral. When these were completed (1424), he worked on a further pair of gates, which were finished in 1452.

Ghirardelli, Domingo [zhiradelee], originally **Domenico** (1817–94) Chocolate manufacturer, born in Rapallo, Italy, the son of a leading chocolatier. In 1837 he travelled to South America, where he established a chocolate trade, eventually settling in Lima, Peru, and then moved on to San Francisco, where he supplied the 1849 gold rush miners with chocolate. He founded his chocolate company in

the city, building it up into one of the largest stores in the W USA. Ghirardelli Square is now a feature of the San Francisco tourist scene, the old store being one of the buildings to survive the 1906 earthquake.

Ghirlandaio, Domenico [geerlandahyoh], originally **Domenico di Tommaso Bigordi** (1449–94) Painter, born in Florence, Italy. He was apprenticed to a goldsmith, a metal garland-maker or *ghirlandaio*. His main works were frescoes, in his native city, notably a series illustrating the lives of the Virgin and the Baptist in the choir of Santa Maria Novella (1490).

Ghose, Aurobindo >> Aurobindo, Sri

Giacometti, Alberto [jiakometee] (1901–66) Sculptor and painter, born in Stampa, Switzerland. He studied at Geneva and worked mainly in Paris, at first under Bourdelle. He joined the Surrealists in 1930, producing many abstract constructions of a symbolic kind, arriving finally at the characteristic 'thin man' bronzes, long spidery statuettes, such as 'Pointing Man' (1947, Tate, London). >> Bourdelle

Giaever, Ivar [jayver] (1929–) Physicist, born in Bergen, Norway. He studied at the Norwegian Institute of Technology, Trondheim, then emigrated to Canada in 1954. After moving in 1956 to the General Electric Research and Development Center in Schenectady, NY, he did research which led to a greater understanding of superconductivity, applying results developed by Leo Esaki. He shared the 1973 Nobel Prize for Physics. >> Esaki; RR1122

Giambologna >> Bologna, Giovanni da

Giannini, Amadeo Peter [jianeenee] (1870–1949) Banker, born in San Jose, CA. The son of immigrant Italian farmers, he entered the produce business in San Francisco, and in 1904 with several partners founded the San Francisco-based Bank of Italy. By 1920 the bank had become one of California's largest, and in 1928 it was organized under the name *Bank of America*. During the Depression era, he received criticism for excessive holdings of California farm mortgages and for encouraging the exploitation of migrant farm workers. He retired in 1934, but continued to head the bank's holding company, Transamerica Corp. In 1927 he donated $1.5 million to the University of California to establish the Giannini Foundation of Agricultural Economics; after his death, much of his fortune went to a foundation for medical research.

Giap, Vo Nguyen [gyap] (1912–) Vietnamese military leader, born in Quang Binh Province. He studied law at Hanoi University, joined the Vietnamese Communist Party, and trained in China. He led the Viet Minh army in revolt against the French, leading to the decisive defeat of their garrison at Dien Bien Phu in 1954. As vice-premier and defence minister of North Vietnam, he masterminded the military strategy that forced the US forces to leave South Vietnam (1973) and led to the reunification of Vietnam in 1975. He was a member of the Politburo from 1976 to 1982.

Giauque, William (Francis) [jeeohk] (1895–1982) Chemist, born in Niagara Falls, Ontario, Canada. He studied at the University of California, Berkeley, becoming professor there in 1934. In 1929 he took part in the discovery of the existence of isotopes of oxygen. Most of his work was devoted to studying matter at temperatures very close to absolute zero (-273·15°C), and he developed a method for the production of extremely low temperatures. He was awarded the Nobel Prize for Chemistry in 1949.

Gibb, Sir Alexander (1872–1958) Civil engineer, born near Dundee, E Scotland, UK. He was in the fifth generation of a family very involved in civil engineering since the 18th-c. He joined the firm of Easton Gibb & Son in 1900, worked on the construction of Rosyth naval dockyard (1909–16), then after five years in government posts set up in practice as a consulting engineer. His firm became one of the world's largest, their work at home and abroad including hydro-electric schemes, bridges, docks, and harbours.

Gibbon, Edward (1737–94) Historian, born in Putney, Surrey, SE England, UK. He studied at Oxford, became a Catholic at 16, and was sent to Lausanne, where he boarded with a Calvinist pastor who wooed him back to Protestantism. After a visit to Rome in 1764 he began to plan for his major work, *The History of the Decline and Fall of the Roman Empire* (5 vols, 1776–88). Left money by his father, he settled in London for the task (1772), in 1774 entering parliament, and becoming commissioner of trade and plantations. After completing his *History*, he spent much of the rest of his life with Lord Sheffield, who published his *Miscellaneous Works* (1796).

Gibbon, Lewis Grassic, pseudonym of **James Leslie Mitchell** (1901–35) Writer, born in Auchterless, Aberdeenshire, NE Scotland, UK. Educated at Stonehaven Academy, he worked as a journalist in Aberdeen, and served in the RAF until 1929. He published the historical novels *Three Go Back* (1932) and *Spartacus* (1933) under his own name, but the three novels *Sunset Song* (1932), *Cloud Howe* (1933), and *Grey Granite* (1934), which form the trilogy *A Scots Quair* appeared under his pseudonym.

Gibbons, Grinling (1648–1721) Sculptor and woodcarver, born in Rotterdam, The Netherlands. He moved to England, UK, where he was appointed by Charles II to the Board of Works, and employed in the chapel at Windsor and in St Paul's London. At Chatsworth, Burghley, and other mansions he executed an immense quantity of carved fruit and flowers, cherubs' heads, and other typical Baroque embellishment.

Gibbons, James (1834–1921) Roman Catholic clergyman, born in Baltimore, MD. He became archbishop of that city in 1877, and a cardinal in 1886. He was largely responsible for the growth of the Roman Catholic Church in the USA. He wrote *The Faith of Our Fathers* (1876), *Our Christian Heritage* (1889), and many other books.

Gibbons, Orlando (1583–1625) Composer, born in Oxford, Oxfordshire, SC England, UK. He studied at Cambridge, and c.1615 was appointed organist of the Chapel Royal, London, and in 1623 of Westminster Abbey. His compositions include services, anthems, and madrigals (notably *The Silver Swan*), and also hymns, fantasies for viols, and music for virginals.

Gibbons, Stella (Dorothea) (1902–89) Writer, born in London, England, UK. She worked as a journalist, and later began a series of successful novels, as well as writing poetry and short stories. Her *Cold Comfort Farm* (1932), a light-hearted satire on melodramatic rural novels, has established itself as a classic of parody.

Gibbs, James (1682–1754) Architect, born in Aberdeen, NE Scotland, UK. He studied under Carlo Fontana, in Italy. A friend and disciple of Wren, he became in 1713 one of the commissioners for building new churches in London. HIs designs included St Mary-le-Strand (1717) and St Martin-in-the-Fields (1726), the latter being perhaps his most influential and attractive work. He was also responsible for St Bartholomew's Hospital (1730). His *Book of Architecture* (1728) helped to spread the Palladian style, and influenced the design of many churches of the colonial period in America. >> Fontana, Carlo; Wren, Christopher

Gibbs, J(osiah) Willard (1839–1903) Mathematician and physicist, born in New Haven, CT. He studied at Yale, becoming the recipient of the first doctorate in engineering awarded in the USA. After studying in Europe for a few years, he returned to Yale in 1869, becoming professor there in 1871. He contributed to the study of thermodynamics; and his most important work, first published as the paper 'On the Equilibrium of Heterogeneous Substances' (1876), established him as a founder of physical chemistry.

Gibbs, William Francis (1886–1967) Naval architect, born in Philadelphia, PA. He studied at Harvard and Columbia, where he graduated in law, but soon changed to naval architecture, where his designs placed great emphasis on safety in the event of collision. In partnership with his brother Frederick he designed and built yachts, luxury liners, and (from 1933) US naval vessels and the 'Liberty Ships' of World War 2. His most famous design was the 53 330 ton *United States*, which regained the Blue Riband of the North Atlantic for the USA in 1952.

Gibbs-Smith, Charles Harvard (1909–81) Aeronautical historian, born in Teddington, Gloucestershire, SWC England, UK. He studied at Harvard, returning to England as instructor in aircraft recognition at the ministry of information during World War 2, where he developed a keen interest in the history of aeronautics. He wrote the definitive *Aviation – an Historical Survey From its Origins to the End of World War 2* (1960) for the Science Museum, where he took up a research fellowship in 1976. He was appointed as the Smithsonian Institution's first Lindbergh professor of aerospace history at the Aerospace Museum, Washington, DC, in 1978.

Gibson, Sir Alexander Drummond (1926–) Conductor, born in Motherwell, North Lanarkshire, C Scotland, UK. He studied at Glasgow University and the Royal College of Music in London. He became principal conductor and artistic director of the Scottish National Orchestra (1959), helped to form Scottish Opera (1962), and as its artistic director was responsible for many notable successes, such as the first complete performance of Berlioz's *Les Troyens* in 1969.

Gibson, Althea (1927–) Tennis player, born in Silver City, SC. She was the first African-American player to achieve success at the highest levels of the game, winning the French and Italian singles championships in 1956, and the British and US titles in 1957 and 1958. She turned professional in 1959, and won the professional singles title in 1960. >> RR1174

Gibson, Charles (Dana) (1867–1944) Illustrator and cartoonist, born in Roxbury, MA. A brilliant black-and-white artist, he drew society cartoons for such periodicals as *Life*, *Scribner's*, *Century*, and *Harper's*. In his celebrated 'Gibson Girl' drawings, he created the idealized prototype of the beautiful, well-bred, American woman.

Gibson, Edmund (1669–1748) Church jurist, born in Bampton, Cumbria, NW England, UK. He studied at Oxford, and became Bishop of Lincoln (1716), then of London (1720). He edited the *Anglo-Saxon Chronicle* and translated Camden's *Britannia*, but he is best known for his great *Codex iuris ecclesiastici Anglicani* (1713, Codex of English Church Law). His aim was to reconcile the clergy and universities to the Hanoverian dynasty.

Gibson, Guy (Penrose) (1918–44) British airman. As a wing-commander in the RAF he led the famous 'dambusters' raid on the Möhne and Eder dams in 1943, for which he received the VC. He was killed during a later operation.

Gibson, James (Jerome) (1904–79) Psychologist, born in McConnelsville, OH. He studied at Princeton and Edinburgh universities, and taught psychology at Smith College (1928–49) and at Cornell (1949–72). During World War 2 he served as director of the Research Unit in Aviation Psychology for the US air force. His influential theory of vision, described in *The Perception of the Visual World* (1950), viewed perception as the direct detection of invariances in the world, requiring neither inference nor the processing of information.

Gibson, John (1790–1866) Sculptor, born in Gyffin, Gwynedd, NW Wales, UK. Apprenticed to a monumental mason, he found a patron in William Roscoe (1753–1831). He went to Rome in 1817, studied under Canova, and lived there permanently. His best works are 'Psyche borne by Zephyrs', 'Hylas surprised by Nymphs', and 'Venus with the Turtle'. The controversial innovation of tinting his figures (eg his Venus) he defended by reference to Greek precedents. >> Canova

Gibson, Josh, nickname **Black Babe Ruth** (1911–47) Baseball player, born in Buena Vista, GA. A legendary hitter, he was barred from major-league baseball because he was an African-American, and could play only in the Negro National League. Playing for the Pittsburgh Homestead Grays and the Pittsburgh Crawfords, it is estimated that he hit more than 950 home runs in his career. In 1972 he was elected to the National Baseball Hall of Fame.

Gibson, Mel, originally **Columcille Gerard Gibson** (1956–) Film actor, born in Peekskill, NY. In 1968 his family emigrated to Australia, where he trained as an actor at the National Institute of Dramatic Art in Sydney, making his film debut in 1977. He made several stage appearances before his film debut in *Summer City* (1977), and became an international star following his leading role in the trio of action-packed *Mad Max* films (1979, 1981, 1985) and the highly successful *Lethal Weapon* series (1987, 1989, 1991). He displayed different facets of his talent in *Tequila Sunrise* (1988) and *Forever Young* (1992), and gave a well-received interpretation of *Hamlet* (1990). He directed and starred in *Braveheart* (1995, Oscar Best Film, Golden Globe). Later films include *Ransom* (1996) and *Conspiracy Theory* (1997).

Gibson, Mike, popular name of **(Cameron) Michael (Henderson) Gibson** (1942–) Rugby union player, born in Belfast. He played as centre and outside half with the North of Ireland, Cambridge University, and the British Lions, appearing a world record 69 times for his country (the most for any International Board nation). He toured with the British Lions in 1966, 1968, and 1971, and made 12 international appearances. He is now a Belfast solicitor.

Gibson, Richard (1615–90) Painter of miniatures. He was a page to Charles I and Henrietta Maria, and the king gave away the bride when he married **Anne Shepherd** (1620–1709), like himself only 1·15 m/3 ft 10 in tall. He later made several portraits of Cromwell and was himself painted by Lely. >> Lely

Gibson, Robert (1935–) Baseball player, born in Omaha, NE. A noted pitcher with the St Louis Cardinals, with whom he started in 1959, he was twice named best pitcher in the National League, and in 1968 became Most Valuable Player in the League on the strength of his exceptionally low earned-run average of 1·12. He set a World Series record of strike-outs against the Detroit Tigers in 1968. >> RR1145

Gide, André (Paul Guillaume) [zheed] (1869–1951) Writer, born in Paris. He was author of over 50 volumes of fiction, poetry, plays, criticism, biography, belles lettres, and translations. Among his best-known works are *Les Nourritures terrestres* (1897, Fruits of the Earth) and *Les Faux Monnayeurs* (1926, The Counterfeiters), his translations of *Oedipus* and *Hamlet*, and his *Journal*. He received the Nobel Prize for Literature in 1947.

Gideon Greatest of the judges of Israel, the son of Joash. He suppressed Baal-worship, and put an end to the seven years' domination of the Midianites by routing them near Mt Gilboa.

Gielgud, Sir (Arthur) John [geelgud] (1904–) Actor and director, born in London, England, UK. Educated in London, he made his debut in 1921 at the Old Vic Theatre, and established a reputation as Hamlet (1929) and in *The Good Companions* (1931). He became a leading Shakespearian actor, directing several of the Shakespeare Memorial Theatre productions. His many film appearances include his role as Disraeli in *The Prime Minister* (1940), *Arthur* (1970, Oscar), and *Prospero's Books* (1991). He was knighted in 1953, and received a special Laurence Olivier Award for his services to the theatre in 1985. His books include an autobiography, *An Actor in his Time* (1979), *Backward Glances* (1989), and *Notes from the Gods* (1994). The London *Globe* theatre was renamed after him in 1994. >> Gielgud, Maina

Gielgud, Maina [geelgud] (1945–) Dancer, artistic director, and teacher, born in London, England, UK, the niece of actor Sir John Gielgud. She studied with many distinguished teachers prior to her 1961 debut with Roland Petit's company, and later danced with Ballet of the 20th Century (1967–71) and the London Festival Ballet (1972–5). She became artistic director of the Australian Ballet (1983–96) and then director of the Royal Danish Ballet. >> Gielgud, John; Petit, Roland

Gierek, Edward [geerek] (1913–) Polish statesman, born in Porabka, Poland. He lived in France (1923–34) during the Pilsudski dictatorship, and joined the French Communist Party in 1931. He was deported to Poland in 1934, and lived in Belgium (1937–48), becoming a member of the Belgian resistance. On his return to Poland in 1948, he joined the ruling Polish United Workers' Party (PUWP), being inducted into its Politburo in 1956 and appointed party boss of Silesia. He became PUWP leader in 1970, when Gomulka resigned after strikes and riots in Gdansk, Gdynia, and Szczecin. Head of the Party's 'technocrat faction', he embarked on an ambitious industrialization programme. This plunged the country heavily into debt and, following a wave of strikes in Warsaw and Gdansk, spearheaded by the 'Solidarity' free trade union movement, he was forced to resign in 1980, and was expelled from the Party in 1981. >> Gomulka; Pilsudski

Gieseking, Walter (Wilhelm) [geezuhking] (1895–1956) Pianist, born of German parents in Lyon, France. He studied in Hanover and made his first public appearance in 1915. After World War 1 he established an international reputation, especially in the works of Debussy and Ravel.

Giffard, Henri [zhifah(r)] (1825–82) Engineer and inventor, born in Paris. He studied at the Collège Bourbon and the Ecole Centrale. In 1852 he built a light 3 hp steam engine, fitted it with an 3·3 m/11 ft propeller, and succeeded in piloting a coal-gas balloon, steered by a rudder, over a distance of 17 mi. This can be considered as the first powered and controlled flight ever achieved, in a craft which was a primitive example of the dirigible or semi-rigid airship. In 1858 he patented a steam injector which became widely used in locomotives and other types of steam engine, and made him a fortune. He continued with his aeronautical experiments, and left his money to the state for humanitarian and scientific purposes.

Gifford, William (1756–1826) Editor and critic, born in Ashburton, Devon, SW England, UK. Orphaned at 12, he secured education at Oxford through patronage. His early works, the *Baviad* (1794), and the *Maeviad* (1796), were satirical attacks against writers who had had an easier start in life. Gifford's editorship of the *Anti-Jacobin* (1797–8) gained him favour with Tory magnates, and he was the first editor of the *Quarterly Review* (1809–24). He possessed much satirical acerbity, but little merit as a poet, and as a critic was unduly biased.

Giggs, Ryan (1973–) Footballer, born in Cardiff. He made his league debut for Manchester United in 1991, and first played for Wales later that year, becoming the youngest-ever Welsh cap. Twice named the Professional Football

Association's Young Player of the Year (1991–2), his honours with Manchester United include the FA Premiership (1993, 1994, 1996, 1997), the FA Cup (1994, 1996), and the Rumbelows (League) Cup (1992).

Gigli, Beniamino [jeelyee] (1890–1957) Tenor, born in Recanati, Italy. He won a scholarship to the Liceo Musicale, Rome, and made his operatic debut in Ponchielli's *La gioconda* in 1914. By 1929 he had won a worldwide reputation as a lyric-dramatic tenor of great vitality, at his best in the works of Verdi and Puccini.

Gilbert, Sir Alfred (1854–1934) Sculptor and goldsmith, born in London, England, UK. He studied in France and Italy, and executed work of remarkable simplicity and grace, including his statue of 'Eros' in Piccadilly Circus, London, and 'Comedy and Tragedy' (1892). He later became professor at the Royal Academy (1900–9).

Gilbert, Cass (1859–1934) Architect, born in Zanesville, OH. He studied at the Massachusetts Institute of Technology. He designed the first tower skyscraper, the 60-storey Woolworth Building in New York City (1912), at that time the tallest building in the world. He also designed the US Customs House in New York City (1907), the Supreme Court Building in Washington, DC (1935), and the campuses of the universities of Minnesota (Minneapolis) and Texas (Austin).

Gilbert, Grove (Karl) (1843–1918) Geologist, born in Rochester, NY. He became chief geologist of the US geological survey (1889), and formulated many of the laws of geological processes. His report on the Henry Mts became the foundation of many modern theories of denudation and river-development. He also published a history of the Niagara R, and introduced such technical terms as *laccolith* and *hanging valley*.

Gilbert, Sir Henry >> **Lawes, Sir John Bennet**

Gilbert, Sir Humphrey (c. 1539–83) English navigator, the half-brother of Sir Walter Raleigh. He served in Ireland (1566–70), and was made Governor of Munster. He then campaigned in Holland (1570–5), and in 1578 led an unsuccessful colonizing expedition to the New World. In a second attempt in 1583 he landed in Newfoundland, taking possession of it for the crown, and established a colony at St John's. >> **Raleigh, Walter**

Gilbert, Sir John (1817–97) Painter and illustrator, born in London, England, UK. Mainly self-taught, he began to exhibit in oil and watercolour in 1836. Known as 'the Scott of painting' he is remembered for his illustrations of Shakespeare, Scott, Cervantes, and other authors, and for his woodcut illustrations in the *Illustrated London News*.

Gilbert, Walter (1932–) Molecular biologist, born in Boston, MA. He studied physics and mathematics at Harvard and Cambridge, then taught physics at Harvard from 1959, before moving to biophysics and from there to molecular biology. He became professor of biophysics at Harvard in 1968. He developed an elegant method for finding the sequence of bases in nucleic acids, for which he shared the 1980 Nobel Prize for Chemistry. >> **RR1123**

Gilbert, William (1544–1603) Physician and physicist, born in Colchester, Essex, SE England, UK. After a period at Cambridge, he was appointed physician to Elizabeth I. He established the magnetic nature of the Earth, and conjectured that terrestrial magnetism and electricity were two allied emanations of a single force. He was the first to use the terms *electricity*, *electric force*, and *electric attraction*. His book, *De magnete* (1600, On the Magnet) is the first major English book in science.

Gilbert, Sir W(illiam) S(chwenck) (1836–1911) Parodist, and librettist of the 'Gilbert and Sullivan' light operas, born in London, England, UK. He studied at London, became a clerk in the privy-council office (1857–62), and

was called to the bar (1864). Failing to attract lucrative briefs, he subsisted on magazine contributions to *Fun*, for which he wrote much humorous verse under his boyhood nickname 'Bab', collected in 1869 as the *Bab Ballads*. He also wrote fairy comedies and serious plays in blank verse. He is remembered for his partnership with Sir Arthur Sullivan, begun in 1871, with whom he wrote 14 popular operas, from *Trial by Jury* (1875) to *The Gondoliers* (1889). The partnership was broken by a quarrel, and on its resolution they wrote little more before Sullivan's death in 1900. He was knighted in 1907. >> **Sullivan, Arthur**

Gilbert and George Avant-garde artists: **Gilbert Proesch** (1943–) and **George Passmore** (1944–). Gilbert studied at the Academy of Art in Munich, George at Dartington Hall and at the Oxford School of Art. They made their name in the late 1960s as performance artists (the 'singing sculptures'), with faces and hands painted gold, holding their poses for hours at a time. More recently they have concentrated on photopieces, assembled from a number of separately framed photographs which key together to make a single whole.

Gilbert of Sempringham, St (c. 1083–1189) Priest, the founder of the Gilbertine Order, born in Sempringham, Lincolnshire, EC England, UK. In 1148 he founded an order of monks and nuns, and lay sisters and brothers. The only mediaeval religious order founded in England, it did not spread beyond England and Scotland, and was dissolved at the Reformation. He was canonized in 1202; feast day 4 February.

Gilbey, Sir Walter (1831–1914) Wine merchant, born in Bishop's Stortford, Hertfordshire, SE England, UK. He was founder of a well-known wine company, a horse-breeder, and an agriculturist.

Gilbreth and Gilbreth Efficiency experts: **Frank (Bunker) Gilbreth** (1868–1924) and **Lillian (Evelyn) Gilbreth**, *née* **Moller** (1878–1972), born in Fairfield, ME, and Oakland, CA, respectively. He began work as an apprentice bricklayer in 1885, and from that time devoted himself to developing time-and-motion studies of industrial processes as a means of increasing efficiency. She was a teacher and psychologist until they married in 1904. Together they laid the foundations of modern scientific management, collaborating on several books and many articles, and serving as consultants to numerous firms in the USA and abroad. She wrote four books on her own, and was a pioneer in making the environment easier for the physically handicapped. They had 12 children, two of whom wrote the popular book and film *Cheaper by the Dozen* (1949–50), recording how the Gilbreths applied efficiency methods at home.

Gilchrist, Ellen [gilkrist] (1935–) Writer, born in Vicksburg, MI. She studied at Vanderbilt University, Millsap College (Jackson, MI), and the University of Arkansas. She has written poetry, short stories, and novels, and is known especially for her satirical treatment of the upper-class world of the southern states of the USA. Her novels include *The Annunciation* (1983), *I Cannot Get You Close Enough* (1990), and *Net of Jewels* (1993).

Gilchrist, Percy Carlyle [gilkrist] (1851–1935) Metallurgist, born in Lyme Regis, Dorset, S England, UK. Educated at the Royal School of Mines, he developed, with his cousin **Sydney Gilchrist Thomas** (1850–85), a new process for smelting iron ore, which removed phosphorus-containing impurities. The *Gilchrist–Thomas process* doubled the potential steel production of the world by making possible the use of the large European phosphoric iron ore fields.

Gildas, St (c. 493–570) Historian and monk, born in the Strathclyde area of Scotland, UK. He lived mostly in Wales, where he became a monk after the death of his wife. He is the writer of *De excidio et conquestu Britanniae* (The Overthrow and Conquest of Britain), probably written between 516 and 547, the only extant history of the Celts, and the only contemporary British version of events from the invasion of the Romans to his own time. Feast day 29 January.

Giles, St, Lat **Aegidius** (?–c. 700) Athenian hermit. According to legend he went to France and built a hermitage, where he was discovered by a Frankish king who was so impressed with his holiness that he built a monastery on the spot (St Gilles) and made him its abbot. He is the patron of lepers, beggars, and cripples. Feast day 1 September.

Giles, Bill, popular name of **William George Giles** (1939–) British weatherman, the head of the Weather Centre at the BBC since 1983. He studied at Bristol College of Science and Technology, joining the Meteorological Office in 1959. He became a radio broadcaster in 1972, and moved to television in 1975. His books include *Weather Observations* (1978) and *The Story of Weather* (1990).

Giles, Carl [jiylz] (1916–95) Cartoonist, born in London, England, UK. He trained as an animator and worked for the film-maker Alexander Korda in 1935. From 1937 he produced his distinctive and popular humorous drawings, first for *Reynolds News*, then (from 1943) for the *Express* newspapers, celebrating the down-to-earth reactions of ordinary British people to great events. >> Korda

Giles, H(erbert) A(llen) (1845–1935) Scholar and linguist, born in Oxford, Oxfordshire, SC England, UK. After a career in the diplomatic service in China (1867–92), he returned to Britain and succeeded Sir Thomas Wade as professor of Chinese at Cambridge University (1897–1932). He modified the romanization system of his predecessor and used it in his *Chinese–English Dictionary* (1892), establishing it as the preferred transliteration system in English-speaking countries until the introduction of pinyin in 1979. >> Wade, Thomas

Giles, William (Ernest Powell) (1835–97) Explorer, born in Bristol, SW England, UK. He was educated at Christ's Hospital, London, emigrated to Australia in 1850, and worked in the Victoria goldfields. Sponsored by Sir Ferdinand Müller, he began to search the outback for good grazing land, discovering L Amadeus (1872) and the Gibson Desert (1874), named after a companion who died there. His journey from Port Augusta to Perth and back (1875–6) is described in his *Australia Twice Traversed* (1889).

Gill, Sir David (1843–1914) Astronomer, born in Aberdeen, NE Scotland, UK. He studied at Aberdeen, and became astronomer at the Cape Observatory (1879–1907). He is noted for his measurements of the distances of the Sun and stars from the Earth, and pioneered the use of photography for charting the heavens.

Gill, (Arthur) Eric (Rowton) [gil] (1882–1940) Carver, engraver, and typographer, born in Brighton, East Sussex, SE England, UK. He trained as an architect, but then took up letter-cutting, masonry, and engraving. After his first exhibition (1911) he maintained a steady output of carvings in stone and wood, engravings, and type designs. Among his main works is 'Prospero and Ariel' (1931) above the entrance to Broadcasting House, London.

Gillars, Mildred, originally **Mildred Elizabeth Sisk** (1901–88) Axis propagandist, born in Portland, ME. She went to Europe in the 1920s, changed her name, and by 1934 was an English-language radio broadcaster in Berlin. During World War 2 she broadcast Nazi propaganda aimed at demoralizing US troops, who nicknamed her 'Axis Sally'. Convicted of treason, she spent 12 years in jail. She was a teacher in later years.

Gillespie, Dizzy [gilespee], popular name of **John Birks**

Gillespie (1917–93) Jazz trumpeter and composer, born in Cheraw, SC. He worked in prominent swing bands (1937–44), including those of Benny Carter and Charlie Barnet. As a band leader, often with Charlie Parker on saxophone, he developed the music known as *bebop*, with dissonant harmonies and polyrythms, a reaction to swing. His own big band (1946–50) was his masterpiece, affording him scope as both soloist and showman. He was immediately recognizable from the unusual shape of his trumpet, with the bell tilted upwards at an angle of 45° – the result of someone accidentally sitting on it in 1953, but to good effect, for when he played it afterwards he discovered that the new shape improved the sound quality, and he had it incorporated into all his trumpets thereafter. His memoirs *To Be or Not to Bop* (with Al Fraser) appeared in 1979. >> Parker, Charlie

Gillett, Frederick Hunting [jilet] (1851–1935) US representative and senator, born in Westfield, MA. He studied at Amherst College and Harvard University, and began practising law in Springfield, MA, in 1877. An assistant state attorney general and state senator, he served as a Republican in the US House of Representatives (1893–1925), where he championed the freedman's civil rights and denounced Tammany Hall's election practices. Elected speaker of the House (1919–25), he won praise for his impartiality from Democrats and Republicans, and he reluctantly gave up the position to run for the US Senate (1925–35) where he supported the World Court.

Gillette, King C(amp) [jilet] (1855–1932) Inventor of the safety razor, born in Fond du Lac, WI. Brought up in Chicago, he became a travelling salesman for a hardware company, before founding his razor blade company in 1903. Later he wrote a series of books on industrial welfare and social reform.

Gillette, William [jilet] (1855–1937) Actor and playwright, born in Hartford, CT. Best known for his authoritative, striking presence in plays that he had himself adapted from other works, he made an extremely successful Sherlock Holmes in 1899, later performing the role in England, and frequently reviving it throughout his life. His original plays include two successful Civil War dramas, *Held by the Enemy* (1866) and *Secret Service* (1896).

Gilliam, Terry [gilyam] (1940–) Artist and film director, born in Minneapolis, MI. Originally known for his fantasy animations in the television series 'Monty Python's Flying Circus' (1969–74), he went on work in film, directing such imaginative adventures as *Jabberwocky* (1977), *The Time Bandits* (1980), *The Adventures of Baron Munchausen* (1988), *The Fisher King* (1991), and *Twelve Monkeys* (1995).

Gilliéron, Jules [zheelyayrõ] (1854–1926) Linguist, born in Neuveville, Switzerland. He studied at the Ecole des Hautes Etudes in Paris, and was professor of Romance dialectology there from 1883 until his death. His dialect atlas, *Atlas linguistiques de la France* (1902–12), provided a basic model for further studies in linguistic geography.

Gillies, Sir Harold (Delf) [gileez] (1882–1960) Plastic surgeon, born in Dunedin, New Zealand. He studied at Wanganui College and Cambridge. In 1920 he published his *Plastic Surgery of the Face*, which established this subject as a recognized branch of medicine. During World War 2 he was responsible for setting up plastic surgery units throughout the country, and was personally in charge of the largest one at Park Prewett Hospital, Basingstoke. In 1957 he published *The Principles and Art of Plastic Surgery*, the standard work on this subject.

Gillies, Sir William George [gileez] (1898–1973) Artist, born in Haddington, East Lothian, E Scotland, UK. He studied at the Edinburgh College of Art, in Italy, and in France. His finely organized interpretations of Scottish landscape (many in watercolour) are well known, and his work is represented in the Tate Gallery. He later became principal of Edinburgh College of Art (1961-6).

Gillray, James [gilray] (1757-1815) Caricaturist, born in London, England, UK. A letter engraver by training, from c.1779 he turned to caricature. He issued about 1500 caricatures of political and social subjects, notably of Napoleon, George III, and leading politicians.

Gilman, Charlotte Anna Perkins, *née* **Perkins**, earlier married name **Stetson** (1860-1935) Feminist and writer, born in Hartford, CT. She studied at Rhode Island School of Design, then moved to California, where she published her first stories. She lectured on women's issues, as well as wider social concerns, and in 1898 wrote *Women and Economics*, now recognized as a feminist landmark. In 1902 she married her cousin **George Gilman**, a New York lawyer. She founded, edited, and wrote for the journal *Forerunner* in 1909. She commited suicide on being told that she was suffering from incurable cancer.

Gilman, Harold (1878-1919) Artist, born in Rode, Somerset, SW England, UK. He studied at the Slade School of Art, London, and in Spain, became associated with the Camden Town Group (1910), and was later the first president of the London Group. Influenced by Pissarro and Van Gogh, he used Fauve colouring to paint interiors and portraits, as in his 'Mrs Mounter' in the Tate Gallery, London. >> Pissarro; Sickert; Van Gogh

Gilmore, Dame Mary Jane (1865-1962) Poet and writer, born near Goulburn, New South Wales, Australia. In 1896 she joined William Lane's Utopian 'New Australia' settlement in Paraguay, South America, but returned when the venture failed. She became the editor of the women's columns in the Sydney *Worker* newspaper for 23 years, and published several books of verse that were socially radical in tone, including *Marri'd and Other Verses* (1910) and *The Wild Swan* (1930). She was created a dame in 1937.

Gilmour, John Scott Lennox (1906-86) Botanist, born in London, England, UK. He was director of the Royal Horticultural Society Gardens, Wisley (1946-51), and director of the Cambridge University Botanic Garden (1951-73). His name has been given to the *Gilmourian* concept of multiple classifications.

Gilpin, Bernard, known as **the Apostle of the North** (1517-83) Clergyman, born in Kentmere Hall, Cumbria, NW England, UK. He studied at Oxford, Louvain, and Paris, and became archdeacon of Durham in 1556. A strong supporter of royal supremacy in the English Church, he defended himself against accusations of heresy, and on Elizabeth I's succession in 1558 was appointed rector of Houghton le Spring. He turned down many offers of promotion, preferring to minister to his parish and to make preaching excursions into the remotest parts of N England, which gave him his byname.

Gilpin, John (1930-) Dancer, born in Southsea, Hampshire, S England, UK. A child actor, he studied at the Rambert School, joining Ballet Rambert in 1945. In 1949 he was a principal with Petit's Ballets de Paris, returning to Britain in 1950 to join the London Festival Ballet, where he became artistic director (1962-5), later returning to dancing and teaching. >> Petit, Roland; Rambert

Gilpin, William (1724-1804) Clergyman, writer, and artist, born in Carlisle, Cumbria, NW England, UK. He studied at Oxford, and in 1777 became vicar of Boldre in Hampshire. A leader of the 18th-c cult of the picturesque, he was the author of works on the scenery of Britain, illustrated by his own aquatint engravings. He is satirized by Combe in *Dr Syntax*. His brother **Sawrey** (1733-1807) was a highly successful animal painter, especially of horses. >> Combe

Gilruth, Robert (Rowe) (1913-) Aeronautical engineer, born in Nashwauk, MN. He studied at the University of Minnesota. In 1958 he was appointed head of the NASA programme which put the first American, John Glenn, into Earth orbit in 1962, and the first men on the Moon in 1969. >> Armstrong, Neil; Glenn, John

Gilson, Etienne (Henry) [zheelsö] (1884-1978) Philosopher and historian, born in Paris. He studied at the Sorbonne, and became professor there (1921-32) and at the Collège de France (1932-51). He was founder of the Pontifical Institute of Mediaeval Studies at Toronto University (1929), and divided his academic year between the two institutions until 1951, thereafter concentrating on Toronto until 1968. He is known especially for his works on mediaeval Christian philosophy.

Gil Vicente >> **Vicente, Gil**

Gimson, Ernest William (1864-1919) Designer, born in Leicester, Leicestershire, C England, UK. He was for a while an architect, and planned a number of buildings around Leicester, but he is best known as a furniture designer specializing in the use of untreated native timbers.

Ginckell or **Ginkel, Godert de** [**ging**kel] (1630-1703) Dutch general, born in Utrecht, The Netherlands. He accompanied William III to England in 1688, and fought at the Battle of the Boyne (1690). As commander-in-chief in Ireland, he defeated the remaining rebels, and was created Earl of Athlone (1692). He later led the Dutch troops under Marlborough. >> Marlborough; William III

Ginola, David [zhinola] (1967-) Footballer, born in Gassin, near St Tropez, France. He played for Paris St Germain, moving to the UK to join Newcastle in 1995, then Tottenham Hotspur in 1997. He had won 15 caps for France, and in 1994 was voted French Footballer of the Year, but he lost his place in the national team after France failed to qualify in the 1994 World Cup.

Ginsberg, Allen (1926-97) Poet of the 'beat' movement, born in Newark, NJ. He studied at Columbia University, where he became friendly with Jack Kerouac, William Burroughs, and others of the movement. *Howl* (1956), his epic poem, was a significant success, and launched him on a high profile career as a public speaker against authoritarianism. Other collections include *Kaddish and Other Poems* (1961), *Reality Sandwiches* (1963), and *Poems All Over The Place: Mostly Seventies* (1978). >> Burroughs, William S; Kerouac

Gioberti, Vicenzo [jiobairtee] (1801-52) Philosopher and statesman, born in Turin, Italy. He was ordained in 1825 and became chaplain to the court of Sardinia, but fell from favour through his radical republican views. He was in exile from 1833, and from Brussels published works advocating a united Italy under the pope. He returned to Italy in 1848 and became premier of Sardinia-Piedmont (1848-9), then ambassador to France. His philosophy centred on the concept of being, and is usually described as *ontologism*.

Giolitti, Giovanni [jioleetee] (1842-1928) Italian statesman and prime minister (1892-3, 1903-5, 1906-9, 1911-14, 1920-1), born in Mondovi, Italy. He studied law at the University of Turin, and entered the civil service in 1860. He became a deputy in the Italian parliament (1882), and was five times prime minister. He introduced universal suffrage and tried unsuccessfully to keep Italy neutral during World War 1. After the war, he introduced vast schemes of social reform. >> RR1065

Giordano, Luca [jiaw(r)dahnoh], known as **Fa Presto** ('Make Haste') (1634-1705) Painter, born in Naples, Italy. He was able to work with extreme rapidity, hence his nickname, and to imitate the great masters. In 1692 he went to Madrid, at the request of Charles II of Spain, to embellish the Escorial.

Giordano, Umberto [jiaw(r)**dah**noh] (1867–1948) Operatic composer, born in Foggia, Italy. He composed several operas, and is best remembered for *Andrea Chenier* (1896) and *Fedora* (1898).

Giorgio, Francesco di >> **Francesco di Giorgio**

Giorgione [jiaw(r)ji**oh**nay], also called **Giorgio da Castelfranco**, originally **Giorgio Barbarelli** (c. 1478–1510) Painter, born in Castelfranco, Italy. He studied under Giovanni Bellini in Venice, where he painted frescoes, though few have survived. A great innovator, he created the small, intimate easel picture and a new treatment of figures in landscape, 'the landscape of mood'. Among the paintings reliably attributed to him are 'The Tempest' (c.1505, Venice) and 'The Sleeping Venus' (c.1510, Dresden). >> Bellini, Giovanni; Titian

Giotto (di Bondone) [ji**o**toh] (c. 1266–1337) Painter and architect, the founder of the Florentine School of painting, born near Vespignano, Italy. His major work was the fresco cycle, 'The Lives of Christ and the Virgin', in the Arena Chapel Padua (1305–8). In 1330–3 he was employed by King Robert in Naples, and in 1334 was appointed Master of Works of the cathedral and city of Florence, where amongst other works he designed the campanile.

Giovanni da Fiesole >> **Angelico, Fra**

Giovanni di Paolo [jioh**vah**nee di **pow**loh], also known as **Giovanni dal Poggio** (c.1403–c.1483) Painter, born in Siena, Italy. Though little is known of his life, many documented works by him have survived, dating from 1426 to c.1475. Like his contemporary Sassetta, he worked in a style which was essentially archaizing, continuing the tradition of Sienese Trecento masters rather than looking to new developments elsewhere. >> Sassetta

Giovanni di Steffano >> **Lanfranco, Giovanni**

Gipps, Sir George (1791–1847) Colonial administrator, born in Ringwould, Kent, SE England, UK. He served in the Royal Engineers before becoming Governor of New South Wales (1838–46). His policy of selling land by auction instead of the colonial office policy of a fixed price showed him to be an unpopular but farsighted opponent of land monopoly. *Gippsland* in Victoria is named after him.

Giraldi, Giambattista [ji**ral**dee], also called **Cynthius** (1504–73) Writer, born in Ferrara, Italy. He was professor of natural philosophy at Florence, and later held the chair of rhetoric at Pavia. He is the author of nine plays in imitation of Seneca, of which *Orbecche* (1541) is regarded as the first modern tragedy on Classical lines to be performed in Italy. His *Ecatommiti* (1565) is a collection of tales which was translated into French and Spanish, and which gave Shakespeare his plots for *Measure for Measure* and *Othello*. >> Seneca (the Younger); Shakespeare, William

Giraldus Cambrensis [ji**ral**dus kam**bren**sis], also known as **Gerald of Wales** or **Gerald de Barri** (c. 1147–1223) Historian and clergyman, born in Manorbier Castle, Carmarthenshire, SW Wales, UK. He was elected Bishop of St David's in 1176, but when Henry II refused to confirm his election, he withdrew to lecture at Paris. Later appointed a royal chaplain, in 1185 he accompanied Prince John to Ireland. He wrote an account of Ireland's natural history and inhabitants, following this with *Expugnatio Hibernica* (c.1189, History of the Conquest of Ireland). In 1188 he travelled through Wales to recruit soldiers for the Third Crusade, and wrote up his observations in the *Itinerarium Cambriae* (1191, Itinerary of Wales).

Girard, Stephen [je**rah**(r)d] (1750–1831) Businessman and philanthropist, born near Bordeaux, France. He went from cabin boy to fleet owner and banker, and settled in Philadelphia in 1769. During the war of 1812 his bank provided most of the finance needed by the US government. He left most of his fortune for social welfare projects, including the Girard College in Philadelphia for male orphans.

Girardon, François [zhirah(r)dõ] (1630–1715) Sculptor, born in Troyes, France. He studied in Rome, and after 1650 settled in Paris and joined the Le Brun group. He worked on decorative sculpture in Louis XIV's galleries, gardens, and palaces, mostly at Versailles, where he is noted for the fountain figures. He also designed the tomb of Richelieu in the Sorbonne. >> Le Brun; Richelieu

Giraud, Henri Honoré [zheeroh] (1879–1949) French soldier, born in Paris. He trained at St Cyr, served in Morocco, and was captured by the Germans during World War 1. After the war he rose to become chief-of-staff of the Moroccan Division. In early 1940 he commanded in turn the French 7th and 9th armies, again suffering capture and internment by the Germans. Escaping his captors in 1942, he was taken to North Africa, where he became commander of the Free French forces. He was co-president of the French Committee of National Liberation (1943–4) with General de Gaulle, and vice-president of the Supreme War Council after the war. >> de Gaulle

Giraudoux, (Hippolyte) Jean [zheerohdoo] (1882–1944) Writer and diplomat, born in Bellac, France. He joined the diplomatic service and was for a time head of the French ministry of information during World War 2. He is chiefly remembered for his plays, mainly fantasies based on Greek myths and biblical lore, satirically treated as commentary on modern life. They include *La Guerre de Troie n'aura pas lieu* (1935, trans Tiger at the Gates), *Ondine* (1939), and *La Folle de Chaillot* (1945, The Mad Woman of Chaillot).

Girtin, Thomas [**ger**tin] (1775–1802) Landscape painter, born in London, England, UK. His landscapes included many on subjects in the N of England and also in France, which he visited in 1802. His works were among the first to exploit water-colour as a true medium, as distinct from a tint for colouring drawings. >> Turner, J M W

Giscard d'Estaing, Valéry [zheeskah(r) daystĩ] (1926–) French statesman and president (1974–81), born in Koblenz, Germany. He was educated in Paris, and worked for the Resistance during World War 2, after which he entered the Ministry of Finance as a civil servant. In 1955 he became an assistant director of the cabinet, finance minister (1962–6), and launched his own Party (National Federation of Independent Republicans). He returned to the finance ministry in 1969, defeated Mitterrand to become president, and was then beaten by Mitterrand in 1981. >> Mitterrand; RR1049

Gish, Lillian, originally **Lillian de Guiche** (1893–1993) Actress, born in Springfield, OH. She started in silent films as an extra under D W Griffith in 1912, and became the girl heroine in all his classics from *The Birth of a Nation* (1915) and *Intolerance* (1916) to *Orphans of the Storm* (1922). After the coming of sound films, she lost interest in the cinema, but continued on the stage, occasionally returning to film and television in character roles, even in the 1970s. >> Griffith, D W

Gissing, George (Robert) (1857–1903) Novelist, born in Wakefield, West Yorkshire, N England, UK. He studied at Manchester, was expelled from the university, travelled to the USA, and returned to work as a tutor in London. *Workers in the Dawn* (1880) was the first of over 20 novels largely presenting realistic portraits of poverty and misery, such as *Born in Exile* (1892) and *The Odd Women* (1893). His best-known novel is *New Grub Street* (1891), a bitter study of corruption in the literary world. *The Diary of George Gissing, Novelist* appeared in 1982.

Gist, George >> **Sequoia**

Giuffre, Jimmy [**joo**free], popular name of **James Peter Giuffre** (1921–) Jazz musician and composer, born in

Dallas, TX. He played clarinet and saxophones with various bands during the 1940s, then for over a decade specialized in the clarinet, developing a distinctive breathy tone. He formed groups of various sizes, early albums including *Ad Lib* (1959), *Jimmy Giuffre With Strings* (1960), and *Free Fall* (1962). He later worked also as a composer, his compositions including several chamber and ballet pieces, and became active in music education.

Giugiaro, Giorgio [jiujahroh] (1938–) Automobile and industrial designer, born in Cuneo, Italy. After working in the 1960s for the bodywork designers Bertone and Ghia, he established his own firm, Ital Design, in 1969. His designs have been for the popular car market, such as the first Volkswagen 'Golf' (1974) and the Fiat 'Panda' (1980) and 'Uno' (1983). Since the late 1970s Ital has extended its scope to product design including cameras for Nikon, sewing machines for Necchi, and watches for Seiko.

Giulio Romano [joolioh romahnoh], originally **Giulio Pippi de' Giannuzzi** (c. 1499–1546) Painter and architect, born in Rome. He assisted Raphael in the execution of several of his later works, and in 1524 went to Mantua, where he drained the marshes and protected the city from floods. He also restored and adorned the Palazzo del Te, the cathedral, and a ducal palace. >> Raphael

Giuseppe del Gesù >> Guarnieri, Giuseppe

Givenchy, Hubert James Marcel Taffin de [zhivãshee] (1927–) Fashion designer, born in Beauvais, France. He attended the Ecole des Beaux-Arts and the Faculté de Droit in Paris. He worked with Jacques Fath (1912–54) in 1944, then with Robert Piguet (1901–53), Lucien Lelong (1889–1958), and Elsa Schiaparelli. He opened his own house in 1952, producing ready-to-wear clothes under his Nouvelle Boutique label. >> Schiaparelli, Elsa

Glackens, William (James) (1870–1938) Painter, born in Philadelphia, PA. After studying in Philadelphia under Robert Henri, he worked in New York City as an illustrator for magazines until about 1905, when he devoted himself to painting. A member of The Eight, who emphasized Realism and Modernism, his own work – such as 'Nude with Apple' (1910) – tended towards Impressionism. >> Henri, Robert

Gladstone, Herbert John Gladstone, 1st Viscount (1854–1930) British statesman, born in Dane End, Hertfordshire, SE England, UK, the youngest son of W E Gladstone. He was Liberal MP for Leeds (1880–1910), became Liberal chief whip in 1899, and home secretary (1905–10). He was appointed first Governor-General of the Union of South Africa (1910–14) and raised to the peerage in 1910. He was head of the War Refugees Association (1914–19), and published his political reminiscences, *After Thirty Years*, in 1928. >> Gladstone, W E

Gladstone, W(illiam) E(wart) (1809–98) British statesman and prime minister (1868–74, 1880–5, 1886, 1892–4), born in Liverpool, Merseyside, NW England, UK. He studied at Oxford, and entered parliament in 1832 as a Conservative, working closely with Peel. From 1834 he held various junior posts, becoming President of the Board of Trade (1843–5). He was Chancellor of the Exchequer in Aberdeen's coalition (1852–5) and again under Palmerston (1859–66). In 1867 he became leader of the Liberal Party, and soon after served his first term as premier. He disestablished and disendowed the Irish Church, and established a system of national education (1870). Frequently in office until his resignation in 1894, he succeeded in carrying out a scheme of parliamentary reform which went a long way towards universal male suffrage. In his last two ministries he introduced bills for Irish Home Rule, but both were defeated. >> Aberdeen; Gladstone, Herbert; Palmerston; Peel; RR1095

Glaisher, James [glaysher] (1809–1903) Meteorologist,

born in London, England, UK. He joined the Ordnance Survey in 1829, and later became chief meteorologist at Greenwich. He made a large number of balloon ascents, once reaching a height of over 11 km/7 mi to study the higher strata of the atmosphere. He compiled dew-point tables and wrote on several scientific subjects.

Glanvill, Joseph (1636–80) Philosopher and clergyman, born in Plymouth, Devon, SW England, UK. After studying at Oxford, he served as vicar of Frome (1662), rector of the Abbey Church in Bath (1666), and prebendary of Worcester (1678). He is known for *The Vanity of Dogmatising* (1661), in which he attacked scholastic philosophy, supported experimental science, and appealed for freedom of thought. He defended the work to the newly established Royal Society, of which he became a fellow in 1664. He also attacked the rationalizing scepticism of those who denied the existence of ghosts, witches, and other apparitions of the spirit. >> Wilkins, John

Glanvill, Ranulf de (?–1190) Jurist, born in Stratford St Andrew, Suffolk, E England, UK. He was an adviser to Henry II, and the reputed author of the earliest treatise on the laws of England, the *Tractatus de legibus et consuetudinibus Angliae* (c.1187, Treatise on the Laws and Customs of England), which describes the procedure of the king's courts. The *Tractus* is a brief but lucid exposition of the law, based on the writs which initiated actions, and is historically very important. >> Henry II (of England)

Glanville-Hicks, Peggy (1912–90) Composer, born in Melbourne, Victoria, Australia. She studied at the Melbourne Conservatory, at the Royal College of Music, London, and with Vaughan Williams and Nadia Boulanger among others. She was music critic of the *New York Herald Tribune* (1948–58), and director of Asian Studies at the Australian Music Centre from 1975. She wrote several operas including *Nausicaa* (1961), and much work for theatre and ballet. >> Boulanger, Nadia; Vaughan Williams

Glas, John (1695–73) Clergyman and founder of a small religious sect, born in Auchtermuchty, Fife, E Scotland, UK. From 1719 he was minister of Tealing near Dundee. Deposed in 1728 for opposing the concept of a national church, he formed a congregation later known as the *Glassites* or *Sandemanians*, based on simple apostolic practice. The latter name was from his son-in-law **Robert Sandeman** (1718–71), through whom his teachings survived and spread to America for a while, until by 1890 the sect had been absorbed into other denominations.

Glaser, Donald A(rthur) [glayzer] (1926–) Physicist, born in Cleveland, OH. He studied at the Case (Cleveland) and California institutes of technology. While working at the University of Michigan (1949–60) he developed the 'bubble chamber' for observing the paths of atomic particles, an achievement for which he was awarded the Nobel Prize for Physics in 1960. He became professor of physics and molecular biology at the University of California, Berkeley, in 1964.

Glaser, Milton [glayzer] (1929–) Graphic designer and illustrator, born in New York City. He studied at Cooper Union, New York City, and also in Italy. Based in New York, he was one of the founders and president of Push Pin Studios (1954–74). He was also a founder of *Push Pin Graphic* magazine (1955–74), and vice-president and design director of the *Village Voice* (1975–7). In 1974 he became president of his own graphics/design firm, Milton Glaser, Inc. The recipient of many awards, he is known for his eclectic experiments with graphics, typefaces, and magazine designs.

Glasgow, Ellen (Anderson Gholson) (1873–1945) Novelist, born in Richmond, VA. From a socially-prominent family, she was the archetypal Southern Belle, apart from her desire to be a successful novelist. Her early works reflected the irony of her situation, and include *The Voice of the People* (1900), and *Virginia* (1913). She obtained critical acclaim in her late middle age, with the publication of *Barren Ground* (1925). Other works include *They Stooped to Folly* (1929), *Vein of Iron* (1935), and *In This Our Life* (1941, Pulitzer).

Glashow, Sheldon (Lee) [gla**show]** (1932–) Physicist, born in New York City. He studied at Cornell, Harvard, Copenhagen, and Geneva universities, and became professor of physics at Harvard in 1967. He was a major contributor to the Glashow–Salam–Weinberg theory explaining electromagnetic and weak nuclear forces, and to the theory of quantum chromodynamics. He shared the Nobel Prize for Physics in 1979. >> Salam; Weinberg

Glaspell, Susan [gla**spel]** (1882–1948) Playwright and novelist, born in Davenport, IA. She studied at Drake University, Des Moines, IA, then worked as a local reporter before concentrating on writing short stories and novels. With her husband, **George Carm Cook** (d.1924), she founded the Provincetown Playhouse (1915), which introduced the plays of Eugene O'Neill. Her novels include *Fidelity* (1915), *Brook Evans* (1928), and *The Fugitive's Return* (1929), but she is best-remembered for her dramatic work, notably *Bernice* (1919), *Inheritors* (1921), and *Alison's House* (1931, Pulitzer), based on the life of Emily Dickinson. >> Dickinson; O'Neill, Eugene

Glass, Carter (1858–1946) US senator, representative, and newspaper publisher, born in Lynchburg, VA. Starting at 14 as a printer's assistant on his father's newspaper, he became an editor, and by 1895 owned three newspapers. An active Democrat, he served in the Virginia Senate and then in the US House of Representatives (1902–18). He was secretary of the Treasury (1918–20), leaving to fill a vacancy in the US Senate, where he served until his death. A fiscal conservative and a defender of states' rights, he often opposed 'New Deal' legislation, but he supported the League of Nations and the US role in World War 2.

Glass, Philip (1937–) Composer, born in Baltimore, MD. He studied with Nadia Boulanger (1964–6) and the Indian musician Ravi Shankar. He is best known for his works *Einstein on the Beach* (1976), *Satyagraha* (1980), *Akhnaten* (1984), and *The Making of the Representative for Planet 8* (1988). Later works include *The Hydrogen Jukebox* (1990) and *Orphee* (1993). >> Boulanger, Nadia; Ravi Shankar

Glauber, Johann Rudolph [glow**ber]** (1604–68) Physician, born in Karlstadt, Germany. He settled in Holland, where he lived through selling medical and other substances. In 1648 he discovered hydrochloric acid, and was probably the first to produce nitric acid. He also discovered *Glauber's salt* (sodium sulphate), the therapeutic virtues of which he greatly exaggerated.

Glazunov, Alexander (Konstantinovich) [glaz**unof]** (1865– 1936) Composer, born in St Petersburg, Russia. He studied under Rimsky-Korsakov, and was director of the Conservatory at St Petersburg (1906–17), when he was given the title of 'People's Artist of the Republic'. Among his compositions are eight symphonies, and works in every branch except opera. In 1928 he emigrated to Paris. >> Rimsky-Korsakov

Gleason, James >> **Abbott, George**

Glemp, Jozef (1929–) Clergyman, born in Inowroclaw, Poland. He spent World War 2 in forced labour on a German-run farm. He was ordained priest in 1956, and became Bishop of Warmia in 1979, succeeding Cardinal Stefan Wyszynski as Archbishop of Gniezno and Warsaw, and Primate of Poland, after the latter's death in 1981. A specialist in civil and canonical law, Glemp was a prominent figure during Poland's internal political unrest. He was made a cardinal early in 1983. >> Wyszynski

Glendower, Owen [glen**dower]**, Welsh **Owain Glyndwr** or **Owain ap Gruffudd** (c. 1354–1416) Welsh chief, born in

Powys, E Wales, UK. He studied law at Westminster, and became esquire to the Earl of Arundel. In 1401 he rebelled against Henry IV, proclaimed himself Prince of Wales, established an independent Welsh parliament, and joined the coalition with Harry Percy (Hotspur) (1364–1403), who was defeated at the Battle of Shrewsbury (1403). He continued to fight for Welsh independence until his death. >> Henry IV (of England)

Glenn, John H(erschel) (1921–) Astronaut, the first American to orbit the Earth, born in Cambridge, OH. He studied at the University of Maryland, joined the US Marine Corps (1943), served in the Pacific during World War 2, and later served in Korea. In 1957 he made the first non-stop supersonic flight from Los Angeles to New York City. He became an astronaut in 1959, and in 1962 made a three-orbit flight in the Friendship 7 space capsule. He resigned from the Marine Corps in 1965, has been a senator from Ohio since 1975, and sought the Democratic nomination for the presidency in 1984 and 1988. >> Gagarin

Glennie, Evelyn (Elizabeth Ann) (1965–) Percussionist, born in Ellon, Aberdeenshire, NE Scotland, UK. Although profoundly deaf, she studied at the Royal Academy of Music, London, winning several prizes, and made her debut recital at the Wigmore Hall in 1986. She has since received international recognition as a percussionist, playing with orchestras all over the world. A composer herself, several pieces have been specially composed for her. She has also worked as a radio and television presenter, and written a volume of autobiography, *Good Vibrations* (1996).

Gleyre, Charles [glair] (1806–74) Painter, born in Chevilly, Switzerland. He studied in Italy, travelled in Greece and Egypt, and took over Delaroche's teaching school in Paris. Monet, Renoir, and Sisley numbered among his pupils. Much of his work is at Lausanne. >> Delaroche; Monet; Renoir, Pierre Auguste; Sisley

Glidden, Joseph (Farwell) (1813–1906) Inventor, born in Charlestown, NH. He worked on the family farm and as a teacher before moving West in 1844 and gradually acquiring large landholdings in Illinois and Texas. He patented an improved type of barbed wire in 1874, but sold his interest in the Barb Fence Co in 1876. By 1880 the factory was turning out 80 million pounds of wire a year, and his invention ultimately fenced in vast areas of the W range.

Glinka, Mikhail (Ivanovich) [gling**ka]** (1804–57) Composer, born in Novospasskoye, Russia. He was a civil servant, but after a visit to Italy began to study music in Berlin. His opera *A Life for the Tsar* (1836, known earlier as *Ivan Susanin*) was followed by *Russlan and Ludmilla* (1842), which pioneered the style of the Russian national school of composers. He left Russia in 1844, and lived in Spain and France, returning home in 1854.

Glock, Sir William (1908–) Music critic, born in London, England, UK. He studied at Cambridge, then studied the piano under Schnabel in Berlin. He joined *The Observer* in 1934 and became its chief music critic (1939–45), while also serving in the RAF. He was director of the Summer School at Dartington (1953–79), editor of the music magazine *The Score* (1949–61), and controller of music at the BBC (1959–72), where he devised the invitation concerts in which new works were performed amid more popular pieces. He was knighted in 1970. >> Schnabel

Gloucester, Prince Henry, Duke of [glos**ter]** (1900–74) Prince of the United Kingdom, the third son of George V. Educated privately and at Eton, he became a captain in the 10th Hussars and was created duke in 1928. In 1935 he married **Lady Alice Montagu-Douglas-Scott**, and they had two children: William (1941–72) and Richard, who succeeded him. He served as Governor-General of Australia (1945–47). >> George V; Gloucester, Richard, Duke of

Gloucester, Humphrey, Duke of [gloster], known as **the Good Duke Humphrey** (1391–1447) Youngest son of Henry IV, and protector during the minority of Henry VI (1422–9). He greatly increased the difficulties of his brother, Bedford, by his greed, irresponsibility, and factious quarrels with their uncle, Cardinal Beaufort. In 1447 he was arrested for high treason at Bury St Edmunds, and five days later was found dead in bed (apparently from natural causes). His patronage of literature led to his nickname. >> Beaufort, Henry; Bedford, Duke of; Henry IV; Henry VI

Gloucester, Prince Richard, Duke of >> **Richard III**

Gloucester, Richard (Alexander Walter George), Duke of [gloster] (1944–) British prince, the younger son of Henry, Duke of Gloucester (the third son of George V). In 1972 he married **Birgitte van Deurs** (1946–); they have one son, **Alexander, Earl of Ulster** (1974–), and two daughters, **Lady Davina Windsor** (1977–) and **Lady Rose Windsor** (1980–). >> Gloucester, Prince Henry

Glubb, Sir John Bagot, known as **Glubb Pasha** (1897–1986) British soldier, born in Preston, Lancashire, NW England, UK. He trained at the Royal Miltary Academy, Woolwich, served in World War 1, and became the first organizer of the native police force in the new state of Iraq (1920). In 1930 he was transferred to British-mandated Transjordan, organizing the Arab Legion's Desert Patrol, and became Legion Commandant (1939). He had immense prestige among the Bedouin, but was dismissed from his post in 1956 following Arab criticism. Knighted in 1956, he then became a writer and lecturer.

Gluck, Christoph (Willibald) [glook] (1714–87) Composer, born in Erasbach, Bavaria. He taught music at Prague, then studied in Vienna and Milan. In 1741 he began to write operas, and after collaborating with the librettist Raniero de Calzabigi (1714–95) he produced such works as *Orfeo ed Euridice* (1762) and *Alceste* (1767). In the late 1770s, Paris was divided into those who supported Gluck's French opera style and those supporting the Italian style of Niccolo Piccinni – the *Gluckists* and *Piccinnists*. Gluck finally conquered with his *Iphigénie en Tauride* (1779), and retired from Paris full of honour. >> Piccinni

Gluckman, (Herman) Max (1911–75) Social anthropologist, born in Johannesburg, South Africa. He studied at Witwatersrand and Oxford, carried out extensive field work among tribes of C and S Africa (1936–44), was director of the Rhodes–Livingstone Institute, Northern Rhodesia (1941–7), and lectured at Oxford (1947–9). He was appointed to the chair of social anthropology at Manchester (1949), becoming research professor in 1971. His studies focused on the political systems of the tribes, analysing the role of conflict in the maintenance of social cohesion.

Glyn, Elinor, *née* **Sutherland** (1864–1943) Writer, born in Jersey, Channel Is. A writer of romantic novels, she started with *The Visits of Elizabeth* (1900), and found fame with *Three Weeks* (1907), a book which gained a reputation for being risqué. She went to Hollywood (1922–7), where her works were glamorized on the screen. She also wrote an autobiography, *Romance Adventure* (1936).

Glyndwr, Owen >> **Glendower, Owen**

Gmelin, Leopold [gmayleen] (1788–1853) Chemist, born in Göttingen, Germany. He was professor of medicine and chemistry at Heidelberg (1817–50). He discovered potassium ferricyanide, known as *Gmelin's salt*, in 1822, introduced the terms *ester* and *ketone* into organic chemistry, and published a textbook of inorganic chemistry (trans 1849). *Gmelin's test* is for the presence of bile pigments.

Gneisenau, August (Wilhelm Anton), Graf (Count) **Neithardt von** [gniyzuhnow] (1760–1831) Prussian general, born in Schildau, Germany. In 1786 he joined the Prussian army, fought at Saalfeld and Jena (1806), helped to reorganize the army after its defeat by Napoleon (1807), and in the war of liberation gave distinguished service at Leipzig (1813). In the Waterloo campaign, as chief of Blücher's staff, he directed the strategy of the Prussian army. >> Blücher; Napoleon; Scharnhorst

Göbbels, Joseph >> **Goebbels, Joseph**

Gobbi, Tito (1915–84) Baritone, born in Bassano del Grappa, Italy. He studied law at Padua, then took up singing in Rome, making his operatic debut in 1935 at Gubbio. He appeared regularly with the Rome Opera from 1938, and soon made an international reputation, especially in Verdian roles such as Falstaff and Don Carlos.

Gobineau, Joseph Arthur, comte de (Count of) [gobinoh] (1816–82) French diplomat and orientalist, born in Bordeaux, France. He was a member of the French diplomatic service (1849–77). He wrote several romances and a history of Persia, but is best known for his *Essai sur l'inégalité des races humaines* (4 vols, 1853–5, Essay on the Inequality of Human Races), arguing that racial composition determines the fate of civilization. He has been called the 'intellectual parent' of Nietzsche. >> Nietzsche

Godard, Jean-Luc [gohdah(r)] (1930–) Film director, born in Paris. Educated in Paris, he was a journalist and film critic before turning director. His first major film *A bout de souffle* (1960, *Breathless*) established him as one of the leaders of *Nouvelle Vague* cinema. He wrote his own film scripts on contemporary and controversial themes, his prolific output including *Vivre sa vie* (1962, trans My Life to Live) and *Weekend* (1968). He then collaborated with other film-makers in the making of politically radical films, but returned to feature films with *Sauve qui peut* (1980, trans Slow Motion), *Detective* (1984), *Je vous salue, Marie* (1985, Hail, Mary), and *Nouvelle Vague* (1990).

Goddard, Robert H(utchings) (1882–1945) Physicist and rocketry pioneer, born in Worcester, MA. He studied at Clark and Princeton universities, becoming professor of physics at Clark (1919–43). He elaborated the theory of rocketry, developing the first successful liquid-fuelled rocket, launched in 1926. In 1929 he launched the first instrumented rocket, and later conducted research for US Navy applications. NASA's Goddard Space Flight Center is named in his honour.

Gödel or **Goedel, Kurt** [goedl] (1906–78) Logician and mathematician, born in Brno, Czech Republic. He taught at Vienna, then emigrated to the USA (1940), where he became a US citizen in 1948, and professor at the Institute of Advanced Study, Princeton, NJ. He showed in 1931 that any formal logical system adequate for number theory must contain propositions not provable in that system (*Gödel's proof*).

Godey, Louis Antoine [gohdee] (1804–78) Publisher, born in New York City. Educated largely in newspaper editorial offices, he was a middle-class tastemaker in fashion, music, and literature, publishing (1930–77) *Godey's Lady's Book*, the largest circulation magazine of its time. Its illustrations not only influenced women's fashion of the time, but later became documents for social historians and prized items for collectors. A publisher also of children's and music journals, he was among the first to copyright magazine contents.

Godfrey, Bob, popular name of **Robert Godfrey** (1921–) Animated cartoon producer/director, born in New South Wales, Australia. He was brought to England as a baby. After training in animation as a background artist, he went on to produce his own cartoons, such as *Polygamous Polonius* (1960), bringing a new bawdy humour to British cartoons. His musical cartoon, *Great*, the life of Isambard Kingdom Brunel, won an Oscar in 1975.

Godfrey of Bouillon [booeeyõ] (c.1061–1100) Duke of Lower Lorraine (1089–95), and leader of the First Crusade, born in Baisy, Belgium. He served under Emperor Henry IV against Rudolph of Swabia, and in 1084 in the expedition against Rome. He was elected one of the principal commanders of the First Crusade, and later became its chief leader. After the capture of Jerusalem (1099) he was proclaimed king, but he refused the crown, accepting only the title Defender of the Holy Sepulchre.

Godfrey of Strasburg >> **Gottfried von Strassburg**

Godiva, Lady [godiyva] (11th-c) An English lady and religious benefactress, who, according to tradition, rode naked through the market place at Coventry, in order to obtain the remission of a heavy tax imposed by her husband, **Leofric, Earl of Chester** (d.1057), upon the townsfolk (1040). The story occurs in the *Chronica* of Roger of Wendover (1235). >> Roger of Wendover

Godolphin, Sidney Godolphin, 1st Earl of [godolfin] (1645–1712) English statesman, born near Helston, Cornwall, SW England, UK. He entered parliament (1668), visited Holland (1678), and was made head of the Treasury and a baron (1684). He stood by James II when William of Orange landed (1668), and voted for a regency; yet in 1689 William reinstated him as First Commissioner of the Treasury. He was ousted in 1696, but made Lord High Treasurer by Anne (1702), and created an earl (1706). His able management of the finances helped Marlborough in the War of the Spanish Succession (1701–13), but court intrigues led to his dismissal in 1710. >> Anne; Marlborough; William III

Godowsky, Leopold [godofskee] (1870–1938) Pianist and composer, born in Soshly, Lithuania. He studied briefly in Berlin when aged 14, then went to the USA, becoming a US citizen in 1891. He worked at the Chicago Conservatory of Music (1895–1900) and was professor at Vienna (1909–14). A master of the keyboard, he also wrote over 400 compositions and transcriptions, including *Triakontameron* (1920).

Godoy, Manuel de [gothoy] (1767–1851) Spanish court favourite, and chief minister (1792–1808) under Charles IV, born in Castuera, Spain. An obscure guards officer, he achieved dictatorial power at the age of 25 through the favour of the Queen, Maria Luisa, whose lover he was. His rule represented a corrupt form of 'enlightened despotism'. In 1795 he assumed the title 'Prince of the Peace', following Spain's defeat by Revolutionary France. In 1796 he allied with France against England – a disastrous move which turned Spain into a virtual French satellite, and contributed massively to her losing her American empire. In 1808 he was overthrown by an alliance of aristocrats and the populace, spending the rest of his life exiled in Rome and in Paris.

Godric, St (c. 1069–1170) Hermit, born in Norfolk, England, UK. He worked as a pedlar, mariner (possibly pirate), pilgrim, and seer. From 1110, and for the rest of his long life, he lived as a hermit in a hut at Finchale, on the R Wear near Durham. A priory was later built on the site. Feast day 21 May.

Godunov, Boris (Fyodorovich) [goduhnof] (c. 1552–1605) Tsar of Russia (1598–1605). Of Tartar stock, he became an intimate friend of Ivan IV (the Terrible), who entrusted to Boris the care of his imbecile elder son, Fyodor. Ivan's younger son, Dmitri, had been banished to the upper Volga, where he died in 1591 – murdered, it was said, at Boris's command. During the reign of Tsar Fyodor (1584–98), Godunov was virtual ruler of the country, with the title of 'the Great Sovereign's brother-in-law', becoming tsar himself on Fyodor's death in 1598. He continued the expansionist policies of Ivan, going to war against both Poland and Sweden. At home, he disposed finally of the

Tartar threat, but was embroiled in the last years of his reign in a civil war against a pretender who claimed to be Dmitri, and who was eventually crowned after Boris's death. >> Dmitri; Ivan IV; RR1085

Godwin, also spelled **Godwine** (?–1053) Anglo-Saxon nobleman and warrior, the father of Harold Godwinsson. He became a favourite of Canute, who made him Earl of Wessex in 1018. In 1042 he helped to raise Edward the Confessor to the throne, and married him to his daughter Edith. He led the struggle against the king's foreign favourites, and Edward revenged himself by banishing Godwin and his sons in 1051. But in 1052 they landed in the S of England and gained so much local support that Edward was forced to grant his demands and reinstate his family. Godwin's son Harold was for a few months Edward's successor. >> Canute; Edward the Confessor; Harold II

Godwin, Edward William (1833–86) Architect and designer, born in Bristol, SW England, UK. He trained as an architect at Bristol. Northampton Town Hall (1861) dates from his early Gothic period. His mainly domestic architecture included the White House in Chelsea (1877) for his friend Whistler. A central figure in the 'Aesthetic Movement', his furniture designs after 1875 were much influenced by the Japanese taste which that movement made fashionable. He also designed textiles and wallpapers. >> Whistler, James McNeill

Godwin, Fay Simmonds (1931–) Photographer, born in Berlin of English parents. Educated in numerous schools worldwide, she began by taking photographs of her two young sons, but has become best known for her landscapes, including Welsh and Scottish scenes. Since 1970 she has worked as a freelance photographer, based in London. Her many publications include *The Oldest Road* (1975, co-authored with J R C Anderson), *The Whisky Roads of Scotland* (1982, with Derek Cooper), and *Our Forbidden Land* (1990).

Godwin, Francis (1562–1633) Clergyman and writer, born in Hannington, Northamptonshire, C England, UK. He studied at Oxford, and became rector of Sampford, Bishop of Llandaff (1601), and Bishop of Hereford (1617). His eight works include *A Catalogue of the Bishops of England* (1601), but he is best known as the author of the first science-fiction romance in English literature, *Man in the Moon or a Voyage Thither, by Domingo Gonsales* (1638).

Godwin, Mary Wollstonecraft >> **Wollstonecraft**

Godwin, William (1756–1836) Political writer and novelist, born in Wisbech, Cambridgeshire, EC England, UK. His major work of social philosophy was *An Enquiry Concerning Political Justice* (1793), which greatly impressed the English Romantics. His masterpiece was the novel *The Adventures of Caleb Williams* (1794). He married Mary Wollstonecraft in 1797. A bookselling business long involved him in difficulties, and in 1833 he was glad to accept the sinecure post of yeoman usher of the Exchequer. >> Wollstonecraft

Godwin-Austen, Henry Haversham (1834–1923) British soldier and surveyor. A lieutenant-colonel, he was attached to the trigonometrical survey of India (1856–77). The second highest mountain in the world, in the Himalayas (also known as K2), was named *Mt Godwin-Austen* after him in 1888.

Goebbels or **Göbels, (Paul) Joseph** [goeblz] (1897–1945) Nazi politician, born in Rheydt, Germany. A deformed foot absolved him from military service, and he attended several universities. He became Hitler's enthusiastic supporter, and was appointed head of the Ministry of Public Enlightenment and Propaganda (1933). A bitter anti-Semite, his gift of mob oratory made him a powerful exponent of the more radical aspects of Nazi philosophy. Wartime conditions greatly expanded his responsibilities and power, and by 1943, while Hitler was running the war, Goebbels was virtually running the country. He retained Hitler's confidence to the last, and in the Berlin bunker he and his wife committed suicide, after taking the lives of their six children. >> Hitler

Goehr, (Peter) Alexander [ger] (1932–) Composer, born in Berlin. Brought to England in 1933, he studied at the Royal Manchester College (1952–5) and in Paris. He was professor of music at Leeds University (1971–6), then at Cambridge, where he is a fellow of Trinity Hall. His compositions include the operas *Arden Must Die* (1967), *Behold the Sun* (1985), and *Arianna* (1995), as well as concertos, cantatas, and chamber music.

Goeppert-Mayer, Maria [goepert mayer], née **Goepert** (1906–72) Physicist, born in Katowice (formerly, Kattowitz), Poland. She studied at Göttingen, then emigrated to the USA, and taught at Johns Hopkins University, where her husband, **Joseph Mayer**, was professor of chemical physics. From 1960 she held a chair at the University of California. She shared the 1963 Nobel Prize for Physics for research on nuclear shell structure. >> RR1122

Goerdeler, Karl Friedrich [goe(r)deler] (1884–1945) German politician, born in Pila (formerly, Schneidemühl), Poland. He served under Hitler as commissar for price control (1934), but resigned his mayoralty of Leipzig in 1937, and became one of the leaders of opposition to Hitler, culminating in Stauffenberg's unsuccessful bomb plot of 20 July 1944, for which Goerdeler was executed together with a number of generals. >> Hitler; Stauffenberg

Goering or **Göring, Hermann (Wilhelm)** [goering] (1893–1946) Nazi politico-military leader, born in Rosenheim, Germany. In the 1914–18 war he fought on the Western Front, then transferred to the air force, and commanded the famous 'Death Squadron'. In 1922 he joined the Nazi Party and was given command of the Hitler storm troopers. He became president of the Reichstag in 1932, and joined the Nazi government in 1933. He founded the Gestapo, setting up the concentration camps for political, racial, and religious suspects. In 1940 he became economic dictator of Germany, and was made Marshal of the Reich, the first and only holder of the rank. As the war went against Germany, his prestige waned. In 1945 he attempted a palace revolution, was condemned to death, but escaped, to be captured by US troops. In 1946 he was sentenced to death at the Nuremberg War Crimes Trial, but before his execution could take place he committed suicide. >> Hitler

Goes, Hugo van der >> **van der Goes, Hugo**

Goethals, George Washington [gohthalz] (1858–1928) Engineer, born in New York City. He trained at West Point, and became an engineer, working on the construction of canals, harbours, and other installations. He was appointed chief engineer for construction of the Panama Canal (1907–14) and, on the opening of the Canal, the first civil governor of the Canal Zone (1914–16).

Goethe, Johann Wolfgang von see panel on p. 382

Goffman, Erving (1922–82) Sociologist, born in Alberta, Canada. He studied at the universities of Toronto and Chicago, then taught at California (1958–68) and Pennsylvania universities. He is best known for his work on patterns of human communication, particularly the way in which people present themselves to each other, and what happens when they deviate from accepted norms. His books include *Asylums* (1961), *Relations in Public* (1972), and *Forms of Talk* (1981). His approach influenced the development of ideas in sociolinguistics.

Gogh, Vincent van >> **van Gogh, Vincent**

Gogol, Nikolai (Vasilievich) [gohgl] (1809–52) Novelist and playwright, born in Sorochintsi, Ukraine. In 1829 he settled in St Petersburg, and became famous through two masterpieces: *Revizor* (1836, The Inspector General), a satire exposing the corruption and vanity of provincial officials, and a novel, *Myortvye dushi* (1842, Dead Souls). He also wrote several short stories. He lived abroad for many years, mostly in Rome (1836–46), but returned to Russia.

Gold, Thomas (1920–) Astronomer, born in Vienna. He studied at Cambridge, and worked with Hermann Bondi and Fred Hoyle on the steady-state theory of the origin of the universe (1948). He became professor of astronomy at Harvard (1957), and director of the Center for Radiophysics and Space Research at Cornell (1959–81). In 1968 he suggested that pulsars are rapidly rotating neutron stars, as was later confirmed. >> Bondi; Hoyle, Fred

Goldberg, Arthur J(oseph) (1908–) Public official, diplomat, and Supreme Court justice, born in Chicago, IL. He practised law privately before serving the Office of Strategic Services during World War 2. He often represented the interests of organized labour in strike negotiations and litigation. After serving as a presidential campaign adviser (1960), he was appointed by President Kennedy to be secretary of labour (1961–2). He served in the US Supreme Court (1962–5), then resigned at the request of President Johnson in order to replace Adlai Stevenson as the US delegate to the UN (1965–8). He ran unsuccessfully for Governor of New York (1970), then taught and practised law in Washington, DC. >> Stevenson, Adlai

Goldberg, Whoopi, originally **Caryn Johnson** (1955–) Film actress, born in New York City. She gained recognition while on tour with her one-woman show, which was adapted for Broadway and became the critically acclaimed *Whoopi Goldberg Show* (1983). She achieved instant fame with her role in *The Color Purple* (1985), for which she received a Golden Globe Award. Her performance in *Ghost* (1990) won her an Oscar for best supporting actress, becoming only the second African-American woman to win this honour. Later films include *Sister Act* (1992), *Made in America* (1993), *Sister Act II* (1994), *Boys on the Side* (1995), and *The Associate* (1996).

Goldblum, Jeff (1952–) Film actor, born in Pittsburgh, PA. He began his stage training at the age of seventeen at the New York City's Neighborhood Playhouse, and within a year had made his debut on Broadway in a musical version of *Two Gentlemen of Verona*. His film debut came with a small part in *Death Wish* (1974), and he has since become well known especially for his roles in science-fiction films, including *The Fly* (1986), *Earth Girls Are Easy* (1989), *Jurassic Park* and its sequel (1993, 1997), and *Independence Day* (1996).

Golding, Louis (1895–1958) Writer, born in Manchester, Greater Manchester, NW England, UK. He studied at Oxford, beginning his writing career while still a student. He wrote many books about Jewish life, of which the best-known is *Magnolia Street* (1932), the story of a typical street in a provincial city whose inhabitants were Jews on one side, Gentiles on the other.

Golding, Sir William (Gerald) (1911–93) Novelist, born near Newquay, Cornwall, SW England, UK. He studied at Oxford, became a teacher, served in the navy in World War 2, then returned to teaching until 1961. *Poems* (1934) was followed by his first novel, *Lord of the Flies* (1954), widely considered to be one of the greatest English-language novels of this century. Other books quickly followed, such as *The Inheritors* (1955), *Pincher Martin* (1956), *Free Fall* (1959), and *The Spire* (1964), each confirming Golding's power to create contemporary myth. Later novels include *Darkness Visible* (1979) and the trilogy *Rites of Passage* (1980, Booker), *Close Quarters* (1987), *Fire Down Below* (1989), republished under the general title *To The Ends of the Earth* in 1991. He

JOHANN WOLFGANG VON GOETHE (1749–1832)

Goethe was born in Frankfurt-am-Main, the first child of Johann Caspar Goethe, a retired lawyer from N Germany, and his wife, Katharine Elisabeth Textor, the daughter of a mayor of Frankfurt. His autobiography, *Dichtung und Wahreit* (1812-22, Poetry and Truth), describes a particularly happy childhood shared closely with his only surviving sibling of seven, his sister Cornelia. Although he would have preferred to read Classics, he was sent to study law (1765–8) at Leipzig, where his father had been before him. His disinclination for law was relieved by a love affair which inspired his first two plays, *Die Laune das Verliebten* (1767, The Mood of the Beloved) and *Die Mitschuldigen* (1768, The Accomplices). He went on to study further at Strasbourg, coming under the influence of Herder, the pioneer of German Romanticism, and dabbling in alchemy, anatomy, and the antiquities.

Returning to Frankfurt in 1771, Goethe immersed himself in literature, though practising as a lawyer. He captured the thwarted spirit of German nationalism with his early *Sturm und Drang* ('Storm and Stress') masterpiece, *Götz von Berlichingen* (1773), which epitomized the man of genius (Götz) at odds with society. He followed up his first triumph with his self-revelatory cautionary novel, *Die Leiden des jungen Werthers* (1774, The Sorrows of Young Werther), which mirrored his hopeless affair with Lotte Buff, the fiancée of a colleague. Werther is made to solve the problem of clashing obligations by nobly and romantically committing suicide. *Clavigo* (1774), a Hamlet-like drama, followed in the same vein, based on Beaumarchais' *Memoires*. His engagement to Lili Schönemann (which did not result in marriage) inspired the love lyrics of 1775.

Perhaps to escape from law, in 1775 Goethe accepted the post of court official and privy councillor to the young duke of the tiny principality of Weimar, where he was to remain until his death. He conscientiously carried out all his state duties, interested himself in a geological survey, and exerted a steadying influence on the inexperienced duke.

He developed a close attachment to Charlotte von Stein, the wife of another court official. His 10-year, platonic relationship with Charlotte served to help his development as a creative writer: he poured out his frustrations in analytical works such as *Die Geschwister* (1776, Brother and Sister).

In 1782 he extended his ongoing scientific research to botany and comparative anatomy; discovering the human intermaxillary bone (1784), and formulating a vertebral theory of the skull. He also made attempts to refute Newton's theory of light. At the same time he was writing the novel, *Wilhelm Meisters Theatralische Sendung* (William Meister's Theatrical Mission), not discovered until 1910, which contains the enigmatic and beautiful poetry of Mignon's songs, epitomizing the best in German romantic poetry.

His visits to Italy (1786–8) cured him of his emotional dependence on Charlotte von Stein and contributed to a greater preoccupation with poetical form, as in the classical verse version of his drama, *Iphigenie* (final form, 1787), and the more modern subjects *Egmont* (1788) and *Tasso* (1790). His love for Italy, coupled with his passion for Christiane Vulpius, whom he eventually married in 1806, found full expression in his poem *Römische Elegien* (1795, Roman Elegies).

From 1794 Goethe formed a close friendship with Schiller, with whom he corresponded about aesthetics until 1805, and carried on a friendly contest in the writing of ballads, which resulted on Goethe's part in the epic idyll *Hermann und Dorothea* (1797). They also wrote for the literary magazine *Horen*.

Goethe's last great period saw the prototype of the favourite German literary composition, the *Bildungsroman* (novel about the spiritual and emotional development of its hero) in *Wilhelm Meisters Lehrjahre* (1795-6, William Meister's Apprenticeship), continued as *Wilhelm Meisters Wanderjahre* (1821–9, William Meister's Travels). Wilhelm Meister became the idol of the German Romantics, of whom Goethe increasingly disapproved. He disliked their enthusiasm for the French Revolution, which he satirized in a number of works, including the epic poem 'Reineke Fuchs' (1793, Reynard the Fox) and the drama *Die natürliche Tochter* (1804, The Natural Daughter). He also condemned their disregard for style, which he attempted to correct by example in his novel *Die Wahlverwandtschaften* (1809, Elected Affinities) and the collection of lyrics inspired by Marianne von Willemer, *West-östlicher Divan* (1819, Divan of East and West).

Goethe's masterpiece was undoubtedly his version of Marlowe's drama of *Faust*, on which he worked for most of his life. Begun in 1775, the first part was published after much revision and Schiller's advice in 1808, and the second part in 1832. Faust, a disillusioned scholar, deserts his 'ivory tower' to seek happiness in real life. To ensure worldly success, he makes a pact with Satan, who brings about the seduction and death of Gretchen, an ordinary village girl. Satan subtly brings Faust, by other such escapades, to the brink of moral degradation.

Goethe took little part in the political upheavals of his time, though Napoleon made a point of meeting him at the Congress of Erfurt in 1803, and Goethe saw in Napoleon the salvation of European civilization. He died in Weimar. During his last years he received a constant stream of visitors to his home from all over the world. He was buried near Schiller in the ducal vault at Weimar, and has since been recognized as a towering influence on German literature.
>> Herder; Schiller; Stein, Charlotte von

was awarded the Nobel Prize for Literature in 1983, and knighted in 1988.

Goldman, Emma, known as **Red Emma** (1869–1940) Anarchist, feminist, and birth control advocate, born in Kaunas, Lithuania. She emigrated to the USA in 1885, and was imprisoned in 1893 for inciting a riot in New York City. Imprisoned again during World War 1 for opposing and obstructing the military draft, she was deported to the Soviet Union in 1919, eventually settling in France.

Goldman, Hetty (1881–1972) Archaeologist, born in New York City. She studied at Bryn Mawr College and Radcliffe, turned to fieldwork while in Athens on a fellowship, and began to specialize in prehistoric archaeology of the Greek and other E Mediterranean peoples. She was one of the first female directors of an archaeological excavation (at Halae, Greece, 1911–14) and went on to direct numerous other excavations for the Fogg Museum and Bryn Mawr in Greece, Asia Minor, and Yugoslavia at sites including Eutresis in Greece (1924–7) and Colophon (1922, 1925) and Tarsus (1934–9, 1947, 1948) in Turkey.

Goldmark, Peter (Carl) (1906–77) Engineer and inventor, born in Budapest, Hungary. He studied at the universities of Vienna and Berlin, and emigrated to the USA in 1933. He worked in the laboratories of the Columbia Broadcasting System (CBS), where he developed the first practical colour television system, used for experimental transmissions in New York City in 1940. He led the team that invented the long-playing record (1948), and later built a special type of camera for the lunar-orbiting space vehicle, which transmitted very high definition pictures of the Moon's surface back to the Earth.

Goldoni, Carlo [gol**doh**nee] (1707–93) Playwright, born in Venice, Italy. He studied for the law, and practised intermittently (1731–48), but his real interest was drama. He discovered he had a talent for comedy, and wrote over 250 comic plays in Italian, French, and the Venetian dialect. He was greatly influenced by Molière and the *commedia dell'arte*. His best-known plays are *La locandiera* (1753, trans Mine Hostess), *I Rusteghi* (1760, which provided the plot for *The School for Fathers*, produced in London in 1946), and *Le baruffe Chiozzotte* (1762, Quarrels at Chioggia). In 1762 he undertook to write for the Italian theatre in Paris, and was attached to the French court until the revolution. >> Molière

Goldschmidt, Berthold [gohld**shmit**] (1903–96) Composer, born in Hamburg, Germany. He had a promising career in Germany, and became artistic adviser at the Berlin City Opera. In 1932 his first opera was premiered at Mannheim: *Der gewaltige Hahnrei* (The Magnificent Cuckold). He fled Nazi Germany to London in 1935 and composed his second string quartet in 1936, expressing the sorrow of his race. An expert on the music of Gustav Mahler, in 1960 he helped to complete Mahler's unfinished 10th symphony, and conducted its first performance in London in 1988. >> Mahler

Goldschmidt, Hans [gohld**shmit**], popular name of **Johann Wilhelm Goldschmidt** (1861–1923) Chemist, born in Berlin. He invented the aluminothermic process for the reduction of certain metallic oxides by the use of a highly inflammable mixture of finely divided aluminium powder and the metal oxide. The high temperatures attained on ignition have led to this process being used to weld iron and steel (the Thermit process).

Goldschmidt, Richard Benedikt [gohld**shmit**] (1878–1958) Biologist and geneticist, born in Frankfurt am Main, Germany. In 1921 he was appointed biological director of the Kaiser-Wilhelm Institute, Berlin, and in 1935 went to the USA, where he became professor of zoology at California University (1936–58). He was the author of the theory that it is not the qualities of the individual genes, but the chromosome molecules, that are decisive factors in heredity. He also stated a theory of intersexuality where an individual begins development in the womb under the influence of one sex factor but ends its development as the other sex.

Goldschmidt, Victor Moritz [gohld**shmit**] (1888–1947) Chemist, the founder of geochemistry, born in Zürich, Switzerland. He studied at Kristiania (now Oslo) University in 1911, where he became the director of the Mineralogical Institute (1914). In 1929 he moved to Göttingen, but returned six years later when the Nazis came to power. In Norway he was imprisoned by the Germans but escaped, eventually reaching England in 1943. His success was in applying physical chemistry to mineralogy. Using X-ray techniques he worked out the crystal structure of over 200 compounds and 75 elements, and made the first tables of ionic radii. In 1929 he postulated what is now known as *Goldschmidt's law* – that the structure of a crystal is determined by the ratio of the numbers of ions, the ratio of their sizes, and polarization properties. This work enabled him to predict in which minerals and rocks various elements could be found.

Goldsmith, Sir James (Michael) (1933–97) Businessman, publisher, and politician, born in Paris. His family left France at the beginning of World War 2, and he was educated in the UK, where after leaving school he built up a range of companies and developed a reputation as a charismatic, risk-taking financier. He lived both in France and the UK, and received a great deal of media attention for his flamboyant public and private lives, to which he responded aggressively, notably in the libel suit against *Private Eye* in the 1970s. In the 1980s he worked chiefly in the USA, then developed environmental and political interests, and was elected a member of the European Parliament for France (1995–7). He was knighted in 1976, and became a controversial figure in the UK when he financed the Referendum Party in the 1997 general election – a campaign he forcefully promoted while suffering from the pancreatic cancer from which he died two months later.

Goldsmith, Oliver (1728–74) Playwright, novelist, and poet, born in Kildare, Ireland. He studied erratically at Dublin, tried law at London then medicine at Edinburgh, drifted to Leyden, and returned penniless in 1756. He practised as a physician in London, held several temporary posts, and took up writing and translating. *The Vicar of Wakefield* (1766) secured his reputation as a novelist, 'The Deserted Village' (1770) as a poet, and *She Stoops to Conquer* (1773) as a dramatist.

Goldstein, Eugen [gohld**stiyn**] (1850–1930) Physicist, born in Gleiwitz, Germany. After studying at the University of Breslaw, he worked at the Potsdam Observatory. He discovered that cathode rays could produce sharp shadows, and that they were emitted perpendicular to the cathode surface, leading to the development of concave cathodes to produce focused rays.

Goldstein, Joseph (Leonard) [gohld**stiyn**] (1940–) Molecular geneticist, born in Sumter, SC. He studied at Texas University in Dallas, carried out research into biomedical genetics at the National Heart Institute at Bethesda, MD (1968–70), and was appointed professor at Texas in 1972. He shared with Michael Brown the 1985 Nobel Prize for Physiology or Medicine for their work in familial hypercholesterolaemia. >> Brown, Michael

Goldthorpe, John Harry (1935–) British sociologist. He studied at London, and taught at Leicester (1957–60) and Cambridge (1960–9) before being elected fellow of Nuffield College, Oxford (1969). He is an authority on the class structure of advanced industrial societies, and has developed a model which distinguishes between 10 main social classes. His studies of relative social mobility indicate that, despite increased prosperity and better education, equality of opportunity between classes in the UK has not improved since 1945.

Goldwater, Barry M(orris) (1909–) Politician and writer, born in Phoenix, AZ. He studied at the University of Arizona, then worked in his family's department store. He became a senator for Arizona in 1952, resigning the seat in 1964 to become the Republican nominee for the presidency, but was defeated by Lyndon Johnson. He returned to the US Senate (1969–87), and was one of the architects of the conservative revival within the Republican Party. *The*

Conscience of a Conservative (1960) is his most notable book. >> Johnson, Lyndon B

Goldwyn, Samuel, originally **Samuel Goldfish** (1882–1974) Film producer, born in Warsaw, Poland. He emigrated to the USA as a child, and helped to found a film company, producing *The Squaw Man* (1913). He founded the Goldwyn Pictures Corporation (1917), Eminent Authors Pictures (1919), and finally Metro-Goldwyn-Mayer (1925), allying himself with United Artists from 1926. His 'film-of-the-book' policy included such films as *Bulldog Drummond* (1929) and *All Quiet on the Western Front* (1930). A colourful personality, many of his remarks have become catch phrases (*Goldwynisms*), such as 'include me out'. >> Mayer

Golgi, Camillo [gol jee] (1843–1926) Cell biologist, born in Corteno, Italy. As professor of pathology at Pavia (1876–1918), he discovered the *Golgi bodies* in animal cells which, through their affinity for metallic salts, become readily visible under the microscope. His work opened up a new field of research into the central nervous system, sense organs, muscles, and glands. He shared the 1906 Nobel Prize for Physiology or Medicine. >> RR1124

Gollancz, Sir Victor [go langks, go lants] (1893–1967) Publisher, writer, and philanthropist, born in London, England, UK. He studied at Oxford, became a teacher, then entered publishing, founding his own firm in 1928. In 1936 he founded the Left Book Club, which had a great influence on the growth of the Labour Party, and after World War 2 founded the Jewish Society for Human Service, and War on Want (1951). He was knighted in 1965.

Golombek, Harry [go lombek] (1911–95) Chess master and writer on chess, born in London, England, UK. He studied at London University, and became editor of *British Chess* (1938–67). Several times British chess champion, he was classed as a master (1948) and a grandmaster (1985), and published numerous books on chess, including *The Encyclopedia of Chess* (1977).

Gomarus, Franciscus, also known as **Francis Gomer** (1563–1641) Calvinist theologian, born in Bruges, Belgium. As divinity professor at Leyden (1594) he became known for his hostility to his colleague, Arminius, with whom he fiercely debated predestination. At the Synod of Dort (1618) he secured the Arminians' expulsion from the Reformed Church. From then until his death he was professor at Groningen. >> Arminius

Gombrich, Sir Ernst (Hans Josef) [gom brik] (1909–   ) Art historian, born in Vienna. He studied at the University of Vienna before emigrating to Britain, where he joined the staff of the Warburg Institute, London (1936), becoming its director and professor of the history of the classical tradition (1959–76). During World War 2 he worked for the BBC Monitoring Service. His books include *The Story of Art* (1950), *Art and Illusion* (1960) – an influential study of the psychology of pictorial representation, *The Sense of Order* (1979), and *New Light on Old Masters* (1986). He was knighted in 1972.

Gompers, Samuel [gom perz] (1850–1924) Labour leader, born in London, England, UK. He went to the USA in 1863, and became a US citizen in 1872. A cigar maker by trade, in 1886 he helped to found the American Federation of Labor, becoming its first president.

Gomułka, Władysław [go mool ka] (1905–82) Polish Communist leader, born in Krosno, Poland. A professional trade unionist, in 1943 he became secretary of the outlawed Communist Party. He was vice-president of the first post-war Polish government (1945–8), but his criticism of the Soviet Union led to his arrest and imprisonment (1951–4). He returned to power as party first secretary in 1956. In 1971, following a political crisis, he resigned office, and spent his remaining years largely in retirement.

Gonçalves, Nuno [gon salves] (fl.1450–72) Portuguese painter. He is recorded, in 1463, as court painter to Alfonso V (ruled 1416–28). He was virtually forgotten until the discovery of his only extant work, an altarpiece for the convent of St Vincent in 1882. This work established him as the most important Portuguese painter of the 15th-c, and the founder of the Portuguese school of painting.

Goncharov, Ivan Alexandrovich [gon charof] (1812–91) Writer, born in Ulyanovsk (formerly, Simbirsk), Russia. He graduated from Moscow University (1834), led an uneventful life in the civil service, and wrote *Oblomov* (1857), a leading work of Russian Realism.

Goncharova, Natalia Sergeyevna [gon charova] (1881–1962) Painter and designer, born in Ladyzhino, Russia. She began as a science student but turned to sculpture c.1898, studying at the Moscow Academy of Art. She started to paint in 1904 and, liking the flat colours and primitive forms of Russian folk art, combined these with the new influences of Cubism and Fauvism. She moved to Geneva in 1915 with her husband Larionov to design for Diaghilev's ballets, and went to Paris in 1921. She took French nationality in 1938. >> Diaghilev; Larionov

Goncourt brothers [gō koor] **Edmond de Goncourt** (1822–96) and **Jules de Goncourt** (1830–70) Novelist collaborators, born in Nancy and Paris, respectively. They began as artists, in 1849 travelling across France for watercolour sketches. They then collaborated in studies of history and art, and took to writing novels, notably *Germinie Lacerteux* (1865) and *Madame Gervaisais* (1869). They are also remembered for their *Journal*, begun in 1851, a detailed record of French social and literary life which Edmond continued for over 40 years. Edmond also founded in his will the Académie Goncourt to foster fiction, and the Goncourt Prize is awarded annually to the author of an outstanding work of French literature.

Góngora y Argote, Luis de [gon gora ee ah(r) goh tay] (1561–1627) Poet, born in Córdoba, Spain. He studied law, but in 1606 took orders and became a prebendary of Córdoba, and eventually chaplain to Philip III (reigned 1598–1621). His earlier writings are elegant and stylish. His later works, consisting for the most part of longer poems such as *Solidades* and *Polifemo* (both 1613), are written in an entirely novel style, which his followers designated *Gongorismo*.

Gonne, Maud >> **MacBride, Maud**

Gonzaga, Luigi, St [gon zah ga], known as **St Aloysius** (1568–91) Jesuit priest, and the patron saint of youth. The eldest son of the Marquis of Castiglione, near Brescia, he renounced his title in order to become a missionary, and entered the Society of Jesus in 1585. When Rome was stricken with plague in 1591, he devoted himself to the care of the sick, but was himself infected and died. He was canonized in 1726, and in 1926 was declared the patron saint of Christian youth by Pope Pius XI. Feast day 21 June.

Gonzales, Pancho [gon zah lez], popular name of **Ricardo Alonzo Gonzales** (1928–95) Tennis player, born in Los Angeles, CA. From an impoverished background, and largely self-taught, he rose to the top in tennis, winning the US singles in 1948 and 1949, and the doubles at both Wimbledon and France in 1949, after which he turned professional. In 1969 he took part in the longest-ever men's singles match at Wimbledon, playing 112 games to defeat fellow-American, Charlie Pasarell. >> RR1173

González, Felipe [gon zah lez] (1942–   ) Spanish statesman and prime minister (1982–96), born in Seville, Spain. He practised as a lawyer, and in 1962 joined the Spanish Socialist Workers' Party (PSOE), then an illegal organization. The Party regained legal status in 1977, three years after he became secretary-general. He persuaded the PSOE to adopt a more moderate policy, and in the 1982 elections they won a substantial majority to become the first left-wing administration since 1936; he was narrowly re-elected in 1993 for a fourth consecutive term of office. >> RR1088

González, Julio [gonzahlez] (1876–1942) Sculptor, born in Barcelona, Spain. Educated at the Escuela de Bellas Artes, in 1900 he went to Paris, joining the avant-garde circle around Picasso. He began as a painter, but in 1927 turned to sculpture, mainly in wrought and welded iron. Like Picasso he was inspired initially by African masks, and worked in a Cubist style, but also had links with Surrealism. His most famous work is 'Montserrat I', a life-size figure of a peasant mother (1936–7), a symbol of popular resistance in the Spanish Civil War.

Gooch, Graham (Alan) (1953–) Cricketer, born in Leytonstone, E Greater London, England, UK. He began his career playing for Essex. His Test Match cricket debut in Australia (1975) was a failure, and prompted him to participate in an unofficial tour of South Africa (1982), resulting in his ban from international cricket for three years. A change of fortune brought him the England captaincy (1988–93) and a notable victory over the West Indies in Jamaica (1989). The leading England Test run-scorer, and most-capped player, he announced his retirement in January 1995, with 8900 runs scored in 118 Tests, at an average of 42·58.

Goodhart, Arthur (Lehman) (1891–1978) Jurist, born in New York City, New York, USA. He studied at the Hotchkiss School and Yale University, then lived most of his life in England, becoming professor of jurisprudence at Oxford, and Master of University College there (1951–63). He is also known for his editorship of the *Law Quarterly Review* (1926–75).

Goodman, Benny, popular name of **Benjamin David Goodman,** nickname **the King of Swing** (1909–86) Clarinettist and bandleader, born in Chicago, IL. A musical prodigy, he was working in dance bands by the age of 13, joining the Ben Pollack Orchestra at 16. He formed his own orchestra in New York City in 1934, and became one of the best-known leaders of the era. Hiring top African-American musicians such as pianist Teddy Wilson and vibraphone-player Lionel Hampton, he successfully defied racial taboos of the time. He led a succession of large and small bands for three decades, occasionally performing as a classical player, and was noted for his technical facility and clean tone. >> Hampton, Lionel; Wilson, Teddy

Goodman, Isador (1909–82) Pianist and composer, born in Cape Town, South Africa. He studied at the Royal College of Music, London, and appeared in concerts in England and Europe before emigrating to Australia in 1930, where he taught at the New South Wales Conservatory. For the next 50 years he performed in recital and as a soloist with leading orchestras, in concert, and for television and radio. In 1944 he wrote his *New Guinean Fantasy* on that island at the height of the battle there. He was a renowned exponent of the Romantic repertoire, and especially of Rachmaninov and Liszt.

Goodman, John (1953–) Film actor, born in St Louis, MO. He became well known for his role as the husband Dan in the television comedy series *Roseanne* (1988–97). His major films include *King Ralph* (1991), *Barton Fink* (1991), and *The Flintstones* (1994).

Goodrich, Samuel Griswold, pseudonym **Peter Parley** (1793–1860) Publisher, born in Ridgefield, CT. He edited in Boston *The Token* (1828–42), to which he contributed moralistic poems, tales, and essays for children. He published some 200 volumes, mostly for the young as 'Peter Parley' books, starting with *The Tales of Peter Parley about America* (1827). He was also consul in Paris (1851–3).

Goodyear, Charles (1800–60) Inventor, born in New Haven, CT. In 1834 he began research into the properties of rubber. Amid poverty and ridicule he pursued the experiments which ended, in 1844, in the invention of vulcanized rubber. This led to the development of the rubber-manufacturing industry and the production of the well-known tyres named after him. Legal battles over patent infringements left him impoverished, and he died in debt.

Goolagong, Yvonne >> **Cawley, Yvonne**

Goons, The >> **Bentine; Milligan; Secombe; Sellars**

Goossens, Eugène (1845–1906) Conductor, born in Bruges, Belgium. He studied at the Brussels Conservatoire and became a conductor of several opera companies in Belgium, France, and Italy before making his name in comic opera with the Carl Rosa Company in Britain from 1873. He founded the Goossens Male Voice Choir in Liverpool in 1894. >> Goossens, Eugène (1867–1958)

Goossens, Eugène (1867–1958) Violinist and conductor, born in Bordeaux, France, the son of Eugène Goossens (1845–1906). He studied at the Brussels Conservatoire and at the Royal Academy of Music, London, and played with the Carl Rosa Company under his father (1884–6) and with the orchestra at Covent Garden (1893–4). He was principal conductor of the Carl Rosa Company (1899–1915). His children were also well-known musicians: **Eugène Goossens** became a conductor and composer, **Léon Goossens** an oboist, and **Marie Goossens** (1894–1991) and **Sidonie Goossens** (1899–) both harpists. >> Goossens, Sir Eugène; Goossens, Léon

Goossens, Sir Eugène (1893–1962) Composer and conductor, born in London, England, UK, the son of Eugène Goossens (1867–1958). He studied in Bruges and London, became associate conductor to Sir Thomas Beecham, then worked in the USA (1923–45) as a conductor of orchestras in Rochester (New York) and Cincinnati (Ohio). As conductor of the Sydney Symphony Orchestra and director of the New South Wales Conservatory (1947–56), he became a major influence on Australian music. His compositions include two operas, a ballet, an oratorio, and two symphonies. He was knighted in 1955. >> Beecham; Goossens, Eugène (1867–1958); Goossens, Léon

Goossens, Léon (1897–1988) Oboist, born in Liverpool, Merseyside, NW England, UK, the son of Eugène Goossens (1867–1958). He studied at the Royal College of Music, London, and held leading posts in most of the major London orchestras, before devoting himself to solo playing and teaching. >> Goossens, Eugène (1867–1958); Goossens, Sir Eugène

Gorbachev, Mikhail Sergeyevich [go(r)bachof] (1931–) Soviet statesman, general secretary of the Communist Party of the Soviet Union (1985–91), and president of the Supreme Soviet of the USSR (1988–91), born in Privolnoye, Russia. He studied at Moscow State University and Stavropos Agricultural Institute, began work as a machine operator (1946), and joined the Communist Party in 1952. He held a variety of senior posts in the Stavropol city and district Party organization (1956–70), and was elected a deputy to the USSR Supreme Soviet (1970) and a member of the Party Central Committee (1971). He became secretary for agriculture (1979–85), a member of the Politburo in 1980, and, on the death of Chernenko, general secretary of the Central Committee (1985–91). In 1988 he also became chairman of the Presidium of the Supreme Soviet, and in 1990, the first (and last) executive president of the USSR. On becoming party general secretary he launched a radical programme of reform and restructuring (*perestroika*) of the Soviet economic and political system. A greater degree of civil liberty, public debate, journalistic and cultural freedom, and a reappraisal of Soviet history was allowed under the policy of *glasnost* (openness of information). In foreign and defence affairs he reduced military expenditure, pursued a policy of detente and nuclear disarmament with the West, and ended the Soviet military occupation of Afghanistan (1989). He briefly survived a coup in August 1991, but was forced to resign following the abolition of the Communist Party and the dissolution of the Soviet Union in December 1991. Since 1992 he has been president of the International Foundation for Socio-Economic and Political Studies (the Gorbachev Foundation). >> Chernenko; Yeltsin; Zaslavskaya

Gorboduc [gaw(r)boduk] A legendary King of Britain, first heard about in Geoffrey of Monmouth's *History*. He was the subject of an early Elizabethan tragedy in Senecan style, written by Norton and Sackville (1561). >> Geoffrey of Monmouth

Gorchakov, Prince Alexander Michaelovich [gaw(r)-cha**kof**] (1798–1883) Russian statesman, born in Khaapsalu, Estonia, the cousin of Prince Michael Gorchakov. He was ambassador at Vienna (1854–6), then succeeded Nesselrode as foreign minister. As chancellor of the empire (1863) he was, until the rise of Bismarck, the most powerful minister in Europe. He secured Austrian neutrality in the Franco-German War of 1870, and in 1871 absolved Russia from the Treaty of Paris (1856). After the conclusion of the Russo-Turkish War, the repudiation of the Treaty of San Stefano, and the signing of the Treaty of Berlin, his influence began to wane, and he retired in 1882. >> Bismarck; Gorchakov, Michael; Nesselrode

Gorchakov, Prince Michael [gaw(r)cha**kof**] (1795–1861) Russian soldier, the cousin of Prince Alexander Gorchakov. He served against the French in the Napoleonic campaign (1812–14), and in the Russo-Turkish War (1828–9). He helped to suppress the Polish revolution of 1831 and the Hungarian insurrection in 1849. He was appointed commander-in-chief in the Crimea (1855), was defeated on the Tchernaya, but recovered his laurels by his gallant defence of Sebastopol. He later became military governor of Poland (1856–61). >> Gorchakov, Alexander Michaelovich

Gordimer, Nadine (1923–) Novelist, born in Springs, South Africa. She has lived in Johannesburg since 1948, and taught in the USA during the early 1970s. In novels such as *A Guest of Honour* (1971, James Tait Black), *The Conservationist* (1974), *Burger's Daughter* (1979), and *A Sport of Nature* (1987), she adopts a liberal approach to problems of race and repression, both in her native country and in other African states. Later books include *My Son's Story* (1990) and *None to Accompany Me* (1994). She was awarded the Nobel Prize for Literature in 1991.

Gordon, Adam Lindsay (1833–70) Poet, born in Fayal in the Azores. He was raised and educated in England. A wild and reckless youth, his father sent him to South Australia, where he became a horsebreaker and amateur steeplechaser. During the next few years he moved several times, published three volumes of poetry without success, suffered a series of mishaps, and finally committed suicide. Much of his best work is collected in *Sea Spray and Smoke Drift* (1867) and *Bush Ballads and Galloping Rhymes* (1870). He is recognized as the first poet to write in an Australian style, and is the only Australian poet honoured in the poets' corner of Westminster Abbey.

Gordon, Charles George (1833–85) British general, born in Woolwich, E Greater London, England, UK. He trained at Woolwich Academy, joined the Royal Engineers in 1852, and in 1855–6 fought in the Crimean War. In 1860 he went to China, where he crushed the Taiping Rebellion, for which he became known as **Chinese Gordon**. In 1877 he was appointed Governor of the Sudan. He resigned in poor health in 1880, but returned in 1884 to relieve Egyptian garrisons which lay in rebel territory. He was besieged at Khartoum for 10 months by the Mahdi's troops, and was killed there two days before a relief force arrived. The incident captured the public imagination, and there are memorials to Gordon in St Paul's Cathedral and elsewhere. >> Mohammed Ahmed

Gordon, David (1936–) Choreographer, born in New York City. He studied painting before he began dancing with James Waring's company in New York City (1958–62). In 1974 he formed his own Pick-Up Company. Several of his works are in the repertories of major US and British classical and modern dance companies.

Gordon, Dexter (Keith) (1923–89) Jazz musician, born in Los Angeles, CA. He was an influential saxophonist and the leader of his own groups from 1945. He won acclaim for his portrayal of a jazz musician in the 1986 film *Round Midnight*.

Gordon, Lord George (1751–93) Anti-Catholic agitator, born in London, England, UK. Educated at Eton, he entered the navy but resigned when refused a command in 1772. Elected MP in 1774, he formed an association aiming for the repeal of the Catholic Relief Act (1778), and led a protest mob to Parliament, causing a major riot with 500 casualties. He was tried for high treason; but was acquitted. He subsequently became a Jew, calling himself **Israel Abraham George Gordon**. In 1787 he was convicted for a libel on Marie Antoinette, and fled to Holland, but he was extradited and imprisoned in Newgate, where he died of gaol fever. >> Erskine

Gordon, Noele (1922–85) Actress, born in London, England, UK. After studying at the Royal Academy of Dramatic Art, London, she worked in repertory and pantomime before such London successes as *Diamond Lil* (1948) and *Brigadoon* (1949–51). She became a household name as the owner of the motel in the television soap-opera, *Crossroads* (1964–81).

Gore, Al(bert) (1948–) US vice-president, born in Washington, DC. He studied at Harvard and Vanderbilt Universities, worked as a journalist, then became a Democratic congressman (1977–85) and senator (1985–92). He was elected vice-president to Bill Clinton in 1992. >> Clinton

Gore, Charles (1853–1932) Anglican clergyman and theologian, born in London, England, UK. He studied at Oxford, where he became a fellow of Trinity College in 1875, and was the first principal of Pusey House in 1884. His contribution to *Lux Mundi* (1889) abandoned the strict tractarian view of biblical inspiration, and his Bampton Lectures (1891) were equally controversial. He founded the Community of the Resurrection at Pusey House in 1892, and became bishop successively of Worcester (1901–4), Birmingham (1904–11), and Oxford (1911–19).

Gore, Spencer Frederick (1878–1914) Painter, born in Epsom, Surrey, SE England, UK. He studied at the Slade School of Art, London, during its most creative period (1896–9), and joined the New English Art Club in 1909. He was a founder member and first president of the Camden Town Group (1911), and became a member of the London Group in 1913. He met Sickert in Dieppe in 1904, and was inspired to paint theatre and music hall subjects, using a quasi-Pointilliste technique learnt from Lucien Pissarro. >> Pissarro, Lucien; Sickert

Górecki, Henryk Mikolaj [go**res**kee] (1933–) Composer, born in Czernica, near Rybnik, Poland. He studied in Paris and at the Katowice Conservatory, and in 1975 was elected provost of the State Higher School of Music, but resigned in protest four years later when the government refused to allow Pope John Paul 2 to visit Katowice. His work, usually based on tragic themes and in very slow tempi, was virtually unknown in the West until 1993, when his *Symphony No. 3: Symphony of Sorrowful Songs* (1973), with texts from a 15th-c monastic song, a folk song, and a prayer scratched on a cell wall by a girl imprisoned by the Gestapo, reached number six in the British best-selling album charts, and sold over half a million copies worldwide. Later works include *Miserere* (1981).

Goren, Charles H(enry) (1901–) Contract bridge expert and writer, born in Philadelphia, PA. He practised as a lawyer in Philadelphia until 1936, when he abandoned law to concentrate on bridge. As a masterful player, he put his knowledge into print with numerous books, and contributed a daily newspaper column, syndicated in the USA.

Gorges, Sir Ferdinando (c. 1566–1647) English proprietor of Maine, born in Wraxall, Somerset, SW England, UK. He founded two Plymouth companies (1606–19 and 1620–35) for planting lands in New England. In 1639 he received a charter constituting him proprietor of Maine, although he never went to America. His grandson sold his rights to Massachusetts in 1677.

Gorgias [gaw(r)jias] (c. 485–c. 380 BC) Greek sophist, sceptical philosopher, and rhetorician, born in Leontini, Sicily. He went to Athens as ambassador in 427 BC and, settling in Greece, won wealth and fame as a teacher of eloquence. In his work *On Nature* he argued that nothing exists; even if something did exist, it could not be known; and even if it could be known it could not be communicated. Plato's dialogue *Gorgias* is written against him.

Göring, Hermann >> **Goering, Hermann**

Goring, Marius [gawring] (1912–) Actor, born in Newport, Isle of Wight, S England, UK. He trained for the stage at the Old Vic dramatic school, and made his professional debut in 1927. Most of his career has been spent on the stage, often on tour throughout Europe, performing also in French and German. He is probably best known as the forensic scientist in the television series *The Expert* (1968–70).

Gorky, Arshile, originally **Vosdanig Manoog Adoian** (1905–48) Painter, born in Khorkom Vari, Turkish Armenia. He emigrated in 1920, and studied at the Rhode Island School of Design and in Boston. He combined ideas and images derived from Surrealism and Biomorphic art, and played a key role in the emergence of the New York school of abstract Expressionists in the 1940s.

Gorky, Maxim, pseudonym of **Alexey Maksimovich Peshkov** (1868–1936) Novelist, born in Nizhni Novgorod (formerly, Gorky), Russia. He held a variety of menial posts before becoming a writer, producing several Romantic short stories, then social novels and plays, notably the drama *Na dne* (1902, The Lower Depths). An autobiographical trilogy (1915–23) contains his best writing. Involved in strikes and imprisoned in 1905, he was an exile in Italy until 1914, then engaged in revolutionary propaganda for the new regime. He was the first president of the Soviet Writers' Union, and a supporter of Stalinism. He died in mysterious circumstances, and may have been the victim of an anti-Soviet plot. >> Zamyatin

Gorshkov, Sergey Georgievich [gaw(r)shkof] (1910–88) Soviet admiral, born in Podolsk, Ukraine. He joined the navy in 1927 and was given command of surface boats in the Black Sea from 1932 onwards, ending World War 2 in charge of a destroyer squadron. He was appointed commander-in-chief of the Soviet navy by Khrushchev in 1956, and under Brezhnev oversaw a massive naval build-up, both surface and underwater, creating a force capable of challenging the West's by the 1970s. He remained in command of the navy until his death. >> Brezhnev; Khrushchev

Gort, John Standish Surtees Prendergast Vereker, 6th Viscount (1886–1946) British soldier, born at Hamsterley Hall, Durham, NE England, UK. He trained at the Royal Military College, Woolwich, served with the Grenadier Guards in World War 1, and was awarded the VC in 1918. He was appointed Chief of the Imperial General Staff in 1938. In World War 2 he was commander-in-chief of the British forces overwhelmed in the initial German victories of 1940. Afterwards he was Governor of Gibraltar (1941–2) and of Malta (1942–4), and was promoted field marshal in 1943. He later became high commissioner for Palestine and Transjordan (1944–5).

Gorton, Sir John Grey (1911–) Australian statesman, and prime minister (1968–71), born in Melbourne, Victoria, Australia. He studied at Oxford, and in 1940 joined the RAAF, but was seriously wounded, and discharged in 1944. He was a Liberal senator for Victoria (1949–68) and a member of the House of Representatives (1968–75). He served in the governments of Sir Robert Menzies and Harold Holt before becoming prime minister. In 1971 he was defeated on a vote of confidence, and resigned in favour of William McMahon, becoming deputy leader of his Party. In 1993 he announced that he was to wed for the second time, at the age of 82. >> Holt; McMahon; Menzies; RR1033

Gorton, Samuel (1592–1677) Colonist and religious leader, born in Gorton, Greater Manchester, NW England, UK. He emigrated to Massachusetts Colony (1637) where, having denied the doctrine of the Trinity and the existence of heaven and hell, he was tried for heresy and banished (1638). He fell foul of other authorities before returning to London in 1644, where he was given a letter of safe conduct by John Rich, 2nd Earl of Warwick, to settle in Rhode Island (1648). He gave the township Shawomet a new name, Warwick, and lived there peacefully with a few faithful *Gortonite* adherents. >> Warwick, John Rich

Gossaert, Jan >> **Mabuse, Jan**

Gosse, Sir Edmund William (1845–1928) Critic, essayist, and translator, born in London, England, UK. He was educated privately, and became assistant librarian in the British Museum (1867–75), then translator to the Board of Trade (1875–1904) and finally librarian to the House of Lords (1904–14). His *Studies in the Literature of Northern Europe* (1879), and other critical works, first introduced Ibsen to English-speaking readers. He is also remembered for his autobiography, *Father and Son* (1907). He was knighted in 1925.

Gosse, William Christie (1842–81) Explorer, born in Hoddesdon, Hertfordshire, SE England, UK. In 1850, his family emigrated to Adelaide, South Australia, where he was educated privately. He joined the South Australian surveyor-general's department, and in 1873 led an expedition from Alice Springs in search of an overland route to Perth. He discovered a massive sandstone monolith which he named Ayers Rock, after Sir Henry Ayers. Although his group was forced to turn back, his maps proved invaluable to Sir John Forrest's successful 1874 expedition from Perth. >> Ayers; Forrest, John

Gotoma >> **Gautama**

Gottfried von Strassburg or **Godfrey of Strasburg** [gotfreed] (fl. 12th-c) German poet. He wrote the masterly German version of the legend of *Tristan and Isolde*, based on the Anglo-Norman poem by Thomas (c.1155). He is also noteworthy as an early exponent of literary criticism, having left appraisals of the work of poets of the period.

Gottlieb, Adolph [gotleeb] (1903–74) Painter, born in New York City. He studied at the Art Students' League in New York City, and also in Paris. He is best known as one of the original and most outstanding of the Abstract Expressionist school of painters. >> de Kooning; Mitchell, Joan; Motherwell; Tworkov

Gottlieb, Robert (Adams) [gotleeb] (1931–) Publisher and editor, born in New York City. He studied at Columbia and Cambridge universities, and became editor-in-chief at Simon and Schuster (1955–68) and at Alfred Knopf (1968–87). He was appointed editor of the *New Yorker* (1987–92).

Gottschalk, Louis Moreau [gotschawk] (1829–69) Composer, born in New Orleans, LA. A keyboard prodigy, he was sent at 13 to study in Paris, where his playing and his compositions were widely admired. He was among the first Americans to feature nationalistic elements in his music, such as the piano piece *Bamboula* (1845), based on a New Orleans slave dance. Highly successful in Europe, he returned to the USA in 1853, and made several tours in the Americas. In 1865 he fled an amatory indiscretion in the USA and spent the rest of his life in South America, where he died of yellow fever.

Gottschalk of Orbais >> **Hincmar**

Gottwald, Klement [gotvald] (1896–1953) Czech prime minister (1946–8) and president (1948–53), born in Dedice, Czech Republic (formerly, Moravia). He joined the Communist Party, becoming secretary-general in 1927. He gained prominence by opposing the Munich Agreement of 1938, and as a Communist leader, became vice-premier in the Czech provisional government in 1945. Prime minister in 1946, in February 1948 he carried out the Communist coup which averted a defeat for his party at the polls, and in June became president. Strong in the support of Moscow, whose line he followed closely, he established a complete dictatorship in Czechoslovakia.

Götz von Berlichingen [goets fon berlikhingen], known as **Götz of the Iron Hand** (1480–1562) Mercenary knight, born in Jagsthausen, Germany. From 1497 onwards he was involved in continual feuds, in which he displayed both lawless daring and chivalrous magnanimity. He lost his hand in the siege of Landshut (1504) and replaced it with one of iron. He fought for different masters in various battles, including in Hungary against the Turks (1542), and for Charles V against the French (1544). He wrote an autobiography, published in 1731, on which Goethe based his drama *Götz von Berlichingen*. >> Goethe

Goudsmit, Samuel (Abraham) [gudsmit] (1902–78) Physicist, born in The Hague, The Netherlands. He studied in Amsterdam and Leyden, and emigrated in 1927 to the USA, where he was professor at Michigan (1932–46) and later worked at the Brookhaven National Laboratory, Long Island (1948–70). Aged 23, he and his fellow-student **George Uhlenbeck** (1900–) had proposed the idea that electrons in atoms can show an effect which they described as electron spin, a novel and important concept which soon proved to be correct. In World War 2 he headed the secret Alsos mission (1944) charged with following German progress in atomic bomb research; this led to the award of the US Medal of Freedom, and to his book *Alsos* (1947).

Goudy, Frederic William [gowdee] (1865–1947) Type designer and printer, born in Bloomington, IL. After learning the printing trade in small shops and working as an accounting clerk in a Chicago bookstore, he devoted himself to typography. His first venture, Camelot Press, failed; a second, Village Press, was suspended after a fire (1908), but revived after World War 1 and a second fire in 1939. He designed many popular typefaces, including two that bear his name (*Goudy Old Style* and *Goudy Modern*), and his books include *A Half Century of Type Design and Typography* (1946).

Gough, Sir Hubert de la Poer [gof] (1870–1963) British soldier, born in Gurteen, Co Waterford, Ireland. He trained at Sandhurst, joined the 16th Lancers, and served in the Boer War, relieving Ladysmith against orders. In Ireland, as commander of the 3rd Cavalry Brigade at the Curragh (1914), he opposed the use of force to impose Home Rule against the Ulster Volunteers. He was rapidly promoted in World War 1, but his command of the Fifth Army at the third Ypres campaign impaired his reputation. He was made a scapegoat for British military failure during the German advance of March 1918. In 1922 he was retired as a full general. He wrote a self-vindication in *Fifth Army* (1931), and was knighted in 1937.

Goujon, Jean [goozhõ] (c. 1510–c. 68) The foremost French sculptor of the 16th-c, probably born in Normandy, France. His finest work is a set of reliefs for the Fountain of the Innocents (1547–9, Louvre). He worked for a while at the Louvre in Paris, but his later career is obscure. He was a Huguenot, but seems to have died before the St Bartholomew massacre (1572).

Gould, Benjamin (Apthorp) (1824–1926) Astronomer, born in Boston, MA. He studied at Harvard and Göttingen, was in charge of the longitude department of the US Coast Survey (1852–67), and director of the Dudley Observatory, Albany (1856–9). He determined the distance between Greenwich, England, and Washington, DC, by using the Atlantic cable to compare simultaneous solar elevations. He was invited to found and direct the Argentinian National Observatory in 1868. He is best known for his star catalogues of the S hemisphere (1884).

Gould, Bryan (Charles) (1939–) Former British politician, now Vice-Chancellor of Waikato University, New Zealand, born in New Zealand. He studied at Auckland University and Oxford, joined the British diplomatic service, but left to teach at Worcester College, Oxford (1968–74). He entered the House of Commons as a Labour MP in 1974, lost his seat in the 1979 general election, but returned in 1983, having spent the intervening four years as a television journalist. His rise in the Labour Party was rapid, and in 1986 he was elected to the shadow Cabinet, but resigned in 1992 (as a leading 'Eurosceptic') over the Party's policy on Europe. He was defeated in a bid for the Party leadership in 1992.

Gould, Chester (1900–85) Strip cartoonist, born in Pawnee, OK. He joined the art staff of the *Chicago American* in 1922, creating his first strip, *Fillum Fables* (1924), then moving to the *Chicago Tribune* to draw *Girl Friends* (1929). He submitted a new idea in continuity strips, *Plainclothes Tracy*, to the *New York Daily News*, who rechristened it *Dick Tracy*. It kept Gould busy until his retirement in 1977.

Gould, Glenn (Herbert) [goold] (1932–82) Pianist, born in Toronto, Ontario, Canada. He studied at the Royal Conservatory of Music, Toronto, before making his debut as a soloist with the Toronto Symphony Orchestra. He then performed extensively in the USA and Europe, but left the concert stage after only 10 years, in 1964. He became a renowned recording artist, particularly of works by Bach, and was known for his innovative radio documentaries, television shows, and occasional writings.

Gould, Jay, popular name of **Jason Gould** (1836–92) Financier, born in Roxbury, NY. He made a survey of parts of the state, engaged in lumbering, and in 1857 became the principal shareholder in a Pennsylvania bank. He began to buy up railroad bonds, started as a broker in New York City (1859), and manipulated shares to seize the presidency of the Erie Railway Co (1868–72). He also tried to corner the gold market, causing the 'Black Friday' stock-market crash of September 1869.

Gould, John (1804–81) Ornithologist and publisher, born in Lyme Regis, Dorset, S England, UK. In 1827 he became curator and preserver (taxidermist) to the new Zoological

Society's museum in London. An accomplished artist, he travelled widely, drawing birds whose skins he collected for the museum. Working with the newly developed technique of lithography, and assisted by his talented wife Elizabeth, née Coxon (d.1841), he produced 18 monumental books of sumptuous bird illustrations, including *Birds of Europe* (5 vols, 1832–7), *Birds of Australia* (7 vols, 1840–8), *Birds of Asia* (1849–83), and *Birds of Great Britain* (5 vols, 1862–73).

Gould, Morton (1913–96) Composer, conductor, and pianist, born in Richmond Hill, NY. He studied at the New York Institute of Musical Art. His music is national in style, and exploits the various aspects of popular music from both North and South America. He has composed symphonies and a variety of works in more popular style, and been a guest conductor for many orchestras.

Gould, Nat, popular name of **Nathaniel Gould** (1857–1919) Sporting journalist and novelist, born in Manchester, Greater Manchester, NW England, UK. He became a sports columnist for a newspaper in Sydney, Australia, and achieved great success with his first novel about the turf, *The Double Event*. He subsequently wrote some 130 thrillers about horse-racing, and an autobiography, *The Magic of Sport* (1909).

Gould, Shane (Elizabeth) (1956–) Swimmer, born in Brisbane, Queensland, Australia. She created Olympic history by being the first and only woman to win three individual gold swimming medals in world record time. She won the World Trophy (Helms) Medal in 1971. In 1972 she held every swimming record from 100 m to 1500 m, and in the same year gave the greatest performance of any Australian at a single Olympics in Munich. She retired in 1973, at the age of 17.

Gould, Stephen Jay (1941–) Palaeontologist, born in New York City. He studied at Antioch College and Columbia University, and became professor of geology at Harvard in 1973. His forceful support for modern views on evolution has been expressed in many articles and books, including *Hen's Teeth and Horses' Toes* (1983).

Gouled Aptidon, Hassan [gooled aptidon] (1916–) President of Djibouti (1977–), born in Djibouti city. He was a representative of French Somaliland in France while becoming increasingly active in the independence movement. He joined the African People's League for Independence (LPAI) in 1967 and, when independence was achieved, became the country's first president. Later LPAI was amalgamated with other parties to become the People's Progress Party, and Djibouti's sole political party. He was re-elected in 1987 for a final six-year term, was faced with armed opposition from the Federation for the Restoration of Unity and Democracy in 1992, and proposed a new multi-party constitution. >> RR1045

Gounod, Charles (François) [goonoh] (1818–93) Composer, born in Paris. He studied at the Paris Conservatoire and in Rome, then became organist of the Eglise des Missions Etrangères, Paris, where his earliest compositions, chiefly polyphonic in style, were performed. His major works include the opera, *Le Médecin malgré lui* (1858, trans The Mock Doctor), and his masterpiece, *Faust* (1859). He also published Masses, hymns, and anthems, and was popular as a songwriter.

Gourment, Rémy de [goormã] (1858–1915) Poet, novelist and critic, born in Bazoches-en-Houlme, France. Having been dismissed from his post at the Bibliothèque Nationale, Paris (1891), because of an allegedly unpatriotic article in *Mercure de France*, of which he was a co-founder, he lived the life of a recluse. His creative work, which was in the Symbolist vogue, includes *Sixtine* (1890, trans Very Woman) and *Un Coeur virginal* (1907, A Virgin Heart).

Gow, Niel (1727–1807) Violinist and songwriter, born in Inver, Perth and Kinross, E Scotland, UK. He composed nearly 100 tunes, and from his collection of Strathspey reels and singular skill with the bow, his name is still a household word in Scotland.

Gower, David (Ivon) (1957–) Cricketer, born in Tunbridge Wells, Kent, SE England, UK. He came to the fore quickly chiefly because of the elegance of his left-handed stroke play. He was captain of England (1984–6, 1989) though without particular success. He became the leading Test run-scorer, with 8231 runs in Test cricket over 117 matches, at an average of 44·25, but he lost this place to Graham Gooch after the final Test against the Australians in August. He retired in 1993 and became a cricket journalist and television commentator. >> Gooch; RR1149

Gower, John (c. 1325–1408) Mediaeval poet, born in Kent, SE England, UK, a friend of Chaucer. His works include many French ballads, written in his youth, and *Vox clamantis*, in Latin elegiacs (1382–4), describing the rising under Wat Tyler. His best-known work is the long English poem, *Confessio amantis* (c.1383), comprising over 100 stories from various sources on the theme of Christian and courtly love. >> Chaucer

Gowers, Sir Ernest (Arthur) (1880–1966) British civil servant, and author of an influential work on English usage. He studied at Cambridge, and was called to the bar in 1906. After a distinguished career in the civil service, he wrote *Plain Words* (1948) and *ABC of Plain Words* (1951) in an attempt to maintain standards of clear English, especially in official prose.

Gowing, Sir Lawrence Burnett (1918–91) Painter and writer on art, born in London, England, UK. He studied at the Euston Road School under William Coldstream, and his Impressionist style was often applied to portraits, such as *Mrs Roberts* (Tate, London). He was professor of fine art in the University of Durham (1948–58), Principal of Chelsea School of Art (1958–65), professor of fine art at Leeds (1967–75), and professor of fine art at University College, London (1975–85). Among his books are studies of Renoir (1947) and Vermeer (1952). >> Coldstream

Gowon, Yakubu (1934–) Nigerian soldier and president (1966–75), born in Garam, Nigeria. He trained in Nigeria and Britain (Sandhurst), and joined the Nigerian army, becoming adjutant-general in 1963 and commander-in-chief in 1966. He led a military takeover in 1966 and became president, but could not prevent a costly civil war which lasted until 1970. In 1975 he was ousted in a bloodless coup while in Kampala. After pursuing academic studies in Britain, he eventually settled in Togo.

Goya (y Lucientes), Francisco (José) de [gohya] (1746–1828) Artist, born in Fuendetodos, Spain. After travelling in Italy, he returned to Spain to design for the Royal Tapestry factory. In 1798 he produced a series of frescoes, incorporating scenes from contemporary life, in the Church of San Antonio de la Florida, Madrid, and over 80 satirical etchings, 'Los caprichos' (1799, The Caprices). He became famous for his portraits, and in 1799 was made court painter to Charles IV, which led to 'The Family of Charles IV' (1800, Prado) and other works. He settled in France in 1824.

Goyathlay >> Geronimo
Goyen, Jan van >> van Goyen, Jan
Gozzi, Carlo, conte (Count) [gotzee] (1720–1806) Playwright, born in Venice, Italy. After a period in the army, he took up writing in Venice. Among his works are several satirical poems and plays, defending the traditions of the *commedia dell' arte* against the innovations of Goldoni and others. His best-known works include the comedy,

Fiaba dell' amore delle tre melarance (1761, The Love of the Three Oranges) and *Turandot* (1762). His brother, **Gasparo Gozzi** (1713–86) was a journal editor and press censor, who also became known for his verse satires. >> Goldoni

Gozzoli, Benozzo [gotsohlee], also called **Benozzo di Lese** (1420–97) Painter, born in Florence, Italy. A pupil of Fra Angelico, in Florence (1456–64) he adorned the Palazzo Medici-Riccardi with scriptural subjects, including his famous 'Journey of the Magi' in which Florentine councillors accompanied by members of the Medici family appear, and painted similar frescoes at Gimignano (1464–7), and in the Campo Santo at Pisa (1468–84). >> Angelico

Graaf, Reinier de [grahf] (1641–73) Physician and anatomist, born in Schoonhoven, The Netherlands. He studied at the University of Angers, practised at Delft, and in 1663 wrote a famous treatise on the pancreas. In 1672 he discovered the follicles of the ovary, which became known as *Graafian follicles*.

Graaff, Robert Van de >> **Van de Graaff, Robert**

Gracchus, Gaius Sempronius [grakus] (c. 159–121 BC) Roman statesman. After the murder of his brother Tiberius Gracchus, he returned to Rome and was elected to the tribuneship in 123 and 122 BC. He renewed his brother's agrarian law and took other measures to control abuses by those in power. By a senatorial intrigue he was rejected from a third tribuneship, and the Senate began to repeal his enactments. He led an illegal demonstration, and a riot ensued in which many of his supporters were slain, and he committed suicide. Much of his legislation survived, and his ideals influenced reforms proposed in the last century of the republic. >> Gracchus, Tiberius Sempronius; Scipio Aemilianus

Gracchus, Tiberius Sempronius [grakus] (168–133 BC) Roman statesman. In 137 he served as quaestor in Spain, where his influence enabled him to save an entire Roman army from destruction by the Numantines. He was concerned at the lack of manpower for the army, traditionally recruited from land-owning peasants, and having been elected tribune in 134, proposed reforms to extend land-ownership among the poor. His measures were strongly disapproved of by wealthy land-owners and he was assassinated while trying to gain re-election as tribune. >> Gracchus, Gaius Sempronius

Grace of Monaco, Princess >> **Kelly, Grace**

Grace, W(illiam) G(ilbert) (1848–1915) Cricketer, born in Downend, South Gloucester, SWC England, UK. By 1864 he was playing cricket for Gloucester County, and was chosen for the Gentlemen *v.* the Players at 16. He practised medicine in Bristol, but his main career was cricket. He toured Canada, the USA, and Australia, twice captaining the English team. His career in first-class cricket (1865–1908) as batsman and bowler brought 126 centuries, 54 896 runs, and 2876 wickets. >> RR1151

Gracián (y Morales), Baltasar [grathyahn] (1601–58) Philosopher and writer, born in Belmonte de Calayatud, Spain. He entered the Jesuit order in 1619 and later became head of the College at Tarragona. His early works, such as *The Man of Discretion* (1646), are all heavily didactic guides to life. He set out his literary ideas on *conceptismo*, the art of conceited writing, in *Subtlety and the Art of Genius* (1642). He is best known, however, for his three-part allegorical novel, *The Critic* (1651, 1653, 1657), in which civilization and society are portrayed through the eyes of a savage.

Grade (of Elstree), Lew Grade, Baron, originally **Louis Winogradsky** (1906–) Theatrical impresario, born near Odessa, Ukraine, the eldest of three brothers who were to dominate British show-business for over 40 years. He arrived in Britain in 1912, accompanied by his parents and

younger brother **Boris Grade**, who became **Baron Bernard Delfont of Stepney** (1909–94). The brothers became dancers, then theatrical agents, along with the youngest brother **Leslie Grade**. Bernard entered theatrical management in 1941, and acquired many properties, notably the London Hippodrome. His many companies embraced theatre, film, television, music, and property interests. From 1958 to 1978 he presented the annual Royal Variety Performance. Lew was an early entrant to the world of commercial television, and became managing director of ATV in 1962. He has headed several large film entertainment and communications companies. He was knighted in 1969 and made a life peer in 1976.

Graebner, (Robert) Fritz [graybner] (1877–1934) Ethnologist, born in Berlin. He studied in Berlin and joined the staff of the Royal Museum of Ethnology in Berlin in 1899, but moved to the Rautenstrauch-Joest Museum in Cologne in 1906 (director in 1925), and became honorary professor at Cologne University in 1926. He is principally known for developing the theory of *Kulturkreise* (culture complex), clusters of diffusing cultural traits which he used to explain cultural similarities and differences. His most important work, *Methode der Ethnologie* (1911, Method of Ethnology), became the cornerstone for the German culture-historical school of ethnology.

Graf, Steffi [grahf] (1969–) Tennis player, born in Brühl, Germany. In 1982 she became the youngest person to receive a World Tennis Association ranking, aged 13, and reached the semi-final of the US Open in 1985. She won the French Open in 1987, and took all four major titles in 1988, as well as the Wimbledon doubles. She beat Natalya Zvereva 6-0 6-0 to win the Australian title, the first shutout in a major final since 1911. She won the Wimbledon title again in 1989, 1991, 1992, 1993, 1995, and 1996. >> RR1173

Grafton, Augustus Henry Fitzroy, 3rd Duke of (1735–1811) British statesman and prime minister (1768–70). He was secretary of state under Rockingham (1765–6), and First Lord of the Treasury under Pitt (1766); but owing to Chatham's illness Grafton had to undertake the duties of premier from September 1767. He resigned in 1770, and later served as Lord Privy Seal under North (1771–5) and in the new Rockingham ministry (1782–3). >> North, Lord; Pitt, William (the Elder); Rockingham; RR1095

Graham, Billy, popular name of **William Franklin Graham, Jr** (1918–) Evangelist, born in Charlotte, NC. He attended Florida Bible Institute, was ordained a Southern Baptist minister in 1939, and quickly gained a reputation as a preacher. During the 1950s he conducted a series of highly organized revivalist campaigns in the USA and UK, and later in South America, the former USSR, and W Europe. A charismatic figure, his campaigns continued to attract large audiences into the 1990s. His books include *Peace with God* (1952), *World Aflame* (1965), and *Storm Warning* (1992).

Graham, Ennis >> **Molesworth, Mary Louisa**

Graham, James >> **Higgins, Jack**

Graham, Sir James Robert George, Bart (1792–1861) British statesman, born in Netherby, Cumbria, NW England, UK. He studied at Oxford, entered parliament as a Whig in 1826, became First Lord of the Admiralty (1830–4), reformed administration of the Navy, and helped draft the electoral reform bill (1832) under Earl Grey. He became home secretary under Peel in 1841, supported the Corn Law Repeal Bill, and resigned (1846) as soon as it was carried. On Peel's death in 1850 he became leader of the Peelites, and was First Lord of the Admiralty in the coalition ministry (1852–5). >> Grey, Charles; Peel

Graham, John of Claverhouse >> **Dundee, Viscount**

Graham, Martha (1894–1991) Dancer, teacher, and choreographer, born in Pittsburgh, PA. She first appeared in vaudeville and revue, and started the Martha Graham School of Contemporary Dance in 1927. She was the most famous exponent of Expressionist modern dance in the USA. Her works dealt with frontier life, as in *Appalachian Spring* (1944), Greek myths, as in *Clytemnestra* (1958), and psychological drama. Her method of dance training has been widely adopted in professional schools. In 1996 the company appeared at the Edinburgh International Festival's 50th anniversary celebrations, performing reconstructions of her early works. >> Hawkins, Erick

Graham, Otto Everett, Jr, nickname **Automatic Otto** (1921–) Quarterback and coach of American football, born in Waukegan, IL. He played various sports, then concentrated on football, playing with the Cleveland Browns from 1946. In 1950, the Browns went into the National Football League, and he led them to championship victories in 1950, 1954, and 1955. He later became head coach of the Washington Redskins (1966–8).

Graham, Thomas (1805–69) Chemist and physcist, born in Glasgow, W Scotland, UK. He was professor of chemistry at Glasgow (1830–7) and London (1837–55), and Master of the Mint (1855–69). One of the founders of physical chemistry, he formulated the law that the diffusion rate of gases is inversely proportional to the square root of their density (*Graham's law*). He also studied the properties of colloids, and devised dialysis for separating colloids from crystalloids.

Graham, W(illiam) S(ydney) (1918–86) Poet, born in Greenock, Inverclyde, WC Scotland, UK. Essentially a Scottish poet, he was much influenced by Continental and American authors, such as Rimbaud and Hart Crane. His early poems brought encouragement and support from T S Eliot, and contain an exotic mix of imagery from industrial and rural scenes. In later work, such as his best-known single volume, *The Nightfishing* (1955), he uses the extended metaphor of the voyage, both inward and outward, to examine language and being. His *Collected Poems* were published in 1979. >> Crane, Hart; Eliot, T S; Rimbaud

Grahame, Kenneth (1859–1932) Writer, born in Edinburgh, EC Scotland, UK. He entered the Bank of England in 1879, became its secretary in 1898, and retired for health reasons in 1908. He wrote several stories for children, the best known being *The Wind in the Willows* (1908), which was dramatized in 1930 by A A Milne as *Toad of Toad Hall*. >> Milne, A A

Grahame-White, Claude (1879–1959) Aviator and engineer, born in Bursledon, Hampshire, S England, UK. He was the first Englishman to be granted a British certificate of proficiency in aviation (1910). In 1909 he founded the first British flying school at Pau, in France, and in 1910 founded his own company to build aircraft. He helped to establish London Aerodrome at Hendon (1911), and published books on the aeroplane and flying.

Grahn, Lucile (1819–1907) Ballerina, born in Copenhagen. Making her official debut in 1829, she studied and worked in the Royal Danish Ballet with Auguste Bournonville until 1839. She then gave guest performances throughout Europe. Retiring from dancing in 1856, she was ballet mistress at the Leipzig State Theatre (1858–61) and the Munich Court Opera (1869–75), where she assisted Richard Wagner in the production of *Das Rheingold* and *Die Meistersinger von Nürnberg*. A street in Munich is named after her. >> Bournonville; Wagner, Richard

Grainger, Percy (Aldridge), originally **George Percy Grainger** (1882–1961) Composer and pianist, born in Melbourne, Victoria, Australia. A child prodigy on piano,

he studied in Melbourne and Frankfurt, and became a travelling virtuoso based in London. After making a sensational US debut (1915) with the piano concerto by his friend Grieg, he remained in the USA for most of the rest of his life. He championed the revival of folk music in such works as 'Molly on the Shore' and 'Shepherd's Hey' (1911), but was also one of the first to compose for electronic instruments. He often returned to Australia, and in 1935 founded the Grainger Museum at Melbourne. >> Grieg, Edvard

Gram, Hans Christian Joachim (1853–1938) Bacteriologist, born in Copenhagen. Professor at Copenhagen, he established in 1884 a microbiological staining method for bacteria, distinguishing the *Gram-positive* from the *Gram-negative*.

Gramme, Zénobe Théophile [gram] (1826–1901) Electrical engineer, born in Jehay-Bodegnée, Belgium. In 1869 he built the first successful direct-current dynamo, which after various improvements he manufactured from 1871; it was the first electric generator to be used commercially, for electroplating as well as electric lighting. In 1873, in partnership with Hippolyte Fontaine, he showed that a dynamo could function in reverse as an electric motor. >> Fontaine, Hippolyte

Grammer, Kelsey (1955–) Actor, born on St Thomas, US Virgin Islands. Brought up in New Jersey and Florida, he trained at the Juilliard School, then acted on stage in theatres across the USA. He is best known for his role as Dr Frasier Crane, originally seen in *Cheers* (1982–93) and *Wings*, and then in *Frasier* (from 1993, 2 Emmies). His first feature film was *Down Periscope* (1996), and he has published a volume of autobiography, *So Far...* (1995).

Gramsci, Antonio [gramskee] (1891–1937) Italian political leader and theoretician, born in Ales, Sardinia. He studied at Turin University, helped found a left-wing paper, *L'ordine nuovo* (1919, The New Order), and was active in promoting workers' councils in factories. Dissatisfied with moderate, reformist Socialism, he helped to establish the Italian Communist Party (1921), which he represented at the Third International in Moscow (1922), and in 1924 he became leader of the Party in parliament. When Mussolini banned the Party, he was arrested and spent the rest of his life in prison (1926–37), where he completed some 30 notebooks of reflections which were published posthumously (*Lettere del carcere*, 1947, Letters from Prison), and are now regarded as one of the most important political texts of this century. >> Mussolini

Granados (y Campiña), Enrique [granahthos] (1867–1916) Composer and pianist, born in Lérida, Spain. He studied at Barcelona and at Paris. A composer of Spanish dances, his *Goyescas* (1911–13) for piano are his most accomplished works. He was drowned when the *Sussex* was torpedoed by the Germans in the English Channel.

Granby, John Manners, Marquess of (1721–70) British army officer, whose reputation was made in the Seven Years' War (1756–63) when he led the British cavalry in a major victory over the French at Warburg (1760). He became a popular hero, and in 1763 was appointed Master-General of the Ordnance.

Grand, Sarah, *née* **Frances Elizabeth Clarke** (1854–1943) Novelist, born of English parents in Donaghadee, Ireland. At the age of 16 she married an army doctor, and later became Mayoress of Bath (1923, 1925–9). Her reputation rests on *The Heavenly Twins* (1893), in which she skilfully handles delicate problems of sexual development, relationships, and disease, and her autobiographical *The Beth Book* (1897). Her later works, including *The Winged Victory* (1916), are advocacies of feminine emancipation.

Grandi, Dino, conte di (Count of) **Mordano** (1895–1988) Italian statesman and diplomat, born in Mordano, near

Bologna. He studied law, and joined the Fascist quadrumvirate during the 1922 March on Rome. He became Mussolini's foreign minister (1929–32), then Italian ambassador in London (1932–9), but was recalled in 1939 after the formation of the Berlin–Rome Axis, and appointed minister of justice. In July 1943 he moved the motion in the Fascist Grand Council which brought about Mussolini's resignation, then fled to Portugal before being sentenced to death in absentia by a Fascist Republican court at Verona. For many years he lived in exile in Brazil, then returned to Italy in 1973 and wrote two acclaimed books, *The Foreign Policy of Italy, 1929–32*, and *My Country*. >> Mussolini

Grange, Kenneth Henry (1929–) Industrial designer, born in London, England, UK. He studied at Willesdon School of Arts and Crafts (1944–7) before working as a technical illustrator. After some years in architectural and design practices, he ran his own design consultancy (1958–71). In 1971 he cofounded the multi-disciplinary practice Pentagram. His product designs are among the most familiar even to those who do not know his name. They include food mixers for Kenwood, cameras for Kodak, locomotives for British Rail, and the unloved parking meter for Venner. He became a royal designer for industry in 1969.

Grange, Red, popular name of **Howard Edward Grange**, nickname **the Galloping Ghost** (1903–91) Player and coach of American football, born in Forksville, PA. His achievements as a running back in the 1920s earned him his byname. He played for Illinois University (1923–5), and signed for the Chicago Bears in 1925. He retired from playing in 1935, and became a sports commentator on radio and television.

Granger, Stewart, originally **James Lablanche Stewart** (1913–93) Film actor, born in London, England, UK. He studied at Epson College and at the Webber-Douglas School of Dramatic Art, then worked in repertory companies and as a film extra before being cast as the romantic lead in *So This Is London* (1938). He assumed his professional name in the 1930s, to avoid confusion with actor James Stewart. The success of the film *The Man In Grey* (1943) swept him to star status in Britain. Later films included *King Solomon's Mines* (1950), *Beau Brummell* (1954), *North to Alaska* (1960), and *The Wild Geese* (1977). He became a US citizen in 1956.

Granit, Ragnar Arthur (1900–) Physiologist, born in Helsinki, Finland. He studied at Helsinki University, and after working at the universities of Pennsylvania and Oxford (1928–31) became professor of neurophysiology at the Karolinska Institute in Stockholm (1940–67), and a Swedish national. He pioneered the study of the neurophysiology of vision by the use of microelectrodes, and shared the 1987 Nobel Prize for Physiology or Medicine. >> RR1124

Grant, Alexander (Marshall) (1925–) Dancer and director, born in Wellington, New Zealand. A scholarship took him to London and the Royal Ballet, Covent Garden, where he was to spend his entire dancing career. A soloist by 1949, he became best known for such character roles as Bottom in Frederick Ashton's *The Dream* (1964). He was director of the Royal Ballet's offshoot, Ballet For All (1971–5), and director of the National Ballet of Canada (1976–83).

Grant, Cary, originally **Archibald Leach** (1904–86) Film actor, born in Bristol, SW England, UK. He went to Hollywood in 1928, played opposite Marlene Dietrich and Mae West, and from the late 1930s developed in leading comedy roles, especially under the direction of Howard Hawks, such as *Bringing Up Baby* (1938) and *His Girl Friday*

(1940). He also provided several memorable performances for Hitchcock in *Suspicion* (1941), *Notorious* (1946), *To Catch a Thief* (1955), and *North by North-West* (1959), but during the 1960s his appearances were fewer. >> Dietrich; Hawks; Hitchcock, Alfred; West, Mae

Grant, Duncan (James Corrow) (1885–1978) Painter, born in Rothiemurchus, Highland, N Scotland, UK. He studied at the Westminster and Slade Schools, in Italy, and in Paris, and was associated with Fry's Omega Workshops, and then with the London Group. His works were mainly landscapes, portraits, and still-life, and he also designed textiles, pottery, and stage scenery. >> Fry, Roger

Grant, James Augustus (1827–92) British soldier and explorer, born in Nairn, Highland, N Scotland, UK. Educated at Marischal College, Aberdeen, he joined the British army, eventually reaching the rank of colonel, and saw service in the Battle of Gujerat, the Indian Mutiny, and the Abyssinian campaign of 1868. He is best known as a colleague of John Hanning Speke, with whom he explored the sources of the Nile (1860–3), keeping a record of significant geographical features and native customs which he published as *A Walk Across Africa* (1864). >> Speke

Grant, Ulysses S(impson) (1822–85) US general and 18th president (1869–77), born in Point Pleasant, OH. He trained at West Point, fought in the Mexican War (1846–8), then settled as a farmer in Missouri. On the outbreak of the Civil War (1861), he rejoined the army and rose rapidly, leading Union forces to victory, first in the Mississippi Valley, then in the final campaigns in Virginia. He accepted the Confederate surrender at Appomattox Court House (1865), and was made a full general in 1866. Elected president in 1868 and 1872, he presided over the reconstruction of the South, but his administration was marred by scandal. He wrote two volumes of memoirs (1885–6), which were highly acclaimed as a contribution to military history. >> RR1097

Granville-Barker, Harley (1877–1946) Actor, playwright, and producer, born in London, England, UK. After a career in acting, he entered theatre management at the Court Theatre (1904) and the Savoy (1907). He wrote several plays himself, such as *The Voysey Inheritance* (1905), collaborated in translations, and wrote a famous series of prefaces to Shakespeare's plays (1927–45).

Granz, Norman (1918–) Concert impresario and record producer, born in Los Angeles, CA. He borrowed money to stage a jazz concert at the Philharmonic Auditorium, and its success led to national and international tours called Jazz at the Philharmonic. His recording companies Clef (1951) and Norgran (1954) originally released his concert recordings. He discovered Oscar Peterson and became his manager, and also managed Ella Fitzgerald. In 1973 he started Pablo Records and quickly established its name by recording Dizzy Gillespie, Count Basie, Duke Ellington, and many others. He is widely recognized as the leading disseminator of jazz music around the world.

Grappelli, Stéphane [grapelee] (1908–97) Jazz violinist, born in Paris. He and Django Reinhardt were the principal soloists in the Quintet of the Hot Club of France (1934–9), the first European jazz band to exert an influence in the USA. Grappelli's suave, piercing violin lines made a perfect foil for Reinhardt's busy guitar. Their partnership ended when Grappelli escaped to England during the Occupation. He returned to Paris in 1948, and continued to make many international appearances. >> Reinhardt, Django

Grass, Günter (Wilhelm) (1927–) Writer, born in Gdańsk, Poland (formerly, Danzig, Germany). He was educated at Danzig Volksschule and Gymnasium, the Academy of Art, Düsseldorf, and the State Academy of Fine Arts, Berlin. He served in World War 2 and was held as a prisoner-of-war. *Die Blechtrommel* (1959, The Tin Drum) was the first of the novels that have made him Germany's greatest living novelist, and it caused a furore in Germany because of its depiction of the Nazis. Intellectual and experimental, his books consistently challenge the status quo and question our reading of the past. Important books are *Katz und Maus* (1961, Cat and Mouse), *Hundejahre* (1963, Dog Years), *Örtlich betäubt* (1969, Local Anaesthetic), and *Der Butt* (1977, The Flounder). Later novels include *Kopfgeburten* (1980, Headbirths) and *Ein weites Feld* (1995, A Wide Field). He worked as a ghost-writer for the leader of the Social Democrats, Willy Brandt, and has published a collection of speeches and essays, 'Der Bürger und seine Stimme' (1974, The Citizen and his Vote). >> Brandt, Willy

Grassmann, Hermann (Günther) (1809–77) Mathematician and philologist, born in Stettin, Germany. He studied at Berlin, and spent most of his life as a teacher there and in Stettin. His book *Die lineale Ausdehnungslehre* (1844, The Theory of Linear Extension) developed a general calculus for vectors. It made little impact during his life, and it is only since his death that its importance has gradually been recognized; it anticipated much later work in quaternions, vectors, tensors, matrices, and differential forms. From 1849 he studied Sanskrit and other ancient Indo-European languages and, unlike his mathematics, his work in Indo-European and Germanic philology met with immediate acceptance.

Gratian [grayshian], in full **Flavius Augustus Gratianus** (359–383) Roman emperor from 375, the son of Valentinian I. In 367 his father made him Augustus in Gaul, and on Valentinian's death he became emperor of the West, which he shared with his brother Valentinian II. He appointed Theodosius emperor in the East on the death of his uncle Valens (378). He was much influenced by St Ambrose, and dropped the phrase *Pontifex Maximus* ('Supreme Priest') from his title as a mark of respect for Christianity. He was eventually overthrown by the usurper Magnus Maximus (ruled W empire, 383–88), and was murdered at Lyon. >> Ambrose; Theodosius I; Valentinian I; RR1084

Gratian [grayshian], also known as **Franciscus Gratianus** (12th-c) Italian jurist and Carmaldulensian monk of Bologna. Between 1139 and 1150 he compiled the collection of canon law known as the *Decretum Gratiani*, which became the basic text for all studies of canon law, and remained the first part of the traditional body of canon law in the Roman Catholic Church until 1917.

Grattan, Henry (1746–1820) Irish statesman, born in Dublin. In 1772 he was called to the Irish bar, and in 1775 entered the Irish parliament, where his oratory made him the leading spokesman for the patriotic party. He secured Irish free trade in 1779, and legislative independence in 1782. He was returned for Dublin in 1790, and in 1805 was elected to the House of Commons, where he fought for Catholic Emancipation.

Graun, Karl Heinrich [grown] (1703/4–59) Composer, born near Torgau, Germany. A singer as well as a composer, he became *Kapellmeister* to Frederick II (1740), and remained with him throughout his career. His works include 32 operas and a 'Passion piece'. >> Frederick II

Graveney, Tom [grayvnee], popular name of **Thomas William Graveney** (1927–) Cricketer and television commentator, born in Riding Mill, Northumberland, NE England, UK. A tall, graceful batsman, he had a patchy Test career; nevertheless, he made 11 Test centuries for England in the course of compiling 4882 runs, recording double centuries against the West Indies at Nottingham in 1957. >> RR1151

Graves, Robert James (1796–1853) Physician, born in Dublin. He studied medicine in Edinburgh, but took his medical degree in 1818 from Dublin. After three years' travel in Europe, he returned to Dublin and was appointed physician to the Meath Hospital. There he reorganized medical teaching along the lines advocated in France, with emphasis on physical examination and systematic note-taking and autopsies. He was an excellent diagnostician, best remembered today for his description of a form of hyperthyroidism (*Graves' disease*), and his *Clinical Lectures on the Practice of Medicine* (1843) won him an international reputation.

Graves, Robert (Ranke) (1895–1985) Poet and novelist, born in London, England, UK. He studied at Oxford, served in the trenches in World War 1, became professor of English at Cairo, and after 1929 lived mainly in Majorca. His best-known novels are *I, Claudius* and its sequel, *Claudius the God* (both 1934), which were adapted for television in 1976. He wrote several autobiographical works, notably *Goodbye to All That* (1929) and *Occupation Writer* (1950), published critical essays, carried out Greek and Latin translations, and was professor of poetry at Oxford (1961–6). His *Collected Poems* (1975) draws on more than 20 volumes.

Gray, Asa (1810–88) Botanist, born in Sauquoit, NY. He trained in medicine, but then took up botany, becoming professor of natural history at Harvard (1842–73), and a strong Darwinian. His main works were the *Flora of North America* (1838–42), which he compiled with John Torrey, and the *Manual of the Botany of the Northern United States* (1848), often known simply as *Gray's Manual*. >> Torrey

Gray, Elisha (1835–1901) Inventor, born in Barnesville, OH. A manufacturer of telegraphic apparatus, his firm became the Western Electric Co. His 60 patents included a multiplex telegraph. He also claimed the invention of the telephone, but lost the patent rights to Alexander Graham Bell after a long legal battle in the US Supreme Court. >> Bell, Alexander Graham

Gray, George Robert (1808–72) Ornithologist and entomologist, born in London, England, UK. Educated at Merchant Taylor's School, he became zoological assistant at the British Museum in 1831, where his first task was cataloguing insects. This led to his publication of *Entomology of Australia* (1833). He is best known for his *Genera of Birds* (3 vols, 1844–49). *Gray's grasshopper warbler* is named after him.

Gray, George William (1926–) Chemist, born in Scotland, UK. He studied at Glasgow and London, and joined the staff of Hull University in 1946, becoming professor of chemistry (1964). His research into liquid crystals took on a new importance in the 1960s when electronics companies realized they could be used to form a visual display, and he succeeded in making the necessary stable liquid crystal.

Gray, Harold (Lincoln) (1894–1968) Cartoonist, born in Kankakee, IL. After serving as an assistant on Sidney Smith's newspaper comic strip, *The Gumps* (1921–4), he created his own strip in 1924, called *Little Orphan Annie*. For the next 45 years, he worked ceaselessly on his widely syndicated strip. Little Orphan Annie was adapted to a hit Broadway musical, *Annie* (1977), and a film based on the musical was released in 1982.

Gray, Milner Connorton (1899–) Graphic designer, born in London, England, UK. He studied at Goldsmith's College, London. He founded with Misha Black the Industrial Design Partnership (1935) and the Design Research Unit (1945). He worked for the ministry of information during World War 2 and was involved in two major exhibitions, 'Britain Can Make It' (1946) and the 'Festival of Britain' (1951). Although he designed in other fields, such as ceramics and furniture, he is best known for his co-ordinated 'corporate identity' schemes for such organizations as Ilford, Austin Reed, ICI, Gilbey, and British Rail. He became a royal designer for industry in 1937. >> Black, Misha

Gray, Simon (James Holliday) (1936–) Playwright, director, and novelist, born on Hayling Island, Hampshire, S England, UK. He studied at Cambridge, and became lecturer in English literature at Queen Mary College, London (1965–85). Many of his plays are set in the world of academics, depicting lonely alienated men rejected by society. His first play, *Wise Child*, was produced in 1967. Later plays include *Otherwise Engaged* (1975), *Quartermaine's Terms* (1981), *Melon* (1987), and *Simply Disconnected* (1996). In *An Unnatural Pursuit* (1985), he describes the suffering endured by a lonely playwright.

Gray, Thomas (1716–71) Poet, born in London, England, UK. He studied at Cambridge, where in 1768 he became professor of history and modern languages. In 1742 he wrote his 'Ode on a Distant Prospect of Eton College', and began his masterpiece, 'Elegy Written in a Country Churchyard' (1751), set at Stoke Poges, Buckinghamshire. He then settled in Cambridge, where he wrote his *Pindaric Odes* (1757).

Graziani, Rodolfo, Marquess of Neghelli [gratsiahnee] (1882–1955) Italian soldier and administrator, born in Filettino, Italy. He served in World War 1, and thereafter in Tripolitania and Cyrenaica. He was Governor of Somaliland (1935–6), and a ruthless Viceroy of Ethiopia (1936–7). In World War 2, as Governor of Libya, he attacked Egypt, was defeated by Wavell (1940–1) and resigned, but after the fall of Mussolini in 1943 re-emerged as minister of defence and head of continuing Fascist armed resistance. He was captured by his own countrymen on the eve of final capitulation in Italy (1945), tried for war crimes, and sentenced in 1950, but released the same year. >> Mussolini; Wavell

Great Elector, The >> **Frederick William**

Greathead, Henry >> **Wouldhave, William**

Greathead, James Henry (1844–96) Civil engineer, born in Grahamstown, South Africa. He went to England in 1859 and studied civil engineering. At the age of 24 he undertook to build a subway under the Thames in London (1869). To penetrate the very difficult water-bearing strata he greatly improved the tunnelling shield designed (1818) by Brunel for the Rotherhithe tunnel. He engaged in various other surface and underground railway contracts including the City and South London Railway tunnels under the Thames (1886), having in 1884 patented further improvements to his shield, incorporating the use of compressed air and forward propulsion by hydraulic jacks, an arrangement that is now in general use in tunnel construction. >> Brunel, Mark Isambard

Greaves, Jimmy, popular name of **James Greaves** (1940–) English footballer and television commentator, born in London, England, UK. He scored 357 goals in 517 league matches with Chelsea, Tottenham Hotspur, and West Ham United. His highly individual style of play made him difficult to fit into a team pattern, and Alf Ramsey felt able to do without him in the World Cup Final of 1966. After his retirement he made a new career as a television sports commentator, and co-presented the popular *Saint and Greavsie Show* (1985–92) with Ian St John. >> Ramsey, Sir Alf; RR1155

Greco, El [grekoh] (Span 'the Greek'), nickname of **Domenikos Theotokopoulos** (1541–1614) Painter, born in Candia, Crete, Greece. He studied in Italy, probably as a pupil of Titian, and is known to have settled in Toledo, Spain, c.1577. He became a portrait painter whose reputation fluctuated because of the suspicion which greeted his characteristic distortions, such as his elongated, flamelike figures. His most famous painting is probably the 'Burial of Count Orgaz' (1586) in the Church of San Tomé, Toledo. Many of his works are in Toledo, where there is also the Museo del Greco. >> Titian

Greeley, Adolphus (Washington) (1844–1935) Arctic explorer, born in Newburyport, MA. During the first International Polar Year in 1881 he was the officer in charge of a US Army expedition to Smith Sound to set up a meteorological station; one of the team travelled to within 396 miles of the Pole, the farthest point reached till then. The relief boat failed to turn up in 1883, and when rescue came in 1884, only six of the party of 25 were still alive. In 1888 he helped form the American Geographical Society.

Greeley, Andrew M(oran) (1928–) Catholic priest and sociologist, born in Oak Park, IL. Ordained in 1954, he studied sociology at the University of Chicago (1962) while doing parish work; he then joined the university's National Opinion Research Center. His studies convinced him that the Catholic hierarchy was out of touch with the attitudes and needs of priests and laity. Besides sociological studies and writings on moral and religious topics, he turned out salty popular novels, increasing his reputation as a maverick within the Church.

Greeley, Horace (1811–72) Editor and politician, born in Amherst, NH. He was editor of the weekly *New Yorker* in 1834, and in 1841 founded the daily New York *Tribune*, of which he was the leading editor until his death, exerting, without concern for popularity, a supreme influence on US opinion. The *Tribune* was at first Whig, then anti-slavery Whig, and finally extreme Republican. He maintained his anti-slavery stance throughout the Civil War. After Lee's surrender he warmly advocated a universal amnesty; but his signing the bail-bond of Jefferson Davis awakened a storm of public indignation. He made a bid in 1872 for the presidency, but died before the election was completed. >> Davis, Jefferson; Lee, Robert E

Green, George (1793–1841) Mathematician and physicist, born in Nottingham, C England, UK. While working as a baker he taught himself mathematics, and in 1828 published a pamphlet, *An Essay on the Application of Mathematical Analysis to the Theories of Electricity and Magnetism*, containing what are now known as *Green's theorem* and *Green's functions*, and introducing the electrical term *potential*. He entered Caius College, Cambridge, in 1833, published several papers on wave motion and optics, and was elected a fellow in 1839.

Green, Henry, pseudonym of **Henry Vincent Yorke** (1905–73) Writer and industrialist, born in Tewkesbury, Gloucestershire, SWC England, UK. He studied at Oxford, and became managing director in his father's engineering company in Birmingham, but pursued a parallel career as a writer, publishing his first book, *Blindness* (1926), while still an undergraduate. Other titles include *Party Going* (1939), *Loving* (1945), and *Doting* (1952), and an autobiographical work, *Pack My Bag: a Self Portrait* (1940). His writing was much admired in Europe.

Green, Julien (Hartridge) (1900–) Writer, born of American parents in Paris. He studied in France and at Virginia University, and was bilingual, but wrote mainly in French. He began a successful series of psychological studies in a melancholy vein with *Mont-Cinère* (1925, trans Avarice House). His other works include *Adrienne Mesurat* (1927, trans The Closed Garden), *Léviathan* (1929, trans The Dark Journey, which won the Harper Prize Novel contest), and his *Journals* I, II, and III (1938–46), *Memories of Happy Days* (1942), and *Memories of Evil Days* (1976). Later works include the novel *Dixie* (1995) and the play *L'étudiant roux* (1993).

Green, Lucinda, *née* **Prior-Palmer** (1953–) Three-day eventer, born in London, England, UK. She is the only person to win the Badminton Horse Trials six times (1973, 1976–7, 1979, 1983–4), and the Badminton and Burghley Horse Trials in the same year, on *George* in 1977. She was individual European champion in 1975 and 1977, and the 1982 world champion on *Regal Realm*, when she also won a team gold medal. She married Australian eventer **David Green** in 1981 (marriage dissolved, 1992). >> RR1153

Greenaway, Kate, popular name of **Catherine Greenaway** (1846–1901) Artist and book-illustrator, born in London, England, UK. She became well known in the 1880s for her coloured portrayals of child life, in such works as *The Birthday Book* (1880). The *Greenaway Medal* is awarded annually for the best British children's book artist.

Greenaway, Peter (1942–) Film-maker and painter, born in London, England, UK. Trained as a painter, he first exhibited at the Lord's Gallery in 1964. Employed at the Central Office of Information (1965–76), he worked as an editor and began making his own short films, gaining a reputation on the international festival circuit with such works as *A Walk Through H* (1978) and *The Falls* (1980), before *The Draughtsman's Contract* (1982) won him critical acclaim and a wider audience. His later works explore such preoccupations as sex, death, decay, and gamesmanship, and include *The Belly of An Architect* (1987), *Drowning By Numbers* (1988), *The Cook, The Thief, His Wife and Her Lover* (1989), *Prospero's Books* (1991), *The Baby of Macon* (1993), and *The Pillow-Book* (1996).

Greene, (Henry) Graham (1904–91) Writer, born in Berkhamsted, Hertfordshire, SE England, UK. He studied at Oxford, converted from Anglicanism to Catholicism, and moved to London, where he became a journalist and then a freelance writer. His early novels, beginning with *The Man Within* (1929), and 'entertainments', such as *Stamboul Train* (1932), use the melodramatic technique of the thriller. In his major novels, central religious issues emerge, first apparent in *Brighton Rock* (1938), and more explicit in *The Power and the Glory* (1940), *The End of the Affair* (1951), and *A Burnt-Out Case* (1961). He also wrote several plays, film scripts (notably, *The Third Man*, 1949), short stories, and essays, as well as three volumes of autobiography. His later works include *Dr Fischer of Geneva* (1980), *Monsignor Quixote* (1982), and *The Tenth Man* (1985). He lived in Antibes, France, for many years. >> Greene, Hugh Carleton

Greene, Sir Hugh Carleton (1910–87) Journalist and television executive, born in Berkhamsted, Hertfordshire, SE England, UK, the brother of Graham Greene. After studying at Oxford he worked in Germany as a foreign correspondent for the *Daily Herald* and later the *Daily Telegraph* (1934–9). In 1940 he joined the BBC to work on propaganda broadcasts to Germany, became controller of broadcasting in the British zone of Germany (1946), and rebuilt the country's peacetime radio service. He worked with the BBC's Overseas Service (1952–6), and became the BBC's first director of news and current affairs (1958–60) before being chosen as director-general (1960–9). He injected fresh vigour into the BBC, encouraging it to compete with Independent Television, and creating a liberal climate in which programme-makers flourished. >> Greene, Graham

Greene, Nathanael (1742–86) US general, born in Warwick, RI. In the American Revolution, he fought (1775–6) at Boston, Trenton, the Brandywine, and Germanton, and in 1780 took command of the Southern army, which had just been defeated by Cornwallis. He was defeated by Cornwallis at Guildford Courthouse (1781), but the victory was so costly that Greene was able to recover South Carolina and Georgia, paving the way for American victory in the South. He was considered second only to Washington as a general. >> Cornwallis; Washington, George

Greene, Robert (1558–92) Playwright, born in Norwich, Norfolk, E England, UK. He studied at Oxford and Cambridge, moved to London, and began to write a stream of plays and romances, his most popular work being the comedy *Friar Bacon and Friar Bungay* (c.1589). He helped to lay the foundations of English drama, and his *Pandosto* (1588) was a source for Shakespeare's *The Winter's Tale*. In his final years, his work grew more serious, and after his death appeared his *A Groat's Worth of Wit bought with a Million of Repentance* (1592), in which he lays bare the wickedness of his former life. >> Shakespeare, William

Greenidge, (Cuthbert) Gordon [**gren**ij] (1951–) West Indian cricketer, born in St Peter, Barbados. An explosive opening batsman, he spent a long time as an English county player with Hampshire, and he averaged 82·23 for the English season of 1984. He scored a century on his Test debut, and holds five West Indian Test partnership records. >> RR1150

Greenough, Horatio [**green**oh] (1805–52) Sculptor and writer, born in Boston, MA. After two years at Harvard he moved to Italy in 1825, where he became a leading member of the American artistic colony there. His principal work is a colossal statue in Classical style of George Washington as Zeus, commissioned for the Capitol rotunda but now in the Smithsonian Institution, Washington, DC. His advanced views on functionalism and freedom from ornament in design, as expressed in his *Travels, Observations and Experience of a Yankee Stonecutter* (1852), probably influenced the architectural ideas of Louis Sullivan and Frank Lloyd Wright. >> Sullivan, Louis; Wright, Frank Lloyd

Greenspan, Alan (1926–) Businessman and financier. He studied at New York University, and became president and chief executive officer of Townsend-Greenspan and Co, New York City (1954–74, 1977–87). His consultancies include the US Treasury and Federal Reserve Board (1971–4), and he was a member of the president's economic policy advisory board (1981–7). He became chairman of the governors of the Federal Reserve System in 1987.

Greenway, Francis Howard (1777–1837) Architect, born in Mangotsfield, near Bristol, SW England, UK. A student of John Nash, he set up his own architecture firm, but went bankrupt. In 1812 he was transported for forgery, arriving in Sydney two years later. Soon given 'ticket-of-leave' (parole), he established himself in practice as an architect. Governor Macquarie appointed him civil architect, and Greenway designed most of the early colony's public buildings. He made effective use of local material, and the best remaining examples of his work, such as St James's Church, Sydney, and St Matthew's Church, Windsor, New South Wales, are elegant examples of the Georgian style. He was depicted on the former Australian $10 note – a considerable distinction for a convicted forger. >> Macquarie; Nash, John

Greenwood, Arthur (1880–1954) British statesman, born in Leeds, West Yorkshire, N England, UK. He studied at Leeds, and was a wartime member of Lloyd George's secretariat. He became an MP in 1922 and deputy leader of the parliamentary Labour Party in 1935, showing himself an outspoken critic of 'appeasement'. In the 1940 government he was minister without portfolio, and 1945 became Lord Privy Seal, but resigned from the government in 1947. He remained treasurer of the Labour Party, of whose national executive he became chairman in 1953. He did much to shape Labour's social policies. >> Lloyd-George, David

Greenwood, Joan (1921–1987) Actress, born in London, England, UK. She studied at the Royal Academy of Dramatic Art, London, before making her stage debut in *Le Malade Imaginaire* (1938). A woman of distinctive style, her husky tones and feline grace allowed her to be witty and sensual in the portrayal of classical roles and contemporary femmes fatales. Her film credits include the influential and enduring Ealing comedies *Whisky Galore* (1948), *Kind Hearts and Coronets* (1949), and *The Man in the White Suit* (1951), as well as *Tom Jones* (1963) and *Little Dorrit* (1987). She married actor **André Morell** in 1960.

Greenwood, Walter (1903–74) Writer, born in Salford, Greater Manchester, NW England, UK. His best-known novel is *Love on the Dole* (1933), inspired by his experiences of unemployment and depression in the early 1930s. It made a considerable impact as a document of the times, and was subsequently dramatized in 1934 and filmed in 1941.

Greer, Germaine (1939–) Feminist, writer, and lecturer, born in Melbourne, Victoria, Australia. She studied at Melbourne, Sydney, and Cambridge universities, and became a lecturer in English at Warwick University (1968–73). Her controversial and highly successful book *The Female Eunuch* (1970) portrayed marriage as a legalized form of slavery for women, and attacked the misrepresentation of female sexuality by male-dominated society. She was director (1979–82) of the Tulsa Center for the Study of Women's Literature, OK, and since 1989 has been special lecturer and unofficial fellow of Newnham College, Cambridge. Later works include *The Change* (1991), a discussion of women, aging, and menopause, and *Slip-shod Sibyls: Recognition, Rejection and the Woman Poet* (1995).

Gregg, John Robert (1867–1948) Publisher, and inventor of a shorthand system, born in Co Monaghan, Ireland. His shorthand system was published in *Light Line Phonography* and *Gregg Shorthand Manual* (1888). He emigrated to the USA in 1893, and established the Gregg Publishing Co. His shorthand system came to be the most widely taught and used in the USA.

Gregg, Sir Norman McAlister (1892–1966) Ophthalmologist, born in Sydney, New South Wales, Australia. He studied at Sydney University, and served with the Royal Australian Medical Corps in World War 1. He later studied ophthalmology in London before returning to Sydney. After an epidemic of German measles there in 1939, his research proved the link between the incidence of that illness in pregnancy and cataracts or blindness in children.

Grégoire, Henri [graygwah(r)] (1750–1831) Clergyman and revolutionary, born near Lunéville, France. Entering the priesthood he became curé of Embermènil in Lorraine. An ardent democrat, he was sent to the States General of 1789 as a deputy of the clergy, where he attached himself to the Third Estate Party, and took a prominent part throughout the revolution, calling for the abolition of the monarchy in 1792. He was the first of his order to take the oaths, and was elected 'constitutional bishop' of Loir-et-Cher. During the de-Christianizing campaign (1793–4) he continued to openly profess his faith. After the 18th Brumaire he became a member of the Corps Législatif, and the Concordat forced him to resign his bishopric.

Gregory, St, known as **the Illuminator** (c. 240–332) Apostle of Armenia, said to have been a Parthian prince who fled from a Persian invasion, and was brought up a Christian in Cappadocia. Returning to Armenia he was taken prisoner by Tiridates III for refusing to condone idolatry. He succeeded in converting the king (301), who then made Christianity the official religion of the state, and Gregory became Patriarch of Armenia. Feast day 30 September.

Gregory I, St, known as **the Great** (c. 540–604) Pope (590–604), a Father of the Church, born in Rome. Appointed praetor of Rome, he left this office (c.575), distributed his wealth among the poor, and withdrew into a monastery of Rome. It was here that he saw some Anglo-Saxon youths in the slave market, and was seized with a longing to convert their country to Christianity. As pope, he was a great administrator, reforming all public services and ritual, and systematizing the sacred chants. In his writings the whole dogmatic system of the modern Church is fully developed. He died in Rome, and was canonized on his death; feast day 12 March. >> Augustine, St (of Canterbury)

Gregory VII, St, originally **Hildebrand** (c. 1020–85) Pope (1073–85), the great representative of the temporal claims of the mediaeval papacy, born near Soana, Italy. He became a cardinal in 1049. As pope, he worked to change the secularized condition of the Church, which led to conflict with the German Emperor Henry IV, who declared Gregory deposed in a diet at Worms (1076), but then yielded to him after excommunication. In 1080 Henry resumed hostilities, appointing an antipope (Clement III), and after a siege took possession of Rome (1084). Gregory was freed by Norman troops, but was forced to withdraw to Salerno, where he died. He was canonized in 1606; feast day 25 May. >> Henry IV (Holy Roman Emperor)

Gregory XIII, originally **Ugo Buoncompagni** (1502–85) Pope (1572–85), born in Bolgona, Italy. He was professor of law at Bologna for several years, settled at Rome in 1539, was one of the theologians of the Council of Trent, and became a cardinal in 1565. As pope, he displayed great zeal for the promotion of education; many of the colleges in Rome were wholly or in part endowed by him. He also corrected the errors of the Julian calendar, and in 1582 introduced the calendar named after him.

Gregory, Augustus Charles (1819–1905) Surveyor and explorer, born in Farnsfield, Nottinghamshire, C England UK. He went to Australia in 1829, joined the Western Australian Survey Department in 1841, and undertook several expeditions to explore the Australian interior. He discovered coal on the Irwin R (1846), and lead on the Murchison R (1848), then headed the Northern Australian Expedition (1855–6), which discovered new pastures along the reverse of the route of Ludwig Leichhardt. He was surveyor general of the new state of Queensland (1859). >> Leichhardt

Gregory, Isabella Augusta, Lady, née Persse (1852–1932) Playwright, born at Roxborough House, Co Galway, Ireland. After her marriage in 1880 to Sir William Henry Gregory, Governor of Ceylon (1872–7), she became an associate of Yeats in the foundation of the Abbey Theatre in Dublin and the Irish Players. For these she wrote a number of short plays, notably *Spreading the News* (1904) and *The Rising of the Moon* (1907). She also wrote Irish legends in dialect and translated Molière. >> Yeats, W B

Gregory, James (1638–75) Mathematician, born in Drumoak, Aberdeen, NE Scotland, UK. He graduated from Aberdeen University and went to London in 1662, and the following year published *Optica promota* (The Advance of Optics), containing a description of the Gregorian reflecting telescope he had invented in 1661. He went to Padua, Italy, and published *Vera circuli et hyperbole quadratura* (1667, The True Squaring of the Circle and of the Hyperbola), making use of convergent infinite series to find the areas of these figures. He became professor of mathematics at St Andrews University (1669–74) and at Edinburgh University (1674–5). Manuscripts discovered after his death showed that he had anticipated several discoveries in number theory, including the Taylor expansion.

Gregory of Nazianzus, St [nazianzus] (c. 329–90) Bishop and theologian, born in Cappadocia, Asia Minor. Educated at Caesarea, Alexandria, and Athens, he became a close friend of Basil the Great, and was made Bishop of Sasima, but withdrew to a life of religious study at Nazianzus. Feast day 2 January (W), 25 or 30 January (E). >> Basil the Great

Gregory of Nyssa, St [nisa] (c. 331–95) Christian theologian, born in Caesarea, Asia Minor. He was consecrated Bishop of Nyssa in Cappadocia by his brother Basil the Great (c.371). Deposed in 376 by the Arian Emperor Valens, he regained office in 378 after Valens's death. An outstanding scholarly defender of orthodoxy, he wrote several theological works, sermons, and epistles. Feast day 9 March. >> Basil the Great

Gregory of Tours, St [toor], originally **Georgius Florentinus** (c. 538–c. 594) Frankish historian, born in Arverna (now Clermont). His recovery from sickness, through a pilgrimage to the grave of St Martin of Tours, led Gregory to devote himself to the Church, and he was elected Bishop of Tours in 573. His *Historia Francorum* is the chief authority for the history of Gaul in the 6th-c. Feast day 17 November. >> Martin, St

Gregory Thaumaturgus [thowmatoorgus] (c. 213–c. 270) Christian apostle of Roman Asia, born in Neocaesarea in Pontus (now N Turkey). He became a disciple of Origen, and was consecrated Bishop of Neocaesarea. His *Ekthesis* (Confession of Faith) is an apology for belief in the Trinity, and a forerunner of the Nicene Creed. His surname means 'wonder worker', from the miracles he is reputed to have performed while preaching. >> Origen

Greig, Tony, popular name of **Antony Greig** (1946–) Cricketer, born in Queenstown, South Africa. A good all-rounder, he captained England in Test matches, scoring 3599 runs and eight centuries. His great height enabled him to bowl sharp medium pace, and he took 141 Test wickets, twice taking ten in a match. He played a leading part in recruiting players from all Test countries to join the rival organization, World Series Cricket, being assembled by the Australian entrepreneur Kerry Packer in 1977, and was stripped of the England captaincy. He later became a commentator with Packer's Channel Nine television station in Australia. >> Packer, Kerry

Grenfell, Joyce (Irene Phipps) (1910–79) Entertainer, born in London, England, UK. She made her debut in *The Little Revue* in 1939 and, after touring hospitals with concert parties during World War 2, appeared in revue until the early 1950s, delivering comic monologues. She later appeared in her own one-woman shows, such as *Joyce Grenfell Requests the Pleasure*. Her monologues exploited the foibles and manners of middle-class schoolmistresses and ageing spinsters. Her books include her autobiography, *Joyce Grenfell Requests the Pleasure* (1976) and *George, Don't Do That* (1977). >> Potter, Stephen

Grenfell, Sir Wilfred (Thomason) (1865–1940) Physician and missionary, born in Parkgate, Cheshire, NWC England, UK. He studied at London University, became a surgeon on a hospital ship serving the North Sea fisheries, and was a member of the Mission to Deep Sea Fishermen. In 1892 he went to Labrador and founded hospitals, orphanages, and other social services, as well as fitting out hospital ships for the fishing grounds. He was knighted in 1927.

Grenville, George (1712–70) British statesman and prime minister (1763–5), born in London, England, UK, the father of William Grenville. He entered parliament in 1741, in 1762 became secretary of state and First Lord of the Admiralty, and in 1763 prime minister. The prosecution of Wilkes and the passing of the American Stamp Act which alienated the American Colonies took place during his ministry. He resigned in 1765. >> Grenville, William; Wilkes, John; RR1095

Grenville, Sir Richard (c. 1542–91) English naval commander, a cousin of Sir Walter Raleigh. He fought in Hungary and Ireland (1566–9), was knighted c.1577, and in 1585 commanded the seven ships carrying 100 English colonists to Roanoke Island, NC. In 1591, as commander of the *Revenge*, he fought alone against a large Spanish fleet off the Azores, dying of wounds on board a Spanish ship. >> Raleigh, Walter

Grenville, William Wyndham Grenville, 1st Baron (1759–1834) British statesman, the son of George Grenville. He studied at Oxford, entered parliament in 1782, and became paymaster-general (1783), home secretary (1790), and foreign secretary (1791). He resigned with Pitt in 1801 on the refusal of George III to agree to Catholic Emancipation. In 1806–7 he formed the coalition 'Government of All the Talents', which abolished the slave trade. >> Grenville, George; Pitt, William (the Younger)

Gresham, Sir Thomas [greshm] (1519–79) Financier, born in London, England, UK. He studied at Cambridge, passed into the Mercers' Company, and in 1551 was employed as 'king's merchant' at Antwerp. He was knighted in 1559, and was for a time ambassador at Brussels. An observation in economics is attributed to him (*Gresham's law*): if there are two coins of equal legal exchange value, and one is suspected to be of lower intrinsic value, the 'bad coin' will tend to drive the other out of circulation, as people will begin to hoard it. He built the Royal Exchange (1566–8), and founded Gresham College.

Gresley, Sir (Herbert) Nigel (1876–1941) Locomotive engineer, born in Edinburgh, EC Scotland, UK. For 30 years from 1911 he was the foremost British locomotive designer of such classic trains as the streamlined 'Silver Jubilee' and 'Coronation' in the mid-1930s. His A4 class Pacific 4–6–2 'Mallard' achieved a world record speed for a steam locomotive of 126 mph in July 1938 which has never been exceeded.

Grétry, André Ernest Modeste [graytree] (1741–1813) Composer, born in Liège, Belgium. After studying in Rome and working for a year in Geneva (1766) he settled in Paris, and composed over 40 comic operas, of which *Le Huron* (1768) and *Lucile* (1769) were the earliest; among the best known are *Raoul* and *Richard cœur-de-lion*. He became inspector of the Conservatoire and a member of the Institute. He published his *Mémoires* in 1796.

Gretzky, Wayne, nickname **the Great One** or **the Great Gretzky** (1961–) Ice-hockey player, born in Brantford, Ontario, Canada. He joined the Edmonton Oilers in 1979, and has scored more goals in a season than any other player (92 in 1981–2). Voted the Most Valuable Player in the National Hockey League nine times, he is the NHL's all-time leading scorer. He transferred to the Los Angeles Kings in 1988 for a record $15 million, and in 1993 agreed a $25·5 million contract, making him the NHL's highest-paid player.

Greuze, Jean Baptiste [groez] (1725–1805) Genre and portrait painter, born in Tournus, France. His first notable works were historical, and after a visit to Italy (1755) he painted Italian subjects; but he is seen at his best in such studies of girls as 'The Broken Pitcher' (c.1773, Louvre) and 'Girl with Doves' (Wallace Collection, London).

Greville, Sir Fulke, 1st Baron Brooke (1554–1628) Poet, born at Beauchamp Court, Warwickshire, C England, UK. He studied at Cambridge, and travelled abroad on diplomatic missions. He wrote several didactic poems, over 100 sonnets, and two tragedies. Knighted in 1597, he was Chancellor of the Exchequer (1614–22), and created baron in 1620. He died after being stabbed by a servant. His life of Sir Philip Sidney appeared in 1652.

Grévy, (François Paul) Jules [grayvee] (1807–91) French

statesman and president (1879–87), born in Mont-sous-Vaudrey, France. As an advocate he acquired distinction in the defence of Republican political prisoners. Vice-president of the Constituent Assembly (1848), he opposed Louis Napoleon, and after the coup retired from politics; but in 1869 he was again returned for Jura. In February 1871 he became president of the National Assembly, and was re-elected in 1876, 1877, and 1879. He was elected president of the Republic in 1879, and elected again in 1885, but, hampered by ministerial difficulties, resigned in December 1887. >> Napoleon III

Grew, Nehemiah (1641–1712) Botanist and physician, born in Atherstone, Warwickshire, C England, UK. He studied at Cambridge and Leyden, and practised medicine at Coventry and London. He is best known as the author of the pioneering *Anatomy of Plants*, where he introduced the idea that the stamen and pistil of flowers correspond to male and female sex organs.

Grey, Dame Beryl, *née* **Groom**, married name **Svenson** (1927–) Ballerina, born in London, England, UK. She won a scholarship to Sadler's Wells Ballet School at the age of nine, and her first solo appearance at Sadler's Wells Theatre was in the part of Sabrina, in *Comus* (1941). The youngest Giselle ever, at the age of 16 she was prima ballerina of the Sadler's Wells Ballet (1942–57), and has also appeared with the Bolshoi Ballet in Russia (1957–8) and the Chinese Ballet in Peking (1964). She was artistic director of the London Festival Ballet (1968–79).

Grey, Charles Grey, 2nd Earl (1764–1845) British statesman and prime minister (1830–4), born in Fallodon, Northumberland, NE England, UK. He studied at Cambridge, became a Whig MP in 1786, and was a leading supporter of parliamentary reform in the 1790s. In 1806 he became First Lord of the Admiralty, foreign secretary, and Leader of the House of Commons. In 1807 he succeeded his father as second Earl Grey. In 1830 he formed a government promising peace, retrenchment, and reform, and after considerable difficulties secured the passage of the 1832 Reform Bill. In the new parliament he carried the Act for the abolition of slavery in the colonies, but was forced to resign following disagreement over the Irish question. >> RR1095

Grey, Sir George (1799–1882) British statesman, born in Gibraltar. He studied at Oxford, but relinquished law after succeeding his father in the baronetcy in 1828. He was MP for Devonport (1832–47), under-secretary for the Colonies (1834–5), judge-advocate (1839), Chancellor of the Duchy of Lancaster (1841), and in 1846 home secretary. During the Chartist disturbances he discharged his duties with vigour and discrimination. He carried the Crown and Government Security Bill, the Alien Bill, and a measure for the further suspension in Ireland of the Habeas Corpus Act (1849). In 1854 he became colonial secretary, and in 1855 took his old post of home secretary.

Grey, Sir George (1812–98) British explorer and administrator, born in Lisbon, Portugal. He made two expeditions to NW Western Australia (1837, 1839), and was appointed Governor of South Australia in 1840. Transferred to New Zealand in 1845, he succeeded in establishing peace between the warring Maoris and British settlers, becoming a pioneer scholar of Maori culture in the process. Knighted in 1848, he was appointed Governor of Cape Colony in 1854, and again helped to restore peace between the natives and settlers. He returned to New Zealand for a second term as governor in 1861, but had less success this time in carrying out his legislative programme. He was a member of the New Zealand House of Representatives (1874–94), and premier (1877–9), before retiring to England.

Grey, Henry George Grey, 3rd Earl (1802–94) British statesman, the son of Charles, 2nd Earl Grey. He entered parliament in 1826 as Lord Howick, became under-secretary for the Colonies in his father's ministry, retired in 1833, but was subsequently under-secretary in the Home Department, and in 1835 secretary for war. In 1845 he succeeded to the peerage, in 1846 became colonial secretary, where he was in favour of local self-government for the colonies, and in 1852 published his *Defence of Lord John Russell's Colonial Policy*. He opposed the Crimean War, and condemned Beaconsfield's Eastern policy. >> Disraeli; Grey, Charles

Grey, Lady Jane (1537–54) Queen of England for nine days in 1553, the eldest daughter of Henry Grey, Marquess of Dorset, and great-granddaughter of Henry VII. In 1553 the Duke of Northumberland, foreseeing the death of Edward VI, aimed to secure the succession by marrying Jane (against her wish) to his fourth son, Lord Guildford Dudley. Three days after Edward's death (9 Jul), she was named as his successor, but was forced to abdicate in favour of Mary, who had popular support. She was imprisoned, and beheaded on Tower Green. >> Dudley, Guildford; Edward VI; Mary Tudor; Ridley, Nicholas (c.1500–55); Warwick, John Dudley; RR1095

Grey, Maria (Georgina), *née* **Shirreff** (1816–1906) Pioneer of women's education in Britain, the sister of Emily Shirreff. She helped to found the National Union for Promoting the Higher Education of Women (1871), which created the Girls' Public Day School Company (later Trust) in 1872, and eventually had some 38 schools which set new academic standards for girls' education. With her sister she revived interest in the work of the German educationist Froebel, and promoted the Froebel Society. She also published a novel and works on women's enfranchisement and education. >> Froebel; Shirreff

Grey, Zane, pseudonym of **Pearl Grey** (1875–1939) Novelist, born in Zanesville, OH. He first worked as a dentist, but after a trip out West in 1904 began to write Westerns. Best known of his 54 books was *Riders of the Purple Sage* (1912), which sold nearly two million copies. He also wrote on big-game fishing and other outdoor pursuits.

Grey Eminence >> **Joseph, Père**

Grieg, Edvard (Hagerup) [greeg] (1843–1907) Composer, born in Bergen, Norway. He studied at Leipzig, where he was much influenced by Schumann's music, then worked in Copenhagen (1863–7), and developed into a strongly national Norwegian composer. After some years teaching and conducting in Christiania, the success of his incidental music for Ibsen's *Peer Gynt* (1876), and a state pension, enabled him to settle near Bergen. His other major works include the A minor piano concerto, orchestral suites, violin sonatas, and numerous songs and piano pieces. >> Schumann, Robert

Grieg, (Johan) Nordahl Brun [greeg] (1902–43) Poet and playwright, born in Bergen, Norway. He studied at Oslo and Oxford, and spent much of his youth travelling, mirrored in his volumes of early poetry. A committed anti-Fascist, he wrote dramas about national freedom, as in *Vår Ære og Vår Makt* (1935, Our Power and Our Glory) and *Nederlaget* (1937, Defeat). During World War 2 he joined the Resistance, escaped to London, and broadcast his patriotic verses back to his homeland. He died when his plane was shot down over Berlin in 1943.

Grien, Hans >> **Baldung, Hans**

Grierson, Sir Herbert John Clifford [greerson] (1866–1960) Critic and scholar, born in Lerwick, Shetland, NE Scotland, UK. He studied at King's College, Aberdeen, and at Oxford, and became professor at Aberdeen (1894–1915) and Edinburgh (1915–35), where he was also elected rector (1936–9). His books include *Metaphysical Poets* (1921), *Milton and Wordsworth* (1937), and *Essays and Addresses* (1940).

Grierson, John [greerson] (1898–1972) Producer of documentary films, born in Kilmadock, Stirling, C Scotland, UK. He studied at Glasgow and Chicago, made his name with *Drifters* (1929), and is regarded as the founder of the British documentary movement. He moved to the GPO Film Unit in 1933 for his most creative period, and in 1938 was invited to set up the Canadian Film Board, with which he remained until 1945.

Grieve, Christopher Murray >> **MacDiarmid, Hugh**

Griffes, Charles Tomlinson [grifuhs] (1884–1920) Composer, born in Elmira, NY. After beginning his music studies in the USA, he studied piano and composition in Berlin, returning in 1907 to teach in a boy's school in Tarrytown, NY, where he remained until his early death. Developing slowly and composing painstakingly, he had begun to achieve a highly colourful and personal style in such works as *Pleasure Dome of Kubla Khan* (1920). He is remembered as the great 'might-have-been' of American music.

Griffin, Bernard (1899–1956) Roman Catholic clergyman, born in Birmingham, West Midlands, C England, UK. He studied at the English and Beda Colleges, Rome, became Archbishop of Westminster in 1943, and was made a cardinal in 1946. He toured postwar Europe and America, and in 1950 was papal legate for the centenary celebrations of the reconstitution of the English hierarchy.

Griffin, Gerald (1803–40) Writer, born in Limerick, Ireland. He wrote for local journals and went to London in 1823, but returned to Limerick in 1838 and joined the Christian Brothers, after burning his manuscripts. His novel, *The Collegians*, was published anonymously in 1829.

Griffin, Walter Burley (1876–1937) Architect and town planner, born in Maywood, IL. He studied at Illinois State University. In 1912 he won an international competition for the design of the new federal capital of Australia, Canberra, and went to Australia to supervise construction. He remained there, designing a number of notable buildings and the eccentric Castlecrag estate in N Sydney. In 1935 he went to India following an invitation to design a library for Lucknow University, and died there two years later.

Griffith, Arthur (1872–1922) Irish nationalist politician, born in Dublin. He worked as a compositor, then as a miner and journalist in South Africa (1896–8), before editing the *United Irishman*. In 1905 he founded *Sinn Féin*, editing it until 1915. He was twice imprisoned, became an MP (1918–22), signed the peace treaty with Britain, and was a moderate president of the Dáil Eireann (1922).

Griffith, D(avid) W(ark) (1875–1948) Pioneer film director, born in Floydsfork, KY. He began with literary ambitions, then turned to film-making, where he experimented with new techniques in photography and production, and brought out two masterpieces, *The Birth of a Nation* (1915) and *Intolerance* (1916). He continued to make films until 1931, but his studio went into artistic decline, and failed in the economic aftermath of the Depression.

Griffith, Hugh (Emrys) (1912–80) Actor, born in Anglesey, NW Wales, UK. He began work as a bank clerk, served in the army during World War 2, then joined what is now the Royal Shakespeare Company. A colourful character actor, probably his most notable performance was as Falstaff (1964). He also received acclaim for his roles in *The Waltz of the Toreadors* (1956) and a New York City production of *Look Homeward Angel* (1957). He won an Oscar for his performance in the motion picture *Ben Hur* (1959).

Griffith, Melanie (1957–   ) Actress, born in New York City. The daughter of Hitchcock actress Tippi Hedren, she made her screen debut in *Night Moves* (1975). She appeared in a number of films as a teenager, then after a gap of four years her adult career commenced with *Body Double* (1984).

Later films include *Bonfire of the Vanities* (1990), *Born Yesterday* (1993), *Reasonable Doubt* (1997), and *Lolita* (1997). >> Hedren

Griffith, Sir Richard John (1784–1878) Geologist and civil engineer, born in Dublin. He studied civil engineering in London and Edinburgh, returned to Ireland in 1808, and became mining engineer to the Royal Dublin Society in 1812 and a government inspector of mines. He published a geological map of Ireland in 1835. As commissioner of valuations after the Irish Valuation Act of 1827 he created *Griffith's valuations* for country rate assessments, and was consulted in all major Irish building projects, including the National Gallery and the Museum of Natural History, Dublin.

Griffith, Samuel Walker (1845–1920) Judge, born in Merthyr Tydfil, S Wales, UK. He emigrated to Australia in 1854 and studied at Sydney University. From 1867 he practised law in Queensland, and became prime minister of that state three times. He was chairman of the Constitutional Committee of the National Australian Convention in 1891, and had a major role in drafting the Australian Commonwealth Constitution. Chief Justice of Queensland from 1893, he was first Chief Justice of the High Court of Australia (1900–19).

Griffiths, James (1890–1975) British statesman and miners' leader, born in Ammanford, Carmarthenshire, SW Wales, UK. A leading official in the miners' union in South Wales, he was elected Labour MP for Llanelli (1936–70). In the Labour governments (1945–51), he was minister of national insurance and secretary of state for the colonies. He argued for a separate Welsh Office, and became the first secretary of state for Wales (1964–6). He was a moderating influence in Labour Party politics during the tensions of the Gaitskell–Bevan disputes in the 1950s. >> Bevan, Aneurin; Gaitskell

Griffiths, Trevor (1935–93) Playwright, born in Manchester, Greater Manchester, NW England, UK. He studied at Manchester, became a teacher, then worked as an education officer for the BBC (1965–72). His plays are social dramas, such as *The Party* (1973), which revolves around a discussion of left-wing politics, and *Comedians* (1975), an angry survey of British social attitudes. Other plays include *Real Dreams* (1987), another angry political piece. He also wrote several plays and screenplays for television, including an adaptation of *Sons and Lovers* (1982).

Grignard, (François Auguste) Victor [greenyah(r)] (1871–1935) Organic chemist, born in Cherbourg, France. He studied chemistry at Lyon, and became professor there in 1919. He introduced the use of organo-magnesium compounds (*Grignard reagents*), which form the basis of the most valuable class of organic synthetic reactions, for which he shared the Nobel Prize for Chemistry in 1912. >> RR1123

Grigorovich, Yuri (Nikolayevich) [grigorovich] (1927–   ) Dancer, artistic director, teacher, and choreographer, born in Leningrad. He trained at the Leningrad Choreographic School before joining the Kirov Ballet as a soloist in 1946. He is best known as a choreographer, his first major ballet, *The Stone Flower* (1957), marking a new stage for Soviet choreography. He became ballet master of the Kirov Ballet (1962), and chief choreographer and artistic director of the Bolshoi Ballet (1964). He was named People's Artist of the Russian SFSR in 1966.

Grigson, Geoffrey (Edward Harvey) (1905–85) Poet, critic, and editor, born in Pelynt, Cornwall, SW England, UK. The founder of the influential magazine *New Verse* (1933–9), his works include volumes of verse, essays, and anthologies. His *Collected Poems, 1924–62* was published in 1963.

Grigson, Sophie, popular name of **Hester Sophia Frances Grigson** (1959–) British cookery writer and broadcaster. She studied at the University of Manchester Institute of Science and Technology and became a cookery correspondent for the *Evening Standard* (1986–93), *The Sunday Express* (1988–91), *The Independent* (1993–4), and *The Sunday Times* (1994–6). Her television programmes for Channel 4 include *Grow Your Greens/Eat Your Greens* (1993) and *Sophie's Meat Course* (1995), and among her books are *Food for Friends*, *Sophie's Table*, and *Travels à la Carte* (with William Black).

Grillparzer, Franz [**gril**pah(r)tzer] (1791–1872) Dramatic poet, born in Vienna. He studied at the University of Vienna, and worked in the imperial civil service (1813–56). He first attracted literary attention with a tragedy, *Die Ahnfrau* (1817, The Ancestress), and was appointed poet to the Hofburgtheater in 1818. He wrote 12 tragedies and one comedy, as well as lyric poetry and a novel. His plays are considered to be some of the best written for the Austrian stage.

Grimald, Nicholas (1519–62) Poet and playwright, born in Cambridgeshire, EC England, UK. He studied at Oxford and Cambridge, became Ridley's chaplain, but recanted under Queen Mary I. He contributed 40 poems to Tottel's *Songes and Sonettes* (1557), known as *Tottel's Miscellany*, and translated Virgil and Cicero. He also wrote two Latin verse tragedies on religious subjects. >> Ridley, Nicholas (c.1500–55); Tottel

Grimaldi, Joseph [**grimal**dee] (1779–1837) Comic actor, singer, and acrobat, born in London, England, UK. From 1800 until his retirement through ill health in 1828, he dominated the stage of Sadler's Wells as the figure of 'Clown' in the English harlequinade. Many of his innovations became distinctive characteristics of the pantomime clown, or 'Joey'. His memoirs were edited by Charles Dickens.

Grimké sisters [**grim**kay] Abolitionists and feminists: **Sarah Moore Grimké** (1792–1873) and **Angelina Emily Grimké** (1805–79), born to a major slaveholding family in Charleston, SC. They rejected their family's way of life and joined the Quakers, who were officially anti-slavery. They moved to Philadelphia and lived quietly, until in 1835 Angelina published a letter in an anti-slavery newspaper, *The Liberator*. They became public figures, and Angelina undertook an unprecedented speaking tour. She resisted efforts to silence her, but gave up public life after her marriage to the abolitionist **Theodore Weld** (1803–95). Sarah lived with the couple thereafter, and the two remained committed to social change. >> Garrison

Grimm brothers Folklorists and philologists: **Jacob Ludwig Carl Grimm** (1785–1863) and **Wilhelm Carl Grimm** (1786–1859), both born in Hanau, Germany. After studying at Marburg, Jacob became a clerk in the War Office at Kassel, and in 1808 librarian to Jerome Bonaparte, King of Westphalia. Wilhelm, in poorer health, remained in Kassel, where he became secretary of the elector's library. He was joined there by Jacob in 1816. Between 1812 and 1822 they published the three volumes known as *Grimm's Fairy Tales* (Ger *Kinder und Hausmärchen*). Jacob's *Deutsche Grammatik* (1819, Germanic Grammar, revised 1822–40) is perhaps the greatest philological work of the age; he also formulated *Grimm's law* of sound changes. In 1829 the two removed to Göttingen, where Jacob became professor and librarian, and Wilhelm under-librarian (professor in 1835). In 1841 they both received professorships at Berlin, and in 1854 began work on their historical dictionary, *Deutsches Wörterbuch*.

Grimmelshausen, Hans Jacob Christoph von [**grim**els-howzen] (c. 1622–76) Writer, born in Gelnhausen, Germany.

He served on the imperial side in the Thirty Years' War, led a wandering life, then settled in Renchen, near Kehl. In later life he wrote a series of novels, the best of them on the model of the Spanish picaresque romances, such as the *Simplicissimus* series (1669–72).

Grimond (of Firth), Jo(seph) Grimond, Baron [**grim**uhnd] (1913–93) British politician, born in St Andrews, Fife, E Scotland, UK. He studied at Oxford, was called to the bar in 1937, served in World War 2, and entered parliament in 1950. Elected leader of the Liberal Party (1956–67), he was largely responsible for the modernizing of both the Party and Liberalism, and called for a 'realignment of the left' of British politics. He served again as Party leader for a short period following the resignation of Jeremy Thorpe (1976), retiring from the House of Commons in 1983, when he was created a life peer. He was also Chancellor of the University of Kent (1970–90). >> Thorpe, Jeremy

Grimthorpe, Edmund Beckett Denison Grimthorpe, Baron (1816–1905) Lawyer, and authority on architecture and horology, born at Carlton Hall, Nottinghamshire, C England, UK. He studied at Cambridge, made a fortune at the bar, then turned his attention to church architecture and clock-making. He helped to design the clock for the tower of the Houses of Parliament, and also for St Paul's Cathedral.

Grinnell, George Bird [**gri**nel] (1849–1938) Naturalist and author, born in Brooklyn, NY. He studied at Yale, and worked as a banker for four years before joining a Black Hills expedition as a naturalist. In 1876 he became an editor with *Forest and Stream* magazine, and as editor-in-chief (1880–1911) made it the country's leading natural history journal. A founder of the Audubon Society (1886) and the New York Zoological Society, he promoted national parks and wildlife preserves. He published several books on Indian lore, hunting, and natural history, as well as a series for boys about the outdoors.

Grinnell, Henry (1799–1874) Shipping merchant, born in New Bedford, MA. He financed an Arctic expedition to search for Sir John Franklin in 1850, and another in 1853–5 under Elisha Kane. *Grinnell Land* is named after him. >> Franklin, John; Kane, Elisha

Gris, Juan [grees], pseudonym of **José Victoriano Gonzàlez** (1887–1927) Painter, born in Madrid. He studied there, and in 1906 went to Paris, where he associated with Picasso and Matisse and became one of the most logical and consistent exponents of Synthetic Cubism. He settled at Boulogne and in 1923 designed the décor for three Diaghilev productions. He also worked as a book illustrator. In most of his paintings, the composition of the picture dictates the deliberate distortion and rearrangement of the subjects, as in *Still Life with Dice* (1922). >> Diaghilev; Matisse; Picasso

Grivas, Georgeios (Theodoros) [**gree**vas] (1898–1974) Greek political leader, born in Trikomo, Cyprus. He commanded a Greek Army division in the Albanian Campaign of 1940–1, and led a secret organization called 'X' during the German occupation of Greece. In 1955 he became head of the underground campaign against British rule in Cyprus (EOKA), calling himself 'Dighenis' after a legendary Greek hero. In 1959, after the Cyprus settlement, he left Cyprus and was promoted general in the Greek army. In 1971 he returned secretly to Cyprus and, as leader of EOKA-B, directed a terrorist campaign for *enosis* (union with Greece) until his death.

Grock, stage name of **Charles Adrien Wettach** (1880–1959) Clown, world-famous for his virtuosity in both circus and theatre, born in Reconvilier, Switzerland. He was particularly known for his clowning with musical instruments, especially using the violin and piano. He wrote several books, including his autobiography, *Die Memoiren des Königs der Crowns* (1956, trans Grock, King of Clowns).

Grofé, Ferde [groh fay] (1892–1972) Composer, born in New York City. He is known for a number of orchestral suites, all named after American places, which are descriptive of the American scene. He orchestrated *Rhapsody in Blue* for Gershwin, and the modern-style orchestra based upon saxophones rather than strings is attributed to him. >> Gershwin, George

Grolier (de Servières), Jean, vicomte d' (Viscount of) Aguisy [grohlyay] (1479–1565) Bibliophile, born in Lyon, France. Educated in Paris, he was attached to the court of Francis I, went to Italy as intendant-general of the army, was long employed in diplomacy at Milan and Rome, and then became treasurer-general of France (1547). He built up a magnificent library of 3000 volumes, which was dispersed in 1675.

Gromyko, Andrei Andreevich [gromeekoh] (1909–89) Soviet statesman and president (1985–8), born near Minsk, Belarus. He studied agriculture and economics, and became a research scientist at the Soviet Academy of Sciences. In 1939 he joined the staff of the Russian embassy in Washington, becoming ambassador in 1943, and after World War 2 was permanent delegate to the UN Security Council (1946–9). As longest-serving foreign minister (1957–85), he was responsible for conducting Soviet relations with the West during the Cold War, presenting an austere and humourless demeanour for which he became notorious in diplomatic circles. He became president in 1985, but retired from office following the 19th Party Conference (1988) and was replaced by Gorbachev. >> Gorbachev; RR1085

Grooms, Red, popular name of **Charles Roger Grooms** (1937–) Sculptor, painter, and performance artist, born in Nashville, TN. He studied at the Art Institute of Chicago, the New School for Social Research, NY, and the Hans Hofmann School, MA, then settled in New York City (1957). He founded Ruckus Productions (1963), a multi-media environmental and performance company, and is known both for his lifesize installations and for his impromptu happenings and other theatrical events.

Groot, Huig de >> **Grotius, Hugo**

Groote, Geert de [groht], Lat **Gerardus Magnus** (1340–84) Priest and reformer, born in Deventer, The Netherlands. He studied for the priesthood in Paris and led a life of excess until 1374 when, following a spiritual conversion, he began to preach against the affluent lifestyle practised by many clergy throughout Holland. About 1376 he founded at Deventer the 'Brethren of Common Life', a teaching order evolved from a centre established to copy manuscripts. The Order had great influence on education in Europe until the advent of the printing press and newer teaching orders; the last house closed in 1811.

Gropius, Walter (Adolph) [grohpius] (1883–1969) Architect, born in Berlin. He studied at Munich, and after serving in World War 1 was appointed director of the Grand Ducal group of schools of art in Weimar, which he reorganized to form the Bauhaus, aiming at a new functional interpretation of the applied arts. His revolutionary methods and bold use of unusual building materials were condemned in Weimar, and the Bauhaus was transferred to Dessau in 1925. When Hitler came to power he moved to London (1934–7), designing factories and housing estates, and then to the USA, where he was professor of architecture at Harvard University (1937–52). He became a US citizen in 1944. >> Velde

Gros, Antoine Jean, Baron [groh] (1771–1835) Historical painter, born in Paris. He studied under Jacques Louis David, and later travelled with Napoleon's armies, acquiring celebrity by producing great pictures of his battles (1797–1811). His works, such as 'Charles V and Francis I' (1812) and 'Embarkation of the Duchess of Angoulême' (1815), combine Classicism and Romanticism. Later he attempted a return to Classicism, found his work ignored, and drowned himself in the Seine. >> David, Jacques Louis

Grose, Francis [grohs] (1731–91) Antiquary, born in Greenford, W Greater London, England, UK. He squandered the family fortune, but applied himself to his *Antiquities of England and Wales* (1773–87). He toured Scotland and Ireland for antiquarian material, but died suddenly in Dublin. Other works include *A Classical Dictionary of the Vulgar Tongue* (1785) and *Treatise on Ancient Armour and Weapons* (1785–9).

Grosman, Tatyana [grohsman], *née* **Aguschewitsch** (1904–82) Printmaker, born in Yekaterinburg, Ukraine. She studied at the Dresden Academy of Arts and Crafts, Germany, and settled in France (1931). She and her husband, **Maurice**, escaped from the Nazis by walking across the Pyrenees to Italy; from there they emigrated to New York City (1943). She founded the Universal Limited Art Editions workshop in East Islip, Long Island (1957), and encouraged several leading New York School artists to take up printmaking.

Gross, Chaim (1904–91) Sculptor and teacher, born in Wolow, Poland. During World War 1 he and his family fled to Budapest (c.1914), and he then emigrated to New York City (1921), where he studied at the Educational Alliance Art School (1921) and the Beaux-Arts (1922–6). He taught at many institutions, and was known for his wood and stone Expressionistic figures, such as 'Strong Woman' (1935).

Gross, Michael [grohs], nickname **the Albatross** (1964–) Swimmer, born in Frankfurt, Germany. An outstanding butterfly and freestyle swimmer, he uses his great height (6 ft 7 in/201 cm) and long arm span to advantage. In 1981–7 he won a record 13 gold medals at the European Championships. He was the world 200 m freestyle and 200 m butterfly champion in 1982 and 1986, and has won three Olympic gold medals: the 100 m butterfly and 200 m freestyle in 1984, and the 200 m butterfly in 1988.

Grosseteste, Robert [grohstest] (c. 1175–1253) Scholar, bishop, and Church reformer, born in Stradbroke, Suffolk, E England, UK. He studied at Oxford and Paris, taught theology at Oxford, then became Bishop of Lincoln in 1235. He undertook the reformation of abuses in the Church, which brought him into conflict both locally and with the papacy.

Grossmith, George [grohsmith] (1847–1912) Comedian and entertainer, born in London, England, UK. From 1877 to 1889 he took leading parts in Gilbert and Sullivans's operas, and with his brother, **Weedon Grossmith** (1853–1919), wrote *Diary of a Nobody* in *Punch* (1892). His son, **George Grossmith** (1874–1935) was a well-known musical-comedy actor, songwriter, and manager of the Gaiety Theatre, London.

Grosz, George [grohs] (1893–1959) Artist, born in Berlin. He studied at Dresden and Berlin, and was associated with the Berlin Dadaists (1917–18). While in Germany he produced a series of bitter, ironic drawings attacking German militarism and the middle classes. He fled to the USA in 1932, and became a US citizen in 1938. He later produced many oil paintings of a symbolic nature.

Grosz, Karoly [grohs] (1930–96) Hungarian politician and prime minister (1987–8), born in Miskolc, Hungary. He began his career as a printer, then worked as a newspaper editor. He joined the ruling Hungarian Socialist Workers'

Party (HSWP) in 1945, and served as Party chief in Budapest (1984–7). He joined the HSWP Politburo in 1985, became prime minister in 1987, and succeeded Kadar as HSWP leader (1988–9). He moved with the times, and became a committed reformer in both the economic and political spheres, seeking to establish in Hungary a new system of 'socialist pluralism'. >> Kadar

Grotius, Hugo [**groh**shius], also found as **Huig de Groot** (1583–1645) Jurist and theologian, born in Delft, The Netherlands. He studied at Leyden, practised in The Hague, and in 1613 was appointed pensionary of Rotterdam. In 1618 religious and political conflicts led to his imprisonment, but he escaped to Paris, where Louis XIII for a time gave him a pension. In 1625 he published his great work on international law, *De jure belli et pacis* (On the Law of War and Peace).

Grotowski, Jerzy [gro**tof**skee] (1933–   ) Theatre director, teacher, and drama theorist, born in Rzeszów, Poland. His work had a major impact on experimental theatre and actor training in the West during the 1960s and 1970s. After studying in Cracow and Moscow, he founded the Theatre of 13 Rows in Opole (1956–64), which moved to Wrocław as the Laboratory Theatre (1965–84). Since 1982 he has lived in the USA.

Grouchy, Emmanuel, Marquis de [grooshee] (1766–1847) French Napoleonic soldier, born in Paris. He greatly distinguished himself in Italy (1798), fought in the Russian campaign of 1812, and after Leipzig, covered the retreat of the French. On Napoleon's escape from Elba, he destroyed the Bourbon opposition in the S of France, and helped to rout Blücher at Ligny, but failed to play an effective part at Waterloo due to misleading orders (1815). After Waterloo, as commander-in-chief of the broken armies of France, he led them skilfully back towards the capital; then, resigning, he retired to the USA. He returned in 1819, and was reinstated as marshal in 1831. >> Blücher

Grove, Sir George (1820–1900) Musicologist, born in London, England, UK. He practised as a civil engineer, then became secretary to the Society of Arts (1849), and secretary and director of the Crystal Palace Company (1852). His major work was as editor of the *Dictionary of Music and Musicians* (1878–89), and he also edited *Macmillan's Magazine* (1868–83) and contributed to biblical study. He was knighted in 1883 on the opening of the Royal College of Music, of which he was director till 1895.

Grove, Sir William Robert (1811–96) Lawyer and physicist, born in Swansea, SC Wales. He graduated at Oxford in 1835, and became a barrister, then turned to electrochemistry, and taught physics. He returned to the law to improve his income, becoming a judge in 1871. In 1842 he made the first fuel cell, generating electric current from a chemical reaction using gases, and the first filament lamp (1845). He also published early ideas on energy conservation. >> Bacon, Francis Thomas

Groves, Sir Charles (1915–92) Conductor, born in London, England, UK. He studied at the Royal College of Music, London. He trained the BBC Chorus (1938–42), conducted the BBC Northern (1944–51), the Bournemouth Symphony (1951–61), and the Royal Liverpool Philharmonic (1963–77) orchestras, and was also musical director of the Welsh and English National Operas (1961–3 and 1978–9 respectively), as well as president of the National Youth Orchestra (1977–92). He became musical director of the Leeds Philharmonic Society in 1988. He was noted for his mastery of the Romantic repertoire and for championing living composers. He was knighted in 1973.

Grubb, Sir Kenneth (George) (1900–80) Anglican missionary and ecumenist, born in Oxton, Nottinghamshire, C England, UK. Following research on religious and social conditions in South America in the 1930s, and wartime service with the ministry of information, he became president of the Church Missionary Society (1944–69), chairman of the Churches Committee on International Affairs (1946–68), and chairman of the House of Laity in the Church Assembly (1959–70). Author of several studies on South America and successive editions of the *World Christian Handbook* (1949–68), he revealed his waspish assessments of himself and others in *A Layman Looks at the Church* (1964) and his autobiography *Crypts of Power* (1971).

Gruen, David >> **Ben-Gurion, David**

Gruenberg, Louis [**groon**berg] (1884–1964) Composer, born near Brest-Litovsk, Belarus. He was taken to the USA at the age of two. A pupil of Busoni, he worked as a concert pianist until 1919, then retired to devote himself to composition. He wrote extensively for orchestra, chamber music combinations, and voices, but is best known for his opera *The Emperor Jones*, based on Eugene O'Neill's play. >> Busoni

Grumman, Leroy (Randle) (1895–1982) Engineer and aircraft pioneer, born in Huntington, NY. He studied engineering at Cornell University, and served as a navy pilot in World War 1. He became general manager of the Loening Aeronautical Corporation (1921–9), thereafter forming his own company. He produced a series of successful navy aircraft which played vital roles in the naval battles in World War 2, and jet fighters after the war. He also built the Lunar Excursion Module (LEM) for the Apollo flights to the Moon.

Grundtvig, N(ikolai) F(rederik) S(everin) [**grunt**vig] (1783–1872) Theologian and poet, born in Udby, Denmark. He studied theology at Copenhagen, wrote some volumes of patriotic poetry, then became a curate in his father's church in 1815. He was soon embroiled in controversy over his criticisms of the rationalist tendency in the Danish Church, and was suspended from preaching in 1825. During three study tours to England he formed the ideas which led to the creation of Folk High Schools, which had a tremendous effect on rural life and education. In 1862 he was made Bishop of Zealand. He is also known as the greatest Scandinavian hymn writer.

Gruner, Elioth [**groo**ner] (1882–1939) Painter, born in Gisborne, New Zealand. Having arrived in Sydney as an infant, he was accepted by Julian Ashton as a pupil in 1894, and later became an assistant at Ashton's Sydney Art School. He won his first Wynne prize, for landscape painting, in 1916, and was to win six more in the next 20 years. Although sometimes criticized for a primness and lack of vitality, his best work captures the special quality of the Australian light, and he is regarded as one of Australia's leading landscape artists. >> Ashton, Julian

Grünewald, Matthias [grünevalt], originally **Mathis Gothardt** (?1470–1528) Artist, architect, and engineer, probably born in Würzburg, Germany. Very little is known of his life, but he was court painter at Mainz (1508–14) and Brandenburg (1515–25), and in 1516 completed the great Isenheim altarpiece (Colmar Museum).

Guangxu or **Kuang-hsu** [gooahngsü], reign-title **Zai Tian** (1871–1908) Ninth emperor of the Qing dynasty (1875–1908), who remained largely under the control of the Empress Dowager Ci-Xi. In 1898, after the defeat of China by Japan (1894–5), he was determined to reform and strengthen China, and threatened to abdicate if not given full authority. He issued a series of reforming edicts; but his attempts to gain power precipitated a coup, after which he was confined to his palace until his mysterious death one day before the death of the Empress Dowager.

Guardi, Francesco [gwah(r)dee] (1712–93) Painter, born in Venice, Italy. A pupil of Canaletto, he was noted for his views of Venice, full of sparkling colour, with an

Impressionist's eye for effects of light, as in the 'View of the Church and Piazza of San Marco' (National Gallery, London). >> Canaletto

Guardia, Fiorello H La >> **La Guardia, Fiorello H**

Guare, John [gwah(r)] (1938–) Playwright, born in New York City. His first success came with *The House of Blue Leaves* (1970), a sardonic comedy about how the pope's visit to New York affects a zookeeper's family. He wrote several plays for Joseph Papp's Public Theater, and had his second major hit with *Six Degrees of Separation* (1990, filmed 1993). >> Papp

Guareschi, Giovanni [gwa**res**kee] (1908–68) Writer and journalist, born in Parma, Italy. He became editor of the Milan magazine *Bertoldo*, and after World War 2 continued in journalism. He achieved fame with his stories of the village priest, beginning with *The Little World of Don Camillo* (1950). The books were illustrated with his own drawings.

Guarini, (Giovanni) Battista [gwa**ree**nee] (1538–1612) Poet, born in Ferrara, Italy. He was entrusted by Duke Alfonso II with diplomatic missions to the Pope, the Emperor, Venice, and Poland. His chief work was the pastoral play, *Il pastor fido* (1585, The Faithful Shepherd), which helped to establish the genre of pastoral drama.

Guarini, Guarino [gwa**ree**nee], originally **Camillo Guarini** (1642–83) Architect, philosopher, and mathematician, born in Modena, Italy. In Rome (1639–47) he studied under Borromini. He designed several churches in Turin, of which the only two survivors are San Lorenzo (1668–80) and Capella della SS Sindone (1668), and the Palazzo Carignano (1679), considered his masterpiece, as well as palaces for Bavaria and Baden, and churches in Paris, Messina, Prague, and Lisbon (known only from his writings). He also published books on mathematics, astronomy, and architecture, and was responsible for the spread of the Baroque style beyond Italy. His influential *Architettura civile* (published posthumously in 1737), concerning the relationship of geometry and architecture, also included a defence of Gothic architecture. >> Borromini

Guarnieri [gwah(r)**nyay**ree], also found as **Giuseppe Guarneri**, known as **Giuseppe del Gesù** (1687–1745) Celebrated violin maker from Cremona, Italy. His byname came from his practice of signing *IHS* (*Jesu hominum salvator*) after his name on his labels. His instruments are noted for their tonal qualities. He was the nephew of **Andrea Guarnieri** (fl.1628–98) who, with his two sons **Giuseppe Guarnieri** (fl.1690–1730) and **Pietro Guarnieri** (fl.1690–1725), also made quality instruments.

Gucci, Guccio [**goo**chee] (1881-1953) Fashion designer, founder of the Gucci firm, born in Florence, Italy. He opened his first shop in Florence in 1920, becoming known for his leather craftsmanship and accessories. His four sons joined the firm, and in 1953 (the year he died) the first overseas shop opened in New York City. His grandson, **Maurizio** (1949–95) oversaw the resurrection of the firm in the 1980s, and became group president in 1989. Following a series of legal and family disputes, the company was sold to the multinational Investcorp in 1993.

Guderian, Heinz (Wilhelm) [gu**der**ian] (1888–1954) German soldier, born in Kulm, Germany. A leading tank expert and exponent of the *Blitzkrieg* theory, he created the panzer armies which overran Poland in 1939 and France in 1940. He commanded the 2nd Panzer Group in Army Group Centre under Bock in the attack on the USSR in June 1941. Recalled after the failure to take Moscow, he was chief of general staff in 1944, and after the anti-Hitler plot in the same year was made commander on the Eastern Front. He wrote *Panzer Leader* (1952). >> Bock

Guedella, Philip [gwe**da**la] (1889–1944) Writer, born in London, England, UK. He studied at Oxford and became a barrister (1913–23). Sometimes described as the most distinguished and certainly the most popular historian of his time, he was the author of *Second Empire* (1922), *Palmerston* (1926), *The Hundred Days* (1934), *The Hundredth Year* (1940), *Two Marshals* (Bazaine and Pétain, 1943), and *Middle East* (1944).

Guercino, Il [eel gwer**chee**noh], nickname of **Giovanni Francesco Barbieri** (1591–1666) Painter of the Bolognese School, born in Cento, Italy. His major work is the ceiling fresco 'Aurora' at the Villa Ludovisi for Pope Gregory XV. After 1642 he became the leading painter of Bologna, where he died. His name means 'the squint-eyed'.

Guericke, Otto von [**gay**rikuh] (1602–86) Physicist, born in Magdeburg, Germany. An engineer in the Swedish army, he later defended his home town in the Thirty Years' War, resulting in his election as one of its four burgomasters in 1646. He improved a water pump so that it would exhaust air from a container, and was able with this air pump to give dramatic demonstrations of pressure reduction (the *Magdeburg hemispheres*). He also made the first recorded electrostatic machine.

Guérin, Camille >> **Calmette, Albert**

Guérin, (Georges) Maurice de [gay**ri**] (1810–39) Poet, born in the Château du Cayla, France. Educated in Paris, he entered the community of Lamennais at Le Chesnay in Brittany (1831), but returned to Paris (1833) when Lamennais was condemned by the pope and the community dissolved. He wrote two major poems, *La Bacchante* and *Le Centaure*, before falling ill with tuberculosis and returning to Cayla (1837). A Guérin cult arose after his death, resulting in the publication of everything he had written, including personal letters.

Guérin, Pierre Narcisse, Baron [gay**ri**] (1774–1833) Historical painter, born in Paris. A skilful painter of Classical subjects but inclined to melodrama, he was appointed professor at the Ecole des Beaux-Arts (1814), where he counted among his pupils Géricault and Delacroix. He was director of the French Academy of Painting in Rome (1822–8). >> Delacroix; Géricault

Guesclin, Bertrand du [gay**kli**] (c. 1320–80) French knight and military leader during the Hundred Years' War, born in La Motte-Broons, France. He entered royal service on the eve of Charles V's accession, and on becoming Constable of France (1370) assumed command of the French armies, reconquering Brittany and most of SW France. He died while besieging Châteauneuf-de-Randon in the Auvergne.

Guest, George >> **Sequoia**

Guevara, Che [gay**vah**ra], popular name of **Ernesto Guevara (de la Serna)** (1928–67) Revolutionary leader, born in Rosario, Argentina. He trained as a doctor (1953), then played an important part in the Cuban revolution (1956–9), after which he held government posts under Castro. He left Cuba in 1965 to become a guerrilla leader in South America, and was captured and executed in Bolivia. His remains were returned to Cuba in 1997. >> Castro

Guggenheim, Marguerite [**gu**genhiym], known as **Peggy** (1898–1979) Art collector and patron, born in New York City, the niece of Solomon R Guggenheim. She studied at the Jacobi School, New York City (1915), became a radical bohemian, and settled in Paris soon after the end of World War 1. She married young, was divorced (1930), then married Max Ernst (1941). She opened a modern art gallery in England, the Guggenheim Jeune (1938), where she exhibited and collected works by avant-garde artists. In 1941 she moved to New York City, opening a new art gallery, Art of This Century (1942). In 1946 she divorced Ernst, moved to Venice, and established a new gallery in her villa there. Her memoirs, *Out of This Century* (1946) and *Confessions of an Art Addict* (1960), were notorious for details of her love life.

Her collection and the Venice gallery were donated to the Solomon R Guggenheim Foundation. >> **Ernst, Max; Guggenheim, Solomon**

Guggenheim, Meyer [**gu**genhiym] (1828–1905) Financier, born in Langnau, Switzerland. He emigrated to the USA in 1848, where he began as a manufacturer of stove polish, then turned to importing and selling Swiss needlework with his own firm. By 1888 he had shifted his interest to the mining and smelting of metals, forming the Philadelphia Smelting and Refining Co. He had seven sons, who carried on his tradition of business success and generous philanthropy. >> **Guggenheim, Solomon**

Guggenheim, Solomon R(obert) [**gu**genhiym] (1861–1949) Businessman and art collector, born in Philadelphia, PA, the son of Meyer Guggenheim. He studied in Zürich, and became a partner in his father's Swiss embroidery import business. He returned to the USA (1889), worked in the family mining industry in Colorado and New Mexico, then moved to the business headquarters in New York City (1895). He was a director of many family companies and a founder of the Yukon Gold Co in Alaska before retiring from business in 1919. With the assistance of Hilla Rebay, he collected important Modernist paintings and established the Solomon R Guggenheim Foundation (1937). This was the source of funds for the temporary Museum of Non-Objective Paintings (1937) and the permanent Solomon R Guggenheim Museum, designed by Frank Lloyd Wright in 1959. >> **Guggenheim, Marguerite/ Meyer; Wright, Frank Lloyd**

Guicciardini, Francesco [gwichiah(r)**dee**nee] (1483–1540) Historian, born in Florence, Italy. He studied at Florence, Ferrara, and Padua, became professor of law there, and also practised as an advocate; but his real field was diplomacy. He became papal governor of Modena and Reggio (1515), Parma (1521), the Romagna (1523), and Bologna (1531). Retiring from the papal service in 1534, he secured the election of Cosimo de' Medici as Duke of Florence; but, disappointed in his hope of high office, he withdrew to Arcetri, and busied himself with his great *Storia d'Italia*, a dispassionate analytical history of Italy from 1494 to 1532. >> **Cosimo de' Medici**

Guidi, Tommaso >> **Masaccio**

Guido d'Arezzo [**gwee**doh da**ret**zoh], also known as **Guido Aretino** (c. 990–c. 1050) Benedictine monk and musical theorist, probably born in Arezzo, Italy. He was a monk at Pomposa, and is supposed to have died as prior of the Camaldolite monastery of Avellana. He contributed much to musical science: the invention of the staff is ascribed to him, and he introduced the system of naming the notes of a scale with syllables.

Guido di Pietro >> **Angelico, Fra**

Guilbert, Yvette [geel**bair**] (1867–1944) Comedienne of stage and screen, born in Paris. She was a penniless seamstress before she turned to acting and won fame for her songs and sketches of all facets of Parisian life. After 1890 she became known for her revivals of old French ballads, and was a popular recording artist from the 1920s. She visited America and founded a school of acting in New York City. She wrote two novels, and *La Chanson de ma vie* (1919, Song of My Life, trans My Memories).

Guillaume, Charles Edouard [geeohm] (1861–1938) Physicist, born in Fleurier, Switzerland. He studied at Neuchâtel, and became director of the Bureau of International Weights and Measures at Sèvres. He discovered a nickel-steel alloy, 'Invar', which does not expand significantly and can therefore be used in precision instruments and standard measures, and was awarded the Nobel Prize for Physics in 1920.

Guillaume de Champeaux >> **Abelard, Peter**

Guillaume de Lorris [geeyohm duh **lo**ris] (c. 1200–?) Poet, born in France – his surname derives from a village near Orléans. He wrote, before 1260, the first part (c.4000 lines) of the encyclopedic *Roman de la Rose* – an allegory presenting love as a garden, the lady as a rose, and the knight as in quest of her favour. The work was widely influential in mediaeval Europe, and was continued a few decades later by Jean de Meung. >> **Jean de Meung**

Guillaume de Machaut [gee**yohm** duh ma**shoh**] (c. 1300–77) Poet and musician, born possibly in Reims, France. He worked successively under the patronage of John of Luxemburg and John II of France. One of the creators of the harmonic art, he wrote a Mass, motets, songs, ballads, and organ music. His poetry greatly influenced Chaucer. >> **Chaucer**

Guillemin, Roger C(harles) L(ouis) [geel**min**] (1924–) Physiologist, born in Dijon, France. He studied at Dijon, Lyon, and Montreal universities, joining Baylor University, TX, in 1953, where he became professor and director of neuroendocrinology (1963–70). Since 1970 he has been at the Salk Institute for Biological Studies. He shared the 1977 Nobel Prize for Physiology or Medicine for his work on the isolation of peptide hormones of the hypothalamus. >> **RR1124**

Guillotin, Joseph Ignace [geeyohti] (1738–1814) Physician and revolutionary, born in Saintes, France. He proposed to the Constituent Assembly, of which he was a deputy, the use of a decapitating instrument as a means of execution. This was adopted in 1791 and named after him (the *guillotine*), though a similar apparatus had been used earlier in Scotland, Germany, and Italy. It was last used in France in 1977.

Guimard, Hector Germain [geemah(r)] (1867–1942) Architect, born in Lyon, France. He was the most important Art Nouveau architect active in Paris between 1890 and World War 1. For his outstanding architectural scheme, the *Castel Béranger* apartment block (1894–8), he designed every aspect of the building and its interiors. He is best known for the famous Paris Métro entrances of the early 1900s, made of cast iron, many of which are still in place.

Guimerá, Angel [geemay**ra**] (1847–1924) Poet and playwright, born in Santa Cruz, Canary Is. Educated in Barcelona, he is regarded as the greatest Catalan dramatist, and a major influence in the Renaixensa movement to revive Catalan literature. His most famous play is *Terra Baixa* (1896, trans Martha of the Lowlands), on which D'Albert based his opera *Tiefland*. >> **Albert, Eugene d'**

Guin, Ursula Le >> **Le Guin, Ursula**

Guinness, Sir Alec (1914–) Actor, born in London, England, UK. He began acting in 1934, and joined the Old Vic company in 1936, rejoining it in 1946 after serving in the Royal Navy. His famous stage performances include Hamlet (1938) and Macbeth (1966). Among his notable films are *Kind Hearts and Coronets* (1949) and *The Lavender Hill Mob* (1951). In 1958 he received an Oscar for his part in the film *The Bridge on the River Kwai*. Later roles include Ben Kenobi in the *Star Wars* series, and Smiley in the television versions of John Le Carré's novels (1979, 1982). He was knighted in 1959 and made a Companion of Honour in 1994.

Guinness, Sir Benjamin Lee (1798–1868) Brewer, born in Dublin, the grandson of **Arthur Guinness** (1725–1803), the founder of Guinness's Brewery (1759). He joined the firm at an early age, and became sole owner at his father's death in 1855. Under him the brand of stout became famous, and the business grew into the largest of its kind in the world. He was the first Lord Mayor of Dublin (1851), became an MP (1865–8), and was created a baronet in 1867.

Guiscard, Robert [geeskah(r)] (c. 1015–85) Norman adventurer, the son of Tancred de Hauteville, who campaigned with his brothers against the Byzantine Greeks, and created a duchy comprising S Italy and Sicily. In 1059 the papacy recognized him as Duke of Apulia, Calabria, and Sicily. He ousted the Byzantines from Calbria by 1060, then conquered Bari (1071) and captured Salerno (1076). In 1081 he crossed the Adriatic, seized Corfu, and defeated the Byzantine Emperor, Alexius Comnenus, at Durazzo. He died at Cephalonia, while advancing on Constantinople. >> Alexius I

Guise, Claude of Lorraine, 1er duc de (1st Duke of) [geez] (1496–1550) French nobleman and soldier, born in the château de Condé-sur-Moselle, France. He fought under Francis I at Marignano in Italy in 1515, but after that campaign remained at home to defend France successfully against the English (1522), and defeated the army of the Holy Roman Emperor, Charles V, at Neufchâteau. He was regent during the captivity of Francis (1525–7), and was created Duke of Guise in 1527. His daughter, Mary of Lorraine, married James V of Scotland. >> Francis I; Guise, 2e duc; Guise, Mary of Lorraine

Guise, Francis, 2e duc de (2nd Duke of) [geez], known as **le Balafré** ('the Scarred') (1519–63) French soldier and statesman, son of Claude, 1st Duke of Guise. He fought at Montmédy (1542) and the siege of Landercies (1543) and Boulogne (1545), where he received a near-fatal wound. He held Metz (1552–3) against Emperor Charles V, and in 1556 commanded the expedition against Naples. Recalled in 1557 to defend the N frontier against the English, he took Calais (1558) and other towns, and brought about the Treaty of Château Cambrésis (1559). He and his brother, **Cardinal Charles of Guise** (1525–74), shared the chief power in the state during the reign of Francis II (1559–60). During the regency of Charles IX, he was besieging Orléans when he was assassinated by a Huguenot. >> Charles V (Emperor); Charles IX; Guise, 1er duc

Guise, Henri, 3e duc de (3rd Duke of) [geez] (1550–88) French soldier and statesman, the son of Francis, 2nd Duke of Guise, known as **le Balafré** like his father. He fought fiercely against the Protestants at Jarnac and Moncontour (1569), and forced Coligny to raise the siege of Poitiers. He was one of the contrivers of the massacre on St Bartholomew's Day (1572), and was the head of the Holy League against the Bourbons (1576). He was ambitious to succeed to the throne of France, but Henry III procured his assassination at Blois. >> Coligny; Guise, 2e duc; Henry III (of France)

Guise, Mary of [geez], also known as **Mary of Lorraine** (1515–60) Daughter of Claude of Lorraine, 1st Duke of Guise. In 1534 she married Louis of Orléans, Duke of Longueville (d.1537), and in 1538 James V of Scotland, at whose death (1542) she was left with one child, Mary, Queen of Scots. During the troubled years that followed, the queen mother acted with wisdom and moderation, but after her accession to the regency in 1554 she allowed the Guises so much influence that the Protestant nobles raised a rebellion (1559), which continued to her death in Edinburgh Castle. >> Guise, 1er duc; James V; Mary, Queen of Scots

Guiteau, Charles >> Garfield, James Abram

Guitry, Sacha [geetree], originally **Alexandre Georges Guitry** (1885–1957) Actor and playwright, born in St Petersburg, Russia, the son of French actor-manager **Lucien Guitry** (1860–1925). He first appeared on stage in Russia with his father's company, and later acted in Paris (1902) and London (1920). He wrote nearly 100 plays, mostly light comedies, many performed in English. He also wrote and directed several films, including *Le Roman d'un tricheur* (1936, trans The Cheat). >> Printemps

Guizot, François (Pierre Guillaume) [geezoh] (1787–1874) Historian and statesman, born in Nîmes, France. He studied law in Paris, but in 1812 became professor of modern history at the Sorbonne. A member of the Doctrinaires under Louis XVIII, he was minister of the interior (1830), and of public instruction (1832). As the king's chief adviser (1840), he relapsed into reactionary methods of government, and escaped to London with Louis-Philippe in 1848. >> Louis XVIII; Louis-Philippe

Gulbenkian, Calouste (Sarkis) [gulbengkian] (1869–1955) Financier, industrialist, and diplomat, born in Scutari, Turkey. He entered his father's oil business in 1888, and became a naturalized British subject in 1902. After a lifetime of oil deals between Europe, the USA, and the Arab countries, he left $70 million and vast art collections to finance an international Gulbenkian Foundation.

Guldberg, Cato Maximilian (1836–1902) Chemist and mathematician, born in Oslo (formerly, Christiania), Norway. He studied at Oslo and later became professor of applied mathematics there. With his brother-in-law, **Peter Waage** (1833–1900), he formulated the chemical law of mass action (1864) governing the speed of reaction and the relative concentrations of the reactants.

Gullit, Ruud [khulit, rood] (1962–) Football player and manager, born in Suriname. The son of a former Suriname international, he began his professional career at age 16 with Haarlem, made his debut for Holland in 1981, and gained honours with Dutch teams Feyenoord and PSV Eindhoven. In 1987 he was named European Footballer of the Year, later joining AC Milan for a then world record £7.5 million fee. He captained Holland to win the European Championships (1988), and with AC Milan won the European Cup (1989, 1990). In 1995 he joined Chelsea, and the next year took over as player-manager, leading his team to FA Cup victory (1996–7).

Gumilev, Nikolay Stepanovich [gumeelyef] (1886–1921) Russian poet, a leader of the Acmeist school which revolted against Symbolism. His exotic and vivid poems include *The Quiver* (1915), with some fine verses of war and adventure, and *The Pyre* and *The Pillar of Fire*, which contain his best pieces. He also wrote criticism, and translated French and English poetry. He was shot as a counter-revolutionary. His wife was the poet Anna Akhmatova. >> Akhmatova

Gumm, Frances >> Garland, Judy

Gundelach, Finn Olav [gundelach] (1925–81) Danish diplomat and European Commissioner, born in Vejle, Denmark. He studied at Århus, joined the Danish Diplomatic Service, and became ambassador to the European Community in 1967, directing the negotiations for Denmark's entry into the Community (1973), and becoming his country's first European commissioner. In 1977 he was made vice-president of the new European Commission, and was given charge of the Common Agricultural Policy.

Gundulf (1024–1108) Norman churchman, and Bishop of Rochester from 1077. A monk at Bec and Caen, in 1070 he followed Lanfranc to England. He built the Tower of London, rebuilt Rochester cathedral, and founded St Bartholomew's hospital in Chatham. The great keep of Rochester castle is also attributed to him. >> Lanfranc

Gunn, Neil (Miller) (1891–1973) Novelist, born in Dunbeath, Highland, N Scotland, UK. He entered the Civil Service in 1907, and became an officer of Customs and Excise in Inverness and elsewhere in Scotland (1911–37). Following the success of *Highland River* (1937) he became a full-time writer. He was at his best when describing the ordinary life and background of a Highland fishing or crofting community, and when interpreting in simple prose the complex character of the Celt. His best-known novel *The Silver Darlings* (1941), was followed by *The Well at the World's End* (1951), *Bloodhunt* (1952), and *The Other Landscape* (1954).

Gunn, Thom(son William) (1929–) Poet, born in Gravesend, Kent, SE England, UK. After studying at Cambridge, he went to California (1954), where he taught English at Stanford and Berkeley. His often erotic poems are written in an intriguing variety of regular and free forms. Volumes include *Fighting Terms* (1954), *Jack Straw's Castle* (1976), *The Passages of Joy* (1982), *The Man With Night Sweats* (1992), and *Shelf Life* (1993).

Gunnarsson, Gunnar (1889–1975) Novelist, born in Valthjófsstadur, Iceland. He went to Denmark in 1907 and wrote *Af Borgslægtens Historie* (1912–14, From the Annals of the House of Borg), which became a best-seller, and was the first Icelandic work to be turned into a feature film. A prolific writer, his acknowledged masterpiece was the autobiographical novel, *Kirken paa Bjerget* (5 vols, 1923–8, The Church on the Mountain, trans in two volumes as Ships in the Sky and The Night and the Dream).

Gunter, Edmund (1581–1626) Mathematician and astronomer, born in Hertfordshire, SE England, UK. He studied at Oxford, became professor of astronomy in Gresham College, London, and invented many measuring instruments that bear his name; *Gunter's chain*, the 22-yard-long, 100-link chain used by surveyors; *Gunter's line*, the forerunner of the modern slide-rule; *Gunter's scale*, a two-foot rule with scales of chords, tangents and logarithmic lines for solving navigational problems; and the portable *Gunter's quadrant*. He made the first observation of the variation of the magnetic compass, and introduced the words *cosine* and *cotangent* into the language of trigonometry.

Gunther, John (1901–70) Writer and journalist, born in Chicago, IL. He was a foreign correspondent for the *Chicago Daily News* and for NBC. He established his reputation with the best-selling *Inside Europe* (1936), followed by a series of similar works in which first-hand material is blended with documentary information to present penetrating social and political studies. Other books include *Death Be Not Proud* (1949) and *A Fragment of Autobiography* (1962).

Gurevich, Mikhail Iosifovich [gooryayvich] (1893–1976) Aircraft designer, born in Rubanshchina, Russia. He graduated in 1925 from the aviation faculty of Kharkov Technological Institute. He was best known for the fighter aircraft produced by the design bureau he headed with Artem Ivanovich Mikoyan, the MiG (from 'Mikoyan and Gurevich') series. >> Mikoyan

Gurley Brown, Helen (1922–) US writer and editor, born in Arkansas. An advertising copywriter, her first book, *Sex and the Single Girl* (1962), became a best seller. She was made editor of *Cosmopolitan* in 1965, and transformed the struggling magazine into an international journal with 14 overseas editions.

Gurney, Edmund (1847–88) Psychical researcher, born in Hersham, Surrey, SE England, UK. He studied at Cambridge, and became one of the founding members of the Society for Psychical Research. He conducted important experimental studies of hypnosis and telepathy, and a statistical survey of hallucinations. His investigation of apparitions, telepathy, and other such phenomena culminated in his classic *Phantasms of the Living* (with F W H Myers and F Podmore, 1886).

Gurney, Sir Goldsworthy (1793–1875) Inventor, born in Treator, Cornwall, SW England, UK. He trained and practised as a surgeon, but became more interested in solving scientific problems. Inspired by Stephenson's *Rocket*, he built a steam-powered carriage which completed a return journey from London to Bath at an average speed of 15 mph. He opened a passenger service, but this drew much opposition from horse-coach operators, and was soon taxed out of existence. He improved the lighting and ventilation in the House of Commons, for which he was knighted in 1863.

Gurney, Ivor (1890–1937) Composer and poet, born in Gloucester, Gloucestershire, SWC England, UK. He studied at the Royal College of Music in London. Gassed and shell-shocked in 1917, he published two volumes of poems from hospital: *Severn and Somme* (1917) and *War's Embers* (1919), and later *Five Elizabethan Songs* (1920). From 1922 he was confined in an asylum, and died in London. Some 300 songs and 900 poems survive, whose quality is increasingly recognized.

Gustafsson, Greta Lovisa >> **Garbo, Greta**

Gustav I, originally **Gustav Eriksson Vasa** (1496–1560) King of Sweden (1523–60), the founder of the Vasa dynasty, born into a gentry family in Lindholmen, Sweden. In 1518 he was carried off to Denmark as a hostage, but escaped to lead a peasant rising against the occupying Danes, capturing Stockholm (1523) and driving the enemy from Sweden. He was elected king by the Diet and, despite several rebellions, his 40-year rule left Sweden a peaceful realm. >> RR1090

Gustav II Adolf or **Gustavus Adolphus** (1594–1632) King of Sweden (1611–32), born in Stockholm, the son of Charles IX. On ascending the throne, he reorganized the government with the assistance of Chancellor Oxenstierna, raised men and money, and recovered his Baltic provinces from Denmark. He ended wars with Russia (1617) and Poland (1629), and carried out major military and economic reforms at home. In 1630 he entered the Thirty Years' War, leading the German Protestants against the Imperialist forces under Wallenstein, and won several victories, notably at Breitenfeld (1631). He was killed during the Swedish victory at Lützen, near Leipzig. >> Oxenstierna; Tilly; Wallenstein; RR1090

Gustav III (1746–92) King of Sweden (1771–92). He reasserted royal power by arresting the council of nobles and declaring a new form of government (1772). He encouraged agriculture, commerce, and science, and granted religious toleration, but also created a secret police system and introduced censorship. He founded the Royal Opera House (1782), the Swedish Academy (1786), and the Royal Dramatic Theatre (1788). Poor harvests and a failing economy created discontent, and as a diversion he launched into a war against Russia (1788–90) that proved unpopular and inconclusive. He was shot by a former army officer during a masked ball at the Royal Opera House. >> RR1090

Gustav IV Adolf (1778–1837) King of Sweden (1792–1809), the son of Gustav III. During his minority, the regent was his uncle Karl, Duke of Sudermania. In the first years of his reign as an absolute monarch, he did much to improve Swedish agriculture with a General Enclosure Act (1803). He joined the European coalition against Napoleon in 1805, but after Russia sided with France in 1807, Sweden was attacked by Denmark. His policies provoked a military coup, and he and his family went into exile in 1809, eventually settling in Switzerland. >> RR1090

Gustav V (1858–1950) King of Sweden (1907–50), born in Stockholm. Shy and reserved by nature, he disliked pomp and spectacle, and refused a coronation ceremony, thus becoming the first 'uncrowned king' on the Swedish throne. He reigned as a popular constitutional monarch, and in World War 2 came to symbolize the unity of the nation. He was the longest-reigning king in Swedish history. >> RR1090

Gustav VI Adolf (1882–1973) King of Sweden (1950–73), born in Stockholm, the son of Gustav V. He studied at the

University of Uppsala, and was respected as a scholar, archaeologist, and authority on Chinese art. During his reign a new constitution was under preparation, and the king worked to transform the crown into a democratic monarchy, which helped to preserve it against political demands for a republic. His eldest son, **Gustav Adolf** (1906–47), having been killed in an air-crash, he was succeeded by his grandson, Carl XVI Gustaf. >> Carl XVI Gustaf; Gustav V; RR1090

Gustavus III (1746–92) King of Sweden (1771–92), born in Stockholm. His reign was known as the 'Gustavian Era' or the age of 'the Swedish Enlightenment'. His first political act was to reassert royal authority, subordinating the parties in the Riksdag and thereby halting the so-called Age of Freedom (1720–71). He followed this with administrative, economic, religious, and press reforms, strengthening the navy, increasing trade, and improving the poor law. A committed patron of the arts, he founded the National Theatre, Opera, and Academy. His involvement in war with Russia (1788–90) produced an aristocratic conspiracy in Finland, the League of Anjala, before the Swedish fleet was finally victorious at Svenskund (1790). He continued to reduce the powers of the nobility, but aristocratic plots continued, and he was shot and mortally wounded by a Swedish army officer. >> RR1090

Gustavus Adolphus >> **Gustav II Adolf**

Guston, Philip [guhstn] (1913–80) Painter, born in Montreal, Quebec, Canada. His family moved to the USA in 1916, and he settled in New York City, where he was involved with the Federal Works of Art Project (1935–40), then taught at Iowa University (1941–5). His work of the 1950s was in the Abstract Expressionist style, but from the late 1960s he introduced brightly coloured and crudely drawn comic-strip characters into his painting.

Gutenberg, Beno [gootenberg] (1889–1960) Geophysicist, born in Darmstadt, Germany. He studied at Darmstadt and Göttingen universities, and taught at Freiberg from 1926. In 1930 he moved to the California Institute of Technology, becoming director of the seismology laboratory in 1947. In 1913 he had proposed that data on earthquake shock waves can be interpreted as showing that the Earth's core is liquid, a novel idea now fully accepted. His name is preserved in the geological term *Gutenberg discontinuity*. >> Richter, Charles

Gutenberg, Johannes (Gensfleisch) [gootnberg] (1400–68) Printer, regarded as the inventor of printing from movable type, born in Mainz, Germany. Between 1430 and 1444 he was in Strasbourg, probably working as a goldsmith, and here he may have begun printing. In Mainz again by 1448 he entered into partnership with Johann Fust, who financed a printing press. This partnership ended in 1455, when Fust sued him for repayment of the loan, and forced him to give up his machinery, leaving him ruined. Aided by Konrad Humery, he was able to set up another press, but little is known of his work thereafter. His best-known book is the 42-line Bible, often called *Gutenberg's Bible* (c.1455). >> Fust

Guthlac, St [guthlak] (c. 673–714) English monk at Repton, Derbyshire, C England, UK in 697, and a hermit at Crowland Abbey in 699, where he lived a life of severe asceticism. Feast day 11 April.

Guthorm or **Guthrum** (?–890) Danish king of East Anglia, and opponent of King Alfred the Great. He led a major Viking invasion of Anglo-Saxon England in 871 (the 'Great Summer Army'), seized East Anglia, and conquered Northumbria and Mercia. He attacked Wessex early in 878 and drove Alfred into hiding in Somerset. By May of that year Alfred had recovered sufficiently to defeat the Danes at the crucial Battle of Edington in Wiltshire. In the ensuing treaty, Guthorm agreed to leave Wessex and accept baptism as a Christian, and he and his army settled down peacefully in East Anglia. >> Alfred

Guthrie, Thomas Anstey >> **Anstey, F**

Guthrie, Sir (William) Tyrone (1900–71) Theatrical director, born in Tunbridge Wells, Kent, SE England, UK. He studied at Oxford, and became director of the Scottish National Players (1926–8) and the Cambridge Festival Theatre (1929–30). He was responsible for many fine productions of Shakespeare at the Old Vic during the 1930s, and became administrator of the Old Vic and Sadler's Wells (1939–45), and director of the Old Vic (1950–1). He often worked abroad, and founded the Tyrone Guthrie Theatre in Minneapolis, MN, in 1963. He was knighted in 1961.

Guthrie, Woody, popular name of **Woodrow Wilson Guthrie** (1912–67) Folksinger and songwriter, born in Okemah, OK. He took to the road during the Great Depression, singing for his meals, and wrote hundreds of songs, lauding migrant workers, pacifists, and underdogs of all kinds. His best-known songs are 'So Long, It's Been Good to Know You' and 'This Land is Your Land'. He helped to form the Almanac Singers, a group that advocated public power at workers' rallies. In 1952, he was hospitalized with Huntington's chorea, and died of it 15 years later, by which time a new generation, including Joan Baez and Bob Dylan, had learned his songs and adopted his causes. >> Baez; Dylan; Seeger

Guthrum >> **Guthorm**

Gutiérrez, Gustavo [gootyaires] (1928–) Liberation theologian and priest, born in Lima, Peru. He studied at Louvain (1951–5) and Lyon (1955–9), before ordination in Lima, becoming professor of theology at the Catholic university there in 1960. His theology is based on responding to the needs of the poor and oppressed rather than on imposing solutions from the outside. This has challenged supporters of the status quo in Latin America and practitioners of academic theology elsewhere. He has written several books, including *A Theology of Liberation* (1971), *The Power of the Poor in History* (1984), *We Drink from Our Own Wells* (1984), and *On Job* (1987).

Guttuso, Renato [gootoosoh] (1912–87) Artist, born in Palermo, Italy. He worked for some time in Milan, and settled in Rome in 1937. He was associated with various anti-Fascist groups from 1942 to 1945, and much of his work reflects this experience. After the war he began to paint dramatic Realist pictures of the lives of the Italian peasants.

Guy, Thomas [giy] (c. 1644–1724) Philanthropist, born in London, England, UK. He began business in 1668 as a bookseller, and then became a printer of Bibles, amassing a fortune of nearly half a million pounds. In 1707 he built and furnished three wards of St Thomas' Hospital, and in 1722 founded the hospital in Southwark which bears his name.

Guy de Lusignan [gee, looseenyá] (?–1194) French crusader. He became King of Jerusalem in 1186 as consort of Sibylla, the daughter of Amalric I, but was defeated and captured at Hattin (1187) by Saladin, who overran most of the kingdom. On the death of his wife in 1190, he fought with Conrad of Montferrat for the throne. He ceded the throne to Richard I of England in 1192, and in exchange received Cyprus, where his family ruled until 1474. >> Richard I; Saladin

Guy of Arezzo >> **Guido d'Arezzo**

Guyon, Jeanne Marie de la Motte [geeyō], *née* **Bouvier** (1648–1717) Mystic, born in Montargis, France. She was married at 16 to the wealthy and elderly Jacques de la Motte Guyon. A widow at 28, she determined to devote her life to the poor and needy, and to the cultivation of spiritual perfection. Between 1681 and 1686 she visited several cities, but had to move on when her Quietist teachings upset the local bishops. She finally settled in Paris, but was arrested for heretical opinions. Released by the intervention of Mme de Maintenon, she continued teaching and was again imprisoned (1695–1702). Her works include *The Short and Very Easy Method of Prayer* (1685, trans title), a mystical interpretation of the Song of Solomon, an autobiography, letters, and some spiritual poetry. >> Maintenon

Guyot, Arnold Henry [geeyoh] (1807–84) Geographer, born in Boudevilliers, Switzerland. He studied at Neuchâtel and in Germany, became professor of geology at Neuchâtel (1839), and studied glaciers in Switzerland with Jean Louis Agassiz. In 1848 he emigrated to the USA, and became professor of physical geography and geology at Princeton (1854), and was in charge of the meteorological department of the Smithsonian Institution. His name is preserved in the geological term *guyot*, a flat-topped sub-ocean mountain. >> Agassiz

Guzmán Blanco, Antonio [goos**mahn**] (1829–99) Venezuelan dictator, born in Carácas. He was vice-president from 1863 to 1868. Driven from office (1868), he headed a revolution which restored him to power (1870), and became dictator, holding the presidency on three occasions (1873–7, 1879–84, 1886–8). He then retired to Paris.

Gwyn or **Gwynne, Nell**, popular name of **Eleanor Gwyn** (c. 1650–87) Mistress of Charles II, possibly born in London, England, UK. Of humble parentage, she lived precariously as an orange girl before going on the boards at Drury Lane, where she quickly established herself as a comedienne. She had at least one son by the king – Charles Beauclerk, Duke of St Albans – and James Beauclerk is often held to have been a second. >> Charles II (of England)

Gwynne-Vaughan, Dame Helen Charlotte Isabella [gwin **vawn**], *née* **Fraser** (1879–1967) Botanist and servicewoman. She studied at King's College, London, and became head and later professor of botany at Birkbeck College, London (1909–44). In World War 1 she was organizer (1917) and later controller of the Women's Army Auxiliary Air Force in France, and commandant of the Women's Royal Auxiliary Air Force (1918–19). In World War 2 she was chief controller of the Women's Auxiliary Territorial Service (1939–41).

Gyllenhammar, Pehr Gustaf [gülenhamer] (1935–   ) Industrialist, born in Gothenburg, Sweden. He studied at Lund University, then took up international law in England, the USA, and Switzerland. He joined the Volvo Motor Co in 1970, becoming its managing director (1971–83), chairman (1983–90), then executive chairman (1990–3). He has written a number of books, including *Jag Tror på Sverige* (1973, I Believe in Sweden).

Gyp [zhip], pseudonym of **Sibylle-Gabrielle-Marie-Antoinette comtesse de Mirabeau de Martel de Joinvil** (1849–1932) Novelist, born at the château of Koëtsal, Brittany, France. She wrote a series of humorous novels, describing fashionable society, of which the best known are *Petit Bob* (1882) and *Mariage de Chiffon* (1894).

Haakon VII [hawkon] (1872–1957) King of Norway (1905–57), born in Charlottenlund, Denmark. He became king when Norway voted herself independent of Sweden in 1905, dispensed with regal pomp, and emerged as the 'people's king'. During World War 2, he carried on Norwegian resistance to Nazi occupation from England. >> RR1079

Haas, Earle C (1885–1981) US physician who invented the tampon. A doctor in Denver, in 1936 he adapted a surgical cotton plug for use as an intravaginal sanitary towel. He patented his design, and marketed it under the name Tampax.

Haavelmo, Trygve [hawvelmoh] (1911–) Econometrician and economist, born in Skedsmo, Norway. In 1947, he became head of a division in the Norwegian ministry of commerce, and in 1948 was appointed professor of political economy and statistics at the University of Oslo. He was awarded the 1989 Nobel Prize for Economics for his contributions to developing the field of econometrics, especially methods to estimate and test quantitative relations.

Hába, Alois [hahba, aloys] (1893–1973) Composer, born in Vyzovice, Czech Republic. He studied in Prague, Vienna, and Berlin, and was made professor at Prague Conservatory in 1924. He composed prolifically, and showed interest in the division of the scale into quarter-tones. His works include an opera, The Mother, and orchestral, chamber, and piano music.

Haber, Fritz [hahber] (1868–1934) Chemist, born in Wrocław, Poland (formerly Breslau, Germany). He studied in Berlin, Heidelberg, and Zürich. Professor of chemistry at Karlsruhe and Berlin, he became known for his invention of the process for making ammonia from the nitrogen in the air. He was awarded the Nobel Prize for Chemistry in 1918.

Habermas, Jürgen [habermas] (1929–) Philosopher and social theorist, born in Düsseldorf, Germany. He studied at Göttingen and Bonn, taught at Heidelberg (1962) and Frankfurt (1964), and became director of the Max Planck Institute (1971). His books include Erkenntnis und Interesse (1968, Knowledge and Human Interests) and Theorie des kommunikatives Handelns (1982, Theory of Communicative Action).

Habib, Philip C(harles) [habeeb] (1920–92) US diplomat, born in New York City. He served in the US army (1942–6) and was a foreign service officer (1949–80). A US delegate to the Vietnam War negotiations in Paris (1968–71), he became ambassador to the Republic of Korea (1971–4), assistant secretary of state for East Asian and Pacific affairs (1974–6), and under-secretary of state for political affairs (1976–8). He left the service due to health reasons, but returned to the diplomatic scene as President Reagan's personal representative to the Middle East (1981–3), where he negotiated for an end to the crisis in Lebanon. >> Reagan

Hácha, Emil [hakha] (1872–1945) Czech politician and president (1938–9), born in Trhové Sviny, Bohemia. He became president following the German annexation of Sudetenland; as such, under duress, he made over the state to Hitler (1939). He was then puppet president of the German protectorate of Bohemia and Moravia (1939–45). >> Hitler; RR1043

Hackett, Sir John (Winthrop) (1910–97) British soldier and academic. After studying at Oxford he was commissioned in the Hussars (1931). In World War 2 he served with distinction, notably with the 4th Parachute Brigade at Arnhem in 1944. He held several post-war commands, culminating in commander-in-chief, British Army of the Rhine, and of the Northern Army Group in 1966. He later became principal of King's College, University of London (1968–75).

Hackman, Gene (1931–) Film actor, born in San Bernardino, CA. Having established himself as a theatre performer, he made his film debut in Mad Dog Coll (1961), and had small roles in many films before earning a Best Supporting Actor Oscar nomination for his performance in Bonnie and Clyde (1967). He won an Oscar for his role as 'Popeye Doyle' in The French Connection (1971, Oscar), and received further Oscar nominations for Mississippi Burning (1989), and Unforgiven (1992). Later films include Wyatt Earp (1994), Get Shorty (1995), and Absolute Power (1997).

Hackworth, Timothy (1786–1850) Locomotive engineer, born in Wylam, Northumberland, NE England, UK. He was manager of the Stockton–Darlington railway (1825–40), and builder of a number of famous engines, including the Royal George and the Sans Pareil, rival of George Stephenson's Rocket. >> Stephenson, George

Hadamard, Jacques (Salomon) [adamah(r)] (1865–1963) Mathematician, born in Versailles, France. He studied in Paris, became lecturer at Bordeaux (1893–7) and the Sorbonne (1897–1909), and was then professor at the Collège de France and the Ecole Polytechnique until his retirement in 1937. He was a leading figure in French mathematics throughout his career, working in complex function theory, differential geometry, and partial differential equations. In 1896 he and the Belgian mathematician, **Charles Jean de la Vallée Poussin** independently proved the definitive form of the prime-number theorem.

Hadas, Moses [hadahs] (1890–1966) Classicist and translator, born in Atlanta, GA. He studied at Emory and Columbia universities, then taught at Columbia (1925–8, 1930–66). His best-known publications include History of Greek Literature (1950) and History of Latin Literature (1952). His translations introduced works in German and Greek to English readers.

Hadden, Briton >> **Luce, Henry R**

Haddon, Alfred Cort (1855–1940) Anthropologist, born in London, England, UK. He studied at Cambridge, and was appointed professor of zoology at Dublin (1880). A visit to the Torres Straits, ostensibly to study coral reefs, led to his interest in the native culture of the region, and he went on to organize the Cambridge Anthropological Expedition to the Torres Straits (1898–9), in which were developed the basic techniques of modern anthropology. He later became reader in ethnology at Cambridge University (1904–25).

Hadfield, Maria >> **Cosway, Richard**

Hadfield, Sir Robert (Abbot) (1858–1940) Metallurgist and industrialist, born in Sheffield, South Yorkshire, N England, UK. The son of a Sheffield steel manufacturer who was a pioneer of steel casting, he was educated locally, taking an interest in science. After taking over the business from his father, he continued to research alloys of steel, and developed manganese steel, an alloy of exceptional durability with many applications in industry. He was knighted in 1908.

Hadlee, Sir Richard (John) (1951–) Cricketer, born in Christchurch, New Zealand. He started his first-class career with Canterbury in 1971–2, made his Test debut in 1973, and scored 3124 Test runs. A right-arm fast bowler, and a left-handed batsman, he also played for Nottinghamshire and Tasmania. New Zealand's best all-round cricketer, in 1988 he surpassed Ian Botham's record of 383 Test wickets, and went on to a total of 431 before retiring in 1990, when he was knighted. >> RR1151

Hadley, John (1682–1744) Mathematician, born in Hertfordshire, SE England, UK. He developed many improvements to the Gregorian reflecting telescope, making it into an accurate instrument for use in astronomy. He also designed a double-reflecting quadrant which became the basis for the sextant.

Hadley, Patrick (Arthur Sheldon) (1899–1973) Composer, born in Cambridge, Cambridgeshire, EC England, UK. He studied at Cambridge and the Royal College of Music, learning composition under Vaughan Williams and conducting from Adrian Boult. He became professor of music at Cambridge (1946–62), where he established excellent male-voice chapel and secular choirs. He wrote his most significant work, a choral symphony entitled *The Hills*, in 1946. >> Boult; Vaughan Williams

Hadow, Sir William Henry [hadoh] (1859–1937) Scholar, educational administrator, and musicologist, born in Ebrington, Gloucestershire, SWC England, UK. He studied at Oxford, where he was successively scholar, lecturer, fellow, tutor, and dean (1889). He was Vice-Chancellor of Sheffield University (1919–30), and as chairman of several committees published a series of reports on education, notably *The Education of the Adolescent* (1926) which called for the re-organization of elementary education, the abandonment of all-age schools, and the creation of secondary modern schools. He was a leading influence in English education at all levels in the 1920s and 1930s.

Hadrian [haydrian], in full **Publius Aelius Hadrianus** (76–138) Roman emperor (117–38), ward, protégé, and successor of the Emperor Trajan, a fellow-Spaniard and relation by marriage. Coming to power in ambiguous circumstances, Hadrian was always unpopular in Rome, and even the object of a serious conspiracy there (118). He spent little of his reign in Rome, but toured the empire, consolidating the frontiers (as in Britain, where he initiated the building of the wall named after him), visiting the provinces, and promoting urban life. >> Trajan; RR1084

Haeckel, Ernst (Heinrich Philipp August) [haykl] (1834–1919) Naturalist, born in Potsdam, Germany. He studied at Würzburg, Berlin, and Vienna, and became professor of zoology at Jena (1862–1909). One of the first to sketch the genealogical tree of animals, he strongly supported Darwin's theories of evolution. >> Darwin, Charles

Háfiz or **Háfez**, pseudonym of **Shams-ed-Din Mohammad** (c. 1326–c. 1390) Lyrical poet, born in Shiraz, Iran. He worked as a religious teacher and wrote commentaries on sacred texts. A member of the mystical sect of Sufi philosophers, his short poems (*ghazals*), all on sensuous subjects, such as love, wine, and flowers, contain an esoteric signification to the initiated.

Hagar [haygah(r)] Biblical character, the maid of Sarah (the wife of Abraham). Due to Sarah's barrenness, Abraham had a son Ishmael by Hagar (*Gen* 16), but Hagar and her son were later expelled into the wilderness by Abraham after Isaac's birth (*Gen* 21). >> Abraham

Hagen, Walter (Charles) [haygn], nickname **the Haig** (1892–1969) Golfer, born in Rochester, NY. At the age of 21 he won the US Open (1914), the first of his 11 major championship titles. A flamboyant personality who insisted on good manners, he is credited with raising the image and social standing of the game. He published an autobiography, *The Walter Hagen Story* (1956). >> RR1158

Haggard, Sir H(enry) Rider (1856–1925) Novelist, born at Bradenham Hall, Norfolk, E England, UK. Educated at Ipswich, he travelled widely in government service in South Africa, before taking up a literary life in England in 1881. *King Solomon's Mines* (1885) made his work known, and was followed by *She* (1887) and several other stories. He was knighted in 1912.

Hague, William (Jefferson) [hayg] (1961–) British statesman. He came to notice at an early age, when at 16 he received a standing ovation after addressing the 1977 Tory Party Conference. He studied at Oxford, where he became president of the Union, joined a firm of management consultants, and was elected an MP in 1989. He acted as parliamentary private secretary to Chancellor of the Exchequer Norman Lamont (1990–3), then became under-secretary (1993–4) and minister of state for social security (1994–5), and minister for Wales (1995–7). He won the leadership of the Conservative Party following John Major's resignation in 1997. >> Lamont, Norman; Major

Hahn, Kurt (Matthias Robert Martin) (1886–1974) Educationist, born in Berlin. He studied at the universities of Berlin, Heidelberg, Freiburg, and Göttingen, fled from Nazi Germany in 1933, and established Gordonstoun School in Moray (Scotland) in 1934, emphasizing physical rather than intellectual activities in education. His ideas influenced the development of such establishments as the Outward Bound Schools (1941) and the Atlantic Colleges (1957).

Hahn, Otto (1879–1968) Physical chemist, born in Frankfurt, Germany. He studied at the University of Marburg, and lectured in Berlin from 1907, becoming director of the Kaiser Wilhelm Institute there in 1927. With Meitner he discovered the radioactive element protactinium (1917), and in 1938 bombarded uranium with neutrons to find the first chemical evidence of nuclear fission products. He was awarded the Nobel Prize for Chemistry in 1944. >> Meitner

Hahnemann, (Christian Friedrich) Samuel [hahnuhman] (1755–1843) Physician and founder of homeopathy, born in Meissen, Germany. He studied at Leipzig, and for 10 years practised medicine. He observed that a medicine administered to a healthy person produced similar symptoms to those of the illness it was intended to cure, and developed his law of 'similars', around which he built his system of homeopathy. He published *Reine Arzneimittellehre* (1811, Precept of Pure Drugs), a homeopathic drug catalogue.

Haidar Ali [hiyder alee], also spelled **Hyder Ali** (1722–82) Muslim ruler of Mysore, born in Budikote, India. Having conquered Calicut and fought the Marathas, he waged two wars against the British, in the first of which (1767–9) he won several gains. In 1779 he and his son, Tippoo, again attacked the British, initially with great success; but in 1781–2 he was defeated. >> Tippoo Sahib

Haig, Alexander (Meigs) [hayg] (1924–) US army officer and statesman, born in Philadelphia, PA. He trained at West Point, studied at Georgetown University, and joined the US army in 1947, serving in Korea (1950–1) and in the Vietnam War (1966–7), and becoming a general in 1973. He then retired from the army to become White House chief-of-staff during the last days of the Nixon presidency. Returning to active duty, he was supreme NATO commander before returning again to civilian life, as president of United Technologies Corporation. He served President Reagan as secretary of state in 1981–2, and sought the Republican nomination for the presidency in 1988. He has been chairman of Worldwide Associates Inc since 1984. >> Reagan

Haig (of Bemersyde), Douglas Haig, 1st Earl [hayg] (1861–1928) British field marshal, born in Edinburgh, EC Scotland, UK. He studied at Oxford and Sandhurst, obtained a commission in the 7th Hussars, and served in

Egypt, South Africa, and India. In 1914 he led the 1st Army Corps in France, and in 1915 became commander of the British Expeditionary Force. He waged a costly and exhausting war of attrition, for which he was much criticized, but led the final successful offensive (Aug 1918). In postwar years he devoted himself to the care of ex-servicemen, organizing the Royal British Legion. His earldom was awarded in 1919.

Haile Selassie I [hiylee selasee], originally **Prince Ras Tafari Makonnen** (1891–1975) Emperor of Ethiopia (1930–6, 1941–74), born near Harer, Ethiopia. He led the revolution in 1916 against Lij Yasu, and became regent and heir to the throne, westernizing the institutions of his country. He settled in England after the Italian conquest of Abyssinia (1935–6), but in 1941 was restored after British liberation. In the early 1960s he helped to establish the Organization of African Unity. The disastrous famine of 1973 led to economic chaos, industrial strikes, and mutiny among the armed forces, and he was deposed (1974) in favour of the crown prince. Accusations of corruption levelled at him and his family have not destroyed the reverence in which he is held by certain groups, notably the Rastafarians. >> RR1048

Hailey, Arthur (1920–) Popular novelist, born in Luton, Bedfordshire, SC England, UK. He became a naturalized Canadian in 1947. He worked in industry and sales before becoming a freelance writer in 1956. He has written many best-selling blockbusters about disasters, several of which have become highly successful films, such as *Hotel* (1965), *Airport* (1968), and *Wheels* (1971). Later novels include *Strong Medicine* (1984), *The Evening News* (1990), and *Detective* (1997).

Hailsham, Quintin (McGarel) Hogg, 2nd Viscount [haylsham] (1907–) British statesman, born in London, England, UK. He studied at Oxford, was called to the bar (1932), and became an MP (1938). He succeeded to his title in 1950, and was First Lord of the Admiralty (1956–7), minister of education (1957), Lord President of the Council (1957–9, 1960–4), chairman of the Conservative Party (1957–9), minister for science and technology (1959–64), and secretary of state for education and science (1964). In 1963 he renounced his peerage and re-entered the House of Commons in an unsuccessful bid to become leader of the Conservative Party. In 1970 he was created a life peer (**Baron Hailsham of Saint Marylebone**) and became Lord Chancellor (1970–4), a post he held again from 1979 until his retirement in 1987.

Hailwood, Mike, popular name of **Stanley Michael Bailey Hailwood** (1940–81) Motor-cyclist, born in Oxford, Oxfordshire, SC England, UK. He took nine world titles: the 250 cc in 1961 and 1966–7, the 350 cc in 1966–7, and the 500 cc in 1962–5, all using Honda or MV Agusta machines. In addition, he won a record 14 Isle of Man Tourist Trophy races between 1961 and 1979. During the 1960s he also had a career in motor racing, but was unable to match his success on two wheels. His awards included the George Medal. He was killed in a car accident near his Birmingham home. >> RR1164

Haitink, Bernard [hiytingk] (1929–) Conductor, born in Amsterdam. He studied at the Amsterdam Conservatory, and was an orchestral violinist before becoming second conductor of The Netherlands Radio Union (1955). He was later conductor of the Amsterdam Concertgebouw Orchestra (from 1961) and of the London Philharmonic (1967–79), and was appointed musical director at Glyndebourne in 1977 (the year he was granted an honorary knighthood) and at Covent Garden in 1987.

Hakluyt, Richard [hakloot] (c. 1552–1616) Geographer, born in Hertfordshire, SE England, UK. He studied at

Oxford, where he lectured in geography, and was ordained some time before 1580. He wrote widely on exploration and navigation, notably his *Principal Navigations, Voyages, and Discoveries of the English Nation* (1589; 3 vols, 1598–1600). He also introduced the use of globes into English schools. Made a prebendary of Westminster in 1602, he is buried in Westminster Abbey. The *Hakluyt Society* was instituted in 1846.

Halas, George (Stanley) (1895–1983) Founder, owner, and coach with the Chicago Bears American football team, born in Chicago, IL. A co-founder of the National Football League (1920), he helped shape the modern professional game, bringing large crowds in to watch the sport for the first time. In 1968 he retired as head coach to the Bears for the fourth and last time. After more than 40 years of coaching, his record showed 320 wins, 147 defeats, and 30 draws.

Halas, John [halas], original surname **Halasz** (1912–95) Animated cartoon producer, born in Budapest. He moved to England in 1936 to work as an animator, met and married Joy Batchelor, and they formed the Halas–Batchelor animation unit (1940). They produced *Animal Farm* (1954), England's first full-length cartoon, and many more films, especially for television. >> Batchelor

Halasz, Gyula >> Brassaï

Haldane, Elizabeth Sanderson [holdayn] (1862–1937) Writer, born in Edinburgh, EC Scotland, UK, the sister of John Scott Haldane and Richard Burdon Haldane. She studied nursing, for a while managed the Royal Infirmary, Edinburgh, and became the first woman justice of the peace in Scotland (1920). She wrote a life of Descartes (1905) and edited his philosophical works, translated Hegel, and wrote commentaries on George Eliot (1927) and Mrs Gaskell (1930). >> Haldane, John Scott; Haldane, Richard Burdon

Haldane, J(ohn) B(urdon) S(anderson) [holdayn] (1892–1964) Biologist and geneticist, born in Oxford, Oxfordshire SC England, UK, the son of John Scott Haldane. He studied at Oxford, became reader in biochemistry at Cambridge (1922–32), and professor of genetics (1933–57) and of biometry (1937–57) at London. He then emigrated to India, adopting Indian nationality, and worked in Calcutta and Orissa. He wrote widely on his subject, and was well known for his popularizations. He was also chairman of the editorial board of the *Daily Worker* (1940–9), but left the British Communist Party in 1956. >> Haldane, John Scott

Haldane, John Scott [holdayn] (1860–1936) Physiologist, born in Edinburgh, EC Scotland, UK. A fellow of New College, Oxford, he made a study of the effects of industrial occupations upon human physiology, especially respiration, and served as director of a mining research laboratory at Birmingham. >> Haldane, Elizabeth Sanderson; Haldane, Richard Burdon

Haldane (of Cloan), Richard Burdon Haldane, 1st Viscount [holdayn] (1856–1928) Jurist, philosopher, and statesman, born in Edinburgh, EC Scotland, UK. He studied at Edinburgh and Göttingen, was called to the bar in 1879, entered parliament in 1885 as a Liberal, and supported the Boer War. He is best known for his period as secretary of state for war (1905–12), when he remodelled the army and founded the Territorials. He was Lord Chancellor (1912–15 and, under Labour, in 1924), and ranked high as a judge. >> Haldane, Elizabeth Sanderson; Haldane, John Scott

Hale, Edward Everett (1822–1909) Unitarian clergyman and writer, born in Roxbury, MA. He started on his father's newspaper, the *Boston Daily Advertiser*, and produced numerous essays, short stories, pamphlets, and novels throughout his life. He became a minister in Roxbury in 1846. He is best remembered for his story 'The Man Without a Country' (1863), which encouraged patriotism during the Civil War. His most popular novels were *In His Name* (1873) and *East and West* (1892). A proponent of the Social Gospel movement, his other works include *Ten Times One is Ten* (1871) which inspired the 'Lend a Hand' clubs.

Hale, George Ellery (1868–1938) Astronomer, born in Chicago, IL. He studied at the Massachusetts Institute of Technology, and became director of the Yerkes Observatory, WI (1892–1904), and at Mt Wilson, CA (1904–23), where he initiated the construction of some of the world's largest telescopes, notably the 5 m *Hale reflecting telescope* on Mt Palomar, CA. His research led to the discovery of magnetic fields within sunspots. The Palomar and Mt Wilson observatories were established under his guidance, and operated jointly (1948–80) as the Hale Observatories.

Hale, Sir Matthew (1609–76) Judge, born in Alderley, Gloucestershire, SWC England, UK. He studied at Oxford, entered Lincoln's Inn in 1628, and in 1637 was called to the bar. A justice of the common pleas from 1654 until Cromwell's death in 1658, after the Restoration (which he zealously promoted) he was made chief-baron of the Exchequer, and in 1671 Chief Justice of the King's Bench. Devout, learned and even-handed, although a believer in witchcraft, he wrote a *History of the Common Law* (1713), a *History of the Pleas of the Crown* (1736), both still important, and the *Prerogatives of the King* (printed 1776), besides religious works.

Hale, Nathan (1755–76) American revolutionary officer, hero, and martyr, born in Coventry, CT. Educated at Yale, he became a school teacher, served in the siege of Boston (1775), and was commissioned captain (1776). He penetrated the British lines on Long Island to obtain information, but was captured by the British and hanged without trial the next day. His statue stands at the headquarters of the CIA at Langley, VA.

Hale, Sarah (Josepha), *née* **Buell** (1788–1879) Writer and first female magazine editor, born in Newport, NH. A widow from 1822, she wrote to support her family. In 1828 she was offered the editorship of the *Ladies' Magazine*, which continued until 1877 under the later title of *Godey's Magazine and Lady's Book*. Other notable works include the critically acclaimed *Woman's Record: or Sketches of All Distinguished Women from 'the Beginning Till AD 1850* (1853–76), *The Ladies' Wreath* (1837), a collection of poetry by women, and a book of *Poems for Our Children* (1830), which contains 'Mary had a Little Lamb'.

Hales, Stephen (1677–1761) Botanist and chemist, born in Bekesbourne, Kent, SE England, UK. He studied theology at Cambridge, and became in 1709 perpetual curate of Teddington. He developed gas-handling methods, discovered that plants take in a part of the air for their nutrition, and measured the pressure of rising sap. His *Vegetable Staticks* (1727) was the foundation of plant physiology. In *Haemastaticks* (1733) he discussed the circulation of the blood and blood pressure.

Halévy, (Jacques François) Fromental (Elié) [alayvee] (1799–1862) Composer, born in Paris. He studied in Paris, and won the Prix de Rome in 1819. His first successful opera was *Clari* (1828), but he is best known for *La Juive* (1835), which established his reputation. Bizet and Gounod studied under him. >> Bizet; Gounod

Halévy, Ludovic [alayvee] (1834–1908) Playwright and novelist, born in Paris. He produced vaudevilles and comedies, and with **Henri Meilhac** (1831–97) wrote libretti for the best-known operettas of Offenbach, and for Bizet's *Carmen*. >> Bizet; Offenbach

Haley, Bill, popular name of **William Haley** (1927–1981) Popular singer and musician, born in Highland Park, MI. With his group 'The Comets' he popularized rock-and-roll in the 1950s. His most famous song, 'Rock Around the Clock', was used in the film *Blackboard Jungle* (1955).

Haliburton, Thomas Chandler (1796–1865) Writer and jurist, born in Windsor, Nova Scotia, Canada. He was called to the bar in 1820, becoming a judge of the Supreme Court in 1842. In 1856 he retired to England. He is best known as the creator of 'Sam Slick', a sort of American 'Sam Weller', originally printed in the Halifax newspaper *Nova Scotian* (1835), later as a book *The Clockmaker, or Sayings and Doings of Samuel Slick of Slickville*, in which such sayings as 'barking up the wrong tree' were first used. He continued with *The Attaché, or Sam Slick in England* (1843–4).

Halifax, Charles Montagu, 1st Earl of (1661–1715) English Whig statesman, born in Horton, Northamptonshire, C England, UK. He studied at Cambridge, became MP for Maldon (1688) and a Lord of the Treasury (1692), establishing the National Debt and the Bank of England (1694). As Chancellor of the Exchequer (1694–5), he introduced a new coinage. In 1697 he was First Lord of the Treasury and Leader of the House of Commons, but resigned when the Tories came to power in 1699, and became Baron Halifax. On Queen Anne's death he was made a member of the Council of Regency, and on George I's arrival (1714) became an earl and prime minister. He was also a patron of letters and a poet.

Halifax, Edward Frederick Lindley Wood, 1st Earl of (2nd creation) (1881–1959) British Conservative statesman, born in Powderham, Devon, SW England, UK. He studied at Oxford, and became (as Baron Irwin 1925) Viceroy of India (1926–31). He was foreign secretary (1938–40) under Neville Chamberlain, whose 'appeasement' policy he implemented, and ambassador to the USA (1941–6). He was created earl in 1944. >> Chamberlain, Neville

Halifax, George Savile, 1st Marquess of (1633–95) English statesman, born in Thornhill, West Yorkshire, N England, UK. He was created viscount (1668) for his share in the Restoration, and in 1672 was made a marquess and Lord Privy Seal. On the accession of James II (1685) he became president of the Council, but was dismissed soon after. He was one of the three Commissioners appointed to treat with William of Orange after he landed in England (1688). He gave allegiance to William and resumed the office of Lord Privy Seal; but, joining the Opposition, resigned his post in 1689.

Hall, Asaph (1829–1907) Astronomer, born in Goshen, CT. He was professor of mathematics at the US Naval Observatory (1863–91), and professor of astronomy at Harvard (1896–1901). In 1877 he discovered the two satellites of Mars, calculated their orbits, and named them Deimos and Phobos.

Hall, Ben(jamin) (1837–65) Bushranger, born in New South Wales, Australia. After arrest in 1862 in connection with a robbery, then acquittal, he was deserted by his wife and young son. He joined the Gardiner gang to rob a bullion coach, was arrested, but released again. Returning home, he discovered it burned down by the police and all his cattle killed. He was now committed to a life of outlawry, and a series of audacious exploits followed, which engaged the sympathies of the locals. However, after the needless shooting of a constable by one of the gang, he decided to change his ways. He retired to a secluded camp, but was betrayed by a companion and died in a hail of police bullets at the age of 28.

Hall, Charles Francis (1821–71) Arctic explorer, born in Rochester, NH. He became interested in the fate of Sir John Franklin whose 1845 expedition to the Northwest

Territories, Canada, had been lost. He made two search expeditions (1860–2, 1864–9), living among the Inuits, and bringing back information and relics of the Franklin journey. In 1871 he sailed in command of the *Polaris* in an attempt to reach the North Pole, and via Smith's Sound made 82° 16' N, the northernmost latitude to date. On the return journey he was taken ill, and died. >> Franklin, John

Hall, Charles (Martin) (1863–1914) Chemist, born in Thompson, OH. He studied at Oberlin College, OH, where in 1886 he discovered (independently of Paul Héroult) the electrolyte method of producing aluminium economically. He helped to found the Aluminum Company of America, of which he became vice-president in 1890. >> Davis, Arthur Vining; Héroult

Hall, G(ranville) Stanley (1844–1924) Psychologist and educationist, born in Ashfield, MA. He studied at Leipzig, then taught at various universities, becoming professor of psychology and pedagogics at Johns Hopkins University in 1882, where he introduced experimental psychology on a laboratory scale. He founded the *American Journal of Psychology* (1887), influenced the development of educational and child psychology in the USA, and became the first president of Clark University (1889–1920).

Hall, Sir James (1761–1832) Geologist, born in Dunglass, East Lothian, E Scotland, UK. He studied at Cambridge and Edinburgh, sought to prove in the laboratory the geological theories of his friend and mentor James Hutton, and so founded experimental geology, artificially producing many of the igneous rocks of Scotland. >> Hutton, James

Hall, James (1811–98) Geologist and palaeontologist, born in Hingham, MA. On the staff of the Rensselaer Polytechnic Institute, NY, he made extensive explorations in the St Lawrence Valley, and was appointed state geologist of New York (1836). He wrote the classic report *Geology of New York* (Part 4, 1843), and contributed to the geosynclinal theory. He was also director of the New York Museum of Natural History (1871–98).

Hall, Joseph (1574–1656) Clergyman and writer, born in Ashby-de-la-Zouch, Leicestershire, C England, UK. He studied at Cambridge, was dean of Worcester (1616), Bishop of Exeter (1627–42), and Bishop of Norwich (1642–7). He was a moral philosopher, and also wrote satires. Among his works are *Contemplations, Christian Meditations, Episcopacy*, and *Mundus alter et idem* (c.1605, The World Different and the Same). His poetical satires *Virgidemiarum* (1597–1602, trans A Harvest of Blows) were described by Pope as 'the best poetry and the truest satire in the English language'. >> Pope, Alexander

Hall, Marguerite Radclyffe (1880–1943) Writer, born in Bournemouth, Dorset, S England, UK. She began as a lyric poet with several volumes of verse, some of which have become songs, but turned to novel writing in 1924 with *The Forge* and *The Unlit Lamp*. Her *Adam's Breed* (1926) won the Femina Vie Heureuse and the James Tait Black prizes, but *The Well of Loneliness* (1928), which embodies a sympathetic approach to female homosexuality, caused a prolonged furore and was banned in Britain for many years.

Hall, Marshall (1790–1857) Physician and physiologist, born in Basford, Nottinghamshire, C England, UK. After studying at Edinburgh, Paris, Göttingen, and Berlin, he settled at Nottingham in 1817, and practised in London from 1826 until 1853. He did important work on reflex action of the spinal system (1833–7); this was rejected by the Royal Society but accepted in other European countries, where later work verified his ideas. His name is also associated with a standard method of restoring suspended respiration. He wrote on diagnosis (1817), the circulation (1831), *Respiration and Irritability* (1832), and other subjects.

Hall, Sir Peter (Reginald Frederick) (1930–) Theatre, opera, and film director, born in Bury St Edmunds, Suffolk, E England, UK. He studied at Cambridge, where he produced and acted in more than 20 plays. After working in repertory and for the Arts Council, he became artistic director of the Elizabethan Theatre Company (1953), director (1955–6) of the London Arts Theatre, and formed his own company, The International Playwrights' Theatre (1957). After several productions at Stratford, he became director of the Royal Shakespeare Company, and remained as managing director of the company's theatres in Stratford and London until 1968. He was also director of the Covent Garden Opera (1969–71), and became successor to Olivier as director of the National Theatre (1973–88). He formed his own production company in 1988, and became artistic director at the Old Vic in 1997. He was knighted in 1977. >> Olivier

Hall, Rodney (1935–) Writer, arts administrator, and musician, born in Solihull, West Midlands, C England, UK. He was educated in England, then at the University of Queensland. He has published widely as a poet, with works such as *Penniless Till Doomsday* (1962) and *Romulus and Remus* (1971), and was influential as *The Australian* newspaper's poetry editor (1967–78). He has also edited some significant collections of Australian poetry. His novels include *The Ship on the Coin* (1972), *Just Relations* (1982, Miles Franklin Award), *Captivity Captive* (1988), *The Second Bridegroom* (1991), and *Island in the Mind* (1997). His narratives are often poetic and epic, and his work reveals a familiarity with a range of myths and legends. He was also chair of the Australia Council (1991–4).

Hall, Willis >> **Waterhouse, Keith**

Halle, Adam de la [ahl], known as **Adam le Bossu** ('Adam the Hunchback') (c. 1250–c. 1306) Poet and composer, born in Arras, France. He was court poet and musician to Robert II of Artois, and followed him to Naples in 1283. He was the originator of French comic opera, with *Le Jeu de Robin et de Marion*, and the partly autobiographical composition *Jeu de la fuellée* (Play of the Greensward). He also wrote poems in mediaeval verse forms.

Hallé, Sir Charles [halay] (1819–95) Pianist and conductor, born in Hagen, Germany. He studied at Darmstadt and Paris, where his reputation was established by his concerts of classical music. Driven to England by the Revolution of 1848, he settled in Manchester, where in 1858 he founded his famous orchestra. He was knighted in 1888.

Halleck, Henry W(ager) (1815–72) US army officer, born in Westernville, NY. He trained at West Point, served in the Mexican War, and in the Civil War (1861–5) was appointed commander of the Missouri (1861). In May 1862 he captured Corinth, in July became general-in-chief, but in March 1864 was superseded by General Grant. Chief-of-staff until 1865, he commanded the military division of the Pacific until 1869, and that of the South until his death. >> Grant, Ulysses S

Haller, Albrecht von [haler] (1708–77) Biologist, anatomist, botanist, physiologist, and poet, born in Bern. He studied at Tübingen and Leyden, and was professor of anatomy, surgery, and medicine in the new university of Göttingen (1736–53). Here he carried out biological experiments leading to the publication of *Elementa physiologiae corporis humani* (8 vols, 1757, Physiological Elements of the Human Body), a major contribution to the understanding of the functioning of the body, which opened the door to modern neurology.

Halley, Edmond [halee, hawlee] (1656–1742) Astronomer and mathematician, born in London, England, UK. He studied at Oxford, but left without taking a degree to undertake cataloguing the stars of the S hemisphere. He published his catalogue in 1687 and was elected a member of the Royal Society, as well as receiving his degree after intercession by the king. He then began a study of planetary orbits, and correctly predicted the return in 1758 of the comet now named after him. He published studies on magnetic variations (1683), trade winds and monsoons (1686), and sea-charts of magnetic variation (1701). He encouraged Isaac Newton to write his celebrated *Principia* (1687), and paid for the publication out of his own pocket. With his *Breslau Table of Mortality* (1693), he laid the actuarial foundations for life insurance and annuities. In 1720 he became astronomer-royal. >> Newton, Isaac

Halliday, M(ichael) A(lexander) K(irkwood) (1925–) Linguist, born in Leeds, West Yorkshire, N England, UK. He studied at London and Cambridge universities, taught Chinese at Cambridge (1954–8) and linguistics at Edinburgh (1958–63), and held professorial posts at universities in Britain and the USA before becoming professor of linguistics at Sydney (1976–87). He is known for his work in theoretical linguistics which led to the development of scale-and-category grammar in the 1960s, and then systemic grammar. >> Firth, J R

Halliwell, Geri >> **Spice Girls, The**

Hallstrom, Sir Edward John Lees (1886–1970) Pioneer of refrigeration, born in Coonamble, New South Wales, Australia. He worked in a furniture factory from the age of 13, later opening his own works to make ice-chests, then wooden cabinets for refrigerators, and he eventually designed and manufactured the first popular domestic Australian refrigerator. He made generous donations to medical research, children's hospitals, and the Taronga zoo in Sydney, becoming an honorary life director of the zoo.

Hals, Frans [hals] (c. 1580–1666) Portrait and genre painter, probably born in Antwerp, Belgium. Among his best-known works are 'The Laughing Cavalier' (1624, Wallace Collection, London) and 'Gypsy Girl' (c.1628–30, Louvre), and several portraits of militia groups, notable for their lively facial expressions, and bold use of colour. After 1640, his mood became more contemplative and sombre, as in 'Man in a Slouch Hat' (c.1660–6, Kassel). For most of his life, he lived in Haarlem.

Halsey, William F(rederick), Jr [holzee], known as **Bull Halsey** (1884–1959) US admiral, born in Elizabeth, NJ. He studied at the US Naval Academy, Annapolis, held destroyer commands in World War 1, qualified as a naval pilot (1934), then commanded the Carrier Division as rear admiral (1938) and vice-admiral (1940). In 1944 he commanded the 3rd Fleet in the battles for the Caroline and Philippine Is, and defeated the Japanese navy at the Battle of Leyte Gulf. Appointed fleet admiral in 1947, he retired in 1949, and became president of International Telecommunications Laboratories (1951–7).

Halsted, William (Stewart) (1852–1922) Surgeon and pioneer of scientific surgery, born in New York City. He studied at the College of Physicians and Surgeons, New York City, and in Vienna. Professor at Johns Hopkins University from 1886, he established there the first surgical school in the USA. He developed a cocaine injection for local anaesthesia, became an addict in the process, was cured, then returned to Johns Hopkins. He devised successful operative techniques, including those for cancer of the breast and inguinal hernia, and pioneered the use of rubber gloves and sterile conditions in surgery.

Halston, public name of **Roy Halston Frowick** (1932-90) Fashion designer, born in Des Moines, IA. He showed his first collection in 1969, creating the vogue for easy-to-wear clothes, and his understated designs earned four Coty Awards. In 1973 he diversified into luggage and cosmetics.

Hamada, Shoji [hamada, shohjee] (1894–1978) Japanese potter, widely recognized as one of the great modern potters. He studied and held a professorship at the Institute of Pottery in Kyoto. He worked primarily in stoneware, using ash or iron glazes producing utilitarian wares in strong, simple shapes brushed with abstract design. >> Leach, Bernard

Hamilcar [hamilkah(r)], known as **Hamilcar Barca** ('Lightning') (c. 270–228 BC) Carthaginian statesman and general at the time of the First Punic War, the father of Hannibal. Following Carthage's defeat in 241 BC, and the loss of her empire in Sicily and Sardinia to Rome, he set about founding a new Carthaginian empire in Spain. Between 237 BC and his death, he conquered most of the S and E of the peninsula. >> Hannibal

Hamilton, Alexander (1757–1804) US statesman, born in the West Indian island of Nevis. He studied at King's (now Columbia) College, New York City, and fought in the American Revolution, becoming Washington's aide-de-camp (1777–81). After the war, he studied law, and in 1782 was returned to Congress. He was instrumental in the movement to establish the USA in its present political form. As secretary to the Treasury (1789–95), he restored the country's finances, and was leader of the Federalist Party until his death. His successful effort to thwart the ambition of his rival, Aaron Burr, led to a duel in New Jersey, in which Hamilton was killed. >> Burr; Washington, George

Hamilton, Chico, originally **Foreststorn Hamilton** (1921–) Musician, born in Los Angeles, CA. He played trumpet with Count Basie, Woody Herman, and other major bands. A talented drummer, prominent in the West Coast 'cool jazz' movement, he first recorded with Slim and Slam in 1941, and worked with Lena Horne for many years. He also provided the drumming for several film soundtracks, including Bing Crosby and Bob Hope's *Road To Bali* (1952). >> Gaillard, Slim; Horne, Lena

Hamilton, Emma, Lady, *née* **Emily Lyon** (c. 1765–1815) Lord Nelson's mistress, probably born in Ness, Cheshire, NWC England, UK. In 1782 she accepted the protection of Charles Greville, to exchange it in 1786 for that of his uncle, Sir William Hamilton, whom she married in 1791. She first met Nelson in 1793, and bore him a daughter, **Horatia** (1801–81). After the death of her husband and Nelson, she became bankrupt, and in 1813 was arrested for debt. The next year she fled to Calais, where she died. >> Hamilton, Sir William (1730–1803); Nelson

Hamilton, Hamish (1900–88) Publisher, the founder of the London publishing house of Hamish Hamilton Ltd, born in Indianapolis, IN. He spent his childhood in Scotland, studied at Cambridge, and joined Harper & Brothers, the New York publishers, as London manager in 1926. In 1931 he founded his own firm, with the support of Harpers, who helped him build up a particularly strong list of US writers. In 1965 he sold his company to Thomson Publications Ltd, who later sold it to Viking-Penguin. He retired as chairman in 1981.

Hamilton, Iain Ellis (1922–) Composer, born in Glasgow, W Scotland, UK. Originally trained as an engineer, in 1947 he entered the Royal College of Music where he won the *prix d'honneur* in 1951 as well as the Royal Philharmonic Society's Prize, and an award from the Koussevitsky Foundation. He emigrated to the USA in 1962, becoming professor of music at Duke University, NC (1962–78), and has produced many orchestral and chamber works, as well as operas including *The Royal Hunt of the Sun* and *The Cataline Conspiracy*.

Hamilton, Sir Ian (Standish Monteith) (1853–1947) British soldier, born in Corfu, Greece. He entered the army

(1873), and served with distinction in Afghanistan (1878) and the Boer Wars (1881, 1899–1901), and was knighted in 1902. In World War 1, as a general, he led the disastrous Gallipoli expedition (1915). Relieved of his command, he later became Lieutenant of the Tower (1918–20).

Hamilton, James Hamilton, 1st Duke of (1606–49) Scottish Royalist commander during the English Civil War. He fought during the Thirty Years' War, leading an army in support of Gustavus Adolphus (1631–2), and later played a conspicuous part in the contest between Charles I and the Covenanters. Created duke in 1643, he led a Scottish army into England (1643), but was defeated by Cromwell at Preston, and beheaded.

Hamilton, Patrick (1503–28) Protomartyr of the Scottish Reformation, born in the diocese of Glasgow, W Scotland, UK. He studied at Paris, Louvain, and St Andrews. Attracted to Lutheranism, he went to Wittenberg in 1527, where he met Luther and Melanchthon, and settled for some months in Marburg, writing (in Latin) a series of theological propositions known as 'Patrick's Places'. Returning to Scotland he was summoned to St Andrews by Archbishop James Beaton, and on a renewed charge of heresy was burned before St Salvator's College. His death did more to extend the Reformation in Scotland than ever his life could have done. >> Beaton, James; Luther; Melanchthon

Hamilton, Richard (1922–) Pop Art painter, born in London, England, UK. He studied at the Royal Academy Schools and the Slade School of Art, London, and taught at the Central School of Art and Crafts, London, and Durham University. During the 1950s he devised and participated in several influential exhibitions, notably 'This is Tomorrow' (1956, London). This introduced the concept of Pop Art, of which he became a leading pioneer.

Hamilton, Scott (1954–) Musician, born in Providence, RI. Influenced by his father's record collection, he played the harmonica professionally at fourteen, and took up the tenor saxophone two years later. He made his record debut in 1977, later forming his own quintet. He never learned to sight-read, and plays a Selmer saxophone that is older than he is.

Hamilton, Thomas (1784–1858) Architect, born in Glasgow, W Scotland, UK. He studied as a mason with his father, beginning independent practice in Edinburgh before 1817. In 1826 he was among the founders of the Royal Scottish Academy, and was a leading figure in the international Greek Revival. His Grecian designs include the Royal College of Physicians Hall (1844–5), Edinburgh. Cumston (Compstone) House, Kirkcudbright (1828), in a Tudor style, and a handful of Gothic church designs, demonstrate his versatility. As a prime mover of the Edinburgh Improvement Act (1827) to create the New Town, he designed the George IV and King's Bridges which followed.

Hamilton, Sir William (1730–1803) Diplomat and anti-quary, born in Scotland, UK. He served in the army (1747–58), and married a Welsh heiress, inheriting her estate when she died (1782). He married Emily Lyon (Emma, Lady Hamilton) in 1791. He was ambassador at Naples (1764–1800), and while there contributed to the excavation of Pompeii, made observations of Vesuvius and Etna, published essays on volcanoes (1782), and wrote on Greek and Roman antiquities. He was knighted in 1772. >> Hamilton, Emma

Hamilton, Sir William (1788–1856) Philosopher, born in Glasgow, W Scotland, UK. He studied at Oxford, and became professor of civil history in Edinburgh in 1821, and of logic and metaphysics in 1836. He published many important articles, mostly in the *Edinburgh Review*, which were collected in 1852 under the title *Discussions on Philosophy and Literature, Education and University Reform*. His articles on German philosophers introduced Kant to the British public. His main work was published posthumously as *Lectures on Metaphysics and Logic* (1859–60). >> Kant

Hamilton, Sir William Rowan (1805–65) Mathematician, the inventor of quaternions, born in Dublin. At the age of nine he knew 13 languages, and at 15 he had read Newton's *Principia*, and begun original investigations. In 1827, while still an undergraduate, he was appointed professor of astronomy at Dublin and Irish Astronomer Royal; in 1835 he was knighted. His first published work was on optics, and he then developed a new approach to dynamics which became of importance in the 20th-c development of quantum mechanics. He introduced quaternions as a new algebraic approach to three-dimensional geometry, and they proved to be the seed of much modern algebra.

Hamlin, Hannibal (1809–91) US statesman and vice-president (1861–5), born in Paris Hill, ME. He practised law (1833–48), was speaker of the Maine House of Representatives, and was returned to Congress in 1842 and 1844. He sat in the US Senate as a Democrat (1848–57), but separated from his Party over his anti-slavery opinions, and was elected Governor of Maine by the Republicans. He returned to the Senate in 1857, and in 1861 became vice-president under Lincoln. After a further period in the Senate (1869–81), he served as minister to Spain (1881–2). >> Lincoln, Abraham

Hamlyn, Paul (Bertrand), Baron, originally **Paul Hamburger** (1926–) British entrepreneur and publisher. Educated in Letchworth, Hertfordshire, SE England, UK, he went into publishing, founding Books for Pleasure (1949), Prints for Pleasure (1960), and Records for Pleasure (1961) under the name of Hamlyn Publishing, which he sold to the International Publishing Corporation (IPC) in 1964. He joined the board of IPC, becoming chairman of IPC Books (1965–70). He co-founded Sundial Publications with David Frost, Conran Octopus with Terence Conran (1983), became chairman of Heinemann Publishing (1985), re-purchased Hamlyn Publishing in 1986, and was appointed chairman of Book Club Associates in 1993. He became a life peer in 1998. >> Conran, Terence; Frost, David

Hammarskjöld, Dag (Hjalmar Agne Carl) [hamershohld] (1905–61) Swedish statesman, and secretary-general of the UN (1953–61), born in Jönköping, Sweden. After teaching at Stockholm University, he was secretary (1935) then chairman (1941–8) of the Bank of Sweden, and Swedish foreign minister (1951–3). At the UN, he helped to set up the Emergency Force in Sinai and Gaza (1956), and worked for conciliation in the Middle East (1957–8). He was awarded the 1961 Nobel Peace Prize after his death in an air crash near Ndola, Zambia, while engaged in negotiations over the Congo crisis.

Hammer, Armand (1899–1990) Businessman, born in New York City. He trained as a physician at Columbia University, and served with the US Army Medical Corps (1918–19). In 1921, he went to Russia to help with an influenza epidemic, but turned to business, dealing with Lenin and other Soviet leaders. He founded the A Hammer Pencil Co in 1925, operating in New York City, London, and Moscow, bought the Occidental Petroleum Corporation of California (1957), and founded Hammer Galleries in New York City (1930). He maintained strong connections with the USSR, acting as US intermediary on a number of occasions, including the Soviet troop withdrawal from Afghanistan (1987). >> Lenin

Hammerin' Hank >> Aaron, Hank

Hammerstein, Oscar, II [hamerstiyn] (1895–1960) Librettist, born in New York City. He wrote the book and lyrics for many operettas and musical comedies. With composer Jerome Kern he wrote *Show Boat* (1927), a landmark of musical theatre, with such songs as 'Ol' Man River' and 'Only Make Believe'. Later, with composer Richard Rodgers, he wrote some of the greatest musicals, including *Oklahoma!* (1943, Pulitzer), *South Pacific* (1949, Pulitzer), *The King and I* (1951), and *The Sound of Music* (1959). **Oscar Hammerstein I** (1847–1919) was his impresario grandfather. >> Kern; Rodgers, Richard

Hammett, (Samuel) Dashiell (1894–1961) Crime writer, born in St Mary's Co, MD. He left school at 14 and took various menial jobs before joining the Pinkerton Detective Agency as an operator. After World War 1 he wrote stories for magazines, developing a style of unsentimental writing which came to be known as 'hard-boiled' fiction. He published two novels, then achieved international fame with his 'private eye' novels *The Maltese Falcon* (1930), made into a classic film starring Humphrey Bogart (1941), and *The Thin Man* (1932), which was also filmed and later made into a television series. >> Hellman

Hammond, Eric (Albert Barratt) (1929–) British trade union leader. He became active in trade union affairs in his early 20s, and rose from shop steward in 1953 to general secretary of the Electrical, Electronics, Telecommunications and Plumbing Union (EETPU) (1984–92). He was a long-time outspoken critic of what he saw as old-fashioned unionism and concluded a number of single-union, 'no strike' agreements with employers, in defiance of Trades Union Congress (TUC) policy. Criticism of him and his union came to a head in 1988 when the EETPU was dismissed from the TUC.

Hammond, Dame Joan (1912– 96) Soprano, born in Christchurch, New Zealand. She studied at the Sydney conservatory, and played violin in the Philharmonic Orchestra there, making her operatic debut in 1929. She toured widely, and became noted particularly for her Puccini roles. She was made a dame in 1974. >> Puccini

Hammond, Walter (1903–65) Cricketer, born in Dover, Kent, SE England, UK. In his long career as a Gloucestershire player he scored over 50 000 runs, of which 7249 were obtained in 85 Tests at an average of 58·45 (almost 3000 of them against Australia). He was a fine bowler and fielder, taking 10 catches in a match against Surrey in 1928, a record that still stands. He also holds the highest average score (563) achieved in a Test series against New Zealand in 1932–3. >> RR1149

Hammond Innes, Ralph [inis] (1913–) Writer and traveller, born in England, UK, of Scottish descent. He worked as a journalist (1934–40) and served in the Royal Artillery (1940–6) before becoming a full-time writer. While researching his adventure stories, he has travelled to many parts of the globe and lived among the local people to ensure authenticity in his works. His books, translated into many languages, include *The Trojan Horse* (1940), *The Lonely Skier* (1947), *Campbell's Kingdom* (1952, filmed), *Atlantic Fury* (1962), and *Levkas Man* (1971, filmed 1981). Later works include *Target Antarctica* (1993) and *Delta Connection* (1996). A keen sailor, he is vice-president of the Association of Sea Training Organizations.

Hammurabi [hamurahbee] (18th-c BC) Amorite king of Babylon (c.1792–1750 BC), best known for his Code of Laws. He is also famous for his military conquests that made Babylon the greatest power in Mesopotamia. >> RR1034

Hamnett, Katharine (1948–) Fashion designer, born in Gravesend, Kent, SE England, UK. She studied fashion at art school in London, then worked as a freelance designer, setting up her own business in 1979. She draws inspiration for designs from workwear, and also from social movements, such as the peace movement, which she supports.

Hampden, John (1594–1643) English parliamentarian and patriot, born in London, England, UK. He studied at Oxford, became a lawyer, and in 1621 an MP. His opposition to Charles I's financial measures led to his imprisonment (1627–8), and in 1634 he became famous for refusing to pay Charles's imposed levy for outfitting the navy ('ship money'). A member of both the Short and the Long Parliaments, he was one of the five members whose attempted seizure by Charles (1642) precipitated the Civil War. He fought for the Parliamentary army at Edgehill and Reading, but was killed at Thame. >> Charles I (of England)

Hampole, Richard Rolle of >> **Rolle of Hampole, Richard**

Hampshire, Susan (1942–) British actress. She was educated in London, made her stage debut in *Expresso Bongo* (1958), and has since taken leading roles in numerous plays and films. She won Emmy awards for best actress as Fleur in the television series *The Forsyte Saga* (1970), Sarah Churchill in *The First Churchills* (1971), and Becky Sharp in *Vanity Fair* (1973). Later series include *The Grand* (1997). She published a volume of autobiography, *Susan's Story* in 1981, in which she writes about her problems with dyslexia, and is also known for her series of *Lucy Jane* books.

Hampson, Frank (1918–85) Strip cartoonist, born in Manchester, Greater Manchester, NW England, UK. Employed as a Post Office telegraph boy, he contributed his first strip to the Post Office staff magazine in 1937. In 1950 he designed a Christian comic for boys, which eventually became the *Eagle*, featuring the adventures of 'Dan Dare, Pilot of the Future', a painted strip which introduced a unique authenticity through Hampson's use of human models and carefully modelled spaceships.

Hampton, Christopher (James) (1946–) British playwright, born in Fayal, Azores. He studied at Oxford; his first play, *When Did You Last See My Mother?* (1964), was produced in London and New York while he was still an undergraduate, and led to his appointment as the Royal Court Theatre's first resident playwright. The Court produced more of his plays, including *Total Eclipse* (1968), *The Philanthropist* (1970), *Savages* (1973), set in Brazil, and *Treats* (1976). His finest play is considered to be *Tales From Hollywood* (1982), but his most commercial success has been *Les Liaisons dangereuses* (1985), adapted from the novel by Laclos. Later works include a semi-autobiographical play, *White Chameleon* (1991), and *Alice's Adventures Under Ground* (1994). >> Laclos

Hampton, Lionel (Leo), nickname **Hamp** (1909–) Jazz musician and bandleader, born in Louisville, KY. Originally a drummer, he was given xylophone tuition while a young man in Chicago. He later introduced the vibraphone into jazz, recording with Louis Armstrong in 1930. A member of Benny Goodman's small groups in the late 1930s, he first formed a permanent big band in 1940, continuing as a leader until the 1980s, taking his entertaining brand of musicianship and showmanship on many overseas tours. >> Armstrong, Louis; Goodman, Benny

Hampton, Wade (1812–1902) Hero of the Confederacy, born in Columbia, SC. He studied law, but devoted himself to managing his extensive family estates. In the Civil War (1861–5) he raised 'Hampton's Legion'. As brigadier-general he commanded a cavalry force (1862–3), was wounded at Gettysburg, received the command of Lee's cavalry in 1864, and in 1865 served in South Carolina against Sherman. He became state governor in 1876, when he was instrumental in restoring white rule to South Carolina, and later became a senator (1878–91). >> Lee, Robert E; Sherman, William Tecumseh

Hamsun, Knut [hamsoon], pseudonym of **Knut Pederson** (1859–1952) Novelist, born in Lom, Norway. Raised on the Lofoten Is with little education, he worked at various odd jobs, and twice visited the USA (1882–4, 1886–8), where he worked as a streetcar attendant in Chicago and a farmhand in North Dakota. He sprang to fame with his novel *Sult* (1890, Hunger), followed by *Mysterier* (1892, Mysteries) and the lyrical *Pan* (1894). His masterpiece is considered *Markens grøde* (1917, Growth of the Soil), which was instrumental in his award of the 1920 Nobel Prize for Literature. A recluse during the inter-war years, he lost popularity during World War 2 for his Nazi sympathies, but his reputation has been largely rehabilitated.

Hanbury-Tenison, Robin (Airling) (1936–) Explorer, writer, and broadcaster, brought up in Ireland. He studied at Oxford, and in 1958 achieved the first land crossing of South America at its widest point. He crossed the Sahara many times by camel (1962–6), and took part in both British Hovercraft expeditions in Amazonas (1968) and trans-Africa (1969). He took part in the British Trans-Americas expedition of 1972, crossing the Darien Gap and writing a report on the impact of the road on the Cuna Indians. He led the Royal Geographical Society's Gunung Mulu (Sarawak) Expedition 1977–8, involving 115 scientists in a multi-disciplinary survey of a tropical forest ecosystem in a newly created national park. Following his travels through South America, his concern for Indian tribes led to him being one of the founding members of Survival International, of which he is now president.

Hancock, John (1737–93) US statesman, born in Braintree, MA. He studied at Harvard, then worked for his uncle, a wealthy merchant who later left him a considerable fortune. A member of the Massachusetts General Court (1769–74), he became president (1775–7) of the Continental Congress, and was the first to sign the Declaration of Independence.

Hancock, Lang(ley) George (1909–92) Australian mining industrialist, born in Perth, Western Australia. In 1934 he leased claims for mining blue asbestos, and developed a processing plant. After making a forced landing in bad weather, he discovered substantial iron ore deposits in the Pilbara region, and concluded mining agreements with a number of companies, thus initiating the growth of Australian extractive industries. He went on to make further discoveries, including Rhodes Ridge, the largest iron ore deposit in the world. He held controversial right-wing views on politics and Aboriginal affairs, and in 1974 formed a secessionist movement in Western Australia with the aim of better political representation. By the late 1980s his personal wealth was estimated to be $A60 million, and the family feuds over the inheritance were much publicized after his death.

Hancock, Herbie, popular name of **Herbert Jeffrey Hancock** (1940–) Pianist and composer, born in Chicago, IL. During the 1960s he worked with such stars as Phil Woods, Miles Davis, the Poynter Sisters, and Stevie Wonder, and greatly influenced pop music with his Blue Note album *Takin' Off* (1962), which featured the hit song 'Water-melon Man'. Later albums include *Dedication* (1974) and *Village Life* (1985). He also arranged and conducted the soundtrack of the film *Blow Up* (1966) and of the Oscar-winning *Round Midnight* (1986).

Hancock, Tony, popular name of **Anthony John Hancock** (1924–68) Comedian, born in Birmingham, West Midlands, C England, UK. After a brief period as a civil servant, he enlisted in the RAF (1942). Overcoming extreme stagefright he tried his hand as a stand-up comic with touring shows before making his professional stage debut in *Wings* (1946). Pantomimes, cabaret, and radio appearances in *Educating Archie* (1951) contributed to his growing popularity, and he made his film debut in *Orders is Orders* (1954). He achieved national fame and popularity with the radio, and later TV, series *Hancock's Half Hour* (1954–61). A chronic alcoholic beset by self-doubt and unable to reconcile his ambition with his talent, he spent his final years in a self-destructive round of aborted projects and unsatisfactory performances, and committed suicide while attempting a comeback on Australian television.

Hancock, Winfield Scott (1824–86) US general, born in Montgomery Co, PA. He trained at West Point, and served through the Mexican War. In 1861, as brigadier-general on the Union side, he organized the Army of the Potomac, was prominent at South Mountain, Antietam, and Fredericksburg, and took command of the 2nd Corps (1863). Distinguished at Gettysburg (1863), he was conspicuous in the battles of the Wilderness, Spottsylvania, and Cold Harbor in 1864. As the popular Democratic candidate for the presidency in 1880, he was narrowly beaten by James Garfield. >> Garfield

Hand, (Billings) Learned (1872–1961) Jurist, born in Albany, NY. He studied at Harvard, practised law in New York City, and in 1909 was appointed a federal judge, holding this position for 52 years until his death. His legal judgments were profound, and extended into all branches of law, having so much influence on the US Supreme Court that, although never appointed to it, he was sometimes called the Supreme Court's 'tenth man'.

Handel, George Frideric (1685–1759) Composer, born in Halle, Germany. He was organist of Halle Cathedral at the age of 17, while also studying law, and worked as a violinist and keyboard player in the Hamburg opera orchestra (1703–6). In Italy (1706–10) he established a great reputation as a keyboard virtuoso, and had considerable success as an operatic composer. He was appointed in 1710 to the court of the Elector of Hanover (later George I of Great Britain). In 1720 he worked at the King's Theatre, London, where he produced a stream of operas, and then developed a new form, the English oratorio, which proved to be highly popular. After a stroke in 1737, he rallied, and afterwards wrote some of his most memorable work, such as *Saul* (1739), *Israel in Egypt* (1739), and *Messiah* (1742). His vast output included over 40 operas, about 20 oratorios, cantatas, sacred music, and orchestral, instrumental, and vocal works. He is buried in Poet's Corner, Westminster Abbey. >> Chrysander

Handley, Tommy, popular name of **Thomas Reginald Handley** (1892–1949) Comedian, born in Liverpool, Merseyside. He served in World War 1, then worked in variety, and in the infancy of radio became known as a regular broadcaster. In 1939 he achieved nationwide fame through his weekly programme *ITMA* (*It's That Man Again*) which, with its mixture of satire, parody, slapstick, and wit, helped to boost wartime morale, and continued as a prime favourite until brought to an untimely end by his sudden death.

Hands, Terry, popular name of **Terence David Hands** (1941–) Stage director, born in Aldershot, Hampshire, S England, UK. He studied at Birmingham University, co-founded the Everyman Theatre, Liverpool (1964), then joined the Royal Shakespeare Company in 1966, where he became an associate director (1967–77), joint artistic director with Trevor Nunn (1978–86), and sole artistic director and chief executive (1986–91). He was consultant director at the Comédie Française (1975–7), and has directed Shakespeare at the Burgtheater in Vienna. >> Nunn

Handy, Charles (Brian) (1932–) Management educator and writer, born in Dublin, Ireland. He studied at Oxford, became a manager in Shell Petroleum (1956–65), then an economist in the City of London. He joined the London Business School in 1968, becoming professor of management development there (1972–7), and 1977–81 was appointed warden of St George's House, Windsor (the Church of England's 'staff college'). His books include *Understanding Organizations* (1976), *Inside Organizations* (1990), and a collection of essays, *Beyond Certainty* (1995).

Handy, W(illiam) C(hristopher) (1873–1958) Blues composer, born in Florence, AL. He studied at Teachers Agricultural and Mechanical College, Huntsville, AL, became a schoolteacher, then joined a minstrel show as a cornet player. In 1903, despite becoming blind, he formed his own band in Memphis, subsequently moving to Chicago and to New York City, where he formed his own publishing company. He was the first to introduce the 'blues' style to printed music, his most famous work being the 'St Louis Blues' (1914). He wrote *Father of the Blues* (1958).

Hani, Chris [hanee], popular name of **Martin Thembisile Hani** (1942–93) South African political leader, born in Cofimvaba, South Africa. His record as guerrilla leader and his charisma made him the most popular African political figure of his generation. He joined the African National Congress (ANC) Youth League at the age of 15, and in 1963 became a member of Umkhonto we Sizwe, the ANC's armed wing. He left the country in 1963, and rose through the ranks of Umkhonto, serving as chief-of-staff between 1987 and 1992. In 1991, he topped the poll for the ANC's National Executive Committee, and was also elected secretary-general of the South African Communist Party. He was shot dead on Easter Saturday by a white right-winger, and his murder triggered massive protests and some rioting.

Hanif Mohammad (1934–) Cricketer, born in Junagadh, India. One of five Test-playing brothers, he made his first-class debut for Karachi at the age of 16. Noted for his dour play, he took 970 minutes to amass 337 runs against the West Indies in 1957–8, and established a world record score of 499 against Bahawalpur in 1959. He made his Test debut at the age of 17, and played in 55 Tests, scoring 3915 runs. He captained Pakistan 11 times between 1964 and 1967.

Hanks, Tom, popular name of **Thomas J Hanks** (1957–) Film actor, born in Oakland, CA. He studied at the California State University, Sacramento, where he worked as stage manager and actor in university productions. He spent three seasons performing the classics with the Great Lakes Shakespeare Festival in Ohio before making his film debut in the thriller *He Know's You're Alone* (1981). After some well received television comedy, he was cast in the film *Splash* (1984), and received an Oscar nomination for his role in *Big* (1988). He gained an Oscar and Golden Globe Award for his character performance as an AIDS victim in *Philadelphia Story* (1993), and won another Oscar for *Forrest Gump* (1994). He made his directorial debut in 1996 with *That Thing You Do!*.

Hanna, Mark, popular name of **Marcus Alonzo Hanna** (1837–1904) Businessman and politician, born in New Lisbon, OH. His family moved to Cleveland, OH, where he started in partnership with his father in coal and iron, becoming a prosperous industrialist. He helped organize the Union National Bank, bought the Cleveland Opera House, invested in Cleveland street railways, and moved into politics to protect his business interests. In favour of William McKinley's high protective tariff sponsorship, he financed the presidential campaign on his behalf, and after McKinley's election he accepted a seat in the US Senate (1897). >> McKinley

Hanna–Barbera [hana bah(r)bera] Animated cartoonists, in partnership for nearly 50 years. **William (Denby) Hanna**

(1910–), born in Melrose, NM, was a structural engineer by training. He turned to cartooning in 1930, and became one of the first directors at the new MGM animation studio in 1937, making Rudolph Dirks's *Captain and the Kids*. He then teamed up with **Joseph (Roland) Barbera** (1911–), born in New York City, who initially worked as an accountant, drawing cartoons for magazines in his spare time. He joined MGM as an artist at the same time as Hanna. Together they created the *Tom and Jerry* cartoons, and produced more than 200 films of the series (1940–57), winning seven Oscars between 1943 and 1952. Working as Hanna-Barbera Productions from 1957, they created numerous television cartoon series using computer animation, including *The Flintstones*, *Yogi Bear*, and *Huckleberry Hound*.

Hannibal [hanibl] (247–182 BC) Carthaginian general and statesman, the son of Hamilcar Barca. As a child, his father made him swear eternal enmity to Rome. He served in Spain under Hamilcar and Hasdrubal (his brother-in-law), and as general brought most of S Spain under his authority (221–219 BC). In the Second Punic War (218–202 BC), he completely wrong-footed the Romans by his bold and unexpected invasion of Italy from the N (with elephants), and thus inflicted a series of heavy defeats on them – at the Ticinus, the R Trebia (218 BC), L Trasimene (217 BC), and Cannae (216 BC). Failure to win over Rome's allies in Italy, plus lack of support from Carthage, severely hampered him, and Rome was still undefeated when he was recalled to Africa in 203 BC to face the invading army of Scipio. Decisively defeated at Zama (202 BC), he turned in the postwar years to political reform; but this raised such opposition that he voluntarily exiled himself, first to Syria, then Crete and finally Bithynia, where he committed suicide to avoid Roman capture. >> Fabius Maximus; Flaminius; Hamilcar; Hasdrubal; Scipio; Scipio Africanus Major

Hanno (fl.5th-c BC) Carthaginian navigator. He undertook a voyage of exploration along the W coast of Africa, and led a fleet of 60 vessels with 30 000 settlers to found Thymaterion (now Kénitra, Morocco). He founded other colonies, and reached Cape Nun or the Bight of Benin. An account of his voyages known as *Periplus of Hanno* survives in a Greek translation.

Hanratty, James [hanratee] (c. 1936–62) Convicted murderer, whose case has remained controversial. He was found guilty of the murder of Michael Gregsten, who was shot while in his car with his lover, Valerie Storie, in a layby on the A6 on 22 August 1961. Hanratty was arrested on 11 October. Storie, who had been raped, and paralysed by several bullets, picked out Hanratty from an identity parade. Hanratty, reportedly a feeble-minded petty criminal, was charged on 14 October. He denied the charge but refused to name his alibis, saying that to do so would be to betray his friends' trust. He then changed the location of his alibi from Liverpool to Rhyl. The jury found him guilty. After he was hanged on 4 April, 1962, several witnesses came forward who said that they believed they had seen him in Rhyl. His case was reopened in 1997.

Hansard, Luke (1752–1828) British printer, who went from Norwich to London, and entered the office of Hughes, printer to the House of Commons, becoming acting manager in 1774, and in 1798 succeeding as sole proprietor of the business. He and his descendants printed the parliamentary reports from 1774 to 1889, a role now performed by HM Stationery Office. In 1943 *Hansard* became the official name for the parliamentary reports.

Hansen, Martin (Jens) Alfred (1909–55) Novelist, born in Stroby, Denmark. He worked on the land and as a teacher, but after 1945 devoted himself to writing. His early novels deal with social problems in the 1930s, and he later developed a more profound style, notably in his psychological novel *Løgneren* (1950, The Liar) and the metaphysical *Orm og Tyr* (1952, The Serpent and the Bull).

Hansom, Joseph Aloysius (1803–82) Inventor and architect, born in York, North Yorkshire, N England, UK. He invented the 'Patent Safety (Hansom) Cab' in 1834. He also designed Birmingham town hall and the Roman Catholic cathedral at Plymouth.

Hanson, Duane (1925–96) Sculptor, born in Alexandria, MN. He studied at the Cranbrook Academy of Art, Bloomfield, MI. He specializes in life-size figures painted realistically and adorned with hats, wristwatches, and other objects. His earlier work was violent (eg 'Abortion', 1966), but he later made mildly satirical pieces, such as 'Woman with Shopping Trolley' (1969) and 'Tourists' (1970).

Hanson, Howard (1896–1981) Composer, born in Wahoo, NE. He was awarded the American Prix de Rome in 1921, and after three years' study in Italy became director of the Eastman School of Music in Rochester, NY, a post he held until 1964. Under his leadership, the School became one of the most important centres of American musical life. His compositions, firmly in the tradition of 19th-c Romanticism, include an opera, *The Merry Mount*, and seven symphonies.

Hanson, Raymond (1913–76) Composer and teacher, born in Sydney, New South Wales, Australia. He studied at the New South Wales Conservatory, to which he returned to lecture from 1948 until his death. His *Trumpet Concerto* is well known, and was one of the first Australian recordings to be released internationally. Other works include operas, a ballet, a symphony, four concertos, chamber music, and film scores.

Hanson-Dyer, Louise Berta Mosson (1884–1962) Music publisher and patron, born in Melbourne, Victoria, Australia. She studied in Edinburgh and at the Royal College of Music, London, and became the centre of Melbourne's musical life, helping establish the British Music Society there in 1921. She established Editions du Oiseau-Lyre, a music-publishing business in Paris in 1927, which set a new standard of music printing, and she became a leader in the revival of early music. Later resident in France, she maintained her links with Australia, and published the works of leading Australian composers. Her considerable Australian estate was left to Melbourne University for music research.

Han Suyin, originally **Elizabeth Kuanghu Chow** (1917–) Novelist and doctor, born in Beijing. She studied medicine at Beijing, Brussels, and London, and practised in Hong Kong until 1964. Her many novels include *Destination Chungking* (1942), *A Many-splendoured Thing* (1952, film 1955), and *Four Faces* (1963). She also wrote a semi-autobiographical and historical trilogy, *The Crippled Tree* (1965), *A Mortal Flower* (1966), and *Birdless Summer* (1968), as well as *The Morning Deluge* (1972), *The Wind in the Tower* (1976), and *Han Suyin's China* (1987). Later works include *Tigers and Butterflies* (1990) and the autobiographical *Wind in my Sleeve* (1992).

Hantzsch, Arthur Rudolf [hanch] (1857–1935) Organic chemist, born in Dresden, Germany. He developed the synthesis of substituted pyridines at the age of 25, and became professor at Zürich, Wurzburg, and Leipzig. He investigated the arrangement of atoms in the molecules of nitrogen compounds and the electrical conductivity of organic compounds, and was a pioneer in spectrophotometry.

Harald I Gormsson, nickname **Harald Bluetooth** (c.910–c.985) King of Denmark from c.940. The son of Gorm the Old and father of Sweyn Forkbeard, he was the first king to unify all the provinces of Denmark under a single crown. He was converted to Christianity in c.960, made Christianity the state religion of Denmark, and made his parents' burial mound at Jelling the site of a Christian church. He strengthened the unity and central administration of the country, and repelled attacks from Norway and Germany. He was eventually deposed in c.985 by his son, Sweyn, and died in exile soon afterwards. >> Sweyn; RR1044

Harald I Halfdanarson, nickname **Harald Fairhair** or **Finehair** (c.860–c.940) King of Norway (c.890–c.942), the first ruler to claim sovereignty over all Norway. The son of Halfdan the Black (King of Vestfold), he fought his way to power with a crushing defeat of his opponents at the naval Battle of Hafursfjord, off Stavanger, in c.890. His authoritarian rule caused many of the old aristocratic families to emigrate W to the Orkneys, Hebrides, and Ireland, and to newly-settled Iceland. >> RR1079

Harald III Sigurdsson, nickname **Harald Hardrada** ('the Ruthless') (1015–66) King of Norway from 1045. The half-brother of Olaf II (St Olaf), he was present at the Battle of Stiklestad in 1030 where St Olaf was killed, and sought refuge in Kiev at the court of Prince Yaroslav the Wise. He fought as a Viking mercenary with the Varangian Guard in Constantinople, and returned to Norway in 1045, shared the throne with his nephew, and became sole king in 1047. After long and unrelenting wars against Sweyn II of Denmark, he invaded England in 1066 to claim the throne after the death of Edward I, but was defeated and killed by Harold II at Stamford Bridge. >> Harold II; Olaf II; Sweyn II; RR1079

Harburg, E Y(ip) (1898–1981) Songwriter, born in New York City of Russian Jewish immigrants. He studied at City College and ran an electrical appliance store. When the Depression closed his business in 1929, he began writing song lyrics, and in 1932 incisively captured the mood of the day with the melancholy lament 'Brother, Can You Spare a Dime?' (with music by Jay Gorney). Almost alone among his colleagues, he was politically active in civil rights groups. In his music, his political convictions were realized in a quiet idealism that a better world was in the offing, as in 'April in Paris' (1932, with Vernon Duke), and his masterwork 'Somewhere Over the Rainbow' (1939, with Harold Arlen). He could also write genuinely funny lyrics, as in 'If I Only Had a Brain' and the other clown songs for *The Wizard of Oz* (1939). In 1947, with Burton Lane, he wrote the Broadway musical *Finian's Rainbow* with such hit songs as 'How Are Things in Glocca Morra' and 'Old Devil Moon'. For reasons unknown, he is the least celebrated of the great songwriters.

Harcourt, Sir William (George Granville Venables Vernon) [hah(r)kaw(r)t] (1827–1904) British statesman, born in York, North Yorkshire, N England, UK. He studied at Cambridge, practised as a lawyer from 1854, taught international law at Cambridge, and entered Parliament in 1868. He was solicitor general (1873–4), home secretary (1880–5), and Chancellor of the Exchequer (1886, 1892–4). On Gladstone's retirement in 1893 he became Leader of the House of Commons. He resigned the Liberal leadership in 1898 but remained a private member of the Party. He is best remembered for his revision of death duties in 1894. >> Gladstone

Harden, Sir Arthur (1865–1940) Chemist, born in Manchester, Greater Manchester, NW England, UK. He studied at Manchester and Erlangen, taught at Manchester University (1888–97), worked in the Jenner (now Lister) Institute from 1897, and became professor of biochemistry at London in 1912. In 1929 he shared the Nobel Prize for Chemistry for his work on alcoholic fermentation and enzymes. He was knighted in 1936. >> RR1123

Hardenberg, Friedrich von >> **Novalis**

Hardenberg, Karl August, Fürst von (Prince of) (1750–1822) Prussian statesman, born in Essenrode, Germany. He studied at Göttingen and Leipzig. After holding appointments in Hanover, Brunswick, Ansbach, and Bayreuth, he became foreign minister in Berlin. His policy was to preserve neutrality in the war between France and Britain; but in 1806, under Napoleon's influence, he was dismissed. In 1810 he was appointed chancellor, and addressed himself to the task of completing the reforms begun by Karl Stein. In the war of liberation he played a prominent part, and after the Treaty of Paris (1814) was made a prince. He reorganized the Council of State (1817), was appointed its president, and drew up the new Prussian system of taxes. To Hardenberg (and Stein), Prussia owed the improvements in her army system, the abolition of serfdom and the privileges of the nobles, the encouragement of municipalities, and the reform of education. >> Stein, Karl

Hardicanute [hah(r)dikan**oot**], also spelled **Harthacnut** (c. 1018–42) King of Denmark (1035–42), and the last Danish King of England (1040–2), the only son of Canute and Emma of Normandy. Canute had intended that Hardicanute should succeed him in both Denmark and England simultaneously, but he was unable to secure his English inheritance until his stepbrother, Harold I, died in 1040. Hardicanute's death without children led to the restoration of the Old English royal line in the person of Edward the Confessor, the only surviving son of Emma and Ethelred the Unready. >> Canute; Edward the Confessor; Ethelred II; Harold I

Hardie, (James) Keir (1856–1915) British politician, born near Holytown, North Lanarkshire, C Scotland, UK. He worked in the mines between the ages of seven and 24, and was victimized as the miners' champion. He became a journalist and the first Labour candidate, entering parliament in 1892. He founded and edited the *Labour Leader*, and was chairman of the Independent Labour Party (founded 1893). Instrumental in the establishment of the Labour Representation Committee, he served as chairman of the Labour Party (1906–8). His strong pacifism led to his becoming isolated within the Party, particularly once World War 1 had broken out.

Harding, Stephen, St (c.1060–1134) Abbot, born in Sherborne, Dorset, S England, UK. Educated at Sherborne Abbey, he joined the Cluniac abbey at Molesme, but was dissatisfied with the lax way of life, and left (1098) with several others to found the monastery of Cîteaux, S of Dijon. He was abbot from 1109, and under him several other abbeys were founded to follow the strict rule he imposed, forming the Cistercian Order. Feast day 16 July.

Harding (of Petherton), John Harding, Baron (1896–1989) British soldier and field-marshal, born in South Petherton, Somerset, SW England, UK. A subaltern in World War 1, he rose to chief-of-staff of the Allied Army in Italy in 1944. As Governor-General of Cyprus (1955–7) during the political and terrorist campaign against Britain, he re-organized the security forces to combat terrorism, re-established order through the imposition of martial law and press control, banished Archbishop Makarios, and, although he failed to bring about a political settlement, was widely respected for his straightforward, soldierly approach. >> Makarios

Harding, Warren G(amaliel) (1865–1923) US statesman and 29th president (1921–3), born in Corsica, OH. He studied at Ohio Central College, then became a journalist and a newspaper owner (the *Marion Daily Star*). He gained a seat in the Ohio State Senate (1899) and the lieutenant-governorship (1902), after which he returned to journalism until 1914, when he was elected to the US Senate. Emerging as a power in the Republican Party, he won its nomination and the presidency in 1920, campaigning against US membership of the League of Nations. He fell ill and died under somewhat mysterious circumstances, during a series of scandals involving corruption among members of his cabinet, the full extent of which was revealed only after his death. >> RR1097

Hardinge (of Lahore), Henry Hardinge, 1st Viscount (1785–1856) British soldier and colonial administrator, born in Wrotham, Kent, SE England, UK. After serving as a soldier (1799–1820) and as an MP (1820–44), he was appointed Governor-General of India (1844–8). He offered employment to educated locals, and attempted to end the practices of suttee and infanticide. He prepared plans for a railway system, and commenced construction of the Ganges canal. During the 1st Sikh War he was second-in-command to Lord Gough, and negotiated the Peace of Lahore (1845). Returning to England he was created viscount, and succeeded Wellington as commander-in-chief (1852), establishing training camps and purchasing improved weapons. He was demoted to field marshal in 1855 during the Crimean War for the poor quality of his commanders. >> Wellington

Hardouin-Mansart, Jules >> **Mansard, Jules**

Hardwick, Philip (1792–1870) Architect, born in London, England, UK. He designed the original Euston railway station, the hall and library of Lincoln's Inn, Goldsmiths' Hall, and Limerick Cathedral.

Hardwicke, Sir Cedric (Webster) (1893–1964) Actor, born in Lye, Hereford and Worcester, WC England, UK. He served in World War 1 and made his name in Birmingham repertory company's productions of Shaw's plays and in *The Barretts of Wimpole Street* (1934). He also played leading roles in a number of films, including *Dreyfus*, *Things to Come* (1931), and *The Winslow Boy* (1948). He was knighted in 1934, and was Cambridge Rede Lecturer in 1936.

Hardy, Sir Alister (Clavering) (1896–1985) Marine biologist, born in Nottingham, Nottinghamshire, C England, UK. He served on the *Discovery* expedition in the Antarctic (1924–8), and in 1928 founded the oceanographic department at Hull University, where he was professor of zoology. Later he became professor of zoology and comparative anatomy at Oxford (1946–61). He made quantitative researches into marine plankton, and invented the continuous plankton recorder, which permitted the detailed study of surface life in the oceans.

Hardy, Bert (1913–95) Photojournalist, born in London, England, UK. He started as a messenger in a photographic agency. Self-taught, he was one of the first to use a Leica 35 mm camera (1938). He was on the staff of *Picture Post* until 1957, except for service as an army photographer from (1942–6), during which he recorded the horrors of the concentration camps. His records of London under the Blitz rank among the finest of the period. Later assignments took him to the Korean and Vietnam Wars. After the closure of *Picture Post* he was in much demand for advertising photography until his retirement in 1967.

Hardy, Godfrey (Harold) (1877–1947) Mathematician, born in Cranleigh, Surrey, SE England, UK. He studied at Cambridge, was professor of geometry at Oxford (1919–30), then returned to Cambridge as professor of pure maths (1931–42). He was an internationally important figure in mathematical analysis, collaborating with John Littlewood in much of his work in analytic number theory. He was greatly influenced by the work of Srinivasa Ramanujan. His mathematical philosophy was described for the layman in his book *A Mathematician's Apology* (1940). In his one venture into applied maths he developed (concurrently with, but independent of, **Wilhelm Weinberg**) the *Hardy–Weinberg law* fundamental to population genetics. >> Littlewood, John; Ramanujan

Hardy, Oliver >> **Laurel and Hardy**

Hardy, Thomas (1840–1928) Novelist and poet, born in Upper Bockhampton, Dorset, S England, UK. After schooling in Dorchester, he studied as an architect, and at 22 moved to London, where he began to write poems expressing his love of rural life. Unable to publish his poetry, he turned to the novel, and found success with *Far from the Madding Crowd* (1874). He then took up writing as a profession, and produced a series of novels, notably *The Return of the Native* (1878), *The Mayor of Casterbridge* (1886), *Tess of the D'Urbervilles* (1891), and *Jude the Obscure* (1896). His main works were all tragedies, increasingly pessimistic in tone, and after *Tess* he was dubbed an atheist. He then took up poetry again, writing several volumes of sardonic lyrics, as well as the moving elegies to his first wife **Emma Gifford** (d.1912), and the epic drama, *The Dynasts* (1903–8). Several of his novels have been filmed, notably *Far from the Madding Crowd* (Schlesinger, 1967) and *Tess* (Polanski, 1979).

Hardy, Sir Thomas (Masterman) (1769–1839) British naval officer, born in Portisham, Dorset, S England, UK. He was closely associated with Nelson, whom he served as flag-captain at the Battle of Trafalgar (1805). He was First Sea Lord (1830), and from 1834 was governor of Greenwich Hospital. He was promoted vice-admiral in 1837. >> Nelson

Hare, David (1947–) Playwright and director, born in London, England, UK. He studied at Cambridge, founded the Portable Theatre (1968), and went on to be resident playwright at the Royal Court (1969–71) and elsewhere. His politically engaged plays include *Slag* (1970), *Teeth 'n Smiles* (1975), *Plenty* (1978), and *Pravda* (1985), this last written in collaboration with Howard Brenton. He has also written several plays for television, including *Licking Hitler* (1978) and *Dreams of Leaving* (1980), and the films *Wetherby* (1985) and *Strapless* (1989). *The Secret Rapture* (1988) won two awards for best play of the year. Later works include *Racing Demon* (1990) and *Amy's View* (1997). >> Brenton

Hare, Robertson (1891–1979) Actor, born in London, England, UK. He built up his reputation as a comedian in the famous 'Aldwych farces', such as *Thark*, *Plunder*, *Rookery Nook*, and *Cuckoo in the Nest*, cast invariably in 'henpecked little man' parts in which his ultimate 'debagging' became proverbial. He also featured in many other stage comedies and films, including *A Funny Thing Happened on the Way to the Forum* (1963).

Hare, William >> **Burke, William**

Hare, William Henry, nickname **Dusty Hare** (1952–) Rugby union player, born in Newark-on-Trent, Nottinghamshire, C England, UK. A sheep farmer, he holds the all-time points-scoring record. When he retired in 1989 he had scored 7337 points. His phenomenal accuracy as a place kicker never deserted him through an 18-year career, during which he won 23 full caps for England.

Harewood, George Henry Hubert Lascelles, 7th Earl of [hah(r)wud] (1923–) Elder son of Princess Mary, and cousin of Queen Elizabeth II, born in Harewood, West Yorkshire, N England, UK. He studied at Cambridge, served as captain in the Grenadier Guards in World War 2, and was a prisoner of war. Since the 1950s he has been much involved in the direction of operatic and arts institutions, such as at Covent Garden, Edinburgh, and Leeds.

Hargrave, Lawrence (1850–1915) Aeronautical pioneer, born in Greenwich, EC Greater London, England, UK. He arrived in Sydney in 1865, and spent five years exploring in New Guinea before being appointed to a post at the Sydney Observatory (1878). He resigned five years later to devote his time to aeronautical experiments. In 1893 he developed the box-kite to produce a wing form used in early aircraft, and in 1894 four tethered kites successfully lifted him 5 m from the ground. He also designed a radial rotary engine in 1899, the predecessor of the engine which drove most aircraft in the early days of aviation. His other projects included wave-driven ships and a one-wheel gyroscopic car.

Hargreaves, James (c. 1720–78) Inventor, probably born in Blackburn, Lancashire, NW England, UK. An illiterate weaver and carpenter, c.1764 he invented the spinning jenny (named after his daughter); but his fellow spinners broke into his house and destroyed his frame (1768). He moved to Nottingham, where he erected a spinning mill, and continued to manufacture yarn until his death.

Harington, Sir Charles Robert (1897–1972) British chemist. He became professor of pathological chemistry at University College, London (1931–42), and director of the National Institute of Medical Research (1942–62). He synthesized thyroxine and published *The Thyroid Gland* (1933).

Harington, Sir John (1561–1612) Courtier and writer, born in Kelston, Somerset, SW England, UK. From Cambridge he went to the court of his godmother, Elizabeth I. His wit brought him into much favour, which he endangered by the freedom of his satires. He is remembered as the metrical translator of Ariosto's *Orlando Furioso* (1591). His other writings include Rabelaisian pamphlets, epigrams, and *The Metamorphosis of Ajax* (1596), containing the earliest design for a water closet, and a *Tract on the Succession to the Crown*. >> Ariosto

Hariot, Thomas >> **Harriot, Thomas**

Harlan, John (Marshall) (1833–1911) Jurist, born in Boyle Co, KY. He studied at Transylvania University and was admitted to the bar in 1853. An unsuccessful candidate for the US House of Representatives in 1858, he was a presidential elector on the Bell–Everett (Constitutional Union) ticket in 1860. Appointed to the Supreme Court, he served 34 years (1877–1911), and is best remembered for defending the Thirteenth and Fourteenth Amendments as upholders of African-American civil rights.

Harland, Sir Edward James (1831–96) British shipbuilder. In 1858 he founded in Belfast the firm which became Harland and Wolff, in whose yard were built many famous Atlantic liners and warships. **Gustav William Wolff** (1834–1913), his partner from 1860, was born in Hamburg, but learned engineering at Liverpool and Manchester.

Harley, Robert, 1st Earl of Oxford (1661–1724) British statesman, born in London, England, UK. He became a lawyer, and a Whig MP in 1689. In 1701 he was elected Speaker, and in 1704 became secretary of state. Shortly after, he became sympathetic to the Tories, and from 1708 worked to undermine the power of the Whigs. In 1710 Godolphin was dismissed, and Harley made Chancellor of the Exchequer, head of the government, and (1711) Earl of Oxford and Lord High Treasurer. The principal act of his administration was the Treaty of Utrecht (1713). In 1714 he was dismissed, and after the Hanoverian succession spent two years in prison. >> Godolphin

Harlow, Jean, originally **Harlean Carpentier**, nickname **the Blonde Bombshell** (1911–37) Film star, born in Kansas City, MO. After a broken childhood, at 16 she moved to Los Angeles, where she became a film extra and worked at the Hal Roach Studios. Signed to a contract by Howard Hughes, she rocketed to fame in *Hell's Angels* (1930), her platinum-blonde hair initiating a craze across the country. Subsequent roles in *Platinum Blonde* (1931), *Red-Headed Woman* (1932), and *Red Dust* (1932), established her as a brazenly sexual screen goddess. Under contract to M-G-M from 1932, she played opposite the studio's top male stars in *Bombshell* (1933) and other films. Her private life caused many a scandal, and she died of uraemic poisoning at the age of 26.

Harlow, Harry (Frederick) (1905–81) Psychologist, born in Fairfield, IA. He studied at Stanford University, taught at Wisconsin University, and became director of the Regional Primate Center there (1961–71). He is known for his pioneering methods of research into the behaviour of captive monkeys.

Harman, Harriet (1950–) British stateswoman. She was educated at York University, became a solicitor, and was legal officer for the National Council of Civil Liberties (1978–82). She became a Labour MP in 1982, held shadow ministerial posts for social services (1984, 1985–7), health (1987–92, 1995–6), the Treasury (1992–4), employment (1994–5), and social security (1996–7), and became secretary of state for social security and minister for women in 1997.

Harmodius [hah(r)**moh**dius] (?–514 BC) Athenian assassin, who with **Aristogeiton** in 514 BC killed Hipparchus, the younger brother of the 'tyrant' Hippias, during the Panathenaic festival. They meant to kill Hippias also, but Harmodius was cut down, and Aristogeiton, who fled, was taken and executed. Subsequently they were regarded as patriotic martyrs, and received divine honours.

Harmsworth, Alfred (Charles William), 1st Viscount Northcliffe (1865–1922) Journalist and newspaper magnate, one of the pioneers of mass circulation journalism, born near Dublin. Brought up in London, he became editor of *Youth*, and with his brother, Harold, founded *Comic Cuts* (1890), the basis for the Amalgamated Press. In 1894 he absorbed the *London Evening News*, published a number of Sunday magazine papers, and in 1896 revolutionized Fleet Street with his *Daily Mail*, introducing popular journalism to the UK. In 1908, he became proprietor of *The Times*. A baronet in 1904, he was created baron in 1906 and viscount in 1917. >> Harmsworth, Harold; King, Cecil

Harmsworth, Harold (Sydney), 1st Viscount Rothermere (1868–1940) Newspaper magnate, born in London, England, UK. Closely associated with his brother, Alfred, he also founded the Glasgow *Daily Record* and in 1915 the *Sunday Pictorial*. He became air minister (1917–18), and after his brother's death acquired control of the *Daily Mail* and *Sunday Dispatch*. A baronet in 1910, he was created baron in 1914 and viscount in 1919. >> Harmsworth, Alfred

Harnack, Adolf (Karl Gustav) von (1851–1930) Protestant Church historian and theologian, born in Dorpat, Germany. He was professor at Leipzig (1876), Giessen (1879), Marburg (1886), and Berlin (1889), where he also became keeper of the Royal (later State) Library (1904–21). His major writings include works on the history of dogma, on early Gospel traditions, and on a reconstruction of the essence of Jesus's teachings.

Harnick, Sheldon (1924–) Songwriter, born in Chicago, IL. He went to New York City as a violinist, and began selling songs to revues. His first real success came when he teamed with composer Jerry Bock (1928–) on *The Body Beautiful* (1958), a musical about boxers. This was followed by *Fiorello* (1959, with Bock), a political satire based loosely on the life of New York Mayor LaGuardia, which was awarded the Pulitzer Prize. His greatest success has been *Fiddler on the Roof* (1964), which includes 'Matchmaker, Matchmaker', 'If I Were a Rich Man', and 'Sunrise, Sunset'.

Harold I, nickname **Harold Harefoot** (c.1016–40) King of England (1037–40), the younger son of Canute and Ælgifu of Northampton. Canute had intended that Hardicanute, his only son by Emma of Normandy, should succeed him

in both Denmark and England. But in view of Hardicanute's absence in Denmark, Harold was accepted in England, first as regent (1035–6), and from 1037 as king. >> Canute; Hardicanute; RR1095

Harold II (c.1022–66) Last Anglo-Saxon king of England (1066), the second son of Earl Godwin. By 1045 he was Earl of East Anglia, and in 1053 succeeded to his father's earldom of Wessex, becoming the right hand of Edward the Confessor. After Edward's death (Jan 1066), Harold, his nominee, was crowned as king. He defeated his brother Tostig and Harold Hardrada, King of Norway, at Stamford Bridge (Sep 1066), but Duke William of Normandy then invaded England, and defeated him near Hastings (14 Oct 1066), where he died, shot through the eye with an arrow. >> Edward the Confessor; Godwin; Harold III; William I (of England)

Harold III >> **Harald III Sigurdsson**

Harper, Edward (1941–) Composer, born in Taunton, Somerset, SW England, UK. A lecturer in music at Edinburgh University, he directs the New Music Group of Scotland. Early works owed much to serial and aleatoric styles, but with the orchestral *Bartók Games* (1972) and a one-act opera *Fanny Rodin* (1975) he evolved a more tonally-based style. Other works include the operas *Hedda Gabler* (1985), *The Mellstock Quire* (1988), a symphony, concertos, choral works, two string quartets, and other chamber and vocal pieces.

Harper, James (1795–1869) Founder member of the publishing firm, Harper & Brothers, born in New York City. He was apprenticed to a printer at 16, and in 1818 with his brother, **John** (1797–1875), began publishing as J & J Harper. His other brothers, **Joseph Wesley** (1801–70), and **Fletcher** (1806–77) joined the firm in 1823 and 1825 respectively. The firm of Harper & Brothers was established in 1833, and went into periodical publishing with several literary and political magazines, including *Harper's New Monthly Magazine* (1850) and *Harper's Bazaar* (1867). The business experienced financial difficulties in 1899, and passed out of family ownership a year later.

Harrelson, Woody (1961–) Actor, born in Midland, TX. He studied at Hanover College, went into the theatre, and became well known for his role as the bartender in the popular television series *Cheers* (1983–93). His feature films include *Indecent Proposal* (1993), *Natural Born Killers* (1994), and *The People vs. Larry Flynt* (1996, Oscar nomination). In 1996 he attracted publicity when he was arrested twice as an activist during events drawing attention to endangered forests.

Harriman, W(illiam) Averell (1891–1986) US statesman and diplomat, born in New York City. He studied at Yale, and became a diplomat, taking up posts as ambassador to the USSR (1943) and to Britain (1946). He was secretary of commerce (1946–8), and special assistant (1950–1) to his close friend, President Truman. He became Governor of New York (1955–8), ambassador-at-large (1961, 1965–9), and US representative at the Vietnam peace talks in Paris (1968). He negotiated the partial nuclear test-ban treaty between the USA and USSR in 1963, and continued to visit the USSR on behalf of the government, making his last visit there at 91. His wife, **Pamela C(hurchill) Harriman** (d. 1997) became vice-chairman of the Atlantic Council and then US ambassador to France. >> Truman

Harriot, Thomas, also spelled **Hariot** (1560–1621) Mathematician and scientist, born in Oxford, Oxfordshire, SC England, UK. He studied at Oxford, became mathematical tutor to Sir Walter Raleigh (1581–5), and was sent to survey Virginia. He corresponded with Johannes Kepler on astronomical matters, observed Halley's comet in 1607, and made observations with the newly discovered telescope from 1609, as early as Galileo. He studied optics, refraction by prisms, and the formation of rainbows. Most of his work was never published and remains in manuscript, although his *Artis analyticae praxis*, a treatise on algebra, was published posthumously in 1631, showing that he had developed an effective algebraic notation for the solution of equations. >> Galileo; Kepler

Harris, Sir Arthur Travers, nickname **Bomber Harris** (1892–1984) British airman, born in Cheltenham, Gloucestershire, SWC England, UK. He served in the Royal Flying Corps in World War 1, and as commander-in-chief of Bomber Command in World War 2 (1942–5) organized mass bomber raids on industrial Germany. He was knighted in 1942, and created a baronet in 1953.

Harris, Barbara (Clementine) (1931–) Social activist, born in Philadelphia, PA. She worked as a public relations executive, becoming director of the Episcopal Publishing Co. In the late 1960s she joined the Church of the Advocate, campaigning for social and civil rights. She was ordained a priest in 1980, and made history when she became the first woman to be consecrated an assistant bishop in the Episcopal Church (1989) – an appointment which was highly controversial within the Anglican Church.

Harris, Frank, pseudonym of **James Thomas Harris** (1856– 1931) Literary editor and journalist, born in Galway, Co Galway, Ireland. He travelled to New York as a teenager, and worked at a series of menial jobs before returning to Europe. As a journalist he gained a considerable reputation on the London literary scene, editing the *Evening News* (1882–6), the *Fortnightly Review* (1886–94), and *Saturday Review* (1894–8). His notoriety as a braggart and liar was epitomized in *My Life and Loves* (4 vols, 1922–7). Other works include short stories, studies of Shakespeare, biographies of Wilde and Shaw, and *Contemporary Portraits* (1915–23).

Harris, Howel (1714–73) Clergyman, the chief organizer of the Methodist Revival in Wales in the 1740s, born in Trefeca, Powys, E Wales, UK. Originally intended for ordination in the Anglican Church, he became a travelling preacher in Wales, capable of gathering large crowds. Refused ordination, he founded his own community at Trefeca. His split with other Methodist leaders, notably Daniel Rowland (1713–90) and William Williams (1717–91), became known as the 'great schism'.

Harris, Jet >> **Shadows, The**

Harris, Joel Chandler (1848–1908) Humorist and dialect writer, born in Eatonton, GA. An apprentice on the *Countryman* weekly, he joined the staff of the Atlanta *Constitution* (1876–1900). His 'Tar Baby' story (1879), and later *Uncle Remus* stories about 'Brer Rabbit' and 'Brer Fox', made him internationally famous, known especially for his distinctive use of Southern African-American folklore and dialect. He edited *Uncle Remus's Magazine* from 1907.

Harris, Julie, originally **Julia Harris** (1925–) Film, stage, and television actress, born in Michigan. Following her Broadway debut in 1945, she rose to stardom through her roles in *The Member of the Wedding* (1950), *The Lark* (1955), and other plays, performances she later filmed. In 1976 she successfully performed a one-woman show as Emily Dickinson in *The Belle of Amherst*, which she later toured, including a season in London. In 1980 she played the lead in *On Golden Pond* on the West coast, and in 1992–3 toured in *Lettice & Lovage*. She wrote the highly acclaimed *Julie Harris Talks to Young Actors* (1972).

Harris, Paul (1868–1947) Lawyer, born in Racine, WI. He was the founder in 1905 of a club for business and professional men, using the name *Rotary* (because the meetings took place at each member's office in turn). This grew into the worldwide organization, Rotary International, whose motto 'Service above Self' embodies the ideals of all service clubs. Women were admitted for the first time in 1987.

Harris, Reg(inald Hargreaves) (1920–92) Track cyclist, born in Bury, Lancashire, NW England, UK. He came to prominence in 1947 when he won the world amateur sprint championship, and followed this with silver medals in sprint and tandem in the 1948 Olympic Games in London. That same year he turned professional, and was world sprint champion (1949–51), and again in 1954, setting records in the process which stood for 20 years. He came out of retirement to take the British sprint championship in 1974, aged 54. He died after suffering a stroke while cycling.

Harris, Richard (1930–) Actor, born in Co Limerick, Republic of Ireland. He studied at the London Academy of Music and Dramatic Art, and immediately joined Joan Littlewood's company in *The Quare Fellow* (1956). He remained with the Littlewood company for some years and became established as a name in the West End production of *The Ginger Man* (1959). He made his screen debut in the comedy *Alive and Kicking* (1958), then became well known for his portrayal of rebel characters such as the rugby player in *This Sporting Life* (1963). Later films include *Camelot* (1967), *A Man Called Horse* (1969), *The Wild Geese* (1978), and *The Field* (1990). >> Littlewood, Joan

Harris, Rolf (1930–) Entertainer and artist, born in Bassendean, Western Australia. He won a radio 'Amateur Hour' competition at the age of 18, and after graduating from the University of Western Australia, went to London in 1952 where he studied art. While there he performed at the Down Under Club, and in 1954 started working for the BBC children's department. He returned to Perth in 1960 to present a children's television programme, and then had commercial success with his recordings. He has since appeared widely on stage and television, and has written popular books.

Harris, Rosemary (1930–) British actress. She made her debut in New York City in 1952, and later appeared with the Bristol Old Vic and the Old Vic in London. She has appeared in over 140 roles in more than 30 years on the English and American stage, including affiliations with some of the great theatre companies on both sides of the Atlantic.

Harris, Roy, popular name of **LeRoy Ellsworth Harris** (1898–1979) Composer, born in Lincoln Co, OK. A truck driver, he turned to music at 24, and after tuition in California won a Guggenheim scholarship, enabling him to study in Paris under Nadia Boulanger. He later held positions in Californian universities as a teacher of composition. His music is ruggedly American in character, as in his symphonic overture *When Johnny Comes Marching Home* (1935). He wrote 16 symphonies, the third being the best known. >> Boulanger, Nadia

Harris, Theodore Wilson (1921–) Novelist, born in New Amsterdam, Guyana. He studied at Queen's College, Georgetown, and worked as a surveyor. In 1959 he moved to London, England. One of the pre-eminent Caribbean writers, his masterpiece is *The Guyana Quartet* (1985, a compilation of novels written 1960–3); starting with a poetic exploration, it evolves into a composite picture of Guyana, its various landscapes and racial communities. Later works include *The Four Banks of the River of Space* (1990) and *Jonestown* (1996).

Harris, Thomas (Lake) (1823–1906) Spiritualist, born in Fenny Stratford, Buckinghamshire, SC England, UK. At the age of three he was taken to America, and in 1843 became a Universalist pastor. In 1850 he set up as a spiritualistic medium, founding the 'Church of the Good Shepherd'

(c.1858) on doctrines compounded of Swedenborg and Fourier. >> Fourier, Charles; Swedenborg

Harrison, Benjamin (1833–1901) US statesman and 23rd president (1889–93), born in North Bend, OH, the grandson of William Henry Harrison. He studied at Miami University, and in 1854 settled as a lawyer in Indianapolis. During the Civil War (1861–5) he fought in Sherman's Atlanta campaign. He was elected a Republican senator for Indiana in 1880. In 1888 he defeated Cleveland on the free trade issue, but lost the popular vote. He failed to gain re-election in 1892, and returned to his law practice in Indianapolis. >> Cleveland, Stephen Grover; Harrison, William Henry; Sherman, William Tecumseh; RR1097

Harrison, George (1943–) Singer, musician, and songwriter, born in Liverpool, Merseyside, NW England, UK. He played lead guitar and sang with the Beatles, and developed an interest in Indian music and Eastern religion, receiving instruction on the sitar from Ravi Shankar, and associating with the religious leader, Maharishi Mahesh Yogi. Following the break-up of the Beatles, he made a solo album, *All Things Must Pass* (1970), which included the gospelly hit 'My Sweet Lord', later the subject of an expensive plagiarism suit. Later solo albums included *Living in the Material World* (1973), *Dark Horse* (1974), and *Somewhere in England* (1981), and he joined with other artists in the 'super-group' The Traveling Wilburys (1988–90), and with Starr and McCartney to produce the Beatles anthology (1995). He formed Dark Horse Records in 1974, and a film company, HandMade Films, in 1978, producing a number of feature films, such as *Monty Python's Life of Brian* (1979), *Time Bandits* (1981, also writing the music and lyrics), *A Private Function* (1984), and *Withnail and I* (1987). He has also written a volume of autobiography, *I Me Mine* >> Beatles, The; Shankar

Harrison, John (1693–1776) Inventor and horologist, born in Foulby, West Yorkshire, N England, UK. By 1726 he had constructed a clock with compensating apparatus for correcting errors due to variations of climate. In 1713 the British government had offered three prizes for the discovery of a method to determine longitude accurately (only possible with very accurate timepieces). After long perseverance he developed a marine chronometer which, in a voyage to Jamaica (1761–2) determined the longitude within two geographical miles. After further trials, he was awarded the first prize (1765–73).

Harrison, Sir Rex, originally **Reginald Carey Harrison** (1908–90) Actor, born in Houghton, Lancashire, NW England, UK. He reached the London stage by 1930, and had his first leading film role in *Storm in a Teacup* (1937). His charming, somewhat blasé style attracted many star comedy parts, such as in *Blithe Spirit* (1945), *The Constant Husband* (1958), and *My Fair Lady* (1964, Oscar).

Harrison, Ross (Granville) (1870–1959) Zoologist, born in Germantown, PA. He was professor of biology at Johns Hopkins (1899–1907) and Yale (1907–38) universities. His observations of animal tissue cultures pioneered modern nerve neurology and physiology, and he also invented methods of tissue grafting which suggested future organ-transplantation techniques.

Harrison, Thomas (1606–60) English Parliamentarian soldier and regicide, born in Newcastle-under-Lyme, Staffordshire, C England, UK. He fought for the parliamentary army in the Civil War (1642–5), commanded the guard which took Charles I from Hurst Castle to London, sat among his judges, and signed his death warrant (1649). He became a member of the Council of State (1651), but was too uncompromising in religion and politics to favour Cromwell's tolerant ideas, and was deprived of his commission, and later imprisoned for his share in plots

hatched by the more irreconcilable bigots. After the Restoration he was arrested and executed. >> Charles I (of England); Cromwell, Oliver

Harrison, Tony (1937–) Poet, born in Leeds, West Yorkshire, N England, UK. After studying in Leeds, and teaching in Nigeria and Prague, he became known with *The Loiners* (1970) and *Palladas* (1975). His combination of classical technique and colloquial language has produced powerful effects in the open sequences *The School of Eloquence* (1978) and *Continuous* (1981), also evident in his vigorous adaptations from French, Greek, and mediaeval drama. Poems on social conflict ('V'. 1985, televised 1987) and the Gulf War ('A Cold Coming', 1991) underline his commitment to public issues, confirmed in *The Gaze of the Gorgon* (1992, Whitbread). Later works include *Poetry or Bust* (1993) and *The Prince's Play* (1996).

Harrison, William Henry (1773–1841) US soldier, statesman, and ninth president (1841), born in Charles City Co, VA. He fought against the Indians, and when Indiana Territory was formed (1800) he was appointed governor. He tried to avoid further Indian wars, but was compelled to suppress Tecumseh's outbreak, which ended in the Battle of Tippecanoe (1811). In the War of 1812 he defeated the British in the Battle of the Thames (1813). In 1816 he was elected to Congress, became a senator in 1824, and president in 1841, but died of pneumonia a month after his inauguration. >> Tecumseh; RR1097

Harrod, Sir (Henry) Roy (Forbes) (1900–78) Economist, born in London, England, UK. He studied at Oxford and, apart from a break (1940–2) for service in World War 2, and as adviser to the International Monetary Fund (1952–3), remained there throughout his career (1922–67). He wrote widely as a biographer and on philosophy and logic, as well as economics. His major contributions to economic theory were developed at the same time and independently of those of Polish-born US economist Evsey Domar, leading to the *Harrod–Domar model* for economic development. >> Domar

Harry, Deborah >> Blondie

Harsanyi, John C (1928–) Economist, born in Budapest. He studied mathematics at Budapest, moved to the USA in 1956, and worked at Stanford and Yale universities before moving to the Haas School of Business at the University of California, Berkeley, in 1964. He shared the Nobel Prize for Economics in 1994 for his contribution to the analysis of equilibria in the theory of non-co-operative games. >> Nash, John F; Selten

Hart, Francis Brett >> Harte, Brett

Hart, Gary, originally **Gary Hartpence** (1936–) US politician, born in Ottawa, KS. He studied at Yale, and established a law practice at Denver, CO. After managing George McGovern's presidential campaign (1970–2), he entered the US Senate in 1974. A 'neo-liberal', seeking to combine social and environmental reform with enhanced economic efficiency, he contested the Democrats' presidential nomination in 1980, and almost defeated Walter Mondale. He retired from the Senate in 1986 to concentrate on a bid for the presidency, which proved unsuccessful. >> McGovern; Mondale

Hart (of South Lanark), Judith (Constance Mary) Hart, Baroness (1924–91) British stateswoman, born in Burnley, Lancashire, NW England, UK. She studied at the London School of Economics, entered the House of Commons in 1959, and joined Harold Wilson's Labour government in 1964, reaching cabinet rank as paymaster-general in 1968. She then had three successful terms as minister of overseas development (1969–70, 1974–5, 1977–9). She was a popular and influential left-winger, with a strong concern for the needs of Third World countries. She was made a dame in 1979, and a life peer in 1988. >> Wilson, Harold

Hart, Lorenz >> **Rodgers, Richard**

Hart, Moss (1904–61) Playwright and director, born in New York City. An office boy to a theatrical producer, his first play, written at 18, was a flop. He then wrote *Once in a Lifetime* (1929) which, fine-tuned by George S Kaufman, became a hit, and started his career as one of the most successful US playwrights. Other works in collaboration with Kaufman include *Merrily We Roll Along* (1934), *You Can't Take It With You* (1936), and *The Man Who Came to Dinner* (1939). *Lady in the Dark* (1941), which he wrote with Kurt Weill and Ira Gershwin, was one of the many successful musical plays he directed. >> Gershwin, Ira; Kaufman, George; Weill

Hart, William S(urrey) (1870–1946) Cowboy hero of silent motion pictures, born in Newburgh, NY. An employee of the New York City post office, he studied acting, and toured the country with numerous troupes before he had Broadway successes in *Ben Hur* (1899), *The Squaw Man* (1905), and *The Virginian* (1907–8). He made his film debut in *The Fugitive* (1913), and went on to enjoy great popularity in a series of Westerns as a defender of justice and the honour of women. He often devised and directed his moralistic adventures, including *Wild Bill Hickok* (1923) and *Tumbleweeds* (1925). He also published several volumes of fiction and an autobiography.

Harte, Bret, pseudonym of **Francis Brett Hart** (1836–1902) Writer, born in Albany, NY. He went to California in 1854, and wrote about the miners in the *Northern Californian* weekly. He later became a clerk at the US Mint in San Francisco (1864–70), during which time he edited the *Californian* and then the *Overland Monthly*. His collection of articles, *The Luck of Roaring Camp* (1870), brought him world fame, and he was contracted to *The Atlantic Monthly* (1871) to write 12 stories a year. He moved to the East coast, where he was lionized, but his work suffered as a consequence. From 1878 he accepted consulships in Europe, never returning to the USA.

Hartford, George Huntington (1833–1917) Grocery store magnate, born in Augusta, ME. After working as a store clerk in Boston, he went to St Louis, where in 1858 he joined a store owned by George F Gilman (1858). The men went to New York City, where they opened the first of their stores known as the Great American Tea Company. The company expanded to other cities, and in 1869 was renamed the Great Atlantic and Pacific Tea Company. Hartford moved to Orange, NJ, where he served as mayor (1879–91). Gilman retired from the business in 1878, but Hartford's sons – **George Ludlum** (1864–1957) and **John Augustine** (1872–1951) – joined the firm, and at Gilman's death (1901) the Hartfords acquired complete ownership. They expanded the variety of items sold, added to the chain, and began to process and manufacture food products for their stores under their own brand name. By 1951 there were 4700 stores in the chain, by then known as the A & P.

Hartley, David (1705–57) Philosopher, physician, and psychologist, born in Armley, West Yorkshire, N England, UK. He studied at Cambridge, at first for the Church, but changed direction and became a successful medical practitioner. His *Observations on Man, his Frame, his Duty and his Expectations* (1749) relates psychology closely to physiology, and develops a theory of the association of sensations with sets of ideas which forms part of an associationist tradition running from Hume through to Mill and Spencer. >> Hartley, David (1731–1813); Hume, David; Mill, John Stuart; Spencer, Herbert

Hartley, David, known as **the Younger** (1731–1813) Inventor and politician, born in Bath, SW England, UK, the son of the philosopher David Hartley. He was a fellow of Merton College, Oxford, and an MP (1774–84). With Benjamin Franklin, he drafted the Treaty of Paris between Britain and the USA in 1783 that ended the American War of Independence. His main claim to fame was his invention of a system of fire-proofing houses. >> Franklin, Benjamin; Hartley, David (1705–57)

Hartley, L(eslie) P(oles) (1895–1972) Writer, born near Peterborough, Cambridgeshire, EC England, UK. His early short stories, such as *Night Fears* (1924), established his reputation as a master of the macabre. Later he turned to depicting psychological relationships, and made a new success with such novels as *The Shrimp and the Anemone* (1944), *The Boat* (1950), and *The Go-Between* (1953).

Hartley, Marsden (1877–1943) Painter and writer, one of the pioneers of American modern art, born in Lewiston, ME. In 1892 he won a scholarship to the Cleveland School of Art, and in 1898 moved to New York City. He visited France and Germany (1912–15), experimenting with the latest styles. Inspired by Kandinsky and Franz Marc, his work became abstract, and he exhibited with the *Blaue Reiter* group. >> Delaunay, Robert; Kandinksy; Marc

Hartline, Haldan (Keffer) (1903–83) Physiologist, born in Bloomsburg, PA. He studied at Johns Hopkins University, then taught at Cornell (1931–49) and Johns Hopkins (1949–53), and became professor of physiology at the Rockefeller University, New York City (1954–74). By the use of very small electrodes applied to cells in the eyes of frogs and crabs, he was able to show how an eye distinguishes shapes. He shared the 1967 Nobel Prize for Physiology or Medicine for work on the neurophysiology of vision. >> RR1124

Hartnell, Sir Norman (1901–78) Fashion designer and court dressmaker, born in London, England, UK. He studied at Cambridge, then started his own business in 1923, receiving the Royal Warrant in 1940. He was president of the Incorporated Society of London Fashion Designers (1946–56). His work included costumes for leading actresses, wartime 'utility' dresses, the Women's Royal Army Corps uniform, and Princess Elizabeth's wedding and coronation gowns. He was knighted in 1977.

Hartnett, Sir Laurence John (1898–1986) Automotive engineer, born in Woking, Surrey, SE England, UK. He was head of General Motors' English subsidiary, Vauxhall, and went to Australia in 1934 to take over GM-Holden, when GM acquired the company established by Sir Edward Wheewall Holden in 1917. His enthusiasm for a locally built mass-produced car, despite the opposition of his New York bosses, won over the Australian government. War production intervened, and the first 'Holden' car appeared in 1946.

Hartono (Kurniawan), Rudy [hah(r)**toh**noh] (1948–) Indonesian badminton player. The winner of a record eight All-England titles (1968–74, 1976), he was also a member of Indonesia's Thomas Cup winning teams in 1970, 1973, 1976, and 1979. He was world champion in 1980.

Hartree, Douglas Rayner (1897–1958) Mathematician and physicist, born in Cambridge, Cambridgeshire, EC England, UK. He graduated from Cambridge after working on the science of anti-aircraft gunnery during World War 1. He was professor of applied mathematics and theoretical physics at Manchester (1929–45), returning to Cambridge as professor of mathematical physics in 1946. His work was mainly on computational methods applied to a wide variety of problems, ranging from atomic physics, where he invented the method of the self-consistent field in quantum mechanics, to the automated control of chemical plants. At Manchester he developed the differential analyser, an analogue computer, and was deeply involved in the early days of the electronic digital computer.

Hartung, Hans (1904–89) Artist, born in Leipzig, Germany. He studied in Basel, Leipzig, Dresden, and Munich. Although in his earlier years he was influenced by the German Impressionists and Expressionists, from 1928 onwards he produced mainly abstract work. During World War 2 he served in the Foreign Legion, and gained French citizenship in 1945. His later paintings, which have made him one of the most famous French abstract painters, show a free calligraphy allied to that of Chinese brushwork.

Harty, Sir (Herbert) Hamilton (1880–1941) Composer, conductor, and pianist, born in Hillsborough, Lisburn, Co Antrim. He conducted the Hallé (1920–33) and other orchestras. His compositions include an *Irish Symphony*, and many songs, and he made well-known arrangements of Handel's *Music for the Royal Fireworks* and *Water Music* suites.

Harun al-Raschid [ha**roon** al ra**sheed**] (766–809) Fifth Abbasid caliph, known to posterity especially from the *Arabian Nights*. He came to the throne on the death of his brother, al-Hadi, with the help of the influential Barmakid family, which he permitted to dominate his early reign, but gradually removed from power. He was a great patron of the arts, enthusiastic in waging war against the Byzantines, but less interested in the detail of central government. He weakened the empire through his attempts to divide it among his three sons.

Harvard, John (1607–38) Colonist, the major benefactor of Harvard College, born in London, England, UK. He studied at Cambridge, and in 1637 went to Charlestown, MA, where he became a freeman of the town and a preacher. He was appointed a member of the committee that helped compile the Body of Liberties. He left his considerable inherited wealth and his collection of theological and classical literature to a new school in nearby New Towne. The Massachusetts General Court named the school Harvard College in 1639.

Harvey, Catherine >> Trollope, Joanna

Harvey, David (1935–) Geographer, born in Gillingham, Kent, SE England, UK. He studied at Cambridge, taught at Bristol University (1961–9), was professor of geography at Johns Hopkins University (1969–86), and professor at Oxford (1987–93), returning to Johns Hopkins as professor of geography and environmental engineering in 1993. He was a founder member of the so-called 'positivist' school, and his book, *Explanation in Geography* (1969), was regarded by adherents of that school as the fundamental reference. He has subsequently become one of its major critics, and his advocacy of 'radical' geography (in which the subject is viewed as a tool of social revolution) crystallized in his book *Social Justice and the City* (1973).

Harvey, Sir John Martin (1863–1944) Actor-manager, born in Wivenhoe, Essex, SE England, UK. He intended to follow in his father's footsteps as a naval architect, but soon developed a preference for the stage, and joined Irving at the Lyceum (1882–96). He also toured the provinces in Shakespeare, and in 1899 under his own management produced at the Lyceum *The Only Way*, adapted from *A Tale of Two Cities*, in which he played Sydney Carton, his most successful role. He became world-famous as a romantic actor and manager. >> Irving, Henry

Harvey, William (1578–1657) Physician who discovered the circulation of the blood, born in Folkestone, Kent, SE England, UK. He studied at Cambridge and Padua, and settled in London as a physician, holding appointments at St Bartholomew's Hospital (1609–43) and from 1615 at the College of Physicians. He was also appointed physician to James I and Charles I. His celebrated treatise, *De motu cordis et sanguinis in animalibus* (On the Motion of the Heart and Blood in Animals), in which the circulation of the blood was first described, was published in 1628. >> Leeuwenhoek

Harvey-Jones, Sir John (Henry) (1929–) Industrial executive, born in Kent, SE England, UK. He trained at Dartmouth Naval College, and served in the navy until 1956. He joined ICI as a work study officer in 1956, rose to be chairman (1982–7), and was largely responsible for reshaping the company. He has since become more well known to the general public through the TV series *Troubleshooter* (1990, 1992, 1995), where he was invited to visit and advise businesses. He has been chairman of Parallax Enterprises since 1987, and was knighted in 1985.

Harwood, Gwen, *née* **Foster** (1920–) Poet, born in Brisbane, Queensland, Australia. She started writing in her late 30s, publishing *Poems* (1963), *Selected Poems* (1975), *The Lion's Bride* (1981), and *Bone Scan* (1990). She has written under a wide range of pseudonyms, but wrote librettos for Larry Sitsky's operas under her own name. She has spent much of her adult life in Tasmania, and many of her poems are set there. Her work, which has been influenced by the philosophy of Wittgenstein, deals with the themes of physical pain and motherhood, and shows a preoccupation with the need for personal fulfilment. She won the Robert Frost Award in 1977 and the Patrick White Literary Award in 1978. >> Sitsky; Wittgenstein

Harwood, Sir Henry (1888–1959) British naval commander. As commander of the South American division, he commanded the British ships at the Battle of the River Plate, in which the German pocket battleship *Graf Spee* was trapped in Montevideo, and later scuttled (Dec 1939). He was made commander-in-chief of the Mediterranean fleet in 1942.

Hasdrubal [**haz**drubal] (?–221 BC) Carthaginian general, son-in-law of Hamilcar, whom he succeeded as commander in Spain in 229 BC. He extended the Carthaginian empire in Spain to the boundary of the R Ebro, using diplomatic negotiations with the Romans rather than military force, and founded Cartagena. He was murdered by a Celtic slave, and succeeded by Hannibal. >> Hamilcar; Hannibal

Hasdrubal [**haz**drubal], known as **Hasdrubal Barca** ('Lightning') (?–207 BC) Carthaginian general, the son of Hamilcar and brother of Hannibal. He was left in command of the Carthaginian army in 218 BC when Hannibal invaded Italy at the start of the 2nd Punic War. He fought successfully against the Roman General Publius Cornelius Scipio and his son Gnaeus Scipio Africanus (218–208 BC). In 207 BC he marched across the Alps to Italy to bring help to his brother, but was intercepted at the R Metaurus and killed. >> Hamilcar; Hannibal; Scipio

Hašek, Jaroslav [**ha**shek] (1883–1923) Novelist and short-story writer, born in Prague. An accomplished practical joker who despised pomposity, he is best known for his novel *The Good Soldier Švejk* (1920–3), a satire on military life and bureaucracy, four volumes of which were completed by his death.

Haselrig, Sir Arthur [**hay**zlrig], also spelled **Hesilrige** (?–1661) English parliamentarian. In 1640 he sat in the Long and Short Parliaments for his native county, Leicestershire, and was one of the five members whose attempted seizure by Charles I in 1642 precipitated the Civil War. He commanded a parliamentary regiment, and in 1647 became Governor of Newcastle upon Tyne. After the Restoration, he died a prisoner in the Tower. >> Charles I (of England)

Hashman, Judy, popular name of **Judith Hashman**, *née* **Devlin** (1935–) Badminton player, born in Winnipeg, Manitoba, Canada. The winner of the singles title at the All-England Championships a record 10 times (1954,

1957–8, 1960–4, 1966–7), she also won seven doubles titles – six with her sister, **Susan Peard** (1940–). She was a member of the US Uber Cup-winning teams in 1957, 1960, and 1963. Her Irish-born father, **Frank Devlin** (1899–1988), won 18 All-England titles. >> RR1143

Hassall, John (1868–1948) Artist and cartoonist, born in Walmer, Kent, SE England, UK. He studied art at Antwerp and Paris, and in 1895 entered the advertising field, becoming the acknowledged pioneer of modern poster design. Among railway posters, his 'Skegness is so bracing' holds the record for longevity and ubiquity. He also illustrated children's books, and drew cartoons for many magazines.

Hassan II (1929–) King of Morocco, born in Rabat, Morocco, the eldest son of Sultan Mulay Mohammed Bin Yusuf, who was proclaimed king as Mohammed V in 1957. Having studied in France at Bordeaux University, Crown Prince Hassan served his father as head of the army and, on his accession as king in 1961, also became prime minister. He suspended parliament and established a royal dictatorship in 1965 after riots in Casablanca. Despite constitutional reforms (1970–2), he retained supreme religious and political authority. His forces occupied Spanish (Western) Sahara in 1957, and he mobilized a large army to check the incursion of Polisario guerrillas across his W Saharan frontier (1976–88). Unrest in the larger towns led Hassan to appoint a coalition 'government of national unity' under a civilian prime minister in 1984. He helped form the Arab Maghreb Union in 1989, and was chairman of its Presidential Council in 1991. >> RR1076

Hassel, Odd (1897–1981) Physical chemist, born in Oslo, Norway. He studied there and in Berlin, and spent his career in Oslo as professor of chemistry (1934–64). In 1943, independently of Sir Derek Barton, he developed the basic ideas of chemical conformational analysis (the study of the three-dimensional geometric structure of molecules), for which he shared with Barton the Nobel Prize for Chemistry in 1969. >> Barton, Derek

Hastings, Francis Rawdon-Hastings, 1st Marquess of (1754–1826) British soldier and colonial administrator, born in Dublin. Educated at Harrow, he fought with distinction in the American War of Independence (1775–81), became active in politics, and in 1813 was made Governor-General of India. Here he warred successfully against the Gurkhas (1814–16) and the Pindaris and Mahrattas (1817–18), purchased Singapore island (1819), encouraged Indian education and the freedom of the press, reformed the law system, and elevated the civil service. In 1821 he resigned after apparently unfounded charges of corruption had been made against him, and from 1824 till his death off Naples he was Governor of Malta.

Hastings, Max Macdonald (1945–) British writer, journalist, and broadcaster. He studied at Oxford, became a journalist for the BBC (1970–3), and from 1973 worked as a freelance journalist and broadcaster, covering conflicts in many parts of the world, including the S Atlantic (1982). He has made a number of television documentaries, including *Cold Comfort Farm* (1985) and *We Are All Green Now* (1990). He became editor (1986) and editor-in-chief (1990) of the *Daily Telegraph*, and editor of *The Evening Standard* (1996).

Hastings, Thomas (1860–1929) Architect, born in Mineola, NY. At the Ecole des Beaux-Arts, Paris, in the early 1880s he met **John Merven Carrére** (1858–1911, born in Rio de Janeiro, Brazil), with whom he later formed a highly successful New York partnership (1885–1915) that became identified with Beaux-Arts architecture in its public and corporate buildings, houses, and country estates. Their work included the New York Public Library (1902–11),

Manhattan Bridge (1904–11), and the Henry Clay Frick House (1913–14). Among the many large office buildings dating from the end of his career is the Standard Oil Building (1926), New York City.

Hastings, Warren (1732–1818) British colonial administrator in India, born in Churchill, Oxfordshire, SC England, UK. Educated at Westminster, he joined the East India Company in 1750, and by 1774 was Governor-General of Bengal. Carrying out several reforms, he made the Company's power paramount in many parts of India. However, wars (1778–84) interfered with trade, and damaged his reputation, and on his return to England in 1784 he was charged with corruption. After a seven-year trial, he was acquitted. The Company made provision for his declining years, which he spent as a country gentleman in Daylesford, Gloucestershire.

Hathaway, Anne >> **Shakespeare, William**

Hatshepsut [hatshepsoot] (c. 1540–c. 1481 BC) Queen of Egypt of the XVIIIth dynasty, the daughter of Thutmose I. She was married to Thutmose II, on whose accession (1516 BC) she became the real ruler. On his death (1503 BC) she acted as regent for his son, Thuthmose III, then had herself crowned as Pharaoh. Maintaining the fiction that she was male, she was represented with the regular pharaonic attributes, including a beard. >> Thutmose III; RR1046

Hattersley, Roy (Sydney George), Lord (1932–) British statesman, born in Sheffield, South Yorkshire, N England, UK. He studied at Hull University, and was a journalist and local authority politician before becoming a Labour MP in 1964. A supporter of Britain's membership of the European Economic Community, he was a minister at the Foreign Office (1974–6), then secretary of state for prices and consumer protection in the Callaghan government (1976–9). He has since been Opposition spokesman on the environment and on home affairs, shadow Chancellor, and deputy leader of the Labour Party (1983–92). He is a regular contributor to newspapers and periodicals. He was created a life peer in 1997.

Hauer, Rutger [hower] (1944–) Film actor, born in Breukelen, The Netherlands. The son of actor parents, he left school early to join an experimental theatre company. His screen debut came in a European film *Turkish Delight* (1973). He made an English-speaking debut in *The Wilby Conspiracy* (1975), but when this failed to establish him in Hollywood, he returned to making European films. International recognition came with his casting as the terrorist in *Nighthawks* (1981) and his role in *Blade Runner* (1982). Later films include *Blind Fury* (1990), *Past Midnight* (1992), *Fatherland* (1994), and *Mr Stitch* (1995).

Haughey, Charles (James) [hokhee] (1925–) Irish statesman and prime minister (1979–81, 1982, 1987–92), born in Castlebar, Co Mayo, Ireland. He studied at Dublin, was called to the bar in 1949, and became a Fianna Fáil MP in 1957. From 1961 he held posts in justice, agriculture, and finance, but was dismissed in 1970 after a quarrel with the prime minister, Jack Lynch. He was subsequently tried and acquitted on a charge of conspiracy to import arms illegally. After two years as minister of health and social welfare, he succeeded Lynch as premier in 1979, was in power again for a nine-month period in 1982, and defeated Garrett Fitzgerald in the 1987 election. He resigned after a phone-tapping scandal. >> Lynch, Jack; RR1064

Hauptman, Herbert (Aaron) [howptman] (1917–) Mathematical physicist, born in New York City. He studied at the City College of New York and Maryland University, then worked in the US Naval Research Laboratories in Washington until 1970, and afterwards at the Medical Foundation of Buffalo. With Jerome Karle he devised new methods for computing molecular structures from X-ray crystal diffraction data. The major advances made led to them sharing the Nobel Prize for Chemistry in 1985. >> Karle

Hauptmann, Bruno Richard >> **Lindbergh, Charles A**

Hauptmann, Gerhart (Johann Robert) [howptman] (1862–1946) Writer, born in Obersalzbrunn, Germany. He studied sculpture in Wrocław, Poland (formerly Breslau, Germany), and Rome before settling in Berlin (1885), where he established a reputation with his first play, *Vor Sonnenaufgang* (1889, trans Before Dawn). He followed this with several other social dramas, such as *Die Weber* (1892, The Weavers). He also wrote several novels, as well as poetry, and was awarded the Nobel Prize for Literature in 1912.

Hauron, Louis Duclos du >> **Duclos du Hauron, Louis**

Hausdorff, Felix [howsdaw(r)f] (1868–1942) Mathematician, born in Wrocław, Poland (formerly Breslau, Germany). He studied at Leipzig and Berlin, and taught at Leipzig (1896–1910). In 1910 he moved to Bonn, where he stayed until, as a Jew, he was forced by the Nazis to resign his chair in 1935; ultimately he committed suicide with his family, to avoid the concentration camps. He is regarded as the founder of point set topology, and his book *Grundzüge der Mengenlehre* (1914) introduced the basic concepts of topological spaces and metric spaces which have since become part of the standard equipment of analysis and topology. His work on set theory continued that of Cantor and Zermelo. >> Cantor, Georg; Zermelo

Hauser, Gayelord (Helmut Eugene Benjamin Gellert) [howzer] (1895–1984) Popular nutritionist, originally from Germany. He emigrated to the USA after World War 1 and set up business in California in 1927, advocating special vegetable diets featuring 'wonder foods' such as brewer's yeast, skimmed milk, wheat germ, and blackstrap molasses. He made a fortune with such best-selling books as *Look Younger, Live Longer* (1950) and *Be Happier, Be Healthier* (1952).

Hauser, Kaspar [howzer] (c. 1812–33) German foundling, a 'wild boy', found in the market place of Nuremberg in May 1828. Though apparently 16 years old, his mind was a blank, and his behaviour that of a little child. He later gave some account of himself, as having lived in a hole, looked after by a man who had brought him to the place where he was found. In 1833 he was discovered with a wound in his side, from which he died. Many have regarded him as an imposter who committed suicide: others, as a person of noble birth who was the victim of a crime.

Haussmann, Georges Eugène, Baron [howsman] (1809–91) Financier and town planner, born in Paris. He entered public service, and under Napoleon III became prefect of the Seine (1853), improving Paris by widening streets, laying out boulevards and parks, and building bridges. He was made baron and senator, but the heavy burden laid upon the citizens led to his dismissal (1870). He was elected to the Chamber of Deputies in 1881.

Hauteclocque, viscomte de >> **Le Clerc, Jacques-Philippe**

Havel, Václav [havl, vahtslaf] (1936–) Playwright, president of Czechoslovakia (1989–92), and president of the Czech Republic (1993–), born in Prague. He studied at the Prague Academy of Dramatic Art, and began work in the theatre as a stagehand, then became resident writer for the Prague 'Theatre on the Balustrade' (1960–9). His work was then judged subversive, and he was imprisoned in 1979 for four years, his plays only being performed abroad. These include *Zahradni slavnost* (1963, The Garden Party), *Spiklenci* (1970, The Conspirators), and *Temptation* (1987). He was imprisoned again in 1989, but was elected

president by direct popular vote in December following the collapse of the hardline Communist Party leadership. He resigned in 1992 in protest at the dissolution of Czechoslovakia, but became president of the new Czech Republic in January 1993. >> RR1043

Havelock (Allan), Sir Henry [havlok] (1795–1857) British soldier, born in Sunderland, Tyne and Wear, NE England, UK. He studied at Charterhouse and the Middle Temple, entered the army a month after Waterloo, and went out to India in 1823. He distinguished himself in the Afghan and Sikh wars, and in 1856 commanded a division in Persia. He led the relief of Cawnpore and Lucknow (1857).

Havergal, William Henry [havergal] (1793–1870) Hymn writer, born in High Wycombe, Buckinghamshire, SC England, UK. He took holy orders at Oxford, composed hymn tunes, chants, and songs, and wrote *History of the Old 100th Tune*. He also published sermons and pamphlets.

Havers (of St Edmundsbury), Robert Michael Oldfield Havers, Baron [hayverz] (1923–92) British lawyer and politician. He studied at Cambridge, saw wartime service in the Royal Navy, was called to the bar in 1948, and made a QC in 1964. Following a successful career as advocate and judge, he entered the House of Commons as MP for Wimbledon (1970). He was solicitor general under Edward Heath (1972–4), and attorney general under Margaret Thatcher (1979–87). He was made a life peer in 1987, and spent a brief period as Lord Chancellor before his retirement in 1988.

Havilland, Geoffrey de >> **de Havilland, Geoffrey**

Havlicek, John [havlichek], nickname **Hondo Havlicek** (1940–) Basketball player, born in Lansing, OH. He studied at Ohio State University, then joined the Boston Celtics in the National Basketball Association. During his career with Boston he played in eight NBA championship teams, averaging 20·8 points per game. He stayed with Boston (1963–78), and was voted Most Valuable Player in the NBA in 1974.

Hawes, Harriet (Ann) Boyd (1871–1945) Archaeologist, educator and social activist, born in Boston, MA. She studied at Smith College, then worked as a nurse in Greece during the Greco–Turkish war. She began to excavate a Minoan site at Kavousi in Crete (1900), and led a large team that excavated the Minoan town of Gournia (1901–5), thereby becoming the first woman to head a major archaeological dig. During World War 1 she organized a unit of Smith College graduates and directed their relief efforts in France (1917–18). She later joined the faculty of Wellesley College (1920–36). Always involved in one political and social cause or another, she worked for women's suffrage, became involved in economic issues during the Depression, and was a strong advocate of an international body to promote peace.

Hawes, Stephen (?–c. 1523) English poet, about whose early life very little is known, except that he was attached to the court from 1502 as groom of the chamber to Henry VII. His chief work is the allegory, 'The Passetyme of Pleasure' (1509), dedicated to the king. He also wrote 'The Example of Virtue' (1504).

Haw-Haw, Lord >> **Joyce, William**

Hawke, Bob, popular name of **Robert (James Lee) Hawke** (1929–) Australian statesman and prime minister (1983–91), born in Bordertown, South Australia. He studied at the universities of Western Australia and Oxford, and worked for the Australian Council of Trade Unions for over 20 years, before becoming a Labor MP in 1980. His party defeated the Liberals in the 1983 election only one month after adopting him as leader. A popular politician, known for his emotional outbursts, he was a skilled negotiator who won praise for his handling of industrial disputes. In 1990 he became the first Labor prime minister to win a fourth term in office, and the party's longest serving prime minister, but his role was challenged by Paul Keating in 1991, who narrowly defeated him in a leadership ballot. Hawke was largely responsible for his party's electoral successes, but many felt that traditional Labor values were discarded under his leadership. >> Keating

Hawke (of Towton), Edward Hawke, Baron (1705–81) British admiral, born in London, England, UK. As a young commander, he fought against the French and Spanish, for which he was knighted (1747). His major victory was against the French at Quiberon Bay (1759), which caused the collapse of their invasion plans. He also became an MP (1747) and First Lord of the Admiralty (1766–71), and was created a baron in 1776.

Hawker, R(obert) S(tephen) (1803–75) Poet, born in Plymouth, Devon, SW England, UK. He studied at Oxford, and in 1834 became vicar of Morwenstowe, on the Cornish coast, where he shared many of the superstitions of his people. He was devoted to animals, many of which accompanied him to church. His first volume *Tendrils by Reuben* appeared anonymously when he was only 18. A local newspaper published his best-known ballad, 'Song of the Western Men', in 1826. Other volumes include *Records of the Western Shore* (1832), *Cornish Ballads* (1869), and *Footprints of Former Men in Far Cornwall* (1870).

Hawkes, Jacquetta (1910–96) British archaeologist and writer. She studied at Cambridge, took part in excavations in Britain, France, and Palestine (1931–40), and was principal of the UK National Commision for UNESCO (1943–9) before taking up writing full-time. She married J B Priestley in 1953, and with him wrote *Journey Down a Rainbow* (1955). Her other works include *The World of the Past* (1963) and *Shell Guide to British Archaeology* (1986). >> Priestley, J B

Hawkesworth, John (c. 1715–73) Writer, born possibly in London, England, UK. In 1744 he succeeded Dr Johnson on the *Gentleman's Magazine*, compiling parliamentary debates. In 1752 he started, with Johnson and others, *The Adventurer*, a periodical to which he made the major contribution. He published a volume of fairy tales (1761), wrote dramatic works including *Edgar and Emmeline* (1761), edited Swift, and prepared a poorly received account of Captain Cook's *Voyages* (1773). >> Johnson, Samuel

Hawking, Stephen (William) (1942–) Theoretical physicist, born in Oxford, Oxfordshire, SC England, UK. He studied at Oxford, then spent his career in Cambridge, holding a chair there from 1977. His work has been concerned with cosmology in a variety of aspects, dealing with black holes, singularities, and the 'big bang' theory of the origin of the universe. His popular writing is also notable, especially *A Brief History of Time* (1988). Later books include *Black Holes and Baby Universes* (1993). His achievement is all the more noteworthy because since the 1960s he has suffered from a neuromotor disease, amyotrophic lateral sclerosis, causing extreme physical disability; he communicates with the aid of a computer. He was made a Companion of Honour in 1989.

Hawkins, Sir Anthony Hope >> Hope, Anthony

Hawkins, Coleman (1901–69) Jazz tenor saxophonist, born in St Joseph, MO; (he claimed 1904 as his birth year). He joined Fletcher Henderson's jazz orchestra in 1923. The performances on romping swing tunes such as 'The Stampede' (1926), and on slow ballads such as 'One Hour' (1929), altered the way the tenor saxophone was played, and popularized the instrument in jazz music. He played widely in Europe (1934–9), and on returning to New York City recorded 'Body and Soul', a jazz landmark. >> Henderson, Fletcher; Russell, Pee Wee

Hawkins, Erick, popular name of **Frederick Hawkins** (1909–94) Dancer, choreographer, and teacher, born in Colorado. He read Greek at Harvard, studied at the School of American Ballet, and joined American Ballet (1935–7) and Ballet Caravan (1936–9). The first man to dance with the Martha Graham company, he created roles in many of her most famous dances until 1951, and married her in 1948 (divorced, 1954). He formed his own company in the mid-1950s, his mainly abstract dances reflecting his natural approach to movement. >> Graham, Martha

Hawkins, Sir John >> Hawkyns, Sir John

Hawks, Howard (Winchester) (1896–1977) Film director, born in Goshen, IN. He studied at Cornell, working as a prop man in Hollywood on vacations. He wrote and directed his first feature, *The Road to Glory* (1926), and was always closely involved with the scripts in his later productions. With the coming of sound films, he had many successes over some 40 years, in such varied genres as airforce dramas (*The Dawn Patrol*, 1930), detection and crime (*The Big Sleep*, 1946), Westerns (*Rio Lobo*, 1970), and comedy (*Man's Favorite Sport?*, 1962).

Hawkshaw, Sir John (1811–91) Civil engineer, born in Leeds, West Yorkshire, N England, UK. He was a mining engineer in Venezuela (1831–4), chief engineer of the Manchester and Leeds Railway (1845–50), and consulting engineer (1850) in the construction of Charing Cross and Cannon Street stations and bridges, and of the Inner Circle underground railway in London. He designed the Narmada bridge in India, was engineer for the Amsterdam ship canal (1862), wrote a decisive report in favour of the chosen route of the Suez Canal (1863), and was one of the engineers of the original Channel Tunnel project (1872–86).

Hawksmoor, Nicholas (1661–1736) Architect, born in East Drayton, Nottinghamshire, C England, UK. His most individual contributions are the London churches, St Mary Woolnoth, St George's (Bloomsbury), and Christ Church (Spitalfields), as well as parts of Queen's College and All Souls, Oxford.

Hawkyns or **Hawkins, Sir John** (1532–95) English sailor, born in Plymouth, Devon, SW England, UK. He was the first Englishman to traffic in slaves (1562) between W Africa and the West Indies, but on his third expedition his fleet was destroyed by the Spanish (1567). He became navy treasurer in 1573, and was knighted for his services against the Armada in 1588. In 1595, with his kinsman Drake, he commanded an expedition to the Spanish Main, but died in Puerto Rico. >> Drake

Hawn, Goldie (Jeanne) [hawn] (1945–) US actress, born in Washington, DC. She became known through her comedy roles in Rowan and Martin's TV review *Laugh In* (1968–70), then won a best supporting actress award for her first film role in *Cactus Flower* (1969). Later films include *There's A Girl in my Soup* (1970), *Private Benjamin* (1980), which she also produced, *Bird on a Wire* (1990), *Housesitter* (1992), *Death Becomes Her* (1992), and *The First Wives Club* (1996). In 1997 she appeared in the film musical *Everyone Says I Love You*.

Haworth, Sir (Walter) Norman [hah(r)th] (1883–1950) Chemist, born in Chorley, Lancashire, NW England, UK. He studied at Manchester and Göttingen, and was professor of organic chemistry at Newcastle (1920–5) and Birmingham (1925–48). He determined the chemical structure of vitamin C and various carbohydrates, for which he shared the Nobel Prize for Chemistry in 1937. He was knighted in 1947. >> RR1123

Hawthorne, Nathaniel (1804–64) Novelist and short-story writer, born in Salem, MA. Educated at Bowdoin College, he shut himself away for 12 years to learn to write fiction. His first novel was amateurish, but later some of the stories gained favourable notice from the London *Athenaeum*, and a volume of them, *Twice-Told Tales*, was published in 1837. His first major success was the novel *The Scarlet Letter* (1850), still the best known of his works. Other books include *The House of the Seven Gables* (1851), *The Snow Image* (1852), and a campaign biography of his old schoolfriend, President Franklin Pierce, on whose inauguration Hawthorne became consul at Liverpool (1853–7). Only belatedly recognized in his own country, he continued to write articles and stories, notably those for the *Atlantic Monthly*, collected as *Our Old Home* (1863).

Hay, John (Milton) (1838–1905) US secretary of state (1898–1905) and writer, born in Salem, IN. He studied at Brown University, became a lawyer, and was private secretary (1861–5) to President Lincoln. After Lincoln's death, he served as a diplomat in Paris, Vienna, and Madrid. He returned to the USA and to journalism in 1870, going on to write poetry, fiction, and a multi-volume biography of Lincoln. He became assistant secretary of state (1878), ambassador to Britain (1897), and secretary of state, best-remembered for the Open Door Policy towards China (1899). >> Lincoln, Abraham

Haydee, Marcia (1939–) Dancer and director, born in Niteroi, Brazil. She trained in Rio de Janeiro, and with the Sadler's Wells Ballet School. She joined the Grand Ballet of Marquis de Cuevas in 1957, and Stuttgart Ballet in 1961, working under the direction of John Cranko, for whom she created roles in *Romeo and Juliet* (1962), *Onegin* (1965), *Carmen* (1971), and *Initials R.B.M.E.* (1972). She has made guest appearances frequently around the world, and worked for major choreographers such as Kenneth MacMillan and Glen Tetley. In 1976 she was appointed artistic director of Stuttgart Ballet. >> Cranko; MacMillan, Kenneth; Tetley

Hayden, Bill, popular name of **William George Hayden** (1933–) Australian statesman, born in Brisbane, Queensland, Australia. He studied at Queensland University, then served in the state civil service (1950–2) and the police (1952–61), before he joined the Australian Labor Party and entered the federal parliament in 1961. He served under Gough Whitlam and replaced him as Party leader in 1977. In 1983 he surrendered the leadership to the more charismatic Bob Hawke, and was foreign minister in his government (1983–8). As Governor-General of Australia (1989–96), he characteristically refused the customary knighthood which accompanies the post, and was rumoured to be Australia's first republican governor-general. >> Hawke, Bob; Whitlam

Hayden, Ferdinand (Vandeveer) (1829–87) Geologist, born in Westfield, MA. After working on surveys in the NW (1853–62), he was professor of geology at Pennsylvania University (1865–72), and was subsequently head of the US geological survey. He was influential in securing the establishment of Yellowstone National Park.

Haydn, Franz Joseph [hiydn] (1732–1809) Composer, born in Rohrau, Austria. Educated at the Cathedral Choir School of St Stephen's, Vienna, he earned his living initially by playing in street orchestras and teaching. He became musical director (1759–60) for Count von Morzin's court musicians, for whom he wrote his earliest symphonies. He entered the service of the Esterházy family as musical director in 1761, staying with them until 1790. He was given great scope for composition, and among his innovations were the four-movement string quartet and the 'classical' symphony. His output was vast, and he earned a major international reputation. His works include 104 symphonies, about 50 concertos, 84 string quartets, 24 stage works, 12 Masses, orchestral divertimenti, keyboard sonatas, and diverse chamber, choral, instrumental, and vocal pieces. >> Haydn, Michael

Haydn, Michael [hiydn] (1737–1806) Composer, born in Rohrau, Austria, the brother of Franz Joseph Haydn. He was a cathedral chorister with Joseph in Vienna, and ultimately became musical director and concert master to the Archbishop in Salzburg, where he remained until his death. Some of his compositions are of considerable merit and charm; and several of his church pieces and instrumental works are still performed. Carl Weber was among his pupils. >> Haydn, Franz Joseph; Weber, Carl

Hayek, Friedrich A(ugust von) [hiyek] (1899–1992) Economist, born in Vienna. He studied in Vienna, became director of the Austrian Institute for Economic Research (1927–31), lectured at Vienna (1929–31), and was appointed professor of economic science at London (1931–50), becoming a British citizen in 1938. He was professor of social and moral science at Chicago (1950–62). Strongly opposed to Keynesianism, he was often called 'the father of monetarism', and believed that government intervention in a free market leads eventually to domestic disaster. He shared the Nobel Prize for Economics in 1974. >> RR1125

Hayem, Georges [ayem] (1841–1920) Physician, born in Paris. He studied medicine in Paris, and became professor of therapy and materia medica in 1879, working for much of his long career at the Hôpital Tenon. He first described the platelets in the blood, and did classic work on the formation and diseases of the red and white blood cells. He also published important accounts of diseases of several organs, including the stomach, liver, heart, and brain.

Hayes, Helen, originally **Helen Hayes Brown** (1900–93) Actress, born in Washington, DC. A successful actress from the age of five, her adult stage productions brought her national popularity, and include *Caesar and Cleopatra* (1925), *The Glass Menagerie* (1956), and *Long Day's Journey into Night* (1971). She received many awards for her work on radio and television, and appeared in several films, including *A Farewell to Arms* (1932), *The Sin of Madelon Claudet* (1931), and *Airport* (1970), winning Oscars for the latter two. The Helen Hayes Theater in New York City was named after her.

Hayes, Isaac Israel (1832–81) Physician and Arctic explorer, born in Chester Co, PA. He studied at the University of Pennsylvania, then volunteered himself as a surgeon, sailing in the Kane expedition (1853–4) searching for the lost Franklin expedition of 1845. Seeking to prove that there were open seas around the North Pole, he led two more expeditions (1860, 1869). His book *The Land of Desolation* (1871–2) describes his sighting of the open polar sea, but it was later deduced that he saw only the Kennedy Channel between Greenland and Ellesmere I. >> Franklin, John; Kane, Elisha

Hayes, Rutherford B(irchard) (1822–93) US statesman and 19th president (1877–81), born in Delaware, OH. He practised as a lawyer at Cincinnati (1849–61), served with distinction in the Civil War, entered Congress as a Republican (1865–7), and became Governor of Ohio (1868–76). Following a dispute over voting returns in the 1876 election, he was awarded all the contested votes by a commission of congressmen and Supreme Court justices. Under his presidency, the country recovered commercial prosperity after the corruption following the Civil War. His policy included reform of the civil service and the conciliation of the Southern states. He chose to serve only one term of office as president, and devoted himself thereafter to humanitarian causes such as prison reform and educating young blacks. >> Tilden, Samuel Jones; RR1097

Haynes, Elwood (1857–1925) Inventor, born in Portland, IN. He trained as an engineer and a chemist, and produced in 1893 a one-horsepower, one-cylinder vehicle, the oldest US automobile in existence (preserved in the Smithsonian Institution). He traded as the Haynes–Apperson Co (1898–1902), then as the Haynes Automobile Co (1905–25). He also patented a number of alloys, including a type of stainless steel (1919), and was the first to use aluminium in an automobile engine.

Haynes, John (1934–) Footballer, born in London, England, UK. He spent his whole career with Fulham. The club's director and later chairman, the comedian Tommy Trinder, persuaded Haynes to stay with Fulham by mak-ing him the first £100-per-week footballer in the his-tory of the British game. A highly gifted and creative inside-forward, he won 56 caps and captained his country 22 times.

Hays, Will(iam Harrison) (1879–1954) Politician and film censor, born in Sullivan, IN. A lawyer by training, he was Republican national chairman (1918–20), and engineered Warren G Harding's presidential campaign. He became US postmaster general (1921–2), then served as the first presi-dent of the Motion Picture Producers and Distributors of America (1922–45). In 1930 he formulated the Production Code, known as the *Hays Code*, which enforced a rigorous code of morality on American films, and which was not superseded until 1966. >> Harding, Warren G

Hayter, Stanley William (1901–88) Artist and engraver, born in London, England, UK. He studied chemistry and geology at King's College, London, and worked for the Anglo-Iranian Oil Company in Abadan (1922–5). He returned to London to exhibit paintings he had completed in the Middle East (1926), then moved to Paris to study art at the Académie Julian, where he learned printmaking and line-engraving. In 1927 he founded a studio in which artists of all nationalities could work together; in 1933 it moved to No 17, Rue Campagne Première, where it became interna-tionally known as Atelier 17. It was moved to New York City (1940–50), then returned to Paris. As a painter, Hayter became one of the earliest members of the Surrealist movement, but it is as a master innovator in printmaking that he made his greatest mark.

Haywood, Eliza, *née* **Fowler** (c. 1693–1756) Novelist, born in London, England, UK. She left her middle-aged clergyman husband, became an actress, and wrote a number of scan-dalous society novels about real people, their names thinly disguised by the use of initials. (The British Museum has the key to their full names.) They include *Memoirs of a Certain Island Adjacent to Utopia* (1725) and *The Secret History of the Present Intrigues of the Court of Caramania* (1727). Pope denounced her in his poem *The Dunciad*. Her periodical, *The Female Spectator* (1744–6), was the first to be written by a woman. >> Pope, Alexander

Haywood, William D(udley), nickname **Big Bill Haywood** (1869–1928) Political activist, born in Salt Lake City, UT. As a young miner he became actively involved in politics, and went on to become leader of the Industrial Workers of the World (IWW). He became nationally known following his acquittal on a murder charge (1907–8). The IWW lent sup-port to striking industries (1909–13) and achieved notable successes, but Haywood was later arrested on treason and sabotage charges. He jumped bail (1921) and fled to Russia, where he worked for the Russian revolutionary govern-ment. His biography, *Bill Haywood's Book* (1929) was pub-lished after his death.

Hayworth, Rita, originally **Margarita Carmen Cansino** (1918–87) Film actress, born into a show business family in New York City. Her nightclub appearances as a Spanish dancer led to a succession of small roles in B-pictures. Blossoming into an international beauty after dyeing her hair red, she partnered both Fred Astaire and Gene Kelly in

musicals of the 1940s, and found her best-known lead in *Gilda* (1946). A pin-up of US serviceman, her Hollywood career was effectively closed by a scandal involving her romance with Aly Khan (1949), whom she later married. During the 1960s she appeared in character parts, often in Europe, including *The Money Trap* (1966) and *The Wrath of God* (1972). Married five times, she suffered from Alzheimer's disease for several years prior to her death. >> Astaire; Kelly, Gene

Hazlitt, William (1778–1830) Essayist, born in Maidstone, Kent, SE England, UK. The son of a Unitarian minister, he took up painting, but was encouraged by Coleridge to write *Principles of Human Action* (1805), and further essays followed. In 1812 he found employment in London as a journalist, and also contributed to the *Edinburgh Review* (1814–20), proving himself to be a deadly controversialist, and a master of epigram, invective, and irony. His best-known essay collections are *Table Talk* (1821) and *The Spirit of the Age* (1825).

Hazzard, Shirley (1931–) Writer, born in Sydney, New South Wales, Australia. She studied in Sydney, and later moved to Manhattan. She has published numerous short stories, often in the *New Yorker* magazine, which were col-lected in *Cliffs of Fall* (1963) and *People in Glass Houses* (1967), a series of satirical sketches about the UN, for which she worked 1952–62. Her novel, *The Transit of Venus* (1980), encompassing a subtle survey of the political and social movements of post-war society, established her as a major contemporary writer. Other novels include *The Evening of the Holiday* (1966) and *The Bay of Noon* (1970), both set in Italy.

H D >> **Doolittle, Hilda**

Head, Bessie (1937–86) Novelist, born in Pietermaritzburg, South Africa. She published all her major work while liv-ing in Botswana from the mid-1960s until her death. Each of her first three novels – *When Rain Clouds Gather* (1968), *Maru* (1971), and *A Question of Power* (1974) – set lonely pro-tagonists in a context of political and sexual oppression. Later works, such as *The Collector of Treasures* (1977) and *Serowe: Village of the Rain Wind* (1981), give literary form to Setswana folk tales and oral tradition.

Head, Sir Henry (1861–1940) Neurologist, born in Stamford Hill, N Greater London, England, UK. He studied at Cambridge and University College Hospital, London. His research into the functions and diseases of the nervous system included making observations on the sensory changes in his own arm after cutting some of the nerves to it. He wrote widely on disorders of speech (aphasia) and other neurological disorders, and edited the journal *Brain* (1910–25).

Heal, Sir Ambrose (1872–1959) Furniture designer, born in London, England, UK. He studied at the Slade School of Art, London, and served an apprenticeship as a cabinet maker before joining the family firm in 1893. He began designing furniture influenced by the Arts and Crafts Movement.

Healey (of Riddlesden), Denis (Winston) Healey, Baron (1917–) British statesman, born in Eltham, Kent, SE England, UK. He studied at Oxford, served in N Africa and Italy (1940–5), then became secretary of the Labour Party's international department, and an MP (1952). He was secretary of state for defence in the Wilson govern-ments of 1964–70, and Chancellor of the Exchequer (1974–9). Unsuccessful in the Labour leadership contests of 1976 and 1980, he became deputy leader (1980–3), nar-rowly fighting off a challenge from Tony Benn in 1981, and in 1983 was appointed shadow foreign minister. He resigned from the shadow Cabinet in 1987, and declined to stand in the 1992 elections. He was created a life peer following his retirement later that year. A keen photographer, he published a selection of his work in *Healey's Eye* (1980). >> Benn, Anthony Wedgwood; Wilson, Harold

Healy, Timothy Michael (1855–1931) Irish Nationalist leader, born in Bantry, Co Cork, Ireland. He sat in parliament (1880–1918), headed in 1890 the revolt against Parnell, and became an Independent Nationalist. He was the first Governor-General of the Irish Free State (1922–8). >> Parnell

Heaney, Seamus (Justin) [heenee, shaymus] (1939–) Poet, born on a farm in Co Londonderry. He studied at Belfast, and moved to Dublin in 1976. Early works such as *Death of a Naturalist* (1966) and *Door into the Dark* (1969) established a deep bond between language and the land. Later volumes (*North*, 1975; *Field Work*, 1979; *Station Island*, 1984) extended this to reveal a problematic political dimension, and the more recent *Haw Lantern* (1987) and *Seeing Things* (1991) confirm him as one of the most significant of contemporary English-language poets. His play *The Cure at Troy* (1990) is a version of Sophocles' *Philoctetes*. He became professor of rhetoric and oratory at Harvard in 1985, and professor of poetry at Oxford in 1989. Volumes of selected poems appeared in 1980 and 1990, and his collection *The Spirit Level* in 1996. He was awarded the Nobel Prize for Literature in 1995.

Hearn, (Patricio) Lafcadio (Tessima Carlos) [hern] (1850–1904) Writer and translator, born on the island of Lefkas, Greece. He was raised in Ireland, England, and France, moved to the USA in 1869, settled first in Cincinnati, then in New Orleans as a journalist and French translator. In 1890 Harpers' *New Monthly Magazine* sent him to Japan to write a series of articles. He stayed there for the rest of his life, becoming a teacher, marrying a Japanese woman, Setsuko Koizumi (1891), and taking citizenship there as **Koizumi Yakumo**. He published a series of books that offered the West its first sympathetic view of Japanese culture, notably *Japan: an Attempt at Interpretation* (1904).

Hearne, Samuel [hern] (1745–92) Explorer of N Canada, born in London, England, UK. He served in the Royal Navy, then joined the Hudson's Bay Company, who sent him to Fort Prince of Wales (Churchill) in 1769. He became the first European to travel overland by canoe and sled to the Arctic Ocean by following the Coppermine R north of the Great Slave Lake (1770). In 1774 he set up the first interior trading post for the company at Cumberland House, then became governor of Fort Prince of Wales. He was taken prisoner by the French in 1782, and taken to France, where he was encouraged to publish an account of his travels. Released in 1783, he returned to Canada, but ill health forced him to return to England in 1787.

Hearns, Thomas [hernz], nicknames **Hit Man** and **Motor City Cobra** (1958–) Boxer, born in Memphis, TN. In 1988 he became the first man to win world titles at four and five different weights, and in 1991 the first to win titles at six different weights: he defeated Pipino Cuevas for the welterweight title (WBA, 1980), Wilfred Benitez for the super-welterweight (WBC, 1982), Roberto Duran for the vacant WBA junior-middleweight title (1984), Dennis Andries for the light-heavyweight (WBC, 1987), Juan Roldan for the middleweight (WBC, 1987), James Kinchen for the super-middleweight (WBO, 1988), and Virgil Hill for the light-heavyweight (WBA, 1991).

Hearst, Patty, popular name of **Patricia (Campbell) Hearst**, married name **Shaw** (1954–) Heiress to William Randolph Hearst's empire, born in San Francisco, CA. The daughter of newspaper tycoon Randolph Hearst (d.1993), she was kidnapped in 1974 by the radical Symbionese Liberation Army. After brainwashing, she assumed the name 'Tania' and joined in their bank robberies. She was captured in 1975, tried, and sentenced to prison in 1976. Paroled in 1979, she married her former bodyguard and wrote an autobiography, *Every Secret Thing* (1982). >> Hearst, William Randolph

Hearst, William Randolph (1863–1951) Newspaper publisher, born in San Francisco, CA. He studied at Harvard, then took over the *San Francisco Examiner* in 1887 from his father. He acquired the *New York Morning Journal* (1895), and launched the *Evening Journal* in 1896. He sensationalized journalism by the introduction of banner headlines and lavish illustrations. Believed by many to have initiated the Spanish–American War of 1898 to encourage sales of his newspaper, he also advocated political assassination in an editorial just months before the assassination of President McKinley. A member of the US House of Representatives (1903–7), he failed in attempts to become mayor and governor of New York. His national chain of newspapers and periodicals grew to include the *Chicago Examiner*, *Boston American*, *Cosmopolitan*, and *Harper's Bazaar*. His life inspired the Orson Welles film *Citizen Kane* (1941). >> Hearst, Patty; McKinley

Heartfield, John, originally **Helmut Herzfelde** (1891–1968) German photomonteur and painter. Together with George Grosz, he was a leading member of the Berlin Dada group in the aftermath of World War 1, producing satirical collages from pasted, superimposed photographs cut from magazines. A lifelong pacifist and staunch Communist, he moved to East Berlin in 1950, and anglicized his name as a gesture of sympathy with America. >> Grosz, George

Heath, Sir Edward (Richard George), known as **Ted Heath** (1916–) British statesman and prime minister (1970–4), born in Broadstairs, Kent, SE England, UK. He studied at Oxford, served in the Royal Artillery in World War 2, and became an MP in 1950. Following a career in the Whip's office (1951–9), he was minister of labour (1959–60), then Lord Privy Seal (1960–3) and the chief negotiator for Britain's entry into the European Economic Community. Elected Leader of the Conservative Party in 1965, he was Leader of the Opposition until his 1970 victory. After a confrontation with the miners' union in 1973, he narrowly lost the two elections of 1974, and in 1975 was replaced as Leader by Mrs Thatcher. He is known for his interests in yachting, having won the 1969 Hobart Ocean race and captained the British entry in the Admiral's Cup races of 1971 and 1979. He is also an accomplished musician, giving organ recitals and conducting at charity concerts. He has continued to play an active part in politics. >> Thatcher; RR1095

Heathcoat, John (1783–1861) Inventor, born in Duffield, Derbyshire, C England, UK. He designed a machine for making lace (patented in 1809), and set up a factory in Nottingham which was destroyed in 1816 by the Luddites. He then moved his business to Tiverton in Devon, installing greatly improved machines. He also invented machinery to make ribbon and net, and devised methods of winding raw silk from cocoons. He later became MP for Tiverton (1832–59).

Heathcoat-Amory, Derick >> **Amory, Derick Heathcoat**

Heaviside, Oliver [heveesiyd] (1850–1925) Physicist, born in London, England, UK. A telegrapher by training, he had to retire because of deafness in 1874, and spent much of his life investigating electricity. He predicted the existence of an ionized gaseous layer (the ionosphere) capable of reflecting radio waves, at the same time as, but independently of, the American Arthur E Kennelly, and made important contributions to the theory of electrical communications. >> Kennelly

Hebb, Donald (Olding) (1904–85) Psychologist, born in Chester, Nova Scotia, Canada. He spent most of his academic career at McGill University, Montreal, where he became an influential theorist concerned with the relation between the brain and behaviour. His most important book *The Organization of Behavior* (1949), was influential in the development of connectionism.

Hebbel, (Christian) Friedrich (1813–63) Playwright, born in Wesselburen, Germany. He studied in Hamburg from 1835, and after stays in Heidelberg, Munich, and Copenhagen, settled in Vienna (1846). His only contemporary play is *Maria Magdalena* (1844), his favourite settings being of a legendary, historical, or biblical character, as in *Herodes und Marianne* (1850) and his masterpiece, the *Nibelungen* trilogy (1862). He constantly portrayed the inherent Hegelian conflict between individuality and humanity as a whole. >> Hegel

Hébert, Jacques René [aybair] (1757–94) French revolutionary extremist who represented the aspirations of the sans-culottes, born in Alençon, France. He became a popular political journalist, assumed the pseudonym **le Père Duchesne** after launching a satirical newspaper of that name (1790), and joined both the Cordelier and Jacobin Clubs. He became a member of the Revolutionary Council, playing a major part in the September Massacres and the overthrow of the monarchy. After denouncing the Committee of Public Safety for its failure to help the poor, he tried to incite a popular uprising, but having incurred the suspicion of Danton and Robespierre, he and 17 of his followers (*Hébertists*) were guillotined. >> Danton; Robespierre; Saint-Just

Hecataeus of Miletus [hekateeus, miyleetus] (fl.6th–5th-c BC) Pioneer Greek historian and geographer. He is known for two works. *Genealogies* (or *Histories*), of which just a few fragments survive, is referred to by Herodotos. *Tour of the World*, of which a larger number of fragments remain, is divided into two parts, Europe and Asia, and describes local customs and curiosities. >> Herodotos

Hecht, Ben (1894–1964) Newspaperman, novelist, and playwright, born in New York City. He worked as a reporter for the *Chicago Journal* (1910–14), then the *Chicago Daily News*, from where he was expelled on the publication of his novel *Fantazius Mallare* (1922), which was attacked on grounds of obscenity. He wrote (often with Charles MacArthur) a number of successful film scripts, including *The Scoundrel* (1935), *Gunga Din* (1938), *Spellbound* (1945), and *Notorious* (1946). His columns written for the New York newspaper *PM* were collected in *1001 Afternoons in New York* (1941).

Heckel, Erich (1883–1970) Painter, born in Döbeln, Germany. He studied architecture at Dresden before turning to painting. He excelled in lithography and the woodcut, as in his *Self-portrait* (1917, Munich). Vilified by the Nazis, he stayed in Berlin and was professor at Karlsruhe (1949–56). He is best known for his paintings of nudes and landscapes, and as a founder member of the Expressionist school, *Die Brücke* ('the Bridge'). >> Kirchner; Schmidt-Rottluff

Heckel, Johann Adam (c. 1812–77) Woodwind instrument maker, born in Germany. In 1831 he established his own workshop near Wiesbaden, and introduced improvements in the structure and key-system of bassoons, which, when standardized, differentiated the German from the French type. His son, **Wilhelm** (1856–1909), and grandsons, **Wilhelm Hermann** (1879–1952) and **August** (1880–1914), carried on the business, which introduced several instrumental novelties, such as the *Heckelphone* (1903).

Hecker, Isaac Thomas (1819–88) Roman Catholic priest, born in New York City. He studied in Europe, became a Catholic in 1844, and was ordained in England as a Redemptorist priest in 1849. Claiming new freedom, he was expelled from that order, but then founded the Paulist Fathers. He greatly extended Catholicism in America, though his tendency to democratize Catholicism created much controversy.

Hedin, Sven Anders [haydeen] (1865–1952) Explorer and geographer, born in Stockholm. He went to Persia as a tutor (1885), and was attached to a Swedish–Norwegian embassy to the Shah in 1890. He made many journeys into uncharted areas, particularly in the Himalayas (1893–8), the Gobi Desert (1899–1902), and Tibet, of which he made the first detailed map (1908). After World War 1 he organized and led the Sino–Swedish Scientific Expedition to the NW provinces of China (1927–33). A gifted writer, his accounts of his journeys achieved much popularity.

Hedley, William (1779–1843) Inventor, born in Newburn, Tyne and Wear, NE England, UK. A colliery official, he patented a design for a railway traction engine using smooth wheels on smooth rails. His locomotive was known as *Puffing Billy*, and was the first commercial steam locomotive, hauling coal trucks a distance of about 5 mi from the mine at Wylam to the dockside at Lemington-on-Tyne.

Hedren, Tippi, originally **Nathalie Hedren** (1935–) Film actress, born in New Ulm, MI. She was discovered by Alfred Hitchcock, who cast her in *The Birds* (1963) and *Marnie* (1964). Later films include *Roar* (1981), which she also produced, *Deadly Spygames* (1989), and *Citizen Ruth* (1996), and she has appeared in several television movies, including *Birds 2: The Land's End* (1994). She now runs an animal preserve near Los Angeles, called The Roar Foundation. She is the mother of Melanie Griffith. >> Griffith

Heemskerck, Maerten van (1498–1574) Portrait and religious painter, born in Heemskerck, The Netherlands. By c.1528 he was working in Haarlem with the Italianate painter Jan van Scorel. Following his lead, van Heemskerck also travelled to Rome (1532–5) where he was greatly attracted to the work of Michelangelo and Raphael. While in Rome he also studied antiquities, and his surviving sketchbooks supply a vivid account of the ancient monuments of the city as they appeared in the 16th-c. >> Michelangelo; Raphael; Scorel

Heenan, John >> **Sayers, Tom**

Heenan, John Carmel (1905–75) Roman Catholic Archbishop of Westminster (1963–75), born in Ilford, E Greater London, England, UK. Educated at Ushaw and the English College, Rome, he was ordained in 1930, became a parish priest in E London, and during World War 2 worked with the BBC, when he was known as the 'Radio Priest'. He became Bishop of Leeds in 1951, Archibishop of Liverpool in 1957, and Archbishop of Westminster in 1963. A convinced ecumenist, he was created a cardinal in 1975.

Heezen, Bruce (Charles) (1924–77) Oceanographer, born in Vinton, IA. He studied at Iowa and Columbia universities. In 1952 he became the first to show the existence and importance of ocean turbidity currents, using the records of failure of the many Atlantic communications cables during the 1929 earthquake. In 1957, with William Ewing, he went on to demonstrate that mid-ocean ridges have a central rift. >> Ewing, William

Heffer, Eric (Samuel) (1922–91) British politician. He worked as a carpenter-joiner until he entered the House of Commons, representing Walton, Liverpool, in 1964. He had joined the Labour Party as a youth, and became Liverpool president (1959–60) and a Liverpool city councillor (1960–6). A traditional Socialist, favouring public ownership, and strongly unilateralist, he distrusted centrist tendencies and had a brief, uncomfortable period as a junior minister (1974–5). He unsuccessfully challenged Roy Hattersley for the deputy leadership in 1988. >> Hattersley

Hefner, Hugh (Marston) (1926–) Editor and publisher of *Playboy* magazine, born in Chicago, IL. He grew up in a family of strict Methodists, studied at Illinois University, and had a variety of jobs. He worked in the subscriptions department of *Esquire* magazine until 1952, when he resigned to start a new magazine. Investing $10 000, he published *Playboy* in 1953, with Marilyn Monroe posing nude. Practical advice on sexual problems, men's talk, and other articles combined to make the magazine a notorious success, and Hefner a conspicuously wealthy man, frequently photographed at his mansion surrounded by a bevy of 'playmates'. His *Playboy* empire extended into real estate, nightclubs (with the 'bunny-girl' hostesses), and sundry products.

Hegel, Georg Wilhelm Friedrich [haygl] (1770–1831) Idealist philosopher, born in Stuttgart, Germany. He studied theology at Tübingen, and in 1801 edited with Schelling the *Kritische Journal der Philosophie* (1802–3, Critical Journal of Philosophy), in which he outlined his system with its emphasis on reason rather than the Romantic intuitionism of Schelling, which he attacked in his first major work, *Phänomenologie des Geistes* (1807, The Phenomenology of the Mind). While headmaster of a Nuremberg school (1808–16) he wrote his *Wissenschaft der Logik* (1812–16, Science of Logic). He then published his *Enzyklopädie der philosophischen Wissenschaften* (1817, trans Encyclopedia of the Philosophical Sciences), in which he set out his tripartite system of logic, philosophy of nature, and mind. He became professor in Heidelberg (1816) and Berlin (1818). His approach, influenced by Kant, rejects the reality of finite and separate objects and minds in space and time, and establishes an underlying, all embracing unity, the Absolute. The quest for greater unity and truth is achieved by the famous dialectic, positing something (*thesis*), denying it (*antithesis*), and combining the two half-truths in a *synthesis* which contains a greater portion of truth in its complexity. His works exerted considerable influence on subsequent European and American philosophy. >> Kant; Schelling

Heidegger, Martin [hiydeger] (1889–1976) Philosopher, born in Messkirch, Germany. He became professor of philosophy at Marburg (1923–8) and Freiburg (1929–45), when he was retired for his connections with the Nazi regime. In his incomplete main work, *Sein und Zeit* (1927, Being and Time), he presents an exhaustive ontological classification of 'being', through the synthesis of the modes of human existence. He disclaimed the title of Existentialist, since he was not only concerned with personal existence and ethical choices but primarily with the ontological problem in general. Nevertheless, he was a key influence in Sartre's Existentialism. >> Sartre

Heifetz, Jascha [hiyfets] (1901–87) Violinist, born in Vilna, Lithuania. He studied violin from the age of three, at nine entered St Petersburg Conservatory, and at 12 toured Russia, Germany, and Scandinavia. After the Russian Revolution he settled in the USA, becoming a US citizen in 1925. He first appeared in Britain in 1920. Among works commissioned by him from leading composers is Walton's violin concerto. >> Walton, William

Heine, (Christian Johann) Heinrich [hiynuh] (1797–1856) Poet and essayist, born in Düsseldorf, Germany, of Jewish parentage. He studied banking and law, and in 1821 began to publish poetry, establishing his reputation with his four-volume *Reisebilder* (1826–7, 1830–1, Pictures of Travel) and *Das Buch der Lieder* (1827, The Book of Songs). In 1825 he became a Christian to secure rights of German citizenship, but this alienated his own people, and his revolutionary opinions made him unemployable in Germany. Going into voluntary exile in Paris after the 1830 revolution, he turned from poetry to politics, and became leader of the cosmopolitan democratic movement, writing widely on French and German culture.

Heinemann, Gustav [hiynuhman] (1899–1976) West German statesman and president (1969–74), born in Schwelm, Germany. He studied at Marburg and Münster, practised as an advocate from 1926, and lectured on law at Cologne (1933–9). After the war he was a founder of the Christian Democratic Union, and was minister of the interior in Adenauer's government (1949–50), resigning over a fundamental difference over defence policy. Heinemann, a pacifist, opposed Germany's re-armament. He formed his own Neutralist Party, but later joined the Social Democratic Party, was elected to the Bundestag (1957) and was minister of justice in Kiesinger's 'Grand Coalition' government from 1966. >> Kiesinger

Heinemann, William [hiynuhman] (1863–1920) Publisher, born in Surbiton, SW Greater London, England, UK. He founded his publishing house in London in 1890, and established its reputation with the works of Stevenson, Kipling, H G Wells, Galsworthy, Somerset Maugham, and Priestley, as well as publishing translations of major works from mainland European authors.

Heinkel, Ernst (Heinrich) [hiyngkel] (1888–1958) Aircraft engineer, born in Grunbach, Germany. He was chief designer of the Albatros Aircraft Company in Berlin before World War 1. He founded the Heinkel-Flugzeugwerke at Warnemünde (1922), making at first seaplanes, and later bombers and fighters which achieved fame in World War 2. He built the first jet plane, the HE-178, in 1939, and also the first rocket-powered aircraft, the HE-176.

Heinz, H(enry) J(ohn) [hiynts] (1844–1919) Food manufacturer, born in Pittsburgh, PA. At age eight he peddled produce from the family garden, at 16 employed others to tend and sell his produce, and in 1876 became co-founder, with his brother and cousin, of F & J Heinz. The business was reorganized as H J Heinz Co in 1888, and he became its president (1905–19). He invented the advertising slogan '57 Varieties' in 1896, promoted the pure food movement in the USA, and was a pioneer in staff welfare work.

Heinze, Sir Bernard Thomas [hiynz] (1894–1982) Conductor and teacher, born in Shepparton, Victoria, Australia. He studied at Melbourne University, at the Royal College of Music, London, in Paris, and Berlin. He was professor of music at Melbourne University (1925–56), and director of the New South Wales Conservatory (1956–66). He was also conductor of the Melbourne Symphony Orchestra (1933–49), and recorded with several other orchestras. From 1932 he was music adviser to the Australian Broadcasting Corporation, with whom he was instrumental in founding symphony orchestras in each Australian state.

Heisei >> Akihito

Heisenberg, Werner (Karl) [hiyznberg] (1901–76) Theoretical physicist, born in Würzburg, Germany. He studied at Munich and Göttingen. After a brief period working with Max Born (1923) and Niels Bohr (1924–7), he became professor of physics at Leipzig (1927–41), director of the Kaiser Wilhelm Institute in Berlin (1941–5), and director of the Max Planck Institute at Göttingen (and from 1958 at Munich). He developed a method of expressing quantum mechanics in matrices (1925), and formulated his revolutionary principle of indeterminacy (the *uncertainty principle*) in 1927. He was awarded the 1932 Nobel Prize for Physics. >> Bohr, Niels; Born

Held, Al (1928–) Painter, born in New York City. He studied at the Art Students' League in New York and in Paris, then returned to New York, and during the 1950s painted in the Abstract Expressionist manner. From 1960 he adopted a more geometric style, painting complex cube-like structures with heavy impasto paint. In the 1980s he turned to acrylic paints, rendering precise and brightly coloured geometric forms in a deep perspectival space.

Helena, St (c. 255–c. 330) Mother of the Roman Emperor Constantine (the Great), born in Bithynia, Asia Minor. The wife of Emperor Constantius Chlorus, she early became a Christian, and when Constantine became emperor he made her empress dowager. In 326, according to tradition, she visited Jerusalem, and founded the basilicas on the Mt of Olives and at Bethlehem. Feast day 18 August (W), 21 May (E). >> Constantius Chlorus; Constantine I (Emperor)

Helfgott, David [**helf**got] (1947–) Pianist, born in Australia. After many competition successes as a child, in 1966 he obtained a place at the Royal College of Music, London, where he is remembered for his acclaimed performance of Rachmaninov's third piano concerto in 1969. Following a nervous breakdown, he spent the next few years in psychiatric hospitals in England and Australia. Since leaving institutional care in 1975, and especially following his marriage in 1984, he has come to cope with a serious mood disorder which has left him with a rapid and repetitive interactional style of speech, and a distinctive mode of playing which is often accompanied by highly audible vocalization. His life-story was dramatized in the film *Shine* (1995). His world tour in 1997 received a generally cool reception from music critics, but the concerts were given sell-out support and enthusiasm from the general public.

Helga, St >> Olga, St

Heliodorus [helio**daw**rus] (fl.3rd-c) Greek romance writer and Sophist, born in Emesa in Syria. One of the earliest Greek novelists, he was the author of *Aethiopica*, which narrates in poetic prose the loves of Theagenes and Chariclea.

Heliogabalus [helioh**gab**alus], divine name of **Caesar Marcus Aurelius Antonius Augustus**, originally **Varius Avitus Bassianus** (204–222) Roman emperor, born in Emesa, Syria. As a child he was appointed high priest of the Syro-Phoenician Sun-god Elagabal, and he assumed the name of that deity. In 218, he was proclaimed emperor by the soldiers. He defeated his rival Macrinus on the borders of Syria and Phoenicia. His brief reign was marked by extravagant homosexual orgies and intolerant promotion of the god Baal. He was murdered by the praetorians in a palace revolution. >> RR1084

Heller, Joseph (1923–) Novelist, born in New York City. He served in the US Army Air Force in World War 2, and studied at New York, Columbia, and Oxford universities. His wartime experience forms the background for his first book, *Catch 22* (1961), which launched him as a successful novelist. The anti-war plot centred on the view that US airmen on dangerous combat missions must be considered insane, but if they seek to be relieved on grounds of mental derangement, they find themselves ineligible, since such a request proves their sanity. Hence 'Catch 22' has come to signify any logical trap or double bind. A sequel, *Closing Time*, appeared in 1994. His other works include *Something Happened* (1974), *God Knows* (1984), and *Picture This* (1988).

Hellman, Lillian (Florence) (1907–84) Playwright, born in New Orleans, LA. She studied at New York and Columbia universities, worked for the New York *Herald Tribune* as a reviewer (1925–8), and read plays for MGM in Hollywood (1927–32). She lived for many years with the detective writer Dashiell Hammett, who encouraged her writing. She had her first stage success with *The Children's Hour* (1934), a controversial play which ran on Broadway for 86 weeks. This was followed by *Days to Come* (1936) and *The Little Foxes* (1939), which was later adapted into a film starring Bette Davis. A left-wing activist, her voice was one of the most persuasive in the modern US theatre. Her autobiographical works include *An Unfinished Woman* (1969) and *Pentimento* (1973). >> Hammett

Helmholtz, Hermann von (1821–94) Physiologist and physicist, born in Potsdam, Germany. He was successively professor of physiology at Königsberg (1849), Bonn (1855), and Heidelberg (1858), and in 1871 became professor of physics in Berlin. He was equally distinguished in physiology, mathematics, and experimental and mathematical physics. His physiological works are principally connected with the eye, the ear, and the nervous system. His work on vision is regarded as fundamental to modern visual science. He invented an ophthalmoscope (1850) independently of Charles Babbage. He is best known for his statement of the law of the conservation of energy, which was more precise and wide-ranging than previous attempts, and well supported with examples of its application. >> Babbage; Wien

Helmont, Jan Baptista van (1579–1644) Chemist, born in Brussels. He studied medicine, mysticism, and chemistry under the influence of Paracelsus, devoting much study to gases, and invented the term *gas*. He was the first to take the melting-point of ice and the boiling-point of water as standards for temperature. Through his experiments he bridged the gap between alchemy and chemistry. >> Paracelsus

Helms, Richard (McGarrah) (1913–) Intelligence officer, born in Pennsylvania. He studied in Switzerland and in the USA at Williams College, becoming a journalist, then joining the US navy in 1942. After World War 2 he joined the newly formed Central Intelligence Agency (CIA), and rose to become the organization's director in 1966. He was dismissed by President Nixon in 1973, and appointed ambassador to Iran (1973–6). In 1977 he was convicted of lying before a congressional committee, but argued that his oath as head of the intelligence service required him to keep secrets from the public. >> Nixon

Héloïse >> Abelard, Peter

Helpmann, Sir Robert (Murray) (1909–86) Dancer, actor, and choreographer, born in Mount Gambier, South Australia, Australia. He made his debut in Adelaide in 1923, studied with Pavlova's touring company in 1929, and in 1931 moved to Britain to study under Ninette de Valois. He was first dancer of the newly founded Sadler's Wells Ballet (1933–50), and became known for his dramatic roles in de Valois' works. His ballets include *Hamlet* (1942) and *Miracle in the Gorbals* (1944), and he also appeared in many films. Joint artistic director of Australian ballet in 1965, he was knighted in 1968. >> Pavlova; Valois

Helst, Bartholomaeus van der (1613–70) Painter, born in Haarlem, The Netherlands. He was joint founder in 1653 of the painters' guild of St Luke at Amsterdam, where he flourished as a portrait painter in the manner of Frans Hals. >> Hals

Helvétius, Claude-Adrien [elvay**syus**] (1715–71) Philosopher, born in Paris. He trained for a financial career, and in 1738 was appointed to the lucrative office of farmer-general. In 1751 he withdrew from public life to the family estate at Voré, where he spent the rest of his life in philosophy, and as host to the Philosophes, a group of French thinkers. In 1758 he published the controversial *De l'esprit*, advancing the view that sensation is the source of all intellectual activity and that self-interest is the motive force of all human action. The book was promptly denounced by the Sorbonne and condemned by the parliament of Paris to be publicly burnt. As a result it was widely read, translated into all the main European languages and, together with his posthumous *De l'homme* (1772), greatly influenced Bentham and the British utilitarians. >> Bentham, Jeremy

Hemans, Felicia Dorothea [hemanz], *née* **Browne** (1793–1835) Poet, born in Liverpool, Merseyside, NW England, UK. She produced a large number of books of verse of all kinds – love lyrics, classical, mythological, sentimental – including *The Siege of Valencia* (1823) and *Records of Women* (1828). She is perhaps best remembered for the poem 'Casabianca', better known as 'The boy stood on the burning deck'.

Hemingway, Ernest (Miller) (1899–1961) Novelist and short-story writer, born in Oak Park, IL. He worked as a reporter for *The Kansas City Star*, served with an ambulance unit in World War 1, was wounded in 1918, and was decorated for heroism. His first important work was a collection of short stories, *In Our Time* (1925), and success came with his novel, *The Sun Also Rises* (1926), inspired by his experience as one of the 'lost generation' of young expatriates in France and Spain after World War 1. Obsessed with war, big-game hunting, and bullfighting, his works include *A Farewell to Arms* (1929), *Death in the Afternoon* (1932), *For Whom the Bell Tolls* (1940), and *The Old Man and the Sea* (1952, Pulitzer). In 1954 he was awarded the Nobel Prize for Literature. A war correspondent in World War 2, he took part in the D-Day landings (1944), and after the Spanish Civil War lived in Cuba, staying there until the 1960 revolution, when he moved to the USA. Married four times, he was subject to depression, and fearing ill health he took his own life with a shotgun.

Hench, Philip (Showalter) (1896–1965) Physician, born in Pittsburgh, PA. He studied at Pittsburgh University, and became head of the department of rheumatics at the Mayo Clinic (Rochester) from 1926, and professor of medicine at Minnesota University from 1947. In 1948 he discovered with Edward C Kendall the use of an adrenal hormone (cortisone) in alleviating the symptoms of rheumatoid arthritis, for which they shared the Nobel Prize for Physiology or Medicine in 1950. >> Kendall, Edward C

Henderson, Fletcher (1897–1952) Pianist, arranger, and jazz bandleader, born in Cuthbert, GA. He graduated in chemistry from Atlanta University, and moved to New York City in 1920 to continue his studies, but was diverted into a musical career, starting as house pianist for publishing and recording companies. In 1924 he put together a big band for what was supposed to be a temporary engagement, but stayed at the head of the orchestra until the mid-1930s, attracting the finest instrumentalists and arrangers of the time. His own orchestrations, and those of Don Redman, set the standard for the swing era. >> Allen, Red; Redman

Henderson, Mary >> **Bridie, James**

Hendrix, Jimi, popular name of **James Marshall Hendrix** (1942–70) Rock guitarist, singer, and songwriter, born in Seattle, WA. He taught himself guitar, and played lead for several rhythm and blues artists. Discovered by Chas Chandler (1938–), who took him to London, he formed the Jimi Hendrix Experience, with Noel Redding (1945–) and Mitch Mitchell (1947–). The band's first single, 'Hey Joe', was an immediate British success, and his adventurous first album, *Are You Experienced?*, was an unexpected international success which paved the way for other psychedelic and experimental rock acts. He died after taking barbiturates and alcohol.

Hendry, Stephen (Gordon) (1969–) Snooker player, born in Edinburgh. He became a professional in 1985, won the Scottish championship in 1986, and went on to dominate the game in the 1990s. By 1997 he had won over 60 major titles worldwide, including six Embassy world championships (1990, 1992–6). He holds the record for the most titles won in a season (9 in 1991–2).

Hengist and **Horsa** Brothers, leaders of the first Anglo-Saxon settlers in Britain, said by Bede to have been invited over by Vortigern, the British king, to fight the Picts in about AD 450. According to the *Anglo-Saxon Chronicle*, Horsa was killed in 455, and Hengist ruled in Kent until his death in 488. >> Vortigern

Henie, Sonja [henee] (1912–69) Ice-skater, born in Oslo. After winning the gold medal in figure-skating at the Olympics of 1928, 1932, and 1936, she turned professional and starred in touring ice-shows. She later went to Hollywood, where she made several films. >> RR1162

Henle, Friedrich Gustav Jakob [henluh] (1809–85) Anatomist and pathologist, born in Fürth, Germany. He studied at Bonn and Berlin, and held professorships at Zürich (1840–4), Heidelberg (1844–52), and Göttingen (1852–85). He was a major influence in the development of histology, his *Allgemeine Anatomie* (1841, Comprehensive Anatomy) being the first systematic treatise of the subject. His *Handbuch der rationellen Pathologie* (1846–53, Handbook of Rational Pathology) marks the beginning of modern pathology. As early as 1840 he was claiming that contagious diseases were caused by parasitic organisms, a theory later proved by one of his students from Göttingen, Robert Koch. >> Koch, Robert

Henlein, Konrad [henliyn] (1898–1945) German politician, born near Liberec, Czech Republic. He was the leader in the agitation on the eve of World War 2 leading in 1938 to Germany's seizure of Sudetenland from Czechoslovakia, and in 1939 to the institution of the German protectorate of Bohemia and Moravia and the dissolution of Czechoslovakia. Gauleiter of Sudetenland (1938) and civil commissioner for Bohemia (1939–45), on Germany's subsequent defeat in the war he committed suicide when in US hands.

Henley, William Ernest (1849–1903) Poet, playwright, critic, and editor, born in Gloucester, Gloucestershire, SWC England, UK. Crippled by tuberculosis as a boy, he spent nearly two years in Edinburgh Infirmary (1873–5), where he had a leg amputated, and wrote *A Book of Verses* (1888) which won him the friendship of R L Stevenson (who used him as a model for Long John Silver in *Treasure Island*). He was a pungent critic, and successfully edited the *Magazine of Art* (1882–6) and the *Scots Observer* (1889), which he renamed the *National Observer*. He was joint compiler of a dictionary of slang (1894–1904), and published several books of verse, including *In Hospital* (1875), which contains his best-known poem, 'Invictus'. >> Stevenson, Robert Louis

Henman, Tim (1974–) Tennis player, born in Oxford, Oxfordshire, SC England, UK. He turned professional in 1993, and his achievements include the British National Championships (singles and men's doubles, 1995–6, singles 1996), an Olympic silver medal in the men's doubles (1996), and the Association of Tennis Professionals Tour title at Sydney (1997). He had become Britain's number one player by early 1997, and reached the singles quarter-finals round at Wimbledon later that year. By the end of August he had reached 21st position in the world listings, but had dropped to second in Britain, behind Greg Rusedski. >> Rusedski

Hennebique, François [onuhbeek] (1842–1921) Civil engineer, born in Neuville-Saint-Vaast, France. He introduced the use of reinforced concrete for the building industry, commencing with flooring slabs in 1879, and progressing to a whole system which he patented in 1892. He built the first reinforced concrete bridge at Viggen in Switzerland in 1894, the first grain elevator at Roubaix in 1895, and the first multi-storey reinforced concrete framed building in Britain, Weaver's Mill at Swansea, in 1898.

Henri (French kings) >> see under **Henry**

Henri, Robert [henree] (1865–1929) Realist painter, born in Cincinnati, OH. He studied at the Pennsylvania Academy and at the Ecole des Beaux Arts in Paris. On his return to Philadelphia he taught at the Women's School of Design (1891–6), and became an ardent advocate of Realism in art, beginning a movement which, in the first decade of the 20th-c, came to be known as the Ashcan school. In 1898 he began teaching at the New York School of Art, in 1908 established his own influential art school in New York City, and formed the group known as 'The Eight'. >> Bellows; Sloan, John

Henrietta Anne, Duchess of Orléans (1644–70) Youngest daughter of Charles I of Great Britain and Henrietta Maria, and sister of Charles II, born in Exeter, Devon, SW England, UK, while the English civil wars were still at their height. Brought up by her mother in France, she married Louis XIV's homosexual brother Philippe, but was also rumoured to have been for a time the mistress of the French king himself. She played an important part in the negotiations of the Secret Treaty of Dover (1670) between Charles and Louis. There were strong rumours that her subsequent death was caused by poison, although it was more probably a case of a ruptured appendix. >> Charles I (of England); Charles II (of England); Henrietta Maria

Henrietta Maria (1609–69) Queen consort of Charles I of England, born in Paris, France, the youngest child of Henry IV of France. She married Charles in 1625, but her French attendants and Roman Catholic beliefs made her unpopular. In 1642, under the threat of impeachment, she fled to Holland and raised funds for the Royalist cause. A year later she landed at Bridlington, and met Charles near Edgehill. At Exeter she gave birth to Henrietta Anne, and a fortnight later she was compelled to flee to France (1644). She paid two visits to England after the Restoration (1660–1, 1662–5), and spent her remaining years in France. >> Charles I (of England); Charles II (of England); Henrietta Anne; Henry IV (of France); James II (of England)

Henry I (of England) (1068–1135) King of England (1100–35) and Duke of Normandy (1106–35), the youngest son of William the Conqueror. Under Henry, the Norman empire attained the height of its power. He conquered Normandy from his brother, Robert Curthose, at the Battle of Tinchebrai (1106), maintained his position on the European mainland, and exercised varying degrees of authority over the King of Scots, the Welsh princes, the Duke of Brittany, and the Counts of Flanders, Boulogne, and Ponthieu. His government of England and Normandy became increasingly centralized and interventionist, with the overriding aim of financing warfare and alliances, and consolidating the unity of the two countries as a single cross-Channel state. His only legitimate son, **William Adelin**, was drowned in 1120, and in 1127 he nominated his daughter Empress **Matilda**, widow of Emperor Henry V of Germany, as his heir for both England and Normandy. But Matilda and her second husband, Geoffrey of Anjou, proved unacceptable to the king's leading subjects. After Henry's death at Lyons-la-Forêt, near Rouen, the crown was seized by Stephen, son of his sister, Adela. >> Matilda; Stephen; William I (of England); RR1095

Henry II (of England) (1133–89) King of England (1154–89), born in Le Mans, France, the son of Empress Matilda, Henry I's daughter and acknowledged heir, by her second husband, Geoffrey of Anjou. Already established as Duke of Normandy (1150) and Count of Anjou (1151), and as Duke of Aquitaine by marriage to Eleanor of Aquitaine (1152), he invaded England in 1153, and was recognized as the lawful successor of the usurper, Stephen. He founded the Angevin or Plantagenet dynasty of English kings, and ruled England as part of a wider Angevin empire. He restored and transformed English governance after the disorders of Stephen's reign. His efforts to restrict clerical independence caused conflict with his former Chancellor Thomas à Becket, Archbishop of Canterbury, which was ended only with Becket's murder (1170). He led a major expedition to Ireland (1171), which resulted in its annexation. The most serious challenge to his power came in 1173–4, when his son, the young Henry, encouraged by Eleanor, rebelled in alliance with Louis VII of France, William I of Scotland, and Count Philip of Flanders. All parts of the king's dominions were threatened, but his enemies were defeated. In 1189 he faced futher disloyalty from his sons, John and Richard, allied with Philip II of France, who overran Maine and Touraine. Henry agreed a peace which recognized Richard as his sole heir for the Angevin empire, and he died shortly afterwards. >> Becket; Eleanor of Aquitaine; John; Matilda; Richard I; Theobald; RR1095

Henry II (of France) (1519–59) King of France (1547–69), born near Paris, the second son of Francis I. In 1533 he married Catherine de' Medici. Soon after his accession, he began to oppress his Protestant subjects. Through the influence of the Guises he formed an alliance with Scotland, and declared war against England, which ended in 1558 with the taking of Calais. He continued the long-standing war against the Emperor Charles V, gaining Toul, Metz, and Verdun, but suffered reverses in Italy and the Low Countries, which led to the Treaty of Cateau-Cambrésis (1559). >> Catherine de' Medici; Diane de France; Francis I; Guise, Francis; RR1049

Henry III (of England) (1207–72) King of England (1216–72), the elder son and successor, at the age of nine, of John. He declared an end to his minority in 1227, and in 1232 stripped the justiciar, Hubert de Burgh, of power. His arbitrary assertion of royal rights conflicted with the principles of Magna Carta, and antagonized many nobles. Although he failed to recover Poitou (N Aquitaine) in 1242, he accepted for his son Edmund the Kingdom of Sicily (1254), then occupied by the Hohenstaufens. This forced him to seek the support of the barons who, under the leadership of the king's brother-in-law, Simon de Montfort, imposed far-reaching reforms by the Provisions of Oxford (1258), which gave them a definite say in government. When Henry sought to restore royal power, the barons rebelled and captured the king at Lewes (1264), but were defeated at Evesham (1265). The Dictum of Kenilworth (1266), though favourable to Henry, urged him to observe Magna Carta. Organized resistance ended in 1267, and the rest of the reign was stable. He was succeeded by his elder son, Edward I. >> Burgh; Montfort, Simon de (Earl of Leicester); RR1095

Henry III (of France) (1551–89) King of France (1574–89), born in Fontainebleau, the third son of Henry II. In 1569 he gained victories over the Huguenots, and took an active share in the massacre of St Bartholomew (1572). In 1573 he was elected to the crown of Poland, but two years later succeeded his brother, Charles IX, on the French throne. His reign was a period of almost incessant civil war between Huguenots and Catholics. In 1588 he engineered the assassination of the Duke of Guise, enraging the Catholic League. He joined forces with the Huguenot Henry of Navarre, and while marching on Paris was assassinated by a fanatical priest. The last of the Valois line, he named Henry of Navarre as his successor. >> Charles IX; Henry II; Henry IV (of France); RR1049

Henry IV (Emperor) (1050–1106) Holy Roman Emperor (1084–1106). He was crowned King of Germany while still an infant (1053), under the regency of his mother. He came of age in 1066, and began to assert his own authority soon afterwards. Twice excommunicated (1076, 1080) by Pope Gregory VII, he attacked Rome and installed an antipope (Clementine III) and had himself proclaimed emperor. Meanwhile, his son Conrad had been elected king in Germany and rebelled unsuccessfully against him. Conrad was replaced by Henry's second son, Henry V, who promptly imprisoned his father and forced him to abdicate. >> Gregory VII; RR1057

Henry IV (of England), originally **Henry Bolingbroke** (1366–1413) King of England (1399–1413), the first king of the House of Lancaster, the son of John of Gaunt. He was surnamed Bolingbroke from his birthplace in Lincolnshire. In 1397 he supported Richard II against the Duke of Gloucester, and was created Duke of Hereford, but was banished in 1398. After landing at Ravenspur, Yorkshire, Henry induced Richard, now deserted, to abdicate in his favour. During his reign, rebellion and lawlessness were rife, and he was constantly hampered by lack of money. Under Owen Glendower the Welsh maintained their independence, and Henry's attack on Scotland in 1400 ended in his defeat. Henry Percy (Hotspur) and his house then joined with the Scots and the Welsh against him, but they were defeated at Shrewsbury (1403). He was a chronic invalid in his later years. >> Glendower; Joan of Navarre; John of Gaunt; Richard II; RR1095

Henry IV (of France), originally **Henry of Navarre** (1553–1610) The first Bourbon king of France (1589–1610), born in Pau, France, the third son of Antoine de Bourbon. Brought up a Calvinist, he led the Huguenot army at the Battle of Jarnac (1569), and became leader of the Protestant Party. He married Marguerite de Valois in 1572. After the massacre of St Bartholomew (1572), he was spared by professing himself a Catholic, and spent three years virtually a prisoner at the French court. In 1576 he escaped, revoked his conversion, and resumed command of the army in continuing opposition to the Guises and the Catholic League. After the murder of Henry III, he succeeded to the throne. In 1593 he became a Catholic again, thereby unifying the country, and by the Edict of Nantes Protestants were granted liberty of conscience. His economic policies, implemented by his minister, Sully, gradually brought new wealth to the country. He was assassinated in Paris by a religious fanatic. >> Guise, Henri; Henry III; Marie de Médicis; Sully, duc de; RR1049

Henry V (of England) (1387–1422) King of England (1413–22), born in Monmouth, Monmouthshire, SE Wales, UK, the eldest son of Henry IV. He fought against Glendower and the Welsh rebels (1402–8), and became Constable of Dover (1409) and Captain of Calais (1410). To this time belong the exaggerated stories of his wild youth. The main effort of his reign was his claim, through his great-grandfather Edward III, to the French crown. In 1415 he invaded France, and won the Battle of Agincourt against great odds. By 1419 Normandy was again under English control, and in 1420 was concluded the 'perpetual peace' of Troyes, under which Henry was recognized as heir to the French throne and Regent of France, and married Charles VI's daughter, Catherine of Valois. >> Catherine of Valois; Edward III; Glendower; Henry IV (of England); RR1095

Henry VI (of England) (1421–71) King of England (1422–61, 1470–1), born in Windsor, Berkshire, S England, UK, the only child of Henry V and Catherine of Valois. During Henry's minority, his uncle John, Duke of Bedford, was Regent of France, and another uncle, Humphrey, Duke of Gloucester, was Lord Protector of England. Henry was crowned King of France in Paris in 1431, two years after his coronation in England. But once the Burgundians had made a separate peace with Charles VII (1435), Henry V's French conquests were progressively eroded, and by 1453 the English retained only Calais. Henry had few kingly qualities, and from 1453 suffered from periodic bouts of insanity. Richard, Duke of York, seized power as Lord Protector in 1454, and defeated the king's army at St Albans in 1455, the first battle of the Wars of the Roses. Fighting resumed in 1459, and although York himself was killed at Wakefield (1460), his heir was proclaimed king as Edward IV after Henry's deposition (1461). In 1464 Henry returned from exile in Scotland to lead the Lancastrian cause, but was captured and imprisoned (1465–70). Richard Neville, Earl of Warwick, restored him to the throne (Oct 1470), his nominal rule ending when Edward IV returned to London (Apr 1471). After the Yorkist victory at Tewkesbury (May 1471), where his only son was killed, Henry was murdered in the Tower. >> Bedford, Duke of; Cade; Charles VII; Edward IV; Gloucester, Humphrey, Duke of; Henry V (of England); Warwick, Earl of; York, 3rd Duke of; William of Waynflete; RR1095

Henry VII (of England) (1457–1509) King of England (1485–1509), born at Pembroke Castle, Pembrokeshire, SW Wales, UK, the grandson of Owen Tudor and Catherine of Valois, the widow of Henry V, and known as Duke of Richmond before his accession. He was the founder of the Tudor dynasty. After the Lancastrian defeat at Tewkesbury (1471), Henry was taken to Brittany, where several Yorkist attempts on his life and liberty were frustrated. In 1485 he landed unopposed at Milford Haven, and defeated Richard III at Bosworth. As king, his policy was to restore peace and prosperity to the country, and this was helped by his marriage of reconciliation with Elizabeth of York. He was also noted for the efficiency of his financial and administrative policies. He firmly dealt with Yorkist plots, such as that led by Perkin Warbeck. Peace was concluded with France, and the marriage of his heir to Catherine of Aragon cemented an alliance with Spain. He was succeeded by his son, Henry VIII. >> Catherine of Valois; Richard III; Warbeck; Woodville; RR1095

Henry VIII (of England) (1491–1547) King (1509–47), born in Greenwich, EC Greater London, England, UK, the second son of Henry VII. Soon after his accession he married **Catherine of Aragon**, his brother Arthur's widow. As a member of the Holy League, he invaded France (1512), winning the Battle of Spurs (1513); and while abroad, the Scots were defeated at Flodden. In 1521 he published a book on the Sacraments in reply to Luther, receiving from the pope the title 'Defender of the Faith'. From 1527 he determined to divorce Catherine, whose children, except for Mary, had died in infancy. He tried to put pressure on the pope by humbling the clergy, and in defiance of the Roman Catholic Church was privately married to **Anne Boleyn** (1533). In 1534 it was enacted that his marriage to Catherine was invalid, and that the king was the sole head of the Church of England. The policy of suppressing the monasteries then began. In 1536 Catherine died, and Anne Boleyn was executed on the grounds of infidelity. Henry then married **Jane Seymour**, who died leaving a son, afterwards Edward VI. In 1540 **Anne of Cleves** became his fourth wife, in the hope of attaching the Protestant interest of Germany; but dislike of her appearance caused him to divorce her speedily. He then married **Catherine Howard** (1540), who two years later was executed on grounds of infidelity (1542). In 1543 his last marriage was to **Catherine Parr**, who survived him. His later years saw further war with France and Scotland, before peace was concluded with France in 1546. He was succeeded by his son as Edward VI. >> Anne of Cleves; Boleyn; Catherine of Aragon; Cromwell, Thomas; Fisher, St John; More,

Thomas; Parr, Catherine; Seymour, Jane; Wolsey, Thomas; RR1095

Henry (1594–1612) Prince of Wales, the eldest son of James I (of England) and Anne of Denmark. Notable for the strict morality of his way of life, in marked contrast to his father, and known to support a vigorously Protestant and anti-Spanish foreign policy, he became the focus for the hopes of those at court with Puritan sympathies. His death, loudly rumoured to be a result of poison, brought nation-wide regret, while the hopes of forward Protestants centred increasingly upon Henry's sister, Elizabeth, and her husband, Frederick V of the Palatinate. >> Elizabeth (1596–1662); James I (of England)

Henry of Blois [blwah] (c. 1099–1171) Clergyman, the younger brother of King Stephen. He was Bishop of Winchester from 1129, and papal legate in England from 1139. He supported Stephen against the Empress Matilda, and went to France after Stephen's death (1154). >> Matilda; Stephen

Henry of Huntingdon (c. 1084–1155) English chronicler, archdeacon of Huntingdon from 1109. In 1139 he visited Rome. He compiled a *Historia Anglorum* down to 1154.

Henry the Fowler (c. 876–936) King of Germany as Henry I from 919. The founder of the Saxon dynasty, he was Duke of Saxony from 912. He brought Swabia and Bavaria into the German confederation, regained Lotharingia (Lorraine, 925), defeated the Wends in 928 and the Hungarians in 933, and seized Schleswig from Denmark in 934. He is said to have been laying bird snares when informed of his election as king, hence his nickname.

Henry the Lion (1129–95) Duke of Saxony (1142–80) and Bavaria (1156–80), the head of the Guelphs. His ambitious designs roused against him a league of princes in 1166, but he retained power through an alliance with Emperor Frederick I Barbarossa. After breaking with Frederick in 1176, he was deprived of most of his lands, and exiled. Ultimately, he was reconciled to Frederick's successor, Henry VI. He encouraged commerce, and founded the city of Munich. >> Frederick I

Henry the Navigator (1394–1460) Portuguese prince, the third son of John I, King of Portugal, and Philippa, daughter of John of Gaunt, Duke of Lancaster. He set up court at Sagres, Algarve, and erected an observatory and school of scientific navigation. He sponsored many exploratory expeditions along the W African coast, and the way was prepared for the discovery of the sea route to India.

Henry, Joseph (1797–1878) Physicist, born in Albany, NY. In 1832 he became professor of natural philosophy at Princeton, and in 1846 first secretary of the Smithsonian Institution. He discovered electrical induction independently of Michael Faraday, constructed the first electromagnetic motor (1829), demonstrated the oscillatory nature of electric discharges (1842), and introduced a system of weather forecasting. The *henry* unit of inductance is named after him. >> Faraday

Henry, Lenny, popular name of **Lenworth George Henry** (1958–) Comedian and actor, born in Dudley, West Midlands, C England, UK. He won the *New Faces Talent Show* in 1975, joined the children's television show *Tiswas*, was one of *Three of a Kind* (1981–3), and went on to star in his own BBC television comedy series the *Lenny Henry Show* (1984–95) and *Chef* (3 series, from 1992). He also hosts the annual BBC *Comic Relief* telethon. He appeared in the film *True Identity* (1991). He has also written a volume of autobiography, *The Quest for the Big Woof* (1991) and a book for children (1995). He is married to Dawn French. >> French, Dawn

Henry, O, pseudonym of **William Sydney Porter** (1862–1910) Writer, master of the short story, born in Greensboro, NC.

Brought up during the post-Civil War depression in the South, he held various jobs before becoming a teller in the First National Bank. Jailed for embezzlement (1898), he started writing short stories in prison under his pseudonym. In 1902 after his release, he moved to New York City, and produced the first of his many volumes, *Cabbages and Kings*, in 1904. His stories provide a romantic and humorous treatment of everyday life, and are noted for their use of coincidence and trick endings. Other collections include *The Voice of the City* (1908), *Whirligigs* (1910), and *Waifs and Strays* (1917, posthumously). Despite enormous success, his life was marred by debts, ill health, and alcoholism.

Henry, Patrick (1736–99) American revolutionary and statesman, born in Studley, VA. After training as a lawyer, he entered the colonial Virginia House of Burgesses, where his oratorical skills won him fame. He was outspoken in his opposition to British policy towards the colonies, particularly on the subject of the Stamp Act (1765), and he made the first speech in the Continental Congress (1774). In 1776 he became governor of independent Virginia, and was four times re-elected. The words 'give me liberty or give me death' are often attributed to him, but are probably apocryphal.

Henry, William (1774–1836) Chemist, born in Manchester, Greater Manchester, NW England, UK. He studied medicine at Edinburgh, and practised in Manchester, but soon devoted himself to chemistry. He formulated the law named after him that the amount of gas absorbed by a liquid varies directly as the pressure of the gas above the liquid, provided no chemical action takes place.

Henryson, Robert [henrison] (c. 1425–1508) Scottish mediaeval poet. He is usually designated a schoolmaster of Dunfermline, and he was certainly a notary in 1478. His works include *The Testament of Cresseid; Robene and Makyne*, the earliest Scottish specimen of pastoral poetry; and a metrical version of 13 *Morall Fabels of Esope*, often viewed as his masterpiece.

Hensen, (Christian Andreas) Viktor (1835–1924) Physiologist, born in Kiel, Germany. He was a professor at Kiel (1871–1911), did research work on embryology, and the anatomy of the organs of sense (the *Hensen duct* in the ear), and investigated in a survey of the Atlantic the production of marine fauna which he named *plankton*.

Henslowe, Philip (c. 1550–1616) Theatre manager, born in Lindfield, West Sussex, S England, UK. Originally a dyer and starchmaker, in 1587 he built of the Rose Theatre on the Bankside, London. From 1591 until his death he was in partnership with Edward Alleyn, who married his stepdaughter. Henslowe's business diary (1598–1609) contains invaluable information about the stage of Shakespeare's day. >> Alleyn; Middleton

Henson, Jim, popular name of **James Maury Henson** (1936–90) Puppeteer, born in Greenville, MS. He lived near Washington, DC, working on a local television station as a puppeteer while studying at Maryland University. His 'Muppets' (Marionettes/puppets) first appeared in a five-minute programme entitled 'Sam and His Friends'. Other commercial and short appearances led to nationwide popularity on the children's television workshop, *Sesame Street* from 1969. Kermit the Frog, Miss Piggy, and friends went on to gain phenomenal success in *The Muppet Show* (1976–81), which reached an estimated 235 million viewers in more than 100 countries, appearing also in a string of films and on a Grammy-winning album (1979). The recipient of numerous Emmy awards, he continued to make television programmes combining live action and increasingly sophisticated puppetry, including *Fraggle Rock* (from 1983) and *The Storyteller* (from 1987).

Henty, G(eorge) A(lfred) (1832–1902) Writer and journalist, born in Trumpington, Cambridgeshire, EC England, UK. He studied at Cambridge, became a special correspondent for the *Morning Advertiser* during the Crimean War, and for the *Standard* in the Franco–Prussian War. He is best known for his 80 historical adventure stories for boys, which sold well in Britain and the USA, including *With Clive in India* (1884) and *With Moore at Corunna* (1898).

Henze, Hans Werner [hentsuh] (1926–) Composer, born in Gütersloh, Germany. He studied at Heidelberg and Paris, and was influenced by Schoenberg, exploring beyond the more conventional uses of the 12-tone system. His more recent works, which include operas, ballets, symphonies, and chamber music, often reflect his left-wing political views. He settled in Italy in 1953, and has taken master classes in composition at the Salzburg Mozarteum since 1961. >> Schoenberg

Hepburn, Audrey, originally **Eda van Heemstra** (1929–93) Actress and film star, born in Brussels, Belgium. She trained as a ballet dancer in Amsterdam, and at the Marie Rambert school in London, making her film and stage debuts in London in 1948. Noticed by the French writer Colette, she was given the lead in the Broadway production of her novel, *Gigi* (1951), and went on to win international acclaim for *Roman Holiday* (1953, Oscar), in which she starred with Gregory Peck. One of the most enchanting stars of the 1950s and 60s, her popular film roles included *Sabrina* (1954), *The Nun's Story* (1959), *Breakfast at Tiffany's* (1961), all Oscar nominations, and *My Fair Lady* (1964). Contrasting roles included *Two for the Road* (1967), and as the blind girl terrorized in *Wait Until Dark* (1967, Oscar nomination). She travelled extensively as a goodwill ambassador for UNICEF. >> Colette

Hepburn, James >> Bothwell, Earl of

Hepburn, Katharine (1909–) Actress, born in Hartford, CT. She studied at Bryn Mawr College, PA, made her professional stage debut in 1928 in Baltimore, and from 1932 attained international fame as a strong character actress. Among many of her outstanding films was *Woman of the Year* (1942), which saw the beginning of a 25-year professional and personal relationship with co-star Spencer Tracy. She won Oscars for *Morning Glory* (1933), *Guess Who's Coming to Dinner?* (1967), *The Lion in Winter* (1968), and *On Golden Pond* (1981), and she is also remembered for her role in *The African Queen* (1952). On Broadway she played Shakespearean roles in the 1950s, and enjoyed enormous success in the stage musical *Coco* (1969). Her television work includes *The Glass Menagerie* (1973), *Love Among the Ruins* (1975), and *Mrs Delafield Wants to Marry* (1986). In 1991 she published *Me: Stories of My Life*. >> Tracy, Spencer

Hepplewhite, George (?–1786) British furniture designer. He seems to have trained as a cabinet-maker with the Lancaster firm of Gillow, and then set up a workshop at St Giles, Cripplegate, in London; but not a single piece of extant furniture is attributable to him. His simple and elegant designs, characterized by the free use of inlaid ornament and the use of shield or heart shapes in chair backs, only became famous with the posthumous publication by his widow of his *Cabinet-Maker and Upholsterer's Guide* (1788), containing nearly 300 designs.

Hepworth, Dame (Jocelyn) Barbara (1903–75) Sculptor, born in Wakefield, West Yorkshire, N England, UK. She studied at the Leeds School of Art (where she befriended Henry Moore, a fellow student), the Royal College of Art, and in Italy. She married, first, the sculptor **John Skeaping** (1901–80), then (1933) the painter Ben Nicholson, who had a strong influence on her work. She was one of the foremost nonfigurative sculptors of her time, notable for the

strength and formal discipline of her carving (as in *Contrapuntal Forms*, exhibited at the Festival of Britain, 1951). Her representational paintings and drawings are of equal power. She was made a dame in 1965. >> Moore, Henry; Nicholson, Ben

Heraclitus or **Heracleitos** [herakliytus] (?–460 BC) Greek philosopher, born in Ephesus. Although only fragments of his writings survive, he seems to have thought that all things are composed of opposites (eg hot/cold, wet/dry). Because the opposites are constantly at strife with one another, all things are in perpetual change. Yet the change is governed by *logos* (Greek: reason), a principle of order and intelligibility.

Heraclius [heraklius] (c. 575–641) Byzantine emperor (610–41), born in Cappadocia, the son of the Roman governor of Africa. Responding to an appeal to free Constantinople from the terror of the tyrant Phocas (ruled 602–10), his father made him leader of a force that ultimately overthrew Phocas and crowned Heraclius emperor. The empire was threatened by the Avars, and by the Persians under Chosroes II (ruled 588–627), who overran Syria, Egypt, and Asia Minor. Heraclius carried out far-reaching reorganizations of the army, the provincial government, and the empire's finances, and made Greek its official language. These reforms enabled him to defeat the Persians in a series of campaigns which restored the lost territories (628–33). However, he failed to resolve the differences between the Orthodox and Monophysite parties in the Church, and from 634 the recent gains in the East were almost completely lost to the Arabs and Islam. >> RR1037

Herbart, Johann Friedrich (1776–1841) Philosopher and educational theorist, born in Oldenburg, Germany. After studying at Jena, he taught in Switzerland (1797–1800), where he became interested in Pestalozzi's educational methods. He was professor of philosophy at Göttingen (1805–8), and at Königsberg as Kant's successor (1809–33), before returning to Göttingen (1833–41). His metaphysics posited a multiplicity of 'reals', and led to a psychology which rejected the notions of faculties and innate ideas, and formed a basis for his pedagogical theories. He encouraged the study of education as a university subject. >> Kant; Pestalozzi

Herbert, Sir A(lan) P(atrick) (1890–1971) British politician and writer, born in Elstead, Surrey, SE England, UK. He studied at Oxford. Having established himself even while at school as a witty writer of verses, he joined *Punch* in 1924. His first theatrical success, *Riverside Nights* (1926), was followed by a series of brilliant libretti for comic operas, including *La Vie Parisienne* (1929) and *Bless the Bride* (1947). He was also the author of several successful novels, notably *The Secret Battle* (1919), *The Water Gipsies* (1930), and *Holy Deadlock* (1934). He became an MP (1935–50), introduced a marriage bill in the House of Commons that became law as the Matrimonial Causes Act (1938), and did much to amend divorce laws in England.

Herbert (of Cherbury), Edward Herbert, Baron (1583–1648) English soldier, statesman, and philosopher, born in Eyton, Shropshire, WC England, UK, the brother of George Herbert. He studied at Oxford, was knighted at James I's coronation, became a member of the Privy Council, and was ambassador to France (1619). He is regarded as the founder of English deism. His main works are *De veritate* (1624, On Truth), *De religione Gentilium* (published 1663, On the Religion of the Gentiles), and his *Autobiography* (published 1764). >> Herbert, George

Herbert, George (1593–1633) Clergyman and poet, born at Montgomery Castle, Powys, E Wales, UK. He studied at Cambridge, where he was public orator (1619), and became an MP before entering the Church (1630), serving as parish priest of Bemerton, Wiltshire. His verse is collected in *The Temple* (1633), and his chief prose work, *A Priest in the Temple*, was published in *Remains* (1652). >> Herbert, Edward

Herbert, Victor (1859–1924) Composer, born in Dublin. A cellist by training, he played in the orchestras of Johann Strauss and the Stuttgart Court before settling in New York City as leading cellist of the Metropolitan Opera Company's Orchestra. His successful comic opera, *Prince Ananias* (1894), was followed by a long series of similar works containing such enduringly popular songs as 'Ah, sweet mystery of life' and 'Kiss me again'. His ambition to succeed as a composer of serious opera resulted in *Natoma* (1911) and *Madeleine* (1914).

Herbert, Wally, popular name of **Walter William Herbert** (1934–) Arctic explorer. Brought up in South Africa and trained at the School of Military Survey, he served with the army in Egypt (1953–4). He was surveyor with the Falkland Is Dependencies Survey (1955–8), and took part in expeditions to Lapland, Svalbard, and Greenland. He participated in the New Zealand Antarctic Expedition (1960–2), and commemorated the 50th anniversary of Amundsen's attainment of the Pole by following his return journey. He led the first surface crossing of the Arctic Ocean (1968–9), lived in the Arctic with his wife and daughter, and made several attempts to circumnavigate Greenland (1978–82). >> Amundsen

Herbert, William, 3rd Earl of Pembroke (1580–1630) English poet. He was a patron of Ben Jonson, Massinger, and Inigo Jones, and a lord chamberlain of the court (1615–30). He became Chancellor of Oxford University in 1617, and Pembroke College is named after him. Shakespeare's 'W H', the 'onlie begetter' of the *Sonnets* has been taken by some to refer to him. >> Jones, Inigo; Jonson; Massinger

Herbert, Zbigniew [**hair**bairt, **zhbig**nev] (1924–) Poet, born in Lvov, Poland. His first collection was *Struna swiatla* (1956, Chords of Light). Later volumes include *Studium przedmiotu* (1961, Study of the Object), *Pan Cogito* (1974, Mr Cogito), and *Raport z oblozonego miasta* (1983, Report from a Besieged City). He has also written plays which have been broadcast in Poland and abroad.

Herder, Johann Gottfried von (1744–1803) Critic and poet, born in Mohrungen, Germany. He studied at Königsberg, and there made the acquaintance of Kant. He was a teacher and pastor in Riga (1764–9), and met Goethe in Strasbourg (1769). He was appointed court preacher at Bückeburg (1770), and first preacher in Weimar (1776). His love for the songs of the people, for unsophisticated human nature, found expression in *Volkslieder* (1778–9, Folk Songs), a treatise on the influence of poetry on manners (1778), in oriental mythological tales, in parables and legends, in his version of the *Cid* (1805), and in several other works. The supreme importance of the historical method is recognized in a work on the origin of language (1772), and especially in his masterpiece, *Ideen zur Geschichte der Menschheit* (1784–91, Outlines of a Philosophy of the History of Man), which is remarkable for its anticipations of evolutionary theories. He is best remembered for the influence he exerted on Goethe and the growing German Romanticism. >> Goethe; Kant

Hereward, known as **Hereward the Wake** (?–c. 1080) Anglo-Saxon thegn who returned from exile to lead the last organized English resistance against the Norman invaders. He held the Isle of Ely against William the Conqueror for nearly a year (1070–1), then disappeared from history, and entered mediaeval outlaw legend as a celebrated opponent of the forces of injustice. >> William I (of England)

Hergé [**her**zhay], Fr [airzhay], pseudonym of **Georges Rémi** (1907–83) Strip cartoonist, the creator of 'Tin-Tin' the boy detective, born in Etterbeek, Belgium. He drew his first strip, *Totor*, for a boy scouts' weekly in 1926. He created the *Tin-Tin* strip for the children's supplement of the newspaper *Le Vingtième Siècle*, using the pseudonym Hergé, a phonetic version of his initials, RG.

Herkomer, Sir Hubert von [**her**komer] (1849–1914) Artist and film pioneer, born in Waal, Germany. He studied art at Southampton, Munich, and the College of Art in South Kensington, and in 1870 settled in London. As well as painting, he worked as an engraver, wood-carver, ironsmith, architect, journalist, playwright, composer, singer, and actor. He was also a pioneer producer/director of British silent films, with his own studio at Bushey, Hertfordshire. He later became professor of fine art at Oxford (1889–94). His portrait paintings included those of Wagner, Ruskin, and Lord Kelvin. He was knighted in 1907.

Herman, Woody, popular name of **Woodrow Charles Herman** (1913–87) Bandleader, alto saxophonist, and jazz clarinettist, born in Milwaukee, WI. He was a member of the band led by Isham Jones, but when this broke up (1936) he took certain key members as the nucleus of his own first band, which became noted for the way it blended saxophones. The Herman Orchestra (or 'Herd') was one of the very few big bands to survive intact beyond the 1950s, continuing to tour throughout the 1970s and 80s.

Hermandszoon, Jakob >> **Arminius, Jacobus**

Hermannsson, Steingrímur (1928–) Icelandic statesman and prime minister (1983–7, 1988–91). He trained as an electrical engineer in the USA, returning to pursue an industrial career. He was director of Iceland's National Research Council (1957–78), and became chairman of the Progressive Party (PP) in 1979. He became a minister in 1978, then prime minister, heading a PP-Independence Party coalition, after which he accepted the foreign affairs portfolio in the government of Thorsteinn Pálsson. He became prime minister again in 1988, but was defeated in the 1991 elections. >> RR1058

Hermes, Georg [**her**mes] (1775–1831) Roman Catholic theologian, born in Dreyerwalde, Germany. He studied at Münster, and became theological professor there (1807) and at Bonn (1819). He sought to combine the Catholic faith and doctrines with Kantian philosophy, and the *Hermesian method* became influential in the Rhineland, but his doctrines were condemned by Pope Gregory XVI in 1835. >> Kant

Hero of Alexandria (1st-c) Greek mathematician and inventor. He devised many machines, among them a fire engine, a water organ, coin-operated devices, and the *aeolipile*, the earliest known steam engine. He showed that the angle of incidence in optics is equal to the angle of reflection, and devised the formula for expressing the area of a triangle in terms of its sides.

Herod [**her**od], known as **the Great** (c. 73–4 BC) King of Judea, the younger son of the Idumaean chieftain, Antipater. He owed his initial appointment as Governor of Galilee (47 BC) to Julius Caesar, his elevation to the kingship of Judea (40 BC) to Marcus Antonius, and his retention in that post after Actium (31 BC) to Octavian, later Augustus. Besides being a loyal and efficient Roman client king, who ruthlessly kept all his subjects in check, he was also an able and far-sighted administrator who did much to develop the economic potential of his kingdom, founding cities, and promoting agricultural projects. Life at court was marked by constant and often bloody infighting between his sister, his various wives, and their many offspring. Undoubtedly he was cruel, and this is reflected in the Gospel account of the Massacre of the Innocents. >> Antipater; Antonius; Augustus; Caesar; RR1065

Herod Agrippa I [herod agripa] (10 BC–AD 44) King of Judaea (41–4), the grandson of Herod the Great. Reared at the court of the Emperor Augustus, Agrippa's early contacts with the imperial family stood him in good stead later on. Caligula gave him two-thirds of the former kingdom of Herod the Great, while Claudius added the remaining third, the Judaean heartland (41). Loved by the Jews, despite being a Roman appointee, and an active Hellenizer, he was no friend to the Christians, executing St James and imprisoning St Peter. >> Augustus; Caligula; Claudius; RR1065

Herod Agrippa II [herod agripa] (c. 27–c. 93) King of Chalcis (49/50–53), ruler of the Ituraean principality (53–c.93), the son of Herod Agrippa I. He was not permitted by Rome to succeed to his father's Judaean kingdom in 44, but given various minor territories to the N, mostly Arab. A supporter of Rome in the Jewish War (66–70), he was rewarded for it afterwards with grants of land in Judaea and public honours in Rome. It was before him that St Paul made his defence and was found innocent. >> Herod Agrippa I; Paul, St; RR1065

Herod Antipas [herod antipas] (?–AD 39) The son of Herod the Great and ruler (tetrarch) of Galilee and Peraea (4–39), after Herod's death. An able client of the Romans, he enjoyed an especially good relationship with the Emperor Tiberias, but fell foul of his successor, Caligula, largely through the machinations of his nephew, Herod Agrippa. In the Christian tradition he looms large as the capricious murderer of John the Baptist. >> Caligula; Herod; Herod Agrippa I; John the Baptist, St

Herodian (?–c.238) Historian, born in Syria. He lived in Rome, and wrote in Greek a history of the Roman emperors in eight books, from the death of Marcus Aurelius (180) to the accession of Gordian III (238).

Herodotos or **Herodotus** [herodotus] (c. 485–425 BC) Greek historian, born in Halicarnassus, Asia Minor. He travelled widely in Asia Minor and the Middle East, and in 443 BC joined the colony of Thurii, from where he visited Sicily and Lower Italy. On his travels, he collected material for his great narrative history, which gave a record of the wars between the Greeks and the Persians. Cicero called him 'the father of history'.

Hérold, Louis Joseph Ferdinand [ayrold] (1791–1833) Composer, born in Paris. He wrote many operas, and is best remembered for his comic operas, such as *Zampa* (1831) and *Le Pré aux clercs* (1832). He also wrote several ballets and piano music.

Heron, Patrick (1920–) Painter, writer, and textile designer, born in Leeds, West Yorkshire, N England, UK. He studied at the Slade School of Art, London. He was art critic for the *New Statesman and Nation* (1947–50), and taught at the Central School of Art, London (1953–6). He has travelled and lectured in Australia, Brazil, and the USA, and has held numerous one-man exhibitions worldwide.

Herophilus [herofilus] (c. 335–c. 280 BC) Greek anatomist, founder of the school of anatomy in Alexandria, born in Chalcedon. He was the first to dissect the human body to compare it with that of other animals. He described the brain, liver, spleen, sexual organs, and nervous system, dividing the latter into sensory and motor.

Héroult, Paul Louis Toussaint [ayroo] (1863–1914) Chemist, born in Thury-Harcourt, France. He studied at the Ecole des Mines, Paris. Working independently of Charles M Hall of the USA he discovered the electrolytic process for the production of aluminium in 1886. He also devised an electric-arc furnace which is widely used in the manufacture of steel. >> Hall, Charles M

Herrera, Francisco [eraya], known as **el Mozo** ('the Younger') (1622–85) Painter, born in Seville, Spain, the son and pupil of Francisco Herrera (the Elder). He worked in Rome, and in 1656 moved back to Seville, where he helped to found the Academy. In 1661 he went to Spain, and became painter to Philip IV in Madrid. His best works are a fresco, 'The Ascension', in the Atocha Church in Madrid, and 'St Francis', in Seville Cathedral. >> Herrera, Francisco (the Elder)

Herrera, Francisco [erayra], known as **el Viejo** ('the Elder') (1576–1656) Painter and engraver, born in Seville, Spain. He painted historical pieces, wine shops, fairs, carnivals, and the like. His early works are in a Mannerist style, but later works, such as 'St Basil' (1637, Louvre), show a transition to a move towards naturalism. >> Herrera, Francisco (the Younger)

Herrick, Robert (1591–1674) Poet, born in London, England, UK. He studied at Cambridge, was ordained in 1623, and worked in Devon, until deprived of his living as a royalist in 1647. His writing, both secular and religious, is mainly collected in *Hesperides* (1648), and includes such well-known lyrics as 'Cherry ripe'. He resumed his living after the Restoration.

Herriman, George (1881–1944) Cartoonist, born in New Orleans, LA. A fall prevented him from continuing as a house painter, and he turned to drawing cartoons. His first strip was *Lariat Pete*, appearing in the San Francisco *Chronicle* (1903). Becoming a sports cartoonist on the *New York Journal* (1904), he launched a daily strip, *Baron Mooch* (1907), replacing it with *The Dingbat Family* in 1910. The family cat, lurking in bottom corners, eventually evolved into *Krazy Kat* (1910), whose painful unrequited love for Ignatz mouse was featured for more than 30 years in Hearst's newspapers. Intellectually acclaimed, the strip remained Herriman's work, and died with him. >> Hearst, William Randolph

Herriot, Edouard [airyoh] (1872–1957) French statesman and prime minister (1924–5, 1932), born in Troyes, France. He became professor at the Lycée Ampère, Lyon, and was mayor there from 1905 until his death. He was minister of transport during World War 1, radical-Socialist premier, and several times president of the Chamber of Deputies, a post which he was holding in 1942 when he became a prisoner of Vichy and of the Nazis. He later became president of the National Assembly (1947–54). A keen supporter of the League of Nations, he nonetheless opposed the whole concept of the European Defence Community, especially German rearmament. He wrote a number of literary and biographical studies, the best known of which are *Madame Récamier* (1904) and *Beethoven* (1932).

Herriot, James, pseudonym of **James Alfred Wight** (1916–95) Veterinary surgeon and writer, born in Glasgow, W Scotland, UK. Beginning in the 1970s, he brought the vet's world to the notice of the public with a number of best-selling books, such as *It Shouldn't Happen to a Vet* and *Vet in a Spin*, as well as several compilations and children's books. Feature films and television series made his work known all over the world, especially the television series *All Creatures Great and Small* (1977–80). The stories prompted a thriving tourist industry based on 'Herriot country', and transformed the public image of his profession, making veterinary medicine one of the most competitive university subjects. In 1992 he was the first recipient of the Chiron Award, created by the British Veterinary Association for exceptional service to the profession.

Herschel, Caroline Lucretia [hershl] (1750–1848) Astronomer, born in Hanover, Germany, the sister of Sir William Herschel. In 1772 she joined her brother in Bath, SW England, UK. Acting as his assistant she did many of the lengthy calculations relating to his observations, and made independent observations, discovering eight comets and several nebulae and clusters of stars. She gave the Royal Society a list of amendments to the *British Catalogue* in 1798, and published a catalogue of 2500 nebulae and star clusters after her return to Germany (1822). >> Herschel, William

Herschel, Sir John Frederick William [hershl] (1792–1871) Astronomer, born in Slough, Berkshire, S England, UK, the son of Sir William Herschel. He studied at Cambridge, and joined with Charles Babbage to found the Analytical Society (1812), introducing Leibniz notation into English mathematics to replace the cumbersome Newtonian symbols. He continued and augmented his father's researches, and spent four years in South Africa to chart the S hemisphere stars (1834–8). He pioneered celestial photography, carried out research on photo-active chemicals and the wave theory of light, and translated from Johann Schiller and the *Iliad*. He was also Master of the Mint (1851–6). >> Herschel, William

Herschel, Sir William (Frederick) [hershl], originally **Friedrich Wilhelm Herschel** (1738–1822) Astronomer, born in Hanover, Germany. He moved to England to escape the French occupation of Hanover (1757), became a music teacher (1766), then took up astronomy and the construction of ever more powerful reflecting telescopes. He discovered the planet Uranus in 1781, and became famous overnight, being appointed private astronomer to George III. He continued his research at Slough, Berkshire, UK, assisted by his sister Caroline and his son John. He greatly added to knowledge of the Solar System, of the Milky Way, and of the nebulae. He was knighted in 1816. >> Herschel, Caroline; Herschel, John

Hersey, John (Richard) (1914–93) Writer, born in Tientsin, China. He studied at Yale, and became a correspondent in the Far East for *Time* magazine (1937–46). Acclaimed for his clever fictionalizing of fact, his early novel, *A Bell for Adano* (1944), won the Pulitzer Prize, and was dramatized and filmed. *Hiroshima* (1946) was the first on-the-spot description of the effects of a nuclear explosion. Other titles include *The War Lover* (1959), *Under the Eye of the Storm* (1967), *The Walnut Door* (1977), and *Antonietta* (1991).

Hershey, A(lfred) D(ay) (1908–97) Biologist, born in Lansing, MI. He studied at Michigan State College, taught at Washington State University, St Louis, then worked in the Carnegie Institution, Washington, DC (1950–74). He became an expert on bacteriophages (viruses that infect bacteria), and in the early 1950s, working with Martha Chase, proved that the DNA of these organisms is their genetic information-carrying component. He shared the 1969 Nobel Prize for Physiology or Medicine with Salvador Luria and Max Delbrück, with whom he had exchanged information. >> Delbrück; Luria, Salvador

Hershey, Barbara (1948–) Film actress, born in Hollywood, CA. She made her film debut in *With Six You Get Egg Roll* (1968), and in 1987 received a Best Actress award at the Cannes film festival for her role in *Shy People*, winning the award again in 1988 for *A World Apart*. Other films include *Hannah and Her Sisters* (1986), *The Last Temptation of Christ* (1988), *Falling Down* (1993), *The Pallbearer* (1996), and *Frogs for Snakes* (1998).

Herskovits, Melville J(ean) [herskovits] (1895–1963) Cultural anthropologist, born in Bellefontaine, OH. He studied at Columbia University, and taught at Northwestern University, IL, (1927–63), where he founded the first US university programme in African studies (1951). An advocate of cultural relativism, he expounded in *Man and His Works* (1948) that all standards of judgment are culturebound.

Hertz, Gustav (Ludwig) (1887–1975) Physicist, born in Hamburg, Germany, the nephew of Heinrich Hertz. He studied at Göttingen, Munich, and Berlin, then taught physics at Berlin (1913–25), where he worked with James Franck on experiments that confirmed quantum theory, and they shared the Nobel Prize for Physics in 1925. After World War 2 he went to the USSR to become head of a research laboratory (1945–54), and returned to East Germany to be director of Karl Marx University, Leipzig (1954–61). >> Franck, James; Hertz, Heinrich

Hertz, Heinrich (Rudolf) (1857–1894) Physicist, born in Hamburg, Germany. He studied under Kirchhoff and Helmholtz in Berlin, and became professor at Bonn in 1889. His main work was on electromagnetic waves (1887), and he was the first to broadcast and receive radio waves. The unit of frequency is named after him. >> Helmholtz; Kirchhoff

Hertzog, J(ames) B(arry) M(unnik) [hertzokh] (1866–1942) South African statesman and prime minister (1924–39), born in Wellington, Cape Colony, South Africa. He studied law at Stellenbosch and Amsterdam, became a Boer general (1899–1902), and was minister of justice (1910) in the first Union government. He founded the Nationalist Party in 1914, advocating complete South African independence, and in World War 1 opposed co-operation with Britain. As premier, in coalition with Labour (1924–9), and with Smuts in a United Party (1933–9), he renounced his earlier secessionism, but on the outbreak of World War 2 declared for neutrality, was defeated, lost office, and in 1940 retired. >> Smuts; RR1088

Hertzsprung, Ejnar [hertshprung] (1873–1967) Astronomer, born in Frederiksberg, Denmark. He trained as a chemical engineer at the Copenhagen Polytechnic. Interested in the chemistry of photography, and in astronomy, he began researching starlight with photographs in 1902, and was appointed as an astronomer at the Potsdam Observatory (1909–19). He had then already shown that for most stars, colour and brightness are related; all later work on the evolution of stars begins with Hertzsprung's work on this relationship. He worked at Leyden University observatory (1919–45), becoming director there in 1935, and remained an active researcher until he was over 90.

Herzberg, Gerhard [hertsberg] (1904–) Physical chemist, born in Hamburg, Germany. He studied at Göttingen and Berlin universities, and taught at Darmstadt before emigrating to Canada in 1935, where he taught at the University of Saskatchewan (1935–45). He was director of the division of pure physics at the National Research Council in Ottawa (1949–69). He greatly developed and used spectroscopic methods for a variety of purposes, including the detailed study of energy levels in atoms and molecules, and the detection of free radicals both in laboratory work and in interstellar space. He was awarded the Nobel Prize for Chemistry in 1971.

Herzl, Theodor [hertsl] (1860–1904) Zionist leader, born in Budapest. He trained as a lawyer in Vienna, then became a journalist and playwright. After reporting the Dreyfus trial (1894), he was converted to Zionism, and in the pamphlet *Judenstaat* (1896, The Jewish State) he called for a world council to discuss the question of a homeland for the Jews, convened the first Zionist Congress at Basel (1897), and became the first president of the World Zionist Organization. >> Dreyfus

Herzog, Werner [hertzog], originally **Werner Stipetic** (1942–) Film director, screenwriter, and producer, born in Sachrang, Germany. He made numerous shorts in the 1960s, and became recognized as a leading member of the New Cinema in Germany with his features *Aguirre, der Zorn Gottes* (1973, Aguirre, Wrath of God) and the story of Kaspar

Hauser (1975). His treatment of *Nosferatu, the Vampyre* (1979) reflected the German silent film Expressionists of the 1920s, but his general themes are metaphysical in character, often with remoteness in time or location, as in *Where the Green Ants Dream* (1984). Later films include *Scream of Stone* (1991). >> Hauser, Kasper; Kinski

Heselrig, Sir Arthur >> **Haselrig, Arthur**

Heseltine, Michael (Ray Dibdin) [heseltiyn] (1933–) British statesman, born in Swansea, SC Wales, UK. He studied at Oxford, and built up a publishing business before becoming an MP in 1966. After holding junior posts in transport (1970), environment (1970–2), and aerospace and shipping (1972–4), he was appointed secretary of state for the environment (1979–83), then defence secretary (1983–6). He resigned from the government in dramatic fashion by walking out of a cabinet meeting over the issue of the takeover of Westland helicopters. He stood unsuccessfully as a candidate in the leadership contest following Mrs Thatcher's resignation (1990). His posts under John Major included environment secretary (1990–2), President of the Board of Trade (1992–5), and first secretary and deputy prime minister (1995–7). He was made a Companion of Honour in 1997. >> Thatcher

Heseltine, Philip Arnold >> **Warlock, Peter**

Hesiod [heesiod] (fl. 8th-c BC) Poet, born in Ascra, Greece. One of the earliest known Greek poets, he is best known for two works. *Works and Days* exalts honest labour and denounces corrupt and unjust judges. *Theogony* contains advice as to the days, lucky or unlucky, for the farmer's work. His poetry is didactic. *Works and Days* gives an invaluable picture of the Greek village community in the 8th-c BC, and the *Theogony* is of importance to the comparative mythologist.

Hess, Germain Henri (1802–50) Chemist, born in Geneva, Switzerland. As professor of chemistry at St Petersburg, he formulated *Hess's law* (1840), which states that the net heat evolved or absorbed in any chemical reaction depends only on the initial and final stages. It was a forerunner of the more complete law of the conservation of energy.

Hess, Dame Myra (1890–1965) Pianist, born in London, England, UK. She studied at the Royal Academy of Music, and was an immediate success on her first public appearance in 1907. During World War 2 she organized the lunchtime concerts in the National Gallery, for which she became a dame in 1941.

Hess, (Walter Richard) Rudolf (1894–1987) German politician, Hitler's deputy as Nazi Party leader, born in Alexandria, Egypt. Educated at Godesberg, he fought in World War 1, then studied at Munich. He joined the Nazi Party in 1920, and became Hitler's close friend and (in 1934) deputy. In 1941, on the eve of Germany's attack on Russia, he flew alone to Scotland to plead the cause of a negotiated Anglo-German peace. He was temporarily imprisoned in the Tower of London, then placed under psychiatric care near Aldershot. At the Nuremberg Trials (1946) he was sentenced to life imprisonment, and remained in Spandau prison, Berlin (after 1966, as the only prisoner) until his death. >> Hitler

Hess, Victor (Francis) (1883–1964) Physicist, born in Waldstein, Austria. He studied at Graz and Vienna universities, then taught at Vienna. He realized during balloon ascents that high-energy radiation in the Earth's atmosphere originated from outer space. For his work on cosmic radiation he shared the 1936 Nobel Prize for Physics. In 1938 he emigrated to the USA to become professor of physics at Fordham University, New York (1938–56). >> RR1122

Hess, Walter Rudolf (1881–1973) Physiologist, born in Frauenfeld, Switzerland. As professor of physiology at Zürich (1917–51) he did much important research on the nervous system, and developed methods of stimulating localized areas of the brain by means of needle electrodes. He shared the 1949 Nobel Prize for Physiology or Medicine. >> RR1124

Hesse, Eva [hes] (1936–70) Sculptor, born in Hamburg, Germany. Her family emigrated to the USA in 1939, and settled in New York City. She studied at the Pratt Institute, New York, and at Cooper Union. From 1965 she worked on a variety of unusual materials, including rubber, plastic, string, and polythene. These were made into hauntingly bizarre objects designed to rest on the floor or against a wall or even be suspended from the ceiling. Her unconventional techniques and imaginative work exerted a strong influence on later sculptors.

Hesse, Hermann [hesuh] (1877–1962) Novelist and poet, born in Calw, Germany. He was a bookseller and antiquarian in Basel (1895–1902), and published his first novel in 1904. His works include *Rosshalde* (1914), *Siddhartha* (1922), *Steppenwolf* (1927), and *Das Glasperlenspiel* (1945, The Glass Bead Game). He was awarded the Nobel Prize for Literature in 1946. From 1911 he lived in Switzerland. His psychological and mystical concerns made him something of a cult figure after his death.

Heston, Charlton, originally **John Charles Carter** (1923–) Actor, born in Evanston, IL. He made his film debut in an amateur production of *Peer Gynt* (1941) and, after air force war service and further theatre experience, his Broadway debut in *Antony and Cleopatra* (1947). In Hollywood from 1950, he portrayed historic or heroic roles in such epics as *The Ten Commandments* (1956), *Ben Hur* (1959, Oscar) and *El Cid* (1961). He displayed his potential as a character actor in *Touch of Evil* (1958), *The War Lord* (1965), and *Will Penny* (1967). Frequently returning to the stage, he also directs for film and television, including *Antony and Cleopatra* (1972, film), and *A Man for All Seasons* (1988, television). Later film appearances include *The Awakening* (1980) and *True Lies* (1994). He has also played a prominent role in US arts, theatre, and film organizations.

Heuss, Theodor [hoys] (1884–1963) First president of the Federal Republic of Germany (1949–59), born in Brackenheim, Germany. He studied at Munich and Berlin, became editor of the political magazine *Hilfe* (1905–12), professor at the Berlin College of Political Science (1920–33), and an MP (1924–8, 1930–2). A prolific author and journalist, he wrote two books denouncing Hitler, and when the latter came to power in 1933, he was dismissed from his chair and his books publicly burned. In 1946 he became a founder member of the Free Democratic Party, and helped to draft the new federal constitution. >> RR1051

Hevelius, Johannes [heveelius] (1611–87) Astronomer, born in Gdansk, Poland. He studied at Leyden, built his own observatory in Gdańsk, and made his own instruments. He catalogued 1564 stars in *Prodromus Astronomiae* (1690), discovered four comets, and was one of the first to observe the transit of Mercury. He gave names to many lunar features in his atlas of the Moon, *Selenographia* (1647).

Hevesy, George Charles de [heveshee] (1885–1966) Chemist, born in Budapest, Hungary. He studied at Berlin and Freiberg, worked at Manchester under Rutherford (1911), then with Paneth at Vienna (1912–20). In 1923 he discovered, with the Dutch physicist **Dirk Coster** (1889–1950), the element hafnium at Copenhagen (Hafnia being the Latin name for the city). He was a professor at Freiburg University from 1926, but during World War 2 went to Sweden, where he became professor at Stockholm. He was awarded the 1943 Nobel Prize for Chemistry for his work on isotopic tracer techniques. >> Paneth; Rutherford, Ernest

Hewett, Dorothy (1923–) Playwright, poet, and novelist, born in Perth, Western Australia. Her plays are mainly epic, Expressionist works that feature music and poetry; her first was the working-class drama *This Old Man Comes Rolling Home* (1967). Others include *The Chapel Perilous* (1971), her most widely performed play, which was banned by the West Australian government for many years, *The Man from Muckinupin* (1979), and *The Fields of Heaven* (1982). *Selected Poems* appeared in 1991. Her only novel is *Bobbin' Up* (1959).

Hewish, Antony (1924–) Radio astronomer, born in Fowey, Cornwall, SW England, UK. He studied at Cambridge and spent his career there, becoming professor of radio astronomy (1971–89). In 1967 he began studies, using a radio telescope of novel design, on the scintillation ('twinkling') of quasars (a class of radio stars). This led him and his student Susan Jocelyn (Burnell) Bell to discover the first radio stars emitting radio signals in regular pulses; named as pulsars, many others have since been discovered. Hewish shared the Nobel Prize for Physics in 1974 with his former teacher, Sir Martin Ryle. >> Bell Burnell; Ryle, Martin

Hewlett-Packard Founders of the Hewlett-Packard electronics and computer equipment company: **William Hewlett** (1913–) and **David Packard** (1912–96) They were fellow students at Stanford University under Fred Terman, and with his encouragement set up an electronics business in a garage in Palo Alto (1938), manufacturing a wide range of specialized measuring equipment. Their hand-held scientific calculator, the HP-35 (1972), was a best seller, and marked the start of personal computing. The garage is now a registered historical landmark, 'The birthplace of Silicon Valley'. >> Jobs; Terman, Fred

Hewson, John (1946–) Australian politician and economist, born in Sydney, New South Wales, Australia. He studied at the University of Sydney and Johns Hopkins University, USA, worked as a consultant to the International Monetary Fund and to a range of business and industrial concerns, and became professor of economics at the University of New South Wales (1978–87). He entered federal politics in 1987, and was shadow minister for finance (1988–9) and shadow treasurer (1989–90), becoming leader of the Liberal Party in 1990 when Andrew Peacock lost the federal election. He was a strong advocate of neo-classical economics. In 1993, to the surprise of many, the Liberal Party lost their fifth successive federal election. Hewson was replaced as leader in 1994, and served as shadow minister for industry in 1994–5. >> Peacock, Andrew

Heyden, Jan van der [hayden] (1637–1712) Painter, born in Gorinchem, The Netherlands. He is best known for his novel and meticulously detailed townscapes of Amsterdam, executed in the 1660s. He was also interested in mechanical inventions, especially of fire-fighting equipment and street lighting, which he depicted in a series of engravings published in book form in 1690 under the title of *Brandspuiten-boek* (Fire Engine Book).

Heydrich, Reinhard [hiydrikh], nickname **the Hangman** (1904–42) Nazi politician and deputy-chief of the Gestapo, born in Halle, Germany. He joined the violent anti-Weimar 'Free Corps' (1918), and served in the navy (1922–31), quitting to join the Nazi Party. He rose to be second-in-command of the secret police, and was charged with subduing Hitler's war-occupied countries, which he did by ordering mass executions. In 1941 he was made deputy-protector of Bohemia and Moravia, but next year was struck down by Czech assassins. In the murderous reprisals, Lidice village was razed and every man put to death. >> Hitler

Heyer, Georgette [hayer] (1902–74) Writer, born in London, England, UK. She studied at Westminster College, London, married in 1925, and travelled in East Africa and Yugoslavia until 1929. Her early work includes historical novels, and fictional studies of real figures in crisis, such as William I. An outstanding authority on the Regency period, she had success with *Regency Buck* (1935), and later novels. She also wrote modern comedy detective novels, such as *Death in the Stocks* (1935), and historical thrillers.

Heyerdahl, Thor [hiyerdahl] (1914–) Anthropologist, born in Larvik, Norway. After studying at Oslo, he served with the free Norwegian forces in World War 2. In 1947 he set out to prove, by sailing a balsa raft (the *Kon-Tiki*) from Peru to Tuamotu I in the S Pacific, that the Peruvian Indians could have settled in Polynesia. His success in the venture, and his archaeological expedition to Easter I, won him popular fame and several awards. In 1970 he sailed from Morocco to the West Indies in a papyrus boat, *Ra II*, and made the journey from Iraq to Djibouti in a reed boat, the *Tigris*, in 1977–8. Among his many publications are *The Maldive Mystery* (1986), *Pyramids of Tucume* (1995, jointly), and *Green was the Earth on the Seventh Day* (1996). >> Lewis, David

Heyhoe Flint, Rachel [hayhoh flint] (1939–) British cricketer. She studied at Dartford College of Physical Education and became a PE teacher. A member of the Women's England Cricket Team (1960–83, captain 1966–77), she captained England to victory in the first women's World Cup in 1973. In the 1976 Test against Australia, she scored 179, a world record for England and the world's fourth highest score by a woman in tests. She also played for the England women's hockey team as goalkeeper in 1964. She later became a journalist and public relations consultant.

Heymans, Corneille Jean François [hiymahns] (1892–1968) Physiologist, born in Ghent, Belgium. He worked at the University of Ghent (1920–68), becoming professor of pharmacology there in 1930. He discovered the regulatory effect on respiration of certain sensory organs, and how blood pressure and its oxygen content are monitored. He was awarded the 1938 Nobel Prize for Physiology or Medicine.

Heyrovsky, Jaroslav [hiyrofskee] (1890–1967) Chemist, born in Prague. He studied at Charles University in Prague, and University College, London, where he worked under Frederick George Donnan (1870–1956), who suggested a line of study which ultimately led to Herovsky's discovery of polarography in 1922. He became professor of physical chemistry at Charles University (1926–54), where he continued to develop and improve his discovery and its application. He was awarded the Nobel Prize for Chemistry in 1959, the first Czech national to gain a Nobel award.

Heysen, Sir (Wilhelm Ernst) Hans (Franz) [hiysen] (1877–1968) Landscape painter, born in Hamburg, Germany. He emigrated to Australia with his parents in 1884. He was sponsored by local businessmen for his tuition at the Adelaide School of Design, and his trip to Europe in 1899, where he studied in Paris and painted in Italy, The Netherlands, and the UK. Primarily a watercolourist, his first important exhibition was in Melbourne, in 1908, and his success grew during the following 20 years. He was knighted in 1959.

Heyward, (Edwin) DuBose (1885–1940) Writer, born in Charleston, SC. He first worked in a hardware store, then as a checker in a cotton warehouse. Although not African-American, he drew on the life of South Carolina African-Americans for much of his writing. He and his wife dramatized his first novel, *Porgy* (1925), and it was the basis for George Gershwin's opera *Porgy and Bess* (1935). He also wrote poetry and other fictional works. >> Gershwin, George

Heywood, John (c. 1497–c. 1575) Epigrammatist, playwright, and musician, born perhaps in London, England, UK. He was a favourite with Henry VIII and with Mary I, to whom he had been music teacher in her youth. He was a devout Catholic, and after the accession of Elizabeth I went to Belgium. He wrote several short plays (interludes), where the individual characters represent classes, such as the Pedlar and the Pardoner. They thus form a link between the old morality plays and modern drama. He is remembered above all, however, for his collections of proverbs and epigrams.

Heywood, Thomas (c. 1574–1641) Playwright and poet, born in Lincolnshire, EC England, UK. He studied at Cambridge, was writing plays by 1596, and by 1633 had shared in the composition of 220 plays, and written 24 of his own, notably his domestic tragedy, *A Woman Killed with Kindness* (1607). He also wrote many pageants, tracts, treatises, and translations.

Hiawatha [hiyawotha], Indian name **Heowenta** (16th-c) Legendary Mohawk leader, born in present-day New York State. Although he is known only through Iroquois mythology and legend, it is now generally accepted that he was a real person who was influential in founding the Five Nations League, or Long House – an alliance of five (later six) Iroquois tribes that ended inter-tribal feuding from c.1550, or earlier, to 1775. Longfellow used Hiawatha's name for the hero of his poem (1855), but set the action in Minnesota, and used only elements of the legendary Hiawatha and other Indian stories for his essentially Romantic tale. >> Longfellow

Hibbert, Eleanor (Alice Burford) (1906–93) Novelist, born in London. She was a prolific writer of romantic novels, writing under several pseudonyms. She began with **Eleanor Burford** (*Daughter of Anna*, 1941), and under the name of **Jean Plaidy** wrote over 40 historical novels, beginning with *Together They Ride* (1945). Her other pseudonyms were **Elbur Ford**, beginning with *The Flesh and the Devil* (1950), **Kathleen Kellow** (*Danse Macabre*, 1952). **Ellalice Tate** (*Queen of Diamonds*, 1958), **Victoria Holt** (*Mistress of Mellyn*, 1961), and **Philippa Carr** (*The Miracle at St Bruno's*, 1972).

Hibbert, Robert (1770–1849) Merchant and philanthropist, born in Jamaica. A slave-owner in Jamaica, he moved to England, UK, and in 1847 founded the Hibbert Trust, whose funds set up the Hibbert Lectures (from 1878), and also aided the *Hibbert Journal* (1920–70).

Hick, John (Harwood) (1922–) Theologian and philosopher of religion, born in Scarborough, North Yorkshire, N England, UK. He studied at Edinburgh University, and was ordained in the Presbyterian Church of England in 1953. After a long teaching career in the USA and Cambridge, he held professorships in Birmingham (1967–82) and at Claremont Graduate School, CA (1979–92, now emeritus). He has produced several standard textbooks and anthologies in the philosophy of religion, and has questioned the status of Christianity among the world religions in such works as *God and the Universe of Faiths* (1973) and *The Myth of God Incarnate* (1977). Later works include *Problems of Religious Pluralism* (1985) and *The Rainbow of Faiths* (1995).

Hickock, Wild Bill >> **Calamity Jane**

Hicks, Elias (1748–1830) Liberal Quaker preacher and abolitionist, born in Hempstead, Long Island, NY. A carpenter by trade, he became a preacher in the American Society of Friends (Quakers) in 1775, and worked for the abolition of slavery. Because of his successful opposition to the adoption of a set creed in 1817, he was held responsible for the subsequent split of the Quakers into Orthodox and *Hicksite* Friends (1827–8), which continued into the 20th-c.

Hicks, Sir John Richard (1904–89) Economist, born in Leamington Spa, Warwickshire, C England, UK. He studied

at Oxford, taught at the London School of Economics (1926–35), and was professor of political economy at Manchester (1938–46) and Oxford (1952–65). He wrote a classic book on the conflict between business-cycle theory and equilibrium theory (*Value and Capital*, 1939), and other works include *A Theory of Economic History* (1969) and *Causality in Economics* (1979). He shared the 1972 Nobel Prize for Economics. >> RR1125

Hideyoshi, Toyotomi [hideyoshee] (1536–98) The second of the three great historical unifiers of Japan, between Nobunaga and Ieyasu Tokugawa, sometimes called 'the Napoleon of Japan'. Unusually, he was an ordinary soldier who rose to become Nobunaga's foremost general. His law forbade all except samurai to carry swords (1588), and he banned Christianity for political reasons (1597). His armies invaded Korea (1592–8), but withdrew after his death at Fushimi Castle, Kyoto. >> Nobunaga; Tokugawa

Higden, Ranulph (c. 1280–1364) Benedictine monk of St Werburgh's monastery in Chester, Cheshire, NWC England, UK. He wrote a Latin *Polychronicon*, a general history from the creation to about 1342, which was continued by others to 1377. An English translation of the *Polychronicon* by John of Trevisa was printed by Caxton in 1482. >> John of Trevisa

Higgins, Alex(ander Gordon), nickname **Hurricane Higgins** (1949–) Snooker player, born in Belfast. He had a tempestuous career after becoming the youngest world champion in 1972, at age 23. A former trainee jockey, he became a professional snooker player in 1971, and won the world title at the first attempt. He won the title for a second time in 1982, and though less successful thereafter he has remained a favourite with snooker fans despite (or because of) his confrontations with the authorities. >> RR1168

Higgins, George (Vincent) (1939–) Novelist, born in Brockton, MA. Called to the Massachusetts bar in 1967, he worked in newspapers before becoming a successful attorney. He used his experience of low life and his observation of criminals at close quarters to telling effect in a spate of acclaimed literary thrillers. *The Friends of Eddie Coyle* (1972) was his first book, and he has published many since, invariably told almost entirely in dialogue and using Boston as a backdrop. Titles include *Kennedy for the Defence* (1980), *Outlaws* (1987), and *Wonderful Years, Wonderful Years* (1988).

Higgins, Jack, pseudonym of **Harry Patterson** (1929–) Writer, born in Newcastle upon Tyne, Tyne and Wear, NE England, UK. He studied at Beckett Park College for Teachers and the London School of Economics. After army service (1947–50) and various occupations including circus hand (1950–8), he became a teacher and college lecturer. He took up full-time writing in 1970, and became a best-selling author with the success of *The Eagle Has Landed* (1975; filmed 1976). Later novels include *Night of the Fox* (1986) and *Year of the Tiger* (1996). He also writes as **Martin Fallon, Hugh Marlowe**, and **James Graham**.

Higginson, Thomas Wentworth (Storrow) (1823–1911) Writer and reformer, born in Cambridge, MA. He studied at Harvard Divinity School, and became a Unitarian minister. Passionate in his opposition to slavery, he engaged in numerous missions to help fugitive slaves. During the Civil War he commanded the first troop of African-American soldiers in the Union army, and out of this experience produced *Army Life in a Black Regiment* (1870). He wrote magazine essays on literary as well as political topics, and discovered the poet Emily Dickinson, co-editing the first published volume of her poetry in 1890. >> Dickinson, Emily

Highsmith, Patricia (1921–95) Writer of detective fiction, born in Fort Worth, TX. She studied at Barnard College and

Columbia University, New York City. Her first novel, *Strangers on a Train* (1949), became famous as a source of Hitchcock's 1957 film of that name, but her best novels are generally held to be those describing the criminal adventures of her psychotic hero, Tom Ripley, beginning with *The Talented Mr Ripley* (1956). Other titles included *Ripley Under Ground* (1971), *Found in the Street* (1986), and *Ripley Under Water* (1991).

Hightower, Rosella (1920–) Ballerina and teacher, born in Ardmore, OK. She studied in Kansas City, MI, before beginning her long career as a leading ballerina with the Ballets Russes (1938–46). She then performed primarily with the Grand Ballet du Marquis de Cuevas (until 1961), touring the world and making guest appearances with various companies. She later directed the Marseille Opera (1969–72), the Ballet de Nancy (1973–74), and from 1980 the Opéra Ballet in Paris.

Hijikata, Tatsumi [hijikahta] (1928–86) Performance artist, born in Akita province, Japan. He was a key figure in the Japanese avant-garde of the 1950s and 1960s, and with **Kazuo Ohno** is credited with the founding of the *butoh* dance-theatre movement, that draws on and yet refutes traditional Japanese *Kabuki* and *Noh* theatre and Western art forms. His 1968 piece *Nikutai No Hanran* (Rebellion of the Body) is acknowledged as one of the most important productions in the development of butoh.

Hilarion, St (c.291–371) Hermit, born in Tabatha, Palestine. He was educated at Alexandria, where he became a Christian. He lived as a hermit in the desert between Gaza and Egypt from 306, and established the first Palestinian monastery (329), then travelled via Egypt and Sicily to Cyprus. Feast day 21 October.

Hilary (of Poitiers), St (c. 315–c. 368) Clergyman, one of the Doctors of the Church, born of pagan parents in Limonum (Poitiers), France. He did not become a Christian until he was advanced in life. About 350 he was elected Bishop of Poitiers, and immediately rose to the first place as an opponent of Arianism. His principal work is that on the Trinity, but his three addresses to Emperor Constantius II are remarkable for the boldness of their language. His feast day marks the beginning of an Oxford term and English law sittings, to which his name is consequently applied. Feast day 13 January. >> Arius

Hilary of Arles, St [ah(r)l] (401–49) Clergyman, born probably in N France. Educated at the Abbey of Lerins, he became Bishop of Arles in 429, and presided at several synods, especially that of Orange in 441, whose proceedings involved him in a serious controversy with Pope Leo the Great. He wrote a life of St Honoratus, which is still extant. Feast day 5 May. >> Leo I

Hilbert, David (1862–1943) Mathematician, born in Königsberg, Germany. He studied at Königsberg and became professor there (1893). He moved to Göttingen in 1895, where he critically examined the foundations of geometry. He made important contributions to the theory of numbers, the theory of invariants and algebraic geometry, and the application of integral equations to physical problems. At the International Congress of Mathematicians in 1900 he listed 23 problems which he regarded as important for contemporary mathematics; the solutions of many of these have led to interesting advances, while others are still unsolved. >> Waerden

Hilda, St (614–680) Abbess, born in Northumberland, NE England, UK. She was baptized by Paulinus in 627, and in 649 became Abbess of Hartlepool. In 657 she founded the monastery at Streaneshalch or Whitby, a house for both nuns and monks. This became a great religious centre for the N of England, and housed the Synod of Whitby in 664. Feast day 17 November. >> Paulinus

Hildebrand, St >> **Gregory VII**

Hildebrand, Adolf [hildebrant] (1847–1921) Sculptor, born in Marburg, Germany. He sought a renaissance of Classical Realism in his public monuments, such as those to Brahms at Meiningen, Bismarck at Bremen, and Schiller at Nuremberg. His *Das Problem der Form* (1893, The Problem of Form) founded a new school of art criticism.

Hildebrandt, Johann Lukas von [hildebrant] (1668–1745) Architect, born in Genoa, Italy. He studied in Rome, joined the Austrian army as a fortifications engineer (1695–1701), then became court engineer in Vienna. His earlier works were heavily influenced by the Italian school, as seen in the Mansfield Fondi garden palace (1697–1715). He gradually developed a more mature style, less Classical and more intuitive, as seen in the Starhemborg-Schönberg garden palace (1705–6), where his mastery of the relationship between house and garden is clear.

Hildegard of Bingen, St (1098–1179) Abbess and mystic, born in Böckelheim, Germany. Educated in a Benedictine convent, she experienced visions from childhood, many of which were considered authentic and recorded. In c.1147 she founded her own convent. Her many writings include works on medicine and natural history, and she also composed poetry and music, and invented a language. Though never formally canonized, she is often listed as a saint, and has her own feast day (17 September), especially recognized in Germany.

Hill, Alfred Francis (1870–1960) Composer, born in Melbourne, Victoria, Australia. He studied at Leipzig Conservatory (1887–91), became conductor of the Wellington Orchestral Society (1891–7), and collected and recorded much Maori music, which influenced his music of the period. He was professor of composition and harmony at the New South Wales Conservatory (1915–35). His work includes 13 symphonies, many of which are orchestrations of his earlier string quartets, 10 operas, a *Maori Rhapsody*, five concertos, and a considerable body of chamber music.

Hill, A(rchibald) V(ivian) (1886–1977) Physiologist, born in Bristol, SW England, UK. He was professor of physiology at Manchester (1920) and University College, London (1923), and research professor of the Royal Society (1926–51). He shared the 1922 Nobel Prize for Physiology or Medicine for his research into heat production in muscle contraction, which helped establish the origin of muscular force. >> RR1124

Hill, Benny, popular name of **Alfred Hawthorne Hill** (1925–92) Comedian, born in Southampton, Hampshire, S England, UK. An enthusiastic performer in school shows, he was a milkman, drummer, and driver before finding employment as an assistant stage manager. During World War 2 he appeared in *Stars in Battledress*, and later followed the traditional comic's route of working-men's clubs, revues, and end-of-the-pier shows. An early convert to the potential of television, he appeared in *Hi There* (1949), and was named TV personality of the year in 1954. He gained national popularity with the saucy *The Benny Hill Show* (1957–66), and spent over two decades writing and performing in top-rated television specials that were seen around the world.

Hill, David Octavius (1802–70) Photographer and painter, born in Perth, Perth and Kinross, E Scotland, UK. In 1843 he was commissioned to paint a commemorative scene of the founding of the Free Church of Scotland, and in order to get accurate details of the many founders, decided to take photographs of them. In this he was helped by the Edinburgh chemist, Robert Adamson, who had experience of the calotype process. The results of their collaboration, some 1500 pictures, are considered to be the finest photographic portraits of the 19th-c. >> Adamson, Robert

Hill, Damon (Graham Devereux) (1960–) Motor-racing driver, the son of Graham Hill. He joined the Williams Formula One team as a test driver in 1991, and drove for Brabham in his first Grand Prix at Silverstone in 1992. He won over 20 grands prix in the next four years, succeeding Nigel Mansell on the Williams team. He took third place in the world championship in 1993, was runner-up in 1994, and won in 1996. >> Hill, Graham; Mansell, Nigel

Hill, Geoffrey (William) (1932–) Poet, born in Bromsgrove, Hereford and Worcester, WC England, UK. He studied at Oxford, taught at the universities of Leeds (1954–80) and Cambridge (1981–8), and became professor at Boston, MA, in 1988. His first volume *For the Unfallen* (1959) introduced a serious and astringent voice, which has commanded increasing authority with *King Log* (1968), *Mercian Hymns* (1971), and *Tenebrae* (1978). His religious preoccupation is fully revealed in *The Mystery of the Charity of Charles Péguy* (1983), and later works include *New and Collected Poems 1952–1992* (1994) and *Canaan* (1996). Among his critical works is *Illuminating the Shadows: Mythic Powers of Film* (1992).

Hill, George (Roy) (1922–) Film director, born in Minneapolis, MN. He had been an actor, a soldier, and a playwright before becoming a film director at the age of forty. His films include *Thoroughly Modern Millie* (1967), *Butch Cassidy and the Sundance Kid* (1969), *Slaughterhouse 5* (1972), and *The World According to Garp* (1982).

Hill, (Norman) Graham (1929–75) Motor-racing driver, born in London, England, UK. He won 14 races from a record 176 starts (since surpassed) between 1958 and 1975, and was world champion in 1962 (in a BRM) and in 1968 (Lotus). He won the Monaco Grand Prix five times (1963–5, 1968–9). In 1975 he started his own racing team, Embassy Racing, but was killed when the plane he was piloting crashed near Hendon, N London. His son, Damon, also went into motor-racing. >> Hill, Damon; RR1165

Hill, James (Jerome) (1838–1916) Railway magnate, born in Guelph, Ontario, Canada. He moved to St Paul, MN, in 1856, where he entered the transportation business. He took over the St Paul–Pacific line and extended it to link with the Canadian system, later gaining control of the Northern Pacific Railroad. He was also active in the construction of the Canadian Pacific Railroad.

Hill, J(oseph) Lister (1894–1984) US senator, born in Montgomery, AL. He served as a Democrat in the US House of Representatives (1923–38) and the US Senate (1939–69), and helped shape the Tennessee Valley Authority Act, the GI bill, and the Hill–Burton Hospital Act.

Hill, Octavia (1838–1912) Housing reformer and founder of the National Trust, born in London, England, UK. She worked among the London poor, and in 1864, supported by Ruskin, commenced her project to improve the homes of people in the slums – methods which were imitated in Europe and the USA. In 1869 she helped to found the Charity Organization Society. A leader of the open-space movement, she was a co-founder in 1895 of the National Trust for Places of Historic Interest or Natural Beauty.

Hill, Patty Smith (1868–1946) Educator and composer, born in Anchorage, KY. Director of the Louisville Training School for Kindergarten and Primary Teachers (1893–1905), she wrote songs for children, one of which became 'Happy Birthday to You'. Joining the Teachers College faculty of Columbia University (1905–35), she initiated curriculum reform, stressing the value of less structured classroom activities and of children's ability to learn through play.

Hill, Rowland (1744–1833) Popular preacher, born in Hawkstone Park, Shropshire, WC England, UK. He studied at Cambridge where, influenced by Methodism, he gave open-air sermons despite opposition from the authorities,

and became an itinerant preacher after his ordination as curate (1773). Receiving an inheritance, he built Surrey Chapel, Blackfriars Rd, London, for his own use. He helped to found the Religious Tract Society and the London Missionary Society, and it is said that the first London Sunday school was his. His *Village Dialogues* (1801) was immensely popular.

Hill, Sir Rowland (1795–1879) Originator of penny postage, born in Kidderminster, Hereford and Worcester, WC England, UK. He became a teacher, and helped to found the Society for the Diffusion of Useful Knowledge (1826). In his *Post-office Reform* (1837), he advocated a low and uniform rate of postage, to be prepaid by stamps, and in 1840 a uniform penny rate was introduced. He became secretary to the Post Office (1854), and was knighted in 1860.

Hillary, Sir Edmund (Percival) (1919–) Mountaineer and explorer, and later writer and lecturer, born in Auckland, New Zealand. As a member of John Hunt's Everest expedition he attained, with Tenzing Norgay, the summit of Mt Everest in 1953, for which he was knighted. As part of the Commonwealth Trans-Antarctic Expedition (1955–8) led by Sir Vivian Fuchs, he and a New Zealand expeditionary party reached the South Pole in 1958. He subsequently established a medical and educational charity, the Himalayan Trust, for the Sherpa peoples of Nepal, which since 1961 has built many schools and two hospitals. His autobiography, *Nothing Venture, Nothing Win*, appeared in 1975. >> Fuchs, Vivian Ernest; Hunt, John; Tenzing

Hillel [hilel], known as **Hillel Hazaken** (the Elder), or **Hillel Hababli** ('the Babylonian') (1st-c BC–1st-c AD) One of the most respected Jewish teachers of his time, probably born in Babylonia. He immigrated to Palestine at about age 40. He founded a school of followers bearing his name, which was frequently in debate with (and often presented more tolerant attitudes than) the contemporary followers of Shammai. Noted for his use of seven rules in expounding Scripture, his views were influential for later rabbinic Judaism. >> Shammai

Hiller, Johann Adam (1728–1804) Composer, born in Wendisch-Ossig, Germany. He studied law at Leipzig University, where he also performed as a singer and flautist. From 1763 he concentrated on composing, and wrote over 30 comic operas, practically creating this genre in Germany. He was also a noted conductor and teacher.

Hiller, Dame Wendy (1912–) Actress, born in Bramhall, Greater Manchester, NW England, UK. She joined the Manchester Repertory Theatre straight from school in 1930, made her London debut in 1935, and her film debut in 1937. Her clarity of diction and spirited personality made her one of Britain's leading stage performers, while her sporadic film career includes performances of distinction in *Separate Tables* (1958, Oscar), *Sons and Lovers* (1960), and *A Man for All Seasons* (1966). Television appearances include *Clochmerle* (1973), *Death of the Heart* (1985), and *The Countess Alice* (1992). She was made a dame in 1975.

Hillery, Patrick (John) (1923–) Irish statesman and president (1976–90), born in Miltown Malbay, Co Clare, Ireland. He studied at Dublin. Following his election as an MP (1951), he held ministerial posts in education (1959–65), industry and commerce (1965–6), and labour (1966–9), then became foreign minister (1969–72). Before becoming president, he served as European Commissioner for social affairs (1973–6). >> RR1064

Hilliard, Nicholas (1547–1619) Court goldsmith and miniaturist, born in Exeter, Devon, SW England, UK. He worked for Elizabeth I and James I, and founded the English school of miniature painting.

Hillier, James (1915–) Physicist, born in Brantford, Ontario, Canada. He studied in Toronto, then moved to the

USA in 1940 and made his career with RCA (the Radio Corporation of America). There he led the group which made the first successful high-resolution electron microscope in 1940. He continued to supervise improvements in RCA's electron microscopes, whose commercial availability after World War 2 revolutionized biology.

Hillier, Tristram Paul (1905–) British artist, born in Beijing. He studied at the Slade School of Art, London, and in Paris. Many of his paintings are of ships and beaches, the earlier ones of a Surrealist character. He has lived much in France, particularly in Dieppe, and his craftmanship and smooth handling of paint are such that his oil paintings are often mistaken for tempera.

Hillman, Sidney (1887–1946) Labour leader, born in Zagare, Lithuania. A labour activist in Russia, he was imprisoned for participation in the abortive revolution of 1905. Upon his release, he emigrated in 1907 to the USA, settling in Chicago. He emerged in the Hart, Schaffner, and Marx strike of 1910 as one of the leaders of the United Garment Workers (UGW), and negotiated a new contract that was regarded as a model of labour-management relations. In 1914 he went to New York City, where he led a split from the UGW that resulted in the formation of the Amalgamated Clothing Workers of America (ACWA). He was elected its first president (1914), an office he held until his death. A founder of the Congress of Industrial Organizations (CIO), he was the first chairman of the CIO's Political Action Committee (1943–6) and a vice-chairman of the newly founded World Federation of Trade Unions (1945–6).

Hilton, Conrad (Nicholson) (1887–1979) Hotelier, born in San Antonio, NM. He became a partner in his father's general store, expanding the business after his father's death, and buying the Mobley Hotel in Cisco. This led to the purchase of other hotels in Texas, and by 1939 he was buying or starting up hotels further afield. The Hilton Hotels Corporation was formed in 1946, becoming the Hilton International Company (1948), one of the world's largest hotel organizations, diversifying in the 1950s to include car-rental and credit-card operations.

Hilton, James (1900–54) Novelist, born in Leigh, Lancashire, NW England, UK. He studied at Cambridge, and quickly established himself as a writer, his first novel, *Catherine Herself*, being published in 1920. His success was dual, for many of his novels were filmed, notably *Lost Horizon* (1933, Hawthornden Prize), and *Goodbye Mr Chips* (1934). He settled in the USA in 1935.

Hilton, Roger (1911–75) Painter, born in Northwood, NW Greater London, England, UK. He trained at the Slade School of Art, London. After spending some time in Paris in the 1930s, he was captured at Dieppe in 1942, and was a prisoner-of-war till 1945. He produced his first abstract paintings in 1950. He won first prize in the John Moores Liverpool Exhibition in 1963, and the UNESCO Prize at the Venice Biennale in 1964.

Himmler, Heinrich (1900–45) German Nazi leader and chief of police, born in Munich, Germany. He joined the Nazi Party in 1925, and in 1929 was made head of the SS (*Schutzstaffel*, protective force), which he developed from Hitler's personal bodyguard into a powerful Party weapon. He also directed the secret police (*Gestapo*), and initiated the systematic liquidation of Jews. In 1943 he became minister of the interior, and in 1944 commander-in-chief of the home forces. He was captured by the Allies, and committed suicide in Lüneburg.

Hinault, Bernard [eenoh] (1954–) Cyclist, born in Yffignac, France. In 1985 he joined Eddy Merckx and Jacques Anquetil as a five-times winner of the Tour de France. He was French pursuit champion in 1974, and turned professional in 1977. In 1982 he won the Tours of Italy and France, and overcame knee surgery in 1983 to win his fifth Tour de France. He retired at 32, and became technical adviser to the Tour de France. >> Anquetil; Merckx; RR1152

Hincmar (c.806–882) Clergyman, born in N France. Educated in the monastery of St Denis, Paris, he became consultant to Louis I and Charles the Bald, and was elected Archbishop of Reims (845). He had disputes with the popes of the day over authority within his dioceses, but is best known for his denunciation of the German theologian **Gottschalk of Orbais** (c.804–c.869) for his predestination doctrines. >> Louis I

Hindemith, Paul [hinduhmit] (1895–1963) Composer, born in Hanau, Germany. He studied at Frankfurt, then played violin in the Rebner Quartet and the Opera Orchestra (1915–23), which he often conducted. His works include operas, concertos, and a wide range of instrumental pieces. He also pioneered *Gebrauchsmusik*, pieces written with specific aims, such as for newsreels and community singing. His music was banned by the Nazis in 1934, and he moved to Turkey, the UK, and the USA. In 1941 he was appointed professor at Yale and in 1953 at Zürich.

Hindenburg, Paul (Ludwig Hans Anton von Beneckendorff und) von [hindenberg] (1847–1934) German general and president (1925–34), born in Posnan, Poland (formerly, Posen, Prussia). Educated at Wahlstatt and Berlin, he fought in the Franco–Prussian War (1870–1), rose to the rank of general (1903), and retired in 1911. Recalled at the outbreak of World War 1, he won victories over the Russians (1914–15), but was forced to direct the German retreat on the Western Front (to the *Hindenburg line*). A national hero, he became the second president of the German Republic in 1925. He was re-elected in 1932, and in 1933 appointed Hitler as chancellor. >> Rennenkampf; Samsonov; RR1051

Hindley, Myra >> Brady, Ian

Hindmarsh, Sir John [hiyndmah(r)sh] (c.1782–1860) British naval officer and administrator, probably born in Chatham, Kent, SE England, UK. He served in the Navy (1796–1815), before being appointed the first governor of South Australia. The vagueness of Hindmarsh's powers led him into conflict with the resident commissioners, which set the tone for his period of office, and he was recalled to London in 1838. He was restored to favour two years later as Lieutenant-Governor of Heligoland.

Hine, Lewis (Wickes) [hiyn] (1874–1940) Photographer, born in Oshkosh, WI. He studied sociology at Chicago and New York universities, making a photographic study of Ellis Island immigrants as an expression of his social concern. In 1909 he published the first of his many photo stories, such as 'Little Spinner in Carolina Cotton Mill', depicting children as young as eight in dangerous work. During World War 1 he documented the plight of refugees for the American Red Cross, and in 1930–1 hung upside down from a crane to photograph the construction of the Empire State Building, 'Men at Work' (1932).

Hines, Earl (Kenneth) [hiynz], nickname **Fatha** ('Father') **Hines** (1905–83) Jazz pianist and bandleader, born in Duquesne, PA. He worked under such leaders as Erskine Tate and Carroll Dickerson, then in association with trumpeter Louis Armstrong (1927–9), with whom he made several recordings now considered jazz classics, notably 'Weather Bird'. Hines formed his own band in 1928, expanding it to a large orchestra resident at the Grand Terrace Ballroom, Chicago. His economical, linear approach to solo improvisation, known as 'trumpet-style piano', had great influence on succeeding jazz pianists. >> Armstrong, Louis

Hingis, Martina [**hing**is] (1981–) Tennis player, born in Kosice, Slovak Republic. She was brought up in Switzerland and, playing for that country, in 1997 became the youngest singles Grand Slam tournament winner of the 20th-century after her victory in the Australian Open, and the youngest-ever world number one when she replaced the injured Steffi Graf. Winner of the 1996 Wimbledon doubles title, she won the singles title in 1997 at the age of 16. >> Graf

Hinkler, Bert (Herbert John Louis) (1892–1933) Aviator, born in Bundaberg, Queensland, Australia. He served in the Royal Naval Air Service in World War 1. In 1928 he created a new England–Australia record, arriving in Darwin, Northern Territory, 16 days after leaving England. In 1931 he flew from the USA to England by way of Jamaica, Brazil, and West Africa, creating another three records on the journey. He crashed and was killed in the Alps while on a solo flight from England to Australia in 1933.

Hinshelwood, Sir Cyril Norman (1897–1967) Chemist, born in London, England, UK. He studied at Oxford, and was professor there from 1937. He did valuable work on the effect of drugs on bacterial cells, and investigated chemical reaction kinetics, for which he shared the Nobel Prize for Chemistry in 1956. A considerable linguist and Classical scholar, he had the unique distinction of being president of both the Royal Society (from 1955) and the Classical Association (in 1960). >> RR1123

Hinsley, Arthur, Cardinal (1865–1943) Roman Catholic clergyman, born in Carlton, North Yorkshire, N England, UK. He studied at the English College, Rome, where he became rector (1917–28) after various posts in England. He was appointed Archbishop of Westminster from 1935, and made a cardinal in 1937. Outspoken in his opposition to the Fascist powers in Germany and Italy, he founded in 1940 an ecumenical politico-religious group called the Sword of the Spirit to rally British churchmen against totalitarianism.

Hinton (of Bankside), Christopher Hinton, Baron (1901–83) Nuclear engineer, born in Tisbury, Wiltshire, S England, UK. He studied at Cambridge, after winning a scholarship while an apprentice in a railway workshop. From 1946, as deputy director of atomic energy production, he constructed the world's first large-scale commercial atomic power station at Calder Hall, Cumbria, opened in 1956. He was knighted in 1951, and created a life peer in 1965.

Hipparchos / Hipparchus [hi**pah**(r)kus] (2nd-c BC) Astronomer, born in Nicaea, Rhodes. He carried out observations at Rhodes, discovered the precession of the equinoxes and the eccentricity of the Sun's path, determined the length of the solar year (to within seven minutes), estimated the distances of the Sun and Moon from the Earth, and drew up a catalogue of 1080 stars. He also fixed the geographical position of places by latitude and longitude, and invented trigonometry.

Hipper, Franz von (1863–1932) German naval officer. He commanded the German scouting groups at the Battles of Dogger Bank (1915) and Jutland (1916). He succeeded as commander-in-chief of the German High Seas fleet in 1918. >> Beatty, David; Jellicoe; Scheer

Hippias of Elis (5th-c BC) Greek Sophist philosopher, a contemporary of Socrates. He was vividly portrayed in Plato's dialogues as a virtuoso performer as teacher, orator, memory man, and polymath. He also discovered a curve used for trisecting a triangle (the quadratrix). Only fragments of his vast literary output have survived. >> Plato; Socrates

Hippius, Zinaida Nikolayevna >> **Merezhkovsky, Dmitry Sergeyevich**

Hippocrates [hi**po**krateez] (c.460–c.377 BC) Physician, known as 'the father of medicine', and associated with the medical profession's *Hippocratic oath*, born on the island of Cos, Greece. The most celebrated physician of antiquity, he gathered together all that was sound in the previous history of medicine. A collection of 70 works, the *Hippocratic corpus*, has been ascribed to him, but very few were written by him, it being more likely that they formed a library at a medical school.

Hippolytus, St [hi**pol**itus] (170–235) Christian leader and antipope in Rome. When Calixtus was elected pope (c.217) he headed a group of dissidents who consecrated him pope in opposition. The schism lasted till 235, when Hippolytus and the successor of Calixtus were both deported to work in the Roman mines in Sardinia, where they died as martyrs. He is generally believed to be the author of a *Refutation of all Heresies* in 10 books, discovered in 1842 in a 14th-c manuscript at Mt Athos. He also wrote a smaller work against heretics extant in a Latin translation. The so-called *Canons of Hippolytus* are more probably Graeco-Egyptian in origin. Feast day (W) 13 August, (E) 30 January.

Hire, Philippe de la [eer] (1640–1718) Engineer, born in Paris. He became a teacher of mathematics at the Collège Royal, and five years later professor at the Royal Academy of Architecture. His most notable work is the *Traité de Méchanique* (1695), in which he correctly analyzed the forces acting at various points in an arch, making use of geometrical techniques now generally known as graphic statics.

Hirohito >> **Showa Tenno**

Hiroshige, Ando [hiroh**shee**gay] (1797–1858) Painter, born in Edo (modern Tokyo). He is celebrated for his impressive landscape colour prints. His 'Fifty-three Stages of the Tokaido' had a great influence on Western Impressionist painters, but heralded the decline of *ukiyo-e* (wood block print design) art.

Hirshhorn, Joseph H(erman) (1899–1981) Financier and art collector, born in Mitvau, Latvia. His family emigrated to New York City in 1907. After studying on his own, he became a stockbroker (1916), amassed a fortune, and liquidated his holdings just prior to the crash of 1929. He made other fortunes in gold and uranium mines in Canada, and invested much of his money in art, especially sculpture. In 1966 he donated his collection to the United States to be administered by the Smithsonian Institution. The Joseph H Hirshhorn Museum and Sculpture Garden in Washington, DC, opened in 1974.

Hirst, Damien (1965–) Avant-garde artist, born in Bristol, SW England, UK. He studied art at Goldsmith's College, London, produced several paintings and mixed-medium sculptures, then became known for his works which made use of parts or all of dead animals, preserved in formalin, such as 'Mother and Child Divided' – four tanks contained the severed halves of a cow and calf. Considerable controversy surrounded the show he organized in London for young artists in 1994, at which one of his works, 'Away from the Flock', consisting of a dead lamb suspended within a tank, became the focus of attention when another artist poured ink into the tank. At the centre of debate over the nature and role of art, he became an established figure after being awarded the Turner Prize in 1995. His 1996 exhibition, 'No Sense of Absolute Corruption' (New York City) contained several large paintings, as well as earlier works.

His, Wilhelm (1831–1904) Biologist, born in Basel, Switzerland. He studied at Berlin and Würzburg, and became professor of anatomy at Basel (1857–72) and Leipzig (1872–1904). He invented the microtome (1865, a device to cut very thin slices for microscopic investigation), and discovered that each nerve fibre is linked to a single nerve cell.

Hislop, Ian (1960–) British writer, editor, and broadcaster. He studied at Oxford, became a television scriptwriter for *Spitting Image* (1984–9), a columnist for *The Listener* (1985–9), and editor of the satirical magazine *Private Eye* (1986–). Presenter of *The Canterbury Tales* series for Channel 4 (1996), he is also a team captain of BBC's popular *Have I Got News For You* (1991–), and has co-written a number of plays for television.

Hiss, Alger [aljer] (1904–96) US State Department official, born in Baltimore, MD. He studied at Johns Hopkins University and Harvard Law School, and reached high office in the State Department. He stood trial twice (1949, 1950) on a charge of perjury, having denied before a Congressional Committee that he had passed secret state documents to Whittaker Chambers, in 1938 an agent for an international Communist spy ring. The case aroused great controversy, but he was convicted at his second trial, and sentenced to five years' imprisonment. He did not return to public life after his release. The justice of his conviction continues to be disputed, but revelations from Soviet archives in 1992 seem to indicate his innocence. >> Chambers, Whittaker

Hitchcock, Sir Alfred (Joseph) (1899–1980) Film director, born in London, England, UK. He studied engineering at London, and began in films as a junior technician in 1920. He directed his first film in 1925, and rose to become an unexcelled master of suspense, internationally recognized for his intricate plots and novel camera techniques. His British films included *The Thirty-Nine Steps* (1935) and *The Lady Vanishes* (1938). His first US film, *Rebecca* (1940), won an Oscar. Later films included *Psycho* (1960), *The Birds* (1963), and *Frenzy* (1972). He was knighted in 1980.

Hitchcock, Lambert (1795–1852) Furniture designer, born in Cheshire, CT. In 1818 he established a furniture factory in Barkhamsted (now Riverton), employing 100 workers for mass production of Hitchcock chairs, now considered collectors' items. He also made the first designer rocking-chair.

Hitchens, Ivon (1893–1979) Painter, born in London, England, UK. He studied at the Royal Academy. Painting in a semi-abstract style with obvious roots in Cubism, he always retained a strongly expressive feeling for natural forms, especially in the wide, horizontal landscapes which he painted from 1936. His first retrospective exhibition was in Leeds in 1945, after which he had many one-man shows in Europe and America.

Hitchings, George (Herbert) (1905–) Chemist, born in Hoquiam, WA. He studied at the University of Washington and at Harvard, where he taught for a while before moving to Western Reserve University (1939). From 1942 he worked at the Burroughs Wellcome Research Laboratories in Tuckahoe, NY, being joined by Gertrude Elion in a major programme of drug development, notably 6-mercaptopurine (6MP) for the treatment of childhood leukaemia, and later other drugs for use in relation to a wide range of diseases, auto-immune disorders, and tissue transplantation. In 1988 they shared, with James Black, the Nobel Prize for Physiology or Medicine. >> Black, James; Elion

Hitler, Adolf, popular name **der Führer** ('the Leader'), see panel on p. 452

Hittorf, Johann Wilhelm (1824–1914) Physicist, born in Bonn, Germany. He became professor of physics and chemistry at Münster (1879–89). He was the first to determine the charge-carrying capacity of ions, which brought greater understanding of electrochemical reactions, and he also studied electrical discharges in gases.

Hjelmslev, Louis (Trolle) [hyelmzlev] (1899–1965) Linguist, born in Copenhagen. He founded the Linguistic Circle of Copenhagen in 1931, and was a co-founder of the journal *Acta Linguistica* in 1939. With associates in Copenhagen, he devised a system of linguistic analysis known as glossematics, based on the study of the distribution of, and the relationships between, the smallest meaningful units of a language (glossemes). This is outlined in his *Prolegomena to a Theory of Language* (1943).

Hoad, Lew(is Alan) [hohd] (1934–94) Tennis player, born in Sydney, New South Wales, Australia. With his doubles partner, Ken Rosewall, he had a meteoric rise to fame, winning the Wimbledon doubles title and a Davis Cup challenge match against the USA before he was 20 years old. He defeated Rosewall in the Wimbledon final of 1956, and won again the following year, but thereafter turned professional and was ineligible by the rules of the time to compete for the game's major honours. >> Rosewall; RR1173

Hoadley, Silas >> **Thomas, Seth**

Hoagland, Mahlon (Bush) [hohgland] (1921–) Biochemist, born in Boston, MA. He studied medicine at Harvard, taught there (1960–7), and became scientific director of the Worcester Foundation for Experimental Biology (1970–85). In the 1950s he isolated t-RNA (transfer RNA), and went on to show in some detail how cells use it to synthesize proteins from amino acids.

Hoare, Sir Richard (1648–1718) Banker, born in London, England, UK. He became a Lombard Street goldsmith (c.1673) and moved (c.1693) to Fleet Street, where he founded the bank which still bears his name. He was Lord Mayor of London in 1713.

Hoare, Sir Samuel (John Gurney), Viscount Templewood of Chelsea (from 1944) (1880–1959) British statesman, born in London, England, UK. He studied at Oxford, entered politics in 1905, and became Conservative MP for Chelsea (1910–44). He was secretary of state for air (1922–9), and as secretary of state for India (1931–5) piloted the India Act through the Commons, despite the opposition of Winston Churchill. In 1935, as foreign secretary, he resigned after criticism of his part in the discussions which led to the abortive Hoare–Laval pact over the Italian invasion of Ethiopia. >> Churchill, Sir Winston; Laval

Hoban, Russell (Conwell) (1925–) Novelist and writer of children's literature, born in Lansdale, PA. He was an illustrator for many years before becoming a writer. *The Mouse and His Child* (1969) is regarded as a modern children's classic. He became known as a novelist with *Turtle Diary* (1975), later books including *Riddley Walker* (1980) and *The Medusa Frequency* (1987). He has also produced some lively picture-books for children, many illustrated by Quentin Blake. >> Blake, Quentin

Hobbema, Meindert [hobema], originally **Meyndert Lubbertsz(oon)** (1638–1709) Landscape painter, probably born in Amsterdam. He studied under Ruysdael, but lacked his master's genius and range, contenting himself with florid, placid, and charming watermill scenes. Nevertheless his masterpiece, 'The Avenue, Middelharnis' (1689, National Gallery, London) is a striking exception, and has greatly influenced modern landscape artists. >> Ruysdael

Hobbes, Thomas (1588–1679) Political philosopher, born in Malmesbury, Wiltshire, S England, UK. He studied at Oxford, then began a long tutorial association with the Cavendish family, through which he travelled widely. After being introduced to Euclidian geometry, he thought to extend its method into a comprehensive science of man and society. Obsessed by the civil disorders of his time, he wrote several works on government. In 1646 he became

ADOLF HITLER (1889–1945)

Hitler was born at Braunau in Upper Austria, the son of an illegitimate father, Alois Hitler (previously Schicklgruber, his mother's name, but legitimized to Hitler, a mis-spelling of Hiedler, in 1867). Alois was a minor customs official married to Klara Pölzl, Hitler's overindulgent mother. He was educated at the secondary schools of Linz and Steyr, and destined by his father for the civil service. Hitler, however, saw himself as a great artist, and disgraced himself in his school-leaving examinations. After his father's death in 1903, he attended a private art school in Munich, but failed twice to pass into the Vienna Academy. Advised to try architecture, he was debarred from that for lack of a school-leaving certificate. He lived by his wits in Vienna (1904–13), making a precarious living by selling bad postcard sketches, beating carpets, and doing odd jobs. He worked only fitfully, and spent his time in passionate political arguments directed at the money-lending Jews and the trade unions. He dodged military service, and in 1913 emigrated to Munich where he found employment as a draughtsman.

In 1914 he volunteered for war service in a Bavarian regiment, rose to the rank of corporal, and was recommended for the award of the Iron Cross for service as a runner on the Western front. At the time of the German surrender in 1918 he was lying wounded in hospital, temporarily blinded by gas. In 1919, while acting as an informer for the army, spying on the activities of small political parties, he became a member of one of them, changing its name to *National sozialistiche Deutsche Arbeiterpartei* (National Socialist German Workers' Party, abbreviated to *Nazi*) in 1920. Its programme was a convenient mixture of mild radicalism, bitter hatred of the politicians who had 'dishonoured Germany' by signing the Treaty of Versailles, and clever exploitation of provincial grievances against the weak federal government.

By 1923 he was strong enough to attempt, with the help of General Ludendorff and other extreme right-wing factions, the overthrow of the Bavarian government. On 9 November the Nazis marched through the streets of Munich, but the police, with whom they thought they had a tacit agreement, machine-gunned the Nazi column. Hitler narrowly escaped serious injury, Goering was badly wounded, and 16 storm troopers were killed. After nine month's imprisonment in Landsberg jail, during which he dictated his autobiography and political manifesto, *Mein Kampf* (1925, My Struggle), to Rudolf Hess, he began with Goebbels to woo the Ruhr industrialists. Although unsuccessful in the presidential elections of 1932 when he stood against Hindenburg, Hitler was made chancellor in January 1933 on the advice of von Papen, who mistakenly thought that he could best be brought to heel inside the Cabinet.

By that time, Hitler had become a magnetic political leader. He soon dispensed with constitutional restraints, silenced all opposition, and successfully engineered the burning of the Reichstag building (1933) – an attack he advertised as a communist plot. He used this pretext to call for a general election in which the police, under Goering, allowed the Nazis full play to break up the meetings of their opponents. Only under these conditions did the Nazi Party achieve a bare majority, and Hitler took on absolute power through the Enabling Acts. He ruthlessly crushed opposition inside his own Party with the purge of June 1934, in which his rival Röhm and hundreds of influential Nazis were murdered at the hands of Hitler's bodyguard, the SS, under Himmler and Heydrich. Hindenburg's convenient demise in August left Hitler sole master of Germany.

Under the pretext of undoing the wrongs of the Versailles Treaty, uniting the German peoples and extending their living-space (*Lebensraum*), he openly rearmed (1935); sent troops into the demilitarized Rhineland zone; established the Rome–Berlin 'axis' (1936) with Mussolini's Italy; created 'Greater Germany' by the invasion of Austria (1938); and, by systematic infiltration and engineered incidents, engendered a favourable situation for an easy absorption of the Sudeten or German-populated borderlands of Czechoslovakia, in which Britain and France acquiesced at Munich (Sep 1938). Renouncing further territorial claims, Hitler nevertheless seized Bohemia and Moravia, took Memel from Lithuania, and demanded from Poland the return of Danzig and free access to East Prussia through the 'Corridor'. Poland's refusal, backed by Britain and France, precipitated World War 2, on 3 September 1939.

Meanwhile Hitler's domestic policy was one of thorough nazification of all aspects of German life, enforced by the Secret State Police (*Gestapo*), and the establishment of concentration camps for political opponents and Jews, who were systematically persecuted. Strategic roads or *Autobahnen* were built, and Schacht's economic policy expanded German exports up to 1936. Goering's 'Guns before Butter' four-year plan boosted armaments and provided for the construction of the Siegfried Line.

Hitler entered the war with the grave misgivings of German High Command, but as his intuitions scored massive triumphs in the first two years, he ignored the advice of military experts more and more. Peace with Russia having been secured by the Molotov–Ribbentrop pact (Aug 1939), he invaded Poland; and after three weeks' *Blitzkrieg* ('lightning war') Poland was divided between Russia and Germany. In 1940 Denmark, Norway, Holland, Belgium, and France were occupied, and the British expelled from France at Dunkirk. But Goering's invincible *Luftwaffe* (the airforce) was routed in the Battle of Britain (Aug–Sep 1940).

Hitler then turned E, entered Romania (Oct 1940), invaded Yugoslavia and Greece (Apr 1941), and, ignoring his pact of convenience with Stalin, attacked Russia. As an ally of Japan, he also found himself at war with the US (Dec 1941). The *Wehrmacht* (army) penetrated to the gates of Moscow and Leningrad, to the Volga, into the Caucasus and, with Italy as an ally from 1940, to North Africa as far as Alexandria. But there the tide turned. Montgomery's victory over Rommel at El Alamein (Oct 1942); and Paulus's grave defeat, through Hitler's misdirection, at Stalingrad (Nov 1942), heralded the Nazi withdrawal from North Africa pursued by the British and Americans (Nov 1942–May 1943). The Allied invasion of Sicily, Italian capitulation (Sep 1943) and engulfing Russian victories (1943-4) followed. The Anglo-American invasion of Normandy and breach of Rommel's 'Atlantic Wall' (Jun 1944) were not effectively countered by Hitler's V1 and V2 guided missile attacks on S England. The Allies were now advancing steadily.

Several plans to assassinate Hitler were made between 1943 and 1944 by German pacifists. He miraculously survived the explosion of a bomb placed at his feet by Colonel Stauffenberg in July 1944, but he purged the army of all suspects, including Rommel, who was given the chance to commit suicide. Rundstedt's counter-offensive against the Allies in the Ardennes (Dec 1944) under Hitler's direction failed, and the invasion of Germany followed. Hitler lived out his fantasies, commanding nonexistent armies from his bunker, the air-raid shelter under the chancellory building in Berlin. At midnight on 28 April, with the Russians only a few hundred yards away, he went through a marriage ceremony with his mistress, Eva Braun, in the presence of Goebbels and his family, who then poisoned themselves. All available evidence suggests that Hitler and his wife committed suicide (Hitler probably by shooting himself and Eva by poison) and had their bodies burnt on 30 April 1945.

>> Braun, Eva; Goebbels; Goering; Hess; Heydrich; Himmler; Hindenburg; Ludendorff; Montgomery; Paulus; Röhm; Rommel; Rundstedt; Schacht; Stalin; Stauffenberg; von Papen

mathematical tutor to the Prince of Wales at the exiled English court in Paris, where he wrote his masterpiece of political philosophy, *Leviathan* (1651). In 1652 he returned to England, submitted to Cromwell, and settled in London. After the Restoration he was given a pension.

Hobbs, Jack, popular name of **Sir John Berry Hobbs** (1882–1963) Cricketer, born in Cambridge, Cambridgeshire, EC England, UK. He played in county cricket for Cambridgeshire (1904) and Surrey (1905–34), and for England (1908–30), when he and **Herbert Sutcliffe** (1894–1978) established themselves as an unrivalled pair of opening batsmen. He made 5410 runs in 61 Test matches (average 56·94), and a record number of 197 centuries and 61 237 runs in first-class cricket. He was the first English cricketer to be knighted, in 1953. >> RR1151

Hobday, Sir Frederick (George Thomas) (1870–1939) British veterinarian. He was principal of the Royal Veterinary College, London (1927–37), and responsible for the 'Farthing Fund' to raise £250 000 for the new College building, opened by George VI in 1937. He is said to have performed **Hobday's operation** (stripping part of the larynx as a remedy for laryngeal hemiplegia) on more than 4000 horses.

Hobday, Peter (1937–) British journalist and broadcaster. Educated at Leicester University, he spent a year with a local newspaper in Wolverhampton, then joined the BBC, working in both radio and television. He became known for his contributions to such programmes as BBC2's *The Money Programme* (1979–81) and *Newsnight* (1980–2), and Radio 4's *Today* (from 1981).

Hobson, Sir Harold (1904–92) Dramatic critic, born in Thorpe Hesley, South Yorkshire, N England, UK. He studied at Oxford, and was an assistant literary editor (1942–7) before becoming drama critic (1947–76) of the *Sunday Times*. He was one of the most influential critics in Britain, championing many new playwrights, including Beckett, Pinter, and Stoppard. He was also drama critic of the *Christian Science Monitor* (1931–74), and a regular member of the radio programme *The Critics*. He wrote a number of books on British and French theatre, an autobiography (*Indirect Journey*, 1978), and a personal history, *Theatre in Britain* (1984). He was knighted in 1977. >> Beckett, Samuel; Pinter; Stoppard

Hobson, Thomas (c. 1544–1631) Carrier and inn-keeper of Cambridge, Cambridgeshire, EC England, UK. For some 50 years he drove a stagecoach the 60 mi from Cambridge to London at breakneck speed. He kept a stable of horses to rent out to students at the university, and required each customer to take the horse nearest the stable door, whatever its quality; hence the expression 'Hobson's choice', meaning no choice at all.

Hoccleve or **Occleve, Thomas** [hokleev] (c. 1368–c. 1450) Poet, born in London, England, UK. He spent his life as a clerk in the privy seal office in London (1378–1425). His chief work, *The Regement of Princes* (1411) is a free but tedious version, in the style of Chaucer, of the *De regimine principum* of Aegidius Romanus (13th-c). *La male regla* (1406, The Male Regimen) is of more value as social history, with its vivid account of night life in Westminster.

Hochhuth, Rolf [hokhhoot] (1931–) Playwright, born in Eschwege, Germany. He studied at Heidelberg and Munich. His play *Der Stellvertreter* (1963, The Representative), focusing on the role of the Pope in World War 2, excited controversy and introduced the fashion for 'documentary drama'. Later plays have touched on other sensitive issues: *Soldaten* (1967, Soldiers) on the war morality of the Allies, and *Juristen* (1980, trans The Legal Profession) on collaboration with the Nazis.

Ho Chi-Minh [hoh chee min], originally **Nguyen That Thanh** (1892–1969) Vietnamese statesman, prime minister (1954–5), and president (1954–69), born in Kim-Lien, North Vietnam. From 1912 he visited London and the USA, and lived in France from 1918, where he was a founder member of the Communist Party. From 1922 he was often in Moscow. He led the Viet Minh independence movement in 1941, and directed the successful military operations against the French (1946–54), becoming President of North Vietnam. He was a leading force in the war between North and South Vietnam during the 1960s. >> RR1099

Hockney, David (1937–) Artist, born in Bradford, West Yorkshire, N England, UK. He studied at Bradford School of Art and the Royal College of Art, London, and was associated with the Pop Art movement from his earliest work. He taught at the University of California, Los Angeles (1965–7), and it was a visit to California that inspired his 'swimming pool' paintings, prompted by his fascination with the representation of water. His later work, often portraits, has become more representational. He has also worked in printmaking and photography, and designed sets and costumes.

Hoddinott, Alun (1929–) Composer, born in Bargoed, Caerphilly, S Wales, UK. He studied in Cardiff, and taught at the College of Music and Drama before joining the music staff at University College, Cardiff in 1959, becoming professor (1967–87, now emeritus). In 1967 he was co-founder of the Cardiff Festival, serving as artistic director (1967–89) and president (1990–). He is a prolific composer of operas, symphonies, concertos, and a large corpus of choral and chamber works.

Hoddle, Glenn (1957–) Football manager and player, born in Hayes, NW Greater London, England, UK. He made his professional debut with Tottenham Hotspur (1976), moved to AS Monaco (1986), and returned to England as player/manager of Swindon Town (1991–3), continuing this dual role at Chelsea (1993–6). He replaced Terry Venables as England's manager in 1996. >> Venables

Hodges, Johnny (1906–70) Jazz alto and soprano saxophonist, born in Cambridge, MA. He joined Duke Ellington's orchestra in 1928, and became an indispensable colour in Ellington's sound palette, staying with him until 1951 and, after leading his own band with moderate success, rejoining in 1955 until his death. Ellington wrote numerous showpieces for Hodges, one of the most distinctive instrumental voices in jazz, such as 'Sophisticated Lady' (1933), 'The Star-Crossed Lovers' (1957), and 'Blues for New Orleans' (1970). Despite their musical intimacy that lasted for 38 years, Hodges and Ellington were not close. At performances when Hodges had been drinking heavily, Ellington often called for three or four of his featured numbers in a row; and Hodges stopped playing soprano saxophone forever, a sound Ellington loved, because Ellington refused him a raise in 1940. >> Ellington, Duke

Hodgkin, Sir Alan (Lloyd) (1914–) Physiologist, born in Banbury, Oxfordshire, SC England, UK. He studied at Cambridge. He worked on the development of radar (1939–45), was a lecturer at Cambridge (1945–52), becoming Royal Society research professor (1952–69), and professor of biophysics at Cambridge (1970–81). With his former student Andrew Huxley he researched the passage of impulses in nerve fibres, for which they shared the 1963 Nobel Prize for Physiology or Medicine. >> Eccles, John Carew; Huxley, Andrew

Hodgkin, Dorothy Mary, *née* **Crowfoot** (1910–94) Chemist, born in Cairo. She studied at Oxford and Cambridge, became a research fellow at Somerville College, Oxford (1936–77), and research professor at the Royal Society (1960–77). A crystallographer of distinction, she was awarded the Nobel Prize for Chemistry in 1964 for her discoveries, by the use of X-ray techniques, of the structure of certain molecules, including penicillin, vitamin B^{12}, and insulin.

Hodgkin, Sir Howard (1932–) Painter, born in London, England, UK. He trained chiefly at Bath Academy of Art, where he later taught (1956–66). His highly personal style has not followed any of the major art movements of recent decades: though at first sight apparently abstract, his paintings are in fact representational, usually of interiors with people captured at a particular moment in time. In 1985 he won the Turner Prize for contemporary British art. He was knighted in 1992. >> RR1127

Hodgkin, Thomas (1798–1866) Physician and pathologist, born in London, England, UK. He studied at Edinburgh, held various posts at Guy's Hospital, and described the glandular disease lymphadenoma, which is named after him (*Hodgkin's disease*).

Hodgkins, Frances Mary (1869–1947) Artist, born in Dunedin, New Zealand. She studied there, and travelled extensively in Europe with long visits to Paris and England. Her paintings, examples of which are in the Tate Gallery and the Victoria and Albert Museum, are characterized by a harmonious use of flat colour, somewhat reminiscent of Matisse. Though older than most of her circle, she was ranked as a leader of contemporary Romanticism. >> Matisse

Hodgkinson, Eaton (1789–1861) Engineer, born in Anderton, Cheshire, NWC England, UK. He had little formal higher education, but became one of the foremost authorities on the strength of materials, by carrying out tests in the engineering works of Sir William Fairbairn. He proposed the *Hodgkinson's beam* as the most efficient form of cast-iron beam (1830), and published a paper *On the Strength of Pillars of Cast Iron and Other Materials* (1840). He also collaborated with Fairbairn and Robert Stephenson on the design of the wrought-iron rectangular tubes within which trains crossed the R Conway and the Menai Straits in N Wales, a significant advance in the theory and practice of structural engineering at the time. >> Fairbairn; Stephenson, Robert

Hodgson, Leonard (1889–1969) Anglican theologian, born in London, England, UK. He taught at Magdalen College, Oxford, and the General Theological Seminary, New York, before returning to Oxford as professor of moral and pastoral theology (1938–54) and then professor of divinity (1944–58). He was also theological secretary to the Commission on Faith and Order of the World Council of Churches, Geneva (1933– 52), and warden of William Temple College, Rugby (1954–66). He wrote some 20 books, including *The Doctrine of the Trinity* (1943) and *The Doctrine of the Atonement* (1951).

Hodgson, Ralph (1871–1962) Poet, born in Yorkshire, N England, UK. He became a journalist in London and editor of *Fry's Magazine*, and a member of the group of poets known as the 'Georgians'. He is best known for three volumes of poems with the recurring theme of nature and England: *The Last Blackbird* (1907), *Eve* (1913), and *Poems* (1917), which contains the polemic against the destruction of animals for feminine vanity in 'To Deck a Woman'. He lectured in Japan (1924–38), then made his home in Ohio, USA. An anthology of his works appeared as *The Skylark and Other Poems* (1958).

Hodja, Enver >> **Hoxha, Enver**

Hodler, Ferdinand (1853–1918) Artist, born in Bern. He was one of the group of Swiss painters whose landscapes influenced the Expressionist artists of the early 20th century. He also painted many symbolic works: in particular, 'Die Nacht' (1890, Night; Kunstmuseum, Bern), engaging with the symbolism of youth and age, solitude, and contemplation, brought him great acclaim throughout Europe.

Hoe, Richard (March) (1812–86) Inventor and industrialist, born in New York City. At the age of 15, he joined his father's firm, which manufactured printing presses, and took over after his father's death. He developed the first successful rotary press, patented in 1847, and used by the *Philadelphia Public Ledger*. An improved model, the *Hoe web perfecting press*, was first used by the *New York Tribune*.

Hofer, Andreas [hohfer] (1767–1810) Tyrolese patriot leader and innkeeper, born in St Leonhard, Austria. In 1808 he called the Tyrolese to arms to expel the French and Bavarians, and twice succeeded in freeing the Tyrol of invaders, but was eventually captured and, on Napoleon's orders, executed. >> Napoleon

Hoff, Jacobus Henricus van't (1852–1911) Chemist, a founder of physical chemistry and stereochemistry, born in Rotterdam, The Netherlands. He studied at Leyden, and became professor of chemistry at Amsterdam (1877), Leipzig (1887), and Berlin (1895). He postulated the asymmetrical nature of bonds formed with carbon atoms, was the first to apply thermodynamics to chemical reactions, discovered that osmotic pressure varies directly with the absolute temperature, and investigated the formation of double salts. He was awarded the first Nobel Prize for Chemistry in 1901. >> Le Bel

Hoff, Ted, popular name of **Marian Edward Hoff** (1937–) Creator of the microprocessor, born in Rochester, NY. He studied at Stanford, and became a researcher for the Intel Co, who were developing an integrated circuit for a Japanese manufacturer of desk-top calculators. With a knowledge of computers (then still very large machines) he designed the computer-on-a-chip microprocessor (1968), which came on the market as the Intel 4004 (1971), starting the microcomputer industry. >> Bushnell, Nolan

Hoffa, Jimmy, popular name of **James R(iddle) Hoffa** (1913–75) Labour leader, born in Brazil, IN. A grocery warehouseman member of the Teamster's Union in 1931, he became vice-president of his Union in 1952, and president in 1957. Following corruption investigations, he was imprisoned in 1967 for attempted bribery of a federal court jury. His sentence was commuted by President Nixon, and he was given parole in 1971, on condition that he resigned as Teamsters' leader. In 1975 he disappeared, and is thought to have been murdered. >> Nixon

Hoffenberg, Sir Raymond (Bill) (1923–) Physician, born in Port Elizabeth, South Africa. He served with South African armed forces in World War 2, qualified in medicine at the University of Cape Town, and taught in the Medical School. In 1967 he was 'banned' by the South African government, and the next year moved to Britain, where he became professor of medicine at Birmingham University (1972–85) and president of Wolfson College, Oxford (1985–93). He has written extensively on endocrinology and metabolism, and has been president of several organizations, including the Mental Health Foundation (1989–). He was knighted in 1984.

Hoffman, Dustin (1937–) Actor, born in Los Angeles, CA. A student at the Pasadena Playhouse, he pursued a career on stage and television in New York City, making his Broadway debut in 1961. His first leading film role was *The Graduate* (1967), and this was followed by a number of similar 'anti-hero' roles: *Midnight Cowboy* (1969), *Little Big Man* (1970), and *Marathon Man* (1976). He found wider scope in *All the President's Men* (1976), *Kramer v. Kramer* (1979, Oscar), and *Tootsie* (1982). He returned to Broadway in *Death of a Salesman* (1984), winning an Emmy for its television reprise (1985). His later films include *Rain Man* (1988, Oscar), *Billy Bathgate* (1991), *Hook* (1991), *Outbreak* (1995), and *American Buffalo* (1996).

Hoffman, Samuel (Kurtz) (1902–) Rocket propulsion engineer, born in Williamsport, PA. He studied at Pennsylvania State University (1925), and became professor of aeronautical engineering there (1945–9). From 1949 he led the team developing rocket engines at North American Aviation, raising their power from an initial 75 000 pounds of thrust to 1·5 million pounds by the mid-1960s. Eight of these engines powered the multi-stage Saturn 5 launching vehicle which in 1969 took US astronauts on the first stage of their journey to the Moon.

Hoffmann, August Heinrich, known as **Hoffman von Fallersleben** (1798–1874) Poet and philologist, born in Fallersleben, Germany. He studied at Göttingen and Bonn, was keeper of the university library of Wrocław, Poland (formerly Breslau, Germany (1823–38)), and professor of German there (1830–42). He is best known for his popular and patriotic *Volkslieder*, including 'Alle Vögel sind schon da' and the song 'Deutschland, Deutschland über Alles' (1841), which became the German national anthem in 1922.

Hoffmann, E(rnst) T(heodor) W(ilhelm), known as **Amadeus** (1776–1822) Writer, composer, music critic, and caricaturist, born in Königsberg, Germany. Trained as a lawyer, he had an unsettled career until 1816, when he attained a high position in the Supreme Court in Berlin. His shorter tales were mostly published in the collections *Phantasiestücke* (1814) and *Nachtstücke* (1817, trans Hoffman's Strange Stories), which was an inspiration for Offenbach's opera *Tales of Hoffmann*, and also for Delibes's *Coppélia*. His longer works include *Elixiere des Teufels* (1816, The Devil's Elixir). His most important opera was *Undine*, and he also composed vocal, chamber, orchestral, and piano works.

Hoffmann, Friedrich (1660–1742) German physician. He was professor of medicine at Halle, and physician to Frederick I of Prussia. He introduced various medicines, including *Hoffmann's drops* and *Hoffmann's anodyne*.

Hoffmann, Josef (1870–1956) Architect, born in Pirnitz, Austria. He studied in Vienna, was a leader of the Vienna 'Secession' group (1899 – seceding from the traditional Viennese style), and in 1903 founded the *Wiener Werkstätte* (Vienna Workshops), devoted to arts and crafts. He himself designed metalwork, glass, and furniture. His main architectural achievements were the white-stuccoed Purkersdorf Sanatorium in Austria (1903–5) and Stoclet House in Brussels (1905–11). He was city architect of Vienna from 1920, and designed the Austrian pavilion for the 1934 Venice Bienniale.

Hoffmann (of Chedworth), Leonard Hubert Hoffmann, Baron (1934–) Judge, born in Cape Town. He was South African College School's Rhodes Scholar at Oxford (1954–7) and a Vinerian Law Scholar (1957). After two years at the Cape Town bar he returned to Britain, and in 1961 was elected Stowell Civil Law Fellow at University College, Oxford. He wrote *The South African Law of Evidence* (1963). He was appointed a QC (1977), a judge in the High Court of Justice (1985), a Lord Justice of Appeal (1992), and a Lord of Appeal in Ordinary (1995). He has twice been director of the English National Opera (1985–90, 1991–4). Knighted in 1985, he was created a life peer in 1995.

Hoffmann, Roald (1937–) Chemist, born in Zloczow, Poland. He moved to the USA in 1949, studied at Columbia and Harvard universities, and worked at Cornell from 1965. While at Harvard he worked with R B Woodward to develop the *Woodward–Hoffmann rules*, which enable the path of an important class of organic reactions to be predicted. He shared the Nobel Prize for Chemistry in 1981. >> Woodward, R B

Hoffnung, Gerard (1925–1959) Cartoonist and musician, born in Berlin, but raised in England. Educated at Highgate School of Arts, he taught art at Stamford School (1945) and Harrow (1948). His first cartoon was published in *Lilliput* magazine while he was still at school (1941). He was staff cartoonist on the London *Evening News* (1947) and after a brief time in New York (1950) returned in 1951 to freelance for *Punch* and others. His interest in music led to his creation of the Hoffnung Music Festivals at the Royal Festival Hall, in which his caricatures came to life and sound. They were also animated by Halas-Batchelor in the television series, *Tales From Hoffnung* (1965).

Hofmann, August Wilhelm von (1818–92) Chemist, born in Giessen, Germany. He became first director of the Royal College of Chemistry in London (1845), and was chemist to the Royal Mint (1856–65). He went to Berlin as professor of chemistry in 1865, founded the German Chemical Society (1868), and was ennobled in 1888. He obtained aniline from coal products, discovered many other organic compounds, including formaldehyde (1867), and devoted much labour to the theory of chemical types. His work was of importance to the aniline-dye industry. >> Perkin

Hofmann, Hans (1880–1966) Painter and art teacher, born in Weissenberg, Germany. He studied painting in Munich, then lived in Paris, where he was influenced by Matisse. He returned to Germany in 1914, opening an art school in Munich. In 1930 he emigrated to the USA, settling in New York City, where he opened the Hans Hofmann School of Fine Art, pioneering the use of improvisatory techniques. >> Matisse

Hofmannsthal, Hugo von [**hof**manztahl] (1874–1929) Poet and playwright, born in Vienna. He early attracted attention by his symbolic, neo-Romantic poems, then wrote several plays, notably *Electra* (1903), the morality play *Jedermann* (1912), and the comedy, *Der Schwierige* (1921, The Difficult Man). He also collaborated with Richard Strauss, for whom he wrote the libretti for *Der Rosenkavalier* (1911) and other works. With Strauss and Max Reinhardt, he founded the Salzburg Festival after World War 1. >> Reinhardt, Max; Strauss, Richard

Hofmeister, Wilhelm (Friedrich Benedikt) [**hohf**myster] (1824–77) Botanist, born in Leipzig, Germany. Although he was completely self-taught, he was appointed professor of botany at Heidelberg (1863), and in 1872 at Tübingen. He did fundamental work on plant embryology, and pioneered the science of comparative plant morphology.

Hofstadter, Richard [**hof**stater] (1916–70) Historian, born in Buffalo, NY. He studied at Buffalo and Columbia universities, then taught at the University of Maryland (1942–6) and at Columbia (1946–70). His popular works on political, social, and intellectual trends in the USA include *The Age of Reform* (1955, Pulitzer), *Anti-Intellectualism in American Life* (1963, Pulitzer), and *The Paranoid Style in American Politics* (1965).

Hofstadter, Robert [**hof**stater] (1915–) Physicist, born in New York City. He taught at Stanford University from 1946, becoming professor of physics there in 1954. He studied the atomic structure of protons and neutrons on the large linear accelerator at Stanford, and determined their electromagnetic form factors. He shared the 1961 Nobel Prize for Physics. >> RR1122

Hogan, Ben(jamin William), nickname **The Hawk** (1912–97) Golfer, born in Dublin, TX. A professional at various country clubs, he fought his way to the top despite financial difficulties, and in 1948 became the first man in 26 years to win all three US major titles. He had a near-fatal car accident in 1949, but amazed everyone by his determination to continue playing, and despite pain from his injuries he returned to win a further three major titles in 1953. He won the US Open four times (1948, 1950–1, 1953) before retiring in 1970 with a grand total of 63 US Professional Golf Association tour victories. A film on his life, *Follow the Sun*, starring Glenn Ford, was made in 1951, and he wrote an influential manual on the game in 1957. >> RR1158

Hogan, Paul (1941–) Comedian and actor, born in Lightning Ridge, New South Wales, Australia. When he appeared on a television talent show as a comedian, his original style proved so popular that he was given his own programme, *The Paul Hogan Show*, which ran for nine years. International fame followed with the successful films *Crocodile Dundee* and *Crocodile Dundee II*. His series of television advertisements for the Australian Tourist Board did much to promote his country, and he has become something of a national folk hero. His 1990 film *Almost an Angel* was less successful, but in 1993 he listed his next film, *Lightning Ridge*, on the Australian Stock Exchange to raise funds – a unique and successful venture.

Hogarth, William [hoh-gah(r)th] (1697–1764) Painter and engraver, born in London, England, UK. By 1720 he had his own business as an engraver, and by the late 1720s as a portrait painter. Tiring of conventional art forms, he began his 'modern moral subjects', such as 'A Rake's Progress' (1733–5), and his masterpiece, the 'Marriage à la Mode' (1743–5, Tate, London). His crowded canvases are full of revealing details and pointed subplots. In 1743 he visited Paris, and followed this with several prints of low life, such as the 'Industry and Idleness' series (1747). >> Thornhill

Hogben, Lancelot (1895–1975) Physiologist and writer, born in Southsea, Hampshire, S England, UK. He studied at Cambridge, and held academic appointments in zoology in England, Scotland, Canada, and South Africa before becoming professor of zoology at Birmingham (1941–7), and then professor of medical statistics (1947–61). He wrote several popular books on scientific subjects, including *Mathematics for the Million* (1936) and *Science for the Citizen* (1938), as well as many specialist publications. In *The Loom of Language* (1943), he set out his version of an international auxiliary language, *Interglossa*.

Hogg, James, known as **the Ettrick Shepherd** (1770–1835) Writer, born near Ettrick, Scottish Borders, SE Scotland, UK. He tended sheep in his youth, and after only a spasmodic education he became a writer of ballads, which achieved some success thanks to the patronage of Walter Scott. He eventually settled in Edinburgh, and wrote several works in verse and prose, notably *The Private Memoirs and Confessions of a Justified Sinner* (1824). >> Scott, Walter

Hogg, Quintin (1845–1903) Philanthropist, born in London, England, UK. Educated at Eton, he went to work in a tea merchant's in a poor area of London. Moved by the plight of the poor children he observed, he determined to improve their lot. With the support of his wife he opened a 'ragged school' for destitute children at Charing Cross, then a Youths' Christian Institute, and in 1882 opened Regent Street Polytechnic to teach various trades. His work did not have any public funding until 1889, when London County Council gave support, leading to the spread of polytechnics.

Hogg, Quinton >> **Hailsham, Viscount**

Hohenheim, Philippus von >> **Paracelsus**

Hohner, Matthias (1833–1902) German mouth-organ manufacturer. In 1857 he established his firm at Trossingen, Württemberg. His five sons added music publishing (1931), the manufacture of accordions, harmonicas, saxophones, and (from 1945) electrical musical instruments, and established an accordion school at Trossingen in 1931, thus making the family business the biggest of its kind.

Hokusai, Katsushika [hokusiy] (1760–1849) Artist and wood engraver, born in Edo (modern Tokyo). He early abandoned traditional styles of engraving for the coloured woodcut designs of the *ukiyo-e* school. His 10 volumes of the *Mangwa* (1814–19, Sketches at Random) depict most facets of Japanese life. He is best known for his 'Hundred Views of Mount Fuji' (1835), many of which are widely known through reproductions in Western homes today. His work greatly influenced the French Impressionists.

Holbein, Hans [holbiyn], known as **the Younger** (1497–1543) Painter, born in Augsburg, Germany, the son of **Hans Holbein the Elder** (c.1460–1524). He studied under his father, worked in Zürich and Lucerne, and from c.1516 was in Basel, where he settled in 1520. His early religious pictures include the celebrated 'Dead Christ' (1521). The 'Dance of Death' woodcuts were designed in 1523–6 (published in 1538). He went to France (1524) and then to England (1526), where he finally settled in 1532. Here there was no demand for religious art, and he painted portraits almost exclusively, notably of Sir Thomas More (to whom he had been introduced by Erasmus), Henry VIII (whose service he entered in 1537), and his wives.

Holberg, Ludvig, Baron (1684–1754) Poet, playwright, and philosopher, born in Bergen, Norway. He was professor at Copenhagen of metaphysics (1717), eloquence (1720), and history (1730). His first notable works were satirical poems, among them *Peder Paars* (1719–20), the earliest classic in Danish. After 1724 he turned to history, producing a history of Denmark, and other works. In 1741 appeared another classic, the satirical comic romance *Nicolai Klimii iter subterraneum* (Niels Klim's Subterranean Journey). He became a baron in 1747.

Holbrooke, Josef (Charles) (1878–1958) Composer of chamber music and opera, born in Croydon, S Greater London, England, UK. He studied at the Royal Academy of Music, was an accomplished pianist, and composed the symphonic poems *Queen Mab* (1904), *The Bells* (1906), and *Apollo and the Seaman* (1908). He also wrote a trilogy of operas based on Welsh legends, the first of which, *The Children of Don* (1912), was performed at Salzburg in 1923. His variation of 'Three Blind Mice' formed his most popular composition.

Holden, Sir Edward Wheewall (1896–1978) Pioneer motor manufacturer, born in Adelaide, South Australia. He joined his father in the manufacture of car body parts, and eventually Holdens became the major Australian producer of bodies for imported chassis, especially from General Motors in the USA. He had studied automation methods in the USA, and rapidly expanded the productivity of the company; by 1929 Holdens was the biggest body builder in the British empire. Through a downturn in demand during the Depression, General Motors acquired Holdens, and he became chairman of the company in 1931.

Holden, William, originally **William Franklin Beadle** (1918–82) Film actor, born in O'Fallon, IL. He took part in radio plays before making his film debut in *Million Dollar Legs* (1939). Later films include *Sunset Boulevard* (1950), *The Wild Bunch* (1969), and *The Network* (1973), and he won a Best Actor Oscar for his role in *Stalag 17* (1953).

Hölderlin, (Johann Christian) Friedrich [hoelderlin] (1770–1843) Poet, born in Lauffen, Germany. He studied theology at Tübingen and philosophy at Jena, and trained as a Lutheran minister, then became a family tutor in Frankfurt. He began to publish, with the help of Schiller, notably the philosophical novel, *Hyperion* (1797–9). He became increasingly schizophrenic, spent a period in an asylum (1806–7), and lived in Tübingen until his death. His difficult Symbolist poetry has been revalued this century by Rilke and Stefan George. >> George, Stefan; Rilke; Schiller

Holiday, Billie (Eleanora), originally **Eleanora Fagan**, nickname **Lady Day** (1915–59) Jazz singer, born in Baltimore, MD. She began recording in 1933, and her wistful voice and remarkable jazz interpretation of popular songs led to work with Benny Goodman and Teddy Wilson. In the late 1930s she worked with the big bands of Count Basie and Artie Shaw, singing such memorable ballads as 'Easy Living' (1937) and 'Yesterdays' (1939), and her recordings have been a major influence on later pop and jazz singers. By the late 1940s she was falling victim to drug addiction, and losing her voice, though not her technique. Her autobiography *Lady Sings the Blues* (1956, actually written by William Dufty) was filmed in 1972. She died while under house arrest in a New York City hospital. >> Basie; Goodman, Benny; Shaw, Artie; Wilson, Teddy

Holinshed, Raphael [holinshed] (?–c. 1580) English chronicler, born apparently of a Cheshire family. He went to London early in Elizabeth I's reign, and became a translator. His compilation of *The Chronicles of England, Scotland, and Ireland* (1577), was a major source for many of Shakespeare's plays. >> Shakespeare, William

Holkeri, Harri [holkeree] (1937–) Finnish politician and prime minister (1987–91), born in Oripaa, Finland. He became politically active as a young man, and was secretary of the Youth League of the centrist National Coalition Party in 1959. He then served as the Party's information secretary (1962–4), research secretary (1964–5) and national secretary (1965–71). He was elected to Helsinki City Council in 1969, and to parliament (Eduskunta) in 1970. He did not stand for re-election when his term as prime minister ended. >> RR1049

Holkham, Leicester of >> **Leicester (of Holkham), Earl of**

Holland, Henry (1746–1806) British architect. Pupil and son-in-law of Lancelot ('Capability') Brown, he designed old Carlton House in London, the original Brighton Pavilion (1786–7), Brook's Club (1776–8), and many other buildings. >> Brown, Lancelot

Holland (of Foxley and of Holland), Henry Richard Vassall Fox, 3rd Baron (1773–1840) British Liberal statesman, born at Winterslow House, Wiltshire, S England, UK. He studied at Oxford, was Lord Privy Seal in the Grenville ministry (1806–7), and Chancellor of the Duchy of Lancaster (1830–4). He worked for reform of the criminal code, attacked the slave trade (although he was himself a West Indian planter), and threw himself wholeheartedly into the the corn-law struggle. >> Grenville, William

Holland, John (Philip) (1840–1914) Inventor, born in Liscannor, Co Clare, Ireland. He studied in Limerick, and taught there until emigrating to the USA in 1873. He continued as a teacher until 1879, and began designing submarines, building the *Fenian Ram* (financed by the Fenian Society), which was launched on the Hudson R in 1881. In 1898 he launched the *Holland VI*, and successfully demonstrated it on and under the Potomac R. It was accepted by the US Navy, and orders from several other governments followed. >> Bushnell, David

Holland, Sir Sidney George (1893–1961) New Zealand politician and prime minister (1949–57), born in Greendale, New Zealand. He was managing director of an engineering company before taking up politics. Entering parliament as a member of the National Party in 1935, he was Leader of the Opposition (1940–9), then premier. He was knighted in 1957. >> RR1078

Hollar, Wenzel or **Wenceslaus** (1607–77) Engraver and etcher, born in Prague. He studied engraving in Frankfurt,

and worked in Germany and Holland before settling in England (1652), where he was appointed 'His Majesty's designer'. He produced two magnificent plates of costume, entitled *Severall Habits of English Women* (1640) and *Theatrum Mulierum* (1643), as well as maps and panoramas, etc, preserved in the British Museum and in the Royal Library, Windsor. His panoramic view of London from Southwark after the Great Fire is one of the most valuable topographical records of the 17th-c.

Hollerith, Herman [holerith] (1860–1929) Inventor, born in Buffalo, NY. He studied at the School of Mines at Columbia University, and worked as a statistician for the US census of 1880. Realizing the need for automation in the recording and processing of such a mass of data, he devised a system based initially on cards with holes punched in them (similar to that developed by Jacquard in 1801). He won a competition for the most efficient data-processing equipment to be used in the 1890 US census, established his own company in 1896, and later merged with two others to become the International Business Machines Corporation (IBM) in 1924. >> Jacquard

Holles (of Ifield), Denzil Holles, Baron [holis] (1599–1680) English statesman, born in Houghton, Nottinghamshire, C England, UK. He entered parliament in 1624, and in 1642 was one of the five members whom Charles I tried to arrest. In the Civil War, he advocated peace, was accused of treason, and fled to Normandy. In 1660 he was spokesman of the commission delegated to recall Charles II at Breda, and in 1661 was created a baron. >> Charles I (of England); Charles II (of England)

Holley, Robert (William) (1922–93) Biochemist, born in Urbana, IL. He studied at Cornell University, where he worked until 1964. He secured the first pure sample of t-RNA (transfer RNA), and by 1965 had determined its structure. In 1968 he moved to the Salk Institute in California. He shared the 1968 Nobel Prize for Physiology or Medicine. >> RR1124

Holliday, Doc, popular name of **John Henry Holliday** (1852–87) Gambler, gunslinger, and dentist, baptised at Griffin, GA. After attending the Pennsylvania College of Dental Surgery (1872), he moved to Dallas, but soon adopted a life of gambling, drinking, and gunfighting. He drifted his way through the West, and in Dodge City befriended Wyatt Earp, later becoming involved in the famous gunfight at the OK Corral, Tombstone (1882), between the Earp brothers and the Clanton gang. He died of tuberculosis a few years later. >> Earp

Hollis, Sir Roger Henry (1905–73) British civil servant. He studied at Oxford, and travelled extensively in China before joining the British counter-intelligence service MI5 in the late 1930s. He was appointed deputy director general in 1953 and director general (1956–65). His name came to public attention when Peter Wright, in *Spycatcher* (1987), argued that Hollis, with Blunt, Burgess, Maclean, and Philby, was a Soviet spy. >> Blunt, Anthony; Burgess, Guy; Maclean, Donald; Philby; Wright, Peter

Holloway, Stanley (1890–1982) Entertainer, born in London, England, UK. He had various occupations before making his London stage debut in *Kissing Time* (1920) and first film appearance in *The Rotters* (1921). He was an original member of The Co-Optimists revue group (1921–30). Popular on radio and in pantomime, he created the monologue characters of Sam Small and the Ramsbottom family, and he was a genial comedy actor in such Ealing film classics as *Passport to Pimlico* (1948), *The Lavender Hill Mob* (1951), and *The Titfield Thunderbolt* (1952). He is perhaps best known for his role of Alfred Dolittle in *My Fair Lady* on Broadway (1956–8) and later on film (1964). He published an autobiography, *Wiv a Little Bit of Luck* (1969).

Hollows, Fred(erick) Cossom (1929–93) Ophthalmologist, born in Dunedin, New Zealand. He studied in New Zealand and in Britain, and became associate professor at the University of New South Wales and chairman of ophthalmology at Prince of Wales Hospital, Sydney. He was famed for his contribution to the prevention and treatment of blinding eye infections, especially trachoma, among Australian Aborigines, Eritreans, and Vietnamese. In Eritrea he trained doctors to perform simple eye surgery, and helped establish a factory to manufacture plastic intra-ocular lenses. He planned similar projects for Vietnam, Bangladesh, Burma, and Nepal. In 1991 he was named Australian of the Year, and in 1993 won the Rotary International Award for Human Understanding.

Holly, Buddy, popular name of **Charles Hardin Holley** (1936–59) Rock singer, songwriter, and guitarist, born in Lubbock, TX. Originally from a country-and-western background, he was also influenced by hill-billy, Mexican, and African-American music. He was the first to add drums and a rhythm-and-blues beat to the basic country style, and his band, The Crickets, was the first to use the now standard rock-and-roll line-up of two guitars, bass, and drums. He left The Crickets in 1958, and was killed when a plane carrying him between concerts crashed. At the time he had released only three US albums. He became an important cult figure, much of his material being released posthumously. His most popular records include 'That'll Be The Day', 'Not Fade Away', 'Peggy Sue', and 'Oh Boy'.

Holm, Hanya, originally **Johanna Kuntze**, *née* **Eckert** (1893–1992) Dancer, choreographer, and teacher, born in Worms, Germany. A pupil of Emile Jacques-Dalcroze, starting in 1921 she worked as both teacher and dancer with Mary Wigman, who in 1931 sent her to New York City to establish the US branch of her school. In 1936 she founded her own studio, and became a key figure in the field of modern dance. She is best known for her choreography for Broadway musicals such as *Kiss Me Kate* (1948) and *My Fair Lady* (1956). >> Jaques-Dalcroze; Wigman

Holm, Ian (1931–) Actor, born in Ilford, E Greater London, England, UK. He was a member of the Shakespeare Memorial Theatre Company at Stratford (1954–5), toured Europe with Laurence Olivier in *Titus Andronicus*, and returned to Stratford in 1957, where he achieved a major success playing Prince Hal, Henry V, and Richard III in *The Wars of The Roses* (1963–4). He won an award for his part in the film *Chariots of Fire* (1981, Cannes, Best Supporting Actor), and among many later films are *Blue Ice* (1993) and *Big Night* (1997). After a period away from the stage, he played a widely acclaimed Lear in Richard Eyre's 1997 production. >> Olivier

Holman, Nat(han) (1896–1995) Basketball player and coach, born in New York City. One of basketball's pioneers, he helped the Original Celtics win 720 out of 795 (1921–8). A coach at City College of New York for 37 years (1920–52, 1955–6, 1959–60), he was elected to basketball's Hall of Fame in 1964.

Holmes, Arthur (1890–1965) Geologist, born in Hebburn, Tyne and Wear, NE England, UK. Professor of geology at Durham (1924–43) and Edinburgh (1943–56), he determined the ages of rocks by measuring their radioactive constituents, and was an early scientific supporter of Alfred Wegener's continental drift theory. He wrote *The Age of the Earth* (1913) and *Principles of Physical Geology* (1944). >> Wegener

Holmes, Larry, nickname **the Easton Assassin** (1949–) Boxer, born in Cuthbert, GA. He beat Ken Norton for the World Boxing Council heavyweight title in 1978, gave it up in 1984, was named International Boxing Federation champion that year, and held the title until 1985, when he finally lost to Michael Spinks in his 49th contest, just one short of Rocky Marciano's record. He lost the return contest with Spinks, and in 1988 challenged Mike Tyson for the title, but was defeated in four rounds. He retired after winning 48 of his 51 contests, 34 by a knockout, then launched a comeback in 1991. >> Marciano; Tyson, Mike; RR1148

Holmes, Oliver Wendell (1809–94) Physician and writer, born in Cambridge, MA. He studied law and medicine at Harvard University, and became professor of anatomy and physiology at Dartmouth College, NH, and professor of anatomy at Harvard (1847–82). In 1842 he made the discovery that puerperal fever was contagious. He is best known for his humorous verse and prose which he began writing as an undergraduate, winning national acclaim with *Old Ironsides* (1830) and his 'Breakfast Table' essays, beginning with 'The Autocrat of the Breakfast Table' (1858). >> Holmes, Oliver Wendell, Jr

Holmes, Oliver Wendell, Jr, nickname **the Great Dissenter** (1841–1935) Judge, born in Boston, MA, the son of writer Oliver Wendell Holmes. He studied at Harvard Law School, then served in the Union army as captain in the Civil War. From 1867 he practised law in Boston, edited Kent's *Commentaries* (1873), became editor of the *American Law Review*, and was appointed professor of law at Harvard (1873–82). He made his reputation with a fundamental book on *The Common Law* (1881). He then became associate justice (1882) and chief justice (1899–1902) of the Supreme Court of Massachusetts, and associate justice of the US Supreme Court (1902–32). He was one of the great judicial figures of his time, and many of his judgments on common law and equity, as well as his dissent on the interpretation of the 14th amendment, have become famous. >> Holmes, Oliver Wendell

Holmes, William Henry (1846–1933) Archaeologist and museum director, born near Cadiz, OH. Trained as an artist, his interests turned to archaeology in 1875 when exploring ancient cliff dwellings in the arid SW with the US Geological Survey. A visit to the Yucatan while he was curator of anthropology at the Field Museum of Natural History, Chicago, stimulated a major contribution to Mesoamerican archaeology, the illustrated *Archaeological Studies among the Ancient Cities of Mexico* (1895–97). He worked at the Smithsonian Institution, Washington, DC, for much of his career, acting as chief of the Bureau of American Ethnology (1902–9) and director of the National Gallery of Art (1920–32).

Holmes a Court, (Michael) Robert Hamilton [hohmz uh kaw(r)t] (1937–90) Entrepreneur, born in South Africa. He studied in South Africa, New Zealand, and at the University of Western Australia, Perth, and became a lawyer. He acquired his first company in 1970, and went on to establish the Bell Group, where he demonstrated his skill in managing takeovers, even making money out of unsuccessful takeover bids such as those for the Ansett Transport Group and Elders. The Bell Group owned the Herald and Weekly Times newspaper group, among numerous other interests, and in 1984 stunned the business world by bidding for BHP, Australia's largest company. The Bell Group was debilitated after the 1987 stock-market crash, but by 1990, when he died, Holmes a Court's private company was recovering well, consolidating his position as one of the wealthiest people in Australia. He had a significant collection of Australian art and was involved in horse breeding and racing. His widow **Janet Holmes a Court** (1944–) became chair of the $400 million family company Heytesbury Holdings after her husband's sudden death.

Holofernes >> **Judith**

Holroyd, Michael (de Courcy Fraser) (1935–) Biographer, born in London, England, UK. He was educated at Eton. His first book was *Hugh Kingsmill: a critical biography* (1964). His two-volume life of Lytton Strachey, *The Unknown Years* (1967) and *The Year of Achievement* (1968), is recognized as a landmark in biographical writing. He has written the official biography of George Bernard Shaw, in five volumes: *The Search for Love* (1988), *The Pursuit of Power* (1989), *The Lure of Fantasy* (1991), *The Last Laugh* and *The Shaw Companion* (both 1992). He married the novelist Margaret Drabble in 1982. >> Drabble, Margaret

Holst, Gustav (Theodore) (1874–1934) Composer, born of Swedish origin in Cheltenham, Gloucestershire, SWC England, UK. He studied at the Royal College of Music, London, but neuritis in his hand prevented him from becoming a concert pianist. From 1905 he taught music at St Paul's School, Hammersmith, and from 1907 at Morley College. He emerged as a major composer with the seven-movement suite *The Planets* (1914–16), and gave up most of his teaching in 1925. Among his other major works are *The Hymn of Jesus* (1917), his comic operas *The Perfect Fool* (1922) and *At the Boar's Head* (1924), and his orchestral tone poem, *Egdon Heath* (1927).

Holt, Harold (Edward) (1908–67) Australian politician and prime minister (1966–7), born in Sydney, New South Wales, Australia. He studied law at Melbourne University, joined the United Australia Party, which was to be replaced by the Liberal Party of Australia, and entered the House of Representatives in 1935. He became deputy leader of his Party in 1956, and leader and prime minister when Robert Menzies retired in 1966. During the Vietnam War he strongly supported the USA with the slogan 'all the way with LBJ'. He died in office while swimming at Portsea, near Melbourne. >> Menzies; RR1033

Holt, Victoria >> Hibbert

Holtby, Winifred (1898–1935) Writer and feminist, born in Rudston, East Riding of Yorkshire, NE England, UK. She studied at Oxford, and was a director from 1926 of *Time and Tide*. She wrote a number of novels, but is chiefly remembered for *South Riding* (1935).

Holub, Miroslav [holoob] (1933–) Poet, born in Plzen, Czech Republic. He studied medicine in Prague, specializing in immunology, and worked at the Max Planck Institute in Freiburg (1968–9). His collections include *Kam tece krev* (1963, Where the Blood Flows), *Udalosti* (1971, Events), and *Naopal* (1982, On the Contrary).

Holyoake, George (Jacob) (1817–1906) Social reformer, born in Birmingham, West Midlands, C England, UK. He taught mathematics, lectured on Owen's socialist system, edited the *Reasoner*, and promoted the bill legalizing secular affirmations. He was the last person imprisoned in England on a charge of atheism (1842). He wrote histories of the co-operative movement and of secularism. >> Owen, Robert

Holyoake, Sir Keith (Jacka) (1904–83) New Zealand statesman and prime minister (1957, 1960–72), born near Pahiatua, New Zealand. He joined the Reform Party (later the New Zealand National Party), and served in the House of Representatives (1932–8). Re-elected in 1943, he became deputy leader of the National Party in 1946, and deputy prime minister in 1949. He was president of the UN Food and Agriculture Conference (1957). On the retirement of Sir Sydney Holland (1957) he became Party leader and prime minister on two occasions. He later served as Governor-General of New Zealand (1977–80), the first politician to hold the post. He was knighted in 1970. >> Holland, Sydney George; RR1078

Homans, George (Caspar) (1910–89) Sociologist, born in Boston, MA. He studied at Cambridge University, UK, and taught at Harvard (1946–80). An authority on the social behaviour of small groups, he posited group behaviour to be the result of individual behaviour, and wrote such books as *The Human Group* (1950), *Sentiments and Activities* (1962), and *Certainties and Doubts* (1987).

Home of the Hirsel, Baron [hyoom], formerly **Sir Alec Douglas-Home**, originally **Alexander Frederick Douglas-Home, 14th Earl of Home** (1903–95) British statesman and prime minister (1963–4), born in London, England, UK. He studied at Oxford, became a Conservative MP in 1931, and was Chamberlain's secretary during the negotiations with Hitler and beyond (1937–40). He became minister of state at the Scottish Office (1951–5), succeeded to the peerage as 14th Earl (1951), and was Commonwealth Relations secretary (1955–60) and foreign secretary (1960–3). After Macmillan's resignation, he astonished everyone by emerging as premier. He made history by renouncing his peerage and fighting a by-election, during which, although premier, he was technically a member of neither House. After the 1964 defeat by the Labour Party, he was leader of the Opposition until replaced in 1965 by Edward Heath, in whose 1970–4 government he was foreign secretary. In 1974 he was made a life peer. >> Douglas-Home, William; Macmillan, Harold; RR1095

Homer, Greek **Homēros** (c.9th-c BC) Greek poet, to whom are attributed the great epics, the *Iliad*, the story of the siege of Troy, and the *Odyssey*, the tale of Ulysses's wanderings. The place of his birth is doubtful, probably a Greek colony on the coast of Asia Minor, and his date, once put as far back as 1200 BC, from the style of the poems attributed to him is now thought to be much later. Arguments have long raged over whether his works are in fact by the same hand, or have their origins in the lays of Homer and his followers (*Homeridae*), and there seems little doubt that the works were originally based on current ballads which were much modified and extended. Of the true Homer, nothing is positively known. The so-called *Homeric hymns* are certainly of a later age.

Homer, Winslow (1836–1910) Painter, born in Boston, MA. After an apprenticeship to a lithographer (1855–7), he began his career as an illustrator for such magazines as *Harper's Weekly* (1859–67), making drawings of routine life at the front during the Civil War. He spent two years (1881–3) at Tynemouth, Tyne and Wear, and began painting maritime scenes. On his return to the USA he continued to depict the sea, latterly at Prouts Neck, an isolated fishing village on the E seaboard, where he spent the rest of his life. His highly original work is often regarded as a reflection of the American pioneering spirit.

Honda, Soichiro (1906–92) Motor cycle and car manufacturer, born in Iwata Gun, Japan. He started as a garage apprentice in 1922 and opened his own garage in 1928. By 1934 he had started a piston-ring production factory. He began producing motor cycles in 1948, and became president of Honda Corporation in the same year, until 1973. He stayed on as a director, and was appointed 'supreme adviser' in 1983.

Hondius, Jodocus, Latin name of **Joost de Hondt** (1563–1612) Flemish cartographer. He emigrated to London c.1584 and moved from there to Amsterdam c.1593. In addition to his own maps of the world and the hemispheres, he engraved much of John Speed's work. >> Speed

Honecker, Erich [honeker] (1912–94) East German statesman and head of state (1976–89), born in Neunkirchen, Germany. Active in the Communist youth movement from an early age, he was involved in underground resistance to Hitler, and was imprisoned for 10 years. Released by Soviet forces, he became the first chairman of the Free German Youth in the German Democratic Republic

(1946–55). He first entered the Politburo in 1958, was elected Party chief in 1971, and became head of state from 1976 to 1989, when he was dismissed as a consequence of the anti-Communist revolution. Charges were brought against him in the new united Germany that he had ordered the killings along the Berlin Wall and GDR Border, but he was allowed to leave for Chile in 1993 on grounds of illness.

Honegger, Arthur [oneger] (1892–1955) Composer, born in Le Havre, France, of Swiss parentage. He studied in Zürich and at the Paris Conservatoire, and after World War 1 became one of the group of Parisian composers known as *Les Six*. His dramatic oratorio *King David* established his reputation in 1921, and *Pacific 231* (1923), his musical picture of a locomotive, won considerable popularity. His other works include five symphonies. >> Auric; Cocteau; Durey; Milhaud; Poulenc; Tailleferre

Honeycombe, (Richard) Gordon (1936–) British writer, playwright, and broadcaster, born in Karachi, India. He studied at Oxford, and was an announcer on Radio Hong Kong while there on National Service (1956–7). He appeared in the BBC programme *That Was the Week that Was* (1962–3), presented *The Late Show* (1978), and has narrated on many documentaries. His non-fiction work includes *The Complete Murders of the Black Museum* (1995). He has also written several plays for stage, radio, and television, but is most widely known for his role as a newscaster with ITN (1965–77) and TV-AM (1985–9).

Hongi Hika [honggee heeka] (1772–1828) Maori war leader, born near Kaikohe, New Zealand. He protected the first missionaries who arrived in New Zealand in 1814. In 1820 he visited England and Australia and acquired muskets. He then waged war on other Maori tribes, thereby severely disrupting traditional political arrangements. This has had an enduring influence on Maori affairs to the present time.

Hongwu [hong woo], also spelled **Hung-wu**, originally **Zhu Yuanzhang** (1328–98) First emperor of the Chinese Ming dynasty (1368–1644), known posthumously as **Taizu**. His rise has few world history parallels. Born into a poor Nanjing family and orphaned at 16, he was in turn Buddhist novice, beggar, White Lotus secret society member, and Red Turban rebel. Setting up his own organization, he seized Nanjing (1356), overran the Yangtze basin, took Beijing, overthrew the Yuan dynasty (1368), established a Ming ('brilliant') dynasty at Nanjing, and took the reign name **Hongwu** ('vast military power'). He then drove the Mongols out of China, Korea, Manchuria, and beyond the Tien Shan. He bloodily suppressed secret societies and subversives, set up a special police with torture prisons, and concentrated all power in his own hands. Grotesque in appearance with a snout-like face, he was known as 'pig emperor': puns about it were risky.

Honorius, Flavius [onawrius] (384–423) Roman Emperor of the West (393–423), the younger son of Theodosius I. A young and feeble ruler, he abandoned Britain to the barbarians, and cowered in Ravenna while Alaric and the Goths besieged and sacked Rome (408–10). From 395 to 408, power was effectively in the hands of Stilicho. >> Alaric; Stilicho

Honorius I [onawrius] (?–638) Pope (625–38). He supported the Christianization of the Anglo-Saxons, sending St Birinus to Wessex, and persuaded the Celtic Church to accept the Roman liturgy and date of Easter. In the Monothelite controversy he abstained from condemning the new doctrines, and for so doing was stigmatized as a heretic at the Council of Constantinople (680).

Hontheim, Johann Nikolaus von [honthiym], pseudonym **Justinus Febronius** (1701–90) Clergyman, theologian, and historian, born in Trier, Germany. He was ordained in Rome (1728), and became professor of law at the University of Trier (1734) and Bishop of Trier (1748). He wrote two works on the history of Trier (1750–7), but is remembered chiefly for a theological essay (1763) in which he propounded a system of Church government combining an exaggerated Gallicanism with the democratic element of Congregationalism (*Febronianism*).

Honthorst, Gerrit van [honthaw(r)st] (1590–1656) Painter, born in Utrecht, The Netherlands. He moved to Italy (c.1610), returning to Holland in 1620, and twice visited England (1620, 1628), where he painted portraits of the royal family. He was fond of painting candle-lit interiors. His brother **William van Honthorst** (1604–66), historical and portrait painter, worked for the court of Berlin (1650–64).

Hooch or **Hoogh, Pieter de** [hohkh] (c.1629–c.1684) Painter, born in Rotterdam, The Netherlands. By 1654 he was living in Delft, and probably came under the influence of Carel Fabritius and his pupil, Vermeer. 'Courtyard of a House in Delft' (1658, National Gallery, London) and the 'Card Players' (royal collection) are among the outstanding examples of the Dutch school of the 17th-c, with their characteristically serene domestic interior or courtyard scenes, warm colouring, and delicate light effects. >> Fabritius; Vermeer, Jan

Hood, Alexander, 1st Viscount Bridport (1727–1814) English naval commander, the brother of Samuel, 1st Viscount Hood. He entered the navy in 1741, and in 1761 recaptured from the French the *Warwick*, a 60-gun ship. During the French Revolutionary Wars he served under Richard, 1st Earl Howe, in the Channel and the Strait of Gibraltar, and took part in the 'Glorious First of June' engagement off Ushant in 1794. He later became commander-in-chief of the Channel fleet (1797–1800). >> Hood, Samuel; Howe, Richard

Hood, John B(ell) (1831–79) US soldier, born in Owingsville, KY. He trained at West Point, commanded the 'Texas Brigade' in the Confederate army, and was wounded at Gaines's Mill, Gettysburg, and Chickamauga. He commanded a corps in the retreat to Atlanta, and in 1864 succeeded Joseph Johnston in command. He had to evacuate the city, leaving the road free for Sherman's march to the sea, then pushed as far north as Nashville; but, defeated by George Henry Thomas, he was relieved of command in 1865 at his own request. He later became a businessman in New Orleans. >> Johnston, Joseph E; Sherman, William Tecumseh; Thomas, George H

Hood, Raymond M(athewson) (1881–1934) Architect, born in Pawtucket, RI. He studied at Massachusetts Institute of Technology before moving to the Ecole des Beaux Arts, Paris, in 1905. In 1922, with **John Mead Howells** (1868–1959), he won the competition for the Chicago Tribune Tower, designed with Gothic details. He became the leading designer of skyscrapers in North America in the following decade. Later works in New York City were designed in a modern, rationalist style, such as the Daily News Building (1929–30), the Rockefeller Center (1930–40), and the McGraw-Hill Building (1931).

Hood (of Whitley), Samuel Hood, 1st Viscount (1724–1816) British admiral, born in Thorncombe, Dorset, S England, UK. He joined the navy in 1741, and fought during the American Revolution, when he defeated the French in the West Indies (1782), for which he was made a baron in the Irish peerage. In 1784 he became an MP, and in 1788 a Lord of the Admiralty. In 1793, he directed the occupation of Toulon and the operations in the Gulf of Lyon. He was created a viscount in 1796. >> Hood, Alexander

Hood, Thomas (1799–1845) Poet and humorist, born in London, England, UK. He achieved recognition when, with **John Hamilton Reynolds** (1794–1852), he published *Odes and Addresses to Great People* (1825). In his *Whims and Oddities* (1826) he showed his graphic talent in 'picture-puns', of which he seems to have been the inventor. In 1844 he started his own *Hood's Monthly Magazine*.

Hooft, Pieter (1581–1647) Poet, playwright, and historian, born in Amsterdam. He wrote lyrical verse early in his career, then plays (*Granida*, 1605; *Baeto*, 1626), and finally turned to the writing of history with his unfinished *Nederlandsze Historien 1555–85* (1642–54), important also for the establishment of the Dutch language.

Hoogh, Pieter de >> **Hooch, Pieter de**

Hook, James (1746–1827) Composer and organist, born in Norwich, Norfolk, E England, UK. He was organist and composer at Marylebone Gardens (1769–73) and at Vauxhall Gardens (1774–1820). He wrote the music for a large number of plays, as well as cantatas, odes, and a vast number of popular songs, including 'The Lass of Richmond Hill'.

Hook, Sidney (1902–89) Philosopher and educationist, born in New York City. He studied at Columbia University, and became professor at New York University (1932–72). He was politically active, first as a spokesman for Marxism, later as a leading Social Democrat. Among his many books are *Towards an Understanding of Karl Marx* (1933) and *Revolution, Reform and Social Justice* (1976).

Hooke, Robert (1635–1703) Chemist and physicist, born in Freshwater, Isle of Wight, S England, UK. He studied at Oxford, became curator of experiments to the Royal Society (1662), and in 1677 was appointed its secretary. He formulated the law governing elasticity (*Hooke's law*), and invented the balance spring for watches. The Gregorian telescope and microscope are materially his inventions, with which he made important observations, many of which were published in his *Micrographia* (1665). >> Wallis, John; Wilkins, John; Willis, Thomas; Wren, Christopher

Hooker, Joseph, nickname **Fighting Joe** (1814–79) US Union general, born in Hadley, MA. He trained at West Point, served in the Mexican War (1846–8), commanded a division of the 3rd corps in the Peninsular campaign of 1862, and compelled the enemy to evacuate Manassas. During the Civil War he opened the battle at Antietam, and earned his nickname at Williamsburg (1862). In 1863 he succeeded Burnside in command of the Army of the Potomac, but was defeated in the Battle of Chancellorsville and superseded by Meade. He accompanied Sherman in his invasion of Georgia, and served until the fall of Atlanta in 1864. >> Burnside, Ambrose Everett; Meade, George G; Sherman, William Tecumseh

Hooker, Sir Joseph (Dalton) (1817–1911) Botanist and traveller, born in Halesworth, Suffolk, E England, UK. He studied at Glasgow University, and eventually succeeded his father as director of the Royal Botanic Gardens at Kew (1865). He was a friend of Darwin, and supported Darwin's theory of evolution. He went on several expeditions which resulted in works on the flora of New Zealand, Antarctica, and India, as well as his *Himalayan Journals* (1854) and his monumental *Genera plantarum*. >> Darwin, Charles; Hooker, William Jackson

Hooker, Richard (1554–1600) Anglican theologian, born in Heavitree, Devon, SW England, UK. He studied at Oxford, was ordained in 1581, and became rector of a parish near Tring. After engaging in doctrinal controversy, he resolved to set forth the basis of Church government, and in 1591 accepted the living of Boscombe near Salisbury, where he began his eight-volume work *Of the Laws of Ecclesiastical Polity* (1594, 1597, 1648, 1662). It is mainly to this work that Anglican theology owes its tone and direction.

Hooker, Sir Stanley George (1907–84) Aero-engine designer, born in the I of Sheppey, Kent, SE England, UK. He studied at Imperial College, London, and Oxford, where he published several papers for the Royal Society on compressible fluid flow. He worked for Rolls–Royce (1938–49), designing superchargers for the Merlin aero-engine, and led them into jet-engine production. He then moved to the Bristol Aeroplane Company, working on Proteus, Olympus (for Concorde), Orpheus, and Pegasus (Harrier) jet engines. He returned from retirement in 1970 to Rolls–Royce to resolve the problems of the RB-211 engine. His autobiography, *Not Much of an Engineer*, was published in 1984.

Hooker, Thomas (1586–1647) Nonconformist preacher, born in Marefield, Leicestershire, C England, UK. He became a fellow of Emmanuel College, Cambridge, then a Puritan lecturer at Chelmsford. In 1631 he went to Holland, then in 1633 emigrated to America and became pastor at Cambridge, MA. He moved with his congregation to Connecticut, and founded the town of Hartford (1636), where in 1638 he told the State Court that the people had the right to choose their own magistrates, an idea much advanced for the age and for which he is sometimes called 'the father of American democracy'.

Hooker, Sir William Jackson (1785–1865) Botanist, born in Norwich, Norfolk, E England, UK. A chance discovery of a rare moss (1805) led him into a career in botany. He collected specimens in Scotland (1806) and Iceland (1809), and wrote his *Recollections of Iceland* (1811). He became professor at Glasgow (1820), and the first director of the Royal Botanic Gardens at Kew (1841), which he developed into the leading botanical institute in the world. >> Hooker, Joseph Dalton

Hookham, Margaret >> **Fonteyn, Dame Margot**

Hooks, Benjamin (Lawson) (1925–) Judge, public official, and civil rights reformer, born in Memphis, TN. A lawyer as well as an ordained minister, he was pastor of the Middle Baptist Church of Memphis (1956–72), and co-founder and vice-president of the Mutual Federal Savings and Loan Association (1955–69). He gained national recognition as the first African-American to serve on the Federal Communications Commission (1972–7), and succeeded Roy Wilkins as executive director of the National Association for the Advancement of Colored People (1977–93). He also served as producer and host of a number of television shows airing racial issues. >> Wilkins, Roy

Hooton, Ernest A(lbert) (1887–1954) Physical anthropologist, born in Clemansville, WI. He studied at Lawrence College and Wisconsin University, then taught anthropology at Harvard (1913–54), where his laboratory became the main US centre for training physical anthropology specialists. In his many popular writings, such as *Apes, Men and Morons* (1937), he introduced the subject to a wide readership. In his research he concentrated on the racial classification of the human species, and on relationships between body build and behaviour, as in *Crime and Man* (1939).

Hoover, Herbert (Clark) (1874–1964) US statesman and 31st president (1929–33), born in West Branch, IA. He studied at Stanford, then worked abroad as an engineer. During and after World War 1 he was associated with the relief of distress in Europe. In 1921 he became secretary of commerce, and in 1928 received the Republican Party's presidential nomination. As president, his opposition to direct governmental assistance for the unemployed after the world slump of 1929 made him unpopular, and he was beaten by Roosevelt in 1932. He assisted Truman with the various American–European economic relief programmes which followed World War 2. The *Hoover Dam* is named after him. >> Roosevelt, Franklin D; Truman, Harry S

Hoover, J(ohn) Edgar (1895–1972) US public servant, born in Washington, DC. He studied law at George Washington University in 1917, after taking evening classes. He entered the Justice Department, becoming special assistant to the attorney general in 1919, and assistant director of the Federal Bureau of Investigation (FBI) in 1921. He became FBI director in 1924, and remained in charge until his death, remodelling it to make it more efficient, and campaigning against city gangster rackets in the inter-war years, and against Communist sympathizers in the post-war period. He was later criticized for abusing his position by engaging in vendettas against liberal activists.

Hoover, William (Henry) (1849–1932) Industrialist, born in Ohio. After running a tannery business (1870–1907), he bought the patent of a light-weight electric cleaning machine from a janitor, James Murray Spangler, and formed the Electric Suction Sweeper Co in 1908 to manufacture and market it throughout the world. The company was renamed Hoover in 1910. >> Booth, Hubert Cecil

Hope, A(lec) D(erwent) (1907–) Poet and critic, born in Cooma, New South Wales, Australia. He studied at Sydney and Oxford, and became professor of literature at the Australian National University. His works include *The Wandering Islands* (1955) and *Poems* (1960). His *Collected Poems* (1972) is one of the major books of Australian verse, and later works include *Ladies from the Sea* (1987) and *Orpheus* (1991).

Hope, Anthony, pseudonym of **Sir Anthony Hope Hawkins** (1863–1933) Writer, born in London, England, UK. He studied at Oxford, and in 1887 was called to the bar; but after the success of his 'Ruritanian' romance *The Prisoner of Zenda* (1894) he turned entirely to writing. He was knighted in 1918.

Hope, Bob, originally **Leslie Townes Hope** (1903–) Comedian, born in London, England, UK. He emigrated with his parents to the USA in 1907. After some years on the stage as a dancer and comedian, he made his first film appearance in *The Big Broadcast of 1938* singing 'Thanks for the Memory', which became his signature tune. In partnership with Bing Crosby and Dorothy Lamour, he appeared in the highly successful *Road to ...* comedies (1940–52), and in many others until the early 1970s. During World War 2 and the Korean and Vietnam Wars he spent much time entertaining the troops in the field. For these activities and for his continued contributions to the industry he was given a special Academy Award on five occasions. >> Crosby, Bing

Hope, Thomas (1769–1831) Connoisseur and antiquarian, born in Amsterdam of English parents. A man of considerable wealth, he travelled widely in Europe and the Near East in his youth, collecting marble artefacts and making drawings of buildings and sculptures. He settled in London c.1796, and introduced the vogue of Egyptian and Roman decoration in his mansion in Duchess St, London. He wrote *House Furniture and Interior Decoration* (1807), and a novel, *Anastasius, or Memoirs of a Modern Greek* (1819), a picaresque tale of an unscrupulous Greek adventurer, which enjoyed great popularity in its time.

Hopf, Heinz (1894–1971) Mathematician, born in Wrocław, Poland (formerly Breslau, Germany). After war service he studied at Berlin and Göttingen universities, where he met the Russian topologist Pavel Alexandrov with whom he wrote the influential *Topologie* (1935). In 1931 he became professor at Zürich. One of Europe's leading topologists, he worked on many aspects of combinatorial topology, including homotopy theory and vector fields. >> Alexandrov

Hopkins, Sir Anthony (1937–) Actor, born in Port Talbot, SC Wales, UK. He trained at the Royal Academy of Dramatic Art, London, and made his stage debut in *The Quare Fellow* (1960) at Manchester. A member of the National Theatre, he appeared there in numerous plays, latterly including *Pravda* (1985), *King Lear* (1986), and *Antony and Cleopatra* (1987). He made his film debut in 1967, and has appeared in *The Lion in Winter* (1968), *The Elephant Man* (1980), *84 Charing Cross Road* (1987), and numerous other films, all acclaimed, but none so widely as his compelling performance as serial murderer Hannibal Lecter in *The Silence of the Lambs* (1991, Oscar). Later films include *Shadowlands* (1994), *Legend of the Fall* (1995), and he made his directorial debut with *August* (1996). On television he won a BAFTA award for *War and Peace* (1972), and Emmies for *The Lindbergh Kidnapping Case* (1976) and *The Bunker* (1981). He won a further BAFTA award for *The Remains of the Day* (1994). He was knighted in 1993.

Hopkins, Sir Frederick (Gowland) (1861–1947) Biochemist, born in Eastbourne, East Sussex, SE England, UK. Professor at Cambridge from 1914, he was a pioneer in the study of accessory food factors, now called vitamins. He was knighted in 1925, and shared the 1929 Nobel Prize for Physiology or Medicine. >> RR1124

Hopkins, Gerard Manley (1844–89) Poet, born in London, England, UK. He studied at Oxford where, influenced by the Oxford Movement, he became a Catholic in 1866. He studied for the priesthood with the Jesuits in North Wales, absorbing the language and poetry of the region; he was ordained in 1877, and became professor of Greek at Dublin (1884). None of his poems was published in his lifetime. His friend and literary executor, Robert Bridges, published an edition in 1918, which was given a very mixed reception, notably to Hopkins' experiments with 'sprung rhythm'; but a new and expanded edition in 1930 was widely acclaimed, and his work became influential. His best-known poems include 'The Wreck of the *Deutschland*' and 'The Windhover'. >> Bridges, Robert

Hopkins, Harry L(loyd) (1890–1946) US administrator, born in Sioux City, IA. He was Federal emergency relief administrator in the depression of 1933, and under Franklin D Roosevelt headed the 'New Deal' projects in the Works Progress Administration (1935–8). He became secretary of commerce (1938–40), and supervised the lend-lease programme in 1941. As Roosevelt's closest confidante and special assistant, he undertook several important missions to Europe during World War 2, and helped to set up the Potsdam Conference (1945). >> Roosevelt, Franklin D

Hopkins, John >> Sternhold, Thomas

Hopkins, Johns (1795–1873) Businessman and philanthropist, born in Anne Arundel Co, MD. He set up a grocery business in Baltimore in 1819, retiring in 1847 with a large fortune from investments in real estate, insurance, and steamships. Besides a public park for Baltimore, he endowed an orphanage for African-American children, a free hospital, and Johns Hopkins University.

Hopkins, Samuel (1721–1803) Theologian, born in Waterbury, CT. He studied at Yale, and was ordained in the Congregationalist Church in 1743. He was pastor in Housatonick (now Great Barrington), MA, until 1769, and then in Newport. A close friend of Jonathan Edwards, his *System of Doctrines* (1793) maintains that all virtue consists of disinterested benevolence, and that all sin is selfishness (*Hopkinsianism*). He was a vigorous opponent of slavery, and raised money to free numerous slaves. >> Edwards, Jonathan

Hopman, Harry, popular name of **Henry Christian Hopman** (1906–85) Tennis player, born in Sydney, New South Wales, Australia. Despite being a talented singles player, he specialized almost exclusively in doubles. He is, however, best known for his captaincy of the Australian Davis Cup side. He was briefly in charge before World War 2, and his return to the post in 1950 saw Australia dominate world men's tennis. Willing to take a chance with young players, he often had players representing Australia in the Davis Cup before they were 20 years old.

Hopper, Dennis (1936–) Film actor and director, born in Dodge City, KS. *Rebel Without A Cause* (1955) is cited as his film debut, although he is credited with an appearance in *Johnny Guitar* (1954). He caused a sensation with the anti-establishment *Easy Rider* (1969), the archetypal 'road' film in which he directed and starred. *Hoosiers* (1986) earned him an Oscar nomination for Best Supporting Actor. Later films include *The American Friend* (1977), *Blue Velvet* (1986), *Speed* (1994), and *Star Truckers* (1997). His films as a director include *Colors* (1988), *The Hot Spot* (1990), and *Chasers* (1994).

Hopper, Edward (1882–1967) Painter, born in Nyack, NY. He studied under Robert Henri (1900–6) and made several trips to Europe (1906–10). He worked mainly as an illustrator until 1924. His paintings are of commonplace urban scenes characterized by a pervasive sense of stillness and isolation, and have had a strong influence on Pop Art and New Realist painters during the second half of the 20th-c. >> Henri

Hoppe-Seyler, Ernst Felix (Immanuel) [hopuh ziyler] (1825–95) Physiological chemist, born in Freiburg im Breisgau, Germany. A pioneer in the application of chemical methods to understand physiological processes, he showed how haemoglobin in the red blood cells binds oxygen, which is subsequently delivered to the tissues. He also investigated the chemical composition and functions of chlorophyll, as well as the chemistry of putrefaction. He taught in Berlin, Tübingen, and Strasbourg, and founded in 1877 *Zeitschrift für physiologische Chemie*, the first biochemical journal.

Horace, in full **Quintus Horatius Flaccus** (65–8 BC) Latin poet and satirist, born near Venusia, Italy. The son of a freed slave, he was educated in Rome and Athens. While in Athens he joined Brutus, and fought at Philippi. Back in Italy, he joined the civil service, but had to write verses to avoid poverty. His earliest works were chiefly satires and lampoons, and through the influence of Virgil he came under the patronage of Maecenas, a minister of Octavianus. Given a farm in the Sabine Hills, he devoted himself to writing, and became the unrivalled lyric poet of his time. He produced his greatest work, the three books of *Odes*, in 19 BC. >> Brutus, Marcus Junius; Maecenas; Virgil

Hordern, Sir Michael (Murray) (1911–95) Actor, born in Berkhamsted, Hertfordshire, SE England, UK. He studied at Brighton College, and made his professional debut in 1937 after a spell in amateur dramatics. Despite being a popular actor for 20 years, he only became a major London star with his appearance in John Mortimer's *The Dock Brief*. A formidable classical actor, he appeared as Malvolio at The Old Vic (1954), as Jonathan Miller's King Lear (1960), and as Prospero in *The Tempest* (1978, Stratford). His outstanding performances in modern roles included Tom Stoppard's *Jumpers* (1972) and Howard Barker's *Stripwell* (1975). He made numerous film and television appearances, notably in the television adaptation of John Mortimer's *Paradise Postponed* (1986). He was knighted in 1983.

Hore-Belisha, Leslie Hore-Belisha, Baron [haw(r) beleesha] (1893–1957) British statesman and barrister, born in Devonport, Devon, SW England, UK. He studied at Oxford, and was called to the bar in 1922. He entered parliament in 1923, and became first chairman of the National Liberal Party (1931). He was minister of transport (1934), drafted a new highway code, and inaugurated driving tests for motorists. As secretary of state for war (1937–40) he carried out several far-ranging and controversial reforms to modernize and democratize the army. He was minister of national insurance in the 1945 'caretaker' government, but lost his seat at the July election. In 1954 he received a peerage. His name is preserved in the *Belisha beacons* he introduced in the UK to mark pedestrian road crossings.

Horkheimer, Max [haw(r)khiymer] (1895–1973) Philosopher and social theorist, born in Stuttgart, Germany. He studied at Frankfurt, where he was director of the Institute for Social Research (1930–3) (the 'Frankfurt school'). He moved with the school to New York City when the Nazis came to power, and returned to Frankfurt in 1950 as professor at the university. He published a series of influential articles in the 1930s, collected in two volumes under the title *Kritische Theorie* (1968).

Hornblower, Jonathan (Carter) (1753–1815) Engineer, born in Chacewater, Cornwall, SW England, UK. As a young man he was employed by Boulton and James Watt to build one of their engines. He determined to improve Watt's design, and by 1781 had obtained a patent for a single-acting compound engine with two cylinders, in which the steam acted expansively and hence much more efficiently. He was judged, however, to have infringed Watt's patent of the separate condenser, and had to abandon further development of his engine. He later patented a rotary type of steam engine which was never built. >> Boulton; Watt; Woolf, Arthur

Hornby, A(lbert) S(idney) (1898–1978) Teacher, grammarian, and lexicographer, born in Chester, Cheshire, NWC England, UK. He is best known for a dictionary he prepared for Japanese students of English, published in Japan in 1942, and later in England as *A Learner's Dictionary of Current English* (1948).

Hornby, Frank (1863–1936) British inventor of the constructional toy. Although he had no formal training in mechanics or engineering, he enjoyed making mechanical toys for his sons in his spare time. To reduce the time needed to make individual parts, he devised and patented (1901) the perforated strips marketed as *Meccano* from 1907. He began production of the model railway, Hornby Trains (1920), and founded Dinky Toys to make model cars in the 1930s.

Horne, Donald (Richmond) (1921–) Writer, academic, and arts administrator, born in New South Wales, Australia. He became associate professor of political science at the University of New South Wales in 1964 (emeritus, 1987). His best-known book is *The Lucky Country* (1964), the title of which has become a common Australian expression, used without the ironic sense originally intended. Other books include *A History of the Australian People* (1985), *The Lucky Country Revisited* (1987), and *Ideas for the Nation* (1989). He was editor of *The Bulletin* (1967–72), chairman of the Australia Council (1985–90), Chancellor of the University of Canberra, and chairman of the Ideas for Australia programme since 1991. A leading member of the Australian Republican Movement, he has written *The Coming Republic* (1992).

Horne, Lena (1917–) Singer and actress, born in Brooklyn, NY. Raised by her actress mother, by the age of 16 she was dancing at Harlem's Cotton Club, becoming a popular singer with bands such as those of Noble Sissle and Teddy Wilson. She performed in the musical *Blackbirds of 1939*, and went into film, becoming the first African-American to be signed to a long-term contract (although her scenes were sometimes excised for distribution in the South). The title song of *Stormy Weather* (1943) became her signature. She was blacklisted in the early 1950s for little more than her friendship with Paul Robeson and her outspokenness about discrimination, but she performed in the musical *Jamaica* (1957) and later made several other films. She toured Europe and the USA as a nightclub singer, spoke out increasingly against racism, and published her autobiography, *Lena* (1965). >> Robeson, Paul; Wilson, Teddy

Horne, Marilyn (Bernice) (1934–) Mezzo-soprano opera singer, born in Bradford, PA. She studied at the University of Southern California, and made her opera debut in *The Bartered Bride* in Los Angeles in 1954. She is noted for her efforts to revive interest in the lesser-known operas of Rossini and Handel.

Horner, Arthur Lewis (1894–1968) Political activist and trade unionist, born in Merthyr Tydfil, S Wales, UK. He worked in a Rhondda coalmine, was a founder-member of the British Communist Party, and stood unsuccessfully for parliament a number of times. He was elected president of the South Wales miners' union in 1936, and general secretary of the National Union in 1946.

Horne-Tooke, John >> **Tooke, John Horne**

Horney, Karen, *née* **Danielsen** (1885–1952) Psychiatrist and psychoanalyst, born near Hamburg, Germany. While still a medical student in Germany, she married a fellow student and they had three children. Her personal life was already under great strain by 1915, and she underwent Freudian analysis with Karl Abraham. She began to take on patients for analysis in 1919, and was affiliated to the Berlin Psychoanalytic Clinic and Institute until 1932, when she joined the Chicago Institute for Psychoanalysis. During the 1920s she began to publish papers that took issue with orthodox Freudianism, particularly in relation to women's particular psychosexuality, and in the 1930s developed theories about the importance of sociocultural factors in human development which, at the time, were considered heretical by many Freudians. In 1934 she moved to New York City, fell out with the orthodox Freudians there, and with other prominent psychoanalysts formed (1941) the Association for the Advancement of Psychoanalysis. Her influential books include *Our Inner Conflicts* (1945) and *Neurosis and Human Growth* (1950). >> Freud, Sigmund

Horniman, Annie E(lizabeth) F(redericka) (1860–1937) Theatre manager and patron, born in London, England, UK. She inherited a large legacy in 1893, and began to invest in the theatre. She financed the first staging of Yeats's *The Land of Heart's Desire*, and Shaw's *Arms and the Man*, and sponsored the building of the Abbey Theatre in Dublin for the Irish National Theatre Society (1904). In 1908 she purchased the Gaiety Theatre in Manchester, to house the repertory company she had founded the previous year. Until the company disbanded (1917) for want of financial success, she put on over 100 new plays by the so-called 'Manchester School', mostly directed by Lewis Casson, who married a member of the company, Sybil Thorndike. >> Casson, Lewis; Shaw, George Bernard; Thorndike, Sybil; Yeats, William Butler

Hornsby, Rogers, nickname **the Rajah** (1896–1963) Baseball player, born in Winters, TX. During his 23-year career as a second baseman (1915–37), mostly with the St Louis Cardinals and Chicago Cubs, he posted a lifetime batting average of ·358, the second highest in major league history. Three times he batted over ·400 in a season, his 1924 average of ·424 being the highest ever in modern major league baseball. An outspoken and controversial player, he also managed the Cardinals, Cubs, Boston Braves, and St Louis

Browns between 1925 and 1953. He was elected to baseball's Hall of Fame in 1942.

Hornung, Ernest William (1866–1921) Writer, born in Middlesbrough, NE England, UK. Brother-in-law of Arthur Conan Doyle, he was the creator of Raffles the gentleman burglar, hero of *The Amateur Cracksman* (1899), *Mr Justice Raffles* (1909), and many other adventure stories. >> Doyle, Arthur Conan

Horowitz, Vladimir [ho̱rovits] (1904–89) Pianist, born in Kiev, Ukraine. He studied in Kiev, made his concert debut when he was 17, and toured widely before settling in the USA and becoming a US citizen. There were long periods of retirement from concert life, but in 1986 he played again in Russia.

Horrocks, Sir Brian (Gwynne) (1895–1985) British general, born in Raniket, India. He trained at Sandhurst, joined the army in 1914, and served in France and Russia. In 1942 he commanded the 9th Armoured Division and then the 13th and 10th Corps in N Africa, where he helped to defeat Rommel. Wounded at Tunis, he headed the 30th Corps during the Allied invasion (1944). He became well known as a military journalist and broadcaster after the war.

Horrocks, Jeremiah (c. 1617–41) Astronomer, born in Toxteth, Merseyside, NW England, UK. He studied at Cambridge, and was ordained in 1639. He was curate of Hoole, Lancashire, where he made the first recorded observation of the transit of Venus (24 Nov 1639, old dating style) which he had predicted. He made other observations, and calculated an improved value for the solar parallax.

Horsa >> **Hengist** and **Horsa**

Horsely, Sir Victor (Alexander Haden) (1857–1916) Physiologist and surgeon, born in London, England, UK. He was professor at the Royal Institution (1891–3), and professor of pathology at University College, London (1893–6). He was the first to remove a spinal tumour. He distinguished himself by his work on the localization of brain function and the improvement of operative techniques to allow brain surgery; and he improved the treatment of myxoedema. He was knighted in 1902, and died of heatstroke on active service in Mesopotamia.

Horta, Victor, Baron (1861–1947) Architect, born in Ghent, Belgium. Trained at the Académie des Beaux-Arts, Brussels, his designs include several works in that city: Maison Tassel (1892–3), which was at the same time individual and contemporary but conscious of tradition; Maison Solray (1894–1900), a luxurious design full of light and movement; and Maison du Peuple (1895–9), a masterpiece in metal, glass, and stone (demolished in 1964). He is considered the originator of Art Nouveau.

Horthy (de Nagybánya), Miklós [haw(r)tee] (1868–1957) Hungarian statesman and regent (1920–44), born in Kenderes, Hungary. He commanded the Austro-Hungarian fleet (1918), and was minister of war in the counter-revolutionary 'White government' (1919), opposing Bela Kun's Communist regime, which he suppressed (1920). He became regent, presiding over a resolutely conservative, authoritarian regime. In World War 2 he supported the Axis Powers until Hungary was overrun by the Germans in 1944. He was imprisoned by the Germans, released by the Allies in 1945, and went to live in Estoril, Portugal. >> Kun; Skorzeny; RR1058

Horwitz brothers >> **Stooges, The Three**

Hoskins, Bob, popular name of **Robert William Hoskins** (1942–) Actor, born in Bury St Edmunds, Suffolk, E England, UK. He sampled numerous other occupations before choosing acting and making his debut in *Romeo and Juliet* (1969) at Stoke-on-Trent. Avidly learning his craft, his notable stage performances include *Richard III* (1971), *The Iceman Cometh* (1976), and *Guys and Dolls* (1981). He achieved widespread public recognition with the television series *Pennies From Heaven* (1978), as the menacing hoodlum in the film *The Long Good Friday* (1980), and the minder in *Mona Lisa* (1986). After several years as a reliable and much-employed supporting actor in films he acquired international stardom with his award-winning performance in *Who Framed Roger Rabbit* (1988). Later films include *Hook* (1991), *Super Mario Bros* (1993), and *The Secret Agent* (1996). He made his directorial debut with *The Raggedy Rawney* (1988).

Hoskins, W(illiam) G(eorge) (1908–92) Historian, born in Exeter, SW England, UK. He studied at Exeter, taught economics at Leicester (1931–41, 1946–48), served on the price regulating committee (1941–5), and joined the history department at Leicester (1948), becoming professor in 1965. He is best known for his book *The Making of the English Landscape* (1955), and for his BBC television series, *Landscapes of England* (1976–8). He was the first to explain the historical evolution of the landscape, and created a new interest in local history.

Hotchkiss, Benjamin (Berkeley) (1826–85) Inventor, born in Watertown, CT. He devised an improved type of cannon shell, the *Hotchkiss revolving-barrel machine gun* (1872), and a magazine rifle (1875) which came to be widely used in the USA, France, and Britain.

Hotspur, Harry >> **Percy**

Hotter, Hans (1909–) Baritone, born in Offenbach-am-Main, Germany. He studied in Munich and, after working as an organist and choirmaster, made his debut as an opera singer in 1930. In 1940 he settled in Munich, but sang frequently in Vienna and Bayreuth, becoming one of the leading Wagnerian baritones of his day. He retired from opera in 1972, but continued to do recital work.

Houdin, (Jean Eugène) Robert [oodī] (1805–71) Conjurer, considered the father of modern conjuring, born in Blois, France. He made mechanical toys and automata in Paris for some years, and gave magical soirées at the Palais Royal (1845–55). In 1856 he was sent by the government to Algiers to destroy the influence of the dervishes by exposing their pretended miracles.

Houdini, Harry [hoodeenee], originally **Erich Weiss** (1874–1926) Magician and escape artist, born in Budapest. His family emigrated to the USA while he was still a child. He could escape from any kind of bonds or container, from prison cells to padlocked underwater boxes. He was a vigorous campaigner against fraudulent mediums, and was president of the Society of American Magicians.

Houdon, Jean Antoine [oodō] (1741–1828) Classical sculptor, born in Versailles, France. He won the *Prix de Rome* in 1761, spent 10 years in Rome, and there executed the colossal figure of 'St Bruno' in Santa Maria degli Angeli. In 1785 he visited America to execute a marble statue of Washington (Richmond, VA). His most famous busts are those of Diderot, Voltaire (foyer of the Théâtre Français, Paris), Napoleon, Catherine the Great, and Rousseau (Louvre). He was appointed professor at the Ecole des Beaux-Arts in 1805.

Hounsfield, Sir Godfrey (Newbold) (1919–) Physicist, born in Newark, Nottinghamshire, C England, UK. He studied in London, and joined Electrical and Musical Industries (EMI) in 1951. Independently of A M Cormack, he developed the method of X-ray computer-assisted tomography (CAT), the first body scanners being made by EMI in the early 1970s. He continued to work on new medical imaging methods, and shared the Nobel Prize for Physiology or Medicine in 1979. He was knighted in 1981. >> RR1124

Houphouët-Boigny, Felix [oofway bwīnyee] (1905–93)

African statesman, the first president of Côte d'Ivoire (Ivory Coast) (1960–93), born in Yamoussoukro, Côte d'Ivoire. He became a doctor, and the leading African politician of French West Africa. He was a member of the French Constituent Assembly (1945–6) and of the National Assembly (1946–59), and held several ministerial posts. He became president when the country was granted independence, was re-elected at every subsequent election, and commenced his seventh term of office in 1990. >> RR1043

House, Edward M(andell) (1858–1938) US diplomat, born in Houston, TX. During and after World War 1 he represented the USA in many conferences, and was long a close associate of President Wilson, helping him to draft terms for peace at the end of the War. He also supported the establishment of the League of Nations. >> **Wilson, Woodrow**

Houseman, John, originally **Jacques Haussman** (1902–89) Stage director, producer, teacher, and actor, born in Bucharest, Romania. Educated in England, he first worked as a producer in New York City in 1934, joining the Federal Theater Project in 1935. With Orson Welles he founded the Mercury Theater (1937), becoming editor of the Mercury Theater of the Air, and producing Welles' famous broadcast adaptation of H G Wells' *The War of the Worlds* (1938). He was artistic director of several US theatres, and taught at the Juilliard School, New York City (1968–76). He also made many film appearances, notably in *The Paper Chase* (1973), and wrote three volumes of autobiography. >> **Welles, Orson**

Housman, A(lfred) E(dward) (1859–1936) Scholar and poet, born near Bromsgrove, Hereford and Worcester, WC England, UK, the brother of Laurence Housman. He studied at Oxford, failed his degree, and entered the Patent Office, but his contributions to learned journals enabled him to return to academic life, and he became professor of Latin at London (1892), then at Cambridge (1911). He is best known for his own poetry, notably *A Shropshire Lad* (1896) and *Last Poems* (1922). He saw himself chiefly as a Latinist, and devoted much of his life to an annotated edition (1903–30) of Manilius. >> **Housman, Laurence**

Housman, Laurence (1865–1959) Writer and playwright, born in Bromsgrove, Hereford and Worcester, WC England, UK, the brother of A E Housman. He studied art at Lambeth and South Kensington, and attracted attention by his illustrations of Meredith's poem, 'Jump-to-Glory Jane'. He is best known for his *Little Plays of St Francis* (1922) and his Victorian biographical 'chamber plays', such as *Angels and Ministers* (1921) and *Victoria Regina* (1937). His autobiography, *The Unexpected Years* (1937), reveals a romantic Victorian figure, a Conservative radical who espoused pacificism and votes for women. >> **Housman, A E**

Houssay, Bernardo Alberto [oosiy] (1887–1971) Physiologist, born in Buenos Aires. He was professor at Buenos Aires until dismissed by President Juan Perón in 1943, and thereafter founded the Institute of Biology and Experimental Medicine, in 1944. He investigated the role of pituitary hormones, and shared the 1947 Nobel Prize for Physiology or Medicine. >> RR1124

Houston, Edwin J(ames) >> **Thomson, Elihu**

Houston, Sam(uel) [hyoostn] (1793–1863) US soldier and statesman, born in Lexington, VA. In his teens he lived for three years among the Cherokee Indians, learning their customs and language. He enlisted in the army in 1813, but resigned in 1818 and studied law. In 1823 he was elected a member of Congress, and in 1827 became Governor of Tennessee. As commander-in-chief in the Texan War, he defeated the Mexicans on the San Jacinto in 1836, and achieved Texan independence. He was elected president of the republic, re-elected in 1841, and on the annexation of

Texas (1845) returned to the US Senate. Elected Governor of Texas in 1859, he opposed secession, was deposed in 1861, and retired to private life. Houston, TX, is named after him.

Houston, Whitney (1963–) Singer and film actress, born in Newark, NJ, USA. She began singing in the local gospel choir, and became a backing singer for Chaka Khan, Lou Rawls, and others. The album *Whitney Houston* (1985) won a Grammy award and included her first US number 1 hit single 'Saving All My Love For You'. Her second album, *Whitney* (1987), entered the UK chart and became the first album by a female artist to debut at number 1. In 1988 she broke a US chart record with seven consecutive number 1 hits, overtaking the previous record of six achieved by The Beatles and The Bee Gees. Her films include *The Bodyguard* (1992) and *The Preacher's Wife* (1996).

Houstoun, Michael (1952–) Pianist, born in Timaru, New Zealand. He first gained international recognition with third place in the 1973 Van Cliburn International Piano Competition. He has also been a major prizewinner in both the Leeds and Tchaikovsky International Piano Competitions. A regular performer on the world concert stage, particularly of the works of Beethoven and Rachmaninov, he has worked from New Zealand since 1981.

Howard, John (Winston) (1939–) Australian statesman and prime minister (1996–), born in Sydney, New South Wales, Australia. Educated at Sydney University, he became a solicitor, and was elected Liberal MP for Bennelong, New South Wales, in 1974. He held ministerial posts in business and trade before becoming Federal Treasurer (1977–83) and deputy-leader (1983–5) then leader of the Liberal Party in Opposition (1985–9,1995–6). He became prime minister following his party's general election victory in 1996.

Howard, Catherine (?–1542) Fifth wife of Henry VIII, a grand-daughter of the 2nd Duke of Norfolk. She was married to the king in the same month as he divorced Anne of Cleves (July 1540). However, after Henry learned of Catherine's alleged premarital affairs (1541), she was arrested for treason, and beheaded in the Tower of London. >> Henry VIII

Howard, Charles, 1st Earl of Nottingham (1536–1624) Lord High Admiral, a cousin of Elizabeth I, who commanded the English fleet against the Spanish Armada (1588). He succeeded to his father's title in 1573, and became Lord High Admiral in 1585. For his role in the Cadiz expedition (1596) he was created an earl, and in 1601 he quelled Essex's rising. >> Essex, 2nd Earl of

Howard, Sir Ebenezer (1850–1928) Founder of the garden city movement, born in London, England, UK. He emigrated to Nebraska in 1872, but returned to England in 1877 and became a parliamentary shorthand-writer. His *Tomorrow* (1898) envisaged self-contained communities with both rural and urban amenities and green belts, and led to the formation in 1899 of the Garden City Association and to the laying out of Letchworth (1903) and Welwyn Garden City (1919) in Hertfordshire. He was knighted in 1927.

Howard, Henry >> **Surrey, Earl of**

Howard, John (1726–90) Prison reformer, born in London, England, UK. While travelling in Europe he was captured by the French, and spent some time in prison at Brest. In 1773 he became high sheriff for Bedfordshire, and began a series of tours in which he investigated the condition of prisons and prisoners. As a result, two acts were passed in 1774, one providing for fixed salaries to jailers, and the other enforcing cleanliness. He died of typhus, contracted while visiting a military hospital in Kherson, Russia. The

Howard League for Penal Reform, founded in 1866, is named after him.

Howard, Leslie, originally **Leslie Howard Stainer** (1893–1943) Actor, born in London, England, UK. He made his film debut in 1914, and turned to the theatre after being invalided home from the Western Front. During the 1930s he had many leading film roles, including *The Scarlet Pimpernel* (1935), *Pygmalion* (1938, co-director), and as Ashley Wilkes in *Gone with the Wind* (1939). He appeared in several British wartime productions, such as *The First of the Few* (1942), and is thought to have been killed when a special mission flight from Lisbon to London was shot down.

Howard, Michael (1941–) British statesman. He studied at Cambridge, where he was president of the Union, and was called to the bar in 1964. He was elected an MP in 1983, and after several junior posts became minister for local government (1987–8), minister for water and planning (1988–90), secretary-of-state for employment (1990–2) and the environment (1992–3), and home secretary (1993–7). He emerged as a contender for the leadership of the Conservative Party following John Major's resignation in 1997, but withdrew after the first ballot. >> Major

Howard, Oliver O(tis) (1830–1909) US soldier, born in Leeds, ME. He trained at West Point, and in the Civil War took command of a regiment of Maine volunteers (1861). In 1864 he commanded the Army of Tennessee, and led the right wing of Sherman's army on the march to the sea. He was commissioner of the Freedmen's Bureau (1865–74), where he did much to help former slaves. He was the first president of Howard University, Washington, DC (1869–74), which was named after him. He then returned to military service, fighting out West against the Indians, and became superintendent at West Point (1880–2). >> Sherman, William Tecumseh

Howard, Thomas, 3rd Duke of Norfolk, Earl of Surrey (1473–1554) English statesman, the son of Thomas Howard, 2nd Duke of Norfolk (1443–1524), and brother-in-law of Henry VII. Howard was Lord High Admiral (1513), and helped defeat the Scots at Flodden Field (1513). He became Lord Lieutenant of Ireland (1520). He was uncle to Anne Boleyn, but as Lord Steward presided over her trial for adultery (1536). He lost influence at court when another niece, Catherine Howard, was beheaded for adultery in 1542. Throughout the reign of Edward VI he was imprisoned on suspicion of the treason for which Henry VIII had executed his eldest son, Henry Howard, Earl of Surrey, in 1547. He was released on the accession of Mary I in 1553. >> Boleyn; Henry VIII; Howard, Catherine; Surrey

Howard, Trevor (Wallace) (1916–88) Actor, born in Cliftonville, Kent, SE England, UK. He trained in London and had a successful stage career until joining the army at the beginning of World War 2. Invalided out in 1944, he turned to films, and sprang to stardom with *Brief Encounter* (1945), followed by *The Third Man* (1949) and *Outcast of the Islands* (1951). His versatile and often eccentric characterizations were regularly in demand for both film and television, with later appearances in *Gandhi* and *The Missionary* (both 1982), *Dust* (1985), and *White Mischief* (1987).

Howe, Elias (1819–67) Inventor, born in Spencer, MA. He worked as a mechanic in Lowell and Boston, where he constructed and patented (1846) the first sewing machine. After an unsuccessful visit to England to introduce his invention, he returned to Boston, where he found his patent had been infringed. Harassed by poverty, he entered on a seven years' war of litigation to protect his rights, was ultimately successful (1854), and amassed a fortune. >> Singer, Isaac Merritt

Howe (of Aberavon), (Richard Edward) Geoffrey Howe, Baron (1926–) British statesman, born in Port

Talbot, SC Wales, UK. He studied at Cambridge, was called to the bar in 1952 and became a Conservative MP in 1964. Knighted in 1970, he became solicitor general (1970–2), minister for trade and consumer affairs (1972–4), Chancellor of the Exchequer (1979–1983), and foreign secretary (1983–9). In 1989 he was made deputy prime minister, Lord President of the Council, and Leader of the House of Commons, but resigned from the government (Nov 1990) in opposition to Mrs Thatcher's hostility towards European monetary union. He was created a life peer in 1992, and a Companion of Honour in 1996. >> Thatcher

Howe, Joseph (1804–73) Canadian statesman, born in Halifax, Nova Scotia, Canada. Proprietor and editor of the Halifax *Nova Scotian*, he became chief commissioner of railways for Nova Scotia (1854), then premier of the province (1863–1870). After federation he entered the first Canadian government at Ottawa as President of the Council, then as secretary of state.

Howe, Julia Ward, *née* **Ward** (1819–1910) Feminist, reformer, and writer, born in New York City. A wealthy banker's daughter, she became a prominent suffragette and abolitionist, and founded the New England Woman Suffrage Association (1868) and the New England Women's Club (1868). She published several volumes of poetry, as well as travel books and a play. Best known for the 'Battle Hymn of the Republic' (published in *Atlantic Monthly*, 1862), she edited *Woman's Journal* (1870–90), and became the first woman to be elected to the American Academy of Arts and Letters (1908). >> Howe, Samuel

Howe, Richard Howe, 1st Earl (1726–99) British admiral, born in London, England, UK, the brother of William Howe. He entered the navy at 13, and distinguished himself in the Seven Years' War (1756–63). He became a Lord of the Admiralty (1763), Treasurer of the Navy (1765), First Lord of the Admiralty (1783), viscount (1782), and earl (1788). In 1776 he was made commander of the British fleet during the American War of Independence. In 1778 he defended the American coast against a superior French force, and in the French Revolutionary Wars defeated the French at 'the Glorious First of June' (1794). >> Howe, William

Howe, Samuel (Gridley) (1801–76) Reformer and philanthropist, born in Boston, MA. He studied at Harvard Medical School, and in the Greek War of Independence organized the medical staff of the Greek army (1824–7). In 1831 he went to Europe to study methods of educating the blind, became involved in the Polish insurrection, and spent six weeks in a Prussian prison. On his return to Boston he established the Perkins School for the Blind, and taught Laura Bridgman, among others. He married Julia Ward in 1843. He was widely known as a campaigner for better education facilities for the mentally ill, the blind, and the deaf. >> Bridgman, Laura; Howe, Julia Ward

Howe, William Howe, 5th Viscount (1729–1814) British soldier who commanded the army in North America during the American Revolution, the brother of Richard Howe. He joined the army in 1746, and served under Wolfe at Louisburg (1758) and Quebec, where he led the famous advance to the Heights of Abraham. He became an MP in 1758. In the American War of Independence his victories included Bunker Hill (1775), the Brandywine (1777), and the capture of New York City (1776). He returned to England, and was made a viscount in 1799. >> Howe, Richard; Putnam, Israel; Wolfe, James

Howells, Herbert (1892–1983) Composer, born in Lydney, Gloucestershire, SWC England, UK. He studied under Stanford at the Royal College of Music, where he became professor of composition (1920). He followed Holst as director of music at St Paul's Girls' School (1936), and

became professor of music at London University (1952–62). He is best known for his choral works, especially the *Hymnus paradisi*, which combine an alert sense of 20th-c musical developments with a firm foundation in the English choral tradition. >> Stanford, Charles

Howells, John Mead >> **Hood, Raymond M**

Howells, William Dean (1837–1920) Writer and critic, born in Martin's Ferry, OH. A typesetter, then a reporter, his early poetry was published in the *Atlantic Monthly*, which he later edited (1871–81). His biography of Lincoln (1860) procured for him the post of US consul in Venice (1861–5). He became the king of critics in America, with his *Easy Chair* column for *Harper's* (1900–20). A great influence on Mark Twain and Henry James, his theories of fiction were expounded in *Criticism and Fiction* (1891). His novels include *Their Wedding Journey* (1872), *The Lady of the Aroostook* (1879), and *A Hazard of New Fortunes* (1890). >> James, Henry; Twain

Howerd, Frankie, originally **Francis Alex Howard** (1922–92) Comedian and actor, born in London, England, UK. He made his debut at the Stage Door Canteen, Piccadilly, London, in 1946, and appeared in revues in London during the 1950s, including *Out of This World* (1950), *Pardon My French* (1953), and *Way Out In Piccadilly* (1960). He occasionally acted in plays, and gave a notable performance in Sondheim's musical, *A Funny Thing Happened on the Way to the Forum*, in 1963. He appeared regularly on television and in films, his most famous role being that of a Roman slave in the television series *Up Pompeii* (1970–1), a series drenched in sexual innuendo. His films include *The Ladykillers* (1956), *Carry On Doctor* (1968), *Up Pompeii* (1971), and *Up the Chastity Belt* (1972). His brand of humour became increasingly appreciated in the 1980s, and he presented several successful television series, including *Frankie Howerd on Campus* (1990).

Hoxha, Enver, also spelled **Hodja** [hoja] (1908–85) Albanian prime minister (1946–54) and Communist Party secretary (1954–85), born in Gjirokastër, Albania. He founded and led the Albanian Communist Party (1941) in the fight for national independence. In 1946 he deposed King Zog (who had fled in 1939), and became head of state. >> Zog I

Hoyland, John (1934–) Painter, born in Sheffield, South Yorkshire, N England, UK. He studied at Sheffield College of Art and at the Royal Academy Schools, and held several teaching posts, including principal lecturer at the Chelsea School of Art. He won an international Young Artists Prize in Tokyo in 1964. In America in the same year he met 'Colour Field' painters such as Morris Louis, and turned to hard-edge abstraction using broad, freely painted rectangles of rich colour. >> Louis, Morris

Hoyle, Edmond (1672–1769) Writer on card games, called 'the father of whist', who lived in London, England, UK. His popular *Short Treatise on Whist* (1742) ran into many editions, and was ultimately incorporated with his manuals on backgammon, brag, quadrille, piquet, and chess into an omnibus volume (1748).

Hoyle, Sir Fred(erick) (1915–) Astronomer, mathematician, astrophysicist, and science fiction writer, born in Bingley, West Yorkshire, N England, UK. He studied at Cambridge, where he taught applied mathematics, became professor of astronomy (1958–72), and founded a world-famous Institute of Theoretical Astronomy. His work on the origin of chemical elements is particularly important. He is a leading proponent of steady-state cosmology, of the notion that viruses come from outer space, and a believer in an extraterrestrial origin for life on Earth. He was knighted in 1972. His scientific works include *Nature of the Universe* (1952) and *Frontiers of Astronomy* (1955). His science fiction writing includes *The*

Black Cloud (1957), *A for Andromeda* (1962, with J Elliot), and *The Molecule Men* (1971, with G Hoyle). His other writing includes stories for children, space serials for television, and two volumes of autobiography, *The Small World of Fred Hoyle* (1966) and *Home is Where the Wind Blows* (1994). >> Fowler, William A

Hoyte, (Hugh) Desmond (1929–) Guyanese statesman and president (1985–92), born in Georgetown, Guyana. He studied at London University and the Middle Temple, taught in a boys' school in Grenada (1955–7), then practised as a lawyer in Guyana. He joined the Socialist People's National Congress Party, and in 1968, two years after Guyana achieved full independence, was elected to the National Assembly. He held a number of ministerial posts before becoming prime minister under Forbes Burnham. On Burnham's death, in 1985, he succeeded him as president. >> Burnham, Forbes; RR1056

Hrdlička, Aleš [**herd**lichka] (1869–1943) Physical anthropologist, born in Humpolec, Czech Republic. He arrived in the USA in 1882, studied medicine and anthropology, and joined the American Museum of Natural History (1899–1903). He then moved to the National Museum of Natural History (1903–43), becoming curator from 1910. His extensive anatomical research led to his being one of the first to argue that North and South American Indians derived from a racial stock that originated in Asia and migrated to the Americas across the Bering Strait.

Hromadka, Josef Luki [**hrom**adka] (1889–1969) Theologian, born in Hodslavice, Czech Republic. He studied at Basel, Heidelberg, Vienna, Prague, and at the United Free Church College, Aberdeen, and was theological professor at Prague (1920–39) and at Princeton Theological Seminary (1939–47). He returned to Czechoslovakia and became dean of the Comenius faculty, Prague, in 1950. Active in the World Council of Churches from its inception, he contributed much to Christian–Marxist dialogue, and received the Lenin Peace Prize in 1958.

Hroswitha [hrohs**vee**ta] (c. 932–1002) German poet and Benedictine nun of Gandersheim near Göttingen. She wrote Latin poems and six prose Terentian comedies, with a religious slant. She is regarded as the first German woman poet.

Hua Guofeng [hwah gwohfeng], also spelled **Hua Kuo-feng** (1920–) Chinese statesman and prime minister (1976–80), born in Jiaocheng, Shanxi province, China. He was vice-governor of Hunan (1958–67), but came under attack during the Cultural Revolution. A member of the Central Committee of the Party from 1969, and of the Politburo from 1973, he became deputy prime minister and minister of public security (1975–6), and in 1976 was made prime minister and chairman of the Central Committee. Under him China adopted a more pragmatic domestic and foreign policy, with emphasis on industrial and educational expansion, and closer relations with Western and Third World countries. He resigned as chairman in 1981. >> RR1040

Hubbard, Elbert (1856–1915) Writer and craft colonist, born in Bloomington, IL. Following years as a successful businessman, he established in 1893 the Roycrofters, a craft community in East Aurora, NY. Following the ideals of William Morris, the artisans produced mission-style furniture and Art Nouveau household accessories in metal and leather. He edited the Roycrofters' monthly *The Philistine*, in which appeared 'A Message to Garcia' (1899), embodying his ideas on a community of workers. >> Morris, William

Hubbard, L(afayette) Ron(ald) (1911–86) Writer, and founder of the Church of Scientology, born in Tilden, NE. He wrote science-fiction stories before his most famous work, *Dianetics: the Modern Science of Mental Health* (1950) became an instant best seller, and the basic text of the Scientology movement. Hubbard, who claimed to have visited heaven twice, was banned (1968) from re-entering Britain amid public concern over his aims and methods. In 1984 he was accused of embezzlement, his Church's tax-exempt status was revoked in the USA, and he withdrew into seclusion.

Hubble, Edwin (Powell) (1889–1953) Astronomer, born in Marshfield, MO. He studied mathematics and astronomy at Chicago University, then law at Oxford. He joined the Kentucky bar in 1913, but left to make astronomy his career. He worked at the Mt Wilson Observatory from 1919, studying nebulae, and in 1924 discovered that there were other galaxies apart from our own. While carrying out studies to classify these galaxies, he discovered in 1929 that the universe is expanding, establishing a ratio between the galaxies' speed of movement and their distance (*Hubble's constant*). The *Hubble Space Telescope* is named after him.

Hubel, David (Hunter) (1926–) Neurophysiologist, born in Windsor, Ontario, Canada. He studied at McGill University, Montreal, and became a US citizen in 1953. He did research at Johns Hopkins University (1954–9), then worked at Harvard. With Torsten Wiesel at Harvard Medical School he investigated the mechanics of visual perception at the cortical level, and they shared the 1981 Nobel Prize for Physiology or Medicine. >> Wiesel

Hubert, St (656–727) Frankish clergyman, the son of the Duke of Guienne. He lived a luxurious life, but was converted to Christianity and in 708 became Bishop of Liège. In art he is represented as a hunter converted by the apparition of a crucifix between the horns of a stag. This story may have been borrowed from St Eustace. Feast day 3rd November.

Hubert, Walter >> **Walter, Hubert**

Huch, Ricarda [hookh] (1864–1947) Writer, historian, and feminist, born in Brunswick, Germany. She studied at Zürich, taught in a girls' school there, travelled extensively in Italy, and finally settled in Munich in 1910. A neo-Romantic, she rejected naturalism, and wrote novels, social and political works, and works on religious themes. The first woman to be admitted to the Prussian Academy of Literature in 1931, she resigned in 1933 over the expulsion of Jewish writers.

Huddleston, (Ernest Urban) Trevor (1913–) Anglican missionary. He studied at Oxford, and was ordained in 1937. He entered the Community of the Resurrection, and in 1943 went to Johannesburg, where he ultimately became provincial of the Order (1949–55). After working in England (1956–60), he became Bishop of Masasi, Tanzania (1960–8), Bishop Suffragan of Stepney until 1978, then Bishop of Mauritius and Archbishop of the Indian Ocean. After his retirement, he returned to London, and became president of the Anti-Apartheid Movement (1981–94).

Hudson, George (1800–71) Financier, born near York, North Yorkshire, N England, UK. He was a linen-draper there until, inheriting £30 000 in 1828, he went into local politics and invested heavily in the North Midland Railway, making York a major railway centre, and became known as 'the railway king'. He bought large estates, was three times Lord Mayor of York, and was elected MP for Sunderland (1845). The railway mania of 1847–8 plunged him into ruin; he was accused of fraud, and lost his fortune and influence.

Hudson, Henry (?–1611) English navigator, who explored the NE coast of North America, making claims for both the English and the Dutch. Nothing is known about his early life. He sailed in search of a passage across the Pole (1607), reached Novaya Zemlya (1608), entered the river which was named after him (1609), and (1610) travelled through the strait and bay which now bear his name. He resolved to winter there, but food ran short, the men mutinied, and he and eight others were cast adrift to die.

Hudson, Manley (Ottmer) (1886–1960) Jurist, born in St Peters, MS. He studied at West Jewell College and at Harvard, where he became a professor. A member of the Permanent Court of Arbitration at The Hague (1933–45), and a judge of the Permanent Court of International Justice (1936–46), he became chairman of the International Law Commission. He wrote and edited many books on international law, as well as the *American Journal of International Law* (1924–60).

Hudson, Rock, originally **Roy Scherer, Jr** (1925–85) Film actor, born in Winnetka, IL. He had had no acting experience before being given his first chance in films, but he underwent intensive grooming to become one of the biggest box-office idols of the 1950s, starring with Doris Day in the comedy hit *Pillow Talk* (1959). Other films include *A Farewell to Arms* (1958), *Tobruk* (1967), and *Ice Station Zebra* (1968). In the 1970s he went on to have a successful television career in *McMillan and Wife*.

Hudson, Sir William (1896–1978) Hydro-electric engineer, born in Nelson, New Zealand. After service in World War 1, he worked for five years on hydro-electric schemes in New Zealand, then worked in Australia until 1930. He was in charge of the Galloway hydro-electric scheme in Scotland (1931–7) before returning to Sydney, eventually to head the Metropolitan Water Board. He then became commissioner of the Snowy Mountains Hydro-Electric Authority Scheme (1949–67), a mammoth engineering project which through his leadership was completed ahead of schedule in 1973.

Hudson, W(illiam) H(enry) (1841–1922) Writer and naturalist, born near Buenos Aires. He moved to England in 1869 and became a British subject in 1900. His early writings concerned the natural history of South America, but he is best known for the account of his rambles in the New Forest in *Hampshire Days* (1903), his romantic novel *Green Mansions* (1904), and the autobiographical *Far Away and Long Ago* (1918). His ornithological works include *Birds in London* (1898), and *The Book of a Naturalist* (1919). A bird sanctuary was created in his memory in Hyde Park, London (1925), and Epstein's sculpture 'Rima' (a character from *Green Mansions*) erected there.

Huggins, Charles B(renton) (1901–) Surgeon, born in Halifax, Nova Scotia, Canada. He studied at Acadia, Harvard, and Michigan universities, from 1927 working at Chicago, where he became professor of surgery in 1936 and head of the Ben May Laboratory for Cancer Research (1951–69). He shared the 1966 Nobel Prize for Physiology or Medicine for work on cancer research, notably his discovery of hormonal treatment for cancer of the prostate gland. >> RR1124

Huggins, Sir William (1824–1910) Astronomer, born in London, England UK. He built an observatory near London (1855), where he invented the stellar spectroscope, which had a major influence on the study of the physical constitution of stars, planets, comets, and nebulae. He discovered that comets emit the light of luminescent carbon gas (1868), and determined the amount of heat that reaches the Earth from some of the stars. He was knighted in 1897.

Hugh, St (c. 1140–1200) Clergyman, born in Avalon, France. Priest at the Grande Chartreuse (1160–70), he was called to England by Henry II to found a Carthusian monastery in Witham, Somerset (1178). He became Bishop of Lincoln (1186), where he fought against the savage forestry laws in the royal forests, and defended the Jews against rioting mobs. He refused to pay taxes to Richard I to finance wars (a significant event in constitutional history), and began the rebuilding of Lincoln cathedral. He was canonized in 1220; feast day 17 November. >> Richard I

Hugh Capet >> **Capet, Hugh**

Hughes, Arthur (1830–1915) Painter, born in London, England, UK. He trained at the Royal Academy Schools, London. During the 1850s he produced several paintings that rank as some of the finest works executed in the precise and richly coloured style of the Pre-Raphaelite Brotherhood. He also, from c.1855, pursued a successful career as an illustrator of the works of Christina Rossetti, among others. >> Rossetti, Christina

Hughes, Charles (Evans) (1862–1948) Jurist and politician, born in Glens Falls, NY. Admitted to the bar in 1884, he became Governor of New York (1907–10) and an associate justice of the US Supreme Court (1910). He ran against Woodrow Wilson as Republican candidate for the presidency in 1916, became secretary of state (1921–5) in the Warren Harding administration, and was appointed Chief Justice (1930–41). He also presided at the Washington Arms Limitation Conference (1921–5) and was a judge of the Permanent Court of International Justice (1928–30). >> Harding, Warren

Hughes, David (Edward) (1831–1900) Inventor, born in London, England, UK. He was brought up in Virginia and became professor of music at Bardston College, Kentucky (1850–3). In 1855 he invented a telegraph typewriter which was widely used throughout the USA and Europe, even up to the 1930s, and in 1878 a carbon microphone, important for telephony, and the precursor of modern carbon microphones. He left a large fortune to London hospitals.

Hughes, Howard (Robard) (1905–76) Millionaire businessman, film producer, film director, and aviator, born in Houston, TX. He studied at the California Institute of Technology, inheriting his father's machine tool company in 1923. In 1926 he ventured into films, producing *Hell's Angels* (1930), *Scarface* (1932), and *The Outlaw* (1941). He also founded his own aircraft company, designing, building, and flying aircraft, and broke several world air speed records (1935–8). His most famous aircraft, the 'Spruce Goose', was an oversized wooden sea-plane designed to carry 750 passengers, which was completed in 1947, but flew only once over a distance of one mile. Throughout his life he shunned publicity, eventually becoming a recluse while still controlling his vast business interests from sealed-off hotel suites, and giving rise to endless rumour and speculation. In 1971 an 'authorized' biography was announced, but the authors were imprisoned for fraud, and the mystery surrounding him continued until his death.

Hughes, (James Mercer) Langston (1902–67) Poet, short-story writer, and playwright, born in Joplin, MO. He studied briefly at Columbia University, but left to explore Harlem. Celebrated early on as a young poet of the Harlem Renaissance, his poetry appeared in *The Crisis* (1923–4) and *The New Negro* (1925). His first prose work, *Not Without Laughter*, appeared in 1930 to some acclaim. His other works include the play *The Mulatto* (produced on Broadway, 1935), and poetry collected in *Shakespeare of Harlem* (1942) and *Ask Your Mama* (1961). He is also well known for his 'Simple Stories' which appeared in the 1950s in comic strips, in books, and on the stage.

Hughes, Owain Arwel (1942–) Conductor, born in Cardiff, S Wales, UK. He studied at University College, Cardiff, and the Royal College of Music, London, and became associate conductor of the BBC Welsh Symphony Orchestra (1980–6) and the Philharmonia Orchestra, London (1985–90), musical director of the Huddersfield

Choral Society (1980–6), and founding artistic director and conductor of the Annual Welsh Proms (1986–). In 1992 he was the creator and musical director of The World Choir (10 000 male voices), and since 1995 has been principal conductor of the Aalborg Symphony Orchestra, Denmark.

Hughes, Richard (Arthur Warren) (1900–76) Writer, born in Weybridge, Surrey, SE England, UK. He studied at Oxford, co-founded and directed the Portmadoc Players (1922–5), and was vice-president of the Welsh National Theatre (1924–36). He wrote the first radio drama, *Danger*, for the BBC (1924), and a collection of poems *Confessio juvenis* (1925). He travelled widely in Europe, America, and the West Indies, and eventually settled in Wales. He co-authored *The Administration of War Production* (1956), one of the official war histories, but he is best known for *A High Wind in Jamaica* (1929, entitled *The Innocent Voyage* in the USA).

Hughes, Robert (Studley Forrest) (1938–) Art critic and writer, born in Sydney, New South Wales, Australia. He studied at the University of Sydney, decided to become an art critic rather than an artist, and was art critic of the *Sydney Observer* (1958–9) and *Nation* (1960–4). Since 1970 he has been senior art critic for *Time* magazine. He was awarded the Frank Jewett Mather Award for Distinguished Art Criticism in 1982 and 1985. He has written many important books on a wide range of subjects, including *The Art of Australia* (1966) and *The Shock of the New* (1980) – a guide to 20th-c art based on the BBC television series. Later works include *The Fatal Shore* (1987), a history of convict transportation to Australia, *The Culture Complaint* (1993), a polemical discussion about 'political correctness' in the USA, and the television series *American Visions* (1996, published 1997), a history of American art.

Hughes, Ted, popular name of **Edward (James) Hughes** (1930–) Poet, born in Mytholmroyd, West Yorkshire, N England, UK. He studied at Cambridge. Best known for his very distinctive animal poems, his first collections were *The Hawk in the Rain* (1957) and *Lupercal* (1960). He married the US poet, Sylvia Plath, in 1954, and after her death edited her collected poems (1981). *Selected Poems, 1957–81* was published in 1982, and he became British poet laureate in 1984. Later works include *Rain Charm for the Duchy* (1992) and *Tales from Ovid* (1997). He has always written a great deal for children, beginning with *Meet My Folks* (1961) and *Earth Owl* (1963). His story *The Iron Man* (1968, *The Iron Giant* in the USA) received a complementary volume, *The Iron Woman*, in 1993. >> Plath, Sylvia

Hughes, Thomas (1822–96) Writer, born in Uffington, Oxfordshire, SC England, UK. He studied at Oxford, was called to the bar (1848), and became a county court judge (1882). A Liberal MP (1865–74), closely associated with the Christian Socialists, he helped to found the Working Men's College (1854), of which he became principal (1872–83). He is primarily remembered as the author of the public school classic, *Tom Brown's Schooldays* (1856), based on his school experiences at Rugby under the head-mastership of Arnold. >> Arnold, Thomas; Kingsley, Charles; Maurice, Frederick Denison

Hughes, William Morris (1862–1952) Australian statesman and prime minister (1915–23), born in London, England, UK. He went to Australia in 1884, entered the New South Wales and Commonwealth parliaments, and became federal prime minister. He was the major proponent of conscription in World War 1, and as Nationalist prime minister represented Australia at the Versailles conference. A founder of the United Australian Party in the early 1930s, he served in successive cabinets until 1941, and remained an MP until his death. >> RR1033

Hugo, Victor (Marie) (1802–85) Writer, born in Besançon, France. Educated in Paris and Madrid, he wrote his first play at the age of 14, and went on to become the most prolific French writer of the 19th-c. His early works include *Odes et Ballades* (1822, 1826), and *Hernani* (1830), the first of the 'five-act lyrics' which compose his drama. The 1830s saw several plays, such as *Marion Delorme* (1831), books of poetry, notably *Les Feuilles d'automne* (1831, Autumn Leaves), and novels, of which the most popular is *Notre Dame de Paris* (1831, trans The Hunchback of Notre Dame). He was elected to the Legislative Assembly, and joined the democratic republicans; but in 1851, after the coup, he fled into exile in Brussels, and in 1852 moved to the Channel Is. There he wrote several major works, notably his books of poems *Les Châtiments* (1853, Punishments) and *Les Contemplations* (1856), and his panoramic novel of social history, *Les Misérables* (1862). He returned to Paris in 1870, was made a senator in 1876, and upon his death was given a national funeral. >> Sue

Hulbert, Jack >> **Courtneidge, Dame Cicely**

Hull, Clark L(eonard) (1884–1952) Psychologist, born in Akron, NY. He studied at Michigan and Wisconsin universities, then taught at Wisconsin and (from 1929) in the Institute of Human Relations at Yale, where he conducted experimental research into behaviour and learning processes. Much of his work was based on reinforcement theory, as seen in such books as *Principles of Behavior* (1943). He developed a rigorous mathematical theory of the learning process that attempted to reduce learned behaviour to a few simple axiomatic principles.

Hull, Cordell (1871–1955) US statesman, born in Overton Co, TN. He studied at Cumberland University, TN, qualified as an attorney, then entered politics, becoming a member of the US House of Representatives (1907–21, 1923–31). Under Franklin Roosevelt he became secretary of state in 1933, and served for the longest term in that office until he retired in 1944, having attended most of the great wartime conferences. He was a strong advocate of maximum aid to the Allies. One of the architects of 'bipartisanship', he received the Nobel Peace Prize in 1944. >> Roosevelt, Franklin D

Hulme, Keri (Ann Ruhi) [hyoom] (1947–) Writer, born in Otautahi, Christchurch, New Zealand. From a novelist with a moderate measure of local recognition, she acquired international renown in 1985 when her story *The Bone People* (1984) was awarded the Booker Prize. Maori themes figure prominently in her work, which also reflects a desire to live in close affinity to the natural environment. Later books include *The Windeater* (1987) and *Bait* (1992).

Hulme, T(homas) E(rnest) [hyoom] (1883–1917) Critic, poet, and philosopher, born in Endon, Staffordshire, C England, UK. He studied at Cambridge, and became a champion of modern abstract art, of the poetic movement known as 'Imagism,' and of the anti-liberal political writings of Georges Sorel, which he translated. Killed in action in France, he left a massive collection of notes, edited by his friend Herbert Read, under the titles *Speculation* (1924) and *More Speculation* (1956), which expose philistinism, and attack what he considered to be weak and outworn liberalism. >> Read, Herbert; Sorel

Hulst, Hendrik van de >> **van de Hulst, Hendrik**

Hulton, Sir Edward (George Warris) (1906–88) Magazine proprietor and journalist, born in Harrogate, North Yorkshire, N England, UK. He studied at Oxford, and was called to the bar. He succeeded to his father's newspaper interests, and became chairman of Hulton Press Ltd. He was the founder of *Picture Post*, a brilliant experiment in journalism which ceased in 1957.

Humboldt, (Friedrich Wilhelm Heinrich) Alexander, Freiherr (Baron) **von** [**hum**bohlt] (1769–1859) Naturalist and geographer, born in Berlin. He studied at Frankfurt, Berlin, Göttingen, and Freiberg, then in 1799 spent five years with **Aimé Bonpland** (1773–1858) exploring South America. He worked mainly in France until 1827, then explored Central Asia. From 1830 he was employed in politcal service. His major work, *Kosmos* (1845–62), endeavours to provide a comprehensive physical picture of the universe. The ocean current off the W coast of South America is named after him.

Humboldt, (Karl) Wilhelm von [**hum**bohlt] (1767–1835) German statesman and philologist, born in Potsdam, Germany. After travelling in Europe, he became a diplomat, and for some years devoted himself to literature. He became Prussian minister at Rome (1801), first minister of public instruction (1808), and minister in Vienna (1810). He was the first to study Basque scientifically, and he also worked on the languages of the East and of the South Sea Is.

Hume, (George) Basil, Cardinal [hyoom] (1923–) Roman Catholic Benedictine monk and cardinal. He studied at Ampleforth, Oxford, and Freibourg, and was ordained in 1950. He became Magister Scholarum of the English Benedictine Congregation (1957–63), and in 1963 Abbot of Ampleforth, where he remained until created Archbishop of Westminster and a cardinal in 1976. His books include *Searching for God* (1977), *Towards a Civilisation of Love* (1988), and *Remaking Europe: The Gospel in a Divided Continent* (1994).

Hume, David [hyoom] (1711–76) Philosopher and historian, born in Edinburgh, EC Scotland, UK. He studied at Edinburgh, took up law, and in 1734 went to La Flèche in Anjou, where he wrote his masterpiece, *A Treatise of Human Nature* (1739–40), consolidating and extending the empiricist legacy of Locke and Berkeley. His views became widely known only when he wrote two volumes of *Essays Moral and Political* (1741–2). He wrote the posthumously published *Dialogues concerning Natural Religion* in the 1750s. His atheism thwarted his applications for professorships at Edinburgh and Glasgow, and he became a tutor, secretary, and keeper of the Advocates' Library in Edinburgh, where he published his popular *Political Discourses* (1752), and his six-volume *History of England* (1754–62). His views inspired Kant to argue for the inadequacy of empiricism. >> Berkeley, George; Kant; Locke, John; Reid, Thomas

Hume, (Andrew) Hamilton [hyoom] (1797–1873) Explorer, born in Parramatta, New South Wales, Australia. From the age of 17 he made several expeditions, discovering the Goulburn and Yass plains (1822) and L Bathurst in S New South Wales, saw part of the Murray R (1824), made the first sighting of Australia's highest mountain, Mt Kosciusko, and received grants of land as reward. In 1828 Hume joined Charles Sturt's expedition which discovered the Darling R, but poor health prevented his continuing, and he settled down to farm his land grants near Yass. He was elected a Fellow of the Royal Geographical Society in 1860. >> Sturt

Hume, John [hyoom] (1937–) Northern Ireland politician, born in Londonderry, Co Londonderry. He studied at the National University of Ireland, and was a founder member of the Credit Union Party, which was a forerunner to the Social Democratic Labour Party (SDLP). He sat in the Northern Ireland parliament (1969–72) and the Northern Ireland Assembly (1972–3), and became widely respected as a moderate, non-violent member of the Catholic community. He became SDLP leader in 1979, and in the same year was elected to the European Parliament. He has represented Foyle in the House of Commons since 1983. In 1993 he and Sinn Féin leader Gerry Adams began a series of discussions, the Hume–Adams peace initiative, intended to bring about an end to violence in Northern Ireland. This helped create the climate for John Major and Albert Reynolds' Downing Street Declaration (1993), setting out general principles for peace talks in Northern Ireland. >> Adams, Gerry

Hume, Joseph (1777–1855) British radical politician, born in Montrose, Angus, E Scotland, UK. He studied medicine at Edinburgh University, and in 1797 became assistant surgeon under the East India Company. After returning to England (1808), he sat in parliament (1812, 1819–55), where his arguments for reform included the legalizing of trade unions, freedom of trade with India, and the abolition of army flogging, naval impressment, and imprisonment for debt.

Hume, Patrick >> Baillie, Grizel

Hummel, Johann Nepomuk (1778–1837) Pianist and composer, born in Pressburg, Austria. He was taught by his father and, when the family moved to Vienna, by Mozart. He began playing in public in 1787, and after a tour of Germany, Denmark, Britain, and Holland he studied composition under Albrechtsberger. In 1804 he became *Kapellmeister* to Prince Esterházy, and later held similar appoint-ments at Stuttgart (1816) and Weimar (1819–37). He wrote several ballets and operas, but was best known for his piano and chamber works, and wrote a manual of piano technique (1828) which had considerable influence. >> Albrechtsberger; Mozart

Humperdinck, Engelbert (1854–1921) Composer, born in Siegburg, Germany. He studied music at Cologne, Frankfurt, Munich, and Berlin, and travelled widely as a teacher. He composed several operas, one of which, *Hänsel und Gretel* (1893), was highly successful.

Humphrey, Duke of Gloucester >> Gloucester, Humphrey, Duke of

Humphrey, Doris (1895–1958) Dancer, choreographer, and teacher, born in Oak Park, IL. She studied a range of dance forms before joining Ruth St Denis to learn an early form of modern dance. In 1928 she formed her own group with Charles Weidman, and toured with performances of her own choreography. She also wrote the key text on dance composition in modern dance, *The Art of Making Dances* (1959). >> Saint Denis, Ruth; Weidman

Humphrey, Hubert H(oratio) (1911–78) US politician, born in Wallace, SD. He studied at Minnesota and Louisiana universities, entered politics as Mayor of Minneapolis in 1945, and was elected senator in 1948. He built up a strong reputation as a liberal, particularly on the civil rights issue, but, as vice-president from 1964 under Johnson, alienated many supporters by defending the policy of continuing the war in Vietnam. Although he won the Democratic presidential nomination in 1968, a substantial minority of Democrats opposed him, and he narrowly lost the election to Nixon. >> Johnson, Lyndon B; Nixon

Humphreys, Emyr (Owen) (1919–) Novelist, poet, and playwright, born in Prestatyn, Denbighshire, NC Wales, UK. He studied at University College, Aberystwyth, where he read history, learned Welsh, and became a nationalist. He has worked as a teacher and a BBC Wales drama producer. He won the Somerset Maugham Award for his novel *Hear and Forgive* (1952), and the Hawthornden Prize for *A Toy Epic* (1958). Later books include *The Triple Net* (1988), *The Crucible of Myth* (1990), *Bonds of Attachment* (1991), and *Unconditional Surrender* (1996).

Humphries, (John) Barry (1934–) Comic performer and satirical writer, born in Melbourne, Victoria, Australia. He studied at Melbourne University, and made his theatrical debut at the Union Theatre, Melbourne (1953–4). In

Britain from 1959, he made his London debut in *The Demon Barber* (1959) and subsequently appeared in *Oliver!* (1960, 1963, 1968). He created the Barry McKenzie comic strip in *Private Eye* (1964–73) and wrote the screenplay for *The Adventures of Barry McKenzie* (1972), in which he also appeared. His many one-man stage shows include *A Nice Night's Entertainment* (1962) and *Back With a Vengeance* (1987–9). He is best known for his characters Sir Les Patterson and 'housewife megastar' Dame Edna Everage, who have frequently appeared on television and in film. His books include *Barry Humphries' Treasury of Australian Kitsch* (1980), *Neglected Poems and Other Creatures* (1991), an autobiography *More Please* (1992), and an autobiographical novel *Women in the Background* (1995). 'Dame Edna' has also written a number of books, including *My Gorgeous Life* (1989).

Hung-wu >> Hongwu

Hunniford, Gloria (1940–) British broadcaster, born in Northern Ireland, UK. She started singing at the age of nine, releasing four records, and during the 1960s became involved in several shows on radio and television, including a weekly broadcast to British forces in Germany (1969–81). She became widely known with her daily radio programme for BBC's Radio 2 (1982–95), while participating in a wide range of shows, including London Weekend Television's *Sunday Sunday* (1982–91) and BBC's *Gloria Live* (1990–3). The recipient of several broadcasting personality awards, she has also written an autobiography, *Gloria* (1994), and a cookbook (1995).

Hunt, Geoff(rey) (1947–) Squash rackets player, born in Victoria, Australia. He was the Australian amateur champion at age 17, the world amateur champion in 1967, 1969, and 1971, and the world Open champion in 1976–7 and 1979–80.

Hunt, Henry, known as **Orator Hunt** (1773–1835) Radical agitator, born in Upavon, Wiltshire, S England, UK. He was a well-to-do farmer who in 1800 became a staunch radical, and spent the rest of his life advocating the repeal of the Corn Laws, democracy, and parliamentary reform. In 1819, on the occasion of the Peterloo massacre, he delivered a speech which cost him three years' imprisonment. He became an MP in 1831.

Hunt, (William) Holman (1827–1910) Painter, born in London, England, UK. He studied at the Royal Academy, shared a studio with Rossetti, and helped inaugurate the Pre-Raphaelite Brotherhood, which aimed at detailed and uncompromising truth to nature. His first public success was 'The Light of the World' (1854, Keble College, Oxford). The influence of several visits to the East appeared in 'The Scapegoat' (1856) and 'The Finding of Christ in the Temple' (1860). His *Pre-Raphaelitism and the Pre-Raphaelite Brotherhood* (1905) is a valuable record of the movement. >> Rossetti, Dante Gabriel

Hunt, James (Simon Wallis) (1947–93) Motor-racing driver and broadcaster, born in London, England, UK. He studied at Wellington College, and planned to take up medicine until he was introduced to motor-racing at 18. From club racing with a Mini, where he earned the nickname 'Hunt the Shunt', he quickly progressed through Formula Three and Two to Formula One with the Hesketh Team, joined McLaren, and won the World Championship in 1976. He retired from racing in 1979, and worked as a motor-racing commentator for the BBC, noted for his candid and pithy comments. >> RR1165

Hunt (of Llanfair Waterdine), (Henry Cecil) John Hunt, Baron (1910–) Mountaineer, born in Marlborough, Wiltshire, S England, UK. A British army officer, he saw military and mountaineering service in India and Europe, and in 1953 led the first successful expedition to Mt Everest. He

also led the British party in the British–Soviet Caucasian mountaineering expedition (1958). He was knighted in 1953, and made a life peer in 1966. >> Hillary

Hunt, (James Henry) Leigh (1784–1859) Poet and essayist, born in Southgate, N Greater London, England, UK. Educated at Christ's Hospital, from 1808 he edited with his brother *The Examiner*, which became a focus of Liberal opinion and attracted leading men of letters, including Byron, Shelley, and Lamb. After travelling with Shelley to Italy, and associating with Byron, he returned to England in 1825. His *Autobiography* (1850) is a valuable picture of the times. >> Byron, George; Keats, John; Shelley, Percy Bysshe

Hunt, Richard Morris (1827–95) Architect, born in Brattleboro, VT. The first American admitted (1846) to the Ecole des Beaux-Arts, Paris, he worked with Hector Martin Lefuel on the Pavillon de la Bibliothèque (1854–5) of the Louvre. He opened a practice (1855) and an atelier in New York City, where he designed numerous houses and public buildings, including the Presbyterian Hospital (1872), the Tribune Building (1873), and Lenox Library (1877), and after the 1880s the luxurious mansions by which he is best remembered, among them Marble House (1892), Newport, RI, and the 225-room Biltmore House (1895), Asheville, NC.

Hunt, William Henry (1790–1864) Painter, a creator of the English school of watercolour painting, born in London, England, UK. He was ranked by Ruskin with the greatest colourists of the school. He chose very simple subjects, such as 'Peaches and Grapes', 'Old Pollard', and 'Wild Flowers'. >> Ruskin

Hunter, Evan >> McBain, Ed

Hunter, John (1728–93) Physiologist and surgeon, born in Long Calderwood, East Kilbride, WC Scotland, UK. He worked in the dissecting room (1748–59) as assistant to his brother, William Hunter, studied surgery at Chelsea Hospital and St Bartholomew's, became house-surgeon at St George's (1756), and lecturer for his brother in the anatomical school. One of his pupils was Edward Jenner. He served in the army as staff-surgeon (1760–3), then started a practice of surgery in London, and devoted much time and money to comparative anatomy. He was appointed surgeon at St George's Hospital (1768), surgeon-extraordinary to George III (1776), and in 1790 surgeon-general to the army. He investigated a large number of subjects, including venereal disease, embryology, inflammation, and gunshot wounds. His *Natural History of Human Teeth* (1771–8) revolutionized dentistry. He is considered to be the founder of scientific surgery. >> Hunter, William; Jenner, Edward

Hunter, William (1718–83) Anatomist and obstetrician, born in Long Calderwood, East Kilbride, WC Scotland, UK, the brother of John Hunter. He studied medicine at Glasgow University, and became a physician in London (1756), also teaching surgery and anatomy. He introduced the practice of dissection of cadavers for medical students. From about 1756 he confined his practice to obstetrics, and was appointed physician-extraordinary to Queen Charlotte (1762). He was appointed the first professor of anatomy to the Royal Academy (1768). Through him obstetrics became a recognized branch of medicine. >> Charlotte Sophia; Hunter, John

Huntingdon, Selina Hastings, Countess of, *née* **Shirley** (1707–91) Methodist leader, born in Staunton Harold, Leicestershire, C England, UK. In 1728 she married the Earl of Huntingdon, but was widowed in 1746. Joining the Methodists in 1739, she made Whitefield her chaplain, and assumed a leadership among his followers, who became known as 'the Countess of Huntingdon's Connexion.' She built a training school for ministers, and many chapels. >> Whitefield

Huntington, Collis P(orter) (1821–1900) Railway pioneer, born in Harwinton, CT. An equipment supplier during the Californian gold rush, he became involved in the construction of the Central Pacific Railway (completed, 1869), as well as the Southern Pacific (1881), of which he became president. His nephew, **Henry Edwards Huntington** (1850–1927), also a railroad executive, acquired an immense art collection and library, which he presented to the nation in 1922, together with his estate at Pasadena, California.

Huntsman, Benjamin (1704–76) Inventor, born in Barton-upon-Humber, North Lincolnshire, EC England, UK. After an apprenticeship to a clockmaker, he established a business in Doncaster making clocks, locks, and scientific instruments. Dissatisfied with the quality of available steel, he developed the crucible, or casting, process which produced a better and more uniform steel with less expenditure of labour and fuel, at a foundry he opened in Sheffield (c.1740). Although a major advance in steel production, crucible steel could be made only in relatively small quantities, and it required the advances of Kelly, Bessemer, and Martin in the mid-19th-c before steel would become a major structural material. >> Bessemer; Kelly, William; Martin, Pierre Emile

Hunyady, János [hoonyodi] (c. 1387–1456) Hungarian statesman and warrior, apparently a Wallach by birth, who was knighted and in 1409 presented by Emperor Sigismund with the Castle of Hunyad in Transylvania. His life was one unbroken crusade against the Turks, whom he defeated in several campaigns, notably in the storming of Belgrade (1456). During the minority of Ladislaus V he acted as Governor of the Kingdom (1446–53). One of his sons, Matthias, became King of Hungary. >> John of Capistrano; Matthias I; Mohammed II; Sigismund

Hurd, Douglas (Richard) [herd] (1930–) British statesman, born in Marlborough, Wiltshire, S England, UK. He studied at Cambridge, and followed a career in the Diplomatic Corps (1952–66) before moving to work in the Conservative Research Department (1966–70). A Conservative MP from 1974, he became Northern Ireland secretary (1984), home secretary (1985), and foreign secretary (1989–95). He stood unsuccessfully as a candidate in the leadership contest following Mrs Thatcher's resignation (1990). He was made a Companion of Honour in 1996. >> Thatcher

Hurst, Sir Cecil (James Barrington) (1870–1963) Lawyer, born at Horsham Park, West Sussex, S England, UK. He studied at Cambridge, became legal adviser to the Foreign Office (1918), worked on the Paris Peace Treaties of 1919, and proposed the Permanent Court of International Justice. He was a judge of this court (1929–46), serving as president (1934–6), and in this capacity greatly strengthened the court's prestige and authority. He was president of the Institute of International Law, and a founder of the *British Yearbook of International Law* in 1919.

Hurston, Zora (Neale) (1903–60) Novelist, born in Eatonville, FL. She studied at Howard University and Barnard College, New York City, then worked under anthropologist Franz Boas, with whom she began a career as a folklorist. Her best-known novel, *Their Eyes Were Watching God* (1937), portrays an independent black woman and folk heroine. Other works include *Tell My Horse* (1938), *Moses, Man of the Mountain* (1939), and an autobiography, *Dust Tracks on a Road* (1942). Alice Walker edited a collection of her writings, *I Love Myself When I Am Laughing* (1979). >> Boas; Walker, Alice

Hurt, John (1940–) Actor, born in Chesterfield, Derbyshire, C England, UK. He trained at the Royal Academy of Dramatic Art and made his stage debut in 1962 at the Arts Theatre, London. He won an Emmy Award for playing the part of Quentin Crisp in the television play *The Naked Civil Servant* (1975), and BAFTA awards for *Midnight Express* (1978) and *The Elephant Man* (1980). Other films include *Alien* (1978), *Nineteen Eighty Four* (1984), and *Rob Roy* (1995).

Hurt, William (1950–) Actor, born in Washington DC, USA. He studied at the Juilliard School in New York City, acted in a succession of off-Broadway productions, then worked in television before making his cinema debut in *Altered States* (1980). He won a Best Actor Oscar for *Kiss of The Spiderwoman* (1985), and Oscar nominations for *Children Of A Lesser God* (1986) and *Broadcast News* (1987). Frequently returning to the stage between films, he won an Obie and Theatre World Award for *My Life* (1977), a Tony nomination for Best Supporting Actor in *Hurlyburly* (1984-5), and the 1988 Spencer Tracy Award. Later films include *Trial By Jury* (1993), *Jane Eyre* (1996), and *Michael* (1996).

Hus, John >> **Huss, John**

Husain, Sadam >> **Hussein, Saddam**

Husák, Gustáv [hoosak] (1913–91) Czechoslovakian politician and president (1975–89), born in Bratislava, Slovak Republic. He trained as a lawyer at the Bratislava Law Faculty, and was a member of the resistance movement during World War 2. After the war he worked for the Slovak Communist Party (SCP) before being imprisoned in 1951 on political grounds. Rehabilitated in 1960, he worked at the Academy of Sciences (1963–8) before becoming first secretary of the SCP and deputy premier in 1968. After the 'Prague Spring' and the Soviet invasion of 1968, he replaced Dubček as leader of the Communist Party of Czechoslovakia (CCP). He became state president in 1975, resigned as party leader in 1987, and was replaced as state president by Vaclav Havel after the CCP regime was overthrown in 1989. >> Dubček; Havel; RR1043

Hu Shih [hoo shee] (1891–1962) Liberal scholar and reformer, born in Chiki, Anhwei, China. He studied at Cornell and Columbia universities, where he became a disciple of the philosopher, John Dewey. He became professor of philosophy at Beijing University (1917–49), where he led the gradualist New Culture movement from 1919, urging the re-examination of China's culture and increased personal liberty, and opposing the increasingly rigid Marxism of Chen Duxiu and Li Dazhao. He wrote extensively on Chinese philosophy, and is also known for his championing of *pai-hua*, the new Chinese vernacular that would make literature accessible to the masses. He served the Nationalist government as ambassador to the USA (1938–42) and the UN (1957), and was president of the Academica Sinaica on Taiwan (1958–62). >> Chen Duxiu; Dewey, John

Huskisson, William (1790–1830) British statesman, born at Birch Moreton Court, Hereford and Worcester, WC England, UK. He was appointed under-secretary in the colonial department (1795), and entered parliament in 1796. He was secretary of the Treasury (1804–9), President of the Board of Trade, treasurer of the navy (1823), and colonial secretary (1827–8). He obtained the removal of restrictions on the trade of the colonies with foreign countries, the removal or reduction of many import duties, and relaxation of the navigation laws, and was an active pioneer of free trade. He received fatal injuries at the opening of the Liverpool and Manchester Railway.

Huss or **Hus, John** (c. 1369–1415) Bohemian religious reformer, born in Husinec, Czech Republic, from which his name derives. In 1398 he lectured on theology at Prague, where he was influenced by the writings of Wycliffe. In 1408 he continued to preach in defiance of a papal bull, and was excommunicated (1411). After writing his main work, *De ecclesia* (1413, On the Church), he was called before a General Council at Constance, and burned after refusing to recant. The anger of his followers in Bohemia led to the Hussite Wars, which lasted until the middle of the 15th-c. >> Sigismund; Wycliffe

Hussein (ibn Talal) [hu**sayn**] (1935–) King of Jordan since 1952, born in Amman. He studied at Alexandria, Harrow, and Sandhurst. He steered a middle course in the face of the political upheavals inside and outside his country, favouring the Western powers, particularly Britain, and pacifying Arab nationalism. After the 1967 war with Israel, the PLO made increasingly frequent raids into Israel from Jordan, their power developing to such an extent that he ordered the Jordanian army to move against them, and after a short civil war (1970), the PLO leadership fled abroad. His decision to cut links with the West Bank (1988) prompted the PLO to establish a government in exile. Alone among the Arab Middle-East States he was forced by domestic pressure to give support to Iraq during the Gulf Conflict (1991), and risked losing Western aid for Jordan. He has been married four times; his second wife, Toni Gardiner, was an Englishwoman, by whom he had an heir, Abdullah, in 1962. >> Hussein, Saddam; RR1069

Hussein, Saddam [hu**sayn**], also spelled **Sadam Husain** (1937–) President of Iraq (1979–), born in Takrit, Iraq. He joined the Arab Baath Socialist Party in 1957, and was sentenced to death in 1959 for the attempted assassination of President Kassem, but escaped to Egypt. He played a prominent part in the 1968 revolution, became vice-president of the ruling Revolutionary Command Council (1969), and sole president in 1979. His attack on Iran in 1980, to gain control of the Strait of Hormuz, led to a war of attrition which ended in 1988, during which he quelled a Kurdish uprising by the widespread use of chemical weapons. He invaded Kuwait in 1990, but was forced to withdraw when he was defeated by a coalition of Arab and Western forces in Operation Desert Storm (1991). For continued breaching of the peace terms he brought further military strikes against his country by the coalition forces early in 1993, and later by the USA for an alleged assassination plot against former President Bush during a visit to Kuwait City. >> Bush, George; RR1063

Hussein ibn Ali [hu**sayn** ibn a**lee**] (1856–1931) King of the Hejaz (1916–24), and founder of the modern Arab Hashemite dynasty, the great-grandfather of King Hussein of Jordan and father of King Faisal I. He was Emir of Mecca (1908–16), and after first siding with the Turks and Germans in World War 1, on the advice of T E Lawrence came over to the side of the Allies, declaring for Arab independence (1916), and was chosen first king of the Hejaz. After provoking the opposition of the Wahabis and Britain, he was forced to abdicate in 1924, and went into exile in Cyprus. >> Faisal I; Hussein; Lawrence, T E; RR1063

Husserl, Edmund (Gustav Albrecht) [hu**serl**] (1859–1938) Philosopher, founder of the school of phenomenology, born in Prossnitz, Czech Republic. He studied mathematics at Berlin and psychology at Vienna, and taught at Halle (1887), Göttingen (1901), and Freiburg (1916). His two-volume *Logische Untersuchungen* (1900–1, Logical Investigations) defended the view of philosophy as an *a priori* discipline, unlike psychology. He developed phenomenology while at Göttingen – an approach which was particularly influential in Germany and the USA, and gave rise to *Gestalt* psychology. >> Koffka; Köhler; Scheler; Wertheimer

Hussey, Obed (1792–1860) Inventor, born in Exeter, ME. He spent his life in the invention, improvement, and manufacture of machines for use in agriculture and light engineering. He achieved his greatest success with a reaping machine patented in 1833, the year before a very similar machine was patented by Cyrus McCormick. Whereas McCormick was prepared to adapt other people's ideas,

Hussey was not, and he eventually lost the competition with McCormick, selling out in 1858. >> McCormick

Huston, Angelica (1951–) Film actress, born in California. She won a Best Supporting Actress Oscar for *Prizzi's Honor* (1985), directed by her father John Huston, and Oscar nominations for *Enemies: A Love Story* (1989) and *The Grifters* (1990). Later films include her role as Morticia in *The Addams Family* (1991) and *Addams Family Values* (1993), *Bitter Moon* (1992), and *Phoenix* (1997). She made a directorial debut with *Bastard Out Of Carolina* (1996). >> Huston, John

Huston, John (Marcellus) [**hyoos**tn] (1906–87) Film director, born in Nevada, MO. He moved to Hollywood in 1930 as a script writer, and in 1941 was given the direction of *The Maltese Falcon*, following this with a series of films for the US army. After the War, several films, such as *The Treasure of the Sierra Madre* (1948, Oscar), *The Asphalt Jungle* (1950), and *The African Queen* (1951), established him as a leading director of action drama, and his imaginative use of colour was given full expression in such films as *Moulin Rouge* (1952) and *Moby Dick* (1956). In 1982 he made the musical, *Annie*.

Hutcheson, Francis (1694–1746) Philosopher, probably born in Drumalig, Co Down. He studied for the Church at Glasgow (1710–16), but then started a successful private academy in Dublin. In 1729 he became professor of moral philosophy at Glasgow. His main work was published posthumously, *A System of Moral Philosophy* (1755), in which he argues that moral distinctions are intuited, rather than arrived at by reasoning. His view of 'the greatest happiness for the greatest number' in judging an action anticipated utilitarianism.

Hutchinson, Anne, *née* **Marbury** (1591–1643) Religious leader and American pioneer, born in Alford, Lincolnshire, EC England, UK. In 1634 she emigrated with her husband to Boston, MA, where she began spreading her own theological ideas. She was tried for heresy and sedition, and banished. With some friends she acquired territory from the Narragansett Indians of Rhode Island, and set up a democracy (1638). After her husband's death (1642), she removed to a new settlement in what is now Pelham Bay in New York State, where she and most of her family were killed by Indians. >> Winthrop, John (1588–1649)

Hutchinson, Sir Jonathan (1828–1913) Surgeon, born in Selby, North Yorkshire, N England, UK. He became surgeon at the London hospital (1859–83) and professor of surgery at the Royal College of Surgeons (1879–83). He is best known for his lifelong study of syphilis, *Hutchinson's triad* being the three symptoms of congenital syphilis which he first described. He was knighted in 1908.

Hutchison, Sir William Oliphant (1889–1970) Artist, born in Collessie, Fife, E Scotland, UK. He studied at Edinburgh and Paris, and is known for his portraits and landscapes. He later became director of the Glasgow School of Art (1933–43).

Hutten, Ulrich von (1488–1523) Humanist, born at the castle of Steckelberg, Germany. He was sent to the Benedictine monastery of Fulda in 1499, but fled from there in 1505. After many travels he was crowned poet laureate by Emperor Maximilian I (1517), entered the service of Albert, Archbishop of Mainz, and shared in the famous satires *Epistolae obscurorum virorum* (Letters of Obscure Men). Eager to see Germany free from foreign and priestly domination, he took part in the campaign of the Swabian League against Ulrich of Württemberg (1519). He supported Luther and was dismissed from the archbishop's service. He was given shelter by Sickingen until Sickingen was killed (1523). Rejected by Erasmus, he finally found a resting place through Zwingli's help on the island of Ufnau in L Zürich. >> Erasmus; Luther; Sickingen; Zwingli

Hutton, James (1726–97) Geologist, born in Edinburgh, EC Scotland, UK. He studied medicine there, at Paris, and at Leyden. In 1754 he devoted himself to agriculture and chemistry in Berwickshire, which led him to mineralogy and geology; in 1768 he moved to Edinburgh. The *Huttonian theory*, emphasizing the igneous origin of many rocks and deprecating the assumption of causes other than those we see still at work, was expounded in *A Theory of the Earth* (1795), which forms the basis of modern geology. >> Hall, James; Werner

Hutton, Len, popular name of **Sir Leonard Hutton** (1916–90) Cricketer, born in Fulneck, West Yorkshire, N England, UK. He was the inspiration of England after World War 2, and skipper of the team which regained the Ashes in 1953. England's first professional captain, he never captained his county, Yorkshire. Playing for England against Australia at the Oval in 1938, he scored a world record 364 runs. Between 1937 and 1955 he scored 6971 Test runs in 79 matches (average 56·67), and during his firstclass career (1934–60) scored 40 140 runs (average 55·51), including 129 centuries. He was knighted in 1954. >> RR1149

Huxley, Aldous (Leonard) (1894–1963) Novelist and essayist, born in Godalming, Surrey, SE England, UK, the grandson of T H Huxley. He studied at Oxford, lived mainly in Italy in the 1920s, (where he met and befriended D H Lawrence) and moved to California in 1937. His early writing included poetry, short stories, and literary journalism, but his reputation was made with his satirical novels *Crome Yellow* (1921) and *Antic Hay* (1923). Later novels include *Point Counter Point* (1928) and, his best-known work, *Brave New World* (1932), where he warns of the dangers of dehumanization in a scientific age. His later writing became more mystical in character, as in *Eyeless in Gaza* (1936) and *Time Must Have a Stop* (1944), while *Island* (1962) is an optimistic Utopia. >> Huxley, Andrew; Huxley, Julian; Huxley, T H; Lawrence, D H; Zamyatin

Huxley, Sir Andrew Fielding (1917–) Physiologist, born in London, England, UK, a grandson of T H Huxley, and half-brother of Aldous and Julian Huxley. He studied at Cambridge, then taught there in the department of physiology (1941–60). He helped to provide a physico-chemical explanation for nerve transmission, and outlined a theory of muscular contraction. He was professor of physiology at London (1960–9) and a Royal Society Research Professor (1969–83). He shared the Nobel Prize for Physiology or Medicine in 1963, and was knighted in 1974. >> Huxley, Aldous; Huxley, Julian; Huxley, T H; RR1124

Huxley, Hugh Esmor (1924–) Molecular biologist, born in Birkenhead, Merseyside, NW England, UK. He studied at Cambridge, worked on radar in World War 2, and turned to biophysics at the Massachusetts Institute of Technology (1952–4) and the Medical Research Council Laboratory of Molecular Biology from 1961. From the 1950s he was the central figure in developing the sliding filament model of muscle contraction. He developed this concept in detail with Jean Hansen, and devised X-ray diffraction and electron microscopy techniques for this work which are also applicable in other studies in physiology. He became professor of biology at Brandeis University, MA, in 1987.

Huxley, Sir Julian (Sorell) (1887–1975) Biologist, born in London, England, UK, the grandson of T H Huxley. He studied at Oxford, became professor of zoology at London (1925–7) and at the Royal Institution (1926–9), and was secretary to the Zoological Society of London (1935–42). He applied his scientific knowledge to political and social problems, formulating a pragmatic ethical theory based on the principle of natural selection. He was the first director-

general of UNESCO (1946–8), and was knighted in 1958. >> Huxley, Aldous; Huxley, Andrew; Huxley, T H

Huxley, T(homas) H(enry) (1825–95) Biologist, born in London, England, UK. He studied medicine at London, worked as a naval surgeon, and developed his interest in natural history during a visit to the Australian coast. In 1854 he was appointed professor of natural history at the Royal School of Mines, and became the foremost expounder of Darwinism, to which he added an anthropological perspective in *Man's Place in Nature* (1863). He also studied fossils, influenced the teaching of science in schools, and wrote essays on theology and philosophy from an 'agnostic' viewpoint, a term he introduced. >> Darwin, Charles; Huxley, Aldous; Huxley, Andrew; Huxley, Julian

Hu Yaobang [hoo yowbang] (1915–89) Chinese politician, born in Hunan province, China. He took part in the Long March (1934–6), and held a number of posts under Deng Xiaoping before becoming head of the Communist Youth League (1952–67). He was purged during the Cultural Revolution (1966–9), then briefly rehabilitated (1975–6), but did not return to high office until 1978, when, through his patron Deng, he joined the Communist Party's Politburo. From head of the secretariat he was promoted to Party leader in 1981, but dismissed in 1987 for his relaxed handling of a wave of student unrest. Popularly revered as a liberal reformer, his death triggered an unprecedented wave of pro-democracy demonstrations. >> Deng Xiaoping

Huygens, Christiaan [hoygenz] (1629–95) Physicist and astronomer, born in The Hague, The Netherlands. He studied at Leyden and Breda, discovered the ring and fourth satellite of Saturn (1655), and made the first pendulum clock (1657). In optics he propounded the wave theory of light, and discovered polarization. He lived in Paris, a member of the Royal Academy of Sciences (1666–81), but as a Protestant felt it prudent to return to The Hague.

Huysmann, Roelof >> **Agricola, Rudolphus**

Huysmans, Joris Karl [hoysmahnz] (1848–1907) Novelist of Dutch origin, born in Paris. His books reflect many aspects of the spiritual and intellectual life of late 19th-c France. His best-known works are *À rebours* (1884, Against the Grain), a study of aesthetic decadence (which influenced Oscar Wilde); the controversial *Là-bas* (1891, Down There), which dealt with devil-worship; and *En route* (1892), an account of his return to Catholicism.

Huysum, Jan van [hoysum] (1682–1749) Painter, born in Amsterdam. He studied under his father, **Justus** (1659–1716), a landscape painter. Jan also painted landscapes, purely conventional in style; but his fruit and flower pieces are distinguished for their exquisite finish.

Hyacinthe, Père [eeasīt], originally **Charles Loyson** (1827–1912) French preacher. He taught philosophy and theology at Avignon and Nantes, gathering enthusiastic audiences to the Madeleine and Notre Dame in Paris. He boldly denounced abuses in the Church, and was excommunicated (1869). He married in 1872, and continued to preach, protesting against the Infallibility Dogma. In 1879 he founded a Gallican Catholic Church in Paris. His writings include *Mon Testament, ma protestation* (1873).

Hyatt, John Wesley (1837–1920) Inventor, born in Starkey, NY. He was apprenticed as a printer, but soon found his real vocation as an inventor. His inventions include a water-filter and the *Hyatt roller bearing*. He is best remembered for discovering the process to make celluloid, which he did while trying to find a substitute for ivory in billiard balls. His discovery laid the foundation for the plastics industry.

Hyde, Anne >> **Anne; Clarendon, Earl of; Mary II**

Hyde, Charles Cheney (1873–1952) Jurist, born in Chicago, IL. He studied at Yale and Harvard, then taught law at Northwestern (1907–25) and Columbia universities (1925–45). He served as solicitor for the US Department of State (1923–5) and was a member of the Permanent Court of Arbitration at The Hague (1951–2). He was an advocate of all military power being within one international security organization. His major work, *International Law, chiefly as Interpreted and Applied by the United States* (1922, revised 1945) is of high authority.

Hyde, Douglas, Ir **Dubhighlas de Hide** (1860–1949) Writer, philologist, and first president of Ireland (1938–45), born in Frenchpark, Co Roscommon, Ireland. He studied at Dublin, and was the founder and first president (1893–1915) of the Gaelic League. Professor of Irish in the National University (1909–32), he wrote *A Literary History of Ireland* (1899), as well as poems, plays, works on history and folklore, in Irish and English.

Hyder Ali >> **Haidar Ali**

Hyne, Charles (John Cutcliffe Wright) (1865–1944) Traveller and writer, born in Bibury, Gloucestershire, SWC England, UK. He is remembered above all as the creator of the fictional character 'Captain Kettle' in several adventure stories.

Hypatia [hiypa**tee**a] (c. 375–415) Neoplatonist philosopher, the daughter of Theon, an astronomer and mathematician of Alexandria. Her learning, wisdom, and high character made her the most influential teacher in Alexandria, her philosophy being an attempt to combine Neoplatonism with Aristotelianism. Associated by many Christians with paganism, she was murdered by a fanatical mob at Alexandria.

Hyperides or **Hypereides** [hiype**riy**deez] (390–322 BC) Athenian orator and statesman. Probably a pupil of Plato and Isocrates, he became a professional speech-writer. He was a supporter of Demosthenes for many years, but in the corruption case involving Harpalus, he was one of Demosthenes' accusers. He promoted the Lamian War against Macedonia (323–22 BC) after the death of Alexander, but was captured and put to death when the Athenians were defeated. >> Demosthenes

Hyrcanus I, John [heer**kay**nus] (2nd-c BC) High priest of Israel, and perhaps also a king subject to Syrian control (c.134–104 BC), the son of the high priest Simon, and in the line of Hasmonean priestly rulers. He consolidated his own hold over Israel, destroyed the Samaritan temple on Mt Gerizim, and forced the Idumeans (residents of S Judea) to adopt Judaism. Eventually he supported the Sadduceans against the Pharisees, who opposed his combination of political and religious leadership.

Hyrcanus II [heer**kay**nus] (?–30 BC) Jewish high priest and ruler. On the death of his father (76 BC) he was appointed high priest by his mother, Alexandra, who ruled Judaea until her death (67 BC). He then warred for power with his younger brother Aristobulus, with varying fortune until Aristobulus died from poisoning (49 BC). In 47 BC Caesar made Antipater Procurator of Judaea with supreme power, and a son of Aristobulus, with Parthian help, captured Hyrcanus, and carried him off to Seleucia. But when Herod the Great, son of Antipater, came to power, the aged Hyrcanus was invited home to Jerusalem. He lived there in peace until, suspected of intriguing against Herod, he was put to death in 30 BC. >> Herod

Iacocca, Lee [yakocha], popular name of **Lido Anthony Iacocca** (1924–) Businessman, born in Allentown, PA. He worked for the Ford Motor Company (1946–78), at first in sales, rising to become president in 1970. In 1978 he joined Chrysler Corporation as president and chief executive officer when the company was in serious financial difficulties, and steered the company back to profitability. He published a best-selling autobiography (with William Kovak), *Iacocca* (1985), and a sequel, *Talking Straight* (1989).

Ibáñez, Vicente Blasco >> **Blasco Ibáñez, Vicente**

Ibárruri (Gómez), Dolores [eebaruree], known as **la Pasionaria** ('The Passionflower') (1895–1989) Spanish politician and orator, born of a Catholic mining family in Gallarta, Spain. She became a member of the Central Committee of the Spanish Communist Party (1930), served as Spanish delegate to the Third International (1933, 1935), and was elected deputy to the Spanish Cortes (1936). With the outbreak of the Civil War (1936), she became the Republic's most emotional and effective propagandist. After the war she took refuge in the USSR, becoming president of the Spanish Communist Party in exile. In 1977 she returned to Spain as Communist deputy for Asturias.

Ibert, Jacques (François Antoine) [eebair] (1890–1962) Composer, born in Paris. He studied in Paris, won the Prix de Rome in 1919, and became director of the French Academy in Rome (1937–55) and of the Opéra-Comique in Paris. His works include seven operas, ballets, cantatas, and chamber music, the orchestral *Divertissement* (1930), based upon his incidental music for Labiche's play, *The Italian Straw Hat*, and the *Escales* (1922) suite.

Ibn Battutah (1304–68) Traveller and writer, born in Tangiers, Morocco. He spent 30 years (1325–54) in travel, covering over 120 000 km (75 000 mi), to all the Muslim countries, visiting Mecca, Persia, Mesopotamia, Asia Minor, Bokhara, S Spain, Timbuktu, India, China, and Sumatra. He then settled in Fez, and dictated the entertaining history of his journeys: *Riḥlāh* (Travels, published in a French translation 1853–8).

Ibn Gabirol >> **Avicebrón**

Ibn Khaldun [ibn khaldoon] (1332–1406) Philosopher, historian, and politician, born in Tunis, modern Tunisia. He held various political positions in Spain, but largely abandoned politics in 1375, and in 1382 went to Cairo, where he became professor and a chief judge. His major work was a monumental history of the Arabs, *Kitab al-ibar*. The influential *Maqaddimah* (Introduction to History) outlined a cyclical theory of history by which nomadic peoples became civilized, attained a peak of culture, were then corrupted by their own success, and were in turn destroyed by another, more vigorous nomadic culture.

Ibn Rushd >> **Averroës**

Ibn Saud, Abdul Aziz [ibn sahood], in full **Ibn Abd al-Rahman al-Saud** (1880–1953) The first king of Saudi Arabia (1932–53), born in Riyadh. He followed his family into exile in 1890 and was brought up in Kuwait. In 1901 he succeeded his father, and set out to reconquer the family domains from the Rashidi rulers, an aim which he achieved with British recognition in 1927. He changed his title from Sultan of Nejd to King of Hejaz and Nejd in 1927, and in 1932 to King of Saudi Arabia. After the discovery of oil (1938), he granted substantial concessions to US oil companies. His son, **Saud** (1902–69) had been prime minister

for three months when he succeeded his father (1953). In 1964 he was peacefully deposed by the council of ministers, and his brother **Faisal** (1904–75) became king, as well as remaining prime minister and minister of foreign affairs. >> Faisal (ibn Abd al-Aziz); RR1086

Ibn Sina >> **Avicenna**

Ibn Zohr >> **Avenzoar**

Ibrahim >> **Abraham**

Ibrahim, Abdullah, formerly **Dollar Brand** (1934–) Jazz pianist, born in Cape Town, South Africa. His group, Jazz Epistles, recorded the country's first black jazz album (1960). He was invited by Duke Ellington (1962) to work in the USA. Since then, he has worked as a soloist and leader in America and Europe, notably in the 1980s with his septet Ekaya ('Home'). He also plays cello, soprano saxophone, and flute, and is remarkable for his jazz interpretations of the melodies and rhythms of his African childhood. He adopted his Muslim name in the 1970s.

Ibrahiz >> **Abraham**

Ibsen, Henrik (Johan) (1828–1906) Playwright and poet, born in Skien, Norway. He worked at theatres in Bergen and Kristiania (Oslo), and wrote several conventional dramas before his first major play, *Kongsemnerne* (1857, The Pretenders). His theatre having gone bankrupt, and angry at Norway's aloofness in the struggle of Denmark with Germany, he went into voluntary exile to Rome, Dresden, and Munich (1864–92). His international reputation began with *Brand* and *Peer Gynt* (1866–7). He regarded his historical drama, *Kejser og Galilaeer* (1873, Emperor and Galilean) as his masterpiece, but his fame rests more on the social plays which followed, notably *Et Dukkehjem* (1879, A Doll's House) and *Gengangere* (1881, Ghosts), which was controversially received. In his last phase he turned more to Symbolism, as in *Vildanden* (1884, The Wild Duck), *Rosmersholm* (1886), and *Bygmester Solness* (1892, trans The Master-Builder). The realism of *Hedda Gabler* (1890) was a solitary escape from Symbolism. He suffered a stroke in 1900 which ended his literary career.

Ibycus [ibikus] (fl.6th-c BC) Greek poet from Rhegium in Italy. He lived at the court of Polycrates, tyrant of Samos, and wrote choral lyrics. Legend has it that he was slain by robbers near Corinth, and as he was dying he called upon a flock of cranes to avenge him. The cranes then hovered over the theatre at Corinth, and one of the murderers exclaimed, 'Behold the avengers of Ibycus!' This led to their conviction. The story is told in Schiller's ballad, *Die Kraniche des Ibykos*. >> Polycrates; Schiller

Icahn, Carl [iykn] (1936–) Arbitrageur and options specialist, born in New York City. A postgraduate student at the New York School of Medicine, he became an apprentice broker with Dreyfus Corporation. An options manager in 1963, he formed his own company in 1968, holding the posts of chairman and chief executive. He has been chairman and chief executive officer of ACF Industries since 1984, and chairman of the airline TWA since 1986.

Ichikawa, Fusaye [ichikahwa] (1893–1981) Japanese politician and feminist. Working as a teacher in Tokyo she helped to found the New Women's Association (c.1920), which successfully fought for women's right to attend political meetings. Impressed by the suffrage movement during a visit to the USA (1921–4), she formed the Women's Suffrage League in Japan (1924). After World War 2 she became head of the New Japan Women's League, which secured the vote for women in 1945. She served in the Japanese Diet (1952–71), where she continued to press for an end to bureaucratic corruption. After defeat in 1971 she was triumphantly returned to parliament in 1975 and 1980.

Ickes, Harold L(eClaire) [ik**eez**] (1874–1952) Lawyer and public official, born in Frankstown Township, PA. He studied at the University of Chicago, reported for Chicago newspapers (1897–1900), and became involved in Republican reform politics and a civic-minded law practice. Prominent in the Progressive Party (1912–16), he changed affiliation, backed Franklin D Roosevelt in 1932, and was appointed interior secretary (1933–46). As public works administration director (1933–9) he angered private utilities by curbing their power and providing low-cost public utilities and housing. During World War 2 he was administrator of solid fuels, petroleum, fisheries, and coal mines. In 1946 he resigned in protest at President Truman's appointment of an oilman as navy undersecretary, but supported Truman's re-election, joining the staff of *The New Republic* in 1949. >> Roosevelt, Franklin D; Truman, Harry S

Ickx, Jacky [iks] (1945–) Motor-racing driver, born in Brussels. He won eight races from 116 starts in Formula One. Outstanding at endurance racing, he won 34 world sports car championship races, and was world champion in 1982–3 (both Porsche). He won the Le Mans 24-hour race a record six times, in 1969 (with Oliver), 1975 (with Bell), 1976 (with van Lennep), 1977 (with Barth and Haywood), and 1981–2 (both with Bell). >> RR1165

Ictinos or **Ictinus** [ik**tiy**nus] (5th-c BC) Greek architect. With **Callicrates** he designed the Parthenon (447–438 BC). He was also architect of the Temple of the Mysteries at Eleusis and the Temple of Apollo Epicurius at Bassae.

Idriess, Ion Llewellyn [id**ruhs**] (1889–1979) Writer, born in Sydney, New South Wales, Australia. After various occupations, which later helped to provide colour for his works, he became a writer. *Lasseter's Last Ride* (1931) was his first success. In the next 40 years he wrote almost one book each year, of which the best known are *Flynn of the Inland* (1932, about Rev John Flynn, founder of the Flying Doctor Service), *The Desert Column* (1932, based on his experiences with the Australian Light Horse during World War 1), *The Cattle King* (1936, the life of Sir Sidney Kidman), and *Onward Australia* (1944). >> Kidman, Sidney

Ignatiev, Nikolay Pavlovich, Count [ig**nat**yef] (1832–1908) Russian diplomat, born in St Petersburg. He entered the diplomatic service (1856), led a mission to C Asia (1858), and negotiated the Treaty of Peking (1860) with China, giving Russia the territory where Vladivostok now stands. He became ambassador at Constantinople (1864), encouraged both the Serbs and the Bulgarians to rebel (unsuccessfully) against the Turks (1876), and was responsible for the Treaty of San Stefano after the Russians defeated the Turks in 1878. Under Alexander III he was minister of the interior (1881), but was dismissed in June 1882.

Ignatius (of Antioch), St [ig**nay**shus] (c. 35–c. 107) One of the apostolic Fathers of the Church, reputedly a disciple of St John, the second Bishop of Antioch. According to Eusebius, he died a martyr in Rome. The *Ignatian Epistles*, whose authenticity was long controversial, were written on his way to Rome after being arrested. They provide valuable information on the nature of the early Church. Feast day 17 October. >> Eusebius of Nicomedia

Ignatius de Loyola, St >> **Loyola, Ignatius of, St**
Ike >> **Eisenhower, Dwight D**
Illingworth, Ray(mond) (1932–) Cricketer and broadcaster, born in Pudsey, West Yorkshire, N England, UK. A proficient batsman and spin-bowler, he captained both Yorkshire and Leicestershire to the county championship.

He won 66 Test caps for England (36 as captain), taking 122 wickets and scoring two Test centuries. From 1979–84 he was manager of Yorkshire, and after retirement became a cricket commentator. He was later appointed Chairman of Selectors, Test and County Cricket Board (1994–6), and manager of the England team (1995–6).

Ilyushin, Sergey Vladimirovich [il**yoo**shin] (1894–1977) Aircraft designer, born in Dilialevo, Russia. After working as an aviation mechanic, he graduated in engineering, and in 1931 took charge of the design of both military and civil aircraft, including the Il-4 long-range bomber, which was important in World War 2. Afterwards his passenger aircraft became the basic Soviet carriers.

Imhotep [im**hoh**tep] (fl.27th-c BC) Egyptian physician and adviser to King Zoser (3rd dynasty). He was probably the architect of the so-called Step Pyramid at Sakkara, near Cairo. In time, he came to be revered as a sage, and during the Saite period (500 BC) he was worshipped as the life-giving son of Ptah, god of Memphis. The Greeks identified him with their own god of healing, Asclepius, because of his reputed knowledge of medicine. Many bronze figures of him have been discovered.

Immelmann, Max (1890–1916) German airman. He laid the foundation of German fighter tactics in World War 1, and originated the *Immelmann turn* – a half-loop followed by a half-roll. He was killed in action.

Imran Khan, in full **Ahmad Khan Niazi Imran** (1952–) Cricketer, born in Lahore, Pakistan. He studied at Oxford, playing in his first Test at 18 while at the university. He was a fast bowler and astute captain who inspired Pakistan's rise to prominence in world cricket. After leading Pakistan to the 1992 World Cup, he retired with a score of 3807 runs and 362 wickets in Test matches. He also played for Sussex and Worcester. He married, with much attendant publicity, in 1995, and has since been developing a career in politics.

Ince, Paul (1967–) Footballer, born in Ilford, Essex, SE England, UK. A midfielder, he played for West Ham, Manchester United, and Inter Milan, signing for Liverpool in 1997. By early 1997 he had won 28 caps playing for England.

Indiana, Robert, originally **Robert Clarke** (1928–) Painter and graphic designer, born in New Castle, IN. He studied art in Indianapolis, in Ithaca, NY, and at the Art Institute of Chicago. Settling in New York City in 1956, he began making hard-edged abstract pictures and stencilled wooden constructions, as part of the early Pop Art movement. His best-known images are based on the letters LOVE, as featured in his first one-man show in New York City (1962). His other word-paintings have included HUG, ERR, and EAT.

Indurain, Miguel [in**duhran**] (1964–) Racing cyclist, born in Villava, Spain. A talented basketball player, he chose cycling as his career and turned professional in 1982. In 1991 he won the first of five successive Tours de France races (1991–5) becoming the first to achieve this distinction, and in 1996 won an Olympic Gold in the time trial. He retired in 1997.

Indy, Vincent d' >> **d'Indy, Vincent**
Inge, William (Motter) [inj] (1913–73) Playwright and novelist, born in Independence, KS. He studied at Kansas University and George Peabody College for Teachers, became a schoolteacher (1937–49), and worked as a drama editor (1943–6) for the St Louis *Star-Times*. Outside the mainstream of American theatre, he is best remembered for *Come Back, Little Sheba* (1950), *Picnic* (1953, Pulitzer), *Bus Stop* (1955), and *The Dark at the Top of the Stairs* (first produced as *Farther off from Heaven* in 1947, and revised in 1957).

Inge, William Ralph [ing], known as **the Gloomy Dean** (1860–1954) Clergyman and theologian, born in Crayke, North Yorkshire, N England, UK. He studied at Cambridge, taught at Eton, and was vicar of All Saints, Kensington, before being appointed professor of divinity at Cambridge (1907). He was dean of St Paul's (1911–34), earning his byname from the pessimism displayed in his sermons and newspaper articles.

Ingenhousz, Jan [eenggenhows] (1730–99) Physician and plant physiologist, born in Breda, The Netherlands. He practised as a doctor in England, then became physician to Empress Maria Theresa. He improved methods of generating static electricity (1766), and was the first to make quantitative measurements of heat conduction in metals. He is best known as the discoverer of photosynthesis (1779).

Ingham, Sir Bernard [ingam] (1932–) Journalist, born in Hebden Bridge, West Yorkshire, N England, UK. He studied at Hebden Bridge Grammar School, then embarked on a career as a journalist, joining the *Hebden Bridge Times* (1948–52), *The Yorkshire Post* and *Yorkshire Evening Post* (1952–62), and *The Guardian* (1962–7). He was a government press adviser (1976) and under-secretary in the Department of Energy (1978–9), becoming nationally known after his appointment as chief press secretary to prime minister Margaret Thatcher (1979–90). He was knighted in 1990.

Inglis, Elsie Maud [inggls] (1864–1917) Surgeon and reformer, born in Naini Tal, India. One of the first women medical students at Edinburgh and Glasgow, she inaugurated the second medical school for women at Edinburgh (1892). Appalled at the lack of maternity facilities and the prejudice held against women doctors by their male colleagues, she founded a maternity hospital in Edinburgh, completely staffed by women (1901). She also founded the Scottish Women's Suffragette Federation (1906), which sent two women ambulance units to France and Serbia in 1915. She set up three military hospitals in Serbia (1916), fell into Austrian hands, and was repatriated, but in 1917 returned to Russia with a voluntary corps, which was withdrawn after the revolution.

Ingoldsby, Thomas >> **Barham, Richard (Harris)**

Ingres, Jean Auguste Dominique [igruh] (1780–1867) Painter, the leading exponent of the Classical tradition in France in the 19th-c, born in Montauban, France. He studied in Paris under David in 1796, and at the Ecole des Beaux-Arts; in 1801 he won the Prix de Rome. He then lived in Rome (1806–20), where he began many of his famous nudes, including 'Baigneuse' (1808, Louvre) and 'La Source' (1807, completed 1856, Musée d'Orsay). He became professor at the Ecole des Beaux-Arts, Paris, and director of the French Academy in Rome. He was made a senator in 1862. >> David, Jacques Louis

Innes, Hammond Ralph >> **Hammond Innes, Ralph**
Innes, Michael >> **Stewart, J I M**
Inness, George [inis] (1825–94) Landscape artist, born near Newburgh, NY. He visited Italy and France, and came under the influence of the Barbizon school. His later, more mystic work sprang from his conversion to Swedenborgianism. Among his best-known paintings are 'Delaware Water Gap' (1861), 'Delaware Valley' (1865), and 'Autumn Oaks' (c.1875), all at the Metropolitan Museum, New York City. >> Swedenborg

Innis, Harold Adams (1894–1952) Political economist and pioneer in communication studies. A veteran of World War 1, he studied at McMaster (Hamilton) and Chicago universities, then taught at the University of Toronto. He introduced the staple thesis of economic development, and argued against continentalism in such works as *The Fur Trade in Canada* (1930) and *The Cod Fisheries* (1940).

Known for the breadth of his reading and theorizing, his influence on later Canadian communication theorists, such as Marshall McLuhan, is notable. >> McLuhan

Innis, (Emile Alfredo) Roy (1934–) Civil rights activist, born in St Croix, US Virgin Isles. Moving to New York City at 14, he dropped out of high school to join the army, then worked in a New York research laboratory (1963–7). He joined the Congress of Racial Equality in 1963, advocating black separatism and community school boards, and became CORE national president in 1968. He promoted community development corporations, founded several African-American business groups, and was co-editor of the *Manhattan Tribune*. Dogged by charges from associates of being too dictatorial, he often took positions that put him at odds with other prominent African-Americans.

Innocent III, originally **Lotario de' Conti di Segni** (1160–1216) Pope (1198–1216), born in Agnagni, Italy. His pontificate is regarded as the high point of the temporal and spiritual supremacy of the Roman see. He judged between rival emperors in Germany, and had Otto IV deposed. He laid England under an interdict, and excommunicated King John for refusing to recognize Stephen Langton as Archbishop of Canterbury. Under him the fourth Lateran Council was held in 1215. >> John; Langton

Inönü, Ismet [inoenü], originally **Mustafa Ismet** (1884–1973) Turkish soldier, prime minister (1923–37, 1961–5), and president (1938–50), born in Izmir, Turkey. He fought in World War 1, then became Atatürk's chief-of-staff in the war against the Greeks (1919–22), defeating them twice at Inönü. As the first premier of the new republic, he introduced many political reforms, and was elected president in 1938 on Atatürk's death. From 1950 he was leader of the Opposition, and became premier again in 1961, resigning in 1965. >> Atatürk; RR1093

Ionesco, Eugène [yoneskoh] (1912–94) Playwright, born in Slatina, Romania. He studied in Bucharest and Paris, where he settled before World War 2. After the success of *La Cantatrice chauve* (1950, trans The Bald Prima Donna), he became a prolific writer of one-act plays which came to be seen as typical examples of the Theatre of the Absurd, such as *Les Chaises* (1952, The Chairs) and *Rhinocéros* (1960). His later, full-length plays centre around a constant, semi-autobiographical figure, Berenger. After 1970, his writing was mainly non-theatrical, including essays, children's stories, and a novel.

Ipatieff, Vladimir Nikolayevich [eepatyef] (1867–1952) Chemist, born in Moscow. An officer in the Russian army, he was professor of chemistry at the Artillery Academy in St Petersburg (1898–1906). He synthesized isoprene, the basic unit of natural rubber, and made contributions to the catalytic chemistry of unsaturated carbons, of great value to the petrochemical industry. During World War 1 he directed Russia's chemical industry. He emigrated to the USA in 1930, and became professor at Northwestern University (1931–5), where he developed a process for making high-octane petrol.

Iqbal, Sir Mohammed [ikbal] (1875–1938) Poet and philosopher, born in Sialkot, Pakistan. He studied at Lahore, Cambridge (where he read law and philosophy), and Munich. On his return to India, he achieved fame through his poetry, whose compelling mysticism and nationalism caused him to be regarded almost as a prophet by Muslims. His efforts to establish a separate Muslim state eventually led to the formation of Pakistan. He was knighted in 1923.

Ireland, John (Nicholson) (1879–1962) Composer, born in Bowdon, Greater Manchester, NW England, UK. He studied under Charles Stanford at the Royal College of Music, London, where he later became a teacher of composition.

He established his reputation with his Violin Sonata in A (1917), and between the wars was a prominent member of the English musical renaissance. He is best known for his picturesque orchestral pieces *The Forgotten Rite* (1913) and *Mai-dun* (1921), the piano concerto (1930), and *These Things Shall Be* (1937) for chorus and orchestra. >> Stanford, Charles

Ireland, William Henry (1777–1835) Forger of Shakespeare, born in London, England, UK. He was articled to a London conveyancer where he had access to old legal documents. Tempted by his father's enthusiasm for Shakespeare, he forged an autograph of the poet on a carefully copied old lease, and gradually more and more documents which his father eventually put on display. Many visitors believed in what they saw, but the material was denounced as a forgery by specialists such as Malone. Ireland then 'found' a new historical play entitled *Vortigern*, which was produced by Sheridan at Drury Lane in 1796, but damned at once. His father finally began to suspect, and Ireland confessed in a public statement (1796) which he later expanded into his *Confessions* (1805). >> Malone

Irenaeus, St [irenayus] (c. 130–c. 200) One of the Christian Fathers of the Greek Church, probably born near Smyrna. A priest of the Graeco–Gaulish Church of Lyon, he became bishop there in 177. A successful missionary bishop, he is chiefly known for his opposition to Gnosticism, his theological writing, and his attempts to prevent a rupture between Eastern and Western Churches over the computing of Easter. Feast day 28 June (W), 23 August (E).

Irene [ireenee] (752–803) Byzantine empress, the wife of the emperor Leo IV. After 780 she ruled as regent for her son, Constantine VI. When Constantine attempted to deprive her of power, she imprisoned and blinded him and her husband's five brothers, and ruled in her own right as emperor from 797. She was deposed and banished to Lesbos in 802. For her part in the restoration of the use of icons (forbidden in 730) at the Council of Nicaea (787), she was recognized as a saint by the Greek Orthodox Church. >> RR1037

Ireton, Henry [iy(r)tn] (1611–51) English soldier, born in Attenborough, Nottinghamshire, C England, UK. He studied at Cambridge, and in the Civil War fought for parliament, serving at Edgehill, Naseby, and the siege of Bristol. Cromwell's son-in-law from 1646, he was one of the most implacable enemies of the king, and signed the warrant for his execution. He accompanied Cromwell to Ireland, and in 1650 became lord deputy. He died of the plague during the siege of Limerick. >> Cromwell, Oliver

Irigoyen, Hipólito [irigoyen], also spelled **Yrigoyen** (1852–1933) Argentine politician and president (1916–22, 1928–30), born in Buenos Aires. He became leader of the Radical Civic Union Party in 1896 and worked for electoral reform, which, when it came in 1912, ushered him into power as the first Radical president of the Argentine. He was elected again in 1928, but deposed by a military coup. >> RR1032

Irons, Jeremy (John) [iyonz] (1948–) Actor, born in Cowes, Isle of Wight, S England, UK. A student with the Bristol Old Vic, he made his London stage debut as John the Baptist in the rock musical *Godspell* (1971–2), and joined the Royal Shakespeare Company. In 1984 he won a Tony award for Best Actor in *The Real Thing*. His role as Charles Ryder in the acclaimed television series *Brideshead Revisited* (1981) made him a household name. His film debut came in *Nijinsky* (1980), and he won a Best Actor Oscar for his performance in *Reversal of Fortune* (1990). Other films include *The Mission* (1985), *Damage* (1993), and *Stealing Beauty* (1996).

Ironside, William Edmund Ironside, Baron (1880–1959) British field marshal, born in Ironside, Aberdeenshire, NE

Scotland, UK. He served as a secret agent disguised as a railwayman in the Boer War, held several staff-appointments in World War 1, and commanded the Archangel expedition against the Bolsheviks (1918). He was Chief of the Imperial General Staff at the outbreak of World War 2, and placed in command of the home defence forces (1940). The *Ironsides*, fast light-armoured vehicles, were named after him. He was made a peer in 1941.

Irvine (of Lairg), Alexander Andrew Mackay Irvine, Baron (1940–) British judge. He studied at Glasgow University and Christ's College, Cambridge, and became a lecturer at the London School of Economics (1965–9). He was called to the bar in 1967, and became a QC (1978) and a deputy judge in the High Court (1987). Appointed shadow Lord Chancellor (1992–7), he became Lord Chancellor in 1997. He was made a life peer in 1987.

Irvine, Andy [ervin], popular name of **Andrew (Robertson) Irvine** (1951–) Rugby union player, born in Edinburgh, EC Scotland, UK. He won 51 caps for Scotland, scored more points in South Africa than any touring Lion had previously done, and was the first player in the world to score more than 300 points in international rugby. He toured with the Lions in 1974, 1977, and 1980. >> RR1167

Irving, Edward (1792–1834) Church of Scotland clergyman, born in Annan, Dumfries and Galloway, SW Scotland, UK. He studied at Edinburgh University, then was invited to the Caledonian Church, Hatton Garden, London (1822), where for a while he enjoyed success as a preacher. In 1825 he began to announce the imminent second advent of Jesus Christ, and to elaborate his views of the Incarnation. Charged with heresy for maintaining the sinfulness of Christ's nature, he was convicted by the London presbytery (1830), ejected from his new church in Regent's Square (1832), and finally deposed (1833). The majority of his congregation adhered to him, and a new communion, the Catholic Apostolic Church, was developed, commonly known as *Irvingite*, though Irving had little to do with its development.

Irving, Sir Henry, originally **John Henry Brodribb** (1838–1905) Actor and theatre manager, born in Keinton-Mandeville, Somerset, SW England, UK. He went on stage in 1865, appeared in Sunderland, Edinburgh, Manchester, and Liverpool, and in 1866 made his London debut at the St James's Theatre. He transferred to the Lyceum (1871), and gained a reputation as the greatest English actor of his time. In 1878 he began a theatrical partnership with Ellen Terry which lasted until 1902. He became the first actor to receive a knighthood (1895). >> Stoker; Terry, Ellen

Irving, John (1942–) Novelist, born in Exeter, NH. A former assistant professor of English at Mount Holyoke College, his first three novels received little attention, but he made his name with *The World According To Garp* (1978, filmed 1982). Later books include *The Hotel New Hampshire* (1981) and *A Prayer for Owen Meany* (1989).

Irving, Washington, pseudonym **Geoffrey Crayon** (1783–1859) Man of letters, born in New York City. He studied law, travelled through Europe, was admitted to the bar in 1806, and began writing in 1807. Under his pseudonym he wrote *The Sketch Book* (1819–20), a miscellany, containing in different styles such items as 'Rip Van Winkle' and 'The Legend of Sleepy Hollow'. He lived in Europe (1815–32), and his stay in Spain (1826–9) produced *Columbus* (1828), *The Companions of Columbus* (1831), and *Conquest of Granada* (1829). He was later appointed US ambassador to Spain (1842–6). >> Paulding

Isaac [iyzak] Biblical character, the son of Abraham by Sarah, through whose line of descent God's promises to Abraham were seen to continue. He was nearly sacrificed by Abraham at God's command (*Gen* 22). He fathered Esau and Jacob by his wife Rebecca, but was deceived into passing his blessing on to his younger son Jacob. >> Abraham; Esau; Jacob

Isaacs, Alick (1921–67) Biologist, born in Glasgow, W Scotland, UK. He studied at Glasgow, and specialised in virology. His work, especially that on influenza, led to his appointment as head of the World Influenza Centre in London from 1950. In 1957, with Swiss virologist Jean Lindenmann he described a novel protein, *interferon*, a natural antiviral agent, whose potential use in therapy has been much studied ever since.

Isaacs, Sir Jeremy (Israel) (1932–) Television executive, born in Glasgow, W Scotland, UK. He studied at Oxford, and became a producer with Granada Television on such current affairs series as *What the Papers Say* and *All Our Yesterdays* (1958–63). He later worked on BBC's *Panorama* (1965), and at Thames Television (1968–78), where he produced *The World at War* (1975). Later programmes include *Ireland: a Television History* (1981) and the brutal drama *A Sense of Freedom* (1981). He served as the first chief executive of Channel 4 (1981–7), vigorously defending its right to offer alternative programming and service minority interests. He became general director of the Royal Opera House in Covent Garden (1988–97), and was knighted in 1996.

Isaacs, Rufus Daniel >> **Reading, 1st Marquess of**

Isaacs, Susan Brierley, *née* **Fairhurst** (1885–1948) Specialist in the education of young children, born in Bromley Cross, Essex, SE England, UK. She studied at Manchester and Cambridge, became a disciple of Freud, and ran an experimental progressive school, Malting House, in Cambridge (1924–7). She was an influential head of the Department of Child Development at the Institute of Education, London (1933–43). She published *Intellectual Growth in Young Children* (1930) and *Social Development of Young Children* (1933), where some of her conclusions challenged the theories of Jean Piaget before it was acceptable to question Piaget's work. She was a powerful influence on the theory and practice of the education of young children between the wars. >> Piaget

Isabella I (of Castile), also known as **Isabella the Catholic** (1451–1504) Queen of Castile (1474–1504), born in Madrigal de las Altas Torras, Spain, the daughter of John II, King of Castile and León. In 1469 she married Ferdinand V of Aragon, with whom she ruled jointly from 1479. During her reign, the Inquisition was introduced (1478), the reconquest of Granada completed (1482–92), and the Jews expelled (1492). She sponsored the voyage of Christopher Columbus to the New World. >> Columbus; Ferdinand the Catholic; RR1088

Isabella of Angoulême [ãgoolem] (?–1246) Queen of England, the consort of King John, whom she married in 1200. In 1214 she was imprisoned by John at Gloucester, and after his death in 1216 returned to France, where she married a former lover, the Comte de la Marche, in 1220. Isabella was the mother of Henry III. Her daughter by John, **Isabella** (1214–41), married Emperor Frederick II. >> John; Henry III (of England)

Isabella of France (1292–1358) Queen of England, the consort of Edward II, and daughter of Philip IV of France. She married Edward in 1308 at Boulogne, but then became the mistress of Roger Mortimer, Earl of March, with whom she overthrew and murdered the king (1327). Her son, Edward III, had Mortimer executed in 1330, and Isabella was sent into retirement, eventually to join an order of nuns. >> Edward II; Edward III

Isabey, Jean Baptiste [eezabay] (1767–1855) Portrait painter and miniaturist, born in Nancy, France. Trained under Jacques Louis David, he painted portraits of revolution notabilities, and afterwards became court painter to Napoleon and the Bourbons. >> David, Jacques Louis

Isaiah [iyziya], Heb **Jeshaiah** (8th-c BC) The first in order of the major Old Testament prophets, the son of Amoz. A citizen of Jerusalem, he began to prophesy c.747 BC, and exercised his office until at least the close of the century. According to tradition, he was martyred.

Isherwood, Christopher (William Bradshaw) (1904–86) Novelist, born in Disley, Cheshire, NWC England, UK. He studied at Repton, Cambridge, and London, and taught English in Germany (1930–3). His best-known novels, *Mr Norris Changes Trains* (1935) and *Goodbye to Berlin* (1939), were based on his experiences in the decadence of post-slump, pre-Hitler Berlin, and later inspired *Cabaret* (musical, 1966; filmed, 1972). In collaboration with Auden, a school friend, he wrote three prose-verse plays with political overtones. He also travelled in China with Auden in 1938, and wrote *Journey to a War* (1939). In 1939 he emigrated to California to work as a scriptwriter, and became a US citizen in 1946. Later novels include *Prater Violet* (1945), *The World in the Evening* (1954), and *Meeting by the River* (1967). >> Auden

Ishiguro, Kazuo [ishigooroh] (1954–) Novelist, born in Japan. He came to Britain to study at the University of Kent before joining Malcolm Bradbury's creative writing course at the University of East Anglia. His third novel, *The Remains of the Day* (1989, filmed 1993), won the Booker Prize and established his reputation. Later books include *The Unconsoled* (1995). >> Bradbury, Malcolm

Ishmael [ishmayel] Biblical character, the son of Abraham by Hagar, his wife's maid. He was expelled into the desert with his mother from Abraham's household after the birth of Isaac. He is purported to have fathered 12 princes, and is considered the ancestor of the Bedouin tribes of the Palestinian deserts (the *Ishmaelites*). Mohammed considered Ishmael and Abraham as ancestors of the Arabs, and as associated with the construction of the Kaba at Mecca. >> Abraham; Hagar; Isaac; Mohammed

Isidore of Seville, St [izidaw(r), sevil] (c. 560–636) Ecclesiastic, encyclopedist, and historian, born either in Seville or Carthagena, Spain. Archbishop of Seville in c.600, his episcopate was notable for the Councils at Seville (618 or 619) and Toledo (633). A voluminous writer, his most influential work was the encyclopedia *Etymologies*. He was canonized in 1598; feast day 4 April.

Islam, Kazi Nazrul [izlam] (1899–1976) Poet, born into extreme poverty in the West Bengali village of Churulia. He rose to fame in the 1920s as a poet and leader of the anti-British movement in India with his poem *The Rebel*. He also published a bimonthly radical magazine, *Dhumketu* (The Comet), which was virulently revolutionary and anti-British in tone, and spent 40 days on hunger-strike in jail. In the 1930s he concentrated more on composing music and songs, and became an actor and radio personality. In 1942 he contracted a brain disease that bereft him of his faculties, including his speech. After the partition, which he had always opposed, he lived in penury until he was brought home in honour to the newly independent state of Bangladesh, and installed as the national poet. A Muslim, he married a Hindu, and was a lifelong advocate of Muslim–Hindu unity. He wrote over 500 devotional Hindu songs.

Islebius, Magister >> **Agricola, Johann**

Ismail Pasha [ismaeel] (1830–95) Khedive of Egypt, born in Cairo. Educated at St Cyr, France, he became Deputy of the Ottoman Sultan (1863), and was granted the title of khedive in 1866. His massive development programme included the building of the Suez Canal, which was opened in splendour in 1869. The accumulation of a large foreign debt led to European intervention; he was deposed by the Ottoman sultan, and replaced by his eldest son, Tewfik. >> Tewfik Pasha; RR1046

Ismay (of Wormington), Hastings Lionel Ismay, Baron, nickname **Pug** (1887–1965) English soldier, born in Naini Tal, India. He trained at Sandhurst, was commissioned in 1905, and served on India's NW Frontier (1908) and in Somaliland in World War 1. He was appointed assistant secretary to the Committee of Imperial Defence (1926–30), and chief-of-staff to Winston Churchill (1940–6), where he participated in most major Allies' conferences. He later became secretary of state for Commonwealth Relations (1951–2), and secretary-general to NATO (1952–7). >> Churchill, Sir Winston

Isocrates [iysokrateez] (436–338 BC) Greek orator and prose writer, born in Athens. In his youth, he joined the circle of Socrates, but abandoned philosophy for speech writing. He then became an influential teacher of oratory (c.390 BC), and presented rhetoric as an essential foundation of education. >> Socrates

Israëls, Jozef [izraelz] (1824–1911) Genre painter, born in Groningen, The Netherlands. He studied at Amsterdam and Paris, where he exhibited in 1855 a historical picture of William the Silent. He soon turned to scenes from humble life, especially the portrayal of fisher folk. He also worked as an etcher.

Issigonis, Alec [iseegohnis], popular name of **Sir Alexander Arnold Constantine Issigonis** (1906–88) Automobile designer, born in Smyrna, Turkey. He settled in Britain in 1923 and studied at Battersea Polytechnic. His early fascination for cars led him to use his talents in the motor industry. He is best known as the designer of the Morris Minor (1948–71), and the revolutionary British Motor Corporation Mini, launched in 1959. He became a royal designer for industry in 1967.

Ito, Hirobumi [eetoh] (1841–1909) Japanese statesman and premier (1885–8, 1892–6, 1898, 1900–1), born in Choshu province, Japan. He visited Europe and the USA on several occasions, drafted the Meiji constitution (1889), and played a major role in abolishing Japanese feudalism and building up the modern state. He was assassinated at Harbin by a supporter of Korean independence.

Itten, Johannes (1888–1967) Painter and teacher, born in Sudern-Linden, Switzerland. He studied art in Stuttgart (1913–16) before moving to Vienna, where he started his own art school. A leading theorist at the Bauhaus (1919–23), he wrote on the theory of colour (*Kunst der Farbe*, 1961) and developed the idea of a compulsory 'preliminary course', based on research into natural forms and the laws of basic design. This has been widely adopted in art schools.

Itúrbide, Agustín de [eetoorbithay] (1783–1824) Mexican general, born in Morelia, Mexico. He became prominent in the movement for Mexican independence, and made himself emperor as Agustin I (1822–3). He was forced to abdicate, travelled in Europe, and was executed on his return to Mexico. >> RR1075

Ivan III, known as **the Great** (1530–84) Grand Prince of Moscow (1462–1505), born in Moscow. He succeeded in ending his city's subjection to the Tartars, and gained control over several Russian principalities. In 1472 he assumed the title of 'Sovereign of all Russia', and adopted the emblem of the two-headed eagle of the Byzantine Empire.

Ivan IV, known as **the Terrible** (1530–84) Grand prince of Moscow (1533–84), born near Moscow, the first to assume the title of 'tsar' (Lat *Caesar*). He subdued Kazan and Astrakhan, made the first inroads into Siberia, and established commercial links with England. In 1564 the treachery

of one of his counsellors caused him to see treachery everywhere, and he embarked on a reign of terror, directed principally at the feudal aristocracy (boyars). He nonetheless did much for Russian culture and commerce. >> RR1085

Ivanov, Lev (Ivanovich) [eevahnof] (1834–1901) Choreographer, teacher, and dancer, born in Moscow. After studying in Moscow and St Petersburg, he joined the Imperial Ballet (1852), becoming principal dancer in 1869. Appointed rehearsal director by Marius Petipa in 1882, he became second ballet master under Petipa in 1885, the year of his choreographic debut, with a new version of *La Fille mal gardée*. His two most celebrated works are Tchaikovsky's *The Nutcracker* (1892), and the second and fourth acts of Tchaikovsky's *Swan Lake* (1895). Despite his achievements, he lived in the shadow of Petipa, and died in poverty. >> Petipa

Ives, Charles E(dward) (1874–1954) Composer, born in Danbury, CT. He studied music at Yale, and worked in insurance till 1930, when he retired due to ill health. His music is firmly based in the American tradition, but at the same time he experimented with dissonances, polytonal harmonies, and conflicting rhythms, anticipating modern European trends. He composed four symphonies, chamber music (including the well-known 2nd piano sonata, the *Concord Sonata*), and many songs. In 1947 he was awarded the Pulitzer Prize for his third symphony (composed in 1904).

Ives, Frederick (Eugene) (1856–1937) Photographer and inventor, born in Litchfield, CT. Apprenticed to a printer as a boy, he was head of the Cornell University photographic library at 18. He experimented with the possibilities of photography as a means of illustration, and invented (1878) and improved (1885) the half-tone process. He later pioneered natural colours for motion pictures (1914).

Ivory, James (Francis) (1928–) Film director and writer, born in Berkeley, CA. With Ismail Merchant he formed Merchant-Ivory Productions in 1961, which became one of the most enduring and productive of independent film associations. International success came with *Shakespeare Wallah* (1965), which he wrote with Ruth Jhabvala, and other films dealing with the clash of cultural sensibilities in India. He went on to direct a series of films based on major works in English literature, such as *The Bostonians* (1984) and *Howard's End* (1992). He also wrote *Bombay Talkie* (1970), and wrote and produced *A Soldier's Daughter Never Cries* (1998). >> Jhabvala; Merchant

Iwasaki, Koyota [eewasahkee] (1879–1945) Japanese tycoon. He studied at Cambridge, and returned to Japan to be vice-president of the Mitsubishi Co, founded by his grandfather in the 1870s. President from 1916, he expanded the company into a commercial group turning over more than 10% of Japan's national income before World War 2, and producing most of the ships, aircraft, and equipment used by the Japanese armed forces in the War.

Iwerks, U B, originally **Ubbe Iwwerks** (1901–71) Animated-cartoon director, born in Kansas City, KS. The animator who put life into Walt Disney's sketches of Mickey Mouse, he began as an apprentice to the Union Bank Note Company (1916). In 1920, in partnership, he set up the Disney–Iwerks Studio, and produced *Laugh-O-Gram* cartoons, followed by *Alice in Cartoonland* (1923). Iwerks joined Disney in California to animate *Oswald the Lucky Rabbit* (1924), then animated the first film to star Mickey Mouse, *Plane Crazy* (1928). He won Oscars in 1959 and 1964 for his technical achievements. He also developed xerographic animation for *The 101 Dalmatians* (1961), and directed special effects for Alfred Hitchcock's *The Birds* (1963).

Izzard, Eddie [ˈizah(r)d] (1962–) British comedian, actor, and writer, born in Aden, Yemen. His family moved to Northern Ireland, then South Wales, and he studied at the University of Sheffield, where he presented his first shows. He worked in street theatre and comedy clubs before devising a theatre act as a stand-up comic, and becoming nationally known through live videos of his major shows at the Ambassadors (1993) and the Albery (1995) in London. He was voted best live stand-up comic in 1993. Other shows include *One Word Improv* (1997) and *Glorious* (1997). He also wrote the television sitcom, *The Cows* (1996), and made some appearances in films, such as *The Secret Agent* (1996).

Jabir ibn Hayyan >> **Geber**

Jack the Ripper Unidentified English murderer, who between August and November 1888 murdered and mutilated five prostitutes in the East End of London. The murderer was never discovered. The affair roused much public disquiet, provoked a violent press campaign against the CID and the home secretary, and resulted in some reform of police methods. Speculation about the murderer's identity was still continuing in the 1990s, fuelled by the publication of his alleged diary in 1993.

Jacklin, Tony, popular name of **Anthony Jacklin** (1944–) Golfer, born in Scunthorpe, North Lincolnshire, EC England, UK. He won the 1969 Open at Royal Lytham (the first British winner for 18 years), and in 1970 won the US Open at Hazeltine, MN (the first British winner for 50 years). He turned professional in 1962, and won the Jacksonville Open in 1968, the first Briton to win on the US Tour. A former Ryder Cup player (1967–80), he was appointed non-playing captain of the European team in (1983–9), and is now director of golf at the San Roque club. >> RR1158

Jackson, Andrew, nickname **Old Hickory** (1767–1845) US statesman and seventh president (1829–37), born in Waxhaw, SC. He trained as a lawyer, and became a member of Congress for Tennessee (1796), a senator (1797), and a judge of its Supreme Court (1798–1804). In the War of 1812 against Britain, he was given command of the South, and his first military fame came from action against Creek Indians. His victory over the British at New Orleans (1815) further enhanced his reputation. His election as president was the result of a campaign in which he gained the support of the mass of voters – a new development in US politics which came to be called 'Jacksonian democracy'. >> Van Buren; RR1097

Jackson, Betty (1940–) Fashion designer, born in Backup, Lancashire, NW England, UK. She studied at the Birmingham College of Art, and became a freelance fashion illustrator (1971–3), design assistant (1973–5), and chief designer with Quorum (1975–81). In 1985 she was British Designer of the Year, and the same year won the British Fashion Council award. She is design director of Betty Jackson Ltd.

Jackson, Glenda (1936–) Actress and politician, born in Birkenhead, Merseyside, NW England, UK. She trained in London, and became a leading member of the Royal Shakespeare Company before appearing in films, winning Oscars for *Women in Love* (1969) and *A Touch of Class* (1973). She continued to portray complex characterizations on stage and screen, such as the poet Stevie Smith, whom she played first in the theatre and then in the film *Stevie* (1979), and made several television appearances. Later films include *Beyond Therapy* (1985), *Business as Usual* (1986), and *The Rainbow* (1989). A director of British Artists in 1983, she became a Labour MP in 1992 after which she devoted herself full-time to politics. In 1997 she was appointed Transport minister in the new Labour government.

Jackson, Gordon (1923–90) Film actor, born in Glasgow, W Scotland, UK. He made his debut in *Foreman Went to France* (1941), and went on to appear in over sixty films, including *The Ipcress File* (1965) and *The Prime of Miss Jean Brodie* (1968). He became a household name through his television work as the butler in *Upstairs, Downstairs* (1970–75) and in *The Professionals* (1977–81).

Jackson, Helen (Maria) Hunt, *née* **Fiske** (1830–85) Writer, born in Amherst, MA. She turned to writing after the deaths of her first husband and two sons, remarried (1875), and settled in Colorado. A campaigner for American Indian rights, she highlighted the injustices of government policy in her book *A Century of Dishonor* (1881). She was appointed to a Federal Commission to investigate the Indian question, and the experience provided material for her successful novel *Ramona* (1884), which aroused social awareness but was acclaimed mainly for its nostalgic portrayal of old California.

Jackson, (George) Holbrook (1874–1948) Bibliophile and literary historian, born in Liverpool, Merseyside, NW England, UK. He helped establish the formidable political and literary *New Age* (1907). He was active in the Fabian Society, and his life-long devotion to William Morris was reflected in various works from his early study to his Morris anthology, *On Art and Socialism* (1947). *The Eighteen Nineties* (1913) established the literary contours of the decade. His later works include the enormous *Anatomy of Bibliomania* (1931) and *Bookman's Holiday* (1945). >> Morris, William

Jackson, Jesse (Louis) (1941–) Clergyman and politician, born in Greenville, NC. He studied at the University of Illinois and Chicago Theological Seminary, and was ordained a Baptist minister in 1968. He was an active participant in the Civil Rights movement, and organized Operation PUSH (People United to Save Humanity) in 1971. In 1984 and 1988 he sought the Democratic nomination for the presidency, winning considerable support, and becoming the first African-American to mount a serious candidacy for the office.

Jackson, John, known as **Gentleman Jackson** (1769–1845) Boxer, born in London, England, UK. He won the English heavyweight boxing championship in 1795, and retired undefeated in 1803 after only three defences of his title. After his retirement he started a school of self-defence in London, where one of his pupils was Lord Byron, who celebrated him in verse. >> Byron, George

Jackson, John Hughlings (1835–1911) Neurologist, born in Green Hammerton, North Yorkshire, N England, UK. Physician at the National Hospital for the Paralysed and Epileptic (1862–1906), and at the London Hospital (1874–94), he investigated unilateral epileptiform seizures, and discovered that certain regions of the brain are associated with certain movements of the limbs.

Jackson, Laura >> **Riding, Laura**

Jackson, Mahalia (1911–72) Gospel singer, born in New Orleans, LA. The daughter of a clergyman, she sang in his choir as a child, later moving to Chicago, where she performed religious songs in Baptist churches. Her strong religious background and the influence of contemporary blues music were unmistakeably evident in her singing style. Two notably successful records were 'Move On Up a Little Higher' and 'Silent Night'. She appeared in the film *Jazz on a Summer's Day*, singing Gospel music.

Jackson, Michael (1958–) Pop singer, born in Gary, IN. With his brothers, Jackie, Tito, Marlon, and Jermaine in the pop group The Jackson Five, later The Jacksons, he knew stardom from the age of 11, and sang on four consecutive Number One hits. Between 1972 and 1975 he also had six solo hits on the Motown record label. In 1977 he played the scarecrow in *The Wiz*, a black remake of the film *The Wizard of Oz*. His first major solo album was *Off The Wall*

(1979), and he consolidated his career with *Thriller* (1982), which sold over 35 million copies and which helped to establish him as one of the major pop superstars of the 1980s. He repeated this success with his album *Bad* (1987), and in 1988 wrote an autobiography *Moonwalk*, which was filmed as *Moonwalker*. Deals in 1991 for handling his album *Dangerous* were the most lucrative in pop history. *HIStory* appeared in 1995. Having been a celebrity since childhood, he developed a reclusive lifestyle in adulthood, though he continues to tour widely. Worldwide publicity surrounded him in 1993, when allegations about his sexual life caused the cancellation of an international tour on health grounds. He married Lisa Marie Presley in 1994, but they divorced in 1996. Later that year he married nurse Debbie Rowe; their son, named Prince Michael, was born in 1997.

Jackson, Milt(on) (1923–) Vibraphone player, born in Detroit, MI. He learned the guitar and piano while at school, taking up xylophone and vibraphone in his teens. He was discovered by Dizzy Gillespie in 1945, which led to his emergence as the most important vibraphone player of the bebop era. In 1952 he was, with **John Lewis** (1920–), a founding member of the Modern Jazz Quartet, which existed until 1974 and re-formed in the 1980s. Jackson's lyrical interpretations, particularly of ballads, kept him in the forefront of jazz through periods of stylistic change. >> Gillespie

Jackson, Reggie, popular name of **Reginald Martinez Jackson**, nickname **Mr October** (1946–) Baseball player, born in Wyncote, PA. He began an athletic career at Arizona State University, but turned to baseball. He joined the Kansas City Athletics (1968–75), establishing himself as a versatile player, with exceptional skill as a hitter. He transferred to the Baltimore Orioles in 1976, then signed for the New York Yankees and (1982) the California Angels, and retired after the 1987 season with 563 home runs. In his later career he also worked as a sports commentator. He was elected to the Baseball Hall of Fame in 1993. >> RR1144

Jackson, Sir Thomas Graham (1835–1924) British architect. He studied under Sir George Gilbert Scott, and was responsible for many restorations of and additions to libraries, public schools, and colleges. His work can be seen at Eton, Harrow, Rugby, the Inner Temple, the Bodleian Library, and the New Examination Schools at Oxford. >> Scott, George Gilbert

Jackson, Thomas Jonathan, nickname **Stonewall Jackson** (1824–63) Confederate general in the American Civil War, born in Clarksburg, WV. In 1851 he became a professor at the Viriginia Military Institute. During the War, he took command of the Confederate troops at Harper's Ferry on the secession of Virginia, and commanded a brigade at Bull Run, where his firm stand gained him his nickname. He showed tactical superiority in the campaign of the Shenandoah Valley (1862), and gained several victories, notably at Cedar Run, Manassas, and Harper's Ferry. He was accidentally killed by his own troops at Chancellorsville.

Jackson, Sir William (Godfrey Fothergill) (1917–) British soldier and historian. He studied at Shrewsbury School, the Royal Military Academy, Woolwich, and Cambridge, and was commissioned in the Royal Engineers (1937). After service in World War 2 he held several senior posts before becoming military historian in the cabinet office (1977–8, 1982–7), and was governor and commander-in-chief at Gibraltar (1978–82). His publications on military historical and strategic subjects include *Attack in the West* (1953), *Seven Roads to Moscow* (1957), *The Battle for Italy* (1967), and *Overlord: Normandy 1944* (1978). Later works include *Britain's Triumph and Decline in the Middle East* (1996). He was knighted in 1971.

Jacob Biblical character, the son of Isaac, and patriarch of the nation Israel. He supplanted his elder brother Esau, obtaining his father Isaac's special blessing and thus being seen as the inheritor of God's promises. He was re-named *Israel* (perhaps meaning 'God strives' or 'he who strives with God') after his struggle with a divine being. By his wives Leah and Rachel and their maids he fathered 12 sons, to whom Jewish tradition traced the 12 tribes of Israel. >> Esau; Isaac; Joseph; Levi; Rachel

Jacob, François [zhakohb] (1920–) Biochemist, born in Nancy, France. He studied at the University of Paris and the Sorbonne, worked at the Pasteur Institute in Paris (from 1950), and was appointed professor of cellular genetics at the Collège de France (1964). With Lwoff and Jacques Monod he conducted research into cell physiology and the structure of genes, for which they were jointly awarded the 1965 Nobel Prize for Physiology or Medicine. >> Lwoff; Monod, Jacques

Jacobi, Carl Gustav Jacob [jakohbee] (1804–51) Mathematician, born in Potsdam, Germany. As professor of mathematics at Königsberg (1827–42), his book *Fundamenta nova* (1829) was the first definitive study of elliptic functions, which he and Niels Henrik Abel had independently discovered. He also made important advances in the study of differential equations, the theory of numbers, and determinants. >> Abel, Niels Henrik

Jacobi, Sir Derek (George) [jakohbee] (1938–) Actor, born in London, England, UK. He studied at Cambridge, made his professional debut in *One Way Pendulum* at Birmingham Repertory Theatre (1961), and joined the National Theatre's inaugural company playing Laertes in *Hamlet* (1963). He was with the Prospect Theatre (1972–8), made his New York debut in *The Suicide* (1980), and joined the Royal Shakespeare Company in 1982. He has made several film and television appearances, of which the most popular was the title role in the television drama serial *I, Claudius* (1977). He gave a highly acclaimed performance in Hugh Whitmore's *Breaking the Code* (1986–7), and appeared in films such as *Dead Again* (1991) and *Hamlet* (1996), but his main work continues to be in the theatre, playing classical roles such as the 'turbulent priest' in Anouilh's *Becket* (1993). In 1995 he became artistic director of the Chichester Festival Theatre. He was knighted in 1994.

Jacobs, David (Lewis) (1926–) British radio and television broadcaster. He began his career as an announcer with the Forces Broadcasting Service (1944–7), and joined the BBC in 1947. He has been a part of British radio and television since then, introducing shows, chairing panel games, and presenting many light and popular music programmes. He was voted top disc jockey on six occasions.

Jacobs, W(illiam) W(ymark) (1863–1943) Short-story writer, born in London, England, UK. He was a post-office official (1883–99), and began writing humorous yarns of seafarers ashore such as *Many Cargoes* (1896), *The Skipper's Wooing* (1897) and *Deep Waters* (1919). He also wrote macabre tales, such as his best-known story, *The Monkey's Paw* (1902).

Jacobsen, Arne [yahkobsen] (1902–71) Architect and designer, born in Copenhagen. He studied at the Royal Danish Academy, where he later became professor of architecture (1956). He won a House of the Future competition in 1929 and became a leading exponent of Modernism. He designed many private houses in the Bellavista resort near Copenhagen; his main public buildings were the SAS skyscraper in Copenhagen (1955) and St Catherine's College, Oxford (1964). He also designed cutlery and textiles, and classic furniture, especially the 'Egg' and 'Swan' chairs for his Royal Hotel in Copenhagen.

Jacobson, Dan (1929–) Novelist and short-story writer, born in South Africa. He studied at the University of Witwatersrand in Johannesburg, then spent some time on a kibbutz in Israel before settling in Britain in 1958. He began writing in the 1950s, with *The Trap* (1955), later novels including *The Beginners* (1966), *The Wonder-Worker* (1973), *Her Story* (1987), and *The God-Fearer* (1993). A volume of autobiography, *Time and Time Again*, appeared in 1985.

Jacobus de Voragine >> **Voragine, Jacobus de**

Jacopo della Quercia [yakohpoh dela kwairchia] (c. 1374–1438) Sculptor, born in Siena, Italy. His greatest works include the city's fountain (the 'Fonte Gaia', executed 1414–19) and the reliefs on the portal of San Petronia, Bologna.

Jacopone da Todi >> **Todi, Jacopone da**

Jacquard, Joseph Marie [zhakah(r)] (1752–1834) Silk-weaver, born in Lyon, France. His invention (1801–8) of the *Jacquard loom*, controlled by punched cards, enabled an ordinary workman to produce the most beautiful patterns in a style previously accomplished only with patience, skill, and labour. But though Napoleon rewarded him with a small pension and the Légion d'Honneur, the silk weavers were long opposed to his machine. At his death his machine was in almost universal use, and his punched card system was adopted in the 20th-c as a control and data input system for many office machines and early digital computers. >> **Vaucanson**

Jacque, Charles Emile [zhak] (1813–94) Painter and etcher, born in Paris. A prominent member of the Barbizon school, he is best known for his paintings of sheep and etchings of rural scenes, many of them in the Louvre.

Jacques, Hattie [jayks], popular name of **Josephine Edwina Jacques** (1924–80) Comic actress, born in Sandgate, Kent, SE England, UK. A factory worker and nurse during World War 2, she made her stage debut in 1944, toured with the Young Vic, and made her first film appearance in 1946. Frequently called upon to play sturdy matrons and bossy figures of authority, she appeared in 14 *Carry On* films, and became a foil to top comedians, performing on radio in *ITMA* (1948–50) and *Educating Archie* (1950–4). On television she played opposite Eric Sykes in various long-running series from 1959 until her death. >> **Sykes**

Jacuzzi, Candido [jakootzee] (1903–86) Inventor, born in Italy. He was an engineer whose infant son suffered from arthritis. In an attempt to relieve the pain by hydrotherapy, he devised a pump that produced a whirlpool effect in a bath, and when his invention became generally available a bath with such a facility was known as a *jacuzzi*.

Jagger, Charles Sargeant (1885–1934) Sculptor, born in Yorkshire, N England, UK. He studied at the Royal College of Art and at Rome, and executed mainly mythological and historical subjects. His most famous work is the 'Royal Artillery Memorial' at Hyde Park Corner, London.

Jagger, Mick, popular name of **Michael Phillip Jagger** (1943–) Singer, born in Dartford, Kent, SE England, UK. He attended the London School of Economics, but left to form his own rock group, The Rolling Stones, together with Keith Richard, Bill Wyman, Charlie Watts, and Brian Jones. Following their debut in London (1962), the group released its first single, 'Come On' (1963). Jagger's unconventional behaviour on stage, and the group's uninhibited lifestyles, cultivated a rebellious image which appealed to a generation of teenagers during the 1960s. He wrote and sang many of their hit singles including 'The Last Time' (1965), 'I Can't Get No Satisfaction' (1965), 'Honky Tonk Woman' (1969), and various albums. He released two solo albums, *She's the Boss* (1985) and *Primitive Cool* (1987). Still popular after three decades, the group released the *Steel Wheels* album (1988), and went on tour (1989). They were still topping album charts in 1991 with the release of *Flashpoint*, and in 1992 he made a film, *Freejack*, with Anthony Hopkins.

Jahangir [yahanggeer], originally **Salim** (1569–1627) Mughal emperor of India (1605–27), born in Fatehpur Sikri, India, the son of Akbar the Great. The earlier part of his reign was a period of peace and great prosperity for the empire, with a steady growth of trade and commerce and a great flowering of the arts. The later part of the reign was characterized by continual rebellions against his rule, principally on behalf of his various sons, and he was able to survive as ruler only by dint of the courage and vigour of the empress, Nur Jahan. He was, however, a just and tolerant man, and a consistent patron of the arts. >> **Akbar the Great; RR1058**

Jahn, Frederick Ludwig [yahn] (1778–1852) Physical educationist, born in Lanz, Germany. After studying at Halle, Göttingen, and Greifswald, he became a teacher and began a programme of physical exercise for his students, inventing most of the equipment that is now standard in gymnasia. He opened the first gymnasium (*Turnplatz*) in Berlin in 1811. An ardent nationalist, he commanded a volunteer corps in the Napoleonic Wars (1813–15), then returned to teaching, publishing *Die deutsche Turnkunst* (1816, trans A Treatise on Gymnastics), but the gymnasia became centres for political gatherings, and they were closed in 1818. He was arrested in 1819, and suffered five years' imprisonment. He is acknowledged as 'the father of gymnastics'.

Jaimini [jiyminee] (c.200 BC) Indian founder of the *Purva-Mimamsa* school of Hindu philosophy, also known as *Vkyasastra*, the study of words, from its concern with correct methods of interpreting the Vedas. Little is known of Jaimini himself, but his *Mimamsa Sutra* emphasizes the need for right action (which presupposes understanding how to acquire valid knowledge) and performing the duties required by the Vedas.

Jakes, Mílos [yahkesh, meelosh] (1922–) Czechoslovakian politician, born in České Chalupy, Czech Republic. Originally an electrical engineer, he joined the Communist Party of Czechoslovakia (CCP) in 1945 and studied in Moscow (1955–8). He supported the Soviet invasion of Czechoslovakia (1968) and later, as head of the CCP's central control commission, oversaw the purge of reformist personnel. He entered the CCP secretariat (1977) and the Politburo (1981), and replaced Husak as Party leader in 1987. He was forced to step down as CCP leader in November 1989, following a series of pro-democracy rallies. >> **Husak; RR1043**

Jakobson, Roman (Osipovich) [yahkobson] (1896–1982) Linguist, born in Moscow. The founder of the Moscow Linguistic Circle (which generated Russian formalism), he moved in 1920 to Czechoslovakia (starting the Prague Linguistic Circle), and finally in 1941 to the USA, where he taught at Harvard and the Massachusetts Institute of Technology until his death. His many books and papers on language have had a great influence on linguistic and literary thought.

Jalal ad-Din ar-Rumi [jalal adin aroomee] (1207–73) Persian lyric poet and mystic, born in Balkh, modern Afghanistan. He settled at Iconium (Konya) in 1226 and founded a sect who, after his death, were known in the West as the Whirling Dervishes. He wrote a great deal of lyrical poetry, including a long epic on Sufi mystical doctrine.

Jamal, Ahmad, originally **Fritz Jones** (1930–) Jazz pianist, born in Pittsburgh, PA. He began playing the piano at three and joined the musicians' union at 14. In 1952 he became the house pianist at the Lounge of the Pershing Hotel in

Chicago with a guitarist and bassist, and his distinctive style, characterized by melodic understatement, harmonic inventiveness, and rhythmic lightness, attracted a small but fervent audience, among them Miles Davis. In 1956–9, Jamal's trio consisted of Israel Crosby on bass and Vernell Fournier on drums, and the three musicians developed a telepathic interplay. A live recording at the Pershing Lounge in 1958 stayed on the national best-selling lists for 108 weeks, one of the greatest popular successes in jazz history. Over the years, his style has become more complex melodically and less lyrical, but his deft touch and subtle shadings remain. >> Davis, Miles

James I (of England) (1566–1625) The first Stuart king of England (1603–25), also king of Scots (1567–1625) as James VI, born in Edinburgh, EC Scotland, UK, the son of Mary, Queen of Scots, and Henry, Lord Darnley. On his mother's forced abdication, he was proclaimed king, and brought up by several regents. When he began to govern for himself, he ruled through his favourites, which caused a rebellion and a period of imprisonment. In 1589 he married **Anne of Denmark**. Hating Puritanism, he managed in 1600 to establish bishops in Scotland. On Elizabeth's death, he ascended the English throne as great-grandson of James IV's English wife, Margaret Tudor. At first well received, his favouritism again brought him unpopularity. >> Anne of Denmark; Margaret Tudor; Mary, Queen of Scots; Moray; RR1095

James I (of Scotland) (1394–1437) King of Scots (1424–37), born in Dunfermline, Fife, E Scotland, UK, the second son of Robert III. After his elder brother David was murdered at Falkland (1402), allegedly by his uncle, the Duke of Albany, James was sent for safety to France, but was captured by the English, and remained a prisoner for 18 years. Albany meanwhile ruled Scotland as governor until his death in 1420, when his son, Murdoch, assumed the regency, and the country rapidly fell into disorder. Once released (1424), James dealt ruthlessly with potential rivals to his authority, executing Murdoch and his family. He brought state finance under his direct control and curtailed the power of the nobles. He improved the administration of justice for the common people, raising his popularity, but he was assassinated by a small group of dissidents led by Sir Robert Stewart. James was the first of many Stewart kings to act as a patron of the arts, and almost certainly wrote the tender, passionate collection of poems, *The Kingis Quair* ('The King's Quire' or book), c.1423–4. >> RR1095

James II (of England) (1633–1701) King of England and Ireland (1685–8), also king of Scotland, as James VII, born in London, England, UK, the second son of Charles I. Nine months before his father's execution, he escaped to Holland. At the Restoration (1660) he was made Lord High Admiral of England, and commanded the fleet in the Dutch Wars; but after becoming a convert to Catholicism he was forced to resign his post. The national ferment occasioned by the Popish Plot (1678) became so formidable that he had to retire to the European mainland, and several unsuccessful attempts were made to exclude him from the succession. During his reign his actions in favour of Catholicism raised general indignation, and William, Prince of Orange, his son-in-law and nephew, was formally asked by leading clerics and landowners to invade. Deserted by ministers and troops, James escaped to France, where he was warmly received by Louis XIV. He made an ineffectual attempt to regain his throne in Ireland, which ended in the Battle of the Boyne (1690), and remained at St Germain until his death. >> Charles I (of England); Churchill, Arabella; Mary of Modena; Stuart, James; William III; RR1095

James II (of Scotland) (1430–60) King of Scots (1437–60), the son of James I. He was six years old at his father's murder, and three rival families vied for power until James was able to assume control after his marriage to **Mary of Gueldres** (1449). He confiscated the estates of the Livingstone family, then quarrelled with William, Earl of Douglas, killed him in a brawl (1450), and confiscated the Douglas estates (1453). A growing stability in domestic politics was made ineffective by his involvement in the English struggles between the houses of York and Lancaster. In 1460 he marched for England with a powerful army, and laid siege to Roxburgh Castle, which had been held by the English for over a century, but was killed by the bursting of a cannon. >> James I (of Scotland); RR1095

James III (1452–88) King of Scots (1460–88), the son of James II. Too young to rule when his father died, the country once again was ruled by assorted persons who wanted power for themselves. James himself began to govern from 1469, but was a weak monarch, and was unable to restore strong central government. A breakdown of relations with England brought war in 1480, and the threat of English invasion resulted in a calculated political demonstration by his nobles, who hanged unpopular royal favourites at Lauder Bridge in 1482. The rebellion which brought about his downfall and death at Sauchieburn resulted from a further crisis of confidence in the king. The eldest of his sons, James, who had appeared with the rebels in the field, succeeded as James IV. >> James II (of Scotland); James IV; RR1095

James IV (1473–1513) King of Scots (1488–1513), the eldest son of James III. He became active in government at his accession, at the age of 15, and gradually exerted his authority over the nobility. In 1503 he married Margaret Tudor, the elder daughter of Henry VII – an alliance which led ultimately to the union of the crowns. However, he adhered to the French alliance when Henry VIII joined the League against France, and was induced to invade England by the French. He was defeated and killed, along with the flower of his nobility, at the Battle of Flodden, Northumberland. >> Henry VIII; James III; Margaret Tudor; RR1095

James V (1512–42) King of Scots (1513–42), the son of James IV. An infant at his father's death, he grew up amid the struggle between the pro-French and pro-English factions in his country. In 1536 he visited France, marrying **Magdeleine**, the daughter of Francis I (1537), and after her death, **Mary of Guise** (1538). War with England followed from the French alliance (1542), and after attempting to invade England he was routed at Solway Moss. He retired to Falkland Palace, Fife, where he died soon after the birth of his daughter Mary (later, Mary, Queen of Scots). >> Guise, Mary of; James IV; Mary, Queen of Scots; RR1095

James, St (the 'brother' of Jesus), also known as **St James the Just** (1st-c) Listed with Joseph, Simon, and Judas (*Matt* 13.55) as a 'brother' of Jesus of Nazareth, and identified as the foremost leader of the Christian community in Jerusalem (*Gal* 1.19, 2.9; *Acts* 15.13). He is not included in lists of the disciples of Jesus, and should not be confused with James, the son of Alphaeus, or James, the son of Zebedee, but he did apparently witness the resurrected Christ (1 *Cor* 15.7). He showed Jewish sympathies over the question of whether Christians must adhere to the Jewish law. According to Josephus, he was martyred by stoning (c.62). Feast day 1 May. >> Jesus Christ; James, St (son of Zebedee)

James, St (the son of Alphaeus), also known as **St James the Less** (1st-c) One of the 12 apostles. He may be the James whose mother Mary is referred to at the crucifixion of Jesus. Feast day 3 May.

James, St (son of Zebedee), also known as **St James the Great** (1st-c) One of Jesus's 12 apostles, often listed with John (his brother) and Peter as part of an inner group closest to Jesus. They were fishermen, among the first called by Jesus, and were with him at his Transfiguration and at Gethsemane. He and his brother John were also called *Boanerges* ('sons of thunder'). According to Acts 12.2, he was martyred under Herod Agrippa I (c.44). Feast day 25 July. >> Herod Agrippa; Jesus Christ; John, St

James, Arthur Lloyd (1884–1943) Phonetician, born in Pentre, Wales. He studied at Cardiff University and at Cambridge, became lecturer in phonetics at University College, London (1920), and professor at the School of Oriental and African Studies (1933). He is chiefly remembered for his *Historical Introduction to French Phonetics* (1929) and for his work with the BBC, whose adviser he was in all matters concerning pronunciation, and whose well-known handbooks on the pronunciation of place names he edited. He committed suicide after killing his wife, as a result of a depressive psychosis brought on by the war.

James, C(yril) L(ionel) R(obert)) (1901–89) Writer and journalist, born in Tunapuna, Trinidad. He studied at Queens Royal College, moved to England in 1933, and was cricket correspondent for *The Manchester Guardian* (1933–5). In America (1938–53) he developed Marxist sympathies, for which he was deported. Perhaps his most influential book was *The Black Jacobins: Toussaint L'Ouverture and the San Domingo Revolution* (1938), but his most popular book was *Beyond the Boundary* (1963), a fusion of anecdote, report, analysis, and comment, in which sport and politics are harmoniously and ingeniously conjugated.

James, Clive (Vivian Leopold) (1939–) Writer, satirist, broadcaster, and critic, born in Sydney, New South Wales, Australia. He studied at the universities of Sydney and Cambridge, and became television critic for the English newspaper *The Observer*. He has published several books of comment and criticism, including *The Metropolitan Critic* (1974) and *Snakecharmers in Texas* (1988). Other writing includes volumes of verse, such as *Other Passports: Poems 1958–85* (1986), three volumes of autobiography, *Unreliable Memoirs* (1980, 1985, 1990), and the novel *The Silver Castle* (1996). His television programmes have been a combination of chat, humour, and commentary, and include *Saturday Night Clive*, as well as a series of 'documentaries' set in cities around the world, such as *Clive James Live in Japan* (1987).

James (of Rusholme), Eric John Francis James, Baron (1909–92) Educational administrator. He studied at Oxford and became assistant master at Winchester (1933–45), high master at Manchester Grammar School (1945–62), and Vice-Chancellor of York University (1962–73). He was chairman of the Committee to Inquire into the Training of Teachers (1970–1) which reported in 1972 (*Teacher Education and Training*). The *James Report* recommended a restructuring of the pattern of teacher training, advocated an all-graduate entry to the profession, and emphasized the importance of in-service education for teachers. He was knighted in 1956, and elevated to the peerage in 1959.

James, Harry (Hagg) (1916–83) Jazz trumpeter and band-leader, born in Albany, GA. He played with Benny Goodman before forming and leading his own band in 1938, and enjoyed success through the 1940s and 1950s; vocalists with the band included Frank Sinatra and Dick Haymes. His many hits included 'One o'Clock Jump' and 'You Made Me Love You'. He married the film actress Betty Grable in 1943.

James, Henry, Snr (1811–82) Religious philosopher, born in Albany, NY. Heir to a large fortune, he left Princeton Theological Seminary in 1837, and abandoned institutional religion. He was at first attracted to Sandemanism, a pietistic sect encountered on a trip to England, but his writings were more permanently influenced by the teachings of Swedenborg, which interpreted human nature as a collective spiritual being identified with God. James became better known as the father of William and Henry James, whose European education he supervised in the 1850s. >> James, Henry; James, William; Swedenborg, Emanuel

James, Henry (1843–1916) Novelist, born in New York City. After a roving youth in America and Europe, he began in 1865 to write literary reviews and short stories. His work as a novelist falls into three periods. In the first he is mainly concerned with the impact of American life on the older European civilization, as in *Roderick Hudson* (1875), *Portrait of a Lady* (1881), and *The Bostonians* (1886). From 1876 he made his home in England, chiefly in London and in Rye, East Sussex. His second period is devoted to purely English subjects, such as *The Tragic Muse* (1890), *What Maisie Knew* (1897), and *The Awkward Age* (1899). He reverts to Anglo-American attitudes in his last period, which includes *The Wings of a Dove* (1902) and his masterpiece, *The Ambassadors* (1903). The acknowledged master of the psychological novel, he was a major influence on 20th-c writing. >> Edel; James, Henry, Snr; James, William; Wharton

James, Jesse (Woodson) (1847–82) Wild West outlaw, born in Centerville, MO. After fighting with a guerrilla group in the Civil War, he and his brother **Frank James** (1843–1915) led numerous bank, train, and stagecoach robberies in and around Missouri, before Jesse was murdered for a reward by Robert Ford, a gang member. Frank gave himself up soon after, stood trial, was released, and lived the rest of his life on the family farm. Jesse's story has been the subject of numerous Hollywood Westerns. >> Quantrill; Younger, Cole

James, M(ontague) R(hodes) (1862–1936) Scholar and writer, born in Goodnestone, Kent, SE England, UK. He studied at Cambridge, where he was elected a fellow of King's College (1887). He was director of the Fitzwilliam Museum (1894–1908), provost of King's College (1905–18), and Vice-Chancellor of Cambridge (1913–15). He catalogued the manuscripts of every Cambridge college, Aberdeen University, and several London libraries, and wrote on the *Apocrypha*, and the art and literature of the Middle Ages. Outside the academic world he is best remembered as a writer of ghost stories, such as *Ghost Stories of an Antiquary* (1904–11) and *Twelve Mediaeval Ghost Stories* (1922).

James, P D, pseudonym of **Phyllis Dorothy White, Baroness James of Holland Park** (1920–) Detective-story writer, born in Oxford, Oxfordshire, SC England, UK. Educated at Cambridge High School, she worked as a National Health Service administrator (1949–68) and at the Home Office (1968–9), first in the Police Department, then in the children's division of the Criminal Department. The experience provided the backgrounds of several of her novels, such as *Shroud for a Nightingale* (1971), *Death of an Expert Witness* (1977), *Innocent Blood* (1980), *A Taste for Death* (1986), *Original Sin* (1994), and *A Certain Justice* (1997). The futuristic novel *The Children of Men* (1992) represents a new departure. She was made a baroness in 1991.

James, William (1842–1910) Philosopher and psychologist, born in New York City, the brother of Henry James. He studied in New York and in Europe, and received a medical degree from Harvard (1869), where he began teaching anatomy and physiology (1873), then philosophy (1879). His books include *The Principles of Psychology* (1890), *The Will to Believe and Other Essays in Popular Philosophy* (1897), and *The*

Varieties of Religious Experience (1902). He helped found the American Society for Psychical Research, and published numerous papers on the subject. >> James, Henry, Snr; James, Henry

Jameson, Sir Leander Starr [jaymsn] (1853–1917) British colonial statesman, born in Edinburgh, EC Scotland, UK. After studying in London, he met Cecil Rhodes at Kimberley diamond mines (1878), and became involved in Rhodes' plan to extend British rule in Africa. He was made administrator for the South Africa Company at Fort Salisbury (1891), and won enormous popularity. During the troubles at Johannesburg between the Uitlanders and the Boer government, he led an attack against the Boers, but was defeated (1896), handed over to the British authorities, and sent back to England. He was sentenced to 15 months' imprisonment, but was released after six. He returned to South Africa, was elected to the Cape Legislative Assembly (1900), and became premier of Cape Colony (1904–8). He helped promote the Union of South Africa, and formed the Unionist Party (1910). He was created a baronet in 1911. >> Rhodes, Cecil John

Jameson, (Margaret) Storm [jaymsn] (1891–1986) Writer, born in Whitby, North Yorkshire, N England, UK. She studied at Leeds University, and took up writing. Her first success was *The Lovely Ship* (1927), which was followed by more than 30 books that maintained her reputation as storyteller and stylist. These include *The Voyage Home* (1930), *Cloudless May* (1943), *The Writer's Situation* (1950), *Last Score* (1961), and *The White Crow* (1968). Her work assisting refugees during World War 2 as president of PEN, an international association of writers, is recorded in *Journey from the North* (1969).

Jamet, Marie [zhamay] (1820–93) French religious, known as Marie Augustine de la Compassion. A St Servan seamstress, she was a founder in 1840 of the Little Sisters of the Poor.

Jamison, Judith [jaymisn] (1943–) Dancer, born in Philadelphia, PA. She studied piano and violin in her home town before making her New York debut as a guest dancer with American Ballet Theater in 1964. She joined Alvin Ailey's American Dance Theater the following year, becoming one of his top soloists. He choreographed the solo *Cry* for her in 1971, and she also starred in the Broadway musical *Sophisticated Ladies* (1981). >> Ailey

Janáček, Leoš [yanachek] (1854–1928) Composer, born in Hukvaldy, Czech Republic. He became choirmaster in Brno, where he eventually settled after studying at Prague and Leipzig, and became professor of composition (1919). Devoted to the Czech folksong tradition, he wrote several operas, a Mass, instrumental chamber pieces, and song cycles.

Jane, Frederick Thomas (1865–1916) Writer, journalist, and artist, born in Upottery, Devon, SW England, UK. He worked first as an artist, then as a naval correspondent on various periodicals. He founded and edited *Jane's Fighting Ships* (1898) and *All the World's Aircraft* (1909), the annuals by which his name is still best known.

Janet, Pierre [zhanay] (1859–1947) Psychologist and neurologist, born in Paris. He studied under Jean Martin Charcot, lectured in philosophy, and became the director of the psychological laboratory at La Salpêtrière hospital in Paris (1899), and professor of psychology at the Sorbonne (1898) and Collège de France (1902). His theory of hysteria, which linked 'dissociation' with a lowering of psychic energy, was described by Sigmund Freud as the first significant psychological theory, based as it was on sound clinical practice. >> Freud, Sigmund

Jannings, Emil, originally **Theodor Friedrich Emil Janenz** (1884–1950) Actor, born in Rorschach, Switzerland. He grew up in Görlitz, Austria, and made his name in Max Reinhardt's company from 1906. He worked in American films (1926–9), and won the first Oscar for his performances in *The Way of All Flesh* (1928) and *The Last Command* (1928). With the advent of sound movies he returned to Germany, where he appeared with Marlene Dietrich in *The Blue Angel* (1930), his most famous film. >> Reinhardt, Max

Jansen, Cornelius (Otto) [jansen], Dutch [yahnsen] (1585–1638) Theologian, founder of the reform movement known as Jansenism, born in Acquoi, The Netherlands. He studied at Utrecht, Louvain, and Paris, became professor of theology at Louvain (1630), and Bishop of Ypres (1636), where he died just after completing his four-volume work, *Augustinus* (published 1640). This sought to prove that the teaching of St Augustine on grace, free will, and predestination was opposed to the teaching of the Jesuit schools. The book was condemned by Pope Urban VIII in 1642, but the controversy raged in France for nearly a century, when a large number of *Jansenists* emigrated to Holland.

Jansky, Karl (Guthe) [yanskee] (1905–50) Radio engineer, born in Norman, OK. He studied at the University of Wisconsin and joined Bell Telephone Laboratories in 1928. His fundamental discovery (1932) was of radio waves from outer space, while working on interference suffered by radio reception. This discovery allowed the development of radio astronomy during the 1950s. The unit of radio emission strength, the *jansky*, is named after him. >> Reber

Janssen, Cornelis [yahnsen], originally **Cornelius Johnson** (1593–1661) Portrait painter, born in London, England, UK, of Dutch parents. He left England in 1643, and lived in Amsterdam. His portraits show the influence of Van Dyck, with whom he worked at the court of Charles I. He is represented in the National Gallery, London, and at Chatsworth. >> van Dyck

Janssen, Pierre (Jules César) [jansen], Fr [zhänsen] (1824–1907) Astronomer, born in Paris. He studied there, became head of the Astrophysical Observatory at Meudon (1876), and greatly advanced spectrum analysis by his observation of the bright line spectrum of the solar atmosphere (1868). He established an observatory on Mont Blanc, and published a pioneering book of photographs of the Sun, *Atlas de photographies solaries* (1904). A crater on the Moon has been named after him.

Jansson, Tove (Marika) [yansn] (1914–) Writer of children's books, and artist, born in Helsinki. Her books for children, featuring the 'Moomintrolls' and illustrated by herself, are as much appreciated by adults. They have reached an international audience and she has been the recipient of many literary prizes. In later years she has written a number of books aimed at adults, such as *Sommarboken* (1972, The Summer Book).

Janszoon, Laurens, also called **Laurens Coster** (c. 1370–c. 1440) Dutch official, sacristan (*Koster*) of the Grote Kerk of Haarlem, credited by some with the invention of printing before Gutenberg. He is said to have printed as early as 1430, but no evidence exists to support the claim, first made over 100 years after his death. >> Gutenberg, Johannes

Januarius, St [janyuahrius], Ital **San Gennaro** (?-c.305) Christian martyr, Bishop of Benevento, believed to have been a victim of the persecution under Diocletian. Two phials kept in Naples cathedral are said to contain his dried blood, believed to liquefy on his feast day and on certain other occasions throughout the year. Feast day 19 September. >> Diocletian

Japheth [jayfeth] Biblical character, one of the sons of Noah who survived the Flood, the brother of Shem and Ham. He is portrayed as the ancestor of peoples in the area of Asia Minor and the Aegean (*Gen* 10). >> Noah

Jaques-Dalcroze, Emile [zhak dalkrohz] (1865–1950) Music teacher and composer, born in Vienna. He studied composition, and became professor of harmony at Geneva, where he originated eurhythmics, a method of expressing the rhythmical aspects of music by physical movement, which had great influence on the development of 20th-c dance. He was head of a school of eurhythmic instruction in Geneva (1914–50), where his pupils included Mary Wigman and Hanya Holm. >> Holm, Hanya; Wigman

Jardine, Al(an) >> **Beach Boys, The**

Jardine, Douglas (Robert) [jah(r)din] (1900–58) Cricketer, born in Mumbai (Bombay), India. He was captain of England during the controversial 'bodyline' tour of Australia (1932–3), where he employed Harold Larwood to bowl extremely fast at the batsman's body, the first use of intimidatory bowling in the game. He wrote a defence of his tactics in *In Quest of the Ashes* (1933). >> Larwood

Jarman, Derek (1942–94) Painter and film maker, born in Northwood, NW Greater London, England, UK. He studied at London University and the Slade School of Art, London, then worked in costume and set design for the Royal Ballet and the film industry. He directed his first feature film, *Sebastiane*, in 1976, and his later (often controversial) works included *Jubilee* (1977), *Caravaggio* (1985), and *The Last of England* (1987). *The Garden* and *Edward II* both appeared in 1991. He also directed pop videos, designed for opera and ballet, and wrote several books, including the autobiographical *Dancing Ledge* (1984).

Jarmusch, Jim [jah(r)mush] (1953–) Film scriptwriter and director, born in Akron, OH. He studied at Columbia University, then went to France, where he discovered European films, became acquainted with Nicholas Ray, and set about making his first film, *Permanent Vacation* (1981). This was never released, and it was his *Stranger Than Paradise* (1984) that gained both critical acclaim and a devoted if small following. *Down by Law* (1986) and *Mystery Train* (1989) increased his reputation as a maker of offbeat films, noted for their 'European sensibility'. Later films include *Night on Earth* (1991).

Jarrell, Randall (1914–65) Poet and critic, born in Nashville, TN. He studied at Vanderbilt University, and taught English literature and creative writing at the University of North Carolina (1947–65). He wrote an early campus novel, *Pictures from an Institution* (1954), and published several volumes of criticism. A dozen volumes from *Blood for a Stranger* (1942) to *The Lost World* (1966) feature in his *Complete Poems* (1971).

Jarry, Alfred [zharee] (1873–1907) Writer, born in Laval, France. Educated at Rennes, his satirical play, *Ubu-Roi*, was first written when he was 15; later rewritten, it was produced in 1896. He wrote short stories, poems, and other plays in a Surrealist style, inventing a logic of the absurd which he called *pataphysique*. He ended his life destitute and alcoholic.

Jaruzelski, General Wojciech (Witold) [yaruzelskee] (1923–) Polish general, prime minister (1981–5), head of state (1985–90), and president (1989–90), born near Lublin, Poland. He became chief of general staff (1965), minister of defence (1968), a member of the Politburo (1971), and prime minister after the resignation of Pinkowski in 1981. Later that year, in an attempt to ease the country's economic problems and to counteract the increasing political influence of the free trade union Solidarity, he declared a state of martial law, which was lifted in 1982. He became president, but in 1990 bowed to pressure to resign as an anachronism from the former Communist regime. >> Wałesa; RR1082

Jason, David (1940–) Actor, born in Edmonton, N Greater London, England, UK. He made his professional debut with the Bromley Repertory in 1965, and then appeared regularly in theatre, but became best known as a television actor. His many series include *Open All Hours* (1976, 1981–5), *Only Fools and Horses* (several series), *A Bit of a Do* (1988–9), *The Darling Buds of May* (1990–3), and *A Touch of Frost* (1992–). He received BAFTAs for Best Actor (1988) and Best Light Entertainment Performer (1990), and he has also had a National Television Special Recognition Award for Lifetime Achievement in Television.

Jaspers, Karl (Theodor) [yasperz] (1883–1969) Philosopher, born in Oldenburg, Germany. He studied medicine at Berlin, Göttingen, and Heidelberg, where he undertook research in a psychiatric clinic, published a textbook on psychopathology (*Allgemeine Psychopathologie*, 1913) and was professor of psychology (1916–20). From 1921 he was professor of philosophy at Heidelberg, until dismissed by the Nazis in 1937. His work was banned but he stayed in Germany, and was awarded the Goethe Prize in 1947 for his uncompromising stand. In 1948 he settled in Basel as a Swiss citizen, and was appointed professor. Among his many works are *Philosophie* (3 vols, 1932), considered his most important writing, and *Die Atombombe und die Zukunft des Menschen* (1958, trans The Future of Mankind), in which he talks of the possibility of a world political union under which all could live and communicate in peace and freedom.

Jastrow, Robert [jastroh] (1925–) Physicist and writer, born in New York City. Involved in the theoretical aspects of space exploration and the early development of NASA, he was director of the Goddard Institute for Space Studies (1961–81). He joined the faculty of Dartmouth College in 1973, and became director of the Mt Wilson Institute, CA in 1990. His books include *Red Giants and White Dwarfs* (1963) and *Journey to the Stars* (1989).

Jaurès, (Auguste Marie Joseph) Jean [zhohres] (1859–1914) Socialist leader, writer, and orator, born in Castres, France. He lectured on philosophy at Toulouse, became a deputy (1885), co-founded the Socialist paper *L'Humanité* (1904), and was the main figure in the founding of the French Socialist Party. He was assassinated in Paris while advocating reconciliation with Germany.

Javacheff, Christo >> **Christo**

Javal, Camille >> **Bardot, Brigitte**

Jawara, Sir Dawda Kairaba [jawahra] (1924–) Gambian statesman, prime minister (1965–70), and president (1970–94), born in Barajally, The Gambia. He studied at Glasgow University, and returned to The Gambia to work in the national veterinary service (1957–60). He entered politics in 1960 and progressed rapidly, becoming minister of education and then premier (1962–5). When full independence was achieved in 1965, he became prime minister, and when in 1970 the country chose republican status he became its first president. He was re-elected in 1992 for his fifth consecutive term of office, having survived an abortive coup against him in 1981, but was ousted in 1994 following a military coup. >> RR1051

Jawlensky, Alexey von [yavlenskee] (1864–1941) Painter, born in Kuslovo, Russia. He studied at St Petersburg Academy and in Munich, and developed his own brightly-coloured Fauvist style by c.1905. After c.1913 he came under Cubist influence, and painted simpler, more geometrical arrangements using more subdued colours.

Jay, John (1745–1829) US statesman and jurist, born in New York City. He studied at King's College (now Columbia University), New York City, and was admitted to the bar (1768). Elected to the Continental Congress (1774–7), he became president of Congress in 1778, secretary for foreign affairs (1784–9), and Chief Justice of the Supreme Court (1789–95). In 1794 he negotiated *Jay's Treaty* with Britain, in an attempt to avoid war. It was unpopular with the US public, and instrumental in the formation of the Democratic-Republicans as an Opposition party. He retired in 1801, after a period as Governor of New York.

Jay, Peter (1937–   ) British writer, broadcaster, and businessman. He studied at Oxford, then worked at the Treasury (1961–7), as a financial journalist (1967–77), and as a presenter for ITV (1972–7). He was ambassador to the USA (1977–9), then returned to television, becoming presenter of TV-AM (1983) and of *A Week in Politics* (1983–6, Channel 4). He has been a senior executive for several organizations, and a member of government, industrial, and charitable advisory committees. He became economics and business editor at the BBC in 1990.

Jayawardene, Junius Richard [jayawah(r)denay] (1906–96) Sri Lankan statesman, prime minister (1977–8), and president (1978–89), born in Colombo. He studied law in Colombo, and became a member of the State Council (1943) and the House of Representatives (1947). He was honorary secretary of the Ceylon National Congress (1940–7), minister of finance (1947–53), and vice-president of the United National Party. He led his Party in Opposition, both as deputy leader (1960–5) and Leader (1970–7), before becoming prime minister and president. >> RR1090

Jean de Meung [zhã duh mõe], or **Jean Clopinel** (c. 1250–1305) Poet and satirist, born in Meung-sur-Loire, France. He flourished in Paris in the reign of Philip IV. He translated many books into French, but his great work is his lengthy continuation (18 000 lines) of the *Roman de la Rose* by Guillaume de Lorris, in which he replaced allegory with satirical pictures of actual life, and an encyclopedic discussion of contemporary learning. >> Guillaume de Lorris

Jeanne d'Arc >> **Joan of Arc, St**
Jeanneret, Charles Edouard >> **Le Corbusier**
Jeans, Sir James (Hopwood) [jeenz] (1877–1946) Astrophysicist and popularizer of science, born in Ormskirk, Lancashire, NW England, UK. He taught at Cambridge (1904–5, 1910–12) and Princeton (1905–9), where he was professor of applied mathematics, then became a research associate at Mt Wilson Observatory, Pasadena until 1944. He made important contributions to the theory of gases, quantum theory, and stellar evolution, and became widely known for his popular exposition of physical and astronomical theories. He was knighted in 1928.

Jefferson, Joseph (1829–1905) Comic actor, born in Philadelphia, PA. He came of theatrical stock, and first appeared on stage at age three. He was for years a strolling actor, until in New York City in 1857 he made a hit as Doctor Pangloss, and in 1858 created the part of Asa Trenchard in *Our American Cousin*. In 1865 he visited London, and at the Adelphi first played his famous part of Rip Van Winkle, a role he maintained until his retirement.

Jefferson, Thomas (1743–1826) US statesman and third president (1801–9), born in Shadwell, VA. He studied at the College of William and Mary, became a lawyer (1767), joined the revolutionary party, and took a prominent part in the first Continental Congress (1774), drafting the Declaration of Independence. He was Governor of Virginia (1779–81), minister in France (1785), and secretary of state (1789). Vice-president under Adams (1797–1801), he then became president. Events of his administration included the war with Tripoli, the Louisiana Purchase (1803), and the prohibition of the slave trade. He retired in 1809, but continued to advise as an elder statesman. He was highly accomplished in architecture, science, the humanities, and education. >> Adams, John; RR1097

Jeffreys (of Wem), George Jeffreys, Baron, known as **Judge Jeffreys** (1648–89) Judge, born in Acton, Wrexham. Called to the bar in 1668, he rose rapidly, was knighted (1677), and became recorder of London (1678). He was active in the Popish Plot prosecutions, became Chief Justice of Chester (1680), baronet (1681), and Chief Justice of the King's Bench (1683). In every state trial he proved a willing tool of the Crown, and was raised to the peerage by James II (1685). His journey to the West Country to try the followers of Monmouth earned his court the name of 'the Bloody Assizes' for its severity. He was Lord Chancellor (1685–8), but on James's flight was imprisoned in the Tower, where he died. >> Charles II (of England); James II (of England); Monmouth, James; Oates, Titus

Jeffreys, Sir Harold (1891–1989) Geophysicist, astronomer, and mathematician, born in Fatfield, Tyne and Wear, NE England, UK. He studied at Cambridge, where he became reader in geophysics (1931–46) and professor of astronomy (1945–58). In a wide-ranging scientific career, he investigated the effect of radioactivity on the cooling of the Earth, and postulated that the Earth's core is liquid. He studied earthquakes and monsoons, made a fresh estimate of the age of the Solar System, and re-calculated the surface temperatures of the outer planets. In mathematics he made contributions to probability theory and operational calculus.

Jeffries, James J(ackson), nickname **the Boilermaker** (1875–1953) Boxer, born in Carroll, OH. He received his nickname because he worked in a boiler factory. He trained as sparring partner to 'Gentleman' Jim Corbett, and in 1899 won the world heavyweight championship by knocking out Bob Fitzsimmons in 11 rounds. He retired undefeated in 1905, but in 1910 was persuaded to return to the ring as the 'great white hope' against the new black champion, Jack Johnson, who knocked him out in the 15th round. >> Corbett, James John; Fitzsimmons; Johnson, Jack

Jeffries, John (1744–1819) Balloonist and physician, born in Boston, MA. A loyalist during the American Revolution, he settled in England and made the first balloon crossing of the English Channel with the French aeronaut Blanchard in 1785. >> Blanchard

Jehu, King of Israel [jeehoo] (9th-c BC) King of Israel (c.842–815 BC). He was a military commander under King Ahab, but after Ahab was killed he led a military coup against Jehoram, Ahab's son, and slaughtered the royal family, including Ahab's wife Jezebel. Having seized the throne for himself, he founded a dynasty that presided over a decline in the fortunes of Israel. >> Ahab; Jezebel; RR1064

Jekyll, Gertrude [jeekl] (1843–1932) Horticulturalist and garden designer, born in London, England, UK. She trained as an artist, but was forced by failing eyesight to abandon painting, and took up garden design (1891). In association with the young architect, Edwin Lutyens, her designs for more than 300 gardens for his buildings had a great influence on promoting colour design in garden planning. She also wrote several books, including *Colour in the Flower Garden* (1918). >> Lutyens, Edwin Landseer

Jellicoe, John Rushworth Jellicoe, 1st Earl [jelikoh] (1859–1935) British admiral, born in Southampton, Hampshire, S England, UK. He became Third Sea Lord (1908), and was commander-in-chief at the outbreak of World War 1. His main engagement was the Battle of Jutland (1916), for which he was much criticized at the time, although it is now accepted he rendered the German high seas fleet ineffective for the remainder of the war.

Promoted to First Sea Lord, he organized the defences against German submarines, and was made Admiral of the Fleet (1919). He later became Governor-General of New Zealand (1920–4), and was created an earl in 1925. >> Hipper; Scheer; Sturdee; Pound, Dudley Pickman Rogers

Jenghiz Khan >> **Genghis Khan**

Jenkins, David (Edward) (1925–) Theologian and clergyman, born in Bromley, S Greater London, England, UK. He studied at Oxford, and was a lecturer in Birmingham and Oxford before being appointed director of *Humanum* studies at the World Council of Churches, Geneva (1969–73). He then became director of the William Temple Foundation, Manchester (1973–8), and professor of theology at Leeds (1979–84). He was appointed Bishop of Durham (1984–94), amidst controversy over his interpretation of the Virgin Birth and the Resurrection. He has published several books, including his recent trilogy, *God, Miracle and the Church of England* (1987), *God, Politics and the Future* (1988), and *God, Jesus and Life in the Spirit* (1988).

Jenkins, Richard Walter >> **Burton, Richard**

Jenkins, Robert (18th-c) English merchant captain, engaged in trading in the West Indies. In 1731 he alleged that his sloop had been boarded by a Spanish *guarda costa* (coastal guard), and that, though no proof of smuggling had been found, he had been tortured, and had his ear torn off. He produced the alleged ear in 1738 in the House of Commons, and so helped to force Walpole into the 'War of Jenkins' Ear' against Spain in 1739, which merged into the War of the Austrian Succession (1740–8). Jenkins served with the East India Company, and for a time as Governor of St Helena. >> Walpole, Robert

Jenkins (of Hillhead), Roy (Harris) Jenkins, Baron (1920–) British statesman, born in Abersychan, Torfaen, SE Wales, UK. He studied at Oxford, became a Labour MP in 1948, and was minister of aviation (1964–5), home secretary (1965–7), Chancellor of the Exchequer (1967–70), deputy leader of the Opposition (1970–2), and again home secretary (1974–6). He resigned as an MP in 1976 to take up the presidency of the European Commission (1977–81). Upon his return to Britain, he co-founded the Social Democratic Party (1981), and became its first leader, standing down after the 1983 election in favour of David Owen. Defeated in the 1987 election, he was given a life peerage and also became Chancellor of Oxford University. >> Owen, David

Jenkinson, Robert Banks >> **Liverpool, Earl of**

Jenner, Edward (1749–1823) Physician, the discoverer of the vaccination for smallpox, born in Berkeley, Gloucestershire, SWC England, UK. After an apprenticeship with a local surgeon, he studied under John Hunter in London, then returned to practise in Berkeley (1773), while remaining a firm friend of Hunter. Having observed how an infection of the mild disease cowpox prevented later attacks of smallpox, in 1796 he inoculated a child with cowpox, then two months later with smallpox, and the child failed to develop the disease. His discovery was violently opposed at first, but within five years vaccination was being practised throughout the civilized world. >> Hunter, John

Jenner, Sir William (1815–98) Physician, born in Chatham, Kent, SE England, UK. He studied at University College, London, where he became professor (1848–79). He became physician in ordinary to Queen Victoria in 1862, and to the Prince of Wales in 1863. He established the difference between typhus and typhoid fevers in 1851.

Jennings, Herbert Spencer (1868–1947) Zoologist, the first to study the behaviour of micro-organisms, born in Tonica, IL. He studied at Harvard, and became professor of experimental zoology (1906) and zoology (1910–38) at Johns Hopkins University. He wrote the standard work *Contributions to the Study of the Behavior of the Lower Organisms* (1919), and investigated heredity and variation in micro-organisms.

Jennings, Pat(rick) (1945–) Footballer, born in Newry, Co Down. Britain's most capped footballer, he played for Northern Ireland 119 times. He started his career with Newry Town before joining Watford, moved to Tottenham Hotspur in 1974, and became their regular goalkeeper for over 10 years before joining Arsenal in 1977. He made a total of 747 Football League appearances, and won several cup-winner's medals. He retired in 1986. >> RR1155

Jennings, Sarah >> **Churchill, Sarah**

Jensen, Georg [yensen] (1866–1935) Silversmith, born in Raadvad, Denmark. Having worked as a sculptor, he founded his smithy in Copenhagen in 1904, and revived the high artistic traditions of Danish silver. He developed modern designs which proved highly popular, enabling his business to expand throughout Europe, and was one of the first to produce high quality, fashionable steel cutlery.

Jensen, (Johannes) Hans (Daniel) [yensen] (1907–73) Physicist, born in Hamburg, Germany. Professor at Hamburg (1936–41) and Hanover (1941–9), in 1949 he became professor of theoretical physics at Heidelberg. He shared the Nobel Prize for Physics in 1963 for research leading to the development of the shell theory for the structure of the atomic nucleus. >> RR1122

Jensen, Johannes Vilhelm [yensen] (1873–1950) Writer and poet, born in Farsø, Denmark. A student of medicine in Copenhagen, he turned to writing. His early works detail his native land and its people, as in *Himmerlandshistorier* (1898–1910), but many of his works, such as *The Forest* and *Madama d'Ora* (1904), are based on his extensive travels in the Far East and America. He wrote many tales under the title *Myter* (Myths), as well as a psychological study of Christian II of Denmark, *Kongens Fald* (1900, The Fall of the King). His best-known work *Den Lange Rejse* (1908–22, The Long Journey), depicting the rise of the human race through time is an expression of Jensen's Darwinism. He was awarded the Nobel Prize for Literature in 1944.

Jepson, Willis (Lyn) (1867–1946 Botanist, born near Vacaville, CA. He spent his career at the University of California, Berkeley (1899–1937), and his works include the classic *A Manual of the Flowering Plants of California* (1925). An outspoken conservationist, he founded the California Botanical Society (1913) and the Save the Redwoods League (1918). A genus of flowering plants, *Jepsonia*, is named after him.

Jeremiah [jeruhmiya] (7th-c BC) Old Testament prophet, whose prophecies are recorded in the *Book of Jeremiah*, born near Jerusalem. He was in Jerusalem during the siege by Nebuchadrezzar II, and was persuaded to flee to Egypt after the assassination of Gedaliah, the governor appointed by the Babylonians for the province of Judah. Jeremiah is said to have been stoned to death by his fellow Jews for constantly rebuking them for idolatry. >> Nebuchadrezzar II

Jerne, Niels K(ai) [yernuh] (1911–94) Immunologist, born in London of Danish parents. He studied at Leyden, worked at the Danish State Serum Institute (1943–55), and later took a medical degree at Copenhagen. He was chief medical officer of the World Health Organization (1956–62), and founding-director of the Institute of Immunology at Basel (1969–80). For his research into the way the immune system in the body creates antibodies against disease, he shared the 1984 Nobel Prize for Physiology or Medicine. >> RR1124

Jeroboam I [jeroboham] (10th-c BC) First king of the divided kingdom of Israel. Solomon made him superintendent of the labours and taxes exacted from his tribe of Ephraim at the construction of the fortifications of Zion. The growing disaffection towards Solomon fostered his ambition, but he was obliged to flee to Egypt. After Solomon's death he headed the successful revolt of the N tribes against Rehoboam, and, as their king, established shrines at Dan and Bethel as rival pilgrimage centres to Jerusalem. He reigned for 22 years. >> Solomon; RR1064

Jerome, St [jerohm], originally **Eusebius Hieronymus** (c. 342–420) Christian ascetic and scholar, born in Stridon, Croatia. After living for a while as a hermit, he was ordained in 379, and became secretary to Pope Damasus (reigned 366–84). He moved to Bethlehem in 386, where he wrote many letters and treatises, and commentaries on the Bible. He is chiefly known for making the first translation of the Bible from Hebrew into Latin (the Vulgate). Feast day 30 September.

Jerome, Jerome K(lapka) [jerohm] (1859–1927) Humorous writer, novelist, and playwright, born in Walsall, Staffordshire, C England, UK. Brought up in London, he was successively a clerk, schoolmaster, reporter, actor, and journalist, then became joint editor of *The Idler* (1892) and started his own weekly, *To-Day*. His novel *Three Men in a Boat* (1889) became a humorous classic.

Jerome of Prague [jerohm] (c. 1365–1416) Religious reformer, born in Prague. He studied at Prague and Oxford. A friend and collaborator of John Huss, he also became a disciple of Wycliffe, and zealously spread his teachings after returning to the European mainland (1401), but in each city the ecclesiastical authorities forced him to move on. From the Sorbonne (1405), he moved to Heidelberg and Cologne (1406), Vienna (1410), and Cracow (1412). He was arrested in Bavaria in 1415, and taken to Constance, where he was condemned as a heretic to burn at the stake. >> Huss; Wycliffe

Jespersen, (Jens) Otto (Harry) [yespersen] (1860–1943) Philologist, born in Randers, Denmark. He studied at Copenhagen, and became professor of English language and literature there (1893–1925), where he revolutionized the teaching of languages. His *Sprogundervisning* (1901, trans How to Teach a Foreign Language) became perhaps the best-known statement of what is now called the 'direct method'. His other books include *Growth and Structure of the English Language* (1905), *A Modern English Grammar on Historical Principles* (1909), and *Philosophy of Grammar* (1924). He also invented an international language, 'Novial', with its own grammar and lexicon.

Jesse, Fryn Tennyson [jesee], popular name of **Friniwyd Tennyson Jesse** (1889–1958) British writer and playwright. She studied painting, but during World War 1 took up journalism, and after the war served on Herbert Hoover's Relief Commission for Europe. She published collected poems, *The Happy Bride* (1920), and remarkable accounts of the trials of Madeleine Smith (1927) and John Christie (1958). She is best known for her novels set in Cornwall, such as *The White Riband* (1921) and *Moonraker* (1927), as well as *A Pin to See a Peepshow* (1934), based on the Thompson–Bywaters murder case.

Jessel, Sir George (1824–83) Judge, born in London, England, UK. He studied at University College, London, and was called to the bar in 1847. He served as a Liberal MP (1868–73), solicitor general (1871–3), and then as Master of the Rolls (1873–83). He gave many judicial opinions of continuing value, and made important contributions to legal principle by reshaping older doctrines, especially of equity.

Jessop, William (1745–1814) Civil engineer, born in Devonport, Devon, SW England, UK. He worked under John Smeaton on canals in Yorkshire and elsewhere. With others he founded the Butterley Iron Works in 1790, and began to manufacture fish-bellied cast-iron rails which

marked an important advance in railway track technology. He was involved as chief engineer on the construction of the Grand Junction Canal with its mile-long tunnel at Blisworth, the Surrey Iron Railway (1802), Avon docks at Bristol, and the West India Docks on the Thames. His works put him in the front rank of early British civil engineers. >> Smeaton, John

Jesus Christ see panel on p. 494

Jevons, William Stanley [jevonz] (1835–82) Economist and logician, born in Liverpool, Merseyside, NW England, UK. He studied chemistry and metallurgy at University College, London, and became assayer to the Mint in Sydney, Australia (1854–9). He returned to England and studied logic under Augustus de Morgan at London, becoming professor of logic at Manchester (1866) and professor of political economy at London (1876). He introduced mathematical methods into economics, was one of the first to use the concept of final or marginal utility as opposed to the classical cost of production theories, and wrote *Theory of Political Economy* (1871), a major work in the development of economic thought. >> de Morgan

Jewel, John (1522–71) Clergyman, born in Berrynarbor, Devon, SW England, UK. He studied at Oxford, and absorbed reformed doctrines early in his career. On Mary I's accession he travelled through Europe, staying in Frankfurt, Zürich, Strasbourg, and Padua, returning to England when Elizabeth I became queen. He was appointed Bishop of Salisbury in 1560, and published his famous *Apologia pro ecclesiae Anglicanae* (Apologia for the English Church) in 1562.

Jewel and Warriss Stage names of **Jimmy Jewel** (1909–95) and **Ben Warriss** (1909–93) Comedy partners, born in Sheffield, South Yorkshire, N England, UK. They were cousins, both of them children of popular entertainers. Warriss made his professional debut at Stockport when he was 10, and went on to play revues and pantomimes. He joined up with Jewel as a double act in Newcastle in 1934, and they quickly achieved success, becoming favourites in pantomimes, and achieving national fame as stars on BBC radio's *Up the Pole* (1947) and as cover stars of the weekly children's comic, *Radio Fun*. They appeared frequently on television in the 1950s, including four Royal Variety performances. They separated in 1966, Jewel continuing with comedy acting, Warriss making occasional theatrical and television appearances.

Jewett, (Theodora) Sara Orne (1849–1909) Novelist, born in South Berwick, ME. She wrote a series of sketches, *The Country of the Pointed Firs* (1896), as well as romantic novels and stories based on the provincial life of her state, such as *A Country Doctor* (1884) and *A White Heron* (1886), and a historical novel, *The Tory Lover* (1901). She was the first president of Vassar College (1862–4).

Jex-Blake, Sophia Louisa (1840–1912) Physician and pioneer of medical education for women, born in Hastings, East Sussex, SE England, UK. She studied at Queen's College for Women, London, and became a tutor in mathematics there (1859–61). She then studied medicine in New York City (1865–8) under Elizabeth Blackwell, continuing her studies at Edinburgh University. With five other women she was allowed to matriculate in 1869, but the university authorities reversed their decision in 1873. She waged a public campaign in London, opened the London School of Medicine for Women (1874), and won her campaign when medical examiners were permitted by law to examine women students (1876). She later founded a medical school in Edinburgh (1886). >> Blackwell, Elizabeth

Jezebel (?–c. 843 BC) Phoenician princess, the daughter of Ethbaal, King of Tyre and Sidon, and wife of King Ahab of Israel (869–850). She introduced Phoenician habits (and

JESUS CHRIST (c. 6/5 B C–c. A D 30/33)

Jesus of Nazareth is the central figure of the Christian faith, whose nature as Son of God and whose redemptive work are fundamental beliefs for adherents of Christianity. 'Christ' became attached to the name Jesus in view of his followers' conviction that he was the Jewish Messiah (*Christ* comes from the Greek meaning 'Anointed One'). According to the accounts of St Matthew and St Luke, he was the first-born son of the Virgin Mary, a member of the tribe of Judah, and the betrothed of Joseph, who was a carpenter, and a descendant of David. St Matthew and St Luke relate that before her marriage to Joseph, Mary was chosen to bear God's son, and conceived through the Holy Spirit while still a virgin.

According to a tradition based on St Luke's Gospel, Jesus was born in a stable in Bethlehem, because arriving there from Joseph's home town, Nazareth, in order to comply with the regulations of a Roman population census, his parents found there was no room for them in any of the local inns. However, this story cannot be historically correct. According to St Matthew, Jesus's birth took place just prior to the demise of Herod the Great (4 BC), but the Roman census referred to by St Luke did not take place before AD 6. (The use of BC and AD is a convention which began in the Middle Ages.) The only sources of information are the four gospels of the New Testament, but it has been estimated that they cover just 50 days in the life of Christ. He is also mentioned in writings by Tacitus Suetonius and Josephus, and in certain anti-Christian Hebrew writings of the time.

Little is written of Jesus's early life. He is believed to have followed Joseph's trade of carpentry. However, we are told how his astonished mother, on seeing him knowledgeably discoursing with the scribes when he was 12, was assured by him that he was about his 'father's business'. Nearly 18 years passed in obscurity, before baptism at the hands of his cousin, John the Baptist, provided a public intimation of Jesus' mission.

After 40 days in the wilderness wrestling successfully with all manner of temptations, he gathered around him 12 disciples (known as the 12 apostles, from Greek *apostello*, 'I send out'), and undertook two missionary journeys through Galilee. He was active mainly in the villages and countryside of Galilee rather than in the towns and cities, and was credited in the gospel records with many miraculous healings and exorcisms. This culminated in the miraculous feeding of the 5000 (*Mark* 4) – an event which, to the authorities, had obvious dangerous political implications. Furthermore, Jesus's association with 'publicans and sinners'; his apparent flouting of traditional religious practices; the performance of miracles on the Sabbath; his driving moneylenders from the temple; and the whole tenor of his revolutionary Sermon on the Mount (*Matt* 5–7), emphasizing love, humility, meekness, and charity – roused the Pharisees (a lay, rule-bound party of Jews). Christ and his disciples sought refuge for a while in the Gentile territories of Tyre and Sidon, where he secretly revealed himself to them as the promised Messiah, and hinted beyond their comprehension at his coming passion, death, and resurrection.

According to Mark, he returned to Jerusalem in triumph, a week before the Passover feast, and took his last supper with his disciples. Betrayed to the authorities by one of them, Judas Iscariot, he was given a hurried trial, and condemned to death by the Sanhedrin, the Jewish religious court. Confirmation of their sentence was required from Pontius Pilate, the Roman procurator, and it was obtained on the grounds of political expediency. Jesus was crucified on the hill of Calvary early on either the Passover or the preceding day (the 'preparation of the Passover'). The year of death is uncertain, but is usually considered to be in AD 30 or 33. He was buried on the same day. The following Sunday, according to all four gospels, he appeared to his disciples who were hiding in an 'upper room', and afterwards to several other followers, among them Mary of Magdala. The history of the Christian Church begins at this point, with the Acts of the Apostles in the New Testament. Accounts of Jesus's resurrection from the dead are preserved in the gospels, the writings of St Paul, and the Acts of the Apostles; Acts and the Gospel of St John also describe Jesus's ascension into heaven.

The New Testament gospels as reliable historical sources for the life of Jesus have been subject to considerable scrutiny in modern Biblical criticism, partly in view of the differences between the gospel accounts themselves. Some scholars have been sceptical about efforts to reconstruct the life of Jesus from the Gospel sources. These have distinguished between the 'Jesus of history' and the 'Christ of faith', counting only the latter as theologically significant. Others have attached greater importance to the historical Jesus for Christian faith, and in particular have made efforts to present a credible hypothesis about the person in terms of the social, political, and cultural situation in Judaism during the early 1st-c.

>> John, St; John the Baptist, St; Joseph, St; Judas Iscariot; Luke, St; Mark, St; Mary (mother of Jesus); Matthew, St; Peter, St; Pontius Pilate

religion) to the capital, Samaria, thus earning the undying enmity of the prophet Elijah and his successors. After Ahab's death, Jezebel was the power behind the throne of her sons until the usurper Jehu seized power in an army coup. He had Jezebel thrown from a window, and trampled her to death under his chariot. >> Ahab; Elijah; Jehu

Jhabvala, Ruth [jabvahla], *née* **Prawer** (1927–) Writer, born in Cologne, Germany, of Polish parents. Her parents emigrated to Britain in 1939. She studied at London University, married a visiting Indian architect, and lived in Delhi (1951–75). Most of her fiction relates to India, taking the viewpoint of an outsider looking in. Significant novels include *To Whom She Will Marry* (1955), *The Householder* (1960), and *Heat and Dust* (1975, Booker). Later novels include *Poet and Dancer* (1993) and *Shards of Memory* (1995). In association with the film makers James Ivory and Ismail Merchant, she has written several accomplished screenplays, among them *Shakespeare Wallah* (1965, with James Ivory) and *A Room with a View* (1986, Oscar). >> Ivory; Merchant

Jhering, Rudolf von [yayring] (1818–92) Jurist, born in Aurich, Germany. He was a teacher of Roman Law at Geissen (1852–68), and at Göttingen from 1872. He founded a school of jurisprudence based on teleological principles, and wrote extensively on Roman law and legal history. He is sometimes regarded as the father of sociological jurisprudence.

Jiang Jieshi [jiang jieshee], or **Chiang Kai-shek** [chang kiy shek] (1887–1975) Revolutionary leader of 20th-c China, the effective head of the Nationalist Republic (1928–49), and head thereafter of the emigré Nationalist Party regime in Taiwan, born into a merchant family in Zhejiang. He interrupted his military education in Japan to return to China and join the Nationalist revolution. In 1918 he joined the separatist revolutionary government of Sun Yixian (Sun Yat-sen) in Canton, where he was appointed commandant of the new Whampoa Military Academy. After Sun's death (1925), he launched an expedition against the warlords and the Beijing government, entering Beijing in 1928, but fixed the Nationalist capital at Nanjing (Nanking). During the ensuing decade the Nationalist Party steadily lost support to the Communists. When Japan launched a campaign to conquer China (1937), Nationalist resistance was weak. Defeated by the Communist forces, he was forced to retreat to Taiwan (1949), where he presided over the beginnings of Taiwan's 'economic miracle'. >> Jiang Jingguo; Mao Zedong; Sun Yixian

Jiang Jingguo [jiang jinggwoh], also spelled **Chiang Ching-kuo** (1918–) Taiwanese prime minister (1972–8) and president (1978–87), born in Chekiang Province, China. The son of Jiang Jieshi, he studied in the Soviet Union during the early 1930s, returning to China with a Russian wife in 1937. After the defeat of Japan in 1945 he held a number of government posts before fleeing with his father and the defeated Kuomintang forces to Taiwan in 1949. He was defence minister (1965–72) before becoming prime minister, and succeeded to the post of Party leader on his father's death in 1975. State president in 1978, in his later years he instituted a progressive programme of political liberalization, which was continued by his successor, Lee Teng-hui. >> Jiang Jieshi; Lee Teng-hui

Jiang Qing [jiang ching], also spelled **Chiang Ch'ing** (1914–91) Chinese politician, born in Zhucheng, Shandong Province, China. She studied at Qingdao University, went to the Chinese Communist Party headquarters at Yenan to study Marxist–Leninist theory (1936), and met the Communist leader, Mao Zedong; she became his third wife in 1939. In the 1960s she began her attacks on bourgeois influences in the arts and literature, and became one of the leaders of the 'Cultural Revolution' (1966–76). She was elected to the Politburo (1969), but after Mao's death (1976) was arrested with three others – the 'Gang of Four' – imprisoned, expelled from the Communist Party, and tried in 1980 on a charge of subverting the government and wrongly arresting, detaining, and torturing numbers of innocent people. She was sentenced to death, though the sentence was later commuted. >> Mao Zedong

Jiang Zemin (1926–) Chinese president (1993–), born in Yangzhou, Jiangsu Province, China. An electrical engineer, he became commercial counsellor at the Chinese embassy in Moscow (1950–6) and during the 1960s and 1970s held a number of posts in the ministries of heavy industry and power. He was elected to the Chinese Communist Party's (CCP) central committee in 1982, and appointed Mayor of Shanghai in 1985. A cautious reformer, loyal to the Party, he was inducted into the Politburo in 1987, and following the Tiananmen Square pro-democracy massacre and the dismissal of Zhao Ziyang, was elected Party leader (1989), and chairman of the Central Military Commission (1990). He has pledged to maintain China's 'open door' economic strategy. >> Zhao Ziyang

Jikaku Daishi >> **Ennin**

Jiménez, Francisco >> **Ximénes, Cardinal**

Jiménez, Juan Ramón [himayneth] (1881–1958) Lyric poet, born in Moguer, Spain. He made his birthplace famous by his delightful story of the young poet and his donkey, *Platero y yo* (1914, Platero and I), one of the classics of modern Spanish literature. He abandoned law studies and settled in Madrid, where he began to write poetry, such as *Sonetos espirituales* (1916, Spiritual Sonnets). In 1936 he left Spain because of the Civil War, and settled in Florida. In his last period he emerged as a major poet, and was awarded the Nobel Prize for Literature in 1956.

Jimmu [jimoe] Legendary Japanese emperor, of divine descent (from Izanagi). He is supposed to have founded the Japanese imperial lineage near modern Kyoto in the Yamato plain.

Jinnah, Muhammad Ali [jina] (1876–1948) Muslim politician and founder of Pakistan, born in Karachi, India (now Pakistan). He studied in Bombay and London, was called to the bar in 1897, and practised in Bombay. He became a member of the Indian National Congress (1906) and the Muslim League (1913), and supported Hindu–Muslim unity until 1930, when he resigned from the Congress in opposition to Gandhi's policy of civil disobedience. His advocacy of a separate state for Muslims led to the creation of Pakistan in 1947, and he became its first governor-general. >> Gandhi, Mahatma

Joachim, St >> **Anne, St**

Joachim of Fiore or **Joachim of Floris** [joh]akim] (c. 1135–1202) Mystic, born in Calabria, Italy. In 1177 he became abbot of the Cistercian monastery of Corazzo, and later founded a stricter Order, the *Ordo Florensis*, which was absorbed by the Cistercians in 1505. He is known for his mystical interpretation of history, recognizing three ages of increasing spirituality: the Age of the Father (the Old Testament), the Age of the Son (the New Testament and the period to 1260), and the Age of the Spirit, a period of perfect liberty, which would emerge thereafter.

Joad, C(yril) E(dwin) M(itchinson) [johd] (1891–1953) Controversialist and popularizer of philosophy, born in Durham, Co Durham, NE England, UK. He studied at Oxford, became a civil servant (1914–30), then joined the philosophy department at Birkbeck College, London. He wrote 47 highly personal books, notably *Guide to Philosophy* (1936), and was a fashionable atheist until his last work, *Recovery of Belief* (1952). He is also remembered for his highly successful BBC Brains Trust intervention, 'It all depends what you mean by ...'.

Joan of Arc, St, Fr **Jeanne d'Arc**, known as **the Maid of Orléans** (c. 1412–31) Traditionally recognized patriot and martyr, who halted the English ascendancy in France during the Hundred Years' War, born into a peasant family in Domrémy, France. At the age of 13 she heard the voices of Sts Michael, Catherine, and Margaret bidding her rescue France from English domination. She was taken to the Dauphin, and eventually allowed to lead the army assembled for the relief of Orléans. Clad in a suit of white armour and flying her own standard, she entered Orléans (1429), forced the English to retire, and took the Dauphin to be crowned Charles VII at Reims. She then set out to relieve Compiègne, but was captured and sold to the English by John of Luxembourg. Put on trial (1431) for heresy and sorcery, she was found guilty by an English-constituted court, and burned. She was canonized in 1920. Recent historical evidence has challenged the traditional account, with the contention that Joan of Arc has been confused with Jehanne, the illegitimate daughter of Queen Isabeau of France and Louis, duc d'Orléans, brother of the king. Feast day 30 May. >> Charles VII; Dunois

Joan of Navarre, also known as **Joanna of Navarre** (c. 1370–1437) Queen consort of Henry IV of England, and stepmother of Henry V. She married first the Duke of Brittany (1386), by whom she had eight children; after his death (1399), she married Henry IV (1402), leaving her older children in Brittany. After Henry's death in 1413, her situation became difficult, because Brittany, ruled by her eldest son John, was hostile to England. She was falsely accused of witchcraft, and imprisoned for three years. >> Henry IV (of England); Henry V (of England)

Jobs, Steven [jobz] (1955–) Computer inventor and entrepreneur, born in San Francisco, CA. He studied at Reed College, Portland, before becoming a computer hobbyist. He was co-founder with ex-Hewlett-Packard engineer **Stephen Wozniak** (1950–), of the Apple Computer Co in a garage in 1976. Their brainchild, the Apple II computer (1977), the first 'open system' machine designed to encourage others to write programs and build add-on hardware for it, helped launch the personal computer, and made their company the fastest growing in US history. In 1985 he left Apple and founded a new company, NeXT Inc. >> Hewlett-Packard

Jochum, Eugen [yokhuhm] (1902–87) Conductor, born in Babenhausen, Germany. He studied in Augsburg (1914–22) and Munich (1922-4), and became musical director of the Hamburg Staatsoper and conductor of the Hamburg Philharmonic Orchestra (1934–49). In 1949 he returned to Munich, where he conducted the Bavarian Radio Symphony Orchestra.

Jodl, Alfred [yohdl] (1890–1946) German general, born in Aachen, Germany. An artillery subaltern in World War 1, he became general of artillery in 1940, the planning genius of the German High Command and Hitler's chief adviser. He was found guilty of war crimes at Nuremberg (1946), and executed. >> Hitler

Joel, Billy (1949–) Singer, songwriter, and pianist, born in Long Island, NY. He played with various bands before beginning his solo career in 1971. He earned a gold disk with the album *Piano Man* (1974), and one of his most popular singles, 'Uptown Girl' (1983), topped the UK charts for five weeks. Later albums include *Stormfront* (1989) and *River of Dreams* (1993).

Joffre, Joseph Jacques Césaire [zhofruh] (1852–1931) French general, born in Rivesaltes, France. He entered the army in 1870, and rose to be French chief-of-staff (1914) and commander-in-chief (1915), carrying out a policy of attrition against the German invaders of France. He was made a marshal of France (1916) and president of the Allied War Council (1917).

Joffrey, Robert, originally **Abdullah Jaffa Bey Kahn** (1930–88) Dancer, choreographer, teacher, and ballet director of Afghan descent, born in Seattle, WA. He studied at the School of American Ballet and New York's High School of Performing Arts, and made his debut in Roland Petit's Ballets de Paris in 1949. He choreographed his first ballet in 1952, and within a few years had formed the Joffrey Ballet, which toured America by the middle of the decade, and achieved international fame. He cultivated a young, energetic image for his company, helping to usher in the US ballet boom of the 1960s, with rock music and multi-media techniques deployed alongside revivals of contemporary classics.

Johanan ben Zakkai, Rabban [yohhanan ben zakiy] (1st-c) Prominent Jewish teacher and leader of the reformulation of Judaism after the fall of Jerusalem (AD 70), who helped to found rabbinic Judaism. His early career was apparently in Galilee, although there are also traditions of his legal disputes with the Sadducees in Jerusalem before its fall. Afterwards he was instrumental in reconstituting the Sanhedrin council in Jabneh.

Johannsen, Wilhelm Ludvig [johhansen] (1857–1927) Botanist and geneticist, born in Copenhagen. He studied in Copenhagen, Germany, and Finland, and worked at the Institute of Agriculture in Copenhagen before becoming professor of agriculture at the university there (1905). His pioneering experiments with princess beans laid the foundation for later developments in the genetics of quantitative characters. The terms *gene*, *phenotype*, and *genotype* are due to him.

Johanson, Donald (Carl) [johhanson] (1943–) Palaeoanthropologist, born in Chicago, IL. A graduate of Chicago University, he worked at the Cleveland Museum of Natural History, where he became curator in 1974. His spectacular finds of fossil hominids 3–4 million years old at Hadar in the Afar triangle of Ethiopia (1972–7) generated worldwide interest. They include 'Lucy', a unique female specimen that is half complete, and the so-called 'First Family', a scattered group containing the remains of 13 individuals. Since 1981 he has been director of the Institute of Human Origins, Berkeley, CA.

John, also known as **John Lackland** (1167–1216) King of England (1199–1216), the youngest son of Henry II, born in Oxford, Oxfordshire, SC England, UK, and one of the least popular monarchs in English history. He tried to seize the crown during Richard I's captivity in Germany (1193–4), but was forgiven and nominated successor by Richard, who thus set aside the rights of Arthur, the son of John's elder brother Geoffrey. Arthur's claims were supported by Philip II of France, and, after Arthur was murdered on John's orders (1203), Philip marched against him with superior forces, conquering all but a portion of Aquitaine (1204–5). In 1206 John refused to receive Stephen Langton as Archbishop of Canterbury, and in 1208 his kingdom was placed under papal interdict. He was then excommunicated (1209), and finally conceded (1213). His oppressive government, and failure to recover Normandy, provoked baronial opposition, which led to demands for constitutional reform. The barons met the king at Runnymede, and forced him to grant the Great Charter (Magna Carta) (Jun 1215), the basis of the English constitution. His repudiation of the Charter precipitated the first Barons' War (1215–17). >> Arthur, Prince; Isabella of Angoulême; Langton, Stephen; Richard I; Walter, Hubert; RR1095

John II, known as **John the Good** (1319–64) King of France (1350–64), the son of Philip VI, born near Le Mans, France. In 1356 he was taken prisoner by Edward the Black Prince at the Battle of Poitiers, and brought to England. After the treaty of Brétigny (1360) he returned home, leaving his second son, the Duke of Anjou, as a hostage. When the duke broke his parole and escaped (1363), John chivalrously returned to London, and died there.

John, St, also known as **John, son of Zebedee** and **John the Evangelist** (1st-c) One of the 12 apostles, the son of Zebedee, and the younger brother of James, a Galilean fisherman. He was one of the inner circle of disciples who were with Jesus at the Transfiguration and Gethsemane. Acts and Galatians also name him as one of the 'pillars' of the early Jerusalem Church. Some traditions represent him as having been slain by the Jews or Herod Agrippa I; but from the 2nd-c he was said to have spent his closing years at Ephesus, dying there at an advanced age, after having written the Apocalypse, the Gospel, and the three Epistles which bear his name (though his authorship of these works has been disputed by modern scholars). Feast day 27 December. >> Herod Agrippa I; James, St (son of Zebedee); Jesus Christ

John, St, Chrysostom >> **Chrysostom, St John**

John XXII, originally **Jacques Duèse** (c.1249–1334) Pope (1316–34), one of the most celebrated of the popes of Avignon, born in Cahors, France. He intervened in the contest for the imperial crown between Louis of Bavaria and Frederick of Austria, supporting the latter. A long contest ensued both in Germany and Italy between the Guelph (papal) party and the Ghibelline (imperial) party. In 1327 Louis entered Italy, was crowned emperor at Rome, and deposed the pope, setting up an anti-pope (1328). Although Guelphic predominance at Rome was later restored, John died at Avignon.

John XXIII, originally **Angelo Giuseppe Roncalli** (1881–1963) Pope (1958–63), born in Sotto il Monte, Italy. He was ordained in 1904, served as a chaplain in World War 1, and was subsequently apostolic delegate to Bulgaria, Turkey, and Greece. Patriarch of Venice in 1953, he was elected pope in 1958 on the 12th ballot. He convened the Second Vatican Council to renew the religious life of the Church and to modernize its teachings, disciplines, and organization, with the aim of eventual unity of all Christians.

John, Augustus (Edwin) (1878–1961) Painter, born in Tenby, Pembrokeshire, SW Wales, UK. He studied in London and Paris, and made an early reputation with his etchings (1900–14). His favourite themes were gypsies, fishing folk, and naturally regal women, as in 'Lyric Fantasy' (1913); and he painted portraits of several political and artistic contemporary figures, such as Shaw, Hardy, and Dylan Thomas. >> John, Gwen

John, Barry (1945–) Rugby union player, born in Cefneithin, Carmarthenshire, SW Wales. One of the greatest outside-halves that Wales has ever produced, he played 25 times for his country, scoring a record 90 points, before retiring at the early age of 27. A devastating player with Llanelli and Cardiff at club level, his elusiveness and skill at dropping goals made him equally effective at international level. On the Lions tour of New Zealand in 1971 he scored 180 points.

John, Sir Elton (Hercules), originally **Reginald Kenneth Dwight** (1947–) Rock singer and pianist, born in Pinner, NW Greater London, England, UK. He played the piano by ear from age four, and studied at the Royal Academy of Music at 11. From 1967, he and Bernie Taupin began writing songs such as 'Rocket Man' (1972) and 'Goodbye Yellow Brick Road' (1973). Their publisher pressed John to perform them, for which he obscured his short, plump, myopic physique in a clownish garb that included huge glasses, sequinned and fringed jump suits, and ermine boots. The top pop star of the 1970s, he later became chairman (1976–90) and then honorary life president (1990–) of the Watford Football Club and a stock-market speculator. Despite health problems in 1993 he continues to perform live across the world. His recording of 'Candle in the Wind '97', sung at the funeral of Princess Diana, became the largest-selling single in history, within a month of its release. He was knighted in 1998. >> Diana, Princess of Wales

John, Gwen (1876–1939) Painter, born in Haverfordwest, Pembrokeshire, SW Wales, the elder sister of Augustus John. She studied at the Slade School, London, before moving to Paris (1904), where she worked as an artist's model, becoming Rodin's mistress c.1906. After converting to Roman Catholicism in 1913 she lived at Meudon, where she became increasingly religious and reclusive. She exhibited with the New English Art Club (1900–11), and her work was included in the Armory Show of 1913. >> John, Augustus; Rodin

John, Otto [yohn] (1909–97) West German ex-security chief, the defendant in a major postwar treason case. In 1944 he was part of the plot against Hitler, after which he escaped to Britain. In 1950 he was appointed to the West German Office for the protection of the constitution. In 1954 he mysteriously disappeared from West Berlin, and later broadcast for the East German Communists. In 1956 he returned to the West, was arrested, tried, and imprisoned. His defence was that he had been drugged, driven to the Communist sector, held prisoner, and forced to make broadcasts until he managed to escape. Released in 1958, he continued to protest his innocence.

John of Austria, Don, Span **Don Juan** (1547–78) Spanish soldier, the illegitimate son of Emperor Charles V, born in Regensburg, Germany. He defeated the Moors in Granada (1570) and the Turks at Lepanto (1571). In 1573 he took Tunis, and was then sent to Milan and (1576) to Holland as viceroy. He planned to marry Mary, Queen of Scots, but died of typhoid at Namur. >> Charles V (Emperor)

John of Beverley, St (?–721) Monk, born in Harpham, East Riding, NE England, UK. After studying at Canterbury, he became a monk at St Hilda's monastery for nuns and monks at Whitby, North Yorkshire. He became Bishop of Hexham (687–705) and Bishop of York (705–17), before retiring to the monastery of Beverley, which he had founded. During his ministry he took an especial interest in the poor and disabled. Feast day 7 May.

John of Capistrano, St [kapis**trah**noh], Ital **Giovanni da Capistrano** (1386–1456) Monk, born in Capistrano, Italy. He studied law and became Governor of Perugia (1412), but was imprisoned after a civil quarrel. After his release (1416) he entered the Franciscan order, and became a famous preacher and promoter of education. In 1451 he was sent to Austria by Pope Nicholas V to counter the teachings of the followers of John Huss. When Belgrade was besieged by Mohammed II in 1456, he helped raise and lead an army to defeat the Turks, but died of the plague while returning from this crusade. He was canonized in 1690; feast day 28 March. >> Hunyady; Huss; Mohammed II

John of Damascus, St, also called **St John Damascene** (c. 675–c. 749) Theologian and hymn writer of the Eastern Church, born in Damascus. He was educated by the Italian monk, Cosmas, and defended the use of images in church worship during the iconoclastic controversy. His later years were spent in a monastery near Jerusalem, where he was ordained. Feast day 4 December.

John of Gaunt (1340–99) Duke of Lancaster, born in Ghent, Belgium, the fourth son of Edward III, and ancestor of Henry IV, V, and VI. In 1359 he married his cousin, **Blanche of Lancaster**, and was created duke in 1362. After her death (1369), he married **Constance**, the daughter of Pedro the Cruel of Castile, and assumed the title of King of Castile, though he failed by his expeditions to oust his rival, Henry of Trastamare. In England he became highly influential as a peacemaker during the troubled reign of Richard II. He was made Duke of Aquitaine by Richard (1390), and sent on several embassies to France. On his second wife's death (1394) he married his mistress, **Catherine Swynford**, by whom he had three sons; from the eldest descended Henry VII. >> Richard II; RR1095

John of Leyden (1509–36) Anabaptist leader, born in Leyden, The Netherlands. He worked as a tailor, merchant, and innkeeper, and became noted as an orator. Turning Anabaptist, he went to Münster, became head of the movement, and set up a 'kingdom of Zion', with polygamy and community of goods. In 1535 the city was taken by the Bishop of Münster, and John and his accomplices were executed.

John of Nepomuk, St (c. 1330–93) Patron saint of Bohemia, born in Nepomuk, Czech Republic. He studied at Prague, and became confessor to Sophia, the wife of Wenceslaus IV (ruled 1378–1419). For refusing to betray the confession of the queen, he was tortured and drowned. He was canonized in 1729; feast day 16 May.

John of Salisbury [**sawlz**bree] (c. 1115–80) Clergyman and scholar, born in Salisbury, Wiltshire, S England, UK. Educated in Paris under Abelard, he was a clerk to Pope Eugenius III and to Archbishop Theobald at Canterbury, but fell into disfavour with Henry II and retired to Reims, where he wrote *Historia pontificalis* (c.1163). He returned to

England and witnessed Thomas à Becket's murder in Canterbury. He became Bishop of Chartres (1176) and took part in the third Lateran Council (1179). A learned classical writer, he also wrote lives of Becket and Anselm. >> Becket; Henry II (of England); Theobald

John of Trevisa (1326–1412) English translator, born in Cornwall, SW England, UK. A fellow of Exeter and Queen's Colleges, Oxford, he became vicar of Berkeley, and canon of Westbury (probably Westbury-on-Trym). He is known for his translations of Higden, Glanville, and Bartholomaeus Anglicus. >> Higden

John of the Cross, St, originally **Juan de Yepes y Álvarez** (1542–91) Christian mystic and poet, the founder with St Teresa of the Discalced Carmelites, born in Fontiveros, Spain. He became a Carmelite monk in 1563, and was ordained in 1567. Imprisoned at Toledo (1577), he wrote a number of poems, such as *Canto espiritual* (Spiritual Canticle), which are highly regarded in Spanish mystical literature. After escaping, he became vicar-provincial of Andalusia (1585–7), and died in seclusion at the monastery of Úbeda. He was canonized in 1726; feast day 14 December. >> Teresa of Avila

John the Baptist, St (1st-c) Prophetic and ascetic figure referred to in the New Testament Gospels and in Josephus's *Antiquities*, the son of a priest named Zechariah; roughly contemporary with Jesus of Nazareth. A story of his birth to Elizabeth, the cousin of Mary the mother of Jesus, is recorded in *Luke* 1. He baptized Jesus and others at the R Jordan, but his baptism seemed mainly to symbolize a warning of the coming judgment of God and the consequent need for repentance. He was executed by Herod Antipas, but the circumstances differ in the accounts of Josephus and the Gospels. He is treated in the New Testament as the forerunner of Christ, and sometimes as a returned Elijah (*Matt* 11.13–14). Feast day 24 June. >> Herod Antipas; Jesus Christ; Josephus

John the Scot >> **Erigena, John Scotus**

John Damascene >> **John of Damascus**

John Paul I, originally **Albino Luciani** (1912–78) Pope (Aug–Sep 1978), born in Forno di Canale, Italy. He studied at the Gregorian University in Rome, and was ordained in 1935. He became a parish priest and teacher in Belluno, vicar-general of the diocese of Vittorio Veneto (1954), a bishop (1958), patriarch of Venice (1969), and a cardinal (1973). He was the first pope to use a double name (from his two immediate predecessors, John XXIII and Paul VI). He died only 33 days later, the shortest pontificate of modern times.

John Paul II, originally **Karol Jozef Wojtyla** (1920–) Pope (1978–), born in Wadowice, Poland, the first non-Italian pope in 450 years. He studied in Poland, was ordained in 1946, and became professor of moral theology at Lublin and Cracow. Archbishop and Metropolitan of Cracow (1964–78), he was created cardinal in 1967. Noted for his energy and analytical ability, his pontificate has seen many foreign visits, in which he has preached to huge audiences. In 1981 he survived an assassination attempt, when he was shot in St Peter's square by a Turkish national, Mehmet Ali Agca, the motives for which have remained unclear. A champion of economic justice and an outspoken defender of the Church in Communist countries, he has been uncompromising on moral issues.

Johns, Jasper (1930–) Painter, sculptor, and print-maker, born in Augusta, GA. He studied at the University of South Carolina, became a painter in New York City in 1952, and was attracted by the Dadaist ideas of Marcel Duchamp. Because conventional art critics placed so much emphasis on 'self expression' and 'originality', he chose to paint flags, targets, maps, and other pre-existing images in a style deliberately clumsy and banal. He was one of the creators of Pop Art. >> Duchamp

Johns, W(illiam) E(arl) (1893–1968) Writer, author of the 'Biggles' stories, born in Hertford, Hertfordshire, SE England, UK. He trained as a surveyor before serving in the Norfolk Yeomanry (1914). He transferred to the Royal Flying Corps, and was shot down and imprisoned; he then escaped, but was recaptured. He retired from the Royal Air Force in 1930, and edited *Popular Flying*, where he first wrote his stories featuring Captain James Bigglesworth ('Biggles'). He went on to write over 70 novels, many of which are still in print.

Johns Hopkins >> **Hopkins, Johns**

Johnson, Alexander Bryan (1786–1867) Philosopher, born in Gosport, Hampshire, S England, UK. He settled in Utica, NY, in 1801, where he enjoyed a successful career in business. He published three philosophical works, *The Philosophy of Human Knowledge* (1828), *A Treatise on Language: or the relation which Words bear to Things* (1836), and *The Meaning of Words* (1854), which can now be seen to anticipate views familiar to the logical positivists and linguistic philosophers of the 20th-c. He also published works on politics, economics, and banking.

Johnson, Amy (1903–41) Pioneer aviator, born in Hull, NE England, UK. She flew solo from England to Australia (1930), to Japan via Siberia (1931), and to Cape Town (1932), making new records in each case. A pilot in Air Transport Auxiliary in World War 2, she was drowned after bailing out over the Thames estuary. >> Mollison

Johnson, Andrew (1808–75) US statesman and 17th president (1865–9), born in Raleigh, NC. With little formal schooling, he became alderman and mayor in Greenville, TN, and a member of the Legislature (1835), State Senate (1841), and Congress (1843). He was made Governor of Tennessee in 1853, and a senator in 1857. During the Civil War he became military governor of Tennessee (1862), US vice-president (1865), and president on Lincoln's assassination (1865). A Democrat, his conciliatory policies were opposed by Congress, who wished to keep the Southern states under military government. He vetoed the congressional measures, was impeached, brought to trial, and acquitted. >> Lincoln, Abraham; Stanton, Edwin; Stevens, Thaddeus; RR1097

Johnson, Ben (1961–) Athlete, born in Falmouth, Jamaica. He moved to Canada in 1976, and in the middle 1980s was the world's fastest sprinter, with Carl Lewis. He was unbeaten in 21 consecutive starts over 100 m, and at the 1988 Seoul Olympics set a new world 100-m record, but was immediately deprived of his gold medal for having taken banned substances in preparation for the Games. >> Lewis, Carl

Johnson, Dame Celia (1908–82) Actress, born in Richmond, SW Greater London, England, UK. Well-established on the stage, she had leading roles in Noel Coward's wartime films *In Which We Serve* (1942) and *This Happy Breed* (1944), and is best remembered for her performance in *Brief Encounter* (1945). Her later film appearances were infrequent, among them *The Prime of Miss Jean Brodie* (1968), but she continued in the theatre and on television until very shortly before her death.

Johnson, Clarence (Leonard), known as **Kelly Johnson** (1910–90) Aircraft designer, born in Ishpeming, MI. He studied aeronautical engineering at the University of Michigan, and went to work for Lockheed Corporation in 1933. Beginning as a tool designer, he held positions as flight test engineer and stress analyst before becoming chief research engineer in 1938. He was involved in designing over 40 aircraft, including the U-2 high-altitude reconnaissance plane, the F-104 Starfighter, and the P-38 Lightning plane, used during World War 2. During his years at Lockheed he was best known for his leadership of the 'Skunk Works', the company's advanced development unit. Awarded the Medal of Freedom in 1964, he retired in 1975, but remained a senior adviser to Lockheed until his death.

Johnson, Eyvind (1900–76) Writer, born near Boden, Sweden. After minimal schooling, and a number of years in mainly manual occupations, he spent most of the 1920s in Paris and Berlin, and began to write. His four-part *Romanen om Olof* (1934–7, The Story of Olof) is the finest of the many working-class autobiographical novels written in Sweden in the 1930s. He was much involved in anti-Nazi causes, and produced a number of novels, especially the *Krilon* series (1941–3), castigating totalitarianism. The same humanitarian values are evident in his later historical novels, particularly *Strändernas Svall* (1946, trans Return to Ithaca), and *Hans Nådes Tid* (1960, trans The Days of his Grace). He shared the 1974 Nobel Prize for Literature with his fellow Swede, Harry Martinson. >> Martinson

Johnson, Hewlett, nickname **the Red Dean** (1874–1966) Clergyman, born in Macclesfield, Cheshire, NWC England, UK. He studied at the universities of Manchester and Oxford, became an engineering apprentice, and did welfare work in the Manchester slums. He joined the Independent Labour Party, entered the Church, and was ordained in 1905. He became dean of Manchester (1924) and dean of Canterbury (1931–63). In 1938 he visited Russia, and became an untiring champion of the Communist state and Marxist policies, which involved him in continuous and vigorous controversy in Britain. He received the Stalin Peace Prize in 1951. His publications include *Christians and Communism* (1956) and the autobiographical *Searching for Light* (1968).

Johnson, Howard (Deering) (1896–1972) Business executive, born in Boston, MA. Uneducated beyond elementary school, he developed 28 flavours of ice-cream for his Wollaston, MA, drugstore soda fountain, and by 1929 was franchising his name and products. He won exclusive catering rights on thousands of miles of East Coast highways, and built the country's largest private food distribution corporation before retiring in 1959.

Johnson, J J, popular name of **James Louis Johnson** (1924–) Jazz trombonist and composer, born in Indianapolis, IN. He took up the trombone at 14 after studying the piano. While working professionally in New York City in the 1940s, he was inspired by the bebop movement; his recordings of the period with Charlie Parker and others show him to be the first slide trombonist to answer the demands of the style for speed, articulation, and harmonic sophistication. From the 1960s he worked largely as a composer for films and televison, but his playing continues to influence modern jazz trombonists. >> Parker, Charlie

Johnson, Jack, popular name of **John Arthur Jackson**, also called **Li'l Arthur** (1878–1946) Boxer, the first African-American world champion (1908–15), born in Galveston, TX. He defeated the Canadian Tommy Burns at Sydney in 1908. His win provoked violent racial prejudice, and a 'Great White Hope' was sought to defeat him – the former champion James J Jeffries – whom he knocked out in the 15th round in a fight in 1910. He lost his title in 1915 to Jess Willard. His relationship with one of the two white women he married led to a conviction under the Mann Act for transporting a white woman across state lines for immoral purposes, and he was a fugitive in Europe for seven years. He died in a car accident, and his life became the subject of a Broadway play, *The Great White Hope* (1968). >> Jeffries, James J

Johnson, James P(rice) (1894–1955) Jazz pianist and composer, born in New Brunswick, NJ. He was given rudimentary piano instruction by his mother, and while still at

school played ragtime with other performers. In 1912 he began a series of piano-playing jobs in cabarets, moviehouses, and dance-halls, eventually becoming the most accomplished player in the post-ragtime 'stride' style. A prolific performer in the 1920s and during the traditional jazz revival of the 1940s, he wrote more than 200 songs (including 'The Charleston') as well as several stage shows, and was a strong influence on such later pianists as Fats Waller and Art Tatum. >> Tatum, Art; Waller

Johnson, James Weldon (1871–1938) Writer and diplomat, born in Jacksonville, FL. He practised at the bar there (1897–1901), and in 1906 was US consul at Puerto Cabello, Venezuela, and at Corinto, Nicaragua (1909–12). He was secretary of the National Association for the Advancement of Colored People (1916–30), and from 1930 was professor of creative literature at Fisk University. He wrote extensively on African-American problems, and compiled collections of African-American poetry.

Johnson, Lyndon B(aines), also known as **LBJ** (1908–73) US statesman and 36th president (1963–9), born in Stonewall, TX. He studied at Southwest Texas State Teachers College, and became a teacher and congressman's secretary before being elected a Democrat representative in 1937. He became a senator in 1948, and an effective leader of the Democratic majority. Vice-president under Kennedy in 1960, he was made president after Kennedy's assassination, and was returned to the post in 1964 with a huge majority. His administration passed the Civil Rights Act (1964) and the Voting Rights Act (1965), which helped the position of African-Americans in US society. However, the escalation of the war in Vietnam led to active protest and growing unpopularity, and after 1969 he retired from active politics. >> McCarthy, Eugene J; RR1097

Johnson, Magic, popular name of **Earvin Johnson** (1959–) Basketball player, born in Lansing, MI. Named the National Basketball Association's Most Valuable Player in 1979, he was a member of NBA championship teams in 1980, 1982, 1985, 1987, and 1988. With the Los Angeles Lakers from 1979, he retired in 1991. His autobiography was called, simply, *Magic* (1983). In 1992 his book *What You Can Do to Avoid AIDS* generated controversy when two of the largest US retailers refused to carry it. >> RR1146

Johnson, Martin W(iggo) (1893–1984) Oceanographer, born in Chandler, SD. He was an associate of the University of Washington (1933–4) before joining the Scripps Institution of Oceanography (1934–61). He made major contributions to biological and military science by investigating invertebrate-produced underwater sounds and acoustic signal reflections.

Johnson, Pamela Hansford (1912–81) Writer, born in London, England, UK. Best known for her portrayal of her native postwar London, her books include *An Avenue of Stone* (1947), *The Unspeakable Skipton* (1958), *A Bonfire* (1981), and several works of nonfiction, such as her study of the Moors murders, *On Iniquity* (1967). In 1950 she married the novelist C P Snow. >> Snow, C P

Johnson, Philip C(ortelyou) (1906–) Architect and theorist, born in Cleveland, OH. A graduate of Harvard, he also studied under Marcel Breuer, and became a proponent of the International Style. He designed his own home, the Glass House, New Canaan, CT (1949–50), on principles of space unification derived from Ludwig Mies van der Rohe, with whom he designed the Seagram Building skyscraper, New York City (1945). Further works include the Amon Carter Museum of Western Art, TX (1961), the New York State Theater, Lincoln Center (1964), and the American Telephone and Telegraph Company building in New York City (1978–84). >> Breuer; Mies van der Rohe

Johnson, Richard M(entor) (1780–1850) Vice-president of the USA (1837–41), born near Louisville, KY. He became a lawyer, and was elected a member of the US House of Representatives (1807–19, 1829–37), the intervening years being spent in the US Senate. He became Democratic vice-president to Martin Van Buren after the elections had not thrown up a majority in the electoral college for any one candidate. >> Van Buren

Johnson, Robert U >> **Muir, John**

Johnson, Samuel, known as **Dr Johnson** (1709–84) Lexicographer, critic, and poet, born in Lichfield, Staffordshire, C England, UK. The son of a bookseller, he studied at Lichfield and Oxford, but left before taking a degree, and became a teacher. In 1737 he went to London, and worked as a journalist. From 1747 he worked for eight years on his *Dictionary of the English Language*, started the moralistic periodical, *The Rambler* (1750), and wrote his prose tale of Abyssinia, *Rasselas* (1759). In 1762 he was given a crown pension, which enabled him to figure as arbiter of letters and social personality, notably in the Literary Club, of which he was a founder member (1764). In 1765 he produced his edition of Shakespeare, from 1772 engaged in political pamphleteering, in 1773 went with Boswell on a tour of Scotland, and later wrote *Lives of the Poets* (1779–81). His reputation as a man and conversationalist outweighs his literary reputation, and for the picture of Johnson in society we are indebted above all to Boswell. >> Boswell; Piozzi

Johnson, Uwe (1934–84) Writer, born in Pomerania (now part of Poland). He studied at Rostock and Leipzig, and left East for West Germany after completing his first novel, *Mutmassungen über Jakob* (Speculations about Jakob) in 1959. His second and third novels, *Das dritte Buch über Achim* (1961, The Third Book about Achim), and *Zwei Ansichten* (1965, Two Views), develop the theme of the relation between the two Germanies. He later moved to university posts in the USA, and then to England, but published no fiction after 1965.

Johnson, Virginia E >> **Masters and Johnson**

Johnson, Walter (Perry), nickname **the Big Train** (1887–1946) Baseball pitcher, born in Humboldt, KN. During his 21-year career with the Washington Senators (1907–27) he won 416 games, the second highest in major league history, and pitched 110 shutouts, a major league record. One of the fastest throwers in the game's history, the right-hander led the league in strikeouts 12 times. He was elected to baseball's Hall of Fame in 1936.

Johnson, Sir William (1715–74) Merchant and colonial administrator, born in Co Meath, Ireland. In 1737 he emigrated to America, and became a fur trader in the Mohawk Valley. By his fairness he acquired great influence with the Indians, married two Indian women, and in the Anglo-French Wars often led the Six Iroquois Nations against the French, notably at Lake George, NY (1755). He was appointed superintendent of Northern Indian Affairs (1756–64). In 1759 he captured Fort Niagara, and in 1760 took part in Amherst's victory against Montreal. >> Amherst, Jeffrey

Johnson, William Eugene, nickname **Pussyfoot** (1862–1945) Reformer and temperance propagandist, born in Coventry, NY. He became a journalist, and later a special officer in the US Indian Service (1908–11), where he received his nickname from his methods of raiding gambling saloons in Indian Territory. He was prominent during the prohibitionist movement in the USA, and lectured for the cause all over Europe. In 1919 he lost an eye when he was struck and dragged from a lecture platform in London by medical students.

Johnson, William H (1901–70) Painter, born in Florence, SC. He went to Harlem at age 17, and for five years studied painting at the National Academy of Design. He then lived mainly in Denmark (he had married a Danish weaver and potter, **Holcha Krake**, in 1930) and Norway, returning to New York City in 1938. In 1943 they lost everything in a fire, then his wife died, and by 1947 he was placed in a mental institution. Virtually all his surviving output (some 800 paintings and watercolours and 400 drawings and prints) was given to the National Museum of American Art in 1967. It is becoming recognized for its original fusion of such disparate influences as van Gogh and African sculpture, Constructivism and African textiles. >> van Gogh

Johnston, Albert Sidney (1803–62) Confederate general, born in Washington, KY. He trained at West Point, joined the Army of Texas, became its head, and in 1838 was appointed secretary of Texas. He served in the Mexican War, and commanded in Utah and on the Pacific (1857–9). In 1861 he resigned to fight for the Confederacy in the Civil War. Appointed to the command of Kentucky and Tennessee, he fortified Bowling Green, retreated to Corinth, and attacked Grant at Shiloh (1862). The Union army was surprised, and the advantage lay with the Confederates until he was mortally wounded. >> Grant, Ulysses S

Johnston, Brian (Alexander) (1912–94) British broadcaster and commentator. He studied at Oxford, and worked in the family coffee business (1934–9), before joining the BBC in 1945. He specialized in cricket commentary on radio and TV, and became a respected commentator on state occasions, such as the royal weddings. He also presented the touring programme *Down Your Way* (1972–87). He wrote many light-hearted books about cricket, including *It's a Funny Game...* (1978).

Johnston, Bruce >> **Beach Boys, The**

Johnston, (William) Denis (1901–84) Playwright, born in Dublin. He studied at Cambridge and Harvard, and was called to the bar in England (1925) and Northern Ireland (1926). His first play, an Expressionistic satire called *Shadowdance*, was rejected by Lady Gregory for the Abbey Theatre. Retitled *The Old Lady Says 'No'*, it became a major success at the Gate Theatre in 1929. He had a further triumph with *The Moon on the Yellow River* (1931) and several other plays over the next three decades. His autobiographical *Nine Rivers from Jordan* (1953) recounted his experiences as a war correspondent.

Johnston, Edward (1872–1944) Calligrapher, born in Uruguay of Scottish parents. He studied at Edinburgh. Instead of practising medicine, for which he had trained, he taught himself the art of lettering, and began to teach others. He taught at the Central School of Fine Arts and Crafts, London (1899–1913), where one of his students was Eric Gill; he also taught at the Royal College of Art. His books, *Writing and Illuminating, and Lettering* (1906) and *Manuscript and Inscription Letters* (1909), were landmarks in the revival and development of calligraphy. >> Gill

Johnston, George Henry, pseudonym **Shane Martin** (1912–70) Writer and journalist, born in Melbourne, Victoria, Australia. He studied at the National Gallery Arts School, Melbourne, worked as a journalist, and became a war correspondent during World War 2, where he gathered much source material. Returning to journalism after the war, he worked in London before making a new home on the Greek island of Hydra, where he wrote several books. He is best known for his semi-autobiographical trilogy *My Brother Jack* (1964), *Clean Straw for Nothing* (1969), and the unfinished *A Cartload of Clay* (1971). He wrote a great deal in collaboration with his wife, **Charmian Clift** (1923–69).

Johnston, Sir Harry Hamilton (1858–1927) Explorer and writer, born in London, England, UK. He spent much of his life travelling in Africa, and learned many African languages. He led the Royal Society's botanical expedition to Kilimanjaro (1884), and as commissioner for South Central Africa made possible British acquisition of Northern Rhodesia and Nyasaland. He wrote books on the Congo and zoology, five novels, and *The Story of My Life* (1923).

Johnston, Joseph E(ggleston) (1807–91) Confederate general, born near Farmville, VA. He trained at West Point, fought in the Seminole and Mexican Wars, and in 1860 was made quartermaster-general. At the outbreak of the Civil War, he resigned to enter the Confederate service, and as brigadier-general took command of the army of the Shenandoah. He supported Beauregard at the first Battle of Bull Run (1861), but after the fall of Vicksburg he was criticised by Jefferson Davis for failing to stem the Union advance, and relieved of his command (1864). Restored in 1865, he surrendered to Sherman. He was elected to Congress in 1877, and was US commissioner of railroads (1885). >> Beauregard; Davis, Jefferson; Sherman, William Tecumseh

Johnstone, William (1897–1981) Painter, born in Denholm, Scottish Borders, SE Scotland, UK. He studied at Edinburgh College of Art and subsequently in Paris. His work in the late 1920s and 1930s shows the influence of Surrealism in its use of rounded semi-abstract images suggestive of dream-like landscapes and human forms. He held a series of teaching posts in London, latterly as principal of the Central School of Arts and Crafts (1947–60).

Joinville, Jean, sieur de (Lord of) [zhwĩveel] (c. 1224–1317) Historian, born in Joinville, France. He became seneschal to the Count of Champagne and King of Navarre, took part in the unfortunate Seventh Crusade (1248–54) of Louis IX, returned with him to France, and lived partly at court, partly on his estates. While imprisoned at Acre with Louis, he composed a Christian manual, his *Credo* (1250). Throughout the Crusade he took notes of events and wrote down his impressions which he fashioned, at the age of almost 80, into his delightful *Histoire de Saint Louis* (1309). >> Louis IX

Joliot-Curie, (Jean) Frédéric [zholyoh küree], originally **Jean Frédéric Joliot** (1900–58) Physical chemist, born in Paris. He studied at the Sorbonne, where in 1925 he became assistant to Marie Curie, and in 1926 married her daughter Irène, with whom he shared the 1935 Nobel Prize for Chemistry. Professor at the Collège de France (1937), he became a strong supporter of the Resistance movement during World War 2, and a member of the Communist Party. After the liberation he became high commissioner for atomic energy (1946–50), a position from which he was dismissed for his political activities. President of the Communist-sponsored World Peace Council, he was awarded the Stalin Peace Prize in 1951. >> Curie; Joliot-Curie, Irène

Joliot-Curie, Irène [zholioh kyooree], née **Curie** (1897–1956) Physical chemist, born in Paris, the daughter of Pierre and Marie Curie. She studied at the Collège Sévigné, and worked as her mother's assistant at the Institut du Radium in Paris. There she met her future husband Frédéric Joliot, with whom she discovered artificial radioactivity in 1934, a major step on the road to nuclear energy. A strong Socialist and an outspoken anti-Fascist, she was under-secretary of state for scientific research in the Popular Front government (1936). She became director of the Institut du Radium (1946–50), and shared with her husband the Nobel Prize for Chemistry in 1935. >> Curie; Joliot-Curie, Frédéric

Jolley, (Monica) Elizabeth (1923–) Writer, born in Birmingham, West Midlands, C England, UK. She was educated at a Quaker boarding school in Birmingham, moved to Perth, Western Australia in 1959, and has lived there ever since, working in a variety of occupations as a nurse, orchardist, and teacher. Her first book was a volume of short stories, *Five Acre Virgin and Other Stories* (1976), which she followed with *Mr Scobie's Riddle* (1982, Age Book of the Year Award), *Miss Peabody's Inheritance* (1983), *The Well* (1986), *My Father's Moon* (1989), and *Cabin Fever* (1990). She has an eye for eccentric, incongruous, and ridiculous characters and situations, but the underlying moral tone is serious and can be disturbing.

Jolson, Al [johlson], originally **Asa Yoelson** (1886–1950) Actor and singer, born in Srednike, Russia. Brought to the USA in 1893, he made his stage debut in 1899, and with his brother toured with circus and minstrel shows. His sentimental songs, such as 'Mammy', 'Sonny Boy', and 'Swanee', delivered on one knee, arms outstretched, brought tears to the eyes of vaudeville audiences in the 1920s. He called himself 'the World's Greatest Entertainer'. In 1927, he starred in *The Jazz Singer*, the first motion picture with sound. Years after his popularity waned, his career revived briefly with the release of the films *The Jolson Story* (1946) and *Jolson Sings Again* (1949).

Joly, John [johlee] (1857–1933) Geologist and physicist, born in Holywood, Co Down. He studied at Trinity College, Dublin, where he became professor of geology and mineralogy in 1897. He invented a photometer in 1888, calculated the age of the Earth (as 100 million years) by measuring the sodium content of the sea, and formulated the theory of thermal cycles based on the radioactive elements in the Earth's crust. With Walter Stevenson he evolved the 'Dublin method' in radiotherapy, and pioneered colour photography, and the radium treatment of cancer. He became a fellow of the Royal Society in 1892.

Jomini, (Antoine) Henri, Baron de [zhomeenee] (1779–1869) French general and writer, born in Payerne, Switzerland. He served as a volunteer in the French army (1798–1800), returned to civilian life, and wrote *Treatise on Grand Military Operations* (1804, trans title). Rejoining the army in 1804, he rose to become chief-of-staff to Marshal Ney (1813), but quit after unjust treatment by a senior officer and joined the Russian army as aide-de-camp to Alexander I (1813) and Nicholas I (1826). He wrote a great history of the wars of the Revolution (1806), a life of Napoleon (1827), and *Summary of the Art of War* (1838, trans title). >> Alexander I (of Russia); Ney; Nicholas I (of Russia)

Jonathan (c. 11th-c BC) Biblical character, the son and heir of Saul (the first king of Israel) and loyal friend of David. He is portrayed in 1 Samuel as a cunning soldier, but he faced conflicting loyalties when he continued his friendship with David in spite of Saul's mounting hostility to David. David succeeded Saul as King of Israel, since Jonathan was killed in the Battle of Gilboa against the Philistines. >> David; Saul

Jones, Allen (1937–) Painter, sculptor, and printmaker, born in Southampton, Hampshire, S England, UK. He studied at Hornsey Art School and at the Royal College of Art. An early Pop artist, he specialized in slick, fetishistic images (high-heeled shoes, stockings, etc) taken from pornographic or glossy fashion magazines.

Jones, Bob, popular name of **Robert Reynolds Jones** (1883–1968) Evangelist, born in Dale County, AL. He conducted revival meetings from the age of 13, and was licensed by the Methodist Church to preach at 15. He studied at Southern University, Greensboro, SC, and began full-time evangelistic work in 1902. To further his brand of fundamentalism, in 1927 he founded Bob Jones University, which from small beginnings in Florida eventually (1947) settled in Greenville, SC, with several thousand students.

Jones, Bobby, popular name of **Robert (Tyre) Jones** (1902–71) Golfer, born in Atlanta, GA. A practising lawyer, he was an amateur golfer throughout his career, winning the (British) Open three times (1926–7, 1930) and the US Open four times (1923, 1926, 1929–30). He also won the US Amateur title five times and the British Amateur title once. In 1930 he took the Amateur and Open titles of both countries, the game's greatest Grand Slam. He was responsible for the founding of the US Masters at Augusta, GA. >> RR1158

Jones, Chuck, popular name of **Charles Jones** (1912–) Animated cartoon director, born in Spokane, WA. His early work included *Daffy and the Dinosaur* (1939), Wile E Coyote, and the Road Runner (*Fast and Furry-ous*, 1949). Pepe le Pew, the amorous skunk, won him his first Oscar with *For Scentimental Reasons* (1951). His Bugs Bunny cartoons include the classic *What's Opera Doc* (1957) and the stereoscopic *Lumber Jack Rabbit* (1954). He won another Oscar with *The Dot and the Line* (1965). For television he created many specials including Kipling's *Rikki-Tikki-Tavi*, winning another Oscar for *A Christmas Carol* (1972).

Jones, Daniel (1881–1967) Phonetician, born in London, England, UK. He was called to the bar in 1907, when he was also appointed lecturer in phonetics at University College, London (professor 1921–49). He collaborated with others in compiling Cantonese (1912), Sechuana (1916), and Sinhalese (1919) phonetic readers. He wrote *An Outline of English Phonetics* (1916), and compiled an *English Pronouncing Dictionary* (1917, 14th edn 1977). His other works included *The Phoneme* (1950), and *Cardinal Vowels* (1956). He was secretary (1928–49) then president (1950–67) of the International Phonetic Association.

Jones, David Michael (1895–1974) Poet, born in Kent, SE England, UK. After art school he served in World War 1, and had an abiding interest in martial matters. His war experience is central to *In Parenthesis* (1937), the first of his two major literary works. *The Anathemata* (1952) is likewise personal, but draws heavily on his religious influences.

Jones, Davy >> **Monkees, The**

Jones, Edward Burne >> **Burne-Jones, Edward Coley**

Jones, Eli Stanley (1884–1973) Missionary to India, born in Baltimore, MD. He went to India as a missionary of the Methodist Episcopal Church in 1907, and later became an itinerant evangelist, declining a bishopric in 1928. Concerned equally for social justice and spirituality, he supported Indian aspirations for independence, and was sensitive to Indian religious traditions. He founded two Christian *ashrams*, one at Sat Tal and the other in Lucknow (where he also founded a psychiatric centre). He wrote nearly 30 books, most notably *The Christ of the Indian Road* (1925).

Jones, (Alfred) Ernest (1879–1958) Psychoanalyst, born in Llwchwy, S Wales. He studied at University College, Cardiff, and qualified as a physician in London. Medical journalism and neurological research brought him into contact with the work of Sigmund Freud. He introduced psychoanalysis into Britain and North America, founded the British Psycho-Analytical Society (1913), as well as the *International Journal of Psycho-Analysis*, which he edited (1920–33). He was professor of psychiatry at Toronto (1909–12) and director of the London Clinic for Psycho-Analysis. Among his numerous works and translations is a psychoanalytical study of *Hamlet and Oedipus*, and an authoritative biography of Freud (1953–7). >> **Freud, Sigmund**

Jones, Gwyn (1907–) Scholar and writer, born in Blackwood, Caerphilly, S Wales, UK. He studied at the University of Wales, and was a schoolmaster and lecturer before becoming professor of English language and literature at the University College of Wales, Aberystwyth (1940–64). His works on Norse history and literature include *The Norse Atlantic Saga* (1964), *A History of the Vikings* (1968), and various translations. His Welsh studies include a translation of the *Mabinogion* (1948), *Welsh Legends and Folk-Tales* (1955), and editions of *Welsh Short Stories* (1956) and *The Oxford Book of Welsh Verse in English* (1977). He has also published several novels and collections of short stories.

Jones, Dame Gwyneth (1936–) Dramatic soprano, born in Pontnewydd, Torfaen, SE Wales. She studied at the Royal College of Music, London, and also in Siena and Zürich. She made her Covent Garden debut in 1963, first sang at the Vienna State Opera in 1966, and subsequently sang at Bayreuth, Munich, La Scala Milan, and other great houses of the world. She is renowned as an interpreter of the heroines of Wagner and Strauss operas.

Jones, Sir Harold Spencer (1890–1960) Astronomer, born in London, England, UK. He studied at Cambridge, and became chief assistant to the Astronomer Royal at Greenwich (1913–23). He then served as astronomer at the Royal Observatory at the Cape of Good Hope (1923–33), before returning to Greenwich to become Astronomer Royal (1933–55). He organized an international project to determine Earth–Sun distance, using a close approach of the asteroid Eros, and improving on previous values. He investigated problems related to the Earth's rotation, introduced a new system of time measurement in astronomy, ephemeris time, and brought about the move of the Royal Observatory from Greenwich to Herstmonceux in East Sussex.

Jones, Henry, pseudonym **Cavendish** (1831–99) Physician and writer, born in London, England, UK. He studied at King's College and St Bartholomew's Hospital, practised as a surgeon (1852–69), and began writing about whist, publishing *Principles of Whist* (1862), and became whist editor of *The Field* magazine (1862). He wrote manuals on many other games, and helped found the All-England Croquet Club (1870).

Jones, Henry Arthur (1851–1929) Playwright, born in Grandborough, Buckinghamshire, SC England, UK. He was in business until 1878, when *Only Round the Corner* was produced at Exeter. His first great hit was a melodrama, *The Silver King* (1882), which he followed with more melodramatic successes. He also wrote and lectured about the theatre, as in *The Renaissance of the English Drama, 1883–94* (1895).

Jones, Inigo (1573–1652) The first of the great English architects, born in London, England, UK. He studied landscape painting in Italy, and from Venice introduced the Palladian style into England. In 1606 James I employed him in arranging the masques of Ben Jonson, and he introduced the proscenium arch and movable scenery to the English stage. In 1615 he became surveyor-general of the royal buildings. He designed the Queen's House at Greenwich (1616–35), the Banqueting House in Whitehall (1619–22), and laid out Covent Garden and Lincoln's Inn Fields, all in London. >> **Jonson, Ben; Russell, Francis**

Jones, Jack, popular name of **James (Larkin) Jones** (1913–93) Trade unionist, born in Liverpool, Merseyside, NW England, UK. He was general secretary of the Transport and General Workers Union (1969–78), favouring the decentralization of trade union power to the local branches, and had some influence on the Labour government's policies of 1974–6. Made a Companion of Honour in 1978, his autobiography, *Union Man*, was published in 1986.

Jones, James (1921–77) Novelist, born in Robinson, IL. He studied at the University of Hawaii, then served in the US army as a sergeant (1939–44), boxed as a welterweight in Golden Gloves tournaments, and was awarded a Purple

Heart. His wartime experience in Hawaii led to *From Here to Eternity* (1951), a classic war novel for which he received a National Book Award. Later work was disappointing, with the exception of *The Thin Red Line* (1962).

Jones, Jennifer >> **Selznick, David O**

Jones, John Paul, originally **John Paul** (1747–92) American naval officer, born in Kirkbean, Dumfries and Galloway, SW Scotland, UK. He made voyages to America, and assumed the name of Jones after escaping from a mutinous crew. In the American War of Independence he was commissioned as a senior lieutenant. In 1778 he cruised into British waters in the *Ranger*, and made a daring descent on the Solway Firth in Scotland. In 1779, as commodore of a French squadron displaying American colours, he threatened Leith, and off Flamborough Head won a hard-fought engagement on the *Bonhomme Richard* against the British Frigate *Serapis*. In 1788 he entered Russian service, and as rear-admiral of the Black Sea fleet fought in the Russo-Turkish war of 1788–9.

Jones, Mary Harris, known as **Mother Jones** (1830–1930) US labour agitator, born in Co Cork, Ireland. She migrated to the USA via Canada, lost her family to an epidemic in 1867, and her home to the Chicago fire of 1871, and thereafter devoted herself to the cause of labour. Homeless after 1880, she travelled to areas of labour strife, especially in the coal industry, and was imprisoned in West Virginia on a charge of conspiracy to murder in 1912, at the age of 82. Freed by a new governor, she returned to labour agitation, which she continued almost until her death.

Jones, Owen (1809–74) Architect and designer, born in London, England, UK. He studied at the Royal Academy, was superintendent of works for the Great Exhibition of 1851 in London, and director of decoration for the Crystal Palace (1852). He also designed St James's Hall in London. He wrote a monumental *Grammar of Ornament* (1856), magnificently illustrated with decorative patterns and motifs from many cultures and periods.

Jones, Robert Edmond (1887–1954) Scene designer, born in Milton, NH. He studied at Harvard, went to Berlin to learn from Max Reinhardt, then returned to the USA to design for a Broadway production of *The Man Who Married A Dumb Wife* by Anatole France. His symbolic use of primary colours and light frame construction, a radical departure in 1915 from the prevailing norms of realism, ushered in a career that was to revolutionize stagecraft in the USA. His simplified designs sought to engage the audience's imagination rather than copy reality and, together with his theoretical work, had an enduring influence. >> **Reinhardt, Max**

Jones, Tom, originally **Thomas Jones Woodward** (1940–) Singer, born in Pontypridd, Rhondda Cynon Taff, S Wales, UK. He began singing as a child, later performing in working-men's clubs, and became known following his hit single, 'It's Not Unusual' (1965), which made UK number 1 and US number 10. His version of 'Green Green Grass of Home' (1966) was his biggest selling single, other hits including 'What's New Pussycat?' (1965), 'Delilah' (1968), 'Love Me Tonight' (1969), and 'She's a Lady' (1971).

Jones, Sir William (1746–94) Orientalist, born in London, England, UK. He studied at Oxford, was called to the bar (1774), became a judge in the Supreme Court in Bengal (1783), and was knighted. He devoted himself to Sanskrit, whose resemblance to Latin and Greek he pointed out in 1787, thus motivating the era of comparative philology.

Jongen, Joseph [yongen] (1873–1953) Composer, born in Liège, Belgium. He studied at the Liège Conservatory, and in Italy, France, and Germany. He won the Belgian *Prix de Rome*, and was professor at Liège Conservatoire until the outbreak of World War 1, when he went to England. He became director of the Brussels Conservatoire (1920–39). He composed

piano, violin, and organ works, the symphonic poem *Lalla Roukh*, an opera, and a ballet.

Jongkind, Johan Barthold [yongkint] (1819–91) Painter, born in Lattrop, The Netherlands. He studied at The Hague, but moved to Paris in 1846, establishing close links with French art. He was a friend of Eugène Boudin, and exhibited with the Barbizon painters. An important precursor of Impressionism, he influenced the young Monet. >> **Boudin; Monet**

Jonson, Ben(jamin) (1572–1637) Playwright, born in London, England, UK. Educated at Westminster School, he worked as a bricklayer, did military service in Flanders, and joined Henslowe's company of players, where he killed a fellow player in a duel. His *Every Man in His Humour*, with Shakespeare in the cast, was performed in 1598. After some less successful works, including two Roman tragedies, he wrote his four chief plays: *Volpone* (1606), *The Silent Woman* (1609), *The Alchemist* (1610), and *Bartholomew Fair* (1614). He wrote several masques before 1625, when the death of James I ended his period of court favour. He was a major influence on 17th-c poets (known as 'the tribe, or sons, of Ben'). >> **Henslowe**

Jónsson, Asgrímur (1876–1958) Landscape painter, born in Rútsstaða-Suðurkot, Iceland. He was the first artist to portray the Icelandic landscapes in all their vivid variety and ethereal colour. He was given a generous state grant to travel and study abroad (1907), where he came into contact with the Impressionists. He turned to water-colours, and to interpreting Icelandic folk-tales. He bequeathed his home in Reykjavík and his private collection of paintings to the nation as an art gallery.

Jónsson, Einar [yohnsn] (1874–1954) Sculptor, born in Galtafell, Iceland. He studied at Copenhagen and in Rome. After extensive travel he settled in Copenhagen (1905), but returned to Iceland in 1914, donating all his works to the nation. He spent two years in the USA making a statue of the first European settler in North America, Thorfinn Karlsefni, for a new sculpture park in Philadelphia, before withdrawing into increasing isolation in his home-cum-museum in Reykjavík.

Jónsson, Finnur [yohnsn] (1892–1989) Painter, born in Strýta, Iceland. He went to study in Copenhagen and discovered a vocation for painting (1921). He joined the Modernist group at Der Sturm gallery, Berlin, and Dresden, where he was much influenced by Oskar Kokoschka. Returning to Iceland he held the first exhibition of abstract art in Reykjavík (1925), causing something of a scandal, and thereafter worked in more traditional styles, painting landscapes and scenes from fishing life. His later paintings showed a return towards abstraction. >> **Kokoschka**

Jooss, Kurt [johs] (1901–79) Dancer, choreographer, teacher, and director, born in Wasseralfingen, Germany. He studied ballet before meeting Laban, with whom he then worked. He was appointed director of the dance department at the Essen Folkwang School in 1927, from which the dance theatre company developed. His best-known work, *The Green Table*, was created in 1932. He left Germany in 1933 for England, where he formed a new group, Ballets Jooss, and toured extensively. He returned to Essen in 1949, and retired in 1969, but his works continue to be mounted by his daughter **Anna Markard** (1931–). >> **Laban**

Joplin, Scott (1868–1917) Pianist and composer, born in Texarkana, AR. Largely self-taught, he became a professional musician in his teens, but later studied music at George Smith College, Sedalia. He gained fame as a pianist in Chicago and St Louis in the 1890s, but he longed for recognition as a serious composer. His 'Maple Leaf Rag' (1899) made ragtime music a national craze, and was the first of his several popular rags. Ragtime experienced a revival in the 1970s, and Joplin's music (especially 'The Entertainer') became more widely known.

Jordaens, Jakob [yawdahns] (1593–1678) Painter, born in Antwerp, Belgium. He became a member of an Antwerp guild in 1616 and from 1630 came under the influence of Rubens, who obtained for him the patronage of the kings of Spain and Sweden. He painted several altarpieces, and became known for his scenes of merry peasant life, such as 'The King Drinks' (1638, Brussels). After Rubens' death he was considered the greatest painter in Antwerp. >> Rubens

Jordan, Barbara (Charline) (1936–96) US representative, born in Houston, TX. She studied at Boston University, then practised law in Houston (1960–7), entering Democratic politics in the Texas Senate (1967–72), and continuing in the US House of Representatives (1973–9). A compelling orator, she electrified the 1976 Democratic convention before illness cut short her political career. She became a professor at the Lyndon B Johnson School of Public Affairs at the University of Texas in Austin.

Jordan, (Marie-Ennemond) Camille [zhawdā] (1838–1922) Mathematician, born in Lyon, France. He became professor at the Ecole Polytechnique (1876–1912) and at the Collège de France. He pioneered group theory, wrote on the theory of linear differential equations, and on the theory of functions, which he applied to the curve which bears his name. His work brought full understanding of the importance of the pioneering work done by Galois. >> Galois

Jordan, Dorothea, *née* **Bland** (1762–1816) Actress, born near Waterford, Ireland. She made her debut in Dublin in 1777, and appeared with great success at Drury Lane in 1785. For nearly 30 years she kept her hold on the public, mainly in comic tomboy roles. Between 1790 and 1811 she was involved with the Duke of Clarence, afterwards William IV, by whom she had 10 of her 15 children. In 1814 she retired to St-Cloud, France. >> William IV

Jordan, Michael (Jeffrey), nickname **Air Jordan** (1963–) Basketball player, born in New York City. He played with the Chicago Bulls from 1984, and was named as the National Basketball Association's Most Valuable Player in 1988, 1991, 1992, 1996, and 1997. A member of the USA Olympic gold medal-winning team in 1984 and 1992, he holds the record for most points in an NBA play-off game (63), against Boston in 1986, and scored over 50 points in a game on 34 occasions. He earned his nickname for his remarkable athleticism. One of the world's most idolized sportsmen, he announced his retirement in 1993, turned to baseball, but returned to the Chicago Bulls in 1995. In addition to his MVP award in 1996, he also took the NBA scoring title for the eighth time to break Wilt Chamberlain's record, and won it again in 1997. Appearances in television commercials led to his role in the Disney part-animated film *Space Jam* (1996). >> RR1146

Jordan, Neil (1950–) Film maker and writer, born in Co Sligo, Ireland. He studied at University College, Dublin, and helped form the Irish Writers Co-operative (1974). His first collection of stories, *Night in Tunisia* (1976), was followed by the acclaimed novels *The Past* (1980) and *The Dreams of the Beast* (1983). He worked as a script consultant on *Excalibur* (1981), made his directorial debut with the thriller *Angel* (1982), and has boldly emphasized the fairy-tale and fantasy elements of such challenging works as *The Company of Wolves* (1984) and *Mona Lisa* (1986). Recently, he has turned his hand to comedy with *High Spirits* (1988) and *We're No Angels* (1989). His study of the legendary Irish patriot *Michael Collins* appeared in 1996.

Jordanes [jaw(r)**dah**neez] (fl.6th-c) Gothic monk and historian.

His chief work was a history of the Goths, *De origine actibusque Getarum* (c.551, On the Origins and Deeds of the Getae), condensed from a lost book by Cassiodorus. It is important as a contemporary source on both the Goths and the Huns. >> Cassiodorus

Jorn, Asger Oluf [yaw(r)n] (1914–73) Painter, born in Jutland, Denmark. He studied art in Paris from 1936 with Léger and Le Corbusier, and in 1948–50 founded the 'Cobra' group (Co[penhagen], Br[ussels], A[msterdam]) which aimed to exploit fantastic imagery derived from the unconscious, not directed by reason. >> Le Corbusier; Léger

Joseph II (1741–90) Holy Roman Emperor (1765–90), born in Vienna, the son of Francis I and Maria Theresa. Until his mother's death (1780) he was co-regent, and his power was limited to the command of the army and the direction of foreign affairs. A sincere enlightened despot, he was known as 'the revolutionary emperor' for his programme of modernization. He was determined to assert Habsburg leadership, but some of his ambitious plans were thwarted variously by the diplomatic obstruction of France, Prussia, the United Provinces, and Britain, by war (with Prussia in 1778–9 and Turkey in 1788), and by insurrection (in The Netherlands in 1787, Hungary in 1789, and the Tyrol in 1790). >> Maria Theresa

Joseph, St (1st-c BC) Husband of the Virgin Mary, a carpenter in Nazareth, who last appeared in the Gospel history when Jesus Christ was 12 years old (*Luke* 2.43). He is never mentioned during Jesus's ministry, and must be assumed to have already died. Feast day 19 March. >> Jesus Christ; Mary

Joseph Biblical character, the subject of many stories (*Gen* 37–50); the 11th son of Jacob, but the first by his wife Rachel. He is depicted as Jacob's favourite son (marked by the gift of a multicoloured coat) who was sold into slavery by his jealous brothers, yet who by prudence and wisdom rose from being a servant to high office in Pharaoh's court, with special responsibility for distributing grain supplies during a time of famine. Eventually he is portrayed as reconciled with his brothers, who came to Egypt to escape the famine. His sons, Ephraim and Manasseh, were blessed by Jacob, and became ancestors of two of the tribes of Israel. >> Jacob

Joseph (of Portsoken), Keith (Sinjohn) Joseph, Baron (1918–94) British statesman, born in London, England, UK. He studied at Oxford, was called to the bar (1946) then became a Conservative MP (1956). A former secretary of state for social services (1970–4) and industry (1979–81), he held the education and science portfolio (1981–6). He was given an overall responsibility for Conservative policy and research in 1975, and with Margaret Thatcher founded the Centre for Policy Studies. He became a life peer in 1987. >> Thatcher

Joseph, Père, known as **l'Eminence grise** ('Grey Eminence'), originally **François Joseph le Clerc du Tremblay** (1577–1638) French diplomat and mystic, born in Paris. He became a Capuchin monk in 1599, and Cardinal Richelieu's secretary in 1611. His nickname derives from his contact with Richelieu (the 'Red Eminence'), for whom he went on several important diplomatic missions, especially during the Thirty Years' War. >> Richelieu

Joseph of Arimathea, St [arima**thee**a] (1st-c) In the New Testament a rich Israelite, a secret disciple of Jesus, and a councillor in Jerusalem. He went to Pontius Pilate and begged the body of Jesus, burying it in his own rock-hewn tomb (*Mark* 15.42–7). He is frequently referred to in later Christian literature, such as the Gospel of Nicodemus. According to legend, he was sent by Philip (the apostle) to Glastonbury, England, where he is recognized as patron. He was also said to have been given the Holy Grail by

Christ, when in prison. Feast day 17 March (W), 31 July (E). >> Jesus Christ; Pilate

Joséphine de Beauharnais, *née* **Marie Josèphe Rose Tascher de la Pagerie** (1763–1814) First wife of Napoleon Bonaparte, and French empress, born in Trois-Ilets, Martinique. In 1779 she married the **Vicomte de Beauharnais** who was executed during the French Revolution (1794). She married Napoleon (1796), and accompanied him on his Italian campaign, but soon returned to Paris. At Malmaison, and afterwards at the Luxembourg and the Tuileries, she attracted round her the most brilliant society of France, and contributed considerably to the establishment of her husband's power. The marriage, being childless, was dissolved in 1809, but she retained the title of empress. >> Napoleon

Josephson, Brian (David) (1940–) Physicist, born in Cardiff. He studied at Cambridge, was elected a fellow of Trinity College (1962), and became professor of physics from 1974. While a research student (1962) he deduced theoretically what is now called the *Josephson effect* at the junction of two superconductors, and for which he shared the 1973 Nobel Prize for Physics. >> RR1122

Josephus, Flavius [johseefus], originally **Joseph ben Matthias** (c. 37–?) Jewish historian and soldier, born in Jerusalem, who commanded a Galilean force during the Jewish Revolt against Rome in 66. He cunningly gained favour upon surrendering to the Romans, and went to Rome, where he produced several writings on Jewish history and religion, including *History of the Jewish War* (75–9) and *Antiquities of the Jews* (93).

Joshua, Heb **Yehoshua** In the Old Testament, the son of Nun, of the tribe of Ephraim, who during the 40 years' wanderings of the Israelites acted as 'minister' or personal attendant of Moses, and upon Moses' death was appointed to lead the people into Canaan. The Book of Joshua is a narrative of the conquest and settlement of Canaan under his leadership. >> Moses

Josiah [johsiya] (7th-c BC) Biblical character, king of Judah (c.639–609 BC), a favourite of the Deuteronomistic historians because of his religious reforms (2 *Kings* 22–3, 2 *Chron* 34–5), allegedly based on the discovery of 'the book of the law' in the 18th year of his reign. He is credited with destroying pagan cults and attempting to centralize worship in Jerusalem and the Temple. He died in battle against the Egyptians at Megiddo.

Josquin des Prez or **Prés** [zhoskï day **pray**] (c.1440–1521) Composer, probably born in Condé, France. Possibly a pupil of Okeghem, he was composer to the Sforza family in Milan and Rome, Louis XII of France, and the Duke of Ferrara. A master of polyphony, he left a number of valuable Masses, motets, and secular vocal works. Charles Burney called him 'the father of modern harmony'. >> Burney, Charles; Okeghem

Joubert, Piet (Petrus Jacobus) [zhoobair] (1831–1900) Afrikaaner soldier and statesman, born in Prince Albert, South Africa. Living in the Transvaal from 1840, he studied law and was elected to parliament in 1860, becoming attorney general (1870) and acting president (1875). In the 1st Boer War (1880–1) he commanded the Transvaal's forces, and defeated the British in 1881. He negotiated the Pretoria Convention (1881), became vice-president in 1883, and opposed Kruger for the presidency over the next 15 years. In the 2nd Boer War (1899–1902) he held command at the outset, but resigned from ill health and died soon afterwards. >> Kruger

Joule, James (Prescott) [jool] (1818–89) Physicist, born in Salford, Greater Manchester, NW England, UK. He studied at Manchester University under John Dalton. In a series of experiments (1843–78) he showed that heat is a form of energy, and established the mechanical equivalent of heat. This formed the basis of the theory of the conservation of energy. He also worked with Lord Kelvin on temperature changes in gases, which led to the founding of the refrigeration industry. His name is preserved in the unit of work, the *joule*. >> Dalton, John; Kelvin

Jourdan, Jean-Baptiste, comte (Count) [zhoordä] (1762–1833) French soldier, born in Limoges, France. He joined the Revolutionary army, and defeated the Austrians at Wattignies (1793) and Fleurus (1794), then drove the Austrians across the Rhine, took Luxembourg, and besieged Mainz. He was defeated at Höchst (1795), and four times (1796–9) by the Archduke Charles of Austria. Napoleon made him marshal (1804) and Governor of Naples (1806). He was defeated by Wellington at Vitoria (1813), and in 1814 transferred his allegiance to Louis XVIII, who made him a count. He supported the Revolution of 1830. >> Louis XVIII; Napoleon; Wellington

Jouvet, Louis [zhoovay] (1887–1951) Actor and theatre/film director, born in Crozon, France. He studied as a pharmacist but took to the stage, touring the USA with Jacques Copeau's company (1918–19). He became stage-manager (1922) and director (1924) of the Comédie des Champs Elysées. He was the first to recognize Giraudoux, all but one of whose plays he produced. In 1934 his company transferred to the Théâtre de l'Athénée, and he became professor at the Paris Conservatoire. >> Giraudoux

Jovian [johvian], in full **Flavius Claudius Jovianus** (c. 331–64) Roman emperor (363–4), appointed by the army in Mesopotamia on Julian's death in battle. He was immediately forced to make a humiliating peace with Shapur II, ceding great tracts of Roman territory to Sassanian Persia, and agreeing to pay a subsidy. >> Julian; Shapur II; RR1084

Jowett, Benjamin (1817–93) Scholar, born in London, England, UK. He studied at Oxford, and spent his career there. Elected a fellow (1838), tutor (1840), and master (1870), he was professor of Greek (1855–93), and Vice-Chancellor of Oxford (1882–6). He is best known for his translations of the *Dialogues* of Plato (1871), Thucydides (1881), the *Politics* of Aristotle (1885), and Plato's *Republic* (1894).

Joyce, Eileen (Alannah) (1912–91) Concert pianist, born in Zeehan, Tasmania, Australia. Discovered by Percy Grainger, she was sent at the age of 15 to study at Leipzig Conservatory. She made her debut with Sir Henry Wood at a promenade concert under his baton (1930). She became a prolific broadcaster, and during the war frequently visited the blitzed towns of Britain with Malcolm Sargent and the London Philharmonic. She is particularly known for her work on film sound-tracks, especially *Brief Encounter*, *The Seventh Veil*, and the film of her childhood, *Wherever She Goes*. >> Grainger; Sargent, Malcolm; Wood, Henry

Joyce, James (Augustine Aloysius) (1882–1941) Writer, born in Dublin. He studied in Dublin, went in 1902 to Paris to study medicine, then took up voice training for a concert career. Back in Dublin, he published a few stories but, unable to make a living by his pen, left for Pola to tutor in English. He started the short-lived Volta Cinema Theatre in 1909, and left Dublin in 1910. He later went to Zürich (1915), where he formed a company of English players, settled in Paris (1920–40), then returned to Zürich, where he died. His early work includes the short stories, *Dubliners* (1914), and *A Portrait of the Artist as a Young Man* (1914–15). His best-known book, *Ulysses*, based on one day in Dublin (16 Jun 1904), appeared in Paris in 1922, but was banned in the UK and USA until 1936. *Work in Progress* began to appear in 1927, and finally emerged as *Finnegans Wake* (1939). His work revolutionized the novel form, partly through the abandonment of ordinary plot for 'stream of consciousness', but more fundamentally through his unprecedented exploration of language. >> Svevo

Joyce, William, nickname **Lord Haw Haw** (1906–46) British traitor, born in New York City. As a child he lived in Ireland, and in 1922 his family emigrated to England. He founded the fanatical British National Socialist Party and fled to Germany before war broke out. Throughout World War 2 he broadcast from Radio Hamburg propaganda against Britain, gaining his nickname from his upper-class drawl. He was captured by the British at Flensburg, and was tried and executed in London.

Joyner-Kersee, Jackie, popular name of **Jacqueline Joyner-Kersee** *née* **Joyner** (1962–   ) Athlete, born in East St Louis, IL. At the Los Angeles Olympics of 1984, she won the heptathlon silver medal. Four years later, at Seoul, she won the gold medal in both heptathlon and long jump. >> RR1138

Juan, Don >> **John of Austria**

Juan Carlos I [hwan **kah(r)**los] (1938–   ) King of Spain (1975–   ), born in Rome, the son of **Don Juan de Borbón y Battenberg, Count of Barcelona** (1908–93), and the grandson of Spain's last ruling monarch, Alfonso XIII. He studied in Switzerland and from 1948 in Spain (by agreement between his father and General Franco). He earned commissions in the army, navy, and air force (1955–9), and studied at the University of Madrid (1959–61). In 1962 he married **Princess Sophia of Greece** (1938–   ), and they have three children. In 1969 Franco named him as his eventual successor, and he was proclaimed king on Franco's death in 1975. Instead of upholding the Franco dictatorship (as had been intended), he decisively presided over Spain's democratization, helping to defeat a military coup (1981) and assuming the role of a constitutional monarch. >> Alfonso XIII; Franco; RR1088

Juárez, Benito Pablo [hwah**res**] (1806–72) Mexican national hero and president (1861–72), born of Indian parents in San Pablo Guelatao, Mexico. His ideas for reform forced him to live in exile (1853–5), but he then joined the Liberal government. During the civil war of 1857–60, he assumed the presidency, and was elected to that office on the Liberal victory (1861). The French invasion under Maximilian forced him to the far N, from where he directed resistance until the defeat of Maximilian, in 1867. >> Maximilian, Ferdinand Joseph; RR1075

Judah [**joo**da] Old Testament figure, the fourth son of Jacob and Leah. He was the founder of the greatest of the 12 tribes of Israel. >> Jacob

Juda Leon >> **Abarbanel**

Judas Iscariot [is**ka**ryot] (1st-c) One of the 12 apostles of Jesus, usually appearing last in the lists in the synoptic Gospels (*Mark* 3.19), identified as the one who betrayed Jesus for 30 pieces of silver by helping to arrange for his arrest at Gethsemane by the Jewish authorities (*Mark* 14.43–6). Other traditions indicate his role as treasurer (*John* 13.29) and his later repentance and suicide (*Matt* 27.3–10, *Acts* 1.16–19). The meaning of *Iscariot* is unclear: it may mean 'man of Keriot' or 'man of falsehood'. The Latin word *sicarius* referred to a curved dagger; and the *sicarii* were a Zealot sect of politically motivated assassins. >> Jesus Christ

Judd, Donald (1928–94) Minimalist artist, born in Excelsior Springs, MO. He studied at the College of William and Mary, Columbia University, and at the Art Student's League. He had metal boxes manufactured to his specification, spray-painted one colour, and stood on the floor. He had therefore only 'minimal' contact with his work, which is deliberately non-imitative, non-expressive, and not 'composed' in any traditional sense. His first one-man show was held in New York City in 1964.

Jude, St or **Thaddeus** (1st-c) One of the 12 Apostles. He is called 'Judas (son) of James' (*Luke* 6.16, *Acts* 1.13), and appears to correspond to the **Thaddeus** mentioned in Mark 3.18 and Matthew 10.3, perhaps to avoid confusion with Judas Iscariot. He is traditionally thought to have preached and healed in Mesopotamia and Persia. Some scholars have considered him the author of the Letter of Jude, who is there described as 'Judas, a servant of Jesus Christ and brother of James', but this identification is disputed. He is traditionally thought to have been martyred in Persia with St Simon, whose feast is held on the same day. Feast day 28 October (W), 19 June or 21 August (E).

Judith Old Testament Jewish heroine. In the Apocryphal Book of Judith, she is portrayed as a widow who made her way into the tent of Holofernes, general of Nebuchadnezzar, cut off his head, and so saved her native town of Bethulia.

Judson, Adoniram (1788–1850) Missionary, born in Malden, MA. He thought of turning playwright, but in 1812, having married, went to Burma as a Baptist missionary, and was a prisoner during the Anglo-Burmese War (1824–6). His Burmese translation of the Bible (1833) was followed by a Burmese–English dictionary (1849).

Jugnauth, Sir Aneerood [**jug**nawt] (1930–   ) Mauritian politician and prime minister (1982–95). After qualifying as a barrister in London (1954), he returned to Mauritius and was elected to the Legislative Council in the period before full independence in 1968. In 1970 he co-founded the Socialist Mauritius Militant Movement (MMM), from which he later broke away to form his own Mauritius Socialist Party (PSM); and in 1982 he became prime minister at the head of a PSM–MMM alliance. In 1983 his Party was reconstituted as the Mauritius Socialist Movement, with a pledge to make the country a republic within the Commonwealth. The 1991 election gave his ruling coalition sufficient majority to pass the bill to sever ties with the British monarchy, effective from 1992. >> RR1075

Jugurtha [ju**goor**tha] (c. 160–104 BC) King of Numidia (118–105 BC), after whom the *Jugurthine War* (112–104 BC) is named. Rome's difficulty in defeating him provided Marius with a launching pad for his career, and led to important reforms in the Roman army. Jugurtha's surrender to Marius's deputy, Sulla, ended the war, but was the starting point of the deadly feud between Marius and Sulla which plunged Rome into civil war 20 years later. >> Marius, Gaius; Sulla

Juin, Alphonse (Pierre) [zhwĩ] (1888–1967) French soldier, born in Bône, Algeria. He trained at St Cyr Military Academy, served with the Moroccan forces during World War 1, and became chief-of-staff in North Africa (1938). He was captured by the Germans (1940), released in 1941, and became military governor of Morocco under the Vichy government. After the Allied invasion of Tunisia, he changed sides, and distinguished himself in the subsequent Italian campaign. He became chief-of-staff of the National Defence Committee in Liberated France (1944–7), and was resident-general in Morocco (1947–51). He was promoted field-marshal in 1952, broke with de Gaulle in 1960 over the Algerian policy, and retired. >> de Gaulle

Julia (39 BC–AD 14) Roman noblewoman, the daughter of Emperor Augustus and Scribonia. She was married at the age of 14 to her cousin Marcellus, and after his death (23 BC) she married Marcus Vipsanius Agrippa (21 BC), who died in 12 BC. Augustus forced his stepson Tiberius to divorce his wife and marry Julia (11 BC). The marriage was unhappy, and Julia began to lead a promiscuous life. Her father Augustus learned of her adulteries, and banished her to the isle of Pandataria (2 BC), and from there to Reggio, where she died of malnutrition when her father, now emperor, withheld her allowance. >> Agrippa, Marcus Vipsanius; Augustus; Tiberius

Julian, in full **Flavius Claudius Julianus**, known as **Julian the Apostate** (332–63) Roman emperor (361–3), the son of a half-brother of Constantine the Great. Appointed deputy emperor in the West by his cousin, Constantius II (355), he served with great distinction on the Rhine, and was proclaimed emperor by his adoring troops in 360. As emperor, he publicly proclaimed himself a pagan (hence his nickname) and initiated a vigorous policy of reviving the old pagan cults, though without persecuting Christians. He was killed in battle against the Sassanid Persians. >> Shapur II; RR1084

Julian, Percy (Lavon) (1899–1975) Chemist and inventor, born in Montgomery, AL. The grandson of a former slave, he studied at DePauw University, IN, and at Harvard, then taught chemistry at Howard University. Denied a professorship at Harvard on account of his race, he returned to DePauw. There in 1935 he synthesized the drug physostigmine, used to treat glaucoma. In 1936 he became director of research for the soya products division of the Glidden Co in Chicago. He and his associates developed scores of soya derivatives, notably cortisone, used in the treatment of arthritis and other afflictions. He left Glidden in 1953 to establish Julian Laboratories. From 1964 until his death he headed the Julian Research Institute, and served as consultant to the National Institute of Arthritis and Metabolic Diseases.

Julian or **Juliana of Norwich** (c. 1342–1413) English mystic who probably lived in isolation outside St Julian's Church, Norwich, E England, UK. Her work, *Sixteen Revelations of Divine Love*, based on a series of visions she received in 1373, has been a lasting influence on theologians stressing the power of the love of God. Her assurance that everything is held in being by the love of God, so that 'all shall be well', and her characterization of the Trinity as Father, Mother, and Lord, has particularly appealed to the contemporary Church.

Juliana, in full **Juliana Louise Emma Marie Wilhelmina** (1909–) Queen of The Netherlands (1948–80), born in The Hague. She studied at Leyden, became a lawyer, and in 1937 married Prince Bernhard zur Lippe-Biesterfeld; they had four daughters. On the German invasion of Holland (1940), Juliana escaped to Britain and later resided in Canada. She returned to Holland in 1945, and became queen on the abdication of her mother, Wilhelmina. She herself abdicated in favour of her eldest daughter, Beatrix. >> Beatrix; Bernhard Leopold; Wilhelmina; RR1077

Julius II, originally **Giuliano della Rovere** (1443–1513) Pope (1503–13), born in Albizuola, Italy, the nephew of Sixtus IV. He became a monk in 1468, was created cardinal by his uncle in 1471, and was endowed with many wealthy estates. While Alexander VI was pope, Giuliano had to go into exile for fear of his life. Once elevated to the papal chair, his public career was mainly devoted to political and military enterprises for the re-establishment of papal sovereignty in its ancient territory, and for the extinction of foreign domination in Italy. He is best known as a liberal patron of the arts; he employed Bramante for the design of St Peter's begun in 1506, had Raphael brought to Rome to decorate his private apartments, and commissioned Michelangelo for the frescoes on the ceiling of the Sistine Chapel, and for his own tomb. His military exploits inspired Erasmus's satire *Julius Exclusus*. >> Alexander VI; Bramante; Michelangelo; Raphael; Sixtus IV

Jumblat, Kemal (1919–77) Lebanese Socialist statesman and hereditary Druze chieftain, born in the Chouf Mts, Lebanon. He founded the Progressive Socialist Party in 1949, held several cabinet posts (1961–4), and was minister of the interior (1969–70). The Syrian intervention on the side of the Christians in 1976 was a response to the increasing

power of his authority in partnership with the Palestinians. He was assassinated in an ambush outside the village of Baaklu in the Chouf Mts. His son **Walid Jumblat** became leader of the Druze after his death.

Jung, Carl (Gustav) [yung] (1875–1961) Psychiatrist, born in Kesswil, Switzerland. He studied medicine at Basel, and worked at the Burghölzli mental clinic in Zürich (1900–9). He met Freud in Vienna in 1907, became his leading collaborator, and was president of the International Psychoanalytic Association (1911–14). He became increasingly critical of Freud's approach, and *Wandlungen und Symbole der Libido* (1911–12, trans The Psychology of the Unconscious) caused a break in 1913. He then developed his own theories, which he called 'analytical psychology' to distinguish them from Freud's psychoanalysis and Adler's individual psychology. Jung's approach included a description of psychological types ('extraversion/introversion'); the exploration of the 'collective unconscious'; and the concept of the psyche as a 'self-regulating system' expressing itself in the process of 'individuation'. He held chairs at Basel and Zürich. >> Adler, Alfred; Freud, Sigmund

Juninho [zhoo**nee**nyo], popular name of **Osvaldo Giroldo Jr** (1973–) Footballer, born in Brazil. A midfielder, he joined Middlesborough in 1995 from São Paulo, moving to Atletico Madrid in 1997. He was Footballer of the Year in 1994, and scored on his international debut for Brazil in 1995.

Junkers, Hugo [**yung**kerz] (1859–1935) Aircraft designer, born in Rheydt, Germany. He was professor of mechanical engineering at Aachen, before establishing an aircraft factory at Dessau (1910). He built the first successful all-metal monoplane, and many of his later aircraft had a corrugated sheet-metal skin. His aircraft played an important part in the *Luftwaffe* during World War 2. After World War 1 he founded aircraft factories at Dessau, Magdeburg, and Stassfurt, which produced many famous planes, both civil and military.

Jussieu, Bernard de [zhüsyoe] (c. 1699–1777) Botanist, born in Lyon, France. He created the botanical garden at Trianon for Louis XV, and adopted a system which has become the basis of modern natural botanical classification. His brother **Antoine** (1686–1758) was a physician and professor at the Jardin des Plantes, Paris. His nephew, **Antoine Laurent** (1748–1836), was also professor at the Jardin, and elaborated his uncle's system in *Genera plantarum* (1778–89).

Just, Ernest E(verett) (1883–1941) Cell biologist, born in Charleston, SC. He was a teacher and researcher at Howard University (1907–41), and also studied at the Woods Hole (MA) Marine Biological Laboratory. He made pioneering contributions to the cytology and embryology of marine organisms, and in 1925 demonstrated the carcinogenic effects of ultraviolet radiation on cells. By 1929, the diminishing number of African-American graduate students, his disenchantment with Howard's attitude towards his need for research facilities, and his feeling that Americans regarded him (an African-American) with more curiosity than respect, caused him to take leave of absence and pursue his studies in Europe.

Justin (Martyr), St (c. 100–c. 165) One of the Fathers of the Church, born in Sichem, Samaria. He was converted to Christianity, studied Stoic and Platonic philosophy, and founded a school of Christian philosophy at Rome, where he wrote two *Apologies* on Christian belief (150–60). He is said to have been martyred at Rome. Feast day 1 June.

Justinian [ju**stin**ian], in full **Flavius Petrus Sabbatius Justinianus** (c. 482–565) Roman emperor (527–65), the protégé of his uncle, the Byzantine emperor, Justin (reigned 518–27). At first co-emperor with Justin, on his death he became sole ruler. Along with his wife Theodora, he presided over the most brilliant period in the history of the late Roman empire. Through his generals, Belisarius and Narses, he recovered N Africa, Spain, and Italy, and carried out a major codification of the Roman law. >> Belisarius; Narses; Theodora; RR1084

Justus of Ghent [yustus], originally **Joos van Wassenhove** (c.1435–c.1480) Painter, who became a member of the painters' guild in Antwerp in 1460, and in 1464 was a master in Ghent. During the mid-1470s he is recorded as being at the court of Federigo da Montefeltro, Duke of Urbino, where he painted his only surviving documented work, *The Institution of the Eucharist* (1472–4). He is also thought to have painted a series of 28 *Famous Men* for the Ducal Palace (c.1476). His work was an important source of knowledge of the Netherlandish oil technique for contemporary Italian painters.

Juvarra or **Juvara, Filippo** [yuvahra] (1678–1736) Architect, born in Messina, Sicily. He studied under Carlo Fontana in Rome (1703–14), and received several commissions for stage designs. Appointed architect to the King of Sicily (1714), he moved to Turin and took charge of its rebuilding and enlargement. Influenced by the Roman Baroque, Bernini, and French planning, his major works include the Palazzo Madama (1718–21), the royal hunting lodge at Stupinigi, outside Turin (1729), and the Church of the Carmine (1732). >> Bernini; Fontana, Carlo

Juvenal, in full **Decimus Junius Juvenalis** (c.55–c.130) Satirist, born in Aquinum, Italy. He served as tribune in the army, in Britain and in Egypt. He is best known for his 16 brilliant satires in verse (c.100–c.127), dealing with life in Roman times under Domitian and his successors. Written from the viewpoint of an angry Stoic moralist, they range from the exposures of unnatural vices, the misery of poverty, and the extravagance of the ruling classes, to the precarious makeshift life of their hangers-on. Dryden's versions of five of Juvenal's satires are among the best of his works. >> Domitian; Dryden

Kabalevsky, Dmitry (Borisovich) [kabalefskee] (1904–87) Composer and pedagogue, born in St Petersburg, Russia. He entered Moscow Conservatory (1925), studied composition with Nikolai Miaskovsky, and taught there himself from 1932. His prolific output included four symphonies, operas, concertos, film scores, and much chamber and piano music. >> Miaskovsky

Kádár, János [kahda(r)] (1912–89) Hungarian statesman, premier (1956–8, 1961–5) and first secretary (1956–88), born in Kapoly, Hungary. He joined the (illegal) Communist Party in 1931, and was arrested several times. He became a member of the Central Committee (1942) and the Politburo (1945), and minister of the interior (1949), but was arrested for anti-Stalinist views (1951–3). When the anti-Soviet uprising broke out in 1956, he was a member of the 'national' government of Imre Nagy, but then formed a puppet government which repressed the uprising. He resigned in 1958, becoming premier again in 1961. His long reign as Party secretary ended in 1988, when he stepped down as leader, and was given the new titular post of Party president. He was removed from this position shortly before his death. >> Nagy, Imre; RR1057

Kael, Pauline [kayl] (1919–) Film critic, born in Petaluma, CA. She studied at the University of California, Berkeley, and became a journalist. She has been movie critic of the *New Yorker* since 1968, and has published several anthologies of her articles, including *Kiss Kiss Bang Bang* (1968), *5001 Nights at the Movies* (1982), and *State of the Art* (1985).

Kafka, Franz [kafka] (1883–1924) Novelist, born in Prague, of German Jewish parents. He studied law, became an official in an insurance company (1907–23), moved to Berlin, but soon after succumbed to tuberculosis. His short stories and essays, such as *Die Verwandlung* (1916, The Metamorphosis), appeared in his lifetime, but his three unfinished novels were published posthumously by his friend Max Brod: *Der Prozess* (1925, The Trial), *Das Schloss* (1926, The Castle), and *Amerika* (1927). He has influenced many authors with his vision of society (often called 'Kafkaesque') as a pointless, schizophrenically rational organization, with tortuous bureaucratic and totalitarian procedures, psychological labyrinths, and masochistic fantasies, into which the bewildered individual has strayed. >> Brod

Kaganovich, Lazar Moiseyevich [kaganohvich] (1893–1991) Russian politician, born near Kiev, Ukraine. He joined the Communist Party in 1911, and after the Revolution became secretary of the Ukrainian Central Committee. In 1928 he became Party secretary in Moscow, and during the 1930s played a prominent role in the forced collectivization programme. He also served as commissar for railways, and was made a deputy chairman of the Council of Ministers in 1947. He opposed Khrushchev's de-Stalinization and attempted to depose him, but failed, and was himself dismissed from the Party in 1957. >> Khrushchev

Kagawa, Toyohiko [kagahwa] (1888–1960) Social reformer and evangelist, born in Kobe, Japan. A convert to Christianity, he was educated at the Presbyterian College in Tokyo, and at Princeton Theological Seminary in the USA. Returning to Japan, he became an evangelist and social worker in the slums of Kobe. He was a leader in the Japanese labour movement, helping to found the Federation of Labour (1918) and the Farmer's Union (1921),

and founded the Anti-War League (1928). After World War 2 he was a leader in the women's suffrage movement, and helped with the process of democratization. He wrote numerous books, including the autobiographical novel *Before the Dawn* (1920).

Kagel, Mauricio Raúl [kaygl] (1931–) Composer, born in Buenos Aires. Prominent in the avant-garde movement, he evolved a fantastically complex serial organization of the elements of music, combined with aleatory elements drawn from random visual patterns, linguistic permutations, electronic sounds, and unconventional percussion instruments. His work often had a strong visual or theatrical aspect.

Kahanamoku, Duke (Paoa) [kahanamohkoo] (1890–1968) Swimmer and surfer, born in Hawaii. He revolutionized sprint swimming by introducing the flutter kick, and for 20 years was an international freestyle champion. A member of Olympic teams from 1912 to 1932, he won gold medals in 1912 and 1920. In addition, he is generally regarded as having introduced surfboarding (practised for centuries by Pacific islanders) to the West, starting with Australia and California in 1912. After a brief movie career, he became sheriff of Honolulu (1932–61).

Kahane, Meir [kahayn], originally **Martin Kahane** (1932–90) Zionist, born in New York City. An orthodox rabbi and life-long Jewish militant, he founded (1963) the anti-Arab Jewish Defense League. After emigrating to Israel in 1971, he founded the extremist Kach Party, banned in 1988 (four years after his controversial election to the Israeli parliament) as racist and undemocratic. He was assassinated in New York City.

Kahlo, Frida [kahloh] (1907–54) Artist, born in Coyoicoán, Mexico City. She began painting while convalescing from a serious road accident at the age of 15, and sent her work to the painter Diego Rivera, whom she later married (1928). Characterized by vibrant imagery, many of her pictures were striking self-portraits. Pain, which dogged her all her life, and the suffering of women, are recurring and indelible themes in her Surrealistic and often shocking pictures. André Breton likened her paintings to 'a ribbon around a bomb' (1938). >> Breton, André; Rivera, Diego

Kahn, Louis I(sadore) (1901–74) Architect, born in Osel, Estonia. He emigrated to the USA in 1905, when he studied at the University of Pennsylvania, then taught at Yale (1947–57) and Pennsylvania (1957–74). He was a pioneer of Functionalist architecture, expressed in a New Brutalist vein, clearly demonstrated in the Richards Medical Research Building, Pennsylvania (1957–61). Further works include the City Tower Municipal Building in Philadelphia, Yale University Art Gallery (1952–4), and the Salk Institute in La Jolla, California (1959–65). >> Venturi, Robert

Kahn, Otto (Herman) (1867–1934) Financier and art patron, born in Mannheim, Germany. He trained as a banker and worked in London, before emigrating in 1893 to New York City, where he formed Kahn, Loeb & Co, an investment banking firm, in 1897. He owed much of his wealth to financing railroads, in particular from helping Edward H Harriman (1848–1909) in his operations. A generous supporter of the arts, Kahn served as chairman (1911–31) and president (1918–34) of the Metropolitan Opera Company. He collected valuable works of art, but suffered huge financial losses in the Depression, and his major art works were sold off to private collectors.

Kain, Karen [kayn] (1951–) Dancer, born in Hamilton, Ontario, Canada. After training with the Canadian National Ballet School she joined the company in 1969, becoming principal dancer in 1970. Canada's most popular ballerina, she has danced the major classical leads as well as interpreting roles in works by contemporary choreographers.

Kaiser, Georg [kiyzer] (1878–1945) Playwright, born in Magdeburg, Germany. He worked in Buenos Aires as a clerk, returned to Germany in ill health, and began to write plays which established him as a leader of the Expressionist movement, such as *Von Morgens bis Mitternachts* (1916, From Morn to Midnight), *Gas I* (1918), and *Gas II* (1920). His work was banned by the Nazis, and he left Germany in 1938.

Kaiser, Henry J(ohn) [kiyzer] (1882–1967) Industrialist, born in Sprout Brook, NY. He worked on major civil engineering projects in the USA, Canada, and the West Indies (1914–33). As manager of seven highly productive shipyards on the Pacific coast during World War 2, he developed revolutionary methods of prefabrication and assembly in shipbuilding, enabling his ships to be constructed and launched within six days. His vast industrial empire included motor, steel, aluminium, and chemical corporations.

Kalashnikov, Mikhail [kalashnikof] (1919–) Russian gun designer. Drafted into the Russian army in 1938, he was seriously wounded in 1941, and while recovering in hospital listened to the complaints of his many fellow patients of the inferiority of the Russian rifle. In response he designed the *Avtomat Kalishnikova*, the AK-47 machine gun, of which over 50 million have been produced.

Kaldor (of Newnham), Nicholas Kaldor, Baron (1908–86) Economist, born in Budapest. He studied in Budapest and at the London School of Economics, where he taught (1932–47). He was chief of the economic planning staff of the US Bombing Survey of Germany (1945), and director of the Research and Planning Division of the Economic Commission for Europe (1947). He was professor of economics at Cambridge (1966–75), economic adviser to the Labour Party, and an outspoken critic of monetarist policies. He was created a peer in 1974.

Kalecki, Michal [kaleskee] (1899–1970) Economist and journalist, born in Lodz, Poland. He studied engineering in Warsaw and Gdansk, and taught himself economics. He worked at the Institute of Statistics, Oxford (1940–5), then became a UN economist (1946–54), and a government economist and teacher of economics in Poland (1955–67). A Marxist, he was critical of both capitalism and socialism. He developed a theory of macroeconomic dynamics, and introduced the new Western methods in economics to the Soviet bloc.

Kalidāsa [kalidahsa] (c.5th-c) Indian poet and dramatist, best known through his drama *Abhijnana-Sakuntala* (The Recognition of Sakuntala). Also attributed to him are two other plays, two epic poems, and a lyric poem.

Kalinin, Mikhail Ivanovich [kaleenin] (1875–1946) Soviet statesman, born in Tver, Russia. He was the formal head of state after the 1917 Revolution and during the years of Stalin's dictatorship (1919–46). A peasant and metalworker, he entered politics as a champion of the peasant class, and won great popularity. He became president of the Soviet Central Executive Committee (1919–38), and of the presidium of the Supreme Soviet (1938–46).

Kalogeropoulos, Maria >> **Callas, Maria**

Kaltenbrunner, Ernst [kaltenbruner] (1903–46) Nazi leader, born in Ried im Innkreis, Austria. He studied at Prague, joined the Nazi Party (1932), and became leader of the Austrian SS (1935). He agreed with Himmler on the establishment of gas-chambers for execution (1942),

became head of the security police (1943), and sent millions of Jews and political suspects to their deaths in concentration camps. He was also responsible for orders sanctioning the murder of prisoners of war. He was condemned by the Nuremberg Tribunal and hanged.

Kamen, Martin (David) (1913–) Biochemist, born in Toronto, Ontario, Canada. He studied at Chicago, and afterwards held posts in a number of US universities. He showed that the oxygen formed in plants by photosynthesis is derived from water (and not from CO_2); discovered the carbon isotope ^{14}C, afterwards much used as a biochemical tracer; studied photosynthetic bacteria and nitrogen-fixing bacteria; and contributed to the discovery of messenger-RNA.

Kamenev, Lev Borisovich [kamyaynef], originally **Lev Borisovich Rosenfeld** (1883–1936) Soviet politician, born in Moscow. He was an active revolutionary from 1901, and was exiled to Siberia in 1915. Liberated during the revolution (1917), he became a member of the Communist Central Committee. Expelled as a Trotskyite in 1927, he was readmitted next year but again expelled in 1932. He was shot after being arrested with Zinoviev for conspiring against Stalin. >> Stalin; Zinoviev

Kamerlingh Onnes, Heike [kamerling awnes] (1853–1926) Physicist, born in Groningen, The Netherlands. He studied at Heidelberg and Groningen, and became professor of physics at Leyden. He was the first to produce liquid helium, and worked in low-temperature physics, discovering the phenomenon of superconductivity. He was awarded the 1913 Nobel Prize for Physics.

Kaminski, David Daniel >> **Kaye, Danny**

Kammerer, Paul (1880–1926) Biologist, born in Vienna. He studied in Vienna, where he joined the Institute of Experimental Biology. He claimed to be able to prove that acquired traits could be inherited, and produced at Cambridge three generations of a species of toad where nuptial pads induced in the first had been inherited by the second and third generations (1923). However, after G K Noble of the American Museum of Natural History examined material preserved from Kammerer's work, and showed that the pads were in fact due to injections of ink, Kammerer shot himself.

Kamp, Peter Van de >> **Van de Kamp, Peter**

Kandinsky, Wasily [kandinskee] or **Vasily Vasilyevich** (1866–1944) Painter, born in Moscow. He spent his childhood in Italy, and his early work was carried out in Paris. In Russia (1914–21) he founded the Russian Academy and became head of the Museum of Modern Art. In 1922 he was in charge of the Weimar Bauhaus. He moved to Paris in 1933, and became a naturalized French citizen in 1939. He had a great influence on young European artists, and was a leader of the *Blaue Reiter* group. >> Hartley, Marsden; Macke; Marc

Kane, Bob, popular name of **Robert Kane** (1916–) Cartoonist and animator, the creator of 'Batman', born in New York City. He studied art at Cooper Union, joined the Max Fleischer Studio as a trainee animator in 1934, and entered the comic book field with the serial *Hiram Hick* in *Wow* (1936). His early strips were humorous, but mystery and menace entered his serial *Peter Pupp* in *Wags* (1937), where a cartoon hero battled a one-eyed super-villain. Working to scripts by his partner, **Bill Finger** (1917–74), he created *Batman* for *Detective Comics* (1939), which caught on rapidly. Kane returned to animation to create *Courageous Cat* (1958) and *Cool McCool* (1969) for television. >> Fleischer

Kane, Elisha (Kent) (1820–57) Physician and Arctic explorer, born in Philadelphia, PA. Entering the US navy as a surgeon, he visited China, the East Indies, Arabia, Egypt, Europe, W Africa, and Mexico. He sailed as surgeon and naturalist with the first expedition (1850–1) in search of Sir John Franklin, who had been missing since 1845. He then commanded a second Arctic expedition (1853–5), which had no greater success. The *Kane Basin* is named after him. >> Franklin, John; Hayes, Isaac; Peabody

Kane, Martin >> **O Cadhain, Máirtín**

Kangxi [kangshee], also spelled **K'ang-hsi**, originally **Xuanye** (1654–1722) Fifth emperor of the Manchurian Qing dynasty, and the second to rule China. He succeeded at the age of eight, and ruled personally at 16, cultivating the image of an ideal Confucian ruler, and stressing traditional morality. He organized the compilation of a Ming history, a 50 000-character dictionary, and (1726) a 5000-volume encyclopedia. He adopted the Western calendar, and permitted an East India Company trading post (1699). A pro-Ming revolt was crushed in the SE (1673–81), and he conquered Outer Mongolia (1696), Taiwan (1683), W Mongolia, and Turkestan (from 1715), and established a Tibetan protectorate (1720). A man of wide personal interests, he published three volumes of essays. >> Qianlong

Kang Youwei [kang yooway], also spelled **K'ang Yu-wei** (1858–1927) Philosopher and historian, the leader of the Hundred Days of Reform in China (1898). Impressed by British administration, he saw equality as a product of Confucianism. In 1895, he organized thousands of young scholars to demand drastic national reforms. The young Emperor Zaitian summoned him to implement reforms as the first step to creating a constitutional monarchy, but the movement was ended when Dowager Empress Ci-Xi seized the emperor, executed six of the young reformers, and punished all who had supported them. Kang escaped to Japan with foreign help, returning to China in 1914. >> Ci-Xi; Liang Qichao; Zai-Tian

Kanhai, Rohan Babulal [kanhiy] (1935–) Cricketer, born in Berbice, Guyana. Small in stature but immensely powerful, he was one of the West Indies' leading batsmen in the 1960s and 1970s. He played in 79 Tests, including 61 consecutive appearances, scoring 6277 runs and 15 centuries (two in the match against Australia at Adelaide in 1960–1). His fiery temper sometimes brought him into confrontation with umpires, but he rendered great service to his country and to Warwickshire, where he played for several seasons.

Kano, Motonobu (1476–1559) Painter, born in Kyoto, Japan. He achieved a synthesis of *kanga* (ink painting in the Chinese style) with the lively colours of *yamato-e* (the Japanese style). Under him the *Kano School* established itself, artistically as well as socially, and became a virtual academy. His most famous works, originally in various sanctuaries and monasteries in Kyoto, now preserved in its National Museum, show the decorative treatment of nature, which became standard for the Kano School.

Kant, Immanuel [kant] (1724–1804) Philosopher, born in Königsberg, Germany. He spent his entire life there, studying at the university, and becoming professor of logic and metaphysics in 1770. His main work, now a philosophical classic, is the *Kritik der reinen Vernunft* (1781, Critique of Pure Reason), in which he provided a response to the empiricism of Hume. His views on ethics are set out in the *Grundlagen zur Metaphysik der Sitten* (1785, Foundations of the Metaphysics of Morals) and the *Kritik der praktischen Vernunft* (1788, Critique of Practical Reason), in which he elaborates on the Categorical Imperative as the supreme principle of morality. In his third and last Critique, the *Kritik der Urteilskraft* (1790, Critique of Judgment), he argued that aesthetic judgments, although universal, do not depend on any property (such as beauty or sublimity) of the object. His thought exerted great influence on subsequent philosophy. >> Hume, David

Kantorovich, Leonid Vitaliyevich [kantorohvich] (1912–86) Economist and mathematician, born in St Petersburg, Russia. He studied there, receiving his doctorate at the age of 18. He was a professor at Leningrad State University (1934–60), director of the mathematical economics laboratory at the Moscow Institute of National Economic Management (1971–6), and from 1976 directed the Institute of System Studies at the Moscow Academy of Sciences. He shared the 1975 Nobel Prize for Economics. >> RR1125

Kan-ying >> **Ganying**

Kao Kang >> **Gao Gang**

Kao-tsu >> **Gaozu**

Kapila [kapila] (fl.550 BC) Indian founder of the Samkhya school of Hindu philosophy. An almost legendary figure, said to have spent the latter half of his life on Sagar I at the mouth of the Ganges, he is held to be the originator of the philosophical system presently expounded in the 3rd–5th-c AD commentary of Iśvarakrishna and the *Samkhya Sutra* (c.1400 AD). It is notable for parallels with Buddhist thought, and for a theory of evolution or constant 'becoming' of the world.

Kapil Dev, Nihanj (1959–) Cricketer, born in Chandigarh, Punjab, India. An all-rounder, he made his first-class debut for Haryana at the age of 16, and played county cricket in England for Northants and Worcester. He led India to victory in the 1983 World Cup, and set a competition record score of 175 not out against Zimbabwe. In 1983 he became the youngest player (at 24 years 68 days) to perform a Test double of 2000 runs and 200 wickets (surpassing Ian Botham). In 1994 he broke Sir Richard Hadlee's record of 431 Test wickets by taking 432 wickets in his 130th Test match. >> Botham; Hadlee; RR1149

Kapitza, Pyotr Leonidovich [kapitza] (1894–1984) Physicist, born in Kronstadt, Russia. He studied at St Petersburg (then Petrograd), and taught there until 1921. He then studied under Rutherford at Cambridge, where he became assistant director of magnetic research at the Cavendish Laboratory (1924–32). He was elected fellow of the Royal Society in 1929. He returned to Russia for a conference, but was prevented from leaving again, and was appointed director of the Institute of Physical Problems. He was dismissed in 1946 for refusing to work on the atomic bomb, but reinstated in 1955. He is known for his work on high-intensity magnetism, low temperature, and the liquefaction of hydrogen and helium. He shared the Nobel Prize for Physics in 1978. >> Rutherford, Ernest; RR1122

Kaplan, Viktor (1876–1934) Engineer and inventor, born in Murz, Austria. Educated as a mechanical engineer at the Technische Hochschule in Vienna, he taught at the equivalent school in Brunn from 1903. He researched turbines powered by a low head of water, and patented the turbine with variable pitch blades which now bears his name (1920) and is widely used in hydro and tidal power schemes throughout the world.

Kapoor, Anish [kapoor] (1954–) Artist and sculptor, born in Bombay, India. He moved to London in 1973, where he studied at the Hornsey College of Art and the Chelsea School of Art, and became a teacher at Wolverhampton Polytechnic (1979) and artist in residence at the Walker Art Gallery, Liverpool (1982). He has exhibited at major venues around the world, and his awards include the Premio Duemila Venice Biennale (1990) and the Turner Prize (1991).

Kaprow, Allen (1927–) Avant-garde artist and theorist, born in Atlantic City, NJ. He studied art under the influential painter and theorist Hans Hofmann, and music under John Cage. Rejecting such traditional values as craftsmanship and permanence, he instead promotes 'happenings', involving spectator participation, and welcoming unplanned developments.

Karageorge, Turk **Karadjordje** ('Black George'), also **Czerny George**, nickname of **George Petrović** (1766–1817) Leader of the Serbians in their struggle for independence, born in Viševac, Serbia. His nickname arose from his dark complexion. He led a revolt against Turkey, and in 1808 was elected governor and recognized as Prince of Serbia by the sultan, Selim III (ruled 1789–1807). When Turkey regained control of Serbia in 1813, Karageorge was exiled. When he tried to return, he was murdered at the instigation of his rival, Prince Milosch (ruled 1815–39).

Karajan, Herbert von [ka**ra**yan] (1908–89) Conductor, born in Salzburg, Austria. He studied there and in Vienna, and conducted at the Städtisches Theater, Ulm (1928–33), at Aachen (1934–8), and at the Berlin Staatsoper (1938–42). After the war he was not permitted to work until 1947, having been a member of the Nazi Party, but in 1955 he was made principal conductor of the Berlin Philharmonic, and it is with this orchestra that he was mainly associated until his resignation in 1989. He also conducted frequently elswhere, and was artistic director of the Salzburg Festival (1956–60) and of the Salzburg Easter Festival (from 1967).

Karamanlis, Konstantinos [karaman**lees**], also spelled **Caramanlis** (1907–) Greek statesman, prime minister (1955–63, 1974–80), and president (1980–5), born in Próti, Greece. A former lawyer, he was elected to parliament in 1935, became minister of public works (1952), then prime minister, and formed his own party, the National Radical Union. During his administration, Greece signed a Treaty of Alliance with Cyprus and Turkey. After his party's election defeat in 1963, he left politics and lived abroad, but returned to become premier again in 1974, when he supervised the restoration of civilian rule after the collapse of the military government. He then served as president. >> RR1054

Karan, Donna (1948–) Fashion designer, born in Forest Hills, NY. She became chief designer with the Anna Klein sportswear company in 1974, and with fellow designer Louis Dell'Olio won the Coty American Fashion Critic's Award in 1977and 1981. She launched the Donna Karan Co in 1984, and DKNY in 1988.

Karl (of Sweden) >> **Charles (of Sweden)**

Karle, Jerome (1918–) Physicist, born in New York City. He studied at the City College of New York, Harvard, and Michigan University. He made his career in the US Naval Research Laboratories in Washington, specializing in diffraction methods for studying the fine structure of crystalline matter. For his major contribution in this field, he shared the Nobel Prize for Chemistry in 1985 with Herbert Hauptman. >> Hauptman

Karloff, Boris, originally **William Henry Pratt** (1887–1969) Film star, born in London, England, UK. He studied at London University, then went to Canada and the USA, aiming for a diplomatic career, and became involved in acting. He spent 10 years in repertory companies, went to Hollywood, and after several silent films made his name as the monster in *Frankenstein* (1931). Apart from a notable performance in a World War 1 story, *The Lost Patrol* (1934), his career was mostly spent in popular horror films, though his performances frequently transcended the crudity of the genre, bringing, as in *Frankenstein*, a depth and pathos to the characterization. He continued to appear in films, on television, and on the stage until his death.

Karlstadt >> **Carlstadt**

Karmal, Babrak (1929–96) Afghan prime minister (1979–81) and president (1979–86). He studied at Kabul University, and was imprisoned for anti-government activity during the early 1950s. He formed the Khalq ('masses') Party (1965) and the breakaway Parcham ('banner') Party (1967), the two groups merging to form the banned People's Democratic Party of Afghanistan (PDPA), with Karmal as deputy leader (1977). After briefly holding office as president and prime minister (1978), he was forced into exile in E Europe until after the Soviet military invasion (1979), returning as president. Karmal's rule was fiercely opposed by the Mujahideen guerrillas, and he was replaced as president and PDPA leader by Najibullah Ahmadzai.

Kármán, Theodore von [kah**(r)**man] (1881–1963) Physicist and aeronautical engineer, sometimes called 'the father of modern aerodynamics', born in Budapest. He studied at Budapest Technical University and at Göttingen, and in 1912 became professor at the University of Aachen and head of its Aeronautical Institute. After visits to the USA in 1926, he became director of the Guggenheim Aeronautical Laboratories (1930–49) and the Jet Propulsion Laboratory (1942–5) at the California Institute of Technology. He became a US citizen in 1936. Several theories bear his name, such as the *Kármán vortex street* (1911).

Karp, David (1922–) Writer, born in New York City. He served in the US army, worked as a journalist, then as a radio, TV, and paperback writer, and emerged as a serious novelist with *One* (1953), an Orwellian condemnation of totalitarianism. Other works include *The Day of the Monkey* (1955), *All Honourable Men* (1956), *The Sleepwalkers* (1960), and *Last Believers* (1964).

Karpov, Anatoly Yevgenyevich [kah**(r)**pof] (1951–) Chess player and world champion (1975–85), born in Zlatoust, Russia. Trained by former world champion Mikhail Botvinnik, he won the world junior championship (1969). He became world champion by default after Bobby Fischer refused to defend his title (1975), and successfully defended his title until losing to Kasparov in a controversial match (1985). He defeated Jan Timman of The Netherlands in an official world championship match in 1993, though publicity for this event and his victory suffered as a result of the independent championship match being played at the same time between Kasparov and Nigel Short. >> Botvinnik; Fischer, Bobby; Kasparov; RR1149

Karrer, Paul [ka**rer**] (1889–1971) Chemist, born in Moscow. He studied at Zürich, where he became professor of organic chemistry (1919). He was the first to isolate vitamins A and K, and produced synthetically vitamins B_2 and E. He shared the Nobel Prize for Chemistry in 1937. >> RR1123

Karsavina, Tamara (Platonovna) [kah(r)**sa**vina] (1885–1978) Ballet dancer, born in St Petersburg, Russia. She trained at the Imperial Ballet School under Cecchetti, joined the Maryinsky Theatre (1902), and became one of the original members of Diaghilev's Ballets Russes, partnering Nijinsky in ballets by Michel Fokine (1909–14). She married an English diplomat and moved with him to London (1918), where she became vice-president of the Royal Academy of Dancing until 1955. She coached Margot Fonteyn, and wrote several books, including the autobiographical *Theatre Street* (1930), *Ballet Technique* (1956), and *Classical Ballet* (1962). >> Cecchetti; Diaghilev; Fokine; Fonteyn; Nijinsky

Karsh, Yousuf (1908–) Portrait photographer, born in Mardin, Turkey. An Armenian in Turkey, he suffered persecution before emigrating to Canada in 1924. He was apprenticed to a Boston portraitist (1928–31), and in 1932 opened his own studio in Ottawa, being appointed official portrait photographer to the Canadian government in 1935. His wartime studies of Winston Churchill and other national leaders were widely reproduced, and he has continued to portray statesmen, artists, and writers throughout the world.

Karski, Jan, original surname **Kozielecki** (1914–) Polish resistance hero, born in Lodz, Poland. A Roman Catholic, he graduated from Lvov University in 1935, worked in diplomatic posts until 1939, then joined the army. Taken prisoner first by the Soviets then by the Germans, he escaped and became a government courier. After discovery by German intelligence, he emigrated to the USA in 1942, where he eventually became a US citizen, a professor at Georgetown University, and a lecturer for the Pentagon and State Department. While in Poland, he secretly toured the Warsaw Ghetto and a concentration camp, gathering evidence of Nazi atrocities against Polish Jews, and was the first to present documented proof of Hitler's extermination policy to Allied leaders in Britain and the USA. Embittered by the Allies' failure to take decisive action, he refused to speak about his activities in the post-war years, but his story became known in 1979, after the writer Elie Wiesel made contact with him, and he is the subject of a biography by E T Wood & S M Jankowski, *One Man Tried to Stop the Holocaust* (1994). He was made an honorary citizen of Israel in 1994.

Kasdan, Lawrence (1949–) Film director, born in Miami Beach, FL. He studied at the University of Michigan and gained a co-writer credit on *The Empire Strikes Back* (1980) before becoming a director with *Body Heat* (1981). Later films include *The Accidental Tourist* (1989), *Grand Canyon* (1991) and *Wyatt Earp* (1996).

Kasparov, Gary (Kimovich) [kas**pah**rof] (1963–) Chess player, born in Baku, Azerbaijan. When he beat Anatoly Karpov for the world title (Nov 1985), he became the youngest world champion, at the age of 22 years 210 days. He has successfully defended his title, and is the highest-ranked active player, with a ranking of 2805. His 1984–5 match with Karpov was the longest in the history of chess. Long-term friction between him and the international chess organization, FIDE, resulted in his establishing the Grandmasters' Association in 1987, and arranging a World Championship match in 1993 without FIDE involvement, in which he defeated Nigel Short of Britain. In 1996 he competed against Deep Blue, the world's best chess-playing computer, winning four of the six games, but in a rematch the following year he was decisively beaten by the machine. His autobiography, *Child of Change* (a reference to Gorbachev's policy of glasnost), appeared in 1987. >> Gorbachev; Karpov; RR1149

Kassem, Abdul Karim (1914–63) Iraqi soldier and revolutionary, born in Baghdad. He joined the army and rose to the rank of brigadier. He led the coup which resulted in the overthrow of the monarchy and the deaths of King Faisal II and the pro-Western prime minister General Nuri Es-Sa'id. Kassem suspended the constitution and established a left-wing military regime, with himself as prime minister and president, but soon found himself increasingly isolated in the Arab world. He survived one assassination attempt, but failed to crush a Kurdish rebellion (1961–3), and was killed in a coup led by Colonel Salem Aref. >> Faisal II

Kastler, Alfred (1902–84) Physicist, born in Guebwiller, Germany. He studied at the Ecole Normale Supérieure, Paris, and worked at Bordeaux, Clermont-Ferrand, and Louvain before returning to the Ecole Normale (1941–68), becoming professor there and director of the physics laboratory. He discovered and developed methods of observing Hertzian resonances in atoms, leading to the development of the maser and laser. He was awarded the Nobel Prize for Physics in 1966.

Kästner, Erich [**kest**ner] (1899–1974) Writer, born in Dresden, Germany. He was a teacher and journalist, then turned to writing poetry and novels. He is best known for his children's books, which include *Emil und die Detektive* (1928,

Emil and the Detectives). After World War 2, he became magazine editor of *Die Neue Zeitung*, and founded a paper for children.

Kastrioti, George >> **Skanderbeg**

Katherine >> **Catherine**

Katz, Alex (1927–) Painter, born in New York City. He studied painting at Cooper Union, New York City, and at Skowhegan School, ME. From 1959 he began making portraits of his friends in a deliberately gauche, naive style, simplifying forms and using a limited palette. These large-scale portraits, which have a directness bordering on kitsch, have been likened to cinematic images of film idols.

Katz, Sir Bernard (1911–) Biophysicist, born in Leipzig, Germany. He studied at Leipzig and London, carried out research in London (1935–9) and Sydney (1939–42), and became professor of biophysics at London (1952–78), then an honorary research fellow. Knighted in 1969, in 1970 he shared the Nobel Prize for Physiology or Medicine for his studies on how transmitter substances are released from nerve terminals. >> RR1124

Kauffmann, (Maria Anna Catharina) Angelica [**kowf**man] (1741–1807) Painter, born in Chur, Switzerland. By the age of 11 she was already an acknowledged painter and musician. She went to London (1766), became a close friend of Reynolds, and a founder member of the Royal Academy (1769). She is best known for her wall paintings for residences designed by Robert Adam. >> Adam, Robert; Reynolds, Joshua

Kaufman, George S(imon) [**kowf**man] (1889–1961) Playwright and director, born in Pittsburgh, PA. In collaboration with Moss Hart he wrote *You Can't Take It With You* (1936, Pulitzer) and *The Man Who Came to Dinner* (1939). Other works include *The Solid Gold Cadillac* (with Howard Teichmann, 1953) and many musicals, some of which have been filmed. He directed much of his work. >> Hart, Moss

Kaufman, Henry [**kowf**man] (1927–) Economist and banker, born in Wenings, Germany. He moved to the USA in 1937. He was assistant chief economist in the research department of the Federal Reserve Bank, New York City (1957–61), then joined Salomon Brothers, becoming a partner in 1967 and managing director in 1981. Chief economist in charge of (among other interests) bond market research and bond portfolio analysis, he wrote *Interest Rates, the Markets, and the New Financial World* in 1986.

Kaufman, Philip (1936–) Film director, born in Chicago, IL. As an independent film-maker he wrote, produced, and directed his first film, *Goldstein* (1964), in collaboration with Benjamin Manaster. He also worked closely with his wife Rose, co-writer on *The Wanderers* (1979) and *Henry and June* (1990), and his son Peter, who produced *Rising Sun* (1993). He wrote the story for *The Outlaw Josey Wales* (1975) and *Raiders of the Lost Ark* (1981). Other films include *Invasion of the Body Snatchers* (1978), *The Unbearable Lightness of Being* (1988), and *China: The Wild East* (1995).

Kaunda, Kenneth (David) [ka**oon**da] (1924–) Zambian statesman and president (1964–91), born in Lubwa, Zambia. He became a teacher in Zambia and Tanganyika (Tanzania), then joined the African National Congress, becoming its secretary-general, and in 1958 founding a development of this organization, the Zambian African National Congress. He was subsequently imprisoned, and the movement banned. Elected president of the United National Independent Party (1960), he played a leading part in his country's independence negotiations, and became the first president of the country. After a failed military coup in 1990, he agreed to multi-party elections in 1991; but lost the presidency to Frederick Chiluba, leader of the Movement for Multi-Party Democracy. >> RR1101

Kaunitz(-Rietberg), Wenzel Anton, Fürst von (Prince of) [**kow**nits **reet**berg] (1711–94) Austrian statesman and chancellor (1793–92), born in Vienna. He distinguished himself at the Congress of Aix-la-Chapelle (1748), and as Austrian ambassador at the French court (1750–2). As chancellor, he instigated the Diplomatic Revolution, and directed Austrian politics for almost 40 years under Maria Theresa and Joseph II. He was a liberal patron of arts and sciences. >> Joseph II; Maria Theresa

Kavanagh, Henry Edward [**ka**vana] (1892–1958) Journalist and scriptwriter, born in Auckland, New Zealand. He went to England in 1914 to study medicine, but turned instead to writing. He wrote scripts for the radio comedy programme *ITMA*, which was extremely popular during World War 2, and whose anarchic humour influenced much subsequent British comedy. His son, **P J Kavanagh** (1931–) wrote a stylish family history, *Finding Connections* (1991). >> Handley, Tommy

Kavanagh, Patrick (Joseph) [**ka**vana] (1904–67) Poet and writer, born near Inniskeen, Co Monaghan, Ireland. He was self-educated, and worked as a peasant farmer before moving to Dublin (1939) to pursue a career as a writer and journalist. He is best known for *The Great Hunger* (1942), a long, angry and passionate poem of farm life, and *Tarry Flynn* (1948), an autobiographical novel, in which he depicts sensitively and convincingly the countryside where he was brought up.

Kawabata, Yasunari (1899–1972) Writer, born in Osaka, Japan. He studied at Tokyo University, and published his first novel, *The Dancer of Izu Province*, in 1925. He experimented with various Western novel forms, but by the mid-1930s returned to traditional Japanese ones. Later novels include *Yukiguni* (1935–48, Snow Country), *Sembazuru* (1949, Thousand Cranes), and *Yama no oto* (1949–54, The Sound of the Mountain). He received the 1968 Nobel Prize for Literature, the first Japanese writer to be given the award.

Kay, John (1704–c. 1764) Inventor, born near Bury, Greater Manchester, NW England, UK. He took charge of his father's woollen mill, made many improvements to the machinery, and obtained a patent for a device for twisting and cording mohair and worsted (1730). In 1733 he patented his flying shuttle, one of the most important inventions in the history of textile machinery. The new shuttle was eagerly adopted by weavers, but they were reluctant to pay the royalties due to him, and the cost of court actions against defaulters nearly ruined him. After his house was ransacked by a mob of textile workers, who feared that his machines would destroy their livelihood, he left England for France (1753), where he is believed to have died a pauper. >> Arkwright

Kay, Ulysses (Simpson) (1917–95) Composer, born in Tucson, Az. One of the first prominent African-American composers, he studied with Hindemith and Hanson, and wrote mildly Modernist works that won numerous prizes. >> Hanson, Howard; Hindemith

Kaye, Danny, originally **David Daniel Kaminski** (1913–87) Stage, film, and television entertainer, born in New York City. A singer and dancer at school and summer camps, he toured extensively in the 1930s, and made his film debut in 1937. His first feature film, *Up in Arms* (1943), was an instant success, and launched him on a career as an international star, noted for his mimicry and tongue-twisting speciality songs. His best-loved films include *The Secret Life of Walter Mitty* (1946), *Hans Christian Andersen* (1952), and *The Court Jester* (1956). As a straight dramatic actor his most accomplished performance was as a concentration camp survivor in the television film *Skokie* (1981). Well known for his fundraising activities for UNICEF, he received a special Academy Award in 1954.

Kaye, Nora, originally **Nora Koreff** (1920–87) Ballerina, born in New York City. She studied at the School of American Ballet and the New York Metropolitan Opera Ballet School. She joined American Ballet Theater at its inception in 1939, and soon became the leading dramatic ballerina of her generation, creating the role of Hagar in Antony Tudor's *Pillar of Fire* (1942), and appearing in other modern ballets as well as the classics. She was a member of New York City Ballet (1951–4), then returned to ABT until her retirement in 1961. She co-founded Ballet of Two Worlds with her choreographer husband **Herbert Ross** (1926–). >> Tudor, Antony

Kay-Shuttleworth, Sir James (Phillips), originally **James Phillips Kay** (1804–77) Physician and educationist, born in Rochdale, Greater Manchester, NW England, UK. He studied and practised medicine, married the heiress of the Shuttleworths of Gawthorpe, and assumed her surname (1842). As secretary to the committee of the Privy Council on Education he was instrumental in establishing a system of government school inspection. The pupil-teacher system originated with him, and he founded his own teacher-training college (1840), which later became St John's College, Battersea.

Kazan, Elia [ka**zan**], originally **Elia Kazanjoglous** (1909–) Stage and film director, born in Istanbul. He studied at Yale, then acted in minor roles on Broadway and in Hollywood before becoming a director of plays and films. With Lee Strasberg, he founded the Actors Studio in 1947. His Broadway productions include the works of Thornton Wilder, Arthur Miller, and Tennessee Williams. Many of his films have a social or political theme, such as *Gentleman's Agreement* (1948, Oscar) and *On the Waterfront* (1954, Oscar). Other notable films include *A Streetcar Named Desire* (1951), *East of Eden* (1955), and *America, America* (1964). His last film was *The Last Tycoon* (1976). He published his autobiography, *My Life*, in 1988, and *Beyond the Aegean* appeared in 1994. >> Loden, Barbara; Strasberg, Lee

Kazantzakis, Nikos [kazan**za**kis] (1883–1957) Writer, born in Heraklion, Crete, Greece. He studied law at Athens, spent some years travelling in Europe and Asia, and published his first novel in 1929. He is best known for the novel *Vios kai politia tou Alexi Zormpa* (1946, trans Zorba the Greek, filmed 1964) and the epic autobiographical narrative poem, *Odissa* (1938, trans The Odyssey, a Modern Sequel).

Kean, Edmund (c. 1789–1833) Actor, born in London, England, UK. He became a strolling player, and after 10 years in the provinces made his first appearance at Drury Lane as Shylock (1814). A period of great success followed as a tragic actor, but because of his irregularities he gradually forfeited public approval, his reputation being finally ruined when he was successfully sued for adultery in 1825.

Keane, Molly, professional name of **Mary Nesta Keane**, pseudonym **M J Farrell** (1904–96) Writer, born in Co Kildare, Ireland. She wrote her first book at the age of 17 under the pseudonym M J Farrell, and wrote 10 novels in the period 1928–52, including *The Rising Tide* (1937), *Two Days in Aragon* (1941), and *Loving Without Tears* (1951), drawing her material from the foibles of her own class. She also wrote plays, such as *Spring Meeting* (1938), *Ducks and Drakes* (1942), and *Dazzling Prospect* (1961). When her husband died at 36 she stopped writing for many years, but *Good Behaviour* (1981, televised 1983), short-listed for the Booker Prize, led to the reprinting of many of her books and a revival of critical appreciation. Later books included *Time After Time* (1983, televised 1986) and *Loving and Giving* (1988).

Kearny, Philip [kah(r)nee] (1814–62) Soldier, born in New York City. He became a cavalry officer, serving on the W frontier, then with the French army in Algiers. He lost his left arm in the Mexican War, and served with the French Imperial Guard at the Battles of Magenta and Solferino (1859). Returning to the USA at the outbreak of the Civil War, he was commissioned a brigadier general in the Union Army of the Potomac, and commanded first a brigade, then a division through some dozen battles, before being killed in action at Chantilly.

Keating, Paul (John) (1944–) Australian statesman and prime minister (1991–6), born in Sydney, New South Wales, Australia. He managed a rock-and-roll band before entering federal parliament as a member of the House of Representatives in 1969. He was minister for Northern Australia in the Whitlam Government in 1975, and president of the New South Wales Labor Party (1979–83). As Treasurer (1983–91), he was the main architect of the government's economic policies, particularly the deregulation of financial markets. After unsuccessfully challenging Bob Hawke as leader, he spent some time as a back-bencher before being elected leader by his party in 1991. In 1993, in the midst of a recession and record high levels of unemployment, he and his party managed to win a general election that was seen as unwinnable. An outspoken republican, known for his razor-sharp tongue, he retired from parliament following the election defeat of 1996. In 1997 he declined the award of Companion to the Order of Australia – the first living former prime minister not to accept the honour. >> Hawke, Bob; Whitlam

Keating, Tom (1918–84) Art restorer and celebrated forger of paintings, born in London, England, UK. The scandal about his fakes of the works of the great masters broke in 1976, when an art expert suggested that a work by Samuel Palmer, which sold at an auction for £9400, was not genuine. Keating admitted that a series of nine pictures, bearing imitations of Samuel Palmer's signature, were in fact drawn by himself, and estimated that there were some 2500 of his fakes in circulation. In 1979 he was put on trial at the Old Bailey for forgery, but charges were eventually dropped because of his deteriorating health. Keating and his work became very popular with the public, who enjoyed the way in which he had fooled art-dealers. >> Palmer, Samuel

Keaton, Buster, popular name of **Joseph Francis Keaton** (1895–1966) Film comedian, born in Piqua, KS. He joined his parents vaudeville act 'The Three Keatons' at the age of 3, developing great acrobatic skill. In 1917 he went to Hollywood, where he made his film debut. Renowned for his inimitable deadpan expression, he starred in and directed such silent classics as *Our Hospitality* (1923), *The Navigator* (1924), and *The General* (1926). His reputation went into eclipse with the advent of talking films until the 1950s, when many of his silent masterpieces were re-released. He also began to appear in character roles in several films, such as *Sunset Boulevard* (1950) and *Limelight* (1952). He received a special Academy Award in 1959.

Keaton, Diane [keeton] (1946–) Film actress, born in Los Angeles, CA. She played opposite Woody Allen in the Broadway production of *Play It Again, Sam* (1969), then went on to star in several of his films, such as *Annie Hall* (1977, Oscar) *Manhattan* (1979), and *Manhatten Murder Mystery* (1993). Other films include *The Godfather* (1972), *Reds* (1981), *Baby Boom* (1987), *First Wives Club* (1996), and *Marvin's Room* (1996, Oscar nomination). Her first major film as a director was *Unstrung Heroes* (1995). >> Allen, Woody

Keaton, Michael (1951–) Actor, born in Caraopolis, PA. He started with Chicago's Second City improvisational group, then went to Los Angeles and appeared in a few film comedies. His breakthrough came with the film *Mr Mom* (1983), and five years later, after *Beetlejuice* (1988) and

Clean and Sober (1988), he was named Best Actor by national film critics. Other films include *Batman* (1989), *Batman Returns* (1992), *Much Ado About Nothing* (1993), and *Multiplicity* (1996).

Keats, Ezra Jack (1916–) Illustrator of children's books, born in New York City. *My Dog Is Lost* (1960) was his first book, but *The Snowy Day* (1962), about a small black boy's adventure in the snow, is the one for which he is best known. Among later books, *Peter's Chair* (1967) was a notable success.

Keats, John (1795–1821) Poet, born in London, England, UK. Educated at Enfield, he became a medical student in London (1815–17). Leigh Hunt introduced him to other young Romantics, including Shelley, and published his first sonnets in the *Examiner* (1816). His first book of poems was published in 1817. His long mythological poem *Endymion* (1818) was fiercely criticized, but he was nonetheless able to produce *Lamia and Other Poems* (1820), a landmark in English poetry, which contains 'The Eve of St Agnes' and 'Lamia', and his major odes. Seriously ill with tuberculosis, he sailed for Italy, and died in Rome. His *Letters* (1848) are among the most celebrated in the language. >> Hunt, Leigh; Shelley, Percy Bysshe

Keble, John [keebl] (1792–1866) Anglican clergyman and poet, born in Fairford, Gloucestershire, SWC England, UK. He studied at Oxford, was ordained in 1816, and became a college tutor (1818–23) and professor of poetry (1831–41). In 1827 his book of poems on the liturgical calendar, *The Christian Year*, was widely circulated. His sermon on 'National apostasy' (1833) began the Oxford Movement, encouraging a return to High Church ideals, and his circle issued the 90 *Tracts for the Times*. In 1835 he moved to the Hampshire living of Hursley, where he remained until his death. Keble College, Oxford, was erected in his memory. >> Newman, John Henry

Kee, Robert (1919–) British broadcaster and writer. He studied at Oxford, joined the RAF, and was shot down over The Netherlands, spending four years in a prisoner-of-war camp. His first novel, *A Crowd Is Not Company* (1947), reflected this experience and won him the Atlantic Award for literature. Other novels include *The Impossible Shore* (1949) and *A Sign of the Times* (1955). He worked for *Picture Post* (1948–51), and was a special correspondent for *The Observer* (1956–7) and *The Sunday Times* (1957–8). Joining the BBC, he worked on *Panorama* (1958–62). The recipient of the Richard Dimbleby Award (1976), his other major television work includes the series *Ireland* (1981), co-founding the breakfast programme for TV-AM (1983), and Channel 4's *Seven Days* (1984–8). His non-fiction books include *The Green Flag* (1972), *Ireland: a History* (1980), *Trial and Error* (1986), and *The Laurel and the Ivy: Parnell and Irish Nationalism* (1993).

Keegan, (Joseph) Kevin (1951–) Footballer, born in Armthorpe, South Yorkshire, N England, UK. He played for Scunthorpe (1966–71), Liverpool (1971–7), Hamburg (1977–80), Southampton (1980–2), and Newcastle (1982–4), and was a lively member of the England side (1973–82, captain from 1976). He received several Cup-winners' medals, and was European Footballer of the Year in 1978 and 1979. He became manager of Newcastle United in 1992, resigning in 1997 to become chief executive of Fulham. >> RR1156

Keeler, Christine (1942–) Former model and showgirl, raised in Wraysbury, Berkshire, S England, UK. She was involved in an affair with a Soviet naval attaché, Ivanov, and the Conservative cabinet minister, John Profumo, which led to Profumo's resignation from politics (1963), the prosecution of her patron Stephen Ward (d.1963) for living off the immoral earnings of Keeler and Mandy Rice Davies, and Ward's eventual suicide. Keeler served a prison sentence for related offences. In the late 1980s, her autobiography, and the film *Scandal* (1989), in which she collaborated, revived interest in the events and raised doubts about the validity of the charges made against her and Ward. >> Profumo; Rice-Davies

Keeler, James (Edward) (1857–1900) Astronomer, born in La Salle, IL. He studied at Johns Hopkins, Heidelberg, and Berlin universities, and became director of the Allegheny Observatory, Pittsburgh (1891–8), then of the Lick Observatory, CA. He established the composition of Saturn's rings (as Maxwell had postulated), and carried out important spectroscopic work on nebulae, discovering 120 000 of them. >> Maxwell, James C

Keilin, David (1887–1963) Biochemist, born in Moscow. He studied in Warsaw, Liège, and Paris, then spent his career in Cambridge, where he was director of the Molteno Institute from 1931, and professor of biology. His ingenious studies of enzymes and animal pigments led to his major discovery, the pigment cytochrome, which occurs in plant and animal cells and has a key role in biochemical oxidation.

Keillor, Garrison [keeler], pseudonym of **Gary Edward Keillor** (1942–) Humorous writer and radio performer, born in Anoka, MN. He studied at Minnesota University, became a radio announcer, then began writing for *The New Yorker*. In 1974 he first hosted the live radio show, 'A Prairie Home Companion', delivering a weekly monologue set in the quiet, fictional mid-western town of Lake Wobegon, 'where all the women are strong, all the men are good looking, and all the children are above average'. When the show closed in 1987 he was celebrated for his wry, deliberate, hypnotic storytelling. His books include *Happy To Be Here* (1981), the best-selling *Lake Wobegon Days* (1985), *Leaving Home* (1987), *We Are Still Married* (1989), and *WLT: A Radio Romance* (1992).

Keino, Kip(choge) [kaynoh] (1940–) Athlete, born in Kipsamo, Kenya. Concentrating on middle-distance events, his most effective range lay between 1500 m and 5000 m. At the 1968 Mexico City Olympics he won the 1500 m, and at Munich in 1972 he won the gold medal for the 3000 steeplechase. In 1965 he established new world records for the 3000 and 5000 m.

Keitel, Wilhelm [kiytl] (1882–1946) German field marshal, born in Helmscherode, Germany. He joined the army in 1901, and became an artillery staff officer in World War 1. An ardent Nazi, he was made chief of the Supreme Command of the Armed Forces (1938). In 1940 he signed the Compiègne armistice with France, and in 1945 was one of the German signatories of surrender in Berlin. He was convicted of war crimes at Nuremberg, and executed.

Keith, Sir Arthur (1866–1955) Physical anthropologist, born in Aberdeen, NE Scotland, UK. Holding doctorates in medicine, science, and law, he became professor at the Royal College of Surgeons, London, professor of physiology at the Royal Institution, London (1918–23), and Rector of Aberdeen University (1930–3). He is best known for his work on fossilized humanoid forms. He wrote *Introduction to the Study of Anthropoid Apes* (1896), *Concerning Man's Origin* (1927), and *New Theory of Human Evolution* (1948).

Kekkonen, Urho K(aleva) [kekonen] (1900–86) Finnish prime minister (1950–3, 1954–6) and president of Finland (1956–81), born in Pielavesi, Finland. He studied law at Helsinki University, and worked in the Ministry of Agriculture before entering parliament as an Agrarian party deputy (1936). Although he had always been hostile to Stalinist Russia, as president he encouraged a policy of cautious friendship with the Soviet Union. At the same time his strict neutrality ensured that he retained the confidence of his Scandinavian neighbours. He supported

Finland's membership of the European Free Trade Association (1961), and was host to the 35-nation European Security Conference in Helsinki (1975). He accepted a Lenin Peace Prize in 1980. His popularity in Finland led to the passage of special legislation enabling him to remain in office until 1984, but his health gave way and he resigned in 1981. >> RR1049

Kekulé von Stradonitz, (Friedrich) August [kaykuhlay fon **shtrad**onits] (1829–1896) Chemist, born in Darmstadt, Germany. He studied at Giessen and Paris, where he met and was influenced by the work of Charles Gerhardt. He became professor at Ghent (1858) and at Bonn (1865), and made a major contribution to organic chemistry by developing structural theories, in particular the cyclic structure of benzene. >> Gerhardt

Keldysh, Mstislav (Vsevoldvich) (1911–78) Mathematician and space programme leader, born in Riga, Latvia. He studied at Moscow, and conducted aeronautical research at Zhukovskii Aero-Hydrodynamics Institute (from 1934) and at Steklow Mathematics Institute (from 1939). He was a leading figure in the development of the theory of rocketry and in the emergence of the USSR in space exploration.

Keller, Hans (1919–85) Musicologist, born in Vienna. He emigrated to England in 1938, and followed a career in musical journalism and analytical criticism. He co-founded the magazine *Music Survey*, wrote for many other journals, served on the BBC staff from 1959, and broadcast frequently. He was influentially erudite upon contemporary music, chamber music, and football.

Keller, Helen (Adams) (1880–1968) Writer, born in Tuscumbia, AL. She lost her sight and hearing after an illness at 19 months, but was educated by Anne Sullivan who taught her to speak, read, and write, and became her lifelong companion. She obtained a degree in 1904, and became distinguished as a lecturer and a writer, publishing her autobiography *The Story of My Life* (1902). It was dramatized by William Gibson in *The Miracle Worker* (1959, Pulitzer, filmed 1962). >> Sullivan, Anne

Kelley, Florence (1859–1932) Feminist and social reformer, born in Philadelphia, PA. She studied at Cornell and Zürich universities, and in 1891 joined Jane Addams's Hull House Settlement in Chicago. She became the first woman factory inspector in Illinois, successfully fighting to reduce working hours and improve methods and conditions of production. Gaining a law degree from Northwestern University (1895), she moved to New York City in 1899, becoming general secretary of the National Consumers' League, and in 1910 was one of the founders of the National Association for the Advancement of Colored People. She helped establish the Women's International League for Peace and Freedom (1919). >> Addams, Jane

Kelley, Oliver Hudson (1826–1913) Farmer, and founder of the Grange, born in Boston, MA. He worked in Illinois and Iowa before moving to Minnesota (1840), where he traded with Dakota Sioux and farmed. In 1864 he became a clerk in the Bureau of Agriculture, and undertook the Bureau's survey of agriculture conditions in Minnesota (1865). In 1867 he and six other men founded the National Grange of the Patrons of Husbandry, with him acting as its secretary. He argued the benefits of the Grange in the agricultural press, and by 1874 there were more than 20 000 Granges. In 1875 he moved his family to Louisville, KY, where he established the Grange secretary's office. In 1878 he resigned his office and became a land speculator in N Florida, founding the town of Carrabelle.

Kellogg, Frank B(illings) (1856–1937) Jurist and statesman, born in Potsdam, NY. After law practice in Minnesota, he became a senator (1917–23), ambassador in

London (1923–5), and secretary of state (1925–9). With Aristide Briand he drew up the Briand–Kellogg Pact (1928) outlawing war, which became the legal basis for the Nuremberg trials (1945–6). He was a judge of the Permanent Court of Justice at the Hague (1930–5), and was awarded the 1929 Nobel Peace Prize. >> Briand

Kellogg, Paul Underwood (1879–1958) Editor and social reformer, born in Kalamazoo, MI. After working as a journalist, he studied at Columbia University, then joined the editorial staff of *Charities*, a magazine devoted to philanthropic activities. In 1907 he left the magazine to commence an in-depth study of every aspect of life in Pittsburgh, the first such social survey of a US urban community, published as the *Pittsburgh Survey* (1910–14). In 1909 he returned to his old magazine, now retitled *Survey*; as its editor (1912–52), he forged it into America's leading journal of social work and a major force in social reform, and during the 1930s he saw many of his concerns addressed by President Franklin D Roosevelt's 'New Deal'. In 1939 he became president of the National Conference of Social Work, and was active in a variety of progressive causes. >> Roosevelt, Franklin D

Kellogg, W(illie) K(eith) (1852–1943) Cereal manufacturer and philanthropist, born in Battle Creek, MI. After working as a broom salesman, he joined with his brother, **Dr John H(arvey) Kellogg** (1852–1943), at Battle Creek Sanitarium during the 1890s to develop a process of cooking, rolling, and toasting wheat and corn into crisp flakes which made a nourishing breakfast cereal for their patients. Soon their *corn flakes* were being sold through the mail, and in 1905, Will formed the Battle Creek Toasted Corn Flake Co. When he renamed it W K Kellogg Co he had to fight a long legal battle with his brother over the right to use the family name. The new product was extensively advertised, and resulted in a revolution in the breakfast-eating habits of the Western world. In 1930 he established the W K Kellogg Foundation, which became one of the leading philanthropic institutions in the USA.

Kellow, Kathleen >> Hibbert

Kelly, Ellsworth (1923–) Artist, born in Newburgh, NY. He studied in Boston and at the Académie des Beaux-Arts in Paris, and lived in France until 1954. From the late 1950s he made his name as a 'hard-edge' abstract painter, using wide, flat areas of strong colour. He is also a sculptor, and made a screen for the Philadelphia Transport Building in 1956.

Kelly, Gene, popular name of **Eugene Curran Kelly** (1912–96) Modern dancer and actor, born in Pittsburgh, PA. A dance instructor with a degree in economics from the University of Pittsburgh, he travelled to New York City, and found employment in the chorus of *Leave it to Me* (1938). His stage success in *Pal Joey* (1939) led to a Hollywood debut in *For Me and My Girl* (1942), followed by a long series of musicals in which he was often co-director and choreographer, such as *An American in Paris* (1951) and *Singin' in the Rain* (1952). In 1951 he received a special Academy Award, and from the 1960s worked mostly as a director, notably of *Hello, Dolly!* (1969). He received an American Film Institute Life Achievement Award in 1985.

Kelly, George A (1905–66) Psychologist, born in Kansas. He studied at several universities, including Edinburgh and Iowa, and taught at Fort Hays Kansas State College prior to World War 2, during which he was an aviation psychologist with the US navy. From 1946 he worked at Ohio State University, leaving to take up a post at Brandeis University in 1965. Best known for his novel approach to the understanding of personality, he devised the repertory grid test, an open-ended method for exploring an individual's 'personal constructs'.

Kelly, Grace (Patricia), married name **Grimaldi, Princess Grace of Monaco** (1929–82) Film actress and princess, born in Philadelphia, PA. After studying at the American Academy of Dramatic Art, she acted in television and on Broadway, and made her film debut in 1951. Her short but highly successful film career as a coolly elegant beauty included such classics as the Western *High Noon* (1952), *Rear Window* (1954), *The Country Girl* (1954, Oscar), *To Catch a Thief* (1955), and *High Society* (1956). In 1956 she married Prince Rainier III of Monaco, and retired from the screen. She was killed in a car accident. >> Rainier III

Kelly, Howard (Atwood) (1858–1943) Surgeon and gynaecologist, born in Camden, NJ. He practised surgery and gynaecology for several years before taking up a post at Pennsylvania University, then at Johns Hopkins Medical School (1889–1919). He pioneered the use of cocaine anaesthesia, developed a number of operations for the kidney and bladder, and played an important role in the development of gynaecology as a surgical speciality separate from obstetrics.

Kelly, Ned, popular name of **Edward Kelly** (1855–80) Outlaw, born in Beveridge, Victoria, Australia. After shooting a policeman who was attempting to arrest his brother, Dan, he fled to the outback, where he was joined by his brother and two others, and formed the Kelly gang. They carried out a series of daring robberies (1878–80) which, coupled with Ned's home-made armour, made them into legendary figures. After a siege at Glenrowan township, he was arrested, taken to Melbourne, and hanged.

Kelly, Petra, originally **Petra Lehmann** (1947–92) German political activist, co-founder of the Green Party, born in Günzburg, Germany. She moved to the USA at the age of 13 when her mother married a US serviceman, and became actively involved in the antiwar and civil rights demonstrations of the 1960s while a student at the American University, Washington. She returned to Germany, joined the Social Democratic Party, but quit in 1979 to help found the Green Party, and was elected to the Bundestag in 1983. She became involved with Gert Bastian, a general who had resigned his commission to take up the Green cause, and her body was found near his in the house they shared. She is believed to have been shot by him before he took his own life.

Kelly, Walt(er Crawford) (1913–73) Animator and strip cartoonist, born in Philadelphia, PA. He joined the Walt Disney studio in Hollywood as an animator in 1935, and moved to comic books in 1941, creating his most famous characters, Albert Alligator and Pogo Possum of Okefenokee Swamp. He became art editor of the *New York Star* (1948), introducing *Pogo* as a daily strip. The serial embraced slapstick, fantasy, and influential political comment, and was later published in several collections. It was the source of the frequently quoted aphorism: 'We have met the enemy and they is us.'

Kelly, William (1811–88) Inventor of the pneumatic process for steelmaking, born in Pittsburgh, PA. With his brother he became involved in the manufacture of wrought-iron articles. He discovered that an air blast directed on or through molten cast iron can remove much of the carbon in it, so that the resulting metal becomes suitable for a wider range of applications than relatively brittle cast iron. He built seven of his 'converters' (1851–6), then heard that Henry Bessemer had been granted a US patent for the same process. As a result, although he managed to build a steel plant in the 1860s, the commercial impact of his discovery was much reduced. >> Bessemer; Huntsman

Kelman, James (1946–) Novelist and short-story writer, born in Glasgow, W Scotland, UK. He published his first book of short stories in 1983, and his first novel, *The Busconductor Hines*, in 1984. Regarded as one of the major talents in contemporary Scottish fiction, he won the Booker Prize in 1994 for *How Late It Was, How Late*.

Kelsen, Hans (1881–1973) Jurist and legal theorist, born in Prague. Professor at Vienna, Cologne, Geneva, Prague, Harvard, and Berkeley, he is best known as the creator of the 'pure theory of law' (*Reine Rechtslehre*, 1934), in which the science of law is required to be exclusively normative and pure, not practical. His work was extremely influential in the 20th-c.

Kelvin (of Largs), William Thomson, 1st Baron (1824–1907) Mathematician and physicist, born in Belfast. He studied at Glasgow and Cambridge, and became professor of natural philosophy at Glasgow (1846). He designed several kinds of electrometer, and his sounding apparatus and compass were widely adopted. In pure science, he carried out fundamental research into thermodynamics, helping to develop the law of the conservation of energy, and the absolute temperature scale (now given in kelvin). He also presented the dynamical theory of heat, developed theorems for the mathematical analysis of electricity and magnetism, and investigated hydrodynamics, particularly wave-motion and vortex-motion. He was created a peer in 1892. >> Joule; Tait, Peter Guthrie

Kemble, Fanny, popular name of **Frances Ann Kemble** (1809–93) Actress, born in London, England, UK, the niece of John Philip Kemble. She made her debut at Covent Garden as Juliet in *Romeo and Juliet*, and created a great sensation. For three years she played leading parts in London, then went with her father to America (1832), where she married a Southern planter. Divorced in 1848, she successfully returned to the stage under her maiden name. >> Kemble, John Philip

Kemble, John Philip (1757–1823) Actor, born in Prescot, Merseyside, NW England, UK. He trained for the priesthood at Sedgley Park, Staffordshire, and the English college at Douai, but became an actor, making his first appearance at Wolverhampton (1776). The success of his sister, Sarah Siddons, gave him the opportunity to play Hamlet at Drury Lane. He continued to play leading tragic characters at Drury Lane for many years, and became Sheridan's manager. He purchased a share of Covent Garden Theatre (1802), became manager, and made his first appearance there as Hamlet (1803). In 1808 the theatre was burned, and on the opening of the new building (1809) the notorious 'Old Price' riots broke out. He retired in 1817, and afterwards settled in Lausanne. His brother, **Charles** (1775–1854), also an actor, was the father of Fanny Kemble. >> Kemble, Fanny; Sheridan, Richard Brinsley; Siddons

Kemp, Lindsay (1939–) Mime artist, dancer, and director, born on the I of Lewis, Western Isles, W Scotland, UK. He trained with the Ballet Rambert, where his teachers included mime artist Marcel Marceau, and launched his colourful career at the 1964 Edinburgh Festival. He has had his own company in various forms since the early 1960s, and has created his own work in camp, extravagant style since then, including *The Parade's Gone By* (1975) and *Cruel Garden* (1977), both for Ballet Rambert, and *Flowers*, *Midsummer Night's Dream* (1979), and *The Big Parade* for his own company. >> Marceau

Kempe, Margery [kemp], *née* **Brunham** (c. 1373–c. 1440) Writer of one of the earliest autobiographies in English, the daughter of a mayor of Lynn. She was the wife of a burgess in Lynn and the mother of 14 children. After a period of insanity she experienced a conversion, and undertook numerous pilgrimages. Between 1432 and 1436 she dictated her spiritual autobiography, *The Book of Margery Kempe*, which recounts her persecution by devils

and men, repeated accusations of Lollardism, and her journeys to Jerusalem, Rome, and Germany. Her book is valuable as a source of contemporary expression. >> Wycliffe

Kempe, Rudolf [kempuh] (1910–76) Conductor, born near Dresden, Germany. He studied at the Musikhochschule in Dresden, and played the oboe in orchestras at Dortmund and Leipzig before making his debut as a conductor in 1935. He then worked at Leipzig and, after the war, at Dresden and Munich. He later appeared frequently at Covent Garden, London, and was principal conductor of the Royal Philharmonic Orchestra (1961–75), then of the BBC Symphony Orchestra until his death.

Kempe, William [kemp] (c. 1550–c. 1603) Clown, who was famous in the Elizabethan theatre, and a member of the Lord Chamberlain's Company at the time they decided to build the Globe theatre (1598). For some unknown reason he left and morris-danced his way to Norwich, publishing an account of his feat in *Nine Daies Wonder* (1600).

Kempis, Thomas à [kempis], originally **Thomas Hemerken** (1379–1471) Religious writer, whose name derives from his birthplace, Kempen, in Germany. He entered the Augustinian convent of Agnietenberg near Zwolle (1400), was ordained in 1413, chosen sub-prior in 1429, and died as superior. His many writings include the influential devotional work *Imitatio Christi* (c.1415–24, The Imitation of Christ).

Kempson, Rachel >> **Redgrave, Michael**

Kemsley, James Gomer Berry, 1st Viscount (1883–1968) Newspaper proprietor, born in Merthyr Tydfil, S Wales. He became chairman of Kemsley Newspapers Ltd in 1937, controlling *The Sunday Times* and other newspapers. He was created a baronet in 1928, raised to the peerage in 1936, and received a viscountcy in 1945. In 1950 he published *The Kemsley Manual of Journalism*.

Ken, Thomas (1637–1711) Clergyman, born in Little Berkhampstead, Hertfordshire, SE England, UK. He became a prebendary of Winchester cathedral (1669), and royal chaplain to Charles II (1680). Appointed Bishop of Bath and Wells (1685), he refused to publish in his diocese the Declaration of Indulgence issued by James II (1688). With seven other bishops he was imprisoned, tried for sedition, and acquitted. After the Revolution of 1688 he refused to swear allegiance to William of Orange, and was deprived of his bishopric. >> James II (of England); William III

Kendal, Felicity (1947–) British actress, born in Olton, West Midlands, C England, UK. Her parents had a travelling theatre company, and she grew up touring India and the Far East, attending various schools in India, and learning stage craft from her parents. She graduated from playing page boys at the age of eight to a number of Shakespearean roles before returning to England in 1965, making her London debut in *Minor Murder* (1967). She is probably best known for her part in the television series *The Good Life* (1974–8) and *The Mistress* (1985–6), but much of her work is in the theatre. In 1993 she appeared in *Arcadia* by Tom Stoppard, and later work includes Peter Hall's production of *Waste* at the Old Vic (1997). >> Briers; Stoppard

Kendall, Edward (Calvin) (1886–1972) Chemist, born in South Norwalk, CT. He studied at Columbia University, then worked at the Mayo Clinic, Rochester (1914–51), where he isolated thyroxin, the active element in the thyroid gland (1915), and adrenal hormones such as cortisone (1935). He shared the 1950 Nobel Prize for Physiology or Medicine with Philip Hench. >> Hench; RR1124

Kendall, Henry W(ay) (1926–) Physicist, born in Boston, MA. He studied at the Massachusetts Institute of Technology, then taught at Stanford (1956–61) before returning to MIT in 1961. He shared the 1990 Nobel Prize for Physics for his experiments confirming the existence of quarks. >> RR1122

Kendrew, Sir John (Cowdery) (1917–97) Biochemist, born in Oxford, Oxfordshire, SC England, UK. He studied at Bristol and Cambridge, where he became a fellow (1947–75), and carried out research into the chemistry of blood. He was co-founder (with Max Perutz) and deputy chairman of the Medical Research Council unit for molecular biology at Cambridge (1946–75). He discovered the structure of the muscle protein myoglobin (1957), and was awarded the 1962 Nobel Prize for Chemistry jointly with Perutz. He was director of the European Molecular Biology Laboratory at Heidelberg (1975–82), and president of St John's College, Oxford (1981–7). He was knighted in 1974. >> Perutz

Keneally, Thomas (Michael) [keneelee] (1935–) Writer, born in Sydney, New South Wales, Australia. Educated at Strathfield, New South Wales, he studied for the priesthood, but left before ordination, becoming a teacher and then a full-time writer. His novels are frequently historical, and include *Gossip from the Forest* (1975), about the armistice negotiations in 1918, and *Schindler's Ark* (1982, Booker, filmed as *Schindler's List* in 1993 by Steven Spielberg), the story of an industrialist who saved the lives of Polish Jews during the early 1940s. He is a prolific writer whose later novels include *Towards Asmara* (1989), *Flying Hero Class* (1991), and *A River Town* (1995). *Our Republic* (1993) expresses his passionate support for the Australian republican cause.

Kennan, George F(rost) (1904–) US diplomat and historian, born in Milwaukee, WI. He studied at Princeton, then joined the foreign service. In 1947 he was appointed director of policy planning, and advocated the policy of 'containment' of the Soviet Union. He served as US ambassador in Moscow (1952–3) and Yugoslavia (1961–3). As professor of history at the Institute for Advanced Study, Princeton (1956–74), he revised his strategic views and called for US 'disengagement' from Europe. He has published numerous books throughout his career, and in 1996 appeared *At a Century's Ending: Reflections 1982–1995*.

Kennaway, James (1928–68) Writer, born in Auchterarder, Perth and Kinross, E Scotland, UK. He studied at Oxford after completing national service. His first novel, *Tunes of Glory* (1956), remains his best known, and was made into a successful film of the same name. *Household Ghosts* (1961) was equally powerful, and was made into a stage-play (1967) and a film (1969) under the title *Country Dance*.

Kennedy, Edward M(oore) (1932–) US politician, born in Brookline, MA, the youngest son of Joseph Kennedy. He studied at Harvard and at Virginia University Law School, was called to the bar in 1959, and elected a Democratic senator for his brother John F Kennedy's Massachusetts seat in 1962. In 1969 he became the youngest-ever majority whip in the US Senate, but his involvement the same year in a car accident at Chappaquidick in which a woman companion (Mary Jo Kopechne) was drowned, dogged his subsequent political career, and caused his withdrawal as a presidential candidate in 1979. >> Kenned/John F/ Joseph/Robert F

Kennedy, Jackie >> **Onassis, Jacqueline Kennedy**

Kennedy, John F(itzgerald), also known as **JFK** (1917–63) US statesman and 35th president (1961–3), born in Brookline, MA, son of Joseph Kennedy. He studied at Harvard, and served as a torpedo boat commander in the Pacific in World War 2. His *Profiles in Courage* (1956) won the Pulitzer Prize. Elected Democratic representative (1947) and senator (1952) for Massachusetts, in 1960 he became the first Catholic, and the youngest person, to be elected president.

His 'new frontier' in social legislation involved a federal desegregation policy in schools and universities, along with Civil Rights reform. He displayed firmness and moderation in foreign policy. In October 1962, at the risk of nuclear war, he induced the Soviet Union to withdraw its missiles from Cuba, and achieved a partial nuclear test ban treaty with the Soviet Union in 1963. On 22 November, he was assassinated by rifle fire while being driven in an open car with his wife Jackie through Dallas, TX. The alleged assassin, Lee Harvey Oswald, was himself shot and killed at point-blank range by Jack Ruby two days later, while under heavy police escort on a jail transfer. >> Kennedy, Edward M/Jackie/Joseph P/Robert F; Oswald, Lee Harvey; Ruby; Warren, Earl; RR1097

Kennedy, Joseph P(atrick) (1888–1969) Multimillionaire businessman, born in Boston, MA, the father of John F, Robert, and Edward Kennedy. He studied at Harvard, then made a large fortune in the 1920s. During the 1930s he was a strong supporter of Roosevelt and the 'New Deal', and became ambassador to Britain (1938–40). After World War 2 he concentrated on fulfilling his ambitions of a political dynasty through his sons. He had married in 1914 Rose Fitzgerald, daughter of a local politician, John F Fitzgerald, also of Irish immigrant descent. They had nine children, at whose political disposal he placed his fortune. The eldest son, **Joseph Patrick** (1915–44), was killed in a flying accident; the others achieved international political fame. >> Fitzgerald, John Francis; Kennedy, Edward M/John F/ Robert F; Roosevelt, Franklin D

Kennedy, Sir Ludovic (Henry Coverley) (1919–) Broadcaster and writer, born in Edinburgh, EC Scotland, UK. He studied at Oxford, and served in the navy in World War 2, before becoming a librarian, lecturer, and later editor of the BBC's *First Reading* (1953–4). On television, he introduced *Profile* (1955–6), was an ITN newscaster (1956–8), hosted *This Week* (1958–60), and contributed to the BBC's *Panorama* (1960–3). He contested the Rochdale by-election as a Liberal in 1958 and the general election of 1959. He has devoted himself to defending victims of alleged injustice. His many notable series include *Your Verdict* (1962), *Your Witness* (1967–70), and *A Life With Crime* (1979). He has also acted as host on *Face the Press* (1968–72), *Tonight* (1976–8), and *Did You See?* (1980–8), among many others. His books include *Ten Rillington Place* (1961) and *The Trial of Stephen Ward* (1964). He published an auto-biography, *On My Way to the Club*, in 1989. He was knighted in 1994.

Kennedy, Nigel (Paul), professional name (from 1997) **Kennedy** (1956–) British violinist. He studied at the Yehudi Menuhin School, London, and the Juilliard School, New York City. He made his debut as a concert soloist in 1977, and has since played with many of the world's major orchestras, and alongside jazz violinist Stéphane Grappelli. He is noted for his unconventional style of dress, as well as for his remarkable playing ability. His recording of Vivaldi's *Four Seasons* held the No 1 spot in the UK Classical Chart for over a year (1989–90). >> Grappelli; Menuhin

Kennedy, Robert F(rancis) (1925–68) US politician, born in Brookline, MA, the third son of Joseph Kennedy. He studied at Harvard and at Virginia University Law School, served at sea (1944–6) in World War 2, was admitted to the bar (1951), and served on the Senate Select Committee on Improper Activities (1957–9), when he prosecuted several top union leaders. An efficient manager of his brother John F Kennedy's presidential campaign, he was an energetic attorney general (1961–4), notable in his dealings with civil rights problems. He became senator for New York in 1965. After winning the Californian Democratic presidential primary election, he was shot at a hotel in Los Angeles. His assassin, Sirhan Sirhan, a 24-year-old Jordanian-born immigrant, was sentenced to the gas chamber in 1969, but was not executed. >> Sirhan; Kennedy, Edward M/John F/Joseph P

Kennedy, William Joseph (1928–) Novelist and screenwriter, born in Albany, NY. He studied at Siena College, NY, and served in the US army (1950–2), before becoming a journalist and eventually a full-time writer. *Ironweed* (1983), his best-known novel, describes the homecoming of a fallen baseball star; Jack Nicholson made an accurate film portrayal, and the book won a Pulitzer Prize. Other titles include *The Ink Truck* (1969), *Legs* (1975), and *Quinns's Book* (1988).

Kennelly, Arthur E(dwin) [ken elee] (1861–1939) Engineer, born in Mumbai (Bombay), India. He went to the USA in 1887, and worked as assistant to Edison. In 1894 he founded a consultancy firm in Philadelphia, where he developed new mathematical analyses of electrical circuits, and in 1902 discovered the ionized layer in the atmosphere, sometimes named after him. >> Edison

Kenneth I, known as **Kenneth MacAlpin** (?–858) King of the Scots of Dal Riata (from 841) and King of the Picts (from c.843). He combined the territories of both peoples in a united kingdom of Scotia (Scotland N of the Forth–Clyde line). >> RR1095

Kennington, Eric Henri (1888–1960) Painter and sculptor, born in London, England, UK. He was an official war artist in both world wars, and in the field of sculpture designed many memorials.

Kenny, Elizabeth, known as **Sister Kenny** (1886–1952) Australian nurse. She began practising as a nurse in the bush-country in Australia (1912), then joined the Australian army nursing corps (1915–19). She developed a new technique for treating poliomyelitis by muscle therapy rather than by immobilization with casts and splints. She established clinics in Australia (1933), Britain (1937), and America (Minneapolis, 1940), and travelled widely to demonstrate her methods. Her autobiography, *And They Shall Walk*, was published in 1943.

Kensett, John (Frederick) (1816–72) Painter, born in Cheshire, CT. He began his career as an engraver, printing maps and banknotes in New York City. In 1840 he travelled in Europe, returning to New York in 1847. From then on he painted the detailed and luminous landscapes which made him a leader of the Hudson River School from 1850–70, as seen in 'Lake George' (1869). >> Bierstadt; Cole, Thomas; Cropsey; Durand, Asher B

Kent, Bruce (1929–) Clergyman and peace campaigner, born in London, England, UK. He studied in Canada and at Oxford University, was ordained in 1958, then served as a curate in London (1958–63) and as a parish priest (1977–80). He was also Catholic chaplain to London University (1966–74) and to Pax Christi (1974–7). He became increasingly involved in the Campaign for Nuclear Disarmament (CND), becoming its general secretary (1980), vice-chairman (1985), and chairman (1987–90). He resigned his ministry (1988), married **Valerie Flessati**, and stood (unsuccessfully) as a Labour Party candidate in the general election of 1992.

Kent, Edward (George Nicholas Paul Patrick), Duke of (1935–) British prince, the eldest son of **George, Duke of Kent**. He was commissioned in the army in 1955, and in 1961 married **Katharine Worsley** (1933–). He retired from the army in 1976. They have three children: **George Philip Nicholas Windsor, the Earl of St Andrews** (1962–), **Helen Marina Lucy, Lady Helen Windsor** (1964–), and **Nicholas Charles Edward Jonathan, Lord Nicholas Windsor** (1970–). George, Earl of St Andrews married **Sylvana Tomaselli** (1957–) and they have one son, **Edward, Lord Downpatrick** (1988–). Lady Helen Windsor married Timothy Taylor to become Lady Helen Taylor; they have two sons, **Columbus George Donald Taylor** (1994–) and **Cassius Edward Taylor** (1996–). >> Alexandra, Princess; Kent, George; Kent, Prince Michael of

Kent, George Edward Alexander Edmund, Duke of (1902–42) Son of King George V and Queen Mary. Educated at Dartmouth Naval College, he served in the foreign office and inspected factories for the home office, the first member of the British royal family to work in the civil service. In 1934 he was created duke, and married **Princess Marina of Greece and Denmark** (1906–68). He was killed on active service, as chief welfare officer of RAF Home Command, when his Sunderland flying-boat crashed in Scotland. >> George V; Kent, Edward, Duke of; Kent, Prince Michael of

Kent, Prince Michael of (1942–) British prince, the younger brother of Edward, Duke of Kent. He married in 1978 **Baroness Marie-Christine Von Reibniz**, and their children are **Frederick Michael George David Louis, Lord Frederick Windsor** (1979–) and **Gabriella Marina Alexandra Ophelia, Lady Gabriella (Ella) Windsor** (1981–). >> Kent, Edward, Duke of

Kent, Rockwell (1882–1971) Artist, born in Tarrytown, NY. He studied with William Merritt Chase in 1900, and became well known as a painter, book designer and illustrator, explorer, writer, sailor, and political activist. His output of wood engravings, lithographs, textiles, oils, and watercolours was inspired by the great outdoors, and he was involved in the organization of the 1910 Exhibition of Independent Artists. He was awarded the Lenin Peace Prize in Moscow in 1967. >> Chase, William Merritt

Kent, William (1685–1748) Painter, landscape gardener, and architect, born in Bridlington, East Riding of Yorkshire, NE England, UK. He studied in Rome, and became the principal exponent of the Palladian style of architecture in England. His buildings include the Horse Guards block in Whitehall, the Royal Mews in Trafalgar Square and the Treasury Buildings. An example of his gardens is at Stowe House in Buckinghamshire, and his artistry is visible in the Gothic screens at Westminster Hall and Gloucester Cathedral, and the interiors of Burlington House and Chiswick House in London.

Kentigern, St, also known as **St Mungo** (Celtic 'My Friend') (c. 518–603) Celtic clergyman. According to legend he was the grandson of a British prince, raised by St Serf in a monastery at Culross, and given by him the name Mungo. He founded a monastery at Cathures (now Glasgow), and in 543 was consecrated Bishop of Cumbria. In 553 he was driven to seek refuge in Wales, where he visited St David, and where he founded another monastery and a bishopric, which still bears the name of his disciple, St Asaph. He was recalled to Scotland by a new king, Rederech Hael, and c.584 was visited by Columba. He was buried in Glasgow Cathedral, which is named after him as St Mungo's. Feast day 13 January.

Kentner, Louis Philip (1905–87) Pianist, born in Karwin, Hungary. He studied from the age of six at the Budapest Royal Academy, and made his debut in Budapest (1916). An acclaimed interpreter of Chopin and Liszt, he also gave first performances of works by Bartók, Kodály, Tippett, Walton, and others. He settled in England in 1935, and was a frequent chamber-music partner of his brother-in-law, Yehudi Menuhin. >> Menuhin

Kenton, Stan(ley Newcomb) (1912–79) Pianist, composer, and bandleader, born in Wichita, KS. He studied piano privately before beginning his professional career in 1934 with a succession of lesser-known big bands. He first formed his own orchestra in 1941, but is more immediately associated with the big band 'progressive' jazz style of the 1950s. His later orchestras were unusual for their five-member trombone sections, and have stood the test of time.

Kentridge, Sydney (1922–) Lawyer, born in Johannesburg, South Africa. He served with South African forces in World War 2, studied at the University of the Witwatersrand and in Oxford, and was admitted to the bar in 1949. He became the leading lawyer for the defence in political trials in South Africa; his notable cases include the Treason Trial (1958–61), the Prisons Trial (1968–9), and the Steve Biko inquest (1977). He was admitted to the bar in England in 1977, and was appointed QC in 1984. He has been a Judge of Appeal in Botswana, and also in Jersey and Guernsey. >> Biko

Kenyatta, Jomo [kenyata], originally **Kamau Ngengi** (c. 1889–1978) Kenyan statesman and president (1964–78), born in Mitumi, Kenya. Educated at a Scots mission school, he studied at London, and became president of the Pan-African Federation. In the late 1940s his Kenya African Union advocated total independence in a unitary state. He was charged with leading the Mau Mau terrorist organization (a charge he denied), and was sentenced to seven years' hard labour in 1952, then exiled. In 1960, while still in detention, he was elected president of the new Kenya African National Union Party. He became an MP in 1961, prime minister in 1963, and President of the Republic of Kenya in 1964. He adopted moderate social and economic policies, and succeeded in conciliating many members of the Kenyan white community. >> RR1070

Kenyon, Dame Kathleen (Mary) (1906–78) Archaeologist, born in London, England, UK. She studied at Oxford, became lecturer in Palestinian archaeology at London University (1948–62), and then principal of St Hugh's College, Oxford (1962–73). She was director of the British School of Archaeology in Jerusalem (1951–66) when she accomplished her major work of excavating Jericho to its Stone Age beginnings, and revealing it to be the oldest known site that has seen continuous human occupation.

Kenzo, in full **Kenzo Takada** (1940–) Fashion designer, born in Kyoto, Japan. After studying art and graduating in Japan, he worked there for a time, but produced freelance collections in Paris from 1964. He started a shop called Jungle Jap in 1970, and is known for his innovative ideas and use of traditional designs. He creates clothes with both oriental and Western influences, and is a trendsetter in the field of knitwear.

Kepler, Johannes (1571–1630) Astronomer, born in Weil-der-Stadt, Germany. He studied at Tübingen, and in 1593 was appointed professor of mathematics at Graz. In c.1596 he commenced a correspondence with Tycho Brahe, who was then in Prague, and from 1600–1 worked with him, showing that planetary motions were far simpler than had been imagined. He announced his first and second laws of planetary motion in *Astronomia nova* (1609, New Astronomy), which formed the groundwork of Isaac Newton's discoveries. His third law was promulgated in *Harmonice mundi* (1619, Harmonies of the World). He succeeded Brahe as court astronomer to Emperor Rudolf II, and in 1628 became astrologer to Albrecht Wallenstein. >> Brahe; Newton, Isaac; Wallenstein

Ker, W(illiam) P(aton) (1855–1923) Scholar, born in Glasgow, W Scotland, UK. He studied at Glasgow and Oxford, and became professor of English at Cardiff (1883–9) and University College, London (1889–1920), and professor of poetry at Oxford in 1920. A talker, lecturer, and writer of prodigious learning and vitality, his books include *Epic and Romance* (1897), *The Dark Ages* (1904), *Essays on Mediaeval Literature* (1905), and *The Art of Poetry* (1923).

Kérékou, Mathieu Ahmed [kayraykoo] (1933–) Benin soldier, politician, and president (1980–91), born in Natitingou, Benin. Trained in France, he served in the French army before joining the army of what was Dahomey, where he took part in a coup which removed the civilian government in 1967. He became army deputy chief (1968), and led the coup which removed the government of Justin Ahomadegbe (1972), established a National Council of the Revolution (CNR), and changed the country's name to Benin. Gradually social and economic stability returned, the CNR was dissolved, and a civilian administration installed. He was elected president in 1980 and re-elected in 1984. In 1987 he resigned from the army as a gesture of his commitment to genuine democracy. He was soundly defeated when the first free elections for 30 years were held in 1991. >> RR1035

Kerensky, Alexander Fyodorovich [kerenskee] (1881–1970) Russian Socialist, born in Ulyanovsk (formerly Simbirsk). He studied law in St Petersburg, and took a leading part in the 1917 revolution, becoming minister of justice (Mar), minister of war (May), and premier (Jul) in the provisional government. He crushed Kornilov's military revolt (Aug), but was deposed (Oct) by the Bolsheviks, and fled to France. In 1940 he went to Australia, and in 1946 to the USA, and wrote several books on the Russian revolution. >> Kornilov

Kerguélen-Trémarec, Yves Joseph de [kairgaylen traymarek] (1745–97) French naval officer and aristocrat, born in Quimper, France. On an unsuccessful voyage of exploration seeking Terra Australis, he discovered a group of islands in the South Indian Ocean to which he gave his name (Kerguélen Is, 1772).

Kermode, Sir (John) Frank [kermohd] (1919–) Literary critic, born in the Isle of Man. He studied at Liverpool University, served in the navy during World War 2, then taught at Durham and Reading, before holding professorial posts at Manchester (1958–65), Bristol (1965–7), University College, London (1967–74), and Cambridge (1974–82), where he was a fellow of King's College (to 1987). His works (which negotiate the boundaries of literary scholarship, theory, and the reader's experience) include *Romantic Image* (1957), *The Sense of an Ending* (1967), *Forms of Attention* (1985), and *Uses of Error* (1991). He was knighted in 1991.

Kern, Jerome (David) (1885–1945) Songwriter and composer, born in New York City. After studying at the New York College of Music, and briefly in London and Heidelberg, he worked as a rehearsal pianist. His first complete score for a musical play, *The Red Petticoat*, was in 1912, followed by a string of successful Broadway shows. His greatest musical was *Show Boat* (1928, book and lyrics by Hammerstein). Among his finest songs are: 'The Way You Look Tonight', 'Smoke Gets in Your Eyes', and 'A Fine Romance'. >> Gershwin, Ira; Hammerstein, Oscar

Kerouac, Jack [kerooak], popular name of **Jean Louis Kerouac** (1922–69) Writer, born in Lowell, MA. Discharged from the navy with a personality problem, he served as a merchant seaman, then took a variety of jobs before publishing his first novel, *The Town and the City* (1950). It was written in a conventional style which he abandoned in *On the Road* (1957), a formless, spontaneous work, expressing the youthful discontent of the 'Beat generation', which he was the first to name. Later works, all in this vein, and all autobiographical in character, include *The Subterraneans* (1958) and *Big Sur* (1962).

Kerr, Clark [kair] (1911–) University president and economist, born in Stony Creek, PN. A widely published labour economist and arbitrator, he presided over rapid growth at the University of California (chancellor 1952–8, president

1958–67), coined the term *multiversity*, and wrote the controversial *Uses of the University* (1963). He also chaired the Carnegie Commission on Higher Education (1967–73).

Kerr, Deborah [kah(r)], popular name of **Deborah Kerr Viertel**, *née* **Deborah Jane Kerr-Trimmer** (1921–) Actress, born in Helensburgh, Argyll and Bute, W Scotland, UK. She trained as a dancer, but took up acting and made her film debut in *Contraband* (1940). Successes in British films *The Life and Death of Colonel Blimp* (1943) and *Black Narcissus* (1947) brought her a Hollywood contract. Invariably cast in well-bred, lady-like roles, she played numerous governesses and nuns, sensationally straying from her established image to play an adulterous wife in *From Here to Eternity* (1953). Nominated six times for an Oscar, she retired from the screen in 1969, returning to the theatre in the 1970s, and to the cinema in *The Assam Garden* (1985). She received a BAFTA special award in 1991, and an honorary Academy Award in 1994.

Kerr, John [kair] (1824–1907) Physicist, born in Ardrossan, North Ayrshire, W Scotland, UK. He studied at Glasgow, where he was an assistant to Lord Kelvin. He then became a lecturer in mathematics at a teachers' training college, where he carried out research on light passing through electromagnetic fields, and discovered the effect that is now named after him. >> Kelvin

Kerr, Sir John (Robert) [kair] (1914–91) Lawyer and administrator, born in Sydney, New South Wales, Australia. He studied at the University of Sydney, was admitted to the bar in 1938, and became a QC in 1953. He was made Chief Justice of New South Wales in 1972, and was appointed Governor-General of Australia in 1974. In 1975, his actions as governor-general made Australian constitutional history: the Coalition opposition had refused to pass the Labor government's budget bill unless a general election was called. To resolve this impasse he exercised the regal 'reserve powers' and sacked the elected prime minister, Gough Whitlam, asking leader of the Liberal opposition, Malcolm Fraser, to form a caretaker government and call a general election. Stepping down as governor-general in 1977, he was named Australian ambassador to UNESCO in 1978, but the ensuing controversy forced him to resign without taking up the appointment. >> Fraser, Malcolm; Whitlam

Kertész, André [kertesh] (1894–1985) Photographer, born in Budapest, Hungary. He started as a photographer in 1912, using glass plates, and served as a photographer with the Hungarian army in World War 1. He moved to Paris, where he was acclaimed for his unposed photographs, and strongly influenced Brassaï and Cartier-Bresson. He went to the USA in 1936, and became a US citizen in 1944. His fashion work in New York City in the 1940s and 1950s became more glossily conventional, and he did not return to a more individual creative style until 1962. >> Cartier-Bresson; Brassaï

Kesey, Ken (Elton) [keezee] (1935–) Writer, born in La Junta, CO. He worked as a ward attendant in a mental hospital, an experience he used to telling effect in *One Flew Over the Cuckoo's Nest* (1962). Filmed in 1975 by Milos Forman, it won five Oscars. After the failure of *Sometimes a Great Notion* (1966), he relinquished 'literature' for 'life'. He served a prison sentence for marijuana possession, and formed the 'Merry Pranksters', whose weird exploits are described at length in Tom Wolfe's *The Electric Kool-Aid Acid Test* (1967). The stories, essays, and poems in *Demon Box* (1986) are also partly autobiographical. A later novel, *Sailor Song*, appeared in 1993.

Kesselring, Albert [keslring] (1885–1960) German air commander in World War 2, born in Markstedt, Germany. He led the *Luftwaffe* attacks on France and (unsuccessfully)

on Britain, in 1943 was made commander-in-chief in Italy, and in 1945 in the West. Condemned to death as a war criminal in 1947, he had his sentence commuted to life imprisonment, but was released in 1952.

Ketch, Jack, popular name of **John Ketch** (?–1686) English hangman and headsman from about 1663. He was notorious for his barbarity and bungling, particularly the executions of Lord Russell (1683) and the Duke of Monmouth (1685, where he took eight strokes of the axe to complete the execution). His name became the popular term for a hangman. >> Monmouth, Duke of; Russell, William

Ketèlbey, Albert William [ketelbee], pseudonym of **Anton Vodorinski** (1875–1959) Composer and conductor, born in Birmingham, West Midlands, C England, UK. Success came early with, for example, a piano sonata written at the age of 11. His light, colourful and tuneful, orchestral pieces had enormous popularity, and included 'In a Monastery Garden', 'In a Persian Market', 'Sanctuary of the Heart', and many others.

Kettering, Charles F(ranklin) (1876–1958) Inventor, born in Loudonville, OH. He developed the first electric cash register (1904), and went on to become co-founder of Dayton Engineering Laboratories (Delco). His notable early invention was the electric starter, which revolutionized the automotive industry. Among his many achievements were advances in aircraft design, fuels, and diesel engines. His lifelong interest in science culminated in the building of the Sloan-Kettering Institute for Cancer Research, and the C F Kettering Foundation.

Kettlewell, Henry (Bernard David) (1907–79) Geneticist and entomologist, born in Howden, Hull, NE England, UK. He studied at Cambridge and St Bartholomew's Hospital, London, and from 1952 held various posts in the genetics unit of the zoology department, Oxford. In his best known research he showed that the dark coloration developed by the peppered moth in industrial areas had a greater survival value than the original light coloration it had in rural areas, thus demonstrating the effectiveness of natural selection as an evolutionary process.

Key, Ellen (Karolina Sophia) (1849–1926) Reformer and educationist, born in Sundsholm, Sweden. She became a teacher in Stockholm (1880–99) when her father lost his fortune. She made her name as a writer with advanced liberal ideas on the feminist movement, child welfare, sex, love, and marriage, in *Barnets Århundrade* (1900, The Century of the Child).

Key, Francis Scott (1779–1843) Lawyer and poet, the writer of 'The Star-Spangled Banner', born in Frederick Co, MD. During the British bombardment of Fort McHenry, Baltimore (1814), which he witnessed from a British man-of-war, he wrote a poem about the lone US flag seen flying over the fort as dawn broke. It was published as 'The Defence of Fort McHenry', and later set to a tune by the English composer, John Stafford Smith ('To Anacreon in Heaven'). In 1931 it was adopted as the US national anthem.

Keyes (of Zeebrugge and of Dover), Roger John Brownlow Keyes, Baron (1872–1945) British admiral, born in Tundiani Fort, India. He entered the navy in 1885, and served with distinction in the Boxer Rebellion (1900), earning rapid promotion to commander. He was chief-of-staff Eastern Mediterranean (1915–16), and in 1918 commanded the Dover Patrol, leading the raids on German U-boat bases at Zeebrugge and Ostend (1918). He was promoted to admiral in 1930. MP for Portsmouth (1934–43), he was recalled in 1940, and appointed director of combined operations (1940–1). His books include *Naval Memoirs* (2 vols, 1934–35) and *Amphibious Warfare and Combined Operations* (1943).

Keynes (of Tilton), John Maynard Keynes, Baron [kaynz] (1883–1946) Economist whose theories have influenced governments on both sides of the Atlantic, born in Cambridge, Cambridgeshire, EC England, UK. He studied at Cambridge, became one of the 'Bloomsbury group', and lectured in economics. In both World Wars he was an adviser to the Treasury, and his views on a planned economy influenced Roosevelt's 'New Deal' administration. The unemployment crises inspired his two great works, *A Treatise on Money* (1930) and the revolutionary *General Theory of Employment, Interest and Money* (1936). He was created a peer in 1942. >> Moore, G E; Roosevelt, Franklin D

Keyser, Hendrik de [kiyzer] (1565–1621) Architect and sculptor, born in Utrecht, The Netherlands. He was appointed stonemason and sculptor for Amsterdam (1594), and municipal architect (1612). Notable sculptural commissions were the tomb of William the Silent in Delft (1614–21) and the bronze statue of Erasmus in Rotterdam (1621). He designed the Amsterdam Exchange and three Amsterdam churches: Zuiderkerk (1603–14), Noorderkerk (1620–2), and his masterpiece, Westerkerk (1620–38).

Khama, Sir Seretse [kahma] (1921–80) Botswana statesman and president (1966–80), born in Serowe, Botswana (formerly, Bechuanaland). He studied at Oxford, became a lawyer, and after marrying an Englishwoman, Ruth Williams, in 1948, was banned from the chieftainship and the territory of the Bamangwato. Allowed to return as a private citizen in 1956, he became active in politics, and was restored to the chieftainship in 1963. He became the first prime minister of Bechuanaland (1965), and the first president of Botswana. He was knighted in 1966. >> RR1036

Khan, Jahangir (1963–) Squash rackets player, born in Karachi, Pakistan. A member of a prolific squash-playing family, he won three world amateur titles (1979, 1983, 1985), a record six World Open titles (1981–5, 1988), and eight consecutive British Open titles (1982–9). He was undefeated from April 1981 to November 1986, when he lost to Ross Norman (Australia) in the World Open final. >> RR1169

Khan, Mohammad Ayub >> Ayub Khan, Mohammad

Khatchaturian, Aram [kachatooryan] (1903–78) Composer, born in Tiflis, Georgia. He was a student of folksong, and an authority on oriental music. His compositions include symphonies, concertos, choral works, and ballet music. An excerpt from his ballet music *Spartacus* topped the popular music charts when used as the theme music for the TV series *The Onedin Line* in the 1970s.

Khayyám, Omar >> Omar Khayyám

Khinchin, Alexander Yakovlevich (1894–1959) Mathematician, born in Kondrovo, Russia. He studied at Moscow University, and became professor there in 1927. With Andrei Kolmogorov he founded the Soviet school of probability theory, and he also worked in analysis, number theory, statistical mechanics, and information theory. >> Kolmogorov

Khomeini, Ayatollah Ruhollah [homaynee] (1900–89) Iranian political and religious leader, born in Khomeyn, Iran. A Shiite Muslim who was bitterly opposed to the pro-Western regime of Shah Mohammed Reza Pahlavi, he was exiled to Turkey and Iraq in 1964, and from Iraq to France in 1978. He returned to Iran amid great popular acclaim in 1979 after the collapse of the Shah's government, and became virtual head of state. Under his leadership, Iran underwent a turbulent 'Islamic Revolution' in which a return was made to the strict observance of Muslim principles and traditions. In 1979, a new Islamic constitution was sanctioned, into which was incorporated his leadership concept of the *Vilayet-i faqih* (Trusteeship of the Jurisconsult). This supreme religious and political position was recognized as belonging to Khomeini, as was the title *Rahbar* (Leader). >> Pahlavi

Khorana, Har Gobind [korahna] (1922–) Molecular biologist, born in Raipur, India. He studied at Punjab, Liverpool, Zürich, and Cambridge universities, and moved to Vancouver in 1952. His work on nucleotide synthesis at Wisconsin (1960–70) was a major contribution to the elucidation of the genetic code, and in 1970 he synthesized the first artificial gene. In 1971 he moved to the Massachusetts Institute of Technology. He shared the Nobel Prize for Physiology or Medicine in 1968. >> RR1124

Khrushchev, Nikita Sergeyevich [khrushchof, khrushchof] (1894–1971) Soviet statesman, first secretary of the Soviet Communist Party (1953–64), and prime minister (1958–64), born in Kalinovka, Ukraine. Joining the Bolshevik Party in 1918, he fought in the Russian civil war and rose rapidly in the Party organization. In 1939 he was made a full member of the Politburo and of the Presidium of the Supreme Soviet. In 1953, six months after the death of Stalin, he became first secretary of the Communist Party of the Soviet Union, and three years later, at the 20th Party Congress, denounced Stalinism and the 'personality cult'. Among the events of his administration were the 1956 Poznan riots and Hungarian uprising, and the failed attempt to install missiles in Cuba (1962). He was deposed in 1964, replaced by Brezhnev and Kosygin, and went into retirement. >> Brezhnev; Kosygin; Stalin; Suslov; RR1085

Khwarizmi, al- >> al-Khwarizmi

Kidd, Michael (1919–) Dancer, choreographer, and director, born in New York City. He studied privately and at the School of American Ballet, appeared on Broadway in 1937, and danced with American Ballet the same year. He later danced with Ballet Caravan (1937–40), Dance Players (1941–2), and American Ballet Theater (1942–7). He then became a successful choreographer of Broadway and Hollywood musicals, including *Guys and Dolls* (1951), *Seven Brides for Seven Brothers* (1954), and *Hello, Dolly!* (1969).

Kidd, William, known as **Captain Kidd** (c. 1645–1701) Privateer and pirate, probably born in Greenock, Inverclyde, WC Scotland, UK. He established himself as a sea captain in New York (1690), saw much privateering service, and gained a high reputation for courage. In 1696 he was commissioned to suppress piracy, and reached Madagascar, but then turned pirate himself. After a 2-years' cruise he returned to the West Indies, ventured to Boston, and was arrested. He was hanged in London.

Kidder, Alfred V(incent) (1885–1963) Archaeologist and pioneer of stratigraphic methods in the USA, born in Marquette, MI. He studied at Harvard, then did fieldwork in Utah, Colorado, and New Mexico (1907–14). His extensive excavations (1915–29) at Pecos, New Mexico, revolutionized American settlement archaeology, and allowed him to develop a chronological sequence for the cultures of the region. From 1929 he undertook major work in Guatemala on Maya archaeology. He later joined the faculty of the Peabody Museum at Harvard (1939–50).

Kidman, Sir Sidney (1857–1935) Pastoralist, born near Adelaide, South Australia. He left home at the age of 13, with five shillings in his pocket and riding a one-eyed horse. In 1886 he bought his first grazing station, and 30 years later he controlled lands greater in area than the whole of England. The ability to move stock to well-watered areas in times of drought, and selling in the best markets, enabled him to withstand the depression years of the 1890s and the Great Drought of 1902. During World War 1 he gave fighter planes to the forces, and made substantial gifts to charities and the government.

Kiefer, Anselm [keefer] (1945–) Avant-garde artist, born in Donaueschingen, Germany. A pupil of Joseph Beuys in Düsseldorf, he makes 'books' from photographs or woodcuts, sometimes cut or worked over. Some critics have seen 'Fascist', others mediaeval or Nordic, symbolism in his work. >> Beuys

Kienholz, Edward [keenhohlts] (1927–94) Avant-garde artist, born in Fairfield, WA. Self-taught, he opened the Now Gallery in Los Angeles in 1956, and co-founded the city's first avant-garde gallery, the Ferus Gallery, in 1957. His 'assemblages' were typically room-size, and incorporated dummies, furniture, bones, rugs, household objects, and quantities of 'blood' arranged to create shockingly violent tableaux.

Kierkegaard, Søren (Aabye) [keerkuhgah(r)d] (1813–55) Philosopher and theologian, a major influence on 20th-c existentialism, born in Copenhagen. He studied theology, philosophy, and literature at Copenhagen, and came to criticize purely speculative systems of thought, such as Hegel's, as irrelevant to existence-making choices. For Hegel's rationalism, Kierkegaard substituted the disjunction *Enten-Eller* (1843, Either/Or). In *Afsluttende Uvidenskabelig Efterskrift* (1846, Concluding Unscientific Postscript), he attacked all philosophical system building, and formulated the thesis that subjectivity is truth.

Kiesinger, Kurt Georg [keesinger] (1904–88) German statesman and chancellor (1966–9), born in Ebingen, Germany. He studied at Berlin and Tübingen, practised as a lawyer (1935–40), and served during World War 2 at the Foreign Office on radio propaganda. Interned after the war until 1947, he was exonerated of Nazi crimes. In 1949 he became a Conservative member of the *Bundestag*, and succeeded Erhard as chancellor. Long a convinced supporter of Adenauer's plans for European unity, he formed with Brandt a government combining the Christian Democratic Union and the Social Democrats, until in 1969 he was succeeded as chancellor by Brandt. >> Adenauer; Brandt, Willy; Erhard

Kilburn, Tom (1921–) Computer scientist, born in Dewsbury, West Yorkshire, N England, UK. He studied at Cambridge, becoming professor of computer science at Manchester (1964–81), and one of the dominant figures in British computer design. After working with Sir Frederic Calland Williams to build the world's first operational stored-program computer in 1948, he directed a series of collaborative ventures with Ferranti Ltd. His design for the ATLAS computer (1962) pioneered many modern concepts in paging, virtual memory, and multiprogramming. >> Williams, Frederick

Kildall, Gary (1942–) US computer software designer. A lecturer at the Naval Postgraduate School in California, he wrote CP/M (Control Program for Microcomputers) in 1974, the first operating system for general use on microcomputers using the Intel 8080 chip, enabling others to write applications programs. It provided a major boost to the micro revolution. >> Hoff, M Edward

Killy, Jean-Claude [keelee] (1943–) Alpine skier, born in Val d'Isère, France. He won the downhill and combined gold medals at the world championship in Chile in 1966; and in 1968, when the Winter Olympics were held almost on his own ground at Grenoble, he won three gold medals for slalom, giant slalom, and downhill. He turned professional immediately afterwards and pursued a highly profitable career as an endorser and later manufacturer of winter sports equipment.

Kilmuir, David Patrick Maxwell Fyfe, 1st Earl of [kilmyoor] (1900–67) British statesman and jurist, born in Aberdeen, NE Scotland, UK. He studied at Edinburgh and Oxford, and became the youngest KC since the time of Charles II in 1934. He sat in the House of Commons (1935–54), was home secretary and minister for Welsh affairs in the 1951 government, and was appointed Lord Chancellor in 1954. He was deputy chief prosecutor at the Nuremberg trial of the principal Nazi war criminals. He was knighted in 1942, made a viscount 1954, and created an earl and Baron Fyfe of Dornoch in 1962.

Kilvert, (Robert) Francis (1840–79) Clergyman and diarist, born near Chippenham, Wiltshire, S England, UK. He was a curate at Clyro in Radnorshire and later vicar of Bredwardine on the Wye. His *Diary* (1870–9), giving a vivid picture of rural life in the Welsh marches, was discovered in 1937 and published in three volumes (1938–40).

Kimberley, John Wodehouse, 1st Earl of (1826–1902) British statesman. He was Lord Privy Seal (1868–70), colonial secretary (1870–4, 1880–2), secretary for India (1882–5, 1886), secretary for India and Lord President of the Council (1892–4), and foreign secretary until 1895. Kimberley in South Africa was named after him.

Kim Il-sung [kim ilsung], originally **Kim Song-ju** (1912–94) North Korean soldier, statesman, prime minister (1948–72), and president (1972–94), born near Pyongyang, Korea. He founded the Korean People's Revolutionary Army in 1932, and led a long struggle against the Japanese. He proclaimed the Republic in 1948, and became effective head of state. He was re-elected president in 1982 and 1986, established a unique personality cult wedded to an isolationist, Stalinist political-economic system, and named his son, **Kim Jong-Il** (1942–), as his successor. >> RR1070

Kimmel, Husband Edward (1882–1968) Naval officer, born in Henderson, KY. At the time of the surprise attack on Pearl Harbor he was the commander-in-chief of the US fleet. He was suspended from command, and a presidential board of inquiry found him guilty of dereliction of duty (1942), but a naval court found no blame or mistakes in his judgment (1944). He published his side of the controversy in *Admiral Kimmel's Story* (1955). >> Nagano

Kim Young-Sam (1927–) South Korean politician and president (1993–), born in Pusan, Korea. He studied at Seoul National University, and was elected to the National Assembly in 1954. A founder member of the Opposition New Democratic Party, he became its president in 1974. His opposition to the Park Chung-Hee regime (1963–79) resulted in his being banned from all political activity (1980). He staged a 23-day pro-democracy hunger strike (1983), and his political ban was formally lifted (1985). He helped form the New Korea Democratic Party (1985) and the centrist Reunification Democratic Party (RDP, 1987). In his 1987 bid for the presidency he came second, behind the governing party's candidate, Roh Tae-Woo. He merged the RDP with the ruling party to form the new Democratic Liberal Party (1990), and was elected president at the end of 1992. >> Roh Tae Woo; RR1070

Kincaid, Thomas (Cassin) [kinkayd] (1888–1972) Naval officer, born in Hanover, NH. He took command of the USS *Enterprise* after Pearl Harbor, and fought in the Battles of the Coral Sea, Midway, and the E Solomons. As Douglas MacArthur's naval commander (1943–5) he participated in the New Guinea and Philippines operations, fought the Battle of Leyte Gulf (1944), and landed US troops in Korea in 1945. >> MacArthur, Douglas

Kindi, al- >> al-Kindi

King, B B, popular name of **Riley B King** (1925–) Blues singer and guitarist, born in Itta Bena, MI. As a disc-jockey in the 1940s he became known as the 'Beale Street Blues Boy', later shortened to B B. In 1950 a recording contract with Modern Records led to a string of rhythm-and-blues hits over the next 10 years. In 1961 he moved to ABC Records, who released what is probably his finest album,

Live At The Regal (1965). His reputation grew considerably in the late 1960s as the blues influence on rock music came to be acknowledged by white audiences. Notable albums include *Confessin' The Blues* (1966), and the Grammy award-winning *There Must Be a Better World Somewhere* (1981).

King, Billie Jean, *née* **Moffat** (1943–) Tennis player, born in Long Beach, CA. She won the women's doubles title at Wimbledon in 1961 (with Karen Hantze Susman) at her first attempt, and between 1961 and 1979 won a record 20 Wimbledon titles, including the singles in 1966–8, 1972–3, and 1975. She also won 13 US titles (including four singles), four French titles (one singles), and two Australian titles (one singles). She was the first president of the Women's Tennis Association in 1974. >> RR1174

King, Carole, originally **Carole Klein** (1942–) Singer and songwriter, born in New York City. With lyricist **Gerry Goffin** she was responsible for dozens of classic pop songs, including their first number 1 hit, 'Will You Love Me Tomorrow' (1960), sung by the Shirelles. She wrote and sang 'It Might As Well Rain Until September' (1962), which reached the US and UK charts. They received the National Academy of Songwriters Lifetime Achievement award in 1988, and were included in the Rock'n'Roll Hall of Fame in New York in 1990.

King, Cecil (Harmsworth) (1901–87) Newspaper proprietor, born in Totteridge, Hertfordshire, SE England, UK, the nephew of the Harmsworth brothers. He joined the *Daily Mirror* in 1926, and became chairman of Daily Mirror Newspapers Ltd and Sunday Pictorial Newspapers Ltd (1951–63), and chairman of the International Publishing Corporation and Reed Paper Group (1963–8). >> Harmsworth

King, Ernest (Joseph) (1878–1956) US admiral, born in Lorain, OH. He trained at the US Naval Academy, Annapolis, and during World War 1 served on the staff of the US Atlantic Fleet (1916–19). He commanded the submarine base at New London (1923–5), and became commander-in-chief of the Atlantic Fleet, with the rank of admiral (1941), and of the US fleet (also 1941). As chief of naval operations (1942–5) he masterminded the carrier-based campaign against the Japanese.

King, Francis (Henry) (1923–) Novelist and short-story writer, born in Switzerland. He studied at Shrewsbury and Oxford, after a childhood spent partly in India, and worked for the British Council in Greece, Egypt, and Japan (1945–64). His novels include *The Dividing Stream* (1951, Somerset Maugham Award), *The Needle* (1975), *Act of Darkness* (1983), *Visiting Cards* (1990), *The Ant Colony* (1991), and *Ash on an Old Man's Sleeve* (1996). His volumes of short stories include *The Japanese Umbrella* (1964) and *Hard Feelings* (1976), and he has also written poetry and travel books.

King, Jessie Marion (1875–1945) Designer and illustrator, born in Bearsden (formerly New Kilpatrick), East Dunbartonshire, WC Scotland, UK. She studied at the Glasgow School of Art and won a travelling scholarship to Italy and Germany. She was an internationally renowned and much sought-after book illustrator, who also designed jewellery and wallpaper, and was greatly involved with batik and pottery.

King, John (1838–72) Traveller, born in Moy, Co Tyrone. He was a member of the Burke and Wills expedition which set out from Melbourne in 1860; four members of the expedition reached the tidal marshes of the Flinders R at the edge of the Gulf of Carpentaria. On the way back, three of them, including Burke and Wills, died of starvation; the fourth man, John King, was given succour by the Aborigines and was eventually found by a relief party six months later, emaciated but alive. He thus became the first white man to traverse the Australian continent from S to N and back again. >> Burke, Robert O'Hara; Wills, William John

King, Larry, originally **Lawrence Harvey Zeiger** (1933–) Talk-show host, born in New York City. After leaving school, he joined a Florida radio station, and in the 1960s hosted local talk-shows. He joined CNN in 1985, taking *Larry King Live* to the top of the ratings by 1992, widely watched for its commentary and debate on contemporary events. He has made many specials, and written several books, starting with *Tell It to the King* (1988) and including *The Best of Larry King Live* (1995).

King, Martin Luther, Jr (1929–68) Clergyman and civil rights campaigner, born in Atlanta, GA, the son of a Baptist pastor. He studied at Morehouse College, Atlanta, Crozer Theological Seminary, PA, and Boston University, and became a leader of the black Civil Rights movement, known for his policy of passive resistance and his acclaimed oratorical skills. In 1964 he received the Kennedy Peace Prize and the Nobel Peace Prize. His greatest success came in challenging the segregation laws of the South. After 1965, he turned his attention to social conditions in the North, which he found less tractable. He was assassinated in Memphis, TN; his assassin, James Earl Ray, was apprehended in London, and in 1969 was sentenced in Memphis to 99 years. A national holiday in King's honour has been recognized in many states since 1986. >> Young, Andrew

King, Stephen (Edwin) (1947–) Novelist, born in Portland, ME. He graduated from the University of Maine in 1970, and became an English teacher (1971–3), turning to full-time writing after the success of his first novel, *Carrie* (1974). He has become known for his vivid treatment of horrific and supernatural themes, later books (many of which have been filmed) including *Salem's Lot* (1975), *The Shining* (1976), *It* (1986), and *Insomnia* (1994). He has also written collections of short stories, and other novels under the name of Richard Bachman.

King, W(illiam) L(yon) Mackenzie (1874–1950) Canadian statesman and prime minster (1921–6, 1926–30, 1935–48), born in Kitchener (formerly Berlin), Ontario, Canada. He studied law at Toronto University, and became an MP (1908), minister of labour (1909–11), and Liberal leader (1919). His view that the dominions should be autonomous communities within the British empire resulted in the Statute of Westminster (1931). He resigned from office in 1948. >> RR1039

King, William Rufus (1786–1853) US statesman, born in Sampson Co, NC. He studied at the University of North Carolina, and became a lawyer. A member of the state legislature for three years, he entered Congress in 1810, was senator for Alabama (1820–44), minister to France (1844–6), senator again (1846–53), and just before his death was elected Democratic vice-president of the USA.

Kingman, Sir John (Frank Charles) (1939–) British academic. He studied at Cambridge, where he became a fellow of Pembroke College, and taught mathematics. He was professor at the University of Sussex (1966–9) and at Oxford (1969–85), before becoming Vice-Chancellor of the University of Bristol in 1985. His books include *The Algebra of Queues* (1966) and *Mathematics of Genetic Diversity* (1980), but his name became more generally known as chairman of the Committee of Inquiry into the Teaching of the English Language (1987–8), which produced the *Kingman Report*, a major influence on changing practices in English language teaching in British schools in the 1990s. He was knighted in 1985. >> Cox, (Charles) Brian

Kingsford Smith, Sir Charles Edward (1897–1935) Pioneer aviator, born in Hamilton, Queensland, Australia. He studied at Sydney Technical College, served in the

Royal Flying Corps (1917), then became an instructor in the Royal Air Force. He joined West Australia Airways (1921), becoming chief pilot in 1924. With Charles Ulm he completed a record-breaking flight round Australia (1927), and in 1928 flew from California to Brisbane via Honolulu and Fiji. He was knighted in 1932. In November 1935 he set off with Thomas Pethybridge from Allahabad, India, on the second leg of an attempt at the England–Australia record, but the plane went missing over the Bay of Bengal. >> Taylor, Patrick Gordon; Ulm

Kingsley, Ben (1943–) Actor, born in Snainton, North Yorkshire, N England, UK. Educated in Manchester, he joined the Royal Shakespeare Company (1970–80, 1985–6), and has appeared in a number of television plays. He is best known for his title role in the film *Gandhi* (1980), for which he won many awards, including an Oscar. Other films include *Testimony* (1987), *The Children* (1990), *Schindler's List* (1993), and *Twelfth Night* (1996). Notable stage performances include Peter Hall's 1997 production of *Waiting for Godot* at the Old Vic, London.

Kingsley, Charles (1819–75) Writer, born in Holne, Devon, SW England, UK. He studied at Cambridge, was ordained in 1842, and lived as curate and rector of Eversley, Hampshire. A 'Christian Socialist', he was much involved in schemes for the improvement of working-class life, and his social novels, such as *Alton Locke* (1850), had great influence at the time. His best-known works are *Westward Ho!* (1855), *Hereward the Wake* (1866), and his children's book, *The Water Babies* (1863). In 1860 he was appointed professor of modern history at Cambridge, and in 1873 chaplain to the queen. >> Kingsley, Mary Henrietta

Kingsley, Mary Henrietta (1862–1900) Traveller and writer, born in London, England, UK, the niece of Charles Kingsley. She was not formally educated, but was a voracious reader in her father's scientific library. She led a secluded life tending her sick parents until they died; she then undertook two remarkable journeys to West Africa (1893–5), to study African religion and law, and was the first European to enter some parts of Gabon. Returning from her second journey in 1895, she wrote *Travels in West Africa* (1897) and *West African Studies* (1899). She later came to be consulted by colonial administrators, for her expertise was wide and her understanding of African culture broad-based. Serving as a nurse in the second Boer War, she died of enteric fever. >> Kingsley, Charles

Kingsmill, Hugh (1889–1949) British writer, critic, and anthologist. He studied at Oxford and Dublin, and became a writer, publishing his first novel, *A Will to Love*, in 1919. He wrote several irreverent biographies, and the satirical fantasy *The Return of William Shakespeare* (1929). His anthologies include *Invective and Abuse* (1929), *Johnson Without Boswell* (1940), and *The Worst of Love* (1931), while with Hesketh Pearson he established a genre of conversational literary journeys through such works as *Skye High* (1937), *This Blessed Plot* (1942), and *Talking of Dick Whittington* (1947). >> Lunn; Pearson, Hesketh

Kinnock, Neil (Gordon) (1942–) British politician, born in Tredegar, Blaenau Gwent, SE Wales, UK. He studied at Cardiff, became a Labour MP in 1970, joined the Labour Party's National Executive Committee (1978), and was chief Opposition spokesman on education (1979–83). A skilful orator, he was elected party leader following Michael Foot in 1983, and resigned as Leader of the Opposition after the 1992 general election. He became a European Commissioner (with responsibility for transport) in 1994. >> Foot, Michael

Kinsey, Alfred (Charles) (1894–1956) Sexologist and zoologist, born in Hoboken, NJ. He studied at Bowdoin College, ME, and at Harvard, becoming professor of zoology at Indiana University from 1920. In 1942 he was the founder-director of the Institute for Sex Research, Bloomington, for the scientific study of human sexual behaviour. He published two controversial studies, *Sexual Behavior in the Human Male* (1948, the so-called 'Kinsey Report') and *Sexual Behavior in the Human Female* (1953).

Kinski, Klaus, originally **Nikolaus Gunther Naksznski** (1926–91) Film actor, born in Zoppot, Poland. In the 1930s his family moved to Germany, where he joined the army in 1942. Soon captured, he spent the rest of the War in a British concentration camp, where he first went on stage. He later played many minor parts in films such as spaghetti Westerns (including Clint Eastwood's *For a Few Dollars More*), then became known for his leading roles in the films of Werner Herzog, such as *Aguirre, the Wrath of God* (1972) and *Fitzcarraldo* (1982). He was also acclaimed for his role in *Nosferatu, the Vampyre* (1979), a remake of the Dracula story. His daughter, **Natassja** (1960–), is also an actress. >> Herzog; Kinski, Natassja

Kinski, Natassja (1960–) Film actress, born in Berlin, Germany, the daughter of Klaus Kinski. She was discovered at the age of fourteen and cast in the film *Wrong Movement* (1975), then trained in New York and London. Her films include *Tess* (1979), *Paris Texas* (1984), *Terminal Velocity* (1994), and *My Two Dads* (1997). >> Kinski, Klaus

Kiphuth, Robert (John Herman) (1890–1967) Physical educator, born in Tonawanda, NY. A highly successful swimming coach, he retired after 41 years at Yale with a 528–12 dual meet record and 38 eastern intercollegiate and 14 national championships. He also coached (1928–48) US Olympic swimming teams. He was awarded the US Medal of Freedom in 1963.

Kipling, (Joseph) Rudyard (1865–1936) Writer, born of British parents in Mumbai (Bombay), India. Educated at boarding school in England, UK, he returned in 1882 to India, where he worked as a journalist. His satirical verses and short stories, such as *Plain Tales From the Hills* (1888) and *Soldiers Three* (1892), won him a reputation in England, to which he returned in 1889 and settled in London. His verse collections *Barrack Room Ballads* (1892) and *The Seven Seas* (1896) were highly successful, as were the two *Jungle Books* (1894–5), which have become classic animal stories. *Kim* appeared in 1901, and the classic *Just So Stories* in 1902. Later works include *Puck of Pook's Hill* (1906) and the autobiographical *Something of Myself* (1937). He was awarded the Nobel Prize for Literature in 1907. >> Thirkell

Kipp, Petrus Jacobus (1808–64) Chemist, born in Utrecht, The Netherlands. He started a business in laboratory apparatus in Delft in 1830. He invented the apparatus called after him for the continuous and automatic production of gases such as carbon dioxide, hydrogen, and hydrogen sulphide. A representation of it appears in the arms of the Dutch Chemical Society. He also invented a method of fixing carbon and pastel drawings.

Kipping, Frederick (Stanley) (1863–1949) Chemist, born in Manchester, Greater Manchester, NW England, UK. He studied at Manchester and in Germany, and worked in Nottingham (1897–1936) as professor of chemistry. He is now best known as the founder of silicone chemistry, although the technical uses for silicones were developed by others from 1940 onwards.

Kirchhoff, Gustav (Robert) [keerkhhohf] (1824–87) Physicist, born in Königsberg, Germany. After lecturing at Berlin (1847), he became professor of physics at Wrocław, Poland (formerly Breslau, Germany) (1850)) and Heidelberg (1854), and of mathematical physics at Berlin (1875). He formulated the laws involved in the mathematical analysis of an electrical network (*Kirchhoff's laws*, 1845). He also investigated heat, and with Bunsen helped to develop the prism spectrometer and the technique of spectrum analysis, used in the discovery of caesium and rubidium (1859). >> Bunsen

Kirchner, Ernst Ludwig [keerkhner] (1880–1938) Artist, born in Aschaffenburg, Germany. He studied architecture at Dresden, then turned to painting, and became the leading spirit in the formation of *Die Brücke* ('The Bridge', 1905–13), the first group of German Expressionists. Many of his works were confiscated as degenerate by the Nazis in 1937, and he committed suicide in 1938. >> Heckel, Erich

Kirk, Alan G(oodrich) (1888–1963) US naval officer and diplomat, born in Philadelphia, PA. He trained at the US Naval Academy, Annapolis, served as naval attaché in London (1939–41), and was promoted rear-admiral in 1941. He commanded the amphibious forces in the invasion of Sicily (1943) and the Western Task Force in the Normandy landing in 1944. He later became ambassador to Belgium (1946–9), the USSR (1949–52), and Taiwan (1962).

Kirk, Norman Eric (1923–74) New Zealand prime minister (1972–4), born in Waimate, New Zealand. He became president of the Labour Party (1964) and was Leader of the Opposition in the House of Representatives (1965–72). As prime minister, he stressed the need for greater economic co-operation with Australia at a time when Britain's entry into the European Economic Community would restrict the British market for New Zealand produce. He was strongly opposed to French nuclear tests in the Pacific (1973). He died in office. >> RR1078

Kirkeby, Per [keerkuhbü] (1939–) Danish painter. He became professor at the Staatliche Hochschule für Bildende Künste, Frankfurt, in 1988. For several years he has been a prominent representative of new, experimental Danish painting. He has also published poetry, essays, and novels, and directed several documentary films.

Kirkland, Gelsey (1952–) Dancer, born in Bethlehem, PA. After studying at the School of American Ballet, she joined New York City Ballet in 1968, becoming a principal in 1972. She moved to the American Ballet Theater in 1975, where she partnered Baryshnikov in one of the decade's most celebrated partnerships. A troubled personal life curtailed her career in the early 1980s, but she made a dramatic and successful comeback in *Swan Lake* with the Royal Ballet in London, where she has settled. >> Baryshnikov

Kirkpatrick, Jeane (Duane Jordan) (1926–) US stateswoman and academic, born in Duncan, OK. She studied at Columbia and Paris universities, then became a research analyst for the state department (1951–3). She concentrated on a career as an academic, at Trinity College and Georgetown University, Washington DC, becoming Georgetown's professor of government in 1978. Noted for her anti-Communist defence stance and advocacy of a new Latin-American and Pacific-orientated diplomatic strategy, she was appointed permanent representative to the UN by President Reagan (1981–5).

Kirkwood, Daniel (1814–95) Astronomer and mathematician, born in Harford, MD. He became professor of mathematics at Delaware (1851) and at Indiana (1856). He explained the unequal distribution of asteroids in the ring system of Saturn as a result of the influence of Jupiter. These interruptions became known as *Kirkwood gaps*.

Kirov, Sergey Mironovich [kirof] (1886–1934) Russian revolutionary and politician, born in Urzhum, Russia. Educated at Kazan, he played an active part in the October Revolution and Civil War, and during the 1920s held a number of leading provincial Party posts. In 1934 he became a full member of the Politburo, and at the 17th Party Congress was elected a secretary of the Central Committee. Later that year he was assassinated at his Leningrad headquarters, possibly at the instigation of Stalin, and his death served as the pretext for a widespread campaign of reprisals. >> Stalin; Zinoviev

Kirstein, Lincoln [kersteen] (1907–96) Writer, impresario, and ballet director, born in Rochester, NY. He studied at Harvard, and became an influential force in the ballet world, best known for recognizing the talents of George Balanchine and taking him to the USA to co-found the School of American Ballet in 1934. Their American Ballet became attached to the Metropolitan Opera in 1935, and at the same time Kirstein ran the touring company, Ballet Caravan. In 1946 they founded the Ballet Society, and in 1948 moved to New York's new City Centre as the directors of what has become one of America's top-ranking companies, New York City Ballet. He was founder editor of *Dance Index Magazine* (1942–8), and wrote many books. >> Balanchine

Kissinger, Henry (Alfred) [kisinjer] (1923–) US secretary of state (1973–6) and academic, born in Fürth, Germany. His family emigrated to the USA in 1938 to escape the Nazi persecution of the Jews. He studied at Harvard, and after war service worked for a number of public agencies before joining the Harvard faculty (1962–71). He became President Nixon's adviser on national security affairs in 1969, was the main US figure in the negotiations to end the Vietnam War (for which he shared the 1973 Nobel Peace Prize), and became secretary of state under Nixon and Ford. His 'shuttle diplomacy' was aimed at bringing about peace between Israel and the Arab states, and resulted in a notable improvement in Israeli–Egyptian relations. After leaving public office (1977), he became professor of diplomacy at Georgetown, and established Kissinger Associates, a consulting firm. His book *Diplomacy* was published in 1994. >> Ford, Gerald R; Le Duc Tho; Nixon

Kitaj, R(onald) B(rooks) [kitazh] (1932–) Painter, born in Cleveland, OH. He was a sailor (1951–5) and travelled extensively. Following army service, he went to Oxford, where he studied art, and in 1960 entered the Royal College of Art, London. An intellectual Pop artist, his oil paintings and pastels demonstrate a mastery of figure drawing, while his economic use of line and the flattened colour recall Oriental art.

Kitazato, Shibasaburo (1852–1931) Bacteriologist, born in Oguni, Japan. He studied in Berlin under Robert Koch, and later founded in Japan an Institute for Infectious Diseases. He discovered the bacillus of bubonic plague (1894), isolated the bacilli of symptomatic anthrax, dysentery, and tetanus, and prepared a diphtheria antitoxin. >> Koch, Robert; Yersin

Kitchener (of Khartoum and of Broome), (Horatio) Herbert Kitchener, 1st Earl (1850–1916) British field marshal, born near Ballylongford, Co Kerry, Ireland. He joined the Royal Engineers in 1871, and served in Palestine (1874), Cyprus (1878), and the Sudan (1883). By the final rout of the Khalifa at Omdurman (1898), he won back the Sudan for Egypt, and was made a peer. Successively chief-of-staff and commander-in-chief in South Africa (1900–2), he brought the Boer War to an end, and was made viscount. He then became commander-in-chief in India (1902–9), consul-general in Egypt (1911), and secretary for war (1914), for which he organized manpower on a vast scale (*Kitchener armies*). He was lost with HMS *Hampshire*, mined off the Orkney Is.

Kitt, Eartha (Mae) (c. 1928–) Entertainer and singer, born in North, SC. She studied at the New York School of the Performing Arts, and made her New York debut as a member of Katherine Dunham's dance troupe in 1945. She toured throughout Europe, and was cast by Orson Welles in his production of *Dr Faustus* (1951). Her vocal vibrancy, fiery personality, and cat-like singing voice made her a top international cabaret attraction and recording artiste. Since her debut in *Casbah* (1948), her film appearances have included *St Louis Blues* (1957) and the documentary *All By Myself* (1982). On television from 1953, she received the Golden Rose of Montreux for *Kaskade* (1962), and was appropriately cast as Catwoman in the series *Batman* (1966). Later theatre work has included a show-stopping appearance in *Follies* (1988–9), and a one-woman show.

Kivi, Aleksis [keevee], pseudonym of **Alexis Stenvall** (1834–72) Playwright and novelist, born in Nurmijärvi, Finland. He wrote penetratingly of Finnish peasant life, notably in *Seitseman Veljesta* (1870, Seven Brothers), and is now recognized as one of his country's greatest writers. He died insane, poverty-stricken, and unrecognized.

Kjarval, Jóhannes (Sveinsson) (1885–1972) Painter, born in Efri-Ey, Iceland. He studied at Reykjavík under Asgrímur Jónsson before going to the Royal Academy in Copenhagen (1912–18). From 1918 he lived in Iceland but travelled widely. Essentially an eccentric Romantic, he had a powerful sense of historical nationalism, and often featured the 'hidden people' of Icelandic folklore. He became the best-loved painter in Iceland. >> Jónsson, Asgrímur

Kjeldahl, Johan G(ustav) C(hristoffer) T(horsager) (1849–1900) Danish chemist. Director of the Carlsberg Laboratory in Copenhagen (1876–1900), he was noted for his analytical methods, and especially for the method of nitrogen determination named after him (1883).

Klammer, Franz (1953–) Alpine skier, born in Mooswald, Austria. He was the Olympic downhill champion in 1976, and the World Cup downhill champion five times (1975–8, 1983). In 1974–84 he won a record 25 World Cup downhill races.

Klaproth, Martin Heinrich [klaproht] (1743–1817) Chemist, born in Wernigerode, Germany. He learnt chemistry as an apprentice to an apothecary, and did much to develop analytical chemistry. He was able to deduce, but not isolate, the elements zirconium, uranium, strontium, and titanium. He was appointed the first professor of chemistry in the new University of Berlin (1810).

Kléber, Jean Baptiste [klaybair] (1753–1800) French soldier, born in Strasbourg, France. He held a commission in the Austrian army (1776–82), and worked as an architect in Belfort before enlisting in the French Revolutionary army (1792). A general by 1793, he led successful campaigns in the French conquest of Belgium, accompanied Napoleon to Egypt, and won the Battle of Mt Tabor (1799). When Napoleon left Egypt he entrusted the chief command to Kléber, who concluded a convention with Sir Sidney Smith for its evacuation; but on Admiral Keith's refusal to ratify it, Kléber resolved to reconquer Egypt, destroyed the Turkish army at Heliopolis, and took Cairo. He tried to conclude a treaty with the Turks, and was assassinated by an Egyptian fanatic in Cairo. >> Napoleon

Klee, Paul [klay] (1879–1940) Artist, born in Münchenbuchsee, near Bern, Switzerland. He studied at Munich and settled there, becoming a member of the *Blaue Reiter* group (1911–12). He then taught at the Bauhaus (1920–32), and after returning to Bern (1933) many of his works were confiscated in Germany. His early work consists of bright watercolours, but after 1919 he worked in oils, producing small-scale, mainly abstract pictures, as in his 'Twittering Machine' (1922, New York). >> Macke

Kleiber, Erich [kliyber] (1890–1956) Conductor, born in Vienna. He studied in Prague, and the age of 33 became director of the Berlin State Opera, holding this post for 12 years until forced by the Nazis to leave Germany. In 1938

he became a citizen of Argentina. After the war he was again appointed director of the Berlin State Opera, until his resignation in 1955.

Klein, Anne (Hannah) [kliyn], originally **Hannah Golofski** (?1921–74) Fashion designer, born in New York City. In 1938 she started as a sketcher on Seventh Avenue. In 1948, Junior Sophisticates was launched, and Anne Klein & Co was established in 1968. She was a noted leader in designing sophisticated, practical sportswear for young women. She early recognized a need for blazers, trousers, and separates, and her designs became particularly popular in the USA.

Klein, Calvin (Richard) [kliyn] (1942–) Fashion designer, born in New York City. He graduated from New York's Fashion Institute of Technology in 1962, gained experience in New York, and set up his own firm in 1968. He quickly achieved recognition, and became known for understatement and the simple but sophisticated style of his clothes, including designer jeans.

Klein, (Christian) Felix [kliyn] (1849–1925) Mathematician, born in Düsseldorf, Germany. He studied at the University of Bonn, and held chairs at Erlangen (1872–5), Munich (1875–80), Leipzig (1880–6), and Göttingen (1886–1913). He worked on geometry, including non-Euclidean geometry, function theory (in which he developed Bernhard Riemann's ideas), and elliptic modular and automorphic functions. His *Erlanger Programm* showed how different geometries could be classified in terms of group theory. He also wrote on the history of mathematics, encouraged links between pure and applied mathematics and engineering, and promoted general mathematical education. >> Riemann

Klein, Lawrence (Robert) [kliyn] (1920–) Economist, born in Omaha, NE. He studied at the University of California, Berkeley, and the Massachusetts Institute of Technology, and became professor at the universities of Chicago (1944–7), Michigan (1949–54), and Pennsylvania (1958–91, now emeritus). He was economic adviser to President Carter (1976–81), and was awarded the 1980 Nobel Prize for Economics for his work on forecasting business fluctuations and portraying economic interrelationships. >> Carter, Jimmy

Klein, Melanie [kliyn] (1882–1960) Austrian child psychoanalyst. She studied under Sigmund Freud, and opened a practice in London. She was the first to use the content and style of children's play to understand their mental processes, a technique now widely used to help troubled children. >> Freud, Anna; Freud, Sigmund

Kleist, (Bernd) Heinrich (Wilhelm) von [kliyst] (1777–1811) Playwright and poet, born in Frankfurt an der Oder, Germany. He left the army in 1799 to study, and soon devoted himself to literature. His best plays are still popular, notably *Prinz Friedrich von Homburg* (1821) and his finest tale, *Michael Kohlhaas* (1810–11). He committed suicide in 1811.

Klemperer, Otto (1885–1973) Conductor, born in Wrocław, Poland (formerly Breslau, Germany). He studied at Frankfurt and Berlin, first appeared as a conductor in 1906, made a name as a champion of modern music, and was appointed director of the Kroll Opera in Berlin (1927–31). Nazism drove him to the USA, where he became director of the Los Angeles Symphony Orchestra (1933–9). In his later years, he concentrated mainly on the German classical and Romantic composers, and was particularly known for his interpretation of Beethoven. He also composed six symphonies, a Mass, and Lieder.

Klerk, F W de >> de Klerk, F W

Klimt, Gustav (1862–1918) Painter, born in Vienna. The leading master of the Vienna *Sezession*, he began with a firm of decorators, painting nondescript murals for museums and theatres, but in 1900-3 he painted some murals for the University of Vienna in a new and shocking Symbolist style which caused great controversy. His portraits combine realistically painted heads with flat abstract backgrounds. >> Schiele

Kline, Franz (Joseph) (1910-62) Artist, born in Wilkes-Barre, PA. He studied at Boston University and at the Hetherley School of Art in London. Throughout the 1940s he worked in a traditional style, painting urban scenery, but after c.1950 he went abstract, using black, irregular shapes on white canvases.

Kline, Kevin (1947–) Film actor, born in St Louis, MO. He studied music at Indiana University, then switched to drama, training at the Juilliard School in New York City. On Broadway he won Tonies for two hit musicals, *On the Twentieth Century* (1978) and *The Pirates of Penzance* (1980). Though known for his dramatic abilities, it was his comic role in *A Fish Called Wanda* (1988) that earned him an Oscar as Best Supporting Actor. Later films include *Chaplin* (1992), *French Kiss* (1995), *Looking for Richard* (1996), and *Fierce Creatures* (1997).

Klinger, Friedrich Maximilian von (1752-1831) Playwright and writer, born in Frankfurt, Germany. He was a poet with a touring theatre company before joining the Russian army as an officer (1780-1811), and became curator of Dorpat University (1803-17). The *Sturm-und-Drang* school was named after one of his tragedies, *Der Wirrwarr, oder Sturm und Drang* (1776, Confusion, or Storm and Stress). He wrote several other plays and some novels.

Klinger, Max (1857-1920) Painter and sculptor, born in Leipzig, Germany. He studied in Karlsruhe, Brussels, and Paris, and excited hostility as well as admiration by his pen drawings and etchings, which were audaciously original in concept and often imbued with macabre realism. Later he turned to painting, and did much work in coloured sculpture, including Beethoven (1902), and an unfinished monument to Richard Wagner.

Klinsmann, Jurgen (1964–) Footballer, born in Groppingen, Germany. A forward, he played in minor league teams from the age of 17, then for VFB Stuttgart, Inter Milan, and AS Monaco, moving to Tottenham Hotspurs in 1994, Bayern Munich in 1995, and back to Tottenham in 1997. He led the German team to victory in the 1996 EUFA cup.

Klint, Kaare (1888-1954) Architect and furniture designer, born in Copenhagen. He placed great emphasis on the function of furniture, and applied ergonomics to his designs. He was one of the initiators of Denmark's prominence in the field of design, partly through his teaching at the Royal Danish Academy of Fine Arts, which he helped to found in 1924. He was made an honorary royal designer for industry in Britain in 1949.

Klippel, Robert Edward (1920–) Sculptor, born in Sydney, New South Wales, Australia. He served in the Royal Australian Navy (1939-45), and later studied, worked, and exhibited in London and Paris. He spent the years 1957-63 in New York City. He was professor of sculpture at the University of Minneapolis (1966-7), after which he returned to Sydney, where he has since lived and worked. His sculptures are intricate and complex, often made of metal 'found objects' welded together (hence the name 'junk sculpture'), although he does also work with wood, plaster, and bronze. He is Australia's senior and best-known sculptor.

Klopstock, Friedrich Gottlieb (1724-1803) Poet, born in Quedlinburg, Germany. Inspired by Virgil and Milton, he began *Der Messias* (The Messiah) as a student at Jena (1745), completing it in 1773. He lived in Copenhagen (1751-71),

then moved to Hamburg. Regarded in his own time as a great religious poet, he helped to inaugurate the golden age of German literature, especially by his lyrics and odes.

Kluckhohn, Clyde K(ay) M(aben) (1905-60) Cultural anthropologist, born in Le Mars, IA. He studied at Princeton, Wisconsin, Vienna and Oxford universities, and in 1935 was appointed to the faculty of Harvard, where he remained for the rest of his career. His abiding research interest was in the culture of the Navaho Indians, on which he wrote many studies, most notably *Navaho Witchcraft* (1944). A major contributor to culture theory, he popularized his views in *Mirror for Man* (1949).

Klug, Sir Aaron [klook] (1926–) Biophysicist, born in Lithuania. He moved to South Africa at the age of three, and later studied at Johannesburg and Cape Town, completing his doctorate at Cambridge. He was a research fellow at Birkbeck College (1953), where he worked with Rosalind Franklin, and became director of the Virus Structure Research Group there (1958-62). He joined the staff of the Medical Research Council Laboratory at Cambridge (1962), becoming its director in 1986. He brought together X-ray diffraction methods, electron microscopy, structural modelling, and symmetry arguments to elucidate the structure of viruses. He was awarded the Nobel Prize for Chemistry in 1982, and knighted in 1988. >> Franklin, Rosalind

Kluge, (Hans) Günther von [klooguh] (1882-1944) German soldier, born in Poznan, Poland. In 1939 he carried out the Nazi occupation of the Polish Corridor, commanded the German armies on the central Russian front (1942), and in July 1944 replaced Rundstedt as commander-in-chief of the Nazi armies in France confronting the Allied invasion, but was himself replaced after failing to stop the advance. He committed suicide after being implicated in the plot to kill Hitler. >> Hitler; Rundstedt

Kneale, Nigel (1922–) Writer and playwright, born on the Isle of Man. He joined the drama department of the BBC in a general capacity, and progressed to writing the serial *The Quatermass Experiment* (1953), an imaginative science-fiction drama, reflecting the paranoia of the day. Its immense popularity led to sequels and feature films. Other TV adaptations *1984*, which caused questions about the BBC to be raised in parliament. His film scripts include *The Abominable Snowman* (1957), *First Men in the Moon* (1964), *The Witches* (1966), and *Halloween III* (1983).

Kneller, Sir Godfrey [kneler], originally **Gottfried Kniller** (1646-1723) Portrait painter, born in Lübeck, Germany. He studied at Amsterdam and in Italy, went to London (1676), and was appointed court painter (1680). He was knighted (1692), and in 1715 made a baronet. His best-known works are his 48 portraits of the Whig 'Kit-Cat Club' (1700-17, National Portrait Gallery, London), and of nine sovereigns.

Kngwarreye, Emily Kame [nuhwaray] (c. 1910-96) Artist, born in Alhalkere, Northern Territory, Australia. The pre-eminent artist of the internationally renowned Utopia group of artists, she first became known by exhibiting with Utopia Women's Batik (1977-88), a group which used non-traditional batik techniques. She began painting in her seventies, working mainly with acrylic paints, and her works now feature in major public and private collections throughout Australia and the USA. A non-English speaking elder of the Alhalkere people, her innovative style is based on Amnatyerre ceremonial body designs and symbols and Dreaming maps, over which she applied her own distinct images. She is known as much for being an Aboriginal artist as a contemporary abstract painter.

Knickerbocker, Harmen Jansen (c. 1650-c. 1716) Colonist, from Friesland, one of the earliest settlers of New Amsterdam (New York). He went to New Amsterdam in 1674 and settled near Albany (1682). A descendant, **Johannes** (1749-1827), was a friend of Washington Irving, who immortalized the name through his *History of New York* by 'Diedrich Knickerbocker' (1809). >> Irving, Washington

Knievel, Evel [kneevel, eevel], professional name of **Robert Craig Knievel** (1938–) Motorcycle stunt performer, born in Butte, MT. He began carrying out motorcycle stunts as a teenager, and after a succession of jobs, from hockey player to safecracker, formed Evel Knievel's Motorcycle Devils in 1965, becoming internationally known for his spectacular and dangerous performances. He later managed the stunt career of his son, **Robbie Knievel**.

Knight, Dame Laura *née* **Johnson** (1877–1970) Artist, born in Long Eaton, Derbyshire, C England, UK. Trained at Nottingham, she produced a long series of oil paintings of the ballet, the circus, and gypsy life, in a lively and forceful style, and also executed a number of watercolour landscapes. She was made a dame in 1929.

Knopf, Alfred A (1892–1984) Publisher, born in New York City. He studied at Columbia University, then worked briefly for a publishing house before founding one under his own name. The firm gained a prestigious reputation for the quality and variety of its literature, and attracted many authors who became Nobel and Pulitzer prizewinners. The company became a subsidiary of Random House in 1966.

Knott, Alan (Philip Eric) (1946–) Cricketer, born in Belvedere, NW Greater London, England, UK. One of a great trio of Kent wicket-keepers (with Leslie Ames and Godfrey Evans), he played in 95 Test matches, and his 269 dismissals are exceeded only by Rodney Marsh of Australia. He was a genuine wicket-keeper–batsman, whose 4389 runs included five centuries. He kept wicket for England in 65 consecutive Test matches. >> Evans, Godfrey; RR1149

Knox, Archibald (1864–1933) Designer, born on the Isle of Man. He studied at Douglas School of Art, and worked part-time in an architectural office. In 1899 he designed silver-work and metalwork for Liberty & Co. By 1900 he was their main designer and the inspiration behind the Celtic revival. Apart from the Cymric (silver) and Tudric (pewter) ranges, he designed carpets, textiles, jewellery, and pottery, as well as teaching for Liberty's.

Knox, Edmund George Valpy, pseudonym **Evoe** (1881–1971) Writer and parodist, the brother of Ronald Knox. He joined the staff of *Punch* in 1921 and became editor (1932–49), contributing articles under his pseudonym. His best work was republished in book form, and includes *Parodies Regained*, *Fiction As She Is Wrote*, *It Occurs to Me*, *Awful Occasions*, *Here's Misery*, and *Folly Calling*. >> Knox, Ronald

Knox, John (c. 1513–72) Protestant reformer, born near Haddington, East Lothian, E Scotland, UK. A Catholic priest, he acted as a notary in Haddington (1540–3), and in 1544 was influenced by George Wishart to work for the Lutheran reformation. After Wishart was burned (1546), Knox joined the reformers defending the castle of St Andrews, and became a minister. After the castle fell to the French, he was kept a prisoner until 1549, then became chaplain to Edward VI, and was consulted over the Second Book of Common Prayer. On Mary's accession (1553), he fled to Dieppe, then to Geneva, where he was much influenced by Calvin. He returned to Scotland in 1555 to preach, and again in 1559, where he won a strong party in favour of reform, and founded the Church of Scotland (1560). He played a lasting part in the composition of *The Scots Confession*, *The First Book of Discipline*, and *The Book of Common Order*. >> Calvin; Mary I; Wishart

Knox, Ronald (Arbuthnott) (1888–1957) Theologian and essayist, born in Birmingham, West Midlands, C England, UK. He studied at Oxford, where he became a lecturer (1910), but resigned in 1917 on being converted to Catholicism. He was then ordained, and appointed Catholic chaplain to the university (1926–39). He wrote an influential translation of the Bible, and several works of apologetics, as well as detective novels. His autobiography, *A Spiritual Aeneid*, appeared in 1918. >> Knox, Edmund George Valpy

Knox-Johnston, Robin, popular name of **Sir William Robert Patrick Knox-Johnston** (1939–) British yachtsman, the first person to circumnavigate the world nonstop and single-handed, 14 June 1968–22 April 1969. He is also holder of the British Sailing Trans Atlantic Record (1986: 10 days, 14 hours, 9 mins), and he co-skippered *Enza* achieving the world's fastest circumnavigation under sail (1994: 74 days, 22 hours, 17 mins, 22 secs). His books include *World of My Own* (1969), *The Columbus Venture* (1991), and *Beyond Jules Verne* (1995). He was knighted in 1995.

Knudsen, William S(ignius), originally **Signius Wilhelm Paul Knudsen** (1879–1948) Industrialist and government official, born in Copenhagen. Emigrating to America at 21, he mastered bicycle and auto-parts production, and when Ford purchased his auto-parts firm, he was soon running assembly-line production for Ford (1913–20). Hired by Ford's arch-rival Chevrolet in 1922, he was outselling Ford by 1927, and became president of General Motors in 1937. He resigned in 1940 to serve on the National Defense Advisory Commission, then with the Office of Production Management, expediting war-related production. He accepted an army commission as lieutenant general to supervise production for the War Department and Army Air Force (1942–5). After the war he worked with the Hupp Corporation. >> Ford, Henry

Knussen, (Stuart) Oliver [noosn] (1952–) Composer and conductor, born in Glasgow, W Scotland, UK. He showed early flair for composition, conducting the London Symphony Orchestra in his first symphony in 1968. Two other symphonies followed, together with numerous orchestral, chamber, and vocal works, and operas including *Where the Wild Things Are*, (1979–83). He became a co-director of the Aldeburgh Festival in 1983.

Knut, Sveinsson >> Canute

Koch, Ed(ward Irving) [koch] (1924–) US politician, born in New York City. He interrupted college to serve in the US army (1943–6), and after the war practised as a lawyer (from 1949). He became a member of the New York City Council (1967–8), then served in the US House of Representatives (1969–74). He was well known as Democratic Mayor of New York (1978–90); his re-election in 1981 was partly due to his success in handling New York's financial problems and saving the city from bankruptcy. In 1982 he lost a bid for the Democratic governorship nomination to Mario Cuomo. Defeated as Democratic candidate for mayor in 1989 by David Dinkins, he returned to practise law. A colourful and outspoken character, he also found a place in the news media as a TV talk-show host and newspaper columnist. >> Cuomo; Dinkins

Koch, (Heinrich Hermann) Robert [kokh, rohbert] (1843–1910) Bacteriologist, born in Klausthal, Germany. He studied at Göttingen, became a physician and surgeon, and settled in Wollstein. He discovered the tuberculosis bacillus (1882), and led a German expedition to Egypt and India, where he discovered the cholera bacillus (1883). He became professor and director of the Hygienic Institute at Berlin (1885), and director of the new Institute for Infectious Diseases (1891). The major figure in medical bacteriology, he was awarded the 1905 Nobel Prize for Physiology or Medicine. >> Cohn; Henle; Kitazato

Köchel, Ludwig Ritter von [koekhel] (1800–77) Musicologist, born in Stein, Austria. He compiled the famous catalogue of Mozart's works, arranging them in chronological order, and giving them the 'K' numbers now commonly used to identify them. >> Mozart

Kocher, Emil [kokher] (1841–1917) Swiss surgeon. He worked at Bern University, and won the 1909 Nobel Prize for Physiology or Medicine for his work on the physiology, pathology, and surgery of the thyroid gland.

Kodály, Zoltán [kohdiy] (1882–1967) Composer, born in Kecskemét, Hungary. He studied at the Budapest Conservatory, where he became professor. Among his best-known works are his *Háry János* suite (1926), and several choral compositions, especially his *Psalmus Hungaricus* (1923) and *Te Deum* (1936). He also published editions of folk songs with Bartók. >> Bartók

Koechlin, Charles (Louis Eugène) [koeshlī] (1867–1950) Composer and writer on music, born in Paris. He studied under Massenet and Fauré at the Paris Conservatoire. He excelled in colourful and inventive orchestration in his symphonies, symphonic poems, choral-orchestral works (including seven based on Kipling's *Jungle Book*), film music, and works inspired by Hollywood, such as the *Seven Stars Symphony*. He also wrote prolifically for a wide range of vocal and chamber combinations. His writings included studies of recent French music and treatises on music theory. >> Fauré, Gabriel; Massenet

Koechlin, Pat >> **Smythe, Pat**

Koestler, Arthur [kestler] (1905–83) Writer and journalist, born in Budapest. He studied science at Vienna, embraced the cause of Zionism, and became a journalist and editor, and a British citizen. His masterpiece is the political novel, *Darkness at Noon* (1940). His nonfiction books and essays deal with politics, scientific creativity, and parapsychology, notably *The Act of Creation* (1964), and he wrote several autobiographical volumes. He and his wife were active members of the Voluntary Euthanasia Society and, after he developed a terminal illness, they committed suicide. He endowed a chair of parapsychology at Edinburgh University.

Koetsu, Hon'ami [kohetsoo] (1558–1637) Calligrapher and designer, born in Kyoto, Japan. He became famous for his raku and lacquer ware, but his numerous interests made him one of the most creative figures in the history of Japanese art, and an artist of tremendously wide achievement. He collaborated with the great master of the later decorative style, **Sotatsu** (1576–1643), and founded Takagamine, a community of artists and craftsmen in N Kyoto which infused the Japanese art world with new vigour.

Koffka, Kurt (1886–1941) Psychologist, born in Berlin. At the University of Geissen (1911–24) he helped to conduct experiments in perception, which led to the founding of the *Gestalt* school of psychology. In 1927 he moved to the USA, becoming professor of psychology at Smith College. >> Husserl; Köhler; Wertheimer

Kohl, Helmut (1930–) German statesman and chancellor (1982–), born in Ludwigshafen-am-Rhein, Germany. He studied at Frankfurt and Heidelberg, became a lawyer, and joined the Christian Democrats. In 1976 he moved to Bonn as a member of the Federal Parliament, became Leader of the Opposition, and his party's candidate for the chancellorship. After the collapse of the Schmidt coalition in 1982, Kohl was installed as interim chancellor, and in the elections of 1983 formed a government which has since adopted a central course between political extremes. After the collapse of East Germany in 1989, he played a key role in German reunification and was elected chancellor of the united Germany in 1990. He is a strong supporter of a united Europe. >> Schmidt, Helmut

Köhler, Georges >> **Milstein, César**

Köhler, Wolfgang [koeler] (1887–1967) Psychologist, born in Tallinn, Estonia. He studied at Berlin, lectured at Frankfurt (1911), and participated in experiments which led to the formation of the school of *Gestalt* psychology. Professor of psychology at Berlin in 1921, he emigrated to the USA in 1935, where he taught at Swarthmore College, PA, until 1955, and at Dartmouth College, New Hampshire, from 1958. >> Husserl; Koffka; Wertheimer

Kohlrausch, Friedrich Wilhelm Georg [kohlrowsh] (1840–1910) Physicist, born in Rinteln, Germany. He was professor of physics at Göttingen and Frankfurt, before becoming professor of physics at Würzburg (1875) and Berlin (1895). He is best known for his research into the properties of electrolytes, determining the transfer velocities of the ions in solution.

Kohr, Leopold (1909–94) Austrian economist and writer. His book *Breakdown of Nations* (1957) advocated a move towards smaller national and industrial groupings at a time most others were proposing larger and larger units. >> Schumacher, E F

Kokhba, Simon bar >> **bar Kokhba, Simon**

Kokoschka, Oskar [kokoshka] (1886–1980) Artist and writer, born in Pöchlarn, Austria. He studied at Vienna, and taught at the Dresden Academy of Art (1919–24). He travelled widely, and painted many Expressionist landscapes in Europe. In 1938 he fled to England, and became naturalized in 1947. From 1953 he lived in Switzerland.

Kolbe, St Maximilian (Maria) [kolbuh] (1894–1941) Franciscan priest, born near Łódź, Poland. He joined the Franciscans in 1907, and studied at the Gregorian University in Rome. In 1917 he founded a devotional association, the Militia of Mary Immaculate, was ordained in 1918, and became director of a religious centre and publishing company. He was arrested by the Gestapo in 1939, and again in 1941, and imprisoned in Auschwitz, where he gave his life in exchange for one of the condemned prisoners, Franciszek Gajowniczek. He was canonized in 1982; feast day 14 August.

Kolbe, (Adolph Wilhelm) Hermann [kolbuh] (1818–84) Scientist, born near Göttingen, Germany. He studied chemistry under Wöhler and Bunsen, succeeded Bunsen as professor at Marburg (1851), and moved to Leipzig (1865–84). An outstanding teacher and experimenter, he did much in the development of organic chemical theory, and was one of the first to synthesize an organic compound from inorganic materials. >> Bunsen; Wöhler

Kolchak, Alexander Vasilevich (1874–1920) Russian admiral and leader of counter-revolutionary (White) forces during the Russian Civil War, born in the Crimea. He fought in the Russo–Japanese War (1904–5), and in 1916 became commander of the Black Sea Fleet. After the 1917 Revolution he established an anti-Bolshevik government in Siberia, and proclaimed himself 'Supreme Ruler' of Russia. He was captured and shot by Red Army forces in Irkutsk.

Kolff, Willem (Johan) (1911–) Physician, the developer of the artificial kidney, born in Leyden, The Netherlands. He studied at Leyden and Groningen universities, constructed his first rotating drum artificial kidney in wartime Holland, and treated his first patient with it in 1943. Since 1950, when he moved to the USA, he has worked primarily at the Cleveland Clinic and Utah University, developing the artificial kidney further. He was also involved in research on the heart-lung machine used during open-heart surgery.

Kollo, René (1937–) Tenor, born in Berlin, Germany. He studied at Berlin and made his debut in Braunschweig in 1965. He spent a period with the Düsseldorf Opera (1967–71), and went on to perform leading Wagnerian roles in Salzburg, Vienna, and the New York Metropolitan Opera.

Kollontai, Alexandra Mikhaylovna [kolontiy], *née* **Domontovitch** (1872–1952) Russian feminist and revolutionary, the world's first female ambassador, born in St Petersburg into an upper-class family. She rejected her privileged upbringing and joined the Russian Social Democratic Party. She travelled widely in the USA, returning to Russia after the Revolution (1917), and becoming commissar for public welfare. In this post she agitated for domestic and social reforms, including collective child care and easier divorce proceedings. Although her private liaisons shocked the Party, she was appointed minister to Norway (1923–5, 1927–30), Mexico (1926–7), and Sweden (1930–45), becoming ambassador in 1943. Her works, such as *The New Morality and the Working Class* (1918), aroused considerable controversy because of their open discussion of such subjects as sexuality and women's place in society. Her autobiography, written in 1926, was not published in Russia.

Kollwitz, Käthe [kolvits], *née* **Schmidt** (1867–1945) Artist and sculptor, born in Königsberg, Germany. She studied in Königsberg, then Berlin, where she married a doctor, Karl Kollwitz, who established a clinic in a poor quarter of the city, giving her an insight into life at the lowest levels of society. She chose serious, tragic subjects, with strong social or political content, such as the 'Weaver's Revolt' (1897–8) and 'The Peasants' War' (1902–8). After her youngest son was killed in battle (1914) she began a sculpture in granite which was later erected in Flanders as a memorial to all the young men killed in the war (1932). She was elected to the Prussian Academy of Arts (the first woman member), becoming head of graphic arts (1928), but was expelled by the Nazis in 1933. Her home and studio with much of her life's work were destroyed by bombs in 1943.

Kolmogorov, Andrey Nikolayevich [kolmogorof] (1903–87) Mathematician, born in Tambov, Russia. He studied at Moscow University, where he became professor in 1931. He worked on the theory of functions of a real variable, functional analysis, mathematical logic, and topology. He also worked in applied mathematics on the theory of turbulence, information theory, and cybernetics. He is particularly remembered for his creation of the axiomatic theory of probability in his book *Grundbegriffe der Wahrscheinlichkeitsrechnung* (1933, Foundations of the Theory of Probability), and for his work with Alexander Khinchin on Markov processes. >> Khinchin

Komenský, Ian >> **Comenius, John Amos**

Komorowski, Tadeusz [komorofskee] (1895–1966) Polish soldier, born in Lwów, Poland. As 'General Bór' he led the heroic but unsuccessful Warsaw rising against the occupying Germans in 1944, and settled in England after World War 2.

Konev, Ivan Stepanovich [konyef] (1897–1973) Soviet military commander and marshal of the Soviet Union (1944), born in Lodeyno, Russia. He was drafted into the Tsarist army in 1916, and joined the Red Army in 1918. During World War 2 he commanded several different fronts against the Germans. He then became commander-in-chief, ground forces (1946–50), first deputy minister of defence, and commander-in-chief of the Warsaw Pact forces (1956–60).

Konigsberg, Allen Stewart >> **Allen, Woody**

Koninck, Philips de (1619–88) Painter, born in Amsterdam. He was possibly a pupil of Rembrandt, and certainly a member of the same artistic circle. He painted portraits, religious subjects, and scenes of everyday life, but his best paintings by far were panoramic landscapes with large areas of sky. >> Rembrandt

Konitz, Lee (1927–) Saxophonist, born in Chicago, IL. A pupil of Lennie Tristano, he became part of the avant-garde school of 'cool jazz' during the 1950s, along with Stan Getz, Gerry Mulligan, and Jimmy Giuffre. In the latter part of the decade he produced a series of acclaimed albums, beginning with *Inside Hi Fi* (1956), later recordings including *Lone-Lee* (1974) and *Art of the Duo* (1983). >> Getz; Giuffre; Mulligan; Tristano

Konwicki, Tadeusz [konviskee, tadayush] (1929–) Dissident writer and film-maker, born in Lithuania. After fighting with guerrilla forces in Lithuania against both German and Russian occupation in World War 2, he moved to Poland, where he made his home, and began to write. His book, *A Minor Apocalypse*, was banned. In the 1950s, *At the Construction Site* was a much prized novel about the Party as an engineer of souls. He was denounced in 1968. His latest book, *Moonrise, Moonrise* (1988), is about the early struggles of the Solidarity movement. His films include *Salto* and *The Last Day*. >> Walesa

Kooning, Willem de >> **de Kooning, Willem**

Koopmans, Tjalling C(harles) (1910–85) Economist, born in 's Graveland, The Netherlands. He studied at Utrecht and Leyden, emigrated to the USA in 1940, and worked for a shipping firm, devising a system to optimize transport costs. He became a US citizen in 1946. He was professor of economics at Chicago (1948–55) and Yale (1955–81), and shared the 1975 Nobel Prize for Economics for his contributions to the theory of optimal allocation of resources. >> RR1125

Köpfel, Wolfgang Fabricius >> **Capito, Wolfgang**

Kopp, Hermann Franz Moritz (1817–92) Chemist, born in Hanau, Germany. Professor of chemistry at Giessen (1843–63) and Heidelberg (1863–90), his studies of the relationship of physical properties to the chemical structure of compounds formed the basis of modern physical organic chemistry. He is also noted for his *Geschichte der Chemie* (1843–7, History of Chemistry).

Koppel, Herman (1908–) Composer and pianist, born in Copenhagen. He studied at the Royal Danish Academy of Music, and has been a professor at the Academy since 1955. He made his debut as a composer in 1929 and as a pianist in 1930. His compositions include seven symphonies, four piano concertos, six string quartets, an opera (*Macbeth*, 1970), a ballet, and music for theatre, film, and radio. He has been awarded several prizes, among them the Ove Christensen honorary prize in 1952 and the Carl Nielsen prize in 1958.

Korbut, Olga (1956–) Gymnast, born in Grodno, Belarus. She captivated the world at the 1972 Olympics at Munich with her lithe grace, and gave gymnastics a new lease of life as a sport. She won a gold medal as a member of the winning Soviet team, as well as individual golds in the beam and floor exercises and silver for the parallel bars. After retiring, she became a coach.

Korda, Sir Alexander, originally **Sándor Laszlo Korda** (1893–1956) Film producer, born in Puszta, Hungary. He began as a journalist in Budapest, became a film producer there, and then in Vienna, Berlin, and Hollywood, where he directed for First National. He moved to the UK, and in 1932 founded London Film Productions and Denham studios. His films include *The Private Life of Henry VIII* (1932), *The Third Man* (1949), and *Richard III* (1956). He was knighted in 1942, the first film-maker to be so honoured.

Koresh, David [koresh] (1960–93) Cult leader, born in Texas. He was the charismatic leader of a heavily armed group of Branch Davidians (a sect which had split away from the Seventh Day Adventist Church in 1959) who were put under siege by federal agents at a ranch in Mount Carmel, Waco, TX, between February and April 1993. The siege ended after a devastating fire in which Koresh and many of his followers were killed.

Kornberg, Arthur (1918–) Biochemist, born in New York City. A graduate in medicine from Rochester University, he was director of enzyme research at the National Institutes of Health (1947–52) and head of the department of microbiology at Washington University (1953–9). He discovered the DNA enzyme polymerase, for which he shared the 1959 Nobel Prize for Physiology or Medicine. In 1959 he was appointed professor at Stanford University, and became the first to synthesize viral DNA (1967). >> RR1124

Korngold, Erich (Wolfgang) (1897–1957) Composer, born in Brünn, Austria. He studied in Vienna, and from the age of 12 had spectacular success there and throughout Germany as a composer of chamber, orchestral, and stage works in late-Romantic vein. His finest operas were *Violanta* (1916) and *Die tote Stadt* (1920, The Dead City). He was professor at the Vienna State Academy of Music (1930), but in 1934 emigrated to Hollywood. Two of his film scores, *Robin Hood* and *Anthony Adverse*, received Oscars. His post-war works included a violin concerto, a cello concerto, and a symphony.

Kornilov, Lavr Georgyevich [kaw(r)neelof] (1870–1918) Russian soldier, a Cossack born in W Siberia. In World War 1 he took command of all troops in August 1917, and marched on St Petersburg. He was accused of trying to set up a military dictatorship, was forced to surrender by Kerensky, and imprisoned. He escaped and organized an anti-Bolshevik force, but fell in battle. >> Kerensky

Korolyov, Sergey (Pavlovich) [korolyof], also spelled **Korolev** (1907–66) Aircraft engineer and rocket designer, born in Zhitomir, Ukraine. Educated at Moscow Higher Technical School, in 1931 he formed the Moscow Group for Investigating Jet Propulsion, which launched the Soviet Union's first liquid-propelled rocket in 1933. By 1949 he was engaged in high-altitude-sounding flights employing rockets. As chief designer of Soviet spacecraft, he directed the Soviet Union's space programme, launching the first artificial satellite (1957), the first manned space flight (1961), the *Vostok* and *Voskhod* manned spacecraft, and the *Cosmos* series of satellites. >> Gagarin

Korzybski, Alfred (Habdank Skarbek) [kaw(r)zibskee] (1879–1950) Scholar and philosopher of language, born in Warsaw. He was sent to the USA in 1915 on a Russian military mission, and remained there after World War 1, becoming a US citizen in 1940. He is best known as the originator of a system of linguistic philosophy and expression (*general semantics*, now written officially as *general-semantics* to stress its status as a unitary term), and he became founder-director of the Institute of General Semantics. His major work on the subject is *Science and Sanity* (1933).

Kościuszko or **Kościusko, Thaddeusz (Andrzej) Bonawentura** [koshchooshkoh] (1746–1817) Polish general and patriot, born near Slonim, Lithuania. Although a captain in the Polish army, he volunteered his services to Benjamin Franklin during the American Revolution, arrived in Philadelphia in 1776, and was commissioned a colonel in the engineers. He made major contributions at Saratoga, Hudson River, and in the Carolinas campaign, and was promoted brigadier-general in 1783. He then returned to Poland (1784), and achieved fame for his defence of Dubienka against a superior force of Russians (1792), and in 1794 became head of the national movement. His defeat of the Russians at Raclawice was followed by a rising in Warsaw. He established a provisional government, but was defeated at Maciejowice (1794) and taken prisoner until 1796. In 1816 he settled in Soleure, Switzerland. His will directed that the 500 acres in Ohio granted him by the US Congress (1797) be sold and the money used to free slaves; instead it was used to found the Colored School of Newark, NJ, one of the earliest schools for African-Americans in the USA.

Kosinski, Jerzy (Nikodem) [kosinskee] (1933–91) Novelist, born in Łódź, Poland. He studied political science at Łódź University, where he taught (1955–7) before emigrating to the USA in 1957 to follow an academic career. His novels espouse a belief in survival at all costs, his characters machinating to make the most of a given situation. His best-known books include *The Painted Bird* (1965), a classic of Holocaust literature, *Steps* (1968), *Being There* (1971), and *Passion Play* (1979).

Kossel, Albrecht (1853–1927) Biochemist, born in Rostock, Germany. He studied at Strasbourg, and became professor of physiology at Marburg (1895–1901) and Heidelberg (1901–23). He investigated the chemistry of cells and of proteins, and the chemical processes in living tissue. He was awarded the Nobel Prize for Physiology or Medicine in 1910. >> Kossel, Walther

Kossel, Walther (1888–1956) German physicist, the son of Albrecht Kossel. Professor of physics at Kiel (1921) and Danzig (1932), he did much research on atomic physics, especially on Röntgen spectra, and was known for his physical theory of chemical valency. >> Kossel, Albrecht

Kossoff, David (1919–) British actor, author, and illustrator. He trained as a commercial artist, worked as a technical illustrator, and became an actor in 1943, joining the BBC Repertory Company (1945–51). He became especially known on stage and film for his portrayal of Jewish characters, and for his short stories based on Jewish traditions and culture. He performed his one-man show, *A Funny Kind of Evening* in many countries, and was well known for his Bible story-telling programmes on radio and television. His books include *Bible Stories Retold by David Kossoff* (1968) and *You Have a Minute, Lord?* (1977).

Kossoff, Leon (1926–) Painter, born in London, England, UK. He studied at St Martin's School of Art, at the Borough Polytechnic (under David Bomberg, 1949–53), and at the Royal College of Art (1953–6). Painting figures in interiors and city views, he follows Bomberg and Soutine in his expressive style, using very thick impasto. His colours were originally sombre, but brightened after c.1975. >> Bomberg; Soutine

Kossuth, Lajos [kosooth, loyosh], also Hung [koshut] (1802–94) Hungarian statesman, a leader of the 1848 Hungarian Revolution, born in Monok, Hungary. He practised law, and became a political journalist, for which he was imprisoned (1837–40). In 1847, he became Leader of the Opposition in the Diet, and in 1848 demanded an independent government for Hungary. At the head of the Committee of National Defence, he was appointed provisional governor of Hungary (1849), but internal dissensions led to his resignation, and he fled to Turkey, and then to England.

Koster, Laurens >> **Janszoon, Laurens**

Kosygin, Alexey Nikolayevich [koseegin] (1904–80) Russian statesman and premier (1964–80), born in St Petersburg, Russia. Educated in Leningrad, he joined the army in 1919, and the Communist Party in 1927. Elected to the Supreme Soviet (1938), he held a variety of industrial posts, becoming a member of the Central Committee (1939–60) and the Politburo (1946–52). Chairman of the State Economic Planning Commission (1959–60), and first deputy prime minister (with Mikoyan) from 1960, he succeeded Khrushchev as chairman of the Council of Ministers in 1964. He resigned in 1980 because of ill health. >> Khrushchev; Mikoyan, Anastas Ivanovich; RR1085

Kotane, Moses [kotahnay] (1905–78) South African politician, born in the Rustenburg district, South Africa. The child of a peasant family, and largely self-taught, in the late 1920s he joined both the African National Congress (ANC) and the Communist Party of South Africa. After study at the Lenin School in Moscow, he served as General Secretary of the Communist Party for 40 years, both while it was a legal organization (the Party was banned in 1950) and also in its underground period after 1953. In 1963 he went into exile, and served on the national executive of the ANC in addition to his Party duties.

Kotzebue, August (Friedrich Ferdinand) von [kotzebyoo] (1761–1819) Playwright, born in Weimar, Germany. He worked in government service in Russia, and wrote about 200 poetic dramas, notably *Menschenhass und Reue* (1789–90, trans The Stranger), as well as tales, satires, and historical works. While on a mission for Emperor Alexander I, he was assassinated in Mannheim by a radical student as an alleged spy. >> Kotzebue, Otto

Kotzebue, Otto [kotzebyoo] (1787–1846) German naval officer and explorer, born in Tallin, Estonia, the son of August von Kotzebue. He accompanied Russian admiral **Baron Adam Johann von Krusenstern** (1770–1846) in the first voyage round the world to be made by Russians (1803–6). He also led an expedition via Cape Horn and Oceania to the Alaskan coast, tried to find a passage across the Arctic Ocean, and discovered *Kotzebue Sound* near Bering Strait (1815–18). He later commanded another round-the-world voyage (1823–6). >> Kotzebue, August von

Koufax, Sandy [kohfaks], popular name of **Sanford Koufax** (1935–) Baseball player, born in New York City. He played in his home town, then in Los Angeles with the Dodgers. His short career reached its peak in the 1960s, and in 1963 he was named Most Valuable Player as the Dodgers beat the New York Yankees in the World Series. Famous for his pitching, in 1965 he again helped the Dodgers to a World Series victory over Minnesota with two consecutive shutouts (where the opposition fail to score a single run). He retired at 31, as a result of arthritis. >> RR1144

Koussevitsky, Serge [koosevitskee], originally **Sergei Alexandrovich Koussevitsky** (1874–1951) Conductor, composer, and double-bass player, born in Vishni-Volotchok, Russia. He founded his own orchestra in Moscow in 1909, and after the revolution was director of the State Symphony Orchestra in Petrograd (St Petersburg). He left Russia in 1920, worked in Paris, and settled in Boston in 1924, remaining conductor of its symphony orchestra for 25 years. He became a US citizen in 1941. A champion of new music, he commissioned and premiered many works which became 20th-c classics. He founded the Berkshire Symphonic Festivals (1934) and the Berkshire Music Centre (1940) at Tanglewood, MA.

Kouwenhoven, William Bennett [kohenhohvn] (1886–1975) Electrical engineer, born in New York City. He studied at the Brooklyn Polytechnic, where he later taught physics. He moved to Washington University in 1913, and the following year to Johns Hopkins, where he became professor of electrical engineering in 1930. In the 1930s he developed the first practical electrical defibrillator, which has since come into general use for the treatment of heartbeat irregularities, and in 1959 introduced the first-aid technique of external heart massage.

Kraepelin, Emil [kraypelin] (1856–1926) Psychiatrist, born in Neustrelitz, Germany. He studied at Würzburg, and did further study under Wundt, whose techniques he later used for research on the effects of alcohol. Professor at Dorpat, Heidelberg, and Munich, he was a pioneer in the psychological study of serious mental diseases (psychoses), which he divided into two groups, manic-depressive and dementia praecox. He compiled a classification of

disorders *Compendium der Psychiatrie* (1883, Compendium of Psychiatry), which he continued to revise throughout his life, and which was very influential at the beginning of the 20th-c.

Krafft-Ebing, Richard, Freiherr von (Baron) [kraft ebing] (1840–1902) Psychiatrist, born in Mannheim, Germany. He studied in Germany and Switzerland, and was professor at Strasbourg and Vienna. Much of his work was on forensic psychiatry and on sexual aberrations. He is best known for *Psychopathia sexualis* (1886).

Kramer, Jack [kraymer], popular name of **John Albert Kramer** (1921–) Tennis player, born in Las Vegas, NV. He won a number of important titles during the early 1940s, and turned professional after winning the Wimbledon singles title in 1947. Arthritis impeded his career, and he later became a successful promoter and television commentator. He was elected to the International Tennis Hall of Fame in 1968. Open tennis began the same year, and he was instrumental in setting up the Grand Prix series and the Masters Championship. He played a major role in establishing the Association of Tennis Professionals, and was its first director (1972). >> RR1173

Kramer, Dame Leonie (Judith) [kraymer] (1924–) Academic, writer, and administrator, born in Melbourne, Victoria, Australia. She studied at Melbourne and Oxford universities, was professor of Australian literature at Sydney (1968–89) then emeritus professor, and in 1991 became chancellor of the university. She has held positions on a number of influential bodies, including the board of the Australian Broadcasting Commission (since 1947, chairman 1981–3) and the Universities Council (1977–86), and is a director of the Australian and New Zealand Banking Group (since 1983). She is a prominent member of the group 'Australians for Constitutional Monarchy', founded in 1992 in response to growing republican sentiment. She was created a dame in 1983.

Krautheimer, Richard [krowthiymer] (1897–) Architectural historian, born in Fuerth, Germany. He taught at Vassar College (1937–52), then at the Institute of Fine Arts, New York University. A specialist in early Christian and mediaeval architecture who later turned to the Baroque period, he was an early exponent of architectural iconography. Among his works is *Corpus basilicarum christianarum Romae* (1937–70).

Kray brothers Convicted British murderers, twin brothers who ran a criminal Mafia-style operation in the East End of London, England, UK in the 1960s: **Ronald Kray** (1933–95) and **Reginald Kray** (1933–). Their gang collected protection money, organized illegal gambling and drinking clubs, and participated in gang warfare. An early attempt to convict them of murder failed. Their activities became increasingly violent, and in the late 1960s Ronnie Kray shot dead a member of a rival gang, and Reggie stabbed another to death because he had threatened his brother. The twins were tried at the Old Bailey in 1969, found guilty, and were sentenced to life imprisonment of not less than 30 years. A campaign to free them in 1987 failed.

Krebs, Sir Hans (Adolf) (1900–81) Physiologist, born in Hildesheim, Germany. He began his research at Freiburg, but was forced to emigrate to England in 1933, where he continued his work at Cambridge, then at Sheffield (1935–54) and Oxford (1954–67). He shared the Nobel Prize for Physiology or Medicine in 1953 for his work on the nature of metabolic processes, the way living creatures obtain energy from food. He was knighted in 1958. >> RR1124

Kreisky, Bruno [kriyskee] (1911–90) Austrian chancellor (1970–83), born in Vienna. He studied at Vienna University, joined the Social Democratic Party of Austria (SPO) as a young man, and was imprisoned for his political activities from 1935 until he escaped to Sweden in 1938. He returned to Austria, and served in the foreign service (1946–51) and the prime minister's office (1951–3). He was increasingly active in party politics, and in 1970 became prime minister in a minority SPO government. He steadily increased his majority in subsequent elections but in 1983, when that majority disappeared, he refused to serve in a coalition and resigned.

Kreisler, Fritz [kriysler] (1875–1962) Violinist, born in Vienna. He began studies at the Vienna Conservatory at the age of seven, later moving to the Paris Conservatoire. He also studied medicine in Vienna, art in Paris and Rome, and became an army officer. From 1889 he became one of the most successful violin virtuosos of his day, and composed violin pieces, a string quartet, and an operetta, *Apple Blossoms* (1919), which was a Broadway success. He became a US citizen in 1943.

Kreitman, Esther >> **Singer, Esther**

Křenek, Ernst [krzhenek] (1900–91) Composer, born in Vienna. He worked with various German theatres as a conductor and director, emigrated to the USA in 1938, and became a US citizen in 1945. He wrote two symphonies, and developed a style which ranged from jazz, as in his opera *Jonny spielt auf* (1927, trans Johnny Strikes Up the Band), which made his name, to serialism, as in *Karl V* (1930–3). After the mid-1950s he adopted various avant-garde idioms.

Kresge, S(ebastian) S(pering) [krezgee] (1867–1966) Merchant and philanthropist, born in Bald Mount, PA. After business school he worked as a book-keeper and a tinware salesman (1890–7), then he bought into J G McCrory's chain stores, opening stores in Memphis and Detroit. In 1899 he bought out the Detroit store to begin the S S Kresge Co, which sold nothing over ten cents, and by the mid-1920s had over 300 stores. In the 1920s he expanded into real estate, and founded the National Vigilance Committee for Prohibition Enforcement and the Kresge Foundation (1924), a philanthropic organization that he endowed with the bulk of his fortune. As chairman of the board after 1925, he continued to play an active role in his company, contributing to the establishment of the K-Mart discount stores (1961) and the Jupiter stores (1963).

Kretzer, Marx (1854–1941) Writer, born in Poznan, Poland (formerly, Posen, East Prussia). He worked in a factory from the age of 13, educated himself, and became a writer whose works reflected his own experiences and the social problems of industrial Berlin. His books include *Die Betrogenen* (1882, The Deceived), *Die Verkommenen* (1883, The Depraved), and *Meister Timpe* (1888, Master Timpe). He has sometimes been called 'the German Zola', on account of his realism. >> Zola

Kreutzer, Rodolphe [kroytzer] (1766–1831) Violinist, born in Versailles, France. He studied with his father, and from 1784 until 1810 was one of the leading concert violinists in Europe. He also taught at the Paris Conservatoire (1793–1826), conducted at the Opera (from 1817), and composed. He became friendly with Beethoven, who dedicated a sonata to him. >> Beethoven

Kripke, Saul [kripkee] (1940–) Philosopher and logician, born in Bay Shore, NY. He studied at Harvard, then taught at Rockefeller University (1968–76) and Princeton (since 1976). As a youthful prodigy he made remarkable technical advances in modal logic, whose wider philosophical implications were later explored in such famous papers as 'Naming and Necessity' (1972).

Krishna Menon, V(engalil) K(rishnan) [krishna menon] (1896–1974) Indian politician and diplomat, born in Kozhikode (formerly Calicut), Malabar, India. He studied

at Madras and London, and became a history teacher and a barrister. In 1929 he was secretary of the India League and the mouthpiece of Indian nationalism in Britain. He was India's first high commissioner in London (1947), and the leader of the Indian delegation to the UN (1952). As defence minister (1957–62), he came into conflict with Pakistan over Kashmir.

Krishnamurti, Jiddu [krishnamoortee] (1895–1986) Theosophist, born in Madras, India. He was educated in England by Annie Besant, who in 1925 proclaimed him the Messiah. Later he rejected this persona, dissolved The World Order of the Star in the East (founded by Dr Besant), and travelled the world teaching and advocating a way of life and thought unconditioned by the narrowness of nationality, race, and religion. He set up the Krishnamurti Foundation, and wrote several books on philosophy and religion. >> Besant, Annie

Kristian X (of Denmark) >> **Christian X**

Kristiansen, Ingrid, *née* **Christensen** (1956–) Athlete, born in Trondheim, Norway. A former cross-country skiing champion, and then an outstanding long-distance runner, she is the only person to hold world best times for the 5000 m, 10 000 m, and marathon, which she achieved in 1985–6. In 1986 she knocked 45·68 s off the world 10 000 m record, and easily won the European title. She has won most of the world's major marathons, including Boston, Chicago, and London, and was the world cross-country champion in 1988.

Kristina (of Sweden) >> **Christina**

Kroc, Ray (1902–84) US founder of the McDonald's chain of fast-food restaurants. A manufacturer of milk-shake machines in the 1950s, he was impressed by the standards of one of his customers, Mac and Dick McDonald, who sold hamburgers, French fries, and milk-shakes from a stand. He bought the rights to operate similar stands, set out strict standards of quality, hygiene, service, and value, and a franchise arrangement of individual restaurant owners. He opened the 100th store in 1959, the first overseas branch in 1967, and a branch in Moscow in 1990.

Kroeber, A(lfred) L(ouis) [krohber] (1876–1960) Cultural anthropologist, born in Hoboken, NJ. He studied under Franz Boas at Columbia University, and went on to build up the anthropology department at the University of California (1901–46, professor from 1919). He made contributions to archaeology with expeditions to Mexico (1924, 1930) and Peru (1925, 1926, 1942). He also maintained an interest in linguistics, pioneering studies of American Indian dialects. His overriding interest was in culture as a whole, shaped by folklore, kinship, and ecological elements. His most influential work, *Anthropology* (1923), helped to establish anthropology as a professional academic discipline. >> Boas

Krogh, (Schack) August (Steenberg) [krawg] (1874–1949) Physiologist, born in Grenå, Denmark. He studied at Copenhagen, and became professor of animal physiology there (1916–45). He researched the process of respiration, gas exchange in the lung, and the supply of oxygen to muscle tissue, discovering the motor-regulating mechanism of capillaries. He was awarded the Nobel Prize for Physiology or Medicine in 1920.

Kropotkin, Pyotr Alexeyevich, Knyaz (Prince) [kropotkin] (1842–1921) Revolutionary and geographer, born in Moscow. The son of a prince, he was educated at the Corps of Pages, St Petersburg. He became an army officer and was stationed in Siberia (1862–7), where he made zoological and geographical studies that won him recognition in scientific circles. In 1871 he renounced his title and devoted himself to a life as a revolutionary. Arrested and imprisoned (1874), he escaped to Switzerland in 1876. Expelled from Switzerland in 1881, he went to France, and was condemned in 1883 to five years' imprisonment for anarchism. Released in 1886, he settled in England until the revolution of 1917 took him back to Russia. He wrote of an anarchy where mutual support and trust in a harmonious society is the central theme, not the lawlessness and chaos more usually associated with the term.

Kroto, Harold [krohtoh] (1939–) Chemist, born in Wisbech, Cambridgeshire, EC England, UK. He studied at the University of Sheffield, moving to the University of Sussex in 1967. He shared the Nobel Prize for Chemistry in 1996 for his contribution to the discovery of fullerenes (1985) >> Curl; Smalley

Kruger, Paul [krooger], in full **Stephanus Johannes Paulus Kruger**, nickname **Oom** ('Uncle') **Paul** (1825–1904) President of the Transvaal (1883–1902), born in Colesberg, Cape Colony, South Africa. With his fellow-Boers he trekked to Natal, the Orange Free State, and the Transvaal, and won such a reputation for cleverness, coolness, and courage that in the first Boer War (1881) he was appointed head of the provisional government. In 1883 he was elected President of the Transvaal and held the post until the Boers submitted to British control in 1902. After the discovery of gold on the Rand, he strove to protect the Boer state, refusing civil rights to the 'Uitlanders', and resisting British power by seeking alternative railway outlets as well as capital and arms from the Germans and the Dutch. During the second Boer War (1899–1902), after weeks as a fugitive, he left for Europe, urging the Boers to fight on. He died in Switzerland. >> Milner, Alfred

Krupp (von Bohlen und Halbach), Alfried (Alwin Felix) (1906–67) Industrialist, born in Essen, Germany. He graduated from Aachen Technical College, and succeeded his father Gustav Krupp to the Krupp empire (1943). He was arrested (1945) and convicted (1947) at Nürnberg for plunder in Nazi-occupied territories, and for employing slave labour under inhuman concentration camp conditions. He was sentenced to 12 years' imprisonment and his property was to be confiscated, but by an amnesty in 1951 he was released and his property restored. He played a prominent part in the West German 'economic miracle', and rebuilt his family fortune. In 1959 he belatedly agreed to pay some compensation to former victims of forced labour, but only to those of Jewish origin. His only son **Arndt** renounced his succession rights and, after Alfried's death, the Krupp industrial family came to an end. >> Krupp, Gustav

Krupp, Bertha >> **Krupp, Gustav**

Krupp, Gustav, originally **Gustav von Bohlen und Halbach** (1870–1950) Industrialist, born in The Hague. He was a Prussian diplomat when he was chosen by Wilhelm II as a suitable husband for **Bertha Krupp** (1886–1957), heiress to the Krupp industrial empire. They married in 1906 and by special imperial edict he was allowed to adopt the name Krupp. He took over the firm, gained the monopoly of German arms manufacture during World War 1, and manufactured the long-range gun for the shelling of Paris, nicknamed 'Big Bertha'. He turned to agricultural machinery and steam engines after the war, gave financial support to Hitler, and connived in secret rearmament, contrary to the Versailles Treaty, after the latter's rise to power in 1933. Hitler's *Lex-Krupp* (1943) confirmed exclusive family ownership for the firm. After World War 2, the Krupp empire was split up by the Allies, but Gustav was too senile to stand trial as a war criminal at Nuremberg. >> Krupp, Alfried

Krusenstern, Baron Adam Johann >> **Kotzebue, Otto**

Krutch, Joseph Wood (1893–1970) Writer, critic, and naturalist, born in Knoxville, TN. He studied at Tennessee and

Columbia, then taught at Columbia (1937–52), published critical studies of Samuel Johnson, Edgar Allen Poe, and Henry David Thoreau, and was drama critic for *The Nation* (1924–52). His study *The Measure of Man* won a National Book Award in 1954. He moved to Tucson, AZ, for his health in 1952, published a number of lyrical works about the life of the desert, and wrote and narrated several television specials about the area.

Kubelík, Rafael (Jeronym) [kubelik] (1914–96) Conductor and composer, born in Býchory, Czech Republic. He studied at Prague Conservatory, and conducted the Czech Philharmonic Orchestra (1936–9, 1942–8). He left Czechoslovakia and settled first in England (1948), then in Switzerland, where he became a citizen in 1973. He was conductor of the Chicago Symphony Orchestra (1950–3) and the Bavarian Radio Orchestra (1961–79), conducted at Covent Garden (1955–8), and was musical director of the New York Metropolitan Opera (1973–4). He has composed five operas, symphonies, concertos, and other works.

Kubitschek (de Oliveira), Juscelino [kubshek] (1902–76) Brazilian statesman and president (1956–61), born in Diamantina, Minas Gerais. He studied medicine at Belo Horizonte, Paris, and Berlin. His government sponsored rapid economic growth, and the dramatic building of a new capital, Brasília. >> RR1036

Kublai Khan [koobliy kahn] (1214–94) Mongol emperor of China (1279–94), the grandson of Genghis Khan. An energetic prince, he suppressed his rivals, adopted the Chinese mode of civilization, encouraged men of letters, and made Buddhism the state religion. He established himself at Cambaluc (modern Beijing), the first foreigner ever to rule in China, and ruled an empire which extended as far as the R Danube. The splendour of his court was legendary. >> Genghis Khan; Polo; RR1040

Kubrick, Stanley [koobrik] (1928–) Screen writer, film producer, and director, born in New York City. He started as a staff photographer with *Look* magazine, before making his directorial debut in documentaries in 1950. He moved to features, and after directing *Spartacus* (1960), went to the UK, where he made a series of unusual features in several film genres: *Lolita* (1962), black comedy in *Dr Strangelove* (1964), psychedelic science fiction in *2001: a Space Odyssey* (1965), urban violence in *A Clockwork Orange* (1971, withdrawn from circulation in Britain at the director's request), a period piece in *Barry Lyndon* (1975), and a horror film, *The Shining* (1980). Later productions have been infrequent, but include the Vietnam saga, *Full Metal Jacket* (1987).

Kudrow, Lisa [kudroh] (1963–) Actor, born in Encino, CA. She studied biology at Vassar College, then took up acting, becoming a member of the Groundlings, a Los Angeles improvisational comedy group. After a range of small parts in television, she became known for her role as Ursula in *Mad About You* (1992–), then achieved a major success as Phoebe Buffay (Ursula's 'twin sister') in the acclaimed television series *Friends* (1994–). Her feature films include *Mother* (1996) and *Romy and Michelle's High School Reunion* (1997).

Kuhn, Richard [koon] (1900–67) Biochemist, born in Vienna. He studied at Munich, was director of the Kaiser Wilhelm Institute, and became professor at Heidelberg University from 1929. He was noted for his work on the structure and synthesis of vitamins A and B_2, and on carotinoids. He was awarded the 1938 Nobel Prize for Chemistry, but was forbidden to accept it by the Nazi government (he received the prize after World War 2).

Kuhn, Thomas (Samuel) [koon] (1922–96) Philosopher and historian of science, born in Cincinnati, OH. He studied physics at Harvard and worked as a physicist, but then became interested in the historical development of science. He is chiefly known through his book, *The Structure of Scientific Revolutions* (1962), which challenged the idea of cumulative, unidirectional scientific progress. He held positions at Harvard, Boston, Berkeley (1958–64), Princeton (1964–79), and the Massachusetts Institute of Technology (from 1979).

Kuhn, Walt(er Francis) [koon] (1877–1949) Painter, born in New York City. He had a varied career as a bicycle shop owner and cartoonist before exhibiting at the Armory Show in New York City (1913). From then on he experimented with different styles, particularly those of French painters such as Cézanne, Matisse, and Picasso. His mature work, which specialized in portraits of clowns and other circus performers, conveyed an emotionally charged, often stoic message, as seen in 'The Blue Clown' (1931).

Kuiper, Gerard (Peter) [kiyper] (1905–73) Astronomer, born in Harenkarspel, The Netherlands. He studied at Leyden, moved to the USA in 1933, and became a US citizen in 1937. He took an appointment at the Lick Observatory, CA, then taught at Harvard (1935–6), and joined the Yerkes Observatory before moving to the McDonald Observatory, TX, in 1939. He discovered two new satellites: Miranda, the fifth satellite of Uranus; and Nereid, the second satellite of Neptune (1948–9). His study of the planetary atmospheres detected carbon dioxide on Mars and methane on Titan, the largest Saturnian satellite. He was involved with the early US space flights, including the Ranger and Mariner missions.

Kummer, Ernst Eduard (1810–93) Mathematician, born in Sorau, Germany. He studied at Halle, and taught at the Gymnasium in Liegnitz (1832–42). He was professor of mathematics at Wrocław, Poland (formerly Breslau, Germany) (1842–55), and at Berlin from 1855. He added to the work of Gauss on the hypergeometric series, and worked in number theory. In trying to prove Pierre de Fermat's last theorem, he introduced 'ideal numbers', later developed by Richard Dedekind into one of the fundamental tools of modern algebra. He also developed the *Kummer surface*, the wave surface in four dimensional space. >> Dedekind; Fermat; Gauss

Kun, Béla (1886–c. 1939) Hungarian political leader and revolutionary, born in Szilágycseh, Hungary. He was a journalist, soldier, and prisoner in Russia, and in 1918 founded the Hungarian Communist Party. In March 1919 he organized a Communist revolution in Budapest, and set up a Soviet republic which succeeded Karolyi's government. It failed to gain popular support, and he was forced to flee for his life in August of that year. After escaping to Vienna he returned to Russia. He is believed to have been killed in a Stalinist purge. >> Horthy

Kundera, Milan [kundaira] (1929–) Novelist, born in Brno, Czech Republic. He studied in Prague, and lectured in cinematographic studies there until he lost his post after the Russian invasion of 1968. His first novel, *Zert* (1967, The Joke), was a satire on Czechoslovakian-style Stalinism. In 1975 he fled to Paris, where he has lived ever since, taking French nationality in 1981. He came to prominence in the West with *Kniha smichu a zapomneni* (1979, The Book of Laughter and Forgetting). *Nesnesitelna lehkost byti* (The Unbearable Lightness of Being) appeared in 1984, and was filmed in 1987. *Immortality* (1991) is set in his adoptive France. Later novels include *Testaments Betrayed* (1995) and *Slowness* (1996).

Küng, Hans (1928–) Roman Catholic theologian, born in Sursee, Switzerland. A professor at Tübingen (1960–96), he has written extensively for fellow theologians and for lay people. His questioning of received interpretations of Catholic doctrine, as in *Justification* (1965), *The Church*

(1967), and *Infallible? An Inquiry* (1971), and his presentations of the Christian faith, as in *On Being a Christian* (1977), *Does God Exist?* (1980), and *Eternal Life?* (1984), aroused controversy both in Germany and with the Vatican authorities, who withdrew his licence to teach as a Catholic theologian in 1979. He defended himself in *Why I Am Still a Christian* (1987). Later works include *Yes to a Global Ethic* (1996). >> Schillebeeckx

Kunitz, Stanley (Jasspon) (1905–) Poet, born in Worcester, MA. He studied at Harvard, and became a literary scholar, teaching poetry at the New School for Social Research, New York City (1950–7), and at Columbia University (from 1963). His first collection of verse was *Intellectual Things* (1930). Success came with *Selected Poems 1928–1958*, which was awarded a Pulitzer Prize in 1959. Later books include *The Testing-Tree* (1971) and *Next to Last Things* (1985).

Kuniyoshi, Yasuo (1893–1953) Painter and graphic artist, born in Okayama, Japan. He emigrated to the USA in 1906, where he studied at the Los Angeles School of Art and Design and at the Art Students League, New York City. He then settled in New York. His later work was marked by sinister fantasy, as seen in the well-known canvas, 'Juggler' (1952).

Kunstler, William M(oses) (1919–95) Lawyer and social activist, born in New York City. He studied at Yale and Columbia, and in 1949 formed a law partnership with his brother. In the early 1960s he began to represent the Congress of Racial Equality, Martin Luther King's Southern Christian Leadership Conference, and the Student Non-Violence Co-ordinating Committee, and became known as the legal voice of 'the Movement' – the more radical groups opposing the Vietnam war, mistreatment of African-Americans, and other perceived flaws in US society. His clients included the Black Panthers, the Catonsville Nine, and the Roman Catholic militants Philip and Daniel Berrigan, but his most celebrated case was that of the Chicago Seven charged with inciting the violence associated with the 1968 Democratic convention. He himself ended up being sentenced to jail for contempt of court (but won on appeal). He also taught at New York University Law School, and published several popular books, including *Beyond a Reasonable Doubt* (1961) and *Deep in My Heart* (1966). >> Berrigan, Daniel/Philip; Dershowitz; King, Martin Luther

Kupka, Frantisěk (1871–1957) Painter, born in Opočno, Czech Republic. He studied art at the Prague and Vienna academies, and at the Ecole des Beaux-Arts, Paris. He settled in France, becoming one of the pioneers of pure abstract painting, a style called Orphism by Apollinaire. >> Apollinaire

Kurath, Gertrude (Prokosch) [koorahth] (1903–92) Musicologist, born in Chicago, IL. She danced and taught professionally as **Tula** (1922–46) before turning to the study of American-Indian dance. She did extensive fieldwork, publishing on Iroquois, Pueblo, Six Nations, and Great Lakes Indian dance, and also contributed to dance theory and notation. In 1962 she founded the Dance Research Center in Ann Arbor, MI.

Kurchatov, Igor (Vasilevich) [koorchatof] (1903–60) Physicist, born in Sim, Russia. He graduated from the Crimean University in Simferopol and went to the Physico-Technical Institute, Leningrad (St Petersburg) where he became director of nuclear physics (1938). He carried out important studies of neutron reactions, and was the leading figure in the building of Russia's first atomic (1949) and thermonuclear (1953) bombs, and the world's first industrial nuclear power plant (1954). He became a member of the Supreme Soviet in 1949.

Kuropatkin, Alexey Nikolaievich [kurohpatkin] (1848–1925) Russian soldier, born a noble of Pskov, Russia. He was chief-of-staff in the Turkish war (1877–8), commander-in-chief in Caucasia (1897), minister of war (1898), and commander-in-chief in Manchuria (1904–5) against the victorious Japanese. He commanded the Russian armies on the Northern Front (Feb–Aug 1916), then was Governor of Turkestan until the Revolution in 1917.

Kurosawa, Akira [kurohsahwa] (1910–   ) Film director, born in Tokyo. He began as a painter, and joined a cinema studio in 1936, making his first feature film (*Sanshiro Sugata*) in 1943. He is renowned for his adaptation of the techniques of the Noh theatre to film-making, in such films as *Rashomon* (1950), which won the Venice Film Festival Prize, and *Shichinin No Samurai* (1954, The Seven Samurai). Also characteristic are his literary adaptations, such as *Kumonosu-Jo* (1957, The Throne of Blood, from *Macbeth*) and *Donzoko* (1957, The Lower Depths, from Gorky). Later films include *Kagemusha* (1980), *Ran* (1985, from *King Lear*), *Dreams* (1990), and *Rhapsody in August* (1991).

Kurtzman, Harvey (1924–93) Strip cartoonist and scriptwriter, born in New York City. He studied art at Cooper Union, and entered comic books drawing *Magno* (1943). He created *Silver Linings* for the *Herald-Tribune*, then *Hey Look* one-pagers for Marvel comics. He became editor of *Frontline Combat* and *Two-Fisted Tales*, and in 1952 created *Mad* as a parody of comic books and characters, later converting it to magazine format. He also created the humour magazines *Trump*, *Humbug*, and *Help*, then the colour strip *Little Annie Fanny* for *Playboy* (1962).

Kurzweil, Raymond C [kertzviyl] (1948–   ) Computer scientist, a pioneer of reading technology, born in New York City. In the 1970s he led the development of the first device capable of carrying out automatic optical character recognition, and followed this with several other machines, including a text-to-speech synthesizer, a flat-bed scanner, a computer music keyboard, and a large vocabulary automatic speech recognizer. In 1982 he founded Kurzweil Music Systems and Kurzweil Applied Intelligence (dealing in automatic speech recognition), and in 1996 became founder-chairman of Kurzweil Educational Systems.

Kusch, Polykarp (1911–93) Physicist, born in Blankenburg, Germany. Taken to the USA as a baby, he became a US citizen in 1922. He studied at Illinois University, and became professor of physics at Columbia (1937–72) and Texas (from 1972). He shared the 1955 Nobel Prize for Physics for his precise determination of the magnetic moment of the electron. >> RR1124

Kuts, Vladimir Petrovich (1927–75) Athlete and middle-distance runner, born in Aleksino, Ukraine. At one time holder of the world record for the 10 000 m and the 5000 m, he won the gold medals for these events in the 1956 Olympics in Melbourne, and was voted the best athlete of the Games.

Kutuzov, Mikhail Ilarionovich, Knyaz (Prince) [kutoozof] (1745–1813) Russian field marshal, born in St Petersburg, Russia. He distinguished himself in the Turkish wars, and in 1805 commanded against the French, but was defeated at Austerlitz. In 1812, as commander-in-chief, he fought Napoleon obstinately at Borodino, and later obtained a major victory over Davout and Ney at Smolensk. >> Davout; Napoleon; Ney

Kuznets, Simon (Smith) (1901–85) Economist and statistician, born in Kharkov, Ukraine. He emigrated to the USA in 1922, studied at Columbia, and investigated business cycles for the National Bureau of Economic Research from 1927. He was professor of economics at Pennsylvania (1930–54), Johns Hopkins (1954–60), and Harvard (1960–71). In his work he combined a concern for facts and measurement with creative and original ideas on economic growth and social change, such as the 20-year *Kuznets cycle* of economic growth. His major publication was *National Income and its Composition, 1919–1938* (2 vols, 1941). He was awarded the Nobel Prize for Economics in 1971.

Kuznetsov, Alexander Vasilievich [kuznetsof] (1929–79) Writer, born in Kiev, Ukraine. He published short stories as early as 1946, but first came to public notice in the USSR with the short novel *Prodolzheniye legendy* (1957, The Continuation of a Legend). He is best known for *Babi Yar* (1966), a novel about the massacre of Ukrainian Jews by the German SS in 1941. He defected to England in 1969, changing his name to **A Anatoli**.

Kyan, John Howard [kiyan] (1774–1850) Inventor, born in Dublin, Ireland. He worked in a brewery in England, and in 1832 invented a patent method of preserving wood, known as the *kyanizing* process. He died in New York City, where he was planning the filtering of the water supply.

Kyd, Thomas (1558–94) Playwright, born in London, England, UK. He was probably educated at the Merchant Taylors' School, and brought up as a scrivener under his father. His tragedies early brought him reputation, especially *The Spanish Tragedy* (c.1592). He has been credited with a share in several plays, and may have written an earlier version of *Hamlet*. Imprisoned in 1593 on a charge of atheism, he died in poverty.

Kylian, Jiri [kilian] (1947–   ) Dancer and choreographer, born in Prague. He trained at the Prague Conservatory, and at the Royal Ballet School, London. He began his choreographic output with Stuttgart Ballet (1970) before moving to the Netherlands Dance Theatre, where he became director in 1978. His many works include *Sinfonietta*, with music by Janáček (1979), the all-male *Soldiers' Mass* (1980), *L'Enfant et les Sortileges* (1984), and three based on Aboriginal culture: *Nomads* (1981), *Stamping Ground* (1982), and *Dreamtime* (1983). In 1996 his company performed at the Edinburgh International Festival's 50th anniversary celebrations.

Kyprianou, Spyros [kipriahnoo] (1932–   ) Cypriot statesman and president (1978–88), born in Limassol, Cyprus. He attended the Greek Gymnasium, Limassol, continued his education at the City of London College, and was called to the bar in 1954. He became secretary to Archbishbop Makarios in London (1952), and returned with him to Cyprus in 1959. He was foreign minister (1961–72), and in 1976 founded the Democratic Front. He became president on the death of Makarios (1977), but despite efforts to find a peaceful solution to the divisions in Cyprus, success always eluded him. >> Makarios III; RR1043

Laar, Pieter van, nickname **i Bamboccio** ('the Cripple') (c. 1590–c. 1658) Artist, born in Harlem, The Netherlands. He is noted for his paintings of country scenes, weddings, wakes, and fairs. He gave his name to the term *bambochades* for genre paintings of bucolic themes.

Labadie, Jean de [labadee] (1610–74) Protestant reformer, born in Bourg, France. A former member of the Jesuits, he became a Pietist and a Calvinist convert in 1650. He preached a return to primitive Christianity in Holland, and was excommunicated from the Reformed Church in 1670, whereupon he moved his Labadist colony to Germany.

Laban, Rudolf von [laybn] (1879–1958) Dancer, choreographer, dance theorist, and notator, born in Bratislava. He studied ballet, acting, and painting in Paris, and from 1910 founded numerous European schools, theatres, and institutions. He was ballet director of Berlin State Opera (1930–4), and created dances for the Berlin Olympic Games in 1936. In England he established the Art of Movement Studio in 1946, now known as the Laban Centre and part of Goldsmiths College, London University. His system of dance notation, *Labanotation*, was published as *Kinetographie Laban* in 1928.

Labé, Louise [labay], originally **Louise Charly**, known as **la Belle Cordière** ('the Lovely Ropemaker') (c. 1524–66) Poet, born in Parcieux, France. Educated in the Renaissance manner, she was also a skilled rider, reputed to have fought, disguised as a knight, at the siege of Perpignan. In 1550 she married a wealthy rope manufacturer, which accounts for her nickname, and in 1555 published a book of love sonnets including 'Débat de Folie et d'Amour'.

Labiche, Eugène [labeesh] (1815–88) Playwright, born in Paris. He was the author of over 100 comedies, farces, and vaudevilles, including *Frisette* (1846), which was the original of *Cox and Box* (1847), by British dramatist **John Maddison Morton** (1811–91), and *Le Voyage de Monsieur Perrichon* (1860).

La Bruyère, Jean de [brooyair] (1645–96) Writer, born in Paris. His only well-known work, *Caractères*, (1688, Characters), consists of two parts: a translation of Theophrastus, and a masterpiece of French literature in the form of a collection of maxims, reflections, and character portraits of the time. He was chosen to aid Jacques Bossuet in educating the dauphin, and also became tutor to the Duc de Bourbon, grandson of the great Condé. >> Bossuet; Condé, Louis II, Prince de; Theophrastus

Lacaille, Nicolas Louis de [lakiy] (1713–62) Astronomer, born in Rumigny, France. From 1750 to 1754 he led an expedition to the Cape of Good Hope, where he was the first to measure the arc of the meridian in South Africa, and compiled a catalogue of nearly 10 000 southern stars, many of which are still referred to by his catalogue numbers.

Lacépède, Bernard de Laville, comte de (Count of) [laseped] (1756–1825) Naturalist and French politician, born in Agen, France. He became curator at the Royal Gardens at Paris in 1785, and at the revolution became professor of natural history at the Jardin des Plantes. He was made a senator in 1799, a minister of state in 1809, and a peer in 1814. He contributed to Buffon's *Histoire naturelle* (Natural History) series, and later published *Histoire naturelle des poissons* (5 vols, 1798–1803, Natural History of Fish). >> Buffon

Lachaise, François d'Aix [lashez] (1624–1709) Jesuit, born at the castle of Aix in Forez, France. Louis XIV selected him as his confessor in 1675, and he retained the post until his death. The cemetery Père Lachaise in Paris is named after him. >> Louis XIV

Lachaise, Gaston [lashez] (1882–1935) Figurative sculptor, born in Paris. He studied at the Ecole des Beaux Arts in Paris (1898–1903). With **Isabel Nagel**, an American who later became his wife, he emigrated to Boston in 1906. He made his name as a portraitist, and as a sculptor of massively proportioned bronze statues of women, reputedly modelled on his wife. His most famous work is 'Standing Woman' (1932, Museum of Modern Art, New York City).

La Chaussée, Pierre Claude Nivelle de [shohsay] (1692–1754) Playwright, born in Paris. *La Comédie larmoyante* (or 'tearful comedy'), as his work was named, had some influence on later writers, including Voltaire. Among his plays are *Préjuge à la mode* (1735, Stylish Prejudice), *Mélanide* (1741), and *L'Ecole des mères* (1744, Mothers' School). >> Voltaire

Lackland, John >> **John** (King)

Laclos, Pierre (Ambroise François) Choderlos de [lakloh] (1741–1803) Novelist and soldier, born in Amiens, France. He spent nearly all his life in the army, but saw no active service until he was 60, and ended his career as a general. His one masterpiece, *Les Liaisons dangereuses* (1782, Dangerous Acquaintances), a novel in epistolary form, became an immediate sensation for its cynical analysis of personal and sexual relationships. It has been successfully adapted for the theatre and several films.

Lacondamine, Charles Marie de [lakŏdameen] (1701–74) Mathematician and scientist, born in Paris. He served in the army, travelled extensively, and was sent to Peru (1735–43) to measure a degree of the meridian. He explored the Amazon, and brought back the poison curare, as well as information on platinum and India rubber.

Lacoste, Robert [lakost] (1898–1989) French Socialist statesman, born in Azerat, France. In World War 2 he began the first Trade Union Resistance Group, and thereafter held various ministerial posts including minister of industrial production (1944), and minister for industry and commerce (1946–7, and 1948). His position as resident minister in Algeria (1956–8) highlighted the ruthless aspect of French post-war politics.

Lacroix, Christian [lakrwah] (1951–) Fashion designer, born in Arles, France. He studied Classics in Montpellier, specializing in French and Italian painting and the history of costume. After working at Hermès and with Guy Paulin, he joined Jean Patou, who showed his first collection in 1982. In 1987 he left Patou and, with other partners, opened the House of Lacroix in Paris. He is known for his ornate and frivolous designs. >> Patou

Lactantius [laktanshius], in full **Lucius Cae(ci)lius Firmianus Lactantius** (c. 240–c. 320) Christian apologist, brought up in North Africa. His principal work is his *Divinarum Institutionum libri vii*, a systematic account of Christian attitudes. He settled as a teacher of rhetoric in Nicomedia, Bithynia, where he witnessed the constancy of the Christian martyrs under the persecution of Diocletian. >> Diocletian

Lacy, Steve, originally **Steven Lackritz** (1934–) Saxophonist, born in New York City. He concentrated entirely on the soprano saxophone, becoming a sideman of some the best soloists during the 1950s. In 1960 he recorded with Thelonius Monk, and *Soprano Today* (1957) was the first of several recordings dedicated to Monk's work. >> Monk

Laënnec, René (Théophile Hyacinthe) [laynek] (1781–1826) Physician, born in Quimper, France. He was the inventor of the stethoscope, with which he studied patients' lung and heart sounds for a three-year period. He published the classic *Traité de l'auscultation mèdiate* (1819, On Mediate Auscultation), and is sometimes called 'the father of thoracic medicine'.

Laestadius, Lars Levi [laystadius] (1800–61) Priest and botanist, born in Arjeplog, Sweden. He was a parson in Karesuando in 1826, where he continued his botanical work. In the early 1840s, he underwent a profound spiritual crisis and began the ecstatic revivalist preaching that had great influence among the Lapps. Today there are some 300 000 *Laestadians* in Finland and 20 000 in Sweden.

La Farge, John (1835–1910) Landscape and ecclesiastical painter, born in New York City. He travelled widely in Europe, and painted pre-Impressionist landscapes and flowers (1860–76). Thereafter he concentrated on murals and stained-glass work in churches, notably 'The Ascension' in the Church of the Ascension, New York City.

Lafayette, Marie Joseph (Paul Yves Roch Gilbert Motier), marquis de [lafiyet] (1757–1834) French soldier and politician, born in Chavagniac, France. He fought in America against the British during the War of Independence (1777–9, 1780–2), and became a hero and friend of Washington. In the National Assembly of 1789 he presented a draft of the declaration of the Rights of Man, based on the US Declaration of Independence. During the French Revolution he was hated by the Jacobins for his moderation. He won the first victories of the Revolutionary Wars, but as Jacobin opposition increased he rode over the frontier to Liège, and was imprisoned by the Austrians until Napoleon obtained his release in 1797. During the Restoration he sat in the Chamber of Deputies (1818–24), became a radical leader of the Opposition (1825–30), and commanded the National Guard in the 1830 Revolution. >> Washington, George; Wayne, Anthony

La Fayette, Marie Madeleine (Pioche de la Vergne), comtesse de (Countess of) [lafiyet], known as **Madame de La Fayette** (1634–93) Novelist and reformer of French romance-writing, born in Paris. She married the Comte de La Fayette in 1655, and played a leading part at the French court. When she was 33 she formed a liaison with La Rochefoucauld which lasted until his death in 1680. Her novels are *Zaïde* (1670) and, recognized as a masterpiece, *La Princesse de Clèves* (1678). >> La Rochefoucauld

Laffite, Jean [lafeet] (?1780–?1825) Pirate, probably born in France. He was in New Orleans by 1809, where he led a band of smugglers and pirates, but he and his men were pardoned by President James Madison after they manned artillery during the Battle of New Orleans (1815). He founded Galveston, Texas, then reverted to piracy. After a US naval force dispersed the colony, he sailed away and passed into legend.

La Follette, Robert M(arion) [la folet] (1855–1925) US politician, born in Primrose, WI. He was a senator from 1905, and became a 'Progressive' candidate for the presidency. He was defeated in 1924, having gained nearly five million votes.

La Fontaine, Jean de [fonten] (1621–95) Poet, born in Château-Thierry, France. He assisted his father, a superintendent of forests, then moved to Paris, and devoted himself to writing. His major works of verse include *Contes et nouvelles en vers* (1664, Tales and Novels in Verse) and *Les Amours de Psyché et de Cupidon* (1669, The Loves of Cupid and Psyche). He is best known for the *Fables choisies mises en vers*

(12 vols, 1668–94), in translation usually called 'La Fontaine's Fables'. In 1684 he presented a *Discours en vers* on his reception by the Academy.

Lafontaine, Sir Louis Hippolyte >> **Baldwin, Robert**

Lafontaine, Oskar [lafonten], nicknames **Red Oskar** and **Ayatollah of the Saarland** (1943–) West German politician, born in Saarlois, Germany. He studied at Bonn University, became leader of the Saar regional branch of the Social Democratic Party (SPD) in 1977, and served as Mayor of Saarbrucken (1976–85). He was elected as minister-president of the Saarland State Assembly in 1985, and in 1987 was appointed a deputy chairman of the SPD's federal organization. His nicknames come from his early reputation for radicalism.

Lagerfeld, Karl [lahgervelt] (1939–) Fashion designer, born in Hamburg, Germany. He was design director at Chanel, and updated the Chanel look. Known for his high quality ready-to-wear clothing, he showed the first collection under his own label in 1984. >> Chanel

Lagerkvist, Pär (Fabian) [lahgerkvist] (1891–1974) Writer, poet, and playwright, born in Växjö, Sweden. He was the most significant figure in Swedish literature in the first half of the 20th-c, and was awarded the Nobel Prize for Literature (1951) for his novel *Barabbas*. His first best seller was the novel *Dvärgen* (1944, The Dwarf), and *The Marriage Feast* (1973) contains English translations of his short stories.

Lagerlöf, Selma (Ottiliana Lovisa) [lahgerloef] (1858–1940) Novelist, born in Mårbacka, Sweden. She was the first woman and the first Swedish writer to receive the Nobel Prize for Literature (1909), and became the first female member of the Swedish Academy (1914). She sprang to fame with her novel *Gösta Berlings saga* (1891, The Story of Gösta Berling), based on the traditions and legends of her native Värmland. She also wrote the children's classic, *Nils Holgerssons Underbara Resa Genom Sverige* (1906–7, trans The Wonderful Adventures of Nils).

Lagrange, Joseph Louis, comte de l'Empire (Count of the Empire) [lagrazh], originally **Giuseppe Luigi Lagrangia** (1736–1813) Mathematician and astronomer, born in Turin, Italy. In 1766 he became director of the Berlin Academy, and published papers on many aspects of number theory, mechanics, the stability of the Solar System, and algebraic equations. His major work was the *Mécanique analytique* (1788, Analytical Mechanics), and he was appointed professor of mathematics at the Ecole Polytechnique, heading the committee reforming the metric system (1795). He was made a senator and a count by Napoleon. The *Lagrangian point* in astronomy, the *Lagrangian function* in mechanics, and several notions in mathematics are all named after him.

La Guardia, Fiorello H(enry) [la gah(r)dia] (1882–1947) US politician and lawyer, born in New York City. He became deputy attorney general (1915–17), sat in Congress (1917–21, 1923–33) as a Republican, and held three terms of office as Mayor of New York City (1933–45). One of the city's airports is named after him. >> Norris, George W

La Guma, Alex [la gooma] (1925–85) Novelist, born in Cape Town, South Africa. He became one of the best-known literary opponents of apartheid. He grew up in the community known as 'Coloured', and from 1956 until 1966 (when he went into exile) was charged with treason, detained several times, placed under house arrest, and banned under the Suppression of Communism Act. His first novel, *A Walk in the Night* (1962), like his subsequent works, combined Realist depictions of the iniquities of apartheid with a Romantic faith in the heroism and humanity of his characters. Later works include *The Stone Country* (1967) and *Time of the Butcherbird* (1979).

Lahm, Frank (Purdy) (1877–1963) Aviator, born in Mansfield, OH. The son of a balloonist, he trained at West Point, served in the cavalry, and transferred to the signal corps in 1907. A pioneer aviator, he trained with Wilbur Wright, and in 1909 became one of the army's first two certified pilots. Lahm organized the US Expeditionary Force in France in 1917, and in the 1930s served as attaché for air in France, Spain, and Belgium. He retired from the service in 1941. >> Wright brothers

Lahr, Bert, originally **Irving Lahreim** (1895–1967) Actor, born in New York City. A comedian with a lovably ugly face, he gagged his way through impossible situations that he created for his characters. After touring in vaudeville with his wife, **Mercides Delpino** (1916–27), he appeared on Broadway in *Hold Everything* (1928). A musical comedy star (1928–64), he also appeared in films (1931–67), notably *The Wizard of Oz* (1939), where he played the Cowardly Lion. In 1956, he played Estragon in *Waiting for Godot*.

Laine, Cleo >> **Dankworth, John**

Laing, Alexander Gordon [lang] (1793–1826) Explorer, born in Edinburgh, EC Scotland, UK. He served with the British army in the West Indies before becoming the first European to reach the ancient city of Timbuktu (1826), while searching for the source of the R Niger in W Africa. After leaving Timbuktu, he was murdered by local tribesmen.

Laing, R(onald) D(avid) [lang] (1927–89) Psychiatrist, born in Glasgow, W Scotland, UK. He studied at the University of Glasgow, where he practised as a psychiatrist (1953–6). He joined the Tavistock Clinic in London in 1957, and the Tavistock Institute for Human Relations in 1960. He is noted for his studies of schizophrenia, and published his revolutionary ideas in *The Divided Self* (1960), which suggested that psychiatrists should not attempt to cure mental illness (a term he repudiated), but should encourage patients to view themselves as going through an enriching experience – a view which came to be called 'anti-psychiatry'. His writings extended from psychiatry into existential philosophy, and later into poetry.

Laird, Macgregor (1808–61) Explorer and merchant, born in Greenock, Inverclyde, WC Scotland, UK. He first travelled to the lower Niger with Richard Lander's last expedition (1832–4), and was the first European to journey up the Benue R. In 1837 he started a transatlantic steamship company, his ship *Sirius* becoming the first to cross the Atlantic entirely under steam in 1854. >> Lander, Richard

Laithwaite, Eric Roberts (1921–97) Electrical engineer and inventor, born in Atherton, Greater Manchester, NW England, UK. He studied at Manchester, and after war service taught there (1950–64), then became professor of heavy electrical engineering at the Imperial College of Science and Technology, London (1964–86, then emeritus). He was also a professor at the Royal Institution (1967–76), where he gave the Christmas lectures in 1966 and 1974. His principal research interest was in the linear motor, a means of propulsion utilizing electro-magnetic forces acting along linear tracks.

Lakatos, Imre (1922–74) Philosopher of mathematics and science, born in Debrecen, Hungary. He moved to England after the Hungarian uprising in 1956, and taught at the London School of Economics, where he became a professor in 1969. His best-known work is *Proofs and Refutations* (1976), a collection of articles demonstrating the creative and informal nature of real mathematical discovery.

Lake, Simon (1866–1945) Engineer and inventor, born in Pleasantville, NJ. Interested in designing underwater vessels, he competed with John Holland's design in 1893, and launched his gasoline-engine-powered *Argonaut*, which became the first submarine to successfully operate in the open sea (1898). He established the Lake Torpedo Boat Co in Bridgeport, CT (1900), and the US government bought his submarine *Seal* in 1911. He also worked as a submarine consultant to the Russian, German, and British governments. >> Holland, John

Laker, Sir Freddie, popular name of **Sir Frederick Alfred Laker** (1922–   ) Business entrepreneur, born in Kent, SE England, UK. Best known as chairman and managing director of Laker Airways (1966–82), he started his career in aviation with Short Brothers, was a member of the Air Transport Auxiliary (1941–6), and a manager with British United Airways (1960–5). In 1966 he headed the successful Laker Airways Ltd, but was severely set back by the failure of the 'Skytrain' project (1982). Since 1992 he has been chairman and managing director of Laker Airways (Bahamas) Ltd. He was knighted in 1978.

Laker, Jim, popular name of **James Charles Laker** (1922–86) Cricketer and broadcaster, born in Bradford, West Yorkshire, N England, UK. He was a member of the Surrey county side which won seven consecutive championships between 1952 and 1958. His off-spinners (along with the bowling of Tony Lock) were a large factor in England's domination of international cricket in the late 1950s. His great season was 1956, when he took 19 of the 20 Australian wickets in the Test Match at Old Trafford. In later years he became a television commentator. >> Lock; RR1149

Lalande, Joseph Jérôme Le Français de [lalãd] (1732–1807) Astronomer, born in Bourg-en-Bresse, France. In 1751 he was sent to Berlin by the French Academy to determine the Moon's parallax. From 1762 he was professor of Astronomy in the Collège de France, and later became director of the Paris Observatory. His chief work is *Traité d'astronomie* (1764), and he also produced the most comprehensive star catalogue of his time (1801).

Lalanne, Maxine [lalan] (1827–86) Etcher and lithographer, born in Bordeaux, France. He worked in Paris from 1852, chiefly producing charcoal drawings, then turned to engraving. In 1866 he began a successful collaboration with the 'House of Cadart', who published his treatise on acid engraving. He transcribed his impressions of the troubles of 1870–1 in a series of plates such as 'The Siege of Paris' and 'Bastion 66'.

Lalić, Susan (Kathryn) [lalich] (1965–   ) British chess player. She first represented England when aged 14, and her achievements include the national girls under-18 championship (1983), the British Ladies Championships (1986, 1990, 1991, 1992), and the Commonwealth Ladies Championships (1988–92). She gained the woman international master title in 1985, and is the only British-born woman to achieve the woman grandmaster title (1988).

Lalique, René [laleek] (1860–1945) Jeweller and designer, born in Ay, France. He studied in Paris and London, and founded his own jewellery firm in Paris in 1885. His glass designs, decorated with relief figures, animals, and flowers, were an important contribution to the Art Nouveau and Art Deco movements.

Lally, Thomas Arthur, comte de (Count of) (1702–66) French general, son of an Irish Jacobite, born in Romans, France. He accompanied Prince Charles Edward to Scotland in 1745, and in 1756 became commander-in-chief in the French East Indies. Active against the British in the Seven Years' War, he was defeated, and capitulated in 1761. On returning to France, he was accused of treachery, and was executed in Paris. In 1778 a royal decree declared the condemnation unjust.

Lalo, (Victor Antoine) Edouard [laloh] (1823–92) Composer, born in Lille, France. His best known musical composition is *Symphonie espagnole* for violin and orchestra.

Other works include his opera, *Le Roi d'Ys*, and the ballet *Namouna*.

Lam, Wilfredo (1902–82) Painter, born in Sagua la Grande, Cuba. He studied in Havana and in Madrid, where he held his first one-man show in 1928. He fused Latin-American, African, and Oceanic elements with the European modern movement, as in *The Jungle* (1943). His numerous exhibitions included one in New York (with Picasso, 1939), and he won the Guggenheim International Award in 1964.

Lamarck, Jean Baptiste (Pierre Antoine) de Monet, Chevalier de [lamah(r)k] (1744–1829) Naturalist and pre-Darwinian evolutionist, born in Bazentin, France. He was an army officer and worked in a bank before developing his interests in medicine and botany, in 1773 publishing the successful *Flore française* (French Flora). In 1774 he became keeper of the royal garden, and in 1793 was made professor of invertebrate zoology at the Museum of Natural History, Paris. His major works were *Philosophie zoologique* (1809), in which he postulated that acquired characters can be inherited by future generations, and *Histoire des animaux sans vertèbres* (1815–22, Natural History of Invertebrate Animals). >> Darwin, Charles; Waddington, C H

Lamartine, Alphonse (Marie Louis) de [lamah(r)teen] (1790–1869) Poet, statesman, and historian, born in Mâcon, France. His best-known work was his first volume of lyrical poems, *Méditations poétiques* (1820). He became a diplomat, a member of the provisional government in the 1848 revolution, and acted as minister of foreign affairs, finally devoting himself to literature. Among his later works are the *Histoire des Girondins* (1847, 8 vols, History of the Girondists), and histories of the French restoration, the 1848 revolution, and other events of his lifetime.

Lamb, Lady Caroline >> **Melbourne, William Lamb, 2nd Viscount**

Lamb, Charles, pseudonym **Elia** (1775–1834) Essayist, born in London, England, UK. He studied at Christ's Hospital, and worked as a clerk for the East India Company (1792–1825). He achieved success through joint publication with his sister, **Mary** (1764–1847), of *Tales from Shakespeare* (1807), and they followed this by other works for children. In 1818 he published his collected verse and prose, and was invited to join the staff of the new *London Magazine*. This led to his best-known works, the series of essays under his pseudonym, the *Essays of Elia* (1823–33).

Lamb, Henry (1883–1960) Painter, born in Adelaide, South Australia. He studied at Manchester University Medical School and at Guy's Hospital before taking up painting. He exhibited with the Camden Town Group, and was an official war artist (1940–4). His best-known work is the portrait of Lytton Strachey (1914, Tate, London).

Lamb, William >> **Melbourne, 2nd Viscount**

Lamb, Willis Eugene, Jr (1913–) Physicist, born in Los Angeles, CA. He was professor of physics at Columbia (1948), Stanford (1951), Oxford (1956), Yale (1962), and Arizona (1974). In 1955 he shared the Nobel Prize for Physics for research that led to refinements in the quantum theories of electromagnetic phenomena. >> RR1122

Lambert, Christopher (1957–) Film actor, born in New York City, and brought up by French parents in Geneva. He began to study acting at the National Conservatory in Paris, but left after three years. He then appeared in a number of French films before starring in *Greystoke: The Legend of Tarzan* (1984). Other films include the *Highlander* series (1985, 1991, 1994), *Mortal Kombat* (1995), and *Arlette* (1997).

Lambert, Constant (1905–51) Composer, conductor, and critic, born in London, England, UK. He studied at the Royal College of Music, London, became conductor of the Sadler's Wells Ballet (1928–47), and was also known as a concert conductor and music critic, notably in *Music Ho!*

(1934). His best-known composition is the choral work in jazz idiom, *The Rio Grande* (1927). Other works include the ballets *Pomona* (1927) and *Horoscope* (1938), and the cantata *Summer's Last Will and Testament* (1936).

Lambert, George Washington Thomas (1873–1930) Painter and sculptor, born in St Petersburg, Russia. He studied in Australia and Paris, and worked in London, where he was successful in portraiture. As official war artist for Australia (World War 1), he later visited Gallipoli to make sketches with C E W Bean, the war historian. He returned to Australia in 1921 and took up sculpture. >> Bean, C E W

Lambert, Johann Heinrich (1728–77) Mathematician, born in Mülhausen, Germany. Largely self-educated, he worked as a secretary and tutor, and in 1764 moved to Berlin, where Frederick the Great became his patron. He was among the first to appreciate the nature of the Milky Way, and in an inconclusive attempt to give a rigorous proof of Euclid's parallel postulate he established several theorems in non-Euclidean geometry. He also demonstrated that pi (π) is an irrational number (1768). The first to show how to measure scientifically the intensity of light (1760), the unit of light intensity is now named after him.

Lambert, John (1619–84) English general, born in Calton, North Yorkshire, N England, UK. He studied law, then joined the parliamentary army in the English Civil War, commanding the cavalry at Marston Moor (1644). He helped to install Oliver Cromwell as protector, but opposed the movement to declare him king, and headed the Cabal which overthrew Richard Cromwell in 1659. Considered the leader of the 'fifth monarchy', or extreme republican party, he suppressed the Royalist insurrection of August 1659, and virtually governed the country with his officers as the 'committee of safety'. At the Restoration (1661) he was tried, and imprisoned on Drake's I, Plymouth, until his death. >> Cromwell, Oliver; Cromwell, Richard

Lambton, John George >> **Durham, Earl of**

Lamennais, Félicité [lamenay], in full **(Hugues-) Félicité (-Robert de) Lamennais** (1782–1854) Priest and writer, born in St-Malo, France. Ordained in 1816, his *Essai sur l'indifférence en mattière de religion* (1818–24, Essay on Indifference towards Religion) brought him acclaim, but later works began to show his readiness to combine Roman Catholicism with political liberalism, and were condemned by the pope in 1832. He was active in the 1848 revolution, and sat in the Constituent Assembly until the coup which established Louis-Napoleon as dictator.

La Mettrie, Julien Offroy de [la metree] (1709–51) Philosopher and physician, born in St-Malo, France. He studied medicine, and in 1742 became surgeon to the Guards in Paris. His *L'Histoire naturelle de l'âme* (1745, Natural History of the Soul) argued that all psychical phenomena were the effects of organic changes in the nervous system – a view which provoked such hostility that the book was publicly burned. Under the protection of Frederick the Great of Prussia, he published many other works expounding his atheist convictions.

Lamming, George Eric (1927–) Novelist, born in Carrington Village, Barbados. He was a teacher before moving to England in 1950, where he hosted a book programme for the BBC West Indian Service. His first novels, with their unfamiliar background and terminology, received a lukewarm reception, but he continued to write about his West Indian experiences, notably *Natives of My Person* (1972).

Lamond, Frederic [lamond], (1868–1948) Pianist and composer, born in Glasgow, W Scotland, UK. A pupil of Bülow and Liszt, he made his debut at Berlin in 1885, and followed this by touring in Europe and America. He excelled in playing Beethoven, and among his own compositions are an overture, a symphony, and several piano works. >> Bülow; Liszt

Lamont, Johann von [lamont] (1805–79) Astronomer, born in Braemar, Aberdeenshire, NE Scotland, UK. He took German nationality, and became director of Bogenhausen Observatory in 1835. He was appointed professor of astronomy at Munich, and is noted for discovering that the magnetic field of the Earth fluctuates in a period of over 10 years. His best-known work is *Handbuch des Erdmagnetismus* (1849, Handbook of Terrestrial Magnetism).

Lamont, Norman [lamont] (1942–) British politician, born in Lerwick, Shetland Is, NE Scotland, UK. He studied at Cambridge, worked for the Conservative Research Department, then became a merchant banker and journalist. He was elected Conservative MP for Kingston-upon-Thames in 1972. Always a staunch supporter of Margaret Thatcher, she appointed him financial secretary to the Treasury (1986) and promoted him to the Cabinet (1989). During November 1990 he managed John Major's successful campaign for the Conservative Party leadership and was rewarded with the post of Chancellor of the Exchequer. However, following his replacement in the 1993 Cabinet reshuffle, he launched an attack on Major's policies. >> Major; Thatcher

L'Amour, Louis (Dearborn) [lamoor], pseudonym **Tex Burns** (1908–88) Novelist, born in Jamestown, ND. He earned his living in a variety of ways, including becoming a deputy sheriff. His first novel about the Wild West, *Hondo* (1953), was an instant success, and he followed it with another 80 novels, including *The Quick and the Dead* and *How the West Was Won* (1963), several of which were made into successful films. He was awarded the Presidential Medal of Freedom in 1984.

Lampedusa, Giuseppe Tomasi, duca di (Duke of) **Palma** [lampedooza] (1896–1957) Novelist, born in Palermo, Sicily. His memorial, his only novel, *Il gattopardo* (1958, The Leopard), was rejected by publishers throughout his life, and published posthumously. It was rapturously received then vilified by the Italian literary establishment, but has subsequently come to be regarded as a masterpiece.

Lancaster, Burt, popular name of **Stephen Burton Lancaster** (1913–94) Film actor, born in New York City. A former circus acrobat, he performed in army shows before making his name in Hollywood. Cast in a succession of tough-guy roles, he increasingly found opportunities to show his dramatic abilities, notably in *From Here to Eternity* (1953), *Elmer Gantry* (1960, Oscar), and *Birdman of Alcatraz* (1962). Later films include *Atlantic City* (1980), *Local Hero* (1983), and *Field of Dreams* (1989).

Lancaster, Duke of >> **John of Gaunt**

Lancaster, Joseph (1778–1838) Educator and Quaker, born in London, England, UK. In 1798 he opened a school in London based on a monitorial system, in which the more able children taught the less able. This led to the founding of the *Lancasterian method*, popular in Europe and, later, North America. The Royal Lancasterian Society was formed in 1808, but Lancaster severed his connections in 1818. He was welcomed in the USA, where he founded more than 60 schools in New York City alone. >> Bell, Andrew

Lancaster, Sir Osbert (1908–86) Cartoonist, writer, and theatrical designer, born in London, England, UK. He studied at Oxford and the Slade School of Art, London. His lifelong passion was architecture, and he worked on *Architectural Review* (1932), writing and illustrating humorous articles. He began drawing pocket-sized front-page cartoons for the *Daily Express* in 1939, creating Lady Maudie Littlehampton and friends. He was knighted in 1975. His autobiography, *All Done From Memory*, was published in 1953.

Lanchester, Elsa >> **Laughton, Charles**

Lanchester, Frederick William (1868–1946) Automobile and aeronautics pioneer, born in London, England, UK. He built the first experimental motor car in Britain (1895), and founded the Lanchester Engine Co in 1899. He was also consultant to Daimler, and in 1907–8 published an important two-volume work on aerodynamics. >> Daimler

Land, Edwin (Herbert) (1909–91) Inventor and physicist, born in Bridgeport, CT. He studied at Harvard, and co-founded laboratories at Boston in 1932, where he produced the light-polarizing filter material 'Polaroid' (1936). His well-known *Land Polaroid* camera (1947) was a self-developing system of instant photography.

Landau, Lev Davidovich [landow], known as **Dev Landau** (1908–68) Physicist, born in Baku, Azerbaijan. He studied at Leningrad University, and with Niels Bohr in Copenhagen, and became professor of physics at Moscow (1937). He received the Nobel Prize for Physics in 1962 for his work on theories of condensed matter, particularly helium. >> Bohr, Niels

Landells, Ebenezer (1808–60) Wood-engraver, born in Newcastle upon Tyne, NE England, UK. In 1841 he originated the humorous magazine *Punch*, worked under Thomas Bewick, and contributed wood engravings to both *Punch* and the *Illustrated London News*. >> Bewick

Lander, Harald, originally **Alfred Bernhardt Stevnsborg** (1905–71) Ballet dancer and choreographer, born in Copenhagen. He trained at the Royal Danish Ballet School and joined the company in 1923. As ballet master (1932–51) he was responsible for the enormous success of the company. From 1953 he was ballet master of the Paris Opéra, and opened a studio in Paris in 1964.

Lander, Richard (1804–34) Explorer, born in Truro, Cornwall, SW England, UK. In 1825 he accompanied Hugh Clapperton to West Africa. There Clapperton died, and Lander published an account of the expedition. In 1830 he and his brother **John** (1807–39) traced the course of the lower Niger. During a third expedition, he was fatally wounded by Niger natives. >> Clapperton

Landers, Ann, pseudonym of **Esther Pauline Friedman** (1918–) Journalist, born in Sioux City, IA. In 1955 she inherited her job as a Chicago-based advice columnist from a previous 'Ann Landers', creating an international institution. She earned a devoted following for her guidance to the perplexed, weathering her own 1975 divorce along the way. She also won many public service awards for her open discussions of medical issues.

Landis, Kenesaw Mountain (1866–1944) Federal judge and baseball commissioner, born in Millville, OH. He was appointed a district judge in Illinois (1907), where in a famous case he imposed a fine of $29 million on the Standard Oil Company over rebate cases (reversed on appeal). After the bribery scandal in the World Series of 1919, his autocratic rule as first commissioner of baseball restored the credibility of the game.

Landon, Alf, originally **Alfred Mossman** (1887–1987) Businessman and politician, born in West Middlesex, PA. In 1912 he founded A M Landon & Co to produce oil, and had become a millionaire by 1929. As Republican Governor of Kansas (1933–7), he supported the New Deal, but opposed labour unions. After losing the 1936 presidential election, he returned to his oil firm. >> Roosevelt, Franklin D

Landor, Walter Savage (1775–1864) Writer, born in Warwick, Warwickshire, C England, UK. He was sent down from both Rugby School and Trinity College, Oxford, but despite this and his difficult character, he became an outstanding classicist. He published *Poems* in 1795, *Examination of Shakespeare* (1834), and *Hellenics* (1847). His best-known work is the prose dialogue *Imaginary Conversations* (1824–9).

Landowska, Wanda (Louise) [landofska] (1877–1959) Harpsichordist and music teacher, born in Warsaw. After studying at Warsaw Conservatory, she became a prominent concert pianist in Europe, was appointed professor of the harpsichord at the Berlin Hochschule (1912), and in 1927 estabished a school for the study of old music near Paris. She emigrated to the USA in 1940, and settled in Connecticut in 1949. She composed and wrote prolifically, her best-known work being *La Musique ancienne* (1908).

Landseer, Sir Edwin (Henry) (1802–73) Artist, born in London, England, UK. Trained by his father to sketch animals from life, he exhibited at the Royal Academy at the age of 13. Dogs and deer were his main subjects, often with the Highlands of Scotland as a backdrop. His paintings include 'Rout of Comus' (1843), and 'Monarch of the Glen' (1851), and he modelled the four bronze lions at the foot of Nelson's Monument in Trafalgar Square (unveiled in 1867). He was knighted in 1850.

Landsteiner, Karl [landstiyner] (1868–1943) Pathologist, born in Vienna. A research assistant at the Pathological Institute, Vienna, he became professor of pathological anatomy from 1909. He worked in the Rockefeller Institute for Medical Research, New York City (1922–43), and received the 1930 Nobel Prize for Physiology or Medicine for his discovery of the human ABO blood-group system. In 1940 he also discovered the Rhesus (Rh) system.

Lane, Sir Allen, originally **Allen Lane Williams** (1902–70) Publisher, born in Bristol, SW England, UK. He studied at Bristol, and was apprenticed in 1919 to The Bodley Head publishing house. He resigned as managing director in 1935 in order to form Penguin Books Ltd, where he began by reprinting novels in paper covers at sixpence each, a revolutionary step in the publishing trade. He was knighted in 1952.

Lane (of St Ippollitts), Geoffrey Dawson Lane, Baron (1918–) British judge. He studied at Cambridge, served in the RAF in World War 2, and was called to the bar in 1946. He became a QC in 1962, and a judge in 1966, a Lord Justice of Appeal (1974–9), and a Lord of Appeal in Ordinary (1979–80). Appointed Lord Chief Justice of England (1980–92), he proved to be a vigorous leader of the courts. He was created a baron in 1979.

Lane, Richard James (1800–82) British engraver. An associate engraver of the Royal Academy (1827), he turned to lithography, reproducing works by Sir Thomas Lawrence, Gainsborough, Landseer, and others. He was also a sculptor. >> Gainsborough; Landseer; Lawrence, Sir Thomas

Lanfranc [lanfrangk] (c. 1005–89) Clergyman, born in Pavia, Italy. Originally a lawyer, he founded a school in Normandy, became a Benedictine monk at Bec, and was later prior there. In 1062 William made him prior of St Stephen's Abbey at Caen, and in 1070 Archbishop of Canterbury.

Lanfranco, Giovanni [lanfrangkoh], known as **Giovanni di Steffano** or **il Cavaliere Giovanni Lanfranchi** (1582–1647) Religious painter, born in Parma, Italy. He was one of the first interpreters of Baroque illusionism, widely influencing and copied by later painters. The best of his work can be seen on the dome of San Andrea della Valle in Rome, and in his paintings for the cathedral at Naples, where he worked from 1633 to 1646.

Lang (of Lambeth), (William) Cosmo Gordon Lang, Baron (1864–1945) Anglican clergyman, born in Fyvie, Aberdeenshire, NE Scotland, UK. Entering the Church of England in 1890, he was a curate at Leeds, dean of divinity at Magdalen College, Oxford, Bishop of Stepney (1901–8), and Canon of St Paul's. In 1908 he was appointed Archbishop of York, and in 1928 Archbishop of Canterbury. He was both counsellor and friend to George VI, who created him a life peer on his retirement in 1942.

Lang, Fritz (1890–1976) Film director, born in Vienna. He studied at the College of Technical Sciences and the Academy of Graphic Arts in Vienna, and intended to paint, but turned to the cinema after working with a film company in Berlin. His early films include *Dr Mabuse, der Spieler* (1922, Dr Mabuse, the Gambler), the first of three Mabuse films (the others in 1932 and 1960), and the futuristic *Metropolis* (1926), with its nightmare vision of urban living. When Hitler came to power in 1933, Goebbels offered Lang the post of head of the German film industry. Lang refused, and the same night fled to Paris, and later to the USA. Among his many films of this period, *Fury* (1936) was acclaimed as a masterpiece. Later films include *You Only Live Once* (1937) and *The Big Heat* (1953). He largely abandoned film-making after 1956. >> Goebbels

Lang, John Dunmore (1799–1878) Australian politician and clergyman, born in Greenock, Inverclyde, WC Scotland, UK. He studied at Glasgow University, arriving in New South Wales in 1823 with a mission to establish Presbyterianism in the new colony, and the foundation stone of Scots Church, Sydney, was laid in the following year. He was also instrumental in persuading the English government to subsidize those who wished to emigrate to Australia.

Langdon, Harry (Philmore) (1884–1944) Comedian, born in Council Bluffs, IA. As a child he appeared in amateur shows, and joined *Dr Belcher's Kickapoo Indian Medicine Show* in 1897. He made his film debut in the serial *The Master Mystery* (1918), and was signed by Mack Sennett for a series of short comedies. He moved on to features and the very popular trio of *Tramp Tramp Tramp* (1926), *The Strong Man* (1926), and *Long Pants* (1927). He is remembered for his character as a baby-faced innocent, handicapped by indecisiveness and bemused by the wider world. His attempts at directing failed, but he continued to work in films until the 1940s. >> Sennett

Lange, David (Russell) [longee] (1942–) New Zealand politician and prime minister (1984–9), born in Otahuhu, Auckland, New Zealand. After qualifying in law at Auckland University, he worked for the underprivileged in Auckland. His election to the House of Representatives in 1977 changed the direction of his life, and he rose rapidly to become leader of the Labour Party in 1983. His non-nuclear defence policy won him the 1984 general election, and made him New Zealand's youngest prime minister of the 20th-c. He and his party were re-elected in 1987, but he resigned in 1989. He was made a Companion of Honour in 1990.

Lange, Dorothea [lang], originally **Dorothea Nutzhorn** (1895–1965) Photographer, born in Hoboken, NJ. She studied at Columbia University, and established a studio in San Francisco in 1919. She is best known for her social records of migrant workers, share-croppers, and tenant farmers in the depression years from 1935, especially her study 'Migrant Mother' (1936). She later worked as a freelance photo-reporter in Asia, South America, and the Middle East (1958–63).

Lange, Jessica [lang] (1949–) Film actress, born in Cloquet, MN. She studied at the University of Michigan and the Opera Comique in Paris. After her first film, the 1976 remake of *King Kong*, she won acclaim for her performance in *The Postman Always Rings Twice* (1981). She received an Oscar nomination as Best Actress for her role in *Frances* (1982), and won the Oscar for Best Supporting Actress in *Tootsie* (1982). Later films include *Cape Fear* (1991) and *Rob Roy* (1995).

Langer, Susanne K(nauth) [languh] (1895–1985) Philosopher and educator, born in New York City. She studied at Radcliffe College, where she taught (1927–42), later holding positions at the University of Delaware, Columbia University, and Connecticut College. Much influenced by Ernst Cassirer, she published important works in aesthetics, often with reference to language, such as *Philosophy in a New Key* (1942), *Problems of Art* (1957), and *Mind: An Essay on Human Feeling* (3 vols, 1967–82). >> Cassirer

Langevin, Paul [lãzhvĩ] (1872–1946) French physicist. He studied under Perrin at the Sorbonne, and worked with Pierre Curie. Professor at the Sorbonne (1909), he was noted for his work on the molecular structure of gases, and for his theory of magnetism. He was the inventor of sonar for submarine detection during World War I. Imprisoned by the Nazis after the occupation of France, he was later released, and managed to escape to Switzerland. After the liberation he returned to Paris. >> Curie; Perrin

Langland, William, also spelled **Langley** (c. 1332–c. 1400) Poet, probably born in Ledbury, Hereford and Worcester, WC England, UK. Little is known about his life, but he is thought to have been a clerk and a minor cleric who lived many years in London in poverty. He is credited with the authorship of the great mediaeval alliterative poem on the theme of spiritual pilgrimage, *Piers Plowman*.

Langley, John Newport (1852–1925) British physiologist. Professor at Cambridge from 1903, he was noted for his research on the sympathetic nervous system. He owned and edited the *Journal of Physiology*.

Langley, Samuel Pierpont (1834–1906) Astronomer and aeronautical pioneer, born in Roxbury, MA. He practised as a civil engineer and architect in Chicago and St Louis, and in 1867 became professor of astronomy at Western University, PA. He invented the bolometer for measuring the Sun's radiant heat, and was the first to build a heavier-than-air flying machine – a steam-powered model aircraft.

Langmuir, Irving [lang̩myoor] (1881–1957) Physical chemist, born in New York City. He studied at Columbia and Göttingen universities, and was attached to the General Electric Company (1909–50), becoming associate director of the research laboratory in 1932. He received the Nobel Prize for Chemistry in 1932 for his work on solid and liquid surfaces. His many inventions include the gas-filled tungsten lamp and atomic hydrogen welding. >> Schaefer

Langton, Stephen (c. 1150–1228) Theologian, probably born in Lincolnshire, EC England, UK. He studied at the University of Paris, was made a cardinal by Pope Innocent III in 1206, and became Archbishop of Canterbury in 1207. His appointment was resisted by King John, and Langton was kept out of the see until 1213, living mostly at Pontigny. He sided warmly with the barons against John, and his name is the first of the subscribing witnesses of Magna Carta. >> Innocent III; John

Langtry, Lillie, popular name of **Emilie Charlotte Langtry**, *née* **Le Breton**, nickname **the Jersey Lily** (1853–1929) Actress, born in Jersey, Channel Is. One of the most noted beauties of her time, she married Edward Langtry in 1874, and was the first society woman to appear on stage. Her beauty brought her to the attention of the Prince of Wales, later Edward VII, and she became his mistress. She managed the Imperial Theatre, which was never successful. Widowed in 1897, she married in 1899 **Hugo Gerald de Bathe**, and became well known as a racehorse owner. >> Edward VII

Lanier, Sidney [laneer] (1842–81) Poet, born in Macon, GA. After a variety of jobs, he became a lecturer in English literature at Johns Hopkins University (1879). He believed in a scientific approach towards poetry-writing, breaking away from traditional metrical techniques and making it more akin to musical composition (he was also a musician), illustrated in later poems such as 'Corn' (1875) and 'The Symphony' (1875). He also wrote a novel and several critical studies.

Lankester, Sir Edwin Ray (1847–1929) Zoologist, born in London, England, UK. He was professor at London University and at Oxford, and director of the Natural History Museum in London (1898–1907). His contributions to zoology include important work in embryology and proto-zoology. He became president of the Marine Biological Association in 1892, and was knighted in 1907.

Lansbury, Angela (Brigid) (1925–   ) Actress, born in London, England, UK. Evacuated to the USA in 1940, she became a US citizen in 1951. Her role in *Gaslight* (1944, Oscar nomination) led to a contract with MGM, and she appeared in such films as *National Velvet* (1944) and *Samson and Delilah* (1949). Later, she made many more films, including *The Manchurian Candidate* (1963, Oscar nomination), *Bedknobs and Broomsticks* (1972), and *Death on the Nile* (1978). She made her Broadway stage debut in *Hotel Paradiso* (1957), and appeared in several musicals, such as *Gypsy* (1974) and *Sweeney Todd* (1979). She also achieved success in the role of Jessica Fletcher in the long-running TV mystery series *Murder She Wrote* (1984–95). In 1991 she won a new generation of fans as the voice of the housekeeper teapot in Disney's animated musical film *Beauty and the Beast*.

Lansbury, George (1859–1940) British politician, born near Lowestoft, Suffolk, E England, UK. Active as a radical since boyhood, he became a convinced socialist in 1890, and a Labour MP in 1910, resigning in 1912 to stand in support of women's suffrage. He was defeated and not re-elected until 1922. He founded and edited the *Daily Herald* (1912–22), and became commissioner of works (1929), and leader of the Labour Party (1931–5).

Lansdowne, Henry Petty-Fitzmaurice, 3rd Marquess of, also known as **Earl of Shelburne** (1780–1863) British statesman. He studied at Cambridge and became MP for Calne. He succeeded Pitt as member for Cambridge University (1806), and also as Chancellor of the Exchequer in the Grenville administration. In 1832, as president of the council, he helped to pass the Reform Bill. In 1852 he was requested to form an administration but declined, serving without office in the Aberdeen coalition. >> Aberdeen; Grenville; Pitt (the Younger)

Lansing, Robert (1864–1928) US statesman and lawyer, born in Watertown, NY. He became an attorney in 1889, and made a name as US counsel in arbitration cases. An authority on international law, he became counsellor for the Department of State in 1914, and was appointed secretary of state in 1915. He attended the Peace Conference in Paris (1919), but resigned in 1920 over the proposal to establish the League of Nations.

Lanston, Tolbert (1844–1913) Inventor, born in Troy, OH. He patented the Monotype, a type-forming and composing machine, in 1887. It was first used commercially in 1897, and revolutionized printing processes.

Lantz, Walter (1900–94) Cartoonist and film animator, born in New Rochelle, NY. An office boy on the *New York American* (1914), he studied cartooning by correspondence course, then started with William Randolph Hearst's animation studio in 1916. He rose to be writer/director/'star' of his own *Dinky Doodle* cartoons, then went to Hollywood, where he took over *Oswald the Lucky Rabbit* (1928), and remained with Universal Pictures for over 50 years. Of the many characters he created, the most popular is *Woody Woodpecker*, whose characteristic laugh was supplied by his wife, actress **Grace Stafford**, (d.1992). >> Hearst

Lanza, Mario, originally **Alfredo Arnold Cocozza** (1921–59) Tenor, born in Philadelphia, PA. Discovered while working in the family's grocery business, he auditioned for Serge Koussevitzky in 1942, and appeared that summer at Tanglewood. His career was interrupted by service in

World War 2, and afterwards he went on to Hollywood to appear in several musicals, including his most famous role in *The Great Caruso* (1951). >> Koussevitsky

Lao She [lau shoe], also known as **Shu Ching-chün** (1899–1966) Writer, born in Beijing. He lectured in Britain, USA, and China, and was influenced by Western writers including Dickens and Swift. His earlier work on humorous stories was later replaced by social concerns. His major novel *Rickshaw Boy* (1937) sympathetically recounted rickshaw-men's lives in the early 20th-c and exposed the dismal existence of republican China's masses. *Cat City* (influenced by *Gulliver's Travels*) was a satirical allegory on the state of China. After 1949 he wrote several plays acceptable to Communist orthodoxy, and *Rickshaw Boy* has been filmed (1984) and serialized on Chinese television. >> Dickens; Swift, Jonathan

Lao-tzu >> **Laozi**

Laozi [lautsee], also spelled **Lao-tzu** or **Lao-tse** ('Old Master') (?6th-c BC) The legendary founder of Chinese Taoism (Daoism). Nothing is known of his life: the oldest biography (c.100 BC) claims he held official rank. He was first mentioned by Zhuangzi. Taoist tradition attributes their classic text, the *Daodejing* (*Tao Te Ching*) to Laozi, but it was written in the 3rd-c BC. By the 2nd-c AD, Taoists claimed he had lived more than once and had travelled to India, where he became the Buddha. (Later he was claimed to have founded Manichaeism.) The Tang emperors (618–906) claimed descent from him. >> Buddha; Zhuangzi

La Pérouse, Jean François de Galaup, comte de (Count of) [la payrooz] (1741–88) Navigator, born near Albi, France. He distinguished himself in the naval war against Britain (1778–83) by destroying the forts of the Hudson's Bay Company. In 1785, in command of an expedition of discovery, he visited the NW coast of America, explored the NE coasts of Asia, and sailed through *La Pérouse Strait* between Sakhalin and Yezo. In 1788 he sailed from Botany Bay, but his two ships were wrecked N of the New Hebrides.

Laplace, Pierre Simon, Marquis de [laplas], also known as **Comte de** (Count of) **Laplace** (1749–1827) Mathematician and astronomer, born in Beaumont-en-Auge, France. He studied at Caen, and became professor of mathematics at the Ecole Militaire, Paris. He applied his mathematical knowledge to physical astronomy, particularly the stability of orbits in the Solar System. His five-volume *Mécanique céleste* (1799–1825, Celestial Mechanics) is a landmark in applied mathematics. In his study of the gravitational attraction of spheroids, he formulated the fundamental differential equation in physics which now bears his name. He entered the Senate in 1799, and was made a peer in 1815. >> Bowditch, Nathaniel; Legendre

Lapworth, Arthur (1872–1941) Chemist, born in Galashiels, Scottish Borders, SE Scotland, UK. He studied at Birmingham and the City and Guilds College, London. After holding a number of senior academic posts, he was appointed professor of organic chemistry at Manchester in 1913, and professor of physical and inorganic chemistry in 1922. He worked on an electronic theory of organic chemical reactions, and classified reagents by charge type, suggesting the existence of alternating electrical polarity along a chain of atoms.

Lapworth, Charles (1842–1920) Geologist, born in Faringdon, Berkshire, SE England, UK. In 1864 he became a teacher in Galashiels, where he did important work on the geology of S Scotland and the NW Highlands. He was professor of geology at Birmingham (1881–1913), and wrote especially on graptolites. The term *Ordovician* was introduced by him.

Lara, Brian (1969–) Cricketer, born in Cantaro, Trinidad, West Indies. He came to prominence in the 1994 season,

when he broke several cricketing records, scoring seven centuries in eight successive innings, and a world record Test innings of 375 for the West Indies against England. He became the world's first batsman to score over 500 runs in one innings in first-class cricket, playing for Warwickshire against Durham.

La Ramée, Marie Louise de >> **Ouida**

Lardner, Dionysius (1793–1859) Scientific writer, born in Dublin. He attracted attention by his works on algebraic geometry (1823) and the calculus (1825), and was elected professor of natural philosophy and astronomy at London University in 1827. He is best known as the originator and editor of *Lardner's Cabinet Cyclopaedia* (133 vols, 1829–49).

Lardner, Ring(gold Wilmer) (1885–1933) Writer, born in Niles, MI. He studied at the Armour Institute of Technology, Chicago, then worked as a reporter on the *South Bend Times* (1905). He became a specialist sportswriter for several important Chicago papers, and published successful collections of stories, such as *You Know Me, Al* (1916) and *How to Write Short Stories* (1924). Between then and 1929 he wrote prolifically in a number of genres, including novels, plays, poetry, and an autobiography, *The Story of a Wonder Man* (1927). Regarded as a gifted satirist, several biographies were published during the 1970s.

Larionov, Mikhail Fyodorovich [larionof] (1881–1964) Painter and stage designer, born in Tiraspol, Ukraine. He studied sculpture and architecture at the Moscow Institute of Painting until 1908. He worked closely with his future wife, **Natalia Goncharova**, and together they developed Rayonism (1912–14), a style akin to Italian Futurism. They held a joint exhibition in Paris 1914, and from 1915 were renowned for their work on ballet designs for Diaghilev. >> Diaghilev; Goncharova

Larivey, Pierre [larivay] (c. 1550–1619) Playwright, born in Champagne, France. As the introducer of Italian-style comedy to the French stage, he foreshadowed Molière. His licentious *Comédies facétieuses* (2 vols, 1579, 1611) were adaptations of existing Italian pieces. >> Molière

Larkin, Philip (Arthur) (1922–85) Poet, librarian, and jazz critic, born in Coventry, West Midlands, C England, UK. He studied at Oxford – an experience on which he based his first novel, *Jill* (1946). *A Girl in Winter* (1947) was his only other novel. His early poems appeared in the anthology, *Poetry from Oxford in Wartime* (1944), and in a collection *The North Ship* (1945). *XX Poems* was published privately in 1950. He became librarian at the University of Hull in 1955, and further collections appeared at regular intervals, including *The Less Deceived* (1955), *The Whitsun Weddings* (1964) and *High Windows* (1974). *Collected Poems* was published posthumously (1988) and became a best seller. His articles on jazz were collected in *All What Jazz?* (1970), and his essays in *Required Writing* (1983). His *Letters* were published in 1992, and the first biography of his life in 1993.

Laroche, Guy [larosh] (1923–89) Fashion designer, born in La Rochelle, France. He worked in millinery, first in Paris, then in New York City, before returning to Paris. In 1957 he started his own business and showed a small collection. By 1961 he was producing both couture and ready-to-wear clothes, achieving a reputation for skilful cutting. From 1966 his designs included menswear.

La Rochefoucauld, François, duc de (Duke of) [la rosh-fookoh] (1613–80) Classical writer, born in Paris. He devoted himself to the cause of the queen, Marie de' Medici, in opposition to Richelieu, and became entangled in a series of love adventures and political intrigues, and was forced to live in exile (1639–42). Involved in the wars of the Frondes, he was wounded at the siege of Paris, and retired to the country after being wounded again in 1652. His *Mémoires*, written in retirement, was published in

1664, but as it gave wide offence he denied its authorship. He is best known for his *Réflexions, ou sentences et maximes morales* (first edition, 1665), commonly known as the *Maximes*, making him the leading exponent of the French literary term *maxime* ('maxim'). >> Marie de' Medicis; Richelieu

Larousse, Pierre (Athanase) [la**roos**] (1817–75) Publisher and lexicographer, born in Toucy, France. He studied at Versailles, became a teacher, and began his linguistic research in Paris in 1840. He wrote several grammars, dictionaries, and other textbooks, notably his *Grand dictionnaire universel du XIXᵉ siècle* (15 vols, 1865–76, Great Universal Dictionary of the Nineteenth Century).

Larrieu, Daniel [laryoe] (1957–) Dancer and choreographer, born in Marseilles, France. He began performing professionally in 1978, and in 1982 formed the three-person company Astrakan that won the Bagnolet international choreographic competition the same year. His biggest success was the underwater modern ballet *Waterproof* (1986), performed in swimming pools to video accompaniment.

Larsen, Henning (1925–) Danish architect. He studied at the Royal Danish Academy in Copenhagen, the Architectural Association in London, and Massachusetts Institute of Technology, and in 1968 became professor of architecture at the Royal Danish Academy. His buildings include the University of Trondheim, the foreign ministry building in Riyadh, Saudi Arabia, and the 1100-seat Compton Verney opera house, near Stratford-upon-Avon, Warwickshire (1989). Later projects include the Danish Design Centre, Copenhagen (1994).

Larsson, Carl (1853–1919) Artist, born in Stockholm. He studied at the Swedish Academy of Arts (1869–76), visited Paris in 1877, and was the centre of the Scandinavian artists' colony in Grez-sur-Loing (1882–4). The series of 26 watercolours entitled *A Home* (1894–9), won him international renown and enormous popularity in Sweden. He also produced monumental historical paintings and was an outstanding illustrator of books.

Lartigue, Jacques Henri (Charles Auguste) [lah(r)**teeg**] (1894–1986) Photographer, born in Curbevoie, France. He adopted an informal approach to the photography of everyday subjects, including experiences in World War 1 and the life of the leisured classes of the 1920s. A one-man show at the New York Museum of Modern Art in 1963 aroused wide interest, and he is noted for his collection, *Diary of a Century* (1970).

Larwood, Harold (1904–95) Cricketer, born in Nuncargate, Nottinghamshire, C England, UK. He played for Nottinghamshire, where he was known for the speed of his opening attack. He bowled 'bodyline' in the 1932–3 tour of Australia when several of the home batsmen were seriously hurt, and diplomatic relations between the two countries were imperilled. Afterwards, feeling that he had not been supported in official quarters, he retired from Test cricket after playing in only 21 matches. He published two memoirs, *Bodyline* (1933) and *The Larwood Story* (1965). In his later life he settled in Australia. >> Jardine

La Salle, St Jean Baptist de (1651–1719) Educational reformer and philanthropist, born in Reims, France. He set up schools for the poor, reformatories, and training colleges for teachers, and was the founder in 1684 (with 12 others) of the Brothers of the Christian Schools, known as the Christian Brothers. He was canonized in 1900; feast day 7 April.

La Salle, René Robert Cavelier, sieur de (Lord of) [la **sal**] (1643–87) Explorer of North America, born in Rouen, France. He settled as a trader near Montreal, and descended the Ohio and Mississippi to the sea (1682), claiming Louisiana for France and naming it after Louis XIV. In 1684 he led an expedition to the Gulf of Mexico, but spent two fruitless years looking for the Misissippi Delta. His followers mutinied, and he was murdered. >> Louis XIV

Las Casas, Bartolomé de [las **kah**sas], known as **the Apostle of the Indians** (1474–1566) Missionary, born in Seville, Spain. He sailed in the third voyage of Columbus (1502) to Hispaniola, was ordained (1512), and travelled to Cuba (1513). His desire to protect the natives from slavery led him to visit the Spanish court on several occasions. Appointed Bishop of Chiapa, he was received (1544) with hostility by the colonists, returned to Spain, and resigned his see (1547). His most important work is the unfinished *Historia de las Indias* (1875–6). >> Columbus

Lasdun, Sir Denys (Louis) (1914–) Architect, born in London, England, UK. He studied at at the Architectural Association School, served with the Royal Engineers in World War 2, and was professor at Leeds University (1962–3). He is renowned for the Royal College of Music (1958–64) in London, the University of East Anglia, Norwich (1962–8), the National Theatre, London (1965–76), the European Investment Bank, Luxembourg (1975), and the Institute of Education (1970–8) in London. He was awarded the Royal Gold Medal of the Royal Institute of British Architects in 1977. His publications include *A Language and a Theme* (1976) and *Architecture in an Age of Scepticism* (1984). He was knighted in 1976 and made a Companion of Honour in 1995.

Lashley, Karl S(pencer) (1890–1958) Psychologist, born in Davis, VA. He studied at Johns Hopkins University, and became professor at the universities of Minnesota (1920–9), Chicago (1929–35), and Harvard (1935–55). In 1942 he also became director of the Yerkes Laboratory for primate biology at Orange Park, FL. He made valuable contributions to the study of localization of brain function, and is often called 'the father of neuropsychology'.

Lasker, Emanuel (1868–1941) Chess player and mathematician, born in Berlinchen, Germany. He won the world championship in 1894, retaining it until 1921, when he was defeated by Capablanca. He studied mathematics at Erlangen University, and formulated a theorem of vector spaces which is known by his name. He left Germany in 1933, and finally settled in the USA, continuing to play chess until his late 60s. >> Capablanca; RR1149

Lasker, Mary, *née* **Woodward** (1900–) Philanthropist, born in Watertown, WI. She worked as an art dealer, then started a dress pattern line called Hollywood Patterns (1932). In 1942 she and her husband **Albert** (1880–1958) founded the Albert and Mary Lasker Foundation, using some of the money from the sale of Albert's successful advertising agency, Lord and Thomas Co. The foundation has influenced and supported medical research and public health initiatives in a number of ways, including the coveted Albert Lasker Medical Research Awards. A pink tulip was named for her to honour her urban beautification efforts in New York City and Washington, DC.

Laski, Harold J(oseph) (1893–1950) Political scientist and socialist, born in Manchester, Greater Manchester, NW England, UK. He studied at Oxford, and lectured at several US universities before joining the London School of Economics (1920), becoming professor of political science in 1926. He was chairman of the Labour Party (1945–6). His political philosophy was a modified Marxism which he expounded in his many books, including *Authority in the Modern State* (1919), *A Grammar of Politics* (1925), and *The American Presidency* (1940). >> Laski, Marghanita

Laski, Marghanita (1915–88) Novelist and critic, born in Manchester, Greater Manchester, NW England, UK, the niece of Harold Laski. She studied at Oxford, and her first novel, *Love on the Supertax*, appeared in 1944. She wrote extensively for newspapers and reviews, and published a number of critical works. Her later novels include *Little Boy Lost* (1949) and *The Victorian Chaise-longue* (1953). >> Laski, Harold

Laslett, (Thomas) Peter (Ruffell) (1915–) British historian. He studied at Cambridge, served in naval intelligence during World War 2, and became a producer for the BBC radio *Talks* programme (1946–9). He returned to Cambridge in 1948, where he established the Cambridge Group for the history of population and social structure (1964), and was reader in politics and the history of social structure (1966–83). He is best known for his book *The World We Have Lost* (1965), and for discovering the lost library of John Locke. >> Locke, John

Lassalle, Ferdinand [laˈsal] (1825–64) Social Democrat, born in Wrocław, Poland (formerly Breslau, Germany). In Berlin (1844–5) he championed the cause of Countess Sophie Hatzfeld's divorce before 36 tribunals, earning financial independence. He took part in the revolution of 1848, during which he met Marx, and for an inflammatory speech got six months in prison. He founded the Universal German Working-Men's Association (the forerunner of the Social Democratic Party) to agitate for universal suffrage. He died shortly after a duel with Count Racowitza of Wallachia over the hand of Helene von Domiges. >> Marx

Lassell, William (1799–1880) Astronomer, born in Bolton, Lancashire, NW England, UK. As an amateur, he built an observatory at Starfield near Liverpool, where he constructed and mounted equatorial reflecting telescopes. He discovered several planetary satellites, including Triton (1846) and Hyperion (1848). He also discovered Ariel and Umbriel, satellites of Uranus (1851). He later became president of the Royal Astronomical Society (1870–2).

Lassus, Orlandus, also known as **Orlando di Lasso** (c. 1532–94) Musician and composer, born in Mons, Belgium. He travelled widely, visiting Italy, England, and France. In 1570 he was ennobled by Maximilian II, and received the knighthood of the Golden Spur (1574). He wrote over 2000 compositions, secular pieces as well as church music, his best-known work being *Psalmi Davidis poenitentiales* (1584).

Latham, Sir John Greig [layˈtham] (1877–1964) Australian statesman and judge, born in Melbourne, Victoria, Australia. He studied at Melbourne University, where he also taught, then practised at the bar and served in World War 1. From 1922 he became attorney general of the Commonwealth, Leader of the Opposition, deputy prime minister (1931–4), and Chief Justice of the High Court of Australia (1935–52). In this office he enhanced the standing of the High Court, keeping it distinct from politics, and favoured Commonwealth power against state power.

Lathrop, Julia (Clifford) [layˈthrop] (1858–1932) Social reformer, born in Rockford, IL. She studied at Vassar College, NY, then joined Jane Addams's Hull House Settlement in Chicago, and was active in promoting welfare for children and the mentally ill. One of the founders of the Chicago Institute of Social Science (1903–4), she was associated with the Chicago School of Philanthropy (1908–20), and was first head of the Federal Children's Bureau (1912). >> Addams, Jane

Latimer, Hugh (c. 1485–1555) Protestant martyr, born in Thurcaston, Leicestershire, C England, UK. In 1510 he was elected a fellow of Clare College, Cambridge, and in 1522 was appointed a university preacher, soon becoming noted for his reformed doctrines. He was made rector of West Kington in Wiltshire, and in 1535 was consecrated as Bishop of Worcester. Twice during Henry VIII's reign he was sent to the Tower, in 1539 and 1546, and under Mary I he was examined at Oxford (1554) and committed to jail.

The next year he was found guilty of heresy, and was burned with Ridley opposite Balliol College. >> Ridley, Nicholas (c.1500–55)

Latimer, Lewis Howard (1848–1928) Inventor and engineer, born in Chelsea, MA. After serving in the US navy during the Civil War, he studied drafting, eventually becoming chief draftsman for both General Electric and Westinghouse. He invented a 'water closet for railroad cars' (1873), and drafted the patent drawings for Alexander Graham Bell's first telephone. In 1881 he devised a method for making a carbon filament for a light bulb made by one of Thomas Edison's competitors, and then supervised that firm's installation of electric lights in New York City, Philadelphia, Montreal, and London. In 1884 he went to work for Edison's company. >> Bell, Alexander Graham; Edison

La Tour, Georges de (1593–1652) Artist, born in Vic-sur-Seille, France. From 1620 he worked at Lunéville and achieved a high reputation. The Duke of Lorraine became his patron, and later Louis XIII accepted a painting by him, liking it so much he had all works by other masters removed from his chambers. La Tour was entirely forgotten until his rediscovery in 1915. He specialized in candle-lit scenes, mostly of religious subjects, such as 'St Joseph the Carpenter' (1645, Louvre).

La Tour, Maurice Quentin de [laˈtoor], also spelled **Latour** (1704–88) Pastellist and portrait painter, born in St Quentin, France. He settled in Paris, where he became immensely popular, and was made portraitist to Louis XV (1750–73). His best works include portraits of Madame de Pompadour, Voltaire, and Rousseau.

Latreille, Pierre André [laˈtray] (1762–1833) Entomologist, born in Brive-la-Gaillarde, France. An ordained priest, he became head of the entomology department at the Muséum National d'Histoire Naturelle, Paris (1799), and professor of natural history. He is best known for his pioneering work on the classification of crustaceans, arachnids, and insects (1829). He has been called 'the father of modern entomology'.

Latrobe, Benjamin (Henry) [laˈtrohb] (1764–1820) Architect and civil engineer, born in Fulneck, West Yorkshire, N England, UK. He trained in England with Cockerell, enjoying a successful practice there before emigrating to the USA (1795), where he introduced the Greek Revival style and was surveyor of public buildings in Washington, DC (1803–17). As an engineer he designed waterworks for the city of Philadelphia (1801), worked on the Washington navy yard, and joined with Robert Fulton in a scheme to build steamboats (1813–15). His most notable work is the Basilica of the Assumption of the Blessed Virgin Mary, Baltimore (begun 1805). >> Cockerell, Samuel Pepys; Fulton

Lattimore, Owen (1900–89) Sinologist and defender of civil liberties, born in Washington, DC. He studied at Harvard before being sent to China to do research. He published narratives of his journeys, notably *Inner Asian Frontiers of China* (1940). He was made political adviser to Jiang Jieshi by Franklin D Roosevelt (1941–2), and became director of Pacific operations in the office of war information. His *Ordeal by Slander* (1950) refers to his being wrongly named as a top Russian agent by Senator Joseph McCarthy. >> Jiang Jieshi; McCarthy, Joseph

Lattre de Tassigny, Jean (Marie Gabriel) de [laˌtruh duh taˈsinyee] (1889–1952) French soldier, born in Mouilleron-en-Pareds, France. He studied at the Jesuit College at Poitiers and at St Cyr, commanded an infantry battalion during World War 1, and was decorated with the Croix de Guerre. In World War 2 he commanded the 14th division against the advancing Germans (1940), then served in

Tunisia. As commander of the French 1st Army, he took part in the Allied liberation of France (1944–5), signing the German surrender. He was responsible for the reorganization of the French army, and was appointed commander-in-chief of Western Union Land Forces under Montgomery in 1948, and in 1950 in French Indo-China. He was posthumously made a marshal of France in 1952. >> Montgomery, Viscount

Latynina, Larisa Semyonovna [lateenina] (1934–) Gymnast born in Kherson, Ukraine. She studied at the Kiev State Institute of Physical Culture, competed in three Olympic Games (1956, 1960, 1964), and was the first woman athlete to win nine gold medals.

Laubach, Frank Charles [lowbak] (1884–1970) Missionary and pioneer of adult basic education, born in Benton, PA. Sent to evangelize the Moro tribespeople of the Philippines (1915), he devised a simple way to combat illiteracy among them. His method and its application in Southern Asia, India, and Latin America are described in such works as *India Shall Be Literate* (1940) and *Thirty Years with the Silent Billion* (1961). His spiritual motivation is expounded in *Letters by a Modern Mystic* (1937) and *Channels of Spiritual Power* (1955).

Laud, William [lawd] (1573–1645) Clergyman and Archbishop of Canterbury, born in Reading, Berkshire, S England, UK. He studied at Oxford, and was ordained in 1601. His learning and industry brought him many patrons, and he rapidly received preferment, becoming King's Chaplain (1611), Bishop of St David's (1621), Bishop of Bath and Wells and a privy councillor (1626), Bishop of London (1628), and Archbishop of Canterbury (1633). With Strafford and Charles I, he worked for absolutism in Church and state. In Scotland, his attempt (1635–7) to anglicize the Church led to the Bishops' Wars. In 1640 the Long Parliament impeached him. He was found guilty, and executed on Tower Hill. >> Charles I (of England); Prynne; Strafford

Lauda, Niki [lowda], popular name of **Nikolas Andreas Lauda** (1949–) Motor-racing driver, born in Vienna. He world champion racing driver in 1975, 1977 and 1984. In 1976 he suffered horrific burns and injuries in the German Grand Prix at the Nürburg Ring. Despite a series of operations, he remained a contender for the 1976 Japanese Grand Prix, but finally declined to race because of adverse weather conditions. He then refuted rumours that he had lost his nerve by winning again in 1977. Going on to drive for Brabham involved a two-year absence from Grand Prix racing. He crowned his come-back with McLaren by winning his third and last Grand Prix championship in 1984. He retired in 1985. >> RR1165

Lauder, Estée [lawder], *née* **Mentzer** (c. 1910–) Businesswoman, born in New York City. From a poor immigrant family, she worked her way up in the cosmetics industry by selling a face cream made by her uncle. She co-founded Estée Lauder Inc with her husband **Joseph Lauder** in 1946, and had great success with the fragrance 'Youth Dew' in the 1950s. She was named one of 100 women of achievement by *Harper's Bazaar* in 1967, and one of the Top Ten outstanding women in business in 1970. She published her autobiography, *Estée: a Success Story*, in 1985. >> Arden, Elizabeth; Rubinstein, Helena

Lauder, Sir Harry (MacLennan) [lawder] (1870–1950) Singer, born in Edinburgh, EC Scotland, UK. He started his career on the music-hall stage as an Irish comedian, but made his name as a singer of Scots songs, many of which were of his own composition, such as 'Roamin' in the Gloamin'. He was knighted in 1919 for his work in organizing entertainments for the troops during World War 1. Some of his biggest successes were in London's famous

music halls, but he was also popular abroad, especially in the USA and Commonwealth countries, which he toured extensively after 1907. He wrote volumes of memoirs, the best known of which is *Roamin' in the Gloamin'* (1928).

Lauder, William [lawder] (c. 1680–1771) Scottish scholar and charlatan. He was a classical scholar, and studied at Edinburgh, but after a series of failures, he sought to prove by blatant forgeries (1747–50) that Milton in writing *Paradise Lost* had plagiarized various 17th-c poets writing in Latin. He was exposed by Bishop John Douglas (1750), and regarded thereafter with great contempt. He retreated in poverty to Barbados, where he became a store-keeper.

Lauderdale, John Maitland, Duke of [lawderdayl] (1616–82) Scottish statesman, born in Lethington, East Lothian, E Scotland, UK. He was an ardent supporter of the Covenanters (1638), and in 1643 became a Scottish Commissioner at Westminster, succeeding his father as second Earl of Lauderdale in 1645. He was taken prisoner at Worcester in 1651, and spent nine years in the Tower, at Windsor, and at Portland. At the Restoration, he became Scottish secretary of state. A member of the Privy Council, he had a seat in the so-called Cabal ministry, and was created a duke in 1672. >> Charles II (of England)

Laue, Max (Theordor Felix) von [lowuh] (1879–1960) Physicist, born near Koblenz, Germany. As professor of physics at Zürich (1912), he worked on X-ray diffraction in crystals, leading to the use of X-rays to study the atomic structure of matter. He supported Einstein's theory of relativity, and investigated quantum theory and the Compton effect. He was appointed director of the Institute for Theoretical Physics in 1919, and director of the Max Planck Institute for Research in Physical Chemistry, Berlin in 1951. He was awarded the 1914 Nobel Prize for Physics. >> Compton, Arthur; Franklin, Rosalind; Wilkins, Maurice

Laughton, Charles [lawtn] (1899–1962) Film and stage actor, born in Scarborough, North Yorkshire, N England, UK. He trained at the Royal Academy of Dramatic Art, London, and first appeared on stage in London in 1926. This was followed by successes in *The Cherry Orchard*, *A Man with Red Hair*, and *Payment Deferred*. He appeared with the Old Vic Company in 1933, played in and produced Shaw's *Don Juan in Hell* and *Major Barbara*, and as a Shakespearean actor gave fine performances in *Macbeth*, *Measure for Measure*, and *King Lear*. He began to act in films in 1932 and among his memorable roles are *The Private Life of Henry VIII* (1932, Oscar), Mr Barrett in *The Barretts of Wimpole Street* (1934), Captain Bligh in *Mutiny on the Bounty* (1935), and Quasimodo in *The Hunchback of Notre Dame* (1939). He was married to the actress **Elsa Lanchester** (1902–86), and became a US citizen in 1950.

Laurana, Luciano [lowrana] (c. 1420–79) Architect, born in Dalmatia. Little is known of his early work or training, but he was in Urbino c.1465, and by 1468 had been appointed architect in chief at the Palazzo Ducal of Federico da Montefeltro. The design of the palace courtyard evidenced his familiarity with recent Renaissance masterpieces in the field, particularly Brunelleschi's Foundling Hospital, Florence. He is recognized as one of the leading figures of 15th-c Italian architecture. >> Brunelleschi

Laurel and Hardy Comedians who formed the first Hollywood film comedy team. The 'thin one', **Stan Laurel** (1890–1965), originally **Arthur Stanley Jefferson**, was born in Ulverston, Lancashire, NW England, UK. He began in a British touring company, went to the USA in 1910, and worked in silent films from 1917. The 'fat one', **Oliver Hardy** (1892–1957), born near Atlanta GA, left college to join a troupe of minstrels before drifting into the film industry. They came together in 1926. They made many full-length feature films, but their best efforts are generally thought to be their early (1927–31) shorts. Their contrasting personalities, general clumsiness, and disaster-packed predicaments made them a universally popular comedy duo.

Lauren, Ralph [loren], originally **Ralph Lifschitz** (1939–) Fashion designer, born in New York City. He attended night school for business studies and worked as a salesman in Bloomingdale's. In 1967 he joined Beau Brummel Neckwear and created the Polo range for men, later including womenswear. He is famous for his American styles, such as the 'prairie look' and 'frontier fashions'.

Laurence or **Lawrence, St**, also **Laurentius** (d.258) Christian martyr, said to have been born in Huesca, Spain. He became a deacon at Rome under Pope St Sixtus II. In the persecution of Valerian he was condemned to death, and the Basilica of San Lorenzo, Rome, was later built over his place of burial. Feast day 10 August. >> Valerian

Laurence, (Jean) Margaret, *née* **Wemyss** (1926–87) Novelist, born in Neepawa, Manitoba, Canada. She graduated from United College (now Winnipeg University) in 1947 – the same year she married John Laurence (separated 1962), a civil engineer. His job took them to England, Somaliland, and Ghana, which inspired her early poetry and travel books. *This Side Jordan* (1960), her first novel, was set in Ghana. She moved to England in 1962 and wrote her famous Manawaka series: *The Stone Angel* (1964), *A Jest of God* (1966), *The Fire-Dwellers* (1969), *A Bird in the House* (1970), and *The Diviners* (1974).

Laurencin, Marie [lorãsĩ] (1883–1956) Painter, born in Paris. She studied at the Académie Humbart and exhibited in the Salon des Indépendents in 1907. Best known for her portraits of women in misty pastel colours, she also illustrated many books with water colours and lithographs.

Laurens, Henri [lohrãs] (1885–1954) Sculptor, born in Paris. He worked as an illustrator, stonemason, and interior decorator before he became involved in sculpting. He was a leading exponent of three-dimensional Cubism, and modelled many works with a marine theme, including 'Bathing Girl' (1947).

Laurent, Auguste [lohrã] (1807–53) Chemist, born in La Folie, France. After eight years as professor in Bordeaux (1838–45) he went to Paris to work with Charles Frédéric Gerhardt. There, he was forced by financial difficulties to become assayer at the Mint from 1848. He propounded the nucleus theory of organic radicals, discovered anthracine, worked on the classification of organic compounds, and gave his name to *Laurent's acid*. >> Gerhardt

Laurie, Piper, originally **Rosetta Jacobs** (1932–) Film actress, born in Detroit, MI. She made her film debut in 1950 with *The Milkman*, later films including *The Hustler* (1961, Oscar nomination), *Carrie* (1976), *Return to Oz* (1985), *Wrestling Ernest Hemingway* (1993), and *The Grass Harp* (1996). Her television series include *The Thorn Birds* (1983), *Twin Peaks* (1990), and *Intensity* (1997), and she received an Emmy for her role in the television production of *Promise* (1986).

Laurier, Sir Wilfrid [loryay] (1841–1919) Canadian statesman and prime minister (1896–1911), born in St Lin, Quebec, Canada. He became a lawyer, a journalist, and a member of the Quebec Legislative Assembly. He entered federal politics in 1874, and became minister of inland revenue (1877), leader of the Liberal Party (1887–1919), and the first French-Canadian to be prime minister of Canada (1896). A firm supporter of self-government for Canada, in his home policy he was an advocate of compromise and free trade with the USA. >> RR1039

Lauterpacht, Sir Hersch [lowterpakht] (1897–1960) Lawyer, born near Lemberg, Germany. He studied in Vienna, moved to England in 1923, and became a law teacher in London, and professor of International Law

at Cambridge (1938–55). He acted for Britain in many international disputes, and became a judge of the International Court of Justice (1954–60).

Lautréamont, comte de (Count of) [lohtrayamõ], pseudonym of **Isidore Ducasse** (1846–70) Poet, born in Montevideo, Uruguay. He went to France as an adolescent, and published the sequence of prose poems *Les Chants de Maldoror* (1868, The Songs of Maldoror). *Poésies* was published in 1870, the year he died in Paris. His work was a significant influence on the Surrealists and other Modernist writers.

Laval, Carl Gustaf Patrik de [laval] (1845–1913) Engineer, scientist, and inventor, born in Blasenborg, Sweden. He became an engineer with the Klosters-Bruck Steel works (1872), invented a centrifugal cream separator in 1878, and made important contributions to the development of the steam turbine (1880–95). >> Parsons, Charles

Laval, Pierre (1883–1945) French statesman and prime minister (1931–2, 1935–6, 1942–4), born in Châteldon, France. He became a lawyer, deputy (1914), and senator (1926), before serving as premier. From a position on the left, he moved rightwards during the late 1930s, and in the Vichy government was Pétain's deputy (1940), then his rival. As prime minister, he openly collaborated with the Germans. Fleeing after the liberation to Germany and Spain, he was brought back, charged with treason, and executed in Paris. >> RR1049

La Vallière, Louise-Françoise de La Baume le Blanc, duchesse de (Duchess of) [la valyair] (1644–1710) Mistress of Louis XIV, born in Tours, France. Brought to court by her mother, she became the king's mistress in 1661 and bore him four children. When the Marquise de Montespan superseded her, she was publicly humiliated, then compensated by being made a duchess (1667). After one escape attempt, she retired to a Carmelite nunnery in Paris (1674), where she lived in penitence for 36 years. >> Louis XIV; Montespan

Laval-Montmorency, François Xavier [laval mõmohrãsee] (1623–1708) Clergyman and missionary, born in Montigny-sur-Avre, France. He was sent as vicar apostolic to Quebec in 1659, and became the first Bishop of Quebec (1674–88). In 1663 he founded the seminary of Quebec, which in 1852 was named Laval University after him.

Lavater, Johann Kaspar [lavater] (1741–1801) Physiognomist, theologian, and writer, born in Zürich, Switzerland. In 1769 he received Protestant orders, and made himself known by a volume of poems, *Schweizerlieder* (1767). He attempted to elevate physiognomy into a science in his *Physiognomische Fragmente* (1775–8, trans Essays on Physiognomy), written with the assistance of Goethe. While tending the wounded at the capture of Zürich by Masséna (1799) he was wounded himself, and later died of his injuries. >> Goethe; Masséna

Laver, James [layver] (1899–1975) Writer and art critic, born in Liverpool, Merseyside, NW England, UK. He won the Newdigate Prize for verse at Oxford in 1921, and later books of verse include *His Last Sebastian* (1922) and *Ladies' Mistakes* (1933). He was assistant keeper, then keeper at the Victoria and Albert Museum (1922–59). His critical books on art include *French Painting and the 19th century* (1937), and *Fragonard* (1956). He also wrote on the history of English costume in *Taste and Fashion* (1937), and other works.

Laver, Rod(ney George) [layver], nickname **the Rockhampton Rocket** (1938–) Tennis player, born in Rockhampton, Queensland, Australia. An aggressive left-handed player, he first won the Wimbledon singles title in 1961, and again in 1962 in the course of a Grand Slam of all the major titles (British, US, French, and Australian). He turned professional in 1962 and won the world singles title five times between 1964 and 1970. In 1968, when Wimbledon went open, he took the title, and won again in the course of another Grand Slam the following year. The first professional to make more than $1 million, he won more money than anyone else until 1978. >> RR1173

Laveran, (Charles Louis) Alphonse [laverã] (1845–1922) Physician and parasitologist, born in Paris. He studied at the Strasbourg faculty of medicine, and became professor of military medicine and epidemic diseases at the military college of Val de Grâce (1874–8, 1884–94). In Algeria, he discovered the blood parasite which caused malaria (1880), and he also did important work on other diseases, including sleeping-sickness and kala-azar. From 1896 until his death he was at the Pasteur Institute at Paris. In 1907 he was awarded the Nobel Prize for Physiology or Medicine.

Lavigerie, Charles (Martial Allemand) [lavizheree] (1825–92) Clergyman, born in Bayonne, France. He studied at Saint-Sulpice, Paris, and was ordained in 1849. In 1863 he was made Bishop of Nancy, in 1867 Archbishop of Algiers, and a cardinal in 1882. As Primate of Africa (1884) he became well known for his missionary work, and founded the Society of Missionaries of Africa, or White Fathers (1868). In 1888 he also founded the Anti-Slavery Society.

Lavin, Mary (1912–96) Short-story writer and novelist, born in East Walpole, MA. Her parents returned to Ireland when she was nine, and she lived there ever since. 'Miss Holland', her first short story, was published in the *Dublin Magazine*, and her first collection, *Tales from Bective Bridge* (1942), was awarded the James Tait Black Memorial Prize. Apart from two early novels – *The House in Clewe Street* (1945) and *Mary O'Grady* (1950) – she concentrated on the short story. Her collections include *A Memory and Other Stories* (1972), *The Shrine and Other Stories* (1977), and *A Family Likeness* (1985).

Lavoisier, Antoine Laurent [lavwazyay] (1743–94) Chemist, born in Paris. To finance his investigations, in 1768 he accepted the office of farmer-general of taxes, and became director of the government powder mills in 1776. In 1788 he showed that air is a mixture of gases which he called *oxygen* and *nitrogen*, thus disproving the earlier theory of phlogiston. His major work is the *Traité élémentaire de chimie* (1789), containing the ideas which set chemistry on its modern path. He also devised the modern method of naming chemical compounds, and was a member of the commission which devised the metric system. Politically a liberal, and despite his many reforms, he was guillotined in Paris on a contrived charge of counter-revolutionary activity. He is now recognized as the founder of modern chemistry.

Law, (Andrew) Bonar [law, boner] (1858–1923) British statesman and prime minister (1922–3), born in New Brunswick, Canada. He studied in Canada and Glasgow, was an iron merchant in Glasgow, became a Unionist MP in 1900, and in 1911 succeeded Balfour as Unionist leader. He acted as colonial secretary (1915-16), a member of the war cabinet, Chancellor of the Exchequer (1916-18), Lord Privy Seal (1919), and from 1916 Leader of the House of Commons. He retired in 1921 through ill health, but returned to serve as premier for several months in 1922-3. >> Balfour, Arthur James; RR1095

Law, Denis (1940–) Footballer, born in Aberdeen, NE Scotland, UK. He never played at senior level in Scotland, his career being spent almost entirely in England. He made his international debut when only 18 years old, and shortly afterwards moved to Manchester City. After the Italian failure with Turin, he returned to Manchester United, the club with which he is indelibly associated.

With them he won every major domestic honour, although injury excluded him from the European Cup success of 1968. >> RR1156

Law, William (1686–1761) Clergyman, born in Kingscliffe, Northamptonshire, C England, UK. He studied at Emmanuel College, Cambridge, where he became a fellow (1711), and was ordained, but was forced to resign on refusing to take the oath of allegiance to George I. He wrote several treatises on Christian ethics and mysticism, notably the *Serious Call to a Devout and Holy Life* (1729), which influenced the Wesleys.

Lawes, Henry (1596–1662) Composer, born in Dinton, Wiltshire, S England, UK. He studied with John Coperaria (c.1570–1626), becoming a gentleman of the Chapel Royal (1626) and royal musician for lutes and voices (1631). He set Milton's *Comus* to music, and also Robert Herrick's verses. He was highly regarded by Milton, who sang his praises in a sonnet. >> Herrick; Milton

Lawes, Sir John Bennet (1814–1900) Agriculturist, born in Rothamsted, Hertfordshire, SE England, UK. From his experiments with plants and crops on his estate developed the artificial fertilizer industry. He set up a factory at Deptford Creek in 1842 for the manufacture of his 'superphosphate'. Even more important than this commercial enterprise was his research into agriculture. Aided by his partner **Sir (Joseph) Henry Gilbert** (1817–1901), he founded the Rothamsted Experimental Station in 1843, elevating the study of agriculture to scientific levels.

Lawler, Ray(mond Evenor) (1921–) Playwright, producer, and actor, born in Melbourne, Victoria, Australia. He was a factory-hand at the age of 13, and had several jobs before joining the National Theatre Company in Melbourne. He gained an international reputation from his first major piece of writing, *Summer of the Seventeenth Doll*, a play of the outback, which he produced in 1956, with himself in the leading role. *Kid Stakes* (1975) and *Other Times* (1977) completed the *Doll* trilogy.

Lawrence, St >> **Laurence, St**

Lawrence D(avid) H(erbert Richard) (1885–1930) Novelist, poet, and essayist, born in Eastwood, Nottinghamshire, C England, UK. He studied at University College, Nottingham, and became a schoolmaster, and the moderate success of his first novel, *The White Peacock* (1911), made him leave teaching and turn to writing. In 1912 he eloped with **Frieda Weekley** (née von Richthofen), the wife of Lawrence's professor at Nottingham. They travelled in Germany, Austria, and Italy (1912–13), and married in 1914 after her divorce. Meanwhile Lawrence had secured his success with *Sons and Lovers* (1913). They returned to England at the outbreak of World War 1. In 1915 he published *The Rainbow*, and was prosecuted for obscenity. He left England in 1919, and after three years' residence in Italy, where he produced *Women in Love* (1920), he settled in Mexico, returning to Italy in 1925. *Lady Chatterley's Lover* (1928) was published privately in Florence, and copies were confiscated in England the next year; it was not published in the UK in unexpurgated form until after a sensational obscenity trial in 1960. Some of his most original writing occurs in his poems, notably *Birds, Beast and Flowers* (1923), and in his *Letters* (7 vols, 1979–93). His other major novels include *Aaron's Rod* (1922), *Kangaroo* (1923), and *The Plumed Serpent* (1926), and his collected poems were published in 1928. Many films have been made from his fiction, notably by Ken Russell. >> Russell, Ken

Lawrence, Ernest (Orlando) (1901-58) Physicist, born in Canton, SD. He studied at South Dakota, Minnesota, and Yale universities, and in 1929 constructed the first cyclotron for the production of artificial radioactivity, fundamental to the development of the atomic bomb. He was professor at Berkeley, CA, from 1930, and in 1936 was appointed first director of the radiation laboratory there. He was awarded the Nobel Prize for Physics in 1939. >> Livingston, M S

Lawrence, Geoffrey, 3rd Baron Trevithin and **1st Baron Oaksey** (1880–1971) British lawyer. He studied at Oxford, and was called to the bar in 1906. He became a judge of the High Court of Justice in 1932, a Lord Justice of Appeal in 1944, and a Lord of Appeal in Ordinary in 1947–57. He was president of the International Tribunal for the trial of war criminals at Nuremberg in 1945, and was distinguished for his fair and impartial conduct of the proceedings. Created Baron Oaksey in 1947, he succeeded his brother in the title of Trevithin in 1959.

Lawrence, Jacob (1917–) Painter, born in Atlantic City, NJ. He studied in New York City at the Art Workshop, Harlem, the Harlem Art Center, and the American Artists School (1937–9). Considered a leading African-American artist, he has worked in gouache and tempera. He is famous for the distinctive flat surfaces of his narrative paintings depicting social problems, as may be seen in 'The Migration of the Negro' (1940–1) and 'Struggle: from the History of the American People' (1955).

Lawrence, James (1781–1813) Naval officer, born in Burlington, NJ. He served with distinction in the Tripolitan War, and won a notable victory over the British ship HMS *Peacock* in 1813. He was defeated and mortally wounded in the HMS *Shannon*–USS *Chesapeake* duel the same year. His famous appeal, 'Don't give up the ship', became a rallying cry for US sailors.

Lawrence, Marjorie (Florence) (1908–79) Operatic soprano, born in Deans Marsh, Victoria, Australia. She studied overseas, and made her operatic debut in 1932 with the Monte Carlo Opera, appearing in Paris the following year. She became a leading Wagnerian soprano at the Metropolitan Opera, New York City (1935–9). In 1941 she contracted poliomyelitis, and subsequently made guest appearances at the Metropolitan Opera in a wheelchair. During World War 2 she travelled extensively to entertain the troops, and later took up teaching at the University of Southern Illinois. Her autobiography was filmed as *Interrupted Melody*.

Lawrence, T(homas) E(dward), known as **Lawrence of Arabia** (1888–1935) Soldier, Arabist, and writer, born in Tremadoc, Gwynedd, N Wales, UK. He studied at Oxford, and became a junior member of the British Museum archaeological team at Carchemish, on the Euphrates (1911–14). In World War 1 he worked for army intelligence in North Africa (1914–16), and in 1916 joined the Arab revolt against the Turks, entering Damascus in October 1918. He was a delegate to the Peace Conference, and later became adviser on Arab affairs to the Colonial Office (1921–2). He withdrew from his legendary fame in 1922 and joined the RAF as an aircraftman under the assumed name of **John Hume Ross**. When his identity was discovered, he joined the Royal Tank Corps in 1923 as **T E Shaw**, transferring back to the RAF in 1925. He was discharged in 1935, and was killed in a motor-cycling accident. His major works were *The Seven Pillars of Wisdom* (for private circulation, 1926), *Revolt in the Desert* (1927), *Crusader Castles* (1936), *Oriental Assembly* (1929), and *The Mint* (1936). >> Hussein ibn Ali

Lawrence, Sir Thomas (1769–1830) Portrait painter, born in Bristol, SW England, UK. The son of an innkeeper, as a child he was famed for his pencil portraits, and by the age of 12 he had his own studio in Bath. His full-length portrait of Queen Charlotte, which he painted at the age of 20, is one of his best works. In 1792 he was patronized by George

III, knighted in 1815, and in 1820 succeeded Benjamin West as president of the Royal Academy. >> West, Benjamin

Lawrence of Arabia >> **Lawrence, T E**

Lawry, Bill [loree], popular name of **William Morris Lawry** (1936–) Cricketer, born in Melbourne, Victoria, Australia. He made a reputation as a left-handed batsman and captain. He took part in several mammoth stands, notably one of 382 with R B Simpson at Bridgetown in 1964–5. In all he played 67 times for Australia, scoring 5234 runs, and recording 13 centuries.

Lawson, Henry (1867–1922) Poet, born in Grenfell, New South Wales, Australia, the son of Louisa Lawson. After his parents' separation, he moved to Sydney with his mother and began writing verse, including such bush ballads as 'Andy's Gone with the Cattle' and 'Roaring Days', and his stories, published by *The Bulletin* from 1888, were immensely popular. In 1895 his collection of prose *While the Billy Boils* was published. His work has received little critical acclaim, although his authentic dramatization of the hardship and comradeship of bush life is recognized. For many he is seen as the national poet. He was given a state funeral when he died. >> Lawson, Louisa

Lawson, Louisa (1848–1920) Suffragist and social reformer, born in Mudgee, New South Wales, Australia, and educated to primary level there. She married Norwegian immigrant Niels Larsen (who later anglicized his name) and lived on many New South Wales goldfields throughout their marriage. They separated after 17 years together, and she moved to Sydney, surrounding herself with radical thinkers and social reformers. In 1888 she founded *Dawn*, Australia's first feminist journal, which elevated women's affairs and promoted women's suffrage. Known also for her famous son, Henry, whom she set on the path of writing, she ended her days in Gladesville Hospital for the Insane. >> Lawson, Henry

Lawson (of Blaby), Nigel, Baron (1932–) British statesman, born in London, England, UK. He studied at Oxford, then worked for various newspapers, including *The Financial Times* and the *Daily Telegraph*, where he was city editor, and also for television (1956–72), and during this time edited the *Spectator* (1966–70). Elected to parliament in 1974, when the Conservatives returned to office he became financial secretary to the Treasury (1979–81), energy secretary (1981–3), and Chancellor of the Exchequer (1983–9). During his time at the Exchequer, Britain saw lower direct taxes, but high interest rates and record trade deficits. He was created a life peer in 1992.

Lawton, Tommy (1919–96) Footballer, born in Bolton, Lancashire, NW England, UK. A successful English centre-forward, his most famous days were with Everton and Arsenal, but he also served Burnley, Chelsea, Notts County, and Brentford. Like most of his generation, he lost almost seven years to World War 2, but his international record was a remarkable 22 goals in 23 matches.

Laxness, Halldór (Gu_jónsson Kiljan) (1902–) Novelist, born in Reykjavík. He travelled in Europe and the USA after World War 1, and became a Catholic before going to Canada and the USA (1927–30), where he was converted to Socialism. His major works include *Salka Valka* (1934), a story of Icelandic fishing folk, and the epic *Sjálfstaet Folk* (1934–5, Independent People). He has also written a number of plays, and adapted some of his own novels for the stage. He was awarded the Nobel Prize for Literature in 1955.

Layamon [layamon] (13th-c) Poet and priest, thought to have lived at Areley Kings, Hereford and Worcester, WC England, UK. He wrote (c.1200) an alliterative verse chronicle, *Brut*, a mythical history of England from the landing of Brutus to the final Saxon victory in 689. His source was Wace's *Brut d'Angleterre*, and *Brut* was important in English versification as the first poem written in Middle English. >> Wace

Layton, Irving Peter, originally **Israel Lazarovitch** (1912–) Poet, born in Romania. He moved to Montreal as an infant. While teaching for many years, he participated actively in local poetry movements, and produced much vital, versatile, and controversial poetry. His first collection was *Here and Now* (1945), and *A Red Carpet for the Sun* (1959) won the Governor-General's Award. Later works include *The Shattered Plinths* (1968) and *A Wild Peculiar Joy* (1982).

Lazarsfeld, Paul (Felix) [lahzersfelt] (1901–76) Sociologist, born in Vienna. After studying at Vienna he taught mathematics and physics in a Viennese secondary school, and statistics in the university department of psychology, setting up a social psychology research centre (1927). The Rockefeller Foundation awarded him a scholarship to the USA (1933), where he became a US citizen. He worked at Newark and Princeton universities, and later at Columbia, where he established the Bureau of Applied Social Research (1945). He retired in 1969. An influential quantitative methodologist, he also wrote about popular culture in mass communications.

Lazarus, Emma (1849–87) Writer, born in New York City. She published striking volumes of poems and translations, including *Admetus and Other Poems* (1871), *Songs of a Semite* (1882), and *By the Waters of Babylon* (1887). She also wrote a prose romance, *Alide: an Episode of Goethe's Life* (1874), and a verse tragedy, *The Spagnaletto* (1876). She is best known for her sonnet, 'The New Colossus' (1883), inscribed in a room in the base of the Statue of Liberty in New York harbour.

LBJ >> **Johnson, Lyndon B**

Leach, Archibald >> **Grant, Cary**

Leach, Bernard (Howell) (1887–1979) Studio potter, born in Hong Kong. He studied at the Slade School of Art, London, and went to Japan at the age of 21. There he took up pottery, becoming the sole pupil of Ogata Kenzan (1911–19). He returned to England in 1920, where with Shoji Hamada he established the Leach pottery at St Ives in Cornwall, where he made earthenware and stoneware. He played a crucial role in promoting handmade pottery which could be appreciated as art. From 1932, he taught at Dartington Hall, Devon. His written works include *A Potter's Book* (1940) and *A Potter's Work* (1967). He was made a Companion of Honour in 1973. >> Hamada

Leach, Sir Edmund (Ronald) (1910–89) Social anthropologist, born in Sidmouth, Devon, SW England, UK. He studied mathematics and engineering at Cambridge, and anthropology at the London School of Economics. After the war he took up a post in anthropology at the London School of Economics (1947–53), and published his first major monograph, *Political Systems of Highland Burma* (1954). He then taught at Cambridge (1957–78), becoming professor in 1972, and Provost of King's College (1966–79). His other publications include *Rethinking Anthropology* (1961) and *Social Anthropology* (1982).

Leach, Johnny, popular name of **John Leach** (1922–) Table tennis player, born in Romford, Essex, SE England, UK. He won the world singles title in 1949 and 1951, and was a member of England's winning Swaythling Cup team in 1953. During 12 years as an England international (1947–59), he represented his country 152 times. He became England's non-playing captain upon retirement, and team manager in 1968, retiring in 1970 to concentrate on his sports goods firm.

Leacock, Stephen (Butler) (1869–1944) Writer and humorist, born in Swanmore, Hampshire, S England, UK.

He studied at Toronto, Canada, becoming head of the economics department at McGill University, Montreal (1908). He wrote several books on his subject, including *The Economic Prosperity of the British Empire* (1931), but it is as a humorist that he became widely known. Among his popular works are *Literary Lapses* (1910), *Winsome Winnie* (1920), and *The Garden of Folly* (1924). *The Boy I Left Behind Me*, an unfinished autobiography, was published in 1946.

Leadbelly, nickname of **Huddie Ledbetter** (c. 1885–1949) Folk-blues musician, born in Mooringsport, LA. In his early life he experienced poverty and violence as he drifted through the South. He was imprisoned for murder (1918), pardoned after six years, then imprisoned again for attempted murder (1930). The folklorists John and Alan Lomax secured his release in 1934, and organized a concert tour and recording contract. His songs highlighted the plight of African-Americans during the Depression. He died penniless, although a number of his songs became standards, notably 'Goodnight, Irene'. >> Lomax

Leahy, William (Daniel) [layhee] (1875–1959) US naval officer and public official, born in Hampton, IA. As a naval commander in World War 1, he became a close friend of assistant secretary of the navy Franklin D Roosevelt. He was chief of naval operations (1937–9), ambassador to Vichy, France (1940–42), and chief-of-staff to President Roosevelt (1942–5) and President Truman (1945–9). He took part in virtually all of the top-level Allied war conferences, and became Admiral of the Fleet in 1944. >> Roosevelt, Franklin D

Leakey, L(ouis) S(eymour) B(azett) [leekee] (1903–72) Archaeologist and physical anthropologist, born in Kabete, Kenya. He studied at Cambridge, took part in several archaeological expeditions in East Africa, and became curator of the Coryndon Memorial Museum at Nairobi (1945–61). His great discoveries took place in East Africa, where in 1959, together with his wife, he unearthed the skull of *Zinjanthropus*. In 1964 he found remains of *Homo habilis*, and in 1967 discovered *Kenyapithecus africanus*. He also unearthed evidence of human habitation in California more than 50 000 years old. >> Leakey, Mary/Richard

Leakey, Mary (Douglas) [leekee], *née* Nicol (1913– 96) Archaeologist, born in London, England, UK. She met and married **L S B Leakey** while preparing drawings for his book *Adam's Ancestors* (1934), and moved to Kenya where she undertook pioneering archaeological research (1937–42). She discovered *Proconsul africanus* (1948) at L Victoria, and with her husband found *Zinjanthropus* (1959) in Tanzania. *Homo habilis* was discovered in 1960, and she found fossilized hominid footprints during her excavation at Laetoli in 1976. Her books included *Olduvai Gorge: My Search for Early Man* (1979) and an autobiography, *Disclosing the Past* (1984). >> Leakey, L S B/Richard

Leakey, Richard (Erskine Frere) [leekee] (1944–) Palaeoanthropologist, born in Nairobi, the second son of L S B and Mary Leakey. From an early age he worked in the field with his parents, and with the archaeologist Glynn Isaac on the E shores of L Turkana (1969–75), discovering crania of *Australopithecus boisei* (1969), *Homo habilis* (1972), and *Homo erectus* (1975). He was appointed administrative director (1968) of the National Museum of Kenya, and director (1974). Since 1989 he has been director of the Wildlife and Conservation Management Service, Kenya. His publications include *Origins* (1977) and *The Making of Mankind* (1981), both with Roger Lewin. >> Leakey, L S B/Mary

Lean, Sir David (1908–91) Film director, born in Croydon, S Greater London, England, UK. Beginning as a clapperboard boy, he gradually progressed to become film editor for *Gaumont Sound News* (1930) and *British Movietone News*

(1931–2), before moving on to fictional features. His co-direction with Noel Coward of *In Which We Serve* (1942), led to a full-scale directorial career, including *Blithe Spirit* (1945), *Brief Encounter* (1945), *Great Expectations* (1946), and *Oliver Twist* (1948). He won Oscars for *Bridge on the River Kwai* (1957) and *Lawrence of Arabia* (1962). In 1965 he made *Dr Zhivago*, followed by *Ryan's Daughter* (1970), and *A Passage to India* (1984). In 1990 he was the first non-American recipient of the American Film Institute Life Achievement Award. >> Coward

Lear, Edward (1812–88) Artist and writer, born in London, England, UK. Employed by the Zoological Society of London and the British Museum as an artist, and later by the 13th Earl of Derby, he travelled widely in Europe, making landscape sketches and oil paintings which he published in several travel books, including *Sketches of Rome* (1842) and *Illustrated Excursions in Italy* (1846). He entertained children with nonsense limericks and verse, illustrated by his own sketches, and published as *A Book of Nonsense* (1846). His other humour includes *Nonsense Songs, Stories, Botany, and Alphabets* (1870), *More Nonsense Rhymes* (1871), and *Laughable Lyrics* (1876).

Lear, William P(owell) (1902–78) Inventor and electronic engineer, born in Hannibal, MO. He joined the US navy at 16 to study radio and electronics. His inventive genius resulted in more than 150 patents in the fields of radio, electronics, aviation, and automobile engineering, including the first car radio, the first commercial radio compass for aircraft, and an automatic pilot for jet aircraft. In 1962 he founded Lear Jet Corporation, which became the largest manufacturer of small private jet planes. Lear Motors Corporation was founded in 1967 to introduce steam-powered cars and buses.

Leavis, F(rank) R(aymond) [leevis] (1895–1978) Literary critic, born in Cambridge, Cambridgeshire, EC England, UK. He studied at Cambridge, returning after service in World War 1 to become a lecturer in English at Emmanuel College (1925), and later a fellow of Downing College (1936–52). He edited the journal *Scrutiny* (1932–53), and wrote several major critical works, notably *New Bearings in English Poetry* (1932), *The Great Tradition* (1948), and *The Common Pursuit* (1952). Throughout his work, much of it shared with his wife **Queenie Dorothy Leavis** (1906–91), he stresses the moral value of literary study, and his re-assessments of such major figures as Joseph Conrad and D H Lawrence were to prove extremely influential.

Leavitt, Henrietta Swan (1868–1921) Astronomer, born in Lancaster, MA. She studied at Radcliffe College, and became a volunteer research assistant at Harvard College Observatory. By 1902 she was head of the department of photographic photometry, where her major work was the discovery of the period–luminosity relationship of Cepheid variable stars (1912). This work proved invaluable in establishing the distance scale of the universe.

Lebed, Alexander (Ivanovich) [ljebed] (1950–) General and politician, born in Novocherkassk, Russia. He served in Afghanistan (1981–2) and the Caucasus (1988–90), and became commander of the 14th Army in Moldova in 1992. After retiring from the army in 1995, he entered politics, coming to international attention during the 1996 presidential elections, when he unexpectedly finished third, with 15% of the vote. He then gave his support to Yeltsin, and was appointed National Security Advisor in the new Yeltsin administration. He acted as chief negotiator in the Chechen conflict later in 1996. After what many observers saw as a power struggle within the Kremlin, Yeltsin dismissed him. He then formed the Russian Popular Republican Party, and announced the continuation of his presidential aspirations.

Le Bel, Joseph Achille [luh **bel**] (1847–1930) Chemist, born in Pechelbronn, France. He studied at the Ecole Polytechnique, and the Sorbonne, became an industrial consultant, and continued research on his private estate. In 1874 he published his account of the asymmetric carbon atom, two months after Jacobus van't Hoff's identical but independent work was published, giving Hoff the priority in this fundamental stereochemical concept. >> Hoff

Lebesgue, Henri (Léon) [luh**beg**] (1875–1941) Mathematician, born in Beauvais, France. He studied at the Ecole Normale Supérieure, and taught at Rennes, Poitiers, the Sorbonne, and the Collège de France. Following the work of Emile Borel and René Baire (1874–1932), he developed the theory of measure and integration which bears his name, and applied it to many problems of analysis, in particular to the theory of Fourier series. >> Borel; Fourier, Joseph

LeBlanc, Matt (1967–) Actor, born in Newton, MA. After leaving school, he took several television commercial parts in New York City, then (1988) trained as an actor. He went to Hollywood, where he played a range of television roles before achieving success as Joey Tribbiani in the acclaimed series *Friends* (1994–). Roles in feature films include *Lookin' Italian* (1994), *Ed* (1996), and *Lost in Space* (1997)

Leblanc, Nicolas [luh**blã**] (1742–1806) Chemist and physician, born in Issoudun, France. He trained as a physician, and became surgeon to the future Duke of Orléans in 1780. He devised a cheap, simple process for making sodium carbonate, essential in making glass, soap, and other chemicals. In 1791 he was granted a patent for his invention, and built a factory for its production. However, his factory was confiscated by the Revolutionary leaders in 1793 (it had been financed by the Duke), and although it was returned to him in 1802 by Napoleon, he had no money to continue, and committed suicide. His process continued to be used on a large scale for a century.

Lebow, Fred (1932–94) US marathon runner and organizer, born in Romania. He emigrated to the USA in 1951, joined the New York Road Runners Club in 1968, and became club president in 1972. By obtaining sponsorship, attracting big name runners, and international television, he turned the New York Marathon into a major event and the prototype for other city marathons. >> Brasher; RR1142

Lebrun, Albert [luh**brõe**] (1871–1950) French statesman, born in Mercy-le-Haut, France. A mining engineer, he studied at the Ecole Polytechnique and the Ecole Nationale Supérieure des Mines. He became a deputy (left-wing Republican) in 1900, minister for the colonies (1911–14), minister for blockade and liberated regions (1917–19), senator (1920), and president of the Senate (1931). The last president of the Third Republic, he surrendered his powers to Pétain in 1940, and went into retirement. >> Pétain

Le Brun, Charles [luh **brõe**] (1619–90) Painter and designer, born in Paris. He studied in Rome for four years under Poussin and Vouet, and for nearly 40 years (1647–83) exercised a despotic influence over French art and artists. He is usually considered to be the founder of the French school of painting. He helped to found the Academy of Painting and Sculpture in 1648, and was the first director of the Gobelins tapestry works in 1662. From 1668 to 1683 he was employed by Louis XIV in the decoration of Versailles. >> Le Vau; Poussin, Nicolas; Vouet

Le Carré, John [luh **ka**ray], pseudonym of **David John Moore Cornwell** (1931–) Novelist, born in Poole, Dorset, S England, UK. He studied at Bern and Oxford universities, taught French and German for two years at Eton, then went into the British Foreign Service as second secretary in

Bonn, and consul in Hamburg. He resigned in 1964 to become a full-time writer. His first published novel, *Call for the Dead* (1961, filmed as *The Deadly Affair*, 1967), introduced his 'anti-hero' George Smiley, who appears in most of his stories. His many popular works include *The Spy Who Came in from the Cold* (1963, Somerset Maugham Award, later filmed), *Tinker, Tailor, Soldier, Spy* (1974, televised 1979), *The Honourable Schoolboy* (1977, James Tait Black), *Smiley's People* (1980, televised 1982), *The Little Drummer Girl* (1983, filmed 1985), *The Russia House* (1989, filmed 1991), *Our Game* (1995), and *The Tailor of Panama* (1996).

Le Chatelier, Henry >> **Chatelier, Henry le**

Lecky, William Edward Hartpole (1838–1903) Historian and philosopher, born in Newton Park, near Dublin. He studied at Trinity College, Dublin, and in 1861 published anonymously *The Leaders of Public Opinion in Ireland* – four essays on Swift, Flood, Grattan, and O'Connell. His other works include *History of England in the 18th Century* (1878–90), *Democracy and Liberty* (1896), and *The Map of Life* (1899). He became MP for Dublin University in 1895, and a privy councillor in 1897.

Leclanché, Georges [luhklǎshay] (1839–82) Chemist, born in Paris. An engineer by training, he gave up work to devote his time on his invention of the *Leclanché battery* (1866), now in a slightly modified form known as a *dry-cell battery*. The Belgian telegraph service made use of it, and he opened a factory for its production.

Le Clerc, Jacques-Philippe [luh klairk], also known as **Philippe-Marie, viscomte de Hauteclocque** or **Jacques-Philippe Leclerc de Hauteclocque** (1902–47) French general and war-time hero, born in Belloy-Saint-Leonard, France. He trained at St Cyr (1924), and in World War 2 served in France (1939–40). Captured twice during the German invasion, he escaped on both occasions, and joined the Free French forces under Charles de Gaulle in England. He became military commander in French Equatorial Africa, and led a force across the desert to join the British 8th Army in 1942. He commanded the French 2nd Armoured Division in Normandy, and liberated Paris in 1944. >> de Gaulle

Leconte de Lisle, Charles Marie René [luhkŏt duh leel] (1818–94) French poet, born on Réunion. After some years of travel he settled down to a literary life in Paris. He exercised a profound influence on younger poets, headed the school called *Parnassiens*, and succeeded to Victor Hugo's chair at the Academy in 1886. His works include *Poésies complètes* (1858), *Poèmes barbares* (1862), and *Poèmes tragiques* (1884). >> Hugo

Lecoq, Jacques [luhkok] (1921–) Mime artist and director, born in Paris. He was an actor with the Compagnie des Comédiens in Grenoble (1945), teacher-director with the Padua University Theatre, Italy (1948), and a member of the Piccolo Theatre in Milan (1951). In 1956 he returned to Paris and established the Ecole Internationale de Mime et de Théâtre. He formed his own company in 1959, and began his research into the various theatrical genres in terms of the actor's physical movement on the stage.

Le Corbusier [luh kaw(r)büsyay], pseudonym of **Charles Edouard Jeanneret** (1887–1965) Architect and artist, born in La Chaux-de-Fonds, Switzerland. He left school at age 13 to learn the trade of engraving watch faces. Encouraged by a local art teacher he taught himself architecture, travelling throughout Europe to observe architectural styles. Settling in Paris in 1917, he met Ozenfant, who introduced him to Purism, and with whom he collaborated in writing several articles under his pseudonym (the name of a relative on his father's side). His main interest was large urban projects and city-planning. Many of his designs were rejected, but they influenced other architects throughout

the world. Examples of his work are the Unité d'habitation, Marseille (1945–50); Chandigarh, the new capital of the Punjab; the Swiss Dormitory in the Cité Universitaire in Paris; and the Exposition Pavilion in Zürich. >> Behrens; Niemeyer; Ozenfant

Ledbetter, Huddie >> **Leadbelly**

Lederberg, Joshua [layderberg] (1925–) Biologist and geneticist, born in Montclair, NJ. He studied biology at Columbia and became professor at Wisconsin (1947–59), Stanford (1959–78), and president of Rockefeller University (1978–90). With Edward Tatum he demonstrated that bacteria can reproduce by a sexual process, thus founding the science of bacterial genetics. He also discovered the process allowing the possibility of genetic engineering. He shared the Nobel Prize for Physiology or Medicine in 1958. >> Beadle; Tatum, Edward L

Lederman, Leon M(ax) [layderman] (1922–) Physicist, born in New York City. He taught and carried out research at Columbia (1951–79), before becoming director of the Fermi National Accelerator Laboratory (1979–89). He shared the 1988 Nobel Prize with Melvin Schwartz (1932–) and Jack Steinberger for their discovery (1960–2) of a new subatomic particle, the muon neutrino. A prolific researcher in particle physics, he retired from Fermi to teach at the University of Chicago in 1989. >> Steinberger

Ledoux, Claude Nicolas [luhdoo] (1736–1806) Architect, born in Dormans-sur-Marne, France. As architect to Louis XVI, his major works include the Château at Louveciennes for Madame du Barry (1771–3), and the Saltworks at Arc-et-Senans (1775–80). In 1785 he was employed by the Fermes-Général to erect 60 tax buildings around Paris, though only a few were built. >> du Barry

Le Duc Tho [lay duhk toh], originally **Phan Dinh Khai** (1911–90) Vietnamese politician, born in Ninh Province, Vietnam. He joined the Communist Party of Indo-China (1929), was exiled by the French (1930–7), and re-arrested and imprisoned (1939–44). After World War 2, he worked for the Communist Party of Vietnam (CPV), entering its Politburo in 1955. For his actions as leader of the Vietnamese delegation to the Paris Conference on Indo-China (1968–73), he was awarded the 1973 Nobel Prize for Peace jointly with Henry Kissinger, but declined to accept it. >> Kissinger

Lee, Andrew >> **Auchinloss, Louis Stanton**

Lee, Ann, known as **Mother Ann** (1736–84) Religious mystic, born in Manchester, Greater Manchester, NW England, UK. In 1758 she joined the 'Shaking Quakers', or 'Shakers', who saw in her the second coming of Christ. Imprisoned in 1770 for street-preaching, she emigrated with her followers to the USA in 1774, and in 1776 founded the parent Shaker settlement.

Lee, Charles (1731–82) American revolutionary soldier, born in Dernhall, Cheshire, NWC England, UK. He went to America in 1773, and joined the Continental army as a major-general at the outbreak of the War of Independence. Captured by the British in 1776, he proposed to them a secret plan for defeating the Americans. Released in an exchange of prisoners in 1778, he was dismissed in 1780.

Lee, Christopher (1922–) Film actor, born in London, England, UK. His gaunt appearance and sinister image led to acclaimed performances in *Dracula* (1958) and its sequels, as well as in a range of other horror movies. Later films include *The Three Musketeers* and its sequel (1973, 1989), *Gremlins 2* (1990), *Funny Man* (1994), and *The Stupids* (1996).

Lee, David M (1931– Physicist, born in Rye, NY. He studied at Yale, then worked at Cornell University, where along with Richardson and Osherhoff in 1972 he contributed to the discovery of the superfluidity of helium-3. They shared the Nobel Prize for Physics in 1996 >> Osherhoff; Richardson, Robert C

Lee, Gypsy Rose, originally **Louise Rose Hovick** (1914–70) Stripper, actress, and writer, born in Seattle, WA. Starting as a four-year-old in vaudeville with her sister, she became the best-known stripper of the 1930s. She made some films (at first as **Louise Hovick**), and wrote two mystery stories as well as an autobiography that was the basis of the musical, *Gypsy*. Stylish and witty, she was briefly (1966) a talk-show host.

Lee, (Nelle) Harper (1926–) Novelist, born in Monroeville, AL. She studied at the University of Alabama, and spent a year at Oxford before becoming a full-time writer. Her first and only novel, *To Kill a Mockingbird* (1960, filmed 1962), a story of racial prejudice set in a Southern town, received a Pulitzer Prize.

Lee, James (Paris) (1831–1904) Inventor, born in Hawick, Scottish Borders, SE Scotland, UK. He emigrated with his parents to Canada, later going from Ontario to Hartford, CT. The *Lee-Enfield* and *Lee-Metford* rifles are based in part on his designs. >> Metford

Lee (of Ashridge), Jennie Lee, Baroness (1904–88) British stateswoman, born in Lochgelly, Fife, E Scotland, UK. She studied at Edinburgh University, and, as a Labour MP for North Lanark at the age of 24, became the youngest member of the House of Commons. A dedicated Socialist, she married Aneurin Bevan (1934). Appointed Britain's first arts minister in 1964, she doubled government funding for the arts, and was instrumental in setting up the Open University. In 1970 she retired from the House of Commons to be made a life peer. She published two autobiographies, *Tomorrow Is a New Day* (1939) and *My Life with Nye* (1980). >> Bevan, Aneurin

Lee, Laurie (1914–97) Writer, born in Slad, Gloucestershire, SWC England, UK. He was educated at the village school there, and worked as a scriptwriter for documentary films during the 1940s. His poetic works included *The Sun My Monument* (1944) and *My Many-Coated Man* (1955). His books *Cider With Rosie* (1959), *As I Walked Out One Midsummer Morning* (1969), and *I Can't Stay Long* (1975) are widely acclaimed for their evocation of a rural childhood and of life in the many countries he had visited. His last book, *A Moment of War* (1991), recalls his experiences during the Spanish Civil War.

Lee, Ming Cho (1930–) Set designer and water colourist, born in Shanghai, China. After early education in Shanghai and Hong Kong, he attended Occidental College in Los Angeles, CA. He served a five-year apprenticeship with Jo Mielziner, and beginning in 1958 went on to make a name for himself with his imaginative sets for scores of productions on and off Broadway, as well as in opera and dance. For many years he was the principal designer for the New York Shakespeare Festival. He has also designed the interiors of theatres and has exhibited his water colours. >> Mielziner, Jo

Lee, Nathaniel (c. 1649–92) English playwright. He studied at Cambridge, failed as an actor because of stagefright, and produced nine or ten tragedies between 1675 and 1682. His best-known play is *The Rival Queens* (1677), and with Dryden he wrote *Oedipus* (1678), and *The Duke of Guise* (1682). >> Dryden

Lee, Robert E(dward) (1807–70) Confederate general, born in Stratford, VA. He trained at West Point, and in the Mexican War became chief engineer of the central army in Mexico (1846). He commanded the US Military Academy (1852–5), was a cavalry officer on the Texan border (1855–9), and in 1861 was made commander-in-chief of the Virginia forces. He was in charge of the defences at Richmond, and defeated Federal forces in the Seven Days' Battles (1862). His

strategy in opposing General Pope, his invasion of Maryland and Pennsylvania, and other achievements are central to the history of the war. In 1865, he surrendered his army to General Grant at Appomattox Courthouse. After the war, he became President of Washington College at Lexington. >> Grant, Ulysses; Pope, John; Sheridan, Philip H; Stuart,

Lee, Spike, popular name of **Shelton Jackson Lee** (1957–) Film-maker, born in Atlanta, GA. At New York University's Institute of Film and Television he gained artistic recognition and a student Oscar for his graduation film, *Joe's Bed-Study Barbershop: We Cut Heads* (1982). *She's Gotta Have It* (1986) established him internationally. Later films, centred around African-American culture, include *School Daze* (1988), *Do the Right Thing* (1989), *Mo' Better Blues* (1990), and *Get on the Bus* (1996).

Lee, Tsung Dao (1926–) Physicist, born in Shanghai, China. He studied at Zhejiang University, won a scholarship to Chicago University in 1946, became a lecturer at the University of California, and from 1956 was professor at Columbia University, as well as a member of the Institute for Advanced Study (1960–3). With Chen Ning Yang he disproved the parity principle, till then considered a fundamental physical law, and they shared the Nobel Prize for Physics in 1957. >> Yang, Chen Ning

Lee, Vernon, pseudonym of **Violet Paget** (1856–1935) Writer, born in Boulogne, France. She travelled widely in her youth and settled in Florence. Studies of Italian and Renaissance art were followed by her philosophical study, *The Beautiful* (1913). She also wrote a collection of essays, and more than 30 books, including *Miss Brown* (3 vols, 1884), *Vital Lies* (1912), and a dramatic trilogy, *Satan the Waster* (1920), giving full rein to her pacifism.

Leech, John (1817–64) Caricaturist, born in London, England, UK. He was educated at Charterhouse, and then studied medicine, but turned to art after publishing *Etchings and Sketchings, By A Pen, Esq* (1835). From 1841 he contributed hundreds of sketches of middle-class life and political cartoons to *Punch*, as well as to the *Illustrated London News* (1856) and *Once a Week* (1859–62). He illustrated several books, including Dickens's *A Christmas Carol* and the sporting novels of R S Surtees.

Leeds, Thomas Osborne, Duke of, also known as **Earl of Danby** (1632–1712) English statesman, the son of a Yorkshire baronet. He entered parliament in 1661, and in 1674 became the Earl of Danby. Against Roman Catholics and Dissenters, he used his influence to secure the marriage of Princess Mary and William of Orange (1677), and negotiated with Louis XIV for bribes to Charles II. He was impeached and imprisoned (1678–84), and in 1688 signed the invitation to William of Orange to seize power from James II. He was rewarded by being made Marquess of Carmarthen and President of the Council, and was created Duke of Leeds in 1694. >> William III

Lee Kuan Yew [lee kwan yoo] (1923–) Singaporean statesman and prime minister (1959–90), born in Singapore City. He studied law at Cambridge and qualified as a barrister in London before returning to Singapore in 1951 to practise. He founded the moderate, anti-Communist People's Action Party in 1954, and entered the Singapore Legislative Assembly in 1955. He became the country's first prime minister in 1959, remained in power for 31 years, and oversaw a successful programme of economic development. He resigned as premier at the end of 1990, but remained in the government as senior minister in the premier's office. >> RR1087

Leese, Sir Oliver (William Hargreaves) (1894–1978) British soldier. He won the DSO in World War 1, and in 1939 became deputy chief-of-staff of the British Expeditionary Force in France. In 1942 he was promoted lieutenant-general, commanded an army corps from El Alamein to Sicily, where he succeeded Montgomery as commander of the Eighth Army, and in November 1944 commanded an army group in Burma. He was appointed Lieutenant of the Tower of London in 1954.

Lee Teng-hui [lee teng wee] (1923–) Taiwanese politician and president (1988–), born in Tamsui, Taiwan. He studied at universities in the USA and Japan, taught economics at the National Taiwan University, and became Mayor of Taipei in 1979. A member of the ruling Kuomintang party, and a protégé of Jiang Jingguo, he became vice-president of Taiwan in 1984, and state president and Kuomintang leader on Jiang's death in 1988. >> Jiang Jingguo; RR1092

Leeuwenhoek, Antonie van [**lay**venhook] (1632–1723) Microscopist, born in Delft, The Netherlands. A clerk in an Amsterdam cloth warehouse until 1650, he returned to Delft, where he made a series of discoveries in relation to the circulation of the blood. He also first detected the fibres of the crystalline lens, the fibrils and striping of muscle, the structure of ivory and hair, the scales of the epidermis, and the distinctive characters of rotifers. >> Harvey, William

Lefanu, Nicola >> **Maconchy, Elizabeth**

Le Fanu, (Joseph) Sheridan [**lef**uhnyoo] (1814–73) Writer and journalist, born in Dublin. He studied at Trinity College, Dublin, and was called to the bar in 1839, but soon abandoned law for journalism. He began writing for the *Dublin University Magazine*, of which he became editor and proprietor (1869), and later bought three Dublin newspapers. Of his 14 novels, the best-known are *The House by the Churchyard* (1863) and *Uncle Silas* (1864).

Lefebvre, Marcel [luh**fair**bruh] (1905–91) Leader of a 'traditionalist' schismatic group within the Roman Catholic Church, born in Tourcoing, France. He studied at the French Seminary in Rome and was ordained in 1929. In the 1930s he was a missionary in Gabon, and became Archbishop of Dakar, Senegal (1948–62). In 1970, objecting to the modernized form of the Catholic liturgy, he formed the 'Priestly Cofraternity of Pius X', and was suspended in 1976. He defied the suspension, and was excommunicated by Pope John Paul II in 1988, thus producing the first formal schism within the Roman Catholic Church since 1870.

Lefrak, Samuel J(ayson) [**lef**rak] (1918–) Real estate developer, born in New York City. He joined his father's Brooklyn construction firm, expanding the Lefrak Organization (as president from 1948 and chairman from 1975) through the construction of such major housing, industrial, and commercial developments as King's Bay Houses, Brooklyn (1957), Lefrak City, Queens (1960), and later urban renewal projects. The owner of 94 000 New York apartments, he was long the City's largest private residential landlord.

Lefschetz, Solomon [**lef**shets] (1884–1972) Mathematician, born in Moscow. He studied engineering in Paris before emigrating to the USA. After losing both his hands in an industrial accident (1910), he was forced to abandon engineering, and turned to mathematics. He took his doctorate in 1911, taught at Kansas University (1913–25), and studied topology at Princeton (1925–53), becoming the leading topologist of his generation in the USA.

Le Gallienne, Eva [luh **gal**yuhn] (1899–1991) Stage actress, born in London, England, UK, the daughter of Richard Le Gallienne. Making her stage debut in London at 15, she moved to the USA the next year and thereafter spent most of her professional career in America, both as a versatile actress in serious plays and as a director and producer. She founded the Civic Repertory Theater in New York City (1926–32), and later the American Repertory Theater Company. In addition to translations and stage adaptations, she published her memoirs and a study of Eleonora Duse. >> Le Gallienne, Richard

Le Gallienne, Richard [luh **gal**yuhn] (1866–1947) Writer, born in Liverpool, NW England, UK, the father of Eva Le Gallienne. In 1891 he became a London journalist, but later lived in New York City. He published many volumes of prose and verse, the best of which are *Quest of the Golden Girl* (1896), *The Romantic Nineties* (1926), and *From a Paris Garret* (1936). >> Le Gallienne, Eva

Legat, Nicolay (1869–1937) Dancer, ballet master, and choreographer, born in St Petersburg, Russia. He trained at the Imperial Ballet School (1888), joined the Maryinsky Theatre, where he was a principal for 20 years, and became director there in 1905. His pupils included Nijinsky. In 1923 he moved to the USA to become ballet master of Diaghilev's company, and finally settled in London, where he established his own school and taught, among others, Margot Fonteyn. >> Diaghilev; Fonteyn; Nijinsky

Legendre, Adrien-Marie [luh**zhãdr**] (1752–1833) Mathematician, born in Paris. He studied at the Collège Mazarin, became professor of mathematics at the Ecole Militaire (1775–80), a member of the Académie des Sciences (1783), and professor at the Ecole Normale (1795). He made major contributions to number theory and elliptical functions, but due to the jealousy of his colleague Laplace, he received little recognition or reward for his work. >> Laplace

Léger, Fernand [**lay**zhay] (1881–1955) Painter, born in Argentan, France. He studied in Paris, and helped to form the Cubist movement, but later developed his own 'aesthetic of the machine' as seen in 'Contrast of Forms' (1913, Philadelphia). He also designed theatre sets, taught at Yale University, and painted murals for the UN building in New York (1952). He collaborated on the first 'art-film', *Le Ballet mécanique*, in 1923, and there is a museum dedicated to his work at Biot on the Côte d'Azur.

Legge, Walter (1906–79) Record producer, a major figure in the European classical record industry, and founder of the Philharmonia Symphony Orchestra, born in London, England, UK. He engaged Fischer-Dieskau, Nicolai Gedda, and his future wife Elisabeth Schwarzkopf for a series of classic recordings of opera under equally famous conductors, and was responsible for the revival of interest in Lieder. >> Fischer-Dieskau; Schwarzkopf, Elisabeth

Legros, Alphonse [luh**groh**] (1837–1911) Painter, born in Dijon, France. After successes with early works in Paris, he moved to London in 1863, and by 1875 was in charge of the etching class at the Royal College. Appointed professor at University College (1875–6), he exercised a strong traditional influence. He produced over 750 etchings, and was noted for his original portraiture, and for his landscape and figure studies.

Le Guin, Ursula [luh gween], *née* **Kroeber** (1929–) Science fiction writer, born in Berkeley, CA. She studied at Radcliffe College and Columbia University, and became a prolific writer both for adults and children. Her 'Hain' novels include *Rocannon's World* (1966) and *The Left Hand of Darkness* (1969). Her 'Earth Sea' trilogy includes *A Wizard of Earthsea* (1968), *The Tombs of Atuan* (1971), and *The Farthest Shore* (1972). Later works include the children's book *Tehanu* (1990).

Lehár, Franz [luh**hah(r)**] (1870–1948) Composer, born in Komárom, Hungary. He studied at the Prague Conservatory, became a conductor in Vienna and wrote a violin concerto, but is best known for his operettas, including *The Count of Luxembourg* (1909), *The Land of Smiles* (1929), and his internationally acclaimed *The Merry Widow* (1905).

Lehman, Adele Lewisohn [**lay**man] (1882–1965) Philanthropist, art collector, and painter, born in New York

City. She studied at Barnard College, and married Arthur Lehman, an investment banker (1901). She became active in the Federation of Jewish Philanthropies, of which he was a founder, and after he died she founded the Arthur Lehman Counselling Service to help people needing psychiatric services. Her philanthropies extended to many activities, from the women's suffrage movement to handicapped children. She and her husband collected Italian art works, many of which became part of various museum collections. She also painted landscapes and still-lifes.

Lehman, Herbert (Henry) [layman] (1878–1963) Banker, politician, and philanthropist, born in New York City. He became a partner in his family's banking business in 1908, and served the government in various capacities during World War 1. He was Lieutenant Governor (1929–33) then Governor of New York (1933–42), and combined fiscal benefits with Liberal legislation. During World War 2 he directed the UN Relief and Rehabilitation Administration (1943–6). He served as a Democrat in the US Senate (1949–57), and was outspoken in his opposition to McCarthyism and in support of civil rights. Among his various philanthropies were child welfare and Jewish resettlement programmes. >> McCarthy, Joseph R

Lehman, Robert [layman] (1891–1969) Banker and art collector, born in New York City. He studied at Yale, joined the family banking business, Lehman Brothers (1919), and became principal partner (1921–64). He financed a variety of major enterprises, such as department stores, airlines, and film and television companies. A generous art patron, his art collection – strong in Gothic tapestries and European paintings – was donated to the Metropolitan Museum of Art in 1969, where it is displayed in a replica of his New York apartment.

Lehmann, Beatrix [layman] (1903–79) Actress, born in Bourne End, Buckinghamshire, SC England, UK, the sister of John and Rosamond Lehmann. Her stage debut was at the Lyric, Hammersmith, in London (1924), and thereafter she appeared in many successful plays. In 1946 she became director-producer of the Arts Council Midland Theatre Company. She also appeared in films, and wrote two novels and several short stories. >> Lehmann, John Frederick/ Rosamond

Lehmann, John (Frederick) [layman] (1907–87) Writer and publisher, born in Bourne End, Buckinghamshire, SC England, UK. He studied at Cambridge, and founded the periodical New Writing (1936–41). He was managing director of the Hogarth Press, and with his sister, Rosamond, ran John Lehmann Ltd (1946–53). In 1954 he inaugurated the London Magazine, which he edited until 1961. His works include Forty Poems (1942), Virginia Woolf and her World (1975), and Rupert Brooke (1980). >> Lehmann, Beatrix/ Rosamond

Lehmann, Lilli [layman] (1848–1929) Soprano, born in Würzburg, Germany. She was taught singing by her mother, and made her debut at Prague in 1865. She sang in Danzig, Lepzig, London, New York City, and elsewhere, and took part in the first performance of Wagner's Ring (1876) at Bayreuth.

Lehmann, Lotte [layman] (1888–1976) Soprano, born in Perleberg, Germany (no relation to Lilli Lehmann). She studied in Berlin, made her debut in Hamburg in 1910, and sang at the Vienna Staatsoper (1914–38). She also appeared frequently at Covent Garden and at the New York Metropolitan, and was noted particularly for her performances in operas by Richard Strauss, including two premieres. She took US nationality, and in 1951 retired to Santa Barbara.

Lehmann, Rosamond (Nina) [layman] (1901–90) Novelist, born in Bourne End, Buckinghamshire, SC England, UK.

She studied at Cambridge, which provided the background for her first novel, Dusty Answer (1927). Other novels include Invitation to the Waltz (1932), The Echoing Grove (1953), and A Sea-Grape Tree (1970), and she also wrote a play, a volume of short stories, and the autobiographical The Swan in the Evening (1967). She later became president of the College of Psychic Studies. >> Lehmann, Beatrix/ John

Leibl, Wilhelm [liybl] (1844–1900) Painter, born in Cologne, Germany. He studied in Paris, being much influenced by Courbet's Realism, and later worked in Munich. Most of his paintings are genre scenes of Bavaria and the lower Alps, although he painted a number of portraits, notably 'Three Women in a Church' (1878–82, Kunsthalle). >> Courbet

Leibniz, Gottfried Wilhelm [liybnits] (1646–1716) Philosopher and mathematician, born in Leipzig, Germany. He studied there and at Altdorf, spent time in Paris and London, and in 1676 became librarian to the Duke of Brunswick at Hanover. He also travelled in Austria and Italy, and went in 1700 to persuade Frederick I of Prussia to found the Prussian Academy of Sciences in Berlin, of which he became the first president. A man of remarkable breadth of knowledge, he made original contributions to optics, mechanics, statistics, logic, and probability theory. He conceived the idea of calculating machines, and of a universal language. He wrote on history, law, and political theory, and his philosophy was the foundation of 18th-c Rationalism. He was involved in a controversy with Isaac Newton over whether he or Newton was the inventor of integral and differential calculus; the Royal Society formally declared for Newton in 1711, but the matter was never really resolved. Unpopular with George of Hanover, he was left behind in 1714 when the Elector moved his court to London (as George I). He died in Hanover two years later, without real recognition and with almost all his work unpublished. >> Bernoulli, Jacques

Leicester, Robert Dudley, Earl of [lester], also known as **Baron Denbigh** and **Sir Robert Dudley** (c.1532–88) Nobleman, the favourite and possibly the lover of Elizabeth I. He became Master of the Horse, Knight of the Garter, a privy councillor, baron, and finally Earl of Leicester (1564). He continued to receive favour in spite of his unpopularity at court and a secret marriage in 1573 to the Dowager Lady Sheffield. In 1578 he bigamously married the widow of Walter, Earl of Essex, yet Elizabeth was only temporarily offended. In 1585 he commanded the expedition to the Low Countries, but was recalled for incompetence in 1587. He was nonetheless appointed in 1588 to command the forces against the Spanish Armada. >> Elizabeth I

Leicester (of Holkham), Thomas William Coke, Earl of [lester, holkam] (1752–1842) Agriculturist, born in London, England, UK. He studied at Eton, and became one of the first agriculturists of England. People visited his estate from all over the world, and special meetings were held at sheep clipping time – called Coke's Clippings – the last of which took place in 1821, lasting three days and attracting 7000 visitors. He became MP for Norfolk at 21, holding the seat for 57 years, and was the one who brought forward the motion to recognize the independence of the American Colonies.

Leichhardt, (Friedrich Wilhelm) Ludwig [liykhhah(r)t] (1813–c.1848) Naturalist and explorer, born in Trebatsch, Germany. He studied at the universities of Berlin and Göttingen, arrived in Sydney in 1842, and mounted an important expedition from Brisbane heading NW in 1844. He had been presumed lost when his arrival back in Sydney in March 1846 caused great excitement. He was forced to turn back from his next expedition, and in 1848 set off on a third trans-continental journey, from which he and his party disappeared without trace. By this time he had become a national hero, and searches were mounted for nearly a century afterwards. >> Burke, Robert O'Hara; Mountford

Leif Eriksson [layv erikson] (fl. 1000) Icelandic explorer, the son of Erik the Red, the first European to reach America. He introduced Christianity to Greenland, and c.1000 discovered land which he named *Vinland* after the vines he found growing there. It is still uncertain where Vinland actually is and whether he was indeed the first to find it. Two Icelandic sagas, *Eiríks Saga* and *Groenlendinga Saga*, tell the story of the Norse discovery and attempted colonization of North America, 500 years before Christopher Columbus arrived in the area. >> Columbus; Erik the Red

Leigh, Mike [lee] (1943–) Playwright and theatre director, born in Salford, Greater Manchester, NW England, UK. He has scripted a distinctive genre based on actors' improvizations around given themes. His most successful work for the theatre has had a second life on film, as in *Bleak Moments* (1970), and on television, as in *Abigail's Party* (1977). Later films include *Life is Sweet* (1990), *Naked* (1993), and *Secrets and Lies* (1996) which won the 1996 Cannes Palme d'Or and received Oscar nominations for best director and best screenplay.

Leigh, Vivien [lee], originally **Vivian Hartley** (1913–67) Actress, born in Darjeeling, India. She had a convent education, then studied at the Royal Academy of Dramatic Art, London. She became an overnight sensation in the comedy *The Mask of Virtue* (1935). She married Laurence Olivier in 1940, and appeared opposite him in numerous classical plays, including *Romeo and Juliet* and *Antony and Cleopatra*. She is best remembered for her Oscar-winning performance as Scarlett O'Hara in the film *Gone With the Wind* (1939). Manic depression and ill health marred her career and her marriage, and she was divorced from Olivier in 1961. >> Olivier

Leigh-Mallory, Sir Trafford [lee] (1892–1944) British air force officer, born in Cheshire, NWC England, UK. He studied at Oxford, and served with the Royal Flying Corps in World War 1. In World War 2 he commanded groups in Fighter Command in the Battle of Britain. He was commander-in-chief of Fighter Command (1942–4), and of Allied expeditionary air forces for the Normandy landings (1944). He was killed in an aircraft accident en route to his new appointment as commander-in-chief of Allied air forces in SE Asia.

Leigh-Pemberton, Robert (Robin) Leigh-Pemberton, Baron [lee pemberton] (1927–) Banker, born in Sittingbourne, Kent, SE England, UK. He studied at Oxford, practised as a lawyer (1954–60), and in 1965 qualified as a chartered accountant. He was a Kent county councillor (1961–77), and also served as a member of several national committees of enquiry. A director then chairman (1977–83) of the National Westminster Bank, he became Governor of the Bank of England in 1983. He was created a life peer in 1993.

Leighton (of Stretton), Frederic Leighton, Baron [laytn] (1830–96) Painter, born in Scarborough, North Yorkshire, N England, UK. He studied and travelled extensively in Europe, and had success in 1855 with his 'Cimabue's Madonna Carried in Procession through Florence'. Several of his paintings became mass best sellers in photogravure reproduction, and he also won distinction as a sculptor. He was made a member of the Royal Academy in 1869, and president in 1878, when he was also knighted. In 1886 he was made a baronet, and a baron just before he died.

Leighton, Kenneth [laytn] (1929–88) Composer and pianist, born in Wakefield, West Yorkshire, N England, UK. After graduating from Oxford, he studied composition in Rome. He taught composition at Edinburgh University from 1956, and from 1970 was professor of music there. His works include choral music, piano concertos, three symphonies, organ and chamber music, and an opera, *Columba* (1981).

Leighton, Margaret [laytn] (1922–76) Actress, born at Barnt Green, West Midlands, C England, UK. She made her stage debut at the Birmingham Repertory Theatre (1938), later joining the Old Vic. Throughout her career she worked regularly in London and on Broadway, making numerous stage, screen, and television appearances. She won Tony Awards for *Separate Tables* (1956) and *The Night of the Iguana* (1962). For *The Go-Between* (1970) she received the award of best supporting actress from the British Society of Film and Television Arts, and won an Emmy for her performance in a television production of *Hamlet* (1970).

Leighton, Robert [laytn] (1611–84) Clergyman, probably born in London, England, UK. He studied at Edinburgh University, spent some years in France, and was ordained in 1641, signing the Covenant two years later. In 1653 he was appointed Principal of Edinburgh University. Soon after the Restoration he was made one of Charles II's new Scottish bishops, and in 1669 he became Archbishop of Glasgow. >> Charles II (of England)

Leino, Eino [leenoh], pseudonym of **Armas Eino Leopold Lönnbohm** (1878–1926) Poet, born in Paltamo, Finland. He studied at Helsinki, and went into journalism as a literary critic. He developed the *Kalevala* metre into a distinctive style of his own, notably in *Helkavirsiä* (1903–16, Whitsongs). He also wrote novels, and made fine translations of classics, including those of Dante and Goethe.

Leinsdorf, Erich [liynzdaw(r)f] (1912–93) Conductor, born in Vienna. After musical studies in Vienna, he became an assistant to Bruno Walter and Toscanini at the Salzburg Festival (1934–7). He moved to New York City in 1938 to conduct at the Metropolitan Opera, and was acclaimed especially for his Wagner. He conducted the Rochester Philharmonic (1947–56), the New York City Opera and Metropolitan (1955–62), and the Boston Symphony (1962–9), the latter his most notable years. He then guest-conducted widely. >> Toscanini; Walter, Bruno

Leiris, Michel [lairees] (1901–90) Writer and anthropologist, born in Paris. After an early involvement with the Surrealist movement (1925–9), he joined the trans-African Dakar–Djibouti expedition (1931–3). He returned to study, combining anthropology with a distinguished career as a literary and art critic. His major works include *L'Afrique Fantôme* (1934, Phantom Africa), and the autobiographical *L'Age d'homme* (1963, Manhood).

Leishman, Sir William Boog [leeshman] (1865–1926) Bacteriologist, born in Glasgow, W Scotland, UK. He became professor of pathology in the Army Medical College, and director-general of the Army Medical Service (1923). He discovered an effective vaccine for inoculation against typhoid, and was also the first to discover the parasite of the disease kala-azar. The bacterium which causes the disease *leishmaniasis* is named after him.

Lejeune, John A(rcher) [luhzhoon] (1867–1942) Marine officer, born in Pointe Coupee Parish, LA. He trained at the US Naval Academy in 1888, served in Panama and the Philippines, and in 1914 led the marine brigade that assisted in the capture of Vera Cruz, Mexico. In 1918, he led the 2nd Infantry Division of the US Expeditionary Force in the Battles of St Mihiel, Blanc Mont, and the Meuse-Argonne. Appointed commandant of the corps in 1920, he developed amphibious doctrine and tactics that were to be applied in the Pacific campaigns of World War 2. He retired in 1929 to become superintendent of the Virginia Military Institute (1929–37).

Leland, Charles (Godfrey) [leeland], pseudonym **Hans Breitmann** (1825–1903) Writer, born in Philadelphia, PA. He graduated at Princeton in 1845, and afterwards studied at Heidelberg, Munich, and Paris. He was admitted to the Philadelphia bar in 1851, but turned to journalism. He gained great popularity with his poems in 'Philadelphia German', the famous *Hans Breitmann Ballads* (1871–95).

Leland, John [leeland] (c. 1506–52) Antiquary, born in London, England, UK. He studied at Cambridge and Oxford. After a stay in Paris he became chaplain to Henry VIII, who in 1533 made him 'king's antiquary', with power to search for records of antiquity in the cathedrals, colleges, abbeys, and priories of England. Most of his papers are in the Bodleian and British Museums, one of his chief works being *The Itinerary*. >> Henry VIII

Leloir, Luis Federico [luh**lwah(r)**] (1906–) Biochemist, born in Paris. He studied in Buenos Aires and at Cambridge, then worked mainly in Argentina, where he set up his own Research Institute in 1947, and discovered how glycogen, the energy storage material, is synthesized in the body (1957). For this work he was awarded the Nobel Prize for Chemistry in 1970, the first Argentinian to be so honoured.

Lely, Sir Peter [leelee], originally **Pieter van der Faes** (1618–80) Painter, born in Soest, The Netherlands. He studied in Haarlem before settling in London in 1641 as a portrait painter. He was patronized by Charles I and Cromwell, and in 1661 was appointed court painter to Charles II, for whom he changed his style of painting. His 'Windsor Beauties' series is collected at Hampton Court, and the 13 Greenwich portraits, 'Admirals' are among his best works. He was knighted in 1679. >> Charles I (of England); Charles II (of England); Cromwell, Oliver

Lemaître, Georges (Henri) [luh**may**truh] (1894–1966) Astrophysicist, born in Charleroi, Belgium. A civil engineer, army officer, and ordained priest, he studied physics at Cambridge and the Massachusetts Institute of Technology. He became professor of the theory of relativity at Louvain (1927), where he did research on cosmic rays and the three-body problem, and proposed (1927) the 'big bang' theory of the origin of the universe, later developed by Gamow and others. >> Gamow

LeMay, Curtis (Emerson) [luh**may**] (1906–) Aviator, born in Columbus, OH. Commissioned in 1928 from the Reserve Officers' Training Corps at Ohio State University, he earned a reputation as an excellent pilot during the 1930s. From August 1944 he commanded the heavy bomber force that carried out long-range attacks on the Japanese home islands, and helped plan the atomic bomb missions of August 1945. He directed the US airlift of supplies to Berlin in 1948, led the Strategic Air Command, and served as Air Force chief-of-staff (1961–5). An outspoken 'hawk' on Vietnam, he ran for vice-president on George Wallace's independent ticket in 1968. >> Wallace, George

Lemieux, Mario [luh**myoe**] (1965–) Ice hockey player, born in Montreal, Canada. A member of the Pittsburgh Penguins from 1984, in 577 National Hockey League matches (to 1993) he scored 477 goals and 697 assists. In 1993, after nine seasons, he was the fifth all-time goal scorer.

Lemmon, Jack, popular name of **John Uhler Lemmon** (1925–) Film and stage actor, born in Boston, MA. He studied at Harvard, served in the navy, and was a singing waiter, before appearing in numerous television plays. Following his film debut in *It Should Happen to You* (1954), he was established as a comedy performer. *Some Like It Hot*

(1959) began a seven-film collaboration with director Billy Wilder. He received great acclaim for his performances, winning Oscars for *Mister Roberts* (1955) and *Save the Tiger* (1973). Later films include *Tribute* (1980), *Missing* (1981), *Dad* (1989), *Glengarry Glen Ross* (1992), and *Out to Sea* (1997). He received the American Film Institute Life Achievement Award in 1988. >> Wilder, Billy

Lemon, Mark (1809–70) Writer and journalist, born in London, England, UK. In 1841 he helped to establish *Punch*, becoming first joint editor (with Henry Mayhew), then sole editor from 1843. He also wrote a farce, followed by several melodramas, operettas, children's stories, essays, a *Jest Book* (1864), and novels – the most notable of which is *Falkner Lyle* (1866). >> Mayhew

Lemonnier, Pierre Charles [luhmonyay] (1715–99) Astronomer, born in Paris. Professor at the Collège Royale from 1746, he greatly advanced astronomical measurement in France, and made 12 observations of Uranus before it came to be recognized as a planet.

Le Nain, Antoine [luh **nã**] (c. 1588–1648) Painter, born in Laon, France, the brother of **Louis** (c.1593–1648) and **Mathieu** (1607–77), who were also painters. All three were resident in Paris by 1630, and Mathieu became painter to the city in 1633. They were all founder members of the French Académie. The brothers worked in harmony, painting portraits and scenes of peasant life, signing their work simply 'Le Nain', so any individual attribution is purely speculative.

Lenard, Philipp (Eduard Anton) [**lay**nah(r)t] (1862–1947) Physicist, born in Pressburg, Hungary. He was professor of physics at the universities of Wrocław, Poland (formerly Breslau, Germany), Aachen, Heidelberg, and Kiel, before returning to Heidelberg (1907–31). His main research concerned the properties of cathode rays, for which he was awarded the Nobel Prize for Physics in 1905.

Lenbach, Franz von [**len**bakh] (1836–1904) Portrait painter, born in Schrobenhausen, Germany. He studied in Munich, travelled in Italy, and was appointed professor in the academy at Weimar, Germany (1862). He copied the great masters, including Rubens and Velazquez, before becoming one of the finest 19th-c German portraitists. His numerous portraits of Bismarck are particularly famous. >> Rubens; Velazquez

Lenclos, Ninon de [lã**kloh**], popular name of **Anne de Lenclos** (1620–1705) Courtesan, born in Paris. Her salon attracted the aristocracy as well as leading literary and political figures, and the most respectable women sent their children to her to acquire taste, style, and manners. Her lovers included the great Condé, and the Duc de La Rochefoucauld. She bore two sons, one of whom, brought up in ignorance of his mother, conceived a passion for her; when informed of their relationship, he committed suicide. >> Condé, Louis; La Rochefoucauld

Lendl, Ivan [**len**dl] (1960–) Tennis player, born in Ostrava, Czech Republic. He became a US citizen in 1992. He dominated male tennis in the 1980s, winning the singles title at the US Open (1985–7), French Open (1984, 1986–7), and Australian Open (1989, 1990), and becoming the Masters champion (1986–7) and the World Championship Tennis champion (1982, 1985). He won 94 singles titles, but failed to win at Wimbledon. He was forced to retire in December 1994 because of a spinal condition. >> RR1175

L'Enfant, Pierre Charles [lãfã] (1754–1825) Architect and city planner, born in Paris. He trained as an artist at the Royal Academy of Painting and Sculpture, Paris, moving to America in 1777 to fight the British in the Revolutionary War. In New York City after 1786, he designed ceremonial and monumental works introducing symbolic and allegorical European decorative motifs to America. At

Washington's invitation, in 1791 he submitted a plan for the new federal capital in the District of Columbia, which became an influential model of urban planning. >> Washington, George

Leng, Virginia (Helen Antoinette), *née* **Holgate** (1955–) Equestrian rider, born in Malta. The European junior champion in 1973, she won the team gold at the senior championship in 1981, 1985, and 1987, and individual titles in 1985 (on *Priceless*), 1987 (on *Night Cap*), and 1989 (on *Master Craftsman*). She won the World Championship team gold in 1982 and 1986, and the individual title in 1986 on *Priceless*. She also won at Badminton (1985, 1989, 1993) and at Burghley (1983–86, 1989). >> RR1153

Lenglen, Suzanne [lãlã] (1899–1938) Tennis player, born in Compiègne, France. She was the woman champion of France (1920–3, 1925–6), and her Wimbledon championships were the women's singles and doubles (1919–23, 1925), and the mixed doubles (1920, 1922, 1925). In 1920 she was Olympic champion. She became a professional in 1926, toured the USA, and retired in 1927 to found the Lenglen School of Tennis in Paris. >> RR1173

Lenin, Vladimir Ilyich, originally **Vladimir Ilyich Ulyanov** (1870–1924) Marxist revolutionary, born in Ulyanovsk (formerly, Simbirsk), Russia. He studied at Kazan and St Petersburg, where he graduated in law. From 1897 to 1900 he was exiled to Siberia for participating in underground revolutionary activities. At the Second Congress of the Russian Social Democratic Labour Party (1903), he caused the split between the Bolshevik and Menshevik factions. Following the February 1917 revolution, he returned to Petrograd (St Petersburg) from Zürich, and urged the immediate seizure of political power by the proletariat under the slogan 'All Power to the Soviets'. In October 1917 he led the Bolshevik revolution and became head of the first Soviet government. At the end of the ensuing Civil War (1918–21), he introduced the New Economic Policy, which his critics in the Party saw as a 'compromise with capitalism' and a retreat from strictly Socialist planning. On his death, his body was embalmed and placed in a mausoleum near the Moscow Kremlin. In 1924 Petrograd was renamed Leningrad in his honour, but since the collapse of Communism the city is once more St Petersburg. >> Plekhanov; Zetkin

Lennon, John (1940–80) Pop star, composer, songwriter, and recording artist, born in Liverpool, Merseyside, NW England, UK. He was the Beatles rhythm guitarist, keyboard player, and vocalist, and a partner in the Lennon–McCartney songwriting team. He married Japanese artist **Yoko Ono** (1933–) – his second marriage – in 1969. Together they invented a form of peace protest by staying in bed while being filmed and interviewed, and the single recorded under the name of The Plastic Ono Band, 'Give Peace a Chance' (1969), became the 'national anthem' for pacifists. He had five more chart singles between 1971–4, but only 'Imagine' (1971) had any immediate impact. On the birth of his son, **Sean** (1975–), he retired from music to become a house-husband. Five years later he recorded '(Just Like) Starting Over', but he was shot and killed by a deranged fan just before its release. His death affected millions of people, record sales soared, and he continues to be admired by new generations of fans. >> Beatles; McCartney

Leno, Dan [leenoh], originally **George Galvin** (1860–1904) Comedian, born in London, England, UK. He began his career as an entertainer at the age of four, and by 18 had become a champion clog-dancer. Ten years later he joined the Augustus Harris management at Drury Lane, where he starred for many years in the annual pantomime. He was the first music hall performer to give a command performance (for Edward VII), in 1901.

Lenoir, Jean Joseph (Etienne) [luhnwah(r)] (1822–1900) Inventor and engineer, born in Mussy-la-Ville, Belgium. By converting a steam engine to burn a mixture of coal-gas and air, and successfully marketing it, he became the inventor of the first practical internal combustion engine (c.1859). He later adapted it to run on liquid fuel, and used it to propel a vehicle he built (1860). He also constructed a boat driven by his engine (1886).

Lenormand, Henri René [luhnaw(r)mã] (1882–1951) Playwright, born in Paris. He was the author of *Le Mangeur de rêves* (1922, The Dream-Eaters), a modern equivalent of *Oedipus Rex*, and other plays in which Freud's theories are adapted to dramatic purposes. He was associated with the Pietoëff company, who used techniques pioneered by Chekhov and Pirandello. He also wrote the enlightening *Confessions of a Playwright* (1952). >> Chekhov; Freud, Sigmund; Pirandello

Le Nôtre, André [luh nohtr] (1613–1700) Landscape architect, born in Paris. The creator of French landscape-gardening, he designed many celebrated European gardens, including those at Versailles and Fontainebleau, and St James's Park and Kensington Gardens in London.

Lenya, Lotte [laynya], originally **Karoline Wilhelmine Blamauer** (1900–81) Actress and cabaret singer, born in Vienna. She studied drama and ballet at Zürich, lived in Berlin from 1920, and came to represent the spirit of that decadent era. In 1926 she married Kurt Weill, starring in many of his works, including *The Little Mahagonny* (1927) and *The Threepenny Opera* (1928, filmed 1931). They fled to Paris in 1933, then to New York City, where she made many stage appearances, and after Weill's death she became the public custodian of his legacy. Later stage appearances included *Brecht on Brecht* (1962) and *Mother Courage* (1972), and her rare film roles included *From Russia with Love* (1963) and *Semi-Tough* (1977). >> Weill

Lenz, Heinrich (Friedrich Emil) [lents] (1804–65) Physicist, born in Tartu (formerly Dorpat), Estonia. He first studied theology, then chemistry and physics at Dorpat. He became professor of physics at St Petersburg Academy of Science (1836), and later, dean of mathematics and physics. He was the first to state the law governing induced current (*Lenz's law*), and is also credited with discovering the dependence of electrical resistance on temperature (Joule's law). >> Joule

Leo III, known as **Leo the Isaurian** (c. 680–741) Byzantine emperor from 717, born in Syria, his byname coming from the region of his birth. He reorganized the army and financial system, and in 718 repelled a formidable attack by the Saracens. In 726 he issued an edict prohibiting the use of images in public worship. In Italy the controversy raised by the edict rent the empire for over a century. In 728 the exarchate of Ravenna was lost, and the E provinces became the prey of the Saracens, over whom he won a great victory in Phrygia.

Leo I, St, known as **the Great** (c. 390–461) Pope (440–61), probably born in Tuscany. One of the most eminent of the Latin Fathers, he summoned the Council of Chalcedon (451), where the intention of his 'Dogmatical Letter', defining the doctrine of the Incarnation, was accepted. He also made treaties with the Huns and Vandals in defence of Rome, and consolidated the primacy of the Roman see. Feast day 10 November (W), 18 February (E).

Leo III, St (c. 750–816) Pope (795–816), born in Rome. In 799, opposition to his election forced him to flee from Rome to the protection of Charlemagne. After returning safely, he crowned Charlemagne Emperor of the West (800), thus initiating the Holy Roman Empire. He was canonized in 1673. Feast day 12 June.

Leo X, originally **Giovanni de' Medici** (1475–1521) Pope

(1513–21), born in Florence, Italy. It is as a patron of learning and art that he is best remembered. He founded a Greek college in Rome and established a Greek press. His vast project for the rebuilding of St Peter's, and his permitting the preaching of an indulgence in order to raise funds, provoked Luther's Reformation. >> Luther; Tetzel

Leo XIII, originally **Vincenzo Giocchino Pecci** (1810–1903) Pope (1878–1903), born in Carpineto, Italy. He studied law, and became papal nuncio in Belgium (1843), Archbishop of Perugia (1846), and a cardinal (1853). He restored the hierarchy in Scotland, resolved political difficulties with Germany, and in 1888 denounced the Irish Plan of Campaign. In 1883 he opened the archives of the Vatican for historical investigations, and made himself known as a poet. The 25th anniversary of his episcopate in 1893 was marked by pilgrimages, addresses, and gifts, as was the 50th anniversary of his priesthood in 1887. In 1896 he issued an encyclical pronouncing Anglican orders invalid.

Leo Africanus, originally **Alhassan ibn Mohammed Alwazzan** (c.1485–c.1554) Traveller and geographer, born in Granada, Spain. He studied at Fés in Morocco, and travelled in N Africa and Asia Minor on commercial and diplomatic missions. Falling into the hands of Venetian corsairs, he was sent to Pope Leo X in Rome, where he lived for 20 years, and accepted Christianity, but later returned to Africa. He wrote *Descrittione dell'Africa* (1550, trans A Geographical Historie of Africa), and for some 400 years it was the chief source of information about Islam.

Leo Hebraeus >> Abarbanel, Isaac ben Jehudah

Leon, Daniel de >> de Leon, Daniel

León, Juan, Ponce de >> Ponce de León, Juan

Leonard, Elmore (John) (1925–) Thriller writer, born in New Orleans, LA. During World War 2 he served in the US navy, and afterwards studied English literature at Detroit. Throughout the 1950s he worked in advertising as a copywriter, but from 1967 concentrated on screenplays and novels. Regarded as the foremost crime writer in America, his books include *Unknown Man No. 89* (1977), *La Brava* (1983), *Touch* (1987), *Get Shorty* (1990, filmed 1995), and *Maximum Bob* (1991).

Leonard, Sir Graham Douglas (1921–) Clergyman, born in London, England, UK. He studied at Oxford, served in World War 2, and was ordained in 1948. He became Bishop of Willesden (1964), Truro (1973), and London (1981–91), and was chair of the Church of England Board for Social Responsibility (1976–83). He opposed the 1970s Anglican–Methodist unity scheme, and as Bishop of London became the focus of opposition to the ordination of women to the priesthood. He was knighted in 1991.

Leonard, 'Sugar' Ray (1956–) US boxer, born in Wilmington, DE. He fought 12 world title fights, and became WBC world welterweight champion in 1977, adding the WBA light middleweight champion in 1981. He is the only boxer to have been world champion at five weights.

Leonardo da Vinci [leeo**nah**(r)doh da **veen**chee] see panel on p. 563

Leonardo of Pisa >> Fibonacci, Leonardo

Leoncavallo, Ruggero [leeonka**va**loh] (1857–1919) Composer, born in Naples, Italy. He studied at Naples Conservatory, and earned his living as a pianist and giving singing lessons. His only major success was the opera *I Pagliacci* (1892). His *La Bohème* suffered by comparison with Puccini's on the same theme. >> Puccini

Leoni, Leone [lay**oh**nee] (1509–90) Goldsmith, medallist, and sculptor, born in Arezzo, Italy. He worked in Milan, Genoa, Brussels, and Madrid, and was the rival of Benvenuto Cellini. His portrait medals often depicted well-known artists, such as Michelangelo, and his bronze busts,

particularly of Charles V and Philip II, had a significant influence on Spanish sculpture. >> Cellini

Leonidas [lee**on**idas] (?–480 BC) King of Sparta (c.491–480 BC), and Greek hero. In 480 BC his small command resisted the vast army of Xerxes, King of Persia, at Thermopylae. After two days he dismissed his troops, and with only his 300-strong Spartan royal guard, fought to the last man. The legend that Spartans never surrender emanated from his heroism. >> RR1055

Leonov, Alexey Arkhipovich [lay**o**nof] (1934–) Astronaut, born near Kemerovo, Russia. He trained at the Chuguyev Air Force Flying School, and joined the astronaut corps in 1959. In 1965 he made the first 'extra-vehicular-activity' (EVA) excursion from the spacecraft Voskhod 2 in orbit round the Earth, 'walking' in space for 10 minutes. In 1975 he took part in the joint US–USSR Apollo-Soyuz space mission.

Leontief, Wassily [lay**on**tyef, va**si**lee] (1906–) Economist, born in St Petersburg, Russia. He studied at Leningrad (St Petersburg) and Berlin universities, taught at Harvard (1931–75), and became director of the Institute of Economic Analysis at New York University (1975–84). He was awarded the 1973 Nobel Prize for Economics for developing the input–output method of economic analysis, used in more than 50 industrialized countries for planning and forecasting.

Leopardi, Giacomo [layoh**pah**(r)dee] (1798–1837) Poet and scholar, born in Recanati, Italy. He was a gifted, congenitally handicapped (hunch-backed) child who by the age of 16 had read all the Latin and Greek classics, and outstripped any tutor found for him. Most of his afflicted life was lived in hopeless despondency and unrequited love, and this became the basis of his superb lyric poetry and prose. Among his most noted works are those collected under the title *I canti* (1831).

Leopold I (Emperor) (1640–1705) Holy Roman Emperor (1658–1705), born in Vienna, the second son of Ferdinand III. He was elected to the crowns of Hungary (1655) and Bohemia (1656), and succeeded to the imperial title in 1658. In 1666 he married his niece, **Margaret Theresa**, and after her death (1673) he took a second Habsburg bride, **Claudia Felicitas**, before his third marriage (1676) to **Eleonore of Palatinate-Neuberg**, by whom he had two sons. Committed to the defence of the power and unity of the House of Habsburg, he faced constant threats from the Ottoman Turks and the King of France, as well as the hostility of the Hungarian nobility. Treaties of neutrality (1667, 1671) between Leopold and Louis XIV of France gave way to military conflict over the Rhine frontier (1674–9, 1686–97), and he took the empire into the Grand Alliance (1701). He died during the War of the Spanish Succession (1701–13) and the Hungarian revolt of Rákóczi (1703–11). >> Louis XIV; Rákóczi

Leopold I (of Belgium) (1790–1865) First king of Belgium (1831–65), born in Coburg, Germany, the son of Francis, Duke of Saxe-Coburg, and uncle of Queen Victoria. In 1816 he married **Charlotte**, daughter of the future George IV of England, and lived in England after her death in 1817. He declined the crown of Greece (1830), but in 1831 he was elected King of the Belgians. His second marriage, to **Marie Louise of Orléans**, daughter of Louis-Philippe, ensured French support for his new kingdom against the Dutch, and he was an influential force in European diplomacy. >> RR1035

Leopold II (of Belgium) (1835–1909) King of Belgium (1865–1909), born in Brussels, the eldest son of Leopold I. He married **Maria Henrietta**, daughter of the Austrian Archduke Joseph in 1853. In 1885 he became king of the independent state of the Congo, which was annexed to

LEONARDO DA VINCI (1452–1519)

Leonardo was the illegitimate son of a Florentine notary and landowner, Ser Piero da Vinci, and a peasant girl Caterina, who later married a local craftsman. He was brought up on his father's estate at Vinci, and received an elementary education. During the 1460s, he was apprenticed to the renowned sculptor, painter, and engineer, Andrea del Verrocchio, with whom he remained for the best part of 10 years, and with whom he painted 'The Baptism of Christ' (c.1474–5, Florence). This painting marks the transition of styles from Early Renaissance (Verrocchio) to High Renaissance (Leonardo). From 1478–82, Leonardo worked from his own studio in Florence, during which time he painted an altarpiece called 'The Adoration of the Kings' (c.1481, Florence).

Despite being offered substantial painting commissions in Florence, he left the city in 1482 to become a painter, engineer, and designer to Ludovico Sforza, Duke of Milan, for 17 years. There his famous 'Last Supper' (1495–7), commissioned jointly by Ludovico and the monks of Sta Maria delle Grazie, was painted on the convent's refectory wall. Owing to dampness, and to the method of tempera painting upon plaster, it soon showed signs of deterioration, yet is still considered one of the masterpieces of world art. Among other paintings commissioned in Milan were portraits of two mistresses of the duke – one of them perhaps Le Belle Ferronnière of the Louvre, the other was of Lucrezia Crivelli. (Scholars disagree about the attribution of these paintings.) He also devised a system of hydraulic irrigation for use on the Lombardy plains, and directed the court pageants. Architecture, mechanics, and the study of anatomy occupied much of his time, and he filled his copious notebooks with mirror-writing. Mathematician Lucas Pacioli's book Divina proportione (1494, Divine Proportion) contained 60 geometrical figures by Leonardo.

After the fall of Duke Ludovico in 1499, Leonardo returned to Florence, where he was received with great acclaim. In 1502, he entered the service of the notorious commander, Cesare Borgia, then Duke of Romagna, as military architect and engineer. In 1503 he returned to Florence and commenced a 'Virgin and Child with St Anne' (c.1501–12), of which only the cartoon (c.1495), now in the Royal Academy, London, was completed. Both he and Michelangelo received commissions to decorate with historical compositions the Sala de Consiglio in the Palazzo di Gran Vecchio. For it, Leonardo depicted 'The Battle of Anghiari' (1503–6), a Florentine victory over Milan, and finished his cartoon; but, having employed a method of painting upon the plaster which proved a failure, he abandoned the work in 1506.

About 1504 he completed his most celebrated easel portrait: 'Mona Lisa' (1503–6, Paris), the wife of Zanoki del Gioconda, hence sometimes known as 'La Gioconda'. An earlier work portrayed the celebrated beauty Ginevra de' Benci (c.1475-78, Vaduz). In 1506 he was employed in Milan by Louis XII of France, making scientific investigations in geology, botany, hydraulics, and a host of other subjects; he did not paint a great deal.

In 1513 he moved to Rome for political reasons, and worked there at the same time as Michelangelo was working on the tomb of Pope Julius. He was lonely, and felt underused, so despite his age (65) he moved again to France with his pupil, Francesco Melzi. In 1516 Francis I bestowed on him a yearly allowance, and assigned to his use for research purposes the Château Cloux near Amboise in France, where he lived until his death.

Among his later works are 'The Virgin of the Rocks', (1494–1508, Paris), a figure of 'St John the Baptist', and a 'St Anne' (Paris).

There is no extant sculpture which can positively be attributed to him, but he may well have designed or been closely associated with three works – three figures over the N door of the Baptistery at Florence, a bronze statuette of horse and rider in the Budapest Museum, and the wax bust of Flora in Berlin.

In his art Leonardo was hardly influenced by the antique at all; his practice was founded upon study of nature, and in particular the study of light and shade. So few in number are the surviving works by his hand that he may be most fully studied in his drawings, of which there are rich collections in Milan, Paris, Florence, and Vienna, as well as in the British Museum and in Windsor Castle, UK. His celebrated Trattato della Pitture (Treatise on Painting, a collection of his manuscripts), was published in 1651; but a more complete collection, discovered by Manzi in the Vatican, was published in 1817.

Leonardo da Vinci cannot be classified singly as a painter, architect, musician, engineer, or sculptor. He had a wide knowledge and understanding, far beyond that of his time, of most of the sciences, including biology, anatomy, physiology, hydrodynamics, mechanics, and aeronautics. His notebooks contain original observations and remarks in these subjects and countless others, showing him to have had an inventiveness of mind and a keeness of observation centuries ahead of his time.

>> Borgia, Cesare; Ludovico Sforza; Michelangelo; Verrocchio

Belgium in 1908. He strengthened his country by military reforms, and under him Belgium flourished, developing commercially and industrially. >> Leopold I; RR1035

Leopold III (1901–83) King of Belgium (1934–51), born in Brussels. He was the son of Albert I, and he married **Princess Astrid of Sweden** in 1926. On his own authority he ordered the capitulation of his army to the Germans (1940), thus opening the way to Dunkirk. He then remained a prisoner in his own palace at Laeken until 1944, and afterwards in Austria. On returning to Belgium in 1945, he was finally forced to abdicate in favour of his son, Baudouin. >> Albert I; Baudouin; RR1035

Leopold, (Rand) Aldo (1887–1948) Conservationist and ecologist, born in Burlington, IA. He grew up as a sportsman and naturalist, studied at Yale, and joined the US Forest Service. Assigned to the Arizona–New Mexico district, he spent 15 years in the field, rising to chief of the district. By 1921 he had begun to campaign for the preservation of wildlife areas for recreational and aesthetic purposes. He was with the US Forest Products Laboratory (1924–8), spent three years surveying game populations, and in 1933 became the first professor of wildlife management at the University of Wisconsin. Over the years he worked out his concept of the 'land ethic', which (in his words) 'enlarges the boundaries of the (human) community to include soils, waters, plants, and animals, or collectively the land'. After retiring from the university he bought a farm in the Wisconsin Dells, where he wrote *A Sand County Almanac* (published posthumously in 1949), the 'bible' of environmental activists of the 1960s and 1970s. >> Brower; Muir, John

Le Parc, Julio [luh **pah(r)k**] (1928–) Artist, born in Mendoza, Argentina. After training in Buenos Aires he moved to Paris in 1958, and helped found the Groupe de Recherche D'art Visuel with Viktor Vasarely. He became particularly interested in the exploitation of light through transparent prisms and cubes. Controversy surrounded his award of the painting prize at the 1966 Venice Biennale, and he is remembered for the Op and Kinetic art movements of the 1960s. >> Vasarely

Le Pen, Jean-Marie [luh **pen**] (1928–) French politician. He graduated in law at Paris before serving in the 1950s as a paratrooper in Indochina and Algeria, where he lost an eye in a street battle. In 1956 he won a National Assembly seat as a right-wing Poujadist. He was connected with the extremist Organisation de l'Armée Sécrète before forming the National Front in 1972. This party, with its extreme right-wing policies, emerged as a new 'fifth force' in French politics in the 1986 Assembly elections, winning 10% of the national vote. A controversial figure and noted demagogue, he unsuccessfully contested the presidency in 1988. >> Poujade

Lepidus, Marcus Aemilius [lepidus] (?–13 /12 BC) Roman statesman. He declared for Julius Caesar against Pompey (49 BC), and Caesar made him dictator of Rome and his colleague in the consulate (46 BC). He supported Marcus Antonius, and became one of the triumvirate with Octavian Augustus and Antonius, with Africa for his province (40–39 BC). He thought he could raise Sicily against Octavian, but his soldiers deserted his cause, and he retired from public life. >> Antonius; Caesar

Lepsius, Karl Richard [lepsius] (1810–44) Egyptologist, born in Naumburg, Germany. He studied Egyptology in Rome, headed an antiquarian expedition to Egypt (1842–5), and in 1846 was appointed professor in Berlin. His *Chronologie der Aegypter* (1849, Egyptian Chronology) laid the foundation for a scientific treatment of early Egyptian history, and *Denkmäler aus Aegypten und Aethiopien* (1859, Egyptian and Ethiopian Monuments) remains a masterpiece. He was a member of the Royal Academy, director of the Egyptian section of the Royal Museum, and chief librarian of the Royal Library at Berlin.

Lermontov, Mikhail Yuryevich [lermontof] (1814–41) Poet and writer, born in Moscow. He attended Moscow University and the military cavalry school of St Petersburg. A poem he wrote in 1837 on the death of Pushkin caused his exile to the Caucasus. Reinstated, he was again banished following a duel with the son of the French ambassador. The scenery of the Caucasus inspired his best poetry, such as 'The Novice' and 'The Demon', and his novel, *A Hero of our Time* (1840), is a masterpiece of prose writing. He was killed in another duel at the age of 27, and much of his fame as the leading Romantic poet was posthumous.

Lerner, Alan J >> Loewe, Frederick

Leroux, Gaston (Louis Alfred) [leroo] (1868–1927) Writer, born in Paris. He was raised in Normandy, and began to write while studying law in Paris. He qualified for the bar, then became a journalist, while writing short stories, poetry, and eventually novels and plays. His first novel, *The Seeking of the Morning Treasures* (trans, 1903) was followed by a series of detective stories. He moved to Nice in 1908, where he wrote his best-known work, *The Phantom of the Opera*, in 1911. Although it attracted little attention in its early days, it became a hit following a Lon Chaney film in 1924. A prolific author, publishing at least a book a year, Leroux would signal the completion of a manuscript by firing a loaded revolver from his balcony.

Lesage, Alain René [luh**sahzh**], also spelled **Le Sage** (1668–1747) Novelist and playwright, born in Sarzeau, France. A poor but well-educated orphan, he studied law in Paris briefly, but married early and sought his fortune in literature. The Abbé de Lionne allowed him a pension and access to a good Spanish library. He became a prolific playwright, sometimes accused of borrowing stories from others. He is best known for the novel *Histoire de Gil Blas de Santillane* (12 vols, 1715–35, The Adventures of Gil Blas of Santillane). As a playwright, his leading work is *Turcaret* (1708).

Le Saux, Graeme [luh **soh**] (1968–) Footballer, born in Jersey, Channel Is, UK. A left back defender, he played in Jersey, then joined Chelsea, later moving to Blackburn Rovers, and returning to Chelsea in 1997. He joined England in 1995, and though an injury kept him out of the team for a while, he had won 14 caps by early 1997.

Lescot, Pierre [leskoh] (c. 1515–78) Architect, born in Paris. He studied architecture, mathematics, and painting. One of the greatest classical architects of his time, among his works are the screen of St Germain l'Auxerrois, the Fontaine des Innocents, and the Hôtel de Ligneris. His masterwork was the rebuilding of the Louvre.

LeSieg, Theo >> Seuss, Dr

Leslie, Charles Robert (1794–1859) Painter, born in London, England, UK. He studied from 1800 in Philadelphia, and returned to England in 1811 to study at the Royal Academy. He was professor of drawing at West Point, NY (1833), and professor of painting at the Royal Academy (1848–52). His paintings were mostly scenes from famous plays and novels.

Leslie, Sir John (1766–1832) Physicist, born in Largo, Fife, E Scotland, UK. He studied at St Andrews and Edinburgh, and travelled as a tutor in America and Europe. He invented a differential thermometer, a hygrometer, and a photometer. In 1805 he was elected to the chair of mathematics at Edinburgh, and transferred to the chair of natural philosophy (physics) in 1819. In 1810 he succeeded in creating artificial ice by freezing water under an air pump. He was knighted in 1832.

Leslie, Sir Shane (John Randolph) (1885–1971) Writer, born in Glaslough, Co Monaghan, Ireland. He studied at Paris and Cambridge universities, visited Russia in 1907, and became friendly with Tolstoy. He became a Roman Catholic in 1908, and unsuccessfully contested Londonderry in 1910. He published poems of some quality, and produced a much praised analysis of the pre-war generation in *The End of a Chapter* (1916). He is also known for his novels, clerical biographies, memoirs, and supernatural short stories. He also investigated the relationship between George IV and Mrs Fitzherbert, from whom he was descended. >> Fitzherbert

L'Esperance, Elise, *née* **Strang** (?1878–1959) Physician, pathologist, and clinic founder, born in Yorktown, NY. Best known for her work in cancer in women and cancer prevention, she founded several New York clinics both individually and with her sister, **May**. Three clinics, staffed entirely by women, provided the first organized attempts to prevent cancer through early diagnosis and testing of healthy-appearing women. The Strang clinics prompted similar cancer-prevention clinics for women nationwide, and made acceptable the 'Pap' smear for diagnosis of cervical cancer. She was affiliated with Cornell University for 40 years (1910–50), and was finally named a full clinical professor of preventive medicine before retiring in the early 1950s. Involved in promoting equality for women in medicine, she was active in several women's medical associations. She was editor of the *Medical Woman's Journal* (1936–41) and the first editor of the *Journal of the American Medical Women's Association* (1946–8).

Lesseps, Ferdinand (Marie), vicomte de (Viscount of) [**les**eeps] (1805–94) French diplomat and entrepreneur, born in Versailles, France. From 1825 he held various diplomatic posts, and in 1854 began his campaign for the construction of a Suez Canal. The works started in 1860, and were completed in 1869. In 1881 his ambitious scheme for a sea-level Panama Canal commenced, but had to be abandoned in 1888. His company was subsequently charged with breach of trust, and Lesseps, then elderly, was sentenced to five years' imprisonment; but the sentence was reversed, and did little to ruin his esteem. He wrote *Histoire du canal de Suez* (1875–9, History of the Suez Canal), and a biography.

Lessing, Doris (May), *née* **Tayler** (1919–) Writer, born in Kermanshah, Iran. She lived on a farm in Rhodesia, and was married and divorced twice (Lessing is her second husband's name). Her first published novel was *The Grass is Singing* (1950), a study of white civilization in Africa, the theme of many early works. Her experiences of life in working-class London after her arrival in 1949 are described in *In Pursuit of the English* (1960). In 1952 she published the first in a series of the important *Martha Quest* novels, *The Children of Violence*, which is semi-autobiographical and, typically, explores political and social undercurrents in contemporary society. Her many other novels include the popular *The Golden Notebook* (1962), and the later books *London Observed* (1992) and *Love, Again* (1996). Her work also includes several collections of short stories, fantasies, and science fiction.

Lessing, Gotthold Ephraim (1729–81) Playwright and man of letters, born in Kamenz, Germany. After studying theology at Leipzig University, he worked as a translator, then continued his studies at Wittenberg (1751). The first German playwright of lasting importance, he produced his classic tragedy *Miss Sara Sampson* in 1755. While secretary to the Governor of Breslau, he wrote his famous *Laokoon* (1766), a critical treatise defining the limits of poetry and the plastic arts. His *Minna von Barnhelm* (1767) was the first German comedy on the grand scale. In 1769 the Duke of Brunswick appointed Lessing as Wolfenbüttel librarian, and in 1772 he wrote another great tragedy, *Emilia Galotti*.

Leszczynski, Stanislaus >> **Stanislaus Leszczynski**

Lethaby, William Richard (1857–1931) Architect and designer, born in Barnstaple, Devon, SW England, UK. He worked in London (1877–87), and was a founder of the Art Workers' Guild (1884) and the Arts and Crafts Exhibition Society (c.1886). He was associated with Ernest Gimson when he designed his most important building, Avon Tyrrell near Salisbury. He was joint principal of The Central School of Arts and Crafts in 1896, and sole principal (1900–12). He also taught at the Royal College of Art. >> Gimson

Letterman, David (1947–) Television talk-show host, born in Indianapolis, IN. He studied at Ball State University, Indiana, then worked as a TV weatherman and on radio before working in New York City as a writer. He became well-known following guest-host appearances on the Johnny Carson Show in 1979–80, hosted a late-night show for MBC from 1982, noted for its irreverent manner and zany comic stunts, then in 1993 joined CBS as host of 'Late Night with David Letterman'.

Letts, Thomas (1803–73) Bookbinder, born in London, England, UK. John Letts founded the Charles Letts family business in 1796. After his death, Thomas began to manu-

facture diaries, and by 1839 was producing 28 varieties. His great great grandson is now chairman of the family business.

Leuchtenberg, Duke of >> **Beauharnais, Eugène**

Leucippus [**loo**sipus] (5th-c BC) Philosopher, born in Miletus, Asia Minor. He was the originator of the atomistic cosmology which Democritus later developed, and which is most fully expounded in Lucretius's great poem 'De rerum natura'. Leucippus is usually credited with two books, *The Great World System* and *On the Mind*, but his theories and writings are not reliably separable from those of Democritus. >> Democritus; Melissus

Leuckart, (Karl Georg Friedrich) Rudolf [**loy**kah(r)t] (1822–98) Zoologist, born in Helmstedt, Germany. He studied at Göttingen, and became professor of zoology at Giessen (1850) and Leipzig (1869). A pioneer of parasitology, his work on classification is important, especially his division of the Radiata into Coelenterata and Echinodermata. He also distinguished himself by his study of the Entozoa.

Leutze, Emanuel (Gottlieb) [**loyt**zuh] (1816–68) Painter, born in Gmünd, Germany. He emigrated to America in 1825, but returned to Europe on several occasions to study. His famous historical paintings have been reproduced countless times, especially 'Washington Crossing the Delaware' (1851). His popular mural, 'Westward the Course of Empire Takes Its Way' (1862), is in the Capitol, Washington, DC.

Levant, Oscar [le**vant**] (1906–72) Pianist and actor, born in Pittsburgh, PA. He studied composition with Schoenberg, but his close friendship with Gershwin was the determining factor in his career, becoming as a pianist one of the foremost Gershwin interpreters. At the same time, he had an active career as a screen and radio humorist and author, his films including *An American in Paris* (1951), and his books including *Memoirs of an Amnesiac* (1965). >> Gershwin, George; Schoenberg

Levassor, Emile >> **Panhard, René**

Le Vau or **Levau, Louis** [luh **voh**] (1612–70) Architect, born in Paris. He produced outstanding Baroque designs for the aristocracy, and the Hôtel Lambert, Paris, stands out particularly for the ingenious use of site. His design of Vaux-le-Vicomte (1657–61), with formal landscape by André Le Nôtre, constituted an influential milestone in French architecture, leading to his Baroque masterpiece of Versailles (from 1661, again with Le Nôtre), designed on a palatial scale for court and government. >> Le Brun; Le Nôtre

Levene, Phoebus (Aaron Theodor) [luh**veen**], originally **Fishel Aaronovich Lenin** (1869–1940) Biochemist, born in Sagor, Russia. He qualified in medicine in St Petersburg in 1891, and in 1905 became a founder member of the Rockefeller Institute in New York City, applying chemistry to biological problems. His work established the nature of the sugar component which defines the two types of nucleic acid (RNA and DNA) before 1930, although it was not until 1953 that newer methods allowed Watson and Crick to deduce the complete structure of the nucleic acids. >> Crick; Watson, James

Lever, Charles (James) [**lee**ver] (1806–72) Writer, born in Dublin. He studied at Trinity College, Dublin, and went to Göttingen to study medicine. His most popular work, *Charles O'Malley*, is a description of his own college life in Dublin. His travels took him to North America and Europe, and he related his experiences in many novels, including *Arthur O'Leary* (1844), *Knight of Gwynne* (1847), and *Luttrel of Arran* (1865). In 1858 he was appointed British vice-consul in Spezia (1858), and promoted to the consulship in Trieste in 1867.

Leverhulme (of the Western Isles), William Hesketh Lever, 1st Viscount [**lee**verhyoom], also known as **Baron**

Leverhulme of Bolton-Le-Moors (1851–1925) Soap-maker and philanthropist, born in Bolton, Greater Manchester, NW England, UK. In 1886, with his brother, **James Darcy Lever**, he started the manufacture of soap from vegetable oils instead of tallow. He turned the small soap works into a national business through skilled advertising and continuous consideration for the customer and his staff, founding the model industrial new town of Port Sunlight. He was made a baron in 1917, and a viscount in 1922. Among his many benefactions, he endowed to Liverpool University a school of tropical medicine, and Lancaster House to the nation.

Leverrier, Urbain Jean Joseph [luhveryay] (1811–77) Astronomer, born in St Lô, France. In 1836 he became teacher of astronomy at the Polytechnique, and 10 years later gained admission to the Academy. From disturbances in the motions of planets he predicted the existence of an undiscovered planet, and calculated the point in the heavens where, a few days afterwards, Neptune was actually discovered by Galle at Berlin (1846). In 1852 Louis Napoleon made him a senator, and in 1854 he became director of the observatory of Paris. >> Galle

Levertov, Denise (1923–97) Poet, born in Ilford, E Greater London, England, UK. Educated at home, she emigrated to the USA in 1948, and became a US citizen in 1955. She was appointed poetry editor of *The Nation* in 1961. Her first collection of verse was published in 1946, and others have appeared steadily. She has been outspoken on many issues, particularly Vietnam and feminism, and her poetry is similarly questioning – notably *With Eyes at the Back of Our Heads* (1959) and *Footprints* (1972). *Selected Poems* appeared in 1986.

Levesque, Rene [luhvek] (1922–87) Journalist, and premier of Quebec, Canada. A minister on Jean Lesage's Liberal team, he resigned in 1968 and founded the Parti Québecois, whose main objective became Quebec sovereignty and the creation of a new form of association with Canada. Levesque was elected premier in 1976, and again in 1981. The Parti Québecois was not able to prevail in a 1980 referendum on sovereignty-association, but passed Bill 101, which formalized the status of French as the official language of Quebec.

Levey, Barnett [leevee] (1798–1837) Australian pioneer, born in the East End of London, England, UK. He arrived in Australia in 1821 to join his brother **Solomon** (1794–1833), who had been transported for stealing a chest of tea, and then pardoned. He was the first free Jewish settler to arrive in the new colony, and was soon in business, dealing in general goods and books. He established one of the first lending libraries in Australia. The first person to be granted a theatre licence in the colony, he opened on a temporary stage in 1832, and built the Theatre Royal in 1833.

Levi [leeviy] Biblical character, the third son of Jacob by his wife Leah. It is debated whether his descendants ever formed one of the 12 tribes of Israel descended from Jacob's sons. Although they were called a tribe, no territory was apparently allocated to them (*Josh* 13.14), and they seem to have been a kind of priestly class. Moses is later depicted as a descendant of Levi. >> Jacob

Levi, Edward Hirsch [leevee] (1911–) Attorney general and university president, born in Chicago, IL. He studied at Chicago, where he began to teach (1936), and returned there in 1945 after serving as special assistant to the US attorney general. He was an advisor to the 'Chicago School' of physicists, and assisted in the drafting of the US Atomic Energy Act (1946), which led to the establishment of the Atomic Energy Commission. Considered a brilliant anti-trust lawyer, he became dean of the University of Chicago Law School (1950–62), university provost (1962–7), and president (1967–75). In the aftermath of the Watergate scandals, he helped to restore Americans' respect for the government by serving as the US attorney general (1975–7).

Levi, Primo [layvee] (1919–87) Writer and chemist, born in Turin, Italy, to Jewish parents. On completing his schooling he enrolled at Turin University to study chemistry. During the war he formed a small guerrilla force, but he was betrayed and despatched to Auschwitz. He was one of the few to survive, and returned to Italy in 1945. All of his novels are attempts to understand the nature of Nazi barbarity and the variety of responses to it evinced by its victims. *Se questo è un Uomo* (1947, If this is a Man), was the first of these. With *La tregua* (1963, The Truce), its sequel, it has acquired the status of a classic work on the concentration camps. His best-known book is *The Periodic Table* (1985), a volume of autobiographical reflections.

Levi-Civita, Tullio [layvee chiveeta] (1873–1941) Mathematician, born in Padua, Italy. He studied in Padua and became professor there in 1897. From about 1900 he worked on the absolute differential calculus (or tensor calculus) which became the essential mathematical tool in Einstein's general relativity theory. He was professor in Rome (1919–38), but was forced to retire by Fascist laws against Jews. >> Einstein

Levi-Montalcini, Rita [layvee montalcheenee] (1909–) Neurophysiologist, born in Rome. Graduating in medicine at Rome when World War 2 began, she had to go into hiding as a non-Aryan; her early research was done in her bedroom on the neuro-embryology of the chick. In the USA for several years from 1947, she discovered nerve growth factor. She retired in 1979 from directing the Rome Cell Biology Laboratory, and shared the Nobel Prize for Physiology or Medicine in 1986 with Stanley Cohen. >> Cohen, Stanley

Levine, James [luhviyn] (1943–) Conductor, born in Cincinnati, OH. From a musical family, he studied piano in childhood, and soloed with the Cincinnati Symphony at the age of 10. After studies in piano and conducting at the Juilliard School, New York City (from 1961), he became assistant conductor of the Cleveland Orchestra. He made his opera debut conducting *Tosca* at the Metropolitan Opera in 1971; two years later he became the house's principal conductor, in 1976 music director, and since 1986 artistic director. He has successfully built the Met orchestra into one of the finest in the world, and guest-conducted orchestras and opera companies internationally.

Levinson, Barry (1942–) Film director and producer, born in Baltimore, MD. He was a comic writer for television before Mel Brooks engaged him as a scriptwriter. He made his directorial debut with *Diner* (1982), which earned him an Oscar nomination for Best Screenplay. Other films include the comedy *Good Morning Vietnam* (1987), *Rain Man* (1988, Oscar), and *Bugsy* (1991). He produced, directed, and wrote *Sleepers* (1996), produced *Donnie Brasco* (1997), and produced/directed *Sphere* (1997) and *Wag the Dog* (1998). >> Brooks

Lévi-Strauss, Claude [layvee strows] (1908–) Social anthropologist, born in Brussels. A graduate in law and philosophy, he became interested in anthropology while lecturing at São Paulo University, Brazil (1934–9). He subsequently worked in the New School for Social Research in New York City before becoming director of studies at the Ecole Pratiques des Hautes Etudes in Paris (1950–74), and professor of social anthropology at the Collège de France (1959). He has been a major influence on contemporary anthropology, establishing a new method for analysing various collective phenomena such as kinship, ritual, and myth.

His major four-volume study, *Mythologiques* (1964–72), studied the systematic ordering behind codes of expression in different cultures.

Lévy-Bruhl, Lucien [layvee brül] (1857–1939) Philosopher and anthropologist, born in Paris. He studied at the École Normale Supérieure, and in 1904 was appointed to a chair in the history of modern philosophy at the Sorbonne. His early work was in moral philosophy, and he published *La Morale et la science des moeurs* (1903, Ethics and Moral Science). He went on to develop a theory of primitive mentality, suggesting that the mentality of primitive people was essentially mystical and prelogical, differing from the rational and logical thought of the modern West. This view drew him into a sharp exchange with Durkheim, and has little support today. >> Durkheim

Lewald, Fanny [layvalt] (1811–89) Writer, born in Königsberg (now Kaliningrad), Germany. In 1845 she met **Adolf Stahr** (1805–76), a Berlin critic, whom she later married. She was an enthusiastic champion of women's rights, which were aired in her early novels, including *Clementine* (1842). She also wrote records of travel in Italy and Great Britain, and published an autobiography. Her later works were family sagas, notably *Die Familie Darner* (3 vols, 1887, The Darner Family).

Lewes, George Henry [loois] (1817–78) Writer, born in London, England, UK. He left school at an early age to enter first a notary's office, then the house of a Russian merchant. In London, after a stay in Germany, he started writing for the *Penny Encyclopaedia* and other journals, edited the *Leader* (1851–4) and founded and edited the *Fortnightly* (1865–6). He was married, with a family, when he began a lifelong affair with George Eliot in 1854. His works, as well as a tragedy and two novels (1841–8), include *The Spanish Drama* (1846), *Life and Works of Goethe* (1855), and *Problems of Life and Mind* (1874–9). >> Eliot, George

Lewis, Alun (1915–44) Writer, born in Cwmaman, Rhondda Cynon Taf, S Wales, UK. He studied at the University College of Wales, Aberystwyth, and at Manchester. A lieutenant in the army, his first work, a volume of short stories about army life, was *The Last Inspection* (1942), followed by a volume of poetry. He died of gunshot wounds at Chittagong during the Burma campaign. Another volume of verse, *Ha! Ha! Among the Trumpets*, was published posthumously in 1945, followed by a collection of short stories and letters, *In the Green Tree* (1948).

Lewis, Sir (William) Arthur (1915–) British economist, born in St Lucia. He was professor of economics at Manchester (1948–58), then became the first president of the University of the West Indies (1959–63). From 1963 until his retirement in 1983 he held a chair in economics at Princetown. In 1979 he shared the Nobel Prize for Economics for work on economic development in the Third World. >> RR1125

Lewis, (Frederick) Carl(ton) (1961–) Track and field athlete, born in Birmingham, AL. An all-round athlete at Houston University (1979–82), he won the world long jump gold medal at the 1981 World Cup, and went on to win three gold medals in the inaugural World Championships in 1983. He emulated Jesse Owens' record by winning four gold medals at the 1984 Olympic Games (100 m, 200 m, 4 × 100 m relay, and long jump), won two more at the 1988 Olympics (100 m, long jump), an unprecedented third consecutive gold medal in the long jump in the 1992 Olympics, and another gold medal for the long jump at the 1996 Games. He was awarded the gold medal for the 100 m in 1988 when Ben Johnson (the winner on the track) was disqualified for drug abuse; but Lewis held the world record in the 100 m for many years. >> Johnson, Ben; RR1133

Lewis, C Day >> **Day-Lewis, C**

Lewis, C(live) S(taples) (1898–1963) Academic, writer, and Christian apologist, born in Belfast. He taught at Oxford (1925–54), and was professor of Mediaeval and Renaissance English at Cambridge from 1954. His novel *The Screwtape Letters* (1942), is the most well known of more than 40 works on Christian apologetics, and *The Lion, the Witch and the Wardrobe* (1950), was the first in the *Chronicles of Narnia*, which has become a classic children's series. His autobiography, *Surprised by Joy* (1955), describes his conversion to Christianity. His brief marriage to **Joy Davidman** (d.1960) was the subject of the successful West End play, *Shadowlands*.

Lewis, David (1919–) Sailor and writer, born in New Zealand. He studied at Leeds University, and practised medicine until the 1960s, when he devoted himself to sailing. In particular, he sought to rediscover the traditional sailing methods of the ancient Polynesians, and to vindicate their reputation as master mariners. He has written numerous books, including *We the Navigators* (1976) and *The Voyaging Stars* (1978), and has opened up a significant area of scholarly research. >> Heyerdahl

Lewis, Edward B (1918–) Developmental biologist, born in Wilkes-Barre, PA. He studied at the California Institute of Technology, where he carried out his research. He shared the Nobel Prize for Physiology or Medicine in 1995 for his research into how genes control early development of the human embryo. Using the fruit fly, he investigated how genes could control development of body segments into specialized organs. >> Nuesslein-Volhard; Wieschaus

Lewis, G(ilbert) N(ewton) (1875–1946) Physical chemist, born in Weymouth, MA. He studied at Nebraska University, Harvard, and in Germany before taking a post as government chemist in the Philippines. He taught at the Massachusetts Institute of Technology (1905–12), then moved to California University (1912–45). He was a pioneer in taking ideas from physics and applying them to chemistry, much of his research focusing on the arrangement of electrons around atomic nuclei.

Lewis, Hywel (David) (1910–) Religious philosopher, born in Llandudno, NW Wales. He held the chair of philosophy at University College, Bangor, before becoming professor of the history and philosophy of religion at King's College, London (1955–77). He has been president of Mind and other learned societies, founder editor of *Religious Studies* (1965–84), and author of many works, including *Our Experience of God* (1959) and *Freedom and Alienation* (1985).

Lewis, Jerry Lee (1935–) Rock singer, country singer, and pianist, born in Ferriday, LA. After working as a session musician at Sun Studios in Memphis, he was invited to record by the label's founder, Sam Phillips. His 1957 recordings 'Whole Lotta Shakin' and 'Great Balls of Fire' became classics of rock, copied by successive generations of musicians. After he married his 14-year-old cousin, Myra, in 1958 (divorced 1971), he was effectively boycotted by television and the pop radio stations. During the 1960s he concentrated on country music, returning to rock-and-roll only in the 1970s.

Lewis, John (jazz player) >> **Jackson, Milt**

Lewis, John L(lewellyn) (1880–1969) Labour leader, born in Lucas, IA. He became president of the United Mine Workers' Union (1920–60), and in 1935 formed a combination of unions, the Congress of Industrial Organizations, of which he was president until 1940. A skilful negotiator, he made the miners' union one of the most powerful in the USA.

Lewis, Martyn (John Dudley) (1945–) British television journalist, presenter, and newsreader. He studied at Trinity College, Dublin, became a presenter with BBC

Belfast (1967–8), moved to HTV Wales (1968–70), and joined ITN (1971), becoming newsreader and foreign correspondent on *News at Ten* and *News at 5.45* (1978–86). His work for the BBC includes presenter of the *One O'Clock News* (1986), *Nine O'Clock News* (1987–94), *Six O'Clock News* (1994–   ), the *Crimebeat* series (1996, 1997), and he hosted *Today's the Day* (1993–7). His books include *Tears and Smiles – The Hospice Handbook* (1989), *Go For It* (annual, 1993–   ), and *Reflections on Success* (1997).

Lewis, Meade, known as **Meade Lux Lewis** (1905–64) Musician, born in Louisville, KY. Originally a violin student, he worked as a pianist in Chicago nightclubs for many years. His recording of 'Honky Tonk Train Blues' (1929) was belatedly very successful (1936), and he became a leading exponent of the boogie-woogie piano during the late 1930s.

Lewis, Meriwether (1774–1809) Explorer, born in Charlotteville, VA. In 1801 he became personal secretary to President Thomas Jefferson, and was invited with his long-time friend William Clark to lead an expedition (1804–6) to explore the lands to the W of the Mississippi, and to keep a detailed journal of his experiences. It was the first overland journey across North America to the Pacific Coast, and one of the longest transcontinental journeys ever undertaken. He became Governor of Louisiana in 1808, and died in a shooting incident on his way to Washington. >> Clark, William; Jefferson, Thomas

Lewis, M(atthew) G(regory), nickname **Monk Lewis** (1775–1818) Novelist, born in London, England, UK. He studied at Oxford and in Germany. In 1794 he was an attaché to The Hague, and it was there he wrote *The Monk* (1796), a Gothic novel which caught the public's attention and inspired his nickname. After the success of his musical drama, *The Castle Spectre* (1798), his concern about the treatment of the slaves on the vast estates he inherited in the West Indies took him there twice, and he subsequently died of yellow fever. His memorable *Journal of a West Indian Proprietor* was published posthumously in 1834.

Lewis, Oscar (1914–70) Anthropologist, born in New York City. He founded in 1948 the anthropology department at the University of Illinois (Urbana), where he spent his career. His powerful best-selling records of the oral histories of Mexican villagers, Mexican and Puerto Rican slum-dwellers, and the Cuban revolution led to his controversial theory of poverty as a transnational subculture, and brought the poor to widespread public attention.

Lewis, Richard, known as **Dic Penderyn** (c. 1807–31) Folk hero, born near Aberavon, Neath and Port Talbot. SC Wales. He was accused of wounding a soldier during the Merthyr Tydfil riots of 1831, found guilty, and publicly executed at Cardiff. Many were convinced of his innocence, and he became a folk hero in South Wales.

Lewis, Saunders (1893–1958) Playwright, poet, and Welsh nationalist, born in Cheshire, NWC England, UK. He studied English and French at Liverpool, became a lecturer in Welsh at University College, Swansea, in 1922, and in 1924 published a study on classical Welsh 18th-c poetry, *A School of Welsh Augustans*. He was co-founder of the Welsh Nationalist Party (later Plaid Cymru) in 1925, and became its president in 1926. Imprisoned for an act of arson (1936), he was dismissed from Swansea and made his living by journalism, teaching, and farming until his appointment in 1952 as lecturer (later senior lecturer) in Welsh at University College, Cardiff. He published many essays, plays, poems, novels, and historical and literary criticism, chiefly in Welsh.

Lewis, (Harry) Sinclair (1885–1951) Novelist, born in Sauk Center, MN. He studied at Yale, became a journalist, and wrote several minor works before *Main Street* (1920)

appeared, the first of a series of best-selling novels satirizing US small-town life. *Babbitt* (1922) still lends its title as a synonym for the small-town middle-class American. He refused the Pulitzer Prize for *Arrowsmith* (1925), but accepted the Nobel Prize for Literature in 1930, being the first US writer to receive it.

Lewis, Sir Thomas (1881–1945) Cardiologist and clinical scientist, born in Cardiff. He trained at University College, Cardiff, and University College Hospital, London, where he remained as a teacher and consultant until his death. He was the first to completely master the use of electrocardiograms, establishing the basic parameters which still govern their interpretation. During his later years he turned his attention to the physiology of cutaneous blood vessels, and the mechanisms of pain. He fought for full-time clinical research posts to investigate clinical science.

Lewis, (Percy) Wyndham [**wind**am] (1882–1957) Artist, writer, and critic, born on a yacht in the Bay of Fundy, Nova Scotia, Canada. He studied at the Slade School of Art, London, and with Ezra Pound founded *Blast* (1914–15), the magazine of the Vorticist school. His writings include the satirical novel *The Apes of God* (1930), and the multi-volume *The Human Age* (1955–6), as well as literary criticism, such as *Men Without Art* (1934), and autobiographical books, such as *Blasting and Bombardiering* (1937). His paintings include works of abstract art, a series of war pictures, and portraits. >> Pound, Ezra

Lewitt, Sol (1928–   ) Minimalist and exponent of Conceptual Art, born in Hartford, CT. He studied at Syracuse University in 1949, and emerged as an abstract artist in the early 1960s. In the 1970s he made Minimalist 'structures', but was already declaring that the concept was more important than the work, and the planning more than the execution, hence his exhibited wall-drawings were afterwards obliterated.

Ley, Willy [lay] (1906–69) Rocket scientist and writer, born in Berlin. After studying science at German universities, he abandoned his plan to be a geologist after reading (1926) a work by the rocket scientist, Hermann Oberth. Ley took the lead in founding the German Society for Space Travel (1927), made it the centre of international activity in rocket research, brought Wernher von Braun and others into the group, and in particular helped develop the liquid-fuel rocket. When the Nazis forced rocket research into military applications, he fled to the USA (1935). Unable to find financial support for rocket research and space travel, he turned to writing about all aspects of science, and became widely known as a popularizer. But he never lost his faith in space travel, writing numerous science fiction and nonfiction accounts, including the award-winning *The Conquest of Space* (1949). He advised film-makers from Fritz Lang to Walt Disney on space travel, and during World War 2 advised Americans on bombs and explosive devices. >> Oberth; von Braun

Leyden, Lucas van >> Lucas van Leyden

Li, Choh Hao [lee] (1913–   ) Biochemist, born in Canton, China. He studied at Nanjing, and from 1935 at Berkeley, where he became professor of biochemistry (1950). His main work was on the pituitary hormones: he isolated adrenocorticotrophic hormone (ACTH), and by 1956 had established its molecular structure. Ten years later he had similar success with the growth hormone, somatotropin, which he synthesized in 1970.

Liang Qichao [leeang cheechow], also spelled **Liang Ch'i-ch'ao** (1873–1929) Chinese reformer. He travelled in the West, was prominent in China's late 19th-c reform movement, and fled to Japan in 1898. He published the journal *Renovated Citizen*, seeking to reappraise Confucianism in the light of Western liberal democracy. Though an influential intellectual, his gradualism was overtaken by events. He opposed Sun Yixian's Socialism, and founded (1913) the anti-Guomindang Democratic Party. He abandoned political activity when his Western illusions were destroyed by World War 1. >> Ci-Xi; Kang Youwei; Sun Yixian

Libau or **Libavius, Andreas** [**lee**bow, li**bay**vius] (c. 1540–1616) Alchemist, born in Halle, Germany. He studied at Jena, became professor of history and poetry there (1586–91), and in the 1590s took a post at Rothenberg an der Taube. His finest work was *Alchymia* (1606, Alchemy), the first modern chemical textbook, which gives an account of a range of chemical methods and substances, and vigorously attacks the ideas of Paracelsus. >> Paracelsus

Libby, Willard (Frank) (1908–80) Chemist, born in Grand Valley, CO. He studied and lectured at Berkeley, CA, and was involved in atom bomb research at Columbia (1941–5). He became professor of chemistry at Chicago (1945–54), a member of the US Atomic Energy Commission (1954–9), and professor of chemistry at Los Angeles (1959–76). He received the Nobel Prize for Chemistry in 1960 for his part in the invention of the carbon-14 method of dating.

Liberace [libuh**rah**chee], also known as **Walter Busterkeys**, originally **Wladziu Valentino Liberace** (1919–87) Entertainer, born in Milwaukee, WI. He appeared as a soloist with the Chicago Symphony Orchestra at 14, and earned a living under his stage name. Over the years he developed an act of popular piano classics performed with a lavish sense of showmanship. His television series, *The Liberace Show* (1952–7), won him an Emmy as Best Male Personality, and he broke all box-office records at Radio City Music Hall in New York City during 1985. His enduring career rested on his live performances and a flamboyant life style, full of piano-shaped swimming pools, glittering candelabra, and sartorial excess. His books include *The Things I Love* (1976).

Li Bo >> Li Po

Lichfield, (Thomas) Patrick (John Anson), 5th Earl of, professional name **Patrick Lichfield** (1939–) British photographer. He went to Sandhurst, served in the Grenadier Guards (1959–62), and became a photographer. He has achieved success in travel and publicity work as well as in many personal royal portraits, and in 1991 produced *Elizabeth R: A Photographic Celebration of 40 Years*. He created the well-known Unipart calendar, and has published many books, including his biography, *Not the Whole Truth* (1986).

Lichtenstein, Roy [**likh**tenstiyn] (1923–97) Painter, born in New York City. He studied at the Art Students' League, New York City (1939), and at Ohio State College, and taught at Ohio State, New York State, and Rutgers universities. From the early 1960s he produced many of the best-known images of American Pop Art, especially frames from comic books complete with speech balloons, enlarged onto canvases and painted in primary colours in a hard-edged style imitated from cheap printing techniques. The huge 'Whaam' (1963, Tate, London) is a typical example.

Lick, James (1796–1876) Financier and philanthropist, born in Fredericksburg, VA. A piano-maker by training, he went to California c.1848 and made a fortune in real estate investment. He founded the Lick Observatory on Mt Hamilton, CA.

Li Dazhao [lee dajow], also spelled **Li Ta-chao** (1888–1927) One of the founders of the Chinese Communist Party, whose interpretation of Marxism as applied to China had a profound influence on Mao Zedong. Appointed head librarian of Beijing University and professor of history (1918), he had the young Mao as a library assistant, and founded one of the first of the Communist study circles

which in 1921 were to form the Communist Party. In 1927, when the Manchurian military leader Chang Tso-lin (1873–1928), then occupying Beijing, raided the Soviet Embassy, Li was captured and executed. >> Mao Zedong

Liddell, Eric (Henry) [**lidl**], nickname **the Flying Scotsman** (1902–45) British athlete and missionary, born in Tientsin, China. He studied at Eltham College, London, and Edinburgh University. At the 1924 Olympics in Paris he won the bronze medal in the 200 m, and then caused a sensation by winning the gold medal in the 400 m (at which he was comparatively inexperienced) in a world record time of 47·6 s. In 1925, having completed his degree in science, and a degree in divinity, he went to China to work as a missionary. During World War 2 he was interned by the Japanese, and not long before the war ended he died of a brain tumour. The story of his athletic triumphs was told in the film *Chariots of Fire* (1981). >> RR1134

Liddell, Henry George [**lidl**] (1811–98) Scholar and lexicographer, born in Bishop Auckland, Co Durham, NE England, UK. He studied at Oxford, was ordained in 1838, and became a tutor at Oxford (1836–45) and headmaster of Westminster School (1846–55). He returned to Christ Church as dean, was vice-chancellor of the university (1870–4), and resigned the deanship in 1891. His major work was co-editing the *Greek–English Lexicon* (1843), and he also wrote a *History of Rome* (1855). His daughter, **Alice**, was the little girl for whom Charles Dodgson, his colleague at Christ Church, wrote *Alice in Wonderland*. >> Carroll, Lewis

Liddell Hart, Sir Basil (Henry) [**lidl** hah(r)t] (1895–1970) Military journalist and theorist, born in Paris. He studied at Cambridge, served in World War 1, and was wounded as an infantry officer. He joined the Army Education Corps, then became military correspondent for the *Daily Telegraph* (1925–35) and *The Times* (1935–9), advocating the principles of modern mobile warfare. He was knighted in 1966.

Liddon, Henry Parry (1829–90) Theologian, born in North Stoneham, Hampshire, S England, UK. He studied at Oxford, was ordained in 1852, and became vice-principal of Cuddesdon Theological College (1854–9), a prebendary of Salisbury (1864), a canon of St Paul's (1870), and professor of exegesis at Oxford until 1882. He strongly opposed the Church Discipline Act of 1874, supported Gladstone's crusade against the Bulgarian atrocities (1876), and was the most able and eloquent exponent of Liberal High Church principles. >> Gladstone, W E

Lidman, Sara (1923–) Writer, born in Missenträsk, Sweden. Tuberculosis interrupted her studies at the University of Uppsala, and she took to writing. Her early widely acclaimed novels include *Tjärdalen* (1953, The Tar Still) and *Hjortonlandet* (1955, Cloudberry Land). Her writing became more overtly political in the 1960s after her experiences of South Africa, Kenya, and Vietnam, but later, in the important series of novels beginning with *Din Tjänare Hör* (1977, Thy Servant Heareth), she returns to her roots and rural life in the north.

Lie, Jonas (Lauritz Idemil) [lee] (1833–1908) Writer, born in Eiker, Norway. He trained as a lawyer but turned to writing after being made bankrupt. His classic novels, which present realistic portrayals of ordinary folk in Norway, include *Den Fremsynte* (1870, The Visionary) and *Lodsen og Hans Hustru* (1874, Lodsen and his Wife). One of Norway's four great men of literature, he also wrote poetry, plays, and fairy-tales, including *Trold* (1891–2, Trolls).

Lie, (Marius) Sophus [lee] (1842–99) Mathematician, born in Nordfjordeide, Norway. He studied at Oslo University, then supported himself by giving private lessons. He became professor of mathematics at Oslo, then succeeded Felix Klein at Leipzig (1886), and returned to Oslo in 1898.

His study of contact transformations arising from partial differential equations led him to develop an extensive theory of continuous groups of transformations, now known as *Lie groups*. This theory has become a central part of 20th-c mathematics, and has important applications in quantum theory. >> Klein, Felix

Lie, Trygve (Halvdan) [lee, **trig**vuh] (1896–1968) Norwegian statesman and UN secretary-general (1946–52), born in Oslo (formerly, Kristiania). He studied at the University of Kristiania, became a Labour member of the Norwegian parliament and held several posts, before having to flee to Britain, where he was Norway's foreign minister-in-exile until 1945. He was elected the first secretary-general of the UN, but resigned in 1952 as a result of Soviet opposition to his support of UN intervention in the Korean War. He later became minister of industry (1963–4), and minister of commerce and shipping from 1964.

Lieber, Francis [lee ber] (1800–72) Political reformer, editor, and political scientist, born in Berlin. Persecuted as a liberal in Prussia, he fled in 1826 and arrived in Boston in 1827. Proposing to translate a German encyclopedia, he so enlarged and revised it that he ended up editing a new *Encyclopedia Americana* (13 vols, 1829–33). He taught at South Carolina (1835–57) and Columbia (1857–72). Two of his works, *Manual of Political Ethics* (1838–9) and *On Civil Liberty and Self-Government* (1853) provided the first thorough analysis of US government since its inception. Known for his ideas on prison reform, he also drafted a *Code for the Government of the Armies of the United States* (1863), which was adopted by the Union army. Essentially the first code of international law governing war, it was later used as the basis for the Hague Convention.

Liebermann, Max [lee berman] (1847–1935) Painter and etcher, born in Berlin. He studied at Weimar and in Paris, where he first won fame as 'disciple of the ugly'. In Germany from 1878, he painted open-air studies and scenes of humble life which were often sentimental. Later, however, his work became more colourful and romantic and, influenced by the French Impressionists, he became the leading painter of that school in his own country.

Liebig, Justus, Freiherr von (Baron) [lee bikh] (1803–73) Chemist, born in Darmstadt, Germany. He studied at Bonn and Erlangen, and in 1822 went to Paris, where he worked with Gay-Lussac. He became professor of chemistry at Giessen (1824) and Munich (1852). He investigated many aspects of organic, animal, and agricultural chemistry, and developed new techniques for carrying out analyses, such as the distillation equipment known as *Liebig's condenser*. He was created baron in 1845. >> Gay-Lussac; Wöhler

Liebknecht, Karl [leeb knekht] (1871–1919) German barrister and politician. A member of the Reichstag (1912–1916), he was imprisoned during World War 1 as an independent, anti-militarist Social Democrat. He was a founder member with Rosa Luxemburg of the German Communist Party (KPD) in 1918, and led an unsuccessful revolt in Berlin, the 'Spartacus League Revolution', in January 1919, during which he was killed by army officers. >> Luxemburg

Lifar, Serge [li fah(r)] (1905–86) Dancer and choreographer, born in Kiev, Ukraine. He was a student and friend of Diaghilev, whose company he joined in 1923. He scored his first triumph as a choreographer in Paris with *Créatures de Prométhée* (1929), and became the guiding genius behind the Paris Opéra (1929–58). He wrote several works on ballet, including a biography of Diaghilev (1940). >> Diaghilev

Ligachev, Yegor Kuzmich [li gachof] (1920–   ) Soviet politician. After training as an engineer, he worked in the Urals region during World War 2, joining the Communist Party in 1944. In 1957 he became Party chief of Akademgorodok.

He was brought to Moscow by Khrushchev (1961), then in 1965 was sent to Tomsk, in W Siberia, where he was regional Party boss for 18 years. He was promoted to the central Party secretariat by Yuri Andropov (1983), becoming ideology secretary (1984), and with the accession to power of Mikhail Gorbachev (1985) he was brought into the Politburo. He initially served as Gorbachev's deputy, but in 1988 he was demoted to the position of agriculture secretary. >> Andropov; Gorbachev

Ligeti, György (Sándor) [li get ee] (1923–   ) Composer, born in Dicsöszent-Márton, Hungary. He studied and later taught at the Budapest Academy of Music. After leaving Hungary in 1956, he worked at the electronics studio in Cologne, then settled in Vienna, where he developed an experimental approach to composition. His first large orchestral work, *Apparitions* (1958–9), made his name widely known. In *Aventures* (1962) he uses his own invented language of speech sounds. He has also written a choral requiem, a cello concerto, and music for harpsichord, organ, and wind and string ensembles.

Liguori, St Alfonso Maria de' [li gwoh ree], also known as **St Alphonsus Liguori** (1696–1787) Theologian, and founder of the Redemptorists, born in Naples, Italy. He abandoned law to take orders, and with 12 companions founded the order of *Liguorians* or Redemptorists (1732). In 1762 he became Bishop of Sant' Agata de' Goti, but he resigned in 1775, and returned to his order. He was canonized in 1839, and declared a Doctor of the Church in 1871. His prolific writings include the notable *Theologia moralis* (1748). Feast day 1 August.

Likert, Rensis [li kert] (1903–81) Psychologist and management theorist, born in Cheyenne, WY. At the University of Michigan (1946–70) he was founding director of the Institute for Social Research (1949–70), working on large organizations and theories of management. His major contributions included the development of a survey methodology that laid the groundwork for probability sampling, the *Likert scale* for measuring attitudes, and a theory of participatory management.

Lilburne, John (c. 1614–57) Pamphleteer and extreme Leveller (Puritan), probably born in Greenwich, EC Greater London, England, UK, but with family origins in Sunderland, Tyne and Wear. In 1638 he imported illegal Puritan literature from Holland, for which he was whipped, and imprisoned until 1640 by the Star Chamber. He was a captain in the Parliamentary army in the Civil War (1642), but resigned in 1645 over the Covenant. He became an indefatigable agitator for the Levellers, demanding greater liberty of conscience and numerous reforms, and was repeatedly imprisoned for his treasonable pamphlets.

Lilienthal, Otto [leel yentahl] (1849–96) Aeronautical inventor and pioneer of gliders, born in Anklam, Prussia. After graduating from the Berlin Trade Academy, he studied bird flight in order to build heavier-than-air flying machines resembling the birdman designs of Leonardo da Vinci. He made hundreds of short flights in his gliders, but crashed to his death near Berlin. >> Leonardo da Vinci

Li Lisan [lee leesan] (1900–67) Chinese politician, and effective head of the Communist Party (1928–30), born in Hunan province, China. He enforced what has since become known as the 'Li Lisan line', in which the Party's weak and undeveloped military forces were used in futile attempts to capture cities. His authoritarian methods alienated his fellow leaders. He was demoted in 1930, and lived in the Soviet Union until 1945. Thereafter he was employed by the Chinese Communist Party in various minor roles.

Lillee, Dennis (Keith) (1949–   ) Cricketer, born in Perth, Western Australia. A renowned fast bowler, he epitomized the move towards the more combative approach to international cricket. He took 355 wickets in 70 Tests, and his attempts to introduce a metal bat (illegal) into Test matches led to well-publicized clashes with the Australian cricketing authorities. >> RR1150

Lillehei, Clarence (Walton) [**lil**hay] (1918–) Thoracic and cardiovascular surgeon, born in Minneapolis, MN. He trained in medicine, physiology, and surgery at Minnesota University, working in the department of surgery there for most of his life, apart from a period (1967–74) at Cornell University Medical Center in New York City. His pioneering work on open-heart surgery began in the early 1950s, before the development of the pump oxygenator made such procedures more reliable.

Lilley, Peter (Bruce) (1943–) British statesman and writer. He studied at Cambridge, and became an investment adviser. He was elected an MP in 1983, then became parliamentary private secretary to Chancellor of the Exchequer Nigel Lawson (1985–7), economic secretary (1987–9) and financial secretary (1989–90) to the Treasury, and secretary-of-state for trade and industry (1990–2) and for social security (1992– –7). He is the author of several books on economic and political affairs. He emerged as a contender for the leadership of the Conservative Party following John Major's resignation in 1997, but withdrew after the first ballot. >> Lawson, Nigel; Major

Lillie, Beatrice (Gladys) (1898–1989) Revue singer, born in Toronto, Ontario, Canada. After an unsuccessful start as a drawing-room ballad singer, she found her true talent in 1914 in music hall and the new vogue of 'intimate revue' which came from Paris. She is particularly remembered for her version of Noel Coward's 'Mad Dogs and Englishmen'. During World War 2 she played to the troops, and was decorated by General de Gaulle. After the War she continued to work on the stage and in films, such as *Thoroughly Modern Millie* (1967).

Lilye or **Lily, William** (c. 1468–1522) Grammarian, born in Odiham, Hampshire, S England, UK. After graduating in the arts at Oxford, he visited Jerusalem, Rhodes, and Italy, and learned Greek from refugees from Constantinople. He was appointed first headmaster of St Paul's School (1512), and was perhaps the first person to teach Greek in London. He wrote *Lily's Grammar*, which after much revision was published as *Eton Latin Grammar* (1758).

Limburg brothers (fl. early 15th-c) **Pol, Jehanequin** and **Herman de Limburg** or **Limbourg** Three brothers, famous Flemish illuminators or miniaturists, of whom comparatively little is known. In 1411 they became court painters to the Duke of Berry, and produced illustrations for his illuminated manuscript *Les Très riches heures du Duc de Berry*, celebrated as one of the greatest masterpieces of the international Gothic style. Other works have been attributed to Pol de Limbourg, including *Heures d'Ailly*.

Limón, José [li**mon**] (1908–72) Dancer, choreographer, and teacher, born in Culiacan, Mexico. With the intention of becoming a painter, he moved to New York City, where he joined the company of Doris Humphrey and Charles Weidman (1930–40). He formed the José Limón Company in 1946, and it became the first American modern dance company to tour Europe, later touring the world with great success. The company continued in New York City after his death. >> Humphrey, Doris; Weidman

Limousin or **Limosin, Léonard** [limoozĩ] (c. 1505–77) Painter in enamel, born in Limoges, France. From one of the most famous families of enamellers working in Limoges, he was the most accomplished. He became court painter to Francis I from 1530, and was appointed head of the royal factory at Limoges. He was also well known for his work in oils.

Linacre, Thomas (c.1460–1524) Physician and scholar, born in Canterbury, Kent, SE England, UK. He studied at Oxford, was elected fellow of All Souls in 1484, and studied to be a physician at Padua. One of the earliest champions of the 'new learning', Erasmus and Sir Thomas More were both taught Greek by him. About 1500 Henry VII made him tutor to Prince Arthur. As king's physician to Henry VII and Henry VIII, he practised in London. In 1518 he founded the Royal College of Physicians, becoming its first president, and took Catholic orders in 1520. >> Henry VII; Henry VIII

Lin Biao or **Lin Piao** [lin byow] (1907–71) Chinese military leader, born in Huang-kang, China. He became one of the leaders of the Chinese Communist Party and a marshal of the Red Army. He was minister of defence from 1959, and in 1968 replaced the disgraced Liu Shaoqi as heir apparent to Mao Zedong. He was one of the promoters of the Cultural Revolution of 1966, and appears to have been a patron of extreme left-wing factions. In 1971, after a political struggle, he was killed in a plane crash in Mongolia, apparently in the course of an attempt to seek refuge in the USSR. >> Liu Shaoqi; Mao Zedong

Lincoln, Abraham see panel on p. 572

Lincoln, Benjamin (1733–1810) Revolutionary soldier, born in Hingham, MA. A major-general in the Continental Army, he reinforced Washington after the defeat on Long Island (1776), and in 1777 received command of the southern department. In 1780, besieged by Clinton in Charleston, he was forced to surrender with some 7000 troops. He took part in the siege of Yorktown (1781), and later became secretary of war (1781–3) and Lieutenant-Governor of Massachusetts (1789). >> Clinton, Henry

Lind, James (1716–94) Physician, born in Edinburgh, EC Scotland, UK. He served in the navy as a surgeon's mate, qualified in medicine at Edinburgh, and became physician at the Haslar naval hospital at Gosport. He is remembered for his research into cases of scurvy aboard ship; and his recommendation to the Royal Navy to issue citrus fruits and juices to sailors eradicated the disease. He also instigated delousing procedures, hospital ships, and distillation of seawater for drinking.

Lind, Jenny, originally **Johanna Maria Lind**, known as **the Swedish Nightingale** (1820–87) Soprano, born in Stockholm. She trained in Stockholm and Paris, made her debut in Stockholm in 1838, and attained great popularity everywhere. After 1856 she lived in England, and became professor of singing at the Royal College of Music (1883–6).

Lindbergh, Charles A(ugustus) [**lind**berg] (1902–74) Aviator, born in Detroit, MI. He worked as an airmail pilot on the St Louis–Chicago run, then in 1927 made the first nonstop solo transatlantic flight, from New York City to Paris, in the monoplane *Spirit of St Louis*. His book of the same name won the Pulitzer Prize in 1954. In 1932 his infant son was kidnapped and murdered, a sensational crime for which **Bruno Richard Hauptmann** was executed (1936), and the Lindberghs retreated to Europe. He later became an aeronautics consultant.

Lindemann, Frederick Alexander >> **Cherwell, Viscount**

Lindgren, Astrid (1907–) Children's novelist, born in Vimmerby, Sweden. She established her reputation with *Pippi Långstrump* (1945, Pippi Longstocking), and followed this with a succession of other popular characters, later turning to folklore with such titles as *Bröderna Lejonhjärta* (1973, The Brothers Lionheart).

Lindley, John (1799–1865) Botanist and horticulturalist, born in Catton, Norfolk, E England, UK. He was appointed assistant secretary to the Horticultural Society of London in 1827, and was professor of botany at University College, London (1829–60). In 1828 he prepared a report on the

ABRAHAM LINCOLN (1809–65)

Lincoln was born in a log cabin near Hodgenville, KY, and after several moves the family settled in SW Indiana in 1816. His education was limited and sporadic; although both of his parents were virtually illiterate, he was encouraged to attend schools organized by wandering teachers, and to read whenever he could. His total formal education amounted, on his own estimation, to less than one year's school attendance. Later he taught himself grammar and mathematics.

In 1832 he served for three months as a volunteer in the Black Hawk War, but saw no action. On his return he was elected to the Illinois State Assembly. In 1836 he qualified as a lawyer, became a junior partner in a Springfield law firm, and began to take a more prominent part in local politics. After one, possibly two love affairs (possibly with Ann Rutledge, and with Mary Owens, to whom he proposed in 1835), he married **Mary Todd** (1818–82) in 1843. They had four sons: **Robert Todd** (1843–1926), **Edward Baker** (1846–50), **William Wallace** (1850–62), and **Thomas 'Tad'** (1853–71). His wife never recovered from the early deaths of Edward and William. Having witnessed Lincoln's assassination and seen Tad die, she was eventually declared insane.

Lincoln's career as a lawyer developed rapidly, and he established his own practice with William H Herndon. After two failed attempts, in 1846 he was elected to the US House of Representatives as a Whig, but served only one term before taking up his law practice again. His return to active politics was precipitated by a crisis in Congress over slavery. In 1854 his political rival, Stephen A Douglas, steered the Kansas–Nebraska Act through Congress, the effect of which was to reopen the whole Louisiana Purchase to slavery. The old Northwest states, including Illinois, were violently opposed to this move, which nullified the anti-slavery feature of the Missouri Compromise (1852).

The anti-Nebraska movement marked the demise of the Whig Party and the emergence of the Republican Party; and Lincoln's active canvassing against the Act won him recognition as the local leader of the movement. Having narrowly missed election to the US Senate, he joined the Republican Party in 1858 and stood against Democrat Senator Douglas for the Illinois seat. The senatorial campaign featured a remarkable series of face-to-face encounters on the issue of slavery, known as the Lincoln–Douglas debates, in which the two candidates took turns to address the same election meetings. Lincoln lost, partly through electoral mismanagement, but the publicity and national stature which he gained during the campaign made possible his presidential nomination in 1860. He won the nomination at the third ballot, and although he undertook no active campaining, beat a divided Democratic Party to become the 16th president.

Announcement of his victory signalled the secession of the Southern states, and by the time of his inauguration (4 May 1861), the Confederate States had seized most of the key government buildings and military forts within their territory. His initial direction of the Civil War was seriously handicapped by his inability to select an effective army commander; only the eventual appointment of Ulysses S Grant led to victory for the Union forces.

The whole of Lincoln's presidency was overshadowed by the bitter Civil War. In addition to having problems with his generals, he presided over a divided and generally incompetent cabinet. However, he maintained his pragmatism in dealings with Congress, despite radical Republican demands for a more aggressive approach to the abolition of slavery and, later, opposition to his conciliatory plans for the reconstruction of the South. On 1 January 1863 he proclaimed the emancipation of all slaves in the Confederate States, and later that year (19 Nov) restated his anti-slavery views in the Gettysburg Address. During his 1864 campaign for re-election he embraced the abolition of slavery.

With Robert E Lee's surrender (9 Apr 1865), the Civil War was effectively ended. On 14 April, Lincoln was shot by an actor, John Wilkes Booth, while attending Ford's Theatre, Washington, DC, with his wife. He died early the following day without recovering consciousness. The manner of his death made him an instant folk hero. During his lifetime he had gained political stature, but he was also hated in many quarters, not least for the use of his executive powers to rule by proclamation, and his imprisonment of suspected opponents without trial. With the perspective of time, he has come to be seen as the saviour of his country and the liberator of slaves, noted for his integrity, fairness, and directness of speech and action.

>> Booth, John Wilkes; Douglas, Stephen A; Grant, Ulysses S; Lee, Robert E

---

royal gardens at Kew which saved them from destruction, and this led to the creation of the Royal Botanic Gardens. The most important of his many publications were those on orchids and *The Vegetable Kingdom* (1846).

Lindrum, Walter (1898–1960) Billiards player, born in Kalgoorlie, Western Australia. Regarded as the world's greatest billiards player, he set the current world record break of 4317 while playing Joe Davis in 1932, at Thurston's Hall, London. He competed in only two world championships (1933–4), and won both. He retired from competitive play in 1950. >> Davis, Joe

Lindsay, Sir David >> **Lyndsay, Sir David**

Lindsay, (Nicholas) Vachel [linzee] (1879–1931) Poet, born in Springfield, IL. He studied painting in Chicago and New York City, and from 1906 travelled America like a troubadour, reciting his very popular ragtime rhymes in return for food and shelter. His irrepressible spirits appear in *General Booth Enters into Heaven* (1913) and *The Congo* (1914). His later volumes of verse were less successful, and while suffering from extreme depression he committed suicide.

Lindwall, Ray(mond Russell) (1921–96) Cricketer, born in Sydney, New South Wales, Australia. With Keith Miller he formed an invincible Australian opening attack in the five years after World War 2. He took 228 wickets in 61 Tests, and also scored more than 1500 runs, with two Test centuries to his name. >> Miller, Keith; RR1150

Lineker, Gary (Winston) [lineker] (1960–) Footballer, journalist, and broadcaster, born in Leicester, Leicestershire, C England, UK. He played for Leicester City (1978–85), Everton (1985–6), FC Barcelona (1986–9), Tóttenham Hotspur (1982–92), and Grampus 8, Nagoya, Japan (1993–4).

He made his England debut in 1984 (captain 1990–2), playing in the 1986 and 1990 World Cups, and also in two European Championships (1988, 1992). He was voted the Professional Footballers' Association Player of the Year (1986) and the Football Writers' Association Player of the Year (1986, 1992). Retiring in 1994, he became a regular presenter of sports programmes for BBC radio and television, a columnist for *The Observer* (1995–   ), and a familiar figure on television commercials.

Link, Edwin (Albert) (1904–81) Inventor and aviation executive, born in Huntington, IN. While working in his father's piano factory, he and his brother built a flight simulator to help them learn to fly. In 1935 he founded Link Aviation Inc, which produced flight simulators and other apparatus. He also invented equipment for deep-sea exploration, including a mobile unmanned television camera.

Linklater, Eric (Robert) (1899–1974) Novelist, born in Dounby, Orkney Is, NE Scotland, UK. He studied medicine and English at Aberdeen, served in World War 1, then became a journalist in Bombay (1925–7), and an English lecturer at Aberdeen. While in the USA (1928–30) he wrote *Poet's Pub* (1929), the first of a series of satirical novels which include *Juan in America* (1931) and *Private Angelo* (1946). Later books include *A Year of Space* (1953) and *Fanfare for a Tin Hat* (1970), which are autobiographical.

Linley, Viscount >> Margaret, Princess

Linnaeus, Carolus [linayus], Swed **Carl von Linné** (1707–78) Botanist, born in Råshult, Sweden. He studied at Lund and Uppsala, where in 1730 he was appointed a botany assistant. He travelled widely on botanical exploration, and is the founder of modern taxonomic botany. His *Systema naturae fundamenta botanica* (1735), *Genera plantarum* (1737), and *Species plantarum* (1753), expound his influential system of classification, based on plant sex organs, and in which names consist of generic and specific elements, with plants grouped hierarchically into genera, classes, and orders. He practised as a physician in Stockholm, and in 1742 became professor of botany at Uppsala. He was ennobled in 1757.

Linowitz, Sol Myron [linohvich] (1913–   ) Lawyer, diplomat, and businessman, born in Trenton, NJ. He studied at Cornell University Law School, then worked in the Office of Price Administration in Washington, and in the Office of the General Council Navy Dept. He joined the Xerox Corporation and became its chairman (1958–66), and in 1969 became a senior partner with an international law firm. In the 1970s he co-negotiated the Panama Canal Treaties of 1977, and was personal ambassador for President Carter during the Middle East negotiations (1979–81). >> Carter, Jimmy

Lin Piao >> Lin Biao

Linton, Ralph (1893–1953) Cultural anthropologist, born in Philadelphia, PA. He studied at Swarthmore College, PA, then at Pennsylvania, Columbia, and Harvard universities. On his return from fieldwork in Polynesia, he joined the Museum of Natural History in Chicago, and became professor of sociology at Wisconsin (1928–37), Columbia (1937–46), and Yale (1946–53). He pioneered the use of the terms *status* and *role* in social science, and exercised an important influence on the development of the culture-and-personality school of anthropology. His major work was *The Study of Man* (1936).

Lin Yü-tang (1895–1976) Writer and philologist, born in Lun-chi, China. He studied at Shanghai, Harvard, and Leipzig, became professor of English at Peking (1923–6), and secretary of the ministry of foreign affairs (1927). He lived mainly in the USA from 1936, and was also Chancellor of Singapore University (1954–5). He is best known for his numerous novels, essays, and anthologies relating to Chinese wisdom and culture, and as co-author of the official romanization plan for the Chinese alphabet.

Lionheart, Richard the >> Richard I

Liouville, Joseph [lyooveel] (1809–82) Mathematician, born in St Omer, France. He studied at the Ecole Polytechnique and the Ecole des Ponts et Chaussées, where he trained as an engineer. He taught at the Ecole Polytechnique, the Collége de France, and the University of Paris. In 1836 he founded the *Journal de Mathématiques*, which he edited for nearly 40 years. His work in analysis continued the study of algebraic function theory begun by Niels Abel and Carl Jacobi, and he studied the theory of differential equations, mathematical physics, and celestial mechanics. >> Abel, Niels Henrik; Jacobi, Carl Gustav

Lipatti, Dinu [lipatee] (1917–50) Pianist and composer, born in Bucharest. He studied in Paris with Cortot and Boulanger, and after World War 2 established an international reputation as a gifted pianist, especially in the works of Chopin. His compositions include a *Symphonie concertante* for two pianos and strings, and a concertino for piano and orchestra. His career was cut short when he died of a rare form of cancer. >> Boulanger, Nadia; Chopin; Cortot

Lipchitz, Jacques [lipshitz], originally **Chaim Jacob Lipchitz** (1891–1973) Sculptor, born in Druskininkai, Lithuania. He studied engineering, then moved to Paris (1909–11), where he started producing Cubist sculpture in 1914. In the 1920s he experimented with abstract forms he called 'transparent sculptures'. Later he developed a more dynamic style which he applied with telling effect to bronze figure and animal compositions. He emigrated to the USA in 1941, by which time he had established an international reputation, and lived in Italy from 1963.

Li Peng [lee peng] (1928–   ) Chinese politician and prime minister (1987–   ), born in Chengdu, China. He trained as a hydro-electric engineer, and was appointed minister of the electric power industry in 1981. He became a vice premier (1983), was elevated to the Politburo (1985), and made prime minister. He sought to retain firm control of the economy, favoured improved relations with the Soviet Union, and took a strong line in facing down the student-led, pro-democracy movement. >> RR1040

Lipman, Maureen (Diane) (1946–   ) Actress and writer, born in Hull, NE England, UK. She studied at the London Academy of Music and Dramatic Art and made her debut in *The Knack* (1969). She has played in a number of West End productions, including *See How They Run* (1984). Television appearances include *Smiley's People*, *Absent Friends*, *Agony*, and *Eskimo Day* (1996), but she is probably best known for her award-winning 'You got an Ology?' British Telecom commercial on television. She has written several humorous books, including *How Was It For You?* (1985), *Thank You For Having Me* (1990), and *You Can Read Me Like a Book* (1995). In 1973 she married the playwright Jack Rosenthal. >> Rosenthal

Lipmann, Fritz (Albert) (1899–1986) Biochemist, born in Königsberg, Germany. He studied medicine at Berlin, and worked in biochemistry at the Carlsberg Institute in Copenhagen (1932–9). In the USA from 1939, he did research at the Massachusetts General Hospital (1941–57), then became professor at Harvard Medical School (1949–57) and at Rockefeller University, New York City (from 1957). He isolated and elucidated the molecular structure of co-enzyme A, for which he shared the 1953 Nobel Prize for Physiology or Medicine. >> RR1124

Li Po [lee poh], also found as **Li Bo** and **Li T'ai Po** (c. 700–762) Poet, born in Szechwan Province, China. He led a dissipated life at the emperor's court, and later was one of a wandering band calling themselves 'The Eight Immortals of the Wine Cup'. Regarded as the greatest poet of China, he wrote colourful verse of wine, women, and nature. It is believed that he was drowned while trying to pluck the Moon from a lake.

Lippershey, Hans or **Jan** [**lip**ershay], also spelled **Lippersheim** (c. 1570–1619) Dutch optician, born in Wesel, Germany. He is one of several spectacle-makers credited with the discovery that the combination of a convex and a concave lens can make distant objects appear nearer. He is believed to be the inventor of the telescope (1608).

Lippi, Filippino [**li**pee] (c. 1458–1504) Painter, born in Florence, Italy. He was the son of Fra Filippo Lippi, and was apprenticed to Botticelli. He completed the frescoes in the Brancacci Chapel, Florence, left unfinished by Masaccio c.1484. Other celebrated series of frescoes were painted by him between 1487 and 1502, the one in the Caraffa Chapel, S Maria sopra Minerva, Rome, being his most influential. 'The Vision of St Bernard' (c.1480–6) is his best-known picture. >> Botticelli; Lippi, Fra Filippo; Masaccio

Lippi, Fra Filippo [**li**pee], known as **Lippo** (c. 1406–69) Religious painter, born in Florence, Italy. In 1424 he became a pupil of Masaccio, who was painting the frescoes in the Brancacci Chapel where Lippi had taken his monastic vows. The style of his master can be seen in his early work, such as in the frescoes, 'The Relaxation of the Carmelite Rule' (c.1432). His greatest work, on the choir walls of Prato Cathedral, was begun in 1452. Between 1452 and 1464 he abducted a nun, **Lucrezia Buti**, and was released from his vows by Pope Pius II in order to marry her. She was the model for many of his fine Madonnas, and the mother of his son, Filippino Lippi. His later works, deeply religious, include the series of 'Nativities'. >> Lippi, Filippino; Masaccio

Lippincott, Joshua (Ballinger) (1813–86) Publisher, born in Juliustown, NJ. He had a bookseller's business in Philadelphia (1834–6), then founded his well-known publishing firm. He started *Lippincott's Magazine* in 1868.

Lippmann, Gabriel (1845–1921) Physicist, born in Hollerich, Luxembourg. Professor of mathematical and experimental physics at the Sorbonne (1886), he invented a capillary electrometer, and produced the first coloured photograph of the spectrum. He was awarded the 1908 Nobel Prize for Physics.

Lippmann, Walter (1889–1974) Journalist, born in New York City. He studied at Harvard, was on the editorial staff of the *New York World* until 1931, then became a special writer for the New York *Herald Tribune*. His daily columns became internationally famous, and he won many awards, including the Pulitzer Prize for International Reporting (1962). Among his best-known books is *The Cold War* (1947).

Lippold, Richard [**li**pohld] (1915–) Sculptor, born in Milwaukee, WI. He studied at Chicago (1933–7), worked as an industrial designer (1937–41), moved to New York City (1944), then settled in Locust Valley, NY. He is known for his constructed wire sculptures, as in 'Variation Number 7: Full Moon' (1950).

Lips, Joest >> **Lipsius, Justus**

Lipscomb, William Nunn, Jr (1919–) Physical chemist, born in Cleveland, OH. He studied at Kentucky University and the California Institute of Technology, and was appointed professor of chemistry at Harvard in 1959. He deduced the molecular structures of a curious group of boron compounds by X-ray crystal diffraction analysis in the 1950s, and went on to develop theories for the chemical bonding in these compounds. He was awarded the Nobel Prize for Chemistry in 1976.

Lipsius, Justus [**lip**sius], also known as **Joest Lips** (1547–1606) Humanist and Classical scholar, born in Issche, Belgium.

Professor of Classics at Jena, Leyden, and Louvain, he was successively Catholic, Lutheran, Calvinist, and once more Catholic. Noted for his essays in moral and political theory, his writings also include important editions of the Latin prose texts of Tacitus (1574) and Seneca (1605). >> Seneca; Tacitus

Lipton, Seymour (1903–86) Sculptor, born in New York City. He studied dentistry at Columbia (1923–7). Without formal training, he began sculpting in 1928, and first exhibited in 1933. Many of his 1930s works are figurative wood carvings, but during the 1940s he began constructing abstract sculptures from sheet lead. From the 1950s he worked primarily in silver-plated nickel on metal.

Lipton, Sir Thomas Johnstone (1850–1931) Businessman and philanthropist, born in Glasgow, W Scotland, UK. After various jobs in the USA he returned to Glasgow, and in 1870 opened the first of his many prosperous grocery shops, which made him a millionaire by the age of 30. He bought tea plantations, rubber estates, factories and packing houses abroad, and many farms and factories at home, creating Lipton Ltd in 1898. A keen yachtsman, he challenged the America's Cup five times with his yachts *Shamrock I–V*, and made generous donations to charities. He was knighted in 1898 and created a baronet in 1902.

Li Shih-chen [lee sheechen] (1518–93) Pharmaceutical naturalist and biologist, regarded as 'the prince of pharmacists', and 'the father of Chinese herbal medicine'. He compiled the *Pen Tshao Kang Mu* (Great Pharmacopoeia), completed in 1578 and published in 1596. It gives an exhaustive description of 1000 plants and 1000 animals, and includes more than 8000 prescriptions.

Lisle, Leconte de >> **Leconte de Lisle**

Lisle, Rouget de >> **Rouget de Lisle**

Lissajous, Jules Antoine [leesazhoo] (1822–80) French physicist. He became professor at the Collège St Louis, Paris, and in 1857 invented the vibration microscope which showed visually the *Lissajous figures* obtained as the resultant of two simple harmonic motions at right angles to one another. His researches extended to acoustics and optics, and his system of optical telegraphy was used during the siege of Paris (1871).

Lissitsky, El(iezer) [**lisit**skee], also spelled **Lissitzky** (1890–1941) Painter and designer, born in Smolensk, Russia. He trained in engineering and architecture at Darmstadt, Germany. In 1919 Chagall appointed him professor of architecture and graphic art at the art school in Vitebsk, where he came under the influence of his colleague, Kasimir Malevich. He produced a series of abstract works, called 'Proun' (1919), in which he combined flat rectilinear forms and dramatic architectonic elements. >> Chagall; Malevich

Lister, Joseph Jackson (1786–1869) Wine merchant and amateur microscopist, born in London, England, UK. A wine merchant with an interest in optics, he developed a method of building lens systems to greatly reduce chromatic and spherical aberrations. In 1826 **James Smith** (d.1870) built a much improved microscope to Lister's design, and this was used a year later to produce the first competent article on histology. Lister was elected a fellow of the Royal Society in 1832. >> Lister, Joseph

Lister (of Lyme Regis), Joseph Lister, Baron (1827–1912) Surgeon, born in Upton, Essex, SE England, UK, the son of Joseph Jackson Lister. He studied at London, and became professor of surgery at Glasgow (1859), Edinburgh (1869), and London (1877). His great work was the introduction (1860) of the use of antiseptic conditions during surgery, which greatly reduced surgical mortality. He was made a baronet in 1883, and a baron in 1897. >> Lister, Joseph Jackson; Semmelweiss

Lister, Samuel Cunliffe, 1st Baron Masham (1815–1906) Inventor, born in Bradford, West Yorkshire, N England, UK. Working in his father's worsted mill at Manningham, he invented a wool-comber in 1845, and made a fortune, at the same time bringing prosperity to Bradford and the wool trade of Australia and New Zealand. Later he spent a quarter of a million pounds developing a machine to spin waste silk, and was nearly bankrupt by the time its success made him a second fortune. A generous benefactor, he presented Bradford with Lister Park, and was created Baron Masham in 1891.

Liston, Sonny, popular name of **Charles Liston** (?1917–70) Boxer, born in St Francis Co, AR. There is a great deal of uncertainty about his early life, and especially his age. It is thought he learned to box while serving two long prison sentences, and began his career in the ring in 1934. He defeated Floyd Patterson to become world heavyweight champion in 1962, but in 1964 lost the title to Cassius Clay (Muhammad Ali). >> Ali, Muhammad; Patterson

Liszt, Franz (1811–86) Composer and pianist, born in Raiding, Hungary. He studied and played at Vienna and Paris, touring widely in Europe as a virtuoso pianist. From 1835 to 1839 he lived with the Comtesse d'Agoult, by whom he had three children. He gave concerts throughout Europe, and in 1847 met Princess Carolyne zu Sayn-Wittgenstein with whom he lived until his death. In 1848 he went to Weimar, where he directed the opera and concerts, composed, and taught. His works include 12 symphonic poems, Masses, two symphonies, and a large number of piano pieces. In 1865 he received minor orders in the Catholic Church, and was known as Abbé. >> Agoult; Smetana

Li Ta-chao >> **Li Dazhao**

Li Tsang >> **Li Zang**

Little, Malcolm >> **Malcolm X**

Little Richard, popular name of **Richard Wayne Penniman** (1932–) Rock-and-roll singer and pianist, born in Macon, GA. Raised as a Seventh-Day Adventist, he sang in church choirs throughout his childhood. Leaving home at 14, he started singing professionally, and became well known on the southern vaudeville circuit. 'Tutti Frutti' (1955) brought him international popularity. Most of his recordings from 1958 to 1964 were of Gospel songs, but in the mid-1960s he made a comeback with 'Whole Lot Of Shaking Goin' On', 'Lawdy Miss Clawdy', and his album *The Rill Thing*.

Littlewood, (Maudie) Joan (1914–) Theatre director, born in London, England, UK. She trained at the Royal Academy of Dramatic Art, London, and with Ewan MacColl founded in Manchester the Theatre of Action (1934) and the Theatre Union (1936). Out of this pioneering work in left-wing, popular theatre was formed the Theatre Workshop in 1945. She directed the first British production for Brecht's *Mother Courage* in Barnstaple in 1955, in which she played the title role, and after settling at the Theatre Royal, Stratford East, her productions included *The Hostage* (1958) and *Oh! What a Lovely War* (1963). >> MacColl, Ewan

Littlewood, John (Edensor) (1885–1977) Mathematician, born in Rochester, Kent, SE England, UK. He studied at Cambridge, lectured in Manchester (1907–10), then returned to Cambridge as a fellow of Trinity, and remained there for the rest of his life. In collaboration with Godfrey Hardy, he wrote papers on summability theory, Tauberian theorems, Fourier series, analytic number theory, and the Riemann zeta-function. He was appointed to the chair of mathematics at Cambridge in 1928. >> Hardy, Godfrey

Littré, (Maximilien) Paul Emile [leetray] (1801–81) Lexicographer and philosopher, born in Paris. He abandoned medicine for philology, and his translation of Hippocrates

procured his election in 1839 to the Academy of Inscriptions. He became an enthusiastic supporter of Auguste Comte, after whose death in 1857 he became the leader of the Positivist school. He published the outstanding *Dictionnaire de la langue française* (1863–72, Dictionary of the French Language), and after some controversy he was admitted to the Académie Française in 1871. >> Comte

Litvinov, Maxim (Maximovich) [litveenof] (1876–1951) Russian politician and diplomat, born in Bialystok, Poland. He joined the Russian Social Democratic Party (1898), was exiled to Siberia (1903), but escaped. At the Revolution he was appointed Bolshevik ambassador in London (1917–8). He became deputy people's commissar for foreign affairs in 1921, then commissar (1930–9), achieving US recognition of Soviet Russia (1934). He was dismissed in 1939, but reinstated after the German invasion of Russia, and became ambassador to the USA (1941–3) and vice-minister of foreign affairs (1943–6).

Liu-Bang >> **Gaozu**

Liu Shaoqi [lyoo showchee], also spelled **Liu Shao-ch'i** (1898–1969) Chinese political leader, born in Ningxiang, Hunan, China. He studied at Changsa and Shanghai, went to Moscow to study, joined the Chinese Communist Party, and became a party labour organizer in Shanghai. He was elected to the Politburo in 1934, became secretary-general of the Party (1943), vice-chairman (1949), and chairman of the People's Republic of China in 1958. During the Cultural Revolution (1966–9) he was denounced, and banished to Hunan province. He reportedly died in detention, but was posthumously rehabilitated in 1980. >> RR1041

Liu Sheng [lyoo shang] (?–113 BC) Chinese prince, the brother of Wudi. His tomb, and that of his consort, **Princess Dou Wan** (d.103 BC), was opened at Mancheng, Hopei, in 1968. Stretching 46 m/170 ft into a hill, it contained 2800 objects, including the famous suits of 4846 jade pieces sewn with gold to prevent body decay (they failed), six carriages, 16 horses, en-suite bathroom with drain, and embroidered curtains. >> Wudi

Liu Xin [lyoo sheen], also spelled **Liu Hsin** (1st-c BC–1st-c AD) Astronomer, and scholar-minister to the Chinese usurper Wang Mang. He antedated Ptolemy's *Almagest* (2nd-c AD) with his astronomical tables, and catalogued 1080 stars in six magnitude categories, and calculated the year at 365 385/1539 days. In AD 4 he organized a national scientific congress attended by 1000 scholars. >> Wang Mang

Li Yuan >> **Gaozu**

Lively, Penelope (Margaret), *née* **Greer** (1933–) Novelist and children's author, born in Cairo. She settled in England, UK and studied at Oxford. Her first books were for children, and include *The Ghost of Thomas Kempe* (1973), *A Stitch in Time* (1976), and *The Revenge of Samuel Stokes* (1981). Her adult novels include *Judgement Day* (1980), *Moon Tiger* (1987, Booker), *City of the Mind* (1991), and *Cleopatra's Sister* (1993). In 1997 appeared a collection of short stories, *Beyond the Blue Mountains*.

Livermore, Mary Ashton, *née* **Rice** (1820–1905) Suffragette and reformer, born in Boston, MA. A teacher by training, in 1845 she married the **Rev Daniel P Livermore**, and became active in the women's suffrage movement. She was founder-editor of *The Agitator* (1869), which was later merged into the *Woman's Journal*.

Liverpool, Robert Banks Jenkinson, 2nd Earl of (1770–1828) British prime minister (1812–27), born in London, England, UK. He studied at Oxford, entered parliament in 1790, and was a member of the India Board (1793–6), Master of the Royal Mint (1799–1801), foreign secretary (1801–4), home secretary (1804–6, 1807–9), and secretary for war and the colonies (1809–12). He succeeded his father as Earl of Liverpool in 1807. As premier, he over-saw the final years of the Napoleonic Wars and the War of 1812–14 with the USA. He resigned after a stroke early in 1827. >> RR1095

Livia Drusilla (58 BC–AD 29) Roman empress, the third wife of the emperor Augustus, whom she married in 39 BC after divorcing her first husband Tiberius Claudius Nero. From her first marriage she had two children: Tiberius and Nero Claudius Drusus. She was influential with Augustus, and conspired maliciously to ensure Tiberius's succession, gaining the nickname 'Ulysses in Petticoats'. Relations with Tiberius after his accession became strained, and when she died he did not execute her will or allow her to be deified. >> Augustus; Drusus Germanicus; Tiberius; RR1084

Livingston, M(ilton) Stanley (1905–86) Physicist, born in Brodhead, WI. He taught and carried on research at Cornell (1934–8), then moved to the Massachusetts Institute of Technology (1938–70). Concurrently he consulted and performed atomic research at Brookhaven, (1946–8), Harvard (1956–67), the Fermi National Accelerator Laboratory (1967–70), and Los Alamos (1950–86). A lifelong leader in atomic particle accelerator design, he developed the first cyclotron with Ernest Lawrence in 1931. >> Lawrence, Ernest

Livingston, Robert R >> **Morey, Samuel**

Livingstone, David (1813–73) Missionary and explorer, born in Blantyre, South Lanarkshire, WC Scotland, UK. After studying medicine in London, he was ordained under the London Missionary Society in 1840, and in 1852–6 was the first European to discover L Ngami, and the Victoria Falls of the Zambezi. He was welcomed home as a hero, and published his *Missionary Travels* (1857). He led an expedition (1858–63) exploring the Zambezi, and discovered Lakes Shirwa and Nyasa. The expedition was recalled, he journeyed as far as Bombay, and returned to England in 1864. He was asked to return to Africa and settle a dispute regarding the sources of the Nile, and in 1867–8 he discovered Lakes Mweru and Bangweulu. On his return to Ujiji after severe illness he was found there by Henry Morton Stanley, sent to look for him by the *New York Herald*. He returned to Bangweulu, but died, and his body was taken for burial in Westminster Abbey. >> Cameron, Verney Lovett; Stanley, Henry Morton; Williams, John (1796–1839)

Livius >> **Livy**

Livius Andronicus [livius andronikus] (fl.3rd-c BC) Writer and playwright, born in Tarentum, Greece. He was taken prisoner during the Roman capture of the city, and sold as a slave in Rome in 272 BC. After he was freed, he earned his living teaching Latin and Greek in Rome, translated the *Odyssey* into Latin Saturnian verse, and wrote tragedies, comedies, and hymns after Greek models. Only fragments of his works have survived, but he remains 'the father of Roman dramatic and epic poetry'.

Livy [livee], in full **Titus Livius** (c. 59 BC–AD 17) Roman historian, born in Patavium, Italy. He settled in Rome sometime before 29 BC, when he began his history of Rome from her foundation to the death of Nero Claudius Drusus (9 BC). This momentous work of 142 books became the foundation of historical writing through to the 18th-c, and placed him at the forefront of Latin writers.

Li Xiannian [lee shanyan] (1905–92) Chinese statesman, born in Hubei province, China. He worked as a carpenter before serving with the Kuomintang (Nationalist) forces (1926–7). After joining the Communist Party in 1927 he established the Oyuwan Soviet (people's republic) in Hubei, participated in the Long March (1934–6), and was a military commander in the war against Japan, and in the

civil war. He was inducted into the Politburo and secretariat in 1956 and 1958, but fell out of favour during the 1966–9 Cultural Revolution. He was rehabilitated, as finance minister, by Zhou Enlai in 1973, and later served as state president under Deng Xiaoping (1983–8). >> Deng Xiaoping; Zhou Enlai

Li Zang [lee tsang], also spelled **Li Tsang** (?–168 BC) Wife of a relatively minor Chinese official of the Han period. Her tomb at Mawangdui, Hunan, was opened in 1972. It contained, besides a well-preserved corpse wrapped in 20 layers of embroidered silk in a painted lacquer coffin, over 1000 other objects, including rolls of silk, lacquered *objets d'art*, clothing and wigs, picnic boxes of food, and her portrait.

Llewellyn (Prince of Wales) >> **Llywelyn**

Llewellyn, Richard [hlooelin], pseudonym of **Richard Dafydd Vivian Llewellyn Lloyd** (1907–83) Writer, born in St David's, Pembrokeshire, SW Wales. He established himself, after service with the regular army and a short spell in the film industry and journalism, as a best-selling novelist with *How Green Was My Valley* (1939), a novel about a Welsh mining village. Later works include *The Flame of Hercules* (1957) and *I Stand on a Quiet Shore* (1982).

Llosa, Mario Vargas [hohsa] (1936–) Novelist, born in Arequipa, Peru. After studying law and literature at home he became a student in Paris and Madrid, building up a reputation as a writer before returning. *The Time of the Hero*, his first novel, published in 1962, so outraged the Peruvian authorities that a 1000 copies were publicly burned. Subsequent novels include his masterpiece *Aunt Julia and the Scriptwriter* (1977), *The War at the End of the World* (1985), and *A Fish in the Water* (1994), and he is heralded as one of the world's greatest novelists, winning many honours. He is also a football commentator, and a candidate for the Peruvian presidency, having declined an offer of the premiership in 1984.

Lloyd, Clive (Hubert) (1944–) Cricketer, born in Georgetown, Guyana. Educated on a scholarship to Chatham High School, Georgetown, he worked as a hospital clerk until his first West Indies Test cap in 1966, then moved to England to play for Haslingden before joining Lancashire (1968–86). A batsman and fielder, he played in 110 Test matches (captain 1974–85), scoring 7515 runs and making 19 centuries. He captained the West Indies, winning the World Cup in 1975 and 1979. >> RR1149

Lloyd, Edward (?–c. 1730) English newspaper founder and coffee-house keeper. From 1688 until 1726 he owned a coffee house in Lombard St, London, after which is named *Lloyd's*, the London society of underwriters. It also became a haunt of merchants and ship-owners, and for them Lloyd started his *Lloyd's News*, later to become *Lloyd's List*, London's oldest daily newspaper, providing an information service on shipping matters.

Lloyd, George Walter Selwyn (1913–) Composer and conductor, born in St Ives, Cornwall, SW England, UK. His 3rd symphony and two operas (*Iernin*, 1935, and *The Serf*, 1938) were well received in London, before he served during World War 2 in the Royal Marines Band, and was severely shell-shocked. Another opera, *John Socman*, followed in 1951, but owing to illness he retired to Devon, and composed only intermittently for a period. With improved health he has produced several other concertos and symphonies.

Lloyd, Harold (Clayton) (1893–1971) Film comedian, born in Burchard, NE. Stagestruck from an early age, he worked extensively as an extra before becoming one of America's most popular daredevil comedians in films such as *High and Dizzy* (1920) and, most famously, *Safety Last* (1923), in which he dangles perilously from the hands of a high-rise clock face. He enjoyed a remarkable run of hits from *Why Worry?* (1923) to *Speedy* (1928), and received an honorary Academy Award in 1952.

Lloyd, Henry Demarest (1847–1903) Journalist and reformer, born in New York City. He studied at Columbia, lectured in economics, was admitted to the bar (1869), and became secretary of the American Free Trade League. He worked on the Chicago *Tribune* as a member of the editorial staff (1872–85). He became dedicated to the exposure of capitalist abuses, and his masterpiece, *Wealth Against Commonwealth* (1894), was a searing indictment of the methods by which John D Rockefeller built up Standard Oil. >> Rockefeller, John D; Tarbell

Lloyd, Marie, originally **Matilda Alice Victoria Wood** (1870–1922) Music-hall singer and entertainer, born in London, England, UK. She made her first appearance at the Royal Eagle Music Hall (later The Grecian) in 1885. Her first great success was with a song called 'The Boy I Love Sits Up in the Gallery', and she became one of the most popular music-hall performers of all time, appearing in music halls in America, South Africa, and Australia. Among her most famous songs was 'My Old Man Said Follow the Van'.

Lloyd, (John) Selwyn >> **Selwyn-Lloyd, Baron**

Lloyd-George (of Dwyfor), David Lloyd George, 1st Earl (1863–1945) British Liberal statesman and prime minister (1916-22), born in Manchester, Greater Manchester, NW England, UK. He studied in Wales, became a solicitor and, in 1890, an MP for Caernarfon Boroughs (a seat he was to hold for 55 years). He was President of the Board of Trade (1905–8) and Chancellor of the Exchequer (1905–15). His 'people's budget' of 1909–10 was rejected by the House of Lords, and led to a constitutional crisis and the Parliament Act of 1911, which removed the Lords' power of veto. He became minister of munitions (1915), secretary for war (1916), and coalition prime minister. After World War 1, he continued as head of a coalition government dominated by Conservatives. He negotiated with Sinn Féin, and conceded the Irish Free State (1921) – a measure which brought his downfall. Following the 1931 general election, he led a 'family' group of Independent Liberal MPs. He was made an earl in 1945. A film about his life, directed by Maurice Elvey and starring Norman Page, was made in 1918, but was then mysteriously suppressed and lost. Rediscovered in 1994, it was restored by the Welsh and National Film Archives, and premiered in 1996. >> Lloyd-George, Gwilym/Megan; RR1095

Lloyd-George (of Dwyfor), Gwilym, 1st Viscount Tenby of Bulford (1894-1967) British statesman, born in Criccieth, Gwynedd. The second son of David Lloyd-George, he entered parliament in 1922, and again from 1929 to 1950, during which term he was parliamentary secretary to the Board of Trade (1939–41) and minister of fuel and power (1942–5). In 1951 he was returned as Liberal-Conservative member for Newcastle North, and was minister of food until 1954. He was minister for Welsh affairs until 1957, when he was created Viscount Tenby of Bulford. >> Lloyd-George, David

Lloyd-George (of Dwyfor), Lady Megan (1902–66) British politician, born in Criccieth, Gwynedd, the younger daughter of David Lloyd-George. She was elected Liberal member of parliament for Anglesey in 1929, and Independent Liberal between 1931 and 1945. Defeated in the election of 1951, in 1955 she joined the Labour Party and became MP for Carmarthen in 1957. >> Lloyd-George, David/Gwilym

Lloyd-Jones, David Martyn (1899–1981) Preacher and writer, born in Newcastle Emlyn, Carmarthenshire, SW Wales. He trained in medicine at London, then entered the Christian ministry. After 11 years in Aberavon, he became colleague and successor to G Campbell Morgan at Westminster Chapel, London, where he preached for 30 years. His published works include *Studies in the Sermon on the Mount* (2 vols, 1959–60).

Lloyd-Webber, Andrew Lloyd Webber, Baron (1948–) Composer, born in London, England, UK. From a distinguished musical family, he had no conventional musical education. With Tim Rice he wrote *Joseph and the Amazing Technicolour Dreamcoat* (1968), and the rock opera *Jesus Christ Superstar* (staged 1970), the LP of which achieved record-breaking sales. He has since composed the music for many West End hits, including *Evita* (1978), *Cats* (1981), and *Starlight Express* (1984). All his shows are sold out for months in advance, and his most recent successes include *The Phantom of the Opera* (1986) and *Aspects of Love* (1989). With the opening of *Sunset Boulevard* in 1993, he had five musicals concurrently in production in London. He wrote the film scores for *Gumshoe* (1971) and *The Odessa File* (1974), and, in a fresh departure, composed a Requiem Mass in 1985. He was knighted in 1992, and received a life peerage in 1997. >> Lloyd Webber, Julian

Lloyd Webber, Julian (1951–) Cellist, born in London, the brother of composer Andrew Lloyd Webber. He studied at the Royal College of Music and with Pierre Fournier in Geneva, and in 1972 made his UK debut. He has since performed with all the major British orchestras, appeared internationally, and made many recordings. His books include *The Young Cellist's Repertoire* (1984), *The Great Cello Solos* (1991), and *Cello Song* (1994). >> Lloyd-Webber, Andrew

Llull or **Lull, Ramón** [lul], Eng **Raymond Lully**, known as **the Enlightened Doctor** (c. 1235–1315) Theologian and mystic, born in Palma, Majorca. He served as a soldier and led a dissolute life, but from 1266 gave himself up to asceticism, became a Franciscan, and went on a spiritual crusade to convert the Mussulmans. His major work is the *Ars magna* (The Great Art), condemned in 1376 for its attempt to link faith and reason, but later viewed more sympathetically. He travelled widely, and was allegedly killed on missionary work in Budia (Bougie), Algeria. His followers, known as *Lullists*, combined religious mysticism with alchemy.

Llywelyn ap Gruffydd [hluhwelin ap grifith] (?–1282) Prince of Gwynedd in North Wales, the grandson of Llywelyn ap Iorwerth. In 1258 he proclaimed himself Prince of Wales, and was recognized by the Treaty of Shrewsbury in 1265. When Edward I succeeded to the English throne in 1272, he was invaded and forced to submit in 1277. In 1282 he rebelled against Edward, but was killed in battle near Builth, and with him Wales lost her political independence. >> Edward I; Llywelyn ap Iorwerth

Llywelyn ap Iorwerth [hluhwelin ap yaw(r)werth], known as **Llywelyn Fawr** ('Llywelyn the Great') (?–1240) Prince of Gwynedd in North Wales. He seized power from his uncle in 1194, and soon had most of N Wales under his control. In 1205 he married Joan, the illegitimate daughter of King John of England. He successfully maintained his independence against King John and Henry III, and extended his kingdom over most of Wales, but by 1223 he had to withdraw to the north. >> John; Henry III (of England); Llywelyn ap Gruffudd

Loach, Kenneth (1936–) Film-maker, born in Nuneaton, Warwickshire, C England, UK. After studying law at Oxford he became an actor, then trained as a television director, and joined the BBC. He directed various early episodes of *Z Cars* (1962) before making his name in the Wednesday Play series, highlighting social problems such as homelessness in *Cathy Come Home* (1966). His first feature film, *Poor Cow*

(1967), was followed by the popular *Kes* (1969). His television documentary series, *Questions of Leadership* (1983), was banned on political grounds. Later works include *Fatherland* (1987), *Hidden Agenda* (1990), *Riff-Raff* (1991), and *Carla's Song* (1996).

Loane, Sir Marcus Lawrence (1911–) Clergyman, born in Tasmania, Australia. He studied at Sydney University, and was ordained in 1935. He was vice-principal (1939–53) and principal (1954–8) of Moore Theological College, Bishop-Coadjutor (1958–66) and Archbishop (1966–82) of Sydney, later serving also as Primate of the Anglican Church in Australia (1978–82).

Lobachevsky, Nikolay Ivanovich [lobachefskee] (1792–1856) Mathematician, born in Nizhni Novgorod, Russia. He became professor at Kazan in 1816, where he spent the rest of his life. In the 1820s he developed a theory of non-Euclidean geometry in which Euclid's parallel postulate did not hold. A similar theory was discovered almost simultaneously and independently by Jénos Bolyai. >> Bolyai; Euclid

L'Obel or **Lobel, Matthias de** [lohbel] (1538–1616) Botanist, born in Lille, France. He studied at the University of Montpelier, later becoming botanist and physician to James I of England. He gave his name to the *Lobelia*.

Lochner, Stefan [lokhner] (c. 1400–1451) Religious painter, born in Meersburg am Bodensee, on L Constance, Germany. He was the principal master of the Cologne school, marking the transition from the Gothic style to Naturalism. His best-known work is the great triptych, 'Adoration of the Kings', in Cologne Cathedral.

Lock, Tony, popular name of **Graham Anthony Richard Lock** (1929–95) Cricketer, born in Limpsfield, Surrey, SE England, UK. His left-arm bowling helped to make Surrey virtually unbeatable at county level in the 1950s. He played 49 Tests for England and took 174 wickets, taking 10 or more wickets in a match on three occasions. His bowling action came under suspicion, but he returned with a satisfactorily remodelled bowling method. He also played for Western Australia and Leicestershire. >> Laker, Jim; RR1151

Locke, Alain (LeRoy) (1886–1954) Educator and writer, born in Philadelphia, PA. The first black Rhodes scholar at Oxford (1907–10), he became professor of philosophy at Howard University (1917). A leader of the Harlem Renaissance, his works include *The Negro in America* (1933).

Locke, Bessie (1865–1952) Pioneer of kindergarten education, born in Arlington (formerly West Cambridge), MA. She attended a private kindergarten, and went on to Columbia University. She founded the National Association for the Promotion of Kindergarten Education (later, the National Kindergarten Association) in 1909, and became chief of the kindergarten division of the US Bureau of Education (1913–19). From 1917 she published influential home education articles for parents, and helped to open over 3000 kindergartens.

Locke, Bobby, popular name of **Arthur D'Arcy Locke** (1917–) Golfer, born in Germiston, South Africa. A slow, methodical player, he won four British Open championships (1949, 1950, 1952 and 1957), and between 1947 and 1950 won 11 events on the US tour circuit. >> RR1157

Locke, John (1632–1704) Philosopher, born in Wrington, Somerset, SW England, UK. He studied at Oxford, and in 1667 joined the household of Lord Ashley, later first Earl of Shaftesbury, as his personal physician and adviser in scientific and political matters. He was elected a fellow of the Royal Society in 1668. He retired to France, but after Shaftesbury's fall and death in 1683 he fled to Holland,

returning to England in 1689, where he declined an ambassadorship, and became commissioner of appeals until 1704. His major philosphical work, the *Essay Concerning Human Understanding* (1689), accepted the possibility of rational demonstration of moral principles and the existence of God, but its denial of innate ideas, and its demonstration that 'all knowledge is founded on and ultimately derives itself from sense... or sensation', was the real starting point of British Empiricism. >> Shaftesbury, 1st Earl of

Locke, Joseph (1805–60) Civil engineer, born in Attercliffe, South Yorkshire, N England, UK. He left school at the age of 13, became articled to George Stephenson in 1823, and began to learn the art of railway civil engineering. After almost 10 years he broke away, and built a large number of important railways in England, Scotland, and Europe. His lines were noted for being straight, and he avoided expensive tunnelling, but in some places the gradients were too steep for economical running. >> Stephenson, George

Locke, Matthew (c. 1630–77) Composer, born in Exeter, Devon, SW England, UK. Collaborating with James Shirley on the masque *Cupid and Death*, he won a reputation as a theatre composer. After composing the music for Charles II's coronation procession, he became composer-in-ordinary to the king. A champion of the 'modern' French style of composition, his works include much incidental music for plays, Latin church music, songs, and chamber works. He also wrote part of *The Siege of Rhodes* (1656), the first English opera. >> Shirley

Lockhart, John Gibson [lokert] (1794–1854) Biographer, novelist, and critic, born in Wishaw, North Lanarkshire, C Scotland, UK. He studied at Glasgow and Oxford, and practised law in Edinburgh before becoming a writer. In 1820 he married **Sophia**, the eldest daughter of Sir Walter Scott, and produced four novels in four years. Lives of Burns and Napoleon followed in 1828 and 1829, and his masterpiece, the *Life of Sir Walter Scott*, in 1837–8 (7 vols). From 1825 until 1853 he was editor of the Tory *Quarterly Review*, and wrote a biography of Robert Burns. >> Scott, Walter

Lockwood, Belva Ann, née **Bennett** (1830–1917) Lawyer and feminist, born in Royalton, NY. She studied at Genesee College, became a teacher, then graduated from the National University Law School in Washington (1873), and was admitted to the bar. A skilled and vigorous supporter of women's rights, she became the first woman to practise before the Supreme Court, and helped to promote various reforms, such as the Equal Pay Act for female civil servants (1872). In 1884 and 1888, as a member of the National Equal Rights Party, she was nominated for the presidency.

Lockwood, Margaret (1916–90) English actress, born in Karachi, Pakistan (formerly India). She studied at the Royal Academy of Dramatic Art, made her film debut in *Lorna Doone* (1935), and starred in the Alfred Hitchcock film *The Lady Vanishes* (1938). In the late 1940s she was Britain's most popular leading lady, appearing regularly in theatre productions. Later films include *Cast a Dark Shadow* (1955) and *The Slipper and the Rose* (1976).

Lockyer, Sir Joseph Norman (1836–1920) Astronomer, born in Rugby, Warwickshire, C England, UK. As a clerk in the War Office (1857–75) he detected and named *helium* in the Sun's chromosphere by daylight (1868), shortly before William Ramsay. He worked in the government science and art department (1875–90), started and edited *Nature* (1869–1920), and was professor of astronomical physics at the Royal College of Science (1908–13). He was knighted in 1897. >> Frankland; Ramsay, William

Loden, Barbara [lohdn] (1932–80) Actress and film director, born in Marion, NC. Commencing her Broadway career in 1957, she enjoyed her greatest success playing the Marilyn Monroe-inspired role in Arthur Miller's *After the Fall* (1964); its director, Elia Kazan, became her (second) husband in 1967. She appeared in a few films and TV dramas, then turned to writing and directing her own films, including *The Frontier Experience* and *Wanda* (1970); the latter gained considerable acclaim for its anticipation of feminist themes. She also directed off-Broadway plays, and before her premature death was starring in and co-directing *Come Back to the Five and Dime, Jimmy Dean*. >> Kazan, Elia

Lodge, David (John) (1935–) Novelist and critic, born in London, England, UK. He studied at University College, London, then taught at Birmingham University (1960–87, then honorary professor). Three early realist novels gave place to parodic fictions in pursuit of literature itself, including *Changing Places* (1975) and *Small World* (1984, televised 1988). The real world returns in *Nice Work* (1988, televised 1989), a rewrite of the 19th-c industrial novel. Later books include *Paradise News* (1991) and *Therapy* (1995). His critical works include *Language of Fiction* (1966), *The Novelist at the Crossroads* (1971), *Write On* (1986), a collection of essays, *After Bakhtin* (1990), and *The Practice of Writing* (1996).

Lodge, George Cabot (1873–1909) Poet, born in Boston, MA, the son of Henry Cabot Lodge. He studied at Harvard (1891–5), in France, and Berlin (1895–7), then became secretary to his father (1897), and to a US Senate committee in Washington, DC. He is known for his sonnets, as in *The Song of the Wave* (1898). >> Lodge, Henry Cabot

Lodge, Henry Cabot (1850–1924) US Republican senator, historian, and biographer, born in Boston, MA. He studied at Harvard, and received the first PhD in political science to be granted there (1876). He became assistant editor of the *North American Review*, but from 1878 his career was mainly political, becoming a member of the US House of Representatives in 1887 and a senator in 1893. He led the opposition to the Treaty of Versailles in 1919, and prevented the USA joining the League of Nations in 1920. >> Lodge, George Cabot

Lodge, Sir Oliver Joseph (1851–1940) Physicist, born in Penkhull, Staffordshire, C England, UK. He studied at the Royal College of Science and at University College, London, and in 1881 became professor of physics at Liverpool. In 1900 he was appointed first principal of the new university at Birmingham. A pioneer of radio-telegraphy, his early experiments showed that radio-frequency waves could be transmitted along electric wires (1888). In 1894 he hypothesised that the Sun emitted radio waves (not proved until 1942). The author of c.140 books, he was one of the leading scholars of his day, also known for his efforts in reconciling the ideas of science, religion, and the paranormal. He was knighted in 1910.

Lodge, Thomas (c. 1558–1625) Playwright, romance writer, and poet, probably born in London, England, UK. He studied at Oxford, then at Lincoln's Inn. Around 1588 he took part in a buccaneering expedition to the Canaries, and wrote the romance, *Rosalynde* (1590), his best-known work, the source of Shakespeare's *As You Like It*. He went on a second freebooting expedition to South America in 1591, and wrote many other works. He is believed to have taken a medical degree at Avignon (1600), and was a physician in Oxford in 1602.

Loeb, Jacques [loeb] (1859–1924) Biologist, born in Mayen, Germany. He studied at Berlin, Munich, and Strasbourg universities, emigrated to the USA in 1891, and after various university appointments became head of the general physiology division at the Rockefeller Institute for Medical Research, New York City (1910–24). He did pioneer work on artificial parthenogenesis, and also carried out research in comparative physiology and psychology.

Loeb, James [lohb] (1867–1933) Banker and scholar, born in New York City. With his fortune he founded the Institute of Musical Art in New York City (1905) and a mental clinic in Munich. A classical scholar himself, in 1910 he provided funds for the publication of the famous Loeb Classical Library of Latin and Greek texts with English translations.

Loesser, Frank (Henry) [lerser] (1910–69) Songwriter and composer, born in New York City. He published his first lyric in 1931, and in 1937 went to Hollywood as a contract writer. With a succession of collaborators he turned out several hit songs including 'Baby, It's Cold Outside'. He branched out into writing his own music, soon achieving international fame with the music and lyrics for *Guys and Dolls* (1950). Later musicals included *The Most Happy Fella* (1956) and *How to Succeed in Business Without Really Trying* (1961).

Loewe, (Johann) Carl (Gottfried) [loevuh] (1796–1869) Composer, born near Halle, Germany. He studied music and theology at Halle, and in 1822 became a musical teacher at Stettin. In 1847 he sang and played before the court in London. He composed operas (of which only one, *The Three Wishes*, was performed), oratorios, symphonies, concertos, duets, and works for piano. He is best known for his dramatic ballads, including his setting of Goethe's *Erlkönig*. He published his autobiography in 1870.

Loewe, Frederick [loh] (1904–88) Composer, born in Berlin. He went to the USA in 1924, and worked as a composer on a number of Broadway musicals. Those he wrote in collaboration with **Alan J Lerner** (1918–86), including *Brigadoon* (1947) and *My Fair Lady* (1956), were particularly successful, as also was the film *Gigi* (1958), for which he wrote the score.

Loewi, Otto [loevee] (1873–1961) Pharmacologist, born in Frankfurt, Germany. He studied at Strasbourg and Munich, and was professor of pharmacology at Graz (1909–38). Forced to leave Nazi Germany in 1938, he became research professor at New York University College of Medicine from 1940. In 1936 he shared the Nobel Prize for Physiology or Medicine for his work on nerve impulses and their chemical transmission. >> RR1124

Loewy, Raymond (Fernand) [lohee] (1893–1987) Industrial designer, born in Paris. He graduated from the University of Paris in electrical engineering (1910), and from the Ecole Lanneau in advanced engineering (1918). In the USA, he was commissioned to redesign the casing for the Gestetner duplicator, and this led to commissions for designing products and graphics for industrial corporations worldwide. His outstanding success ranges from the design of Lucky Strike cigarette packs to Apollo and Skylab spacecraft.

Löffler, Friedrich August Johannes [loefler] (1852–1915) Bacteriologist, born in Frankfurt an der Oder, Germany. He studied medicine at Würzburg, started as a military surgeon, became professor at Greifswald (1888), and from 1913 was director of the Koch Institute for Infectious Diseases in Berlin. He first cultured the diphtheria bacillus (1884), discovered the causal organism of glanders and swine erysipelas (1886), isolated an organism causing food poisoning, and prepared a vaccine against foot-and-mouth disease (1899).

Lofting, Hugh (John) (1886–1947) Children's novelist, born in Maidenhead, Berkshire, S England, UK. He trained as a civil engineer, worked in Africa, the West Indies, and Canada, then settled in New York City to become a writer. He created the immensely successful Dr Dolittle books from letters he wrote to his children from the front lines in World War 1. There were a dozen Dolittle books, which he also illustrated, and although he tired of his hero – once attempting to abandon him on the Moon – his popularity was such that his readers demanded his return.

Logan, James (1674–1751) Colonial statesman, Quaker, and scholar, born in Lurgan, Co Armagh. He became William Penn's secretary, and arrived in Pennsylvania in 1699. He advised Penn's descendants for 50 years, and was chief justice of the colony's Supreme Court (1731–9). He pursued scholarly interests in botany, and published *M T Cicero's Cato Major* (1744). >> Penn

Logan, James, originally **Tahgahjute** [tagajoot] (?1723–80) American Indian leader, (probably named for the Quaker, James Logan), born in Sunbury (formerly Shamokin), PA. He was a friend of the white settlers until his family were killed at the Yellow Creek Massacre (Ohio, 1774). Dedicating himself to revenge, he refused to attend a peace meeting. Instead he allegedly sent a reply that was quoted in newspapers (and later used by Thomas Jefferson), including the eloquent plaint: 'There runs not a drop of my blood in the veins of any other living creature...Who is there to mourn for Logan? Not one!' Logan continued to attack white settlements, and during the revolution brought scalps and prisoners to the British at Detroit. He was killed by a fellow-Indian near L Erie.

Logan, John A(lexander) (1826–86) US soldier and legislator, born in Jackson County, IL. He graduated in law at Louisville, served in the Mexican War, was called to the bar in 1852, and was elected to Congress as a Democrat in 1858. He raised an Illinois regiment in the Civil War, and retired at its close as major-general. Returned to Congress as a Republican in 1866, he was repeatedly chosen as a senator.

Lo Guangzhong [loe gwangjong], also spelled **Lo Kuan-chung** (1330–1400) Writer, born in Hangzhou, China. He is probably associated with two of the four great Ming-period novels. *The Romance of the Three Kingdoms* is a fictionalized vividly vernacular narrative of the 2nd–3rd-c struggles between three rival states after the Han period. The text was not published until 1522, and quickly became a popular item of Chinese fiction in East Asia. *The Water Margin*, or *Men of the Marshes*, recounts the (partly true) adventures of 108 outlaws who in the 1120s executed savage retaliation against authority for wrongs experienced by themselves and others, dying one by one in the process. The book was banned by Qing rulers. A translation by Pearl Buck, *All Men Are Brothers*, was published in 1933. >> Buck

Loisy, Alfred Firmin [lwazee] (1857–1940) Theologian, born in Ambrières, France. He was ordained priest in 1879, and in 1881 became professor of holy scripture at the Institut Catholique, where he incurred the disfavour of the Church and was dismissed in 1893. In 1900 he was appointed lecturer at the Sorbonne, but resigned after his biblical criticisms were condemned by Pope Pius X in 1903. His controversial books included *L'Evangile et l'Eglise* (1902, The Gospel and the Church), and for subsequent works of the same kind he was excommunicated in 1908. He was professor of history of religion in the Collège de France (1909–32).

Lomax, Alan (1915–) Ethnomusicologist, born in Austin, TX. He studied at Harvard, Texas, and Columbia universities before accompanying his father on a tour of prisons in the deep South, where they discovered blues singer Leadbelly. Lomax devoted his life to the study of folk and blues music. In 1938 he interviewed Jelly Roll Morton, obtaining an oral record of early jazz which appeared both in printed and recorded form. Among his notable publications is *Cantometrics: a Handbook and Training Method* (1976). >> Leadbelly; Morton, Jelly Roll

Lombard, Carole, originally **Jane Alice Peters** (1908–42) Actress, born in Fort Wayne, IN. Later resident in California, she was talent-spotted and cast in the film *A Perfect Crime* (1921). After her studies she returned to film-making, signed a long-term contract with Paramount in 1930, revealed a comic flair in *Twentieth Century* (1934), and made the perfect heroine of screwball comedies such as *My Man Godfrey* (1936). Married to Clark Gable in 1939, she was one of Hollywood's most popular stars at the time of her death in an air crash. >> Gable, Clark

Lombard, Peter, known as **Magister Sententiarum** ('Master of Sentences') (c. 1100–60) Theologian, born near Novara, Italy. He studied in Bologna, at Reims, and in Paris, and, after holding a chair of theology there, became Bishop of Paris (1159). He was generally styled 'Master of Sentences', because of his collection of sentences from Augustine and others on points of Christian doctrine, with objections and replies. The theological doctors of Paris in 1300 denounced some of his teachings as heretical, but his work became the standard textbook of Catholic theology until the Reformation.

Lombardi, Vince(nt Thomas) [lombah(r)dee] (1913–70) Coach of American football, born in New York City. Although a noted offensive guard in his playing days with Fordham University, he was better known as a coach. He started in professional leagues by coaching offence for the New York Giants (1954–9), but his best work was done with the Green Bay Packers from Wisconsin (1959–69), with whom he lifted five league titles and took them successfully to two Super Bowls (1967–8).

Lombardo, Pietro [lombah(r)doh] (c. 1435–1515) Sculptor and architect, born in Carona, Italy. After working in Padua, and probably Florence, he settled in Venice c.1467, and became the head of the major sculpture workshop of the day. With the assistance of his sons, Tullio and Antonio, he was responsible for both the architecture and sculptural decoration of Santa Maria dei Miracoli (1481–9), one of the finest Renaissance buildings in Venice. He also designed many monuments, including the tomb of Dante in Ravenna.

Lombroso, Cesare [lombrohsoh] (1836–1909) Founder of the science of criminology, born in Verona, Italy. After working as an army surgeon, he became professor of mental diseases at Pavia, director of an asylum at Pesaro, and professor of forensic medicine (1876), psychiatry (1896), and criminal anthropology (1906) at Turin. His theory (now discredited) postulated the existence of a criminal type distinguishable from a normal person.

Lomonosov, Mikhail Vasilyevich [lomonohsof] (1711–65) Scientist and linguistic reformer, born in Denisovka, Russia. He studied at St Petersburg, then at Marburg in Germany under the philosopher Christian von Wolff. He became professor of chemistry at St Petersburg Academy of Sciences in 1745, where he set up the first chemical laboratory in Russia, and in 1755 he founded Moscow University. His writings include works on rhetoric, grammar, and Russian history, and his greatest contribution to Russian culture was his systematization of the grammar and orthography. >> Wolff, Christian von

Lomu, Jonah [lohmoo] (1975–) Rugby union player, born in Mangere, New Zealand, of Tongan parents. A brilliant athlete while at school, he played rugby league, then switched to union, being selected for the New Zealand All Blacks in 1994. He became internationally known as a member of the World Cup squad in 1995, when his massive physique (1.95 m/6 ft 5 in; 119 kg/266 lb) made him an awesome opponent. A serious kidney disorder kept him out of the game for over a year, but he returned to international rugby in November 1997.

London, Fritz (Wolfgang) (1900–54) Physicist, born in Wrocław, Poland (formerly Breslau, Germany). He studied at Frankfurt and Munich, then did research in philosophy at Bonn. He worked at Zürich, and devised the quantum theory of the chemical bond with Walter Heitler (1927). In 1930 he calculated the non-polar component of forces between molecules, now called *Van de Waals* or *London forces*. With his brother Heinz he fled from Germany in 1933 to the Clarendon Laboratory, Oxford, where they published major papers on conductivity, giving the *London equations* (1935). Fritz moved to Duke University in the USA as professor of chemistry (1939–54), and became a US citizen in 1945. >> London, Heinz

London, Heinz (1907–70) Physicist, born in Bonn, Germany. He studied at the universities of Bonn, Berlin, Munich, and Breslau where he studied under Francis Simon. With his brother Fritz he fled from Germany in 1933, and joined Simon's group at the Clarendon Laboratory, Oxford, working together on conductivity. He moved to Bristol, was briefly interned in 1940, then released to work on the development of the atomic bomb. In 1946 he joined the Atomic Energy Research Establishment at Harwell. >> London, Fritz; Simon, Francis Eugen

London, Jack, pseudonym of **John Griffith Chaney** (1876–1916) Novelist, born in San Francisco, CA. Deserted by his father, he educated himself at public libraries, gained admittance to the University of California, but left to seek his fortune in the Klondike gold rush (1897). He returned and made a living by writing prolifically, including the highly successful *The Call of the Wild* (1903), the more serious political novel *The Iron Heel* (1907), and several autobiographical tales, notably *John Barleycorn* (1913).

Lonergan, Bernard (Joseph Francis) (1904–85) Jesuit theologian and philosopher, born in Buckingham, Quebec, Canada. He entered the Society of Jesus in 1922, and was appointed professor of systematic theology at the Gregorian University, Rome (1954–65). The findings of his massive and seminal studies are summarized in *Philosophy of God, and Theology* (1973) and *Understanding and Being* (1980). His other interests in theology and the history of ideas were explored in occasional papers, assembled in his *Collections* (1967, 1974, 1985).

Long, Earl K(emp) (1895–1960) US politician, born near Winnfield, LA, the brother of Huey Long. He continued his brother's method of corrupt administration, coupled with sound social legislation, as Lieutenant-Governor (1936–8) and Governor (1939–40, 1948–52, 1956–60) of Louisiana. Suffering from paranoid schizophrenia, he was at his wife's request placed in a mental hospital in 1959, and forcibly detained there with police help until, using his powers as governor, he dismissed the mental hospital superintendent and appointed politically favourable medical officers. >> Long, Huey

Long, George Washington De >> **De Long, George Washington**

Long, Huey (Pierce), nickname **Kingfish** (1893–1935) US politician, born in Winnfield, LA. A lawyer by profession, he became Governor of Louisiana (1928–31) and a US senator (1930–5). He became notorious for his corruption and demagoguery. He secured the wrath of the rich and support of the poor by his intensive 'Share the Wealth' social services and public works programmes, but also squandered public funds on extravagant personal projects, including the construction of a marble and bronze statehouse at Baton Rouge. He was assassinated by the son of a man he had vilified. >> Long, Earl K; Talmadge

Long, Richard (1945–) 'Land artist', born in Bristol, SW England, UK. He takes country walks, which he considers works of art in themselves, sometimes marking a place with a simple 'sculpture', such as a circle of stones, or a shallow trench, and afterwards exhibits photographs,

maps, and texts. He held his first one-man show in Dusseldorf, 1968, leading to many more worldwide. He won the 1989 Turner Prize. >> RR1127

Longchamp, William de [**long**shā] (d.1197) English clergyman and statesman. He was a lowly-born favourite of Richard I, who in 1189–90 made him chancellor, Bishop of Ely, and joint justiciar of England. In 1191 he was made papal legate, but because of his arrogance he had to withdraw to Normandy. He regained Richard's favour by arranging a ransom to free him from Germany, and was retained as chancellor. >> Richard I

Longfellow, Henry Wadsworth (1807–82) Poet, born in Portland, ME. He studied at Bowdoin College in Brunswick, ME, and as a gifted translator was sent to Europe to qualify for a chair of foreign languages. On his return, he was unable to settle, and when offered a professorship at Harvard he accepted it as another opportunity to go abroad. After the early death of his wife in 1835, he returned and became professor of modern languages and literature at Harvard (1836–54). During this period he remarried, and published many works, notably the immensely successful *Ballads and Other Poems* (1841), including 'The Wreck of the Hesperus'. His most popular work, 'Hiawatha', with its distinctive 'Indian drum' rhythm, was published in 1855, and in 1863 appeared *Tales of a Wayside Inn*, which included the famous 'Paul Revere's Ride'.

Longhi, Pietro [**long**gee], originally **Pietro Falca** (1702–85) Painter, born in Venice, Italy. He excelled in small-scale satirical pictures of Venetian life. Most of his work is in Venetian public collections, but the National Gallery, London, has three, of which the best known is 'Rhinoceros in an Arena'. His son **Alessandro** (1733–1813) was also a painter, and some of his portraits are now attributed to his father.

Longinus, Dionysius [lon**jiy**nus] (c. 213–73) Greek Neoplatonic rhetorician and philosopher. He taught rhetoric in Athens, settled at Palmyra, and became chief counsellor to Queen Zenobia, for which Emperor Aurelian beheaded him. He is the supposed author of the treatise on excellence in literature, *On the Sublime*, which influenced many Neoclassical writers, such as Dryden and Pope. >> Zenobia

Longman, Thomas (1699–1755) Publisher, born in Bristol, SW England, UK. He bought a bookselling business in Paternoster Row, London, in 1724, and shared in publishing such works as Ephraim Chambers's *Cyclopaedia*, and Johnson's *Dictionary*. He was the founder of the British publishing house that still bears his name.

Longstreet, James (1821–1904) US soldier, born in Edgefield District, SC. He fought in the Mexican War (1846–8), but resigned from the US army at the outbreak of the Civil War (1861–5) to join the Confederates. He fought in both Battles of Bull Run (1861, 1862) and at Gettysburg (1863), and surrendered with Lee at Appomattox Courthouse in 1865. He later became ambassador to Turkey (1880–1).

Longuett-Higgins, (Hugh) Christopher [**long**gee **hi**ginz] (1923–) Theoretical chemist and neuropsychologist, born in Lenham, Kent, SE England, UK. He studied at Oxford, and after university posts in the USA and London, he became professor of theoretical chemistry at Cambridge (1954–67), then professor at Edinburgh (1968–74), and at the Centre for Research in Perception and Cognition, Sussex (1974–88, emeritus 1989). He made contributions to theories of chemical bonding from the 1940s, but later worked on language acquisition, music perception, and speech analysis.

Longus (fl.3rd-c) Greek writer, the author of the Greek prose romance *Daphnis and Chloë*. The first pastoral romance known, it is the most popular of the Greek erotic romances, dealing with the relationship of two foundlings from Lesbos who eventually marry.

Lönnrot, Elias [loenrot] (1802–84) Philologist and folklorist, born in Sammatti, Finland. He studied medicine at Helsinki, and was district medical officer in Kajana for 20 years. As a result of his folklore researches, he was appointed professor of Finnish at Helsinki (1853–62). His major achievement was the epic poem of ancient life in the far north, the *Kalevala* (1835, 1849).

Lonsdale, Hugh Cecil Lowther, 5th Earl of (1857–1944) English sportsman. A landowner in Cumberland, he was a noted huntsman, steeplechaser, yachtsman, and boxer. As president of the National Sporting Club he founded and presented the *Lonsdale belts* for boxing in 1909.

Lonsdale, Dame Kathleen, *née* **Yardley** (1903–71) Crystallographer, born in Newbridge, Co Kildare, Ireland. She studied physics at Bedford College, London, and spent the next 20 years in the research team of William Bragg based at the Royal Institution. She worked at University College, London, as professor of chemistry and head of the department of crystallography (1946–68). From the 1920s she applied X-ray crystal diffraction to determine chemical structures. In 1945 the Royal Society agreed to elect women fellows, and she became the first female FRS. She was created a dame in 1956. >> Bragg, William Henry

Loon, Hendrik Willem van >> **van Loon, Hendrik Willem**

Loos, Adolf [loos] (1870–1933) Architect and writer on design, born in Brno, Czech Republic. After studying architecture in Dresden, and visiting America (1893–6), he settled in Vienna in 1896. One of the major architects of the 'Modern Movement', he is particularly remembered for articulating the view that ornament is decadent, and argues against modern civilized design. His designs reflect this view, notably the Villa Karma, Clarens, Switzerland (1904–6).

Lope de Vega >> **Vega, Lope de**

Lopez, Nancy [lohpez] (1957–) Golfer, born in Torrance, CA. After an outstanding career in amateur golf, she turned professional in 1977 and won the Ladies' Professional Golf Association (LPGA) championship the following year. She was voted LPGA player of the year four times (1978–9, 1985, 1988). She is married to former baseball star, **Ray Knight**.

Lopukhov, Fyodor [lopookof] (1886–1973) Dancer, choreographer, and teacher, born in St Petersburg, Russia. He studied at the Imperial Ballet Academy before joining the Maryinsky Theatre. He started choreographing in 1916, and set the foundation of Neoclassical and modern dance in Russia. His most influential ballet was *Dance Symphony* (1923), and he was artistic director of the Kirov, Maly Theatre, and Bolshoi Ballet companies.

Lorant, Stefan (1901–97) Pioneer photo-journalist, born in Budapest. He studied at Budapest, and became editor of the *Muenchner Illustrierte Presse* in Munich (1928–33), using photographs to make political comments which led to his imprisonment by the Nazis (1933). Released through the efforts of Hungarian journalists, he fled to Britain and founded *Weekly Illustrated* (1934) and *Picture Post* (1938). He moved to the USA in 1940, and published a number of photographic books, including *Sieg Heil: an Illustrated History of Germany from Bismarck to Hitler* (1974).

Lorca, Federico García [law(r)ka, gah(r)**see**a] (1899–1936) Poet, born in Fuente Vaqueros, Spain. A gifted musician, he studied law at Granada, to please his father, but soon turned to the arts, and after publishing a promising book of prose, entered the residence of scholars at Madrid. His *Canciones* (1927, Songs), *Romancero Gitano* (1928, 1935, The

Gypsy Ballads), and tragic poems place him among the greatest of 20th-c poets. He also wrote successful prose plays, including the trilogy *Bodas de Sangre* (1933, Blood Wedding), *Yerma* (1934), and *La Casa de Bernarda Alba* (1936, The House of Bernarda Alba). He was assassinated in the Spanish Civil War at Granada.

Lord, Thomas (1755–1832) Sportsman, born in Thirsk, North Yorkshire, N England, UK. He was founder of Lord's Cricket Ground in London, first opening a cricket ground in Dorset Square in London in 1787, which became the home of the Marylebone Cricket Club (MCC), the regulating body of English cricket, and also the county ground of Middlesex. It was moved to its present site at St John's Wood in 1814.

Loren, Sophia [loren], originally **Sofia Scicolone** (1934–) Actress, born in Rome. An illegitimate child from a poor home in Naples, she became a teenage beauty queen and model. Her film debut was as an extra. She came under contract to film producer **Carlo Ponti** (1912–), later her husband, and blossomed as an actress. An international career followed and she won an Oscar for *La Ciociara*, (1961, trans Two Women). Frequently appearing with Marcello Mastroianni, her many films include *The Millionairess* (1961) and *Marriage Italian Style* (1964). In 1979 she published *Sophia Loren: Living and Loving* (with A E Hotchner) which was filmed for television as *Sophia Loren: Her Own Story* (1980), in which she played herself and her mother. She received an honorary Academy Award in 1991. >> Mastroianni

Lorente de No, Rafael [lorentay] (1902–) Neurophysiologist, born in Zaraguza, Spain. He studied at Madrid, and after several years in the Cajal Institute in Madrid, and at Santander, joined the Rockefeller Institute in New York City (1936). His research covered a wide range of neurophysiological and neuroanatomical problems, including the co-ordination of eye movements and the functional anatomy of neurone networks.

Lorentz, Hendrik Antoon [lohrents] (1853–1928) Physicist, born in Arnhem, The Netherlands. He studied at Leyden and became professor of mathematical physics there (1878), and from 1923 directed research at the Taylor Institute, Haarlem. He clarified the electromagnetic theory of James Clerk Maxwell, and introduced the concept of local time while working on the Michelson–Morley experiment. In 1902 he was awarded, with Pieter Zeeman, the Nobel Prize for Physics for his theory of electromagnetic radiation. Their work led to Einstein's theory of special relativity. >> Einstein; Maxwell, James Clerk; Zeeman

Lorenz, Edward N(orton) [lorens] (1917–) Meteorologist, born in West Hartford, CT. Working at the Massachusetts Institute of Technology from 1946, he was the first to describe what is known as 'deterministic chaos' as a shaper of weather, and was the originator of the term 'the butterfly effect' – the flapping wings of a butterfly in China could alter the weather over America a few days later. Among other major meteorology awards, he received the 1991 Kyoto Prize. >> Feigenbaum; May, Robert

Lorenz, Konrad (Zacharias) [lohrents] (1903–89) Zoologist and ethologist, born in Vienna. He studied medicine at Vienna, and became professor at the Albertus University in Königsberg, headed the Institute of Comparative Ethology at Altenberg, established a comparative ethology department in the Max Planck Institute, and became its co-director in 1954. The founder of ethology, his studies have led to a deeper understanding of behaviour patterns in animals, notably imprinting in young birds. In his book *On Aggression* (1963) he argued that aggressive behaviour in humans may be modified or channelled, but in other animals it is purely survival motivated. *King Solomon's Ring* (1949) and *Man Meets Dog* (1950) also enjoyed wide popularity. He shared the 1973 Nobel Prize for Physiology or Medicine. >> RR1124

Lorenzetti, Ambrogio [loren**ze**tee] (c. 1280–c. 1348) Painter born in Siena, Italy. Probably taught by his brother Pietro, he worked in Cortona and Florence, and is best known for his allegorical frescoes in the Palazzo Pubblico at Siena, symbolizing the effects of good and bad government. His 'Annunciation' is also at Siena. >> Lorenzetti, Pietro

Lorenzetti, Pietro [loren**ze**tee] (c. 1280–c. 1348) Painter from Siena, Italy. Probably a pupil of Duccio, he was one of the liveliest of the early Sienese painters. He also worked at Arezzo (the polyptych in S Maria della Pieve) and Assisi, where he painted dramatic frescoes of 'The Passion' in the Lower Church of S Francis. His 'Madonna' (1340) is in the Uffizi Gallery. >> Duccio di Buoninsegna; Lorenzetti, Ambrogio

Lorenzo [lo**ren**zoh], known as **il Monaco** ('the Monk'), originally **Piero di Giovanni** (c. 1370–c. 1425) Painter, born in Siena, Italy. By 1391 he was a monk in the Camaldolite monastery of S Maria degli Angeli, Florence, and his great altarpiece, 'The Coronation of the Virgin' (1414, now in the Uffizi) was painted for the high altar there. His graceful, linear, Gothic style epitomizes the last phase of mediaeval art before the onset of the Renaissance.

Lorenzo de' Medici [lo**ren**zoh day **may**deechee], known as **the Magnificent** (1449–92) Florentine ruler, born in Florence, Italy, the son of Pietro I Medici and grandson of Cosimo de' Medici. He succeeded as head of the family upon the death of his father in 1469, and was an able if autocratic ruler, who made Florence the leading state in Italy. In 1478 he thwarted an attempt by malcontents, with the encouragement of Pope Sixtus IV, to overthrow the Medici, although the rising led to the assassination of his brother, **Giuliano** (1453–78). A distinguished lyric poet, he was, in the words of Macchiavelli, 'the greatest patron of literature and art that any prince has ever been'. >> Cosimo de' Medici; Sixtus IV; RR1067

Lorjou, Bernard [law(r)zhoo] (1908–) Painter, born in Blois, France. He was the founder of the *L'Homme Témoin* group in 1949. Among a number of large satirical paintings is his 'Atomic Age' (1951).

Lorrain, Claude >> **Claude Lorrain**

Lorre, Peter [lo**ree**], originally **László Löwenstein** (1904–64) Actor, born in Rosenberg, Hungary. A student in Vienna, he acted in repertory theatre, gave one-man performances and readings, and gained international fame as the psychotic child murderer in the German silent-film classic *M* (1931). He left Germany in 1933, making his way to Hollywood, where he was succesfully cast in many sinister parts, including *Mad Love* (1935), *Crime and Punishment* (1935), and *Casablanca* (1942). He also played the part of the Japanese detective in the *Mr Moto* films.

Lorris, Guillaume de >> **Guillaume de Lorris**

Losey, Joseph (Walton) [**loh**see] (1909–84) Film director, born in La Crosse, WI. He attended Dartmouth College, NH, and Harvard, and worked first as a show-business reporter before becoming a stage director on Broadway. His early films centred on controversial topics, and when he came to be suspected of Communist activities he left Hollywood for England (1952). Working anonymously at first, he went on to direct a number of successful films, including *The Servant* (1963), *Modesty Blaise* (1966), *Accident* (1967), and *The Go-Between*, which won the Cannes Film Festival in 1971. From the mid-1970s he worked mainly in France, where his last film was *La Truite* (1982, The Trout).

Lothrop, Harriet Mulford, *née* **Stone**, pseudonym **Margaret Sidney** (1844–1924) Writer, born in New Haven,

CT. She attended private school in New Haven, married **Daniel Lothrop**, founder of the Lothrop publishing company (1881), and settled in the former home of Louisa May Alcott and Nathaniel Hawthorne in Concord, MA. She is remembered, among many other works, for the *Five Little Peppers and How They Grew* (1881) series for children.

Loti, Pierre >> **Viaud, Louis Marie Julien**

Lotto, Lorenzo (c. 1480–1556) Religious painter, born in Venice, Italy. He worked in Treviso, Bergamo, Venice, and Rome, and became known for his altarpieces and portraits. In 1554 he became a lay brother in the Loreto monastery.

Lotze, Rudolf Hermann [**lots**uh] (1817–81) Philosopher, born in Bautzen, Germany. He studied medicine and philosophy at Leipzig, and went on to become professor of philosophy at Leipzig (1842–4), Göttingen (1844–80), and Berlin (1880–1). He first became known as a physiologist, opposing the popular doctrine of 'vitalism', and helped to found the science of physiological psychology, but he is best known for his religious philosophy, Theistic Idealism, expounded in *Mikrokosmos* (3 vols, 1856–8).

Loudon, John Claudius [**low**dn] (1783–1843) Horticultural writer and architect, born in Cambuslang, South Lanarkshire, WC Scotland, UK. Apprenticed to a landscape gardener, he worked in London, and founded and edited *The Gardener's Magazine* (1826–43) and *Architectural Magazine* (1834). He was a major influence in London landscape and domestic architecture, and his major work was *Arboretum et fruticetum Brittanicum* (8 vols, 1838).

Louganis, Greg(ory) [**looga**nis] (1960–) Diver, born in El Cajon, CA. In the 1983 world diving championships, his routine won him more than 700 points for his 11 dives, the first man to achieve such a score. He was Olympic champion (1984, 1988), platform world champion (1978, 1982, 1986), and springboard champion (1982, 1986).

Louis I, known as **the Pious** (778–840) King of Aquitaine (781–814) and emperor of the Western or Carolingian empire (814–40), the son of Charlemagne. His reign was marked by reforms of the Church in collaboration with the monk St Benedict of Aniane, and for the raids of the Norsemen in the NW of the empire, especially the Seine and Scheldt basins. After his death the empire disintegrated while his sons fought for supremacy. >> Charlemagne; RR1049

Louis II (1845–86) King of Bavaria (1864–86), born in Nymphenburg, Germany, the son of Maximilian II. A German patriot of romantic disposition, he devoted himself to patronage of Wagner and his music. Siding with Prussia (1870–1) against France, he took Bavaria into the new German Reich. Later he adopted the life of a recluse, and in 1886 was declared insane; shortly after, he drowned himself in the Starnberger L, near his castle of Berg.

Louis IX, St (1214–70) King of France (1226–70), born in Poissy, near Paris, the son of Louis VIII. By his victories he compelled Henry III of England to acknowledge French suzerainty in Guienne (1259). He led the Seventh Crusade (1248), but was defeated in Egypt, taken prisoner, and ransomed. After returning to France (1254), he carried out several legal reforms, and fostered learning, the arts, and literature. He embarked on a new Crusade in 1270, and died of plague at Tunis. He was canonized in 1297; feast day 25 August. >> Henry III (of England); RR1049

Louis XI (1423–83) King of France (1461–83), born in Bourges, France. He made two unsuccessful attempts to depose his father, Charles VII, but eventually succeeded to the throne on his father's death. During his reign he broke the power of the nobility, led by Charles the Bold of Burgundy, who was killed in 1477. By 1483 he had succeeded in uniting most of France under one crown (with the exception of Brittany), and laid the foundations for absolute monarchy in France. He patronized the arts and sciences, and founded three universities. >> Charles VII; RR1049

Louis XII (1462–1515) King of France (1498–1515), born in Blois, France, the son of Charles, duc d'Orléans, to whose title he succeeded in 1465. He commanded the French troops at Asti during Charles VIII's invasion of Italy (1494–5), before succeeding him to the French throne (1498), and marrying his widow, Anne of Brittany. He proved a popular ruler, concerned to provide justice and avoid oppressive taxation. His Italian ambitions brought him into diplomatic and military involvement with Ferdinand II of Aragon, who finally outmanoeuvred Louis with the formation of the Holy League (1511). Meanwhile, Louis had foiled the Emperor Maximilian's dynastic designs on Brittany, but paid the price when his forces were driven from Italy (1512), and was then defeated by an Anglo–Imperial alliance at the Battle of Guinegate (1513). To guarantee peace, Louis married Mary Tudor, the sister of Henry VIII (1515), but died in Paris shortly afterwards. >> Anne of Brittany; Ferdinand the Catholic; Mary Tudor; Maximilian I; Sforza, Ludovico; RR1049

Louis XIII (1601–43) King of France (1610–43), born in Fontainebleau, France, the eldest son of Henry IV and Marie de Médicis. He succeeded to the throne on the assassination of his father (1610), but was excluded from power, even after he came of age (1614), by the queen regent. She arranged Louis' marriage to Anne of Austria, the daughter of Philip III of Spain (1615). In 1617 Louis took over the reins of government, and exiled Marie de Médicis to Blois (1619–20). By 1624 he was entirely dependent upon the political acumen of Richelieu, who became his chief minister. Various plots to oust the Cardinal were foiled by the king's loyalty to his minister, whose domestic and foreign policies seemed to fulfil the royal ambition for great achievements. Louis' later years were enhanced by French military victories in the Thirty Years' War against the Habsburgs, and by the birth of two sons in 1638 and 1640, including the future Louis XIV. >> Anne of Austria; Marie de Médicis; Richelieu; RR1049

Louis XIV, known as **le Roi soleil** ('the Sun King') (1638–1715) King of France (1643–1715), born in St Germain-en-Laye, France, the son of Louis XIII, whom he succeeded at the age of five. During his minority (1643–51) France was ruled by his mother, Anne of Austria, and her chief minister, Cardinal Mazarin. In 1660 Louis married the Infanta Maria Theresa, the elder daughter of Philip IV of Spain, through whom he was later to claim the Spanish succession for his second grandson. In 1661 he assumed sole responsibility for government, advised by various royal councils. His obsession with France's greatness led him into aggressive foreign and commercial policies, particularly against the Dutch. His patronage of the Catholic Stuarts also led to the hostility of England after 1689; but his major political rivals were the Austrian Habsburgs, particularly Leopold I. From 1665 Louis tried to take possession of the Spanish Netherlands, but later became obsessed with the acquisition of the whole Spanish inheritance. His attempt to create a Franco–Spanish Bourbon bloc led to the formation of the Grand Alliance of England, the United Provinces, and the Habsburg empire, and resulted in the War of the Spanish Sucession (1701–13). In later years Louis was beset by other problems. His determination to preserve the unity of the French state and the independence of the French Church led him into conflict with the Jansenists, the Huguenots, and the papacy, with damaging repercussions. His old age was overshadowed by military disaster and the financial ravages of prolonged warfare. Yet Louis was the greatest monarch of his age, who established the parameters of successful absolutism. In addition, his long reign marked the cultural ascendancy of France within Europe, symbolized by the Palace of Versailles. He was succeeded by his great-grandson as Louis XV. >> Colbert, Jean Baptiste; Condé, Louis II de Bourbon; Fouquet, Nicholas; Jansen; La Vallière; Leopold I (Emperor); Louvois; Maintenon; Montespan; RR1049

Louis XV, known as **Louis le Bien-Aimé** ('Louis the Well-Beloved') (1710–74) King of France (1715–74), born in Versailles, France, the son of Louis, duc de Bourgogne and Marie-Adelaide of Savoy, and the great-grandson of Louis XIV, whom he succeeded at the age of five. His reign coincided with the great age of decorative art in the Rococo mode (dubbed the *Louis XV style*). Until he came of age (1723) he was guided by the regent, Philippe d'Orléans, and then by the Duc de Bourbon, who negotiated a marriage alliance with **Maria Leczczynska**, daughter of the deposed King Stanislas I of Poland. In 1726 Bourbon was replaced by the king's former tutor, the elderly Fleury, who skilfully steered the French state until his death (1744). Thereafter Louis vowed to rule without a First Minister, but allowed the government to drift into the hands of ministerial factions, while indulging in secret diplomatic activity, distinct from official policy, through his own network of agents. This system – *le secret du roi* – brought confusion to French foreign policy in the years prior to the Diplomatic Revolution (1748–56), and obscured the country's interests overseas. Instead, France was drawn into a trio of continental wars during Louis's reign, which culminated in the loss of the French colonies in America and India (1763). In 1771 Louis tried to introduce reforms, but these came too late to staunch the decline in royal authority. He was succeeded by his grandson, Louis XVI. >> Choiseul; du Barry; Fleury; Louis XIV; Pompadour; RR1049

Louis XVI (1754–93) King of France (1774–93), born in Versailles, France, the third son of the dauphin Louis and Maria Josepha of Saxony, and the grandson of Louis XV, whom he succeeded in 1774. He was married in 1770 to the Archduchess Marie Antoinette, daughter of the Habsburg Empress Maria Theresa, to strengthen the Franco–Austrian alliance. He failed to give consistent support to ministers who tried to reform the outmoded financial and social structures of the country, such as Turgot (1774–6) and Necker (1776–81). He allowed France to became involved in the War of American Independence (1778–83), which exacerbated the national debt. Meanwhile, Marie Antoinette's propensity for frivolous conduct and scandal helped to discredit the monarchy. To avert the deepening social and economic crisis, he agreed in 1789 to summon the States General. However, encouraged by the queen, he resisted demands from the National Assembly for sweeping reforms, and in October was brought with his family from Versailles to Paris as hostage to the revolutionary movement. Their attempted flight to Varennes (Jun 1791) branded the royal pair as traitors. Louis reluctantly approved the new constitution (Sep 1791), but his moral authority had collapsed. In August 1792 an insurrection suspended Louis's constitutional position, and in September the monarchy was abolished. He was tried before the National Convention for conspiracy with foreign powers, and was guillotined in Paris. >> Marie Antoinette; Necker; Turgot; RR1049

Louis (Charles) XVII (1785–95) Titular King of France (1793–5), born in Versailles, France, the second son of Louis XVI and heir to the throne from June 1789. After the execution of his father (Jan 1793) he remained in the

Temple prison in Paris. His death there dealt a blow to the hopes of Royalists and constitutional monarchists. The secrecy surrounding his last months led to rumours of his escape, and produced several claimants to his title. >> RR1049

Louis XVIII, originally **Louis Stanislas Xavier, comte de** (Count of) **Provence** (1755–1824) King of France in name from 1795 and in fact from 1814, born in Versailles, France, the younger brother of Louis XVI. He fled from Paris in June 1791, finally taking refuge in England, becoming the focal point for the Royalist cause. On Napoleon's downfall (1814) he re-entered Paris, and promised a Constitutional Charter. His restoration was interrupted by Napoleon's return from Elba, but after Waterloo (1815) he again regained his throne. His reign was marked by the introduction of parliamentary government with a limited franchise. >> Charles X; Jourdan; Napoleon; RR1049

Louis, Joe [loois], popular name of **Joseph Louis Barrow**, nickname **the Brown Bomber** (1914–81) Boxer, born in Lafayette, AL. He was the US amateur light-heavyweight champion in 1934, and turned professional the same year. He beat James J Braddock for the world heavyweight title in 1937, and held the title for a record 12 years, making a record 25 defences. He retired in 1949, but made a comeback in 1950. He lost the world title fight to **Ezzard Charles** (1921–75), and had his last fight against Rocky Marciano in 1951. In all, he won 67 of his 70 professional fights. >> Braddock, James J; Marciano

Louis, Morris, originally **Morris Bernstein** (1912–62) Painter, born in Baltimore, MD. He studied at the Maryland Institute of Fine and Applied Arts (1929–33), in the early 1950s being influenced by Jackson Pollock and the New York Action Painters. His later work shows an individual use of colour, and he came to be associated with the New York school of Abstract Expressionism. >> Pollock

Louis Napoleon >> **Napoleon III**

Louis-Philippe [fileep], known as **the Citizen King** (1773–1850) King of the French (1830–48), born in Paris, the eldest son of the duc d'Orléans, Philippe Egalité. At the Revolution he entered the National Guard, and with his father renounced his titles to demonstrate his progressive sympathies. He joined the Jacobin Club (1790), and fought in the Army of the North before deserting to the Austrians (1793). He lived in Switzerland (1793–4), the USA, and England (1800–9), and in 1809 moved to Sicily and married **Marie Amélie**, daughter of Ferdinand I of Naples and Sicily. He returned to France in 1814, but fled to England again in the Hundred Days. On the eve of Charles X's abdication (1830) he was elected lieutenant-general of the kingdom, and after the Revolution was given the title of King of the French. He strengthened his power by steering a middle course with the help of the upper bourgeoisie; but political corruption and industrial and agrarian depression (1846) caused discontent, and united the radicals in a cry for electoral reform. When the Paris mob rose (1848), he abdicated, and escaped to England. >> Fieschi; Guizot; Orléans, Louis Philippe Joseph, Duc d'; Talleyrand; RR1049

Loutherbourg, Philip James de [lootherboorg] (1740–1812) Stage designer and illustrator, born in Fulda, Germany. He studied at Strasbourg, and after working in Paris was hired by Garrick as artistic adviser at the Drury Lane theatre, London (1771–81). His innovations in scene design and particularly in stage lighting laid the foundations for the development of pictorial illusion and the picture-frame concept in stagecraft. He abandoned theatre in 1781 to develop and exhibit his Eidophusikon, a model stage displaying panoramic transformations through the use of transparencies and coloured plates. >> Garrick

Louvel, Pierre Louis >> **Berry, Charles Ferdinand**

L'Ouverture, Toussaint >> **Toussaint L'Ouverture**

Louvois, François Michel le Tellier, marquis de [loovwah] (1641–91) French statesman, and secretary of state for war under Louis XIV, born in Paris. He proved an energetic minister in the War of Devolution (1668), reforming and strengthening the army. His work bore fruit in the Dutch War, ending with the Peace of Nijmegen (1678). He was recognized as a brilliant administrator and the king's most influential minister in the years 1683–91. >> Louis XIV

Louÿs, Pierre [lwee], pseudonym of **Pierre Louis** (1870–1925) Poet and novelist, born in Ghent, Belgium. In Paris he founded *Le Conque* (1891), a literary review in which he published his first poems, most of which later appeared in *Astarté* (1891). His lyrics, based on the Greek form which he so much admired, are masterpieces of style, and in 1896 his novel *Aphrodite* brought him considerable fame. This was followed by his psychological novel *La Femme et le pantin* (1898, Woman and Puppet).

Love, Mike >> **Beach Boys, The**

Lovecraft, H(oward) P(hillips) (1890–1937) Science fiction writer and poet, born in Providence, RI. Educated at local schools, he supported himself by ghost writing. From 1923 he was a regular contributor to *Weird Tales*. His cult following, particularly in America and France, can be traced to the 60 or so horrific 'Cthulhu Mythos' stories. His novellas included *The Case of Charles Dexter Ward* (1928) and *At the Mountains of Madness* (1931).

Lovejoy, Arthur O(ncken) (1873–1963) Philosopher, born in Berlin. He studied at Berkeley, Harvard, and the Sorbonne, and after holding various teaching positions in America became professor of philosophy at Johns Hopkins University (1910–38). He was co-founder (in 1938) and first editor of the *Journal of the History of Ideas*, and effectively invented the discipline under that title. His method of detailed 'philosophical semantics', investigating the history of key terms and concepts, is best exemplified in *The Great Chain of Being: a Study of the History of an Idea* (1936).

Lovelace, Augusta Ada King, Countess of, *née* **Byron** (1815–52) Writer, mathematician, and socialite, the daughter of Lord Byron. She taught herself geometry, and was trained in astronomy and mathematics. She owes much of her fame to her friendship with Charles Babbage, the computer pioneer. She translated and annotated an article on his Analytical Engine written by an Italian mathematician, L F Menabrea, adding many explanatory notes of her own. In 1983 the high-level universal computer programming language, ADA, was named in her honour. >> Babbage; Byron, George

Lovelace, Richard (1618–57) English Cavalier poet. He studied at Oxford, SC England, UK, and in 1642 was imprisoned for presenting to the House of Commons a petition from the royalists of Kent 'for the restoring the king to his rights', and was released on bail. He spent his estate in the king's cause, assisted the French in 1646 to capture Dunkirk from the Spaniards, and was flung into jail on returning to England in 1648. In jail he revised his poems, including 'To Althea, from Prison', and in 1649 published his collection of poems, *Lucasta*. >> Charles I (of England)

Lovell, Sir (Alfred Charles) Bernard (1913–) Astronomer, born in Oldland Common, Gloucestershire, SWC England, UK. He studied at Bristol, and became professor of radio astronomy at Manchester (1951–80, then emeritus), and director of Jodrell Bank experimental station (now the Nuffield Radio Astronomy Laboratories). He gave the radio Reith Lectures in 1958, taking for his subject *The Individual and the Universe*. He has written several books on radio astronomy and on its relevance to life and civilization today. His works include *Radio Astronomy* (1951), *The Story of Jodrell Bank* (1968), and *Voice of the Universe* (1987). He was knighted in 1961.

Lovell, James A(rthur) (1928–) Astronaut, born in Cleveland, OH. After attending the Naval Academy, Annapolis, he became a test pilot, and in 1963 was selected for the manned space programme. He was crew member of several historic flights: Gemini 7 (1965), Gemini 12 (1966), and Apollo 8 (1968). As commander of the unsuccessful Apollo 13 Moon mission (1970) he returned the spacecraft safely to Earth following a potentially disastrous explosion on board. He was appointed deputy director of the Johnson Space Center, Houston, in 1971.

Lovelock, Jack, popular name of **John Edward Lovelock** (1910–49) Athlete, born in Temuka, New Zealand. He studied medicine at Otago University before going to Oxford University as a Rhodes scholar. In 1932 he set a British record for the mile, in 1933 a world record for that distance, and at the Berlin Olympics in 1936 a world record of 3 min 47·8 s for the 1500 m. A notably relaxed runner, he owed much of his success to his mastery of tactics. It has been said that he was the first major athlete to run with his head as well as his legs.

Lovelock, James (Ephraim) (1919–) British scientist. He studied at Manchester and London, worked at the National Institute for Medical Research (1941–61), was professor of chemistry at Baylor University, TX (1961–4), and then worked as an independent scientist. He is best known as the originator of the 'Gaia hypothesis', a controversial ecological idea that considers the Earth as a single living entity, in his book *Gaia* (1979). Later books include *Gaia: The Practical Science of Planetary Medicine* (1991).

Low, Sir David (Alexander Cecil) (1891–1963) Political cartoonist, born in Dunedin, New Zealand. After working for several newspapers in New Zealand and for the *Bulletin of Sydney*, he joined the *Star* in London, then the *Evening Standard* in 1927, for which he drew some of his most successful cartoons. His work ridiculed all political parties, notably with his character 'Colonel Blimp', whose name has been incorporated into the English language. From 1950 he worked for the *Daily Herald*, and from 1953 with *The (Manchester) Guardian*. He produced volumes of collected cartoons, including *Low and I* (1923), *A Cartoon History of the War* (1941), and *Low's Company* (1952). He was knighted in 1962.

Lowe, Arthur (1914–82) Actor, born in Hayfield, Derbyshire, C England, UK. Becoming a salesman after leaving school, he served in the armed forces (1939–45), ultimately appearing with their entertainments division. He made his London stage debut in *Larger Than Life* (1950), and his film debut in *London Belongs to Me* (1948). His subsequent theatre work included *The Pajama Game* (1955), but it was television that brought him his greatest popularity, first as Mr Swindley in *Coronation Street* (1960–5), then as the bumbling Captain Mainwaring in *Dad's Army* (1968–77).

Lowell, A(bbott) Lawrence (1856–1943) Lawyer and educator, born in Boston, MA, the brother of Amy and Percival Lowell. He studied at Harvard, qualified in law in 1880, practised in Boston (1880–97), then lectured in law at Harvard and became professor of government there (1900). While president of Harvard (1909–33), he doubled enrolment and trebled the faculty. >> Lowell, Amy/Percival

Lowell, Amy (1874–1925) Imagist poet, born in Brookline, MA, the sister of Percival and A Lawrence Lowell. Privately educated, an unconventional member of the great Lowell dynasty, she began to write poetry in her late 20s, producing volumes of free verse which she named 'unrhymed cadence' and 'polyphonic prose', as in *Sword*

Blades and Poppy Seed (1914). She also wrote several critical volumes, and a biography of Keats. >> Lowell, A Lawrence/Percival

Lowell, Francis Cabot (1775–1817) Textile manufacturer, born in Newburyport, MA. He worked in the import-export trade and observed textile machinery in Lancashire while on a visit to England (1810–12). On his return, with the assistance of his brother-in-law Patrick Tracy Jackson, Paul Moody, and Nathan Appleton, he started the Boston Manufacturing Co (1813) in Waltham, MA, the first mill to combine all the operations of making finished cloth from raw cotton. He died prematurely, and his partners named their new factory town, Lowell, MA, after him.

Lowell, James Russell (1819–91) Poet, essayist, and diplomat, born in Cambridge, MA. He studied at Harvard, then published two volumes of poetry, helped to edit *The Pioneer*, and in 1846, at the outbreak of the Mexican War, started work on what was to become *The Biglow Papers* (1848), a poem denouncing the pro-slavery party and the government. In 1855 he was appointed professor of modern languages and literature at Harvard, went to Europe to finish his studies, and edited the *Atlantic Monthly* from 1857. The second series of *Biglow Papers* appeared in 1867. He was later appointed US minister to Spain (1877–80) and Britain (1880–5).

Lowell, Percival (1855–1916) Astronomer, born in Boston, MA, the brother of Amy and A Lawrence Lowell. He studied at Harvard, and established the Flagstaff (now Lowell) Observatory in Arizona (1894). He is best known for his observations of Mars, which were intended to prove the existence of artificial Martian canals, and for his prediction of the existence of the planet Pluto (discovered by Clyde William Tombaugh in 1930). >> Lowell, A Lawrence/Amy; Tombaugh

Lowell, Robert (Traill Spence), Jr (1917–77) Poet, born in Boston, MA. He studied at Harvard, but left to study poetry, criticism, and classics under John Crowe Ransom at Kenyon College, OH. During World War 2 he was a conscientious objector, and served five months of a prison sentence. In 1940 he married the writer Jean Stafford, and during their turbulent relationship published his first collection – the self-critical autobiographical *Land of Unlikeness* (1944). His widely acclaimed second volume, *Lord Weary's Castle* (1946), was awarded the Pulitzer Prize in 1947, and he was accorded the status of a major poet. He divorced in 1948, and married twice more. Other confessional volumes followed, including *Life Studies* (1959) and *The Dolphin* (1973). >> Ransom; Stafford

Lower, Richard (1631–91) Physician and physiologist, born in Tremeer, Cornwall, SW England, UK. He studied at Oxford, and worked with Thomas Willis in London. With Robert Hooke he collaborated in a series of experiments on the role of the lungs in changing the colour of the blood. His *Tractatus de corde* (1669, Treatise on the Heart) was a major work on pulmonary and cardiovascular anatomy and physiology. He also conducted experiments in blood transfusion. >> Hooke; Willis; Thomas

Lowie, Robert Harry [**loh**ee] (1883–1957) Cultural anthropologist, born in Vienna. He grew up in New York City, and studied anthropology at Columbia University under Franz Boas. He joined the staff of the American Museum (1907–17), then went to the University of California, becoming professor of anthropology (1921–50). He made several ethnographic studies of North American Indian societies, publishing *Social Life of the Crow Indians* (1912) and *The Crow Indians* (1935). His most influential general works included *Primitive Society* (1920) and *Social Organization* (1948). >> Boas

Lowry, L(aurence) S(tephen) [**low**ree] (1887–1976) Artist, born in Manchester, Greater Manchester, NW England, UK.

He worked as a clerk in the city all his life, but studied art in his spare time, and from 1939 produced many pictures of the Lancashire industrial scene which became immensely popular after his death, mainly in brilliant whites and greys, peopled with scurrying stick-like men and women.

Lowry, (Clarence) Malcolm [lowree] (1909–57) Novelist, born in New Brighton, Merseyside, NW England, UK. He left school to go to sea and, after an 18-month journey to the East, returned to England, where he studied at Cambridge. His reputation is based on *Under the Volcano* (1947), a novel set in Mexico, where he lived in 1936–7. He also wrote *Ultramarine* (1933), based on his first sea voyage, and several other novels published posthumously, such as *Dark is the Grave Wherein My Friend Is Laid* (1968). He spent most of his writing years in British Columbia, Canada, but died in England, where he lived from 1954.

Lowry, Thomas Martin >> **Brønsted, Johannes**

Lowth, Robert [lowth] (1710–87) Clergyman and scholar, born in Winchester, Hampshire, S England, UK. In 1741 he became professor of poetry at Oxford, in 1766 Bishop of St David's and of Oxford, and in 1777 Bishop of London. His publications include a *Life of William of Wykeham* (1758) and a new translation of Isaiah. He was one of the first to treat the Bible poetry as literature in its own right. His highly prescriptive English grammar was extremely influential on the subsequent course of English language teaching in British schools.

Lowther, Hugh Cecil >> **Lonsdale, 5th Earl of**

Loy, Myrna [loy] (1905–93) Film actress, born in Helena, MT. She began her career as a dancer, moved into silent films, and made her debut in 1925 in *Pretty Ladies*, the next year starring in *Don Juan*. For nearly a decade she played a series of exotic female roles, then developed a bright and witty persona in films throughout the 1930s and 1940s, such as *The Thin Man* (1934), *The Great Ziegfeld* (1936), and *Too Hot to Handle* (1938). She worked with the Red Cross during World War 2, then returned to full-time film-making, and starred in *The Best Years of Our Lives* (1946). Known as the 'Queen of Hollywood', she continued to appear in films until the early 1980s, and received an honorary Oscar in 1991.

Loyola, Ignatius of, St [loyohla], originally **Iñigo López de Recalde** (1491 or 1495–1556) Theologian and founder of the Jesuits, born in his ancestral castle of Loyola in the Basque province Guipúzcao. He became a soldier, was wounded, and while convalescing read the lives of Christ and the saints. In 1522 he went on a pilgrimage to Jerusalem, studied in Alcalá, Salamanca, and Paris, and in 1534 founded with six associates the Society of Jesus. Ordained in 1537, he went to Rome in 1539, where the new order was approved by the Pope. He wrote the influential *Spiritual Exercises*, and was canonized in 1622; feast day 31 July. >> Francis Xavier, St

Loyson, Charles >> **Hyacinthe, Père**

Lü, Empress [lü] (?–180 BC) Consort of the first Han dynasty Chinese emperor, Gaozu, and dowager empress after his death (195 BC). She tried to ensure her own family's succession, but after her death all were murdered, and Wendi, Gaozu's son, acceded. >> Gaozu; Wendi

Lubbers, Ruud (Franz Marie) (1939–) Dutch statesman and prime minister (1982–94). He studied at Erasmus University, Rotterdam, and joined the family engineering business of Lubbers Hollandia. He made rapid progress after entering politics, becoming minister of economic affairs in 1973, and in 1982, at the age of 43, prime minister leading a Christian Democratic Appeal coalition. This continued as the main party in a new coalition formed after the 1989 elections. >> RR1077

Lubbock, Sir John, 1st Baron Avebury (1834–1913) Archaeologist, biologist, and politician, born in London, England, UK. He became an MP in 1870, and initiated over a dozen Acts of Parliament, including Bank Holidays ('St Lubbock's Days') in 1871. In science his work was on human prehistory in Europe, and also on social insects, where he devised new methods of study.

Lubbock, Percy (1879–1965) Critic and biographer, born in London, England, UK. He became librarian of Magdalene College, Cambridge (1906–8). Among his writings are *The Craft of Fiction* (1920), *Earlham* (1922), a book of personal childhood memories, and studies of Pepys (1909) and Edith Wharton (1947).

Lubetkin, Berthold [lubetkin] (1901–90) Architect, born in Tbilisi. He studied in Moscow, then in Paris, where he was influenced by Le Corbusier. In 1931 he moved to London and set up his own firm, Tecton. His major works include the Penguin Pool at London Zoo (1933), and Highpoint in Hampstead (1935), a block of high-rise flats which was praised by Le Corbusier as creating a new quality of high-rise housing. His Finsbury Health Centre (1938), a social experiment, is still in use as intended today. >> Le Corbusier

Lubin, David [loobin] (1849–1919) Agriculturalist, born in Klodowa, Poland (formerly Russia). His family settled in New York City in 1855. In 1884, on a visit to Palestine, he had a vision that his life should serve justice. He took up the cause of agriculture, and fought the railroads over practices that benefited the middlemen over the growers. In 1896, at the International Agricultural Congress in Budapest, he realized that justice for the American farmer depended on justice for all farmers. For 12 years he sought a sovereign state to support an International Institute of Agriculture; in 1910 Italy agreed, and the Institute's treaty was ratified by 46 nations. He was the US delegate to the Institute until his death.

Lubitsch, Ernst [loobich] (1892–1947) Film director, born in Berlin. A teenage actor in Max Reinhardt's theatre company, he then starred as 'Meyer' in a popular slapstick series before beginning his directorial career. He was invited to Hollywood by Mary Pickford, whom he directed in *Rosita* (1923), and stayed on to become an acknowledged master of light, sophisticated sex comedies graced with 'the Lubitsch touch' of elegance, including *Forbidden Paradise* (1924) and *Heaven Can Wait* (1943). He received an honorary Academy Award in 1947. >> Pickford; Reinhardt, Max

Lübke, Heinrich [lübkuh] (1894–1972) German statesman and president (1959–69), born in Westphalia, Germany. He helped to found the Christian Democratic Party in Westphalia after World War 2, entered the Bundestag in 1949, and was minister of food, agriculture, and forestry (1953–9). In 1959 he succeeded Theodor Heuss as president of the German Federal Republic. >> Heuss; RR1051

Luca da Cortona >> **Signorelli, Luca**

Lucan [lookn], in full **Marcus Annaeus Lucanus** (39–65) Roman poet, born in Córdoba, Spain. The nephew of the philosopher Seneca the Younger, he studied in Rome and in Athens, and was recalled to Rome by Emperor Nero, who made him quaestor and augur. In 62 he published the first three books of his epic *Pharsalia* on the civil war between Pompey and Caesar. After the emperor forbade him to write poetry, he joined the conspiracy of Piso against Nero, but was betrayed and compelled to commit suicide. >> Nero; Seneca; Lucius Annaeus

Lucan, George Charles Bingham, Earl of [lookn] (1800–88) British soldier, born in London, England, UK. He accompanied the Russians as a volunteer against the Turks in 1828, and succeeded as third earl in 1839. As commander of cavalry in the Crimean War (1853–6), he passed on the disastrous order for the Charge of the Light Brigade at Balaclava (1854), and later fought at Inkermann. He was promoted fieldmarshal in 1887.

Lucan, Richard John Bingham, 7th Earl of [lookn], known as **Lord Lucan** (1934–?) British aristocrat, and alleged murderer. He disappeared following events on the evening of 7 November 1974, when police found the body of the Lucan family's nanny, Sandra Rivett, in a mail-bag in the basement of Lady Lucan's house. Lady Lucan told police that she had gone downstairs to find the nanny when a man, whom she identified as her estranged husband, had attacked her, claiming that he had mistaken the nanny for her and had killed her. The police failed to trace Lucan, who had amassed large gambling debts and who had fought for and lost custody of his children. In June 1975 the coroner's jury charged Lord Lucan with the murder. Speculation about Lucan's whereabouts and about events that night continues to this day.

Lucaris or **Lukaris, Cyril** [lukahris] (1572–1638) Orthodox theologian, born in Candia, Crete, Greece. He studied in Venice, Padua, and Geneva, and by 1621 had become Patriarch of Constantinople. He opened negotiations with the Calvinists of England and Holland with a view to union and the reform of the Greek Church, and presented the Alexandrian Codex to Charles I. The Jesuits five times brought about his deposition, and are supposed by the Greeks to have instigated his murder by the Turks in 1637.

Lucas, Colin Anderson (1906–) Architect, born in London, England, UK. He studied at Cambridge, and in 1930 designed a house in Bourne End, Buckinghamshire, which was the first English example of the domestic use of monolithic reinforced concrete. Subsequent designs (1933–9) played an important part in the development in England of the ideas of the European modern movement in architecture. He was a founder member of the MARS group of architects.

Lucas, Edward Verrall (1868–1938) Essayist and biographer, born in Eltham, Kent, SE England, UK. He became a bookseller's assistant, then a reporter, contributor to, and assistant editor of *Punch*, and finally a publisher. He compiled anthologies, wrote novels (the best of which was probably *Over Bemerton's*, 1908), books of travel, and about 30 volumes of light essays. An authority on Lamb, he wrote a life of this author in 1905.

Lucas, F(rank) L(awrence) (1894–1967) Critic and poet, born in Hipperholme, West Yorkshire, N England, UK. A fellow of King's College, Cambridge, he wrote many scholarly works of criticism, including *Seneca and Elizabethan Tragedy* (1922) and *Eight Victorian Poets* (1930). Among his volumes of poetry are *Time and Memory* (1929) and *Ariadne* (1932). He also wrote plays, novels, and popular translations of Greek drama and poetry.

Lucas, Robert E, Jr (1939–) Economist, born in Yakima, WA. He studied at the University of Chicago, taught at Carnegie Mellon University (1963–74), then returned to Chicago,. He won the Nobel Prize for Economics in 1995 for developing and applying the hypothesis of rational expectations in macroeconomic analysis. He is known for his 'Lucas critique' (1976), showing that shifts in economic policy often produce a completely different outcome if people adapt their expectations to new policy stances.

Lucas, Victoria >> **Plath, Sylvia**

Lucas van Leyden [laydn], or **Lucas Jacobsz** (1494–1533) Painter and engraver, born in Leyden, The Netherlands. He practised almost every branch of painting, his most notable works including the triptych of 'The Last Judgement' (1526) and 'Blind Man of Jericho Healed by Christ' (1531). As an engraver he is believed to have been the first to etch on copper rather than iron, and ranks almost with Albrecht Dürer, by whom he was much influenced. >> Dürer

Luce, Clare Boothe, *née* **Boothe** (1903–87) Playwright, editor, and public figure, born in New York City. Privately educated, she became associate editor of *Vogue* (1930), and associate editor and managing editor of *Vanity Fair* (1930–4), and was the author of several Broadway successes including *The Women* (1936) and *Kiss the Boys Goodbye* (1938). She divorced her first husband, and married millionaire publisher Henry Luce in 1935, with whom she became a major influence in the Republican Party. She was US ambassador to Italy (1953–7), and the first woman to receive the Sylvanus Thayer Award for distinguished civil service. >> Luce, Henry R

Luce, Henry R(obinson) (1898–1967) Magazine publisher and editor, born in Shandong, China. He studied at Yale, and with Briton Hadden founded the weekly news magazine *Time* in 1923. In 1929, when Hadden died, he launched the business magazine *Fortune*, and later the popular picture magazine *Life* (1936). His empire made him a millionaire, and he became the most powerful figure in American journalism. He married playwright and editor Clare Boothe in 1935, and together they were a major influence in national politics. >> Luce, Clare Boothe

Lucian [looshan] (c. 117–c. 180) Rhetorician, born in Samosata, Syria. He practised as an advocate in Antioch, travelling widely in Asia Minor, Greece, Italy, and Gaul. He then settled in Athens, where he devoted himself to philosophy, and produced a new form of literature – humorous dialogue. His satires include *Dialogues of the Gods* and *Dialogues of the Dead*. His ironic *True History* describes a journey to the Moon, and inspired a number of imaginary voyages. In his later years, he spent some time attached to the court in Alexandria.

Luciano, Lucky [loosiahnoh], popular name of **Charles Luciano**, originally **Salvatore Lucania** (1897–1962) Gangster, born in Lercara Friddi, Sicily, Italy. He moved with his family to New York City in 1906, and was soon an active criminal. He became the chief of New York organized crime, founding his empire on narcotics-peddling, extortion, and prostitution. For years he managed to evade arrest, but he was tried and imprisoned in 1936. However, he retained control, initiated a reorganization of crime, and set up the Crime Syndicate of Mafia families. In 1946 he was deported to Italy. >> Valachi

Lucid, Shannon [loosid] (1943–) US astronaut and biochemist. In 1996 she set a new record for the longest US space mission (188 days) in orbit aboard the *Mir* space station. The distance she travelled during that time was equivalent to roughly half the distance between the Earth and the Sun. She became the first woman to be awarded the Congressional Space Medal of Honor.

Lucilius, Gaius [loosilius] (c. 180–102 BC) Satirist, born in Suessa Aurunca, Italy. He wrote 30 books of *Satires*, of which only fragments remain. Written in hexameters, they give a critical insight into his times, and were the first works in the style of critical observation that we have come to know as true satire. >> Scipio, Aemilianus

Lucretia [lookreesha] (6th-c BC) Roman heroine, the wife of Lucius Tarquinius Collatinus who, according to legend, was raped by Sextus, the son of Tarquinius Superbus. She incited her father and husband to take an oath of vengeance against the Tarquins, then committed suicide by plunging a knife into her heart. The incident led to the expulsion of the Tarquins from Rome, and the tale has formed the basis of several works, notably Shakespeare's *Rape of Lucrece* and the opera *The Rape of Lucretia* by Benjamin Britten. >> Brutus, Lucius Junius

Lucretius [loo**kree**shus], in full **Titus Lucretius Carus** (1st-c BC) Roman poet and philosopher. His major work is the six-volume hexameter poem *De rerum natura* (On the Nature of Things), in which he tried to popularize the philosophical theories of Democritus and Epicurus on the origin of the universe, denouncing religious belief as the one great source of human wickedness and misery. Little is known about his life, but one story recounts that a love potion given to him by his wife Lucilia sent him insane, and that he committed suicide. >> Democritus; Epicurus

Lucullus, Lucius Licinius [loo**ku**lus] (c. 110–57 BC) Roman politican and general, famous for his victories over Mithridates VI, and also for his enormous wealth, luxurious lifestyle, and patronage of the arts. He is believed to have introduced the cherry to Italy from Asia Minor, the scene of his greatest military triumphs and administrative reforms. The term *Lucullan* has since been used as an epithet for luxurious living.

Lucy, St (?–303) Christian martyr, the patron saint of virgins and of the blind. According to legend, she was a virgin denounced as a Christian by a rejected suitor, and martyred under Diocletian at Syracuse. Feast day 13 December. >> Diocletian

Lucy, Sir Thomas (1532–1600) Squire, member of parliament, and justice of the peace, born near Stratford-upon-Avon, Warwickshire, C England, UK. He married an heiress at the age of 16, and was knighted in 1565. He is said to have prosecuted Shakespeare for stealing deer from Charlecote Park, and may have been caricatured as Shakespeare's Justice Shallow in *The Merry Wives of Windsor*. >> Shakespeare, William

Ludd, Ned (fl.1779) Farm labourer from Leicestershire, C England, UK. It is not known whether he really existed, but legend has it that he destroyed some stocking frames about 1782, and it is from him that the *Luddite* rioters (1812–18) took their name, in their quest to destroy machinery which was displacing their work as craftsmen.

Ludendorff, Erich von [**lu**dendaw(r)f] (1865–1937) General, born near Poznan, Poland (formerly Russia). He became chief-of-staff under Hindenburg, defeated the Russians at Tannenberg (1914), and conducted the 1918 offensives on the Western Front. In 1923 he was a leader in the unsuccessful Hitler putsch at Munich, but was acquitted of treason. He became a Nazi, but from 1925 led a minority party of his own. >> Hindenburg; Hitler

Ludlow, Edmund (c. 1617–92) English politician, born in Maiden Bradley, Wiltshire, S England, UK. During the Civil War he served under Sir William Waller and Thomas Fairfax, and was returned for Wiltshire in 1646. Elected to the council of state, he was sent to Ireland as lieutenant-general of horse in 1651, but refused to recognize Cromwell's protectorate. He was member for Hindon in 1659, urged the restoration of the Rump Parliament, was nominated by John Lambert to the Committee of Safety, and strove in vain to reunite the Republicans. After the Restoration he escaped to Vevey in Switzerland. >> Cromwell, Oliver; Fairfax; Waller, William

Ludmila, St [lud**mi**la] (c. 860–921) Patron saint of Bohemia, born near Melník, Bohemia. She married the first Christian Czech prince, **Borivoj**, and pioneered the establishment of Christianity. She was murdered by her heathen daughter-in-law, Drahomira, the mother of Wenceslaus, whom Ludmila had raised as a Christian. Feast day 16 September. >> Wenceslaus

Ludwig II [**lud**veekh], nickname **Mad King Ludwig** (1845–86) King of Bavaria (1864–86), born in Munich, the son of Maximilian II. A German patriot of Romantic disposition, he devoted himself to patronage of Wagner and his music, and built Neuschwanstein castle in the Bavarian mountains.

Siding with Prussia (1870–1) against France, he took Bavaria into the new German Reich. Later he adopted the life of a recluse, and in 1886 was declared insane; shortly after, he drowned himself in the Starnberger L, near his castle of Berg. >> Wagner, Richard

Ludwig, Carl F(riedrich) W(ilhelm) [**lud**veekh] (1816–95) Physiologist, born in Witzenhausen, Germany. Professor at Leipzig (1865–95), he did pioneer research on glandular secretions, and his invention of the mercurial blood-gas pump revealed the role of oxygen and other gases in the bloodstream. He also invented the kymograph (1847) for recording changes in blood pressure, and was the first to keep animal organs alive in vitro (1856).

Ludwig, Christa [**lud**vik] (1924–) Mezzo-soprano, born in Berlin, Germany. She made her operatic debut in *Die Fledermaus* (1946) in Frankfurt, Germany, and went on to be particularly associated with the operas of Mozart and Richard Strauss. >> Mozart; Strauss

Ludwig, Emil [**lud**veekh], pseudonym of **Emil Ludwig Cohn** (1881–1948) Writer, born in Wrocław, Poland (formerly Breslau, Germany). He studied law, but wrote plays and poems, and after World War 1 wrote the novel *Diana* (1918–19). He became popular as a new-style biographer, emphasizing the personality of his subjects, including (English translations) *Napoleon* (1927), *Bismarck* (1927), *Goethe* (1928), and the controversial biography of Christ, *The Son of Man* (1928).

Lugard (of Abinger), Frederick John Dealtry, Baron (1858–1945) British soldier and colonial administrator, born in Fort St George, Madras, India. He served in the Sudan and Burma, and commanded an expedition against slavers in Nyasaland (1888). He was responsible for Uganda becoming a British protectorate in 1894, and became commissioner in the Nigerian hinterland (1897), and high commissioner for N Nigeria (1900–7). He was appointed Governor of Hong Kong from 1907, returned to Nigeria as governor of the two protectorates, becoming governor-general (1914–19) on their amalgamation.

Lugosi, Bela [lu**goh**see], popular name of **Bela Ferenc Denzso Blasko** (1884–1956) Actor, born in Lugos, Romania (formerly Hungary). A student at the Academy of Performing Arts in Budapest, he made his stage debut in 1902, and his film debut in *A Leopard* (1917). He enjoyed his greatest success on Broadway as *Dracula* (1927), a role he repeated on film in 1931, which brought him international fame. He soon found himself typecast in low-budget horror films, and died in poverty and obscurity, as a drug addict. At his own request he was buried in the cloak he wore in *Dracula*.

Lukács, Georg or **György** [**loo**kach] (1885–1971) Marxist philosopher and critic, born in Budapest. He took a degree in jurisprudence at Budapest (1906), then studied at Berlin and Heidelberg. He became a member of the Hungarian Communist Party in 1918, spent several years in Vienna (1919–29) and Moscow (1933–45), then returned to Budapest to a chair of aesthetics. He was a major figure in the articulation of the Marxist theory of literature and Socialist Realism, especially through his work on the novel, as in *Die Theorie des Romans* (1916, trans 1971, The Theory of the Novel).

Lukaris, Cyril >> Lucaris, Cyril

Luke, St (1st-c) New Testament evangelist, a Gentile Christian, perhaps 'the beloved physician' and companion of St Paul (*Col* 4.14, *Phil* 24), but this is disputed. Church tradition made him a native of Antioch in Syria, and a martyr. He is first named as author of the third Gospel in the 2nd-c, and tradition has ever since ascribed to him both that work and the Acts of the Apostles. Feast day 18 October. >> Paul, St

Lull, Ramón >> Llull, Ramón

Lully, Jean Baptiste [loolee], originally **Giovanni Battista Lulli** (1632–87) Composer, born in Florence, Italy. He came as a boy to Paris, and after much ambitious intriguing was made operatic director by Louis XIV in 1672. With Philippe Quinault (1635–88) as librettist, he composed many operas in which he made the ballet an essential part, including *Phaéton*, *Isis*, and *Acis et Galatée*. He also wrote church music, dance music, and pastorals. He died of blood poisoning after striking his foot with his conducting stick.

Lully, Raymond >> **Llull, Ramón**

Lumet, Sidney [loomet] (1924–) Film director, born in Philadelphia, PA. Originally a child actor, then a TV director, he made his first feature film in 1957 – *Twelve Angry Men*. Known for making films that combine popular elements with serious themes, his greatest commercial triumph was *Network* (1976). Other works include *The Pawnbroker* (1965), *Murder on the Orient Express* (1974), *Dog Day Afternoon* (1975), and *The Verdict* (1982). Among later films are *Q & A* (1991), *Guilty as Sin* (1993), and *Night Falls on Manhattan* (1996).

Lumière brothers [lümyair] Chemists, born in Besançon, France: **Auguste (Marie Louis) Lumière** (1862–1954) and **Louis (Jean) Lumière** (1864–1948) Manufacturers of photographic materials, in 1893 they developed a cine camera, the *cinématographe*, and showed the first motion pictures using film projection in 1895. They also invented the Autochrome screen plate for colour photography in 1903, producing the first film newsreels, and the first 'movie', *La Sortie des usines Lumière* (1895, trans Workers Leaving the Lumière Factory).

Lumumba, Patrice (Hemery) [lumumba] (1925–61) Congolese statesman and prime minister (1960), born in Katako Kombé, Congo. He studied at a Protestant mission school, wrote essays and poems, and became an accountant. He was imprisoned for embezzlement, and on his release became active in politics, founding and leading the Congolese National Movement. When the Congo became an independent republic in June 1960 he was made premier. Almost immediately the country was plunged into chaos by warring factions, and after being deposed in September 1960, he was assassinated in 1961, becoming a national hero.

Lunceford, Jimmie, popular name of **James Melvin Lunceford** (1902–47) Jazz dance-band leader, born in Fulton, MO. As a child he became a proficient player of wind instruments, but preferred conducting to playing. He began a career as a professional bandleader in 1929, and enjoyed success during the 1930s and early 1940s.

Lunn, Sir Arnold (Henry Moore) (1888–1974) British alpine ski pioneer and Roman Catholic apologist, born in Madras, India, the son of the travel-bureau pioneer **Sir Henry Lunn** (1859–1939), and brother of the writer Hugh Kingsmill. He is remembered for his debates about Catholicism (as a Methodist) with Ronald Knox, for his classic account of his conversion, *Now I See* (1933), and later for his debates (as a Catholic) with C E M Joad, and others. An accomplished skier, he founded the Ski Club of Great Britain and the Alpine Ski Club, invented slalom gates, and obtained Olympic recognition for the modern Alpine slalom race and downhill races. He founded the *British Ski Year Book* in 1919, and edited it for more than 50 years. He was knighted in 1952. >> **Kingsmill**

Lunt, Alfred (1892–1977) and **Fontanne, Lynne**, originally **Lillie Louise Fontanne** (1887–1983) Acting partnership, born in Milwaukee, WI, and Woodford, Essex, SE England, UK, respectively. He studied at Carroll College, Waukesha, abandoned early plans to be an architect, and made his stage debut in 1912 with the Castle Square Theatre Company in Boston, MA. She studied in England with Ellen Terry, then moved to the USA in 1916, meeting Lunt that year when they both appeared in *A Young Man's Fancy*. They were married in 1922, and from 1924 became a popular husband-and-wife team, known especially for their performances in Noel Coward's plays, such as *Design for Living* (1933). Broadway's Lunt–Fontanne Theatre, opened in 1958, was named in the couple's honour, and in 1964 they received the US Medal of Freedom. >> **Coward; Terry, Ellen**

Lupino, Ida [lupeenoh] (1914 /18–95) Actress and director, born in London, England, UK, the daughter of popular comedian **Stanley Lupino** (1893–1942). She trained at the Royal Academy of Dramatic Art, London, and made her film debut in *Her First Affair* (1932). She moved to Hollywood in 1933, and made several films for Warner Brothers, notably *High Sierra* (1941), *Ladies in Retirement* (1941), and *The Hard Way* (1942), for which she was voted best actress by the New York film critics. She later formed her own film company, and worked increasingly as a director of motion pictures and for television.

Lupus >> **Wulfstan**

Luria, Alexander Romanovich [looria] (1902–77) Psychologist, born in Kazan, Russia. He studied at the Moscow Medical Institute, and from 1945 taught at Moscow State University, carrying out extensive researches into the effects of brain injuries that had been sustained by people during World War 2. One of the founders of neuropsychology, he established and became head of the neuropsychology unit at the university in 1967. His books include *The Man with a Shattered World* (trans 1972) and *The Working Brain* (trans 1973).

Luria, Salvador (Edward) [looria] (1912–91) Biologist, born in Turin, Italy. He studied at the Institute of Radium in Paris, and in the USA worked with Max Delbrück and Alfred Hershey on the role of DNA in the viruses that infect bacteria. With them he was joint recipient of the 1969 Nobel Prize for Physiology or Medicine. >> **Delbrück; Hershey**

Lurie, Alison [looree] (1926–) Novelist, born in Chicago, IL. She studied at Radcliff College, and from 1968 taught at Cornell University, specializing in children's literature. She won a Pulitzer Prize for her novel *Foreign Affairs* (1985). Other novels include *Imaginary Friends* (1967), *The War Between the Tates* (1974), and *The Truth About Lorin Jones* (1988).

Lushan, An [looshan], also spelled **Lu-shan** (?–757) Chinese general under the Tang dynasty in China (618–907), of Turkish origin. He overthrew the crown, and established the short-lived Yan dynasty (755–7). He was patronized by Yang Guifei, mistress to Emperor Xuanzong (ruled 712–55), who adopted him as her son. Controlling 160 000 troops as commandant of three NE regions, he revolted in 755, capturing Luoyang and Changan (Xian). The emperor fled and Yang was executed. An Lushan made himself emperor on Xuanzong's abdication (755), but was murdered by his own son (757). >> **Xuanzong**

Lusignan, Guy of >> **Guy de Lusignan**

Luther, Martin see panel on p. 591

Luthuli or **Lutuli, Albert (John Mvumbi)** [lutooleе] (c. 1899–1967) Resistance leader, born in Zimbabwe (formerly Rhodesia). He studied at an American mission school, and was a teacher before being elected tribal chief of Groutville, KwaZulu Natal. Deposed for anti-apartheid activities, he became president-general of the African National Congress (1952–60), and was a defendant in the Johannesburg treason trial (1956–7). He was awarded the 1960 Nobel Peace Prize for his unswerving opposition to racial violence, and was elected rector of Glasgow University (1962), but severe restrictions imposed by the

MARTIN LUTHER (1483–1546)

Luther was born in Eisleben, Germany, the son of Hans Luther, who worked in the copper mines, and his wife Margarethe. He went to school at Magdeburg and Eisenach, and entered the University of Erfurt in 1501, graduating with a BA in 1502 and an MA in 1505. His father wished him to be a lawyer, but Luther was drawn to the study of the Scriptures, and spent three years in the Augustinian monastery at Erfurt. In 1507 he was ordained a priest, and went to the University of Wittenberg, where he lectured on philosophy and the Scriptures, becoming a powerful and influential preacher.

On a mission to Rome in 1510–11 he was appalled by the corruption he found there. Money was greatly needed at the time for the rebuilding of St Peter's, and papal emissaries sought everywhere to raise funds by the sale of indulgences. The system was grossly abused, and Luther's indignation at the shameless traffic, carried on in particular by the Dominican Johann Tetzel, became irrepressible. As professor of biblical exegesis at Wittenberg (1512–46), he began to preach the doctrine of salvation by faith rather than works; and on 31 October 1517 drew up a list of 95 theses on indulgences denying the pope any right to forgive sins, and nailed them on the church door at Wittenberg. Tetzel retreated from Saxony to Frankfurt-an-der-Oder, where he published a set of counter-theses and burnt Luther's. The Wittenberg students retaliated by burning Tetzel's, and in 1518 Luther was joined in his views by Melanchthon.

The pope, Leo X, at first took little notice of this disturbance, but in 1518 summoned Luther to Rome to answer for his theses. His university and the elector interfered, and ineffective negotiations were undertaken by Cardinal Cajetan and by Miltitz, envoy of the pope to the Saxon court. The scholar Johann Eck and Luther held a memorable disputation at Leipzig (1519); and Luther began to attack the papal system more boldly. In 1520 he published his famous address *An den christlichen Adel deutscher Nation* (Address to the Christian Nobility of the German Nation), followed by a treatise *De captivitate Babylonica ecclesiae praeludium* (A Prelude concerning the Babylonian Captivity of the Church), which also attacked the doctrinal system of the Church of Rome.

A papal bull containing 41 theses was issued against him. He burned it before a multitude of doctors, students, and citizens in Wittenberg. He was excommunicated, and Charles V, Holy Roman Emperor, convened the first Diet at Worms in 1521, before which Luther was called to retract his teachings. Luther refused to relent. An order was issued for the destruction of his books, and he was put under the ban of the Empire. On his return from Worms he was seized, at the instigation of the elector of Saxony, and lodged (for his own protection) in the Wartburg, the elector's fortress. During the year he spent there, he translated the Scriptures and composed his cogent controversial treatise, 'Refutation of the Argument of Latomus'.

Civil unrest called Luther back to Wittenberg in 1522. He rebuked the unruly elements, and made a stand against lawlessness on the one hand, and tyranny on the other. In the same year Luther published his acrimonious reply to Henry VIII's attack on him in *Assertio septem sacramentorum adversus Martinum Lutherum* (1521) about the nature of the seven sacraments.

A divergence had gradually taken place also between the views of the Humanist scholar Erasmus and Luther. There was an open breach in 1525, when Erasmus published *De libero arbitrio* (1524, Discourse on Free Will), and Luther followed with *De Servo arbitrio* (Concerning the Bondage of Will). In the same year he married Katherine von Bora, a nun who had withdrawn from convent life.

In 1529 he engaged with the controversial question of transubstantiation in the famous conference at Marburg with Zwingli and other Swiss theologians; he obstinately maintained his view that Christ is present in the bread and wine of the Eucharist. The drawing up of his theological views in the Augsburg Confession (1530) by Melanchthon, ably representing Luther at the Diet of Augsburg, marks the culmination of the German Reformation.

Luther died in Eisleben, and was buried at Wittenberg. Endowed with broad human sympathies, massive energy, manly and affectionate simplicity, and a rich, if sometimes coarse, humour, he was undoubtedly a spiritual genius. His intuitions of divine truth were bold, vivid, and penetrating, if not necessarily philosophical and comprehensive; and he possessed the power of kindling other souls with the fire of his own convictions. His voluminous works include *Von den guten Wercken* (1520, Of Good Works), and *Widder die hymelischen Propheten von den Bildern und Sacrament* (1525, Against the Heavenly Prophets in the Matter of Images and Sacraments). His commentaries on Galatians and the Psalms are still read; and his hymns such as 'Ein feste Burg ist unser Gott' (A Mighty Fortress Is Our God) have an enduring power. >> Bora; Eck; Erasmus; Melanchthon; Tetzel; Zwingli

South African government prevented him from leaving Natal. In 1962 he published *Let My People Go*.

Lutosławski, Witold [lootoh**slav**skee] (1913–94) Composer and conductor, born in Warsaw. He studied at Warsaw Conservatory with Mailiszewski, and his first internationally applauded work was *Concerto for Orchestra* (1954). He travelled and taught widely in W Europe and the USA, being honoured with many awards. From a huge, varied output, his orchestral works stand to the fore, including *Symphonic Variations* (1938), a cello concerto (1970), and a piano concerto (1988).

Lutuli, Albert John >> **Luthuli, Albert John**

Lutyens, Sir Edwin Landseer [**lut**yenz] (1869–1944) Architect, born in London, England, UK. He studied at the London Royal College of Art, and became known as a designer of country houses. His best-known projects are the Cenotaph, Whitehall (1919–20), and the laying out of the Indian capital New Delhi, with its spectacular Viceroy's House (1912–30). He was knighted in 1918. His project for a Roman Catholic cathedral in Liverpool was incomplete at his death. >> Jekyll; Lutyens, Elizabeth

Lutyens, (Agnes) Elizabeth [**lut**yenz] (1906–83) Composer, born in London, England, UK. The daughter of Sir Edwin Lutyens, she studied in Paris and at the Royal College of Music. She was one of the first British composers to adopt the 12-tone technique, notably with the *Chamber Concerto No 1* (1939). Her chamber opera *Infidelio* (1954) and cantata

De Amore (1957) were not performed until 1973, but she then became accepted as a leading British composer. Her work includes the chamber opera *The Pit* (1947), *Quincunx* (1959), and *Vision of Youth* (1970). >> Lutyens, Edwin

Luwum, Janani (1922–77) Anglican clergyman and archbishop, born in East Acholi, Uganda. He became a teacher, was converted to Christianity in 1948, and ordained in the Anglican Church. He was theological college principal and Bishop of Northern Uganda, before election in 1974 as Archbishop of Uganda, where in 1971 Idi Amin had established a reign of terror. He spoke out fearlessly on behalf of victims and the oppressed, and at Amin's instigation (some say by his hand) he was shot dead, and Anglicans in Kampala were forbidden to hold a memorial service for him. >> Amin

Luxembourg, François Henri de Montmorency-Bouteville, duc de [lüksäboor] (1628–95) French soldier, born in Paris. A hunchback and of small stature, he was brought up by his aunt, mother of the Great Condé, prepared for a military career, and adhered to Condé through the wars of the Fronde. After 1659 he was pardoned by Louis XIV, who created him Duc de Luxembourg (1661), and in 1667 he served in Franche-Comté, successfully invading Holland in 1672. During the war he stormed Valenciennes, was made a marshal in 1675, commanded in Flanders in 1690, and defeated the Allies at Fleurus in 1690. He twice more routed his old opponent, now King William III of Britain, at Steinkirk (1692) and Neerwinden (1693). >> Condé, Louis II de Bourbon; William III

Luxemburg, Rosa (1871–1919) Revolutionary, born in Russian Poland. She became a German citizen in 1895, and emigrated to Zürich in 1889, where she studied law and political economy. With the German politician Karl Liebknecht she formed the Spartacus League, which later became the German Communist Party. She was arrested and murdered during the Spartacus revolt in Berlin. >> Liebknecht

Luxon, Benjamin (1937–) Baritone, born in Camborne, Cornwall, SW England, UK. He studied at the Guildhall School of Music, London, and was a teacher before becoming a professional singer in 1963. His major roles include *Eugene Onegin*, *Don Giovanni*, and *Julius Caesar*.

Lu Xun [loo shün], also spelled **Lu-hsün** or **Lu-hsin** (1881–1936) Writer and revolutionary, born in Shaoxing, China. He studied as a doctor, but by 1913 was professor of Chinese literature at the National Peking University and National Normal University for Women. In 1926 he became professor at Amoy University, and later dean of the College of Arts and Letters at Yixian University, Canton. His career as an author began with his famous short story, 'Diary of a Madman' (1918), followed in 1921 by *The True Story of Ah Q*, his most successful book, translated into many languages. A revolutionary hero, he was posthumously adopted by the Chinese Communists as an exemplar of Socialist Realism.

Lvov, Prince Georgy Yevgenyevich [lvof] (1861–1925) Russian statesman and social reformer, born in Popovka, Russia. He studied law at Moscow and worked in the civil service, briefly becoming head of the provisional government in the revolution of 1917. Kerensky succeeded him, and he was arrested by the Bolsheviks, but he escaped and fled, eventually to live in Paris. >> Kerensky

Lwoff, André (Michael) [lwof] (1902–94) Biochemist, born in Ainay-le-Chateau, France. He studied at the University of Paris, worked in the Pasteur Institute in Paris from 1921, was a member of the Resistance in World War 2, and became professor of microbiology at the Sorbonne from 1959. He researched the genetics of bacterial viruses and demonstrated the process of lysogeny, with implications for cancer research. He shared the Nobel Prize for Physiology or Medicine in 1965. >> RR1124

Lyautey, Louis Hubert Gonzalve [lyohtay] (1854–1934) French soldier and colonial administrator, born in Nancy, France. He held administrative posts in Algeria, Tongking, and Madagascar (under Galliéni), where he reformed the administration. But his most brilliant work was done in Morocco, where he was resident commissary-general (1912–25), with a break as French minister of war (1916–17). He established firm French authority, and developed Casablanca as a seaport. >> Galliéni

Lycurgus [liːkoorgus] (c.7th-c BC) Traditional, possibly legendary, law-giver of Sparta, who is said to have instigated the Spartan ideals of harsh military discipline. There is much dispute over his existence, but some scholars claim his measures were instrumental in preventing a second helot revolt, and that he delineated the powers of the two traditional organs of the Spartan government.

Lycurgus [liːkoorgus] (c. 390–c. 325 BC) Athenian orator and statesman. A supporter of Demosthenes, as manager of the public revenue he distinguished himself by his integrity, and through his public architectural works. Only one complete speech, *Against Leocrates*, and a fragment of his orations have survived. >> Demosthenes (c.383–322 BC)

Lydgate, John [lidgayt] (c. 1370–c. 1451) Monk and poet, born in Lidgate, Suffolk, E England, UK. He may have studied at Oxford and Cambridge. He became a Benedictine monk at Bury St Edmunds, and in 1423 was made prior of Hatfield Broad Oak, Essex. A court poet, his longer moralistic works include the *Troy Book*, the *Siege of Thebes*, and the *Fall of Princes*.

Lydiard, Arthur Leslie (1917–) Athletics coach and author, born in Auckland, New Zealand. A marathon runner, he later achieved fame as the coach of many successful middle-distance runners, such as Peter Snell. His method emphasized building up strength through distance running before developing speed. From 1960 he popularized the habit of jogging as a means of avoiding cardiac problems. Among his books are *Run to the Top* (1960), *Run for Your Life* (1965), and *Running the Lydiard Way* (1978). >> Snell, Peter

Lyell, Sir Charles [liyl] (1797–1875) Geologist, born in Kinnordy, Angus, E Scotland, UK. He studied law at Oxford, but turned to geology, becoming professor of geology at King's College, London (1832–3). His *Principles of Geology* (1830–3) taught that the greatest geological changes might have been produced by forces still at work, and *The Geological Evidences of the Antiquity of Man* (1863) startled the public in its unbiased attitude towards Charles Darwin. He was knighted in 1848, and made a baronet in 1864. >> Darwin, Charles

Lyle, Sandy [liyl], popular name of **Alexander Walter Barr Lyle** (1958–) Golfer, born in Shrewsbury, Shropshire, WC England, UK. His major championship successes have been the European Open in 1979, the French Open in 1981, the British Open in 1985, and the US Masters Championship in 1988. An extremely long hitter, he has largely been responsible, with Nick Faldo, for the revival of British professional golf at world level. >> Faldo; RR1157

Lyly, John [liːlee] (c. 1554–1606) Writer, born in the Weald of Kent, SE England, UK. He studied at Oxford and Cambridge, and was MP for a while (1597–1601). He is remembered for the style of his writing, as seen in his two-part prose romance *Euphues* (1578, 1580). This work gave rise to the term *euphuism*, referring to an artificial and extremely elegant language, with much use made of complex similes and antithesis.

Lynam, Desmond (Michael) [**liy**nam] (1942–) British sports broadcaster. He studied at Brighton Business College, then worked in insurance before becoming a freelance journalist and local radio reporter. He joined the BBC in 1969 as a sports presenter and commentator, moving to television in 1978, where he became nationally known for his contributions to such programmes as *Grandstand*, *Sportsnight*, and *Match of the Day*. He has also presented *Holiday* (from 1988) and *How Do They Do That?* (from 1994) for BBC television. Several times Sports Presenter of the Year, he received the BAFTA Richard Dimbleby Award in 1995. His books include accounts of the 1986 Commonwealth Games, the 1988 Olympics, and the 1992 Olympics.

Lynch, Benny (1913–46) Boxer, born in Glasgow, W Scotland, UK. In 1935 he became the first Scot to hold a world title, taking the National Boxing Association/International Boxing Union version of the world flyweight title. From 1937 to 1938 he was undisputed world champion, but he forfeited the title when he failed to make the weight for a title bout against Jacky Jurich of the USA. During his career he won 82 out of 110 bouts.

Lynch, David (1946–) Film director, born in Missoula, MT. He studied at the Corcoran School of Art, Washington, DC, took up painting in Boston and Philadelphia, then studied at the American Film Institute in Los Angeles. His first film, *Eraserhead* (1977), gained him recognition and a reputation for the bizarre. This was followed by *The Elephant Man* (1980) and *Blue Velvet* (1986), for which he won an Oscar nomination for best director. He is probably best known for the cult television series *Twin Peaks* (1990–1), which he co-wrote; shown on US and British prime-time television, it successfully challenged traditional mainstream programming. *Wild at Heart* (1990) won the Palme d'Or at the Cannes Film Festival. Later films include *Lost Highway* (1997).

Lynch, Edmund C >> Merrill, Charles E

Lynch, Jack, popular name of **John Lynch** (1917–) Irish statesman and prime minister (1966–73, 1977–9), born in Cork, Co Cork, Ireland. Following a career in the Department of Justice (1936), he was called to the bar (1945). Elected an MP in 1948, he held ministerial posts in lands (1951), the Gaeltacht (1957), education (1957–9), industry and commerce (1959–65), and finance (1965–6), before becoming prime minister. Perceived as a strong supporter of the Catholic minority in Ulster, he drew criticism from both Ulster and mainland Britain. He lost the premiership in 1973, regaining it four years later, but in 1979 resigned both the post and the leadership of Fianna Fáil. He retired from politics in 1981. >> RR1064

Lynd, Robert (Staughton) (1892–1970) and **Helen Lynd**, *née* **Merrill** (1894–1982) Sociology authors, born in New Albany, IN, and La Grange, IL, respectively. He worked at research institutions until 1931, then taught at Columbia University. She taught at Sarah Lawrence College, Bronxville (1929–64). They were married in 1921, and together conducted a sociological study of Muncie, IN, on which they based two successful books: *Middletown: a Study in Contemporary American Culture* (1929) and *Middletown in Transition: a Study in Cultural Conflicts* (1937).

Lyndsay or **Lindsay, Sir David** [**lind**zee] (c. 1486–1555) Poet, born probably near Cupar, Fife, E Scotland, UK. For two centuries he was the poet of the Scottish people, and his poems were said to have done more for the Reformation in Scotland than all the sermons of Knox. The earliest and most poetic of his writings is the allegorical

The Dreme (1528). His most remarkable work was *The Satyre of the Thrie Estaitis*, a dramatic work first performed at Linlithgow in 1540, and revived with great success at the Edinburgh Festivals of 1948 and 1959, and several times thereafter.

Lynen, Feodor (Felix Konrad) [**lee**nen] (1911–79) Biochemist, born in Munich, Germany. He studied at Munich, became head of biochemistry there, and director of the Max Planck Institute for Cell Chemistry and Biochemistry (1945–79). For his work in lipid biochemistry on the formation of the cholesterol molecule, and discovering the biochemistry of the vitamin biotin, he shared the 1964 Nobel Prize for Physiology or Medicine. >> RR1124

Lyngstad, Anni-Frid >> Abba

Lyon, John (?–1592) Philanthropist, and yeoman landowner of the estate of Preston, Middlesex, regarded as the founder of the great public school of Harrow. Relatively prosperous but childless, he used his money for the endowment of local charities. In 1572 he obtained a royal charter from Elizabeth I for the pre-Reformation school at Harrow, which he supported with endowments to guarantee its continuation. In 1590 he drew up statutes and a course of Classical education for the school.

Lyon, John (1962–) Boxer, born in St Helens, Merseyside, NW England, UK. An outstanding amateur boxer, he is the only man to win eight Amateur Boxing Association titles– the light-flyweight title in 1981–4, and the flyweight title in 1986–9. He also won the 1986 Commonwealth Games flyweight title.

Lyons, Sir John (1932–) Linguist, born in Manchester, Greater Manchester, NW England, UK. He studied at Cambridge, taught at London (1957–61) and Cambridge (1961–4), then became professor of linguistics at Edinburgh (1964–76) and Sussex (1976–84), and Master of Trinity Hall, Cambridge (1984–). A specialist in semantics and linguistic theory, his major publications include *Semantics* (2 vols, 1977), *Language, Meaning and Context* (1980), and *Linguistic Semantics* (1995). He was knighted in 1987.

Lyons, Sir Joseph (1848–1917) Businessman, born in London, England, UK. He first studied art, and invented a stereoscope before joining with three friends to establish a teashop in Piccadilly. He became head of one of the largest catering businesses in Britain – J Lyons and Co Ltd.

Lyons, Joseph Aloysius (1879–1939) Australian statesman and prime minister (1932–9), born in Stanley, Tasmania, Australia. He studied at Tasmania University, became a teacher, entered politics in 1909 as Labor member in the Tasmanian House of Assembly, held the post of minister of education and railways (1914–16), and was premier (1923–9). In the federal parliament he became postmaster-general, minister of public works, and treasurer. In 1931 he broke away and founded and led an Opposition party, the United Australian Party. As prime minister he saw the country's economic recovery after the years of the Depression. >> RR1033

Lyot, Bernard (Ferdinand) [lyoh] (1897–1952) Astronomer, born in Paris. He studied engineering at the Ecole Supérieure d'Electricité, and worked at the Paris Observatory at Meudon from 1920. In 1930 he invented the coronagraph, a device which allows the Sun's corona to be observed without a total solar eclipse. He achieved this by creating an artificial eclipse inside a telescope. He also pioneered the study of the polarization of light reflected from the surface of the Moon and of the planets.

Lysander [lis**an**der] (?–395 BC) Greek political leader and naval commander. He commanded the Spartan fleet which defeated the Athenians at Aegospotami (405 BC), and in 404 BC took Athens, thus ending the Peloponnesian War.

Lysenko, Trofim Denisovich [lisengkoh] (1898–1976) Geneticist and agronomist, born in Karlovka, Ukraine. He developed a doctrine, compounded of Darwinism and the work of Michurin, that heredity can be changed by good husbandry. As director of the Institute of Genetics of the Soviet Academy of Sciences (1940–65), he declared the accepted Mendelian theory erroneous, and ruthlessly silenced any Soviet geneticists who opposed him. He was dismissed by Khrushchev in 1965, having gravely hampered scientific and agricultural progress in the USSR. >> Darwin, Charles; Mendel; Michurin; Vavilov

Lysias [lisias] (c. 445–c. 380 BC) Greek orator, the son of a rich Syracusan. Educated at Thurii in Italy, he settled in Athens c.440 BC. The Thirty Tyrants in 404 BC stripped him and his brother Polemarchus of their wealth, and killed Polemarchus. The first use to which Lysias put his eloquence was in 'Against Eratosthenes' to prosecute the tyrant chiefly to blame for his brother's murder. He then practised with success as a writer of speeches for litigants. His family home in Athens is portrayed in Plato's *Republic*.

Lysimachus [lisimakus] (c. 355–281 BC) Macedonian general of Alexander the Great. He acted as his bodyguard during the conquest of Asia, and became King of Thrace, to which he later added NW Asia Minor and Macedonia. He was defeated and killed at Koroupedion by Seleucus. >> Alexander the Great; Antigonus I; Arsinoë; Seleucus

Lysippos or **Lysippus of Sicyon** [lisipus] (4th-c BC) Greek sculptor. Originally a metal worker, he developed his own style of sculpture, and is said to have made more than 1500 bronzes and introduced a new naturalism. He made several portrait busts of Alexander the Great.

Lyttelton, Humphrey [litltuhn] (1921–) Jazz trumpeter and bandleader, born in Windsor, Berkshire, S England, UK. He formed a band in 1948, and became the leading figure in the British revival of traditional jazz. His group expanded to an octet, emulating Ellington's early ensembles, and then modernized even further, to the horror of many fans of traditional jazz. He responded with a satirical book *I Play As I Please* (1954). He retained his stature, and increased the tolerance for more modern jazz styles in Britain. On BBC Radio he has hosted *The Best of Jazz* for many years, and has been chairman of the panel game *I'm Sorry I Haven't a Clue* since 1972.

Lyttleton, Oliver >> **Chandos, 1st Viscount**

Lytton (of Knebworth), Edward George Earle Bulwer-Lytton, Baron [litn] (1803–73) Writer and statesman, born in London, England, UK. He took early to poetry, and in 1820 published *Ismael and other Poems*. At Cambridge (1822–5) he won the Chancellor's Gold Medal for a poem. His enormous output, extremely popular during his lifetime, includes the novel *The Last Days of Pompeii* (1834), his play *Money* (1840), and the epic poem 'King Arthur' (1848–9). MP for St Ives (1831–41), he was created a baronet in 1838, and in 1843 succeeded to the Knebworth estate. He re-entered parliament as member for Hertfordshire in 1852, and in 1858–9 was colonial secretary. In 1866 he was raised to the peerage.

Lytton, (Edward) Robert Bulwer-Lytton, 1st Earl of, pseudonym **Owen Meredith** (1831–91) Poet and statesman, born in London, England, UK. He studied at Bonn, and in 1849 went to Washington as attaché and private secretary to his uncle, **Henry Bulwer** (1801–72). He subsequently held diplomatic posts all over Europe, before succeeding his father as second Lord Lytton in 1873. He became minister at Lisbon (1874), Viceroy of India (1876–80), Earl of Lytton (1800), and in 1887 ambassador to Paris. His works, published mostly under his pseudonym, include novels, poems, and translations from Serbian. His *Indian Administration* (1899) and his *Letters* (1906) were both edited by his daughter, **Lady Betty Balfour**.

Lyubimov, Yuri [lyubeemof] (1917–) Russian theatre director. He joined the Vakhtangov Theatre Company in Moscow after World War 2, and after the tremendous acclaim for his production of Brecht's *The Good Woman of Setzuan*, was appointed director of the Taganka Theatre, Moscow (1964). At the Taganka his productions included Molière's *Tartuffe* (1969) and a modern-dress *Hamlet* in 1974. He fell from favour, was fired from his theatre, expelled from the Party, and deprived of his Soviet citizenship. He subsequently worked on several productions outside the Soviet Union, but returned in 1988.

Ma, Yo-Yo (1955–) Cellist, born in Paris. Coming to New York City with his family at age seven, he enrolled at the Juilliard School, New York City at nine, and after studies at Harvard ascended rapidly to the highest rank of international soloists. He is noted for his warmth of playing, superlative technique, a repertoire stretching from Bach to the moderns, and an energetic stage presence.

Maazel, Lorin (Varencove) [mahzel] (1930–) Conductor, born to American parents in Neuilly, France. Brought to the USA as a child, he was a prodigy as a violinist, pianist, and conductor, conducting the New York Philharmonic at age 12. He studied at the University of Pittsburgh, making his professional debut as a violinist in 1945 and as a conductor in 1953. He directed the Deutsche Oper, Berlin (1965–71), the Cleveland Orchestra (1972–82), the Vienna Staatsoper (1982–4), and the Pittsburgh Symphony Orchestra (1988–96).

Mabillon, Jean [mabeeyõ] (1632–1707) Scholar and historian, born near Reims, France. He became a Benedictine monk in 1654, and from 1664 worked in the abbey of St Germain-des-Prés in Paris. Considered the founder of Latin palaeography, he edited St Bernard's works (1667) and wrote a history of his order (9 vols, 1668–1702).

Mabo, Eddie Koiki [mahboh] (1940–92) Traditional leader of the Meriam people of Murray I in Torres Strait, Australia. In 1982, with four other Meriam people, he began legal proceedings against the Queensland government, seeking recognition of their traditional ownership of the island and its surrounding seas. He persisted with the case, and in 1992 the High Court of Australia held that the Australian common law recognizes a form of native title, making it a landmark case which overturned the 18th-c notion of *terra nullius*. The victory for Eddie Mabo was posthumous, but the decision was so controversial that his case rapidly became a cause célèbre.

Mabon >> **Abraham, William**

Mabuse, Jan [mabüz], originally **Jan Gossaert** or **Jenni Gossart** (c.1478–c.1532) Painter, born in Maubeuge, France. In 1503 he entered the painters' guild of St Luke in Antwerp, and accompanied Philip of Burgundy to Italy (1508–9), where he was greatly influenced by the High Renaissance style. He was the first artist to introduce the Italian style to Holland, and his works in that genre include 'Hercules and Deianeira' (1517, Birmingham). He was also a well-known portraitist.

McAdam, John Loudon (1756–1836) Inventor of macadamized roads, born in Ayr, South Ayrshire, SW Scotland, UK. He went to New York City in 1770, where he made a fortune in his uncle's counting-house. On his return in 1783 he bought an estate and started experimenting with new methods of road construction. In 1816 he was appointed surveyor to the Bristol Turnpike Trust, re-made the roads there with crushed stone bound with gravel, and raised the carriageway to improve drainage. In 1827 he was made surveyor-general of metropolitan roads in Great Britain, and his *macadam surfaces* were adopted in many other countries.

McAleese, Mary [makalees] (1951–) President of Ireland (1997–), born in Belfast, Northern Ireland. She studied at Queen's University, Belfast, moving in 1975 to Trinity College, Dublin as professor of criminal law. She also worked as a television journalist (1979–81), and in the 1980s became known as an outspoken campaigner for a wide range of social causes. In 1987 she moved into university administration at Queen's, becoming the first woman and Catholic pro-vice-chancellor in 1994. Despite her northern background, she became the presidential successor to Mary Robinson in the 1997 election. >> Robinson, Mary

McAliskey, Bernadette (Josephine) [muhkaliskee], *née* **Devlin** (1947–) Northern Irish political activist, brought up in Dungannon, Co Tyrone. She studied at Queen's University, Belfast, and became the youngest MP in the House of Commons since William Pitt when she was elected as an Independent Unity candidate in 1969. Her aggressive political style led to her arrest while leading Catholic rioters in the Bogside, and she was sentenced to nine months' imprisonment. In 1971 she lost Catholic support when she gave birth to an illegitimate child; she married two years later and was defeated in the 1974 general election. She was a co-founder of the Irish Republican Socialist Party.

McAnally, Ray(mond) [makanalee] (1926–89) Actor, born in Buncrana, Co Donegal, Ireland. A member of Dublin's Abbey Theatre from 1947, he had appeared in some 150 productions there by 1963. He made his London debut in 1962, and subsequent West End appearances included *Who's Afraid of Virginia Woolf?* (1964). On film he won international acclaim and a BAFTA award for his performance as the papal envoy in *The Mission* (1986), and was acclaimed for his part in *My Left Foot* (1989). A veteran of over 500 television productions, he won BAFTA awards for *A Perfect Spy* (1988) and *A Very British Coup* (1989).

MacArthur, Douglas (1880–1964) US general, born in Little Rock, AR. He trained at West Point, joined the US army engineers, and in World War 1 served with distinction in France. In 1941 he became commanding general of the US armed forces in the Far East, and from Australia directed the recapture of the SW Pacific (1942–5). He formally accepted the Japanese surrender, and commanded the occupation of Japan (1945–51), introducing a new constitution. In 1950 he led the UN forces in the Korean War, defeating the North Korean army, but was relieved of command when he tried to continue the war against China. >> Kincaid; Yamashita

Macarthur, Elizabeth, *née* **Veale** (1766–1850) Australian pioneer, born in Bridgerule, Devon, SW England, UK. She married John Macarthur in 1788 and emigrated to New South Wales. During her husband's prolonged absences, she introduced the merino sheep to the area, and experimented in the breeding of sheep for fine wool which led to the establishment of the Australian wool industry. >> Macarthur, John

Macarthur, John (1767–1834) Pioneer and wool merchant, born in Stoke Damerel, Devonshire, SW England, UK. In 1789 he emigrated to Australia, where he became leader of the settlers in New South Wales. He inspired the Rum Rebellion (1808–10) in which British soldiers mutinied and imprisoned the governor, William Bligh. He was banished to England in 1810, but returned in 1816 and made a fortune in the wool trade. He later became a member of the New South Wales Legislative Council (1825–32). >> Bligh; Macarthur, Elizabeth

Macarthur, Robert (Helmer) (1930–72) Ecologist, born in Toronto, Ontario, Canada. He studied mathematics at Yale, changed to zoology, and from 1965 was professor of biology at Princeton. His early work on birds led him to devise methods for quantifying ecological factors. He categorized animals as 'R' species (opportunistic, rapid reproduction and development, short lives, high mortality), and 'K' species (larger, slowly developing, more stable). In 1962 he showed that natural selection principles apply to both groups.

Macaulay, Dame (Emilie) Rose (1881–1958) Novelist, essayist, and poet, born in Rugby, Warwickshire, C England, UK. She read history at Oxford, where she wrote her first book. She won a considerable reputation as a social satirist, with such novels as *Dangerous Ages* (1921). Her best-known novel is *The Towers of Trebizond* (1956). Two posthumous volumes, *Letters to a Friend* (1961–2), describe her return to Anglicanism. She was made a dame in 1958.

Macaulay (of Rothley), Thomas Babington Macaulay, Baron [muh**kaw**lee] (1800–59) Essayist and historian, born in Rothley Temple, Leicestershire, C England, UK. He was educated privately and at Cambridge, where he became a fellow. Called to the bar in 1826, he had no liking for his profession, and turned to literature. He also became an MP (1830), and established his powers as an orator in the Reform Bill debates. After a period in Bengal (1834–80), he became secretary of war (1839–41), and wrote the highly popular *Lays of Ancient Rome* (1842). His major work, the *History of England from the Accession of James II*, was published between 1848 and 1861, the fifth volume unfinished. He became a peer in 1857.

McAuley, Catherine [muh**kaw**lee] (1787–1841) Founder of a religious order, born in Dublin. She was left money by her protestant foster-parents, and founded the Roman Catholic House of Mercy, an institution for educating the poor. She took her vows in 1831, and founded the order of the Sisters of Mercy.

McBain, Ed, pseudonym of **Evan Hunter**, originally **Salvatore A Lambino** (1926–) Novelist, born in New York City. He was educated in New York, served in the US navy, and became a teacher before concentrating on his career as a novelist. He is renowned for his '87th Precinct' thrillers, written under his pseudonym. Under his own name, his works generally deal with social problems. He is best known for *The Blackboard Jungle* (1954), acclaimed for its realism and topicality. Later books include *Sons* (1969), *Walk Proud* (1978), and *Privileged Conversation* (1996).

McBean, Angus (Rowland) (1904–90) Stage photographer, born in Newbridge, Monmouth, Monmouthshire, SE Wales. He studied at Newport, and started as a full-time theatrical photographer in 1934, becoming noted for his individual approach to portraiture. He used elaborate settings, photographic montage, collage, and double-exposure to achieve a Surrealistic interpretation of character. In later years he applied his creativity to pop music.

Macbeth (c. 1005–57) King of Scots (1040–57), the legend of whose life was the basis of Shakespeare's play. The *mormaer* (provincial ruler) of Moray, he became king after slaying Duncan I in battle near Elgin, and in 1050 went on a pilgrimage to Rome. He was defeated and killed by Duncan's son, Malcolm Canmore, at Lumphanan, Aberdeenshire. >> Malcolm III; RR1095

Macbeth, Ann (1875–1948) Embroideress, born in Little Bolton, Greater Manchester, NW England, UK. She studied at Glasgow School of Art (1897–1900), and was a member of its staff from 1901 to 1920, latterly as head of the embroidery department. She was influential in advocating new methods of teaching embroidery, and wrote an instruction manual called *Educational Needlecraft*. She had many ecclesiastical commissions, and her embroidered panels decorate many Glasgow interiors.

McBey, James [muh**kbay**] (1883–1959) Artist and etcher, born in Newburgh, Aberdeenshire, NE Scotland, UK. After working in a bank, he left to become an artist, producing his first etching in 1902. Entirely self-taught, he became

well known as a master of British etching. He travelled extensively in Europe, N Africa, and America, and was a war artist in France and with the Australian Camel Patrol in Egypt and Palestine during World War 1.

MacBride, Maud, *née* **Gonne** (1865–1953) Irish nationalist and actress, born in Aldershot, Surrey, SE England, UK. She became an agitator for the cause of Irish independence, one of the founders of Sinn Féin, and edited a nationalist newspaper in Paris. Her acting involved her with W B Yeats, who wished to marry her, and who made her the heroine of his first play, but she married **Major John MacBride**, who fought against the British in the Boer War and was executed as a rebel in 1916. Their son **Sean** (1904–) was foreign minister of the Irish Republic (1948–51), and was awarded the Nobel Peace Prize in 1974. >> Yeats

McBride, Willie John, popular name of **William John McBride** (1940–) Rugby union player, born in Toomebridge, Co Antrim. A man of virtually one club, he was with Ballymena from 1962, and within 10 years had won 45 caps and made four Lions tours. Tall and massively built, he won a total of 63 caps and played in 17 Tests on five Lions tours, then retired from top-class rugby, and became interested in the management of international teams.

MacBryde, Robert [muh**kbriyd**] (1913–66) Painter, born in Ayr, South Ayrshire, SW Scotland, UK. He worked in industry for five years before studying at the Glasgow School of Art, and later worked with Robert Colquhoun, painting brilliantly-coloured Cubist lifes and, later, brooding Expressionist figures. >> Colquhoun

MacCaig, Norman (Alexander) [muh**kayg**] (1910–96) Poet, born in Edinburgh, EC Scotland, UK. He read Classics at University there, and was a primary school teacher for nearly 40 years. The first fellow in creative writing at Edinburgh University (1967–9), he then lectured in English studies at Stirling University (1970–7). The leading Scottish poet of his generation writing in English, he was awarded the Queen's Gold Medal for Poetry in 1986. His collections of quick, imagistic, and philosophic poems include *Riding Lights* (1955), *A Round of Applause* (1962), *The White Bird* (1973), and *Voice-Over* (1988). His *Collected Poems* were published in 1985 (revised 1990).

McCarroll, Tony >> Oasis

McCarthy, Eugene J(oseph) (1916–) US politician, born in Watkins, MN. He studied at St John's University, MN, and Minnesota University, then taught at St John's (1940–3) before working in military intelligence during World War 2, after which he was elected to the US House of Representatives (1948). He became nationally known when he challenged President Lyndon B Johnson in the race for the Democratic presidential nomination (1968), a decision which ultimately led to Johnson's withdrawal. McCarthy was eventually defeated by Robert F Kennedy. In 1971 he turned to writing, producing works of non-fiction, poetry, and children's stories. >> Johnson, Lyndon B; Kennedy, Robert F

McCarthy, Joseph R(aymond) (1909–57) US Republican politician and inquisitor, born in Grand Chute, WI. He studied at Marquette University, Milwaukee, became a circuit judge in 1939, and after war service was elected senator (1945). He achieved fame for his unsubstantiated accusations, in the early 1950s, that 250 Communists had infiltrated the State Department, and in 1953 became chairman of the powerful Permanent Subcommittee on Investigations. By hectoring cross-examination and damaging innuendo he arraigned many innocent citizens and officials, overreaching himself when he came into direct conflict with the army. The kind of anti-Communist witch-hunt he instigated became known as *McCarthyism*. Formally condemned by the US Senate, he lost most of his remaining Republican support. >> Cohn, Roy M; Lattimore

McCarthy, Mary (Therese) (1912–89) Writer and critic, born in Seattle, WA. Orphaned at the age of six, she was brought up by relatives. She studied at Vassar College, NY, then worked as a publisher's editor, theatre critic, and teacher before writing her first novel, *The Company She Keeps* (1942). Other novels include *The Groves of Academe* (1952) and *The Group* (1963). She also published critical works, travel books, and the autobiographical *Memories of a Catholic Girlhood* (1957).

McCartney, Sir Paul [muhkah(r)tnee] (1942–) Musician, songwriter, and composer, born in Liverpool, Merseyside, NW England, UK. The Beatles' bass guitarist, vocalist, and member of the Lennon–McCartney songwriting team, he made his debut as a soloist with the album *McCartney* (1970), heralding the break-up of the group. In 1971 he formed the band Wings (disbanded in 1981) with his wife **Linda** (1942–). 'Mull of Kintyre' (1977) became the biggest-selling UK single (2·5 million). In 1979 he was declared the most successful composer of all time: by 1978 he had written or co-written 43 songs that sold over a million copies each. Later albums included *Band on the Run* (1973), *Wings Over America* (1977), *Give My Regards To Broad Street* (1984), *Tripping the Live Fantastic* (1990), and *Flaming Pie* (1997), and his music attracted numerous Grammy awards. 'Ebony and Ivory', recorded with Stevie Wonder, was an international hit of the year in 1982. He has performed at concerts all over the world, gaining a place in the Guinness Book of Records for playing before the largest-paid attendance (1990, Rio de Janeiro). He wrote and produced the film/video featuring 'We All Stand Together' (1984), which has become a perennial Christmas favourite. His *Liverpool Oratorio* (written in association with Carl Davis) was performed by the Royal Liverpool Philharmonic Orchestra in 1991, and he has since continued to develop his interests as a classical composer, notably in *Standing Stone* (1997). He collaborated with Harrison and Starr in the retrospective Beatles' anthology in 1995. He wrote the books *All You Need Is Love* (1968) and *Paul McCartney In His Own Words* (1976), and wrote, produced, and composed the music for a successful animated film, *Rupert and the Frog Song* (1984, BAFTA). He was knighted in 1997. ➤ Beatles, The; Davis, Carl; Lennon; Wonder

McCay, Winsor (Zezic) [muhkay], pseudonym **Silas** (1867–1934) Cartoonist and film animator, born in Spring Lake, MI. He worked as an illustrator on various newspapers before joining the *New York Herald* to make his first successful strip, *Dreams of a Rarebit Fiend* (1904), which was filmed by Edison. He drew under his pseudonym, but used his own name for the successful *Little Nemo in Slumberland* (1905). His animated films include *Gertie the Dinosaur* (1914) and *The Sinking of the Lusitania* (1918), the first dramatic/documentary cartoon.

McClellan, George B(rinton) (1826–85) US Union general in the American Civil War, born in Philadelphia, PA. He trained at West Point, fought in the Mexican War, then worked on military engineering projects. When the War began, he drove the enemy out of West Virginia, and was called to Washington to reorganize the Army of the Potomac. His Peninsular Campaign in Virginia ended disastrously at Richmond (1862). He forced Lee to retreat at Antietam, but failed to follow up his advantage, and was recalled. In 1864 he opposed Lincoln for the presidency, and in 1877 was elected governor of New Jersey. ➤ Lee, Robert E; Stuart, Jeb

McClintock, Barbara (1902–92) Geneticist and biologist, born in Hartford, CT. She studied at Cornell, where she later taught (1927–31). Working at the Cold Spring Harbor Laboratory from the 1940s, she discovered and studied a new class of mutant genes in corn, concluding that the function of some genes is to control other genes, and that they can move on the chromosome to do this. She was awarded the National Medal of Science (1970), the first MacArthur Laureate Award (1981), and received the first unshared Nobel Prize for Physiology or Medicine to be awarded to a woman (1983). A biography detailing her pioneering work *A Feeling for the Organism* appeared in 1983.

McCloy, John (Jay) (1895–1989) Lawyer and government official, born in Philadelphia, PA. A corporate lawyer and presidential advisor, he served as assistant secretary of war (1941–5). President of the World Bank (1947–9) and US High Commissioner of Germany (1949–50), he oversaw Germany's return to statehood. After serving as chairman of the Chase Bank (1953–60), he became principal negotiator on the President's Disarmament Committee (1961–74).

McClung, Nellie (Letitia), *née* **Mooney** (1873–1951) Suffragist, writer, and public speaker, born in Chatsworth, Ontario, Canada. Educated in Manitoba, she rose to prominence through the Women's Christian Temperance Union and the suffrage movement, and was elected to the Alberta Legislative Assembly (1921–6).

McClure, Sir Robert (John le Mesurier) [muhkloor] (1807–73) Explorer, born in Wexford, Co Wexford, Ireland. He joined the navy in 1824, and served in an expedition to the Arctic in 1836. He was with the Franklin expedition (1848–9), and again in 1850, when he commanded a ship that penetrated E to the coast of Banks Land, where he was icebound for nearly two years. Rescued by another ship which had travelled from the W, he thus became the first person to navigate the Northwest Passage. The McClure Strait is named after him. ➤ Franklin, John

McColgan, Liz [muhkolgan], popular name of **Elizabeth McColgan**, *née* **Lynch** (1964–) Athlete, born in Dundee, E Scotland, UK. She studied in Dundee and at the University of Alabama. Her athletic achievements in the 10 000 m include gold medals at the Commonwealth Games (1986, 1990), gold at the World Championships (1991), and silver at the Olympics (1988). She also won the silver for the 3000 m at the Indoor World Championships (1989), and was winner of the New York Marathon (1991) and the London Marathon (1996). She was voted Sportswriters' Athlete of the Year (1988, 1991) and BBC Sports Personality of the Year (1991).

MacColl, Dugald Sutherland (1859–1948) Painter and art historian, born in Glasgow, W Scotland, UK. He studied at London and Oxford, and after travelling Europe studying works of art, established a reputation as a critic, and brought out his *Nineteenth Century Art* in 1902. As keeper of the London Tate Gallery (1906–11) and of the Wallace Collection (1911–24), he instituted many reforms.

MacColl, Ewan, pseudonym of **James Miller** (1915–89) Folk-singer, composer, and writer, born in Salford, Greater Manchester, NW England, UK. As a playwright, he collaborated with Joan Littlewood in forming the experimental Theatre Workshop in the 1940s, and reviving street theatre. Later he became a pioneer of the British folk-music revival. His series of Radio Ballads, begun in 1957, combining contemporary social comment with traditional musical forms, had a powerful influence on songwriting and performing in subsequent decades. As a collector of traditional folk-song, he has published several anthologies. Among his own compositions are 'Dirty Old Town', 'Freeborn Man', and 'The First Time Ever I Saw Your Face'. ➤ Littlewood, Joan

McCollum, Elmer (Verner) [muhkoluhm] (1879–1967) Biochemist, born in Fort Scott, KS. He studied at Yale, and became professor of biochemistry at Johns Hopkins University (1917–44). In 1913 he showed that more than one vitamin was necessary for normal animal growth, classifying these as vitamins A (fat-soluble) and B (water-soluble), and in 1920 added the rickets-preventative factor, D. His book *Newer Knowledge of Nutrition* (1918) was a standard text for some years.

McCormack, John (Francis) (1884–1945) Tenor, born in Athlone, near Dublin. He studied in Milan, made his London debut in 1905, and was engaged by Covent Garden opera for the 1905–6 season, appearing also in oratorio and as a *Lieder* singer. As an Irish nationalist, he did not appear in England during World War 1, but took US citizenship in 1919, and turned to popular sentimental songs. He was raised to the papal peerage as a count in 1928.

McCormack, Mark (Hume) (1930–) Sports agent, promoter, and lawyer, born in Chicago, IL. He studied at Princeton and Yale, and was called to the bar in 1957. A keen golfer, he offered to arrange exhibitions for Arnold Palmer, and founded the International Management Group (IMG) in 1962. His agency quickly grew into the largest company of its kind, handling the sponsorship deals and promotion of numerous sports stars and other personalities. IMG was used by the Catholic Church in Britain to market the pope's visit in 1982, and it handles almost all aspects of the Wimbledon championships.

McCormick, Cyrus (Hall) (1809–84) Inventor of the reaper, born in Rockbridge Co, VA. He continued experiments begun by his father, and produced a successful model in 1831, at the age of 22. He made his first sale in 1840, and moved to Chicago in 1847, where he manufactured more than six million harvesting machines during his lifetime. His McCormick Harvesting Machine Co became in 1902 the International Harvester Co, with his son **Cyrus Hall, Jr** (1859–1936) as first president and chairman of the board. >> Bell, Patrick; Hussey

McCracken, Esther (Helen), *née* **Armstrong** (1902–71) Playwright and actress, born in Newcastle upon Tyne, Tyne and Wear, NE England, UK. She acted with the Newcastle Repertory Company (1924–37), and had her first play produced in 1936, but it was with *Quiet Wedding* (1938) that her reputation was made as a writer of domestic comedy. Other successes were *Quiet Weekend* (1941) and *No Medals* (1944).

McCracken, James (1927–88) Tenor, born in Gary, IN. He started life as a steelworker, but his potential as a singer was spotted during service with the US navy. He made his operatic debut as Rodolfo in Puccini's *La Bohème* in 1952, but his 1959 performance as Verdi's *Otello* in Europe marked a turning point in his career. In 1963 he returned to America to become one of the Metropolitan Opera's leading tenors, and was internationally acclaimed in the 1960s, particularly for his Otello.

MacCready, Paul (Beattie) [muh**kree**dee] (1925–) Aeronautical engineer and inventor, born in New Haven, CT. He was the designer of the ultra-light aircraft *Gossamer Condor*, which in 1977 made the first man-powered flight over a one-mile course. Its successor, *Gossamer Albatross*, in 1979 crossed the 23 mi of the English Channel in just under three hours at a height of only a few feet, propelled and piloted by US racing cyclist, Bryan Allen.

McCubbin, Frederick (1855–1917) Landscape painter, born in Melbourne, Victoria, Australia. A part-time artist, working in his father's bakery until 1877, he became teacher of drawing at the National Gallery of Victoria's Art School in 1886, a position which he held until his death. With other painters, including Tom Roberts, he established the first of the artist camps which became the Heidelberg school of Australian painting. Also a successful portraitist, he exhibited in London and Paris in 1897. >> Roberts, Tom

McCullers, (Lula) Carson, *née* **Smith** (1917–67) Writer, born in Columbus, GA. She studied at Columbia and New York universities. She married and divorced Reeves McCullers twice (1937–41, 1945–8). From the age of 29, paralysis of one side confined her to a wheelchair. Her work reflects the sadness of lonely people, and her first book, *The Heart Is a Lonely Hunter* (1940), about a deaf mute, distinguished her immediately as a novelist of note. She wrote the best and the bulk of her work in a six-year burst through World War 2, including the novella *The Ballad of the Sad Café* (1951), which was dramatized by Edward Albee. >> Albee

McCullough, Colleen [muh**kuh**luh] (1937–) Novelist, born in Wellington, New South Wales, Australia. She studied in Sydney and London, and pursued a career as a neurophysiologist in Sydney, London, and Yale University Medical School. She then moved to Norfolk I in the South Pacific (1979) and became a best-selling novelist. Her books include *Tim* (1974), *The Thorn Birds* (1977), which sold 20 million copies, *A Creed for the Third Millennium* (1985), *The First Man in Rome* (1990), and *The Grass Crown* (1991).

MacDiarmid, Hugh [muh**der**mid], pseudonym of **Christopher Murray Grieve** (1892–1978) Poet, born in Langholm, Dumfries and Galloway, SW Scotland, UK. He became a pupil-teacher at Broughton Higher Grade School in Edinburgh before turning to journalism. After World War 1, he married, settled as a journalist in Montrose, and edited anthologies of contemporary Scottish writing. After publishing his outstanding early lyrical verse, *Sangschaw* (1925) and *Penny Wheep* (1926), he established himself as the leader of a vigorous Scottish Renaissance with *A Drunk Man Looks at the Thistle* (1926), full of political, metaphysical, and nationalistic reflections on the Scottish predicament. He became professor of literature at the Royal Scottish Academy (1974), and president of the Poetry Society (1976). He was a founder member of the Scottish Nationalist Party, and an active Communist.

MacDonagh, Donagh [muh**don**a] (1912–68) Playwright, born in Dublin, the son of Thomas MacDonagh. He was orphaned by his father's execution, and the drowning of his mother in an attempt to plant the tricolour on an island in Dublin Bay. He studied at University College, Dublin, became a barrister in 1935, and was made a district justice in 1941. A hunchback, he won success as a writer of the exuberant *Happy as Larry* (1946), and other plays including *Step-in-the-Hollow* (1957). He was a highly acclaimed broadcaster, and co-edited *The Oxford Book of Irish Verse* (1958). >> MacDonagh, Thomas

MacDonagh, Thomas [muh**don**a] (1878–1916) Poet, critic, and nationalist, born in Cloughjordan, Co Tipperary, Ireland. He helped P H Pearse to found St Enda's College, Dublin (1908), and published poems, original works, and translations from the Irish. In 1914 he founded the Irish Theatre with Joseph Plunkett and Edward Martyn (1859–1923). An outstanding critic of English literature, his works include *Literature in Ireland* and *Thomas Campion*. He took part in the Irish Volunteers, was very belatedly drawn into preparations for the Easter Rising of 1916, commanded at Jacob's Factory in the fighting, and was executed. Yeats wrote his epitaph in 'Easter 1916'. >> MacDonagh, Donagh

MacDonald, Dwight (1906–82) Writer and film critic, born in New York City. While still a student at Yale he became a literary editor, and worked for *Fortune* (1929–36), the business magazine. A social and political commentator, he wrote regularly for *Partisan Review*, was a staff writer for the *New Yorker* (1951–71), and film critic for *Esquire* (1960–6). His essays were collected in several books, including *The Memoirs of a Revolutionist* (1957) and *Against the American Grain* (1963).

MacDonald, Elaine (1943–) Dancer, born in Tadcaster, North Yorkshire, N England, UK. She trained at the Royal Ballet School, joining Western Ballet Theatre in 1964, and moving with the company to Glasgow when it became Scottish Ballet in the late 1960s. A dancer of international standard, she created many roles for the choreographer/ director Peter Darrell, including *Sun into Darkness* (1966) and *Mary Queen of Scots* (1976). She was made artistic controller of the company in 1988, and left to teach in 1989. Since 1993 she has been director of the Creative Dance Artists Trust.

Macdonald, Flora (1722–90) Scottish heroine, born in South Uist, Western Isles, W Scotland, UK. After the rebellion of 1745, she conducted the Young Pretender, Charles Edward Stuart, disguised as 'Betty Burke', to safety in Skye. For this she was imprisoned in the Tower of London, but released in 1747. She married in 1750, and in 1774 emigrated to North Carolina, where her husband fought in the War of Independence. When he was captured, Flora returned to Scotland in 1779, and her husband rejoined her there in 1781. >> Stuart, Charles

MacDonald, Jeanette (1907–65) Soprano, born in Philadelphia, PA. Five years after her 1920 debut in a Broadway chorus, she began appearing in films. Though she sang occasionally in opera, she was best known for roles opposite Nelson Eddy (1901–67) in film operettas such as *Naughty Marietta* (1935) and *Rose Marie* (1936).

Macdonald, Sir John A(lexander) (1815–91) Canadian statesman and prime minister (1857–8, 1864, 1867–73, 1878–91), born in Glasgow. His family emigrated in 1820, and he was educated in law at Kingston. Entering politics in 1843, he became leader of the Conservative Party, and joint premier in 1856. He was instrumental in bringing about the confederation of Canada, and in 1867 formed the first government of the new Dominion. The 'Pacific scandal' brought down his government in 1874, but he regained the premiership in 1878. >> Cartier, Georges Etienne; RR1039

MacDonald, (James) Ramsay (1866–1937) British statesman and prime minister (1924, 1929–31, 1931–5), born in Lossiemouth, Moray, NE Scotland, UK. He had little formal education, worked as a clerk, then joined the Independent Labour Party in 1894, eventually becoming its leader (1911–14, 1922–31). He became an MP in 1906, and was prime minister and foreign secretary of the first British Labour government. He met the financial crisis of 1931 by forming a largely Conservative 'National' government, most of his party opposing; and in 1931 reconstructed it after a general election. Defeated by Shinwell in 1935, he returned to parliament in 1936, and became Lord President. >> Shinwell; RR1095

MacDonald, (John) Ross, pseudonym **Kenneth Millar** (1915–83) Thriller writer, born in Los Gatos, CA. He studied at the University of Western Ontario, and became a college teacher. From the 1950s he lived in S California. His books include *The Moving Target* (1949), *The Galton Case* (1959), and *The Blue Hammer* (1976). Many of his novels have been filmed.

McDonald, Trevor (1939–) Television journalist and newscaster, born in Trinidad. He worked in the media in Trinidad in the 1960s, joining the Caribbean section of the World Service in London in 1969. He became a reporter for ITN in 1973, then a sports correspondent (1978), diplomatic correspondent (1980), and diplomatic editor (1987). After doing some newscasting for ITN and Channel Four, he joined ITN's *News at Ten* in 1990, and became a nationally known personality. His books include biographies of cricketers Clive Lloyd (1985) and Viv Richards (1987) and a volume of autobiography, *Fortunate Circumstances* (1993).

McDonald-Wright, Stanton >> Russell, Morgan

McDonnell, James S(mith) (1899–1980) Aircraft manufacturer, and pioneer in space technology, born in Denver, CO. After studying aeronautical engineering at the Massachusetts Institute of Technology, he became a test pilot, stress analyst, and chief engineer, before setting up his own company in 1928. This led to the founding of the McDonnell Aircraft Corporation (1939), which was to produce successful military and naval aircraft, including the famous F-4 Phantom. In 1967 the company was merged with the Douglas Co, and became the McDonnell Douglas Corporation. >> Douglas, Donald

McDougall, William [muhkdoogl] (1871–1938) Psychologist, born in Chadderton, Lancashire, NW England, UK. After studying at Manchester, Cambridge, and Göttingen universities, in 1898 he accompanied an anthropological expedition to the Torres Strait. He held academic posts at both Oxford and Cambridge, and in 1920 went to Harvard as professor of psychology. In 1927 he transferred to Duke University, NC, where he conducted experiments in parapsychology. Influential in establishing experimental and physiological psychology, he expounded his theories in the well-known *Introduction to Social Psychology* (1908). >> Rhine

McDowell, Edward (Alexander) (1860–1908) Composer and pianist, born in New York City. He studied in Paris, Wiesbaden, and Frankfurt, and in 1881 was appointed head teacher of pianoforte at Darmstadt. At the invitation of Liszt, he played his first piano concerto in Zürich in 1882. He returned to the USA in 1888, and became head of the department of music at Columbia University (1896–1904). He composed extensively for orchestra, voices, and piano, and is best remembered for some of his small-scale piano pieces, such as *Woodland Sketches* and *Sea Pieces*. >> Liszt

McEnroe, John (Patrick) [makenroh] (1959–) Tennis player, born in Wiesbaden, Germany. He trained at Port Washington Tennis Academy in New York State, and at 18 became the youngest man to reach the Wimbledon semifinals (1977). He won four US Open singles titles (1979–81, 1984) and three Wimbledon singles titles (1981, 1983-4), and was an invaluable member of the US Davis Cup team between 1978 and 1985. He was also Grand Prix winner in 1979 and 1984–5, and World Championship Tennis champion in 1979, 1981, and 1983–4. His skill as a player was often overshadowed by his fierce emotional outbursts on court and frequent wrangling with umpires, which always attracted the attention of the media, and which led to professional censure on several occasions. He married film actress **Tatum O'Neill** (1963–) in 1986, but they separated in 1993. >> RR1173

McEwan, Ian (Russell) [muhkyooan] (1948–) Novelist and short-story writer, born in Aldershot, Hampshire, S England, UK. He attracted immediate attention with two collections of short stories, *First Love, Last Rites* (1975) and *In Between The Sheets* (1977), and a novella, *The Cement Garden* (1978). His novels include *A Child in Time* (1987), *The Innocent* (1990), and *Black Dogs* (1992), and he has also written screenplays, notably for *The Ploughman's Lunch* (1983).

MacEwen, Sir William [muhkyooan] (1848–1924) Neurosurgeon, born in Glasgow, W Scotland, UK. His interest in surgery was stimulated by Joseph Lister, then professor of surgery at Glasgow University. He adopted and extended Lister's antiseptic surgical techniques and pioneered operations on the brain for tumours, abscesses, and trauma. In addition, he operated on bones, introducing methods of implanting small grafts to replace missing portions of bones in the limbs. In 1892 he was appointed to the chair which Lister had held when MacEwen was a student. >> Lister, Joseph

McGahern, John [muhgah(r)n] (1934–) Novelist and short-story writer, born in Dublin, Republic of Ireland. His novels include *The Barracks* (1963), *The Leave Taking* (1975), and *Amongst Women* (1990). A volume of *Collected Stories* appeared in 1992.

McGee, Thomas D'Arcy (1825–68) Writer and politician, born in Carlingford, Co Louth, Ireland. After a Catholic education, he worked briefly in Quebec and Boston, wrote fiction, and supported a variety of romantic causes. He returned to Ireland in 1845, where he was identified with the Young Ireland *Nation*. After the abortive rebellion of 1848 he fled to the USA, where he established the *American Celt* and the *New Era* newspapers. He took Canadian citizenship, became an MP in 1858, and was minister of agriculture (1864–8). He was assassinated in Ottawa at the time of his opposition to a threatened Fenian invasion of Canada. His published works include *A Popular History of Ireland* (1862–9) and *Poems* (1869).

McGill, Donald, pseudonym of **Fraser Gould** (1875–1962) Comic postcard artist, born in London, England, UK. A junior to a naval architect, he studied cartooning by correspondence course. In 1905 he sold his first comic card for six shillings to Asher's Pictorial Postcards – two million copies were sold. Famous for his outsize women in bathing costumes, paddling alongside weedy henpecked husbands, and for the double meanings in his captions, he did not receive critical attention until 1941. He is estimated to have drawn 500 cards a year over 50 years.

McGill, James (1744–1813) Entrepreneur and philanthropist, born in Glasgow, W Scotland, UK. He emigrated to Canada in the 1770s, and made a fortune in the NW fur trade and in Montreal. He bequeathed land and money to found McGill College, Montreal, which became McGill University in 1821.

MacGill, Patrick (1890–1963) Navvy, novelist, and poet, born in the Glenties, Co Donegal, Ireland. Sold into servitude by his farming parents, he escaped, working as a farm-labourer and a navvy. He wrote verses, and worked on the London *Daily Express* before being adopted as secretary by Canon John Neale Dalton of Windsor. He published his semi-autobiographical novel *Children of the Dead End* (1914), and this was followed by many other successful books. He married **Margaret Gibbons** (who published stories as **Mrs Patrick MacGill**), and went to the USA in 1930, where he declined into poverty, and developed multiple sclerosis.

MacGill-Eain, Somhairle >> **Maclean, Sorley**

MacGillivray, James Pittendrigh [muhgilivray] (1856–1938) Sculptor and poet, born in Inverurie, Aberdeenshire, NE Scotland, UK. He studied under William Brodie and John Mossman, and was appointed the King's Sculptor in Ordinary for Scotland in 1921. His major sculptures include the huge statue of Robert Burns in Irvine, and the Knox statue in St Giles's Cathedral, Edinburgh.

McGonagall, William [muhgonagl] (1830–1902) Scottish poet and novelist, the son of an immigrant Irish weaver. He spent some of his childhood in the Orkneys, and in Dundee. He did some acting at Dundee's Royal Theatre, and in 1877 began to write poems, the best-known of which is 'The Tay Bridge Disaster' (1880). From then on he travelled in C Scotland, giving readings and selling his poetry in broadsheets, and was lionized by the legal and student fraternity. His poems are uniformly bad, but possess a disarming innocence and a calypso-like disregard for metre which still never fail to entertain.

McGovern, George S(tanley) [muhguhvern] (1922–) US politician, born in Avon, SD. During World War II, he served with distinction in the Army Air Force. He studied at Northwestern University, and became professor of history and government at Dakota Wesleyan University. He was a Democratic member of the US House of Representatives (1956–61), and senator for South Dakota from 1963. He sought the Democratic presidential nomination in 1968, and opposed Nixon in the 1972 presidential election, but was defeated. He tried again for the presidential nomination in 1984, but withdrew. >> Nixon

McGrath, John (Peter) (1935–) Playwright and theatre director, born in Birkenhead, Merseyside, NW England, UK. Between 1958 and 1961 he was a television director with the BBC, and wrote scripts for *Z Cars*. He founded the 7:84 Theatre Company in 1971, and was their artistic director until 1988. Among the numerous popular political plays he has written are *Fish in the Sea* (1975), *Yobbo Nowt* (1978), and *Swings and Roundabouts* (1981). Later works include: *John Brown's Body* (1990), *Watching for Dolphins* (1991), *The Wicked Old Man* (1992), and *The Last of the MacEachans* (1996).

McGraw, John (Joseph), nickname **the Little Napoleon** (1873–1934) Baseball player manager, born in Truxton, NY. During a 16-year career as a third baseman (1891–1906), mostly with the famous Baltimore Orioles of the 1890s, he compiled a lifetime batting average of ·334. After managing Baltimore for three years, he was manager of the New York Giants for 31 years (1902–32), winning ten league pennants, three world championships and more major league games (2840) than any manager except Connie Mack. He was elected to the Baseball Hall of Fame in 1937. >> Mack, Connie

Macgregor, Douglas (1906–64) US industrial psychologist. He studied at Harvard, and taught there (1935–7) before moving to the Massachusetts Institute of Technology, where he helped set up an Industrial Relations section. He was president of Antioch College (1948–54), and returned to MIT to become the first Sloan Fellows professor (1962). His highly regarded book, *The Human Side of Enterprise* (1960), discussed two contrasting theories of motivation at work, which he called 'Theory X and Theory Y'.

McGregor, Sir Ian (Kinloch) (1912–) Business executive, born in Kinlochleven, Highland, N Scotland, UK. He studied at Glasgow and the Royal College of Science and Technology, then developed his business career in the USA, returning in 1977 as deputy chairman of British Leyland, working with Sir Michael Edwardes. He was appointed chairman of the British Steel Corporation in 1980, and chairman of the National Coal Board (1983–6). Both industries required drastic cutbacks to survive, which he carried out despite strong trade union opposition. He was knighted in 1986. >> Edwardes

MacGregor, Robert >> **Rob Roy**

McGuffey, William (Holmes) [muhguhfee] (1800–73) Educator, born near Claysville, PA. Largely self-educated through secondary school, he became (1845–73) a professor of moral philosophy at the University of Virginia. He compiled the famous *McGuffey Readers*, six elementary schoolbooks (1836–57) that sold 122 million copies and became standard texts for generations of 19th-c US children.

McGuigan, Paul >> **Oasis**

Mach, Ernst [mahk] (1838–1916) Physicist and philosopher, born in Turas, Austria. He studied at Vienna University, and became professor of mathematics at Graz in 1864, and of physics at Prague (1867) and Vienna (1895). His experimental work has proved of great importance in aeronautical design and the science of projectiles, and his name has been given to a unit of velocity (the *Mach number* – the ratio of speed of object to the speed of sound in the medium in which the object is moving), and to the angle of a shock wave to the direction of motion (the *Mach angle*). His writings greatly influenced Einstein, and laid the foundations of logical positivism. >> Einstein

Machado, (y Ruiz) Antonio [ma**shah**thoh] (1875–1939) Poet and playwright, born in Seville, Spain. He studied at the Sorbonne, became a French teacher, and wrote lyrics characterized by a nostalgic melancholy, among them *Soledades, galerías y otros poemas* (1907), and *Campos de Castilla* (1912). With his brother **Manuel** (1874–1947), he also wrote several plays.

Machaut, Guillaume de >> Guillaume de Machaut

Machel, Samora Moïsés [ma**shel**] (1933–86) Leader of the guerrilla campaign against Portuguese rule in Mozambique, and first president of Mozambique (1975–86). He studied at a Catholic mission school, and worked as a hospital nurse, rising to a senior position. He was commander-in-chief of the army of Frente de Libertação de Moçambique (FRELIMO) (1966–70), president of FRELIMO from 1970, and became president of the country at its independence. Although a Marxist, he established warm relations with Western governments, and attempted an accommodation with the South African regime. >> Chissano

Machiavelli, Niccolò (di Bernardo dei) [makia**vel**ee] (1469–1527) Italian statesman, writer, and political theorist, born in Florence, Italy. Little is known of his early life, but he travelled on several missions in Europe for the Republic of Florence (1498–1512). On the restoration of the Medici, he was arrested on a charge of conspiracy (1513) and, though pardoned, was obliged to withdraw from public life. He devoted himself to literature, writing historical treatises, poetry, short stories, and comedies. His masterpiece is *Il Principe* (1532, The Prince), whose main theme is that all means may be used in order to maintain authority. It was condemned by the pope, and its viewpoint gave rise to the adjective *machiavellian*. His writings were not published until 1782. >> Medici

MacIndoe, Sir Archibald [muh**kin**doh] (1900–60) Plastic surgeon, born in Dunedin, New Zealand. He studied at Otago, the Mayo Clinic, and St Bartholomew's Hospital, and was the most eminent pupil of Harold Gillies. He won fame during World War 2 as surgeon-in-charge at the Queen Victoria Hospital, East Grinstead, West Sussex, where he became known for his work on the faces and limbs of severely injured airmen. >> Gillies, Harold

Macintosh, Charles (1766–1843) Manufacturing chemist, born in Glasgow, W Scotland, UK. While trying to find uses for the waste products from gasworks, he developed in 1823 a method of waterproofing cloth, which resulted in the manufacture of the raincoat, or *macintosh*.

McIntyre, Sir Donald (Conroy) (1934–) Opera singer, born in Auckland, New Zealand. A bass baritone, he made his debut in Cardiff in 1959 as Zaccaria in Verdi's *Nabucco*. Based at Bayreuth (1967–81), he established himself as one of the world's leading Wagnerian singers, while also developing a wide repertoire drawn from the works of other composers. He was knighted in 1992.

Mack, Connie, originally **Cornelius Alexander McGillicuddy** (1862–1956) Baseball player and manager, born in East Brookfield, MA. He was catcher with various teams (1886–1916), and began his managerial career at Pittsburgh (1894–6). He moved on to Philadelphia in 1901, and stayed for 50 years. He holds the record for most years managing (53), most games won (3776), and most games lost (4025). He won World Championships in 1910–11, 1913, and 1929–30, and in 1937 was elected to the Baseball Hall of Fame.

McKay, Claude [muh**kiy**], originally **Festus Claudius McKay**, pseudonym **Eli Edwards** (1889–1948) Writer, born in Sunny Ville, Jamaica. He had already published two volumes in Jamaican dialect before he arrived in the USA to study at

Tuskegee Institute, AL (1912) and Kansas State (1912–14). He moved to New York City and began to publish his poems under his pseudonym. By this time he was having an influence on 'Harlem Renaissance', and was also widely respected internationally. He lived abroad (1922–34), returning to New York in poor health. In addition to his major work, *Harlem Shadows* (1922), he wrote novels, such as *Home to Harlem* (1928), short stories, an autobiography, and the sociological study, *Harlem: Negro Metropolis* (1940).

Mackay, Fulton [muh**kiy**] (1922–87) Actor, born in Paisley, Renfrewshire, W Scotland, UK. He was a member of the Citizens' Theatre, Glasgow (1949–51, 1953–8), and of the Old Vic company (1962–3). As a director of the Scottish Actors Company, he appeared in numerous productions, made several television and film appearances, and is probably best remembered for playing the role of Mr Mackay, the officious prison warder, in the 1970s television series, *Porridge*.

McKay, Heather [muh**kiy**], *née* **Blundell** (1941–) Squash player, born in Queanbeyan, New South Wales, Australia. During her career she completely dominated the game, from 1962 to 1979 winning every competition she entered. She won the British squash championship for 16 consecutive years (1962–77), and also regularly won the Australian championship (1960–73).

Mackay (of Clashfern), James Peter Hymers Mackay, Baron [muh**kiy**] (1927–) Jurist, born in the village of Scourie, Highland, N Scotland, UK. He studied mathematics and physics at Edinburgh, and taught mathematics at St Andrews University, then switched to law, and was called to the bar in 1955. In 1965 he became a QC, specializing in tax law. He was made Lord Advocate for Scotland, and became a life peer in 1979. As Lord Chancellor (1987–97), he created consternation among the English bar by proposing radical reforms of the profession.

Macke, August [**mah**kuh] (1887–1914) Painter, born in Meschede, Germany. He studied at Düsseldorf, and designed stage scenery. Profoundly influenced by Matisse, whose work he saw in Munich in 1910, he founded the *Blaue Reiter* group together with Franz Marc. He was a sensitive colourist, working in watercolour as well as oil, and painted the kind of subject-matter favoured by the Impressionists – figures in a park, street scenes, children, and animals (eg 'The Zoo', 1912). He was killed in action in Champagne, France. >> Kandinsky; Klee; Marc; Matisse

McKellen, Sir Ian (Murray) [muh**kel**en] (1939–) Actor, born in Burnley, Lancashire, NW England, UK. He played in several repertory theatres before making his London debut in 1964. He joined the National Theatre in 1965, the touring Prospect Theatre Company in 1968, and with Edward Petherbridge founded the Actors' Company in 1972. He played many memorable parts for the Royal Shakespeare Company (1974–8), including the title role of the 1976 Trevor Nunn production of *Macbeth* with Judi Dench. His film roles include John Profumo in *Scandal* (1988), *Richard III* (1995), and *Cold Comfort Farm* (1996), and he is also known for his solo recitals on a wide range of themes. He was knighted in 1991. >> Dench, Judi

McKenna, Siobhan [muh**ke**na, shuh**vawn**], originally **Siobhan Giollamhuire Nic Cionnaith** (1923–86) Actress, born in Belfast. She studied at University College, Galway, and made her stage debut at the Gaelic-language An Taibhdhearc Theatre (1940). She performed with the Abbey Theatre, Dublin (1943–6), and after her London debut (1947) she worked in Britain and North America. Her role as Pegeen Mike in *The Playboy of the Western World* at the Edinburgh Theatre Festival (1951) brought her international fame. An intensely dramatic actress, she is particularly remembered for her performance as *Saint Joan* in London (1954). Throughout her career she worked primarily on the Irish stage, and was appointed to the Council of State of the Republic of Ireland in 1975.

Mackenzie, Sir Alexander (c. 1755–1820) Explorer and fur-trader, born in Stornoway, Western Isles, W Scotland, UK. In 1779 he joined the Northwest Fur Company, and in 1788 established Fort Chipewayan on L Athabasca. From there he discovered the Mackenzie R (1789), followed it to the sea, and became the first European to cross the Rockies to the Pacific (1792–3). He was knighted in 1802.

Mackenzie, Sir (Edward Montague) Compton (1883–1972) Writer, born in West Hartlepool, Co Durham, NE England, UK. He studied at Oxford, and began on the stage, but turned to literature, publishing his first novel in 1911. He served at Gallipoli in World War 1, and in 1917 became director of the Aegean Intelligence Service in Syria. He wrote a large number of novels, notably *Sinister Street* (1913–14) and *Whisky Galore* (1947). He lived in Scotland after 1928, and became a strong nationalist. He was knighted in 1951. >> Compton, Fay; Trog

Mackenzie, Henry (1745–1831) Writer, born in Edinburgh, EC Scotland, UK. He studied at Edinburgh University, became a crown attorney in the Scottish Court of Exchequer (1765), and in 1804 was made comptroller of taxes. His sentimental novel *The Man of Feeling*, which was published in 1771, secured his standing in Scottish literary circles, and was followed by more than 100 other novels, plays, and biographies, notably on Burns. His memoirs and anecdotes were published as *Anecdotes and Egotisms* (1927).

McKenzie, Julia (1941–) Actress and singer. An outstanding interpreter of the work of Stephen Sondheim, her London musical appearances include *Maggie May* (1965), *Cole* (1974), *Guys and Dolls* (1982), *Into the Woods* (1990), and *Sweeney Todd* (1993). She is also known for her TV roles, such as in *French Fields* (1989–91). She has also appeared in many plays, notably Alan Ayckbourn's *The Norman Conquests* (1974), *Ten Times Table* (1979), and *Woman in Mind* (1986). >> Sondheim

Mackenzie, William Lyon (1795–1861) Politician, born in Dundee, E Scotland, UK. He emigrated to Canada in 1820, established the *Colonial Advocate* in 1824, and entered politics in 1828. In 1837 he published in his paper a declaration of Canadian independence, headed a band of reform-minded insurgents, and after a skirmish with a superior force, fled to the USA, where he was imprisoned. He returned to Canada in 1849, becoming a journalist and MP (1850–8).

Mackenzie King, William Lyon >> **King, William Lyon Mackenzie**

Mackenzie Stuart (of Dean), Alexander John Mackenzie Stuart, Baron (1924–) Judge, born in Aberdeen, NE Scotland, UK. He studied at Cambridge and Edinburgh, and practised at the Scottish bar. He became a judge of the Court of Session in 1972, and was the first British judge appointed to the Court of Justice of the European Communities (1972–88, president 1984–8).

Mackerras, Sir (Alan) Charles (MacLaurin) [muhkeras] (1925–) Conductor, born in Schenectady, NY. He played oboe with the Sydney Symphony Orchestra (1943–6), was a staff conductor at Sadler's Wells Opera (1949–53), and returned there in 1970 as musical director, having established an international reputation. Subsequent conducting posts have included the BBC Symphony Orchestra, Sydney Symphony Orchestra, Royal Liverpool Philharmonic Orchestra, and Welsh National Opera (musical director, 1987–92). He was principal guest conductor, Scottish

Chamber Orchestra (1992–5), and with the Czech Philharmonic from 1996. A noted scholar of the music of Janáček, he was knighted in 1979.

Mckillop, Mary Helen [muhkilop], known as **Mother Mary of the Cross** (1842–1909) Religious, born in Fitzroy, Queensland, Australia. With Father Tenison-Woods she founded in 1866 the Society of the Sisters of St Joseph of the Sacred Heart in Penola, South Australia. Excommunicated in 1871, she was reinstated two years later by Pope Pius IX, who approved the Sisterhood. In 1875 she was confirmed as superior-general of the order. The case for her beatification was made in 1925, and in 1975 her cause was formally introduced by the Vatican, when it was announced that she would become Australia's first saint. She was declared venerable by Pope John Paul II in 1992, and her beatification was approved in 1993.

McKim, Charles Follen (1847–1909) Architect, born in Isabella Furnace, PA. He studied at Harvard and the Ecole des Beaux-Arts, Paris. The addition of Stanford White to his partnership with William Rutherford Mead launched McKim, Mead & White in 1879, designers of more than 1000 public, commercial, and residential buildings. McKim was an elegant Classical designer; his work includes the Boston Public Library (1887–95) and the Pierpont Morgan Library (1902–7), New York City. >> White, Stanford

Mackinder, Sir Halford John [muhkinder] (1861–1947) Geographer and politician, born in Gainsborough, Lincolnshire, EC England, UK. He studied at Oxford, and laid the foundations of British academic geography there, and later at Reading and the London School of Economics. He held numerous senior university appointments, became an MP (1910–22), and was British high commissioner for South Russia (1919–20). Knighted in 1920, he became chairman of the Imperial Shipping Committee (1920–45) and of the Imperial Economic Committee (1926–41).

McKinley, William (1843–1901) US statesman and 25th president (1897–1901), born in Niles, OH. He served in the Civil War, then became a lawyer. He was elected to Congress in 1877, and in 1891 was made Governor of Ohio, his name being identified with the high protective tariff carried in the *McKinley Bill* of 1890. He secured a large majority in the presidential elections of 1896 and 1900 as the representative of a gold standard and high tariffs. In his first term the war with Spain (1898) took place, with the conquest of Cuba and the Philippines. At the beginning of his second term, he was shot by an anarchist at Buffalo, and died a few days later. >> RR1097

MacKinnon, Catharine (1946–) Legal scholar, born in Minneapolis, MN. She studied at Smith College (1969) and Yale (1977), and began to focus on women's social and legal inequality, publishing a landmark study, *Sexual Harassment of Working Women: a Case of Sex Discrimination* (1979). Her other, more controversial focus has been to urge that pornography be recognized as another form of sex discrimination. She has also pioneered the approach to law from the perspective of women's experience of sex inequality, addressing such other gender-related issues as rape and abortion. Her later publications include *Feminism Unmodified*, (1987). Throughout these years of public engagement (1977–89), she practised law and taught at several law schools before accepting a tenured post at the University of Michigan (1989–).

MacKinnon, Donald MacKenzie (1913–94) Philosopher of religion, born in Oban, Argyll and Bute, W Scotland, UK. He studied at Oxford, where he was a fellow of Keble College (1937–47). Professor of moral philosophy at Aberdeen (1947–60), and of the philosophy of religion at Cambridge (1960–78), he explored the relations between theology, metaphysics, and moral philosophy, championing realism over idealism. His 1965–6 Gifford lectures were published as *The Problem of Metaphysics* (1974). His books include *Themes in Theology* (1988).

Mackintosh, Sir Cameron (Anthony) (1946–) British impresario. Following a childhood ambition to stage musical shows, he became a stage hand at the Theatre Royal, Drury Lane, London, in the early 1960s. He produced his first musical in 1969, and in association with the Arts Council supplied road-show musicals to regional theatres in the 1970s. He agreed to finance Lloyd Webber's *Cats*, and has subsequently produced, in London and New York City, such musicals as *Little Shop of Horrors* (1983), *Les Misérables* (1985), *Phantom of the Opera* (1986), and *Miss Saigon* (1989). Later London productions include *Moby Dick* (1992) and *Martin Guerre* (1996). He was knighted in 1996.

Mackintosh, Charles Rennie (1868–1928) Architect, designer, and painter, born in Glasgow, W Scotland, UK. He attended evening classes at Glasgow School of Art, joined the established firm of Honeyman and Kepple in 1889, and in 1900 married **Margaret Mackintosh** (1865–1933), with whom he worked in close collaboration. He became a leader of the 'Glasgow Style', a movement related to Art Nouveau. His work exercised considerable influence on European design, and included the Glasgow School of Art (1896–1909), and Hill House in Helensburgh (1902–6). His designs included detailed interiors, textiles, furniture, and metalwork. His work was exhibited at the Vienna Secession Exhibition in 1900, and in his later years he turned to painting, producing a series of watercolours (1923–7). He left Glasgow in 1914, and eventually settled in London.

Mackintosh, Elizabeth Daviot, pseudonyms **Josephine Tey** and **Gordon Daviot** (1896–1952) Novelist and playwright, born in Inverness, Highland, N Scotland, UK. She taught physical education before the success of her first novel, *The Man in the Queue* (1929). Under the pseudonym of Gordon Daviot she wrote more serious works, including the historical drama, *Richard of Bordeaux* (1932), which was staged with great success in London and New York. As Josephine Tey she wrote many popular detective novels, including *Miss Pym Disposes* (1947) and *The Franchise Affair* (1949).

Mackmurdo, Arthur Heygate (1851–1942) Architect and designer, born in London, England, UK. After studying architecture, he was influenced by his friends John Ruskin and William Morris, and became a member of the Arts and Crafts movement. In 1875 he set up in architectural practice, and in 1882 was a founder of the Century Guild, a group which designed for all aspects of interiors. He also designed furniture, textiles, metalwork, and for print. His design for the title page of his book, *Wren's City Churches* (1883), is often seen as a forerunner of Art Nouveau. >> Morris, William; Ruskin

McKnight Kauffer, Edward [kowfer] (1890–1954) Poster designer, illustrator, and artist, born in the USA. He trained as a painter, moving to England, UK in 1914. In 1921 he gave up painting for commercial art, and designed posters for the Underground Railway Co, London Transport Board, Shell-Mex, BP, The Great Western Railway, and many others. He also illustrated a number of books, including *Don Quixote* (1930) and T S Eliot's *Triumphal March* (1931).

MacLaine, Shirley, stage name of **Shirley Maclean Beaty** (1934–) Actress, born in Richmond, VA. She took dancing lessons in childhood, and entered show business as a teenager when she joined the chorus of *Oklahoma* in New York City (1950). An understudy on *The Pajama Game* (1954), she moved centre stage when the star broke her leg. Her performance earned her a long-term contract, and she

made her film debut in *The Trouble with Harry* (1955). Her performances were acclaimed in *Irma La Douce* (1963) and *Sweet Charity* (1969), and she won an Oscar for *Terms of Endearment* (1983), a sequel, *The Evening Star*, appearing in 1997. Other films include *Steel Magnolias* (1989) and *Postcards from the Edge* (1990). >> Beatty, Warren

McLaughlin, Audrey (1936–) Canadian politician, born in Dutton, Ontario, Canada. She has been an MP for the Yukon Territory since 1987, and leader of the federal New Democratic Party since 1989.

McLaughlin, Isabel [muhgloklin] (1903–) Painter, born in Oshawa, Ontario, Canada. She studied at the Ontario College of Art, then in Toronto and Paris, and has become one of Canada's leading women artists, a past president of the Canadian Group of Painters. She is known for her highly imaginary paintings depicting botanical studies, noted for their bright colours, vibrant brush strokes, and strong sense of design. She is benefactor and patron of the Robert McLaughlin Art Gallery in Oshawa.

McLaughlin, John [muhglokhlin] (1942–) Electric guitarist and composer, born in Doncaster, South Yorkshire, N England, UK. He played with British blues, rock, and free-jazz groups before moving to the USA. In 1969 he played with Miles Davis on two influential jazz-rock albums, *Bitches Brew* and *In a Silent Way*, and from 1971 led the Mahavishnu Orchestra, starting a movement of jazz and rock fusion with Indian rhythms. He has since developed this theme, often using acoustic guitar and working in trio settings. >> Davis, Miles

Maclaurin, Colin [muhklorin] (1698–1746) Mathematician, born in Kilmodan, Argyll and Bute, W Scotland, UK. He studied at Glasgow, became professor at Aberdeen (1717), and in 1725 was appointed to the chair of mathematics at Edinburgh. His best-known work, *Treatise on Fluxions* (1742) gave a systematic account of Newton's approach to the calculus, taking a geometric point of view rather than the analytical one used in mainland Europe. >> Newton, Isaac

Maclean, Alistair [muhklayn] (1922–87) Writer, born in Glasgow, W Scotland, UK. He studied at Glasgow University, served in the Royal Navy (1941–46) and, while a schoolteacher, won a short-story competition held by the *Glasgow Herald*. At the suggestion of William Collins, the publishers, he produced a full-length novel, *HMS Ulysses* (1955), and this epic story of wartime bravery became an immediate best seller. He followed it with *The Guns of Navarone* in 1957, and turned to full-time writing. One of the most successful and prolific writers of adventure stories, many of his books were made into films, including *Ice Station Zebra* (1963), *Where Eagles Dare* (1967), and *Puppet on a Chain* (1969).

Maclean, Donald (Duart) [muhklayn] (1913–83) British traitor, born in London, England, UK. He studied at Cambridge at the same time as Anthony Blunt, Guy Burgess, and Kim Philby, and was similarly influenced by Communism. He joined the diplomatic service in 1934, and was recruited by Soviet intelligence as an agent. In 1950, he became head of the American Department of the Foreign Office, where he had access to highly classified information, especially about the progress of the war in Korea. He was warned by Philby (1951) that he was under suspicion, and disappeared with Burgess, reappearing in Russia in 1956; later (1979) it transpired that he had escaped with the help of Blunt. >> Blunt, Anthony; Burgess, Guy; Philby

Maclean, Sorley [muhklayn], Gaelic **Somhairle MacGill-Eain** (1911–96) Gaelic poet, born at Osgaig, I of Raasay, off Skye, Highland, N Scotland, UK. He read English at Edinburgh University (1929–33), and by the end of the 1930s was an established figure on the Scottish literary scene. In 1940 he published *Seventeen Poems for Sixpence*, which he produced with Robert Garioch, and in 1943, *Dàin do Eimhir* (Poems to Eimhir), addressed to the legendary Eimhir of the early Irish sagas. A teacher and headmaster until his retirement in 1972, his major collection of poems, *Reothairt is Contraigh* (Spring Tide and Neap Tide), appeared in 1977. Translations of his work from Gaelic (often made by himself) have been issued in bilingual editions all over the world. >> Garioch

Maclehose, Agnes [**mak**lhohz], *née* **Craig** (1759–1841) Scots literary figure, the daughter of an Edinburgh surgeon. She met Robert Burns at a party in Edinburgh in 1787, and subsequently carried on the well-known correspondence with him under the name of **Clarinda**. A number of Burns's poems and songs were dedicated to her. >> Burns, Robert

Macleish, Archibald [muhk**leesh**] (1892–1982) Poet, born in Glencoe, IL. He studied at Yale and Harvard, was librarian of Congress (1939–44), and became professor of rhetoric at Harvard (1949–62). His first volumes of poetry appeared in 1917, and he won Pulitzer Prizes for *Conquistador* (1932), *Collected Poems 1917–52* (1953), and his social drama in modern verse, *J B* (1959). A strong supporter of Franklin D Roosevelt, he was assistant secretary of state (1944–5). >> Roosevelt, Franklin D

MacLennan, (John) Hugh (1907–90) Novelist and essayist, born in Nova Scotia, Canada. He studied at Dalhousie, Oxford, and Princeton universities, then taught at McGill (1967–79). A highly esteemed writer, he was the first major English-speaking novelist to attempt to portray Canada's national character and regional relationships. He won the Governor-General's Award three times for fiction – *Two Solitudes* (1945), *The Precipice* (1948), and *The Watch that Ends the Night* (1959) – and twice for non-fiction, with *Cross Country* and *Thirty and Three*.

McLennan, Sir John (Cunningham) (1867–1935) Physicist, born in Ingersoll, Ontario, Canada. He studied at the University of Toronto, and also at the Cavendish Laboratory in Cambridge, England. He spent most of his career at Toronto (1907–31), where he carried out leading research in radioactivity, spectroscopy, and low-temperature physics. In England from 1932, he investigated the use of radium to treat cancer. He was knighted in 1935.

Maclennan, Robert (Adam Ross) (1936–) British politician, born in Glasgow, W Scotland, UK. He studied at Oxford, Cambridge, and Columbia University, New York, before being called to the bar in 1962. He entered parliament as Labour member for Caithness and Sutherland in 1966 and has represented it ever since. A founder member of the Social Democratic Party, he came to prominence in 1987 when David Owen resigned the leadership, and he offered himself as caretaker leader until the terms of the merger had been agreed. He then became a leading member of the new Party, the Social and Liberal Democrats, under Paddy Ashdown, becoming Party president in 1994. >> Ashdown, Paddy; Owen, David

MacLeod (of Fuinary), George (Fielden) MacLeod, Baron [muhk**lowd**] (1895–1991) Clergyman, born in Glasgow, W Scotland, UK. He studied at Oxford and Edinburgh, becoming minister of St Cuthbert's in Edinburgh (1926–30), then minister at Govan in Glasgow (1930–8). He founded the Iona Community, and as moderator of the General Assembly (1957–8) supported the controversial scheme to introduce bishops into the kirk. Well known as a writer and broadcaster, he was strongly left-wing. He succeeded to the baronetcy in 1924, and in 1967 was created a life peer.

Macleod, Iain (Norman) [muhk**lowd**] (1913–70) British statesman, born in Skipton, North Yorkshire, N England, UK. He studied at Cambridge, became a Conservative MP

(1950), minister of health (1952–5), minister of labour (1955–9), secretary of state for the Colonies (1959–61), and chairman of the Conservative Party (1961–3). Refusing to serve under Home, he spent two years editing the *Spectator* (1963–5). Highly popular, and a gifted speaker, he was appointed shadow Chancellor (1965–70) under Heath, and after the Conservative victory (1970) became Chancellor of the Exchequer. However, a month later he died suddenly at the age of 57. >> Heath; Home of the Hirsel

Macleod, J(ohn) J(ames) R(ickard) [muhk**lowd**] (1876–1935) Physiologist, born in Clunie, Perth and Kinross, E Scotland, UK. He studied at Aberdeen, Leipzig, and Cambridge, and became professor of physiology at Cleveland, OH (1903), Toronto (1918), and Aberdeen (1928). In 1922 he discovered insulin with Sir Frederick Banting and Charles Best, and shared the 1923 Nobel Prize for Physiology or Medicine. >> Banting; Best, Charles

Mac Liammóir, Micheál [muhk**leea**mer] (1899–1978) Actor, painter, and writer, born in Cork, Co Cork, Ireland. His family moved to London, and he became a successful child actor. He studied art at the Slade School of Art, London, and inspired by Beardsley became a painter and designer. With his lifelong friend, Hilton Edwards (1903–82), he founded the Gate Theatre Company in Dublin (1928). He wrote distinguished fiction, plays, and memoirs in Irish and in English, and in the 1960s his one-man shows brought him an international reputation, including *The Importance of Being Oscar* (1960) about Wilde's life. His most famous film appearance was as Iago in Orson Welles' *Othello* (1949). >> Beardsley; Wilde, Oscar

Maclise, Daniel [muhk**leez**] (1806–70) Painter, born in Cork, Co Cork, Ireland. He trained at the Cork School of Art and at the school of the Royal Academy in London. He is noted for the frescoes in the Royal Gallery of the House of Lords: 'The Meeting of Wellington and Blücher' (1861) and 'The Death of Nelson' (1864). He was also known as an illustrator of books for Tennyson and Dickens. His sketches of contemporaries in *Fraser's Magazine* (1830–8) were published in 1874 and 1883.

McLuhan, (Herbert) Marshall [muhk**loo**an] (1911–80) Writer, born in Edmonton, Alberta, Canada. He studied English literature at the universities of Manitoba and Cambridge. In 1946 he became professor at St Michael's College, Toronto, and in 1963 was appointed director of the University of Toronto's Centre for Culture and Technology. He held controversial views on the effect of the communication media, claiming that it is the media, not the information and ideas which they disseminate, that influence society. His books include *The Gutenberg Galaxy* (1962), *Understanding Media* (1964), *The Medium is the Message* (with Q Fiore, 1967), and *Counter-Blast* (1970).

Maclure, William [muhk**loor**] (1763–1840) Geologist, born in Ayr, South Ayrshire, SW Scotland, UK. Educated privately, he travelled to New York City and made a considerable fortune as a merchant. He travelled widely, studying geology, and helped to found the Academy of Natural Sciences in Philadelphia, becoming its president (1817–40). His *Observations on the Geology of the United States* (1817) gives the first full account of its subject. His later writing supported the ideas on evolution offered by Lamarck, and opposed Werner's theory of the exclusively sedimentary origin of primitive rock. >> Lamarck; Werner

Macmahon, Marie Edme Patrice Maurice de, duc de (Duke of) **Magenta** [makmahon] (1808–93) Marshal and second president of the Third Republic (1873–9), born in Sully, France. He was a commander in the Crimean War (1854–6), and for his services in the Italian campaign (1859) was made marshal and a duke. In the Franco-Prussian War (1870–1) he was defeated at Wörth, and surrendered at

Sedan. After the war he suppressed the Commune (1871), and succeeded Thiers as president. Failing to assume dictatorial powers, he resigned in 1879, thus ensuring the supremacy of parliament. >> Thiers

McMahon, Sir William [muhk**mahn**] (1908–88) Australian statesman and prime minister (1971–2), born in Sydney, New South Wales, Australia. He studied at the university there, and qualified and practised as a solicitor. After service in World War 2 he became active in the Liberal Party and was elected to the House of Representatives in 1949. He held a variety of posts in the administrations of Sir Robert Menzies, Harold Holt, and John Gorton, until he took over the premiership when Gorton lost a vote of confidence in 1971. The following year the Liberals lost the general election, but he continued to lead his party until 1977, when he was knighted. >> Gorton, John Grey

McManaman, Steve [muhk**ma**naman] (1972–) Footballer, born in Liverpool, Merseyside, NW England, UK. A midfielder, he served an apprenticeship at Liverpool, then joined the club. By early 1997 he had won 18 caps playing for England.

MacMaster, John (Bach) (1852–1932) Social historian, born in New York City. He studied civil engineering at the City College of New York, but his interest in the Civil War and the pioneers of the American West led to his becoming professor of American history at Pennsylvania University (1883–1920). His chief work was *A History of the People of the United States from the Revolution to the Civil War* (8 vols, 1883–1913).

Macmillan, Daniel (1813–57) and **Alexander Macmillan** (1818–96) Booksellers and publishers, brothers, born in Upper Corrie, I of Arran, and Irvine, North Ayrshire, Scotland, UK respectively. Daniel was apprenticed to booksellers in Scotland and Cambridge from the age of 11 when his father died, and in 1843 he and his brother Alexander opened a bookshop in London. In Cambridge they started publishing textbooks (1844), then novels, including *Westward Ho!* and *Tom Brown's Schooldays*. In the year after Daniel's death the firm opened a branch in London, and by 1893 had become a limited company, with Daniel's son, **Frederick** (1851–1936), as chairman. >> Macmillan, Harold

McMillan, Edwin (Mattison) (1907–91) Physical chemist, born in Redondo Beach, CA. He studied at Princeton University, and became professor of physics at the University of California, Berkeley (1946–73). He shared with Glenn Seaborg the 1951 Nobel Prize for Chemistry for his part in the discovery of the transuranic elements. >> Abelson; Seaborg

Macmillan, (Maurice) Harold, 1st Earl of Stockton (1894–1986) British statesman and prime minister (1957–63), born in London, England, UK, the grandson of Daniel Macmillan. He studied at Oxford, and became a Conservative MP in 1924. He was minister of housing (1951–4), minister of defence (1954–5), foreign secretary (1955), and Chancellor of the Exchequer (1955–7), and succeeded Eden as premier. He gained unexpected popularity with his infectious enthusiasm, effective domestic policy ('most of our people have never had it so good'), and resolute foreign policy, and he was re-elected in 1959. After several political setbacks, he resigned through ill health in 1963, and left the House of Commons in 1964. He became Chancellor of Oxford University in 1960, and was made an earl on his 90th birthday in 1984. >> Eden; MacMillan, Daniel; RR1095

Macmillan, Sir Kenneth (1929–92) Ballet dancer, choreographer, and ballet company director, born in Dunfermline, Fife, E Scotland, UK. He joined the Sadler's Wells Theatre Ballet in 1946, and began to choreograph in 1953. He

directed the Berlin Opera (1966–9), and became artistic director of the Royal Ballet in 1970, and its principal choreographer in 1977. His works include *Romeo and Juliet* (1965), *Manon* (1974), and *Meyerling* (1978). He was knighted in 1983.

Macmillan, Kirkpatrick (1813–78) Blacksmith, born near Thornhill, Dumfries and Galloway, SW Scotland, UK. In 1837 he built a 'dandy' horse – a kind of bicycle on which the rider pushed himself along with his feet. Two years later he had applied the crank to his machine to make the world's first pedal cycle, with wooden frame and iron-tyred wheels. His invention was never patented, and for many years it was credited to one of his imitators, Gavin Dalzell.

McMillan, Margaret (1860–1931) Educational reformer, born in New York City, New York, USA, and brought up near Inverness, NE Scotland, UK. She agitated ceaselessly in the industrial N of England for medical inspection and school clinics. In 1902 she joined her sister **Rachel** (1859–1917) in London, where they opened the first school clinic (1908) and the first open-air nursery school (1914). After Rachel's death, the Rachel McMillan Training College for nursery and infant teachers was established as a memorial.

McNaghten or **M'Naghten, Daniel** [muhk**nawt**n] (fl. 19th-c) British murderer. He was tried in 1843 for the murder of Edward Drummond, private secretary to Sir Robert Peel. The question of his sanity arose, and whether he knew the nature of his act. As a result the *McNaghten Rules*, on the criminal responsibility of the insane, state in English law that: (*a*) every person is presumed sane until the contrary is proved, and (*b*) it must be clearly proved that at the time of committing the act, the accused was labouring under such a defect of reason as not to know the nature of the act, or that he or she was doing wrong.

Macnaghten, Edward, Lord [muhk**nawt**n] (1830–1913) Judge, born in London, England, UK. He studied at Trinity College, Dublin, and Cambridge, where he was distinguished in both Classics and rowing. He became an MP in 1880, declined the home secretaryship and a judgeship, and was then appointed direct from the bar in 1887 to be a Lord of Appeal in Ordinary. He was a leader in reforming professional legal education.

McNamara, Frank (1917–57) US businessman and innovator. Credit cards had been issued to customers by individual businesses in the USA since the 1920s. When he found himself without cash in a restaurant, but with a bill to pay, he conceived the idea of a credit card issued by a finance company to be used in a variety of outlets. He persuaded 27 Manhattan restaurants to join his scheme, and launched the Diners Club Card in 1950, gaining 42 000 members in the first year, and initiating the credit card industry.

Macnamara, Dame (Annie) Jean (1899–1968) Physician, born in Beechworth, Victoria, Australia. She studied at Melbourne University, worked in local hospitals, and during the poliomyelitis epidemic of 1925 tested the use of immune serum. Later, with Sir Macfarlane Burnet, she found that there was more than one strain of the polio virus, a discovery which led to the development of the Salk vaccine. She was also involved in the controversial introduction of myxomatosis as a means of controlling the rabbit population of Australia in 1951. >> Burnet; Salk

McNamara, Robert S(trange) (1916–) US Democratic politician and businessman, born in San Francisco, CA. After service in the air force (1943–6), he worked his way up in the Ford Motor Co to president by 1960, and in 1961 joined the Kennedy administration as secretary of defense, being particularly involved in the Vietnam War. In 1968 he resigned to become president of the World

Bank (a post he held until 1981). In the 1980s he emerged as a critic of the nuclear arms race, and among his publications are *Blundering into Disaster* (1987) and *In Retrospect: The Tragedy and Lessons of Vietnam* (1995). >> Kennedy, John F

McNaught, William [muhk**nawt**] (1813–81) Engineer and inventor, born in Paisley, Renfrewshire, W Scotland, UK. He was apprenticed to marine engineer Robert Napier, and attended classes at the Andersonian Institution in Glasgow. He joined his father in the manufacture of steam-engine components, and in 1845 conceived the idea of adding to an existing engine a smaller second cylinder, operating at a higher pressure and exhausting spent steam into the original cylinder, where its remaining energy could be utilized, creating a 'compound engine'. For many years this process was called *McNaughting*.

MacNeice, Louis [muhk**nees**] (1907–63) Poet, born in Belfast. He studied at Oxford, and became a lecturer in Classics at Birmingham (1930–6), and in Greek at the University of London (1936–40). He was closely associated with the new British left-wing poets of the 1930s, especially Auden, with whom he wrote *Letters from Iceland* (1937). Other volumes include *Blind Fireworks* (1929), *Collected Poems* (1949), and *Solstices* (1961). He was the author of several verse plays for radio, notably *The Dark Tower* (1947), as well as translations of Aeschylus and of Goethe's *Faust*. >> Auden

McNeile, Herman Cyril >> **Sapper**

MacNeill, John or **Eoin** (1867–1945) Historian and nationalist, born in Glenarm, Co Antrim, Northern Ireland. He studied in Belfast, and made himself an authority on Old Irish. He ultimately became professor of early Irish history at University College, Dublin (1908–45), his books including *Celtic Ireland* (1921). In 1913 he led the Irish Volunteers, but after the Dublin Rising he was interned. He later played a part in organizing the new Sinn Féin Party, becoming MP for Derry. He supported the Anglo-Irish Treaty, was minister for education, and delegate for his government to the Boundary Commission, but after the revision of Irish partition in the Catholics' favour he resigned, and the boundary was left unchanged.

Maconchy, Dame Elizabeth [muhk**ong**kee] (1907–) Composer, born in Broxbourne, Hertfordshire, SE England, UK. She studied under Vaughan Williams at the Royal College of Music, then went to Prague, where her first major work, a piano concerto, was performed in 1930. Her most characteristic work is in the field of chamber music, and among her best-known compositions are her *Symphony* (1953) and the overture *Proud Thames* (1953). She has also written choral, operatic, and ballet music, as well as orchestral works and songs. She was made a dame in 1987. She married writer **William Richard LeFanu** in 1930; their daughter, **Nicola (Frances) LeFanu** (1947–), is also a composer. >> Vaughan Williams

Macphail, Agnes [muhk**fayl**], *née* **Campbell** (1890–1954) Suffragette and politician, Canada's first woman MP, born in Grey Co, Ontario, Canada. A schoolteacher, she became involved with the women's suffrage movement, and was elected MP for the United Farmers of Ontario (1921–40). She was a leader of the Co-operative Commonwealth Federation of Canada, and represented Canada in the Assembly of the League of Nations.

McPhee, John (Angus) (1931–) Writer, born in Princeton, NJ. He graduated from Princeton (1953), studied in the UK at Cambridge (1953–4), then became a television playwright for *Robert Montgomery Presents* (1955–7), co-editor of *Time* magazine (1957–64), and a staff writer for the *New Yorker* (from 1964). His non-fiction books cover wide-ranging subjects, including a series on geology beginning with *Basin and Range* (1981).

McPherson, Aimée Semple, *née* **Kennedy** (1890–1944) Pentecostal evangelist and healer, born near Ingersoll, Ontario, Canada. Widowed shortly after her first marriage, she became hugely successful as an evangelist. In 1918 she founded the Foursquare Gospel Movement in Los Angeles, and for nearly two decades conducted a flamboyant preaching and healing ministry in the Angelus Temple, which cost her followers $1·5 million to construct. She had her own radio station, Bible school, and magazine. She married three more times, had many legal actions against her, and mysteriously disappeared for five weeks in 1926, claiming to have been kidnapped.

Macpherson, James (1736–96) Poet, born in Ruthven, Highland, N Scotland, UK. He studied at King's College and Marischal College, Aberdeen, and became a schoolteacher and poet. In 1760 he was commissioned by the Faculty of Advocates in Edinburgh to tour the Highlands in search of material relating to the legendary hero Fingal, as told by his son, Ossian. He published his work in 1762 as *Fingal: an Ancient Epic Poem in Six Books*, followed by *Temora, an Epic Poem, in Eight Books* (1763). They were received with huge acclaim, but a storm of controversy soon arose about their authenticity. It appears that he used only about 15 genuine pieces of original verse which he altered and amended, and invented the rest to create an epic form for them.

Macquarie, Lachlan [muhk**wo**ree] (1761–1824) Soldier and colonial administrator, born on the I of Ulva, Argyll and Bute, W Scotland, UK. He joined the Black Watch in 1777, and after service in North America, India, and Egypt, was appointed Governor of New South Wales following the deposition of Bligh. The colony, populated largely by convicts, and exploited by monopolists, was raised by his administration to a state of prosperity. In 1821, political chicanery by the monopolists and his own ill health compelled him to return to Britain. Known as 'the father of Australia' he has given his name to the Lachlan and Macquarie rivers, and to Macquarie I. >> Bligh

Macquarrie, John [muhk**wo**ree] (1919–) Theologian and philosopher of religion, born in Renfrew, Renfrewshire, W Scotland, UK. A lecturer at Glasgow (1953–62), and professor at Union Theological Seminary, New York (1962–70) and Oxford (1970–86), he has written extensively across the whole field of theology. Out of his many works the influence of Bultmann and Tillich may be traced in *An Existentialist Theology* (1955) and *Principles of Christian Theology* (1966), and his more catholic works include *Paths in Spirituality* (1972) and *Theology, Church and Ministry* (1986). Later books include *Heidegger and Christianity* (1994) and *The Mediators* (1995). >> Bultmann; Tillich

McQueen, (Terence) Steve(n) (1930–80) Film actor, born in Slater, MO. After periods in a reform school and in the marines, he trained at the Neighbourhood Playhouse and Uta Hagen School, New York City. He made his film debut as an extra in *Somebody Up There Likes Me* (1956). The television Western series *Wanted Dead or Alive* (1958) revealed his film potential, and led to a co-starring role in *The Magnificent Seven* (1960). He became the archetypal 1960s cinema hero/rebel with his performances in *The Great Escape* (1963), *The Cincinnati Kid* (1965), and *Bullitt* (1968). He was married (1973–8) to actress **Ali McGraw** (1938–), and died after a long struggle with cancer.

Macrae, (John) Duncan [muhk**ray**] (1905–67) British actor. He studied at Glasgow University, and was a teacher before becoming a full-time actor. He made his first London appearance in 1945, and his performances ranged from Ibsen and Shakespeare to pantomime, television, and film, but he became known especially as a Scottish actor. His association with the Citizens' Theatre in Glasgow dated from its opening production in 1943, and with the playwright and critic T M Watson, he ran a touring company (1952–5).

Macready, William Charles [muhkreedee] (1793–1873) Actor, born in London, England, UK. He made his debut at Birmingham in 1810, and in 1816 appeared at Covent Garden, developing his acting techniques which later became a major influence on modern stagecraft. In 1837 he was appointed manager of Covent Garden, and extended his techniques to production. After two seasons he moved to Drury Lane (1841–3), then played in the provinces, Paris and America. His last visit to the USA was marked by terrible riots (1849), in which 22 people died, as a result of a feud started by the US actor Edwin Forrest. >> Forrest, Edwin

Macrobius, Ambrosius Theodosius [makrohbius] (5th-c) Roman writer and Neoplatonist philosopher, probably born in Africa. He wrote a commentary on Cicero's *Somnium Scipionis*, and *Saturnaliorum conviviorum libri septem*, a series of historical, mythological, and critical dialogues.

MacSwiney, Terence [muhksweenee] (1879–1920) Irish nationalist, born in Cork, Co Cork, Ireland. He trained as an accountant, and wrote poetry and plays before becoming a major influence in forming the Irish Volunteers in Cork in 1913. He accepted MacNeill's countermanding of the Easter Rising in 1916, and was elected Sinn Féin MP for West Cork in 1918. In 1920 he was elected Lord Mayor of Cork, and was arrested the following August, being sentenced by court-martial to two years' imprisonment. Transferred to Brixton Prison, he died after a 74-day hunger strike which had aroused worldwide sympathy. Among those deeply influenced by his sacrifice was the future Ho Chi-Minh, then working in the kitchens of the Ritz Hotel, London. >> Ho Chi-Minh; MacNeill

McTaggart, David (1932–) Canadian conservationist. A former businessman, he volunteered to sail his yacht into the French nuclear-testing area in the Pacific on behalf of Greenpeace, a Vancouver-based conservation group, to prevent a nuclear weapon test taking place. He subsequently took an active part in other Greenpeace campaigns, and formed Greenpeace International (1979) as an alliance of national Greenpeace groups.

McTaggart, John (McTaggart Ellis) (1866–1925) Philosopher, born in London, England, UK. He taught at Cambridge (1897–1923). His systematic metaphysics is set out in *The Nature of Existence* (2 vols, 1921, and posthumously 1927). He is regarded as the most important of the Anglo-Hegelian or Idealistic philosophers who dominated British and American thought in the late 19th-c and early 20th-c.

McVeigh, Timothy (James) [muhkvay] (1968–) Convicted perpetrator of the 1995 Oklahoma City bombing, born in Pendleton, NY. He joined the army in 1988, took part in Operation Desert Storm, and was discharged in 1991. He became internationally known when he was charged with the bombing of the Alfred P Murrah US government building in Oklahoma City in 1995, in which 168 people died. At his trial in 1997, a Denver jury found him guilty of conspiracy and murder, and he was sentenced to death by lethal injection, although a series of appeals was expected to follow.

McWhirter, Norris (Dewar) (1925–) British publisher, writer, journalist, and broadcaster. He studied at Oxford, and became chairman of the family business (1955–86). With his twin brother **Ross McWhirter** (1925–75) he founded an information service, McWhirter Twins Ltd (1950). They were invited by the managing director of Guinness Breweries to compile a book of records to settle arguments in public houses, and the first edition of *The*

Guinness Book of Records was published in 1954. Norris was editor (1954–86), and is director of Guinness Publications Ltd. A sports journalist (1951–67), he has also been a television sports commentator (1960–72), and co-presenter of *The Record Breakers* (1972–94). Ross was assassinated by IRA terrorists.

Madariaga (y Rojo), Salvador de [mathariahga] (1886–1978) Writer, scholar, and diplomat, born in La Coruña, Spain. He studied at Madrid and Paris, and became a journalist in London (1916–21), a member of the League of Nations secretariat (1922–7), professor of Spanish studies at Oxford (1928–31), and Spanish ambassador to the USA (1931) and France (1932–4). During 1933 he was briefly minister of education in the Spanish Republican government. An opponent of the Franco regime, he was in exile 1936–76. He wrote many historical works, especially on Spain and Spanish-America, including *Latin America between the Eagle and the Bear* (1962, trans title).

Maderna, Bruno [madairna] (1920–73) Composer and conductor, born in Venice, Italy. A child prodigy violinist and conductor, he went on to study composition and conducting. Early in his musical career he composed for films and radio, and taught at the Venice Conservatory, then in 1955 he began to do research into the possibilities of electronic music, founding with Luciano Berio the Studio di Fonologia Musicale of Italian Radio. He became music director of Milan Radio, and wrote pieces for combinations of live and taped music, such as *Compositions in Three Tempi*, and a number of pieces for electronic music, such as *Dimensions II* (1960). >> Berio

Maderna or **Maderno, Carlo** [madairna] (1556–1629) Architect, born in Bissone, Italy. He started as assistant to his uncle, Domenico Fontana, and became the leading exponent of the early Baroque in Rome, producing bold and vigorous innovative designs. In 1603 he was appointed architect to St Peter's, where he lengthened the nave and added a massive facade (1606–12). Other notable works include S Susanna (1597–1603), and the revolutionary Palazzo Barberini, Rome (1628–38), completed by Borromini and Bernini. >> Bernini; Borromini; Fontana, Domenico

Madero, Francisco (Indalécio) [mathayroh] (1873–1913) Revolutionary and president of Mexico (1911–13), born in Parras, Mexico. He studied at the University of California at Berkeley, unsuccessfully opposed Porfirio Díaz's local candidates in 1904, and in 1908 published *La sucesión presidencial en 1910* (The Presidential Succession in 1910), which launched his presidential campaign. His popularity grew rapidly, and Díaz imprisoned him and many of his supporters. He escaped to the USA in 1910, led a military campaign that captured Ciudad Juarez, and the dictatorship crumbled. Once elected president, he faced a succession of revolts, and in 1913 he and his vice-president were murdered following a military coup led by General Victoriano Huerta. >> Díaz, Porfirio; RR1075

Madhva [mahdva] (14th-c) Kanarese Brahmin philosopher, born near Mangalore, S India. After study in Trivandrum, Banaras, and elsewhere, he settled in Udipi, and is traditionally held to have vanished in mid-lecture in 1317, retiring to the Himalayas. Taking Ramanuja's side against Sankara, he promoted *dvaita* or dualistic *Vedanta*, allowing for the separate existence of the Divine, human souls, and matter. His belief that some souls were eternally damned suggests Christian influence on his thinking. >> Ramanuja; Sankara

Madison, Dolly, *née* **Payne Todd** (1768–1849) US first lady, born in New Garden, NC. Her first husband having died, she married James Madison in 1794. Extremely popular as first lady, she was a great asset to Madison's political career. In 1814, she saved many state papers and a portrait of George Washington from the advancing British soldiers. In later life she retained a place in Washington society, and was granted a lifelong seat on the floor of the US House of Representatives. >> Madison, James

Madison, James (1751–1836) US statesman and fourth president (1809–17), born in Port Conway, VA. He studied at the College of New Jersey (Princeton University), and entered politics in 1776. He played a major role in the Constitutional Convention of 1787, becoming known as 'the father of the Constitution', and he collaborated in the writing of *The Federalist Papers*. Elected to the first national Congress, he became a leader of the Jeffersonian Republican Party. He was secretary of state under Jefferson, and president for two terms from 1809. His period in office saw the Napoleonic Wars and the conflict with Britain (the War of 1812). >> Jefferson, Thomas; Madison, Dolly; RR1097

Madoc [**ma**dog] (12th-c) Legendary Welsh prince, long believed by his countrymen to have discovered America in 1170. The story is in Hakluyt's *Voyages* (1582) and Lloyd and Powell's *Cambria* (1584). The essay by Thomas Stephens written in 1858 for the Eisteddfod, and published in 1893, proved it to be baseless. >> Hakluyt

Madonna, in full **Madonna Louise Ciccone** (1958–) Pop singer, born in Rochester, MI. She trained as a dancer at Michigan University before moving to New York City, where she began her professional career as a backing singer to a number of New York groups. She hired Michael Jackson's manager prior to releasing *Madonna* (1983), an album which included five US hit singles. Subsequent albums have included *Like a Virgin* (1984), *True Blue*, and *You Can Dance* (1987). She has also acted in films, including *Desperately Seeking Susan* (1985), *Shanghai Surprise* (1986), and *Evita* (1996). Her defiant and raunchy stage appearances became an important role model for teenagers in the 1980s and 1990s, and her international success has been secured by clever promotion and image-making. This was reinforced in several media in the early 1990s, with the publication of a controversial collection of erotic photographs of herself in *Sex* (1992), alongside a new album, *Erotica*, and a new film, *Body of Evidence*.

Maecenas, Gaius (Cilnius) [mi**see**nas] (?–8 BC) Roman politician of ancient Etruscan lineage, who together with Agrippa played a key role in the rise to power of Octavian/Augustus, and his establishment of the empire after 31 BC. Besides being a trusted counsellor and diplomatic agent, he also helped the new regime by his judicious patronage of the arts, encouraging such poets as Horace, Virgil, and Propertius. >> Augustus; Horace; Propertius; Virgil

Maes, Nicholas [mays] (1634–93) Painter, born in Dordrecht, The Netherlands. He studied in Rembrandt's studio in Amsterdam (c.1648–50), returning to Dordrecht by 1654. He specialized in small genre subjects, especially kitchen scenes (eg 'Woman Scraping Parsnips' 1655, National Gallery, London) and old women praying. After a visit to Antwerp (c.1665), he turned to portraiture in a style derived from van Dyck. >> Rembrandt; van Dyck

Maeterlinck, Maurice (Polydore Marie Bernard) [**may**-terlingk], also known as **comte** (Count) **Maeterlinck** (1862–1949) Playwright, born in Ghent, Belgium. He studied law at Ghent University, became a disciple of the Symbolist movement, and in 1889 produced his first volume of poetry, *Les Serres chaudes* (Hot House Blooms). His masterpiece was the prose-play *Pelléas et Mélisande* (1892), on which Debussy based his opera. He wrote many other plays, which have been widely translated, and was awarded the Nobel Prize for Literature in 1911.

Magdalene, St Mary >> **Mary Magdalene, St**

Magellan, Ferdinand [ma**je**lan] (c. 1480–1521) Navigator, born in Sabrosa or Porto, Portugal. After serving in the East Indies and Morocco, he offered his services to Spain. He sailed from Seville (1519) around the foot of South America (Cape of the Virgins) to reach the ocean which he named the Pacific (1520). He was killed in the Philippines, but his ships continued back to Spain (1522), thus completing the first circumnavigation of the world. The *Strait of Magellan* is named after him. >> Cano, Juan Sebastian del

Magendie, François [mazh**ä**dee] (1783–1855) Physiologist and physician, born in Bordeaux, France. As professor of anatomy in the Collège de France (1831), he studied nerve physiology and the veins, and was the first to experiment on hypersensitivity to foreign substances (anaphylaxis). His research demonstrated the functional differences in the spinal nerves, and the effects of drugs on the body.

Maginot, André (Louis René) [**ma**zhinoh] (1877–1932) French statesman, born in Paris. He was first elected to the Chamber in 1910. As minister of war (1922–4, 1926–31) he pursued a policy of military defence, and began the system of frontier fortifications facing Germany which was named the *Maginot Line* after him.

Magnani, Anna [man**yah**nee] (1908–73) Actress, born in Alexandria, Egypt. Raised in poverty, she first made her living as a nightclub singer, but married the director Goffredo Alessandrini (annulled 1950) and worked in films from 1934, achieving recognition in Rossellini's *Roma città aperta* (1945, Rome, Open City). She received an Oscar for her first Hollywood film *The Rose Tattoo* (1955), but much of her later work was for the Italian stage and television, although she appeared in Fellini's *Roma* (1972). She died unexpectedly following a minor operation. >> Rossellini

Magnus, Heinrich Gustav (1802–70) German physicist. As professor of chemistry at Berlin University he made important discoveries in the fields of acids and gases, and in 1853 he described the *Magnus effect* – the sideways force experienced by a spinning ball which is responsible for the swerving of golf or tennis balls when hit with a slice.

Magnusson, Magnus (1929–) Writer and broadcaster, born in Edinburgh, EC Scotland, UK of Icelandic parents. He studied at Oxford, and became a journalist, then a broadcaster. He is chiefly known for presenting a wide range of radio and television programmes, such as *Chronicle*, *Tonight* and, most famously, the annual series of *Mastermind* (1972–97). His books include *Introducing Archaeology* (1972), *Vikings!* (1980), and *Treasures of Scotland* (1981), and he has translated many books from Icelandic (with Hermann Pálsson). He was the editor of the 5th edition of the *Chambers Biographical Dictionary* (1990). He was Rector of Edinburgh University (1975–8), and has been much involved with heritage and conservation organizations.

Magoun, Horace (Winchell) (1907–) Neuroscientist, born in Philadelphia, PA. He studied at Rhode Island State College and at Northwestern University Medical School, teaching there and at Johns Hopkins University before moving in 1950 to the University of California, Los Angeles. He did important work on many neurological and psychopharmacological topics, and was one of the leaders in the new field of neuroscience.

Magritte, René (François Ghislain) [ma**greet**] (1898–1967) Surrealist painter, born in Lessines, Belgium. He studied at the Académie Royale des Beaux-Arts (1916–18) in Brussels, and became a wallpaper designer and commercial artist. He was a leading member of the newly formed Belgian Surrealist group (1924), and produced works of dreamlike incongruity, such as 'Rape', in which he substitutes a torso for a face. His major paintings include 'The Wind and the

Song' (1928-9) and 'The Human Condition' (1934, 1935). He was acclaimed in the US as an early innovator of the Pop Art of the 1960s.

Mahan, Alfred Thayer [ma**han**] (1840-1914) Naval officer and writer, born in West Point, NY. He served in the Civil War and carried out 20 years of routine sea duty before becoming a lecturer at the new Naval War College (1885). He twice served as the College's president (1886-9, 1892-3), and published numerous influential books, such as *The Influence of Sea Power upon History: 1660-1783* (1890). He was publicly honoured by the British government, and thoroughly studied by German naval officers. Elected president of the American Historical Association in 1902, he became a rear-admiral on the retired list in 1906.

Mahathir bin Mohamad [ma**hateer**] (1925-) Malaysian statesman and prime minister, (1981-), born in Alur Setar, Malaysia. He practised as a doctor (1957-64) before being elected to the House of Representatives as a United Malays' National Organisation (UMNO) candidate. He won support through his affirmative action in favour of *bumiputras* (ethnic Malays) and a more Islamic social policy. After holding several ministerial posts, he was appointed UMNO leader and prime minister in 1979, immediately launching a new economic policy, emulating Japanese industrialization. He was re-elected in 1982, 1986, and 1990.

Mahdi >> Mohammed Ahmed

Mahfouz, Naguib [ma**fooz**] (1911-) Novelist, born in Cairo. He graduated from Cairo University in 1934 and held administrative posts, but by 1939 had already written three novels. His later work was somewhat overshadowed by the notoriety surrounding *The Children of Gebelawi* (1961), serialized in the magazine *Al-Ahram*, which portrays average Egyptians living the lives of Cain and Abel, Moses, Jesus, and Mohammed. It was banned throughout the Arab world, except Lebanon. He was awarded the Nobel Prize for Literature in 1988, but his work is still unavailable in many Middle Eastern countries on account of his outspoken support for President Sadat's Camp David peace treaty with Israel. In 1994 he survived an attack on his life by Islamic fundamentalists, and in 1996 published *Echoes of the Autobiography* (trans title). >> Sadat

Mahler, Gustav (1860-1911) Composer, born in Kalist, Czech Republic (formerly Bohemia). He studied at the Vienna Conservatory, and worked as a conductor, becoming artistic director of the Vienna Court Opera in 1897. He resigned after 12 years to devote himself to composition and the concert patform. His mature works consist entirely of songs and nine large-scale symphonies, with a 10th left unfinished. He is best known for the song-symphony *Das Lied von der Erde* (1908-9, The Song of the Earth). >> Goldschmidt, Berthold; Walter, Bruno

Mahmud of Ghazna [mah**mood**] (971-1030) Muslim Afghan conqueror of India. The son of **Sebuktigin**, a Turkish slave who became ruler of Ghazna (modern Afghanistan), he succeeded to the throne in 997. He invaded India 17 times between 1001 and 1026, and created an empire that included Punjab and much of Persia. A great patron of the arts, he made Ghazna a remarkable cultural centre.

Mahmut II >> Abd-ul-Medjid
Mahomet >> Mohammed

Mahon, Derek [mahn] (1941-) Poet, born in Belfast. He was educated at Belfast Institute and Trinity College, Dublin, and was a teacher before turning to journalism and other writing. Drawn to squalid landscapes and desperate situations, his acknowledged influences are Louis MacNeice and W H Auden. *Twelve Poems* was published in 1965, since when there have been a number of others,

including *The Hunt by Night* (1982) and *A Kensington Notebook* (1984). *Selected Poems* appeared in 1991. >> Auden; MacNeice

Mahony, Francis Sylvester [ma**hoh**nee], pseudonym **Father Prout** (1804-66) Priest and humorous writer, born in Cork, Co Cork, Ireland. He became a Jesuit priest, but was expelled from the order for a late-night frolic, and was ordained a priest at Lucca in 1832. He moved to London in 1834, forsook his calling for journalism and poetry, and contributed to *Fraser's Magazine* and *Bentley's Miscellany*. He is remembered as author of the poems 'The Bells of Shandon' and 'The Lady of Lee'.

Mahy, Margaret [**may**hee] (1936-) Children's author, born in Whangarei, New Zealand. A librarian with a taste for writing, she published her first story in 1961, and by 1993 had published 110 books. Since 1986, with *The Trickster*, the settings of her stories have increasingly had a more distinctively New Zealand flavour. She has twice won the Carnegie Award for children's literature.

Maier, Ulrike [**miy**er] (1965-94) Skier, born in Austria. She won the world Supergiant slalom skiing championship twice before her fatal accident during a practice run at Garmisch-Partenkirchen. She was the first women skier to be killed in a World Cup race.

Mailer, Norman [**may**ler] (1923-) Novelist and journalist, born in Long Branch, NJ. He studied at Harvard, and served in the Pacific in World War 2. His first novel, *The Naked and the Dead* (1948), became a best seller, and established him as a leading novelist of his generation. His miscellany of pieces, *Advertisements for Myself* (1959), also attracted considerable interest. As a protester he was prominent throughout the 1960s, publishing *Armies of the Night* (1968, Pulitzer), whose subject is the 1967 protest march on the Pentagon. Later books include *Ancient Evenings* (1983), *Tough Guys Don't Dance* (1984), *Harlot's Ghost* (1991), and *Oswald's Tale* (1995).

Maillart, Ella Kini [mayah(r)] (1903-97) Travel writer, born in Geneva, Switzerland. An accomplished sailor, hockeyplayer, and skier, she taught in Wales, worked on an archaeological dig in Crete, and studied film production in Moscow. In 1932 she crossed Russian Turkestan and wrote of her travels in both French and English. In 1934 she went to Mongolia to report on the Japanese invasion for *Petite Parisien*, and returned via Peking across Tibet and into Kashmir with Peter Fleming, described in *Forbidden Journey* (1937). She worked and journeyed in Iran and Afghanistan, and lived in an ashram in S India under the tutelage of Sri Ramama. She was one of the first travellers into Nepal when it opened in 1949, and wrote *The Land of the Sherpas* (1955). >> Ramana Maharishi

Maillart, Robert [mayah(r)] (1872-1940) Civil engineer, born in Bern. He studied at the Zürich Polytechnic, worked with Hennebique, then set up on his own. He was one of the first to work on three-hinged, reinforced concrete arch bridges in the Swiss Alps, designing some remarkable examples, including the bridge over the Inn at Zuoz (1901) and the spectacular curving Schwandbach Bridge at Schwarzenburg (1933). He also designed many industrial buildings in which he used a 'mushroom' column, supporting a flat, two-way reinforced floor slab. >> Hennebique

Maillet, Antonine [mayay] (1929-) Novelist, born in Buctouche, New Brunswick, Canada. Her novels are rooted in the geography, history, and people of Acadia, and after the success of *La Sagouine* (1971) and *Pelagie-La-Charrette* (1979), she dominated contemporary Acadian literature. The Prix Goncourt was awarded to her for *Pelagie-La-Charrette*, bringing her overnight fame in France.

Maillol, Aristide (Joseph Bonaventure) [ma**yol**] (1861-1944) Sculptor, born in Banyuls-sur-Mer, France. He studied at the Ecole des Beaux-Arts, and spent some years designing tapestries. The latter half of his life was devoted to the representation of the nude female figure in a style of monumental simplicity and classical serenity, such as 'Mediterranean' (c.1901, Museum of Modern Art, New York City) and 'Night' (1902, Dina Vierny Collection, Paris).

Maiman, Theodore H(arold) [miyman] (1927–) Physicist, born in Los Angeles, CA. He studied physics at Colorado and Stanford universities, and joined Hughes Research Laboratories, Miami, in 1955. He was much interested in the maser, devised in 1953 to produce coherent microwave radiation. He improved its design, and by 1960 devised the first working laser, which gave coherent visible light. From the 1960s he founded companies to develop laser devices, and in 1977 joined TRW Electronics of California. >> Schawlow; Townes

Maimonides, Moses [miymonideez], originally **Moses ben Maimon** (1138–1204) Philosopher, born in Córdoba, Spain. He studied Aristotelian philosophy and Greek medicine from Arab teachers, and migrated to Egypt, where he became physician to Saladin. A major influence on Jewish thought, he wrote an important commentary on the Mishna, and a great philosophical work, the *Dalalat al-ha'irin* (1190, Guide of the Perplexed), arguing for the reconciliation of Greek philosophy and religion.

Mainbocher [maynboshay], originally **Main Rousseau Bocher** (c. 1890–1976) Fashion designer, born in Chicago, IL. He studied and worked in Chicago, and after service in World War 1 stayed on in Paris, eventually becoming a fashion artist with *Harper's Bazaar* and editor of French *Vogue*. He started his couture house in Paris in 1930. One of his creations was the wedding dress designed for Mrs Wallis Simpson, the Duchess of Windsor (1937). He opened a salon for ready-to-wear clothes in New York City in 1940, but returned to Europe in 1971. >> Windsor, Wallis Warfield

Maintenon, Françoise d'Aubigné, Marquise de (Marchioness of) [mĩtenõ], (1635–1719) Second wife of Louis XIV of France, born in Niort, France. Orphaned, she married her guardian, the crippled poet Paul Scarron in 1652, and on his death was reduced to poverty. In 1669 she discreetly took charge of the king's two sons by her friend Mme de Montespan, and became the king's mistress. By 1674 the king had enabled her to purchase the estate of Maintenon, near Paris, which was converted to a marquisate. After the queen's death (1683), Louis married her secretly. She was accused of having great influence over him, especially over the persecution of Protestants. On his death in 1715 she retired to the educational institution for poor noblewomen which she had founded at St Cyr (1686). >> Louis XIV; Montespan; Scarron

Mairet, Ethel [mairet] (1872–1952) English weaver. After visiting Ceylon (1903–6), she worked with Charles Robert Ashbee and the Guild of Handicrafts, and established 'Gospels', her workshop based at Ditchling, East Sussex, which became a creative centre for many weavers from all over the world. She also wrote a great deal, revealing a desire for rethinking the educational approach to handweaving, and a reassessment of its relationship to powerloom production. >> Ashbee

Maitani, Lorenzo [miytahnee] (c.1275–1330) Sculptor and architect, born in Orvieto, Italy. In 1310 he was put in charge of the works at Orvieto Cathedral, and the reliefs on the façade of the Cathedral are attributed to him.

Maitland, F(rederic) W(illiam) (1850–1906) Jurist and historian of English law, born in London. He studied at Trinity College, Cambridge (1873–6) and Lincoln's Inn, and was called to the bar in 1876. After practising law he became reader in English law (1884) and professor (1888) at Cambridge. His contribution was to apply historical and comparative methods to the study of English institutions, and with Frederick Pollock he wrote the classic *The History of English Law before the Time of Edward I* (1895). In 1887 he co-founded the Selden Society for the study of English law.

Maitland (of Lethington), William (c. 1528–73) Scottish statesman, probably born in Lethington, East Lothian, E Scotland, UK. In 1558 he became secretary of state to the queen-regent, Mary of Guise. He represented Mary, Queen of Scots, at the court of Elizabeth, but made her his enemy by his connivance at Rizzio's murder in 1566. He was also privy to the murder of Darnley, and was one of the commissioners who presented to Elizabeth an indictment of Mary in 1568. Accused of plotting against his colleagues, he was imprisoned in Edinburgh Castle, and later died in prison at Leith. >> Darnley; Guise, Mary of; Mary, Queen of Scots; Rizzio

Major, John (1943–) British statesman and prime minister (1990–7), born in London, England, UK. He had a career in banking before becoming Conservative MP for Huntingdonshire in 1979. He entered Margaret Thatcher's government as a junior minister in 1981, and rose to become Treasury chief secretary under Chancellor Nigel Lawson in 1987. Thereafter, having caught the eye of the prime minister, his progress was spectacular. In 1989 he replaced Sir Geoffrey Howe as foreign secretary, then the same year returned to the Treasury as Chancellor, when Lawson dramatically resigned. He remained loyal to Thatcher in the first round of the 1990 Conservative Party leadership election; then, when she stood down, and indicated that he was her preferred candidate, he ran successfully against Michael Heseltine and Douglas Hurd to become prime minister. He resigned as leader of the Conservative party after they lost the 1997 general election. >> Lawson; Thatcher; RR1095

Makarios III [makaryos], originally **Mihail Khristodoulou Mouskos** (1913–77) Archbishop and primate of the Orthodox Church of Cyprus, and president of Cyprus (1960–74, 1974–7), born in Ano Panciyia, Cyprus. He was ordained priest in 1946, elected Bishop of Kition in 1948, and became archbishop in 1950. He reorganized the *enosis* (union) movement, was arrested and detained in 1956, but returned to a tumultuous welcome in 1959 to become chief Greek-Cypriot Minister in the new Greek–Turkish provisional government. Later that year he was elected president. A short-lived coup removed him briefly from power in 1974. On his death, the posts of archbishop and head of state were separated. >> Harding, John; RR1043

Makarova, Nataliya (Romanovna) [makahrova] (1940–) Ballerina, born in St Petersburg, Russia. After studying in St Petersburg, she joined the Kirov Ballet and became one of their top ballerinas. She defected to the West while touring with the Kirov in London. She joined the American Ballet Theatre in New York City, and became a guest dancer with the Royal Ballet, Covent Garden, and other companies. Best known for her *Giselle* with the Kirov, she was one of the greatest classical dancers, and also created roles for contemporary choreographers. She formed her own company in 1980.

Makeba, Miriam [makayba] (1932–) Singer, born in Johannesburg, South Africa. Exiled from South Africa because of her political views, she settled in the USA, where she became the first African performer to gain an international following, and played a vital role in introducing the sounds and rhythms of traditional African song to the West. She is best known for her recordings of 'click' songs from S Africa. Her marriage in the late 1960s to the militant black leader, Stokely Carmichael, effectively ended her career in the USA. >> Carmichael, Stokely

Malachy, St [malakhee], originally **Máel Máedoc úa Morgair** (c. 1094–1148) Monk and reformer, born in Armagh, Co Armagh. He became Abbot of Bangor (1121), Bishop of Connor (1125) and Archbishop of Armagh (1134). He substituted Roman for Celtic liturgy, and renewed the use of the sacraments. In 1139 he journeyed to Rome, visiting St Bernard at Clairvaux, and introduced the Cistercian Order into Ireland on his return in 1142. In 1190 he became the first Irishman to be canonized. Feast day 3 November. >> Bernard of Clairvaux

Malamud, Bernard [malamuhd] (1914–86) Novelist and writer of short stories, born in New York City. He studied at Columbia University, and taught at Oregon State University (1949–61) and Bennington College, VT (1961–86). His novels reflect his keen interest in Jewish-American life, notably in *The Assistant* (1957) and *God's Grace* (1982), and in his short stories, including *The Stories of Bernard Malamud* (1983). *The Fixer* (1966) won the Pulitzer Prize and the National Book Award.

Malan, Daniel (François) [malan] (1874–1959) South African statesman and prime minister (1948–54), born in Riebeek West, South Africa. He studied at Victoria College, Stellenbosch, and Utrecht University, and in 1905 joined the ministry of the Dutch Reformed Church, but left to become editor of *Die Burger* (1915), the Nationalist newspaper. He became an MP in 1918, and in 1924 held the portfolios of the interior, education, and public health. He broke with Hertzog in 1934, and formed the Purified (Afrikaans *Gesuiwerde*) National Party. In 1939 Herzog resigned from the government, and joined Malan in the Reunited (Afrikaans *Herenigde*) National Party. He was Leader of the Opposition, and in 1948 became premier and minister for external affairs, introducing the controversial apartheid policy. He was a strong believer in a strict white supremacy and a rigidly hierarchical society. >> Hertzog; Suzman; RR1088

Malatesta, Enrico [malatesta] (1853–1932) Anarchist, born in Campania, Italy. He studied medicine at Naples University but was expelled for encouraging student unrest. To demonstrate his beliefs, he gave away his personal wealth, and worked as an electrician in cities around Europe, at the same time organizing anarchist revolutionary groups. He was imprisoned many times, sentenced to death on three occasions, and spent more than half his adult life in exile. He settled in London in 1900, advocating peaceful opposition to authority, and survived an attempt to deport him, in 1911, for alleged complicity with the Sidney St anarchists who had killed three policemen. He returned to Italy in 1913.

Malcolm III, nickname **Malcolm Canmore** ('Big Head') (c.1031–93) King of Scots (1058–93), the son of Duncan I, who was slain by Macbeth in 1040. He returned from exile in 1054, and conquered S Scotland; but he did not become king until he had defeated and killed Macbeth (1057) and disposed of Macbeth's stepson, Lulach (1058). He married as his second wife the English Princess Margaret (later St Margaret), sister of Edgar the Ætheling, and launched five invasions of England between 1061 and his death in a skirmish near Alnwick, Northumberland. >> Macbeth; Margaret (of Scotland); RR1095

Malcolm, George (John) (1917–97) Harpsichordist and conductor, born in London, England, UK. He studied at the Royal College of Music and at Oxford, and was Master of the Music at Westminster Cathedral (1947–59), after which he earned a wide reputation as a freelance harpsichord soloist and a conductor. He was made a papal Knight of the Order of St Gregory in 1970.

Malcolm X, originally **Malcolm Little** (1925–65) African-American nationalist leader, born in Omaha, NE. Imprisoned for burglary in 1946, he was converted to the Black Muslim sect led by Elijah Muhammad. On his release in 1953, he assumed his new name, and won a large following on speaking tours on behalf of the sect, pressing for black separatism and the use of violence in self-defence. In 1964, following a trip to Mecca, his views changed, and he founded the Organization of Afro-American Unity. A factional feud ensued, culminating in his assassination by Black Muslim enemies during a rally in Harlem. >> Muhammad

Malebranche, Nicolas [malbräsh] (1638–1715) Philosopher, born in Paris. He joined the Catholic Oratorians in 1660, and studied theology until Descartes' works drew him to philosophy. His major work is *De la recherche de la vérité* (1674, Search after Truth), which defends many of Descartes' views, but explains all causal interaction between mind and body by a theory of divine intervention known as *occasionalism*. >> Descartes

Malenkov, Georgiy Maksimilianovich [malyenkof] (1902–88) Soviet statesman and prime minister (1953–5), born in Orenburg, Russia. He joined the Communist Party in 1920 and was involved in the collectivization of agriculture and the purges of the 1930s under Stalin. He became a member of the Politburo and deputy prime minister in 1946, succeeding Stalin as Party first secretary and prime minister in 1953. He resigned in 1955, admitting responsibility for the failure of Soviet agricultural policy, and in 1957 was sent to Kazakhstan as manager of a hydroelectric plant. >> RR1085

Malesherbes, Chrétien (Guillaume de Lamoignon) de [malzairb] (1721–94) French statesman, born in Paris. He became a counsellor of the *Parlement* of Paris (1744), and was made chief censor of the press (1750). At Louis XVI's accession (1774) he became secretary of state for the royal household, instituting prison and legal reforms in tandem with Turgot's economic improvements. He resigned in 1776 on the eve of Turgot's dismissal. Despite his reforming zeal, he was mistrusted as an aristocrat during the Revolution. Arrested as a Royalist (1794), he was guillotined in Paris. >> Louis XVI; Turgot

Malevich, Kazimir (Severinovich) [malayevich] (1878–1935) Painter and designer, born in Kiev, Ukraine. He studied in Moscow in 1902 and, together with Mondrian, was one of the earliest pioneers of pure abstraction, founding the Suprematist movement. He claimed to have painted the first totally abstract picture, a black square on a white background, as early as 1913. Certainly he was exhibiting similar work by 1915, and went on to paint a series entitled 'White on White'. >> Mondrian; Pevsner, Antoine

Malherbe, François de [malairb] (1555–1628) Poet, born in Caen, France. He studied at Basel and Heidelberg universities, ingratiated himself with Henry IV (of France), and received a pension. He was an industrious writer, producing odes, songs, epigrams, epistles, translations, and criticisms, and founded the literary tradition of classicism.

Malik, Jacob Alexandrovich (1906–80) Soviet politician, born in the Ukraine. Said to be one of Stalin's favourite juniors, he was ambassador to Japan (1942–45), and deputy foreign minister in 1946. In 1948 he succeeded Andrei Gromyko as Soviet spokesman at the UN, and was ambassador to Britain (1953–60). From 1960 he was again deputy foreign minister, serving a second term as ambassador to the UN (1968–76). >> Gromyko; Stalin

Malina, Judith >> Beck, Julian

Malinovsky, Rodion Yakovlevich [malinofskee] (1898–1967) Soviet soldier and statesman, born in Odessa, Ukraine. He joined the Red Army after the Revolution (1917), and was major-general at the time of the Nazi invasion in 1941. He commanded the forces which liberated Rostov, Kharkov, and the Dnepr basin, and led the Russian advance on Budapest and into Austria (1944–5). When Russia declared war on Japan, he took a leading part in the Manchurian campaign. He later became Khrushchev's minister of defence (1957–67). >> Khrushchev

Malinowski, Bronislaw (Kasper) [mali**nof**skee] (1884–1942) Anthropologist, born in Kraków, Poland. He studied at the Jagiellonian University, Kraków, and at Leipzig, went to London in 1910, and taught at the London School of Economics, where he became a professor (1927). In 1938 he went to the USA, where he accepted a post at Yale. He was the pioneer of 'participant observation' as a method of fieldwork (notably in the Trobriand Is), and a major proponent of functionalism in anthropology. >> Seligman

Malipiero, (Gian) Francesco [mali**pyay**roh] (1882–1973) Composer, born in Venice, Italy. He studied in Vienna, Venice, and Bologna, visited Paris, and became professor of composition at the Parma Conservatory (1921), and director of institutes at Padua and Venice (1939–52). He wrote symphonic, operatic, vocal, and chamber music, and edited Monteverdi and Vivaldi.

Malkovich, John [**mal**kovich] (1953–) Film actor, born in Christopher, IL. He studied at the University of Illinois, then joined the Steppenwolf theatre company in Chicago. He won an Oscar nomination for Best Supporting Actor for his role in *Places in The Heart* (1984). Other films include *Empire of the Sun* (1987), *Dangerous Liaisons*, and *Con Air* (1997).

Mallarmé, Stéphane [malah(r)**may**] (1842–98) Symbolist poet, born in Paris. He taught English in Paris and elsewhere, visiting England on several occasions. He translated the poems of Poe, and in his own writing became a leader of the Symbolist school. His works included *Hérodiade* (1864), *L'Après-midi d'un faune* (1865), which inspired Debussy's prelude, and the remarkable experimental poem, *Un Coup de dés* (1914, A Dice Throw).

Malle, Louis [mal] (1932–95) Film director, born in Thumeries, France. He studied political science at the Jesuit College, Fontainebleau, and the Sorbonne, after which he entered the Institut des Hautes Etudes Cinématographiques (1950). His first feature film was *Ascenseur pour l'échafaud* (1957, trans Frantic) for which he won the Prix Delluc. The success of his second film *Les Amants* (1958, The Lovers) brought recognition, and he went on to establish an international reputation, receiving critical acclaim for such works as *Calcutta* (1969), *Le Souffle au coeur* (1971, trans Dearest Love), and *Atlantic City* (1980). Later films included *Au Revoir les enfants* (1987, Goodbye, Children) and *Damage* (1993). He married actress **Candice Bergen** (1946–) in 1980.

Mallowan, Sir Max (Edgar Lucien) [**mal**ohan] (1904–78) Archaeologist, born in London, England, UK. He studied Classics at Oxford, and was apprenticed to Leonard Woolley at Ur (1925–31), where he met novelist Agatha Christie, whom he married in 1930. He excavated for the British Museum at Arpachiyah, Chagar Bazar, and Tell Brak (1932–8). As professor of W Asiatic archaeology at London University (1947–60), he excavated in the Near East, principally at Nimrud, with striking results described in detail in *Nimrud and its Remains* (1970). Agatha Christie's *Come, Tell Me How You Live* (1946) is an account of his digging in Syria (1934–8), and his own autobiography, *Mallowan's Memoirs*, appeared in 1977. He was knighted in 1968. >> Christie, Agatha; Woolley, Leonard

Malmesbury, William of >> **William of Malmesbury**

Malone, Edmund (1741–1812) Scholar, and editor of Shakespeare, born in Dublin, Ireland. He graduated from Trinity College, Dublin, devoted himself to literary work in London,

and his 11-volume edition of Shakespeare (1790) was warmly received. He denounced the Shakespeare forgeries of William Henry Ireland, and left behind a large mass of materials for *The Variorum Shakespeare*, edited in 1821 by James Boswell (the Younger, 1778–1822). >> Ireland, William Henry; Shakespeare, William

Malory, Sir Thomas (?–1471) Writer, known for his work *Le Morte d'Arthur* (The Death of Arthur). From Caxton's preface, we are told that Malory was a knight, that he finished his work in the ninth year of the reign of Edward IV (1461–70), and that he 'reduced' it from some French book. Probably he was the Sir Thomas Malory of Newbold Revel, Warwickshire, whose quarrels with a neighbouring priory and (probably) Lancastrian politics brought him imprisonment. >> Caxton

Malouf, David [ma**loof**] (1934–) Novelist, born in Brisbane, Queensland, Australia. He studied at Queensland University, teaching there and at Sydney. Previously concentrating on poetry, his first novel was *Johnno* (1975). He became a full-time writer in 1978, and in 1979 was awarded the New South Wales Premier's Literary Award for *An Imaginary Life* (1978). Other novels include *Fly Away Peter* (1982), *Harland's Half Acre* (1984), *The Great World* (1991, Miles Franklin Award), *Remembering Babylon* (1993), which was shortlisted for the Booker Prize, and won the 1996 IMPAC Dublin Literary Award, and *Conversation at Curlow Creek* (1997).

Malpighi, Marcello [mal**pee**gee] (1628–94) Anatomist, born near Bologna, Italy. He studied medicine at Bologna, became professor at Pisa, Messina, and Bologna, and from 1691 was chief physician to Pope Innocent XII. The founder of microscopic anatomy, he described the major types of plant and animal structures, and did investigative work, notably on silkworms and the embryology of chicks.

Malraux, André (Georges) [mal**roh**] (1901–76) Statesman and novelist, born in Paris. He studied oriental languages and spent much time in China, where he worked for the Guomindang and was active in the 1927 revolution. He also fought in the Spanish Civil War, and in World War 2 escaped from a prison camp to join the French resistance. He was minister of information in de Gaulle's government (1945–6), and minister of cultural affairs (1960–9). He is known for his novels, notably *La Condition humaine* (1933, trans Man's Fate; Prix Goncourt) and *L'Espoir* (1937, trans Man's Hope). >> de Gaulle

Malthus, Thomas Robert (1766–1834) Economist, born near Dorking, Surrey, SE England, UK. He studied at Cambridge, and was ordained in 1797. In 1798 he published anonymously his *Essay on the Principle of Population*, which argued that the population has a natural tendency to increase faster than the means of subsistence, and that efforts should be made to cut the birth rate, either by self-restraint or birth control– a view which later was widely misrepresented under the name of *Malthusianism*. In 1805 he became professor of political economy in the East India College at Haileybury, where he wrote *Principles of Political Economy* (1820) and other works.

Malus, Etienne Louis [ma**lüs**] (1775–1812) Physicist, born in Paris. A military engineer in Napoleon's army (1796–1801), he carried out research in optics and discovered the polarization of light by reflection. His paper explaining the theory of double refraction in crystals won him the Institute's Prize in 1810.

Mamet, David (Alan) [**ma**met] (1947–) Playwright, screenplay writer, and film director, born in Chicago, IL. He studied at Goddard College, VT, then became an actor in New York City. His plays, such as *American Buffalo* (1976) and *Speed the Plow* (1987), address the psychological and ethical issues that confront modern urban society. Other works include the plays *The Woods* (1977), and *The Old Neighborhood* (1990), the screenplays *The Postman Always Rings Twice* (1981) and *The Untouchables* (1986), the films (as director) *House of Games* (1986) and *Homicide* (1991), and the novel *The Village* (1994). In 1984 he was awarded the Pulitzer Prize for Drama for *Glengarry Glen Ross*.

Man, Paul de >> **de Man, Paul**

Manasseh [manasuh] Biblical king of Judah, the eldest son of Joseph who was adopted and blessed by Jacob. He was the eponymous ancestor of one of the 12 tribes of Israel, who later became the Jewish people. >> Jacob

Manasseh [manasuh] (7th-c BC) Biblical king of Judah (696–642 BC), the son of Hezekiah, whom he succeeded. He earned an evil name for idolatry and wickedness until he was taken captive by the Assyrians in Babylon, when he repented. *The Prayer of Manasseh* is apocryphal.

Manasseh ben Israel [manasuh] (1604–57) Scholar, born in Lisbon. He was taken early to Amsterdam, where he became chief rabbi at the age of 18 in 1622, and set up the first printing press in Holland (1626). He later went to England (1655–7), securing from Cromwell the readmission of the Jews. He wrote important works in Hebrew, Spanish, and Latin, and in English a *Humble Address* to Cromwell, *A Declaration*, and *Vindiciae Judaeorum*. >> Cromwell, Oliver

Manchester, Edward Montagu, 2nd Earl of (1602–71) Parliamentary soldier, born in London, England, UK. He studied at Cambridge, accompanied Prince Charles to Spain (1623), and was raised to the House of Lords as Viscount Mandeville (1626). In 1642 he was impeached by the king, acquitted, and succeeded his father as 2nd Earl. In the Civil War he served under Essex at Edgehill. He defeated the royalists at Newbury, but Cromwell accused him of military incompetence. Deprived of his command (1645), he opposed the trial of the king, protested against the Commonwealth, and was made Lord Chamberlain at the Restoration (1660). >> Charles I (of England); Cromwell, Oliver

Manchester, William (1922–) Novelist, foreign correspondent, and contemporary historian, born in Attleboro, MA. His major work is *The Death of the President* (1967), written at the request of the Kennedy family. A landmark in reportage, it received mixed reviews and sold in millions, but has subsequently been superseded as new evidence on the assassination of President Kennedy has emerged. >> Kennedy, John F

Mancini, Henry [manseenee], popular name of **Enrico Mancini** (1924–94) Composer, born in Cleveland, OH. His studies at the Juilliard School of Music, New York City, were interrupted by World War 2, but while in service he met Glenn Miller, later joining his band as an arranger and pianist. His Oscar-winning compositions include the songs 'Moon River' (1961) and 'Days of Wine and Roses' (1962), and the film scores for *Breakfast at Tiffany's* (1961) and *Victor/Victoria* (1982). Other hits include theme tunes for the *Pink Panther* film and the *Peter Gunn* television series. During his career he composed more than 80 film scores and won 20 Grammy Awards. >> Miller, Glenn

Mandela, Nelson (Rolihlahla) [mandela] (1918–) South African statesman and president (1994–), born in Transkei, South Africa. He was a lawyer in Johannesburg, then joined the African National Congress in 1944. For the next 20 years he directed a campaign of defiance against the South African government and its racist policies, orchestrating in 1961 a three-day national strike. In 1964 he was sentenced to life imprisonment for political offences. He continued to be such a potent symbol of black resistance that the 1980s saw a co-ordinated international campaign for his release. His wife Winnie was also frequently subjected to restrictions on her personal freedom.

He was released from prison in 1990, after President F W de Klerk had unbanned the ANC, removed restrictions on political groups, and suspended executions. Mandela immediately urged foreign powers not to reduce their pressure on the South African government for constitutional reform. He was elected president of the African National Congress in 1991. He and his wife separated in 1992, and in 1993 he shared the Nobel Prize for Peace with de Klerk for their work towards dismantling apartheid. He was awarded the Order of Merit in 1995. >> de Klerk; Mandela, Winnie

Mandela, Winnie [mandela], also **Madikizela-Mandela**, popular name of **Nomzano Zaniewe Winnifred Mandela** (1934–) Former wife of Nelson Mandela, born in Bizana, South Africa. After qualifying as a social worker, she married Mandela in 1958. Her first arrest took place three months later, and in 1962 she was banned for the first time. For the next 20 years she was banned, restricted, detained, and jailed a number of times. In 1990, when her husband was released from prison, she took an increasingly prominent role in the African National Congress (ANC), until her conviction on charges of kidnapping and assault. In 1992, the Mandelas separated. She continued to operate as a militant and maverick figure under ANC colours, making a political comeback in late 1993, and given a role in the 1994 government as deputy minister for arts, culture, science, and technology (dismissed in 1995). A controversial and charismatic figure, she figured prominently in the proceedings of the Truth and Reconciliation Commission in 1997. >> Mandela, Nelson

Mandelbrot, Benoit (1924–) Mathematician, born in Warsaw. He studied at the Ecole Polytechnique, Paris, and at the California Institute of Technology, then became professor of mathematics at Geneva (1955–7) and the Ecole Polytechnique (1957–8). He joined IBM in 1958, and became professor of mathematics at Yale in 1987. A central figure in the development of fractals, his book *The Fractal Geometry of Nature* (1982) demonstrated the potential application of fractals to natural phenomena.

Mandelson, Peter [mandelson] (1954–) Politician, born in London, S England, UK. He studied at Oxford, became a television producer for *Weekend World* (1982–5), and was then appointed Labour Party Director for Campaigns and Communications. Elected as MP for Hartlepool in 1992, he became an Opposition whip (1994), and shadow Civil Service spokesman (1995). In 1996 he worked exclusively on the Labour Party election campaign, and in the 1997 Labour government became a Minister without Portfolio – an influential member of the cabinet, responsible for assisting the prime minister in co-ordinating, implementing, and presenting government policy. His grandfather was Herbert Morrison. >> Morrison, Herbert

Mandelstam, Osip [manduhlstam] (1891–1938) Poet, born in Warsaw. His early success with *Kamen* (1913, Stone), *Tristia* (1922, Sad Things), and *Stikhotvorenia 1921–25* (1928, Poems) was followed by arrest (1934) by the Soviet authorities. His death was reported from Siberia in 1938. His *Sobranie sochineny* (Collected Works) were published in three volumes (1964–71), and his wife, **Nadezhda** (1899–1980), wrote their story in *Hope Against Hope* (1970).

Mandeville, Bernard [mandevil] (1670–1733) Physician and satirist, born in Dort, The Netherlands. He trained as a doctor at Leyden in 1691, and settled in London in medical practice. He is known as the author of a short work in doggerel verse originally entitled *The Grumbling Hive* (1705), and finally *The Fable of the Bees* (1723). The book was condemned by the grand jury of Middlesex.

Mandeville, Geoffrey de, 1st Earl of Essex [mandevil] (?–1144) English baron. A cruel man, he succeeded his father as constable of the Tower c.1130, and proved a traitor alternately to King Stephen and Empress Matilda. He took finally to plundering in the Cambridgeshire fens, was besieged by Stephen, and killed. >> Matilda; Stephen

Mandeville, Jehan de or **Sir John** [**man**devil] (14th-c) The name assigned to the compiler of a famous book of travels (*The Voyage and Travels of Sir John Mandeville, Knight*), published apparently in 1366, and soon translated from the French into all European tongues. It may have been written by a physician, **Jehan de Bourgogne**, otherwise **Jehan à la Barbe**, who died in Liège in 1372, and who is said to have revealed on his death-bed his real name of Mandeville (or Maundevylle), explaining that he had had to flee from his native England for a homicide. Some scholars, however, attribute it to **Jean d'Outremeuse**, a Frenchman.

Mandeville, Viscount >> **Manchester, 2nd Earl of**

Manen, Hans van (1932–) Ballet dancer, choreographer, and director, born in Nieuwer, The Netherlands. He joined Ballet Recital in 1952, moving to Amsterdam Opera Ballet in 1959, and became one of the founding members of Netherlands Dance Theatre (NDT), and its artistic director. In 1973 he left to join the Dutch National Ballet as choreographer and ballet master. His work for NDT includes *Symphony in Three Movements* (1963), *Septet Extra* (1973), and *Songs Without Words* (1977).

Manet, Edouard [manay] (1832–83) Painter, born in Paris. Intended for a legal career, he became an artist, and exhibited at the Salon in 1861. His 'Dejeuner sur l'herbe' (1863, Luncheon on the Grass), which scandalized the traditional Classicists, was rejected, and although the equally provocative 'Olympia' was accepted in 1865, the Salon remained hostile, and Manet's genius was not recognized until after his death. He exhibited in the *Salon des Refusés*, and helped to form the group out of which the Impressionist movement arose. >> Morisot

Manetho [**man**ethoh] (fl.c.300 BC) Egyptian historian. He was high-priest of Heliopolis, and wrote in Greek a history of the 30 dynasties from mythical times to 323 BC. Portions have been preserved in the works of Julius Africanus (AD 300), Eusebius of Caesarea, and George Syncellus (AD 800). >> Eusebius of Caesarea

Mangan, James Clarence (1803–49) Poet, born in Dublin. He worked as a lawyer's clerk, and later found employment in the library of Trinity College, Dublin. He published English versions of Irish poems in *The Poets and Poetry of Munster* (1849), notably 'My Dark Rosaleen', 'The Nameless One', and 'The Woman of Three Cows'. Subject to melancholia, he became an opium addict, and died of cholera.

Mangeshkar, Lata [man**gesh**kah(r)] (1928–) Indian singer. She became a singer as a child to help support her family when her father died. In 1948 she was engaged to provide the singing voice of actresses in Indian musical films, and had made over 30 000 recordings for more than 2000 films by the time she retired in 1984. She made several visits to London in the 1980s, performing to sell-out audiences in Wembley Stadium.

Manichaeus or **Mani** [mani**kee**us, **mah**nee], known as **the Apostle of Light** (c. 215–276) Religious leader, born in Ecbatana, Persia. He was the founder of *Manichaeism*, a dualistic religion which offered salvation through the acquisition of special knowledge of spiritual truth ('illumination'). In c.245 he began to proclaim his new religion at the court of the Persian king, Sapor (Shahpur) I. He travelled widely, but eventually King Bahram I abandoned him to his Zoroastrian enemies, who crucified him.

Mankiewicz, Joseph L(eo) [**mang**kuhvich] (1909–93 Film director, born in Wilkes-Barre, PA. After working as a junior writer at Paramount Studios, then as a screenwriter,

he became a producer with MGM. He made his directorial debut with the Gothic thriller *Dragonwyck* (1946), and became a double Oscar winner for the script and direction of *A Letter To Three Wives* (1949) and *All About Eve* (1950). His adaptation of *Sleuth* (1972) earned him a Best Director Oscar nomination.

Mankowitz, (Cyril) Wolf [**mang**kohvits] (1924–) Writer, playwright, and antique dealer, born in London, England, UK. He studied at Cambridge. His publications in the art domain include a study of Josiah Wedgwood, and *The Concise Encyclopedia of English Pottery and Porcelain* (1957). His fiction includes the novel *A Kid for Two Farthings* (1953), the play *The Bespoke Overcoat* (1954), the films *The Millionairess* (1960), *The Long, the Short, and the Tall* (1961), and *Casino Royale* (1967), and the musicals *Expresso Bongo* (1958–9), *Pickwick* (1963), and *Stand and Deliver!* (1972). Later works include the novels *Gioconda* (1987) and *A Night with Casanova* (1991). >> Wedgwood

Manley, Delariviere often called, incorrectly, **Mary** (1663–1724) Writer, born in Jersey, Channel Is, UK. After her first marriage to **Sir Roger Manley** (d.1687), she was unsuspectingly lured into a bigamous marriage with her cousin, **John Manley** of Truro, MP, who soon deserted her. She went to England, where she had success with the publication of her letters. In 1696 she wrote plays, and chronicles disguised as fiction, especially the scandalous anti-Whig *The New Atalantis* (1709). In 1711 she succeeded Swift as editor of *The Examiner*. She also wrote a fictional 'biography', *The Adventures of Rivella* (1714). >> Swift, Jonathan

Manley, Michael (Norman) (1923–97) Jamaican politician and prime minister (1972–80, 1989–92), born in Kingston, Jamaica. He served in the Royal Canadian air force, studied at the London School of Economics, and spent some time as a journalist before returning to Jamaica. In the 1950s he became a leader of the National Workers' Union, sat in the Senate (1962–7), was elected to the House of Representatives, and became leader of the People's National Party in 1969. As prime minister, he embarked on a radical, Socialist programme, cooling relations with the USA. Despite rising unemployment, he was re-elected in 1976, defeated in 1980 and 1983, and returned to power in 1989, but was succeeded in 1992 by Percival Patterson. >> RR1068

Mann, Heinrich (1871–1950) Novelist, born in Lübeck, Germany, the brother of Thomas Mann. After the death of his wealthy father, he became financially independent and settled in Berlin and France. He is best known for the macabre novel, *Professor Unrat* (1904), describing the moral degradation of an outwardly respectable schoolmaster, which was translated and filmed as *The Blue Angel* (1930). Other works include *Die kleine Stadt* (1909, The Little Town) and an autobiography (1945–6). >> Mann, Thomas

Mann, Horace (1796–1859) Educationist, 'the father of American public education', born in Franklin, MA. He entered the Massachusetts legislature in 1827, and was president of the state Senate. As secretary of the board of education (1837–48), he reorganized public-school teaching, and was responsible for setting up the first normal school in the USA (1839). He became a member of the US House of Representatives (1848–53), and president of Antioch College, OH (1852–9).

Mann, Thomas (1875–1955) Novelist, born in Lübeck, Germany. He left school at 19, and spent some time at Munich University before becoming a writer, like his brother Heinrich. His early masterpiece, *Buddenbrooks* (1901), traced the decline of a family over four generations. He produced several short stories and novellas, such as *Der Tod in Venedig* (1913, Death in Venice; filmed, 1971), and then wrote *Der Zauberberg* (1924, The Magic Mountain), for which he was awarded the Nobel Prize for Literature in 1929. He left Germany for Switzerland in 1933, settling in the USA in 1936. He returned to Switzerland in 1947, and produced his greatest work, a modern version of the mediaeval legend, *Doktor Faustus* (1947). >> Fontane; Mann, Heinrich

Mannerheim, Carl Gustav (Emil), vapaaherra (Baron) [**man**erhiym] (1867–1951) Finnish soldier, statesman, and president (1944–6), born in Villnäs, Finland. When Finland declared independence (1918), he became supreme commander and regent. Defeated in the presidential election of 1919, he retired into private life, returning as commander-in-chief against the Russians in the Winter War of 1939–40. He continued to command the Finnish forces until 1944, when he became president of the Finnish Republic. >> RR1049

Manners, John >> **Granby, Marquess of**

Mannheim, Karl [**man**hiym] (1893–1947) Sociologist, born in Budapest. He studied at Budapest and Strasbourg, became a lecturer at Heidelberg (1925), and was appointed professor of sociology and political economy at Frankfurt (1930). He fled to England (1933), where he joined the London School of Economics, and in 1945 became professor of sociology and philosophy of education at the London University Institute of Education. He is known primarily for his contribution to the sociology of knowledge, of which he was one of the founders.

Manning, Henry Edward, Cardinal (1808–92) Roman Catholic clergyman, born in Totteridge, Hertfordshire, SE England, UK. He studied at Oxford, became a priest in the Church of England (1833), converted to Catholicism in 1851, and in 1865 was appointed Archbishop of Westminster. At the Council of 1870, he was a zealous supporter of the infallibility dogma. Appointed cardinal in 1875, he continued as a leader of the Ultramontanes.

Manning, Olivia (1911–80) Novelist, born in Portsmouth, Hampshire, S England, UK. She trained at art school, then went to London, publishing her first novel, *The Wind Changes*, in 1937. She married in 1939, and went abroad with her husband, British Council lecturer, then BBC producer **Reginald Donald Smith**. Her experiences formed the basis of her 'Balkan Trilogy', comprising *The Great Fortune* (1960), *The Spoilt City* (1962), and *Friends and Heroes* (1965). This and the 'Levant Trilogy' (1978–80) form a single narrative entitled *Fortunes of War* which Anthony Burgess described as 'the finest fictional record of the war produced by a British writer'. >> Burgess, Anthony

Mannion, Wilfred (1918–) Footballer, born in Yorkshire, N England, UK. Although his career was spent with two unfashionable clubs (Middlesbrough and Hull City), he was an integral part of the great English national side of the late 1940s, scoring one goal for every four league matches he played.

Mannix, Daniel (1864–1963) Roman Catholic clergyman, born in Ráth Luirc, Co Cork, Ireland. Ordained at Maynooth in 1890, he became president of the college in 1903. He went to Australia in 1913 as coadjutor in Melbourne, succeeding as archbishop in 1917. He opposed conscription, and attacked the government for lack of aid to Church schools. Despite the controversy this caused, he was responsible for establishing nearly 200 schools and more than 100 parishes.

Mannyng, Robert, also known as **Robert of Brunne** (?–c.1338) Chronicler and poet, born in Bourne, Lincolnshire, EC England, UK. In 1288 he entered the nearby Gilbertine monastery of Sempringham. His chief work is the poem *Handlynge Synne* (c.1303), a landmark in the transition from early to later Middle English, and a colourful picture of contemporary life. His chronicle *The Story of England*

(1338) is a literary work of historical fiction.

Mansard or **Mansart, François** [māsah(r)] (1598–1666) Architect, born in Paris. He brought a simplified adaptation of the Baroque style into use in France. His first major work, the N wing of the Château de Blois, featured the double-angled high-pitched roof which now bears his name. His churches include Sainte-Marie de Chaillot, Sainte-Marie de la Visitation, and Val-de-Grâce, and he built or remodelled several notable buildings in Paris and elsewhere. >> Mansard, Jules Hardouin

Mansard or **Mansart, Jules Hardouin** [māsah(r)] (1645–1708) Architect, born in Paris, the great-nephew and possibly pupil of François Mansard. He became chief architect to Louis XIV, and designed many notable buildings, which represent the nearest that French architecture approached to the Baroque. He extended Le Vau's garden facade at Versailles (1678), built the domed chapel of the Invalides (1680–91), and laid out the Place Vendôme in Paris (1698). >> Mansard, François

Mansbridge, Albert (1876–1952) Adult educator, born in Gloucester, Gloucestershire, SWC England, UK. He left school aged 14, but after attending classes at King's College, London, he became an evening-class teacher under the London School Board. He was instrumental in the formation of the Workers' Educational Association, of which he become general secretary (1905), and the National Central Library (1916).

Mansell, Nigel [**man**sl] (1954–) Motor-racing driver, born in Birmingham, West Midlands, C England, UK. He entered Formula 1 racing in 1980. From 176 Grand Prix starts, he won 29 races from 26 pole positions. In 1992 he retired from Formula 1 racing after winning the driver's championship with eight wins. He joined the Haas-Newman Indy car racing team in the USA, becoming Indy car champion in 1993, his first year, briefly returned to Formula 1 in 1995, driving for McLaren, then retired.

Mansfield, Katherine, pseudonym of **Kathleen Mansfield Murry**, *née* **Beauchamp** (1888–1923) Short-story writer, born in Wellington, New Zealand. She studied at Queen's College, London, then took up music for two years in New Zealand before returning to London to pursue a literary career. In 1918, after some traumatic early experiences that marked her work, she married writer John Middleton Murry. Her first major work was *Prelude* (1917), a recreation of the New Zealand of her childhood. *Bliss, and Other Stories* (1920), containing the classic stories 'Je ne parle pas francais' and 'Prelude', confirmed her standing as an original and innovative writer, influenced by Chekhov. The only other collection published before her premature death from tuberculosis was *The Garden Party, and Other Stories* (1922). Posthumous works include *Poems* (1923), *Something Childish, and Other Stories* (1924), and her revealing *Journal* (1927) and *Letters* (1928). >> Chekhov; Murry

Mansfield, Jayne, originally **Vera Jayne Palmer** (1933–67) Film actress, born in Bryn Mawr, PA. She made her debut in *Underwater* (1954), and became known for her striking looks in such films as *The Female Jungle* (1955) and *The Girl Can't Help It* (1956). In *Will Success Spoil Rock Hunter* (1956), she reprised a part she had created on stage.

Mansfield (of Caen Wood), William Murray, 1st Earl of (1705–93) Judge, born in Scone, Perth and Kinross, E Scotland, UK. He studied at Oxford, was called to the bar, and acquired an extensive practice. He was appointed solicitor general (1742), became MP for Boroughbridge, and was appointed attorney general in 1754. In 1756 he became Chief Justice of the King's Bench, a member of the cabinet, and Baron Mansfield. His judgments were influential, and he made important contributions to international law, but his opinions were unpopular, and during the Gordon riots of 1780 his house was burned. He was created an earl in 1776, and resigned his office in 1788.

Manship, Paul (Howard) (1885–1966) Sculptor, born in St Paul, MN. He studied in New York City and Philadelphia, and attended the American Academy in Rome (1908–12), where he was greatly influenced by antique sculpture. He then returned to the USA, and became renowned for his bronze figurative sculptures, which drew heavily on Roman and Greek sources. His many important commissions include the gilded 'Prometheus Fountain' (1934) for the Rockefeller Center, New York City.

Manson, Charles (1934–) Cult leader, born in Cincinnati, OH. Released from prison in 1967, he set up a commune based on free love and devotion to himself. Members of his cult conducted a series of grisly murders in California in 1969, including that of actress **Sharon Tate** (1943–69). He and his accomplices were sentenced to death, but were spared the death penalty due to a Supreme Court ruling against capital punishment.

Manson, Sir Patrick, nickname **Mosquito Manson** (1844–1922) Physician, born in Old Meldrum, Aberdeenshire, NE Scotland, UK. He practised medicine in China (1871), and in Hong Kong (1883) started a school of medicine that became the University of Hong Kong. He became medical adviser to the Colonial Office, and in 1899 helped to found the London School of Tropical Medicine. He received his nickname from his pioneer work with Sir Ronald Ross, being the first to argue that the mosquito was host to the malaria parasite (1877). >> Ross, Ronald

Manstein, (Fritz) Erich von [**man**shtiyn] (1887–1973) German field marshal, born in Berlin. At the outset of World War 2 he became chief-of-staff to Rundstedt in the Polish campaign, and in France was the architect of Hitler's *Blitzkrieg*. In 1941 he was given command of an army corps on the Eastern Front, and after the disaster of Stalingrad, staged a successful counter-attack at Kharkov, though he failed to relieve Paulus's Sixth Army. Imprisoned as a war criminal in 1945, he was released in 1953. >> Paulus; Rundstedt

Mansur, al- [man**soor**], in full **Abua Jafar Abd Allah al-Mansur ibn Muhammad** (c. 710–75) Second caliph of the Abbasid dynasty. He held important military commands during the struggle against the Umayyads under his brother **al-Saffah**, whom he succeeded in 754. An astute politician, he defeated several revolts, establishing a firm government dominated by the Abbasid family, and founding a new capital for the empire, Baghdad (762). He overcame considerable opposition to ensure the succession of his own son, **Mahdi**, and died while leading his fifth pilgrimage to Mecca.

Mantegna, Andrea [man**ten**ya] (c. 1431–1506) Painter, born in Vicenza, Italy. He was apprenticed to the tailor-painter Francesco Squarcione in Padua, and seems to have been adopted by him. In 1459 he was persuaded by Ludovico Gonzaga, Duke of Mantua, to work for him. His most important works were nine tempera pictures of 'The Triumph of Caesar' (1482–92), which were acquired by Charles I and are now at Hampton Court, and his decoration of the ceiling of the Camera degli Sposi in Mantua. >> Squarcione

Mantle, Mickey (Charles) (1931–95) Baseball player, born in Spavinaw, OK. A great centrefielder, baserunner, and hitter, he was a member of the renowned New York Yankees team of the 1950s and 1960s. He once hit a home run measured at a record 177 m/565 ft. The American League's Most Valuable Player in 1956, he won a rare Triple Crown in batting, home runs, and runs batted in. He was elected to the Baseball Hall of Fame in 1974. >> RR1144

Manucci, Aldo >> **Aldus Manutius**

Manuel I >> **Emanuel I**

Manuel, Nikolaus (1484–1530) Painter, poet, and reformer, born in Bern. A painter of stained glass, he changed over to orthodox media and produced biblical and mythological pictures in the Renaissance style, often showing the influence of Baldung in his tendency towards the macabre. He held several government offices, was a member of the Great Council, and wrote satirical verse. >> Baldung

Manuzio, Aldo >> **Aldus Manutius**

Manzoni, Alessandro [mant**soh**nee] (1785–1873) Novelist and poet, born in Milan, Italy. He published his first poems in 1806, and spent the next few years writing sacred lyrics and a treatise on the religious basis of morality. The work which gave him European fame is his historical novel, *I promessi sposi* (1825–7, The Betrothed), one of the most notable works of fiction in Italian literature. He was a strong advocate of a united Italy, and became a senator of the kingdom in 1860. When he died he was given a state funeral. Verdi composed his *Requiem* in Manzoni's honour. >> Verdi

Manzú, Giacomo [man**zoo**] (1908–91) Sculptor, born in Bergamo, Italy. He studied at the Fantoni Trade School, and in 1930 was commissioned to make religious reliefs and saints for the Catholic University of Milan. He taught sculpture in Milan (1940) and Turin (c.1940–5), and revived Classical techniques of relief sculpture in bronze, such as the bronze doors of St Peter's in Rome (1950). His series of cardinals in their tall mitres (more than 50 made after 1936) are executed in various sizes.

Mao Dun [mow dun], also spelled **Mao Tun**, pseudonym of **Shen Yen-ping** (1896–1981) Writer, born in Ch'ing-chen, China. He studied at Beijing University, and was a founder-member of the Literary Research Society, and editor of the (trans titles) *Short Story Monthly* (1921–3) and the *Hankow National Daily*. In 1930 he helped to organize the influential League of Left-Wing Writers, and his major works include a best-selling novel, *Ziye* (1932, Midnight). After the Communists came to power in 1949 he was China's first minister of culture (1949–65), and founder-editor of the literary journal *People's Literature* (1949–53). During the Cultural Revolution he was kept under house arrest in Beijing (1966–78).

Mao Zedong [mow dzuhdoong], also spelled **Mao Tse-tung** see panel on p. 617

Maradona, Diego [mara**do**na] (1960–) Footballer, born in Lanus, Argentina. He became Argentina's youngest ever international in 1977, transferred to Boca Juniors for £1 million as a teenager, and in 1982 became the world's most expensive footballer when he joined Barcelona for £5 million. He broke the record again in 1984 when the Italian club Napoli paid £6·9 million for him. He captained Argentina to their second World Cup in 1986, only for his career to founder amid accusations of drug-taking. Following a 15-month ban, he returned by popular demand, though without a club, to the World Cup side as captain in 1994, but was again suspended from the team following a positive drug test. He signed for Santos in 1995.

Marat, Jean Paul [mara] (1743–93) French revolutionary politician, born in Boudry, Switzerland. He studied medicine at Bordeaux, and lived in Paris, Holland, Newcastle, and London. At the Revolution he became a member of the Cordelier Club, and established the radical paper *L'Ami du peuple* (The Friend of the People). His virulence provoked hatred, and he was several times forced into hiding. Elected to the National Convention, he became a leader of the Mountain, and advocated radical reforms. After the king's death he was locked in a struggle with the

MAO ZEDONG (1893–1976)

Mao was born in the village of Shaoshan in the Hunan Province of China, the son of a peasant who had become an affluent farmer. He left the family farm at the age of 13 to study in Changsha, where he was introduced to Western ideas. After graduating from a teachers' training college there, he went to the University of Beijing, where he came under the influence of Li Dazhao. He took a leading part in the May Fourth Movement (student protests against the Paris Peace Conference's decision to hand over German gains in Shandong Province, formerly Chinese, to Japan), then became a Marxist and a founding member of the Chinese Communist Party (1921).

During the first Communist alliance with the Nationalist Party (Jul 1921), he worked in the Kuomintang Executive Bureau in Shanghai. Between 1924–25 he concentrated on political work among the peasants of his native province, and advocated a rural revolution, creating a soviet in Jiangxi Province in 1928. After the break with the Nationalists in 1927, the Communists were driven from the cities; so with the assistance of Zhu De he evolved the guerrilla tactics of the 'people's war'. In 1934 the Nationalist government was at last able to destroy the Jiangxi Soviet, and in the subsequent Long March the Communist forces retreated to Shanxi to set up a new base.

In 1936, under the increasing threat of Japanese invasion, the Nationalists renewed their alliance with the Communists. Mao then restored and vastly increased the political and military power of his Party. His claim to share in the government led to civil war; and by employing rural-based guerrilla warfare (his slogan being 'political power grows through the barrel of a gun') the regime of Jiang Jieshi was ousted from the Chinese mainland. The new People's Republic of China was proclaimed (1 Oct 1949) with Mao as both Chairman of the Chinese Communist Party and President of the Republic.

Mao's ideas were set out in *New Democracy* (1940). At first he followed the Soviet model of economic development and social change. The Party was organized along strict centralist, hierarchical lines, and increasingly became a vehicle for personal dictatorship. In domestic terms he pursued a radical and far-reaching attempt to transform traditional Chinese society and its economy, using thought reform, indoctrination, and the psychological transformation of the masses. Then, in 1958, he launched his 'Great Leap Forward', which encouraged the rapid advancement of industrial and agricultural industry, harnessing surplus rural labour organized into huge communes. The failure of the Great Leap lost him most of his influence, but by 1965, with China's armed forces securely in the hands of his ally Lin Biao, he launched the Cultural Revolution; the Great Leap strategy was revived (with caution) when the left wing was victorious in the ensuing political struggles (1965–71). Mao's ideas were popularized during the Cultural Revolution by 'The Little Red Book' or *Mao Zedong on People's War* (1967).

During his final years he was beset by deteriorating health. His political grip weakened, and he died in Beijing after a prolonged illness. Following his death, his third wife (whom he married in 1939), the politician and actress Jiang Qing made an unsuccessful attempt to seize power and was arrested and imprisoned with three others – the 'Gang of Four'. A strong reaction set in against the excessive collectivism and egalitarianism which had emerged. Nonetheless, Mao's anti-Stalinist emphasis on rural industry and on local initiative was retained and developed by his successors. Since his death, however, his use of the masses for political purposes, his economic reforms, and his conception of political power have been increasingly criticized inside and outside China.
>> Jiang Jieshi; Jiang Qing; Li Dazhao; Zhu De

Girondins, and was fatally stabbed in his bath by a Girondin supporter, Charlotte Corday; thereafter he was hailed as a martyr. >> Corday

Maratti, Carlo [ma**rah**tee] (1625–1713) Painter, born in Camerano, Italy. He studied in Rome, and his first work attracted many commissions for altarpieces, including 'The Virgin with SS Charles and Ignatius' (c.1685, S Maria in Vallicella, Rome). A leader of the 17th-c Baroque school, he also painted many notable canvasses and frescoes in Rome, and became a noted portraitist.

Marc, Franz (1880–1916) Artist, born in Munich, Germany. He studied in Munich, Italy, and France, and with Kandinsky founded *Der Blaue Reiter* (The Blue Rider) Expressionist group in Munich in 1911. Most of his paintings were of animals, such as the famous 'Tower of the Blue Horses' (1911, Walker Art Center, Minneapolis), portrayed in forceful colours. >> Macke; Kandinsky; Klee

Marcantonio [mah(r)kan**toh**nioh], in full **Marcantonio Raimondi** (1480–1534) Engraver, born in Bologna, Italy. At first a goldsmith, he moved to Rome in 1510 and became an engraver of other artists' works, especially those of Raphael and Michelangelo. >> Michelangelo; Raphael

Marceau, Marcel [mah(r)**soh**] (1923–) Mime artist, born in Strasbourg, France. He studied at the Ecole des Beaux-Arts in Paris, and with Etienne Decroux. In 1948 he founded the Compagnie de Mime Marcel Marceau, developing the art of mime, becoming himself the leading exponent. His white-faced character, Bip, is famous from his appearances on stage and television throughout the world, and among the many original performances he has devised are the mime-drama *Don Juan* (1964), and the ballet *Candide* (1971). He has also created about 100 pantomimes, such as *The Creation of the World*. In 1978 he became head of the Ecole de Mimodrame Marcel Marceau. >> Decroux

Marcel, Gabriel (Honoré) [mah(r)**sel**] (1889–1973) Existentialist philosopher and playwright, born in Paris. He studied philosophy at the Sorbonne, but made his living as a freelance writer, teacher, editor, and critic. In 1929 he became a Catholic, and came reluctantly to accept the label 'Christian existentialist', partly in order to contrast his views with those of Sartre. His philosophical works tend to have a personal, meditative character, as in *Journal métaphysique* (1927). His plays include *Un Homme de Dieu* (1925, A Man of God) and *La Dimension Florestan* (1956, The Florestan Dimension). >> Sartre

Marcello, Benedetto [mah(r)**che**loh] (1686–1739) Composer, born in Venice, Italy. He was a judge of the Venetian Republic and a member of the Council of Forty, and afterwards held offices at Pola and Brescia. As a composer he is noted for his *Estro poetico armonico* (1724–7), an eight-volume collection of settings for 50 of the Psalms of David, his oratorio *Le quattro stagioni* (1731, The Four Seasons), and his keyboard and instrumental sonatas. He wrote the satirical *Il teatro alla moda* (1720).

Marcellus, Marcus Claudius [mah(r)**sel**us] (c. 268–208 BC) Roman general of the time of the Second Punic War. Nicknamed the 'Sword of Rome', his main exploits were the defeat of the Insubrian Gauls (222 BC) and the capture of Syracuse (212 BC)

Marcellus, Marcus Claudius [mah(r)**sel**us] (42–23 BC) Nephew of the Emperor Augustus by his sister Octavia, and his first intended successor. His early death was widely regarded as a national calamity

March, Francis (Andrew) (1825–1911) Philologist, born in Millbury, MA. Educated at Amherst College, he studied law in New York City, was admitted to the bar in 1850, and became professor of English language and comparative philology at Lafayette College, Easton, PA (1857–1906). Regarded as the founder of comparative Anglo-Saxon linguistics, his publications included the monumental *Comparative Grammar of the Anglo-Saxon Language* (1870).

Marchais, Georges (René Louis) [mah(r)she] (1920–97) Political leader, born in La Hoguette, France. A former metal-worker, he joined the French Communist Party in 1947, becoming its general secretary in 1972. Under his leadership the Party joined the Socialist Party, but the union was severed in 1977. He unsuccessfully contested the 1981 presidential election.

Marchand, Jean Baptiste [mah(r)shã] (1863–1934) Soldier and explorer, born in Thoissey, France. He joined the army at 20, explored the Niger, W Sudan, and Ivory Coast, and caused a Franco-British crisis in 1898 by hoisting the tricolor at Fashoda on the White Nile. As a general he distinguished himself in World War 1.

Marciano, Rocky [mah(r)si**ah**noh], originally **Rocco Francis Marchegiano**, nickname **the Rock from Brockton** (1923–69) Heavyweight boxing champion, born in Brockton, MA. He first took up boxing as a serviceman in Britain during World War 2, turned professional in 1947, and made his name when he defeated the former world champion, Joe Louis, in 1951. He won the world title from Jersey Joe Walcott the following year, and when he retired in 1956 was the only undefeated world heavyweight champion, with a professional record of 49 bouts and 49 victories, including 43 by knockout. He died in an air-crash in Newton, IA. >> Louis, Joe

Marcion [**mah(r)**shuhn] (c.100–c.165) Christian Gnostic believer. A wealthy shipowner of Sinope in Pontus, in c.140 he went to Rome, where he founded the *Marcionites* in 144. He was expelled from the Church as a heretic the same year, but his Gnostic sect flourished during the 2nd-c.

Marconi, Guglielmo [mah(r)**koh**nee] (1874–1937) Physicist and inventor, born in Bologna, Italy. He studied at the Technical Institute of Livorno, and started experimenting with a device to convert electromagnetic waves into electricity. His first successful experiments in wireless telegraphy were made at Bologna in 1895, and in 1899 he erected a wireless station at La Spezia, and formed the Marconi Telegraph Co in London. In 1898 he transmitted signals across the English Channel, and in 1901 across the Atlantic. He later developed short-wave radio equipment, and established a worldwide radio telegraph network for the British government. He shared the 1909 Nobel Prize for Physics. >> Popov; RR1122

Marco Polo >> **Polo, Marco**

Marcos, Ferdinand (Edralin) [**mah(r)**kos] (1917–89) Philippines statesman and president (1965–86), born in Ilocos Norte, Philippines. He trained as a lawyer, and as a politician obtained considerable US support as an anti-Commu-

nist. His regime as president was marked by increasing repression, misuse of foreign financial aid, and political murders (notably the assassination of Benigno Aquino in 1983). He declared martial law in 1972, but was overthrown in 1986 by a popular front led by Corazon Aquino. He went into exile in Hawaii, where he, and his wife **Imelda** (1930–   ), fought against demands from US courts investigating charges of financial mismanagement and corruption. His body was returned to the Philippines for burial in 1993, and soon afterwards Imelda was convicted of corruption and sentenced to 18 years imprisonment. She was released on bail and appealed against her sentence. Still commanding a great deal of popular support, she was re-elected to congress for Leyte province in 1996. >> Aquino; RR1081

Marcus Aurelius Antoninus (121–180) >> **Aurelius**

Marcus Aurelius Antoninus (188–217) >> **Caracalla**

Marcuse, Herbert [mah(r)**kooz**uh] (1898–1979) Marxist philosopher, born in Berlin. He studied at Berlin and Freiburg, and became an influential figure in the Frankfurt School. He fled to Geneva in 1933, and after World War 2 moved to the USA, working in intelligence. He later held posts at Columbia (1951), Harvard (1952), Brandeis (1954), and California, San Diego (1965–76). His books include *Reason and Revolution* (1941) and *Eros and Civilization* (1955).

Marden, Brice (1938–   ) Painter, born in Bronxville, NY. He studied in Boston and Yale, and by 1965 was producing uniformly coloured canvases of horizontal and vertical formats. From 1968 he made two- and three-panel canvases, each of contrasting monochromatic colour. His paintings of the 1980s involved crossing diagonal and vertical lines.

Mare, Walter de la >> **de la Mare, Walter**

Marenzio, Luca [ma**ren**zioh] (1553–99) Composer, born near Brescia, Republic of Venice (modern Italy). He was probably a choirboy at Brescia before becoming a prolific writer of madrigals. He was in service with Cardinal Luigi d'Este of Rome (1578–86), then worked in Florence and Poland, before becoming a musician at the papal court in Rome.

Marey, Etienne Jules [maray] (1830–1903) Physiologist, born in Beaune, France. Professor at the Collège de France (from 1868), he pioneered scientific cinematography with his studies of animal movement (1887–1900). He invented a number of improvements in camera design, and succeeded in reducing exposure time to the region of 1/25 000 of a second for the purpose of photographing the flight of insects.

Margaret (of Scotland), St (c. 1046–93) Scottish queen, born in Hungary. She moved to England, but after the Norman Conquest fled to Scotland with her younger brother, Edgar the Ætheling. She married the Scottish king, Malcolm Canmore, and did much to civilize the realm, and to assimilate the old Celtic Church to the rest of Christendom. She was canonized in 1250. Feast day 16 November or 19 June. >> Edgar the Ætheling; Malcolm III; RR1095

Margaret (Rose), Princess (1930–   ) British princess, born at Glamis Castle, Angus, E Scotland, UK, the second daughter of George VI and sister of Elizabeth II. In 1955, when she was third in succession to the throne, she denied rumours of her possible marriage to **Group-Captain Peter Townsend** (a divorcé), amid a great deal of publicity and concern that a constitutional crisis could be precipitated by such a marriage. In 1960 she married Antony Armstrong-Jones (divorced, 1978), who was created Viscount Linley and Earl of Snowdon in 1961. The former title devolved upon their son, **David Albert Charles** (1961–   ), who married Serena Alleyne Stanhope in 1993. They also have a daughter, **Sarah Frances Elizabeth** (1964–   ), who married Daniel Chatto in 1994, and they have a son, **Samuel David Benedict Chatto** (1996–   ). >> Elizabeth II; George VI; Snowdon

Margaret of Angoulême [āgoolem], also known as **Margaret of Navarre** (1492–1549) Queen of Navarre, born in Angoulême, France. The sister of Francis I of France, she married first the **Duke of Alençon** (d.1525) and then, in 1527, **Henry d'Albret** (titular king of Navarre). With a strong interest in Renaissance learning, she was much influenced by Erasmus and the religious reformers of the Meaux circle, who looked to her for patronage and protection. She encouraged agriculture, learning, and the arts, and her court was the most intellectual in Europe. The patron of men of letters, including the heretical poet Clément Marot, she was a prolific writer of long devotional poems, dramas, secular poems, and the celebrated *Heptaméron* (published posthumously, 1558–9), a collection of stories on the theme of love. >> Francis I; Erasmus; Marot

Margaret of Anjou [āzhoo] (1430–82) Queen of England, probably born in Pont-à-Mousson, France. The daughter of René of Anjou, she was married to Henry VI of England in 1445. Owing to his mental weakness she was in effect sovereign, and the war of 1449, in which Normandy was lost, was laid by the English to her charge. In the Wars of the Roses, after a brave struggle of nearly 20 years, she was finally defeated at Tewkesbury (1471), and imprisoned for four years in the Tower, until ransomed by Louis XI. She then retired to France, where she died in poverty. >> Henry VI (of England);York, Richard, 3rd Duke of

Margaret of Navarre >> **Margaret of Angoulême**

Margaret Tudor (1489–1541) Queen of Scotland, born in London, England, UK, the eldest daughter of Henry VII. She became the wife of James IV of Scotland (1503), and the mother of James V, for whom she acted as regent. After James IV's death in 1513 she married twice again, to the Earl of Angus (1514), and Lord Methven (1527). She was much involved in the political intrigues between the pro-French and pro-English factions in Scotland. Her great-grandson was James VI of Scotland and I of England. >> RR1095

Margareta or **Margaret** (1353–1412) Queen of Denmark, Norway, and Sweden, born in Søborg, Denmark. She became Queen of Denmark in 1375, on the death of her father, Waldemar IV, without male heirs; by the death of her husband Haakon VI in 1380, she became ruler of Norway; and in 1388 she aided a rising of Swedish nobles against their king, Albert of Mecklenburg, and became Queen of Sweden. She had her infant cousin, Eric of Pomerania, crowned king of the three kingdoms at Kalmar in 1397, but remained the real ruler of Scandinavia until her death. >> RR1044

Marggraf, Andreas Sigismund [mah(r)graf] (1709–82) Chemist, born in Berlin. He worked with his father, an apothecary, in Berlin, studied in several German cities, and became director of the chemical laboratory at the German Academy of Sciences, Berlin (1754–60). He introduced the use of the microscope in chemical research, but is noted particularly for the discovery of sugar in sugar-beet (1747), and so prepared the way for the sugar-beet industry.

Margrethe II [mah(r)gretuh] (1940–) Queen of Denmark, born in Copenhagen, the daughter of Frederick IX, whom she succeeded in 1972. She studied at Copenhagen, Aarhus, Cambridge, Paris, and London, and qualified as an archaeologist. In 1967 she married a French diplomat, **comte Henri de Laborde de Monpezat**, now **Prince Henrik** of Denmark. Their children are the heir apparent, **Prince Frederik André Henrik Christian** (1968–), and **Prince Joachim Holger Waldemar Christian** (1969–). >> RR1044

Marguerite d'Angoulême >> **Margaret of Angoulême**

Maria de' Medici >> **Marie de Médicis**

Marianus Scotus [mariahnus skohtus] (1028–c.1083) Chronicler, born in Ireland. Banished from Ireland for breaking monastic rules, he entered a Benedictine monastery at Cologne (1052–8), was ordained priest in 1059, and became a recluse at Fulda and at Mainz. He wrote *Chronicon Universale*, the story of the world from the Creation to 1082. >> Florence of Worcester

Maria Theresa (1717–80) Archduchess of Austria, and Queen of Hungary and Bohemia (1740–80), born in Vienna, the daughter of Emperor Charles VI (ruled 1711–40). In 1736 she married **Francis, Duke of Lorraine**, and in 1740 succeeded her father in the hereditary Habsburg lands. Her claim, however, led to the War of the Austrian Succession, during which she lost Silesia to Prussia. She received the Hungarian crown (1741), and in 1745 her husband was elected Holy Roman Emperor. Although her foreign minister, Kaunitz, tried to isolate Prussia by diplomatic means, military conflict was renewed in the Seven Years' War, and by 1763 she was finally forced to recognize the status quo of 1756. In her later years she strove to maintain international peace, and reluctantly accepted the partition of Poland (1772). Of her 10 surviving children, the eldest son succeeded her as Joseph II. >> Joseph II; Kaunitz

Marie, Pierre (1853–1940) Neurologist, born in Paris. He studied under Jean Charcot at the Salpêtrière Hospital, Paris (1885) and is noted for his contribution to the modern science of endocrinology. He served as professor of neurology at the University of Paris (1907–25). >> Charcot, Jean

Marie Antoinette (Josèphe Jeanne) (1755–93) Queen of France, born in Vienna, the daughter of Maria Theresa and Francis I. She was married to the Dauphin, afterwards Louis XVI (1770), to strengthen the Franco-Austrian alliance, and exerted a growing influence over him. Capricious and frivolous, she aroused criticism by her extravagance, disregard for conventions, devotion to the interests of Austria, and opposition to reform. From the outbreak of the French Revolution, she resisted the advice of constitutional monarchists (eg Mirabeau), and helped to alienate the monarchy from the people. In 1791 she and Louis tried to escape from the Tuileries to her native Austria, but were apprehended at Varennes and imprisoned in Paris. After the king's execution, she was arraigned before the Tribunal and guillotined. >> Louis XVI; Maria Theresa; Mirabeau

Marie de France (12th-c) Poet, born in Normandy, France. She spent much of her life in England, where she wrote several verse narratives based on Celtic stories. Her *Lais*, dedicated to 'a noble king' (probably Henry II), were a landmark in French literature.

Marie de Médicis [maydeesees], Ital **Maria de' Medici** [maydichee] (1573–1642) Queen consort of Henry IV of France, born in Florence, Italy, the daughter of Francesco de' Medici, Grand Duke of Tuscany. She married Henry in 1600, following his divorce from his first wife Margaret, and gave birth to a son (later Louis XIII) in 1601. After her husband's death (1610) she acted as regent, but her capricious behaviour and dependence on favourites led to her confinement in Blois when Louis assumed royal power in 1617. She continued to intrigue against Louis and her former protégé, Richelieu, who had become the king's adviser. She was banished to Compiègne, but escaped to Brussels (1631). Her last years were spent in poverty. >> Henry IV (of France); Louis XIII; Sully

Marie Louise (1791–1847) Empress of France, born in Vienna, the daughter of the Holy Roman Emperor, Francis II. She married Napoleon in 1810 (after his divorce from Joséphine), and in 1811 bore him a son, who was created King of Rome and who became Napoleon II. On Napoleon's abdication she returned to Austria. By the Treaty of Fontainebleau (1814) she was awarded the Duchies of Para, Piacenza, and Guastalla in Italy. >> Francis II; Metternich; Napoleon I; Napoleon II; Schwarzenberg

Marin, John [marin] (1870–1953) Artist, born in Rutherford, NY. He trained and worked as an architect before studying art at Pennsylvania Academy, Philadelphia, and the Art Students League of New York. After travelling in Europe (1905–10), he was involved in the Stieglitz circle, an avant-garde movement. Well known for his water-colours and etchings in an extremely individual style, his early work was in the manner of Whistler, but his later works are adapted from Cubist concepts. >> Whistler, James McNeill

Marin, Maguy [mari] (1951–) Dancer and choreographer, born in Toulouse, France. Having studied dance as a child, she secured her first job with the Strasbourg Opera Ballet before continuing to train at the Mudra school in Brussels. She joined Maurice Béjart's Ballet of the 20th Century in the mid-1970s. In 1978 she founded her own troupe, which in 1981 became the resident company of Creteil, a Paris suburb. She has choreographed for several major European companies, including the Paris Opéra Ballet, Dutch National Ballet and, most notably, a 1985 version of *Cinderella* for Lyon Opéra Ballet. >> Béjart

Marina, Princess >> **Kent, George, Duke of**

Marinetti, Filippo (Tommaso) Emilio [marinetee] (1876–1944) Italian writer, born in Alexandria, Egypt. He studied in Paris and Genoa, then worked as a journalist in Milan. He published the original Futurist manifesto in *Figaro* in 1909. In his writings he glorified war, the machine age, speed and 'dynamism', and condemned all traditional forms of literature and art. In 1919 he became a Fascist. His publications include *Le futurisme* (1911) and *Teatro sintetico futurista* (1916, Synthetic Futurist Theatre). >> Nevinson; Severini

Marini, Marino [mareenee] (1901–80) Sculptor and painter, born in Pistoia, Italy. He studied in Florence, and taught at the Scuola d'Arte di Villa Reale, Monza (1929–40), before moving to Milan, where he was professor at Brera Academy (1940–70). His work, mainly in bronze, was figurative, his best-known theme being the horse and rider. He liked to combine different techniques, including colour, as in 'Dancer' (1949–54). He also executed portraits of Stravinsky, Chagall, Henry Miller, and others.

Marino, Dan [mareenoh] (1961–) Player of American football, born in Pittsburgh, PA. An outstanding quarterback with the Miami Dolphins, in the 1984 season he gained 5084 yards passing, to create a National Football League record. He completed a record 29 passes in the 1985 Super Bowl, and in 1986 established a record for the most passes completed in a season, 378.

Mario, Giovanni Matteo (1810–83) Tenor, born in Cagliari, Italy. An officer in the Piedmontese Guard, he left the army in 1836 and moved to Paris, where he studied voice at the Paris Conservatory. He made his debut in 1838 in *Robert le diable*, and became immediately successful. There followed a long series of operatic triumphs in Paris, London, St Petersburg, and America, and he married the singer **Giulia Grisi** (1811–69). After his retirement he lost his fortune through disastrous speculations.

Marion, Francis (c. 1732–95) US soldier, born in Berkeley Co, SC. A planter, he fought against the Cherokees in 1759 and 1761, and led 'irregulars' in several engagements during the Revolution. He commanded the remaining resistance in South Carolina after the colonials' loss at Camden, and used guerrilla tactics to strike at British and Loyalist forces. After the war, he served in the South Carolina Senate, and commanded Fort Johnson in Charleston harbour (1784–90).

Mariotte, Edme (1620–84) Physicist and priest, born in Dijon, France. One of the earliest members of the Academy of Sciences, he wrote on percussion, air and its pressure, the movements of fluid bodies and of pendulums, and colours. He coined the word *barometer* in his *Discours de la nature de l'air* (1676) in which he independently stated Boyle's law of 1662 (long known in France as *Mariotte's law*). >> Boyle, Robert

Marisol, (Escobar) [marisol] (1930–) Sculptor, painter, and graphic artist, born in Paris. Of Venezuelan parents, she studied in Paris (1949), settled in New York City (1950), and studied at the Art Students League (1950), the New School (1951–4), and the Hans Hofmann School (1951–4). She is known for her witty satirical carvings and assemblages in wood, plaster, paint, and other materials, such as 'Woman and Dog' (1964).

Maritain, Jacques [mareetĩ] (1882–1973) Philosopher and diplomat, born in Paris. He studied in Paris and Heidelberg, and converted to Catholicism in 1906. He was professor at the Institut Catholique in Paris (1914–40), and taught mainly in North America, at Toronto, Columbia, Chicago, and Princeton universities (1948–60). As French ambassador to the Vatican (1945–8), he later became a strong opponent of the Vatican Council and the neo-Modernist movement. His main works include *Les Degrés du savoir* (1932, The Degree of Knowledge), *Art et scolastique* (1920, Art and Scholasticism), and *La Philosophie morale* (1960, Moral Philosophy).

Marius, Gaius (c. 157–86 BC) Roman general and politician, born in Arpinum. Of comparatively humble extraction, his military talents and ruthless ambition enabled him to rise to the very top in Rome, where he held an unprecedented number of consulships (seven), and married into the heart of the aristocracy – the Julian gens. Famous in his lifetime for his victories over Jugurtha (105 BC), the Teutones (102 BC), and the Cimbri (101 BC), it was by his army reforms that he made his greatest impact on the state. His final years were dominated by his rivalry with Sulla. The violence with which he recaptured Rome for Cinna from the forces backing Sulla (87 BC) permanently damaged his reputation. >> Cinna; Sertorius; Sulla

Marius, Simon (1573–1624) Astronomer, born in Gunzenhausen, Germany. A pupil of Tycho Brahe, in 1609 he claimed to have discovered the four satellites of Jupiter independently of Galileo. He named them Io, Europa, Ganymede, and Callisto, but other astronomers merely numbered them, as they did not recognize his claim to discovery. He was one of the earliest users of a telescope, and the first to observe by this means the Andromeda nebula (1612). >> Brahe, Tycho; Galileo

Marivaux, Pierre (Carlet de Chamblain de) [mareevoh] (1688–1763) Playwright and novelist, born in Paris. Trained as a lawyer, he published his first play at the age of 20. He wrote several comedies, of which his best is *Le Jeu de l'amour et du hasard* (1730, The Game of Love and Chance). His best-known novel, *La Vie de Marianne* (1731–41, The Life of Marianne) was never finished, and is marked by an affected style which has been dubbed *Marivaudage*. Although he became director of the Académie Française in 1759, his work was not fully appreciated until after his death.

Mark, St, also called **John Mark** (fl. 1st-c) Christian disciple. He is described in the New Testament as 'John whose surname was Mark' (*Acts* 12.12, 25), and a helper of the apostles Barnabas and Paul during their first missionary journey. He is often considered the Mark who is accredited in 2nd-c traditions with the writing of the second Gospel, described by Papias (early 2nd-c bishop in Asia Minor) as the 'interpreter of Peter'. Feast day 25 April.

Mark Antony >> **Antonius, Marcus**

Markard, Anna >> **Jooss, Kurt**

Markievicz, Constance (Georgine), Countess [mah(r)-**kyay**vich], née **Gore-Booth** (1868–1927) Irish nationalist, born in London, England. UK. She married the Polish Count Casimir Markievicz, fought in the Easter Rising (1916), and was sentenced to death, but reprieved. Elected the first British woman MP in 1918, she did not take her seat, but was a member of the Dáil from 1923.

Markov, Andrey Andreyevich [mah(r)kof] (1856–1922) Mathematician, born in Ryazan, Russia. He studied at St Petersburg, where he became professor (1893–1905), before going into self-imposed exile in the town of Zaraisk. A student of Pafnuty Chebyshev, he worked on number theory and probability theory. His name is best known for the concept of the *Markov chain*, a series of events in which the probability of a given event occurring depends only on the immediately previous event. This has since found many applications in physics, biology, and linguistics. >> **Chebyshev**

Markova, Dame Alicia [mah(r)**koh**va], originally **Lilian Alicia Marks** (1910–   ) Prima ballerina, born in London, England, UK. She danced with Ballets Russes in 1924, and on her return to Britain appeared for the Camargo Society and the Vic-Wells Ballet. There followed a period of partnership with Anton Dolin which led to the establishment of the Markova–Dolin Company in 1935. They made guest appearances together around the world, and were famed for their interpretation of *Giselle*. She was created a dame in 1963, became a director of the Metropolitan Opera Ballet (1963–9), and took up an appointment as professor of ballet and the performing arts at the University of Cincinnati in 1970. In 1986 she became president of the London Festival Ballet. >> **Dolin**

Markowitz, Harry M [mah(r)kovits] (1927–   ) Economist, born in Chicago, IL. He taught at Los Angeles, Pennsylvania, and Rutgers universities, and at Baruch College, New York City (from 1982). He was also chairman of the board at Consolidated Analysis Centers (1963–8) and president of Arbitrage Management Co (1969–72). He shared the 1990 Nobel Prize for Economics for developing the theory of the rational behaviour involved in portfolio selection under uncertainty.

Marks (of Broughton), Simon Marks, Baron (1888–1964) Businessman, born in Leeds, West Yorkshire, N England, UK. In 1907 he inherited the 60 Marks and Spencer penny bazaars which his father **Michael Marks**, with Thomas Spencer, had built up from 1884. In collaboration with Israel (later Lord) Seiff, he developed Marks and Spencer, with its pioneering policy of 'Don't ask the price – it's a penny', into a major retail chain. 'Marks and Sparks' used their considerable purchasing power to encourage British clothing manufacturers to achieve demanding standards, and their 'St Michael' brand label became a guarantee of high quality at a reasonable price. >> **Sieff**

Marlborough, John Churchill, 1st Duke of [mah(r)lbruh] (1650–1722) English general, born in Ashe, Devon, SW England, UK. He was commissioned in the Guards (1667), and further promoted when in 1678 he married **Sarah Jennings**, an attendant of Princess Anne. On James II's accession (1685), he was elevated to an English barony and given the rank of general. He took a leading part in quelling Monmouth's rebellion at Sedgemoor, but deserted to the Prince of Orange in 1688, serving the Protestant cause in campaigns in Ireland and Flanders. Under Queen Anne he was appointed supreme commander of the British forces in the War of the Spanish Succession, and he became captain-general of the Allied armies. His military flair and organization skils resulted in several great victories – Donauwörth and Blenheim (1704), Ramillies (1706), Oudenaarde and the capture of Lille (1708) – for which he was richly rewarded with Blenheim Palace and a dukedom. Forced by political interests to align himself with the Whig war party (1708), his influence waned, and when his wife fell from royal favour the Tories pressed for his downfall. He was dismissed on charges of embezzling, and left England for continental Europe (1712), returning after George's accession (1714). >> **Anne; Churchill, Sarah; Monmouth; Vendôme; Villars; William III**

Marley, Bob, popular name of **Robert Nesta Marley** (1945–81) Singer, guitarist, and composer of reggae music, born near Kingston, Jamaica. He made his first record at the age of 19, and in 1965 formed the vocal trio, The Wailers, with Peter Tosh and Bunny Livingstone. Their music developed political themes with an artless lyricism and infectious rhythm, and in the 1970s Marley brought it around the world. He was a disciple of Rastafarianism, and a charismatic spokesman not only for his religion but also his culture and generation. His albums include *Catch a Fire* (1972), and *Uprising* (1980), and his most famous songs include 'No Woman, No Cry' and 'I Shot the Sheriff'.

Marlowe, Christopher (1564–93) Playwright, born in Canterbury, Kent, SE England, UK. He studied there and at Cambridge, and was the most significant of Shakespeare's predecessors in English drama. His *Tamburlaine the Great* (c.1587) shows his discovery of the strength and variety of blank verse, and this was followed by *The Jew of Malta* (c.1590), *The Tragical History of Dr Faustus* (c.1592), partly written by others, and *Edward II* (c.1592). He wrote several translations and poems, such as the unfinished *Hero and Leander*, and much of his other work has been handed down in fragments. He led an irregular life, and was on the point of being arrested for disseminating atheistic opinions when he was fatally stabbed, under mysterious circumstances, apparently in a tavern brawl in Deptford; research suggests he was murdered by an agent of Walsingham, for reasons unknown. >> **Watson, Thomas**

Marlowe, Hugh >> **Higgins, Jack**

Marot, Clément [maroh] (c.1497–1544) Poet, born in Cahors, France. He entered the service of Margaret of Angoulême, was wounded at the Battle of Pavia in 1525, and was then imprisoned briefly on a charge of heresy. He made many enemies with his witty satires, and in 1535 fled first to Navarre, and later to the court of the Duchess of Ferrara. He returned to Paris in 1536, and began to translate the Psalms into French, but he was accused of heresy by the Sorbonne, and again had to flee in 1543. One of the celebrated poets of the French Renaissance, his work included elegies, epistles, rondeaux, ballads, sonnets, madrigals, epigrams, and nonsense verses.

Marquand, J(ohn) P(hillips) [mah(r)**kwond**] (1893–1960) Novelist, born in Wilmingon, DE. He studied at Harvard, served with the military, became a war correspondent, and later wrote advertising copy. For many years he was a writer of popular stories for magazines, featuring the Japanese detective Mr Moto; but he is best known for a series of novels which gently satirized affluent middle-class American life, including *The Late George Apley* (1937), *Wickford Point* (1939), and *Point of No Return* (1949).

Marquet, (Pierre) Albert [mah(r)kay] (1875–1947) Artist, born in Bordeaux, France. He studied under Gustave Moreau, and was one of the original Fauves. After initial hardships, he became primarily an Impressionist landscape painter and travelled widely, painting many pictures of Le Havre, Algiers, and the Seine, such as his 'Pont neuf'. >> **Matisse; Moreau, Gustave; Vlaminck**

Marquette, Jacques [mah(r)ket] (1637–75) Jesuit missionary and explorer, born in Laon, France. He was sent in 1666 to North America, where he brought Christianity to the Ottawa Indians around L Superior. He also went on the expedition which discovered and explored the Mississippi (1673).

Márquez, Felipe González >> **González, Felipe Márquez**

Márquez, Gabriel García [mah(r)kez] (1928–) Novelist, born in Aracataca, Colombia. He studied law and journalism at Bogotá and Cartagena, and began writing while working as a journalist in Europe (1950–65), publishing his first novel, *La hojarasca* (trans *Leaf Storm*) in 1955. His masterpiece is *Cien años de soledad* (1967, *One Hundred Years of Solitude*). Later works include *El amor en los tiempos del cólera* (1985, *Love in a Time of Cholera*), *Of Love and Other Demons* (1995), and *Noticia de un secuestro* (1996). He received the Nobel Prize for Literature in 1982.

Marquis, Don(ald Robert Perry) [mah(r)kwis] (1878–1937) Novelist, playwright, and poet, born in Walnut, IL. He studied at Knox College, Galesburg, IL, and became a well-known literary journalist in New York City, writing for *The Sun*. He achieved fame as a comic writer in his column 'The Sun Dial' with the popular *archy and mehitabel* (1927), and *archys life of mehitabel* (1933), which follow the fortunes of Archy the cockroach who cannot reach the typewriter's shift key (hence the lower-case titles), and Mehitabel, an alley cat. Among his other works are poetry, prose, and plays, including *The Old Soak* (1916, dramatized 1926).

Marriner, Sir Neville (1924–) Conductor, born in Lincoln, Lincolnshire, EC England, UK. He studied at the Royal College of Music and the Paris Conservatory, played violin with the London Philharmonia and the London Symphony Orchestra, then turned to conducting. He has held posts with the Los Angeles Chamber Orchestra (1968–77), the Minnesota Orchestra (1979–86), and the Stuttgart Radio Symphony Orchestra (1984–9). Since 1956 he has been founder-director of the Academy of St Martin-in-the-Fields chamber ensemble. He was knighted in 1985.

Marrison, Warren (1896–1980) US electrical engineer. He was employed by Bell Telecommunications Laboratories to investigate the use of quartz crystals in long-distance telephone and radio transmissions (c.1923), and was involved in timed observations of the total eclipse of the Sun in 1925. He combined his experiences in 1929, producing the first quartz-controlled electric clock.

Marryat, Frederick (1792–1848) Naval officer and novelist, born in London, England, UK. After a life at sea, including commanding the *Ariadne* (1828), he retired and wrote novels based on his experiences, of which some of the best known are *Frank Mildmay* (1829), *Peter Simple* (1833), and *Mr Midshipman Easy* (1836). He toured the USA and wrote other books before settling in Langham, Norfolk, where he spent his days farming and writing stories for children. His best-known work is *The Children of the New Forest* (1847).

Marsalis, Wynton [mah(r)sahlis] (1961–) Trumpeter and composer, born in New Orleans, LA. At 14 he performed Haydn's trumpet concerto with the New Orleans Philharmonic Orchestra – the first of many engagements as a classical virtuoso – and went on to study at the Berkshire Music Center, MA, and the Juilliard School, New York City. Recruited in 1980 to Art Blakey's Jazz Messengers (along with his brother, **Branford** (1960–), on tenor and soprano saxophones), he left in 1982 to lead the first of a succession of small groups. He won Grammy awards in 1984 for both a jazz and a classical recording, and in 1997 was awarded the Pulitzer Prize for Music. >> Blakey

Marsden, Samuel (1764–1838) Clergyman, magistrate, and farmer, born in Farsley, West Yorkshire, N England, UK. He arrived in New South Wales as assistant chaplain in 1794, and farmed at Parramatta, where he was also appointed magistrate. His harsh measures towards Irish convicts in 1800 earned him the title of 'the flogging parson'. A pioneer breeder of sheep for wool production, in 1807 he took the first commercial consignment of Australian wool to England. He made seven missionary journeys to New Zealand, and conducted the first Christian service in that country at Rangihoua, Bay of Islands, in 1814.

Marsh, James (1789–1846) British chemist. An expert on poisons, he worked at the Royal Arsenal, Woolwich, and assisted Michael Faraday at the Military Academy. He invented the standard test for arsenic, which has been given his name. >> Faraday

Marsh, Dame Ngaio (Edith) [niyoh] (1899–1982) Detective-story writer, born in Christchurch, New Zealand. She moved to England, UK in 1928, and published her first novel, *A Man Lay Dead* (1934). It was followed by a series of novels and short stories featuring Superintendent Roderick Alleyn of Scotland Yard. These include *Vintage Murder* (1937), *Opening Night* (1951), and *Black as He's Painted* (1974). She was made a dame in 1948.

Marsh, O(thniel) C(harles) (1831–99) Palaeontologist, born in Lockport, NY. He studied at Yale and in Germany, then taught at Yale (1866–99) and became chief vertebrate palaeontologist (1882–92) of the US Geological Survey. He discovered more than 1000 fossil vertebrates, amassing extensive collections for Yale's Peabody Museum. His classification of extinct vertebrates helped confirm Darwinian theories of evolution, and occasioned a fierce rivalry with Edward Drinker Cope. He described 80 new species of dinosaurs, and the first fossil serpents and flying reptiles found in W America. He also established the reptilian origin of birds, the evolution of the horse, and the presence of early primates in North America. >> Cope; Darwin, Charles

Marsh, Reginald (1898–1954) US painter, born in Paris. His parents were American artists who returned to America in 1900. He studied at Yale, became a cartoonist and illustrator for periodicals, and lived in New York City. Known for his water colours and egg tempera paintings of contemporary urban life, he combined the Baroque with a Realistic style, as seen in 'The Bowery' (1930) and 'Negroes on Rockaway Beach' (1934).

Marshal, William, 1st Earl of Pembroke (and Strigul) (c. 1146–1219) Knight, and regent of England (1216–19), a nephew of the Earl of Salisbury. He won a military reputation fighting the French, supported Henry II against Richard I, and went on a crusade to the Holy Land. Pardoned by Richard, he was made an earl, appointed a justiciar, and shared the marshalcy of England with his brother, **John**, until the latter's death gave him full office. He saw further fighting in Normandy (1196–9), supported the new king (John) but spent the years 1207–12 in Ireland, returning to become the king's chief adviser. After John's death in 1216, he was appointed regent for the nine-year-old Henry III, and as such concluded a peace treaty with the French. >> John; Henry II (of England); Henry III (of England); RR1095

Marshall, George C(atlett) (1880–1959) US soldier and statesman, born in Uniontown, PA. He studied at the Virginia Military Institute, and was commissioned in 1901. As chief-of-staff (1939–45) he directed the US army throughout World War 2. After two years in China as special representative of the president, he became secretary of state (1947–9), and originated the *Marshall Aid* plan for the post-war reconstruction of Europe. He was awarded the Nobel Peace Prize in 1953. >> Edward V

Marshall, John (1755–1835) Jurist, born in Germantown, VA. He studied law, but served in the Continental army in the American Revolution (1775–9). In 1788 he was elected to the Constitutional Convention, and in 1799 to Congress. He became Chief Justice of the USA (1801–35), during which time he dominated the Supreme Court, and established the US doctrine of judicial review.

Marshall, Sir John Hubert (1876–1958) Archaeologist and administrator, born in Chester, Cheshire, NWC England, UK. He studied Classics at Cambridge and excavated in Greece, before being appointed director-general of archaeology in India (1902–31). He reorganized the Indian Archaeological Survey, and worked at the city of Taxila in the Himalayan foothills (1913–33), and at the Buddhist religious centres of Sanchi and Sarnath. His excavations at Mohenjo-daro and Harappa in the Indus Valley in the 1920s revealed for the first time the antiquity of Indian civilization. He was knighted in 1914.

Marshall, Paule (1929–) Writer, born in New York City. Her parents emigrated from Barbados during World War 1, and she grew up in Brooklyn during the Depression. She graduated from Brooklyn College and worked for *Our World Magazine*. Her first novel, *Brown Girl, Brownstones* (1959), is regarded as a classic of African-American literature. Later books include *The Chosen Place* (1969), *The Timeless People* (1969), and *Praisesong for the Widow* (1983).

Marshall, Peter (1902–49) Presbyterian clergyman, born in Coatbridge, North Lanarkshire, C Scotland, UK. Educated at the mining college there, he served in the navy before being called to the ministry. He graduated from Columbia Theological Seminary, Decatur, GA, and served pastorates in the South before his appointment in 1937 to the historic New York Avenue Presbyterian Church in Washington, DC. In 1948 he became chaplain to the US Senate. Much in demand as a speaker, he also wrote *Mr Jones, Meet the Master* (1949), and after his premature death was the subject of a film, *A Man Called Peter*, based on his wife's biography of him.

Marshall, Thurgood (1908–93) Judge, born in Baltimore, MD. He studied at Lincoln University and Howard University Law School, then began work for the National Association for the Advancement of Colored People (1936), becoming head of its legal staff (1940). As an attorney he won a historic victory in the case of *Brown v. Board of Education of Topeka* (1954) which declared that racial segregation in public schools was unconstitutional. Further notable successes followed in cases concerning prejudice against African-Americans. He was nominated to the US Court of Appeals (1961), named solicitor general (1965), and became the first African-American member of the Supreme Court (1967–91). >> Warren, Earl

Marsilius of Padua [mah(r)**sil**ius] (c.1275–c.1342) Political theorist and philosopher, born in Padua, Italy. He was rector of the University of Paris from 1313, where he lectured on natural philosophy, engaged in medical research, and involved himself in Italian politics. In 1324 he completed *Defensor pacis*, a political treatise which argued against the temporal power of clergy and pope. When the authorship of the work became known, he was forced to flee Paris (1326). Excommunicated by Pope John XXII, he took refuge at the court of Louis of Bavaria in Munich.

Mars-Jones, Adam (1954–) Novelist and film critic, born in London, England, UK. He studied at Cambridge University, and became a columnist for *The Independent* in 1986. His novels include *The Darker Proof* (1987), *Monopolies of Loss* (1992), and *The Waters of Thirst* (1993).

Marston, John (1576–1634) Playwright and satirist, born in Wardington, Oxfordshire, SC England, UK. He studied at Oxford, and wrote several plays which were published between 1602 and 1607, notably *The Malcontent* (1604), and

Eastward Ho! (1605), a satirical comedy written in conjunction with Chapman and Jonson. In 1607 he gave up playwriting, took orders (1609), and held the living of Christ Church, Hampshire (1616–31). >> Chapman, George; Jonson

Martel, Charles >> **Charles Martel**

Martel, Sir Giffard Le Quesne [mah(r)**tel**] (1889–1958) British soldier. During World War 1 he aided in the development of the first tanks, and in 1925 was responsible for the construction of the first one-man tank. In 1940 he commanded the Royal Armoured Corps, and in 1943 headed the British military mission in Moscow.

Martel de Janville, comtesse de >> **Gyp**

Martin, Henry or **Harry** (1602–80) Parliamentary judge and regicide, born in Oxford, Oxfordshire, SC England, UK. He studied at Oxford, was a prominent member of the Long Parliament, but was expelled from it (1643–6) as an extremist. He fought in the parliamentary army, then returned to parliament, sat on Charles I's trial, and signed his death warrant. After the Restoration he was imprisoned at Chepstow Castle (1660) for the remainder of his life. >> Charles I (of England)

Martens, Conrad (1801–78) Landscape painter, born in London, England, UK. He studied in London, and in 1833 was appointed by the commander of HMS *Beagle*, Robert Fitzroy, as a topographer for the voyage with Charles Darwin from Rio de Janeiro to Valparaiso. In 1835 he arrived in Sydney, where he set up a studio and began teaching. His favourite subject was Sydney harbour, and a set of lithographs, 'Sketches of Sydney', was published in 1850–1. In 1863 he obtained a post in the parliamentary library, which he held for the rest of his life. >> Darwin, Charles; Fitzroy, Robert

Martens, Wilfried (1936–) Belgian statesman and prime minister (1979–81, 1981–92). He studied at Louvain University, and was adviser to two governments (1965 and 1966), before becoming minister for community problems (1968). He was president of the Dutch-speaking Social Christian Party (1972–9), when he became prime minister at the head of a coalition. He then continued in office, apart from a brief break in 1981, heading no fewer than six coalition governments.

Martial, in full **Marcus Valerius Martialis** (c.40–c.104) Latin poet and epigrammatist, born in Spain. He went to Rome in 64, and became a client of the influential Spanish house of the Senecas, through which he found a patron in Calpurnius Piso. He is remembered for his 12 books of epigrams, mainly satirical comments on contemporary events and society. >> Seneca

Martin, St (c.316–c.400) Patron saint of France, born in Sabaria, Pannonia. He studied at Pavia, travelled to Gaul, and founded the first monastery near Poitiers in c.360. He became famous for his sanctity and as a worker of miracles. He was drawn by force from his retreat in 371–2, and made Bishop of Tours, but chose to live in a new monastery which he founded at Marmoutier, near Tours. Feast day 11 (W) or 12 November (E).

Martin, Agnes (1912–) Painter, born in Maklin, Saskatchewan, Canada. After studying at Columbia University in the 1940s she started to paint in a style called 'biomorphic abstraction'. In 1959 she began painting the repetitive abstract grids of vertical and horizontal lines which have preoccupied her ever since. She held an exhibition at the Institute of Contemporary Art, Pennsylvania University, in 1973.

Martin, A(rcher) J(ohn) P(orter) (1910–) Biochemist, born in London, England, UK. He studied at Cambridge, and worked for the Wool Industry Research Association in Leeds (1938–46), the Medical Research Council (1948–59), the Abbotsbury Laboratories (1959–70), and the Wellcome Research Laboratories (1970–3). He later held university appointments at Sussex, Houston, and Lausanne. His work on nutrition led him to the study of protein structure, and the development of partition chromatography to separate and analyze proteins, for which he shared the 1952 Nobel Prize for Chemistry with his colleague, Richard Synge. From 1953 he worked on gas-liquid chromatography as another analytical technique. >> Synge

Martin, Frank [mah(r)tĩ] (1890–1974) Composer and pianist, born in Geneva, Switzerland. He studied at Geneva Conservatory, and in 1928 was appointed professor at the Jaques-Dalcroze Institute in Geneva. His works include the oratorios *Golgotha* and *In terra pax*, a Mass, and the cantata *Le Vin herbé*, based upon the legend of Tristan and Isolde, as well as incidental music and works for orchestra and chamber combinations.

Martin, Glenn L(uther) (1886–1955) Aircraft manufacturer, born in Macksburg, IA. He studied at Kansas Wesleyan University, Salina, built his first glider in California in 1905, and by 1909 had built and flown his first powered aircraft. In 1912 he flew his seaplane from near Los Angeles to Catalina I and back (32 mi), and in 1913 invented a bomb sight and a free-fall parachute. The production of the MB-1 bomber at his factory at Cleveland in 1918 established him as one of the leading military aircraft manufacturers in the USA. In 1929 he moved to Baltimore, producing such famous aircraft as the B-10 bomber and the China Clipper flying boat. During World War 2 his factory created the B-26 Marauder, Mariner, and Mars flying boats.

Martin, (Basil) Kingsley (1897–1969) Journalist, born in London, England, UK. He studied at Cambridge and Princeton, and taught at the London School of Economics (1923–7), after which he entered journalism, working on the *Manchester Guardian* (1927–31). As editor of the *New Statesman and Nation* (1932–62), he transformed it into a strongly self-assured weekly journal of Socialist opinion. Khrushchev and John Foster Dulles replied in its columns to an open letter it published from Bertrand Russell on the Cold War. >> Dulles, John Foster; Khrushchev; Russell, Bertrand

Martin, Paul [mah(r)tĩ] (1864–1942) Photographer, born in Herbenville, France. Employed as a wood-engraver, he was an amateur photographer who used a concealed camera to record working people in the streets of London and on holiday at the seaside (1888–98). His *London by Gaslight* (1896) was recognized by the Royal Photographic Society, and his records have been much used in this century to represent the realities of late-Victorian everyday life.

Martin, Pierre Emile [mah(r)tĩ] (1824–1915) Metallurgist, born in Bourges, France. In his father's iron and steel works, he devised an improved method of producing high-quality steel in an open-hearth furnace using the heat-regeneration process introduced by Siemens. The products of the Siemens–Martin process won a gold medal at the Paris Exhibition of 1867, and the open-hearth furnace became the major source of the world's steel. Martin spent his later years in poverty while others profited from his process, until in 1907 an international benefit fund restored his finances to a level of modest comfort. >> Siemens, William

Martin, Richard (1754–1834) Lawyer and humanitarian, born in Dublin. He studied at Cambridge, became an MP for Galway (1801–26), and in 1822 sponsored a bill to make the cruel treatment of cattle illegal, the first legislation of its kind. Through his efforts the Royal Society for the Prevention of Cruelty to Animals was formed.

Martin, Steve (1945–) Film actor, born in Waco, TX. As a

comedy writer for television he won an Emmy Award for *The Smothers Brothers Comedy Hour* (1968) and a nomination for *Van Dyke and Company* (1975). He made his film debut in *The Absent Minded Waiter* (1977), which received an Oscar nomination for best short film. An inspired performance of lunacy in *All Of Me* (1984) brought him a New York Film Critics' Best Actor Award. Later films include *Parenthood* (1989), *Housesitter* (1992), *Father of the Bride* and its sequel (1991, 1995), and *Sergeant Bilko* (1996).

Martin, Violet Florence, pseudonym **Martin Ross** (1862–1915) Writer, born in Co Galway, Ireland. She is known chiefly for a series of novels written in collaboration with her cousin Edith Somerville, such as *An Irish Cousin* (1889). She also wrote travel books about the Irish countryside and two autobiographical works, *Some Irish Yesterdays* (1906) and *Strayaways* (1920). >> Somerville, Edith

Martín de Porres, St [pohres] (1579–1639) South American saint, who spent his entire life in the Dominican Order in Lima, Peru, ministering to the sick and poor. He was also noted for his way with animals. Beatified in 1837, he was canonized in 1962. He is the patron saint of social justice. Feast day 3 November.

Martin du Gard, Roger [mah(r)tĩ dü gah(r)] (1881–1958) Novelist, born in Neuilly, France. He is best known for his eight-novel series, *Les Thibault* (1922–40), dealing with family life during the first decades of the present century. Author also of several plays, he was awarded the Nobel Prize for Literature in 1937.

Martineau, Harriet [mah(r)tinoh] (1802–76) Writer, born in Norwich, Norfolk, E England, UK. In 1821 she began writing articles and short stories then, when obliged her to earn her living, she became a successful social, economic, and historical writer, with titles including *Illustrations of Political Economy* (25 vols, 1832–4) and *Poor Laws and Paupers Illustrated* (1833–4). After a visit to the USA (1834–6) she published *Society in America* (1837), as well as two novels. In 1853 she translated and condensed Comte's *Philosophie positive*. She also wrote for the daily and weekly press, and the larger reviews.

Martinelli, Giovanni [mah(r)tinelee] (1885-1969) Tenor, born in Montagnana, Italy. He played in a regimental band before making his debut as a singer in Rossini's *Stabat Mater* (1910) in Milan. He was engaged by Puccini to sing in the European premiere of *La Fanciulla del West* (1911), and became a member of the New York Metropolitan Opera (1913–46).

Martinet, Jean [mah(r)teenay] (?–1672) French army officer. He won renown as a military engineer and tactician, devising forms of battle manoeuvre, pontoon bridges, and a type of copper assault boat used in Louis XIV's Dutch campaign. He became notorious for his stringent and brutal forms of discipline, and this led to the common use of the word *martinet*. He was killed by his troops at the siege of Duisberg.

Martínez Ruiz, José >> **Azorín**

Martínez Sierra, Gregorio [mah(r)teeneth syayra] (1881–1947) Novelist and playwright, born in Madrid. A theatre manager and producer, he was also a publisher and prolific writer who did much to revive Spanish theatre. His masterpiece is the play *Canción de cuna* (1911, The Cradle Song), which was also popular in Britain and America. Much of his writing was done in collaboration with his wife **María** (1874–1974), whose feminist opinions find expression in some of the plays, and who wrote a book on their work together, *Gregorio y yo* (1953, Gregory and I).

Martini, Simone [mah(r)teenee] (c.1284–1344) Painter, born in Siena, Italy. A pupil of Duccio, he was the most important artist of the 14th-c Sienese school, notable for his grace of line and exquisite colour. He worked in Assisi

(1333–9), and at the papal court at Avignon (1339–44). His 'Annunciation' is in the Uffizi Gallery. >> Duccio di Buoninsegna

Martins, Peter (1946–) Ballet dancer, born in Copenhagen. He trained at the Royal Danish Ballet School from the age of eight, and made his debut in Edinburgh with the New York City Ballet. He joined the company two years later, creating roles for George Balanchine, and forming a successful partnership with Kay Mezzo. In the late 1970s he returned to the Royal Danish Ballet. He retired from performance in 1983, and shared the directorship of the New York City Ballet with Jerome Robbins. >> Balanchine; Robbins, Jerome

Martinson, Harry (Edmund) (1904–78) Poet and novelist, born in Jäshög, Sweden. After a harsh childhood as parish orphan, he went to sea as a stoker in 1919 and travelled worldwide, before making his name as a poet. His autobiographical novels include *Nässlorna blomma* (1935, Flowering Nettle), and *Vägen ut* (1936, The Way Out). His poetic space epic, *Aniara* (1956), was set to music as an opera by Karl-Birger Blomdahl. He was elected to the Swedish Academy in 1949, and he shared the 1974 Nobel Prize for Literature. >> Blomdahl; RR1123

Martinů, Bohuslav [mah(r)tinoo] (1890–1959) Composer, born in Polička, Czech Republic. Expelled from the Prague Conservatory, he was readmitted in 1920, studying under Suk, before working in Paris. He fled to America in 1941, and produced a number of important works, including his first symphony, commissioned by Koussevitzky for the Boston Symphony Orchestra (1942). A prolific composer, he ranges from 18th-c orchestral works to modern programme pieces evoked by unusual stimuli such as football (*Half Time*) or aeroplanes (*Thunderbolt P 47*). His operas include the miniature *Comedy on a Bridge*. >> Suk; Koussevitzky

Marty, Martin (Emil) (1928–) Religious historian and scholar, born in West Point, NE. He had an extensive theological training before taking a doctorate at Chicago. Ordained in the Lutheran Church in 1952, he ministered in Illinois, and was appointed professor of the history of modern Christianity at Chicago in 1963. Among his many books are *A Short History of Christianity* (1959) and *Protestantism in the United States* (1985).

Marvell, Andrew [mah(r)vl] (1621–78) Poet, born in Winestead, Hull, NE England, UK. He studied at Cambridge, travelled widely in Europe (1642–6), worked as a tutor, and became Milton's assistant (1657). He is remembered for his pastoral and garden poems, notably 'To His Coy Mistress'. After becoming an MP (1659), his writing was devoted to pamphlets and satires attacking intolerance and arbitrary government. >> Milton

Marvin, Hank >> Shadows, The

Marx, Karl (Heinrich) (1818–83) Founder of international communism, born in Trier, Germany. He studied law at Bonn and Berlin, but took up history, Hegelian philosophy, and Feuerbach's materialism. He edited a radical newspaper, and after it was suppressed he moved to Paris (1843) and Brussels (1845). There, with Engels as his closest collaborator and disciple, he reorganized the Communist League, which met in London in 1847. In 1848 he finalized the *Communist Manifesto*, which attacked the state as the instrument of oppression, and religion and culture as ideologies of the capitalist class. He was expelled from Brussels, and in 1849 settled in London, where he studied economics, and wrote the first volume of his major work, *Das Kapital* (1867, two further volumes were added in 1884 and 1894). He was a leading figure in the First International from 1864 until its demise in 1872. The last decade of his life was marked by increasing ill health. He is buried in Highgate Cemetery, London. >> Engels; Feuerbach; Vico

Marx Brothers Family of film comedians, born in New York City, comprising Julius (1895–1977), or **Groucho**; Leonard (1891–1961), or **Chico**; Arthur (1893–1961), or **Harpo**; and Herbert (1901–79), or **Zeppo**. They began their stage career in vaudeville in a team called the Six Musical Mascots that included their mother, **Minnie** (d.1929), and an aunt; another brother, Milton (?1897–1977), known as **Gummo**, left the act early on. They later appeared as the Four Nightingales, and finally as the Marx Brothers. Their main reputation was made in a series of films, such as *Animal Crackers* and *Monkey Business* (both 1932). Herbert retired from films in 1935, and the others had further successes, such as *A Day at the Races* (1937). Each had a well-defined stencil: Groucho with his wisecracks; Chico, the pianist with his own technique; and Harpo, the dumb clown and harp maestro. The team broke up in 1949, and the brothers then pursued individual careers.

Mary (mother of Jesus), also known as **Our Lady** or **the Blessed Virgin Mary** (?–c. 63) Mother of Jesus Christ. In the New Testament she is most prominent in the stories of Jesus's birth (in the Gospels of Matthew and Luke), where the conception of Jesus is said to be 'of the Holy Spirit' (*Matt* 1.18), and she is described as betrothed to Joseph. She only occasionally appears in Jesus's ministry, but (*John* 19.25) she was present at Jesus's crucifixion, and was committed by him to the care of the disciple, John. According to the Acts of the Apostles, she remained in Jerusalem during the early years of the Church, and tradition places her tomb in Jerusalem. She has become a subject of devotion in her own right, especially in Roman Catholic doctrine and worship, and apocryphal traditions were attached to her in works such as the *Gospel of Mary* and *Gospel of the Birth of Mary*. The belief that her body was taken up into heaven is celebrated in the festival of the Assumption, defined as Roman Catholic dogma in 1950. Her Immaculate Conception has been a dogma since 1854. Belief in the apparitions of the Virgin at Lourdes, Fatima, Medugorje and in several other places attracts many thousands of pilgrims each year. In Roman Catholic and Orthodox Christianity, she holds a special place as an intermediary between believers and God. >> Jesus Christ; Joseph, St

Mary I, Tudor (1516–58) Queen of England and Ireland (1553–8), born in Greenwich, EC Greater London, England, UK, the daughter of Henry VIII by his first wife, Catherine of Aragon. She was a devout Catholic, and during the reign of Edward, her half brother, she lived in retirement, refusing to conform to the new religion. Despite Northumberland's conspiracy to prevent her succession on Edward's death (1553), she relied on the support of the country, entered London, and ousted Lady Jane Grey. Thereafter she proceeded cautiously, repealing anti-Catholic legislation and reviving Catholic practices, but her intention was to restore papal supremacy with the assistance of Cardinal Pole, and to cement a Catholic union with Philip II of Spain. These aspirations provoked Wyatt's rebellion, followed by the execution of Jane Grey and the imprisonment of Mary's half-sister, Elizabeth, on suspicion of complicity. Mary's unpopular marriage to Philip (1554) was followed by the persecution of some 300 Protestants, which earned her the name of 'Bloody Mary' in Protestant hagiography, though her direct responsibility is unproven. She died broken by childlessness, sickness, grief at her husband's departure from England, and the loss of Calais to the French. >> Cranmer; Edward VI; Grey, Lady Jane; Henry VIII; Latimer; Philip II (of Spain); Vivés; Wyatt, Thomas (the Younger); RR1095

Mary II (1662–94) Queen of Britain and Ireland from 1689, born in St James's Palace, London, England, UK, the daughter of the Duke of York (later James II) and his first wife,

Anne Hyde (1638–71). She was married in 1677 to her first cousin, William, Stadtholder of the United Netherlands, who in November 1688 landed in Torbay with an Anglo-Dutch army in response to an invitation from seven Whig peers hostile to the arbitrary rule of James II. When James fled to France, she came to London from Holland and was proclaimed queen, sharing the throne with her husband, who became William III. Both sovereigns accepted the constitutional revolution implicit in the Declaration of Rights. She was content to leave executive authority with William (except when he was abroad or campaigning in Ireland), but she was largely responsible for raising the moral standard of court life, and enjoyed a popularity which her husband never attained. She died of smallpox, and left no children. >> James II (of England); William III; RR1095

Mary, Queen of Scots (1542–87) see panel

Mary of Modena, née **Maria Beatrice d'Este** (1658–1718) Queen of Britain and Ireland (1685–88), the second wife of James II. The only daughter of Alfonso IV, Duke of Modena, she married James in 1673 when he was Duke of York. They lost five daughters and a son in infancy, but in 1688 she gave birth to James Francis Edward Stuart (the future 'Old Pretender'). When William of Orange (the future William III) landed in England later that year, she escaped to France with her infant son, to be joined there later by her deposed husband. She spent the rest of her life at St Germain. >> James II (of England); Stuart, James; William III

Mary of Teck, in full **Victoria Mary Augusta Louise Olga Pauline Claudine Agnes** (1867–1953) Queen-consort of Great Britain, the wife of George V, born in Kensington Palace, London, England, UK, the only daughter of Francis, Duke of Teck, and Princess Mary Adelaide of Cambridge, a grand-daughter of George III. In 1891 she accepted a marriage proposal from the Duke of Clarence, who within six weeks died from pneumonia. She then married his brother, the Duke of York, in 1893. After his accession (as

---

MARY, QUEEN OF SCOTS (1542–87)

Mary was the daughter and only child of James V of Scotland by his second wife, a French woman called Mary of Guise. While James lay on his deathbed at Falkland, Mary was born at Linlithgow Palace, West Lothian, Scotland. She became queen upon his death when she was a week old, and Henry VIII attempted to betrothe her to his son, Prince Edward of England, in order to establish control of her and Scotland. The betrothal was annulled by the Scottish parliament, precipitating war with England. After the Scots' defeat at Pinkie (1547) she was sent by her mother to France. There she was brought up at the glittering French court of Henry II, where she excelled at hunting and dancing, and was carefully educated in the manner of a Frenchwoman. She married the Dauphin (1558), later Francis II, but was widowed at 18 (1560), and became the dowager Queen of France with her own estates and a substantial income.

Her presence was increasingly called for in Scotland, where the death of her mother (1560) had left the country in a highly fluid and dangerous political state. Effective power was in the hands of the Protestant Lords of the Congregation, who had held an illegal parliament to implement the Reformation and ban the authority of the pope. Mary therefore returned to Scotland in 1561. A Protestant riot threatened the first mass held in her private chapel at Holyrood, and a religious standstill was imposed, which in effect banned the mass to all but the Queen and her household.

Ambitious for the English throne, in 1565 she married her cousin, Henry Stuart, Lord Darnley, a grandson of Margaret Tudor. However, disgusted by his debauchery, she soon became alienated from him. The vicious murder, in her presence, of Rizzio, her Italian secretary, by Darnley and a group of Protestant nobles (Mar 1566), confirmed her insecurity. The birth of a son (Jun 1566), the future James VI, failed to reconcile her to Darnley. While ill with smallpox, Darnley was mysteriously killed in an explosion at Kirk o' Field (1567). The chief suspect was the Earl of Bothwell, who underwent a mock trial and was acquitted. Mary's involvement is unclear, but shortly afterwards she was carried off by Bothwell, who had divorced the wife he had only recently married. Mary publicly pardoned his seizure of her person, created him Duke of Orkney, and three months after her husband's death married the man most people regarded as his murderer.

This fatal step united her nobles in arms against her. Her army melted away without striking a blow on the field of Carberry, and nothing was left to her but surrender to the confederate lords. She was constrained at Loch Leven by a minority of the most radical of the Protestant nobles under Morton, and made to sign an act of abdication in favour of her son who, five days afterwards, was crowned as James VI. After escaping, she raised an army, but was defeated again by the confederate lords at Langside (1568). Placing herself under the protection of Queen Elizabeth, she found herself instead in an English prison. She would remain Elizabeth's prisoner for the rest of her life.

The presence of Mary in England was a constant source of unease to Elizabeth and her advisers. She had a claim to the English throne through Darnley, and a large Catholic minority naturally looked to Mary as the likely restorer of the old faith. Yet her position as guest or prisoner was always ambiguous. Plot followed plot in England, though after that of Ridolfi (1571), few if any posed any real threat. The last by Anthony Babington in 1586, was known to Walsingham's agents from the outset. Letters from Mary seemingly approving Elizabeth's death passed along a postal route which went via Walsingham, who opened them himself. Mainly on the evidence of copies of these letters, Mary was brought to trial in 1586. Early in 1587 Elizabeth signed her death warrant, and she was executed at Fotheringay Castle. Buried at Peterborough, in 1612 her body was moved to Henry VII's chapel at Westminster, where it still lies.

Mary's beauty and personal accomplishments have never been disputed. She spoke or read in six languages, sang well, played various musical instruments, and had a library which included the largest collection of Italian and French poetry in Scotland. The portrayals of her after 1571 largely fall into one of two types: Catholic martyr or papist plotter, making all the more difficult a proper assessment of Mary as Queen of Scots.

>> Babington; Bothwell; Darnley; Elizabeth I; Rizzio; Walsingham

---

George V) in 1910, she accompanied him to Delhi as Empress of India for the historically unique Coronation Durbar of December 1911. Although by nature stiff and reserved, she was more sympathetic to changing habits than her husband, whom she helped to mould into a 'people's king'. After the abdication of her eldest son, Edward VIII, she once again strengthened the popular appeal of the monarchy throughout the reign of her second son, George VI, whom she survived by 13 months. >> Edward VIII; George V; George VI

Mary Magdalene, St [**mag**dalen] (1st-c) Disciple of Jesus. Very little is known about her; *Magdalene* possibly means 'of Magdala', in Galilee. Luke (8.2) reports that Jesus exorcised seven evil spirits from her; thereafter she appears only in the narratives of Jesus's passion and resurrection where, seemingly with other women, she appears at the Cross and later at the empty tomb. John (20) relates a private encounter with the resurrected Jesus. Her identification with Mary, the sister of Martha (*John* 11–12), is very tenuous. Feast day 22 July. >> Jesus Christ

Mary Tudor (1495/6–1533) Royal princess, the daughter of Henry VII. She was betrothed to Archduke Charles of Austria in 1507, but when her brother, Henry VIII, succeeded to the throne he renounced the match, and arranged her marriage with Louis XII of France (1514). Following Louis' death (1515), Mary secretly married Charles Brandon, Duke of Suffolk, with whom she had been in love for several years. One of their daughters became the mother of Lady Jane Grey, who was titular queen of England for nine days (1553). >> Grey, Lady Jane; Henry VII; Henry VIII; Louis XII

Masaccio [ma**sa**chio], originally **Tommaso de Giovanni di Simone Guidi** (1401–28) Painter and pioneer of the Renaissance, born in Castel San Giovanni di Altura, Duchy of Milan. In his short life he brought about a revolution in the dramatic and realistic representation of biblical events. This was recognized by his contemporaries, and had a great influence on Michelangelo and through him on the entire 16th-c. His greatest work is the fresco cycle in the Brancacci Chapel of the Church of S Maria del Carmine in Florence (1424–7). >> Lippi, Filippino; Masolino

Masaryk, Jan (Garrigue) [ma**sa**rik] (1886–1948) Diplomat and statesman, born in Prague, the son of Tomáš Masaryk. He entered the diplomatic service, and was Czechoslovak ambassador in London (1925–38). In 1941 he was appointed foreign minister of the Czechoslovak government in exile, becoming a popular broadcaster to his home country during the war. He returned with President Beneš to Prague in 1945, remaining in office. In 1948 his body was found beneath the open window of the foreign ministry in Prague, and it was assumed he had killed himself in protest at the Stalinization of his homeland. >> Beneš; Masaryk, Tomáš

Masaryk, Tomáš (Garrigue) [ma**sa**rik] (1850–1937) Founder-president of the Czechoslovakian Republic (1918–35), born in Hodonin, Czech Republic. He was a professor of philosophy in Prague (1882–1914), supported Czech national causes in parliament in Vienna (1891–3, 1907–14), and exposed as forgeries documents intended by the Habsburg authorities to discredit the political leaders of the Slav minorities. In 1914 he escaped to London, where he became chairman of the Czech National Council, organizing the Czech independence movement. He was re-elected president on three occasions, before retiring in his mid-80s. >> Masaryk, Jan; RR1043

Mascagni, Pietro [ma**skan**yee] (1863–1945) Composer, born in Livorno, Italy. After leaving the Milan Conservatory prematurely (disliking the discipline there), he joined a travelling opera company. In 1890 he produced the brilliantly successful one-act opera, *Cavalleria rusticana*. His many later operas failed to repeat this success, though arias and intermezzi from them are still performed. >> Verga

Mascall, E(ric) L(ionel) (1905–) Anglo-Catholic theologian and writer. He read mathematics at Cambridge, and was ordained priest in 1932. After a few years in parish work he became sub-warden of Lincoln Theological College, where he remained for eight years. He then taught philosophy of religion at Oxford (1946–62), and became professor of historical theology at King's College, London (1962–73, then emeritus). His books *He Who Is* (1943) and *Existence and Analogy* (1949) have acquired the character of textbooks on natural theology. Later works include *Christian Theology and Natural Science* (Oxford Bampton Lectures, 1956) on the relations of theology and science, the ecumenical *The Recovery of Unity* (1958), and *The Triune God* (1986).

Masefield, John (1878–1967) Poet and novelist, born in Ledbury, Hereford and Worcester, WC England, UK. Trained for the merchant service, he served his apprenticeship on a sailing ship. Ill health drove him ashore, and after three years in New York he returned to England to become a writer in 1897, first making his mark as a journalist. His earliest and best-known poetical work, *Salt Water Ballads* (containing 'Sea Fever'), appeared in 1902. His finest narrative poem is probably 'Reynard the Fox' (1919), and other works include the novels *Sard Harker* (1924) and *The Hawbucks* (1929), and the plays *The Trial of Jesus* (1925) and *The Coming of Christ* (1928). He became poet laureate in 1930.

Masham, Lady Abigail, *née* **Hill** (?–1734) Queen Anne's confidante, the cousin of Sarah Churchill, Duchess of Marlborough, through whose influence she entered the royal household. In 1707 she married Samuel (later Baron) Masham. A subtle intriguer and strongly Tory, she gradually turned the queen against the Marlboroughs, and in 1710 superseded her cousin as the queen's confidante and the power behind the throne. >> Anne; Churchill, Sarah

Masire, Quett (Ketumile Joni) (1925–) [ma**seer**] Politician and president of Botswana (1980–). He began a journalistic career before entering politics, through the Bangwaketse Tribal Council and then the Legislative Council. In 1962, with Seretse Khama, he was a founder member of the Botswana Democratic Party, and in 1965 became deputy prime minister. When full independence was achieved in 1966 he became vice-president, and in 1980, president. He continued his predecessor's policy of non-alignment, and helped Botswana become one of the most politically stable nations in Africa. >> Khama; RR1036

Maskelyne, John Nevil [**mas**kelin] (1839–1917) Magician, born in Cheltenham, Gloucestershire, SWC England, UK. He trained as a watchmaker, and built 'magic boxes' and automata which he used in his entertainments. He joined forces with **George Cooke** (d.1904) and they appeared together, first at Cheltenham, then at the Crystal Palace, in 1865. In 1873 they leased the Egyptian Hall for three months, but their tenancy lasted for 31 years. Maskelyne then moved his 'Home of Magic' to the St George's Hall in 1905, with **David Devant** (1868–1941) as his partner. He devoted much energy to exposing spiritualistic frauds.

Maskelyne, Nevil [**mas**kelin] (1732–1811) Astronomer, born in London, England, UK. He studied at Cambridge, was ordained, and became rector of Shrawardine, Shropshire (1775–82), then of North Runcton, Norfolk. His interest in astronomy led to his election to the Royal Society (1758), and after a voyage to Jamaica he produced the *British Mariner's Guide* (1763). He was appointed Astronomer Royal, and published the first volume of the *Nautical*

Almanac (1765). He improved methods and instruments of observation, invented the prismatic micrometer, and in 1774 measured the Earth's density.

Maslow, Abraham (Harold) (1908–70) Psychologist, born in Brooklyn, NY. A professor at Brooklyn College (1937–51) and Brandeis University (1951–61), he is regarded as the founder of humanistic psychology. His seminal *Motivation and Personality* (1954) explored the new humanistic model, and introduced such psychological concepts as the need hierarchy, self-actualization, and peak experience.

Masolino (da Panicale) [masohleenoh], originally **Tommaso di Cristoforo Fini** (1383–c. 1447) Painter, born in Panicale, Romagna. He matriculated in the Florentine Guild in 1423. His early style, close to the Gothic manner of Lorenzo Monaco, yielded briefly to the influence of the more realistic art of Masaccio, with whom he worked on the frescoes of the Life of St Peter in the Brancacci Chapel of the Church of S Maria del Carmine in Florence. His greatest work is the fresco cycle in the Baptistery and Collegiata of Castiglione d'Olona near Como (1430s), which were discovered only in 1843. >> Lorenzo; Masaccio

Mason, A(lfred) E(dward) W(oodley) (1865–1948) Novelist, born in London, England, UK. He studied at Oxford, became a successful actor, and subsequently combined writing with politics, as Liberal MP for Coventry (1906–10). His first published novel was *A Romance of Wastdale* (1895). *Four Feathers* (1902) captured the popular imagination, and *The Broken Road* (1907) cemented his success. With *At the Villa Rose* (1910) he started writing detective novels, and introduced his ingenious Inspector Hanaud. Several of his books have been filmed.

Mason, Charles (1730–87) Astronomer, known for the 'Mason–Dixon Line' in the USA. As an assistant at Greenwich Observatory, with the English surveyor **Jeremiah Dixon** (d.1777), he observed the transit of Venus at the Cape of Good Hope in 1761. From 1763 to 1767 Mason and Dixon were engaged to survey the boundary between Maryland and Pennsylvania, and end an 80-year-old dispute. They reached a point 224 mi W of the Delaware R, but were prevented from further work by Indians. The survey was completed by others, but the boundary was given their name.

Mason, Daniel (Gregory) (1873–1953) Composer, born in Brookline, MA. He studied under Vincent d'Indy in Paris, and became a leading exponent of Neoclassical composition in the USA. He wrote books on American musical conditions and a study of Beethoven's string quartets. He composed three symphonies, the last of which is a study of Abraham Lincoln, and a considerable amount of chamber music. >> d'Indy

Mason, James (1909–84) Actor, born in Huddersfield, West Yorkshire, N England, UK. He studied architecture, then made his stage debut in 1931. He appeared at the Old Vic and with the Gate Company in Dublin before making his film debut in 1935. He became one of the most prolific, distinguished, and reliable of cinema actors. He was nominated for an Oscar for *A Star Is Born* (1954), *Georgy Girl* (1966), and *The Verdict* (1982). Other respected performances from more than 100 films include *Lolita* (1962) and *The Shooting Party* (1984).

Massaddiq, Mohammed >> **Mosaddeq, Mohammed**

Masséna, André [masayna] (1758–1817) French general of the Revolutionary and Napoleonic Wars, born in Nice, France. He distinguished himself in Napoleon's Italian campaign (1796–7), defeating the Russians at Zürich (1799), and successfully defending Genoa (1800). He was created a marshal of the empire in 1804, took command of the army in Italy, and after further successes was made

Duke of Rivoli (1807). After the Austrian campaign (1809) he was made Prince of Essling. However, forced to retreat in the Iberian Peninsula by Wellington's forces, he was relieved of his command (1810). >> Napoleon I; Suvorov; Wellington

Massenet, Jules (Emile Frédéric) [masenay] (1842–1912) Composer, born in Montaud, France. He studied at the Paris Conservatoire, where he was professor (1878–96). He made his name with the comic opera *Don César de Bazan* (1872). Other operas followed, including *Manon* (1884), considered by many to be his masterpiece, *Le Cid* (1885), and *Werther* (1892). Among his other works are oratorios, orchestral suites, music for piano, and songs.

Massey, Raymond (Hart) (1896–1983) Actor, born in Toronto, Ontario, Canada, the brother of Vincent Massey. He made his stage debut in 1922, and played Lincoln in *Abe Lincoln* (1938–9). On film he played leading parts in more than 60 films, including *Arsenic and Old Lace* and *East of Eden*. He is remembered for his long-running television role as 'Dr Gillespie' in the *Dr Kildare* series during the 1960s. >> Massey, Vincent

Massey, (Charles) Vincent (1887–1967) Canadian statesman, diplomat, and governor-general, born in Toronto, Ontario, Canada, the brother of Raymond Massey. He joined the Liberal Cabinet after World War 1, and became Canada's first minister in Washington (1926–30), high commissioner to Britain (1935–46), and Governor-General of Canada (1952–9). >> Massey, Raymond

Massey, William Ferguson (1856–1925) New Zealand statesman and prime minister (1912–25), born in Limavady, Co Londonderry. He emigrated to New Zealand in 1870 and became a farmer, taking the leadership of farming associations. Elected to the House of Representatives (1894) as a Conservative, he became Leader of the Opposition (1894–1912), and then prime minister. He held this office until his death, leading the coalition during World War 1. >> RR1078

Massine, Léonide [maseen], originally **Leonid Fyodorovich Miassin** (1896–1979) Ballet dancer and choreographer, born in Moscow. He trained with the Imperial ballet school at St Petersburg, then became principal dancer, replacing Nijinsky in Diaghilev's Ballets Russes, and going on to choreograph such acclaimed works as *La Boutique fantasque* (1919) and *Parade* (1917). He settled in Europe, working independently for various companies, including Sadler's Wells and Ballets des Champs Elysées. He appeared in the ballet films *The Red Shoes* (1948) and *The Tales of Hoffmann* (1950). >> Diaghilev; Nijinsky

Massinger, Philip (1583–1640) Playwright, born near Salisbury, Wiltshire, S England, UK. After leaving Oxford without a degree, he became a playwright apprenticed to Henslowe. Much of his work after 1613 is in collaboration with others, especially Fletcher. *The City Madam* (1632) and *A New Way to Pay Old Debts* (1633) are among his best-known satirical comedies. >> Fletcher, John; Henslowe

Masson, André [masõ] (1896-1987) Painter and graphic artist, born in Balagny-sur-Thérain, France. He studied at the Académie Royale des Beaux-Arts, Brussels, was a member of the Surrealist group in the 1920s, and became a leading figure in French art. He was a leading practitioner of 'automatic' drawing – a technique of spontaneous composition which tried to capture unconscious feelings and images, using such materials as glue and sand, or squeezing paint tubes directly onto a canvas.

Massys or **Matsys, Jan** [masiys, matsiys] (1509–75) Painter, born probably in Louvain, Belgium, the son of Quentin Massys. An imitator of his father, he worked in Antwerp, becoming Master of the Guild in 1531. He was banished for heresy in 1543, and spent 15 years in Italy. His brother,

Cornelius Massys (1513–79), was also a painter. >> Massys, Quentin

Massys or **Matsys, Quentin** [masees] (c. 1466–c. 1530) Painter, born in Louvain, Belgium. In 1491 he joined the painters' Guild of St Luke in Antwerp. His paintings are mostly religious and genre pictures, treated with a reverent spirit, but with decided touches of Realism (as in 'The Banker and His Wife'). He also ranks high as a portrait painter, his best works including a portrait of Erasmus. >> Massys, Jan

Masters, Edgar Lee (1869–1950) Poet and novelist, born in Garnett, KS. He studied at Knox College, Galesborough, IL, was admitted to the bar in 1891, and became a successful lawyer in Chicago. His most memorable work is the *Spoon River Anthology* (1915), a book of epitaphs in free verse in the form of monologues about a small town community.

Masters and Johnson Human sexuality researchers and authors: **William H(owell) Masters** (1915–) and **Virginia E(shelman) Johnson** (1925–), born in Cleveland, OH, and Springfield, MO, respectively. He studied medicine at Rochester University, joined Washington University School of Medicine (St Louis) in 1947, and began his research work into sexuality in 1954. She studied at University of Missouri, and began work with Masters as a research associate in 1957. In 1964 they established the Reproductive Biology Research Foundation, where the study of the psychology and physiology of sexual intercourse was carried out using volunteer subjects under laboratory conditions. They published *Human Sexual Response* in 1966, which became an international best seller. They continue to publish sexual studies, including *Human Sexual Inadequacy* (1970) and *On Sex and Human Loving* (1986). They married in 1971 and divorced in 1991.

Mastroianni, Marcello [mastroyahnee] (1924–96) Actor, born in Fontana Liri, Italy. A survivor of a wartime Nazi labour camp, he studied at the University of Rome, was involved in amateur dramatics and, sponsored by the university, joined a leading theatrical troupe. He made his film debut in 1947, and by 1960 was established as an international star with his role in Fellini's *La dolce vita*. Co-starring in many films with Sophia Loren, he received Oscar nominations for *Divorzio all'Italiano* (1962, Divorce, Italian Style), *Una giornata particolare* (1977, A Special Day), and *Oci ciornie* (1987, Dark Eyes). His last film was *Three Lives and Only One Death* (1996). >> Fellini; Loren

Mata Hari [mahta hahree], (Malay 'sun'), pseudonym of **Margaretha Geertruide MacLeod**, *née* **Zelle** (1876–1917) Spy, born in Leeuwarden, The Netherlands. She became a dancer in France (1905), had many lovers – several in high military and governmental positions (on both sides during the war) – and, found guilty of espionage for the Germans, was shot in Paris. Her name has become synonymous with the alluring female spy.

Mather, Cotton [mather] (1663–1728) Colonial minister and writer, born in Boston, MA. He studied at Harvard, and became a colleague to his father, Increase Mather, at the Second Church, Boston, succeeding him in 1683. His reputation suffered because of his involvement in the Salem witchcraft trials of 1692, but he nevertheless supported smallpox inoculation and other progressive ideas. A polymath, he reported on American botany, and was one of the earliest New England historians. >> Mather, Increase

Mather, Increase [mather] (1639–1723) Congregational minister and writer, born in Dorchester, MA. He studied at Harvard and Dublin, and was put in charge of Great Torrington, Devon; but in 1661, finding it impossible to conform, he returned to America, and from 1664 until his death was pastor of the Second Church, Boston. He also became president of Harvard (1681–1701). He published

no fewer than 136 separate works, including *Remarkable Providences* (1684) and a *History of the War with the Indians* (1676). Sent to England in 1689 to lay colonial grievances before the king, he obtained a new charter from William III. >> Mather, Cotton

Mathewson, Christy, popular name of **Christopher Mathewson** (1880–1925) Baseball player, born in Factoryville, PA. An outstanding right-handed pitcher, he played 17 seasons (1900–16) for the New York Giants (now the San Francisco Giants), and holds the record (with Grover Alexander) of 373 wins. He won more than 30 games in three successive seasons, and struck out 2499 batters in his career. He was one of the first five players to be elected to the Baseball Hall of Fame in 1936. >> Alexander, Grover

Mathieu, Georges [matyoe] (1921–) Painter, born in Boulogne, France. He took a degree in literature, and began to paint in 1942, settling in Paris in 1947, and exhibiting there and in New York City. He developed a form of lyric, nongeometrical abstraction, in close sympathy with the American neo-Expressionists.

Matilda, also called **Maud** (1102–67) English princess, born in London, England, UK, the only daughter of Henry I. In 1114 she married Emperor Henry V, but returned to England after his death in 1125, and was acknowledged as the heir to the English throne. She married Geoffrey Plantagenet of Anjou (1128), by whom she had a son, the future Henry II of England. When Henry I died (1135), his nephew Stephen of Blois seized the throne, and in 1139 Matilda invaded England from Anjou. After capturing Stephen, she declared herself 'Lady of the English', but was never crowned. Stephen gradually regained control, and in 1148 Matilda left England for Normandy. >> Henry I (of England); Henry II (of England); Stephen

Matisse, Henri (Emile Benoît) [matees] (1869–1954) Painter, born in Le Cateau, France. He studied law in Paris, then worked as a lawyer's clerk. An interest in art came unexpectedly in his 20s, and in 1892 he took classes in Paris, first at the Académie Julian, then at the Ecole des Beaux-Arts. From 1904 he was the leader of the Fauves (Fr 'wild beasts', the name given by a hostile critic), and although he painted several pictures influenced by Cubism and Impressionism, his most characteristic paintings display a bold use of brilliant areas of primary colour, organized within a rhythmic two-dimensional design. During the early 1930s he travelled in Europe and the USA, and in 1949–51 he decorated a Dominican chapel at Vence, near Nice. >> Derain; Marquet; Rouault; Vlaminck

Matsys, Jan >> **Massys, Jan**

Matsys, Quentin >> **Massys, Quentin**

Matteotti, Giacomo [matiotee] (1885–1924) Italian politician, born in Fratta Polesine, Italy. A member of the Italian Chamber of Deputies, he began to organize the United Socialist Party (1921), and was an outspoken opponent of Mussolini's Fascists (1922–4). His protests against Fascist election outrages led to his murder in 1924, provoking a crisis which nearly brought the Fascist regime to an end. >> Mussolini

Matthau, Walter [matow], originally **Walter Matuschanskavasky** (1920–) Film actor, born in New York City. The son of Russian-Jewish immigrants, he studied at the New School for Social Research Dramatic Workshop, began working in Yiddish theatre, and made his Broadway debut in 1948. His film debut was in *The Kentuckian* (1955), and for many years he was cast as a villain. It was the 1967 Neil Simon comedy film *The Odd Couple* which pushed him into major film parts. Later films include *Hello ·Dolly* (1969), *Cactus Flower* (1969), *Pirates* (1986), *I.Q.* (1995), and *Out to Sea* (1997).

Matthew, St (1st-c) One of the 12 apostles in the New Testament. He was a tax gatherer before becoming a disciple of Jesus, and is identified with Levi (in *Mark* 2.14 and *Luke* 5.27). According to tradition he was the author of the first Gospel, a missionary to the Hebrews in Judaea, Ethiopia, and Persia, and suffered martyrdom, but nothing is known with certainty about his life. Feast day 21 September (W) or 16 November (E). >> Jesus Christ

Matthew Corvinus >> **Matthias I**

Matthew Paris (c. 1200–59) Chronicler and Benedictine monk. He entered the monastery at St Albans, Hertfordshire, SE England, UK in 1217, and became abbey chronicler there in 1236. His main work is the *Chronica majora*, the fullest available account of events in England between 1236 and 1259, and which also included interesting details of many other European countries. He is especially famous for his maps and drawings.

Matthews, (James) Brander (1852–1929) Writer, born in New Orleans, LA. He studied at Columbia University, where he later became professor of literature (1892–1900), and was also appointed the first US professor of dramatic literature (1900–24). During his career he worked as an editor, essayist, drama critic, and novelist, these works being the foundation of the Brander Matthews Dramatic Museum at Columbia University.

Matthews, Sir Stanley (1915–) Footballer, born in Hanley, Staffordshire, C England, UK. He started his sporting career with Stoke City in 1931, before a controversial transfer to Blackpool in 1947. Medals eluded him until 1953, when he played a significant role in the Football Association Cup Final. He returned to Stoke in 1961, and continued to play First Division football until after he was 50. He played for England 54 times, was twice Footballer of the Year (1948, 1963), and was the inaugural winner of the European Footballer of the Year Award in 1956. He later managed Port Vale, and was knighted in 1965. >> RR1156

Matthias I, known as **Matthew Corvinus**, Hung **Mátyás Corvin** (c. 1443–90) King of Hungary (1458–90), born in Koloszvár, Hungary, the second son of János Hunyady. He drove back the Turks, and made himself master of Bosnia (1462), Moldavia and Wallachia (1467), Moravia, Silesia, and Lusatia (1478), Vienna, and a large part of Austria proper (1485). His rule was arbitrary and his taxes heavy, but he greatly encouraged arts and letters, founded the Corvina library, promoted industry, and reformed finances and the system of justice. >> Hunyady

Matthias, Bernard (Teo) (1918–) Physicist, born in Frankfurt, Germany. He studied at Rome University, and the Federal Institute of Technology, Zürich, before moving to the USA in 1947. After a period with Bell Telephones, he was appointed professor of physics at the University of California, San Diego. In his search for new superconducting materials, he discovered that alloys of metals with five or seven valence electrons were the most effective. His work was a useful advance in the period before ceramic superconductors were found in the late 1980s.

Matthias, William (James) (1934–92) Composer, born in Whitland, Pembrokeshire, SW Wales. He studied in London, and became lecturer (1959–68) and professor (1970–88, then research professor) at University College, Bangor. His works include an opera, *The Servants* (1980), three symphonies, several concertos, and much chamber, choral, and church music. Among his choral works is an anthem written for the wedding ceremony of the Prince and Princess of Wales (1981). He was artistic director of the North Wales Music Festival from 1972 until his death.

Matthiessen, Peter [mathesen] (1927–) Novelist, travel writer, naturalist, and explorer, born in New York City. He made anthropological and natural history expeditions to Alaska, the Canadian Northwest Territories, Peru, New Guinea, Africa, Nicaragua, and Nepal. The author of six novels and a number of ecological and natural history studies, he won the National Book Award with the best-selling *The Snow Leopard* (1978), his account of a trek across the Tibetan plateau to the Crystal Mountain.

Matzeliger, Jan Earnst [matzeliger] (1852–89) Inventor, born in Dutch Guiana. The child of a black mother and white father, he emigrated to the USA c.1872. Although uneducated, he invented a shoe-making machine (1891) and shoe-nailing machine (1896) which revolutionized the shoe industry. His inventions formed the basis of the United Shoe Machinery Corporation.

Mauchly, John W(illiam) [mawklee] (1907–80) Physicist and inventor, born in Cincinnati, OH. He studied physics at Johns Hopkins University, and after a few years in teaching joined J Presper Eckert at the University of Pennsylvania (1943) in the development of ENIAC, one of the first modern computers. Following ENIAC they built EDVAC, an Electronic Discrete Variable Automatic Computer, and finally UNIVAC, a Universal Automatic Computer, first used in 1951 by the US Census Bureau. The success of these machines played a large part in launching the computer revolution in the second half of the 20th-c. >> Eckert

Maud, Empress >> **Matilda**

Maudling, Reginald (1917–79) British Conservative statesman, born in London, England, UK. He studied at Oxford, was called to the bar (1940), and served in the air force during World War 2. He entered parliament in 1950, became minister of supply (1953–7), paymaster-general (1957–9), President of the Board of Trade (1959–61), colonial secretary (1961), Chancellor of the Exchequer (1962–4), and deputy leader of the Opposition in 1964. In 1970 he became home secretary in the Heath government, but resigned in 1972 when he became implicated in the bankruptcy proceedings of architect John Poulson.

Maudslay, Henry [mawdzlee] (1771–1831) Engineer, and inventor of improvements for the metal lathe, born in Woolwich, Kent, SE England, UK. He learned his job as apprentice to Joseph Bramah, set up on his own in 1797, and invented various types of machinery, including a screw-cutting lathe. He also invented the slide rest, and a method of desalinating sea water. With **Joshua Field** (1757–1863), he began producing marine engines, and started the firm of Maudslay, Sons & Field (1810). >> Bramah

Maudsley, Henry [mawdzlee] (1835–1918) Psychiatrist, born in Giggleswick, North Yorkshire, N England, UK. He was physician to the Manchester Asylum, and professor of medical jurisprudence at University College (1869–79). The Maudsley Hospital, Denmark Hill, London, is named after him.

Mauger, Ivan (Gerald) [mawger] (1939–) Speedway rider, born in Christchurch, New Zealand. He rode for Wimbledon, Rye House, Eastbourne, Newcastle, Belle Vue, Exeter, and Hull between 1957 and 1982, and won the world individual title a record six times (1968–70, 1972, 1977, 1979). He also won two pairs world titles, four team titles, and the world long-track title twice. >> RR1169

Maugham, W(illiam) Somerset [mawm] (1874–1965) Novelist, playwright, and short-story writer, born in Paris. Orphaned at 10, he studied at Canterbury and Heidelberg, qualifying as a surgeon at St Thomas's Hospital, London. His first novel, *Liza of Lambeth* (1897), was a minor success, and he turned to writing full-time. Four of his plays ran simultaneously in London in 1908, and he wrote many others, notably *The Moon and Sixpence* (1919), *The Circle* (1921), *East of Suez* (1922), and *Cakes and Ale* (1930). His novels include the semi-autobiographical *Of Human Bondage* (1915). He is best known for his short stories, particularly 'Rain', originally published in the collection, *The Trembling of a Leaf* (1921). *The Complete Short Stories* (3 vols) was published in 1951.

Maundeville / Maundevylle >> Mandeville, Sir John

Maupassant, (Henri René Albert) Guy de [mohpasā] (1850–93) Novelist, born probably at the Château de Miromesnil, Dieppe, France. He studied at Rouen, and spent his life in Normandy. After serving as a soldier and a government clerk, he took to writing, encouraged by Flaubert, a friend of his mother's. His stories range from the short tale to the full-length novel. His first success, *Boule de suif* (1880, Ball of Fat), led to his being in great demand by newspapers. There followed about 300 stories and several novels, including *Une Vie* (1883, trans A Woman's Life), and the supposedly autobiographical *Bel-Ami* (1885). His stories 'Le Horla' (Hallucination) and 'La Peur' (Fear) describe madness and fear with a horrifying accuracy which foreshadows the insanity which beset Maupassant in 1892, when he was committed to an asylum in Paris. >> Flaubert

Maupertuis, Pierre Louis Moreau de [mohpertwee] (1698–1759) Mathematician, born in St Malo, France. A member of the Académie of Sciences from 1731, he led the French Academicians sent to Lapland in 1736 to measure the length of a degree of the meridian, in order to verify Newton's theories of the shape of the Earth. Frederick II made him president of the Berlin Academy in 1746. Maupertuis is best known for his 'principle of least action' in mechanics, and formed a theory of heredity which was a century ahead of its time. >> Newton, Isaac

Maupin, Armistead (1944–) Novelist, born in Washington DC. He attended the University of North Carolina, and after serving as a naval officer in Vietnam he settled in California in 1971. The six volumes of his *Tales of the City* sequence (beginning in 1978) have been praised for their unsentimental portrait of gay lifestyle on the US West Coast.

Mauriac, François [mohriak] (1885–1970) Novelist, born in Bordeaux, France. He studied at Bordeaux, was of strict Roman Catholic parentage, and became regarded as the leading novelist of that faith. He started as a poet, publishing his first volume of verse in 1909. His novels explore temptation, sin, and redemption, and include *Le Baiser au lépreux* (1922, The Kiss to the Leper) and *Le Noeud de vipères* (1932, Viper's Tangle). He was awarded the 1952 Nobel Prize for Literature.

Maurice, (John) Frederick Denison (1805–72) Theologian and writer, born in Normanston, Suffolk, E England, UK. He studied at Cambridge, left in 1827 without a degree, and began a literary career in London. He wrote one novel, *Eustace Conway*, and for a time edited the *Athenaeum*. He took orders in the Church of England, and became chaplain to Lincoln's Inn (1841–60). He became professor of literature (1840) at King's College, London (1840), then of theology, and at Cambridge was professor of moral philosophy (1866). With Thomas Hughes and Charles Kingsley he founded the Christian Socialism movement, and he was the founder and first principal of the Working Man's College (1854). >> Hughes, Thomas; Kingsley, Charles

Maurice, Prinz van Oranje, Graaf van Nassau (Prince of Orange, Count of Nassau) (1567–1625) Stadtholder of the United Provinces of the Netherlands, born in Dilenburg, the son of William the Silent. He was elected stadtholder of Holland and Zeeland (1587) and later (1589) of Utrecht, Overyssel, and Gelderland, also becoming captain-general of the armies of the United Provinces during their War of Independence from Spain. He checked the Spanish advance, and by his steady offensive (1590–1606) liberated the N provinces. He became Prince of Orange in 1618, on the death of his elder brother. In the renewed conflict with the Habsburgs, he commanded the new republic, seeking help from England and France (1624). >> Barneveldt; William I (of The Netherlands)

Maurier, du >> du Maurier

Maurin, Peter >> Day, Dorothy

Maurois, André [mohrwah], pseudonym of **Emile Herzog** (1885–1967) Writer and biographer, born in Elbeuf, France. During World War 1 he was a liaison officer with the British army, and began his literary career with a book of shrewd and affectionate observation of British character, *Les Silences du Colonel Bramble* (1918, The Silences of Colonel Bramble). His many biographies include studies of Shelley (1923), Disraeli (1927), Voltaire (1935), and Proust (1949).

Mauroy, Pierre [mohrwah] (1928–) French politician and prime minister (1981–4). He was a teacher before becoming involved with trade unionism and Socialist politics, and was prominent in the creation of a new French Socialist Party in 1971. He became Mayor of Lille in 1973, and was elected to the National Assembly in the same year. A close ally of Mitterrand, Mauroy acted as his spokesman during the Socialists' successful election campaign. >> Mitterrand; RR1049

Maurras, Charles [mohra] (1868–1952) Journalist and critic, born in Martigues, France. A student of philosophy at Paris, he was established as an avant-garde journalist by 1894. From 1908, in *Action française*, he wrote articles which wielded a powerful influence on the youth of the country. he was imprisoned for violent attacks on the government in 1936. At the fall of France in 1940 he supported the Vichy government. In 1945, he was brought to trial and sentenced to life imprisonment, but was released, on medical grounds, just before he died.

Maury, Matthew (Fontaine) [mawree] (1806–73) Naval officer and hydrographer, born in Spotsylvania, VA. He entered the US navy in 1825, and voyaged round the world (1826–30). After an accident in 1839, he was appointed in 1842 superintendent of the hydrographical office at Washington, and in 1844 of the observatory. There he wrote his *Physical Geography of the Sea* (1856), and his works on the Gulf Stream, ocean currents, and Great Circle sailing. He became an officer of the Confederate navy, and later professor of physics at Lexington.

Mauser, (Peter) Paul von [mowzer] (1838–1914) Fire-arm inventor, born in Oberndorf, Germany. With his brother **Wilhelm** (1834–82) he was responsible for the improved needle-gun (adopted by the German army in 1871) and for the improved breech-loading cannon. He produced the *Mauser magazine-rifle* in 1897.

Mausolus >> Artemisia II

Mauss, Marcel [mohs] (1872–1950) Sociologist and anthropologist, born in Epinal, France. He studied philosophy at Bordeaux, and the history of religion at Paris. In 1902 he became professor of primitive religion at the Ecole Pratique des Hautes Etudes, Paris, and in 1925 was co-founder of the Institute of Ethnology at Paris University. From 1931 to 1939 he was at the Collège de France. After World War 1, he devoted himself to editing the work of the *Année* school and to writing his masterpiece, *Essai sur le don* (1925, Essay on the Gift), in which he demonstrated the importance of gift exchange in primitive social organization.

Mauve, Anton [mowvuh] (1838–88) Painter, born in Zaandam, The Netherlands. Regarded as one of the greatest landscapists of his time, he was influenced by Corot and Milet, and painted country scenes. From 1878 he lived in

Laren, where he founded the Dutch Barbizon school. >> Corot; Millet

Mavor, Osborne Henry >> **Bridie, James**

Maw, (John) Nicholas (1935–) Composer, born in Grantham, Lincolnshire, EC England, UK. He studied in London (1955–8) and Paris (1958–9), taught at Cambridge and Yale universities, and became professor of music at Milton Avery Graduate School of Arts, Bard College, NY, in 1990. His music, traditional in idiom but original in expression, includes two operas – *One Man Show* (1964) and *The Rising of the Moon* (1970) – two string quartets, and many orchestral works.

Mawson, Sir Douglas (1882–1958) Explorer and geologist, born in Shipley, West Yorkshire, N England, UK. He studied at Sydney, was appointed to the scientific staff of Ernest Shackleton's Antarctic expedition (1907), and with T W E David discovered the South Magnetic Pole. From 1911 to 1914 he was leader of the Australasian Antarctic expedition, which charted 2000 mi of coast; he was knighted on his return. He also led the joint British–Australian–New Zealand expedition to the Antarctic (1929–31). >> Shackleton

Max, Adolphe (1869–1939) Belgian politician and statesman, born in Brussels. First a journalist, then an accountant, he became burgomaster of Brussels in 1909. When the German troops approached Brussels in August 1914, he boldly drove to meet them and opened negotiations. He defended the rights of the Belgian population against the invaders, and was imprisoned. He refused an offer of freedom which carried the condition that he went to Switzerland and desisted from anti-German agitation. In November 1918 he returned to Belgium, was elected to the House of Representatives, and became a minister of state.

Maxim, Sir Hiram (Stevens) (1840–1916) Inventor and engineer, born in Sangerville, ME. He became a coachbuilder in an engineering works in Fitchburg, MA (1865), and from 1867 took out patents for a wide range of inventions, including electric lamps and gas equipment. An interest in automatic weapons took him to England in 1881, where he perfected the *Maxim machine-gun* in 1883. He also invented a pneumatic gun, a smokeless powder, a mousetrap, and carbon filaments for light bulbs.

Maximilian I (1459–1519) Holy Roman Emperor (1493–1519), born as Archduke of Austria in Weiner Neustadt, Austria, the eldest son of Emperor Frederick III and Eleanor of Portugal. Elected King of the Romans (1486), he inherited the Habsburg territories and assumed the imperial title in 1493. He pursued an ambitious foreign policy, based on dynastic alliances, with far-reaching results for Habsburg power. His marriage to Mary of Burgundy brought his family the Burgundian inheritance, including Holland, followed by union with the Spanish kingdoms of Castile and Aragon when the Spanish crown passed to his grandson, Charles (1516). A double marriage treaty between the Habsburgs and the Jagiellons (1506) eventually brought the union of Austria–Bohemia–Hungary (1526). He was involved in conflict with the Flemish, the Swiss, the German princes, and especially with the Valois kings of France. Financial difficulties weakened his campaigns, and he was later forced to cede Milan (1504) to Louis XII. He incurred the hostility of the Venetians and, despite the League of Cambrai (1508), suffered defeat. He was succeeded by his grandson, as Charles V. >> Charles V (Emperor); Louis XII; RR1057

Maximilian, Ferdinand Joseph (1832–67) Emperor of Mexico (1864–7), born in Vienna, the younger brother of Emperor Francis Joseph, and an archduke of Austria. In 1863, he accepted the offer of the crown of Mexico, supported by France. When Napoleon III withdrew his troops, he refused to abdicate, and made a brave defence at Querétaro, but was betrayed and executed. >> Francis Joseph; Juárez; Napoleon III; RR1075

Max-Müller, Friedrich >> **Müller, Max**

Maxwell, James C(lerk) (1831–79) Physicist, born in Edinburgh, EC Scotland, UK. He studied at Edinburgh and Cambridge, became professor at Aberdeen (1856) and London (1860), and was the first professor of experimental physics at Cambridge (1871), where he organized the Cavendish Laboratory. In 1873 he published his great *Treatise on Electricity and Magnetism*, which gives a mathematical treatment to Faraday's theory of electrical and magnetic forces. He also contributed to the study of colour vision, and to the kinetic theory of gases, but his greatest work was his theory of electromagnetic radiation, which established him as the leading theoretical physicist of the century. >> Faraday; Keeler, James; Tsiolkovsky

Maxwell, (Ian) Robert, originally **Ludvik Hoch** (1923–91) Publisher and politician, born in Slatinske Dòly, Czech Republic. Self-educated, he served in World War 2 before founding the Pergamon Press. A former Labour MP (1964–70), he had many business interests, including film production and television. He became chairman of the Mirror group of newspapers in 1984, but was forced to float the company on the London stock market in 1991. Following his death in mysterious circumstances (his body was found in the sea near the Canary Is, after he disappeared from his luxury yacht), it transpired that he had secretly siphoned large sums of money from two of his companies, and from employee pension funds, to preserve his financial empire.

Maxwell, Vera, *née* **Huppé** (1901–96) Fashion designer, born in New York City. She was a dancer with the Metropolitan Opera Ballet (1919–24), then became interested in designing. Dubbed the 'American Chanel', she was one of the first US designers to introduce sportswear for women. She founded her own company in 1947. >> Chanel

Maxwell Davies, Sir Peter >> **Davies, Sir Peter Maxwell**

May, Peter (Barker Howard) (1929–94) Cricketer and administrator, born in Reading, Berkshire, S England, UK. He studied at Cambridge, and was one of the last great amateur cricketers, first capped for Surrey in 1950. He played in 66 Tests for England (41 as captain), scoring 4537 runs at an average of 46·77, and in all first-class matches scored 27 592 runs, at an average of 51, including 85 centuries. His highest score, 285 not out, at the Edgbaston Test in 1957, was at the time a record by an English captain. With Colin Cowdrey of Kent, he set up the record fourth-wicket Test partnership of 411 against the West Indies at Edgbaston in 1957. He later became chairman of the England Cricket Selection Committee (1982–8). >> Cowdrey; Ramadhin

May, Phil(ip William) (1864–1903) Caricaturist, born in Wortley, West Yorkshire, N England, UK. Orphaned at the age of nine, he endured years of poverty before he became poster artist and cartoonist of the *St Stephen's Review*. He went to Australia, and on his return in 1890 established himself with contributions to *Punch* (of which he was a staff member from 1896) and other periodicals. He excelled in depicting East London types, and brought a new simplicity of line to popular cartooning.

May, Sir Robert McCredie (1936–) Australian scientist. He studied at Sydney University, taught maths at Harvard (1959–61), physics at Sydney (1962–73), and was professor of biology and zoology at Princeton (1973–88), before moving to Oxford. He is one of a growing number of scientists who have contributed to chaos theory, his work having applications in ecology and public health. Since 1995 he has been chief scientific adviser to the government. He was knighted in 1996. >> Feigenbaum; Lorenz

Mayakovsky, Vladimir (Vladimirovich) [miyakofskee] (1893–1930) Poet and playwright, born in Bagdadi, Georgia. He began writing at an early age, and was regarded as the leader of the Futurist school. During the Russian Revolution (1917) he emerged as the propaganda mouthpiece of the Bolsheviks. His plays include *Misteriya-Buff* (1918, Mystery-Bouffe), and the satirical *Klop* (1929, The Bedbug) and *Banya* (1930, The Bath-House). Towards the end of his life he was severely castigated by more orthodox Soviet writers and critics for his outspoken criticism of bureaucracy and his unconventional opinions on art, and this appears to have contributed towards his suicide.

Maybach, Wilhelm [maybakh] (1846–1929) Inventor and car manufacturer, born in Heilbronn, Germany. He joined Gottlieb Daimler in 1869 as a draughtsman, and became his partner in 1882 when he established a factory near Stuttgart. He was responsible for an innovation that was crucial to the development of high-speed petrol engines suitable for motor cars, the float-feed carburettor (1893), as well as improvements in timing, gearing, and steering. He left Daimler in 1907 and set up his own works at Friedrichshafen (1909), where he made engines for Zeppelin airships, and (1922–39) luxury Maybach cars. >> Daimler

Mayer, Louis B(urt) [mayer], originally **Eliezer Mayer** (1885–1957) Film mogul, born in Minsk, Belarus. In 1907 he purchased a house in Haverhill, MA, refurbished it as a nickelodeon, and opened one of the earliest custom-designed cinemas. He later acquired a chain of theatres in New England, moving into film production with the formation of Metro Films (1915) and Louis B Mayer Productions (1917), which later joined with Sam Goldwyn to form Metro–Goldwyn–Mayer in 1924. The first vice-president in charge of production, he was instrumental in the creation of Hollywood as a dream factory and the establishment of the star system, with such successes as *Ben Hur* (1926), *Grand Hotel* (1932), the Andy Hardy series, *Ninotchka* (1939), and countless others. He received an honorary Academy Award in 1950. >> Goldwyn

Mayhew, Henry (1812–87) Writer, born in London, England, UK. He ran away from Westminster School, and collaborated with his brother **Augustus** (1826–75) in writing numerous successful novels, such as *The Good Genius that Turns Everything to Gold* (1847) and *Whom to Marry* (1848). He wrote on many subjects, his best-known work being the classic social survey, *London Labour and the London Poor* (4 vols, 1851–62). Another brother, **Horace** (1816–72), was also a collaborator. In 1841, with Mark Lemon, Henry founded the humorous magazine, *Punch*. >> Lemon

Mayo, Charles Horace [mayoh] (1865–1939) Surgeon, born in Rochester, MN. He studied at Chicago Medical College, went into private practice with his father, and made a special study of goitre. In 1905, he helped his brother William James Mayo to organize at Rochester the Mayo Clinic, which their father had founded. >> Mayo, William James

Mayo, Henry Thomas [mayoh] (1856–1937) US naval officer, born in Burlington, VT. He was the central American figure in the Tampico Incident of 1914 that led to the US naval capture of Veracruz, Mexico. He later commanded the Atlantic Fleet (1916–19), and was in charge of all naval forces in Atlantic and European waters during World War 1. In 1917 he represented the USA at the Allied naval conference in London.

Mayo, Katherine [mayoh] (1868–1940) Journalist, born in Ridgeway, PA. She is remembered for her books exposing social evils, especially *Isles of Fear* (1925), condemning US administration of the Philippines, and *Mother India* (1927), a forthright indictment of child marriage and other customs.

Mayo, William James [mayoh] (1861–1939) Surgeon, born in Le Sueur, MN. He studied at the University of Michigan, and was in private practice with his father before becoming a specialist in stomach surgery. He established the Mayo Clinic with his brother Charles Horace Mayo at St Mary's Hospital, Rochester, MN, and in 1915 set up the Mayo Foundation for Medical Education and Research. >> Mayo, Charles Horace

Mayr, Ernst (Walter) [mayer] (1904–) Zoologist, born in Kempten, Germany. He studied at Berlin, and became professor of zoology at Harvard (1953–75). His early work was on the ornithology of the Pacific, leading three scientific expeditions to New Guinea and the Solomon Is (1928–30), but in his later career he was best known for his neo-Darwinian views on evolution, as developed in such books as *Animal Species and Evolution* (1963) and *Evolution and the Diversity of Life* (1976). >> Darwin, Charles

Mays, Willie (Howard), nickname **the Say Hey Kid** (1931–) Baseball player, born in Westfield, AL. He played for the New York (1951–7) and San Francisco (1958–72) Giants, and the New York Mets (1972–3). A magnificent fielder, batter, and baserunner, only he and Hank Aaron have performed the baseball double of more than 3000 hits and 600 home runs. He was twice voted the Most Valuable Player (1954, 1965), and became the Baseball Player of the Decade (1960–9). He was elected to the Baseball Hall of Fame in 1979. >> Aaron, Hank; RR1144

Mazarin, Jules [mazari], known as **Cardinal Mazarin**, originally **Giulio Raimondo Mazzarino** (1602–61) Neapolitan clergyman, diplomat, and statesman, born in Pescine, Italy. He studied at Rome and in Spain, became papal nuncio to the French court (1634–6) and entered the service of Louis XIII in 1639. Through the influence of Richelieu he was elevated to cardinal, succeeding his mentor as first minister in 1642. After Louis' death (1643), he retained his authority under the queen-regent, Anne of Austria. Blamed by many for the civil disturbances of the Frondes, he twice fled the kingdom, and returned to Paris in 1653 after the nobles' revolt had been suppressed. His foreign policy was more fruitful: he concluded the Peace of Westphalia (1648), whose terms increased French prestige, and negotiated the Treaty of the Pyrenees (1659), ending the prolonged Franco–Spanish conflict. He was a patron of the arts and learning, founding the Royal Academy of Painting and Sculpture (1648) and building up an important library in Paris. >> Anne of Austria; Fouquet; Retz, Cardinal de; Richelieu; Turenne

Mazzini, Giuseppe [matseenee] (1805–72) Patriot and republican, born in Genoa, Italy. He was trained as a lawyer, and became an ardent liberal, founding the Young Italy Association (1833). Expelled from France, he travelled Europe advocating republicanism and insurrection. In 1848 he became involved in the Lombard revolt, and collaborated with Garibaldi in attempting to keep the patriotic struggle alive in the Alps. In 1849 he became one of the triumvirate governing the Roman Republic, overthrown after two months by French intervention. During the events of 1859–60 he and his supporters worked strenuously but vainly to make the new Italy a republic. >> Garibaldi

Mbeki, Thabo (Mvuyelwa) [mbekee] (1942–) Leader (from 1997) of the African National Congress (ANC), born in Idutywa, South Africa. He joined the ANC Youth League as a teenager, and in 1959 was expelled from school for political activities. By the time his father, **Govan Mbeki** (1910–), was sentenced to life at the Rivonia Trial of

1964, Thabo was in exile. He then studied in England and the USSR. Elected to the National Executive Committee of the ANC in 1975, he became one of its most influential leaders. After the organization was unbanned in 1990, he returned to South Africa, and played a major role in the negotiations for a new political dispensation. In 1994 he was appointed first deputy president in Nelson Mandela's administration.

Mbiti, John Samuel [mbitee] (1931–) Theologian, born in Kenya. He taught theology and comparative religion at Makere University College, Uganda, before becoming director of the World Council of Churches Ecumenical Institute, Bossey, Switzerland (1972–80). He now teaches Christianity and African religions at Bern University and is a pastor in Burgdorf, Switzerland. His books include *African Religions and Philosophy* (1969) and *Bible and Theology in African Christianity* (1987).

Mboya, Tom [mboya], popular name of **Thomas Joseph Mboya** (1930–69) Kenyan statesman and nationalist leader, born in Kilima Mbogo, Kenya. He studied at Mangu, joined the Kenya African Union, and after this Party was suppressed became secretary of the Kenya Federation of Labour and a campaigner for independence. In 1960 he was general secretary of Kenyatta's Kenya African National Union, and became minister of labour (1962–3), minister of justice (1963–4), and minister of economic development and planning (1964–9). He was assassinated in Nairobi in 1969. >> Kenyatta

Mead, George Herbert (1863–1931) Social psychologist, born in South Hadley, MA. He studied at Harvard, Leipzig, and Berlin, taught at Michigan University (1891–4), then moved to the philosophy department at Chicago (1894–1931). His main interest lay in the theory of the mind, the notion of the self, and how this is developed through communication with others. His work gave rise to Symbolic Interactionism, a social science approach concerned with the meanings that people give to the world, and how these are worked out through interpersonal interaction. His main works, published shortly after his death, are *Mind, Self and Society* (1934) and *The Philosophy of the Act* (1938).

Mead, Margaret (1901–78) Anthropologist, born in Philadelphia, PA. She studied at Columbia University under Franz Boas, then carried out a number of field studies in the Pacific, writing both academic and popular books, such as *Coming of Age in Samoa* (1928). She held a position for many years at the American Museum of Natural History, but increasingly became a freelance media heavyweight, one of the most famous women of her generation, particularly well known for her views on educational and social issues. >> Boas

Meade, George G(ordon) (1815–72) US army officer, born in Cadiz, Spain. He trained at West Point, and served against the Seminoles and in the Mexican War. In the American Civil War (1861–5) he distinguished himself at Antietam and Fredericksburg (1862), and in 1863 commanded the Army of the Potomac, defeating Lee at Gettysburg. >> Hooker, Joseph; Lee, Robert E

Meade, James Edward (1907–95) Economist, born in Swanage, Dorset, S England, UK. He worked for the League of Nations in the 1930s, and was a member, then director, of the economic section of the Cabinet Office (1940–6). He then became professor of economics at London School of Economics (1947–57) and of political economics at Cambridge (1957–68). A prolific writer, his principal contributions have been in the area of international trade, including *The Theory of International Economic Policy* (2 vols, 1951–5). He shared the 1977 Nobel Prize for Economics. >> RR1125

Meade, Richard (John Hannay) (1938–) Equestrian rider, born in Chepstow, Monmouthshire, SE Wales. One of Britain's most successful Olympians, he won three gold medals – the Three-day Event team golds in 1968 and 1972, and the individual title in 1972 (on *Laurieston*). He also won world championship team gold medals (1970, 1982), European championship team gold medals (1967, 1971, 1981), Burghley in 1964 (on *Barberry*), and Badminton in 1970 (on *The Poacher*) and 1982 (on *Speculator III*). >> RR1153

Meads, Colin (Earl), nickname **Pine Tree** (1936–) Rugby union player, born in Cambridge, New Zealand. A lock forward, he wore the All Black jersey in 133 representative matches, including a national record 55 in Test matches between 1957 and 1971. He then became a sheep farmer.

Meale, Richard Graham (1932–) Composer, conductor, and teacher, born in Sydney, New South Wales, Australia. He studied at the New South Wales Conservatory and the University of California, where he researched the music of Japan, Java, and Bali. Returning to Australia he made an immediate impact with his compositions *Los Alboradas* (1963) and *Homage to Garcia Lorca* (1964). From 1969 he was reader in music at Adelaide University. His first opera *Voss* (1982), with a libretto by David Malouf based on the novel by Patrick White, demonstrates the strength of his orchestral and vocal writing, and is part of the Australian Opera's repertoire. His second opera, *Mer de Glace*, again with a libretto by Malouf, was premiered in 1991. >> Malouf

Meany, George [meenee] (1894–1980) Labour leader, born in New York City. Active first in the plumber's union, then in the New York State Federation of Labor, he was elected secretary-treasurer of the American Federation of Labor (AFL) in 1939. He became its president in 1952, and later was president of the combined organization, AFL-CIO (1955–80).

Mechnikov or **Metchnikoff, Ilya** [mechnikof] (1845–1916) Biologist, born in Ivanovka, Ukraine. He became professor of zoology and comparative anatomy at Odessa (1870), and in 1888 joined Pasteur in Paris. He shared the 1908 Nobel Prize for Physiology or Medicine for his work on immunology, in which he discovered the cells (*phagocytes*) which devour infective organisms. >> Pasteur

Medawar, Sir Peter (Brian) [medawah(r)] (1915–87) Zoologist and one of the world's leading immunologists, born in Rio de Janeiro, Brazil. He studied zoology at Oxford, was appointed professor of zoology at Birmingham University (1947–51) and professor of comparative anatomy at University College, London (1951–62), where he pioneered experiments in the prevention of rejection in transplant operations. He was director of the National Institute for Medical Research from 1962. In 1960 he shared the Nobel Prize for Physiology or Medicine for researches on immunological tolerance in relation to skin and organ grafting. He was also well known for his writing on scientific method, as in *The Art of the Soluble* (1967). >> RR1124

Medici >> **Catherine de' Medici; Clement I; Cosimo de' Medici; Lorenzo de' Medici; Leo X; Marie de Médecis; Pius IV**

Medina-Sidonia, Alonso Pérez de Guzmán, duque de (Duke of) [medeena sidohnia] (1550–1619) Commander of the Spanish Armada, and captain-general of Andalusia, born in Sanlúcar, Spain. A distinguished administrator with a good record in conquest of Portugal, he was appointed to command the Great Armada in the Enterprise of England on the death of the Marquis of Santa Cruz (1588). After successfully navigating the Armada up the English Channel to rendezvous with Parma off the Dutch coast, he was thwarted by the latter's failure to break out, by the action of the English fleet, and by adverse weather conditions. He returned to Spain around the N of Britain, and continued in royal service to the Spanish Navy. >> Drake; Howard, Charles

Medlicott, William Norton (1900–87) Diplomatic historian, born in London, England, UK. He studied at University College, London, became lecturer at Swansea (1926–39), professor of history at Exeter (1939–53), and Stevenson professor of international history at the London School of Economics (1953–67). He was known especially for his studies of the Bismarck period in international relations, and of British diplomacy in the 20th-c.

Mee, Arthur (1875–1943) Journalist, editor, and writer, born in Stapleford, Nottinghamshire, C England, UK. He was most widely known for his *Children's Encyclopaedia* (1908) and *Children's Newspaper*. He also wrote a wide range of popular works on history, science, and geography.

Mee, Margaret (Ursula) (1909–88) British botanical artist and traveller. She trained at the Camberwell School of Art, and first visited the Amazon forests when she was 47. Ten years later, having settled in Brazil, she began her outstanding career as a botanical artist, travelling extensively in the Brazilian Amazonia, and collecting new species and painting many others, some of which have since become extinct. The Margaret Mee Amazon trust was set up in 1988 to draw attention to the area's ecological crisis.

Meegeren, Han van >> **van Meegeren, Han**

Meehan, Tony >> **Shadows, The**

Meer, Simon van der >> **van der Meer, Simon**

Megasthenes [megastheneez] (c. 350–c. 290 BC) Greek historian. He was ambassador (306–298 BC) at the Indian court of Sandrakottos or Chandragupta, where he gathered materials for *Indica*, from which Arrian, Strabo, and others borrowed. >> Arrian; Chandragupta; Strabo

Mège Mouriés, Hippolyte [mezh moories] (1817–80) Chemist and inventor, born in Draguignan, France. He patented margarine in its original form in 1869, winning the prize offered by the French government for an economical butter substitute. His margarine was manufactured from tallow, and it was not until F Boudet patented a process for emulsifying it with skimmed milk and water in 1872 that it could be made sufficiently palatable to be a commercial success.

Mehemet Ali >> **Mohammed Ali**

Mehmet Ali Agca >> **John Paul II**

Mehta, Ved (Parkash) [mayta] (1934–) Writer, born in Lahore, India. Blind from the age of eight, he went to the USA for his education when he was 15, and attended the Arkansas School for the Blind at Little Rock, and Pomona College, before going to Oxford and Harvard universities. While at Pomona he published his first book, the autobiography *Face to Face* (1957). He has had a distinguished career as a journalist, contributing chiefly to *The New Yorker*. Employing amanuenses, he has written biographies, stories, essays, and portraits of India, including *The New India* (1978) and *Rajiv Gandhi and Rama's Kingdom* (1995). His enduring achievement, however, is *Continents of Exile*, an acclaimed series of autobiographical books (1972–89). He became a US citizen in 1975.

Mehta, Zubin [mayta] (1936–) Conductor, born in Mumbai (Bombay), India. Born into a musical family, he later studied music in Vienna. He became associate conductor of the Royal Liverpool Philharmonic (1958), and went on to be conductor and musical director of many prestigious orchestras, notably the Los Angeles Philharmonic (1962–78) and the New York Philharmonic (1978–91). He is now the musical director (for life) of the Israel Philharmonic Orchestra.

Meighen, Arthur [meeuhn] (1874–1960) Canadian statesman and prime minister (1920, 1921, 1926), born in Anderson, Ontario, Canada. He became a lawyer, and sat in the Canadian House of Commons as a liberal Conservative (1908–26). He was solicitor general (1913), secretary of state (1917), and minister of the interior (1917), and succeeded Robert Borden as leader of the Conservatives in 1920. A brilliant parliamentary debater, his skill helped to carry the controversial Military Service Bill in 1917. He later became a minister without portfolio (1932–5) and a senator (1932–41). >> Borden, Robert; RR1039

Meigs, Montgomery C(unningham) [megz] (1816–92) Engineer, born in Augusta, GA. He attended the University of Pennsylvania (1831) and the US Military Academy (1836), after which he was assigned to the engineers corps. During the Civil War he was quartermaster general in the Union army, and later continued in this role to supervise the construction of several important buildings and public works in Washington, DC, notably, the Washington Aqueduct, the Cabin John Bridge, and the Pennsylvania Avenue Bridge. The Old Pension Building (1883) is his best-known work.

Meiji Tenno >> **Mutsuhito**

Meikle, Andrew [meekl] (1719–1811) Millwright and inventor, born in Houston Mill, East Lothian, E Scotland, UK. He inherited his father's mill, and invented the fantail (1750), a machine for dressing grain (1768), and the spring sail (1772). His most significant invention was a drum threshing machine which could be worked by wind, water, horse, or (some years later) steam power. He obtained a patent in 1788 and built a factory, but derived very little financial return.

Meilhac, Henri >> **Halévy, Ludovic**

Meillet, Antoine [mayay] (1866–1936) Philologist, born in Moulins, France. A great authority on Indo-European languages, he was professor at the Ecole des Hautes Etudes (1891–1906), and at the Collège de France from 1906. His standard works encompass Old Slavonic, Greek, Armenian, Old Persian, comparative Indo-European grammar, and linguistic theory.

Meinhof, Ulrike (Marie) [miynhof] (1934–76) Terrorist, born in Oldenburg, Germany. While studying at Marburg, she campaigned for German nuclear disarmament, and became a respected left-wing journalist. After an interview with the imprisoned arsonist, Andreas Baader, she became committed to the use of violence to secure radical social change. In May 1970, she helped free Baader, and they headed an underground urban guerrilla organization which conducted brutal terrorist attacks against the post-war West German materialist order. She was arrested in 1972, and in 1974 was sentenced to eight years' imprisonment. She committed suicide in Stammheim high-security prison. >> Baader, Andreas

Meir, Golda [mayeer], originally **Goldie Myerson**, *née* **Mabovitch** (1898–1978) Israeli stateswoman and prime minister (1969–74), born in Kiev, Ukraine. Brought up in Milwaukee, WI, from 1906, she became a teacher and an active Zionist. After her marriage to **Morris Myerson** (1917), she emigrated to a kibbutz in Palestine in 1921, and became a leading figure in the Labour movement. She was Israeli ambassador to the Soviet Union (1948–9), minister of labour (1949–56), then Hebraized her name when appointed foreign minister (1956–66). As prime minister, her efforts for peace in the Middle East were halted by the fourth Arab–Israeli War (1973), and she was forced to resign as a result of Israeli losses. >> RR1064

Mei Sheng [may sheng] (?–140 BC) Chinese poet. He is often credited with the introduction of the five-character line, and for this reason is sometimes called 'the father of modern Chinese poetry'.

Meissonier, (Jean Louis) Ernest [maysonyay] (1815–91) Painter, born in Lyon, France. His works were largely of military and historical scenes, painted with careful attention to detail, including several of the Napoleonic era.

Meitner, Lise [**miyt**ner] (1878–1968) Physicist, born in Vienna. She studied at Vienna, and became a professor in Berlin (1926–38), where she was also a member of the Kaiser Wilhelm Institute for Chemistry (1907–38). In 1917 she shared with Otto Hahn the discovery of the radioactive element protactinium, and became known for her work on nuclear physics. In 1938 she fled from Nazi Germany to the Nobel Physical Institute, Sweden, moving from there to the Royal Swedish Academy of Engineering Sciences, Stockholm, in 1947. With her nephew Frisch she devised the idea of nuclear fission in late 1938. She retired to England in 1960. >> Frisch, Otto; Hahn, Otto

Mela, Pomponius [**mee**la] (fl. 43) Latin geographer, born in Tingentera, Spain. He was the author of *De situ orbis* (3 vols, A Description of the World), largely borrowing from Greek sources.

Melanchthon, Philipp [me**langk**thon], originally **Philipp Schwartzerd** (1497–1560) Protestant reformer, born in Bretten, Germany. His name is a Greek translation of his German surname, 'black earth'. He studied at Heidelberg and Tübingen, and in 1516 became professor of Greek at Wittenberg and Luther's fellow worker. His *Loci communes* (1512) is the first great Protestant work on dogmatic theology. He also composed the Augsburg Confession (1530). >> Camerarius; Hamilton, Patrick; Luther

Melba, Dame Nellie, professional name of **Helen Armstrong**, *née* **Mitchell** (1861–1931) Prima donna, born in Melbourne, Victoria, Australia, from which she took her name. A talented pianist, she studied singing after her marriage in 1882. She appeared at Covent Garden in 1888, and the purity of her coloratura soprano voice won her worldwide fame. She was created a dame in 1918. 'Peach Melba' and 'Melba toast' were named after her.

Melbourne, William Lamb, 2nd Viscount (1779–1848) British statesman and prime minister (1834, 1835–41), born in London, England, UK. He studied at Cambridge and Glasgow, became a Whig MP in 1805, and was made chief secretary for Ireland (1827–8). Succeeding as second viscount (1828), he became home secretary (1830–4) under Grey. He formed a close, almost avuncular relationship with the young Queen Victoria. Defeated in the election of 1841, he resigned and thereafter took little part in public affairs. His wife wrote novels as **Lady Caroline Lamb** (1785–1828), who was notorious for her 9-months' devotion (1812–13) to Lord Byron. >> Byron, George; Grey, Charles; RR1095

Melchett, Baron >> **Mond, Ludwig**

Melchior, Lauritz (Lebrecht Hommel) (1890–1973) Tenor, born in Copenhagen. His career began as a baritone (in *Pagliacci*, 1913), then from 1918 he appeared as a tenor, making his Covent Garden debut in 1924. One of the foremost Wagnerian singers of the century, he sang at Bayreuth (1924–31) and regularly at the New York Metropolitan (1926–50).

Meleager [meli**ay**jer] (fl. 80 BC) Greek poet and epigrammatist, from Gadara, Syria. He was the author of 128 short elegiac poems, and many epigrams, contained in his anthology *Stephanos* (Garland). They comprise the core of the large collection of Greek writings known as the Greek Anthology.

Méliès, Georges [**may**lyes] (1861–1938) Illusionist and film maker, born in Paris. He made his name in Paris as a stage magician. Immediately after the invention of the cinema, he began making short films, and from 1895 was a pioneer in trick cinematography to present magical effects. His films include *Voyage to the Moon* (1902) and *20,000 Leagues Under the Sea* (1907). He fell into obscurity after 1913, and died in poverty.

Melissus [me**li**suhs] (5th-c BC) Greek philosopher and statesman. He commanded the Samian fleet which defeated the Athenians under Pericles in 441 BC. He was probably a pupil of Parmenides of Elea, and wrote a book entitled *On Nature*, which elaborated Parmenides' views on the properties of reality. It had most influence on the atomists, Democritus, and Leucippus, in their response to Eleatic doctrines. >> Leucippus; Parmenides; Pericles

Mellanby, Kenneth (1908–93) Entomologist and environmentalist, born in Barrhead, East Renfrewshire, W Scotland, UK. He studied at Cambridge and London, and his early career was in medical entomology at the London School of Hygiene and Tropical Medicine. In 1955 he was appointed head of the entomology department at Rothamsted Experimental Station, and in 1961 founded and directed the Nature Conservancy's experimental station at Monks Wood, Huntingdon. Here he led research into the deleterious effects of pesticides on the environment, and advocated the advantages of biological control of insect pests. He founded the leading journal *Environmental Pollution* in 1970.

Mellitus of Canterbury, St [**me**litus] (?–624) Christian leader, born in Rome, Italy. He may have been abbot of St Andrew's monastery in Rome, before beginning missionary work under Pope Gregory I, who sent him in 601 to England to assist Augustine, the Archbishop of Canterbury. His mission was to convert Saxon places of pagan worship into Christian churches. He was consecrated as the first Bishop of London (c.604) and became the third Archbishop of Canterbury (619–624). Feast day 24 April. >> Augustine, St (of Canterbury); Gregory I

Mellon, Andrew W(illiam) (1855–1937) Financier, philanthropist, and statesman, born in Pittsburgh, PA. Trained as a lawyer, he entered his father's banking house in 1874, became its president, and made a reputation for himself as an industrial magnate, becoming one of the richest men in the USA by the early 1920s. Entering politics, he was secretary of the Treasury (1921–32) under presidents Harding, Coolidge, and Hoover, and made controversial fiscal reforms, drastically reducing taxation of the wealthy. He endowed the National Gallery of Art at Washington, DC. >> Mellon, Paul

Mellon, Paul (1907–) Art collector and philanthropist, born in Pittsburgh, PA, the son of Andrew Mellon. He studied at Yale and Cambridge universities, then presided over his father's Washington art collection (1937–9). As chairman of two foundations set up to dispense the family fortune, he made generous gifts to several universities. Yale received his $35 million collection of British and French art in 1966. He also served as president of the National Gallery of Art (1963–79). >> Mellon, Andrew

Mellor, David (John) (1949–) British statesman. He studied at Cambridge, and was called to the bar in 1972. He was elected Conservative MP for Putney in 1979, and after holding various junior posts became minister of state at the Home Office (1986–7, 1989–90), Foreign and Commonwealth Office (1987–8), and the Department of Health (1988–9). He was minister for the arts in 1990, then chief secretary to the Treasury (1990–2) and secretary of state for national heritage (1992). His political career ended when he was forced to resign from the government in 1992 following revelations about an extra-marital affair. He has since presented a football programme on BBC's Radio 5, and was voted BBC Radio Personality of the Year in 1995. He failed to retain his seat in the 1997 election, but later that year was appointed head of a football Task Force by the Labour minister for sport.

Melmoth, Sebastian >> **Wilde, Oscar**

Melville, Andrew (1545–c. 1622) Presbyterian religious reformer, born in Baldovie, Angus, E Scotland, UK. He studied at St Andrews and Paris, and in 1568 became professor at Geneva. He was principal of Glasgow University (1574–80), then of St Mary's College, St Andrews. He had an important share in drawing up the controversial *Second Book of Discipline*. He succeeded John Knox in trying to preserve the independence of the Church from state control, heading in 1606 a deputation to remonstrate with King James I in London; but, having ridiculed the service in the Chapel Royal, he was sent to the Tower. He was released in 1611 to take a professorship in France. >> Knox, John

Melville, Herman (1819–91) Novelist, born in New York City. He became a bank clerk, but left in search of adventure, and joined a whaling ship bound for the South Seas (1841). His journeys were the subject matter for his first novels, *Typee* (1846) and *Omoo* (1847). In 1847 he married, and after three years in New York City took a farm near Pittsfield, MA. During this period he wrote his masterpiece, *Moby-Dick* (1851), a classic among sea stories. After 1857, he wrote only some poetry, leaving his long story *Billy Budd, Foretopman* in manuscript. Now regarded as one of America's greatest novelists, he was not so acclaimed during his life; even *Moby-Dick* was unappreciated.

Memlinc or **Memling, Hans** [memling] (c.1435–1494) Religious painter, born in Seligenstadt, Germany. He lived mostly in Bruges, and was probably a pupil of Rogier van der Weyden. His works include the triptych of the 'Madonna Enthroned' at Chatsworth (1468), and the 'Marriage of St Catherine' (1479) and the 'Shrine of St Ursula' (1489), both at Bruges. He was also an original and creative portrait painter. >> Weyden

Menaechmus [menekmus] (4th-c BC) Greek mathematician. One of the tutors of Alexander the Great, he was the first to investigate conics as sections of a cone. >> Alexander the Great

Menander [menander] (c. 343–291 BC) Greek comic playwright, born in Athens. He wrote more than 100 comedies, but only a few fragments of his work were known until 1906, when a papyrus containing 1328 lines from four different plays was discovered in Egypt. In 1957, however, the complete text of the comedy *Dyskolos* ('The Bad-Tempered Man') was brought to light in Geneva.

Menander (1894–1958) >> **Morgan, Charles Langbridge**

Menas, St >> **Abu Mena**

Menchik-Stevenson, Vera (Francevna), *née* **Menchik** (1906–44) Chess player, born in Moscow. She became a British citizen on her marriage in 1937. Recognized as the finest of all female chess players, she held the world title from 1927 (the first champion) to 1944, when she was killed during a London air-raid. >> RR1149

Mencius [menshius], Latin name **Meng-tzu** (Master Meng) (c. 371–c. 289 BC) Philosopher and sage, born in Shantung, China. He founded a school modelled on that of Confucius, and travelled China for some 20 years searching for a ruler to implement Confucian moral and political ideals. The search was unsuccessful, but his conversations with rulers, disciples, and others are recorded in a book of sayings compiled after his death (*Book of Meng-tzu*). His ethical system was based on the belief that human beings are innately and instinctively good, but require the proper conditions and support for moral growth. He also made many practical recommendations about taxes, road maintenance, and poor law.

Mencken, H(enry) L(ouis) (1880–1956) Philologist, editor, and satirist, born in Baltimore, MD. He studied at Baltimore Polytechnic, became a journalist and literary critic, and greatly influenced the US literary scene in the 1920s. His major work, *The American Language*, was first published in 1918, and in 1924 he founded the *American Mercury*, editing it until 1933.

Mendel, Gregor (Johann) (1822–84) Biologist and botanist, born in Heinzendorf, Austria. Entering an Augustinian cloister in 1843, he was ordained a priest in 1847. After studying science at Vienna (1851–3), he became abbot at Brno (1868). He researched the inheritance characters in plants, especially edible peas, and his experiments in hybridity in plants led to the formulation of his laws of segregation and independent assortment. His principle of factorial inheritance and the quantitative investigation of single characters have provided the basis for modern genetics. >> Correns

Mendeleyev, Dmitri Ivanovich [mendelayef] (1834–1907) Chemist, born in Tobolsk, Russia. He became a teacher, then studied at Odessa, St Petersburg, and Heidelberg, becoming professor of chemistry at St Petersburg from 1866. He devised the periodic classification (or table) of chemical elements, by which he predicted the existence of several elements which were subsequently discovered. Element No 101 (*mendelevium*) is named after him.

Mendelsohn, Erich [mendlsuhn] (1887–1953) Architect, born in Allenstein, Germany. He studied architecture at Munich, and attracted attention with his architectural sketches during World War 1. He was commissioned to design the Einstein Tower in Potsdam (1919–21), as well as factories and department stores, and became noted for his use of modern materials (particularly expanses of glass) and construction methods. In 1933 he fled to England to work, and also carried out commissions in Palestine, notably the Hebrew University at Jerusalem. From 1945 he lived in San Francisco, continuing with the design of hospitals, synagogues, and community centres.

Mendelssohn, Moses [mendelsuhn] (1729–86) Philosopher, literary critic, and biblical scholar, born in Dessau, Germany. He studied at Berlin and became the partner to a silk manufacturer. A zealous defender of enlightened monotheism, he was an apostle of deism. His major works include *Phädon* (1767), on the immortality of the soul, and *Jerusalem* (1783). >> Mendelssohn, Felix

Mendelssohn(-Bartholdy), (Jakob Ludwig) Felix [mendlsuhn] (1809–47) Composer, born in Hamburg, Germany, the grandson of Moses Mendelssohn. He studied piano and compostion in Berlin, making his first public appearance at the age of nine. A prolific composer even as a boy, among his early successes was the *Midsummer Night's Dream* overture (1826). In London in 1829 he conducted his C minor symphony. A tour of Scotland inspired him with the *Hebrides* overture and the *Scottish Symphony*. He founded an Academy of Arts at Berlin in 1841, and a music school at Leipzig in 1843. Other major works include his oratorios *St Paul* (1836) and *Elijah* (1846). >> Mendelssohn, Moses

Menderes, Adnan [menderez] (1899–1961) Turkish statesman and prime minister (1950–60), born near Aydin, Turkey. Though educated for the law, he became a farmer, and entered politics in 1932. In 1945 he became one of the leaders of the new Democratic Party, and was made prime minister when it came to power in 1950. Re-elected in 1954 and 1957, in May 1960 he was deposed and superseded after an army coup. He appeared as defendant with over 500 officials of his former Democratic Party administration at the Yassiada trials (1960–1), was sentenced to death, and hanged. >> RR1093

Mendes, Chico [mendez] (1944–88) Brazilian rubber tapper who organized resistance to the wholesale exploitation of the Amazon. He formed an alliance between the tappers and their former enemies, the Amazonian Indians, to fight against the deforesters. He was shot and killed in December 1988, but his work had attracted worldwide attention, and the fight against deforestation goes on.

Mendès-France, Pierre [mendez fräs] (1907–82) French statesman and prime minister (1954–5), born in Paris. A lawyer, he entered parliament in 1932, and in 1941 escaped to join the Free French forces in England. He was minister for national economy under Charles de Gaulle in 1945, and became a prominent member of the Radical Party. As prime minister, he ended the war in Indo-China, but his government was defeated on its N African policy. A firm critic of de Gaulle, he lost his seat in the 1958 election. >> de Gaulle; RR1049

Menem, Carlos (Saul) [menem] (1935–) Argentinian politician and prime minister (1989–), born in Anillaco, Argentina. While studying for the legal profession he became politically active in the Peronist movement (the Justice Party), founding the Youth Group in 1955. He was elected president of the Party in La Rioja (1963), and in the same year unsuccessfully contested the governorship of the province, eventually being elected in 1983 and re-elected in 1987. In 1989 he defeated the Radical Union Party candidate for the presidency. Despite inflammatory speeches during the election campaign, he declared a wish to resume normal diplomatic relations with the United Kingdom regarding the future of the Falkland Is. In 1992, after the resignation of his senior officials because of corruption allegations, he claimed he was the target of a smear campaign by the Opposition. >> RR1032

Mengele, Josef [menggele] (1911–79) Physician, born in Günzburg, Germany. He studied philosophy in Munich, where he encountered the racial ideology of Alfred Rosenberg. He later studied medicine at the University of Frankfurt, after which he joined the Institute for Hereditary Biology and Racial Hygiene (1934). An ardent Nazi, he served as medical officer with the Waffen SS during World War 2, and was appointed chief doctor at the Auschwitz concentration camp where Jews were selected for labour, extermination, or medical experimentation. He became known as 'the Angel of Death'. After the war he escaped, reportedly surfacing in South America (1949); it is believed that he befriended another Nazi, Wolfgang Gerhard, in Brazil (1961). A team of forensic experts determined that Mengele assumed Gerhard's identity when he died and was buried under that name. >> Rosenberg, Alfred

Mengistu, Haile Mariam [menggistoo] (1937–) Ethiopian soldier, politician, and president (1987–91), born in the Harar region, Ethiopia. He studied at Holetu military academy, and joined the Ethiopian army, rising to the rank of colonel. He took part in the 1974 coup which removed Emperor Haile Selassie, then in 1977 led another coup which ousted the military regime. Despite Ethiopia's perilous economy, guerrilla fighting, and frequent droughts throughout the 1970s and 1980s, he managed to retain power with help from Russia and the West. In 1987 he sanctioned the return of one-party civilian rule under the Marxist–Leninist Workers Party, with himself as president. In 1991 when rebel groups closed in on Addis Ababa, he fled the country, and his government fell. >> Haile Selassie; RR1048

Mengs, Anton Raphael (1728–79) Painter, born in Aussig, Germany. He studied under his father at Dresden, eventually settled at Rome, and directed a school of painting. A close friend of Winckelmann, he became the most famous of the early Neoclassical painters. In Madrid (1761–70, 1773–6) he decorated the dome of the grand salon in the royal palace with the 'Apotheosis of the Emperor Trajan'. >> Winckelmann

Mengzi / Meng-tzu >> **Mencius**

Menken, Adah Isaacs (1835–68) Actress, born near New Orleans, LA. After the deaths of her stepfather and her first husband, she supported herself as a dancer and circus rider, before making her acting debut in 1857. She appeared throughout the USA in *Mazeppa* (1861), almost naked, and bound to a wild horse on stage, which brought her considerable notoriety. She was paid £500 a performance (the highest ever salary for an actress) to do the same in London. She became the idol of literary men, including Dickens, Rossetti, and Swinburne, and was involved in many scandalous alliances, in and out of marriage.

Mennin, Peter (1923–83) Composer, born in Erie, PA. He studied at the Eastman College of Music, then taught at the Juilliard School, New York City (1947–58), became its president (1962–83), and was also director of the Peabody Conservatory in Baltimore (1958–62). He rapidly established himself as a composer of large-scale works, composing nine symphonies, including *The Cycle* – a choral work to his own text.

Menno Simons (1496–1561) Anabaptist leader, born in Witmarsum, The Netherlands. Ordained a Roman Catholic priest in 1524, he withdrew from the Church under the influence of Lutheran thought in 1536. He was made an elder at Groningen in 1537, and organized Anabaptist groups in N Europe that were persecuted by Catholics and Protestants alike. The evangelical *Mennonite* sect was named after him.

Menon, Krishna >> **Krishna Menon**

Menotti, Gian Carlo [menotee] (1911–) Composer, born in Cadegliano, Italy. He studied in Milan, then emigrated to the USA. A student in Philadelphia, he achieved international fame with a series of operas that began with *Amelia Goes to the Ball* (1937). *The Consul* (1950) and *The Saint of Bleecker Street* (1954) both won Pulitzer Prizes. *Amahl and the Night Visitors* (1951) was a successful television opera. In 1958 he founded the Festival of Two Worlds in Spoleto. Later works include a symphony (1976), a Mass, *O Pulchritudo* (1979), and several other operas.

Menuhin, Yehudi Menuhin, Baron [menyooin] (1916–) Violinist, born in New York City, New York, USA. He achieved fame at the age of seven when he appeared as soloist with the San Francisco Symphony Orchestra. This was followed by appearances all over the world as a prodigy, and after 18 months' retirement for study, he continued his career as a virtuoso, winning international renown especially for his interpretation of Bartók and Elgar. Largely based in Switzerland and England after World War 2, he conducted as often as he played. In 1962 he founded a school for musically gifted children near London. He was awarded an honorary knighthood in 1965, took British nationality in 1985, and was made a member of the Order of Merit in 1987 and a life peer in 1993. >> Kennedy, Nigel; Kentner

Menzel, Donald (Howard) (1901–76) Astrophysicist, born in Florence, CO. He studied at the universities of Denver and Princeton, then joined the staff of the Lick Observatory, CA, and was appointed director of the Harvard College Observatory (1954–66). He did valuable work on planetary atmospheres and on the composition of the Sun.

Menzies, Sir Robert Gordon [menzees] (1894–1978) Australian statesman and prime minister (1939–41, 1949–66), born in Jeparit, Victoria, Australia. He studied in Melbourne, practised as a barrister before entering politics, became a member of the Victoria parliament (1928), a KC (1929), and moved to the Federal House of Representatives (1934). He was Commonwealth attorney general (1935–9), then became prime minister. He again took office as premier of the coalition government in 1949, which he led for the next 25 years, maintaining strong political links with Britain and cultivating a close economic and military alliance with the USA. In 1956 he headed the Five Nations Committee, which sought to come to a settlement with Nasser on the question of Suez. He was knighted in 1963. >> Nasser; RR1033

Mercator, Gerardus [mer**kay**ter], originally **Gerhard Kremer** or **Cremer** (1512–94) Mathematician, geographer, and map-maker, born in Rupelmonde, Belgium. He graduated at Louvain, and by the time he was 24 was proficient as an engraver, calligrapher, and scientific-instrument maker. He is best known for introducing the map projection to aid navigators (1569) which bears his name, and which has been used for nautical charts ever since. In 1585 he was the first to use the word *atlas* to describe a book of maps (completed by his son in 1595), with a cover drawing of Atlas holding a globe on his shoulders.

Mercé, Antonia >> **Argentina, La**

Mercer, Cecil William >> **Yates, Dornford**

Mercer, David (1928–80) Playwright, born in Wakefield, West Yorkshire, N England, UK. He left school at 14, coming back to study painting, then took a degree in fine arts at Durham (1953). After a period as a teacher, he became a full-time writer in the early 1960s. Winner of the 1965 *Evening Standard* Award for most promising playwright, his stage work includes *Ride a Cock Horse* (1965) and *Cousin Vladimir* (1978). His screenplays include *Morgan* (1965), and *Providence* (1977). He continued to address issues of personal alienation and the class system in later television plays such as *Huggy Bear* (1976) and *Rod of Iron* (1980).

Mercer, Joe, popular name of **Joseph Mercer** (1914–90) Footballer and manager, born in Ellesmere Port, Cheshire, NWC England, UK. Already an established player with Everton when war broke out in 1939, he began a new career with Arsenal in 1946, with whom he gained two more championship medals and an FA Cup-winners' medal. He was chosen Player of the Year in 1950 when 35 years old. With Aston Villa and Manchester City he was a highly successful manager, and he had a spell later as caretaker of the England side. >> RR1156

Mercer, John (1791–1866) Dye chemist, born near Blackburn, Lancashire, NW England, UK. Almost entirely self-educated, he made many important discoveries connected with dyeing and calico printing. He is chiefly known for his invention of *mercerization* – a process by which cotton is given a silky lustre resembling silk.

Mercer, Johnny, popular name of **John H Mercer** (1909–76) Singer and composer, born in Savannah, GA. He came to prominence during the 1930s as a singer, lyricist, and composer. He founded Capitol Records in 1942, and collaborated with popular composers to produce numerous hit songs, such as 'Jeepers Creepers' and 'That Old Black Magic'. He won Oscars for several of his lyrics, including 'In the Cool, Cool, Cool of the Evening' (1951), 'Days of Wine and Roses' (1961), and 'Moon River' (1962). He contributed to many Broadway musicals and Hollywood films, and was the first president of the Songwriter's Hall of Fame.

Merchant, Ismail, originally **Ismail Noormohamed Abdul Rehman** (1936–) Film producer, born in Mumbai (Bombay), India. In 1961 he collaborated with James Ivory in setting up a film production company, Merchant-Ivory Productions. They made their first film, *The Householder*, in 1963, and achieved international success with *Shakespeare Wallah* (1995). Later works include *The Bostonians* (1984), the Oscar-nominated *A Room With A View* (1985), *Howards End* (1992), *The Remains of the Day* (1993), and *Surviving Picasso*

(1996). He has also worked as a director, his films including *The Proprietor* (1996) >> Ivory; Jhabvala

Merck, George W(ilhelm Emanuel) (1894–1957) Chemicals executive, born in New York City. He studied at Harvard, then in 1915 joined Merck & Co, the family chemical firm, becoming its president (1925–50) and chairman (1949–57). He developed the aggressive research programme that shifted Merck's focus to pharmaceuticals and made it a leader in manufacturing vitamins, sulfa drugs, and cortisone. He directed the War Research Service during World War 2.

Merckx, Eddy [merks], nickname **the Cannibal** (1945–) Racing cyclist, born in Woluwe St Pierre, Belgium. He won the Tour de France a record-equalling five times (1969–72, 1974), the Tour of Italy five times, and all the major classics, including the Milan–San Remo race, seven times. World Amateur Road Race champion in 1964, he won the professional title three times. He won more races (445) and more classics than any other rider. He retired in 1978 and established his own bicycle manufacturing company. >> RR1152

Mercouri, Melina [mer**koo**ree], originally **Anna Amalia Mercouri** (1923–94) Film actress, born in Athens. She began in films in 1955, and found international fame in 1960 in *Never on Sunday*. Always politically involved, she was exiled from Greece (1967–74), during which time she played in several British and US productions, such as *Topkapi* (1964) and *Gaily, Gaily* (1969). She returned to be elected to parliament in 1977, and became minister of culture from 1981.

Mercredi, Ovide [**mair**kredee] (1946–) Canadian aboriginal affairs activist, born in Grand Rapids, Manitoba, Canada. A Cree Indian, he studied law at the University of Manitoba, and practised as a criminal lawyer. A leading advocate of native people's rights, he supported a policy of nonviolent civil activism, and became National Chief of the Assembly of First Nations in 1991. His book, *In the Rapids: Navigating the Future of First Nations* appeared in 1993.

Mercury, Freddie, originally **Frederick Bulsara** (1946–91) British pop star, born in Zanzibar. His family moved to England in 1959, where he studied design and began singing with small groups. He formed the heavy metal group Queen in 1971, and this quickly became known for its combination of flamboyant musical technique and visual impact, seen to best effect in the promotional video released for the six-minute hit 'Bohemian Rhapsody' in 1975. The group remained popular for two decades, and were seen in some notable performances, such as the 1985 Live Aid concert. A day before his death, he made a public announcement that he had AIDS. When 'Bohemian Rhapsody' was re-released as a tribute to him, it again reached the No 1 spot in the British charts.

Meredith, George (1828–1909) Writer, born in Portsmouth, Hampshire, S England, UK. He was educated privately and in Germany, and on his return to London rejected a career in law. Although his best-known work, *The Ordeal of Richard Feverel*, was written in 1859, he achieved no real literary success to begin with, and lived in poverty, forced to eke out a living by becoming a manuscript reader. Later works, such as *The Egoist* (1879) and *Diana of the Crossways* (1885), brought him financial reward. His main poetic work is *Modern Love* (1862), based partly on his first, unhappy marriage. Other books include *Evan Harrington* (1860), *Harry Richmond* (1871), and *Beauchamp's Career* (1875). His prose works include *Poems and Lyrics of the Joy of Earth* (1883). He was awarded the Order of Merit in 1905, and enjoyed much recognition towards the end of his life.

Meredith, Owen >> **Lytton, Edward Robert Bulwer**

Merezhkovsky, Dmitry Sergeyevich [merezhofskee] (1865–1941) Novelist, critic, and poet, born in St Petersburg, Russia. He studied at university there, then became a writer, producing the historical trilogy, *Khristos i Antikhrist* (1896–1905), Christ and Antichrist, *The Death of the Gods*, *The Forerunner*, *Peter and Alexis* (trans titles), and books on Tolstoy, Ibsen, and Gogol. He opposed the Revolution in 1917, and fled to Paris in 1919 with his wife, **Zinaida Nikolayevna Hippius** (1870–1945), also a poet, novelist, and critic.

Mergenthaler, Ottmar [mergentahler] (1854–99) Inventor of the Linotype machine, born in Hachtel, Germany. Apprenticed to a watchmaker, his interest was in engineering, which he learned through evening classes. After emigrating to the USA in 1872, he worked in a machine shop belonging to a relative, where he developed the famous Linotype typesetting machine in 1886, and worked on many other inventions.

Mérimée, Prosper [mayreemay] (1803–70) Writer, born in Paris. He studied law, visited Spain in 1830, and held posts under the ministries of the navy, commerce, and the interior. He was appointed inspector-general of historical remains in France in 1833, and became a senator in 1853. He wrote novels and short stories, archaeological and historical dissertations, and travel stories, all of which display exact learning, keen observation, and humour. Among his novels are *Colomba* (1840), *Carmen* (1845, popularized by Bizet's opera), and *La Chambre bleue* (1872, The Blue Room). He also wrote plays, and the famous *Lettres á une inconnue* (1873, Letters to an Unknown Girl).

Merleau-Ponty, Maurice [mairloh pōtee] (1908–61) Philosopher, born in Rochefort-sur-mer, France. He studied in Paris, taught in various lycées, and served as an army officer in World War 2, before holding professorships at Lyon (1948) and Paris (from 1949). He helped Sartre and de Beauvoir found the journal *Les Temps Modernes* in 1945, and was a fellow-traveller with Sartre in the Communist Party in the early post-war years. His two main philosophical works are *La Structure du comportement* (1942, The Structure of Behaviour) and *Phénoménologie de la perception* (1945, Phenomenology of Perception) which investigate the nature of consciousness, and reject the extremes of both behaviouristic psychology and subjectivist accounts. >> de Beauvoir; Sartre

Merneptah [mernepta] (13th-c BC) King of Egypt (1236–1223 BC), the son of Rameses II. He is famous principally for his great victory near Memphis over the Libyans and Sea Peoples (1232 BC).

Merovech or **Merovius** [merohvius] (5th-c) Frankish ruler, the father of Childeric I (who died c.481) and grandfather of Clovis I. Little is known of his life except that the *Merovingian* dynasty is traditionally held to have taken its name from him. >> Clovis I

Merriam, Clinton Hart (1855–1942) Naturalist, zoologist, and early conservationist, born in New York City. A physician by training, he became head of the US Bureau of Biological Survey (1885–1910, later known as the Fish and Wildlife Service). He wrote on grizzly bears, brown bears, and the birds of Connecticut, but his most important work was his *Life Zones and Crop Zones of the United States* (1898). He helped in the foundation of the National Geographic Society (1888).

Merrick, Joseph >> **Treves, Frederick**

Merrifield, (Robert) Bruce (1921–) Organic chemist, born in Fort Worth, TX. He studied at the University of California, Los Angeles, and from 1949 worked at the Rockefeller Institute for Medical Research, New York City. There he devised (1959–62) the important and now much-used 'solid phase' method for synthesizing peptides and proteins from amino acids, for which he received the Nobel Prize for Chemistry in 1984.

Merrill, Charles E(dward) (1885–1956) Investment banker, born in Green Cove Springs, FL. After various jobs, he joined a commercial paper house in New York City, then with **Edmund C Lynch** started his own investment banking firm of Merrill Lynch, specializing in underwriting the securities of chain stores. Through innovative advertising techniques, the Company introduced stocks and bonds to America's growing middle-class, and became one of the largest brokerage firms in the USA.

Merrill, Frank (Dow) (1903–55) US soldier, born in Hopkinton, MA. He served as an intelligence officer early in World War 2 before being assigned to raise the volunteer unit known as *Merrill's marauders*, which fought in the Burma jungle behind the Japanese lines (1943–4). >> Wingate

Merrill, Helen, originally **Helen Milcetic** (1930–) Jazz singer, born in New York City. She sang with the Earl Hines Sextet in 1952, and made a wide range of recordings during the following decade. Her albums include *The Complete Helen Merrill on Mercury* (1959), and *The Artistry of Helen Merrill* (1968).

Merrill, Robert (1917–) Baritone, born in New York City. He sang popular music before making his operatic debut in 1944, joining the Metropolitan Opera in 1945 and remaining a favourite there for 30 years. He also appeared in recitals, with orchestras, in films, and in musical comedy.

Merriman, Brian (1747–1805) Irish Gaelic poet, born in Ennistymon, Co Clare, Ireland. He became a schoolteacher and small farmer in Feakle, later (1790) marrying and settling as a mathematics teacher in Limerick. He was author of the epic *Cúirt an Mheáin Oidhche* (c.1786, The Midnight Court). The poem was banned in all English translations after Irish independence, but the Irish language itself was deemed incapable of having a corrupting influence. Liberal (and ribald) Irish intellectuals have established an annual Merriman Summer School, convening in August in Clare.

Mersenne, Marin [mairsen] (1588–1648) Mathematician and scientist, born in Oize, France. He became a Minim Friar in 1611, and lived in Paris. Devoting himself to science, he corresponded with all the leading scientists of his day, including Descartes, Fermat, Pascal, and Hobbes, acting as a clearing house for scientific information. A pioneer in the theory of prime numbers, he also experimented with the pendulum and found the law relating its length and period of oscillation, studied the acoustics of vibrating strings and organ pipes, and measured the speed of sound. He also wrote on music, mathematics, optics, and philosophy.

Merton, Robert K(ing) (1910–) Sociologist, born in Philadelphia, PA. He studied at Temple and Harvard, going on to teach at Harvard (1934–9), Tulane (1939–41), and Columbia universities (1941–79). He was also associate director of the Bureau of Applied Social Research. He is regarded as the founder of the sociology of science, in which he developed an analysis of the norms guiding scientists' behaviour, the competition and reward system in science, and how both of these operate in historical and contemporary contexts. His main works include *Social Theory and Social Structure* (1949) and *The Sociology of Science* (1973).

Merton, Thomas (1915–68) Catholic monk and writer, born in Prades, France. He studied and taught English at Columbia University, became a convert to Roman Catholicism, and in 1941 joined the Trappist order at Our Lady of Gethsemane Abbey, Kentucky. His best-selling autobiography, *The Seven Storey Mountain* (1946), prompted many to become monks, and brought him international fame. His other works ranged from personal journals and poetry to social criticism. His growing interest in Eastern spirituality led him to attend a conference in Bangkok, where he was accidentally electrocuted by a faulty fan.

Merton, Walter de (?–1277) Clergyman, probably born in Surrey, SE England, UK. In 1264 he founded Merton College, Oxford, the prototype of the collegiate system in English universities. He was Bishop of Rochester from 1274.

Merwin, W(illiam) S(tanley) (1927–) Poet, born in New York City. He studied at Princeton, tutored Robert Graves' son in Majorca (1950), and has been based in England, France, and Hawaii. He is known for his plays, prose parables, and translations as well as for his Surrealist poetry, as in *Opening the Hands* (1983). Later works include *Travels: Poems* (1993). He received the Pulitzer Prize for *The Carrier of Ladders* (1970). >> Graves, Robert

Meselson, Matthew (Stanley) (1930–) Molecular biologist, born in Denver, CO. He studied chemistry at the California Institute of Technology, and was professor of biology at Harvard from 1964. In 1957, with **Franklin Stahl** (1929–), he carried out some ingenious experiments which both verified Watson and Crick's ideas on the way the double helix of the DNA molecule carries genetic information, and provided new information on the details. >> Crick; Watson, James

Mesmer, Franz Anton [mezmer] (1734–1815) Physician, born near Constance, Austria. He studied and practised medicine at Vienna, and c.1772 took up the idea that there exists a power which he called 'animal magnetism'. This led to the founding of *mesmerism*, precursor of hypnotism in modern psychotherapy. In 1778 he went to Paris, where he created a sensation curing diseases at seances. In 1785, when a learned commission denounced him as an imposter, he retired to Switzerland.

Messager, André (Charles Prosper) [mesazhay] (1853–1929) Composer and conductor, born in Montluçon, France. He was artistic director of Covent Garden Theatre, London (1901–7), and director of Opéra Comique, Paris (1898–1903, 1919–20). His operettas were popular in England as well as France, and include *La Bearnaise* (1885), *Madame Chrysanthème* (1893), and *Monsieur Beaucaire* (1919). He also wrote piano pieces and several ballets, notably *Les Deux pigeons* (1886, The Two Pigeons).

Messalina, Valeria [mesaleena] (c. 22–c. 48) Third wife of the emperor Claudius, whom she married at the age of 14. She bore him two children, Octavia (wife of Nero) and Britannicus. She instigated a reign of terror during which many senators were put to death, but her end came when Narcissus (secretary to Claudius) convinced Claudius that in his absence she had married Gaius Silius and was plotting against him. Her name has become a byword for avarice, lust, and cruelty. >> Britannicus; Claudius

Messerer, Asaf (1903–) Ballet dancer, teacher and choreographer, born in Vilnius. He studied with Mikhail Mordkin at the Bolshoi Ballet School, graduating in 1921 to join the company. A versatile principal, he retired from dancing in 1954 to concentrate on teaching, the element of his work for which he is best known. His choreography includes *Football Player* (1924) and *Ballet School* (1962). >> Mordkin

Messerschmitt, Willy [mesershmit], popular name of **Wilhelm Messerschmitt** (1898–1978) Aircraft engineer and designer, born in Frankfurt, Germany. He studied at the Munich Institute of Technology, and in 1926 joined the Bayerische Flugzeugwerke as its chief designer and engineer. In 1938 the company became the Messerschmitt-Aitken-Gesellschaft, producing military aircraft. His Me109 set a world speed record in 1939, and during World War 2 he supplied the Luftwaffe with its foremost types of combat aircraft. In 1944 he produced the Me262 fighter, the first jet-plane flown in combat.

Messiaen, Olivier (Eugène Prosper Charles) [mesiä] (1908–92) Composer and organist, born in Avignon, France. He studied at the Paris Conservatoire, where his teachers included Paul Dukas. He became professor at the Schola Cantorum (1936–9) and (after a period of war-time imprisonment) professor of harmony at the Paris Conservatoire in 1941. He composed extensively for organ, orchestra, voice, and piano, and made frequent use of new instruments. His music was motivated by religious mysticism, and he is best known for *Vingt regards sur l'enfant Jésus* (1944, Twenty Looks at the Infant Jesus), and the mammoth *Turangalila* symphony. His great interest in birdsong proved the stimulus for several works, including the *Catalogue d'oiseaux* for piano (1956–8). >> Dukas

Messier, Charles [mesyay] (1730–1817) Astronomer, born in Badonviller, France. He had a keen interest in comets, discovering 15, and is mainly remembered for the *Messier Catalogue* (1784), containing 103 star clusters, nebulae, and galaxies. Objects were given alphanumeric names (M1, M2, etc) – a convention which continues to be used in astronomy.

Messmer, Otto (1894–1985) Animator, born in New Jersey. He contributed joke cartoons to *Life* magazine (1914), and entered animation in 1916, scripting and animating many films, including the *Charlie Chaplin* cartoons (1917). In 1920 he created *Feline Follies*, making Felix the Cat the first cartoon film star to win international fame; one of the many spin-offs was a comic strip for newspaper syndication (1923) which he drew in his spare time. Felix failed to make the transition to sound, but Messmer continued the strip until 1954.

Mestral, Georges de >> de Mestral, Georges

Meštrović, Ivan [meshtrohvich] (1883–1962) Sculptor, born in Vrpolje, Slavonia, Croatia. Apprenticed to a marble-cutter, he eventually studied in Vienna and Paris, where he became a friend of Rodin. He designed the national temple at Kosovo (1907–12) and the colossal *Monument to the Unknown Soldier* in Belgrade (1934). He lived in England during World War 2, and executed many portrait busts, including that of Sir Thomas Beecham. After the war he emigrated to the USA, becoming a US citizen in 1954, and professor of fine arts at Notre Dame University in 1955. >> Rodin

Metastasio, Pietro [metastahzioh], originally **Pietro Armando Dominico Trapassi** (1698–1782) Poet, born in Rome. A gift for versifying attracted the attention of Fian Vincenzo Gravin, a man of letters who educated him, and left him his fortune (1718). He gained his reputation by his masque *The Garden of Hesperides* (1722), wrote the libretti for 27 operas, including Mozart's *Clemenza di Tito*, and became court poet at Vienna in 1729.

Metaxas, Ioannis [metaksas] (1871–1941) General and dictator of Greece (1936–41), born in Ithaka. He fought against the Turks in 1897, studied military science in Germany, and in 1913 became chief of the general staff. On the fall of Constantine I in 1917 he fled to Italy, but returned with him in 1921. In 1935 he became deputy prime minister, and as premier in 1936 established a Fascist dictatorship. He led the resistance to the Italian invasion of Greece in 1940, and remained in office until his death. >> Constantine I; RR1054

Metcalf, John, known as **Blind Jack of Knaresborough** (1717–1810) British engineer. He lost his sight at six, but became an outstanding athlete and horseman. During the 1745 Jacobite rising he fought at Falkirk and Culloden (1746), set up a stagecoach between York and

Knaresborough, and from 1765 constructed 185 mi of road, and numerous bridges, in Lancashire and Yorkshire.

Metchnikoff, Ilya >> **Mechnikov**

Metford, William Ellis (1824–99) Engineer and inventor, born in Taunton, Somerset, SW England, UK. He invented an explosive rifle bullet which was outlawed by the St Petersburg Convention of 1869. He then worked on the design of a breech-loading rifle (1871), which was adapted by the American James Lee as the Lee-Metford rifle, and adopted by the British War Office in 1888. >> Lee, James

Metheny, Pat (1954–) Guitarist and composer, born in Lee's Summit, Kansas City, MO. He formed his own group, producing an album a year over a decade, beginning with *Bright Size Life* (1976). He also wrote the score for the John Schlesinger film *The Falcon And The Snowman* (1985).

Methodius, St >> **Cyril and Methodius, Saints**

Methuen, Sir Algernon (Methuen Marshall) [methyooen], originally **Stedman** (1856–1924) Publisher, born in London, England, UK. He was a teacher of classics and French (1880–95), and began publishing as a sideline with Methuen & Co in 1889 to market his own textbooks. His first publishing success was Kipling's *Barrack-Room Ballads* (1892), and he also published works of Belloc, R L Stevenson, and Oscar Wilde. He was created a baronet in 1916.

Metternich, Klemens (Wenzel Nepomuk Lothar), Fürst von (Prince of) [meternikh] (1773–1859) Austrian statesman, born in Coblenz, Germany. He studied at Strasburg and Mainz, was attached to the Austrian embassy at The Hague, and became Austrian minister at Dresden, Berlin, and Paris. In 1809 he was appointed Austrian foreign minister, and negotiated the marriage between Napoleon and Marie Louise. He took a prominent part in the Congress of Vienna, and between 1815 and 1848 was the most powerful influence for conservatism in Europe, contributing much to the tension that produced the upheaval of 1848. After the fall of the imperial government in that year, he fled to England, and in 1851 retired to his castle of Johannesberg on the Rhine. >> Marie Louise; Napoleon I

Mettrie, Julien de la >> **La Mettrie, Julien Offroy de**

Meung, Jean de >> **Jean de Meung**

Meyer, Adolf [miyer] (1866–1950) Psychiatrist, born in Niederweningen, Switzerland. After medical and psychiatric training in Zürich and elsewhere, he emigrated to the USA in 1892, and held posts in a number of universities and psychiatric hospitals, including Johns Hopkins Medical School (1910–41). He sought to integrate psychiatry and medicine, seeing mental disorder as the consequence of unsuccessful adjustment patterns.

Meyer, (Julius) Lothar [miyer] (1830–95) Chemist, born in Varel, Germany. Although trained as a physician, he became the first professor of chemistry at Tübingen in 1876. He discovered the periodic law independently of Dmitri Mendeleyev in 1869, and showed that atomic volumes were functions of atomic weights. >> Mendeleyev

Meyer, Viktor [miyer] (1848–97) Chemist, born in Berlin. He studied under Bunsen at Heidelberg University, became professor at Zürich, Göttingen, and finally at Heidelberg (1889). He discovered and investigated thiophene and the oximes. >> Bunsen

Meyerbeer, Giacomo [miyerbayer], originally **Jakob Liebmann Meyer Beer** (1791–1864) Operatic composer, born in Berlin. At seven he played Mozart's D-minor piano concerto in public, and at 15 was received into the house of Abt Vogler at Darmstadt. He attracted attention as a pianist in Vienna, and after studying in Italy produced operas in the new style (Rossini's), which were well

received. He lived mostly in Berlin (1824–31), then studied French opera, writing the highly successful *Robert le Diable* (1831) and *Huguenots* (1836). He was appointed *Kapellmeister* at Berlin (1842), and continued to write successfully. >> Rossini

Meyerhof, Otto Fritz [miyerhohf] (1884–1951) Physiologist, born in Hanover, Germany. He studied at Heidelberg, and became professor at Kiel (1918–24), director of the physiology department at the Kaiser Wilhelm Institute for Biology (1924–9), and professor at Heidelberg (1930–8). He shared the 1922 Nobel Prize for Physiology or Medicine for his work on the metabolism of muscles. Forced to leave Nazi Germany in 1938, he continued his work in France, and in 1940 fled to America, where he was professor at Pennsylvania University. >> RR1124

Meyerhold, Vsevolod Emilievich [miyerhohld] (1874–c.1940) Actor and director, born in Penza, Russia. He joined the Moscow Art Theatre as an actor, and was appointed by Stanislavsky as director of the new Studio on Povarskaya Street in 1905. He later became director of the Theatre of the Revolution (1922–4) and of the Meyerhold Theatre (1923–38). He was arrested in 1939 after delivering a defiant speech at a theatre conference, and either died in a labour camp or was executed.

Meynell, Alice (Christiana Gertrude), *née* **Thompson** (1847–1922) Essayist and poet, born in London, England, UK. She spent her childhood on the mainland of Europe, and became a convert to Catholicism. Her volumes of essays include *The Colour of Life* (1896) and *Hearts of Controversy* (1917). She published several collections of her own poems, starting in 1875 with *Preludes*. In 1877 she married **Wilfrid Meynell** (1852–1948), author and journalist, with whom she launched the journal *Merry England* (1883–95), for which she wrote many essays. >> Thompson, Francis

Meyrink, Gustav [miyringk] (1868–1932) Writer, born in Vienna. He translated Dickens and wrote satirical novels with a strong element of the fantastic and grotesque. Among the best known are *Der Golem* (1915) and *Walpurgisnacht* (1917).

Mialaret, Adèle >> **Michelet, Jules**

Miaskovsky, Nikolay Yakovlevich [miyaskofskee] (1881–1950) Composer, born near Warsaw. Originally a military engineer, he studied under Rimsky-Korsakov, and after army service (1914–21) he became an influential professor of composition at Moscow Conservatory. Among his works are 27 symphonies, orchestral pieces, concertos for violin and cello, 13 string quartets, songs, and nine piano sonatas. >> Rimsky-Korsakov

Micah [miyka], also known as **Micheas** (735–665 BC) One of the 12 so-called 'minor' prophets of the Hebrew Bible, a native of Moresheth Gath in SW Judah. He prophesied during the reigns of Jotham, Ahaz, and Hezekiah, being a younger contemporary of Isaiah, Hosea, and Amos. His writings attack social injustices against the poorer classes, and he is known for predicting the punishment of Samaria and Jerusalem because of the sins of their people. >> Amos; Isaiah

Michael VIII Palaeologus [payleeologus] (c. 1224–1282) Byzantine emperor (1261–82), born in Nicaea into the Greek nobility. He rose to be a successful general in the empire of Nicaea. In 1258 he became a regent for, and soon co-ruler with, the eight-year-old emperor, John IV Lascaris, whom he later had blinded and imprisoned. In 1261 he became emperor of Constantinople, incurring the enmity of the papacy and Charles of Anjou (1227–85) who aimed to re-establish the Latin empire. The forced reunion of the Orthodox Church with Rome aroused great discontent among his subjects but warded off attacks until 1281. The hostile Pope Martin IV (pontiff 1281–5) proclaimed a crusade against him, but Michael incited discontent in Sicily, which was invaded by his allies the Aragonese, thereby ending the Angevin threat. >> RR1038

Michael (1921–) King of Romania (1927–30, 1940–7), born in Sinaia, Romania, the son of Carol II. He first succeeded to the throne on the death of his grandfather Ferdinand I, his father having renounced his own claims in 1925. In 1930 he was supplanted by his father (reigned 1930–40), but was again made king in 1940 when the Germans gained control of Romania. In 1944 he played a considerable part in the overthrow of the dictatorship of Antonescu. He announced the acceptance of the Allied peace terms, and declared war on Germany. Forced in 1945 to accept a Communist-dominated government, he was later compelled to abdicate (1947), and has since lived in exile near Geneva. >> Antonescu; Carol II; RR1084

Michael, George, originally **Yorgos Kyriatou Panayiotou** (1963–) Singer and songwriter, born in Finchley, NW Greater London, England, UK. A partner with **Andrew Ridgeley** (1963–) of the band Wham!, he released his debut solo single 'Careless Whisper' in 1985, which reached number 1 in the UK charts, while Wham!'s popularity continued to rise. In 1985 he became the youngest ever recipient of the Ivor Novello Songwriter of the Year award (he won it again in 1989). His second solo single 'A Different Corner' (1986) topped the UK charts before the final Wham! concert. His debut solo album, *Faith*, topped the UK and US charts, staying in the US charts for over a year.

Michaelis, Leonor [meekaylis] (1875–1949) Biochemist, born in Berlin. He was professor in Berlin (1908–22) and the Nagoya Medical School in Japan (1922–6), then went to the USA to Johns Hopkins University (1926–9) and the Rockefeller Institute (1929–40). He made early deductions on enzyme action, and is especially known for the *Michaelis–Menten equation* on enzyme-catalysed reactions.

Michael Romanov [rohmanof] (1596–1645) Tsar of Russia (1613–45), the great-nephew of Ivan IV. He was the founder of the Romanov dynasty that ruled Russia until the revolution of 1917. Elected by the boyars after a successful revolt against the Poles, he brought an end to the Time of Troubles that had plagued Russia since the death of Boris Godunov in 1605. He concluded peace with Sweden (1617) and Poland (1618). He left the business of government largely in the hands of his father, the patriarch Filaret (Philaret) (**Fedor Nikitch Romanov**, c.1554/5–1633), who reorganized the army and industry with the help of experts from abroad, and consolidated the system of serfdom. >> Godunov; Ivan IV; RR1085

Micheas >> **Micah**

Michel, Claude >> **Clodion**

Michelangeli, Arturo Benedetti [meekelanjelee] (1920–95) Pianist, born in Brescia, Italy. He studied in Brescia and Milan, and won the International Music Competition in Geneva in 1939. After war service in the Italian air force, he acquired a legendary reputation as a virtuoso in the postwar years, enhanced by the rarity of his public performances, and became highly regarded as a teacher.

Michelangelo [miyklanjeloh], in full **Michelangelo di Lodovico Buonarroti Simoni** (1475–1564) Sculptor, painter, and poet, born in Caprese, Italy. As a boy he was placed in the care of a stonemason at Settignano, and in 1488 spent three years in Florence with Ghirlandaio. He received the patronage of Lorenzo de' Medici, and after his death (1492) spent three years in Bologna. His 'Cupid' was bought by Cardinal San Giorgio, who summoned him to Rome (1496), where he stayed for four years. He then returned to Florence, where he sculpted the marble 'David'. Though

he did not wholly neglect painting, his genius was essentially plastic, and he was far more interested in form than in colour. In 1503 Julius II summoned him back to Rome, where he was commissioned to design the pope's tomb; but interruptions and quarrels left him able to complete only a fragment. Instead, he was ordered to decorate the ceiling of the Sistine Chapel with paintings, which he did with reluctance (1508–12). In 1528 danger to Florence forced him to the science of fortification, and when the city was besieged (1529) he was foremost in its defence. His last pictorial achievement was 'The Last Judgement' (1537), and the next year he was appointed architect of St Peter's, to which he devoted himself until his death. >> Ghirlandaio; Lorenzo de' Medici

Michelangelo Merisi >> **Caravaggio**

Michelet, Jules [meeshlay] (1798–1874) Historian, born in Paris. He lectured on history at the Ecole Normale, and was appointed professor of history at the Collège de France (1838–51). The greatest of his many historical works is his monumental *Histoire de France* (24 vols, 1833–67). By refusing to swear allegiance to Louis Napoleon he lost his appointments, and henceforth worked mostly in Brittany and the Riviera. His second wife, **Adèle Mialaret**, collaborated with him in several nature books, including *L'Oiseau* (1856) and *La Mer* (1861).

Michelin, André [michelin], Fr [meeshlī] (1853–1931) Tyre manufacturer, born in Paris. He and his younger brother **Edouard** (1859–1940) established the Michelin tyre company in 1888, and were the first to use demountable pneumatic tyres on motor cars. They also initiated the production of high-quality road maps and guide books.

Michell, John (1724–93) Geologist, born in Nottinghamshire, C England, UK. A fellow of Queen's College, Cambridge, and professor of geology (1762–64), he described a method of magnetization, founded the science of seismology, and is credited with the invention of the torsion balance.

Michelozzi (di Bartolommeo) [meekelotsee] (1396–1472) Architect and sculptor, born in Florence, Italy. He was associated with Ghiberti on his famous bronze doors for the baptistery there, and collaborated with Donatello in several major sculpture groups, including monuments to John XXIII (the anti-pope), and Cardinal Brancacci (1427). He was court architect to Cosimo de' Medici, with whom he was in exile at Venice, where he designed a number of buildings. One of his finest works is the Ricardi Palace in Florence. >> Cosimo de' Medici; Donatello; Ghiberti

Michelson, A(lbert) A(braham) [mikelsn] (1852–1931) Physicist, born in Strzelno, Poland. His family emigrated to the USA in 1854. He trained at the Naval Academy, Annapolis, MD, studied physics at various centres in Europe, and became professor of physics at Chicago from 1892. He established the speed of light as a fundamental constant, and in 1907 became the first US scientist to be awarded the Nobel Prize for Physics. He invented an interferometer and an echelon grating, and did important work on the spectrum, but is chiefly remembered for the *Michelson–Morley* experiment (1887) to determine ether drift, the negative result of which set Albert Einstein on the road to the theory of relativity. >> Einstein, Albert; Morley, Edward Williams

Michie, Donald [michee] (1923–) Specialist in artificial intelligence, born in Rangoon, Burma. He studied at Oxford, and worked on the Colossus code-breaking project in World War 2. After a career in experimental genetics, he developed the study of machine intelligence at Edinburgh University as director of experimental programming (1963–6), and professor of machine intelligence (1967–84, now emeritus). He is editor-in-chief of the *Machine Intelligence* series, and became chief scientist at the Turing Institute (1986–92), which he founded in Glasgow in 1984. In publications such as *On Machine Intelligence* (1974) and *The Creative Computer* (1984) he has argued that computer systems are able to generate new knowledge.

Michurin, Ivan Vladimirovich [mi**choor**in] (1855–1935) Horticulturist, born near Dolgoye, Russia. At his private orchard at Koslov, which became a state institution, he developed many new varieties of fruit and berries. His theory of cross-breeding, which postulated the idea that acquired characteristics were heritable, became state doctrine amid much controversy. >> Lysenko

Mickiewicz, Adam (Bernard) [mits**kyay**vich] (1798–1855) The national poet of Poland, born near Novogrodek, Lithuania. He studied at Wilno, and published his first poems in 1822. After travelling in Germany, France, and Italy, he wrote his masterpiece, the epic *Pan Tadeusz* (1834, Thaddeus). He taught at Lausanne and Paris, and in 1853 went to Italy to organize the Polish legion.

Micklewhite, Maurice >> **Caine, Michael**

Middleton, Thomas (c. 1570–1627) Playwright, probably born in London, England, UK. After spending two years at Oxford and writing verse, he wrote plays for producer Philip Henslowe, collaborating with Dekker on plays such as *The Honest Whore* (1604), a comedy. In 1620 he was appointed city chronologer, commissioned to write and produce the Lord Mayors' pageants. His stage masterpieces include *Women Beware Women* (c.1621) and *The Changeling* (1622, with William Rowley). >> Dekker; Henslowe; Rowley, William

Midgley, Thomas, Jr (1889–1944) Engineer and inventor, born in Beaver Falls, PA. He studied engineering at Cornell University. During World War 1, on the staff of Dayton (OH) Engineering Laboratories (1916–23), he worked on the problem of 'knocking' in petrol engines, and by 1921 found tetraethyl lead to be effective as an additive to petrol, used with 1,2-dibromoethane to reduce lead oxide deposits in the engine. As president of Ethyl Corporation from 1923, he introduced Freon-12 as a non-toxic non-inflammable agent for domestic refrigerators. He also devised the octane number method of rating petrol quality.

Midler, Bette [bet] (1945–   ) Comedienne and actress, born in Honolulu, HI. After studying drama at the University of Hawaii she was hired as a film extra, and made her stage debut in New York City in 1966. She then developed a popular nightclub act as a chanteuse and purveyor of outrageously bawdy comic routines. Her album *The Divine Miss M* (1974) won her a Grammy award as Best New Artist, and the same year she received a Tony award for her record-breaking Broadway show. Her dramatic performance in the film *The Rose* (1979) earned her an Oscar nomination, and she has since enjoyed considerable commercial success in a string of films including *Outrageous Fortune* (1987), *Big Business* (1988), *Scenes from a Mall* (1991), *The First Wives Club* (1996), and *That Old Feeling* (1997).

Mielziner, Jo [meel**zee**ner] (1901–1976) US set and theatre designer, born in Paris. He designed the sets for over 400 Broadway plays, most of the major productions from the 1930s to the 1950s. Turning his back on the earlier tradition of theatrical realism, he often employed mere suggestions of settings, using scrims and isolated scenic units to create further effects. His use of lighting to change the dramatic focus from one scene to another has been described as 'cinematic'. He was the designer of the Washington Square Theatre and the Vivian Beaumont Theatre at Lincoln Center with Eero Saarinen. >> Saarinen, Eero

Mies van der Rohe, Ludwig [mees van duh **roh**uh], also spelled **Miës**, originally **Ludwig Mies** (1886–1969) Architect and designer, born in Aachen, Germany. A pioneer of glass skyscrapers, he designed high-rise flats for the Weissenhof Exhibition in 1927, and the German Pavilion for the Barcelona International Exposition (1929). He also designed tubular-steel furniture, particularly the 'Barcelona chair'. He was director of the Bauhaus in Dessau (1930–3), before becoming professor of architecture at the Illinois Institute of Technology in Chicago (1937–58). Among his major works are the two glass apartment towers on Lake Shore Drive in Chicago, the Seagram Building in New York City (1956–8), and the Public Library in Washington, DC (1967).

Mihailović, Dragoljub [mi**hiyl**ohvich], nickname **Drazha** (1893–1946) Serbian soldier, born in Ivanjica, Serbia. After World War 1, he rose to the rank of colonel in the Yugoslav army. In 1941 when Germany occupied Yugoslavia, he remained in the mountains and organized resistance, forming groups (Chetniks) to wage guerrilla warfare. He became minister of war for the Yugoslavian goverment in exile (1943), then allied himself with the Germans, and then with the Italians in order to fight the Communists. After the war he was captured and executed by the Tito government for collaboration.

Mikan, George (Lawrence) [**miy**kn] (1924–   ) Basketball player, born in Joliet, IL. He studied at Chicago, then played with Minneapolis in the National Basketball Association (1948–56), winning the championship five times. He led the NBA in points-scoring three times. At 6 ft 10 in tall, he set the stage for the big men who now dominate the sport, and helped launch basketball into a new era. He resigned in 1969, continuing as a successful lawyer. >> RR1146

Mikoyan, Anastas Ivanovich [mikoy**an**] (1895–1978) Politician, born in Sanain, Armenia, the brother of Artem Ivanovich Mikoyan. He studied theology, then joined the Bolsheviks in 1915. A member of the Central Committee in 1922, he supported Stalin against Trotsky, and in 1926 became minister of trade, doing much to improve Soviet standards of living, and introducing several ideas from the West. He was vice-chairman of the Council of Ministers (1955–64), and President of the Presidium of the Supreme Soviet (1964–5). >> Mikoyan, Artem Ivanovich; Stalin; Trotsky

Mikoyan, Artem Ivanovich [mikoy**an**] (1905–70) Aircraft designer, born in Sanain, Armenia, the brother of Anastas Ivanovich Mikoyan. He was a metal-worker, and served in the Red Army before graduating from the NE Zhukovsky Air Force Academy (1936). He was best known for the MiG fighter aircraft produced by the design bureau he headed with Gurevich, including the MiG-1 (1940), and the MiG-3 (1941), both single-engine fighters used in World War 2, and the MiG-21 (1967) single-turbojet Mach 2 fighter interceptor, on which design the world's first supersonic passenger aircraft, the Tu-144, was based. >> Gurevich; Mikoyan, Anastas Ivanovich

Milanov, Zinka [mi**lah**nof] (1906-89) Soprano, born in Zagreb. She studied in Zagreb, Prague, and New York City, made her debut as Leonora in *Il Trovatore* (1927), and became principal soprano with the Zagreb Opera (1928–35). In 1937 she sang in Verdi's *Requiem* at the Salzburg Festival under Toscanini, and appeared in *Il Trovatore* at the New York Metropolitan Opera.

Miles, Bernard (James) Miles, Baron (1907–91) Actor, stage director, and founder of the Mermaid Theatre, born in Uxbridge, W Greater London, England, UK. His career as an actor flourished from the 1930s onward, but it was as the founder of the Mermaid Theatre that he made his greatest contribution to the British theatre. In 1951 he founded a small private theatre in the grounds of his home at St John's Wood, London; it was re-erected in the City of London, and in 1959 a permanent, professional

Mermaid Theatre, financed by public subscription, was built at Puddle Dock, Blackfriars. He was knighted in 1969.

Miles, Nelson (Appleton) (1839–1925) US soldier, born in Westminster, MA. A clerk in a crockery store when the Civil War broke out, he fought in the Army of the Potomac, ending the war as a brigadier general. After the war, he was Confederate President Jefferson Davis's jailer at Fortress Monroe, VA, and was criticized for keeping Davis shackled in his cell. He then fought the Indians on the W frontier (1869–91), capturing Chief Joseph (1877) and Geronimo (1886); but his reputation never recovered from allowing the massacre at Wounded Knee (1890). He became commander-in-chief of the army in 1895, and led the US forces that occupied Puerto Rico in 1898. >> Davis, Jefferson; Geronimo

Milgram, Stanley (1933–84) Psychologist, born in New York City. He studied at Harvard, then taught at Yale (1960–3) and the City University of New York (1967–84). He became concerned to understand how apparently ordinary people in Nazi Germany had committed the atrocities of the Holocaust, so he examined what factors would influence the tendency of people to obey orders in an artificial situation where they were given to believe (wrongly) that they were administering electric shocks to other experimental subjects. The most striking result of this study was that the vast majority of people were prepared to do so in the cause of 'science' when requested by an authoritarian figure. The results are published in his most famous research programme, *Obedience to Authority: an Experimental View* (1974).

Milhaud, Darius [meeoh] (1892–1974) Composer, born in Aix-en-Provence, France. He studied under Widor and d'Indy at the Paris Conservatoire. While attached to the French Embassy at Rio de Janeiro (1917–18), he met the playwright Paul Claudel, with whom he frequently collaborated, as on the opera *Christopher Columbus*. Returning to France, he was for a while a member of *Les Six*. He was professor of music at Mills College, California (1940–7), and taught at the Paris Conservatoire from 1947. His ballets include the jazz ballet *La Création du monde* (1923, The Creation of the World), and he composed several operas, much incidental music for plays, symphonies, and orchestral, choral, and chamber works. >> Auric; Claudel, Paul; Cocteau; d'Indy; Durey; Honegger; Poulenc; Widor

Milken, Michael (Robert) (1946–) Investment entrepreneur, born in California. He studied at the University of California, Berkeley, and joined Drexel, Burnham, Lambert in 1970. He led the firm into the 1980s, using high-risk, high-yield bonds to finance corporate takeovers. Condemned by some for virtually inventing these 'junk bonds' – bonds secured by little more than the future promises of the very companies the bonds were being used to take over – he was praised by others for shaking up complacent US businesses. In 1989 he admitted to fraud and racketeering charges, and was imprisoned until 1993.

Mill, James (1773–1836) Philosopher, historian, and economist, the father of John Stuart Mill, born in Northwater Bridge, Angus, E Scotland, UK. He studied for the ministry at Edinburgh, and became a teacher, then a journalist. A disciple and friend of Jeremy Bentham, he was an enthusiastic proponent of utilitarianism, and took a leading part in the founding of University College, London (1825). His first major publication was the *History of British India* (1817–18), which secured him a permanent position with the East India Co, where he rose to become head of the Examiner's Office in 1830. He continued writing utilitarian essays for such publications as the *Westminster Review* and the *Encyclopaedia Britannica*, and wrote *Analysis of the Phenomenon of the Human Mind* (1829), his main philosophical work,

which provides a psychological basis for utilitarianism. >> Bentham, Jeremy; Mill, John Stuart

Mill, John Stuart (1806–73) Empiricist philosopher and social reformer, born in London, England, UK. His father James Mill was responsible for his education, and in 1823 he began a career under his father at the India Office, where he advanced to become head of his department. One of the major intellectual figures of the 19th-c, he was leader of the Benthamite utilitarian movement, helped form the Utilitarian Society, was a major contributor to the *Westminster Review*, and became a regular participant in the London Debating Society. He published his major work, *A System of Logic*, in 1843. In 1851 he married **Harriet Taylor**, who helped him draft the brilliant essay *On Liberty* (1859), the most popular of all his works. His other main works include *Utilitarianism* (1863) and *Three Essays on Religion* (1874). He was elected to parliament in 1865, campaigning for women's suffrage and liberalism. >> Mill, James

Millais, Sir John Everett [milay] (1829–96) Painter, born in Southampton, Hampshire, S England, UK. He studied at the Royal Academy from the age of 11, and became a founder member of the Pre-Raphaelite Brotherhood, his works in this style including the controversial 'Christ in the House of His Parents' (1850, Tate, London). His later works were largely portraits, and some landscapes, and he also became well known for his woodcut illustrations for magazines. He became a baronet in 1885. A late painting, 'Bubbles' (1886), achieved huge popularity. >> Hunt, William Holman; Patmore; Rossetti, Dante Gabriel

Millar, Kenneth >> **MacDonald, Ross**

Millay, Edna St Vincent [milay] (1892–1950) Poet, born in Rockland, ME. Her first poem was published when she was a student at Vassar College, NY. Moving to Greenwich Village, then at its height as a meeting place for artists and writers, she published *A Few Figs from Thistles* (1920), from which the line 'My candle burns at both ends' came to represent youthful escapades. In 1923 came *The Harp Weaver and Other Poems*, for which she was awarded a Pulitzer Prize. She published many other works, including three verse plays, and wrote the libretto for the successful American opera, *The King's Henchman* (1927).

Mille, De >> **De Mille**

Miller, Arthur (1915–) Playwright, born in New York City. After his father's ruin in the Depression, he worked to pay for his education at the University of Michigan, where he began writing plays. He achieved recognition with *All My Sons* (1947), but *Death of a Salesman* (1949) won the Pulitzer Prize and brought him international fame. This and *The Crucible* (1953) have been performed all over the world, making him America's most well-known playwright. His brief marriage to Marilyn Monroe, from whom he was divorced in 1961, and his brush with the authorities over early Communist sympathies, helped bring him considerable publicity. He wrote many other plays, a screenplay, short stories, and a collection of theatre essays. His autobiography *Timebends* was published in 1987. >> Monroe, Marilyn

Miller, (Alton) Glenn (1904–44) Trombonist and bandleader, born in Clarinda, IA. He studied at Colorado, joined the Ben Pollack Band before completing his studies, then moved to New York City in 1928, where he worked as a freelance musician and arranger. From 1937 he led a succession of popular dance orchestras, and joined the US Army Air Force in 1942, forming the US Air Force band to entertain the troops. He achieved a distinctive sound with a saxophone–clarinet combination, his many successes including 'Moonlight Serenade' (his theme song), 'Little Brown Jug', and 'In the Mood' (1939). While the band was stationed in Europe, he was a passenger in a small aircraft lost without trace over the English Channel. Several theories have been proposed for the disappearance, such as bad weather, but records have suggested that his aircraft may have been hit by bombs jettisoned over the Channel by Allied bombers returning from a mission aborted through bad weather. The big band sound he created has continued to be performed with great popularity since his death, and the film *The Glenn Miller Story* (1953) has kept his memory alive.

Miller, Henry (Valentine) (1891–1980) Writer, born in New York City. With money from his father, which was intended to finance him through Cornell, he travelled throughout SW USA and Alaska. In 1930 he moved to France for nine years, during which time he published *Tropic of Cancer* (1934) and *Tropic of Capricorn* (1938), much of which is autobiographical and explicitly sexual. American editions of the *Tropics* were not published until the early 1960s, but he became one of the most widely read US authors. Other books include *Black Spring* (1936), *The Air-Conditioned Nightmare* (1945), and *The Rosy Crucifixion* trilogy (1965).

Miller, Joaquin, pseudonym of **Cincinnatus Hiner Miller** (1837–1913) Poet, born in Liberty, IN. He settled in the Old West after practising law in Oregon. A flamboyant character, at one time he owned a newspaper and a pony express, and took the name Joaquin from a Mexican brigand. After a brief spell in the UK, where he was much admired, he settled in California from 1877 as a fruit-grower. His best-known poem is 'Columbus', with the familiar refrain 'On, sail on!'. His other works include *Songs of the Sierras* (1871) and *The Danites in the Sierras* (1881).

Miller, Jonathan (Wolfe) (1934–) Actor and director, born in London, England, UK, He qualified as a doctor at Cambridge, and his career has combined medical research with contributions to stage and television. He came to public attention as part of the *Beyond the Fringe* team (1961–4), and in 1962 he directed John Osborne's *Under Plain Cover* at the Royal Court, which led to work in New York City, and an associate directorship of the National Theatre (1973–5), as well as much freelance work. From 1964 to 1965 he was editor and presenter of the BBC Television arts programme, *Monitor*. From 1974 he specialized in productions for the English National Opera and other major companies, and was artistic director at the Old Vic, London (1988–90). He wrote and presented the BBC television series *The Body in Question* (1977) and *States of Mind* (1982), and in 1985 became a research fellow in neuropsychology at Sussex University. He has written several books, including *Subsequent Performances* (1986). >> Cook, Peter; Moore, Dudley

Miller, Keith (Ross) (1919–) Cricketer, born in Melbourne, Victoria, Australia. In the great Don Bradman Test side of 1948, he established himself as the world's leading all-rounder of the time. During his career he scored 2598 runs in 55 Test matches, including seven centuries, and took 170 wickets. After retirement he became a sports journalist. >> Bradman

Miller, Merton (1923–) Economist, born in Boston, MA. He taught at the Carnegie Institute of Technology, and in 1961 moved to Chicago University. In 1990 he shared the Nobel Prize for Economics for his contributions in applying economic theory to the field of corporate finance.

Miller, Stanley Lloyd (1930–) Chemist, born in Oakland, CA. He studied at California University and taught there from 1960. His most familiar work concerns the possible origin of life on Earth. He passed electric discharges (similar to miniature thunderstorms) through a mixture of those gases which probably formed the early planetary atmosphere. After some days, analysis showed the presence

of some typical organic substances, including amino acids and urea.

Miller, William (1781–1849) Religious leader, born in Pittsfield, MA. A New York farmer, he believed that the Second Coming of Christ was imminent in 1843 or 1844, and founded the religious sect of Second Adventists or *Millerites*. His followers organized the Seventh Day Adventist Church in 1863. >> White, Ellen Gould

Milles, Carl (Wilhelm Emil) [milz], original surname **Andersson** (1875–1955) Sculptor, born in Uppsala, Sweden. He studied in Paris, and won recognition with the competition for the Sten Sture monument near Uppsala (completed 1925). His other monuments include the Gustav I Vasa statue, and he was especially renowned as a designer of fountains. Much of his work is in the USA, where he settled in 1931, becoming a US citizen in 1945. Noteworthy examples are *Wedding of the Rivers* (1940) in St Louis, and *St Martin of Tours* (1955) in Kansas City.

Millet, Jean François [meeay] (1814–75) Painter, born in Gruchy, France. He farmed with his peasant father before being placed with a painter at Cherbourg. In 1837 he worked under Delaroche in Paris, achieving recognition at the Salon in 1844. Later he settled in Barbizon, painting the rustic life of France with sympathetic power. His famous 'Sower' was completed in 1850. His 'Peasants Grafting' (1855) was followed by 'The Gleaners' (1857), and other masterpieces. He also produced charcoal drawings of high quality, and etched a few plates. He received little public notice, but after the Great Exhibition in Paris (1867) he was awarded the *Légion d'honneur*. >> Delaroche

Milligan, Spike, popular name of **Terence Alan Milligan** (1918–) Humorist, born in Ahmadnagar, India. A singer and trumpeter, he made his radio debut in *Opportunity Knocks* (1949), and co-wrote and performed in *The Goon Show* (1951–9). His unique perspective on the world, allied to an irrepressible sense of the ridiculous, has been expressed in all the artistic media and has left an indelible influence on British humour. As well as numerous stage and television appearances, and small roles in feature films, he has published a variety of children's books, poetry, and comic novels including *Puckoon* (1963), *Adolf Hitler, My Part in His Downfall* (1971), and an autobiography, *Where Have All the Bullets Gone?* (1985). In 1995 appeared *Spike Milligan: A Celebration*. >> Bentine; Secombe; Sellers

Millikan, Robert (Andrews) (1868–1953) Physicist, born in Morrison, IL. He studied at Columbia University, Oberlin College, Berlin, and Göttingen, taught physics at Chicago University (1896–1921), then became head of California Institute of Technology. He determined the charge on the electron, for which he was awarded the Nobel Prize for Physics in 1923, and did important work on cosmic rays, showing them to come from space.

Mills, Charles Wright (1916–62) Sociologist, born in Waco, TX. He studied at the universities of Texas and Wisconsin, taught at Wisconsin and Maryland, and was professor at Columbia (1946–62). One of the most controversial figures in American social science, he was strongly critical of mainstream US sociology, and was something of an outcast from academic life; but his writings attracted a large popular audience, and he had an important influence on the American New Left.

Mills, Enos (Abijah) (1870–1922) Naturalist and writer, born near Kansas City, KS. A frail child, he went to Colorado for his health, settling in a cabin at the foot of Long's Peak mountain. He began studying nature, became a writer, lecturer, and mountain guide, and in 1901 opened the Long Peak Inn, a haven for nature lovers. His lobbying efforts led to the establishment of the Rocky Mountain National Park in 1915.

Mills, Hayley (1946–) Film actress, born in London, England, UK. From an acting family, she made her film debut in *Tiger Bay* (1959) with her father, John Mills. She won a special Oscar for her part in *Pollyanna* (1960), and went on to star in such films as *The Parent Trap* (1961), *Whistle Down The Wind* (1961), and *Endless Night* (1971), as well as several television movies, including *Parent Trap II* (1986) and its two sequels (both 1989). >> Mills

Mills, Sir John (Lewis Ernest Watts) (1908–) Actor and director, born in Felixstowe, Suffolk, E England, UK. He first appeared on stage in 1929, becoming a popular actor in light comedies and musicals in the 1930s. He was best known as a film star, appearing in many patriotic war films as well as such epics as *Scott of the Antarctic* (1948), *The Colditz Story* (1954), and *Oh! What a Lovely War* (1969). For two generations of film audiences he represented the figure of a fundamentally decent and reliable Englishman, and took few unsympathetic roles. He was awarded an Oscar for his role as the village idiot in *Ryan's Daughter* (1970), and appeared in *Gandhi* (1982) and *A Woman of Substance* (1986). His stage career indicates a wider acting range, including *The Petition* at the National Theatre in 1986. He was knighted in 1976, and is the father of actresses **Juliet** and **Hayley**. >> Mills, Hayley; Mills, Juliet

Mills, Juliet (Maryon) (1941–) Film actress, born in London, England, UK. She appeared in several films as a baby and young child, beginning with *In Which We Serve* (1942), and made her debut as an adult in *No My Darling Daughter* (1961). Later films include *Carry on Jack* (1964), *Oh! What a Lovely War* (1969), and *Jonathan Livingston Seagull* (1973), as well as several television movies, such as *Waxwork II* (1992) and *A Stranger in the Mirror* (1993).

Mills, Martin >> **Boyd, Martin**

Mills, Wilbur (Daigh) (1909–92) US representative, born in Kensett, AR. He studied at Harvard, and became a Democratic county and probate judge in White Co, AR (1934–8), before going to the US House of Representatives (1939–77). He chaired the powerful Committee on Ways and Means (1957–73) and the Joint Committee on Internal Revenue before personal scandal forced him to resign. In 1977 he became a tax consultant for the Washington office of a New York law firm.

Milne, A(lan) A(lexander) (1882–1956) Writer, born in London, England, UK. He studied at Cambridge, where he edited the undergraduate magazine *Granta*. He joined the staff of *Punch* as assistant editor, and became well known for his light essays and comedies, notably *Wurzel-Flummery* (1917), *Mr Pim Passes By* (1919), and *The Dover Road* (1922). In 1924 he achieved world fame with his book of children's verse, *When We Were Very Young*, written for his son, Christopher Robin, who was immortalized with his toy bear Winnie-the-Pooh in further children's classics such as *Winnie-the-Pooh* (1926), *Now We Are Six* (1927), and *The House at Pooh Corner* (1928), later made into a series of successful cartoon films.

Milne, David Brown (1882–1953) Artist and writer, born in Ontario, Canada. He first received recognition for his work in oil and watercolour in the USA. Impressionism, and particularly the work of Claude Monet, was his greatest influence, and his own paintings endowed the simplest subjects – houses, barns, flowers, trees, and still-lifes – with majestic stature. Many consider his drypoints, made by a method he invented, his finest work. His autobiography (1974), journals, and letters offer a store of artistic observations unparalleled in Canadian art. >> Monet

Milne, Edward Arthur (1896–1950) Astrophysicist, born in Hull, NE England, UK. Assistant director of the Cambridge Solar Physics Observatory (1920–4), he became professor of mathematics at Manchester (1924–8) and Oxford (from 1928). He made notable contributions to the study of cosmic dynamics, and estimated the age of the universe to be c.2 thousand million years.

Milner, Alfred Milner, 1st Viscount (1854–1925) British statesman, born in Bonn, Germany. He studied at Oxford, and became assistant editor of the *Pall Mall Gazette*, private secretary to the Chancellor of the Exchequer, and under-secretary of finance in Egypt (1889), where he wrote *England in Egypt* (1892). He was chairman of the Board of Inland Revenue (1892–7), for which he was knighted in 1895. As Governor of Cape Colony (1897–1901) he negotiated with Kruger at Bloemfontein (1899), giving an ultimatum which led to the second Boer War. He later became Governor of the Transvaal and Orange River Colony (1901–5) and high commissioner for South Africa (1897–1905), receiving a barony (1901) and a viscountcy (1902) for his services in the Boer War. In 1916 he entered the War Cabinet, later becoming secretary for war (1918–19) and colonial secretary (1919–21). >> Kruger

Milner, Brenda Atkinson, *née* **Langford** (1918–) British psychologist. She studied at Cambridge and at McGill University, Montreal, then taught at Montreal and McGill universities before becoming head of the Neuropsychology Research Unit at the Montreal Neurological Institute (1953). Much of her research into brain function has also had application to the clinic, particularly in relation to the surgical treatment of temporal-lobe epilepsy.

Milnes, Richard Monckton, 1st Baron Houghton (1809–85) Politician and man of letters, born in London, England, UK. He studied at Cambridge, and was MP for Pontefract from 1837 until he entered the House of Lords in 1863. A patron of young writers, he was one of the first to recognize Swinburne's genius, and secured the poet laureateship for Tennyson (1850). He championed oppressed nationalities, liberty of conscience, fugitive slaves, and the rights of women and carried a bill for establishing reformatories (1846). As well as his poetry and essays, he published *Life, Letters and Remains of Keats* (1848). He held cabinet rank (1905–16, 1931), and was British ambassador in Paris (1922–8). >> Swinburne, Algernon Charles; Tennyson

Milo of Croton [miyloh, meeloh] (6th-c BC) Legendary Greek wrestler from the Greek colony of Croton in S Italy. He won the wrestling contest at five successive Olympic Games, and swept the board at all other festivals. A man of huge stature, he boasted that no one had ever brought him to his knees. It is said that he carried a live ox upon his shoulders through the stadium at Olympia, then ate it all in a single day. He played a leading part in the military defeat of Sybaris in 511 BC. Tradition has it that in his old age he tried to split a tree, which closed upon his hands and held him there until he was devoured by wolves.

Miłosz, Czeslaw [meewosh, chezhwof] (1911–) Poet and man of letters, born in Szetejnie, Lithuania. A founder of the catastrophist school of Polish poetry, co-founder of the literary periodical *Zagary*, and author of a book of essays called *The Captive Mind* (trans title), he was a leader of the avant garde before World War 2. During the War he worked for the Warsaw underground, then became a member of the Polish diplomatic service (1946–50). Rejecting the Communist government, he exiled himself to Paris to write (1951–60), then emigrated to America, becoming professor of Slavic languages and literature at the University of California, Berkeley. His books include *Hymn of the Pearl* (1981) and *Hymn of the Earth* (1986) (trans titles). A selection of his wartime essays, *Legends of Modernity* (trans title), appeared in 1996. He was awarded the Nobel Prize for Literature in 1980.

Milstein, César [**mil**stiyn] (1927–) Molecular biologist and immunologist, born in Bahía Blanca, Argentina. He studied at Buenos Aires University and at Cambridge, then joined the Medical Research Council Laboratory of Molecular Biology in Cambridge in 1963. He worked on antibody research, and in 1975 developed monoclonal antibodies with **Georges Köhler** (1946–95), which revolutionized biological research, and for which they shared the 1984 Nobel Prize for Physiology or Medicine. >> RR1124

Milstein, Nathan (Mironovich) [**mil**stiyn] (1904–92) Violinist, born in Odessa, Ukraine. He began his concert career there in 1919, soon playing with Horowitz and Piatigorsky. He left Russia in 1925, gave recitals in Paris, and made his US debut under Stokowski in 1929. He became a US citizen in 1942. >> Horowitz; Piatigorsky; Stokowski

Miltiades, the Younger [mil**tiy**adeez] (c. 550–489 BC) Athenian general and statesman. From an immensely wealthy family, he was reduced to becoming a vassal of Darius I of Persia, and accompanied him on his Scythian expedition (c.514). He returned to Athens in 493, and masterminded the Greek victory against the Persians at Marathon (490). He was the father of Cimon by the Thracian princess, Hegesipyle. >> Cimon; Darius I

Milton, John (1608–74) Poet, born in London, England, UK. He studied at Cambridge, and spent six years of studious leisure at Horton, which he regarded as preparation for his life's work as a poet. There he wrote *L'Allegro* and *Il Penseroso* (1632), *Comus* (1633), and *Lycidas* (1637). He concluded his formal education with a visit to Italy (1638–9). The fame of his Latin poems had preceded him, and he was received in the academies with distinction. His revolutionary ardour during the Civil War silenced his poetic outpourings for 20 years, except for occasional sonnets, most of which were published in a volume of *Poems* in 1645. On his return to London in 1639 he emerged as the polemical champion of the revolution in a series of pamphlets against episcopacy (1642), on divorce (1643), in defence of the liberty of the press, *Areopagitica* (1644), and in support of the regicides (1649), and became official apologist for the Commonwealth. Blind from 1652, after the Restoration he went into hiding for a short period, then devoted himself wholly to poetry, becoming widely esteemed as a poet second only to Shakespeare. The theme of his epic sacred masterpiece, *Paradise Lost* had been in his mind since 1641. The first three books reflect the triumph of the godly; the last of the 12, written in 1663, are tinged with despair – as if to acknowledge that God's kingdom is not of this world. It was followed by *Paradise Regained* and *Samson Agonistes* (both 1671).

Mindszenty, József, Cardinal [mind**sen**tee], (1892–1975) Roman Catholic clergyman, born in Mindszent, Hungary. Primate of Hungary (1945), and created cardinal (1946), he became internationally known in 1948 when, having refused to let the Catholic schools be secularized, he was arrested and charged with treason by the Communist government in Budapest, and sentenced to life imprisonment. Temporarily released in the wake of the 1956 uprising, he was granted asylum in the US legation at Budapest, where he remained as a voluntary prisoner until 1971, when he went to Rome. He criticized the Vatican's policy towards Hungary, and was asked by Pope Paul VI to resign his primacy. He settled in Vienna, and spent his last years in a Hungarian religious community.

Mingus, Charlie [**ming**guhs], popular name of **Charles Mingus** (1922–79) Jazz bassist, composer, and bandleader, born in Nogales, AZ. He played the cello with the Los Angeles Junior Philharmonic Orchestra before becoming a bassist with traditional-style bands. As a child, he had sung Gospel music, and his later work as a leader and composer brought elements of this background together with modern and avant-garde ideas. During the 1940s, he worked with big bands, and from 1953 led groups called the 'Jazz Workshop', which experimented with atonality and other devices of European symphonic music. His most powerful and individualistic music came later, such as *Wednesday Night Prayer Meeting* (1959) and *Fables of Faubus* (1960).

Minkowski, Hermann [ming**kof**skee] (1864–1909) Mathematician, born near Kaunas, Lithuania. He was professor at Königsberg (1895), Zürich (1896), where he taught Einstein, and Göttingen (1902). He discovered a new branch of number theory, the geometry of numbers, and gave a precise mathematical description of space-time as it appears in Einstein's relativity theory. >> Einstein

Minnelli, Liza (May) [mi**nel**ee] (1946–) Singer and actress, born in Los Angeles, CA, the daughter of Vincente Minnelli and Judy Garland. She first appeared on screen in her mother's film *In the Good Old Summertime* (1949), and became the youngest-ever actress to win a Tony award, for *Flora, the Red Menace* (1965). On television and in cabaret, her vocal talents and emotional rendition of plaintive songs earned comparisons with her mother. Dramatic roles in such films as *Charlie Bubbles* (1967), *The Sterile Cuckoo* (1969), and *Tell Me that You Love Me, Junie Moon* (1970) revealed her as a skilled portrayer of social outcasts. She won an Oscar for *Cabaret* (1972), and a television special, *Liza with a Z* (1972), confirmed her many talents. Subsequent dramatic appearances include *New York, New York* (1977), *Stepping Out* (1991), the *Arthur* films with Dudley Moore, and on television *West Side Waltz* (1995). >> Garland, Judy; Minnelli, Vincente

Minnelli, Vincente [mi**nel**ee] (1910–86) Film director, born in Chicago, IL, the husband of Judy Garland. He left school at 16, and by 1933 was art director of Radio City Music Hall. He became a Broadway director in 1935, and went to Hollywood in 1940, becoming an outstanding director of film musicals of sweeping scope and lavish visual style. His best-known works include *The Clock* (1945), *Kismet* (1955), and *Gigi* (1958, Oscar). >> Garland, Judy; Minnelli, Liza

Minogue, Kylie [mi**nohg**] (1968–) Singer and actress, born in Melbourne, Victoria, Australia. She began acting in TV at age 12 in the soap opera *Skyways*, but achieved fame around the world some years later for her role in the soap opera *Neighbours*. In 1987 she began a successful recording career, and her 1988 single 'I Should Be So Lucky', had huge sales. Numerous hit singles in Europe, Australia, and Japan followed. All 15 of the singles she has released in Britain have reached the Top 10.

Minot, George (Richards) [**mi**ynuht] (1885–1950) Physician, born in Boston, MA. Professor of medicine at Harvard (1928–48), he first introduced, with William P Murphy, a diet of raw liver in the treatment of pernicious anaemia, which led to the preparation of vitamin B_{12}. They shared the 1934 Nobel Prize for Physiology or Medicine. >> Murphy, William P; Whipple, George H

Minter, Alan (1951–) Boxer, born in Crawley, Surrey, SE England, UK. He held the European middleweight title (1977, 1978–9) and the British crown (1975–7, 1977–8), becoming world champion in 1980.

Mintoff, Dom(inic) (1916–) Maltese statesman and prime minister (1955–8, 1971–84), born in Cospicua, Malta. He studied at Malta and Oxford universities, afterwards becoming a civil engineer. In 1947 he joined the Malta Labour Party, and in the first Labour government was minister of works and deputy prime minister. As premier from

1955, his demands for independence and the accompanying political agitation over the transfer of the naval dockyard to a commercial concern led directly to the suspension of Malta's constitution in 1959. He resigned in 1958 to lead the Malta Liberation Movement, and became Leader of the Opposition in 1962. In a second term as prime minister again (1971–84), he followed a policy of moving away from British influence. >> RR1075

Minton, (Francis) John (1917–57) Artist, born in Cambridge, Cambridgeshire, EC England, UK. He studied in London and Paris, and from 1943 to 1956 taught at various London art schools. He was noted for his book illustrations and his brilliant watercolours, and also as a designer of textiles and wallpaper.

Minton, Thomas (1765–1836) Pottery and china manufacturer, born in Shrewsbury, Shropshire, WC England, UK, founder of the firm which bears his name. Originally trained as a transfer-print engraver, he worked for Josiah Spode before he set up his own business in Stoke-on-Trent (1789), producing copperplates for transfer-printing in blue underglaze. He is reputed to have invented the willow pattern. In 1793 he built a pottery works at Stoke, producing fine bone china, much of it tableware decorated with finely painted flowers and fruit. His son, **Herbert** (1793–1858), was his partner between 1817 and 1836, and succeeded him. >> Spode

Minton, Yvonne (Fay) (1938–) Mezzo-soprano, born in Sydney, New South Wales, Australia. She attended the New South Wales Conservatory, then studied in London, where in 1961 she won the Kathleen Ferrier Prize. She made her operatic debut in 1964 at the Royal Opera House, Covent Garden, where she has since been resident artist. A guest member of the Cologne Opera since 1969, and guest artist with the New York Metropolitan Opera, the Chicago, Paris, and Australian opera companies, she is noted for her Octavian in Strauss's *Rosenkavalier*, and for her Wagnerian roles.

Mirabeau, Honoré Gabriel Riqueti, comte de (Count of) [meeraboh] (1749–91) Revolutionary politician and orator, born in Bignon, France. At 17 he entered a cavalry regiment, but was imprisoned on several occasions for his disorderly behaviour. While hiding in Amsterdam, having eloped with a young married woman, he wrote the sensational *Essai sur le despotisme* (Essay on Despotism). Sentenced to death, he was imprisoned at Vincennes in 1777 for over three years, where he wrote his famous *Essai sur les lettres de cachet* (2 vols, 1782). Elected to the Estates General by the Third Estate of Marseilles (1780), his political acumen made him a force in the National Assembly, while his audacity and eloquence endeared him to the people. He advocated a constitutional monarchy on the English model, but failed to convince Louis XVI. As the popular movement progressed, his views were also rejected by the revolutionaries. He was nonetheless elected president of the Assembly in 1791, but died soon afterwards. >> Louis XVI; Marie Antoinette

Mirabilis, Doctor >> **Bacon, Roger**

Mirandola, Pico della >> **Pico della Mirandola**

Miró, Joán [meeroh, hwan] (1893–1983) Artist, born in Barcelona, Spain. After an unhappy period as a clerk, he studied in Paris and Barcelona, and exhibited with the Surrealists in 1925. In his early years he had great admiration for primitive Catalan art and the Art Nouveau forms of Gaudí's architecture. In 1920 he settled in Paris and invented a manner of painting using curvilinear, fantastical forms which suggest all kinds of dreamlike situations. His paintings are predominantly abstract, and his humorous fantasy makes play with a restricted range of pure colours and dancing shapes, as in 'Catalan Landscape'

(1923–4, New York City). His other work includes ballet sets, sculptures, murals, and tapestries. >> Gaudi

Mirren, Helen (1945–) Actress, born in London, England, UK. A member of the Royal Shakespeare Company, she appeared in a wide range of classical theatre roles, and won the Best Actress award at the Cannes Film Festival for *Cal* (1984). Later films include *The Cook, The Thief, His Wife and Her Lover* (1989), *The Madness of King George* (1994), and *Some Mother's Son* (1997). Her role as Jane Tennison in the television series *Prime Suspect* made her a household name in the UK.

Mirrlees, James (Alexander) (1914–96) Economist, born in Minnigaff, Dumfries and Galloway, SW Scotland, UK. He studied mathematics at Edinburgh and Cambridge, then taught at Oxford (1969–95) and Cambridge. He shared the Nobel Prize for Economics in 1996 for his work in analyzing the consequences of incomplete financial information >> Vickrey

Mirza Ali Mohammed >> **Bab-ed-Din**

Mirza Huseyn Ali >> **Baha-Allah**

Mirza Muhammad >> **Siraj ud Daula**

Mises, Richard von [meezes] (1883–1953) Mathematician and philosopher, born in Lember, Austria. He was professor at Dresden, Berlin, Istanbul, and (from 1939) Harvard. An authority in aerodynamics and hydrodynamics, he set out in *Wahrscheinlichkeit, Statistik und Wahrheit* (1928, Probability, Statistics and Truth) a frequency theory of probability which has had a wide influence, though not acceptance.

Mishima, Yukio, pseudonym of **Hiraoka Kimitake** (1925–70) Writer, born in Tokyo. He studied at Tokyo University, became a civil servant, then embarked on a prolific writing career which, as well as 40 novels, produced poetry, essays, and modern *Kabuki* and *Noh* drama. His first major work was *Confessions of a Mask* (1949) which dealt with his discovery of his own homosexuality, and the ways in which he attempted to conceal it. His great tetralogy, *Sea of Fertility* (1965–70) with a central theme of reincarnation, spanned Japanese life and events in the 20th-c. Passionately interested in the chivalrous traditions of imperial Japan, he believed implicitly in the ideal of a heroic destiny. He became an expert in the martial arts of *karate* and *kendo*, and in 1968 founded the Shield Society, a group of a 100 youths dedicated to a revival of *Bushido*, the Samurai knightly code of honour. In 1970 he publicly committed suicide by disembowelling himself with his sword after a carefully staged token attempt to rouse the nation to a return to pre-war nationalist ideals.

Missoni, Tai Otavio [misohnee] (1921–) Knitwear designer, born in Yugoslavia. He founded the Missoni company in Milan with his wife, Rosita, in 1953. At first manufacturing knitwear to be sold under other labels, they later created, under their own label, innovative knitwear notable for its sophistication and distinctive colours and patterns.

Mistinguett [meestiget], originally **Jeanne Marie Bourgeois** (1875–1956) Dancer, singer, and actress, born in Enghien-les-Bains, France. Making her debut in 1895, she became the most popular French music-hall artiste of the first three decades of the century, reaching the height of success with Maurice Chevalier at the Folies Bergère. >> Chevalier

Mistral, Frédéric [meestral] (1830–1914) Poet, born in Maillane, France. He became a founder of the Provençal renaissance movement (the *Félibrige* school), and is best known for his long narrative poems, such as *Miréio* (1859) and *Calendau* (1861), and for his Provençal French dictionary (1878–86). He was awarded the Nobel Prize for Literature in 1904.

Mistral, Gabriela [mee**stral**], pseudonym of **Lucila Godoy de Alcayaga** (1889–1957) Poet, diplomat, and teacher, born in Vicuña, Chile. A teacher from the age of 15, she taught at Columbia University, Vassar College, and in Puerto Rico, and combined her writing with a career as a diplomat and cultural minister. She established herself as a poet with 'Sonetos de la muerte' (1914, Sonnets of Death), taking her name from Gabriele d'Annunzio and Frédéric Mistral. Her poem 'Dolor' from the collection *Desolación* (1922, Desolation) is based on the suicide of her lover. She never married, and her work is inspired by a Romantic preoccupation with sorrow and death. She was awarded the Nobel Prize for Literature in 1945.

Mita, Ciriaco de >> **de Mita, Ciriaco**

Mitchell, Arthur (1934–) Dancer, choreographer, and director, born in New York City. He trained at the School of American Ballet, and in 1956 joined New York City Ballet, creating roles in Balanchine's *Agon* (1957) and *A Midsummer Night's Dream* (1962). The first African-American principal dancer to join that company, his dream was to found his own group in order to develop opportunities for fellow black dancers. The Dance Theater of Harlem made its debut in 1971 with resounding success, quickly growing to a company of international standing. >> **Balanchine**

Mitchell, Billy, popular name of **William Mitchell** (1879–1936) Aviation pioneer, born in Nice, France. Beginning his army career in the USA in the signal service, he became an early enthusiast for flying, and commanded the US air forces in World War 1. He foresaw the development and importance of air power in warfare, but his outspoken criticism of those who did not share his convictions resulted in a court martial which suspended him from duty. His resignation followed, and he spent the rest of his life lecturing and writing in support of his ideas. His vindication came with World War 2, and he was posthumously promoted and decorated.

Mitchell, James Fitz Allan (1931–) Prime minister of St Vincent and the Grenadines (1972–4, 1984–). He trained and worked as an agronomist (1958–65), then bought and managed an hotel in Bequia, St Vincent. He entered politics through the St Vincent Labour Party, and in the pre-independence period served as minister of trade (1967–72). He was then premier (1972–4), heading the People's Political Party. In 1975 he founded the New Democratic Party and, as its leader, became prime minister. He was re-elected in 1989. >> **RR1086**

Mitchell, James Leslie >> **Gibbon, Lewis Grassic**

Mitchell, Joan (1926–) Painter, born in Chicago, IL. She studied for two years at Smith College, then transferred to the Art Institute of Chicago so as to paint full time. Coming to New York City in 1947, she became one of the early Abstract Expressionists. In 1959 she moved to Paris, then in 1967 to Vetheuil, a village near Paris where Monet once lived (1878–81). She continued to paint in the Abstract Expressionist manner, and in her attempts to convey the realm of nature – as in 'No Birds' (1987–8) or 'Wind' (1990) – she seemed to echo French Impressionism. >> **Gottlieb, Adolf; de Kooning; Motherwell; Tworkov**

Mitchell, John (Newton) (1913–88) Lawyer and US cabinet member, born in Detroit, MI. A wealthy New York investment lawyer (1936–68), he specialized in municipal bonds. President Nixon's 1968 campaign manager and attorney general (1969–73), he used illegal surveillance methods against student radicals and African-American activists. Convicted of obstruction of justice in the Watergate investigation, he served two years in prison (1977–9). >> **Nixon**

Mitchell, Joni, *née* **Roberta Joan Anderson** (1943–) Singer and songwriter, born in McLeod, Alberta, Canada. Her compositions, highly original and personal in their lyrical imagery, first attracted attention among folk-music audiences in Toronto while she was still in her teens. She moved to the USA in the mid-1960s, and in 1968 recorded her first album, *Joni Mitchell* (1968). Other highly successful albums followed, including *Clouds*, *Ladies of the Canyon* (1969), and *Blue* (1970). Many of her songs, notably 'Both Sides Now' (1971), have been recorded by other singers.

Mitchell, Lucy, *née* **Sprague** (1878–1967) Educationist, born in Chicago, IL. She studied at Radcliffe College, then went to California, where in 1906 she became dean of women and assistant professor of English at the University of California, Berkeley. After her marriage in 1912 to **Wesley Clair Mitchell**, an economist, the couple moved to New York City, where she concentrated on the education of children. With the support of her cousin, **Elizabeth Sprague Coolidge**, she co-founded in 1916 the Bureau of Educational Experiments, and directed it until 1956; by 1950 it had become the Bank Street College of Education. She also co-founded (1931) the Co-operative School for Teachers.

Mitchell, Margaret (1900–49) Novelist, born in Atlanta, GA. She studied for a medical career, but turned to journalism, writing for *The Atlanta Journal* (1922–6). After her marriage to **John R Marsh** in 1925, and an injury to her ankle which forced her retirement, she began the 10-year task of writing her only novel, *Gone with the Wind* (1936), which won the Pulitzer Prize, sold over 25 million copies, was translated into 30 languages, and was the subject of an Oscar-winning-film (1939).

Mitchell, Sir Peter (Chalmers) (1864–1945) Zoologist and journalist, born in Dunfermline, Fife, E Scotland, UK. He started his career as a lecturer at Oxford and London, and in 1903 was elected secretary of the Zoological Society. He inaugurated a period of prosperity at the London Zoo, and was responsible for the Mappin terraces, Whipsnade, the Aquarium, and other improvements. He wrote a number of books on zoological subjects, including *The Nature of Man* (1904) and *Materialism and Vitalism in Biology* (1930).

Mitchell, Peter (Dennis) (1920–92) Biochemist, born in Mitcham, SW Greater London, England, UK. He studied at Cambridge, then taught there (1943–55) and at Edinburgh (1955–63), before creating his own research institute, the Glynn Research Laboratories, at Bodmin, Cornwall, in 1964 (from 1987 the Glynn Research Institute). In the 1960s he proposed an entirely novel theory of the way energy is generated at the molecular level in biochemical cells. Although at first greeted with extreme scepticism, his views became widely accepted, and his position was formally established by the award of the Nobel Prize for Chemistry in 1978.

Mitchell, R(eginald) J(oseph) (1895–1937) Aircraft designer, born in Talke, Staffordshire, C England, UK. Trained as an engineer, he joined the Vickers Armstrong Supermarine Co in 1916, where he soon became chief designer. He designed sea-planes that won many of the Schneider trophy races (1922–31) and from them evolved the famous Spitfire, whose triumph in World War 2 he did not live to see.

Mitchell, S(ilas) Weir (1829–1914) Physician and writer, born in Philadelphia, PA. He studied at Pennsylvania and Jefferson Medical College, and became a surgeon in the Union army during the Civil War. He specialized in nervous diseases, and pioneered the application of psychology to medicine. As well as a host of psychological and historical novels and poems, he wrote medical texts, including the popular *Fat and Blood* (1877), which became a best seller.

Mitchell, Sir Thomas Livingstone (1792–1855) Explorer,

born in Craigend, Renfrewshire, W Scotland, UK. After service in the Peninsular War, from 1828 he became surveyor-general of New South Wales. In four expeditions (1831, 1835, 1836, 1845–7) he did much to explore eastern and tropical Australia, especially the Murray, Glenelg, and Barcoo rivers.

Mitchell, Warren (1926–) Actor, born in London, England, UK. After studying at Oxford, he trained at the Royal Academy of Dramatic Art, London, and made his first appearance at the Finsbury Park Open Air Theatre in 1950. He won great acclaim for his interpretation of Willy Loman in Arthur Miller's *Death of a Salesman* at the National Theatre in 1979. He is most widely known for playing the character of Alf Garnett, a garrulous, foul-mouthed, right-wing Cockney, in the BBC television series *Till Death Us Do Part* (1966–78). A spin-off stage show, *The Thoughts of Chairman Alf*, starring Mitchell, opened at the Theatre Royal, Stratford East, in 1976, and the character returned in a further television series, *In Sickness and In Health* (1985–6), which was repeated in 1993. Later BBC television appearances include *Wall of Silence* (1995) and *Death of a Salesman* (1996).

Mitchison, Naomi (Mary Margaret), *née* **Haldane** (1897–) Writer, born in Edinburgh, EC Scotland, UK. Educated at the Dragon School, Oxford, she won instant attention with her brilliant and personal evocations of Greece and Sparta in such novels as *The Conquered* (1923), *When the Bough Breaks* (1924), *Cloud Cuckoo Land* (1925), and *Black Sparta* (1928). In 1931 came the erudite *Corn King and Spring Queen*, which brought to life the civilizations of ancient Egypt, Scythia, and the Middle East. She has travelled widely, and in 1963 was made Tribal Adviser and Mother to the Bakgatla of Botswana.

Mitchum, Robert (1917–97) Film actor, born in Bridgeport, CT. After a youth spent as a labourer, vagrant, and professional boxer, he went to Hollywood, where he found employment in the film industry as an extra (1943). A prolific leading man particularly associated with the post-war film noir thriller, his laconic, heavy-lidded manner was deceptively casual, disguising a potent screen presence. His films included *Out of the Past* (1947), *Night of the Hunter* (1955), *The Sundowners* (1960), and *Farewell My Lovely* (1975, as Philip Marlowe). Among later films were *Mr North* (1988), *Cape Fear* (1991), and *Dead Man* (1996). He also appeared in several television films and series.

Mitford, Diana >> Mosley, Oswald

Mitford, Jessica (Lucy) (1917–96) Writer, the sister of Diana, Nancy, and Unity Mitford. She wrote *Hons and Rebels* (1960), her autobiography and story of the unconventional Mitford childhood. She went to the USA in 1939, became a Communist, and married in 1943. Later books included *The American Way of Death* (1963), *The Trial of Dr Spock* (1970), *The Making of a Muckraker* (1979), and *Grace Had an English Heart: the Story of Grace Darling* (1988). >> Mitford, Diana/Nancy/Unity

Mitford, Mary Russell (1787–1855) Essayist and playwright, born in Alresford, Hampshire, S England, UK. At the age of 10 she won £20 000 in a lottery, with which her father built a house and sent her to school in Chelsea. They had to move to a labourer's cottage when her father's extravagance ruined them, and thereafter she earned a living as a writer to support him and pay his gambling debts. Her gift was for charming sketches of country manners, scenery, and character, which after appearing in magazines were collected as *Our Village* (5 vols, 1824–32). She received a civil list pension in 1837, which was increased on her father's death from subscriptions raised to pay his debts.

Mitford, Nancy (Freeman) (1904–73) Writer, born in London, England, UK, the sister of Diana, Jessica, and Unity Mitford. Educated at home, she established a reputation with her witty novels such as *Pursuit of Love* (1945) and *Love in a Cold Climate* (1949). After the war she settled in France and wrote major biographies, including *Madame de Pompadour* (1953), *Voltaire in Love* (1957), and *Frederick the Great* (1970). As one of the essayists in *Noblesse Oblige*, edited by herself (1956), she popularized the famous 'U' (upper-class) and 'non-U' classification of linguistic usage and behaviour. >> Mitford, Diana/Jessica/Unity

Mitford, Unity (Valkyrie) (1914–48) Socialite, the daughter of the 2nd Baron Redesdale, and sister of Diana, Jessica, and Nancy Mitford. She was notorious for her associations with Hitler and other leading Nazis in Germany, but returned to Britain during World War 2 in January 1940, suffering from a gunshot wound. >> Mitford, Diana/Jessica/Nancy

Mithridates VI (Eupator) [mithri**dah**teez], also spelled **Mithradates**, known as **the Great** (?–63 BC) King of Pontus (c.115–63 BC), a Hellenized ruler of Iranian extraction in the Black Sea area, whose attempts to expand his empire over Cappadocia and Bithynia led to a series of wars (the Mithridatic Wars) with Rome (88–66 BC). Though worsted by Sulla (c.86 BC) and Lucullus (72–71 BC), he was not finally defeated until Pompey took over the E command (66 BC). He avoided capture, but later took his own life. >> Lucullus; Sulla; Pompey the Great

Mitropoulos, Dimitri [mi**tro**pulos] (1896–1960) Conductor, born in Athens. He trained in Athens, then held conducting posts in Berlin and Paris before making his US debut with the Boston Symphony in 1936. He conducted the Minneapolis Symphony (1937–49), then became co-conductor of the New York Philharmonic and its principal conductor (1951–7). Known also as a pianist and composer, he was noted for his remarkable technical abilities and for his advocacy of progressive composers.

Mitterrand, François (Maurice Marie) [meetuh**rã**] (1916–96) French statesman and president (1981–95), born in Jarnac, France. He studied law and politics at the University of Paris. During World War 2 he served with the French forces, was wounded and captured, but escaped and joined the French resistance. He was a deputy in the French National Assembly almost continuously from 1946, representing the constituency of Nievre (near Dijon), and held ministerial posts in 11 centrist governments (1947–58). He opposed de Gaulle's creation of the Fifth Republic, and lost his assembly seat in the 1958 election. For many years he remained a stubborn opponent of de Gaulle. He worked for unification of the French Left, and became secretary of the Socialist Party in 1971. Following his victory in 1981, he embarked on a programme of nationalization and job creation in an attempt to combat stagnation and unemployment. He was re-elected president in 1988, but defeated by Jacques Chirac in 1995. >> de Gaulle; RR1049

Miyake, Issey [mee**yah**kay] (1938–) Fashion designer, born in Hiroshima, Japan. After studying at Tama Art University in Toyko, he spent six years in Paris and New York City fashion houses. He showed his first collection in Tokyo in 1963, and founded his studio there in 1971. His first subsequent show was in New York City the same year, followed by one in Paris in 1973. His distinctive style combines Eastern and Western influences in garments which have an almost theatrical quality. Loose fitting, but with dramatic often asymmetric outline, his clothes achieve richness by varied textures, weaves, and patterns rather than by colour.

Mnouchkine, Arianne [**nush**keen] (1938–) French stage director and playwright. She studied at Paris and London universities, and founded the Association Théâtrale des Etudiants de Paris at the Sorbonne (1959), putting on plays, and organizing workshops and lectures. In 1963 she founded the Théâtre du Soleil as a theatre co-operative. The early productions were influenced by the teachings of Stanislavsky, and their first major success came with a production of Arnold Wesker's *The Kitchen* in 1967. *1789*, first produced in 1970, is one of the company's best-known works. >> Stanislavsky

Mo, Timothy (Peter) [moh] (1950–) Novelist, born in Hong Kong. He studied at Oxford University, attracting attention with his first novel, *The Monkey King* (1978), set in Hong Kong, followed by *Sweet And Sour* (1982), a densely realistic portrait of London's Chinese community. Later novels include *The Redundancy of Courage* (1991), and *Brownout on Breadfruit Boulevard* (1995).

Moberg, (Carl Artur) Vilhelm [moh]berg] (1898–1973) Writer, born in Algutsboda, Sweden. From a family of crofters, his unfinished *Min Svenska Historia 1–2* (1970–1, My Swedish History) looks at history from the viewpoint of the illiterate classes. His best-known work is the series of novels that deal with the 19th-c mass migration of Swedes to the USA, including *Utvandrarna* (1949, The Emigrants), and *Sista Brevet till Sverige* (1959, Last Letter to Sweden). He was a popular playwright, and several of his novels, notably *The Emigrants*, have been filmed.

Möbius, August Ferdinand [moe]bius] (1790–1868) Mathematician, born in Schulpforta, Germany. As professor at Leipzig he worked on analytical geometry, topology, and theoretical astronomy, but is chiefly known for the discovery of the *Möbius strip* (a one-sided surface formed by giving a rectangular strip a half-twist, then joining the ends together) and the *Möbius net*, important in projective geometry. He also introduced barycentric co-ordinates into geometry.

Mobutu, Sese Seko [mo**boo**too], originally **Joseph Désiré Mobutu** (1930–97) Zairean politician and president (1965–97), born in Lisala, Democratic Republic of Congo (formerly, Zaire, and earlier, Belgian Congo). He rose quickly to become commander in the Belgian army at the age of 30 with the rank of colonel. In 1958 he joined Lumumba's Congolese National Movement Party. In 1960, immediately after independence, the government in Leopoldville was so indecisive in its dealings with dissidents in Katanga province that Mobutu stepped in and took over, five months later handing back power to the civilian government. After the civil war of 1963–5 he again took over, but this time retained power. As president, with a new constitution and a new name for his country, he adopted a new name for himself and the rank of marshal. His regime was harsh and highly personalized. He was forced to stand down in May 1997 following an uprising led by Laurent Kabila. >> Lumumba; RR1100

Modigliani, Amedeo [mohdeel**yah**nee] (1884–1920) Painter and sculptor of the modern school of Paris, born in Livorno, Italy. His early work was influenced by the painters of the Italian Renaissance, and in Paris by Toulouse-Lautrec and the Fauves. In 1909, encouraged by the Rumanian sculptor Brancusi, he produced a number of elongated stone heads in African style. He continued to use this style when he resumed painting, with a series of richly coloured, elongated portraits. In 1918 in Paris he opened his first one-man show, which included some very frank nudes, and the exhibition was closed for indecency on the first day. His health was delicate, and his life was marred by poverty, drink, and drug addiction. It was only after his death that he obtained recognition, and the prices of his paintings soared. >> Brancusi; Toulouse-Lautrec

Modigliani, Franco [mohdeel**yah**nee] (1918–) US economist, born in Rome. Having taken a law degree in Rome in 1939, he held professorships at a number of small institutions in the USA (1942–8), then at Illinois (1949–52), Carnegie-Mellon (1952–60), and Northwestern (1960–2) universities, and at Massachusetts Institute of Technology (from 1962). He was awarded the 1985 Nobel Prize for Economics for his work on two fundamental theories – personal saving and corporate finance.

Moe, Jörgen >> **Asbjörnsen, Peter Christian**

Moeran, Ernest John [**moor**an] (1894–1950) Composer, born in Heston, SE Greater London, England, UK. He was a pupil at the Royal College of Music, London, and after service in World War 1 he studied under John Ireland. As well as his orchestral *Rhapsody* (1924), he composed a large number of songs, a symphony, and concertos for violin, piano, and cello. >> Ireland, John

Moffatt, James (1870–1944) Theologian and scholar, born in Glasgow, W Scotland, UK. Ordained a minister of the Free Church of Scotland in 1896, he became professor at Mansfield College, Oxford (1911–14) and the United Free Church College, Glasgow (1914–27), then professor of church history at Union Theological Seminary, New York City (1927–39). His most famous work is the translation of the Bible into modern English: his New Testament was published in 1913, and his Old Testament in 1924.

Mohammad Reza Pahlavi >> **Pahlavi, Mohammad Reza**

Mohammed or **Mahomet** (Western forms of Arabic **Muhammad**) see panel on p. 653

Mohammed II or **Mehmet II**, known as **the Conqueror** (1432–81) Sultan of Turkey (1451–81), and founder of the Ottoman empire, born in Adrianople. He took Constantinople in 1453, renaming it Istanbul, thus extinguishing the Byzantine empire and giving the Turks their commanding position on the Bosphorus. Checked by Janos Hunyady at Belgrade in 1456, he nevertheless annexed most of Serbia, all of Greece, and most of the Aegean Is. He threatened Venetian territory, was repelled from Rhodes by the Knights of St John (1479), and took Otranto (1480). He died in a campaign against Persia. >> Hunyady; John of Capistrano; RR1093

Mohammed Ahmed, known as **the Mahdi** (1844–85) African political leader, born in Dongola, Sudan. He was in the Egyptian Civil Service, then became a slave trader, and finally a relentless and successful rebel against Egyptian rule in E Sudan, becoming known as the Mahdi, or Muslim messiah. He made El Obeid his capital in 1883, and annihilated an Egyptian army under **William Hicks** ('Hicks Pasha', 1830–83). In 1885 Khartoum was taken, and General Gordon killed. >> Gordon, Charles George

Mohammed Ali or **Mehemet Ali** (c.1769–1849) Governor and later viceroy of Egypt (1805–49), the founder of the Egyptian royal family which endured until the 1953 revolution. He was sent to Egypt with a Turkish–Albanian force on the French invasion in 1798, and after the departure of the French, supported Egypt against the Mamluks. As viceroy he massacred the Mamluks (1811), and formed a regular army. In 1816 he reduced part of Arabia through the generalship of his adopted son **Ibrahim Pasha** (1789–1848), in 1820 he annexed Nubia, and his troops occupied Morea and Crete against the Greeks (1821–8). In 1831 Ibrahim began the conquest of Syria, and the victory at Nezib (1839) might have elevated his father to the throne of Constantinople; but the quadruple alliance in 1840, the fall of Acre to the British, and the consequent evacuation of Syria compelled him to limit his ambition to Egypt.

Moholy-Nagy, László [**moh**hoy **nodj**] (1895–1946) Artist and photographer, born in Bácsborsód, Hungary. He

MOHAMMED (c. 570–c. 632)

Mohammed was born in Mecca, the son of Abdallah, a poor merchant of the powerful tribe of Quaraysh, hereditary guardians of the shrine in Mecca. Orphaned at six, he was brought up by his grandfather and uncle, Abu Talib, who trained him to be a merchant. At the age of c.25 he led the caravans of a rich widow, Khadija (d.619), of the Asad clan, who was so impressed by him that she offered him marriage and financial security. She is believed to have been c.40 when they met, but she bore him six children. These included their daughters Umm Kulthum, who married Uthman, the 3rd caliph; and Fatima, who married Mohammed's second cousin, Ali, the 4th Caliph, and founded the Fatimid dynasty. Mohammed's marriage liberated him from the unfortunate financial circumstances of his childhood and made him financially independent. It also caused him to reflect deeply about the inequalities in Mecca society, which he saw to be changing into a trade-driven society with no place in it for the unfortunate.

While continuing as a merchant, Mohammed became increasingly concerned about the polytheism and superstition of the Meccans and other Arabs, some of whom worshipped idols. Also at that time, in S Arabia, the Jewish religion and Christianity flourished in some communities. Becoming interested in the Bible and the books of the Jews, he grew familiar with the teachings of Jesus Christ and his prophets, furthering his growing conviction that there was only one true God.

He was increasingly drawn to religious contemplation, and in c.610, when he was 40, the angel Gabriel appeared to him on Mt Hira, near Mecca, and told him he was the messenger of God. About four years later (c.613), he was told to come forward publicly as a preacher. His teaching was collected and written down (c.650) as the Koran (Recitation) revealed to him by God.

When his wife and uncle died (both in c.619), Mohammed was reduced to poverty, having lost the protection of his family's clan, but began to attract converts amongst pilgrims to Mecca from the town of Yathrib, an agricultural community to the N. By 622, the position of Mohammed and his small band of devoted followers in Mecca had become untenable. There was much persecution of those propounding the new religion, which came to be called *Islam* ('surrender' – to the will of God). Its followers were called *Muslims* or *Moslems* ('those who have surrendered'). They were saved by an invitation from the people of Yathrib, who hoped Mohammed would arbitrate in the feuds that racked their community. Mohammed travelled there, and this emigration, the *Hegira*, marks the beginning of the Muslim era: 622 is the year from which the Muslim calendar begins. The name of the town was changed from Yathrib to Medina, 'The city of the Prophet'.

In the first year of the Hegira, Mohammed was prompted to go to war with the enemies of Islam – in particular the Meccans – in the name of God, to protect and spread the faith. In 623 his Muslims attacked Meccan forces, but he was severely wounded in the battle Uhud (625). This reversal failed to dent his faith, and in 627 he repelled a Meccan siege of Medina. By 629 he was able to take control of Mecca, which recognized him as chief and prophet. By 630 he had control over all Arabia.

In 632 he undertook his last pilgrimage to Mecca. He fell ill soon after his return that same year, and died in June at the home of his favourite of nine wives, Aïshah, the daughter of one of his first followers, Abu Bakr. His tomb in the mosque at Medina is venerated throughout Islam, as is the sacred city of Mecca. Courageous and resolute, during his lifetime Mohammed founded a state and a worldwide religion that today numbers over 700 million Muslims and provides the basis for Arab unity.

>> Abu Bakr; Aïshah; Ali; Fatima; Uthman

studied law in Budapest, painted with Dada and Constructionist groups in Vienna and Berlin (1919–23), and produced his first 'photograms' (non-representational photographic images made directly without a camera) in 1923. He joined the Bauhaus under Walter Gropius in 1925. He was quickly recognized as a leading avant-garde artist in the New Photographers movement in Europe (1925–35), his work including film-making and typography integrated with photographic illustration. He was invited to the USA in 1937 to head the New Bauhaus school in Chicago, later the Institute of Design. Here he taught photography, becoming a US citizen shortly before his death. >> Gropius

Mohorovičić, Andrija [mohhorohvuhchich] (1857–1936) Geophysicist, born in Volosko, Croatia. He studied at Prague University, and became professor at the Zagreb Technical School in 1891, and later at Zagreb University. In 1909, when studying the seismographic records of the earthquake in the Kulpa Valley, he noted that some waves arrived earlier than others and reasoned that they had travelled through two different layers of the Earth. He deduced that the Earth's crust must overlay a denser mantle, and calculated the depth of this transition (the *Mohorovičić*, or *Moho, discontinuity*) to be about 30 km. The depth of the Moho has now been extensively mapped using reflection seismic techniques. >> Oldham

Mohs, Friedrich [mohz] (1773–1839) Mineralogist, born in Gernrode, Germany. He became successively professor at Graz, Freiburg, and Vienna. The *Mohs scale* for measuring mineral hardness, introduced in 1812, is still in use, rating talc as hardness 1, and diamond as hardness 10. He wrote *The Natural History System of Mineralogy* (1821) and *Treatise on Mineralogy* (3 vols, 1825).

Moi, Daniel Arap [moy] (1924–) Kenyan politician and president (1978–), born in the Rift Valley Province, Kenya. He was educated at mission schools, then worked as a teacher (1949–57). In 1957 he was elected to the Legislative Council as a member of the Kenya African Democratic Union. He served as a minister from 1961, and became vice-president under Kenyatta in 1967. When Kenyatta died in 1978, few people expected him to be capable of surviving under that enormous shadow, but, adopting the motto *nyayo* (footsteps to freedom), he gradually asserted his authority. He purged the army, launched a development plan, and in 1982 made the Kenyan African National Union the only legally permitted party. Despite his increasingly firm style of government, he was re-elected in 1983 and 1988. In late 1992 he held multi-party elections, which he won, though they were followed by some accusations of ballot-rigging. >> Kenyatta; RR1070

Moiseiwitsch, Benno [moyzayvich] (1890–1963) Pianist, born in Odessa, Ukraine. He studied at the Imperial

Academy of Music, Odessa, where he won the Rubinstein Prize at the age of nine, and subsequently studied in Vienna. Rapidly winning recognition as an exponent of the music of the Romantic composers, he first appeared in Britain in 1908, and took British nationality in 1937.

Moiseyev, Igor Alexandrovich [moy**say**ef] (1906–) Dancer, choreographer, and ballet director, born in Kiev, Ukraine. He studied privately and at the Bolshoi Ballet School, graduating in 1924 into the main company, where he remained, as character soloist and choreographer, until 1939. He accepted the directorship of the new dance department of the Moscow Theatre for Folk Art in 1936, and formed a professional folk dance company the following year, developing simple steps and primitive patterns into full theatrical expression. This ensemble has since toured the world, amassing a vast repertoire of dances from other nations. As a choreographer, he is best known for creating scenes from daily life and genre pieces. In 1967 he founded the State Ensemble of Classical Ballet.

Moissan, (Ferdinand Frédéric) Henri [mwasā] (1852–1907) Chemist, born in Paris. He studied at the Muséum d'Histoire Naturelle and the Ecole de Pharmacie in Paris, and became professor of toxicology at the School of Pharmacy in Paris (1886), and of inorganic chemistry at the Sorbonne (1900). He was awarded the Nobel Prize for Chemistry in 1906 for his work isolating the element fluorine and for the development of the electric furnace. He discovered carborundum, and was able to produce tiny artificial diamonds in his laboratory.

Moivre, Abraham de >> de Moivre, Abraham

Mokanna (Arabic 'the Veiled One'), nickname of **Hakim ben Atta** (?–778) Arab prophet, the founder of a sect in the Persian province of Khorasan. Ostensibly to protect onlookers from the dazzling rays from his divine countenance, but actually to conceal the loss of an eye, he wore a veil. Setting himself up as a reincarnation of God, he gathered enough followers to seize several fortified places, but the caliph Almahdi, son of Almansur, took his stronghold of Kash (778) after a long siege. With the remnant of his army, Mokanna took poison. His story is the subject of one of the poems in Thomas Moore's *Lalla Rookh*.

Molesworth, Mary Louisa, *née* **Stewart**, pseudonym **Ennis Graham** (1839–1921) British novelist and writer of children's stories, born in Rotterdam, The Netherlands. Of Scottish parentage, she spent her childhood in Manchester, Scotland, and Switzerland. She wrote novels under her pseudonym, but she is best known as a writer of stories for children, such as *The Cuckoo Clock* (1877), *The Carved Lions* (1895), and *Peterkin* (1902).

Molière [molyair], pseudonym of **Jean Baptiste Poquelin** (1622–73) Playwright, born in Paris. He studied with the Jesuits at the Collège de Clermont. In 1643 he embarked on a theatrical venture under the title of L'Illustre Théâtre, which lasted for over three years in Paris. The company then proceeded to the provinces, and had sufficient success to keep going from 1646 to 1658, obtaining the patronage of Philippe d'Orléans. In 1658 he played before the king, and organized a regular theatre. From the publication of *Les Précieuses ridicules* (1659, trans The Affected Young Ladies), no year passed without at least one major dramatic achievement, such as *L'Ecole des femmes* (1622, The School for Wives), *Tartuffe* (1664), *Le Misanthrope* (1666, The Misanthropist), and *Le Bourgeois Gentilhomme* (1670). Widely recognized as one of the greatest French dramatists, many of his plays have also been translated for performances in English theatres, giving him a considerable reputation abroad.

Molina, Luis de [moh**lee**na] (1535–1600) Jesuit theologian, born in Cuenca, Spain. He studied at Coimbra, and was professor of theology in Evora for 20 years. His principal writings include the celebrated treatise on grace and free will *Concordia liberi arbitrii cum gratiae donis* (1588, The Harmony of Free Will with Gifts of Grace). He asserts that predestination to eternal happiness or punishment is consequent on God's foreknowledge of the free determination of human will. This view (*Molinism*) was attacked as a revival of Pelagianism, causing the dispute between Molinists and Thomists. A papal decree in 1607 permitted both opinions.

Molina, Mario (Jose) (1943–) Physical chemist, born in Mexico City. He studied at the University of California, Berkeley (1968–72), then worked at the University of California, Irvine (1973–9), the Jet Propulsion Laboratory (1983–9), and the Massachusetts Institute of Technology (from 1989). With Sherwood Rowland, he studied the effect of man-made compounds on the Earth's upper atmosphere, particularly the chlorofluorocarbons that he warned were depleting the ozone layer, and shared the 1995 Nobel Prize for Physics with Paul Crutzen and Sherwood Rowland. >> Crutzen; Rowland, Sherwood

Molina, Tirso de >> Tirso de Molina

Mollet, Guy (Alcide) [molay] (1905–75) French politician and prime minister (1956–7), born in Flers-de-l'Orne, France. An English teacher, he was a member of the resistance in World War 2. In 1946 he became Mayor of Arras, an MP, secretary-general of the Socialist Party, and a cabinet minister in the Léon Blum government. In 1949 he became a delegate to the Consultative Assembly of the Council of Europe, and its president in 1955. He became prime minister in February 1956, survived the international crisis over the Anglo-French intervention in Suez, but fell from office in May 1957 after staying in power longer than any French premier since the war. In 1959 he was elected a senator of the French Community. >> Blum, Léon; Eden; RR1049

Mollison, James (1931–) Arts administrator, born in Melbourne, Victoria, Australia. Trained as a schoolteacher, he became director of Gallery A in Toorak, Melbourne (1964–5), director of the Ballarat Gallery (1967–8), acting director and then director of the Australian National Gallery (1971–89), and director of the National Gallery of Victoria (1989–95). He is the author of *Renaissance Art* (1968), the jointly written *Albert Tucker* (1982), and *A Singular Vision: the Work of Fred Williams* (1988). Responsible for much of the outstanding Australian and international collection in the Australian National Gallery, he is known for his promotion of contemporary Australian artists and Aboriginal art.

Mollison, James (Allan) (1905–59) Aviator, born in Glasgow, W Scotland, UK. A consultant engineer by profession, he was commissioned into the RAF (1923), and won fame for his record flight, Australia–England (1931) in 8 days 19 hours and 28 minutes. In 1932 he married Amy Johnson (divorced, 1938). He made the first solo E–W crossing of the N Atlantic (1932), and in February 1933 the first England–South America flight. With his wife, he made the first flight across the Atlantic to the USA (1933), and the first flight to India (1934). >> Johnson, Amy

Molnár, Ferenc [**mohl**nah(r), **fe**rents] (1878–1952) Novelist and playwright, born in Budapest. He trained as a lawyer, but became a journalist and war correspondent. He had considerable success with his short stories, but is best known for his novel *The Paul Street Boys* (1907), and his plays *The Devil* (1907), *Liliom* (1909), and *The Good Fairy* (1930), all of which have achieved success in English translation.

Molotov, Vyacheslav Mikhailovich [**mo**lotof], originally **Vyacheslav Mikhailovich Skriabin** (1890–1986) Russian statesman and prime minister (1930–41), born in Kukaida, Russia. An international figure from 1939, when he became foreign minister (1939–49, 1953–6), he was Stalin's chief adviser at Teheran and Yalta, and was present at the founding of the UN (1945). After World War 2, he emerged as the uncompromising champion of world Sovietism; his *nyet* ('no') at meetings of the UN became a byword, and fostered the Cold War. He resigned in 1956, and was demoted by Krushchev. In the 1960s he retired to his home near Moscow. His name is preserved in *Molotov cocktail* – a bottle of inflammable liquid used as a weapon – which he put into production during World War 2. >> Stalin; RR1085

Moltke, Helmuth (Johannes Ludwig) von [**molt**kuh] (1848–1916) German soldier, born in Gersdorff, Germany. Like his uncle, Count Helmuth von Moltke, he rose to chief of the general staff (in 1906), but in World War 1, after losing control of his armies at the Battle of the Marne in September 1914, he was superseded by Falkenhayn. >> Falkenhayn; Moltke, Helmuth (Karl Bernhard)

Moltke, Helmuth (Karl Bernhard), Graf von (Count of) [**molt**kuh] (1800–91) Field marshal, born in Parchim, Germany (formerly, Prussia). He entered Prussian service in 1822, and became chief of the general staff in Berlin (1858–88). His reorganization of the Prussian army led to success in the wars with Denmark (1863–4), Austria (1866), and France (1870–1). >> Moltke, Helmuth (Johannes Ludwig)

Moltmann, Jürgen (1926–) Theologian, born in Hamburg, Germany. He became a professor at the universities of Wuppertal (1958–63), Bonn (1963–7), and Tübingen (1967–). Probably the most significant Protestant theologian of the 20th-c since Karl Barth, his support of a theology of hope marked a reaction against the individualistic existential approach of Rudolf Bultmann, and a revival in Protestant theology of concern for the social nature of Christian faith in the modern world. >> Barth, Karl; Bultmann

Molyneux, Edward (Henry) [**mol**inyoo] (1891–1974) Fashion designer, born in London, England, UK. After studying art, he worked for Lucile in London and abroad. After service as a captain in the British army in World War 1, in which he lost an eye, he opened his own couture house in Paris in 1919, with branches in London, Monte Carlo, Cannes, and Biarritz. He became famous for the elegant simplicity of his tailored suits with pleated skirts, and for his evening wear.

Mommsen, (Christian Matthias) Theodor (1817–1903) Historian, born in Garding, Germany. He studied jurisprudence at Kiel, examined Roman inscriptions in France and Italy for the Berlin Academy (1844–7), and held a chair of law at Leipzig (1848–50). In 1852 he became professor of Roman law at Zürich, in 1854 at Wrocław, Poland (formerly Breslau, Germany), and in 1858 professor of ancient history at Berlin. He edited the monumental *Corpus inscriptionum Latinarum*, helped to edit the *Monumenta Germaniae historica*, and from 1873–95 was permanent secretary of the Academy. In 1882 he was tried and acquitted on a charge of slandering Bismarck in an election speech. His greatest works remain his *History of Rome* (3 vols, 1854–5) and *The Roman Provinces* (1885) (trans titles). He was awarded the Nobel Prize for Literature in 1902. >> Bismarck

Momoh, Joseph Saidu (1937–) Sierra Leonese soldier, politician, and president (1985–92) of Sierra Leone, born in Binkolo, Sierra Leone. He was trained at military schools in Ghana, Britain, and Nigeria, before being commissioned in the Sierra Leone army in 1963, rising to army commander with the rank of major-general (1983). In 1985, when the president, Siaka Stevens, announced his retirement, Momoh was endorsed by Sierra Leone's only political party, the All-People's Congress, as the sole presi-

dential candidate. When he took office he disassociated himself from the policies of his predecessor, pledging to fight corruption and improve the economy. He was ousted in a military coup (1992) led by a young army officer, **Captain Valentine E M Strasser** (1965–). >> Stevens, Siaka; RR1087

Mompesson, William (1639–1709) Rector of Eyam, Derbyshire, C England, UK, where in 1665–6 the plague (brought from London in a box of infected cloths) carried off 267 of his 350 parishioners. He persuaded his people to confine themselves entirely to the parish, and the disease was not spread. In 1669 he became rector of Eakring, Nottinghamshire, and in 1676 was made a prebendary of Southwell.

Monash, Sir John (1865–1931) Australian soldier, born in Melbourne, Victoria, Australia. He studied at Scotch College and Melbourne University, practised as a civil engineer, and also held a commission in the Australian Citizen Force (1887). He commanded the 4th Australian Brigade at Gallipoli (1914–15), the 3rd Australian Division in France (1916), and the Australian Corps as lieutenant-general (1918). Recognized as one of the outstanding generals of World War 1, he was noted for the meticulous preparation and planning of his operations.

Monboddo, James Burnett, Lord [mon**bod**oh] (1714–99) Judge and pioneer anthropologist, born in Monboddo, Aberdeenshire, NE Scotland, UK. He studied at Aberdeen, Edinburgh, and Gröningen, was called to the Scottish bar, and in 1767 was raised to the bench as Lord Monboddo. His *Origin and Progress of Language* (6 vols, 1773–92) is a learned but eccentric production, but his theory of human affinity with monkeys anticipated Darwin and the modern science of anthropology. >> Darwin, Charles

Monceau, Henri-Louis Duhamel du >> **Duhamel du Monceau, Henri-Louis**

Monck, George >> **Monk, George**

Monckton, Lionel (1861–1924) Composer, born in London, England, UK. Prominent as an amateur while at Oxford, he turned to composition, and contributed songs to many of the shows of **George Edwardes** (1852–1915), at the Gaiety Theatre and elsewhere in London. He was composer of several musical comedies, of which *The Quaker Girl* and *The Country Girl* were popular.

Monckton (of Brenchley), Walter Turner Monckton, 1st Viscount (1891–1965) Lawyer and statesman, born in Plaxtol, Kent, SE England, UK. He studied at Oxford, was called to the bar (1919), and became attorney general to the Prince of Wales (1932), in which capacity he was adviser to him (as Edward VIII) in the abdication crisis of 1936. He held many legal offices, and in World War 2 was director-general of the Ministry of Information, and in the 1945 caretaker government acted as solicitor general. A Conservative MP for Bristol West from 1951 until his elevation to the peerage in 1957, he was minister of labour (1951–5), minister of defence (1955–6) and paymaster-general (1956–7). >> Edward VIII

Monczer, Thomas >> **Müntzer, Thomas**

Mond, Alfred Moritz, Baron Melchett (1868–1930) Industrialist and statesman, born in Farnsworth, Cheshire, NWC England, UK, the son of Ludwig Mond. After some years in industry and as chairman of the Mond Nickel Co, he became a Liberal MP (1906–28), the first commissioner of works (1916–21) and minister of health (1922). In 1926 he helped to form ICI (Imperial Chemical Industries Ltd), of which he became chairman. A powerful advocate of industrial co-operation, in 1927 he instituted the Mond–Turner conference with the Trades Union Council, which suggested the formation of a national industrial council. >> Mond, Ludwig

Mond, Ludwig (1839–1909) Chemist and industrialist, born in Kassel, Germany. Settling in England in 1864, he perfected at Widnes a sulphur recovery process. He founded in 1873, with John Tomlinson Brunner, a great alkali-works at Winnington, Cheshire, and made discoveries in nickel manufacture. In 1896 he gave to the Royal Institution for the nation a physico-chemical laboratory costing £100 000. >> Mond, Alfred Moritz

Mondale, Walter F(rederick) (1928–) US politician and vice-president (1977–81), born in Ceylon, MN. He studied at the University of Minnesota Law School, and made his reputation as a local Democrat in his home state, before serving in the US Senate (1964–76). He was selected as Jimmy Carter's running-mate in the 1976 presidential election, and served as an active vice-president, but was defeated with Carter in their bid for re-election in 1980. In 1984 he was the Democratic presidential nominee, but was crushingly defeated by the Republican, Ronald Reagan. Following this reverse, Mondale retired from national politics to resume his law practice, and in 1993 became ambassador to Japan. >> Carter, Jimmy; Reagan

Mondrian, Piet [**mon**drian], originally **Pieter Cornelis Mondriaan** (1872–1944) Artist, born in Amersfoort, The Netherlands. One of the founders of the *De Stijl* movement, he began by painting landscapes in a traditional sombre Dutch manner, but after moving to Paris in 1909 he came under the influence of Matisse and Cubism. He then began painting still-lifes, becoming increasingly abstract. During World War 1 he concentrated on rectilinear compositions which depend for their beauty on the simple relationships between the coloured areas. His work has been a major influence on all purely abstract painters, and he is considered the leader of Neoplasticism. >> Matisse; Oud

Monet, Claude [monay] (1840–1926) Painter, born in Paris. He spent his youth in Le Havre, where he met Boudin, who encouraged him to work in the open air. Moving to Paris, he associated with Renoir, Pissarro, and Sisley, and exhibited with them at the first Impressionist Exhibition in 1874; one of his works at this exhibition, 'Impression: soleil levant' (Impression: Sunrise, 1872, Paris), gave the name to the movement. Later he worked much in Argenteuil. With Pissarro, Monet is recognized as being one of the creators of Impressionism, and he was one of its most consistent exponents. He visited England, The Netherlands, and Venice, and spent his life expressing his instinctive way of seeing the most subtle nuances of colour, atmosphere, and light in landscape. Apart from many sea and river scenes, he also executed several series of paintings of subjects under different aspects of light, such as 'Haystacks' (1890–1, Chicago) and the almost abstract 'Water Lilies' (the Orangerie, Paris). >> Boudin; Pissarro, Camille; Renoir, Pierre Auguste; Sisley

Monge, Gaspard, comte de (Count of) **Péluse** [mōzh] (1746–1818) Mathematician, physicist, and founder of descriptive geometry, born in Beaune, France. He was professor of mathematics at Mézières (1768), and professor of hydraulics at the Lycée in Paris (1780). He helped to found the Ecole Polytechnique (1794), and became professor of mathematics there. The following year there appeared his *Leçons de géométrie descriptive*, in which he stated his principles regarding the general application of geometry to the arts of construction (descriptive geometry). During the Revolution he was minister for the navy, and in charge of the national manufacture of arms and gunpowder. He was made a senator (1805), but lost his honours at the Restoration, and died in poverty.

Monica, St >> **Augustine** (of Hippo)**, St**

Monier-Williams, Sir Monier, originally **Monier Williams** (1819–99) Sanskrit scholar, born in Mumbai (Bombay), India. He studied at London and Oxford universities, became professor of Sanskrit at Haileybury (1844–58), master at Cheltenham (1858–60), and professor of Sanskrit at Oxford (1860). He was knighted in 1886 at the opening of the Indian Institute, which was established mainly through his energy, and completed in 1896. His books include Sanskrit grammars and dictionaries, editions of Sanskrit texts, and books on India.

Moniz, António Egas >> **Egas Moniz, António**

Monk or **Monck, George, 1st Duke of Albemarle** (1608–70) General, born in Great Potheridge, Devon, SW England, UK. He fought in the Low Countries, and with the Royalists in Scotland, then joined the Commonwealth cause and served successfully in Ireland, Scotland, and in the first Dutch War (1652–4). He feared a return to Civil War during and after Richard Cromwell's regime (1658–9), and was instrumental (as commander of the army in Scotland) in bringing about the restoration of Charles II, for which which he was created Duke of Albemarle. >> Charles II (of England); Cromwell, Richard

Monk, Maria (c. 1817–50) Impostor, born in Quebec, Canada. She pretended in 1835 to have escaped from cruel treatment in a nunnery at Montreal, and published *Awful Disclosures by Maria Monk* (1836) and *Further Disclosures* (1837), before being exposed as a fake.

Monk, Meredith (1943–) Dancer, choreographer, and musician, born in Lima, Peru. The daughter of a professional singer, she began composing music as a teenager. She was briefly associated with the experimental Judson Dance Theater in the mid-1960s, but broke away to develop multimedia music/theatre/dance events of her own, later featuring her own company, The House (formed in 1968). These frequently occur in unconventional venues (such as churches, museums, or car parks) and use film, props, sound, gestures and other movement, public history, and personal myth.

Monk, Thelonious (Sphere) (1917–82) Jazz pianist and composer, born in Rocky Mount, NC. He worked as a free-lance musician, and studied briefly at the Juilliard School, New York City. He worked under a succession of leaders in New York City (1939–45), and first recorded while playing with the Coleman Hawkins Sextet in 1944. He formed his own small group in 1947, and from that time performed chiefly with small groups. Although once called the 'High Priest of Bebop', and credited with helping to create the jazz style of the 1940s, his angular, idiosyncratic melodies stood apart from the main currents of the day, and some of his audiences never quite caught up with him. His most memorable compositions include 'Round Midnight' (1947) and 'Criss Cross' (1951). >> Gillespie; Hawkins, Coleman

Monkees, The US pop group, formed in 1966 with members **Davy Jones** (1946– , vocals, guitar), **Mike Nesmith** (1942– , vocals, guitar), **Peter Tork** (1944– , vocals, keyboards, bass guitar), and **Micky Dolenz** (1945– , drums). Created by the producers of the successful television show of the same name, the music was actually played by session musicians. Their first single, 'Last Train To Clarkesville' (1966), reached US number 1, and their second, 'I'm A Believer' (1966), written by Neil Diamond, was a transatlantic number 1 hit. In 1967 Nesmith insisted that The Monkees be allowed to play on their own records. Success continued until they finally split up in 1970. The group performed in a revival tour in 1996.

Monmouth, James Scott, Duke of (1649–85) Illegitimate son of Charles II of England, born in Rotterdam, The Netherlands. He was created Duke of Monmouth in 1663, and became captain-general in 1670. He had substantial popular support, and as a Protestant became a focus of opposition to James II. After the discovery of the Rye House Plot (1683), he fled to the Low Countries. In 1685 he landed at Lyme Regis, and asserted his right to the crown. He was defeated at the Battle of Sedgemoor, captured, and beheaded in London. >> Charles II (of England); Ketch; Marlborough; Walter, Lucy

Monnet, Jean [monay] (1888–1979) French statesman, born in Cognac, France. He was educated locally, and in 1914 entered the Ministry of Commerce. A distinguished economist and expert in financial affairs, he became in 1947 commissioner-general of the 'Plan de modernisation et d'équipement de la France' (the *Monnet plan*). He was awarded the Prix Wateler de la Paix (1951), became president of the European Coal and Steel High Authority (1952–5), and in 1956 was president of the Action Committee for the United States of Europe.

Monod, André Théodore [monoh] (1902–) Naturalist and explorer, born in Rouen, France. He studied at the Sorbonne, and made extensive botanical and geological studies of remote regions of the Sahara. His most memorable trans-Saharan crossing of 560 mi was by camel from Wadan, Mauritania, to Arawan, Mali, made by laying down advance depots of food and water. He subsequently became director of the Institut Français d'Afrique Noire (1938–64), and dean of the Faculty of Sciences at Dakar University, Senegal.

Monod, Jacques (Lucien) [monoh] (1910–76) Biochemist, born in Paris. He studied at Paris University, served in the French Resistance during World War 2, then joined the Pasteur Institute in Paris. He became head of the cellular biochemistry department in 1954, and director in 1971, as well as professor of molecular biology at the Collège de France from 1967. With François Jacob he discovered genes that regulate other genes (*operons*), for which they shared the 1965 Nobel Prize for Physiology or Medicine with André Lwoff. >> Jacob, François; Lwoff

Monroe, Harriet (1860–1936) Poet and critic, born in Chicago, IL. From an influential family, she was educated at the Visitation Convent, Washington, DC, then worked as an art and drama critic. In 1912 she founded the highly respected magazine *Poetry*, which was influential in publicizing the work of Lindsay, Eliot, Pound, and Frost, among others. She wrote the 'Columbian Ode' for the Chicago World's Columbian Exposition (1892), celebrating the 400th anniversary of the West's 'discovery' of America.

Monroe, James (1758–1831) US statesman and fifth president (1817–25), born in Westmoreland Co, VA. After serving in the Revolution he entered politics, becoming a member of the US Senate (1790–4). He was governor of Virginia (1799–1802), and in 1803 helped to negotiate the Louisiana Purchase. In 1811 he was again Governor of Virginia, then secretary of state (1811–17), and also secretary of war (1814–15). In 1816 he was elected president, and in 1820 re-elected almost unanimously. His most popular acts were the recognition of the Spanish American republics, and the promulgation in a message to Congress (1823) of the *Monroe Doctrine*, embodying the principle 'that the American continents ... are henceforth not to be considered as subjects for future colonization by any European power'. >> Adams, John Quincy; RR1097

Monroe, Marilyn, stage name of **Norma Jean Mortenson** or **Baker** (1926–62) Film star, born in Los Angeles, CA. After a childhood spent largely in foster homes, she became a photographer's model in 1946. Following small film parts, she starred as a beautiful, sexy 'dumb blonde' in such films as *How to Marry a Millionaire* and *Gentlemen Prefer Blondes* (both 1953). Wanting more serious roles, she studied at Lee Strasberg's Actors' Studio, and went on to win acclaim in *Bus Stop* (1956) and *The Misfits* (1961), written for

her by her third husband, Arthur Miller. She went to London to make *The Prince and the Showgirl* (1957) with Sir Laurence Olivier. Divorced from Miller in 1961, her death in 1962 from an overdose of sleeping pills shocked the world, and has become a symbol of Hollywood's ruthless exploitation of beauty and youth. Media investigations into the circumstances surrounding her death have continued into the 1990s. >> DiMaggio; Miller, Arthur; Strasberg

Monsarrat, Nicholas (John Turney) [monsarat] (1910–79) Novelist, born in Liverpool, Merseyside, NW England, UK. He studied at Cambridge, abandoned law for literature, and wrote three novels, and a play, *The Visitors*, which reached the London stage. During World War 2 he served in the navy, and out of his experiences emerged his best-selling novel, *The Cruel Sea* (1951, filmed 1953). *The Story of Esther Costello* (1953) repeated that success, followed by *The Tribe That Lost Its Head* (1956) and *The Pillow Fight* (1965). He settled in Ottawa, Canada, as director of the UK Information Office (1953–6), after holding a similar post in South Africa. He wrote a two-volume autobiography *Life is a Four-Letter Word* (1966, 1970).

Mont, Allen B Du >> Du Mont, Allen B

Montagna, Bartolomeo [montanya] (c. 1450–1523) Painter, born in Brescia, Italy. He probably studied at Venice under Giovanni Bellini and Carpaccio. He founded a school of painting at Vicenza, and is best known for the altarpiece in S Michele at Vicenza (1499, Milan). >> Bellini, Giovanni; Carpaccio

Montagnier, Luc [mõtanyay] (1932–) French virologist. Working at the Institut Pasteur in Paris in 1983, he discovered a retrovirus he called LAV, suspected of causing AIDS. **Robert Gallo** (1937–), working in the USA, claimed in 1984 that he had discovered the virus earlier, and had named it HTLV-3. The virus is now known as HIV (Human Immune-deficiency Virus), and Montagnier and Gallo are listed as co-discoverers.

Montagu >> Halifax, Charles; Manchester, Edward; Sandwich, Edward / John

Montagu, (Montague Francis) Ashley [montagyoo] (1905–) Anthropologist, born in London, England, UK. He studied at London, Florence, and Columbia universities, held posts at the Wellcome History Museum in London, New York University, Hahnemann Medical College, PA, and Rutgers University, NJ (1949–55). Throughout his work on human biosocial evolution, he has argued strongly against the view that cultural phenomena are genetically determined. Best known as the author of UNESCO's 'Statement on Race' (1950), his many publications include *The Elephant Man* (1971) and *Growing Young* (1981).

Montagu, Elizabeth [montagyoo], *née* **Robinson** (1720–1800) Writer and society leader, born in York, North Yorkshire, N England, UK. In 1742 she married Edward Montagu, grandson of the 1st Earl of Sandwich, thus became a cousin by marriage to Lady Mary Wortley Montagu. She established a salon in Mayfair which became the heart of London social and literary life. The members became known as 'Bluestockings', from the way several of them dressed. >> Montagu, Mary Wortley

Montagu, George [montagyoo] (1753–1815) Naturalist and British soldier, born at Lackham House, Wiltshire, S England, UK. A failed career in the army and a disastrous marriage that led to the loss of his estates turned his attention to ornithology. He moved to Devon, where he produced his notable *Ornithological Dictionary; or Alphabetical Synopsis of British Birds* (2 vols, 1802). *Montagu's harrier* is named after him.

Montagu, Lady Mary Wortley [montagyoo], *née* **Pierrepont** (1689–1762) Writer, born in London, England, UK. The daughter of the Earl of Kingston, she married Edward Wortley Montague in 1712, and lived in London. A poet and essayist as well as a feminist and a beauty, she gained a brilliant reputation among literary figures. While in Constantinople with her husband, she wrote her entertaining *Letters* describing Eastern life. She also brought the smallpox inoculation from Turkey, introducing it to England, her own beauty having been marked by an attack while she was a young woman.

Montaigne, Michel (Eyquem) de [mõten] (1533–92) Essayist and courtier, born at Château de Montaigne, Périgord, France. He spoke no language but Latin until he was six, received his early education at Bordeaux, then studied law. He obtained a post in connection with the *parlement* of Bordeaux, and for 13 years was a city counsellor, later becoming mayor. A translation (1569) of the *Natural History* of a 15th-c professor at Toulouse was his first attempt at literature, and supplied the text for his *Apologie de Raymon Sebond*. In 1571 he succeeded to the family estate at Montaigne, and lived the life of a country gentleman, varied by visits to Paris and a tour in Germany, Switzerland, and Italy. He is remembered for his *Essais* (1572–80, 1588) on the new ideas and personalities of the time, which introduced a new literary genre to accommodate what Matthew Arnold was later to call 'the dialogue of the mind with itself'. Quoted by Shakespeare, imitated by Bacon, and incorporated into the discourse of the novel, Montaigne's essays have provided a major contribution to literary history. >> Arnold, Matthew; Bacon, Francis (1561–1626)

Montale, Eugenio [montahlay] (1896–1981) Poet, born in Genoa, Italy. He was the leading poet of the modern Italian 'Hermetic' school, and his primary concern was with language and personalities of the time, which his works include *Ossi di seppia* (1925, Cuttlefish Bones), *Le occasioni* (1939, The Occasions), *La bufera e altro* (1956, The Storm, and Other Poems), *Satura* (1962), and *Xenia* (1966). He was awarded the Nobel Prize for Literature in 1975. >> Quasimodo; Ungaretti

Montalembert, Charles (Forbes René), comte de (Count of) [mõalãbair] (1810–70) French historian and politician, born in London, England, UK. Educated at Fulham and the Collège Ste Barbe, in 1830 he helped Lamennais and others publish *L'Avenir* (The Future), a liberal newspaper, but it was condemned by the pope. In 1835 he was outspoken in defence of the liberty of the press, and in 1848 against tyranny, and after the Revolution he was elected a member of the National Assembly. His greatest work was *Les Moines d'occident* (7 vols, 1860–77, Monks of the West). >> Lamennais

Montana, Joe [montana], popular name of **Joseph C Montana, Jr** (1956–) Player of American football, born in Monongahela, PA. A former Notre Dame quarterback, he led the San Francisco 49ers to victories in four Super Bowls during the 1980s. An inspirational leader and talented passer, he was named the National Football League's most valuable player in 1989. >> RR1155

Montand, Yves [mõtã, eev], originally **Ivo Livi** (1921–91) Actor-singer, born in Monsummano Alto, Italy. He worked at a variety of jobs before performing as a singer and impressionist in Marseilles and Paris. A protégé of Edith Piaf, he made his film debut with her in *Etoile sans lumière* (1946, Star Without Light). He appeared in *Le Salaire de la peur* (1953, The Wages of Fear), and ventured abroad for such films as *Let's Make Love* (1960). His acting reputation was enhanced by an association with the director Constantin Costa-Gavras in such films as *Z* (1968) and *L'Aveu* (1970, The Confession). He was married to actress **Simone Signoret** from 1951 until her death in 1985. In the 1980s he became a distinguished elder statesman of the

French film industry, his films including *Jean de Florette* and *Manon des sources* (both 1986). >> Piaf; Signoret

Montcalm (de Saint Véran), Louis Joseph de Montcalm-Grozon, marquis de [mõkalm] (1712–59) French general, born in Condiac, France. During the Seven Years' War he took command of the French troops in Canada (176), and captured the British post of Oswego and Fort William Henry. In 1758 he defended Ticonderoga, and proceeded to the defence of Quebec, where he died in the battle against General Wolfe on the Plains of Abraham. >> Wolfe, James

Montefiore, Sir Moses (Haim) [montefyohray] (1784– 1885) Philanthropist, born in Livorno, Italy. He retired with a fortune from stockbroking in 1824, and from 1829 was prominent in the struggle for Jewish equality. After long exclusion and repeated re-election, he was admitted sheriff of London in 1837. Between 1827 and 1875 he made seven journeys to Palestine in the interests of his oppressed co-religionists in Poland, Russia, Rumania, and Damascus. He was knighted in 1837, and became a baronet in 1846.

Montesi, Wilma [montayzee] (1932–53) Fashion model, the daughter of a Roman carpenter. The finding of her body on the beach near Ostia in April 1953 led to prolonged investigations involving sensational allegations of drug and sex orgies in Roman society. After four years of debate, scandal, arrests, re-arrests and libel suits, the Venice trial in 1957 of the son of a former Italian foreign minister, a self-styled marquis, and a former Rome police chief for complicity in her death, ended in their acquittal after many conflicts of evidence. The trial left the mystery unsolved, but exposed corruption in high public places and helped to bring about the downfall of the government in 1955.

Montespan, Françoise Athenaïs de Rochechouart, marquise de (Marchioness of) [mõtespã] (1641–1707) Mistress of Louis XIV, born in Tonnay-Charente, France, the daughter of the Duc de Mortemart. In 1663 she married the Marquis de Montespan, and joined the household of Queen Maria Theresa as lady-in-waiting. She became the king's mistress in c.1667, and after her marriage was annulled (1674), was given official recognition of her position. She bore the king seven children, who were legitimized (1673). Supplanted first by Mlle de Fontanges and later by Mme de Maintenon, she left court in 1687 and retired to the convent of Saint-Joseph in Paris, eventually becoming the superior. >> Louis XIV; Maintenon

Montesquieu, Charles Louis de Secondat, Baron de la Brède et de [mõteskyoe] (1689–1755) Philosopher and jurist, born at Château La Brède near Bordeaux, France. Educated at Bordeaux, he became an advocate, but turned to scientific research and literary work. He settled in Paris (1726), then spent some years travelling and studying political and social institutions. His best-known work is the comparative study of legal and political issues, *De l'esprit des lois* (1748, The Spirit of Laws), which was a major influence on 18th-c Europe.

Montessori, Maria [montesawree] (1870–1952) Physician and educationist, born in Rome. She studied at Rome, where she was the first woman in Italy to graduate in medicine. Later, she joined the psychiatric clinic, and became interested in the problems of mentally handicapped children. She opened her first 'children's house' in 1907, developing a system of education for children of three to six, based on freedom of movement, the provision of considerable choice for pupils, and the use of specially designed activities and equipment. *Montessori schools* were also later developed for older children throughout the world.

Monteux, Pierre [mōtoe] (1875–1964) Conductor, born in Paris. He trained at the Paris Conservatoire, where he began his career as a viola player. He conducted Diaghilev's Ballets Russes in Paris (1911–14, 1917), and in 1914 organized the 'Concerts Monteux', whose programmes gave prominence to new French and Russian music. Founding and directing the Orchestre Symphonique de Paris, in 1936 he took over the newly organized San Francisco Symphony Orchestra, and in 1941 established a summer school for student conductors at Hanover, NH. From 1960 until his death he was principal conductor of the London Symphony Orchestra, and became one of the 20th-c's leading conductors, his interpretations equally admired in ballet, opera, and symphonic music.

Monteverdi, Claudio [montayvairdee] (1567–1643) Composer, born in Cremona, Italy. A proficient violist, he learned the art of composition in Cremona, publishing a set of three-part choral pieces at the age of 15. About 1590 he was appointed court musician to the Duke of Mantua, whose *maestro di capella* he became in 1602, moving on to a similar post at St Mark's, Venice, in 1613, where he remained until his death. His eight books of madrigals, which appeared at regular intervals between 1587 and 1638, show his originality and pioneering spirit. The two surviving operas of his later period, *Il Ritorno d'Ulisse* (1641, The Return of Ulysses) and *L'Incoronazione di Poppea* (1642, The Coronation of Poppaea), both written when he was well past 70, show development towards the Baroque style and foreshadow the use of the *leitmotif*. His greatest contribution to church music is the *Mass* and *Vespers of the Blessed Virgin* (1610), which contained tone colours and harmonies well in advance of his time.

Montez, Lola [montez], originally **Marie Dolores Eliza Rosanna Gilbert** (1818–61) Dancer, born in Limerick, Ireland. An outstanding beauty, she trained to be a Spanish dancer, and appeared at Her Majesty's Theatre in London. While touring Europe, she went to Munich (1846), where she soon won over the eccentric artist-king, Ludwig I of Bavaria (reigned 1825–48), with whom she had a scandalous affair that greatly boosted her career as a dancer. After a tour of the USA she settled in California, where she lectured on fashion and beauty, but she never regained her former standing, and died in poverty.

Montezuma II [montezooma] (1466–1520) The last Aztec emperor (1502–20). A distinguished warrior and legislator, he died during the Spanish conquest of Hernán Cortés. One of his descendants was viceroy of Mexico (1697–1701). >> Cortés

Montfaucon, Bernard de [mōfohsō] (1655–1741) Scholar and monk, born in Soulage, France, the founder of the science of palaeography. A Benedictine monk at Saint-Maur, he went to Paris to edit the Latin works of the Greek Fathers of the Church, and published *Palaeographia Graeca* (1708, Greek Palaeography), the first work to be based on a study of manuscript handwriting. He also published editions of Athanasius and St John Chrysostom.

Montfort, Simon de (c. 1160–1218) Norman crusader, born in Toulouse, France. He took part in the 4th Crusade (1202–4), and also undertook a crusade against the Albingenses in 1208. He was killed at the siege of Toulouse.

Montfort, Simon de, Earl of Leicester (c. 1208–1265) English statesman and soldier, born in Montfort, France. Well received by Henry III of England in 1230, he was confirmed in his title and estates in 1232, and in 1238 married the king's youngest sister, **Eleanor**. As the king's deputy in Gascony (1248), he put down disaffection with a heavy hand. He returned to England in 1253, became the leader of the barons in their opposition to the king, and defeated him at Lewes (1264). He then became virtual ruler of England, calling a parliament in 1265; but the barons soon grew dissatisfied with his rule, and the king's army defeated him at Evesham, where he was killed. >> Henry III (of England)

Montgolfier brothers [mōgolfyay] Aeronautical inventors: **Joseph Michel Montgolfier** (1740–1810) and **Jacques Etienne Montgolfier** (1745–99), born in Annonay, France. In 1782 they constructed a balloon whose bag was lifted by lighting a cauldron of paper beneath it, thus heating and rarifying the air it contained. A flight of 9 km/5½ mi, at 3000 ft, carrying Pilatre de Rozier and the Marquis d'Arlandes, was achieved in 1783 – the world's first manned flight. Further experiments were frustrated by the outbreak of the French Revolution. >> Séguin

Montgomery (of Alamein), Bernard Law Montgomery, 1st Viscount (1887–1976) British field marshal, born in London, England, UK. He trained at Sandhurst, and was commissioned into the Royal Warwickshire Regiment in 1908. In World War 2, he gained renown as arguably the best British field commander since Wellington. A controversial and outspoken figure, he was nevertheless a 'soldier's general', able to establish a remarkable rapport with his troops. He commanded the 8th Army in N Africa, and defeated Rommel at El Alamein (1942). He played a key role in the invasion of Sicily and Italy (1943), and was appointed commander-in-chief, ground forces, for the Allied invasion of Normandy (1944). In 1945, German forces in NW Germany, The Netherlands, and Denmark surrendered to him on Lünenberg Heath. Appointed field marshal (1944) and viscount (1946), he served successively as Chief of the Imperial General Staff (1946–8) and deputy supreme commander of NATO forces in Europe (1951–8). His books include *History of Warfare* (1968).

Montgomery, L(ucy) M(aud) (1874–1942) Novelist, raised in Cavendish, Prince Edward Island, Canada. She was earning money as a writer by the 1890s. Her first book was the phenomenally successful *Anne of Green Gables* (1908), after which she published several sequels. Her works are sometimes highly satirical; at her best she captures memorably the mysteries and terrors of early childhood, as in *Magic for Marigold* (1929). She married the Rev Ewan MacDonald in 1911, and moved to Ontario. At her death she left 10 volumes of unpublished personal diaries (1889–1942), whose publication began in 1985.

Montgomery, Wes, popular name of **John Leslie Montgomery** (1925–68) Jazz musician, born in Indianapolis, IN. A highly influential guitarist, with a distinctively mellow sound, he recorded from 1957 with his brothers **Monk (William) Montgomery** (1921–82, bassist) and **Buddy (Charles) Montgomery** (1930– , vibes) as The Montgomery Brothers. He made commercial big band albums in the mid-1960s, and appeared on television with Herb Alpert and his Tijuana Brass.

Montherlant, Henri (Marie Joseph Millon) de [mōtairlã] (1896–1972) Novelist and playwright, born in Paris. He was severely wounded in World War 1, after which he travelled in Spain, Africa, and Italy. His major work is a four-novel cycle, beginning with *Les jeunes filles* and *Pitié pour les femmes* (1936, published together as Pity for Women). After 1942 he wrote several plays, including *Malatesta* (1946) and *Don Juan* (1958).

Montholon, Charles Tristan, marquis de [mōtolō] (1783–1853) French soldier and diplomat, born in Paris. He joined the army in 1798, served in the navy and cavalry, was wounded in 1809, and in the same year was appointed Napoleon's chamberlain. He was promoted general in 1811, becoming Napoleon's aide-de-camp at Waterloo

(1815). He accompanied him to St Helena, and published memoirs dictated by him (8 vols, 1822–5). Condemned in 1840 to 20 years' imprisonment for helping Louis Napoleon's attempted seizure of power, he was liberated in 1848. >> Napoleon I; Napoleon III

Monti, Eugenio [**mon**tee] (1928–) Bobsleigh driver, born in Dobbiaco, Italy. The winner of a record six Olympic bobsleighing medals, he won golds in the two- and four-man events at the 1968 Games, after winning the silver in both events in 1956, and the bronze in 1964. He was also a member of 11 Italian world championship winning teams between 1957 and 1968. After retiring in 1968, he was appointed manager to the Italian national team. >> RR1147

Montini, Giovanni Battista >> **Paul VI**

Montpensier, Anne Marie Louise d'Orléans, duchesse de (Duchess of) [mõpãsyay], known as **la Grande Mademoiselle** (1627–93) Niece of Louis XIII, born in Paris. She inherited a huge fortune from her mother, but was thwarted in her desire to marry Louis XIV or Ferdinand III. She supported her father, Gaston de France, duc d'Orléans, and Condé in the revolt of the Fronde (1651–2), where she commanded an army that occupied Orléans and later the Bastille. After a period in disgrace she returned to the court and secretly married the **Comte de Lauzun** (c.1681), a captain in the king's bodyguard. The marriage was unhappy, and they separated in 1684. She published her memoirs, and two novellas, and her last years were spent in religious duties. >> **Condé, Louis II de Bourbon**

Montrose, James Graham, 1st Marquess of (1612–50) Scottish soldier and royalist. He studied at St Andrews and travelled in Europe, returning in 1637, and was one of the four noblemen who drew up the National Covenant in support of Presbyterianism. He served in the Covenanter army in 1640, but transferred his allegiance to Charles I, and led the Royalist army to victory at Tippermuir (1644). After the Royalist defeat at Naseby (1645), his army became disaffected, and his remaining force was defeated at Philiphaugh. He fled to Europe, returning to Scotland after Charles's execution to avenge his death; but his army was largely lost by shipwreck, and the remnant defeated at Invercharron (1650). He was taken prisoner, and hanged in Edinburgh. >> **Charles I (of England)**

Monty Python, in full **Monty Python's Flying Circus** >> **Cleese; Palin**

Moodie, Susanna, née **Strickland** (1803–85) Writer, born in Bungay, Suffolk, E England, UK. She married in 1831, and moved to Canada the following year. She came from a literary family – her sister, and neighbour in Canada, was the writer **Catherine Parr Traill** (1802–99) – and among her many literary works are poems, stories for children, and sketches. Her best-known work concerns her life in Cobourg, Ontario, *Roughing It in the Bush: or, Life in Canada* (1852). Along with later memoirs and novels, this is marked by humour, frankness, and a dramatic and keen observation unusual in the literature of emigration and settlement.

Moody, Dwight L(yman) (1837–99) Evangelist, born in Northfield, MA. A shoe salesman in Boston, in 1856 he went to Chicago to engage in missionary work, and founded the Moody Church. In 1870 he was joined by **Ira David Sankey** (1840–1908). In 1873 and 1883 they visited Great Britain as evangelists, Moody preaching and Sankey singing; afterwards they worked together in America. In 1899 he founded the Moody Bible Institute in Chicago.

Moon, William (1818–94) Inventor, born in Kent, SE England, UK. Partially blind from the age of four, he became totally blind in 1840 and began to teach blind children. Dissatisfied with existing systems of embossed type,

he invented (in 1845) a system based on Roman capitals (*Moon type*), and later a stereotype plate for use with his type. Although requiring more space, his type is easier to learn than Braille for those who have become blind late in life, and is still widely used. >> **Braille**

Mooney, Edward (Francis) (1882–1958) Roman Catholic clergyman, born in Mt Savage, MD. Ordained in 1909, he was a theology professor, seminary spiritual director, and Vatican diplomat before becoming Bishop of Rochester, NY (1933). As an official of the National Catholic Welfare Conference, he was a major Catholic spokesman on social issues. Named Archbishop of Detroit (1937) and made a cardinal (1946), he promoted workers' rights and bolstered church finances.

Moorcroft, William (1872–1945) Potter, born in Staffordshire, C England, UK. In 1913 he set up his own firm in Burslem, producing a range of white-bodied ceramics decorated with stylized flowers and leaves, titled 'Florian Ware'. More colourful were his 'Hazledene' (landscape and trees) and 'Claremont' (toadstools). His main interest, however, was the flambé glaze, and he won many prizes for his work in Paris, Brussels, and America. In 1928 he was appointed Potter to the Crown.

Moore, Archie, originally **Archibald Lee Wright**, nickname **the Mongoose** (1913/16–) Boxer, born in Benoit, MI. His actual date of birth is uncertain (by his own account), but he is still the oldest man to hold a world title; he also reigned longer than any light-heavyweight champion – nine years, one month. He was 39 (or 36) when he beat Joey Maxim for the light-heavyweight title in 1952. He had 228 professional bouts and won 194, knocking out a record 141 opponents. He lost to Cassius Clay in 1962, and retired in 1965. >> **Ali, Muhammad**

Moore, Bernard (1850–1935) Potter, born in Staffordshire, C England, UK. He succeeded his father in the firm of Moore Brothers, where he traded with his brother until the sale of the business in 1905. He then set up his own business (1905–15), where he was joined by his son. As a chemist he was particularly interested in glazes, and his experiments led him to produce a series of rouge flambés, turquoise, sang-de-boeuf, crystalline, and aventurine glazes as well as fine lustres. He worked as a technical consultant with many British, European, and American companies. He was greatly concerned with health risks to pottery workers, and delivered an influential paper to the Ceramic Society in 1932 suggesting changes in production to minimize lung disease.

Moore, Bobby, popular name of **Robert Frederick Chelsea Moore** (1941–93) Footballer, born in London, England, UK. In a long career with West Ham United (1958–74) and later Fulham (1974–7), he played 1000 matches at senior level, receiving an FA Cup-winner's Medal in 1964 and a European Cup-winner's Medal in 1965. He was capped a record 108 times (107 in succession), 90 of them as captain. He played in the World Cup finals in Chile in 1962, and captained the victorious England side in the 1966 World Cup. >> RR1155

Moore, Brian (1921–) Writer, born in Belfast. After World War 2 he became a journalist and adopted Canadian citizenship. He spent time in New York before moving to California. He is particularly admired for his portrayal of women, as seen in *The Lonely Passion of Judith Hearne* (1955, filmed 1987). *The Great Victorian Collection* (1975) was awarded the James Tait Black Memorial Prize, and both *The Doctor's Wife* (1976) and *Black Robe* (1985) were short-listed for the Booker Prize. Later books include *The Colour of Blood* (1987), *No Other Life* (1993), and *The Statement* (1995). The play *Lies of Silence* (1990, filmed 1991) is an exile's view of the troubles in Northern Ireland.

Moore, Clement (Clarke) (1779–1863) Educator, Hebraist, and poet, born in New York City. He studied at Columbia College, (1798), became a Hebrew scholar, and was a founder of the General Theological Seminary, New York City (1823–50). He is generally known for a poem written for his children, 'A Visit From St. Nicholas' (1822), later known as 'The Night Before Christmas'. His other claim to fame is that in 1807 he discovered Lorenzo da Ponte, the librettist of three of Mozart's greatest operas, in a New York City bookstore, and was instrumental in launching da Ponte's new career as a teacher of Italian language and literature. >> da Ponte, Lorenzo

Moore, Demi, originally **Demetria Guynes** (1962–) Film actress, born in Roswell, NM. She worked in television before she made her film debut in *Choices* (1981), but her major breakthrough came with *St Elmo's Fire* (1984). Later films include *Ghost* (1990), *Indecent Proposal* (1992), *The Scarlet Letter* (1995), and *Striptease* (1996). She married actor Bruce Willis in 1987. >> Willis, Bruce

Moore, Dudley (Stuart John) (1935–) Actor, comedian, and musician, born in London, England, UK. He studied at Oxford. Small in stature but big in personality he was one of the successful *Beyond the Fringe* team (1960–64). He joined Peter Cook for the TV series *Not Only... but also* (1964–70), and starred in several films including *10* (1979), *Arthur* (1981), *Santa Claus – The Movie* (1985), *Arthur 2 – On the Rocks* (1988), and *Crazy People* (1990). An accomplished musician, he has performed for radio and TV with his own jazz piano trio, and has composed for several films and plays. In 1991 he co-presented the television series *Orchestra!* (1991) with Sir Georg Solti. >> Cook, Peter; Miller, Jonathan; Solti

Moore, Edward (1712–57) Playwright, born in Abingdon, Berkshire, SE England, UK. He turned to writing plays when his business as a linen-draper failed. The comedy *Gil Blas* (1751), based on Lesage, and the tragedy *The Gamester* (1753), are his best-known productions. He also edited the weekly journal *The World* (1753–7).

Moore, Francis (1657–c. 1715) Astrologer, born in Bridgnorth, Shropshire, WC England, UK. In 1700 he published *Vox Stellarum* (Voices of the Stars), which later became known as *Old Moore's Almanac*, and continues to be published annually, prophesying events of the following year.

Moore, George (Augustus) (1852–1933) Writer, born in Ballyglass, Co Mayo, Ireland. Groomed for the army, he lived a bohemian life in London until his father's death in 1870 left him free to become a dilettante artist and writer in Paris. A novelist of the Realist school, he introduced this type of fiction into England, notably with *Esther Waters* (1894). During the Boer War he sought exile in Ireland, and turned his attention away from sordid realism, as in *A Drama in Muslin* (1886) and the stories in *The Untilled Field* (1903). He returned to England in 1911, where he wrote confessions and memoirs, including the *Hail and Farewell* trilogy (1911–14), which satirically portrays his friendships (particularly with Yeats) during the setting up of the Abbey Theatre in Dublin. He turned in his last phase to romanticize history, beginning with the masterpiece *The Brook Kerith* (1916), and *Héloïse and Abelard* (1921). >> Yeats, William Butler

Moore, G(eorge) E(dward) (1873–1958) Philosopher, born in London, England, UK. He studied at Dulwich College and Cambridge, and left classics for philosophy, where he first embraced then rejected the claims of Hegelian idealism. His major ethical work was *Principia Ethica* (1903), in which he argued against the naturalistic fallacy. At Cambridge he became a lecturer in moral science (1911), and professor of mental philosophy and logic (1925–39). He was a leading influence on the Bloomsbury group. He also edited the journal *Mind* (1921–47), and

made it the major English-language journal in the field. >> Bell, Vanessa; Keynes; Virginia; Strachey, Lytton; Woolf, Leonard/Virginia

Moore, Gerald (1899–1987) Pianoforte accompanist, born in Watford, Hertfordshire, SE England. He studied music at Toronto, and established himself as an outstanding accompanist of the world's leading singers and instrumentalists. He was a regular performer at international music festivals, and a notable lecturer and television broadcaster on music.

Moore, Henry (Spencer) (1898–1986) Sculptor, born in Castleford, West Yorkshire, N England, UK. He studied at the Royal College of Art, London, where he taught sculpture (1924–31), moving to the Chelsea School of Art (1931–9). Recognized as one of the most original and powerful modern sculptors, his style is based on the organic forms and undulations found in landscape and natural rocks, and influenced by primitive African and Mexican art. He achieved the spatial, three-dimensional quality of sculpture by the piercing of his figures. Principal commissions included the 'Madonna and Child' in St Matthew's Church, Northampton (1943–4), the decorative frieze (1952) on the Time Life building, London, and the monumental female reclining figures for the UNESCO building in Paris (1958) and the Lincoln Center in New York City (1965). Major collections can be seen at the Henry Moore Sculpture Center, Toronto, The Tate Gallery, London, and at his home in Much Hadham, Hertfordshire. >> Hepworth

Moore, Sir (John) Jeremy (1928–) British soldier. From Cheltenham College he joined the Royal Marines at the age of 19 as a probationary second-lieutenant. He saw service in Britain, Brunei, and Australia in a variety of roles, including that of commandant of the Royal Military School of Music. By 1979 he had reached the rank of major-general in the commando forces, and in 1982, when the decision was taken to recapture the Falkland Is from Argentina, he was made commander of land forces. His success in the brief campaign brought him unexpected fame as well as a knighthood in 1982. He retired from the forces in 1983. >> Galtieri

Moore, Sir John (1761–1809) British soldier, born in Glasgow, W Scotland, UK. From 1794 he served in many countries in Europe and in the West Indies, but is remembered for his command of the English army in Spain (1808–9), where he was forced to retreat to Coruña. There he defeated a French attack, but was mortally wounded (as recounted in the poem by Wolfe). >> Stanhope, Hester Lucy; Wolfe, Charles

Moore, Marianne (Craig) (1887–1972) Poet, born in St Louis, MO. She studied at Bryn Mawr College, PA, and taught at Carlisle Commercial College before becoming a branch librarian in New York City (1921–5). She contributed to *The Egoist* from 1915, and edited *The Dial* from 1926 until its demise in 1929. She was acquainted with such seminal Modernists as Pound and T S Eliot, and associated with the Greenwich Village group, Idiosyncratic. A consummate stylist, and unmistakably modern, her first publication was *Poems* (1921). *Selected Poems* appeared in 1935, and *Complete Poems* in 1967.

Moore, Mary Tyler (1936–) Actress, born in New York City. Trained as a dancer, she became the Happy Hotpoint Pixie in a series of television commercials in 1955. Small acting roles followed, and she made her film debut in 1961. *The Dick Van Dyke Show* (1961–6) highlighted her talent for domestic comedy, and won her Emmies in 1964 and 1965. Her small-screen popularity was used to launch a multi-media career on Broadway with *Breakfast at Tiffanys* (1966) and in the cinema, but she returned to television with *The Mary Tyler Moore Show* (1970–7), winning Emmies in 1973, 1974, and 1976. She subsequently won an Emmy for *First, You Cry* (1978), a Tony for *Whose Life Is It Anyway?* (1980), and an Oscar nomination for *Ordinary People* (1980). MTM Enterprises, formed with her second husband **Grant Tinker** in 1970, has been responsible for such television series as *Hill Street Blues*. >> Van Dyke, Dick

Moore, Patrick (Alfred Caldwell) (1923–) British amateur astronomer, writer, broadcaster, and musician. He was educated at home due to childhood illness. He is best known as the enthusiastic and knowledgeable presenter of the long-running BBC television programme *The Sky at Night* (1957–). He is an accomplished xylophone player, and has composed several works, including *Perseus and Andromeda* (1975). The recipient of many awards for his services to astronomy, he has published over 60 books, including *The Amateur Astronomer* (1970), *The A–Z of Astronomy* (1986), *Mission to the Planets* (1990), and *Teach Yourself Astronomy* (1995).

Moore, Roger (George) (1927–) Film star, born in London, England, UK. An art school student of painting, he made his film debut as an extra in 1945, and appeared in small roles on stage and in films prior to army service. He appeared on Broadway in *A Pin to See the Peepshow* (1953) and in the Hollywood film *The Last Time I Saw Paris* (1954). On television he won stardom as the action-man hero of such series as *Ivanhoe* (1958), *The Alaskans* (1960–1), and *The Persuaders* (1972–3), but most especially, *The Saint* (1962–9). His own wittiest critic, he brought a lightweight insouciance to the role of James Bond in seven films between *Live and Let Die* (1973) and *A View to a Kill* (1985).

Moore, Stanford (1913–82) Biochemist, born in Chicago, IL. He studied chemistry at Vanderbilt and Wisconsin universities, and spent his career at the Rockefeller Institute, New York City (1939–82). In the 1950s, with William Stein, he devised a general method for finding the identity of the number of amino acids in protein molecules. By 1958 they had developed an ingenious automated analyser to carry out all the steps of the analysis of the structure of RNA on a small sample. They shared the Nobel Prize for Chemistry in 1972, and later devised a method of analysing DNA. >> Stein, William; RR1172

Moore, Thomas (1779–1852) Poet, born in Dublin. He studied at Trinity College, Dublin, and the Middle Temple. His best-known work, *Irish Melodies* (1807–34), including such memorable poems as 'The Last Rose of Summer', was set to music and aroused sympathy for the Irish nationalists among London's nobility. His reputation at that time was on a par with that of Byron and Scott, and he was paid the then phenomenal sum of £3000 by Longmans for his narrative poem *Lalla Rookh* (1817). The recipient of Byron's memoirs, he burned them (with publisher John Murray), and later edited the *Letters and Journals of Lord Byron* (1830). >> Byron, George

Moorer, Thomas H(inman) (1912–) US naval officer, born in Mount Willing, AL. During World War 2 he narrowly escaped death twice – his airplane was shot down and the ship that rescued him was torpedoed (1942). He was commander of the Atlantic Fleet (1965–7), chief of naval operations (1967–70), and chairman of the joint chiefs-of-staff (1970–4) before he retired in 1974.

Moores, Sir John (1896–1993) Businessman, born in Eccles, Greater Manchester, NW England, UK. He founded Littlewoods football pools in 1923, distributing 4000 coupons by hand in Liverpool. Following a visit to America, he established a mail-order business in Britain (1932), and opened the first store in the Littlewoods chain in 1937. When Liverpool Polytechnic was awarded university status in 1992, it took the name of Liverpool John Moores University.

Moors Murderers >> Brady, Ian
Mor, Anthonis >> More, Sir Anthony
Morandi, Giorgio [moran̄dee] (1890–1964) Painter, born in Bologna, Italy. He studied at the Academy of Fine Arts, Bologna, where he later taught (1930–56). Although influenced by the Italian Metaphysical painters (c.1918–19), he concentrated on landscapes, portraits, and above all still-life. His arrangements of everyday objects on a tabletop were painted in subdued tones, and with a simplicity of form reminiscent of Cézanne. He won the Grand Prix for Painting at the Venice Biennale in 1948, and other honours followed. >> Cézanne

Morant, Harry Harbord [morant], originally **Edwin Henry Murrant**, nickname **Breaker Morant** (1865–1902) Adventurer and minor poet, born probably in Bridgwater, Somerset, SW England, UK. He arrived in N Queensland in 1883, and the following year married **Daisy May O'Dwyer**, later Daisy Bates. About this time he changed his name, and ranged about Queensland and New South Wales earning a living by his undoubted skills as a rider and horse-breaker. Under his pseudonym he contributed ballads and bush verse to the Sydney magazine *The Bulletin* from 1891, writing some 60 poems. In 1899 he enlisted in the Australian contingent sailing for the Boer Wars. In South Africa, after the murder and mutilation by the Boers of a close friend, Morant and a companion were court martialled and executed by a firing squad for their retaliation against the surrendering Boers. >> Bates, Daisy May

Morata, Olympia [morahta] (1526–55) Italian humanist scholar and poet. She gave public lectures at the age of 15. In 1548 she married the German physician **Andreas Grundler**, followed him to Germany, became a Protestant, and died penniless. She left numerous Latin and Greek poems, a treatise on Cicero, dialogues, and letters.

Moravia, Alberto [morayvia], pseudonym of **Alberto Pincherle** (1907–90) Novelist and short-story writer, born in Rome. He became a journalist, travelled extensively, and lived for a time in the USA. His first novel was a major success, *Gli indifferenti* (1929, trans The Time of Indifference), portraying in a fatalistic way the preoccupation with sex and money of bourgeois Roman society. Later works include *La disubbidienza* (1948, Disobedience), *Racconti romani* (1954, Roman Tales), and *La Vita Interiore* (1978, trans Time of Desecration).

Moray, James Stuart, Earl of [muhree] (1531–70) Regent of Scotland (1567–70), the illegitimate son of James V of Scotland, and half-brother of Mary, Queen of Scots. He acted as Mary's chief adviser (1560), but supported John Knox and opposed Mary's marriage to Darnley. After an attempted coup, he was outlawed and took refuge in England (1565). Pardoned the following year, he became regent for Mary's baby son, James VI, when she abdicated (1567), and defeated her army at Langside (1568). His Protestant and pro-English policies alienated some Scots nobles, and he was killed at Linlithgow by one of Mary's supporters. >> Darnley; James I (of England); James V; Knox, John; Mary, Queen of Scots

Mordecai [maw(r)dekiy] (c.5th-c BC) Biblical hero. He is described in the Book of Esther as a Jew in exile in Persia, who cared for his orphaned cousin Esther and gained the favour of King Xerxes after uncovering a plot against him. He used his subsequent influence to protect Jews from an edict issued against them. The event is commemorated by the annual Jewish feast of Purim. >> Xerxes I

Mordkin, Mikhail (1880–1944) Ballet dancer, teacher, and director, born in Moscow. After graduating from the Bolshoi Ballet School in 1899, he became soloist and then ballet master of the company. His career in the West was launched with his appearance in Diaghilev's 1909 Paris season, from which he went on to tour with Anna Pavlova. After touring the USA with his own group, he returned to the Bolshoi in 1912, becoming director in 1917. The October Revolution sent him back to the USA, where he settled and became a pioneer of American ballet. He became best known for his teaching, with such stars as Judy Garland and Katharine Hepburn among his pupils. >> Diaghilev; Garland, Judy; Hepburn, Katharine; Pavlova

More, Sir Anthony [moor], originally **Anthonis Mor**, also known as **Antonio Moro** (c. 1519–75) Portrait painter, born in Utrecht, The Netherlands. In 1547 he entered the Antwerp Guild of St Luke. He visited Italy, Spain, and (1553) England. An eminent portraitist, he painted Queen Mary I for her bridegroom, Philip II of Spain, for which it is believed he was knighted. From c.1568 he lived in Antwerp.

More, Hannah [moor] (1745–1833) Playwright and religious writer, born in Fishponds, Bristol, SW England, UK. Educated at a boarding school run by her sisters, she was jilted by her fiancé, then went to London in 1774, where she joined the 'Blue Stocking' coterie of Elizabeth Montagu and her friends. She wrote two tragedies for David Garrick: *Percy* (1777), and *The Fatal Secret* (1779). Her religious views caused her to withdraw from society to Cowslip Green near Bristol, where she did much to improve the condition of the poor, and published religious poems. Her moral tracts for the poor, *Village Politics by Will Chip* (1793), led to the founding of the Religious Tracts Society. >> Garrick; Montagu, Elizabeth

More, Henry [moor] (1614–87) Philosopher and theologian, born in Grantham, Lincolnshire, EC England, UK. He studied at Cambridge, where he remained all his life, and became a leading figure in the circle of 'Cambridge Platonists' which included Whichcote and Cudworth. He devoted himself entirely to study, despite the turbulent political times in which he lived, and developed a particular affinity for Plato, Plotinus, and Descartes. He wrote in prose verse, his main works being *Philosophical Poems* (1647), *The Immortality of the Soul* (1659), and *Divine Dialogues* (1668). >> Cudworth; Whichcote

More, Sir Thomas [moor], also **St Thomas More** (1478–1535) English statesman and scholar, born in London, England, UK. He studied at Oxford, became a lawyer, then spent four years in a Carthusian monastery to test his vocation for the priesthood. He did not take holy orders, and under Henry VIII became Master of Requests (1514), Treasurer of the Exchequer (1521), and Chancellor of the Duchy of Lancaster (1525). On the fall of Wolsey (1529), he was appointed Lord Chancellor, but resigned in 1532 following his opposition to Henry's break with the Roman Catholic Church. On refusing to recognize Henry as head of the English Church, he was imprisoned and beheaded. A leading humanist scholar, as revealed in his Latin *Utopia* (1516) and many other works, he was canonized in 1935; feast day 22 June. >> Henry VIII; Wolsey

Moreau, Gustave [moroh] (1826–98) Painter, born in Paris. He studied at the Ecole des Beaux-Arts, where he was appointed professor of painting in 1892. He was an eccentric Symbolist who painted colourful but usually rather sinister scenes from ancient mythology and the Bible, as in 'Salome' (1876).

Moreau, Jeanne [moroh] (1928–) Actress and director, born in Paris. A pupil at the Conservatoire National d'Art Dramatique, she made her stage and film debuts in 1948. An association with the directors of the French New Wave brought her recognition as an intense, hypnotic film actress. Her most famous films include *Jules et Jim* (1961), *Journal d'une femme de chambre* (1964, Diary of a Chambermaid), *La Mariée etait en noir* (1967, The Bride Wore Black), and *Viva Maria* (1965). Occasional English-language ventures

met with little acclaim, but she proved herself a formidable director with *Lumière* (1976) and *L'Adolescente* (1978). She returned to the screen in the 1990s with *Nikita* (1990) and *The Proprietor* (1996).

Moreau, (Jean) Victor (Marie) [moroh] (1763–1813) French general in the Napoleonic Wars, born in Morlaix, France. He studied law, but in 1789 commanded the volunteers from Rennes, and in 1794 was made a general of division. He drove the Austrians back to the Danube, but was forced to retreat, and later deprived of his command (1797). He declined the dictatorship of Sieyès, but lent his assistance to Napoleon in the coup of 18th Brumaire. He gained victories over the Austrians in 1800, winning the Battle of Hohenlinden. Napoleon accused him of sharing in the royalist plot against him, and sentenced him to two years' imprisonment (1804), but the sentence was commuted to banishment, and he settled in New Jersey. In 1813 he accompanied the Russian attack on Dresden, but died following wounds received in the battle. >> Napoleon; Sieyès; Suvorov

Morecambe, Eric, originally **Eric Bartholomew** (1926–84) Comedian, born in Morecambe, Lancashire, NW England, UK. Having appeared in working men's clubs since the age of 11, he teamed up in 1943 with fellow entertainer, **Ernie Wise** (originally **Ernest Wiseman**) (1925–). They made their West End debut in the revue *Strike a New Note* in 1943. In 1947 they teamed up again and, as **Morecambe and Wise**, subsequently became the finest British comedy double-act for many years, working in music-hall, summer-shows, pantomimes, radio, films, and television. In 1968, Morecambe had a heart attack; they reduced their workload, concentrating on their television shows – programmes of sketches interspersed with the double-act routine. Their films, such as *The Magnificent Two* (1967), were not successful; the small screen and the stage were their media, and quick-fire repartee their true forte.

Morel >> **Deschamps, Eustache**

Morelli, Giovanni [morelee] (1816–91) Art critic, born in Verona, Italy. He studied natural philosophy and medicine at Munich University. Active in the Italian liberation movement, in 1861 he became a deputy for Bergamo in the first free Italian parliament, and later a senator (1873). From that year he began writing art criticism and, in 1880, published in German *Italian Masters in German Galleries* (trans 1883). This was followed by *Critical Studies of Italian Painters* (1890–3, also originally in German). His criticism concentrated on attribution, which he claimed to have reduced to scientific principles – the *Morellian method*. He was also instrumental in the passing of an act, later named after him, which gave state protection to important works of art.

Moresby, John [maw(r)zbee] (1830–1922) Naval commander and explorer, born in Allerton, Somerset, SW England, UK. He conducted exploration and survey work in New Guinea, where he discovered the fine natural harbour now fronted by Port Moresby, which was named after him.

Morey, Samuel [mawree] (1762–1843) Inventor, born in Hebron, CT. He built up a successful business in timber and sawmills, and acted as a consulting engineer for the construction of locks on the Bellows Falls Canal. After 1790, he and his older brother became interested in steam navigation, and built a series of paddle-wheel steamboats, but in spite of encouragement and financial support from US lawyer and congressman **Robert R Livingston** (1746–1813) none of them were commercially successful. Morey took out more than 20 patents in all, such as his American Water Burner (1817–18), which was ridiculed when it appeared, but was a precursor of the water-gas process widely used half a century later. >> Fulton

Morgagni, Giovanni Battista [maw(r)**gan**yee] (1682–1771) Physician, born in Forli, Italy. He studied at Bologna, worked as an anatomical demonstrator, and became professor of medicine at Padua in 1711. In his writings, he correlated pathological lesions with symptoms in over 700 cases, and is traditionally considered to be the founder of the science of pathological anatomy, 'the father of morbid anatomy'.

Morgan, Agnes Fay, originally **Jane Agnes Fay** (1884–1968) Biochemist and nutritionist, born in Peoria, IL. She studied at Chicago, then taught (1915–54) at the University of California, Berkeley. A founder of the science of nutrition, her research focused on the analysis of nutrients in foods, the stability of vitamins and proteins during food processing, and the physiological effects of vitamin deficiencies. Especially noteworthy was her discovery of the role of pantothenic acid in adrenal function and pigmentation.

Morgan, Augustus De >> **De Morgan, Augustus**

Morgan, Charles (Langbridge), pseudonym **Menander** (1894–1958) Writer, born in Bromley, S Greater London, England, UK. After serving in the navy, he went to Oxford University, where he published *The Gunroom* (1919) on his early experiences, and became a well-known personality. He joined the editorial staff of *The Times* in 1921, and was their principal drama critic (1926–39). Under his pseudonym he also wrote for *The Times Literary Supplement* critical essays called *Reflections in a Mirror*, which were later (1944–5) collected in two series. His novel *Portrait in a Mirror* (1929), won the Femina Vie Heureuse Prize; *The Fountain* (1932) won the Hawthornden Prize; and *The Voyage* (1940) won the James Tait Black Memorial Prize. He also wrote plays, such as *The River Line* (1952) and *The Burning Glass* (1953).

Morgan, Edwin (George) (1920–) Poet, born in Glasgow, W Scotland, UK. He studied at Glasgow University, where he later taught literature. He is a versatile writer, having produced both powerful 'social' poems (the Glasgow Sonnets in *From Glasgow to Saturn*, 1973) as well as much experimental writing, including concrete and computer poems. His work is well represented in *Poems of Thirty Years* (1982). Later works include *You: Anti-War Poetry* (1991) and *Collected Poems* (1996).

Morgan, Sir Henry (c.1635–88) Buccaneer, born in Llanrumney, S Wales. Kidnapped as a child in Bristol and shipped to Barbados, he joined the buccaneers, leading many raids against the Spanish and Dutch in the West Indies and Central America. His most famous exploit was the sacking of Porto Bello and Panama (1671). Transported to London under arrest (1672) to placate the Spanish, he was subsequently knighted (1674) on the renewal of hostilities. He moved to Jamaica, where he became a wealthy planter and deputy-governor.

Morgan, John Hunt (1825–64) Confederate guerrilla leader, born in Huntsville, AL. He joined the army in 1846 and saw action in the Mexican War. During the 1850s he ran a business, but enlisted in the Confederate army in 1861, attaining the rank of captain. He led the *Morgan raiders* in a series of raids on Union supply lines, and was promoted to colonel and then brigadier-general. He is remembered for his attacks in Indiana and Ohio (1863), the farthest N a Confederate force penetrated during the Civil War. He was killed in action.

Morgan, J(ohn) P(ierpont) (1837–1913) Banker, financier, and art collector, born in Hartford, CT. The son of the financier **John Spencer Morgan** (1813–90), he built his father's firm into the most powerful private banking house in the USA. His house financed the Federal Reserve system in the depression of 1895, developed the railroad system, and formed the US Steel Corporation (1901). He compiled one of the greatest private art collections of his day, which he bequeathed to the Metropolitan Museum of Art in New York City. He was also noted for his extensive philanthropic benefactions. His son, **John Pierpont Jr** (1867–1943), succeeded him, and raised loans for Britain during World War 1.

Morgan, Thomas Hunt (1866–1945) Geneticist and biologist, born in Lexington, KY. He studied zoology at Kentucky State College and Johns Hopkins University, and became professor of experimental zoology at Columbia (1904–28) and the California Institute of Technology (1928–45). He carried out experiments with the *Drosophila* fruit fly, and established a chromosome theory of heredity involving genes for specific tasks aligned on chromosomes, which earned him the 1933 Nobel Prize for Physiology or Medicine.

Morgan, William de >> **de Morgan, William**

Morganwg, Iolo >> **Williams, Edward**

Morison, James (1816–93) Clergyman, born in Bathgate, West Lothian, EC Scotland, UK. Minister of Kilmarnock in 1840, he was suspended by the United Secession Church in 1841 for preaching universal atonement, and in 1843, with three other ministers, founded the Evangelical Union of Congregational churches.

Morison, Stanley (1889–1967) Typographer and scholar, born in Wanstead, Essex, SE England, UK. A clerk in London, he became typographical adviser to Cambridge University Press (1923–44, 1947–59) and to the Monotype Corporation (from 1923). On the staff of *The Times* from 1929, he designed the Times New Roman type, introduced in 1932. He edited *The Times Literary Supplement* (1945–7), and was the author of many works on typography and calligraphy. He also edited the history of *The Times* (1935–52), and in 1961 was appointed to the editorial board of the *Encylopaedia Britannica*.

Morisot, Berthe (Marie Pauline) [morisoh] (1841–95) Painter and printmaker, born in Bourges, France, the grand-daughter of Fragonard. The leading female exponent of Impressionism, she painted chiefly women and children. Her early work shows the influence of Corot, who was her friend and mentor, but her later style owes more to Renoir. She herself exercised an influence on Manet, whose brother Eugène she married. >> Corot; Fragonard; Manet; Renoir; Pierre Auguste

Morita, Akio [mor**ee**ta] (1921–) Manufacturer, born in Nagoya, Japan. With Masaru Ibuka he founded, after World War 2, the electronics firm which since 1958 has been known as Sony. Like many Japanese companies, Sony has been at the forefront of technological developments and has had a strong design policy. Among its most important products have been early tape recorders for the domestic market (c.1950), advanced television equipment, and the 'Walkman' range of radios and cassette players, first produced in 1980.

Morley, Christopher (Darlington) (1890–1957) Novelist and essayist, born in Haverford, PA. He was a Rhodes scholar at Oxford, then joined the editorial staff of Doubleday's (1913–17), and made popular literary contributions to numerous periodicals such as the New York *Evening Post* and the *Saturday Review of Literature*. His varied works included *Parnassus on Wheels* (1917), *Swiss Family Manhattan* (1932), and *The Ironing Board* (1949).

Morley, Edward Williams (1838–1923) Chemist and physicist, born in Newark, NJ. He was taught at home, and studied at Williams College. He became a Congregational minister, like his father, but taught science at the college which became Western Reserve University, OH (1869–1906). His early research was on the oxygen content of air, and he also studied the relative atomic mass of oxygen (measured to within 1 in 10 000). He worked with Albert Abraham Michelson in their famous experiments to detect the 'ether-drift' (1887). >> Michelson

Morley, John Morley, 1st Viscount (1838–1923) Journalist, biographer, and statesman, born in Blackburn, Lancashire, NW England, UK. He studied at Oxford, and was called to the bar, but chose literature as a profession. He edited the *Fortnightly Review* (1867–82) and the *Pall Mall Gazette* (1880–3). A firm supporter of Gladstone, he was an MP (1883–1908) until his elevation to the peerage, and served as Irish secretary (1886, 1892–5). He later became secretary for India (1905–10), then Lord President of the Council from 1910 until the outbreak of World War 1. His writings include biographies of Voltaire (1872), Rousseau (1876), Diderot (1878), and Gladstone (4 vols, 1903). >> Gladstone, W E

Morley, Robert (1908–92) Actor and writer, born in Semley, Wiltshire, S England, UK. He trained in London, and appeared on the London and Broadway stages. In his film career, from 1938, he played many individual character parts, including the title role in *Oscar Wilde* (1960). His appearances continued into the 1980s, with *Loophole* (1980) and *Sky High* (1986). He was well known for his edited collections, such as *Robert Morley's Book of Bricks* (1979), and humorous anecdotal writing, such as *Morley Matters* (1980).

Morley, Thomas (1557/8–1602) Composer, born in Norwich, Norfolk, E England, UK. A pupil of William Byrd, he became organist at St Paul's Cathedral, and from 1592 was a Gentleman of the Chapel Royal. He is best known for *A Plaine and Easie Introduction to Practicall Musicke* (1597), written in entertaining dialogue with the purpose of encouraging part-singing for pleasure; also for his volumes of madrigals and canzonets, which include such evergreen favourites as 'Now is the month of maying', 'My bonny lass she smileth', and 'It was a lover and his lass'. He was compiler of the collection, in honour of Elizabeth I, called *The Triumphes of Oriana* (1603). >> Byrd, William (1543–1623)

Mornay, Philippe de, seigneur du (Lord of) **Plessay-Marly** (1549–1623) French Huguenot leader and polemicist, born in Buhy, France. Converted to Protestantism in 1560, he was nicknamed the 'Pope of the Huguenots' for his role in the Wars of Religion (1562–98). A trusted counsellor of Henry of Navarre, he undertook many embassies for the Protestant cause; however, he lost the king's favour after Henry's conversion to Catholicism (1593) and played no further part in national affairs.

Morny, Charles Auguste Louis Joseph, duc de (Duke of) [maw(r)nee] (1811–65) Nobleman, born in Paris, believed to be the illegitimate son of Queen Hortense and the Comte de Flahaut, and so half-brother to Napoleon III. Adopted by the Comte de Morny, he served in Algeria, but soon left the army, and in 1838 became a manufacturer of beet sugar, making his fortune with that and other speculations. Chosen a deputy in 1842, he quickly became prominent in financial questions. After 1848 he supported Louis Napoleon, took a leading part in the coup, and became minister of the interior. He later became president of the *corps législatif* (1854–65), and was ambassador to Russia (1856–7). >> Beauharnais, Hortense Eugénie Cécile; Napoleon III

Moro, Aldo [moroh] (1916–78) Italian statesman and prime minister (1963–4, 1964–6, 1966–8, 1974–6, 1976), born in Maglie, Italy. He was professor of law at the University of Bari, and published several books on legal subjects. After World War 2 he was elected deputy to the Constituent Assembly and to the Legislature and held various cabinet posts. He took office as secretary of the Christian Democrats (1959) and, although leader of the centrist group within the Party, was sympathetic to the Socialists. He was Italian premier on five occasions, then became Leader of the Christian Democrats (1976), which afforded him powerful influence in Italian politics. Red Brigade left-wing terrorists kidnapped him in Rome in 1978 and subsequently murdered him. >> RR1065

Moro, Antonio >> **More, Sir Anthony**

Moroni, Giovanni Battista [morohnee] (1525–78) Portraitist, born in Albino, Italy. His work was almost always confined to portraiture, making him unique among the artists of the Italian Renaissance. His well-known work in oils, 'The Tailor', is in the National Gallery, London.

Morphy, Paul (Charles) (1837–84) Chess player, born in New Orleans, LA. He had a meteoric chess career (1857–9), during the period when he was called to the bar at 19, but not allowed to practise until he was 21. He won the US championship and beat the strongest masters in Europe, establishing himself as unofficial world champion (the championship not being instituted until 1886). When no other player in the world would take up his challenge, he retired from competitive chess. Attempts to commence his legal career were unsuccessful, and he suffered from bouts of delusion and paranoia until his death.

Morris, Arthur (Robert) (1922–) Cricketer, born in Sydney, New South Wales, Australia. An opening batsman for Australia, he was capped 46 times, and his 3533 Test runs (average 46·48) included 12 centuries. Twice he made two centuries in the same Test match.

Morris, Desmond (John) (1928–) British zoologist and writer. He studied at Birmingham and Oxford, then did research into animal behaviour under Nikolaas Tinbergen. His later career as head of Granada TV's Film Unit at London Zoo (1956–9), and curator of mammals for the Zoological Society (1959–67), developed his interest in the explanation and demonstration of animal behaviour to the public. Already the author of scientific papers, his study of human behaviour in *The Naked Ape* (1967) became a best seller, popularizing sociology and zoology, and was followed by many television programmes on animal and social behaviour. His other books include *The Human Zoo* (1969), *Manwatching* (1977), *The Soccer Tribe* (1981), *Catwatching* and *Dogwatching* (both 1986), *Animal-Watching* (1990), and *Illustrated Babywatching* (1995). >> Tinbergen, Nikolaas

Morris, George Pope (1802–64) Journalist and poet, born in Philadelphia, PA. In 1823 he founded the *New York Mirror* and became its editor (1824–42). He later edited the *Evening Mirror* and the *Home Journal* (1846–64). He published many poems, including the celebrated 'Woodman, Spare that Tree'.

Morris, Gouverneur (1752–1816) US statesman, born in Morrisania, NY. Admitted to the bar in 1771, he lost a leg in an accident in 1780, but went on to become assistant in the Finance Department (1781–85), where he was instrumental in the introduction of a decimal monetary system. In 1787 he took a seat in the convention that framed the US constitution. The greater part of 1791 he spent in England as Washington's agent, and until 1794 was US minister to France. Returning to America in 1798, he became a member of the US Senate (1800–3), before retiring from his public career. >> Washington, George

Morris, Sir Lewis (1833–1907) Poet and barrister, born in Carmarthen, Carmarthenshire, SW Wales. He studied at Oxford, and became a lawyer. His main literary works were *Songs of Two Worlds* (3 vols, 1872–5), followed in 1876 by *The Epic of Hades*. Much of his verse and drama draws on incidents in Welsh history and mythology. In the later stages of his career he campaigned for the fostering of higher education in Wales and the establishment of a national university. He was knighted in 1895.

Morris, Mark (1956–) Dancer and choreographer, born in Seattle, WA. His training included ballet, flamenco, and Balkan folk dance. He danced for several important modern choreographers before making an informal New York City debut with his company in 1980. He has designed dances for his own and other companies, as well as for opera, and in 1988 the Mark Morris Dance Group began a permanent residency at Théâtre de le Monnaie in Brussels. In 1996 his company performed at the Edinburgh International Festival's 50th anniversary celebrations.

Morris, Robert (1734–1806) Financier and statesman, born in Liverpool, Merseyside, NW England, UK. He joined his father in Maryland in 1747, then worked in the shipping industry in Philadelphia. A member of the Continental Congress (1775–8), he was a signatory of the Declaration of Independence. Known as the 'Financier of the American Revolution', he organized the finance for Washington's military supplies, and in 1782 founded the Bank of North America. He died a bankrupt. >> Washington, George

Morris, Robert (1931–) Sculptor and mixed media artist, born in Kansas City, MO. He studied engineering and art, and after moving to San Francisco in 1950 became active as a painter and in improvisatory theatre. He settled in New York City in 1961, specializing in minimalist works, earthwork projects, and scatter pieces.

Morris, Robert L(yle) (1942–) Psychologist, born in Canonsburg, PA. He studied at the University of Pittsburgh and Duke University. In 1985 he was appointed the first Koestler professor of parapsychology at the University of Edinburgh. >> Koestler

Morris, William (1834–96) Craftsman, poet, and political activist, born in Walthamstow, NC Greater London, England, UK. Educated at Marlborough College, he studied for holy orders at Oxford, but renounced the Church, studied architecture, then became a professional painter (1857–62). In 1861, after designing and furnishing his marital home, he founded the firm of Morris, Marshall, Faulkner & Co, which revolutionized the art of house decoration and furniture in England. His literary career began with a volume of poetry. He visited Iceland twice (1871, 1873), and was inspired to write *The Story of Sigurd the Volsung and the Fall of the Nibelungs* (4 vols, 1876), regarded as the greatest of his many works. His belief that the excellence of mediaeval arts and crafts was destroyed by Victorian mass-production and capitalism led him to join the Social Democratic Federation in 1883, and he subsequently organized the Socialist League. In 1890 he founded the Kelmscott Press at Hammersmith, issuing his own works and reprints of classics. >> Brangwyn; Brown, Ford Madox; Burne-Jones; Cobden-Sanderson; Crane, Walter; Hubbard, Elbert; Mackmurdo; Webb, Philip

Morris-Jones, Sir John, originally **John Jones** (1864–1929) Scholar, poet, and teacher, born in Llandrygarn, Anglesey, NW Wales, UK. He studied at Oxford, and became the first professor of Welsh at the University College of North Wales, Bangor. His devotion to the Welsh language and literature, through teaching and writing, helped restore classical standards to Welsh poetry. Works include *A Welsh Grammar, Historical and Comparative* (1913), *Cerdd Dafod* (1925, The Art of Poetry), and *Orgraff yr Iaith Gymraeg* (1928, The Orthography of the Welsh Language). The unfinished *Welsh Syntax* (1931) was published posthumously.

Morrison, Arthur (1863–1945) Novelist and short-story writer, born in London, England, UK. He became clerk to the People's Palace in Mile End Road, London, then a journalist on the *National Observer*, for which he wrote a series of stories published as *Tales of Mean Streets* (1894). His powerfully realistic novels of London slum life include *A Child of the Jago* (1896), which is believed to have accelerated changes in British housing legislation and the elimination of the worst of the slums. He also wrote detective stories featuring the private investigator, Martin Hewett.

Morrison (of Lambeth), Herbert Stanley Morrison, Baron (1888–1965) British statesman, born in London, England, UK. Largely self-educated, he helped to found the London Labour Party, and became its secretary in 1915. As leader of the London County Council from 1934, he grouped together London's passenger transport system, and much of the credit for the 'Green Belt' was due to him. First elected an MP in 1923, in Churchill's War Cabinet he was home secretary and minister of home security. A powerful figure in the postwar social revolution, he was deputy prime minister (1945–51), Lord President of the Council, and Leader of the House of Commons. In 1951 he became deputy Leader of the Opposition, but was defeated by Hugh Gaitskell in the contest for the leadership of the Labour Party in 1955. He was created a life peer in 1959. >> Churchill, Sir Winston; Gaitskell

Morrison, Marion Michael >> Wayne, John

Morrison, Richard James >> Zadkiel

Morrison, Toni, *née* **Chloe Anthony Wofford** (1931–) Novelist, born in Lorain, OH. She studied at Howard and Cornell universities, then taught at Howard before moving to New York City in 1965. She worked in publishing as a senior editor at Random House before becoming a novelist. She explores in rich vocabulary and cold-blooded detail the story of rural African-Americans. Her early titles include *The Bluest Eye* (1970) and *Song of Solomon* (1977). Two later novels, *Tar Baby* (1981) and *Beloved* (1988, Pulitzer), confirmed her as one of the most important novelists of her generation, and she received the Nobel Prize for Literature in 1993. Her novel *Jazz* appeared in the same year.

Morrison, Van, popular name of **George Ivan Morrison** (1945–) Singer, musician, and songwriter, born in Belfast, Northern Ireland, UK. After leaving school, he played guitar and later saxophone in several teenage groups, making his first recordings as a member of Them during the 1960s. His first solo hit was 'Brown-Eyed Girl' (1967) and a year later he released the highly acclaimed, surreal album *Astral Weeks*; other successes of that period including *Moondance* (1970) and *Tupelo Honey* (1971). In the 1980s his work developed a more mystical dimension. He continued to record into the 1990s, with such albums as *Enlightenment* (1990) and *The Healing Game* (1997).

Morse, Samuel F(inley) B(reese) (1791–1872) Artist, and inventor of the telegraph and Morse code, born in Charlestown, MA. He graduated from Yale in 1810, and studied painting in England. Founder and first president of the National Academy of Design in New York City (1826), he taught art at New York University from 1832. Interested in chemistry and electricity, in 1832 he conceived the idea of a magnetic telegraph, which he exhibited to Congress in 1837, and attempted in vain to patent in Europe. He struggled on with scanty means until 1843, when Congress voted him $30 000 for an experimental telegraph line between Washington and Baltimore, built by Ezra Cornell, over which he sent the historic message, 'What hath God wrought?' on 24 May 1844. His system, widely adopted, then brought him honours and rewards. >> Cornell, Ezra

Morshead, Sir Leslie James [**moorz**hed] (1889–1959) Australian military commander, born in Ballarat, Victoria, Australia. He enlisted in the Australian Imperial Forces in 1914, commanded a company at Gallipoli, and later a batallion on the Western Front. In World War 2 he commanded the 18th Brigade in the Middle East, and led the 9th Division at Tobruk during the siege of 1941 and at the Battles of El Alamein. He returned to Australia to lead the New Guinea Force, taking command of the First Australian Corps. He ended the war in 1945 as commander of the Australian and USA task force in Borneo.

Mort, Thomas Sutcliffe (1816–78) Businessman and pioneer of refrigeration, born in Bolton, Lancashire, NW England, UK. He went to Sydney in 1838 as agent for an English firm. In 1854 he constructed a dry dock at Balmain, Sydney, a venture in which half of the company shares were held by his employees. As well as shipbuilding, the first Australian railway locomotive was built there in 1870. He established a scientific farm at Bodalla, New South Wales, building a model community for his workers. His experience there in the wastage of perishable foods led to an interest in refrigeration, and he built a large freezing plant at Darling Harbour, Sydney, in 1875.

Mortara, Edgar [maw(r)**tah**ra] (1852–1940) Italian religious, born into a Jewish family, and the unwitting principal in the celebrated 'Mortara' case. In 1858 he was carried off from his parents by the Archbishop of Bologna, on the grounds that he had been secretly baptized when seriously ill as an infant, by a Catholic maidservant. The refusal of the authorities to give him up to his parents excited great indignation in Britain. Eventually he was discovered in Rome in 1870. He retained his Christian faith, and became an Augustinian monk.

Mortensen, Erik (1926–) Danish fashion designer. In 1948 he joined the Balmain fashion house in Paris, becoming the artistic director in 1960. He took over the management of the fashion house after the death of Pierre Balmain in 1982. He was awarded the Golden Thimble of the French Haute Couture in 1983 and 1987. >> Balmain

Mortenson, Norma Jean >> **Monroe, Marilyn**

Mortier, Edouard Adolphe Casimir Joseph, duc de Trevise (Duke of Treviso) [maw(r)tyay] (1768–1835) French soldier who fought in the Revolutionary and Napoleonic Wars, born in Cateau-Cambrésis, France. Promoted to general (1799) and Marshal of the Empire (1804), he campaigned in Germany, Russia, and Spain. He was prime minister and minister of war (1834–5) under Louis Philippe, at whose side he was killed during an assassination attempt on the king's life in Paris.

Mortimer, John (Clifford) (1923–) Playwright, novelist, and barrister, born in London, England, UK. He studied at Oxford, and was called to the bar in 1948, and became a QC in 1966, participating in several celebrated civil cases. He came to public prominence as a dramatist with his one-act play *The Dock Brief* (1957). An autobiographical play, *A Voyage Round My Father* (1970), was filmed for television in 1982. He has made notable translations, especially of Feydeau, and written several TV screenplays, including *I, Claudius* (1976) and *Brideshead Revisited* (1981). His series of novels featuring the disreputable barrister, Horace Rumpole, were adapted for television as *Rumpole of the Bailey*, and won him the British television writer of the year award in 1980. His other novels include *Paradise Postponed* (1985), *Summer's Lease* (1988), and *Under the Hammer* (1994). He was married to novelist **Penelope Mortimer** (1918–) from 1949 to 1972. A volume of autobiography, *Clinging to the Wreckage*, appeared in 1982.

Mortimer, Roger, Earl of March >> **Edward II / III**

Morton, H(enry) V(ollam) (1892–1979) Travel writer, born in Birmingham, West Midlands, C England, UK. He began his career on the staff of the *Birmingham Gazette* in 1910, becoming assistant editor in 1912. After the success of *The Heart of London* (1925) and *In Search of England* (1927), he devoted himself to travel writing, becoming known for his 'In Search of ...' titles. He travelled extensively, writing about the British Isles as well as the Middle East (1941),

South Africa (1948), where he finally settled, Spain (1954), Rome (1957), and the Holy Land (1961).

Morton, James Douglas, 4th Earl of (c. 1516–81) Regent of Scotland (1572–8) for James VI. Although a Protestant, he was made Lord High Chancellor by Mary Stuart (1563); yet he was involved in the murders of Rizzio (1566) and Darnley (1567), and played an important part in the overthrow of the queen. He joined the hostile noble confederacy, leading its forces at Carberry Hill and Langside, and succeeded Moray as regent. However, his high-handed treatment of the nobles and Presbyterian clergy caused his downfall (1581). He was arraigned for his part in Darnley's murder, and executed at Edinburgh. >> Darnley; James I (of England); Mary, Queen of Scots; Rizzio

Morton, Jelly Roll, popular name of **Ferdinand Joseph La Menthe Morton** (1885–1941) Jazz pianist, composer, and bandleader, born in Gulfport, LA. He worked as a gambler and pimp as well as a piano entertainer. His genius as a jazz pioneer is revealed in the recordings he made (1923–9) while living in Chicago. His unaccompanied piano solos made best sellers of such tunes as 'King Porter Stomp', 'Wolverine Blues', and 'Jelly Roll Blues'. His orchestral arrangements for his band, the Red Hot Peppers, blended lyricism with stomping rhythms, and ensemble subtlety with improvisation. He died, all but forgotten, in Los Angeles, but his recordings were rediscovered with considerable fanfare a few years later. >> Lomax

Morton, John (c. 1420–1500) Statesman and cardinal, probably born in Milborne St Andrew, Dorset, S England, UK. He practised as a lawyer, and strongly supported Henry VI, but after the Battle of Tewkesbury made his peace with Edward IV, and became Master of the Rolls (1473) and Bishop of Ely (1479). Richard III imprisoned him in 1483, but he escaped, and after the accession of Henry VII was made Archbishop of Canterbury (1486), Chancellor (1487), and a cardinal (1493). >> Edward IV; Henry VII; Richard III

Morton, John Cameron (Andrieu Bingham Michael), pseudonym **Beachcomber** (1893–1979) British writer and journalist. After serving in World War 1, he took up writing and published many books of humour, fantasy, and satire, as well as a number of historical works, including several on the French Revolution. From 1924 to 1975 he contributed a regular humorous column, 'By the Way', to the *Daily Express* under his pseudonym.

Morton, John Maddison >> **Labiche, Eugène**

Morton, Levi (Parsons) (1824–1920) Banker and US vice-president (1889–93), born in Shoreham, VT. He began as a country storekeeper's assistant, and in 1863 founded banking-houses in New York City and London. He was returned to Congress as a Republican (1878–80), became minister to France (1881–5), was elected vice-president under Harrison, and served as Governor of New York State (1895–7). >> Harrison, Benjamin; Rose, John

Morton, William (Thomas Green) (1819–68) Dental surgeon, the first to administer ether as an anaesthetic, born in Charlton, MA. He practised in Boston from 1844, tried ether out on a dental patient in 1846, then demonstrated its use with a patient undergoing a surgical operation, while a medical student at Harvard. He engaged in a battle over the exclusive rights for its use, which was to continue for the rest of his life.

Mosaddeq, Mohammed [**mo**sadek], also spelled **Massaddiq** or **Mossadegh** (1880–1967) Iranian statesman and president (1951–3), born in Tehran. He studied at Lausanne University, and became a lawyer. He held various ministerial positions in Iran in the 1920s, retired to private life in 1925, then returned to politics in 1944. A strong advocate of nationalism, he directed his attack on the Anglo-Iranian

Oil Co, which by his Oil Nationalization Act of 1951 he claimed to have expropriated. His government was overthrown by a royalist uprising in 1953, and he was imprisoned. Released in 1956, he remained under house arrest for the rest of his life. >> RR1063

Mosby, John Singleton (1833–1916) US soldier and lawyer, born in Edgemont, VA. As a student at the University of Virginia, he shot a fellow student, then while in jail began to read law under his defence lawyer. He joined the Confederate forces in Virginia, leading hit-and-run raids against scattered outposts of the Federals, who viewed him as an outlaw. (His most famous incident involved his surprising Union General Edwin Stoughton in bed and slapping him on the behind.) He was noted for his gray cape, lined with scarlet, and the large ostrich plume on his hat. He briefly served as US consul in Hong Kong, and practised law in California, then returned to Virginia to a long career as a lawyer.

Moschino, Franco [mo**skee**noh] (1950-95) Fashion designer, born in Abbiategrasso, Italy. He studied painting at the Academy of Fine Arts, Milan, and afterwards worked as a freelance illustrator in the fashion industry. He started his own company Moonshadow in 1983, with designs inspired by the Surrealist movement of the 1920s.

Mosconi, Willie [mos**koh**nee], popular name of **William Joseph Mosconi** (1913–93) Pocket billiards player, born in Philadelphia, PA. After pocketing $75 in a Depression tournament, he took the first of many world titles in 1941. A tireless promoter of the game, he was technical adviser for the movie *The Hustler* (1961), and wrote *Willie Mosconi on Pocket Billiards* (1959).

Moseley, Harry [**mohz**lee], popular name of **Henry Gwyn Jeffreys Moseley** (1887–1915) Physicist, born in Weymouth, Dorset, S England, UK. He studied at Oxford, then worked under Ernest Rutherford at Manchester University (1910–14). He worked on radioactivity, determining by means of X-ray spectra the atomic numbers of the elements (*Moseley's law*), the basis of 20th-c atomic and nuclear physics. He also predicted the unknown element hafnium. He was killed in action in Turkey at the age of 27. >> Rutherford, Ernest

Moser-Pröll, Annemarie [**moh**zer **proel**], *née* **Pröll** (1953–) Alpine skier, born in Kleinarl, Austria. She won a women's record 62 World Cup races (1970–9), and was overall champion (1979), downhill champion (1978, 1979), Olympic downhill champion (1980), world combined champion (1972, 1978), and world downhill champion (1974, 1978, 1980). She temporarily retired in 1975–6, after her marriage, and finally retired after the 1980 Olympics.

Moses [**moh**ziz] (c. 13th-c BC) Major character of Israelite history, portrayed in the Book of Exodus as the leader of the deliverance of Hebrew slaves from Egypt and the recipient of the Ten Commandments at Mt Sinai. In Exodus, stories about his early life depict his escape from death as an infant by being hidden in the bulrushes, his upbringing in the Egyptian court, his flight to Midian, and his divine call to lead the Hebrews out of Egypt. Stories of this deliverance describe Moses predicting a series of miraculous plagues designed to persuade the Pharaoh to release the Hebrews, the Passover narrative, and the miraculous escape led by Moses through the 'sea of reeds'. Traditions then describe Moses' leadership of the Israelites during their 40 years of wilderness wandering, and his death E of the Jordan R before the Hebrews entered Canaan, the Promised Land. He was traditionally considered the author of the five books of the Law, the Pentateuch of the Hebrew Bible, but this is doubted by modern scholars.

Moses, Sir Charles Joseph Alfred (1900–88) Broadcaster and administrator, born in Bolton, Lancashire, NW England, UK. He trained at Sandhurst, emigrated to Australia in 1922, and in 1930 became an announcer with the then Australian Broadcasting Company. He rose to be general manager of the ABC (1935–65), during which time he pioneered broadcasting to schools and rural areas, introduced an independent news service and national television, and established ABC symphony orchestras in each state. He joined the Australian Imperial Forces in 1940, and escaped after the fall of Singapore in 1942 to serve in New Guinea. On retiring from the ABC in 1965, he became secretary-general of the Asian Broadcasting Union until 1976.

Moses, Ed(win Corley) (1955–) Hurdler, born in Dayton, OH. Between August 1977 and June 1987 he ran a record 122 races without defeat. He was the World Cup gold medal winner at the 400 m hurdles in 1977, 1979, and 1981, the world champion in 1983, and Olympic champion in 1976 and 1984, only the US boycott of the 1980 Olympic games preventing a possible hat trick. He won the bronze medal at the 1988 Olympics. Between 1976 and 1983 he broke the world record four times. >> RR1136

Moses, Grandma, popular name of **Anna Mary Robertson Moses** (1860–1961) Artist, born in Greenwich, NY. She began to paint childhood country scenes at about the age of 75, when arthritis made it difficult for her to sew, such as 'Catching the Thanksgiving Turkey' and 'Over the River to Grandma's House'. She had her first show in New York City in 1940, and achieved popular success throughout the USA.

Moses, Robert (1888–1981) US public official, born in New Haven, CT. He studied at Yale, Oxford, and Columbia universities, and became chief-of-staff of the New York State reconstruction committee in 1919, and commissioner of the City Parks in 1934. An eminent and committed spokesman for parks and limited-access roads, he is thought to be responsible for much of the modern appearance of New York City. His impersonal and grandiose projects became unpopular in the 1950s and 1960s.

Moses Ben Maimon >> Maimonides

Moshoeshoe [moshwe**shwe**], also spelled **Mshweshwe** (c.1796–1870) African statesman, the founder of the modern state of Lesotho, born in N Basutoland. The chief of a Sotho clan, he moved to a mountain stronghold during the period of warfare and migrations caused by the rise of Shaka's Zulu kingdom. Through a blend of warfare and diplomacy, he created and defended a kingdom in the face of pressure from the Boer republic of the Orange Free State. Basutoland was annexed to the Cape Colony, but in 1884 became a British protectorate, and in 1964 an independent nation state. >> Shaka

Moshoeshoe II [moshwe**shwe**], originally **Constantine Bereng Seeiso** (1938–96) King of Lesotho (1966–90, 1994–96). He studied at Oxford, was installed as Paramount Chief of the Basotho people (1960), and proclaimed king when Lesotho became independent six years later. His desire for political involvement led to his being twice placed under house arrest, and in 1970 an eight-month exile in The Netherlands ended when Moshoeshoe agreed to take no further part in the country's politics. A military coup in 1986 replaced the government with a military council with the king as nominal executive head. When Moshoeshoe refused to sanction certain changes in 1990, he was forced to abdicate in favour of his son, **Letsie III**, but returned as king in 1994. >> RR1072

Mosley, Nicholas [**mohz**lee], **Baron Ravensdale** (1923–) Writer, born in London, England, UK. He studied at Oxford, joined the army (1942–6), and published his first novel, *Spaces of the Dark* in 1951. Later novels include *The Rainbearers* (1955), *Accident* (1966, filmed by Joseph Losey in 1967), *Hopeful Monsters* (1990, Whitbread Prize), and *Children of Darkness and Light* (1996). Other works include a 2-volume biography of his parents, Sir Oswald and Lady Cynthia

Mosley (1982–3), and a volume of autobiography, *Efforts at Truth* (1995). >> Losey; Mosley, Oswald

Mosley, Sir Oswald (Ernald) [mohzlee] (1896–1980) Politician, born in London, England, UK. He was successively a Conservative, Independent, and Labour MP, and a member of the 1929 Labour government. He resigned from Labour and founded the New Party (1931). Following a visit to Italy, he joined the British Union of Fascists, of which he became leader, and which is remembered for its anti-Semitic violence in the East End of London and its support for Hitler. Detained under the Defence Regulations during World War 2, he founded another racialist party, the Union Movement, in 1948. His second wife (in 1936) was a member of the Mitford family, **Diana Mitford** (1910–). >> Mitford, Jessica/Nancy/Unity

Moss, Stirling (1929–) Motor-racing driver, born in London, England, UK. He won many major races in the 1950s, including the British Grand Prix (twice), the Mille Miglia, and the Targa Florio. He never won a world title, though he was runner-up to Fangio (1955–7) and to Mike Hawthorn (1958). He won 16 races from 66 starts (1951–61). A bad crash at Goodwood in 1962 ended his career. He then became a journalist and broadcaster, returning to saloon car racing in 1980. >> Fangio

Mossadegh, Mohammed >> Mosaddeq, Mohammed

Mössbauer, Rudolph (Ludwig) [mocsbower] (1929–) Physicist, born in Munich, Germany. He discovered the recoil-free adsorption and subsequent re-emission of gamma rays by matter – the *Mössbauer effect*, for which he shared the 1961 Nobel Prize for Physics. He became professor of experimental physics at the Technische Hochschule, Munich, in 1964, and was a visiting professor of physics at the Californian Institute of Technology. >> RR1122

Most, Johann Joseph (1846–1906) Anarchist, born in Augsburg, Germany. He edited Socialist newpapers in Switzerland and Germany (1868–78), was elected twice to the German parliament, wrote many pamphlets and labour songs, and was expelled from Austria and Germany. Turning anarchist, he was expelled from the German Socialist Party (1880). Emigrating to America in 1882, he was greeted as a radical martyr and travelled extensively, advocating a violent overthrow of capitalists and the ruling class. He became the leader of an extreme faction of US anarchists, and composed the declaration adopted by the Pittsburgh Convention (1883) to become the manifesto of Communist anarchism in America. Imprisoned several times for inciting violence (1886–1901), he later repudiated violent intervention, and lost his influence.

Mostel, Zero [mostel], originally **Samuel Joel Mostel** (1915–77) Actor, singer, and artist, born in New York City. He began work as an artist, and to supplement his income entertained in nightclubs. Radio and film work followed, and he established a successful theatre career, particularly in comedy roles, appearing in *Rhinoceros* (1961) and the musicals *A Funny Thing Happened on the Way to the Forum* (1962) and *Fiddler on the Roof* (1964). He played several of his theatrical roles in films.

Mother Ann >> Lee, Ann

Motherwell, Robert (Burns) (1915–91) Artist, born in Aberdeen, WA. He briefly attended the California School of Fine Arts in San Francisco, and studied philosophy at Stanford, Harvard, Grenoble, and Columbia universities. He wrote a good deal on the theory of modern art, and helped found the Abstract Expressionist group in New York City in the 1940s. His interest in Freud and psychoanalysis led him to spontaneous painting, his huge images often resembling semi-automatic doodles of a kind that the Surrealists had explored. He married the artist Helen Frankenthaler in 1955. >> de Kooning; Frankenthaler; Freud, Sigmund; Gottlieb; Mitchell, Joan; Tworkov

Mott, John R(aleigh) (1865–1955) Religious leader and social worker, born in Livingston Manor, NY. A Methodist layman, he became known the world over by his work for the Young Men's Christian Association (1915–31), the Student Volunteer Movement (1888–1920), and the World Missionary Council (1941–2). He shared the 1946 Nobel Prize for Peace. >> RR1125

Mott, Lucretia, *née* **Coffin** (1793–1880) Feminist and reformer, born in Nantucket, MA. Educated at a Friends' boarding school, she became a teacher, earning half the salary of her male colleagues, which prompted her interest in women's rights. She married fellow-teacher **James Mott** in 1811, and together they campaigned against slavery, offering refuge to runaway slaves after the Fugitive Slave Law of 1850. With Elizabeth Stanton she organized the first Woman's Rights Convention in 1848, from which time she remained prominent and active in the feminist movement. >> Stanton, Elizabeth

Mott, Sir Nevill F(rancis) (1905–96) Physicist, born in Leeds, West Yorkshire, N England, UK. He studied at Cambridge, and became a lecturer and fellow there, working with Ernest Rutherford. He later became professor at Bristol, and in 1954 at Cambridge. He shared the 1977 Nobel Prize for Physics for his independent work on the electronic properties of disordered materials. One of the major theoretical physicists of this century, he was influential in showing how to model the complexity of physical problems such as fracture of metals and electronic processes in disordered semiconductors. He was knighted in 1962. >> Rutherford, Ernest; RR1122

Mottelson, Ben R(oy) (1926–) Physicist, born in Chicago, IL. He studied at Purdue and Harvard universities, and moved to the Institute of Theoretical Physics in Copenhagen (now the Neils Bohr Institute) on a travelling fellowship, where he worked with Aage Bohr on the problem of combining the two models of the atomic nuclei. They secured experimental evidence in support of Leo James Rainwater's collective model of the atomic nucleus, and all three shared the 1975 Nobel Prize for Physics. >> Bohr, Aage; Rainwater

Mottram, R(alph) H(ale) (1883–1971) Novelist, born in Norwich, Norfolk, E England, UK. He began his working life as a banker. Galsworthy, with whom he became friends in 1904, encouraged him to write, but he did not achieve recognition until the publication of *Spanish Farm* (1924) and its sequels, *Sixty-Four, Ninety-Four* (1925) and *The Crime at Vanderlynden* (1926). Many of his later novels are set in East Anglia. >> Galsworthy

Moule, Charles (Francis Digby) (1908–) British biblical scholar, born in Hanchow, China. He studied at Cambridge and was ordained into the Anglican Church in 1933. After several curacies and theological appointments he returned to Cambridge as lecturer, before becoming professor of divinity (1951–76). One of the most versatile scholars of his time, his many books include *An Idiom Book of New Testament Greek* (1953), *The Holy Spirit* (1978), and *Essays in New Testament Interpretation* (1982).

Moulins, Master of [moolī] (c. 1460–c. 1529) The name given to an unknown French artist whose principal work was the triptych in Moulins Cathedral of the 'Virgin and Child'. He is regarded as the most accomplished French artist of the time. The influence of Hugo van der Goes can be seen in his vividly coloured and realistic paintings, and some authorities identify him as Jean Perreal or Jean de Paris, court painter to Charles VIII. >> van der Goes

Mountbatten, Edwina (Cynthia Annette) Mountbatten, Countess of, *née* **Ashley** (1901–60) Wife of Louis, Earl Mountbatten of Burma, whom she married in 1922. She rendered distinguished service during the London blitz (1940–2) to the Red Cross and St John Ambulance Brigade, of which she became superintendent-in-chief in 1942. As Vicereine of India (1947), her work in social welfare brought her the friendship of Gandhi and Nehru. She died suddenly on an official tour of Borneo for the St John Ambulance Brigade. >> Gandhi; Mountbatten (of Burma); Nehru, Jawaharlal

Mountbatten, Prince Louis Alexander, 1st Marquess of Milford Haven, originally **Prince Louis of Battenberg** (1854–1921) British naval commander, born in Graz, Austria, the son of Prince Alexander of Hesse. He became a naturalized British subject and entered the Royal Navy in 1868. He served with distinction as a commodore in the Mediterranean fleet, and as director of naval intelligence. He was First Sea Lord at the outbreak of World War 1, but was forced to resign because of anti-German prejudice. By royal command he gave up his German titles in 1917, changed the family name from Battenberg to Mountbatten, and was created Marquess of Milford Haven. He was promoted admiral in 1919. >> Mountbatten (of Burma)

Mountbatten (of Burma), Louis (Francis Albert Victor Nicholas) Mountbatten, 1st Earl (1900–79) British Admiral of the Fleet and statesman, born in Windsor, Berkshire, S England, UK, the younger son of Prince Louis of Battenberg and Princess Victoria of Hesse, the granddaughter of Queen Victoria. He trained at Dartmouth, and joined the Royal Navy in 1916. In World War 2 he became chief of Combined Operations Command (1942), and played a key role in preparations for D-Day. In 1943 he was appointed supreme commander in SE Asia, where he defeated the Japanese offensive into India (1944), and worked closely with Slim to reconquer Burma (1945). He received the Japanese surrender at Singapore, and in 1947 was sworn in as last Viceroy of India prior to independence. Created an earl in 1947, he returned to the Admiralty, and became First Sea Lord (1954) and chief of the defence staff (1959). Retiring in 1965, he remained in the public eye, and was assassinated by Irish terrorists while fishing off Mullaghmore near his summer home, Classiebawn Castle, Co Sligo, Ireland. >> Mountbatten, Edwina/Philip; Slim

Mountbatten, Prince Philip >> **Edinburgh, Duke of**

Mountcastle, Vernon (Benjamin) (1918–) Neurophysiologist, born in Shelbyville, KY. He trained at Johns Hopkins University School of Medicine, where he joined the faculty in 1946. His research has been concerned with neural mechanisms in sensation and perception, and his book (with G M Edelman), *The Mindful Brain* (1978), has been influential. >> Edelman

Mountevans, Edward (Ratcliffe Garth Russell) Evans, Baron (1881–1957) British naval commander. He entered the Royal Navy in 1897, and was second-in-command to Scott's Antarctic expedition (1910–13). In Word War 1 he fought at Jutland, and in command of HMS *Broke* scored an outstanding victory over four German destroyers. In 1929 he was appointed rear-admiral commanding the Royal Australian Navy. He later became commander-in-chief of the Africa station and deputy high commissioner of the British Protectorates, where his actions against Chief Tshkedi Khama of Bechuanaland were criticized. Recalled in 1939, he served in World War 2 as London Regional Commissioner. >> Jellicoe; Scott, R F

Mountford, Charles Pearcy (1890–1976) Ethnologist, writer, and film director, born in Hallett, South Australia. As a mechanic for the post office he was brought into contact with the Aborigines, and became an expert on their way of life. He led an expedition in search of the lost explorer Ludwig Leichhardt (1937), and between 1938 and 1960 led 10 expeditions into C Australia. In 1948 he was leader of expeditions into Arnhem Land and to Melville I,

for the National Geographic Society of the USA. Beginning with *Brown Men and Red Sand* (1948), he wrote a series of books, illustrated with his own photographs, about the Aborigines and their culture. >> Leichhardt

Mountjoy, Charles Blount, Lord >> **Blount, Charles**

Mouskouri, Nana [mus**koo**ree] (1936–) Singer, born in Athens. She had her first record in Greece in 1959, and went on to record 'The White Rose of Athens' (1962), which became a major European hit. In the early 1970s she had a series of hit albums in the UK.

Moussorgsky, Modest (Petrovich) [mus**aw(r)**gskee], also spelled **Mussorgsky** or **Musorgsky** (1839–81) Composer, born in Karevo, Russia. He was educated for the army, but resigned his commission in 1858 and began the serious study of music under Balakirev. His masterpiece is the opera *Boris Godunov*, first performed in St Petersburg in 1874; his piano suite *Pictures from an Exhibition* (1874) has also kept a firm place in the concert repertoire. Other operas and large-scale works remained uncompleted as the composer sank into the chronic alcoholism which hastened his early death. His friend Rimsky-Korsakov undertook the task of musical executor, arranged or completed many of his unfinished works, and rearranged some of the finished ones. >> Balakirev; Rimsky-Korsakov

Mowatt, Marina / Zenouska >> **Alexandra, Princess**

Moynihan (of Leeds), Berkeley George Andrew Moynihan, Baron (1865–1936) Surgeon, born in Malta. He held various posts at the Leeds General Infirmary, specializing in the techniques of abdominal, gastric, and pancreatic operations, and became professor at Leeds in 1909. The driving impulse of his life was the promotion of scientific surgery, and he set out his doctrine in his *Abdominal Operations* (1905). He formed the Moynihan Chirurgical Club, was active in starting the Association of Surgeons of Great Britain and Ireland, and was also a leader of the movement to found the *British Journal of Surgery*.

Moynihan, Daniel P(atrick) (1927–) Academic and politician, born in Tulsa, OK. He studied at the City College of New York and Tufts University, then taught at Syracuse, Harvard, and the Massachusetts Institute of Technology. He served in the administrations of Presidents Johnson and Nixon, acquiring notoriety as the author of *The Negro Family: the Case for National Action* (1965). He was ambassador to India (1973–4), and won a seat in the US Senate as a Democrat in 1976.

Moynihan, Rodrigo (1910–) British painter. He studied at the Slade School of Art, London, and joined the London Group in 1933. He was an official war artist (1943–4), and professor of painting at the Royal College of Art (1948–57). Most of his works are of an Impressionist nature, with soft tones, such as his portrait of Elizabeth II, 'Princess Elizabeth', but he later changed to non-figurative painting.

Mozart, Wolfgang Amadeus see panel on p. 671

Mphahlele, Es'kia [mpah**lay**lay], popular name of **Ezekiel Mphahlele** (1919–) Novelist, autobiographer, and critic, born in Pretoria, South Africa. His ghetto childhood bulks large in his autobiography, *Down Second Avenue* (1959). He spent the years 1957 to 1978 in Nigeria, France, Kenya, Zambia, and the USA. By the time he published a second volume of autobiography, *Afrika My Music* (1984), he had also written four volumes of short stories and three novels. His influential criticism includes *The African Image* (1962), a pioneering analysis of African literature in its political context. He returned to South Africa in 1978.

Mtshali, Oswald Mbuyiseni [m**chah**lee] (1940–) Poet, born in Vryheid, South Africa. He was one of the wave of 'township poets' whose angry verse in the 1970s broke a decade of black creative silence. He published *Sounds of a Cowhide Drum* in 1971. These poems, in forceful language, conveyed the harshness of ghetto life to a stunned white readership. Later works include *Fireflames* (1980).

Muawiyah I [mwawiya] (c. 602–680) First Umayyad caliph (661–80). He opposed the Prophet Mohammed until the conquest of Mecca in 630, then became his secretary. Under the second caliph, Omar, he took part in the conquest of Syria and was made governor in 640. He rebelled against the fourth caliph, Ali, for the murder of his kins-

---

WOLFGANG AMADEUS MOZART (1756–91)

Mozart was born in Salzburg, Austria, the son of composer, musical author, and violinist, Leopold Mozart and his wife, Anna Maria Pertl. His given names were Johann Chrysostom Wolfgang Theophilus, the last of which is Gottlieb in German, and Amadeus in Latin. He used Wolfgang and Amadeus in his signature, so he is generally known by these two names.

He displayed marked musical gifts very early, playing the keyboard confidently when aged four, composing his first pieces for it aged five, and quickly mastering the violin. Leopold was keen to exhibit his son's extraordinary talents, along with those of his gifted pianist-daughter, **Maria-Anna** (called Nannerl) (1751–1829), and he undertook a series of tours across Europe with them when Mozart was just six years old.

In 1767 the family went for five months to Vienna, where Mozart wrote an *opera buffa* (comic opera) for the Emperor, *La finta semplice* (trans, the Pretend Simpleton); and a *Singspiel* (a German-language opera with some spoken dialogue), *Bastien und Bastienne* (1769), commissioned by Dr Franz Anton Mesmer. However, in Vienna the Italian musicians at court, including the composer Antonio Salieri, made it difficult for him to produce his operas. He returned to Salzburg, and was appointed honorary *Konzertmeister* to Archbishop Sigismund von Schrattenbach.

There followed three extended visits by father and son to Italy (1770–2). Musical experience gained on these tours helped mould Mozart's style, especially in dramatic music. He was prolific, writing sacred vocal pieces and instrumental works too. By 1772 he had written about 25 symphonies (some are lost), and his first quartets. Further quartets and symphonies followed during and after a visit to Vienna in 1773, when he came into contact with Haydn's music. Between 1775–6 he composed two operas: *La finta giardiniera* (trans The Lady Who Disguised Herself as a Gardener) and *Il re pastore* (The Shepherd King); five violin concertos; the Haffner Serenade, and masses for the Salzburg Court Chapel. Bach, Haydn, Handel, and the Italian composers were all major influences on him at the time.

Unhappy with the austere and unmusical Archbishop Colloredo of Salzburg, who was appointed at the death of Sigismund, Mozart left his service in 1777 and, travelling with his mother, sought employment elsewhere. They stayed at Mannheim, where he composed some piano concertos and flute quartets, and fell in love with a coloratura soprano, Aloysia Weber. In 1778 his mother died in Paris. He composed the Paris symphony the same year. His father then persuaded him to return to Salzburg. Mozart visited the Webers on his way back to find that Aloysia seemed to have forgotten him entirely.

Back in Salzburg, Mozart reluctantly accepted the post of court organist (1779). At this time he composed the Coronation Mass (1779), the Sinfonia Concertante in E Flat Major for Violin, Viola and Orchestra, and the Serenade in D Major. In 1780 he received an important commission from Munich, the *opera seria* (serious opera) *Idomeneo*. In 1781 Colloredo summoned Mozart to Vienna for the coronation of Emperor Joseph II. Again, he left the archbishop's service, this time after a stormy scene, but remained in Vienna, which became his home for the rest of his short, full life.

Aloysia Weber had married a court actor and Mozart had turned his attentions to her sister **Constanze**, whom he married in 1782 – the year of his *Singspiel, Die Entführung aus dem Serail* (The Abduction from the Harem). Married life was humorous and happy, but financially insecure. Mozart eked out his income by teaching. They had six children, two of whom survived. He became a Freemason in 1784, and in the same year he produced six piano concertos. In 1785 he composed a futher three, and in 1786 three more. These marked the rich flowering of his maturity, along with the six quartets dedicated to Haydn; the Linz and Prague symphonies; and the three Italian comic masterpieces composed to libretti by Lorenzo da Ponte: *Le nozze di Figaro* (1786, The Marriage of Figaro, after Beaumarchais), *Don Giovanni* (first performed in Prague, 1787), and *Così fan tutte* (1790, trans Thus All Women). The string quintets in C major and G minor (1787), the last three symphonies (1788) – including his masterpiece of counterpoint, the Symphony no.41 in C Major, the Jupiter – the quartets for the King of Prussia, and a clarinet quintet mark the peak of his instrumental powers.

The letters to fellow Masons in his last three years make sad reading, reflecting his countless anxieties about finance or health. He hoped for new commissions or a court post on the accession of Emperor Leopold II, but nothing was forthcoming. In 1791 he applied unsuccessfully for the post of *Kapellmeister* of St Stephen's Cathedral. His last complete works were the masonic *Singspiel, Die Zauberflöte* (1791, The Magic Flute); an opera seria, *La clemenze di Tito* (1791, The mercy of Tito), and a clarinet concerto for Leopold's coronation. Commissioned by an unknown stranger to compose the Requiem Mass, Mozart became obsessed with the idea that it was for his own death, and he died before the work was finished after a three-week fever. No convincing evidence about the cause of death has come to light, although there has been much speculation about it. Deeply in debt at the time of his death, Mozart did not live long enough to enjoy the financial rewards from the success of *The Magic Flute*, and was buried unattended in a pauper's grave.

Mozart's facility, grace, and polish; his innate sense of phrasing, and gift of melodic beauty; his ability to create vital characters by music in opera; his mastery of form, and the richness of his harmony all contribute to his excellence in every genre of the music of his day. His works were catalogued by Ludwig Köchel in 1862, and are now referred to by their numbers in his catalogue as 'K numbers'.

>> Beaumarchais; Haydn; Köchel; Leopold II; Lorenzo da Ponte; Mesmer; Salieri

---

man, the caliph Uthman, and fought him at the indecisive Battle of Siffin (657). With the help of Amr ibn al-As he gained control of Egypt, and after the assassination of Ali in 661 took over the caliphate, thus founding the Umayyad dynasty, and moved the capital to Damascus. >> Ali; Amr ibn al-As; Omar; Uthman

Mubarak, (Mohammed) Hosni (Said) [mubarak] (1928–) Egyptian statesman and president (1981–), born in al-Minufiyah, Egypt. A former pilot and flying instructor who rose to become commander of the Egyptian Air Force, he was vice-president under Anwar Sadat from 1975 until the latter's assassination in 1981. The only candidate for the presidency, he pledged to continue Sadat's domestic and international policies, including firm treatment of Muslim extremists, and the peace process with Israel. >> Sadat; RR1046

Mucha, Alphonse (Maria) (1860-1939) Painter and designer, born in Moravia, Czech Republic. He became known for his Art Nouveau style poster designs, especially those made in Paris in the 1890s for Sarah Bernhardt. He also designed sets, costumes, and jewellery. >> Bernhardt

Mueller, Erwin (Wilhelm) [müler] (1911-77) Physicist, born in Berlin. He studied engineering in Berlin, then worked for industrial laboratories and at the Fritz Haber Institute until 1952, when he joined the Pennsylvania State University. He became a US citizen in 1962. In 1936 he invented the field-emission microscope, and in 1951 the field-ion microscope, which gave the first photographs affording a direct view of atoms and some heat-stable molecules.

Mueller, Sir Ferdinand (Jakob Heinrich) von, Baron [müler] (1825-96) Explorer and botanist, born in Rostock, Germany. After emigrating to Australia in 1847, he was appointed government botanist for the state of Victoria in 1853, and travelled extensively, building up a valuable collection of native flora. He explored Western Australia and Tasmania, promoted expeditions into New Guinea, and was a member of the first Australian Antarctic Exploration committee. He sponsored a fund for an expedition in search of the lost explorer Leichhardt, and he organized the 1875 trip into the central desert by Giles. He published a large number of scientific works on the plants of Australia. >> Giles, Ernest; Leichhardt

Mueller, George E [muhler] (1918–) US engineer. He trained as an electrical engineer, was involved in the production and launch of the first US space probe, Pioneer One (1957), and supervised the development of the first US intercontinental ballistic missiles. He was in charge of the NASA manned space flight and Moon programme (1963-9), and responsible for the successful landings on the Moon.

Mugabe, Robert (Gabriel) [mugahbay] (1924–) First prime minister (1980–) and president (1987–) of Zimbabwe, born in Kutama, Zimbabwe (formerly, Southern Rhodesia). Largely self-educated, he became a teacher in 1942. After short periods in the National Democratic Party and Zimbabwe African People's Union (ZAPU), he was briefly detained, but escaped to co-found, with Ndabaningi Sithole, the Zimbabwe African National Union (ZANU). After a 10-year detention in Rhodesia (1964-74) he spent five years in Mozambique gathering support in preparation for Zimbabwe's independence in 1980. His ZANU and the ZAPU forces of Joshua Nkomo united in 1976 to form the Patriotic Front, and later, a coalition government. Though Mugabe formerly espoused a pragmatic Marxism and declared his intention of turning Zimbabwe into a one-party state, multi-party elections were held in 1990 (which he won), and his party dropped all references to 'Marxism-Leninism' from its constitution in 1991. >> Muzorewa; Nkomo; Sithole; RR1101

Muggeridge, Malcolm (1903-90) Journalist and sage, born in London, England, UK. A lecturer at the Egyptian University in Cairo (1927-30), he joined the Manchester Guardian (1930-3), was assistant editor of the Calcutta Statesman (1934-5), and joined the editorial staff of the Evening Standard. Serving with the Intelligence Corps during World War 2, he received the Legion of Honour and the Croix de Guerre. Resuming his journalistic career, he worked with the Daily Telegraph (1946-52), and was editor of Punch (1953-7). He contributed regularly to the television programme Panorama (1953-60), and had his own series Appointment With ... (1960-1) and Let Me Speak (1964-5). Later television appearances include the autobiographical Muggeridge Ancient and Modern (1981), and he wrote Chronicle of Wasted Time (1982), and other books. A controversial rector of Edinburgh University (1967-8), he resigned over student liberalism. He characterized his life as a spiritual journey towards a greater understanding of faith, and in 1982 became a Roman Catholic.

Muggleton, Lodowick (1609-98) Sectarian, born in London, England, UK. With his cousin, **John Reeve** (1608-58), he presented himself as the messenger of a new divine dispensation in 1652, founded the sect of Muggletonians, and published a Spiritual Transcendental Treatise (1652). They held that the Devil became incarnate in Eve, and denied the Holy Trinity. Muggleton was imprisoned for blasphemy in 1677.

Muhammad >> Mohammed

Muhammad, Elijah, originally **Elijah Poole** (1897-1975) Religious movement leader, born near Sandersville, GA. The son of former slaves and sharecroppers, he left home at 16 and went to Detroit. Having had his own spiritual revelation about 1930, he fell in with the Nation of Islam, a movement founded by W D Fard. When Fard disappeared from Detroit in 1934, Poole took over, changed his name, proclaimed himself the 'Messenger of Allah', and made a national movement out of the Black Muslims, arguing for separation of the races, and scorning attempts of the civil rights movement to bring about integration. He also stressed the need for African-Americans to establish their own economic power-base, and he required strict obedience to certain tenets of Islam. When he died, his son **Wallace** took over, leading the movement closer to traditional Islam and changing its name to the World Community of Islam in the West. >> Farrakhan; Malcolm X

Muhlenberg, Frederick Augustus (Conrad) [myoolenberg] (1750-1801) US representative and clergyman, born in Trappe, PA. Sent to school in Germany as a teenager, he returned to Philadelphia in 1770 to become a Lutheran minister, and spent three years at Christ Church in New York. His career as a clergyman ended in 1779, when he was appointed to the Continental Congress. After a three-year term, he continued in local political offices, and presided over his state's convention, ratifying the new US constitution (1787). A Federalist (1789-97), he served as speaker during the first three Congresses. Shortly before he died he gave his support to the Republican Party, which appointed him receiver-general of the Pennsylvania Land Office.

Muir, Edwin [myoor] (1887-1959) Poet and critic, born in Deerness, Orkney Is, NE Scotland, UK. Educated in Kirkwall, he moved to Glasgow at 14, and in 1919 married the novelist **Willa Anderson** (1890-1970), with whom he settled in London. They travelled in mainland Europe (1921-4), where they collaborated in notable translations of Kafka and other authors. He also worked in Rome, Scotland, and Harvard (1955-6, as professor of poetry). His poems appeared in eight slim volumes, dating from 1925, notably in The Voyage (1946) and The Labyrinth (1949). His other writing includes a controversial study of John Knox, studies on D H Lawrence, and an autobiography (1954).

Muir, Frank [myoor] (1920–98) Writer and broadcaster, born in London, England, UK. He served in the RAF (1940–6), and joined Denis Norden to become one of the best-known teams of comedy script-writers (1947–64), contributing to many shows on radio and television. After a short period in television management he returned to facing the camera in *Call My Bluff* (1970), and began the radio series *Frank Muir Goes into...* (1971). With Norden he has published a number of books on the theme *My Word*, such as *The Complete and Utter 'My Word!' Collection* (1983), and by himself a series of children's books based on the dog 'What-a-Mess'. >> Norden, Denis

Muir, Jean (Elizabeth) [myoor] (1933–95) Fashion designer, born in London, England, UK. Educated at Dame Harper School, Bedford, she started as a salesgirl with Liberty's in London in 1950, then moved to Jaeger in 1956. In 1961 she worked on her own as Jane & Jane, establishing in 1966 her own company, Jean Muir. Her clothes are noted for classic shapes, softness, and fluidity.

Muir, John [myoor] (1838–1914) Explorer, naturalist and conservationist, considered the father of the modern environment movement, born in Dunbar, East Lothian, E Scotland, UK. He studied at Wisconsin University, and was an ingenious inventor, but concentrated on natural history after an industrial accident in 1867 in which he nearly lost an eye. With his friend **Robert U Johnson** (1853–1937) he campaigned for a national park in California. In 1890 Congress approved a bill creating the Yosemite National Park. However, active opposition to the Park's ideals did not cease, and it needed a decade of Muir's vigorous oratory and article-writing, and President Roosevelt's support, before the idea of wildlife conservation became widely accepted. His writings include *The Mountains of California* (1894) and *Steep Trails* (1918), and he was founder-president of the Sierra Club conservation organization (1892). In Alaska he discovered the glacier later named for him. The Muir Woods National Monument in California was established in 1908, and the John Muir Trust to acquire wild land in Britain in 1984. >> Brower, David; Olmsted; Roosevelt, Franklin D

Muirhead, (Litellus) Russell (1896–1976) British editor and traveller. He studied at Cambridge, and in 1930 became editor of the 'Blue Guides' to Europe. His other editorial work included scientific journals and the Penguin guides to England and Wales (1938–49). He was also the author of numerous travel books and articles.

Mujibar Rahman >> **Rahman, Mujibur**

Mulcaster, Richard [muhlkaster] (c. 1530–1611) Educationist, probably born in Cumbria, NW England, UK. He studied at Cambridge and Oxford, was a brilliant Greek and Oriental scholar, and became first headmaster of Merchant Taylors School. He advocated university training for teachers, and other reforms well in advance of his time. In 1582 he published his famous *The First Part of the Elementairie*, which included a list of 7000 words in his proposed reformed spellings.

Muldoon, Paul (1951–) Poet, born in Moy, Co Armagh, Northern Ireland. He studied at Queen's University, Belfast, where Seamus Heaney was among his teachers. His works include *New Weather* (1973), *Selected Poems* (1986), and *Madoc: A Mystery* (1990). He has also edited a controversial anthology, *Contemporary Irish Poetry* (1986). >> Heaney

Muldoon, Sir Robert (David) [muhldoon] (1921–92) New Zealand statesman and prime minister (1975–84), born in Auckland, New Zealand. He served as an infantryman in World War 2 before becoming an accountant and president of the New Zealand Institute of Cost Accountants. He was first elected to parliament (as a National Party MP) in 1960, and after five years as minister of finance became

deputy prime minister. From 1974 he was Party leader and Leader of the Opposition, and led the National Party to victory in the 1975 elections. After serving as prime minister, he gave up leadership of the National Party, but remained an MP until 1991, and served as shadow foreign affairs spokesman. He was knighted in 1984. >> RR1078

Müller, Hermann (Joseph) [müler] (1890–1967) Geneticist, born in New York City. He studied at Columbia University, and held appointments at the universities of Texas (1920–32), Moscow (1933–7), Edinburgh (1938–40), and Indiana (from 1945). He was awarded the 1946 Nobel prize for Physiology or Medicine for his discovery of the use of X-rays to induce genetic mutations. He was much concerned about the possible harmful effects of radiation on human genes, and advocated the use of sperm banks to preserve and maintain the human gene pool.

Müller, Johannes >> **Regiomontanus**

Müller, Karl (Alexander) [müler] (1927–) Physicist, born in Basel, Switzerland. He studied at the Swiss Federal Institute of Technology, worked at the Batelle Institute in Geneva, then (1963) joined the IBM Zürich Research Laboratory at Rüschlikon. A specialist in oxides, he was joined by Georg Bednorz in 1982 to study superconductivity in these materials. In 1986 they demonstrated that some mixed-phase oxides would superconduct above 30 K, and by 1987 related materials were found to show the effect up to 90 K, at a temperature which offered novel possibilities in practical electronics. They shared the Nobel Prize for Physics in 1987. >> Bednorz, Georg

Müller, (Friedrich) Max [müler] (1823–1900) Philologist and orientalist, born in Dessau, Germany. He studied at Dessau, Leipzig, and Berlin, and took up Sanskrit and its kindred sciences of philology and religion. In Paris, he began to prepare an edition of the *Rigveda*, the sacred hymns of the Hindus. He visited England in 1846 to examine the manuscripts, and in 1847 the East India Company commissioned him to edit and publish it at their expense (1849–74). He was appointed professor of modern languages at Oxford (1854) and professor of comparative philology (1868 onwards), a study he did more than anyone else to promote in Britain. Among his most notable works was the *Sacred Books of the East* (51 vols, 1879–1910).

Müller, Paul Hermann [müler] (1899–1965) Chemist, born in Olten, Switzerland. As research chemist for the J R Geigy company, in 1939 he synthesized DDT (dichlorodiphenyl-trichloroethane) and demonstrated its insecticidal properties. He received the Nobel Prize for Physiology or Medicine in 1948, but use of DDT has now been discontinued (and banned) in many countries.

Mulligan, Gerry, popular name of **Gerald Joseph Mulligan** (1927–96) Jazz musician, born in New York City. He was one of many white jazz musicians to emerge in the USA after World War 2. He moved to California in 1952, and formed his own quartet. A technically accomplished musician, he experimented to produce a distinctive sound which proved popular and commercially successful. His motion pictures include *Jazz on a Summer's Day, I Want to Live* (both 1958), and *The Subterraneans* (1960).

Mulliken, Robert (Sanderson) (1896–1986) Chemist and physicist, born in Newburyport, MA. He studied at the Massachusetts Institute of Technology and the University of Chicago, then taught briefly at New York (1926–8), before settling as a professor at Chicago. He was awarded the Nobel Prize for Chemistry in 1966 for his work on chemical bonds and the electronic structure of molecules.

Mulready, William [muhlreedee] (1786–1863) Painter, born in Ennis, Co Clare, Ireland. He studied at the Royal Academy, London, and specialized in genre paintings, becoming best known for his rural scenes such as 'Interior of an English Cottage' (1828). He also worked at portraiture and book illustration, and designed the first penny-postage envelope.

Mulroney, (Martin) Brian (1939–) Canadian politician and prime minister (1984–93), born in Baie Comeau, Quebec, Canada. He attended St Francis Xavier University in Nova Scotia, and studied law at Laval University, taking up a career first in law, then in business. He became leader of the Progressive Conservative Party in 1983, and won a landslide election victory in 1984. He negotiated a free trade agreement with the USA in 1988. His period in office was marked by controversial proposals regarding the position of French-speaking Quebec. He resigned in 1993 when the party's popularity was at an all-time low. >> RR1039

Mumford, Lewis (1895–1990) Sociologist and writer, born in Flushing, NY. He studied at the City College of New York, became a literary critic and journal editor, and began to write on architecture and urbanization in such works as *The Story of Utopias* (1922) and *The City in History* (1961), stressing the unhappy effects of technology on society. A prolific author, his academic posts included the chair of city and regional planning at the University of Pennsylvania (1951–9).

Munch, Edvard [mungk] (1863–1944) Painter, born in Löten, Norway. He studied in Oslo, travelled in Europe, and finally settled in Norway in 1908. In Paris he came under the influence of Gauguin. He was obsessed by subjects such as death and love, which he illustrated in an Expressionist Symbolic style, using bright colours and a tortuously curved design, as in 'The Scream' (1893). His engravings influenced *die Brücke* in Germany. >> Gauguin

Münchhausen, (Karl Friedrich Hieronymus), Freiherr von (Baron) [munch howzen] (1720–97) Soldier, born in Bodenwerder, Germany. Proverbial as the narrator of ridiculously exaggerated exploits, he served in Russian campaigns against the Turks. A collection of stories attributed to him was first published in English as *Baron Munchhausen's Narrative of his Marvellous Travels and Campaigns in Russia* (1785) by **Rudolf Erich Raspe** (1737–94). In medicine, *Münchhausen's syndrome* describes individuals who present themselves at different hospitals with different but spurious physical complaints.

Mungo, St >> **Kentigern, St**

Munk, Kaj (Harald Leininger) (1898–1944) Playwright, priest, and patriot, born in Maribo, Denmark. He studied theology at Copenhagen University, and as priest of a small parish in Jutland wrote heroic and religious plays that led the Danish dramatic revival in the 1930s. His first play was *En Idealist* (1928), followed by *Cant* (1931), *Henrik VIII* (1931), *Ordet* (1932, The Word), and *Han sidder ved smeltedigien* (1938, He Sits by the Melting-Pot). During World War 2 he became one of the spiritual leaders of the Danish Resistance. In 1943 he wrote a patriotic drama, *Niels Ebbeson*. His sermons attracted many to the Resistance, and he was killed by the Nazis in 1944.

Munnings, Sir Alfred (1878–1959) Painter, born in Suffolk, E England, UK. A specialist in the painting of horses and sporting pictures, he became president of the Royal Academy (1944–9). His work is in many public galleries. He was well known for his forthright criticism of modern art.

Munro, Alice [muhn roh] (1931–) Short-story writer and novelist, born in Wingham, Ontario, Canada. She studied at the University of Western Ontario, and wrote short stories from an early age. Her novel, *Lives of Girls and Women*, appeared in 1971. Her short stories, published for many years without being collected, are recognized as among the finest of the day. Invariably set in rural and semi-rural Ontario, the landscape of her childhood, the collections include *Dance of the Happy Shades* (1968), *The Progress of Love* (1987), and *Friend of My Youth* (1990).

Munro, H(ector) H(ugh) [muhn roh], pseudonym **Saki** (1870–1916) Novelist and short-story writer, born in Akyab, Myanmar (formerly, Burma). Educated in England at Bedford Grammar School, he returned to Burma and joined the police force in 1893. He went to London in 1896, took up writing for the *Westminster Gazette*, and from 1902 was the Balkans correspondent for the *Morning Post*. He is best known for his short stories, humorous, satiric, supernatural, and macabre, which are highly individual, full of eccentric wit and unconventional situations. Collections include *Reginald* (1904) and *Beasts and Superbeasts* (1914). His novels *The Unbearable Bassington* (1912) and *When William Came* (1913) show his gifts as a social satirist of his contemporary upper-class Edwardian world. He was killed on the Western Front during World War 1, having volunteered for active service despite being over 40.

Munthe, Axel (Martin Fredrik) [mun tuh] (1857–1949) Physician and writer, born in Oskarshamn, Sweden. He studied at Uppsala, Montpellier, and Paris, practised as a physician and psychiatrist in Paris and Rome, and became Swedish court physician. He then retired to Capri, where he wrote his best-selling autobiography, *The Story of San Michele* (1929).

Müntzer, Thomas [münt ser], also spelled **Münzer** or **Monczer** (c. 1489–1525) Religious reformer and Anabaptist, born in Stolberg, Germany. He studied theology, and in 1520 began to preach at Zwickau. His socialism and mystical doctrines soon brought him into collision with the authorities. After preaching widely, in 1525 he was elected pastor of the Anabaptists at Mülhausen, where his communistic ideas soon aroused the whole country. He joined the Peasants' Revolt (1524–5), but was defeated at Frankenhausen, and executed a few days later.

Muqaddasi [mukadasee] (945–88) Arab geographer, and pioneer of fieldwork, born in Jerusalem. He travelled widely, and described Muslim lands in a geographical compendium published in 985.

Murasaki, Shikibu [murasah kee] (978–c. 1031) Lady of the court, and writer, born in Kyoto, Japan. She wrote the world's earliest surviving long novel, also considered the greatest Japanese literary work, *Genji Monogatari* or *The Tale of Genji* (first translated into English by Arthur Waley, 6 vols, 1925–33).

Murat, Joachim [mürah] (1767–1815) French marshal and king of Naples (1808–15), born in La Bastide-Fortunière, France. He enlisted in the cavalry on the eve of the French Revolution (1787), and was promoted to general of division in the Egyptian campaign (1799). He married Napoleon's sister, Caroline, after helping him become First Consul. He failed to gain the Spanish crown (1808), and was proclaimed King of the Two Sicilies. After taking part in the Russian campaign, he won Dresden and fought at Leipzig, but concluded a treaty with the Austrians, hoping to save his kingdom. On Napoleon's return from Elba, he recommenced war against Austria, but was twice defeated, and failed to recover Naples. He was captured and executed at Pizzo, Calabria. >> Bonaparte, Caroline; Napoleon I

Murchison, Sir Roderick Impey (1792–1871) Geologist, born in Tarradale, Highland, N Scotland, UK. After leaving the army in 1816, he devoted himself to geology. He established the Silurian system (1835) and, with Adam Sedgwick, the Devonian system. From 1840 to 1845 he carried out a geological survey of the Russian empire. Struck with the resemblance between the Ural mountains and Australian chains, he predicted the discovery of gold in Australia (1844). *Murchison Falls* (Uganda) and *Murchison R* (Western Australia) are named after him. In 1855 he was made director-general of the Geological Survey, and director of the Royal School of Mines. >> Sedgwick

Murdoch, Dame (Jean) Iris (1919–) Novelist and philosopher, born in Dublin. She studied at Oxford, then worked at the Treasury (1938–42) and for a UN relief organization (1944–6). She was fellow and tutor in philosophy at Oxford (1948–63), and took up novel-writing as a hobby. A prolific writer, she has produced a series of succeful books exploring complex human relationships with subtlety and humour, such as *Under the Net* (1954), *The Bell* (1958), *The Black Prince* (1973), *The Sea, The Sea* (1978, Booker), *The Philospher's Pupil* (1983), *The Message to the Planet* (1989), and *Jackson's Dilemma* (1995). She has also written plays and several philosophical and critical studies, including *Sartre* (1953). Many themes are recapitulated in *Metaphysics as a Guide to Morals* (1992). She was made a dame in 1987.

Murdoch, Lachlan (Keith) (1971–) Media executive, born in London, the son of Rupert Murdoch. He graduated in philosophy from Princeton University, and became general manager of Queensland Newspapers, part of News Limited, the Australian company which itself is the original arm of the News Corporation empire. In 1995 he became publisher of *The Australian* newspaper, and his meteoric rise continued, so that by 1997 he was the executive chairman of News Limited. One of a trio of possible heirs to Rupert, Lachlan is the only sibling with a seat on News Corporation's board. >> Murdoch, Rupert

Murdoch, (Keith) Rupert (1931–) Media proprietor, born in Melbourne, Victoria, Australia. He studied at Oxford, then worked for two years on the *Daily Express*, returning to Australia in 1952, where he inherited *The News* in Adelaide on the death of his father. He built a substantial newspaper and magazine publishing empire in Australia, the USA, Hong Kong, and the UK, including the *News of the World* and the *Sun* which, boosted by his 'page three' feature, maintained its lead in the circulation war. In 1981 his company, News International, acquired *The Times* and *The Sunday Times* after a bitter struggle. He moved into the American market in 1976 with the purchase of the New York *Post*, then acquired The New York Magazine Company, whose titles include *The New York Magazine*, *New West*, and *Village Voice*. He also has major business interests in other media industries, especially television, films and publishing, on three continents. He became a US citizen in 1985. >> Murdoch, Lachlan

Murdock, George P(eter) (1897–1985) Cultural anthropologist, born in Meriden, CT. He studied at Yale, and taught there (1928–60) and at Pittsburgh (1960–71). He initiated the cross-cultural survey, later known as the 'human relations area files', as an instrument of sociological and anthropological generalization. His best-known work is *Social Structure* (1949), in which he focused on family and kinship organization, seeking sets of functionally interrelated traits in a wide range of societies.

Murdock, William (1754–1839) Engineer, and pioneer of coal gas for lighting, born in Old Cumnock, East Ayrshire, SW Scotland, UK. He worked with Boulton and James Watt of Birmingham, and was sent to Cornwall to erect mining engines. At his home in Redruth he constructed the model of a high-pressure engine to run on wheels (1784), introduced labour-saving machinery, a new method of wheel rotation, an oscillating engine (1785), and a steam-gun. He also improved Watt's engine. His distillation of coal gas began at Redruth in 1792, when he lit his own home with it, but it was not until 1803 that Boulton's engineering works at Soho had gas lighting. >> Boulton; Watt, James

Murfree, Mary Noailles >> **Craddock, Charles Egbert**

Murger, (Louis) Henri [mürzhay] (1822–61) Writer, born in Paris. He began life as a notary's clerk, devoted his time to literature, and led the life of privation and adventure described in his first novel, *Scènes de la vie de Bohème* (1845),

the basis of Puccini's opera *La Bohème*. During his later years he led a dissipated life, writing slowly and fitfully. His other works include *Le Pays Latin* (1861, The Latin Country) and a great deal of poetry. >> Puccini

Murillo, Bartolomé Esteban [mooreelyoh] (1618–82) Painter, born in Seville, Spain. In 1645 he painted 11 remarkable pictures for the convent of San Francisco, which made his name. He founded the Academy of Seville (1660), of which he became first president. He frequently chose the Immaculate Conception or the Assumption of the Virgin as a subject, and treated them much alike. His pictures fall into two groups – scenes from low life, such as gipsies and beggar children (mostly early works), and religious paintings. In 1681 he fell from a scaffold when painting an altarpiece at Cadiz, and died soon after.

Murnau, F W [moornow], pseudonym of **Friedrich Wilhelm Plumpe** (1888–1931) Film director, born in Bielefeld, Germany. He studied at Berlin and Heidelberg, and was influenced by Max Reinhardt. After World War 1, he made his directorial debut with *Der Knabe in Blau* (1919, The Boy in Blue). Experimenting with the mobility of the camera, his expressive use of light and shade heightened the menace in such macabre works as *Der Januskopf* (1920, Janus-Faced) and *Nosferatu* (1922). After a successful trio of films with actor Emil Jannings, including *Der letzte Mann* (1924, trans The Last Laugh), he moved to America and made *Sunrise* (1927), which won three of the first-ever Oscars. He had just completed the much-praised South Seas documentary *Tabu* (1931) before his death in a car crash. >> Jannings; Reinhardt, Max

Murphy, Eddie, popular name of **Edward Reagan Murphy** (1961–) Comic performer, born in New York City. A popular prankster and mimic at school, he hosted a talent show at the Roosevelt Youth Center in 1976 and subsequently decided to pursue a career in show-business. He first came to national prominence on the television show *Saturday Night Live* (1980–4). A charismatic, self-confident humorist, his debut in the film *48 Hrs* (1982) was followed by an unbroken string of box-office hits including *Trading Places* (1983), *Beverly Hills Cop* (1984, and its sequel, 1987), *Coming to America* (1988). Later films include *Big Baby* (1991), *The Nutty Professor* (1996), and *Metro* (1997). His best-selling albums include *Eddie Murphy Comedian* (1982) and *How Could it Be?* (1984). He made his directorial debut with *Harlem Nights* (1989).

Murphy, Graeme (1951–) Ballet dancer, choreographer, and ballet director, born in Melbourne, Victoria, Australia. He trained at the Australian Ballet School in New York City, and at Sadler's Wells, then worked as a freelance choreographer before rejoining Australian Ballet as dancer and resident choreographer. Appointed director of the Sydney Dance Company in 1976, he gained international stardom by creating dances which feature a sexy, eclectic range of subjects and styles, all rooted in the classical idiom, one of the best known being *Poppy* (1978), based on the life of Jean Cocteau. In 1988 he created *Vast*, an Australian bicentennial performance featuring many Australian dance companies. He later directed *Turandot* (1990) and *Salome* (1993) for the Australian Opera.

Murphy, Lionel (Keith) (1922–86) Lawyer and politician, born in Sydney, New South Wales, Australia. He studied chemistry at the University of Sydney, but turned to law. Unusually, he was admitted to the New South Wales bar in 1947 before graduating as a lawyer from the University of Sydney in 1949. He was elected as Labor senator for New South Wales in the 1962 Federal Parliament, became Opposition leader in 1967, and was appointed attorney-general in 1972. He oversaw several items of landmark legislation, including the Family Law Act, the Law Reform

Commission, the Trade Practices Act, and the Human Rights Commission. In 1975 he was appointed to the High Court of Australia, where he made many progressive decisions. Accused in 1984 of having attempted to pervert the course of justice, he was exonerated in 1986, but died soon after. A controversial figure who challenged political and legal boundaries, the impact of his reforms on Australian society is widely acknowledged.

Murphy, Thomas Bernard (1935–) Playwright, born in Tuam, Co Galway, Ireland. His first play, *A Whistle in the Dark*, was produced in England in 1961, and from then until 1970 he lived and wrote in London. His major works date from his return to Ireland, and include *The Sanctuary Lamp* (1975), *The Blue Macushla* (1980), *The Gigli Concert* (1983), and *Bailegangaire* (1985).

Murphy, William P(arry) (1892–1987) Haematologist, born in Stoughton, WI. He was a staff member of several New England hospitals before starting private practice in Brookline, MA (1923–87), concurrently working at Peter Bent Brigham Hospital, Boston (1923–73), and Harvard Medical School (1923–58). Inspired by the work of Whipple, and in conjunction with Minot, he shared the 1934 Nobel Prize for Physiology or Medicine for devising dietary liver and liver extract therapy for patients with pernicious anaemia. >> Minot, George; Whipple, George H

Murrant, Harry >> **Morant, Harry**

Murray, (George) Gilbert (Aimé) (1866–1957) Classical scholar and writer, born in Sydney, New South Wales, Australia. He studied at Oxford, and was appointed professor of Greek at Glasgow (1889) and at Oxford (1908). His work as a Classical historian and translator of Greek playwrights brought him acclaim as 'the foremost Greek scholar of our time'. His celebrated verse translations of Greek plays, including *The Trojan Women*, *Medea*, and *Electra*, were performed at London's Court Theatre from 1902. His many works on Classics include *History of Ancient Greek Literature* (1897) and *Five Stages of Greek Religion* (1913). As a lifelong Liberal, he stood for parliament, unsuccessfully, six times. President of the League of Nations Union (1923–38), he was the first president of the UN Association General Council.

Murray, Sir James (Augustus Henry) (1837–1915) Philologist and lexicographer, born in Denholm, Scottish Borders, SE Scotland, UK. A grammar school teacher (1855–85), his *Dialects of the Southern Counties of Scotland* (1873) established his reputation. The great work of his life, the editing of the *New English Dictionary* (later called the *Oxford English Dictionary*), was begun at Mill Hill in 1879, and completed in 1928 at Oxford. He edited about half the work, but he created the organization and the inspiration for its completion. He was knighted in 1908.

Murray, Joseph E(dward) (1919–) Surgeon, born in Milford, MA. Trained as a plastic surgeon, he joined Peter Bent Brigham Hospital, Boston (now Brigham and Women's Hospital) (1951–86), became interested in treatments for kidney failure, and performed the first human kidney transplant between identical twins in 1954. After investigating the effects of immunosuppressant drugs, he performed the first human kidney transplant from an unrelated donor in 1962. He became professor of surgery at Harvard (1970–), returning to plastic surgery at the Children's Hospital Medical Center, Boston (1972–85). He shared the Nobel Prize for Physiology or Medicine in 1990. >> RR1124

Murray, Keith (Bay Pearce) (1892–1991) Architect and designer, born in Auckland, New Zealand. He began designing glass in England in the 1930s, moving to silver and then to ceramics, principally for Josiah Wedgwood & Sons. His hallmarks were simple, functional, clean shapes relying a great deal on turned grooves and stepped sur-

faces. These were executed in black basalt or earthenware with matt glaze effects in cream, green, or straw colours. He exhibited widely, including a one-man show at the Medici Gallery in 1935, and the Triennial in Milan in 1933.

Murray, Len, popular name of **Baron Lionel Murray of Telford** (1922–) Trade union leader, born in Hadley, Shropshire, WC England, UK. He studied at London and Oxford, and joined the staff of the Trades Union Congress (TUC) in 1947. He progressed from the economic department to become assistant general secretary (1969–73), then general secretary (1973–84). He played a major role in the 'social contract' partnership between the TUC and the Labour governments of Harold Wilson and James Callaghan (1974–8) but, from 1979, had an unhappy relationship with the Conservative administration of Margaret Thatcher. He was made a life peer in 1985. >> Callaghan, James; Thatcher; Wilson, Harold

Murray, Les(lie Allen) (1938–) Poet, born in Nabiac, New South Wales, Australia. His childhood and adolescence were spent on a dairy farm, and he studied at Sydney University. He has worked mostly as a freelance writer, contributing literary journalism to newspapers and magazines. His poetry, which has made him one of Australia's leading literary figures, is revered for its evocation of rural life, though its personal style and often polemical tone are also noted. Significant collections include *The Ilex Tree* (1965), *The People's Otherworld* (1983), *Dog Fox Field* (1990), and *Subhuman Redneck Poems* (1996, T S Eliot Prize).

Murray, Lindley (1745–1826) Grammarian, born in Swatara Creek, PA. He practised law, made his fortune in New York City during the War of Independence and then, for health reasons, retired to England in 1784, buying an estate near York. His *English Grammar* (1795) was for long the standard text, and was followed by *English Exercises*, the *English Reader*, and various religious works.

Murray, Matthew (1765–1826) Inventor and mechanical engineer, born near Newcastle upon Tyne, Tyne and Wear, NE England, UK. Apprenticed to a blacksmith, he moved to Leeds as a qualified mechanic in 1788. He devised and patented several improvements in flax spinning machinery before establishing his own engineering works in 1795, where he manufactured textile machinery and also steam engines of his own design. When Watt's master patent for the separate condenser steam engine expired in 1800, he was one of the first to make significant improvements, his designs being smaller, lighter, more efficient, and easier to assemble. >> Watt, James

Murray, William Staite (1881–1962) British potter. He started work on a bulb plantation in The Netherlands and spent 10 years there, but returned to England in 1908. He learnt his craft as a potter at Camberwell School of Art, and began working as an individual potter at Yeoman's Row in South Kensington in 1919. He worked at Brockley in Kent and Bray in Berkshire, then started teaching at the Royal College, where he became head of the Pottery School in 1926. He taught pottery as a fine art medium, attributing to it the same importance as is usually given to painting and sculpture. He lived in Rhodesia from 1940.

Murrow, Ed(ward Egbert) R(oscoe) (1908–65) Journalist and broadcaster, born in Greensboro, NC. He first visited Europe as assistant director of the Institute of International Education (1932–5). Joining CBS in 1935, he returned to Europe in 1937, and became a compassionate conveyor of the wartime spirit in Britain. In postwar America he became a producer and presenter of such hard-hitting, current affairs programmes as *See It Now* (1951–8) and *Person to Person* (1953–60). Committed to the pursuit of truth and excellence, his questioning of Senator McCarthy in 1954 contributed to the latter's fall from grace. He received five Emmy Awards (1953–8), then retired from television journalism to head the United States Information Agency (1961–4). >> McCarthy, Joseph R

Murry, John Middleton (1889–1957) Writer and critic, born in London, England, UK. He studied at Oxford, and became editor of *Rhythm*. He then edited the *Athenaeum* (1919–21), and wrote poetry and many volumes of essays and criticism which had a strong influence on the young intellectuals of the 1920s. In 1918 he married Katherine Mansfield, and introduced her work in the *Adelphi*, another literary magazine, of which he was founder and editor (1923–48). He produced posthumous selections from Katherine Mansfield's letters and diaries, and a biography in 1932. He became a pacifist, and edited *Peace News* (1940–6). Towards the end of his life he became interested in agriculture, starting a community farm in Norfolk. His major works include critical studies on *Keats and Shakespeare* (1925), his friend *D H Lawrence* (1931), *William Blake* (1933), and *Swift* (1954). >> Mansfield, Katherine

Musaeus [moozeeus] (5th–6th-c) One of the Greek poets who preserved the legend of Hero and Leander in the poem of the same name. Also attributed to Ovid, *Hero and Leander* was adapted by several later writers, notably Christopher Marlowe. >> Marlowe

Museveni, Yoweri Kaguta [moosevaynee] (1945–) Soldier, politician, and president of Uganda (1986–). He studied at Dar es Salaam University, then worked for President Milton Obote until his overthrow by Idi Amin (1971). From exile in Tanzania he formed the Front for National Salvation, and took part in the defeat of Amin in 1979. He became minister of defence (1979–80), but was in disagreement with Obote, who returned to the presidency in 1980 with the help of Tanzanian troops. When they withdrew in 1982, a virtual civil war ensued, and reasonable normality did not return until 1986 when Museveni became president. >> RR1094

Musgrave, Thea (1928–) Composer, born in Edinburgh, EC Scotland, UK. She studied at Edinburgh University, the Paris Conservatoire, and with Nadia Boulanger. Her early work was largely Scottish in inspiration, but in the late 1950s became more abstract, and she has used serial and aleatory devices. Her music includes the dramatic choral work *The Five Ages of Man* (1963), a full-length ballet, *Beauty and the Beast* (1968), and the chamber opera *The Voice of Ariadne* (1972–3), based on a story by Henry James. Later works include the orchestral pieces *The Seasons* (1988) and *Rainbow* (1990), and an oboe concerto, *Helios* (1995). >> Boulanger, Nadia

Mushet, David (1772–1847) Iron-master, born in Dalkeith, Midlothian, EC Scotland, UK. He discovered black band ironstone at Calder Ironworks near Glasgow in 1801, and maintained against strong opposition that it was suitable for smelting. After the invention (1828) of the hot blast process by **James Beaumont Neilson** (1792–1865) it became widely used in the Scottish iron industry. He showed that non-phosphoric oxides of iron could be used to make better quality wrought iron, patented a process for making cast steel from wrought iron, and discovered the beneficial effects of adding manganese to iron and steel. >> Mushet, Robert Forester

Mushet, Robert Forester (1811–91) Metallurgist, born in Coleford, Gloucestershire, SWC England, UK, the son of David Mushet. In 1856 Henry Bessemer patented his new steel-making process, but it was soon found that it could not be applied to the majority of iron ores. Only through Mushet's discovery, also patented in 1856, of the beneficial effects of adding ferro-manganese to the blown steel, did the Bessemer process become a profitable commercial success. Ironically, Mushet's patent was allowed to lapse, and

he derived little benefit from his discovery. His invention in 1868 of a self-hardening tungsten alloy steel was the forerunner of a whole family of tool steels. >> Bessemer; Mushet, David

Musial, Stan(ley Frank) [myoozial], nickname **Stan the Man** (1920–) Baseball player, born in Donora, PA. He spent his entire career with the St Louis Cardinals, making his debut in 1941. He topped the National League's batting list seven times (1943–57), and was three times the Most Valuable Player of the Year. He retired in 1962 with a ·331 batting average, 475 home runs, and a then National League record of 3630 hits to his credit. >> RR1144

Musil, Robert (Elder von) [moosil] (1880–1942) Novelist, born in Klagenfurt, Austria. He was trained as a scientist (he invented a chromatometer) and as a philosopher. During World War 1 he was an officer, and drew on his experience for *Die Verwirrungen des Zöglings Törless* (1906, trans Young Törless), a story of life inside a military academy. *Der Mann ohne Eigenschaften* (1930–42, The Man Without Qualities, 1969), his unfinished masterpiece, depicting a society on the brink of an abyss, is widely acknowledged as one of the great novels of the century.

Muskie, Edmund S(ixtus) (1914–96) US lawyer and statesman, born in Rumford, ME. He studied at Bates College and Cornell University, and after war service and private law practice entered the Maine legislature in 1947. He became Governor of Maine (1955–9), then state senator (1959–80), resigning to accept appointment as secretary of state under President Carter. He was Democratic candidate for the vice-presidency in 1968. >> Carter, Jimmy

Musorgski, Modest >> **Moussorgsky, Modest**

Muspratt, James >> **Gamble, Josias Christopher**

Musset, (Louis Charles) Alfred de [müsay] (1810–57) Poet and playwright, born in Paris. After studying first the law, then medicine, he published his first collection of poems, *Contes d'Espagne et d'Italie* (1830, Tales of Spain and Italy). This won the approval of Victor Hugo, who accepted him into his *Cénacle*, the inner shrine of militant Romanticism, even though Musset had already begun to poke gentle fun at the movement. His first excursion into drama failed, and from then on he conceived an 'armchair theatre' with plays intended for reading only. In 1833 Musset met George Sand, and there began the stormy love affair which, according to his autobiographical poem *La Confession d'un enfant du siècle* (1835, The Confession of a Child of the Age), coloured much of his work after that date. His *Nuits* (1835–7, Nights), trace the emotional upheaval of his love for George Sand from despair to final resignation. >> Hugo; Sand

Mussolini, Benito (Amilcare Andrea), known as **il Duce** ('the Leader') (1883–1945) Prime minister of Italy (1922–43) and dictator, born in Predappio, Romagna. From a poor family, he was expelled from two schools for knife-assaults on other students, and soon became one of Italy's most intelligent and menacing young Socialists. He broke with the Italian Socialist Party after advocating Italian intervention in World War 1. In 1919 he helped found the *Fasci di Combattimento* as a would-be revolutionary force, and in 1922 became prime minister, his success symbolized by the March on Rome (Oct 1922). By 1925 he had established himself as dictator. His rule saw the replacement of parliamentarism by a 'Corporate State' and an officially totalitarian system; the establishment of the Vatican state (1929); the annexation of Abyssinia (1935–6) and Albania (1939); and the formation of the Axis with Germany. His declaration of war on Britain and France exposed Italy's military unpreparedness, and was followed by a series of defeats in N and E Africa and in the Balkans. Following the Allied invasion of Sicily (Jun 1943), and with his supporters deserting him, he was overthrown and arrested (Jul 1943).

Rescued from imprisonment by German paratroopers, he was placed in charge of the puppet Italian Social Repbulic, but in 1945 he was captured by the Italian Resistance and shot, his body being exposed to insult in Como and Milan. >> Ciano; de Bono, Emilio; Farinacci; Gentile; Grandi; Matteotti; Skorzeny; RR1065

Mussorgsky, Modest >> **Moussorgsky, Modest**

Muste, A(braham) J(ohn), originally **Abraham Johannes Muste**, known as **A J** (1885–1967) Labour leader and pacifist, born in Zierikzee, The Netherlands. His family moved to the USA in 1891, where he became a minister of the Dutch Reformed Church of America (1909–14), then of the Congregational Church (1914–18) and of the Society of Friends (1918–26). During World War 1 he became involved with the anti-war movement, joined the Quaker-sponsored pacifist group, the Fellowship of Reconciliation (FOR), and became executive secretary of the Amalgamated Textile Workers (1919–21) and director of Brookwood Labor College (1921–33), where he helped to train labour activists ('Musteites'). As executive secretary of the American Workers Party (1933–5) and the Workers Party of the United States (1935–6), he supported strike actions, and developed a Marxist revolutionary stance. A mystical experience brought him back to Christian pacifism, advocating non-violence, and he became director of the Labor Temple (1937–40), and executive secretary of the FOR (1940–53), adopting radical methods of civil disobedience. During the 1950s he was active in several civil rights and world peace movements, and in the 1960s was one of the leaders of opposition to the Vietnam War. Sometimes called 'America's Gandhi', he was a leading influence on 20th-c social movements in the USA. >> Gandhi, Mahatma

Mutsuhito [mutsuheetoh]], **Meiji Tenno** (1852–1912) Emperor of Japan (1867–1912) who became the symbol of Japan's modernization, born in Kyoto, Japan, son of the titular Emperor, Komei, whom he succeeded. Within a year he had overthrown the last of the shoguns, who had exercised dictatorial authority in Japan for 700 years. His long reign saw the rapid political and military westernization of Japan. The feudal system was abolished in 1871; most restrictions on foreign trade were removed; a constitution providing for an advisory cabinet and an imperial Diet was promulgated in 1889; and a navy was created on the British model and an army on the German. Military success against China in 1894 and 1895 was followed by Japan's victories in the Russo–Japanese War (1904–5), and by the economic penetration of Korea and Manchuria.

Muybridge, Eadweard [moybrij], originally **Edward James Muggeridge** (1830–1904) Photographer and inventor, born in Kingston-on-Thames, SW Greater London, England, UK. He emigrated to California in 1852, and became a professional photographer, then chief photographer to the US government. He was commissioned to take a series of action photographs to prove that a trotting horse has all its feet off the ground at times. This he achieved in 1877 when faster photographic plates became available. In 1880 he devised the zoopraxiscope to show his picture sequences, achieving a rudimentary kind of cinematography in his Zoopraxographical Hall in Chicago (1893), which was hailed as the world's first motion picture theatre. He returned to England following his retirement in 1900.

Muzorewa, Abel (Tendekayi) [muzoraywa] (1925–) Clergyman and politician, born in Umtali, South Africa. Ordained in 1953, he studied in the USA and in 1968 became the first black bishop of the United Methodist Church. In 1971 he became president of the African National Council

(ANC), a non-violent organization intended to pave the way for an internal settlement of the political situation in Rhodesia. In 1975 the ANC split into two factions – the gradualists, led by Muzorewa, working for a transition to majority rule, and the more extreme elements, led by Joshua Nkomo. Muzorewa was prime minister of 'Zimbabwe Rhodesia' for six months in 1979, but after independence his movement was defeated by the parties of Robert Mugabe and Joshua Nkomo. >> Mugabe; Nkomo

Mwinyi, (Ndugu) Ali Hassan [mweenyee] (1925–) Tanzanian statesman and president (1985–95), born in Zanzibar. He trained as a teacher on the island and in Britain, before returning to hold progressively important posts in teaching. He then joined the ministry of education and, after working in a trading corporation on the mainland, entered the government of Julius Nyerere. He held a variety of ministerial and ambassadorial posts until, in 1985, he succeeded Nyerere as president of the United Republic of Tanzania. >> Nyerere; RR1092

Myers, F(rederic) W(illiam) H(enry) (1843–1901) Poet and essayist, born in Keswick, Cumbria, NW England, UK. A classical scholar, he studied at Cambridge, and became a school inspector (1872–1900). He wrote poems (collected 1921), essays, a book on *Wordsworth* (1881), and *Human Personality and its Survival of Bodily Death* (1903). He was one of the founders of the Society for Psychical Research.

Myles na Gopaleen >> **O'Brien, Flann**

Mylonas, George [miylohnas] (1898–1988) Archaeologist, born in Smyrna, Greece. He taught for many years in the USA, and became president of the Archaeological Society of America; he was also secretary-general of the Greek Historical Society. His main excavation was at the Outer Grave Circle at Mycenae, and before that the Neolithic material at Olyathus, and the small Bronze Age site at Ayios Kosmas, near Athens airport. He was also responsible for the building of a new museum at Mycenae.

Myrdal, Alva [merdal], *née* **Reimer** (1902–86) Sociologist, stateswoman, and peace reformer, born in Uppsala, Sweden. She studied at the universities of Uppsala, Stockholm, and Geneva, and married Gunnar Myrdal. She was director of the UN department of social sciences (1950–6), and Swedish ambassador to India, Burma, and Ceylon (1955–61). Elected to parliament in 1962, she acted as Swedish representative on the UN Disarmament Committee (1962–73). As minister for disarmament and Church affairs (1966–73), she played a prominent part in the international peace movement. She was awarded the 1980 Albert Einstein Peace Prize, and in 1982 shared the Nobel Peace Prize. >> Myrdal, Gunnar; RR1125

Myrdal, (Karl) Gunnar [merdal] (1898–1987) Economist, politician, and international civil servant, born in Gustafs Dalecarlia, Sweden. He studied at Stockholm, where he became professor of political economy (1933). He wrote a classic study of race relations in the USA (*An American Dilemma*, 1944), then was minister of trade and commerce in Sweden (1945–7), and executive secretary of the UN Economic Commission for Europe (1947–57). His later works include *The Challenge of Affluence* (1963). He was awarded the 1974 Nobel Prize for Economics, principally for his work on the critical application of economic theory of Third World countries. >> Myrdal, Alva

Myron [miyron] (fl.c. 480–440 BC) Sculptor, born in Eleutherae, Greece. A contemporary of Phidias, he lived mostly in Athens. He worked in bronze, and is best known for his studies of athletes in action, particularly the celebrated 'Discobolos' and 'Marsyas'. >> Phidias

Nabokov, Vladimir [naˈbohkof] (1899–1977) Writer, born in St Petersburg, Russia. He went to school in St Petersburg, and when his family emigrated to Berlin in 1919 he studied at Cambridge. He then rejoined his family, living in Berlin for the next 15 years. There he had his first literary success, a translation of some of Heine's songs, and he published his first novels, all written in Russian, beginning with *Mashenka* (1926). After a time in Paris (1937–40), he emigrated to the USA, where he took out US citizenship in 1945 and taught at Wellesley College and Cornell University. Writing now in English, he published many short stories and novels, including the controversial *Lolita* (1955, filmed 1962), dealing with the desire of a middle-aged intellectual for a 12-year-old girl, which brought him fame and wealth, and allowed him to abandon teaching and devote himself full time to writing. Other works include *The Real Life of Sebastian Knight* (1941), *Bend Sinister* (1947), *Pale Fire* (1962), and *Ada* (1969), as well as his lyrical autobiography *Speak, Memory* (1967). Among 20th-c novelists he is highly regarded for his linguistic versatility and intellectual range. His critical approach is illustrated by the collection *Lectures on Literature* (1980).

Nadar [nadah(r)], pseudonym of **Gaspard Félix Tournachon** (1820–1910) Writer, artist, and photographer, born in Paris. He studied medicine, but became a journalist, and in 1852 published a series of caricatures, some of which were based on his photographs. In 1853 he opened a photographic studio which became a favourite haunt of the intelligentsia, and for many years produced intimate and natural studies of distinguished literary and artistic contemporaries, in 1886 presenting the first 'photo-interview' – a sequence of photographs accompanied by caption quotations from the subject. Among other innovations he proposed the use of aerial photographs for map-making, and in 1858 took the first photographs from a balloon, the city of Paris.

Nadel, S(iegfried) F(rederick) [nahdl] (1903–56) Social anthropologist, born in Vienna. He studied psychology and philosophy at Vienna University before moving to the London School of Economics to study anthropology under Malinowski. He taught at Durham (1948–50), then became professor at Canberra University, Australia (1950–6). He carried out fieldwork among the Nupe in N Nigeria (1934–6) and the Nuba of the Sudan (1938–40). However, his major contribution to anthropology was theoretical, as seen in *The Foundations of Social Anthropology* (1951) and *The Theory of Social Structure* (1957). >> Malinowski

Nadelman, Elie [naydlman] (1882–1946) Sculptor, born in Warsaw. He studied at Warsaw Art Academy, left Poland in 1904, and settled in Paris. His drawings and sculptures after 1906 reveal a simplification of forms and stylization close to Cubism, but also show an affinity with antique sculpture. In 1914 he moved to the USA, taking a studio in New York City. There he produced a number of unusual painted figure sculptures in wood. He became a US citizen in 1927, and from the 1930s worked extensively in ceramics.

Nader, Ralph [nayder] (1934–) Lawyer and consumer activist, born in Winsted, CT. He studied at Princeton and Harvard, and was admitted to the Connecticut bar in 1959. Since then he has campaigned for improved consumer rights and protection, encouraging the establishment of powerful civic interest lobbies of which the US Congress, state legislatures, and corporate executives have had to take note. His best-seller about the automobile industry, *Unsafe at Any Speed* (1965), led to the passing of improved car safety regulations in 1966. He became head of the Public Citizen Foundation in 1980. His other books include *The Menace of Atomic Energy* (1977), *Who's Poisoning America?* (1981), and *Winning the Insurance Game* (1990).

Nadir Shah, Mohammed (c. 1880–1933) King of Afghanistan (1929–33). As commander-in-chief to Amanullah Khan, he played a prominent role in the 1919 Afghan War against Britain which secured the country's full independence in 1922. He subsequently fell into disfavour, and was forced to live in exile in France. In 1929, with British diplomatic support, he returned to Kabul and seized the throne, immediately embarking on a programme of economic and social modernization. These reforms, however, alienated the Muslim clergy, and in 1933 he was assassinated. He was succeeded by his son, Mohammed Zahir Shah. >> Amanullah Khan; Zahir Shah; RR1031

Naevius, Gnaeus [neevius] (c. 264–c. 194 BC) Poet and playwright, probably born in Campania. He served in the first Punic War (264–241 BC), and started producing his own plays in 235. A plebeian, for 30 years he satirized the Roman nobles in his plays, and was compelled to leave Rome, ultimately retiring to Utica in Africa. Fragments of an epic, *De bello Punico*, are extant.

Nagano, Osami [nagahnoh] (1880–1947) Admiral of the Japanese navy, born in Kochi, Japan. He studied law at Harvard, and served as naval attaché in Washington (1920–3). Promoted rear-admiral in 1928, he was superintendent of the Naval Academy (1928–9). As head of the Japanese delegation to the 2nd London Naval Conference (1935–6), he advocated the expansion of Japanese naval power. He was navy minister (1936–7), commander-in-chief of the combined fleet (1937), and as chief of naval general staff (1941–4) he planned and ordered the attack on Pearl Harbor in December 1941. He died while on trial for war crimes. >> Kimmel

Nagarjuna [nagah(r)juna] (c. 150–c. 250) Indian Buddhist monk-philosopher. He was the founder of the Madhyamika or Middle Path school of Buddhism.

Nagel, Ernest [naygl] (1901–85) Philosopher of science, born in Nové Město, Czech Republic. He emigrated to the USA, became a US citizen in 1919, and taught philosophy at Columbia University (1931–70). He published widely on the philosophy of science, his best-known works being *An Introduction to Logic and Scientific Method* (1934, with M R Cohen), *Logic without Metaphysics* (1957), and *The Structure of Science* (1961).

Nagle, Kelvin [naygl] (1920–) Golfer, born in Sydney, New South Wales, Australia. After winning the Australian Open in 1959, he won the British Open in 1960 and came second two years later. He was also second in the US Open of 1965. He represented Australia in their World Cup side on nine occasions between 1954 and 1966, taking part in two trophy-winning sides. He set up a record low aggregate of 260 (64–65–66–65) when winning the Irish Hospitals event in 1961, and continued to be a formidable golfer even in his 50s, taking the World Senior title in 1971. >> RR1158

Naguib, Mohammed [nageeb] (1901–84) Egyptian general and president (1952–4), born in Khartoum. As general of an army division in 1952 he carried out a coup in Cairo which banished Farouk I and initiated the 'Egyptian Revolution'. Taking first the offices of commander-in-chief and prime minister, he abolished the monarchy in 1952 and became president of the republic. He was deposed in 1954 and succeeded by Nasser. >> Farouk I; Nasser; RR1046

Nagy, Imre [noj, **im**ray] (1895–1958) Hungarian statesman and prime minister (1953–5), born in Kaposvar, Hungary. He had a minor post in the Béla Kun revolutionary government in Hungary. He then went to Moscow (1929), and became a member of the Institute for Agrarian Sciences. Returning with the Red Army (1944), he was minister of agriculture, and as premier introduced milder political control. When Soviet forces began to put down the 1956 revolution, he appealed to the world for help, but was displaced by the Soviet puppet, János Kádár, and executed in Budapest. >> Kádár; Kun; RR1057

Nahum [**nay**huhm] (7th-c BC) Old Testament minor prophet. He seems to have been an Israelite or Judaean who had been a captive in Nineveh, and prophesied the destruction of Nineveh by the Medes in 612 BC.

Nahyan, Zayed ibn Sultan al-Shaykh [na**yahn**] (?1918–) President of the United Arab Emirates (1971–), raised as a desert nomad. He was governor of the province of Abu Dhabi, one of seven Trucial States on the S shores of the Persian Gulf and the Gulf of Oman, which were under British protection, until in 1969 he deposed his brother, Sheikh Shakhbut, and became emir. When the States decided to federate as the United Arab Emirates in 1971, he became president of its Supreme Council, and was re-elected in 1986. >> RR1094

Naidoo, Jay (Jayaseelan) [**niy**doo] (1954–) South African labour leader and opponent of apartheid, born in Durban, South Africa. In 1979 he became a trade union organizer, and rose to prominence in the labour movement. When the Congress of South African Trade Unions (COSATU) was founded in 1985, he was elected general secretary. In this capacity he played a leading role during the mass-based protest politics of the 1980s, and led COSATU into formal alliance with the African National Congress and the South African Communist Party. From December 1990, he was active in the negotiations for a new political dispensation in South Africa.

Naidu, Sarojini [**niy**doo], née **Chattopadhyay** (1879–1949) Feminist and poet, born in Hyderabad, India. She studied at Madras, London, and Cambridge, and became known as 'the nightingale of India'. She published three volumes of lyric verse: *The Golden Threshold* (1905), *The Bird of Time* (1912), and *The Broken Wing* (1915). She organized flood-relief in Hyderabad (1908), and lectured and campaigned on feminism, particularly the abolition of purdah. Associated with Mahatma Gandhi, she was imprisoned several times for civil disobedience incidents, and took part in the negotiations leading to independence. She was the first Indian woman to be president of the Indian National Congress (1925) and to be appointed an Indian state governor (1947). >> Gandhi, Mahatma

Nain, Antoine le >> **le Nain, Antoine**

Naipaul, Sir V(idiadhar) S(urajprasad) [niy**pawl**] (1932–) Novelist, born in Chaguanas, Trinidad. He studied at Port of Spain, and Oxford, became editor of *Caribbean Voices* for the BBC, and was a journalist, before publishing his first novel, *The Mystic Masseur* in 1957. The book which made his name was *A House for Mr Biswas* (1961), a satire spanning three Trinidadian generations. Thereafter the Caribbean figured less prominently in his work, which grew steadily darker and more complex, as seen in *In a Free State* (1971, Booker) and *A Bend in the River* (1979), a re-creation of what it is like to live under an African dictatorship. *The Enigma of Arrival* (1987) returns the scene to England. Later novels include *A Way in the World* (1994).

He has also written several travel books, including *An Area of Darkness: an Experience of India* (1964) and *Among the Believers: an Islamic Journey* (1981). He was knighted in 1990.

Naismith, James A [**nay**smith] (1861–1939) Physical educationist, born in Almonte, Ontario, Canada. He was originator of the game of basketball in 1891 at the YMCA college in Springfield, MA. The game was designed to bridge the gap between the baseball and American football season. He studied at McGill University, taught at the YMCA, Denver, CO (1895–8), and the University of Kansas (1898–1937), and attended the Berlin Olympics of 1936, at which basketball was elevated to the status of an Olympic sport.

Najibullah, Mohammad [naji**bul**a] (1947–96) Afghan Communist leader and president (1987–92), born in Kabul. He studied at Kabul University, joined the Communist People's Democratic Party of Afghanistan in 1965, and was twice imprisoned for political activities during the 1960s and 1970s. In 1986 he replaced Babrak Karmal as Party leader, and was formally elected state president in 1987. He promulgated a non-Marxist constitution which enshrined a multi-party system, and a dominant position for Islam. However, his hold over power became imperilled following the withdrawal of Soviet military forces in 1989, and after a period of unceasing opposition from Mujahideen guerrillas, his regime collapsed in 1992. He was executed by the *taliban* (army of students), Sep 1996, when they took control of Kabul. >> Karmal; RR1031

Nakasone, Yasuhiro [naka**soh**nay] (1918–) Japanese statesman and prime minister (1982–7), born in Takasaki, Japan. He studied at Tokyo University, was a junior naval officer in World War 2, and entered the ministry of home affairs in 1945. Elected to the Diet at age 29 for the Liberal–Democratic (Conservative) Party, he held a range of ministerial posts (1959–82). As premier, he supported the renewal of the US–Japan Security Treaty, and maintained close relations with President Ronald Reagan. >> Reagan; RR1068

Namath, Joe, popular name of **Joseph William Namath**, nickname **Broadway Joe** (1943–) Player of American football, born in Beaver Falls, PA. He joined the New York Jets from the unbeaten University of Alabama team in 1965, and became one of the leading quarterbacks in the 1960s. His lifestyle outside football attracted a great deal of publicity, hence his nickname. After his retirement (1978), he remained in the public eye, with appearances in films and on television. >> RR1155

Namatjira, Albert [namat**jeer**a] (1902–59) Artist, born in Hermannsberg Lutheran mission, near Alice Springs, Northern Territory, Australia, a member of the Aranda Aboriginal people. He achieved wide fame almost overnight for his European-influenced watercolour landscapes. In 1957 he was in the unique position of being made an Australian citizen, 10 years before other Aboriginal people. Divided by two cultures, his last years became a nightmare. A retrospective exhibition of his work was held in Alice Springs in 1984.

Namier, Sir Lewis (Bernstein) [**naym**yer], originally **Ludwik Bernstein Niemirowski** (1888–1960) Historian, born near Warsaw. He moved to England in 1906, studied at Oxford, and took British nationality. He became professor of modern history at Manchester (1931–52), creating a school of history in which the emphasis was on the detailed analysis of events and institutions, particularly parliamentary elections, so as to reveal the motivation of the individuals involved in them. One of his most important works is *The Structure of Politics at the Accession of George II* (1929).

Nanak [na̱nak], known as **Guru Nanak** (1469–1539) Religious leader, the founder of Sikhism, born near Lahore, India. A Hindu by birth and belief, he travelled widely to Hindu and Muslim centres in search of spiritual truth. He settled in Kartarpur, in the Punjab, where he attracted many followers. His doctrine, set out later in the *Adi-Granth*, sought a fusion of Brahmanism and Islam on the grounds that both were monotheistic, although his own ideas leaned rather towards pantheism.

Nana Sahib [na̱na sa̱heeb], originally **Brahmin Dundhu Panth** (c.1820–c.1859) Prominent rebel of the Indian Mutiny, the adopted son of the ex-peshwa of the Mahrattas **Baji Rao II** (1796–1818). At the outbreak of the Indian Mutiny (1857) he became the leader of the Sepoys in Cawnpore, and organized the massacre of the British residents. After the collapse of the rebellion he escaped into Nepal, and died in the hills some time later. >> Tantia Topi

Nannerl >> **Mozart, Wolfgang Amadeus**

Nanni, di Banco (c. 1380–1421) Sculptor, one of the most important artists of the early Renaissance, born in Florence, Italy. He was recorded as a member of the Stonemasons' Guild in 1405, and was working with his father shortly thereafter on the Porta della Mandorla of Florence cathedral. He contributed statues to three of the niches on the guild hall Orsanmichele; his best work here was the group of 'Four Crowned Saints', which shows strong classical influence. However, in his most important later commission, the relief of the 'Assumption of the Virgin' above the Porta della Mandorla (1414–21), he returned to a more Gothic manner.

Nansen, Fridtjof [fri̱tyof] (1861–1930) Explorer, born near Oslo, Norway. He studied at Oslo University and later at Naples. In 1882 he made a voyage into the Arctic regions in the sealer *Viking*, and on his return was made keeper of the natural history department of the museum at Bergen. In 1888 he journeyed across Greenland E–W, but his great achievement was his scheme for reaching the North Pole by letting his ship, *The Fram*, get frozen into the ice N of Siberia (1883) and drift with a current setting towards Greenland; the boat reached 84°4', and after a further voyage on foot, he achieved 86°14', the highest latitude then attained. The first Norwegian ambassador in London (1906–8), he was awarded the Nobel Prize for Peace for Russian relief work (1922), and he did much for the League of Nations.

Naomi >> **Ruth**

Napier, Sir Charles [na̱ypyer] (1786–1860) British naval commander, born near Falkirk, C Scotland, UK. He went to sea at 13, received his first command in 1808, and served in the Napoleonic Wars and against the US in 1812. As commander of the Portuguese navy, he destroyed Don Miguel's fleet (1833). With the British he was second-in-command in Syria (1840–4), and took part in the capture of Beirut and Acre. As commander of the Baltic Fleet at the beginning of the Crimean War (1854), he refused to attack Kronstadt and was recalled in disgrace. He later sat in parliament, and worked to reform the naval administration.

Napier, Sir Charles James [na̱ypyer] (1782–1853) British soldier, the conqueror of Sind (now part of Pakistan), born in London, England, UK. He served in Ireland during the rebellion, in Portugal (1810), against the USA (1813), and in the storming of Cambrai (1815). In 1841 he was ordered to India to command in the war with Sind, and at the Battle of Meeanee (1843) broke the power of the amirs. He is said to have informed the authorities of his victory by sending the punning telegram *Peccavi* (Latin for 'I have sinned').

Napier, John [na̱ypyer] (1550–1617) Mathematician, the inventor of logarithms, born at Merchiston Castle, Edinburgh, EC Scotland, UK. He studied at St Andrews,

travelled in Europe, then settled down to a life of literary and scientific study. He described his famous invention in *Mirifici logarithmorum canonis descriptio* (1614, Description of the Marvellous Canon of Logarithms), and also devised a calculating machine, using a set of rods called *Napier's bones*.

Napier (of Magdala), Robert (Cornelius) Napier, 1st Baron [na̱ypyer] (1810–90) British field marshal, born in Colombo, Sri Lanka (formerly Ceylon). He studied at Addiscombe, and entered the Bengal Engineers in 1826. He served in the campaigns in India, distinguished himself at the siege of Lucknow (1857), then in the Chinese war (1860) and the expedition in Abyssinia (1868). In 1870 he became commander-in-chief in India and a member of the Indian Council, and was subsequently Governor of Gibraltar, field marshal, and Constable of the Tower.

Napoleon I, Fr **Napoléon Bonaparte**, Ital **Napoleone Buonaparte** see panel on p. 682

Napoleon II, in full **François Charles Joseph Bonaparte** (1811–32) Son of Napoleon I by the Archduchess Marie Louise, born in Paris. He was styled King of Rome at his birth. After his father's abdication he was brought up in Austria, and in 1818 given the title of the Duke of Reichstadt, though allowed no active political role. >> Marie Louise; Napoleon I

Napoleon III, until 1852 **Louis Napoleon**, originally **Charles Louis Napoleon Bonaparte** (1808–73) Third son of Louis Bonaparte, king of Holland (the brother of Napoleon I) and Hortense Beauharnais; the president of the Second French Republic (1848–52) and emperor of the French (1852–70), born in Paris. After the death of Napoleon II he became the head of the Napoleonic dynasty. He made two abortive attempts on the French throne (1836, 1840), for which he was imprisoned. He escaped to England (1846), but when the Bonapartist tide swept France after the 1848 revolution he was elected first to the Assembly and then to the presidency (1848). Engineering the dissolution of the constitution, he assumed the title of emperor, and in 1853 married **Eugénie de Montijo de Guzman** (1826–1920), a Spanish countess, who bore him a son, the Prince Imperial, **Eugène Louis Jean Joseph Napoleon** (1856). He actively encouraged economic expansion and the modernization of Paris, while externally the Second Empire coincided with the Crimean conflict (1854–6), the expeditions to China (1857–60), the annexation (1860) of Savoy and Nice, and the ill-starred intervention in Mexico (1861–7). Encouraged by the empress, he unwisely declared war on Prussia in 1870, and suffered humiliating defeat, culminating in the Battle of Sedan. Confined at Wilhelmshohe until 1871, he went into exile in England. >> Bonaparte, Louis; Montholon; Morny; Napoleon II; Orsini; RR1049

Narayan, R(asipuram) K(irishnaswamy) [na̱riyan] (1906–) Novelist and short-story writer, born in Madras, India. He studied there and at Maharaja's College in Mysore. His first novel, *Swami and Friends* (1935), and its successors, including *Mr Sampath* (1949), *The Vendor of Sweets* (1967), and *A Tiger for Malgudi* (1983) are set in the enchanting fictional territory of 'Malgudi'. His novel *The Guide* (1958) won him the National Prize of the Indian Literary Academy. He has also published stories, travel books, books for children, and essays. One of the most highly acclaimed Indian novelists of his generation, his publication in Britain was brought about by Graham Greene. Later works include the novels *Talkative Man* (1986), *The World of Nagaraj* (1990), and *The Grandmother's Tale* (1993). His autobiography, *My Days*, was published in 1975. >> Greene, Graham

Narses [na̱h(r)seez] (c. 478–573) Persian statesman and general, born in Armenia. He rose in the imperial household

NAPOLEON (1769–1821)

Napoleon Bonaparte, originally **Napoleon Buonaparte**, was born in Ajaccio, Corsica, the second son of Carlo (d.1785), a lawyer, and Letizia Ramolino – resistance workers who had joined a revolt against the Genoese government of the island. He went to school in France, entering the military academy at Brienne, then the Ecole Militaire in Paris (1784), and received a commission as a second lieutenant in the artillery.

The French Revolution began in 1789, and France went to war with Austria in 1792. In 1793, Napoleon and his family fled the civil war in Corsica (where he had returned in 1792), and he rejoined his regiment in Nice. Showing early promise, he was put in charge of the barrage at the siege of Toulon, where his role in breaking the siege and forcing the withdrawal of Admiral Hood earned him favourable reports to the Convention. He was promoted to brigadier-general in 1793, and appointed artillery commander of the Army of Italy in 1794. Although imprisoned because of a former association with army commissioner Augustin de Robespierre, the brother of the deposed instigator of the Reign of Terror, he was released through the influence of the political commissar at Toulon.

Napoleon was then appointed to the planning section of the Committee of Public Safety, and given second command, and later command, of the Army of the Interior in 1795. The same year, called upon to defend the deputies of the National Convention against the attack of a mob of Royalist sympathizers, he dispersed the group with the celebrated 'whiff of grapeshot'. He was appointed by the Directory to command the Army of Italy in 1796. Before departing on this campaign, he married Joséphine de Beauharnais, widow of the guillotined Vicomte Alexandre de Beauharnais. It was at this point that he changed the spelling of his name, to avoid drawing attention to his Italian origin.

Having been promoted over the heads of older officers, his unbroken run of victories over the armies of both Austria and Piedmont established his credibility as a commander, while his concern for his previously ill-equipped soldiers won their loyalty. During the storming of a bridge at Lodi, he fought alongside his troops, and earned from them the nickname of 'the little corporal'. Despite conflicts with the Directory over his ambitious strategic initiatives, he was allowed to take all of Italy and to conclude the Treaty of Campo Formio with Austria in 1797. By 1798 only Britain remained at war with France, and he was appointed commander of the Army of England. Without control of the sea, however, Napoleon did not consider an attack on England feasible. Instead he suggested attacking British interests elsewhere.

The Directory approved his campaign to capture Egypt, as a launching point for an attack on British interests in India. Napoleon's Army of the Orient arrived at Alexandria in a French fleet in 1798. He defeated the Egyptian armies, but lost his fleet to Nelson at the Battle of the Nile in Abu Qir (Aboukir) Bay. There was then a lengthy stalemate, with the victorious French army penned into Egypt by the royal navy blockade. However, after learning of the increasingly serious situation in France, now at war with a coalition of several European nations, Napoleon abandoned his army in Egypt, evaded the blockade, and returned to France almost alone (1799). There he became part of the plot to replace the Directory, leading to the Coup of 18–19 Brumaire (9–10 Nov 1799). He assumed the role of First Consul and, with the visible support of the army, effectively became dictator.

His first priority was the defence of France against the coalition forces of Europe. He reorganized his armies, defeating Austria at Marengo and Hohenlinden (1800). A Concordat with Pope Pius VII re-established the Roman Catholic Church in France. The Treaty of Amiens (1802) then ended the Revolutionary Wars. Having been made First Consul for life, he took an active part in organizing French law (the Napoleonic Code), and achieved popular appeal by returning France to economic stability. When hostilities recommenced he began preparations for the invasion of Britain. After foiling a Royalist plot to kidnap him, he was proclaimed emperor in 1804, and crowned in Notre Dame Cathedral.

Napoleon's conduct of the wars was characterized by his

in Constantinople to be keeper of the privy purse to Justinian I. In 538 he was sent to Italy, but recalled the next year. In 552 Belisarius was recalled from Italy, and Narses succeeded him, defeated the Ostrogoths, took possession of Rome, and completely extinguished the Gothic power in Italy. Justinian appointed him prefect of Italy in 554, but he was charged with avarice, and on Justinian's death he was deprived of his office. >> Belisarius; Justinian

Nash, John (1752–1835) Architect, born in London, England, UK. He trained as an architect, practised in London, and gained a reputation by his country-house designs. He came to the notice of the Prince of Wales (the future George IV), and was engaged to plan the layout of the new Regent's Park and its environs of curved terraces (1811–25). He laid out Regent Street to link the Park with Westminster, built Carlton House Terrace, and laid out Trafalgar Square and St James's Park. He recreated Buckingham Palace from old Buckingham House, designed the Marble Arch which originally stood in front of it (moved to its present site in 1851), and rebuilt Brighton Pavilion in Oriental style. On the strength of a patent for improvements to the arches and piers of bridges (1797), he claimed much of the credit for introducing steel girders.

Nash, John F (1928–) Economist, born in Bluefield, WV. He studied at the Carnegie Institute of Technology and Princeton University, moved to MIT, then returned to Princeton. He shared the Nobel Prize for Economics in 1994 for his contribution to the analysis of equilibria in the theory of non-co-operative games. >> Harsanyi; Selten

Nash, (Frederic) Ogden (1902–71) Humorous writer, born in Rye, NY. He studied at Harvard, then tried teaching, editing, selling bonds, and copy writing, before his poetry became successful enough for him to make a living from it. Taking outrageous liberties with the English language ('I would live all my life in nonchalance and insouciance / Were it not for making a living, which is rather a nouciance'), he soon became the most popular modern versifier, frequently published in the *New Yorker*, whose sophisticated tone he enormous personal energy and his ability to manoeuvre and concentrate his forces rapidly. The high regard in which his troops held him was due in no small measure to his conspicuous personal courage. In 1803–5 he was fighting the British; but in 1805 Britain organized a coalition of Austria, Russia, Sweden, and Naples against France. Among his greatest victories were the defeat of the Austrians at Ulm (1805) and of a joint Austro-Russian army at Austerlitz (1805). But while he remained pre-eminent on the European mainland, his plans to invade England remained thwarted by a powerful Royal Navy, and in 1805 his fleet was destroyed at Trafalgar, though his great enemy, Nelson, was killed in the battle.

By 1807 Napoleon controlled an empire which stretched from the Elbe in the N across the whole of Italy, and from the Pyrenees to the Dalmatian coast. He was also King of Italy, Mediator of the Swiss Confederation, and Protector of the Confederation of the Rhine. He had appointed his brothers as kings over the conquered territories: Jérôme of the newly created Westphalia, Joseph of Naples, and Louis of Holland. Having lost the initiative at sea, he sought to impose a commercial blockade on Britain along the Atlantic coast, the so-called 'Continental system'. He also occupied Spain and Portugal, thus initiating the Peninsular Wars (1808–14). In the E, he defeated the Austrians at Wagram.

The empress Joséphine had been unable to produce the heir Napoleon so earnestly wanted. He therefore divorced her and, as part of the harsh peace terms exacted from the Austrians under the Treaty of Schöbrunn (1809), he took the emperor's 19-year-old daughter Marie-Louise as his wife; a son, François Charles Joseph Napoleon was born in 1811.

Jealous of Russia's power, and suspicious of the Tsar Alexander as as ally, Napoleon commenced a campaign to invade Russia, defeating the Russians at Borodino (1812). His advance over burnt earth and occupation of a deserted Moscow (1812), while exposing his overextended lines of supply and communication to continual harassment by the Russians, was a major blunder. This was compounded by his desire to avoid the creation of rivals to his own position by selecting generals for their ability to carry out his specific orders rather than for their initiative.

With war on two widely separated fronts, Napoleon's poor delegation became apparent. In the Peninsular War, Wellesley drove the French out of Spain, and in the east Napoleon was forced into a costly retreat from Moscow. He returned to Paris in an attempt to hold together an empire threatened on all sides by defecting former allies, and rife with rumours of his death. He suffered a major defeat by an allied force near Leipzig at the Battle of the Nations (1813), and the following year the allies took Paris. He abdicated in favour of his son in April and attempted to poison himself (1814). The succession was rejected by the French Senate, which forced him to abdicate unconditionally and reinstated the Bourbon dynasty in the person of Louis XVIII.

Napoleon, aged 44, was exiled to Elba, where he threw himself into reviving the ailing economy of his island 'kingdom'. However, when the government of Louis XVIII failed to pay him the pension promised under the Treaty of Paris (1814), and when denied access to his wife and son, he grew resentful. Encouraged by rumours of the unpopularity of the new monarchy, he escaped from Elba, and landed in France with 1500 men. Marching on Paris, he collected devotees on the way, and entered the city in triumph (Mar 1815), forcing Louis XVIII to take refuge in Holland. Over the following 100 days he raised a Grand Army with the aim of striking against the now dispersed allied armies. Despite a victory at Ligny against Blücher (16 Jun) he was decisively defeated by Wellington at Waterloo (18 Jun). Shortly after, he abdicated in favour of his son, surrendering to the British to avoid the revenge of the returning Bourbons.

He was exiled to the Atlantic island of St Helena. Marie-Louise never contacted him, and secretly married again, not waiting for Napoleon's death. He died of a stomach illness, probably cancer, a few years later. In 1840 his body was returned to Paris, and interred in the Hôtel des Invalides.

>> Blücher; Bonaparte, Jérôme / Joseph / Louis; Joséphine; Nelson, Horatio; Ney; Wellington

helped establish. His subject-matter was the everyday life of middle-class America, which he described in a witty and acute manner, in an idiosyncratic style involving long digressions and striking rhyme schemes. He published many collections, including *Hard Lines* (1931) and *Parents Keep Out: Elderly Poems for Youngerly Readers* (1951).

Nash, Paul (1899–1946) Painter, born in London, England, UK. He studied at St Paul's and the Slade School of Art, London, and became an official war artist in 1917 (remembered particularly for his poignant 'Menin Road', 1919). Developing a style which reduced form to bare essentials, he won renown as a landscape painter, and also practised scene painting, commercial design, and book illustration. For a while he taught at the Royal College of Art. In 1939 he again filled the role of war artist, this time for the Air Ministry and the Ministry of Information, producing such pictures as 'Battle of Britain' and 'Totes Meer' (1940–1, Tate, London). Shortly before his death he turned to a very individual style of flower painting.

Nash, Richard, nickname **Beau Nash** (1674–1762) Dandy, born in Swansea, SC Wales. He studied at Oxford, held a commission in the army, and in 1693 entered the Middle Temple. He then made a shifty living by gambling, but in 1704 became master of ceremonies at Bath, where he conducted the public balls with a splendour never before witnessed. His reforms in manners, his influence in improving the streets and buildings, and his leadership in fashion helped to transform Bath into a fashionable holiday centre. Although he died a pauper, he was buried in pomp in Bath Abbey.

Nash, Sir Walter (1882–1968) New Zealand politician and prime minister (1957–60), born in Kidderminster, Worcester, WC England, UK. From 1919 to 1960 he served on the national executive of the New Zealand Labour Party, encouraging the adoption of a moderate reform programme in the Christian Socialist tradition. An MP from 1929, he held numerous ministerial appointments from 1936 onwards, and in World War 2 was deputy prime minister, heading a special mission to the USA (1942–4). He became prime minister with a government possessing a majority of only one, so his period in office saw few political innovations. >> RR1078

Nashe or **Nash, Thomas** (1567–1601) Playwright and satirist, born in Lowestoft, Suffolk, E England, UK. He studied at Cambridge, travelled in Europe, then went to London as a writer, where he plunged into the Martin Marprelate controversy, displaying a talent for vituperation, and attacking the Puritans in *Pierce Penilesse, his Supplication to the Divell* (1592). Other works include the satirical masque, *Summer's Last Will and Testament* (1592), and the picaresque tale, *The Unfortunate Traveller* (1594). His play *The Isle of Dogs* (1597), now lost, drew such attention to abuses in the state that it was suppressed, the theatre closed, and he was thrown into the Fleet prison.

Nasier, Alcofribas >> **Rabelais, François**

Nasmyth, James [**nay**smith] (1808–90) Engineer, born in Edinburgh, EC Scotland, UK. From boyhood he showed a talent for mechanics, building successful model steam engines while still at school. He started in business at Manchester (1834), and established at Patricroft the Bridgewater Foundry (1836). He devised and patented a steam hammer to assist with forging work (1842), and it became a major tool in the Industrial Revolution. Among his other inventions were a steam pile-driver, a planing machine, and a hydraulic punching machine.

Nasser, Gamal Abdel (1918–70) Egyptian statesman, prime minister (1954–6), and president (1956–70), born in Alexandria. An army officer, he became dissatisfied with the corruption of the Farouk regime, and was involved in the military coup of 1952. He assumed the premiership in 1954, and then presidential powers, deposing his fellow officer, General Mohammed Neguib. Officially elected president in 1956, he nationalized the Suez Canal, which prompted Britain and France to seek his forcible overthrow, gaining Israeli co-operation in the invasion of Sinai. In 1958 he created a federation with Syria (the United Arab Republic), but Syria withdrew in 1961. After the six-day Arab–Israeli War (1967), heavy losses on the Arab side led to his resignation, but he was persuaded to stay on, and died still in office. >> Dayan; Eden; Farouk I; Mollet; RR1046

Nast, Condé (Montrose) (1873–1942) Publisher, born in New York City. After working for *Collier's Weekly* (1898–1907) he bought *Vogue*, then a small New York society magazine, transforming it into America's premier fashion magazine. He then turned *Vanity Fair* into a sophisticated magazine for all that was stylish, and eventually owned a stable of high-class magazines including *House and Garden*, British and French *Vogue*, and *Glamour*. Nearly ruined in the Depression, he spent his last years struggling to regain his early prosperity.

Nast, Thomas (1840–1902) Cartoonist, born in Landau, Germany. When he was five, his family migrated to the USA, where he studied at the Academy of Design in New York City. He became a draftsman for *Frank Leslie's Illustrated Newspaper* at 15, and in 1861 was engaged by *Harper's Weekly* (1861–6), where he defined the genre of the political cartoon. His crusade against the corrupt New York political machine known as the Tweed Ring in 1871 resulted in the removal from office of virtually every member of Tammany Hall. He also created such cartoon icons as the Republican elephant, the Democratic donkey, and helped form the American notion of Santa Claus.

Nathan, Isaac [**nay**than] (1790–1864) Composer and music teacher, born in Canterbury, Kent, SE England, UK. Musical librarian to King George IV, he was a friend of the poet Byron, whose *Hebrew Melodies* (1815) Nathan set to

music inspired by Jewish chants. He moved to Australia in 1841, where he became choirmaster of St Mary's Cathedral, Sydney. He published *Australia the Wide and Free* (1842), as well as the first opera to be composed and performed in Australia, *Don John of Austria* (1847). He also composed a dramatic scena, *Leichhardt's Grave*, and in 1849 published *The Southern Euphrosyne*, which included the first harmonizations of aboriginal music. >> Byron, George

Nathanael [na**than**ial], (Heb 'God has given') (fl. 1st-c) New Testament character, who appears only in *John* (1.45–51 and 21.2). He is said to have been brought to Jesus by Philip, and is one of the first to confess Jesus as 'Son of God, King of Israel'. He does not appear by this name in any list of disciples in the synoptic Gospels, however; possibly he was not one of the 12 or even a historical individual at all, despite some attempts to identify him with Bartholomew or Matthew in the synoptic lists of the 12 disciples. >> Jesus Christ; Philip, St

Nathans, Daniel [**nay**thanz] (1928–) Microbiologist, born in Wilmington, DE. He studied at the University of Delaware and at Washington University, St Louis, and became professor at Johns Hopkins University from 1962. He pioneered research on the use of restriction enzymes which had been isolated by Hamilton Smith to fragment DNA molecules, and they shared the 1978 Nobel Prize for Physiology or Medicine. >> Smith, Hamilton

Nation, Carry (Amelia), *née* **Moore** (1846–1911) Temperance agitator, born in Garrard Co, KY. Trained as a teacher, she entered the temperance movement in 1890. A large, powerful woman of volcanic emotions, she went on hymn-singing, saloon-smashing expeditions with a hatchet in many US cities, attacking what she considered to be illegal drinking places. Frequently imprisoned and fined for breach of the peace, she would sell her hatchets as souvenirs to raise money.

Natta, Giulio (1903–79) Chemist, born in Imperia, Italy. Professor at Pavia, Rome, and Turin, from 1939 he held the chair of industrial chemistry at the Milan Institute of Technology. Making use of catalysts developed by Karl Ziegler, he carried out research on polymers which led to important commercial developments in plastics and other industrial chemicals. He and Ziegler shared the Nobel Prize for Chemistry in 1963. >> Ziegler

Nattier, Jean Marc [na**tyay**] (1685–1766) Artist, born in Paris. He executed historical pictures and portraits, including those of Peter the Great and Empress Catherine II of Russia, but after losing his money in the John Law financial crisis (the 'Mississippi bubble') he took up the fashionable stereotyped style of court portraiture now labelled *le portrait Nattier* for the court of Louis XV.

Naughtie, (Alexander) James [**nokh**tee] (1951–) Journalist and broadcaster, born in Scotland. He studied at Aberdeen University and Syracuse University, NY, then worked on various British newspapers, including *The Scotsman* (1977–84) and *The Guardian* (1984–8). He then became presenter of the BBC's *The World At One* (1988–94), and joined the team of *Today* in 1994. He has also presented several documentary series, such as *A Nearby Country* (1991) and *The Thin Blue Line* (1993), and was Sony Radio Awards Personality of the Year in 1991.

Nauman, Bruce (1941–) Sculptor, born in Fort Wayne, IN. He studied mathematics and art at Wisconsin University. In the 1960s he became a leading exponent of Conceptual Art, using neon lights and holograms in addition to producing minimalist sculptures from more conventional materials. Since 1970 he has worked chiefly with fibreglass and wood, exploring the relationship between sculpture and the gallery space.

Navier, Claude (Louis Marie Henri) [na**vyay**] (1785–

1836) Civil engineer, born in Dijon, France. He studied at the Ecole Polytechnique and the Ecole des Ponts et Chaussées, and for much of his life taught at one or other of these schools, being principally occupied in developing the theoretical basis of structural mechanics and the strength of materials, as well as the work done by machines. He is mostly remembered for the *Navier–Stokes equation* (with George Stokes) describing the mechanics of a viscous fluid, relating changes in the velocity of the fluid to the pressure and viscous forces acting on it. >> Stokes

Navratilova, Martina [navratilohva] (1956–) Tennis player, born in Prague. For three years she played for Czechoslovakia in the Federation Cup, but in 1975 defected to the USA and turned professional, becoming a US citizen in 1981. Her rivalry with Chris Evert was one of the great features of the game from 1975. The winner of a record nine singles titles at Wimbledon (1978–9, 1982–7, 1990), she won 167 singles titles (including 18 Grand Slam events) and 165 doubles titles with her partner Pam Shriver (including 37 Grand Slam events), becoming the most prolific winner in women's tennis. In 1994 she retired from competitive singles tennis. She has become known as a spokeswoman on several social issues, notably gay rights, animal rights, and ecology, as well as on issues to do with the status of women and young players in tennis. >> RR1173

Naylor, Eliot >> **Frankau, Pamela**
Nazianzus, Gregory of >> **Gregory of Nazianzus**
Nazimova, Alla [nazimohva], originally **Alla Leventon** (1879–1945) Actress, born in Yalta, Ukraine. She studied in Moscow under Stanislavsky, and made her debut with the Paul Orleneff Company in St Petersburg in 1904, with whom she visited the USA. Such was the impression she made that she was asked to learn English to appear in New York City as Hedda Gabler in 1905. In 1910 she rechristened the 39th Street Theatre 'The Nazimova', and became a highly popular dramatic actress, specializing in the plays of Ibsen, Turgenev, Chekhov, and O'Neill. She also had a successful period in films, which included *Camille, A Doll's House*, and her own *Salomé*, based on the Beardsley illustrations to Wilde's play. >> Beardsley; Stanislavsky; Wilde, Oscar

Nazor, Vladimir [nasaw(r)] (1876–1949) Croatian poet, born in Postire on the island of Brač. He wrote lyrics, ballads, epic poems, and dramatic works in a style similar to the Symbolists. His works include *Slav Legends* (1900), *Lirika* (1910), *Carmen Vitae*, an anthology (1922), and a diary of his experiences with the Yugoslav partisans in World War 2.

Nazrul Islam, Kazi >> **Islam, Kazi Nazrul**
Neagle, Dame Anna, originally **Marjorie Robertson** (1904–86) Actress, born in London, England, UK. She studied dance as a child, and was a chorus girl before graduating to leading roles and making her film debut in 1930. Under the tutelage of director **Herbert Wilcox** (1892–1977), who became her husband in 1943, she emerged as a major star of historical film dramas such as *Victoria, the Great* (1937), *Odette* (1950), and *The Lady With the Lamp* (1951). A series of musicals opposite Michael Wilding made her Britain's top box-office attraction, but she retired from the screen in 1958. She retained the affection of British audiences with appearances in such theatrical candyfloss as *Charlie Girl* (1965–71), *No, No, Nanette* (1973), and *My Fair Lady* (1978–9). She was created a dame in 1969.

Neale, John Mason (1818–66) Hymnologist, born in London, England, UK. He studied at Cambridge, and became warden of Sackville College, East Grinstead. An advanced High Churchman, he wrote many books on Church history, but is remembered chiefly for his hymns, and many of his translations are cherished worldwide. Among his best-

known pieces are 'Jerusalem the golden' and 'O happy band of pilgrims'. >> Bernard of Morval

Nearchus [neeah(r)kus] (4th-c BC) Macedonian general, originally from Crete. He settled in Amphipolis during the reign of Philip II of Macedon, and became the companion of the young Alexander the Great. In 330 BC he became Governor of Lycia, and in 329 joined Alexander in Bactria with a body of Greek mercenaries, and took part in the Indian campaigns. Having built a fleet on the Hydaspes (Jhelum), Alexander gave Nearchus the command. He left the Indus in November 325, and, skirting the coast, reached Susa in February 324. His narrative is preserved in the *Indica* of Arrian. >> Alexander the Great; Arrian

Nebuchadnezzar II [nebookadnezer], also spelled **Nebuchadrezzar** (c. 630–562 BC) King of Babylon (605–562 BC). He succeeded his father Nabopolassar, and during his 43-year reign recovered the long-lost provinces of the kingdom, once more making Babylon a supreme nation. He not only restored the empire and rebuilt Babylon, but almost every temple throughout the land underwent restoration at his hands. Every mound opened by explorers has contained bricks, cylinders, or tablets inscribed with his name. In 597 he captured Jerusalem, and in 586 destroyed the city, removing most of the inhabitants to Chaldea. >> RR1034

Necker, Jacques (1732–1804) Statesman and financier, born in Geneva, Switzerland. Initially a banker's clerk, he moved to Paris (1762), founded a bank, and became a wealthy speculator. In 1776–7 he was director of the French Treasury and director-general of finances. He attempted some administrative reforms, but tried to finance French involvement in the War of American Independence by heavy borrowing, while concealing the large state deficit. He was dismissed in 1781, but recalled in 1788 to deal with the impending financial crisis. He summoned the States General, but his proposals for social and constitutional change aroused royal opposition, and he was dismissed. His dismissal helped to provoke the public disorder that ended in the storming of the Bastille, and he was hastily recalled in 1789, but resigned the following year.

Nedreaas, Torborg [nedrias] (1906–) Novelist, born in Bergen, Norway. She turned to writing late in life, after World War 2. A left-wing feminist, her books highlight social life and class struggle in Norwegian urban society. Especially powerful are (trans titles) *Music from a Blue Well* (1960) and *At the Next New Moon* (1971).

Needham, Joseph [needam] (1900–95) Historian of science, born in London, England, UK. He studied at Cambridge, where he taught (1924–66), becoming Master of Gonville and Caius College (1966–76) and director of the Needham Research Institute (1976–90). He trained as a biochemist, and published a pioneering *History of Embryology* (1934) before developing a consuming interest in the Chinese tradition of science, technology, and medicine. His major work is the multi-volume series *Science and Civilisation in China* (from 1956).

Néel, Louis Eugène Félix [nayel] (1904–) Physicist, born in Lyon, France. A graduate of the Ecole Normale Supérieure, he was professor of physics at Strasbourg University (1937–40). In 1940 he moved to Grenoble and became director of the Centre for Nuclear Studies there in 1956. His research was concerned with magnetism in solids, which led to the development of the 'memories' in computers. He has also studied the past history of the Earth's magnetic field. He shared the Nobel Prize for Physics in 1970. >> RR1122

Ne'eman, Yuval (1925–) Physicist and politician, born in Tel Aviv, Israel. Active against the British in Palestine (1946–7), he became a captain in the Israeli Defence Force

(1947), deputy director of defence intelligence (1955–7), and defence attaché in London (1958–60). He was professor of physics at Tel Aviv (1965–73), then at the University of Texas, Austin, and in 1979 director of the Sackler Institute of Advanced Studies. He became a member of the Knesset in 1981, and has held ministerial posts in the areas of science and development. In physics he has worked on the role of symmetry in particle physics, and co-authored the influential book *The Eight-Fold Way* with Murray Gell-Mann.

Neer, Aernout or **Aert van der** (1603 /4–77) Painter, born in Amsterdam. He specialized in moonlit canal and river scenes. Although his paintings are now regarded as major works of the Dutch school, he received little recognition in his own time. In 1658 he gave up painting in order to open a wineshop. He was no more successful in this venture, and returned to painting in 1662 after being declared bankrupt. Two of his sons became artists: **Eglon** (1634–1703) and **Jan** (1638–65).

Neeson, Liam (1952–) Film actor, born in Ballymena, Northern Ireland. He performed with the Abbey Theatre, Dublin, and the Lyric Players Theatre, Belfast, making his film debut in *Excalibur* (1981). He received an Oscar nomination for his role as Schindler in *Schindler's List* (1993), and went on to play the title roles in *Rob Roy* (1995) and *Michael Collins* (1996).

Nefertiti [neferteetee] (14th-c BC) Egyptian queen, the consort of Akhenaton, by whom she had six children, and whose new religious cult of the Sun god Aton she supported. She is immortalized in the beautiful sculptured head found at Amarna in 1912, now in the Berlin Museum. Little is known of her background, but she is believed to have been an Asian princess from Mitanni. >> Akhenaton

Negus, Arthur (George) [nayguhs] (1903–85) Broadcaster and antiques expert, born in Reading, Berkshire, S England, UK. He took over the family antiques business in 1920, and in 1946 joined the Gloucester firm of fine art auctioneers, Bruton, Knowles & Co, becoming a partner in 1972. Asked to expound on the merits and value of antiques for television, he became a regular panel member on the series *Going for a Song* (1966–76). His avuncular manner, wry humour, and expertise made him a popular broadcaster in such series as *Arthur Negus Enjoys* (1982) and *The Antiques Roadshow* (1982–3). His books include *Going for a Song: English Furniture* (1969) and *A Life Among Antiques* (1982).

Nehemiah [nehemiya] (5th-c BC) Old Testament prophet. He was cupbearer to Artaxerxes Longimanus, who in 444 BC gave him full powers to act as Governor of Judaea. He had the walls of Jerusalem rebuilt, and repopulated the city by drafts from the surrounding districts. In 432 he revisited Jerusalem, and carried out reforms which came to be among the most characteristic features of post-exilic Judaism. The canonical book of Nehemiah originally formed the closing chapters of the undivided work, Chronicles–Ezra–Nehemiah. >> Artaxerxes I

Nehru, Jawaharlal [nairoo], known as **Pandit** ('Teacher') **Nehru** (1889–1964) Indian statesman and prime minister (1947–64), born in Allahabad, India, the son of Motilal Nehru. He studied at Cambridge, became a lawyer, and served in the Allahabad High Court. He joined the Indian Congress Committee (1918), was influenced by Gandhi, and was imprisoned several times by the British. In 1929 he was elected president of the Indian National Congress. He became India's first prime minister and minister of external affairs (1947), and followed a policy of neutrality during the Cold War. He introduced a policy of industrialization, reorganized the states on a linguistic basis, and brought the dispute with Pakistan over Kashmir to a peaceful solution. >> Gandhi, Indira; Gandhi, Mahatma; Pandit; RR1058

Nehru, Motilal [nairoo] (1861–1931) Nationalist leader of India, lawyer, and journalist, born in Delhi, the father of Jawaharlal Nehru. He became a follower of Mahatma Gandhi in 1919, founded the *Independent* of Allahabad, and became the first president of the reconstructed Indian National Congress. >> Gandhi; Nehru, Jawaharlal

Neill, A(lexander) S(utherland) (1883–1973) Educationist and writer, born in Kingsmuir, Fife, E Scotland, UK. He studied at Edinburgh, taught in many different schools, and was editor of *New Era* (1920–1). He started a community school near Salzburg, which eventually settled as Summerhill School in Leiston, Suffolk (1927), a co-educational progressive school that 'began as an experiment and became a demonstration'. Summerhill became a school for children, especially Americans, from higher income groups. Many pupils were 'difficult' and Neill spent a lot of time in psychotherapy, at first called 'private lessons'. He was the most extreme and radical of British progressive schoolmasters and a great publicist, publishing over 20 books, from *A Dominie's Log* (1916) to *Neill! Neill! Orange Peel!* (1973).

Neill, Sam, originally **Nigel Neill** (1948–) Actor, born in Northern Ireland. He moved to New Zealand with his family at the age of seven, and studied at the University of Canterbury. He joined the New Zealand National Film Unit as an actor and director, and moved to Australia in the 1970s, starring in films such as *My Brilliant Career* (1979). Since then he has featured in many Australian and international films, including *Evil Angels* (1988, also known as *A Cry in the Dark*), *The Hunt for Red October* (1990), *Until the End of the World* (1991), Jane Campion's *The Piano* (1993), and *Children of the Revolution* (1997).

Neilson, Donald, originally **Donald Nappey** (1936–) Convicted murderer and kidnapper, born near Bradford, West Yorkshire, N England, UK. He was convicted of four murders, three of which occurred in 1974 when the victims interrupted him as he was robbing their houses. Because of the black hood he wore as a disguise, he became known as 'the Black Panther'. Three murders were followed by a kidnapping. Seventeen-year-old Lesley Whittle was taken from her home in January 1974, and a ransom demand of £50 000 was accompanied by a death-threat. Lesley's body was found at the bottom of a ventilation shaft two months later. Neilson evaded the police until late 1975, when a security guard he had shot and wounded was able to provide a description. He received life-sentences for the murders and 21 years for kidnapping.

Neilson, James Beaumont >> **Mushet, David**

Neiman, LeRoy [neeman, leeroy] (1927–) Illustrator, born in St. Paul, MN. He studied at the Art Institute of Chicago (1946–50) and the University of Illinois (1951). Based in New York City, he specialized as a sports artist, and in 1972 was named the official artist for the Olympic Games. He was given the Olympic Artist of the Century Award in 1979.

Neisser, Ulric (Richard Gustav) [niyser] (1928–) Psychologist, born in Kiel, Germany. He studied at Harvard, then taught at Brandeis, Cornell, and Emory universities. The modern growth of cognitive psychology received a major boost from the publication in 1967 of the first (and most influential) of his books, *Cognitive Psychology*. In his later writings he became critical of the methodology of much cognitive psychology, faulting it for being 'ecologically invalid'.

Nelson, (John) Byron, Jr (1912–) Golfer, born in Fort Worth, TX. He won a record 18 tournaments on the US Professional Golfers Association (PGA) tour in 1945, 11 of them successive, and also won the US Open (1939), the US PGA Championship (1940, 1945), and the US Masters (1937, 1942) – a total of 54 US Tour events. He captained the 1965 US Ryder Cup team at Birkdale, and became a notable golf teacher and broadcaster after he retired from tournament play. >> RR1158

Nelson, George (1907–86) Designer, architect, and writer, born in Hartford, CT. After graduating in architecture he travelled in Europe during the early 1930s, familiarizing himself with the work of the 'Modern Movement'. Its influ-ence is evident in his design work, the best known being his range of wall storage furniture (1946) for the manufacturer Herman Miller, whose design policy he directed. He was editor of *Architectural Forum* (1935–44), and wrote widely on design and architectural subjects.

Nelson, Horatio see panel below

HORATIO NELSON (1758–1805)

Nelson was born at the Rectory of Burnham Thorpe, Norfolk, E England, UK, the son of the village rector Edmund Nelson and his wife Catherine. He attended schools at Norwich and North Walsham before entering the Royal Navy at Chatham in 1770. Under the patronage of an uncle, Captain Maurice Suckling, his naval experience widened rapidly; first by his attachment to a Caribbean-bound merchant ship, and in 1773 by an arduous expedition to the Arctic. A voyage to India followed, but he had to be invalided home after a near fatal malarial fever which left him with recurrent partial paralysis for the rest of his life, in addition to his incurable sea-sickness.

In 1779 at the age of 20, he became captain of a frigate ship in the West Indies, and during the American War served under Admiral Robert Digby and later Lord Samuel Hood. In 1784 he returned to the West Indies to enforce the Navigation Acts prohibiting direct trade between the new American States and the remaining British colonies. His rigid and direct enforcement of the law soon brought him into conflict with the traders, his commander-in-chief, and the Governor of the Leeward Is. However, their attempts to have Nelson removed or court-martialled rebounded on them following his successful petitions to the Admiralty and King George III.

While on the island of Nevis, Nelson met and, in 1787, married **Frances (Fanny) Nisbet** (1761–1831), a widow with a son, Josiah. Returning to England, he found himself out of favour both with the Admiralty, which was embarrassed by his zealous execution of duty in the West Indies, and with George III for associating with his disreputable son, Prince William Henry. He was refused another ship, but five years later was recalled at the outbreak of the Revolutionary Wars (1792–1802) with France. In 1794 he was given the task of securing Corsica as a Mediterranean base for the Royal Navy. While in Naples gathering recruits, he met William Harrison who, in his capacity as British minister, helped Nelson. The campaign was a major success but, during the attack on Calvi, he was blinded in the right eye by stone splinters from a parapet struck by an enemy shell. Despite his injury, he returned to duty the following day.

On leaving the Mediterranean, the British fleet encountered a Spanish fleet off Cape St Vincent, and inflicted a decisive defeat (1797). Much of the credit for the success of the heavily outgunned British fleet was due to Nelson's bold and unorthodox tactics, for which he recieved a knighthood. Later promoted to rear-admiral, he held the blockade of Cadiz before being detached to Santa Cruz in the Canary Is. His ill-founded mission to capture rumoured Spanish treasure ships failed when all element of surprise was lost. His right arm was shattered by grapeshot, and had to be amputated.

In 1798 he was sent on a reconnaisance mission to locate the French fleet. It was eventually found in Abu Qir (Aboukir) Bay near Alexandria, where he executed a daring attack as night fell. The British fleet inflicted a massive defeat (the Battle of the Nile), leaving Napoleon's army stranded in Egypt. Nelson, who had again been wounded, returned to Naples, there to be nursed by Emma, the wife of Sir William Hamilton. He was raised to the peerage as Baron Nelson of the Nile, and appointed principal military adviser to the Court of Ferdinand IV, King of the Two Sicilies. This period was marked by controversy. His advice to send an army to recapture Rome from the French resulted in a humiliating defeat, while his public affair with Lady Hamilton exposed him to criticism. In 1800 he relinquished his command because of ill health, and escorted the Hamiltons overland to England.

Following his return, estrangement from his wife soon resulted in separation. With Emma pregnant with their daughter Horatia, and faced with difficult financial circumstances, he applied for active service. In 1801 he was promoted to vice-admiral and appointed second-in-command to Admiral Sir Hyde Parker in an expedition to break the 'armed neutrality' of the Baltic States. The fleet sailed for Denmark and, despite the irresolute Parker, engaged the Danish fleet at anchor off Copenhagen. During the course of battle, which inflicted heavy losses on both sides, Nelson ignored Parker's signal to disengage from the fighting by putting his telescope up to his blind eye and claiming that he had seen no such signal. An hour later the battle was won. He was appointed commander-in-chief of the fleet following Parker's recall, and elevated to viscount.

Renewed hostilities with France saw his return to active service as commander-in-chief of the Mediterranean fleet on board the flagship HMS *Victory*. In this capacity, his questionable tactics in enforcing a loose blockade of the French-held ports, encouraging the enemy to leave the port and fight, allowed a French fleet under Admiral Villeneuve to escape from Toulon (Jan 1805). A futile chase ensued across the Atlantic to the West Indies and back. This was part of Napoleon's plan to decoy the Royal Navy from the Channel in order to allow him to invade England unmolested. However, Napoleon's combined Spanish and French fleet sweeping through the channel to cover for the invasion was devastated by Nelson's eventual engagement of Villeneuve's fleet off Cape Trafalgar (21 Oct 1805).

At the height of the battle, and with victory in sight, Nelson was mortally wounded as he paced the quarter-deck with Captain Hardy; he died some three hours later as the battle ended, and his body was brought back to England. He was buried in St Paul's Cathedral, and a column erected to his memory in Trafalgar Square. Despite the adulation he received after his death, Emma was ignored, and died in abject poverty in Calais nine years later. Horatia, however, returned to Norfolk, and married a clergyman.

>> Hamilton, Emma; Hardy, Thomas Masterman; Hood, Samuel; Napoleon; Villeneuve

---

Nelson, Thomas (1780–1861) Publisher, born in Edinburgh, EC Scotland, UK. He established his publishing company in 1798. His son **William** (1816–87) entered the business in 1835, and did much to improve the city of Edinburgh, including the restoration of Parliament House. Another son, **Thomas** (1822–92), is credited with the invention of a rotary press (1850), and established an office in London (1844). Specializing in tracts, educational books, and affordable reprints, the company's authors included John Buchan.

Nelson, Willie Country singer, songwriter, and guitarist, born in Abbott, TX. After writing and recording many country-music hits in the 1960s, he gained a wider audience in the 1970s with such albums as *Shotgun Willie* (1972) and *Stardust* (1978). Success continued in the 1980s through further collaborations with Waylon Jennings, Merle Haggard, and other country stars, and albums like *Always on my Mind* prospering in the pop music market.

Nemerov, Howard (Stanley) [**ne**merof] (1920–91) Poet, born in New York City. He studied at Harvard, then taught at several institutions, including Bennington (1948–66) and Washington University, St. Louis (from 1967). He was named consultant in poetry (1963–4) and poet laureate by the Library of Congress (1988), and is known for his literary prose works and blank verse, as in *Collected Poems* (1977). *Trying Conclusions: New and Selected Poems 1961–91* appeared in 1991.

Nemirovich-Danchenko, Vladimir (Ivanovich) [**ne**mirohvich dan**cheng**koh] (1858–1943) Theatre director, writer, and teacher, born in Ozurgety, Russia. Co-founder with Stanislavsky of the Moscow Art Theatre, he became sole director following the latter's death in 1938. Among his most notable productions were *The Brothers Karamazov* (1910) and *Nikolai Stavrogin* (1913). After 1919, his interest in opera led to some of his most original work as a director. >> Stanislavsky

Nenni, Pietro [**ne**nee] (1891–1980) Italian statesman, born in Faenza, Italy. An agitator at 17, as editor of *Avanti* he was exiled by the Fascists (1926). He became secretary-general of the Italian Socialist Party (1944), vice-premier in the Gasperi coalition cabinet (1945–6), and foreign minister (1946–7). His pro-Soviet party did not break finally with the Communists till 1956. In 1963 Nenni became deputy prime minister in the coalition government, including Social Democrats and Socialists. He succeeded in his long-standing aim of uniting the two groups as the United Socialist Party (1966), but in the 1968 elections the Socialists withdrew from the coalition. He was foreign minister in a new coalition from December 1968, but resigned in July 1969. >> Gasperi

Nennius (fl. 769) Writer, from Wales, reputedly the author of the early Latin compilation known as the *Historia Britonum*, an account of British history from the time of Julius Caesar to towards the end of the 7th-c. The book gives a mythical version of the origins of the Britons, and recounts the Roman occupation, the settlement of the Saxons, and King Arthur's 12 victories. Although it contains material of doubtful historical significance, its real value lies in its preservation of material needed for the study of early Celtic literature in general, and the Arthurian legend in particular.

Neot, St [**nee**ot] (?–877) Anglo-Saxon monk. According to mediaeval legends, he was a monk of Glastonbury who became a hermit in Cornwall, and is said to have been visited by Alfred the Great. His relics are thought to have been taken to St Neots in Cambridgeshire. Feast day 31 July. >> Alfred

Nepomuk, St John of >> **John of Nepomuk, St**

Nepos, Cornelius [**nee**pos] (c. 99–25 BC) Roman historian, a native of Pavia or Hostilia. He wrote a lost universal history in three books (*Chronica*), and a series of *Lives of Famous Men* (*De viris illustribus*), of which only 25 (mainly Greek warriors and statesmen) survive – untrustworthy, but written in a clear and elegant style. He also wrote love poems and a book of anecdotes (*Exempla*), and lives of the elder Cato, Atticus, and Thrasybulus.

Neri, St Philip [**nair**ee] (1515–95) Mystic, born in Florence, Italy, the founder of the Oratory. He went to Rome at the age of 18, and for many years spent most of his time in works of charity and instruction, and in solitary prayer. In 1551 he became a priest, and gathered around him a following of disciples which became the Congregation of the Oratory (1564), and later received the approbation of the pope. The community was finally established at Vallicella, where he built a new church (Chiesa Nuova) on the site of Santa Maria. He was canonized in 1622; feast day 26 May.

Nernst, Walther Hermann (1864–1941) Physical chemist, born in Briesen, Germany. He was professor of chemistry in Göttingen (1891), Berlin (1905), and director of the Berlin Physical Institute in 1925. He proposed the heat theorem (the third law of thermodynamics) in 1906, investigated the specific heat of solids at low temperature in connection with quantum theory, and also proposed the atom chain-reaction theory in photochemistry. He was awarded the Nobel Prize for Chemistry in 1920.

Nero [**nee**roh], in full **Nero Claudius Caesar**, originally **Lucius Domitius Ahenobarbus** (37–68) Emperor of Rome (54–68), the son of Gnaeus Domitius Ahenobarbus and the younger Agrippina, daughter of Germanicus. He owed his name and position to the driving ambition of his mother, who engineered his adoption by the Emperor Claudius, her fourth husband. Initially his reign was good, thanks to his three main advisers: his mother, the philosopher Seneca, and the Praetorian Prefect Burrus. But after her murder (59), and their fall from favour, Nero, more interested in sex, singing, acting, and chariot-racing than government, neglected affairs of state, and corruption set in. He was blamed for the Great Fire of Rome (64), despite assiduous attempts to make scapegoats of the Christians. A major plot to overthrow him (the Conspiracy of Piso) was formed (65) but detected, and Rome had to endure three more years of tyranny before he was toppled from power by the army, and forced to commit suicide. >> Agrippina (the Younger); Claudius; Galba; Otho; Seneca; RR1084

Neruda, Pablo (Neftali Reyes) [ne**roo**tha] (1904–73) Poet, born in Parral, Chile. He studied at Santiago, and made his name with *Veinte poemas de amor y una canción desesperada* (1924, Twenty Love Poems and a Song of Despair). From 1927 he held diplomatic posts in various East Asian and European countries. Returning to Chile (1943), he joined the Communist Party, and was elected to the Senate (1945). He travelled in Russia and China (1948–52), and was later the Chilean ambassador in Paris (1970–2). His other works include *Residencia en la tierra* (1925–31, Residence on Earth) and *Canto general* (1950, General Song). He was awarded the Nobel Prize for Literature in 1971.

Nerva, Marcus Cocceius [**nair**va] (c. 32–98) Emperor of Rome (96–98), elected by the Senate after the assassination of Domitianus. One of the 'five good emperors', he rejected terrorism and introduced liberal reforms, but lacked military support, and had to adopt Trajan as his successor. >> Trajan; RR1084

Nervi, Pier Luigi [**nair**vee] (1891–1979) Architect and engineer, born in Sondrio, Italy. After graduating as an engineer, he set up as a building contractor. His many works include the Berta Stadium in Florence (1930–2) and a complex of exhibition halls in Turin (1948–50). He achieved an international reputation with his designs for the two

Olympic stadia in Rome (1960), in which bold and imaginative use is made of concrete for roofing in the large areas. He also designed San Francisco cathedral (1970). He was professor at Rome from 1947 to 1961.

Nesbit, E(dith), maiden name and pseudonym of **Mrs Hubert Bland** (1858–1924) Writer, born in London, England, UK. She was educated at a French convent, and began her literary career by writing poetry, having met the Rossettis and their friends. She is best remembered for her children's stories, which reacted against the moralizing then prevalent. They include *The Story of the Treasure Seekers* (1899), *The Would-be-Goods* (1901), and *The Railway Children* (1906, filmed 1970). She also wrote novels and ghost stories. >> Rossetti, Gabriele

Nesmith, Mike >> **Monkees, The**

Nesselrode, Karl (Robert) Vasilyevich, Graf (Count) [neselr**oh**duh] (1780–1862) Russian statesman, born in Lisbon, the son of the Russian ambassador. He represented Russia at the Congress of Vienna (1814–15), and was one of the most active diplomats of the Holy Alliance. He became foreign minister (1822), and dominated Russian foreign policy for 30 years. His Balkan policy of trying to curb France's influence over the Ottoman empire contributed to the outbreak of the Crimean War (1853).

Nestorius [ne**staw**rius] (?–c. 451) Ecclesiastic, a native of Germanicia in N Syria. As a priest he became so eminent for his zeal, ascetic life, and eloquence that he was selected as patriarch of Constantinople (428). When the presbyter Anastasius denied that the Virgin Mary could be truly called the Mother of God, Nestorius warmly defended him, and so emphasized the distinction of the divine and human natures that antagonists accused him of holding that there were two persons in Christ. A controversy ensued, and at a general council in Ephesus in 431 he was deposed. He was confined in a monastery, then banished. >> Theodore of Mopsuestia

Netaji >> **Bose, Subhas Chandra**

Netanyahu, Benjamin [netany**a**hoo], nicknamed in Israel **Bibi** (1949–) Israeli politician and prime minister (1996–), born in Tel Aviv, Israel. His family moved to the USA when he was a child, and he was educated at Harvard and MIT. He joined the Israeli embassy in Washington, became Israel's ambassador to the UN, and was elected to the Israeli parliament in 1988, becoming leader of the Likud Party in 1993. A hard-liner on security issues, he campaigned on a platform of peace with security, and defeated Shimon Peres by a narrow margin in the 1996 elections. >> Peres

Neumann, St John (Nepomucene) [**noy**man] (1811–60) Catholic prelate and saint, born in Prachatice, Czech Republic (formerly Bohemia). After seminary studies he emigrated, virtually penniless, to New York City, where he was accepted for ordination in 1836. Following pastoral work in the Buffalo region, he took vows as a Redemptorist (1842), served in Baltimore and Pittsburgh, and was a Redemptorist vice-provincial (1847–51). As Bishop of Philadelphia (from 1852), he was well known as a preacher, retreat master, and champion of the poor. Admired for sanctity in his lifetime, he was beatified in 1963 and canonized in 1977; feast day 5 January.

Neumann, (Johann) Balthasar [**noy**man] (1687–1753) Architect, born in Eger, Germany. He was at first a military engineer in the service of the Archbishop of Würzburg, but after visiting Paris and absorbing new ideas, he became professor of architecture at Würzburg. Many outstanding examples of the Baroque style were designed by him, notably the Würzburg Palace and Schloss Bruchsal.

Neumann, John Von >> **Von Neumann, John**

Neumeier, John [**noy**mayer] (1942–) Ballet dancer, chor-

eographer, and artistic director, born in Milwaukee, WI. A choreographer with a large European following and a strong attachment to Germany, he danced with Stuttgart Ballet (1963–9) before assuming leadership of Frankfurt Ballet (1969–73) and Hamburg Ballet (since 1973). He is known for the acrobatically expressive contemporary ballets which match the grand themes and important composers he favours in his work.

Neurath, Konstantin, Freiherr von (Baron) [**noy**raht] (1873–1956) German statesman, born in Klein-Glattbach, Germany. After consular service, he joined the German Embassy in Istanbul, and became ambassador to Italy (1921) and to Britain (1930). He was Hitler's foreign minister (1933–8), and the Reich protector of the Czech territories of Bohemia and Moravia (1939–43). At the Nuremberg trial he was sentenced to 15 years' imprisonment for war crimes, but released in 1954. >> Hitler

Neurath, Otto [**noy**raht] (1882–1945) Philosopher and social theorist, born in Vienna. A member of the influential 'Vienna Circle', he was particularly associated with 'physicalism', which aimed to establish an entirely materialist foundation of knowledge. His best philosophical work was published in the group's journal *Erkenntnis*, but he also wrote books on sociology, education, and social policy, including *International Picture Language* (1936) and *Modern Man in the Making* (1939). Active in public affairs as an independent Marxist, he was an energetic organizer, and was involved with such diverse bodies as the Carnegie Endowment for International Peace (1911–13), and the International Unity of Science movement (1934–40). >> Carnap; Popper; Schlick; von Wright

Nevelson, Louise, *née* **Berliawsky** (1899–1988) Sculptor and printmaker, born in Kiev. Her family settled in Portland, ME, in 1905. She studied at the Art Students' League in New York City (1929–33) and with the influential theorist Hans Hofmann in Munich. In 1932 she worked as an assistant to the Mexican mural-painter Diego Rivera. She is best known for her 'environmental' sculptures – abstract, wooden, box-like shapes stacked up to form walls and painted white or gold. In 1966 she began to use 'plexiglas' and aluminium. >> Hofmann, Hans; Rivera, Diego

Neville, Richard >> **Warwick, Richard Neville, Earl of**

Nevinson, Christopher (Richard Wynne) (1889–1946) Artist, born in London, England, UK. He studied at the Slade School of Art, London, and became a leader of the pre-1914 avant garde, joining Emilio Marinetti as co-signatory of the Futurist Manifesto, published in England in 1914. He volunteered for the Red Cross and was discharged in 1916, but returned the following year as an artist attached to the Bureau of Information. Many of his most famous works reflect his experiences at the front. After the war he moved away from Futurism to paint, in a poetic manner, New York, Paris, and the English landscape. >> Marinetti

Newbery, John (1713–67) Publisher and bookseller, born in Berkshire, S England, UK. He settled in London in c.1744 as a seller of books and patent medicines. He was the first to publish books specifically for children, and was part-author of some of the best of them, notably *Goody Two-Shoes*. In 1758 he started the *Universal Chronicle*, or *Weekly Gazette*, in which the 'Idler' appeared. In the *Public Ledger* (1760) appeared Goldsmith's 'Citizen of the World'. Since 1922 the Newbery Medal has been awarded annually for the best American children's book.

Newbigin, James Edward Lesslie [**nyoo**bigin] (1909–) Missionary and theologian, born in Northumberland, NE England, UK. He went to Madras as a Church of Scotland missionary (1936) and spent most of the next 38 years in S India, being appointed Bishop of Madurai and Ramnad (1947–59) and Bishop of Madras (1965–74), in the Church of

S India. In his retirement he lectured at the Selly Oak Colleges, was appointed moderator of the United Reformed Church (1978–9), and became a parish minister in Birmingham. He wrote on the uniqueness of Christianity, and on Christian responses to secularism in modern Western culture.

Newbolt, Sir Henry (John) (1862–1938) Poet, born in Bilston, Staffordshire, C England, UK. He studied at Oxford, became a barrister, and published novels. He is best known, however, for his sea songs – *Admirals All* (1897), which contained 'Drake's Drum', *The Island Race* (1898), *Songs of the Sea*, and others. In World War 1 he was controller of telecommunications and an official war historian, and published *The Naval History of the Great War* (1920).

Newby, Eric (1919–) Travel writer, born in London, England, UK. He worked briefly in advertising, before joining a Finnish four-masted bark in 1938, an adventure described in *The Last Grain Race* (1956). In 1942 he was captured off Sicily while trying to rejoin the submarine from which he had landed to attack a German airfield. For some years he worked in the rag trade, which he eagerly left to take *A Short Walk in the Hindu Kush* (1958), and in 1963 he made a 1200-mi descent of the Ganges, described in *Slowly Down the Ganges* (1966). Later he became travel editor of *The Observer*. Other significant books are *Love and War in the Apennines* (1971), *The Big Red Train Ride* (1978), *Love and War in the Apennines* (1971), *What the Traveller Saw* (1989), and *A Merry Dance Around the World* (1995).

Newcastle, Duke of >> **Cavendish, William; Pelham, Thomas**

Newcomb, Simon [nyookuhm] (1835–1909) Astronomer and mathematician, born in Wallace, Nova Scotia, Canada. He moved to America in his teens and studied at the Lawrence Scientific School, Harvard. Appointed a professor of mathematics by the US navy in 1861, he was assigned to the Naval Observatory in Washington, DC, and later became professor at Johns Hopkins University (1884–94, 1898–1900). His major contribution was the calculation of all the known positions and motions of the bodies of the Solar System and the major celestial reference objects. He also did pioneer work in calculating the Sun's parallax and determining the velocity of light. He also published popular texts, such as *Reminiscences of an Astronomer* (1903), and three novels, and became the first president of the American Astronomical Society (1899–1905).

Newcombe, John (1944–) Tennis player, born in Sydney, New South Wales, Australia. He won Wimbledon in 1967, the last year of amateur competition, and went on to win again in 1970 and 1971. As part of an outstanding doubles team with Tony Roache, he won the Wimbledon doubles competition in 1965 and 1968–70. He was also the Australian singles champion in 1973 and 1975. Since retiring from the game, he has worked as a tennis coach and commentator. >> RR1173

Newcomen, Thomas [nyookuhmen] (1663–1729) Inventor, born in Dartmouth, Devon, SW England, UK. A blacksmith by trade, he developed a piston engine using steam at atmospheric pressure and the vacuum created when the steam was condensed to pump water from mines. In 1698 he began working with Thomas Savery, who had just patented a high pressure steam engine. Together they constructed practical working engines that were widely used in collieries. >> Savery

Newdigate, Sir Roger [nyoodigayt] (1719–1806) Antiquary, born in Arbury, Warwickshire, C England, UK. He was MP for Middlesex (1741–77) and Oxford University (1750–80). He built up a famous collection of antiquities, and endowed the *Newdigate Prize* for English verse at Oxford, winners of

which have included John Ruskin, Matthew Arnold, Laurence Binyon, and John Buchan.

Ne Win, U [nay win], also known as **Shu Maung** (1911–) Burmese politician and prime minister of Burma (1958–60, 1962–74). He studied at Rangoon University, and in World War 2 became chief-of-staff in the collaborationist army after the Japanese invasion of Burma, but joined the Allied forces later in the war. He held senior military and cabinet posts after Burma's independence (1948), before becoming caretaker prime minister (1958–60). In 1962, following a military coup, he ruled the country as chairman of the revolutionary council and became state president in 1974. In 1981, he dominated political affairs as chairman of the ruling Burma Socialist Programme Party, but was forced to step down in 1988. >> RR1076

Newlands, John (Alexander Reina) (1837–98) Chemist, born in London, England, UK. He worked in a sugar refinery at the Victoria Docks, London. He was the first to arrange the elements in order of atomic number and to see the connection between every eighth. This 'law of octaves' brought him ridicule at the time (1864), but it was the first idea of a periodic law, and in 1887 the Royal Society awarded him its Davy Medal in recognition of his work.

Newman, Barnett (1905–70) Painter, born in New York City. He studied at the Art Students' League in the 1920s, and later taught at the universities of Saskatchewan (1959) and Pennsylvania (1962–4). One of the Abstract Impressionists, he developed a simple, single-image style, and became a founder of the 'Subject of the Artist' school (1948). His series of 14 paintings, 'Stations of the Cross', was exhibited in New York City in 1966. >> Motherwell

Newman, Ernest (1868–1959) Music critic, born in Liverpool, Merseyside, NW England, UK. He was successively music critic of the *Manchester Guardian*, the *Birmingham Post*, and *The Sunday Times* (from 1920). His writings are noted for their wit and elegance, and for their strict factual accuracy. He is best known for his far-reaching studies of Wagner, notably his biography of Wagner (4 vols, 1933–7). >> Wagner, Richard

Newman, Francis William (1805–97) Scholar, born in London, England, UK. He studied at Oxford, and was elected to a fellowship at Balliol College. He went as an unsectarian missionary to Baghdad (1830–3), then returned to England and became classical tutor at Bristol College (1834), professor at Manchester New College (1840), and professor of Latin at University College, London (1846–69). In religion he took a position directly opposite that of his brother (John Henry Newman), being eager for a religion including whatever is best in all the historical religions. *Phases of Faith* (1853) is the best-known of his works. >> Newman, John Henry

Newman, John Henry, Cardinal (1801–90) Theologian, born in London, England, UK, into a Calvinist family. He studied at Oxford, became a fellow of Oriel College, and was ordained in 1824. He was a vigorous member of the Oxford Movement, composing a number of its tracts, notably Tract 90, which argued that the intention of the Thirty-nine Articles was Catholic in spirit. This led to the end of the Movement, and his own conversion to Catholicism (1845). He went to Rome, and joined the Oratorians, returning to set up his own community in Birmingham. He published several essays, lectures, and sermons, as well as a spiritual autobiography, *Apologia pro vita sua* (1864, Apology for His Life). A moderate in the controversies of the Vatican Council, he was made a cardinal in 1879. >> Keble; Newman, Francis William; Pusey; Tait, Archibald Campbell

Newman, Nanette (1939–) British actress and writer. She trained at the Italia Conti Stage School and the Royal

Academy of Dramatic Art, London, and appeared as a child in several films for the Children's Film Foundation. In 1959 she married Bryan Forbes, and has appeared in a number of his films, including *The L-Shaped Room* (1962), *The Raging Moon* (1971), and *The Stepford Wives* (1974). She was a frequent member of the panel on the television quiz shows *Call My Bluff* and *What's My Line*, and had her own series *The Fun Food Factory*. She has written many popular books, such as *God Bless Love* (1972, reprinted 16 times), *Fun Food Feasts* (1978), *Charlie the Noisy Caterpillar* (1989), and *There's a Bear in the Classroom* (1996). >> Forbes, Bryan

Newman, Paul (Leonard) (1925–) Film actor and director, born in Cleveland, OH. He turned to acting after a knee injury ended a promising sports career. Studying at the Yale School of Drama and the Actor's Studio in New York City, he made his film debut in 1954, and became one of the key stars of his generation, portraying idealistic rebels in such popular films as *Cool Hand Luke* (1967) and *Butch Cassidy and the Sundance Kid* (1969). He later pursued interests in motor-racing, politics, and food production, but returned as a powerful character actor and director of such sensitive works as *The Glass Menagerie* (1987). He has been nominated seven times for an Academy Award, receiving a special Oscar for his services to film in 1986, and winning a Best Actor Award for *The Color of Money* the same year. Later films include *Mr and Mrs Bridge* (1990) and *Nobody's Fool* (1995). He married the actress Joanne Woodward in 1958. >> Strasberg; Woodward, Joanne

Newman, Randy (1944–) Singer and songwriter, born in Los Angeles, CA. He established himself as a major songwriter, with something of a cult following, before his debut vocal album *Randy Newman* (1968). Later albums included *Sail Away* (1972) and *Little Criminals* (1978), and in 1979 he released one of the first digitally recorded albums, *Born Again*. He has also composed film scores, such as *Cold Turkey* (1970), *The Natural* (1984), and *Awakenings* (1990).

Newnes, Sir George (1851–1910) Publisher and politician, born in Matlock, Derbyshire, C England, UK. He was educated at Shireland Hall, Warwickshire, and the City of London School. He founded *Tit-Bits* (1881), the *Strand Magazine* (1891), the *Westminster Gazette* (1873), *Country Life* (1897), the *Wide World Magazine* (1898), and others. He was MP for the Newmarket division (1885–95).

Newton, Sir Isaac see panel on p. 692

Nexø, Martin Andersen [**nek**soe] (1869–1954) Novelist, born in Copenhagen. He spent his boyhood on the I of Bornholm, near Nexø (from where he took his name). A shepherd then a shoemaker, with the help of a patron he became a teacher, and from 1901 supported himself by writing. In 1906 he won fame throughout Europe with his major novel *Pelle Erobreren* (1915–17, Pelle the Conqueror), describing his life of poverty, and the growth of the Labour movement with which he became involved. His other major work is *Ditte Mennskebarn* (1920–2, Ditte, Daughter of Man).

Ney, Michel, duc d' (Duke of) Elchingen [nay] (1769–1815) French marshal, born in Saarlouis, France. He fought in the Revolutionary Wars, became a general of division (1799), and a marshal of the empire. Created Duke of Elchingen (1805), he distinguished himself at Jena (1806), Eylau, and Friedland (1807). He commanded the third corps of the Grand Army in the Russian campaign (1813), for which he received the title of Prince of Moskowa. After Napoleon's abdication (1814), he accepted the Bourbon restoration, but instead of obeying orders to retake Bonaparte (1815), Ney deserted to his side and led the centre at Waterloo. On Louis XVIII's second restoration, he was condemned for high treason, and shot in Paris. >> Kutuzov; Napoleon I; Wellington

Ngata, Sir Apirana Turupa Nohopari [**nggah**ta] (1874–

1950) New Zealand statesman and Maori scholar, born in Te Araroa, New Zealand. He studied at Canterbury and Auckland universities, and became a lawyer, an MP (1906–43), and a cabinet minister (1928–36). He worked for the economic development of Maori land and for a revival of interest in Maori culture. He was knighted in 1927.

Ngugi wa Thiong'o [**ngoo**gee wa **tyong**goh], formerly **James Ngugi** (1938–) Writer, born in Limuru, Kenya. He studied at Makerere and Leeds universities, and taught English at Nairobi University, where he became chairman of the department of literature (1972–7). His award-winning novel *Weep Not, Child* (1964) was the first novel in English by an East African. The theme of Kenya's struggle for independence is further explored in later novels, *The River Between* (1965), *A Grain of Wheat* (1967), and *Petals of Blood* (1977). He then gave up using English as the medium for his fiction (though continuing to use it for translation and other purposes), arguing that the continuing use of local languages (Kikuyu, in his case) was a prerequisite for political reform. He wrote several plays, notably *The Trial of Dedan Kimathi* (1977), and co-wrote *Ngaahika Ndeenda* (I Will Marry When I Want), which led to his year-long detention without trial (1978). His ordeal is described in *Detained* (1981). He has lived in exile since 1982. In 1996 he received the Fonlon-Nichols Award, given annually for excellence in African creative writing and contributions to the struggle for human rights and freedom of expression.

Nguyen Van Linh [ngooyen van lin] (1914–) Vietnamese politician. He joined the anti-colonial Thanh Nien, a forerunner of the Communist Party of Vietnam (CPV), in Haiphong in 1929, and spent much of his subsequent Party career in the S, gaining a reputation as a pragmatic reformer. A member of CPV's Politburo and secretariat (1976–81), he was CPV leader (1986–91). Under his leadership there was notable economic liberalization, and he undertook a phased withdrawal of Vietnamese troops from Cambodia and Laos.

Niarchos, Stavros (Spyros) [**nyah(r)**kos] (1909–96) Shipowner, born in Athens. He served during World War 2 in the Royal Hellenic navy, then became controller of one of the largest independent fleets in the world, pioneering the construction of supertankers, in competition with his brother-in-law Aristotle Onassis. He was also a major art collector. >> Onassis

Niccola Pisano >> Pisano, Nicola

Nicholas I (1796–1855) Tsar of Russia (1825–55), born near St Petersburg, Russia, the third son of Paul I. An absolute despot, he engaged in wars with Persia and Turkey, suppressed a rising in Poland, and attempted to Russianize all the inhabitants of the empire. He helped to quell the 1848 Hungarian insurrection, and drew closer the alliance with Prussia. The re-establishment of the French empire confirmed these alliances, and led him to think of absorbing Turkey, but the opposition of Britain and France brought on the Crimean War, during which he died. >> Alexander II (of Russia); RR1085

Nicholas II (1868–1918) The last tsar of Russia (1895–1917), born near St Petersburg, Russia, the son of Alexander III. His reign was marked by the alliance with France, an entente with Britain, a disastrous war with Japan (1904–5), and the establishment of the national assembly, or Duma (1906). He took command of the Russian armies against the Central Powers in 1915. Forced to abdicate at the Revolution, he was shot with his family at Yekaterinburg by the Red Guards. >> Alexander III (of Russia); Alexandra Feodorovna; Anastasia; RR1085

Nicholas, St (4th-c) Bishop of Myra, Lucia, and patron saint of Russia, widely associated with the feast of Christmas. He was imprisoned under Diocletian and released under

SIR ISAAC NEWTON (1642–1727)

Isaac Newton was born in Woolsthorpe, Lincolnshire, EC England, UK, a premature infant not expected to live. His father (of the same name) had died just 3 months before. His mother, Hannah Ayscough Newton, remarried when he was three, and left him with his grandmother until her second husband died, in 1653, when Newton was 11. He was educated at King's School, Grantham, and it was assumed he would continue in the farming tradition of his family, but finally his mother was convinced that he should be prepared for entry to university, and in 1661 he went up to Trinity College, Cambridge, as a poor scholar who would have to earn his keep by doing menial tasks for the Fellows.

Newton showed no particular promise in his early years at Cambridge, but Isaac Barrow, who held the Lucasian chair of mathematics, gave him much encouragment. Newton took his degree without distinction (in 1665), and would have prepared for his MA, but in 1664 the Great Plague broke out in London, and the university was closed down the following year.

At home during the plague years, he studied the nature of light and the construction of telescopes. By a variety of experiments upon sunlight refracted through a prism, he concluded that rays of light which differ in colour, differ also in refrangibility – a discovery which suggested that the indistinctness of the image formed by the object-glass of telescopes was due to the different-coloured rays of light being brought to a focus at different distances. He concluded (rightly for an object-glass consisting of a single lens) that it was impossible to produce a distinct image, and was thus led to the construction of reflecting telescopes, perfected by William Herschel and the Earl of Rosse. At the same time, he was working out his ideas on planetary motion.

On his return to Cambridge (1667), Newton became a Fellow of Trinity College, and, in 1668, took his MA. In the following year, Isaac Barrow resigned his chair in favour of his young pupil. Newton's lecture series resulted in an essay which later formed Book 1 of *Opticks*.

A falling apple had posed in Newton's mind the question of whether the force exerted by the Earth in making the apple fall was the same force that made the Moon 'fall' towards the Earth, and so pull it in to an elliptical orbit round the Earth. Calculations showed him that it did, but it was not until 1684, after an exchange of letters with Robert Hooke, that Newton was fully in command of the dynamic principles involved. In that same year, Edmond Halley visited Newton to try to work through some planetary questions. To his surprise, Newton told him that the force between Sun and planets, resulting in an elliptical orbit, operated according to an inverse square law and that he had proved it. He later sent a small treatise on the subject to Halley. Halley persuaded Newton to write a book and, after much antagonism between Newton and Hooke, who demanded credit for discovering the inverse-square law of attraction, the book appeared in 1687 under the title *Philosophiae naturalis principia mathematica* (The Mathematical Principles of Natural Philosophy).

This important work, which had remained unpublished for years, established Newton as the greatest of all physical scientists. Its impact was immense. Newton had rewritten the whole science of moving bodies. He completed what the late mediaeval physicists had begun and Galileo had tried to bring to fruition; and his three 'laws of motion' formed the basis of all further work.

Meanwhile, the part Newton took in defending the rights of the university against the illegal encroachments of James II procured him a seat in the Convention Parliament (1689–90). In 1696 he was appointed warden of the Mint, at a time when the government had debased the coinage, and a strong, incorruptible man was needed to deal with counterfeiters. He became master of the Mint from 1699, having shown himself to be a brilliant administrator. He again sat in parliament in 1701 for his university, and in 1704 published *Opticks* in English, which he had refused to do until Hooke, his old enemy, was dead.

Much of Newton's life was spent in conflict with other scientists, particulary Hooke, Leibnitz, and Flamsteed, and he sought revenge for slights real or imagined by deleting references to their help from his work. He always took criticism very badly, responding furiously – an anxiety which has often been explained in terms of his abandonment as a child – and showed signs all through his life of a persecution mania. A breakdown in 1693 heralded the end of his scientific work. Knighted in 1705, his last years were spent under the care of his niece. He never married, but was at his happiest in the role of patron to younger scientists and, from 1703, as a tyrannical president of the Royal Society.
>> Barrow, Isaac; Flamsteed; Halley; Herschel, William; Hooke; Leibniz; Rosse

Constantine, and his supposed relics were conveyed to Bari in 1087. He is the patron of youth, merchants, sailors, travellers, and thieves. His identification with Father Christmas began in Europe, and spread to America, where the name was altered to *Santa Claus*. The tradition of exchanging gifts on Christmas Day derives from a legend of his benevolence. Feast day 6 December. >> Constantine I (Emperor); Diocletian

Nicholas I, St, known as **the Great** (c. 820–867) Pope (858–67), born in Rome. He asserted the supremacy of the Church against secular rulers such as Lothair, King of Lorraine (whose divorce he forbade) and Church leaders such as Hincmar, Archbishop of Reims. He had problems with the Eastern Church, however, particularly with Photius, whom he tried to depose as Patriarch of Constantinople, leading to the Photian schism. Feast day 13 November. >> Hincmar; Photius

Nicholas, Grand-Duke, Russ **Nikolay Nikolayevich** (1856–1929) Russian army officer, born in St Petersburg, Russia, the nephew of Alexander II. In World War 1 he was Russian commander-in-chief against Germany and Austria, and commander-in-chief in the Caucasus (1915–17). After 1919 he lived in France, heading the unity of anti-Communist emigrés. >> Alexander II (of Russia)

Nicholas or **Nicolaus of Cusa** [kyooza] (1401–64) Cardinal and philospher, born in Cusa, Germany. He studied at Heidelberg and Padua, and took a prominent part in the Council of Basel. Ordained in 1440, he became a cardinal in 1448, and as papal legate visited Constantinople to promote the union of the Eastern and Western Churches. A Renaissance scientist in advance of his time, he wrote on astronomy, mathematics, philosophy, and biology.

Nicholls, Sir Douglas (Ralph) (1906–88) Aboriginal clergyman, activist, and administrator, born near Echuca, Victoria, Australia. Reared and educated on a mission station, he worked on the land until his football skills took him to Melbourne where, in 1935, he became the first Aborigine to represent his state in football. As pastor, he established an Aborigines' mission at Fitzroy in 1943, and worked actively for Aboriginal advancement. He became the first Aborigine to be knighted (1972). In December 1976 he was appointed Governor of South Australia, but relinquished the position due to ill health four months later.

Nichols, Mike, originally **Michael Igor Peschkowsky** (1931–) Film and theatre director, born in Berlin. A US citizen from 1944, he studied at the University of Chicago, and took up acting with Lee Strasberg. After making a name for himself as one half of a satirical duo with Elaine May, he made a highly successful directing debut on Broadway with *Barefoot in the Park* (1963). He received seven Tony Awards for his theatre work, which included *The Odd Couple* (1965) and *The Real Thing* (1984). He also directed the hit musical, *Annie* (1977). He directed his first film, *Who's Afraid of Virginia Woolf?*, in 1966. His films offer sardonic portraits of American life, social mores, and sexual politics, and include *The Graduate* (1967, Oscar), *Catch 22* (1970), *Working Girl* (1988), *Regarding Henry* (1991), and *The Birdcage* (1996). >> Strasberg

Nichols, Peter (Richard) (1927–) Playwright, born in Bristol, SW England, UK. He worked as an actor and schoolteacher before he began writing television plays in the early 1960s. His first stage success came with *A Day In The Death Of Joe Egg* (1967, filmed 1971). Other works include the screenplays *Catch Us If You Can* (1965) and *Georgy Girl* (1967), and the plays *Privates on Parade* (1977, filmed 1983), *A Piece of My Mind* (1986), and *Blue Murder* (1995).

Nicholson, Ben (1894–1982) Artist, born in Denham, Buckinghamshire, SC England, UK, the son of Sir William Nicholson. He exhibited with the Paris Abstraction-Création group (1933–4) and at the Venice Biennale (1954). He designed a mural panel for the Festival of Britain (1951), and executed another for the Time Life building in London (1952). As one of the leading abstract artists, he gained an international reputation, and won the first Guggenheim Award in 1957. Although he produced a number of purely geometrical paintings and reliefs, in general he used conventional still-life objects as a starting point for his finely drawn and subtly balanced and coloured variations. Three times married, his second wife was Barbara Hepworth. >> Hepworth; Nicholson, Sir William Newzam Prior

Nicholson, Jack (1937–) Film actor, born in Neptune, NJ. An office boy at MGM, he worked with the Players Ring Theater before making his film debut in 1958. A supporting role in *Easy Rider* (1969) brought him belated critical recognition. His intense charisma and acute sense of humour have illuminated a wide range of characters in such diverse films as *Chinatown* (1974), *The Shining* (1980), and *Prizzi's Honor* (1985). He has also written scripts, and occasionally directs. Nominated many times for an Academy Award, he won Oscars for *One Flew Over the Cuckoo's Nest* (1975) and *Terms of Endearment* (1983). Later film credits include *The Witches of Eastwick* (1987), *Batman* (1989), *The Two Jakes* (1990), *Wolf* (1994), and *Mars Attacks!* (1996).

Nicholson, Seth Barnes (1891–1963) Astronomer, born in Springfield, IL. He studied at Drake University, IA, and the University of California, then joined the staff of the Mt Wilson Observatory (1915–57). He is remembered for his discovery of the 9th, 10th, 11th, and 12th satellites of Jupiter.

Nicholson, William (1753–1815) Chemist, born in London, England, UK. A waterworks engineer for Portsmouth and Gosport, he invented the hydrometer named after him, and also a machine for printing on linen. In association with **Anthony Carlisle** (1768–1840) he constructed the first voltaic pile in England, and in so doing discovered that water could be dissociated by electricity (1800). In 1797 he founded the *Journal of Natural Philosophy, Chemistry and the Arts*, commonly known as 'Nicholson's Journal'.

Nicholson, Sir William Newzam Prior, pseudonym **W Beggarstaff** (1872–1949) Artist, born in Newark, Nottinghamshire, C England, UK, the father of Ben Nicholson. He studied in Paris and was influenced by Whistler and Manet. He became a fashionable portrait painter, but is principally remembered for the posters produced with his brother-in-law, **James Pryde** (1866–1941) under their joint-pseudonym of J and W Beggarstaff, for his woodcut book illustrations, and for his glowing still-life paintings (such as 'Mushrooms', Tate, London). >> Manet; Nicholson, Ben; Whistler, James McNeill

Nicias [nisias] (?–413 BC) Wealthy politician and general, from Athens, prominent during the Peloponnesian War. A political moderate, he was opposed to the strident warmongering of Cleon and Alcibiades, and arranged the short-lived peace named after him (421 BC). Appointed commander in Sicily (416 BC), his lack of sympathy with his mission, along with bad luck, ill health, and sheer incompetence, led to the total destruction of the Athenian forces, and his own death at the hands of the Syracusans. >> Alcibiades; Cleon; Demosthenes (d.413 BC)

Nicklaus, Jack (William) [niklows] (1940–) Golfer, born in Columbus, OH. He won the US Amateur title in 1959 and 1961, then turned professional. Runner-up to Arnold Palmer in the 1960 US Open, as amateur, he has since won all the world's major tournaments: the (British) Open (1966, 1970, 1978), the US Open (1962, 1967, 1972, 1980), the US Professional Golfers Association tournament a record-equalling five times (1963, 1971, 1973, 1975, 1980), and the US Masters six times (1963, 1965–6, 1972, 1975, 1986). His win in 1986 was at the age of 46 years 82 days, the oldest winner of the event. His 18 professional majors is a world record. He continues to play, but is also involved in golf course and golf club design. >> RR1157

Nicol, William (1768–1851) Geologist and physicist, born in Edinburgh, EC Scotland, UK. He lectured in natural philosophy at Edinburgh, and in 1828 invented the *Nicol prism*, which utilizes the doubly refracting property of Iceland spar, and which proved invaluable in the investigation of polarized light. He also devised a new method of preparing thin sections of rocks for the microscope, but his reluctance to publish delayed their use for some 40 years, until Sorby and others introduced them into petrology. >> Sorby

Nicolai, (Carl) Otto (Ehrenfried) [nikoliy] (1810–49) Composer, born in Königsberg, Germany. He studied in Berlin and Rome, becoming court conductor in Vienna (1841) and conductor of the Berlin Opera (1847). His opera *The Merry Wives of Windsor* was produced just before he died.

Nicolaus >> **Nicholas of Cusa**

Nicole, Pierre >> **Arnauld, Antoine**

Nicolle, Charles (Jules Henri) [neekol] (1866–1936) Physician and bacteriologist, born in Rouen, France. A pupil of Louis Pasteur, he became director of the Pasteur Institute at Tunis (1903), and professor at the Collège de France (1932).

He discovered that the body louse is a transmitter of typhus fever, and in 1928 was awarded the Nobel Prize for Physiology or Medicine. >> Pasteur

Nicolson, Sir Harold (George) (1886–1968) British diplomat, writer, and critic, born in Teheran, where his father was British chargé d'affaires. He studied at Oxford, and had a distinguished career as a diplomat, entering the service in 1909, and holding posts in Madrid, Constantinople, Teheran, and Berlin until his resignation in 1929, when he turned to journalism. In 1913 he married Vita Sackville-West, and later became National Liberal MP for West Leicester (1935–45). Highly regarded as a literary critic, he wrote several biographies, including those of Tennyson, Swinburne, and the official biography of George V, as well as books on history, politics, and manners. >> Sackville-West

Nicot, Jean [neekoh] (1530–1600) Diplomat and scholar, born in Nîmes, France. He became French ambassador in Lisbon (1559–61), and in 1561 introduced into France from Portugal the tobacco plant, called after him *Nicotiana*. The word *nicotine* derives from his name. He also compiled one of the first French dictionaries (1606).

Nidetch, Jean [niydich] (1923–) Entrepreneur who founded Weight Watchers, born in Brooklyn, NY. When she began a diet devised by the Obesity Clinic of the New York Department of Health (1961), she found it effective, but had difficulty in keeping to its guidelines. To help her persevere she formed a mutual support group with several overweight friends, and out of this group grew Weight Watchers International, taken over by Heinz in 1978.

Niebuhr, Barthold Georg [neeboor] (1776–1831) Historian, born in Copenhagen. He studied at Kiel, London, and Edinburgh, in 1816 became Prussian ambassador at the Vatican, and on his return in 1823 lectured at Bonn. His main work, the *Römische Geschichte* (1811–32, History of Rome), based on the constructive analysis of historical source material, marked him out as a founder of the 19th-c school of German historical scholarship.

Niebuhr, H(elmut) Richard [neeboor] (1894–1962) Protestant theologian, born in Wright City, MO, the brother of Reinhold Niebuhr. He studied at Elmhurst College, IL, and at Washington and Yale universities, becoming professor of theology and Christian ethics at Yale in 1931. Like his brother, he had enormous influence on generations of students. His classic study, *The Meaning of Revelation* (1941), was followed by several books advocating critical reflection on the relation between faith and moral action and on the quest for a Christian transformation of society ('theological existentialism'). >> Niebuhr, Reinhold

Niebuhr, Reinhold [neeboor] (1892–1971) Theologian, born in Wright City, MO, the brother of Helmut Richard Niebuhr. He studied at Elmhurst College, IL, Eden Theological Seminary, and Yale Divinity School, and became an evangelical pastor in working-class Detroit (1915–28) and professor of Christian ethics in the Union Theological Seminary, New York City (1928–60). An advocate of Christian Realism, he was a political activist with the Socialists and then the Democratic Party, and after World War 2 was influential in the US State Department. Among his many writings are *Moral Man and Immoral Society* (1932) and *The Irony of American History* (1952). >> Niebuhr, H(elmut) Richard

Nielsen, A(rthur) C(harles) [neelsen] (1897–1980) Businessman and market-researcher, born in Chicago, IL. He attended the engineering school at Wisconsin University and worked briefly as an engineer. He founded the A C Nielsen Co in 1923, and gained success by analysing retail drug and food sales. The company began researching radio programme ratings (1942), and later established a national television rating service (1950). The system became popularly known as the *Nielsen Ratings*.

Nielsen, Carl (August) [neelsen] (1865–1931) Composer, born in Nørre-Lyndelse, Denmark. He studied at the Copenhagen Conservatory (1884–6), and became conductor at the Royal Theatre (1908–14) and with the Copenhagen Musical Society (1915–27). He is particularly known for his six symphonies, and he also wrote concertos, choral and chamber music, the tragic opera *Saul and David* (1902), the comic opera *Masquerade* (1906), and a huge organ work, *Commotio* (1931).

Niemeyer, Oscar [neemiyer] (1907–) Architect, born in Rio de Janeiro, Brazil. He studied at the National School of Fine Arts in Brazil and began work in the office of Lucio Costa (1935). From 1936 to 1943 he joined Costa and others to design the ministry of education and public health buildings in Rio, including a period with Le Corbusier as consultant architect. With Costa he designed the Brazilian Pavilion at the New York World Fair (1939). He became architectural adviser to Nova Cap, serving as its chief architect (1957–9), co-ordinating the development of Brasilia. Further major works are the Exhibition Hall in São Paolo (1953), and the President's Palace, Law Courts and Cathedrals in Brasilia. He was awarded the Lenin Peace Prize in 1963. >> Costa, Lucio; Le Corbusier; Seidler

Niemöller, (Friedrich Gustav Emil) Martin [neemoeler] (1892–1984) Lutheran pastor and outspoken opponent of Hitler, born in Lippstadt, Germany. He was a leading submarine commander in World War 1, then studied theology, and was ordained in 1924, becoming pastor at Berlin-Dahlem in 1931. Summoned with other Protestant Church leaders before Hitler, he publicly opposed the Nazi regime, and was arrested and placed in various concentration camps (1937–45). Released by Allied forces in 1945, he was responsible for the 'Declaration of Guilt' by the German Churches for not opposing Hitler more strenuously, but he also condemned the abuses of the de-Nazification courts. A controversial pacifist, he later became president of the Evangelical Chuch in Hesse and Nassau (1947), and president of the World Council of Churches (1961). >> Hitler

Niepce, (Joseph) Nicéphore [nyeps] (1765–1833) Chemist, born in Chalon-sur-Saône, France. One of the inventors of photography, he served in the army, and in 1795 became administrator of Nice. At Chalon in 1801 he devoted himself to chemistry, and at length succeeded in producing a permanent photographic image on metal (1826), said to be the world's first. From 1829 he co-operated with Louis Daguerre in further research. >> Daguerre

Nietzsche, Friedrich (Wilhelm) [neechuh] (1844–1900) Philosopher and critic, born in Röcken, Germany. He was a strongly religious child and a brilliant undergraduate, accepting the chair of classical philology at Basel (1869–79) before graduating. Influenced by Schopenhauer, he dedicated his first book, *Die Geburt der Tragödie* (1872, The Birth of Tragedy) to his friend Wagner, whose operas he regarded as the true successors to Greek tragedy. He determined to give his age new values, Schopenhauer's 'will to power' serving as the basic principle. His major work, *Also sprach Zarathustra* (1883–5, Thus Spake Zarathustra) develops the idea of the *Übermensch* 'overman'. Much of his esoteric doctrine appealed to the Nazis, and he was a major influence on existentialism. In 1889 he had a mental breakdown, from which he never recovered. >> Schopenhauer; Wagner, Richard

Nieuwland, Julius (Arthur) [nyooland] (1878–1936) Chemist, born in Hansbeke, Belgium. His family emigrated to the USA in 1880. He studied at Notre Dame University, IN, was ordained a Roman Catholic priest in 1903, and later became professor of botany (1904–18) and organic chemistry (1918–36) at Notre Dame. His researches led to the production of the first commercially successful synthetic rubber, neoprene, in 1932.

Nightingale, Florence, known as **the Lady of the Lamp** (1820–1910) Hospital reformer, born in Florence, Italy. Raised in England, she trained as a nurse at Kaiserswerth and Paris, and in the Crimean War, after the Battle of Alma (1854), led a party of 38 nurses to organize a nursing department at Scutari. There she found grossly inadequate sanitation, but she soon established better conditions and had 10 000 wounded under her care. She returned to England in 1856, where she formed an institution for the training of nurses at St Thomas' Hospital, and spent several years on army sanitary reform, the improvement of nursing, and public health in India.

Nijinska, Bronislava [nizhinska] (1891–1972) Ballet dancer and choreographer, born in Minsk, Belarus, the sister of Vaslav Nijinsky. She studied at St Petersburg, and became a soloist with the Maryinski company. She danced with the Diaghilev company in Paris and London (1909–14) before returning to Russia during World War 1, where she danced and started a school in Kiev. She joined Diaghilev in 1921 as principal choreographer. After working in Buenos Aires and Paris, she briefly formed her own company (1932), and after 1938 lived and worked mainly in the USA. Two works have been revived, and are highly regarded: *Le Noces* (1923) and *Les Biches* (1924). >> Nijinsky

Nijinsky, Vaslav [nizhinskee] (1890–1950) Ballet dancer, born in Kiev, Ukraine. Considered one of the greatest male dancers of the 20th-c, he was, like his sister Bronislava Nijinska, trained at the Imperial Ballet School in St Petersburg, and first appeared in ballet at the Maryinski Theatre. As the leading dancer in Diaghilev's Ballets Russes, taken to Paris in 1909, he became phenomenally successful, and in 1911 he appeared as Petrouchka in the first perfomance of Stravinsky's ballet. His choreographic portfolio is slim but has two high points, *L'Après-midi d'un faune* (1912, Afternoon of a Fawn), and *Sacre du printemps* (1913, The Rite of Spring), which at the time was regarded as outrageous in its subversion of conventional ballet and its use of Stravinsky's rhythmically complex score. He married in 1913, and was interned in Hungary during the early part of World War 1. He rejoined Diaghilev for a world tour, but retired in 1917 when he was diagnosed a paranoid schizophrenic. >> Diaghilev; Nijinska

Nikodim, Boris Georgyevich Rotov [nikohdeem] (1928–78) Orthodox clergyman, and metropolitan of Leningrad, born in Frolovo, Russia. He entered the Orthodox monastery at Ryazan, and assumed the name of Nikodim when made deacon in 1947. He combined parochial work with studies at Leningrad, and was archimandrite in charge of the Russian Orthodox Mission in Jerusalem. In 1960 he became Bishop of Podolsk and head of foreign relations of the Russian Church, which he led into the World Council of Churches amid great acclaim in 1961. At the age of 34, he was appointed metropolitan, and became known at ecumenical meetings all over the world. He collapsed and died during an audience with Pope John Paul I in the Vatican.

Nikolais, Alwin (1912–93) Choreographer, born in Southington, CT. A puppeteer, and a pianist for silent films, he turned to dance, studying with Hanya Holm. Moving to New York City in 1948, he founded his own dance company, the Nikolais Dance Theater, in 1951. His style was idiosyncratic, and uninhibited by conventional artistic boundaries. He designed his own sets and became, in 1963, the first artist to use the Moog Synthesizer. >> Holm, Hanya

Nikolayevich, Nikolay, Grand Duke >> **Nicholas, Grand Duke**

Niland, D'Arcy (Francis) [niyland] (1919–67) Writer, born in Glen Innes, New South Wales, Australia. After his early years working in the bush, he went to Sydney and in 1942 married the New Zealand writer Ruth Park, after which he settled down to writing. Between 1949 and 1952 he won many prizes for short stories and novels, and in 1955 achieved international fame with his novel *The Shiralee*. This was followed by *Call Me When the Cross Turns Over* (1957) and four more novels. He also wrote radio and television plays, and hundreds of short stories, some of which were published in four books between 1961 and 1966. >> Park, Ruth

Niles, Daniel (Thambyrajah) (1908–70) Ecumenical leader and evangelist, born near Jaffna, Sri Lanka. A fourth-generation Tamil Christian, he became increasingly involved in the developing ecumenical movement. The youngest delegate at the 1938 International Missionary Council Tambaram Conference, he was appointed a president of the World Council of Churches after Uppsala (1968), and at the time of his death was chairman of the East Asian Christian Conference and president of the Methodist Church in Ceylon. He wrote 45 hymns for the *EACC Hymnal* (1963), and these, along with the posthumous *A Testament of Faith* (1972), convey the spirit of his many books.

Nilsen, Dennis (1948–) British convicted murderer. He admitted the murder and mutilation of between 12 and 16 young men in England between 1978 and 1983. He was sentenced to life imprisonment, with a recommendation that he serve a minimum of 25 years on six counts of murder and two of attempted murder.

Nilsson, (Märta) Birgit (1922–) Operatic soprano, born in Karup, Sweden. She studied at the Stockholm Royal Academy of Music. Following her debut in 1946, she sang with the Stockholm Royal Opera (1947–51), and at Bayreuth Festivals (1953–70). She was the leading Wagnerian soprano of that period, having a voice of exceptional power, stamina, and intense personality. She sang at most of the great houses and festivals of the world, and her repertoire included Verdi, Puccini, and Strauss. She retired from the stage in 1982. >> Wagner, Richard

Nilsson, Lennart (1922–) Photographer, born in Sweden. He worked as a freelance press photographer, and gained respect for several portraits such as *Sweden in Profiles* (1954), but went on to pioneer microfilm showing the anatomy of plants and animals. He is best known for his microbiological and medical photography, notably combining the techniques of endoscopy and photography to film inside the human body, which enabled him to produce pictures of the human fetus in the womb from conception to birth. His pictorial record *Ett Barn Blir Till* (1965, trans The Everyday Miracle: a Child is Born) won him the American National Press Association Picture of the Year Award.

Nimitz, Chester W(illiam) [nimits] (1885–1966) US admiral, born in Fredericksburg, TX. He graduated from the US Naval Academy in 1905, served mainly in submarines, and by 1938 had risen to the rank of rear-admiral. Chief of the Bureau of Navigation at the outset of World War 2 (1939–41), he commanded the US Pacific fleet and Pacific Ocean areas (1941–5), contributing to the defeat of Japan. He was made a fleet admiral in 1944, and signed the Japanese surrender documents for the USA on board the USS *Missouri* in Tokyo Bay (1945). Later posts include chief of naval operations (1945–7), and special assistant to the secretary of the navy (1947–9).

Nimoy, Leonard [nimoy] (1931–) Actor, director, and producer, born in Boston, MA. He studied at Boston College, moved to Los Angeles and joined a theatre group. His film work began in 1951, with *Queen for a Day*, but he eventually came to be identified in the public mind with the half-Vulcan/half-human character of Spock in the *Star Trek* series (1966–9). When the series was reprised as feature films (1979–91), he produced the third and fourth instalments, and scripted the fourth. In addition to many other acting roles in theatre, film, and television, he has worked as a director, his films including *Three Men and a Baby* (1987) and *Holy Matrimony* (1994). He has also written several books, including several combinations of poetry and photography, as well as the book-pair *I Am Not Spock* (1975), in which he tried to break away from his screen image, and *I Am Spock* (1995), in which he accepted it.

Nin, Anaïs [neen, **an**aees] (1903–77) Novelist and short-story writer, born in Neuilly, France. She studied in New York City, then returned to Paris, where she became acquainted with many well-known writers and artists, and began to write herself. Her early work includes a study of D H Lawrence (1932) and several novels, as well as a collection of short stories, *Under a Glass Bell* (1944). However, her somewhat controversial reputation as an artist and seminal figure in the new feminism of the 1970s rests on her *Journals* (1966–83). Spanning the years 1931 to 1974 they are a record of an era, as well as a passionate, explicit, and candid account of one woman's voyage of self-discovery.

Ninagawa, Yukio (1935–) Stage director, born in Japan. He studied at the Seihari Theatre Company, and emerged as a leading light in Japanese avant-garde theatre with his work at Toyko's Small Basement Theatre. In 1974, he staged *Romeo and Juliet* as his first production for the Toho Company, followed by a series of classical works and numerous Japanese plays. In 1985 he created a sensation at the Edinburgh Festival with a vibrant, colourful, violent, Samurai-influenced production of *Macbeth*, followed by an open-air production in a Georgian courtyard of Euripides' *Medea* in 1986. Both productions were subsequently seen at the National Theatre in London, for which Ninagawa won the 1987 Olivier Award for director of the year.

Ninian, St, also called **Ringan** (fl. 390) Missionary, and the earliest-known Christian leader in Scotland. He was consecrated bishop by the pope (394) and sent as an apostle to the W parts of Britain. On his way home from Rome he visited St Martin of Tours, who supplied him with masons, and to whom he later dedicated his Church. He selected Wigtownshire for the site of a monastery and church, called Candida Casa, which was built c.400. Successful in converting the S Picts, he died at Whithorn and was buried there, though other sources suggest he may have withdrawn to Ireland. Feast day 16 September. >> Martin, St

Nipkow, Paul [**nip**kof] (1860–1940) Engineer and inventor, born in Lauenburg, Germany. One of the pioneers of television, he invented in 1884 the *Nipkow disc*, a mechanical scanning device consisting of a revolving disc with a spiral pattern of apertures. In use until 1932, it was superseded by electronic scanning.

Nirenberg, Marshall (Warren) (1927–) Biochemist, born in New York City. He studied at Michigan University, then worked from 1957 at the National Institutes of Health, Bethesda, MD. He attacked the problem of the genetic code by synthesizing a nucleic acid with a known base sequence, and then finding which amino acid it converted to protein. With his success, Har Gobind Khorana and others soon completed the task of deciphering the full code. He shared the Nobel Prize for Physiology or Medicine in 1968. >> Khorana; RR1124

Niro, Robert De >> **De Niro, Robert**

Nivelle, Robert [neevel] (1857–1924) French soldier, born in Tulle, France. He was an artillery colonel in 1914, and made his name when in command of the army of Verdun

by recapturing Douaumont and other forts (1916). He was commander-in-chief for several months (1916–17), but his Aisne offensive failed, and he was superseded by Pétain. >> Pétain

Niven, David, popular name of **James David Graham Nevins** (1909–83) Actor, born in Kirriemuir, Angus, E Scotland, UK. He trained at Sandhurst, served in the army, and had a variety of jobs before he arrived in Hollywood, where he joined the social set led by Errol Flynn and Clark Gable, and worked as an extra in *Mutiny on the Bounty* (1935). Signed by Samuel Goldwyn, he developed into a polished light comedian and gallant hero in such films as *The Charge of the Light Brigade* (1936) and *The Dawn Patrol* (1938). After service as an army officer in World War 2, he spent 30 years as an urbane leading man, perfectly cast as the gentlemanly voyager Phineas Fogg in *Around the World in 80 Days* (1956), and winning an Oscar for *Separate Tables* (1958). An inimitable raconteur, he published two volumes of lighthearted autobiography: *The Moon's a Balloon* (1972) and *Bring on the Empty Horses* (1975). >> Flynn, Errol; Gable, Clark

Niven, Frederick John (1878–1944) Novelist, born in Valparaiso, Chile. Educated in Scotland, he travelled widely in South America and worked as a journalist (1898–1914). He wrote more than 30 novels, mostly set in Glasgow or Canada, where he lived after World War 1. His major work was a trilogy on Canadian settlement, comprising *The Flying Years*, *Mine Inheritance*, and *The Transplanted* (1935–44).

Nixon, Richard M(ilhous) (1913–94) US statesman and 37th president (1969–74), born in Yorba Linda, CA. He studied at Whittier College and Duke University, became a lawyer, served in the US navy, and was elected to the US House of Representatives in 1946. He became senator in 1950, and vice-president under Eisenhower (1953–61). In 1959 on a visit to Moscow he achieved notoriety by his outspoken exchanges with Nikita Khrushchev. As the Republican candidate, he lost the presidential election (1960) to John F Kennedy by a tiny margin. Standing for the governorship of California in 1962, he was again defeated. He won the presidential election in 1968 by a small margin, and was re-elected in 1972 by a large majority. His presidency saw the end of the Vietnam War, imposed wage and price controls, and presidential visits to China. During an official investigation into a break-in attempt in June 1972 at the Democratic National Committee's headquarters in the Watergate Hotel, Washington, he lost credibility by at first claiming executive privilege for senior White House officials to prevent them being questioned, and by refusing to hand over tapes of relevant conversations. He resigned in August 1974 under the threat of impeachment, after several leading members of his government had been found guilty of being involved in the Watergate scandal. The following month he was given a full pardon by President Gerald Ford. >> Eisenhower; Ford, Gerald R; Mitchell, John; Khrushchev; RR1097

Nizer, Louis [**niy**zer] (1902–94) Lawyer and writer, born in London, England, UK. His family moved to the USA when he was three. Noted for his oratorical skills as a youth, he studied at Columbia, formed the law firm Phillips, Nizer, Benjamin & Krim in 1926, and remained with it throughout his career. He represented many companies and entertainers in the film industry, and became a recognized authority on contracts, copyright, and plagiarism law. A man of many talents, he was a caricaturist and painter, wrote the words and music of songs, was much in demand as a toastmaster, and published several books, including *My Life in Court* (1961) and *The Jury Returns* (1966).

Nkomo, Joshua (Mqabuko Nyongolo) [**nkoh**moh] (1917–) Zimbabwean statesman, born in Semokwe,

Zimbabwe. Educated mainly in South Africa, he became a member of the African National Congress in 1952, and president of the Zimbabwe African People's Union (ZAPU) in 1961. There followed a long period during which he was placed under government restrictions, but in 1976 he formed the Popular Front with Robert Mugabe to press for black majority rule in an independent Zimbabwe, and was given a Cabinet post in the Mugabe government in 1980. However, tension between his party and Mugabe's led to his dismissal in 1982. Although Nkomo's native Matabeleland continued to harbour dissidents from Mugabe's rule, some reconciliation was achieved as Zimbabwe moved towards a one-party state. >> Mugabe; Muzorewa; RR1101

Nkrumah, Kwame [**nkroo**ma] (1909–72) Ghanaian statesman, prime minister (1957–60), and president (1960–6), born in Nkroful, Ghana (formerly, Gold Coast). He studied in both the USA (Lincoln University) and the UK (London School of Economics), returning to the Gold Coast in 1947, and in 1949 formed the nationalist Convention People's Party. In 1950 he was imprisoned, but elected to parliament while still in jail. Released in 1951, he became leader of business in the Assembly, and then premier. Called 'the Gandhi of Africa', he was a significant leader both of the movement against white domination and of pan-African feeling. He was the moving spirit behind the Charter of African States (1961). Economic reforms led to political opposition and several attempts on his life, interference with the judiciary, and the formation of a one-party state in 1964. His regime was overthrown by a military coup during his absence in China, and he sought asylum in Guinea, where he was given the status of co-head of state. >> Gandhi, Mahatma; RR1053

Noah [**noh**uh] Biblical character, depicted as the son of Lamech. He is described as a 'righteous man' who was given divine instruction to build an ark in which he, his immediate family, and a selection of animals were saved from a widespread flood over the Earth (*Gen* 6–9). In the Table of Nations (*Gen* 10), Noah's sons (Japheth, Ham, and Shem) are depicted as the ancestors of all the nations on Earth. A similar flood legend was told of a Babylonian character, Utanapishtim, in the Gilgamesh epic. >> Shem

Nobel, Alfred Bernhard [noh**bel**] (1833–96) Chemist and industrialist, the inventor of dynamite and the founder of the Nobel Prizes, born in Stockholm. He moved to Russia as a child, studied chemistry in Paris, worked in the USA (1852–6) under John Ericsson, and settled in Sweden in 1859. An explosives expert like his father, in 1866 he invented a safe and manageable form of nitroglycerin he called *dynamite*, and later, smokeless gunpowder and (1875) gelignite. He helped to create an industrial empire manufacturing many of his other inventions, and amassed a huge fortune, much of which he left to endow annual prizes (first awarded in 1901) for physics, chemistry, physiology or medicine, literature, and peace. (A sixth prize, for economics, was instituted in his honour in 1969.) >> Ericsson; Suttner; RR1122

Nobile, Umberto [noh**bilay**] (1885–1978) Aviator, born in Lauro, Italy. He became an aeronautical engineer and built the airships *Norge* and *Italia*. He flew across the North Pole in the *Norge* with Amundsen and Ellsworth in 1926. A general in the Italian air force and professor of aeronautical engineering at Naples, in 1928 he was wrecked in the airship *Italia* when returning from the North Pole, and was judged to be responsible for the disaster. He resigned his commission, but was later reinstated. >> Amundsen; Ellsworth, Lincoln

Nobili, Leopoldo [noh**bilee**] (1784–1835) Physicist, born in Italy. Professor of physics at Florence, he invented the thermopile used in measuring radiant heat, and the astatic galvanometer.

Noble, Adrian (Keith) (1950–) British stage director. He studied at Bristol University and the Drama Centre in London, and worked for two years in community and young people's theatre in Birmingham. He became an associate director of the Bristol Old Vic (1976–9), and joined the Royal Shakespeare Company in 1980 as a resident director, becoming an associate director (1982–90), and artistic director in 1991.

Nobunaga, Oda [nobu**nah**ga] (1534–82) The first of the three great historical unifiers of Japan, followed by Hideyoshi and Tokugawa, born into a noble family near Nagoya. He became a general, and occupied the old capital, Kyoto, in 1568, destroying the power of the Buddhist Church, and favouring Christianity as a counter-balance. He built Azuchi Castle, near Kyoto, as his headquarters. He was assassinated by one of his own generals, in Kyoto. >> Hideyoshi; Tokugawa

Noddack, Ida Eva (1896–) Chemist, born in Germany. Working with her husband, **Walter Karl Friedrich** (1893–1960), she discovered the elements masurium and rhenium in 1925.

Noel-Baker (of the City of Derby), Philip (John) Noel-Baker, Baron (1889–1982) British statesman, born in London, England, UK. He studied at Cambridge, and captained the British Olympic team in 1912, where he won a silver medal in the 1500 m. He served on the secretariat of the League of Nations (1919–22), became professor of international relations at London (1924–9), and was elected a Labour MP (1929–31, 1936–70). He was secretary of state for air (1946–7) and of commonwealth relations (1947–50), and minister of fuel and power (1950–1). A lifelong campaigner for peace through multilateral disarmament, he was awarded the Nobel Peace Prize in 1959, and created a life peer in 1977.

Noether, (Amalie) Emmy [**noe**ter] (1882–1935) Mathematician, born in Erlangen, Germany. She studied at Erlangen and Göttingen. Though invited to Göttingen in 1915 by David Hilbert, as a woman she could not hold a full academic post at that time, but worked there in a semi-honorary capacity until she emigrated to the USA in 1933 to Bryn Mawr and Princeton. One of the leading figures in the development of abstract algebra, the theory of *Noetherian rings* has been an important subject of later research. >> Hilbert

Noguchi, Hideyo [no**goo**chee] (1876–1928) Bacteriologist, born in Inawashiro, Japan. He studied at Tokyo Medical College, and from 1900 worked in the USA, first at the University of Pennsylvania, then (from 1904) at the Rockefeller Institute for Medical Research, New York City. He made important discoveries in the cause and treatment of syphilis, and also of yellow fever, from which he died.

Noguchi, Isamu [no**goo**chee] (1904–88) Sculptor, born in Los Angeles, CA. Brought up in Japan, he studied medicine at Columbia University, then moved to New York City, where he attended sculpture classes. A Guggenheim fellowship permitted him to study with Brancusi in Paris (1927–9). He returned to New York City and made stylized sculptures, but from 1940 his work moved closer to Surrealism, incorporating the interrelation of bone and stone. From the mid-1940s he became one of the best-known US sculptors, gaining worldwide commissions for large-scale public sculptures, such as the fountain for the Detroit Civic Center Plaza (1975). >> Brancusi

Noke, Charles John (1858–1941) Ceramic specialist, modeller, and designer, born in Worcester, Hereford and Worcester, WC England, UK. He joined Doulton & Co in 1889 as head modeller, was later responsible for many Parian ware figures, and became instrumental in introducing the

Holbein and Rembrandt wares. In 1914 he became art director at Doulton's in Burslem, where he experimented with reproducing red *rouge flambé* and *sang-de-boeuf* glazes from the Sung, Ming, and early Ching dynasties.

Nolan, Sir Sidney (Robert) (1917–92) Painter, born in Melbourne, Victoria, Australia. Largely self-taught, he took up full-time painting in 1938 and made his name with a series of 'Ned Kelly' paintings begun in 1946, following this with an 'explorer' series. He first went to Europe in 1950, and although he has worked in Italy, Greece, and Africa, he remains best known for his Australian paintings. He also designed the Covent Garden productions *The Rite of Spring* (1962), *Samson and Delilah* (1981), and the Australian Opera's *Il Trovatore* (1983), has illustrated books by Robert Lowell and Benjamin Britten, and published a volume of poems, drawings and paintings, *Paradise Garden* (1972). He was knighted in 1981.

Noland, Kenneth (1924–) Painter, born in Asheville, NC. He studied at Black Mountain College (1946–8). Influenced initially by Klee and Matisse and by the New York Action Painters, he developed his own kind of hard-edge minimalist abstract painting in the late 1950s. He restricts his shapes to circles, ovals, chevrons, and (after c.1966) horizontal stripes. His 'plaid' paintings date from c.1971. >> Klee; Matisse

Nolde, Emil [nolduh], pseudonym of **Emil Hansen** (1867–1956) Artist and printmaker, born in Nolde, Germany. One of the most important Expressionist painters, he was briefly a member of the Expressionist *die Brücke* (1906–7), but produced his own powerful 'blood and soil' style of distorted forms in violent religious pictures such as 'The Life of Christ' (1911–12). He also produced a large number of etchings, lithographs, and woodcuts. >> Heckel; Kirchner; Pechstein

Nollekens, Joseph [nolekenz] (1737–1823) Neoclassical sculptor, born in London, England, UK. He worked in Rome for 10 years from 1760, and became a member of the Royal Academy in 1772. He executed likenesses of most of his famous contemporaries, including Garrick, Sterne, Goldsmith, Johnson, Fox, Pitt, and George III.

Nollet, Jean Antoine (1700–70) Abbé and physicist, born in France. First professor of physics at the Collège de Navarre, in Paris, in 1748, he discovered osmosis (1748), invented an electroscope, and made an improved Leyden jar.

Nolte, Nick (1940–) Film actor, born in Omaha, NB. He was thirty-five before he made his debut in the television mini-series *Rich Man, Poor Man* (1976), and achieved commercial success in *48 Hours* (1982). Later films include *Down and Out in Beverly Hills* (1986), *The Prince of Tides* (1991), *Lorenzo's Oil* (1992), *Jefferson in Paris* (1995), *Mulholland Falls* (1996), and *The Best of Enemies* (1998).

Nono, Luigi [nohnoh] (1924–90) Composer, born in Venice, Italy. He studied at the Venice Conservatoire under Malipiero and Maderna, with whom he and Luciano Berio helped to establish Italy in the forefront of contemporary music. He worked for a time at the electronic studio in Darmstadt, and became a leading composer of electronic, aleatory, and serial music. A strongly politically committed artist, *Il canto sospeso* (1956, The Suspended Song), based on the letters of victims of wartime oppression, brought him to international notice. His other works include *Intolleranza* (1961, Intolerance) and *Canto per il Vietnam* (1973, A Song for Vietnam). >> Berio; Maderna; Malipiero

Noonuccal, Oodgeroo [nunuhkl, ujuhroo], originally **Kath(leen Jean Mary) Walker** (1920–93) Poet and Aboriginal rights activist, born in Brisbane, Queensland, Australia. She was brought up with the Noonuccal tribe on Stradbroke I, Queensland, where many of the old Aboriginal customs survived. She became the first Aboriginal writer to be published in English, with her collection of poems *We Are Going* (1964), followed by *The Dawn is at Hand* (1966). She published a book of stories in traditional Aboriginal form, *Stradbroke Dreamtime* (1972). She visited the USA on a Fulbright Scholarship (1978–9), lecturing on Aboriginal rights, and was active on many Aboriginal interest committees including the Aboriginal Arts Board. She ran a Centre for Aboriginal Culture on Stradbroke I, for children of all races, and adopted her tribal name.

Nordal, Sigurður (Johannesson) (1886–1974) Scholar, born in Vatnsdalur, Iceland. He studied at Copenhagen and Oxford, and became professor of Old Icelandic literature at the new University of Iceland (1918–45), and professor of poetry at Harvard (1931–2). He was Icelandic ambassador to Denmark (1951–7). His *Islenzk Menning I* (1942, Icelandic Culture I), had a profound impact, and he founded the *Islenzk Fornrit* series of literary editions of the sagas. He also published some poetry, a play, and a collection of short stories.

Norden, Carl (Lucas) (1880–1965) Mechanical engineer, born in Semarang, Java. He emigrated to the USA from Switzerland in 1904, worked for Sperry Gyroscope (1911–17), but formed his own company in 1915. In 1911 he developed the first gyrostabilizing equipment for US ships, and became known for his contributions to military hardware. In 1927 he produced the first Norden bombsight, which allowed precision bombing.

Norden, Denis (1922–) British script-writer and broadcaster. He was educated in London, and with Frank Muir formed a comedy script-writing duo (1947–64). They contributed to many shows, including *Take It From Here* (1947–58) and *Bedtime with Braden* (1950–4), and have been resident on many panel shows, such as *My Word* (from 1956) and *My Music* (from 1967), and co-operated in writing a number of books. From 1964 he worked as a solo writer for films and television, especially *It'll Be Alright on the Night* (1977–94), which he also presented. >> Braden, Bernard; Muir, Frank

Nordenskjöld, Nils (Adolf Erik), Baron [naw(r)denshoel] (1832–1901) Arctic navigator, born in Helsinki. A naturalized Swede, he made several expeditions to Spitsbergen, mapping the S of the island. After two preliminary trips proving the navigability of the Kara Sea, he accomplished the navigation of the Northeast Passage (on the *Vega*) from the Atlantic to the Pacific along the N coast of Asia (1878–79). He later made two expeditions to Greenland. >> Nordenskjöld, Otto

Nordenskjöld, (Nils) Otto (Gustaf) [naw(r)denshoel] (1869–1928) Explorer and geologist, born in Småland, Sweden, the nephew of Baron Nils Nordenskjöld. He accompanied expeditions to Patagonia, Klondike, Alaska, and Greenland. In 1901 he led a Swedish party on *Antarctic* to the Antarctic Peninsula area; *Antarctic* was crushed by ice, but they were rescued by the *Uruguay*. In 1920–1 he explored the Andes. He was appointed professor of geography at Gothenburg University in 1905, and principal of Gothenburg University Business School in 1923. >> Nordenskjöld, Nils

Nörgård, Per [noe(r)gaw(r)d] (1932–) Composer, born in Denmark. He studied at the Royal Danish Academy of Music, and continued his studies in Paris. His compositions include operas, symphonies, and ballet and chamber music. He wrote the music for the Oscar-winning Danish film *Babette's Feast* (1987).

Noriega, Manuel (Antonio) [noriayga] (1939–) Soldier and politician, born in Panama City. He studied at the university there and at a military school in Peru. The ruling force behind the Panamanian presidents (1983–9), he had been recruited by the CIA in the late 1960s, and supported by the US government until 1987. Alleging his involvement in drug trafficking, the US authorities ordered his arrest in 1989: 13 000 US troops invaded Panama to support the 12 000 already there. He surrendered in January 1990 after taking refuge for 10 days in the Vatican nunciature. He was taken to the USA for trial, found guilty in 1992, and sentenced to 40 years imprisonment.

Norman, Barry (Leslie) (1933–) British writer and television film critic. In 1973 he joined BBC television as host of *Film '73* and has since regularly written and presented the show (1973–81, 1983–97). He also wrote and presented the series *The Hollywood Greats* (1977–9, 1984–5) and *Talking Pictures* (1988). His books include *100 Best Films of the Century* (1992) and *The Mickey Mouse Affair* (1995). In 1990 he was voted Radio Times Columnist of the Year, and in 1995 was given a special award by the London Film Critics Circle and was honoured with a Special Achievement Award by the Guild of Provincial Film Writers.

Norman, Greg(ory John), nickname **the Great White Shark** (1955–) Golfer, born in Mount Isa, Queensland, Australia. A professional golfer since 1976, and rated the world's top player in 1986, he has won the Australian Open (1980, 1985, 1987), the (British) Open (1986, 1993), and the World Match Play Championship (1986). With more than 50 victories worldwide, golf has made him a multi-millionaire.

Norman, Jessye (1945–) Soprano, born in Augusta, GA. Winning a scholarship to study voice, she graduated from Howard University, and studied further at Michigan. She made her operatic debut in *Tannhäuser* at Berlin (1969), and in *Aïda* at both La Scala and Covent Garden in 1972. She has since toured widely at music festivals and concerts, and is widely admired in opera and concert music for her beauty of tone, breadth of register, and mastery of dynamic range.

Norris, George W(illiam) (1861–1944) US politician, born in Sandusky, OH. He studied law at Northern Indiana Normal School (now Valparaiso University), became a district judge, and was elected as a US Republican to the House of Representatives (1902–12). He was senator for Nebraska (1912–43), voted against entry into World War 1, and was irreconcilably opposed to the Versailles Treaty. He sponsored the Norris–La Guardia Anti-injunction Act (1932), and broke with his Party on the issue of public ownership of water power. His hopes were realized under the 'New Deal', and the Tennessee Valley Authority's first dam was named in his honour. >> La Guardia

Norris, Kathleen, *née* **Thompson** (1880–1966) Novelist, born in San Francisco, CA. She began writing stories, and published her first novel, *Mother*, in 1911. Her later popular works include *Certain People of Importance* (1922) and *Over at the Crowleys* (1946).

Norrish, Ronald (George Wreyford) (1897–1978) Chemist, born in Cambridge, Cambridgeshire, EC England, UK. He studied at Cambridge, and was professor of physical chemistry there (1937–65). His research was in the field of photochemistry and chemical kinetics. He collaborated with George Porter to develop flash photolysis and kinetic spectroscopy for the investigation of very fast reactions, and they shared the 1967 Nobel Prize for Chemistry. >> Porter, George; RR1123

North, Frederick, 8th Baron North (1732–92) British statesman and prime minister (1770–82), born in London, England, UK. He became a Lord of the Treasury (1759) and Chancellor of the Exchequer (1767), and as prime minister brought George III a period of political stability. He was widely criticized both for failing to avert the Declaration of Independence by the North American colonies (1776) and for failing to defeat them in the subsequent war (1776–83).

He annoyed the king by resigning in 1782, then formed a coalition with his former Whig opponent, Fox (1783), but it did not survive royal hostility. After this coalition was dismissed (1783), he remained an Opposition politician until his death. >> Fox, Charles James; George III; RR1095

North, John Dudley (1893–1968) Applied mathematician, aircraft engineer, and designer, born in London, England, UK. At 20 he became Claude Grahame-White's chief engineer at his flying school at Hendon, moving in 1917 to Boulton Paul Aircraft Ltd, of which he eventually became chairman and managing director. His aircraft included the Grahame-White Popular, Type XIII, and for Boulton Paul the Bobolink, Phoenix, and Defiant. His company specialized in hydraulic gun turrets and, later, power controls. He contributed significant papers on cybernetics, operational research, and ergonomics to the Royal Aeronautical Society. >> Grahame-White

North, Marianne (1830–90) British flower painter. At the age of 40, after the death of her father, she set off to paint colourful and exotic flowers in many countries. Encouraged by Sir Joseph Dalton Hooker, she gave her valuable collection to Kew Gardens, where they can be seen in a gallery, opened in 1882, which bears her name. >> Hooker, Joseph Dalton

North, Oliver (1943–) US soldier, born in San Antonio, TX. He trained at the US Naval College, Annapolis, and during the Vietnam War led a counter-insurgency marines platoon, winning a Silver Star and Purple Heart. Appointed a deputy-director of the National Security Council by President Reagan in 1981, he played a key role in a series of controversial military and security actions. Implicated in the Irangate scandal, involving the supply of arms to Iran in exchange for US hostages, and the operation of a secret slush fund to aid the Contra guerrillas in Nicaragua, he was forced to resign in 1986. Found guilty on three of 12 charges arising from the affair, he was given a three-year suspended jail sentence, and fined $150 000. >> Casey, William J; Poindexter

North, Robert (1945–) Ballet dancer and choreographer, born in Charleston, SC. In 1965 he joined the Royal Ballet School, going on to become one of the founding members of London Contemporary Dance Theatre. He spent 12 years with that company as dancer and choreographer. Early work includes *Still Life* (1975), *Scriabin Preludes and Studies* (1978), and *Troy Game* (1974), arguably his best work. He was made artistic director of Ballet Rambert (1981–6), then began working as a freelance choreographer. He later joined the Gothenburg Ballet as artistic director (1991–6).

North, Sir Thomas (?1535–?1601) Translator, born in London, England, UK. He is known for his translation of Plutarch's *Lives of the Noble Grecians and Romans* in 1579, from which Shakespeare drew his knowledge of ancient history. >> Amyot; Shakespeare, William

Northcliffe, Lord >> **Harmsworth, Alfred**

Northcote, (Thomas) James (1746–1831) Painter, born in Plymouth, Devon, SW England, UK. A pupil and assistant of Reynolds, he painted portraits and historical pictures, among them the well-known 'Princes in the Tower' and 'Prince Arthur and Hubert'. He is also remembered by Hazlitt's *Conversations with Northcote*. >> Hazlitt; Reynolds, Joshua

Northrop, John Howard (1891–1987) Biochemist, born in Yonkers, NY. He studied at Columbia University, and became professor of bacteriology at California in 1949. He discovered the fermentation process for the manufacture of acetone, and did valuable work on enzymes, successfully crystallizing pepsin and showing it to be a protein (1930). He shared the 1946 Nobel Prize for Chemistry. >> RR1123

Northrop, John K(nudsen) (1895–1981) Aircraft designer and manufacturer, born in Newark, NJ. He began as a project engineer for the Loughead Aircraft Co in 1916, continued with Douglas Aircraft Co, and was a co-founder and chief engineer of the Lockheed Aircraft Co of Burbank, CA (1927–8). He was vice-president and chief engineer of the Northrop Corporation, a subsidiary of Douglas Aircraft (1933–7), and became president and director of engineering of Northrop Aircraft Inc (1939–52). His company built military planes such as the P-61 Black Widow night fighter and the F-89 Scorpion jet and fighter.

Northumberland, Duke of >> **Warwick, John Dudley**

Norton, Caroline (Elizabeth Sarah), *née* **Sheridan** (1808–77) Writer and reformer, born in London, England, UK, the grand-daughter of Richard Brinsley Sheridan. In 1827 she married a dissolute barrister, the **Hon George Chapple Norton** (1800–75), and had three sons. She took up writing to support the family, and published a successful book of verse, *The Sorrows of Rosalie* (1829). In 1836 she separated from her husband, who brought an action of adultery against Lord Melbourne (which was defeated), obtained custody of the children, and tried to obtain the profit from her books. Her protests led to improvements in the legal status of women in relation to infant custody (1839) and marriage and divorce (1857). >> **Melbourne, 2nd Viscount**

Norton, Charles (Eliot) (1828–1908) Editor, writer, and teacher, born in Cambridge, MA. A cosmopolitan man of letters and a profoundly influential teacher, he edited the works of Dante, Carlyle, and other writers. He helped found *The Nation* (1865), and pioneered the teaching of art history at Harvard (1873–97).

Norton, Mary (1903–92) Children's novelist, born in Leighton Buzzard, Bedfordshire, SC England, UK. Educated in a convent school, she married and lived in Portugal after a brief career as an actress. She turned to writing as a means of support in the USA during World War 2. Her first books were *The Magic Bedknob* (1943), and *Bonfires and Broomsticks* (1947), re-issued in 1970 as *Bedknobs and Broomsticks* (filmed by Walt Disney Studios in 1971), but she is best known for the series of books beginning with *The Borrowers* (1952, Carnegie Medal), about a family of tiny people who live under the floorboards.

Norton, Thomas (1532–84) Lawyer and poet, born in London, England, UK. He was a successful lawyer, an MP, and a zealous Protestant who translated Calvin's *Christianae religionis institutio* (1561). With Sackville he was joint author of the tragedy *Gorboduc*, which was performed before Elizabeth I in 1562. >> **Sackville**

Norway, Nevil Shute >> **Shute, Nevil**

Nossal, Sir Gustav (Joseph Victor) (1931–) Immunologist, born in Bad Ischl, Austria. He studied at the universities of Sydney and Melbourne, and was appointed research fellow at the Walter and Eliza Hall Institute of Medical Research (1957), deputy director (1961), and director (1965. He was also professor of medical biology at Melbourne University. In 1978 he gave the ABC's Boyer Lecture, entitled 'Nature's Defences'. His discovery of the 'one cell–one antibody' rule is crucial to modern work in immunology.

Nostradamus [nostradahmus], Latin name of **Michel de Notredame** (1503–66) Physician and astrologer, born in St Rémy, France. He became doctor of medicine in 1529, and practised in Agen, Lyon, and other places. He set himself up as a prophet in c.1547. His *Centuries* of predictions in rhymed quatrains (two collections, 1555–8), expressed generally in obscure and enigmatical terms, brought their author a great reputation. Charles IX on his accession appointed him physician-in-ordinary.

Nott, Sir John (William Frederic) (1932–) British states-man and merchant banker, born in Bideford, Devon, SW England, UK. He studied at Cambridge, entered the House of Commmons in 1960 as Conservative member for St Ives, Cornwall, and was a junior Treasury minister in the government of Edward Heath (1972–4). In Margaret Thatcher's administration he was trade secretary (1979–81), and then defence secretary (1981–3), his period of office including the Falklands War. He left the House of Commons with a knighthood in 1983, and became chairman and chief executive of Lazard Brothers, the merchant bankers (1985–90).

Novak, Kim, originally **Marilyn Pauline Novak** (1933–) Film actress, born in Chicago, IL. She made her screen debut in *The French Line* (1954), then starred in *The Pushover* (1954), and soon became a leading box-office attraction of the 1950s – perhaps the last of the 'sex goddesses' produced by the Hollywood star system. Her films include *The Man With The Golden Arm* (1955), *Pal Joey* (1957), *Vertigo* (1958), *The Amorous Adventures of Moll Flanders* (1965), and *The Mirror Crack'd* (1980). She was largely absent from the screen in the 1980s, following her marriage, but still takes occasional roles, as in *Liebestraum* (1991).

Novak, Michael [nohvak] (1933–) Lay theologian, economist, and political philosopher, born in Johnstown, PA. He studied at the Holy Cross Seminary at the University of Notre Dame, MA, and the Gregorian University in Rome, but left the Congregation of Holy Cross in 1960 soon after his ordination to the priesthood, and was accepted into Harvard on a graduate fellowship later that year. His books include *The Open Church* (1964) and *The Spirit of Democratic Capitalism* (1982). In 1981 he was appointed US ambassador for the UN Human Rights Commission, and in 1994 received the Templeton Prize for Progress in Religion.

Novák, Vitezslav [nohvak] (1870–1949) Composer, born in Kamenitz, Czech Republic. A pupil of Dvořák, he studied at Prague Conservatory, later becoming professor there (1909–20). His many compositions, which include operas and ballets, show the influence of his native folk melody. >> **Dvořák**

Novalis [nohvalis], pseudonym of **Friedrich Leopold von Hardenberg** (1772–1801) Romantic poet and novelist, born in Oberwiederstedt, Germany. At Weissenfels (1795) he fell in love with a girl whose early death left a lasting impression upon him, and in whose memory he wrote the prose lyrics of *Hymnen an die Nacht* (1800, Hymns to the Night). He also published *Geistliche Lieder* (1799, Sacred Songs). He left two philosophical Romances, both incomplete, *Heinrich von Ofterdingen* and *Die Lehrlinge zu Sais* (The Novices of Sais). He is sometimes called 'the prophet of Romanticism'.

Novatian [nohvayshn] (3rd-c) Theologian and anti-pope, born in Rome. Converted to Christianity, he was ordained a priest. In 251, soon after the persecution under Emperor Decius, a controversy arose about the status of those who fell away during persecution. Pope Cornelius (251–53) defended indulgence towards the lapsed. Novatian was chosen by a small party and ordained bishop in opposition to Cornelius, denying the lawfulness of readmitting the lapsed to communion. He was excommunicated at a synod in 251, but in spite of persecution the sect survived into the 6th-c.

Novello, Ivor [noveloh], originally **David Ivor Davies** (1893–1951) Actor, composer, songwriter, and playwright, born in Cardiff. He studied at Oxford, where he was a chorister. His song 'Keep the Home Fires Burning' was one of the most popular of World War 1. He first appeared on the regular stage in London in 1921 and enjoyed great popularity, his most successful and characteristic works being his 'Ruritanian' musical plays such as *Glamorous Night* (1935), *The Dancing Years* (1939), and *King's Rhapsody* (1949).

Novello, Vincent [no<u>ve</u>loh] (1781–1861) Organist, composer, and music publisher, born in London, England, UK. He arranged the publication of two volumes of sacred music (1811), which was the start of the publishing house of Novello & Co. He was a founder-member of the Philharmonic Society (1813), and subsequently its pianist and conductor. His compositions improved church music, and he was a painstaking editor of unpublished works.

Noverre, Jean-Georges [novair] (1727–1810) Dancer, choreographer, and ballet master, born in Paris. He claimed the invention of the notion of the *ballet d'action*, which is commonly identified as one of the greatest influences on ballet as it is known and practised today. Although he studied dance, he eventually opted for a career as a choreographer. He was ballet master at the Paris Opéra Comique (1754), the royal court theatre of Württemberg (now the Stuttgart Ballet, 1760–6), and the Paris Opéra (1776–9). He also worked extensively in Lyon, Vienna, and Milan.

Novotný, Antonin [<u>no</u>votnee] (1904–75) Czech politician and president (1957–68), born near Prague. A Communist from 1921, he was imprisoned by the Nazis (1941–5), and became first secretary of the Czechoslovak Communist Party, and virtual dictator in 1953. A dedicated Stalinist, his state planning on the needs of heavy industry brought an economic recession (1961), and his unpopularity forced him to make token concessions from 1962 onwards. He was succeeded as first secretary by the reformist Slovak, Alexander Dubček (1968), and resigned the presidency two months later. >> Dubček; RR1043

Noyes, Alfred [noyz] (1880–1958) Poet, born in Wolverhampton, West Midlands, C England, UK. His first book of poetry was completed while studying at Oxford, which he left without taking a degree. His most successful work deals with the sea and the Elizabethan tradition, notably the epic *Drake* (1908). Having married an American, he travelled in the USA, and became visiting professor of poetry at Princeton (1914–23). In 1922 appeared *The Torchbearers*, a panegyric in blank verse on the hitherto comparatively unsung men of science. He published literary essays in *Some Aspects of Modern Poetry* (1924), a defence of traditionalism, and he also wrote plays, and studies of William Morris and Voltaire.

Noyes, Eliot [noyz] (1910–77) Designer and architect, born in Boston, MA. As a student of architecture he came under the influence of Gropius, Breuer, and Le Corbusier. In 1940 he set up the Department of Industrial Design at the Museum of Modern Art, New York City. After working for the American stage designer and architect Norman Bel Geddes, he established his own practice in 1947. He worked for major companies such as Westinghouse, Mobil and, most notably, IBM, for which he became consultant design director. At his death it was said that 'objects the world over were his monument'. >> Bel Geddes; Breuer; Gropius; Le Corbusier

Nu, U [noo] ('uncle'), originally **Thakin Nu** (1907–95) Burmese statesman and prime minister (1948–56, 1957–8, 1960–2), born in Wakema, Myanmar (formerly, Burma). He studied at Rangoon University, and came to prominence through student political movements (1934). Imprisoned by the British for sedition (1940), he was released by the Japanese and served in Ba Maw's puppet administration. In 1946 he became president of the Burmese Constituent Assembly, and then the first prime minister of the independent Burmese Republic. He was finally overthrown by a military coup in 1962, and imprisoned, but released in 1966. He then lived abroad organizing resistance to the military regime, but returned to Burma in 1980 to become a Buddhist monk. Following the uprising in 1988, he formed an Alliance for Peace and Democracy, which led to his house arrest until 1992. >> RR1076

Nuesslein-Volhard, Christiane [nüsliyn folhaht] (1942–) Developmental biologist, born in Magdeburg, Germany. She studied at the University of Tübingen, where she joined the Max-Planck Institute for Developmental Biology. She shared the Nobel Prize for Physiology or Medicine in 1995 for her research into how genes control early development of the human embryo. Using the fruit fly, her contribution, in collaboration with Wieschaus, was to identify a number of genes which determine the body plan and formation of body segments. She was the first German woman to receive a science Nobel Prize. >> Lewis, Edward; Wieschaus

Nuffield, William Richard Morris, 1st Viscount (1877–1963) Motor magnate and philanthropist, born in Worcester, Hereford and Worcester, WC England, UK. He started in the bicycle repair business, and was the first British manufacturer to develop the mass production of cheap cars (Morris). He was made a baronet in 1929 and a viscount in 1934. He used part of his vast fortune to benefit hospitals, charities, and Oxford University. In 1937 he endowed Nuffield College, Oxford, and in 1943 established the Nuffield Foundation for medical, scientific, and social research.

Nujoma, Sam Daniel [nujohma] (1929–) Namibian nationalist leader, and first president of independent Namibia (1990–), born in Ongandjern, Namibia. Educated at a Finnish missionary school in Windhoek, he entered active politics in 1958, founding the South West Africa People's Organisation of Namibia. Exiled in 1960 and again in 1966, he established a military wing, the People's Liberation Army of Namibia, in the mid-1960s, and his long struggle for Namibia's independence eventually bore fruit in 1989. >> RR1077

Numa Pompilius [nyooma pompilius] (c.700 BC) The second of Rome's early kings. According to tradition he ruled from 715 to 673 BC. He is described as a peaceful ruler, and was credited with organizing the religious life of the community. >> RR1084

Nunn, Trevor (Robert) (1940–) Stage director, born in Ipswich, Suffolk, E England, UK. He studied at Cambridge, then joined the Belgrade Theatre, Coventry, as a trainee director, and moved to the Royal Shakespeare Company in 1965. In 1968 he succeeded Peter Hall as the company's artistic director, being joined as co-artistic director by Terry Hands 10 years later. He has directed many outstanding productions for the Royal Shakespeare Company (RSC), and during his directorship (1968–87) the RSC took many strides forward, including the opening of two new theatres in Stratford: The Other Place (1974) and The Swan (1986). He has also directed the Andrew Lloyd Webber musicals *Cats* (1981), *Starlight Express* (1984), and *Aspects of Love* (1989). He was appointed director of the Royal National Theatre from 1997. >> Hands

Nureyev, Rudolf (Hametovich) [noorayef] (1938–93) Ballet dancer, born in Irkutsk, Russia. He studied at the Leningrad Choreographic School, and became a soloist with the Kirov Ballet. While touring with the Ballet in 1961, he obtained political asylum in Paris, and became an Austrian citizen in 1982. He made his debut at Covent Garden with the Royal Ballet in 1962, and became Fonteyn's regular partner. His virtuosity and expressiveness made him one of the greatest male dancers of the 1960s, in both classical and modern ballets. He began to choreograph and dance for many European companies, and became ballet director of the Paris Opéra (1983–9) and principal choreographer (1989–92). In his later years he also began to conduct, leading orchestras in the USA, Europe, and the former Soviet Union. His autobiography, *Nureyev*, appeared in 1962. >> Fonteyn

Nurmi, Paavo (Johannes) [**noor**mee] (1897–1973) Athlete, born in Turku, Finland. He won nine gold medals at three Olympic Games (1920–8), and set 22 world records at distances ranging from 1500 m to 10 000 m. His first world record was in 1921, when he clocked 30 min 40·2 sec for the 10 000 m. He retired from racing in 1933. His statue stands outside the Helsinki Olympic Stadium. >> RR1135

Nuvolari, Tazio [noovoh**lah**ree] (1892–1953) Italian motor-racing driver, considered by many to have been the greatest of the pre-war years. He joined the Alfa Romeo team in 1930, and scored many wins, often against superior cars. He won the 1935 German Grand Prix in a four-year old Alfa Romeo, despite the presence of new Mercedes-Benz and Auto Union cars.

Nyerere, Julius (Kambarage) [nye**rair**ay] (1922–) Tanzanian statesman and president (1962–85), born in Butiama, Tanzania (formerly, Tanganyika). He became a teacher at Makerere, then studied at Edinburgh. He reorganized the nationalists into the Tanganyika African National Union (1954), of which he became president, and in 1960 became chief minister. He was premier when Tanganyika was granted internal self-government (1961), and was made president on independence (1962). In 1964 he negotiated the union of Tanganyika and Zanzibar as Tanzania. He led his country on a path of Socialism and self-reliance, but his policies failed, and he retired in 1985. >> Mwinyi; RR1092

Nyman, Michael [**niy**man] (1944–) Pianist and composer, born in London. He formed the Michael Nyman Band in 1977, for which he composed several works characterized by highly charged, stylized, rhythmical chord progressions, much influenced by Purcell, in which his own piano playing is a driving force. His compositions include scores for the films of Peter Greenaway, and for the films *Carrington* and *The Piano*, as well as a chamber opera *The Man Who Mistook His Wife for a Hat* (1986). Later works include string quartets, and concertos for piano (1994) and trombone (1995). >> Greenaway, Peter

Oakeshott, Michael Joseph (1901–90) Philosopher and political theorist, born in Harpenden, Hertfordshire, SE England, UK. He studied at Cambridge, taught there (1929–49), and was professor of political science at the London School of Economics (1950–69). His first and main philosophical work was *Experience and its Modes* (1933), written broadly from within the English idealist tradition. This view of human experience and conduct is developed in his political theory, which tends to be conservative, pragmatic, and sceptical of systematization and ideology.

Oakley, Annie, popular name of **Phoebe Anne Oakley Moses** (1860–1926) Rodeo star and sharp-shooter, born in Darke Co, OH. She learned to shoot at an early age, and married **Frank E Butler** in 1876 after beating him in a shooting match. They formed a trick-shooting act, and from 1885 toured widely with the Buffalo Bill Wild West Show. A tiny woman just under five feet tall, from 30 paces she shot cigarettes from her husband's lips and the lips of Kaiser Wilhelm II, and through the pips of a playing card tossed in the air. 'Annie Oakley' became a synonym for a complimentary ticket, because of the hole traditionally punched in it. Her story was fictionalized in the Irving Berlin musical comedy *Annie Get Your Gun* (1946), starring Ethel Merman.

Oaksey, Baron >> **Lawrence, Geoffrey**

Oasis British pop group, formed in 1992 with five members, all but one from Manchester: **Liam Gallagher** (1972– , vocals), **Noel Gallagher** (1967– , lead guitar, backing vocals, songwriter), **Paul 'Bonehead' Arthurs** (1965– , rhythm guitar), **Paul 'Guigsy' McGuigan** (1971– , bass guitar), and **Tony McCarroll** (drums), replaced in 1995 by **Alan White** (1972– , born in London). Their first single, 'Supersonic' (1994), became an immediate number 1 hit, and was followed by a series of hits, such as 'Shakermaker' (1994), 'Wonderwall' (1995), 'Don't Look Back in Anger' (1996), and 'D'You Know What I Mean' (1997). Their first album, *Definitely Maybe* (1994) was the fastest selling debut album in British pop history, later albums including *What's The Story (Morning Glory)* (1995) and *Be Here Now* (1997). The group rose to become the leading band of the 1990s, touring widely, the flamboyant personal lives of the Gallagher brothers attracting the kind of media attention that had not been since the Beatles (with whom – along with God – they readily compared themselves). >> Beatles

Oates, Joyce Carol (1938–) Novelist and essayist, born in Lockport, NY. She studied at Syracuse University and at the University of Wisconsin, taught English at Detroit (1961–7), then became professor of English at Windsor, Ontario. Her first novel was *With Shuddering Fall* (1964), and *Them* (1969), her fourth novel, won a National Book award. Later books include *Marya: A Life* (1986), *What I Lived For* (1994), and *We Were the Mulvaneys* (1996). She has published poetry, essays, and criticism, and her short-story collections include *The Wheel of Love* (1970).

Oates, Lawrence (Edward Grace) (1880–1912) Explorer, born in London, England, UK. He studied at Eton, joined the army, and served in South Africa. In 1910 he joined Scott's Antarctic Expedition in charge of the ponies, and was one of the party of five to reach the South Pole in 1912. On the return journey the explorers became weatherbound. Lamed by severe frostbite, and convinced that his condition would fatally handicap his companions' prospect of survival, he walked out into the blizzard, sacrificing his life. His last words have become famous: 'I am just going outside, I may be some time'. >> Scott, R F

Oates, Titus (1649–1705) Conspirator and perjurer, born in Oakham, Leicestershire, C England, UK. He studied at Cambridge, and took Anglican orders, but was dismissed from his curacy for misconduct. Having feigned conversion to catholicism and attended Jesuit seminaries on the continent, in 1677 he made public details of a fictitious Jesuit plot to murder Charles II and restore catholicism. This 'Popish Plot' caused widespread panic, and at least 35 innocent people were tried and executed for complicity in it; but suspicion of Oates gradually grew and two years later he was found guilty of perjury, flogged, and imprisoned for life. The Revolution of 1688 set him at liberty, and he was granted a pension. >> Jeffreys, George

Oatley, Sir Charles (1904–96) Electronic engineer and inventor, born in Frome, Somerset, SW England, UK. He studied at Cambridge, and joined the staff of King's College, London. During World War 2 he was a member of the Radar Research and Development Establishment, and in 1945 he returned to Cambridge, becoming professor of electrical engineering (1960). From 1948 his research was concentrated on the development of the scanning electron microscope, capable of producing three-dimensional images at magnifications of 100 000 or more. >> Hillier; Ruska; Zworykin

Obadiah [ohbadiya], also called **Abdias** One of the 12 so-called 'minor' prophets of the Old Testament. Nothing is known of him except for his name, which means 'servant of God'. His prohecies are contained in the shortest book of the Old Testament. The work may have originated soon after the fall of Jerusalem in 587/6 BC, but it is not always seen as a unified composition deriving from one time. It prophesies the fall of Edom in retribution for taking sides against Jerusalem, predicting judgment on the nations and the restoration of Israel at the final day of the Lord.

Obel, Matthias de l' >> **L'Obel, Matthias de**

Oberth, Hermann (Julius) [ohbairt] (1894–1990) Astrophysicist, born in Sibiu, Hungary. He studied in Munich, and abandoned a medical career for mathematics and astronomy. His first book, *Die Rakete zu den Planetenrämen* (1923, The Rocket into Interplanetary Space), established his reputation, and in 1928 he was elected president of the German Society for Space Travel. In World War 2 he worked at the experimental rocket centre at Peenemünde, and later assisted Wernher von Braun in developing space rockets in the USA (1955–61). He has been called 'the father of German rocketry'. >> von Braun

Obote, (Apollo) Milton [obohtay] (1924–) Ugandan statesman, prime minister (1962–71), and president (1967–71, 1981–5), born in Lango, Uganda. He studied at Makerere College, Kampala, he was elected to the legislative council (1957), and founded the Uganda People's Congress (1960). At independence in 1962 he became the new nation's first prime minister. In 1966 he mounted a coup, declared a republic, and made himself executive president. In 1971 he was, in turn, deposed by Idi Amin, and took refuge in Tanzania. After Amin's removal in 1979, he was re-elected president in 1981. Ousted by Brigadier Basilio Okello in 1985, he was granted political asylum in Zambia. >> Amin; RR1094

O'Brien, (Donal) Conor (Dermod David Donat) Cruise (1917–) Historian, critic, and Irish statesman, born in Dublin. He studied at Dublin, and became an outstanding historian and critic. His best-known work is *To*

Katanga and Back (1962), an autobiographical narrative of the Congo crisis of 1961. An MP from 1969, he became minister for posts and telegraphs (1973–7). He was subsequently editor-in-chief of *The Observer*, as well as the author of studies on Albert Camus and Edmund Burke.

O'Brien, Edna (1932–) Novelist and short-story writer, born in Tuamgraney, Co Clare, Ireland. She studied at the Pharmaceutical College of Dublin, and practised pharmacy briefly before becoming a writer. Much of her writing is concerned with the position of women in society – their lack of fulfilment and the repressive nature of their upbringing. Her celebrated books include *The Country Girls* (1960), *Girls in Their Married Bliss* (1963), and *August Is a Wicked Month* (1965). *The Collected Edna O'Brien*, containing nine novels, was published in 1978. Later works include *Time and Tide* (1992), *House of Splendid Isolation* (1994), and *Down by the River* (1996). Her short stories are also highly regarded, the best from several collections appearing in *The Fanatic Heart* (1985), and in 1990 she published *Lantern Slides*.

O'Brien, Flann, pseudonym of **Brian O'Nolan**, also known as **Myles na Gopaleen** (1911–66) Writer and journalist, born in Strabane, Co Tyrone. He studied at Dublin, and his first and major novel was *At Swim-Two-Birds* (1939). A civil servant, he contributed a column to the *Irish Times* for some 20 years under his Irish pseudonym. Best known as an idiosyncratic newspaper columnist, various anthologies appeared after his death – *The Best of Myles* (1968), *The Various Lives of Keats and Chapman and the Brother* (1976), and *Myles From Dublin* (1985).

O'Brien, Jeremiah (1744–1818) Revolutionary hero, born in Kittery, ME. He ably defended Machias, ME (then part of Massachusetts), against British vessels, and captured HMS *Margaretta* in what was counted as the first naval battle of the Revolution. He commanded privateers (1777–80), and was captured and briefly imprisoned in England (1780).

O'Brien, Kate (1897–1974) Playwright and novelist, born in Limerick, Co Limerick, Ireland. She studied at Dublin, and began a career in London as a playwright when she was 30, publishing her prizewinning *Without My Cloak* in 1931. Other works include *Mary Lavelle* (1936), *The Land of Spices* (1941), and *As Music and Splendour* (1958). A remarkable observer of life, her novels are best understood by an appreciation of her consciousness of a lesbian sexual identity.

O'Brien, (Michael) Vincent (1917–) Horse trainer, born in Churchtown, Co Cork, Ireland. He made an immediate impact on the post-war English National Hunt scene with *Cottage Rake*, which won the Cheltenham Gold Cup in three consecutive years from 1948. On the flat he trained, in 1966, the winners of the Oaks, the 1000 Guineas, the Eclipse Stakes, and the Champion Stakes. In 1977, his horse, *The Minstrel*, won the Derby, the Irish Derby, and the King George VI, and Queen Elizabeth Stakes.

O'Brien, William (1852–1928) Journalist and nationalist, born in Mallow, Co Cork, Ireland. He studied at Queen's College, Cork, became editor of the weekly *United Ireland*, and sat in parliament as a Nationalist (1883–95). Several times prosecuted, and imprisoned for two years, he later returned to parliament (1900–18), founded the United Irish League (1898), and the All-for-Ireland League (1910).

O'Brien, William Smith (1803–64) Irish nationalist, born in Dromoland, Co Clare, Ireland. He studied at Cambridge, was Conservative MP for Ennis (1825) and Co Limerick (1835) and, though a Protestant, supported the Catholic claims as a Whig. In 1848 he urged the formation of a National Guard and a national rebellion, which ended ludicrously in a battle in the widow McCormack's cabbage garden at Ballingarry in Co Tipperary. Arrested and sentenced,

he served five years in Tasmania, released in 1854 on condition of not returning to Ireland. In 1856 he received an unconditional pardon, but took no further part in politics.

O'Bryan, William (1778–1868) Nonconformist clergyman, born in Gunwen, Cornwall, SW England, UK. He quarrelled with the Methodists, and in 1815 founded a new Methodist communion, the (Arminian) Bible Christians, or *Bryanites*. In 1831 he went to the USA as an itinerant preacher.

O'Byrne, Dermot >> **Bax, Sir Arnold**

O Cadhain, Máirtín [oh kayn, mah(r)tin], Eng **Martin Kane** (1906–70) Gaelic novelist, born in Galway, Ireland. A schoolteacher, he lost his job when he joined the Irish Republican Army in the 1930s as a recruiting officer. Interned during World War 2 in the Curragh Camp, Kildare, he published Irish short stories, followed in 1949 by his masterpiece, *Cré na Cille*, a ruthless social analysis of rural community ill-feeling, revealed by the conversations and monologues of the corpses in the local graveyard. An official translator of Irish parliamentary debates from 1949, he was fluent in eight languages. He became lecturer in modern Irish in Trinity College, Dublin (1956), then professor (1969).

O'Casey, Sean, originally **John Casey** (1880–1964) Playwright, born in Dublin. From an impoverished Protestant family, he suffered from poor health during his boyhood. Trachoma permanently damaged his eyesight and interrupted his education. During years of physical hardship in labouring work, he became involved with the Irish Citizen Army, but resigned in 1914 in protest against its anti-Union attitudes. His first publication was a broadside, *The Story of Thomas Ashe* (1917), about a friend in the Citizen Army who died on hunger strike, but he was already interested in the work of the Abbey Theatre. After rejecting at least three of his plays, the Abbey staged *The Shadow of a Gunman* (1923) and *Juno and the Paycock* (1924). Later he became more experimental and impressionistic. His anti-war drama *The Plough and the Stars* (1926) provoked a full-scale riot, and caused him to leave Ireland for good. Other works include *The Silver Tassie* (1929), *Cockadoodle Dandy* (1949), and *The Bishop's Bonfire* (1955). He also wrote essays, such as *The Flying Wasp* (1936), and was awarded the Hawthornden Prize in 1926.

Occam, William >> **William of Ockham**

Occleve, Thomas >> **Hoccleve, Thomas**

Ochino, Bernardino [ohkeenoh] (1487–1564) Protestant reformer, born in Siena, Italy. He changed from the Franciscans to the Capuchins (1534), becoming vicar-general of the order after four years. Summoned to Rome to answer for evangelical tendencies (1542), he fled to Calvin in Geneva. In 1545 he became preacher to the Italians in Augsburg. Invited to England, he was pastor to the Italian exiles and a prebend in Canterbury. At Mary I's accession (1553) he fled to Switzerland, but the publication of *Thirty Dialogues* led to his being banished. >> **Calvin, John**

Ochoa, Severo [ohchoha] (1905–93) Biochemist, born in Luarca, Spain. He studied medicine at Madrid University, then carried out research at Heidelberg and Oxford. He emigrated to the USA in 1941, joining the staff of the New York University Medicine School. His work on the biological synthesis of nucleic activities brought him a share of the 1959 Nobel Prize for Physiology or Medicine. >> RR1124

Ockeghem, Jean d' >> **Okeghem, Jean d'**

Ockham, William of >> **William of Ockham**

O'Connell, Daniel, known as **the Liberator** (1775–1847) Irish Catholic political leader, born near Cahirciveen, Co Kerry, Ireland. He became a lawyer, and in 1823 formed the Catholic Association, which successfully fought elections against the landlords. His election as MP for Co Clare precipitated a crisis in Wellington's government, which eventually granted Catholic Emancipation (1829), enabling him to take his seat in the Commons. In 1840 he founded the Repeal Association, and agitation to end the union with Britain increased. In 1844 he was imprisoned for 14 weeks on charge of sedition. In conflict with the Young Ireland movement (1846), and failing in health, he left Ireland in 1847. >> Wellington

O'Connor, Feargus Edward (1794–1855) Chartist leader, born in Connorville, Co Cork, Ireland. He studied at Dublin, became a lawyer, and entered parliament in 1832. Estranged from O'Connell, he devoted himself to the cause of the working classes in England. His Leeds *Northern Star* (1837) became the most influential Chartist newspaper. He attempted, without great success, to unify the Chartist movement via the National Charter Association (1842), and presented himself as leader of the Chartist cause. Elected MP for Nottingham in 1847, in 1852 insanity caused his withdrawal from public life.

O'Connor, (Mary) Flannery (1925–64) Writer, born in Savannah, GA. She studied at the University of Iowa, and was brought up a Roman Catholic in the Bible-belt of the Deep South. *Wise Blood* (1952), the first of her two novels, is a bizarre tragi-comedy, and its theme of vocation is taken up again in her second, *The Violent Bear It Away* (1960). Regarded as one of the finest short-story writers of her generation, her collections include *A Good Man Is Hard To Find, and Other Stories* (1955) and *Everything That Rises Must Converge* (1965). She was crippled for more than 10 years by lupus erythematosus, from which she died.

O'Connor, Frank, pseudonym of **Michael O'Donovan** (1903–66) Short-story writer, novelist and playwright, born in Cork, Co Cork, Ireland. From a poor family, he worked as a railway clerk and a librarian, and was imprisoned briefly for his involvement with the IRA. A director of the Abbey Theatre, Dublin, in the 1930s, he was a visiting professor at several universities in the USA, and became popular for his short stories published in *The New Yorker* (1945–61). His volumes include *Guests of the Nation* (1931), *Crab Apple Jelly* (1944), and *Collected Stories* (1981). He also wrote critical studies, and a biography of Michael Collins, *The Big Fellow* (1937).

O'Connor, Sandra Day, *née* **Day** (1930–) Jurist, the first female justice of the US Supreme Court, born in El Paso, TX. She studied law and was admitted to the bar in California, but then took up practice in Arizona, where she became assistant attorney-general (1965–9) and then a state senator. She was a Superior Court judge of Maricopa Co (1974–9) and a judge of the Arizona Court of Appeals (1979–81) before being named an Associate Justice of the Supreme Court in 1981.

Octavia (c. 69 BC–11 BC) Sister of the emperor Augustus, distinguished for her beauty and virtue. On the death of her first husband, **Marcellus**, in 40 BC she consented to marry Mark Antony to reconcile him and her brother; but in 32 BC Antony divorced her and forsook her for Cleopatra. >> Antonius; Augustus

Octavian >> **Augustus**

O'Day, Anita (1919–) Jazz vocalist, born in Chicago, IL. She sang with the Max Miller combo (1939) and the Gene Krupa band (1941–3), with whom she had several hit records including 'Just A Little Bit South Of North Carolina' and 'Georgia On My Mind'. She also worked with Duke Ellington and Benny Goodman, and appeared in the films *The Gene Krupa Story* (1959) and *Jazz on a Summer's Day* (1960). She had another hit with 'Tennessee Waltz' (1951), and recorded several albums, include *Sings Jazz* (1952) and *Live at the City* (1979).

Odets, Clifford [oh**dets**] (1906–63) Playwright and actor, born in Philadelphia, PA. In 1931 he joined the Group

Theater, New York City, becoming a leading US playwright in the 1930s. His works are marked by a strong social conscience, and grow largely from the conditions of the Great Depression. They include *Waiting for Lefty*, *Till the Day I Die* (both 1935), and *Golden Boy* (1937). His film scripts include *The General Died at Dawn* (1936), *None but the Lonely Heart* (1944, which he directed), and *The Big Knife* (1955).

Odette, popular name of **Odette Hallowes**, formerly **Churchill** (to 1955) and **Sansom** (to 1946), née **Brailly** (1912–95) French wartime resistance heroine, born in Amiens, France. Brought up in France, she married an Englishman in 1931 and moved to London. Through responding to a BBC appeal in 1942 for information about the coast of N Europe, she came to the attention of the French section of the Special Operations Executive, who trained her, and sent her to France as an agent. Arrested by the Germans in 1943, she was tortured by the Gestapo in Paris, and sent to Ravensbruck concentration camp. Awarded the George Cross in 1946, her wartime exploits were retold in a successful film, *Odette* (1950), starring Anna Neagle, which made her and her then husband, Peter Churchill, national figures. >> Neagle

Odling, William (1829–1921) Chemist, born in London, England, UK. Professor of chemistry at Oxford, he classified the silicates, and put forward suggestions with regard to atomic weights which made O = 16 instead of 8.

Odo [**oh**doh] (c. 1036–97) Anglo-Norman clergyman, Bishop of Bayeux, and half-brother of William I. He fought at the Battle of Hastings (1066) and was created Earl of Kent. He played a conspicuous part under William in English history, and was regent during his absences in Normandy, but left England after rebelling against William II. He rebuilt Bayeux Cathedral, and may have commissioned the Bayeux tapestry. >> William I (of England); William II (of England)

Odoacer [ohdoh**ay**ser], also found as **Odovacar** (?–493) Germanic warrior who destroyed the W Roman empire, and became the first barbarian king of Italy (476–93). An able ruler, he was challenged and overthrown by the Ostrogothic King Theodoric (489–93) at the instigation of the E Roman Emperor, Zeno. >> Theodoric

O'Donnell, Peadar or **Peter** (1893–1986) Revolutionary and writer, born in Meenmore, Co Donegal, Ireland. He became a guerrilla republican leader, opposed the 1921 Anglo-Irish Treaty, was captured in Civil War fighting, and escaped after a 41-day hunger-strike. Editor of *An Phoblacht*, the official IRA newspaper, he left the IRA in 1934, and fought for the Spanish Republic (1936–7). His editorship of the literary monthly, *The Bell* (1946–54), was invaluable in furthering Irish writing, and his finest work was probably the novel *Islanders* (1927).

O'Donovan, Michael >> **O'Connor, Frank**

Odovacar >> **Odoacer**

O'Duffy, Eimar Ultan (1893–1935) Satirical playwright and novelist, born in Dublin. He trained in dentistry at Dublin, but embraced the new Irish revolutionary cultural nationalism under the influence of Thomas MacDonagh and Joseph Plunkett, who published and produced his first play, *The Walls of Athens*, and whose Irish Theatre also staged his *The Phoenix on the Roof* (1915). He broke with them on the Easter Rising of 1916 where, as an Irish volunteer loyal to John MacNeill, he was one of the couriers who tried to transmit the order countermanding it. His other works include the novel *The Wasted Island* (1919). >> MacDonagh, Thomas; MacNeill

Oe, Kenzaburo [oh**ay**] (1935–) Novelist and short-story writer, born in Shikoku, Japan. He studied French at the University of Tokyo, and became known for his short stories capturing the mood of postwar Japan, such as *The Catch*

(trans 1959, Akutagawa Prize). His major books include *Hiroshima Notes* (1965; trans 1981), *A Personal Matter* (1964; trans 1968), *The Silent Cry* (1967, trans 1974, Tanizaki Prize), and *A Healing Family* (trans 1996). He received the Nobel Prize for Literature in 1994.

Oeben, Jean François >> **Riesener, Jean Henri**

Oecolampadius, John [eekohlampadius], Latinized Greek form of **Johannes Hüssgen**, **Huszgen** or **Hausschein** (1482–1531) Clergyman and scholar, born in Weinsberg, Germany. He studied at Heidelberg, became tutor to the sons of the Elector Palatine, and subsequently preacher at Weinsberg (1510) and Basel (1515), where Erasmus employed him on his Greek New Testament. In 1520 he entered a monastery, but under Luther's influence became a reformer at Basel in 1522 as preacher and professor of theology. >> **Erasmus; Luther**

Oehlenschläger, Adam Gottlob [oelenshlayger] (1779–1850) Poet and playwright, born in Vesterbro, Denmark. He studied law at Copenhagen, but turned to writing, becoming the leader of the Danish Romantic movement. His fame rests mainly on his 24 tragedies, beginning with *Hakon Jarl* (1807), based on the life of a national hero. In 1810 he was made professor of aesthetics at Copenhagen.

Oersted, Hans Christian [oe(r)sted] (1777–1851) Physicist, born in Rudkøbing, Denmark. He became a professor at Copenhagen (1806), where in 1820 he discovered the magnetic effect of an electric current. The unit of magnetic field strength is named after him.

Oerter, Al(fred) [erter] (1936–) Athlete and discus-thrower, born in Astoria, NY. An outstanding Olympic competitor, he won four consecutive gold medals for the discus, at Melbourne (1956), Rome (1960), Tokyo (1964), and Mexico (1968), breaking the Olympic record each time. No other athlete has dominated an event so overwhelmingly for so long. >> RR1137

O'Faolain, Sean [ohfaylen], pseudonym of **Sean Whelan** (1900–91) Writer, born in Dublin. He studied at the National University of Ireland, and at Harvard, and lectured in America before returning to Ireland to teach. He attracted attention with a novel, *A Nest of Simple Folk* (1933), and produced an edition of translations from Gaelic – *The Silver Branch* (1938). He never quite repeated his success with later novels, but wrote many biographies, including *Daniel O'Connell* (1938), *De Valera* (1939), and *The Great O'Neill* (1942), this last being a life of the 2nd Earl of Tyrone.

Offa (?–796) King of Mercia (757–96). He was the greatest Anglo-Saxon ruler in the 8th-c, treated as an equal by Charlemagne. He asserted his authority over all the kingdoms S of the Humber, and regarded their rulers as subordinate provincial governors. He was responsible for constructing Offa's Dyke, stretching for 70 mi along the Welsh border, and established a new currency based on the silver penny which, with numerous changes of design, remained the standard coin of England for many centuries. His reign represents an important but flawed attempt to unify England, with the Mercian supremacy collapsing soon after his death.

Offenbach, Jacques [ofenbahkh], originally **Jacob Eberst** (1819–80) Composer, born in Cologne, Germany. He moved to Paris in 1833, directing the Théâtre-Français orchestra in 1848, and becoming manager of the *Bouffes-Parisiens* in 1855. He composed many light, lively operettas, such as *Orphée aux enfers* (1858, trans Orpheus in the Underworld). He also produced one grand opera, *Les contes d'Hoffmann* (The Tales of Hoffmann), which was not produced until 1881, after his death. >> **Hoffman, E T W**

O'Flaherty, Liam (1897–1984) Writer, born on Inishmore in the Aran Is, Co Galway, Ireland. He studied at Rockwell College, Tipperary, and University College, Dublin, and

fought in the British army during World War 1, and with the Republicans in the Irish Civil War. He went to London in 1922 to become a writer, and published his first novels, *Thy Neighbour's Wife* (1923) and *The Black Soul* (1924). *The Informer* (1926) won the James Tait Black Memorial Prize and was a popular success. A leading figure of the Irish Renaissance, he has also published collections of short stories.

Ogden, C(harles) K(ay) (1889–1957) Linguistic reformer, born in Fleetwood, Lancashire, NW England, UK. He studied classics at Cambridge, was founder-editor of the *Cambridge Magazine* (1912–22), and founder in 1917 of the Orthological Institute. In the 1920s he conceived the idea of 'Basic English', a simplified system of English as an international language with a restricted vocabulary of 850 words, which he developed with the help of I A Richards. >> **Richards, I A**

Ogdon, John (Andrew Howard) (1937–89) Pianist, born in Mansfield Woodhouse, Nottinghamshire, C England, UK. He studied in Manchester, and in 1962 was joint prize-winner in the Tchaikovsky Competition in Moscow. He had a powerful technique, a remarkable memory, and a huge repertory. He also composed, his works including a piano concerto. Illness forced him to give up playing for several years.

Ogilby, John [ohgilbee] (1600–76) Topographer, printer, and map-maker, born in Edinburgh, EC Scotland, UK. A dancing teacher and theatre owner, he lost everything in the Civil War, but after the Restoration obtained court recognition and became a London publisher. The great fire of 1666 destroyed his stock but got him the job of surveying the gutted sites in the city. He established a thriving printing house and was appointed 'king's cosmographer and geographic printer'. His most important publications were engravings of maps and atlases, including Africa (1670), America (1671), and Asia (1673), and a road atlas of Britain (1675), unfinished at his death.

Ogilvie, St John (1579/80–1615) Jesuit priest and martyr, born in Banff, Aberdeenshire, NE Scotland, UK. He worked in Edinburgh, Glasgow, and Renfrew, and was hanged at Glasgow Cross for his defence of the spiritual supremacy of the pope. Beatified in 1927 and finally canonized in 1976, he is the only officially recognized martyr in post-Reformation Scotland. Feast day 10 March.

Ogilvie, Angus / James >> **Alexandra, Princess**

Ogilvie Thompson, Julian (1934–) Businessman, born in Cape Town, South Africa. He studied at Diocesan College, Rondebosch, and became a personal assistant to Harry Oppenheimer at Anglo American Corporation of SA, South Africa's largest corporation. Formerly chairman of De Beer's Consolidated Mines, and Minorco SA, he became chairman of Anglo American in 1990. He is also a governor of the Urban Foundation. >> **Oppenheimer, Harry Frederick**

Oglethorpe, James Edward (1696–1785) Army officer, born in London, England, UK. He sat in parliament (1722–54), and in 1732 founded the colony of Georgia in North America, where debtors from English jails and persecuted Austrian Protestants could find refuge. War with Spain was declared in 1739. He invaded Florida (1740), and repulsed a Spanish invasion of Georgia (1742). In 1743 he left the colony to repel malicious charges. He was tried and acquitted after the 1745 Jacobite Rising for failing as major-general to overtake Prince Charles Stuart's army. >> **Stuart, Charles; Wesley, Charles; Wesley, John**

O'Gorman, Juan (1905–82) Architect, born in Mexico City. He trained in Mexico City, studied painting under Diego Rivera, then worked as a draughtsman and as director of the Town Planning Administration, beginning independent practice in 1934. His masterpieces include the windowless, mosaic-covered Library of the National University of Mexico in Mexico City (1952, in collaboration), and his own house (now demolished) which was part-cave and harmonized with the volcanic rocks surrounding it. In later years, disillusioned, he turned to painting. He died by his own hand, being unable to work because of a heart condition. >> Rivera

O'Hara, Frank, popular name of **Francis Russell O'Hara** (1926–66) Poet and art critic, born in Baltimore, MD. He studied at the New England Conservatory of Music in Boston, Harvard, and the University of Michigan. He worked for the Museum of Modern Art from 1951, and as an editor for art magazines (1954–64). He wrote plays and art criticism, and is noted for his Surrealist poetry, as in *Selected Poems* (1973).

O'Hara, John (Henry) (1905–70) Novelist and short-story writer, born in Pottsville, PA. When his father died, instead of going to Yale as planned, he travelled and became a reporter in New York City. His first novel was *Appointment in Samarra* (1934); its naturalistic account of three days that culminate in the suicide of Julian English, a victim of his own reckless sexual appetite, made it a quick success. His best-known works – *Butterfield 8* (1935) and *Pal Joey* (1940) – became film and stage successes. His short-story collections include *The Doctor's Son* (1935) and *Waiting for Winter* (1967).

O'Higgins, Bernardo, known as **the Liberator of Chile** (1778–1842) Revolutionary, and first president of the Republic of Chile (1817–23), born in Chillán, Chile. He was the illegitimate son of **Ambrosio O'Higgins** (c.1720–1801), the Irish-born viceroy of Chile (1789) and of Peru (1795). He played a great part in the Chilean revolt of 1810–17, and became president, but was deposed after a revolution and retired to Peru. >> RR1039

Ohlin, Bertil (Gotthard) (1899–1979) Economist and politician, born in Klippan, Sweden. He studied in Sweden and at Harvard, and became professor at Copenhagen (1925–30) and Stockholm (1930–65). He was a member of the Swedish parliament (1938–70), and leader of the Liberal Party (1944–67). He shared the 1977 Nobel Prize for Economics for his work on the dynamics of trade. >> RR1125

Ohm, Georg Simon (1787–1854) Physicist, born in Erlangen, Bavaria. He became professor at Nuremburg (1833–49) and Munich (1849–54), after a long struggle to get due recognition for the importance of his work. *Ohm's law* had been published in 1827 as a result of his research in electricity, and the measure of resistance is now called the *ohm*.

Ohno, Kazuo >> **Hijikata, Tatsumi**

Oistrakh, David (Fyodorovitch) [oystrak] (1908–74) Violinist, born in Odessa, Ukraine. He studied at Odessa Conservatory, graduating in 1926. In 1928 he went to Moscow, and began to teach at the Conservatory there in 1934, being appointed professor in 1939. He made concert tours in Europe and America, and was awarded the Stalin Prize in 1945 and the Lenin Prize in 1960.

O'Keeffe, Georgia (1887–1986) Painter, born on a farm in Sun Prairie, WI. She studied at the Art Institute of Chicago (1905–6) and at the Art Students' League in New York City (1907–8), where she met photographer Alfred Stieglitz, whom she married in 1924. As early as 1915 she pioneered abstract art in the USA (such as 'Blue and Green Music', 1919), but later moved towards a more figurative style, painting flowers and architectural subjects, frequently with a Surrealist flavour. In her later years, she painted a great deal in New Mexico, and many paintings came from her worldwide travels. >> Stieglitz

Okeghem [okegem] or **Ockeghem, Jean d'** (c. 1430–c. 1495) Composer, probably born in Termonde, Belgium. He had become a court musician to Charles VII of France

by 1452, and treasurer of the abbey of St Martin at Tours (1459). He was also *Kapellmeister* to Louis XI. He played an important part in the stylistic development of church music in the 15th-c, and was renowned as a teacher. His works include 14 Masses, and several motets and songs.

O'Kelly, Sean T(homas), Gaelic **Seán Tómas O Ceallaigh** (1882–1966) Irish statesman and president (1945–59), born in Dublin. A pioneer in the Sinn Féin movement and the Gaelic League, he fought in the Easter Rising (1916) and was imprisoned. Elected to the first Dáil in 1918, he became speaker (1919–21), minister for local government (1932–9) and minister for finance and education (1939–45). He was president of the Irish Republic from 1945, and was re-elected without opposition in 1952. >> RR1064

Okri, Ben [okree] (1959–) Novelist and short-story writer, born in Minna, Nigeria. He studied in Nigeria, then at the University of Essex, UK. His first books were the autobiographical novels *Flowers and Shadows* (1980) and *The Landscapes Within* (1981). Later works include two books of short stories (1986, 1988) and the novels *The Famished Road* (1991, Booker Prize), *Dangerous Love* (1996), and *A Way of Being Free* (1997). A book of poems, *An African Elegy*, appeared in 1992.

Olaf I Tryggvason (c. 965–c. 1000) King of Norway (995–c.1000), the great-grandson of Harald I. He was the most spectacular Viking of his time and the subject of much legend. Brought up at the court of Prince Vladimir I of Russia, he was a Viking mercenary in the Baltic at the age of 18. He led the Viking army that defeated the Anglo-Saxons at the celebrated Battle of Maldon in Essex (991). He returned to harry England in a huge expedition led by the King of Denmark, Sweyn Forkbeard (994). Converted to Christianity, he seized the throne for himself (995) and attempted to convert Norway to Christianity by force. Overwhelmed by a combined Danish and Swedish fleet at the Battle of Svold in 1000, he leapt overboard and was never seen again. >> Harald I Halfdanarson; Sweyn; Vladimir; RR1079

Olaf II Haraldsson, also called **St Olaf** (c. 995–1030) King of Norway (1014–30), the half-brother of Harald III (Hardrada). He became a Viking mercenary in the Baltic at the age of 12, going on to England, Frisia, and Spain. In England in 1010 he took part in a celebrated attack when London Bridge was torn down with grappling irons. He was converted to Christianity in Normandy in 1013, and returned to Norway in 1014, where he seized the throne and worked hard to complete the conversion of Norway begun by Olaf I Tryggvason and establish the Church. In 1028, faced by rebellion abetted from Denmark, he was forced to flee to Russia for safety. In 1030 he came back in an attempt to regain his crown, but was defeated and killed at the Battle of Stiklestad. Within 12 months he was regarded as a national hero and the patron saint of Norway. Feast day 29 July. >> Harald III Sigurdsson; Olaf I Tryggvason; RR1079

Olaf III Haraldsson (?–1093) King of Norway (1067–93), the son of Harald III (Hardrada). He was at the Battle of Stamford Bridge in Yorkshire in 1066 when his father was defeated and killed by Harold II of England, but was allowed to return to Norway with the survivors of the Norwegian invasion force, and assumed the throne of Norway the following year. His long reign was marked by unbroken peace and prosperity in Norway. >> Harald III Sigurdsson; Harold II; RR1079

Olah, George A [ola] (1927–) Chemist, born in Budapest. He studied at the Technical University of Budapest, and worked at the Hungarian Academy of Sciences, but left Hungary in 1956 for Canada, then the USA. He taught at Case Western Reserve University (1965–77), then moved to the University of Southern California, Los Angeles, becoming director of the Loker Hydrocarbon Research Institute in 1991. He received the 1994 Nobel Prize for Chemistry for the study of hydrocarbons, and of new ways to use them, identifying an intermediate stage of short-lived compounds ('carbocations') in organic chemical reactions.

Olav V [ohlaf] (1903–91) King of Norway (1957–91), born near Sandringham, Norfolk, E England, UK, the son and successor of Haakon VII and Maud, daughter of Edward VII of Britain. He studied in Norway and at Oxford, and was an outstanding sportsman and Olympic yachtsman in his youth. He stayed in Norway when it was invaded by Germany in 1940, and was appointed head of the Norwegian armed forces. Later he escaped with his father to England, returning in 1945. In 1929 he married **Princess Martha of Sweden** (1901–54), and had two daughters and a son, **Harald** (1937–), who succeeded to the Norwegian throne as Harald V in 1991. >> Haakon VII; RR1079

Olbers, (Heinrich) Wilhelm (Matthäus) (1758–1840) Physician and astronomer, born in Arbergen, Germany. While practising medicine at Bremen, he calculated the orbit of the comet of 1779, discovered the minor planets Pallas (1802) and Vesta (1807), and discovered five comets (all but one already observed at Paris). He also invented a method for calculating the velocity of falling stars.

Olbrich, Josef (Maria) [olbrikh] (1867-1908) Austrian architect, born in Opava, Czech Republic (formerly, Troppau, Silesia). A pupil of Otto Wagner, he was co-founder of the Vienna *Sezession*, and designed the building in Vienna which housed its exhibitions (1898–99). Among his other buildings was the Hochzeitsturm (1907, Marriage Tower) in Darmstadt, Germany. >> Wagner

Olcott, Henry Steel (1832–1907) Theosophist, born in Orange, NJ. A lawyer by training, he studied theosophy under Madame Blavatsky, and was founder president of the Theosophical Society in 1875. He travelled to India and Ceylon with her (1879–84), but they fell out in 1885. He opened schools for untouchables in India, and became an associate of Annie Besant. >> Besant, Annie; Blavatsky

Oldcastle, Sir John, nickname **Good Lord Cobham** (c.1378–1417) Lollard leader and knight of England, born in Hereford and Worcester, WC England, UK. After serving in the Scottish and Welsh wars, and becoming an intimate of Henry V when Prince of Wales, he was tried and convicted on charges of heresy in 1413. He escaped from the Tower, and conspired with other Lollards to capture Henry V at Eltham Palace, Kent, and take control of London. The rising was abortive. He remained free until caught near Welshpool in 1417, and was hanged and burned. Shakespeare's Falstaff is based partly on him. >> Henry V

Oldenbarneveldt, Jan van >> **Barneveldt, Jan van Olden**

Oldenburg, Claes (Thure) (1929–) Sculptor, born in Stockholm. He studied at Yale and the Art Institute of Chicago before moving to New York City in 1956, where he became part of the milieu from which Pop Art developed. In 1963 he introduced soft sculptures of normally hard objects such as light switches, for which he became best known. His projects for huge monuments in public places have occasionally been realized, as in the 'Colossal Ashtray with Fagends' at the Pompidou Centre, Paris.

Oldfield, (Berna Eli) Barney (1878–1946) Motor-racing driver, born in Wauseon, OH. One of motor-racing's pioneers, he began as a bicycle racer. He was the first to race a car a mile a minute (1903), driving Henry Ford's famous '999' racer. A colourful showman who specialized in short 'match' races on dirt tracks, he also established a land speed record in 1910 for a one-mile distance at over 131 mph.

Oldfield, Bruce (1950–) Fashion designer, born in London, England, UK. He taught art, then studied fashion in Kent (1968–71) and in London (1972–3), after which he became a freelance designer. He designed for Bendel's store in New York City, and sold sketches to Yves Saint Laurent. He showed his first collection in London in 1975. He designs evening dresses for members of the royal family and film-stars, as well as making ready-to-wear clothes. >> Saint Laurent

Oldham, Richard Dixon [ohldam] (1858–1936) Geologist and seismologist, the discoverer of the Earth's core, born in Dublin. He studied at the Royal School of Mines, was a member of the Geological Survey of India (1878–1903), and became director of the Indian Museum in Calcutta (from 1903). His report on the Assam earthquake of June 1897 distinguished for the first time between primary and secondary seismic waves. In 1906 he established from seismographic records the existence of the Earth's core. >> Mohorovičić

Oldman, Gary (1959–) Film actor, born in London, England, UK. He was a member of the Glasgow Citizen's Theatre, and became known following his portrayal of punk rocker Sid Vicious in the film *Sid and Nancy* (1986) and of playwright Joe Orton in *Prick Up Your Ears* (1987). Later films include *Bram Stoker's Dracula* (1992), the role of Beethoven in *Immortal Beloved* (1994), *Basquiat* (1996), and *The Fifth Element* (1997).

Ole Luk-Oie >> **Swinton, Ernest Dunlop**

Olga, St, also called **St Helga** (c. 890–969) Russian saint, the wife of prince Igor of Kiev. She ruled Kiev during the minority of her son (945–64). She was baptized at Constantinople (c.957) and, returning to Russia, laboured to bring Christianity to Russia. She was opposed by her son, but her grandson, St Vladimir I, continued her efforts. Feast day 11 July. >> Vladimir I

Oliphant, Margaret, *née* **Wilson** (1828–97) Novelist, born in Wallyford, East Lothian, E Scotland, UK. She wrote from an early age, and married her cousin, **Francis Oliphant**. Widowed in 1859, she wrote from then on to support her own and her brother's children. Her first novel, *Mrs Margaret Maitland* (1849), began a prolific career in literature extending to more than 100 books and some 200 contributions to *Blackwood's Magazine*. From *The Chronicles of Carlingford*, a series of novels dealing with Scottish life, *Salem Chapel* (1863) and *Miss Marjoribanks* (1866) received particular praise. She also wrote histories and biographies, including *Annals of a Publishing House: William Blackwood and His Sons* (1897).

Oliphant, Sir Mark, in full **Marcus Laurence Elwin Oliphant** (1901–) Nuclear physicist, born in Adelaide, South Australia. He studied there and at Cambridge, where he did valuable work on the nuclear disintegration of lithium. Professor at Birmingham (1937), he designed and built a 60-in cyclotron. He worked on the atomic bomb project at Los Alamos (1943–5), but later strongly argued against the US monopoly of atomic secrets. He became Australian representative of the UN Atomic Energy Commission in 1946, designed a proton-synchrotron for the Australian government, and was appointed research professor at Canberra (1950–63). He was knighted in 1959, and became Governor of South Australia in 1971–6.

Olivares, Gaspar de Guzman y Pimental, conde-duque de (Count-Duke of) [olivahrez] (1587–1645) Spanish statesman, favourite and chief minister (1623–43) of Philip IV (reigned 1621–65), born in Rome. He cultivated the arts, and tried to moderate Spain's anachronistic administration and to build up military resources, but his introduction of the Union of Arms brought revolts in Portugal and Catalonia (1640–3). He took Spain into renewed conflict with the United Provinces and challenged France over the Mantuan Succession (1628–31) and in the Thirty Years' War (1635–48). After the Spanish fleet was destroyed at the Battle of the Downs (1639) and Roussillon was overrun by the French, he was dismissed (1643), and went into exile in Toro.

Oliver, King, popular name of **Joseph Oliver** (1885–1938) Cornettist, composer, and bandleader, born in Abend, LA. Raised in New Orleans, his first instrument was the trombone, and as a youth he played in various parade bands as well as in early jazz groups. He then moved to Chicago, where in 1922 he formed his Creole Jazz Band, and is remembered for his discovery of Louis Armstrong. Although Oliver worked as a musician until 1937, he made no recordings after 1931, when he developed severe dental problems, and he faded into obscurity. His compositions, such as 'Dippermouth Blues' and 'Dr Jazz', have become part of the standard traditional repertoire. >> Allen, Red; Armstrong, Louis

Olivetti, Adriano [olivetee] (1901–60) Manufacturer, born in Ivrea, Italy. After a period in the USA where he was sent to assimilate the methods of mass production, he returned to transform the manufacturing methods of the typewriter firm founded by his father **Camillo Olivetti** (1868–1943). He increased production, and established a strong design policy which embraced products, graphics, and the architecture of the company's buildings. His strong social concerns, for which he was widely noted, led him to provide housing and facilities of a high standard for his employees.

Olivier (of Brighton), Laurence (Kerr) Olivier, Baron (1907–89) Actor, producer, and director, born in Dorking, Surrey, SE England, UK. He trained in London, and began his career at Birmingham in 1926, joining the Old Vic, London, in 1937. He played all the great Shakespearean roles, while his versatility was underlined by his virtuoso display in *The Entertainer* (1957) as a broken-down low comedian. After war service he became co-director of the Old Vic (1944). His films include *Henry V*, *Hamlet*, and *Richard III*. Divorced from his first wife, **Jill Esmond** in 1940, in the same year he married English actress **Vivien Leigh**. They were divorced in 1960, and in 1961 he married English actress **Joan Plowright**. He became first director of the Chichester Theatre Festival (1962) and of the National Theatre (1963–73). After 1974 he appeared chiefly in films and on television, notably in *Brideshead Revisited* (1982) and *King Lear* (1983). He was knighted in 1947, and made a life peer in 1970. >> Leigh, Vivien; Plowright

Olmsted, Frederick (Law) (1822–1903) Landscape architect, born in Hartford, CT. After a limited education because of an eye problem, he attended Yale University to study science and engineering, then became a journalist. An interest in landscape led to his appointment as architect-in-chief of the improvement scheme for Central Park, New York City. He was thereafter commissioned to design other important public park schemes, including those at Brooklyn, Philadelphia, and Belle Isle Park, Detroit, as well as the grounds surrounding Washington, DC, and the campus at Berkeley, University of California. He worked to have Yosemite created a state reservation, and was among those proposing a system of protected wilderness areas for the USA. >> Muir, John; Vaux

Olsen, Ken(neth) (1926–   ) US computer designer and engineer. He was a member of the team at the Massachusett Institute of Technology that built Whirlwind, the first 'real-time' computer (1951). He subsequently formed his own company, DEC, to manufacture mini-computers (1964).

Olson, Harry (Ferdinand) (1901–82) Radio engineer and inventor, born in Mount Pleasant, IA. He studied at the University of Iowa, then joined the RCA laboratories in 1928, his first invention being a directional microphone. In the late 1940s he carried out a series of tests which established the standards for high-fidelity sound reproduction, then in 1955 developed the first electronic music synthesizer with which **Charles Wuorinen** (1938–   ) produced his composition *Time's Encomium* (1970, Pulitzer). He held over 100 US patents for acoustic devices and systems.

Olympias (c. 375–316 BC) Wife of Philip II of Macedon, mother of Alexander the Great, and daughter of Neoptolemus of Epirus. When Philip married Cleopatra, niece of Attalus, she left Macedon and ruled Epirus by herself, and is said to have murdered Cleopatra after Philip was assassinated (336 BC). Alexander died in 323 BC, and she returned to Macedon, where she secured the death of his half-brother and successor, and made Alexander's posthumous son, Alexander IV, king. Eventually Cassander besieged her in Pydna, and she was killed by relatives of those she had put to death. >> Alexander the Great; Cassander; Philip II (of Macedon)

Omar or **Umar** [ohmah(r)] (c. 581–644) The second caliph. He was father of one of Mohammed's wives, and succeeded Abu-Bakr in 634. With his generals he built up an empire comprising Persia, Syria, and all North Africa. He was assassinated in Medina by a Persian slave. >> Abu-Bakr; Aïshah; Mohammed

Omar Khayyám [kayam], also spelled **Umar Khayyám** (c. 1050–c. 1122) Poet, mathematician, and astronomer, born in Nishapur, Persia. Summoned to Merv by the sultan, he reformed the Muslim calendar, and was known to the Western world as a mathematician, until in 1859 Edward FitzGerald published a translation of his *Rubáiyát* ('Quatrains'). The work is now regarded as an anthology of which little or nothing may be by Omar.

Onassis, Aristotle (Socrates) [ohnasis] (1906–75) Millionaire shipowner, born in Smyrna, Turkey. At 16 he left Smyrna for Greece as a refugee, and from there went to Buenos Aires, where he made a fortune in tobacco and was for a time Greek consul. Buying his first ships (1932–3), he built up one of the world's largest independent fleets, and was a pioneer in the construction of super-tankers. His first marriage, to **Athina**, daughter of Stavros Livanos, a Greek ship-owner, ended in divorce (1960). He then had a long relationship with Maria Callas, and in 1968 married Jacqueline Kennedy. >> Callas; Niarchos; Onassis, Jacqueline Kennedy

Onassis, Jacqueline Kennedy, *née* **Jacqueline Lee Bouvier**, popularly known as **Jackie Kennedy** (1929–94) US first lady (1961–3), born in Southampton, NY. She studied at Vassar College, the Sorbonne, and Washington University, and worked as a reporter before marrying John F Kennedy in 1953. She was not always comfortable with the demands of being the wife of a Kennedy and a politician, but as first lady she promoted her personal agenda of the arts, history, and high style. Her first child was stillborn, and she lost an infant in 1963, but they had two other children, **Caroline** (1957–   ) and **John** (1960–   ). Her stoic behaviour at Kennedy's death and funeral enhanced her standing with the public, but she stunned the world when in 1968 she married the Greek millionaire shipping magnate, Aristotle Onassis. For some years she was the world's premier celebrity, but after Onassis's death (1975), she worked in New York publishing, first with Viking Press (1975–7), then with Doubleday (1978–94), and went about her private rounds of family, the arts, and social engagements. >> Kennedy, John F; Onassis

Ondaatje, Michael [ondachee] (1943–   ) Poet, novelist, and editor, born in Colombo, Sri Lanka. He moved to Canada in 1962, studied at Bishop's University in Quebec, the

University of Toronto, and Queen's University, Kingston, Ontario, then became a university lecturer. Among his first books of poetry is *Rat Jelly* (1973). *The Collected Works of Billy the Kid* (1970), a factual and fictional account of the notorious outlaw, won a Governor-General's Award, as did a later book of poems, *There's a Trick with a Knife I'm Learning to Do* (1979). *Running in the Family* (1982) tells of the life of his family in colonial Ceylon, and his novel *The English Patient* was co-winner of the Booker Prize in 1992 (filmed 1996, Oscar). His work characteristically blends the factual and imaginary, has a cinematic quality, and depends on an imagery of exoticism. >> Unsworth

O'Neal, (Patrick) Ryan (1941–) Film actor, born in Los Angeles, CA. He became well known as Rodney Harrison in the television series *Peyton Place*, a character he played for nearly five years. His films include *Love Story* (1970), *Paper Moon* (1973), *Irreconcilable Differences* (1984), *Chances Are* (1989), *Faithful* (1996), and *Hacks* (1997).

O'Neill, Eugene (Gladstone) (1888–1953) Playwright, born in New York City. Born into a volatile theatrical family, his education was fragmented, and for six years he went to sea, living the life of a tramp at docksides, and making an attempt at suicide. After a spell in a sanatorium recovering from tuberculosis, he began writing plays as a means of making sense of his disturbed emotions. He was sent to study play-writing at Harvard (1914), and joined the Provincetown Players in 1915, for whom *Beyond the Horizon* (1920, Pulitzer) was written. The most widely produced and translated US playwright of his time, he gained three more Pulitzer Prizes – for *Anna Christie* (1922), *Strange Interlude* (1928), and his masterpiece *Long Day's Journey Into Night* (published posthumously, 1956). Other classics include *Desire Under The Elms* (1924), *Mourning Becomes Electra* (1931), and *The Iceman Cometh* (1946). He was awarded the Nobel Prize for Literature in 1936, the first US dramatist to be thus honoured. >> Glaspell

O'Neill, Hugh, 3rd Baron of Dungannon, 2nd Earl of Tyrone (1540–1616) Irish rebel leader who petitioned Spain for help in expelling the English from Ireland. He led a victorious attack, destroying the English force at Yellow Ford on Blackwater (1598), but was defeated by Blount (1601–2). In 1603 he fled to the Spanish Netherlands with Rory O'Donnell (1575–1608), and died an exile in Rome. >> Blount

O'Neill, Jonjo, popular name of **John Joseph O'Neill** (1952–) National Hunt jockey, born in Castletownroche, Co Cork, Ireland. Following an unsuccessful spell in the stable of Sir Gordon Richards, he became freelance and concentrated on the National Hunt. He twice became champion jockey (1977–8, 1979–80), riding 148 winners in one season. >> Richards, Gordon

O'Neill (of the Maine), Terence (Marne) O'Neill, Baron (1914–90) Northern Ireland politician and prime minister (1963–9), born in Co Antrim. He studied at Eton, and served in the Irish Guards during World War 2. A member of the Northern Ireland parliament (1946–70), he held junior posts before becoming minister for home affairs (1956), minister of finance (1956–63), then prime minister. A supporter of closer cross-border links with the Republic, he angered many Unionists. Following a general election in 1969, dissension in the Unionist Party increased, and he resigned the premiership soon after. Made a life peer in 1970, he continued to speak out on Northern Ireland issues.

O'Neill, Tip, popular name of **Thomas Phillip O'Neill, Jr** (1912–94) US representative, born in Cambridge, MA. He studied at Boston College, then went into insurance, at the same time becoming actively involved in Democratic politics. He was elected to the Massachusetts House (1936–52),

and became its youngest speaker (1947) before going to the US House of Representatives (1953–1987). He pushed liberal legislation while protecting his working-class constituents from budget cuts. In 1968 he supported Eugene McCarthy's anti-war candidacy, and as majority leader in 1973 voted to cut off funding of the air war in Vietnam. Elected speaker (1977–87), he failed to muster an uneasy Democratic alliance of aging Southern committee chairmen and impatient young liberals to resist President Reagan's Conservative agenda. >> McCarthy, Eugene J; Reagan

Ong, Walter (Jackson) (1912–) Catholic scholar and educator, born in Kansas City, MO. He studied at Harvard, became a Jesuit priest, and won esteem for his wide ranging studies in Renaissance literature, modern poetry, and criticism. He taught from 1959 at St Louis University. His books include *The Barbarian Within* (1962) and *The Presence of the Word* (1967).

Onions, C(harles) T(albut) (1873–1965) Scholar and lexicographer, born in Edgbaston, West Midlands, C England, UK. He was commissioned to revise and complete the *Shorter Oxford English Dictionary*, eventually published in 1933 and which he continued to revise and enlarge until 1959. Reader in English philology at Oxford University (1927–49), and editor of the journal *Medium Aevum* (1932–56), his last great work was as leader of the team which produced the *Oxford Dictionary of English Etymology* (1966). >> Burchfield, Robert

Onnes, Heike Kamerlingh >> **Kamerlingh Onnes, Heike**

Ono, Yoko >> **Lennon, John**

O'Nolan Brian >> **O'Brien, Flann**

Onsager, Lars [onsager] (1903–76) Physical chemist, born in Oslo (formerly, Christiania), Norway. He studied at the Norwegian Institute of Technology and under Debye at Zürich, and in 1928 he went to Yale, where he studied and then taught for the rest of his career (1934–72). He became a US citizen in 1945. His researches in solution chemistry and in chemical thermodynamics led to him receiving the Nobel Prize for Chemistry in 1968. >> Debye

Oort, Jan Hendrik [aw(r)t] (1900–92) Astronomer, born in Franeker, The Netherlands. He worked mainly in Leyden Observatory from 1924 (director 1945–70). He proved that our Galaxy is rotating (1927), and calculated the distance of the Sun from the centre of the Galaxy and the period of its orbit. In 1950 he suggested the existence of a sphere of incipient cometary material surrounding the Solar System. He proposed that comets detached themselves from this *Oort cloud*, and went into orbits about the Sun. The existence of the 'Oort cloud' became generally accepted by astronomers.

Oosting, Henry J(ohn) [oosting] (1903–68) Botanist, born in Holland, MI. He taught at the University of Minnesota (1927–32), then moved to Duke University (1932–63), conducting full-time research after retiring from academic duties. He was an authority on the plant ecology of E USA, including Maine forest birches and the effects of salt spray on the vegetation of the North Carolina coastal dunes.

Opel, Fritz von [ohpel] (1899–1971) Automotive industrialist, born in Rüsselsheim, Germany. He worked for his grandfather's manufacturing firm, which began experimenting with rocket propulsion for automobiles and aircraft (1898). The world's first rocket-propelled car was the Opel-Rak 1 (1928), followed by the Opel-Rak 2, which he himself test-drove. He also piloted the second rocket airplane to fly.

Ophuls or **Opüls, Max** [opüls], originally **Max Oppenheimer** (1902–57) Film director, born in Saarbrücken, Germany, who chose French nationality in the plebiscite of 1934. He worked in films from 1930, first in Germany and later in France. In 1941 he emigrated to the USA, and in 1947–9 made *The Exile*, *Caught*, and *The Reckless Moment*. He then returned to France, where he made his greatest successes, *La Ronde* (1950) and *Lola Montez* (1955).

Opie, John [**oh**pee] (1716–1807) Portraitist and historical painter, born in St Agnes, Cornwall, SW England, UK. His portraits interested his teacher **John Wolcot** (1738–1819, pseudonym **Peter Pindar**), by whom he was taken to London in 1789 to become the 'Cornish Wonder'. He became renowned as a portraitist of contemporary figures, and also painted historical pictures like the well-known 'Murder of Rizzio' (1787). He became professor of painting at the Royal Academy in 1805.

Opie, Peter (Mason) (1918–82) and **Opie, Iona (Margaret Balfour)** (1923–) *née* **Archibald** [**oh**pee] British children's literature specialists, folklorists and anthologists. They married in 1943, and the birth of their first child prompted them to study the folklore of childhood. They published *The Oxford Book of Nursery Rhymes* in 1951, acknowledged widely for its scholarship as well as its sense of humour. They subsequently amassed a peerless collection of children's books, which is now housed in the Bodleian Library. Later works by Iona Opie include *The Singing Game* (1985), *A Dictionary of Superstitions* (1989), *The People in the Playground* (1993), and *Children's Games with Things* (1997).

Opitz (von Boberfeld), Martin (1597–1639) Poet, born in Bunzlau, Germany. He studied at Frankfurt, Heidelberg, and Leyden, served several German princes, and became historiographer to Władysław IV of Poland. He wrote in a scholarly and stilted style which influenced German poetry for 200 years, and introduced Renaissance poetic thinking into Germany.

Oppenheim, E(dward) Phillips [openhiym] (1866–1946) Novelist, born in London, England, UK. He worked in his father's leather business, but after the popularity of his first espionage novels, a wealthy US business bought the company, making him a director, and leaving him free to write. His highly successful novels included *Kingdom of the Blind* (1917), *The Great Impersonation* (1920), and *Envoy Extraordinary* (1937).

Oppenheimer, Sir Ernest [openhiymer] (1880–1957) Mining magnate, politician, and philanthropist, born in Friedberg, Germany. From the age of 17 he worked for a London firm of diamond merchants and, sent out to Kimberley as their representative in 1902, soon became one of the leaders of the diamond industry. In 1917, with John Pierpoint Morgan Jr, he formed the Anglo-American Corporation of South Africa, and at the time of his death his interests extended over 95% of the world's supply of diamonds. He became Mayor of Kimberley (1912–15) and an MP (1924–38). A philanthropist and public figure, he was knighted in 1921. >> Morgan, John Pierpoint; Oppenheimer, Harry

Oppenheimer, Harry (Frederick) [openhiymer] (1908–) Industrialist, born in Kimberley, South Africa, the son of Sir Ernest Oppenheimer. He studied at Oxford, and succeeded his father as chairman of Anglo-American (1957–83). As an MP (from 1947) he was a critic of the South African government's policy of apartheid. His son, **Nicholas Frederick** (1945–), born in Johannesburg and educated at Oxford, was chairman of de Beers (1984–5). >> Ogilvie Thompson; Oppenheimer, Ernest

Oppenheimer, J(ulius) Robert [openhiymer] (1904–67) Nuclear physicist, born in New York City. He studied at Harvard, Cambridge, Göttingen, Leyden, and Zürich universities, then taught physics at the California Institute of Technology (1929). In 1942 he joined the atom bomb project, and became director of the Los Alamos laboratory

(1943–5). He was chairman of the advisory committee to the US Atomic Energy Commission (1946–52), and in 1947 became director and professor of physics at the Institute for Advanced Study, Princeton. In 1953 he was suspended from secret nuclear research by a security review board for his past Communist associations, although many people disagreed with the charges brought against him. He delivered the BBC Reith Lectures (1953), and received the Enrico Fermi Award in 1963.

Opüls, Max >> **Ophüls, Max**

O'Rane, Patricia >> **Dark, Eleanor**

Orange, Princes of >> **William I** (of The Netherlands); **William III**

Orbison, Roy (1936–88) Country-pop singer and songwriter, born in Vernon, TX. He began playing in public at the age of eight on local radio stations, and was discovered in his early teens by the record producer Norman Petty. Moving to the Sun record label, he had his first minor success in 1956, then spent four years writing for other artists. He re-emerged with the hit single 'Only The Lonely' (written for Elvis Presley) in 1960, and this was followed by a succession of smash hits inluding 'Cryin'' (1961), 'Blue Bayou', 'In Dreams' (both 1963), and 'Oh, Pretty Woman' (1964). The death of his wife in a motorcycle accident (1966), and of two of his sons in a fire (1968), coincided with a 10-year low period in his career, but a series of revivals of his songs by other artists, and the patronage of a younger generation of musicians, helped to reverse his fortunes. Tributes to his music continue long after his sudden death from a heart-attack.

Orcagna [aw(r)**kan**ya], originally **Andrea de Cione** (c.1308–c. 1368) Painter, sculptor, and architect, born in Florence, Italy. A member of a family of painters, his greatest paintings are frescoes, an altarpiece in Santa Maria Nobella, and the 'Coronation of the Virgin' (National Gallery, London). Many consider him second in the 14th-c only to Giotto, who influenced him. >> Giotto

Orchardson, Sir William Quiller (1832–1910) Painter, born in Edinburgh, EC Scotland, UK. He studied at the Trustees' Academy, and went to London in 1862. He is best known for historical and social subject paintings. Particularly famous is the scene of Napoleon on board the *Bellerophon* (1880, London).

Orczy, Emma, Baroness [**awt**see, **awk**see] (1865–1947) Novelist and playwright, born in Tarna-Eörs, Hungary. *The Scarlet Pimpernel* (1905) was the first success in her long writing career. It was followed by many popular adventure romances, including *The Elusive Pimpernel* (1908).

Orellana, Francisco de [orel**yah**na] (c.1490–c.1546) Explorer, born in Trujillo, Spain. He went to Peru with Francisco Pizarro. After crossing the Andes in 1541, he descended the Amazon R to its mouth. The river's original name was Rio Santa Maria de la Mar Dulce; but Orellana is said to have renamed it after an attack by a tribe in which he believed women, like the Amazons of Greek mythology, were fighting alongside men. >> Pizarro, Francisco

Orff, Carl (1895–1982) Composer, born in Munich, Germany. He studied at Munich, where he helped found the Günther music school (1925). The influence of Stravinsky is apparent in his compositions. He is best known for his operatic setting of a 13th-c poem, *Carmina Burana* (1937). Later works include *Oedipus* (1959) and *Prometheus* (1966). >> Stravinsky

Orfila, Mathieu (Joseph Bonaventure) [aw(r)**fee**la] (1787–1853) Chemist, founder of toxicology, born in Mahon, Minorca. He studied at Valencia, Barcelona, and Paris, where he subsequently worked. In 1811 he lectured on chemistry, botany, and anatomy. In 1813 appeared his celebrated *Traité de toxicologie générale* (Treatise on General Toxicology). He later became professor of medical jurisprudence (1819), and of chemistry (1823).

Orford, Earl of >> **Walpole, Horace / Robert**

O Riain, Liam P >> **Ryan, William Patrick**

Origen [orijen] (c. 185–c. 254) Christian biblical scholar and theologian of Alexandria, Egypt, who became head of the catechetical school in Alexandria. He was a layman until c.230, when he was ordained in Palestine. Exiled from Alexandria by Bishop Demetrius, he established a new school in Caesarea. He was imprisoned and tortured during the persecution under Decius in 250. His writings were prolific, but his views on the unity of God and speculations about the salvation of the devil were condemned by Church Councils in the 5th–6th-c. >> **Decius**

Orlando di Lasso >> **Lassus, Orlandus**

Orléans, Charles, duc d' (Duke of) [aw(r)layā] (1391–1465) French soldier, nobleman, and poet, born in Paris, France. In 1406 he married his cousin Isabella, the widow of Richard II of England. He commanded at Agincourt (1415), and was taken prisoner and carried to England, where he lived for 25 years, composing courtly poetry in French and English. Ransomed in 1440, he then maintained a kind of literary court at Blois. His son became Louis XII.

Orléans, Jean d' >> **Dunois, Jean d'Orléans**

Orléans, Louis Philippe Joseph, duc d' (Duke of) [aw(r)layā], known as **Philippe Egalité** ('equality') (1747–93) Bourbon prince, born in Saint-Cloud, France, the cousin of Louis XVI and father of Louis Philippe. He became the Duc de Chartres in 1752, and inherited his father's title in 1785. At the Revolution he proved a strong supporter of the Third Estate against the privileged orders, and in 1792 renounced his title of nobility for his popular name. At the Convention he voted for the king's death, but was himself arrested, after the defection of his eldest son to the Austrians (1793), and guillotined. >> **Louis XVI; Louis-Philippe**

Orm (fl.c.1200) Monk and spelling reformer, probably born in Lincolnshire, EC England, UK. He invented an orthography based on phonetic principles, in which he wrote the *Ormulum*, a series of homilies in verse on the Gospel history.

Ormandy, Eugene [aw(r)mandee], originally **Jenö Ormandy** (1899–1985) Conductor, born in Budapest. A child prodigy, he studied the violin in Budapest, became an orchestral player in Berlin, then emigrated to the USA (1921), and became a US citizen (1927). He took up conducting, and headed the Minneapolis Symphony (1931–6) before taking the podium of the Philadelphia Orchestra in 1936 (for two years co-conductor with Stokowski). He remained at that post until his retirement in 1980, maintaining the voluptuousness of sound for which the orchestra was both praised and criticized.

Ormond, John (1923–90) Poet and film-maker, born in Dunvant, Swansea. He studied at University College, Swansea, trained as a journalist, and joined BBC Wales in 1957 as a director and producer of documentary films, including studies of Welsh painters and writers such as Ceri Richards, Dylan Thomas, Alun Lewis, and R S Thomas. He also established a reputation as an Anglo-Welsh poet.

Ornstein, Leo (1895–) Composer, born in Kremenchug, Ukraine. A child prodigy at the piano, his parents settled in the USA in 1906, and he made his US debut at 16. In the years following 1915, he composed much music that placed him among the avant garde, and he has had considerable influence upon younger American composers, with renewed interest in his work in the 1970s. His later works, which include a symphony and various pieces of piano music, are more traditional in style.

Orosius, Paulus [orohzius] (5th-c) Priest and historian, probably born in Braga, Spain. He visited Augustine in 415, and went to study under Jerome at Bethlehem. He was

the author of the first Christian history of the world, *Historiarum adversus Paganos*, from the Creation to 417, a favourite textbook during the Middle Ages. It was translated into Anglo-Saxon by King Alfred. >> **Alfred; Augustine, St (of Hippo); Jerome, St**

Orozco, José Clemente [oroskoh] (1883–1949) Painter, born in Ciudad Guzmán, Mexico. He studied engineering and architectural drawing in Mexico City, and art at the Academia San Carlos. One of the greatest mural painters of the 20th-c, he decorated many public buildings in Mexico and the USA. His powerful Realistic style, verging on caricature, was a vehicle for revolutionary Socialist ideas – his murals in the Rockefeller Center, New York, were later destroyed.

Orr, Bobby, popular name of **Robert Gordon Orr** (1948–) Ice hockey player, born in Parry Sound, Ontario, Canada. The highest goal-scorer ever in North American National League hockey, he played mainly with the Boston Bruins, and became that city's greatest-ever sporting hero, but by the time he moved to Chicago Black Hawks in the 1976–7 season (for a contract reputed to be worth $3 000 000), his career was already almost over. Six major leg operations compelled him to retire in 1979.

Orr, John Boyd >> **Boyd Orr, John**

Orsini, Felice [aw(r)seenee] (1819–58) Revolutionary, born in Meldola, Italy. He was early initiated into secret societies, and in 1844 was sentenced at Rome to the galleys, amnestied, and again imprisoned for political plots. In 1853 he was shipped by the Sardinian government to England, where he joined the Young Italy movement and formed close relations with Mazzini. In 1857 he made an unsuccessful attempt in Paris to assassinate Napoleon III by throwing a bomb under his carriage; the action killed 10 others and injured over 100. He was arrested and executed. >> **Mazzini; Napoleon III**

Örsted, Niels-Henning [oe(r)sted] (1946–) Jazz double-bass player, born in Denmark. He has played with Oscar Peterson, Dexter Gordon, Sonny Rollins, Dizzy Gillespie, Kenny Drew, Count Basie, Ella Fitzgerald and others, and has performed on several hundred recordings, including *Jaywalkin*, *Trio I*, and *Trio II*. In 1977 he was voted the 'World's Best Bass Player' by *Melody Maker* magazine.

Ortega (Saavedra), Daniel [aw(r)tayga] (1945–) Nicaraguan guerrilla leader and president (1984–90), born in La Libertad, Nicaragua. He studied at the University of Central America, Managua, and joined the Sandinista National Liberation Front in 1963, becoming national director in 1966. He was imprisoned for seven years for urban guerrilla bank raids, and played a major part in the overthrow of Anastasio Somoza in 1979, becoming president in 1984. By 1989 there were encouraging signs of peace being achieved, but he lost the 1990 general election to Violeta Chamorro. >> **Somoza; RR1078**

Ortega y Gasset, José [aw(r)tayga ee gaset] (1883–1955) Philosopher and existentialist humanist, born in Madrid. He studied at Madrid and in Germany, and became professor of metaphysics at Madrid (1910). His critical writings on modern authors made him an influential figure, and his *La rebelión de las masas* (1930, The Revolt of the Masses) foreshadowed the Civil War. He lived in voluntary exile in South America and Portugal (1936–48).

Ortelius [aw(r)teelius], Latin name of **Abraham Ortels** (1527–98) Cartographer and engraver, born in Antwerp, Belgium. He was trained as an engraver, and became interested in map-making in c.1560. His *Theatrum orbis terrarum* (1570, trans Epitome of the Theatre of the World) was the first great atlas.

Orton, Joe, popular name of **John Kingsley Orton** (1933–67) Playwright and actor, born in Leicester, Leicestershire, C

England, UK, and trained at the Royal Academy of Dramatic Art, London. His exuberant tastelessness established him as a pioneer of a style of black farce. His play *What the Butler Saw* (1969) carried the farce tradition of threatened adultery into the forbidden realms of incest and sexual violence. Two years before its performance he was bloodily murdered by his male lover, who subsequently took his own life. Other works include *Entertaining Mr Sloane* (1964) and *Loot* (1966).

Orwell, George, pseudonym of **Eric Arthur Blair** (1903–50) Novelist and essayist, born in Motihari, Bengal, India. He studied at Eton, and served in Burma in the Indian Imperial Police (1922–7), but rejected the political injustice of imperial life (recounted in the novel *Burmese Days*, 1934) to live as a beggar in the East End of London, which became the subject for his book *Down and Out in Paris and London* (1933). Similarly researched experiences led to the writing of *A Clergyman's Daughter* (1935), *Keep the Aspidistra Flying* (1936), *The Road to Wigan Pier* (1937), *Homage to Catalonia* (1938) and *The Lion and the Unicorn* (1941). During World War 2, he was war correspondent for the BBC and the *Observer*, and wrote for the *Tribune*. His intellectual honesty motivated his biting satire of Communist ideology in *Animal Farm* (1945) – a masterpiece which was overshadowed only by his novel *1984* (1949), a classic pessimistic satire about the threat of political tyranny. >> Zamyatin

Ory, Kid, popular name of **Edward Ory** (1886–1973) Trombonist and composer, born in Laplace, LA. He rose to fame as leader of a well-known New Orleans jazz band (1911), later forming a new band in Los Angeles (1919). During the 1920s he made numerous records, playing with such popular jazz musicians as King Oliver, Louis Armstrong, and Jelly Roll Morton, and is remembered for his composition, 'Muskrat Ramble' (1926). He retired in 1930, made a successful comeback in 1939, and appeared in the films *New Orleans* (1947) and *The Benny Goodman Story* (1956).

O'Ryan, W P >> **Ryan, William Patrick**

Osborn, Henry Fairfield (1857–1935) Zoologist and palaeontologist, born in Fairfield, CT. He studied at Princeton, and became professor of zoology at Columbia University (1891–1910), then research professor. He is best known for his work at the American Museum of Natural History in New York City, where he was curator of vertebrate palaeontology (1891–1910) and president (1908–33). He revolutionized museum display with innovative instructional techniques, and popularized palaeontology.

Osborne, John (James) (1929–94) Playwright, film producer, and actor, born in London, England, UK. Educated at public school in Devon, he was briefly a copywriter, and he wrote his first plays while working as an actor in repertory theatres. *Look Back in Anger* (1956, filmed 1958), his first play as sole author, established him as the first of the 'Angry Young Men'. *The Entertainer* (1957, filmed 1959), confirmed his position as the leading young exponent of British social drama. Among other works are *Luther* (1960, filmed 1971), *Inadmissible Evidence* (1964, filmed 1965), and *West of Suez* (1971), while *Déjàvu* (1991) rediscovers Jimmy Porter a generation later. He also wrote the screenplay of *Tom Jones* (1964, Oscar), and two volumes of outspoken and acerbic autobiography, *A Better Class of Person* (1981, televised 1985) and *Almost a Gentleman* (1991).

Osborne, Thomas >> **Leeds, Duke of**

Osbourne, Lloyd (1868–1947) Writer, born in San Francisco, CA, the stepson of Robert Louis Stevenson. He collaborated with Stevenson on several books, including *The Wrong Box* (1889), *The Wrecker* (1892), and *The Ebb Tide* (1894). He became US vice-consul in Samoa, and published several books of his own, including *An Intimate Portrait of RLS* (1925). >> Stevenson, Robert Louis

Osceola [oskeeohla], also known as **Powell** (c. 1800–38) Semi-nole Indian leader, born in Georgia. Although not a chief, he took the lead in opposing all efforts to remove the Seminole from their Florida homeland. His warriors' killing of a US agent in 1835 touched off the second Seminole War, and he led his people in actively resisting the Federal forces. He was seized under a flag of truce and imprisoned in Fort Moultrie, SC, where he died.

O'Shane, Pat(ricia) June (1941–) Magistrate, born in Mossman, Queensland, Australia. She studied at the University of New South Wales, and in 1978 became the first person of Aboriginal descent to be called to the bar. In 1981 she became head of the New South Wales State Ministry of Aboriginal Affairs. She was appointed a magistrate in the local courts of New South Wales in 1986, and has made a number of progressive, well-publicized decisions concerning women and Aboriginal people.

Osherhoff, Douglas D [osherhof] (1945–) Physicist, born in Aberdeen, WA. He studied at Cornell University, working under Lee and Richardson as part of the team which in 1972 discovered the superfluidity of helium-3. He shared the Nobel Prize for Physics in 1996. >> Lee, David M; Richardson, Robert C

Osman >> **Uthman**

Osman I (1258–1324) Founder of the Ottoman Turkish empire, born in Bithynia. The son of a border chief, he founded a small Turkish state in Asia Minor called *Osmanli* (Ottoman). On the overthrow of the Seljuk sultanate of Iconium in 1299 by the Mongols, he gradually subdued a great part of Asia Minor.

Osmonds, The US pop vocal group, formed in 1959 with members **Alan** (1949–), **Wayne** (1951–), **Merrill** (1953–), Jay (1955–), **Donny** (1957–), **Marie** (1959–), and **Jimmy** (1963–). The group had been formed as a barber-shop style harmony quartet by the four older sons of a devoted Mormon family. Joined by the younger members of the family, they went on to become one of the most successful acts of the 1970s. 'One Bad Apple' (1971) topped the US music charts for 5 weeks, and their debut album *Osmonds* (1971) earned them a gold disk. They later pursued parallel solo careers, with Donny being the most successful.

Osmund, St (?–1099) Norman clergyman, nephew and chaplain to William I. He became Chancellor of England (1072) and helped to compile the *Domesday Book*. From 1078 he was Bishop of Salisbury, where he established the so-called 'Use of Sarum', a version of the Latin liturgy of worship. Feast day 4 December. >> William I (of England)

Ossietzky, Carl von [osyetskee] (1888–1938) Pacifist and writer, born in Hamburg, Germany. A reluctant conscript in the German army in World War 1, he was co-founder of *Nie wieder Krieg* (1922, No More War), and editor of the weekly *Weltbühne*, which exposed German military leaders' secret rearmament activities. Convicted of treason in 1931, his sentence was commuted, but when Hitler became chancellor he was arrested and sent to Papenburg concentration camp (1933). While he was in prison hospital he was awarded the 1935 Nobel Prize for Peace, the implications of which angered Hitler, who decreed in 1937 that no German could accept a Nobel Prize. He died of tuberculosis while under prison conditions in a private hospital.

Ostade, Adriaen van [ostahduh] (1610–85) Painter and engraver, born in Haarlem, The Netherlands. He was a pupil of Frans Hals, and his use of chiaroscuro shows the influence of Rembrandt. His subjects are taken mostly from everyday life, for example tavern scenes, farmyards, markets, and village greens. His 'Alchemist' is in the National Gallery. His brother **Isaak** (1621–49) treated similar subjects, but excelled at winter scenes and landscapes. >> Hals; Rembrandt

Ostwald, (Friedrich) Wilhelm (1853–1932) Chemist, born in Riga, Latvia. He studied at Dorpat, and taught at Riga before becoming professor at Leipzig (1887–1906). He discovered the dilution law which bears his name, and invented a process for making nitric acid by the oxidation of ammonia. He also developed a new theory of colour. He was awarded the 1909 Nobel Prize for Chemistry for his work on catalytic reactions.

Oswald, St (c. 605–642) Anglo-Saxon king of Northumbria (633–41), the son of Ethelfrith of Benicia. Having been converted at Iona, he established Christianity in Northumbria with St Aidan's help. He fell in battle with the pagan King Penda. Feast day 5 August. >> Aidan; Penda

Oswald, Lee Harvey (1939–1963) Alleged killer of President John F Kennedy, born in New Orleans, LA. A Marxist and former US marine, he lived for a while in the USSR (1959–62). He was arrested some hours after Kennedy's assassination (22 November 1963) on a charge of murdering a police officer in another incident. The following day he was also charged with the murder of President Kennedy. Before he could come to trial, he was shot at close range by nightclub owner Jack Ruby. The Warren Commission held him to be responsible for the assassination, although the belief that he was part of a conspiracy still persists. >> Kennedy, John F; Ruby

Otaka, Tadaaki [ohtaka] (1947–) Japanese conductor. He studied at the Toho Gakuen School of Music and the Vienna Hochschule, and was a student with the NHK (Japanese Broadcasting Corporation) Symphony Orchestra (1968–70), making his professional debut with the NHK (1971), and his US debut in 1985. He became conductor of the Tokyo Philharmonic Orchestra (1971–91, laureate 1991–), principal conductor of the BBC National Orchestra of Wales (1987–95, laureate 1996–), and music adviser and principal conductor of the Kioi Sinfonietta, Japan (1995–).

Otake, Eiko (1952–) and **Otake, Koma** (1948–) [ohtahkay] Dance-theatre artists, from Japan, now resident in New York City. They met in 1971 as law and political science students who joined *butoh* master Tatsumi Hijikata's company in Toyko, later studied with Kazuo Uhno, and developed a partnership in which they perform and choreograph only their own work. In 1972 they studied in Hanover with Mary Wigman, making their US debut in 1976, since when they have regularly toured North America and Europe. >> Hijikata; Wigman

Otho, Marcus Salvius [othoh] (32–69) Roman emperor for three months (69). Emperor Nero took Otho's wife for his mistress, and later married her. He was sent to govern Lusitania (58–68), and joined Galba in his revolt against Nero (68). When he was not proclaimed Galba's successor, he rose against the new emperor, who was slain. Otho was recognized as emperor everywhere except in Germany. Aulus Vitellius marched on Italy, defeated Otho's forces, and Otho committed suicide. >> Galba; Nero; Vitellius; RR1084

Otis, Elisha (Graves) [ohtis] (1811–61) Inventor, born in Halifax, VT. A master mechanic in a bedstead factory, he was put in charge of the construction of a new factory at Yonkers, NY. There he designed a spring-operated safety device which would hold lifting platforms securely if there was any failure of tension in the rope (1853). He opened a shop, patented his 'elevator', and exhibited it dramatically in a rope-cutting incident at an Exposition in New York City in 1854, after which orders came in rapidly for passenger as well as goods lifts. He also patented a new type of steam-powered lift in 1861.

Otis, James [ohtis] (1725–83) US politician, born in West Barnstable, MA. A leader of the Boston bar, he became advocate-general in 1760, when the revenue officers demanded his assistance in obtaining from the superior court general search warrants in quest of smuggled goods. He refused, resigned, and appeared in defence of popular rights. In 1761, elected to the Massachusetts Assembly, he was prominent in resistance to the revenue acts, but in 1769 was struck by a crown officer in a dispute, and lost his already precarious sanity. He was killed by lightning. His fame chiefly rests on *The Rights of the Colonies Asserted* (1764). >> Warren, Mercy Otis

O'Toole, Peter (Seamus) (1932–) Actor, born in Connemara, Co Galway, Ireland. A journalist and member of the submarine service, he attended the Royal Academy of Dramatic Art, London, before joining the Bristol Old Vic, where he made his professional debut in 1955. West End success and a season with the Royal Shakespeare Company established his stage reputation, while his performance in *Lawrence of Arabia* (1962) made him an international film star. Adept at drama, comedy, or musicals, he has tackled many of the great classical roles, frequently being cast as mercurial or eccentric characters. Nominated seven times for an Oscar, his films include *The Lion in Winter* (1968), *Goodbye Mr Chips* (1969), *The Stunt Man* (1980), *My Favourite Year* (1982), *The Last Emperor* (1987), and *Rebecca's Daughters* (1991).

Ott, Mel, popular name of **Melvin Thomas Ott** (1909–58) Baseball player, born in Gretna, LA. He was a player and later manager with the New York Giants in the National League for 22 years (1926–48). In that time he played 2732 games and hit 511 home runs. After arriving at the club at 17, he went on to play in three World Series (1933, 1936, 1937) and twice scored six runs in a single game (1934 and 1944). He became manager of New York in 1942.

Otto I, known as **the Great** (912–73) King of the Germans (from 936) and Holy Roman Emperor (from 962). He subdued many turbulent tribes, maintained almost supreme power in Italy, and encouraged Christian missions to Scandinavian and Slavonic lands. >> Adelaide, St; RR1057

Otto, Nikolaus (August) (1832–91) Engineer, born near Schlangenbad, Germany. In 1876 he built the first internal combustion engine that operated on a four-stroke cycle, now generally known as the *Otto cycle*, even though the principle of four-stroke operation had been patented in 1862 by the French engineer **Alphonse Eugène Beau de Rochas** (1815–93).

Otto, Rudolf (1869–1937) Protestant theologian and philosopher, born in Peine, Germany. A professor at Göttingen and Wrocław, Poland (formerly Breslau, Germany) before settling in Marburg in 1917, he studied non-Christian religions in order to define religion in a new way. In *Das Heilige* (1917, The Idea of the Holy) he describes religious experience as inspiring both awe and a promise of exaltation and bliss. His other books include *India's Religion of Grace and Christianity* (1930) and *Mysticism East and West* (1932).

Otway, Thomas (1652–85) Playwright, born in Trotton, West Sussex, S England, UK. He studied at Oxford, but left without a degree, then failed as an actor and became a writer. He translated Racine and Molière, and wrote Restoration comedies, but his best-known works are the tragedies *The Orphan* (1680) and his masterpiece *Venice Preserved, or a Plot Discovered* (1682).

Oud, Jacobus Johannes Pieter [owd] (1890–1963) Architect, born in Purmerend, The Netherlands. He studied at the Delft Technical University, collaborated with Mondrian and others in launching the review *De Stijl*, and became a pioneer of the modern architectural style based on simplified forms and pure planes. Appointed city architect at Rotterdam in 1918, he designed a number of striking buildings, including municipal housing blocks such as the Kiefhoek Estate in Amsterdam (1925–7). >> Mondrian

Oughtred, William [awtred] (1575–1660) Mathematician, born in Eton, Buckinghamshire, SC England, UK. He studied at Cambridge, and wrote extensively on mathematics, notably *Clavis mathematica* (1631), a textbook on arithmetic and algebra in which he introduced many new symbols. He invented the slide rule, making first a circular model, then the more familiar rectilinear form in c.1633.

Ouida [weeda], pseudonym of **Marie Louise de la Ramée** (1839–1908) Novelist, born in Bury St Edmunds, Suffolk, E England, UK. Her pen-name was a childish mispronunciation of Louise. She studied in Paris, settled in London, and began contributing stories to magazines. Her first novel was *Held in Bondage* (1863), followed by *Strathmore* (1865), and she was soon established as a best-selling writer of hothouse romances with powerful narratives. She spent much time in Italy, settling in Florence (1874), where she lived lavishly. She wrote almost 50 books, mainly novels, but also animal stories, essays, and tales for children. Eventually her royalties dried up, she fell into debt, and her last years were spent in destitution.

Ouimet, Francis (1893–1967) Golfer, born in Brookline, MA. He recorded the first major success in US golfing history when he defeated Harry Vardon and Ted Ray in a play-off for the US Open of 1913, and broke the British stranglehold on top-level events. He was a member of every Walker Cup team from 1922 to 1949, either as player or non-playing captain, and in 1951 became the first foreigner ever to be made captain of the Royal and Ancient golf club at St Andrews. >> Vardon; RR1158

Our Lady >> **Mary** (mother of Jesus)

Overbeck, Johann Friedrich (1789–1869) Painter, born in Lübeck, Germany. He studied art in Vienna (1806–10), and led the group of German artists known as the Nazarenes, or Lucas Brotherhood, which went to Rome (1810). He painted in fresco as well as oil, mainly religious and historical subjects, notably the 'Rose Miracle of St Francis' (1829, Portiuncula Chapel at Assisi).

Ovett, Steve [ohvet], popular name of **Steven Michael James Ovett** (1955–) Athlete, born in Brighton, East Sussex, SE England, UK. Gold medallist in the 800 m at the 1980 Olympics, he also won a bronze in the 1500 m. He broke the world record at 1500 m (three times), at one mile (twice) and at two miles. An outspoken and sometimes controversial figure, he occasionally upset the press, but remained generally popular with his fellow athletes and the spectators. As his competitive career faded he began a new role as a television commentator. >> RR1135

Ovid [ovid], in full **Publius Ovidius Naso** (43 BC–AD 17) Latin poet, born in Sulmo, Italy. He trained as a lawyer, but devoted himself to poetry, and visited Athens. His first success was the tragedy *Medea*, followed by *Heroides*, love letters from legendary heroines to their lords. His major poems are the three-book *Ars amatoria* (Art of Love) and the 15-book *Metamorphoses* (Transformations). With its startling insights into psychological states and symbolism, this is one of the most influential works from antiquity. In AD 8 he was banished, for some reason unknown, to Tomi on the Black Sea.

Owain Glyndwr >> **Glendower, Owen**

Owen, Alun (Davies) (1926–94) Playwright, born in Liverpool, Merseyside, NW England, UK. He began as an actor in Birmingham, then became a prolific writer for television and radio. His works include *The Rough and Ready Lot* (1958), *Progress to the Park* (1959), and a musical collaboration with Lionel Bart, *Maggie May* (1964).

Owen (of the City of Plymouth), David (Anthony Llewellyn), Baron (1938–) British statesman, born in Plymouth, Devon, SW England, UK. He studied at Cambridge and London, trained in medicine, then became Labour MP for Plymouth (1966). He was under-secretary to the navy (1968), secretary for health (1974–6), and foreign secretary (1977–9). One of the so-called 'Gang of Four' who formed the Social Democratic Party (SDP) in 1981, he succeeded Roy Jenkins as its leader in 1983. Following the Alliance's disappointing result in the 1987 general election, he opposed Liberal leader David Steel over the question of the merger of the two parties. In 1988, after the SDP voted to accept merger, he led the smaller section of the Party to an independent existence. He retired from parliament and was created a peer in 1992. With Cyrus Vance he was appointed by the UN to try to establish peace between the warring factions in former Yugoslavia (1992–3). He was made a Companion of Honour in 1994. >> Jenkins, Roy; Steel; Vance

Owen, Robert (1771–1858) Social and educational reformer, born in Newtown, Powys. Apprenticed to a draper, in 1800 he became manager and part owner of the New Lanark cotton mills, Lanarkshire, where he set up a social welfare programme, and established a 'model community'. His socialistic theories were put to the test in other experimental communities, such as at Orbiston, near Glasgow, and New Harmony in Indiana, but all were unsuccessful. He was later active in the trade-union movement, and in 1852 became a spiritualist. >> Owen, Robert Dale; Say, Thomas

Owen, Robert Dale (1801–77) Social reformer, born in Glasgow, W Scotland, UK. In 1825 he accompanied his father Robert Owen to America to help set up the New Harmony colony in Indiana. In 1829 he moved to New York City, where he edited the *Free Inquirer*. In 1832 he became a member of the Indiana legislature, and entered Congress in 1843. He later became US ambassador to India (1855–8). An advocate of emancipation of slaves, he wrote *The Policy of Emancipation* (1863) and *The Wrong Slavery* (1864). >> Owen, Robert; Wright, Frances

Owen, Wilfred (1893–1918) Poet, born near Oswestry, Shropshire, WC England, UK. He studied at the Birkenhead Institute and at Shrewsbury Technical School, left England to teach English in Bordeaux (1913), and began to write. Wounded in World War 1, he was sent to recuperate near Edinburgh, where he met Siegfried Sassoon, who encouraged his poetry writing. His poems, expressing a horror of the cruelty and waste of war, were first collected in 1920 by Sassoon and reappeared in 1931 with a memoir by Edmund Blunden. Several were set to music by Britten in his *War Requiem* (1962). *The Collected Poems* were published in 1963. He was killed in action on the Western Front on his return to France, a week before the armistice. >> Blunden; Britten; Sassoon

Owen Glendower >> **Glendower, Owen**

Owens, Jesse (James Cleveland) (1913–80) Athlete, born in Danville, AL. Within 45 min on 25 May 1935 at Ann Arbor, MI, he set five world records (100 yd, long jump, 220 yd, 220 yd hurdles, and 200 m hurdles). His long-jump record of 26 ft 8¼ in stood for 25 years. In 1936 he showed his dominance at the Berlin Olympics, much to Hitler's annoyance, when he won four gold medals, a feat equalled only in 1984 by Carl Lewis. >> Lewis, Carl; RR1134

Oxenstierna or **Oxenstern, Axel Gustafsson, Greve** (Count) [oksensherna, oksenstern] (1583–1654) Swedish statesman, born near Uppsala, Sweden. From 1612 he served as chancellor, and negotiated peace with Denmark, Russia, and Poland; and though he sought to prevent Gustavus Adolphus from plunging into the Thirty Years' War, he supported the war effort, even after the king's death (1632). During most of the minority of Queen Christina he was effective ruler of the country (1636–44), vindicating his policies by the terms of the Peace of Westphalia (1648). >> Christina; Gustavus II

Oxford, Earl of >> **Asquith, Herbert Henry**

Oz, Amos (1939–) Novelist, born in Jerusalem, Israel. He studied at the Hebrew University there and at Oxford, served in the Israeli army, and worked part-time as a schoolteacher as well as a writer. His novels describe the tensions of life in modern Israel, and include (trans titles) *Elsewhere, Perhaps* (1966), *My Michael* (1968), *In the Land of Israel* (1982), and *Don't Call it Night* (1995).

Özal, Turgut [oezal] (1927–93) Turkish politician and president (1989–93), born in Malatya, Turkey. He studied at Istanbul Technical University, and became under-secretary for state planning (1967). From 1971 he worked for the World Bank, joined the office of Prime Minister Bülent Ecevit (1979), and in 1980 was deputy prime minister within the military regime. He founded the Islamic, right-of-centre Motherland Party in 1983, and led it to victory in the elections. In the 1987 general election he retained his majority, and in 1989 became Turkey's first civilian president for 30 years. >> Ecevit

Ozawa, Seiji [ozahwa] (1935–) Conductor, born in Hoten, China. Trained in Japan, Paris, and the USA, he then conducted the Toronto and San Francisco Symphonies, before beginning in 1973 his long tenure as conductor of the Boston Symphony.

Ozenfant, Amédée [ohzãfã] (1886–1966) Artist, born in St Quentin, France. He was the leader of the Purist movement in Paris, and published a manifesto of Purism with Le Corbusier in 1919. They published an avant-garde magazine, *Esprit nouveau* (1921–5, New Spirit), and collaborated in writing *Après le Cubisme* (1918, After Cubism) and *La Peinture moderne* (1925, Modern Painting). His still-lifes based on this theory reduce vases and jugs to a static counterpoint of two-dimensional shapes. He founded art schools in London (1935) and New York (1938). His publications include *Art* (1928) and his diaries for the years 1931–4. >> Le Corbusier

Ozick, Cynthia (1928–) Novelist and short-story writer, born in New York City. She studied at New York and Ohio State universities, publishing her first novel, *Trust*, in 1966. Her fiction explores the dilemmas of being Jewish in a Christian world, and she is perhaps best known as a writer of short stories, including *The Pagan Rabbi and Other Stories* (1971), *Bloodshed and Three Novellas* (1976), and *The Shawl* (1991).

Ozu, Yasujiro [ohzoo] (1903–63) Film director, born in Tokyo. An inveterate cinema-goer as a youngster, he joined the industry as an assistant cameraman. As a director, in the 1930s he conceived the *shomin-geki* genre of films, dealing with lower middle-class family life. A precise and rigorous cinematic stylist, his films offered gentle, compassionate portraits laced with humour and, latterly, underlying tragedy. An internationally prominent director, his most widely seen work includes *Banshun* (1949, Late Spring), *Ochazuke No Aji* (1952, The Flavour of Green Tea Over Rice), and *Ohayo* (1959, Good Morning!).

Paasikivi, Juo Kusti [**pah**sikivee] (1870–1956) Finnish statesman, prime minister (1918, 1944–6), and president (1946–56), born in Tampere, Finland. He became Conservative prime minister after the civil war in 1918, recognized the need for friendly relations with Russia, and took part in all Finnish–Soviet negotiations. He sought to avoid war in September 1939, conducted the armistice negotiations, later becoming prime minister again and president. >> RR1049

Pabst, G(eorg) W(ilhelm) (1895–1967) Film director, born in Raudnitz, Czech Republic (formerly, Germany). He began directing in 1923, and his darkly realistic, almost documentary style was acclaimed in *Die Liebe der Jeanne Ney* (1927, The Love of Jeanne Ney). Other works include his pacifist *Westfront 1918* (1930) and his great co-production with France, *Kameradschaft* (1931, Comradeship), all examples of the New Realism. After World War 2 he continued to direct for a few years, recreating the last days of Hitler in *Der letzte Akt* (1955, The Last Act).

Pachelbel, Johann [**pa**khelbel] (c. 1653–1706) Composer and organist, born in Nuremberg, Germany. He held a variety of organist's posts before he returned to Nuremberg as organist of St Sebald's Church (1695). His works, which include six suites for two violins, and organ fugues, profoundly influenced J S Bach. His best-known composition is the Canon in D Major. >> Bach, J S

Pacher, Michael [**pah**kher] (c. 1435–98) Painter and woodcarver, born in the Tyrol, Austria. He was one of the earliest artists to bring Italian Renaissance ideas into N Europe. He may have travelled to Italy, for his paintings show the influence of Italian artists in their convincing foreshortening and perspective. His masterpiece was the high altar for the Church of St Wolfgang on the Abersee (1481), depicting the life of the Virgin Mary and the legend of St Wolfgang.

Pachomius, St [pa**koh**mius] (4th-c) Founder of communal monasticism, from Egypt. He superseded the system of solitary reclusive life by founding (AD c.318), the first monastery on the island of Tabenna on the Nile, with its properly regulated communal life and rule. He founded 10 other monasteries, including two convents for women. Feast day 9 May.

Pacino, Al(berto) [pa**chee**noh] (1940–   ) Film actor, born in New York City. He studied at the Herbert Berghov Studio under Charles Laughton, and at the Actors Studio, and is renowned for his detailed and thoroughly researched acting style. His first main role came as Michael in *The Godfather* (1972), which he followed with acclaimed performances in *Serpico* (1973) and *The Godfather, Part II* (1974). Later films include *Scarface* (1983), *Sea of Love* (1989), *The Godfather, Part III* (1990), *Scent of a Woman* (1992, Oscar), *Looking for Richard* (1996), in which he also made his directorial debut, and *Donnie Brasco* (1997). >> Laughton

Packer, Sir (Douglas) Frank (Hewson) (1906–74) Newspaper proprietor, born in Sydney, New South Wales, Australia. He became a cadet reporter on his father's *Daily Guardian* (1923), and established the magazine *Australian Women's Weekly* (1933). The success of the magazine led to the formation of the Australian Consolidated Press group, publishers of the Sydney *Daily Telegraph* (sold to Rupert Murdoch in 1972), *The Bulletin* magazine, and television and radio interests. >> Murdoch, Rupert; Packer, Kerry

Packer, Kerry (Francis Bullmore) (1937–   ) Media proprietor, born in Sydney, New South Wales, Australia. He inherited the Australian Consolidated Press (ACP) group from his father, Sir Frank Packer. In the 1977–8 season he created 'World Series Cricket', contracting the leading Test cricketers for a knock-out series of one-day matches and 'Super-Tests', played in colourful costume and often under floodlights, sole television rights for which were held by ACP's Channel Nine. This led to disputes with national cricket bodies, and provoked many legal battles, before a *modus operandi* was established. He sold Channel Nine to Alan Bond at the height of the 1987 boom for $A1 billion, only to buy it back in 1990 for a fraction of that amount. He has pastoral, mining, manufacturing, and property investments, and is assumed to be the richest person in Australia. >> Bond, Alan; Packer, Frank

Paderewski, Ignacy (Jan) [paduh**refs**kee] (1860–1941) Pianist, composer, and patriot, born in Kurylowka, Poland. He studied at Warsaw, becoming professor at the Conservatory in 1878. In 1884 he taught at the Strasbourg Conservatory, and became a virtuoso pianist, appearing throughout Europe and America. He became director of Warsaw Conservatory in 1909. In 1919 he was asked to be the first premier of Poland, but soon retired from politics, went to live in Switzerland, and resumed concert work.

Padilla, Juan de [pa**deel**ya] (c. 1490–1521) Spanish revolutionary leader and popular hero, born in Toledo, Spain. He was commandant of Saragossa under Charles V, headed an insurrection against the intolerable taxation, and after some success was defeated and beheaded. His wife **Maria** (d.1531) held Toledo against the royal forces for a time (1521–2), then fled to Portugal.

Páez, José Antonio [paez] (1790–1873) Venezuelan general and president (1831–5, 1839–43, 1861–3), born in Aragua, Venezuela. He commanded forces of *llaneros* ('cowboys') in the war of independence as principal lieutenant of Simón Bolívar. On the break-up of Gran Colombia, he became president. >> Bolívar; RR1099

Paganini, Niccolo [paga**nee**nee] (1782–1840) Violin virtuoso, born in Genoa, Italy. He gave his first concert in 1793, began touring professionally in Italy in 1805, and created a sensation in Austria, Germany, Paris, and London (1828–31). Much admired for his dexterity and technical brilliance, he revolutionized violin technique, his innovations including the use of stopped harmonics. He published several concertos and, in 1820, the celebrated *24 Capricci*.

Page, Sir Frederick Handley (1885–1962) Pioneer aircraft designer and engineer, born in Cheltenham, Gloucestershire, SWC England, UK. In 1909 he founded the firm of aeronautical engineers which bears his name. His twin-engined 0/400 (1918) was one of the earliest heavy bombers, and his Hampden and Halifax bombers were used in World War 2. His civil aircraft include the Hannibal, Hermes, and Herald transports. He was knighted in 1942.

Paget, Sir James [pa**jet**] (1814–99) Physician and pathologist, born in Yarmouth, Isle of Wight, S England, UK. One of the founders of modern pathology, he studied at St Bartholomew's Hospital, London, where he became full surgeon in 1861. He discovered the cause of trichinosis, and described the breast cancer known as *Paget's disease*, and the bone disease *osteitis deformans* known as *Paget's disease of the bone*. He was one of the pioneers of the technique of surgical removal of myeloid sarcoma rather than amputation of the affected limb. He was made a baronet in 1871.

Paget, Violet >> **Lee, Vernon**

Pahlavi, Mohammad Reza [**pah**lavee] (1919–80) Shah of Persia, born in Tehran, Iran, who succeeded on the abdication of his father, Reza Shah (1878–1944), in 1941. His reign was for many years marked by social reforms and a movement away from the old-fashioned despotic concept of the monarchy, but during the later 1970s the economic situation deteriorated, social inequalities worsened, and protest at western-style 'decadence' grew among the religious fundamentalists. He lost control of the situation, was forced to leave the country, and a revolutionary government was formed under Ayatollah Khomeini. He was in the USA for medical treatment when the Iranian government seized the US embassy in Teheran and held many of its staff hostage for over a year, demanding his return to Iran. He made his final residence in Egypt at the invitation of President Sadat. >> Khomeini; Soraya; RR1063

Paige, Elaine (1951–) Actress and singer, born in London, England, UK. She joined the West End cast of *Hair* in 1969, but it was her performances in *Jesus Christ Superstar* (1972) and *Billy* (1974) that established her as a musical actress. She appeared at Chichester Festival Theatre, and at Stratford East, before she became a star as *Evita* in 1978. Later shows include *Cats* (1981), *Chess* (1986), *Anything Goes* (1989), *Piaf* (1993), and *Sunset Boulevard* at the Adelphi, London (1994–5), and New York (1996).

Paige, Satchel, popular name of **Leroy Robert Paige** (?1906–82) Baseball player, born in Mobile, AL. A legend in his time, he was one of the first African-Americans to make a breakthrough into the major leagues. As pitcher, he enjoyed success in the Negro leagues (1925–47) before moving into the majors with the Cleveland Indians, whom he helped to win the 1948 World Series.

Paine, Thomas (1737–1809) Revolutionary philosopher and writer, born in Thetford, Norfolk, E England, UK. A corset-maker from the age of 13, he became a sailor, a schoolmaster, and an exciseman. In 1774 he sailed for Philadelphia, where his pamphlet *Common Sense* (1776) argued for complete independence. He served with the US army, and was made secretary to the Committee of Foreign Affairs. In 1787 he returned to England, where he wrote *The Rights of Man* (1791–2) in support of the French Revolution. Arraigned for treason, he fled to Paris, where he was elected a Deputy to the National Convention, but imprisoned for his proposal to offer the king asylum in the USA. At this time he wrote *The Age of Reason*, in favour of deism. Released in 1796, he returned to the USA in 1802.

Paisley, Bob [**payz**lee], popular name of **Robert Paisley** (1919–96) Football manager, born in Hetton-le-Hole, Durham, NE England, UK. A player with the amateur side Bishop Auckland, he joined Liverpool in 1939, and spent nearly 50 years at the club. It was during his spell as manager (1974–83) that Liverpool enjoyed their greatest years, and became the most successful club side in England. Manager of the Year on six occasions, he continued to be involved with the club as director and adviser.

Paisley, Rev Ian (Richard Kyle) [**payz**lee] (1926–) Militant Protestant clergyman and politician, born in Armagh, Co Armagh. Ordained in 1946, he formed his own Church (the Free Presbyterian Church of Ulster) in 1951, and from the 1960s became deeply involved in Ulster politics. He founded the Protestant Unionist Party and stood as its MP for four years until 1974, and has since been the Democratic Unionist MP for North Antrim. He is a member of the European Parliament since 1970. A rousing orator, he is strongly pro-British, fiercely opposed to the IRA, Roman Catholicism, and the unification of Ireland.

Palach, Jan [**pa**lakh] (1948–69) Czech philosophy student. As a protest against the invasion of Czechoslovakia by Warsaw

Pact forces (Aug 1968), he burnt himself to death in Wenceslas Square, Prague in January 1969. He became a hero and symbol of hope, and was mourned by thousands. Huge popular demonstrations marking the 20th anniversary of his death were held in Prague in 1989.

Palade, George E(mil) [pa**lad**] (1912–) Cell biologist, born in Iasi, Romania. He trained as a doctor in Bucharest, and was professor of anatomy there until he moved to the USA in 1946, where he became a US citizen in 1952. He worked under Albert Claude at the Rockefeller Institute, New York City (1946–72), and from 1972 headed cell biology at Yale Medical School. His work on the fine structure of cells as revealed by electron microscopy led him in 1956 to discover the small organelles within cells, called ribosomes, in which RNA synthesizes protein. He shared the 1974 Nobel Prize for Physiology or Medicine. >> Claude, Albert; RR1124

Palestrina, Giovanni Pierluigi da [pale**stree**na] (c. 1525–94) Composer, born in Palestrina, Italy. At Rome he learned composition and organ playing, and became organist and *maestro di canto* at the cathedral of St Agapit, Palestrina (1544). In 1551 he became master of the Julian choir at St Peter's, the first of several appointments in Rome. The most distinguished composer of the Renaissance, he composed over 100 Masses, motets, hymns, and other church pieces, and in 1577 began a revision of the Gradual (which he later abandoned).

Paley, William (1743–1805) Theologian, born in Peterborough, Northamptonshire, C England, UK. He was fellow and tutor of Christ's College, Cambridge (1768–76), and became archdeacon of Carlisle (1782) and subdean of Lincoln (1795). In 1790 he published his most original work, *Horae Paulinae*, the aim of which was to prove the improbability of the hypothesis that the New Testament is a cunningly devised fable. In 1802 he published his most popular work, *Natural Theology, or Evidences of the Existence and Attributes of the Deity*.

Palgrave, Francis Turner [**pal**grayv] (1824–97) Poet and critic, born in Great Yarmouth, Norfolk, E England, UK. He studied at Oxford, and after a variety of posts in education and administration became professor of poetry there (1886–95). He is best kown as the editor of the *Golden Treasury of Songs and Lyrical Poems* (1861), known to generations of schoolchildren as 'Palgrave's Golden Treasury'.

Palin, Michael (Edward) [**pay**lin] (1943–) Script-writer and actor, born in Sheffield, Yorkshire, N England, UK. He studied at Oxford, then joined the BBC team writing and acting in *Monty Python's Flying Circus* (1969–74). He was also involved in *Ripping Yarns* (1976–80), and he co-wrote and acted in the Monty Python films, such as *The Meaning of Life* (1982). He won a BAFTA award for his acting in *A Fish Called Wanda* (1988) and appeared in the not-quite-sequel *Fierce Creatures* (1997). A versatile writer, his works include a play, *The Weekend* (1994), and a novel, *Hemingway's Chair* (1995). He has also presented a popular series of travel documentaries for BBC TV, beginning with *Around the World in Eighty Days* (1989), following this with a journey from North to South Pole along the 30° meridian (1992), and another around the Pacific rim (1997). >> Cleese

Palissy, Bernard [paleesee] (c. 1510–90) Potter, born in Agen, France. He began as a glass-painter, then settled in Saintes (1539), where he devised new techniques for glazing earthenware. His products, bearing in high-relief plants and animals coloured to represent nature, soon made him famous, and although imprisoned as a Huguenot in 1562, he was speedily released and taken into royal favour. In c.1565 he established his workshop at the Tuileries, and was specially exempted from the St Bartholomew's Day massacre (1572). In 1588 he was again arrested as a Huguenot, and died in prison. >> Charles IX

Palladio, Andrea [paladioh], originally **Andrea di Pietro della Gondola** (1508–80) Architect, born in Vicenza, Italy. He founded modern Italian architecture, as distinguished from the earlier Italian Renaissance. The *Palladian* style, modelled on the ancient Roman, can be seen in many places and villas in the Vicenza region, notably the Villa Rotonda (1550–1). *I quattro libri dell' architettura* (1570, The Four Books of Architecture) greatly influenced his successors.

Pallas, Peter Simon (1741–1811) Naturalist, born in Berlin. After studying medicine, he was appointed professor of natural history at the Imperial Academy of Sciences, St Petersburg. He spent six years (1768–74) exploring the Urals, the Kirghiz Steppes, the Altai Range, part of Siberia, and the steppes of the Volga, returning with an extraordinary treasure of specimens. He wrote a series of works on the geography, ethnography, flora, and fauna of the regions he had visited, *Reise durch verschiedene Provinzen des Russischen Reichs* (1771–76, Journey Through Various Provinces of the Russian Empire). Several birds, including *Pallas's sandgrouse*, are named after him.

Palma, Jacopo [palma], also called **Palma Vecchio** ('Old Palma') (c. 1480–1528) Painter of the Venetian School, born in Serinalta, Italy. He is particularly remembered for the ample blonde women who appear in many of his works, which were often sacred subjects or portrait groups, notably 'Three Sisters' (Staatliche Kunstsammlungen, Dresden). His brother's grandson, **Jacopo** (1544–1628), called **il Giovane** ('the Younger'), was a prolific painter of religious pictures in a style influenced by Tintoretto and late Titian. >> Tintoretto; Titian

Palme, (Sven) Olof [palmuh] (1927–86) Swedish politician and prime minister (1969–76, 1982–6), born in Stockholm. He studied in the USA at Kenyon College, then took up law at Stockholm University. He joined the Social Democratic Labour Party (SAP) in 1949, entered the government in 1963 and held several ministerial posts before assuming the leadership of the Party and becoming prime minister. Although losing his parliamentary majority in 1971, he successfully carried out major constitutional reforms, but was defeated in 1976 over taxation proposals to fund the welfare system. He was returned to power, heading a minority government in 1982, and was re-elected in 1985, but was shot and killed while walking home with his wife after a visit to a cinema. >> RR1090

Palmer, Arnold (Daniel) (1929–) Golfer, born in Latrobe, PA. US Amateur champion in 1954, he won the Canadian Open (1955), the (British) Open (1961–2), the US Open (1960), and the US Masters (1958, 1960, 1962, 1964). The first golfer (1968) to win $1 million in his career, he has been credited with turning golf from an exclusive sport into a popular pastime. >> McCormack, Mark; RR1157

Palmer, Daniel (David) (1845–1913) Osteopath and founder of chiropractic, born in Toronto, Ontario, Canada. In 1895 he settled at Davenport, IA, where he first practised spinal adjustment, and founded the Palmer School of Chiropractic in 1898. Later he established a college of chiropractic in Portland, OR.

Palmer, Geoffrey (Winston Russell) (1942–) New Zealand prime minister (1989–90), born in Nelson, New Zealand. He studied at Victoria University, Wellington, taught law in the USA and New Zealand, then entered the House of Representatives as Labour Party member for Christchurch in 1979. By 1984 he had become attorney general and deputy prime minister, and succeeded David Lange as prime minister. He proved an unpopular leader, and was forced by his Party to resign just one month before the 1990 general election. >> Lange, David; RR1078

Palmer, Nettie, popular name of **Janet Gertrude Palmer Higgins** (1885–1964) Writer and critic, born in Bendigo,

Victoria, Australia. She studied in Melbourne and London, where she married Vance Palmer. Her prolific literary journalism in the 1920s and 1930s was extremely important in the development of Australian literary culture. She was a familiar broadcaster on ABC radio in the 1940s and 1950s, and was well known in international literary circles. She published two volumes of poetry, books of criticism including *Modern Australian Literature 1900–23*, a study of Henry Handel Richardson, and various histories and memoirs. A vigorous promoter of Australian writing, she also edited a number of anthologies. >> Palmer, Vance

Palmer, Samuel (1805–81) Landscape painter and etcher, born in London, England, UK. He produced chiefly watercolours in a mystical and imaginative style derived from his friend William Blake, as in 'Repose of the Holy Family' (1824). From 1826 to 1835 he lived in Shoreham, Kent, where he was part of the group which called itself *The Ancients*. He later visited Italy and began producing more academic, conventional work, and was forgotten until the neo-Romantics rediscovered him during World War 2. >> Blake, William

Palmer, Vance (1885–1959) Writer and critic, born in Bundaberg, Queensland, Australia. He rejected the notion of a university education and chose to travel widely instead. A leading member of the Pioneer Players theatre group, he published poetry but was better known as a novelist, publishing a number of outback novels including *The Passage* (1930). By the 1940s he had a reputation as a pre-eminent cultural figure, and wrote a number of essays and literary and historical studies. Vance and Nettie Palmer were a remarkable literary partnership of great importance to Australia's cultural life. >> Palmer, Nettie

Palmerston (of Palmerston), Henry John Temple, 3rd Viscount (1784–1865) British statesman and Liberal prime minister (1855-8, 1859–65), born in Broadlands, Hampshire, S England, UK. He studied at Edinburgh and Cambridge, became a Tory MP in 1807, served as secretary of war (1809–28), joined the Whigs (1830), and was three times foreign secretary (1830–4, 1835–41, 1846–51). His brusque speed, assertive manner, and robust defences of what he considered to be British interests abroad secured him the name of 'Firebrand Palmerston'. A more comfortable nickname was **Pam**, and his frequently xenophobic foreign policy won him substantial popular support in Britain. Home secretary in Aberdeen's coalition (1852), he became premier in 1855, when he vigorously prosecuted the Crimean War with Russia. >> Aberdeen; RR1095

Panaetius [paneeshus] (c. 185–c. 110 BC) Stoic philosopher, from Rhodes. He taught in Athens and Rome, and became head of the Stoa in Athens (129 BC). His writings are now lost, but he was an important figure in the popularization of Stoicism in Rome. He was a friend of the younger Scipio, and his ethical and political works were an important source for Cicero's influential treatise, *De officiis*. >> Cicero; Scipio Aemilianus

Pancras, St (?–304) Christian martyr, the son of a heathen noble of Phrygia, one of the patron saints of children. He was baptized in Rome, but immediately afterwards was slain in the Diocletian persecutions while only a young boy. Feast day 12 May. >> Diocletian

Pander, Christian Heinrich (1794–1865) Anatomist, the father of embryology, born in Riga, Latvia. At Würzburg with Karl Ernst von Baer he did valuable research on chick development in the egg, with particular regard to the embryonic layers now called by his name. He published his findings in 1817, accompanied a Russian mission to Bokhara as a naturalist (1820), and was elected a member of the St Petersburg Academy of Sciences (1826). >> Baer

Pandit, Vijaya Lakshmi, *née* **Swarup Kumari Nehru** (1900–90) Indian diplomat, born in Allahabad, India, the sister of Nehru. She was active in the nationalist movement, and was three times imprisoned. In the Legislative Assembly of the United Provinces (later, Utter Pradesh) she was minister for local self-government and public health (1937–9), the first Indian woman to hold a cabinet post. Leader of the Indian UN delegation (1946–8, 1952–3), she also held several ambassadorial posts (1947–51). In 1953, she became the first woman president of the UN General Assembly, and was Indian High Commissioner in London (1954–61). >> Nehru, Jawaharlal

Pandulf, Cardinal (?–1226) Papal legate, born in Rome. He was the commissioner sent by Innocent III to King John of England after his excommunication to receive his submission (1213). He returned to England as legate (1218–21), was made Bishop of Norwich (1218), and exercised great authority during the minority of Henry III (1216–27). >> Henry III (of England); Innocent III; John

Paneth, Friedrich Adolf [**pa**net] (1887–1958) Chemist, born in Vienna. He studied at Munich, Glasgow, and Vienna, and taught at Hamburg, Berlin, and Königsberg, before moving to England in 1933. He worked at Imperial College, London, and Durham University, where he was appointed professor of chemistry (1939). In 1953 he returned to Germany and the directorship of the Max Planck Institute. With George de Hevesy he developed the concept of radioactive tracers (1912–13), and from the 1920s used them to establish the age of rocks and meteorites by their helium content, and to detect novel metal hydrides and short-lived free radicals. >> Hevesy

Panhard, René [panah(r)] (1841–1908) Engineer and inventor, a pioneer of the motor industry, born in Paris. With **Emile Levassor** (1843–97), his partner from 1886, he was the first to mount an internal combustion engine on a chassis (1891). He founded the Panhard Company.

Panini [**pah**ninee] (5th–7th-c BC) Grammarian, born in India. He was the author of the *Astadhyayi* (Eight Lectures), a grammar of Sanskrit comprising 4000 aphoristic statements which provide the rules of word-formation and, to a lesser extent, sentence structure. His work forms the basis of all later Sanskrit grammars, and also exercised some influence in the development of modern linguistic theory.

Panizzi, Sir Anthony [**pa**neetsee], originally **Antonio Genesio Maria Panizzi** (1797–1879) Bibliographer, born in Brescello, Italy. An advocate by training, he fled to Liverpool after the 1821 revolution, and in 1828 became professor of Italian at University College, London. In 1831 he was appointed assistant librarian, and later chief librarian (1856–66) of the British Museum, where he showed great administrative ability, undertook a new catalogue, and designed the famous Reading Room.

Pankhurst, Emmeline, *née* **Goulden** (1857–1928) Suffragette, born in Manchester, Greater Manchester, NW England, UK. In 1879 she married **Richard Marsden Pankhurst** (d.1898), a radical Manchester barrister who had been the author of the first women's suffrage bill in Britain and of the Married Women's Property Acts of 1870 and 1882. She founded the Women's Franchise League (1889), and in 1903, with her daughter **Christabel Harriette** (1880–1958), the Women's Social and Political Union. From 1905 she fought for women's suffrage by violent means, on several occasions being arrested and going on hunger strike. After the outbreak of World War 1, she worked instead for the industrial mobilization of women. Of her daughters and fellow workers, **Dame Christabel** turned later to preaching Christ's Second Coming; and **Sylvia** (1882–1960) diverged to pacifism, internationalism, and Labour politics. >> Davison; Fawcett, Millicent; Smyth

Panofsky, Erwin [**pa**nofskee] (1892–1968) Art historian, born in Hanover, Germany. He studied at Berlin, Munich, and Freiburg universities, taught at the University of Hamburg (1921–32), and worked as a librarian. He fled from Nazi Germany to New York City in 1934, and from 1935 taught at the Institute for Advanced Study, Princeton. Although best known for developing the iconological approach to art – a method of interpreting the meaning of works of art by an analysis of the symbolism, history, and other non-aesthetic aspects of the subject matter – he had an interest in a wide variety of subjects from the history of movies and the detective story to the works of Mozart. His major works include *Preface to Studies in Iconology* (1939) and *Meaning in the Visual Arts* (1955).

Panov, Valeri [**pa**nof] (1938–) Ballet dancer, born in Vitebsk, Belarus. Trained in St Petersburg (formerly, Leningrad), he made his debut with the Maly Theatre Ballet in 1957, then moved to the Kirov (1964–72). His reputation as a virtuoso performer grew, as he created roles in both classical works and new ballets. He became known internationally when refused emigration papers by the Soviet authorities, who eventually allowed him to resettle in Israel in 1974. From that time he made guest appearances with companies around the world. His choreography includes *Sacré du printemps* (1978, The Rite of Spring), *Cinderella* (1977), and *The Idiot* (1979).

Paola, St Francis of >> **Francis of Paola, St**

Paolozzi, Sir Eduardo (Luigi) [pow**lot**see] (1924–) Sculptor and printmaker, born in Edinburgh, EC Scotland, UK. He studied at Edinburgh College of Art and at the Slade School of Art, London. His early work was influenced by the Dadaists and Surrealists in Paris in the 1940s, but his more mature sculptures in bronze and steel often resemble stylized robotic figures, such as 'Medea' (1964). He also engaged in print-making and textile design, and was elected to the Royal Academy in 1979. He was knighted in 1989.

Papa Doc >> **Duvalier, François**

Papandreou, Andreas (Georgios) [papan**dray**oo] (1919–96) Greek politician and prime minister (1981–9), born in Chios, Greece, the son of Georgios Papandreou. He studied at Athens University and Harvard, became a US citizen in 1944, made a brilliant academic career, then returned to Greece as director of the Centre for Economic Research in Athens (1961–4) and economic adviser to the Bank of Greece, resuming his Greek citizenship. Imprisoned and exiled after the military coup in 1967, he returned in 1974, and founded the Pan-Hellenic Liberation (later Socialist) Movement. He was Leader of the Opposition from 1977, and in 1981 became Greece's first Socialist prime minister. He was re-elected in 1985, and resigned after the 1989 general election. >> Papandreou, Georgios; RR1054

Papandreou, Georgios [papan**dray**oo] (1888–1968) Greek Republican statesman and prime minister (1944–5, 1963, 1964–5), born in Kaléntzi, Greece. A lawyer by training, he moved into politics, holding office in several administrations, including the brief period when the monarchy was temporarily removed (1923–5). He escaped during the German occupation, and returned in 1944 to head a coalition government, but was suspected by the army because of his Socialist credentials, and remained in office for only a few weeks. He then founded the Centre Union Party (1961), and returned as prime minister. A disagreement with King Constantine II led to his resignation, and in 1967, when a coup established a military regime, he was placed under house arrest. >> Papandreou, Andreas; RR1054

Papanek, Victor [**pa**panek] (1925–) Designer, teacher, and writer, born in Vienna. In developing countries he has specialized in design appropriate to local materials and technology, and worked on programmes to further the interests of these countries. In the Western context he has demonstrated particular concern for the handicapped. He is best known for his book, *Design for the Real World* (1971).

Papanicolaou, George (Nicholas) [papaniko**low**] (1883–1962) Physiologist and microscopist, born in Kimi, Greece. He studied at Athens and Munich universities, and for most of his career was associated with Cornell Medical College, New York City. His research on reproductive physiology led him to discover that he could identify cancer cells in samples taken from the cervixes of women with cervical cancer. He subsequently pioneered the techniques, now called *Papanicolaou's stain*, or the *pap smear*, of routine microscopical examination of exfoliated cells for the early detection of cervical and other forms of cancer.

Papen, Franz von [**pa**pen] (1879–1969) German politician, born in Werl, Germany. He was military attaché in Mexico and Washington, chief-of-staff with a Turkish army, and took to Centre Party politics. As Hindenburg's chancellor (1932) he suppressed the Prussian Socialist government, and as Hitler's vice-chancellor (1933–4) signed a concordat with Rome. He later became ambassador to Austria (1936–8) and Turkey (1939– 44). Taken prisoner in 1945, he was acquitted at the Nuremberg Trials. >> Hindenburg; Hitler

Papin, Denis [papĭ] (1647–c. 1712) Physicist, born in Blois, France. He helped Christiaan Huygens and then Robert Boyle in their experiments. He invented the steam digester (1679), forerunner of the domestic pressure cooker, and in c.1690 made a working model of an atmospheric condensing steam engine, on principles later developed by Thomas Newcomen and James Watt. >> Boyle, Robert; Huygens; Newcomen; Watt

Papineau, Louis Joseph [papeenoh] (1786–1871) French-Canadian leader, born in Montreal, Quebec, Canada. He was speaker of the House of Assembly for Lower Canada (1815–37), opposed the union with Upper Canada, and agitated against the imperial government. At the rebellion of 1837 a warrant was issued against him for high treason. He escaped to Paris, but returned to Canada after the general amnesty of 1844.

Papp, Joe, originally **Joseph Papirofsky** (1921–91) Stage director and producer, born in New York City. Following acting and backstage experience, he formed a Shakespeare Workshop which in 1954 started performing free shows in Central Park; in 1960 this Workshop officially became the New York Shakespeare Festival. A permanent open-air theatre, the Delacorte, was built in the Park for the company in 1962. In 1967 he founded the off-Broadway Public Theater, dedicated to new work by US writers, opening with the original production of the rock musical, *Hair*. He was later director of the theatres at the Lincoln Center (1973–8).

Pappus of Alexandria (4th-c) Greek mathematician, whose eight-book *Synagoge* (Collection) is extant in an incomplete form. Some of our knowledge of ancient Greek mathematics derives exclusively from his work.

Paracelsus [para**sel**sus], originally **Philippus Aureolus Theophrastus Bombastus von Hohenheim** (1493–1541) Alchemist and physician, born in Einsiedeln, Switzerland. He travelled widely in Europe and the Middle East, learning about alchemy, and acquiring great fame as a medical practitioner (1526). He became town physician and lecturer at Basel (1527), but his controversial views caused his exile in 1538. He travelled through Europe until settling at Salzburg in 1541. He established the use of chemistry in medicine, gave the most up-to-date description of syphilis, and was the first to argue that small doses of what makes people ill can also cure them.

Parbo, Sir Arvi Hillar [**pah(r)**boh] (1926–   ) Industrialist, born in Tallinn, Estonia. He emigrated to Australia (1949) and studied at the University of Adelaide. He joined the Western Mining Corporation as an underground surveyor, and later became a technical assistant, general manager (1968–71), manager (1971–88), and chairman (1974–91). He led the Western Mining Corporation through its expansion into gold, and is seen as a leader in the Australian mining industry. He was chairman of BHP, Australia's biggest company (1989–92), and has been the chairman of Alcoa since 1978. He received the gold medal of the Institute of Mining and Metallurgy, London, in 1983. He was knighted in 1978.

Parc, Julio Le >> Le Parc, Julio

Pardo Bazán, Emilia, condesa de (Countess of) [**pah(r)**tho ba**thahn**] (1852–1921) Novelist, born in La Coruña, Spain. The centre of a literary controversy in Spain when she championed Naturalism, her first novel was *Pascual Lopez* (1879). Her best-known works include *Los pazos de Ulloa* (1886, trans The Son of a Bondswoman), and *La madre naturaleza* (1887, Mother Nature). An ardent feminist, she also wrote plays, short stories, and literary criticism, and became professor of Romance literature at Madrid from 1916.

Paré, Ambroise [paray] (c. 1510–1590) Surgeon, 'the father of modern surgery', born in Bourg-Hersent, France. Apprenticed to a barber-surgeon, he studied anatomy and surgery, joined the army as a surgeon (1537), and became surgeon to Henry II, Francis II, Charles IX, and Henry III. He improved the treatment of gunshot wounds, was one of the first to cease the automatic castration of hernia patients, and substituted ligature of the arteries for cauterization with a red-hot iron after amputation.

Parer, Damien [**pa**rer] (1912–44) News photographer, born in Malvern, Victoria, Australia. Trained for the priesthood, he developed an interest in cinematography. In 1940 he became an official cameraman with the 2nd Australian Imperial Forces and went to the Middle East, filming the action at the siege of Tobruk, and later worked in Greece, Syria, and New Guinea. He shot a number of documentary films in the heat of battle, and his *Kokoda Front* (1942) was the first Australian film to win an Oscar. In 1943 he joined the US troops for the liberation of the Pacific, and was killed while filming their landing at Peleliu, Caroline Is.

Pareto, Vilfredo [pa**ray**toh] (1848–1923) Economist and sociologist, born in Paris. Brought up in Italy, he studied at Turin University, became an engineer, and directed a railway company in Italy. He then studied philosophy and politics, and became professor of political economy at Lausanne from 1893. He wrote several influential textbooks on the subject, in which he demonstrated a mathematical approach. In sociology, his *Trattato di sociologica generale* (1916, trans The Mind and Society) enquired into the nature of individual and social action; it presented a theory of the superiority of an elite class which anticipated some of the principles of Fascism.

Paris, Matthew >> Matthew Paris

Park, Maud May, *née* **Wood** (1871–1955) Suffrage leader, born in Boston, MA. She studied at Radcliffe College, joined the Massachusetts Woman Suffrage Association, and became co-founder of the Boston Equal Suffrage Association for Good Government. With Inez Gillmore she founded the College Equal Suffrage League (from 1901), aiming to involve young women in the fight for equality. An efficient, strong-minded campaigner, she helped to bring about the 19th Amendment (1920), thus securing the vote for women. She became first president of the League of Women Voters (1920–4), and shortly afterwards head of the Women's Joint Congressional Committee. >> Paul, Alice

Park, Mungo (1771–1806) Explorer of Africa, born in Foulshiels, Scottish Borders, SE Scotland, UK. He became a surgeon at Edinburgh, and in 1792 served on an expedition to Sumatra. In 1795–6 he made a journey along the Niger R, as recounted in *Travels in the Interior of Africa* (1799). He settled as a surgeon in Peebles, then in 1805 undertook another journey to the Niger. They reached Bussa, where he was drowned following an attack by natives.

Park, Robert E(zra) (1864–1944) Sociologist, born in Harveyville, PA. He studied at the universities of Minnesota and Michigan, then worked as a newspaper reporter before returning to study at Harvard, Strasbourg, and Heidelberg. From 1905 he worked as publicity officer for Booker T Washington. He taught at Chicago University (1913–33), then at Fisk University, TN (1936–43). He played a formative part in the founding of urban sociology, as well as making important contributions to the study of race relations. He created the Chicago school of sociology, which was characterized by the use of the participant observation methods that he pioneered. >> Washington, Booker T

Park, Ruth (c.1923–) Writer, born in Auckland, New Zealand. She went to Australia in 1942 and married the author D'Arcy Niland. Her first success was with the novel *The Harp in the South* (1947), a story of slum life in Sydney which has been translated into 10 languages, and forms a trilogy with *Poor Man's Orange* (1949) and *Missus* (1986). Her work includes several other novels, as well as short stories, and scripts for film, television, and radio. She created the popular *Muddle-Headed Wombat* series of children's books, and has written fiction for adolescent readers. Her best-selling autobiography *A Fence Around the Cuckoo* was published in 1992. >> Niland

Parker, Alan (1944–) Film director, born in London, England, UK. He began his career in advertising, then progressed via script writing to directing short films. He made his feature-length cinema debut with *Bugsy Malone* (1976). Later films include *Midnight Express* (1978), *Fame* (1979), *The Commitments* (1991), and *Evita* (1996).

Parker, Bonnie >> **Bonnie and Clyde**

Parker, Charlie, popular name of **Charles (Christopher) Parker**, nickname **Bird** or **Yardbird** (1920–55) Jazz saxophonist, born in Kansas City, KS. He worked with Jay McShann's orchestra, and his first recordings in 1941 already reveal technical grace on the alto saxophone and melodic inventiveness. In New York City, he joined Dizzy Gillespie, Thelonious Monk, and other musicians in expanding the harmonic basis for jazz. The new music, called 'bebop', developed an adventuresome young audience at the end of World War 2. He began using heroin as a teenager, and died at 34. In 1988 the film, *Bird*, directed by Clint Eastwood, presented an entertaining but sanitized version of his life. >> Gillespie; Monk, Thelonious; Young, Lester

Parker, Dorothy, *née* **Rothschild** (1893–1967) Journalist and short-story writer, born in West End, NJ. Educated at a convent, in 1916 she sold some of her poetry to the editor of *Vogue*, and was given an editorial position on the magazine. She became drama critic of *Vanity Fair* (1917–20), and was at her most trenchant in book reviews and stories in the early issues (1927–33) of the *The New Yorker*, a magazine whose character she did much to form. Her work continued to appear in the magazine at irregular intervals until 1955. Her reviews were collected in *A Month of Saturdays* (1971). She also wrote for *Esquire*, and published poems and sketches. Her poems appeared in *Not So Deep as a Well* (1936) and *Enough Rope* (1926), which became a best seller. Her short stories were collected in *Here Lies* (1939).

Parker, Matthew (1504–75) The second Protestant Archbishop of Canterbury, born in Norwich, Norfolk, E England, UK. He was chaplain to Anne Boleyn (1535), and held several church posts, becoming dean of Lincoln. Deprived of his preferments by Queen Mary, he was made Archbishop of Canterbury by Elizabeth I (1559). He strove to bring about more general conformity, adopting a middle road between Catholic and Puritan extremes, and was in charge of the formulation of the Thirty-nine Articles. >> Boleyn; Elizabeth I; Mary I

Parker, Robert LeRoy >> **Cassidy, Butch**

Parkes, Alexander (1813–90) Chemist and inventor, born in Birmingham, West Midlands, C England, UK. He was noted for his inventions in connection with electroplating, in the course of which he even electroplated a spider's web. He invented xylonite (a form of celluloid), first patented in 1855.

Parkes, Sir Henry (1815–96) Australian statesman, born in Stoneleigh, Warwickshire, C England, UK. He emigrated to New South Wales in 1839, and became a well-known journalist in Sydney. A member of the colonial parliament in 1854, from 1872 he was five times premier of New South Wales. Knighted in 1877, he helped draft a consitution for a federated Australia (1891).

Parkinson, Cecil (Edward) (1932–) British statesman, born in Carnforth, Lancashire, NW England, UK. He studied at Cambridge, qualified as an accountant, and in 1970 became a Conservative MP. In 1979 he was appointed trade minister by Margaret Thatcher, then became paymaster-general and Conservative Party national chairman (1981–3), Chancellor of the Duchy of Lancaster (1982–3), and secretary of state for trade and industry (1983). In 1983, he was forced to resign from the Cabinet and as Party chairman following the news of the pregnancy of his mistress, Sarah Keays, which resulted in the birth of his illegitimate daughter. He returned to the Cabinet in 1987 as secretary of state for energy, and was transport secretary from 1989, until surrendering office in the Cabinet reshuffle that followed John Major's election in 1990. After the Conservative government's 1997 general election defeat, Parkinson was elected Party chairman for a second time. >> Major; Thatcher

Parkinson, C(yril) Northcote (1909–93) Political scientist, born in Barnard Castle, Durham, NE England, UK. He studied at Cambridge, and at Kings College, London, then became professor of history at the University of Malaya (1950–8), and a visiting professor at Harvard and Illinois. He wrote many works on historical, political, and economic subjects, but achieved wider renown by his serio-comic tilt at bureaucratic malpractices in *Parkinson's Law: the Pursuit of Progress* (1957). 'Parkinson's law' – that work expands to fill the time available for its completion, and subordinates multiply at a fixed rate, regardless of the amount of work produced – has passed into the language.

Parkinson, James (1755–1824) British physician and amateur palaeontologist. In 1817 he gave the first description of paralysis agitans, or *Parkinson's disease*. He had already (1812) described appendicitis and perforation, and was the first to recognize the latter condition as a cause of death.

Parkinson, Michael (1935–) British journalist and broadcaster. He was educated in Barnsley, South Yorkshire, N England, UK, and became a journalist working for local and national papers. He has produced and presented several television programmes, and is best known as the host of his own chat show *Parkinson* (BBC, 1971–82). His many sporting publications include *Sporting Profiles* (1995), and in the same year he was voted Sports Feature Writer of the Year in the British Sports Journalism Awards.

Parkinson, Norman, originally **Ronald William Parkinson Smith** (1913–90) Photographer, born in London, England, UK. He was educated at Westminster School, London, and became apprenticed as a photographer. He opened his own studio in 1934, and became one of Britain's favourite portrait and fashion artists, with his work widely used in quality magazines. In the 1950s his advertising work took him to exotic locations all over the world, and he settled in Tobago in 1963, regularly returning to Britain and the USA for exhibitions and awards.

Parley, Peter >> **Goodrich, Samuel Griswold**

Parmenides [pah(r)**men**ideez] (c. 515–c. 445 BC) The most influential of the Presocratic philosophers, a native of the Greek settlement of Elea in S Italy, and founder of the Eleatic school. He is the first philosopher to insist on a distinction between the world of appearances and reality. >> Eucleides of Megara; Melissus

Parmigianino [pah(r)mijia**nee**noh], also called **Parmigiano**, originally **Girolamo Francesco Maria Mazzola** (1503–40) Painter of the Lombard school, born in Parma, Italy. He began to paint in Parma, moving to Rome in 1523, but was forced to flee to Bologna when the city was sacked in 1527. At Bologna he painted his famous Madonna altarpiece for the nuns of St Margaret before returning to Parma in 1531.

Parnell, Charles Stewart [pah(r)**nel**] (1846–91) Irish politician, born in Avondale, Co Wicklow, Ireland. He studied at Cambridge, and in 1875 became an MP, supporting Home Rule, and gained great popularity in Ireland by his audacity in the use of obstructive parliamentary tactics. In 1879 he was elected president of the Irish National Land League, and in 1886 allied with the Liberals in support of Gladstone's Home Rule Bill. He remained an influential figure until 1890, when following his affair with Katherine O'Shea, he was cited as co-respondent in a divorce case, and forced to retire as leader of the Irish nationalists. >> Gladstone, W E

Parr, Catherine (1512–48) Sixth wife of Henry VIII, the daughter of Sir Thomas Parr of Kendal. She first married Edward Borough, then Lord Latimer, and in 1543 became Queen of England by marrying Henry VIII. A learned, tolerant, and tactful woman, she persuaded Henry to restore the succession to his daughters, Mary I and Elizabeth, and showed her stepchildren much kindness. Very soon after Henry's death (1547) she married a former suitor, Lord Thomas Seymour of Sudeley, but died in childbirth the following year. >> Henry VIII; Seymour, Thomas

Parr, Thomas, known as **Old Parr** (? 1483–1635) Centenarian, born, according to tradition, in 1483. He was a Shropshire farm-servant, and when 120 years old married his second wife, and till his 130th year performed all his usual work. In his 152nd year his fame had reached London, and he was induced to journey there to see Charles I, where he was treated at court so royally that he died.

Parra, Violeta [**par**a] (1917–67) Internationally celebrated Chilean folklorist, songwriter, and singer, born in San Carlos, Chile. She had a varied career, including a period in Paris (1961–5), and her work inspired the New Chilean Song movement of the later 1960s.

Parrhasios or **Parrhasius** [pah(r)**has**ius] (c. 5 th-c) Painter, born in Ephesus, Ionia. He worked in Athens and, according to tradition, was the greatest painter of ancient Greece. His drawings on parchment and on wood were used for purposes of study by later painters. His works are mostly of mythological groups.

Parrish, (Frederick) Maxfield (1870–1966) Illustrator and painter, born in Philadelphia, PA. He studied at the Pennsylvania Academy of the Fine Arts (1891–3), later joining the well-known art colony in Cornish, NH (1898). He became famous for his technically skilled and highly decorative illustrations, book-covers, murals, and best-selling colour prints such as 'Daybreak' (1920). Retiring from illustration in the 1930s, he spent the rest of his life painting rural landscapes, reproduced on calendars and greeting cards.

Parry, Sir (Charles) Hubert (Hastings) (1848–1918) Composer, born in Bournemouth, Dorset, S England, UK. He studied at Oxford, was professor at the Royal College of Music (1883), and in 1895 became its director. He composed three oratorios, an opera, five symphonies, and many other works, but is best known for his unison chorus 'Jerusalem' (1916), words by William Blake, sung as an unofficial anthem at the end of each season of Promenade Concerts in London.

Parry, Joseph (1841–1903) Musician, born in Merthyr Tydfil, S Wales. He studied at the Royal Academy of Music, London, and became professor at University College, Cardiff. He composed oratorios, operas, and songs, and became one of the leading hymn-writers in the Welsh tradition, his best-known hymn tune being 'Aberystwyth'.

Parry, Sir William Edward (1790–1855) Arctic navigator, born in Bath, SW England, UK. He served in the navy, and was sent in 1810 to the Arctic regions to protect the whale fisheries. He took command in five expeditions to the Arctic regions (1818–27) which reached further N than anyone had done before. In 1829 he was knighted, and in 1837 was made controller of a department of the navy. He was subsequently superintendent of Haslar (1846), rear-admiral (1852), and Governor of Greenwich Hospital (1853).

Parsons, Sir Charles (Algernon) (1854–1931) Engineer, born in London, England, UK. He studied at Dublin and Cambridge, became an engineering apprentice, and in 1884 developed the high-speed steam turbine. He also built the first turbine-driven steamship, the *Turbinia*, in 1897. >> Curtis, Charles; Laval, Carl Gustav Patrik de

Parsons, Robert (1546–1610) Jesuit, born in Nether Stowey, Somerset, SW England, UK. He became a fellow and tutor of Balliol College, Oxford, but, because of his Catholic leanings, his enemies secured his forced retirement in 1574. He then converted to Catholicism, and in Rome entered the Society of Jesus (1575), becoming a priest in 1578. With Edmund Campion he masterminded a secret Jesuit mission in England (1580), baffled all the attempts of government to catch him, and escaped to the European mainland a year later. He then directed the Jesuit ministry from Europe until 1588, when he was sent to Spain to establish seminaries for English priests. >> Campion, Edmund

Parsons, Talcott [**tawl**cot] (1902–79) Sociologist, born in Colorado Springs, CO. He studied at Amherst College, the London School of Economics, and Heidelberg University, and became one of the most prominent US sociologists, based throughout his career at Harvard. He developed a functionalist analysis of social systems through his principal publications, *The Structure of Social Action* (1939) and *The Social System* (1951).

Partridge, Eric (Honeywood) (1894–1979) Lexicographer, born in Waimata Alley, New Zealand. He studied at Queensland and Oxford universities, was elected Queensland travelling fellow at Oxford after World War 1, and briefly lectured at Manchester and London universities (1925–7). For most of his life he worked as a freelance writer, carrying out a vast amount of painstaking personal research into the history and meaning of words. He is best known for his specialized studies of slang and other aspects of colloquial language. His works in this field include the pioneering *Dictionary of Slang and Unconventional English* (1937), *Usage and Abusage* (1947), and *A Dictionary of the Underworld, British and American* (1950), as well as many individual essays on the history and usage of English words.

Pascal, Blaise [pas**kal**] (1623–62) Mathematician, physicist, theologian, and man-of-letters, born in Clermont-Ferrand, France. He invented a calculating machine (1647), and later the barometer, the hydraulic press, and the syringe. Until 1654 he spent his time between mathematics and the social round in Paris, but a mystical experience that year led him to join his sister, who was a member of the Jansenist convent at Port-Royal, where he defended Jansenism against the Jesuits in *Lettres provinciales* (1656–7). Fragments jotted down for a case book of Christian truth were discovered after his death and published as the *Pensées* (1669, Thoughts). >> Arnauld, Antoine; Desargues; Fermat

Pashukanis, Evgeny Bronislavitch (1894–c. 1937) Legal philosopher, born in Russia. More influential outside Russia than any other Marxist legal philosopher, he was the author of *General Theory of Law and Marxism* (1924), which led to his appointment as People's Commissar for Justice in 1936. He argued that law embodied a concept of the individual which corresponded to the individual involved as buyer or seller in market exchange. This approach made him unpopular with Stalin, and he disappeared in 1937. >> Stalin

Pašić, Nikola [pa**sheetch**] (c.1846–1926) Serbian statesman, born in Zaječar, Yugoslavia. Condemned to death in 1883 for his part in the plot against King Milan, he survived on the accession of King Peter to be prime minister of Serbia (five times, from 1891) and later of Yugoslavia (1921–4, 1924–6), which he helped to found.

Pasionaria, La >> Ibárruri, Dolores

Pasmore, (Edwin John) Victor (1908–) Artist, born in Chelsham, Surrey, SE England, UK. Largely self-taught, he was one of the founders of the London 'Euston Road School' (1937). He became an art teacher, and after World War 2 began to paint in a highly abstract style, in which colour is often primarily used to suggest relief. His works include *Rectangular Motif* (1949) and *Inland Sea* (1950, Tate, London).

Pasolini, Pier Paolo [pasoh**lee**nee] (1922–75) Film director and writer, born in Bologna, Italy. He became a Marxist following World War 2, moved to Rome, and began to write sordid novels of slum life in the city. In the 1950s he also worked as a scriptwriter and actor. He made his debut as a director in 1961, and became known for controversial, bawdy literary adaptations such as *Il Vangelo secondo Matteo* (1964, The Gospel According to St Matthew), *Il Decamerone* (1971, The Decameron), and *The Canterbury Tales* (1973). He was murdered, probably as the result of a homosexual encounter.

Passfield, Baron >> Webb, Sidney James

Passmore, George >> Gilbert and George

Passmore, John (1914–) Philosopher, born in Manly, New South Wales, Australia. He studied at Sydney University, and held academic posts there, before becoming professor of philosophy at Otago University, New Zealand. In 1955 he returned as reader in philosophy at the Australian National University's Institute of Advanced Studies, Canberra, and held the chair (1959–79). Regarded as a principal exponent of the 'Andersonian' school of philosophy, he was president of the Australian Academy of the Humanities (1975–7), and his publications include the classic *A Hundred Years of Philosophy* (1957).

Passy, Paul (Edouard) (1859–1940) Philologist and phonetician, born in Versailles, France. An advocate of phonetic spelling, he was one of the founders of the Phonetic Teachers' Association (later the International Phonetic Association) in 1886, and assistant professor of phonetics at the Sorbonne.

Pasternak, Boris (Leonidovich) [**pas**ternak] (1890–1960) Lyric poet, novelist, and translator, born in Moscow. He studied law and musical composition, then switched to philosophy. He wrote autobiographical and political poetry, and some outstanding short stories, some of which were collected in *The Childhood of Lyuvers* (1924). Unable to publish his own poetry during the years under Stalin, he became the official translator into Russian of Shakespeare, Verlaine, and Goethe. He caused a political earthquake with his first novel, *Dr Zhivago*, which was banned in the Soviet Union, but became an international success after its publication in Italy in 1957. A fragmentary, poet's novel, it describes with intense feeling the Russian revolution as it impinged upon one individual. Expelled from the Soviet Writers' Union, he had to take the unprecedented step of refusing the 1958 Nobel Prize for Literature.

Pasteur, Louis [pas**ter**] (1822–95) Chemist and microbiologist, born in Dôle, France. He studied at Besançon and Paris universities, and held academic posts at Strasbourg, Lille, and Paris, where in 1867 he became professor of chemistry at the Sorbonne. He established that putrefaction and fermentation were caused by micro-organisms, thus providing an impetus to microbiology. In a famous experiment in 1881, he showed that sheep and cows 'vaccinated' with the attenuated bacilli of anthrax received protection against the disease. In 1888 the Institut Pasteur was founded at Paris for the treatment of rabies, and he worked there until his death. >> Fracastoro; Roux, Emile

Patanjali [pa**tan**jalee] (2nd-c BC) A pseudonym attributed to the author (or one of the authors) of the *Yoga* system of Hindu philosophy. The four books of the *Yoga Sutra*, extant versions dating from the 3rd-c AD but drawing on earlier traditions, expound the moral and physical disciplines necessary for attaining absolute freedom of the self.

Pataudi, Iftikhar Ali, Nawab of [pa**tow**dee] (1910–52) Cricketer, born in Bhopal, India. He studied at Oxford, played cricket with Worcester, and was first capped by England on the controversial 'bodyline' tour of Australia under D R Jardine (1932–3), where he made a century on his first Test appearance. After World War 2 he captained India on their visit to England in 1946. He made seven Test centuries in all, and retired due to ill health. >> Jardine; Pataudi, Mansur Ali

Pataudi, Mansur Ali, Nawab of [pa**tow**dee] (1941–) Cricketer, born in Bhopal, India, the son of Iftikhar Ali Pataudi. Despite the loss of an eye in a car crash, he captained the Indian Test team. He made 2793 runs in his Test career, scoring six centuries, and his captaincy gave his team the self-confidence which took India to a leading place among the world's cricketing nations. >> Pataudi, Iftikhar Ali

Patenier, Joachim (de) [**pat**enyay], also spelled **Patinir** or **Patinier** (c. 1485–1524) Painter, probably born in Bouvignes, Belgium. Little is known of his early life, although it has been suggested that he studied under Hieronymus Bosch. In 1515 he is recorded as a member of the Antwerp painters' guild. He was arguably the first Western artist to paint scenes in which the natural world, while not the whole subject of the painting, clearly dominates the religious narrative. >> Bosch, Hieronymus

Pater, Walter (Horatio) [**pay**ter] (1839–94) Critic and essayist, born in London, England, UK. He studied at Canterbury and Oxford, where he worked as a scholar, and became known with his *Studies in the History of the Renaissance* (1873). His philosophical romance, *Marius the Epicurean* (1885), appealed to a wider audience, dealing with the spread of Christianity in the days of catacombs. He developed a highly polished prose style, and exercised considerable influence on the aesthetic movements of his time.

Paterson, A(ndrew) B(arton), nickname **Banjo Paterson** (1864–1941) Journalist and poet, born near Orange, New South Wales, Australia. A World War 2 correspondent, he was the author of several books of light verse, including *The Animals Noah Forgot* (1933), but is best known as the author of 'Waltzing Matilda', adapted from a traditional ditty, which became Australia's national song.

Paterson, William (1658–1719) Financier and founder of the Bank of England, born in Tinwald, Dumfries and Galloway, SW Scotland, UK. He spent some years trading in the West Indies, and then promoted a scheme for a colony in Darien, Central America. After making a fortune by commerce in London, he founded the Bank of England, and was one of its first directors (1694). He sailed with the expedition to Darien (1698), and after its failure returned in ill health to England (1699). In 1715 the government awarded him an indemnity for his Darien losses.

Pathé, Charles [pathay], Fr [patay] (1863–1957) Film pioneer, born in Paris. In 1896 he founded Société Pathé Frères with his brothers **Emile**, **Théophile**, and **Jacques**, first for cinema presentation, but expanding into manufacture. By 1912 it had become one of the largest film production organizations in the world, including a hand-coloured stencil process, *Pathécolor*. They introduced the newsreel in France in 1909, and shortly after in the USA and Britain, as well as the screen magazine *Pathé Pictorial*. Charles retired in 1929, but the company continued, and in England became Associated British Pathé Ltd (1949).

Patinier / Patinir, Joachim >> **Patenier, Joachim**

Patmore, Coventry (Kersey Dighton) (1823–96) Poet, born in Woodford, Essex, SE England, UK. He was assistant librarian at the British Museum, and associated with the Pre-Raphaelite Brotherhood. His major work, *The Angel in the House* (1854–62), describing married love, was followed by the death of his wife **Emily** in 1862, and his conversion to Catholicism under the influence of **Marianne**, who became his second wife. Thereafter he wrote mainly on mystical or religious themes, as in *the Unknown Eros* (1877). >> **Millais**

Paton, Alan (Stewart) [paytn] (1903–88) Writer and educator, born in Pietermaritzburg, South Africa. He studied at the University of Natal, began work as a teacher, and became principal of the Diepkloof Reformatory for young offenders (1935), where he was known for the success of his enlightened methods. From his deep concern with the racial problem in South Africa sprang several novels, notably *Cry, the Beloved Country* (1948), *Too Late the Phalarope* (1953), and *Ah, but Your Land is Beautiful* (1981). Also an acclaimed biographer, he was president of the Liberal Association of South Africa (1953–68).

Patou, Jean [patoo] (1880–1936) Fashion designer, born in Normandy, France. The son of a prosperous tanner, in 1907 he joined an uncle who dealt in furs. He opened Maison Parry in Paris (1912), and in 1913 sold his collection outright to a US buyer. After war service, he successfully opened again as couturier in 1919. He was noted for his designs for sports stars, actresses, and society ladies, and for his perfume, 'Joy'.

Patrick, St (c. 385–461) Apostle of Ireland, born (perhaps) in South Wales. At 16 he was carried to Ireland by pirates, and sold to an Antrim chief. Six years later he escaped and became a monk in France. Ordained a bishop at 45, he then became a missionary to Ireland (432), travelling widely among the chiefs, and in 454 fixed his see at Armagh. He died at Saul (Saulpatrick), and was probably buried at Armagh. The only authentic literary remains of the saint are his *Confession*, and a letter addressed to a British chieftain, Coroticus. Feast day 17 March.

Patten, Chris(topher Francis) (1944–) British politician, born in London, England, UK. He studied at Oxford, joined the Conservative Party's research department, worked in the Cabinet office, and became personal assistant to the party chairman (1972–4). When the Conservatives returned to power in 1979, he held a number of non-Cabinet posts, then became minister for overseas development (1986), secretary of state for the environment (1989), and party chairman (1991). Credited with master-minding the Tory victory in the 1992 election, he lost his own seat and was appointed Governor of Hong Kong (1992–7), where his proposals (1993) for greater democracy brought him into conflict with the Chinese government. He was made a Companion of Honour in 1998.

Patterson, Floyd (1935–) Boxer, born in Waco, TX. He grew up in New York City, ending up in a correctional institution, where he took up boxing. He won the gold medal in the middleweight class in the 1952 Olympics. Turning professional, he knocked out Archie Moore in 1956 to take the heavyweight title. He successfully defended it four times before losing it to Ingemar Johansson of Sweden in 1959. He then knocked out Johansson in a bout in 1960, thereby becoming the first heavyweight champion to regain his title. He defeated Johansson again in 1961, but lost the title for good to Sonny Liston in 1962. He continued to box for another decade. >> **Moore, Archie; Liston; RR1148**

Patterson, Harry >> **Higgins, Jack**

Patti, Adelina (1843–1919) Singer, born in Madrid. At seven she sang in New York, and there made her debut in 1859. She appeared in London in 1861. Her voice was an unusually high, rich, ringing soprano, and she is best remembered for her comedy roles, notably in Rossini's *The Barber of Seville*. She made her home in Craig-y-nos Castle, near Swansea, and in 1898 became a naturalized British citizen.

Pattison, Dorothy (Wyndlow) (1832–78) British philanthropist and nurse. In 1861 she became schoolmistress at Little Woolston near Bletchley, and in 1864 joined the Sisterhood of the Good Samaritan at Coatham near Redcar. As **Sister Dora** she became a nurse at Walsall, and in 1877 was appointed head of the municipal epidemic hospital at Walsall (mainly for smallpox).

Patton, George S(mith) (1885–1945) US general, born in San Gabriel, CA. Trained at West Point, he became one of the most daring and flamboyant US combat commanders of World War 2. He played a key role in the Allied invasion of French N Africa (1942), led the US 7th Army in its assault on Sicily (1943), commanded the 3rd Army in the invasion of France, and contained the German counter-offensive in the Ardennes (1944). He was fatally injured in a motor accident.

Paul (1754–1801) Tsar of Russia (1796–1801), born in St Petersburg, Russia, the second son of Peter III and Catherine II. His father's murder and his mother's neglect exerted a baneful influence on his character, and after succeeding his mother to the throne he soon revealed his violent temper and lack of capacity, and irritated his subjects by vexatious regulations. He suddenly declared for the Second Coalition Allies against France (1798), and sent an army of 56 000 into Italy. He sent a second army to co-operate with the Austrians, retired from the alliance, quarrelled with England, and entered into close alliance with Napoleon. After his convention with Sweden and Denmark, England sent a fleet into the Baltic under Nelson to dissolve the coalition (1801). His own officers conspired to compel him to abdicate, and in a scuffle he was strangled. >> **Catherine II; Napoleon I**

Paul I (of Greece) (1901–64) King of the Hellenes (1947–64), born in Athens. In 1922 he served with the Greek navy against the Turks; but in 1924, when a Republic was proclaimed, went into exile, returning to Greece as crown prince in 1935. In World War 2 he served with the Greek general staff in the Albanian campaign, and was in exile in London (1941–6). His reign covered the latter half of the Greek Civil War (1946–9) and its difficult aftermath. During the early 1960s his personal role, and that of his wife Queen Frederika, became sources of bitter political contoversy.

Paul, St, originally **Saul of Tarsus** see panel below

Paul III, originally **Alessandro Farnese** (1468–1549) Pope (1534–49), born in Canino, Italy. The first of the popes of the Counter-Reformation, in 1538 he issued the bull of excommunication and deposition against Henry VIII of England, and also the bull instituting the Order of the Jesuits in 1540. He summoned the Council of Trent in 1545.

Paul VI, originally **Giovanni Battista Montini** (1897–1978) Pope (1963–78), born in Concesio, Italy. He graduated at the Gregorian University of Rome, was ordained in 1920, and entered the Vatican diplomatic service, where he remained until 1944. He was then appointed Archbishop of Milan, in which important diocese he became known for his liberal views and support of social reform. Made a cardinal in 1958, he succeeded John XXIII, many of whose opinions he shared. He travelled more widely than any previous pope, and initiated important advances in the move towards Christian unity.

Paul, Alice (1885–1977) Feminist and social reformer, born in Moorestown, NJ. She studied at Pennsylvania University, then spent some years in England, becoming involved in the militant branch of the suffrage movement, and was several times arrested and imprisoned. Back in the USA (from 1912) she formed the Congressional Union for Woman Suffrage (later the National Woman's Party), her magnetic, forceful personality attracting wide support and equally wide mistrust. She devoted her whole career to fighting for equal rights for women, in particular for the 19th Amendment, and in 1928 founded the World Party for Equal Rights for Women. >> Park, Maud May

Paul, Charles Kegan (1828–1902) Writer and publisher, born in White Laekington, Somerset, SW England, UK. He studied at Oxford, became a chaplain at Eton (1852), and vicar at Sturminster Hall (1862). He wrote religious works and edited the *New Quarterly Magazine*, but in 1874 left the Church, taking over a publishing firm in 1877 which became C Kegan Paul & Co. Among his first publications were the monthly *Nineteenth Century*, and the works of G W Cox, Tennyson, Meredith, and Stevenson. He became a Roman Catholic and published *Biographical Sketches* (1883), works on religion, and translations from Goethe and Pascal.

Paul, Jean >> **Richter, Johann Paul Friedrich**

Paul, Les, originally **Lester Polfus** (1915–) Musician, and inventor of the solid-body electric guitar, born in Waukesha, WI. Well known as a jazz guitarist, he took his design to the Gibson Guitar Company in 1947. The 'Gibson Les Paul' became a firm favourite of rock band musicians, and originals are highly prized possessions. He pioneered over-dubbing, multi-tracking (as on *Lover*, 1948), and built the first eight-track tape recorder, used in making many hit records with his wife, **Mary Ford** (1928–77), in the 1950s, including *Vaya con Dios* (1953, No 1 for 11 weeks).

Paul, Lewis (?–1759) Inventor, son of a Huguenot refugee in England. He invented the first power roller-spinning machine in conjunction with John Wyatt (1700–66), which was a failure commercially, though the idea was later used by Arkwright. In 1738 he invented a carding machine which was used in Lancashire after his death, and in 1758 he patented another type of spinning machine. >> Arkwright

---

ST PAUL (?AD 10–65/7)

Paul was born of Jewish parents at Tarsus, Cilicia (now in Turkey), and was originally known as Saul of Tarsus. At the age of c.14, he trained as a rabbi under Gamaliel at Jerusalem, also acquiring the trade of tent-maker, but he was proud of his Roman citizenship and preferred the use of his Roman name Paulus to the Jewish Saul. A rigorous Pharisee (lay, rule-bound Jew), he was a strong persecutor of the Christian Church, and was on his way to Damascus, against the followers of the martyred Stephen, when he saw a blinding light and heard the voice of Jesus saying 'Saul, Saul, why do you persecute me?' This vision converted him into a fervent adherent of the new faith, and it became his life's work to preach the Christian Gospel to non-Jews, changing him from a bitter enemy of Christianity to its greatest missionary.

After several months of contemplation in Nabatea he began to preach the Christian message, and undertook his first mission journeys to Cyprus, Antioch of Pisidia, Iconium, Lystra, and Derbe. Around 48–51, he addressed an apostolic conference in Jerusalem on the disputed issues of how Gentiles and Jews were to be admitted to the Church, and a form of resolution was apparently reached which allowed him to continue his mission to the Gentiles. The precise chronology of his missionary activities is confused, but tradition has it that his second mission journey led him, with Silas, again to Asia Minor and through Galatia and Phrygia to Macedonia and Achaia – where, in Corinth, he was especially successful. A year and a half later he was again in Jerusalem and Antioch, and then undertook a third mission journey – to Galatia and Phrygia. Driven from Ephesus, he visited Achaia and Macedonia again, and by way of Miletus returned by sea to Jerusalem.

In Jerusalem the fanaticism of the Jews was roused against him, and led to disturbances. He was brought to Caesarea to be tried before Felix the procurator. After two years' imprisonment, he was brought before Felix's successor M Porcius Festus. Using his right as a Roman citizen, Paul 'appealed to Caesar', and in the spring of 60 arrived in Rome, where he spent two years a prisoner, but in his own hired house. He was eventually executed by Nero – probably at the end of the two years' captivity, though tradition has him escaping to visit Spain and other countries.

Paul's influence was decisive in extending Christianity beyond the Jewish perimeters of the Church at Jerusalem. The Pauline Epistles formed the basis of all subsequent theology. The ancient Church recognized 13 of the Epistles as Paul's, but did not unanimously regard Hebrews as his. The order of the Epistles is certainly not chronological, though it is difficult to fix the succession. All but the most destructive modern critics accept unhesitatingly as Paul's the Epistles to the Galatians, Romans, and Corinthians (1 and 2), but a considerable body of scholars dispute the Pauline authorship of the Pastoral Epistles, Thessalonians 2 and Ephesians, and some also dispute Colossians and Philippians. >> Jesus Christ; Nero; Peter, St; Stephen, St

Paul, Oom/Uncle >> **Kruger, Paul**

Paul, Vincent de >> **Vincent de Paul**

Paula, St Francesco di >> **Francis of Paola, St**

Paulding, James (Kirke) (1778–1860) Writer, born in Putnam Co, NY. He was a friend and associate of Washington Irving, with whom he founded the periodical *Salmagundi* (1807–8), and during the War of 1812 published the *Diverting History of John Bull and Brother Jonathan*. In 1814 a more serious work, *The United States and England*, gained him an appointment on the Board of Naval Commissioners. He also wrote *Westward Ho!* (1832), a *Life of Washington* (1835), and a defence of *Slavery in the United States* (1836). He later became secretary of the navy (1838–41). >> Irving, Washington

Pauli, Wolfgang [**pow**lee] (1900–58) Theoretical physicist, born in Vienna. He studied under Arnold Sommerfeld in Munich and Niels Bohr in Copenhagen, then taught at Hamburg and Zürich (1928–55, apart from a wartime period at the Institute for Advanced Study, Princeton, 1940–6). He formulated the 'exclusion principle' (1924) in atomic physics, and in 1931 postulated the existence of an electrically neutral particle (the neutrino), later confirmed by Fermi. He was awarded the 1945 Nobel Prize for Physics, and became a US citizen in 1946, later returning to Zürich. >> Bohr, Niels; Sommerfeld

Paulin, Tom [**paw**lin] (1949–) Poet, born in Leeds, West Yorkshire, N England, UK. He grew up in Belfast, and studied at the universities of Hull and Oxford. His central themes are the Irish predicament, and in particular Protestant identity, beginning with *A Sense of Justice* (1977). Later books include *The Riot Act* (1985) and *Seize the Fire* (1990), and he has also edited the Faber books of political verse (1986) and vernacular verse (1990). He is also known in the UK as a contributor to television discussion programmes on the arts.

Pauling, Linus (Carl) [**paw**ling] (1901–94) Chemist, born in Portland, OR. He studied at Oregon State University and the California Institute of Technology, and at several centres in Europe, and became professor of chemistry at the California Institute of Technology in 1927. He applied quantum theory to chemistry, and was awarded the Nobel Prize for Chemistry in 1954 for his contributions to the theory of valency. His work on molecular structure (mainly using X-ray diffraction) revolutionized both inorganic chemistry and biochemistry. He became a controversial figure from 1955 as the leading scientific critic of US nuclear deterrent policy, forcibly setting out his views in *No More War* (1958). Awarded the Nobel Prize for Peace in 1962, he was the first person to have received two full Nobel Prizes.

Paulinus [**paw**liynus] (?–644) Roman Catholic missionary, and first archbishop of York. Sent to England with St Augustine in 601, he was consecrated bishop in 625 and went N with Princess Æthelburh of Kent on her marriage to the pagan King Edwin of Northumbria. He baptized Edwin and all his court in York at Easter, 627, and was made Bishop of York, becoming archbishop in 633. Edwin's death at the hands of the pagan Penda of Mercia and Cadwallon of Wales in 633 drove him back to Kent, where he was appointed Bishop of Rochester. >> Edwin

Paulinus of Nola, St [**paw**liynus], in full **Pontius Meropius Anicius Paulinus** (353–431) Bishop and writer, born in Bordeaux, France. He accepted Christian baptism (c.389) and settled in Nola in Italy, where he became known for his charity and his rigid asceticism. He was consecrated Bishop of Nola in c.409, and is remembered for his *Carmina* and for his epistles to Augustine, Jerome, Sulpicius Severus, and Ausonius. Feast day 22 June.

Paulus, Friedrich [**pow**lus] (1890–1957) German soldier and tank specialist, born in Breitenau, Germany. He served in World War 1, and by 1940 was deputy chief of the general staff. As commander of the 6th Army he led the attack on Stalingrad (1942), but was trapped in the city by a Russian counter-attack. Totally cut off, he and his troops held out for three months before capitulating in February 1943. Released from captivity in 1953, he became a lecturer on military affairs under the East German Communist government. >> Zhukhov

Pausanias [paw**say**nias] (5th-c BC) Greek soldier, and regent of Sparta, the nephew of Leonidas. He commanded the Greek forces at Plataea (479 BC), where the Persians were routed. He then compelled the Thebans to give up the chiefs of the Persian party, and treated the Athenians and other Greeks haughtily. Capturing the Cyprian cities and Byzantium, he negotiated with Xerxes in the hope of becoming ruler under him of all Greece, and was twice recalled for treachery. He tried to stir up the helots, was betrayed, and fled to a temple of Athena on the Spartan acropolis, where he was walled up and taken out only when dying of hunger (c.470 BC). >> Leonidas; Xerxes; RR1055

Pausanias [paw**say**nias] (2nd-c) Geographer and historian, probably born in Lydia, Greece. He travelled through almost all of Greece, Macedonia, and Italy, and also through part of Asia and Africa. From his observations and research he composed an *Itinerary* of Greece, describing the different parts of that country and the monuments of art.

Pavarotti, Luciano [pava**ro**tee] (1935–) Tenor, born in Modena, Italy. He abandoned a career in school-teaching to become a singer, and won the international competition at the Teatro Reggio Emilia in 1961, making his operatic debut there in *La Bohème* the same year. He took part in the La Scala tour of Europe in 1963–4, toured Australia with Joan Sutherland in *Lucia di Lammermoor* in 1965, and made his US debut in 1968. His voice and performance are very much in the powerful style of the traditional Italian tenor. He is now internationally known as a concert performer, and has achieved a large popular following through his recordings and television appearances. He appeared in the film *Yes, Giorgio* in 1981, and published a volume of autobiography the same year. >> Sutherland, Joan

Pavese, Cesare [pa**vay**zay] (1908–50) Writer, born in Cuneo, Italy. He worked as a translator and publisher before turning to writing. His short stories, such as *La bella estate* (1949, The Beautiful Summer), were well-received, but he is best known for his novel *La luna e i falò* (1950, The Moon and the Bonfires). His unsentimental celebration of Italian rural life exerted a strong influence on later Italian fiction and film making.

Pavlov, Ivan Petrovich [**pav**lov] (1849–1936) Physiologist, born in Ryazan, Russia. He studied medicine at St Petersburg, conducted research in Wrocław, Poland (formerly Breslau, Germany) and Leipzig, and returned to St Petersburg, where he became professor (1890) and director of the Institute of Experimental Medicine (1913). He worked on the physiology of circulation and digestion, and from 1902 studied what later became known as *Pavlovian conditioning* (or classical conditioning) in animals, summarizing this work in *Lectures on Conditioned Reflexes* (1926). A major influence on the development of behaviourism in psychology, he was awarded the Nobel Prize for Physiology or Medicine in 1904.

Pavlova, Anna [**pav**lova] (1881–1931) Ballerina, born in St Petersburg. She trained at the Imperial Ballet School there, and became world famous, creating roles in work by Fokine, in particular *The Dying Swan* (1905). After a period with Diaghilev's Ballets Russes, she began touring Europe with her own company (1909). She choreographed over a dozen works, of which the best known are *Snowflakes* (1915) and *Autumn Leaves* (1918). She did much to create the stereotyped image of the ballerina which persists today. >> Diaghilev; Fokine

Paxman, Jeremy (Dickson) (1950–) British television presenter and journalist. He studied at Cambridge, then joined BBC 1 as presenter on *Tonight* (1977–9), *Panorama* (1979–84), the *Six O'Clock News* (1985–6), and *Breakfast Time* (1986–9). Programmes on BBC 2 include *Newsnight* (1989–), on which he developed a reputation as a tough but fair interviewer, *Did You See?* (1991–3), and *University Challenge* (1994–). He received the BAFTA Richard Dimbleby Award in 1996. A regular contributor to newspapers and magazines, his books include *Fish, Fishing and the Meaning of Life* (1994).

Paxton, Sir Joseph (1801–65) Gardener and architect, born near Woburn, Bedfordshire, SC England, UK. He was a working gardener to the Duke of Devonshire, at Chiswick and Chatsworth, where he remodelled the gardens, and built the conservatory and lily house. He designed a revolutionary building of prefabricated sections of cast-iron and glass for the Great Exhibition of 1851 (nicknamed 'the Crystal Palace'), which he re-erected in Sydenham in 1854. It was destroyed by fire in 1936.

Paxton, Steve (1939–) Experimental dancer and choreographer, born in Tucson, AZ. His training included three years with Merce Cunningham and a year with José Limón. Involved with the Judson Dance Theater, he performed works by Yvonne Rainer and Trisha Brown. He was a founding member of the experimental Grand Union, and in 1972 invented the dance form known as *contact improvization*, which has now been absorbed into the choreography of dancers the world over. Though one of the most important dancers of his generation, he is one of the most reclusive, performing rarely, and usually alone. >> Brown, Trisha; Cunningham, Merce; Limón; Rainer

Payton, Walter (1954–) Player of American football, born in Columbia, MS. In his career with the Chicago Bears (1975–88), he rushed for 16 726 yards, a National Football League record. In one game (1977) he rushed for a record 275 yards. His record of 125 touchdowns (1975–87) is second only to that of Jim Brown. >> Brown, Jim

Paz, Octavio (1914–) Poet, born in Mexico City. He studied at the National University of Mexico, and fought on the Republican side in the Spanish Civil War. A career diplomat, he served as the Mexican ambassador to India (1962–8), and taught at Texas, Harvard, and Cambridge universities. He is a writer of great energy and versatility, with 30 volumes from 1933; his *Collected Poems* (1957–87), in Spanish and English, were published in 1988. He has also written important prose works, notably *Tiempo Nublado* (1984, trans One Earth, Four or Five Worlds), and later works include *The Double Flame: Essays on Love and Eroticism* (1996). He received the Nobel Prize for Literature in 1990.

Paz Estenssoro, Victor [pahs estensawroh] (1907–) Bolivian politician, revolutionary, and president (1952–6, 1960–4, 1985–9), born in Tarija, Bolivia. He studied at the University Mayor de San Andres, and held a number of financial posts before entering politics in the 1930s, and in 1942 founding the National Revolutionary Movement. He went into exile in 1946, returning to win the presidency in 1952. He was re-elected in 1960 and again in 1985, returning from near-retirement at the age of 77. During a long career he was Bolivian ambassador in London (1956–9) and a professor at London University (1966). >> RR1036

Peabody, George (1795–1869) Merchant, financier, and philanthropist, born in Peabody, MA. He became a partner in a Baltimore dry-goods store in 1815, then established himself in London in 1837 as a merchant and banker, raising loans for US causes. In his lifetime he gave away a fortune for philanthropic purposes. He fitted out Kane's Arctic expedition to search for Franklin, and founded and endowed the Peabody Institutes in Baltimore and Peabody, and the Peabody Museums at Yale and Harvard. He also set up the Peabody Education Fund, and built working men's tenements in London. >> Kane, Elisha

Peacock, Andrew (Sharp) (1939–) Australian statesman, born in Melbourne, Victoria, Australia. He studied at Melbourne, and practised law before becoming a Liberal MP in 1966. He was foreign minister (1975–80) and minister for industrial relations (1980–1), but resigned from the government in 1981 over differences with prime minister Malcolm Fraser, and unsuccessfully challenged him for the Liberal leadership a year later. He eventually succeeded Fraser after the Liberals lost the 1983 general election. He was succeeded as Leader of the Opposition by John Howard, but resumed the position in 1989, then resigned after losing the 1990 election. He remained a prominent figure in Australian politics, and became Australian ambassador to the USA in 1997. >> Fraser, Malcolm; RR1033

Peacock, Thomas Love (1785–1866) Novelist and poet, born in Weymouth, Dorset, S England, UK. He entered the service of the East India Company in 1819 after producing three satirical romances, *Headlong Hall* (1816), *Melincourt* (1817), and *Nightmare Abbey* (1818), and later produced four other works along similar lines. In each case a company of humorists meet in a country house, and the satire arises from their conversation rather than from character or plot.

Peake, Mervyn (Laurence) (1911–68) Writer and artist, born in Kuling, China, where his father was a missionary. Educated in China and Kent, he became a painter, and taught at the Westminster School of Art. He is best known for his Gothic fantasy trilogy of novels, *Titus Groan* (1946), *Gormenghast* (1950), and *Titus Alone* (1959), and for the novel *Mr Pye* (1953). He also published books of verse, and illustrated several classics, including *The Ancient Mariner*, and children's books.

Peale, Charles Willson (1741–1827) Painter, born in Queen Annes Co, MD. He began his career as a saddler and silversmith, before becoming well known as a portraitist. A staunch Democrat, he was for a time a member of the Pennsylvania Assembly (1779–80). His Portrait Gallery of the Heroes of the Revolution in 1782 was the first art gallery in America, and in 1786 he founded the Peale Museum of Natural History and Technology. Prolific in all his ventures, he had 17 children, all of whom he named after great artists of the past, and many of whom became painters in their own right.

Peale, Norman Vincent (1898–1993) Christian Reformed pastor and writer, born in Bowersville, OH. He studied at Ohio Wesleyan and Boston universities, was ordained as a Methodist Episcopal minister in 1922, and held three pastorates before beginning his long ministry at Marble Collegiate Reformed Church, New York City (1932–84). He established a psychiatric clinic, the American Foundation of Religion and Psychiatry, next door to his church. He wrote the best seller, *The Power of Positive Thinking* (1952), and was much in demand as a lecturer on public affairs.

Peano, Giuseppe [payahnoh] (1858–1932) Mathematician, born in Cuneo, Italy. He taught at the University of Turin, and was known for his work on mathematical logic. The symbolism he invented was the basis of that used by Bertrand Russell and Alfred Whitehead in *Principia*

mathematica. He also promoted Interlingua, a universal language based on uninflected Latin. >> Russell, Bertrand; Whitehead, Alfred North

Pearce, Richard William (1877–1953) Inventor and pioneer aviator, born in Waitohi, New Zealand. A farmer with an interest in mechanics, he began building an aeroplane in c.1899. In 1903, at Waitohi, from level ground, without the use of ramps, slopes, or catapults, he flew for a distance of possibly 137 m/150 yd. Of the seven powered take-offs made anywhere in the world, before that of the Wright brothers, this was the most successful. The first British subject to leave the ground in a powered aircraft, he subsequently abandoned his experiments with flight, but continued to design machinery. >> Wright brothers

Pearce, Stuart (1962–) Footballer, born in London, SE England, UK. A left back, he played for Wealdstone and Coventry City before moving to Nottingham Forest in 1985, where he also acted for a time as player/manager. A member of the World Cup team in 1990, and of the European Cup teams in 1992 and 1996, by early 1997 he had won 73 caps for England.

Peard, Susan >> Hashman, Judy

Pearlstein, Philip [**perl**stiyn] (1924–) Painter, born in Pittsburgh, PA. Following army service (1943–6), he worked as a graphic designer, and in 1949 moved to New York City. In the 1950s he produced bold landscapes, but from 1960 made detailed studies of the male and female nude. His work emphasizes the impersonal aspect of the subject, often omitting the head of his model to concentrate on an unidealized representation of the naked body.

Pears, Sir Peter (Neville Luard) [peerz] (1910–86) Tenor, born in Farnham, Surrey, SE England, UK. He was organ scholar at Oxford, then studied singing at the Royal College of Music (1933–4). He toured the USA and Europe with Benjamin Britten, and in 1943 joined Sadler's Wells. After the success of *Peter Grimes* (1945), he joined Britten in the English Opera Group, and was co-founder with him of the Aldeburgh Festival (1948). Knighted in 1978, he was noted for his understanding of modern works. >> Britten

Pearse, Patrick (or **Pádraic**) **Henry** [peers] (1879–1916) Writer, educationist, and nationalist, born in Dublin. He wrote poems, short stories, and plays in English and Irish. A leader of the Gaelic revival, he joined the Gaelic League in 1895, became editor of its journal, and lectured in Irish at University College. In 1915 he joined the Irish Republican Brotherhood, and in the 1916 Easter Rising was commander-in-chief of the insurgents, and proclaimed president of the provisional government. After the revolt had been quelled he was arrested, court-martialled, and shot, along with his brother **William**. >> de Valera

Pearson, Sir Cyril (Arthur) (1866–1921) Newspaper and periodical proprietor, born in Wookey, Somerset, SW England, UK. He studied at Winchester, and became a journalist, producing *Pearson's Weekly* in 1890, as well as various other periodicals. In 1900 he became associated with newspapers, founding the *Daily Express*, and amalgamating the *St James Gazette* with the *Evening Standard*. He established St Dunstan's home for blinded soldiers, and was president of the National Institution for the Blind.

Pearson, Gerald (Leondus) (1905–) Physicist, born in Minneapolis, MN. He led the team at Bell Telecommunication Laboratories that developed the first practical solar battery in 1954, originally intended for operating communications equipment in remote terrestrial locations. The space programme greatly enhanced their importance and their efficiency.

Pearson, Hesketh (1887–1964) Biographer, born in Hawford, Hereford and Worcester, WC England, UK. He worked in a shipping office before beginning a successful stage career as an actor and director (1911). In 1931 he started to write popular and racy biographies, including *Gilbert and Sullivan* (1935), *Oscar Wilde* (1946), *Dizzy* (Disraeli, 1951), and *Charles II* (1960).

Pearson, Karl (1857–1936) Mathematician and scientist, born in London, England, UK. He turned from the law to mathematics, becoming professor of applied mathematics at University College, London, and professor of eugenics. He published *The Grammar of Science* (1892), and works on eugenics, mathematics, and biometrics. Motivated by the study of evolution and heredity, he was a founder of modern statistical theory, and his work established statistics as a subject in its own right. He also founded and edited the journal *Biometrika* (1901–36).

Pearson, Lester B(owles) (1897–1972) Canadian statesman and prime minister (1963–8), born in Newtonbrook, Ontario, Canada. He studied at Toronto and Oxford universities, and was leader of the Canadian delegation to the UN, becoming president of the General Assembly (1952–3). Minister of external affairs (1948–57), his efforts to resolve the Suez Crisis were rewarded with the Nobel Peace Prize in 1957. As Liberal prime minister, he introduced a comprehensive pension plan, socialized medicine, and the maple-leaf flag. >> Nasser; RR1039

Peary, Robert (Edwin) [**peer**ee] (1856–1920) Naval commander and explorer, born in Cresson Springs, PA. He made eight Arctic voyages to Greenland, all starting from the W coast of Greenland. He crossed the Greenland ice-sheet to the E coast in 1892 and 1895. In 1900 he reached and named Cape Morris Jessup, the N tip of Greenland. In 1906 he reached 87° 6′ N lat, and on 6 April 1909 attained the North Pole. His claim to be first to reach the North Pole was disputed by his fellow explorer Frederick Cook,who claimed to have reached the Pole in 1908, though doubt still exists about whether Cook actually reached 90°N. >> Cook, Frederick

Pease, Francis (Gladheim) (1881–1938) Astronomer and designer of optical instruments, born in Cambridge, MA. He was observer and optician at Yerkes Observatory, WI (1901–4), and instrument-maker at the Mount Wilson Observatory, Pasadena (1908–13), where he designed the 100-inch telescope, as well as the 50 ft interferometer telescope by means of which he gained direct measurements of star diameters. He was also involved in the design of the 200-inch Palomar telescope.

Pechstein, Max [**pekh**shtiyn] (1881–1955) Painter and print-maker, born in Zwickau, Germany. He studied in Dresden, where he joined the avant-garde *Die Brücke* group in 1906. From 1908 he helped found the rival *Neue Sezession* in Berlin, and developed a colourful style indebted to Matisse and to the Fauvists. He taught at the Berlin Academy from 1923 until he was dismissed by the Nazis in 1933. He was reinstated in 1945. >> Kirchner; Matisse; Nolde

Peck, (Eldred) Gregory (1916–) Film star, born in La Jolla, CA. After two years with the Neighbourhood Playhouse in New York City, his Broadway debut in 1942 led to a flood of film offers. One of the first major independent post-war film stars, his good looks and soft-spoken manner were used to portray many men of action and everyday citizens distinguished by their sense of decency. Nominated five times for an Oscar, he received the Award for his portrayal of a liberal Southern lawyer in *To Kill a Mockingbird* (1962). Among his best-known films are *Spellbound* (1945), *Twelve O'Clock High* (1949), *The Gunfighter* (1950), and *The Omen* (1976), and later appearances include *Old Gringo* (1989) and *Cape Fear* (1991). He also produced films, including *The Trial of the Catonsville Nine* (1972), an anti-Vietnam war drama reflecting his own off-screen involvement with liberal causes and support of the Democratic Party.

Peckinpah, Sam [**pe**kinpah] (1925–84) Film director, born in Fresno, CA. He started work on television Westerns, and directed his first feature, *The Deadly Companions*, in 1961. He portrayed a harshly realistic view of the lawless US West, accentuating the inherent violence, as in *Major Dundee* (1965) and *The Wild Bunch* (1969). His personal life was equally turbulent, his heavy drinking and quarrels with the studios restricting his creative output in his later years, and although he retired to a mountain retreat in 1978, he died in Los Angeles not long after.

Pecock, Reginald [**pee**kok] (c. 1395–c. 1460) Theologian and writer, born in Laugharne, Carmarthenshire, SW Wales, UK. A fellow of Oxford, he was ordained (1421), became Bishop of St Asaph (1444–50), and Bishop of Chichester (1450–58). Involved in several theological controversies of the day, he compiled many treatises in English. In 1457 he was denounced for having written in English, and for making reason paramount to the authority of the old doctors. Condemned as a heretic, he chose to recant, and was deprived of his office.

Pedersen, Holger [**pay**dersn] (1867–1953) Linguist, born in Gelballe, Denmark. He studied at Copenhagen University, where he became professor of linguistics. A prolific writer of books and articles on language science, he is chiefly remembered for his work in the field of comparative Celtic grammar, notably *Vergleichende Grammatik der keltischen Sprachen* (2 vols, 1909–13, Comparative Grammar of the Celtic Languages) and the *Concise Comparative Celtic Grammar* (1937).

Pederson, Charles J (1904–89) Chemist, born in Fusan, Korea. He moved to the USA in 1927, and became a research chemist at DuPont (1927–69). He developed the compounds called *Crown ethers* in the 1960s, initiating a field known as *host–guest chemistry*. He shared the Nobel Prize for Chemistry in 1987.

Pedro I (1798–1834) Emperor of Brazil (1822–31), born in Lisbon, the second son of John VI of Portugal (reigned 1816–26). He fled to Brazil with his parents on Napoleon's invasion, and became prince-regent of Brazil on his father's return to Portugal (1821). A liberal in outlook, he declared for Brazilian independence in 1822, and was crowned as Emperor Pedro I in 1826. The new empire did not start smoothly, and in 1831 he abdicated and withdrew to Portugal, where he had succeeded his father as Pedro IV (1826), but abdicated that throne in favour of his daughter, Maria. >> RR1036

Peel, Sir Robert (1788–1850) British statesman and prime minister (1834–5, 1841–6), born near Bury, Lancashire, NW England, UK. He studied at Oxford, and became a Tory MP in 1809. He was made secretary for Ireland (1812–18), where he displayed a strong anti-Catholic spirit, and was fiercely attacked by O'Connell, earning the nickname 'Orange Peel'. As home secretary (1822–7, 1828–30), he carried through the Catholic Emancipation Act and reorganized the London police force (who became known as *Peelers* or *Bobbies*). As prime minister, his second ministry concentrated upon economic reforms, but his decision to phase out agricultural protection by repealing the Corn Laws (1846) split his party and precipitated his resignation. He remained in parliament as leader of the *Peelites* (1846–50), until a riding accident caused his death. >> Aberdeen; Bentinck, George; Gladstone, W E; O'Connell; RR1095

Peele, George (c. 1558–96) Elizabethan playwright, born in London, England, UK. He studied at Oxford, then moved to London, where for 17 years he lived a Bohemian life as actor, poet, and playwright. His best-known works are *The*

Arraignment of Paris (1584), a dramatic pastoral containing ingenious flatteries of Elizabeth, the historical play *Edward I* (1593), and the popular play *The Old Wives' Tale* (1595).

Péguy, Charles Pierre [**pay**gee] (1873–1914) Poet and publisher, born in Orléans, France. A scholarship student, educated at the Ecole Normale, he intended to teach philosophy but became a fervent Socialist, reflected in his first version of *Jeanne d'Arc* (1897). Caught up in the Dreyfus affair, his bookshop became a centre for political agitation, and he also published the influential literary journal, *Cahiers de la quinzaine* (Fortnightly Notebooks). His important works of poetry include *Le Mystère des Saints Innocents* (1912). >> Dreyfus

Pei, I(eoh) M(eng) [pay] (1917–) Architect, born in Canton, China. He emigrated to the USA in 1935, where he studied at the Massachusetts Institute of Technology. He became a US citizen in 1954, and the following year founded his own firm. His principal projects include Mile High Center, Denver, the 60-storey John Hancock Tower, Boston, and the glass pyramids at the Louvre, Paris. A controversial, adventurous designer, he was awarded the 1983 Pritzker Prize for architecture.

Pei, Mario (Andrew) [pay] (1901–1978) Linguist, born in Rome. He moved to the USA as a child, and later studied languages at Columbia University. A gifted linguist, he joined the university in 1937, and became professor of Romance philology (1952–70). His books include *Languages for War and Peace* (1943) and a *Dictionary of Linguistics* (1954). Several of his introductory books, such as *The Story of English* (1952), were successful in providing the general public with a greater understanding of language study.

Peierls, Sir Rudolph (Ernest) [piylz] (1907–95) Physicist, born in Berlin. He studied at Berlin, Munich, and Leipzig, becoming Pauli's assistant at Zürich. He travelled widely before becoming a professor at Birmingham (1937–63), Oxford (1963–74), and the University of Washington, Seattle (1974–7). He applied quantum theory to solids and to magnetic effects, and then turned to nuclear physics. In 1940 with Frisch he reported to the British government that an atomic bomb based on uranium fission was feasible, and worked on this (the Manhattan project) throughout World War 2. >> Frisch, Otto; Pauli

Peirce, Charles Sanders [peers] (1839–1914) Philosopher, logician, and mathematician, born in Cambridge, MA. He studied at Harvard, and worked for the US Coast and Geodetic Survey from 1861. In 1879 he became a lecturer in logic at Johns Hopkins University, but left in 1894 to devote the rest of his life to private study. His enormous output of papers was collected and published posthumously in eight volumes (1931–58). A pioneer in the development of modern, formal logic and the logic of relations, he is best known as the founder of pragmatism, which he later named 'pragmaticism' to distinguish it from the work of William James. His theory of meaning helped establish the field of semiotics. >> James, William

Peisistratos >> Pisistratus

Pelagius [pe**lay**jius] (c. 360–c. 420) British or Irish monk. He settled in Rome c.400, where he disputed with St Augustine on the nature of grace and original sin. His view that salvation can be achieved by the exercise of human powers (*Pelagianism*) was condemned as heretical by Church Councils in 416 and 418, and he was excommunicated and banished from Rome. Nothing more is known of him after that date.

Pelé [**pe**lay], popular name of **Edson Arantes do Nascimento** (1940–) Footballer, widely held to be the best player in the game's history, born in Três Corações, Brazil. He made his international debut at 16, and at 17 appeared for Brazil in the 1958 World Cup Final, scoring two goals in the 4–2 win over Sweden. He won a second winner's medal in 1962, and a third in 1970. His first-class career was spent at Santos (1955–74), then with the New York Cosmos (1975–7). He appeared in 1363 first-class games (1955–77) and scored 1281 goals. In Brazil, he is a national hero. He was appointed a sports minister in the Brazilian cabinet in 1994, and received an honorary British knighthood in 1997. >> RR1155

Pelham, Henry [**pel**am] (1696–1754) British statesman and prime minister (1743–54), born in London, England, UK, the younger brother of Thomas Pelham. He took an active part in suppressing the Jacobite Rising of 1715, became secretary for war in 1724, and was a zealous supporter of Walpole. Events during his ministry (reconstructed in 1744 as the 'broad-bottom administration') were the Austrian Succession War, the Jacobite Rising of 1745, the Financial Bill of 1750, the reform of the calendar, and the Earl of Hardwicke's Marriage Act. >> Pelham, Thomas; Walpole, Robert; RR1095

Pelham (-Holles), Thomas, 1st Duke of Newcastle [**pel**am] (1693–1768) British statesman and prime minister (1754–6, 1757–62), the brother of Henry Pelham. He became Earl of Clare (1714) and Duke of Newcastle (1715). A Whig and a supporter of Walpole, he was appointed secretary of state in 1724, and held the office for 30 years. Extremely influential during the reigns of George I and II, in 1757 he was in coalition with Pitt during the Seven Years' War, but resigned after hostility from the new king, George III. >> Pelham, Henry; Pitt, William; RR1095

Pell, John (1610–85) Mathematician and clergyman, born in Southwick, West Sussex, S England, UK. He studied at Cambridge, and was appointed professor of mathematics at Amsterdam in 1643, and lecturer at the New College, Breda, in 1646. Employed by Oliver Cromwell, he went to Switzerland in an attempt to persuade Swiss Protestants to join a Continental Protestant league led by England. In 1661 he became rector at Fobbing in Essex, and in 1663 vicar of Laindon. He is remembered chiefly for the equation named after him, and for introducing the division sign ('÷') into England. >> Cromwell, Oliver

Pelletier, Pierre Joseph [peltyay] (1788–1842) Chemist, born in Paris. Professor and later director at the Ecole de Pharmacie in Paris, with Joseph Bienaimé Caventou he discovered strychnine, quinine, brucine, and other alkaloids. He was responsible for the naming of chlorophyll. >> Caventou

Pelopidas [pe**lo**pidas] (c. 410–364 BC) Theban general and statesman. Together with his friend Epaminondas, he established the short-lived Theban hegemony over Greece in the 360s BC. After playing a prominent part in the Theban victory over Sparta at Leuctra (371 BC), he subsequently operated mainly to the N of Greece in Thessaly and Macedonia. He was killed in battle against Alexander of Pherae. >> Epaminondas

Peltier, Jean Charles Athanase [peltyay] (1785–1845) Physicist, born in Ham, France. Originally a clockmaker, he retired at 30 to devote himself to scientific matters, and discovered the thermoelectric reduction of temperature now known as the *Peltier effect*, and later used by Heinrich Lenz as a method of freezing water. >> Lenz

Pelton, Lester (Allen) (1829–1918) Inventor and engineer, born in Vermillion, OH. He was a carpenter when he joined the gold rush to California in 1849. He became interested in the water-wheels used to drive mining machinery, and devised an improved type of undershot wheel powered by a jet of water striking pairs of hemispherical cups. He was granted a patent in 1880, later selling the rights to the Pelton Water Wheel Company of San Francisco. *Pelton*

wheels are in use all over the world for high-head hydro power generation, at efficiencies approaching 90%.

Pemberton, Sir Max (1863–1950) Writer, born in Birmingham, West Midlands, C England, UK. He studied at Cambridge, and was editor of *Chums* (1892–3) and of *Cassell's Magazine* (1894–1906). He wrote reviews and plays, and produced a succession of historical romances, including *Impregnable City* (1895) and *The Mad King Dies* (1928). He founded the London School of Journalism, and in 1920 became a director of Northcliffe newspapers, two years later publishing a biography of Lord Northcliffe. >> Northcliffe

Pembroke, Earl of >> **Marshal, William**

Pen, Jean-Marie Le >> **Le Pen, Jean-Marie**

Penck, Albrecht (1858–1945) Geographer and geologist, born in Leipzig, Germany. He studied at Leipzig, and was appointed to a professorship of physical geography at Vienna (1885–1906) and Berlin (1906–26). He examined the sequence of past Ice Ages, providing a basis for later work on the European Pleistocene. In 1894 he produced his classic *Morphology of the Earth's Surface*. He identified six topographic forms, and is believed to have introduced the term *geomorphology*.

Penda (c. 575–655) King of Mercia (c.632–55). He established mastery over the English Midlands, and was frequently at war with the kings of Northumbria. His forces defeated and killed Edwin at Hatfield in Yorkshire (633), and also Edwin's successor, Oswald, when he invaded Penda's territories (642); but Penda was himself slain in battle near Leeds while campaigning against Oswald's successor, Oswiu. >> Cadwallon; Edwin; Oswald

Penderecki, Krzysztof [pen**dres**kee] (1933–) Composer, born in Debica, Poland. He studied at Kraków Conservatory, and became a leading composer of the Polish avant garde, exercising considerable influence as a teacher. He first attracted international attention with his *Threnody for the Victims of Hiroshima* (1960). Later works include the opera *The Devils of Loudon* (1969), two further operas, a St Luke Passion, and several other orchestral and vocal compositions.

Pendleton, Don(ald Eugene) (1927–95) Author, born in Little Rock, AK. An aerospace engineer, who turned to full-time writing at the age of 40, he contributed to many popular genres, including science fiction and mystery, but is best known for his series of 38 'Executioner' novels, starring Mack Bolan. Launched in 1969 with *War Against the Mafia*, the series led to the emergence of a new genre of 'action/adventure' writing in the 1970s, especially popular in North America. He also published under the names of Dan Britain and Stephan Gregory.

Penfield, Wilder Graves (1891–1976) Neurosurgeon, born in Spokane, WA. He studied at Oxford and Johns Hopkins universities, and made further scientific studies in Oxford and Spain. He carried out experimental neurosurgical work mostly at the Montreal Neurological Institute, of which he was the first director (1934–60). An outstanding practical neurosurgeon, he is best known for his experimental work on the exposed brains of living human beings, which pioneered understanding of the causes of symptoms of brain disease such as epilepsy. He became a naturalized Canadian citizen in 1934. Following his retirement in 1960, he began a second career as a novelist and biographer.

Peniakoff, Vladimir [**pen**yakof], nickname **Popski** (1897–1951) British soldier, born in Belgium. Educated in England, he joined the British army, and from 1940 to 1942 served with the Long Range Desert Group and the Libyan Arab Force. In October 1942, with the sanction of the army, he formed his own force, 'Popski's Private Army', which carried out spectacular raids behind the German lines. He rose to the rank of lieutenant-colonel, and was decorated for bravery by Britain, France, and Belgium. His book, *Private Army*, appeared in 1950.

Penn, William (1644–1718) Quaker reformer and colonialist, the founder of Pennsylvania, born in London, England, UK. Sent down from Oxford for refusing to conform to the restored Anglican Church, he joined the Quakers in 1666, was imprisoned for his writings (1668), and while in the Tower wrote the most popular of his books, *No Cross, No Crown*. In 1681 he obtained a grant of land in North America, which he called Pennsylvania in honour of his father, Admiral Sir William Penn (1621–70). He sailed in 1682, and governed the colony for two years. After his return, he supported James II, and worked for religious tolerance. In 1699 he made a second visit to Pennsylvania, where his constitution had proved unworkable, and much had to be altered. After a permanent Charter was agreed (1701), he returned to England, where he remained until his death.

Penney, J(ames) C(ash) (1875–1971) Retailer and philanthropist, born in Hamilton, MO. He worked in a local dry goods store in Colorado, then moved to Wyoming, where he opened his own store in 1904 and by 1911 owned a chain of 22 stores. He went public in 1927, giving all managers shares of stock, and including all employees in profit-sharing. By 1971, J C Penney's had 1660 stores and had become the second largest non-food retailer in the USA. A devout Christian – he published *50 Years with the Golden Rule* (1950) – he gave generously to his favourite charities and maintained an active role in his company until his death.

Penney, William (George) Penney, Baron (1909–91) Physicist, born in Gibraltar. Professor of mathematics at the Imperial College of Science, London, he became well known for his research work on nuclear weapons, and was an observer when the atomic bomb was dropped on Nagasaki. He became director of the Atomic Weapons Research Establishment at Aldermaston (1953–9), and was chairman (1964–7) of the UK Atomic Energy Authority.

Penniman, Richard Wayne >> **Little Richard**

Pennington, Mary Engle (1872–1952) Chemist and refrigeration specialist, born in Nashville, TN. She studied at the University of Pennsylvania, started her own laboratory for bacteriological analyses in Philadelphia (1898), lectured at the Women's Medical College of Pennsylvania, and became head of the city health department's laboratory. Her pioneer work in methods of preserving dairy products, particularly by refrigeration, led to her becoming head of the US Department of Agriculture's new Food Research Laboratory (1908–19). Among her several practical innovations was the design of refrigerated railroad cars. After 1919 she worked in private industry and as a consultant food preservationist.

Pennington, Michael (Vivian Fyfe) (1943–) British actor. He studied at Cambridge, appeared at the Royal Court Theatre, London, and several other theatres, and became a leading Shakespearian actor, spending seven years with the Royal Shakespeare Company (1974–81). He joined the National Theatre in 1984, and in 1986 co-founded, with the stage director Michael Bogdanov, the English Shakespeare Company, becoming co-artistic director (1986–93). >> Bogdanov

Penrose, Sir Roland (Algernon) (1900–84) Painter, connoisseur, and art collector, born in London, England, UK. He studied at Cambridge, lived in Paris (1922–35), and began to collect Cubist and Surrealist art. In 1936 he organized the International Surrealist Exhibition in London, and in 1947 founded the Institute of Contemporary Arts. His friendship with Picasso led to his writing the standard biography (1958) and organizing a major exhibition of his work at the London Tate in 1960. >> Picasso

Penzias, Arno (Allan) [**pen**zias] (1933–) Astrophysicist, born in Munich, Germany. A refugee with his family from Nazi Germany, he studied at Colombia University, joining the Bell Telephone Laboratories in 1961. In 1964 he and his colleague Robert Wilson, exploring the Milky Way with a radio telescope, discovered cosmic microwave background radiation – a discovery which has provided some of the strongest evidence for the 'big bang' theory for the origin of the universe. They shared the Nobel Prize for Physics in 1978. >> Dicke; Wilson, Robert (Woodrow); RR1122

Pepin III, known as **Pepin the Short** (c. 714–68) King of the Franks (751–68), founder of the Frankish dynasty of the Carolingians, the father of Charlemagne. The son of Charles Martel, he was chosen king after the deposition of Childeric, the last of the Merovingians. He led an army into Italy (754), and defeated the Lombards. The rest of his life was spent in wars against the Saxons and Saracens. >> Charlemagne; Charles Martel; Willibrord; Zacharias; RR1049

Peploe, Samuel John (1871–1935) Artist, born in Edinburgh, EC Scotland, UK. An established painter, he went to Paris in 1911, and returned to Edinburgh to remodel his style in accordance with Fauve colouring and Cézannesque analysis of form. His later still-life paintings brought him fame as a colourist.

Pepper, Art(hur Edward) (1925–82) Saxophone player and composer, born in Gardena, CA. A freelance musician, he played with Buddy Rich, and recorded with Shorty Rogers, Mel Tormé, Miles Davis, and others. Albums from his own groups during the 1950s include *Popo* (1951) and *Meets the Rhythm Section* (1957), and after dealing with a drug problem he made a comeback in the 1970s with such albums as *Art Pepper Today* (1978). He co -wrote (with his wife) an autobiography, *Straight Life* (1979), and was the subject of the film *Notes From A Jazz Survivor* (1981).

Pepusch, Johann Christoph [pe**poosh**] (1667–1752) Composer and musical theorist, born in Berlin. He was appointed to the Prussian court at the age of 14, subsequently emigrating to Holland and settling in London in his early 30s. Best known as the arranger of the music for John Gay's *The Beggar's Opera* from popular and traditional sources, he was a prolific composer of music for the theatre and Church, as well as of instrumental works. >> Gay

Pepys, Samuel [peeps] (1633–1703) Diarist and naval administrator, born in London, England, UK. He studied at Cambridge, rose rapidly in the naval service, and became secretary to the Admiralty in 1672. He lost his office and was imprisoned because of his alleged complicity in the Popish Plot (1679), but was reappointed in 1684 and in that same year became president of the Royal Society. At the Revolution (1688) he was again removed from office. The celebrated diary, which ran from 1 January 1660 to 31 May 1669, the year his wife died and his eyesight failed him, is of interest both as the personal record (and confessions) of a man of abounding love of life, and for the vivid picture it gives of contemporary life, including naval administration and Court intrigue. The highlights are probably the Great Plague (1665–6), the Great Fire of London (1666), and the arrival of the Dutch fleet (1665–7). It was written in cipher, and not decoded until 1825. >> Oates, Titus

Perahia, Murray [puh**riy**a] (1947–) Pianist, born in New York City. He won the prestigious Leeds International Competition in 1972, and soon entered the highest ranks of international soloists. He is especially admired for his Mozart performances. In 1981–9 he was co-artistic director of the Aldeburgh Festival.

Perceval, John de Burgh (1923–) Ceramic artist and painter, born in Bruce Rock, Western Australia. A self-taught artist, in 1939 he joined the Australian Army Survey Corps, where he met artists such as Sydney Nolan. After being exhibited in Melbourne, some of Perceval's paintings were reproduced in the avant-garde periodical, *Angry Penguins*. He travelled to Europe, and returned in 1965 to take up the first creative arts fellowship at the Australian National University, Canberra. >> Nolan

Perceval, Spencer (1762–1812) British statesman and prime minister (1809–12), born in London, England, UK. He studied at Cambridge, was called to the bar (1786), and became an MP in 1796. He was solicitor general (1801), attorney general (1802), and Chancellor of the Exchequer (1807), before becoming premier. An efficient administrator, his Tory government was firmly established when he was shot while entering the lobby of the House of Commons by a bankrupt Liverpool broker, John Bellingham, who was later hanged for the murder. >> RR1095

Percy, Thomas (1729–1811) Antiquarian, poet, and bishop, born in Bridgnorth, Shropshire, WC England, UK. He studied at Oxford, became chaplain to the Duke of Northumberland and George III, Dean of Carlisle (1778), and Bishop of Dromore (1782). As a man of letters his fame rests on his *Reliques of Ancient English Poetry* (1765), largely compiled from a 17th-c manuscript of mediaeval ballads and other material found in a house in Shifnal, Shropshire, and much 'restored' by him. Other works include *Runic Poetry Translated from the Icelandic Language* (1763), a group of five poems actually translated from Latin versions, and a ballad, *The Hermit of Warkworth* (1771).

Percy, Walker (1916–90) Novelist, born in Birmingham, AL. He studied at North Carolina and Columbia universities, intending to make medicine his career, but had to abandon it for a literary career when he contracted tuberculosis. His first novel, *The Moviegoer* (1961), won a National Book Award. A philosophical writer, his novels are firmly grounded in comic social observation, and include *The Last Gentleman* (1966), *The Second Coming* (1980), and *The Thanatos Syndrome* (1987).

Perdiccas [perdikas] (c. 365–321 BC) Macedonian general, the second-in-command to Alexander the Great. He became virtually regent of the empire after Alexander's death, but was soon murdered by mutineers from his own army. >> Alexander the Great

Perdue, Frank(lin Parsons) (1920–) Food executive, born in Salisbury, MD. He left college to join his father's chicken farm in Salisbury in 1939, succeeding him as president (1952), and transforming Perdue Farms into one of the country's largest poultry processors. In 1971 he revolutionized chicken merchandising by labelling what had previously been an anonymous product and by starring in an extensive national advertising campaign. He retired in 1988.

Peregrinus (de Maricourt), Petrus [peregriynus], also called **Peter of Maricourt** or **Peter the Pilgrim** (13th-c) Scientist and soldier, born in Picardy, France. A crusader (his Latin name means 'pilgrim'), he was the first to mark the ends of a round natural magnet and call them poles. He also invented a compass with a graduated scale.

Pereira, Valdir >> Didi

Perelman, S(ydney) J(oseph) (1904–79) Humorous writer, born in New York City. He studied at Brown University, and contributed to magazines until the publication of *Dawn Ginsbergh's Revenge* (1929), which brought him fame. He went to Hollywood and wrote scripts for, among others, the Marx Brothers. From 1931 he began to write for the *New Yorker*, later publishing his material in book form. His writing is remarkable for its linguistic dexterity and ingenuity – at its best in *Crazy Like a Fox* (1944) and *Westward Ha! or, Around the World in 80 Clichés* (1948). *The Most of S J Perelman* was published in 1958.

Peres, Shimon [perez], originally **Shimon Perski** (1923–) Israeli statesman and prime minister (1984–6, 1995–6), born in Wolożyn, Poland. He was raised on a kibbutz, but studied at New York and Harvard universities. In 1948 he became head of naval services in the new state of Israel, and later director-general of the defence ministry (1953–9). In 1959 he was elected to the Knesset, and became minister of defence (1974–7), chairman of the Labour Party, and Leader of the Opposition (1977). He then entered into a unique power-sharing agreement with the leader of the Consolidation Party (Likud), Yitzhak Shamir, becoming prime minister from 1984 to 1986, when Shamir took over. After the inconclusive 1988 general election, Peres eventually rejoined Shamir in a new coalition, which collapsed in 1990. He then opposed Shamir's government until replaced as Labour Party leader by Itzhak Rabin (1992), and shared the Nobel Peace Prize with him in 1994. In 1995–6 Peres served a second term as prime minister. >> Rabin; Shamir; RR1064

Pérez de Ayala, Ramón [pereth, ayahla] (1881–1962) Novelist, poet, and critic, born in Oviedo, Spain. He first attracted attention with his poetry when *La Paz del sendero* (The Peace of the Path) was published in 1904. A sequel volume appeared in 1916 under the title *El Sendero innumerable*. As a novelist he combines realism with beauty, best shown in the philosophical *Belarmino y Apolonio* (1921). Other novels include *Tigre Juan* (1924), which with *El Curandero de ru honra* appeared in English as *Tiger Juan* (1933).

Pérez de Cuellar, Javier [perez duh kwayah(r)] (1920–) Peruvian diplomat, and secretary-general of the UN (1982–91), born in Lima. He studied at Lima University, and embarked on a career in the Peruvian diplomatic service, representing his country at the first UN assembly in 1946. As secretary-general, he played a prominent role in trying to secure a peaceful solution to the Falklands crisis, a ceasefire in the Iran-Iraq War, the release of the Iranian hostages in 1991, and the achievement of independence for Namibia.

Pérez Galdós, Benito [perez galdos] (1843–1920) Novelist and playwright, born in Las Palmas, Canary Is, Spain. He switched from law to journalism, and then to writing historical novels. Regarded as Spain's greatest novelist after Cervantes, his 46 short *Episodios nacionales* (National Episodes) give a vivid picture of 19th-c Spain from the viewpoint of the people. Some of his longer novels have been translated, including *Doña Perfecta*. His plays, many of them based on his novels, have also been successful. >> Cervantes

Pergolesi, Giovanni Battista [pergolayzee] (1710–36) Composer, born in Jesi, Italy. He attended the Conservatorio dei Poveri di Gesù Cristo at Naples, became a violinist, and in 1732 was appointed *maestro di cappella* to the Prince of Naples. His comic intermezzo *La serva padrona* (1732) was highly popular, and influenced the development of *opera buffa*. He wrote much church music, and in 1736 left Naples for a Capuchin monastery at Pozzuoli, where he composed his great *Stabat Mater*.

Peri, Jacopo [payree] (1561–1633) Composer, born in Rome. Attached to the Medici family in Florence, he became the leading composer in a group whose aim was to restore the true principles of Greek tragic declamation. Experimenting in an instrumentally accompanied declamatory style, he wrote *Dafne* (1597–89) and *Euridice* (1600), with libretti by the poet **Ottavio Rinuccini** (1562–1621), which have been historically accepted as the first genuine operas. >> Medici

Periander [periander] (c. 625–585 BC) Tyrant of Corinth, successor to his father, Cypselus. Under him, Corinth's power and position in the Greek world developed further, and he cultivated extensive links with foreign rulers. Later tradition remembered him as an example of a repressive tyrant, yet he was also included in the canon of the Seven Wise Men of Greece. The tyranny came to an end soon after his death. >> Cypselus

Pericles [perikleez] (c. 495–429 BC) General and statesman, of the aristocratic Alcmaeonid family, who presided over the 'Golden Age' of Athens, and was virtually its uncrowned king (443–429 BC). Politically a radical, he helped push through the constitutional reforms that brought about full Athenian democracy (462–461 BC). A staunch opponent of Sparta, it was his unremitting hostility to her and her allies that brought about the Peloponnesian War (431–404 BC). Renowned for his oratory, his 'Funeral Speech' (431/430 BC), as recorded by Thucydides, is an impassioned apologia for Athens' democratic principles and system of government. >> Sophocles; Thucydides

Perkin, Sir William Henry (1838–1907) Chemist, born in London, England, UK. He worked as an assistant to August Hofmann at the Royal College of Chemistry, London. In 1856 he made the discovery of a mauve substance with dyeing properties, which led to the foundation of the aniline dye industry. >> Hofmann, August Wilhelm von

Perkins, Anthony (1932–92) Actor, born in New York City. He studied at Columbia University, and made his film debut in 1953 while still a student. After several early films, such as *Friendly Persuasion* (1956), he achieved international fame as the maniacal Norman Bates in Hitchcock's *Psycho* (1960), with its three sequels (1983, 1986, 1990). Although he played many other parts on stage and screen, this role was the peak of his career. >> Hitchcock

Perkins, Charles (Nelson) (1936–) Bureaucrat and activist, born in Australia of Arunta and European descent. He studied at the University of Sydney, becoming the first Aborigine to graduate from a university. He was a leader of the Aboriginal movement in the 1960s, his 'freedom rides' bringing injustice to Aboriginal people to public attention. He was chairman of the Aboriginal Development Commission (1981–4) and permanent head of the department of Aboriginal Affairs in Canberra (1984–9). He has been a member of the Australia Council Aboriginal Arts Committee since 1990.

Perkins, Francis (1882–1965) Social reformer and politician, born in Boston, MA. She studied at Pennsylvania and Columbia universities, became secretary of the New York Consumers' League (1910–12), then achieved several legislative successes as secretary of the Committee on Safety of the City of New York. In 1918 she became the first woman member of the New York State Industrial Commission (chairman 1926, commissioner 1929). She joined the Democratic Party, and for 30 years played a significant role in introducing women's issues into Party policy. She was appointed US secretary of labor (1933–45), and made an enormous contribution to women's rights in her supervision of the 'New Deal' labour regulations, which included the Social Security Act (1935) and the Wages and Hours Act (1938).

Perkins, Jacob (1766–1849) Mechanical engineer and inventor, born in Newburyport, MA. Apprenticed to a goldsmith, he was a prolific inventor. He is best known for making counterfeiting more difficult by developing steel plates that could be used in place of copper in the engraving process, thus enabling much more complicated patterns to be used for bank-notes. With a partner, he established an engraving factory in England, which in 1840 printed the first penny postage stamps.

Perkins, Kieren (John) (1973–) Swimmer, born in Brisbane, Queensland, Australia. He won the silver medal in the 1500 m at the 1990 Commonwealth Games, and set four world records in the year leading up to the 1992 Barcelona Olympics, where he won the 1500m freestyle final, breaking the world record in the process. He won a gold medal for the same race at the Olympic Games in 1996.

Perkins, Maxwell (Evarts) (1884–1947) Editor and publisher, born in New York City. He joined Charles Scribner's as an editor in 1914, later holding various corporate offices there. He showed a genius for recognizing and fostering talent, publishing early works by F Scott Fitzgerald, Thomas Wolfe, Ernest Hemingway, and others.

Perl, Martin (Lewis) (1927–) Physicist, born in Brooklyn, NY. He studied at Columbia University (1955), taught at the University of Michigan (1955–63), then joined Stanford University (1963). His study of elementary particles led to his detection of the tau lepton – a short-lived, heavy-weight cousin of the electron, and one of the fundamental building blocks of matter. He shared the 1995 Nobel Prize for Physics with Frederick Reines. >> Reines

Perlman, Itzhak (1945–) Violinist, born in Tel Aviv, the son of Polish immigrants. Crippled by polio as a child, he took up the violin with enthusiasm, playing in public from the age of nine. He studied at the Juilliard School, New York City, and made his debut at Carnegie Hall in 1963, and in London in 1968. He is a noted chamber music player, and has recorded almost all the standard violin works.

Permeke, Constant [permaykuh] (1886–1951) Painter and sculptor, born in Antwerp, Belgium. He studied at Bruges and Ghent, and later settled in Laethem-Saint-Martin, where he became the leader of the modern Belgian Expressionist school. After 1936, he concentrated primarily on the sculpture of nudes and torsos.

Perón, (Maria) Eva (Duarte de) [peron], known as **Evita** (1919–52) The second wife of Argentinian President Juan Perón, born in Los Toldos, Argentina. A radio and screen actress before her marriage in 1945, she became a powerful political influence and the mainstay of the Perón government. She was idolized by the poor, and after her death in Buenos Aires, support for her husband waned. Her body was stolen, taken to Europe, and kept in secret until 1976. The successful musical *Evita* (1979) was based on her life. >> Perón, Juan

Perón, Isabelita [peron], popular name of **Maria Estela Perón** *née* **Martínez Cartas** (1931–) President of Argentina (1974–6), born in La Rioja Province, Argentina. She was a dancer, who became the third wife of Juan Domingo Perón in 1961, living with him in Spain until his return to Argentina as president in 1973, when she was made vice-president. She took over the presidency at his death in 1974, but her inadequacy in office led to a military take-over in 1976. She was imprisoned for five years on a charge of abuse of public property, and on her release in 1981 settled in Madrid. >> Perón, Juan

Perón, Juan (Domingo) [peron] (1895–1974) Argentinian soldier and president (1946–55, 1973–4), born in Lobos, Buenos Aires. He took a leading part in the army coup of 1943, gained widespread support through his social reforms, and became president in 1946. He was deposed and exiled in 1955, having antagonized the Church, the armed forces, and many of his former Labour supporters. He returned in triumph in 1973, and won an overwhelming electoral victory, but died the following year. >> Peron, Eva; Peron, Isabelita; RR1032

Perosi, Lorenzo [perohsee] (1872–1956) Priest and composer, born in Tortona, Italy. Ordained a priest, he was the author of *The Resurrection of Lazarus*, *The Passion of Christ*, and other oratorios. He was organist at Monte Cassino and St Mark's, Venice, then chapelmaster at the Sistine Chapel, Rome.

Perot, (Henry) Ross [peroh] (1930–) Businessman and politician, born in Texarkana, TX. After working as a salesman with IBM, he founded the Electronic Data Systems Corporation Inc, Dallas, in 1962, which grew to have over 50 000 employees. He was its chairman and chief executive (1982–6) until a buy-out by General Motors. He became internationally known when he stood as an independent candidate in the 1992 US presidential election. He withdrew in July, but then re-entered the campaign three weeks before the election, on the grounds that neither of the main candidates had addressed the need to reduce the federal deficit. Though attracting a great deal of popular support, he received no electoral votes. He stood again in the 1996 elections, with similar results.

Pérouse, comte de la >> **La Pérouse, comte de**

Perrault, Charles [peroh] (1628–1703) Writer, born in Paris. He became a lawyer, and in 1663 was a secretary to Colbert. He wrote several poems, and engaged in debate over the relative merits of the ancients and the moderns, but is best known for his eight fairy tales, the *Contes de ma mère l'oye* (1697, Tales of Mother Goose), which included 'The Sleeping Beauty' and 'Red Riding Hood'. >> Colbert

Perrin, Jean (Baptiste) [perī] (1870–1942) Physicist, born in Lille, France. He studied at the Ecole Normale Supérieure, and from 1910 was professor of physical chemistry at the University of Paris. For his research in molecular physics and radioactivity, and for his discovery of the equilibrium of sedimentation, he was awarded the 1926 Nobel Prize for Physics.

Perronet, Jean Rodolphe [peronay] (1708–94) Civil engineer, born in Suresnes, France. After training as an architect and working as a civil engineer in French government service, he was appointed in 1747 the first director of the newly–created Ecole des Ponts et Chaussées. He built a number of outstanding masonry arch bridges, including the Pont de Neuilly and the Pont de la Concorde in Paris, setting new standards of aesthetic and engineering design.

Perry, (Mary) Antoinette (1888–1946) Actress and director, born in Denver, CO. She had a long career on the stage from 1905 and as a director from 1928. In 1941 she founded the American Theatre Wing. The annual 'Tony' Awards of the New York theatre are named after her.

Perry, Fred(erick John) (1909–95) Lawn tennis and table tennis player, born in Stockport, Greater Manchester, NW England, UK. He won the world table tennis title (1929) and the men's lawn tennis singles title at Wimbledon (1934–6), the last British male champion. He also won the singles title at the French, Australian, and US championships, and was the first man to win all four major titles. He later became a US citizen, and served with the US armed forces. A notable writer, after retiring he was also proprietor of a sports goods firm. >> RR1173

Perry, Matthew Galbraith (1794–1858) US naval officer, born in South Kingston, RI, the younger brother of Oliver Hazard Perry. He entered the navy in 1809 and served in the War of 1812. He became a captain in 1837, and commanded the first US steam warship, the USS *Fulton*. He also commanded the Africa Squadron (1843–6) and the Home Squadron during the last phase of the Mexican War (1847–8). In 1852 he led the naval expedition to Japan which forced it to accept diplomatic relations and trade with the USA. >> Perry, Oliver Hazard

Perry, Matthew (1969–) Actor, born in Williamstown, MA. He moved with his mother to Ottawa as a child, and became an accomplished teenage tennis-player, but after

moving to Los Angeles, he opted for acting. He had a variety of parts in television sitcoms, eventually achieving success with his role as Chandler Bing in the acclaimed television series *Friends* (1994–). Roles in feature films include *Fools Rush In* (1997) and *Edwards and Hunt: The First American Road Trip* (1997).

Perry, Oliver Hazard (1785–1819) US naval officer, born in South Kingston, RI. During the War of 1812, he led the US Fleet against the British fleet. He defeated a British squadron on L Erie in 1813, during which he sent a famous message to General William Henry Harrison, 'We have met the enemy and they are ours'. In 1819 he commanded a squadron sent to Venezuela, where he died of yellow fever. >> Harrison, William Henry; Perry, Matthew Galbraith

Perse, Saint-John >> **Saint-John Perse**

Pershing, John J(oseph), nickname **Black Jack** (1860–1948) US general, born in Laclede, MO. At first a schoolteacher, he went to West Point, becoming military instructor there and at Nebraska University. He served on frontier duty against the Sioux and Apache Indians (1886–98), in the Cuban War in 1898, during the Moro insurgencies in the Philippines (1903), in the Japanese army during the Russo–Japanese War (1904–5), and in Mexico in 1916. In 1917 he was appointed commander-in-chief of the US Expeditionary Force in Europe, and later became chief-of-staff of the US army (1921–4).

Persius, in full **Aulus Persius Flaccus** (34–62) Satirist, born of a distinguished equestrian family in Volaterrae, Etruria. He was educated in Rome, where he came under Stoic influence. He wrote fastidiously and sparingly, leaving at his death only six admirable satires, the whole not exceeding 650 hexameter lines. These were published by his friend Caesius Bassus after his death. Dryden and others have translated them into verse.

Perthes, Jacques Boucher de >> **Boucher de Perthes, Jacques**

Perugino [perujeenoh] (Ital 'the Perugian'), originally **Pietro di Cristoforo Vannucci** (c. 1450–1523) Painter, born in Città della Pieve, Umbria. He established himself in Perugia, and had Raphael as a pupil in Florence (1486–99). He painted several frescoes in the Sistine Chapel, Rome, notably 'Christ Giving the Keys to Peter' (1481–2). >> Pinturicchio; Raphael

Perutz, Max (Ferdinand) [peruhts] (1914–) Scientist, born in Vienna. He studied at Vienna and Cambridge, and worked at the Cavendish Laboratory on the molecular stucture of haemoglobin, using the technique of X-ray diffraction. He became director of the Medical Research Council's unit for molecular biology, shared the Nobel Prize for Chemistry in 1962, and was awarded the Order of Merit in 1988. >> Kendrew

Peruzzi, Baldassare (Tommaso) [perutsee] (1481–1536) Architect, probably born in Siena. In 1503 he went to Rome, where he designed the Villa Farnesina and the Ossoli Palace, and painted frescoes in the Church of S Maria della Pace (1516). After a short period as city architect in Siena, he returned to Rome in 1535 and designed the Palazzo Massimo.

Pestalozzi, Johann Heinrich [pestalotsee] (1746–1827) Educationist, and pioneer of mass education for poor children, born in Zürich, Switzerland. He worked as a farmer (1769), then tried to educate waifs and strays in his home (1774). After several failed attempts, he managed to open a school at Berthoud (Burgdorf), where he wrote *Wie Gertrud ihre Kinder lehrt* (1801, How Gertrude Educates her Children), the recognized exposition of the Pestalozzian method, in which the process of education is seen as a gradual unfolding, prompted by observation, of the children's innate facilities. *Pestalozzi International Children's Villages* have been established at Trogen, Switzerland (1946) and Sedlescombe, Surrey, UK (1958).

Pétain, (Henri) Philippe (Omer) [paytĩ] (1856–1951) French soldier and statesman, born in Cauchy-à-la-Tour, France. During World War 1 he became a national hero for his defence of Verdun (1916), and was made commander-in-chief (1917) and marshal of France (1918). When France collapsed in 1940, he negotiated the armistice with Germany and Italy, and became chief-of-state, establishing his government at Vichy. His aim to unite France under the slogan 'Work, Family and Country', and keep it out of the war, involved active collaboration with Germany. After the liberation, he was tried in the French courts, his death sentence for treason being commuted to life imprisonment on the Ile d'Yeu, where he died. His role remains controversial, and some still regard him as a patriot.

Peter I, known as **the Great** (1672–1725) Tsar of Russia (1682–1721) and emperor (1721–5), born in Moscow, the son of Tsar Alexey and his second wife Natalia Naryshkin. He was joint tsar with his mentally retarded half-brother, Ivan, under the regency of their sister, Sophia (1682–9). On Ivan's death (1696) he became sole tsar, and embarked on a series of sweeping military, fiscal, administrative, educational, cultural, and ecclesiastical reforms, many of them based on W European models. All classes of society suffered from the impact of the reforms and the brutality of their implementation; his own son, Alexis, died under torture (1718), suspected of leading a conspiracy against his father. Peter fought major wars with the Ottoman empire, Persia, and in particular Sweden, which Russia defeated in the Great Northern War. This victory established Russia as a major European power, and gained a maritime exit on the Baltic, where Peter founded his new capital, St Petersburg. He failed to name a successor, and was succeeded by his wife, Catherine I. >> Alexey I Mihailovitch; Alexis; Catherine I; Elizabeth; Sophia Alexeyevna; RR1085

Peter I (of Serbia) (1844–1921) King of Serbia, born in Belgrade, the son of Prince Alexander Karadjordjević (reigned 1842–59). He fought in the French army in the Franco-Prussian war (1870–1), and was elected King of Serbia in 1903. In World War 1 he accompanied his army into exile in Greece in 1916. He returned to Belgrade in 1918, and was proclaimed titular king of the Serbs, Croats, and Slovenes until his death, although his second son, Alexander (later Alexander I), was regent. >> Alexander I (of Yugoslavia); RR1100

Peter II (1923–70) King of Yugoslavia (1934–45), born in Belgrade, the son of Alexander I. He was at school in England when his father was assassinated in 1934. His uncle, **Prince Paul Karadjordjević** (1873–1976), a nephew of Peter I, was regent until 1941 when he was ousted by pro-Allied army officers, who declared King Peter of age and he assumed sovereignty. The subsequent German attack on Yugoslavia forced him to go into exile within three weeks. He set up a government-in-exile in London, but lost his throne when Yugoslavia became a communist dictatorship in 1945. King Peter never abdicated, and there was no referendum on the monarchy. From then on he lived in France, Italy, and briefly in the USA. >> Alexander I (of Yugoslavia); RR1100

Peter, St, originally **Simon** or **Simeon bar Jona** ('son of Jona') (1st-c) One of the 12 apostles of Jesus Christ, at first a fisherman living in Capernaum. He was renamed by Jesus as **Cephas** (Peter, meaning 'rock') in view of his leadership amongst the disciples. In the Gospels he is often the spokesman for the other disciples, and leader of the inner group which accompanied Jesus at the Transfiguration and Gethsemane. Immediately after Jesus's resurrection and ascension, Peter appears also as the leader of the

Christian community in Jerusalem. Later he may have engaged in missionary work outside Palestine, certainly visiting Antioch, but little is directly known of these activities. Tradition says that he was executed with his head downward in Rome. His presence in Rome is uncertain, but he is regarded by the Roman Catholic Church as the first Bishop of Rome. Two New Testament letters bear his name, but the authenticity of both is often disputed. Other apocryphal writings also exist in his name, such as the Acts of Peter and the Apocalypse of Peter. Feast day 29 June. >> Jesus Christ

Peter Damian, St >> **Damiani, Pietro**

Peter Lombard >> **Lombard, Peter**

Peter the Hermit (c. 1050–c. 1115) Monk, a preacher of the first Crusade, born in Amiens, France. He served as a soldier, became a monk, and in 1095 preached throughout Europe, generating enthusiastic support for the Crusade. He led the second army, which reached Asia Minor, but was defeated by the Turks at Nicaea. He then accompanied the fifth army in 1096, which reached Jerusalem.

Peter the Pilgrim >> **Peregrinus, Petrus**

Peters, Mary (Elizabeth) (1939–) Athlete, born in Halewood, Lancashire, NW England, UK. She started competing in the pentathlon at the age of 17. She won the gold medal at her third Olympics in 1972, at the age of 33, setting a new world record (4801 points). She was also the Commonwealth champion twice, winning the shot as well in the 1970 Games. She campaigned for more sports facilities in Northern Ireland, and an athletics stadium in Belfast is now named after her. >> RR1139

Peterson, Oscar (Emmanuel) (1925–) Jazz pianist and composer, born in Montreal, Quebec, Canada. He could already play the piano when he began formal studies at six, his extraordinary keyboard facility winning him numerous awards and making him a local celebrity. In 1949 he became an international star when he joined a concert tour called 'Jazz at the Philharmonic' in New York. He travels globally, and has recorded both as a soloist and accompanist more than any other musician.

Peterson, Roger Tory (1908–96) Ornithologist, born in Jamestown, NY. He studied at the Art Students League and the National Academy of Design in New York City, then taught art and science in Brookline, MA. After publishing his best-selling *Field Guide to the Birds* (1934), he became art editor for *Audubon* magazine (1934–43). During World War 2, the Army Air Force adapted his bird-spotting methods to aircraft identification. His field guides, books, and other work gave him wide influence in building up popular awareness of wildlife conservation and environmental protection. He founded the Roger Tory Peterson Institute for the study of Natural History in 1986.

Petipa, Marius [peteepa] (1818–1910) Ballet-master and choreographer, credited with the development of Russian classical ballet, born in Marseille, France. After touring France, Spain, and the USA, he went to St Petersburg in 1847 to dance with the Imperial Theatre. There he staged his first ballet, *Pharaoh's Daughter* (1858), setting the style of *ballet à grand spectacle* which was to dominate Russian ballet for the rest of the century. In 1869 he became ballet-master, creating 50 original ballets and restagings, the most famous being Tchaikovsky's *The Sleeping Beauty* (1890).

Petit, Alexis (Thérèse) [puhtee] (1791–1820) Physicist, born in Vesoul, France. Professor at the Lycée Bonaparte, he enunciated with Pierre Louis Dulong the *law of Dulong and Petit*, that for all elements the product of the specific heat and the atomic weight is the same. >> Dulong

Petit, Roland [puhtee] (1924–) Choreographer and dancer, born in Paris. He trained at the Paris Opéra Ballet, and became its leading dancer (1943). In 1948 he founded

Ballets de Paris de Roland Petit, which toured widely in Europe and the USA. He created a repertory of new ballet, and was also responsible for the ballet sequences in the film *Hans Christian Andersen* (1952), danced by his wife, **Zizi (Renée) Jeanmaire** (1924–). In 1972 he founded the Ballet de Marseille, and became its director.

Petitot, Jean [puhteetoh] (1607–91) Painter of enamel miniatures, born in Geneva, Switzerland. After some years in Italy, he went to England and obtained the patronage of Charles I. After the king's execution he moved to Paris, where Louis XIV gave him lodgings in the Louvre and a share in his patronage. His remarkable works included many portaits of the king, most being based on larger paintings done by other artists.

Petöfi, Sandor >> **Arany, János**

Pétomane, Le >> **Pujol, Joseph**

Petrarch [petrah(r)k], in full **Francesco Petrarca** (1304–74) Poet and scholar, born in Arezzo, Italy. He studied at Bologna and Avignon, where he became a clergyman. In 1327 at Avignon he first saw Laura (possibly Laure de Noves, married in 1325 to Hugo de Sade), who inspired him with a passion which has become proverbial for its constancy and purity. As the fame of his learnings grew, royal courts competed for his presence, and in 1341 he was crowned poet laureate at Rome. The earliest of the great Renaissance humanists, he wrote widely on the classics, but he is best known for the series of love poems addressed to Laura, the *Canzoniere*. He left Avignon in 1353 after Laura's death, and lived the rest of his life in N Italy. His writing proved to be a major influence on many authors, notably Chaucer. >> **Chaucer**

Petrie, Sir (William Matthew) Flinders [peetree] (1853–1942) Archaeologist and Egyptologist, born in Charlton, Kent, SE England, UK. He surveyed Stonehenge (1874–7), but turned entirely to Egyptology from 1881, beginning by surveying the pyramids and temples of Giza and excavating the mounds of Tanis and Naucratis. The author of more than 100 books, renowned for his energy and spartan tastes, he became the first Edwards professor of archaeology at London (1892–1933), continuing excavations in Egypt and Palestine until well into his 80s.

Petronio, Stephen [petrohnioh] (1956–) Dancer and choreographer, born in Nutley, NJ. He was studying medicine at college when a chance visit to a dance class changed the course of his life. He trained in contact improvisation with Steve Paxton and also with such leading modern dance experimentalists as Yvonne Rainer and Trisha Brown. He began choreographing while still a member of Brown's company (1979–86), then headed his own troupe. >> **Brown, Trisha; Paxton, Steve; Rainer**

Petronius Arbiter [petrohnius ah(r)bitair] (1st-c) Latin writer, supposed to be the Gaius Petronius whom Tacitus called *arbiter elegantiae* (arbiter of taste) at the court of Nero. He is generally believed to be the author of *Satyricon*, a satirical romance in prose and verse about the licentious life of the upper class in S Italy, fragments of which have been preserved. Accused of conspiring against Nero, he committed suicide. >> **Nero; Tacitus**

Petrosian, Tigran V(artanovich) [petrohzian] (1929–84) Chess player, and world champion (1963–9), born in Tbilisi, Georgia (formerly, USSR). He won the title from Mikhail Botvinnik in 1963, and made one successful defence before losing it to Boris Spassky in 1969. >> **Botvinnik; Spassky; RR1149**

Petrovitch, Alexey >> **Alexis**

Petrov-Vodkin, Kuzma Sergeyevich [petrof vodkin] (1878–1939) Painter, born in Khvalynsk, Russia. Initially trained as an icon painter, he later studied painting in St Petersburg and Moscow, then travelled in Africa. After the

1917 Revolution, the titles of his paintings reflect new concerns, such as 'The Year 1918 in Petrograd' (1920) and 'Workers' (1926). His importance rests mainly on his influence as a teacher of the first generation of Soviet painters at the Leningrad Art Academy.

Pettit, Bob, popular name of **Robert E Lee Pettit** (1932–) Basketball player, born in Baton Rouge, LA. He studied at Louisiana State University, joined the Milwaukee (later the St Louis) Hawks in the National Basketball Association (NBA) in 1954, and stayed with the franchise right through to 1965. He led the NBA in both scoring (twice) and rebounding, helping the Hawks to one championship. Throughout his career he averaged 26·4 points per game, and was twice voted the NBA's Most Valuable Player. >> RR1146

Petty, Sir William (1623–87) Economist, born in Romsey, Hampshire, S England, UK. He went to sea, then studied medicine at Leyden, Paris, and Oxford. He taught anatomy at Oxford, and music at Gresham College, London. Appointed physician to the army in Ireland (1652), he executed a fresh survey of the Irish lands forfeited in 1641, and started ironworks, lead-mines, sea-fisheries, and other industries on estates he bought in SW Ireland. He was made surveyor-general of Ireland by Charles II. His most significant economic work was *Treatise on Taxes* (1662).

Pétursson, Hallgrímur [payterson] (1614–74) Devotional poet, pastor, and hymn-writer, born in Hólar, Iceland. He became pastor of the church at Saurbaer in the W of Iceland (1651), where he wrote his masterpiece, *Passion Hymns* (1666), a cycle of 50 meditations on the Crucifixion. They remain the most popular devotional works in Iceland, and the new cathedral in Reykjavík is named after him.

Peuerbach, Georg von >> **Purbach, Georg von**

Pevsner, Antoine (1886–1962) Constructivist sculptor and painter, born in Oryol, Russia. In Moscow he helped to form the Suprematist group, but in 1920 he broke away from the Suprematists, and issued the *Realist Manifesto* with his brother. This ultimately caused their exile from Russia, and he migrated to Paris. Several of his completely nonfigurative constructions (mainly in copper and bronze) are in the Museum of Modern Art, New York City. >> **Gabo; Malevich**

Pevsner, Sir Nikolaus (Bernhard Leon) (1902–83) Art historian, born in Leipzig, Germany. He was lecturer in art at Göttingen University until the Nazis came to power (1933), when he fled to Britain and became an authority on English architecture. He wrote the enormously popular book, *An Outline of European Architecture* (1942), and became art editor of Penguin Books (1949). He produced the monumental series for Penguin Books, *The Buildings of England* (50 vols, 1951–74), and was professor of fine art at Cambridge (1949–55). He was knighted in 1969.

Pfeiffer, Michelle [fiyfer] (1958–) Film actress, born in Santa Ana, CA. A winner of the Miss Orange County beauty pageant, she had a variety of film and television roles before impressing audiences with her performance in *Scarface* (1983). She won acclaim for her role in *The Witches of Eastwick* (1987) and *Married to the Mob* (1988), and gained a Best Supporting Actress Oscar nomination for *Dangerous Liaisons* (1988), and a Best Actress Oscar nomination for *The Fabulous Baker Boys* (1989). Other films include *Frankie and Johnny* (1991), *Batman Returns* (1992), *Up Close and Personal* (1996), and *One Fine Day* (1997).

Pfitzner, Hans (Erich) (1869–1949) Composer, born in Moscow. He taught in various German conservatories, and conducted in Berlin, Munich, and Strasbourg. He composed *Palestrina* (1917) and other operas, as well as choral, orchestral, and chamber music.

Phaedrus or **Phaeder** [feedrus, feeder] (1st-c) The translator of Aesop's fables into Latin verse, born a slave in Macedonia. He went to Italy, where he was the freedman of Emperor Augustus. He published five books of fables, many his own invention, which were still widely read in mediaeval Europe. >> Aesop

Phalaris [falaris] (?–554 BC) Tyrant of Acragas (modern Agrigento) in Sicily, notorious for his cruelty. On his overthrow, he suffered the same fate as his former victims: he was roasted alive in a bronze bull.

Pheidippides [fiydipideez] (5th-c BC) Long-distance runner from Greece. He was sent to Sparta to ask for aid against the Persians before the Battle of Marathon in 490 BC, and is reputed to have covered 150 mi in two days. Legend has confused him with the man who ran from the battlefield of Marathon to bring news of the victory to Athens. >> RR1141

Phidias [fiydias] (5th-c BC) The greatest sculptor of Greece, born in Athens. He received from Pericles a commission to execute the chief statues for the city, and became superintendent of all public works. He constructed the Propylaea and the Parthenon, carving the gold and ivory 'Athena' there and the 'Zeus' at Olympia. Charged by his enemies with appropriating gold from the statue, he disappeared from Athens, presumably into exile. >> Pericles

Philaretus >> Geulincx, Arnold

Philby, Kim, popular name of **Harold Adrian Russell Philby** (1912–88) British traitor, born in Ambala, India. He studied at Cambridge, where, like Burgess, Maclean, and Blunt, he became a Communist. Already recruited as a Soviet agent, he was employed by the British Secret Intelligence Service (1940–51) as head of anti-Communist counter-espionage. He later became first secretary of the British embassy in Washington, working in liaison with the CIA (1949–51). From 1956 he worked in Beirut as a journalist, passing on to the Soviets information provided by the British. In 1963 he disappeared to Russia, where he was granted citizenship. >> Blunt, Anthony; Burgess, Guy; Maclean, Donald

Philidor, François André, originally **François André Danican** (1726–95) Composer of operas, and chess master, born in Dreux, France. A member of a prominent musical family, he was destined to a career as composer and arranger, but at 18 switched to chess competitions, establishing himself by giving public exhibitions throughout Europe of his ability to defeat two opponents simultaneously while blindfolded. He wrote the first book to lay down the theoretical and strategic principles of chess. His 1765 adaptation of Fielding's *Tom Jones* was the most popular of his 21 operas.

Philip II (of France), known as **Philip Augustus** (1165–1223) King of France (1179–1223), born in Paris, the son of Louis VII (reigned 1137–79). His reign formed a key period in the development of the mediaeval kingdom of France. He embarked on the Third Crusade in 1190, but returned the following year to concentrate on attacking the continental lands of the Angevin kings of England. By the time he died, Capetian power was firmly established over most of France. >> Saladin

Philip II (of Macedon) (382–336 BC) King of Macedon (359–336 BC), the father of Alexander the Great. He used his military and diplomatic skills first to create a powerful unified state at home (359–353 BC), then to make himself the master of the whole of independent Greece. His decisive victory at Chaeronea (338 BC) established Macedonian hegemony there for good. The planned Macedonian conquest of Persia, aborted by his assassination in 336 BC, was eventually carried out by his son. >> Alexander the Great; Olympias

Philip II (of Spain) (1527–98) King of Spain (1556–98) and Portugal (as Philip I, 1580–98), born in Valladolid, the only son of Emperor Charles V and Isabella of Portugal.

Following the death of his first wife, **Maria of Portugal**, at the birth of their son, Don Carlos (1545), he married **Mary I** of England (1554), becoming joint sovereign of England. Before Mary's death (1558) he had inherited the Habsburg possessions in Italy, the Netherlands, Spain, and the New World. To seal the end of the Valois–Habsburg conflict he married **Elizabeth of France**, who bore him two daughters. His brief fourth marriage to his cousin **Anna of Austria** (1570) produced another son, the future Philip III. As the champion of the Counter-Reformation, he tried to destroy infidels and heretics alike. He sought to crush Protestantism, first in the Low Countries (from 1568), then in England and France. The destruction of the Armada (1588) and the continuing revolt of the Netherlands, along with domestic economic problems and internal unrest, suggest a reign marked by failure. However, among his political achievements were the curbing of Ottoman seapower after the Battle of Lepanto (1571) and the conquest of Portugal (1580). >> Charles V (Emperor); Mary I; William I (of the Netherlands)

Philip III, known as **Philip the Good** (1396–1467) Duke of Burgundy (1419–67), born in Dijon, France, the grandson of Philip the Bold. He at first recognized Henry V of England as heir to the French crown, but concluded a separate peace with the French in 1435. Philip created one of the most powerful states in later mediaeval Europe. A committed crusader, he maintained a fleet for operations against the Ottoman Turks.

Philip V (1683–1746) First Bourbon king of Spain (1700–46), born in Versailles, France, the grandson of Louis XIV and Maria Theresa, and great-grandson of Philip IV of Spain. After a long struggle with the rival Habsburg candidate for the Spanish succession, Philip gained the throne at the Peace of Utrecht (1713), but lost the Spanish Netherlands and Italian lands. Twice married, he fell under the influence of his second wife, **Elizabeth Farnese of Parma**, whose desire to secure Italian possessions for her sons brought Spain into conflict with Austria, Great Britain, France, and the United Provinces. >> Vendôme

Philip VI (1293–1350) First Valois king of France (1328–50), the nephew of Philip IV, who became king on the death of Charles IV. His right was denied by Edward III of England, son of the daughter of Philip IV, who declared that females, though excluded from the succession by the Salic law, could transmit their right to their children. The Hundred Years' War with England thus began (1337), and in 1346 Edward III landed in Normandy, defeating Philip at Crécy, just as the Black Death was about to spread through France. >> Edward III

Philip, St (1st-c) One of the disciples of Jesus, listed among the 12 (in *Mark* 3.14 and *Acts* 1). He is especially prominent in John's Gospel, where he is said to come from Bethsaida in Galilee, leads Nathanael to Jesus (1.43), is present at the feeding of the 5000 (6.1), and brings 'the Greeks' to Jesus (12.21). His later career is unknown, but traditions suggest he was martyred on a cross. He is probably not the same person as Philip 'the Evangelist' (*Acts* 6.5). Feast day 3 May (W) or 14 November (E). >> Jesus Christ; Nathanael

Philip (?–1676) American-Indian chief (Indian name, Metacomet), the son of Massoit, chief of the Wampanoag Indians of Massachusetts. He led a confederation of tribes against the European settlers (1675–6), but was shot on the battlefield by one of his own braves. His wife and nine-year-old son, along with hundreds of his people, were sold into slavery by the victorious colonists.

Philip, Prince >> Edinburgh, Duke of

Philip Neri, St >> Neri, St Philip

Philippa of Hainault [enoh] (c. 1314–1369) Queen consort of England, who married her second cousin Edward III at

York in 1327. She brought Flemish weavers to England, encouraged coal-mining, and made the French poet and historian Jean Froissart her secretary. She is said to have roused the English troops before the defeat of the Scots at the Battle of Neville's Cross in 1346, and to have interceded with Edward for mercy for the burgesses of Calais after the long siege in 1347. Queen's College, Oxford, founded by Philippa's chaplain in 1341, was named after her. >> Edward III; Froissart

Philips, Anton (1874–1951) Dutch businessman. A salesman for the light-bulb manufacturing business founded by his brother, he travelled throughout Europe before World War 1 seeking a market for their products. He took over the company in 1921, began mass production of one of the first radio sets, and built the company into a major manufacturer of electrical domestic equipment.

Philips, Katherine, also known by her maiden name **Katherine Fowler** (1631–64) Poet, born in London, England, UK. The first English woman poet to have her work published, she organized a salon for the discussion of poetry and religion. She became known by the admiring title 'Matchless Orinda', and was made the subject of several verses. Her own work includes verses prefixed to Vaughan's *Poems* (1651), a translation of Corneille's *Pompée* (performed in 1663), and a posthumous collection of verses (1667).

Philipson, Sir Robin, popular name of **Sir Robert James Philipson** (1916–92) Painter, born in Broughton-in-Furness, Cumbria, NW England, UK. He studied at Edinburgh College of Art, where he later became head of drawing and painting (1960–82). Like many Scottish artists of his generation, he handled paint freely and colours boldly, but always retained a precise figurative element in his work. He was president of the Royal Scottish Academy (1973–83).

Phillip, Arthur (1738–1814) Admiral, founder and first governor of New South Wales, born in London, England, UK. He trained at Greenwich, joined the navy in 1755, saw service in the Mediterranean, and was at the taking of Havana. In 1787 he was appointed commander of the 'First Fleet' carrying convicts to Australia, and founded a penal colony settlement at Sydney the following year. He left in poor health in 1792, and was made vice-admiral in 1810.

Phillips, David (Graham) (1867–1911) Pro-feminist novelist and journalist, born in Madison, IN. He played a part in the 'muckraker' movement of reform-minded journalism in the early 20th-c. He also wrote powerfully in favour of the emancipation of women, notably in his novels *The Plum Tree* (1905) and *Susan Lennox: Her Fall and Rise* (1917). Although best-remembered for his devoted service to the cause of women's rights, he was assassinated by a lunatic who regarded his efforts in this direction as contributing to female moral depravity.

Phillips, John >> Smith, William

Phillips, John Bertram (1906–82) Bible translator, writer, and broadcaster, born in London, England, UK. He was made famous by *Letters to Young Churches* (1947), translations of Paul's epistles begun in 1941 to encourage his church youth club, and in due course by the complete *New Testament in Modern English* (1958). He wrote a dozen best sellers, including *Your God is Too Small* (1952), *A Man Called Jesus* (1959), and *Ring of Truth: a Translator's Testimony* (1967).

Phillips, Mark, Captain (1948–) Former husband of Princess Anne, and a noted horseman. He trained at Sandhurst, and joined the Queen's Dragoon Guards in 1969. In 1973 he married Princess Anne (now the Princess Royal), but was divorced from her in 1992. He was a regular member of the British equestrian team (1970–6), and won many team events, including the gold medal at the Olympic Games in Munich in 1972. >> Anne (Elizabeth Alice Louise), Princess

Phillips, Peter / Zara >> Anne (Elizabeth Alice Louise), Princess

Phillpotts, Eden (1862–1960) British novelist, playwright, and poet, born in Mount Aboo, India. Educated in Devon, SW England, UK, he remained associated with the county for most of his life. He was the author of well over 200 books, the best of them being novels about Dartmoor, such as *Children in the Mist* (1898), *The Secret Woman* (1905), and *Widecombe Fair* (1913). With his daughter, **Adelaide**, he collaborated in two successful comedies, *The Farmer's Wife* (1924) and *Yellow Sands* (1926).

Philo [fiyloh] (2nd-c) Byzantine scientist. He wrote a treatise on military engineering, of which some fragments remain. He was probably the first to record the contraction of air in a globe over water when a candle is burnt in it.

Philo Judaeus [fiyloh judayus] (c. 20 BC–c.AD 40) Hellenistic Jewish philosopher, born in Alexandria. His work brought together Greek philosophy and the Hebrew Scriptures. His commentaries on the Pentateuch interpret it according to the philosophical ideas of Plato and Aristotle; their doctrines in turn were modified by him in the light of Scripture. In c.40 he headed a deputation to Emperor Caligula in support of Jewish rights. >> Aristotle; Caligula; Plato

Philostratus, Flavius [filostratus] (c. 170–245) Greek sophist. He studied at Athens, and established himself in Rome, where he wrote an idealized life of Apollonius of Tyana, the bright *Lives of the Sophists*, and the amatory *Epistles*. The *Heroicon* and the *Imagines*, a description of 34 paintings on mythological themes supposedly in a villa near Naples, are now ascribed to his son-in-law, **Philostratus the Lemnian**; and further *Imagines* to a third and related **Philostratus**, probably a grandson.

Phintias >> Damon and Pythias

Phipps, Sir William (1651–95) Colonial governor, born in Pemmaquid, ME. He was successively shepherd, carpenter, and trader, and in 1687 recovered £300 000 from a wrecked Spanish ship off the Bahamas. This gained him a knighthood and the appointment as provost-marshal of New England. In 1690 he captured Port Royal (now Annapolis) in Nova Scotia, but failed in 1691 in a naval attack upon Quebec. In 1692 he became governor of Massachusetts.

Phiz >> Browne, Hablot Knight

Phocion [fohshion] (c. 402–318 BC) Athenian soldier. He commanded a division of the Athenian fleet at Naxos (376 BC), helped to conquer Cyprus for Artaxerxes III (351 BC), crushed the Macedonian party in Euboea (341 BC), and the following year forced Philip II to evacuate the Chersonesus. After the murder of Philip (336 BC) he struggled at Athens to repress the reckless desire for war. On the death of Alexander (323 BC), he vainly endeavoured to prevent the Athenians from going to war with Antipater, regent in Macedon. During a brief return to democracy in Athens, he was put to death on a charge of treason. >> Demosthenes (c.383–322 BC); Philip II (of Macedon)

Phoenix, River (1970–93) Film actor, born in Madras, OR. He made his film debut in *Explorers* (1985), and received a Best Actor Oscar nomination for his role in *Running on Empty* (1988). Later films include *Indiana Jones and the Last Crusade* (1989) and *Love You To Death* (1990). He was finishing the filming of *Dark Blood*, when he collapsed and died from a massive drug overdose.

Phomvihane, Kaysone (1920–92) Laotian prime minister (1975–91), born in Savannakhet province, Laos. He studied at Hanoi University, fought with the anti-French forces in Vietnam after World War 2, and joined the exiled Free Lao Front (Neo Lao Issara) nationalist movement in Bangkok in

1945. He later joined the Communist Pathet Lao, becoming its leader in 1955. He became prime minister of the newly formed People's Democratic Republic of Laos and general secretary of the Lao People's Revolutionary Party. Initially he attempted to follow a radical Socialist programme, but later began a policy of economic and political liberalization.>> RR1071

Photius, St [fohtius] (c. 820–91) Patriarch of Constantinople (858–67, 877–86), born in Constantinople (Istanbul). On the deposition of Ignatius from the patriarchate, he was hurried through all the stages of holy orders, and installed in his stead. In 862, Pope Nicholas I called a Council at Rome, which declared Photius's election invalid, and reinstated Ignatius. Supported by the emperor, Photius withdrew from the communion of Rome. He was then deposed and reinstated on several occasions, before in 886 being finally exiled to Armenia. Feast day 6 February (E). >> Nicholas I

Phryne [friynee] (4th-c BC) Greek courtesan of antiquity, who reputedly was Praxiteles' model for his statue of Aphrodite. Accused of profaning the Eleusinian Mysteries, she was defended by the orator Hyperides, who threw off her robe, showing her loveliness, and so gained the verdict. >> Hyperides; Praxiteles

Piaf, Edith [peeaf], popular name of **Edith Giovanna Gassion** (1915–63) Singer, born in Paris. Abandoned by her mother at birth and raised by her grandmother, she was blinded for four years by meningitis, and it was her father, an acrobat, who encouraged her to sing. She started her career by singing in the streets, graduating to cabaret, and becoming known as *Piaf*, from the Parisian slang for 'sparrow'. She appeared in plays and films, but it was for her songs, with their undercurrent of sadness and nostalgia, that she became legendary, travelling widely in Europe and America. Despite her phenomenal success, her life was marred by unhappiness and illness. Among her best-remembered songs are 'La vie en rose', and 'Non, je ne regrette rien'.

Piaget, Jean [pyahzhay] (1896–1980) Psychologist and pioneer in the study of child intelligence, born in Neuchâtel, Switzerland. After studying zoology he turned to psychology, became professor of psychology at Geneva University (1929–54), director of the Centre d'Epistémologie Génétique, and a director of the Institut des Sciences de l'Education. He is best known for his research on the development of cognitive functions in children, in such pioneering studies as *La Naissance de l'intelligence chez l'enfant* (1948, The Origins of Intelligence in Children). >> Isaacs

Piatigorsky, Gregor [pyatigaw(r)skee] (1903–76) Cellist, born in Dnepropetrovsk (formerly, Yekaterinoslav), Ukraine. He gave concerts throughout Russia at the age of nine, and studied at the Moscow Conservatory. He was principal cellist of the Moscow Imperial Opera (1919–21), first cellist with the Warsaw (1921–3) and Berlin (1924–8) Philharmonic Orchestras, then embarked on a solo career. After touring internationally, he made his US debut in 1929. Recital partners included Horowitz and Rachmaninov, and many works were composed for him. A US citizen from 1942, he taught at at the Curtis Institute, Philadelphia, and at several universities. >> Horowitz; Rachmaninov

Piazzi, Giuseppe [pyatsee] (1746–1826) Astronomer, born in Ponte di Valtellina, Italy. He became a Theatine monk, professor of theology in Rome (1779), and professor of mathematics at the Academy of Palermo (1780). He set up an observatory at Palermo in 1789, published a catalogue of the stars (1803, 1814), and discovered and named the first minor planet, Ceres.

Picabia, Francis [pikahbia] (1879–1953) Painter, born in Paris. He was one of the most anarchistic of modern artists, involved in Cubism, Dadaism, and Surrealism. He helped to intoduce Dadaism to New York in 1915. His anti-art productions, often portraying senseless machinery, include 'Parade Amoureuse' (1917) and many of the cover designs for the American anti-art magazine *291*, which he edited.

Picard, (Charles) Emile [peekah(r)] (1856–1941) Mathematician, born in Paris. Professor at the Sorbonne (1886–97), and president of the French Academy of Science (1910), he was especially noted for his work in complex analysis, and integral and differential equations.

Picard, Jean [peekah(r)] (1620–82) Astronomer, born in La Flèche, France. In 1645 he became professor in the Collège de France and helped to found the Paris Observatory. He made the first accurate measurement of a degree of a meridian, and thus arrived at an estimate of the radius of the Earth. He visited Tycho Brahe's observatory on the island of Hven, and determined its latitude and longitude. >> Brahe

Picasso, Pablo [pikasoh] see panel on p. 741

Piccard, Auguste (Antoine) [peekah(r)] (1884–1962) Physicist, born in Basel, Switzerland, the twin brother of Jean Piccard. He studied at Zürich, and became professor of applied physics at Brussels (1922), and held posts at Lausanne, Chicago, and Minnesota universities. In 1932 he ascended in a balloon 16 940 m/55 563 ft into the stratosphere, and in 1948 explored the ocean depths off West Africa in a bathyscaphe of his own design. >> Piccard, Jean

Piccard, Jean (Felix) [peekah(r)] (1884–1963) Chemist, born in Basel, Switzerland, the twin brother of Auguste Piccard. He took a chemical engineering degree at the Swiss Institute of Technology in 1907, taught at Munich, Lausanne, and Chicago universities, and became professor emeritus of aeronautical engineering at Minnesota University (1936–52). His chief interest was in the exploration of the stratosphere, and he designed and ascended (with his wife) in a balloon from Dearborn, Detroit, in 1934, to a height of 11 mi, collecting valuable data concerning cosmic rays. He became a US citizen in 1931. >> Piccard, Auguste

Piccaver, Alfred (1884–1958) Tenor, born in Long Sutton, Somerset, SW England, UK. He studied in New York, made his debut in Prague (1907), and was the leading tenor at Vienna (1910–37), singing Beethoven, Wagner, Verdi, and Puccini roles. He taught in Vienna from 1955.

Piccinni, Niccola [peecheenee] (1728–1800) Composer, born in Bari, Italy. He studied at Naples, and wrote over 100 operas as well as oratorios and church music. In 1766 he was summoned to Paris, and became the representative of the musical party opposed to Gluck. >> Gluck

Pick, Frank (1878–1941) Administrator and design patron, born in Spalding, Lincolnshire, EC England, UK. A solicitor by training, he joined the London Underground Electric Railways in 1906 as assistant to the general manager, rapidly becoming vice-chairman of the London passenger transport board (1933–40). His vision transformed London Transport into a unified modern system. A founder-member of the Design and Industries Association, he employed some of the best artistic and design talents available.

Pickering, Edward Charles (1846–1919) Astronomer, born in Boston, MA, the brother of William Henry Pickering. He studied at Harvard, and became professor of physics at the Massachusetts Institute of Technology. In 1876 he was appointed professor of astronomy and director of the observatory at Harvard, where his work was concerned with stellar photometry and classification of spectra of the stars. He invented the meridian photometer. >> Pickering, William Henry

Pickering, Sir George (1904–80) Clinician who pioneered the study of blood pressure, born in Whalton, Northumberland, NE England, UK. He studied at Cambridge and St

PABLO PICASSO (1881–1973)

Picasso was born in Málaga, Andalusia, the son of José Ruiz Blasco, an art teacher, and Maria Picasso López. His father tutored him in the early years. At the age of 14, he entered the Academy at Barcelona and painted 'Girl with Bare Feet' (1895, Paris). Two years later he transferred to Madrid for advanced training; but he was unimpressed by his tutition, and spent a great deal of time in cafés and brothels.

In 1898 he won a gold medal for 'Customs of Aragon', which was exhibited in his native town. In 1901 he set up a studio in Montmartre. By now a master of the traditional forms of art, as shown by such works as 'Gypsy Girl on the Beach' (1898), he absorbed the neo-Impressionist influences of the Paris school of Toulouse-Lautrec, Degas, and Vuillard, seen in such works as 'Longchamp' (1901) and 'The Blue Room' (1901), but soon began to develop his own idiom. He also admired the work of Goya and El Greco. After illness in 1898 he retired to the country. On his return, he rejected traditional art, and began using his mother's maiden name.

During his Blue Period (1901–4), he produced a series of striking studies of the poor in haunting attitudes often of despair and gloom. This gave way to the bright, life-affirming Rose Period (1904–6). In 1904 Picasso entered into a relationship with Fernande Oliver, who inspired many of his pre-Cubist works, such as the painting 'Woman with Loaves' (1906, Philadelphia) and his sculpture 'Head of a Woman' (1909, several casts). Pink shadows became browner in his remarkable portrait of Gertrude Stein (1906, New York), and 'La Toilette' (1906, Buffalo).

His interest in sculpture and his new enthusiasm for black art are reflected in the transitional painting 'Two Nudes' (1906). This heralded his epoch-making controversial break with tradition in 'Les Demoiselles d'Avignon' (1906–7, New York), the first full-blown example of analytical Cubism – an attempt to render three-dimensions without resorting to perspective. Its exclusive emphasis on formal, geometrical criteria contrasted sharply with the cult of colour espoused by the Fauvists, of whom Braque was one before joining forces with Picasso in 1909. Between them they developed Cubism through its various phases: analytic (1909–11),

synthetic (1912–14), hermetic, and rococo. Along with paint, the works of these phases demonstrate the use of collage techniques. The 'Ma Jolie' series of pictures (1911-12, Paris), after the music-hall song score which appears in them, are examples of the last phase, coinciding with Picasso's new love, Eva (Marcelle Humbert). The outbreak of war in 1914 separated the two friends. Eva died in 1915, and Picasso painted 'Harlequin' (Barcelona) as an outlet for his grief.

From 1917 Picasso became associated with Diaghilev's Russian Ballet, designing costumes and sets for *Parade* (1917) – during which time he met his future wife, **Olga Kokhloven**, a dancer – *Le Tricorne* (1919), *Cuadro Flamenco* (1921), *Pulcinella* (1920), and *Le Train bleu* (1924), in both Cubist and Neoclassical styles. The grotesque facial and bodily distortions of the 'Three Dancers' (1925, London) foreshadows his major work, the immense canvas of 'Guernica' (1937, Madrid), which expressed in synthetic Cubism his horror at the bombing of this Basque town during the Civil War. On a wider scale, it expresses a horror of war in general, as well as his compassion and hope for its victims. He then became director of the Prado Gallery, Madrid (1936–9). During World War 2 he was mostly in Paris, and after the liberation joined the Communists. However, neither 'Guernica' nor his portrait of Stalin (1953) commended him to the Party.

Picasso lived to be 92, and died at Mougins, in France. He had left his wife in 1931, and had a succession of mistresses who were a source of inspiration to him, and whom he used as models. He married the last of them, **Jacqueline Roque**, in 1961. He created more than 50 000 works, and during his last years (1966–73) produced three important series of drawings, including 347 untitled engravings (1968). His 90th birthday was celebrated by an exhibition of eight of his works in the Louvre, Paris, in the place where the 'Mona Lisa' normally hangs. He also designed stage sets for Cocteau and Petit, illustrated translations of classical texts, experimented in sculpture, ceramics, and lithography, allowed his canvas to be filmed while at work, and wrote a play (1941) and two collections of poetry (1935–6). The dominant figure of early 20th-c art, he was above all the great innovator.

\>> Braque; Cocteau; Degas; Diaghilev; Goya; Greco, El; Petit, Roland; Toulouse-Lautrec; Vuillard

---

Thomas', then with Sir Thomas Lewis at University College Hospital in London, where Lewis infused in him a love of clinical research. He worked at St Mary's Hospital and, from 1956, as professor of medicine at Oxford. He did important experimental work on the mechanism of pain in peptic ulcer, and on the physiological causes and epidemiology of high blood pressure in human populations. >> Lewis, Thomas

Pickering, William H(ayward) (1910–   ) Rocket scientist, born in Wellington, New Zealand. He studied in the USA, and in 1944 joined the Jet Propulsion Laboratory, which he went on to direct (1954–76). He oversaw the first orbit of the Earth by a US satellite (1958), the first US soft landings on the Moon, the first mission to orbit Mars (Mariner IX) and the first missions to Venus and Mercury (Mariner X).

Pickering, William Henry (1858–1938) Astronomer, born in Boston, MA. In 1919 he discovered Phoebe, the ninth satellite of Saturn. He was in charge of an observation station at Arequipa, Peru, and from 1900 was director of a station at Mandeville, Jamaica. In 1919 he predicted the existence of a ninth planet in the Solar System (Pluto, discovered in 1930). >> Pickering, Edward Charles; Tombaugh

Pickett, George Edward (1825–75) US soldier, born in Richmond, VA. He trained at West Point, served in the Mexican War (1846–7), and later fought Indians on the frontier. He entered Confederate service in the Civil War, and was promoted to major-general. At Gettysburg he was ordered to form the brigades for one last desperate charge across an open field; the Confederates suffered disastrous casualties while being repulsed, and thereafter the action became known as *Pickett's charge*. He continued to see action right to the end of the War, after which he became an insurance agent in Virginia.

Pickford, Mary, originally **Gladys Mary Smith** (1893–1979) Actress, born in Toronto, Ontario, Canada. She first appeared on the stage at the age of five, and made her film debut in

1909. Her beauty and ingenuous charm won her the title of 'The World's Sweetheart', her many successful films including *Rebecca of Sunnybrook Farm* (1917), *Poor Little Rich Girl* (1917), and *The Taming of the Shrew* (1929). She made her first talkie, *Coquette*, in 1929, and retired from the screen in 1933. She founded United Artists Film Corporation in 1919. Her second husband was Douglas Fairbanks, Snr. >> Fairbanks, Douglas, Snr

Pico della Mirandola, Giovanni, comte (Count) [**pee**koh, mi**ran**dola] (1463–94) Renaissance philosopher, born in Mirandola, Italy. He studied in Italy and France, and in 1486 offered to defend 900 theses on Christian theology at Rome, but the debate was forbidden on the grounds that some of the theses were heretical (a charge from which he was absolved in 1493). His philosophy was an attempt to reconcile Platonic and Aristotelian ontological doctrines. He also wrote Latin epistles and elegies, a series of Italian sonnets, and a major study of free will, *De hominis dignitate oratio* (1486, Oration on the Dignity of Man).

Pieck, Wilhelm [peek] (1876–1960) East German politician and president (1949–60), born near Berlin. Originally a carpenter, he helped found the Spartacus League (1915) and the German Communist Party (1918), leading the unsuccessful 'Spartacus uprising' in Berlin in 1919. Elected as a Communist to the Reichstag (1928), he was forced into exile in 1933, and fled to Moscow where he became secretary of the Comintern (1935). In 1945 he returned to Berlin, founded the dominant Socialist Unity Party (1946), and from 1949 until his death served as president of East Germany.

Pierce, Franklin (1804–69) US statesman and 14th president (1853–7), born in Hillsborough, NH. Admitted to the bar in 1827, he was elected to Congress as a Jacksonian Democrat, and in 1837 to the US Senate. He advocated the annexation of Texas with or without slavery, and was made brigadier-general in the Mexican War. Elected president in 1853, he defended slavery and the fugitive slave law. Among the events of his administration was the repeal of the Missouri Compromise and the passing of the Kansas–Nebraska Act, which kindled a flame that ultimately led to the Civil War. The unpopularity of this Act led to his enforced retirement from politics in 1857. >> RR1097

Pierce, John Robinson (1910–) Electrical engineer, born in Des Moines, IA. He studied at the California Institute of Technology, then worked in the Bell Telephone Laboratories (1936–71), returning to Caltech as professor of engineering. A man of wide scientific interests, he made important discoveries in the fields of microwaves, radar, and pulse-code modulation. In the 1950s he was one of the first to see the possibilities of satellite communication, taking a leading part in the development work that resulted in the launch of *Echo* in 1960 and *Telstar* in 1962.

Piero della Francesca [**pyay**roh, fran**chays**ka] (c. 1420–92) Painter, born in Borgo San Sepolcro, Italy. His major work is a series of frescoes illustrating 'The Legend of the True Cross' (1452–66) in the choir of S Francesco at Arezzo. An unfinished 'Nativity' in the London National Gallery shows some Flemish influence.

Piero di Cosimo [**pyair**oh di **kohz**imoh], originally **Piero di Lorenzo** (c. 1462–c. 1521) Painter, born in Florence, Italy. He was a pupil of Cosimo Rosselli, whose name he adopted. His later style was influenced by Signorelli and Leonardo da Vinci, and among his best-known works are 'The Death of Procris' (c.1500, National Gallery, London) and 'The Rescue of Andromeda' (c.1515, Uffizi). >> Leonardo da Vinci; Signorelli

Pierre, Abbé [pyair], originally **Henri Antoine Groués** (1912–) Priest, born in Lyon, France. He served with distinction during World War 2, becoming a member of the Resistance movement in 1942. Elected a deputy in the Constituent Assembly after the war, he resigned to concentrate on helping the homeless of Paris (1951). Forming his band of Companions of Emmaus, he provided, with little monetary assistance, at least a minimum of shelter for hundreds of families, and finally secured the aid of the French government in dealing with this problem.

Pigalle, Jean Baptiste [peegal] (1714–85) Sculptor, born in Paris. Extremely popular in his day, he was patronized by Louis XV and Madame de Pompadour. His works include a statue of Voltaire and the tomb of Marshal Maurice de Saxe in Strasbourg. His 'Vénus, l'amour et l'amitié' (Venus, Love and Friendship) is in the Louvre.

Piggott, Lester (Keith) (1935–) Flat racing jockey, born in Wantage, Berkshire, S England, UK. He rode his first winner at the age of 12, and his first Epsom Derby winner, *Never Say Die*, in 1954. He subsequently rode a record nine winners of the race, and a record 29 Classic winners between 1954 and 1985. During his career he rode 4349 winners in Britain (1948–85), a figure bettered only by Gordon Richards, and was champion jockey 11 times. After retiring, he took up training at Newmarket, but was imprisoned (1987–8) for tax offences, then returned to the saddle in 1990 and won his 30th Classic, the 2000 Guineas, in 1992. >> RR1160

Pike, Kenneth (Lee) (1912–) Linguist and anthropologist, born in Woodstock, CT. After graduating in theology in 1933, he became involved in linguistic studies through the Summer Institute of Linguistics, whose purpose is to study previously unwritten languages with the aim of producing translations of the Bible in them. Professor of linguistics at the University of Michigan (1948–79), he developed the system of linguistic analysis known as *tagmemics*. Among his many books are *Phonetics* (1943) and *Language in Relation to a Unified Theory of the Structure of Human Behavior* (1954–60).

Pike, Zebulon (Montgomery) (1779–1813) US army officer and explorer, born in Lamberton, NJ. While serving as an army lieutenant he was sent to explore the territory around the Arkansas and Red Rivers. His party encountered a mountain peak at the foot of the Rocky Mountains, Colorado, later named *Pike's Peak*. He attained the rank of brigadier, and was killed in action while attacking York in the War of 1812.

Pilate, Pontius [**pon**shus], Lat **Pontius Pilatus** (1st-c) Roman prefect of Judaea. He was appointed by Tiberius in c.26, having charge of the state and the occupying military forces, but subordinate to the legate of Syria. Although based in Caesarea, he also resided in Jerusalem. He caused unrest by his use of Temple funds to build an aqueduct, by his temporary location of Roman standards in Jerusalem, and by his slaughter of Samaritans in 36 (for which he was recalled). His fame rests entirely on his role in the story of Jesus of Nazareth, permitting his execution by crucifixion at the prompting of the Jewish authorities. >> Jesus Christ

Pilbeam, David Roger (1940–) Physical anthropologist, born in Brighton, East Sussex, SE England, UK. He trained at Cambridge and Yale, and became professor at Harvard. A leading student of human and primate evolution, his many publications include *Evolution of Man* (1970) and *The Ascent of Man* (1972).

Pile, Sir Frederick Alfred (1884–1976) British soldier. In World War 1 he won the DSO and the MC, and throughout World War 2 commanded Britain's anti-aircraft defences. In 1945 he was appointed director-general of the ministry of works.

Pilger, John (Richard) [**pil**jer] (1939–) Journalist and documentary film-maker, born in Sydney, New South Wales, Australia. A provocative and controversial journalist who has worked mainly in Britain, he has twice won the British Journalist of the Year award and is a winner of the UNESCO Peace Prize. His film *Year Zero* (1979) exposed the atrocities of Pol Pot to the world. Later films include *Vietnam: The Last Battle* (1995) and *Inside Burma: Land of Fear* (1996). He has published collections of his writings, including *Heroes* (1986), and his book *The Secret Country* (1989) is a critical appraisal of the position of Aboriginal people in Australia. >> Pol Pot

Pilkington, Sir Alastair, originally **Lionel Alexander Bethune Pilkington** (1920–95) Glass manufacturer, born in Newbury, Berkshire, S England, UK. He studied at Cambridge, joined the family firm of glass-makers, and in 1952 conceived the idea of float glass as a method of manufacturing plate glass without having to grind it to achieve a satisfactory finish. His team successfully introduced the new technique of pouring glass straight from the furnace on to the surface of a bath of molten tin. Director of Pilkington plc (formerly Pilkington Brothers) of St Helens in 1955, he became president of the firm in 1985. He was knighted in 1970, and acted as Pro-Chancellor of Lancaster University (1980–90).

Pillsbury, Charles Alfred (1842–99) Flour miller, born in Warner, NH. In 1869, shortly after joining his uncle, John Sargent Pillsbury, in Minneapolis, he bought into a flour mill. An innovative manager and marketer, he acquired new milling technology, and organized C A Pillsbury & Co in 1872. By the early 1900s the Pillsbury flour mills were the largest such enterprise in the world. He also served as a state senator (1878–85).

Pilnyak, Boris, pseudonym **Boris Andreyevich Vogau** (1894–?1937) Writer, born in Mozhaisk, Russia. He wrote novels and short stories, including (trans titles) *The Naked Year* (1922) and *The Volga Flows Down to the Caspian Sea* (1930). An anti-Communist, he fell into disfavour with the authorities, and he and his works disappeared. It later came to light that he was arrested in 1937, and died shortly afterwards.

Pilon, Germain [peelō] (1537–90) Sculptor, born in Paris. Among his great monumental works are the statues at the tomb of Henry II and Catherine de' Medici at St Denis, and the bronze 'Cardinal René de Biraque' in the Louvre. In these, in contrast with his earlier more conventional work, such as 'The Three Graces', his sharp observation of nature enabled him to produce figures which are both more realistic and more emotional. He also produced skilful medals, especially of the French royal family.

Piłsudski, Józef (Klemens) [pilsudskee] (1867–1935) Polish marshal, statesman, and first president (1918–22), born near Vilna, Poland. Often imprisoned in the cause of Polish independence, he became leader of the Polish Socialist Party (1892), and formed a band of troops which fought on the side of Austria during World War 1. He declared Poland's independence in 1918, and became the country's first president. Following a military coup in 1926, he refused the post of president, but served as a powerful minister of defence in the new government.

Pinchback, Pinckney (Benton Stewart) (1837–1921) US politician and Union army officer, born in Macon, GA. The son of a white planter and a slave mother, as a child he was released from bondage by his father, and subsequently worked on river steamboats. He later served as a Union officer in the American Civil War, but encountered prejudice and resigned his commission. After the War he returned South, entered politics, and was elected to the state Senate (1868). Although he played a leading role in Louisiana politics during the Reconstruction period (1865–77), and received strong electoral support, his attempts to gain seats in Congress and the US Senate were unsuccessful. In later life he studied law, was admitted to the bar, and practised in Washington, DC.

Pinchbeck, Christopher (c. 1670–1732) Clockmaker and toymaker, from London, England, UK. He invented the gold-coloured alloy of copper and zinc for making imitation gold watches, which has since been given his name. His son, **Christopher** (c.1710–38), was an inventor of such things as astronomical clocks, automatic pneumatic brakes, and patent candle snuffers.

Pinckney, Charles (Cotesworth) (1746–1825) US statesman, born in Charleston, SC. He studied at Oxford and at Caen Military Academy, then settled as a barrister in Charleston. He was Washington's aide-de-camp at Brandywine and Germantown, but was taken prisoner at the surrender of Charleston (1780). A member of the Constitutional Convention (1787), he introduced the clause forbidding religious tests. In 1796 he was appointed minister to France, but the French Directory refused to receive him. He was twice Federalist candidate for the presidency (1804, 1808). >> Pinckney, Thomas; Washington, George

Pinckney, Thomas (1750–1828) US diplomat and soldier, born in Charleston, SC, the brother of Charles Pinckney. He studied law in London, then returned to South Carolina and served with distinction in the Revolution. He became Governor of South Carolina (1787–9) and ambassador to Great Britain (1792–6). He negotiated the San Lorenzo or *Pinckney Treaty* with Spain, which established territorial and traffic rights on the Mississippi R (1795), and served as a Federalist in the US House of Representatives (1797–1801). He was a major-general in the War of 1812. >> Pinckney, Charles

Pincus, Gregory (Goodwin) (1903–67) Physiologist, born in Woodbine, NJ. He studied at Cornell, Harvard, Cambridge, and Berlin universities, then founded his own consultancy in experimental biology at Shrewsbury, MA. In 1951, impressed by the work of the birth-control campaigner, Margaret Sanger, he began research into the nature of reproduction, and found that some of the new synthetic hormones controlled fertility effectively. Field trials in 1954 were successful, leading to the development of the contraceptive pill. >> Chang; Sanger, Margaret

Pindar (c. 522–c. 440 BC) The chief lyric poet of Greece, born near Thebes. He studied in Athens, and became famous as a composer of odes for people in all parts of the Greek world. Although he wrote for all kinds of circumstances, only his *Epinikia* (Triumphal Odes) have survived entire, four books celebrating the victories won in the Olympian, Pythian, Nemean, and Isthmian games.

Pindar, Peter >> **Opie, John**

Pindling, Sir Lynden O(scar) (1930–) Bahamian prime minister (1973–92), born in the Bahamas. He studied at London University, and practised as a lawyer before becoming centrally involved in politics, eventually as leader of the Progressive Liberal Party. He became prime minister in 1969, and led his country to full independence within the Commonwealth in 1973. He was re-elected in 1977, 1982, and 1987. When his Party was soundly defeated in the 1992 election, he resigned as leader. >> RR1034

Pinel, Philippe >> **Tuke, William**

Pinero, Sir Arthur (Wing) [pi**nair**oh] (1855–1934) Playwright, born in London, England, UK. He studied law, but in 1874 made his debut on the stage in Edinburgh, and in 1875 joined the Lyceum Company. He wrote several farces, but is best known for his social dramas, notably *The Second Mrs Tanqueray* (1893), which made him the most successful playwright of his day. He was knighted in 1909.

Pinin Farina >> **Farina, Battista**

Pinkerton, Allan (1819–84) Detective, born in Glasgow, W Scotland, UK. He was a Chartist who in 1842 settled in Dundee, IL, became a detective and deputy-sheriff, and in 1850 founded the Pinkerton National Detective Agency. He headed a Federal intelligence network during the Civil War, and his agency later took a leading part in breaking up the Molly Maguires and in policing other labour disputes.

Pinkham, Lydia (Estes) [pingkham] (1819–83) Manufacturer, born in Lynn, MA. A young schoolteacher in Lynn, she became a member of the Female Anti-Slavery Society and a lifelong friend of Frederick Douglass. She took up various causes, including temperence and phrenology, until she married Isaac Pinkham in 1843. In 1875 Isaac went bankrupt speculating on real estate, and Lydia began selling a herbal remedy she had concocted called 'Mrs Lydia E Pinkham's Vegetable Compound'. She did not live long enough to see it achieve its phenomenal success, but for some 50 years it was one of the most popular patent medicines in America. It was promoted especially for 'women's weakness', but the American Medical Association dismissed all its claims as fraudulent. >> Douglass, Frederick

Pinochet (Ugarte), Augusto [peenohshay] (1915–) Chilean dictator (1973–90), born in Valparaíso, Chile. A career army officer, he led the military coup overthrowing the Allende government in 1973, establishing himself at the head of the ensuing military regime. In 1980 he enacted a constitution giving himself an eight-year presidential term (1981–9). A plebiscite held in 1988 rejected his candidacy as president beyond 1990. He retained his post as commander-in-chief of the army. >> Allende, Salvador

Pinter, Harold (1930–) Playwright and director, born in London, England, UK. He became a repertory actor, first writing poetry, then turning to drama with *The Room* (1957). His first major play, *The Birthday Party* (1958), was badly received, but was revived after the success of *The Caretaker* (1960, film 1963), and has been televised twice (1960, 1987) and filmed (1968). Other plays include *The Homecoming* (1965), *Old Times* (1971), and *No Man's Land* (1975). His television play *The Lover* (1963) won the Italia Prize. Early screenplays include *The Servant* (1962), *The Pumpkin Eaters* (1963), *Accident* (1967), and *The Go-Between* (1969). His work is highly regarded for the way it uses the unspoken meaning behind inconsequential everyday talk to induce an atmosphere of menace. Closely associated with the director Peter Hall, he became an associate director of the National Theatre after Hall became director in 1973. He wrote a number of filmscripts during the 1980s, including *The French Lieutenant's Woman* (1981) and *Reunion* (1989), as well as several short plays, such as *A Kind of Alaska* (1982) and *Mountain Language* (1988), in which there is an explicit commitment to radical political causes. A major new play, *Moonlight*, was produced in 1993, and in 1996 appeared *Ashes to Ashes*. >> Fraser, Antonia; Hall, Peter

Pinturicchio [pintureekyoh], originally **Bernardino di Betto Vagio** (1454–1513) Painter, born in Perugia, Italy. As assistant to Perugino, he worked on the frescoes in the Sistine Chapel at Rome. He himself painted frescoes in several Roman churches, the Vatican Library, and in churches in Orvieto, Siena, and elsewhere. A delight in brilliant colour and ornamental detail is evident in his lavish decorative schemes. >> Perugino

Pinza, Ezio, originally **Fortunio Pinza** (1892–1957) Bass singer, born in Rome. After gaining fame in Italy he became a favourite at the Metropolitan Opera, New York City (1926–48). He later appeared in Broadway shows and films, including *South Pacific*.

Pinzón, Vicente Yáñez [peenthon] (c.1460–c.1524) Discoverer of Brazil, born in Palos, Spain. He commanded the *Nina* in the first expedition of Columbus (1492), and his brother, **Martin**, commanded the *Pinta*. In 1499 he sailed on his own account, and in 1500 landed near Pernambuco on the Brazil coast, which he followed N to the Orinoco. He was made Governor of Brazil by Ferdinand V and Isabella of Castile. >> Columbus

Piombo, Sebastiano del [pyomboh] ('of the Seal'), originally **Sebastiano del Luciani** (1485–1547) Painter, born in Venice, Italy. His surname arose because he was sealer of briefs to Pope Clement VII (1523). He studied under Giovanni Bellini and Giorgione, and went to Rome in c.1510, where he worked in conjunction with Michelangelo. In 1519 he painted his masterpiece, 'The Raising of Lazarus' (National Gallery, London). He was also an accomplished portrait painter. >> Bellini, Giovani; Giorgione; Michelangelo

Piozzi, Hester Lynch [pyotsee], previously **Harriet Lynch Thrale** *née* **Salusbury** (1741–1821) Writer, born near Pwllheli, Gwynedd. In 1763 she married Henry Thrale, a prosperous brewer. Dr Samuel Johnson conceived an extraordinary affection for her, and lived in her house at Streatham Place for over 16 years. Thrale also esteemed Johnson, and made him one of his four executors. Thrale died in 1781, and in 1784 the brewery was sold. The widow then became attached to the Italian musician **Gabriel Piozzi**, whom she married in 1784 – with Johnson feeling somewhat slighted as a consequence. She wrote poems and published *Anecdotes of Dr Johnson* (1786) and *Letters to and from Dr Johnson* (1788). >> Johnson, Samuel

Piper, Charles V(ancouver) (1867–1926) Agronomist, born in Victoria, British Columbia, Canada. His parents moved S to Washington soon after he was born. He studied at the University of Washington, then taught botany at the State College of Washington, Pullman (1893–1903). His collection and classification of plants in Washington, Idaho, and Oregon led to a series of classic books, such as *Flora of the State of Washington* (1906). As director of the office of forage crops for the US Department of Agriculture (1903–26), he sought grass samples worldwide to replace the poor Johnson grass. The sudan grass he found was drought resistant, and has remained vitally important for American hay crops.

Piper, John (1903–92) Artist, born in Epsom, Surrey, SE England, UK. An abstract artist in the 1930s, he developed a representational style, as seen in his pictures of war damage and his topographical pictures, notably the watercolours of Windsor Castle commissioned by the Queen (1941–2). He is also known for his theatre sets, as well as the stained glass design in Coventry Cathedral.

Piper, Leonora E (1857–1950) US medium, discovered in 1885 by William James. Mrs Piper's trance speech and writing were studied extensively (1885–1911) by James and other members of the American and British Societies for Psychical Research. She became for William James his 'white crow', when he became convinced of the paranormal origin of some of her trance utterances.

Piper, Otto (1891–) Theologian, born in Lichte, Germany. A student in Jena, Marburg, Paris, and Göttingen, he taught at Göttingen and Münster. In 1933 he fled from Nazi Germany to Britain and then the USA, where he became professor of New Testament at Princeton from 1941. He advocated a 'biblical realism' which neither took Scripture literally nor ignored its teaching, but sought to be true to the writers' intentions. His books include *The Biblical View of Sex and Marriage* (1960).

Piper, Watty >> **Bragg, Mabel Caroline**

Piper, William (Thomas) (1881–1970) Aircraft manufacturer, born in Knapps Creek, NY. He studied at Harvard, then worked in construction and for his family's Pennsylvania oil business. In 1931 he took over a bankrupt aircraft company and began producing small affordable planes, 'Cubs', for ordinary people. During his lifetime, the Piper Aircraft Corporation produced more aircraft than any other company.

Pippi, Giulio >> **Giulio Romano**

Piquet, Nelson [**pee**kay], originally **Nelson Souto Maior** (1952–) Motor-racing driver, born in Rio de Janeiro, Brazil. He changed his name so that his parents would not find out about his racing exploits. He was British Formula Three champion in 1978, and world champion in 1981, 1983 (both Brabham), and 1987 (Williams). He won 23 grand prix between 1978 and a serious accident in 1991.

Pirandello, Luigi [piran**del**oh] (1867–1936) Playwright, novelist, and short-story writer, born in Girgenti, Sicily, Italy. He studied philology at Rome and Bonn, becoming a lecturer in literature at Rome (1897–1922). After writing powerful and realistic novels and short stories, such as *Il fu Mattia Pascal* (1903, The Late Mattia Pascal), he turned to the theatre and became a leading exponent of contemporary drama. Among his plays are *Sei personaggi in cerca d'autore* (1921, Six Characters in Search of an Author), *Enrico IV* (1922, Henry IV) and *Come tu mi vuoi* (1930, As You Desire Me). In 1925 he established a theatre of his own in Rome, the Teatro d'Arte, and his company took his plays all over Europe. Many of his later plays have been filmed. In 1934 he was awarded the Nobel Prize for Literature.

Piranesi, Giambattista [pira**nay**zee], or **Giovanni Battista** (1720–78) Architect and copper-engraver of Roman antiquities, born in Mestre, near Venice, Italy. He went to Rome in 1740 as a draftsman for the Venetian ambassador, and settled there permanently in 1745. He studied with the leading printmakers and developed his own techniques, producing innumerable etchings of the city both in ancient times and in his own day.

Pire, Dominique (Georges) [peer] (1910–69) Dominican priest, born in Dinant, Belgium. He lectured in moral philosophy at Louvain (1937–47) and was awarded the Croix de Guerre for resistance work as priest and intelligence officer in World War 2. After the war he devoted himself to helping refugees and displaced persons, and was awarded the 1958 Nobel Prize for Peace for his scheme of 'European villages', including the 'Anne Frank village' in Germany for elderly refugees and destitute children.

Pirenne, Henri [peeren] (1862–1935) Historian of Belgium and mediaeval Europe, born in Verviers, Belgium. He studied mediaeval history at the universities of Liège, Leipzig, Berlin, and Paris, and became professor of mediaeval and Belgian history at Ghent (1886–1930). His *Economic and Social History of Mediaeval Europe* (1936) summarizes his life's work, and his seven-volume *Histoire de Belgique* (1900–32) is a classic exposition of his country's history.

Pirie, (Douglas Alastair) Gordon (1931–91) Athlete, born in Leeds, West Yorkshire, N England, UK. A middle-distance runner who at various times held the world records for 3000 m and 5000 m, he never produced his top form during the Olympics, and his best performance was a silver medal in the 5000 m in Melbourne in 1956.

Pirie, Norman Wingate (1907–97) British biochemist. He studied at Cambridge, and taught there (1932–40) before joining the Rothamsted Experimental Station (1940–73), becoming head of the biochemistry department in 1947. With **Sir Frederick Bawden** (1908–72) he isolated in 1936 the tobacco mosaic virus in crystalline form, the first scientist to do so for any virus, and an important step on the road to the understanding of DNA and RNA. He was elected a Fellow of the Royal Society (1949). >> **Stanley, Wendell**

Pisanello, Antonio [peesa**nel**oh], originally **Antonio Pisano** (c. 1395–1455) Court painter, born in Pisa, Italy. The foremost draughtsman of his day, his drawings are marked by an accurate observation of reality, and a naturalism which contrasts with the stylized manner of his great contemporary, Gentile da Fabriano. These drawings became models for later Renaissance artists. His most famous picture is 'The Vision of Saint Eustace', but his frescoes have all been lost except for two in Verona. He was also considered the greatest medallist of his time. >> **Fabriano**

Pisano, Andrea [pee**sah**noh], also known as **Andrea da Pontedera** (c. 1270–1349) Sculptor, born in Pontedera, Italy. He became famous as a worker in bronze and a sculptor in marble, settling in Florence. In 1337 he succeeded Giotto as chief artist in the cathedral at Florence, and later became chief artist in the cathedral at Orvieto (1347), working on reliefs and statues.

Pisano, Giovanni [pee**sah**noh] (c. 1250–c. 1320) Sculptor and architect, born in Pisa, Italy, the son of Nicola Pisano. He worked with his father on the pulpit in Siena, the fountain in Perugia, and the facade of Siena Cathedral (1284–6) on which were positioned a number of expressive life-size statues. He also sculpted figures for the entrance to the Baptistery at Pisa (now in the Museo Nazionale), and made a number of free-standing Madonnas, the most famous of which is in the Arena Chapel, Padua. Undoubtedly the greatest sculptor of his day in the Italian Gothic tradition, his innovations pointed the way to Renaissance sculptural ideals. >> **Pisano, Nicola**

Pisano, Nicola [pee**sah**noh] (c. 1225–78/84) Sculptor, architect, and engineer, probably born in Apulia, Italy. His first great work was the sculpted panels for the pulpit in the Baptistery in Pisa, finished in 1260, whose powerful dramatic composition was carved in high relief. He collaborated with his son Giovanni on a pulpit for the cathedral at Siena, and on the Fontana Maggiore in Perugia. Although working in a traditional Gothic style, he studied classical sculpture, and incorporated this into his own work. >> **Pisano, Giovanni**

Piscator, Erwin [pis**kah**ter] (1893–1966) Theatre director, born in Ulm, Germany. He studied at the König School of Dramatic Art, and at the university, becoming first an actor then a director. He was the first to use the term *epic theatre* to describe a theatre composed of short, episodic plays with political ambitions, and pioneered staging techniques using films and mechanical devices. He opened his own theatre in Berlin in 1926. He went to New York City in 1938, where he became head of the Dramatic Department of the New School for Social Research, and in 1962 was appointed director of the West Berlin new Volksbühne Theatre.

Pisistratus [piy**sis**tratus], also spelled **Peisistratos** (c.600–527 BC) Tyrant of Athens (561–c.556 BC, 546–527 BC). A moderate and far-sighted ruler, he did much to improve the lot of the small farmer in Attica, and to boost Athenian trade abroad, especially in the Black Sea area. A patron of the arts, he invited the leading Greek poets of the day to settle in Athens, where he set about fostering a sense of national unity by instituting or expanding great religious and cultural festivals. He was succeeded by his sons Hippias and Hipparchus, the so-called *Pisistratidae*, but the dynasty was overthrown in 510 BC. >> **Anacreon; Harmodius**

Pissarro, Camille [pee**sah**roh] (1830–1903) Impressionist artist, born in St Thomas, Danish West Indies. He went to Paris (1855), where he was much influenced by Corot's landscapes. Most of his works were painted in the countryside round Paris, such as 'Boulevard Montmartre' (1897, National Gallery, London). The leader of the original

Impressionists, he was the only one to exhibit at all eight of the Group exhibitions in Paris from 1874 to 1886. He also experimented with Divisionism. >> Corot; Monet; Pissarro, Lucien

Pissarro, Lucien [peesaroh] (1863–1944) Painter, designer, wood-engraver, and printer, the son of Camille Pissarro. He went to England in 1890, where he founded the Eragny press (1894), designed types, and painted landscapes in the Divisionist manner. >> Pissarro, Camille

Piston, Walter (Hamor) (1894–1976) Composer, born in Rockland, ME. He trained as an artist, and first took a serious interest in music as a student at Harvard. He later studied in Paris under Nadia Boulanger, returning to Harvard as professor of music. He produced textbooks on harmony, counterpoint, and orchestration. His compositions are in a modern, Neoclassical style that includes elements from jazz and popular music. >> Boulanger, Nadia

Pitcairn, Robert (c. 1745–1770) British sailor. He was a midshipman on board the *Swallow* in July 1767 when he was the first to sight the island now named after him. In 1789, Pitcairn I was to become the refuge of the *Bounty* mutineers. >> Christian, Fletcher

Pitman, Benjamin (1822–1910) Educationist and pioneer of shorthand in the USA, born in Trowbridge, Wiltshire, S England, UK, the brother of Sir Isaac Pitman. In 1852 he was sent to the USA by his brother to teach his shorthand system there, and he established the Phonographic Institute in Cincinnati (1853). He invented an electrochemical process of relief engraving (1855), and taught at Cincinnati Art School from 1873. >> Pitman, Isaac

Pitman, Sir Isaac (1813–97) Educationist, and inventor of a shorthand system, born in Trowbridge, Wiltshire, S England, UK. First a clerk, he became a schoolmaster at Barton-on-Humber, and at Wotton-under-Edge, where he issued his *Stenographic Sound Hand* (1837). Dismissed from Wotton because he had joined the New Jerusalem (Swedenborgian) Church, he established a Phonetic Institute for teaching shorthand in Bath (1839). In 1842 he brought out the *Phonetic Journal*, and in 1845 opened premises in London. He was knighted in 1894. >> Pitman, Benjamin; Swedenborg

Pitney, Gene (1941–) Singer and songwriter, born in Hartford, CT. His first hit as a writer came with 'Rubber Ball' (1961), recorded by Bobby Vee. He also wrote 'Hello Mary Lou', a hit for Ricky Nelson in 1961, and one of his most revived songs. Among his hits as a singer were 'I Wanna Love My Life Away' (1961), '24 Hours From Tulsa' (1963), and 'Something's Gotten Hold Of My Heart' (1967).

Pitot, Henri [peetoh] (1695–1771) Hydraulic and civil engineer, born in Aramon, France. He had little formal education, but became laboratory assistant to the great physicist Réaumur in 1723. He developed a particular interest in hydraulic engineering, was appointed superintendent of the Canal du Midi, and constructed an aqueduct for the water supply of Montpellier. In 1730 he invented the device now known as the *Pitot tube*, by means of which the relative velocity of a fluid past the orifice of the tube may be measured. >> Réaumur

Pitt, Thomas (1653–1726) Merchant, born in Blandford St Mary, Dorset, S England, UK. He became a wealthy East India merchant, Governor of Madras, and purchaser of the *Pitt diamond*, which he sold in 1717 to the French regent to become one of the state jewels of France. He was the grandfather of William Pitt, the Elder. >> Pitt, William, Earl of Chatham

Pitt, William, 1st Earl of Chatham, also known as **Pitt the Elder** (1708–78) Statesman and orator, born in London, England, UK. He studied at Oxford, joined the army (1731), then entered Parliament for the family borough of Old Sarum (1735). He led the young 'Patriot' Whigs, and in 1756 became nominally secretary of state, but virtually premier. The king's enmity led him to resign in 1757, but public demand caused his recall. Again compelled to resign when his Cabinet refused to declare war with Spain (1761), he vigorously attacked the peace terms of the Treaty of Paris (1763) as too generous to France. He formed a new ministry in 1766, but ill health contributed to his resignation in 1768. >> Pelham, Thomas; Pitt, Thomas; Pitt, William (the Younger)

Pitt, William, also known as **Pitt the Younger** (1759–1806) British statesman and prime minister (1783–1801, 1804–6), the second son of William Pitt, Earl of Chatham. He studied law at Cambridge, but then became an MP (1781), his first post being Chancellor of the Exchequer under Shelburne (1782). He became First Lord of the Treasury 1783, and accepted the premiership after the collapse of the short-lived Portland government, at the age of 24, to become Britain's youngest prime minister. His first ministry lasted for 18 years, during which he carried through important reforms, his policy being influenced by the political economy of Adam Smith. He negotiated coalitions against France (1793, 1798), but these had little success. After the Irish rebellion of 1798, he proposed a legislative union which would be followed by Catholic emancipation. The union was effected in 1800, but Pitt resigned office in 1801 rather than contest George III's hostility to emancipation. He was persuaded to return to office in 1804, in the face of the mounting Napoleonic threat, formed a coalition with Russia, Austria, and Sweden, and with the defeat of the French at Trafalgar (1805) was hailed as the saviour of Europe. He drank very heavily, and this contributed to his early death while still prime minister. >> Bentinck, 3rd Duke of Portland; Chatham; Pitt, William, Earl of Chatham; Shelburne; Smith, Adam; RR1095

Pittacus of Mytilene [mituhleenee] (650–570 BC) Statesman from ancient Greece, one of the Seven Wise Men of Greece. As a commander in the war against Athens for Sigium, he was distinguished for killing Phrynon single-handedly. His experience, according to the ancients, was embodied in 'know thine opportunity' and other aphorisms.

Pitter, Ruth (1897–1992) Poet, born in Ilford, E Greater London, England, UK. Encouraged by Hilaire Belloc, her work drew mainly upon the beauty of natural things. In 1955 she was awarded the Queen's Gold Medal for Poetry, having already won the Hawthornden Prize in 1936. Her volumes include *First and Second Poems* (1927), *A Mad Lady's Garland* (1934), and *End of Drought* (1975). >> Belloc

Pitt-Rivers, Augustus (Henry Lane-Fox) (1827–1900) British soldier and archaeologist, born at Hope Hall, Yorkshire, N England, UK. He trained at Sandhurst, was a promoter of the Hythe school of musketry, and rose to the rank of lieutenant-general (1882). In 1880, he inherited Wiltshire estates, rich in Romano-British and Saxon remains, from his great-uncle, Lord Rivers, and devoted himself to archaeology, evolving a new scientific approach to excavation which became a model for later workers. He became the first inspector of ancient monuments in 1882.

Pius IV, originally **Giovanni Angelo Medici** (1499–1565) Pope (1559–65), born in Milan, Italy. He became Archbishop of Requsa in 1547, and a cardinal in 1549. He brought to a close the deliberations of the Council of Trent, and issued the Creed of Pius IV (the Tridentine Creed) in 1564. He reformed the sacred college of cardinals, instituted the Index of Forbidden Books, and encouraged St Teresa of Avila. A notable patron of the arts, he built many public buildings and patronized Michelangelo. >> Michelangelo; Teresa of Avila

Pius V, St, originally **Michele Ghislieri** (1504–72) Pope (1566–72), born near Alessandria, Italy. He became a bishop in 1556, and a cardinal in 1557. As pope he implemented the decrees of the Council of Trent (1545–63), excommunicated Elizabeth I (1570), and organized the expedition against the Turks, that resulted in the naval engagement of Lepanto (1571). He was canonized in 1712. Feast day 30 April. >> Elizabeth I

Pius VI, originally **Giovanni Angelo Braschi** (1717–99) Pope (1775–99), born in Cesena, Italy. He became a cardinal in 1773. As pope he failed to restrain the reforming Emperor Joseph from curtailing papal privileges. The confiscation of Church property in France during the French Revolution was followed by the murder of the French agent in Rome (1793), which gave the Directory an excuse to attack Italy. Napoleon took possession of several provinces, which were formally surrendered by Pius in 1797. The murder of a member of the French embassy was then avenged by Berthier's taking possession of Rome. Pius was expelled from Rome, seized by the French (1799), and died soon after. >> Berthier; Napoleon I

Pius VII, originally **Gregorio Barnaba Chiaramonti** (1742–1823) Pope (1800–23), born in Cesena, Italy. He became a cardinal in 1785. He arranged a concordat with Napoleon, and in 1804 was compelled to consecrate him as emperor. In 1809 the French annexed the Papal States. Pius was removed to Grenoble, then to Fontainebleau, and forced to sign a new concordat sanctioning the annexation. The fall of Napoleon (1814) allowed his return to Rome, and papal territory was restored by the Congress of Vienna. >> Napoleon I

Pius IX, known as **Pio Nono**, originally **Giovanni Maria Mastai-Ferretti** (1792–1878) Pope (1846–78), born in Senigallia, Italy. He became Archbishop of Spoleto in 1827, and a cardinal in 1840. He introduced several reforms, but after the 1848 revolutions (during which he was forced to flee from Rome) he became progressively more conservative, and condemned modernism in theology. He decreed the dogma of the Immaculate Conception in 1854, and called the Vatican Council (1869–79), which proclaimed papal infallibility. He refused to recognize the new state of Italy, into which Rome was incorporated in 1870, after which he lived a voluntary 'prisoner' within the Vatican until his death. His pontificate is the longest in papal history.

Pius X, St, originally **Giuseppe Sarto** (1835–1914) Pope (1903–14), born in Riese, Italy. Ordained in 1858, he became Bishop of Mantua (1884), cardinal and patriarch of Venice (1893), and in 1903 was elected pope. He condemned theological modernism and revolutionary movements in his encyclical *Pascendi* (1907), but was a champion of social reforms. He reformed the liturgy, re-codified canon law, and was canonized in 1954. Feast day 21 August.

Pius XI, originally **Ambrogio Damiano Achille Ratti** (1857–1939) Pope (1922–39), born in Desio, Italy. A great linguist and scholar, he was librarian of the Ambrosian (Milan) and Vatican libraries. He became Cardinal Archbishop of Milan in 1921. As pope, he signed the Lateran Treaty (1929), which brought into existence the Vatican State, and made concordats with many countries.

Pius XII, originally **Eugenio Maria Guiseppe Giovanni Pacelli** (1876–1958) Pope (1939–58), born in Rome. Ordained in 1899, he became a papal diplomat, cardinal (1929), and secretary of state to the Holy See. Under his leadership during World War 2 the Vatican did much humanitarian work, notably for prisoners of war and refugees. There has been continuing controversy, however, over his attitude to the treatment of Jews in Nazi Germany, critics arguing that he could have used his influence with Catholic Germany to prevent the massacres, others that any attempt to do so would have proved futile and might have worsened the situation. In the post-war years he was particularly concerned with the plight of persecuted churchmen in Communist countries.

Pivot, Bernard [peevoh] (1935–) French literary critic and broadcaster. Originally a journalist, he became famous as the host of the French television programme *Apostrophes* (1975–90), and the organizer of *Les championnats d'orthographe* spelling contests.

Pizarro, Francisco [peethahroh] (c. 1478–1541) Conquistador, born in Trujillo, Spain. He served in Italy, and with the expedition which discovered the Pacific (1513). In 1526 he and Almagro sailed for Peru, and in 1531 began the conquest of the Incas. He killed the Inca king, Atahualpa, then worked to consolidate the new empire, founding Lima (1535) and other cities. In 1537, dissension with Almagro over the control of Cuzco led to conflict. Too old to take the field himself, Pizarro entrusted the command of his forces to his brothers, who defeated and executed Almagro soon afterwards. In revenge Almagro's followers assassinated Pizarro. >> Almagro; Atahualpa; Orellana; Pizarro, Gonzalo

Pizarro, Gonzalo [peethahroh] (c. 1506–48) Spanish conquistador, born in Trujillo, Spain, the half-brother of Francisco Pizarro. He accompanied him in the conquest of Peru (1531–3), and was made Governor of Quito. In 1539 he undertook an expedition to the E of Quito, and endured fearful hardships and starvation, only 90 out of 350 Spaniards returning with him in 1542. In 1544 the new viceroy, Vela, arrived in Peru to enforce the new laws instigated by the King of Spain. The local Spaniards entreated Pizarro to protect their interests, and he was declared Governor of Peru. He defeated and killed the viceroy in 1546, then Pedro de la Gasca was sent to Peru to restore order. Pizarro defeated a force sent against him, and met Gasca near Cuzco (1548), but his forces deserted him, and he was beheaded. >> Pizarro, Francisco

Pizzetti, Ildebrando [pitsetee] (1880–1968) Composer, born in Parma, Italy. He studied at Parma Conservatory, and in 1908 became professor at the Instituto Musicale, Florence. He was director there from 1917 until 1924, when he became director of the Giuseppe Verdi Conservatory, Milan. He composed extensively in all forms, winning a particular reputation for opera with *Fedra* (1912) and *Debora e Jaele* (1923). In 1936 he became professor at the Accademia di Sancta Cecilia, Rome.

Pizzey, Erin Patria Margaret >> **Shapiro, Erin Patria Margaret**

Plaatje, Sol(omon Tshekisho) [pliykee] (1879–1932) Writer and South African political figure, born in Boshof, South Africa. He was a versatile intellectual and politician, an author, journalist, linguist, and polemicist. Proficient in at least eight languages, he established the first Tswana-language newspaper, published collections of Tswana proverbs, translated four Shakespeare plays into Tswana, and wrote a novel, *Mhudi* (1930). He is perhaps best remembered for his graphic *Native Life in South Africa* (1916), a moving appeal against the 1913 Land Act. He was a founder member of the African National Congress, and that body's first secretary-general.

Plaidy, Jean >> **Hibbert**

Planchon, Roger [plãshõ] (1931–) Theatre director, playwright, and actor, born in the Ardèche, France. He founded a theatre company in a disused printing works in Lyon in 1952, moving to the Théâtre de la Cité in Villeurbanne in 1957. His company was the recipient of the title, subsidy, and touring obligations of the Théâtre National Populaire in 1972.

Planck, Max (Karl Ernst Ludwig) (1858–1947) Theoretical physicist, born in Kiel, Germany. He studied at Munich and

Berlin, where he became professor of theoretical physics (1889–1926). His work on the law of thermodynamics and black body radiation led him to abandon classical Newtonian principles and introduce the quantum theory (1900), for which he was awarded the Nobel Prize for Physics in 1918. Several research institutes now carry his name. >> Stefan; Wien

Planté, Gaston [plãtay] (1834–89) Physicist, born in Orthy, France. A lecture assistant in physics at the Conservatoire des Arts et Métiers (1854), he became professor at the Association Polytechnique pour le Développement de l'Instruction Populaire in Paris from 1860. His experiments, begun in 1859, led to the production of a battery which could store electrical energy, and which was later improved and widely used in cars.

Plantin, Christophe [plãtĩ] (c. 1520–89) Printer, and publisher of the Antwerp Polyglot Bible, born in St Avertin, France. He settled as a bookbinder in Antwerp (1549), and six years later took up printing. His *Biblia Polyglotta* (1569–73), Latin, Hebrew and Dutch Bibles, and editions of the classics are all famous. His printing-houses in Antwerp, Leyden, and Paris were carried on by his sons-in-law, and his office in Antwerp, bought by the city in 1876, is now the Musée Plantin.

Plantinga, Alvin (1932–) Philosopher of religion, born in Ann Arbor, MI. A professor at Calvin College, Grand Rapids (1963–82) and the University of Notre Dame, IN (1982–), his works include *God, Freedom and Evil* (1974) and *Does God have a Nature?* (1980). He argues that God's existence is no less probable than our own, that it can be supported by the ontological argument, and that belief in His goodness is tenable despite the fact of evil.

Plaskett, John Stanley (1865–1941) Astronomer, born in Woodstock, Ontario, Canada. At the Dominion Observatory, Ottawa, his work included research in spectroscopy and improvements in the design of the spectrograph. In 1918 the Dominion astrophysical observatory was built at Victoria to accommodate a huge telescope with a 72-in reflector which he had designed. Director there until 1935, he discovered the largest known star, which was named after him.

Plateau, Joseph Antoine Ferdinand [platoh] (1801–83) Physicist, born in Brussels. He was professor of physics at Ghent from 1835. In his study of optics he damaged his eyesight by looking into the Sun for 20 seconds in order to find out the effect on the eye. By 1840 he was blind but, with help, continued his scientific work. He was the discoverer of the tiny second drop, named after him, which always follows the main drop of a liquid falling from a surface.

Plater, Alan (Frederick) [playter] (1935–) Playwright, born in Jarrow-on-Tyne, Tyne and Wear, NE England, UK. Trained as an architect, his writing was first published in *Punch* (1958). He became a regular writer for *Z Cars* (1963–5), *Softly Softly* (1966–76), and other television series. His television plays include *Close the Coalhouse Door* (1968) and *The Land of Green Ginger* (1974). His screenplays include the film *The Virgin and the Gypsy* (1969) and *It Shouldn't Happen to a Vet* (1974), and the television adaptations *The Barchester Chronicles* (1981) and *Fortunes of War* (1987). Among plays written for the theatre are a jazz musical *Rent Party* (1989) and *I Thought I Heard a Rustling* (1991). He has also written novels, notably *The Beiderbecke Affair* (1985), *The Beiderbecke Tapes* (1986), and *The Beiderbecke Connection* (1992), based on his television series.

Plath, Sylvia (1932–63) Poet, born in Boston, MA. Driven by a desire to write, she won a Fulbright Fellowship to Newnham College, Cambridge, in 1956, where she studied English, and met and married Ted Hughes. After some time spent teaching in the USA, they settled in England,

first in London, then in Devon, but separated in 1962. Her severe depressions drove her to suicide. Often termed a 'confessional poet', her earlier, highly controlled work gave way to a poetry of visionary expression and personal intensity, which has since come to be highly regarded. Her collections include *A Winter Ship* (1960), which was published anonymously, *The Colossus* (1960) and, posthumously, *Ariel* (1965), and *Winter Trees* (1972). Her collected poems were edited by Ted Hughes in 1981. Her only novel, *The Bell Jar* (1963), was published under the pseudonym **Victoria Lucas** just before her death. >> Hughes, Ted; Sexton, Ann

Platière, Jean Marie Roland de la >> **Roland de la Platière, Jean Marie**

Plato see panel on p. 749

Platt, David (Andrew) (1966–) Footballer, born in Chadderton, Greater Manchester, NW England, UK. A midfielder, he played for Crewe Alexandra, Aston Villa, Bari, Juventus, and Sampdoria, before moving to Arsenal in 1995. A former England captain (1994–6), by early 1997 he had won 62 caps for England. He was the Professional Footballers' Association Player of the Year in 1990.

Plautus, Titus Maccius [plawtus] (c. 250–184 BC) Comic playwright, born in Sarsina, Italy. He worked in the theatre, then in foreign trade, before beginning to write plays (c.224 BC). About 130 plays have been attributed to him, but many are thought to be the work of earlier playwrights which he revised. Varro limited the geniune comedies to 21, and these 'Varronian comedies' are the ones which have survived. Extremely popular, and still being performed five centuries later, the plays are full of robust life and vigorous dialogue, and influenced many other playwrights, such as Shakespeare and Molière. >> Varro, Marcus Terentius

Player, Gary (Jim) (1935–) Golfer, born in Johannesburg, South Africa. He is one of only four golfers to win each of the four Grand Slam events. His first major success was the 1959 (British) Open, a title he also won in 1968 and 1974. He was the first non-American for 45 years to win the US Open (1965), and the first to win the US Professional Golfers Association title (1962, regained 1972) and the US Masters (1961, regained 1974, 1978). He won the South African Open 12 times, and the world match-play title a record five times. He now breeds horses in South Africa, and is a leading member of the US Seniors Tour. >> RR1157

Playfair, John (1748–1819) Mathematician and geologist, born in Benvie, Dundee, E Scotland, UK. He studied at St Andrews University, became joint professor of mathematics at Edinburgh (1785), and professor of natural philosophy (1805). He wrote an important textbook on geometry, and also investigated glaciation and the formation of river valleys. >> Playfair, William Henry

Playfair, William Henry (1789–1857) Architect, born in London, England, UK, the nephew of John Playfair. He was brought up in Edinburgh, and designed many of Edinburgh's most prominent buildings, including the National Gallery of Scotland, the Royal Scottish Academy, the National Monument on the Calton Hill, Surgeon's Hall, and Donaldson's Hospital. >> Playfair, John

Playford, Sir Thomas (1896–1981) Australian politician, born at Norton Summit, South Australia. He served with the Australian Imperial Forces during World War 1 at Gallipoli and in France. In 1933 he was elected to the South Australian House of Assembly, entering the ministry in 1938 and becoming premier of South Australia the same year. He remained premier until 1965, and was knighted in 1957.

Pleasence, Sir Donald [plezuhns] (1919–95) Actor, born in Worksop, Nottinghamshire, C England, UK. He made his

PLATO (c. 428–347 B C)

Plato was born, probably in Athens, into a distinguished and wealthy aristocratic family, the son of Ariston and Perictione. Little is known of his early life. Any youthful political ambitions must have withered as he witnessed the decline of imperial Athens after the death of the statesman Pericles in 428 BC; the excesses of the conservative faction, with which he had family connections; the ensuing civil strife, and the equally punitive reaction of the restored democracy, which condemned to death his great friend and mentor, Socrates, in 399 BC. Plato immortalized the story of Socrates' trial and last days in three of his dialogues: the *Apology*, the *Crito*, and the *Phaedo*, where his profound affection and respect for Socrates come through vividly.

After the 'execution' of Socrates, he and other followers took temporary refuge at Megara with the philosopher Euclides, and he then travelled widely in Greece, Egypt, the Greek cities in Italy (where he no doubt encountered Pythagoreans), and Sicily (where he made friends with Dion, brother-in-law of Dionysus I, the ruler of Syracuse). He returned to Athens in c.387 BC and founded the Academy, which became a famous centre for philosophical, mathematical, and scientific research, and over which he presided for the rest of his life. He visited Sicily again in 367 BC, at Dion's request, with the intention of training Dionysus II to become a philosopher-statesman, but despite a second visit in 361–60 BC, which placed him in some personal danger, the attempt failed completely.

Plato's writings consist of some 30 philosophical dialogues and a series of *Letters*, of which the Seventh is the most important (biographically and philosophically), and only the Seventh and Eighth are likely to be genuine. The dialogues are conventionally divided into three groups: early, middle, and late – though the exact relative chronology of individual dialogues is a vexed and probably insoluble problem of scholarship.

The early 'Socratic' dialogues have Socrates as the principal character, usually portrayed interrogating his unfortunate interlocutors about the definition of different moral virtues (eg piety in the *Euthyphro*, and courage in the *Laches*). Their initially confident assertions are shown to be confused and contradictory, and all parties end up sharing Socrates' professed perplexity.

The middle dialogues show the character 'Socrates' expressing more positive, systematic views, which are usually taken to be Plato's own. This group includes the most dramatic and literary of the dialogues, the *Symposium*, *Gorgias*, *Phaedo*, and *Republic*, and presents such famous Platonic doctrines as the theory of knowledge as recollection; the immortality of the soul; the tripartite division of the soul, and above all the theory of *forms* (or ideas). This contrasts the transient material world of *particulars* (objects merely of perception, opinion, and belief) with the timeless unchanging world of *forms* (the true objects of knowledge). The *Republic* also describes Plato's celebrated political utopia, ruled by philosopher-kings who have mastered the discipline of *dialectic* and studied the hierarchy of the forms, including its apex: the form of the Good. The details of this visionary state: the rigid class structure of workers, soldiers, and rulers; the education of the rulers (both men and women); common ownership of property; allegiance to the state overruling that to family; the totalitarian powers of the state – all these have been variously idealized, attacked, misinterpreted, and imitated in subsequent political theory and literature. Nonetheless, the *Republic* remains one of the most compelling and influential works in the history of philosophy.

The third group of 'late' dialogues is generally less literary in form, and represents a series of sustained and highly sophisticated criticisms of the metaphysical and logical assumptions of Plato's doctrines of the middle period. The *Parmenides*, *Theaetetus*, and *Sophist* in particular have attracted the interest of contemporary analytical philosophers, and contain some of Plato's most demanding and original work. Taken as a whole, his philosophy has had a pervasive and incalculable influence on almost every period and tradition, rivalled only by that of his greatest pupil, Aristotle.
>> Aristotle; Socrates

---

first appearance in Jersey in 1939, served in the RAF during World War 2, and returned to the stage in 1946. He worked at various repertory theatres, including Birmingham and the Bristol Old Vic, but scored a huge success as the malevolent tramp, Davies, in Harold Pinter's *The Caretaker* (1960). From the 1960s, his London stage appearances were rare, but he made many TV appearances, including *The Barchester Chronicles* (1982), and was in constant demand for film work, often as a villain, as in *Dr Crippen* (1962), *Cul-de-Sac* (1966), and many others, known for his piercing stare, menacing voice, and bald head. He was knighted in 1994.

Plekhanov, Georgiy Valentinovich [plekahnof] (1856–1918) Marxist philosopher, historian, and journalist, 'the father of Russian Marxism', born in Gundalovka, Russia. He left Russia in 1880, and in 1883 founded the first Russian Marxist group (the Liberation Labour Group) in Geneva, where he remained until 1917. He was a major intellectual influence on the young Lenin, but sided with the Mensheviks against Lenin's Bolsheviks, and denounced the October Revolution. >> Lenin

Plessner, Helmuth (1892–) Philosopher and social theorist, born in Wiesbaden, Germany. He studied zoology, medicine, and philosophy at Freiburg, Heidelberg, and Berlin. He was professor at Cologne (1926–34), then moved to Groningen in Holland to escape the Nazis, but was expelled from there in 1942. He returned to Groningen in 1946, and moved to Göttingen in 1951. He helped found the new discipline of 'philosophical anthropology', as expounded in such works as *Die Einheit der Sinne* (1923, The Unity of the Senses), and also wrote on social philosophy and the origins of Fascism. >> Scheler

Pleydell-Bouverie, Katherine [playdl booveree] (1895–1985) British potter. She studied at the Central School of Arts and Crafts, London, then with Bernard Leach at St Ives, Cornwall. She established a pottery in Wiltshire, producing domestic wares in stoneware, experimenting with wood and vegetable ash glazes. In 1946 she established an oil-fired kiln in Kilmington Manor near Warminster, where her output consisted of a series of unique small works often decorated with vertical ribbing. >> Leach, Bernard

Plimsoll, Samuel (1824–98) Social reformer, known as 'the sailors' friend', born in Bristol, SW England, UK. He became an MP in 1868, and having accumulated a large file on the unseaworthiness of ships, caused the Merchant Shipping Act (1876) to be passed. Every owner was ordered to mark upon the side of a ship a circular disc, with a horizontal line drawn through its centre (the *Plimsoll line*), down to which the vessel might be loaded. This convention was legally enforced in 1894.

Pliny (the Elder), in full **Gaius Plinius Secundus** (23–79) Roman scholar, born in Novum Comum (now Como), Gaul. He studied at Rome, served in the army in Germany, and later settled in Como, where he devoted himself to study and writing. Nero appointed him procurator in Spain, and through his brother-in-law's death (71) he became guardian of his nephew Pliny (the Younger), whom he adopted. He continued his studies, and wrote a 37-volume encyclopedia, the *Historia naturalis* (77, Natural History), his only work to survive. In 79 he was in command of the Roman fleet when the great eruption of Vesuvius was at its height. He landed at Stabiae (Castellamare), to observe more closely, and was killed by volcanic fumes. >> Pliny (the Younger)

Pliny (the Younger), in full **Gaius Plinius Caecilius Secundus** (c. 62–c. 114) Roman writer and administrator, born in Novum Comum (now Como), Gaul, the nephew and adopted son of Pliny the Elder. He became a lawyer and a highly proficient orator, much in demand. He served as a military tribune in Syria, and progressed to be quaestor, praetor, and (100) consul, holding several posts throughout the empire. He was the master of epistolary style, his many letters providing an insight into the life of the upper class in the 1st-c. >> Pliny (the Elder)

Plisetskaya, Maya (Mikhaylovna) [plisetskiya] (1925–) Ballerina, born in Moscow. The niece of Asaf Messerer, she trained at the Bolshoi school, and was made a principal immediately on joining the company in 1943. Celebrated for her classical roles, she came to represent the epitome of the Bolshoi style. Best known for the role Alberto Alonso created for her in *Carmen Suite* (1967), she also danced in Roland Petit's company in *La Rose malade* (1973), and in Maurice Béjart's company in 1979. >> Béjart; Messerer; Petit, Roland

Plomer, William (Charles Franklyn) [pluhmer] (1903–73) Writer, born in Pietersburg, South Africa. He studied at Rugby, farmed and traded in South Africa, and with Laurens van der Post and Roy Campbell started the magazine, *Voorslag* ('Whiplash'), which attacked racism in South Africa. The magazine was soon silenced, and he left the country. He lived in Greece and Japan before returning to England, where during World War 2 he served at the Admiralty. A senior editor with Jonathan Cape, his own works include the novels *Turbott Wolfe* (1926), *Sado* (1931), and *Ali the Lion* (1936), collections of short stories *I Speak of Africa* (1928) and *Paper Houses* (1929), and *Collected Poems* (1960). >> Campbell, Roy; van der Post

Plotinus [plotiynus] (c. 205–70) Philosopher, the founder of Neoplatonism, probably born in Lycopolis, Egypt. He studied in Alexandria and Persia, and settled in Rome (244), where he became a popular lecturer, advocating asceticism and the contemplative life. When 60, he attempted to found a platonic 'Republic' in Campania, but died in Minturnae. His 54 works were edited by his pupil, Porphyry, who arranged them in six groups of nine books, or *Enneads*. He greatly influenced early Christian theology. >> Porphyry

Plowden, Bridget Hortia, Lady, *née* **Richmond** (1907–) British educationist. She was educated at Downe House, and in 1933 married **Edwin Noel Plowden** (1907–), who was created Baron Plowden in 1959. The first woman to chair the Central Advisory Council for Education (1963–6), she also chaired the Independent Broadcasting Authority (1975–80) and the Training Commission (1983–8). Her government report, *Children and their Primary Schools* (1967), argued that education must be concerned with the whole family, and that increased resources were needed for nursery education and for areas starved of new investment. The *Plowden Report* marked a watershed in the development of English primary education.

Plowright, Joan (1929–) Actress, born in Brigg, Lincolnshire, EC England, UK. Trained at the Laban Art of Movement Studio, Manchester, and the Old Vic Theatre School, she became a member of the English Stage Company at the Royal Court Theatre, London, in 1956. There she played opposite Laurence Olivier, whom she married in 1961. She played Jean Rice in Osborne's *The Entertainer* (1957) and Beattie in Arnold Wesker's *Roots* (1959), and in 1963 joined the National Theatre in its first season. A formidably talented classical actress, she has also appeared on television and in films, including *The Entertainer* (1960), *The Dressmaker* (1988), *Avalon* (1991), *Enchanted April* (1993, Golden Globe), and *Picasso* (1995). She has also worked as a stage producer and director. >> Olivier

Plücker, Julius [plüker] (1801–68) Mathematician and physicist, born in Eberfeld, Germany. He studied at Heidelberg, Berlin, and Paris, and held professorships at Halle and Bonn. He investigated diamagnetism, originated the idea of spectrum analysis, and in 1859 discovered cathode rays, produced by electrical discharges in gases at low pressures. His mathematical work was concerned with line geometry and algebraic curves.

Plume, Thomas (1630–1704) Theologian, born in Maldon, Essex, SE England, UK. He studied at Cambridge, and became vicar of Greenwich from 1658, and archdeacon of Rochester from 1679. He endowed an observatory and the Plumian chair of astronomy and experimental philosophy at Cambridge, and bequeathed his extensive library to the town of Maldon, where it still exists intact.

Plumer, Herbert Charles Onslow (1857–1932) British soldier and colonial administrator. He served in Sudan (1884) and led the Rhodesian relief force to Mafeking (1900). In World War 1 he distinguished himself as commander of the 2nd Army of the British Expeditionary Force (1915–18), notably at the great attack on Messines, and was also in command of the Italian Expeditionary Force (1917–18). He was made a field marshal in 1919, and became Governor of Malta (1919–24) and high commissioner for Palestine (1925–8).

Plutarch [plootah(r)k], Gr **Ploutarchos** (c. 46–c. 120) Historian, biographer, and philosopher, born in Chaeronea, Boeotia, Greece. He studied in Athens and made several visits to Rome, where he gave public lectures in philosophy. His extant writings comprise *Opera moralia*, a series of essays on ethical, political, religious, and other topics, and several historical works, notably *Bioi paralleloi* (Parallel Lives), a gallery of 46 portraits of the great characters of preceding ages, each book consisting of a Greek and a Roman figure, sharing some resemblance. North's translation of his work into English (1579) was the source of Shakespeare's Roman plays. >> North, Thomas

Pocahontas [pohkahontas], personal name **Matoaka** (1595–1617) American-Indian princess, born near Jamestown, VA, the daughter of Powhatan. An American folk heroine, she helped maintain peace between the colonists and Indians, and saved the life of English adventurer John Smith when he was at the mercy of her tribe. In 1612 she embraced Christianity and was baptized **Rebecca**. The following year she married **John Rolfe** (1585–1622), and in

1616 came with him to England, where she was received by royalty. She died of smallpox. >> Powhatan; Smith, John

Podgorniy, Nikolay Victorovich [pod**gaw(r)**nee] (1903–) Soviet statesman, party official, and chairman of the Presidium of the Supreme Soviet (1965–77), born in Karlovka, Ukraine. In 1930 he joined the Communist Party, and after World War 2 took a leading role in the economic reconstruction of the liberated Ukraine. He held various senior posts (1950–65), and after the dismissal of Khrushchev (1964) became chairman of the Presidium. He was relieved of his office in 1977 and replaced by Brezhnev, since when he has lived in retirement. >> Brezhnev; Khrushchev

Poe, Edgar Allan (1809–49) Poet and story writer, born in Boston, MA. Orphaned by the age of three, he was adopted by John Allan (1815–20) and brought up partly in England, UK. He began to write poetry, publishing *Tamerlane and other Poems* in 1827. He became a journalist in Richmond, VA, then settled in Philadelphia, PA, where he worked for literary magazines. He published *Tales of the Grotesque and Arabesque* in 1840, and several short stories, notably 'The Murders in the Rue Morgue' (1841), the first detective story. His weird and fantastic stories, dwelling by choice on the horrible, were both original and influential. In 1844 he moved to New York City, where his poem 'The Raven' (1845) won him immediate fame. His wife died in 1847, after which he wrote little. He became mentally disturbed, and attempted suicide in 1848.

Poelzig, Hans [**poel**tsikh] (1869–1936) Expressionist architect, born in Berlin. He joined the Prussian ministry of works in 1899, becoming professor of architecture at the Academy of Arts in Breslau in 1900 (subsequently director). Between 1916 and 1920 he served as city architect of Dresden. Later works include the fine Expressionistic remodelling of the Grosses Schauspielhaus, Berlin (1919).

Poggio (Bracciolini), Giovanni Francesco [**po**jioh] (1380–1459) Florentine humanist, born in Terranuova, Italy. His research took him to many European libraries, where he recovered the manuscripts of several Classical Latin writers. In 1453 he retired to Florence, and became chancellor and historiographer to the republic. His writings include letters, moral essays, invectives, and most notably the *Liber facetiarum*, a collection of humorous stories, mainly against monks and secular clergy.

Pohl, Frederik (1919–) Science-fiction writer, born in New York City. In 1938 he became a founder-member of a group of left-wing science fiction writers known as the Futurists. He served in the air force in World War 2, worked as a literary agent, and edited various science fiction magazines (1953–69). He describes his own multifarious books as 'cautionary literature', seeing science fiction as a kind of alarm signal. His vast output of novels, stories, and anthologies includes *The Space Merchants* (1953) and *Gladiator-at-Law* (1955).

Poincaré, (Jules) Henri [pwīkaray] (1854–1912) Mathematician, born in Nancy, France, the cousin of Raymond Poincaré. He studied at Paris, where he became professor in 1881. He was eminent in physics, mechanics, and astronomy, and contributed to many fields of mathematics. He created the theory of automorphic functions, using new ideas from group theory, non-Euclidean geometry, and complex function theory. The origins of the theory of chaos are in a famous paper of 1889 on real differential equations and celestial mechanics. Many of the basic ideas in modern topology, triangulation, and homology are due to him. He gave influential lecture courses on such topics as thermodynamics, and almost anticipated Einsteins's theory of special relativity, showing that the Lorentz transformations

form a group. In his last years he published several books on the philosophy of science and scientific method, and was also well known for his popular expositions of science. >> Einstein; Lorentz; Poincaré, Raymond

Poincaré, Raymond (Nicolas Landry) [pwīkaray] (1860–1934) French statesman, prime minister (1912–13, 1922–4, 1926–9), and president (1913–20), born in Bar-le-Duc, France. He studied law, then became a deputy (1887) and senator (1903), held ministerial posts in public instruction, foreign affairs, and finance, was three times premier, and president of the Third Republic during World War 1. He occupied the Ruhr in 1923, and his national union ministry averted ruin in 1926. >> Poincaré, Henri; RR1049

Poindexter, John (Marlan) [**poyn**dekster] (1936–) US naval officer and statesman, born in Washington, IN. He studied at the US Naval Academy and the California Institute of Technology, and became chief of naval operations during the 1970s. In 1981 he joined President Reagan's National Security Council, becoming National Security Adviser in 1985. He resigned the following year, together with his assistant, Oliver North, in the aftermath of the 'Irangate' scandal. Retiring from the navy as a rear-admiral in 1987, he was convicted in 1990 by a Federal court on charges of conspiracy, obstructing Congressional inquiries, and lying to Congress. >> North, Oliver; Reagan

Poiré, Emmanuel >> **Caran d'Ache**

Poiret, Paul [pwaray] (1879–1944) Fashion designer, born in Paris. The son of a cloth merchant, he started to make sketches and sell them, eventually joining Jacques Doucet in 1896, and later Worth. In 1904 he set up on his own. He loosened and softened women's clothes, producing a more natural outline; his 'hobble' skirt became famous. In 1914 he was the first president of Le Syndicat de Défence de la Grande Couture Française, formed to protect the copyright of couturiers. >> Worth

Poisson, Siméon Denis [pwasō] (1781–1840) Mathematician, born in Pithiviers, France. He studied medicine, then turned to mathematics, studying under Laplace and Lagrange, and became professor at the Ecole Polytechnique in 1806. He is known for his research into celestial mechanics, electromagnetism, and also probability, where he established the law governing the distribution of rare and randomly occurring events (the *Poisson distribution*). >> Lagrange; Laplace

Poitier, Sidney [**pwa**tyay] (1924–) Actor and director, born in Miami, FL. A student at the American Negro Theater in New York City, he appeared on stage and in films before making his Hollywood debut in 1950. Cast mainly in supporting roles, he won an Oscar for *Lilies of the Field* (1963), and became the cinema's first African-American superstar. Handsome and unassuming, he brought dignity to the portrayal of noble and intelligent characters in such films as *In the Heat of the Night* (1967) and *Guess Who's Coming to Dinner* (1967). During the 1970s he also began to direct, producing a number of lowbrow comedies such as *Stir Crazy* (1980) and *Ghost Dad* (1990). He returned to acting after a 10-year absence, appearing in *Shoot to Kill* (1988), *Little Nikita* (1988), *Sneakers* (1992), and *One Man, One Vote* (1997).

Polano, Fra / Pietro Soave >> **Sarpi, Pietro**

Polanski, Roman [po**lan**skee] (1933–) Polish film-maker, born in Paris. An actor on radio and in the theatre, he attended the State Film School in Łódź (1954–9), making a number of short films. His feature-length debut, *Nóz w Wodzie* (1962, Knife in the Water), brought him international recognition, and he later worked in London, Paris and Los Angeles on such films as *Repulsion* (1965), *Rosemary's Baby* (1968), *Tess* (1979), *Frantic* (1988), and *Bitter Moon* (1992). A traumatic life that includes his internment in a German concentration camp, where his mother died, and the horrifying murder of his second wife, actress **Sharon Tate** (1943–69), has been reflected in his artistic concern with alienation, and the understanding of evil. On stage, he has directed *Lulu* (1974) and *Rigoletto* (1976) and acted in *Amadeus* (1981) and *Metamorphosis* (1988). >> Manson, Charles

Polanyi, Michael [po**lan**yee] (1891–1976) Physical chemist and social philosopher, born in Budapest. He studied there and at Karlsruhe, lectured at Berlin, emigrated to Britain after Hitler's rise to power, and was professor of physical chemistry (1933–48) and of social studies (1948–58) at Manchester. He did notable work on reaction kinetics and crystal structure, and wrote much on the freedom of scientific thought, philosophy of science, and social science.

Polding, John Bede [**pohl**ding] (1794–1877) First Roman Catholic bishop of Australia, born in Liverpool, Merseyside, NW England, UK. Ordained in 1819, he arrived in Sydney in 1835 and consecrated St Mary's as his cathedral in the following year. In 1842 he was made Archbishop of Sydney and Metropolitan of Australia, positions he was to hold until his retirement in 1875. He oversaw the growth of the Catholic Church in Australia into 12 dioceses, under a strong central administration.

Pole, Reginald, Cardinal (1500–58) Roman Catholic archbishop, born in Stourton Castle, Staffordshire, C England, UK. He studied at Oxford and Padua, received several Church posts, and was at first high in Henry VIII's favour; but after opposing the king on divorce, he left for Italy, and lost all his preferments. In 1536 the pope made him a cardinal, and he served on a commision that looked at abuses within the Church, recommending reforms in *Consilium de emendanda ecclesia* (1537, Plan for Church Reform). In 1554, in the reign of Mary I, he returned to England as papal legate. He became one of her most powerful advisers, returned the country to Rome, and became Archbishop of Canterbury. >> Henry VIII; Mary I

Poliakoff, Stephen [**pol**yakof] (1952–) Playwright and film director, born in London, England, UK. He studied at Cambridge, and started to write plays as a teenager. A run of his plays produced by the Bush Theatre, including *Hitting Town* and *City Sugar* (both 1975) established him as a prolific, original playwright with an instinct for powerful contemporary metaphors. He was writer-in-residence at the National Theatre (1976–7), and had several plays produced by the Royal Shakespeare Company, including *Shout Across the River* (1978), *Breaking the Silence* (1984), and *Playing with Trains* (1989). Later plays include *Sienna Red* (1992) and *Blinded by the Sun* (1996), and he wrote and directed the film *Close My Eyes* (1991).

Polignac, Auguste Jules Armand Marie, prince de [poleenyak] (1780–1847) French statesman, born in Versailles, France. Arrested for conspiring against Napoleon (1804), he became a peer at the Bourbon Restoration. A committed exponent of papal and royal authority, he received the title of prince from the pope in 1820. English ambassador in 1823, he became in 1829 head of the last Bourbon ministry, which promulgated the St Cloud Ordinances that cost Charles X his throne (1830). He was imprisoned until 1836, then lived in exile in England, returning in 1845 to Paris. >> Charles X

Politian [po**li**shan], originally **Angelo Ambrogini** (1454–94) Humanist, scholar, and poet, born in Montepulciano, Italy. By 17 he had begun the translation of the *Iliad* into Latin hexameters, and through the friendship of Lorenzo de' Medici (whose sons he taught) he was soon recognized as the leading Italian scholar. Appointed canon of Florence in 1480, he became professor of Greek and Latin at Florence (1482–6). Among his works are Latin translations of a long series of Greek authors, an edition of the *Pandects* of Justinian, and *Orfeo* (1480), the first secular drama in Italian. >> Lorenzo de' Medici

Polk, James K(nox) (1795–1849) US statesman and 11th president (1845–9), born in Mecklenburg Co, NC. Admitted to the bar in 1820, he entered Congress as a Democrat (1825), and became Governor of Tennessee (1839). During his presidency, Texas was admitted to the Union (1845), and after the Mexican War (1846–7) the USA acquired California and New Mexico. The Oregon boundary was settled by a compromise with England. He also condemned the anti-slavery agitation, and was committed to states' rights, a revenue tariff, and an independent treasury. >> Polk, Leonidas; RR1097

Polk, Leonidas (1806–64) US soldier and bishop, born in Raleigh, NC, a cousin of James K Polk. He trained at West Point, and held a commission in the artillery. He was ordained in the Protestant Episcopal Church (1831), consecrated Bishop of Arkansas (1838), and from 1841 until his death was Bishop of Louisiana. He founded the University of the South in 1860. A major-general in the Civil War (1861–5), he forced Grant to retire at Belmont (1861), fought at Shiloh and Corinth, and conducted the retreat from Kentucky. After Chickamauga, where he commanded the right wing, he was relieved of his command. Reappointed in 1863, he was fatally wounded at Pine Mountain. >> Grant, Ulysses S; Polk, James K

Pollack, Sydney (1934–) Film director and producer, born in South Bend, IN. He began as an actor, moved to television directing, and made his debut as a feature film director with *Slender Thread* (1965). His films include *They Shoot Horses Don't They?* (1969) and *Sabrina* (1995), and he received an Oscar nomination for Best Director in 1982 for *Tootsie*, and won two Oscars (as Best Director and Best Producer) in 1985 for *Out of Africa*.

Pollaiuolo, Antonio [poliy**wo**loh] (c. 1432–98) Goldsmith, medallist, metal-caster, and painter, born in Florence, Italy. He cast sepulchral monuments in St Peter's in Rome for Popes Sixtus IV and Innocent VIII. One of the first painters to study anatomy and apply it to his art, he was skilled in suggesting movement. His brother **Piero** (1443–96) was associated with him in his work.

Pollard, Albert Frederick (1869–1948) Historian, born in Ryde, Isle of Wight, S England, UK. He studied at Oxford, and became a fellow of All Souls College (1908–36). He was assistant editor of *The Dictionary of National Biography*, and later professor of Constitutional History at London University (1903–31), founding in 1920 its Institute of Historical Research. Among his many historical works are lives of Henry VIII (1902), Thomas Cranmer (1904), and Wolsey (1929), and *Factors in American History* (1925). He founded the Historical Association in 1906, and was editor of *History* (1916–22).

Pollard, Alfred William (1859–1944) Scholar and bibliographer, born in London, England, UK. He studied at Oxford, and became an assistant at the British Museum (from 1883), and keeper (1919–24). He was reader in bibliography at Cambridge (1915–19), and professor at King's College, London (1919–32). An authority on Chaucer and Shakespeare, his work included *A Chaucer Primer* (1893) and *Shakespeare's Fight with the Pirates* (1917). He was largely responsible for the *Short Title Catalogue of Books Printed in England, Scotland and Ireland 1475–1640* (1926).

Pollio, Gaius Asinius [po**li**oh] (76 BC–AD 4) Roman orator, poet, and soldier. In the Civil War against Pompey he sided with Caesar. In 39 BC he commanded in Spain, and was appointed by Marcus Antonius to settle the veterans on the lands assigned them, saving Virgil's property from confiscation. He founded the first public library in Rome, and was the patron of Virgil and Horace. His orations, tragedies, and history of the civil wars have perished save for a few fragments. >> Antonius; Caesar; Horace; Virgil

Pollitt, Harry (1890–1960) Communist politician, born in Droylesden, Lancashire, NW England, UK. He worked in a cotton mill at 12 and joined the Independent Labour Party at 16. He was secretary of the National Minority Movement (1924–9), secretary of the Communist Party of Great Britain (1929–56), and its chairman thereafter. A stormy demagogue, he was imprisoned for seditious libel in 1925, and deported from Belfast in 1933. During the Spanish Civil War he helped to found the British battalion of the International Brigade.

Pollock, (Paul) Jackson (1912–56) Artist, born in Cody, WY. He studied at the Art Students' League in New York City, and became the first exponent of Action Painting in America. His art developed from Surrealism to abstract art and the first drip paintings of 1947. This technique he continued with increasing violence and often on huge canvases, as in *One*, which is 17 ft long. Other striking works include *No. 32*, and the black and white *Echo and Blue Poles*. He was killed in a motor accident.

Polo, Marco (1254–1324) Merchant and traveller, born in Venice, Italy. After a previous visit to Kublai Khan in China (1260–9), his father and uncle made a second journey (1271–5), taking Marco with them. He became an envoy in Kublai Khan's service, and served as Governor of Yangzhou. He left China in 1292, returned to Venice (1295), and fought against the Genoese, but was captured. During his imprisonment, he compiled an account of his travels, *Il milione* (trans The Travels of Marco Polo), which became widely read. >> Kublai Khan

Pol Pot [pol **pot**], also called **Saloth Sar** (1926–   ) Cambodian politician and prime minister (1976–9), born in Kompong Thom Province, Cambodia. He was active in the anti-French resistance under Ho Chi-Minh, and in 1964 joined the pro-Chinese Communist Party. He then studied in Paris (1949–53), worked as a teacher (1954–63), and became leader of the Khmer Rouge guerrillas, defeating Lon Nol's military goverment in 1976. As prime minister, he set up a totalitarian regime which caused the death, imprisonment, or exile of millions. Overthrown in 1979, when the Vietnamese invaded Cambodia, he withdrew to the mountains to lead the Khmer Rouge forces. He announced his retirement in 1985, but continued to be an influential figure within the movement. In 1997 he was captured by his former comrades, and after a show trial deep in the Cambodian jungle he was condemned to life imprisonment. >> Ho Chi-Minh; Sihanouk; RR1038

Polybius [po**li**bius] (c. 200–c. 120 BC) Greek politician, diplomat, and historian, from Megalopolis in the Peloponnese, who wrote of the rise of Rome to world power status (264–146 BC). Only five of the original books survive. The 18 years he spent in Rome as a political hostage (168–150 BC) gave him a unique insight into Roman affairs, and led to lasting friendships with some of the great figures of the day, notably Scipio Aemilianus. >> Scipio Aemilianus

Polycarp, St (c. 69–c. 155) Greek bishop of Smyrna who bridges the little-known period between the age of his master, the apostle John, and that of his own disciple, Irenaeus. His only extant writing is the *Epistle to the Philippians*, incomplete in the original Greek, but complete in a Latin translation. He visited Rome to discuss the question of the timing of Easter, and was martyred on his return to Smyrna – an event graphically described in an early document, *The Martyrdom of Polycarp*. Feast day 23 February. >> Irenaeus; John, St

Polyclitus or **Polycleitos** [poli**kliy**tus] (5th-c BC) Greek sculptor from Samos, a contemporary of Phidias, known for his

statues of athletes, which were often copied. One of his greatest works is the bronze *Doryphorus* ('Spear Bearer').

Polycrates [poli**kr**ateez] (6th-c BC) Tyrant of Samos (540–522 BC). One of the earliest of Greek tyrants, he turned Samos into a major naval power, the ally of Egypt, Cyrene, and later Persia, and made her the cultural centre of the E Aegean. Among the poets who enjoyed his patronage was Anacreon. >> Anacreon

Polygnotos or **Polygnotus** [poli**g**nohtus] (5th-c BC) Greek painter, born on the I of Thasos. He was innovative in giving life and character to painting, principally by arranging figures in a 'landscape' rather than on the traditional baseline of earlier works. His monumental wall paintings were in Athens, Delphi, and Plataea.

Pombal, Sebastião (José) de Carvalho (e Mello), marquês de (Marquess of) [po**bal**] (1699–1782) Portuguese statesman and chief minister (1756–77), born near Coimbra, Portugal. He became ambassador to London (1739) and Vienna (1745), and secretary of foreign affairs (1750). He showed great resourcefulness in replanning the city of Lisbon following the disastrous earthquake of 1755, and became chief minister. He opposed Church influence, reorganized the army, and improved agriculture, commerce, and finance. He was made count (1758) and marquess (1770), but fell from office on the accession of Maria I (reigned 1777–1816).

Pompadour, Jeanne Antoinette Poisson, marquise de (Marchioness of) [**pom**padoor], known as **Madame de Pompadour** (1721–64) Mistress of Louis XV, born in Paris. A woman of remarkable grace, beauty, and wit, she became a queen of fashion, and attracted the eye of the king at a ball. Installed at Versailles (1745), and ennobled as marquise de Pompadour, she assumed the entire control of public affairs, and for 20 years swayed state policy, appointing her own favourites. She founded the royal porcelain factory at Sèvres, and was a lavish patroness of architecture, the arts, and literature. She was largely blamed for the French defeats in the Seven Years' War. >> Louis XV

Pompey [**pom**pee], in full **Gnaeus Pompeius Magnus**, known as **Pompey the Great** (106–48 BC) Roman politician and general of the late Republic, whose outstanding military talents, as shown by his victories over the Marians (83–82 BC), Sertorius (77 BC), Spartacus (71 BC), the pirates (67 BC), and Mithridates VI (66 BC), put him at the forefront of Roman politics from an early age. He was also an organizer of genius, and his settlement of the East after the Mithridatic Wars (63 BC) established the pattern of Roman administration there for well over a century. Consistently outmanoeuvred in the 50s BC by Julius Caesar, he was finally defeated by him in the Battle of Pharsalus (48 BC), and was assassinated in Egypt shortly after. >> Caesar, Julius; Mithridates VI; Sertorius; Spartacus

Pompidou, Georges (Jean Raymond) [pō**peedoo**] (1911–74) French statesman, prime minister (1962, 1962–6, 1966–7, 1967–8), and president (1969–74), born in Montboudif, France. He trained as an administrator, joined de Gaulle's staff in 1944, and held various government posts from 1946. He helped to draft the constitution for the Fifth Republic (1959), negotiated a settlement in Algeria (1961), and played a key role in resolving the political crisis of 1968. Dismissed by his increasingly jealous patron, Charles de Gaulle, he was elected president following the latter's resignation. The Pompidou Centre in Paris is named after him. >> de Gaulle; RR1049

Ponce de León, Juan [**pon**thay thay lay**on**] (1460–1521) Explorer, born in San Servas, Spain. A page at the Aragonese court, he was a member of Columbus's second expedition (1493) and served as deputy to Ovando (1508–9), exploring and settling Puerto Rico (1510). In 1513 he discovered Florida and, while acting governor, occupied Trinidad, but failed to conquer his new subjects, the Carib Indians. On a second expedition to Florida (1521) he returned to Cuba, where he died from a poisoned-arrow wound. >> Columbus

Poniatoff, Alexander [**pon**yatof] (1892–1980) US electronics engineer and inventor. Born in Russia, he served as a pilot in the Russian navy before emigrating to the USA in the 1920s. He founded the Ampex Co, making sound recording equipment, and built the first video recorder in 1956.

Poniatowski, Stanislaw >> **Stanislaw II Poniatowski**

Pons, Lily (Alice Joséphine) [ponz] (1898–1976) Soprano, born in Draguignan, France. A dramatic coloratura, she excelled in opera, achieving immense success in Paris, London, South America and, especially, at the New York Metropolitan (1931–61). She also sang in films, and during World War 2 toured North Africa and the Far East.

Ponselle, Rosa [pon**sel**], originally **Rosa Ponzillo** (1897–1981) Soprano, born in Meridan, CT. Her career began in vaudeville. At Caruso's suggestion she appeared as Leonora in *La forza del destino* at the New York Metropolitan (1918), where she sang in leading French and Italian grand opera roles until 1937, also appearing at Covent Garden (1929–31). She later taught and directed opera in Baltimore. >> Caruso

Ponsonby, Sarah >> **Butler, Lady Eleanor**

Pont, Pierre Samuel Du >> **Du Pont, Pierre Samuel**

Pontecorvo, Guido [pontay**kaw(r)**voh] (1907–93) Geneticist, born in Pisa, Italy. He studied at the universities of Pisa, Edinburgh, and Leicester. At the Institute of Animal Genetics in Edinburgh (from 1938), he co-discovered the parasexual cycle in fungi (1950), which allows genetic analysis of asexual fungi. Soon afterwards he proposed that the gene is the unit of function in genetics. He was appointed to the first chair of genetics at Glasgow (1955–68), then moved to London, where he worked at the Imperial Cancer Research Fund Laboratories (1968–75).

Pontedera, Andrea da >> **Pisano, Andrea**

Ponti, Carlo >> **Loren, Sophia**

Ponti, Gio [**pon**tee] (1891–1979) Architect and designer, born in Milan, Italy. His best-known architectural work, the Pirelli Building, Milan (1955–9, with Pier Luigi Nervi), is notable for its hexagonal plan. He also designed costumes and scenery for La Scala Opera, Milan. >> Nervi

Pontiac [**pon**tiak] (c. 1720–69) Chief of the Ottawa Indians from 1755. In 1763 he organized a multi-tribal rising against the English garrisons (*Pontiac's War* or *Conspiracy*, 1763–4), and for five months besieged Detroit, but concluded a peace treaty in 1766. He was murdered by an Illinois Indian, and his death was avenged by the near-annihilation of the Illinois tribe. >> Putnam, Israel

Pontius Pilatus >> **Pilate, Pontius**

Pontormo, Jacopo da [pon**taw(r)**moh], originally **Jacopo Carrucci** (1494–1557) Painter, born in Pontormo, Italy. A pupil of Andrea del Sarto and other masters, his works include several frescoes, notably of the Passion (1522–5) in the Certosa near Florence. His masterpiece is 'The Deposition' (c.1525), a chapel altarpiece in Santa Felicità, Florence. >> Sarto

Pontryagin, Lev Semyonovich [pont**ryah**gin] (1908–88) Mathematician, born in Moscow. The loss of his sight in an accident at the age of 14 did not prevent him from graduating from Moscow University, where he became professor in 1935. One of the leading Russian topologists, he worked on topological groups and their character theory, on duality in algebraic topology, and on differential equations with applications to optimal control. His book, *Topological Groups* (trans 1939), is still a standard work.

Pope, Alexander (1688–1744) Poet, born in London, England, UK, to a Roman Catholic family in the year of the Protestant Revolution. In 1700 the family settled at Binfield, Berkshire. Debarred from university because of his religion, and largely self-taught, he suffered from poor health caused by tuberculosis, and asthma, and had a curvature of the spine, his resulting diminutive stature (4 ft 6 in) providing a target for critics, since he was frequently engaged in literary vendettas. He became well known as a satirical poet, and a master of the heroic couplet, notably in *The Rape of the Lock* (1712–14). He turned to translation with the *Iliad* (1715–20), whose success enabled him to set up a home in Twickenham, but he was forced to remove himself from London following further anti-Catholic measures after the Jacobite rebellion of 1715. However, he formed a friendship with his neighbour, Lady Mary Wortley Montagu, which was very important to him but soured after 1723. There he wrote his major poem, *The Dunciad* (1728, continued 1742), the *Epistle to Doctor Arbuthnot* (1735), the philosophical *Essay on Man* (1733–4), and a series of satires imitating the epistles of Horace (1733–8). >> Gay, John; Montagu, Lady Mary Wortley; Winchilsea

Pope, John (1822–92) US soldier, born in Louisville, KY. He trained at West Point, and served with the engineers in Florida (1842–4) and in the Mexican War. As brigadier-general in the Civil War (1861–5) he drove the guerrillas out of Missouri (1861). As major-general he commanded the Army of the Mississippi (1862) and then that of Virginia, but was defeated at the second Battle of Bull Run (1862). Transferred to Minnesota, he kept the Indians in check, and held commands until he retired in 1886.

Pope, Sir William Jackson (1870–1939) Chemist, born in London, England, UK. He studied chemistry at Finsbury Technical College and the Central Institution, London (Imperial College). He became head of chemistry at Goldsmith's College, London, then professor of chemistry at Manchester, and in 1908 at Cambridge. He demonstrated that in an optically active compound the asymmetric centres could be due to elements other than carbon. He also showed that compounds containing no asymmetric atoms could still be optically active.

Pope-Hennessy, Sir John (1913–) Art historian, born in London, England, UK. He studied at Oxford, worked for the Victoria and Albert Museum from 1938, then held many academic and curatorial posts, including professorships of fine art at Oxford (1956–7), Cambridge (1964–5), and New York University (from 1977). He was director of the Victoria and Albert Museum (1967–73) and of the British Museum, (1974–6). A leading authority on Italian Renaissance art, his books include studies of Sienese painting and a series of authoritative volumes on Italian sculpture. He was knighted in 1971.

Popielusko, Jerzy [popye**wus**koh], popular name of **Alfons Popielusko** (1947–84) Priest, born in Okopy, Poland. Serving in Warsaw parishes after ordination, he became an outspoken supporter of the Solidarity trade union, especially when it was banned in 1981. His sermons at 'Masses for the Country' regularly held in St Stanislaw Kostka Church were widely acclaimed. He ignored harassment and resisted official moves to have him silenced, but was kidnapped and murdered by the secret police in 1984.

Popov, Alexander Stepanovich [**po**pof] (1859–1905) Physicist, born in Turinskiye Rudniki, Russia. He studied at St Petersburg, and taught at the Navy's Torpedo School, returning to St Petersburg as professor in 1901. Independently of Guglielmo Marconi, he is acclaimed in Russia as the inventor of wireless telegraphy (1896). He was the first to use a suspended wire as an aerial. >> Marconi

Popova, Liubov Sergeyevna [popohva], *née* **Eding** (1889–1924) Painter and stage designer, born near Moscow. After studying in Paris (1912–13) she returned to Russia, where she met Tatlin, the founder of Soviet Constructivism. In the year before her death she designed textiles for the First State Textile Print Factory, Moscow, where she was given a memorial exhibition in 1924. Her work was especially important for its exploration of abstract colour values. >> Tatlin

Popp, Lucia (1939–93) Austrian lyric soprano, born in the Czech Republic. She studied at the music academy in Bratislava, and made her debut there as Queen of the Night in Mozart's *Magic Flute* (1963). She became the principal soprano with the Vienna State Opera, and made appearances at Salzburg, Covent Garden, London, and the New York Metropolitan Opera.

Poppaea Sabina [popaya sabeena] (?–65) Roman society beauty and voluptuary who before her marriage to the Emperor Nero (62) had been the wife of his playboy friend, the future Emperor Otho. She shared the then fashionable interest in Judaism, and has been thought by many to have encouraged Nero in his vicious attack on the Christians in the aftermath of the Fire of Rome (64).

Popper, Sir Karl (Raimund) (1902–94) Philosopher, born in Vienna. He studied at Vienna University, where he associated with the 'Vienna Circle' of philosophers, though he was strongly critical of their logical positivism. In 1935 he published his first book on scientific methodology, *Die Logik der Forschung* (1934, The Logic of Scientific Discovery). He left Vienna during Hitler's rise to power, lectured in New Zealand (1937–45), finally becoming professor of logic and scientific method at London (1949–69). Later books include *The Open Society and its Enemies* (1945), a polemic directed against all systems with totalitarian implications, particularly Marxism, and *The Poverty of Historicism* (1957). He was knighted in 1965.

Popski >> **Peniakoff, Vladimir**

Poquelin, Jean Baptiste >> **Molière**

Porphyry [paw(r)fuhree] (c. 233–304) Neoplatonist philosopher, born in Tyre or Batanea. After studying at Athens he went to Rome (c.263), where he studied under Plotinus, becoming his disciple and biographer. He wrote a celebrated treatise against the Christians, of which only fragments remain. His most influential work was the *Isagoge*, a commentary on Aristotle's *Categories*, widely used in the Middle Ages. >> Aristotle; Plotinus

Porres, St Martín de >> **Martín de Porres, St**

Porsche, Ferdinand [paw(r)shuh] (1875–1951) Automobile designer, born in Hafersdorf, Germany. He designed cars for Daimler and Auto Union, then set up his own studio, and in 1934 produced the plans for a revolutionary type of cheap car with the engine in the rear, to which the Nazis gave the name *Volkswagen* ('people's car'). The Porsche sports car was introduced in 1950.

Porsenna, Lars [paw(r)sena] (6th-c BC) Etruscan ruler of Clusium. According to Roman patriotic tradition he laid siege to Rome after the overthrow in 510 BC of Tarquinius Superbus, but was prevented from capturing the city by the heroism of Horatius Cocles defending the bridge across the Tiber. However, this tradition may conceal a temporary occupation of Rome by Porsenna. >> Tarquinius Superbus

Porta, Baccio della >> **Bartolommeo, Fra**

Porta, Giacomo della (c. 1541–1604) Architect, the most important of the late 16th-c, born in Rome. A pupil of Vignola, he is best known for the cupola of St Peter's and his work on the Palazzo Farnese, left unfinished by Michelangelo. He was also responsible for some of the fountains of Rome, and designed many palaces, notably the Villa Aldobrandini (1598–1604). >> Michelangelo; Vignola

Portal (of Hungerford), Charles Frederick Algernon Portal, 1st Viscount (1893–1971) Chief of British air staff during World War 2, born in Hungerford, Berkshire, S England, UK. He studied at Oxford, joined the Royal Engineers (1914), and was commissioned, then served in the Royal Flying Corps (1915–18). Promoted air vice-marshal in 1937, he became director of organization at the Air Ministry (1937–8), commander-in-chief of Bomber Command (1940), and chief of air staff (1940–6). After the War he was controller of the Atomic Energy Authority (1946–51), and became chairman of the British Aircraft Corporation in 1960. He was created a baron in 1945, and viscount in 1946.

Porter, Cole (1892–1964) Composer, born in Peru, IN. He studied law at Harvard before entering the Schola Cantorum in Paris. Attracted to musical comedy, he composed lyrics and music for many stage successes. In 1937 he was severely hurt in a riding accident, leaving him in permanent pain, but he continued to compose, reaching the height of his success with *Kiss Me Kate* (1948) and *Can-Can* (1953). His highly personal style and dramatic sense is illustrated by such popular songs as 'Night and Day' (1932), 'Begin the Beguine' (1935), and 'Ev'ry Time We Say Goodbye' (1944).

Porter, David Dixon (1813–91) US naval officer, born in Chester, PA. He accompanied his father against the pirates in the West Indies, and served in the Mexican War (1846–8). In the Civil War, as commander of the federal mortar flotilla, he bombarded the New Orleans forts (1862), and with the Mississippi squadron he passed the batteries of Vicksburg, and bombarded the city. In 1864 he took Fort Fisher. Superintendent till 1869 of Annapolis Naval Academy, he was made admiral of the navy in 1870.

Porter, Eleanor, *née* **Hodgman** (1868–1920) Novelist, born in Littleton, NH. She studied music at the New England Conservatory before publishing her first novels, which included *Cross Currents* (1907) and *Miss Billy* (1911). *Pollyanna* (1913) was an immediate success, and has retained its popularity. A sequel, *Pollyanna Grows Up*, was published in 1915. Two volumes of short stories, *The Tangled Threads* and *Across the Years*, were published posthumously in 1924.

Porter, Eric (Richard) (1928–95) Actor, born in London, England, UK. He made his first appearance in 1945 at the Arts Theatre, Cambridge, then worked in repertory in London and Birmingham, and joined John Gielgud's company at the Lyric Theatre (1952–3). Both a classical and modern actor, he appeared with the Royal Shakespeare Company and the National Theatre, notably as Big Daddy in Tennessee Williams's *Cat on a Hot Tin Roof* (1988), and as King Lear in Jonathan Miller's revival at the Old Vic (1989). He made several film and television appearances, notably as Soames Forsyte in the BBC television series, *The Forsyte Saga*.

Porter, Sir George (1920–) Physical chemist, born in Stainforth, North Yorkshire, N England, UK. He studied at Leeds, and worked with radar as a naval officer in World War 2. In 1945 he moved to Cambridge, where he studied very fast reactions in gases, using a combination of electronic and spectroscopic techniques. He was awarded the Nobel Prize for Chemistry in 1967. He became Director of the Royal Institution (1966–85), and President of the Royal Society (1985–90), continuing his work on ultra-rapid chemical reactions. >> Norrish

Porter, Jane (1776–1850) Novelist, born in Durham, Co Durham, NE England, UK. She had a great reputation as the author of historical romances, which enjoyed considerable success in their day. Her reputation was made with *Thaddeus of Warsaw* (1803), one of the earliest examples of the historical novel, and she was even more successful with *The Scottish Chiefs* (1810).

Porter, Katherine Anne (1890–1980) Short-story writer and novelist, born in Indian Creek, TX. Educated in a convent, she worked as a journalist and teacher in Mexico. Her first book of stories, *Flowering Judas* (1930), was followed by *Pale Horse, Pale Rider* (1939). She is also known for a long allegorical novel, *The Ship of Fools* (1962), about a journey from Mexico to Germany on the eve of Hitler's rise to power. *The Collected Stories of Katherine Anne Porter* (1965) received both the Pulitzer Prize and the National Book Award.

Porter, Michael (c. 1947–) Management theorist, born in Ann Arbor, MI. Trained as an economist at Princeton and Harvard Business School, he became a lecturer at Harvard (1973) and subsequently professor (1982). In 1983 he founded Monitor Co Inc, a strategic consulting organization. He was in great demand throughout the 1980s as a lecturer and consultant to many leading US and UK organizations. His book *Competitive Analysis* (1980) has been translated into 13 languages, and has had over 30 printings.

Porter, Peter (Neville Frederick) (1929–) Poet, born in Brisbane, Queensland, Australia. He studied at Brisbane University, then worked as a journalist before coming to England in 1951. His collections *Once Bitten, Twice Bitten* (1961) and *Poems Ancient and Modern* (1964) are descriptive and satirical of Britain in the 1960s, while later volumes such as *The Cost of Seriousness* (1978) and *The Automatic Oracle* (1987) are more reflective and elegiac. His *Collected Poems* appeared in 1983, and consolidated his international reputation. A later collection, *Dragons in their Pleasant Palaces*, appeared in 1997. He is well known in Britain as a reviewer and broadcaster.

Porter, Rodney Robert (1917–85) Biochemist, born in Liverpool, Merseyside, NW England, UK. He studied there and at Cambridge, worked at the National Institute for Medical Research (1949–60), St Mary's Hospital Medical School, London (1960–7), and became professor at Oxford (1967). His work on antibodies from 1949, together with studies by Gerald Edelman and others, enabled him to propose an overall molecular structure for antibodies. His ideas helped to link the biochemistry of antibodies with immunology, and he shared the Nobel Prize for Physiology or Medicine with Gerald Edelman in 1972. >> Edelman

Porter, William S >> Henry, O

Portillo, Michael (Denzil Xavier) [paw(r)tilow] (1953–) British Conservative statesman. He studied in Cambridge, and became an MP in 1984. After several appointments as a special adviser to government departments, he became minister of state for transport (1988–90) and the environment (1990–2), chief secretary for the Treasury (1992–4), secretary of state for employment (1994–5), and defence secretary (1995–7). He lost his seat in the 1997 general election.

Posidonius or **Poseidonius** [posidohnius], (c. 135–c. 51 BC) Greek Stoic philosopher, scientist, and polymath, born in Apamea, Syria. He studied at Athens as a pupil of Panaetius, spent many years on travel and scientific research in Europe and Africa, then settled in Rhodes. In 86 BC he was sent as an envoy to Rome, where he became a friend of Cicero and other leading figures. He wrote on an enormous range of subjects, and made important contributions to the development of Stoic doctrines. >> Cicero; Panaetius

Post, Emily, *née* **Price** (1872–1960) Authority on etiquette, born in Baltimore, MD. She wrote society fiction and essays before writing her classic *Etiquette – The Blue Book of Social Usage* (1922). In her 10 editions of *Etiquette*, and her syndicated etiquette column and radio show, she defined good manners for millions of Americans, dispensing relaxed yet serious advice that was striking in its flexible response to changing social mores.

Post, Laurens van der >> van der Post, Laurens

Post, Wiley (1900–35) Pioneer aviator, born in Grand Saline, TX. In the early 1920s he was a mechanic, stunt parachutist, and wingwalker. In 1931 he left New York City in a Lockheed Vega monoplane, with the Australian Harold Gatty as navigator, to fly around the world, taking 8 days, 15 hr, 51 min. He gained instant fame, toppling Zeppelin's previous record of 21 days. In 1933 he made the first solo flight round the world, taking 7 days, 18 hr, 49 min. He was killed in an air crash in Alaska. >> Gatty, Harold; Zeppelin

Potemkin, Grigoriy Alexandrovich [potyomkin] (1739–91) Russian field marshal, born near Smolensk, Russia. He entered the Russian army, attracted the notice of Catherine II, and became her intimate favourite, heavily influencing Russian foreign policy. There is some reason to believe they were secretly married. He distinguished himself in the Russo–Turkish Wars (1768–74, 1787–92), during which Russia gained the Crimea and the N coast of the Black Sea. >> Catherine II

Pott, Percivall (1714–88) Surgeon, born in London, England, UK. He became assistant and then senior surgeon at St Bartholomew's Hospital, where he introduced many improvements to make surgery more humane. He wrote *Fractures and Dislocations* (1765), in which he described a compound leg fracture suffered by himself, still called *Pott's fracture*, and gave a clinical account of tuberculosis of the spine called *Pott's disease*.

Potter, (Helen) Beatrix (1866–1943) Writer and illustrator of books for children, born in London, England, UK. A repressed child, she grew up longing for the country and animals. She taught herself to draw and paint, and her famous characters started as sketches of pet animals dressed as human beings, along with letters to amuse a sick child, which she privately published as *The Tale of Peter Rabbit* (1900) and *The Tailor of Gloucester* (1902). A publisher reprinted them, and she became the outstanding writer and artist of picture-story books of her time, widely translated and reprinted. *Peter Rabbit*, *Jemima Puddle-Duck*, *Mrs Tiggy-Winkle*, *Benjamin Bunny*, and her other creations have become classics of children's literature. In 1913 she married **William Heelis**, stopped writing, and spent the rest of her life raising Herdwick sheep.

Potter, Dennis (Christopher George) (1935–94) Playwright, born in the Forest of Dean, Gloucestershire, SWC England, UK. He studied at Oxford, and was a journalist and TV critic before he began writing plays. Although he wrote for the stage (*Sufficient Carbohydrate*, 1984), his first success was *Vote, Vote, Vote for Nigel Barton* (1965). Other plays include *Brimstone and Treacle* (1976), *Blue Remembered Hills* (1979, BAFTA), *Cream in my Coffee* (1982, Prix Italia), *The Singing Detective* (1986), and *Lipstick on Your Collar* (1993). Several dealt with controversial topics, such as the treatment of the self-doubting Christ in *Son of Man* (1969). His work was often technically innovative, as in *Pennies from Heaven* (1978), which required the actors to mime to popular songs of the 1920s and 1930s that intercut the action. His work includes a novel, *Hide and Seek* (1973). He completed *Karaoke* and *Cold Lazarus* just before his death.

Potter, Paul (1625–54) Painter and etcher, born in Enkhuizen, The Netherlands. He worked in Delft and The Hague, moving in 1652 to Amsterdam. His best pictures are small pastoral scenes with animal figures, but he also painted large pictures, notably the life-size 'Young Bull' (1647, The Hague).

Potter, Philip (1921–) Ecumenical leader, born in Roseau, Dominica. After studying law, and pastoring a Methodist church in Haiti, he became secretary of the youth department of the World Council of Churches (1954). Appointed Methodist Missionary Society (London) field secretary for

Africa and the West Indies (1960–7), and chairman of the World Student Christian Federation (1960–8), he was promoted director of World Mission and Evangelism (1967–72), then became general secretary (1972–84) of the World Council of Churches.

Potter, Stephen (Meredith) (1900–69) British writer and radio producer. He joined the BBC in 1938, and was co-author with Joyce Grenfell of the *How* series. He wrote a novel, *The Young Man* (1929), and an educational study, *The Muse in Chains* (1937), but made his name with a series of humorous books on the art of demoralizing the opposition – *The Theory and Practice of Gamesmanship; or the Art of Winning Games Without Actually Cheating* (1947), *One-Upmanship* (1952), and *Supermanship* (1958). >> Grenfell, Joyce

Poujade, Pierre [poozhad] (1920–) Political leader, born in St Céré, France. After serving in World War 2, he became a publisher and bookseller. In 1951 he was elected a member of the St Céré municipal council, and in 1954 he organized his *Poujadist* movement (a union for the defence of tradesmen and artisans) as a protest against the French tax system. His party had successes in the 1956 elections to the National Assembly.

Poulenc, Francis [poolāk] (1899–1963) Composer, born in Paris. He became a member of *Les Six*, and was prominent in the reaction against Impressionism. His works include much chamber music and the ballet *Les Biches*, produced by Diaghilev in 1924; but he is best known for his considerable output of songs, such as *Fêtes galantes* (1943). >> Auric; Cocteau; Durey; Honegger; Milhaud; Tailleferre

Poulsen, Valdemar (1869–1942) Electrical engineer, born in Copenhagen. Working for the Copenhagen Telephone Company, he invented the telegraphone, a wire recording device, forerunner of magnetic tape recorders (1898). In 1903 he also invented an arc generator for use in wireless telegraphy.

Pound, (Alfred) Dudley Pickman Rogers (1877–1943) British naval commander. He became captain in 1914, commanded with distinction the battleship *Colossus* at the Battle of Jutland (1916), and for the remainder of World War 1 directed operations at the Admiralty. Promoted to the rank of rear-admiral, he was commander-in-chief of the Mediterranean fleet (1936–9), becoming in 1939 Admiral of the Fleet and First Sea Lord. >> Jellicoe

Pound, Ezra (Loomis) (1885–1972) Poet and critic, born in Hailey, ID. He studied chiefly at the University of Pennsylvania, then travelled widely in Europe, working as a journalist and editor. He became part of literary movements in London, where his publications included *Personae* (1909) and *Homage to Sextus Propertius* (1919). From 1924 he made his home in Italy, where he caused resentment by making pro-Fascist broadcasts in the early stages of World War 2. In 1945 he was escorted back to the USA and indicted for treason, but judged insane, and placed in an asylum. Released in 1958, he returned to Italy. He was an experimental poet, whom T S Eliot regarded as the motivating force behind modern poetry. His main work is *The Cantos*, a loosely knit series of poems, which he began during World War 1, and which were published in many instalments (1930–59). >> Eliot, T S; Lewis, Wyndham

Pound, Roscoe (1870–1964) Jurist and botanist, born in Lincoln, NE. He studied at Nebraska University and Harvard Law School, eventually becoming professor of law at Harvard (1910–37). A teacher of jurisprudence, his theories have had a universal effect. His many legal writings include *Law and Morals* (1924) and *Jurisprudence* (5 vols, 1959). An authority also on botany, he was largely responsible for the botanical survey of Nebraska. A rare lichen is named after him.

Pounds, John (1766–1839) Shoemaker, born in Portsmouth, Hampshire, S England, UK. Physically handicapped, he became an unpaid teacher of poor children, and is regarded as the founder of what came to be called 'ragged schools' in England and Scotland.

Poussin, Charles de la Vallée >> **Hadamard, Jacques**

Poussin, Gaspard >> **Dughet, Gaspard**

Poussin, Nicolas [poosī] (1594–1665) Painter, born near Les Andelys, France. He went to Rome in 1624, and spent the rest of his life there, apart from a short visit (1640–2) to Paris. The greatest master of French Classicism, deeply influenced by Raphael and the Antique, his masterpieces include two sets of the 'Seven Sacraments'. >> Champaigne; Dughet; Raphael

Powderly, Terence V(incent) (1849–1924) Labour leader, born in Carbondale, PA. A trade-unionist, he joined the secret oath-bound Knights of Labor in 1874, becoming its grand master workman in 1879, and then its general master workman (1883–93). He sought to encourage constructive relations between labour and management, and saw the Knights mushroom to almost a million members by 1886. After its decline, he became commissioner-general of immigration (1897–1902), and head of the division of information in the Immigration Bureau (1907–21).

Powell, Adam Clayton, Jr (1908–72) US representative and minister, born in New Haven, CT. He studied at Columbia University, and became minister at Harlem's Abyssinian Baptist Church (1931). He was elected to New York's City Council in 1941, and served as a Democrat in the US House of Representatives (1945–69), where he fought to outlaw Jim Crow laws, and became chairman of the House Committee on Education and Labor (1960–7). His absentee rate and eight-year legal battle with a Harlem woman who sued him for libel lost him support in Congress. When he moved to Bimini in 1966 to escape payment, the House voted to exclude him from Congress. After paying libel charges, he returned in 1969, vindicated by a Supreme Court decision that his exclusion had been invalid; however, he was defeated in 1970 by Charles Rangel.

Powell, Anthony (Dymoke) (1905–) Novelist, born in London, England, UK. He studied at Oxford, worked in publishing and journalism before World War 2, and by 1936 had published four satirical novels, beginning with *Afternoon Men* (1931). After the war he began the series of novels he called *A Dance to the Music of Time* (1951–75) – 12 volumes, covering 50 years of British upper middle-class life and attitudes. *At Lady Molly's* (1957) won the James Tait Black Memorial Prize, and *Temporary Kings* (1973) won the W H Smith Literary Award. He has also published four volumes of memoirs under the general title *To Keep the Ball Rolling* (1976–82). Later books include the novel *The Fisher King* (1986) and a volume of criticism, *Under Review* (1992). He was made a Companion of Honour in 1988.

Powell, Baden >> **Baden-Powell, Robert**

Powell, Bud, popular name of **Earl Powell** (1924–66) Jazz pianist, born in New York City. Playing from the age of six, he became involved with the modern jazz movement in the 1940s, with encouragement from Thelonious Monk. A head injury sustained in an attack heralded a series of visits to mental hospitals; nevertheless, he was the most influential jazz pianist of his time. He was the first choice to work and record with top New York players until he moved to Paris (1959–64), where he led a trio featuring US expatriate drummer, Kenny Clarke. >> Monk, Thelonious

Powell, Cecil (Frank) (1903–69) Physicist, born in Tonbridge, Kent, SE England, UK. He was professor of physics at Bristol (1948–63), and director of the Wills Physics Laboratory, Bristol from 1964. He is best known for his work on the photography of nuclear processes, for which he was awarded the Nobel Prize for Physics in 1950.

Powell, Colin (Luther) (1937–) US army general, born in New York City. He studied at the City College of New York, and took an army commission, later serving in Vietnam (1962–3, 1968–9). After holding a series of senior commands, he was appointed head of the National Security Council by President Reagan (1987–9), took over the Army Forces Command, and was made chairman of the joint chiefs-of-staff by President Bush (1989–), the first African-American officer to receive this distinction. He had overall responsibility for the US military operation against Iraq in 1990–1. Britain awarded him an honorary knighthood in 1993. >> Schwarzkopf, H Norman

Powell, (John) Enoch (1912–) British statesman, born in Birmingham, West Midlands, C England, UK. He studied at Cambridge, was professor of Greek at Sydney (1937–9), and became a Conservative MP in 1950. He held several junior posts before becoming minister of health (1960–3). His outspoken attitude on the issues of non-white immigration and racial integration came to national attention in 1968, and as a consequence of this he was dismissed from the shadow Cabinet. He was elected an Ulster Unionist MP in October 1974, losing his seat in 1987. His many publications include works on Herodotos, books of poetry (collected works, 1990), and general socio-political texts, such as *A Nation Not Afraid* (1965), *Medicine and Politics* (1966), and *No Easy Answers* (1973). In 1994 appeared *The Evolution of the Gospel*.

Powell, Michael (1905–90) Film director, scriptwriter, and producer, born in Bekesbourne, Kent, SE England, UK. He worked as a director on minor productions in the 1930s, and co-directed on *The Thief of Baghdad* (1940) for Korda, who introduced him to the Hungarian scriptwriter, **Emeric Pressburger** (1902–88). Powell and Pressburger formed The Archers Company in 1942, and for more than 10 years made a series of unusual and original features, many with an exceptional use of colour, such as *Black Narcissus* (1947) and *The Tales of Hoffman* (1951). After the break-up of the partnership, Powell's productions were infrequent, including the controversial *Peeping Tom* (1960) and *The Boy Who Turned Yellow* (1972), from a script by Pressburger.

Powell, Robert (1944–) Actor, born in Salford, Lancashire, NW England, UK. He worked in repertory, appeared with the Royal Shakespeare Company, and toured with the Bristol Old Vic. He became widely known through his role in the television series *Jude the Obscure* (1971), and for his title role in the Franco Zeffirelli film for television, *Jesus of Nazareth* (1977). His feature film roles include *Secrets* (1971), *The Thirty-Nine Steps* (1978), *Frankenstein* (1984), and *The Mystery of Edwin Drood* (1993). Later television work includes *The Detectives* (1989) – reprised in a 1992 comedy series with Jasper Carrot – and *The First Circle* (1991).

Powhatan [powhatan] (?–1618) American Indian chief of the confederacy of Tidewater tribes of New England. Despite considerable provocation, he managed to maintain an uneasy peace with white settlers in Virginia. His daughter, Pocahontas, was carried off by settlers in 1609, but married a white colonist with her father's consent. Powhatan was succeeded by his more warlike brother, **Opechancanough** (c.1550–1644). >> Pocahontas

Powys, John Cowper [powis] (1872–1964) Writer and critic, born in Shirley, Derbyshire, C England, UK, the brother of Llewelyn and Theodore Francis Powys. He studied at Cambridge, then worked as a teacher and lecturer, much of the time in the USA. He wrote poetry and essays, but is best known for his long novels on West Country and historical themes, such as *A Glastonbury Romance* (1932) and *Owen Glendower* (1940). >> Powys, Llewelyn; Powys, T F

Powys, Llewelyn [powis] (1884–1939) Essayist and novelist, born in Dorchester, Dorset, S England, UK, the brother of John and Theodore Francis Powys. He studied at Cambridge, and worked as a journalist in New York City (1920–5), but suffered from recurrent tuberculosis which caused him to spend some years in Switzerland and Kenya. His works include *Ebony and Ivory* (1922), *Apples be Ripe* (1930), *Confessions of Two Brothers* (1916, with his brother John), and *Skin for Skin* (1925), an account of his time in Swiss sanatoria. >> Powys, John Cowper; Powys, T F

Powys, T(heodore) F(rancis) [powis] (1875–1953) Novelist and short-story writer, born in Dorchester, Dorset, S England, UK, the brother of John and Llewelyn Powys. He lived in seclusion and wrote original and eccentric novels, of which the best known is *Mr Weston's Good Wine* (1927). Others include *Mr Tasker's Gods* (1925), *Captain's Patch* (1935), and *Goat Green* (1937). >> Powys, John Cowper; Powys, Llewelyn

Poynings, Sir Edward (1459–1521) English soldier and diplomat, probably born in London, England, UK. He took part in a rebellion against Richard III, escaped to the European mainland, later returning to England with the Earl of Richmond (Henry VII). He became Governor of Calais in 1493, and in 1494 went to Ireland as deputy-governor for Prince Henry (Henry VIII). He is best remembered for *Poyning's laws*, subjecting the Irish Parliament to the control of the English king and privy council. >> Richard III; Henry VII

Poynter, Sir Edward John (1836–1919) Painter, born in Paris. He studied at Westminster and Ipswich, then in Rome and Paris. He was professor at University College, London (1871), art director at South Kensington (1876–81), director of the National Gallery (1894–1905), and president of the Royal Academy (1896). Among his works are 'The Ides of March' (1883), 'The Visit of the Queen of Sheba to Solomon' (1891), and the portrait of Lillie Langtry bequeathed in her will to the Jersey Museum. In 1869–70 he designed the cartoons for a mosaic of St George in the Houses of Parliament.

Praagh, Peggy van >> van Praagh, Peggy

Praetorius, Michael [pritawrius] (1571–1621) Composer, born in Creuzburg, Germany. He studied in Torgau, Frankfurt an der Oder, and Zerbst, and became court organist and (from 1604) *Kapellmeister* at the court of Wolfenbüttel. As well as being one of the most prolific composers of his time (especially of church music), he wrote an important treatise, *Syntagma musicum* (1614–20).

Prandtl, Ludwig [prantl] (1875–1953) Physicist, and pioneer of the science of aerodynamics, born in Freising, Germany. He studied mechanical engineering in Munich, and although destined for a career in elasticity, his interest was redirected to aerodynamics. In this field he made outstanding contributions to boundary layer theory, airship profiles, supersonic flow, wing theory, and turbulence. He was director of technical physics at the University of Göttingen (1904–53), and director of the Kaiser Wilhelm Institute for fluid mechanics from 1925. >> Lanchester

Prasad, Rajendra [prasad] (1884–1963) Indian statesman and first president (1950–62), born in Zeradei, India. He studied law, but left legal practice to become a follower of Mahatma Gandhi. A member of the Working Committee of the All-India Congress in 1922, he was president of the Congress several times between 1934 and 1948. In 1946 he was appointed minister for food and agriculture, and president of the Indian Constituent Assembly, becoming president of the Republic in 1950. He wrote several books, including *India Divided at the Feet of Mahatma Gandhi*. >> Gandhi, Mahatma; RR1058

Pratchett, Terry (1948–) Author, born in Beaconsfield, Buckinghamshire, SC England, UK. He is best known for his series of fantasy novels, Discworld, which began in 1983 with *The Colour of Magic* and which had reached a twentieth novel, *Hogfather* in 1996. Other works include the 'Truckers' trilogy (called the 'Bromeliad' trilogy in the USA), and a series of Johnny Maxwell novels. Several books have been adapted for stage and television.

Pratt, William Henry >> **Karloff, Boris**

Praxiteles [praksiteleez] (4th-c BC) Sculptor from Athens, considered one of the greatest of Greek sculptors. His works have almost all perished, though his 'Hermes Carrying the Boy Dionysus' was found at Olympia in 1877. Several of his statues are known from Roman copies. >> Phryne

Pré, Jacqueline du >> **du Pré, Jacqueline**

Preece, Sir William Henry (1834–1913) Electrical engineer, born in Bryn Helen, Gwynedd. He studied at the Royal Institution, London, and was attached to the Post Office (1870), where he became engineer-in-chief and finally consulting engineer. A pioneer of wireless telegraphy and telephony, he also improved the system of railway signalling, and introduced the first telephones to Great Britain.

Pregl, Fritz [praygl] (1869–1930) Chemist, born in Laibach, Austria. He studied at the University of Graz, with which he was associated for most of his life, and where he became director of the Medico-Chemical Institute (1913). He was specially noted for developing microchemical methods of analysis, for which he was awarded the Nobel Prize for Physics in 1923.

Prelog, Vladimir (1906–) Organic chemist, born in Sarajevo, Bosnia and Herzegovina. He studied at the Prague Institute of Technology, then worked as an industrial chemist, before moving to Zagreb University. In 1941, when the Germans invaded Yugoslavia, he taught at the Federal Institute of Technology in Zürich, and became professor of chemistry (1950–76). Following his notable work in organic chemistry, and especially in stereochemistry, he shared the Nobel Prize for Chemistry in 1975. >> RR1123

Premadasa, Ranasinghe (1924–93) Statesman, prime minister (1978–89), and president (1989–93) of Sri Lanka, born in North Colombo, Sri Lanka. He studied at St Joseph's College, Colombo, was elected to parliament in 1960, and served as chief whip of the United National Party (1965–8, 1970–7), minister of local government (1968–70), and leader of the house (1977–8), before becoming prime minister under President Jayawardene. As prime minister, he implemented a popular housebuilding and poverty alleviation programme, and as president he faced mounting civil unrest and deteriorating relations with India. He was assassinated in a suicide bomb attack during the May Day parade through the capital. >> Jayawardene; RR1090

Preminger, Otto [preminjer] (1906–86) Film director and producer, born in Vienna. He studied law at Vienna University, then became a theatre director there, and directed his first film in 1931. He emigrated to the USA in 1935, and became a US citizen in 1943. After some years of directing on the Broadway stage, he made *Laura* (1944), a *film noir*, often considered his best film. In the 1950s he made good use of the new wide-screen technology in such productions as *Carmen Jones* (1954) and *Bonjour Tristesse* (1959). Later films included *Porgy and Bess* (1959), *Anatomy of a Murder* (1959), *Exodus* (1960), and *The Human Factor* (1979).

Prendergast, Maurice (Brazil) (1859–1924) Painter, born in St John's, Newfoundland, Canada. His family moved to Boston in 1861. He studied at the Académie Julien, Paris (1891–95), then returned to Boston, where he set up an art studio. He made sporadic trips to Europe as his reputation as an artist grew, and was a member of The Eight (1908). He experimented with style, but his work always had an Impressionistic vitality, as in 'Central Park' (1900).

Prés, Josquin >> **Josquin, des Prez**

Prescott, John (Leslie) (1938–) British politician, born in Prestatyn, Denbighshire. He served in the merchant navy (1955–63), and studied at Oxford and Hull universities. In 1968 he became an officer of the National Union of Seamen, and a Labour MP in 1970. Although opposed to Britain's membership of the European Community, he was elected to the European Parliament in 1975, and became leader of the Labour group (1976–9). In the shadow cabinet he was spokesman for employment, energy, and transport, and he became deputy leader of the party in 1994. In the 1997 Labour government, he was appointed deputy prime minister and secretary of state for the Environment and Transport, with extra responsibilities for regional policy.

Presley, Elvis (Aron) (1935–77) Rock singer, born in Tupelo, MS. He began singing in his church choir and taught himself to play the guitar, his early models being black Gospel and blues singers. In 1953 he recorded some sides for Sun Records in Memphis, TN, which came to the attention of the entrepreneur, Colonel Tom Parker, and led to aggressive promotion of Presley's career. In 1956 'Heartbreak Hotel' sold millions of copies, and his performances, featuring much hip-swaying, incited hysteria in teenagers and outrage in their parents. He served two years in the US army in Germany, and became increasingly reclusive on his return to civilian life. He made 45 records that sold in the millions, including 'Hound Dog', 'Love Me Tender', and 'Jailhouse Rock'. His Hollywood films such as *Loving You* (1957), *King Creole* (1958), and *GI Blues* (1960) became enormous moneymakers. Suffering from obesity and narcotics-dependence, he died at Graceland, his Memphis mansion, which is now a souvenir shrine for his many fans.

Press, Frank (1924–) Seismologist and government science advisor, born in New York City. He taught at Columbia University, the California Institute of Technology, and the Massachusetts Institute of Technology, and became president of the National Academy of Science in 1981. While in California he and his colleagues first identified the 'free oscillations' of the Earth – the persistent global vibrations arising from earthquakes and other geological disturbances. He was also a consultant to several national bodies, and director of the US Office of Science and Technology Policy (1977–81).

Pressburger, Emeric >> **Powell, Michael**

Preston, Margaret Rose (1875–1963) Artist and teacher, born in Port Adelaide, South Australia. She studied in Sydney and Melbourne, and at the Government Art School for Women in Munich, and travelled widely in Europe, the South Pacific, Asia, Africa, and India. An active champion of Aboriginal painting, its influence is clearly seen in her still-lifes of Australian flowers, and her wood and linocut engravings.

Pretender, Old / Young >> **Stuart, Prince James / Prince Charles**

Pretorius, Andries (Wilhelmus Jacobus) [pretawrius] (1799–1853) Afrikaner leader, born in Graaff-Reinet, South Africa (then Cape Colony). A prosperous farmer, he joined the Great Trek of 1835 into Natal, where he was chosen commandant-general. He later accepted British rule, but after differences with the governor he trekked again, this time across the Vaal. Eventually the British recognized the

Transvaal Republic, later the South African Republic, whose new capital was named Pretoria after him. >> Pretorius, Marthinus

Pretorius, Marthinus (Wessel) [pretawrius] (1819–1901) Afrikaner soldier and statesman, president of the South African Republic (1857–71), born in Graaff-Reinet, South Africa, the son of Andries Pretorius. He succeeded his father as commandant-general in 1853, and was elected president of the South African Republic, and of the Orange Free State (1859–63). He fought against the British again in 1877, until the independence of the Republic was recognized (1881), then retired. >> Pretorius, Andries

Prévert, Jacques [prayvair] (1900–77) Poet, born in Neuilly-sur-Seine, France. He was involved with the Surrealists, and wrote songs, pieces for cabaret, and scenarios for Renoir, as well as the screenplay for the celebrated film, *Les Enfants du Paradis* (1946, The Children of Paradise). The piquant mixture of wit and sentiment in his poetry proved very popular; collections include *Paroles* (1946, Words), *La Pluie et le beau temps* (1955, Rain and Fine Weather), and *Choses et autres* (1972, Things and Others).

Previn, André (George) [previn] (1929–) Conductor and composer, born in Berlin. His family fled from Nazi Germany to the USA in 1938. He studied music mainly in California and Paris, spent some years as a jazz pianist, and became musical director of symphony orchestras at Houston (1967–9), London (1968–79), Pittsburgh (1976–86), and Los Angeles (1986–9). He became composer laureate of the London Symphony Orchestra in 1991, and conductor laureate the following year. He has composed musicals, film scores, and orchestral works, and achieved popular success both on television and in the concert hall by bringing classical music to the attention of a wide public. His books include *Music Face to Face* (1971) and *André Previn's Guide to Music* (1983). He was given an honorary knighthood in 1996.

Prévost, (Antoine François), l'Abbé [prayvoh] (1697–1763) Novelist, born in Hesdin, France. He spent some years in the army, became a Benedictine monk, then lived in exile in England and Holland. He wrote many novels and translations, but is best known for *Manon Lescaut* (1731), originally published as the final part of a seven-volume novel. Having returned to France by 1735, he was appointed honorary chaplain to the Prince de Conti.

Prévost, Eugène Marcel [prayvoh] (1862–1941) Novelist, born in Paris. A civil engineer, he worked in a tobacco factory until 1891. From the age of 25 he wrote in his leisure hours. Many of his novels and plays have been translated, including *Cousin Laura*, *Frédérique*, and *Léa*.

Prey, Hermann (1929–) Baritone, born in Berlin. Equally distinguished as an interpreter of *lieder* and in stage roles, he sang at the Hamburg Opera (1953–60) and made his debut in *Tannhäuser* at Bayreuth (1956), and the New York Metropolitan (1960). He excelled in the Mozart repertoire, and is accomplished in 20th-c German composers from Berg to Henze. His autobiography is called *First Night Fever* (1986).

Prez, Josquin de >> **Josquin des Pres**

Price, George (Cadle) (1919–) Politician and prime minister of Belize (1981–4, 1989–93). He studied in Belize City and the USA, was elected to the Belize City Council (1947), and founded the People's United Party (PUP) (1950). Partial self-government was achieved in 1954 and he became prime minister, leading his country (which changed its name from British Honduras in 1973) to full independence in 1981. In 1984 PUP's 30 years of rule ended when the general election was won by the United Democratic Party, but he unexpectedly returned to power in 1989. >> RR1035

Price, H(enry) H(abberley) (1899–1985) Philosopher, born in Neath, SC Wales. He studied at Oxford, where he became professor of logic (1935–59). His first and major work was *Perception* (1932), in which he argued against causal theories of perception. He also wrote on religion, parapsychology, and psychic phenomena.

Price, (Mary Violet) Leontyne (1927–) Soprano, born in Laurel, MS. She studied at the Juilliard School, New York City. A notable Bess (1952–4) in Gershwin's *Porgy and Bess*, she was the first black opera singer on television, in *Tosca* for NBC (1955). An outstanding Verdi singer, she was also much associated with Barber's music. >> Barber

Price, Nick, popular name of **Nicholas Raymond Leige Price** (1957–) Golfer, born in Durban, South Africa. His family moved to Zimbabwe, where he began playing golf as a child. At age 17 he won the Junior World Tournament in San Diego, and turned professional in 1977. Notable wins include the PGA World Series (1983), the United States PGA Championship (1992, 1994), and the British Open (1994). He finished the 1994 PGA tour as top money winner, having earned nearly $1.5 million. >> RR1158

Price, Richard (1723–91) Moral philosopher and Unitarian minister, born in Tynton, Monmouthshire, SE Wales, UK. A preacher in London, he established his reputation with the *Review of the Principal Questions in Morals* (1758). He was admitted to the Royal Society in 1765 for his work on probability. His *Observations on Reversionary Payments* (1771) helped to establish a scientific system for life-insurance and pensions. Among his many other influential books is *An Appeal to the Public on the Subject of the National Debt* (1772).

Price, Vincent (Leonard) (1911–93) Actor and writer, born in St Louis, MO. He travelled in Europe, studied at Yale, and became an actor. He made his screen debut in 1938, and after many minor roles he began to perform in low-budget horror movies such as *House of Wax* (1953), achieving his first major success with *The Fall of the House of Usher* (1960). Known for his distinctive, low-pitched, creaky, atmospheric voice, and his quizzical, mock-serious facial expressions, he went on to star in a series of acclaimed Gothic horror movies, such as *The Pit and the Pendulum* (1961) and *The Abominable Dr Phibes* (1971). He abandoned films in the mid-1970s, going on to present cookery programmes for television – he wrote *A Treasury of Great Recipes* (1965) with his second wife, Mary Grant – but he had two last roles in *The Whales of August* (1987) and *Edward Scissorhands* (1991).

Prichard, Katharine Susannah (1883–1969) Writer, born in Levuka, Fiji. She studied in Melbourne, and worked as a journalist there and in London, where she published her first novel, *The Pioneers* (1915). In 1916 she returned to Australia, and produced 12 novels, many poems, plays and short stories, and an autobiography. Notable titles include *Coonardoo* (1929), and the Australian goldfields trilogy: *The Roaring Nineties* (1946), *Golden Miles* (1948), and *Winged Seeds* (1950).

Pride, Sir Thomas (?–1658) English parliamentarian during the Civil War, born (possibly) near Glastonbury, Somerset, SW England, UK. Little is known of his early life. He commanded a regiment at Naseby (1645), and served in Scotland. When the House of Commons indicated it might effect a settlement with Charles I, he was appointed by the army (1648) to expel its Presbyterian Royalist members (*Pride's Purge*). He sat among the king's judges, and signed the death warrant. He was knighted by Cromwell in 1656. >> Charles I (of England)

Priest, Oscar Stanton De >> **De Priest, Oscar Stanton**

Priestley, J(ohn) B(oynton) (1894–1984) Writer, born in Bradford, West Yorkshire, N England, UK. He studied at Bradford and Cambridge, made a reputation with his critical writings, and gained wide popularity from his novel,

The Good Companions (1929). It was followed by other humorous novels, such as Angel Pavement (1930), and he established his reputation as a playwright with Dangerous Corner (1932), Time and the Conways (1937), and other plays on space-time themes, as well as popular comedies, such as Laburnum Grove (1933). He married the archaeologist Jacquetta Hawkes in 1953. He refused both a knighthood and a peerage, but accepted the Order of Merit in 1977. >> Hawkes

Priestley, Joseph (1733–1804) Chemist and clergyman, born in Fieldhead, West Yorkshire, N England, UK. In 1755 he became a Presbyterian minister, and after moving to Leeds in 1767 took up the study of chemistry. He is best known for his research into the chemistry of gases, and for his discovery of oxygen. He also wrote an English grammar and books on education and politics. His controversial views on religion and political theory (he was a supporter of the French Revolution) led him in 1794 to leave in fear of his life for America, where he was well received. >> Cooper, Thomas

Prigogine, Ilya [prigogeenay] (1917–) Physical chemist, born in Moscow. He moved to Belgium at the age of 12, studied in Brussels, and became a professor there in 1951. He was also founder-director of the Center for Statistical Mechanics and Thermodynamics at Texas (1967). For his contributions to nonequilibrium thermodynamics he was awarded the Nobel Prize for Chemistry in 1977. His popular books include Order out of Chaos (1979) and From Being to Becoming (1980).

Primo de Rivera (y Orbaneja), Miguel [preemoh the rivera] (1870–1930) Spanish general, born in Jerez de la Frontera, Spain. He served in Cuba, the Philippines, and Morocco, and in 1923 led a military coup, inaugurating a dictatorship which lasted until 1930. During 1928–9 he lost the support of the army, the ruling class, and King Alfonso XIII, and in 1930 gave up power. His son, **José Antonio Primo de Rivera** (1903–36), founded the Spanish Fascist Party (Falange Española) in 1933, and was executed by the Republicans in 1936. >> Alfonso XIII

Primus, Pearl [preemus] (1919–94) Dancer, choreographer, anthropologist, and teacher, born in Trinidad. She studied at Hunter College, New York City, joining the New Dance Group, and making her debut in 1941. Her first solo recital followed two years later, and in 1944 the first appearance of her own group. She continued to present concerts, and choreographed on Broadway, but her real direction lay in dance and anthropological research in Africa. A teacher at Hunter College, she became director of the Art Center of Black African Culture in Nigeria.

Prince, Hal, popular name of **Harold Smith Prince** (1928–) Stage director and producer, born in New York City. A stage manager on Broadway, he became a successful producer and director of stage musicals. His first production was The Pajama Game (1954), and other memorable shows include West Side Story (1957), Fiddler on the Roof (1964), and Cabaret (1968). He has maintained a long association with Stephen Sondheim, producing and directing many of the composer's shows, including Sweeney Todd (1979). He also directed Evita (1978) and The Phantom of the Opera (1986) for Andrew Lloyd Webber. >> Lloyd Webber; Sondheim

Prince, stage name of **Prince Roger Nelson** (1958–) Pop-singer and composer, born in Minneapolis, MN. Named after the Prince Roger Trio, a jazz band in which his father was a pianist, he was signed to Warner Brother Records as a teenager, and released For You in 1978. Subsequent albums included Prince (1979), Dirty Mind (1980), and Controversy (1981), which attracted increasing controversy with their tendency to mix religious and overtly sexual themes. International success followed the release of 1999

(1982), the film and album Purple Rain (1984), and Batman (1989) confirmed him as one of America's most commercially successful pop artists.

Princip, Gavrilo [prin tsip] (1894–1918) Nationalist and revolutionary, born in Obljaj, Bosnia. He was a member of a secret Serbian terrorist organization known as the 'Black Hand', dedicated to the achievement of independence for the South Slav peoples from the Austro-Hungarian empire. In June 1914, he and a group of young zealots assassinated Archduke Francis Ferdinand of Austria and his wife Sophie on a visit to Sarajevo. The murder precipitated World War 1, Austria declaring war on Serbia in July. Princip died in an Austrian prison. >> Francis Ferdinand

Pringle, Mia (Lilly) Kellmer (1920–83) Educational psychologist, born in Vienna. She studied at King's and Birkbeck Colleges, London, and taught in primary schools until she was appointed psychologist in the Hertfordshire School Psychology and Child Guidance Service (1945–50), deputy head of the Child Study Centre (1954–63), and lecturer (senior lecturer from 1960) in educational psychology at Birmingham University (1950–63). She was director of the National Children's Bureau (1963–81), and her many publications, such as Psychological Approaches to Child Abuse (1980), have greatly influenced parent–child relationships.

Printemps, Yvonne [prītā] (1894–77) Actress, born in Ermont, France. She made her first appearance at the Théâtre Cigale, Paris, in 1908, and appeared regularly in revue and musical comedy until 1916, when she began to work with **Sacha Guitry**, whom she subsequently married. She appeared in London and New York, and in 1937 returned to Paris as manager of the Théâtre la Michodière, with her second husband, the actor **Pierre Fresnay** (1897–1973). >> Guitry

Prior, Matthew (1664–1721) Diplomat and poet, born in Wimborne, Dorset, S England, UK. He studied at Cambridge, became an MP (1700), and carried out diplomatic work in Holland, being instrumental in concluding the Treaty of Utrecht (1713). He wrote several political and philosophical poems, but is best known for his light occasional verse collected as Poems on Several Occasions (1709).

Priscian [prishian], Lat **Priscianus** (6th-c) Latin grammarian, born in Caesarea. At the beginning of the 6th-c he taught Latin at Constantinople. As well as his 18-volume Institutiones grammaticae, which was influential in the Middle Ages, he wrote six smaller grammatical treatises and two hexameter poems.

Priscillian [prisilian] (c. 340–385) Christian bishop, born in Trier, Gaul (modern Germany). He was excommunicated by a synod at Saragossa in 380, then tolerated, but ultimately executed – the first case of capital punishment for heresy in the history of the Church. The Priscillian doctrine, said to have been brought to Spain from Egypt, contained Gnostic and Manichaean elements, and was based on dualism.

Pritchett, Sir V(ictor) S(awdon) (1900–97) Writer and critic, born in Ipswich, Suffolk, E England, UK. He studied in London, became a foreign newspaper correspondent in France, Morocco, and Spain, and published his first novel, Claire Drummer, in 1929. He became known for his critical works, such as The Living Novel (1946), short stories, and travel books. He was knighted in 1975, and also published two volumes of autobiography, A Cab at the Door (1968) and Midnight Oil (1973). He was made a Companion of Honour in 1993.

Proclus [prohklus] (c. 412–85) Greek Neoplatonist philosopher, born in Constantinople. He studied at Alexandria and Athens, and became the last head of Plato's Academy. His approach, based on Plotinus, combined the Roman, Syrian and Alexandrian schools of thought in Greek philosophy into one theological metaphysic. His works were translated into Arabic and Latin, and were influential in the Middle Ages. >> Plotinus

Procop(ius) >> **Prokop**

Procopius [pro**koh**pius] (c. 499–565) Byzantine historian, born in Caesarea (now in Israel). He studied law, and accompanied Belisarius against the Persians (526), the Vandals in Africa (533), and the Ostrogoths in Italy (536). He was highly honoured by Justinian, and seems to have been appointed prefect of Constantinople in 562. His principal works are histories of the Persian, Vandal, and Gothic wars, and an attack on the court of Justinian. >> Belisarius; Justinian

Procter, Mike, popular name of **Michael John Procter** (1946–) Cricketer, born in Durban, South Africa. His Test career was restricted by the sporting ban imposed on South Africa, and he had to be content with a place in English county cricket. In first-class cricket he scored 48 centuries, six of them in succession, and made a hat-trick on four occasions. Highly individual in style, he was for many years the mainstay of Gloucestershire cricket.

Proesch, Gilbert >> **Gilbert and George**

Profumo, John (Dennis) [pro**fyoo**moh] (1915–) British statesman. He studied at Oxford, and became a Conservative MP (1940). He held several government posts before becoming minister of state for foreign affairs (1959–60) and secretary of state for war (1960–3). He resigned in 1963 as a result of a scandal following his admission that he had earlier been guilty of a grave misdemeanour in deceiving the House of Commons about the nature of his relationship with Christine Keeler, who was at the time also involved with a Russian diplomat. He later engaged in a great deal of social and charitable work, and was chairman (1982–5) and president (1985–) of Toynbee Hall, London. >> Denning; Keeler, Christine

Prokhorov, Alexander Mikhailovich [pro**ko**rof] (1916–) Physicist, born in Atherton, Queensland, Australia. His family returned to the Soviet Union after the Revolution, and he became professor at Lebedev Physics Institute, Moscow, where he worked on the principles of lasers with Nikolai Basov. They shared the Nobel Prize for Physics in 1964. >> Basov; RR1122

Prokofiev, Sergey Sergeyevitch [proh**ko**fief] (1891–1953) Composer, born in Sontsovka, Ukraine. He began to compose at the age of five, studied at the St Petersburg Conservatory, and won a reputation as a virtuoso pianist. During World War 1 he lived in London, then moved to the USA, returning to the USSR in 1934. He wrote many occasional works for official celebrations, in addition to popular pieces such as *Peter and the Wolf* (1936) and film music. His works have a vast range, including seven symphonies, nine concertos, ballets, operas, suites, cantatas, sonatas, and songs.

Prokop or **Procop(ius)** [**proh**kop, pro**koh**pius], known as **the Bald** or **the Great** (c. 1380–1434) Bohemian Hussite leader, a follower of Žiška, and on his death, the leader of the Taborites. He carried out raids into Silesia, Saxony, and Franconia, and repeatedly defeated German armies. With his colleague, **Prokop (the Younger)**, he fell in battle in Lipany, Hungary. >> Žiška

Prony, Gaspard François Clair Marie Riche, baron de [**proh**nee] (1755–1839) Civil engineer, born in Chamelet, France. He studied at the Ecole des Ponts et Chaussées, and became assistant to Perronet in Paris, for whom he undertook some analyses of masonry arch bridges, and in 1805 he was appointed inspector-general of roads and bridges. He is most noted for the equations he developed dealing with the flow of water, and for the *Prony brake* (1821) which measures the power of an engine under test. >> Perronet

Propertius, Sextus [pro**per**shius] (c. 48–c. 15 BC) Latin elegiac poet, probably born in Asisium (Assisi), Italy. He travelled to Rome (c.34 BC), where he became a poet, winning the favour of Maecenas and Emperor Augustus. The central figure of his inspiration was his mistress, to whom he devoted the first of his four surviving books, *Cynthia*. Much of his work was published after his death, in Rome. >> Augustus; Maecenas

Prost, Alain [prost], nickname **the Professor** (1955–) Motor-racing driver, born in St Chamond, France. He was the first Frenchman to win the world title. He won in 1985–6 (both for McLaren–Porsche), was runner-up in 1983–4 and 1988, and won again in 1989 (for Maclaren–Honda) and 1993, when he announced his retirement. During his Formula 1 career he won 44 races from 184 starts, and his 699·5 championship points is a world record. >> RR1165

Protagoras [proh**tag**oras] (c. 490–421 BC) The earliest self-proclaimed Greek Sophist, born in Abdera, Greece. He taught mainly in Athens, presenting a system of practical wisdom fitted to train people for citizen's duties, and based on the doctrine that 'man is the measure of all things'. His doctrine that all beliefs are true was examined in great detail and rejected by Plato. All his works are lost except a fragment of his treatise *On the Gods*. >> Plato

Proudhon, Pierre Joseph [proodõ] (1809–65) Socialist and political theorist, born in Besançon, France. In Paris he wrote his first important book, *Qu'est-ce que la propriété?* (1840, What is Property?), affirming the bold paradox 'property is theft', because it involves the exploitation of the labour of others. He then published his greatest work, the *Système des contradictions économiques* (1846, System of Economic Contradictions). During the 1848 Revolution, the violence of his utterances brought him three years' imprisonment, and after further arrest (1858) he retired to Belgium. He was amnestied in 1860.

Proulx, Edna Annie [proo] (1935–) Novelist, born in Norwich, CT. She studied at the University of Vermont (1969) and Sir George Williams University, Montreal (1973). Married and divorced three times, she regularly wrote for magazines to support her family, and in 1988 her collected stories were published as *Heart Songs and Other Stories*. She turned to novel writing with *Postcards* (1992), and won the Pulitzer Prize for her second book, *The Shipping News* (1994). Later works include *Accordion Crimes* (1996).

Proust, Joseph Louis [proost] (1754–1826) Chemist, born in Angers, France. He was director of the royal laboratory in Madrid (1789–1808), but returned to France after the fall of his patron, Charles IV, and the destruction of the laboratory by the French. He developed the law of constant proportion for a chemical compound, known as *Proust's law*, over which he was in a controversy with Claude Berthollet lasting eight years, and which gave valuable support to Dalton's work on chemical compounds. >> Berthollet; Dalton, John

Proust, Marcel [proost] (1871–1922) Novelist, born in Auteuil, France. A semi-invalid from asthma, he was looked after by his mother, and her death in 1905 caused him to withdraw from society, living in a sound-proofed flat, and giving himself over entirely to introspection. He then devoted himself to writing, and in 1912 produced the first part of his 13-volume masterpiece, *A la recherche du temps perdu* (trans Remembrance of Things Past). The second volume of this work, delayed by World War 1, won the Prix Goncourt in 1919. The next volumes brought him an international reputation, and he was able to complete the last six volumes (but not revise them) before his death. His massive novel, exploring the power of the memory and the unconscious, as well as the nature of writing itself, has been profoundly influential.

Prout, Father >> **Mahony, Francis Sylvester**

Prout, Samuel [prowt] (1783–1852) Watercolour painter, born in Plymouth, Devon, SW England, UK. Elected to the Watercolour Society in 1815, his numerous elementary drawing-books influenced many. He was famed for his picturesque views of buildings and streets, and admired by Ruskin. >> Ruskin

Prout, William [prowt] (1785–1850) Chemist and physiologist, born in Horton, Gloucestershire, SWC England, UK. He studied at Edinburgh University, and practised in London from 1812. He is noteworthy for his discovery of the presence of hydrochloric acid in the stomach, and for his 'Hypothesis' (1815), which stated that the relative atomic masses of all elements are whole number multiples of that of hydrogen, which is a primary substance. Although later shown to be incorrect, modern science does accept the hydrogen nucleus (the proton) as a kind of primary substance.

Prudentius [pru**den**shius], in full **Aurelius Clemens Prudentius** (348–c. 410) Christian poet, born in Caesaraugusta, Spain. He practised as a pleader, acted as civil and criminal judge, and afterwards received high office at the imperial court. In his later years he devoted himself to the composition of religious poetry, including *Cathemerinon liber*, a series of 12 hymns, and *Hamartigeneia*, on the origin of evil.

Prudhomme, Paul [proo**duhm**] (1940–) Chef, born in Opelousas, LA. In his early teens he set off on a 12-year apprenticeship with chefs around the USA, then returned to Louisiana and started the first of several restaurants, Big Daddy's Patio. In 1979, he and his wife, **K Hinrichs Prudhomme**, opened K-Paul's Louisiana Kitchen in New Orleans, which became widely known for both its traditional cajun and creole cooking and his own innovations. His reputation was furthered through frequent television appearances, cooking videos, and best-selling cookbooks, such as *Paul Prudhomme's Louisiana Kitchen* (1984). He also markets his line of Magic Seasoning Blends and seasoned and smoked meats.

Prud'hon, Pierre Paul [prüdõ] (1758–1823) Painter, born in Cluny, France. He studied in Dijon, trained with engravers in Paris, and went to Rome. He returned to work in a refined style not in accord with revolutionary Paris. Patronized, however, by the empresses of Napoleon, he was made court painter, and among his best work is a portrait of Joséphine.

Pryde, James >> **Nicholson, William Newzam Prior**

Prynne, William [prin] (1600–69) Puritan pamphleteer, born in Swanswick, Somerset, SW England, UK. He studied at Oxford, and was called to the bar, but was early drawn into controversy. In 1633 appeared his *Histrio-Mastix: the Players Scourge*, which contained an apparent attack on the queen (Henrietta Maria); for this he was tortured, fined, and imprisoned. Released in 1640 by the Long Parliament, he prosecuted Laud (1644), and became an MP (1648). Purged from the House in 1650, he was again imprisoned (1650–2). After Cromwell's death he returned to parliament as a Royalist, for which he was made Keeper of the Tower Records. >> Laud

Prys-Jones, Arthur Glyn [prees] (1888–1987) Poet, born in Denbigh, Denbighshire. He studied at Oxford, became a teacher, and edited the first anthology of Anglo-Welsh poetry, *Welsh Poets* (1917). He published six volumes of his own, including *Poems of Wales* (1923), *High Heritage* (1969), and *Valedictory Verses* (1978). The doyen of Anglo-Welsh writers, he was president of the Welsh Academy from 1970 until his death.

Przhevalski, Nikolay Mikhailovich [pshuh**val**skee] (1839–88) Traveller, born near Smolensk, Russia. From 1867 he made important journeys in Mongolia, Turkestan, and Tibet, reaching to within 160 mi of Lhasa. He explored the upper Hwang-ho, reaching as far as Kiachta. During his travels he amassed a valuable collection of plants and animals, including a wild camel and the wild horse which now bears his name.

Ptolemy I Soter ('Saviour') [**tol**emee] (c. 366–c. 283 BC) Macedonian general in the army of Alexander the Great, who became ruler of Egypt after Alexander's death (323 BC). In 304 BC he adopted the royal title, and thus founded the Ptolemaic dynasty. An able ruler, he secured control over Palestine, Cyprus, and parts of Asia Minor, and placed his regime everywhere on a sound military and financial basis. In 305 BC he defended the Rhodians against Demetrius, and received from them the title of *Soter*. Abroad, the empire was maintained, and in Egypt, Alexandria (with its royally founded museum and library) became the chief centre for learning in the Mediterranean world. On his abdication in 285 BC, he was succeeded by his son as Ptolemy II Philadelphus. >> Ptolemy II; RR1055

Ptolemy II Philadelphus [**tol**emee] (308–246 BC) King of Egypt (283–246 BC), the son and successor of Ptolemy I, Soter. Under him the power of Egypt attained its greatest height. He was generally successful in his external wars, founded the Museum and Library, purchased many valuable manuscripts of Greek literature, and attracted leading Greek intellectuals to his court. The Egyptian history of Manetho was dedicated to him, but the story that he commissioned the Greek translation of the Hebrew Scriptures (the Septuagint) is open to doubt. >> Antiochus II; Arsinoë; Ptolemy I; RR1046

Ptolemy [**tol**emee], in full **Claudius Ptolemaeus** [tole**may**us] (fl.127–145) Greek astronomer and geographer, who worked in the great library in Alexandria. Considered the greatest astronomer of late antiquity, his book known as *Almagest* ('the greatest') is the most important compendium of astronomy produced until the 16th-c. His system, an Earth-centred universe (the *Ptolemaic system*), held sway until dislodged by Copernicus. He also compiled a *Geographia*, containing a catalogue of places with latitude and longitude, wrote on the musical scale and chronology, and constructed several maps, including a map of the world. >> Copernicus

Pucci, Emilio, marchese (Marquess) **di Barsento** [**poo**chee] (1914–92) Fashion designer, born in Naples, Italy. He studied in Italy and the USA, gaining a doctorate in political science in 1941. A member of the Italian ski team (1934), in 1947 he was photographed wearing ski clothes he had designed. He then began to create and sell clothes for women, opening his couture house in 1950, and becoming famous for his use of bold patterns and brilliant colour. He became a member of the Italian parliament in 1965.

Puccini, Giacomo (Antonio Domenico Michele Secondo Maria) [pu**chee**nee] (1858–1924) Operatic composer, born in Lucca, Italy. An organist and choirmaster, his first compositions were for the Church. In 1880 he attended the Milan Conservatory. His first great success was *Manon Lescaut* (1893), but this was eclipsed by *La Bohème* (1896), *Tosca* (1900), and *Madame Butterfly* (1904). His last opera, *Turandot*, was left unfinished at his death.

Pucelle, Jean [püsel] or **Pucello, Johan** (c. 1300–c. 1355) French painter who ran an important workshop in Paris from the 1320s onwards, specializing in illuminated manuscripts. The 'Belleville Breviary' (Bibliothèque Nationale, Paris) and the 'Hours of Jeanne d'Evreux' (Metropolitan Museum, New York City) are among the greatest masterpieces of early French painting, fusing Italian Renaissance with traditional French elements.

Pucello, Johan >> **Pucelle, Jean**

Pudovkin, Vsevoled (Illarianovich) [pudofkin] (1893–1953) Film director and writer, born in Penza, Russia. He joined the State Institute for Cinematography in Moscow, and in his first feature, *Mat* (1926, Mother), applied his concepts of montage and cross-cutting in editing. There followed the silent classics, *Konets Sankt-Peterburga* (1927, The End of St Petersburg) and *Potomok Chingis-Khan* (1928, trans Storm Over Asia), and sound films such as *Dezertir* (1933, Deserter). Much of his work portrays heroic characters in the context of historical turmoil. His books and lectures also had great international influence.

Puffendorf, Samuel, Freiherr (Baron) **von**, also spelled **Pufendorf** (1632–94) Jurist and historian, born in Dorfchemnitz, Germany. After studies at Leipzig and at Jena, he was tutor at the home of the Swedish ambassador at Copenhagen when war broke out, and was imprisoned. Among his great works is *De jure naturae et gentium* (1672, Of the Law of Nature and Nations). Appointed Swedish historiographer to Charles XI, he published a history of Sweden, and in 1688 the Elector of Brandenburg invited him to Berlin to write the history of Frederick William, the Great Elector.

Pugachov, Yemelyan Ivanovich [pugachef], also spelled **Pugachov** (1726–75) Russian Cossack, pretender to the Russian throne, and leader of a mass rebellion against Catherine II (1773–5), born in Zimoveyskaya-na-Donu, Russia. He proclaimed himself to be Peter III, Catherine's murdered husband, and promised to restore ancient freedoms. The rebellion was marked by great ferocity, and Pugachev's name later became a byword for the spirit of peasant revolution in Russia. He was captured in 1774 and taken to Moscow, where he was tortured and executed. >> Catherine II

Pugachov >> **Pugachev**

Puget, Pierre [püzhay] (1620–94) Sculptor, painter, and architect, born in Marseilles, France. He did most of his architectural work in Marseilles. His painting can be seen on the ceilings of the Berberini Palace in Rome and the Pitti Palace in Florence. Examples of his sculpture are in the Louvre, notably 'Hercules', 'Milo of Crotona', 'Alexander', and 'Diogenes'.

Pugh, Clifton Ernest (1924–90) Artist, born in Richmond, Victoria, Australia. He studied at the Art School of the National Gallery of Victoria, Melbourne, had his first major exhibition in 1957, and made his mark with exhibitions at the Whitechapel and Tate Galleries, London, in the early 1960s. His paintings divide into two genres: his love of native Australian wildlife, reflected in his 'bush' paintings, and his perceptive portraits of academics and politicians.

Pugin, Augustus (Welby Northmore) [pyoojin] (1812–52) Architect, born in London, England, UK. Trained by his father, he worked with Charles Barry, designing a large part of the decoration and sculpture for the new Houses of Parliament (begun 1840). He became a Catholic (c.1833), and most of his plans were made for churches within that faith, such as the Catholic cathedral at Birmingham. He did much to revive Gothic architecture in England. >> Barry, Charles

Pujol, Joseph [püzhol], known as **le Pétomane** ('the manic farter') (1857–1945) Entertainer, born in Marseilles, France. A music-hall entertainer whose fame was based on his phenomenal capacity for farting, by drawing in air through his rectum and expelling it. He moved to Paris in 1892, topped the bill at the Moulin Rouge, and in 1895 opened his own theatre, the Pompadour.

Pulaski, Kazimierz [pulaskee] (1748–79) Nobleman and soldier, born in Winiary, Poland. He fought against Russia, and was outlawed at the partition of Poland (1772). In 1777 he went to America, and for his conduct at Brandywine was given a brigade of cavalry. In 1778 he organized *Pulaski's legion*, entered Charleston in 1779, and held it until it was relieved. He was mortally wounded at the siege of Savannah.

Pulitzer, Joseph [poolitser] (1847–1911) Newspaper proprietor, born in Makó, Hungary. In 1864 he emigrated and joined the US army. Discharged the following year, he moved penniless to St Louis. There he became a reporter, was elected to the State legislature, and began to acquire and revitalize old newspapers. The acquisition of the *New York World* (1883) sealed his success, and he became wealthy. He endowed the Columbia University School of Journalism, and in his will established annual Pulitzer Prizes in the fields of literature, drama, history, music, and journalism. >> RR1128

Pullman, George (Mortimer) (1831–97) Inventor and businessman, born in Brocton, NY. A cabinet-maker, he became a contractor in Chicago and a storekeeper in Colorado, before designing a Pullman railroad sleeping-car (1865). The Pullman Palace Car Co was formed in 1867, and in 1868 he introduced dining-cars. In 1880 he founded Pullman City for his workers, since absorbed by Chicago.

Pupin, Michael (Idvorsky) [pyoopeen] (1858–1935) Physicist and inventor, born in Idvor, Hungary. A penniless immigrant, he studied at Columbia University, and became professor of electromechanics there (1901–31). He devised a system of multiplex telegraphy, the fluoroscope, and the *Pupin inductance coil*, which made long-distance telephony practical by amplifying the signal at intervals along the line without distortion. His autobiography, *From Immigrant to Inventor* (1923), won the Pulitzer Prize.

Purbach or **Peuerbach, Georg von** [poorbakh] (1423–61) Astronomer and mathematician, born in Austria. Considered to be the first great modern astronomer, he was teacher of Regiomontanus. Court astrologer to Frederick III and professor at Vienna, he is thought to have been the first to introduce sines into trigonometry. >> Regiomontanus

Purcell, E(dward) M(ills) [persel] (1912–) Physicist, born in Taylorville, IL. He studied at Purdue, Karlsruhe, and Harvard universities, worked on microwave radar at Massachusetts Institute of Technology during World War 2, and was appointed professor of physics at Harvard (1949). He developed nuclear magnetic resonance methods of analysis which have become a major tool in chemistry, and was the first to detect the interstellar microwave radiation predicted by van der Hulst. He shared the Nobel Prize for Physics in 1952 for his work on the magnetic moments of atomic particles. >> van der Hulst; RR1122

Purcell, Henry [persel], earlier [**per**sel] (1659–95) Composer, born in London, England, UK. He was a Chapel Royal chorister, and held posts as organist there and at Westminster Abbey, as well as becoming keeper of the king's instruments (1683). Though his harpsichord pieces and his trio-sonatas for violins and continuo have retained their popularity, he is best known for his vocal and choral works. In his official capacity he produced a number of pieces in celebration of royal birthdays, St Cecilia's Day, and other occasions. He also wrote a great deal of incidental stage music, including *The Fairy Queen* (1692) and *The Tempest* (1695), and an opera, *Dido and Aeneas* (1689). Of his many songs, 'Nymphs and Shepherds' is probably the best known. >> Clarke, Jeremiah

Purcell, William Gray >> **Elmslie, George Grant**

Purchas, Samuel (1577–1626) Compiler of travel books, born in Thaxted, Essex, SE England, UK. He studied at Cambridge, then became vicar of Eastwood (1604) and rector of St Martin's, Ludgate (1614). His great works were *Purchas his Pilgrimage, or Relations of the World in all Ages* (1613) and *Hakluytus Posthumus, or Purchas his Pilgrimes* (1625), based on the papers of Hakluyt and archives of the East India Company. >> Hakluyt

Purdy, James (1923–) Novelist, playwright, and poet, born in Ohio. He studied at the universities of Chicago and Puebla (Mexico), then worked as an interpreter and teacher. He became known following his first collection of short stories, *Color of Darkness* (1957). His novels include *Malcolm* (1959), *Eustace Chisholm* (1967), a trilogy, *Sleepers in Moon-Crowned Valleys* (1970–81), and *Garments the Living Wear* (1989).

Purkinje, Johannes (Evangelista) [**poor**kinyay] (1787–1869) Histologist and physiologist, born in Libochovice, Czech Republic. He graduated in 1818 with a thesis on vision, which gained him the friendship and support of Goethe. Helped by this, he became professor in Wrocław, Poland (formerly Breslau, Germany) and later at Prague. An early user of the improved compound microscope, he discovered a number of new and important microscopic anatomical structures, some of which are named after him. He was also a very early user of the microtome for cutting sections. >> Goethe

Pusey, E(dward) B(ouverie) [**pyoo**zee] (1800–82) Theologian, born in Pusey, Berkshire, S England, UK. He studied at Oxford, where he became professor of Hebrew in 1828, retaining the position until his death. His main aim was to prevent the spread of Rationalism in England, and he joined Newman in the Oxford Movement (1833), contributing several tracts, notably those on baptism and the Eucharist. After Newman's conversion, he became the leader of the Movement, defending his own position in several publications. >> Newman, John Henry

Pushkin, Alexander Sergeyevich [**push**kin] (1799–1837) Poet, born in Moscow. In 1817 he entered government service, but his liberalism caused his exile to S Russia (1820) until after the accession of Nicholas I (1826). Hailed in Russia as its greatest poet, his first success was the romantic poem 'Ruslan and Lyudmila' (1820), followed by the verse novel *Eugene Onegin* (1828), the historical tragedy *Boris Godunov* (1831), and several other large-scale works. He also wrote many lyrical poems, tales, and essays, and was appointed Russian historiographer. His marriage (1831) to **Nikolayevna Goncharova** proved unhappy and led to his early death, defending his wife's honour in a duel with her brother-in-law, brought about by his enemies at court.

Puskas, Ferenc [**pus**kas, **fe**rents] (1927–) Footballer, born in Budapest. A member of the great Hungarian side of the early 1950s, he was severely criticized for playing in the final of the 1954 World Cup tournament when his fitness was in doubt, and was blamed for the defeat by West Germany. After the invasion of Hungary by the Russians in 1956, he signed for Real Madrid, and achieved the unique distinction of scoring four goals and three goals in two separate European Cup finals. As a coach, he took the Greek side Panathinaikos to the European Cup final.

Putnam, Frederic Ward (1839–1915) Archaeologist and ethnographer, born in Salem, MA. He trained as a zoologist, and was appointed curator of the Peabody Museum at Harvard (1875–1909), becoming professor of American archaeology and ethnology from 1887, then curator of anthropology at the American Museum of Natural History from 1894. Pioneering the study of archaeological remains of native Americans, he led field expeditions to Ohio, New Jersey, the American southwest, Mexico, and South America.

Putnam, George Palmer (1814–72) Publisher, born in Brunswick, ME. He went to London in 1840 and opened a branch bookshop selling American books. In 1848 he returned to the USA and founded a book-publishing business, established in 1866 as the firm of G P Putnam & Sons. In 1853 he founded *Putnam's Monthly Magazine*.

Putnam, Hilary (1926–) Philosopher, born in Chicago, IL. He held teaching positions at Northwestern University and Princeton, and became professor of the philosophy of science at the Massachusetts Institute of Technology (1961–5) and professor of philosophy at Harvard in 1965. He argues strongly for a conception of philosophy that makes it essential to a responsible view of the real world and our place in it. His books include *Meaning and the Moral Sciences* (1978) and *Reason, Truth and History* (1982).

Putnam, Israel (1718–90) American revolutionary soldier, born in Danvers, MA. A captain in the French and Indian War (1755–63), he was tortured by the Indians, given command of a regiment in 1759, and in 1762 went on the West India campaign. In 1764 he helped to relieve Detroit, then besieged by Pontiac. Given command of the forces of Connecticut in 1775, then of New York, he was defeated by Howe (1776) at Brooklyn Heights. In 1777 he was appointed to the defence of the Highlands of the Hudson. >> Howe, William; Pontiac

Putnam, Rufus (1738–1824) American revolutionary soldier, born in Sutton, MA. He served against the French (1757–60), and in the American War of Independence commanded a regiment, becoming brigadier-general in 1783. In 1788 he founded Marietta, OH, and in 1789 was appointed a judge of the Supreme Court of the Northwest Territory. He later became surveyor-general of the United States (1793–1803).

Puttnam, David (Terence), Lord (1941–) Film-maker, born in London, England, UK. A very successful background in advertising and photography led him to produce his first feature film *S.W.A.L.K* (1969). Subsequently he helped encourage new directorial talents with stylish, low-budget features such as *Bugsy Malone* (1976) and *The Duellists* (1977). *Chariots of Fire* (1981), which won four Oscars, epitomized the type of intelligent, humanist drama he wanted to make, and its international commercial appeal allowed him to progress to larger scale explorations of human and moral dilemmas in such films as *Local Hero* (1983), *The Killing Fields* (1984), and *The Mission* (1986). In 1986 he became chairman and chief executive of Columbia Pictures, but returned to Britain after a year. Later films include *Memphis Belle* (1990), *Meeting Venus* (1991), *Being Human* (1994), and *Le Confessional* (1995). He was knighted in 1995, and received a life peerage in 1997.

Puvis de Chavannes, Pierre (Cécile) [püvee duh sha**van**] (1824–98) Painter, born in Lyon, France. He is best known for his murals on public buildings, notably of the life of St Geneviève in the Panthéon, Paris, and the large allegorical works such as 'Work' and 'Peace' on the staircase of the Musée de Picardie, Amiens.

Puyi, Pu Yi, or **P'u-i** [pooyee], personal name of the **Xuantong** Emperor (1906–67) Last emperor of China (1908–12) and the first of Manchukuo (1934–5), born in Beijing. Emperor at the age of two, after the 1912 revolution he was given a pension and a summer palace. Known in the West as **Henry Puyi**, in 1932 he was called from private life by the Japanese to be provincial dictator of Manchukuo, under the name of **Kangde**. Taken prisoner by the Russians in 1945, he was tried in China as a war criminal (1950), pardoned (1959), and became a private citizen. The story of his life was made into a successful film (*The Last Emperor*) in 1988. >> RR1040

Puzo, Mario [**poo**zoh] (1920–) Novelist, born in New York

City. He studied at Columbia University, served in the US air force during World War 2, and worked for 20 years as an administrative assistant in government offices. His first novel was *The Dark Arena* (1955), but he is best known for his epic mafia story *The Godfather* (1969, film 1972), which became a best seller.

Pye, John David (1932–) Zoologist, born in Mansfield, Nottinghamshire, C England, UK. He studied at the University College of Wales, Aberystwyth, and Bedford College, London. He taught zoology at King's College, London (1964–73), then joined Queen Mary College, becoming professor there (1973–91, now emeritus). His principal research has been into the use of ultrasound by animals, particularly the echolocation used by bats to obtain food and avoid obstacles while flying, but the applications of his work have raised the possibility of controlling the social behaviour of insects, in particular those which are pests.

Pyke, Magnus (1908–92) Food scientist and broadcaster, born in London, England, UK. He studied at Montreal and London, researched nutrition under wartime conditions for the Ministry of Food (1941–5), and worked in the distilling industry (1949–73). His lively and slightly eccentric manner, along with a gift for communicating scientific knowledge, led to his selection as a host for the television science series *Don't Ask Me* (1974–80). He wrote a number of scientific books for the layman, including *Butter-side Up* (1976) and *Red Rag to a Bull* (1983).

Pyle, Ernie, popular name of **Ernest Taylor Pyle** (1900–45) Journalist, born near Dana, IN. He held a variety of reporting and editorial jobs, then in the late 1930s devoted himself to reporting, especially as a correspondent in Latin America. During World War 2 he accompanied Allied forces in the invasions of North Africa, Italy, and Normandy, and reported from the front lines with personal stories of soldiers and their lives. His reports, collected in *Here Is Your War* (1943) and *Brave Men* (1944), won great popularity and earned him a Pulitzer Prize. He was killed by Japanese gunfire during the US landing on Okinawa, and became a national hero.

Pym, Barbara (Mary Crampton) (1913–80) Novelist, born in Oswestry, Shropshire, WC England, UK. She studied at Liverpool and Oxford universities, and for most of her adult life worked at the International African Institute in London. She is best known for her series of satirical novels on English middle-class society, including *Excellent Woman* (1952) and *Quartet in Autumn* (1977).

Pym (of Sandy), Francis (Leslie) Pym, Baron [pim] (1922–) British statesman. He studied at Cambridge, and was a Conservative MP from 1961, his advancement coming through the whips' office, before being appointed secretary of state for Northern Ireland (1973–4). He was defence secretary (1979–81), and foreign secretary during the Falklands Crisis of 1982. Dropped from the government following the Conservatives' 1983 election victory, it seemed that he might lead an anti-Thatcher faction within the Conservative Party, but support for his 'Centre Forward' group failed to coalesce, and he accepted a life peerage in 1987. >> Thatcher

Pym, John [pim] (1584–1643) English politician, born in Brymore, Somerset, SW England, UK. He left Oxford without taking a degree, studied law, and entered parliament

(1614). In 1641 he took a leading part in the impeachment of Strafford, helped to draw up the Grand Remonstrance, and in 1642 was one of the five members whom Charles I singled out by name. He stayed in London during the Civil War, and died soon after being appointed lieutenant of the Ordnance. >> Charles I (of England); Strafford

Pynchon, Thomas [pin chon] (1937–) Novelist, born in Glen Cove, NY. He studied at Cornell, then worked as a technical writer for Boeing before leaving to write fiction. His novels, such as *V* (1963), *The Crying of Lot 49* (1966), *Gravity's Rainbow* (1973, National Book Award), and *Vineland* (1992) all display a preoccupation with codes, quests, and coincidences that determines the form of the narrative. An experimentalist, esoteric and elusive, his books largely abandon the normal conventions of the novel. He has also written several short stories, published in *Slow Learner* (1984), which also contains a revealing essay on his acknowledged influences.

Pynson, Richard [pin son] (?–1530) Printer, born in Normandy, France. He studied at the University of Paris, learned printing in Normandy, and practised his trade in England. In 1497 his edition of the Latin poet Terence appeared, the first classic to be printed in London. He became printer to Henry VIII (1508), and introduced roman type in England (1509).

Pyrrho [pi roh] (c. 360–c. 270 BC) Philosopher, born in Elis, Greece. His opinions are known from the writings of his pupil, Timon. He taught that we can know nothing of the nature of things, but that the best attitude of mind is suspense of judgment, which brings with it calmness of mind. *Pyrrhonism* is often regarded as the foundation of scepticism.

Pyrrhus [pi rus] (c. 318–272 BC) King of Epirus (modern Albania) (307–303 BC, 297–272 BC), an ambitious ruler whose aim was to revive the empire of his second cousin, Alexander the Great. Unsuccessful in this goal (283 BC), he turned to the West, where he became embroiled in Italian affairs and hence conflict with Rome. Though he won two battles (280–279 BC), his losses, particularly at Asculum (279 BC), were so great that they gave rise to the phrase *Pyrrhic victory*. >> Antigonus II Gonatus

Pythagoras [piy thag oras] (6th-c BC) Philosopher and mathematician, born in Samos, Greece. He settled at Crotona, S Italy (c.530 BC) where he founded a moral and religious school. He eventually fled from there because of persecution, settling at Megapontum in Lucania. *Pythagoreanism* was first a way of life, of moral abstinence and purification, not solely a philosophy; its teaching included the doctrine of the transmigration of souls between successive bodies. The famous geometrical theorem attributed to him was probably developed later by members of the Pythagorean school, which is best known for its studies of the relations between numbers. Pythagorean thought exerted considerable influence on Plato's doctrines. >> Plato

Pytheas [pith ias] (4th-c BC) Mariner, born in Massilia (Marseille), Gaul. He sailed past Spain, Gaul, and the E coast of Britain (c.330 BC), and reached the island of 'Thule', six days' sail from N Britain (possibly Iceland). His account of the voyage is lost, but referred to by several later writers.

Pythias (of Syracuse) >> **Damon and Pythias**

Qaboos bin Said [ka**boos**] (1940–) Sultan of Oman (1970–), born in Muscat, Oman, the son of Said bin Taimar, and the 14th descendant of the ruling dynasty of the Albusaid family. He studied in England and trained at Sandhurst, from where his father recalled him and kept him prisoner for six years. In 1970 he overthrew his father in a bloodless coup and assumed the sultanship. He proceeded to pursue more liberal and expansionist policies, while maintaining an international position of strict non-alignment. >> RR1079

Qaddafi, Muammar >> **Gaddafi, Muammar**

Qianlong [chyan lung], also spelled **Ch'ien-Lung** (1711–99) Seventh emperor of the Manchurian Qing (Ch'ing) dynasty, and the fourth to rule China. He succeeded at the age of 24. Wanting to be thought the greatest ruler in China's history, he ordered (1773) a great literary catalogue by 15 000 scribes (36 000 vols), studied painting and calligraphy, wrote 42 000 poems, published notes on his studies (1736) and a prose/verse collection (1737), patronized the arts and scholarship, and built a sumptuous summer palace. After three major campaigns (1755–9) he annexed E Turkestan (re-named Xinjiang, 'New Dominion'), conquered Burma (1769) and Nepal (1790–1), and suppressed revolt in Taiwan. This expensive foreign policy, allied to governmental corruption, provoked a rebellion which he was unable to suppress, and he abdicated in 1795. >> Kangxi

Qin Shihuangdi [**chin** shihwang**dee**], also spelled **Ch'in Shih Huang-ti** (259–210 BC) First true emperor of China, who forcibly unified much of modern China following the decline of the Zhou dynasty. His achievements in unifying, centralizing, and bureaucratizing China may have been influenced by those of Darius I of Persia, and followed precepts laid out by the legalist philosopher Xunzi. Aided by his chief minister Li Si he consolidated N defences into a Great Wall, and drove the Xiongnu (Huns) from S of the Yellow R. He conquered the S, built canals and roads, divided China into 36 military prefectures, destroyed feudalism, and disarmed nobles. He also standardized Chinese script, and harmonized axle lengths, weights, measures, and laws. His principal palace, accommodating 10 000, was connected to 270 others by a covered road network. He was buried in a starry mausoleum with 6000 life-size terracotta guards. The tomb has been excavated since 1974. >> Darius I; Sima Qian

Quaid, Dennis [kwayd] (1954–) Film actor, born in Houston, TX. He appeared in a number of small films before *The Right Stuff* (1983) established him as a leading man. He proved his versatility in such films as *Innerspace* (1987), *The Big Easy* (1987), and *Postcards from The Edge* (1990). Later films include *Wyatt Earp* (1994) and *Going West In America* (1996). His television work includes the highly rated *Bill* (1980) and its sequel *Bill: On His Own* (1983).

Quant, Mary [kwont] (1934–) Fashion designer, inventor of the mini-skirt and hot pants, born in London, England, UK. She studied at Goldsmith's College of Art and designed hats for the fashionable Danish milliner, Erik. She began fashion design when she opened a small boutique in Chelsea in 1955, and married one of her partners, **Alexander Plunket Greene**. Her designs were an immediate success, and within seven years she had expanded to the USA and Europe, heading a multi-million dollar business. The geometric simplicity of her designs, especially the mini-skirt, and the originality of her colours, became an essential feature of the new young Chelsea look. In the 1970s she extended into cosmetics and textile design. She received the British Fashion Council's Hall of Fame Award in 1990.

Quantrill, William (Clarke) [**kwont**ril] (1837–65) Guerrilla chief and soldier, born in Canal Dover, OH. He lived on the frontier as a gambler and thief, then settled in the area. When the Civil War broke out, he formed a group of irregulars, known as *Quantrill's Raiders*, which included Jesse James, that robbed mail coaches, fought skirmishes, and attacked Union communities – the most notorious raid being the massacre of some 150 free-soilers in Lawrence, KS (1863). As the war was ending, he set out for Washington, DC, evidently to assassinate President Lincoln, but Federal troops mortally wounded him in Kentucky. >> James, Jesse; Younger, Cole

Quantz, Johann Joachim (1697–1773) Flautist and composer, born near Göttingen, Germany. He spent many years in the service of the King of Saxony, toured extensively in Italy, France, and England, and became teacher of Frederick II, and later his court composer. Author of a treatise on flute-playing, he composed some 300 concertos for one or two flutes as well as a vast quantity of other music for this instrument. >> Frederick II (of Prussia)

Quarles, Francis [kwaw(r)lz] (1592–1644) Religious poet, born near Romford, Essex, SE England, UK. He studied at Cambridge and London, and was successively cup-bearer to the Princess Elizabeth (1613), secretary to Archbishop Ussher (c.1629), and chronologer to the City of London (1639). A royalist and churchman, many of his books and manuscripts were destroyed during the Civil War. His best-known work is the emblem book (a series of symbolic pictures with verse commentary) called *Emblems* (1635), and a prose book of aphorisms, *Enchyridion* (1640). >> Ussher

Quarton, Enguerrand [kah(r)tõ], also found as **Charonton** or **Charrenton** (15th-c) Gothic religious painter, born in Laon, France. Documents relating to six of his important paintings survive, one of which, for a Coronation of the Virgin, is one of the most complete and interesting documents of early French art. His style united French and Italian influences, and some have attributed to him, on stylistic grounds, the most famous of 15th-c French paintings, the 'Pietà' of Villeneuve-lès-Avignon.

Quasimodo, Salvatore [kwazee**moh**doh] (1901–68) Poet, born in Syracuse, Sicily. He studied at Palermo and Rome, became an engineer, then turned to writing, becoming professor of literature in Milan. His early work was Symbolist in character, as in *Ed è subito sera* (1942, And Suddenly It's Evening), and he became a leader of the 'hermetic' poets. After World War 2 his poetry dealt largely with social issues and a deep concern with the fate of Italy, as in *La vita non è sogno* (1949, Life is not a Dream). >> Montale; Ungaretti

Quayle, Sir Anthony [kwayl] (1913–89) Actor and director, born in Ainsdale, Lancashire, NW England, UK. He trained at the Royal Academy of Dramatic Art, London, and started in vaudeville, graduating to the Old Vic Company in 1932. After World War 2 he joined the Shakespeare Memorial Theatre Company at Stratford-upon-Avon as actor and theatre director (1948–56), where he elevated the company to international standing, and provided much of the foundation work for the creation of the Royal Shakespeare Company (1960). In Europe and America he appeared in several contemporary plays now established as classics, and also had a successful screen career, with roles in many major films, such as *Lawrence of Arabia* (1962). He founded the Compass Theatre Company in 1982.

Quayle, (James) Dan(forth) [kwayl] (1947–) US politician and vice-president (1989–93), born in Indianapolis, IN. He studied at DePauw and Indiana universities, then worked as a lawyer, journalist, and public official, becoming a member of the Congress (1977–81) and US Senate (1981–8). He was elected vice-president under George Bush in 1988. >> Bush, George

Queen, Ellery Pseudonym of two writers of crime fiction, **Frederick Dannay** (1905–82) and his cousin **Manfred B Lee** (1905–71), both born in New York City. As businessmen they entered for a detective-story competition, and won with *The Roman Hat Mystery* (1929). From then on they concentrated on detective fiction, using Ellery Queen both as pseudonym and as the name of their detective. They also wrote under the pseudonym **Barnaby Ross**, featuring the detective Drury Lane. In 1941 they founded *Ellery Queen's Mystery Magazine*.

Queensberry, Sir John Sholto Douglas, 8th Marquess of (1844–1900) British aristocrat, a keen patron of boxing, who supervised the formulation in 1867 of new rules to govern that sport, since known as the *Queensberry Rules*. In 1895 he was tried and acquitted for publishing a defamatory libel on Oscar Wilde – an event which led to Wilde's trial and imprisonment. >> Chambers, John Graham; Douglas, Lord Alfred; Wilde, Oscar

Queneau, Raymond [kenoh] (1903–76) Novelist and poet, born in Le Havre, France. He studied at the Sorbonne. The best of his poetry is contained in *Les Ziaux* (1943) and *Si tu t'imagines* (1952, If You Suppose). His novels include *Le Chiendent* (1933, The Bark Tree) and *Zazie dans le métro* (1959, Zazie in the Metro, filmed 1960), and are often self-reflective, anticipating some of the devices of the *nouveau roman*.

Quennell, Sir Peter (Courtney) [kwenel] (1905–93) Biographer, born in Bickley, SE Greater London, England, UK. He studied at Oxford, became professor of English at Tokyo for a year, then returned to London as a writer. Author of several books of verse and a novel, and editor of the *Cornhill Magazine* (1944–51), he is best known for his many biographical studies, including those of Byron (1935, 1941), Ruskin (1949), Shakespeare (1963), and Pope (1968). He also edited many volumes of literary studies. He was knighted in 1992.

Quercetanus >> Duchesne, André

Quercia, Jacopo della >> Jacopo della Quercia

Quesada, Elwood (Richard) [kesahda] (1904–) Aviator, born in Washington, DC. During World War 2, he commanded the 9th Fighter Command in England (1943) and, as head of the 9th Tactical Air Command, directed thousands of sorties in preparation for the Allied landings in Normandy in 1944. He retired from the service in 1951, and in 1959 became the first head of the newly formed Federal Aviation Administration.

Quesada, Gonzalo Jiménez de [kaysahtha] (c. 1497–1579) Conquistador, born in Córdoba or Granada, Spain. Appointed magistrate at Santa Marta, in 1536 he headed an expedition, and after many hardships and loss of men conquered the Chibchas in the E. This he called New Granada, and its chief town Santa Fé de Bogotá. In 1569, during a later expedition in search of El Dorado, he reached the R Guaviare not far from the point where it meets the Orinoco.

Quesnay, François [kenay] (1694–1774) Physician and economist, born in Mérey, France. He studied medicine at

Paris, and by his death had risen to be first physician to the king. His fame depends chiefly on his essays in political economy. He became a leader of the *Economistes*, also called the Physiocratic School, and contributed to Diderot's *Encyclopédie*. >> Diderot

Quesnel, Pasquier [kenel] (1634–1719) Jansenist theologian, born in Paris. He studied at the Sorbonne, and in 1662 became director of the Paris Oratory, where he wrote *Nouveau Testament en français avec des réflexions morales* (1687–94, New Testament in French with Thoughts on Morality). Having refused to condemn Jansenism in 1684, he fled to Brussels. Hostility to his work led to his imprisonment (1703), but he escaped to Amsterdam.

Quevedo y Villegas, Francisco Gómez de [kevaythoh ee veelyaygas] (1580–1645) Spanish writer, born in Madrid. He studied at Alcalá and Valladolid universities, and was a distinguished poet, but chose a political career, becoming counsellor to the Duke of Osuna (1613–20). One of the most prolific Spanish poets, his greatest work remains the brilliant picaresque novel, *La vida del buscón* (1626, The Life of a Scoundrel).

Quezon, Manuel (Luis) [kayson] (1878–1944) First Philippine president (1935–44), born in Baler, Philippines. He studied at Manila, and went to Washington as one of the resident Philippine commissioners (1909). President of the Philippine Senate (1916–35), he was elected the first president of the Philippine Commonwealth, establishing a highly centralized government. He displayed great courage during the Japanese onslaught on General MacArthur's defences in 1941, refusing to evacuate to the USA until appealed to by President Roosevelt. The new capital of the Philippines on the island of Luzon is named after him. >> MacArthur, Douglas; RR1081

Quiller-Couch, Sir Arthur [kwiler kooch], pseudonym **Q** (1863–1944) Man of letters, born in Bodmin, Cornwall, SW England, UK. He studied at Oxford, where he became a lecturer in classics (1886–7), then moved to Cambridge (1912) as professor of English literature. He edited *The Oxford Book of English Verse* (1900), and published several volumes of essays and criticism. He also wrote poems, short stories, and several humorous novels. He was knighted in 1910.

Quilter, Roger (1877–1953) Composer, born in Brighton, East Sussex, SE England, UK. He studied in Germany and lived entirely by composing, holding no official posts and making few public appearances. His works include an opera (*Julia*), a radio opera (*The Blue Boar*), and the *Children's Overture*, based on nursery tunes, but he is best known for his songs.

Quinault, Philippe >> Lully, Jean Baptiste

Quincey, Thomas de >> de Quincey, Thomas

Quincy, Josiah (1772–1864) US statesman, born in Boston, MA. He studied at Harvard, was called to the bar in 1793, and became a leading member of the Federalist Party. Elected in 1804 to Congress, he denounced slavery, and distinguished himself as an orator. He declined re-election to Congress (1812), but became a member of the Massachusetts legislature, served as Mayor of Boston (1823–8), and was President of Harvard (1829–45).

Quine, Willard Van Orman [kwiyn] (1908–) Philosopher and logician, born in Akron, OH. He studied at Prague, Oxford, and Harvard, and became professor of philosophy at Harvard (1948–78, now emeritus). Much influenced by Carnap, the Vienna Circle, and the empiricist tradition, he went on to make his own distinctive and original contributions to philosophy. His philosophy of language challenges the standard distinctions between analysis and synthetic truths and between science and metaphysics. His books include *Mathematical Logic* (1940), *Word and Object* (1960), *The Roots of Reference* (1974), *The Logic of Sequences* (1990), and *From Stimulus to Science* (1995). >> Carnap

Quinet, Edgar [keenay] (1803–75) Poet, historian, and politician, born in Bourg-en-Bresse, France. He studied at Strasbourg, Geneva, Paris, and Heidelberg. His first major work was a translation of Herder's *Philosophy of History* (1825), and his reputation was established with the epic poem *Ahasvérus* (1833). Appointed professor of foreign literature at Lyon (1839), his lectures caused so much excitement that the government suppressed them in 1846, and after the coup he was exiled. His historical works include *La Révolution religieuse au XIXe siècle* (1857, The Religious Revolution in the 19th-c), *Histoire de la campagne de 1815* (1862, History of the 1815 Campaign), and *La Révolution* (1865).

Quintana, Manuel José [keentahna] (1772–1857) Poet and advocate, born in Madrid, where his house became a resort of advanced liberals. Besides his classic *Vidas de los Españoles célèbres* (1807–34, Lives of Famous Spaniards), he published tragedies and poetry written in a classical style, the best of which are his odes, ardently patriotic yet restrained. On the restoration of Ferdinand VII he was imprisoned (1814–20), but recanted, and by 1833 had become tutor to the future Queen Isabella II (reigned 1833–70). He was crowned national poet by Isabella in 1855.

Quintero, Serafin Alvarez >> **Alvarez Quintero, Serafin**

Quintilian [kwintilian], in full **Marcus Fabius Quintilianus** (c.35–c.100) Roman rhetorician, born in Calagurris, Spain. He studied oratory at Rome, returned there in 68, and became eminent as a pleader and state teacher of the oratorical art. His reputation rests securely on his great work, *Institutio Oratoria* (Education of an Orator), a complete system of rhetoric in 12 books.

Quirk, (Charles) Randolph, Baron (1920–) Grammarian and writer on the English language, born in the Isle of Man. He was educated at University College, London, where he lectured in English (1947–54), then taught at Durham (1954–60). He returned to a chair at University College (1960–81), where he also directed the Survey of English Usage. Major grammars in which he was involved are *A Grammar of Contemporary English* (1972) and *A Comprehensive Grammar of the English Language* (1985). He was also Vice-Chancellor of London University (1981–5). He was made a life peer in 1994.

Quisling, Vidkun (Abraham Lauritz Jonsson) [kwizling] (1887–1945) Diplomat and fascist leader, born in Fyresdal, Norway. He was an army major, a League of Nations official, had the care of British interests in Russia (1927–9), and was defence minister in Norway (1931–3). In 1933 he founded the *Nasjonal Samling* (National Party) in imitation of the German National Socialist Party, and became puppet prime minister in occupied Norway. He gave himself up in May 1945, was tried and executed. His name has since been used for anyone who aids an enemy.

Qu Yuan or **Chü Yüan** [choo yooan] (3rd-c BC) The earliest named Chinese poet, of royal ancestry. His work is characterized by rich lyricism and philosophical depth. His major work, the 374-line *Li Sao* ('Encountering Sadness') may be an allegory on his own life: a minister to royalty, he had been banished. His suicide by drowning is commemorated in the Chinese Dragon Boat Festival.

Raab, Julius (1891–1964) Austrian statesman and chancellor (1953–61), born in St Pölten, Austria. He became an engineer, was a Christian Socialist member of the Austrian Diet (1927–34), and federal minister of trade and transport (1938). He retired from politics during the Nazi regime. In 1945 he was one of the founders of the People's Party, becoming its chairman (1951–60).

RAB >> **Butler, R A, Baron**

Rabban Sauma [raban sowma] (c.1225–c.1300) The first Chinese known to have visited Europe, born in Beijing. A Nestorian Christian, he was sent (fruitlessly) by the Mongol court via Baghdad and Trebizond to establish an anti-Arab alliance with Europe. He met the emperor in Byzantium, and the Pope in Rome. At Naples he watched a naval battle, and saw Vesuvius erupt. In Paris he met Philip IV, and at Bordeaux gave communion to Edward I of England. He kept a record of his many experiences. >> **Edward I**

Rabelais, François [rabelay], pseudonym (an anagram of his name) **Alcofribas Nasier** (?1494–?1553) Satirist, physician, and humanist, born in or near Chinon, France. After a period with a Franciscan order, he studied medicine at Montpellier, and became a physician at Lyon. Here he began the sequence of books for which he is remembered, beginning with the comic and satirical *Pantagruel* (1532) and *Gargantua* (1534), published under his pseudonym, and both highly successful, though condemned by the Church for their unorthodox ideas and mockery of religious practices. In 1546 he published his *Tiers Livre* (1546, Third Book) under his own name. It was again condemned, and he fled to Metz, where for a while he practised medicine. He later published a *Quart Livre* (1552, Fourth Book), and there is a *Cinquiesme Livre* (1564, Fifth Book), published after his death, whose authorship is uncertain.

Rabi, Isidor (Isaac) [rahbee] (1898–1988) Physicist, born in Rymanow, Austria. His family moved to New York City in 1899, and he studied at Cornell and Columbia universities, becoming professor of physics at Columbia in 1937. An authority on nuclear physics and quantum mechanics, in 1944 he was awarded the Nobel Prize for Physics for his precision work on neutrons.

Rabin, Itzhak [rabeen] (1922–95) Israeli soldier, statesman, and prime minister (1974–7, 1992–5), born in Jerusalem. After studies at agricultural school he embarked on an army career, completing his training in Britain. He fought in the War of Independence (1948–9), and represented the Israeli Defence Forces at the armistice in Rhodes. He rose to become chief-of-staff in 1964, heading the armed forces during the Six-Day War (1967). After serving as ambassador to the USA (1968–73) he became Labour Party leader and prime minister, resigning in 1977 when involved in a scandal over accounts he kept in the USA. He later served as defence minister (1984–90), was re-elected as Labour Party leader in 1992, and became prime minister again later that year. He shared the Nobel Peace Prize in 1994. He was assassinated by Yigal Amir, a 27-year old right-wing Israeli law student. >> **RR1064**

Rabinowitz, Solomon J >> **Aleichem, Sholem**

Rabuka, Sitiveni [rabooka] (1948–93) Fijian soldier, politician, and prime minister (1992–3), born near Suva, Fiji. He trained at Sandhurst, served with the UN peacekeeping force in Lebanon, and returned to Fiji with the rank of colonel. After the 1987 elections, which resulted in an Indian-dominated coalition government, he staged a coup

and set up his own provisional government. The country was declared a republic, and prime minister Mara was reinstated, but Rabuka retained control of the security forces and internal affairs. As leader of the Fijian Political Party with the rank of major-general, he became prime minister following the elections in 1992, but died in office. >> **RR1049**

Rachel Biblical character, the daughter of Laban and wife of Jacob, and the mother of Joseph and Benjamin. According to *Genesis* 29, Jacob worked 14 years to earn Rachel as his wife, after having once been tricked into taking her elder sister Leah. At first, Rachel was said to be barren, but she died when giving birth to her second son, Benjamin. >> **Jacob; Joseph**

Rachman, Peter [rakman] (1919–62) Property developer and landlord, born in Poland. He survived persecution as a Jew by the Nazis, and moved to Britain in 1946. After working in a factory he began to acquire property in London, letting rooms at exorbitant rents to prostitutes and West Indian tenants, whom no-one else would house. By 1959, many of his tenants took him to tribunal, and he was obliged to sell off his properties. He achieved notoriety after his death, when his creditors and family hunted in vain for his 'missing million'. His name has given rise to the term *Rachmanism*, the exploitation of poor tenants by unscrupulous landlords.

Rachmaninov, Sergey Vasilyevich [rakhmaninof], also spelled **Rachmaninoff** and **Rakhmaninov** (1873–1943) Composer and pianist, born in Nizhni Novgorod, Russia. He studied at St Petersburg and at Moscow, where he won the gold medal for composition. Having fled from the Russian Revolution, he settled in the USA (1918). He wrote operas, orchestral works, and songs, but is best known for his piano music, which includes four concertos, the popular *Prelude in C Sharp Minor*, and his last major work, the *Rhapsody on a Theme of Paganini* (1934) for piano and orchestra.

Racine, Jean (Baptiste) [raseen] (1639–99) Dramatic poet, born in La Ferté-Milon, France. He studied at Beauvais and Port Royal, then went to Paris, where his verses quickly made him known. He began to write plays in 1664, his major verse tragedies including *Andromaque* (1667), *Britannicus* (1669), *Bajazet* (1672), *Phèdre* (1677), and *Bérénice* (1679). Widely regarded as the master of tragic pathos, he then left the theatre, married, and lived in domestic retirement. He later wrote two religious plays on Old Testament subjects, *Esther* (1689) and *Athalie* (1691).

Rackham, Arthur [rakam] (1867–1939) Artist, born in London, England, UK. A water-colourist and book illustrator, he was well known for his typically Romantic and grotesque pictures in books of fairy tales, such as *Peter Pan* (1906), and his own work, *The Arthur Rackham Fairy Book* (1933).

Radcliffe, Ann, *née* **Ward** (1764–1823) Novelist, born in London, England, UK. She lived a retired life, and became well known for her Gothic novels, notably *The Romance of the Forest* (1791), *The Mysteries of Udolpho* (1794), and *The Italian* (1797). Her contemporary reputation was considerable, and she influenced Byron, Shelley, and others, many of whom imitated her 'gothick romances'. >> **Byron, George; Shelley, Percy Bysshe**

Radcliffe, Cyril John, Viscount (1899–1978) British lawyer. He was director-general of the ministry of information (1941–5), became a Lord of Appeal in Ordinary (1949) and a life peer, and in 1962 was created viscount. He was chairman of many commissions and committees, notably those on taxation of profits and income, and on the frontier between India and Pakistan. In 1956, as constitutional commissioner for Cyprus, he drew up a constitution for the future of the island.

Radcliffe, John (1650–1714) Physician, born in Wakefield, West Yorkshire, N England, UK. He studied at Oxford, and became the most popular physician of his time in London. Despite being a Jacobite, he attended William III and Queen Mary. In 1713 he was elected MP for Buckingham. He bequeathed the bulk of his large property to form the Radcliffe Library, Infirmary, and Observatory at Oxford.

Radcliffe-Brown, A(lfred) R(eginald) (1881–1955) Social anthropologist, born in Birmingham, West Midlands, C England, UK. After studying at Cambridge, he carried out field research in the Andaman Is (1906–8) and Australia (1910–11), which served as a basis for his later works on *The Andaman Islanders* (1922) and *The Social Organization of Australian Tribes* (1930–1). He became professor of anthropology at Cape Town (1920) and Sydney (1926), and later was professor at Chicago and Oxford. One of the principal architects of modern social anthropology, his major contribution was more theoretical than ethnographic, and his concern throughout was to emulate the methods of natural science.

Radde, Gustav Ferdinand Richard [rahduh] (1831–1903) Naturalist, ornithologist, and explorer, born in Gdańsk, Poland (formerly, Danzig, Germany). Trained as an apothecary, he abandoned his career for a study of natural history. He travelled widely in the Caucasus and surrounding regions, and became director of a museum he established in Tiflis. He wrote *Ornis Caucasica* (1884) and many other works. *Radde's warbler* and *Radde's accentor* are named after him.

Radek, Karl Bernhardovich [rahdek], originally **Karl Sobelsohn** (1885–?1939) Russian revolutionary and politician, born in Lwow, Ukraine. He studied at Kraków and Bern, and became a journalist. He organized the German Communists during their revolution (1918), and was imprisoned (1919). Returning to the Soviet Union, he became a leading member of the Communist International, but lost standing with his growing distrust of extremist tactics. He was charged as a Trotsky supporter, and expelled from the Party (1927–30). In 1937 he was a victim of one of Stalin's show trials. >> Stalin; Trotsky

Radetzky, Joseph, Graf (Count) **von** [radetskee] (1766–1858) Military reformer, born in Trebnitz, Czech Republic (formerly, Bohemia). He fought against the Turks (1788–9) and in nearly all the wars between the Austrians and the French. He was appointed commander-in-chief in Lombardy (1831), and promoted field marshal in 1836. In 1848 he was driven out of Milan by the insurgents, but held Verona and Mantua for the Habsburgs. Defeated at Goito, he won a victory at Custozza (1848), and re-entered Milan. In 1849 he almost destroyed the Sardinian army at Novara, forced Venice to surrender, and until 1857 again ruled the Lombardo-Venetian territories.

Radford, Arthur (William) (1896–1973) US naval officer, born in Chicago, IL. He commanded a carrier group which played a notable role in the Gilbert and Marshall Is campaigns. He later became vice-chief of naval operations (1948–9), commander of the Pacific Fleet (1949–53), and chairman of the joint chiefs-of-staff (1953–7).

Radhakrishnan, Sir Sarvepalli [rahdakrishnan] (1888–1975) Indian philosopher, statesman, and president (1962–7), born in Tiruttani, Madras, India. He studied at Madras, taught at Mysore and Calcutta universities, and became professor of Eastern religions and ethics at Oxford (1936–52). In 1946 he was chief Indian delegate to UNESCO, becoming its chairman in 1949. A member of the Indian

Assembly in 1947, he was Indian ambassador to the Soviet Union (1949), vice-president of India (1952–62), then president. He was knighted in 1931. >> RR1058

Radiguet, Raymond [radeegay] (1903–23) Novelist and poet, born in Saint-Maur, France. A precocious protégé of Jean Cocteau, he took Paris by storm with his poetry and drama as a teenager, but is best known for his masterpieces *Le Diable au Corps* (1923, The Devil in the Flesh) and *Le Bal du Comte d'Orgel* (1924, trans Count Orgel Opens the Ball). He led a dissipated life and died of typhoid. >> Cocteau

Radzinowicz, Sir Leon [rajinovich] (1906–) Criminologist, born in Poland. He taught law in Poland before coming to England, where he directed the department of criminal science at Cambridge (1946–59) and taught as professor of criminology from 1959. He wrote a major *History of English Criminal Law* (5 vols, 1948), and edited many works on criminal science. He was knighted in 1970.

Rae, John [ray] (1813–93) Arctic traveller, born near Stromness, Orkney Is, NE Scotland, UK. He studied medicine at Edinburgh, and in 1833 became doctor to the Hudson Bay Co. In 1846–7 he made two exploring expeditions to the Canadian Arctic, and in 1848 he accompanied Sir John Richardson on a search voyage for Franklin's lost expedition. On a further journey which he commanded (1853–4), he met the Eskimos who gave definite news of Franklin's expedition and its probable fate. Known for his physical strength, he walked more than 23 000 mi on his travels. In 1860 he surveyed a telegraph line to America from England, and in 1864 made a telegraph survey from Winnipeg over the Rocky Mts. >> Franklin, John; Richardson, John

Raeburn, Sir Henry [raybern] (1756–1823) Portrait painter, born near Edinburgh, EC Scotland, UK. He first produced watercolour miniatures, then worked in oils. After his marriage to a wealthy widow, he studied in Rome (1785–7), then settled in Edinburgh, where he painted the leading members of Edinburgh society in a typically bold, strongly shadowed style. He was knighted in 1822.

Raeder, Erich [rayder] (1876–1960) German grand admiral, born in Wandsbek, Germany. He joined the navy in 1894, and became a chief-of-staff during World War 1. In 1928 he was made commander-in-chief of the navy, and encouraged the building of submarines and capital warships despite the ban imposed by the Treaty of Versailles. He became grand admiral in 1939, but disagreed with Hitler on the deployment of the navy and was removed from command in 1943. At the Nuremberg Trials (1946), he was sentenced to life imprisonment, but released in 1955. >> Hitler

Raemaekers, Louis [rahmakerz] (1869–1956) Political cartoonist and artist, born in Roermond, The Netherlands. He started painting landscapes and portraits, then in 1907 his first political cartoons appeared. He joined the *Telegraaf* in 1909, and attained worldwide fame by 1915 with his striking anti-German war cartoons.

Raffaello Sanzio >> Raphael

Raffles, Sir (Thomas) Stamford (1781–1826) Colonial adminstrator, born at sea, off Port Morant, Jamaica. He had limited formal schooling, became a clerk in the East India Company, and after studying by himself gained a position as assistant secretary in Penang. He quickly rose to become Lieutenant-Governor of Java (1811–16), where he completely reformed the administration. In 1816 ill health brought him home to England, where he was knighted. As Lieutenant-Governor of Bengkulu (1818–23), he established a settlement at Singapore, and was thus largely responsible for the development of the British empire in the Far East.

Rafsanjani, Ali Akbar Hashemi [rafsanjahnee] (1934–) Iranian politician and president (1989–), born in Rafsanjan,

Iran. He supported Khomeini after the latter's exile in 1963, and became a wealthy property speculator in the 1970s. After the 1979 revolution, he helped to found the ruling Islamic Republican Party, and in 1980 was chosen as Speaker of the Majlis (Lower House), representing the moderates who favour improved relations with the West. In the 1980s he was the most influential figure in Iran after Khomeini, and his successor. Since he became president, his policies have become more radical. >> Khomeini; RR1063

Ragaz, Leonhard (1862–1945) Reformed pastor and social activist, born in Canton-Graubünden, Switzerland. He studied at Basel, Jena, and Berlin, was ordained in 1890, and encountered opposition through his profound social concern. In World War 1 he denounced violence as an evil solution, later rejecting Fascism, Nazism, and Communism. Visiting the USA, he found the status of black people 'utterly offensive'. In 1921 he resigned his theological chair at Zürich 'to represent Christ in poverty', and established an educational centre for working people.

Raglan (of Raglan), Lord Fitzroy James Henry Somerset, Baron (1788–1855) British general, born at Badminton, Gloucestershire, SWC England, UK, the son of the Duke of Beaufort. He joined the army in 1804, fought at Waterloo (1815), became an MP, and was made a baron in 1852. In 1854 he led an ill-prepared force against the Russians in the Crimea, but though victorious at Alma did not follow up his advantage. His ambiguous order led to the Charge of the Light Brigade (1854) at Balaclava. His name was given to the *raglan sleeve*, which came into use in the 1850s.

Rahere (?–1144) Clergyman of Frankish descent, the founder of St Bartholomew's Hospital in London. On a pilgrimage to Rome he suffered an attack of malarial fever. During his convalescence he made a vow to build a hospital, and on his return to London he was granted the site at Smithfield by Henry I. In 1123 the building of St Bartholomew's Hospital and Church was begun. In charge of the hospital until 1137, he retired in that year to the priory.

Rahman, Shaikh Mujibur [rahman] (1920–75) First prime minister (1972–5) and president (1975) of Bangladesh, born in Tongipara, Bangladesh (formerly East Bengal). After studying law at Dacca, he helped found the Awami League (1949). In 1954 he was elected to the East Pakistan Provincial Assembly, and took an opposition role during the 1960s. In 1966 he was arrested and imprisoned for two years for provoking separatism. After winning an overall majority in the Pakistani elections of 1970, but being denied office, he launched a non-co-operation campaign which escalated into civil war and the creation of Bangladesh. After becoming president in 1975, he and his wife were assassinated in a military coup. >> RR1034

Rahner, Karl (1904–84) Roman Catholic theologian, born in Freiburg, Germany. He studied at Freiburg and Innsbruck, and taught at Innsbruck, Munich, and Münster. In his voluminous writings (such as his multivolume *Theological Investigations*), he uses insights of the philosophy of existentialism while remaining true to the tradition of Aquinas. He played a major role as a consultant at the Second Vatican Council (1962–6).

Raibolini, Francesco >> **Francia**

Raikes, Robert [rayks] (1735–1811) Philanthropist and pioneer of the Sunday-School movement, born in Gloucester, Gloucestershire, SWC England, UK. In 1757 he succeeded his father as proprietor of the *Gloucester Journal*. His pity for the misery and ignorance of many children in his native city led him to start a Sunday school (1780) where they might learn to read and repeat the Catechism. He lived to see such schools spread throughout England.

Raimondi, Marcantonio >> **Marcantonio**

Raimu [remü], stage name of **Jules Auguste César Muraire** (1883–1946) Actor, born in Toulon, France. A child entertainer, he worked in mime and as a croupier before moving to Paris, making his film debut in 1912. He appeared throughout the 1920s in revues, operettas, and comedies before creating the character of César in *Marius* (1929), which he repeated on film in 1931. Able to combine pathos and humour in his portrayals of the dignified French working man, his films include *Fanny* (1932) and *Un Carnet de Bal* (1937).

Raine, Craig (Anthony) (1944–) Poet, born in Shildon, Co Durham, NE England, UK. He studied at Oxford University and lectured there before becoming poetry editor at Faber and Faber (1981–91). He published his first book, *The Onion, Memory*, in 1978. Later books include *Rich* (1984), *Selected Poetry* (1992), and *Clay: Whereabouts Unknown* (1996). He also wrote the libretto for *The Electrification of the Soviet Union* (1986), an opera by Nigel Osborne, commissioned by Glyndebourne.

Raine, Kathleen (Jessie) (1908–) Poet, born in Ilford, E Greater London, England, UK. Brought up partly in Northumberland, she went on to study at Girton College, Cambridge. Her first collection, *Stone and Flower* (1943), was illustrated by Barbara Hepworth. Later books include *The Year One* (1952), *Collected Poems* (1981), and *Living With Mystery: Poems 1987–91* (1992). She also published three volumes of autobiography (1973, 1975, 1977), several works of literary criticism, and founded the review *Temenos* in 1981. >> Hepworth

Rainer, Yvonne (1934–) Experimental dancer, choreographer, and film-maker, born in San Francisco, CA. One of the greatest influences on post-modern dance, she became involved with the radical Judson Dance Theater, for which she was the most prolific choreographer. *Trio A* (part of the larger work *The Mind is a Muscle*), her signature piece, was made to be performed by anyone of any age, whether trained or not.

Rainier III [raynyay], in full **Rainier Louis Henri Maxence Bertrand de Grimaldi** (1923–) Prince of Monaco (1949–), born in Monaco. In 1956 he married film actress Grace Kelly. They had two daughters, **Princess Caroline Louise Marguerite** (1957–) and **Princess Stephanie Marie Elisabeth** (1965–), and a son, **Prince Albert Alexandre Louis Pierre** (1958–). >> Kelly, Grace

Rainwater, (Leo) James (1917–) Physicist, born in Council, ID. He studied at the California Institute of Technology and Columbia University, and contributed to the Manhattan Project on the atomic bomb during World War 2. He became professor of physics at Columbia University and was director of the Nevis Cyclotron Laboratory there (1951–3, 1956–61). He unified two theoretical models of the atomic nucleus, and shared the Nobel Prize for Physics in 1975 with Aage Bohr and Ben Roy Mottelson. >> Bohr, Aage; Mottelson

Rainy, Robert (1826–1906) Theologian, born in Glasgow, W Scotland, UK. He studied at Glasgow and at New College in Edinburgh, and became a Free Church minister in Huntly (1851) and Edinburgh (1854). From 1862 to 1900 he was professor of Church history in the New (Free Church) College in Edinburgh, becoming its principal in 1874. He organized the union of the Free and United Presbyterian Churches in 1900 as the United Free Church of Scotland, and became the first moderator of its General Assembly.

Raitz, Vladimir Gavrilovich [ryts] (1922–) British travel consultant and entrepreneur. He studied at London, and worked as a journalist (1943–8). On holiday in Corsica he was asked by a camp owner to encourage British holiday-makers to come the following year. Having calculated he could charter an aircraft and provide an all-in two-week holiday in Corsica for less than the normal return air-fare, he set up Horizon Holidays, and initiated the package holiday industry. He left Horizon in 1974 after it was taken over by Clarkson's.

Raja Ram Mohan Rai >> **Rammohun Roy**

Rakhmaninov, Sergei >> **Rachmaninov**

Raleigh, Sir Walter [rawlee, ralee], also spelled **Ralegh** (1552–1618) Courtier, navigator, and writer, born in Hayes Barton, Devon, SW England, UK. He studied at Oxford, and became prime favourite of Elizabeth I. He was knighted in 1584, and that year sent the first of three expeditions to America. After the arrival of the Earl of Essex at court, he lost influence, and spent some years in Ireland. On his return, Elizabeth discovered his love affair with Bessy Throckmorton, one of her maids-of-honour, and he was committed to the Tower. On his release, he married Bessy, and lived at Sherborne. He took little part in the intrigues at the close of Elizabeth's reign, but his enemies turned James I against him, and he was imprisoned (1603), his death sentence being commuted to life imprisonment. While in the Tower, he wrote his *History of the World* (1614) and several other works. Released in 1616, he made an expedition to the Orinoco in search of a gold-mine, which was a failure. His death sentence was invoked, and he was executed. >> Elizabeth I; Essex, 2nd Earl of; White, John

Raleigh, Sir Walter (Alexander) [rawlee, ralee] (1861–1922) Scholar, critic, and essayist, born in London, England, UK. He was professor of English literature at Liverpool (1899), Glasgow (1900), and Oxford (from 1904). Among his writings are *The English Novel* (1891), *Milton* (1900), *Wordsworth* (1903), and *Shakespeare* (1907). He was knighted in 1911.

Ralph de Coggeshall >> **Coggeshall, Ralph de**

Ramadhin, Sonny [ramadin] (1930–   ) Cricketer, born in Trinidad. With Valentine he formed a devastating spin attack in the West Indies Test sides of the 1950s. In 43 Tests he took 188 wickets, on one occasion taking 10 wickets in a match. At Birmingham in 1957 he bowled more balls (774) than any other bowler in the history of Test cricket. In later years he played county cricket with Lancashire. >> Valentine, Alfred

Ramakrishna [ramakrishna], originally **Gadadhar Chatterjee** (1836–86) Hindu religious teacher, born in the Hooghly district of Bengal, India, the son of a poor Brahmin family with little formal education. He became a priest at Dakshineswar Kali temple, near Calcutta, eventually forming his own religious order. He believed in self-realization and God-realization – expressing God by the way one lives and worships – and taught that all religions were different paths to the same goal. His most noteworthy disciple was Vivekananda. Several books of his sayings were later published by his followers. >> Vivekananda

Ramal, Walter >> **de la Mare, Walter**

Raman, Sir Chandrasekhara (Venkata) [rahman] (1888–1970) Physicist, born in Trichinopoly, India. He studied at Madras, and became professor of physics at Calcutta (1917–33) and director of the Indian Institute of Science at Bangalore. In 1929 he was knighted, and in 1930 awarded the Nobel Prize for Physics for his discoveries relating to the scattering of light (the *Raman effect*).

Ramana Maharishi [ramahna maharishee] (1879–1950) Philosopher, born in Madurai, India. At the age of 17 a religious experience led him to become a hermit at the holy mountain of Arunachala, where he remained until his death. Much of the time he lived in caves and avoided publicity, but he later allowed devotees to establish an *ashram*. His philosophy of seeking self-knowledge through integration of the personality in the 'cave of the heart' became

known to Westerners through the books of Paul Brunton as well as his own *Collected Works* (1969) and other anthologies.

Ramanuja [ramahnuja] (traditionally c. 1017–1137) Hindu theologian and philosopher, born in Sriperumbudur, Tamil Nadu, India. He organized temple worship, founded centres to disseminate his doctrine of devotion to Visnu and Siva, and provided the intellectual basis for the practice of *bhakti*, or devotional worship.

Ramanujan, Srinivasa [ramahnujan] (1887–1920) Mathematician, born in Erode, India. The child of poor parents, he taught himself from an elementary English textbook. Although he attended college, he did not graduate. While working as a clerk, he was persuaded to send over 100 theorems that he had discovered to Godfrey Hardy at Cambridge, including results on elliptic integrals, partitions, and analytic number theory. Hardy was so impressed that he arranged for him to come to Cambridge in 1914. He was the first Indian to be elected a Fellow of the Royal Society. >> Hardy, Godfrey

Ramaphosa, Cyril (Matamela) [ramapohza] (1952–   ) South African politician and trade unionist, born in Johannesburg, South Africa. He entered politics as a student at the University of the North, and was detained for the first time in 1974. He qualified as a lawyer, and worked initially in the legal department of a trade union grouping. In 1982 he was elected as the first general secretary of the National Union of Mineworkers, which rapidly grew to become the largest trade union in South Africa. He played a prominent part in the protest politics of the 1980s, and in 1991 became the secretary-general of the African National Congress, resigning in 1996. He was perhaps the Congress's most effective representative during the complex sequence of formal negotiations that began in December 1991.

Ramazzini, Bernardino [ramatseenee] (1633–1714) Physician and pioneer of occupational health, born in Capri, Italy. He studied at Parma University, practised medicine near Rome, then settled in Modena, where he became professor of medicine (1682–1700). He moved to Padua in 1700. His major work *De morbis artificum diatriba* (1700, trans Diseases of Workers), was the first systematic treatise on occupational diseases, and includes many shrewd observations about environmental hazards (such as exposure to lead by potters and painters). He also made important observations on epidemics in human beings and animals.

Rambert, Dame Marie [rombair], originally **Cyvia Rambam** (1888–1982) Ballet dancer and teacher, born in Warsaw. She was sent to Paris to study medicine, but became involved in artistic circles and instead took up dancing. In 1913 she worked on Stravinsky's *Rite of Spring* with Diaghilev's Ballets Russes. She moved to London, where she became a British citizen (1918). From 1926 she formed small companies to present classical and new ballets, promoting collaboration between painters, musicians, and choreographers. In 1935 she formed the Ballet Rambert, and remained closely associated with it through its change to a modern dance company in the 1960s. A strong supporter of young British choreographers, dancers, and designers, she was created a dame in 1962. >> Ashton, Frederick; Diaghilev; Tudor, Antony; van Praagh

Rambouillet, Catherine de Vivonne, marquise de (Marchioness of) [rãbweeyay] (1588–1665) French noblewoman, born in Rome, the daughter of Jean de Vivonne, marquis de Pisani. At the age of 12 she was married to the son of the Marquis de Rambouillet, who succeeded to the title in 1611. From the beginning she disliked the coarseness of the French court. Virtuous and spiritual, for 50 years she gathered together in the famous Hôtel de Rambouillet the talent and wit of France culled from both the nobility and the literary world. >> Scudéry; Vaugelas

Rame, Franca >> **Fo, Dario**

Rameau, Jean Philippe [ramoh] (1683–1764) Composer, born in Dijon, France. He became an organist, and in 1722 settled in Paris, where he published his *Traité de l'harmonie* (1722, Treatise on Harmony), a work of fundamental importance in the history of musical style. He wrote many operas, notably *Hippolyte et Aricie* (1733) and *Castor et Pollux* (1737), as well as ballets, harpsichord pieces, and vocal music.

Ramée, de la >> **Ouida; Ramus, Petrus**

Rameses or **Ramses II** [ramzeez], known as **the Great** (13th-c BC) King of Egypt (1304–1237 BC), whose long and prosperous reign marks the last great peak of Egyptian power. Despite his doubtful victory over the Hittites at Kadesh in N Syria (1299 BC), he managed to stabilize his frontier against them, making peace with them (1283 BC) and later marrying a Hittite princess (1270 BC). An enthusiastic builder, he has left innumerable monuments, among them the great sandstone temples at Abu Simbel. >> RR1046

Rameses or **Ramses III** [ram(e)seez] (12th-c BC) King of Egypt (1198–1166 BC), famous primarily for his great victory over the Sea Peoples, invaders from Asia Minor and the Aegean Is. Tradition identifies him with the pharaoh who oppressed the Hebrews of the Exodus.

Rammohun Roy or **Raja Ram Mohan Rai** (1774–1833) Religious reformer, born in Bengal of high Brahman ancestry. He came early to question his ancestral faith, and studied Buddhism in Tibet. He published various works in Persian, Arabic, and Sanskrit, with the aim of uprooting idolatry, and helped in the abolition of sati. He issued an English abridgment of the *Vedanta*, and published *The Precepts of Jesus* (1820) and pamphlets hostile both to Hinduism and to Christian Trinitarianism. In 1828 he began the Brahmo Samaj Association, and in 1830 the Emperor of Delhi bestowed on him the title of raja.

Ramón y Cajal, Santiago [ramon ee kahal] (1852–1934) Physician and histologist, born in Petilla de Aragon, Spain. He studied at Saragossa University, and became professor at Valencia (1881–6), Barcelona (1886–92), and Madrid (1892–1922). He was specially noted for his work on the brain and nerves, isolating the neuron and discovering how nerve impulses are transmitted to brain cells. In 1906 he shared the Nobel Prize for Physiology or Medicine. >> RR1124

Ramos-Horta, José [ramos haw(r)ta] (1950–) East Timorese activist. He was exiled by the Portuguese in 1970 for his support of the independence movement in East Timor, then returned to take part in the civil war (1972–5), becoming a guerrilla member of Fretilin. He withdrew to Australia following the invasion by Indonesia in 1975, becoming East Timor's international spokesman, and has since sought international support for a peaceful solution. He was awarded the Nobel Prize for Peace in 1996. >> Belo

Ramphal, Sir Shridath Surrendranath [ramfal], known as **Sonny Ramphal** (1928–) Guyanese lawyer and diplomat, born in Guyana. He studied law at King's College, London, and was called to the bar in 1951. He returned to the West Indies, and from 1952 held increasingly responsible posts in Guyana and the West Indies before becoming Guyana's foreign minister and attorney general in 1972, and justice minister in 1973. He later became secretary-general of the Commonwealth (1975–89), and co-chairman of the Commission on Global Governance from 1992. He was knighted in 1970.

Rampling, Charlotte (1946–) Film actress, born in Sturmer, Essex, SE England, UK. She made her debut in *The Knack, and How to Get It* (1965), and became known following her supporting role in *Georgy Girl* (1966). Later films include *Stardust Memories* (1980), *Angel Heart* (1987), *Time is Money* (1994), and *Invasion of Privacy* (1996).

Rams, Dieter (1932–) Product designer, born in Wiesbaden, Germany. Although he trained and worked as an architect, he is best known as the chief designer for Braun AG (since 1955). In association initially with Hans Gugelot, of the Hochschule für Gestaltung ('High School for Design') in Ulm, he transformed the company's product range. His food mixers, record players and radios, shavers, hair driers, and clocks are all examples of rational and unadorned modern design. He was made an honorary royal designer for industry in 1968.

Ramsay, Allan (c.1685–1758) Poet, born in Leadhills, South Lanarkshire, WC Scotland, UK. He was known as a poet by 1718, having issued several short humorous satires. His works include the pastoral comedy, *The Gentle Shepherd* (1725), and an edited collection of Scots poetry, *The Evergreen* (1724). >> Ramsay, Allan (1713–84)

Ramsay, Allan (1713–84) Artist, born in Edinburgh, EC Scotland, UK, the son of the poet Allan Ramsay. He trained in Italy, worked first in Edinburgh, and settled in London in 1762. Well known for his portraits of women, in 1767 he was appointed portrait painter to George III. >> Ramsay, Allan (c.1685–1758)

Ramsay, Sir Bertram (Home) (1883–1945) Naval officer, born in London, England, UK. He entered the Royal Navy as a cadet in 1898, and served as a destroyer commander in the Dover Patrol in World War 1. He resigned from the navy after a disagreement in 1938, but was recalled to service on the outbreak of World War 2 and served as flag officer, Dover (1939–42). He directed the Dunkirk evacuation of 338 000 Allied troops in 1940, commanded the British naval forces for the Allied invasion of Sicily (1943), and in 1944 was Allied naval commander-in-chief for the Normandy landings. He was killed in an aircraft accident.

Ramsay, James Andrew Broun >> **Dalhousie, Marquess of**

Ramsay, Sir William (1852–1916) Chemist, born in Glasgow, W Scotland, UK. He studied at Heidelberg, and became professor of chemistry at Bristol (1880–7) and University College, London (1887–1912). In conjunction with Lord Rayleigh he discovered argon in 1894. Later he identified helium, neon, krypton, and xenon, and was awarded the Nobel Prize for Chemistry in 1904. >> Lockyer; Rayleigh; Travers, Morris William

Ramsey, Sir Alf(red) (1922–) Footballer and manager, born in Dagenham, E Greater London, England, UK. He played with Southampton and Tottenham Hotspur, and as manager took Ipswich Town to the 2nd and 1st Division championships in successive years (1961, 1962). As manager of England (1963–74), his team won the World Cup in 1966.

Ramsey, Frank (Plumpton) (1903–30) Philosopher and mathematician, born in Cambridge, Cambridgeshire, EC England, UK. He read mathematics at Cambridge, and went on to be elected fellow of King's College when he was only 21. In his tragically short life (he died after an operation) he made outstanding contributions to philosophy, logic, mathematics, and economics, to an extent which was only properly recognized years after his death. The best of his work is collected in *Philosophical Papers* (edited by D H Mellor, 1990).

Ramsey, Ian (Thomas) (1915–72) Anglican bishop, and philosopher of religion, born in Kearsley, Lancashire, NW England, UK. He taught at Cambridge from 1941, became a professor at Oxford (1951), and was appointed Bishop of Durham (1966). He was respected both as a diocesan bishop and for his intellectual contribution to the Church of England's Board for Social Responsibility, Doctrine Commission, and the committee on religious education that produced *The Fourth R* (1970). His philosophical works include *Models and Mystery* (1964) and *Models for Divine Activity* (1973).

Ramsey (of Canterbury), (Arthur) Michael Ramsey, Baron (1904–88) Archbishop of Canterbury (1961–74), born in Cambridge, Cambridgeshire, EC England, UK. He studied theology at Cambridge, was ordained in 1928, and became professor at Durham (1940–50) and Cambridge (1950–2). He was Bishop of Durham (1952–6) and Archbishop of York (1956–61). As Archbishop of Canterbury he worked for Church unity, making a historic visit to Pope Paul VI in the Vatican in 1966, but was disappointed in his attempts to forge a reconciliation with the Methodist Church. His books include *The Resurrection of Christ* (1945) and *Be Still and Know* (1982). He retired in 1974, and was given a life peerage. >> Paul VI

Ramsey, Norman F(oster), Jr (1915–) Physicist, born in Washington, DC. He studied at Columbia University and Cambridge, then taught at Illinois and Columbia universities before joining Harvard in 1947. Influenced by his graduate adviser, Rabi, he pursued his interest in the energy levels of atoms, his research leading to the development of the caesium atomic clock (1960). He shared the 1989 Nobel Prize for Physics. >> Rabi; RR1122

Ram Singh [rahm sing] (1816–85) Sikh philosopher and reformer, born in Bhaini, India. As a boy, he was a member of the Namdhari movement, of which he later became leader. Having entered the army of Ranjit Singh, he formed a sect to rejuvenate Sikhism. He built up a *khalsa*, or private army, and prophesised that British rule would be broken. Following attacks on Muslims in 1872, he was exiled to Rangoon as a state prisoner.

Ramus, Petrus [ramü], Lat name of **Pierre de la Ramée** (1515–72) Humanist, born in Cuts, France. Educated in Paris, he became a lecturer on Classical authors, and undertook to reform the science of logic. His attempts excited much hostility among the Aristotelians, and his *Dialectic* (1543) was suppressed; but in 1551 he became professor of philosophy at the Collège de France. He later became a Protestant (c.1561), fled from Paris, and travelled in Germany and Switzerland. Returning to France in 1571, he was killed in the massacre of St Bartholomew. >> Charles IX

Ramuz, Charles Ferdinand [ramüz] (1878–1947) Writer, born in Cully, Switzerland. He spent some time in Paris before World War 1, and his first book *Le Petit Village* (The Little Village), appeared in 1903. One of the best-known French-Swiss writers of the century, his prose style and descriptive power won him wide admiration and repute. Most of his works were written after he was 40, and include *Beauté sur la terre* (1927, Beauty on Earth), and *Présence de la mort* (1922, trans The Triumph of Death).

Rancé, Armand Jean Le Bouthillier de [rãsay] (1626–1700) Abbot, founder of the Trappists, born in Paris. He became abbot of the Cistercian abbey of La Trappe in 1662. Affected by the tragic deaths of two of his friends, he undertook a reform of his monastery, and finally established a religious order whose principles were perpetual prayer and austere self-denial. Intellectual work was forbidden, and only manual labour was allowed. He wrote of his order in the controversial *Traité de la sainteté et des devoirs de la vie monastique* (1683, Treatise on Holiness and the Duties of the Monastic Life).

Rand, Ayn [iyn] (1905–82) Writer and philosopher, born in St Petersburg, Russia. She studied at the University of Leningrad, then fled to the USA, becoming a citizen in 1931. Starting as a screenwriter and playwright, she eventually won fame for her novels, such as *The Fountainhead* (1943) – also made into a film she scripted – and *Atlas Shrugged* (1957), which explains her original philosophy, Objectivism. This philosophy, which advocates reason, egoism, and individualism, is also presented in such non-fiction works as *The Virtue of Selfishness* (1964) and *Introduction to Objectivist Epistemology* (1979). It has been systematically presented in *Objectivism: The Philosophy of Ayn Rand* (1991) by Leonard Peikoff, her intellectual heir, and is promoted worldwide by the Ayn Rand Institute, founded in 1985.

Randall, James Ryder (1839–1908) Poet, born in Baltimore, MD. He was first a teacher, then a journalist. His lyrics, which in the Civil War (1861–5) gave powerful aid to the Southern cause, include 'Maryland, My Maryland', 'Stonewall Jackson', and 'There's Life in the Old Land Yet'.

Randall, John (1905–84) British physicist. With his colleague **Harry Boot** (1917–83), working in the physics department of Birmingham University, he invented the cavity magnetron to generate radio waves of very short wavelength (less than 10 cms), essential for radar, in 1940. Their device is now also used in microwave cookers.

Randolph, A(sa) Philip (1889–1979) Labour leader and civil rights activist, born in Crescent City, FL. He studied at City College, New York, co-founded an employment agency and the African-American labour monthly, the *Messenger* (1917), and built the first successful African-American trade union, the Brotherhood of Sleeping Car Porters (1925). He influenced President Truman to desegregate the armed forces in 1948, formed the Negro American Labor Council in 1960, and directed the civil rights march on Washington (1963). >> Truman

Randolph, Edmund (Jennings) (1753–1813) US statesman, born in Williamsburg, VA. Educated at William and Mary College, he studied law with his father, becoming Governor of Virginia (1786–8) during the framing of the US constitution. He was working on a codification of the state laws of Virginia when Washington appointed him attorney general (1789). In 1794 he was made secretary of state, but an accusation of bribery forced his resignation in 1795. He resumed law practice at Richmond, VA, and was chief counsel for Aaron Burr at his treason trial. >> Burr

Randolph, John, known as **John Randolph of Roanoke** (1773–1833) US politician, born in Prince George Co, VA. In 1799 he entered Congress, where he became distinguished for his eloquence, serving until 1829. He was the Democratic leader of the US House of Representatives, but quarrelled with Jefferson and opposed the War of 1812; he also opposed the Missouri Compromise and Nullification. He later helped draft a new Virginia constitution (1829). >> Jefferson, Thomas

Randolph, Sir Thomas (?–1332) Soldier and statesman, the nephew of King Robert I of Scotland, who created him Earl of Moray. He recaptured Edinburgh Castle from the English (1314), commanded a division at Bannockburn, took Berwick (1318), won the victory of Mitton (1319), reinvaded England (1320, 1327), and was guardian of the kingdom after the death of Bruce in 1329. >> Bruce, Robert

Randolph, Thomas (1605–35) Poet and playwright, born in Newnham-cum-Badby, Northamptonshire, C England, UK. He studied at Cambridge, where he was elected a fellow, and soon began to write, gaining the friendship of Ben Jonson and leading a boisterous life. He left a number of bright, fanciful poems, and six plays, including *Aristippus, or the Jovial Philosopher* (c.1626), *The Muses' Looking-glass* (1630), and *Hey for Honesty* (1651). >> Jonson

Ranjit Singh [ranjit sing], known as **the Lion of the Punjab** (1780–1839) Sikh ruler, born in Budrukhan, India. Succeeding his father as ruler of Lahore, he fought to unite all the Sikh provinces, and, with the help of a modernized army trained by Western soldiers, became the most powerful ruler in India. In 1813 he procured the Koh-i-noor diamond from an Afghan prince, as the price of assistance in war. >> RR1062

Ranjitsinhji, Prince [ran jitsinjee] (1872–1933) Indian nobleman and cricketer, born in Sarodar, India. After studying at Cambridge University, he became a star batsman (with C B Fry) for Sussex and England. He succeeded as Jam Sahib of Nawanagar in 1906, becoming maharaja in 1918, and did much to modernize and improve conditions in his home state. >> Fry, Charles Burgess

Rank (of Sutton Scotney), J(oseph) Arthur Rank, Baron (1888–1972) Film magnate, born in Hull, NE England, UK. He became chairman of many film companies, including Gaumont-British and Cinema-Television, and did much to promote the British film industry at a time when Hollywood seemed to have the monopoly, owning a chain of 600 cinemas, and being active in film production, exhibition, and distribution. An active supporter of the Methodist Church, he was keenly interested in social problems. He was made a life peer in 1957.

Ranke, Leopold von [rangkuh] (1795–1886) Historian, born in Wiehe, Germany. He studied at Halle and Berlin, and became a teacher. A work on the Romance and Teutonic peoples in the Reformation period, and another criticizing contemporary historians, procured his call to Berlin as a professor of history (1825–71). A prolific writer on many aspects of European history, his major work was *History of the Popes in the 16th and 17th Centuries* (1834–7, trans title).

Rankin, Dame Annabelle (Jane Mary) (1908–86) Australian stateswoman, born in Brisbane, Queensland, Australia. She became the first Queensland woman to enter federal politics, as a senator for the state in 1946. The first woman whip in the British Commonwealth, serving as Opposition whip (1947–9) and government whip (1951–66), she was also the first Australian woman of ministerial rank, holding the housing portfolio (1966–71), and Australia's first woman head of a diplomatic mission, as high commissioner to New Zealand (1971–4). She was created a dame in 1957.

Rankin, Jeannette (1880–1973) Feminist and pacifist, born near Missoula, MT. She studied at Montana University and the New York School of Philanthropy, and became the first female member of Congress, entering the US House of Representatives as a Republican (1917–19, 1941–3). She was instrumental in the adoption of the first bill granting married women independent citizenship. She worked for the National Council for the Prevention of War (1928–39), and led the Jeannette Rankin March on Capitol Hill, Washington (1968), to protest against the Vietnam War.

Rankine, William (John Macquorn) [rangkin] (1820–72) Engineer and scientist, born in Edinburgh, EC Scotland, UK. In 1855 he was appointed to the chair of engineering at Glasgow. Elected a fellow of the Royal Society in 1853, his works on the steam engine, machinery, shipbuilding, and applied mechanics became standard textbooks. He also did much for the new science of thermodynamics and the theories of elasticity and of waves.

Ransom, John Crowe (1888–1974) Poet and critic, born in Pulaski, TN. He studied at Oxford, then had a long association with Kenyon College (1937–58), and was formative in the founding of the *Kenyon Review* and the 'New' school of criticism. His work includes *Poems About God* (1919), and the critical books *God Without Thunder* (1930) and *The New Criticism* (1941).

Ransome, Arthur (Mitchell) (1884–1967) Writer, born in Leeds, West Yorkshire, N England, UK. He studied at Rugby, worked for a publisher, and became a war correspondent in World War 1, covering the Russian Revolution. After a stormy relationship with his first wife, they divorced in 1924, and he married Trotsky's secretary, **Evgenia Shelepin**, with whom he fled from Russia. He wrote critical works and travel books before making his name with books for young readers, notably *Swallows and Amazons* (1931). >> Trotsky

Rantzen, Esther (Louise) (1940–) Television presenter and producer, born in Berkhamsted, Hertfordshire, SE England, UK. She studied at Oxford, and joined the BBC in 1963, making sound effects for radio drama. She went on to be a researcher, then reporter, and during 1973–94 produced and presented *That's Life*, a populist consumer programme. She has campaigned against issues of child abuse and drug problems in a variety of documentaries, such as *Childwatch* (1987), and founded the charity 'Childline'. In 1988 she received the Richard Dimbleby Award for her contributions to factual television. She married broadcaster **Desmond Wilcox** (1931–) in 1977, their joint publications including *Kill the Chocolate Biscuit* (1981) and *Baby Love* (1987). Since 1995 she has presented the talk-show *Esther*.

Raoult, François Marie [rahoo] (1830–1901) Chemist, born in Fournes, France. He studied at Paris, and in 1870 became professor of chemistry at Grenoble. He discovered the law (named after him) which relates the vapour pressure of a solution to the number of molecules of solute dissolved in it.

Raphael [raf ael], in full **Raffaello Sanzio** (1483–1520) Painter, born in Urbino, Italy. He studied at Perugia under Perugino, whose style is reflected in his earliest paintings, such as 'The Crucifixion' (c.1503, National Gallery, London). In c.1504 he went to Florence, where he was strongly influenced by Leonardo and Michelangelo. He completed several Madonnas, as well as such works as 'The Holy Family' (Madrid) and 'The Deposition' (1507, Borghese). In 1508 he went to Rome, where he produced his greatest works, including the frescoes in the papal apartments of the Vatican, and the cartoons for the tapestries of the Sistine Chapel. In 1514 he succeeded Bramante as architect of St Peter's. His last work, 'The Transfiguration' (Vatican), was nearly finished when he died. >> Bramante; Leonardo da Vinci; Michelangelo; Perugino

Rapp, George (1770–1847) Religious leader, founder of the American Harmony Society, born in Württemberg, Germany. A linen-weaver by trade, he became leader of a group of separatists who emigrated to W Pennsylvania and Indiana, where they established settlements named Harmony. The community of Harmonites (or *Rappites*) sought to amass wealth for the Lord's use, practised rigid economy, self-denial, and celibacy, and came to own property and shares worth millions of dollars. After his death, the community dwindled.

Rask, Rasmus (Kristian) (1787–1832) Founder of historical comparative linguistics, born in Braendekilde, Denmark. He began as assistant keeper of the library at the University of Copenhagen, then became professor of literary history (1825), oriental languages (1828), and Icelandic (1831). His *Essay on the Origin of the Ancient Scandinavian or Icelandic Tongue* (1818) opened up the science of comparative philology. He was one of the first to recognize that the Celtic languages are Indo-European, and he anticipated Grimm in formulating the consonant shift in Germanic languages. >> Grimm brothers

Rasmussen, Knud (Johan Victor) [raz musen] (1879–1933) Explorer and ethnologist, born in Jacobshavn, Greenland. From 1902 onwards he directed several expeditions to Greenland in support of the theory that the Inuit and the North American Indians were both descended from migratory tribes from Asia. In 1910 he established Thule base on Cape York, and crossed by dog-sledge from Greenland to the Bering Strait (1921–4).

Rasp, Charles (1846–1907) Prospector, born in Stuttgart, Germany. Illness forced him to emigrate to Australia in 1869, and he became a boundary rider in New South Wales, at a time when considerable discoveries of tin were being made. He pegged the very first claim on the 'Broken Hill' in 1883. Two years later further tests indicated not tin but rich silver ore. The Broken Hill Proprietory Company was formed, and he became a rich man. Now known as BHP Ltd, the company is the largest industrial company in Australia, with wealth founded on lead, coal, iron ore, and silver.

Raspe, Rudolf Erich >> **Münchhausen, Baron von**

Rasputin, Grigoriy [ras**pyoo**tin] (? 1871–1916) Peasant and self-styled religious 'elder' (*starets*), born in Pokrovskoye, Russia. A member of the schismatic sect of *Khlysty* ('flagellants'), he was introduced into the royal household, where he quickly gained the confidence of the emperor (Nicholas II) and empress by his ability to control through hypnosis the bleeding of the haemophiliac heir to the throne, Tsarevich Alexey. He was also a notorious lecher and drunkard, and created a public scandal through the combination of his sexual and alcoholic excesses, and his political influence in securing the appointment of government ministers. He was murdered by a clique of aristocrats, led by Prince Felix Yusupov, a distant relative of the Tsar. >> Nicholas II

Ras Tafari Makonnen, Prince >> **Haile Selassie I**

Rastrick, John (Urpeth) (1780–1856) Civil and mechanical engineer, born in Morpeth, Northumberland, NE England, UK. Articled to his father, from c.1801 he gained experience with several firms of iron-founders, and designed and built the cast-iron bridge over the Wye at Chepstow (1815–16). He was engineer of the Stratford & Moreton horse-drawn railway (1822), and in 1826, with George Stephenson, supported the use of steam locomotives on the Liverpool & Manchester railway. His locomotive, the *Stourbridge Lion*, was the first to run in North America. His greatest achievement was the London & Brighton railway, opened in 1841, which included the 37-span Ouse viaduct and three major tunnels. >> Stephenson, George

Ratcliffe, Derek (1929–   ) British conservationist. He joined the Nature Conservancy in 1956, becoming its chief scientist (1973–89). His main work is the *Nature Conservation Revue* (1977), cataloguing the prime examples of habitat in the British Is in need of protection. He was also responsible, through his study of the effects of pesticides on the peregrine falcon, for the restriction and eventual ban on the use of organochlorine insecticides.

Rathbone, Basil (Philip St John) (1892–1967) British actor, born in Johannesburg, South Africa. He made his film debut in *The Fruitful Vine* (1921), and went on to become a major star of the 1930s, with roles in several films from literature, such as *David Copperfield* (1935), *Anna Karenina* (1935), and *Romeo and Juliet* (1936). A character actor who specialized in villains, he also played Sherlock Holmes in several films.

Rathbone, Eleanor (Florence) (1872–1946) Feminist and social reformer, born in Liverpool, Merseyside, NW England, UK. She read classics at Oxford, and became the dominant British advocate for family allowances. She was a leader in the constitutional movement for female suffrage, and as an independent member of Liverpool city council from 1909 she worked vigorously in the housing campaign between the wars. Elected as independent MP for the Combined English Universities, she fought for many causes, including franchise for Indian women, attacked the appeasement of Hitler, and was an enthusiastic proponent of Zionism.

Rathbone, Harold Stewart (1858–1929) British painter, designer, and poet. He founded the Della Robbia Pottery with the sculptor, Conrad Dressler, in Birkenhead (1893), producing a wide range of architectural and domestic earthenware. Items were decorated with sgraffito and elaborate modelled relief decoration inspired by Italian maiolica. The pottery merged with a firm of ecclesiastical sculptors in 1900, and went into liquidation in 1906.

Rathenau, Walther [**raht**enow] (1867–1922) Industrialist and statesman, born in Berlin. He organized German war industries during World War 1, and in 1921, as minister of reconstruction, and after February 1922 as foreign minister, dealt with reparations. His attempts to negotiate a reparations agreement with the victorious Allies, and the fact that he was Jewish, made him extremely unpopular in nationalist circles, and he was murdered by extremists. >> Behrens

Rather, Dan [**ra**ther] (1931–   ) Television news presenter and writer, born in Wharton TX. Educated at Sam Houston State Teachers College, he became a television journalist for CBS in Dallas, then White House correspondent and London bureau chief (1963–74), becoming nationally known for his reports on such major events as the Kennedy assassination, Vietnam, and the Watergate affair. His national profile grew when he became co-editor of *60 Minutes* (1975–81), and he went on to become anchor of *CBS Evening News* (from 1981). He has been involved in many other TV specials, and has written several books on television journalism.

Rathke, Martin H(einrich) [**raht**kuh] (1793–1860) Biologist, born in Danzig, Germany. He was a medical practitioner before becoming professor of physiology at Dorpat (1829) and Königsberg (1835). In 1829 he discovered gill-slits and gill-arches in embryo birds and mammals. *Rathke's pocket* is the name given to the small pit on the dorsal side of the oral cavity of developing vertebrates.

Ratsiraka, Didier (1936–   ) President of Madagascar (1975–93, 1997–   ), born in Vatomandry, Madagascar. He studied in Madagascar and France, served in the navy (1963–70), and was military attaché in Paris. Following independence (1960) there were frequent clashes between the country's two main ethnic groups, the highland Merina and the coastal Cotiers, and in 1972 the army, representing the Merina, took control. Martial law was imposed in 1975, and when this was lifted, Ratsiraka, a Cotier, was elected president under a new constitution. In 1976 he formed the Advance Guard of the Malagasy Revolution, which became the nucleus of a one-party state, but discontent, particularly among the Merina, remained. He was defeated by Albert Zafy in the presidential elections in 1993, but was proclaimed president again in 1997 after reversing the result in the 1996 elections. >> RR1073

Rattigan, Sir Terence (Mervyn) (1911–77) Playwright, born in London, England, UK. He studied at Oxford, and scored a great success with his comedy *French Without Tears* (1936). Several later works were acclaimed, notably *The Winslow Boy* (1946), *The Browning Version* (1948), *Separate Tables* (1954), and *Ross* (1960). He was knighted in 1971.

Rattle, Sir Simon (Denis) (1955–   ) Conductor, born in Liverpool, Merseyside, NW England, UK. He won the Bournemouth International Conducting Competition at the age of 17, and made his London debut at both the Royal Albert and Festival Halls in 1976. He was assistant conductor of the BBC Scottish Symphony Orchestra (1977–80), then joined the City of Birmingham Symphony Orchestra as principal conductor (1980), becoming music director there (from 1991), and has been principal guest conductor of the Los Angeles Philharmonic since 1981. He was knighted in 1994.

Rau, Johannes [row] (1931–) West German politician, born in Wuppertal, Germany. He joined the Social Democratic Party (SPD) and was elected to the Diet of his home *Land* ('state') in 1958. He served as chairman of the SPD's parliamentary group (1967–70), and as minister of science and research (1970–8), before becoming its minister-president in 1978. He was elected Federal Party deputy chairman in 1982 and chancellor-candidate for the 1987 Bundestag election. However, the Party was heavily defeated, and he then concentrated on his work as *Land* premier.

Rauschenberg, Robert [rowshenberg] (1925–) Avant-garde artist, born in Port Arthur, TX. He studied art at the Kansas City Art Institute, in Paris, and at Black Mountain College, NC. His collages and 'combines' incorporate a variety of rubbish (rusty metal, old tyres, stuffed birds, fragments of clothing, etc) splashed with paint. Sometimes categorized as a Pop artist, his work has strong affinities with Dadaism, and with the 'ready-mades' of Duchamp. >> Duchamp

Ravel, Maurice [ravel] (1875–1937) Composer, born in Ciboure, France. He studied under Fauré at the Paris Conservatoire, and won recognition with the *Pavane pour une infante défunte* (1899, Pavane for a Dead Princess). He wrote several successful piano pieces, *Rapsodie espagnole* (1908, Spanish Rhapsody), and the music for the Diaghilev ballet *Daphnis et Chloé* (first performed, 1912). After World War 1, in which he saw active service, his works included the 'choreographic poem' *La Valse* (1920), the opera *L'Enfant et les sortilèges* (1925, The Child and the Enchantments), and *Boléro* (1928), intended as a miniature ballet. >> Fauré, Gabriel

Raven, Simon (Arthur Noël) (1927–) Novelist, playwright, and journalist, born in Leicester, Leicestershire, C England, UK. He studied at King's College, Cambridge, served in the army, then turned to writing, producing his first novel, *The Feathers of Death*, in 1959. His most notable work is *Alms for Oblivion* (1964–76), a series of novels portraying the mid-20th-c English upper classes, and this was followed by another sequence, *The First-born of Egypt* (1984–92). Television dramatizations of well-known works include *Point Counter Point* (1968), *The Way We Live Now* (1969), *The Pallisers* (1974), *Edward and Mrs Simpson* (1978), and *The Blackheath Poisonings* (1993). A regular newspaper contributor, he has also written an autobiography, *Shadows on the Grass* (1982), and several other books of memoirs.

Ravilious, Eric William (1903–42) Artist, designer, and illustrator, born in London, England, UK. He studied at Eastbourne School of Art and the Royal College of Art, and became a designer for J Wedgwood & Sons, his patterns including the travel series, coronation mugs, and Christmas tableware. As a wood engraver, he illustrated many books, including *Twelfth Night* (1932) and *Elm Angel* (1930). During the late 1930s he turned increasingly to watercolour painting and colour lithography. He was appointed official war artist in 1940, and was lost on air patrol.

Ravitch, Diane, *née* **Silvers** (1938–) Educator and historian, born in Houston, TX. An educational historian at Teachers College, Columbia (from 1975), she was appointed assistant secretary of education in 1991. She helped define the neo-Conservative agenda for school reform in such works as *The Troubled Crusade* (1983) and *What Do Our Seventeen-Year Olds Know?* (co-authored, 1987).

Rawlings, Jerry J(ohn) (1947–) Ghanaian leader (1979, 1981–) and president (1992–), born in Accra. He was at the centre of a coup in 1979, returning power to a civilian government a few months later. Despite being forcibly retired from the armed forces and discredited by the government he helped instal, his popularity remained high, and he returned with his Armed Forces Revolutionary Council to seize power again at the end of 1981. Under pressure from aid donors to institute democratic reforms, in 1992 he announced a return to multi-party elections and was elected as president. >> RR1053

Rawlings, Marjorie, *née* **Kinnan** (1896–1953) Writer, born in Washington, DC. She studied at the University of Wisconsin, Madison (1918), worked as a publicist in New York City (1918–19), wrote verses for a United Features syndicate (1926–8), and settled in Florida (1928), first in Cross Creek and later in St Augustine (1941). Her first novel for young readers, *The Yearling* (1938), won the Pulitzer Prize.

Rawlinson, Sir Henry Creswicke (1810–95) Diplomat and Assyriologist, born in Chadlington, Oxfordshire, SC England, UK. He entered military service with the East India Company in 1827. He helped to reorganize the Persian army (1833–9), at the same time studying cuneiform inscriptions, and translating Darius's Behistun inscription. Appointed political agent at Kandahar (1840) and consul at Baghdad (1843), he made excavations and collections. A director of the East India Company in 1856, he became British minister in Persia (1859–60), an MP (1858, 1865–8), and a member of the Council of India (1858–9, 1868–95). He wrote books on cuneiform inscriptions, the Russian question, and a *History of Assyria* (1852). >> Rawlinson, Henry Seymour

Rawlinson, Henry Seymour Rawlinson, Baron (1864–1925) British soldier, the eldest son of Sir Henry Creswicke Rawlinson. He served in Burma, Sudan, and South Africa. In World War 1 he commanded the 4th Army at the Somme (1916), and broke the Hindenburg line near Amiens (1918). He was commander-in-chief in India from 1920. >> Rawlinson, Henry Creswicke

Rawls, John (1921–) Philosopher, born in Baltimore, MD. He studied at Princeton, and taught at Princeton and Cornell before going to Harvard as professor in 1962. His best-known work is *A Theory of Justice* (1971).

Rawsthorne, Alan (1905–71) Composer, born in Haslingden, Lancashire, NW England, UK. He trained as a dentist, then turned to music, studying in Manchester and Berlin. He settled in London in 1935, and wrote a wide range of works, including three symphonies, eight concertos, choral and chamber music, and several film scores.

Ray, James Earl >> **King, Martin Luther**

Ray, John (1627–1705) Naturalist, born in Black Notley, Essex, SE England, UK. He studied at Cambridge, where he became a fellow of Trinity College (1649), but lost his post at the Restoration for religious reasons. With a pupil, **Francis Willoughby** (1635–72), he travelled widely in Europe studying botany and zoology. His classification of plants, with its emphasis on the species as the basic unit, was the foundation of modern taxonomy, his major work being the three-volume *Historia Plantarum* (1686–1704).

Ray, Man, originally **Emanuel Rudnitsky** (1890–1976) Painter, photographer, and film-maker, born in Philadelphia, PA. He studied art in New York City, became a major figure in the development of Modernism, and co-founder of the New York Dadaist movement. He experimented with new techniques in painting and photography, became interested in filming, and in France made Surrealist films such as *Anemic Cinema* (1924) with Marcel Duchamp. During the 1930s he published and exhibited photographs and *rayographs* (photographic images made without a camera). >> Duchamp

Ray, Satyajit [riy] (1921–92) Film director, born in Calcutta, India. He studied at Santiniketan University, then worked as a commercial artist while writing screenplays. His first film, *Pather Panchali* (1954, On the Road), was undertaken in his spare time with very limited finance. Its international success at the Cannes Film Festival allowed him to complete the trilogy with *Aparajito* (1956, The Unvanquished) and *Apu Sansar* (1959, The World of Apu), and he continued as India's leading film-maker. Later features include *The Kingdom of Diamonds* (1980), *Pickoo* (1982), *The Home and The World* (1984), and *An Enemy of the People* (1989). He received an Academy Lifetime Achievement Award in 1991.

Rayburn, Sam(uel Taliaferro) (1882–1961) US representative, born in Roane Co, TN. A farm boy, he worked his way through Mayo Normal College, then studied law. A powerful Democrat in the Texas house (1906–12), he rose to prominence in the US House of Representatives (1913–61) on the Committee on Interstate and Foreign Commerce, and became speaker of the House (1940–61). A Southern populist, he sponsored 'New Deal' legislation, including the Securities and Exchange Act of 1934 to regulate Wall Street. He supported Roosevelt's and Truman's foreign policies, but his policy of moderation and compromise during the 1950s ultimately alienated liberal Democrats, who backed John Kennedy in 1960. >> Kennedy, John F; Roosevelt, Franklin D; Truman

Rayleigh, John William Strutt, 3rd Baron [raylee] (1842–1919) Physicist, born near Maldon, Essex, SE England, UK. He studied at Cambridge, and was elected a fellow of Trinity College in 1866. He succeeded his father as third baron in 1873. He became professor of experimental physics at Cambridge (1879–84), professor of natural philosophy at the Royal Institution, London (1888–1905), and president of the Royal Society (1905–8). His work included valuable studies and research on vibratory motion, the theory of sound, and the wave theory of light (*Rayleigh scattering*). With Sir William Ramsay he was the discoverer of argon (1894). He was awarded the Nobel Prize for Physics in 1904, and became Chancellor of Cambridge University in 1908. >> Ramsay, William; Rayleigh, 4th Baron

Rayleigh, Robert John Strutt, 4th Baron [raylee] (1875–1947) Physicist, born at Terling Place, Essex, SE England, UK, the son of Lord Rayleigh. He became professor of physics at the Imperial College of Science (1908–19). Noted for his work on rock radioactivity, he became a fellow of the Royal Society in 1905 and a Rumford medallist. His writings include two biographies – one of his father, the other of Sir Joseph Thomson. >> Rayleigh, 3rd Baron

Raymond, Alex(ander Gillespie) (1905–56) Strip cartoonist, born in New Rochelle, NY. After a brief career in finance, he studied at the Grand Central School of Art, and became an assistant on a cartoon strip. From 1930 he was with the King Features Syndicate and created a number of outstandingly popular adventure strips, including *Jungle Jim* and the science-fiction adventurer *Flash Gordon* (both 1934). In 1946 he created *Rip Kirby*, the intellectual detective.

Rayner, Claire (Berenice), pseudonyms **Ruth Martin, Sheila Brandon, Ann Lynton** (1931–) British writer, broadcaster, and agony aunt. She trained as a nurse and midwife in London, and followed a nursing career until becoming a medical correspondent for a women's magazine, both as **Ruth Martin** (1966–75) and under her own name (1975–87). She contributed to an advice column to national newspapers (1973–91), and has made many appearances on radio and television to advise on family problems. She has published several books dealing with sex, marriage, motherhood, and family health, and a number of novels, including *Cottage Hospital* (1963, as **Sheila Brandon**), *The House on the Fen* (1967), *The Burning Summer* (1972), *Postscripts* (1990), and *Fourth Attempt* (1996).

Razi >> **Rhazes**

Razin, Stepan Timofeyevich [razeen], known as **Stenka Razin** (c. 1630–71) Russian Cossack, and leader of a Cossack and peasant revolt (1670–1) directed against the boyars and landowning nobility. In April 1671 he was captured, taken to Moscow and publicly executed. He became a folk-hero celebrated in later legend and song as the embodiment of popular rebellion against authority.

Read, Sir Herbert (1893–1968) Poet and art critic, born near Kirkby Moorside, North Yorkshire, N England, UK. He was an assistant keeper at the Victoria and Albert Museum, London, then professor of fine art at Edinburgh (1931–3). He held several other academic posts, and became known as a poet and a writer on aesthetics in such works as *The Meaning of Art* (1931) and *The Philosophy of Modern Art* (1946). His *Collected Poems* were published in 1946. He was also director of the first major British design consultancy, the Design Research Unit. He was knighted in 1953. >> Hulme

Reade, Charles (1814–84) Novelist and playwright, born in Ipsden House, Oxfordshire, SC England, UK. He studied at Oxford, and was called to the bar in 1843, but never practised. He first tried to write for the stage in 1850, producing about 13 dramas. His life after 1852 is a succession of plays by which he lost money, and novels that won profit and fame. These novels illustrate social injustice and cruelty in one form or another, and his writing is realistic and vivid. They include *Peg Woffington* (1852), *Hard Cash* (1863), and *A Woman-hater* (1877). His masterpiece was his long historical novel of the 15th-c, *The Cloister and the Hearth* (1861).

Reading, Rufus Daniel Isaacs, 1st Marquess of [reding] (1860–1935) Jurist and statesman, born in London, England, UK. He studied in London, Brussels, and Hanover, entered parliament as Liberal member for Reading in 1904, and also gained a reputation as an advocate. In 1910 he was appointed solicitor general and later attorney general, and became a member of the Cabinet in 1912. Appointed Lord Chief Justice in 1913, he was special envoy to the USA in World War 1, British ambassador in Washington (1918–21), and Viceroy of India (1921–6). Created marquess on his return, he took charge of many business concerns, including the chairmanship of United Newspapers Ltd and the presidency of Imperial Chemical Industries.

Reagan, Ronald (Wilson) [raygn] (1911–) US statesman and 40th president (1981–9), and former film and television actor, born in Tampico, IL. He studied at Eureka College, IL, became a radio sports announcer, went to Hollywood (1937), and made over 50 films, beginning with *Love Is On the Air* (1937). Although originally a Democrat and supporter of liberal causes, he became increasingly anti-Communist, and in 1962 joined the Republican Party as an extreme right-winger. He became Governor of California in 1966, and stood unsuccessfully for the Republican presidential nomination in 1968 and 1976. In 1980 he defeated Jimmy Carter, and won a second term in 1984, defeating Walter Mondale. He introduced a major programme of economic change aimed at reducing government spending and inflation, took a strong anti-Communist stand, especially in the Middle East and Central America, and introduced the Strategic Defence Initiative. In 1981 he was wounded in an assassination attempt. During his second term, he backed off from his previous attitude of confrontation with the USSR, reaching a major arms-reduction accord with Soviet leader Gorbachev. His domestic popularity remained high throughout his presidency, despite charges of corruption against his aides, and his inability to get much of his programme through Congress. >> Carter, Jimmy; Gorbachev; RR1097

Réard, Louis [rayah(r)] (1897–1984) French designer. He designed the modern two-piece swimsuit, which he named after the nuclear test site in the Pacific, Bikini Atoll (1946).

Reardon, Ray(mond) [reerdn] (1932–) Snooker player, born in Tredegar, Blaenau Gwent. SE Wales, UK. The first of the great snooker players of the modern era, he was dominant in the 1970s. Welsh amateur champion six times (1950–5), he turned professional in 1968, after careers as a miner and policeman. He was world professional champion six times (1970, 1973–6, 1978), and until 1982 was top of the snooker ratings. >> RR1168

Réaumur, René Antoine Ferchault de [rayohmür] (1683–1757) Polymath, born in La Rochelle, France. He carried out research in metallurgy and glassmaking, and produced a major work on entomology. His thermometer (with spirit instead of mercury) has 80 degrees between the freezing-point and boiling-point.

Reber, Grote [rayber] (1911–) Radio astronomer, born in Wheaton, IL. Already an enthusiastic radio ham, he studied at the Illinois Institute of Technology. After Jansky's discovery of weak radio noise originating outside the Solar System, he built the first radio telescope, 31 ft in diameter, in his own back yard (1937), and for several years he was the only radio astronomer in the world. He found that the radio map of the sky is quite different to that produced by conventional telescopes. >> Jansky

Rebuck, Gail (Ruth) [reebuhk], married name **Gould** (1952–) Publisher, born in London, SE England, UK. She studied at the University of Sussex, and entered publishing in 1975, first joining Grisewood & Dempsey, then moving to Robert Nicholson Publications (1976) and the Hamlyn Group (1978). Appointed publishing director at Century Publishing in 1982, she stayed with the company when it became Century Hutchinson (1985) and also when this was taken over by Random House (1989), and in 1991 became chair and chief executive of Random House UK.

Récamier, (Jeanne Françoise) Julie (Adélaide) [ruh-kamyay], *née* **Bernard** (1777–1849) Hostess, born in Lyon, France. Her salon became a fashionable meeting place, especially for former Royalists and those opposed to Napoleon. When her husband was financially ruined, she was forced to leave Paris (1805), returning in 1815. The most distinguished friend of her later years was Chateaubriand. >> Chateaubriand

Recorde, Robert [rekaw(r)d] (c. 1510–58) Mathematician, born in Tenby, Pembrokeshire, SW Wales. He studied at Oxford and Cambridge, then practised medicine in London. He wrote the first English textbooks on elementary arithmetic and algebra, which became the standard works in Elizabethan England, including *The Ground of Artes* (1543) and *The Whetstone of Witte* (1557). He was in charge of mines in Ireland, but died in prison after losing a lawsuit brought against him by the Duke of Pembroke.

Redding, Otis (1941–67) Soul singer, born in Dawson, GA. As a high-school student in Macon, GA, he was so impressed by the success of the local luminary, Little Richard, that he decided to become a full-time performer. His early work, including 'Shout Bamalama' (1960), was heavily influenced by Richard's frantic style. An appearance at the Monterey pop festival in 1967 secured his popularity, but he died in a plane crash in December of that year. The posthumously released ballad 'Dock of the Bay' became his first Number 1 US hit early in 1968. Several of his songs, including 'I've Been Loving You Too Long' (1965), 'Try a Little Tenderness', and 'Mr Pitiful' (1965), are now regarded as classics of their style. >> Little Richard

Redfield, Robert (1897–1958) Cultural anthropologist, born in Chicago, IL. He studied law at Chicago and Harvard universities, then a trip to Mexico inspired him to change to anthropology. He conducted field research in an Aztec community near Mexico City (1926), on which he based the acclaimed *Tepoztlán, a Mexican Village* (1930). From 1930 he was a research associate for the Carnegie Institute, Washington, DC, becoming professor of anthropology at Chicago (1934–58). A leading theorist in the study of peasant societies, he continued his field research in Central America, introducing the concept of the 'folk–urban continuum'.

Redford, (Charles) Robert (1937–) Actor and director, born in Santa Barbara, CA. He dropped out of college to study art and acting, and good performances on Broadway and on television led to engagements in Hollywood, but without great success until the film version of his stage role in *Barefoot in the Park* (1968). After this, major star parts followed regularly, as in *Butch Cassidy and the Sundance Kid* (1969), *The Sting* (1973), *All the President's Men* (1976), and *Out of Africa* (1985). Later films include *Indecent Proposal* (1993) and *Up Close and Personal* (1996). As a director he made the Olympics-based skiing film *Downhill Racer* in 1969, was awarded an Oscar for *Ordinary People* (1980), and directed *A River Runs Through It* (1993), acclaimed for its cinematography. He established the Sundance Institute in 1981 to encourage new talent and the creation of independent feature films.

Redgrave, Sir Michael (Scudamore) (1908–85) Actor, born in Bristol, SW England, UK. He studied at Cambridge, became a teacher, and began his acting career at the Liverpool Playhouse in 1934. His many notable stage performances included Richard II (1951), Prospero (1952), Antony (1953), and Uncle Vanya (1962), and he also had a distinguished film career, starting with his appearance in Hitchcock's *The Lady Vanishes* (1938). He was knighted in 1959, and his autobiography *In My Mind's Eye* appeared in 1983. He married the actress **Rachel Kempson** (1910–) in 1935, and their three children are all actors; **Vanessa**, **Corin** (1939–), and **Lynn** (1944–). >> Redgrave, Vanessa

Redgrave, Richard (1804–88) Subject painter, born in London. Inspector-general of art schools from 1857, he was much involved with the circle of Sir Henry Cole, and edited the *Journal of Design and Manufactures*. With his brother **Samuel** (1802–76) he wrote *A Century of English Painters* (1866) and Samuel also wrote *Dictionary of Artists of the English School* (1874). >> Cole, Henry

Redgrave, Vanessa (1937–) Actress, born in London, the daughter of actor Michael Redgrave. She trained at the Central School of Speech and Drama, London, joined the Royal Shakespeare Company in the 1960s, and took the lead in several feature films, including *Morgan, a Suitable Case for Treatment* (1966), *The Devils* (1971), and *Julia* (1977, Oscar). Later film appearances include *The Bostonians* (1983), *Prick Up Your Ears* (1987), *The Ballad of the Sad Cafe* (1991), *Howard's End* (1992), *Wall of Silence* (1993), and *Mission Impossible* (1996). She is also well known for her active support of left-wing causes. >> Redgrave, Michael

Redi, Francesco [raydee] (1626–97) Physician and poet, born in Arezzo, Italy. He studied at Florence and Pisa, and became physician to the dukes of Tuscany. He wrote a book on animal parasites, and proved by a series of experiments that maggots cannot form spontaneously on meat which has been covered. As a poet, his chief work is *Bacco in Toscana* (1685, Bacchus in Tuscany).

Redman, Don(ald Matthew) (1900–64) Saxophonist, arranger, and bandleader, born in Piedmont, WV. Able to play a wide range of wind instruments while still at school, he studied at the Boston Conservatory, and began to work professionally as a clarinettist, alto saxophonist, and arranger. In the mid-1920s he created a distinctive style for the Fletcher Henderson Orchestra. His principles of swing-style orchestration, heard in recordings by McKinney's Cotton Pickers and his own band (1931–40), influenced nearly every important jazz composer of the era, and continue to be respected in big band music. >> Henderson, Fletcher

Redmond, John (Edward) (1856–1918) Irish politician, born in Dublin. He was called to the bar in 1886, and entered parliament in 1881. A champion of Home Rule, he became chairman of the Nationalist Party in 1900. He declined a seat in Asquith's coalition ministry (1915), but supported the War. He deplored the Irish rebellion, and opposed Sinn Féin.

Redon, Odilon [ruhdõ] (1840–1916) Artist, born in Bordeaux, France. He is usually regarded as a pioneer Surrealist, because of his use of dream images in his work. He made many charcoal drawings and lithographs, but after 1900 painted, especially in pastel, pictures of flowers and portraits in intense colour. >> Gérome

Redpath, Anne (1895–1965) Painter, born in Galashiels, Scottish Borders, SE Scotland, UK. She studied at Edinburgh Art College, then lived in France (1919–34). One of the most important modern Scottish artists, her paintings in oil and watercolour show great richness of colour and vigorous technique.

Redpath, Jean (1937–) Folk-singer, born in Edinburgh, EC Scotland, UK. She became involved in folk music while studying at Edinburgh University. In 1961 she emigrated to the USA, where her outstanding ability, particularly as an interpreter of traditional Scots ballads and the songs of Robert Burns, was quickly recognized. She made her mark at academic level, too, and for several years lectured in music at Wesleyan University. >> Burns, Robert

Redwood, John (1951–) British politician, born in Dover, Kent, SE England, UK. Educated at Oxford, he worked with a merchant bank before being appointed head of Margaret Thatcher's Policy Unit in 1983. Elected Conservative MP for Wokingham in 1987, he became a junior minister in the Department of Trade and Industry before being made secretary of state for Wales (1993–5). He came to national attention when he resigned from the Cabinet in 1995 in order to challenge John Major as leader of the Conservative Party, expressing the views of the party's right wing in relation to such matters as public spending and European Union. His vigorous campaign attracted unexpected levels of support, and he was a strong but ultimately unsuccessful contender for leadership of his party, following Major's resignation in 1997. >> Major; Thatcher

Reed, Sir Carol (1906–76) Film director, born in London, England, UK. He studied at Canterbury, and became an actor and director, joining the cinema in 1930. He produced or directed major films, such as *Kipps* (1941), *The Fallen Idol* (1948), and *Oliver!* (1968, Oscar), but is best known for *The Third Man* (1949), depicting the sinister underworld of postwar, partitioned Vienna, based on the book by Graham Greene. He was knighted in 1952. >> Greene, Graham; Reed, Oliver

Reed, Lou, originally **Louis Firbank** (1944–) Rock singer, guitarist, and songwriter, born in Long Island, NY. He was a member of The Velvet Underground, a band which was closely associated with Andy Warhol. After the group split up in 1970, he moved to England to record *Lou Reed* (1972). His 1973 album, *Transformer*, included 'Walk On The Wild Side', a paean to transsexuality which somehow bypassed radio censorship to become the first Top 10 hit of his career. Subsequent albums have included *Rock 'n' Roll Animal* (1974), *Street Hassle* (1978), and *New Sensations* (1984). >> Warhol

Reed, (Robert) Oliver (1938–) Film actor, born in London, England, UK, the nephew of Sir Carol Reed. Educated at Ewel Castle, he became known through his role as Bill Sykes in Carol Reed's musical, *Oliver!* (1968). His many films include *Women in Love* (1969), *The Devils* (1971), *Three Musketeers* (1974), *Second Chance* (1983), *Treasure Island* (1990), and *Funny Bones* (1995). Often in the public eye for his behaviour off as well as on screen, a volume of autobiography, *Reed All About Me*, appeared in 1979. >> Reed, Carol

Reed, Talbot Baines (1852–93) Writer of books for boys, born in London, England, UK. He became head of his father's firm of typefounders, and wrote books on the history of printing. His robust, moral, but entertaining school stories first appeared in the *Boy's Own Paper*. They include *The Fifth Form at St Dominic's* (1881), *The Master of the Shell* (1887), and *Cockhouse at Fellsgarth* (1891).

Reed, Walter (1851–1902) Army surgeon, born in Belroi, VA. He entered the medical corps in 1875, and was appointed professor of bacteriology in the Army Medical College, Washington, DC, in 1893. Investigations carried out by him in 1900 proved that the transmission of yellow fever was by mosquitoes, and his research led to the eventual eradication of this disease from Cuba. The Walter Reed Hospital in Washington is named after him.

Rees, Lloyd Frederick (1895–1988) Artist, born in Yeronga, Queensland, Australia. He worked in Sydney Ure Smith's studio in Sydney from 1917. His early drawings, meticulous in draughtsmanship and Romantic in style, were etched or lithographed, and in 1931 he held his first exhibition, in Sydney. He turned to oils, and in 1942 the Art Gallery of New South Wales held a retrospective exhibition of his work, with another in 1969. He made several journeys to Europe, and the influence of the Italian landscape lightened the tone of his oils. >> Ure Smith

Rees-Mogg (of Hinton Blewitt), William Rees-Mogg, Baron (1928–) Journalist, born in Bristol, SW England, UK. He studied at Charterhouse and Oxford, and joined *The Financial Times* in 1952, becoming chief leader writer and assistant editor. In 1960 he moved to *The Sunday Times* as city editor, and became deputy editor in 1964. He then became editor of *The Times* (1967–81), by which time he had become an accepted establishment figure, on the boards of several companies. In 1988 he was appointed to head the new, controversial, Broadcasting Standards Council. Knighted in 1981, he was created a life peer in 1988.

Reeve, Christopher (1952–) Film actor, born in New York City. He had various stage and television roles before becoming universally known as the star of *Superman* and its sequels (1978, 1980, 1983, 1987). Later films include *Noises Off* (1992) and *Morning Glory* (1994). In 1994 he became wheel-chair bound following a horse-riding accident, but acted again in *Village of the Damned* (1995) and various television productions. He is also much involved in campaigns supporting handicapped children.

Reeve, Clara (1729–1807) Novelist of the Gothic school, born in Ipswich, Suffolk, E England, UK. She translated John Barclay's *Argenis* (1772), and wrote *The Champion of Virtue, a Gothic Story* (1777), renamed *The Old English Baron*, which was avowedly an imitation of Walpole's *The Castle of Otranto*. She wrote four other novels, as well as *The Progress of Romance* (1785). >> Walpole, Horace

Reeve, John >> Muggleton, Lodowick

Reeves, Keanu [keeahnoo] (1965–) Film actor, born in Beirut, Lebanon. He acted in several Canadian television plays, and had a small part in *Youngblood* (1986) before gaining attention for his performance in *The River's Edge* (1986). *Bill and Ted's Excellent Adventure* (1989), and its sequel, *Bill and Ted's Bogus Journey* (1991), brought him international recognition. Later films include *Much Ado*

About Nothing (1993), *Little Buddha* (1994), *Johnny Mnemonic* (1995), and *Feeling Minnesota* (1996).

Reeves, Sir Paul Alfred (1932–) Clergyman, born in Wellington, New Zealand. He studied at the universities of Victoria (Wellington) and Oxford, was ordained an Anglican priest in 1958, and became Bishop of Waiapu (1971–9). He was subsequently Bishop of Auckland (1979–85) and Primate and Archbishop of New Zealand (1980–5) before becoming Governor-General of New Zealand (1985–90), the first Maori to hold any of those positions. He then became the Anglican Consultative Council representative to the UN (1991–3). He was knighted in 1985.

Regan, Donald (Thomas) [**ree**gn] (1918–) US politician, born in Cambridge, MA. He studied English and economics at Harvard, served as a marine in World War 2, then joined Merrill Lynch, rising to become its president in 1968, and building the company into America's largest securities brokerage corporation. Appointed Treasury secretary in 1981, he became White House chief-of-staff in 1985, but was forced to resign two years later as a result of criticism of his role in the 'Irangate Affair' (1985–6). >> North, Oliver

Regener, Erich [**ray**gener] (1881–1955) German physicist. Professor of physics at Berlin and Stuttgart, he was dismissed for political reasons in 1937, but reinstated in 1946. He is known for his pioneering work on cosmic rays, and for his research on the stratosphere.

Reger, Max [**ray**ger], popular name of **Johann Baptist Joseph Maximilian Reger** (1873–1916) Composer, born in Brand, Germany. He studied at Weiden, taught music at Wiesbaden and Munich, and became director of music at Leipzig University (1907), then professor (1908). He composed organ music, piano concertos, choral works, and songs.

Regiomontanus [rejiohmon**tay**nus], Lat name of **Johannes Müller** (1436–76) Mathematician and astronomer, born in Königsberg (Lat *Mons Regius*, hence his pseudonym), Germany. He studied at Vienna, and in 1471 settled in Nuremberg. He established the study of algebra and trigonometry in Germany, and wrote on a variety of applied topics. In 1474 he was summoned to Rome by Sixtus IV to help reform the calendar.

Régnier, Henri (François Joseph) de [raynyay] (1864–1936) Symbolist poet, novelist, and critic, born in Honfleur, France. He studied law in Paris, then turned to letters. His *Poèmes anciens et romanesques* (1890) revealed him as a Symbolist, though later he returned to more traditional versification. In both poetry and prose his style and mood were admirably suited to evocation of the past, and expressive of a melancholy disillusionment induced by the passage of time. Other poetical works include *Lendemains* (1885, Tomorrows) and *La Sandale ailée* (1906, The Winged Sandal). His novels, mainly concerned with France and Italy in the 17th-c and 18th-c, include *La Peur de l'amour* (1907, Fear of Love) and *La Pécheresse* (1912, The Sinner).

Regulus, Marcus Atilius [**reg**yulus] (3rd-c BC) Roman general and statesman of the First Punic War, whose heroic death at the hands of the Carthaginians earned him legendary status. After capture by the Carthaginians, he was sent to Rome on parole to sue for peace. Having dissuaded the Senate from agreeing to their terms, he voluntarily returned to Carthage, where he was tortured to death.

Regulus or **Rule, St** (4th-c) According to legend, a monk of Constantinople or Bishop of Patras, who in 347 moved to Muckross or Kilrimont (St Andrews), bringing relics of St Andrew from the East. He may possibly be identified with an Irish St Riagail of the 6th-c.

Rehnquist, William H(ubbs) [**ren**kwist] (1924–) Jurist, born in Milwaukee, WI. He studied at Harvard and the

Stanford Law School, then practised law, and became active in the Republican Party. In his post as head of the Office of Legal Council in the justice department (1969), he supported such controversial measures as pre-trial detention and wire-tapping, impressing President Nixon, who appointed him Associate Justice of the Supreme Court in 1972. In 1986 he was appointed Chief Justice, and after 1989, when a 'new right' majority had been established by President Reagan, he framed a series of conservative rulings on abortion, affirmative action, and capital punishment. >> Nixon; Reagan

Reich, Steve [riykh] (1936–) Composer, born in New York City. He studied at the Juilliard School, New York City, and at Mills College, and in 1965 formed a New York ensemble. Strongly influenced by Stravinsky, jazz, African and Balinese music, and his training in drumming, he has evolved a style of vigorous tonality, repetitive contrapuntal patterns, and percussive virtuosity. He uses a variety of vocal and instrumental timbres, including taped and electronic effects. >> Riley, Terry; Stravinsky

Reich, Wilhelm [riykh] (1897–1957) Psychoanalyst, born in Dobrzcynica, Austria. He became a practising psychoanalyst while still a medical student in Vienna, but broke from the Freudian school, developing a theory in which neuroses resulted from repressed, undissipated feelings or sexual energy. In *The Function of Orgasm* (1927), and other works, he expounded on the necessity of regular orgasms for the mental health of both men and women. He was expelled from the German Communist Party in 1933 and the International Psychoanalytical Association in 1934, and emigrated to the USA in 1939. He established the pseudo-scientific 'Orgone' Institute, but died in gaol after being prosecuted for promoting a fraudulent treatment. During the sexual revolution of the 1960s, he became something of a cult figure in the USA. His other works include *Character Analysis* (1933) and *The Sexual Revolution* (1936–45).

Reicha, Antonín [**riy**kha] (1770–1836) Composer, teacher, and music theorist, born in Prague. From 1785 he played flute with the Electoral orchestra at Bonn, taught piano in Hamburg (1794–9), then moved to Paris, where he had two symphonies performed. He lived in Vienna (1801–8) and subsequently in Paris, where his pupils included Liszt, Berlioz, Franck, and Gounod. His use of counterpoint and instrumental sonority was highly original, as seen in his *36 Fugues* and his use of timpani chords. His 24 quintets for woodwind have remained popular. >> Beethoven; Berlioz; Franck, César; Gounod; Liszt

Reichenbach, Georg (Friedrich) von [**riykh**enbakh] (1772–1826) Engineer, instrument-maker, and inventor, born in Durlach, Germany. He trained at the School of Army Engineers in Mannheim, and spent the next two years in England studying the latest advances in engineering and scientific instrument-making. Returning to Germany, he designed improved muskets and cannon for the Bavarian army, and in 1804 established a firm in Munich for the manufacture of precision instruments which became famous among astronomers and surveyors for their high quality. In his later years he turned to hydraulic engineering and built a pipeline 67 mi long, in the course of which he used eleven hydraulic rams to pump salt water to a height of 1200 ft.

Reichenbach, Hans [**riykh**enbakh] (1891–1953) Philosopher of science, born in Hamburg, Germany. He became professor of philosophy at Berlin (1926–33), Istanbul (1933–8) and Los Angeles (from 1938). He was an early associate of the Vienna School of logical positivists, and with Rudolph Carnap founded the journal *Erkenntnis* in 1930 (which reappeared in 1975 in the USA). He made an important technical contribution to probability theory, in which two truth tables are replaced by the multivalued concept of 'weight', and wrote widely on logic and the philosophical bases of science in such works as *Theory of Probability* (1935) and *Philosophy of Space and Time* (1978) (trans titles). >> Carnap; Neurath, Otto; Schlick; von Wright

Reichenbach, Karl, Freiherr (Baron) **von** [riykhenbakh] (1788–1869) Natural philosopher and industrialist, born in Stuttgart, Germany. He discovered paraffin (1830) and creosote (1833), and after studying animal magnetism discovered, as he thought, a new force which he called *Od*, intermediate between electricity, magnetism, heat, and light, and recognizable only by the nerves of sensitive persons. He wrote on the geology of Moravia, on magnetism, and several works on 'odic force' (1852–58).

Reichstadt, Duke of >> **Napoleon II**

Reichstein, Tadeusz [riykhshtiyn] (1897–1996) Chemist, born in Włocławek, Poland. He studied at Zürich, and held posts at the Federal Institute of Technology there, and at the University of Basel. For his research on the adrenal hormones, he shared the 1950 Nobel Prize for Physiology or Medicine. >> RR1124

Reid, Beryl (1920–96) Comedienne and actress, born in Hereford, Hereford and Worcester, WC England, UK. She made her first stage appearance at a concert party in 1936. The radio series *Educating Archie* (1952–6) established her in the comic character of schoolgirl Monica, and her other creations include the Midlands teddy-girl Marlene. *The Killing of Sister George* (1965) brought her recognition as a serious actress, and she won a Tony award for its Broadway production (1966), repeating her role on film (1968). In demand for eccentric character roles, her films include *Star!* (1968) and *Entertaining Mr Sloane* (1969). She received a British Academy Award for her role in the television series *Smiley's People* (1982). An autobiography, *So Much Love*, appeared in 1984.

Reid, Sir Bob, popular name of **Sir Robert Paul Reid** (1934–) Industrial executive, born in Scotland, UK. He joined Shell when he left St Andrews University in 1956, and worked in overseas subsidiaries until 1983, when he returned to the UK. He became chairman and chief executive of Shell UK (1985–90), and as chairman of the British Institute of Management (1988–90), he took a leading role in the reshaping of management education. He later served as chairman of the British Railways Board (1990–5), and was knighted in 1990.

Reid, Sir George (Houstoun) (1845–1918) Australian statesman and prime minister (1904–5), born in Johnstone, Renfrewshire. He arrived in Australia with his parents in 1852, studied law, and in 1878 became secretary to the attorney general of New South Wales. In 1880 he was elected to the Legislative Assembly of NSW, becoming premier of the state (1894–9). He was Leader of the Opposition in the House of Representatives (1901), and served briefly as prime minister. He was Australia's first high commissioner to London, and then took up the seat for Hanover Square in the British House of Commons, which he held until his death. >> RR1033

Reid, John (Richard) (1928–) Cricketer, born in Auckland, New Zealand. For almost 15 years he was the batting lynchpin in a weak New Zealand Test side. Six of his 39 first-class centuries were made in Tests, for which he was selected 58 times. He took part in four record Test stands for New Zealand, including the highest-ever partnership for the third wicket – 222 unbroken with Bert Sutcliffe against India at Delhi in 1955–6.

Reid, (Thomas) Mayne, Captain (1818–83) Writer of boys' stories, born in Ballyroney, Co Down, Northern Ireland, UK. He was intended for the Presbyterian ministry but, at the age of 19, went to America, where he spent several adventurous years, becoming a captain in the Mexican War. After his return to Europe in 1849, he settled in England and drew on his American experiences in his popular novels for boys, notably *The Rifle Rangers, or, Adventures in Southern Mexico* (1850), *The Maroon* (1862), *The Headless Horseman* (1866), and *The Castaways* (1870).

Reid, Thomas (1710–96) Philosopher, born in Strachan, Aberdeenshire, NE Scotland, UK. He studied at Aberdeen, becoming professor there in 1751, and later at Glasgow (1764–80). He was leader of the 'Scottish' school, which rejected the scepticism of David Hume. His main publications include *Essays on the Intellectual Powers of Man* (1785) and *Essays on the Active Powers of Man* (1788). >> Hume, David; Stewart, Dugald

Reik, Theodor [riyk] (1888–1969) Psychoanalyst, born in Vienna. He became a close friend and protégé of Sigmund Freud after they met in 1910. He studied at Vienna, where he practised as a psychoanalyst (1918–28), then taught at the Berlin Psychoanalytic Institute until 1933, when he fled the Nazis to The Hague. In 1938 he emigrated to the USA, establishing a private practice in New York City, and becoming a US citizen in 1944. In 1946 he established the National Psychological Association for Psychoanalysis when the American Psychoanalytic Association refused him full membership due to his not being a physician. He emphasized the role of intuition in treatment, and diverged from certain orthodox Freudian views, but maintained his friendship with Freud until the latter's death. His many works include *Listening With the Third Ear* (1948) and *Curiosities of the Self* (1965). >> Freud, Sigmund

Reiner, Fritz [riyner] (1888–1963) Conductor, born in Budapest. He conducted opera in Budapest and Dresden before coming to the USA in 1922 to take over the Cincinnati Symphony Orchestra. In 1931 he taught at the Curtis Institute, then joined the Pittsburgh Symphony Orchestra (1938–48). After several seasons with the Metropolitan Opera in New York City, he found his greatest acclaim leading the Chicago Symphony Orchestra (1953–62).

Reiner, Rob [riyner] (1945–) Film actor, director, and producer, born in New York City. He appeared in a number of small films before becoming known for his role in *All in the Family* (1971–8, 2 Emmies), later roles including *Postcards from the Edge* (1990), *Sleepless in Seattle* (1993), and *The First Wives Club* (1996). He made his directorial debut in 1984 with *This Is Spinal Tap*, and acted as producer as well as director for several other films, notably *When Harry Met Sally* (1989) and *Ghosts of Mississippi* (1996).

Reines, Frederick (1918–) Physicist, born in Paterson, NJ. He studied at New York University (1944), worked on the atomic bomb at Los Alamos (1944–9), taught at Case Western Institute of Technology (1959–66), then joined the University of California, Irvine (1966–88). For his discovery of the free neutrino, one of the basic particles of the universe, he shared the 1995 Nobel Prize for Physics with Martin Perl. >> Perl

Reinhardt, Ad(olf Frederick) [riynhah(r)t] (1913–67) Painter and critic, born in Buffalo, NY. He studied at the National Academy of Design, New York City (1936), then joined the American Abstract Artists, an avant-garde association which promoted hard-edge abstraction. He later restricted his paintings to monochrome, in an attempt to eliminate all meaning from his work, and became influential with the Minimal artists of the 1960s.

Reinhardt, Django [riynhah(r)t], popular name of **Jean Baptiste Reinhardt** (1910–53) Jazz guitarist, born in Liverchies, Belgium. He was born in the family caravan in a Rom (gypsy) community, and taught himself the guitar. At 18, injury in a fire caused the fusing of the fourth and fifth fingers of his left hand, but he simply devised a new chording method for his guitar, and continued to play. He played in the Quintet of the Hot Club of France with Stephane Grappelli (1934-9), producing many renowned recordings, and became the first European jazz musician to influence the music. >> Grappelli

Reinhardt, Max [riynhah(r)t], originally **Max Goldmann** (1873-1943) Theatre director, born in Baden, Germany. An introverted child, he was sent to drama school, and was a shy actor before turning to directing at the Kleines Theatre in Berlin (1902). He became famous overnight with his 1905 production of *A Midsummer Night's Dream*. An innovator in theatre art and technique, his work often involved spectacular, large-scale productions, as in *The Miracle* (London, 1911), which used over 2000 actors. As co-founder of the Salzburg Festival (1920), he left Germany in 1933, and moved to Hollywood, where he opened a theatre workshop. >> Hofmannsthal

Reischauer, Edwin O(ldfather) [riyshower] (1910-90) US diplomat and scholar, born in Tokyo, Japan. The son of an American missionary, he was raised in Japan, then studied at Oberlin College and Harvard. An expert on Japanese language, culture, and politics, he taught at Harvard (1938-81), and collaborated with John K Fairbank on two classic textbooks, *East Asia: the Great Tradition* (1960) and *East Asia: the Modern Transformation* (1965). He became ambassador to Japan (1961-6), when Japan criticized escalating US military involvement in Vietnam, and was an opponent of the Vietnam War, and an early advocate of restoring diplomatic relations with Communist China. >> Fairbank

Reisner, George (Andrew) [riyzner] (1867-1942) Egyptologist, born in Indianapolis, IN. He studied law at Harvard, then Egyptology in Berlin, returning to Harvard to teach Egyptology (1905-42). For the Egyptian government he directed the important campaign to survey Nubian monuments threatened by the raising of the first Aswan dam (1907-9), returning (1916-23) to explore the pyramids of Meroe and Napata. His outstanding discovery (1925) was the tomb of Queen Hetepheres, mother of Cheops, the only major find of jewellery and furniture surviving from the Old Kingdom. >> Cheops

Reith (of Stonehaven), John (Charles Walsham) Reith, Baron [reeth] (1889-1971) British statesman and engineer, born in Stonehaven, Aberdeenshire, NE Scotland, UK. He studied at Glasgow, entered the field of radio communication, and became the first general manager of the BBC (1922), then its director-general (1927-38). He was the architect of public service broadcasting in the UK. He became an MP in 1940, and was minister of works and buildings (1940-2). The BBC inaugurated the Reith Lectures in 1948 in honour of his influence on broadcasting, and he was created a baron in 1940.

Reitz, Dana [riyts] (1948-) Dancer and choreographer, born in New York City. She was in Japan prior to studying dance theatre at the University of Michigan. In New York City she studied classical ballet and *t'ai chi chuan*, became a member of Twyla Tharp's and Laura Dean's companies, and began choreographing in 1973. Best known as a soloist, she has collaborated with other dancers, musicians, and lighting designers, making a notable contribution to Wilson and Glass's opera, *Einstein on the Beach* (1976). >> Dean, Laura; Glass, Philip; Tharp; Wilson, Robert

Reizenstein, Franz [riyzenshtiyn] (1911-68) Composer and pianist, born in Nuremberg, Germany. He studied under Paul Hindemith, and in 1934 moved to England, where he was a pupil of Vaughan Williams. Among his compositions are cello, piano, and violin concertos, the cantata *Voices by Night*, two radio operas, and chamber and piano music. >> Hindemith; Vaughan Williams

Remak, Robert (1815-65) Physician and pioneer in electrotherapy for the treatment of nervous diseases, born in Posen, Germany. He studied at the University of Berlin, went into medical practice, and assisted at the university in an unpaid capacity because, as a Jew, he was not allowed to teach. He discovered the *fibres of Remak* (1830), and the nerve cells in the heart now called *Remak's ganglia* (1844). He finally became the first Jew to teach at the university (1847), but his promotion to assistant professor in 1859 did not reflect his eminence. >> Virchow

Remarque, Erich Maria [ruhmah(r)k] (1898-1970) Novelist, born in Osnabrück, Germany. He served in World War 1, and worked as a sports journalist while writing his famous war novel, *All Quiet on the Western Front* (1929). An immediate international success, it was filmed in 1930. Other titles, none of which were as critically acclaimed, include its sequel, *The Road Back* (1931). His novels were banned by the Nazis (1933), and in 1939 he emigrated to the USA, where he wrote more novels, married the film star **Paulette Goddard** (1911-90), and became a naturalized citizen. Later novels include *The Black Obelisk* (1957) and *The Night in Lisbon* (1962).

Rembrandt (Harmenszoon van Rijn) [rembrant] see panel on p. 785

Rémi, Georges >> Hergé

Remington, Eliphalet (1793-1861) Firearms manufacturer and inventor, born in Suffield, CT. While still a young man he made for himself a flintlock rifle which, although not original, was very accurate. In 1828 he built a factory beside the Erie Canal, and pioneered several improvements in small arms manufacture, including a method of straightening gun barrels and the first successful cast steel rifle barrel in the USA.

Remington, Frederic (Sackrider) (1861-1909) Painter, sculptor, and illustrator, born in Canton, NY. He studied at the Yale Art School (1878-9) and the Art Students League, New York City (c.1885), then moved West and became a cowboy and rancher. Offered a commission to illustrate Geronimo's Apache campaign for *Harper's Weekly* (1882), he began his career as a painter of the American West. He recorded the Indian Wars of 1890-91, created his first bronze sculpture, 'Bronco Buster' (1895), and wrote and illustrated several books that recounted his adventures.

Remington, Philo (1816-89) Inventor, born in Litchfield, NY, the son of the inventor, **Eliphalet Remington** (1793-1861). He entered his father's small-arms factory, and for 25 years superintended the mechanical department. As president of the company from 1860, he perfected the Remington breech-loading rifle.

Remizov, Alexey Mikhaylovich [remizof] (1877-1957) Writer, born in Moscow. Expelled from the University of Moscow for taking part in student riots, he lived in St Petersburg, becoming involved with the Symbolists, but left Russia at the Revolution, going first to Berlin and finally settling in Paris. His writing is full of national pride and a deep love of old Russian traditions and folklore, and contains realism, fantasy, and humour. His main works are the novels (trans titles) *The Pond*, *The Clock*, *Fifth Pestilence*, and *Sisters of the Cross*, as well as several legends, plays, and short stories.

Remy, St [ruhmee], Latin **St Remigius** (c. 437-533) Bishop of Reims, who is traditionally said to have converted Clovis I, King of the Franks, to Christianity, thus advancing the cause of Christianity in that country. He is also believed to have baptized about 3000 of the king's soldiers. Feast day October 1. >> Clovis I

Renan, (Joseph) Ernest [ruhnã] (1823-92) Philosopher and historian, born in Tréguier, France. Trained for the Church, he abandoned the traditional Catholic faith after

REMBRANDT (1606–69)

Rembrandt Harmenszoon van Rijn was born in Leiden, The Netherlands, the son of Harmen Gerritszoon, a miller, and Neeltje van Suydtbroeck, the daughter of a banker. He was the penultimate of nine children, and received a classical education at the Leiden Latin School. He was sent to Leiden University, but left shortly afterwards to develop his talent for painting and drawing. He studied art under Jacob van Swanenburch in Leiden for three years, then moved to Amsterdam. There in 1623 he was apprenticed to Pieter Lastman (1583–1633), who taught him how to create modern historical and religious scenes in the Italian style, after Caravaggio, in which (unusual in a Dutch Protestant) Rembrandt was very interested. During this period he also mastered the fundamentals of etching.

By 1627 Rembrandt had returned to Leiden, where he began to work closely with a fellow-student of Lastman's, Jan Lievens (1607–74). Declining to go to Italy for further studies, as would have been expected of an artist at this stage in his career, he studied moods and emotions through self-portraiture in etching, drawing, and painting. He also executed history paintings which were highly esteemed, and fetched large sums of money. In 1631 he moved to Amsterdam, where he ran a large studio and took numerous pupils. His natural style, expressed in two portraits 'Nicolaes Ruts' (c.1631, New York) and 'Maarten Looten' (1632, Los Angeles), brought him immediate success. Another important commemorative work, 'The Anatomy Lesson of Dr Nicolaes Tulp' (1632, Amsterdam), established him as the city's leading portraitist of the 1630s.

A close association with Amsterdam art dealer Hendrick van Uylenburgh in the early 1630s led to Rembrandt starting an extensive art collection, and also to his meeting with **Saskia van Uylenburgh** (1612–42), Hendrick's cousin, whom he married in 1634. Socially his superior, Saskia's large inheritance, together with Rembrandt's earnings, allowed them to live in considerable style in a fashionable area of Amsterdam. She featured in many of his portraits of the time. The marriage was only to last until 1642, when Saskia died, shortly after the birth of her fourth and only surviving child, **Titus** (1641). In that same year Rembrandt completed his masterpiece 'The Night Watch' (1640–2, Amsterdam), a dramatically lit, dynamically composed group of a local militia band; it was followed by other important commissions. A relationship with Titus' nurse, Geertghe Dircx, who had been engaged at the time of Saskia's death, ended acrimoniously when Rembrandt took **Hendrickje Stoffels** (c.1615–63) as his mistress (1649). She was the model for 'Bathsheba' (1654, Paris). Geertghe sued him for breach of promise, and he was never able to marry Henrickje under the terms of Saskia's will. Nonetheless, they had a daughter, **Cornelia** (1654), and they lived together for the rest of her life, despite Hendrickje being officially warned by the Church council for sinfully living with Rembrandt without being married. His extravagance, especially as a collector, led to his bankruptcy in 1656, but he continued to work with undiminished energy.

Rembrandt's last years were spent in relative simplicity. His circle of friends no longer included influential people, but was generally drawn from the lower middle-classes. He continued to teach pupils at his home, and was internationally renowned. He died in Amsterdam, surviving his son by almost a year. His preserved works number over 650 oil paintings, 1400 drawings and studies, and 300 etchings; but his portraits and self-portraits (c.60) are widely acknowledged as his greatest achievements.
>> Caravaggio

---

studying Greek and Hebrew biblical criticism. His appointment as professor of Hebrew at the Collège de France in 1861 was not confirmed until 1870 because of his controversial *La Vie de Jèsus* (1863, The Life of Jesus), which undermined the supernatural aspects of Christ's life and his teachings. It was the first of a monumental series on the origins of Christianity, which also included books on the Apostles (1866), St Paul (1869), and Marcus Aurelius (1882).

Renaud, Madelaine >> **Barrault, Louis**

Renaudot, Théophraste [ruhnohdoh] (1586–1653) Physician and journalist, founder of the first French newspaper, born in Loudoun, France. He settled in Paris in 1624 and was physician to the king. Appointed commissary general for the poor, he started an information agency for them, and in 1631 founded the regular journal, *Gazette de France*. He opened a medical clinic in 1635, with free dispensaries, and also opened the first pawnshop (1637).

Renault, Louis [renoh] (1877–1944) Automobile manufacturer, born in Paris. Together with his brothers he built a series of small cars and formed the Société Renault Frères (1898). He began racing, but turned to manufacturing and produced the *Renault tank* (1918). During the German occupation of France in World War 2 the factory continued to produce military equipment, leading to his imprisonment on collaboration charges. He died while awaiting trial. His automobile company became the largest in France, and was later nationalized.

Rendell (of Babergh), Ruth Rendell, Baroness [rendl], originally **Ruth Barbara Grasemann**, occasional pseudonym **Barbara Vine** (1930–) Detective-story writer, born in London, England, UK. She went to school in Loughton, Essex, and spent some time as a journalist and managing director of a local newspaper before publishing her first novel *From Doon with Death* in 1964. Several of her detective stories feature Chief Inspector Wexford (such as *Shake Hands Forever*, 1975, and *Simisola*, 1994), and she has also written mystery thrillers (such as *A Judgement in Stone*, 1977) and books of short stories. Books written under her pseudonym include *The House of Stairs* (1988), *Gallowglass* (1990), and *The Brimstone Wedding* (1995). Many of her stories have now been filmed or televised, notably in the series *The Ruth Rendell Mysteries*. She received the Arts Council National Book Award for Genre Fiction in 1981. In 1997 she received a life peerage.

René, France-Albert [ruhnay] (1935–) Seychelles statesman and president (1977–). He studied in the Seychelles, Switzerland, and London, and was called to the bar in 1957. On returning to the Seychelles, he threw himself into politics, establishing the Seychelles People's United Party, a Socialist grouping, in 1964. In 1970 he pressed for full independence for the Seychelles, and became prime minister in a coalition with president James Mancham. While Mancham was abroad, René staged a coup, made himself president, and created a one-party state. Since then he has followed a non-nuclear policy of non-alignment, and resisted several attempts to remove him. >> RR1087

Renfrew (of Kaimsthorn), (Andrew) Colin Renfrew, Baron (1937–) Archaeologist, born in Stockton-on-Tees, Durham, NE England, UK. He studied at Cambridge. His work has ranged widely, but exhibits a central preoccupation with the nature of cultural change in prehistory. He has excavated in Greece (1964–76) and Orkney (1972–4), notably at the chambered tomb of Quanterness. He became professor of archaeology at Cambridge in 1981, and Master of Jesus College, Cambridge, in 1986. His books include *The Emergence of Civilization* (1972), *The Archaeology of Cult* (1985), and *The Cycladic Spirit* (1991). He has also contributed to several pioneering archaeological programmes on BBC television, notably in the *Chronicle* series. He was made a life peer in 1991.

Reni, Guido [**ray**nee] (1575–1642) Baroque painter, born near Bologna, Italy. He studied in Bologna, and worked both there and in Rome. The fresco painted for the Borghese garden house, 'Aurora and the Hours' (1613–14) is usually regarded as his masterpiece, but some critics rank higher the unfinished 'Nativity' in San Martino, Naples. He later settled again in Bologna.

Rennenkampf, Pavel Karlovich von (1853–1918) Russian cavalry officer, of Baltic German origins. He commanded a force in the Russo-Japanese War (1904–5). During World War I, in command of the 1st Army, he defeated the German 8th Army at Insterburg and Gumbinnen (Aug 1914), but was decisively defeated by Hindenburg at Tannenberg a few days later. He was appointed Governor of St Petersburg in 1915, and commander-in-chief of the Northern Front in 1916. After the October Revolution he was shot by the Bolsheviks. >> Hindenburg

Renner, Karl (1870–1950) Austrian statesman, chancellor (1918–20, 1945), and president (1945–50), born in Unter-Tannowitz, Austria. He trained as a lawyer, joined the Austrian Social Democratic Party, and became the first chancellor of the Austrian Republic. Imprisoned as a Socialist leader, following the brief civil war (Feb 1934), he was chancellor again after World War 2, and first president of the new republic. >> RR1033

Rennie, John (1761–1821) Civil engineer, born in Phantassie, East Lothian, E Scotland, UK. He studied at Edinburgh University, entered the employment of Boulton & Watt (1784), set up in London as an engineer (1791), and soon became famous as a bridge-builder – building Kelso, Leeds, Musselburgh, Newton Stewart, Boston, New Galloway, and the old Southwark and Waterloo Bridges, and designing London Bridge. He made many important canals, drained fens, designed the docks in London and several other ports, and improved others. He also constructed the celebrated breakwater at Plymouth (1811–41). >> Boulton; Watt

Renoir, Jean [renwah(r)] (1894–1979) Film director, born in Paris, the son of Pierre Auguste Renoir. After serving in World War 1 (where he won the Croix de Guerre), he studied ceramics, then began writing screenplays, and turned to film-making. His version of Zola's *Nana* (1926), *La Grande Illusion* (1937, The Great Illusion), *La Règle du Jeu* (1939, The Rules of the Game), *The Diary of a Chambermaid* (1946), and *Le Déjeuner sur l'herbe* (1959, Lunch on the Grass) are among the masterpieces of the cinema. He left France in 1941 during the German invasion, and became a US citizen. His last films were *Le Caporal épinglé* (1962, The Vanishing Corporal) and *Le Petit théâtre de Jean Renoir* (1969, The Little Theatre of Jean Renoir). He received an honorary Academy Award in 1975. >> Cartier-Bresson; Renoir, Pierre Auguste

Renoir, Pierre Auguste [ruhn**wah**] (1841–1919) Impressionist artist, born in Limoges, France. He first painted porcelain and fans, began to paint in the open air c.1864, and from 1870 obtained several commissions for portraits. He exhibited with the Impressionists (1874–9, 1882). His picture of sunlight filtering through leaves – *Le Moulin de la Galette* (1876, Louvre) – epitomizes his colourful, happy art. His visit to Italy in 1880 was followed by a series of 'Bathers' in a more cold and Classical style. He then returned to reds, orange, and gold to portray nudes in sunlight, a style which he continued to develop until his death. >> Renoir, Jean

Renshaw, Willie, popular name of **William (Charles) Renshaw** (1861–1904) Tennis player, the first great tennis champion, born in Cheltenham, Gloucestershire, SWC England, UK. He started playing at Cheltenham School with his twin brother **Ernest Renshaw** (1861–99), who also became a champion. Willie was Wimbledon singles champion in 1881–6 and 1899, and won the All-England doubles title with Ernest in 1884–6 and 1888–9. >> RR1173

Rensselaer, Stephen Van >> **Van Rensselaer, Stephen**

Renta, Oscar de la >> **de la Renta, Oscar**

Repin, Ilya Yefimovich [re**peen**] (1844–1930) Painter, born in Chuguyev, Ukraine. Trained as an icon painter, and then at the St Petersburg Academy, he became professor of painting there (1893–1907). The major representative of naturalism in Russia during the second half of the 19th-c, he gained popularity with paintings such as 'The Reply of the Cossacks of Zaporoguus to Sultan Mahmoud IV', which his contemporaries saw as a symbol of the Russian people throwing off their chains; but he also painted portraits of famous contemporaries, such as Mussorgsky (1881) and Tolstoy (1887).

Repton, Humphrey (1752–1818) Landscape designer, born in Bury St Edmunds, Suffolk, E England, UK. The successor to Lancelot 'Capability' Brown, he completed the change from formal gardens of the early 18th-c to the 'picturesque'. He designed gardens at Uppark in Sussex and Sheringham Hall in Norfolk, and wrote *Observations on the Theory and Practice of Landscape Gardening* (1803). >> Brown, Lancelot

Reshevsky, Samuel (Herman) [re**shef**skee] (1911–92) Chess player, born in Ozorkow, Poland. His family emigrated to America when he was eight, and he was seven times the US champion. His world-title hopes were stalled by World War 2, then by Soviet-dominated candidates' matches, and he was eclipsed by Bobby Fischer in 1957. He later worked as an investment analyst and insurance salesman. >> Fischer, Bobby

Resnais, Alain [ruhnay] (1922–) Film director, born in Vannes, France. He studied in Paris, and made a series of prize-winning short documentaries, such as *Van Gogh* (1948, Oscar) and *Guernica* (1950). His first feature film was *Hiroshima mon amour* (1959, Hiroshima, my Love), and this was followed by the controversial *L'Année dernière à Marienbad* (1961, Last Year at Marienbad), hailed as a Surrealistic and dreamlike masterpiece by some, as a confused and tedious failure by others. His later films include *Mon Oncle d'Amérique* (1980, My American Uncle), *La vie est un roman* (1983, Life is a Novel), *L'Amour à mort* (1984, Love Until Death), *Mélo* (1986), and *Smoking/No Smoking* (1993).

Resolutus, Doctor >> **Baconthorpe, John**

Respighi, Ottorino [res**pee**gee] (1879–1936) Composer, born in Bologna, Italy. He studied at Bologna and St Petersburg, and in 1913 became professor of composition at the St Cecilia Academy in Rome. His works include nine operas, the symphonic poems *Fontane di Roma* (1916, Fountains of Rome) and *Pini di Roma* (1924, Pines of Rome), and the ballet *La Boutique fantasque*, produced by Diaghilev in 1919. >> Diaghilev

Restif, Nicolas Edme [resteef], known as **Restif de la Bretonne** (1734–1806) Writer, born in Sacy, France. His many voluminous and licentious novels, such as *Le Paysan perverti* (1776, The Perverted Peasant), give a vividly truthful picture of 18th-c French life, and entitle him to be considered as a forerunner of Realism. His own not unsullied life he described in the 16-volume *Monsieur Nicolas* (1794–7). He also wrote on social reform.

Retz (Jean François Paul de Gondi), Cardinal de (1614–79) Clergyman, born in Montmirail, France. He plotted against Mazarin, and exploited the Parlementary Fronde (1648) to further his own interests and the power of the Church. After transferring his allegiance between the rebel factions and the crown, he received a cardinal's hat, though in 1652 he was imprisoned on Louis XIV's personal orders. After making peace with Louis (1662), he received the abbacy of St Denis. In his last years he wrote his *Mémoires*, a classic in 17th-c French literature. >> Mazarin

Retz, Gilles de Laval, Baron de, also spelled **Rais** or **Raiz** (1404–40) Breton nobleman, born in Champtocé, France. He fought by the side of Joan of Arc at Orléans, and became Marshal of France at 25, but soon retired to his estates, where for over 10 years he is alleged to have indulged in satanism and the most infamous orgies. He was hanged and burned at Nantes, after being tried and condemned for heresy. >> Joan of Arc

Reuter, Paul Julius, Freiherr (Baron) **von** [royter], originally **Israel Beer Josaphat** (1816–99) Founder of the first news agency, born in Kassel, Germany. Of Jewish parentage, he became a Christian and adopted his new name in 1844. He published political pamphlets, moved to Paris during the revolution (1848), and sent news items back to German newspapers via a pigeon carrier service (1850). He developed the idea of a telegraphic news service, and in 1851 moved his headquarters to London, becoming a naturalized British subject. His news service extended worldwide with the development of undersea cables. He was created a baron in 1871.

Reuther, Walter (Philip) [royter] (1907–70) Trade-union leader, born in Wheeling, WV. Apprenticed to a tool and die maker, he rose to become president of the American Auto Workers' Union. From 1935 he began to organize the automobile workers into what later became the largest union in the world, and fought against Communist influence in trade unionism.

Revans, Reginald William (1907–) Management consultant, born in London, England, UK. He studied at London and Cambridge, and was an Olympic athlete in 1928. As deputy chief officer of Essex (1935–45) and as director of education in the coal industry (1945–50), he pioneered 'action learning', founding the Action Learning Trust in 1977. He argued that management skills are better learnt by managers reviewing and questioning their experience with their peers, than by studying programmed information. He was professor of industrial administration at Manchester University (1955–65), then worked as a consultant in many overseas countries, and after retirement retained a connection with Manchester, becoming a professorial fellow in action learning in 1986.

Revelle, Roger [revel] (1909–) Oceanographer and sociologist, born in Seattle, WA. He worked mainly at the Scripps Institution of Oceanography at La Jolla (1931–64). As a result of his geophysical studies of the Pacific Ocean, he contributed to the theory of sea-floor spreading. He later became professor of population policy at Harvard (1964–76).

Revels, Hiram R(hoades) (1822–1901) Clergyman and educator, born in Fayetteville, NC. He was ordained a minister in the African Methodist Episcopal Church (1845), and became principal of a school for African-Americans in Baltimore. During the Civil War he devoted himself to the

education and religious welfare of African-American soldiers. Later, he reluctantly entered politics, but succeeded in becoming the first African-American citizen to be elected to the US Senate (1870–1). He was appointed president of Alcorn Agricultural and Mechanical College, which offered higher education for African-Americans, remaining there until retirement.

Revere, Paul [reveer] (1735–1818) US patriot, born in Boston, MA. A silversmith and copperplate printer, he was one of the party that destroyed the tea in Boston harbour (1773), and was at the head of a secret society formed to watch the British. On 18 April 1775, the night before Lexington and Concord, he started out for Concord, where arms were secreted. He was turned back by a British patrol, and his mission was completed by Dr Samuel Prescott (1751–?77). It was Revere, however, whom the poet Longfellow immortalized for the 'midnight ride'. >> Longfellow

Revie, Don [revee] (1927–89) Footballer and manager, born near Middlesbrough, NE England, UK. UK Footballer of the Year in 1955, he won an FA Cup Medal the following year with Manchester City. In 1961 he was appointed player-manager of Leeds United, and over the next 13 years transformed the struggling club into a powerful force in British football, taking all the major honours. He succeeded Sir Alf Ramsey as England team manager in 1974, but abruptly abandoned the job in 1977 to take up a coaching post in the Middle East. He died of motor neurone disease. >> Ramsey, Alf

Revson, Charles (Haskell) (1906–75) Business executive, born in Boston, MA. With two partners he founded Revlon Inc in 1932, becoming its president (1932–62) and chairman (1962–75). Revlon introduced opaque nail polish and matching colours for lips and nails. Largely through Revson's flair for new product development and magazine advertising, it became the largest retail cosmetics and fragrance company in the USA.

Reyes, Alfonso [rayes] (1889–1959) Literary scholar, poet, and diplomat, born in Monterrey, Mexico. He studied law, entered the diplomatic sevice (1913), served in Spain (1920–7), and was periodically ambassador to Argentina and Brazil. Over the years he established himself as a literary scholar of great authority, producing both academic and creative works including *Visión de Anáhuac* (1917, Vision of Anáhuac), *El plano oblicuo* (1920, The Oblique Plane), and *Reloj de sol* (1926, Sundial). Upon retirement as a diplomat (1939), he was generally regarded as the century's master of Mexican letters.

Reymont, Władysław (Stanisław) (1868–1925) Novelist, born in Kobiele Wielkie, Poland. His works include *Chłopi* (4 vols, 1904–9, The Peasants) and *Ziemia obiecana* (1899, The Promised Land), best known as a film in different language versions. He was awarded the Nobel Prize for Literature in 1924.

Reynaud, Paul [raynoh] (1878–1966) French statesman and prime minister (1940), born in Barcelonnette, France. Originally a barrister, he held many French government posts, and was premier (Apr to Jun) during the fall of France in 1940. He resigned rather than agree to an armistice with Germany, and was imprisoned by the Germans for the duration of World War 2. Afterwards he re-entered politics until losing his seat in 1962, and was a delegate to the Council of Europe (1949). >> RR1049

Reynolds, Albert (1933–) Irish statesman and prime minister (1992–4), born in Roosky, Co Roscommon, Ireland. He became an MP in 1977, and held several ministerial offices from 1979, including minister of finance (1988), under Charles Haughey, but was dismissed in 1991 after being involved in an attempt to gain Haughey's resignation. He became prime minister in the 1992 elections, but his party (Fianna Fáil) lost its majority, forcing the formation of a coalition with the Labour Party in 1993. He lost the support of the Labour Party in November 1994, and was forced to resign. >> Haughey

Reynolds, John Hamilton >> **Hood, Thomas**

Reynolds, Sir Joshua [renuhldz] (1723–92) Portrait painter, born in Plympton, Devon, SW England, UK. He studied art in London, and also in Rome (1749–52), then established himself in London, and by 1760 was at the height of his fame as a portrait painter. His works include 'Dr Samuel Johnson' (c.1756, National Portrait Gallery, London) and 'Sarah Siddons as the Tragic Muse' (1784, San Marino, CA). He became the first president of the Royal Academy (1768), and was knighted in 1769. He left well over 2000 works, from which 700 engravings have been made. >> Kauffmann; Romney, George

Reynolds, Osborne [renuhldz] (1842–1912) Engineer, born in Belfast, Northern Ireland, UK. He studied at Cambridge, became the first professor of engineering at Manchester (1868), and a Royal Society gold medallist (1888). Best known for his work in hydrodynamics and hydraulics, he greatly improved centrifugal pumps. The *Reynolds number*, a dimensionless ratio characterizing the dynamic state of a fluid, takes its name from him.

Rhazes or **Razi** [rayzeez, rayzee], in full **Abu Bakr Muhammad ibn Zakariya ar-Razi** (10th-c) Physician and alchemist, who lived in Baghdad. Considered the greatest physician of the Arab world, he gave full accounts of smallpox and measles, and wrote an immense Graeco-Arabic encyclopedia. This was translated into Latin, and had considerable influence on medical science in the Middle Ages.

Rhee, Syngman (1875–1965) Korean statesman and president of South Korea (1948–60), born near Kaesong, Korea. Imprisoned (1897–1904) for his part in an independence campaign, he later went to the USA, returning to Japanese-annexed Korea in 1910. After the unsuccessful rising of 1919, he became president of the exiled Korean Provisional Government. On Japan's surrender (1945) he returned to become the first elected president of South Korea. Re-elected for a fourth term (1960), he was obliged to resign after a month following major riots and the resignation of his cabinet. He went into exile in Honolulu. >> RR1070

Rheticus [retikus], originally **Georg Joachim von Lauchen** (1514–76) Astronomer and mathematician, born in Feldkirch, Austria. He became professor of mathematics and astronomy at Wittenberg from 1536. He is noted for his trigonometrical tables, some of which went to 15 decimal places. For a time he worked with Copernicus, whose *De revolutionibus orbium coelestium* he was instrumental in publishing. His own *Narratio prima de libris revolutionum Copernici* (1540) was the first account of the Copernican theory. >> Copernicus

Rhine, J(oseph) B(anks) (1895–1980) Psychologist, the pioneer of parapsychology, born in Juniáta, PA. He studied botany at Chicago, switched to psychology under William McDougall at Duke University, and in 1937 became professor of psychology there, co-founding the Parapsychology Laboratory (1930). He later founded the Institute of Parapsychology in Durham, NC (1964). His laboratory-devised experiments involving packs of specially designed cards attempted to establish the phenomena of extrasensory perception and telepathy on a statistical basis. >> McDougall

Rhodes, Cecil (John) (1853–1902) British colonial statesman, and prime minister of Cape Colony, South Africa (1890–6), born in Bishop's Stortford, Hertfordshire, SE England, UK. Suffering from a lung weakness, he was sent for his health to a brother's cotton farm in South Africa; he subsquently made a fortune at the Kimberley diamond diggings, and amalgamated the several diamond companies to form the De Beers Consolidated Mines Co (1888). Dividing his time between Kimberley and England, he studied at Oxford, and entered the Cape House of Assembly, securing Bechuanaland as a protectorate (1884) and the charter for the British South Africa Company (1889), whose territory was later to be named Rhodesia after him. He became prime minister of Cape Colony, but was forced to resign in 1896 because of complications arising from the Jameson raid. He was a conspicuous figure during the Boer War (1899–1902), when he organized the defences of Kimberley. His will founded scholarships at Oxford for Americans, Germans, and colonials (*Rhodes scholars*). >> Jameson, Leander Starr

Rhodes, Wilfred (1877–1973) Cricketer, born in Kirkheaton, West Yorkshire, N England, UK. He played for Yorkshire and England, and during his career (1898–1930) took a world record 4187 wickets and scored 39 722 runs. He took 100 wickets in a season 23 times, and performed the 'double' of 1000 runs and 100 wickets 16 times – first-class cricket records. The oldest man to play Test cricket, he was 52 years 165 days when he played for England against the West Indies at Kingston in April 1930. >> RR1151

Rhodes, Zandra (1940–) Fashion designer, born in Chatham, Kent, SE England, UK. She studied textile printing and lithography at Medway College of Art, then won a scholarship to the Royal College of Art. She designed and printed textiles and, with others, opened the Fulham Road Clothes Shop in 1967, afterwards setting up on her own. She showed her first collection in 1969, and is noted for her distinctive, exotic designs in floating chiffons and silks. In London in 1975 she co-founded Zandra Rhodes (UK) Ltd and Zandra Rhodes (Shops) Ltd, and began licensing her name in the USA, Australia, and Japan. In addition to innovative clothes design, she expanded into cosmetics, jewellery, and home furnishings.

Rhondda (of Llanwern), David Alfred Thomas, 1st Viscount [rontha] (1856–1918) Coal mine owner, financier, and politician, born in Ysgyborwen, Rhondda, Cynon Taf, S Wales. He studied at Cambridge, and became Liberal MP for Merthyr Tydfil (1888–1910). During World War 1, he was sent to the USA by Lloyd George to negotiate the supply of munitions to Britain. His success led to a peerage, and was followed by an equally successful period as minister of food (1917–18), with the introduction of wartime food rationing.

Rhys, Ernest (Percival) [rees] (1859–1946) Editor and writer, born in London, England, UK. He spent much of his youth in Carmarthen and became a mining engineer. Abandoning this for a writing career in 1886, he was first a freelance, then on the staff of Walter Scott's publishing house, Constable's, for whom he edited the Camelot Classics series. He is best-remembered as editor of the Everyman Library of Classics, the first volume of the 983 published during his lifetime appearing in 1906. >> Scott, Walter

Rhys, Jean [rees], pseudonym of **Gwen Williams** (1894–1979) Novelist, born in Roseau, Dominica. She moved to England in 1910 to train at the Royal Academy of Dramatic Art, London, but her father's death after only one term obliged her to join a touring theatre company. After World War 1, she lived in Paris, where she wrote short stories and several novels on the theme of female vulnerability, including *The Left Bank* (1927), *After Leaving Mr Mackenzie* (1930), and *Good Morning Midnight* (1939). Returning to Cornwall, she lived in retirement for nearly 30 years, then published in 1966 her best-known novel, *Wide Sargasso Sea*, a 'prequel' to Charlotte Bronte's *Jane Eyre*. Further short stories followed in 1968 and 1976, and an autobiography, *Smile Please*, was published posthumously in 1979.

Ribalta, Francisco [reebalta] (1565–1628) Painter, born in Castellón de la Plana, Spain. He studied in Rome, and settled in Valencia under the patronage of the archbishop, Juan de Ribera. A major influence on later Spanish painters, he was the first Spanish *tenebroso* – a painter who emphasizes darkness rather than light. His works include 'The Last Supper' and 'Christ Embracing St Bernard' (Prado, Madrid).

Ribbentrop, Joachim von [ribentrop] (1893–1946) German statesman, born in Wesel, Germany. He became a member of the National Socialist Party in 1932 and, as Hitler's adviser in foreign affairs, was responsible for the Anglo-German naval pact (1935). He became ambassador to Britain (1936) and foreign minister (1938–45). Captured by the British in 1945, he was condemned and executed at Nuremberg. >> Hitler

Ribera, José or **Jusepe de** [reevera], known as **Lo Spagnoletto** ('the Little Spaniard') (1588–1656) Painter and etcher, born in Játiva, Spain. He settled in Naples, and became court painter there. He is noted for the often gruesome realism with which he treated religious and mythological subjects, such as the martyrdom of the saints, as well as portraits, such as 'Portrait of a Bearded Woman' (1631, Spain). Later works were calmer and more subtle, and include his paintings of the Passion.

Ricardo, David [rikah(r)doh] (1772–1823) Political economist, born in London, England, UK. He set up in business as a young man, and by 1814 had made a fortune. In 1817 appeared the work on which his reputation chiefly rests, *Principles of Political Economy and Taxation*. In 1819 he became an MP, and was influential in the free-trade movement.

Ricardo, Sir Harry (Ralph) [rikah(r)doh] (1885–1974) Mechanical engineer, born in London, England, UK. He studied at Cambridge, where he designed and built several small petrol engines, and began to work on the problems of ignition, combustion, and detonation. He soon recognized the importance of the type of fuel in avoiding detonation or 'knocking', and this led to the use of octane numbers to measure the anti-knock properties of petrols. His improved design of the combustion chamber in side-valve engines has been universally adopted.

Ricci, Nina, originally **Maria Nielli** (1883–1970) Fashion designer, born in Turin, Italy. She became an apprentice in a Paris couture house in 1900, joined Raffin in 1908, and stayed with him for 20 years, eventually becoming his partner. She showed her first collection in 1932, and her fragrances in 1941, and developed a wide range of further products in cosmetics, furs, and fashion accessories. After her retirement in 1959, the firm continued to grow, and by the mid-1990s it had boutiques in over 130 countries.

Ricci, Marco [reechee] (1676–1730) Painter, born in Belluno, Italy. He was a pupil of his uncle, Sebastiano Ricci, based in Venice, but travelled extensively. He was brought to England by the Earl of Manchester (1708), and seems to have worked mostly on the design of stage scenery for the opera. In 1710 he returned to Venice to bring his uncle to England, where they worked together (1712–16). Little is known of his later career. >> Ricci, Sebastiano

Ricci, Matteo [reechee] (1552–1610) Founder of the Jesuit missions in China, born in Macerata, Italy. He studied at Rome, then travelled to India, where he was ordained (1580), and went on to China in 1582. He mastered Chinese, wrote works to a standard which received much commendation from the Chinese literati, and met with great success as a missionary.

Ricci, Sebastiano [reechee] (1659–1734) Painter, born in Belluno, Italy. He trained in Venice, and after extensive travel in Italy worked for two years in Vienna (1701–3). In 1712 he travelled to England, via Holland, with his nephew Marco Ricci. The only complete work to survive from this time is a 'Resurrection' in the apse of Chelsea Hospital chapel. His colourful style influenced the young Tiepolo. >> Ricci, Marco; Tiepolo

Riccio, David >> Rizzio, David

Rice, Elmer, originally **Elmer Reizenstein** (1892–1967) Playwright, born in New York City. He studied law before becoming a playwright, and used his legal knowledge in several plays, as well as in various disputes with theatres and in causes he served – from Marxism to the American Civil Liberties Union. His best-known work is *The Adding Machine* (1923), an Expressionist play about the dehumanization of people.

Rice, (Henry) Grantland (1880–1954) Sportswriter, born in Murfreesboro, TN. He studied at Vanderbilt University, began as a reporter with the *Nashville News* (1901), joined the *New York Mail* in 1910, then joined the *New York Tribune* (later the *Herald Tribune*) (1911–30). After leaving the *Tribune*, he wrote a widely syndicated column, 'The Sportlight', made a series of short films on sports, and was in charge of selecting the All-American football team for *Collier's* magazine (1926–54). Considered the dean of US sportswriters, his columns included some of the sport's most memorable phrases, including those describing Notre Dame's football backfield as 'The Four Horsemen'.

Rice, (Edmund) Ignatius (1762–1844) Philanthropist and religious founder, born near Callan, Co Kilkenny, Ireland. A wealthy provision merchant in Waterford, he retired from business on the death of his wife (1789) and devoted himself to good works. He founded a school in Waterford for poor boys (1802), and many others elsewhere. In 1808 he took religious vows, and founded the order now known as the Christian Brothers (sanctioned by the pope in 1820). He was superior-general of the order as Brother Ignatius until 1838.

Rice, Tim, popular name of **Sir Timothy Miles Bindon Rice** (1944–) Lyricist, writer, and broadcaster, born in Buckinghamshire, SC England, UK. He studied at Lancing College, then took up law, but left a lawyer's firm to join the EMI recording company. He has co-written lyrics on many award winning records, has appeared on numerous radio and TV quiz shows, and written several books. He is best known for writing the lyrics to music by Andrew Lloyd Webber for *Joseph and the Amazing Technicolour Dreamcoat* (1968), followed by *Jesus Christ Superstar* (1971) and *Evita* (1978). Later works include the lyrics for *Chess* (1984), *Cricket* (1986), *Starmania* (1991), and *Beauty and the Beast* (1997). He was knighted in 1994. >> Lloyd Webber

Rice-Davies, Mandy, popular name of **Marilyn Rice-Davies** (1944–) Model and showgirl, born in Wales, UK. After leaving school, she worked in a department store, did some modelling, then moved to London, becoming a showgirl at Murray's Cabaret Club. Here she met and became close to Christine Keeler and, through the osteopath Stephen Ward, was introduced to influential London society. As a witness at Ward's trial for living off the immoral earnings of Keeler and Rice-Davies, in reply to a suggestion that Lord Astor denied knowing her, she gave the celebrated retort: 'He would, wouldn't he?' After the trial she moved to Israel, where she established two night clubs, then published an autobiography, and returned to live in London. >> Keeler, Christine; Profumo

Rich, Adrienne (Cecile) (1929–) Poet, born in Baltimore, MD. She studied at Radcliffe College, lived briefly in The Netherlands, then taught at several institutions, notably at Cornell from 1981. Based in New York City, she won many awards, and became known for her highly personal poetry, as in *Diving into the Wreck: Poems 1971–2* (1973). Later works include *An Atlas of the Difficult World: Poems 1988–1991* (1991).

Rich, Barbara >> **Riding, Laura**

Rich, Buddy, originally **Bernard Rich** (1917–87) Drummer and bandleader, born in New York City. A child prodigy, he made his debut with his parents when he was 18 months old, toured Australia when he was six, and was one of the highest paid child performers of the 1930s. Known for his virtuoso drumming, he played with several leading bands of the 'big band era', including a period with his own band (1945–7), and formed a very successful second band in 1966, making several hit albums beginning with *Swinging New Big Band* (1966).

Rich, Edmund >> **Edmund, St**

Richard I, known as **Richard Coeur de Lion** or **Richard the Lionheart** (1157–99) King of England (1189–99), born in Oxford, Oxfordshire, SC England, UK, the third son of Henry II and Eleanor of Aquitaine. Of his 10-year reign, he spent only five months in England, devoting himself to crusading and defending the Angevin lands in France. Already recognized as an outstanding soldier, he took Messina (1190), Cyprus, and Acre (1191) during the Third Crusade, and advanced to within sight of Jerusalem. On the return journey, he was arrested in Vienna (1192), and remained a prisoner of the German Emperor Henry VI until he agreed to be ransomed (1194). The rest of his reign was occupied in warfare against Philip II of France, while the government of England was conducted by the justiciar, Hubert Walter. Richard was mortally wounded while besieging the castle of Châlus, Aquitaine. >> Eleanor of Aquitaine; Henry II (of England); Longchamp; Philip II (of France); Saladin; Walter, Hubert; RR1095

Richard II (1367–1400) King of England (1377–99), born in Bordeaux, France, the younger son of Edward the Black Prince, who succeeded his grandfather, Edward III, at the age of 10. He displayed great bravery in confronting the rebels in London during the Peasants' Revolt (1381); but already parliament was concerned about his favourites, and the reign was dominated by the struggle between Richard's desire to act independently, and the magnates' concern to curb his power. He quarrelled with his uncle, John of Gaunt, and his main supporters were found guilty of treason in the 'Merciless Parliament' of 1388. After Richard had declared an end to his minority (1389), he built up a stronger following, and during 1397–8 took his revenge by having the Earl of Arundel executed, the Duke of Gloucester murdered, and several lords banished, the exiles including Gaunt's son, Henry Bolingbroke (later Henry IV). His final act of oppression was to confiscate the Lancastrian estates after Gaunt's death (1399). Having failed to restrain the king by constitutional means, the magnates resolved to unseat him from the throne. Bolingbroke invaded England unopposed, and Richard was deposed in his favour (Sep 1399). He died in Pontefract Castle, Yorkshire, possibly of starvation. >> Edward the Black Prince; Henry IV (of England); John of Gaunt; RR1095

Richard III (1452–85) King of England (1483–5), born in Fotheringay Castle, Northamptonshire, C England, UK, the youngest son of Richard, Duke of York. He was created Duke of Gloucester by his brother, Edward IV, in 1461, accompanied him into exile (1470), and played a key role in his restoration (1471). Rewarded with part of the Neville inheritance, he exercised viceregal powers in N England, and in 1482 recaptured Berwick-upon-Tweed from the Scots. When Edward died (1483) and was succeeded by his under-age son, Edward V, Richard acted first as protector, but within three months, he had overthrown the Woodvilles (relations of Edward IV's queen), seen to the execution of Lord Hastings (c.1430–83), and had himself proclaimed and crowned as the rightful king. Young Edward and his brother were probably murdered in the Tower on Richard's orders (though not all historians agree). He tried to stabilize his position, but failed to win broad-based support. His rival Henry Tudor (later Henry VII), confronted him in battle at Bosworth Field, and Richard died fighting bravely against heavy odds. Though ruthless, he was not the absolute monster Tudor historians portrayed him to be, nor is there proof he was a hunchback. >> Edward IV; Henry VII; RR1095

Richard, Cliff, popular name of **Sir Harry Roger Webb** (1940–) Pop-singer, born in Lucknow, India. He moved to England at the age of eight, began his professional career playing with the Dick Teague Group, and formed his own band in 1958. Originally called The Drifters, the group changed its name to The Shadows to avoid confusion with a US vocal group of the same name. Following the success of 'Living Doll' (1959), The Shadows were hailed as Britain's answer to American rock. He made a series of family musical films during the 1960s, including *Expresso Bongo* (1960), *The Young Ones* (1961), and *Summer Holiday* (1962), and played the leading role in the musicals *Time* (1986) and *Heathcliff* (1996). Following his conversion to Christianity, his clean-cut image damaged his reputation with rock fans, but he has nevertheless become a British entertainment institution. His many recorded albums have included *21 Today* (1961), *Rock and Roll Juvenile* (1979) and *Love Songs* (1981), *Silver*, released in 1983 to celebrate 25 years as a recording artist, and *Mistletoe and Wine* which topped the charts for four weeks at Christmas in 1988. He was knighted in 1995. >> Shadows, The

Richard, Joseph Henri Maurice, nickname **Rocket** (1921–) Ice hockey player, born in Montreal, Quebec, Canada. He joined the Montreal Canadians in 1942, and in 1944–5 made a record total score of 50 goals in 50 games. He won the Hart Trophy in 1947. His fierce competitiveness brought him a great following and, after an incident in March 1955 which caused his suspension for the rest of the year, there was violence and rioting on the streets. He retired in 1960, with a National Hockey League tally of 544 goals, a record at the time.

Richards, Alun (1929–) Novelist, short-story writer, and playwright, born in Pontypridd, Rhondda Cynon Taff, S Wales. He studied at University College, Swansea, and worked as a probation officer, sailor, and teacher. His novels include *The Elephant You Gave Me* (1963), *A Woman of Experience* (1969), and *Barque Whisper* (1979). He has also published two collections of short stories, *Dai Country* (1973) and *The Former Miss Merthyr Tydfil* (1976). He is well-known for his adaptation for television of *The Onedin Line*.

Richards, Ceri (1903–71) Artist, born in Dunvant, Swansea. He studied at Swansea School of Art and the Royal College of Art, holding his first one-man show at Swansea (1930). Influenced by the Surrealists, he joined the London Group (1937), then taught at Chelsea School of Art (1945–55), the Slade School of Art (1956–61), and the Royal College (1961–2). He also designed opera sets, stained-glass windows, and vestments.

Richards, Dickinson (Woodruff) (1895–1973) Physician, born in Orange, NJ. He studied at Yale, specializing in cardiology, then taught at Columbia University (1928–61), where he became professor of medicine in 1947. With André Cournand he developed the technique of cardiac catheterization introduced by Werner Forssmann. All three shared the 1956 Nobel Prize for Physiology or Medicine. >> Cournand; Forssmann

Richards, Ellen Henrietta, née **Swallow** (1842–1911) Chemist, sanitation engineer, and educator, born in Dunstable, MA. The first woman admitted to the Massachusetts Institute of Technology, she became a leader in the movement to educate women in the sciences, setting up programmes in Boston public schools and at MIT, where she taught sanitary chemistry (1884–1911). After conducting a survey of Massachusetts' inland waterways (1878–90), she established the first programme in sanitary engineering at MIT. She was also a leader in establishing a scientific basis for home economics.

Richards, Frank, pseudonym of **Charles (Harold St John) Hamilton** (1875–1961) Children's writer, born in London, England, UK. Educated privately, he wrote stories for magazines and comics while still a schoolboy. As a professional writer, he produced 70 000 words a week under various pseudonyms for *Gem*, *Magnet*, and other papers. He created 'Billy Bunter' and 'Greyfriars School' for *The Magnet*, and after World War 2, wrote numerous books about 'Billy Bunter' and 'Tom Merry', becoming the most prolific author in the history of juvenile fiction.

Richards, Sir Gordon (1904–86) Jockey and trainer, born in Oakengates, Shropshire, WC England, UK. Between 1921 and 1954 he rode a record 4870 winners in Britain, and was champion jockey a record 26 times (1925–53). On 12 occasions he rode 200 winners in a season, and his 269 winners in 1947 remains a record. He won 14 English Classics (1930–53), and rode 12 consecutive winners (1933), including all six at Chepstow. He won his only Epsom Derby in 1953 on *Pinza*, six days after receiving a knighthood. He took up training after retirement in 1954. >> RR1161

Richards, I(vor) A(rmstrong) (1893–1979) Literary critic and scholar, who pioneered the detailed critical study of literary texts in the 20th-c, born in Sandbach, Cheshire, NWC England, UK. With C K Ogden he wrote *The Meaning of Meaning* in 1923. His later books include the influential *Principles of Literary Criticism* (1924) and *Practical Criticism* (1929). During the 1930s he helped to develop Basic English, worked in China (1929–30, 1936–8), and became professor of English at Harvard (1944), where his publications included poetry as well as critical essays. >> Ogden

Richards, Keith >> **Rolling Stones, The**

Richards, Theodore (William) (1868–1928) Chemist, born in Germantown, PA. He studied at Haverford College and at Harvard, where he became professor of chemistry in 1901. He carried out important investigations in thermochemistry and thermodynamics, but is best known for his work on atomic weights which indicated the existence of isotopes. He was awarded the 1914 Nobel Prize for Chemistry.

Richards, Viv, popular name of **Isaac Vivian Alexander Richards** (1952–) Cricket player, born in Antigua. In 1976 he scored a record 1710 Test runs in one calendar year. He captained the West Indies (1985–91), and scored 8540 runs in 121 Test matches, including 24 centuries. In England he played county cricket for Somerset (1974–86) and Glamorgan (1990–3). >> RR1149

Richardson, Dorothy M(iller) (1873–1957) Novelist, born in Abingdon, Berkshire, S England, UK. In 1895 she moved to London and worked as a teacher, clerk, and dentist's assistant. An affair with H G Wells led to a miscarriage and a near-collapse in 1907. She started her writing career with works on the Quakers and George Fox (1914). Her first novel, *Pointed Roofs* (1915), was the first of her well-known 12-volume sequence entitled *Pilgrimage*, culminating with *Clear Horizon* (1935) and *Dimple Hill* (1938). She was the first exponent of the 'stream of consciousness' style later made famous by Virginia Woolf. >> Wells, H G; Woolf, Virginia

Richardson, Elliot (Lee) (1920–) Lawyer and cabinet member, born in Boston, MA. He became Lieutenant-Governor of Massachusetts (1965–7) and state attorney general (1967–9), then served as Nixon's secretary of

health, education, and welfare (1970–3), and briefly as secretary of defense (1973). He became US attorney general in 1973, but resigned in protest at the firing of Watergate prosecutor, Archibald Cox. Secretary of commerce (1976–7), he was the chief US negotiator for the international Law of the Sea (1978–80), before returning to private practice. He is the only man in US history to have held four different cabinet posts. >> Nixon, Richard

Richardson, Henry Handel, pseudonym of **Ethel Florence Lindesay Robertson**, née **Richardson** (1870–1946) Novelist, born in Melbourne, Victoria, Australia. She travelled and studied in Europe, and after her marriage to **John George Robertson** (1895) lived in Strasbourg and then England (1904). She attained distinction with the third part of her trilogy which was published as *The Fortunes of Richard Mahony* (1929).

Richardson, Henry Hobson (1838–86) Architect, born in Priestley Plantation, LA. Educated at Harvard, he studied architecture in Paris, and initiated the Romanesque revival in the USA, leading to a distinctively American style of architecture. He designed a number of churches, especially Trinity Church, Boston (1872–7), the Allegheny Co Buildings in Pittsburgh, and halls of residence at Harvard (1879–84).

Richardson, Sir John (1787–1865) Naturalist and explorer, born in Dumfries, Dumfries and Galloway, SW Scotland, UK. A surgeon in the Royal Navy (1807–55), he served in the Arctic expeditions of Parry and Franklin (1819–22, 1825–7), and the Franklin search expedition of 1848–9. He wrote *Fauna Boreali-Americana* (1829–37) and *Ichthyology of the Voyage of HMS Erebus and Terror* (1844–8), and made major contributions to the knowledge of ichthyology of the Indo-Pacific region. >> Franklin, John; Parry, William Edward; Rae

Richardson, Miranda (1958–) Actress, born in Southport, Lancashire, NW England, UK. She made her West End debut in *Moving* (1980–1), and her film debut in *Dance With a Stranger* (1985). Later films include *Empire of The Sun* (1987), *Damage* (1992, BAFTA for Best Supporting Actress), *Tom and Viv* (1994), and *The Apostle* (1997). She also appeared as Queen Elizabeth in the television comedy series *Blackadder* (1990).

Richardson, Sir Owen Willans (1879–1959) Physicist, born in Dewsbury, West Yorkshire, N England, UK. He studied at Cambridge, and at the Cavendish Laboratory he began his work on *thermionics*, a term he coined to describe the phenomenon of the emission of electricity from hot bodies; for this work he was awarded the Nobel Prize for Physics in 1928. He was appointed professor of physics at King's College, London (1914), and was Yarrow research professor of the Royal Society (1924–44).

Richardson, Sir Ralph (David) (1902–83) Actor, born in Cheltenham, Gloucestershire, SWC England, UK. He made his debut at the Little Theatre, Brighton (1921), and gained an early reputation with the Birmingham Repertory Theatre, which he joined in 1926. His association with the Old Vic Company commenced in 1930, and he was asked to lead its postwar revival. His many stage appearances include *West of Suez* (1971), *The Cherry Orchard* (1978), and *The Understanding* (1982), and he had major roles in such films as *Anna Karenina* (1948), *The Heiress*, Oh! What a Lovely War (1969), *A Doll's House* (1973), and *Invitation to the Wedding* (1983). He was knighted in 1947.

Richardson, Robert C (1937–) Physicist, born in Washington, DC. He studied at Duke University, then moved to Cornell, where with Lee and Osherhoff he contributed to the discovery of the superfluidity of helium-3. He shared the Nobel Prize for Physics in 1996. >> Lee, David M; Osherhoff

Richardson, Samuel (1689–1761) Novelist, born in Mackworth, Derbyshire, C England, UK. He was apprenticed to a printer, married his master's daughter, and set up in business for himself in London, where he became the centre of a wide circle of friends. *Pamela* (1740), his first novel, is 'a series of familiar letters now first published in order to cultivate the Principles of Virtue and Religion', and this was the aim of all his works. He also wrote *Clarissa* (1748), published in seven volumes, and *Sir Charles Grandison* (1754). In using the epistolary method (which suggested authenticity at a time when mere fiction was frowned upon), he helped to develop the dramatic scope of the novel, then little regarded as a literary form.

Richardson, Tony, popular name of **Cecil Antonio Richardson** (1928–91) Stage and film director, born in Shipley, West Yorkshire, N England, UK. He studied at Oxford, and worked for the BBC before entering the theatre. His reputation was established with the Royal Court Theatre production of *Look Back in Anger* (1956), a play representative of the emerging generation of 'Angry Young Men'. During the 1950s his experimental productions stimulated a revival of creative vitality on the British stage. He co-founded Woodfall Film Productions Ltd (1958), and notable films include *Saturday Night and Sunday Morning* (1960), *A Taste of Honey* (1961), *The Loneliness of the Long Distance Runner* (1962), and *Tom Jones* (1963), for which he won an Oscar for best director. Later films include *The Charge of the Light Brigade* (1968) and *Ned Kelly* (1970), and in the 1980s he directed several television films, such as *Phantom of the Opera* (1989) and *Blue Sky* (1990).

Richelieu, Armand Jean du Plessis, Cardinal, duc de (Duke of) [**reesh**lyoe] (1585–1642) French statesman and first minister of France (1624–42), born in Richelieu, France. A protégé of the queen mother, Marie de Medicis, he became minister of state (1624), and as chief minister was the effective ruler of France. His twin aims, to secure universal obedience to the Bourbon monarchy and to enhance France's international prestige, were achieved at the expense of recalcitrant groups in French society. His principal achievement was to check Habsburg power, ultimately by sending armies into the Spanish Netherlands, Alsace, Lorraine, and Roussillon. He founded the French Academy in 1634. >> Louis XIII; Marie de Medicis

Richepin, Jean [reeshpĩ] (1849–1926) Poet, playwright and novelist, born in Médéa, Algeria. He gave up the study of medicine to study literature at the Ecole Normale. His first book of poems, *La Chanson des gueux* (1876, Song of the Poor), caused his imprisonment for its coarse language. Other works of poetry include *Les Caresses* (1877, Caresses), *Les Blasphèmes* (1884, Blasphemies), and *La Mer* (1886, The Sea). He was elected to the Académie Français in 1908, later becoming a director.

Richie, Lionel (1949–) Singer and songwriter, born in Tuskegee, AL. A founder member of the Commodores, his debut solo album *Lionel Richie* (1982) was a US number 3 hit, and 'Truly', a ballad from that album, reached US number 1, winning him a Grammy award. He performed one of his most popular hits, 'All Night Long' (1983), at the closing ceremony of the 1984 Los Angeles Olympic Games. He co-wrote the famine relief song 'We Are The World' with Michael Jackson in 1993. Later albums include *Louder Than Words* (1996). >> Jackson, Michael

Richler, Mordecai (1931–) Writer, born in Montreal, Quebec, Canada. He was brought up in Montreal's Jewish ghetto, attended university in Montreal, then lived in Paris (1951–2). His best-known novel is *The Apprenticeship of Duddy Kravitz* (1959), which was later filmed, although *St Urbain's Horseman* (1971) is a more ambitious work. Later books include *Solomon Gursky was Here* (1989). He has also written essays, scripts for cinema, radio, and television, and a memoir, *This Year in Jerusalem* (1994).

Richmond, Henry Tudor, Duke of >> **Henry VII**

Richter, Burton (1931–) Particle physicist, born in New York City. He studied at the Massachusetts Institute of Technology, and became a professor at Stanford in 1967. Largely responsible for the Stanford Positron–Electron Accelerating Ring, he led a team which discovered the J/psi hadron, for which he shared the 1976 Nobel Prize for Physics with Ting, who independently made the same discovery at the same time. >> Ting

Richter, Charles (Francis) (1900–85) Seismologist, born near Hamilton, OH. He studied at the University of Southern California and at the California Institute of Technology, where he taught from 1936. With Beno Gutenberg he devised the scale of earthquake strength which now bears his name (1927–35). >> Gutenberg, Beno

Richter, Hans (1843–1916) Conductor, born in Raab, Hungary. He studied at Vienna, became conductor at Munich, Budapest, and Vienna, gave a series of annual concerts in London (1879–97), and was conductor of the Hallé Orchestra (1897–1911). He was an authority on the music of Wagner, with whom he was closely associated in the Bayreuth festivals. >> Wagner, Richard

Richter, Johann Paul (Friedrich), pseudonym **Jean Paul** (1763–1825) Novelist and humorist, born in Wunsiedel, Germany. He studied theology in Leipzig, then turned to literature, and after several years struggling to publish, began to teach (1787). He produced a wide range of works, achieving success with such romances as *Die unsichtbare Loge* (1793, The Invisible Lodge), *Hesperus* (1795), and the four-volume *Titan* (1800–3).

Richter, Sviatoslav (Teofilovich) (1915–97) Pianist, born in Zhitomir, Ukraine. He studied at the Moscow Conservatory (1937–42), and won the Stalin Prize in 1949. He made extensive concert tours, with a wide repertoire, and was associated with the music festivals at Aldeburgh and Spoleto.

Richthofen, Manfred, Freiherr (Baron) **von**, nickname **the Red Baron** (1882–1918) German airman, born in Wrocław, Poland (formerly Breslau, Germany). At first in the cavalry, he later joined the German air force and, during World War 1, became commander of the 11th Chasing Squadron, more commonly known as 'Richthofen's Flying Circus' because of their decorated, scarlet aircraft. He was noted for his high number (80) of aerial victories. He was shot down behind the British lines.

Richthofen, Ferdinand (Paul Wilhelm), Baron von [**rikh**thohfn] (1833–1905) Geographer, geologist, and traveller, born in Karlsruhe, Germany. He studied at Wrocław, Poland (formerly Breslau, Germany) and Berlin, in 1860 accompanied a Prussian expedition to E Asia, then travelled in Java, Siam, Burma, California (1863–8), China, and Japan (1868–72). After his return he became professor of geology at Bonn (1875), and of geography at Leipzig (1883) and at Berlin (1886), his research helping to develop the field of geomorphology.

Rickenbacker, Eddie, popular name of **Edward Vernon Rickenbacker** (1890–1973) Aviator and World War 1 ace, born in Columbus, OH. His pre-war skill as a motor-racing-car driver earned him the position of chauffeur to General Pershing, but he applied for aviation duties. In four months of combat flying he scored 26 victories, and received a hero's welcome in the USA and the Congressional Medal of Honor. He returned to motor racing, forming the Rickenbacker Motor Co (1921). He was vice-president and sales director of the Fokker Aircraft Co, then joined Eastern Air Lines in 1934 as a pilot, becoming its president and general manager in 1938 (chairman, 1959).

Rickert, Heinrich (1863–1936) Philosopher, born in Danzig, Germany. He was a pupil of **Wilhelm Windelband** (1848–1915), and founded with him the Baden school of neo-Kantianism. He became professor at Freiburg (1894) and Heidelberg (1916), and argued for a *Kulturwissenschaft* ('science of culture') which could be an objective science of those universal concepts (such as religion, art, and law) that emerge from the multiplicity of individual cultures and societies. His views were a great influence on, among others, Max Weber. >> Weber, Max

Rickey, Branch (Wesley) (1881–1965) Baseball manager and administrator, born in Stockdale, OH. In 1919, as manager of the St Louis Cardinals, he introduced the 'farm system' whereby major league clubs linked themselves to lower-grade clubs to develop their own young players; this brought his team four world championships and made them the most profitable in baseball. While manager of the Brooklyn Dodgers (1942–50) he signed the first black player in major league baseball, Jackie Robinson. >> Robinson, Jackie

Rickman, Alan (1946–) British actor. He studied at Chelsea School of Art, the Royal College of Art, and the Royal Academy of Dramatic Art, London, and played a wide range of theatre roles during the 1980s, including seasons at the RSC in 1978–9 and 1985–6. He has since become well known for his film work, beginning with *Die Hard* (1988), and including *Truly, Madly, Deeply* (1991), *Robin Hood, Prince of Thieves* (1991, BAFTA Best Supporting Actor), *Close My Eyes* (1991), *Mesmer* (1993), *Sense and Sensibility* (1996), *Michael Collins* (1996) and *Rasputin* (1996, Emmy).

Rickover, Hyman G(eorge) (1900–86) Naval engineering officer, born in Makov, Ukraine. Brought up in Chicago, he studied at the US Naval Academy and Columbia University. He led the team that successfully adapted nuclear reactors as a means of ship propulsion, the first vessel so equipped being the US submarine *Nautilus*, launched in 1954.

Ricoeur, Paul [reekoe(r)] (1913–) Philosopher, born in Valence, France. He studied at the University of Paris, and became professor at Strasbourg (1948–56), Paris-Nanterre (1956–70), and Chicago (1970). He has been an influential figure in French and Anglo–American philosophy, engaging critically with various contemporary methodologies – structuralism, phenomenology, psychoanalysis, and hermeneutics – across a whole range of problems. His publications include *Philosophie de la volonté* (3 vols, 1950–60, Philosophy of the Will) and *La Métaphore vive* (1975, The Living Metaphor).

Riddell, William Renwick (1852–1945) Judge and legal historian. He studied at Cobourg Collegiate Institute, Victoria University, and Syracuse University, and was judge of the High Court of Ontario from 1906, and of the Supreme Court of Canada from 1917. A prolific writer, he made notable contributions to Canadian history, particularly legal history, such as *The Legal Profession of Upper Canada in Its Early Years* (1916) and *The Bar and the Courts of the Province of Upper Canada or Ontario* (1928).

Ride, Sally (Kristen) (1951–) Astronaut, the first US woman in space, born in Los Angeles, CA. She studied at Stanford University, and achieved national ranking as a tennis player, but chose not to follow this as a career. In 1978 she was selected as an astronaut candidate by NASA, and became a mission specialist on future space-shuttle flight crews. She was selected to serve on a six-day flight of the orbiter *Challenger* in 1983.

Rideal, Sir Eric Keightley [riydl] (1890–1974) British chemist. He worked at Cambridge (1930–46), the Royal Institution, London (1946–9), and London University (1950–5). He studied colloids and catalysis, and devised the *Rideal–Walker test* for the germicidal power of a disinfectant.

Ridgeley, Andrew >> **Michael, George**

Ridgeway, John (1938–) British trans-Atlantic oarsman and explorer. He studied at the Nautical College, Pangbourne, and served in the Merchant Navy, before doing his national service with the Royal Engineers. After two years at the Royal Military Academy, Sandhurst, he was commissioned into the Parachute Regiment and served in Canada, Norway, Greece, the Gulf, Kenya, and Malaysia. In 1966 he rowed the Atlantic in 92 days from the USA to Eire with Chay Blyth. He then sailed the Atlantic single-handed to South America, led an expedition that followed the R Amazon from source to sea, and another which crossed the Chilean ice-cap. He participated in the Round the World Race (1977–8) with a team from the School of Adventure run from his home at Ardmore in Scotland, and in 1992 led a team canoeing around Cape Horn. >> Blyth, Chay

Ridgway, Matthew B(unker) (1895–1993) US soldier, born in Fort Monroe, VA. He trained at West Point, and commanded the 82nd Airborne Division in Sicily (1943) and Normandy (1944), the 18th Airborne Corps in the North West Europe campaign (1944–5), and the US 8th Army in UN operations in Korea (1950). He succeeded Douglas MacArthur in command of US and UN forces (1951), and was supreme Allied commander in Europe in succession to Eisenhower (1952–3), and chief of US army staff (1953). >> Eisenhower; MacArthur

Ridgway, Robert (1850–1929) Ornithologist, born in Mount Carmel, IL. Curator of birds at the US National Museum, he devised a colour system for bird identification. His books included *A History of North American Birds* (1874–84) and *The Birds of Middle and North America* (8 vols, 1901–19).

Riding, Laura, *née* **Reichenthal**, pseudonyms **Barbara Rich** and **Madeleine Vara** (1901–91) Poet, critic, novelist, and polemicist, born in New York City. She studied at Cornell, and published her first collection of verse, *The Close Chaplet*, in 1926. She was associated with Robert Graves, with whom she collaborated on several projects, including *A Survey of Modernist Poetry* (1927). In 1941 she married **Schuyler B Jackson**, editor of *Time*, and signed herself **Laura (Riding) Jackson**. Her *Collected Poems* appeared in 1938. Other critical and literary works include *Contemporaries and Snobs* (1918), *Anarchism Is Not Enough* (1928), and *Experts are Puzzled* (1930). >> Graves, Robert

Ridley, Nicholas (c. 1500–1555) Protestant martyr, born near Haltwhistle, Northumberland, NE England, UK. Educated at Cambridge, he was ordained c.1524, and studied in Paris and Louvain (1527–30). He then held a variety of posts, including chaplain to Cranmer and Henry VIII, and Bishop of Rochester (1547). An ardent reformer, he became Bishop of London (1550), and helped Cranmer prepare the Thirty-nine Articles. On the death of Edward VI he espoused the cause of Lady Jane Grey, was imprisoned, and executed. >> Cranmer, Thomas; Grey, Lady Jane

Ridley (of Liddesdale), Nicholas Ridley, Baron (1929–93) British statesman, born in Newcastle upon Tyne, Tyne and Wear, NE England, UK. He studied at Oxford, and embarked on an industrial career, then moved into politics, becoming a Conservative MP in 1959. He held junior ministerial posts, and in 1979 joined the Margaret Thatcher government, entering the cabinet as secretary of state for transport (1983–6). Regarded as one of Mrs Thatcher's closest allies, he was moved from the department of the environment (1986–9), where he had responsibility for the controversial 'poll tax', to the department of trade and industry (1989–90). He resigned after making controversial remarks about the European Commission and Germany's role in Europe. He was created a life peer in 1992. >> Thatcher

Ridolfo, Roberto di [riˈdolfoh], also known as **Roberto Ridolfi** (1531–1612) Florentine conspirator, born in Florence, Italy. A businessman in London, in 1570 he organized a Roman Catholic plot, supported by Spain, to marry Mary, Queen of Scots, to Thomas Howard, 4th Duke of Norfolk, and overthrow Elizabeth I. The plot was discovered when an emissary was seized, but Ridolfo was abroad at the time, and returned to Italy, where he became a senator. >> Elizabeth I; Mary, Queen of Scots

Rie, Dame Lucie [ree] (1902–95) Studio potter, born in Vienna. Trained at the *Kunstgewerbeschule*, in 1938 she moved as a refugee to England, where she shared a workshop with Hans Coper, producing ceramic jewellery and buttons while continuing her individual work. She later produced stoneware, tin-glazed earthenware, and porcelain pots, with a precision and technical control that has influenced many of today's leading potters. A retrospective exhibition of her work was held at Norwich in 1981. She was created a dame in 1991. >> Coper

Riefenstahl, Leni [reefenshtahl], popular name of **Berta Helene Amalie Riefenstahl** (1902–) Film-maker, born in Berlin. After acting in several films she formed her own company, and made *Triumph des Willens* (1935, Triumph of the Will), a compelling record of a Nazi rally at Nuremberg. It vividly illustrated Hitler's charismatic appeal, but tainted her career, prompting criticism that she had glorified the event. *Olympia* (1938), her epic documentary of the Berlin Olympic Games, was given a gala premiere on Hitler's 49th birthday. In the 1970s she published several photographic studies of Africa.

Riegger, Wallingford [reeger] (1885–1961) Composer, born in Albany, GA. He studied at Cornell University, the Institute of Musical Art, New York City, and Berlin, and went on to hold posts at Drake University and Ithaca Conservatory, NY. His works, which show the influence of Schoenberg's '12-note' system and his German training, received little attention until the performance of his third symphony in 1948, after which he was increasingly recognized. He wrote extensively for orchestra and for chamber music combinations. >> Schoenberg

Riel, Louis [ree-el] (1844–85) Canadian political leader, born in Red River Settlement, Rupert's Land, Canada. He succeeded his father as a leader of the Métis, and headed the Red River Rebellion in 1869–70. As president of the provisional government, he was able to secure better terms for the new province of Manitoba in the Confederation. Following a period of exile in the USA, he returned to lead a second uprising of Métis (1885), in what is now Saskatchewan. His subsequent arrest and trial led to his execution.

Riemann, (Georg Friedrich) Bernhard [reeman] (1826–66) Mathematician, born in Breselenz, Germany. He studied at Göttingen and Berlin universities, and became professor of mathematics at Göttingen (1859). His early work was on the theory of functions, but he is best remembered for his development of non-Euclidian geometry, important in modern physics and relativity theory. His profound conjecture (the *Riemann hypothesis*) about the behaviour of the zeta (or Riemann) function, which he showed determines the distribution of the prime numbers, has resisted proof since its publication in 1857.

Riemerschmid, Richard [reemershmit] (1868–1957) Architect and designer, born in Munich, Germany. In 1897, after varied experience, he founded *Werkstätten* ('craft workshops') for which he designed functional and simple furniture, suitable for mass production. A major figure and influence in the development of 20th-c German design and industry, his enormous output over almost 50 years included architecture, furniture and interiors, glass and ceramics, cutlery, light-fittings, and graphics.

Rienzi, Cola di [rienzee], also spelled **Rienzo** (1313–54) Italian patriot, born in Rome. In 1347 he incited the citizens to rise against the rule of the nobles. The senators were driven out, and he was made tribune. Papal authority then turned against him, and he fled from Rome. He returned in 1354, and tried to re-establish his position, but was killed in a rising against him. Wagner's opera on his story was completed in 1840. >> Wagner, Richard

Riesener, Jean Henri [reezener] (1734–1806) Cabinet-maker, born in Gladbeck, Münster. In 1754, he joined the workshop of **Jean François Oeben** (c.1715–63) in Paris, taking charge on Oeben's death. A master of marquetry and ebony work, he became the best known cabinet-maker in France. He completed the famous 'king's desk' for Louis XV, and was favoured by the court of Louis XVI from 1774.

Riesman, David [reezman] (1909–) Sociologist, born in Philadelphia, PA. He studied at Harvard, then worked as a clerk, teacher, and assistant district attorney before becoming professor at the University of Chicago (1946–58) and then at Harvard. His most notable work is the co-authored study of the urban middle class, *The Lonely Crowd* (1950).

Riesz, Frigyes [rees] (1880–1956) Mathematician, born in Györ, Hungary. He studied at Zürich, Budapest, and Göttingen, and taught at the University of Kolozsvár (Cluj) from 1911. He worked in functional analysis, integral equations, and subharmonic functions, and developed a new approach to the Lebesgue integral. He published the important textbook *Leçons d'analyse fonctionnelle* (1952, Lessons of Functional Analysis). >> Lebesgue

Rietveld, Gerrit Thomas [reetfelt] (1888–1964) Architect and furniture designer, born in Utrecht, The Netherlands. He started as a woodworker, opening his own cabinet-making workshop in Utrecht in 1911. After studying architecture, he began to design his own furniture, notably the 'red-and-blue' chair (1918). His architectural work includes the Schröder House in Utrecht (1924), exhibiting the rectilinear quality and use of colour associated with the *De Stijl* movement, and the Van Gogh Museum, Amsterdam, completed posthumously in 1973.

Rieu, Emile Victor [ryoe] (1887–1972) Editor and translator, born in London, England, UK. A classical scholar, he formed the habit of translating aloud to his wife, and it was her interest in the *Odyssey* that encouraged him to start on his own version. It was offered to Allen Lane, the Penguin paperback publisher, and was published in 1946. It became the cornerstone of the new Penguin Classics, of which Rieu became editor. By his retirement in 1964, *The Odyssey* had sold over two million copies.

Rifkind, Sir Malcolm (Leslie) (1946–) British Conservative statesman, born in Edinburgh, EC Scotland, UK. He studied at Edinburgh, was called to the bar in 1970, and was elected an MP in 1974. After a ministerial post in the Foreign and Commonwealth office (1983–6), he became secretary of state for Scotland (1986–90), transport (1990–2), defence (1992–5), and foreign secretary (1995–7). He lost his seat in the 1997 general election, the year he received a knighthood.

Rigg, Dame Diana (1938–) Actress, born in Doncaster, S Yorkshire, N England, UK. She studied at the Royal Academy of Dramatic Art and joined the Royal Shakespeare Company at Stratford (1959–64). After playing Emma Peel in the popular *The Avengers* television series, she joined the National Theatre (1972), making regular appearances during the 1970s. In New York her role in *Medea* (1993–4) earned her a Tony Award. Among her films are *Evil Under the Sun* (1982) and *A Good Man in Africa* (1994), and her television work includes *Mother Love* (BAFTA Award). She was made a dame in 1994.

Riley, Bridget (1931–) Artist, born in London, England, UK. She studied at Goldsmith's College of Art (1949–52) and the Royal College of Art (1952–5). Her first one-woman exhibition was in London at Gallery One in 1962, followed by others worldwide. She is a leading practitioner of Op Art, manipulating overall flat patterns, originally in black and white but later in colour, using repeated shapes or undulating lines, often creating an illusion of movement, as seen in 'Fall' (1963, Tate, London). She was the first English painter to win the major painting prize at the Venice Biennale (1968).

Riley, James Whitcomb, known as **the Hoosier poet** (1849–1916) Poet, known as the poet of the common people, born in Greenfield, IN. As a boy he was an entertainer, assisting medicine vendors. He made his name contributing homely dialect poems to the *Indianapolis Journal* (1877–85). He published several volumes, and is well known for his poems about children, including 'Little Orfant Annie'.

Riley, Terry (1935–) Composer, born in Colfax, CA. He studied at the University of California, financing himself by playing jazz in local bars. His compositions include *In C* (1964), first performed by an ensemble including Steve Reich, *Reed Streams* (1966), and *A Rainbow in Curved Air* (1968). >> Reich, Steve

Rilke, Rainer Maria [**ril**kuh] (1875–1926) Lyric poet, born in Prague. He studied at Prague, Munich, and Berlin. His three-part poem cycle, *Das Stundenbuch* (1905, The Book of Hours), written after visiting Russia, shows the deep influence of Russian Pietism. Mysticism was abandoned for the aesthetic ideal in *Gedichte* (1907–8, Poems), seen also in his two major works, *Die Sonnette an Orpheus* (Sonnets to Orpheus) and *Duineser Elegien* (Duino Elegies), both written in 1923.

Rimbaud, (Jean Nicolas) Arthur [**ri**boh] (1854–91) Poet, born in Charleville, France. He published his first book of poems in 1870, following this with his most popular work *Le Bateau ivre* (1871, The Drunken Boat). In 1871, Verlaine invited him to Paris, where they led a life of ill repute together. Before the relationship ended (1873), Rimbaud wrote *Les Illuminations* (1872), a series of prose and verse poems, which show him to be a precursor of Symbolism. Disappointed at the cold reception given to his *Une Saison en enfer* (1873, A Season in Hell), he stopped writing, and spent the rest of his life wandering in Europe and Africa. >> Starkie; Verlaine

Rimet, Jules [reemay] (1873–1956) French football administrator. He founded the Red Star Club of Paris, became president of the French football league (1910), and was president of the French Football Federation (1919–49). He promoted the Fédération Internationale de Football Association (FIFA), of which he was president (1921–56), and founded the World Cup competition (1930), his name being added to the title in 1946.

Rimini, Francesca da >> **Francesca da Rimini**

Rimsky-Korsakov, Nikolai (Andreyevich) [**rim**skee **kaw(r)**sakof] (1844–1908) Composer, born in Tikhvin, Russia. Educated at the naval academy in St Petersburg, his early musical education was perfunctory, but his interest was kindled after meeting Balakirev in 1861. He sailed as a midshipman on a sailing ship (1862–5), after which he wrote his first symphony (1865). In 1871 he was made a professor at the St Petersburg Conservatory, where he was able to develop his technique. He produced three great orchestral masterpieces, *Capriccio Espagnol*, *Easter Festival*, and *Scheherazade* (1887–8), but his main works after that were operas, such as *The Golden Cockerel* (1907). Ever conscious of his earlier technical shortcomings, he rewrote almost all his early work. He also edited and completed works by Borodin and Mussorgsky. >> Balakirev; Borodin; Mussorgsky

Ringan, St >> **Ninian, St**

Rinuccini, Ottavio >> **Peri, Jacopo**

Ripley, George (1802–80) Social reformer and literary critic, born in Greenfield, MA. A graduate of Harvard, he was a Unitarian pastor in Boston until 1841. He joined in the Transcendental movement, founded *The Dial* in 1840, and organized and led the idealistic communal experiment at Brook Farm, near Boston (1841–7). He edited *The Harbinger* (1845–9), and became literary critic for the *New York Tribune* (1849–80). In 1850 he founded *Harper's New Monthly Magazine*, and was joint-editor of the *New American Cyclopaedia* (1858–63).

Ripley, Robert, originally **LeRoy Ripley** (1893–1949) Illustrator, cartoonist, and writer, born in Santa Rosa, CA. He began as a tombstone polisher, worked on newspapers in San Francisco (1909–13), and moved to New York City to work for the *Globe* (1913). He changed his first name and began his *Believe It or Not!* cartoons of oddities (1918). His syndicated feature made him wealthy, and he lived on an island in Long Island Sound he called Bion, an acronym of *Believe It or Not!*.

Rippon (of Hexham), (Aubrey) Geoffrey (Frederick) Rippon, Baron (1924– 96) British statesman. He studied at Oxford, qualified as a barrister, became a Conservative MP in 1955, and served in the governments of Harold Macmillan, Alec Douglas-Home, and Edward Heath. A committed European, he led the UK delegation to the Council of Europe and the Western European Union (1967–70). He left the House of Commons in 1987 to concentrate on business interests, and was made a life peer.

Ritchie, Anne Isabella, Lady (1837–1919) Writer, born in London, England, UK, the daughter of William Makepeace Thackeray. A close companion of her father, she contributed valuable personal reminiscences to an 1898–9 edition of his works, and also wrote memoirs of their contemporaries, such as Tennyson and Ruskin. Her novels include *The Village on the Cliff* (1867) and *Old Kensington* (1873). >> Thackeray

Ritchie-Calder, Peter, Baron >> **Calder, (Peter) Ritchie**

Rits, Jacob (August) (1849–1914) Journalist and social critic, born in Ribe, Denmark. He became a police reporter on the New York *Tribune* (1877–88) and the New York *Sun* (1888–99). His horrifying description of immigrant poverty in New York City in 1890, *How the Other Half Lives*, was the first use of photographic evidence in social reportage. An enthusiastic champion of the reforms of Theodore Roosevelt, he wrote a study of him, and was active in the movement for small parks and playgrounds, in tenement housing, and school reform. >> Roosevelt, Theodore

Ritter, Carl (1779–1859) Geographer, born in Quedlinburg, Germany. He became professor of geography at Berlin (1829), and director of studies of the Military School. He laid the foundations of modern scientific geography, his most important work, *Die Erkunde* (1817, Earth Science), stressing the relation between people and their natural environment.

Rivera, Diego [rivayra] (1886–1957) Painter, born in Guanajuato, Mexico. In 1921 he began a series of murals in public buildings depicting the life and history of the Mexican people. He also executed frescoes in the USA (1930–4), mainly of industrial life. His art is a blend of folk art and revolutionary propaganda, with overtones of Byzantine and Aztec symbolism. >> Kahlo; Nevelson

Rivero, Miguel Primo de >> **Primo de Rivera, Miguel**

Rivers, Augustus Pitt- >> **Pitt-Rivers, Augustus**

Rivers, Joan, professional name of **Joan Alexandra Molinsky** (1933–) Comedienne and writer, born in Larchmont, NY.

She appeared as a film extra in 1951, and after graduating from college, became a fashion co-ordinator. She had parts in minor plays before working with the Chicago improvisational troupe Second City (1961–2), where she developed her acid-comedy routines. Success came with an appearance on *The Tonight Show* in 1965. She made her Las Vegas debut in 1969, wrote a regular column in the *Chicago Tribune* (1973–6), and became the regular guest host of *The Tonight Show* (1983–6). She hosted *The Late Show* (1986–7) and *Hollywood Squares* (from 1987), and has also directed films, recorded albums, and written books, including *Having a Baby Can Be a Scream* (1974).

Rivers, Larry, originally **Larry Grossberg** (1923–) Painter and sculptor, born in New York City. A professional musician, he studied at the Juilliard School of Music (1944–5) before studying art with Hans Hoffmann (1947–8). Based in Southampton, Long Island, since 1953, he became a teacher at several schools. He is known for ironic historical works, such as 'Washington Crossing the Delaware' (1953, New York City), and realistic paintings such as 'Double Portrait of Birdie' (1955, New York City), and has also worked as a sculptor, specializing in figure studies. An Abstract Expressionist as well as a predecessor of Pop Art, he is respected for his versatility as an artist.

Rivers, W(illiam) H(alse) R(ivers) (1864–1922) Anthropologist and medical psychologist, born near Chatham, Kent, SE England, UK. He studied medicine, but lectured at Cambridge in neurophysiology and psychology. He took part in the Cambridge University expedition to the Torres Straits (1898–9), and subsequently worked among the Todas of India and in Melanesia, publishing the well-known *The Todas* (1906). His *Instinct and the Unconscious* (1920) sought to construct a theory of the unconscious based on the conflict of instinct, censorship, and reason.

Rix, Brian, popular name of **Brian Norman Roger Rix, Lord Rix of Whitehall and of Hornsea** (1924–) Actor and manager, born in Cottingham, East Riding of Yorkshire unitary authority, NE England, UK. He studied in York, joined the Donald Wolfit players in 1943, served with the RAF, and formed his own company in Ilkley, Yorkshire (1948) and in Margate (1949). He established a reputation for farce at the Whitehall Theatre with productions of *Reluctant Heroes* (1950), *Dry Rot* (1954), *Simple Spymen* (1958), *One for the Pot* (1961), and *Chase Me Comrade* (1964). After a further series of successful farces at the Garrick and Cambridge Theatres, he left the stage for charity work with the mentally handicapped and became chairman of Mencap in 1988. He has published two volumes of autobiography, *My Farce from My Elbow* (1975) and *Farce About Face* (1989). He was knighted in 1986 and became a life peer in 1992.

Rizzio, David [ritsioh], also spelled **Riccio** (?1533–1566) Courtier and musician, born in Pancalieri, Italy. After travelling to Scotland with the Duke of Savoy's embassy, he entered the service of Mary, Queen of Scots (1561), became her favourite, and was made her French secretary in 1564. He negotiated her marriage with Darnley (1565), who became jealous of his influence, and plotted his death with a group of nobles, including Morton and Ruthven. Rizzio was dragged from the queen's presence and murdered. >> Darnley; Mary, Queen of Scots; Morton, James Douglas; Ruthven

Roach, Hal, popular name of **Harald Eugene Roach** (1892–92) Film-maker, born in Elmira, NY. After an adventurous life as a mule-skinner and gold prospector in Alaska, he entered the film industry as a stuntman and extra in 1911. He began producing short comedy films, becoming an expert in the mechanics of slapstick, and helped to foster the careers of Laurel and Hardy. He also devised the series of Our Gang films, and won Oscars for *The Music Box* (1932)

and *Bored of Education* (1936). His range of full-length productions includes *Way Out West* (1937), *Of Mice and Men* (1939), and *One Million BC* (1940), which he co-directed. After World War 2 he diversified into television production. His final film was the compilation feature *The Crazy World of Laurel and Hardy* (1967), and in 1984 he received a special Academy Award. >> Laurel and Hardy

Roach, Max (1924–) Jazz drummer, bandleader, and composer, born in New Land, NC. He has played with many of the pioneers of 'bop' and modern jazz, including Dizzy Gillespie, Coleman Hawkins, Charlie Parker, Lester Young, and Miles Davis. He is also a teacher of music, and professor of music at the University of Massachusetts.

Robards, Jason [rohbah(r)dz], known as **Robards Jr** (1922–) Actor, born in Chicago, IL. He made his New York City debut in 1947 as the back end of a cow, going on to become an understudy and stage-manager. One of the greatest interpreters of O'Neill's work, in 1956 he won critical acclaim for his legendary performances in *The Iceman Cometh* and *Long Day's Journey into Night* (1956). He joined the Stratford Festival Company, Ontario, in 1958. He has appeared in several films and television dramas, but is primarily recognized as a stage actor. >> Bacall; O'Neill, Eugene

Robbe-Grillet, Alain [rob greeyay] (1922–) Novelist, born in Brest, France. He studied in Paris, and worked as an agronomist, then in a publishing house. After his first novel, *Les Gommes* (1953, The Erasers), he emerged as the leader of the *nouveau roman* group, contributing to the genre such novels as *Le Voyeur* (1955, The Voyeur) and *La Jalousie* (1959, Jealousy), and the theoretical work *Pour un nouveau roman* (1963, Towards the New Novel). Later novels include *Un Régicide* (1978) and *Les Derniers jours de Corinthe* (1994). He has also written essays and film scenarios, notably *L'Année dernière à Marienbad* (1961, Last Year at Marienbad).

Robbia, Luca della (c. 1400–82) Sculptor, born in Florence, Italy. Between 1431 and 1440 he executed 10 unequalled panels of angels and dancing boys for the cathedral there, for whose sacristy he also made a bronze door with 10 panels of figures in relief (1448–67). He is also known for his figures in terracotta, including medallions and reliefs, white or coloured. He established a business producing glazed terracottas which was carried on by his nephew **Andrea della Robbia** (1435–1525) and Andrea's son **Giovanni della Robbia** (1469–c.1529).

Robbins, Frederick (Chapman) (1916–) Physiologist and paediatrician, born in Auburn, AL. He studied at Harvard and served in the US Army's medical laboratory virus section during World War 2. He then joined Enders and Weller at the Children's Hospital, Boston, where he helped devise techniques for cultivating the poliomyelitis virus. He was professor of paediatrics at Case Western Reserve University, Cleveland (1952–80), and shared the 1954 Nobel Prize for Physiology or Medicine. >> Enders; Weller

Robbins, Harold (1916–97) Writer, born in New York City. At 15 he dropped out of George Washington High School, left his foster parents, and eventually became an inventory clerk in a grocery store. During the Depression he showed entrepreneurial flair by buying up crops and selling options to canning companies, and the canning contracts to wholesale grocers. He was a millionaire by the time he was 20, but speculation in sugar before the outbreak of World War 2 relieved him of his fortune. He became interested in writing and, drawing on his knowledge of street life, high finance, and Hollywood, produced a string of earthy best sellers including *Never Love a Stranger* (1948), *A Stone for Danny Fisher* (1952), and *The Carpetbaggers* (1961), which sold six million copies throughout the 1960s.

Later novels include *Dreams Die First* (1977), *Descent from Xanadu* (1984), *The Piranhas* (1991), *The Stallion* (1996), and *Tycoon*, and he completed *Wishing Well* just before his death.

Robbins, Jerome (1918–) Dancer and choreographer, born in New York City. He studied ballet and modern dance, worked initially as an actor, then joined the American Ballet Theater (1940). He became associate director then director of New York City Ballet (1949–59), and joint ballet master (1983–9). His collaboration with Leonard Bernstein resulted in his most famous musical, *West Side Story* (1957), for which he won two Oscars in the 1961 Hollywood version. Other Broadway successes included *Gypsy* (1959) and *Fiddler on the Roof* (1964), and later works include *Watermill* (1972), *Glass Pieces* (1983), and (with Mikhail Baryshnikov) *A Suite of Dances* (1994). >> Bernstein, Leonard; Martins

Robbins (of Clare Market), Lionel Charles Robbins, Baron (1898–1984) Economist and educationist, born in Sipson, S Greater London, England, UK. Professor at the London School of Economics (1929–61), he directed the economic section of the War Cabinet, then became chairman of the *Financial Times* (until 1970). He also chaired the *Robbins Committee* on the expansion of higher education in the UK (1961–4). His best-known work is *An Essay on the Nature and Significance of Economic Science* (1932). He became a life peer in 1959, and a Companion of Honour in 1968.

Robbins, Tim (1958–) Film actor, director, and writer, born in West Govina, CA. He grew up in New York City, moved to Los Angeles in 1981, and helped found the Actors Gang, an alternative theatre group. To fund this venture he took roles in such films as *Fraternity Vacation* (1985) and *Howard the Duck* (1986). He wrote, directed, and composed the songs for the critically acclaimed *Bob Roberts* (1992). Later films include (as actor) *The Shawshank Redemption* (1994) and *The Moviegoer* (1998) and (as producer, director, and writer) *Dead Man Walking* (1995).

Robens (of Woldingham), Alfred Robens, Baron (1910–) Trade unionist and industrialist, born in Manchester, Greater Manchester, NW England, UK. He became a trade union officer of the Union of Distributive and Allied Workers (1935–45). He became a Labour MP (1945–60), and for six months in 1951 was a member of the Cabinet as minister of labour and national service. Created a life peer in 1961, he is particularly remembered as chairman of the National Coal Board (1961–71).

Robert I >> **Bruce, Robert**

Robert II (1316–90) King of Scots (1371–90), the son of Walter, hereditary steward of Scotland. He acted as sole regent during the exile and captivity of David II. On David's death, he became king in right of his descent from his maternal grandfather, Robert I, and founded the Stuart royal dynasty. >> David II; RR1095

Robert of Brunne >> **Mannyng, Robert**

Robert Bellarmine, St >> **Bellarmine, St Robert**

Robert Curthose (c. 1054–1134) Duke of Normandy, the eldest son of William I, the Conqueror. On William's death (1087) Robert succeeded only to Normandy, while England passed to the second son, William Rufus. A protracted struggle between the two brothers was interrupted by Robert's participation in the First Crusade (1096–1101), and in his absence the throne of England was seized by his younger brother Henry I on the death of Rufus. In 1106 Henry invaded Normandy, and Robert was captured at the Battle of Tinchebray. He spent the rest of his life a prisoner. >> Henry I (of England); William I (of England); William II (of England)

Roberti, Ercole (Grandi d'Antonio) de' [ro**bair**tee, **air**kolay] (c. 1450–1496) Painter, born in Ferrara, Italy. His 'Madonna and Child with Saints' (1480, Brera, Milan) and

'Pietà' (Walker, Liverpool) are characteristic of his work, which is less austere than that of his contemporaries of the Ferrarese school. >> Tura

Roberts, Sir Charles G(eorge) D(ouglas) (1860–1943) Writer and naturalist, born in Douglas, New Brunswick, Canada. He studied at Fredericton University, and became a professor at King's College, Nova Scotia (1885–95), and settled in New York as an editor, joining the Canadian army at the outbreak of World War 1. An outstanding lyric poet, his books include *Orion and Other Poems* (1880) and *In Divers Tones* (1887). He excelled in nature studies, such as *The Feet of the Furtive* (1912) and *Eyes of the Wilderness* (1933), and he also wrote a history of Canada, *Canada in Flanders* (1918).

Roberts (of Kandahar, Pretoria, and Waterford), Frederick Sleigh Roberts, 1st Earl (1832–1914) British field marshal, born in Cawnpore, India. He trained at Sandhurst, and took an active part in the Indian Mutiny, winning the VC in 1858. He became commander-in-chief in India (1885–93), and served as supreme commander in South Africa during the Boer War, relieving Kimberley (1900). He was created earl in 1901, and died while visiting troops in the field in France.

Roberts, Sir Gilbert (1899–1978) Civil engineer, born in London, England, UK. He studied at the City and Guilds of London Institute, assisted Ralph Freeman on the design of the Sydney Harbour bridge, then joined Sir William Arrol & Co in Glasgow, where he became director and chief engineer, extending the uses of welding and high-tensile steels in bridges and other structures. In 1949 he joined Freeman, Fox & Partners, and was put in charge of the design of the Forth, Severn, Auckland Harbour, Bosphorus (Turkey), and Humber bridges, as well as radio telescopes, goliath cranes, and many other steel structures. >> Freeman

Roberts, Julia (1967–) US film actress, born in Smyrna, Georgia. She made her screen debut in *Baja Oklahoma* (1988), and became well known following *Mystic Pizza* (1988) and *Steel Magnolias* (1989, Oscar nomination for Best Supporting Actress). Later films include *Pretty Woman* (1990), *Hook* (1991), *The Pelican Brief* (1993), and *Michael Collins* (1996). In 1997 she appeared in *My Best Friend's Wedding* and the musical film *Everyone Says I Love You*.

Roberts, Kate (1891–1985) Novelist and short-story writer, born in Rhosgadfan, Gwynedd. She studied at the University College of North Wales, Bangor, and is regarded as the most distinguished prose writer in Welsh this century. Among her works is *O Gors y Bryniau* (1925, From the Swamp of the Hills), *Traed mewn Cyffion* (1936, Feet in Chains), and *Y Byw Sy'n Cysgu* (1956, The Living Sleep).

Roberts, (Granville) Oral (1918–) Evangelist and faith healer, born in Ada, OK. Ordained at 18 in the Pentecostal Holiness Church, he gained a reputation for faith healing, and when he founded Oral Roberts University in Tulsa (1967), the state governor attended, and Roman Catholics and Jews were among its backers. Flamboyant and enterprising, he is known for his weekly national TV programme, a radio station, and a mass circulation monthly magazine. His writings include *Don't Give Up* (1980).

Roberts, Richard (1789–1864) Inventor, born in Carreghova, Mid Glamorgan. An uneducated quarry worker, he had extraordinary mechanical skills, and went on to work for John Wilkinson and Henry Maudslay. In 1816 he established his own machine-tool business in Manchester, where he built one of the first metal-planing machines. His firm of Sharp, Roberts and Company manufactured a spinning mule as well as railway locomotives, beginning with the *Experiment* for the Liverpool & Manchester Railway in 1833. Although he continued to be a versatile inventor, he had little business acumen, and died impoverished. >> Maudslay; Wilkinson, John

Roberts, Sir Stephen Henry (1901–71) Historian, born in Maldon, Victoria, Australia. He studied at Melbourne University, London, and Paris, then joined Melbourne University, and wrote his first book, *History of Australian Land Settlement* (1923). In 1929 he became professor of history at Sydney. His *History of Modern Europe* (1933), *The Problems of Modern France* (1937), and *The House that Hitler Built* (1937) brought him wider attention, and he became a radio and newspaper commentator during World War 2. In 1947 he was appointed Vice-Chancellor of Sydney University, and principal from 1955.

Roberts, Tom (1856–1931) Painter, born in Dorchester, Dorset, S England, UK. He emigrated as a child, and studied at the Carlton School of Design and at the National Gallery School, both in Melbourne, before returning to London to attend the Royal Academy Schools. His best work, which deals with pioneering life in the bush, was produced in Australia in the late 1880s and 1890s. He was commissioned to paint the official opening of the first Australian federal parliament, a subject which required over 250 individual portraits. >> McCubbin

Roberts, William Patrick (1895–1980) Artist, born in London, England, UK. He was associated with Roger Fry, Wyndham Lewis (as a Vorticist), and the London group, and in both World Wars was an official war artist. His art was then devoted to the portrayal of Cockney characters in a very formal Cubist style, with a certain satirical emphasis. >> Fry, Roger; Lewis, Wyndham

Roberts-Austen, Sir William (Chandler) (1843–1902) Metallurgist, born in London, England, UK. In 1880 he was appointed professor at the Royal School of Mines, two years later becoming chemist and assayer at the Mint. A pioneer of alloy research, he demonstrated the possibility of diffusion occurring between a sheet of gold and a block of lead. He also invented the automatic recording pyrometer. He was knighted in 1899.

Robertson, Ethel Florence Lindesay >> **Richardson, Henry Handel**

Robertson, George (Islay MacNeill) (1946–) British statesman, born in Dunoon, Argyll, and Bute, W Scotland, UK. He studied at Dundee University, became Scottish organizer of the General and Municipal Workers' Union (1969–78), and was elected an MP in 1978. He was the opposition spokesman on Scotland (1979–80), defence (1980–1), and foreign and commonwealth affairs (1981–93), then joined the shadow cabinet, and was spokesman on Scotland (1993–7). He became defence secretary in the 1997 Labour government.

Robertson, Jeannie (1908–75) Folk singer, born in Aberdeen, NE Scotland, UK. She was virtually unknown beyond the NE of Scotland until discovered in 1953 by Scottish folklorist Hamish Henderson (1919–). Her huge repertoire of classic traditional ballads and other songs, together with her powerful and magnetic singing style, exerted a profound influence on the folk-music revival. Although she lived most of her life in Aberdeen, she belonged to the 'travelling folk', whose music was passed down orally from generation to generation, and she represented an important link with this ancient culture.

Robertson, Sir William Robert (1860–1933) British soldier, born in Welbourn, Lincolnshire, EC England, UK. He enlisted as a private in 1877 and rose to be field marshal in 1920. In World War 1 he was quarter-master general (later chief of general staff) of the British Expeditionary Force, and became Chief of the Imperial General Staff (1915–18). He wrote his autobiography, *From Private to Field-Marshal* in 1921.

Robeson, Paul (Bustill) [rohbsn] (1898–1976) Singer and actor, born in Princeton, NJ. He was admitted to the US bar before embarking on a stage career in New York City in 1921, appearing in Britain in 1922. Success as an African-American actor was matched by popularity as a singer, and he appeared in works ranging from *Show Boat* to plays by O'Neill and Shakespeare. He was known particularly for his Othello, a part which he first played in London in 1930. He toured widely giving song recitals, notably of black spirituals, and appeared in numerous films. In the 1950s his outspoken opposition to racial discrimination, and his Communist sympathies, led to professional ostracism at home, and he retired from public life in the 1960s.

Robespierre, Maximilien François Marie Isidore de [rohbspyair] (1758–94) French revolutionary leader, born in Arras, France. He became a lawyer, was elected to the States General (1789), became a prominent member of the Jacobin Club, and emerged in the National Assembly as a popular radical, known as 'the Incorruptible'. In 1791 he was public accuser, and in 1792 presented a petition to the Legislative Assembly for a Revolutionary Tribunal. Elected first deputy for Paris in the National Convention, he emerged as leader of the Mountain, strenuously opposed to the Girondins, whom he helped to destroy. In 1793 he became a member of the Committee of Public Safety, and for three months dominated the country, introducing the Reign of Terror and the cult of the Supreme Being. But as his ruthless exercise of power increased, his popularity waned. He was attacked in the Convention, arrested, and guillotined on the orders of the Revolutionary Tribunal. >> Barras; Carrier, Jean Baptiste; Collot d'Herbois; Couthon; Danton; Saint-Just

Robey, Sir George [rohbee], originally **George Edward Wade** (1869–1954) Comedian, born in Herne Hill, Kent, SE England, UK. He first appeared on the stage in 1891, made a name for himself in musical shows such as *The Bing Boys* (1916), and later emerged as a Shakespearean actor in the part of Falstaff. He was famous for his bowler hat, black coat, hooked stick, and thickly painted eyebrows. He was knighted in 1954.

Robin Hood Legendary 13th-c outlaw who lived in Sherwood Forest in the N Midlands, England, celebrated in ballads dating from the 14th-c. He protected the poor, and outwitted, robbed, or killed the wealthy and unscrupulous officials of Church and state. The legend may have had its origins in the popular discontent that led to the Peasants' Revolt of 1381.

Robins, Benjamin (1707–51) Mathematician and father of the art of gunnery, born in Bath, SW England, UK. A teacher of mathematics in London, he carried out experiments on the air resistance of projectiles, studied fortification, and invented the ballistic pendulum, which for the first time allowed the measurement of muzzle velocities. His *New Principles of Gunnery* (1742) laid the groundwork for modern field-artillery.

Robinson, Arthur Howard (1915–) Geographer, born in Montreal, Quebec, Canada. He studied at Miami and Wisconsin universities, then taught at Wisconsin (1936–8) and Ohio State (1938–41), and became chief of the map division at the Office of Strategic Services (1941–6). Professor of geography at Wisconsin (1945–80), he is internationally known for his major cartographic textbooks, notably *Elements of Cartography*.

Robinson, Bill 'Bojangles', originally **Luther Robinson**, nickname **the King of Tapology** (1878–1949) Tap dancer, born in Richmond, VA. He began dancing professionally at age eight in Louisville, KY, then moved to New York City in 1891 to dance in the popular musical, *The South Before the War*. He first performed on Broadway in 1928, becoming the first African-American to star in the Ziegfeld Follies. He appeared in four films with Shirley Temple, including *The Little Colonel* (1935); although extremely popular in their day, these films would later be criticized for forcing him into the role of a shuffling servant. A star of the movie *Stormy Weather* (1943), he was one of the first performers to tap dance on his toes (as opposed to flat-footed), and is credited with originating the routine of tapping up and down stairs. >> Temple, Shirley

Robinson, Brooks (Calbert), Jr (1937–) Baseball player, born in Little Rock, AR. A highly proficient batter who hit more than 250 home runs and over 1300 runs batted in, he is recognized as the greatest third baseman to date. He won the Golden Glove in that position for 15 consecutive years from 1960, and was named as the American League's Most Valuable Player in 1960 and the Outstanding Player of the 1970 World Series. >> RR1144

Robinson, Edward (1749–1863) Biblical scholar, born in Southington, CT. He studied in Germany, and became professor of theology at Andover (1830–7) and at the Union Theological Seminary, New York City (1837–63). In 1838 he explored Palestine and Syria, and established himself as the father of biblical geography with the publication of *Biblical Researches in Palestine and Adjacent Countries* (1841).

Robinson, Edward G, originally **Emanuel Goldenberg** (1893–1973) Film actor, born in Bucharest, Romania. His family emigrated to the USA in 1903, and he studied at the American Academy of Dramatic Arts in New York City. He started in silent films, but became famous with his vivid portrayal of a vicious gangster in *Little Caesar* (1930). He brought magnetism and a refreshing humanity to a rogues' gallery of larcenous hoodlums in such films as *The Whole Town's Talking* (1935) and *Key Largo* (1948). His support of democratic causes brought disfavour at the time of the McCarthy witch-hunts. Subsequently he continued in strong character parts, such as in *Double Indemnity* (1944) and *All My Sons* (1948), many of his later appearances being in international co-productions, such as *The Cincinnati Kid* (1965). His autobiography, *All My Yesterdays*, was published in 1973, and he was posthumously awarded a special Academy Award the same year.

Robinson, Edwin Arlington (1869–1935) Poet, born in Head Tide, ME. He was brought up in the town of Gardiner, ME, which provided the background for 'Tilbury Town', the fictional New England village setting of his best poetry. He studied at Harvard, and went to New York City to find work. He made his name with an early collection of poetry *The Children of the Night* (1897), and was three times a Pulitzer prizewinner, for his *Collected Poems* (1922), *The Man Who Died Twice* (1924), and *Tristram* (1927), one of his several modern renditions of Arthurian legends.

Robinson, (William) Heath (1872–1944) Artist, cartoonist, and book-illustrator, born in London, England, UK. He trained at the Islington School of Art, and in 1897 illustrated an edition of *Don Quixote*, the first of many works, including editions of *The Arabian Nights* (1899), *Twelfth Night* (1908) and *Water Babies* (1915). His fame rests mainly on his humorous drawings – in his ability to poke fun at the machine age with intricate drawings of countless 'Heath Robinson contraptions' of absurd and fantastic design to perform simple and practical operations, such as the raising of one's hat, the shuffling and dealing of cards, or the recovering of a collar-stud which has slipped down the wearer's back.

Robinson, Henry Crabb (1775–1867) Journalist and diarist, born in Bury St Edmunds, Suffolk, E England, UK. He was articled to an attorney (1790–5), then travelled in Germany and studied at Jena University. He joined *The Times* in 1807 as a foreign correspondent, and covered the Peninsular War as a war correspondent, the first of his kind (1808–9). His valuable diaries (first published 1869) describe life with the major figures of the Romantic period, including

Coleridge, Wordsworth, and Lamb. He was one of the founders of London University (1828), and of the Athenaeum Club in London.

Robinson, Henry Peach (1830–1901) Photographer, born in Ludlow, Shropshire, WC England, UK. He opened a studio at Leamington Spa in 1857, but tired of formal portraiture and moved to 'high art photography', creating literary and narrative genre scenes in the mid-Victorian style, often by composites of several separate images of costumed models and painted settings. Although criticized for artificiality, he exercised considerable influence until the end of the century, and was a founder member of the Linked Ring (1892), an association of photographers seeking artistic creation.

Robinson, Joan V(iolet), née **Maurice** (1903–83) Economist, born in Camberley, Surrey, SE England, UK. She studied at Cambridge, and taught there (1931–71), in 1965 succeeding her husband **(Edward) Austin (Gossidge) Robinson** (1897–1993) as professor of economics. She was one of the most influential economic theorists of her time, and a leader of the Cambridge school, which developed macro-economic theories of growth and distribution, based on the work of Keynes. >> Keynes

Robinson, Jackie, popular name of **Jack Roosevelt Robinson** (1919–72) Baseball player, the first African-American player to play major league baseball, born in Cairo, GA. Excelling in sports at the University of California, Los Angeles, he became a star infielder and outfielder for the Brooklyn Dodgers (1947–56). Largely responsible for the acceptance of black athletes in professional sports, he led the Dodgers to six National League pennants and one World Series, in 1955. He was Rookie of the Year in 1947, and league batting champion and Most Valuable Player in 1949. >> Rickey; RR1144

Robinson, John (c. 1576–1625) Clergyman, pastor of the Pilgrim Fathers, born in Sturton-le-Steeple, Nottinghamshire, C England, UK. He studied at Cambridge, held a curacy at Norwich, became a Separatist, and in 1608 escaped to Leyden, where he established a Church (1609). In 1620, after a memorable sermon, he saw part of his congregation set sail in the *Speedwell* for Plymouth, where they joined the *Mayflower*.

Robinson, John (Arthur Thomas) (1919–83) Anglican clergyman and theologian, born in Canterbury, Kent, SE England, UK. He studied at Cambridge, and lectured there until his appointment as Bishop of Woolwich (1959–69). In 1963 he published *Honest to God*, which he described as an attempt to explain the Christian faith to modern society. It scandalized the Conservatives, became a best seller, and blocked his chances of further ecclesiastical advancement. He also made weighty – and more orthodox – contributions to biblical studies in other volumes, including *Jesus and His Coming* (1957), *The Human Face of God* (1973), and *Redating the New Testament* (1976).

Robinson, (Esmé Stuart) Lennox (1886–1958) Playwright, born in Douglas, Co Cork, Ireland. His first play, *The Clancy Game*, was produced in 1908 at the Abbey Theatre, Dublin, where he was appointed manager in 1910 and then director (1923–56). Other plays include *The Cross Roads* (1909), *The Dreamers* (1915), and *The White-Headed Boy* (1920). He also compiled volumes of Irish verse, including the Irish *Golden Treasury* (1925), and edited Lady Gregory's *Journals* (1946).

Robinson, Mary, née **Bourke** (1944–) Irish Labour politician and president (1990–7), born in Ballina, Mayo, Ireland. She was born into a Roman Catholic family but chose to attend the predominately protestant Trinity College. She left the Labour Party in protest against the Anglo-Irish Agreement (1985), then returned to run for president of Ireland. Against all the odds she defeated Brian Lenihan of the Fianna Fáil Party to take office as Ireland's first female president. In 1997 she chose not to seek a second term in office, and became the UN High Commissioner for Human Rights. >> McAleese

Robinson, (Arthur Napoleon) Raymond (1926–) Prime minister of Trinidad and Tobago (1986–91) and president (1997–). He studied in Trinidad and at Oxford, and qualified as a barrister. Returning to the West Indies he became politically active, and at independence (1967) was deputy leader of the moderate, centrist People's Nationalist Movement (PNM). In 1984, with other colleagues, he broke away to form a left-of-centre coalition which became the National Alliance for Reconstruction (NAR). In the 1986 general election this swept the PNM from power, making Robinson prime minister. He survived an attempted coup in 1990 when he was taken prisoner and treated badly. Freed by loyal troops, he continued to govern the country in a period of unrest. Calling an early general election, his party suffered a humiliating defeat, and he resigned at the end of 1991. In 1997 he became the country's first head of state to be elected. >> RR1093

Robinson, Sir Robert (1886–1975) Chemist, born near Chesterfield, Derbyshire, C England, UK. He studied at Manchester University, and taught at Sydney, Liverpool, St Andrews, Manchester, London, and Oxford universities, becoming Waynflete professor at Oxford (1930–55). He is particularly noted for his work on plant pigments, alkaloids, and other natural products, and in the development of penicillin. Knighted in 1939, he was president of the Royal Society (1945–50) and was awarded the Nobel Prize for Chemistry in 1947. >> Birch

Robinson, Smokey, popular name of **William Robinson** (1940–) Singer, songwriter, and producer, born in Detroit, MI. The lead singer with The Miracles (1959–72), he also wrote and arranged for young artists on the Tamla Motown record label, and in 1961 became vice-president of the company. With the Miracles he had his first big US hit in 'Shop Around' (1961). 'Tears of a Clown' (1970) topped both the US and UK music charts, and became their most successful single. He left to pursue a solo career after a farewell tour in 1972. In 1991 he received the Heritage Award for outstanding career achievements in music and entertainment at the 5th annual Soul Train awards.

Robinson, Sugar Ray, originally **Walker Smith** (1920–89) Professional boxer, born in Detroit, MI. He held the world welterweight title (1946–51) and the world middleweight title (1950–1). He lost the middleweight title to Randolph Turpin in 1951, but soon regained it. He was a professional boxer for 20 years but bore few, if any, visible signs of his calling. Very popular in Europe, he travelled in considerable style with a large entourage. >> Turpin, Randolph

Robinson, William (1838–1935) Gardener and horticultural writer, born in Co Down, Ireland. He worked as a gardener in Ireland, and in 1861 went to the Royal Botanic Society's gardens at Regent's Park, London. An exponent of natural rather than formal gardens, he published 18 books, including *Gleanings from French Gardens* (1868), *Alpine Flowers for English Gardens* (1870), and *The English Flower Garden* (1883), and founded and edited three horticultural journals: *The Garden* (1872), *Gardening Illustrated* (1879), and *Flora and Sylva* (1903).

Rob Roy (Gaelic 'Red Robert'), nickname of **Robert MacGregor** or **Campbell** (1671–1734) Highland outlaw, born in Buchanan, Stirling, C Scotland, UK. Initially he was a grazier, but by 1712 he was in debt to James Graham, 1st Duke of Montrose, and began a life of briganding, chiefly at the expense of Montrose. He was distrusted by both sides during the Jacobite rebellion (1715), stealing from both

without favour. After the rebellion he continued to raid Montrose, and was eventually captured and imprisoned in London. He was pardoned in 1727 while facing deportation. His life was romanticized in the novel by Sir Walter Scott. >> Scott, Walter

Robson, Dame Flora (McKenzie) (1902–84) Actress, born in South Shields, Durham, NE England, UK. She studied at the Royal Academy of Dramatic Art, London, and first appeared at the Shaftesbury Theatre, London, in 1921. She gained fame mainly in historical roles in plays and films, such as Queen Elizabeth in *Fire over England* (1931), and Thérèse Raquin in *Guilty* (1944). She consolidated her reputation with memorable stage performances in Shaw's *Captain Brassbound's Conversion* (1948) and Ibsen's *Ghosts* (1958). She appeared in more than 60 films, and was created a dame in 1960.

Rocard, Michel [rokah(r)] (1930–) French statesman and prime minister (1988–91), born near Paris. He trained at the Ecole National d'Administration, and began his career in 1958 as an inspector of finances. In 1967 he became leader of the radical Unified Socialist Party, standing as its presidential candidate in 1969 and being elected to the National Assembly in the same year. He joined the Socialist Party in 1973, emerging as leader of its moderate Social Democratic wing, and unsuccessfully challenged François Mitterrand for the Party's presidential nomination in 1981. After serving as minister of planning and regional development (1981–3) and agriculture (1983–5), he resigned, but in 1988 was appointed prime minister by Mitterrand. His continuing moderateness brought an end to his premiership, and he was replaced by the left-winger, Edith Cresson. >> Cresson; Mitterrand; RR1049

Rochas, Beau de >> **Otto, Nikolaus**

Rochas, Marcel [rosha] (1902–55) Fashion designer, born in Paris. He set up a couture house in Paris in 1925, launching his first fragrances in 1931, and the sheepskin jacket in 1942. He set up a range of companies in perfumes and fashion during the late 1940s. The couture house closed upon his death in 1955, but his wife Hélène took over the perfume department until she left the company in 1989.

Roche, Mazo de la >> **de la Roche, Mazo**

Rochefoucauld, François de La >> **La Rochefoucauld, François**

Rochester, John Wilmot, 2nd Earl of (1647–80) Courtier and poet, born in Ditchley, Oxfordshire, England, UK. He studied at Oxford, and was a prominent figure in court. In 1665 he showed conspicuous courage against the Dutch. A patron of the arts, he married a wealthy heiress (1667) and plunged into a life of debauchery, yet wrote excellent letters, satires (particularly 'A Satyr against Mankind', 1675), and bacchanalian and amatory songs and verses. Finally he was said to be moved to a death-bed repentance by Bishop Burnet. Among the best of his poems are imitations of Horace and Boileau, *Verses to Lord Mulgrave*, and *Verses upon Nothing*.

Rockefeller, David [rokuhfeler] (1915–) Banker and philanthropist, born in New York City, the brother of Nelson Rockefeller. He studied at Harvard and the University of Chicago and, after World War 2, joined Chase National Bank (now Chase Manhattan), rising to be chief executive officer (1969–80). He worked to further US investment in developing countries, wrote extensively on banking management, and chaired the Council on Foreign Relations (1951–70). He headed the Rockefeller Institute for Medical Research for many years, and was said to enjoy beetle collecting as a favourite hobby. >> Rockefeller, John D, Jr; Rockefeller, Nelson A

Rockefeller, John D(avison) [rokuhfeler] (1839–1937) Industrialist and philanthropist, born in Richford, NY.

After high school he went into the business world, and showed a talent for organization. In 1875 he founded with his brother **William Rockefeller** (1841–1922) the Standard Oil Company, securing control of the US oil trade. In the late 19th-c his power came under strong public criticism. He withdrew from active business in 1897, and devoted the rest of his life to philanthropy. He gave over $500 million in aid of medical research, universities, and churches, and established in 1913 the Rockefeller Foundation 'to promote the well-being of mankind'. One of his sons, **John D Rockefeller Jr** (1874–1960) built the Rockefeller Center. >> Lloyd, Henry Demarest

Rockefeller, John D(avison), Jr [rokuhfeler] (1874–1960) Philanthropist, born in Cleveland, OH, the son of John D Rockefeller. He studied at Brown University, entered his father's business, and from 1910 concentrated on the development of philanthropic institutions. He became chairman of the Rockefeller Institute of Medical Research, built the Rockefeller Center in New York City (1939), and restored colonial Williamsburg in Virginia. His gift of land in New York City was instrumental in the siting of the UN headquarters there. >> Rockefeller, John D

Rockefeller, Laurance (Spelman) [rokuhfeler] (1910–   ) Business executive and conservationist, born in New York City, the son of John D Rockefeller, Jr. He studied at Princeton, became involved in commercial aviation, and managed several family enterprises, including the Rockefeller Center entertainment and business complex. As director of the non-profit-making Jackson Hole Preserve, he oversaw the donation of 33 000 acres of Rockefeller land to the Grand Teton National Park. He later headed the Citizens Advisory Committee on Environmental Quality (1969–73). >> Rockefeller, John D

Rockefeller, Nelson A(ldrich) [rokuhfeler] (1908–79) US statesman and vice-president (1974–7), born in Bar Harbor, ME, the third son of John D Rockefeller, Jr. He studied at Dartmouth College, worked in his father's businesses, and became director of Creole Petroleum. He was Governor of New York State (1958–73), sought the Republican presidential nomination in 1960, 1964, and 1968, and was elected vice-president under President Ford. He was the founder and president of the Museum of Primitive Art, which in 1982 was incorporated into the Metropolitan Museum of Art, New York City. >> Ford, Gerald R; Rockefeller, David; Rockefeller, John D, Jr; RR1097

Rockingham, Charles Watson Wentworth, 2nd Marquess of (1730–82) British statesman and prime minister (1765–6, 1782). Created Earl of Malton in 1750, he served as gentleman of the bedchamber to George II and George III. As leader of a prominent Whig Opposition group, he was called upon to form a ministry in 1765. He repealed the Stamp Act, affecting the American colonies, then court intrigues caused his resignation. He opposed Britain's war against the colonists. His was the most consistent Opposition Whig group to George III's government in the 1760s and 1770s, and leading spokesmen, such as Fox and Burke, were adherents. He died soon after taking office as prime minister for the second time. >> Burke, Edmund; Fox, Charles James; George II (of Great Britain); George III; RR1095

Rockne, Knute (Kenneth) [roknee] (1888–1931) Coach of American football, born in Voss, Norway. His family emigrated to the USA in 1893. He graduated from Notre Dame in 1914, and became head football coach there shortly after the end of World War 1. A humorous personality, he dominated American college football, having markedly changed the emphasis from sheer physical brawn to pace, elusiveness, and ball handling. He died in an air crash. >> RR1155

Rockwell, George Lincoln (1918–67) Political extremist, born in Bloomington, IL. A gifted illustrator, he managed an advertising agency in Portland, ME. He served in the Korean War and then, influenced by anti-Semite Gerald L K Smith, founded the American Nazi Party (1958). A white supremacist who blamed Jews for the worldwide Communist movement, he called for their extermination along with the deportation of all blacks, and staged many provocative demonstrations. He was discharged from the navy reserves for his actions (1960) and ran for Governor of Virginia (1965). He was assassinated by John Patler, a disaffected former member of his Party.

Rockwell, Norman (Percevel) (1894–1978) Illustrator, born in New York City. He studied at the Chase School of Art, the National Academy of Design (1909), and the Art Students League (1910). Using oils, he developed a realistic technique, idealizing small-town America. He was an illustrator for major periodicals, such as *St. Nicholas*, *Collier's*, *Life*, *Judge*, *Look*, and most importantly *The Saturday Evening Post* (1916–63). He also produced calendars for Brown & Bigelow (1924–76), advertisements, and illustrated such classics as *Tom Sawyer* and *Huckleberry Finn*.

Rodbertus, Johann Karl [rodbertus] (1805–75) Economist and politician, born in Greifswald, Germany (formerly Swedish Pomerania). He held law appointments under the Prussian government, but in 1836 settled down on his estate. In 1848 he entered the Prussian National Assembly, and in 1849 he carried the Frankfurt constitution. The founder of scientific Socialism, he held that the socialist ideal would come gradually according to the natural laws of change and progress, and that the state would own all land and capital, and superintend the distribution of all products of labour.

Rodchenko, Alexander Mikhailovich [rodchengkoh] (1891–1956) Painter, designer, and photographer, born in St Petersburg, Russia. He trained at the Kazan Art School, and met Tatlin and the young Russian avant garde. After the revolution he worked for the People's Commissariat of Enlightenment, and taught at the Moscow Proletkult School (1918–26). His most original works were his abstract spatial constructions and his documentary photographs of the new Communist society. >> Tatlin

Roddenberry, Gene, popular name of **Eugene Wesley Roddenberry** (1921–91) Writer, and film and television producer, born in El Paso, TX. He joined the Army Air Corps and served as a bomber pilot (1941–6) and as a crash investigator (1946–9). As an airline pilot (1949–53), he survived an aircrash in the Syrian desert. He moved to Los Angeles, joined the police, wrote scripts in his spare time for *Dragnet*, and became a full-time writer, contributing to several series including *Highway Patrol* and *Dr Kildare*. Always interested in science-fiction, he is best known as the creator and producer of *Star Trek*, and the originator of the phrase 'Beam me up, Scottie'.

Roddick, Anita (Lucia) (1943–   ) Retail entrepreneur, born in Brighton, East Sussex, SE England, UK. She worked in her Italian parents' ice-cream parlour, trained as a drama teacher, and became intrigued by the idea of selling cosmetics in much the same way as a greengrocer would sell vegetables. In 1976 she opened a small shop in a back street of Brighton selling beauty products made from natural products, not tested on animals, and supplied in refillable containers. Her growing commitment to ecology and the Third World brought the Body Shop chain a profit of £6 million in the 1980s, and the company has over 100 stores in the UK (many of them franchised), and twice this number overseas. She has received many awards, including the International Banksia Environmental Award (1993) and the Botwinick Prize in Business Ethics (1994).

Rodgers, Bill, popular name of **Lord William Thomas Rodgers of Quarry Bank** (1928–) British statesman, born in Liverpool, Merseyside, NW England, UK. He studied at Oxford, served as general secretary of the Fabian Society (1953–60), and became a Labour MP in 1962. He held a succession of posts, culminating in that of transport secretary (1976–9). With Roy Jenkins, David Owen, and Shirley Williams, he left Labour to form the Social Democratic Party (SDP) in 1981, and became influential as SDP vice-president (1982–7). Despite expressing support for the SDP–Liberal merger of 1987–8, he resigned to become director-general of the Royal Institute of British Architects. He was given a life peerage in 1992. >> Jenkins, Roy; Owen, David; Williams, Shirley

Rodgers, Richard (1902–79) Composer, born in New York City. He left Columbia University to study composition at the Institute of Musical Art (now the Juilliard School, New York City). With the lyricist **Lorenz Hart** (1895–1942) his first professional success was the *Garrick Gaieties* (1925). Other successes included *Babes in Arms* (1937), with the songs 'The Lady Is a Tramp' and 'My Funny Valentine'; *The Boys from Syracuse* (1938), with 'Falling in Love with Love'; and *Pal Joey* 1940, with 'Bewitched, Bothered and Bewildered'. After Hart's death (1943) he collaborated in a spectacular series of hit musicals with Oscar Hammerstein II, especially *Oklahoma!* (1943, Pulitzer). Other successes were *South Pacific* (1949, Pulitzer), *The King and I* (1951), and *The Sound of Music* (1959). >> Hammerstein

Rodin, (René François) Auguste [rohdĩ] (1840–1917) Sculptor, born in Paris. He trained in Paris and Brussels, and began to produce sculptures which, with their varying surfaces and finishes, resembled the Impressionist painters' effects of light and shade. The great 'La Porte de l'enfer' (The Gate of Hell) was commissioned for the Musée des Arts Décoratifs in 1880, and during the next 30 years he was mainly engaged on the 186 figures for these bronze doors. He also worked on the monument 'Les Bourgeois de Calais' (1884–6, New York City, The Burghers of Calais), which was finally dedicated in 1895. Among his other works is 'Le Penseur' (1904, The Thinker), in front of the Panthéon in Paris. >> Claudel, Camille; John, Gwen

Rodney, George Brydges Rodney, Baron (1718–92) British naval commander, born in London, England, UK. He entered the navy in 1732, had a brilliant share in Hawke's victory against the French off Cape Finisterre (1747), and was appointed Governor of Newfoundland in 1749. In 1759 he destroyed the French flotilla gathering for the invasion of England. He was appointed commander-in-chief on the Leeward Is station (1761), where he captured Martinique, St Lucia, and Grenada (1762). He captured a Spanish convoy off Cape Finisterre, and a few days later defeated another squadron off Cape St Vincent (1780). Dutch islands in the West Indies, used as a base for American contraband trade, fell to him in 1781, and in 1782 he was victorious over the French off Dominica. He was created baron on his return to England. >> Hawke, Edward

Rodnina, Irina [rodneena] (1949–) Figure skater, born in Moscow. She won the pairs title at three Olympics – 1972 (with Alexei Ulanov), 1976, and 1980 (both with Alexandr Zaitsev) – and won four world titles with Ulanov (1969–72) and six with Zaitsev (1973–8). During the same years she won the corresponding European titles. She married Zaitsev in 1975, retired in 1980, and trained to be an astronaut. >> RR1162

Rodrigo, Joaquín [rodreegoh] (1902–) Composer, born in Sagunto, Spain. He began musical studies when a child, despite the handicap of blindness. He is best known for his compositions for guitar, and following the successful first performance of his work *Concierto de Aranjuez* in Barcelona (1940), he became generally regarded as the leading post-Civil War Spanish composer.

Rodzinski, Artur [rodzinskee] (1892–1958) Conductor, born in Spalato, Dalmatia. He conducted in Europe before being invited to the USA in 1925 by Leopold Stokowski to assist at the Philadelphia Orchestra. He went on to conduct the Los Angeles Philharmonic (1929–33), Cleveland (1933–43), New York Philharmonic (1943–7), and Chicago Symphony (1947–8) orchestras. His musicianship was admired, but temperamental clashes in the latter two posts led him to return to Europe in his last years. >> Stokowski

Roe, Sir (Edwin) Alliot Verdon (1877–1958) Aircraft manufacturer, born near Manchester, Greater Manchester, NW England, UK. After an apprenticeship in a locomotive works he went to sea as an engineer for three years. Returning home with an interest in flying, he built a biplane in Brooklands (1907), being the first Englishman to design, build, and fly his own aircraft. With his brother **Humphrey Verdon Roe** (1878–1949), he formed A V Roe & Co in 1910, producing the famous AVRO 504 bomber/trainer type that set a standard for design for many years. He sold out to Armstrong Siddeley in 1928 and formed Saunders–Roe to build flying boats at Cowes. He was knighted in 1929.

Roebling, John Augustus [rohbling] (1806–69) Civil engineer, born in Mühlhausen, Germany. He studied at Berlin Polytechnic, emigrated to the USA in 1831, and took up work as a canal engineer. He proposed the replacement of hemp tow-ropes with wire ropes, and developed the machinery to produce the ropes, the first to be made in America. As demand increased, he turned his attention to suspension bridges, completing the first to use his wire ropes in 1846. He built the pioneer railway suspension bridge at Niagara Falls (1851–5, replaced 1897), and was supervising construction of the Brooklyn Bridge when an injury to his foot resulted in tetanus, from which he died. His son **Washington Augustus Roebling** (1837–1926) succeeded him as chief engineer of the Brooklyn Bridge project, and saw it through to completion in 1883.

Roebuck, Alvah >> Sears, R W

Roeg, Nicolas (Jack) (1928–) Film director, born in London, England, UK. A noted cinematographer in the 1960s, his directorial career began in collaboration with Donald Cammell on *Performance* (1970). He made his debut as solo director with *Walkabout* (1971). Other films include *The Man Who Fell to Earth* (1976), *The Witches* (1990), *Hotel Paradise* (1995), and *Two Deaths* (1996).

Roehm, Ernst >> Röhm, Ernst

Roentgen, Wilhelm Konrad von >> Röntgen

Roethke, Theodore (Huebner) [retkuh] (1908–63) Poet, born in Saginaw, MI. He studied at Michigan and Harvard universities, then taught at Pennsylvania State, Bennington, and Washington. It was not until the publication of his fourth volume, *The Waking* (1953, Pulitzer) that he became widely known. *Words for the Wind* (1958) is a selection from his first four books; his *Collected Poems* appeared posthumously in 1968.

Roger of Wendover (?–1236) Chronicler, and Benedictine monk at the monastery of St Albans. He revised and extended the abbey chronicle from the Creation to the year 1235, under the title *Flores historiarum* (Flowers of History). The section from 1188 to 1235 is believed to be Roger's first-hand account. The chronicle was later extended by Matthew Paris. >> Matthew Paris

Roger of Taizé, Brother, originally **Roger Louis Schutz-Marsauche** (1915–) Founder of the Taizé Community, born in Provence, France. In 1940 he went to Taizé, between Cluny and Citeaux, to establish a community devoted to reconciliation and peace in Church and society. Since 1949, when the first seven brothers took their vows, thousands of pilgrims have been attracted, especially young people drawn there by the distinctive worship in the Church of Reconciliation, built in 1962. His publications include *The Dynamic of the Provisional* (1965), *Violent for Peace* (1968), and several volumes of extracts from his journal.

Rogers, Bruce (1870–1957) Typographer and book designer, born in Linnwood, IN. Trained as an artist, in 1895 he moved to Boston to the Riverside Press, and from 1900 worked in their new limited editions department. Among his typeface designs are the Montaigne (1901) and the Centaur (1915). He became advisor to the Cambridge University Press, UK (1916), the Harvard University Press (1919–34), and the Oxford University Press, where he designed the Oxford Lectern Bible (1935).

Rogers, Carl R(ansom) (1902–87) Psychotherapist, born in Oak Park, IL. He studied psychology at Columbia University Teachers College (1931), taught at Chicago University (1945–57), and produced the book *Client-centered Therapy* (1951). This form of psychotherapy led to open therapy sessions and encounter groups in which patients talk out their problems under the supervision of a passive therapist. He was also a notable pioneer in carrying out systematic evaluations of the efficacy of psychotherapy. He later became resident fellow at the Western Behavioral Science Institute (1964–8) and the Center for Studies of the Person, both at La Jolla, CA (1968–87).

Rogers, Claude (1907–79) Artist, born in London, England, UK. He studied and lectured at the Slade School of Art, London, was professor of fine art at Reading University (1963–72), and president of the London Group (1952–65). With Victor Pasmore and William Coldstream he founded the Euston Road School in 1937. >> Coldstream; Pasmore

Rogers, Ginger, originally **Virginia Katherine McMath** (1911–95) Film actress, born in Independence, MO. She made her professional debut at age 14 with Eddie Foy's vaudeville troupe, and by 1928 was appearing with her first husband, **Jack Pepper**, as a vaudeville song-and-dance team. She made her screen debut in *Young Man in Manhattan* (1930). She and Fred Astaire were not given star billing when they first danced together in *Flying Down to Rio* (1933), but they stole the picture and went on to make nine other films. She won an Oscar for best actress in *Kitty Foyle* (1940). Appearing in films until the mid-1960s, she found a new public when she took over the lead in such musicals as *Hello, Dolly!* and *Mame*. >> Astaire

Rogers, John (c.1500–55) Protestant reformer, born in Aston, Staffordshire, C England, UK. A rector in London (1532–34), he embraced the Reformed doctrines at Antwerp and Wittenberg. He helped to prepare a revised translation of the Bible, pseudonymously called 'Thomas Matthew's Bible' (1537). He returned to England in 1548, preached at St Paul's Cross against Romanism (1553), just after Mary's accession, and was burned as a heretic. >> Mary I

Rogers, Randolph (1825–92) Sculptor, born in Waterloo, NY. He studied in Florence and Rome, and lived in Rome from 1885. His statues include 'Ruth' (Metropolitan Museum) and 'Lincoln' (Philadelphia). He is best known for his 'Columbus Doors' of the Capitol in Washington, DC, and the heroic figure of 'Michigan' on the Detroit monument.

Rogers (of Riverside), Richard Rogers, Lord (1933–) British architect, born in Florence, Italy. He studied at the Architectural Association, London, and was a founder member of Team 4 with Norman Foster. Like Foster, he was concerned with advanced technology in architecture, and pushed the limits of design through exhaustive research. Two important works have caused widespread praise and controversy: the Beaubourg or Pompidou Centre, Paris (1971–9), with Renzo Piano, a large open interior space clothed in highly coloured services; and Lloyds of London (1979–85), a masterful and dramatic exercise in steel and glass, which exemplifies his architectural optimism. He was created a life peer in 1996. >> Foster, Norman

Rogers, Will(iam Penn Adair) (1879–1935) Humorous actor, born in Oolagah, OK. From 1902 he was 'The Cherokee Kid' in a variety of Wild West shows. He became a regular attraction at the Ziegfeld *Midnight Frolic* (1915), by which time his act had grown to include homespun philosophy and rustic ruminations. He appeared, with moderate success, in silent features, wrote for the *Saturday Evening Post*, made frequent radio broadcasts, and came to personify the common man offering simple sagacity to the great and powerful. Films like *State Fair* (1933) and *Steamboat Round the Bend* (1935) catapulted him to the top of cinema popularity polls. At the time of his death in a plane crash, he was widely regarded as an irreplaceable American folk hero.

Rogers, William Pierce (1913–) US Republican politician, born in Norfolk, NY. He studied at the University of Colgate and Cornell University law school, and was assistant district attorney in New York City under Dewey. In 1957 he became attorney general in the Eisenhower government, in which capacity he played a leading role in drafting the Civil Rights Act of 1957. In 1967 he was a delegate to the UN, and was secretary of state in the Nixon administration (1969–73). >> Dewey, Thomas; Nixon

Roget, Peter Mark [rozhay] (1779–1869) Physician and scholar, creator of *Roget's Thesaurus*, born in London, England, UK. He studied medicine at Edinburgh, became physician to the Manchester Infirmary (1804), physician to the Northern Dispensary, London (1808), and Fullerian professor of physiology at the Royal Institution (1833–6). He was also secretary of the Royal Society (1827–49), and an original member of the Senate of London University. He is best known for his *Thesaurus of English Words and Phrases* (1852), which he wrote after his retirement from medical practice.

Rogier van der Weyden >> Weyden, Rogier van der

Rohde, Ruth [rohd], née **Bryan** (1885–1954) Diplomat and feminist, born in Jacksonville, IL. From a political family, she studied at Nebraska University. Her second husband was invalided and, to support her family, she took to public speaking, in 1926 entering politics as a Democrat in Florida. In 1928 she ran for Congress, winning a victory on feminist grounds, resulting in an amendment to the Cable Act, and continued to campaign for women's rights. She was appointed US minister to Denmark (1933–6), the first US diplomatic post ever held by a woman. Returning to the USA, she helped to draft the United States Charter.

Rohe, Ludwig Mies van der >> Mies van der Rohe, Ludwig

Rohlfs, (Friedrich) Gerhard (1831–96) Explorer, born in Vegesack, Germany. He studied medicine, and joined the Foreign Legion in Algeria (1855). After learning Arabic he explored Morocco, disguised as an Arab, and reached Fezzan in the Sahara. He crossed Africa from the Mediterranean to the Gulf of Guinea (1865–6), the first known European to do so, and in 1874 he crossed the Sahara again, from Tripoli to Egypt. In 1885 he was appointed German consul to Zanzibar.

Röhm, Ernst [roem], also spelled **Roehm** (1887–1934) Nazi leader, born in Munich, Germany. He became an early supporter of Hitler, and the organizer and commander of the stormtroopers ('Brownshirts' and 'Blackshirts'). He became state commissar of Bavaria, but in 1934 his plans to increase the power of this force led to his execution on Hitler's orders. >> Hitler

Rohmer, Sax, pseudonym of **Arthur Sarsfield Ward** (c.1883–1959) Writer of mystery stories, born in Birmingham, West Midlands, C England, UK. Interested in things Egyptian, he found literary fame with his sinister, sardonic, oriental, criminal genius villain, Fu Manchu, whose doings were told in many spine-chilling tales, including *Dr Fu Manchu* (1913), *The Yellow Claw* (1915), *Moon of Madness* (1927), and *Re-enter Fu Manchu* (1957).

Roh Tae-Woo [roh tay woo] (1932–) South Korean statesman and president (1988–92), born in Sinyong, Kyongsang, South Korea. He studied at the Korean Military Academy (1951–5), became commanding general of the Capital Security Command in 1979, and helped General Chun seize power in the coup of 1979–80. Retiring from the army in 1981, he became minister for national security and foreign affairs (1981–2), and minister for home affairs (from 1982). Elected chairman of the ruling Democratic Justice Party (1985), his political reforms helped restore democracy to the country, and he was elected president. In 1996 he was found guilty of treason and corruption, and imprisoned, but was released at the end of 1997. >> Chun Doo-Hwan; Kim Young-Sam; RR1070

Rokitansky, Karl, Freiherr (Baron) **von** [rokitanskee] (1804–78) Pathologist, born in Königgrätz, Austria. Professor of pathological anatomy at Vienna (1834–75), he personally performed 30 000 autopsies, was one of the founders of modern pathological anatomy, and established the New Vienna School as an internationally known medical centre. He wrote the great *Handbuch der pathologischen Anatomie* (1842–6, Treatise of Pathological Anatomy).

Rokossovsky, Konstantin [rokosofskee] (1896–1968) Soviet military commander, born in Velikiye Lukie, Russia. He served in World War 1, and joined the Red Guards in 1917. In World War 2 he defended Moscow, played a leading part in the Battle of Stalingrad (1943), recaptured Orel and Warsaw, and led the Russian race for Berlin. Promoted to marshal of the Soviet Union (1944), he was appointed Polish minister of defence (1949), but was forced to resign when Gomulka became premier in 1956. A national hero, he thereafter held various posts, including that of defence minister. >> Gomulka

Roland [rolã] (?–778) Semi-legendary French knight, hero of the *Chanson de Roland* (11th-c, Song of Roland). The most celebrated of the Paladins of Charlemagne, he is said to have been the nephew of Charlemagne, and the ideal of a Christian knight. The only evidence for his historical existence is a passage in Einhard's *Life of Charlemagne* (c.830–3), which refers to Roland as having fallen at Roncesvalle. Boiardo's *Orlando Innamorato* and Ariosto's *Orlando Furioso* depart widely from the old traditions. >> Ariosto; Boiardo; Charlemagne

Roland de la Platière, Jean Marie [platyair] (1734–93) Industrial scientist, born in Thizy, France. He became inspector of manufacturing in Amiens (1780), married **Marie Jeanne Phlipon** in 1780, and moved to Lyon, where he wrote on manufacturing and economics. In 1791 they went to Paris, and through the influence of his wife he became minister of the interior (1792), but was dismissed three months later by Louis XVI after a disagreement about the national guard. He was re-instated after the monarchy was overthrown, but as a Girondist fell foul of Robespierre. He escaped from Paris, but his wife was arrested and guillotined, and he committed suicide.

Rolf, Ida (1896–1979) US biological chemist, physician, and specialist in alternative medicine. He developed a system of deep massage known as *rolfing* or *structural integration*, designed to break down abnormal connective tissue formed as the result of defective posture and thereby allow readjustment.

Rolfe, Frederick William (Serafino Austin Lewis Mary), pseudonym **Baron Corvo** (1860–1913) Novelist and essayist, born in London, England, UK. A convert to Roman Catholicism, his life was shattered by his rejection from the novitiate for the Roman priesthood at the Scots College in Rome; but it prompted his most famous work, *Hadrian the Seventh* (1904), in which a self-modelled priest is unexpectedly chosen for the papacy. His other major work is *The Desire and Pursuit of the Whole*, published in 1934.

Rolfe, John >> Pocahontas

Rolland, Romain [rolã] (1866–1944) Writer, born in Clamecy, France. He studied in Paris and Rome, and in 1910 became professor of the history of music at the Sorbonne. He resigned in 1912 to devote himself to writing, published several biographies and a 10-volume novel, *Jean-Christophe* (1904–12), and in 1915 was awarded the Nobel Prize for Literature. He lived in Switzerland until 1938, completing another novel cycle, several plays, and many pieces of music criticism. On his return to France he became a mouthpiece of the opposition to Fascism and the Nazis, and his later works contain much political and social writing.

Rolle (of Hampole), Richard [rohl] (c. 1290–1349) Hermit, mystic, and poet, born in Thornton, West Yorkshire, N England, UK. He studied at Oxford, but at 19 became a hermit, first at Dalton and then at Hampole, near Doncaster. He wrote lyrics, meditations, and religious works in Latin and English, and translated and expounded the Psalms.

Rolling Stones, The Rock group, members **Mick Jagger** (1943–) vocals, **Keith Richards** (1943–) guitar, **Bill Wyman** (1941–) bass, **Charlie Watts** (1942–) drums, **Ron Wood** (1947–) guitar, former member **Brian Jones** (1944–69) guitar, one of the longest-running and most successful popular music groups to emerge in the 1960s. They first performed together in 1962. At first, they were very much in the shadow of The Beatles, but their less boyish, more rebellious style together with their more aggressive music soon won them a large following. Although their uninhibited life styles and overtly sexual lyrics often hit the headlines, it was the excellence of their compositions (usually by Jagger and Richard) that ensured their continuing success. Among their early hits were 'The Last Time' and 'Satisfaction'. Later albums include *Exile on Main Street* (1972) and *Tattoo You* (1981).

Rollins, Sonny, popular name of **Theodore Walter Rollins** (1930–) Jazz saxophonist and composer, born in New York City. He learned to play piano, alto saxophone, and tenor saxophone while at school, and early on worked and recorded with major bebop figures such as Charlie Parker and Miles Davis. From the mid-1950s he emerged as an important voice in the 'hard bop' movement. His use of calypso themes reflects his roots in the Virgin Is, and he is considered one of the most powerful improvisers on tenor and soprano saxophones. >> Davis, Miles; Parker, Charlie

Rollo, originally **Hrolf** (c. 860–c. 932) Viking leader. He secured from Charles III of France in 911 a large district on condition of being baptized and becoming Charles's vassal. This grant was the nucleus of the Duchy of Normandy.

Rolls, C(harles) S(tewart) (1877–1910) Motorist and aeronaut, born in London, England, UK. He studied at Cambridge, and from 1895 experimented with the earliest motor cars, forming a partnership with Henry Royce in 1906 for their production. In 1906 he crossed the English Channel by balloon, and in 1910 made the first return crossing by aeroplane. Soon afterwards, he died in a flying accident, the first British pilot to do so. >> Royce, Henry

Romains, Jules [romĩ], pseudonym of **Louis Farigoule** (1885–1972) Writer, born in Saint-Julien-Chapteuil, France. He studied at Paris, and became a teacher, but established his name with his poems *La Vie unanime* (1908, The Unanimous Life), and brought about the Unanimist school, devoted to a belief in universal brotherhood and group consciousness. He became a full-time writer from 1919, and remained prominent in French literature, his best-known works being the comedy *Knock, ou le triomphe de la médecine* (1923, Dr Knock, or the Triumph of Medicine) and the cycle of novels, *Les Hommes de bonne volonté* (27 vols, 1932–46, Men of Good Will), covering the early 20th-c era of French life.

Romano, Giulio >> **Giulio Romano**

Romanova, Grand Duchess Anastasia >> **Anastasia**

Romanus, Clemens >> **Clement I, St**

Romberg, Sigmund (1887–1951) Composer of operettas, born in Nagykanizsa, Hungary. He trained in Vienna as an engineer, also studying violin and composition. He settled in the USA in 1909, and in New York City introduced the use of dance bands in restaurants. Of more than 70 works, his most famous were *Blossom Time* (1921), *The Student Prince* (1924), *The Desert Song* (1926), and *The New Moon* (1928).

Romer, Alfred Sherwood (1894–1973) Palaeontologist, born in White Plains, NY. He studied at Columbia University, and became professor of biology at Chicago (1923–34) and Harvard (1934–65). An authority on the evolutionary history of vertebrates, he used his own and other collections of fossils to trace the evolution of fishes to terrestrial vertebrates, as recorded in his book *The Vertebrate Story* (1959).

Rømer, Ole (Christensen) [roemer] (1644–1710) Astronomer, born in Århus, Denmark. While working at the Royal Observatory in Paris (1672–81) he used eclipses of Jupiter's satellites to make the first determination of the velocity of light (1675), which he calculated to be 225 000 km per sec (140 000 mi per sec). 20th-c measurements give the speed as 299 793 km per sec (186 282 mi per sec).

Romero (y Galdames), Oscar (Arnulfo) [roh**mair**oh] (1917–80) Roman Catholic clergyman, born in Ciudad Barrios, El Salvador. Ordained in 1942, he was made bishop in 1970 and archbishop in 1977. An outspoken critic of the government, he was shot down during Mass a year after he was nominated for the Nobel Peace Prize. Some of his 'Thoughts' appeared in translation as *The Church Is All of You* (1984).

Romilly, Sir Samuel (1757–1818) Lawyer and law reformer, born in London, England, UK. Called to the bar in 1783, he served as chancellor of Durham (1805–15). Appointed solicitor general in 1806, he entered parliament and was knighted in the same year. He worked to reduce the severity of English criminal law, notably to end capital punishment for minor felonies. He also took part in anti-slavery agitation, and opposed the suspension of the Habeas Corpus Act and the spy system. His works include *Observations on the Criminal Law of England* (1810).

Rommel, Erwin (Johannes Eugen) (1891–1944) German field marshal, born in Heidenheim, Germany. He studied at Tübingen, fought in World War 1, taught at Dresden Military Academy, and became an early Nazi sympathizer. He commanded Hitler's headquarters guard during the early occupations, and led a Panzer division during the 1940 invasion of France. He then commanded the Afrika Korps, where he achieved major successes. Eventually driven into retreat by a strongly reinforced Eighth Army, he was withdrawn, a sick man, from North Africa, and appointed to an Army Corps command in France. Returning home wounded in 1944, he condoned the plot against Hitler's life. After its discovery, he committed suicide.

Romney, George [rom**nee**, ruhm**nee**] (1734–1802) Painter, born in Dalton-in-Furness, Lancashire, NW England, UK. From 1757 he set up as a portrait painter, leaving his family

and moving to London in 1762. Apart from two visits to France, and two years residence in Italy (1773–5), he stayed in Cavendish Square, where his reputation rivalled that of Reynolds. His many pictures of Lady Hamilton are particularly well known. >> **Reynolds, Joshua**

Romney, George (Wilcken) (1907–95) US politician and businessman, born in Chihuahua, Mexico, the son of Mormon missionaries. His family moved to the USA when he was five, and he studied at the Utah and George Washington universities. He worked his way up in the automobile industry, becoming president and chairman of American Motors Corporation (1954–62). Republican Governor of Michigan (1963–9), he was regarded as the front runner for the Republican presidential nomination in 1968, until he committed a gaffe by stating that the US leaders in Vietnam tried to 'brainwash' him. President Nixon nevertheless appointed him secretary of housing and urban development (1969–73). He later headed the National Center for Voluntary Action, and held high positions in the Church of Jesus Christ of Latter-day Saints.

Romulus Augustulus >> **Augustulus**

Ronald, Sir Landon, originally **Landon Russell** (1873–1938) Conductor, composer, and pianist, born in London, England, UK. He toured with Nellie Melba, conducted the New Symphony Orchestra, notably in Elgar, Strauss, and Tchaikovsky, and was principal of the Guildhall School of Music (1910–37). He wrote many songs, including 'Down in the Forest Something Stirred'. He was knighted in 1922. >> **Melba**

Ronaldo (Luiz Nazario de Lima) [ro**nal**doh] (1976–) Footballer, born in Bento Ribero, Brazil. A forward, he played for Cruzeiro, Brazil, then PSV Eindhoven and Barcelona, moving to Inter Milan in 1997. While at Barcelona he scored a Spanish league record of 34 goals in a season, his team also winning the European cup-winners cup and the Spanish cup final. He won the International Footballer of the Year poll in 1996–7.

Ronay, Egon [ro**nay**, ee**gon**] (1920–) Gastronome and writer, born in Hungary. He studied law at Budapest, and trained as a chef at home and in London before becoming manager of the family group of restaurants in Hungary. He emigrated to England in 1946 and opened his own restaurant in London (1952–5). He founded the annual *Egon Ronay's Guide to Hotels and Restaurants* in 1956, and subsequently similar guides to pubs, ski resorts, and various other places of interest to tourists in Britain and Europe.

Roncalli, Angelo Giuseppe >> **John XXIII**

Ronsard, Pierre de [rôsah(r)] (1524–85) Renaissance poet, born in La Possonnière, France. He trained as a page, but became deaf, and took up writing, studying for seven years at the Collège de Coqueret, and becoming a leader of the *Pléiade* group. His early works include *Odes* (1550) and *Amours* (1552), and he later wrote two bitter reflections on the political and economic state of the country. He was highly successful in his lifetime, but his fame suffered an eclipse after his death until the growth of the Romantic movement in the 19th-c.

Röntgen, Wilhelm Konrad von [roent**guhn**], also spelled **Roentgen** (1845–1923) Physicist, born in Lennep, Germany. He studied at Zürich, and became professor of physics at Strasbourg (1876–9), Giessen (1879–88), Würzburg (1888–1900), and Munich (1900–20). In 1895 he discovered the electromagnetic rays which he called *X-rays*, for which he received the first Nobel Prize for Physics in 1901.

Roon, Albrecht (Theodor Emil), Graf (Count) **von** (1803–79) Prussian army officer, born near Kolberg, Poland. He became war minister (1859–73), and with Bismarck's support effectively reorganized the army. This helped make possible Prussian victories in the Danish,

Austrian, and Franco–Prussian Wars of the 1860s and 1870s. >> **Bismarck**

Rooney, Mickey, originally **Joe Yule, Jr** (1920–) Film actor, born in New York City. A child actor from a vaudeville family, he became known for his roles in the Mickey McGuire (1927–33) and Andy Hardy (1937–8) series. In an up-and-down career, his film roles include *A Midsummer Night's Dream* (1935), *Boy's Town* (1938, Special Oscar), *Babes in Arms* (1939), *Summer Holiday* (1948), and *Breakfast at Tiffany's* (1961). He was married eight times, including once to film actress Ava Gardner. He returned to the stage in 1979 with the musical *Sugar Babes*, gained a Best Supporting Actor Oscar nomination for his role in *The Black Stallion* (1979), and won an Emmy for his television role in *Bill* (1982). Later films include *Erik the Viking* (1989), *Making Waves* (1994), and *Long Road Home* (1996), and he wrote and acted in *The Legend of O B Taggart* (1995).

Roosevelt, (Anna) Eleanor [rohzuhvelt, roozvelt] (1884–1962) Diplomat and humanitarian, born in New York City, the niece of Theodore Roosevelt and the wife of Franklin D Roosevelt, her distant cousin, whom she married in 1905. She took up extensive political work during her husband's illness from polio, and proved herself an invaluable adviser to him when he became president. In 1941 she was appointed assistant director of the office of civilian defence. After her husband's death in 1945 she extended the scope of her activities, and was a delegate to the UN Assembly (1946), US representative at the General Assembly (1946–52), and chair of the UN Human Rights Commission (1947–51). >> **Roosevelt, Franklin D; Roosevelt, Theodore**

Roosevelt, Franklin D(elano) [rohzuhvelt, roozvelt], nickname **FDR** (1882–1945) US statesman and 32nd president (1933–45), born in Hyde Park, NY. He became a lawyer (1907), a New York State senator (1910–13), and assistant secretary of the navy (1913–20). He was Democratic candidate for the vice-presidency in 1920, and Governor of New York (1928–32), although stricken with paralysis (polio) in 1921. As president, he met the economic crisis with his 'New Deal' for national recovery (1933), and became the only president to be re-elected three times. He strove in vain to ward off war, modified the USA's neutrality to favour the Allies, and was brought in by Japan's action at Pearl Harbor (1941). He met with Churchill and Stalin at Teheran (1943) and Yalta (1945), but died at Warm Springs, GA, where he had long gone for treatment, three weeks before the German surrender. >> **Byrns; Churchill, Sir Winston; Stalin; RR1097**

Roosevelt, Theodore [rohzuhvelt, roozvelt], known as **Teddy Roosevelt** (1858–1919) US Republican statesman and 26th president (1901–9), born in New York City. He studied at Harvard, and became leader of the New York legislature (1884). In 1898 he raised a volunteer cavalry ('Roosevelt's Roughriders') in the Cuban War, and came back to be Governor of New York State (1898–1900). Elected vice-president in 1900, he became president on the death (by assassination) of McKinley, and was re-elected in 1904. He was awarded the Nobel Peace Prize in 1906 for mediating the end of the Russo–Japanese War. An expansionist, he insisted on a strong navy and the regulation of trusts and monopolies, promoted the construction of the Panama Canal, and introduced a 'Square Deal' policy for social reform. As Progressive candidate for the presidency in 1912, he was defeated by Wilson. He worked vigorously during World War 1 pressing for America's intervention. >> **McKinley; Wilson, Woodrow; RR1097**

Root, Elihu (1845–1937) Jurist and statesman, born in Clinton, NY. He studied law at New York University, and practised in New York City. He became US secretary of war (1899–1904), and secretary of state (1905–9), and was awarded the Nobel Prize for Peace in 1912 for his promotion of international arbitration. He participated in the founding of the League of Nations.

Root, John Wellborn >> **Burnham, Daniel H**

Roper, Elmo (Burns), Jr (1900–71) Public opinion analyst, born in Hebron, NE. A retailer and salesman, he turned to market research and, founding his own New York firm (1934), pioneered modern public opinion polling techniques. He published *Fortune's* public opinion surveys (1935–50), broadcast the first live analysis of election returns (on CBS, 1940), and wrote a syndicated newspaper column, 'What People are Thinking'. He retired in 1966.

Rorem, Ned (1923–) Composer and writer, born in Richmond, IN. After studies at the Juilliard School, New York City, he spent the greater part of the 1950s in Paris, where he was much influenced by contemporary French culture. As well as a rich corpus of songs, he has composed three symphonies and much other orchestral music, six operas, concertos, and ballets, as well as theatrical, choral, and chamber music. He has also published essays, diaries, and critical works.

Rorschach, Hermann [raw(r)shahkh] (1884–1922) Psychiatrist and neurologist, born in Zürich, Switzerland. He devised a diagnostic procedure for mental disorders based upon the patient's interpretation of a series of standardized ink blots (the *Rorschach test*). His work received little attention until after his death.

Rorty, Richard (McKay) (1931–) Philosopher, born in New York City. He studied at Chicago and Yale universities, and taught at Yale, Wellesley College, and Princeton, before becoming professor of humanities at Virginia University from 1982. In 1979 he published the controversial *Philosophy and the Mirror of Nature*, which mounted a forceful and dramatic attack on the foundationalist, metaphysical aspirations of traditional philosophy.

Rosa, Carl (August Nicolas) [rohza], original surname **Rose** (1842–89) Impresario and violinist, born in Hamburg, Germany. He became *konzertmeister* there in 1863, and appeared in London as a soloist in 1866. In 1873 he founded the Carl Rosa Opera Company, giving a great impulse to opera sung in English, and also to operas by English composers.

Rosa, Salvator [rohza] (1615–73) Painter, born near Naples, Italy. He became famous in Rome for his talents as painter, etcher, actor, and poet, but he made powerful enemies by his satires, and withdrew to Florence, returning to Rome after nine years. He owes his reputation mainly to his landscapes of wild and savage scenes.

Roscellinus, Johannes [roseliynus] (c.1050–c.1120) Scholar, probably born in Compiègne, France. He studied at Soissons, and is considered to be the founder of Nominalism. His most famous pupil was Abelard. In 1092 the Council of Soissons condemned his teaching as implicitly involving the negation of the doctrine of the Trinity. >> **Abelard**

Roscius [roshius], in full **Quintus Roscius Gallus** (c.134–62 BC) Roman comic actor, a slave by birth. He became the greatest comic actor in Rome, and was freed from slavery by the dictator, Sulla. He gave Cicero lessons in elocution, and was defended by him in a lawsuit. >> **Cicero; Sulla**

Rose, Billy, professional name of **William Samuel Rosenberg** (1899–1966) Composer of popular music, born in New York City. During World War 1 he worked as a chief stenographer. He became a prolific song writer during the 1920s, his many hits including 'It's Only a Paper Moon', 'Me and My Shadow', and 'Without a Song'. He produced the musical *Carmen Jones* (1943) and several other stage shows, and became known for his city night-spots, notably Billy Rose's Music Hall.

Rose, Sir John (1820–88) Canadian diplomat, born in Turriff, Aberdeenshire, NE Scotland, UK. He studied in Aberdeen, emigrated to Canada (1836), and was called to the Montreal bar (1842). He acquired numerous directorates, became a close political associate of John A Macdonald, and was drawn into Anglo-American arbitration in deciding Oregon-related questions (1863–9). At the same time he formed a partnership with Levi Morton in London. He played a critical part in adjusting British–American relations after the American Civil War. >> MacDonald, John A; Morton, Levi

Rose, Lionel (Edmund) (1948–) Bantamweight boxer, born in Warragul, Victoria, Australia. Inspired by the success of Jimmy Carruthers, and determined to emulate him, he won the world championship in 1968, becoming the first Aborigine to hold a world title. He defeated Britain's Alan Rudkin on points over 15 rounds at Melbourne, in which the Commonwealth title was also at stake, but in 1969 lost his title to Ruben Olivares. >> Carruthers

Rose, (Iain) Murray (1939–) Swimmer, born in Birmingham, West Midlands, C England, UK. At the 1956 Melbourne Olympics he became the youngest-ever triple gold medallist in swimming, with wins in the 400 m and 1500 m freestyle and the relay team. In Rome in 1960 he became the first swimmer to successfully defend the 400 m title. He received the Helms Foundation World Trophy in 1962, and for three or four years had no serious rivals.

Rose, Pete(r Edward) (1942–) Baseball player and manager, born in Cincinnati, OH. He surpassed Ty Cobb's 57-year-old record of 4191 base hits in 1985, and was the National League's Most Valuable Player in 1973. In his career (1963–86), spent mainly with the Cincinnati Reds, he had a record 4256 base hits. He was banned from baseball while Cincinnati manager in 1989 after an investigation into alleged gambling offences which resulted in a prison sentence. >> Cobb; RR1144

Rose, William (Cumming) (1887–1984) Biochemist, born in Greenville, SC. He studied at Yale, and spent his career at Illinois University. From the 1930s he studied mammalian nutrition. In one series of experiments he replaced all protein by amino acids, and so found that not all 20 of them are essential for a given species; in the rat, 10 are essential (including threonine, which he discovered in 1936). In the adult human diet, only eight are essential, as he showed by experiments using student volunteers.

Roseanne, popular name of **Roseanne Barr** (1952–) Actor and producer, born in Salt Lake City, UT. After an unsettled youth, and a period during the early 1980s as a stand-up comedy performer, she made a breakthrough into television, hosting a number of specials and series, and becoming especially known for her realistic, unglamorized sitcom *Roseanne* (1988–97). Her film credits include *She-Devil* (1989), *The Final Nightmare* (1991), and *Blue in the Face* (1995). She has also written two autobiographical books, *Roseanne: My Life as a Woman* (1989) and *My Lives* (1994).

Rosebery, Archibald Philip Primrose, 5th Earl of (1847–1929) British statesman and prime minister (1894–5), born in London, England, UK. He studied at Oxford, succeeded to the earldom in 1868, and after holding various educational and political posts, became foreign secretary (1886, 1892–4) under Gladstone, whom he succeeded as premier for a brief period before the Liberals lost the election of 1895. He was noted for his racehorse stables, and in his later years as a biographer of British statesmen. >> Gladstone, W E; RR1095

Rosecrans, William S(tarke) [**rohz**krans] (1819–98) US soldier and politician, born in Kingston, OH. At the outbreak of the Civil War (1861–5) he succeeded McClellan, and kept Lee out of Western Virginia. In 1862 he commanded a division at the siege of Corinth, and after its capture commanded the Army of the Mississippi, defeated General Sterling Price (1809–67) at Iuka, and defended Corinth against Price and General Earl Van Dorn (1820–63). He won through in the battles at Stone River (1862–3) against Bragg, but Bragg defeated him at Chickamauga. Superseded by Grant, he repelled Price's invasion of Missouri (1864). He later became minister to Mexico (1868–9), a member for California of the US House of Representatives (1881–5), and registrar of the US treasury (1885–93). >> Bragg, Braxton; Lee, Robert E; McClellan

Rose-Innes, Sir James [**in**is] (1855–1942) Judge, born in Uitenkage, South Africa. He studied at the University of the Cape of Good Hope, became attorney general (1890–3, 1900–2), and then judge president (later Chief Justice) of the Supreme Court of the Transvaal (1902–10), judge of appeal (1910–14), and Chief Justice of the Union of South Africa (1914–27). He advocated a liberal policy towards the Bantu, and his opinions were notable for his willingness to rely on both the English and Roman–Dutch traditions in South African law.

Rosenbach, A(braham) S(imon) W(olf) [**roh**zenbak] (1876–1952) Book dealer and collector, born in Philadelphia, PA. He studied at the University of Pennsylvania, then joined his brother **Philip** in the antique business (1902), branching out to sell rare books and manuscripts. As a dealer, he helped assemble the volumes at the core of such institutions as the Huntington Library and the Folger Shakespeare Library. He also became one of the world's major collectors, and wrote several books, such as *A Book Hunter's Holiday* (1936).

Rosenberg, Alfred [**roh**zenberg] (1893–1946) German politician, born in Reval, Estonia. An avid supporter of National Socialism, he joined the Party in 1920, edited Nazi journals, for a time directed the Party's foreign policy (1933), and in 1934 was given control of its cultural and political education policy. In *The Myth of the 20th Century* (1930) he expounded the extreme Nazi doctrines which he later put into practice in E Europe, for which crime he was hanged at Nuremberg in 1946.

Rosenberg [**roh**zenberg] Alleged spies: **Julius Rosenberg** (1918–53) and **Ethel Rosenberg** (1915–53), husband and wife, both born in New York City. They were part of a transatlantic spy ring uncovered after the trial of Klaus Fuchs in Britain. Julius was an engineer with the US Army Signal Corps, and Ethel's brother, David Greenglass, worked at the nuclear research station at Los Alamos. They were convicted of passing on atomic secrets through an intermediary to the Soviet vice-consul. Greenglass turned witness for the prosecution and saved his life. The Rosenbergs were sentenced to death in 1951 and, despite numerous appeals from many West European countries and three stays of execution, were executed at Sing Sing prison, NY. There was great controversy over the case, as many people felt that they were the victims of the witch-hunt atmosphere in the USA in the early 1950s. >> Fuchs, Klaus

Rosenfeld, Lev Borisovich >> **Kamenev, Lev Borisovich**

Rosenquist, James (Albert) (1933–) Painter, born in Grand Falls, ND. He studied at the Minneapolis School of Art (1948), at Minnesota University (1952–4), and at the Art Students' League (1955). He began as an abstract painter, but c.1960 took to Pop Art and painted enlarged bits and pieces of unrelated everyday objects. He held an exhibition at the Whitney Museum of American Art in 1972.

Rosenthal, Jack (Morris) [**roh**zentahl] (1931–) Playwright, born in Manchester, Greater Manchester, NW England, UK. He studied at Sheffield University, joined Granada Television in 1956, and made his professional writing debut with 150 episodes of *Coronation Street* (1961–9). He created the series *The Lovers!* (1970), followed by individual plays such as *The Evacuees* (1975), *Barmitzvah Boy* (1976), *The Knowledge* (1979), *Day to Remember* (1986), *Sleeping Sickness* (1991), and *Eskimo Day* (1996). His film scripts include *Lucky Star* (1980) and *Yentl* (1983, in collaboration with Barbra Streisand), and his stage work includes *Smash!* (1981) and *Our Gracie* (1983). In 1973 he married the actress Maureen Lipman. >> Lipman; Streisand

Rosenzweig, Franz [**roh**zentsvIyk] (1886–1929) Jewish theologian, born in Kassel, Germany. He first studied medicine, then switched to modern history and philosophy. He reacted against German Idealism, and expounded an existential approach that emphasized the experience and interests of the individual. A critical religious experience in 1913 caused him to reaffirm his Jewishness and devote the rest of his life to the study and practice of Judaism. His major work was *Der Stern der Erlösung* (1921, The Star of Redemption).

Rosewall, Ken(neth Ronald) (1934–) Tennis player, born in Sydney, New South Wales, Australia. He is regarded as the best player never to have won the Wimbledon singles title, although playing in three finals. In the course of a brilliant career he won every other major title, including the US title twice, and with Lew Hoad he won the British, US, French, and Australian doubles titles in 1956, the year in which he turned professional. He won the professional world championship in 1971 and 1972. >> Hoad; RR1175

Rosmini(-Serbati), Antonio [roz**mee**nee] (1797–1855) Theologian and philosopher, born in Rovereto, Austria. Ordained in 1821, he founded the Institute of the Fathers of Charity in 1828. He later developed an interest in political affairs, became an adviser to Pope Pius IX (1848), and worked for a federation of the Italian states under the pope as permanent president, embodied in his *La constituzione secondo la giustizia sociale* (1848, Constitution according to Social Justice). He fell into disfavour, and several of his works were prohibited in 1849 by the Congregation of the Index.

Rosny [rohnee] Pseudonym of the brothers **Joseph Henri Boëx** (1856–1940) and **Séraphin Justin François Boëx** (1859–1948), French novelists, born in Brussels. Their vast output of social novels, naturalistic in character, includes *L'Immolation* (1887) and *L'Impérieuse Bonté* (1905). After they separated in 1908, the older Rosny wrote *L'Appel au bonheur* (1919), and *La Vie amoureuse de Balzac* (1930); the younger wrote *La Courtesane passionée* (1925) and *La Pantine* (1929).

Ross, Barnaby >> **Queen, Ellery**

Ross, Diana (1944–) Singer, born in Detroit, MI. For ten years she was the lead singer with The Supremes, the most successful female trio of the 1960s. Her debut solo single, 'Reach Out and Touch' (1970), was a major hit, as was her next record 'Ain't No Mountain High Enough' (1970). In 1972 she made her film debut, and won an Oscar nomination for her performance as Billie Holiday in *Lady Sings The Blues*. Later albums include *Diana* (1980) and *The Force Behind the Power* (1991).

Ross, Harold (Wallace) (1892–1951) Newspaper editor, born in Aspen, CO. He left high school at 13 to become a reporter for the *Salt Lake City Tribune*, and in 1910 was with the *Marysville Appeal* in California. He worked for a variety of newspapers until 1917, when he enlisted in the Railway Engineer Corps of the US army, becoming editor of *Stars and Stripes*. From 1925 he was founder-editor of the *New Yorker*.

Ross, Herbert >> **Kaye, Nora**

Ross, Sir James Clark (1800–62) Polar explorer, born in London, England, UK. He discovered the north magnetic pole in 1831, then commanded an expedition to the Antarctic seas (1839–43), where the *Ross Barrier*, *Sea*, and *Island* are named after him. He was knighted in 1843. >> Ross, John

Ross, Sir John (1777–1856) British naval officer, and Arctic explorer, born at Balsaroch, Dumfries and Galloway, SW Scotland, UK. In 1818 he led an expedition, including his nephew Sir James Clark Ross and Sir Edward Sabine, in search of the Northwest Passage. In 1829–33 he led another such expedition with Sir Felix Booth (1775–1850), during which he discovered and named Boothia Peninsula, King William Land, and the Gulf of Boothia. His ship was crushed in the ice (1832), and the party were eventually rescued by whalers (1833). In 1850 he made an unsuccessful attempt to discover the fate of Sir John Franklin. >> Franklin, John; Ross, James Clark; Sabine, Edward

Ross, Martin >> **Martin, Violet Florence**

Ross, Nick, popular name of **Nicholas David Ross** (1947–) British broadcaster and journalist. He studied at Queen's University, Belfast, and joined the BBC in Northern Ireland in 1971. Moving to London, he became a reporter on such programmes as *World At One*, *Today*, and *Newsdesk*, becoming nationally known for his investigative reporting in *Call Nick Ross* (from 1987). He has also presented a wide range of news and discussion television programmes, notably *Crimewatch UK* (from 1984) and *Westminster with Nick Ross* (from 1994). He has also been much involved in work on social issues, such as medical ethics, crime, and road safety.

Ross, Sir Ronald (1857–1932) Physician, born in Almora, India. He studied medicine at St Bartholomew's, and joined the Indian Medical Service (1881–99). He became professor of tropical medicine at Liverpool, and directed the Ross Institute for Tropical Diseases from 1926. He received the 1902 Nobel Prize for Physiology or Medicine for his discovery of the malaria parasite and subsequent work on the natural history of the disease.

Rossby, Carl-Gustaf (Arvid) (1898–1957) Meteorologist, born in Stockholm. He studied at Stockholm University, and joined the Bergen Geophysical Institute in 1919. He moved to the USA in 1926, becoming a US citizen in 1938. He became professor of meteorology at the Massachusetts Institute of Technology in 1928, moving to Chicago in 1941, and returning to Stockholm in 1950. In 1940 he demonstrated the large-scale undulatory disturbances, now known as *Rossby waves*, in the flow of the westerly winds in the upper atmosphere. He also showed that the strength of these winds has an important influence on global weather, and is credited with the discovery of the jet stream. His ideas did much to create modern weather-prediction methods.

Rossellini, Isabella [rose**lee**nee] (1952–) Film actress, born in Rome, the daughter of Roberto Rossellini and Ingrid Bergman. She worked as a translator and journalist before making her first film appearance in 1976, playing a small part in her mother's film *A Matter of Time*. She appeared in several European television dramas before her starring role in the Italian film *Il Prato* (1979, The Meadow), then concentrated on a modelling career with the cosmetics firm Lançome for a number of years. Later films include *Death Becomes Her* (1992), *Immortal Beloved* (1994), *Big Night* (1996) and *The Funeral* (1997). >> Bergman, Ingrid; Rossellini, Roberto

Rossellini, Roberto [rose**lee**nee] (1906–77) Film director, born in Rome. His first independent film was *Roma, città apperta* (1945, Rome, Open City), made while it was still under German occupation, often with hidden cameras in a style which came to be known as 'neo-Realism'. It was followed by *Paisà* (1946, Paisan) and *Germania, anno zero* (1947, Germany, Year Zero). Later films on spiritual themes, and his liaison with Ingrid Bergman, were condemned by the Catholic Church in the USA, but another war-time story, *Il generale della Rovere* (1959, General della Rovere), restored his popularity. He later produced several television documentaries on historical figures, such as Louis XIV and Socrates. >> Bergman, Ingrid; Rossellini, Isabella

Rossellino, Antonio [rose**lee**noh] (1427–79) Renaissance sculptor, born in Florence, Italy, the youngest brother and pupil of Bernardo Rossellino. He is best known for sculptural reliefs of the Madonna and Child, and portrait busts, most notably that of the Florentine 'Matteo Palmieri' (1468). His style is less austere than his brother's, and his preference for suggesting movement is well demonstrated in his most important monument, the tomb of the Cardinal of Portugal (1466) in San Miniato al Monte, Florence. >> Rossellino, Bernardo

Rossellino, Bernardo [rose**lee**noh] (1409–64) Architect and sculptor, born in Florence, Italy, the brother and teacher of Antonio Rossellino. As an architect he worked under Leon Battista Alberti, executing his designs for the Church of Santa Maria Novella, Florence. His most complete architectural work is the palace and cathedral of Pienza. His sculptural masterpiece is the tomb of Chancellor Leonardo Bruni (1450) in S Croce, Florence, which in its austere Classical style is the epitome of Italian Renaissance art. >> Alberti, Leon Battista; Rossellino, Antonio

Rossetti, Christina (Georgina) [ro**zet**ee] (1830–94) Poet, born in London, England, UK, the daughter of Gabriele Rossetti. A devout Anglican, and influenced by the Oxford Movement, she wrote mainly religious poetry, such as *Goblin Market and Other Poems* (1862). By the 1880s, recurrent bouts of illness had made her an invalid, but she continued to write, later works including *A Pageant and Other Poems* (1881) and *The Face of the Deep* (1892). Her work displays the influence of the Pre-Raphaelite artistic movement, which her brother helped to found. >> Rossetti, Dante Gabriel/Gabriele/William Michael

Rossetti, Dante Gabriel [ro**zet**ee] (1828–82) Poet and painter, born in London, England, UK, the elder son of Gabriele Rossetti. He trained at the Royal Academy in London, and helped to form the Pre-Raphaelite Brotherhood (c.1850), which aimed to return to pre-Renaissance art forms involving vivid colour and detail. His early work was on religious themes, such as 'The Annunciation' (1850, Tate, London); his later manner became more secular, and more ornate in style. The death of his wife in 1862, and adverse criticism of his poetry, turned him into a recluse, but *Ballads and Sonnets* (1881) contains some of his best work. >> Hunt, William Holman; Rossetti, Christina/Gabriele/William Michael

Rossetti, Gabriele [ro**zet**ee] (1783–1854) Poet, scholar, and revolutionary, born in Vasto, Italy. He is best known as the father of four exceptionally talented children, three of whom have entries in this volume; the fourth (and eldest) was **Maria Francesca** (1827–76). Besides writing poetry he was a close student of Dante, whose *Inferno* he maintained was chiefly political and anti-papal. After the restoration of Ferdinand I to Naples, he joined the Carbonari secret society, and greeted the constitution demanded by the patriots in 1820 with a spirited verse, which heralded his death sentence. He fled to London (1824), where he became professor of Italian at the new University of London. >> Rossetti, Christina/Dante Gabriel/William Michael

Rossetti, William Michael [ro**zet**ee] (1829–1919) Art critic and man of letters, born in London, England, UK, the younger son of Gabriele Rossetti. He started as an official in the Inland Revenue, and became art critic of the *Spectator* from 1850. He wrote biographies of Shelley and Keats, and published editions of Coleridge, Milton, Blake, and Whitman. Like all his family he was devoted to the study of Dante, whose *Inferno* he translated. >> Rossetti, Christina/Dante Gabriel/Gabriele

Rossi, Bruno (1905–) Physicist, born in Venice, Italy. In 1940 he became professor of physics at Cornell University. His work includes the study of cosmic rays, showing them to be positively charged particles, and the development of X-ray astronomy.

Rossi, Giovanni Battista de (1822–94) Archaeologist, born in Rome. He is known for his research on the Christian catacombs of St Callistus in Rome, and has been called 'the founder of Christian archaeology'.

Rossini, Gioacchino (Antonio) [ro**see**nee] (1792–1868) Composer, born in Pesaro, Italy. He studied in Bologna, and began to write comic operas. Among his early successes were *Tancredi* (1813) and *L'Italiana in Algeri* (1813, The Italian Girl in Algiers), and in 1816 he produced his masterpiece, *Il barbiere di Siviglia* (The Barber of Seville). As director of the Italian Theatre in Paris (1823), he adapted several of his works to French taste, and wrote *Guillaume Tell* (1829, William Tell). In 1836 he retired to Bologna and took charge of the Liceo, which he raised to a high position in the world of music. The revolutionary disturbances in 1847 drove him to Florence, and he returned in 1855 to Paris. Later works include his *Stabat Mater* (1841) and the *Petite messe solennelle* (1863). His overtures in particular have continued to be highly popular items in concert programmes.

Rossiter, Leonard (1926–84) Actor, born in Liverpool, Merseyside, NW England, UK. Originally an insurance clerk, he first appeared on stage in Preston, made his London debut in 1957, and his Broadway debut in 1963. His film debut was in *A Kind of Loving* (1962), and he subsequently appeared in *Billy Liar* (1963), and *King Rat* (1965). His theatre work included *Banana Box* (1973), which was adapted as the television series *Rising Damp* (1974–8), bringing him great acclaim. His comic talents were further employed on television in *The Fall and Rise of Reginald Perrin* (1976–80), in a variety of stage appearances, including *Loot* (1984), and in films, such as *Water* (1985).

Rosso, Fiorentino, originally **Giovanni Battista de Jacopo di Gasparre** (1495–1540) Painter, born in Florence, Italy. Trained under Andrea del Sarto, his angular, tortured style owes more to Michelangelo. A leading exponent of the Mannerist style, and founder of the Fontainebleau school, his most famous work is 'The Deposition' (1521, Volterra). >> Michelangelo; Sarto

Rostand, Edmond [ros**tã**] (1868–1918) Poet and playwright, born in Marseille, France. After some early poetry, he achieved international and enduring fame with his play, *Cyrano de Bergerac* (1897, filmed 1950, 1990), the story of the gifted nobleman who felt no-one could love him because of his enormous nose. This was followed by several other verse-plays, such as *L'Aiglon* (1900, The Eaglet) and *Chantecler* (1910).

Rostow, Walt (Whitman) (1916–) Economist, born in New York City. He studied at Yale and Oxford universities, served with the US army, and became assistant chief of the German-Austrian economic division of the State Department. He taught at Oxford and Cambridge, then at the Massachusetts Institute of Technology Center for International Studies (1950–60), and was special adviser to presidents Kennedy (1961–3) and Johnson (1966–9). In

1969 he became professor of economics and history at Texas. He is best known for his theory that societies pass through five stages of economic growth, and his publications include *The World Economy: History and Prospect* (1978). >> Johnson, Lyndon B; Kennedy, John F

Rostropovich, Mstislav Leopoldovich [rostro**poh**vich] (1927–) Cellist and composer, born in Baku, Azerbaijan (formerly, USSR). He studied at the Moscow Conservatory (1943–8), where he later became professor of cello (1956). In 1975, while in the USA, he and his wife decided not to return to the USSR, and he became musical director and conductor of the National Symphony Orchestra, Washington, DC (1977–94). He formed a close friendship with Benjamin Britten, who wrote several cello works for him. He was made an honorary knight in 1987. His wife is the soprano, **Galina Vishnevskaya** (1926–). >> Britten

Rotblat, Joseph (1908–) Physicist and anti-nuclear activist, born in Warsaw. Educated in Poland, he moved to Liverpool University in 1939, then participated in the atomic bomb project in the USA. After the war, he became a British citizen, working first at Liverpool (1945–9) then at St Bartholomew's Hospital, London (1950–76), and devoting himself to the peaceful application of nuclear physics, chiefly in relation to medicine. In 1955 he joined a group of scientists arguing for an end to nuclear weapons, and helped to found the annual series of conferences on arms control in Pugwash, Nova Scotia in 1957 (the Pugwash Conferences), acting first as secretary-general (1957–73) and later as president (from 1988). His books include *Science and World Affairs* (1962), *Scientists in the Quest for Peace* (1972), and *A World at the Crossroads* (1994). He received the Nobel Peace Prize, along with the Conferences, in 1995.

Roth, Henry (1906–95) Novelist, born of Jewish parents in Tysmenica, Austria–Hungary, and taken to New York City in 1907. He was educated at the City College there, and worked as a precision metal grinder in New York and Boston. From 1946 he lived in Maine and New Mexico. His only novel, *Call It Sleep* (1934), is a classic treatment of Jewish immigrant life and childhood.

Roth, Joseph (1894–1939) Novelist, short-story writer, and critic, born in Brod, Slovenia (formerly, Brody, Austria–Hungary). He studied at Lemberg and Vienna, served in the Austrian army, then worked as a journalist in Vienna and Berlin, emigrating to Paris in 1933. His novels include *Radetzkymarsch* (1932, Radetzky March), *Die Kapuzinergruft* (1938, The Capuchin Tomb), and the posthumously published *Der stumme Prophet* (1966, The Silent Prophet).

Roth, Philip (Milton) (1933–) Novelist, born in Newark, NJ. He studied at the University of Chicago, and taught there for a while. His first book *Goodbye, Columbus* (1959), consisted of a novella and five short stories, and gained him the National Book Award in 1960. Jewish-American life in particular, and modern American society in general, are the subjects of his subsequent comedies of manners, which include *Letting Go* (1962), the notorious 'masturbation' novel *Portnoy's Complaint* (1969), and *My Life as a Man* (1974). Later novels record the history of a central character Nathan Zuckerman, in the trilogy *Zuckerman Bound* (1989), while fact and fiction are elaborately interwoven in *The Facts: a Novelist's Autobiography* (1988) and *Deceptions* (1990). Other books include *Operation Shylock: A Confession* (1993) and *American Pastoral* (1997). He was married to the actress Claire Bloom (dissolved, 1995). >> Bloom, Claire

Rothacker, Erich [**rot**aker] (1888–1965) Philosopher, born in Pforzheim, Germany. He was a leading exponent of philosophical anthropology, which aims to construct a coherent picture of human beings in their biological, cultural and social aspects. His main works include *Probleme der Kulturanthropologie* (1948, Problems of Cultural Anthro-

pology) and *Philosophische Anthropologie* (1966, Philosophical Anthropology).

Rotheim, Erik [**rot**hiym] (1898–1938) Norwegian inventor. He filed the first patent for an aerosol-type dispenser in 1926. He later modified his original design, specifying a spray nozzle, and used hydrocarbons as the propellant gas.

Rothenstein, Sir John (Knewstub Maurice) [**roth**enstiyn] (1901–92) Art historian, born in London, England, UK, the son of Sir William Rothenstein. He studied at Oxford and London, taught in the USA (1927–9), and became director of Leeds and Sheffield city art galleries (1932–8). He was then appointed director and keeper of the Tate Gallery, retiring in 1964. His many works on art include *Modern English Painters* (1952–73), and his autobiography (3 vols, 1965, 1966, 1970). >> Rothenstein, William

Rothenstein, Sir William [**roth**enstiyn] (1872–1945) Artist, born in Bradford, West Yorkshire, N England, UK. He studied at the Slade School of Art, London, and in Paris, won fame as a portrait painter, and became principal of the Royal College of Art. He was an official war artist in both world wars. >> Rothenstein, John

Rothermere, Viscount >> Harmsworth, Harold Sydney

Rothko, Mark, originally **Marcus Rothkowitz** (1903–70) Painter, born in Dvinsk, Russia. His family emigrated to the USA in 1913. He studied for a while at Yale, then travelled the USA until settling in New York City in 1925, where he took up painting. Largely self-taught as an artist, he held his first one-man show in 1933. During the 1940s he was influenced by Surrealism, but by the early 1950s he had evolved his own peaceful and meditative form of Abstract Expressionism, staining huge canvases with rectangular blocks of pure colour.

Rothschild, Meyer (Amschel), Eng [**roths**chiyld], Ger [**roht**shilt] (1743–1812) Financier, the founder of a banking dynasty, born in Frankfurt, Germany. The family name comes from the 'Red shield' (Ger *roter schild*) hung on the wall of an ancestor's dwelling. He began as a moneylender, and became the financial adviser of the Landgrave of Hesse. The house transmitted money from the English government to Wellington in Spain, paid the British subsidies to Continental princes, and negotiated loans for Denmark (1804–12). His five sons continued the firm, establishing branches in other countries, and negotiated many of the great government loans of the 19th-c.

Rothschild, Nathaniel Mayer Victor Rothschild, 3rd Baron (1910–90) Administrator, born in London, England, UK. He served in military intelligence (1939–45), then spent two years with the British Overseas Airways Corporation. He was chairman of the Agricultural Research Council (1948–58), assistant director of the department of zoology at Cambridge (1950–70), and research director/co-ordinator of Shell UK. From 1971–4 he was in government service as director-general of the central policy review staff.

Rothwell, Evelyn >> Barbirolli, John

Rouault, Georges (Henri) [roo-oh] (1871–1958) Painter and engraver, born in Paris. He was apprenticed to a stained-glass designer in 1885, and retained the art's glowing colours, outlined with black, in his paintings of clowns, prostitutes, and biblical characters. He joined the Fauves c.1904, and held his first one-man show in 1910. During the two World Wars he worked on a series of religious engravings, and also designed ballet sets and tapestries. >> Matisse

Roubillac, Louis François [roobeeyak], also spelled **Roubiliac** (1702–1762) Sculptor, born in Lyon, France. He studied in Paris, and settled in London (c.1730). His statue of Handel for Vauxhall Gardens (1738) first made him popular, and he completed statues of Newton, at Cambridge (1755), Shakespeare (1758, British Museum), and others.

Rouget de Lisle, Claude Joseph [roozhay duh leel] (1760–1836) French army officer, born in Lons-le-Saunier, France. He wrote and composed the *Marseillaise* when stationed in 1792 as captain of engineers at Strasbourg. Its original name was 'Chant de guerre de l'armée du Rhin' (War Song of the Rhine Army), but it became known in Paris when it was sung by volunteers from Marseille during the French Revolution.

Roughead, William (1870–1952) Criminologist, from Edinburgh, EC Scotland, UK. As a legal apprentice in 1889 he began a lifelong fascination with murder. In 1906 the *Trial of Dr Pritchard* was the first of his 10 volumes in the 'Notable British Trials' series. Harshly moralistic towards the guilty, he also proved a formidable critic where he believed justice had erred. His edition of the Oscar Slater trial (1909, Slater [1873–1948] was wrongly accused and convicted of murder on the dubious evidence of witnesses who thought they saw him leaving the scene of the crime) was of major value in obtaining Slater's ultimate pardon (1928).

Rourke, Mickey, originally **Philip Andre Rourke, Jr** (1956–) Film actor, born in Schenectady, NY. He studied acting in New York City, and became known for his performances in *Body Heat* (1981), *Diner* (1982), and *The Pope of Greenwich Village* (1984). Later films include *Bullet* (1995), *Exit in Red* (1996), and *Double Team* (1997).

Rous, (Francis) Peyton [rows] (1879–1970) Pathologist, born in Baltimore, MD. He studied medicine at Johns Hopkins University, then worked at the Rockefeller Institute for Medical Research to the age of 90, studying cancer. He devised culture methods for viruses and for cancerous cells. The *Rous chicken sarcoma*, which he discovered in 1911, remains the best-known example (as well as the first) of a cancer produced by a virus. He shared the 1966 Nobel Prize for Physiology or Medicine. >> RR1124

Rousseau, Henri Julien Félix [roosoh], known as **le Douanier** ('the Customs Officer') (1844–1910) Primitive painter, born in Laval, France. He worked for many years as a minor customs official, hence his nickname. Retiring in 1885, he spent his time painting and copying at the Louvre, and exhibited for several years at the Salon des Indépendants. He produced painstaking portraits, exotic imaginary landscapes, and dreams, such as 'Sleeping Gypsy' (1897, New York City).

Rousseau, Jean Jacques [roosoh] (1712–78) Political philosopher, educationist, and essayist, born in Geneva, Switzerland. Largely self-taught, he carried on a variety of menial occupations, until after he moved to Paris in 1741, where he came to know Diderot and the *encyclopédistes*. In 1754 he wrote *Discours sur l'origine de l'inégalité et les fondements parmi les hommes* (1755, Discourse on the Origin and Foundations of Inequality Amongst Men), emphasizing the natural goodness of human beings, and the corrupting influences of institutionalized life. He later moved to Luxembourg (1757), where he wrote his masterpiece, *Du contrat social* (1762, The Social Contract), a great influence on French revolutionary thought, introducing the slogan 'Liberty, Equality, Fraternity'. The same year he published his major work on education, *Emile*, in novel form, but its views on monarchy and governmental institutions forced him to flee to Switzerland, and then England, at the invitation of David Hume. There he wrote most of his *Confessions* (published posthumously, 1782). He returned to Paris in 1767, where he continued to write, but gradually became insane. >> Diderot; Hume, David

Rousseau, (Pierre Etienne) Théodore [roosoh] (1812–67) Landscape painter, born in Paris. He studied the old masters in the Louvre, and by 1833 had begun sketching in the Forest of Fontainebleau. His 'Forest of Compiègne' (1834)

was bought by the Duc d'Orléans, but some 12 years of discouragement followed. During the 1840s he settled at Barbizon, where he worked with a group of other painters, becoming leader of the Barbizon school. From the 1850s his work became increasingly accepted. >> Troyon

Roussel, Albert (Charles Paul Marie) [roosel] (1869–1937) Composer, born in Tourcoing, France. He joined the navy at 18, but resigned his commission at 25 to study music in Paris, joining the Schola Cantorum under Vincent d'Indy (1896). A journey to the Far East gave him an interest in Oriental music, which inspired the choral *Evocations* (1912) and the opera *Padmavati*, begun in 1914 and completed after World War 1. His works include ballets, notably *Le Festin de l'araignée* (1912, The Spider's Feast) and *Bacchus et Ariane* (1931), four symphonies, and numerous choral and orchestral works. >> d'Indy

Roussel, Ker Xavier [roosel] (1867–1944) Artist, born in Lorry-les-Metz, France. He was a member of *Les Nabis*, and associated with Bonnard, Vuillard, and Denis. He is best known for his classical subjects portrayed in typical French landscapes, using the Impressionist palette. >> Bonnard, Pierre; Denis, Maurice; Vallotton; Vuillard

Rout, Ettie Annie [rowt] (1877–1936) Journalist and social reformer, born in Hobart, Australia. She moved to New Zealand in 1885, and found fame during World War 1 through her campaign to control venereal disease among New Zealand troops in Europe. A friend of Marie Stopes, she later turned her attention to the sexual education of women. She wrote six books, including *Safe Marriage* (1922) and *The Morality of Birth Control* (1925). >> Stopes, Marie

Routledge, George [rowtlij] (1812–88) Publisher, born in Brampton, Cumbria, NW England, UK. He went to London in 1833, and started up as a bookseller (1836) and publisher (1843). He later took his two brothers-in-law, W H and Frederick Warne (1825–1901), into partnership.

Roux, (Pierre Paul) Emile [roo] (1853–1933) Bacteriologist, born in Confolens, France. He studied at Clermont-Ferrand, became assistant to Pasteur, and was appointed his successor (1905–18). In 1894 he helped to discover diphtheria antitoxin, and also worked on rabies and anthrax. >> Pasteur; Yersin

Roux, Wilhelm [roo] (1850–1924) Anatomist and physiologist, born in Jena, Germany. He studied at Jena, Berlin, and Strasbourg, and became professor at Wrocław, Poland (formerly Breslau, Germany) (1886)), Innsbruck (1889), and Halle (1895). He was one of the first to do extensive practical and theoretical work on experimental embryology (his *Entwicklungsmechanik*, or developmental mechanics).

Rowan, Carl (Thomas) (1925–) Journalist, born in Ravenscroft, TN. One of the most prominent contemporary black journalists, he was a prizewinning reporter for the *Minneapolis Tribune* (1950–61), and later (from 1965) became a nationally syndicated columnist, as well as a radio commentator and a panelist on television public affairs programmes. He also served as ambassador to Finland (1963–4) and as director of the US Information Agency (1964–5).

Rowbotham, Sheila [rohbotham] (1943–) Social historian and feminist, born in Leeds, West Yorkshire, N England, UK. She studied at Oxford, and became involved in the women's movement in the late 1960s. An active Socialist, she wrote for several Socialist papers, and provoked controversy with *Beyond the Fragments: Feminism and the Making of Socialism* (1979, with Segal and Wainwright). Among her most important historical works are *Women, Resistance and Revolution* (1972) and *Hidden from History* (1973).

Rowe, Nicholas [roh] (1674–1718) Poet and playwright, born in Little Barford, Bedfordshire, SC England, UK. He studied at Westminster, and became a lawyer, but from 1692 devoted himself to literature. Three of his plays became very popular: *Tamerlane* (1702), *The Fair Penitent* (1703), and *Jane Shore* (1714). The name of his character Lothario (in *The Fair Penitent*) is still used to describe a fashionable rake. He was the first to publish a critical edition of Shakespeare (1709–10). In 1715 he was appointed poet laureate and a surveyor of customs in London.

Rowland, Henry Augustus (1848–1901) Physicist, born in Honesdale, PA. The first professor of physics at Johns Hopkins University (1875–1901), he invented the concave diffraction grating used in spectroscopy, discovered the magnetic effect of a moving electric charge, and improved on the values of the ohm and the mechanical equivalent of heat.

Rowland, (Frank) Sherwood (1927–) Physical chemist, born in Delaware, OH. He studied at the University of Chicago (1952), taught at Princeton and the University of Kansas, then joined the University of California, Irvine (1964). In 1974, with Mario Molina, he predicted the destruction of ozone in the Earth's atmosphere as a by-product of using chlorofluorocarbons as a refrigerant and aerosol propellant – a prediction confirmed in 1985 when the British Antarctic Survey discovered the hole in the ozone layer over the South Pole. They shared the 1995 Nobel Prize for Chemistry with Paul Crutzen. >> Molina; Crutzen

Rowland, Tiny, originally **Rowland W Furhop** (1917–) Financier, born in India. He joined Lonrho (London and Rhodesian Mining and Land Company) in 1961, and became chief executive and managing director. In 1983 he became chairman of *The Observer* newspaper, which he sold to *The Guardian* in 1993. He stepped down from Lonrho in 1994, following a bitter battle for control of the company with German property tycoon Dieter Bock.

Rowlandson, Thomas (1756–1827) Caricaturist, born in London, England, UK. He studied in London and Paris, then travelled widely in Britain, and became a specialist in humorous watercolours commenting on the social scene. Some of his best-known works are his illustrations to the 'Dr Syntax' series (1812–21) and 'The English Dance of Death' (1815–16).

Rowley, Thomas >> **Chatterton, Thomas**

Rowley, William (c. 1585–c. 1642) Actor and playwright, born in London, England, UK. Little is known about him, except that he collaborated with Dekker, Middleton, Heywood, Webster, Massinger, and Ford. Four plays published with his name are extant: *All's Lost by Lust*, a tragedy (c.1620); *A New Wonder, a Woman Never Vext* (1632); *A Match at Midnight* (1633); and *A Shoomaker a Gentleman* (1638). >> Dekker; Ford, John; Heywood, Thomas; Massinger; Middleton; Webster, John

Rowling, Sir Wallace Edward, known as **Bill Rowling** (1927–95) New Zealand statesman and prime minister (1974–5), born in Motueka, New Zealand. He studied at Canterbury University, joined the New Zealand army, and served in the education corps before becoming active in the Labour Party. He entered parliament in 1962, and was finance minister in the administration of Norman Kirk. When Kirk died in 1974, he succeeded him as prime minister until the National Party returned to power. He was then appointed ambassador to the USA. >> Kirk, Norman; RR1078

Rowntree, B(enjamin) Seebohm (1871–1954) Manufacturer and philanthropist, born in York, North Yorkshire, N England, UK, the son of Joseph Rowntree. He was chairman of the family chocolate firm (1925–41), and introduced enlightened schemes of worker-participation. He devoted his life to the study of social problems and welfare, and

wrote many books, including *Poverty: a Study of Town Life* (1901), *Poverty and Progress* (1941), and *Poverty and the Welfare State* (1951). >> Rowntree, Joseph

Rowntree, Joseph (1836–1925) Quaker industrialist and reformer, born in York, North Yorkshire, N England, UK, the son of Joseph Rowntree, a Quaker grocer. With his brother, **Henry Isaac** (d.1883), he became a partner in a cocoa manufacturing firm in York in 1869, and built up welfare organizations for his employees. >> Rowntree, B Seebohm

Rowse, A(lfred) L(eslie) [rows] (1903–97) Historian, born in St Austell, Cornwall, SW England, UK. He studied at Oxford, became a fellow of All Souls College, and wrote many works on English history, including *Tudor Cornwall* (1941), *The Use of History* (1946), and *The England of Elizabeth* (1950). He also wrote some poetry, much of it on Cornwall, and many literary works, including several on aspects of Shakespeare, a life of Marlowe (1964), and his own autobiography, *A Cornishman at Oxford* (1965). He was made a Companion of Honour in 1997.

Roy, Rammohun >> **Rammohun Roy**

Royal, The Princess >> **Anne, Princess**

Royce, Sir (Frederick) Henry (1863–1933) Engineer, born in Alwalton, Cambridgeshire, EC England, UK. He began as a railway apprentice, but became interested in electricity and motor engineering, founding the firm of Royce Ltd in Manchester (1884). He made his first car in 1904, and his meeting with C S Rolls in that year led to the formation of Rolls–Royce, Ltd (1906). He was created a baronet in 1930. >> Rolls

Royce, Josiah (1855–1916) Philosopher, born in Grass Valley, CA. He trained as an engineer, then switched to philosophy, studying in Germany and at Johns Hopkins University (under Peirce). He taught philosophy at Harvard from 1882. Much influenced by Hegel, he developed a philosophy of Idealism, emphasizing the importance of the individual in *Religious Aspects of Philosophy* (1885) and *The World and the Individual* (1900–1). He also wrote on mathematical logic, social ethics, psychology, and religion. >> Hegel; Peirce

Royden, Agnes Maud (1876–1956) Social worker and preacher, born in Liverpool, Merseyside, NW England, UK. She studied at Oxford, and was prominent in the women's suffrage movement. From 1917 to 1920 she was assistant at the City Temple, and published, amongst others, *Woman and the Sovereign State*, *The Church and Woman*, and *Modern Sex Ideals*.

Rozanov, Vasily Vasilyevich [rozahnof] (1856–1919) Writer, thinker, and critic, born in Vetluga, Russia. A teacher in provincial schools, he came to prominence in 1894 with a critical study of the 'Grand Inquisitor' chapter in Dostoevsky's *The Brothers Karamazov*. Though a Christian, in his prolific writings he criticized contemporary standards from a Nietzschean standpoint. Much of his work is highly introspective, and his literary reputation is firmly based on the two books of fragments and essays, *Solitaria* (1912) and (trans title) *Fallen Leaves* (1913, 1915). >> Nietzsche

Rozeanu, Angelica [roziahnoo], *née* **Adelstein** (1921–) Table tennis player, born in Romania. She won 12 world titles between 1950 and 1956, including the singles title a record six times in succession (1950–5), and was a member of the Romanian Corbillon Cup winning team (1950–1, 1953, 1955–6). She was made a Master of Sport, and appointed to the Romanian Olympic Commission. Upon her retirement in 1960, she emigrated to Israel.

Rózsa, Miklós (Nicholas) [rowsha] (1907–95) Composer, born in Budapest. A child prodigy on the violin, he studied at Leipzig University, and composed symphonies and ballet music in Paris and London before being commissioned to write his first film score for *Knight Without Armour* (1937). He settled in Hollywood in 1939, and later concentrated on accompaniments to historical epics, including *Quo Vadis* (1951) and *El Cid* (1961). He received Oscars for *Spellbound* (1945), *A Double Life* (1947), and *Ben Hur* (1959).

Rubbia, Carlo (1934–) Physicist, born in Gorizia, Italy. He studied at Pisa, Rome, and Columbia universities, and from 1960 headed the team at CERN (the European Organisation for Nuclear Research) in Geneva using the proton-antiproton collider. In 1972 he became professor of physics at Harvard, and in 1989 director-general of the European Organization for Nuclear Research. He shared the Nobel Prize for Physics in 1984 with Simon van der Meer for their work leading to the discovery of the W and Z sub-atomic particles. >> van der Meer

Rubbra, Edmund (1901–86) Composer, born in Northampton, Northamptonshire, C England, UK. He studied at Reading and London, and developed an interest in the polyphonic music of the 16th–17th-c. He wrote 11 symphonies, chamber, choral and orchestral music, songs, and solo instrumental works. He taught at Oxford (1947–68), and became professor of composition at the Guildhall School of Music (1961–74).

Rubens, Bernice (Ruth) (1928–) Novelist and director of documentary films, born in Cardiff, S Wales, UK. She studied at the University of Wales, later becoming a Fellow of University College, Cardiff. She was a film-maker of distinction before she chose a full-time writing career, beginning with *Set on Edge* (1960). Later novels include *The Elected Member* (1970, Booker Prize), *Brothers* (1987), and *Yesterday in the Back Lane* (1995).

Rubens, (Peter Paul) [**roo**benz] (1577–1640) Painter, born in Siegen, Germany. He was educated at Antwerp, and was intended for the law, but began to study art, travelling to Venice in 1600. He entered the service of the Duke of Mantua, and was sent to Spain as a diplomat (1605). There he executed many portraits and works on historical subjects. He then travelled in Italy, producing work much influenced by the Italian Renaissance, and in 1608 settled in Antwerp, becoming court painter to the Archduke Albert. His triptych 'The Descent from the Cross' (1611–14) in Antwerp Cathedral is one of his early masterpieces. He became a prolific and renowned painter, and in 1622 was invited to France by Marie de Médicis, for whom he painted 21 large subjects on her life and regency (Louvre). He was sent on a diplomatic mission to Philip IV of Spain (1628), and there executed some 40 works. The following year he became envoy to Charles I of England, where his paintings included 'Peace and War' (National Gallery, London). He was knighted by both Charles I and Philip IV. In 1630 he retired to Steen, where he engaged in landscape painting. >> Charles I (of England); Marie de Médicis

Rubik, Ernö [**roo**bik] (1944–) Architect, and creator of *Rubik's cube*, born in Budapest. He studied at the Technical University in Budapest, and became a teacher at the School of Industrial Design there. In 1974 he conceived the idea of a multi-coloured puzzle cube, divided into nine other cubes, each of which will pivot. There are millions of combinations, but only one possible way of getting all six sides to form a different colour. The cube was patented in 1975, and had become a world craze by the late 1970s. He has created other puzzles, though none have captured the public imagination in the same way.

Rubin, Robert E [**roo**bin] (1938–) US statesman, born in New York City. Educated at Harvard, Yale, and the London School of Economics, he became a lawyer, and joined the firm of Goldman, Sachs & Co in New York City (1966–93, co-chairman, 1990–2). He then joined the White House as assistant to the president for economic policy (1993–5), directing the activities of the National Economic Council. He became secretary of the Treasury in 1995, and was reappointed to this post in Clinton's 1997 administration. >> Clinton, Bill

Rubinstein, Anton (Grigoryevich) [**roo**binstiyn] (1829–94) Pianist and composer, born in Vykhvatinets, Russia. He studied in Berlin and Vienna, and settled in St Petersburg (1848), where he taught music and took a part in founding the Conservatory, of which he was director (1862–7). He made concert tours in Europe and the USA, gaining widespread acclaim. His compositions include operas, oratorios, and piano concertos. His brother **Nikolay** (1835–81) founded Moscow Conservatory.

Rubinstein, Artur [**roo**binstiyn] (1887–1982) Pianist, born in Łódź, Poland. He made public appearances from the age of six, and his European debut in Berlin at 13. He studied at the Warsaw Conservatory, then in Berlin, and moved to the USA during World War 2, becoming a US citizen in 1946. He continued to perform there with enormous success, making over 200 recordings.

Rubinstein, Helena [**roo**binstiyn] (1870–1965) Beautician and business executive, born in Cracow, Poland. She attended medical school in Cracow, then moved in the 1890s to Australia, where she opened the country's first beauty salon in Melbourne (1902). Her face cream, formulated according to a family recipe, made her fortune. She studied with European dermatologists, and opened salons in London (1908) and Paris (1912). In 1915 she emigrated to New York City and launched an international business empire. She set cosmetic trends, introducing waterproof mascara, foundation make-up, and all-day spa treatments, stressing the scientific preparation of her products and the instruction of clients in their use. Her success was spiced by a 50-year feud with arch-rival Elizabeth Arden. Her many philanthropies included the endowment of a contemporary art museum in Israel and a medical research foundation. >> Arden, Elizabeth

Rublyov or **Rublev, Andrey** [rub**lyof**] (c.1360–c.1430) Painter, born in Russia. Little is known about his life or works, but he is generally regarded as the greatest of Russian icon painters. He became a monk and was an assistant of the Greek painter Theothanes, with whom he worked in Moscow from 1405. In 1422 he returned to Troitsky-Sergieva, where he is traditionally believed to have produced his most famous work, the icon of the Old Testament Trinity, represented by three graceful angels.

Ruby, Jack L, originally **Jacob Rubenstein** (1911–67) Assassin, born in Chicago, IL. He came from a broken home, and engaged in petty crimes, served in the air force (1943–6), and operated nightclubs and dance halls in Dallas, TX. Two days after the assassination of President John F Kennedy, he shot and killed Lee Harvey Oswald, the alleged assassin of the president. Despite many attempts to link Ruby to some conspiracy, it is generally believed that he acted on his own. He was sentenced to death in 1964, but died while awaiting a second trial. >> Kennedy, John F; Oswald, Lee Harvey

Rudbeck, Olof (1630–1702) Anatomist, botanist, writer, and architect, born in Sweden. He studied at Uppsala and Leyden, was appointed professor of medicine at Uppsala in 1660, and discovered the lymphatic system (1652) simultaneously with the Danish physician **Thomas Bartholin** (1616–80). He planned a vast illustrated work on all known plants, but his manuscripts and wood blocks were destroyed in the great Uppsala fire of 1702. The botanical genus *Rudbeckia* is named after him. He also achieved fame throughout Europe with his literary work *Atlantikan* (1675–98).

Rudkin, Margaret, née **Fogarty** (1897–1967) Businesswoman, born in New York City. She worked in a brokerage house in New York, and in 1923 married one of the firm's partners. In 1929 the Rudkins developed an estate in Connecticut, naming it Pepperidge Farm after its black gum trees. In 1937, to help her asthmatic son, she began baking bread using stone-ground whole wheat and other 'pure' ingredients. Her son improved, and the allergist's suggestion that she bake for other patients began a mail-order business. By 1938 she was selling 4000 loaves a week of Pepperidge Farm Bread, and she later opened bakeries in Pennsylvania and Illinois. In 1960 she sold Pepperidge Farm to Campbell Soups, continuing to run the farm as an independent subsidiary. She published *The Margaret Rudkin Pepperidge Farm Cookbook* in 1963 and, with her son installed as president, retired three years later.

Rudolf I (1218–91) German king (1273–91), the founder of the Habsburg sovereign and imperial dynasty, born in Schloss Limburg, Germany. He increased his possessions by inheritance and marriage until he was the most powerful prince in Swabia. Chosen king by the electors, he was recognized by the pope in 1274.

Rudolph, Wilma (Glodean) (1940–94) Sprinter, born in St Bethlehem, TN. Overcoming childhood polio, she came to prominence as a teenager as part of an athletics team known as the 'Tennessee Belles'. As a 16-year-old she won a bronze medal at Melbourne in the 1956 Olympic Games, and at Rome in 1960 won the 100 m, 200 m, and sprint relay events, making her the first US woman to win three gold medals for track and field events. She retired in 1964. >> RR1137

Rue, Warren de la >> de la Rue, Warren

Ruether, Rosemary Radford [roother] (1936–) Theologian, born in Minneapolis, MN. Professor of applied theology at Garrett–Evangelical theological seminary, Evanston, she has written extensively on women and theological issues. Her books analyze the effects of male bias in official Church theology, and seek to affirm the feminine dimension of religion and the importance of women's experience. They include *Sexism and God-Talk* (1983).

Ruggles, Carl (1876–1971) Composer, born in Marion, MA. He was the founder of the Winona Symphony Orchestra, MA (1912), and taught composition at Miami University (1938–43). His radical modernity and individuality met largely with incomprehension, and in later years he concentrated on painting. He destroyed many of his early works, but the best-known and longest of those which survive is the 17-minute orchestral *Sun-treader* (1926–31).

Ruggles-Brise, Sir Evelyn (John) (1857–1935) Prison reformer, born in Finchingfield, Essex, SE England, UK. A civil servant, he was appointed chairman of the Prison Commission (1895–1921). He visited the USA (1897) to study the reformatory system, and on his return brought together a group of young prisoners at Borstal, Kent, where he implemented 'Borstal detention' for young offenders. In 1908, an act was passed allowing magistrates to prescribe such detention. He was knighted in 1902.

Ruïsdael, Jacob van >> Ruysdael, Jacob van

Ruiz, José Martínez >> Azorín

Rukeyser, Muriel [rookiyzer] (1913–80) Writer, born in New York City. She studied at Vassar College and Columbia University (1930–2), taught at Sarah Lawrence (1946, 1956–67), and became a social activist and feminist poet, themes expressed in *The Collected Poems of Muriel Rukeyser* (1979). She also wrote screenplays, and was a playwright, translator, and a writer of children's books.

Rule, St >> Regulus, St

Rumford, Count >> Thompson, Benjamin

Ruml, Beardsley [ruhml] (1894–1960) Public official, born in Cedar Rapids, IA. He joined R H Macy and Co (1934–49, chairman 1945–9) and the New York's Federal Reserve Bank (direc-

tor 1937–47, chairman 1941–7), and acted as a 'New Deal' adviser. He devised the federal tax witholding system (1943), and was instrumental in establishing the International Monetary Fund (1944). >> Roosevelt, Franklin D

Rummell, Joseph (Francis) (1876–1964) Roman Catholic clergyman, born in Baden, Germany. His family emigrated to the USA when he was six. He served in New York before becoming Bishop of Omaha (1928) and Archbishop of New Orleans (1935–62). He became best known for his stand in the 1950s against racial segregation in school, eventually desegregating all Catholic schools in the New Orleans archdiocese.

Rumsey, James (1743–92) Engineer and inventor, born in Cecil Co, MD. His steamboat, propelled by the ejection of water from the stern, was exhibited on the Potomac in 1787, and was one of the earliest constructed. He died in London while preparing a second version for exhibition on the Thames.

Runcie (of Cuddesdon), Robert (Alexander Kennedy) Runcie, Baron [ruhnsee] (1921–) Archbishop of Canterbury (1980–91), born in Crosby, Lancashire, NW England, UK. He studied at Oxford and Cambridge, served in the Scots Guards during World War 2, and was ordained in 1951. He was Bishop of St Albans for 10 years before becoming Archbishop of Canterbury. His period as archbishop was marked by a papal visit to Canterbury, the war with Argentina, ongoing controversies over homosexuality and women in the Church, and his highly acclaimed chairmanship of the Lambeth Conference in 1987. His books include *Windows onto God* (1983) and *The Unity we Seek* (1989). He was created a life peer in 1991.

Runciman, Lord Walter Runciman, 1st Viscount (1870–1949) British statesman. He entered the House of Commons as a Liberal in 1899, and held a number of ministerial posts in Liberal and coalition administrations from 1908 to 1939. He is remembered for his mission to Czechoslovakia in 1938 to persuade the government to make concessions to Nazi Germany as part of Britain's 'appeasement strategy'. >> Chamberlain, Neville

Runcorn, (Stanley) Keith (1922–95) Geophysicist, born in Southport, Lancashire, NW England, UK. He studied at Cambridge, worked at the Radar Research Establishment (1943–6), held posts in physics at Manchester (1946–9) and geophysics at Cambridge and Los Angeles (1949–55), and became professor of physics at Newcastle University (1956–88). He is best known for his studies of terrestrial magnetism, by which he helped to confirm the theory of continental drift. >> Wegener

Rundstedt, (Karl Rudolf) Gerd von [rundshtet] (1875–1953) German field marshal, born in Aschersleben, Germany. He served in World War 1, and in the early 1930s became military commander of Berlin. In 1939 he directed the attacks on Poland and France. Checked in the Ukraine in 1941, he was relieved of his command, but in 1942 was given a new command in France. He was recalled after the success of the 1944 Allied invasion, but returned to direct the Ardennes offensive. War crimes proceedings against him were dropped on the grounds of his ill health.

Runeberg, Johan Ludvig [roonuhberg] (1804–77) Finnish poet, writing in Swedish, born in Jakobstad, Finland. His first poems appeared in 1830, and he became known for his epic poems, notably *Elgskyttarne* (1832, The Moose Hunters) and *Hanna* (1836). His major work is the verse romance based on Scandinavian legend, *King Fjala* (1844). One of his poems became Finland's national anthem.

Runyon, (Alfred) Damon (1884–1946) Writer and journalist, born in Manhattan, KS. After service in the Spanish–American War (1898) he turned to journalism and sports reporting for the *New York American*, and then to feature-writing with syndicated columns. His short stories, written in a racy style with liberal use of American slang and jargon, and depicting life in underworld New York City and on Broadway, won him enormous popularity. His famous collection, *Guys and Dolls* (1931), was the basis of a successful musical (1950) and film (1955). Other books include *Blue Plate Special* (1934) and *Take it Easy* (1938). From 1941 he worked as a film producer.

Rupert, Prince, also known as **Rupert of the Rhine** (1619–82) Royalist commander in the English Civil War, born in Prague, the third son of the Elector Palatine Frederick V and Elizabeth, the daughter of James I of England. A notable cavalry leader, he won several victories in the major battles of the war, but was defeated at Marston Moor (1644), and after his surrender of Bristol he was dismissed by Charles I. Banished by parliament, he led the small Royalist fleet until it was routed by Blake (1650). He escaped to the West Indies, returning to Europe in 1653, and lived in Germany until the Restoration. >> Blake, Robert; Charles I (of England); Cromwell, Oliver

Rupert, Anthony Edward (1916–) Financier, patron of the arts, and leading conservationist, born in Graff-Reiner, South Africa. He trained as a chemist at Pretoria University, then taught there before turning to a business career. He is the founder and retired chairman of the Rembrandt Group of Companies, and the doyen of Afrikaans language business. He became Chancellor of the University of Pretoria, and director of the SA Reserve Bank. He has received international recognition for services rendered to the conservation of fauna and flora, and has written widely on South African issues.

Rüppell, (Wilhelm Peter) Eduard (Simon) [rüpel] (1794–1884) Zoologist and explorer, born in Frankfurt, Germany. He studied at Pavia and Genoa, and went on major expeditions to the Sudan (1821–7) and Ethiopia (1830–4). He published extensive maps and scientific accounts of his travels, including the monumental *Reise in Abyssynien* (1838–40, Travels in Abyssinia). *Rüppell's warbler* is named after him.

Rusedski, Greg [ruzetskee] (1973–) Tennis player, born in Montreal, Quebec, Canada. A prominent junior player in Canada, winning six junior titles (1985–90), he then turned professional, winning tournaments at Newport (1993), Seoul (1995), and Beijing (1996). He became a British subject in 1995, and the first British player to finish in the world's top 50 since John Lloyd in 1985. A left-handed player, known for his very fast serves, by the end of 1997 he had reached number 5 in the world listings, and moved ahead of Tim Henman to become British number 1. >> Henman

Rush, Benjamin (1745–1813) Physician and politician, born in Byberry, PA. He studied medicine at Edinburgh and Paris, and became professor of chemistry at the universities of Philadelphia (1769) and Pennsylvania (1791). Elected a member of the Continental Congress, he signed the Declaration of Independence (1776). In 1777 he was appointed surgeon-general, and later physician-general, of the Continental army. In 1799 he became treasurer of the US Mint. One of the first to argue that mental disorders could be treated as well as could physical ones, he wrote a famous treatise on psychiatry, *Medical Inquiries and Observations upon the Diseases of the Mind* (1812).

Rush, Geoffrey (1951–) Actor, born in Toowoomba, Queensland, Australia. He trained at the Lecoq School in Paris, and was known for 25 years predominantly as a theatre actor in Australia, working with the Queensland, Sydney, and Melbourne Theatre Companies, and particularly remembered for his role in Gogol's *Diary of a Madman*. He became known internationally for his role as David

Helfgott in the 1996 film *Shine*, for which he won, in 1997, the Academy, Golden Globe, BAFTA, and Australian Film Institute Awards for Best Actor, as well as critics awards in New York, Los Angeles, and Boston. >> Helfgott

Rush, Ian (1961–) Footballer, born in St Asaph, Denbighshire. After playing one season with Chester, he moved to Liverpool in 1981, and scored heavily (110 goals in 182 league matches). He won all the major honours in British football, and the European Cup Medal in 1984. He played for Juventus (1986–8) before returning to Liverpool, then joined Leeds United in 1996, and moved to Newcastle United the following year. He has been a regular member of the Welsh international team since 1980. >> RR1156

Rush, Richard (1780–1859) Lawyer, public official, and diplomat, born in Philadelphia, PA, the son of Benjamin Rush. He studied at the College of New Jersey (now Princeton), was admitted to the bar, and served as attorney general of Pennsylvania (1811), comptroller of the US treasury (1811–14), US attorney general (1814), interim secretary-of-state (1817), and minister to Great Britain (1817–25). His reports from London assisted in the formation of the Monroe Doctrine. He ran unsuccessfully for vice-president on the John Quincy Adams ticket in 1828, then retired from political life. However, he returned to public service to become minister to France (1847–9). >> Adams, John Quincey; Monroe, James; Rush, Benjamin

Rushdie, (Ahmad) Salman (1947–) Writer, born in Mumbai (Bombay), India, of Muslim parents. He emigrated to Britain in 1965, and studied at Cambridge. He worked as an actor and an advertising copywriter before becoming a writer, producing his first novel, *Grimus*, in 1975. He became widely known after the publication of his second novel, *Midnight's Children* (1981, Booker, James Tait Black prizes), a fantasia of Indian history in the 20th-c. This was followed in 1983 by *Shame*, set in Pakistan. *The Satanic Verses* (1988, Whitbread) caused worldwide controversy because of its treatment of Islam from a secular point of view, and in 1989 he was forced to go into hiding because of a sentence of death passed on him by Ayatollah Khomeini of Iran. Ten years later the case was still unresolved, despite various high-level appeals. His later books include a novel for children, *Haroun and the Sea of Stories* (1990), a book of essays, *Imaginary Homelands* (1991), and the novels *East, West* (1994) and *The Moor's Last Sigh* (1995, Whitbread). >> Khomeini

Rusk, (David) Dean (1909–94) US secretary of state (1961–9), born in Cherokee Co, GA. He studied at Davidson College and at Oxford, and in 1934 was appointed associate professor of government at Mills College, Oakland, CA. After World War 2, he held various governmental posts: special assistant to the secretary of war (1946–7), assistant secretary of state for UN affairs, deputy under-secretary of state, and assistant secretary for Far Eastern Affairs (1950–1). In 1952 he was appointed president of the Rockefeller Foundation, and from 1961 was secretary of state under Kennedy, in which capacity he played a major role in handling the Cuban crisis of 1962. He retained the post under the Johnson administration, retiring in 1969. After leaving public service, he became professor of international law at the University of Georgia. >> Johnson, Lyndon B; Kennedy, John F

Rusk, Howard A(rchibald) (1903–89) Physician and writer, born in Brookfield, MO. He studied at Pennsylvania, then joined the medical faculty at Washington (1929–42), specializing in rehabilitation. In World War 2 he enlisted in the army, and continued this work at the Jefferson Barracks hospital in Missouri. At New York University in 1946 he started the first comprehensive rehabilitation programme in the world; in 1948 it became the Institute of Rehabilitation Medicine. A columnist for the *New York Times* (1948–69), he also wrote an autobiography, *A World to Care For* (1972).

Ruska, Ernst (1906–88) Physicist, born in Heidelberg, Germany. He studied high voltage and vacuum methods at Munich and Berlin, and from 1928 worked on the development of the electron microscope. His transmission electron microscope achieved up to $10^6\times$, compared with $2000\times$ for a good optical microscope, and its commercial availability (from 1938 onwards) revolutionized biology. He was awarded the 1986 Nobel Prize for Physics.

Ruskin, John (1819–1900) Writer and art critic, born in London, England, UK. He studied at Oxford, and after graduating met Turner, and championed his painting in his first critical work, *Modern Painters* (1843–60). This book, along with *The Seven Lamps of Architecture* (1848) and *The Stones of Venice* (1851–3), made him the critic of the day, and his social criticism gave him the status of a moral guide or prophet. *Unto This Last* (1860) is said to have influenced Gandhi. He became professor of fine art at Oxford in 1870, and founded several educational institutions. His last work was an unfinished autobiography, *Praeterita* (1886–8). >> Gandhi, Mahatma; Turner, J M W

Russell, Anna, originally **Claudia Anna Russell-Brown** (1911–) Singer and musical satirist, born in London, England, UK. She studied singing at the Royal College of Music, London. She worked as a folk singer for the BBC (1935–40), and in various roles with the Canadian Broadcasting Corporation (1942–6), before making her debut as a concert comedienne in New York City (1948). She took her show to many cities throughout the world (1948–60), and was resident in Australia (1968–75) before returning to Canada.

Russell, Bertrand (Arthur William) Russell, 3rd Earl (1872–1970) Philosopher and mathematician, born in Trelleck, Monmouthshire, SE Wales, UK. He studied at Cambridge, where he became a fellow of Trinity College in 1895. Concerned to defend the objectivity of mathematics, he pointed out a contradiction in Frege's system, published his own *Principles of Mathematics* (1903), and collaborated with A N Whitehead in *Principia mathematica* (1910–13). In 1907 he offered himself as a Liberal candidate, but was turned down for his 'free-thinking'. In 1916 his pacifism lost him his fellowship (restored in 1944), and in 1918 he served six months in prison. From the 1920s he lived by lecturing and journalism, and became increasingly controversial. He visited the Soviet Union, was professor at Peking (1920–1), and with his wife started a progressive school near Petersfield (1927). He succeeded to his brother's title in 1931. The evils of Fascism led him to renounce pacifism in 1939. Later works included *An Enquiry into Meaning and Truth* (1940) and *Human Knowledge* (1948). After 1949 he became a champion of nuclear disarmament, and engaged in unprecedented correspondence with several world leaders. One of the most important influences on 20th-c analytic philosophy, he was awarded the Nobel Prize for Literature in 1950, and wrote an *Autobiography* (1967–69) remarkable for its openess and objectivity. >> Frege; Peano; Whitehead, Alfred North; Zermelo

Russell, Bill, popular name of **William Felton Russell** (1934–) Basketball player, born in Monroe, LA. He played with the Boston Celtics (1956–69), winning 11 NBA championships in 13 seasons. 6 ft 10 in tall, he is considered one of the greatest 'big men' in the sport. A member of 11 National Basketball Association championship teams, he went on to become the Celtics coach, the first black coach of a major sports team. Five times voted Most Valuable Player in the NBA, he also worked as a sports commentator for American network television. >> RR1146

Russell, Charles Taze, known as **Pastor Russell** (1852–1916) Religious leader, the founder of what is commonly called the Bible Student Movement, born in Pittsburgh, PA. As a Congregationalist, he struggled with the concept of eternal torment, his subsequent Bible studies leading him to conclude that the Biblical hell is oblivion, that the Millennium began in 1874, and that a period of social and political upheaval would lead to a peaceable kingdom on Earth. After his death, many followers abandoned his Watch Tower Bible and Tract Society (1879), which under the leadership of Joseph Rutherford moved in other directions and ultimately became known as Jehovah's Witnesses (1931).

Russell, Sir Edward John (1872–1965) Agriculturist, born in Frampton-on-Severn, Gloucestershire, SWC England, UK. He studied chemistry at Manchester, then became interested in agricultural science. In 1912 he was appointed director of the Rothamsted Experimental Station, and contributed to its rising status. He published his classic *Soil Conditions and Plant Growth* in 1912.

Russell, Francis, 4th Earl of Bedford (1593–1641) English nobleman, the son of William, Baron Russell. With the help of Inigo Jones he developed Covent Garden and built the mansion of Woburn. He also continued the fen drainage scheme initiated by his father, and known as the Bedford Level. >> Jones, Inigo; Russell, Baron

Russell, Frederick Stratten (1897–1984) Marine biologist, born in Dorset, S England, UK. He studied at Cambridge and served with distinction in the Royal Naval Air Service during World War 1. After the war he joined the staff of the Plymouth Laboratory, of which he eventually became director. He is best known for his work on medusae and plankton, the latter being instrumental in elucidating the movement of water masses in the ocean (distinguished by their characteristic plankton) and allowing the prediction of annual variation in fishes of commercial importance.

Russell, George William, pseudonym Æ (1867–1935) Poet and mystic, born in Lurgan, Co Armagh. He studied at the Metropolitan School of Art, met Yeats, and became interested in theosophy. He worked as a draper's clerk, and published his first book, *Homeward: Songs by the Way* (1894), which made him a recognized figure in the Irish literary renaissance. He was editor of the *Irish Homestead*, later called the *Irish Statesman* (1906–30). His best-known book is *The Candle of Vision* (1918), an expression of his religious philosophy. Other works include volumes of verse, such as *The Divine Vision* (1903) and *Midsummer Eve* (1928). >> Yeats, William Butler

Russell, Sir (Sydney) Gordon (1892–1980) Furniture designer, born in London, England, UK. In 1923 he started a furniture-making business in Hereford and Worcester, in the Cotswold Arts and Crafts tradition. With his brother **Dick** (1903–81), Gordon Russell Ltd went on to produce some of the finest modern furniture of the 1930s. In World War 2 he was chairman of the panel responsible for 'Utility' furniture (1943–7), and was director of the Council of Industrial Design (the Design Council) during its formative years (1947–59). He was elected a royal designer for industry in 1940.

Russell, Henry Norris (1877–1957) Astronomer, born in Oyster Bay, NY. He graduated from Princeton with the highest grade then recorded, earned his doctorate there, then worked at Cambridge (1900–5). He returned to Princeton, becoming professor of astronomy in 1911. Independently of Hertzsprung, he discovered the relationship between stellar absolute magnitude and spectral type, and represented the results in the Hertzsprung–Russell diagram, first published in 1913. >> Hertzsprung

Russell, Jack, popular name of **John Russell** (1795–1883)

Clergyman, born in Dartmouth, Devon, SW England, UK. He studied at Oxford, became curate of Swymbridge near Barnstaple (1832–80), and master of foxhounds. He developed the West Country smooth-haired, short-legged terrier, since named after him.

Russell, (Ernestine) Jane (Geraldine) (1921–) Film actress, born in Bernidji, MN. Discovered by Howard Hughes, she made her first film, *Outlaw*, in 1940, but because of censorship problems it was not released until 1946. Known for her striking looks, she became one of the leading Hollywood sex symbols of the 1950s, her other films including *Paleface* (1948) and *Gentlemen Prefer Blondes* (1953), *Waco* (1966), and *Darker Than Amber* (1970). >> Hughes, Howard

Russell, John, 1st Earl of Bedford (c. 1486–1555) English courtier. He became a gentleman usher to Henry VIII, was entrusted with several diplomatic missions, and later held many court appointments, including those of Comptroller of the Household and Lord Privy Seal. Among the rich possessions which he amassed were the abbeys of Woburn and Tavistock, and the London properties of Covent Garden and Long Acre. Created earl in 1550, he led the mission to Spain in 1554 which escorted Philip home to marry Mary I. >> Henry VIII; Mary I

Russell (of Kingston Russell), John Russell, 1st Earl, known as **Lord John Russell** (1792–1878) British statesman and prime minister (1846–52, 1865–6), born in London, England, UK. He studied at Edinburgh, and became an MP in 1813. He was home secretary (1835–9) and secretary for war (1839–41), and became Liberal prime minister after the Conservative Party split over the repeal of the Corn Laws (1846). In Aberdeen's coalition of 1852 he was foreign secretary and Leader of the House of Commons. He lost popularity over alleged incompetent management of the Crimean War, and retired (1855), but became foreign secretary again in the second Palmerston administration (1859), and was made an earl in 1861. On Palmerston's death, he again became premier, resigning in 1866. >> Aberdeen; Palmerston

Russell, John Robert, 13th Duke of Bedford (1917–) British nobleman. He was estranged from his family at an early age, and lived for a while in a Bloomsbury boarding house until, having been invalided out of the Coldstream Guards in 1940, he became a house agent, journalist, and farmer in South Africa. After succeeding to the title he became well known for his energetic and successful efforts to keep Woburn Abbey for the family, by running it commercially with popular amenities and amusements.

Russell, John Scott (1808–82) Engineer and naval architect, born near Glasgow, W Scotland, UK. He studied at Glasgow University, became professor of natural philosophy at Edinburgh (1832), and researched the effect of water waves on ships' hulls, designing hulls for the Scottish shipbuilding industry. He moved to London in 1844, and helped design many ships, including the *Great Eastern* (1856) and HMS *Warrior* (1860), the first ironclad battleship.

Russell, Ken, popular name of **Henry Kenneth Alfred Russell** (1927–) Film director, born in Southampton, Hampshire, S England, UK. In 1955 he made some documentary shorts which earned him a freelance assignment with BBC Television, for whom he produced experimental studies of Debussy, Isadora Duncan, Delius, and Richard Strauss, which gradually abandoned naturalism. He turned to feature films with *Women in Love* (1969), but continued with musically inspired themes in *The Music Lovers* (1971) and *Mahler* (1974). Other productions include *The Devils* (1971), *Savage Messiah* (1972), *Gothic* (1987), *The Rainbow* (1989), and for television *Lady Chatterley* (1993).

Russell, Kurt (1951–) Film actor, born in Springfield, MA. A child performer, he appeared in a number of television and film roles before deciding to play professional baseball. After an injury he returned to the screen in a television film *Elvis* (1979), and had his first feature role in *Escape From New York* (1981). Later films include *Backdraft* (1991), *Stargate* (1994), *Escape From LA* (1996), and *Breakdown* (1997).

Russell, Morgan (1886–1953) Painter, born in New York City. He moved to Paris in 1906 and studied briefly with Matisse. In 1912 he and the US painter **Stanton McDonald-Wright** (1890–1973) developed the theory of Synchromist colour, in which colour was given precedence over descriptive form. One of his best-known works in this genre is 'Synchromy in Orange: To Form' (1913–14). From 1920 he reverted to figurative painting. >> Matisse

Russell, Pee Wee, popular name of **Charles Ellsworth Russell** (1906–69) Jazz clarinet player, born in Maple Wood, MO. He travelled the American Midwest with bands from age 16. In 1925, he worked in St Louis with Frankie Trumbauer (1901–56) and Bix Beiderbecke, and thereafter was associated with their coterie of Chicago-based Dixielanders. As part of the entrepreneurial troupe of Eddie Condon (1905–73) for nearly two decades, he played frequently at Nick's famous Dixieland bar in Greenwich Village, in concerts at Carnegie Hall, and on network radio broadcasts. He played the clarinet in short staccato bursts and was perilously spontaneous, winding around in his solos like a maze. In the 1960s, when jazz was freeing its forms and exploring new modalities, he was discovered by a younger audience. He played with Thelonious Monk at the Newport Jazz Festival in 1963, fronted a pianoless quartet, and recorded with a large orchestra (*The Spirit of '67* in 1967). Coleman Hawkins, his colleague for more than 40 years, said, 'He's always been way out, but they didn't have a name for it then'. >> Beiderbecke; Ellington; Hawkins, Coleman; Monk, Thelonious

Russell, William, Lord (1639–83) English Whig politician. He studied at Cambridge, travelled in Europe, and at the Restoration became an MP. A supporter of Shaftesbury, and a leading member of the movement to exclude James II from the succession, he was arrested with others for participation in the Rye House Plot (1683), found guilty by a packed jury, and beheaded. >> Ketch; James II (of England)

Russell, Sir William Howard (1821–1907) War correspondent and writer, born near Tallaght, Co Dublin, Ireland. He studied at Trinity College, Dublin, joined *The Times* (1843), and was called to the bar in 1850, but never practised. From the Crimea (1854–5) he wrote the famous despatches (collected 1856) which opened the eyes of the British to the sufferings of the soldiers. Among his other assignments were the Indian Mutiny (1858), the American Civil War (1861), and the Austro-Prussian War (1866). He established the *Army and Navy Gazette* (1860), and wrote several books, including a novel, *The Adventures of Dr Brady* (1868), *Hesperothen* (1882), and *A Visit to Chile* (1890).

Russell (of Thornhaugh), William Russell, Baron (c. 1558–1613) English statesman. He became Governor of Flushing (1587–8), and Lord Deputy of Ireland (1594–7). His experience of lowland drainage methods while in the former post led him to initiate reclamation work in the Cambridgeshire fens. >> Russell, Francis

Russell, Willy, popular name of **William Martin Russell** (1947–) Playwright, born in Whiston, Lancashire, NW England, UK. He gained popularity with his cheerful but sharp portrayal of Liverpudlian life in such comedies as *Stags and Hens* (1978) and such musicals as *John, Paul, George, Ringo and Bert* (1974). Among his best-known plays are *Educating Rita* (1979), *Blood Brothers* (1983), and *Shirley Valentine* (1986).

Rust, Mathias (1968–) German aviator. He achieved worldwide fame in May 1987 when he landed his light aircraft in Red Square in the heart of Moscow, having been undetected on a flight from Finland. His exploit led to the immediate dismissal of defence minister, Marshal Sergei Sokolov. Rust was sentenced to four years' imprisonment, but was released in August 1988 and flown home as a goodwill humanitarian gesture by the Gorbachev administration. >> Gorbachev

Rustin, Bayard (1910–87) Institute head and civil rights activist, born in West Chester, PA. He studied at colleges in Cheyney State, PA, and Wilberforce, OH, joined the Young Communist League (1936), and became an organizer (1938). In 1941 he left the Communist Party and joined the Fellowship of Reconciliation, a non-violent anti-war group. He served several jail terms for conscientious objection during World War 2, for demonstrating in the American Indian independence movement, and for participating in a North Carolina 'freedom ride' (1947). In 1955 he joined the Southern Christian Leadership Conference as Martin Luther King's special assistant, serving as the organizational co-ordinator for the March on Washington in 1963. He then became executive director of the newly founded A Philip Randolph Institute (1964–87). >> King, Martin Luther

Rutebeuf [rütuhboef] (c. 1245–c. 1285) French poet, whose name may have been a pseudonym. He was the author of the semi-liturgical drama, *Miracle de Théophile* (c.1260, a prototype of the Faust story), a monologue by a quack doctor (the *Dit de L'Herberie*), and humorous verse stories (*faibliaux*).

Ruth Biblical character described in the Book of Ruth as a woman from Moab who, after the death of her husband, refused to abandon her widowed mother-in-law Naomi, accompanying her back to Naomi's home town of Bethlehem. Her loyalty was rewarded when Naomi managed to arrange Ruth's marriage to Boaz, a wealthy kinsman of Naomi's deceased husband, and their son was said to be the grandfather of David. >> David

Ruth, Babe, popular name of **George Herman Ruth**, nicknames **the Babe**, **the Bambino**, **the Sultan of Swat** (1895–1948) Baseball player, born in Baltimore, MD. He started his career as a pitcher with the Boston Red Sox in 1914, joined the New York Yankees in 1920, and hit a record 54 home runs in that season. He bettered the record to 60 in 1927, a figure which stood until 1961. In the 1926 World Series he became the first man to hit three home runs in one game. When he retired in 1935 he had hit 714 home runs, a figure not bettered until 1974. Yankee Stadium is affectionately known as 'The House that Ruth Built' because of the increased income he brought to the club during his career. *The Babe Ruth Story* was filmed in 1948, and *The Babe* in 1991.

Rutherford (of Nelson), Ernest Rutherford, 1st Baron (1871–1937) Physicist, a pioneer of subatomic physics, born near Nelson, New Zealand. He studied at Christchurch University, moved to Cambridge (1895), and in 1898 became professor of physics at McGill, Canada, where with Frederick Soddy he proposed that radioactivity results from the disintegration of atoms (1903). In 1907 he became professor at Manchester, developing the modern conception of the atom. In 1919 he became professor at Cambridge and director of the Cavendish Laboratory. He received the Nobel Prize for Chemistry in 1908, was knighted in 1914, and made a peer in 1931. >> Chadwick, James; Moseley, Henry Gwyn Jeffreys; Soddy

Rutherford, Dame Margaret (1892–1972) Theatre and film actress, born in London, England, UK. She made her stage debut in 1925 at the Old Vic theatre, and gained fame as a character actress and comedienne, her gallery of eccentrics including 'Miss Prism' in *The Importance of Being Earnest* (stage 1939, film 1952) and 'Miss Whitchurch' in *The Happiest Days of Your Life* (stage 1948, film 1950). She also scored a success as Agatha Christie's 'Miss Marple' in a series of films from 1962. She won an Oscar for her role in *The VIPs* in 1964, and was created a dame in 1967.

Ruthven, William, 1st Earl of Gowrie (c. 1541–84) Scottish nobleman, created Earl of Gowrie in 1581. He was involved in the murder of David Rizzio (1566), and later was the custodian of Mary, Queen of Scots, during her captivity at Loch Leven (1567–8). In 1582 he kidnapped the boy king, James VI, taking him to Castle Ruthven near Perth, for which he was first pardoned and then ordered to leave the country, but was beheaded at Stirling for his part in a conspiracy to take Stirling Castle. >> James I (of England); Mary, Queen of Scots; Rizzio

Ruysdael, Jacob van [roysdahl], also spelled **Ruisdael** (c.1628–82) Landscape painter, born in Haarlem, The Netherlands. He became a member of the Haarlem painters' guild (1648), and moved to Amsterdam (c.1657), thereafter travelling in Holland and Germany. His best works are country landscapes, and he also excelled in cloud effects, particularly in his seascapes.

Ruyter, Michiel Adriaanszoon de [royter] (1607–76) Dutch naval commander, born in Flushing, The Netherlands. He went to sea at nine, and by 1635 had become a merchant captain. In the Dutch Wars with England he had considerable success as a naval commander, defeating the English in the 'Four Days' Battle' off Dunkirk (1666), and destroying much of the English fleet at Medway (1667), and the larger Anglo-French fleets at Solebay (1672) and off Ostend and Kijkduin (1673), thus preventing an English invasion of the Dutch Republic. In 1675 he sailed for the Mediterranean to help the Spaniards against the French, but was mortally wounded in a battle in the Bay of Catania, off Sicily. >> Duquesne

Ružička, Leopold (Stephen) (1887–1976) Chemist, born in Vukovar, Croatia. He became professor of chemistry at Utrecht (1926) and at Zürich (1929). He made the earliest synthesis of musk, worked on higher terpenes and steroids, and was the first to synthesize sex hormones, for which he shared the Nobel Prize for Chemistry in 1939. >> RR1123

Ryan, Desmond (1893–1964) Socialist and historian, born in London, England, UK, the son of William Patrick Ryan. Educated at Patrick Pearse's school, St Enda's, he became Pearse's secretary, and wrote studies of Pearse and James Connolly. He supported the Anglo–Irish treaty, but left in disgust at the Civil War, and wrote novels in London, including *Invisible Army* (1932) and *St Eustace and the Albatross* (1934). He returned to Dublin in the 1940s, produced *The Rising* (1946), and became editor of *Devoy's Post Bag* (1948, 1953). >> Pearse; Ryan, William Patrick

Ryan, Elizabeth (1892–1979) Tennis player, born in Anaheim, CA. She won 19 Wimbledon titles (12 doubles and seven mixed doubles), a record which stood from 1934 until 1979, when it was surpassed by Billie Jean King. Six of her women's doubles titles were with Suzanne Lenglen. >> King, Billie Jean; Lenglen; RR1173

Ryan, Meg (1963–) Film actress, born in Fairfield, CN. After roles on stage and in television soaps, she appeared in *Top Gun* (1985), and became well known for her performance in *When Harry Met Sally* (1989). Later films include *The Doors* (1991), *Sleepless in Seattle* (1993), *French Kiss* (1995), which she also co-produced, and *Addicted to Love* (1997).

Ryan, (Lynn) Nolan (1947–) Baseball player, born in Refugio, TX. He is regarded as one of the fastest pitchers ever seen in major league baseball, one of his pitches being timed at 162·3 kph/100·9 mph. He started his career with the New York Mets in 1966, then played for the California

Angels, the Houston Astros and in 1993 was with the Texas Rangers until his retirement at the end of the season. He has compiled more strikeouts (5668 to April 1993) and no-hitters (seven) than any player in baseball history. His season total of 383 strikeouts in 1973 is an all-time record.

Ryan, William Patrick, also known as **Liam P O Riain** and **W P O'Ryan** (1867–1942) Journalist and historian, born in Templemore, Co Tipperary, Ireland. He worked in London as a journalist, but returned to Ireland to edit the *Irish Peasant* and other journals (1906–11), before going back to London as assistant editor of the *Daily Herald*. His contemporary histories include *The Irish Literary Revival* (1894) and *The Irish Labour Movement* (1919). In later life he wrote in Irish, his works including a study of European contributions to Gaelic scholarship, *Gaelachas i Gléin* (1933). >> Ryan, Desmond

Rydberg, Johannes Robert [rŭdberg] (1854–1919) Physicist, born in Halmstad, Sweden. He studied at the University of Lund, and became a lecturer there (1882), then professor (1901–19). Best known for his theoretical studies of spectral series, he developed a formula for spectral lines, incorporating the *Rydberg constant*, named after him.

Ryder, Albert (Pinkham) (1847–1917) Romantic painter, born in the whaling town of New Bedford, MA, and always deeply attached to the sea. He worked slowly, producing only 165 pictures in a personal but richly imaginative style, as in 'Siegfried and the Rhine Maidens' (1888–91, National Gallery of Art, Washington, DC).

Ryder, Samuel (1859–1936) Businessman, born in Cheshire, NWC England, UK, the son of a nurseryman. He built up a prosperous business in St Albans, mainly through selling penny packets of seeds. In 1927 he donated the *Ryder Cup*, the trophy of the international golf match known by the same name, played by professional teams of British (now European) and American golfers.

Ryder (of Warsaw), Sue Ryder, Baroness (1923–) Philanthropist, born in Leeds, West Yorkshire, N England, UK. Educated at Benenden School in Kent, she nursed in occupied Europe in World War 2. As a result of her experiences there, she established the Sue Ryder Foundation, begun at Cavendish, Suffolk, in 1953, which now comprises 80 centres worldwide, offering residential care for the sick and disabled. In some countries projects function under the auspices of the Ryder–Cheshire Foundation, which linked her work with that of her husband, Leonard Cheshire. She was created a life peer in 1979. >> Cheshire

Ryder, Winona [winohna] (1971–) Film actress, born in Winona, MI. She attended the American Conservatory Theatre in San Francisco, and made her film debut in *Lucas* (1986), and went on to star in *Beetlejuice* (1988), *Heathers* (1989), *Edward Scissorhands* (1990), and *Mermaids* (1990). She received a Best Supporting Actress Oscar nomination for *The Age of Innocence* (1993), and a Best Actress nomination for her role as Jo in *Little Women* (1995). Other films include *Looking For Richard* (1996) and *The Crucible* (1996).

Rykov, Alexey Ivanovich [reekof] (1881–1938) Russian revolutionary and politician, born in Saratov, Russia. He studied at Kazan University. He helped organize the October Revolution in Petrograd, and was appointed People's Commissar for Internal Affairs in the first Soviet government. He held a number of senior government and party posts (1919–37), becoming a member of the Politburo (1919–29). In 1928, with Bukharin and others, he led the 'right opposition' against Stalin's economic policies. In 1937 he was arrested for alleged anti-Party activities, and shot some months later. >> Bukharin

Rylands, John (1801–88) Textile manufacturer and merchant, born in St Helens, Merseyside, NW England, UK. In 1899 his widow established the John Rylands Library in Manchester.

Ryle, Gilbert (1900–76) Philosopher, born in Brighton, East Sussex, SE England, UK. He studied at Brighton and Oxford, where he was a tutor, served in World War 2, then became professor of metaphysical philosophy at Oxford (1945–68) and editor of *Mind* (1947–71). He was an influential defender of linguistic or 'ordinary language' philosophy, and is best known for his book *The Concept of Mind* (1949), which argued against the mind/body dualism ('the ghost in the machine') proposed by Descartes. >> Descartes; Ryle, Martin

Ryle, Sir Martin (1918–84) Radio astronomer, born in Brighton, East Sussex, SE England, UK, the nephew of Gilbert Ryle. He studied at Oxford, and worked from 1945 on radio physics at the Cavendish Laboratory, Cambridge, becoming professor of radio astronomy (1959–82). His development of interferometers for radio astronomy enabled him to survey the most distant radio sources. In 1961 he challenged the generally accepted steady-state theory of the universe, and paved the way for renewed interest in the expanding-universe theory. He was knighted in 1966, appointed astronomer royal in 1972, and shared the Nobel Prize for Physics in 1974 with his former pupil, Antony Hewish. >> Hewish; Ryle, Gilbert

Rymer, Thomas (1641–1713) Critic and historian, born in Northallerton, North Yorkshire, N England, UK. He studied at Cambridge and entered Gray's Inn in 1666. He published translations, critical discussions on poetry, dramas, and works on history, and in 1692 was appointed royal historiographer. His critical works include *The Tragedies of the Last Age Consider'd* (1678) and *A Short View of Tragedy* (1693). He is chiefly remembered as the compiler of the collection of historical materials known as the *Foedera* (20 vols, 1704–35).

Rysbrack, John Michael [riysbrak] (c.1694–1770) Sculptor, born in Antwerp, Belgium. He settled in London in 1720. Among his works are the monument to Sir Isaac Newton in Westminster Abbey (1731), statues of William III, Queen Anne, and George II, and busts of Gay, Rowe, Pope, Sir Robert Walpole, and others.

Ryun, Jim [riyuhn], popular name of **James Ryun** (1947–) Athlete, born in Wichita, KS. In 1966, while still in his teens, he set a world record time of 3 min 51·3 s for the mile. The following year he established a world record in the 1500 m, clocking 3 min 33·1 s. Never as successful in top-class competition as he was against the clock, he failed to take the gold medal at the Olympic Games of 1964, 1968, and 1972. He turned professional shortly after the 1972 Games.

Ryzhkov, Nikolay Ivanovich [rushkof] (1929–) Soviet statesman and prime minister (1985–90), born in the Urals, Russia. He studied at the Urals Polytechnic in Yekaterinburg (formerly, Sverdlovsk), and worked his way up to become head of the Uralmash engineering conglomerate, the largest industrial enterprise in the Soviet Union. A member of the Communist Party of the Soviet Union from 1956, he was brought to Moscow in 1975 as first deputy minister for heavy transport and machine building. He was the first deputy chairman of Gosplan (1979), and became head of economic affairs (1982). Brought into the Politburo by Gorbachev as chairman of the Council of Ministers in 1985, he suffered a heart attack in 1990, and was replaced. >> Gorbachev

Saadi >> **Sadi**

Saarinen, Eero (1910–61) Architect and furniture designer, born in Kirkkonummi, Finland. He went to the USA in 1923 with his architect father Eliel Saarinen, then studied sculpture in Paris (1929–30) and architecture at Yale (1930–4). He became a US citizen in 1940. His designs for Expressionist modern buildings include the Trans-World Airlines Kennedy Terminal, New York City (1956–62). >> Eames; Saarinen, Eliel

Saarinen, (Gottlieb) Eliel (1873–1950) Architect, born in Rantasalmi, Finland. The leading architect in his native country, he designed the Helsinki railway station (1904–14), and in 1923 emigrated to the USA. He designed the buildings for the Cranbrook Academy of Art, near Detroit, becoming its president (1932–48). An opponent of skyscrapers, he formed a partnership with his son, Eero Saarinen, and designed many churches, including the Christ Lutheran Church in Minneapolis. >> Saarinen, Eero

Saatchi & Saatchi [sahchee] Advertisers: **Charles Saatchi** (1943–) and **Maurice Saatchi** (1946–), born in Iraq. They immigrated to England with their father in 1947, and set up their advertising agency in 1970. They quickly gained fame with advertisements such as a pregnant man to promote contraception, and were engaged by the Conservative Party in 1978 to create election posters and slogans. They bought out three US agencies in the 1980s to become the world's largest agency, but suffered badly in the stock market crash at the end of the decade. In 1995, following a controversial share option package, chairman Maurice Saatchi left the company, and set up a new agency.

Sabatier, Paul [sabatyay] (1854–1941) Chemist, born in Carcassonne, France. He studied at the Ecole Normale Supérieure and the Collège de France, and became professor (1884–1905) and dean (1905–30) at Toulouse. He did notable work in catalysis, discovering processes important for the margarine, oil hydrogenation, and synthetic methanol industries, and shared the 1912 Nobel Prize for Chemistry. >> RR1123

Sabatini, Rafael [sabateenee] (1875–1950) Writer, born in Jesi, Italy. Writing in English, he first made his name as an author of historical romances with *The Tavern Knight* (1904). He settled in England, UK in 1905, and wrote many tales, including *The Sea Hawk* (1915), *Scaramouche* (1921), and *Captain Blood* (1922), as well as historical biographies and a study of Torquemada (1913).

Sabin, A(lbert) B(ruce) [saybin] (1906–93) Microbiologist, born in Białystok, Poland. He moved to the USA in 1921, and became a US citizen in 1930. He studied at New York University, then held a research post at the Rockefeller Institute, New York City, and became professor of research paediatrics at the University of Cincinatti (1946–60, then emeritus). He later held research consultancy posts at the University of South Carolina (1974–82) and the Fogarty International Center, MD (1984–6). He is best known for his research into a live virus as a polio vaccine, which works by causing a harmless infection of the intestinal tract, stimulating immunity to natural infection without causing disease. This replaced the Salk vaccine, as it gives longer-lasting immunity, and may be given orally. >> Salk

Sabine, Sir Edward [sabin] (1788–1883) Physicist, astronomer, and explorer, born in Dublin. He studied at Marlow and the Royal Military Academy at Woolwich, was commissioned in the Royal Artillery, and served until 1877, retiring as a general. He was appointed astronomer on John Ross's expedition to find the Northwest Passage (1818) and on Parry's Arctic expedition (1819–20). He conducted valuable pendulum experiments to determine the shape of the Earth at Spitzbergen and in tropical Africa (1821–3), and devoted the rest of his life to work on terrestrial magnetism, discovering a relationship between sunspots and magnetic disturbances on Earth. >> Parry, William Edward; Ross, Sir John

Sabine, Wallace Clement (Ware) [sabin] (1868–1919) Physicist, the founder of architectural acoustics, born in Richwood, OH. He studied at Ohio State University, then taught at Harvard, where he worked for the rest of his life. A specialist in the acoustic problems of buildings, by 1898 he had devised the *Sabine law*, that the product of the reverberation time multiplied by the total absorptivity of the room is proportional to the volume of the room. He advised on the projected new Boston Symphony Hall (1898–1900), and became much in demand to advise on architectural acoustics.

Sacchi, Andrea [sachee] (1599–1661) Painter, born in Netturo, near Rome. A pupil of Francesco Albani, he upheld the Classical tradition in Roman painting. His works include 'The Vision of St Romuald' (1640, Vatican) and 'Miracle of Saint Gregory' (1625–7, Vatican), painted for Pope Urban VIII, and religious works in many Roman churches. >> Albani

Sacco and Vanzetti [sakoh, vanzetee] **Nicola Sacco** (1891–1927) and **Bartolomeo Vanzetti** (1888–1927) Political radicals, the chief figures in an American *cause célèbre* which had worldwide reverberations. Accused of a payroll murder and robbery in Massachusetts in 1920, they were found guilty, and seven years later were executed in spite of conflicting and circumstantial evidence, and the confession of another man to the crime. Both had been anarchists, and the suspicion that this had provoked deliberate injustice aroused an international outcry.

Sacher-Masoch, Leopold von [zahkher mahzokh] (1836–95) Lawyer and writer, born in Lemberg, Austria. He wrote many short stories and novels, including *Der Don Juan von Kolomea* (1866), depicting the life of small-town Polish Jews. The term *masochism* was coined for the form of eroticism he describes in his later works.

Sacheverell, Henry [sasheverel] (c. 1674–1724) Political preacher, born in Marlborough, Wiltshire, S England, UK. He studied at Oxford, and began to preach sermons attacking Whigs, moderate Tories, and dissenters. In 1709 he delivered a sermon at St Paul's, attacking the Whig minister, Godolphin, with such rancour that Sacheverell was impeached before the House of Lords (1710), found guilty, and suspended from preaching for three years. The Godolphin ministry fell that same summer, and in 1713 he was selected by the House of Commons to preach the Restoration sermon. >> Godolphin

Sacheverell, William [sasheverel] (1638–91) English politician, sometimes called the 'First Whig'. He studied law, and entered the House of Commons as member for Derbyshire (1670). He became one of the leaders of the anti-Court party, instrumental in framing the Test Act, which overthrew Charles II's Cabal ministry. Defeated in the 1685 election, he sat in the Convention parliament of 1689 which offered the throne to William III. >> Charles II (of England)

Sachs, Hans [zahkhs] (1494–1576) Poet, playwright, and composer, born in Nuremberg, Germany. He was trained as a shoemaker, and travelled through Germany (1511–16) practising his craft and frequenting the schools of the *Meistersinger* ('mastersingers', professional songwriters). He wrote over 6300 pieces, some celebrating the Reformation, others dealing with common life and manners in a vigorous, humorous style. His life and work were celebrated by Wagner in his opera dedicated to Sachs, *Die Meistersinger von Nürnberg* (1868, The Meistersinger of Nuremberg). >> Wagner, (Wilhelm) Richard

Sachs, (Ferdinand Gustav) Julius von (1832–97) Botanist, born in Wrocław, Poland (formerly Breslau, Germany). He studied at the University of Prague, became botany lecturer at an agricultural college near Bonn, and professor of botany at Würzburg from 1698. There he carried out important experiments, especially on the influence of light and heat upon plants, and the organic activities of vegetable growth. He exerted widespread influence through his *Lehrbuch der Botanik* (1868) and its English translation, *Textbook of Botany* (1875).

Sachs, Nelly (Leonie) [zahkhs] (1891–1970) Poet and playwright, born in Berlin. Of Jewish descent, she fled from Nazi Germany in 1940, settled in Stockholm, and took Swedish nationality. Her best-known play is *Eli: ein Mysterienspiel vom Leiden Israels* (1951, Eli: a Mystery Play of the Sufferings of Israel). She shared the Nobel Prize for Literature in 1966. >> RR1123

Sacks, Oliver (Wolf) (1933–) Neurologist, born in London, UK. Educated at Oxford, he trained as a doctor at Middlesex Hospital, London, then studied neurology at the University of California, Los Angeles. After taking up an appointment in New York City, he worked with a group of patients who had contracted a form of sleeping sickness, and became internationally known following his account of the tragically brief cure they experienced after receiving treatment with L-dopa, *Awakenings* (1973; filmed, 1990). His insights into unusual syndromes, along with an appealing literary style, resulted in a series of bestselling books, such as *The Man who Mistook his Wife for a Hat* (1986) and *Anthropologist on Mars* (1995).

Sackville, Thomas, 1st Earl of Dorset (1536–1608) English statesman and poet, born in Buckhurst, Sussex, England, UK. He became a lawyer and entered parliament (1558), then collaborated with Thomas Norton (1532–84) in the tragedy *Gorboduc* (1561), the first English play in blank verse. Knighted in 1567, he later became a diplomat in Europe, Lord High Treasurer (1599), and an earl (1604).

Sackville-West, Vita, popular name of **Victoria Mary Sackville-West** (1892–1962) Poet and novelist, born at Knole, Kent, SE England, UK. Educated privately, she started writing as a child. Her work expresses her closeness to the countryside where she lived, notably in the long poem, 'The Land' (1926). Her best-known novels are *The Edwardians* (1930) and *All Passion Spent* (1931). In 1913 she married diplomat and critic Harold Nicolson, a marriage which endured despite their homosexual affairs. *Passenger to Teheran* (1926) records their years in Persia. Her friendship with Virginia Woolf occasioned the latter's *Orlando* (1928). She wrote a weekly gardening column for *The Observer* for many years. >> Nicolson; Woolf, Virginia

Sadam Husain >> Hussein, Saddam

Sadat, (Mohammed) Anwar el- [sadat] (1918–81) Egyptian statesman and president (1970–81), born in the Tala district, Egypt. He trained for the army in Cairo, and in 1952 was a member of the coup deposing King Farouk. After becoming president, he temporarily assumed the post of prime minister (1973–4), after which he sought settlement of the conflict with Israel. He met the Israeli premier in Jerusalem (1977) and at Camp David, USA, in 1978, and the same year he and Begin were jointly awarded the Nobel Peace Prize. Following criticism by other Arab statesmen and hard-line Muslims, he was assassinated in Cairo by extremists. >> Begin; Farouk I; RR1046

Saddam Hussein >> Hussein, Saddam

Sade, Marquis de [sahd], popular name of **Donatien Alphonse François, comte** (Count) **de Sade** (1740–1814) Writer, born in Paris. He studied at Paris, served in the army, and was in 1772 condemned to death at Aix for his cruelty and sexual perversions. He escaped, but was later imprisoned at Vincennes (1777) and in the Bastille (1784), where he wrote *Les 120 Journées de Sodome* (c.1784, The 120 Days of Sodom). After his release (1790), he wrote the licentious novels *Justine* (1791), *La Philosophie dans le boudoir* (1795, Philosophy in the Bedroom), and *Juliette* (1797). He died insane, his name providing the language with the word *sadism*.

Sadi or **Saadi**, assumed name of **Sheikh Muslih Addin** (c. 1184–?1292) Poet, born in Iran. He studied at Baghdad, travelled much, and was taken prisoner by the Crusaders near Jerusalem, but was ransomed by a merchant of Aleppo, who gave him his daughter in marriage. The catalogue of his works comprises 22 different kinds of writings in prose and verse. The most celebrated are a series of moral and religious works, *Gulistan* (Rose Garden), *Bostan* (Orchard Garden), and *Pend-Nameh* (Book of Instructions).

Sadler, Sir Michael Ernest (1861–1943) Pioneer of secondary education, born in Barnsley, South Yorkshire, N England, UK. He studied at Oxford, and was secretary of the Oxford University Extension (1885–95) and steward of Christ Church, Oxford (1886–95). In 1895 he joined the government Education Department as Director of Special Inquiries and Reports, forming a powerful research bureau that was internationally known. He became Vice-Chancellor of the University of Leeds (1911–17, 1919–23), and transformed the university from a little-known college to a major institution. He also served as Master of University College, Oxford (1923–34). He was knighted in 1919.

Sadler, Michael Thomas (1780–1835) Factory reformer, born in Snelston, Derbyshire, C England, UK. An importer of Irish linen in Leeds, he sat as a Tory MP (1829–32) and wrote copiously on Irish social questions. He was a leader of the factory reform movement, and promoted the Factory Act of 1833, which reduced the working-hours in textile mills for children and young people.

Saenredam, Pieter Jansz(oon) [sanredam] (1597–1665) Painter, born in Assendelft, The Netherlands. The son of an engraver, he trained in Haarlem, and may have been inspired by Jacob van Campen's architectural drawings. He is the acknowledged master of paintings of church interiors. Unlike previous architectural paintings, his works are precisely drawn images of known and identifiable churches, such as 'View in the Nieuwe Kerk at Haarlem' (1652, Haarlem). >> Campen

Safire, William [safiyr] (1929–) Journalist, born in New York City. A former public relations writer, and a speechwriter and special assistant to President Nixon, he became a Washington-based columnist for the *New York Times* in 1973. He won the Pulitzer Prize for commentary in 1978, and went on to become a national figure known for his weekly column devoted to language matters. >> Nixon

Sagan, Carl (Edward) [saygn] (1934–96) Astronomer and writer, born in New York City. He studied at the universities of Chicago and California (Berkeley), taught at Berkeley, Stanford, Harvard, and the Smithsonian Institute, and became professor of astronomy and space science at Cornell (1970). He worked on the physics and chemistry of planetary atmospheres and surfaces, and investigated the origin of life on Earth and the possibility of extraterrestrial life. Through such books as *Cosmic Connection* (1973) and a television programme, *Cosmos*, he did much to popularize this aspect of science.

Sagan, Françoise [sagã], pseudonym of **Françoise Quoirez** (1935–) Novelist, born in Paris. Educated privately, at the age of 18 she wrote, in only four weeks, the best-selling *Bonjour tristesse* (1954, Good Morning Sadness), followed by *Un Certain Sourire* (1956, A Certain Smile). Both novels are direct testaments of adolescent wisdom and precocity, written with the economy of a remarkable literary style. Her many later novels, including *Aimez-vous Brahms?* (1959, Do You Like Brahms?, filmed in 1961 as *Goodbye Again*), have had a mixed critical reception. She has also written several plays, and a ballet, *La Chamade* (1966). In 1993 appeared *Oeuvres*, a volume of collected works.

Saha, Meghnad (1894–1956) Astrophysicist, born near Dacca, India. He studied at Presidency College, Calcutta, visited Europe on a travelling scholarship, became professor at Allahabad University (1923), and was elected a fellow of the Royal Society in 1927. He worked on the thermal ionization that occurs in the extremely hot atmosphere of stars, and in 1920 demonstrated that elements in stars are ionized in proportion to their temperature, as defined in *Saha's equation*. In 1938 he was appointed professor of physics at Calcutta, where he was instrumental in the creation of the Calcutta Institute of Nuclear Physics.

Sahlins, Marshall David (1930–) Cultural anthropologist, born in Chicago, IL. He studied at Michigan and Columbia universities, and became professor of anthropology at Michigan in 1964, and later professor at Chicago. He has made major contributions in the field of Oceanic ethnography, cultural evolution, economic anthropology, and the analysis of symbolism. In his early work, such as *Evolution and Culture* (1960), he presented a materialist and progressivist view of cultural evolution. In *Culture and Practical Reason* (1976), he inverts this perspective, insisting on the autonomy of cultural systems.

Said, Edward W(adi) [saeed] (1935–) Writer and political commentator, born in Jerusalem, Israel. He studied at Cairo, Princeton, and Harvard universities, then joined the English department at Columbia. He has become one of the major Palestinian spokesmen in the debate on the future of the Middle East, and took part in the 1988 gathering that declared the existence of an independent Palestinian state.

Sailer, Toni (Anton) [ziyler] (1935–) Alpine skier, born in Kitzbühel, Austria. In 1956, he became the first man to win all three Olympic skiing titles (downhill, slalom, giant slalom). He was the world combined champion (1956, 1958) and the world downhill and giant slalom champion (1958). He later became an actor and singer, a hotel owner, and an investor in a textile business.

Sainsbury (of Drury Lane), Alan John Sainsbury, Baron [saynzbree] (1902–) Retailer, born in London, England, UK. Educated at Haileybury, in 1921 he joined the family grocery business, founded by his grandparents. He became chairman (1956–67), and since then has been joint president of J Sainsbury plc with his younger brother, **Sir Robert** (1906–). He was created a life peer in 1962. His elder son, **Sir John Davan** (1927–), has been chairman of the company since 1969. Sir Robert's son, **David John** (1940–), became deputy chairman in 1988.

Saint, Eva Marie (1924–) Film actress, born in Newark, NJ. She studied at the University of Ohio, and had done a little work on radio, television, and Broadway before Elia Kazan cast her in *On the Waterfront* (1954), for which she won a Best Supporting Actress Oscar. Other films include

North by Northwest (1959), *Exodus* (1960), *Loving* (1970), and *The Last Days of Patton* (1986). >> Kazan

Saint-Denis, Michel (Jacques Duchesne) [sī duhnee] (1897–1971) Theatre director, actor, and teacher, born in Beauvais, France. In 1931 he founded the Compagnie des Quinze, and directed numerous influential productions. When this company disbanded, he settled in England, founding with George Devine and others the London Theatre Studio (1936). His influence on British theatre continued with his work for the Old Vic (1947–52) and later with the Royal Shakespeare Company, where he became a director in 1962. He was appointed director of the Comédie de l'Est in 1952. >> Devine

Saint Denis, Ruth, originally **Ruth Dennis** (1879–1968) Dancer, director, choreographer, and teacher, born in Somerville, NJ. She formed the *Denishawn* partnership with Ted Shawn, and became known, first in Europe, for exotic, colourful, Eastern dances such as *Rhada* (1906). She married Shawn in 1914, and founded a school and company with him in 1915, which was frequented by many Hollywood stars. Fusing all manner of dance forms together, the company toured the USA until it folded in 1931, when the couple separated. She continued to dance into her 80s. >> Shawn

Sainte-Beuve, Charles Augustin [sīt boev] (1804–69) Literary critic, born in Boulogne, France. He studied at Paris, trained in medicine, then turned to writing. He produced several volumes of poetry, and in the *Revue de Paris* (1829) began his *Causeries*, longer critical articles on French literature. His major works include several books of 'portraits' of literary contemporaries. His single novel, *Volupté*, appeared in 1835. In 1840 he became keeper of the Mazarin Library, and in 1848 professor of French literature at Liège. Nominated a senator in 1865, his speeches in favour of liberty of thought earned him great popularity.

Sainte-Claire Deville, Henri Etienne [sīt klair duhveel] (1818–81) Chemist, born in St Thomas, West Indies. He studied medicine in Paris but was soon attracted to chemistry. By 1851 he had become professor of chemistry at the Ecole Normale in Paris, and shortly afterwards professor at the Sorbonne. It was he who first produced aluminium (1855) and platinum in commercial quantities, by reduction of chlorides with sodium metal. His interest in high temperature reactions led to the discovery of reversible changes in relative molecular mass with temperature, which he termed *dissociations*.

Saint-Evremond, Charles Marguetel de Saint Denis, seigneur de (Lord of) [sīt ayvruhmõ] (1610–1703) Writer and wit, born in St Denis le Gast, France. He fought at Rocroi, Freiburg, and Nördlingen, was steadily loyal throughout the Frondes, but in 1661 fled by way of Holland to England on the discovery of his witty and sarcastic letter to François de Bonne Créqui (?1624–89) on the Peace of the Pyrenees. Warmly received by Charles II, he spent most of the rest of his life in London, delighting the world with his wit. His works include the satire, *La Comédie des académistes* (1644).

Saint-Exupéry, Antoine (Marie Roger) de [sīt egzüpayree] (1900–44) Airman and writer, born in Lyon, France. A commercial and wartime pilot, his philosophy of 'heroic action' is found in such novels as *Vol de nuit* (1931, Night Flight). He is also known for his popular children's fable for adults, *Le Petit Prince* (1943, The Little Prince). He was declared missing after a flight to North Africa in World War 2.

Saint-Gaudens, Augustus [saynt gawdnz] (1848–1907) Sculptor, born in Dublin. Taken to the USA as a baby, he was trained as a cameo-cutter, then studied sculpture in Paris and Rome, where he was influenced by the Italian Renaissance. He returned to the USA in 1873, and became the foremost and most honoured sculptor of his time. His major works include Lincoln in Lincoln Park, Chicago, and the Mrs Henry Adams Memorial in Rock Creek Cemetery, Washington, DC.

Saint John, Henry >> Bolingbroke, 1st Viscount

Saint-John Perse, pseudonym of **Marie René Auguste Alexis Saint-Léger Léger** (1887–1975) Poet and diplomat, born in St Léger des Feuilles, Guadeloupe. He studied at Bordeaux, and after many adventures entered the French foreign ministry (1904). He became secretary-general (1933), was dismissed, and deprived of French citizenship by the Vichy government (1940), and fled to the USA, where he became a consultant on French literature in the Library of Congress. The best known of his earlier works is the long poem *Anabase* (1924). Later works include *Exile* (1942), *Pluies* (1944), *Amers* (1957) and *Chroniques* (1960). He was awarded the Nobel Prize for Literature in 1960.

Saint Joseph, John Kenneth Sinclair (1912–94) Aerial photographer and archaeologist, born in Hereford and Worcester, WC England, UK. He studied at Cambridge, and was successively curator, director, and professor of aerial photographic studies there (1948–80). Trained as a geologist, he became involved in the development of a unique university department with its own aircraft, pilot, and servicing facilities, establishing a valuable photographic archive. The often spectacular results were published in the *Journal of Roman Studies* (1951–77), the journal *Antiquity* (1964–80), and in a sequence of books.

Saint-Just, Louis (Antoine Léon Florelle) de [sī zhüst] (1767–94) French revolutionary, born in Decize, France. He studied at Soissons and Reims, then studied law, and while in Paris began to write poetry and essays, notably *L'Esprit de la révolution* (1791, Spirit of the Revolution). He was elected to the National Convention (1792), attracted notice by his fierce tirades against the king, and as a devoted follower of Robespierre was sent on diplomatic and military missions. He joined the Committee of Public Safety (1793), contributing to the destruction of Danton and Hébert, became president of the Convention (1794), and sponsored the radical Ventôse Laws, redistributing property to the poor. He was guillotined with Robespierre in the Thermidorian Reaction. >> Danton; Hébert; Robespierre

Saint Laurent, Louis (Stephen) [sī lohrã] (1882–1973) Canadian statesman and prime minister (1948–57), born in Compton, Quebec, Canada. He trained as a lawyer in Quebec, and entered the Dominion parliament in 1941 as a Liberal. He was minister of justice and attorney general (1941–6) and minister of external affairs (1946–8). In 1948 he became leader of the Liberal Party and prime minister, but resigned as leader after his Party's defeat in the 1957 election. >> RR1039

Saint-Laurent, Yves (Henri Donat Mathieu) [sī lohrã] (1936–   ) Fashion designer, born in Oran, Algeria. He studied in Paris, graduating in modern languages, and was employed by Dior in 1955 after winning an International Wool Secretariat design competition. On Dior's death in 1957, he took over the house. In 1962 he opened his own house, and launched the first of his 160 Rive Gauche boutiques (1966), selling ready-to-wear clothes, a trend which many other designers were to follow. He also creates costumes for theatre, ballet, and films, and in 1985 was awarded a Best Fashion Designer Oscar. >> Dior

Saint-Léger, Alexis >> Saint-John Perse

Saint Leger, Barry [selinjer, saynt lejer] (1737–89) British army colonel, who fought in the American Revolution. He is best known as the founder of the Classic horse race at Doncaster, South Yorkshire. First run in 1776, it was named after him in 1778 (always with the latter pronunciation). >> RR1160

Saint-Léon, (Charles Victor) Arthur [sī layō] (1821–71) Dancer, choreographer, and violinist, born in Paris. He studied with his father, a ballet master in Stuttgart, before making his debut dancing and playing the violin in Munich at 14. He later danced and staged ballets all over Europe (1845–51), often with and for his wife, the ballerina **Fanny Cerrito** (1817–1909), whom he married in 1845 (separated, 1851). He was ballet master with the St Petersburg Imperial Theatre (1859–69) and Paris Opéra (1863–70). He staged his most famous ballet, *Coppelia*, in 1870.

Saint Martin, Alexis >> Beaumont, William

Saint-Saëns, (Charles) Camille [sī säs] (1835–1921) Composer and music critic, born in Paris. He began to compose at five, and studied at the Paris Conservatoire, writing his first symphony in 1853. He was a distinguished pianist and organist, and in 1871 helped to found the Société Nationale de Musique. He wrote four further symphonies, 13 operas, of which the best known is *Samson et Dalila* (1877), and the popular *Carnaval des animaux* (1886, Carnival of the Animals). He also wrote piano, violin, and cello concertos, church music (including his *Messe solennelle*, 1855), chamber music, and songs.

Saintsbury, George Edward Bateman [saynts bree] (1845–1933) Literary critic and scholar, born in Southampton, Hampshire, S England, UK. He studied at Oxford, and became a schoolmaster (1868–76) before establishing himself as one of the most active critics of the day, contributing to all the major magazines and encyclopedias. Among his books are histories of literature, studies of Dryden, Marlborough, Sir Walter Scott, Matthew Arnold, and Thackeray. From 1895 to 1915 he was professor of rhetoric and English literature at Edinburgh. Later works include *The Peace of the Augustans* (1916), *A History of the French Novel* (1917–19), *Notes on a Cellar-book* (1920), and *Scrapbooks* (1922–4).

Saint-Simon, Claude Henri de Rouvroy, comte de (Count of) [sī seemō] (1760–1825) Social reformer, the founder of French Socialism, born in Paris. He served in the American War of Independence, and during the French Revolution was imprisoned as an aristocrat. Lavish expenditure reduced him to poverty, and he turned to writing. His writing was a reaction against the savagery of the revolutionary period, and proclaimed a brotherhood of man in which science and technology would become a new spiritual authority. His books include *Du système industriel* (1821, On the Industrial System) and *Nouveau christianisme* (1825, New Christianity). In his later years, he relied on family and friends to survive, and lost an eye following an attempted suicide in 1823.

Saint-Simon, Louis de Rouvroy, duc de (Duke of) [sī seemō] (1675–1755) Writer, born in Paris. After some time in the army, he joined the court of Louis XIV, and from the 1690s kept a journal, published as his *Mémoires* (1752), giving impressions and descriptions of court life up to 1723.

Saint Vincent, John Jervis, Earl (1735–1823) British naval commander, born in Stone, Staffordshire, C England, UK. He entered the navy in 1749, and was made a commander after the Quebec expedition of 1759. He fought at Brest (1778) and in the West Indies (1793), and commanded the Mediterranean fleet (1795). In 1797, during preparations for the invasion of England by French, Dutch, and Spanish fleets, he intercepted them off Cape St Vincent and completely defeated them. Created Earl St Vincent, he was forced by ill health to return home in 1799. As First Lord of the Admiralty (1801–4), he made significant reforms, then resumed the Channel command (1806–7).

Sakharov, Andrey [sakarof] (1921–89) Physicist, born in Moscow. He studied in Moscow, joined the nuclear weapons research group (1948), and is usually credited with a critical role in developing the Soviet hydrogen bomb. He became a full member of the Academy of Sciences in 1953. In 1958 he openly opposed nuclear weapon tests, thereafter supporting East–West co-operation and human rights, and in 1975 was awarded the Nobel Peace Prize. Exiled to Nizhni Novgorod (formerly, Gorky) in 1980 as a leading dissident, he lived under poor conditions until released in 1986 and restored to favour. He was elected to the Congress of People's Deputies in 1989. >> Bonner

Saki >> **Munro, H H**

Saladin [saladin], in full **Salah ed-din Yussuf ibn Ayub** (1137–93) Sultan of Egypt and Syria, the leader of the Muslims against the crusaders in Palestine, born in Tekrit, Mesopotamia. He entered the service of Nur ed-din, Emir of Syria, and on his death (1174) proclaimed himself sultan, asserted his authority over Mesopotamia, and received the homage of the Seljuk princes of Asia Minor. His remaining years were occupied in wars with the Christians, whom he defeated near Tiberias in 1187, recapturing almost all their fortified places in Syria. The Third Crusade, headed by the kings of France and England, captured Acre in 1191, and he was defeated. >> Frederick I; Philip II (of France); Richard I

Salam, Abdus (1926–96) Theoretical physicist, born in Jhang Maghhiana, Pakistan. He studied at Punjab University and Cambridge, and became professor of mathematics at the Government College of Lahore and at Punjab University (1951–4). He lectured at Cambridge (1954–6), and became professor of theoretical physics at Imperial College, London (1957), and founder-director of the International Centre of Theoretical Physics in Trieste (1964). In 1979 he shared the Nobel Prize for Physics with Steven Weinberg and Sheldon Glashow. Independently each had produced a theory explaining both the weak nuclear force and electromagnetic interactions between elementary particles; their predictions were confirmed experimentally in the 1970s and 1980s. >> Glashow; Weinberg

Salazar, António de Oliviera [salazah(r)] (1889–1970) Portuguese dictator (1932–68), born near Coimbra, Portugal, where he studied law, and taught economics. In 1928 he became minister of finance, with extensive powers. As premier, he introduced a new, authoritarian regime, the *Estado Novo* ('New State'). He was also minister of war (1936–44) and of foreign affairs (1936–47) during the delicate period of the Spanish Civil War. He retired following a stroke in 1968. >> Soares; RR1082

Salchow, (Karl Emil Julius) Ulrich [salkoh] (1877–1949) Swedish figure skater, born in Copenhagen. The first man to win an Olympic gold medal for this sport (1908), he was a record 10 times world champion (1901–5, 1906–11) and nine times European title holder between 1898 and 1913. He was the originator of a type of jump performed in the free-style element of figure skating, and since named after him.

Saleh, Ali Abdullah [sale] (1942–) North Yemeni soldier and president (1978–90), and president of the Republic of Yemen (1990–). A colonel in the army of the Yemen Arab Republic, he took part in the 1974 coup when Colonel Ibrahim al-Hamadi seized power, with rumours that the monarchy was to be restored. Hamadi was assassinated in 1977 and Colonel Hussein al-Ghashmi took over, only to be killed by a South Yemen terrorist bomb in 1978. Against this background of violence Saleh became president. Under his leadership, the war with South Yemen was ended, and the two countries agreed to eventual re-union. >> RR1099

Sales, Francis of >> **Francis of Sales, St**

Salieri, Antonio [salyayree] (1750–1825) Composer, born in Verona, Italy. He arrived in Vienna at 16, and worked there for the rest of his life, becoming court composer (1774) and *Hofkapellmeister* (1788). He wrote over 40 operas, an oratorio, and Masses, and became a famous rival of Mozart. >> Mozart

Salinger, J(erome) D(avid) [salinjer] (1919–) Novelist and short-story writer, born in New York City. Educated at public schools, he studied for a while at New York and Columbia universities, and after serving in the army in World War 2 devoted himself to writing. He graduated from popular magazines to the *New Yorker*, but his fame rests on *The Catcher in the Rye* (1951), his only and enduringly popular novel (which sells 250 000 copies annually). Its hero plays truant from boarding-school and goes to New York, where he tries in vain to lose his virginity. Written in a slick and slangy first-person narrative, it provoked a hostile response from some critics, but this did not prevent it becoming a college set text. His small collections of short stories include *Franny and Zooey* (1961), and two long short stories, *Raise High the Roof Beam, Carpenters* and *Seymour: an Introduction* (1963). He has become a recluse in his later years, living in New Hampshire, but allowed publication of *Hapworth 16, 1924* (first published in 1965) as a novella in 1997.

Salisbury, Marquess of >> **Cecil, Robert**

Salisbury, Sir Edward James [sawlzbree] (1886–1978) Botanist, born in Harpenden, Hertfordshire, SE England, UK. He studied at University College London, where he became reader in plant ecology (1924–9) and professor of botany (1929–45). He was director of the Royal Botanic Gardens, Kew (1943–56), and wrote *The Reproductive Capacity of Plants* (1942), *Weeds and Aliens* (1966), and *The Living Garden* (1935).

Salisbury, John of >> **John of Salisbury**

Salk, Jonas E(dward) [sawlk] (1914–95) Virologist, discoverer of the first vaccine against poliomyelitis, born in New York City. He studied at New York University College of Medicine, worked on an influenza vaccine at Michigan (1942–4), and later became director of virus research (1947–9) and professor (1949–54) at Pittsburgh. In 1953–4 he prepared inactivated poliomyelitis vaccine, given by injections, which (after some controversy) was successfully tested. He was a founding director of the Salk Institute, CA, in 1975. >> Enders; Sabin

Salle, Jean Baptiste de La >> **La Salle, St Jean Baptiste de**

Sallé, Marie [salay] (1707–56) Dancer, born in Paris. A child performer, the daughter of an acrobat, she appeared in London in pantomime, making her Paris debut in 1718. She first performed with the Paris Opéra in 1727. One of the pioneers of dance without masks or elaborate hairstyles, she also created roles of her own, notably in *Pygmalion* (1733).

Sallinen, Aulis (1935–) Composer, born in Salmi, Finland. He studied at the Sibelius Academy (1955–60), and later taught there (1963–76). His works include four operas – *The Horseman* (1975), *The Red Line* (1978), *The King Goes Forth to France* (1984), and *Kullervo* (for the new Helsinki opera house). He has also written a wide range of orchestral works (including six symphonies), chamber music, concertos, songs, and choral music, all in an eclectic, adventurous but mainly tonal idiom.

Sallust, in full **Gaius Sallustius Crispus** (86–34 BC) Historian and Roman politician, born in Amiternum, Samnium. A tribune in 52 BC, his licentiousness caused his expulsion from the Senate in 50 BC. He was restored to senatorial rank in 47 BC, and he served in the African campaign. His governorship of Numidia (46–44 BC) was sullied by oppression and extortion, the funds from which he used to create the famous Sallustian Gardens. In his retirement he wrote his important histories, the *Bellum Catalinae* (43–42 BC), and the *Bellum Jugurthinum* (41–40 BC).

Salome [sa](loh)mee] (1st-c) The traditional name of the daughter of Herodias. She danced before Herod Antipas (*Mark* 6.17–28), and was offered a reward. At her mother's instigation, she was given the head of John the Baptist. However, the incident is not recorded in the historical account by Josephus. >> Herod Antipas; John the Baptist, St; Josephus

Salote Tupou III [sa**loh**tay] (1900–65) Queen of Tonga, who succeeded her father, King George Tupou II, in 1918. She is remembered in Britain for her colourful and engaging presence during her visit for the coronation of Elizabeth II in 1953. >> Taufa'ahau Tupou IV; RR1093

Saloth Sar >> **Pol Pot**

Salt, Sir Titus (1803–76) Manufacturer and benefactor, born in Morley, West Yorkshire, N England, UK. He was a wool stapler at Bradford, started wool-spinning in 1834, and was the first to manufacture alpaca fabrics in England. Around his factories near Bradford he built the model village of Saltaire (1853). He was Mayor of Bradford (1848), its Liberal MP (1859–61), and he was created a baronet in 1869.

Salten, Felix [**sawl**tn], pseudonym of **Siegmund Salzmann** (1869–1945) Novelist and essayist, born in Budapest. He lived in Vienna, but settled in Switzerland after fleeing from the Nazis. He became a theatre critic, but is known especially for his animal stories, particularly *Bambi* (1929) which, in translation and filmed by Walt Disney, achieved great popularity in America and Britain. He also wrote *Florian, the Emperor's Stallion* (1934) and *Bambi's Children* (1940).

Salvator Rosa >> **Rosa, Salvator**

Salvi, Niccolò or **Nicola** (1697–1751) Sculptor, born in Rome. He trained in architecture and painting, and is noted for his late Roman Baroque masterpiece, the *Fontana di Trevi* (Trevi Fountain), Rome. It was completed in 1762, after his death.

Salviati, Cecchino [salvi**ah**tee, ke**chee**noh], originally **Francesco de' Rossi** (1510–63) Painter, born in Florence, Italy. He was a pupil of Andrea del Sarto and a close friend of Vasari. Around 1530 he entered the service of Cardinal Giovanni Salviati, whose name he adopted. He travelled and worked extensively in Rome, Venice, and Florence. His best frescoes include those in the Palazzo Vecchio, Florence (1544–8), and in the Palazzo Farnese, Rome (1555). One of the major Italian Mannerist painters, his work is characterized by strong colour, complex figure arrangements, and spatial ambiguity. >> Sarto; Vasari

Samson (c.11th-c BC) Biblical character, a legendary hero of the tribe of Dan, purportedly the last of Israel's tribal leaders ('judges') prior to Samuel and the establishment of the monarchy under Saul. Stories (*Jud* 13–16) tell of his great strength, his battles against the Philistines, his 20-year rule, and his fatal infatuation with Delilah. When she cut his hair, breaking his Nazirite vow, he lost his strength, and was held by the Philistines until his hair grew back and he pulled down their temple upon them. >> Saul; Solomon

Samsonov, Alexander [**sam**sonof] (1859–1914) Russian soldier. He commanded a force in the Russo-Japanese War (1904–5), and in World War 1 commanded the army which invaded East Prussia in August 1914. He was decisively defeated by Hindenburg at the Battle of Tannenburg, and committed suicide. >> Hindenburg

Samsova, Galina (1937–) Ballet dancer and director, born in Russia. She studied at the State Ballet School, Kiev,

joined the Kiev Opera House (1956–60), and became principal dancer with the National Ballet of Canada (1961–4), the London Festival Ballet (1964–73), the New London Ballet (1973–8), and Sadlers Wells Royal Ballet (1980–90, also as a teacher). In 1991 she was appointed artistic director of the Scottish Ballet.

Samudragupta [sa**mud**ragupta] (?–c. 380) North Indian emperor with a reputation as a warrior, poet, and musician. He epitomized the ideal king of the golden age of Hindu history.

Samuel (Heb probably 'name of God') (11th-c BC) Biblical character, the last of the judges and first of the prophets, the son of Elkanah and his wife Hannah. He was an Ephraimite who was dedicated to the priesthood as a child by a Nazirite vow. After the defeat of Israel and loss of the Ark of the Covenant to the Philistines, he tried to keep the tribal confederation together, moving in a circuit among Israel's shrines. He presided, apparently reluctantly, over Saul's election as the first king of Israel, but later criticized Saul for assuming priestly prerogatives and disobeying divine instructions given to him. Samuel finally anointed David as Saul's successor, rather than Saul's own son, Jonathan. >> David; Saul

Samuel (of Mt Carmel and Toxteth), Herbert Louis Samuel, 1st Viscount (1870–1963) Liberal statesman and philosophical writer, born in Liverpool, Merseyside, NW England, UK. He studied at Oxford, and was a social worker before he entered parliament in 1902. He held various offices, including that of Chancellor of the Duchy of Lancaster (1909), postmaster-general (1910, 1915), and home secretary (1916, 1931–2). He was also high commissioner for Palestine (1920–5). His philosophical works include *Practical Ethics* (1935), *Belief and Action* (1937), and *In Search of Reality* (1957).

Samuelson, Paul (Anthony) (1915–) Economist and journalist, born in Gary, IN. He studied at Chicago and Harvard universities, and became professor at the Massachusetts Institute of Technology (1940–85). His classic publication, *Foundations of Economic Analysis* (1947), is a treatise on his work in economic theory, for which he was awarded the Nobel Prize for Economics in 1970.

Samuelsson, Bengt Ingemar (1934–) Biochemist, born in Halmstad, Sweden. He studied at Stockholm University, where he became a professor in 1967. He shared with Bergström the 1982 Nobel Prize for Physiology or Medicine for discoveries concerning prostaglandins and related substances. >> Bergström; RR1124

Sanchez, Francisco (c. 1550–1623) Physician and philosopher, probably from Braga in Portugal. He became professor of philosophy (1585) and then medicine (1612) at Toulouse. His main work is a study of philosophical scepticism, *Quod nihil scitur* (1576, That Nothing is Known, published in 1581), which is a radical critique of Aristotle and argues that true knowledge is impossible; we must settle for the limited information available from careful experiment and observation.

Sanctorius [sangk**taw**rius], Latin name of **Santorio Santorio** (1561–1636) Physician and friend of Galileo, born in Capodistria, Italy. He studied at Padua, and in 1611 became professor of theoretical medicine there. He invented the clinical thermometer, a pulsimeter, a hygrometer, and other instruments, but he is best known for his investigations into the fluctuations of the body's weight under different conditions. >> Galileo

Sand, George [sã, zhaw(r)zh], pseudonym of **Armandine Aurore Lucile Dudevant**, *née* **Dupin** (1804–76) Writer, born in Paris. She left her husband (Baron Dudevant) and family in 1831, and returned to Paris to take up literature, becoming the companion of several poets, artists, philosophers, and politicians. After 1848 she settled at Nohant, where she spent the rest of her life in literary activity, varied by travel. Her first novel, *Indiana* (1832), was followed by over 100 books, the most successful being those describing rustic life, such as *François le champi* (1848). She also wrote plays, autobiographical works (notably about her notorious affairs with de Musset and Chopin), and letters. >> Agoult; Chopin, Frédéric; Musset

Sandage, Allan Rex (1926–   ) Astronomer, born in Iowa City, IA. He studied at Illinois University and California Institute of Technology before joining the Hale Observatories. In 1960 he made the first optical identification of a quasar. With a junior colleague, Thomas Matthews, he found a faint optical object at the same location as the quasar 3C 48, and noted that it had a very unusual spectrum (soon shown by Maarten Schmidt to be the result of a massive red shift). Sandage went on to identify many more quasars through this peculiarity of their spectra, and showed that most quasars are not radio emitters. >> Schmidt, Maarten

Sanday, Edgar >> **Faure, Edgar**

Sandburg, Carl (1878–1967) Poet, born in Galesburg, IL. After trying various jobs, fighting in the Spanish–American War, and graduating from Lombard College, he became a journalist in Chicago, and started to write for *Poetry*. His work reflects industrial America, and includes *Chicago Poems* (1915) and *Good Morning, America* (1928). His *Complete Poems* gained him the Pulitzer Prize in 1950. Interested in American folksongs, he published a collection in *The American Songbag* (1927). His popular two-part biography, *Abraham Lincoln: the Prairie Years* (1926) and *Abraham Lincoln: the War Years* (1939), won the Pulitzer Prize in history (1940).

Sandby, Paul (1725–1809) Painter, born in Nottingham, Nottinghamshire, C England, UK, the brother of Thomas Sandby. He has been called the father of the watercolour school. His career began as a draughtsman, but later, living at Windsor with his brother, he made many drawings of Windsor and Eton. His watercolours, outlined with the pen and only finished with colour, take the purely monochrome drawing of this school one step forward. He was an original member of the Royal Academy. >> Sandby, Thomas

Sandby, Thomas (1721–98) Artist and architect, born in Nottingham, Nottinghamshire, C England, UK, the brother of Paul Sandby. He ran an academy in Nottingham with his brother, and became private secretary and draughtsman to William Augustus, Duke of Cumberland. He was deputy ranger of Windsor Park from 1746, and became the first professor of architecture to the Royal Academy (1770). He built Lincoln's Inn Fields (1776), and was joint architect of His Majesty's Works with James Adam (1777). >> Adam, Robert; Sandby, Paul

Sandeman, Robert >> **Glas, John**

Sander, August (1876–1964) Photographer, born in Herdorf, Germany. He studied painting in Dresden, and opened studios in Linz and Cologne. For many years he planned and worked towards a documentary study, *Men in the 20th Century*. He published the first part, *Faces of Our Times*, in 1929, but his social realism was discouraged by the Nazi Ministry of Culture in 1934, and he published little thereafter. What little surviving material there is has provided penetrating portraits of German life in the early part of the century.

Sandino, Augusto César [sandeenoh] (1895–1934) Nicaraguan revolutionary, born in Niquinohome (or La Victoria), Nicaragua. He led guerrilla resistance to USA occupation forces after 1926, and was later murdered, on the orders of Somoza, near Managua. The Nicaraguan revolutionaries of 1979 (later known as *Sandinistas*) took him as their principal hero. >> Somoza

Sands, Bobby, popular name of **Robert Sands** (1954–81) Irish revolutionary, born in Belfast. He joined the IRA in 1972, and was sentenced to five years' imprisonment for possession of guns (1973). In 1977 he was sentenced to 14 years after the bombing of a furniture factory. In 1981, while at Long Kesh prison, Northern Ireland, he went on hunger-strike in protest against the authorities' refusal to treat himself and his fellow-IRA prisoners as 'political'. He died after 66 days, the first of 10 to die on hunger-strike that summer.

Sandwich, Edward Montagu, 1st Earl of (1625–72) British admiral, born in Barnwell, Northamptonshire, C England, UK. In the Civil War he fought on the parliamentary side as a soldier at Marston Moor (1644), sat in parliament (1645–8), shared the command of the fleet with Blake from 1653, and fought in the first Dutch War. For services in the restoration of the monarchy (1660), he was appointed Admiral of the Narrow Seas. As ambassador to Spain (1666–9), he helped to negotiate Charles II's marriage, and escorted Catherine of Braganza to England. In the third Dutch War (1672–8) he fought in the Battle of Southwold Bay, and was blown up with his flagship, the *Royal James*. >> Blake, Robert; Catherine of Braganza; Charles II (of England)

Sandwich, John Montagu, 4th Earl of (1718–92) British politician, remembered as the inventor of *sandwiches*, which he devised in order to eat while playing around the clock at a gaming-table. He was First Lord of the Admiralty under both Henry Pelham and Lord North (1748–51, 1771–82), and was frequently attacked for corruption. >> North, Frederick; Pelham, Henry

Sandys, Duncan >> **Duncan-Sandys**

Sandys, George [sandz] (1578–1664) Colonist and traveller, born near York, North Yorkshire, N England, UK. He studied at Oxford, travelled in Europe and the Middle East, and wrote *Relation of a Journey* (4 vols, 1615). In America he acted as treasurer of the colony of Virginia (1621–31) and made an important verse translation of Ovid's *Metamorphoses* (1626), upon which his reputation largely rests. He also wrote poetic versions of the *Psalms* (1636), the *Song of Solomon* (1641), and a translation of Hugo Grotius's *Christ's Passion* (1640).

Sangallo, Antonio (Giamberti) da [sanggahloh], known as **the Younger** (1483–1546) Architect and engineer, born in Florence, Italy. He was the most notable of a family of architects, the nephew of **Giuliano** (c.1445–1516) and **Antonio (the Elder)** (1455–1535), with whom he trained. From 1516 he served as assistant to Raphael at St Peter's, becoming chief architect in 1539. The foremost architect of the High Renaissance in Rome, his works include the Palazzo Palma-Baldassini, Rome (c.1520), and his great masterpiece, the Palazzo Farnese, Rome (1534–46), which was completed by Michelangelo. Also a military engineer, he designed the fortifications around Rome. >> Raphael

Sanger, Frederick (1918–   ) Biochemist, born in Rendcombe, Gloucestershire, SWC England, UK. He studied in Cambridge, and worked there throughout his career, after 1951 at the Medical Research Council Unit. By the mid-1950s he had secured a notable success through experimental work which revealed the full sequence of the 51 amino acids in insulin, for which he was awarded the Nobel Prize for Chemistry in 1958. He then worked on the problems of the nucleic acids, and devised new methods to elucidate molecular structures for these also. His Nobel Prize for Chemistry in 1980 made him the first to receive two such awards.

Sanger, Margaret (Louise), *née* **Higgins** (1883–1966) Social reformer and founder of the birth control movement, born in Corning, NY. Educated at Claverack College, she became a trained nurse. Appalled by the high rates of infant and maternal mortality in a poor area of New York City, she published a radical feminist magazine, *The Woman Rebel* (1914), with advice on contraception. She started the first US birth-control clinic in New York City in 1916, but was charged with creating a 'public nuisance', and imprisoned for 30 days. After a world tour, she founded the American Birth Control League in 1921. Her many books include *What Every Mother Should Know* (1917) and *My Fight for Birth Control* (1931). >> Pincus

Sanguinetti Cairolo, Julio María [sanggwi**ne**tee] (1936–) Uruguayan statesman and president (1984–90). A member of the long-established, progressive Colorado Party, he was elected to the Assembly in 1962, then headed the ministries of labour and industry, and education and culture (1969–73). The oppressive regime of Juan Maria Bordaberry (1972–6) was forcibly removed, and military rule imposed, before democratic government was restored in 1984. He was then elected president, but was defeated in 1990 by Luis Alberto Lacalle Herrera. >> RR1098

Sankara [**sang**kara, **shang**kara] (?700–?750) Hindu philosopher and theologian, born in Kalati, Kerala. The author of commentaries on the Hindu Scriptures, and founder of monastic centres in different parts of India, he is the most famous exponent of *Advaita* (the Vedanta school of Hindu philosophy), and the source of the main currents of modern Hindu thought. In this approach, Brahma alone has true existence, and the goal of the self is to become one with the Divine. His views were strongly opposed by Ramanuja and his successors. >> Ramanuja

Sankey. Ira David >> **Moody, Dwight Lyman**

San Martín, José de [san mah(r)**teen**] (1778–1850) South American patriot, born in Yapeyú, Argentina. He played a major role in winning independence from Spain for Argentina, Chile, and Peru. In 1817 he led an army across the Andes into Chile, defeating the Spanish at Chacubuco (1817) and Maipó (1818). He then captured Lima, and became Protector of Peru (1821), but resigned the following year after failing to reach an agreement with Bolívar, and died an exile in France. >> Bolívar

Sanmichele, Michele [sanmi**ke**lee] (1484–1559) Architect and military engineer, born in San Michele, Italy. Initially a pupil of his father and uncle, he went to Rome, where he came to be regarded as the successor of Bramante. He was master builder of the cathedral of Orvieto (1509–28), and was employed as military architect for Venice (from 1535). Noted for his treatment of military fortifications, his most important works include the Porta Nuova (1533–40) and the Porta S Zeno (1541). >> Bramante

Sansovino [sanso**vee**noh], originally **Andrea Contucci** (1460–1529) Religious sculptor, born in Monte Sansovino, Italy. He worked in Florence, in Portugal at the court of John II, and in Rome. Some of his work survives, including the identical tombs of Cardinal Ascanio Sforza and Girolamo Basso della Rovere, at S Maria del Popolo in Rome (1509). >> Sansovino, Jacopo

Sansovino, Jacopo [sanso**vee**noh], originally **Jacopo Tatti** (1486–1570) Sculptor and architect, born in Florence, Italy. He was a pupil of Andrea Contucci Sansovino, from whom he took his name, and was responsible for bringing the High Renaissance style of his native Florence to Venice. From 1529 he was chief architect in Venice, where he is noted for several buildings, notably the Library of St Mark's (1540s). His early sculptures include the 'Bacchus' (c.1514, Bargello, Florence), and the 'Madonna del Parto' (c.1519, S Agostino, Rome); later works include the two monumental statues, 'Mars' and 'Neptune' (1554–6, Doge's Palace, Venice). >> Sansovino

Santa Anna, Antonio López de (1797–1876) Mexican soldier, president (1833–6, 1846–7, 1853–5), and dictator (1839, 1841–5), born in Jalapa, Mexico. Following the Texas revolt (1836), he defeated Texan forces at the Alamo, but was then routed at San Jacinto R, and imprisoned for eight months. He was recalled from exile in 1846 to be president during the war with the USA, and was twice defeated in the field. He was again recalled by a revolution in 1853, and appointed president for life, but in 1855 he was driven from the country. In 1867, after the death of Maximilian, he tried to effect a landing, but was captured and sentenced to death, then allowed to retire to New York. He returned at the amnesty of 1872. >> Maximilian, Ferdinand-Joseph; Scott, Winfield; RR1075

Santamaria, Bartholomew Augustine [santama**ree**a] (1915–) Political writer, born in West Brunswick, Victoria, Australia. He studied law at Melbourne University, became involved with several Catholic organizations, and served as president of the Catholic Social Movement (1943), director of Catholic Action (1947), and president of the National Civic Council (1957). He was a leading force against Communist influence in Australia, and in the establishment of the Democratic Labor Party. His writings include *The Price of Freedom* (1964) and *The Defence of Australia* (1970).

Santander, Francisco de Paula [santan**dair**] (1792–1840) Colombian statesman, born in Rosario de Cúcuta, New Granada (modern Colombia). He took part in the Spanish-American Wars of Independence, acted as vice-president of Grancolombia (1821–7) during Bolívar's campaigns, and was president of New Granada in 1832–7. >> Bolívar; RR1041

Santayana, George [santa**yah**na], originally **Jorge Augustín Nicolás Ruiz de Santayana** (1863–1952) Philosopher, poet, and novelist, born in Madrid. He moved to Boston in 1872, and was educated at Harvard, where he became professor of philosophy (1907–12), while retaining his Spanish nationality. His writing career began as a poet with *Sonnets and Other Verses* (1894), but he later became known as a philosopher and stylist, in such works as *The Life of Reason* (5 vols, 1905–6), *Realms of Being* (4 vols, 1927–40), and his novel *The Last Puritan* (1935). He moved to Europe in 1912, stayed in Oxford during World War 1, then settled in Rome.

Santer, Jacques [sã**tair**] (1937–) Statesman, prime minister of Luxembourg (1984–95), and president of the European Commission (1995–), born in Wasserbillig, Luxembourg. He studied law at the universities of Strasbourg and Paris, and attended the Institute of Political Science in Paris. Entering politics, he became secretary to the Christian Social People's Party (1966–72), secretary-general (1972–4), and president (1974–82). In 1975 he became a member of the European Parliament, and in 1984 was elected Luxembourg's prime minister, serving three successive terms in office. He became president of the European Commission as a compromise choice, after Britain vetoed the selection of Belgian prime minister Jean-Luc Dehaene.

Santos-Dumont, Alberto [**san**tos doo**mont**] (1873–1932) Aviation pioneer, born in Santos Dumont (formerly, Palmyra), Brazil. He studied in France, where he spent most of his life. After a balloon ascent in 1898, he built an airship in which he made the first flight from St Cloud round the Eiffel Tower and back (1901). Two years later he built the first airship station, at Neuilly. He then experimented with heavier-than-air machines, and eventually achieved the first officially observed powered flight in Europe (1906), in a plane constructed on the principle of the box-kite. In 1909 he succeeded in building a light monoplane, a forerunner of modern light aircraft.

Sapir, Edward [sa**peer**] (1884–1939) Linguist and anthropologist, born in Lauenburg, Germany. His family moved to the USA when he was a child, and he studied ethnology and American Indian languages at Columbia University, where he was influenced by Franz Boas. One of the founders of ethnolinguistics, he is best known for his work on the languages of the North American Indians. His insights into the effect that the grammatical structure and vocabulary of a language may have on the way its speakers perceive the world were developed by his pupil Benjamin Lee Whorf, and came to be known as the *Sapir–Whorf hypothesis*. After working at the Canadian National Museum (1910–25), he became professor of anthropology and linguistics at Chicago (1925–31) and Yale (1931–9). >> Boas; Whorf

Sapor II >> **Shapur II**

Sapper, pseudonym of **Herman Cyril McNeile** (1888–1937) Novelist, born in Bodmin, Cornwall, SW England, UK. He trained as a soldier before achieving fame as the creator of 'Bulldog' Drummond, the aggressively patriotic hero of a series of thrillers written between 1920 and 1937. *The Final Count* (1926) is a typical example.

Sappho [**sa**foh] (c. 610–c. 580 BC) Greek poet, born in Lesbos. The most celebrated female poet of antiquity, she wrote lyrics unsurpassed for depth of feeling, passion, and grace. Only two of her odes are extant in full, but many fragments have been found in Egypt. She is said to have plunged into the sea from the Leucadian rock because Phaon did not return her love, but this event seems to have no historical foundation. Tradition also represents her as exceptionally immoral, but this too has been disputed.

Sarah or **Sarai** (Heb 'princess') Biblical character, the wife and half-sister of Abraham, who is portrayed (*Gen* 12–23) as having accompanied him from Ur to Canaan. On account of her beauty, she posed as Abraham's sister before Pharaoh in Egypt and Abimelech in Gerar, since their desire for her might have endangered her husband's life. Long barren, she is said to have eventually given birth to Isaac in her old age as God promised. She is said to have died at age 127 in Kiriath-arba. >> Abraham; Isaac

Sarandon, Susan [sa**ran**don], originally **Susan Abigail Tomalin** (1946–) Film actress, born in New York City. Educated at the Catholic University of America, Washington, she began her screen career in *Joe* (1970), and became well known after her role in *The Rocky Horror Picture Show* (1975). Later films include *The Witches of Eastwick* (1987), *Thelma and Louise* (1991), *Dead Man Walking* (1995, Oscar), and *James and the Giant Peach* (1996). A commitment to political activism brought her into the public eye in 1993, when she and co-star Tim Robbins interrupted the Academy Awards ceremony in order to draw attention to the situation of HIV-positive Haitian refugees.

Sarasate (y Navascué), Pablo (Martín Melitón) [sara**sah**tay] (1844–1908) Violinist and composer, born in Pamplona, Spain. He gave his first performance at the age of eight, and later studied at the Paris Conservatoire, where he was a star pupil. In 1859 he began to give concert tours, which brought him world fame. One of the greatest violinists of his day, many prominent composers wrote pieces for him.

Sardanapalus [sah(r)da**nap**alus] (7th-c BC) Legendary Assyrian king, notorious for his effeminacy and sensual lifestyle. He probably represents an amalgam of at least three Assyrian rulers, one of them being Assurbanipal. >> Assurbanipal

Sardou, Victorien [sah(r)doo] (1831–1908) Playwright, born in Paris. His first efforts were failures, but after his marriage he met the actress **Virginie Déjazet** (1798–1875), for whom he wrote several plays, and his work became

widely known in Europe and the USA. His plays include *Les Pattes de mouche* (1860, trans A Scrap of Paper), *La Tosca* (1887), on which Puccini's opera is based, and over 60 others, many written for Sarah Bernhardt. >> Bernhardt

Sargent, John Singer [**sah**(r)jnt] (1856–1925) Painter, born in Florence, Italy. He studied at Florence and Paris, where he first gained recognition, but most of his work was done in England, where he became the most fashionable portrait painter of his age. He had to leave Paris following a furore about his décolleté portrait 'Mme Gautreau' (1885), and he travelled much to the USA, where he became a US citizen in 1876. As well as portraits, he worked on decorative paintings for public buildings, such as 'The Evolution of Religion' (1890–1910) for Boston Public Library.

Sargent, Sir (Harold) Malcolm (Watts) [**sah**(r)jnt] (1895–1967) Conductor, born in Ashford, Kent, SE England, UK. Originally an organist, he first appeared as a conductor when his *Impression on a Windy Day* was performed at a Promenade Concert in 1921. He conducted the Royal Choral Society from 1928, the Liverpool Philharmonic Orchestra (1942–8), and the BBC Symphony Orchestra (1950–7). From 1948 he was in charge of the London Promenade Concerts. His sense of occasion and unfailing panache won him great popularity at home and abroad. He was knighted in 1947.

Sargeson, Frank [**sah**(r)jeson], pseudonym of **Norris Frank Davey** (1902–83) Short-story writer and novelist, born in Hamilton, Waikato, New Zealand. He qualified as a lawyer but did not practise. He took various menial jobs, but his main energy was devoted to writing novels and short stories. He made his name with collections of short stories such as *Conversations with My Uncle* (1936), *A Man and His Wife* (1940), and *That Summer and Other Stories* (1946), satirizing the provincial attitudes of his surroundings. His novels include *I Saw in My Dream* (1949), *The Hangover* (1967), and *Man of England Now* (1972).

Sarich, Ralph [**sa**rich] (c. 1939–) Inventor, born in Perth, Western Australia. Apprenticed as a fitter and turner, he studied engineering through correspondence courses and at night school. In 1972 he developed a working model of an orbital two-stroke reciprocating piston engine. The following year, with support from Broken Hill Propriety (BHP Ltd), he founded a company to market the engine, which was developed under licence by Ford and General Motors in the USA, and by Mercury for marine applications.

Sarney (Costa), Jose (1930–) Brazilian soldier and president (1985–90), born in Maranhao state, Brazil. Elected to the State Assembly at 20, he became governor (1965), and then president of the Social Democratic Party (1970). With the introduction of open elections in 1985, he became deputy to Tancredo Neves, the country's first civilian leader for 21 years, taking up the presidency on Neves' death a few months later. >> RR1036

Sarnoff, David (1891–1971) US entrepreneur, born in Minsk, Belarus. Working for Marconi, he was the radio operator who picked up the *Titanic*'s distress calls (1912). He proposed the construction of Marconi radio music boxes, became general manager of the Radio Corporation of America (RCA) in 1921, set up the NBC radio network, ordered the construction of the RCA building in the Rockefeller Center, and set up the first US television service (1939).

Saroyan, William [sa**roy**an] (1908–81) Writer, born in Fresno, CA. He left school at 15, and began writing short stories in the late 1920s. His first volume, *The Daring Young Man on the Flying Trapeze* (1934), was a great success, and was followed by a number of highly original novels and plays. He was awarded (but declined) the Pulitzer Prize for his play *The Time of Your Life* (1939). Among later works are the novel *The Human Comedy* (1943) and the memoir *Places Where I've Done Time* (1975).

Sarpi, Pietro [sah(r)pee], pseudonym **Pietro Soave Polano**, also known as **Fra Paolo** (1552–1623) Historian, theologian, and patriot, born in Venice, Italy. He entered the Servite Order in 1565, and became vicar-general in 1599. He studied a wide range of subjects, and is credited with various anatomical discoveries. He was the champion of Venice in the dispute with Pope Paul V (reigned 1605–21) over the immunity of clergy from the jurisdiction of civil tribunals, resisting the intrusion of Rome in the internal affairs of the Republic. Excommunicated and seriously wounded by assassins, he turned to writing his great *Istoria del Concilio Tridentino* (1619, History of the Council of Trent), published in London.

Sarrail, Maurice Paul Emmanuel [sariy] (1856–1929) French soldier, born in Carcassonne, France. In World War 1 he led the 3rd Army at the Battle of the Marne (1914), and from 1915 to 1917 commanded the Allied forces in the East (Salonica), where he deposed Constantine I of Greece. He was high commissioner in Syria (1924–5), but was recalled after the bombardment of Damascus during a rising. >> Constantine I (of Greece)

Sarraute, Nathalie [saroht], *née* **Nathalie Ilyanova Tcherniak** (1902–) Writer, born in Ivanova, Russia. Her parents settled in France when she was a child, and she studied at the Sorbonne, at Oxford, and in Berlin before becoming a member of the French bar (1926–41). Her first book was a collection of sketches on bourgeois life, *Tropismes* (1939, Tropisms), in which she rejected traditional plot development. Known and widely translated as the leading theorist of the *nouveau roman* ('new novel'), she developed her views in such novels as *Portrait d'un Inconnu* (1947, Portrait of a Man Unknown), *Le Planétarium* (1959, The Planetarium), and *Les Fruits d'or* (1963, The Golden Fruits). Later works include *Collected Plays* (1981), *Tu ne t'aimes pas* (1989, You Don't Love Yourself), and *ICI* (1995).

Sarsfield, Patrick (?–1693) Soldier, born in Lucan, Co Dublin, Ireland. He joined the English Life Guards, and in 1685 fought against Monmouth at Sedgemoor. In 1688 he was defeated at Wincanton, and crossed over to Ireland. Created Earl of Lucan by James II (his title was recognized only by the Jacobites), he drove the English out of Sligo, and was present at the Boyne (1690) and Aughrim (1691). He defended Limerick, and on its capitulation in 1691 left Ireland under amnesty and entered the French service in the Irish Brigade. He fought at Steenkirk (1692), and was mortally wounded at Neerwinden. >> James II (of England)

Sarto, Andrea del [sah(r)toh], originally **Andrea d'Agnolo**, or **Andrea Vannucchi** (1486–1531) Painter, born in Florence, Italy, the son of a tailor (It *sarto* 'tailor'). He was engaged by the Servites to paint a series of frescoes for their Church of the Annunciation (1509–14), and a second series was next painted for the Recollets. Many of his most celebrated pictures are in Florence. >> Franciabigio

Sarton, George (Alfred Leon) (1884–1956) Historian of science, born in Ghent, Belgium. He studied at the university there, and emigrated to the USA in 1915. He taught at Harvard (1920–51), latterly as professor of the history of science. He became the dominant figure of his subject, founding its principal journal, *Isis*, in 1912, and *Osiris* in 1936. His monumental *Introduction to the History of Science* (3 vols, 1927–48) reaches to the 14th-c; later volumes were incomplete at his death. His many books and articles largely shaped the subject as a separate dicipline.

Sartre, Jean-Paul [sahtr] (1905–80) Existentialist philosopher and writer, born in Paris. He taught philosophy at Le Havre, Paris, and Berlin, was imprisoned in Germany (1941), and after his release joined the resistance in Paris. In 1945 he emerged as the leading light of the left-bank intellectual life of Paris. His novels include the trilogy, *Les Chemins de la liberté* (1945–9, Paths of Freedom), and he also wrote (especially after the war) a large number of plays, such as *Huis clos* (1944, trans In Camera/No Exit) and *Le Diable et le bon Dieu* (1951, trans Lucifer and the Lord). His philosophy is presented in *L'Etre et le néant* (1943, Being and Nothingness). In 1964 he published his autobiography *Les Mots* (Words), and was awarded (but declined) the Nobel Prize for Literature. In the later 1960s he became heavily involved in opposition to US policies in Vietnam, and supported student rebellion in 1968. >> de Beauvoir, Simone; Heidegger

Sassau-Nguesso, Denis [sasoh ngwesoh] (1943–) Congolese soldier, politician, and president (1979–92). A member of the left-wing Congolese Labour Party, he became president of the Congo after his predecessor had been assassinated in a coup. He handed over real power to his own Congolese Labour Party's central committee. He was successful in strengthening the Congo's relationship with France and the USA in preference to maintaining its traditional ties with the USSR. At a national conference in 1991 he was severely criticized for gross mismanagement of oil revenues, was implicated in political assassinations, and had his executive powers curtailed. He was soundly defeated in presidential elections in 1992. >> RR1042

Sassetta, originally **Stefano do Giovanni** (?–c. 1450) Painter, probably born in Siena, Italy. Though trained in the late 14th-c Sienese manner, he was receptive to the diverse contemporary developments of both the International Gothic style and the Florentine Early Renaissance. These influences he blended into a unique, highly inventive style, full of narrative interest. His finest work was the altarpiece of St Francis (1437–44), painted for S Francesco, Borgo San Sepolcro, but now dispersed. Some of the finest predella panels are in the National Gallery in London.

Sassoon, Siegfried (Lorraine) [sasoon] (1886–1967) Poet and novelist, born in Brenchley, Kent, SE England, UK. World War 1, in which he served, gave him a hatred of war, fiercely expressed in his *Counterattack* (1918) and *Satirical Poems* (1926). He also wrote several autobiographical works, such as *Memoirs of a Fox-Hunting Man* (1928). His later poetry was increasingly devotional, and he became a Catholic in 1957. >> Owen, Wilfred

Satie, Erik (Alfred Leslie) [satee] (1866–1925) Composer, born in Honfleur, France. He worked as a cafe pianist, and studied erratically in Paris, not beginning to compose seriously until after he was 40. He wrote ballets, lyric dramas, and whimsical pieces which were in violent revolt against musical orthodoxy, and influenced Debussy, Ravel, and others. >> Debussy; Ravel

Saud, Ibn >> **Ibn Saud**

Sauer, Carl O(rtwin) [sower] (1889–1975) Geographer, born in Warrenton, MO. He studied at Northwestern and Chicago universities, and became professor at Michigan (1915–22), where he made vital and practical contributions to the improved use of land in Michigan State. He then became professor of geography at the University of California, Berkeley (1923–54), researching the historical geography of Latin America and the relationships between human societies and plants.

Saul [sawl] (11th-c BC) Biblical character, the first king to be elected by the Israelites. He conquered the Philistines, Ammonites, and Amalekites, became jealous of David, his son-in-law, and was ultimately engaged in a feud with the priestly class. Eventually, Samuel secretly anointed David king, and Saul fell in battle with the Philistines on Mt Gilboa. >> David; Samuel

Saunders, Dame Cicely (Mary Strode) (1918–)
Founder of the modern hospice movement, born in
London, England, UK. She studied at Oxford, and trained
at St Thomas's Hospital Medical School and the Nightingale School of Nursing. She became founder (1967), medical director (1967–85), and chairman (from 1985) of St
Christopher's Hospice, Sydenham. She promotes the principle of dying with dignity, maintaining that death is a natural process and can be eased by sensitive nursing and
effective pain-control. She has received many awards for
her pioneering work, and has written and edited a number
of books on her subject.

Saunders, Jennifer (1958–) British comedy writer and
actress. Trained at the Central School of Speech and
Drama, London, she teamed up with Dawn French in a
comedy act, taking it from clubs to theatre (*An Evening with
French and Saunders*, 1989), and making a successful breakthrough into television with 'The Comic Strip Presents ...'
(1990), 'Girls on Top' and five series of 'French and Saunders'.
She became internationally known following the success
of her comedy series *Absolutely Fabulous* (1993–5; Emmy,
1993), starring herself and Joanna Lumley, which generated a US version in 1995.

Saussure, Ferdinand de [sohsür] (1857–1913) Linguist,
the founder of modern linguistics, born in Geneva,
Switzerland. He taught historical linguistics at Paris
(1881–91), and became professor of Indo-European linguistics and Sanskrit (1901–13) and of general linguistics
(1907–13) at Geneva. The work by which he is best known,
the *Cours de linguistique générale* (1916, Course in General
Linguistics) was compiled from the lecture notes of his students after his death. His focus on language as an 'underlying system' inspired a great deal of later semiology and
structuralism.

Saussure, Horace Bénédict de [sohsür] (1740–99)
Physicist and geologist, born in Geneva, Switzerland. He
became professor of physics and philosophy at Geneva
(1762–88), travelled in Germany, Italy, and England, and
crossed the Alps by several routes. He was the first traveller
to ascend Mont Blanc (1787). A pioneer in the study of mineralogy, botany, geology, and meteorology, his invaluable
observations are recorded in *Voyages dans les Alpes* (1779–96,
Travels in the Alps). He devised the hair hygrometer and
other instruments. The mineral *saussurite* is named after
him, and he introduced the term *geology* into scientific
nomenclature.

Savage, Michael Joseph (1872–1940) New Zealand statesman and prime minister (1935–40), born in Benalla,
Victoria, Australia. He emigrated to New Zealand in 1907.
An MP from 1919, he became leader of the Labour Party in
1933 and then prime minister. As leader of the first Labour
government, he presided over a notable set of social
reforms. He died in office. >> RR1078

Savage, Richard (c. 1697–1743) English poet and satirist.
He declared himself the illegitimate son of the 4th Earl
Rivers, led a dissipated life, and came to prominence as the
subject of a biography by Dr Samuel Johnson (1744). His
work includes *Miscellaneous Poems* (1728), *The Convocation*
(1717), and the notable poem 'The Wanderer' (1729).

Savarin, Anthelme Brillat >> **Brillat-Savarin, Anthelme**

Savart, Félix [savah(r)] (1791–1841) Physician and physicist, born in Mézières, France. He taught physics in Paris,
and invented *Savart's wheel* for measuring tonal vibrations,
and the *Savart quartz plate* for studying the polarization of
light. With Jean Baptiste Biot he discovered the law
(named after them) governing the relationship of a magnetic field around a conductor to the current producing it.
>> Biot

Savery, Thomas (c. 1650–1715) Engineer, born in Shilstone,
Devon, SW England, UK. He developed and patented a
device for pumping water out of mines (1698), using steam
pressure admitted to a closed chamber containing water.
When the steam had forced the water to a higher level, the
steam was condensed, creating a vacuum which drew up
more water from below through a valve, refilling the
closed chamber for the process to be repeated. This was
the first practical steam engine, and he manufactured several until he joined with Newcomen to help develop
Newcomen's more efficient and practical steam piston
engine. >> Newcomen

Savi, Paolo (1798–1871) Naturalist and zoologist, born in
Pisa, Italy. He studied physics and natural science at Pisa,
and soon became professor of natural history (zoology
from 1840) at Pisa University, and also director of the Pisa
Museum. He extended the museum considerably, and
became a senator in 1862. His great work, *Ornitologia Italiana*,
was published posthumously (1873–6). *Savi's warbler* is
named after him.

Savigny, Friedrich Karl von [saveenyee] (1779–1861) Jurist,
born in Frankfurt, Germany. He studied at Göttingen and
Marburg universities, became a law professor at Marburg
(1803), and published a treatise on the Roman law of possession that won him European fame. In 1808 he was professor at Landshut University, and from 1810 at Berlin,
where he became one of the most influential members of
the faculty. He attacked the call for a German Civil Code,
and was leader of the historical school of jurists, contending that law evolved from the spirit of a people and was not
made for them. His works include a treatise on the history
of Roman law (1815–31), the foundation of the modern
study of mediaeval law.

Savile, Sir Henry [savil] (1549–1622) Scholar and courtier,
born in Bradley, West Yorkshire, N England, UK. He studied at Oxford, became a fellow of Merton College, Oxford,
was appointed warden of Merton in 1585, and provost of
Eton in 1596. He translated part of the histories of Tacitus
(1591) and the *Cyropaedia* of Xenophon. He also published
the first edition of St John Chrysostom (1610–13). He
helped Sir Thomas Bodley in the founding of the Bodleian
Library, and in 1619 he founded the Savilian chairs of
mathematics and astronomy at Oxford. >> Bodley

Savile, Jimmy [savil], popular name of **Sir James Wilson
Vincent Savile** (1926–) Television and radio personality,
born in Leeds, West Yorkshire, N England, UK. A former
miner, he achieved fame as a radio disc-jockey and television personality, with regular appearances on *Top of the
Pops* from 1963. On television he has hosted *Jim'll Fix It*
since 1975, helping to realize the dreams of ordinary people. His flamboyant style contrasts with his other role as a
voluntary helper at Leeds Infirmary and elsewhere; he has
used his nationwide prominence and popularity to raise
huge sums of money for deserving causes (such as £12 million to rebuild the National Spinal Injuries Centre at Stoke
Mandeville). He has written two volumes of autobiography, *As It Happens* (1975) and *Love Is an Uphill Thing* (1976). He
was knighted in 1990.

Savimbi, Jonas [savimbee] (1934–) Angolan soldier and
politician, the leader of the Union for the Total
Independence of Angola (UNITA) since its formation in
1966. He studied at Lausanne University, moved to Lusaka,
and was active in the struggle for independence from
Portugal which developed into civil war (1961). He led the
Popular Union of Angola, and was foreign minister of the
government in exile (1962–4). UNITA fought against the
Portuguese until 1974, but after independence under the
Marxist President Neto, Savimbi instituted a civil war
from bases close to the Namibian border, supported by

South Africa, until negotiations brought the war to an end, allowing elections to be held in 1992. Fighting resumed after the election when the result was inconclusive. >> dos Santos

Savonarola, Girolamo [savona**roh**la] (1452–98) Religious and political reformer, born in Ferrara, Italy. He became a Dominican at Bologna in 1474, and after an initial failure, came to be recognized as an inspiring preacher. He was vicar-general of the Dominicans in Tuscany (1493), and his preaching began to point towards a political revolution as the means of restoring religion and morality. When a republic was established in Florence (1494), he was its guiding spirit, fostering a Christian commonwealth, with stringent laws governing the repression of vice and frivolity. His denunciations of the abuses of Church and government leaders made him many enemies, including Pope Alexander VI, who summoned him to Rome (1495) to answer a charge of heresy. He disregarded the order, was excommunicated in 1497, and burned in Florence. >> Alexander VI

Savundra, Emil, originally **Michael Marion Emil Anecletus Savundranayagam** (1923–76) Convicted swindler and fraudster, born in Sri Lanka. He gave himself the title 'Doctor', and perpetrated huge financial swindles in Costa Rica, Goa, Ghana, China, and Britain. He is best known in Britain for the crash of his Fire, Auto and Marine Insurance Co, which left 400 000 British motorists without insurance cover in 1966. In an attempt to defend his actions he made a television appearance on *The Frost Programme*. He was arrested and sentenced to eight years' imprisonment (1968), and freed in 1974.

Sawchuk, Terry, popular name of **Terrance (Gordon) Sawchuck** (1929–70) Ice hockey player, born in Winnipeg, Manitoba, Canada. One of the game's greatest goaltenders, he started his career with the Detroit Red Wings in 1950, and later played for the Boston Bruins, Toronto Maple Leafs, Los Angeles Kings, and New York Rangers. His 103 shutouts are a National Hockey League record. He appeared in 971 games (1950–70), a record for a goaltender. He was largely responsible for the crouched stance subsequently adopted by other goaltenders.

Sax, Antoine Joseph, also known as **Adolphe Sax** (1814–94) Musician and inventor, born in Dinant, France. With his father he invented (patented 1845) a valved brass wind-instrument he called the sax-horn, also the saxophone, the saxtromba, and the sax-tuba. He moved to Paris to promote his inventions, and in 1857 was appointed as an instructor at the Paris Conservatoire. He failed to make a commercial success of his products, was involved in lengthy lawsuits with other instrument makers, and died in poverty.

Saxby, Joseph >> **Dolmetsch, Carl**

Saxe, (Hermann) Maurice, comte de (Count of), usually called **Marshal de Saxe** (1696–1750) Marshal of France, born in Goslar, Germany, the illegitimate son of Augustus II, King of Poland, formerly Elector of Saxony. He served in the French army in the War of the Polish Succession (1733–8), and in the War of the Austrian Succession (1740–8) invaded Bohemia, taking Prague by storm. In 1744 Louis XV appointed him commander in Flanders, where he won victories at Fontenoy (1745), Raucoux (1746), and Lauffeld (1747), and was promoted Marshal of France. After the war he retired. >> Augustus II

Saxe-Coburg-Gotha, Alfred Ernest Albert, Prince of [saks **koh**berg **go**tha] (1844–1900) Second son of Queen Victoria, born at Windsor Castle, Berkshire, S England, UK. He studied at Bonn and Edinburgh before entering the Royal Navy in 1858. In 1866 he was created Duke of Edinburgh, and in 1874 married the Russian **Grand Duchess Marie Alexandrovna** (1853–1920). In 1893 he succeeded his uncle as reigning Duke of Saxe-Coburg-Gotha. During World War 1, the other members of the British royal family abandoned the name Saxe-Coburg-Gotha in favour of Windsor, as a means of asserting the Englishness of royalty and playing down the extent of its German blood. >> Victoria

Saxo Grammaticus (Lat 'the Scholar') (c. 1140–1206) Danish chronicler, born in Zealand, Denmark. He was secretary to Archbishop Absalon of Lund, at whose request he wrote the *Gesta Danorum*, a Latin history of the Danes, in 16 books. The work is partly legendary and partly historical. >> Absalon

Saxton, Christopher, (c. 1544–c. 1611) Surveyor and cartographer, probably born in Sowood, West Yorkshire, N England, UK. He may have studied at Cambridge University. He was commissioned by Elizabeth I to carry out the first survey of all the counties of England and Wales, and worked under the patronage of Thomas Seckford, Master of the Queen's Requests. His atlas (1579) was the first national atlas of any country, and he is often called 'the father of English cartography'.

Say, J(ean) B(aptiste) [say] (1767–1832) Political economist, born in Lyon, France. From 1794 he edited a magazine centred on the French Revolution. A member of the tribunate in 1799, he resigned in 1804 in protest against the arbitrary tendencies of the consular government. He later became professor of industrial economy at the Conservatoire des Arts et Métiers (1817–30), and of political economy at the Collège de France (1830–2). The author of the major *Traité d'économie politique* (1803, A Treatise on Political Economy), he is best remembered for *Say's law*, which expounds the idea of supply creating its own demand, and the automatic adjustment of under- or over-production.

Say, Thomas (1787–1834) Naturalist and entomologist, born in Philadelphia, PA. He made expeditions to the Rocky Mountains, Minnesota, Florida, Georgia, and Mexico (1818–29), and was the author of *American Entomology* (1824–8) and *American Conchology* (1830–4). He was professor at the University of Pennsylvania (1822–8), but joined in Robert Owen's experimental Utopian settlement at New Harmony, IN (1826–7), and settled in the town after the break-up of the community. >> Owen, Robert

Sayce, Archibald H(enry) (1845–1933) Philologist, born in Gloucester, Gloucestershire, SWC England, UK. He studied at Oxford, where he became professor of Assyriology (1891–1919). A member of the Old Testament Revision Company, he wrote on biblical criticism and Assyriology, including an *Assyrian Grammar* (1872), *Principles of Comparative Philology* (1874–75), *The Monuments of the Hittites* (1881), and *The Early History of the Hebrews* (1897).

Sayers, Dorothy L(eigh) (1893–1957) Writer, born in Oxford, Oxfordshire, SC England, UK. She studied at Oxford, and became a celebrated writer of detective stories. Beginning with *Clouds of Witness* (1926), she related the adventures of her hero Lord Peter Wimsey in various accurately observed milieux – such as advertising in *Murder Must Advertise* (1933) and bell-ringing in *The Nine Tailors* (1934). She then earned a reputation as a leading Christian apologist with her plays, radio broadcasts, and essays.

Sayers, Gale (1943–) Player of American football, born in Wichita, KS. Running back with the Chicago Bears (1965–72), he held numerous records, and was elected to the sport's Hall of Fame in 1977. He once scored six touchdowns in a single game (1965). After retiring from the sport, he became a coach, and also went into business as a computer company executive.

Sayers, James (1912–) British physicist. He studied at Belfast and Cambridge, where he became a fellow of St John's (1941–6). A member of the British team associated with the Manhattan atomic bomb project (1943–5), he became professor of electron physics at Birmingham (1946–72). In 1949 he was given a government award for his work on the cavity magnetron valve, which was of great importance in the development of radar.

Sayers, Peig [peg] (1873–1958) Gaelic story-teller, born in Dunquin, Co Kerry, Ireland. She lived most of her life on the Great Blasket I. The disappearance of Gaelic from most parts of Ireland made her powers of recollection and her hold on traditional narratives deeply respected by scholars. Her prose is recorded in *Peig* (1935, edited by Máire Ní Chinnéide) and *Machtnamh Sean-Mná* (1939, An Old Woman's Reflections, translated 1962).

Sayers, Tom, known as **the Little Wonder** and **the Napoleon of the Prize Ring** (1826–65) Boxer, born in London, England, UK. A bricklayer, he took up boxing in 1849, and became English heavyweight champion in 1857 despite weighing only 11 stone, which would be normal for a middleweight. Throughout his career he lost only one fight. His last and most famous contest was with the US champion John Heenan for the first world championship title; the fight lasted 2 hr 6 min, and was declared a draw after 42 rounds.

Scales, Prunella (Margaret Rumney) (1932–) Actress, born in Abinger, Surrey. Educated in Eastbourne, she trained at the Old Vic Theatre School and the Herbert Berghof Studio, New York City. She played in repertory in various British cities, and has made numerous appearances in the West End, including *Hay Fever* (1968), *When We Are Married* (1986), and *The School for Scandal* (1990). On television she played opposite John Cleese in the comedy series *Fawlty Towers* (1975, 1978), and starred in *After Henry* (1988, 1990). A widely acclaimed performance is her solo role in *An Evening with Queen Victoria*, where she spans Victoria's life from teenage princess to old age with a minimum of make-up and costume change. Recent work includes the play *The Matchmaker* (1993), the film *Wolf* (1994), and *The Rector's Wife* (1994) for Channel 4. >> Cleese; West Timothy

Scaliger, Joseph Justus [skalijer] (1540–1609) Scholar, born in Agen, France, the son of Julius Caesar Scaliger. He studied in Paris, became a Protestant, and travelled widely in Europe, becoming professor at Leyden in 1593. One of the most erudite scholars of his day, a classical linguist and historian, he is best known for his *Opus de emendatione temporum* (1583), a study of earlier methods of calculating time. >> Scaliger, Julius Caesar

Scaliger, Julius Caesar [skalijer], originally **Benedetto Bordone** (1484–1558) Humanist scholar, born in Riva, Italy. He studied medicine at Padua, became a French citizen in 1528, and settled in Agen, where he wrote learned works on grammar, philosophy, botany, zoology, and literary criticism. Titles include *De plantis* (1556) and his best-known work, *Poetice* (1561). >> Scaliger, Joseph Justus

Scarfe, Gerald (1936–) Cartoonist, born in London, UK. His cartoons, based on extreme distortion in the tradition of Gillray (eg Mick Jagger's lips are drawn larger than the rest of his face), have appeared in *Punch*, *Private Eye*, and elsewhere, especially *The Sunday Times* since 1967. Appointed artist to the *New Yorker* from 1993, he has also worked as a theatrical designer and animated film director, notably with *Hercules* (1997). He is married to actress Jane Asher. >> Asher; Gillray; Jagger

Scargill, Arthur (1938–) Trade unionist, born in Leeds, West Yorkshire, N England, UK. He became president of the National Union of Mineworkers in 1982, and a member of the Trades Union Congress General Council. He is primarily known for his strong, Socialist defence of British miners that has often brought his union into conflict with the government, most particularly during the miners' strike (1984–5), and when British Coal announced the closure of most deep-mine collieries in 1992.

Scarlatti, (Pietro) Alessandro (Gaspare) [skah(r)latee] (1660–1725) Composer, born in Palermo, Sicily. He produced his first opera in Rome (1679), where he became *maestro di cappella* to Queen Christina of Sweden. He was musical director at the court in Naples (1683–1702, 1709–25), and became a leading figure in Italian opera. He reputedly wrote over 100 operas, of which 40 survive complete, the most famous being *Tigrane* (1715). He also wrote 10 Masses, c.700 cantatas, and oratorios, motets, and madrigals. >> Scarlatti, Domenico

Scarlatti, (Giuseppe) Domenico [skah(r)latee] (1685–1757) Composer, born in Naples, Italy, the son of Alessandro Scarlatti. From 1711 he was *maestro di cappella* in Rome to the Queen of Poland, for whom he composed several operas, and he also served in Lisbon and Madrid. As choirmaster of St Peter's, Rome (1714–19), he wrote much church music. He was a skilled harpsichordist, and is mainly remembered for the 555 sonatas written for this instrument. >> Scarlatti, Alessandro

Scarron, Paul [skarõ] (1610–60) Writer, born in Paris. During his 20s the onset of paralysis forced him to take up writing for a living, and he produced many sonnets, madrigals, songs, epistles, and satires. He is best known for his realistic novel, *Le Roman comique* (1651–7, The Comic Novel). In 1652 he married Françoise d'Aubigné (later, Madame de Maintenon). >> Maintenon

Scarry, Richard (McClure) (1919–94) Illustrator and writer of children's books, born in Boston, MA. He studied at Boston Museum School of Fine Arts, then served in the US army in the Mediterranean and North Africa. Didactic, detailed, and scatty, his output was prolific, and he was hugely popular with children tolerant of his formulaic approach. Typical titles are *What Do People Do All Day?* (1968) and *Hop Aboard, Here We Go!* (1972).

Schacht, (Horace Greely) Hjalmar [shahkht] (1877–1970) Financier, born in Tinglev, Germany. In 1923 he became president of the Reichsbank, and founded a new currency which ended the inflation of the mark. He was minister of economics (1934–7), but in 1939 was dismissed from his bank office for disagreeing with Hitler over rearmament expenditure. Interned by the Nazis, he was acquitted at Nuremberg. In 1953 he set up his own bank in Düsseldorf.

Schaefer, Vincent (Joseph) [shayfer] (1906–93) Physicist, born in Schenectady, NY. He graduated from the Davey Institute of Tree Surgery in 1928, and went as assistant to Irving Langmuir at the research laboratories of the General Electric Company. During World War 2 he worked on the problem of icing on aeroplane wings, which led him in 1946 to demonstrate for the first time the possibility of inducing rainfall by seeding clouds with dry ice. He later became professor of physics (1959–64) and of atmospheric science (1964–76) at the State University of New York. >> Langmuir

Schall (von Bell), (Johann) Adam [shahl] (1591–1666) Jesuit missionary and astronomer, born in Cologne, Germany. He studied astronomy in Rome, and went to China in 1622, where he was appointed to translate astronomical books and reform the Chinese calendar. After 1644 he became head of the Imperial Board of Astronomy, and adviser to the young emperor Shun-chih (ruled 1644–61), who allowed him to build a church in Peking (1650). On the death of the emperor, he was accused of plotting against him, and sentenced to death. An earthquake the following day led to his sentence being commuted. Two years after his death he was vindicated.

Schally, Andrew Victor [shalee] (1926–) Biochemist, born in Wilno, Poland. He studied at the National Institute for Medical Research in London, and McGill University in Montreal, and worked at the Baylor Medical School (1957–62) and Tulane University (from 1962). He discovered and synthesized the hormones produced by the hypothalamus that control the pituitary gland, for which he shared the 1977 Nobel Prize for Physiology or Medicine. >> RR1124

Scharnhorst, Gerhard Johann David von [shah(r)n-haw(r)st] (1755–1813) Prussian general and military reformer, born in Bordenau, Germany. He worked with Gneisenau to reform the Prussian army after its defeat by Napoleon, served as chief-of-staff to Blücher, and was fatally wounded fighting the French at Lützen. >> Blücher; Gneisenau; Napoleon I

Scharwenka, Xaver [shah(r)vengka] (1850–1924) Pianist and composer, born near Posen, Germany. In 1881 he started a music school in Berlin, and spent the years 1891–98 in New York City directing the Scharwenka Music School. He composed symphonies, piano concertos, and Polish dances.

Schaudinn, Fritz (Richard) [showdin] (1871–1906) Zoologist and microbiologist, born in Röseningken, Germany. He studied philology at Berlin, but turned to zoology, and after research work in Berlin became director of the department of protozoological research at the Institute for Tropical Diseases, Hamburg (1904). He demonstrated the amoebic nature of tropical dysentery, and discovered the spirochaete *Treponema Pallidum* which causes syphilis (1905).

Schaufuss, Peter [showfus] (1949–) Ballet dancer and director, born in Copenhagen. His parents were principals with the Royal Danish Ballet, where he trained from the age of seven. In 1964 he moved to Canada to become soloist with the National Ballet of Canada. He returned less than two years later, and danced for various companies, including the London Festival Ballet (1970) and New York City Ballet (1974–7), then returned to Canada as principal (1977–83). He became artistic director of the London Festival Ballet (1984–90), and director of ballet at Deutsche Oper, Berlin (1990–3) and the *Royal Danish Ballet* (1994–5).

Schawlow, Arthur (Leonard) [showloh] (1921–) Physicist, born in Mount Vernon, NY. He studied at Toronto and Columbia universities, worked at Bell Telephone Laboratories (1951–61), then became professor at Stanford, CA. With his brother-in-law, Charles Townes, he devised the laser, although the first working model was made by Maiman in 1960. He shared the 1981 Nobel Prize for Physics for his work in spectroscopy. >> Maiman; Townes; RR1122

Scheel, Walter [shayl] (1919–) West German statesman and president (1974–9), born in Solingen, Germany. After serving in the *Luftwaffe* in World War 2 he went into business, joined the Free Democratic Party, and was elected to the Bundestag in 1953. He was minister for economic co-operation (1961–6) and foreign minister (1969–74), and in 1970 negotiated treaties with the USSR and Poland.

Scheele, Carl Wilhelm [sheeluh] (1742–86) Chemist, born in Stralsund, Germany. He was apprenticed to an apothecary at Gothenburg, and worked as an apothecary at Malmö, Stockholm, Uppsala, and Köping. Experimenting in his spare time, he probably discovered more new substances than any other experimenter, but did not publish his results immediately, and thus did not receive the same acclaim as others who made similar discoveries later but published before him. Among his major discoveries were

oxygen (1772), which he called 'fire air', chlorine (1774), glycerine, and hydrogen sulphide, as well as several types of acid. He was elected to the Stockholm Royal Academy of Sciences in 1777.

Scheer, Reinhard [sheer] (1863–1928) German naval commander, born in Obernkirchen, Germany. He went to sea as a naval cadet in torpedo craft. As vice-admiral he commanded the 2nd Battle Squadron of the German High Seas fleet at the outset of World War 1. He succeeded as commander-in-chief in 1916, and was in command at the indecisive Battle of Jutland (1916). He briefly became chief of the admiralty staff in 1918, before his retirement. >> Beatty; Hipper; Jellicoe

Scheidemann, Philipp [shiyduhman] (1865–1939) Social Democratic politician, born in Kassel, Germany. A journalist, he joined the Reichstag in 1903. He became minister of finance and colonies in the provisional government of 1918, and was the first chancellor of the republic in 1919. He was the subject of a failed assassination attempt in 1922.

Scheler, Max [shayler] (1874–1928) Philosopher and social theorist, born in Munich. He taught at the universities of Jena (1900–6), Munich (1907–10), Cologne (1919–27), and Frankfurt (1928). Influenced by Husserl, he developed a distinctive version of phenomenology which he set out in his major work, *Der Formalismus in der Ethik und die materiale Wertethik* (1921, Formalism in Ethics and the Material Value Ethics). He also did influential work in the sociology of knowledge. >> Husserl

Schelling, Friedrich (Wilhelm Joseph) von [sheling] (1775–1854) Philosopher, born in Leonberg, Germany. He studied at Tübingen and Leipzig, became professor at Jena (1798–1803), Würzburg (1803–8), and Erlangen (1820–7), and from 1806 was secretary of the Royal Academy at Munich. He moved to a chair at Berlin in 1841. His early work, influenced by Fichte and Kant, culminated in his *System des transzendentalen Idealismus* (1800, System of Transcendental Idealism), an important influence on Romanticism. >> Fichte; Kant

Schepisi, Fred [skepsee] (1939–) Film director, born in Melbourne, Victoria, Australia. As a teenager, he worked in an advertising agency, and by 1966 had bought the company and was making documentaries and commercials. His first major feature, *The Devil's Playground* (1976), reflecting his early experiences with Catholicism, established him as one of the industry's most promising talents. After *The Chant of Jimmie Blacksmith* (1978), a true story of racism based on the novel by Thomas Keneally (1935–), he moved to the USA where his fascination with myth and superstition was seen in *Barbarosa* (1982), and *The Iceman* (1984). Other titles include *Roxanne* (1987), *A Cry in the Dark* (1988, known as *Evil Angels* in Australia), *The Russia House* (1991), based on a John Le Carré novel, and *Six Degrees of Separation* (1993). >> Le Carré

Schiaparelli, Elsa [skyaparelee] (1896–1973) Fashion designer, born in Rome. After studying philosophy, she lived in the USA, working as a film script writer, then went to Paris in 1920. She designed and wore a black sweater knitted with a white bow, as a result of which she received orders from a US store, which started her in business. Her designs were inventive and sensational, and she was noted for her use of colour, including 'shocking pink', and her original use of traditional fabrics. She featured zippers and buttons, and made outrageous hats.

Schiaparelli, Giovanni (Virginio) [skyaparelee] (1835–1910) Astronomer, born in Savigliano, Italy. He studied at Berlin and at Pulkova, Russia, and became director of Brera Observatory, Milan. He observed meteors and double stars, discovered the asteroid Hesperia, and termed vague linear features on Mars as 'canali' (1877).

Schiele, Egon [**shee**luh] (1890–1918) Painter, born in Tulln, Austria. He studied at the Vienna Academy of Fine Arts in 1906, met Klimt in 1907, and developed a powerful form of Expressionism in which figures, often naked and emaciated and drawn with hard outlines, fill the canvas with awkward, anguished gestures. In 1912 he was arrested, and some of his work was destroyed by the police. He died in the influenza epidemic of 1918. >> Klimt

Schillebeeckx, Edward (Cornelis Florentius Alfons) [**skil**ebeeks] (1914–) Theologian, born in Antwerp, Belgium. Professor of dogmatics and the history of theology at Nijmegen, The Netherlands (1958–83), his publications have ranged widely across the whole field of theology, from sacraments (*Christ the Sacrament*, 1963), to the presentation of the Gospel in contemporary society (*Jesus in Our Western Culture*, 1987). Like Hans Küng, he has attracted Vatican investigations for questioning received interpretations of doctrine and Church order, as in *The Church with a Human Face* (1985). >> Küng

Schiller, (Johann Christoph) Friedrich (von) [**shil**er] (1759–1805) Historian, playwright, and poet, born in Marbach, Germany. He attended a military academy, and became an army surgeon in Stuttgart, where he began to write *Sturm und Drang* ('storm and stress') verse and plays. The revolutionary appeal of his first play, *Die Räuber* (1781, The Robbers), made it an instant success. He later settled in Dresden, where his works included the poem *An die Freude* (Ode to Joy, later set to music by Beethoven in his Choral Symphony). He became professor of history at Jena in 1788. His last decade was highly productive, including the dramatic trilogy, *Wallenstein* (1796–9), the greatest German historical drama *Maria Stuart* (1800), and *Wilhelm Tell* (1804). >> Hölderlin

Schimper, Andreas (Franz Wilhelm) [**shim**per] (1856–1901) German botanist, born in Strasbourg, France. He studied at the University of Strasbourg, was a fellow at Johns Hopkins (1880–1), then became professor at Bonn (to 1898) and Basel (1898–1901). Widely travelled, he was noted as a plant geographer, and divided the continents into floral regions. He established in 1880 that starch is a source of stored energy for plants.

Schinkel, Karl Friedrich [**shing**kl] (1781–1841) Architect, born in Neuruppin, Germany. He studied at Berlin and in Italy, became state architect of Prussia (1815), and director of public works (1830). He designed a wide range of buildings, in Classical style, and introduced new streets and squares in Berlin. He also became known as a painter, illustrator, and furniture and stage designer.

Schirach, Baldur von [**shee**rakh] (1907–74) Nazi politician, born in Berlin. He studied at the University of Munich, became a party member in 1925, a member of the Reichstag (1932), and founded and organized the Hitler Youth (1933), of which he was leader until his appointment as *Gauleiter* of Vienna in 1940. Captured in Austria in 1945 and tried before the Nuremberg Tribunal, he was found guilty of participating in the mass deportation of Jews, and was sentenced to 20 years' imprisonment. He was released from Spandau prison in 1966.

Schlegel, August Wilhelm von [**shlay**gl] (1767–1845) Poet and critic, born in Hanover, Germany. He studied theology at Göttingen, but soon turned to literature, settling in Jena, where he became professor of literature and fine art (1798). He then lectured at Berlin (1801–4), and from 1818 until his death was professor of literature at Bonn. He is famous for his translations of Shakespeare and other authors, and for founding Sanskrit studies in Germany. He was a leading figure of the Romantic movement. >> Schlegel, Karl Wilhelm Friedrich von

Schlegel, Karl Wilhelm Friedrich von [**shlay**gl] (1772–

1829) Writer and critic, born in Hanover, Germany, the brother of August von Schlegel. He studied at Göttingen and Leipzig, and became closely associated with his brother, with whom he edited the journal *Das Athenaeum*. He wrote widely on comparative literature and philology, his works inspiring the early German Romantic movement. >> Schlegel, August Wilhelm von

Schleicher, August [**shliy**kher] (1821–68) Philologist, born in Meiningen, Germany. He studied at Tübingen University, taught classical philology and the comparative study of Greek and Latin at Prague (1850–7), and was professor at Jena (1857–68). Living among the peasants of Lithuania in 1852, he was the first to study an Indo-European language from speech. His major work is *A Compendium of the Comparative Grammar of the Indo-European, Sanskrit, Greek and Latin Languages* (1861–2, trans title).

Schleicher, Kurt von [**shliy**kher] (1882–1934) German soldier and politician, the chief enemy of Hitler, born in Brandenburg, Germany. He was on the general staff during World War 1. As minister of war in von Papen's government of 1932, he succeeded him as chancellor, but his failure to obtain dictatorial control provided Hitler with his opportunity to seize power in 1933, and Schleicher and his wife were murdered. >> Hitler; Papen

Schleiermacher, Friedrich (Ernst Daniel) [**shliy**ermahkher] (1768–1834) Theologian and philosopher, born in Wrocław, Poland (formerly Breslau, Germany). He studied at Halle, became a preacher in Berlin (1796), and was professor at Halle (1804–6) and Berlin (from 1810). He was a leader of the movement which led to the union in 1817 of the Lutheran and Reformed Churches in Prussia. His most important work is *Der Christliche Glaube* (1821–2, The Christian Faith), and he also wrote on Christian ethics, a life of Jesus, sermons, and letters. He is generally held to be the founder of modern Protestant theology.

Schlemmer, Oskar [**shlem**er] (1888–1943) Painter, sculptor, designer, dancer, and theorist, born in Stuttgart, Germany. He was on the faculty of the Bauhaus (1919–33), where he developed his notions of theatre as a mix of colour, light, form, space, and motion. Using puppet-like human figures as the centrepiece, he called his experimental productions 'architectonic dances'. The best-known was 'Triadic Ballet' (three versions: 1911, 1916, 1922).

Schlesinger, Arthur M(eier) [**shlez**injer] (1888–1965) Historian, born in Xenia, OH. He studied at Columbia University, and taught at Ohio State, Iowa, and (from 1924) Harvard universities. His most important work is *New Viewpoints in American History* (1922), in which he emphasized social and cultural history. This concern, together with his interest in the history of urban growth, was a new departure in US historiography. His *History of American Life* (13 vols, 1928–43) was an attempt to describe all aspects of human life in America. He also established the Schlesinger Library on the History of Women, at Cambridge, MA. >> Schlesinger, Arthur M, Jr

Schlesinger, Arthur M(eier), Jr [**shlez**injer] (1917–) Historian, born in Columbus, OH, the son of Arthur M Schlesinger. He studied at Harvard and Cambridge, and was professor of history at Harvard (1954–61) before becoming special assistant to President Kennedy (1961–3). His publications include *The Age of Jackson* (1945) and *A Thousand Days: John F Kennedy in the White House* (1965) (both Pulitzer Prizes). He later became professor of humanities at the City University of New York (1966–95, now emeritus) and president of the American Institute of Arts and Letters (1981). >> Kennedy, John F; Schlesinger, Arthur M

Schlesinger, John [**shlez**injer] (1926–) Film director, born in London, England, UK. He directed art documentary films for television, and made his first feature film of contemporary social realism, *A Kind of Loving*, in 1962, followed by *Billy Liar* (1963). His interpretation of Hardy's *Far from the Madding Crowd* (1967), the downbeat urban *Midnight Cowboy* (1969, Oscar), and the sensitive *Sunday, Bloody Sunday* (1971) showed his width of range. Later productions in the USA explored political responsibilities, such as *Day of the Locust* (1975), *Marathon Man* (1976), and *Yanks* (1979). Films of the 1980s include *Honky Tonk Freeway* (1980), *Believers* (1987), and *Madame Sousatka* (1989). Later titles include *Pacific Heights* (1990), *The Innocent* (1993), and *Cold Comfort Farm* (1996). He has also directed for stage and opera.

Schlick, Moritz [shlik] (1882–1936) Philosopher, one of the leaders of the Vienna Circle of logical positivists, born in Berlin. He studied physics at Heidelberg, Lausanne, and Berlin, taught at Rostock and Kiel, and from 1922 was professor of inductive sciences at Vienna. An early exponent of Einstein's relativity theories, his major works include *Allgemeine Erkenntnislehre* (1918, General Theory of Knowledge) and *Fragen der Ethik* (1930, Problems of Ethics). He was shot down on the steps of the university by a deranged student. >> Carnap; Neurath; Popper; Schutz; von Wright

Schlieffen, Alfred, Graf von (Count of) [shleefn] (1833–1913) Prussian field marshal, born in Berlin. He entered the army in 1854, and rose to become chief of general staff (1891–1905). He advocated the plan, which bears his name (1895), on which German tactics were unsuccessfully based in World War 1. He envisaged a German breakthrough in Belgium and the defeat of France within six weeks by a major right-wheel flanking movement through The Netherlands, cutting off Paris from the sea, holding off the Russians meanwhile with secondary forces.

Schliemann, Heinrich [shleeman] (1822–90) Archaeologist, born in Neubukow, Germany. After a successful business career, he retired early to realize his ambition of finding the site of the Homeric poems by excavating the tell at Hisarlik in Asia Minor, the traditional site of Troy. From 1871 he discovered nine superimposed city sites, one containing a considerable treasure (found 1873) which he over-hastily identified as Priam's. He also excavated several other Greek sites, including Mycenae (1876) and Tiryns (1884).

Schlüter, Poul (Holmskov) [shlüter] (1929–) Danish politician and prime minister (1982–93). After studying at Aarhus and Copenhagen universities he had a successful career in the law, became leader of the Conservative Youth movement in 1944, and national leader seven years later. He joined the executive committee of the Conservative People's Party in 1964, and became chairman (1972). His 1982 premiership of a centre-right coalition survived the 1987 and 1990 elections, after which he reconstituted the coalition with Liberal support. >> RR1044

Schmelzer, Johann Heinrich [shmeltser] (1623–80) Composer, born in Scheibbs, Austria. He was trained as a musician in the emperor's service, and won fame throughout Europe as a violinist. In 1679 he became *Kapellmeister* to Leopold I, but the following year died of the plague in Prague, where the court had fled from the great epidemic in Vienna. The first to adapt the tunes of the Viennese street musicians and Tyrolean peasants to the more sophisticated instrumental styles of the court, he is often regarded as the true father of the Viennese waltz.

Schmidt, Bernhard Voldemar [shmit] (1879–1935) Astronomer, born in Naissaar, Estonia. He studied at an engineering school in Mittweida, Germany, where he remained until 1926, helping to instal a small observatory. He became a staff member at Hamburg observatory (1926), and in 1929 devised a new mirror system for reflecting telescopes which overcame previous problems of aberration of the image, and which is now widely used in astronomy.

Schmidt, Franz [shmit] (1874–1939) Composer, born in Pressburg, Austria. He studied under Anton Bruckner, played cello in the Vienna Philharmonic Orchestra (1896–1911), and was a distinguished teacher at various Viennese institutions (1901–37). He continued the style of Austro-German lavish late-Romanticism in his four symphonies, an oratorio, the operas *Notre Dame* (Vienna, 1914) and *Fredigundis* (Berlin, 1922), two piano concertos for the left-hand alone, and chamber and organ music. >> Bruckner

Schmidt, Helmut (Heinrich Waldemar) [shmit] (1918–) West German statesman and chancellor (1974–82), born in Hamburg, Germany. After service in World War 2, he studied at Hamburg, joined the Social Democratic Party in 1946, and became a member of the Bundestag in 1953. He was minister of defence (1969–72), and of finance (1972–4), in which role he created a firm basis for Germany's continued economic growth. He succeeded Brandt as chancellor, describing his aim as the 'political unification of Europe in partnership with the United States'. >> Brandt, Willy

Schmidt, Maarten [shmit] (1929–) Astronomer, born in Groningen, The Netherlands. He studied at Groningen and Leyden, moved to the California Institute of Technology in 1959, and became director of the Hale Observatories in 1978. He studied the spectrum of an optically identified quasar, and discovered that the peculiarities of its spectrum were caused by a massive red shift, which appeared to be receding at nearly 16% of the speed of light. Such high velocities are now interpreted as implying that quasars are very distant objects. He also found that the number of quasars increases with distance from Earth, providing evidence for the 'big bang' theory for the origin of the universe. >> Sandage

Schmidt, Wilhelm [shmit] (1868–1954) Ethnologist, born in Hörde, Germany. Ordained a Roman Catholic priest in 1892, he studied oriental languages at Berlin University (1893–5), and became professor in the St Gabriel Mission Seminary at Mödling, where he remained until 1938. He also taught at Vienna and Fribourg. Influenced by Fritz Graebner, he sought to develop and refine Graebner's system of *Kulturkreise* or trait clusters, proposing a theory of devolution to counter that of cultural evolution. In 1906 he founded the journal *Anthropos*. >> Graebner

Schmidt-Rottluff, Karl [shmit rotluhf] (1884–1976) Painter and print-maker, born in Rottluff, Germany. He began as an architectural student in Dresden, and became one of the founder members of the avant-garde group of painters known as *Die Brücke* (1905). He developed a harsh, angular style which is well exemplified in his powerful wood-cuts such as 'Woman with Hat' (1905). >> Heckel; Kirchner; Nolde; Pechstein

Schnabel, Artur [shnahbl] (1882–1951) Pianist and composer, born in Lipnik, Austria. He made his debut at the age of eight. He taught in Berlin, making frequent concert appearances throughout Europe and America, and with the advent of the Nazi government settled first in Switzerland, then in the USA from 1939. He was an authoritative player of a small range of German classics – notably Beethoven, Mozart, and Schubert. His compositions include chamber music and piano works, and a piano concerto.

Schnittke, Alfred [shnitkuh] (1934–) Composer, born near Saratov, Russia. He studied composition at Moscow Conservatory (1953–8), and taught there from 1962 to 1972. His prolific output has attracted more Western attention than any Soviet composer since Shostakovich. It is characterized by bold eclectic flair, and frequent reference to music of the past and to popular styles such as jazz.

His compositions include four symphonies, concertos, ballets, film scores, and chamber, vocal, choral, and piano works. >> Shostakovich

Schnitzer, Eduard >> **Emin Pasha**

Schnitzler, Arthur [shnitsler] (1862–1931) Playwright and novelist, born in Vienna. He was a physician before he turned playwright, writing highly psychological, often strongly erotic short plays and novels. They include his one-act play cycles *Anatol* (1893) and *Reigen* (1900, filmed as *La Ronde*, 1950).

Schoenberg, Arnold [shoenberg], also spelled **Schönberg** (1874–1951) Composer, born in Vienna. He was largely self-taught, and in his 20s lived by orchestrating operettas while composing such early works as the string sextet *Verklärte Nacht* (1899, Transfigured Night). His search for a personal musical style emerged in these works, which were not well received: his *Chamber Symphony* caused a riot at its first performance in 1907 through its abandonment of the traditional concept of tonality. He became known for his concept of '12-note' or 'serial' music, used in most of his later works. At the end of World War 1 he taught in Vienna and Berlin, until exiled by the Nazi government in 1933. He settled in California, and took US nationality in 1941.

Schoenheimer, Rudolf [shoenhiymer] (1898–1941) Biochemist, born in Berlin. He studied at Berlin, taught at Leipzig and Freiburg, then moved to the USA in 1933. Working at Columbia University with Urey, he used two new isotopes to trace biochemical pathways. The methods he pioneered have since been used with a variety of isotopic tracers for a range of biochemical studies. He committed suicide at the height of his career. >> Urey

Schöffer, Peter [shoefer] (c. 1425–1502) Printer, born in Gernsheim, Germany. He studied in Paris, then became an apprentice to Gutenberg. With his father-in-law, Johann Fust, he took over and ran the printing works. They completed the Gutenberg Bible (1456), and in 1457 issued the *Mainz Psalter*, the first work on which the name of the printer and date of publication appears. >> Fust; Gutenberg, Johannes

Scholes, Percy Alfred [skohlz] (1877–1958) Musicologist, born in Leeds, West Yorkshire, N England, UK. He studied at Oxford, then lectured there and at Manchester, London, and Cambridge. Appointed music critic to *The Observer* (1920–5), he became the first music adviser to the BBC, and edited *The Oxford Companion to Music* (1938). His reputation as a musicologist rests on his authorship of *The Puritans and Music* (1934) and *The Life of Dr Burney* (1948).

Scholl, William (1882–1968) US physician and businessman. After learning the trade of shoemaking he went to medical college, then returned to the shoe industry. He patented an arch support and founded his manufacturing company (1904), bringing a scientific basis to shoe fitting. His company later expanded into a wide range of foot products.

Schomberg, Frederick Hermann, Duke of [shomberg] (1615–90) Soldier of fortune, born in Heidelberg, Germany. During the Thirty Years War he fought for the Dutch (1634–7), then served with the French army (1652–4), and with the Portuguese (1660–8). He became a French citizen (1668) and, though a Protestant, obtained a marshal's baton in 1675. After the revocation of the Edict of Nantes (1685), he retired to Portugal and afterwards took service under the Elector of Brandenburg. He commanded under William of Orange (William III) in the English expedition (1688), became a naturalized English citizen, and was created Duke of Schomberg (1689). As commander-in-chief in Ireland, he conducted the Ulster campaign, but was killed at the Boyne. >> William III

Schomburgk, Sir Robert Hermann [shomboork] (1804–65) Explorer and surveyor, born in Freyburg am der Unstrut, Germany. He went to the USA in 1829, and surveyed Anegada, one of the British Virgin Is (1831). Sent by the Royal Geographical Society to explore British Guiana (1835), he discovered the giant Victoria Regia lily. He was employed to draw the *Schomburgk line* marking the boundary of British Guiana (1841–3). Knighted on his return in 1844, he became British consul in San Domingo (1848–57) and Siam (1857–64).

Schönberg, Arnold >> **Schoenberg, Arnold**

Schongauer or **Schön, Martin** [shongower, shoen] (1450–91) Painter and engraver, born in Colmar, France. He may have studied at the University of Leipzig. Many religious paintings attributed to him have not been authenticated, but well over 100 of his engraved plates have survived, including 'The Passion of Christ' and 'The Wise and Foolish Virgins'. His famous 'Madonna of the Rose Garden' altarpiece (1473, Colmar, S Martin) is regarded as one of the best early representations of the Virgin, and shows Flemish influence.

Schoolcraft, Henry Rowe (1793–1864) Ethnologist, born in Albany Co, NY. In 1820 he went with Lewis Cass to L Superior as geologist, and became Indian agent for the tribes round the lakes (1822). He married a woman of Indian blood (1823), made a special study of her tribe, and negotiated treaties by which the government acquired substantial areas of N Michigan. In 1832 he commanded an expedition which discovered the sources of the Mississippi. His most important ethnological work is *Information Respecting the Indian Tribes of the US* (6 vols, 1851–7). >> Cass

Schopenhauer, Arthur [shohpenhower] (1788–1860) Philosopher, born in Gdańsk, Poland. He studied at Göttingen and Berlin, then taught at Berlin (1820), where he boldly held his lectures at the same times as Hegel, whose ideas he rejected; but he failed to attract students. He then lived in retirement as a scholar at Frankfurt. His chief work, *Die Welt als Wille und Vorstellung* (1819, The World as Will and Idea), emphasizes the central role of human will as the creative, primary factor in understanding. His conception of the will as a blind, irrational force led him to a rejection of Enlightenment doctrines and to pessimism. He eventually attracted attention with a collection of diverse essays and aphoristic writings, published under the title of *Parerga und Paralipomena* (1851), and subsequently influenced not only existentialism and other philosophical movements, but a range of writers and artists, such as Wagner, Tolstoy, Proust, and Mann. >> Hegel; Nietzsche

Schott, Otto >> **Abbe, Ernst**

Schouten, Willem Corneliszoon [showten] (c. 1580–1625) Navigator, born in Hoorn, The Netherlands. In the service of the East India Company, he was the first to traverse Drake Passage in 1615. He discovered Cape Horn in 1616, which he named after his birthplace.

Schreiber, Lady Charlotte Elizabeth [shriyber], née **Bertie** (1812–95) Scholar and collector, born in Uffington, Lincolnshire, EC England, UK. She became interested in the literature of Wales after her marriage in 1833 to **Sir Josiah John Guest** (1785–1852), of Merthyr Tydfil. After his death she married (1855) **Charles Schreiber**, former MP for Cheltenham and Poole. Best known for her part in translating and editing *The Mabinogion* (1838–49), she was also a collector of fans, playing cards, and china, which she bequeathed to the British Museum and the Victoria and Albert Museum.

Schreiner, Olive (Emilie Albertina) [shriyner], pseudonym **Ralph Iron** (1855–1920) Writer, born in Wittebergen, South Africa. Largely self-educated, she went to England

(1881–9), working as a governess, while she wrote her successful *The Story of an African Farm* (1883), the first sustained, imaginative work in English to come from Africa. In her later work she became a passionate propagandist for women's rights, pro-Boer loyalty, and pacifism, as in *Woman and Labour* (1911).

Schrieffer, John (Robert) [shreefer] (1931–) Physicist, born in Oak Park, IL. He studied at the Massachusetts Institute of Technology and Illinois University, then taught at Chicago, Illinois, Pennsylvania, Cornell (1969–75), and California (Santa Barbara) universities. Collaboration with John Bardeen and Leon Cooper led to the BCS (Bardeen–Cooper–Schrieffer) theory of superconductivity, for which all three shared the 1972 Nobel Prize for Physics. >> Bardeen; Cooper, Leon

Schrödinger, Erwin [shroedinger] (1887–1961) Physicist, born in Vienna. He taught at Stuttgart, Wrocław, Poland (formerly Breslau, Germany), Zürich, Berlin, Oxford (1933–8), and Dublin (1940–56), after which he retired to Vienna. He originated the study of the wave behaviour of matter within quantum mechanics with his celebrated wave equation (1926), which is as important to science at the subatomic level as Newton's laws of motion are to mechanics in the normal-size world. A versatile scientist, he also made significant contributions to molecular biology, and philosophy. He shared the Nobel Prize for Physics in 1933. His books include *What is Life?* (1946) and *Science and Man* (1958). >> RR1122

Schubert, Franz (Peter) [shoobert] (1797–1828) Composer, born in Vienna. At 11 he became a member of the chapel choir at the imperial court, and with little formal training began to compose. From 1817 he lived precariously as a composer and teacher, until he formed an association with the operatic baritone, **Johann Michael Vogl** (1768–1840), with whom he founded the successful 'Schubertiads' – private and public accompanied recitals of his songs – which made them known throughout Vienna. His major works include the Trout Piano Quintet (1819), his C major symphony (1825), and his B minor symphony (1822), known as the 'Unfinished'. He is particularly remembered as the greatest exponent of German songs (*Lieder*), which number c.600. He also wrote a great deal of choral and chamber music.

Schultz, Theodore (William) [shults] (1902–) Economist, born in Arlington, SD. He studied at South Dakota State College and Wisconsin University, then taught at Iowa State College (1930–43) and the University of Chicago (1943–72). He shared the 1979 Nobel Prize for Economics for his work stressing the importance of the human factor in agriculture. >> RR1125

Schultze, Max (Johann Sigismund) [shultzuh] (1825–74) Zoologist, born in Freiburg, Germany. He studied at Greifswald and Berlin, and taught zoology at Bonn from 1859. His best-known work is on unicellular organisms. In 1861 he argued that cells in general contain a nucleus and protoplasm as 'the basis of life' and that a boundary membrane is not always present. His duplicity theory of vision of 1866, based on his study of the retina of birds, ascribed separate functions to the retinal rods and cones, and was a step towards later theories of vision.

Schulz, Charles (Monroe) [shults] (1922–) Strip cartoonist, the creator of *Peanuts*, born in Minneapolis, MN. Learning cartooning from a correspondence course, he worked as a freelancer for a religious magazine and the *Saturday Evening Post* (1947). He submitted a sample strip about children entitled *Li'l Folks* to many newspapers before United Features accepted it, retitling it *Peanuts* (1950). It became one of the world's most successful strips, and has been adapted for television and stage. Schulz based the Charlie Brown character on himself.

Schumacher, E F [shoomaker] (1911–77) German economist. He was interned in Britain while studying at Oxford at the outbreak of World War 2. After the war he served as economic adviser to the British Control Commission in Germany (1946–50), and with the National Coal Board (1950–70). His concern for the Third World was expressed in his book *Small Is Beautiful* (1973), and he founded the Intermediate Technology Group to develop tools and ideas appropriate to the culture and traditions of the people using them.

Schumacher, Kurt (Ernst Karl) [shoomakher] (1895–1953) German statesman, born in Kulm, Germany. He studied law and political science at the universities of Leipzig and Berlin, and from 1930 to 1933 was a member of the Reichstag and of the executive of the Social Democratic parliamentary group. An outspoken opponent of National Socialism, he spent 10 years in Nazi concentration camps (1933–43), where he showed outstanding courage. In 1946 he became chairman of the Social Democratic Party and of the parliamentary group of the Bundestag.

Schumacher, Michael [shoomaker] (1969–) Motor-racing driver, born in Hürth-Hermuhlheim, Germany. He began racing karts at the age of five, became German and European Senior Kart champion in 1987, moved up to Formula Ford (1988) and Formula Three (1989), and won the German F3 Championship in 1990. He made his F1 debut with Jordan in 1990, but was immediately given a place in the Benetton team, with whom he became world champion in 1994 and 1995. He joined the (unusually) struggling Ferrari team in 1996, and achieved second place in the 1997 championship, but lost this position following an enquiry into a driving incident in which his car hit Villeneuve's. >> Villeneuve

Schuman, Robert [shooman] (1886–1963) French statesman and prime minister (1947–8), born in Luxembourg. He held several government posts after World War 2, and as foreign minister (1948–52) proposed the *Schuman plan* (1950) for pooling the coal and steel resources of West Europe, which came to fruition in the European Coal and Steel Community. He was president of the EEC Assembly (1958–60). >> RR1049

Schuman, William (Howard) [shooman] (1910–92) Composer, born in New York City. He studied under Roy Harris and at Salzburg, winning in 1943 the first Pulitzer Prize to be awarded to a composer. In 1945 he became president of the Juilliard School, New York City. He composed 10 symphonies, concertos for piano and violin, and several ballets, as well as choral and orchestral works. >> Harris, Roy

Schumann, Clara (Josephine) [shooman], née **Wieck** (1819–96) Pianist and composer, born in Leipzig, Germany. She gave her first concert at 11, and published four of her Polonaises the following year. Her compositions include chamber music, songs, and many piano works, including a concerto. She married Robert Schumann in 1840, and from 1878 was principal piano teacher in the Conservatory at Frankfurt. >> Schumann, Robert

Schumann, Elisabeth [shooman] (1885–1952) Operatic soprano and *Lieder* singer, born in Merseburg, Germany. In 1919 she was engaged by Richard Strauss for the Vienna State Opera, and sang in his and Mozart's operas all over the world, making her London debut in 1924. She later concentrated more on *Lieder* by such composers as Schubert, Hugo Wolf, and Richard Strauss. She left Austria in 1936, and became a US citizen in 1944. >> Strauss, Richard

Schumann, Robert (Alexander) [shooman] (1810–56) Composer, born in Zwickau, Germany. He studied law at Leipzig, then turned to music, and particularly the piano, but after injuring a finger in 1832, he gave up performing for writing and composing. He produced a large number of compositions, until 1840 almost all for the piano. He then married Clara, the daughter of his piano teacher, Friedrich Wieck, after much opposition from her father, and under her influence began to write orchestral works, notably his A minor piano concerto (1845) and four symphonies. He also wrote chamber music and a large number of songs (*Lieder*), in addition to his continuing piano compositions. In 1843 he was appointed professor at the new Leipzig Conservatory, but mental illness caused him soon to leave, and he moved to Dresden, then Düsseldorf (1850), where he attempted suicide (1854). He died in a sanatorium in Endenich (now part of Bonn). >> Schumann, Clara

Schumann-Heink, Ernestine [shooman hiyngk], *née* **Rossler** (1861–1936) Contralto, born near Prague. Having come to fame in Europe, especially for her Wagnerian roles, she made her US debut in Chicago in 1898, singing regularly with the Metropolitan Opera until 1932. A US citizen since 1905, she remained in the USA during World War 1 and demonstrated her patriotism while sons of her different marriages fought on opposite sides. She made one film, *Here's to Romance* (1935), but died before she could continue with her plans for a film career.

Schurz, Carl [shoorts] (1829–1906) Journalist and political reformer, born in Liblar, Germany. Imprisoned after the revolution of 1848, he escaped and arrived in the USA in 1852. He became a politician, lecturer, major-general in the Civil War, journalist, senator (1869–75), and secretary of the interior (1877–81). In the 1880s he was editor of the *New York Evening Post* and *The Nation*, and he wrote Lives of Henry Clay (1887) and Lincoln (1889).

Schuschnigg, Kurt von [shushnik] (1897–1977) Austrian statesman and chancellor (1934–8), born in Riva, Italy (formerly Austria–Hungary). He served in World War 1, practised law, was elected a Christian Socialist Deputy (1927), and became minister of justice (1932) and of education (1933). His attempt to prevent Hitler occupying Austria led to his imprisonment until 1945. He then lived in the USA, where he became professor of political science at St Louis University (1948–67), before returning to Austria (1967), and writing *Im Kampf gegen Hitler* (1969, trans The Brutal Takeover).

Schuster, Sir Arthur [shuster] (1851–1934) Physicist, born in Frankfurt, Germany. He studied at Heidelberg and Cambridge, and became professor of applied mathematics (1881) and physics (1888–1907) at Manchester. He carried out important pioneer work in spectroscopy and terrestrial magnetism. The *Schuster–Smith magnetometer* is the standard instrument for measuring the Earth's magnetic force. He led the eclipse expedition to Siam in 1875.

Schutz, Alfred [shuts] (1899–1959) Social philosopher, born in Vienna. He emigrated to the USA, and continued his banking career in New York City from 1939, becoming professor in the New School of Social Research there in 1952. He reacted against the positivism and behaviourism of the Vienna Circle, and developed a phenomenological, descriptive sociology which assumes that the sociologists are themselves a factor in whatever they investigate. His main work is *Die sinnhafte Aufbau der sozialen Welt* (1932, The Phenomenology of the Social World). >> Schlick

Schütz, Heinrich [shüts], Lat **Heinricus Sagittarius** (1585–1672) Composer, born in Köstritz, Germany. He studied under Gabrieli in Venice (1609), and was appointed *Hofkapellmeister* in Dresden (1617), where he introduced Italian-type music, and styles of performance such as instrumentally accompanied choral compositions, as in his *Psalms of David* (1619). Regarded as the founder of the Baroque school of German music, a visit to Italy in 1628 acquainted him with more recent developments, and from 1633 until his return to Dresden in 1641 he travelled between various courts, including those at Copenhagen and Hanover. His compositions

include church music, psalms, motets, passions, a German requiem, and the first German opera, *Dafne*, produced in Torgau in 1627. >> Gabrieli, Giovanni

Schuyler, Philip John [skÿler] (1733–1804) US soldier and politician, born in Albany, NY. He was a member of the Colonial Assembly from 1768, and delegate to the Continental Congress of 1775. As major-general of the northern department of New York, he was preparing to invade Canada when ill health compelled him to tender his resignation (1779). Besides acting as commissioner for Indian affairs, he sat in Congress (1777–81), and became state senator (1780–97), US senator (1789–91, 1797–8), and surveyor-general of New York (from 1782).

Schwann, Theodor [shvahn] (1810–82) Physiologist, born in Neuss, Germany. He studied medicine at Berlin University, and became professor at Louvain (1838) and Liège (1848). He discovered the enzyme pepsin, investigated muscle contraction, demonstrated the role of micro-organisms in putrefaction, and extended the cell theory (previously applied to plants) to animal tissues, thus founding modern histology.

Schwartz, Delmore [shvaw(r)ts] (1913–66) Poet, short-story writer, and critic, born in New York City. He studied at New York University, then taught at Harvard, Princeton, New York, and Syracuse universities. He was influential among Jewish writers after World War 2, and secured fame with his first book of stories and poems, *In Dreams Begin Responsibilities* (1938). His collection of short stories, *The World is a Wedding* (1948), deals with the problems of Jewish life in America.

Schwarz, Harvey (Fisher) [shvaw(r)ts] (1905–88) Electrical engineer, co-inventor of the Decca radio-navigation system for ships and aircraft, born in Edwardsville, IL. He studied at Washington University, St Louis, then worked for the General Electric Co, before the Brunswick Radio Corporation sent him to Britain in 1932 to design radios and radiograms for manufacture in the UK. During World War 2, working for Decca, he helped to develop a prototype radio-navigation system that was put into operation for the first time during the D-Day landings in 1944.

Schwarzenberg, Karl Philipp, Fürst zu (Prince of) [shvah(r)tsenberg] (1771–1820) Austrian soldier and diplomat, born in Vienna. He entered the army in 1787, and in the War of the Second Coalition (1792–1802) distinguished himself at Hohenlinden (1800). As ambassador to Russia when Austria declared war on France (1809), he took part in the defeat at Wagram. After the peace treaty, he conducted the negotiations for the marriage between Napoleon and Marie Louise of Austria (1810). Napoleon appointed him general of the Austrian contingent in the invasion of Russia in 1812, and when Austria turned on Napoleon, he commanded the allied armies which won the Battles of Dresden and Leipzig in 1813. >> Marie Louise; Napoleon I

Schwarzenberg, Felix (Ludwig Johann Friedrich) [shvah(r)tsenberg] (1800–52) Austrian statesman, born in Krumau, Austria. During the 1848 Revolution, he was made prime minister, and created a centralized, absolutist, imperial state. He then sought Russian military aid to suppress the Hungarian rebellion (1849), and demonstrated Austrian superiority over Prussia at the Olmütz Convention (1850). His bold initiatives temporarily restored Habsburg domination of European affairs.

Schwarzenegger, Arnold [shvaw(r)tseneger] (1947–) US film actor, born near Graz, Austria. He took up body-building at the age of 14, winning several Mr Universe and Mr Olympia titles, then starred in a body-building documentary, *Pumping Iron* (1977). He had various small film roles before he was cast in *Stay Hungry* (1976), for which he received a Golden Globe as best newcomer. In the 1980s he became established as the leading figure in a new genre of muscular action films, beginning with *Conan the Barbarian* (1982) and *Conan the Destroyer* (1984), which became increasingly technological and violent with *The Terminator* (1984) and *Total Recall* (1990). A more humane side to his roles also emerged in such films as *Twins* (1988), *Terminator 2: Judgment Day* (1991), *Last Action Hero* (1992), and *Junior* (1994). Later films include *Batman and Robin* (1997). He became an American citizen in 1983.

Schwarzkopf, (Olga Maria) Elisabeth (Friederike) [shvah(r)tskopf] (1915–) Soprano, born in Janotschin, Poland. She studied at Berlin, where she made her debut in 1938, and sang in the Vienna State Opera (1944–8) and at Covent Garden (1949–52). She first specialized in coloratura roles, and later appeared more as a lyric soprano, especially in recitals of *Lieder*. >> Legge

Schwarzkopf, H Norman [shvah(r)tskopf], nickname **Stormin' Norman** (1934–) US general, born in Trenton, NJ. He trained at Valley Forge and West Point, after which he studied guided-missile engineering at the University of Southern California. He served in Vietnam, was promoted to general (1983), and made commander-in-chief of the US Central Command at MacDill Air Force Base in Florida (1988). He is remembered for his role as commander of the Allied forces that liberated Kuwait from the Iraqi occupation led by Saddam Hussein in August, 1990. In 'Operation Desert Storm', Schwarzkopf distinguished himself as a brilliant strategist, and was noted for his expertise in handling press briefings. He retired from active duty in 1991 and began writing his autobiography. >> Hussein, Saddam; Powell, Colin

Schwarzschild, Karl [shvah(r)tsshild] (1873–1916) Theoretical astrophysicist, born in Frankfurt, Germany. He computed exact solutions of Einstein's field equations in general relativity – work which led directly to modern research on black holes. The *Schwarzschild radius* is the critical radius at which an object becomes a black hole if collapsed or compressed indefinitely. At this radius the escape velocity is the speed of light. Its value is 9 mm/0·35 in for Earth, 3 km/1·9 mi for the Sun.

Schweitzer, Albert [shv**iy**tser] (1875–1965) Medical missionary, theologian, musician, and philosopher, born in Kaysersberg, Germany. He studied at Strasbourg, Paris, and Berlin, and in 1896 made his famous decision that he would live for science and art until he was 30, then devote his life to serving humanity. He became a curate at Strasbourg (1899), taught at the university (1902), and was appointed principal of the theological college (1903). His religious writing includes *Von Reimarus zu Wrede* (1906, trans The Quest of the Historical Jesus), and major works on St Paul. True to his vow, despite his international reputation in music and theology, he began to study medicine in 1905, and after qualifying (1913), set out with his newly-married wife to set up a hospital to fight leprosy and sleeping sickness at Lambaréné, French Equatorial Africa, where he remained for the rest of his life, apart from fundraising visits and occasional lectures in Europe. He was awarded the Nobel Peace Prize in 1952.

Schwenkfeld (von Ossig), Kaspar [shvengkfelt] (1489–1561) Writer and preacher, born in Ossig, Germany. He served at various German courts, and c.1525 developed a form of Protestantism. His doctrines resembled those of the Quakers, and brought him banishment and persecution, but he gained disciples everywhere. Most of his works were burned by both Protestants and Catholics. Some of his persecuted followers (most numerous in Silesia and Swabia) emigrated to Holland. In 1734, 40 families emigrated to England, and from there to Pennsylvania, where they formed the *Schwenkfelder Church*.

Schwimmer, David [shwim er] (1966–) Actor and director, born in New York City. He studied theatre and speech at Northwestern University, then co-founded Chicago's Lookingglass Theatre Company, where he has directed a number of productions. He played several small roles in television series, eventually becoming well known for his role as Ross Geller in the acclaimed television series *Friends* (1994–). Roles in feature films include *Crossing the Bridge* (1992 and *The Pallbearer* (1996).

Schwimmer, Rosika [shvim er] (1877–1948) Feminist and pacifist, born in Budapest. As a journalist she was active in the Hungarian women's movement, and was a co-founder of a feminist-pacifist group. She became vice-president of the Women's International League for Peace and Freedom, and was Hungarian minister to Switzerland (1918–19). In 1920, fleeing from the country's anti-Semitic leadership, she emigrated to the USA, where she continued to campaign for pacifism.

Schwinger, Julian (Seymour) [shwing ger] (1918–94) Physicist, born in New York City. A child prodigy, he received his doctorate from Columbia when he was 21, then worked at the universities of California, Berkeley (1939–41), Harvard (1945–72), and California, Los Angeles (from 1972). He shared the 1965 Nobel Prize for Physics for his independent work on quantum electrodynamics. >> RR1122

Schwitters, Kurt [shvi terz] (1887–1948) Artist, born in Hanover, Germany. He studied at the Dresden Academy, and painted abstract pictures before joining the Dadaists. His best-known contribution to the movement was 'Merz', a name he gave to a form of collage using such everyday detritus, such as broken glass, tram tickets, and scraps of paper picked up in the street. From 1920 onwards he slowly built from bits and pieces of rubbish a three-dimensional construction which he called his 'Merzbau', and which filled the house before being destroyed in an air raid in 1943. In 1937 he fled from Nazi Germany to Norway, then in 1940 to England. >> Arp; Duchamp; Ernst; Picabia; Ray, Man

Sciascia, Leonardo [shiashia] (1921–89) Novelist, born in Racalmuto, Sicily. A teacher and politician, he took Sicily for the focus of his writing, and his themes embrace its society past and present, which he saw as exemplifying the political, social, and spiritual tensions to be found on the wider stage of Europe. His novels include *Le parrocchie di Regalpetra* (1956, trans Salt in the Wound), *Candido* (1977), *Il Consiglio d'Egitto* (1963, The Council of Egypt), and *A ciascuno il suo* (1968, To Each His Own).

Scicolone, Sofia >> Loren, Sophia

Scipio Africanus [skipioh], in full **Publius Cornelius Scipio Africanus**, also called **Scipio Africanus Major** (236–c. 183 BC) Innovative Roman general of the Second Punic War, whose victory at Ilipa (206 BC) forced the Carthaginians out of Spain, and whose defeat of Hannibal at Zama (202 BC) broke the power of Carthage altogether. Honoured for this with the title **Africanus**, he remained in the forefront of affairs until forced into retirement by his political enemies of the 180s. >> Antiochus III; Hannibal; Hasdrubal

Scipio Aemilianus [skipioh aymiliahnus], in full **Scipio Aemilianus Publius Cornelius**, also called **Scipio Africanus Minor** (185–129 BC) Roman statesman, general, and orator, the adopted grandson of Scipio Africanus Major. He is famous primarily for the sack of Carthage in the Third Punic War (146 BC), the destruction of Numantia (133 BC), and his patronage of the arts. Members of the so-called *Scipionic circle* included the historian Polybius, the Stoic Panaetius, the poet Lucilius, and the playwright Terence. His opposition to the reforms of the Gracchi may have been the cause of his sudden death, possibly by poison. >> Gracchus, Gaius; Lucilius; Panaetius; Polybius; Terence

Scofield, (David) Paul [skohfeeld] (1922–   ) Actor, born in Hurstpierpoint, West Sussex, England, UK. He studied at the Croydon Repertory School and the London Mask Theatre before making his professional debut in 1940. At Stratford-upon-Avon in the 1940s, he began to distinguish himself in Shakespearian roles, and later starred in Peter Brook's production of *King Lear* (1962, subsequently filmed) and in *Othello* (National Theatre, 1980). His Sir Thomas More in Bolt's *A Man For All Seasons* (Globe Theatre, London, 1960, filmed 1966) remains one of the great performances in post-war British theatre, and work in plays by contemporary playwrights, such as Hampton's *Savages* (1973) and Shaffer's *Amadeus* (1979), give evidence of his range and versatility. Later film credits include *The Crucible* (1996).

Scopas [skohpas] (c.4th-c BC) Sculptor, from the Greek island of Paros. One of the three major artists of the 4th-c, he is traditionally believed to have worked on the Temple of Athena Alea at Tegea, the temple of Artemis at Ephesus, and the Mausoleum at Halicarnassus.

Scorel, Jan van [skorel] (1495–1562) Painter, architect, and engineer, born in Schoorel, The Netherlands. He trained in Amsterdam, and by 1517 was working in Utrecht. He made extensive travels in Europe, and was influenced by the work of Giorgione in Venice. After a pilgrimage to Jerusalem, he returned to Italy in 1521. In Rome, Pope Adrian VI appointed him inspector of the Belvedere, and sat for a portrait (1523). He studied the work of Michelangelo and Raphael, returned to Utrecht in 1524, and established the style of the Italian Renaissance in Holland. Noted particularly for his portraiture, his group portraits of pilgrims to Jerusalem can be seen at Utrecht and Haarlem. >> Giorgione

Scoresby, William (1789–1857) Arctic explorer, born near Whitby, North Yorkshire, N England, UK. As a boy he went with his father to the whaling grounds in the Arctic. He studied at Edinburgh University, and published *The Arctic Regions* (1820), the first scientific accounts of the Arctic seas and lands. In 1822 he surveyed 400 mi of the E coast of Greenland. He later studied at Cambridge, and was ordained in 1825. In 1856 he gathered valuable data on terrestrial magnetism while voyaging to Australia.

Scorsese, Martin [skaw(r)sayzee] (1942–   ) Film director, writer, and producer, born in Flushing, Long Island, NY. He studied film at New York University, then made commercials and worked as a film editor before returning to direction with *Boxcar Bertha* (1972). Considered one of the foremost directors of his generation, his work has sought to illuminate masculine aggression and sexual inequality, and he has frequently questioned traditional American values. His many films include *Alice Doesn't Live Here Anymore* (1974), *Taxi Driver* (1976), *Raging Bull* (1980), the controversial *The Last Temptation of Christ* (1988), *GoodFellas* (1990), *The Age of Innocence* (1993), and *Casino* (1995).

Scott, Alexander (c.1525–c.1584) Lyrical poet from Scotland, UK. Little is known of his early life, but he is regarded as one of the last of the *makaris* (poets of the 14th-c who used the old Scottish metrical forms). He wrote 35 short poems, which appear in the Bannatyne Manuscript (1568).

Scott, C(harles) P(restwich) (1846–1932) Newspaper editor, born in Bath, SW England, UK. He studied at Oxford, and became editor of the *Manchester Guardian* (known as *The Guardian* since 1959) at the age of 26. He raised it to a hugely respected rival of *The Times* by independent and often controversial editorial policies, such as opposition to the Boer War, and by his high literary standards. He was also a Liberal MP (1895–1906). He bought *The Guardian* in 1905, just after the death of his wife, and devoted his life to it. He retired in 1929 and left the newspaper to his younger son, who drowned four months later.

Scott, Cyril Meir (1879–1970) Composer, born in Oxton, Cheshire, NWC England, UK. As a child he studied the piano in Frankfurt, later returning there to study composition. His works won a hearing in London at the turn of the century, and in 1913 he was able to introduce his music to Vienna. His opera, *The Alchemist*, had its first performance in Essen in 1925. He composed three symphonies, piano, violin, and cello concertos, and numerous choral and orchestral works, but is best known for his piano pieces and songs.

Scott, Dred (c. 1795–c. 1858) Slave, born in Southampton Co, VA. He made legal and constitutional history in the *Dred Scott Case* (1848–57), which sought to obtain his freedom on the ground that his master took him from Missouri (a slave state) to Illinois (a free state). The Supreme Court ruled against him, but the decision served to increase anti-slavery agitation in the North. He was soon emancipated, and became a hotel porter in St Louis, MO. >> Taney

Scott, Dunkinfield Henry (1854–1934) Botanist, born in London, England, UK, the son of George Gilbert Scott. He studied at Oxford and Würzburg universities, became assistant professor at the Royal College of Science, and in 1892 keeper of Jodrell Laboratory, Kew, devoting himself to plant anatomy and later to palaeobotany. He collaborated with **William Crawford Williamson** (1816–95) in a number of notable studies of fossil plants, and established in 1904 the class Pteridospermeae. >> Scott, George Gilbert

Scott, Francis George (1880–1958) Composer, born in Hawick, Scottish Borders, SE Scotland, UK. He studied at the universities of Edinburgh and Durham, and in Paris under the symphonic composer Jean Jules Amiable Roger-Ducasse (1873–1954). He lectured in music at Jordanhill Training College for Teachers, Glasgow (1925–46). His *Scottish Lyrics* (5 vols, 1921–39) comprise original settings of songs by Dunbar, Burns, and other poets. Primarily a song composer, he wrote the orchestral suite *The Seven Deadly Sins*, and other orchestral works.

Scott, George C(ampbell) (1927–   ) Film actor, born in Wise, VA. He studied at the University of Missouri and served in the Marines before becoming a theatre actor. He made his film debut in *The Hanging Tree* (1959), other early roles including *The Hustler* (1961) and *Dr Strangelove* (1963). He won an Oscar for *Patton* (1969), but refused to accept it (the first actor to do so), and also refused the Emmy he won for *The Price* (1970). Later films include *Dick Tracy* (1989), *Malice* (1993), and *Country Justice* (1997), as well as appearances in several television productions.

Scott, Sir George Gilbert (1811–78) Architect, born in Gawcott, Buckinghamshire, SC England, UK. He studied in London, and influenced by Pugin became the leading practical architect of the British Gothic revival, responsible for the building or restoration of many ecclesiastical and civil buildings, such as the Albert Memorial (1862–3), St Pancras Station and Hotel in London (1865), and Glasgow University (1865). He became professor of architecture at the Royal Academy in 1868, and was knighted in 1872. >> Pugin; Street; Scott, Dunkinfield Henry; Scott, Giles Gilbert

Scott, Sir Giles Gilbert (1880–1960) Architect, born in London, England, UK, the grandson of George Gilbert Scott. He studied at Beaumont College, designed the Anglican cathedral in Liverpool (begun 1904), and was knighted after the consecration ceremony in 1924. He designed many public buildings, including the new Bodleian Library at Oxford (1936–46), the new Cambridge University Library (1931–4), and the new Waterloo Bridge (1939–45). >> Scott, George Gilbert

Scott, Mackay Hugh Baillie (1865–1945) Architect and designer, born in Kent, SE England, UK. He designed the decoration for the palace of the Grand Duke of Hesse at Darmstadt, which was carried out by the Guild of Handicraft in consultation with Ashbee in 1898. In 1901 he gave up his practice in Douglas, and moved to Bedford. His furniture is simple, solid, bold, and generally decorated with a degree of Art Nouveau ornamentation. He went on to design numerous houses in Britain and Europe before retiring in 1939. >> Ashbee

Scott, Michael (1907–83) British missionary and political activist. He served in a London parish and as chaplain in India (1935–9), where he collaborated with the Communists. Invalided out of the RAF in 1941, he served in various missions in South Africa (1943–50). No longer associating with Communists, he exposed the atrocities in the Bethal farming area and in the Transvaal, defended the Basutos against wrongful arrest, and brought the case of the dispossessed Herero tribe before the UN.

Scott, Paul (Mark) (1920–78) Novelist, born in London, England, UK. He studied in London, then served with the Indian army in India and Malaya (1943–6), and worked as a literary agent until 1960. His reputation is based on four novels collectively known as *The Raj Quartet* (1966–74), comprising *The Jewel in the Crown* (1966), *The Day of the Scorpion* (1968), *The Towers of Silence* (1972), and *A Division of the Spoils* (1974), in which he gave an exhaustive account of the British withdrawal from India. This quartet was adapted for the Granada television series *The Jewel in the Crown* (1982).

Scott, Sir Percy Moreton (1853–1924) British naval commander and gunnery expert, born in London, England, UK. He entered the Royal Navy in 1866 and saw active service in Ashanti (Ghana), Egypt, South Africa, and China. Retiring in 1909, he returned to active service as gunnery adviser to the fleet, and commanded the anti-aircraft defences of London (1915–18). He foresaw the importance of air power at sea, and his methods and inventions transformed naval gunnery.

Scott, Sir Peter (Markham) (1909–89) Artist, ornithologist, and broadcaster, born in London, England, UK, the son of Robert Falcon Scott. An Olympic sportsman (dinghy sailing), he served in the navy in World War 2. He began to exhibit his paintings of bird scenes in 1933, and after the war led several ornithological expeditions (Iceland, 1951, 1953; Australasia and the Pacific, 1956–7). His writing and television programmes helped to popularize natural history, and he received a knighthood in 1973. >> Scott, R F

Scott, Ridley (1937–) Film director, born in South Shields, NE England, UK. He graduated from set designing to directing episodes of television series, such as *Z Cars*, and also commercials, before making his first feature film *The Duellists* (1977). Later films include *Alien* (1979) and *Blade Runner* (1982), and he received an Oscar nomination for *Thelma and Louise* (1991). He acted as both producer and director for *White Squall* (1996) and *G I Joe* (1997).

Scott, R(obert) F(alcon) (1868–1912) Antarctic explorer, born in Devonport, Devon, SW England, UK. He joined the navy in 1881, and commanded the National Antarctic Expedition (1901–4) which explored the Ross Sea area, and discovered King Edward VII Land. In 1910 he led a second expedition to the South Pole (17 Jan 1912), only to discover that the Norwegian expedition under Amundsen had beaten them by a month. All members of his party died, their bodies and diaries being found by a search party eight months later. He was posthumously knighted, and the Scott Polar Research Institute at Cambridge was founded in his memory. >> Amundsen; Oates, Laurence; Scott, Peter; Shackleton; Wilson, Edward A

Scott, Ronnie (1927–96) Jazz saxophonist and night club owner, born in London, England, UK. After visiting New York as a member of the band aboard the *Queen Mary*, he returned to England and disseminated the modern bebop style. He had been a soloist in several great European jazz orchestras, as well as a leader in his own right. In 1959 he opened a club in London's Soho district, and this quickly became an international jazz centre.

Scott, Sheila, originally **Sheila Christine Hopkins** (1927–88) Aviator, born in Worcester, Hereford and Worcester, WC England, UK. A nurse and an actress, she took up flying as a result of a dare, winning trophies a year later in 1960. In 1966 she broke the around-the-world record with the longest solo flight of 49 910 km/31 014 mi. She again broke world records in 1967 flying across the Atlantic, and won the *Daily Mail* Transatlantic Air Race in 1969. She was the first to fly a light aircraft solo over the North Pole, equator to equator. Her books *On Top of the World* (1973) and *Bare Feet in the Sky* (1974) describe her flying career, which broke more than 100 world records.

Scott, Sir Walter (1771–1832) Novelist and poet, born in Edinburgh, EC Scotland, UK. He studied in Edinburgh, trained as a lawyer (1792), and began to write ballads in 1796, though his first major publication did not appear until 1802: *The Border Minstrelsy*. His ballads made him the most popular author of the day, and were followed by other romances, such as *The Lady of the Lake* (1810). He then turned to historical novels, which fall into three groups: those set in the background of Scottish history, from *Waverley* (1814) to *A Legend of Montrose* (1819); a group which takes up themes from the Middle Ages and Reformation times, from *Ivanhoe* (1819) to *The Talisman* (1825); and his remaining books, from *Woodstock* (1826) until his death. His last years were spent in immense labours for his publishers, much of it hack editorial work, in an attempt to recover from bankruptcy following the collapse of his publishing ventures in 1826. His journal is an important record of this period of his life. He was created a baronet in 1820. >> Ballantyne, James; Constable, Archibald; Edgeworth; Lockhart; Rhys, Ernest Percival; Surtees, Robert

Scott, William (1913–89) Painter, born in Greenock, Inverclyde, WC Scotland, UK. He studied at Belfast College of Art and at the Royal Academy Schools. After World War 2 he taught at Bath Academy of Art (1946–56). He visited Canada and New York in 1953, meeting Jackson Pollock and other leading Abstract Expressionists. His preferred subject was still-life, painted in a simplified, nearly abstract way. >> Pollock

Scott, Winfield (1786–1866) US soldier, born in Petersburg, VA. Admitted to the bar in 1807, he obtained a commission as an artillery captain in 1808. As major-general, he framed the 'General Regulations', and helped to settle the disputed boundary line of Maine and New Brunswick (1839). He succeeded to the chief command of the army in 1841, took Vera Cruz (1847), put Santa Anna to flight, and entered the Mexican capital in triumph (1847). An unsuccessful Whig candidate for the presidency (1852), he retained nominal command of the army until 1861. >> Santa Anna

Scotus >> **Duns Scotus; Erigena**

Scriabin, Alexander Nikolayevich [skryahbyin] (1872–1915) Composer and pianist, born in Moscow. He studied at the Moscow Conservatory, and became professor of the pianoforte (1898–1904). His compositions include three symphonies, two tone poems, and 10 sonatas. After 1900 his involvement with theosophy influenced several of his compositions, such as *Prometheus* (1910), which was performed to the accompaniment of coloured lights.

Scribe, (Augustin) Eugène [skreeb] (1791–1861) Playwright, born in Paris. The master of the 'well-made' play, after 1816 his productions became so popular that he established a theatre workshop in which numerous *collaborateurs* worked under his supervision, turning out plays by 'mass-production' methods. The best known are *Le Verre d'eau* (1840, The Glass of Water), *Adrienne Lecouvreur* (1848), and *Bataille des dames* (1851, Battle of the Ladies). He also wrote novels and composed the libretti for 60 operas.

Scriblerus >> Arbuthnot, John

Scribner, Charles, originally **Charles Scrivener** (1821–71) Publisher, born in New York City. He graduated from Princeton in 1840, and in 1846 founded with Isaac Baker (d.1850) the New York publishing firm of Baker & Scribner, which was called Charles Scribner's Sons from 1878. He founded *Scribner's Monthly* (1870–81), which later became *Scribner's Magazine* (1887–1939). His three sons continued the business.

Scrutton, Sir Thomas Edward (1856–1934) Legal textwriter and judge, born in London, England, UK. He studied at London University, and after an outstanding academic career developed a busy practice in commercial cases, and wrote *The Contract of Affreightment as Expressed in Charter-parties and Bills of Lading* (1886). A century later this is still the standard text, while several of his other legal works remain useful. He was a judge of the King's Bench Division (1910–16) and of the Court of Appeal (1916–34).

Scudéry, Madeleine de [skoodayree] (1607–1701) Novelist, born in Le Havre, France. With her brother she was accepted into the literary society of Mme de Rambouillet's salon (1639), and had replaced her by the 1640s. Her best-known work is the 10-volume *Artamène, ou le Grand Cyrus* (1649–59), written with her brother, followed by *Clélie* (10 vols, 1654–60). Her last novel was *Mathilde d'Anguilon* (1667). She was satirized by Molière in *Les précieuses ridicules* (1659). >> Molière; Rambouillet

Sculthorpe, Peter Joshua (1929–) Composer, born in Launceston, Tasmania, Australia. He studied at the Conservatory of Melbourne University, and later in Oxford with Egon Wellesz and Edmund Rubbra. His work is much influenced by the vast spaces of the Australian landscape, and the sounds and rhythms of Asia and the Pacific, and includes the continuing *Irkanda* series, four *Sun Music* pieces, the operas *Rites of Passage* (1974) and *Quiros* (1982). Other major works include a cello requiem (1979), a piano concerto (1983), and *Child of Australia* (1987) – a setting of text by Thomas Keneally (1935–) for Australia's bicentennial celebrations. >> Rubbra; Wellesz

Seaborg, Glenn T(heodore) (1912–) Nuclear chemist, born in Ishpeming, MI. He studied at the University of California at Los Angeles and Berkeley, becoming professor of chemistry at Berkeley in 1945, and was part of the team which discovered the transuranic elements plutonium (1940), americium, and curium (1944). By bombarding the last two with alpha rays he produced the elements berkelium and californium in 1950. He shared the 1951 Nobel Prize for Chemistry with Edwin McMillan, and later became chairman of the US Atomic Energy Commission (1961–71). The 106th element was named seaborgium in his honour in 1994 – the first chemist to have an element named after him in his lifetime. >> McMillan

Seabury, Samuel (1729–96) Clergyman, born in Groton, CT. He graduated at Yale in 1748, studied medicine at Edinburgh, and received orders in the Church of England in 1753. In 1757 he became rector of Jamaica, Long Island, and in 1767 of Westchester, NY. Despite imprisonment for his loyalty to Britain through the War of American Independence as a royalist army chaplain, he was elected the first Episcopal Bishop of Connecticut and Rhode Island in 1785.

Seaga, Edward (Philip George) (1930–) Jamaican politician and prime minister (1980–9), born in the USA. He went to school in Kingston, Jamaica, then studied at Harvard, and was on the staff of the University of the West Indies before joining the Jamaica Labour Party, becoming its leader in 1974. He entered the House of Representatives in 1962 and held a government post before becoming Leader of the Opposition. In 1980 he had a resounding win over the People's National Party, and became prime minister. >> RR1068

Seagram, Joseph Emm (1848–1919) Distiller, turfman, and Canadian politician. He was founder of the world's largest producer and marketer of distilled spirits and wines, and owner and breeder of an unprecedented 15 Queen's/King's Plate horse-race winners. One of Canada's most prominent gentleman entrepreneurs, he was also Conservative Party MP for Waterloo North (1896–1908).

Seaman, David (1963–) Footballer, born in Rotherham, South Yorkshire, N England, UK. A goalkeeper, he played for Peterborough, Birmingham, and Queens Park Rangers, before moving to Arsenal in 1989. He established himself as the England goalkeeper under Terry Venables, and by early 1997 had won 32 caps. >> Venables

Searle, Humphrey [serl] (1915–82) Composer, born in Oxford, Oxfordshire, SC England, UK. He studied at the Royal College of Music, London, and in Vienna with Webern, and became musical adviser to Sadler's Wells Ballet (1951–7). He wrote *Twentieth Century Counterpoint*, and a study of the music of Liszt. An exponent of the '12-note system', his compositions include five symphonies, two piano concertos, and three operas, including *Hamlet* (1968). He also composed a trilogy of works for speaker, chorus, and orchestra to words by Edith Sitwell and James Joyce. >> Joyce, James; Sitwell, Edith; Webern

Searle, John [serl] (1932–) Philosopher, born in Denver, CO. He taught at Oxford (1956–9), and since 1959 has been professor of philosophy at the University of California, Berkeley. He has expounded a distinctive approach to the study of language and mind, which has greatly influenced linguists as well as philosophers, and is also known for his work on the theory of speech acts. He wrote a famous account of the student riots in California, *The Campus War* (1971), and delivered the Reith lectures on *Minds, Brains, and Science* in 1984.

Searle, Ronald (William Fordham) [serl] (1920–) Artist, born in Cambridge, Cambridgeshire, EC England, UK. He served in World War 2, and the drawings he made during his three years' imprisonment by the Japanese helped to establish his reputation as a serious artist. After the war he became widely known as the creator of the macabre schoolgirls of 'St Trinian's'. He settled in France in 1961. He also designed animated films, such as *Dick Deadeye* (1975), and produced the animated sequences for *Those Magnificent Men in Their Flying Machines* (1965).

Sears, R(ichard) W(arren) (1863–1914) Founder of a mail-order jewellery business, born in Stewartville, MN. He founded the R W Sears Watch Co in 1886, moved to Chicago, hired **Alvah Roebuck** as a watch repairer, and published a mail-order catalogue offering jewellery (1887). The men formed a partnership and established Sears, Roebuck & Co, which expanded into a huge retail business, Roebuck later selling his interest in the firm to Sears (1895). The company was subsequently reorganized and, following a disagreement, Sears resigned as president (1909).

Seastrom, Victor >> Sjöström, Victor

Seaver, Tom, popular name of **George Thomas Seaver**, nickname **Tom Terrific** (1944–) Baseball pitcher, born in

Fresno, CA. During his 20-year career (1967–86), primarily with the New York Mets and Cincinnati Reds, the right-hander won 311 games and the Cy Young Award three times (1969, 1973, 1975). He was elected to baseball's Hall of Fame in 1992. >> RR1145

Sebastian, St (?–288) Roman martyr, a native of Narbonne. He was a captain of the praetorian guard, and secretly a Christian. When his belief was discovered, Diocletian ordered his death by arrows; but the archers did not quite kill him, and he was nursed back to life. When he up-braided the tyrant for his cruelty, he was beaten to death with rods. Feast day 20 January. >> Diocletian

Sebastiano del Piombo >> **Piombo, Sebastiano del**

Sebuktigin >> **Mahmud of Ghazna**

Secchi, Pietro Angelo [sekee] (1818–78) Astronomer, born in Reggio nell'Emilia, Italy. Trained as a Jesuit priest, he lectured in physics and mathematics at the Jesuit College in Loreto. When the Jesuits were expelled from Rome in 1848 he became professor of physics at George-town University, Washington, DC, but was allowed to return in 1849 to become director of the observatory at the Collegio Romano. He originated the classification of stars by spectrum analysis.

Secombe, Sir Harry (Donald) [seekm] (1921–) Comedian, singer, and media personality, born in Swansea, SC Wales. A choir boy and office worker, he made his stage debut in 1946 before becoming a regular on the radio show *Variety Bandbox* (1947). An exuberant comic, he was a member of *The Goons* (1951–9), a radio show whose lunacy had a wide-reaching influence. Besides countless variety shows, his stage appearances include *Humpty Dumpty* (1959), *Pickwick* (1963), and *The Four Musketeers* (1967), and his films include *Oliver!* (1968) and *Song of Norway* (1970). As a writer he con-tributed regularly to *Punch*, and his fiction includes *Twice Brightly* (1974), *Katy and the Nurgla* (1978), and *The Nurgla's Magic Tear* (1990). A professional singer with dozens of albums to his credit, he hosted the religious television series *Highway* (from 1983). He was knighted in 1981, and a volume of autobiography, *Arias and Raspberries*, appeared in 1989. >> Bentine; Milligan; Sellars

Seddon, Richard John, nickname **King Dick** (1845–1906) New Zealand statesman and prime minister (1893–1906), born in Eccleston, Lancashire, NW England, UK. He settled in New Zealand in 1866 and entered parliament in 1879. As prime minister he led a Liberal Party government remembered for its social legislation, such as the intro-duction of old-age pensions. He died at sea, while return-ing to New Zealand from Australia. >> RR1078

Sedges, John >> **Buck, Pearl S**

Sedgman, Frank (1927–) Tennis player, born in Mont Albert, Victoria, Australia. In 1951 he defeated Jaroslav Drobny in the Wimbledon singles final, becoming the first Australian to win there since World War 2. The Australian team regained the Davis Cup from the USA in 1950, and only lost it on his turning professional in 1953. His game was based on the modern style of heavy and early volley-ing, and he influenced the careers of such younger players as Lew Hoad. >> Drobny; Hoad; RR1173

Sedgwick, Adam (1785–1873) Geologist, born in Dent, Cumbria, NW England, UK. He studied mathematics at Cambridge, and became professor of geology there in 1818. In 1835 he calculated the stratigraphic succession of fossil-bearing rocks in North Wales, naming the oldest of them the *Cambrian period*. His best-known work was on *British Palaeozoic Fossils* (1854). With Sir Roderick Murchi-son he studied the Alps and the Lake District, and ident-ified the Devonian system in SW England. He strongly opposed Darwin's *Origin of Species*. >> Darwin, Charles; Murchison

Seebeck, Thomas Johann (1770–1831) Physicist, born in Tallin, Estonia. He studied medicine at Berlin and the University of Göttingen, then abandoned medical practice for research in physics. A member of the Berlin Academy, in 1822 he showed that if a circuit is made of a loop of two metals with two junctions, then when the junctions are at different temperatures a current flows; he had thus dis-covered the thermoelectric effect, now much used in ther-mocouples for temperature measurement.

Seefried, Irmgard [zayfreet] (1919–88) Soprano, born in Köngetried, Germany. She lived in Austria, and became famous for her performances with Vienna State Opera, especially in the operas of Mozart and Richard Strauss.

Seeger, Pete(r) (1919–) Folk-singer and songwriter, born in New York City. He studied sociology at Harvard before becoming a professional musician in the late 1930s. In 1940, along with Woody Guthrie, he formed the Almanac Singers, and started the 'protest' movement in contempo-rary folk-music. His later group, the Weavers, carried on this tradition. A popular solo artist, his left-wing politics caused him to be blacklisted for many years. His best-known songs include 'Where Have All the Flowers Gone?', 'If I Had a Hammer', and 'Little Boxes'. >> Guthrie

Seferiades, George [seferyahdeez], also called **Giorgios** or **George Seferis** (1900–71) Poet and diplomat, born in Izmir (formerly, Smyrna), Turkey. He studied at Athens and the Sorbonne, and served as ambassador to the Lebanon (1953–7) and the UK (1957–62). He wrote lyrical poetry, col-lected in *The Turning Point* (1931), *Mythistorema* (1935), and others, and translated T S Eliot's *The Waste Land* into Greek. The most distinguished Greek poet of the 1930s, he intro-duced symbolism into modern literature, and in 1963 was awarded the Nobel Prize for Literature.

Segal, George [seegl] (1924–) Sculptor, born in New York City. He studied at New York and Rutgers universi-ties, began to work as a painter, then switched to sculp-ture. He is best known for his life-sized plaster figures, cast from life and usually unpainted, which exist as ghostly presences within the environments he creates for them with real objects, such as 'Girl in a Doorway' (1969).

Segal, George [seegal] (1934–) Film actor, born in New York City. He studied at the University of Columbia, and started in the theatre off-Broadway. He had his first major film part in *Invitation to a Gunfighter* (1964). Other films include *A Touch of Class* (1973), *Look Who's Talking* (1989), *The Feminine Touch* (1994), and *The Babysitter* (1995).

Segar, Elzie (Crisler) [seeger] (1894–1938) Strip cartoon-ist, the creator of *Popeye*, born in Chester, IL. He took a cor-respondence course in cartooning, and worked on the daily strip, *Charlie Chaplin's Comic Capers* (1916). In New York City he started *Thimble Theater* (1919), a strip about Olive Oyl and her brother Castor. Popeye the Sailor appeared as a character 10 years later, and quickly became internation-ally popular as a weedy hero, who wins Olive Oyl by the powers given him by eating spinach. The subject of numer-ous animated cartoon films, Popeye's statue was erected in Crystal City, a major spinach-growing centre.

Seghers, Hercules [saygerz] (c. 1589–c. 1635) Painter, born in Haarlem, The Netherlands. He may have studied in Amsterdam. He was author of some of the grandest and most romantic mountain landscapes of the 17th-c (influ-encing Rembrandt, who collected his work), yet fewer than 15 pictures survive. Most of his works are original and powerful etchings, but even these are rare. He was last recorded in 1633, living in The Hague. >> Rembrandt

Segonzac, André Dunoyer de [suhgōzak] (1884–1974) Painter and engraver, born in Boussy-Saint-Antoine, France. He was influenced by Courbet and Corot, and pro-duced many delicate watercolour landscapes, etchings, and illustrations. His series of engravings of 'Beaches' was published in 1935. >> Courbet

Segovia, Andrés [seg**oh**via] (1894–1987) Guitarist, born in Linares, Spain. Largely self-taught, he gave his first concert in 1909, and quickly gained an international reputation. Influenced by the Spanish nationalist composers, he evolved a revolutionary guitar technique permitting the performance of a wide range of music, and many modern composers wrote works for him. He was created Marquis of Salobrena by royal decree in 1981.

Segrave, Sir Henry (O'Neal de Hane) [see**grayv**] (1896–1930) Motor-racing driver, born in Baltimore, MD. He trained at Sandhurst, and served in the Royal Flying Corps in World War 1. Wounded in 1916, he became technical secretary to the air minister. A leading postwar racing driver, he helped to design the Sunbeam car, in which he broke the land speed record at 203·9 mph, raising this to 231 mph in 1929. He was killed in his boat *Miss England* on L Windermere, on a trial run following one in which he had set a new world water speed record of 98·76 mph. He was knighted in 1929.

Segrè, Emilio (Gino) [se**gray**] (1905–89) Physicist, born in Tivoli, Italy. He studied at Rome University, becoming an assistant professor in 1932. Appointed director of physics at Palermo (1936), he was dismissed by the Fascist government while on a tour of America, where he remained (1938). He joined the University of California, Berkeley, and became a US citizen in 1944. He helped to develop the atomic bomb at Los Alamos, and shared the 1959 Nobel Prize for Physics with Owen Chamberlain for the discovery of the antiproton (1955). >> Chamberlain, Owen

Séguin, Marc [say**gĩ**], known as **the Elder** (1786–1875) Mechanical and civil engineer, born in Annonay, France. He was taught science informally by his uncle Joseph Montgolfier, and maintained an interest throughout his life in such problems as the mechanical equivalent of heat. His principal achievements were in engineering, notably his association with the development of wire-rope suspension bridges from 1825 onwards, and his invention of the multi-tubular (fire-tube) boiler, which he patented in 1827, and which was used by George Stephenson in his *Rocket* locomotive. >> Montgolfier brothers; Stephenson, George

Segundo, Juan Luis [se**goon**doh] (1925–) Jesuit liberation theologian, born in Montevideo. After studying in Argentina and Europe, he became director of the Pedro Fabbro Institute of socio-religious research in Montevideo. He advocates employing a 'hermeneutical circle', in which the questioning of prevailing ideological and theological assumptions that govern the received way of interpreting Scripture leads to new understanding. His major exposition of liberation theology is *Jesus of Nazareth Yesterday and Today* (5 vols, 1984–8).

Seiber, Mátyás [**shiy**ber] (1905–60) Composer, born in Budapest. He studied at Budapest under Kodály, became professor of jazz (1928–33) at Frankfurt, and in 1935 settled in Britain as a teacher. He gained only belated recognition as a composer, his works including chamber music, piano pieces, and songs. He was killed in a motor accident in South Africa. >> Kodály

Seidler, Harry [**siyd**ler] (1923–) Architect, born in Vienna. He studied at the Vasa Institute in Vienna, and later at Harvard, under Gropius. He worked in New York, and later with Oscar Niemeyer in Brazil, before setting up a practice in Sydney, Australia (1948). His first design, for a private house, won the Sulman Medal three years later, since when he has won many awards for public and private buildings. He has worked in Mexico and Hong Kong, and designed the Australian embassy in Paris. Responsible for much of the Sydney skyline, his work there includes the

award-winning Australia Square tower, and Grosvenor Place, which won him his fifth Sulman Medal in 1990. >> Gropius; Niemeyer

Seifert, Jaroslav [**siy**fert] (1901–86) Poet, born in Prague. His first collection was *Mêsto v slzáck* (1921, City of Tears). Later works include *Zhasnête svêtla* (1938, Put Out The Lights), and the appearance of the post-war volume *Přílba hlíny* (1945, A Helmet of Earth) established him as the national poet. He refused all compromise after the Communist takeover in 1948, and *Morový sloup* (1977, trans The Prague Column) had to be published abroad. He was awarded the Nobel Prize for Literature in 1984.

Sejanus [se**jay**nus] (?–31) Prefect of the Praetorian Guard (14–31), and all-powerful at Rome after the Emperor Tiberius's retirement to Capri (26). He systematically eliminated possible successors to Tiberius, such as Agrippina's sons, so that he himself might wield supreme power after Tiberius's death as regent for his young grandson Gemellus. His plans, however, were made known to Tiberius, and his fall from grace was sudden and spectacular. >> Agrippina (the Elder); Tiberius

Selcraig, Alexander >> **Selkirk, Alexander**

Selden, John (1584–1654) Historian and antiquary, born in Salvington, West Sussex, S England, UK. He studied at Oxford and London, became a lawyer (1612), entered parliament in 1623, and in 1628 helped to draw up the Petition of Rights, for which he was imprisoned until 1634. He entered the Long Parliament in 1640, but after the execution of Charles I he took little part in public matters. His best-known book, *Table Talk*, was published after his death (1689). >> Charles I (of England)

Seles, Monica [se**lesh**] (1973–) Tennis player, born in Novi Sad, Yugoslavia. In 1990 she became the youngest woman to win a 'Grand Slam' singles title this century, winning the French Championship at 16 years 169 days (a record broken by Hingis in 1997). She was also the youngest player to win the Australian Open in 1991, and before she reached 18 she had won three out of four Grand Slam singles titles. In 1993 she was unable to play for some months following an incident on court in which she was stabbed by a deranged fan of Steffi Graf. She became a US citizen in 1994. >> Hingis

Seleucus I Nicator ('Conqueror') [si**loo**kus, niy**kay**ter] (c.358–281 BC) Macedonian general of Alexander the Great, and founder of the Seleucid dynasty. He rose from being satrap of Babylonia (321 BC) to being the ruler of an empire which stretched from Asia Minor to India. To hold his unwieldy empire together, he founded a new, more central capital at Antioch in N Syria (300 BC). >> Alexander the Great; Antigonus I; Antiochus I

Selfridge, Harry Gordon (c. 1864–1947) Businessman, born in Ripon, WI. Educated privately, he joined a trading firm in Chicago and brought new ideas and great organizing ability into the business, being made a junior partner in 1892. While visiting London in 1906 he bought a site in Oxford St, and built the large store which now bears his name (opened 1909). He became a British citizen in 1937.

Seligman, C(harles) G(abriel) (1873–1940) Anthropologist, born in London, England, UK. He trained as a physician in London, then joined the Cambridge Anthropological Expedition to the Torres Straits (1898–9), and carried out subsequent field research in New Guinea, Ceylon, and the Sudan. His principal works include *The Veddas (Ceylon)* (1911) and *Pagan Tribes of the Nilotic Sudan* (1932), both co-authored with his wife. His appointment in 1913 to the first chair of ethnology at London University turned his interests towards anthropology. He pioneered the application of a psychoanalytic approach, influencing the work of Malinowski and Evans-Pritchard. >> Evans-Pritchard; Malinowski

Selkirk, Alexander, also spelled **Selcraig** (1676–1721) Sailor whose story suggested that of Defoe's *Robinson Crusoe*, born in Largo, Fife, E Scotland, UK. He joined the South Sea buccaneers, quarrelled with his captain, and at his own request was put ashore on Juan Fernández I, off the coast of Chile (1704). He lived there alone until 1709, when he was discovered and brought back to Britain. He returned to Largo in 1712, before returning to a life at sea.

Sellars, Peter (1958–) Stage director, born in Pittsburgh, PA. He studied at Harvard, became director of the Boston Shakespeare Company (1983–4), and directed the American National Theater at the Kennedy Center in Washington, DC (1984–6), where his radical staging of Sophocles' *Ajax* divided audiences and critics. He is internationally recognized as a daringly innovative director of opera, setting his productions in the cultural landscape of 20th-c America.

Sellers, Peter (1925–80) Actor and comedian, born in Southsea, Hampshire, S England, UK. After a spell as a stand-up comic and impressionist, he moved into radio. His meeting with Spike Milligan heralded *The Goon Show* (1951–9), which revolutionized British radio comedy. He made his film debut in 1951, and became one of the stalwarts of British film comedy, appearing in *The Ladykillers* (1955), *I'm All Right Jack* (1959), and *Only Two Can Play* (1962). *Lolita* (1962) and *Dr Strangelove* (1963) established his international reputation, and his popularity was unrivalled as the incompetent Inspector Clouseau in a series of films that began with *The Pink Panther* (1963) and extended beyond his death to *The Trail of the Pink Panther* (1982). He received an Oscar nomination for *Being There* (1980). >> Milligan

Sellin, Thorsten (Johan) (1896–) Educator and criminologist, born in Ornskoldsvik, Sweden. He emigrated to America (1915) to study, and taught chiefly at the University of Pennsylvania (1920–68). He advised the Census Bureau on criminal statistics (1931–46), helped construct the Swedish Penal Code (1946–7), was a member of the Prison Labor Compact Authority (1934), and became president of the International Penal and Penitentiary Foundation (1965–71). He wrote several books, including *Culture, Conflict and Crime* (1938).

Selous, Frederick Courtenay [suhloos] (1815–1917) Explorer and big-game hunter, born in London, England, UK. He first visited South Africa in 1871, travelled from Cape Town to Matabeleland (Zimbabwe), and later spent almost 20 years exploring and hunting in the country between the Transvaal of South Africa and the Congo basin. In 1890 he was in the service of the British South African Company, and helped bring the district of Manicaland under British control. His books include *Sunshine and Storm in Rhodesia* (1896), an account of the Matabele War. The Selous National Park in Tanzania is named after him.

Selten, Reinhard [zelten] (1930–) Economist, born in Wrocław, Poland (formerly Breslau, Germany). He studied mathematics at Frankfurt-am-Main, and later worked at universities in California, Berlin, and Bielefeld before moving to the Rheinische Friedrich-Wilhelms University in Bonn in 1984. He shared the Nobel Prize for Economics in 1994 for his contribution to the analysis of equilibria in the theory of non-co-operative games. >> Harsanyi; Nash, John F

Selwyn, George Augustus [selwin] (1809–78) Anglican churchman, born in London, England, UK. He studied at Cambridge, where he rowed in the first university boat race (1829). In 1841 he was consecrated the first (and only) Bishop of New Zealand and Melanesia, and was largely responsible for the organization of the Church of New Zealand. Returning to England, he was appointed Bishop of Lichfield (1867), and initiated the first diocesan conference at which the laity were duly represented (1868). Selwyn College, Cambridge, was founded in his memory (1882).

Selwyn-Lloyd, (John) Selwyn (Brooke) Lloyd, Baron [selwin loyd] (1904–78) British statesman, born in Liverpool, Merseyside, NW England, UK. He studied at Cambridge, became a barrister, and practised in Liverpool. He entered local government, served in World War 2, and became a Conservative MP in 1945. He was appointed minister of state (1951), supply (1954–5), and defence (1955), and as foreign secretary (1955–60) he defended Eden's policy on Suez. He later became Chancellor of the Exchequer, introducing the 'pay pause' (1960–2), Lord Privy Seal and Leader of the House (1963–4), and Speaker of the House of Commons (1971–6). He was created a life peer in 1976. >> Eden

Selye, Hans (Hugo Bruno) [saylee] (1907–82) Physician, born in Vienna. He studied in Prague, Paris, and Rome before emigrating to North America in the 1930s. After a decade at McGill University in Montreal (1933–45), he became director of the Institute for Experimental Medicine and Surgery at the French-language University of Montreal (1945). He was best known for his 'stress-general adaptation syndrome', an attempt to link stress and anxiety and their biochemical and physiological consequences to many modern human disorders.

Selznick, David O(liver) (1902–65) Cinema mogul, born in Pittsburgh, OH. He worked for his father in film distribution and promotion, and as a story editor and associate producer at MGM and Paramount. He was appointed vice-president in charge of production at RKO when the studio created such films as *King Kong* (1933). In 1936 he formed his own company, producing *A Star Is Born* (1937) and his greatest achievement, the enduring screen adaptation of *Gone With the Wind* (1939), for which he received an Oscar. Among the stars he created was **Jennifer Jones** (1919–), who also appeared in his last co-production, *A Farewell to Arms* (1957), and to whom he was married from 1949 until his death.

Semenov, Nikolay Nikolayevich [semyonof] (1896–1986) Physical chemist, born in Saratov, Russia. He studied at St Petersburg and became assistant director at the Leningrad Physical Technical Institute (1920–31). He was appointed director of the newly created Institute of Chemical Physics of the Academy of Sciences in Moscow, where he remained until shortly before his death. An expert in molecular physics, he carried out important research on the kinetics of gas reactions, for which he shared the Nobel Prize for Chemistry in 1956, the first Soviet citizen ever to receive a Nobel Prize. >> RR1123

Semiramis [semiramis] (9th-c BC) Semi-legendary Queen of Assyria, the wife of Ninus, with whom she is supposed to have founded Babylon. The historical germ of the story seems to be the three years' regency of Sammu-ramat (811–808 BC), widow of Shamshi-Adad V, but the details are legendary, derived from Ctesias and the Greek historians, with elements of the Astarte myth. >> Ctesias

Semmelweiss, Ignaz Philipp [zemelviys] (1818–65) Physician, born in Buda, Hungary. He studied at the universities of Pest and Vienna. As assistant in the obstetric clinic at Vienna (from 1844) he sought a reason for the heavy mortality rate of women suffering 'childbed' or puerperal fever. His findings showed that the infection was carried by medical students from one patient to another, so he introduced antisepsis by the washing of their hands in a chlorinated lime. Although this dramatically reduced the mortality rate, his views were not accepted until after his death, when Joseph Lister applauded his findings. Ironically he died from an infection of his hand, caused as a result of an operation he performed. >> Lister, Joseph

Semmes, Raphael [semz] (1809–77) Confederate naval officer, born in Charles Co, MD. He joined the US navy in 1826, and was called to the bar in 1834. On the outbreak of the Civil War he first commanded the confederate raider *Sumter*, and then the *Alabama*, with which he captured 82 vessels, nearly all of which were sunk or burned. In 1864, the *Alabama* was sunk in action off Cherbourg by the US cruiser *Kearsarge*, but he escaped.

Sen, Amartya Kumar (1933–) Economist, born in India. He studied at Calcutta and Cambridge universities, and became a fellow of Trinity College, Cambridge (1957–63). He held professorial posts at New Delhi University (1963–71), the London School of Economics (1971–7), and Oxford (1977–88), then moved to Harvard. He is noted for his work on the nature of poverty and famine.

Senanayake, Don Stephen [senaniykee] (1884–1952) First prime minister of Sri Lanka (1947–52), born in Colombo. He studied in Colombo, then worked on his father's rubber estate. Entering the Legislative Council in 1922, he founded the co-operative society movement in 1923, and was elected to the State Council in 1931, where he was minister of agriculture for 15 years. Following independence, he became prime minister, as well as minister of defence and external affairs. >> RR1090

Sendak, Maurice (Bernard) (1928–) Illustrator and writer of children's books, born in New York City. He trained at the Art Students' League, worked as a window-dresser, encountered classic illustrators in a toy store, and was commissioned by a publisher to illustrate *The Wonderful Farm* (1951) by Marcel Aymé. For *A Hole Is To Dig* (1952) he produced humorous, unsentimental drawings, and in 1956 came *Kenny's Window*, the first book he both illustrated and wrote. *Where the Wild Things Are* (1963, Caldecott Medal) made him internationally famous, followed by *In The Night Kitchen* (1970). Later books include *Seven Little Monsters* (1977) and *We are all in the Dumps with Jack and Guy* (1993). He also collaborated on opera production, such as *The Magic Flute* (Mozart), produced in Houston in 1980.

Senebier, Jean [senebyay] (1742–1809) Botanist and pastor, born in Geneva, Switzerland. He studied theology, and was ordained in 1765. He was pastor of a church at Chancy, Switzerland (1769), then city librarian of Geneva from 1773. He studied botany, and in 1782 first demonstrated the basic principle of photosynthesis, which he published in *Physiologie végétale* (1800). He also wrote an important literary work on Geneva (1786).

Seneca, Lucius Annaeus [seneka], known as **the Elder** (c.55 BC–c.AD 40) Roman rhetorician, born in Córdoba, Spain. Besides a history of Rome, now lost, he wrote several works on oratory. Parts of his *Colores controversiae* and *Suasoriae* have survived. >> Seneca (the Younger)

Seneca, Lucius Annaeus [seneka], known as **Seneca the Younger** (c. 5 BC–AD 65) Roman philosopher, statesman, and writer, born in Córdoba, Spain, the son of Seneca (the Elder). Banished to Corsica (41–9) by Claudius, on a charge of adultery, he was recalled by Agrippina, who entrusted him with the education of her son, Nero. Made consul by Nero in 57, his high moral aims gradually incurred the emperor's displeasure, and he withdrew from public life. Drawn into conspiracy, he was condemned, and committed suicide in Rome. The publication of his *Tenne Tragedies* in 1581 was important in the evolution of Elizabethan drama, which took from them the five-act division, as well as the horrors and the rhetoric. >> Nero; Seneca (the Elder)

Senefelder, Aloys [zaynefelder, alohis]] (1771–1834) Inventor, born in Prague. He became an actor and playwright and, while trying to engrave printing plates to publish his plays, accidentally discovered the technique of lithography by using a grease pencil on limestone (1796). After various trials he opened an establishment of his own in Offenbach-am-Main, and later in Munich to train others in the process.

Senghor, Léopold Sédar [sāgaw(r)] (1906–) Senegalese statesman and first president (1960–80), born in Joal, Senegal. He became a teacher, writer, and politician, a member of the French Constituent Assembly in 1945, deputy for Senegal in the French National Assembly (1948–58), and president following his country's independence. He has also won several literary awards as a poet. >> RR1087

Senna, Ayrton, in full **Ayrton Senna da Silva** (1960–94) Motor racing driver, born in São Paulo, Brazil. He began racing karts when he was four, moved to Formula Three racing in Britain in 1981, and joined a Formula One team in 1984. In a career marked by an agressive competitiveness and rivalry (especially with Alain Prost), he became World Formula One champion 1988, 1990, and 1991, and had 41 Grand Prix victories (second only to Alain Prost). He also built up a major business in São Paulo marketing a range of Senna products. He was killed during the 1994 San Marino Grand Prix. >> Prost

Sennacherib [senakerib] (8th–7th-c BC) King of Assyria (704–681 BC), the son of Sargon II and grandfather of Assurbanipal. He was an able ruler, whose fame rests mainly on his conquest of Babylon (689 BC) and his rebuilding of Nineveh. He figures prominently in the Bible, because of his attack on Jerusalem. >> Assurbanipal; Esarhaddon; RR1032

Sennett, Mack, originally **Michael** or **Mikall Sinnott** (1880–1960) Film director, producer, and actor, born in Richmond, Quebec, Canada. He worked as a comic in burlesque companies, and from 1908 in silent films. He later formed his own company, and made hundreds of shorts, establishing a whole generation of players and a tradition of knockabout slapstick under the name of Keystone Komics (1912) and later the Sennett Bathing Beauties (1920). He was given a special Academy Award in 1937 for his long contribution to film comedy. >> Swanson

Senusrit >> **Sesostris**

Sequoia or **Sequoyah** [sekwoya], also known as **George Gist** or **Guest** (c. 1770–1843) Cherokee Indian Leader, born in Taskigi, NC. Probably the son of Nathaniel Gist, a British trader, and a Cherokee mother, he was a major figure behind the decision of the Cherokee to adopt as much as possible of the white culture, while retaining their own identity. He personally invented an alphabet for their language.

Serao, Matilde [sayrow] (1856–1927) Novelist, and newspaper editor, born in Patras, Greece. She graduated as a teacher in Naples, worked in a telegraph office, and started writing articles for newspapers (1876–8). She wrote about 40 novels of Neapolitan life, including *Il paese di cuccagna* (1890, The Land of Cockayne), and *Il romanzo della fanciulla* (1886, trans A Girl's Romance). In 1904 she founded the influential daily newspaper *Il Giorno*, which she edited for the rest of her life.

Seraphicus, Doctor >> **Bonaventure, St**

Sergeyev-Tsensky, Sergey [sergayeftsenskee] (1875–1958) Novelist, born in Tambov province, Russia. From a Dostoevskian passion for morbid characterization, as in *The Tundra* (1902), he developed greater simplicity of style and social sense in his major 10-volume novel sequence, *Transfiguration* (1914–40; Stalin Prize, 1942).

Serkin, Peter (1947–) Pianist, born in New York City, the son of Rudolf Serkin. He made his public debut at age 10, and from his teens had an active career as a recitalist and performer with orchestras. For some time he concentrated on contemporary music, and was co-founder of the new-music quartet, Tashi. Later he returned to performing the whole range of piano repertoire. >> Serkin, Rudolf

Serkin, Rudolf (1903–91) Pianist, born in Eger, Austria. He studied composition with Schoenberg in Vienna, and made his debut there in 1915. He settled in the USA in 1939, and directed the Curtis Institute, Philadelphia (1968–76). He founded the Marlboro School of Music (1949) and the Marlboro Music Festival (1950). >> Schoenberg; Serkin, Peter

Serling, Rod (1924–75) Television script-writer, born in Syracuse, NY. He studied at Antioch College, then began writing radio scripts before securing a radio staff job in Cincinnati. The author of over 200 television plays, he first wrote for television in 1951, and won the first of six Emmy Awards for *Patterns* (1955). He created, wrote, and hosted the popular anthology series *The Twilight Zone* (1959–64) and *Night Gallery* (1970–3), and frequently narrated documentaries on scientific and nature subjects.

Serlio, Sebastiano [sairlioh] (1475–1554) Architect and painter, born in Bologna, Italy. After training there, he moved to Rome in 1514 to study with Baldassare Peruzzi. He moved to Venice in 1527, and in 1540 was called to France by Francis I. More influential than his architecture was his treatise on Italian architecture, *Regole generali di architettura* (1537–51, and posthumously 1575), which was widely consulted, and later published in English, German, and Dutch editions. >> Peruzzi

Serote, Mongane Wally [serohtay] (1944–) Poet and novelist, born in Sophiatown, South Africa. An influential figure in the 'politics of culture' in South Africa, he became one of the 'township poets' of the 1970s, whose angry verse broke a decade of African creative silence. His first volume of verse, *Yakhal 'inkomo* (1972), was followed by four others, and in 1981 he published a novel, *To Every Birth Its Blood*. He lived in exile for much of the 1970s and 1980s, and after his return to South Africa in 1990 headed the Department of Art and Culture of the African National Congress.

Serra, Richard (1939–) Sculptor, born in San Francisco, CA. He studied art at California (Berkeley) and Yale universities, then went to Paris and Florence before settling in New York City. In the late 1960s he produced a series of films, and began manufacturing austere minimalist works from sheet steel, iron, and lead. Notable are the long arcs of sheet metal which can span city squares, and the cubic structures composed of massive metal plates balanced vertically against one another. Public commissions for such works have made him a controversial but highly influential artist.

Serra, Junipero [hooneeperoh] (1713–84) Missionary, born in Petra, Majorca. He entered the Franciscan Order in 1730, and arrived in Mexico City in 1750. He founded nine missions (including San Diego and San Francisco) in present-day California, and was responsible for the baptism of over 6000 Indians. He was beatified by the Roman Catholic Church in 1988.

Serre, Jean-Pierre [sair] (1926–) Mathematician, born in Bages, France. He studied at the Ecole Normale Supérieure, then worked at the Centre National de la Recherche Scientifique and the University of Nancy, becoming professor at the Collège de France in 1956. He has carried out research in homotopy theory, algebraic geometry, class field theory, group theory, and number theory, and in 1954 he was awarded the Fields Medal (the mathematical equivalent of the Nobel Prize).

Sertorius, Quintus [sertawrius] (123–72 BC) Roman soldier, born in Nursia. He fought with Marius in Gaul (102 BC) and supported him against Sulla. In 83 BC, as praetor, he was given Spain as his province. In 80 BC he headed a successful rising of natives and Roman exiles against Rome, holding out against Sulla's commanders (including Pompey) for eight years until he was assassinated by his chief lieutenant. >> Marius, Gaius; Pompey; Sulla

Servan-Schreiber, Jean-Jacques [sairvã shriybair] (1924–) French politician and journalist, born in Paris. During World War 2 he distinguished himself as a pilot with the Free French Army. He worked for the newspaper *Le Monde* (1948–53), then founded and ran *L'Express* (1953–70). Recalled into the army (1956), he was court-martialled upon the publication of his first book, *Lieutenant en Algérie* (1957, Lieutenant in Algeria) which exposed French wartime atrocities. The Radical Party appointed him secretary general (1969–71) and president (1971–5, 1977–9). He was elected to the National Assembly (1970), served as minister of reforms, and co-founded the Mouvement Réformateur (Reform Movement) in 1972.

Servetus, Michael [servaytus] (1511–53) Theologian and physician, born in Tudela, Spain. He studied law, worked largely in France and Switzerland, and while studying medicine at Paris discovered the pulmonary circulation of the blood. In his theological writings he denied the Trinity and the divinity of Christ, and angered both Catholics and Protestants. He escaped the Inquisition, but was burnt by Calvin in Geneva for heresy. >> Calvin

Service, Robert W(illiam) (1874–1958) Poet, born in Preston, Lancashire, NW England, UK. He emigrated to Canada in 1894, travelled as a reporter for the *Toronto Star*, and served as an ambulance driver in World War 1. Known as 'the Canadian Kipling', he wrote popular ballads, such as 'Rhymes of a Rolling Stone' (1912) and 'The Shooting of Dan McGrew'. He also wrote novels, of which *Ploughman of the Moon* (1945) and *Harper of Heaven* (1948) are autobiographical.

Sesostris [sesostris], also known as **Senusrit** According to Greek legend, an Egyptian monarch who invaded Libya, Arabia, Thrace, and Scythia, subdued Ethiopia, placed a fleet on the Red Sea, and extended his dominion to India. He was possibly Sesostris I (c.1980–1935 BC), II (c.1906–1887 BC), and III (c.1887–1849 BC) compounded into one heroic figure.

Sesshu, Toyo [seshoo] (1420–1506) Painter and priest, born in Akahama, Japan. He was educated as a Zen monk at the Shokokuji in Kyoto, where the teaching of the artist, Shubun (died c.1445), became the determining factor of his career. He travelled in China (1467–9), and his style shows the influence of Chinese painting. His knowledge of Zen Buddhism and communion with nature allowed him to renew the traditional lyricism of Japanese landscapes, and he came to be the greatest Japanese painter of his time. His major works include 'Four Seasons Landscape' (four scrolls, c.1470–90, Tokyo National Museum).

Sessions, Roger (Huntingdon) (1896–1985) Composer, born in New York City. He studied at Harvard and Yale universities, and also under Ernest Bloch, then spent some time in Europe. He later taught in the USA, working at the universities of Princeton (1935–45, 1953–65) and California, Berkeley (1945–52), and at the Juilliard School, New York City (from 1965). His compositions include eight symphonies, a violin concerto, piano and chamber music, two operas, and a Concerto for Orchestra (1981, Pulitzer). >> Bloch, Ernest

Seth, Vikram (1952–) Novelist, poet, and travel-writer, born in Calcutta, India. He studied at Oxford, Stanford, and Nanjing universities. In 1983 he won the Thomas Cook Travel Book award for *From Heaven Lake*, an account of his journey through Sinkiang and Tibet to Nepal. His novel *A Suitable Boy* (1993), one of the longest works of fiction in English, examines the lives of four families against the background of a turbulent post-independence India. His poetry collections include *Mappings* (1980) and *Beastly Tales from Here and There* (1992).

Seton, St Elizabeth Ann [seetn], *née* **Bayley** (1774–1821) The first native-born saint of the USA, born in New York City. She married into a wealthy trading family, and in 1797 founded the Society for the Relief of Poor Widows with Small Children. In 1803 she was widowed herself, with five children. She converted to Catholicism, founded a Catholic elementary school in Baltimore, and in 1809 founded the USA's first religious order, the Sisters of Charity. She was beatified by Pope John XXIII in 1963, and canonized in 1975. Feast day 4 January.

Seton, Ernest Thompson [seetn], originally **Ernest Evan Thompson** (1860–1946) Naturalist, writer, and illustrator, born in South Shields, Durham, NE England, UK. He emigrated to Canada with his family in 1866, studied art, then returned to his first love, natural history, writing and illustrating a series of books about birds and animals, notably *Wild Animals I Have Known* (1898). He was a strong proponent of conservation and of preserving Indian culture and woodcraft skills. A founder of the Boy Scouts of America (1910), he resigned as chief scout in 1915 to protest against former President Theodore Roosevelt's campaign to 'militarize' scouting. >> Roosevelt, Theodore

Seurat, Georges (Pierre) [soerah] (1859–91) Artist, born in Paris. He studied and set up a studio in Paris, where he became known for such works as 'Une Baignade' (A Bather, 1883–4, Tate, London), and 'Un Dimanche d'été à la Grande-Jatte' (1884–6, Chicago, Sunday Afternoon on the Grande Jatte), painted in a Divisionist style. His colour theories were influential, but his main achievement was the marrying of an Impressionist palette to Classical composition.

Seuss, Dr, pseudonym of **Theodor Seuss Geisel**, other pseudonyms **Theo LeSieg** and **Rosetta Stone** (1904–91) Writer and illustrator of children's books, born in Springfield, MA. He studied at Dartmouth College, NH, did postgraduate work at Oxford and the Sorbonne, worked as an illustrator and humorist for US periodicals, then became a writer and animator in Hollywood, settling in La Jolla, CA. He wrote the screenplay for the award-winning animated cartoon *Gerald McBoing Boing* (1950). His famous series of 'Beginner Books' started with *The Cat in the Hat* (1957) and *Yertle the Turtle* (1958). By 1970, 30 million copies had been sold in the USA, and Seuss had become synonymous with learning to read. His books for adults include *You're Only Old Once!* (1986) and *Oh, the Places You'll Go!* (1990).

Severin, (Giles) Timothy (1940–) British historian, traveller, and writer. He studied mediaeval Asian exploration at Oxford, and has recreated many voyages following the routes of early explorers and navigators, using vessels reconstructed to the original specifications. These include the voyages of St Brendan, the legendary Irish monk, from W Ireland to North America; Sinbad, whose seven long voyages in an Arab dhow took him from Oman to China; and the early Greek quests of Jason and Ulysses in a bronze-age galleon. He has written books on these and other projects, such as *The Brendan Voyage* (1978), *In Search of Genghis Khan* (1991), and *The China Voyage* (1994).

Severini, Gino [severeenee] (1883–1966) Artist, born in Cortona, Italy. He studied in Rome and Paris, and signed the first Futurist manifesto in 1910. After 1914 he reverted to a more representational style, which he used in fresco and mosaic work, particularly in a number of Swiss and Italian churches. From 1940 onwards he adopted a decorative Cubist manner. >> Balla; Boccioni; Marinetti

Severus, Lucius Septimius [severus] (c. 146–211) Roman emperor (193–211), the founder of the Severan dynasty (193–235), and the first Roman emperor to be born in Africa (at Leptis Magna, of Romanized Punic stock). Declared emperor by the army in 193, he spent the early years of his reign securing his position against his rivals. Once established, he proved to be an able administrator, effecting many reforms, and showing a particularly close interest in the army and the law. His final years were spent in Britain, trying unsuccessfully to restore order in the N of the province. >> Didius Julianus; RR1084

Sévigné, Madame de [sayveenyay], *née* **Marie de Rabutin-Chantal** (1626–96) Writer, born in Paris. She was a member of French court society, and after the marriage of her daughter in 1669 she began a series of letters, lasting over 25 years, recounting the inner history of her time in great detail, and in a natural, colloquial style. The letters were published posthumously (1725).

Seward, Sir Albert Charles [sooerd] (1863–1941) Palaeobotanist, born in Lancaster, Lancashire, NW England, UK. He studied at Cambridge and Manchester, and was professor of botany at Cambridge (1906–36). He is best known for his work on *English Wealden Flora* (1894–95), *Jurassic Flora* (1900–3), and a panoramic survey, *Plant Life Through the Ages* (1931).

Seward, Anna [sooerd], known as **the Swan of Lichfield** (1747–1809) Poet, born in Eyam, Derbyshire, C England, UK. She lived from the age of 10 at Lichfield, where her father, himself a poet, became a canon. He died in 1790, but she continued to live on in the bishop's palace, and wrote poetry. Her best known work is the poetical novel *Louisa* (1784), which was popular for its sentiment. Her poems were edited by Sir Walter Scott in 1810, with a memoir.

Seward, William H(enry) [sooerd] (1801–72) US statesman, born in Florida, NY. In 1849 he was elected to the US Senate, and became one of the new Republican Party leaders. As Lincoln's secretary of state (1861–9), he negotiated the purchase of the territory of Alaska from Russia (1867). In the 'Trent affair' during the Civil War he advised that the Confederate envoys should be given up to England. He protested against the fitting out of the *Alabama* and similar vessels in British ports, and supported President Johnson's reconstruction policy. >> Johnson, Andrew; Lincoln, Abraham

Sewell, Anna [syooel] (1820–78) Novelist, born in Great Yarmouth, Norfolk. An invalid for most of her life, she wrote *Black Beauty* (1877), the story of a horse, written as a plea for the more humane treatment of animals. It is perhaps the most famous fictional work about horses (filmed, 1946, 1971).

Sexton, Ann, *née* **Harvey** (1928–74) Poet, born in Newton, MA. A confessional poet in the mould of her friend, Sylvia Plath, her main subjects are her depression and mental illness, and her various roles as a woman. She taught at Boston (1969–71) and Colgate (1971–2) universities. *To Bedlam and Part Way Back* (1962) was her first collection of poetry. Others include *Love Poems* (1969) and *The Death Notebooks* (1974). The *Complete Poems* were published in 1981, seven years after she committed suicide. >> Plath

Sexton, Thomas (1848–1932) Irish nationalist politician, born in Ballygannon, Co Waterford, Ireland. He worked as a railway clerk before becoming leader-writer on the *Nation*. He was elected MP for Sligo as Home Rule supporter of Parnell in 1880, captured West Belfast in 1886, and was defeated there in 1892 after the Parnell split. Lord Mayor of Dublin (1888–9), he became MP for Kerry North (1892–6). He controlled the leading Home Rule daily newspaper, the *Freeman's Journal*, from 1892 to 1912. >> Parnell

Sextus Empiricus [em**pi**rikus] (early 3rd-c) Greek philosopher and physician, active at Alexandria and Athens, who is the main source of information for the Sceptical school of philosophy. Little is known of his life, but his extant writings, *Outlines of Pyrrhonism* and *Against the Dogmatists*, had an enormous influence when they were rediscovered and published in Latin translations in the 1560s.

Seymour, Edward >> **Somerset, Duke of**

Seymour, Jane [see**moor**] (c.1509–37) Third queen of Henry VIII, the mother of Edward VI, and the sister of Protector Somerset. She was a lady-in-waiting to Henry's first two wives, and married him 11 days after the execution of Anne Boleyn. She died soon after the birth of her son. >> Edward VI; Henry VIII

Seymour, Lynn [see**moor**] (1939–) Ballet dancer, born in Wainwright, Alberta, Canada. Trained in Vancouver, she went to England and spent two years at the Royal Ballet School, making her debut in 1956 with the Sadler's Wells branch of the company. She is best known for her passionate interpretations of the choreography of MacMillan and Ashton, notably her role in Ashton's *A Month in the Country* (1976). She became the artistic director of the Bavarian State Opera (1978–81), and thereafter concentrated on a career in popular music. >> Ashton, Frederick; MacMillan, Kenneth

Seymour (of Sudeley), Thomas Seymour, Baron [see**moor**] (c. 1508–1549) English soldier and statesman, the brother-in-law of Henry VIII through marriage to Jane Seymour. He became high admiral of England in 1547, and in the same year married the dowager queen **Catherine Parr**, widow of Henry VIII. He sought by intrigue to obtain power, and after his wife's death in 1548 he tried to marry Princess Elizabeth. He was executed for treason by his brother (the Lord Protector for Edward VI). >> Seymour, Jane; Somerset, Edward Seymour

Seymour, William >> **Stuart, Arabella**

Seyss-Inquart, Arthur [**siys ingk**wah(r)t] (1892–1946) Nazi leader, born in Stannern, Austria-Hungary. Chancellor of Austria during the *Anschluss* (1938), he was appointed commissioner for The Netherlands in 1940, where he ruthlessly recruited slave labour. In 1945 he was captured by the Canadians, tried at Nuremberg, and executed for war crimes.

Sforza, Ludovico [**sfaw(r)t**sa], known as **the Moor** (1451–1508) Ruler of Naples, born in Vigevano, Italy. From 1476 he acted as regent for his nephew Gian Galeazzo Sforza (1469–94), but expelled him in 1481 and usurped the dukedom for himself. He made an alliance with Lorenzo de' Medici of Florence and, under his rule, Milan became the most glittering court in Europe. He was a patron of Leonardo da Vinci. He helped to defeat the attempts of Charles VIII of France to secure Naples, but in 1499 was expelled by Louis XII and imprisoned in France, where he died. >> Leonardo da Vinci; Lorenzo de' Medici

Sgambati, Giovanni [sgam**bah**tee] (1841–1914) Composer and pianist, born in Rome. A student of Liszt, he formed an orchestra in Rome, where he conducted performances of the works of Beethoven and Liszt, the first in Italy. In 1876 he helped to found the first public music school in Rome. His compositions include two symphonies, a requiem Mass, chamber music, and piano music. >> Liszt

Shackleton, Sir Ernest Henry (1874–1922) Explorer, born in Kilkea, Co Kildare, Ireland. He was a junior officer in Scott's National Antarctic Expedition (1901–3), and nearly reached the South Pole in his own expedition of 1909. In 1915 his ship *Endurance* was crushed in the ice, and he and five others made a perilous journey of 1300 km/800 mi to bring relief for the crew. Knighted in 1909, he died at South Georgia during a fourth expedition. >> Scott R F; Wilkins, George

Shadows, The British instrumental rock group, formed in 1958 with original members **Hank Marvin** (1941– , lead guitar), **Bruce Welch** (1941– , rhythm guitar), **Brian Bennett** (1940– , drums), **Jet Harris** (1939– , bass), and **Tony Meehan** (1943– , drums). Created to back singer Cliff Richard, they played on numerous hit records, and performed with him in concert and in his films. Although they continued to play and tour with Richard, in 1960 they became an independent group, and were an instant success with Marvin's resonant guitar sound and their trademark 'shadow's step', a three-step dance movement. Their single 'Apache' (1960) was an international hit, and their debut album *The Shadows* (1961) was a UK number 1 hit for six weeks. >> Richard, Cliff

Shadwell, Thomas (c.1642–92) Playwright, born in Brandon, Norfolk, E England, UK. He studied at Cambridge, became a lawyer, and found success with his first satirical comedy, *The Sullen Lovers* (1668), and such later 'comedies of manners' as *Epsom-Wells* (1672). He carried on a literary feud with Dryden, whom he satirized, and who attacked him in turn in *MacFlecknoe* (1684) and other poems. He succeeded Dryden as Poet Laureate in 1689. >> Dryden

Shaffer, Peter (Levin) (1926–) Playwright, born in Liverpool, Merseyside, NW England, UK. He studied at Cambridge, and worked as a librarian and music critic before the immediate success of his first play, *Five Finger Exercise* (1958–60). This was followed by the comedies *The Private Ear* (filmed 1966) and *The Public Eye* (filmed 1972), both produced at the Globe in 1962. *The Royal Hunt of the Sun* (1964) was the first National Theatre hit with a contemporary play. Other notable works include *Lettice and Lovage* (1987), *Equus* (1973–4, filmed 1977), *Amadeus* (1979), which received several awards, including an Academy Award for the filmed version (1984), and *The Gift of the Gorgon* (1992).

Shaftesbury, Anthony Ashley Cooper, 1st Earl of [**shahfts**bree] (1621–83) English statesman, born in Wimborne St Giles, Dorset, S England, UK. He studied at Oxford, became a member of the Short Parliament (1640) and of the Barebones Parliament (1653), and was made one of Cromwell's Council of State, but from 1655 was in Opposition. At the Restoration he became a baron and Chancellor of the Exchequer (1661–72), a member of the Cabal (1667), an earl (1672), and Lord Chancellor (1672–3). He was dismissed in 1673, and led the opposition to the succession of James, Duke of York (later James II). Charged with treason in 1681, he was acquitted, but fled to Holland in 1682. >> Charles II (of England); Cromwell, Oliver; James II (of England); Shaftesbury, 3rd Earl

Shaftesbury, Anthony Ashley Cooper, 3rd Earl of [**shahfts**bree] (1671–1713) Philosopher, born in London, England, UK, the grandson of the 1st Earl of Shaftesbury. He studied in London and Winchester, and entered parliament in 1695, but ill health drove him from politics to literature. He is best known for his essays, collected as *Characteristics of Men, Manners, Opinions, Times* (1711). He was one of the leading English deists, with a considerable influence in Europe. He succeeded to the earldom in 1699, and in 1711 moved to Naples. >> Shaftesbury, 1st Earl

Shaftesbury, Anthony Ashley Cooper, 7th Earl of [**shahfts**bree] (1801–85) Factory reformer and philanthropist, born in London, England, UK. He studied at Oxford, entered parliament in 1826, and became the main spokesman of the factory reform movement. He piloted successive factory acts (1847, 1859) through parliament, regulated conditions in the coal mines (1842), and provided lodging houses for the poor (1851). A leader of the evangelical movement within the Church of England, he succeeded to his earldom in 1851.

Shagall, Marc >> **Chagall, Marc**

Shah Jahan [jahahn] (1592–1666) Mughal emperor of India (1628–58), born in Lahore, Pakistan. His reign saw two wars in the Deccan (1636, 1655), the subjugation of Bijapur and Golconda (1636), and attacks on the Uzbegs and Persians. A ruthless but able ruler, the magnificence of his court was unequalled. His buildings included the Taj Mahal, the tomb of his beloved third wife, **Mumtaz Mahal** (1592–1631). From 1658 he was held prisoner by his son Aurangzeb. >> Aurangzeb; RR1059

Shahn, Ben(jamin) (1898–1969) Painter, born in Kaunas, Lithuania. He emigrated to New York City in 1906, and studied painting in night school. In 1922 he visited several art centres in Europe, and came under the influence of Rouault. His 23 satirical gouache paintings on the trial of the Italian anarchists Sacco and Vanzetti (1932), and the 15 paintings of Tom Mooney, the labour leader (1933), earned him the title of 'the American Hogarth'. He was the first painter to deliver the Charles Eliot Norton Lectures at Harvard (1958). >> Rouault

Shaka [shahka] (c. 1788–1828) African ruler, born near Melmoth, KwaZulu Natal, South Africa. He was a highly successful military ruler, who intensified the centralization of Zulu power, adapted the weapons and tactics of local warfare, and set about the incorporation of neighbouring peoples. The rise of the Zulu kingdom under Shaka was associated with a series of wars and population movements known as the *difagane*. He was killed by his half-brother Dingane. He remains an enigmatic and contentious figure, the subject of novels and films, and his career is a much debated issue in South African history. >> Moshoeshoe

Shakespeare, John (c. 1530–1601) Glover and wool dealer, born in Snitterfield, near Stratford, Warwickshire, C England, UK, the father of William Shakespeare. After his apprenticeship, he set up a business in Stratford, was elected burgess in 1559, and six years later became an alderman. In 1568 he was made bailiff (mayor) of Stratford and a justice of the peace. His wool business failed (1576–7), and at times he dared not leave the house for fear of being arrested for debt. In 1592 he was rescued by his son William, whose earnings in the London theatre were enough to restore the family's position, and in 1596 he was awarded a coat of arms, and died a gentleman. >> Shakespeare, William

Shakespeare, William see panel on p. 851

Shalyapin, Fyodor (Ivanovich) [shalyapeen], often spelled **Chaliapin** (1873–1938) Bass, born near Kazan, Russia. He was largely self-taught, but after a short period of study in Tbilisi (1892–3) he made his way as an opera singer, becoming well known through the roles he sang with the Marmontov Company after 1896. Among his most famous roles was that of Boris Godunov in Musorgsky's opera. He left Russia in 1921, and died in Paris.

Shamir, Yitzhak [shameer], originally **Yitzhak Jazernicki** (1915–) Zionist leader and prime minister of Israel (1983–4, 1986–92), born in Ruzinoy, Poland. He studied law at Warsaw University and at the Hebrew University of Jerusalem, and in his 20s became a founder member of the Israel Freedom Fighters, a terrorist group later known as the Stern Gang. He was arrested by the British in 1941 and exiled to Eritrea in 1946, but given asylum in France. He returned to the new state of Israel (1948), and entered the Knesset in 1973. He was foreign minister (1980–3), before taking over the leadership of the right-wing Likud Party, and becoming prime minister. From 1984 he shared an uneasy coalition with the Labour leader Shimon Peres, and was re-elected in 1988, but lost his position when Labour under Rabin won the 1992 election. >> Peres; Rabin; RR1064

Shammai [shamiy] (c.1st-c BC–AD1st-c) Jewish scholar and Pharisaic leader, apparently a native of Jerusalem. He was the head of a famous school of Torah scholars, whose interpretation of the Law was often in conflict with the equally famous school led by Hillel. Relatively little is known of Shammai himself, except that his legal judgments were often considered severe and literalistic, compared to Hillel's. Both are often referred to in Mishnah. >> Hillel

Shankar, Ravi [shangkah(r)] (1920–) Sitarist, born in Benares, India. He is widely regarded as India's most important musician, not only because of his virtuoso playing, but also as a teacher and composer. After years of intensive musical study, he set up schools of Indian music, founded the National Orchestra of India, and in the mid-1950s became the first Indian instrumentalist to undertake an international tour. He found himself in demand in the West as a performer and teacher in all areas of music – from the Edinburgh International Festival to the jazz and rock worlds. George Harrison of the Beatles was one of his pupils. He has written several film scores, the most notable being for Satyajit Ray's trilogy, *Apu*. >> Beatles, The; Ray, Satyajit

Shankly, Bill, popular name of **William Shankly** (1913–81) Footballer and manager, born in Scotland, UK. As a player he won an FA Cup Medal with Preston North End, and five Scotland caps. As a post-war manager he found success with Liverpool (1959–74), after unremarkable spells with Carlisle, Grimsby, Workington, and Huddersfield. He created a team which was not only highly successful in Britain and Europe, but which encouraged individual expression and communicated great exhilaration to the spectators.

Shannon, Claude E(lwood) (1916–) Mathematician and pioneer of communication theory, born in Gaylord, MI. He studied at Michigan and at the Massachusetts Institute of Technology, and in 1938 published a seminal paper on the application of symbolic logic to relay circuits, which helped transform circuit design from an art into a science. He worked at the Bell Telephone Laboratories (1941–72) in the area of information theory, and wrote *The Mathematical Theory of Communication* (1949) with Warren Weaver.

Shapiro, Erin Patria Margaret, formerly **Pizzey**, *née* **Carney** (1939–) British writer and campaigner for women's rights. She founded the first Shelter for Battered Wives and their children in London (1971), and campaigned for legal protection and resources to help women and children to escape from violent men. Her book *Scream Quietly or the Neighbours Will Hear* encouraged national discussion of what had previously been a hidden problem. Her later book, *Prone to Violence* (1982), suggesting some women are responsible for the violent treatment they suffer, damaged her image as a defender of battered women.

Shapiro, Karl (Jay) [shapeeroh] (1913–) Writer, born in Baltimore, MD. He studied at the University of Virginia, Johns Hopkins, and Pratt Library School, Baltimore, then taught at many institutions, notably at the University of California, Davis (from 1968). He is noted for his mastery of poetic forms, as seen in *Collected Poems 1940–77* (1978), and he was awarded the Pulitzer Prize for *V-Letter and Other Poems* (1944). He also edited literary periodicals (1950–66), and has written literary criticism and a novel.

Shapley, Harlow (1885–1972) Astrophysicist, born in Nashville, MO. He first worked as a newspaper crime reporter before going to the University of Missouri, where he switched from journalism to astronomy. From 1914 he worked at the Mt Wilson Observatory and later became director of Harvard University Observatory (1921–52). He demonstrated that the Milky Way is much larger than had

WILLIAM SHAKESPEARE (1564–1616)

William Shakespeare was born in Stratford-upon-Avon, Warwickshire, C England, UK, the eldest son of John Shakespeare, glover and wool dealer, and his wife Mary Arden. Shakespeare's works display a direct knowledge of classical Latin literature, including texts closely studied by pupils in Elizabethan grammar schools, and he is assumed to have been educated at Stratford Grammar School – his father's civic status entitled him to send William there free of charge. He may have spent the years 1580–2 as a teacher for the Roman Catholic Houghton family in Lancashire. In 1582, when he was 18, he married **Anne Hathaway** in Stratford. She was eight years older than him, and she bore him a daughter, **Susannah**, within six months. Twins were born in 1585; a son **Hamnet** and a daughter **Judith**. Hamnet died in 1596, aged 11.

Little is known about Shakespeare's life immediately after 1582, but it seems probable that he joined a company of players as an actor and playwright, and had probably been a member of several such companies, in London and on tour in the provinces, before joining Strange's Men by 1592. In 1593 the London theatres were closed because of the plague. Shakespeare produced two narrative poems, 'Venus and Adonis' and 'The Rape of Lucrece', which indicates an ambition to secure noble patronage, possibly prompted by the uncertain outlook in the professional theatre.

The next year the theatres reopened, and Shakespeare emerges as a significant member of the Chamberlain's Men, who had their own playhouse in Shoreditch, named The Theatre. The Chamberlain's Men became the leading company, frequently performing at Queen Elizabeth's court, and presenting almost all of the most significant plays of the time. The dates of Shakespeare's earlier plays are uncertain. External evidence is lacking, and their variety in form and style makes assumptions about development difficult. One scholarly view holds *Titus Andronicus* to be the first, written in 1586, with *Romeo and Juliet* as his 10th play in 1591, whereas others suppose *King Henry VI* to be first between 1591–2. However, *The Two Gentlemen of Verona* and *The Taming of the Shrew* have also been proposed as his first play. At any rate, it is agreed that by 1597 Shakespeare had written *The Taming of the Shrew*, *The Comedy of Errors*, *Two Gentlemen of Verona*, *Love's Labour's Lost*, *A Midsummer Night's Dream* (1595–6), *Titus Andronicus*, *Richard III*, *Romeo and Juliet* (1595–6), *King Henry VI* (Parts 1–3), *King John* (1594–6), and *Richard II* (1595).

Shakespeare's sonnets, some in existence by 1598, and all published in 1609, fall into two groups; all those clearly addressed to a man are among the first 126; all those clearly addressed to a woman (the 'dark lady') follow. Many books have been written attempting to identify the supposed real persons behind this great poetic sequence, but until the statement by the publisher is explained – that Mr W.H. is 'the only begetter' of the poems – we are unlikely to be able to pin down any names of real persons inhabiting the world of the sonnets, or even be sure there is any autobiographical basis for them.

Living not far from The Theatre, Shakespeare kept up a steady rate of composition, averaging two plays a year. In 1597 appeared *The Merchant of Venice*, *King Henry IV*, Part I, and *The Merry Wives of Windsor*; during 1598–9 *King Henry IV*, Part 2 and *Much Ado About Nothing*. Then in 1599 the Chamberlain's Men dismantled their theatre building and reassembled it on the S bank of the Thames in Southwark, renaming it the Globe. It seems probable that *King Henry V* was the first Shakespeare play performed there, closely followed by *As You Like It*.

Shakespeare's success as a shareholder in the company is marked by his buying a substantial house in Stratford, called New Place, for £60, in 1597. His father had applied for a grant of arms in 1596, and was said to be 'of good wealth', being worth £500. The grant of arms entitled him to the style of a gentlemen, an honour that would descend in due course to his eldest son. Ironically, Shakespeare's only son died within two months.

The accession of King James I in 1603 brought the acting company new and great benefits. The king immediately conferred his royal patronage on Shakespeare and his fellow sharers in the company, now renamed the King's Men. The next phase of Shakespeare's writing shows great diversity as well as originality. He produced the great sequence of tragedies: *Julius Caesar* (1599), *Hamlet* (1601), *Othello* (1604), *King Lear* (1605-6), *Macbeth* (1606), *Anthony and Cleopatra* (1606-7), and *Coriolanus* (1607–8). After his romantic comedy *Twelfth Night* (1601) came the darker plays *Troilus and Cressida* (1601–2), *All's Well That Ends Well* (1602–3), and *Measure for Measure* (1604).

Shakespeare expected his plays to be performed outdoors at the Globe Theatre and on provincial stages when on tour, but also indoors for court performance before the monarchy (or, as with *The Merry Wives of Windsor*, after a court ceremony); so there would have been little adjustment needed to stage his plays in the indoor playhouse, the Blackfriars Theatre, when it was acquired by the King's Men in 1608. The company now used both indoor and outdoor playhouses in London.

Pericles, first performed at court (1606–8), was the first of several romance tragi-comedies that followed. *Cymbeline* was performed probably at both the Globe and Blackfriars in 1609, then *The Winter's Tale* and *The Tempest* in 1611. Shakespeare collaborated with John Fletcher on *King Henry VIII* and *The Two Noble Kinsmen* in 1613, and there are also signs of a collaborator in *Pericles*. Scholars still argue about the degree of collaboration in several plays, including *Timon of Athens* and *Macbeth*, but the idea that Shakespeare frequently collaborated is now generally discounted.

Shakespeare is supposed to have returned to Stratford for the rest of his life. A number of his plays were published in quarto editions during his lifetime (some of these editions apparently derive from playhouse adaptations), and after his death a folio edition – the famous 'First Folio' – was published in 1623 (the year Anne Hathaway died). There are important and difficult questions associated with the provenance of these texts, especially since none of Shakespeare's original dramatic manuscripts has survived. But what has survived is universally recognized as great literature. The plays have been translated into many languages and are regularly performed all over the world; indeed in the 20th-c a number of the more neglected plays have been rediscovered through theatrical performance. The subject of Shakespeare himself, and his works, also continues to stimulate research by scholars, performance by actors, and new plays and novels by authors.
>> Fletcher, John; Henslowe

been supposed, and that the Solar System is located on the Galaxy's edge, not at its centre. He also did notable work on photometry and spectroscopy.

Shapur or **Sapor II** [sha**poor**], known as **the Great** (309–79) King of Persia (309–79). He was declared king at his birth by the Persian nobility, and ruled with the help of regents until the age of 16. Under him the Sassanian empire reached its zenith. He successfully challenged Roman control of the Middle East, forcing Jovian to cede five provinces to him (363), and establishing Persian control over Armenia. >> Jovian

Sharif, Omar [sha**reef**], originally **Michael Shalhouz** (1932–) Film actor, born in Alexandria, Egypt. He made his Egyptian film debut in 1953, becoming a top male star in the country, before attracting international attention for his role in *Lawrence of Arabia* (1962). Later films include *Doctor Zhivago* (1965, Golden Globe), *Funny Girl* (1968), *The Tamarind Seed* (1974), *Return to Eden* (1982), and *The Mirror Has Two Faces* (1996), and he appeared in the 1996 television production of *Gulliver's Travels*. He has published an autobiography, *The Eternal Male* (1977), and is also renowned as a bridge player.

Sharman, Helen (Patricia) (1963–) Britain's first astronaut, born in Sheffield, South Yorkshire, N England, UK. She studied chemistry at Sheffield University, then worked in electrical engineering and confectionery research. In 1989 she responded to an advertisement asking for trainee astronauts, and was eventually selected from over 13,000 applicants to be the British member of the Russian scientific space mission, Project Juno (May 1991), spending eight days in space. She has since become well known as a lecturer and broadcaster in science education; her book *The Space Place* appeared in 1997.

Sharp, Cecil (James) (1859–1924) Collector of folk songs and dances, born in London, England, UK. He studied at Cambridge, became a lawyer, then turned to music. He published several collections of British and US folk material, and in 1911 founded the Folk-Dance Society. His work is commemorated by Cecil Sharp House, London, the headquarters of the society.

Sharp, Sir Percival (1867–1953) British educationist. He studied at Cambridge, became a teacher, and rose to be head of Bowerham School, Lancashire (1898–1902). He became secretary for education at St Helen's (1905–14), and director of education at Newcastle upon Tyne (1914–19) and Sheffield (1919–32). As secretary of the Association of Education Committees (1933–44), he played a prominent part in the development of English education in the first half of this century.

Sharpe, Tom, popular name of **Thomas Ridley Sharpe** (1928–) Novelist, born in London, England, UK. He studied at Cambridge and did his National Service in the Marines before going to South Africa in 1951, from where he was deported in 1961. He was a lecturer in history at the Cambridge College of Arts and Technology (1963–71) before turning to full-time writing, beginning with *Riotous Assembly* (1971). Later novels include *Indecent Exposure* (1973), *Porterhouse Blue* (1974), a series introducing the character of Wilt (from 1976), and *The Midden* (1996).

Sharpe, William F (1934–) Economist, born in Cambridge, MA. He taught at Washington, Irvine, and Stanford (from 1970) universities. He shared the 1990 Nobel Prize for Economics for his contributions to the corporate finance field, particularly his studies in financial decision-making under uncertainty.

Shastri, Lal (Bahadur) [shas**tree**] (1904–66) Indian statesman and prime minister (1964–6), born in Mughalsarai, Uttar Pradesh, India. He joined the independence movement at 16, and was often imprisoned by the British. He

excelled as a Congress Party official, and in Nehru's Cabinet became minister of transport (1957), commerce (1958), and home affairs (1960). He succeeded Nehru as premier, but died in office from a heart attack, the day after signing a 'no war' agreement with Pakistan. >> Nehru, Jawaharlal; RR1058

Shatner, William (1931–) Actor and writer, born in Montreal, Canada. Educated at McGill University, he became a stage actor in Canada and New York, from 1956 obtaining roles in films and television series. He became internationally known following the cult success of the *Star Trek* television series (1966–9), in which he played Captain James T(iberius) Kirk. He reprised the role in several feature film sequels, directing as well as acting in *Star Trek V: The Final Frontier* (1989). He has also written a number of science-fiction books, starting with *Tek War, Tek Lab* (1989).

Shaw, Anna Howard (1847–1919) Suffragist, born in Newcastle upon Tyne, Tyne and Wear, NE England, UK. Her family emigrated to the USA in 1851, and in 1880 she became the first woman to be ordained as a Methodist preacher. In 1886 she graduated from Boston University as a doctor, but decided to devote herself entirely to the cause of women's suffrage. An eloquent, powerful lecturer, she campaigned widely. She was president of the National American Woman Suffrage Association (1904–15), and head of the Women's Committee of the Council of National Defense during World War 1. She published her autobiography, *The Story of a Pioneer*, in 1915. >> Anthony, Susan; Beard, Mary Ritter; Catt; Stanton

Shaw, Artie, originally **Arthur Arshawsky** (1910–) Clarinet player and bandleader, born in New York City. He turned professional in 1925, and gained popularity during the 1930s, becoming internationally known after recording 'Begin the Beguine' (Cole Porter). Although a gifted jazz musician, his public appearances were erratic, and died away during the 1950s. He wrote an autobiography, *The Trouble with Cinderella* in 1952. He married eight times, always to a well-known beauty, including actresses Lana Turner, Ava Gardner, and Evelyn Keyes.

Shaw, Geoffrey Turton >> **Shaw, Martin Fallus**

Shaw, George Bernard (1856–1950) Playwright, essayist, and pamphleteer, born in Dublin, Ireland. In 1876 he left office-work in Ireland and moved to London, England. In 1882 he turned to socialism, joined the committee of the Fabian Society, and became known as a journalist, writing music and drama criticism, and publishing critical essays. He began to write plays in 1885, and among his early successes were *Arms and the Man* (1894), *Candida* (1897), and *The Devil's Disciple* (1897). There followed *Man and Superman* (1905), *Major Barbara* (1905), *The Doctor's Dilemma* (1906), and several others, displaying an increasing range of subject matter. Later plays include the 'religious pantomime' *Androcles and the Lion* (1912), and the 'anti-romantic' comedy *Pygmalion* (1913), adapted as the musical play *My Fair Lady*, in 1956 (filmed, 1964). After World War 1 followed *Heartbreak House* (1919), *Back to Methuselah* (1921), and *Saint Joan* (1923). He wrote over 40 plays, and continued to write them even in his 90s. He was also passionately interested in the question of spelling reform, wrote most of his own work in shorthand, and left money in his will for the devising of a new English alphabet on phonetic principles (which came to be called *Shavian*). In 1935 he was awarded the Nobel Prize for Literature. >> Webb, Sydney James; Wells, H G

Shaw, Henry Wheeler >> **Billings, Josh**

Shaw, Martin Fallus (1876–1958) Composer, born in London, England, UK. He studied under Charles Stanford at the Royal College of Music, composed the ballad opera,

Mr Pepys (1926), with Clifford Bax, and set T S Eliot's poems to music. He is best known for his songs, and as co-editor of national songbooks with his brother, **Geoffrey Turton** (1879–1943). He also co-edited *Songs of Praise* and *The Oxford Carol Book* with Vaughan Williams. >> Eliot, T S; Stanford, Charles; Vaughan Williams

Shaw, Sir (William) Napier (1854–1945) Meteorologist, born in Birmingham, West Midlands, C England, UK. He was assistant director of the Cavendish Laboratory (1877–1906), director of the Meteorological Office, London (1907–20), and the first professor of meteorology at the Royal College of Science in 1920. He introduced the use of the millibar as a unit of atmospheric pressure, and helped to establish the 'polar front' theory of cyclones propounded by Bjerknes. He was knighted in 1915. >> Bjerknes

Shaw, (Richard) Norman (1831–1912) Architect, born in Edinburgh, EC Scotland, UK. He studied in London, where he practised. He was a leader of the trend away from Victorian style back to traditional Georgian design, as in New Scotland Yard (1888) and the Piccadilly Hotel (1905).

Shaw, Percy (1890–1976) British inventor. While operating a small road repair business in Halifax, West Yorkshire, he devised the idea of self-cleaning, reflective road studs ('cat's eyes'). He set up a factory to manufacture them, and became a millionaire.

Shawcross (of Friston), Hartley William Shawcross, Baron (1902–) Jurist, born in Giessen, Germany. He studied at Dulwich College, was called to the bar at Gray's Inn in 1925, and lectured at Liverpool University (1927–34). After World War 2, he was attorney general (1945–51) and President of the Board of Trade (1951). He established an international legal reputation as chief British prosecutor at the Nuremberg Trials (1945–6), led the investigations of the Lynskey Tribunal (1948), and prosecuted in the Fuchs atom spy case (1950). He was knighted in 1945. He resigned his parliamentary seat in 1958, and was created a life peer in 1959. >> Fuchs, Klaus

Shawn, Ted, popular name of **Edwin Myers Shawn** (1891–1972) Dancer and director, born in Kansas City, MO. He studied theology, and began dancing after suffering diphtheria. In 1914 he met and married Ruth St Denis, and in 1915 they founded *Denishawn*, a dance school favoured by the Hollywood studios, which branched out across America with a wide-ranging curriculum. When the couple separated in 1931, he founded his own group, who toured with dance inspired by native American and Aboriginal work. >> Saint Denis

Shays, Daniel (1747–1825) US soldier, probably born in Hopkinton, MA. During the American War of Independence (1775–83) he served against the British, and was commissioned. In 1786 he led an insurrection by the farmers in W Massachusetts against the US government, which was imposing heavy taxation and mortgages. After raiding the arsenal at Springfield, MA, the insurrectionists were routed at Petersham (1787), and Shays was condemned to death, but pardoned (1788).

Shcharansky, Natan [sharanskee], originally **Anatoly Borisovich Shcharansky** (1948–) Soviet dissident, born in Donetsk, Ukraine. A brilliant mathematician disillusioned with Soviet society, he applied for a visa to emigrate to Israel (1973). This was repeatedly refused, he was harrassed by the KGB, and in 1977 was sentenced to 13 years in a labour colony for allegedly spying on behalf of the CIA. Released in 1986 as part of an East–West 'spy' exchange, he joined his wife in Israel, where he assumed his new name. In 1989 he was nominated as Israeli ambassador to the UN.

Shearer, Moira, originally **Moira Shearer King** (1926–) Ballerina and actress, born in Dunfermline, Fife, E Scotland, UK. She studied at the Sadler's Wells Ballet School, joined the Sadler's Wells Theatre Ballet (1942), and gained ballerina status (1944). She danced leading roles in both classical and modern ballets, her notable performances including *Cinderella* (1948), *Promenade* (1943), and *Clock Symphony* (1948). As an actress she appeared on stage and screen, but is especially remembered for her role in the film *The Red Shoes* (1948).

Shearer, Alan (1970–) England footballer, born in Newcastle-upon Tyne, Tyne & Wear, NE England, UK. He played for Southampton (1988–92), then transferred to Blackburn Rovers (1992–6) at a then record British fee of £3.2 million. He transferred to Newcastle United in 1996 for a world record fee of £15 million. By June 1997 he had a tally of 213 league goals. He joined the England squad in 1992, becoming captain in 1996, and by the end of that year had won 31 caps. He was named 1994 Footballer of the Year and 1995 Professional Footballers' Association Player of the Year.

Shearing, George (1919–) Jazz pianist, bandleader, and composer, born in London, England, UK. Blind from birth, he had some success touring and on radio in Britain, before moving to the USA in the late 1940s. There he gained worldwide fame through his recordings and his lush 'locked hands' style of piano-playing. His compositions include 'Lullaby of Birdland' and 'September in the Rain'.

Sheba, Queen of [sheeba] (c.10th-c BC) Monarch mentioned in the Bible (1 *Kings* 10 and 2 *Chron* 9), perhaps from SW Arabia (modern Yemen), although placed by some in N Arabia. She is said to have journeyed to Jerusalem to test the wisdom of Solomon and to exchange gifts, though this may imply a trade pact. The story depicts the splendour of Solomon's court. >> Solomon

Sheeler, Charles (1883–1965) Painter and photographer, born in Philadelphia, PA. He studied at the School of Industrial Art, Philadelphia, and the Pennsylvania Academy of Fine Arts. From 1912 he worked as an industrial photographer, moving towards creative industrial records, and in 1927 was commissioned to record the building of the Ford Motor installation at River Rouge, MI (1927). Widely acclaimed for this, he became staff photographer at the New York Museum of Modern Art (1942–5), but came to regard photography as a basis for his abstract-realistic paintings and graphic work. >> Strand

Sheen, Charlie, originally **Carlos Irwin Estevez** (1965–) Film actor, born in New York City. He made his first film appearance at the age of nine in his father's film *The Execution of Private Slovik* (1972). His adult film debut was in *Red Dawn* (1984), but it was the Oscar-winning film *Platoon* (1986), about the war in Vietnam, which proved to be his breakthrough picture. Later films include *Wall Street* (1987), *Hot Shots!* and its sequel (1991, 1993), *The Three Musketeers* (1993), *The Arrival* (1996), and *Shadow Conspiracy* (1997). He is the son of Martin Sheen. >> Sheen, Martin

Sheen, Fulton (John) (1895–1979) Roman Catholic clergyman and broadcaster, born in El Paso, IL. Educated at the Catholic University of America, he was ordained in 1919, and returned there to teach philosophy (1926–59) before becoming national director of the Society for the Propagation of the Faith. Meanwhile he became known internationally as a broadcaster on the 'Catholic Hour' (1930–52) and with the TV programme 'Life is Worth Living' (1952–65). He was Auxiliary Bishop of New York (1951–65) and Bishop of Rochester (1966–9).

Sheen, Martin, originally **Ramon Estevez** (1940–) Film actor, born in Dayton, OH. He worked in the theatre before beginning a film career in *Catch 22* (1970). Later films include *Apocalypse Now* (1979), *Wall Street* (1983), *The American President* (1995), and *Hostile Waters* (1997). Known for his support of liberal causes, he narrated *Broken Arrow* (1985), an Oscar-winning documentary about the Navajo nation, and helped narrate the letter-from-Vietnam documentary *Dear America* (1987). He is the father of Charlie Sheen. >> Sheen, Charlie

Shelburne, Earl of >> **Lansdowne, Marquess of**

Shelburne, William Petty Fitzmaurice, 2nd Earl of (1737–1805) British statesman and prime minister (1782–3), born in Dublin, Ireland. He studied at Oxford, entered parliament, succeeded to his earldom in 1761, and became President of the Board of Trade (1763) and secretary of state (1766). Made premier on the death of Rockingham, he resigned when outvoted by the coalition between Fox and North. In 1784 he was made Marquess of Lansdowne. >> Fox, Charles James; North, Frederick; Rockingham, Marquess of; RR1095

Sheldon, Gilbert (1598–1677) English clergyman. Chaplain to Charles I, and warden of All Souls, Oxford (1626–48), he was ejected by the Parliamentarians. At the Restoration in 1660 he was appointed Bishop of London, and in 1663 became Archbishop of Canterbury. He built the Sheldonian Theatre at Oxford (1669). >> Charles I (of England)

Shelley, Mary (Wollstonecraft), *née* **Godwin** (1797–1851) Writer, born in London, England, UK, the daughter of William Godwin and Mary Wollstonecraft. She eloped with Percy Bysshe Shelley in 1814, and married him two years later. She wrote several novels, notably *Frankenstein, or the Modern Prometheus* (1818), travel books, and journals, and edited Shelley's poems and other works (1823) after his death. >> Godwin, William; Shelley, Percy Bysshe; Wollstonecraft

Shelley, Percy Bysshe [bish] (1792–1822) Poet, born at Field Place, near Horsham, West Sussex, S England, UK. He studied at Oxford, but was expelled for his pamphlet, *The Necessity of Atheism* (1811). He eloped to Scotland with Harriet Westbrook, married her and settled in Keswick, where he was influenced by William Godwin, and wrote his revolutionary poem *Queen Mab* (1813). He formed a liaison with Godwin's daughter, Mary, with whom he eloped (1814), and whom he married in 1816 after learning that Harriet had committed suicide. From 1818 he lived in Italy, touring with his family and friends. There he met Byron, and wrote the bulk of his poetry, including odes, lyrics, and the verse drama *Prometheus Unbound* (1818–19). During this tour, he was drowned in the Bay of Spezia near Livorno. >> Byron, George; Godwin, William; Shelley, Mary; Trelawny

Shelton, Ian (1958–) Canadian astronomer. While working as a technician, responsible for running a small S observatory in the Chilean mountains for the University of Toronto, he recognized and identified a celestial phenomenon now known as Supernova Shelton 1987A – an exploding star located 170 000 light years from Earth.

Shem Biblical character, the eldest son of Noah, the brother of Ham and Japeth. He is said to have escaped the flood with his father and brothers, and to have lived 600 years. His descendants are listed (in *Gen* 10), and he is depicted as the legendary father of 'Semitic' peoples, meant to include the Hebrews. >> Noah

Shen Kua [shen kwah] (1031–95) Administrator, engineer, and scientist, born in Qiantang, China. As director of the astronomical bureau from 1072, he improved methods of computation and the design of several observational devices. In 1075 he constructed a series of relief maps of China's N frontier area, and designed fortifications as defences against nomadic invaders. In 1082 he was forced by intrigue to resign from his government posts, and occupied his last years in the writing of *Brush Talks from Dream Brook* (trans title), a remarkable compilation of about 600 observations which has become one of the most important sources of information on early science and technology.

Shenstone, William (1714–63) Poet, born in Leasowes, Shropshire, WC England, UK. He studied at Oxford, and in 1735 inherited the estate of the Leasowes, where he spent most of his income on 'landscape gardening' (a term he originated) to turn it into a show garden. In 1737 he published his best-known poem, 'The Schoolmistress', written in imitation of Spenser. He published *The Judgement of Hercules* in 1741. His *Pastoral Ballad* (1755) was commended by Gray and Johnson. >> Gray, Thomas; Johnson, Samuel; Spenser

Shepard, Alan B(artlett) (1923–) Astronaut, the first American in space, born in East Derry, NH. He trained at the US Naval Academy (1945), and from 1947 flew jet aircraft on test and training missions. One of the original seven NASA astronauts, on 5 May 1961, 23 days after Yuri Gagarin's historic orbit of the Earth, he was launched in *Freedom 7* by a Redstone rocket vehicle, on a ballistic suborbital trajectory to a height of 116 mi, landing 302 mi downrange after a 15-min flight. He was director of astronaut training at NASA (1965–74), and commanded the Apollo 14 lunar mission in 1971. >> Gagarin

Shepard, Ernest (Howard) (1879–1976) Artist and cartoonist, born in London, England, UK. He worked for *Punch* magazine, but made his name with his illustrations for children's books such as A A Milne's *Winnie the Pooh* (1926) and Kenneth Grahame's *The Wind in the Willows* (1931).

Shepard, Sam, popular name of **Samuel Shepard Rogers** (1943–) Playwright and actor, born in Fort Sheridan, IL. He studied agriculture, but joined a touring group and moved to New York City (1963), where his first plays were produced by Theater Genesis. He was resident playwright at the Magic Theater, San Francisco, from 1974. His works include *The Tooth of Crime* (1972), *Killer's Head* (1975), *Curse of the Starving Class* (1976), and *Buried Child* (1978, Pulitzer). He returned to acting later in the 1970s. Other works include the plays *A Lie of the Mind* (1985), which was very successful in the USA, *States of Shock* (1988), and *Simpatico* (1994), and the screenplay *Paris, Texas* (1984).

Shepherd, Cybill (1950–) Film actress, born in Memphis, TN. She was a successful model before her critically acclaimed film debut in *The Last Picture Show* (1971), following this with *The Heartbreak Kid* (1973) and *Taxi Driver* (1976). She also starred with Bruce Willis in the long-running television series *Moonlighting* (1985–9). Later films include *Once Upon a Crime* (1992) and *Married To It* (1993), and the television sitcom *Cybill*. >> Willis

Sheppard, David (Stuart), Baron (1929–) Anglican clergyman, and former cricketer, born in Reigate, Surrey, SE England, UK. He studied at Cambridge, and worked in London's East End as warden of the Mayflower Family Centre, Canning Town (1957–69). He was Bishop of Woolwich before becoming Bishop of Liverpool in 1975. There his profound social concern, the remarkable rapport in which he and his Roman Catholic counterpart worked together, and perhaps also his past record as a former Sussex (1953) and England (1954) cricket captain, made a lasting impact on the city. His books include *Parson's Pitch* (1964), *Built as a City* (1974), and *Bias to the Poor* (1983). He became a life peer in 1998. >> Worlock

Sheppard, Dick, popular name of **Hugh Richard Lawrie Sheppard** (1880–1937) Anglican clergyman and pacifist, born in Windsor, Berkshire, S England, UK. A popular preacher with distinctly modern views on the Christian life, he was a pioneer of religious broadcasting. Vicar of St Martin-in-the-Fields, London (1914–27), he published *The Human Parson* (1927) and *The Impatience of a Parson* (1927). He later became dean of Canterbury (1929–31), and canon of St Paul's Cathedral (1934–7). An ardent pacifist, he founded the Peace Pledge Union in 1936.

Sheppard, Jack, popular name of **John Sheppard** (1702–24) Thief, born in London, England, UK. Brought up in a workhouse, his father having died, he became involved with prostitutes and thieves, and turned to petty crime. The subject of numerous ballads and popular plays, he was imprisoned four times, and made four spectacular escapes, even when manacled to the floor of his cell in solitary confinement. After his fifth arrest and imprisonment he was hanged, reputedly before a gathering of 200 000 people.

Sheppard, Kate, popular name of **Catherine Wilson Sheppard** (1848–1934) Suffragist, born in Liverpool, Merseyside, NW England, UK. She emigrated to New Zealand in 1869. She possessed a strong sense of social responsibility, allied to the belief that women should be entitled to participate fully in political affairs. In 1887 she became an officer of the Women's Christian Temperance Union, and from that position led a nation-wide struggle for the enfranchisement of women. Her campaign succeeded in 1893, when New Zealand became the first country in the world to give women the vote.

Sher, Antony [shair] (1949–) Actor, writer, and painter, born in Cape Town, South Africa. He moved to England in 1968 and studied at the Webber-Douglas Academy of Dramatic Art. He appeared in plays at the Royal Court Theatre, including David Hare's *Teeth 'n' Smiles* in 1975, and joined the Royal Shakespeare Company in 1982. His Fool in *King Lear* was the first of his innovative creations of Shakespearian characters. An exciting actor to watch, in his role as *Richard III* (1984) he used crutches, and as Shylock in *The Merchant of Venice* (1987) he was an immensely powerful stage presence. He has appeared occasionally in television drama, notably in *The History Man* (1981). His books include *The Year of the King* (1985), an account of his work on *Richard III*, *Woza Shakespeare!* (with Gregory Doran), and the novels *The Indoor Boy* (1991) and *Cheap Lives* (1995). Later roles include Disraeli in the film *Mrs Brown* (1997) and Cyrano de Bergerac in the Royal Shakespeare Company's production (1997).

Sherard, Robert Harborough, originally **Robert Harborough Kennedy** (1861–1943) Biographer and defender of Oscar Wilde, the great-grandson of William Wordsworth. He lived most of his life in France and Corsica, and wrote lives of Zola, Daudet, and Maupassant, all of whom he had known. He befriended Oscar Wilde in 1883 and, although deeply shocked by the Wilde scandal, stood by him and wrote several books and pamphlets in his favour, most notably *Oscar Wilde: the Story of an Unhappy Friendship* (1902). >> Wilde, Oscar

Sheraton, Thomas (1751–1806) Cabinet maker, born in Stockton-on-Tees, Durham, NE England, UK. He settled in London c.1790, wrote a *Cabinetmaker and Upholsterer's Drawing Book* (1794), and produced a range of Neoclassical designs which had a wide influence on contemporary taste in furniture.

Sherbrooke (of Sherbrooke), Robert Lowe, Viscount (1811–92) Liberal politician, born in Bingham, Nottinghamshire, C England, UK. He studied at Oxford, and was called to the bar in 1842, when he emigrated to Australia and became prominent as a lawyer and politician. He returned to England in 1850, wrote editorials for *The Times*, and sat in the House of Commons (1852–80). He is best remembered for his defeat of the Reform Bill of 1866, which caused the fall of the Liberal Government. He was Chancellor of the Exchequer under Gladstone, and in 1873 he became home secretary. He was created a viscount in 1880. >> Gladstone, W E

Shere Ali [shair ahlee] (1825–79) Amir of Afghanistan (1863–79), the younger son of Dost Mohammed. Disagree-

ments with his half-brothers arose after he succeeded as amir, which kept Afghanistan in anarchy. He fled to Kandahar, and regained possession of Kabul in 1868 with assistance from the Viceroy of India, Sir John Lawrence. In 1879 his eldest son, Yakub Khan, rebelled, but was captured and imprisoned. Shere Ali's refusal to receive a British mission (1878) led to the second Anglo-Afghan war (1878–80). After severe fighting, he fled to Turkestan, where he died. >> RR1031

Sheridan, Philip H(enry) (1831–88) US general, born in Albany, NY. He trained at West Point, and commanded a Union division at the beginning of the Civil War, taking part in many campaigns. In 1864 he was given command of the Army of the Shenandoah, turning the valley into a barren waste and defeating General Lee. He had a further victory at Five Forks in 1865, and was active in the final battle which led to Lee's surrender. >> Lee, Robert E

Sheridan, Richard Brinsley (Butler) (1751–1816) Playwright, born in Dublin, Ireland. He studied at Harrow, turned immediately to writing, and settled in London. In 1775 appeared the highly successful comedy of manners, *The Rivals*, and this was followed by several other comedies and farces, notably *The School for Scandal* (1777). He became manager of Drury Lane Theatre in 1778, and a Whig MP (1780–1812). He proved to be a great parliamentary orator, and held various junior offices. The extravagances of his second wife, and the burning down of his theatre in 1809, caused him grave hardship, and he died in poverty.

Sheriff, Lawrence (?–1567) Philanthropist, born in Rugby, Warwickshire, C England, UK. A grocer in London, he became the founder of Rugby School (1567), by his bequest and endowment of estates, including his own house. The school became the model public (fee-paying) school for boys for many generations afterwards. The game of rugby football originated there. >> Ellis, William Webb

Sheringham, Teddy (1966–) Footballer, born in Walthamstow NC Greater London, England, UK. A forward, he played for Millwall, Aldershot, Nottingham Forest, and Tottenham Hotspurs, signing for Manchester United in 1997. By early 1997 he had won 22 caps playing for England.

Sherman, Roger (1721–93) US statesman, born in Newton, MA. He lived in Connecticut from 1743. First elected to the State Assembly in 1755, he became a judge of the superior court (1766–89) and Mayor of New Haven (1784–93). A signatory of the Declaration of Independence, as a delegate to the Convention of 1787 he took a prominent part in the debates on the Constitution.

Sherman, William Tecumseh (1820–91) US general, born in Lancaster, OH. Trained at West Point, he became a general in the Union army during the Civil War. His most famous campaign was in 1864, when he captured Atlanta, and commenced his famous 'March to the Sea', with 65 000 men, which divided the Confederate forces. After capturing Savannah, he moved N through the Carolinas, gaining further victories which helped to bring forward the Confederate surrender. >> Hampton, Wade; Hood, John B; Howard, Oliver O

Sherriff, R(obert) C(edric) (1896–1975) Playwright and scriptwriter, born in Hampton Wick, Surrey, SE England, UK. He worked in his father's insurance company after leaving school, and as a claims adjuster after World War 1. Drawing on his wartime experiences, he wrote *Journey's End* (1929), based on life in a dugout on the Western Front. It became an immediate success in London, running for nearly 600 performances, and was staged all over the world. None of his later plays achieved the same impact, but he wrote the scripts for many films, including *The Invisible Man* (1933), *Goodbye Mr Chips* (1939), and *The Dambusters* (1955).

Sherrin, Ned, popular name of **Edward George Sherrin** (1931–) Producer, director, theatre critic, and writer for stage and screen, born in Low Ham, Somerset, SW England, UK. He studied at Oxford, joined the BBC (1957), and became known through producing and directing the satirical revue, *That Was The Week That Was* (1962–3). He has produced a number of plays on stage and television, directed and appeared in *Side by Side by Sondheim* (1976), co-wrote the script of *Ziegfeld* (1988), and is a popular member of radio and television panel programmes.

Sherrington, Sir Charles Scott (1857–1952) Physiologist, born in London, England, UK. He studied at Cambridge and Berlin, taught at London University, where he became professor of pathology (1891–5), and was then professor of physiology at Liverpool (1895–1913) and Oxford (1913–35). His research on the nervous system was a landmark in modern physiology. Knighted in 1922, he shared the Nobel Prize for Physiology or Medicine in 1932. >> RR1124

Sherwood, Robert E(mmet) (1896–1955) Playwright and writer, born in New Rochelle, NY. He wrote his first play, *Barnum Was Right*, while at Harvard, and after service in World War 1 became editor of *Life* (1924–8) and a member of Dorothy Parker's celebrated Algonquin Round Table. He was awarded four Pulitzer Prizes, the first three for drama – *Idiot's Delight*, (1936), *Abe Lincoln in Illinois* (1939), and *There Shall be No Night* (1941) – and the last for his biographical *Roosevelt and Hopkins* (1949). >> Parker, Dorothy

Shevardnadze, Eduard Amvrosiyevich [shevernadze] (1928–) Georgian head of state (1992–) and former Soviet statesman, born in Mamati, Georgia. He studied at the Kutaisi Pedagogical Institute, joined the Communist Party of the Soviet Union in 1948, and worked in the Komsomol Youth League during the 1950s and the Georgian interior ministry during the 1960s, where he gained a reputation as an opponent of corruption. He became Party chief in 1972, and introduced agricultural experiments. In 1978 he was inducted into the Politburo as a candidate member, and in 1985 was promoted by the new Soviet leader, Mikhail Gorbachev, to full Politburo status and appointed foreign minister. He resigned in 1990, expressing concern over some of Gorbachev's decisions and warning of dictatorship. He helped defeat the attempted coup in August 1991, and was briefly foreign minister again at the end of that year. He then returned to Georgia, which had become an independent republic following the break-up of the Soviet Union (1991), and was elected Chairman of the State Council in December 1992, but was unable to prevent the country's slide into civil war. >> Gorbachev; RR1051

Shih Huangdi >> **Qin Shihuangdi**

Shillibeer, George (1797–1866) Pioneer of London omnibuses, born in London, England, UK. He established a coach-building business in Paris in 1825, and from 1829 ran the first London service from the City to Paddington.

Shilton, Peter (1949–) Footballer, born in Leicester, Leicestershire, C England, UK. Starting his career with Leicester City at the age of 16, he also played for Stoke City, Nottingham Forest, Southampton, and Derby County. For the first four clubs he established a record by making over 100 league appearances for each of them. He made his international debut for England in 1970, and became the first England goalkeeper to gain 100 caps. He has won all the major honours in the game, including League championship and European Cup medals. In 1989 he set a new record by winning his 109th cap against Denmark, thus topping the record of Bobby Moore. >> Moore, Bobby

Shinwell, Emmanuel Shinwell, Baron, popularly known as **Manny Shinwell** (1884–1986) British statesman, born in London, England, UK. A 'street-corner socialist' in Glasgow, he became a Labour MP in 1922, held junior office in the interwar Labour governments, and in the postwar Labour government was minister of fuel and power, nationalizing the mines (1946), secretary of state for war (1947), and minister of defence (1950–1). Well known for his party political belligerence, in his later years he mellowed into a back-bench 'elder statesman'. He was awarded a life peerage in 1970. He wrote several autobiographical works, including *I've Lived Through It All* (1973).

Shipley, Jenny (1952–) New Zealand politician and prime minister (1997–), born in Gore, New Zealand. She studied at Christchurch Teachers College, worked as a primary school teacher, then entered politics, becoming an MP for the (conservative) National Party in 1987. Her ministerial portfolios included social welfare (1990–3), health (1993–6), women's affairs (1990–6, 1997), and transport (1997). She became the country's first woman prime minister following the retirement of Jim Bolger. >> Bolger

Shipton, Eric (Earle) (1907–77) British mountaineer. He spent many years climbing in E and C Africa, and obtained much of his knowledge of the East during his terms as consul-general in Kashgar (1940–2, 1946–8) and Kunming (1949–51). Between 1933 and 1951 he either led or was a member of five expeditions to Mt Everest, and helped pave the way for the successful expedition of 1953.

Shipton, Mother, popular name of **Ursula Southiel** (1488–c.1560) Witch, born near Knaresborough, North Yorkshire, N England, UK. At the age of 24 she married **Tony Shipton**, a builder. According to S Baker, who edited her 'prophecies' (1797), she lived beyond 70. A book in 1684 by Richard Head tells how she was carried off by the devil, and bore him an imp. A small British moth, with wing-markings resembling a witch's face, is named after her.

Shirer, William L(awrence) (1904–93) Journalist, broadcaster, and historian, born in Chicago, IL. After working as a newspaper correspondent in Europe, he joined CBS in 1937 and broadcast on the momentous events in Europe from both sides until 1940. He wrote a column for the New York *Herald Tribune* (1942–8). His history, *The Rise and Fall of the Third Reich* (1960), won the National Book Award.

Shirley, James (1596–1666) Playwright, born in London, England, UK. He studied at Oxford and Cambridge, took holy orders, and in 1623 was appointed headmaster of the grammar school in St Albans. He moved to London (c.1624) and became a playwright. Before the parliamentary closure of the theatres in 1642, he had completed at least 36 plays and was the leading working dramatist in London. His works include the comedies *The Witty Fair One* (1628) and *The Lady of Pleasure* (1635), and the tragedies *The Traitor* (1631) and *The Cardinal* (1641).

Shirley-Quirk, John (1931–) Bass-baritone, born in Liverpool, Merseyside, NW England, UK. He studied at Liverpool University, and made his professional debut in 1961. A noted Lieder and operatic singer, his appearances include *Eugene Onegin* at Glyndbourne and *Elegy For Young Lovers* with the Scottish Opera. He made his first appearance at the Metropolitan Opera, New York, in 1974.

Shirreff, Emily Anne Eliza (1814–97) British pioneer of women's education. With her sister, Maria Georgina Grey, she wrote *Thoughts on Self-Culture, Addressed to Women* (1850), and published works on kindergartens and the Froebel system. She founded the National Union for the Higher Education of Women (1872), and was mistress of Girton College, Cambridge (1870–97). >> Grey, Maria Georgina

Shockley, William B(radford) (1910–89) Physicist, born in London, England, UK. He studied at the California Institute of Technology and Harvard, began work with Bell Telephone Laboratories in 1936, and became professor of engineering at Stanford in 1963. During World War 2 he directed US research on antisubmarine warfare. In 1947 he helped devise the point-contact transistor. He then devised the junction transistor, which heralded a revolution in radio, TV, and computer circuitry. He shared the Nobel Prize for Physics in 1956 with John Bardeen and Walter Brattain. In his later years Shockley provoked outrage with his racist comments and sterilization schemes for people of low IQ. >> Bardeen; Brattain

Shoemaker, Willie, popular name of **William Lee Shoemaker**, nickname **the Shoe** (1931–) Racing jockey and trainer, born in Fabens, TX. Only 149·8 cm/4 ft 11 in tall, and weighing 43 kg/95 lb, he won more races than any other jockey – nearly 9000 winners between 1949 and his retirement in 1989. In 1953 he rode a world record 485 winners in one season. He was severely injured in a car accident in 1991, but survived to become a trainer. >> RR1161

Shoenberg, Isaac (1880–1963) British electrical engineer, born in Russia. He became research director of Electrical and Musical Industries (EMI) in 1931, and initiated a programme of development of electronic television in preference to John Logie Baird's system. This led to the BBC's high definition service, which commenced broadcasting in November 1936. >> Baird

Sholes, Christopher Latham [shohlz] (1819–1890) Inventor, born near Mooresburg, PA. An apprentice printer at first, he later worked as a newspaper editor and government official. His best-known invention is the typewriter, which he developed with fellow inventors Carlos Glidden and Samuel Soulé. A patent was granted in 1868, which Sholes sold to the Remington Arms Company, who then marketed the first Remington Typewriter.

Sholokhov, Mikhail Alexandrovich [sholokhof] (1905–84) Novelist, born near Veshenskaya, Russia. After serving in the Red Army (1920), he became a writer, best known for his novel tetralogy *Tikhy Don* (1928–40, And Quietly Flows the Don, trans 1960), and other novels of Cossack life. He received the Nobel Prize for Literature in 1965.

Shore, Jane (?–c.1527) Mistress of Edward IV, born in London, England, UK. She married **William Shore**, a goldsmith, but in 1470 became the mistress of Edward IV. Her husband abandoned her, but she lived till Edward's death in 1483 in luxury. Thereafter she became the mistress of Thomas Grey, 1st Marquess of Dorset. A liaison with William, Lord Hastings, alienated her from Richard III just before he seized power (1483), and he forced her to do public penance. She never recovered, and died a beggar. >> Edward IV; Richard III

Shore, Peter (David) (1924–) British statesman. He studied at Cambridge, joined the Labour Party in 1948, and headed its research department for five years before becoming an MP in 1964. He held several government posts, then served as secretary of state for economic affairs (1967–9), for trade (1974–6), and for the environment (1976–9). After unsuccessfully contesting the Party leadership in 1983, he became shadow Leader of the House of Commons (1983–7) before returning to the back benches.

Short, Clare (1946–) British stateswoman. She studied at Keele and Leeds universities, and after working as a civil servant and in local community organizations, became an MP in 1983. She was the opposition spokesperson on employment (1985–8), social security (1988–91), environmental protection (1992–3), and women (1993–5), then joined the shadow cabinet (1995), and was spokesperson on transport (1995–6) and overseas development (1996–7). She became secretary-of-state for international development in the 1997 Labour government.

Short, Sir Frank (1857–1945) Artist, born in Stourbridge, West Midlands, C England, UK. He studied in London, and became a master of all the engraving processes. Head of

the Engraving School at the Royal College of Art, he spent a great deal of time interpreting other masters, in particular Turner's 'Liber Studiorum'. He was president of the Royal Society of Painter Etchers (1910–39).

Short, Nigel (1965–) Chess player, born in Atherton, Lancashire, NW England, UK. He won the British Championship in 1977, became an international master in 1980, and in 1984 was the UK's youngest ever grandmaster. In 1993 he beat Jan Timmen to become the first UK grandmaster to qualify for a World Championship match, but was defeated by Kasparov. He resigned from FIDE (the international chess organization) in 1993 and with Kasparov formed the Professional Chess Association. >> Kasparov

Shorter, Frank (1947–) US marathon runner, born in Munich, Germany. He won the 1972 Olympic title, and took the silver medal at the 1976 Games. His first Olympic gold came in only his sixth marathon. A track runner before stepping up to marathon distance, his success helped inspire the running and jogging boom in the USA. He went on to a career as a television sports commentator.

Shorter, Wayne (1933–) Jazz saxophonist, born in Newark, NJ. He studied music at New York University, then played with the Art Blakey Jazz Messengers (1959–63) and Miles Davis (1964–70), during the period of the trumpeter's first experiments in electric jazz-rock fusion. He then co-founded the quintet Weather Report, which performed from 1971 until the mid-1980s. Since then, he has continued in the electric jazz style, playing tenor and soprano saxophones at the head of small combos. >> Blakey; Davis, Miles

Shorthouse, Joseph Henry (1834–1903) Novelist, born in Birmingham, West Midlands, C England, UK. He was a Quaker who converted to the Church of England, and his major work, a philosophical romance entitled *John Inglesant* (1881), revealed an insight into religious conflicts. His other works include *The Little Schoolmaster Mark* (1883–4), *Sir Percival* (1886), *A Teacher of the Violin* (1888), and *Blanche, Lady Falaise* (1891).

Shostakovich, Dmitri Dmitriyevich [shostakohvich] (1906–75) Composer, born in St Petersburg, Russia. He studied at the Conservatory there, and composed his first symphony in 1925. His music was at first highly successful, but his operas and ballets were later criticized by government and press for a failure to observe the principles of 'Soviet realism'. He was reinstated by his fifth symphony (1937), and subsequently composed prolifically in all forms. He wrote 15 symphonies, as well as violin, piano, and cello concertos, chamber music, and choral works.

Shotoku Taishi [shotohkoo tiyshee] (574–622) Japanese Yamato period ruler. A member of the Soga ruling clan, he was regent to Empress Suiko (c.592–628). Influenced by Chinese culture, he sent four embassies to the Sui court in China. His patronage of Buddhism, including importing Korean monks, and extensive temple building, aided its ascendancy from c.600.

Showa Tenno ('Emperor') **Hirohito** [shoha tenoh hirohheetoh] (1901–89) Emperor of Japan (1926–89), the 124th in direct lineage, born in Tokyo. His reign was marked by rapid militarization and aggressive wars against China (1931–2, 1937–45) and against the USA and Britain (1941–5), which ended with the two atomic bombs on Hiroshima and Nagasaki. Under US occupation, in 1946 Hirohito renounced his legendary divinity and most of his powers to become a democratic constitutional monarch. >> RR1068

Shrapnel, Henry (1761–1842) British artillery officer, who retired from active service as a lieutenant-general in 1825. In c.1793 he invented the *shrapnel shell*, an anti-personnel device which exploded while in flight, scattering lethal lead shot and other material.

Shu Ching-Chün >> Lao She

Shull, Clarence G (1915–) Physicist, born in Pittsburgh, PA. He studied at New York University, later moving to Oak Ridge National Laboratory (1946–55) and to MIT. He shared the Nobel Prize for Physics in 1994 for his work in the field of neutron scattering. >> Brockhouse

Shultz, George P(ratt) (1920–) US statesman, born in New York City. He studied at Princeton and the Massachusetts Institute of Technology, then taught at MIT and Chicago, where he became dean of the Graduate School of Business. He was named secretary of labour by President Nixon (1969), and went on to hold a number of high governmental posts before returning to private life in 1974. In 1982 President Reagan made him secretary of state, a post he retained for the rest of the Reagan presidency. >> Nixon; Reagan

Shumway, Norman (Edward) (1923–) Cardiac surgeon, born in Kalamazoo, MI. He studied at Vanderbilt and Minnesota universities, then joined the faculty at the Stanford University School of Medicine in 1958, where he and his team have been active in many aspects of cardiovascular surgery, including cardiac transplantation. He did much of the early experimental work in the field, before heart transplants were attempted in human beings, and performed the first adult heart transplant in the USA in 1968.

Shuster, Joseph, >> **Siegel and Shuster**

Shute, Nevil, pseudonym of **Nevil Shute Norway** (1899–1960) Writer, born in London, England, UK. He studied at Oxford, became an aeronautical engineer, and began to write novels in 1926. After World War 2, he emigrated to Australia, which became the setting for most of his later books, notably *A Town Like Alice* (1949) and *On the Beach* (1957), which were both made into successful films. He published his autobiography, *Slide Rule*, in 1954.

Sibelius, Jean (Julius Christian) [sibaylius] (1865–1957) Composer, born in Tavastehus, Finland. He turned from law to music, studying at the Helsinki Conservatory, Berlin, and Vienna. A passionate nationalist, he wrote a series of symphonic poems based on episodes in the Finnish epic *Kalevala*. From 1897 a state grant enabled him to devote himself entirely to composition, and his seven symphonies (he destroyed his eighth), symphonic poems – notably *Finlandia* (1899) – and violin concerto won great international as well as national popularity.

Sibley, Dame Antoinette (1939–) Dancer, born in Bromley, S Greater London, England, UK. She trained with the Royal Ballet, and appeared as a soloist for the first time in 1956 when, due to illness, she stepped into the main role of *Swan Lake*. It was an unprecedented casting move which brought her fame overnight. Her partnership with Anthony Dowell was one of enchanting compatibility, leading them to be dubbed 'the Golden Pair'. A dancer of great sensuality and beauty, her roles in Frederick Ashton's *The Dream* and Kenneth MacMillan's *Manon* are among her most celebrated. A knee injury forced an early retirement in 1976. She became president of the Royal Academy of Dancing in 1991, and was made a dame in 1996. >> Dowell

Sica, Vittorio de >> **de Sica, Vittorio**

Sickert, Walter (Richard) (1860–1942) Artist, born in Munich, Germany. After three years on the English stage, he turned to art, studying in London and Paris, where he met Degas, and used his techniques to illustrate music-hall interiors and London life. The Camden Town Group (later the London Group) was formed under his leadership (c.1910), and he became a major influence on later English painters. >> Degas; Gilman, Harold; Gore, Spencer Frederick

Sickingen, Franz von (1481–1523) Knight, born in Ebernburg, Germany. A member of the *Reichsritterschaft* (the class of free knights), he acquired considerable wealth fighting campaigns against cities, such as at Worms (1513), and Metz (1518). A champion of the poorer classes, he became a prominent leader of the early Reformation in Germany, declaring war against the Archbishop of Trier. He was defeated and died in his last stronghold at Landstuhl. >> Hutten

Siddons, Sarah, *née* **Kemble** (1755–1831) Actress, born in Brecon, Powys, E Wales, UK. She was a member of the theatre company run by her father, Roger Kemble, from her earliest childhood, and in 1773 married her fellow actor, **William Siddons** (1744–1808). She gained a great reputation in the provinces, and after playing at Drury Lane in 1782 became the unquestioned queen of the stage, unmatched as a tragic actress. She retired in 1812. >> Kemble, John Philip

Sidgwick, Henry (1838–1900) Philosopher, born in Skipton, North Yorkshire, N England, UK. He studied at Cambridge, where he became a fellow of Trinity College (1859) and professor of moral philosophy (1883). His best-known work, *Methods of Ethics* (1874), develops the utilitarian theories of John Stuart Mill. He was also active in promoting higher education for women, notably in the founding of Newnham College, Cambridge, in 1880. He was a founder and the first president of the Society for Psychical Research (1882). >> Mill, John Stuart

Sidgwick, Nevil Vincent (1873–1952) Chemist, born in Oxford, Oxfordshire, SC England, UK. He studied science and classics at Oxford, where in 1901 he became professor of chemistry. He is known for his work on molecular structure and his formulation of a theory of valency. His greatest contribution was to compile much work done by others into a coherent and unified account which clarified old ideas and pointed the way to new ones. He was awarded the Royal Society's Royal Medal in 1937.

Sidmouth (of Sidmouth), Henry Addington, 1st Viscount [sidmuhth] (1757–1844) British statesman and prime minister (1801–4), born in London, England, UK. He studied at Oxford, left law for politics, and became an MP in 1783. He was speaker of the House (1789–1801) when, upon Pitt's resignation, he was invited to form a Tory ministry. His administration negotiated the Peace of Amiens (1802), which held for barely a year. His government ended in 1804, when he was created a viscount. He later became home secretary under Liverpool (1812–21), unpopular for coercive measures such as the Six Acts of 1819. >> RR1095

Sidney, Algernon (1622–83) English politician, born in Penshurst, Kent, SE England, UK. He became a cavalry officer in the English Civil War on the parliamentary side, and was wounded at Marston Moor (1644). In 1645 he entered parliament, and served as governor in several cities. An extreme Republican, he resented Cromwell's usurpation of power, and retired to Penshurst (1653–9). After the Restoration he lived on the European mainland, but in 1677 was pardoned and returned to England. In 1683 he was implicated on very little evidence in the Rye House Plot, and beheaded. >> Russell, Lord William

Sidney, Margaret >> **Lothrop, Harriet Mulford**

Sidney, Sir Philip (1554–86) Poet, born in Penshurst, Kent, SE England, UK. He studied at Oxford, and perhaps also at Cambridge, then travelled in Europe (1572–5). He gained Elizabeth I's displeasure when he advised her against a projected marriage plan, and in 1580 left the court. Knighted in 1583, he was sent to Holland to assist in the struggle against Spain, and was fatally wounded at Zutphen. His literary work, written in 1578–82, was not published until after his death. It includes the unfinished pastoral romance, *Arcadia*, the *Defence of Poesie*, and a sonnet cycle, *Astrophel and Stella*. He is also known for the patronage he bestowed on poets, as shown by the dedication in Spenser's *The Shepheardes Calendar* (1579). >> Spenser

Siebold, Karl Theodor Ernst von [zeebolt] (1804–85) Zoologist, born in Würzburg, Germany, the brother of Philipp Franz von Siebold. He studied at Berlin and Göttingen universities, and was professor at Erlangen, Freiburg, Wrocław, Poland (formerly Breslau, Germany), and Munich. He carried out research on invertebrates, and made significant contributions to parasitology. He founded the *Zeitschrift für wissenschaftliche Zoologie* (Journal of Scientific Zoology). >> Siebold, Philip Franz von

Siebold, Philipp Franz von [zeebolt] (1796–1866) Physician and botanist, born in Würzburg, Germany. He became medical officer to the Dutch in Batavia (now Djakarta), Java, and was stationed at a Dutch outpost in Nagasaki from 1823 to 1829, when he was expelled for obtaining too much information about Japan. He was largely responsible for the introduction of Western medicine into Japan, and Japanese plants into European gardens. In collaboration with German and Dutch scientists he published important works on the flora and fauna of Japan. >> Siebold, Karl Theodor Ernst

Sieff (of Brimpton), Israel Moses Sieff, Baron [seef] (1889–1972) Commercial executive, born in Manchester, Greater Manchester, NW England, UK. He was a schoolfellow of Simon Marks, and each married the other's sister. Together they developed Marks and Spencer. He was joint managing director of the company (1926–67) and succeeded Lord Marks as chairman (1964–7). His younger son, **Marcus Joseph** (1913–), who took a life peerage in 1980 as Lord Sieff of Brimpton, was chairman of Marks and Spencer from 1972 to 1984, when he became president of the company. >> Marks, Simon

Siegbahn, Kai (Manne Börje) [seegbahn] (1918–) Physicist, born in Lund, Sweden, the son of Manne Siegbahn. He studied at Stockholm, was professor of physics at the Royal Institute of Technology, Stockholm, until 1954, then moved to Uppsala University. He devised the technique of ESCA (electron spectroscopy for chemical analysis), and also worked on the related technique of ultraviolet photoelectron spectroscopy. He shared the Nobel Prize for Physics in 1981. >> Siegbahn, Manne; RR1122

Siegbahn, (Karl) Manne (Georg) [seegbahn] (1886–1978) Physicist, born in Örebro, Sweden. He was professor at Lund (1920), Uppsala (1923), and the Royal Academy of Sciences, and director of the Nobel Institute for Physics at Stockholm from 1937. He discovered the M series in X-ray spectroscopy, for which he was awarded the Nobel Prize for Physics in 1924. He also constructed a vacuum spectrograph. >> Siegbahn, Kai

Siegel and Shuster [seegl, shuster] **Jerry Siegel** (1914–96), born in Cleveland, OH, and **Joseph Shuster** (1914–92), born in Toronto, Ontario, Canada. Strip cartoonists, creators of the world's most popular comic-book hero, *Superman*. They met in high school, where they published their own science fiction magazine. After a series of strips for various comic books, they created *Superman* for Action Comics in 1938. It became an instant success, leading to huge spin-offs in films and television. The partners had no copyright on the characters in the strip, and failed to benefit until the owners (Warner Communications) agreed, after protracted lawsuits, to pay them a comfortable pension in 1975.

Siegen, Ludwig von [zeegen] (1609–c. 1675) Painter, engraver, and inventor, born in Utrecht, The Netherlands. He lived in Amsterdam in the 1640s, where he is thought to have been influenced by Rembrandt. In 1642 he invented the mezzotint process, sending a portrait of Amelia Elizabeth of Bohemia to the landgrave with a letter stating that the invention was his. He also disclosed his invention to Prince Rupert at Brussels in 1654. Only a handful of his prints are in existence.

Sielmann, Heinz [zeelman] (1917–) Naturalist and nature film photographer, born in Königsberg, Germany. He began to make films in 1938, and won the German Oscar for documentary films three years running (1953–5). He evolved techniques enabling him to film the inside of animal lairs and birds' nests, which revolutionized the study of animal behaviour.

Siemens, (Ernst) Werner von [zeemens] (1816–92) Electrical engineer, born in Lenthe, Germany (formerly, Prussia), the brother of William (Wilhelm) Siemens. In 1834 he entered the Prussian artillery, and in 1844 took charge of the artillery workshops at Berlin. He developed the telegraphic system in Prussia, devised several forms of galvanometer, and determined the electrical resistance of different substances. He founded a telegraph manufacturing firm (Siemens & Halske) in 1847, and was ennobled in 1888. >> Siemens, William

Siemens, Sir (Charles) William [zeemens], originally **Karl Wilhelm Siemens** (1823–83) Electrical engineer, born in Lenthe, Germany, the brother of Werner von Siemens. He studied at Göttingen University, and visited England in 1843 to introduce a process for electro-gilding invented by his brother. He subsequently settled there as an inventor himself, and made a fortune starting with his water meter (1851). He patented an open hearth furnace (1861), and from 1858, as managing partner of the London branch of his brother's telegraph manufacturing firm, Siemens & Halske, was responsible for the development of the first telegraph cable from Britain to America. >> Siemens, Werner von

Sienkiewicz, Henryk (Adam Alexander Pius) [shengkyayvich] (1846–1916) Novelist, born in Wola Okrzejska, Poland. He studied at Warsaw, travelled in the USA, and in the 1870s began to write articles, short stories, and novels. His major work was a war trilogy about 17th-c Poland, beginning with *Ogniem i mieczem* (1884, With Fire and Sword), but his most widely known book is the story of Rome under Nero, *Quo Vadis?* (1896), several times filmed, notably in 1951 by Mervyn Le Roy (1900–87). He received the Nobel Prize for Literature in 1905.

Sierpinski, Wacław [serpinskee] (1882–1969) Mathematician, born in Warsaw. He studied at Warsaw University, where he became professor of mathematics (1919–60). The leader of the Polish school of set theorists and topologists, he was a prolific author, publishing more than 700 research papers on set theory, topology, number theory, and logic, and several books. In 1919 he founded the still-important journal *Fundamenta mathematicae* to publish work in these areas.

Sierra, Gregorio Martínez >> **Martínez Sierra, Gregorio**

Sieyès, Emmanuel Joseph, comte de (Count of) [syayes], also known as **Abbé Sieyès** (1748–1836) French political theorist and clergyman, born in Fréjus, France. His pamphlet, *Qu'est-ce que le tiers-état?* (1789, What is the Third Estate?) stimulated bourgeois awareness and won him great popularity. He became a member of the National Convention, and later served on the Committee of Public Safety (1795) and in the Directory. In 1799, he helped to organize the revolution of 18th Brumaire, becoming a member of the Consulate. When Napoleon assumed supreme power, his authority waned, and he withdrew to his esates. He was exiled at the Restoration (1815), and lived in Brussels until 1830, returning after the July Revolution to Paris. >> Napoleon; Moreau, Victor

Sigismund (1368–1437) Holy Roman Emperor (1433–7), probably born in Nuremberg, Germany, the son of Charles IV.

He became King of Hungary (1387), Germany (1411), and Bohemia (1419). In 1396 he was defeated by the Ottoman Turks at Nicopolis, but later conquered Bosnia, Herzegovina, and Serbia. As emperor, he induced the Pope to call the Council of Constance to end the Hussite schism (1414), but made no effort to uphold the safe conduct he had granted to John Huss, and permitted him to be burned. As a result, his succession in Bohemia was opposed by the Hussites. >> Bayezit; Huss; Ziska; RR1057

Signac, Paul [seenyak] (1863–1935) Artist, born in Paris. He exhibited in 1884 with the Impressionists, and was later involved in the neo-Impressionist movement. With Seurat he developed Divisionism (but using mosaic-like patches of pure colour rather than Seurat's pointillist dots), mainly in seascapes. In his writing he sought to establish a scientific basis for his theories. >> Seurat

Signorelli, Luca [seenyawrelee], also known as **Luca da Cortona** (c. 1441–1523) Painter, born in Cortona, Italy. He painted many frescoes at Loreto, Rome, Florence, Siena, Cortona, and Orvieto, where the cathedral contains his greatest work, the frescoes of 'The Preaching of Anti-Christ' and 'The Last Judgment' (1500–4). He was one of the painters summoned by the Pope in 1508 to adorn the Vatican, and dismissed to make way for Raphael. >> Raphael

Signoret, Simone [seenyawray], originally **Simone Kaminker** (1921–85) Actress, born in Wiesbaden, Germany, and raised by French parents in Paris. She left her job as a typist to become a film extra in *Le Prince Charmant* (1942), and soon graduated to leading roles. Frequently cast as a prostitute or courtesan, her warmth and sensuality found international favour in such films as *La Ronde* (1950), *Casque d'Or* (1952), and *Les Diaboliques* (1954). She won British and American Academy Awards for *Room at the Top* (1959), and gained further distinction for *Ship of Fools* (1965). Married to actor Yves Montand from 1951, she matured into one of France's most distinguished character actresses, in films such as *Le Chat* (1971) and *Madame Rosa* (1977). >> Montand

Sigurdsson, Jón [seegoordson] (1811–79) Scholar and statesman, born in Hrafnseyri, Iceland. He studied at the University of Copenhagen, became archivist of the Royal Norse Archaeological Society (1847–65), and edited several historical works. The leader of the movement to secure political autonomy and freedom of trade from Denmark, he took part in discussion that led to Christian IX (reigned 1863–1906) restoring the ancient Althing (parliament) as a consultative assembly, and later became its speaker. When full independence was finally achieved in 1944, his birthday was chosen as Iceland's National Day.

Sigurjónsson, Jóhann [seegoorjohnson] (1880–1919) Playwright and poet, born in Laxamýri, Iceland. He studied veterinary science in Copenhagen before turning to literature, writing simultaneously in Danish and Icelandic in order to gain a wider audience. He used Icelandic folk-tale motifs for his major play, *Fjalla-Eyvindur* (1911, Eyvind of the Mountains), which took Copenhagen by storm, was produced in England and the USA, and made into a film. The first Icelandic writer in modern times to achieve international recognition, his other plays include *Dr Rung* (1908), *Bonden á Hrauni* (1908, The Farmer at Hraun), and *Logneren* (1917, The Liar).

Sihanouk, Prince Norodom [seeanook] (1922–) Cambodian leader, born in Phnom Penh. He was King of Cambodia (1941–55), chief of state (1960–70, and of the Khmer Republic 1975–6), prime minister on several occasions between 1952 and 1968, president of the government in exile (1970–5, 1982–91), president (1991–3), and once again king (1993–). He studied in Vietnam and Paris, was elected king in 1941, and negotiated the country's independence from France (1949–53). He abdicated in 1955 in favour of his father, in order to become an elected leader under the new constitution. As prime minister, and from 1960 head of state, he steered a neutralist course during the Vietnam War. In 1970 he was deposed in a right-wing military coup led by Lon Nol, fled to Beijing (Peking), and formed a joint resistance front with Pol Pot which successfully overthrew Lon Nol in 1975. Re-appointed head of state, he was ousted a year later by the Communist Khmer Rouge leadership. In 1982 he was elected president of the new government-in-exile. He returned to Cambodia in November 1991 as president of the Supreme National Council, after the signing of a peace treaty ended 13 years of civil war, and was crowned king under the new constitution in 1993. >> Pol Pot; RR1038

Sikorski, Władysław (Eugeniusz) [sikaw(r)skee] (1881–1943) Polish general, statesman, and prime minister (1922–3), born in Galicia (part of modern Poland). He studied at Kraków and Lvóv, fought in the Russian–Polish War (1920–1), became commander-in-chief (1921), and premier. After Piłsudski's coup (1926) he retired and wrote a military history in Paris. He returned to Poland in 1938, but on being refused a command, fled to France, becoming commander of the Free Polish forces, and from 1940 was premier of the Polish government in exile in London. He was killed in an air crash. A national hero, his body was returned to Poland in 1993, and given a state funeral. >> Piłsudski; RR1082

Sikorsky, Igor (Ivan) [sikaw(r)skee] (1889–1972) Aeronautical engineer, the inventor of the helicopter, born in Kiev, Ukraine. He began experimenting with building helicopters in 1909, but shelved his work due to lack of experience and money, and turned to aircraft. He built and flew the first four-engined aeroplane in 1913. He emigrated to the USA in 1919, and became a US citizen in 1928. He founded the Sikorsky Aero Engineering Corporation (1923), merging the company into the United Aircraft Corporation. The recipient of the highest awards and medals for aviation, he built several flying-boats, including the *American Clipper* (1931), and in 1939 developed the first successful helicopter, the VS-300.

Silas >> **McCay, Winsor**

Silhouette, Etienne de (1709–67) French statesman. A parsimonious minister of finance in 1759, his hobby was the cutting out of paper profile portraits, which came to be called *silhouettes*. The phrase *à la Silhouette* also came to be known as 'on the cheap'.

Silius Italicus [silius italikus], in full **Tiberius Catius Asconius Silius Italicus** (c. 25–101) Roman poet and politician. He became a prominent orator in the Roman courts, was made consul in 68, and then proconsul in Asia (77), after which time he lived in retirement on his rich estates near Naples, and became a patron of literature and the arts. He was the author of the longest surviving Latin poem, *Punica*, an epic in 17 books on the 2nd Punic War (218–201 BC). Having contracted an incurable disease, he starved himself to death.

Sillanpää, Frans Eemil [silanpah] (1888–1964) Novelist, born in Hämeenkyrö, Finland. The foremost Finnish writer of his time, he was the son of a peasant farmer. His major works were *Hurskas kurjuus* (1919, Meek Heritage), a novel about the Finnish civil war, and *Nuorena nukkunut* (1931, Fallen Asleep When Young) about the collapse of traditional values in Finland. He was awarded the 1939 Nobel Prize for Literature.

Silliman, Benjamin >> **Dana, James D**

Sillitoe, Alan [silitoh] (1928–) Novelist, born in Nottingham, Nottinghamshire, C England, UK. Before serving in the Royal Air Force, he worked in a bicycle factory for several years, which provided the subject for his first and most popular novel, *Saturday Night and Sunday Morning* (1958). Later novels include *A Tree on Fire* (1967), *A Start in Life* (1970), *Life Goes On* (1985), *Leonard's War* (1991), *Snowstop* (1993), and *Leading the Blind* (1995). His story *The Loneliness of the Long Distance Runner* (1959) was filmed in 1962. He has also written a number of books of poetry, and books for children, several starring the character 'Marmalade Jim'. An autobiography, *Life Without Armour*, appeared in 1995.

Sills, Beverley, stage name of **Belle Miriam Silverman** (1929–) Operatic soprano, born in New York City. After a varied and remarkable career as a child star, she made her operatic debut in 1947, subsequently appearing throughout the USA and Europe. A dramatically gifted coloratura, she retired from the stage in 1979, becoming general director of New York City Opera. An autobiography, *Bubbles: a Self-Portrait*, appeared in 1976.

Silone, Ignazio [silohnay], pseudonym of **Secondo Tranquilli** (1900–78) Novelist, born in Aquilo, Italy. He studied in Abruzzi and Rome. Active in the struggle against Fascism, he escaped to Switzerland in 1941, returning to Italy in 1944. *Fontamara* (1933) describes the interplay between the peasants of Abruzzi and their Fascist governors. Later novels include *Pane e vino* (1937, Bread and wine) and *Il seme sotto la neve* (1941, The Seed Beneath the Snow).

Silvers, Phil, popular name of **Philip Silver** (1912–85) Comic actor, born in New York City. He made his professional debut in 1925, and his Broadway debut in 1939. Signed to a contract with MGM, he appeared as bald, bespectacled, hapless suitors and friends of the leading man in such films as *Tom, Dick and Harry* (1941) and *Cover Girl* (1944). After World War 2, he enjoyed several Broadway hits, including *Top Banana* (1951, Tony). The television series *The Phil Silvers Show* (1955–9) earned him three Emmy Awards and established him irrevocably as Sergeant Bilko, forever pursuing get-rich-quick schemes with fast-talking bravado. He achieved further Broadway success in *A Funny Thing Happened on the Way to the Forum* (1972, Tony).

Silvia, originally **Silvia Renate Sommerlath** (1943–) Queen of Sweden (1976–), born in Heidelberg, Germany, the daughter of a West German businessman and his Brazilian wife. She studied at the Interpreters' School in Munich, graduating in 1969 as an interpreter in Spanish. In 1971 she was appointed chief hostess in the Organization Committee for the Olympic Games in Munich (1972), where she met Carl Gustaf, then heir to the Swedish throne. They were married in 1976. >> Carl XVI Gustaf; RR1090

Sim, Alastair (1900–76) Actor, born in Edinburgh, EC Scotland, UK. Destined to follow in the family tailoring business, he instead became a lecturer in elocution at Edinburgh University (1925–30), and made his professional stage debut in a London production of *Othello* (1930). Further stage work, including a season with the Old Vic, led to his film debut in *Riverside Murder* (1935). A distinctive and popular comic performer, his numerous films include *Green for Danger* (1946), *Stage Fright* (1949), *Scrooge* (1951), *An Inspector Calls* (1954) and *The Belles of St Trinians* (1954). On stage he appeared in *The Tempest* (1962), *Too True To Be Good* (1965), and *Dandy Dick* (1973), among many others.

Sima Guang [seema gwang], also spelled **Ssu-ma Kuang** (1019–86) Chinese statesman-historian, opponent of the reformer Wang Anshi. His *Comprehensive Mirror for Aid in Government* gives not only complete dynastic coverage of Chinese history 403 BC–AD 959, but also details on ordinary lifestyles. Written 1066–84, its 600-character first draft filled two rooms of his house. A later (1189) abridgement

by the philosopher Zhu Xi was widely used in China until modern times. >> Wang Anshi; Zhu Xi

Simak, Clifford (Donald) (1904–88) Science fiction writer, born in Milville, WI. During the Depression he became a journalist in Michigan, then joined the Minneapolis *Star*, to which he contributed a weekly science column for the rest of his life. He started publishing science fiction stories in 1931. His major work was the story sequence *The City* (1952), a chronicle in which dogs and robots take over a world abandoned by people.

Sima Qian [seema chyan] or **Ssu-ma Ch'ien** (c. 145–c. 87 BC) Historian, born in Lung-men, China. He succeeded his father Ssu-ma T'an (?–110 BC) in 110 BC as grand historian, but incurred the emperor's wrath for taking the part of a friend who, in command of a military expedition, had surrendered to the enemy. Imprisoned and destined for execution, he was castrated instead, perhaps to enable him to complete his work. He is chiefly remembered for the *Shih Chi*, the first history of China compiled as dynastic histories, in which annals of the principal events are supplemented by princely and other biographies, as well as notes on economic and institutional history.

Simenon, Georges (Joseph Christian) [seemenõ] (1903–89) Master of the crime novel, born in Liège, Belgium. He began as a journalist, then moved to Paris in 1922, where he wrote serious psychological novels as well as detective stories. He was one of the most prolific authors of his day, producing over 500 novels under a variety of pseudonyms. He revolutionized detective fiction with his tough, morbidly psychological Inspector Maigret series, beginning in 1933, which has provided several films and television series. Autobiographical writings include *When I Was Old* (trans 1971) and *Intimate Memoirs* (trans 1984).

Simeon, Charles (1759–1836) Evangelical clergyman, born in Reading, Berkshire, S England, UK. A fellow of King's College, Cambridge, he was appointed perpetual curate there (1783–1836). A renowned preacher, he led the evangelical revival in the Church of England, and helped form the Church Missionary Society (1797).

Simeon Stylites, St [stiyliyteez] (387–459) The earliest of the Christian ascetic 'pillar' saints. After living nine years in a Syrian monastery without leaving his cell, he became revered as a miracle-worker. To separate himself from the people, c.420 he established himself on top of a pillar c.20 m/70 ft high at Telanessa, near Antioch, where he spent the rest of his life preaching to crowds. He had many imitators, known as *stylites*. Feast day 5 January (W), September (E).

Simmel, Georg (1858–1918) Sociologist and philosopher, born in Berlin. He studied at Berlin University, where he became a lecturer in 1885, teaching philosophy and ethics, and in 1900 was appointed professor of the new discipline of sociology. In 1914 he moved to a chair in philosophy at Strasbourg, where he remained until his death. Instrumental in establishing sociology as a social science, he also wrote extensively on philosophy in such works as *Philosophie des Geldes* (1900, Philosophy of Money).

Simmonds, Kennedy A(lphonse) (1936–) Prime minister of St Kitts and Nevis (1983–95). He studied medicine at the University of the West Indies, worked in hospitals in Jamaica, the Bahamas, and the USA, and returned in 1964 to establish his own practice. He entered politics, and in 1965 founded the People's Action Movement (PAM) as an alternative to the Labour Party. After a series of unsuccessful elections, in 1980 the PAM won enough seats in the Assembly to form a coalition government with the Nevis Reformation Party. Full independence from Anguilla was achieved in 1983, he became prime minister, and his coalition party was re-elected in 1984 and 1989. >> RR1086

Simmons, Jean (1929–) Film actress, born in London, England, UK. She made her first film appearance in *Give Up The Moon* (1942), and had minor parts in a number of British films before going to Hollywood in 1950, where she became a leading star of the following decade. Her films include *The Robe* (1953), *Guys and Dolls* (1955), *The Big Country* (1958), and *Spartacus* (1960), and during the 1980s she appeared in several television productions, including *The Thorn Birds* (1983) and *Great Expectations* (1989).

Simms, William Gilmore (1806–70) Writer, born in Charleston, CA. After a precocious childhood, he edited a magazine and published a volume of poetry at 19, and was admitted to the bar aged 21. Best known for his historical novels, his most popular work was *The Yemassee* (1835). His 'revolutionary series' (1835–67) started with *The Partisan*, and he also published short stories, poetry, biographies, and criticism. He was an apologist for slavery and the South.

Simnel, Lambert (c. 1475–c. 1535) Pretender to the throne, the son of a joiner. Exploited by Roger Simon, a priest from Oxford, because of his resemblance to Edward IV, he was coached to impersonate one of his sons imprisoned in the Tower. He was set up in Ireland in 1487 as, first, a son of Edward IV, and then as the Duke of Clarence's son, Edward, Earl of Warwick (1475–99). He had some success, and was crowned at Dublin as Edward VI, but after landing in Lancashire with 2000 German mercenaries he was defeated at Stoke Field, Nottinghamshire. After imprisonment, he was employed in the royal kitchens. >> Clarence; Edward IV; Edward V

Simon, Claude (Eugène Henri) [seemō] (1913–) Novelist, born in Tananarive, Madagascar. He was educated at Paris, Oxford, and Cambridge universities, fought in World War 2, and later earned a living producing wine at Salses. His novels include *Le Vent* (1957, The Wind), *L'Herbe* (1958, The Grass), and – part of a four-volume cycle – *La Route des Flandres* (1960, The Flanders Road). He received the Nobel Prize for Literature in 1985.

Simon, Sir Francis (Eugen) (1893–1956) Physicist, born in Berlin. He studied at the universities of Munich, Göttingen, and Berlin, and served in World War 1. Nazism forced him to leave his chair at Wrocław, Poland (formerly Breslau, Germany), and he moved to the Clarendon Laboratory, Oxford at the invitation of Frederick Lindemann (Lord Cherwell). He became reader in thermodynamics in 1935, and succeeded Lindemann as professor in 1956. He verified experimentally the third law of thermodynamics, and under his influence Oxford became a centre for low-temperature physics. >> Cherwell

Simon, Herbert (Alexander) (1916–) Economist, born in Milwaukee, WI. He studied at the University of Chicago, then held chairs at Illinois Institute of Technology (1946–9) and Carnegie–Mellon University (from 1949). A man of wide talents, who has written on psychology and computers as well as on economics and political science, he was awarded the Nobel Prize for Economics in 1978.

Simon (of Stackpole Elidor), John (Allsebrook) Simon, 1st Viscount (1873–1954) British statesman and lawyer, born in Manchester, Greater Manchester, NW England, UK. He studied at Edinburgh and Oxford, entered parliament in 1906, and was knighted in 1910. He was attorney general (1913–15) and home secretary (1915–16), before resigning from the Cabinet for his opposition to conscription. Deserting the Liberals to form the Liberal National Party, he supported MacDonald's coalition governments and became foreign secretary (1931–5), home secretary in the Conservative government (1935–7), Chancellor of the Exchequer (1937–40), and Lord Chancellor in Churchill's wartime coalition (1940–5). He was created a viscount in 1940. >> Churchill, Sir Winston; MacDonald, Ramsay

Simon, (Marvin) Neil (1927–) Playwright, born in New York City. His prolific career began with revue sketches written with his brother. His first Broadway Show, *Catch a Star!*, opened in 1955, and a series of long-running successes followed in the 1960s, including *Barefoot in the Park* (1963) and *The Odd Couple* (1965). His later work includes *The Sunshine Boys* (1972), *California Suite* (1976), *Biloxi Blues* (1985, Tony), *Lost in Yonkers* (1991, Pulitzer, Tony), and *London Suite* (1995). He has also written the film scripts for several of his stage plays.

Simon, Paul (1941–) Singer, songwriter, and guitarist, born in Newark, NJ. He teamed up with Art Garfunkel at the age of 15 when they were known as Tom and Gerry, but he also pursued a solo career, under various pseudonyms, before 'The Sound Of Silence' (1965) brought them their first major success as a duo, Simon and Garfunkel. In 1968 the film *The Graduate* became one of the first major films to use rock music in its soundtrack, using songs written by Simon (notably, 'Mrs Robinson', which became a hit), and they had a major success with the album *Bridge Over Troubled Water* (1970). After splitting from Garfunkel, he returned to a solo career, releasing his album *Paul Simon* in 1972. *Graceland* (1986), which featured the work of several African musicians, was one of the most successful albums of the 1980s. There have been occasional reunion concerts with Garfunkel. >> Garfunkel

Simone, Nina, stage name of **Eunice Waymon** (1933–) Jazz singer, pianist, and songwriter, born in Tryon, NC. She moved to Philadelphia at 17, and supported herself teaching piano and accompanying singers. Her first record (1958) included two hits, a melodramatic 'I Loves You, Porgy', and a lilting 'My Baby Just Cares for Me'. She used her smoky contralto voice to great dramatic effect singing protest songs in the 1960s, and she could turn concert audiences into clenched-fist activists with 'Mississippi Goddam', a tough song about racism. She also sought out poetic songs for her repertoire, and set poetry to music, memorably with African-American poets in 'Compensation' by Paul Laurence Dunbar and 'Backlash Blues', and 'Young, Gifted and Black' by Langston Hughes. She was arrested (1978) for withholding taxes in 1971–3 in protest at her government's undeclared war in Vietnam.

Simonides of Ceos [siymonideez, seeos] (c. 556–c. 468 BC) Poet, born in Iulis on the island of Ceos. He travelled extensively, and lived many years in Athens. When Persia invaded Greece he devoted his powers to celebrating the heroes and the battles of that struggle in elegies, epigrams, odes, and dirges. He was believed to be the first Greek poet who wrote for fees. >> Bacchylides

Simon Magus [maygus], Eng **Simon the Magician** (1st-c) Practitioner of magic arts, who appears in Samaria c.37, well known for his sorceries. With Peter's condemnation of his offer to buy the gift of the Holy Ghost, and Simon's submission, the narrative of *Acts* (8.9–24) leaves him. Later Christian authors bring him to Rome and make him the author of heresies. The term *simony* derives from his name.

Simonov, Konstantin Mikhailovich [seemonof] (1915–79) Russian writer and journalist. He achieved a considerable reputation with his historical poem about Alexander Nevski, his poems of World War 2, the novel *Days and Nights* about the defence of Stalingrad, and the play *The Russians*. He was awarded the Stalin Prize three times.

Simpson, Sir George (c. 1787–1860) Explorer and administrator, born in Lochbroom, Highland, N Scotland, UK. He was governor of the territory belonging to the Hudson's Bay Co (1821–56), where he developed an unprecedented knowledge of the fur trade. In 1828 he made an overland journey around the world. *Simpson's Falls* and *Cape George Simpson* are named after him. He was knighted in 1841 for his contribution to Arctic discoveries.

Simpson, Sir George (Clarke) (1878–1965) Meteorologist, born in Derby, Derbyshire, C England, UK. He became a lecturer at Manchester University (1905), was Scott's meteorologist on the Antarctic expedition (1910), and investigated the causes of lightning. He was elected president of the Royal Meteorological Society (1940–2). >> Scott, R F

Simpson, George Gaylord (1902–84) Palaeontologist, born in Chicago, IL. He studied at the universities of Colorado and Yale, joined the American Museum of Natural History in New York City in 1927, then taught at Harvard (1959–70). Now widely regarded as this century's leading palaeontologist, he travelled extensively for his studies on fossil mammals. He was a central figure in the fusion of genetics and palaeontology to form modern Darwinism, which owes much to his influential books *Tempo and Mode in Evolution* (1944) and *The Major Features of Evolution* (1949).

Simpson, Sir James Young (1811–70) Obstetrician, born in Bathgate, West Lothian, EC Scotland, UK. He trained in Edinburgh, where he became professor of midwifery in 1840. He introduced chloroform as an anaesthetic, and was the first to use it as an anaesthetic in labour. He was created a baronet in 1866. >> Blackwell, Emily

Simpson, N(orman) F(rederick) (1919–) Playwright, born in London, England, UK. He worked in a bank and served in the Intelligence Corps in World War 2 before becoming an adult education lecturer. The success of *A Resounding Tinkle*, a zany disruption of middle-class normality, in a competition organized by *The Observer* in 1957 brought him to prominence. His absurdist approach is also seen in *One-Way Pendulum* (1959). Written during the brief popularity of the Theatre of the Absurd in Britain, his work belongs to a comic tradition illustrated by *The Goon Show* and *Monty Python*.

Simpson, O(renthal) J(ames) (1947–) Player of American football, born in San Francisco, CA. He joined the Buffalo Bills in 1968, and led the League as top rusher four times (1972–6). He rushed for a record 2002 yards in 1973, and in 1975 had a then record 23 touchdowns in one season. He became a successful broadcaster, and there was widespread shock in the USA when in 1994 he was arrested on a charge of murdering his ex-wife and her male friend. His court case achieved unprecedented media publicity in 1995, the jury acquitting him later that year. In 1997 a civil trial jury found him responsible for the murders and damages were awarded against him.

Simpson, Robert (Wilfred Levick) (1921–97) Composer and writer, born in Leamington, Warwickshire, C England, UK. He studied with Herbert Howells, and was a BBC music producer in London (1951–80). His works include 11 symphonies, 14 string quartets, concertos for piano and flute, as well as a great deal of chamber music, and published studies of Nielsen and Bruckner. >> Howells, Herbert

Simpson, Thomas (1710–61) Mathematician, born in Nuneaton, Warwickshire, C England, UK. He became professor of mathematics at Woolwich (1743), and published a long series of works (1737–57) on algebra, trigonometry, chance, and other topics.

Simpson, Thomas (1938–67) Cyclist, born in Easington, Durham, NE England, UK. In 1962 he became the first Briton ever to wear the leader's yellow jersey in the Tour de France. Known as **Major Tom** to the French, he led the race for just one day. During the 1967 Tour de France he died from heart failure while riding the 13th stage, the climb of Mont Ventoux. A memorial stone was built near the spot where he died.

Simpson, Wallis Warfield >> **Windsor, Duchess of**

Sims, William (Sowden) (1858–1936) US naval officer, born in Port Hope, Ontario, Canada. He trained at the US Naval Academy, served in China during international action against the Boxer rebellion (1900), and was a naval attaché in Paris and St Petersburg. In World War 1 he was president of the US Naval War College (1914–17), and made a distinguished contribution to Anglo-American action against the U-boat campaign as commander of US Naval Forces in Europe, devising a convoy system to protect merchant shipping.

Sinatra, Frank, popular name of **Francis Albert Sinatra** (1915–) Singer and film actor, born in Hoboken, NJ. Now widely recognized as one of the greatest singers of popular songs, he became known in the 1940s. With the Tommy Dorsey orchestra (1940–2) his hit records included 'I'll Never Smile Again' and 'Without A Song', and he starred on radio and in movies, most notably *Anchors Aweigh* (1945). Then his appeal diminished. He was all but forgotten by 1953, when his memorable acting in the movie *From Here to Eternity* won an Oscar and revived his career. Several choice roles in films followed, such as *High Society* (1956) and *The Manchurian Candidate* (1962), and his revival as an actor led to new opportunities as a singer. He produced his masterworks in a series of recordings (1956–65), especially the albums *Songs for Swinging Lovers* (1956), *Come Fly With Me* (1959), and the recordings 'That's Life' (1966), and 'My Way' (1969). His personal life has always proved noteworthy, with turbulent marriages to Ava Gardner and Mia Farrow, among others, and alleged Mafia connections.

Sinclair, Sir Clive (Marles) (1940–) British electronic engineer and inventor. He worked for three years as a publisher's editor before launching his electronics research and manufacturing company in 1962, which developed and successfully marketed a wide range of calculators, miniature television sets, and personal computers. He later embarked on the manufacture of a small three-wheeled 'personal transport' vehicle, the C5, powered by a washing-machine motor and rechargeable batteries. It was widely condemned as unsafe and impractical, and its failure led to a period of retrenchment in Sinclair's business activities. He was knighted in 1983.

Sinclair, Sir Keith (1922–93) Historian and author, born in Auckland, New Zealand. He taught history at the University of Auckland (1947–86), and established New Zealand history as an object of scholarly study in its own right, rather than as a branch of British imperial history. Among his books are *A History of New Zealand* (1954) and *Half Way Round the Harbour* (1993).

Sinclair, Upton (Beall) (1878–1968) Novelist and social reformer, born in Baltimore, MD. He studied at New York and Columbia universities, and became a journalist. He horrified the world with his exposure of meat-packing conditions in Chicago in his novel *The Jungle* (1906). Later novels such as *Metropolis* (1908), *Oil!* (1927), and *Boston* (1928) were increasingly moulded by his socialist beliefs. For many years prominent in Californian politics, he attempted to found a communistic community in Englewood, NJ (1907). He also wrote a monumental 11-volume series about 'Lanny Budd', starting with *World's End* (1940) and including *Dragon's Teeth* (1942, Pulitzer).

Sinden, Sir Donald (Alfred) (1923–) Actor, born in Plymouth, Devon, SW England, UK. He first appeared in 1942 with a touring company taking comedy to the armed forces. After the war he joined the Shakespeare Memorial Theatre Company at Stratford-upon-Avon (1946) and the Old Vic Company (1948). Under contract to Rank (1952–60), he appeared in 23 films, including *The Cruel Sea* and *Doctor in the House*. Known for his comedy work, he also gave acclaimed performances in the classics, notably with the Royal Shakespeare Company as Richard Plantagnet in *Henry VI* (*The Wars of the Roses*, 1963), *Lear* (1977), and *Othello* (1979). Television series include *Two's Company*, *Our Man From St Mark's*, and *Never the Twain*. He was knighted in 1997.

Singer, Esther, married name **Kreitman** (1892–) Yiddish novelist, born in Radzymin, Poland, the sister of Isaac Bashevis and Israel Joshua Singer. Her *Der sheydim tants* was published in Warsaw in 1936, and translated 10 years later as *Deborah*. >> Singer, Isaac Bashevis/ I J

Singer, Isaac Bashevis (1904–91) Yiddish writer, born in Radzymin, Poland. He studied in Warsaw, emigrating to the USA in 1935, where he worked as a journalist for the *Jewish Daily Forward*. He became a US citizen in 1943. He set his novels and short stories among the Jews of Poland, Germany, and America, combining a deep psychological insight with dramatic and visual impact. His novels include *The Family Moskat* (1950), *The Manor* (1967), *The Estate* (1970), and *Enemies: a Love Story* (1972), and he also wrote short stories and stories for children. He was awarded the Nobel Prize for Literature in 1978. >> Singer, Esther/ I J

Singer, Isaac (Merritt) (1811–75) Inventor and manufacturer of sewing machines, born in Pittstown, NY. He patented a rock drill in 1839, a carving machine in 1849, and at Boston in 1852 an improved single-thread, chain-stitch sewing machine, incorporating some features of Howe's machine. His company quickly became the largest producer of sewing machines in the world. >> Howe, Elias

Singer, I(srael) J(oshua) (1893–1944) Yiddish writer, born in Bilgorai, Poland, the brother of Isaac Bashevis and Esther Singer. He studied in Warsaw, and after World War 1 became a journalist in Kiev. He was foreign correspondent in Warsaw for the New York *Jewish Daily Forward*, for which he continued to write after emigrating to the USA in 1933. His novels have been widely translated, and include *The Brothers Ashkenazi* (1936), *The River Breaks Up* (1938), and *East of Eden* (1939). >> Singer, Esther/Isaac Bashevis

Singer, Peter (Albert David) (1946–) Philosopher, born in Melbourne, Victoria, Australia. He was educated at the universities of Melbourne and Oxford, then taught at New York University before becoming professor of philosophy at Monash University in 1977, where he is associated with the Centre for Human Bioethics. His writing focuses on ethics, particularly in relation to animals and the environment. Also known also as a political activist, his best known works, *Animal Liberation* (1977) and *Practical Ethics* (1979), were still exercising influence in the 1990s.

Singh, V(ishwanath) P(ratap) (1931–) Indian statesman and prime minister (1989–90), born in Allahabad, India. He studied at Poona and Allahabad universities, and was elected to the Federal Parliament as a Congress Party representative in 1971. He served under Indira Gandhi and Rajiv Gandhi as minister of commerce (1976–7), finance (1984–6), and defence (1986–7), but on exposing the Bofors arms scandal, he was sacked from the government and Congress. He made a comeback as head of the Vanseta Dal coalition, and became prime minister. Plagued by political crises, he was defeated on a vote of confidence the following year. >> Gandhi, Indira; Gandhi, Rajiv; RR1058

Siqueiros, David Alfaro [sikayros] (1896–1974) Mural painter, born in Chihuahua, Mexico. He helped to launch the review *El Machete* in Mexico City in 1922, and was imprisoned for revolutionary activities (1930). He was later expelled from the USA, and during the 1930s worked in South America. One of the principal figures in 20th-c Mexican mural painting, he was notable for his experiments with modern synthetic materials.

Siraj-ud-Daula [siraj ud dowla], originally **Mirza Muhammad** (c. 1732–57) Ruler of Bengal under the nominal suzerainty of the Mughal empire. He came into conflict with the British over their fortification of Calcutta, and marched on the city in 1756. The British surrender led to the infamous Black Hole, for which he was held responsible. Following the recapture of Calcutta, the British under Clive joined forces with his general, Mir Jafar, and defeated him at Plassey in 1857. He fled to Murshidabad, but was captured and executed. >> Clive

Sirhan, (Bishara) Sirhan [sirhahn] (c. 1943–) Assassin of Senator Robert Kennedy, born in Palestine. He was a refugee whose family settled in Pasadena, CA, in 1956, having fled from Israeli bombings in Beirut. When Robert Kennedy, who was running for the presidential nomination in 1968, took an overtly pro-Israeli stance in order to gain Jewish votes, Sirhan was enraged and shot him. At his trial, he said that Kennedy's repeated promises of arms for Israel 'burned him up'. He was found guilty of premeditated murder of the first degree, and the death penalty was recommended. Senator Edward Kennedy's plea for lenience led to this sentence being commuted to life imprisonment. >> Kennedy, Edward/Robert

Sisley, Alfred [seeslay] (1839–99) Impressionist painter and etcher, born in Paris, of English ancestry. After training in Paris, he painted landscapes almost exclusively, particularly in the valleys of the Seine, Loire, and Thames, and was noted for his subtle treatment of skies. His works began to sell only after his death.

Sithole, Reverend Ndabaningi [sitohlay] (1920–) Zimbabwean politician and clergyman, born in Nyamandhlovu, Zimbabwe (formerly, Rhodesia). He began as a teacher, and after studying in the USA (1955–8) became a Congregationalist minister, and joined the National Democratic Party. He became president of the Zimbabwe African National Union in 1963. An advocate of violent resistance by Black African nationalists, he joined Mugabe in his struggle against Nkomo. After a period of detention in the 1960s, he was eclipsed by Mugabe, and later moved into a close political alliance with Bishop Muzorewa. >> Mugabe; Muzorewa; Nkomo

Sitsky, Larry (1934–) Composer, pianist, and teacher, born in Tientsin, China. He emigrated to Australia with his parents at 17, and engaged in postgraduate studies at the New South Wales Conservatory, Sydney (1956–8) and the San Francisco Conservatory (1959–61). After a period in Queensland, he joined the Canberra School of Music in 1966, where he became head of keyboard studies, then head of the Department of Composition and Electronic Music (1978; since 1983, the Department of Composition). He won the Advance Australia Award for his work in 1989, was made professor in 1994, and in 1996 he became resident composer at the International String School in Melbourne. A prolific composer in many genres, his major works include the operas *The Fall of the House of Usher* (1965), *Lenz* (1970), *The Golem* (1980), and incidental music to *Faust* (1996), 10 concertos (to 1997), and a wide range of orchestral, instrumental, chamber, vocal, and choral music. He has also published widely in the field of musicology. >> Harwood, Gwen

Sitter, Willem de (1872–1934) Astronomer, born in Sneek, The Netherlands. He studied at Groningen, and became director and professor of astronomy at Leyden (1908). He computed the size of the universe as 2000 million light years in radius, containing about 80 000 million galaxies. He disputed Einstein's concept of 'matter with no motion', and characterized the universe as an expanding curved space–time continuum of 'motion with no matter'. >> Einstein

Sitting Bull, Sioux name **Tatanka Iyotake** (1834–90) Warrior and chief of the Dakota Sioux, born near Grand River, SD. He was a leader in the Sioux War (1876–7), and led the defeat of Custer and his men at the Little Big Horn (1876). He escaped to Canada, but surrendered in 1881. After touring with Buffalo Bill's Wild West Show, he returned to his people, and was present in 1890 when the army suppressed the 'ghost dance' messianic religious movement. He was killed during the army's action. >> Crazy Horse; Custer

Sitwell, Dame Edith (1887–1964) Poet, born in Scarborough, North Yorkshire, N England, UK, the sister of Osbert and Sacheverell Sitwell. She first attracted notice through editing an annual anthology of new poetry, *Wheels* (1916–21). Her own experimental poetry was controversially received with *Façade* (1922), which (with Walton's music) was given a stormy public reading in London. She became a Catholic in 1955, after which her works reflect a deeper religious symbolism, as in *The Outcasts* (1962). She was created a dame in 1954. Her autobiography, *Taken Care Of*, was published posthumously in 1965. >> Searle, Humphrey; Sitwell, Osbert/ Sacheverel; Walton, William

Sitwell, Sir Osbert (1892–1969) Writer, born in London, England, UK, the brother of Edith and Sacheverell Sitwell. He studied at Eton, served in World War 1, began writing poetry, and acquired notoriety with his satirical novel of the Scarborough social scene, *Before the Bombardment* (1927). He is best known for his five-volume autobiographical series, beginning with *Left Hand: Right Hand* (1944). Other collections of essays include *Penny Foolish* (1935) and *Pound Wise* (1963). He became a baronet in 1942. >> Sitwell, Edith/Sacheverel

Sitwell, Sir Sacheverell [sa**shev**erell] (1897–1988) Poet and art critic, born in Scarborough, North Yorkshire, N England, UK, the brother of Edith and Osbert Sitwell. He studied at Eton, served in the army, then travelled in Spain and Italy, where he began to write books on art and architecture, such as *Southern Baroque Art* (1924). His many volumes of poetry cover a period of over 30 years, from *The People's Palace* (1918) to *An Indian Summer* (1982). He became a baronet on the death of his brother, Osbert, in 1969. >> Sitwell, Edith/Osbert

Sivaji [si**vah**jee] (c. 1627–80) Founder of the Maratha Kingdom in W India, born in Shivner, Poona. He campaigned against the Mughals, and was enthroned as an independent ruler in 1674. Renowned as a military leader, social reformer, and advocate of religious tolerance, his last years were made difficult by internal problems and pressure from outside enemies.

Six, Les >> Auric; Durey; Honegger; Milhaud; Poulenc; Tailleferre

Sixtus IV, originally **Francesco della Rovere** (1414–84) Pope (1471–84), a former Franciscan preacher, born in Cella Ligure, Italy. He fostered learning, and built the *Sistine Chapel* and the *Sistine bridge*. His nepotism led to many abuses, and he is said to have been involved in the Pazzi conspiracy against the Medici at Florence. >> Lorenzo de' Medici

Sjöström, Victor [**sjoe**strom], also known as **Victor Seastrom** (1879–1960) Film actor and director, born in Silbodal, Sweden. Trained as an actor, he joined the film company Svenska Bio in 1912. His successes as actor/director included *Ingeborg Holm* (1913), *Terje Vigen* (1918), and *Körkarlen* (1920, The Phantom Carriage), where his psychological portrayal of David Holm and use of double exposure were landmarks in cinematic acting. His ability to adapt classic Swedish writers to the screen gave Swedish cinema popular appeal. He later went to Hollywood (1923–30), where his best-known films were *The Scarlet*

Letter (1926) and *The Wind* (1928). He did not adapt well to sound cinema, and directed only two films after returning home. As an actor, however, he created several memorable parts, notably in *Wild Strawberries* (1957).

Skalkottas, Nikos or **Nikolaus** [skal**ko**tas] (1904–49) Composer, born in Khalkis, Greece. He studied at the Athens Conservatory and in Berlin, where he was a pupil of Weill and Schoenberg, then earned his living as an orchestral violinist in Athens. His works, dating mostly from the period 1935–45, show a complex use of serial techniques, and exploit Greek and Balkan folk elements, but were not much performed until after his death. >> Schoenberg; Weill

Skallagrímsson, Egill (c. 910–990) Poet and warrior, born in Iceland. His father had emigrated to Iceland after falling foul of King Harald of Norway, and Egill became a professional Viking and court-poet. He fought in the service of King Athelstan of England at the Battle of Brunanburh (937), fell out with King Erik Blood-Axe Haraldsson of Norway, but visited him when he was king in the city of York in 948. There he only escaped execution by composing a eulogy in Erik's honour, the *Höfuðlausn* (Head Ransom). In 960 he lost two young sons, and composed the greatest lament in Old Icelandic poetry, *Sonatorrek* (On the Loss of Sons). He is the hero of *Egils saga*, probably written by his descendant, Snorri Sturluson. >> Athelstan; Harald I Halfdanarson; Sturluson

Skanderbeg [**skan**derbek], nickname of **George Castriota** or **Kastrioti** (1405–68) Albanian patriot, the son of a prince of Emathia. Carried away by Ottoman Turks at the age of seven, he was brought up a Muslim, and became a favourite commander of Sultan Murad II (ruled 1421–51), who gave him his nickname, a combination of *Iskander* ('Alexander') and the rank of Bey. In 1443 he changed sides, renounced Islam, and drove the Turks from Albania. For 20 years he maintained Albanian independence, but after his death opposition to the Turks collapsed.

Skeaping, John >> Hepworth, Barbara

Skeat, W(alter) W(illiam) (1835–1912) Philologist, born in London, England, UK. He studied at Christ's College, Cambridge, where he became a fellow in 1860, and professor of Anglo-Saxon (1878). He was founder and first director of the Dialect Society (1873), and made a major contribution to English philology, editing several important texts. His main works include the *Etymological English Dictionary* (1879–82), *Principles of English Etymology* (1887–91), and *Chaucer* (6 vols, 1894–5).

Skelton, John (c.1460–1529) Satirical poet, born in Norfolk, E England, UK. He studied at Oxford and Cambridge universities, was tutor to Prince Henry (the future Henry VIII), took holy orders in 1498, and became rector of Diss in 1502, but seems to have been suspended in 1511 for having a concubine or wife. He had produced some translations and elegies in 1489, but began to write satirical vernacular poetry, overflowing with grotesque words and images and unrestrained joviality, as in *The Bowge of Courte* (c.1499), *Colyn Cloute* (1522), and *Why come ye nat to courte* (1522).

Skelton, Red, popular name of **Richard Bernard Skelton** (1913–97) Entertainer, born in Vincennes, IN. As a child he toured the midwest in a medicine show, and later gained fame as a variety performer of stage, radio, television, and films. He was voted the outstanding new radio star in 1941, and is remembered for the NBC television programme *The Red Skelton Show* (1951–71). He gave a farewell performance at Carnegie Hall in 1990.

Skinner, B(urrhus) F(rederic) (1904–90) Psychologist, born in Susquehanna, PA. He studied at Harvard, teaching there (1931–6, 1947–74, then emeritus) and also at

Minnesota University (1936–45). A leading behaviourist, he was a proponent of operant conditioning, and the inventor of the *Skinner box* for facilitiating experimental observations. His main scientific works include *The Behavior of Organisms* (1938) and *Verbal Behavior* (1957), but his social and political views have reached a wider public through *Walden Two* (1948) and *Beyond Freedom and Dignity* (1971).

Skinner, James (1778–1841) Soldier of Eurasian origin in the Indian army. Under General Lord Lake (1744–1808), he formed *Skinner's Horse*, one of the most famous regiments in India. His rank of lieutenant-colonel was not recognized in London until 1827. With the fabulous wealth of 30 years' looting, and several wives, he settled in Delhi and his country seat nearby. He wrote books in flawless Persian on the princes, castes, and tribes of the region, and built a mosque, a temple, and the Church of St James in Delhi.

Skobtsova, Maria [skobt**soh**va] (1891–1945) Russian Orthodox nun, born in Riga, Latvia. She was the first woman to enrol at the Ecclesiastical Academy at St Petersburg. She later escaped Bolshevik excesses by going to France, where she began work with the Russian Orthodox Student Christian Movement, and in 1932, despite having had two divorces, became a nun. Unconventional and radical, she worked among society's cast-offs, whom she fed and housed. Arrested by the Nazis in wartime Paris, she was sent to Ravensbrück concentration camp (1943), where she brought Christian light and hope despite appalling conditions. She was gassed in 1945, reportedly going voluntarily 'in order to help her companions to die'.

Skorzeny, Otto [skaw(r)**tsay**nee] (1908–75) Austrian soldier, born in Vienna. He joined the Nazi Party in 1930, was mobilized into the SS, and fought in France, Serbia, and Russia (1939–43). He was noted for his commando-style operations in World War 2. He freed Mussolini from internment in a mountain hotel on the Gran Sasso Range (1943), and abducted Horthy, the Regent of Hungary (1944), but failed to capture Tito. During the German counter-offensive in the Ardennes (1944), he carried out widespread sabotage behind Allied lines. He was tried at Nuremberg as a war criminal, but was acquitted (1947). >> Horthy; Mussolini; Tito

Skram, (Bertha) Amalie, *née* **Alver** (1846 /7–1905) Novelist, born in Bergen, Norway. After an unhappy childhood, she made a disappointing marriage to an older man, which ended in divorce (1878). She worked as a critic and short-story writer, then in 1884 married a Danish writer, **Erik Skram**. The pessimism of her writing seems to reflect her early experiences, and much of her work also concerns unhappy marriages. Her tetralogy, *Hellemyrsfoket* (1887–90, People of Hellemyr), is a Norwegian classic of Naturalism, and outlines the emotional deterioration of a family over four generations. Other works include *Constance Ring* (1885), and *Profesor Hieronymus* (1895).

Skriabin, Alexander >> **Scriabin, Alexander**

Skum, Nils Nilsson [skoom] (1872–1951) Artist of the Sami (Lapp) people. Born into a nomadic family of reindeer hunters, he was the first of his people to draw pictures, but using the traditional inspiration of Sami craftwork. His paintings form one of the first comprehensive studies of traditional Sami life.

Slade, Felix (1790–1868) Antiquary and art collector, born in Halsteads, Yorkshire, N England, UK. He bequeathed his engravings and Venetian glass to the British Museum, and founded art professorships at Oxford and Cambridge, as well as the Slade School of Art, London.

Slater, Christian (1969–) Film actor, born in New York City. He had a small role in a television soap opera when he was eight, and by the age of nine he was in the touring company of *The Music Man*. He made his film debut in *The Legend of Billy Jean* (1985), and became known after his role as the young monk in *The Name of the Rose* (1986). Later films include *Robin Hood: Prince of Thieves* (1991), *Murder in the First* (1995), and *Bed of Roses* (1996).

Slater, Samuel (1768–1835) Mechanical engineer, the founder of the US cotton industry, born in Belper, Derbyshire, C England, UK. Apprenticed to Jedediah Strutt, he gained a detailed knowledge of the most advanced textile machinery and its operation. Britain had made both the export of machinery or data, and the emigration of textile workers, illegal; nevertheless, attracted by bounties offered by the USA, he emigrated under an assumed name in 1789, and was able to build up-to-date spinning machines for a struggling cotton mill in Rhode Island. He became a partner in the firm of Almy, Brown & Slater, whose prosperity laid the foundation for the success of the US cotton textile industry.

Sleep, Wayne (1948–) Dancer and choreographer, born in Plymouth, Devon, SW England, UK. He joined the Royal Ballet School at 12, and graduated in 1966. Promoted to principal dancer in 1973, his small stature, extrovert personality, and technical prowess landed him choice roles in such ballets as Frederick Ashton's *A Month in the Country* (1976) and Kenneth MacMillan's *Manon* (1974). His talents extend to the musical stage, cinema, and television. He appeared as 'Squirrel Nutkin' and one of the 'Bad Mice' in the 1971 film *Tales of Beatrix Potter*, and was in the original production of *Cats* (1981). In 1980 he formed his own touring group, Dash, and later adapted *The Hot Shoe Show* (1983–4) into a fast-paced, live revue.

Slessor, Sir John (Cotesworth) (1897–1979) British air-marshal, born in Rhanikhet, India. Educated at Haileybury, he served in the Royal Flying Corps in World War 1 and was awarded the MC. He was an instructor at the RAF Staff College (1924–5) and at Camberley (1931–4). During World War 2 he was commander-in-chief of Coastal Command (1943) and of the Mediterranean theatre (1944–5). Promoted air marshal in 1940, he became chief of the air staff after the War (1950–2). His often original, penetrating, and unorthodox views on nuclear strategy are expressed in *Strategy for the West* (1954) and *The Great Deterrent* (1957). He was knighted in 1948.

Slessor, Kenneth (Adolf) (1901–71) Poet and journalist, born in Orange, New South Wales, Australia. He was editor of *Smith's Weekly* before being appointed as a World War 2 correspondent (1940–4). His best-known poem is 'Beach Burial', a tribute to Australian troops who fought during the War. He published several books of verse, including *Poems* (1957). He also edited the 1945 collection in the series 'Australian Poetry', and co-edited *The Penguin Book of Australian Verse* (1958).

Slessor, Mary (1848–1915) Presbyterian missionary, born in Aberdeen, NE Scotland, UK. She worked as a mill girl in Dundee from childhood but, conceiving a burning ambition to become a missionary, was accepted by the United Presbyterian Church for teaching in Calabar, Nigeria (1876). There she spent many years of devoted work among the natives, who called her 'Great Mother'.

Slevogt, Max [slay**fohkht**] (1868–1932) Impressionist painter and engraver, born in Landshut, Germany. He studied in Munich and Berlin (where he later taught at the Academy), and worked with the Impressionist Louis Corinth. His works comprise murals of historical scenes, landscapes, and portraits. >> Corinth

Slim (of Yarralumia and of Bishopston), William (Joseph) Slim, 1st Viscount (1891–1970) British field marshal, born in Bristol, SW England, UK. Educated in Birmingham, he joined the army at the outbreak of World War 1, and served in Gallipoli and Mesopotamia. In World

War 2, his greatest achievement was to lead his reorganized forces, the famous 14th 'Forgotten Army', to victory over the Japanese in Burma. He was Chief of the Imperial General Staff (1948–52), and a highly successful Governor-General of Australia (1953–60). Knighted in 1944, he became a viscount in 1960. >> Mountbatten (of Burma); Wingate

Slipher, Vesto Melvin (1875–1969) Astronomer, born in Mulberry, IN. He studied at Indiana University, then worked for over 50 years at the Lowell Observatory, AZ (from 1901), becoming its director in 1926. He used spectroscopic techniques to measure the Doppler shift in light reflected from the edges of planetary discs, thereby determining the periods of rotation of Uranus, Jupiter, Saturn, Venus, and Mars in 1912. He also discovered the general recession of galaxies (outside the Local Group) from our own galaxy, a result later seen to be in accord with the idea of an expanding universe.

Sloan, Alfred P(ritchard), Jr (1875–1966) Industrialist and philanthropist, born in New Haven, CT. From 1920 he worked with Pierre Du Pont to reorganize and restructure General Motors, becoming its president in 1924 and later chairman of the board (1937–56). Under his guidance the company became one of the largest industrial corporations in the world. A noted philanthropist, he founded the Alfred P Sloan Foundation in 1937, and the Sloan–Kettering Institute for Cancer Research in 1945. His autobiography, *My Years with General Motors* (1964), is a classic in management literature. >> Du Pont

Sloan, John (French) (1871–1951) Artist, born in Lock Haven, PA. He studied at Philadelphia Spring Garden Institute and Pennsylvania Academy of Fine Arts, and worked as a commercial artist and newspaper art reporter. Influenced by Robert Henri, and a member of 'The Eight', he produced a series of intimate warm-hearted etchings based on New York City life, which gave rise to the name 'Ashcan school'. Throughout his career he continued to project his individual visual documentation of life in the metropolis, placing him in the forefront of the American Realist tradition. >> Bellows; Henri

Sloane, Sir Hans (1660–1753) Physician, born in Killyleagh, Co Down. He studied in London and in France, and settled in London as a physician, but spent 1685–6 in Jamaica, collecting a herbarium of 800 species. His museum and library of 50 000 volumes and 3560 manuscripts formed the nucleus of the British Museum.

Slocum, Joshua [slohkm] (1844–c.1910) Mariner, the first man to sail round the world single-handed, born in Wilmot Township, Nova Scotia, Canada. He joined the crew of a trading vessel and spent most of his life at sea. In 1895 he set out from Boston without capital on the sloop *Spray* for the first solo cruise around the world, arriving back at Newport in 1898, having supported himself by lecturing on the way. He wrote his classic story *Sailing Alone Around the World* in 1899. In 1909 he set out once more, but was not heard of again, and was presumed shipwrecked, although the *Spray* was never found.

Slovo, Joe [slohvoh] (1926–95) South African political leader, born in Lithuania. He moved to South Africa as a child, and became one of the most influential white South Africans associated with the national liberation movement. He qualified as a lawyer, and became an active member of the Communist Party in the 1940s. He left the country in June 1963, and continued to work for the Communist Party and the African National Congress (ANC). He held high office in both organizations, and also served as chief-of-staff of Umkhonto we Sizwe, the armed wing of the ANC (1985–7). He returned to South Africa in 1990, and played a major role in the negotiations for a new dispensation. In 1994 he was appointed minister for housing in Mandela's first cabinet. >> First; Mandela, Nelson

Sluter, Claus or **Claes** [slooter] (c. 1350–c. 1405) Sculptor, probably born in Haarlem, The Netherlands. He went to Dijon under the patronage of Philip the Bold of Burgundy. His chief works are the porch sculptures of the Carthusian house of Champmol near Dijon, and the tomb of Philip the Bold.

Smalley, Richard E (1943–) Chemist, born in Akron, OH. He studied at Princeton University, then moved to Rice University, Houston, in 1976. He shared the Nobel Prize for Chemistry in 1996 for his contribution to the discovery of fullerenes (1985). >> Curl; Kroto

Smeaton, Bruce (James) (1938–) Composer for film and television, born in Brighton, Victoria, Australia. His work for major feature films is internationally recognized, and has won many awards; titles include *Picnic at Hanging Rock* (1975) and *The Chant of Jimmie Blacksmith* (1978). For television he composed the music for *A Town Like Alice* (1981) and *Naked under Capricorn* (1988). Other works include a cello concerto, music for brass, chamber music, and a ballet.

Smeaton, John (1724–94) Civil engineer, born in Austhorpe, West Yorkshire, N England, UK. In c.1750 he moved to London as a mathematical-instrument maker. Elected Fellow of the Royal Society in 1753, he won the Copley Medal for his research into the mechanics of water-wheels and windmills. He made his reputation with a design for the third Eddystone lighthouse (1756–9), using dovetailed blocks of stone. His technique became standard; the lighthouse remained in use until 1877, and was re-erected on Plymouth Hoe as a memorial. His other chief engineering works include Ramsgate Harbour (1774), the Forth and Clyde Canal, and bridges at Coldstream and Perth.

Smellie, William (1740–95) Editor, printer, and antiquary, born in Edinburgh, EC Scotland, UK. Educated at the High School, he was apprenticed to a printer in 1752. In 1765 he set up his own printing business and, with Andrew Bell (1726–1809) and Colin MacFarquhar (?1745–?93), produced the first edition of the *Encyclopaedia Britannica* (1768–71), much of which was later ascribed to him. A founder member of the Society of Antiquities in 1780, he helped prepare the first statistical account of Scotland.

Smetana, Bedřich [smetana] (1824–84) Composer, born in Litomyšl, Czech Republic (formerly, Bohemia). He studied in Prague, and in 1848 opened a music school with the financial support of Liszt. He became conductor of the Philharmonic Orchestra in Göteborg, Sweden, in 1856. Returning to Prague in 1861, he was instrumental in establishing the national opera house. His compositions, intensely national in character, include nine operas, notably *Prodaná nevěsta* (1866, The Bartered Bride), and many chamber and orchestal works, including the series of symphonic poems *Má vlast* (1874–9, My Country). Overwork destroyed his health, and in 1874 he became deaf, though he continued to compose until a mental breakdown in 1883. >> Liszt

Smiles, Samuel (1812–1904) Writer and social reformer, born in Haddington, East Lothian, E Scotland, UK. He studied at Edinburgh, and settled as a surgeon in Leeds, but left medicine for journalism, editing the *Leeds Times* (1838–42), and becoming involved in railway companies until 1866. His main work was a guide to self-improvement, *Self-Help* (1859), with its short lives of great men and the admonition 'Do thou likewise'. He also wrote many biographical and moral books.

Smirke, Sir Robert (1781–1867) British architect, the son of **Robert Smirke** (1752–1845), painter and book-illustrator.

Architect to the board of works, his public buildings are usually Classical, his domestic architecture Gothic. Covent Garden Theatre (1809) was his first great undertaking; the British Museum (1823–47) his best known. He also designed the General Post Office (1824–9) and the College of Physicians (1825). His brother, **Sydney** (1799–1877), completed the west wing of the Museum and the reading room (1854), and rebuilt the Carlton Club (1857).

Smith, Adam (1723–90) Economist and philosopher, born in Kirkcaldy, Fife, E Scotland, UK. He studied at Glasgow and Oxford, and became professor of logic at Glasgow (1751), but took up the chair of moral philosophy the following year. In 1776 he moved to London, where he published *An Inquiry into the Nature and Causes of the Wealth of Nations* (1776), the first major work of political economy. This examined in detail the consequences of economic freedom, such as division of labour, the function of markets, and the international implications of a *laissez-faire* economy. His appointment as commissioner of customs in 1778 took him back to Edinburgh. >> Pitt, William (the Younger)

Smith, Alfred E(manuel), also called **Al Smith** (1873–1944) US politician, born in New York City. He worked in a fish market to support his widowed mother, and joined the New York City Democratic political organization as an investigator. He rose to be Governor of New York State (1919–20, 1923–8), and was the first Roman Catholic to run for the presidency, but was beaten by Herbert Hoover in the 1928 election. >> Hoover, Herbert

Smith, Bessie, nickname **Empress of the Blues** (c. 1898–1937) Blues singer, born in Chattanooga, TN. She began her career in the modest circuit of vaudeville tents and small theatres, but her magnificent voice, blues-based repertoire, and vivacious stage presence soon gained her recognition as one of the outstanding African-American artistes of her day. She made a series of recordings throughout the 1920s, accompanied by leading jazz musicians, including Louis Armstrong, and these are regarded as classic blues statements. She starred in the 1929 film, *St Louis Blues*. The circumstances surrounding her death following a car crash were recorded in Edward Albee's play *The Death of Bessie Smith* (1960). >> Armstrong, Louis

Smith, David R(oland) (1906–65) Sculptor, born in Decatur, IN. He learnt how to cut and shape metal in a car factory, then from 1926 studied under the Czech abstract painter Jan Matulka at the Art Students' League in New York City. His first welded-steel sculptures, inspired by magazine photographs of similar work by Picasso, date from 1932. During the 1930s he assimilated avant-garde European styles, eventually producing nonrepresentational works such as the 'Zig' series (1960).

Smith, Dodie, pseudonym **C L Anthony** (1896–1990) Playwright, novelist, and theatre producer, born in Whitefield, Greater Manchester, NW England, UK. Educated in London, she studied at the Royal Academy of Drama and Art. She started as an actress, but turned to writing, producing such successful plays as *Dear Octopus* (1938). She is also known for her children's book *The Hundred and One Dalmatians* (1956), made into a popular Disney cartoon film (1961) and revived as a 'live' action film (1996).

Smith, Florence Margaret >> **Smith, Stevie**

Smith, George (1824–1901) Publisher, born in London, England, UK. He joined his father's firm of Smith & Elder in 1838, and became head in 1846. He founded the *Cornhill Magazine* in 1860 with Thackeray as editor, and the *Pall Mall Gazette* in 1865. He published the works of George Eliot, the Brownings, Mrs Gaskell, Trollope, and others. He also published the *Dictionary of National Biography* (63 vols, 1885–1900). >> Thackeray

Smith, Gerrit (1797–1874) Reformer and philanthropist, born in Utica, NY. From a wealthy family, he built one of the first temperance hotels in the USA. An abolitionist, he provided financial backing for John Brown's anti-slavery crusades, and was a leader in the organization of the anti-slavery Liberal Party. Nominated for the presidency, he was elected to the US House of Representatives in 1852, but resigned his seat in 1854. >> Brown, John

Smith, Hamilton (Othanel) (1931–) Molecular biologist, born in New York City. He graduated from Johns Hopkins Medical School, where he carried out genetic research (from 1967) and became professor of microbiology (1973). In the 1970s he obtained enzymes from bacteria which would split genes to give genetically active fragments; these 'restriction enzymes' allowed the possibility of genetic engineering of a new kind, as well as providing a tool for DNA sequencing. He shared the 1978 Nobel Prize for Physiology or Medicine with Werner Arber and Daniel Nathans. >> Arber, Werner; Nathans

Smith, (Robert) Harvey (1938–) Show-jumper, born in Bingley, West Yorkshire, N England, UK. He won the British championships, and the British Grand Prix, on several occasions, and represented Britain in the 1968 Mexico City Olympics and at Munich in 1972. Horses most closely associated with him include *Salvador*, *O'Malley*, *Mattie Brown*, *Farmer's Boy*, and *Harvester*. With the increasing prominence and popularity of show-jumping, Smith became a well-known figure, parodying the blunt, bluff, Yorkshireman. He has written two books, *Show Jumping with Harvey Smith* (1979) and *Bedside Jumping* (1985).

Smith, Henry Edward >> **Smith, William Henry**

Smith, Henry (John Stephen) (1826–83) Mathematician, born in Dublin, Ireland. He studied at Balliol College, Oxford, where he became a fellow, and in 1860 professor of geometry. The greatest authority of his day on the theory of numbers, he also wrote on elliptic functions and modern geometry.

Smith, Horace >> **Wesson, Daniel Baird**

Smith, Ian (Douglas) (1919–) Rhodesian politician and prime minister (1964–79), born in Selukwe, Zimbabwe (formerly Rhodesia). He studied in Rhodesia and South Africa, fought in World War 2, and became an MP in 1948. In 1961 he was a founder of the Rhodesian Front, dedicated to immediate independence without African majority rule. As premier, he unilaterally declared independence (UDI, 1965), which resulted in the imposition of increasingly severe economic sanctions by the UN at Britain's request. After an intensive guerrilla war, he created an 'internal settlement', and Muzorewa's caretaker government made him a member of the Transitional Executive Council of 1978–9 to prepare for the transfer of power. The internal settlement was overturned by the Lancaster House Agreement, and he was elected an MP under Mugabe's government, where he continued to be a vigorous opponent of the one-party state. >> Mugabe; Muzorewa; Soames; Wilson, Harold

Smith, James (microscopist) >> **Lister, Joseph Jackson**

Smith, Jedediah (Strong) (1799–1831) Fur trader and explorer, born in Jericho, NY. He went to St Louis to trade furs, and undertook two major explorations in the Far SW of North America in the Central Rockies and Columbia R areas (1823–30). Later he became the first white man to reach California overland across the Sierra Nevada Mts and Great Basin to the Pacific. He was killed by Comanche Indians while leading a wagon train to Santa Fe.

Smith, John (1580–1631) Adventurer, born in Willoughby, Lincolnshire, EC England, UK. He fought in France and Hungary, where he was captured by the Turks and sold as a slave. After escaping to Russia, he joined an expedition to colonize Virginia (1607), and was saved from death by Pocahontas. His energy in dealing with the Indians led to his being elected president of the colony (1608–9). He wrote valuable accounts of his travels, and produced several important maps. >> Pocahontas

Smith, John (1938–94) British politician, born in Dalmally, Argyll and Bute, W Scotland, UK. He studied at Glasgow University, was called to the Scottish bar in 1967, and made a QC in 1983. He became a Labour MP in 1970, held junior government posts under Harold Wilson, and in 1978 was appointed secretary of trade and industry by James Callaghan. From 1979 he was Opposition Front Bench spokesman on trade, energy, and employment, consolidating his reputation on becoming shadow Chancellor of the Exchequer in 1988. A heart attack in the same year seemed to threaten his career, but he made a full recovery in 1989, and succeeded Neil Kinnock as Labour leader after the 1992 general election. A highly respected figure, his unexpected death after a further heart attack in 1994 caused an unusually strong sense of national loss. >> Kinnock

Smith, John Stafford (1750–1836) Composer, and musical scholar, born in Gloucester, Gloucestershire, SWC England, UK. He wrote vocal music, and the tune of 'The Star-spangled Banner'.

Smith, Joseph (1805–44) Founder of the Church of Jesus Christ of Latter-day Saints (the Mormons), born in Sharon, VT. He received his first 'call' as a prophet at Manchester, NY, in 1820. Later he was told of a sacred religious record on golden plates, with two stones which should help to translate it, and in 1827 this was delivered into his hands. In the *Book of Mormon* (1830), Christ is said to have appeared and established his Church in the New World. Smith claimed to have received authority from St John the Baptist and the apostles to be the instrument of the Church's re-establishment. Despite ridicule and hostility, the new Church rapidly gained converts. He founded Nauvoo, IL, in 1840, becoming mayor. Violence followed events surrounding his announcement as a candidate for the US presidency. He was imprisoned for conspiracy, and killed by a mob which broke into a jail in Carthage, IL, where he and his brother Hyram were awaiting trial. >> Young, Brigham

Smith, Keith >> **Smith, Ross**

Smith, Logan Pearsall (1865–1946) Writer, born in Millville, NJ. He studied at Harvard and Oxford, settled in England, UK and took British nationality in 1913. He produced critical editions of several authors, wrote *Milton and His Modern Critics* (1941), but is best remembered for his essays, collected in *All Trivia* (1933) and *Reperusals and Re-collections* (1936), and his short stories.

Smith, Maggie, popular name of **Dame Margaret Natalie Smith** (1934–) Actress, born in Ilford, E Greater London, England, UK. A student at the Oxford Playhouse School, she made her stage debut with the Oxford University Dramatic Society in 1952, and appeared in New York City as one of the *New Faces of '56*. Gaining increasing critical esteem for her performances, she joined the National Theatre, where she played in *Othello* (1963), *Hay Fever* (1966), and *The Three Sisters* (1970), among others. Her film debut in 1958 was followed by such films as *The VIPs* (1963), *The Pumpkin Eater* (1964), and *The Prime of Miss Jean Brodie* (1969, Oscar). Later stage work includes *Virginia* (1980) and *Lettice and Lovage* (1988, Tony). She received an Oscar for her role in *California Suite* (1978), and BAFTA awards for her roles in *A Private Function* (1984), *A Room With a View* (1986), and *The Lonely Passion of Judith Hearne* (1987). Later film appearances include *The Secret Garden* (1993), *The First Wives Club* (1996), and *Washington Square* (1997). She was created a dame in 1990.

Smith, Maria Ann (c.1801–70) Orchardist, born in Australia. In the 1860s she was growing various seedlings in her orchard in Eastwood, near Sydney, and experimented with a hardy French crab-apple from the cooler climate of Tasmania. From this was developed the late-ripening *Granny Smith* apple which, because of its excellent keeping qualities, formed for many years the bulk of Australia's apple exports.

Smith, Sir Matthew Arnold Bracy (1879–1959) Artist, born in Halifax, West Yorkshire, N England, UK. He studied at the Slade School of Art, London, and first went to Paris in 1910, when he met Matisse and the Fauves. In 1915 he exhibited with the London Group, and he later painted much in Provence. >> Gilman, Harold; Matisse

Smith, Robert Holbrook >> **Wilson, William Griffith**

Smith, Rodney, known as **Gypsy Smith** (1860–1947) Evangelist, born of nomadic gypsy parents near Epping Forest, Essex, SE England, UK. He was converted at a Primitive Methodist meeting in 1876. Soon afterwards he joined William Booth, and became one of the first officers in the newly formed Salvation Army. He left the Army in 1882 to carry on his evangelism under the auspices of the Free Church, preaching forcefully in America, Australia, and elsewhere, as well as in Britain. >> Booth, William

Smith, Sir Ross Macpherson (1892–1922) Aviator, born in Semaphore, South Australia. The most decorated pilot of the Australian Flying Corps, which he joined in 1916, he was the first pilot to fly over Jerusalem, when he took T E Lawrence to meet Sharif Nazir. After the war he flew a Handley-Page bomber from Cairo to Calcutta, a record distance of nearly 2400 mi, to survey an air route from England to Australia. In 1919 for a £10 000 prize, he and his brother **Keith** (1890–1955) flew from London to Darwin in 28 days in a Vickers Vimy bi-plane, a feat for which they were both knighted. He was killed in a trial flight of a Vickers Viking amphibian plane. >> Lawrence, T E

Smith, Sophia (1796–1870) Philanthropist, born in Hartfield, MA. Inheriting her brother's fortune, on her pastor's advice she willed this money to be used to found a women's college. Smith College, Northampton, MA, was opened in 1875.

Smith, Stevie, pseudonym of **Florence Margaret Smith** (1902–71) Poet and novelist, born in Hull, NE England, UK. Educated in London, she worked in publishing, then began to write herself. In 1935 she took her first collection of poems to a publisher, who rejected them and advised her to try a novel. The result was *Novel on Yellow Paper* (1936), a largely autobiographical monologue in a humorous conversational style. Her first book of poetry, *A Good Time Was Had By All* was published in 1937, and she gradually acquired a reputation as an eccentrically humorous poet on serious themes. Later books include *Not Waving but Drowning* (1957), *The Frog Prince* (1966), and *Scorpion* (1972).

Smith, Sydney (1771–1845) Clergyman, essayist, and wit, born in Woodford, Essex, SE England, UK. He studied at New College, Oxford, where he became a fellow. He was ordained in 1794, and while serving in Edinburgh he helped to found the *Edinburgh Review* (1802). In 1803 he moved to London, where he made his mark as a preacher, and lectured at the Royal Institution on moral philosophy (1804–6). After various livings, he was appointed canon of St Paul's (1831). His writings include several collections of articles, letters, and pamphlets on a wide variety of themes.

Smith, Sir Sydney Alfred (1883–1969) Forensic medical expert, born in Roxburgh, New Zealand. He studied at Victoria College, Wellington, and Edinburgh University, was medical officer of health for New Zealand, professor of forensic medicine at Cairo, and from 1917 principal medico-legal expert for the Egyptian government. He later became professor of forensic medicine at Edinburgh (1928–53) and dean of the medical faculty from 1931, playing a foremost part in the medical and ballistic aspects of crime detection. >> Smith, Sydney Goodsir

Smith, Sydney Goodsir (1915–75) Poet, born in Wellington, New Zealand, the son of Sydney Alfred Smith. He moved to Edinburgh in 1928 when his father was appointed a professor there. He studied at Edinburgh and Oxford universities, and established a record as one of the best modern Lallans poets with such works as *Skail Wind* (1941), *Under the Eildon Tree* (1948), and *So Late into the Night* (1952). He also wrote a comic novel, *Carotid Cornucopius* (1947). >> Smith, Sydney Alfred

Smith, Theobald (1859–1934) Microbiologist and immunologist, born in Albany, NY. He studied at Cornell, and came to be associated with several US institutions, including Harvard (professor, 1896–1915) and the Rockefeller Institute for Medical Research (1915–29). He first implicated an insect vector in the spread of disease when he showed that Texas cattle fever is spread by ticks. He worked on human and bovine tuberculosis, laid the scientific foundations for a cholera vaccine, improved the production of smallpox vaccine, diphtheria and tetanus antitoxins, and established precise techniques for the bacteriological examination of water, milk, and sewage.

Smith, Tommie (1944–) Sprinter, born in Clarksville, TN. He set world records for both the 220 yd and the 200 m in 1966, and was a member of the US team which broke the world record for the 4 × 400 m relay. In the 1968 Olympics at Mexico City he won the gold medal in the 200 m in a world record time of 19·8 s, but caused considerable controversy by giving the Black Power salute while standing on the victor's rostrum. After retirement, he became a coach at Santa Monica College, CA, and then at Oberlin College, OH. >> RR1134

Smith, William (1769–1839) Civil engineer, born in Churchill, Oxfordshire, SC England, UK. In 1794 he was appointed engineer to the Somerset Coal Canal and began his study of the strata of England, introducing the law of strata identified by fossils. His work as a geological engineer involved him in canal and colliery projects throughout the country, and the restoration of the hot springs at Bath. His epoch-making Geological Map of England (1815) was followed by 21 coloured maps of the geology of the English counties (1819–24), in which he was assisted by his nephew, **John Phillips** (1800–74). He was awarded the first Wollaston Medal (1831).

Smith, Sir William (1854–1914) Businessman, and founder of the Boys' Brigade, born near Thurso, Highland, N Scotland, UK. An active worker in the Free College Church, Glasgow, and a member of the Lanarkshire Volunteers from 1874, he was well embarked on a successful career in commerce when he began his movement for 'the advancement of Christ's Kingdom among Boys' in 1883. The organization instilled habits of discipline, provided recreation through camps and other pursuits, and was firmly based on Christian principles. By 1897 the movement had spread to every continent.

Smith, W(illiam) Eugene (1918–78) Photojournalist, born in Wichita, KS. He left Notre Dame University to work for *Newsweek* magazine in 1937. A photographer with *Life* (1939–41) and a war correspondent (1942–54), his photo essays focused on life in small villages in many parts of the world. In 1971 he captured the suffering of Japanese families poisoned by eating fish contaminated by mercury originating from waste dumped at sea.

Smith, William Henry (1792–1865) British newsagent. He entered the newsagent's business of his father in the Strand, London (1812), and aided by his brother, **Henry Edward**, expanded it into the largest in Britain by making extensive use of railways and fast carts for country deliveries. The business later went to his son. >> Smith, W(illiam) H(enry)

Smith, W(illiam) H(enry) (1825–91) Newsagent, bookseller and statesman, born in London, England, UK, the son of William Henry Smith. He became his father's partner in 1846, and later assumed full control. The business steadily expanded, and in 1849 secured the privilege of selling books and newspapers at railway stations. He entered parliament in 1868, was financial secretary of the Treasury (1874–7), First Lord of the Admiralty (1877–80), and secretary for war (1885). In the second Salisbury ministry he was First Lord of the Treasury and Leader of the House of Commons until his death. >> Smith, William Henry

Smithson, James Louis Macie (1765–1829) Chemist, and founder of the Smithsonian Institution, born in Paris, France, an illegitimate son of Sir Hugh Smithson Percy, 1st Duke of Northumberland. He studied chemistry and mineralogy at Oxford, and was admitted to the Royal Society at 22. It seems that resentment over the circumstances of his birth led him in 1826 to make the endowment of his fortune, largely inherited from his mother's family, for the founding of the Smithsonian Institution in Washington, DC. He wrote that his name should 'live in the memory of man when the titles of the Northumberlands and Percys are extinct and forgotten'. The Institution was established by an Act of Congress in 1846, and opened in 1855.

Smithson, Robert (1938–73) Land artist, born in Passaic, NJ. He studied at the Art Students' League (1955–6) and the Brooklyn Museum School. He took up Minimal Art in the 1960s, but from c.1966 began to exhibit his 'non-sites' – maps of sites he had visited, together with samples of rocks and soil. He is best known for such earthworks as the 'Spiral Jetty on the Great Salt Lake, Utah' (1970). He was killed in a plane crash while taking photographs of one of his earthworks in Texas.

Smollett, Tobias (George) (1721–71) Novelist, born in Cardross, Argyll and Bute, W Scotland, UK. He studied medicine at Glasgow University, served on the Cartagena expedition in 1741, and settled in London as a surgeon in 1744. He turned to writing, achieving success with his first works, the picaresque novels *The Adventures of Roderick Random* (1748) and *The Adventures of Peregrine Pickle* (1751). He spent several years in journal editing, translating, and writing historical and travel works. He retired to Italy in 1768, and completed his masterpiece, *Humphry Clinker* (1771), just before he died.

Smuts, Jan (Christiaan) (1870–1950) South African general, statesman, and prime minister (1919–24, 1939–48), born in Malmesbury, Cape Colony, South Africa. He studied at Cambridge, became a lawyer, fought in the second Boer War (1899–1902), and entered the House of Assembly in 1907. He held several cabinet posts, led campaigns against the Germans in South West Africa and Tanganyika, was a member of the Imperial War Cabinet in World War 1, and succeeded Botha as premier. He was a significant figure at Versailles, and was instrumental in the founding of the League of Nations. As minister of justice under Hertzog, his coalition with the Nationalists in 1934 produced the United Party, and he became premier again in 1939. >> Botha, Louis; Hertzog; RR1088

Smyslov, Vasily Vasiliyevich [smislof] (1921–) Chess player, and world champion (1957–58), born in Moscow. He made chess his career after narrowly failing an audition for the Bolshoi Opera in 1950. After drawing a world championship match against Botvinnik in 1954, which allowed the holder to retain his title, he beat the same player in 1957, only to relinquish the championship in the 1958 re-match. >> Botvinnik; RR1149

Smyth, Dame Ethel Mary (1858–1944) Composer and suffragette, born in London, England, UK. She studied at Leipzig, and composed a Mass in D Minor, symphonies, choral works, and several operas, such as *The Wreckers* (1906) and *The Boatswain's Mate* (1916). As a crusader for women's suffrage she composed the battle-song of the Women's Social and Political Union ('The March of the Women', 1911). She was created a dame in 1922.

Smythe, Francis Sydney (1900–49) Mountaineer, born in Maidstone, Kent, SE England, UK. He was a member of three Everest expeditions (1933, 1936, 1938), and shared the world's altitude climbing record. As a member of the Swiss Kanchenjunga expedition, he was the first to climb the Himalayan peak, Kamet, in 1931. During World War 2 he led the Commando Mountain Warfare School. His many books, illustrated by his fine mountain photography, include *Kamet Conquered* (1932), *Camp Six* (1937), and *Over Welsh Hills* (1941).

Smythe, Pat(ricia), married name **Koechlin** (1928–96) Show jumper, born in Switzerland. She won the European championship four times on *Flanagan* (1957, 1961–3), and in 1956 was the first woman to ride in the Olympic Games, winning a bronze medal in the team event. She won the Queen Elizabeth II Cup on *Mr Pollard* in 1958. She rode very little after her marriage in 1963.

Smythe, Reg(inald Smith) (1917–) Strip cartoonist, the creator of *Andy Capp*, born in Hartlepool, Cleveland, NE England, UK. He was a butcher's errand boy (1931), and became a regular soldier. After World War 2 he joined the Post Office, and freelanced cartoons to the *Daily Mirror*, who invited him to contribute a regular strip for their new Northern edition in 1958. *Andy Capp*, the adventures of a feisty little layabout, fonder of beer than of his wife, became the most popular British strip of all time, and the first British one to be syndicated worldwide. *Andy Capp* was adapted as a stage musical and television series starring James Bolam in 1987.

Smythson, Robert (c. 1535–1614) English architect. Trained as a mason, his first recorded work was at Longleat (1568), which he may have designed. His masterpiece was Wollaton Hall, Nottingham (1580–8), a mock mediaeval castle, made up of classical and Flemish Mannerist elements. He developed a new vertical plan, with the great hall set transversely, which revolutionized the spatial possibilities of contemporary buildings. He settled in Wollaton, which has led the nearby country houses, Worksop Manor, Balborough (1585), and Hardwick Hall, Derbyshire (1591–7) to be attributed to him.

Snagge, John (Derrick Mordaunt) (1904–96) British broadcaster. He studied at Oxford, and joined the BBC as an assistant station director in 1924. He became an announcer in 1928, worked in outside broadcasts (1933–9), then held a series of senior posts in programme presentation, retiring from the BBC in 1965. He provided the commentary on the Oxford and Cambridge Boat Race for half a century (1931–80). More than anyone else, his voice came to represent the traditional values of the BBC.

Snead, Sam(uel Jackson), nickname **Slammin' Sammy** (1912–) Golfer, born in Hot Springs, VA. He was the winner of a record 81 tournaments on the US Professional Golfers Association Tour between 1936 and 1965. Professional since 1934, he is credited with 135 victories worldwide. He won the (British) Open in 1946, the US PGA Championship in 1942, 1949, and 1951, and the US Masters in 1949, 1952, and 1954. His six Senior Championships (1964–5, 1967, 1970, 1972–3) are a record. >> RR1157

Snell, George (Davis) (1903–96) Immunologist, born in Bradford, MA. He studied at Harvard and the University of Texas, then worked at the Jackson Laboratory, Bar Harbour, ME (1935–73), conducting experiments in immunology that did much to make future organ transplants possible. He shared the 1980 Nobel Prize for Physiology or Medicine. >> RR1124

Snell, Peter (1938–) Athlete, born in Opunake, Taranaki, New Zealand. He was a surprise winner of the Olympic 800 m in 1960, but then went on to win gold in both the 800 m and 1500 m in the 1964 Olympics. He also achieved the Commonwealth Games 'double' in 1962, and set world records at 800 m and one mile (twice). In 1962 he broke the world mile record at Wanganui, New Zealand, on an outdated all-grass track, to become his country's first sub-four-minute miler. >> Lydiard; RR1135

Snell, Willebrod van Roijen, Lat **Snellius** (1580–1626) Mathematician, born in The Netherlands. He was professor of mathematics at Leyden (1613), and discovered the law of refraction known as *Snell's law*. He extensively developed the use of triangulation in surveying.

Snorri Sturluson >> **Sturluson, Snorri**

Snow, C(harles) P(ercy) Snow, Baron (1905–80) Novelist and physicist, born in Leicester, Leicestershire, C England, UK. He studied at Leicester and at Cambridge, where he became a fellow of Christ's College (1930–50). He was the author of a cycle of successful novels portraying English life from 1920 onwards, starting with *Strangers and Brothers* (1940), and including *The Masters* (1951), *The New Men* (1954), and *Corridors of Power* (1964). His controversial *The Two Cultures and the Scientific Revolution* (1959) discussed the dichotomy between science and literature, and his belief in closer contact between them. He married the novelist Pamela Hansford Johnson in 1950, was knighted in 1957, and became a life peer in 1964. >> Johnson, Pamela Hansford

Snow, John (1813–58) Anaesthetist and epidemiologist, born in York, North Yorkshire, N England, UK. From 1836 he practised medicine in London, and during the cholera outbreaks of 1848 and 1854 carried out epidemiological investigations, tracing one local outbreak to a well in Soho into which raw sewage seeped. He also implicated the Thames, into which many of London's sewers drained, and from which much of London's domestic water was obtained. Also a pioneer anaesthetist, he did experimental work on ether and chloroform, and devised apparatus to administer anaesthetics. As physician to Queen Victoria in 1853, he administered chloroform to her during the birth of Prince Leopold.

Snow, Peter (John) (1938–) Broadcaster and writer, born in Dublin. He studied at Oxford, joined the army, then became a newscaster and reporter for ITN (1962–6), and a diplomatic and defence correspondent (1966–79), joining the BBC as presenter of *Newsnight* in 1979. He has also become known as the co-presenter of the general elections from 1974, increasingly identified with the 'swingometer' coverage of the results as they are announced. His books include a biography of Saddam Hussein (1972).

Snowdon, Antony Armstrong-Jones, 1st Earl of (1930–) Photographer and designer, born in London, England, UK. He studied at Cambridge, and married Princess Margaret in 1960 (divorced 1978). A freelance photojournalist since 1951, he designed the Aviary of the London Zoo in 1965, and in recent years has devoted much effort to presenting the conditions of the handicapped, both in photographic studies and in television documentaries. >> Margaret, Princess

Snyder, Gary (Sherman) (1930–) Poet, born in San Francisco, CA. He studied at Reed College, OR, Indiana

University, and the University of California, Berkeley, then tried various jobs before beginning to write. He is associated with the Beat poets. From the outset he identified with the natural world and the values of simple living and hard physical work. His writing is also informed with his interest in Asian religious practices and literary traditions. *Turtle Island* (1975) was awarded a Pulitzer Prize. In 1996 appeared *Mountains and Rivers Without End*, a poem cycle some thirty years in the writing. >> Ginsberg; Kerouac

Snyders, Frans (1579–1657) Painter, born in Antwerp, Belgium. He specialized in still-life and animals, often assisting Rubens and other painters. He became court painter to the Governor of the Low Countries, for whom he painted some of his finest hunting scenes. >> Rubens

Soames (of Fletching), (Arthur) Christopher (John) Soames, Baron (1920–87) British statesman. He trained at Sandhurst, served with the Coldstream Guards during World War 2, and in 1947 entered politics after marrying **Mary**, the daughter of Sir Winston Churchill. He became a Conservative MP in 1950, and held junior ministerial posts before becoming secretary of state for war (1958–60). Between 1960 and 1977 he served as agriculture minister, ambassador to France, and as a member of the European Commission. Made a life peer in 1979, he assumed the office of Lord President and Leader of the House of Lords, and was chosen by Margaret Thatcher to oversee Rhodesia's transition to Zimbabwe in 1980. >> Churchill, Sir Winston; Smith, Ian; Thatcher

Soane, Sir John (1753–1837) Architect, born in Goring, Oxfordshire, SC England, UK. He trained in London, visited Italy (1777–80), held several government posts, and became professor of architecture at the Royal Academy (1806). His designs include the Bank of England (1792–1833, now rebuilt), and Dulwich College Art Gallery (1811–14). His house at Lincoln's Inn Fields has become a museum.

Soares, Mario (Alberto Nobre Lopez) [swahresh] (1924–) Portuguese politician, prime minister (1976–8, 1983–5), and president (1986–96), born in Lisbon. He studied at Lisbon and Paris, became politically active in the Democratic Socialist movement from his early 20s, and was imprisoned on 12 occasions. In 1968 he was deported by Salazar, and lived in exile in Paris (1970–4), then returned to co-found the Social Democratic Party. He was elected to the Assembly and was soon brought into the government. In 1986 he became Portugal's first civilian president for 60 years, and was re-elected in 1991. >> Salazar; RR1082

Sobers, Gary [sohberz], popular name of **Sir Garfield St Aubrun Sobers** (1936–) Cricketer, born in Barbados. A great West Indian all-rounder, he is the only man to score 8000 Test runs and take 200 wickets. During his career (1953–74) he scored 28 315 runs in first-class cricket (average 54·87) and took 1043 wickets (average 27·74). Against Pakistan at Kingston in 1958 he scored a Test cricket world record 365 not out, which stood until 1994. Playing for Nottinghamshire against Glamorgan at Swansea in 1968, he scored a record 36 runs in one (six-ball) over. He retired in 1974, and was knighted the following year. >> Lara; RR1149

Sobukwe, Robert Mangaliso [soh**boo**kway] (1924–78) African nationalist leader, born in Graaff-Reinet, South Africa. He was the co-founder and first president of the Pan African Congress, the main rival to the African National Congress (ANC) as opponent of the apartheid regime. His political involvement began while he was at the University of Fort Hare, when he joined the ANC Youth League. In 1958 he broke with the ANC on 'Africanist' grounds, advocating African political self-sufficiency, and hostile to alliance with leftists of other races. He was jailed in 1960,

and detained on Robben I (1963–9) under legislation (nicknamed the 'Sobukwe clause') used only against him. After his release from prison, he lived a further nine years under house arrest and stringent restrictions.

Socinus, Faustus [sosiynus], Ital **Fausto Paulo Sozini** (1539–1604) Protestant reformer, whose work heralded the founding of the *Socinian* sect, born in Siena, Italy. He studied theology at Basel, where he developed the anti-Trinitarian doctrines of his uncle, Laelius Socinus. He became secretary to Duke Orsini in Florence (1563–75). In 1578, on the publication of his *De Jesu Christo Servatore*, he narrowly escaped assassination, and moved to Poland, where he became leader of an anti-Trinitarian branch of the Reformed Church in Cracow. At the synod of Bresz in 1588 he argued against all the chief Christian dogmas. In 1590 he was denounced by the Inquisition, and became destitute. >> Socinus, Laelius

Socinus, Laelius [sosiynus], Ital **Lelio (Francesco Maria) Sozini** (1525–62) Protestant reformer, born in Siena, Italy. He trained as a lawyer at Padua, then turned to biblical studies. He travelled widely in Europe, settling in Zürich (1548). His anti-Trinitarian views were developed by his nephew into a doctrine known as *Socinianism*. >> Socinus, Faustus

Socrates [sokrateez] (469–399 BC) Greek philosopher, born in Athens. Little is known of his early life. By Plato's account, he devoted his last 30 years to convincing the Athenians that their opinions about moral matters could not bear the weight of critical scrutiny. His technique, the *Socratic method*, was to ask for definitions of such morally significant concepts as piety and justice, and to elicit contradictions from the responses, thus exposing the ignorance of the responder and motivating deeper enquiry into the concepts. His profession to know none of the answers himself is ironic: he most probably held the doctrines that human excellence is a kind of knowledge; thus, that all wrongdoing is based on ignorance, that no one desires bad things; and that it is worse to do injustice than to suffer it. He was tried on charges of impiety and corruption of youth by zealous defenders of a restored democracy in Athens. Found guilty, he was put to death by drinking hemlock. His personality and his doctrines were immortalized in Plato's dialogues; his influence on Western philosophy is incalculable. >> Antisthenes; Archelaus; Plato

Soddy, Frederick (1877–1956) Radiochemist, born in Eastbourne, East Sussex, SE England, UK. He studied in Wales and at Oxford, and held posts at Montreal, Glasgow, Aberdeen, and Oxford, where he was professor of chemistry (1919–36). In 1913 he discovered forms of the same element with identical chemical qualities but different atomic weights (which he called *isotopes*), for which he received the Nobel Prize for Chemistry in 1921.

Söderberg, Hjalmar (Erik Fredrik) [soederberg] (1849–1941) Novelist and short-story writer, born in Stockholm. He wrote several collections of witty short stories, such as *Historietter* (1898), and novels of upper-middle-class life in Stockholm, such as *Förvillelser* (1895, Aberrations), *Martin Bircks Ungdom* (1901, The Youth of Martin Birck), and *Doktor Glas* (1905). His plays include *Gertrud* (1905).

Söderblom, Nathan [soederblom] (1866–1931) Lutheran archbishop, born in Trönö, Sweden. He studied at Uppsala, and was ordained in 1893. He was Lutheran minister of the Swedish Church in Paris, and became professor of history of religion at Uppsala (1901) and Leipzig (1912). In 1914 he was appointed Archbishop of Uppsala and Primate of the Swedish Lutheran Church. A leader in the ecumenical movement, he wrote several works on comparative religion, and was the principal promoter of the Life and Work movement. He was awarded the Nobel Peace Prize in 1930.

Södergran, Edith (Irene) [soedergran] (1892–1923) Expressionist poet, born in St Petersburg, Russia. Regarded as the originator of the Swedish–Finnish Modernist movement with her first collection, *Dikter* (1916, Poems), she contracted tuberculosis at 16 and never fully recovered. Her best-known work is *Landet som Icke Är* (The Non-Existent Country), published posthumously in 1925.

Söderström, Elisabeth Anna [soederstroem] (1927–   ) Soprano, born in Sweden. She studied at the Stockholm Opera School, and was engaged by the Royal Opera, Stockholm (1950). She appeared at Glyndebourne in 1957, the Metropolitan Opera Company in 1959, and Covent Garden in 1960, and subsequently sang in all the leading international opera houses. In the 1959 season she sang all three leading female roles in *Der Rosenkavelier*.

Sodoma, il ('The Sodomite'), originally **Giovanni Antonio Bazzi** (1477–1549) Religious and historical painter, born in Vercelli, Duchy of Savoy. A Lombard, he painted frescoes in Monte Oliveto Maggiore near Siena, before being called to the Vatican in 1508, where he began to paint the fresco of 'The Marriage of Alexander and Roxane' in the Villa Farnesina. He was later superseded by Raphael. A known homosexual, his name is likely to have been started as a joke, but was adopted by him as his professional name. >> Raphael

Soeharto >> **Suharto**

Soekarno, Achmad >> **Sukarno**

Sokolow, Anna [sokoloh] (1912–   ) Dancer, choreographer, and teacher, born in Hartford, CT. She studied at the School of American Ballet and Metropolitan Opera Ballet School, and became one of Martha Graham's original dancers (1930–9). Choreographing from 1934, she founded her own troupe and, in 1939, the first modern dance company in Mexico, La Paloma Azul. She has also conducted pioneering collaborations with experimental jazz composers. >> Graham, Martha

Solal, Martial (1927–   ) Jazz pianist and composer, born in Algiers. He played in Paris from the 1940s, often with visiting American musicians, and recorded with Lee Konitz, Hampton Hawes, Stephane Grappelli, and others. Highly regarded by critics, his compositions include 'Suite in D Flat' for jazz quartet in 1959, and 'Concerto' (1981) for jazz trio and orchestra. He presided over the first Martial Solal International Jazz Piano Competition in 1989.

Solario, Antonio [solahrioh], nickname **lo Zingaro** ('the Gypsy') (c.1382–1455) Painter, born in Civita, in the Abruzzi, Italy. Originally a blacksmith, he painted frescoes in the Benedictine monastery at Naples.

Solomon (Hebrew Bible) (10th-c BC) King of Israel, the second son of David and Bathsheba. His outwardly splendid reign (described in 1 *Kings* 1–11 and 2 *Chron* 1–10) saw the expansion of the kingdom and the building of the great Temple in Jerusalem. But high taxation and alliances with heathen courts bred discontent, which later brought the disruption of the kingdom under his son, Rehoboam. Solomon was credited with extraordinary wisdom, and became a legendary figure in Judaism, so that his name became attached to several biblical and extra-canonical writings. >> David; Jeroboam; RR1064

Solomon (music), professional name of **Solomon Cutner** (1902–88) Pianist, born in London, England, UK. After appearing with great success as a child prodigy, he retired for further study, and won a high reputation as a performer of the works of Beethoven, Brahms, and some of the modern composers. He did not tour as extensively as most players, and was forced to retire after a stroke in 1965.

Solomon, John (William) (1931–   ) British croquet player. He made his international debut against New Zealand in 1950 at age 19, and never missed an England Test Match between 1950 and 1973. He won a record 10 Open Croquet Championships (1953, 1956, 1959, 1961, 1963–8), the Men's Championship 10 times between 1951 and 1972, the Open Doubles Championship 10 times (all with Edmond Cotter) between 1954 and 1969, and the Mixed Doubles title once (with Freda Oddie) in 1954. He was winner of the President's Cup a record nine times.

Solon [sohlon] (7th–6th-c BC) Athenian statesman, lawgiver, and poet. As chief archon, he enacted many economic, constitutional, and legal reforms, and paved the way for the development of democracy at Athens, and her emergence as a great trading state. Enslavement for debt was abolished, a new currency instituted, and citizenship granted to foreign craftsmen settling in Athens. Wealth rather than birth was made the criterion for participation in political life, and Draco's inhumane legal code was largely repealed. >> Draco

Solovyev, Vladimir Sergeyevich [solevyof] (1853–1900) Philosopher, theologian, and poet, born in Moscow. Educated at his Orthodox home, he took his doctorate at Moscow. He proposed a universal Christianity which would unite the Catholic and Orthodox churches, and attempted a synthesis of religious philosophy with science. His main works include (trans titles) *The Crisis of Western Philosophy: Against the Positivists* (1874) and *The Meaning of Love* (1894).

Solow, Robert (Merton) [soloh] (1924–   ) Economist, born in New York City. He studied at Harvard, and became professor at the Massachusetts Institute of Technology in 1958. He was awarded the 1987 Nobel Prize for Economics for his 'study of the factors which permit production growth and increased welfare'.

Solti, Sir Georg [sholtee] (1912–97) Conductor, born in Budapest. World War 2 forced him to give up his post as conductor of the Budapest Opera, and he worked in Switzerland until 1946, when he became director at the Munich Staatsoper (until 1952), at Frankfurt (1952–61), and Covent Garden, London (1961–71). He conducted the Chicago Symphony Orchestra (1969–91) and the London Philharmonic (1979–83, then emeritus), and later became artistic director of the Salzburg Easter Festival (1992–3). He was granted an honorary knighthood in 1971, and took British nationality in 1972.

Solvay, Ernest (1838–1922) Industrial chemist, born in Rebecq-Rognon, Belgium. He worked in his father's salt-making business, then at a gasworks. While there he solved the problems of large-scale commercial production of sodium carbonate (1863) used in the manufacture of glass and soap. His findings made him a considerable fortune, and he founded various institutes of scientific research.

Solzhenitsyn, Alexander (Isayevich) [solzhenitsin] (1918–   ) Writer, born in Kislovodsk, Russia. Educated at Rostov in mathematics and physics, he fought in World War 2, and was imprisoned (1945–53) for unfavourable comment on Stalin's conduct of the war. On his release, he became a teacher, and started to write. His first novel (trans titles), *One Day in the Life of Ivan Denisovich* (1962), set in a prison camp, was acclaimed both in the USSR and the West; but his subsequent denunciation of Soviet censorship led to the banning of his later, semi-autobiographical novels, *Cancer Ward* (1968) and *The First Circle* (1968). He was expelled from the Soviet Writers' Union in 1969, and awarded the Nobel Prize for Literature in 1970 (received in 1974). His later books include *The Gulag Archipelago* (1973–8), a factual account of the Stalinist terror, for which he was arrested and exiled (1974). He lived in the USA, where in 1975 he became an honorary fellow of the Hoover

Institution on War, Revolution, and Peace. He was awarded the Templeton Prize for Progress in Religion in 1983, and the Russian State Literature Prize in 1990. He returned to Russia in 1994, and the following year published *The Russian Question at the End of the Twentieth Century*.

Somers, Sir George [suhmerz] (1554–1610) English colonist, a founder of the South Virginia Company. In 1610 he was commander of a fleet of settlers which was shipwrecked on the Bermudas (originally known as the *Somers Is*), and claimed the islands for the British crown.

Somers (of Evesham), John Somers, Baron [suhmerz] (1651–1716) English statesman, born in Worcester, Hereford and Worcester, WC England, UK. He studied at Oxford, and became a lawyer (1676) and a Whig MP (1689). He helped to draft the Declaration of Rights (1689), and after the Revolution of 1688 held several posts under William III, culminating as Lord Chancellor (1697). William's most trusted minister, he was the object of frequent attacks, which led to his impeachment (and acquittal) in 1701. He was president of the Privy Council under Anne (1708–14). >> William III

Somerset, Edward >> **Worcester, Marquess of**

Somerset, Edward Seymour, Duke of, known as **Protector Somerset** (c. 1506–52) English soldier and statesman, the brother of Jane Seymour. He enjoyed high office under his brother-in-law, Henry VIII, and led the invading English army that devastated S Scotland and Edinburgh in the 'Rough Wooing' of 1543–4. On Henry's death in 1547 he was named Protector of England during the minority of Edward VI. He defeated a Scottish army at Pinkie (1547), and furthered the Reformation with the first Book of Common Prayer (1549). In 1549 he had his younger brother, Thomas Seymour, beheaded for attempting to marry the future Queen Elizabeth, and soon he himself was indicted for overambition, deposed by John Dudley, Earl of Warwick (1549), and eventually executed. >> Edward VI; Seymour, Jane; Seymour, Thomas; Warwick, John Dudley

Somervell, Sir Arthur (1863–1937) Composer, born in Windermere, Cumbria, NW England, UK. He is known for the cantata *The Forsaken Merman*, *Thalassa*, a symphony, children's operettas, and for his collection of English folksongs.

Somerville, Edith (Anna Oenone), published under the name **Somerville and Ross** (1858–1949) Novelist, born in Corfu, the daughter of an army officer. As a baby, she returned to her family home in Co Cork, Ireland. She studied painting in London, Düsseldorf, and Paris, and became a magazine illustrator. With her cousin, Violet Florence Martin (pseudonym, Martin Ross), she began a literary partnership under their pseudonym. Starting with *An Irish Cousin* (1889), they completed 14 works together, including *The Real Charlotte* (1894), *Some Experiences of an Irish RM* (1899), and *In Mr Knox's Country* (1915). After Violet's death in 1915, Edith continued to write under their pseudonym, producing *Irish Memoirs* (1917) and *The Big House at Inver* (1925). >> Martin, Violet Florence

Somerville, Sir James (Fownes) (1882–1949) British naval commander. As a radio communications specialist he served in the Dardanelles (1915) and in the Grand Fleet (1915–18). In the West Indies (1938–9), he was invalided home with suspected tuberculosis, but recalled to the active list in 1940. As vice-admiral in the Mediterranean, he sank the French ships at Oran (1940), shelled Genoa (1941), helped in the sinking of the *Bismarck* (1941), and took part in the Malta convoy battle (1941). After the entry of the Japanese into the War, he became commander-in-chief of the British fleet in the Indian Ocean. In 1945 he was promoted Admiral of the Fleet.

Somerville, Mary, *née* **Fairfax** (1780–1872) Scientific writer,

born in Jedburgh, Scottish Borders, SE Scotland, UK. She lived in London from 1816, where she moved in intellectual and scientific circles, and corresponded with foreign scientists. In 1831 she published *The Mechanism of the Heavens*, an account for the general reader of Pierre Simon Laplace's *Mécanique céleste*. This had great success, and she wrote several further expository works on science. She supported the emancipation and education of women, and *Somerville College* (1879) at Oxford is named after her. >> Laplace

Sommerfeld, Arnold (Johannes Wilhelm) [zomerfelt] (1868–1951) Physicist, born in Königsberg, Germany. He studied at Königsberg and became professor of mathematics at Clausthal (1897), and professor of physics at Aachen (1900) and Munich (1906). With Felix Klein he developed the theory of the gyroscope. He researched into a variety of problems, including X-ray and electron diffraction, and radio waves. He is best known for his work on the Bohr atomic model, and the notion of elliptical rather than circular electron orbits. >> Bohr, Aage; Klein, Felix

Somoza (García), Anastasio [somohza] (1896–1956) Nicaraguan dictator, born in San Marcos, Nicaragua. He studied in the USA. As chief of the National Guard, he established himself in supreme power in the early 1930s, and retained power until assassinated. His sons **Luis Somoza Debayle** (1923–67) and **Anastasio Somoza Debayle** (1925–80) continued dynastic control of Nicaragua until the 1979 revolution. >> Ortega; Sandino; RR1078

Sondheim, Stephen (Joshua) [sondhiym] (1930–) Composer and lyricist, born in New York City. As a young man, he studied lyric-writing with Oscar Hammerstein II, and wrote incidental music for *Girls of Summer* (1956), before earning his first success with the lyrics for Bernstein's *West Side Story* (1957). His own highly successful musicals, including *A Funny Thing Happened on the Way to the Forum* (1962), *A Little Night Music* (1972), *Sweeney Todd* (1979), and *Sunday in the Park with George* (1984, Pulitzer) have contributed greatly to the revival of the musical in the USA. Later works include *Assassins* (1991) and *Passion* (1994). >> Bernstein, Leonard; Hammerstein; Prince, Harold

Song Ziwen [sung tseewen], also spelled **Sung Tsu-wen** or **Soong Tse-wen**, abbreviated as **Soong, T V** (1894–1971) Chinese diplomat and financier, born in Shanghai, China. His sister **Song Qingling** (c.1892–1981) married Sun Yatsen, and through this Song became closely associated with the Nationalist Party. He provided the financial stability which made possible the 1926 Northern Expedition that reunited China under the Nationalists. A second sister, **Song Meiling** (c.1899–) married Jiang Jieshi in 1927. Song served as finance minister of the new government until 1931. When the Nationalist government was overthrown in 1949, he moved to the USA. >> Jiang Jieshi; Sun Yatsen

Sonnino, (Giorgio) Sidney, barone (Baron) [soneenoh] (1847–1922) Italian statesman, and prime minister of the Kingdom of Italy (1906, 1909–10), born in Pisa, Italy, of an English mother. He entered parliament in 1880, and became finance minister (1893–96). As prime minister he was unable to conciliate parliament, and as foreign minister (1914–20) denounced the Triple Alliance and brought Italy into the European War (1915). >> RR1065

Son of Sam >> **Berkowitz, David**

Sontag, Susan [sontag] (1933–) Critic, born in New York City. She graduated from the University of Chicago when she was 18, and went on to Harvard. Though she has written novels and stories, she is best known for her innovative essays, for which she has been dubbed a 'new intellectual'. Her influential books include *The Style of Radical Will* (1969), *On Photography* (1976), and *Illness as Metaphor* (1978). Later essays include *AIDS and its Metaphors* (1989) and *Howard Hodgkin: Paintings* (1995).

Soong, Mayling / Tse-ven >> **Song, Ziwen**

Soper, Donald (Oliver) Soper, Baron [sohper] (1903–) Methodist minister, born in London, England, UK. Widely known for his open-air speaking on London's Tower Hill, he became superintendent of the West London Mission in 1936, and has written many books on Christianity and social questions, and particularly on international issues from the pacifist angle. He was made a life peer in 1965, and was still preaching at Tower Hill on his 90th birthday.

Sophia Alexeyevna [sohfeea aleksayevna] (1657–1704) Regent of Russia (1682–9), born in Moscow, the daughter of Tsar Alexey I Mihailovitch and his first wife, Maria Miloslavskaya. On the death of her brother, Tsar Fyodor Alexeyevich (1682), she opposed the accession of her half-brother, Peter (the future Peter the Great), and took advantage of a popular uprising in Moscow to press the candidature of her mentally deficient brother, Ivan. A compromise was reached whereby both Ivan (V) and Peter were proclaimed joint tsars, with Sophia as regent. Supported by leading boyars, she became the *de facto* ruler of Russia. A faction of the nobility succeeded in removing her from power in 1689, and (apart from a failed attempt to regain power in 1698) she spent the rest of her life in a convent in Moscow. >> Alexey I Mihailovitch; Peter I (of Russia); RR1085

Sophia of Greece >> **Juan Carlos I**

Sophocles [sofokleez] (c. 496–406 BC) Greek tragic playwright, born in Colonus Hippius. He wrote 123 plays, of which only seven survive, all written after his victory over Aeschylus in a dramatic contest in 468 BC: *Ajax, Electra, Women of Trachis, Philoctetes,* and his three major plays *Oedipus Rex, Oedipus at Colonus,* and *Antigone.* He played an important part in Athenian public life, and assisted Pericles in the war against the Samians (440 BC). >> Aeschylus; Pericles

Sophonisba [sofohnizba] (?–c. 204 BC) Noblewoman, the daughter of a Carthaginian general. She was betrothed to the Numidian prince Masinissa, but for reasons of state during the 2nd Punic War (218–202 BC) married his rival, Syphax. In 203 Syphax was defeated by a Roman army led by Masinissa, who took Sophonisba captive and married her. The Romans objected to this marriage, and Masinissa gave her up, but delivered poison to her to prevent her being sent as a captive to Rome. Corneille, Voltaire, and Alfieri have written tragedies around this theme.

Sopwith, Sir Thomas (Octave Murdoch) (1888–1989) Aircraft designer and sportsman, born in London, England, UK. He won a prize for the longest flight across the English Channel in 1910, and founded the Sopwith Aviation Co in 1912, building many of the aircraft used in World War 1, such as the Sopwith Camel. Chairman of the Hawker-Siddeley Group from 1935, and president from 1963, he was knighted in 1953.

Sorabji, Kaikhosru Shapurji [sorabjee], originally **Leon Dudley Sorabji** (1892/5–1988) Composer, pianist, and polemical essayist, born in Chingford, Essex, SE England, UK, of Parsi and Spanish–Sicilian descent. Largely self-taught, his works are often epic, such as *Opus clavicembalisticum* (1930), a work of four hours duration in three parts. In addition to piano music, he wrote concertos, organ works, choral music and songs. His witty and outspoken critical writings were collected in *Around Music* (1932) and *Mi contra fa* (1947). During 1940–76 he prohibited publication or performance of his works, making them available only through his own recordings.

Soraya [soriya], in full **Princess Soraya Esfandiari Bakhtiari** (1932–) Ex-queen of Persia, born in Isfahan, Iran, of Persian and German parents. She was educated at Isfahan, and later in England and Switzerland, and became queen of Persia on her marriage to Muhammad Reza Shah Pahlavi (1951). The marriage was dissolved in 1958. >> Pahlavi

Sorbon, Robert de [saw(r)bõ] (1201–74) Theologian, and founder of the Sorbonne, born in Sorbon, France. He studied in Reims and Paris, and in 1251 was appointed canon of Cambria. In 1258 he became canon of Paris and chaplain to the court, thus acting as confessor to Louis IX. He founded the Maison de Sorbonne in 1259, a theological college for the poor, which has since become one of the most prestigious colleges of the University of Paris.

Sorby, Henry Clifton (1826–1908) Geologist and metallurgist, born in Woodbourne, South Yorkshire, N England, UK. He was the first to study rocks in thin sections under the microscope (1849), and he adapted the technique to study metals. He also wrote on biology, architecture, and Egyptian hieroglyphics.

Sorel, Georges (1847–1922) Social philosopher, born in Cherbourg, France. He was trained as an engineer, and worked in the government department of bridges and roads (1870–92). He became interested in philosophy and social theory when he was 40, and left his job for study. His best-known work is *Réflexions sur la violence* (1908, Reflections on Violence), in which he argued that serious political opposition must also resort to violence, and that Socialism would only be achieved by confrontation and revolution. >> Hulme

Sörensen, Sören (Peter Lauritz) [soerensen] (1868–1939) Danish biochemist. He studied chemistry at Copenhagen, and was director of chemistry at the Carlsberg Laboratory from 1901. He did pioneer work on hydrogen-ion concentration, and in 1909 invented the pH scale for measuring acidity.

Sorokin, Pitirim A(lexandrovich) [sorohkin] (1889–1968) Sociologist, born in Turia, Russia. After a varied career as factory hand, journalist, tutor, and cabinet minister (1917), he became professor of sociology at Petrograd (St Petersburg) (1919–22), specializing in the study of the social structure of rural communities. Banished by the Soviet government in 1922, he became professor at Minnesota (1924–30) and (1930–64) Harvard, where he founded the department of sociology.

Sorolla y Bastida, Joaquin [sorolya ee basteetha] (1863–1923) Painter, born in Valencia, Spain. He became one of the leading Spanish Impressionists, known especially for his sunlight effects, as in 'Swimmers' and 'Beaching the Boat' (Metropolitan, New York City).

Soros, George [sawros] (1930–) Financier, born in Budapest. He was a member of a prosperous Jewish family who moved to London in 1947. He studied at the London School of Economics, joined the merchant bank Singer & Friedlander, and in 1956 went to New York City, working as a financial analyst. In 1969 he set up the Quantum Fund, which grew rapidly from his daring speculations, and in 1979 he began to establish a network of Soros Foundations, mainly in Eastern Europe, to advance opportunities in education and business.

Sorsa, (Taisto) Kalevi (1930–) Finnish statesman and prime minister (1972–5, 1977–9, 1982–7), born in Keuruu, Finland. He studied at what is now the University of Tampere, and worked in publishing with the UN and in the ministry of education, before moving into politics. He was secretary-general of the Social Democratic Party in 1969, and its president in 1975. He entered parliament in 1970, and served as foreign minister (1972, 1975–6). After his third term as prime minister, he became deputy prime minister of the coalition in 1987. >> RR1049

Sosigenes of Alexandria [sosijeneez] (1st-c BC) Astronomer and mathematician who advised Julius Caesar on calendar reform. He recommended a year of 365·25 days, and inserted an extra 67 days into the year 46 BC to bring the months back in register with the seasons. >> Caesar, Julius

Sotatsu >> **Koetsu, Hon'ami**

Sotheby, John [suhthebee] (1740–1807) Auctioneer and antiquarian. He was the nephew of Samuel Baker, who founded the first sale room in Britain exclusively for books, manuscripts, and prints at Covent Garden in 1744. He became a director of the firm (1780–1800), then known as Leigh & Sotheby, which was transferred to the Strand in 1803.

Soto, Hernando / Fernando de >> **de Soto, Fernando**

Sottsass, Ettore, Jr (1917–) Architect and designer, born in Innsbruck, Austria. He trained as an architect in Turin, moved to Milan, and set up his own design office in 1946, becoming involved in the reconstruction of N Italian towns. As an industrial designer he is closely associated with the firm of Olivetti (from 1958), for which he designed several typewriters and other office equipment. His departure from mainstream design in the 1970s culminated in his leading role in the Memphis group (1981).

Soufflot, Jacques Germain [soofloh] (1713–80) Architect, born in Irancy, France. He trained in Italy (1731–8), and became the leading French exponent of Neoclassicism. He designed the Panthéon and the Ecole de Droit in Paris, the Hôtel Dien in Lyon, and the Cathedral in Rennes.

Soult, Nicolas Jean de Dieu [soolt] (1769–1851) French marshal, born in Saint-Amans-la-Bastide, France. Created marshal of France by Napoleon in 1804, he led the French armies in the Peninsular War (1808–14) until defeated at Toulouse (1814). A skilled opportunist, he turned Royalist after Napoleon's abdication, but joined him in the Hundred Days, acting as his chief-of-staff at Waterloo. Exiled at the Second Restoration (1815) until 1819, he was gradually restored to all his honours, and presided over three ministries of Louis Philippe (1832–4, 1839–40, 1840–7), and once again professed himself to be a republican when Louis was overthrown in 1848. >> Louis Philippe; Napoleon

Souphanouvong, Prince [soofanoovong] (1909–95) Laotian politician and state president (1975–87), born in Luang Prabang, Laos. He studied engineering in Paris, returned to his home country in 1938 to enter Nationalist politics. He founded the Lao Independence Front with Chinese backing to fight French rule and, in 1954, the ruling rightist Lao Issara. With the country's emergence as a Socialist republic (1975), he was given the honorific post of state president. >> RR1071

Sousa, John Philip [sooza] (1854–1932) Composer and bandmaster, born in Washington, DC. His early training as a conductor was gained with theatre orchestras, and in 1880 he became conductor of the US Marine Band. His own band, formed 12 years later, won an international reputation. As well as more than a 100 popular marches, including 'The Stars and Stripes Forever' (1896) and 'The Liberty Bell' (1893), he composed 10 comic operas, the most successful of which was El Capitan (1896). He also invented the *sousaphone*.

Soustelle, Jacques (-Emile) [soostel] (1912–90) French politician and anthropologist, born in Montpellier, France. He studied at the Ecole Normale Supérieure and the Sorbonne (1937), and began a career in anthropology, becoming assistant director of the Musée d'Homme in Paris (1937–9). He turned to politics, and during World War 2 joined the Free French government, later holding a number of posts, including Governor-General of Algeria (1955). Leader of the Gaullist group in the National Assembly (1956–8), he was instrumental in the return to power of General de Gaulle, but later broke with him over

the question of Algerian independence. Soustelle resigned, and was charged with plotting against the state. He remained in exile until the general amnesty of 1968, when he returned to France and became director of studies at the Ecole Pratique des Hautes Etudes. >> de Gaulle

Soutar, William [sooter] (1898–1943) Poet, born in Perth, Perth and Kinross, E Scotland, UK. Educated at Perth Academy, he was conscripted into the Royal Navy (1916–19), then studied medicine and English at Edinburgh. His first volume of verse, published anonymously, was *Gleanings by an Undergraduate* (1923), followed by *Conflict* (1931). In 1933 he published his first volume of verse in Scots, *Seeds in the Wind*, for children. This was followed by his *Poems in Scots* (1935) and *Riddles in Scots* (1937), which gave him a permanent place in the Scottish literary revival. His remarkable *Diaries of a Dying Man* (1954) were written during a long and crippling illness, and mark him as an outstanding diarist.

South, Robert (1634–1716) High Church theologian, born in London, England, UK. He studied at Oxford, was ordained in 1658, and in 1660 was appointed public orator of Oxford. His vigorous sermons, full of mockery of the Puritans, delighted the restored Royalists. He became domestic chaplain to Clarendon, prebendary of Westminster in 1663, canon of Christ Church in 1670, and rector of Islip in 1678, but his outspokenness prevented any further preferment.

Southampton, Henry Wriothesley, 3rd Earl of [rothslee] (1573–1624) Courtier, born in Cowdray, Sussex. He was known as a patron of poets, notably of Shakespeare, who dedicated to him both *Venus and Adonis* (1593) and *The Rape of Lucrece* (1594). He became involved in the rebellion of Essex (1600), and was imprisoned, but released by James I. He died while in charge of English volunteers against Spain in Holland. >> Essex, 2nd Earl of

Southcott, Joanna (c. 1750–1814) Religious fanatic, born in Dorset, S England, UK. In c.1792 she declared herself to be the woman (predicted in *Rev* 12) who would give birth to the second Prince of Peace. She went to London, where she obtained a great following, but died soon after the predicted date of the birth. Her followers, who believed she would rise again, were still to be found at the beginning of the 20th-c.

Southerne, Thomas [suhthern] (1660–1746) Playwright, born in Oxmantown, Dublin, Ireland. From Trinity College, Dublin, he passed to the Middle Temple, London, England, UK, and in 1682 began his career as a playwright with a performance at the Drury Lane Theatre. Between 1685 and 1688 he was in the army, but thereafter he wrote many plays, contributed to John Dryden's works for a time, was much admired by fellow writers, and helped younger playwrights learn their craft. His two most successful works were tragedies based on novels by Aphra Behn: *The Fatal Marriage* (1694), and *Oroonoko* (1696). >> Dryden

Southey, Robert [suhthee] (1774–1843) Writer, born in Bristol, SW England, UK. He studed at Oxford, left without a degree, then studied law and settled in Keswick, where he was associated with Wordsworth and Coleridge. Originally a radical in politics, his views mellowed, and in 1809 he began to contribute to the Tory *Quarterly Review*. His literary output was considerable, and many of his short poems are familiar, such as 'Inchcape Rock' and 'After Blenheim'. Although made poet laureate in 1813, his prose became more widely known than his poetry, and included a life of Nelson, a naval history, and his letters. >> Coleridge, Hartley/Samuel Taylor/Sara; de Quincey; Wordsworth, William

Southwell, Robert (1561–95) Poet and martyr, born in Horsham, Norfolk, E England, UK. He studied at Douai and Rome, and was ordained as a Jesuit in 1584. He travelled to England as a missionary in 1586, aiding persecuted

Catholics, but was betrayed, tortured, and executed. Beatified in 1929, he is known for his devotional lyrics (such as 'The Burning Babe'), and for several prose treatises and epistles.

Soutine, Chaim [sooteen, khiym] (1893–1943) Artist, born in Smilovich, Belarus. He studied at Vilna, and went to Paris in 1911, where he became known for his paintings of carcases, and for his series of 'Choirboys' (1927). After his death he was recognized as a leading Expressionist painter.

Sowerby, Leo (1895–1968) Composer and organist, born in Grand Rapids, MI. He studied in Chicago and Rome, and became a teacher at the American Conservatory of Music in Chicago. His music, which includes a wide range of symphonies, concertos, and choral works, employs a traditional European style in works often evocative of American scenes, such as *Prairie* (1929), an orchestral tone poem.

Soyinka, Wole [soyingka, wolay], popular name of **Akinwande Oluwole Soyinka** (1934–) Writer, born near Abeokuta, Nigeria. He studied at Ibadan and Leeds, and became a play-reader at the Royal Court Theatre, where his first play, *The Invention*, was performed in 1955. After returning to Ibadan in 1959, he founded two theatre companies, and built up a new Nigerian drama, in English but using the words, music, and dance of the traditional festivals. His writing is deeply concerned with the tension between old and new in modern Africa. His poetic collection *A Shuttle in the Crypt* (1972) appeared after his release in 1969 from two years political detention. His first novel *The Interpreters* (1965), was called the first really modern African novel. *The Open Sore of a Continent*, his personal examination of the Nigerian crisis, appeared in 1996. He became professor of comparative literature at Ife in 1972, and professor of African studies and theatre at Cornell University in 1988. He was awarded the Nobel Prize for Literature in 1986.

Spaak, Paul Henri (1899–1972) Belgian statesman and prime minister (1938–9, 1946, 1947–9), born in Schaerbeek, Belgium. He became the first Socialist premier of his country, and foreign minister with the government-in-exile during World War 2. After his later periods as premier, he was again foreign minister (1954–7, 1961–8), in which role he became one of the founding fathers of the EEC, and secretary-general of NATO (1957–61). >> RR1035

Spaatz, Carl, nickname **Tooey Spaatz** (1891–1974) Aviator, born in Boyertown, PA. He trained at West Point, and in World War 1 shot down three German aircraft as commander of the 31st Aero Squadron in France. In 1941 he became chief of air staff, went on to command the air arm in North Africa and Sicily, and became chief of the Strategic Air Force, Europe, in 1944. After the end of the European war he commanded the air force in the Pacific, directing the firebombing and atomic bombing of Japanese cities (1945). He became first chief-of-staff of the independent air force in 1947 and retired the following year.

Spader, James (1960–) Film actor, born in Boston, MA. He studied acting at the Michael Chekov Studio, New York City, and made his film debut with *Endless Love* (1981). He became well known after *sex, lies, and videotape* (1989), for which he won the Best Actor award at the Cannes Film Festival. Later films include *Storyville* (1992), *Stargate* (1994), *Crash* (1997), and *Keys to Tulsa* (1997).

Spagnoletto, Lo >> **Ribera, Jusepe de**

Spahn, Warren (Edward) (1921–) Baseball player, born in Buffalo, NY. He holds the record for games won by a left-handed pitcher (363), and the record for a left-hander of winning 20 or more games in each of 13 seasons. He played for the Boston Braves in the National League (1942–52), then moved with the team to Milwaukee (1953–64). In

1965 he played for two other NL teams, New York and San Francisco. He was elected to the Baseball Hall of Fame in 1973. >> RR1145

Spallanzani, Lazaro [spalantsahnee] (1729–99) Physiologist, born in Modena, Italy. Ordained in 1757, he studied law at Bologna, then switched to physics. He was professor at Reggio College (1754), Modena (1760), and Pavia (1769 onwards). His work centred on regeneration and reproduction in a wide range of animals, including snails and amphibians, and he carried out successful transplantation experiments. Despite his belief in the preformation theory and his misconceptions about the nature of semen, he was the first to use artificial insemination on small animals, and on a dog.

Spark, Dame Muriel (Sarah) (1918–) Writer, born in Edinburgh, EC Scotland, UK. Educated in Edinburgh, she became editor of *Poetry Review* (1947–9), and published poetry, short stories, and critical biographies, including works on Wordsworth, Mary Shelley, and Emily Brontë. She is best known for her novels, notably *Memento Mori* (1959), *The Ballad of Peckham Rye* (1960), and especially *The Prime of Miss Jean Brodie* (1961, filmed 1969). Other books include *The Mandelbaum Gate* (1965, James Tait Black), *The Driver's Seat* (1970, filmed 1974), *A Far Cry from Kensington* (1988), *Symposium* (1990), and *Reality and Dreams* (1996), as well as her stories, collected in 1986. An autobiography, *Curriculum Vitae*, appeared in 1992. She lives in Italy, and was made a dame in 1993.

Spartacus [spah(r)takus] (?–71 BC) Thracian-born slave and gladiator at Capua, who led the most serious slave uprising in the history of Rome (73–71 BC). With a huge army of slaves and dispossessed, he inflicted numerous defeats on the Roman armies sent against him, until defeated and killed by Crassus. His supporters were crucified wholesale, their bodies left hanging along the Appian Way to act as a deterrent to other would-be rebels. >> **Crassus, Marcus Licinius; Pompey**

Spassky, Boris Vasilyevich (1937–) Chess player, and world champion (1969–72), born in Leningrad, Russia. He learned to play chess in a children's home when he was evacuated during World War 2. He became international master in 1953, and junior world champion in 1955. He gained the world championship against Tigran Petrosian in 1969, and lost it to Bobby Fischer in Reykjavík (1972). In 1992 they held a re-match in the former Yugoslavia, playing part in Montenegro and part in Serbia; Fischer defeated Spassky in both sections. >> **Fischer, Bobby; Petrosian; RR1149**

Speaight, Robert William [spayt] (1904–76) British writer and actor. He performed most of the major Shakespearean roles for the Old Vic Company from 1930, and played Becket in Eliot's *Murder in the Cathedral* at the Canterbury Festival (1935). He wrote many biographies, including *Hilaire Belloc* (1956), edited Belloc's correspondence (1958), and published works on drama.

Speaker, Tris(tram E), nickname **the Grey Eagle** (1888–1958) Baseball player, born in Hubbard, TX. During his 22-year career (1907–28), mostly with the Boston Red Sox and Cleveland Indians, he was considered the greatest defensive center fielder in the game's history. A solid left-handed hitter, he posted a lifetime batting average of ·344, and holds the major league record for most doubles (793) in a career. He managed the Indians (1919–26), and took them to their first pennant and World Series (1920). He was elected to baseball's Hall of Fame in 1937.

Spearman, Charles Edward (1863–1945) British psychologist, born in London, England, UK. He studied in Leipzig, then returned to London, where he became professor of mind and logic at University College. He was a pioneer of the statistical technique of factor analysis, and played a considerable role in the early development of intelligence testing.

Spector, Phil (1940–) Record producer, born in New York City. In the 1960s he developed a distinctive 'wall of sound' style using echo-effects and other innovative recording techniques; hits by such groups as the Ronettes (with his wife Ronnie Spector), the Crystals, and Darlene Love made him a millionaire in his early 20s. The Righteous Brothers' 'You've Lost That Loving Feeling' was his last major single success, in 1965. Later he worked with the Beatles and with ex-Beatles John Lennon and George Harrison. His *Christmas Album* remains a festive classic.

Spedding, Frank (Harold) (1902–84) Inorganic chemist, born in Hamilton, Ontario, Canada. He spent his working career at Iowa State University. He devised a method for purifying uranium metal in quantity in World War 2, and *Spedding's eggs* formed the core of Fermi's first atomic pile, set up in Chicago in 1942. Thereafter he worked on the problem of separating the closely similar lanthanides, and devised an ion-exchange chromatographic method for this purpose, which was also suitable for the separation of the actinides (transuranium elements). >> Fermi

Spee, Maximilian (Johannes Maria Hubert), Graf von (Count of) [shpay] (1861–1914) German naval commander, born in Copenhagen. He entered the imperial German navy in 1878, and in 1908 became chief-of-staff of the North Sea Command. At the outbreak of World War 1 (1914) he was in command of a commerce-raiding force in the Pacific. Off Coronel (Chile) he sank the British warships *Good Hope* and *Monmouth*. The same year he arrived at the Falklands, but he and his ships were taken by surprise and sunk by a reinforced British squadron under Sturdee. >> Sturdee

Speed, John (1552–1629) Antiquary and cartographer, born in Cheshire, NWC England, UK. He began as a tailor, but his considerable historical learning brought him patronage, and he was able to publish his 54 *Maps of England and Wales* (1608–10) and other works.

Speer, Albert [shpeer] (1905–81) Architect and Nazi government official, born in Mannheim, Germany. He joined the Nazi Party in 1931, became Hitler's chief architect in 1934, and was minister of armaments in 1942. Always more concerned with technology and administration than ideology, he openly opposed Hitler in the final months of the war, and was the only Nazi leader at Nuremberg to admit responsibility for the regime's actions. He was imprisoned for 20 years in Spandau, Berlin, and after his release in 1966 became a writer. >> Hitler; Speer

Speidel, Hans [shpiydl] (1897–) German soldier, born in Württemberg, Germany. He served in World War 1, and by 1939 was senior staff officer. As Rommel's chief-of-staff during the Allied invasion of Europe (1944), he was imprisoned after the anti-Hitler bomb plot. In 1951 he became military adviser to the West German government. His NATO appointment as commander-in-chief of land forces, C Europe (1957–63), aroused wide controversy. >> Rommel

Speight, Johnny [spayt] (1920–) Comic writer, born in London, England, UK. A milkman, insurance salesman, and member of a jazz band, he began writing after World War 2 for comedians such as Frankie Howerd, Arthur Haynes, and Morecambe and Wise. He made his mark on television with the creation of the loud-mouthed, working-class bigot, Alf Garnett, in the controversial series *Till Death Do Us Part* (1964–74), which took the Screenwriters' Guild Awards in 1966, 1967, and 1968. His other television series include *Spooner's Patch* (1979–82), *In Sickness and In Health* (1985), and *The Nineteenth Hole* (1989). >> Howerd; Morecambe

Speke, John Hanning (1827–64) Explorer, born in Bideford, Devon, SW England, UK. He served in India, and in 1854 went with Burton to search for the equatorial lakes of Africa. They discovered L Tanganyika (1858), then Speke travelled on alone, finding the lake he named Victoria, and saw in it the headwaters of the Nile. Back in England, his claims to have discovered the source of the Nile were doubted, and so a second expedition set out (1860–3). On his return, his claims were again challenged, and he was about to defend his discovery when he was killed in a shooting accident. >> Baker, Samuel; Burton, Richard Francis; Grant, James Augustus

Spelling, Aaron (1928–) Television producer, born in Dallas, TX. He moved to Hollywood as an actor and writer for popular television, producing his first international hit, *Starsky and Hutch*, in 1975. Several other successful productions followed, notably *Charlie's Angels* (1976–81), *Cagney and Lacey*, *Hart to Hart*, *Dynasty* (1981–9), and *Savannah* (1996–).

Spellman, Francis (Joseph) (1889–1967) Roman Catholic clergyman, born in Whitman, MA. Ordained in 1916 after studies in Rome, he became auxiliary Bishop of Boston (1932), Archbishop of New York (1939), and a cardinal (1946). A strong administrator and influential leader, he was a religious conservative and ardent anti-Communist. His writings include a best-selling novel, *The Foundling* (1951).

Spemann, Hans [shpayman] (1869–1941) Embryologist, born in Stuttgart, Germany. He studied in Stuttgart and Heidelberg, was professor at Rostock (1908–14), director of the Kaiser Wilhelm Institute of Biology in Berlin (1914–19), and professor at Freiburg (1919–35). He worked on embryonic development, discovering the function of certain tissues, and received the 1935 Nobel Prize for Physiology or Medicine.

Spence, Sir Basil (Urwin) (1907–76) Architect, born in Mumbai (Bombay), India. He studied at Edinburgh and London, and gradually emerged as the leading postwar British architect, with his fresh approach to new university buildings, the pavilion for the Festival of Britain (1951), and most famously the new Coventry Cathedral (1951), which boldly merged new and traditional structural methods. He was professor of architecture at Leeds (1955–6) and at the Royal Academy (1961–8). He was knighted in 1960.

Spence, Catherine Helen (1825–1910) Writer and feminist, born near Melrose, Scottish Borders, SE Scotland, UK. She arrived in Adelaide in 1839 with her parents, and later worked as a governess. *Clare Morrison* (1854) was the first novel of Australian life written by a woman, and she followed it with four more novels. Her early preoccupation with social problems, especially of the destitute and the young, led her more into the public arena, and she made lecture tours in Britain and the USA. In 1897 she became Australia's first woman political candidate.

Spence, (James) Lewis Thomas Chalmers (1874–1955) Writer, born in Dundee, E Scotland, UK. He studied dentistry, but turned to writing, and in 1899 became a sub-editor on *The Scotsman* newspaper, and subsequently the *British Weekly* (1906–9). Some of his poetry is collected in *The Phoenix* (1924) and *Weirds and Vanities* (1927). An authority on folklore and mythology, he wrote numerous books on the subject. He was one of the founder members of the National Party of Scotland (1928).

Spencer, Sir (Walter) Baldwin (1860–1929) Anthropologist and biologist, born in Stretford, Lancashire, NW England, UK. He studied at Oxford, and became professor of biology at the University of Melbourne (1887). In 1894 he joined Horn's expedition to C Australia where, with

Francis James Gillen, he began a collaborative study of the local Aboriginal tribes, resulting in *The Native Tribes of Central Australia* (1899), the popular account *Wandering in the Wilds of Australia* (1928), and other works. He was knighted in 1916.

Spencer, Herbert (1820–1903) Evolutionary philosopher, born in Derby, Derbyshire, C England, UK. He became a civil engineer for a railway in 1837, but engaged extensively in journalism. A firm (pre-Darwinian) believer in evolution, his main work is the nine-volume *System of Synthetic Philosophy* (1862–93), which brought together biology, psychology, sociology, and ethics. He was a leading advocate of 'Social Darwinism'. >> Darwin, Charles

Spencer, Sir Stanley (1891–1959) Artist, born in Cookham, Berkshire, S England, UK. He studied in London, then lived and worked mainly at Cookham. During 1926–33 he executed murals (using his war experiences) in the Oratory of All Souls, Burghclere. He produced many purely realistic landscapes, but his main works interpret the Bible in terms of everyday life, such as 'Resurrection: Port Glasgow' (1950, Tate, London). He was knighted in 1959.

Spencer-Churchill, Baroness >> Churchill, Winston

Spender, Sir Stephen (Harold) (1909–95) Poet and critic, born in London, England, UK. He studied at Oxford, and became one of the group of modern poets with Auden and Day-Lewis in the 1930s. His many poetic works include *Poems from Spain* (1939), *Ruins and Visions* (1942), and *The Generous Days* (1971). His *Collected Poems, 1928–85* were published in 1985. He was co-editor of *Horizon* (1939–41) and *Encounter* (1953–67), co-founder of *Index on Censorship* in 1971, and professor of English at University College, London (1970–7). He was knighted in 1983. >> Auden; Day-Lewis, Cecil

Spengler, Oswald [shpenggler] (1880–1936) Philosopher of history, born in Blankenburg, Germany. He studied at Halle, Munich, and Berlin, and taught mathematics before devoting himself entirely to the morbidly prophetic *Der Untergang des Abendlandes* (2 vols, 1918–22, The Decline of the West), which argues that all cultures are subject to the same cycle of growth and decay in accordance with predetermined 'historical destiny'. His views greatly encouraged the Nazis, though he never became one himself.

Spens, Sir Will(iam) (1882–1962) Educational administrator, born in Glasgow, W Scotland, UK. He studied at Cambridge, and was Master of Corpus Christi College there (1927–52). As chairman of the Consultative Committee on Education from 1934, he produced the report on *Secondary Education (Grammar Schools and Technical High Schools)* (1938), which recommended the raising of the school-leaving age to 15, and a widening of the provision of secondary education. His views paved the way for the *Norwood Report* (1943) and the Education Act of 1944.

Spenser, Edmund (?1552–99) Poet, born in London, England, UK. He studied at Cambridge, and obtained a place in Leicester's household, which led to a friendship with Sir Philip Sidney and a circle of wits (the *Areopagus*). His first original work was a sequence of pastoral poems, *The Shepheards Calendar* (1579). In 1580 he became secretary to the lord deputy in Ireland, and for his services was given Kilcolman Castle, Co Cork, where he settled in 1586. Here he began his major work, *The Faerie Queene*, using a nine-line verse pattern which later came to be called the *Spenserian stanza*. The first three books, dedicated to Elizabeth I, were published in 1590, and the second three in 1596, but the poem was left unfinished at his death. >> Sidney, Philip

Speransky, Mikhail Mikhaylovich, Graf (Count) [speranskee] (1772–1839) Russian statesman and reformer, born in Cherkutino, Russia. Destined to be a clergyman, he

was given the surname Speransky ('hope') by an uncle, and became secretary to Prince Kurakin (1795), then adviser to Tsar Alexander I (1807). In 1809 he produced a plan for the reorganization of the Russian structure of government on the Napoleonic model, but was dismissed when Napoleon invaded Russia (1812). Under Nicholas I he was restored to power, and was responsible for the trial and conviction of the Decembrist conspirators of 1825. He also prepared the *Complete Collection of the Laws of the Russian Empire* (44 vols, 1830). >> Alexander I (of Russia)

Speranza >> Wilde, Jane Francesca

Sperry, Elmer Ambrose (1860–1930) Inventor and electrical engineer, born in Cortland, NY. He invented dozens of new devices, including a dynamo, arc-light, and searchlight. His chief inventions were the gyroscopic compass (1911) and stabilizers for ships and aeroplanes. He also devised an electrolytic process for obtaining pure caustic soda from salt.

Sperry, Roger (Wolcott) (1913–94) Neuroscientist, born in Hartford, CT. He studied at Chicago University, then worked at Harvard, the Yerkes Laboratory of Primate Biology (1941–6), and Chicago University (1946–53), becoming professor of psychobiology at the California Institute of Technology (1954–84). He first made his name in the field of developmental neurobiology, and in the 1950s and 1960s pioneered surgical and experimental behavioural investigations. He shared the 1981 Nobel Prize for Physiology or Medicine. >> RR1124

Speusippus [spyoosipus] (?–339 /338 BC) Philosopher, who lived in Athens. He was Plato's nephew, and succeeded him as head of the Academy in 348. He produced a large corpus of writings, but only one fragment of this work, on Pythagorean numbers, survives. >> Plato

Speyr, Adrienne von >> Balthasar, Hans Urs von

Spice Girls, The British pop singing group, with members **Victoria ('Vicki') Addams**, known as 'Posh Spice' (1975–), born in Hertfordshire; **Melanie Jayne Chisholm**, or 'Mel(anie) C', known as 'Sporty Spice' (1975–), born in Liverpool; **Melanie Janine Brown**, or 'Mel(anie) B', known as 'Scary Spice' (1975–), born in Yorkshire; **Emma Lee Bunton**, or 'Emma', known as 'Baby Spice' (1976–), born in Finchley, N London; and **Geri Estelle Halliwell**, or 'Geri', known as 'Ginger Spice' (1972–), born in Watford, Hertfordshire. From earlier careers as dancers, singers, or models, they came together in 1996, their first record, 'Wannabe!', becoming a number 1 hit in the UK. Later hits 'Say You'll Be There' (1996), '2 Become 1' (1996), and 'Who Do You Think You Are' (1997). The group made a feature film, *Spiceworld – the Movie*, in 1997.

Spielberg, Steven [speelberg] (1947–) Film-maker, born in Cincinnati, OH. An amateur film-maker as a child, he became one of the youngest television directors at Universal Studios. A highly praised television film, *Duel* (1972), brought him the opportunity to direct for the cinema, and a string of hits have made him the most commercially successful director of all time. His films have explored primeval fears, as in *Jaws* (1975), or expressed childlike wonder at the marvels of this world and beyond, as in *Close Encounters of the Third Kind* (1977) and *E.T.* (1982). Later films include literary adaptations, such as *The Color Purple* (1985) and *Empire of the Sun* (1987), as well as the continuing adventures of his dare-devil hero, Indiana Jones, in such films as *Raiders of the Lost Ark* (1981) and *Indiana Jones and the Temple of Doom* (1984). Imaginative fantasy is dominant in his version of Peter Pan, *Hook* (1991), *Jurassic Park* (1993), and its sequel *The Lost World: Jurassic Park* (1997). *Schindler's List* (1993, Oscar) also received the 1994 BAFTA award for best director and best film. His company (Amblin') has produced several other successful films, notably *Back to the*

Future (1985) and its two sequels, and *Who Framed Roger Rabbit* (1988).

Spies-Kjaer, Janni [spiys **kyair**] (1962–) Danish businesswoman. In 1983 she married **Simon Spies**, the charismatic and unconventional founder of Spies Travel (who died in 1984), and she became the owner of Scandinavia's largest group of tour operators, the Spies Concern and the Tjaereborg Concern. One of Scandinavia's richest women, she married again in 1988.

Spillane, Mickey [spi**layn**], pseudonym of **Frank Morrison Spillane** (1918–) Detective fiction writer, born in New York City. During the late 1940s and early 1950s, under his pseudonym, he wrote a series of successful novels featuring detective Mike Hammer. *The Girl Hunters* (1962) was made into a film for which Spillane both wrote the script and acted as Hammer. In later novels he introduced the character Tiger Mann. His work contained elements of violence, sadism, and sexual immorality which some readers found disturbing, but his literary style and forceful main characters gained popular appeal, and the mixture translated readily to film. Later novels include *The Last Cop Out* (1973) and *The Day the Sea Rolled Back* (1981).

Spilsbury, Sir Bernard (Henry) (1877–1947) Pathologist, born in Leamington Hastings, Warwickshire, C England, UK. He studied at Oxford and St Mary's Hospital, London, and specialized in the new science of forensic pathology. He made his name at the trial of Crippen (1910), and was appointed pathologist to the Home Office. As expert witness for the Crown, he was involved in many notable murder trials. >> Crippen

Spinello Aretino [spi**nel**oh are**tee**noh], originally **Spinello di Luca Spinelli** (c. 1346–1410) Painter, born in Arezzo, Italy. He spent nearly all his life between there and Florence. His principal frescoes were done for San Miniato, in Florence, for the *campo santo* of Pisa, and for the municipal buildings of Siena.

Spink, Ian (1947–) Dancer, choreographer, and director, born in Melbourne, Victoria, Australia. He joined the Australian Ballet in 1969, and left ballet in 1974 to perform with the Dance Company of New South Wales (now Sydney Dance Company). He moved to England in 1977, where he formed the Ian Spink Group, but it was in partnership with Siobhan Davies and Richard Alston in Second Stride (founded 1982) that he first found success there. He became sole artistic director in 1987. Up-beat and theatrical, his popular work includes *Weighing the Heart* (1987) and *Dancing and Shouting* (1988). >> Alston; Davies, Siobhan

Spinola, Ambrogio di Filippo, marqués de (Marquess of) **Los Balbases** [spi**noh**la] (1569–1630) Soldier in Spanish service, born in Genoa, Italy. In 1602 he raised and maintained at his own cost 9000 troops, and served against Maurice of Nassau in the Spanish Netherlands. In 1603 he besieged Ostend, which fell in 1604 after one year's siege. Early in the Thirty Years' War (1618–48) he was in Germany, subduing the Lower Palatinate, but he was recalled to Holland to fight once more against Maurice of Nassau, who died of fever while attempting to relieve Breda. Breda fell to Spinola in 1625, but soon afterwards he was forced to resign through ill health. >> Maurice

Spinoza, Baruch or **Benedictus de** [spi**noh**za] (1632–77) Philosopher and theologian, born in Amsterdam. His deep interest in optics, the new astronomy, and Cartesian philosophy made him unpopular, and he was expelled from the Jewish community in 1656. His major works include the *Tractatus theologico-politicus* (1670), which despite its anonymity made him famous, and his *Ethica* (published posthumously, 1677). In 1673 he refused the professorship of philosophy at Heidelberg, in order to keep his independence.

Spitteler, Carl (Friedrich Georg) [**shpit**eler] (1845–1924) Poet and novelist, born in Liestal, Switzerland. He studied at Basel, Zürich, and Heidelberg, and became a tutor in Russia, and a teacher and journalist in Switzerland. *Der Olympische Frühling* (1900–5, The Olympic Spring) is his great mythological epic, for which he was awarded the Nobel Prize for Literature in 1919. His most mature work is *Prometheus der Dulder* (1924, Prometheus the Long-suffering). As well as poetry, he wrote tales, essays, and reminiscences.

Spitz, Mark (Andrew) (1950–) Swimmer, born in Modesto, CA. He trained at the Santa Clara Swim Club, and studied at Indiana University (1972). He won two gold medals at the Mexico City Olympic Games (1968) in team events. His outstanding achievement came at the Munich Olympic Games (1972), when he became the first athlete to win seven gold medals at one Games, four of which were for individual events. He turned professional in 1972, and also appeared in several films.

Spitzer, Lyman, Jr (1914–97) Astrophysicist, born in Toledo, OH. He studied at Yale and Princeton, and became professor of astronomy at Princeton (1947–79). His interest in energy generation in stars led to his early attempt to achieve controlled thermonuclear fusion, for which he devised a method of containing a plasma in a magnetic field; the principle continues to form part of experimentation in this area.

Spock, Benjamin (McLane), popular name **Dr Spock** (1903–) Paediatrician, born in New Haven, CT. He studied at Yale (where he became a star oarsman and rowed in the 1924 Olympics) and Columbia University. He qualified as a doctor, having trained in both paediatrics and psychiatry, and started a practice in Manhattan in 1933. His book, *The Common Sense Book of Baby and Child Care* (1946), urging parents to adopt a more flexible and understanding attitude to child-care, made his name a household word, and sold more than 30 million copies (6th edn as *Dr Spock's Baby and Child Care*, 1992). He resigned from his psychiatry and child development work at Western Reserve, Cleveland, OH (1955–67), to devote himself to pacifism, and in 1994 published *A Better World for Our Children*.

Spode, Josiah [spohd] (1755–1827) Potter, born in Stoke-on-Trent, Staffordshire, C England, UK. After working as a china retailer in London, he inherited the pottery founded c.1770 by his father, **Josiah Spode** (1733–97). The business flourished under his direction, and was renowned for transfer-printed earthenware, stoneware, and superbly decorated bone-china. In 1806 he was appointed potter to the Prince of Wales. In 1833 the factory was acquired by William Taylor Copeland and Thomas Garrett, and in c.1845 it introduced Parian porcelain figures, which resembled marble. >> Copeland

Spoerli, Heinz [**sper**lee] (1941–) Dancer, choreographer, and ballet director, born in Basel, Switzerland. He studied at the School of American Ballet and the London Dance Centre, then joined Basel Ballet (1960–3), Cologne Ballet (1963–6), Royal Winnipeg Ballet (1966–7), Les Grands Ballets Canadiens (1967–71), and Geneva Ballet (1971–3). As director of Basel Ballet from 1973, he improved what was strictly a provincial ballet company attached to the state opera into one of the best of Europe's smaller dance ensembles.

Spofforth, Frederick Robert, nickname **the Demon** (1853–1926) Cricketer, born in Sydney, New South Wales, Australia. Reputed the greatest bowler in the history of the game, in 1878 he took 11 wickets for 20 runs against the MCC, and during 1884 took 218 wickets in first-class cricket, with a bowling average of 12·53.

Spohr, Louis [shpohr], originally **Ludwig Spohr** (1784–1859) Composer, violinist, and conductor, born in Brunswick,

Germany. Largely self-taught, he became court conductor at Kassel (1822–57), and is remembered chiefly as a composer for the violin, for which he wrote 17 concertos. He also composed nine symphonies, 11 operas, and other choral and chamber works.

Spontini, Gasparo (Luigi Pacifico) [sponteenee] (1774–1851) Composer, born in Maiolati, Italy. He studied at the Conservatorio de Turchini in Naples, and his first opera *Li puntigli delle donne* (Women's Points of Honour) was well-received in Rome in 1796. He continued with comic operas, then in 1803 settled in Paris, where his major work, the opera *La Vestale* (1807, The Vestal Virgin) was greeted with enthusiasm. In 1812 he was appointed by Frederick William III of Prussia as director of music at Berlin, where he stayed until the king's death in 1840.

Spooner, William Archibald (1844–1930) Anglican clergyman and educationist, dean (1876–89) and warden (1903–24) of New College, Oxford. As an albino he suffered all his life from weak eyesight, but surmounted his disabilities with heroism, and earned a reputation for kindness. His name is associated with a nervous tendency to transpose initial letters or half-syllables in speech, the *spoonerism* (eg 'a half-warmed fish' for 'a half-formed wish').

Spottiswoode, William (1825–83) Mathematician, physicist, and publisher, born in London, England, UK. He studied at Oxford, where he lectured in mathematics, and in 1846 succeeded his father as head of the printing house of Eyre & Spottiswoode. He did original work in polarization of light and electrical discharge in rarefied gases, and wrote a mathematical treatise on determinants.

Sprague, Frank (Julian) (1857–1934) Electrical engineer and inventor, born in Milford, CT. A US Naval Academy graduate, he served in the US navy, then worked for a year with Edison before setting up the Sprague Electric Railway and Motor Co. He developed a new type of motor for trams (1887), and by 1890 his company was absorbed by the Edison General Electric Co. In 1895 he perfected a system of control for multiple-unit trains, which he later developed into an automatic train control system. >> Edison

Spring, Dick, popular name of **Richard Spring** (1950–) Irish statesman. He studied at Trinity College Dublin, and was called to the bar in 1975. He became a member of the Dáil in 1981, and quickly rose to be leader of the Labour Party (1981–97) and deputy prime minister (1982–7, 1993–7). He was minister of state in the departments of justice (1981–2), the environment (1982–3), and energy (1983–7), and became well known abroad following his appointment as minister for foreign affairs (1993–7).

Spring, Howard (1889–1965) Novelist, born in Cardiff. He started as an errand boy, became a newspaper reporter and literary critic, and established himself as a writer with his best-selling *Oh Absalom* (1938), renamed *My Son, My Son*. Other novels include *Fame is the Spur* (1940), *Dunkerleys* (1946), *These Lovers Fled Away* (1955), and *Time and the Hour* (1957), as well as three autobiographical works.

Springfield, Dusty, originally **Mary O'Brien** (1939–) Pop singer, born in London, England, UK. She was originally part of The Springfields, a vocal/guitar trio singing folk and country music. Her debut solo single 'I Only Want To Be With You' (1964) was a UK hit, and marked a move towards a Motown-influenced style; it was the first record to be played on BBC's television show 'Top Of The Pops'. Her debut album, *A Girl Called Dusty*, reached number 6 in the charts. Her career declined following a move to the USA in the 1970s, but in 1987 she achieved a successful comeback as guest vocalist on The Pet Shop Boy hit single 'What Have I Done To Deserve This', and a later album, *Reputations* (1990), reached number 18 in the UK music charts. She has acquired something of a cult following, as part of the renewed interest in music of the 1960s.

Springsteen, Bruce (1949–) Rock singer and guitarist, born in Freehold, NJ. In 1973, having travelled with obscure bands such as Doctor Zoom and the Sonic Boom, he signed with Columbia Records and released his first recording amid unprecedented hype, being featured on the front covers of both *Time* and *Newsweek* in the same week. In the event, his ascent to stardom was more gradual, and more merited. In 1976, he released a hit in 'Born to Run', a raucous song, roughly sung, with memorable, streetwise images in the lyric. Other hits with similar virtues followed, and by the mid-1980s he had become the world's most popular white rock star. His albums include *The River* (1980), *Born in the USA* (1985), and *Tunnel of Love* (1987).

Spruance, Raymond (Ames) (1885–1969) US naval officer, born in Baltimore, MD. Trained at the US Naval Academy, he became a specialist in gunnery. He commanded the USS *Mississippi* in 1938, and led Task Force 16 at the decisive Battle of Midway (1942). He played an important part in the planning and execution of massive amphibious operations, supported by carrier-borne and shore-based aircraft, notably as commander of the 5th Fleet (1944–5). He was president of the US Naval War College (1946–8), and US ambassador to the Philippines (1952–5).

Spurgeon, C(harles) H(addon) (1834–92) Baptist preacher, born in Kelvedon, Essex, SE England, UK. In 1854 he became pastor of the New Park Street Chapel, London. He drew such a large congregation with his often humorous sermons that the Metropolitan Tabernacle, seating 6000, was erected for him (1859–61). In 1887 he withdrew from the Baptist Union because of its increasingly liberal attitude. Apart from 50 popular volumes of sermons, he wrote collections of pithy sayings in *John Ploughman's Talk* (1869) and many other works.

Spurr, Josiah (Edward) (1870–1950) Geologist, born in Gloucester, MA. He was mining engineer to the Sultan of Turkey (1901), geologist in the US geological survey (1902), and eventually professor of geology at Rollins College (1930–2). As a result of his work, the age of the Tertiary period has been estimated at 45 to 60 million years. His explorations in Alaska (1896, 1898) were commemorated by the naming of Mt Spurr. He also did considerable research on lunar topography and geology.

Squarcione, Francesco [skwah(r)**choh**nay] (1397–c. 1468) Painter, and founder of the Paduan school, born in Padua, Italy. His work shows the influence of the early Florentine Renaissance style, and his extant works include a Madonna in the Staatliche Museen Preußischer Kulturbesitz, Berlin, and panels and frescoes for the Church of S Francesco in Padua. >> Mantegna

Squier, E(phraim) G(eorge) [**skwiy**er] (1821–88) Archaeologist, born in Bethlehem, NH. A newspaper editor in the 1840s, he surveyed with physician Edwin Hamilton Davis the native American burial mounds and earthworks of the Mississippi Valley, publishing the results in the earliest classic of North American archaeology, *Ancient Monuments of the Mississippi Valley* (1848). He later became a diplomat, recounting his experiences in Nicaragua and Peru in two popular books.

Squire, Sir J(ohn) C(ollings) (1882–1958) Writer, and journalist, born in Plymouth, Devon, SW England, UK. He studied at Cambridge, and became literary editor of the *New Statesman* (1913) and founder editor of the *London Mercury* (1919–34). His work is composed of light verse and parody, as in *Steps to Parnassus* (1913) and *Tricks of the Trade* (1917). He co-wrote the successful play *Berkeley Square*

(1926) with J L Balderston, and his other works include criticisms and short stories. He was knighted in 1933.

Ssu-ma Ch'ien >> **Sima Qian**

Staal, Marguerite Jeanne, baronne de (Baroness), *née* **Cordier**, pseudonym **Marguerite Delaunay** (1684–1750) Writer of memoirs, born in Paris. The daughter of a poor Parisian painter, she chose to use her mother's name, Delaunay. Her devotion to her employer, the Duchesse de Maine, brought her two years in the Bastille, where she had a love affair with the Chevalier de Menil. In 1735 she married the **Baron de Staal**. Her *Mémoires* (1755) describe the world of the regency, and her *Oeuvres complètes* (Complete Works) appeared in 1821.

Stabler, Harold (1872–1945) Designer and craftsman, born at Levens, Cumbria, NW England, UK. Trained as a woodworker, he studied metalwork at Keswick School of Art, and taught there before moving to London in the early 1900s, joining the staff at the Sir John Cass Technical Institute. He was an instructor at the Royal College of Art (1912–26), and served on the first council of the Design and Industrial Association in 1915. With his wife, **Phoebe Stabler**, he designed and produced ceramic figures and groups, decorative and architectural details, enamels, and jewellery. He became a partner in the Poole pottery firm of Carter & Co in 1921, which changed its name to Carter, Stabler & Adams.

Stacpoole, Henry de Vere (1863–1951) Physician and writer, born in Dun Laoghaire (formerly Kingstown), Co Dublin, Ireland. He studied at Malvern College and St George's and St Mary's Hospitals, London, and made several voyages as a ship's doctor. He was the author of many popular novels, including *The Blue Lagoon* (1909), *The Pearl Fishers* (1915), and *Green Coral* (1935). He wrote his autobiography in *Men and Mice* (1942 and 1945).

Staël, Madame de [stahl], popular name of **Anne Louise Germaine Necker, Baroness of Staël-Holstein** (1766–1817) Writer, born in Paris, the daughter of the financier, Jacques Necker. Both before and after the French Revolution, her *salon* became a centre of political discussion. In 1803 she was forced to leave Paris, and visited Weimar, Berlin, and Vienna, returning to France at intervals. She wrote novels, plays, essays, historical and critical works, and political memoirs, becoming known with her *Lettres* (1788, Letters) on Rousseau, and achieving European fame with her romantic novel, *Corinne* (1807). Her major work, *De L'Allemagne* (On Germany), was published in London in 1813. >> Necker

Staël, Nicolas de [stahl] (1914–55) Painter, born in St Petersburg, Russia. He studied in Brussels, travelled in Spain and Italy, and worked in Paris. His paintings were mainly abstract, and he made inspired use of rectangular patches of colour. His later pictures were more representational and in subdued colours.

Stafford, Grace >> **Lantz, Walter**

Stafford, Jean (1915–79) Short-story writer and novelist, born in Covina, CA. She studied at Colorado University, worked on the *Southern Review*, and taught at Flushing College. *Boston Adventure*, her first novel, was published in 1944 to great praise; *The Mountain Lion*, her second, appeared in 1947. She taught throughout the 1960s and published short stories, children's books, and an interview with the mother of Lee Harvey Oswald, *A Mother in History* (1966). One of America's most admired short-story writers, her *Collected Stories* appeared in 1969, and won a Pulitzer Prize. >> Oswald, Lee Harvey

Stafford-Clark, Max (1941–) Theatre director, born in Cambridge, Cambridgeshire, EC England, UK. He began his career as associate director of the Traverse Theatre, Edinburgh, in 1966, becoming artistic director there

(1968–70). He then became director of the Traverse Theatre Workshop Company (1970–4), when he co-founded the Joint Stock Theatre Company, becoming artistic director in 1993. He was also artistic director of the English Stage Company at the Royal Court Theatre, London (1979–93).

Stagnelius, Erik Johan [stag**neel**ius] (1793–1823) Romantic poet, born on the island of Öland, Sweden. He studied at Uppsala, and became a civil servant in Stockholm. Little is known of his life, but his works show that he was constantly torn between idealism and eroticism. They include the epic *Vladimir den Store* (1817, Vladimir the Great), plays such as *Martyrerna* (1821, The Martyrs), and lyric poetry, much of it found in *Liljan i Saron* (1821, Lilies in Sharon). His works were collected posthumously, when he became the most influential of Swedish Romantics.

Stahl, Franklin >> **Meselson, Matthew**

Stahl, Georg Ernst [shtahl] (1660–1734) Physician and chemist, born in Ansbach, Germany. He became professor of medicine at Halle (1694), and personal physician (1714) to the King of Prussia. He expounded the phlogiston theory of combustion, and believed that animism played a part in the phenomenon of living organisms.

Ståhlberg, Kaarlo Juho [**stawl**berg] (1865–1952) Lawyer, politician, and first president of Finland (1919–25), born in Suomussalmi, Finland. Professor of law at Helsinki (1908–18), and a member of the Finnish Diet (1908–17), he drafted the Finnish constitution of 1919. >> RR1049

Stahr, Adolf >> **Lewald, Fanny**

Stainer, Sir John (1840–1901) Composer, born in London, England, UK. At 16 he was organist at St Michael's College, Tenbury, then served as organist at St Paul's (1872–88). He founded the Musical Association (1874), was knighted in 1888, and became professor of music at Oxford (1889–1901). He wrote cantatas and church music, notably *The Crucifixion* (1887).

Stakhanov, Alexey Grigorievich [sta**khahn**of] (1906–77) Coalminer, and legendary worker, from Sergo (renamed Stakhanov in 1978), Ukraine. In 1935 he started an incentive scheme for exceptional output and efficiency by individual steel workers, coalminers, and others. Such prize workers were called *Stakhanovites*.

Stalin, Joseph see panel on p. 883

Stallone, Sylvester [sta**lohn**] (1946–) Film actor, director, and writer, born in New York City. He studied drama at the University of Miami, and suddenly became known through the success of his first film *Rocky* (1976, 2 Oscars), which he also wrote. Later films established him as an action-film hero, notably the *Rocky* sequels (1979, 1982, 1985, 1990), *First Blood* (1981), *Rambo* and its sequels (1985, 1988), whose title added a word to the language, and *Cliffhanger* (1992). Other films include *Assassins* (1995), *Judge Dredd* (1995), *Daylight* (1996), and *The Hunter* (1997). He wrote and directed the Rocky sequels, *Paradise Alley* (1978), and *Staying Alive* (1983, which he also produced), and has written the screenplays for several of his other films.

Stamitz, Carl (Philipp) [**shtam**its] (1745–1801) Composer and violinist, born in Mannheim, Germany. He studied under his father, and was a travelling instrumentalist in Paris, London, St Petersburg, Prague, and Nuremberg. In 1794 he became conductor of the orchestra at Jena. He wrote 80 symphonies, one of which was for a double orchestra, and concertos for violin, viola, cello, flute, oboe, clarinet, and harpsichord. >> Stamitz, Johann

Stamitz, Johann (Wenzel Anton) [**shtam**its] (1717–57) Violinist and composer, born in Havlíčkův Brod, Czech Republic. He became concert master at the Mannheim court in 1745, where he developed sonata form, and trained the orchestra to a level of perfection unrivalled in

JOSEPH STALIN (1879–1953)

Stalin (an adopted name meaning 'man of steel') was born Iosif Vissarionovich Dzhugashvili at Gori, Georgia, the son of a cobbler, Vissarion Ivanovich Dzhugashvili, a drunkard who beat him badly and frequently. He left the family to work in Tbilisi when Joseph was young. His mother, Ekaterina Gheladze, supported herself and her son (her other three children died young and Joseph was effectively an only child) by taking in washing. She managed, despite great hardship, to send Joseph to school and then on to Tiflis Orthodox Theological Seminary in Tbilisi, hoping he would become a priest. However, he was expelled from there in 1899, officially for not attending an exam, but more probably for propagating Marxism. Joining a Georgian Social Democratic organization (1898), he became active in the revolutionary underground, and was seven times arrested, repeatedly imprisoned, and twice exiled to Siberia between 1902–13. During those years he changed his name, and became more closely identified with revolutionary Marxism. He escaped many times from captivity. Also at this time his intimacy with Lenin and Bukharin grew, as did his disparagement of Trotsky. In 1912, he was co-opted on to the illegal Bolshevik Central Committee. Later he also edited the new Bolshevik paper, *Pravda* (Truth).

As a leading Bolshevik, he played an active role in the October Revolution (1917). He became People's Commissar for Nationalities in the first Soviet government, and a member of the Communist Party Politburo, although his activities throughout the counter-revolution and the war with Poland were confined to organizing a Red 'terror' in Tsaritsin (later renamed Stalingrad). With his appointment as General Secretary to the Party Central Committee in 1922, a post he held until his death, he began to build up the power that would ensure his control of the situation after Lenin's death (1924). He also occupied other key positions which enabled him to build up enormous personal power in the Party and government apparatus. He pursued a policy of building 'socialism in one country', and gradually isolated and disgraced his political rivals, notably Trotsky.

His reorganization of the Soviet's resources (1928), with its successive five-year plans, suffered many industrial setbacks. He encountered stubborn resistance in the field of agriculture, where the Kulaks, the peasant proprietors, steadfastly refused to accept his principle of 'collectivization', or forced industrialization of the economy. The measures taken by the dictator to discipline those who opposed his will involved the death by execution or famine of up to 10 million peasants (1932–3). Between 1934 and 1938 he inaugurated a massive purge of the Party, government, armed forces, and intelligentsia, in which millions of so-called 'enemies of the people' were imprisoned, exiled, or shot.

Red Army forces and material went to the support of the Spanish Communist government in 1936, although Stalin was careful not to commit himself too deeply. After the Munich crisis, he guilefully protracted Franco-British negotiations for Russian support in the event of war, until they ended in Stalin signing the Non-Aggression Pact with Hitler (1939), which bought the Soviet Union two years' respite from involvement in World War 2.

After the German invasion (1941), the USSR became a member of the Grand Alliance, and Stalin, as war leader, assumed the title of *generalissimo*. He took part in the conferences of Teheran, Yalta, and Potsdam, which resulted in Soviet military and political control over the liberated countries of post-war E and C Europe. From 1945 until his death he resumed his repressive measures at home, and conducted foreign policies which contributed to the Cold War between the Soviet Union and the West.

Stalin had little interest in family life, although he married twice. His first wife (**Ekaterina Svanidze**, married c.1904) died three years after their marriage, and left a son, **Jacob**, whom Stalin despised. His second wife (**Nadezhda Alliluyeva**, married 1919) attempted to moderate his politics, but she died by suicide, leaving a daughter, **Svetlana**, and an alcoholic son, **Vasily**. Increasingly paranoid, Stalin himself died suddenly, in somewhat mysterious circumstances, after announcing his intention of arresting Jewish doctors in the Kremlin. The cause of death announced was brain haemorrhage.

Stalin was posthumously denounced by Khrushchev at the 20th Party Congress (1956) for crimes against the Party, and for building a 'cult of personality'. In 1961 his body was removed from the Lenin Mausoleum, where it had been displayed since his death, and buried near the Kremlin. Under Gorbachev many of Stalin's victims were rehabilitated, and the whole phenomenon of 'Stalinism' officially condemned by the authorities.
>> Bukharin; Khrushchev; Lenin; Trotsky

Europe. His works include 74 symphonies, several concertos, chamber music, and a Mass. He founded a school of symphonists which had a profound influence on Mozart. >> Stamitz, Carl

Stamp, Sir (Lawrence) Dudley (1898–1966) Geographer, born in London, England, UK. He studied at King's College, London, did fieldwork in Burma, and became professor of geology and geography at Rangoon in 1923. He became reader at the London School of Economics in 1926, and later professor of geography there (1945–58). He founded and worked on the British Land Utilization Survey until after World War 2, and both during and after the War was adviser to the government on many land-related topics.

Stamp (of Shortlands), Josiah Charles Stamp, Baron (1880–1941) Economist, born in London, England, UK. He served on the Dawes Committee on German reparations, was chairman of the London, Midland & Scottish Railway, and director of Nobel Industries, and on the outbreak of World War 2 was made economic adviser to the government. An expert on taxation, he wrote on this and other financial subjects. He was killed in an air-raid. >> Dawes, Charles G

Stamp, Terence (1939–) Film actor, born in London, England, UK. He made his film debut as the martyred hero of *Billy Budd* (1962, Oscar nomination), and went on to appear in several major productions, such as *The Collector* (1965) and *Far From the Madding Crowd* (1967), before withdrawing in disillusion from Hollywood in 1969 and going to live in England. He returned to the screen as the indomitable Zod in *Superman: The Movie* (1978), later films including *Company of Wolves* (1985), *Wall Street* (1987), *The Real McCoy* (1993), and *The Adventures of Priscilla, Queen of the*

Desert (1994). He made his directorial debut with *Stranger In the House* (1992), and he has also written an autobiography, *Coming Attractions* (1988).

Standish, Myles (c. 1584–1656) Colonist, probably born in Ormskirk, Lancashire, NW England, UK. After serving in Holland, he sailed with the *Mayflower* in 1620, and became military head of the first American settlement at Plymouth, and treasurer of the colony (1644–9).

Stanford, Sir Charles (Villiers) (1852–1924) Composer, born in Dublin. He studied at Cambridge, Leipzig, and Berlin, and became organist at Trinity College (1872–93), professor in the Royal College of Music (1883), and professor of music at Cambridge (1887). He wrote several major choral works, six operas, seven symphonies, and a great deal of chamber music, songs, and English Church music. He was knighted in 1901.

Stanford, (Amasa) Leland (1824–93) Railway magnate, born in Watervliet, NY. In 1856 he settled in San Francisco, became president of the Central Pacific Co, and superintended the construction of the line. He was Governor of California (1861–3) and a US senator (from 1885). In memory of their only son, he and his wife founded and endowed Leland Stanford Junior University (now Stanford University) at Palo Alto in 1891.

Stanhope, Charles Stanhope, 3rd Earl (1753–1816) British politician and scientist, born in London, England, UK. He studied at Geneva, married Lady Hester Pitt, sister of William Pitt the Younger, in 1774, and became an MP in 1780. He broke with Pitt over the French Revolution, and advocated peace with Napoleon, becoming a 'minority of one'. As a scientist he invented a microscope lens that bears his name, two calculating machines, the first hand-operated iron printing press, and a process of stereotyping adopted in 1805 by the Clarendon Press in Oxford. He also experimented with electricity, and wrote *Principles of Electricity* (1779). >> Pitt, William (the Younger); Stanhope, Hester Lucy

Stanhope, Lady Hester Lucy (1776–1839) British traveller, the eldest daughter of Charles, 3rd Earl Stanhope. In 1803, until his death in 1806, she stayed with her uncle, William Pitt, as mistress of his household. On Pitt's death the king gave her a pension, but she missed the excitement of public life. After the deaths in 1809 of her brother and Sir John Moore, whom she loved, she left England (1810), and in 1814 settled on Mt Lebanon. She adopted Eastern manners, dabbled in politics, and became a figurehead of the mountain community. >> Moore, Sir John; Stanhope, Charles

Stanhope, James Stanhope, 1st Earl [stanuhp] (1675–1721) British soldier and statesman, born in Paris. He entered parliament as a Whig in 1701, and commanded in Spain during the War of the Spanish Succession (1701–13). He was secretary of state for foreign affairs under George I, and became his chief minister in 1717.

Stanhope, Philip Dormer >> **Chesterfield, 4th Earl of**

Stanier, Sir William Arthur (1876–1965) Mechanical engineer, born in Swindon, Wiltshire, S England, UK. He began as an apprentice at the Great Western Railway works there in 1892, and ended his railway career as chief mechanical engineer of the London, Midland & Scottish Railway (1932–42). During that time he brought out many successful locomotive designs, including in 1937 the 4-6-2 'Coronation' class, at first streamlined and later in conventional form with distinctive tapered boilers.

Stanislavsky [stanislavskee], originally **Konstantin Sergeyevich Alexeyev** (1863–1938) Actor, theatre director, and teacher, born in Moscow. As a talented amateur actor, he co-founded the Moscow Society of Art and Literature (1888), and in 1898 helped to found the Moscow Arts

Theatre. His work with this influential company, and his teaching on acting, proved to be a major contribution to 20th-c theatre. His system remains the basis of much Western actor-training and practice. >> Nemirovich-Danchenko; Strasberg

Stanisław I Leszczyński [stanislav leshinskee] (1677–1766) King of Poland (1704–9, 1733–5), born in Lwow, Ukraine. After his election in 1704, he was driven out by Peter the Great, under the influence of Charles XII of Sweden. Re-elected in 1733, he lost the War of the Polish Succession, and formally abdicated in 1736, receiving the Duchies of Lorraine and Bar. >> Charles XII; Peter I (of Russia); RR1082

Stanisław II Poniatowski [stanislav, ponyatofskee] (1732–98) Last king of Poland (1764–95), born in Wolczyn, Poland. He travelled to St Petersburg in 1757, and became a favourite of the future empress, Catherine II. Through her influence he was elected king, but was unable to stop the partitions of Poland (1772, 1793). Despite the rebellion of Kosciusko, the country was partitioned again in 1795, and he abdicated. >> Catherine II; Kosciusko; RR1082

Stanley, Edward Geoffrey Smith >> **Derby, 14th Earl of**

Stanley, Sir Henry Morton, originally **John Rowlands** (1841–1904) Explorer and journalist, born in Denbigh, Denbighshire. Abandoned as a child in a workhouse, in 1859 he went as cabin boy to New Orleans, where he was adopted by a merchant who bestowed his own name on the young man. In 1867 he joined the *New York Herald*, and as its special correspondent he travelled to Abyssinia and Spain. Instructed to 'find Livingstone' in Africa (1869), he left Zanzibar for Tanganyika (1871) and encountered Livingstone at Ujiji. In 1874 Stanley led a second expedition which explored L Tanganyika, and traced the Congo to the sea. On a third expedition (1879), he founded the Congo Free State, and a further expedition went to the aid of Emin Pasha in the Sudan (1887–9). He became a US citizen in 1885, but returned to Britain (1890), re-naturalized in 1892, and became an MP (1895–1900). He was knighted in 1899. >> Emin Pasha; Livingstone

Stanley, John (1713–86) Composer, born in London, England, UK. Blinded in an accident at two, his musical talent was such that he became organist at All Hallows, Bread Street, at the age of 11. Later he held posts at St Andrew's, Holborn, and at the Inner Temple. His compositions, which include the oratorios *Zimri* and *The Fall of Egypt*, cantatas, organ voluntaries, concerti grossi, and instrumental sonatas, have won increasing recognition, and today he is regarded as one of the greatest of 18th-c English composers.

Stanley, Wendell (Meredith) (1904–71) Biochemist, born in Ridgeville, IN. He studied at Illinois University, joining the Rockefeller Insitute at Princeton in 1931, where he did important work on the chemical nature of viruses. He isolated and crystallized the tobacco mosaic virus, and worked on sterols and stereo-isomerism. He later became professor of molecular biology and of biochemistry at California, Berkeley (1948–71). He shared the 1946 Nobel Prize for Chemistry. >> Pirie, Norman Wingate; RR1123

Stanley, William (1858–1916) Electrical engineer, born in New York City. After working for Maxim, he set up on his own and invented the transformer (1885). His work also included a long-range transmission system for alternating current. >> Maxim

Stansfield, Grace >> **Fields, Dame Gracie**

Stansgate (of Stansgate), William Wedgwood Benn, 1st Viscount (1877–1960) British statesman. He was a Liberal MP (1906–27), then joined the Labour Party, and was elected for North Aberdeen (1928). He served as secretary for India (1929–31) and secretary for air (1945–6). He was created a viscount in 1941. >> Benn, Anthony Wedgwood

Stanton, Edwin (McMasters) (1814–69) Lawyer and public official, born in Steubenville, OH. A lawyer who pioneered the temporary insanity defence, he served as attorney general under President Buchanan (1860–1) and (although a Democrat) secretary of war (1862–68) under Presidents Lincoln and Johnson. Although he greatly exceeded his authority both during and after the Civil War, he is credited with establishing effective civilian control of the armed forces. Disagreements with Johnson led to his expulsion from the Cabinet, which became the immediate provocation for Johnson's impeachment. President Grant appointed him to the Supreme Court in 1869, but he died before joining the Court. >> Johnson, Andrew

Stanton, Elizabeth, *née* **Cady** (1815–1902) Social reformer and women's suffrage leader, born in Johnstown, NY. At her wedding in 1840 she insisted on dropping the word 'obey' from the marriage vows. In 1848, with Lucretia Mott, she organized the first women's rights convention at Seneca Falls, NY, which launched the women's suffrage movement. With Susan B Anthony she founded the National Woman Suffrage Movement in 1869. >> Anthony, Susan B; Mott, Lucretia

Stanton, Harry Dean (1926–) Film actor, born in West Irvine, KY. After serving in the navy, he studied at the University of Kentucky and the Pasadena Playhouse. A solid supporting actor, he appeared in numerous feature films, many of them Westerns, before starring in *Paris, Texas* (1984). Later films include *The Last Temptation of Christ* (1988), *Hostages* (1992), and *Never Talk To Strangers* (1995).

Stanwyck, Barbara, originally **Ruby Stevens** (1907–90) Actress, born in New York City. A working girl from the age of 13, she became a dancer, appearing in the *Ziegfeld Follies of 1923*, and made her stage debut in 1926 and her film debut in 1927. Established as a major star in the 1930s, she is best remembered for her portrayal of pioneering women in such Westerns as *Annie Oakley* (1935) and *Union Pacific* (1939). Active in radio and television, she enjoyed a long-running series, *The Big Valley* (1965–9). She received a special Academy Award in 1982.

Stapleton, Maureen (1925–) Actress, born in New York City. A major interpreter of the plays of Tennessee Williams, her role as Serafina in *The Rose Tattoo* (1951) brought her great acclaim. She followed with Flora in *Twenty-Seven Wagons Full of Cotton* (1955), Lady Torrance in *Orpheus Descending* (1957), and the turbulent Amanda Wingfield in a revival of *The Glass Menagerie* in 1965. Acclaimed as one of the great US stage actresses, she has also appeared in a number of films.

Stapleton, Ruth, *née* **Carter** (1929–83) Evangelist and faith healer, born in Plains, GA, the younger sister of President Jimmy Carter. She co-operated with other Christians, including Roman Catholics, and used her graduate training in psychology in a remarkable ministry which stressed the necessity for inner healing. In the 1976 presidential campaign she addressed the National Press Club in Washington, DC, largely on her brother's behalf – reportedly the first time that it had listened to a woman preacher. >> Carter, Jimmy

Stark, Dame Freya (Madeline) (1893–1993) Writer and traveller, born in Paris. She studied at London University, worked on the *Baghdad Times*, and mapped the *Valley of the Assassins* in Luristan (published 1934). During World War 2 she worked for the ministry of information in Aden and Cairo, and founded the Brotherhood of Freedom. She trav-

elled extensively, financed by her writings, which include *The Southern Gates of Arabia* (1938), *Dust in the Lion's Paw* (1961), and *The Journey's Echo* (1963).

Stark, Harold (Raynsford) (1880–1972) US naval officer, born in Wilkes-Barre, PA. Trained at the US Naval Academy, he served in a destroyer flotilla (1914–15). As chief of naval operations (1939–42), he was relieved after Pearl Harbor (1942), and became commander of US Naval Forces Europe (1942–3) with headquarters in London, where he made a great contribution to the success of Allied Operations in the European theatre.

Stark, Johannes [shtah(r)k] (1874–1957) Physicist, born in Schickenhof, Germany. He studied at Munich, and became professor at Griefswald and Würzburg. In 1913 he discovered the effect, named after him, concerning the splitting of spectrum lines by subjecting the light source to a strong electrostatic field. He was awarded the Nobel Prize for Physics in 1919. A supporter of Hitler, in 1947 he was sentenced to four years in a labour camp by a denazification group.

Stark, John (1782–1822) American Revolutionary soldier, born in Londonderry, NH. He saw service in the French and Indian War (1754–9), and in the American War of Independence (1775–83) served at Bunker Hill (1775) and won a victory at Bennington (1777). He was a member of the court martial which condemned John André. >> André

Starkie, Enid Mary (1897–1970) Critic of French literature, born in Killiney, Co Dublin, Ireland. She studied at Dublin, Oxford, and the Sorbonne, and taught modern languages at Exeter and Oxford. She wrote perceptively on Baudelaire (1933) and Gide (1954), played a major part in establishing the poetic reputation of Arthur Rimbaud (1938), and published two major volumes on Flaubert (1967, 1971). In 1951 she campaigned successfully to have the quinquennially-elected professor of poetry at Oxford be a poet rather than a critic, whereby C S Lewis was defeated by C Day Lewis.

Starley, James (1830–81) Inventor, born in Albourne, West Sussex, S England, UK. He worked in a factory in Coventry, manufacturing sewing-machines and bicycles, and invented a new, improved sewing-machine and the 'Coventry' tricycle. He also invented the 'Ariel' geared bicycle in 1871, which became a standard bicycle design.

Starling, Ernest Henry (1866–1927) Physiologist, born in London, England, UK. He was lecturer in physiology at Guy's Hospital and later professor at University College (1899–1923). He introduced the term *hormones* for the internal secretions of the ductless glands and, with Sir William Bayliss, discovered the intestinal hormone *secretin* (1902). His studies of cardiovascular physiology did much to elucidate the physiology of the blood circulation. >> Bayliss

Starr, (Myra) Belle, *née* **Shirley** (1848–89) Bandit queen, born at or near Carthage, MO. Her brothers were killed while fighting with Quantrill's Raiders in the Civil War and in gunfights. She was romantically linked with Thomas Coleman Younger, James H Reed, Sam Starr, a Cherokee, and Jim July, also a Cherokee. Said to be 'the leader of a band of horse thieves', she was convicted once in 1883 by 'Hanging Judge' Parker. On other ocassions, she defended herself and her companions with great legal skill. She was shot down by an unknown assassin, and immortalized in popular literature. >> Quantrill; Younger, Cole

Starr, Ringo, originally **Richard Starkey** (1940–) Drummer, singer, songwriter, and actor, born in Liverpool, Merseyside, NW England, UK. He replaced Pete Best as the Beatles' drummer, and following the group's break-up in 1970 embarked on a solo career with the albums *Sentimental Journey* (1970), *Beaucoups of Blues* (1971), and *Ringo* (1973). He continued to record into the 1980s, with albums such as *Stop and Smell the Roses* (1981), then built up his 'All Starrs' band, which toured in 1989, 1992, 1995, and 1997. His wry, deadpan humour was a major feature of the Beatles' films, and he continued as an actor as early as 1968, in *Candy*, following this with *The Magic Christian* (1969). Later films include *Blindman* (1972), *That'll Be The Day* (1973), *Lisztomania* (1975), *Stardust* (1975), and *Alice Through the Looking Glass* (1985), and in 1973 he produced the horror spoof, *Son of Dracula*. He later became more involved with general show-business concerns, but joined the remaining Beatles in producing their anthology in 1995. >> Beatles, The

Stassen, Harold (Edward) (1907–) US state governor, born in Dakota City, MN. He studied at Minnesota, then practised law in St Paul, MN, serving as county attorney (1930–8). He became Governor of Minnesota (1939–43), and served in World War 2 as an aide to Admiral Halsey (1943–5). Highly regarded as a young liberal Republican, he lost the 1948 presidential nomination to Thomas Dewey, so settled for becoming president of the University of Pennsylvania (1948–53). He directed disarmament studies for Eisenhower (1955–58), then practised law in Philadelphia. >> Dewey, Thomas; Eisenhower; Halsey

Statham, (John) Brian [staythm] (1930–) Cricketer, born in Gorton, Greater Manchester, NW England, UK. A fast bowler, he took 252 Test wickets for England in 70 appearances, and 2260 in his first-class career. For almost 20 years he was a Lancashire stalwart, and took 100 wickets in a season on 13 occasions. >> RR1150

Statius [stayshius], in full **Publius Papinius Statius** (c.45–96) Epic and lyric poet, born in Naples, Italy. He won a poetry prize in Naples, and went to Rome, where he flourished as a court poet and a brilliant improviser until 94, when he retired to Naples. His major work was the *Thebaïd*, an epic in 12 books on the struggle between the brothers Eteocles and Polynices of Thebes. Of another epic, the *Achilleïs*, only a fragment remains. His collection of occasional poems, *Silvae*, describes the life style of the fashionable classes.

Statler, Ellsworth (Milton) (1863–1928) Hotel owner, born in Somerset Co, PA. He began work as a hotel bellboy, studied hotel management, and advanced to restaurant owner. He moved to Buffalo in 1896, and when the town was chosen to host the Pan-American Exposition (1901) he seized the opportunity to build his first hotel. From its success he built the Statler Hotel (1904) and established the Statler chain. His hotels gained a reputation for comfort and convenience, his personal slogan being 'The customer is always right'.

Staudinger, Hermann [shtowdinger] (1881–1965) Chemist, born in Worms, Germany. He studied at Halle, and became professor at Freiburg (1926–40), then research director (1940–51). He was awarded the Nobel Prize for Chemistry in 1953 for his research in macro-molecular chemistry, which contributed to the development of plastics.

Stauffenberg, Claus, Graf von (Count of) [shtowfnberg] (1907–44) German soldier, born in Jettingen, Germany. Initially welcoming the advent to power of Hitler, he quickly became alienated by Nazi brutality. He was a colonel on the German general staff in 1944, and placed the bomb in the unsuccessful attempt to assassinate Hitler at Rastenburg (20 Jul 1944). He was shot next day. >> Hitler; Rommel

Stavisky, (Serge) Alexandre [staviskee] (?1886–1934) Swindler, born in Kiev, Ukraine. He went to Paris in 1900 and was naturalized in 1914. He floated a series of fraudulent companies, and in 1933 was discovered to be handling bonds to the value of more than 500 million francs on behalf of the municipal pawnshop in Bayonne. He fled to Chamonix, and probably committed suicide; but in the meantime the affair had revealed widespread corruption in the government, business, the judiciary, and the police, and precipitated the fall (1934) of the prime minister, Camille Chautemps.

Stead, Christina Ellen (1902–83) Novelist, born in Sydney, New South Wales, Australia. She trained as a teacher, and travelled widely, living in France, the USA, and London. In the 1940s she was a screenwriter for MGM in Hollywood, and in 1952 she married the novelist **William Blake**. Her first collection of short stories, *The Salzburg Tales*, was published in 1934, followed in the same year by the novel *Seven Poor Men of Sydney*. Her best-known work, *The Man Who Loved Children* (1940, revised 1965), deals with the conflict between love and independence within marriage.

Stebbins, George (Ledyard) (1906–) Botanist, born in Lawrence, NY. He studied biology at Harvard, and spent most of his career at the University of California, Davis (1950–73), where he established the department of genetics. He was the first to apply modern ideas of evolution to botany, as expounded in his *Variation and Evolution in Plants* (1950). From the 1940s he used artificially induced polyploidy to create fertile hybrids, of value both in taxonomy and in economic plant breeding.

Steel (of Aikwood), David (Martin Scott), Lord (1938–) British politician, born in Kirkcaldy, Fife, E Scotland, UK. He studied in Kenya and at Edinburgh, and became an MP in 1965. He sponsored a controversial bill to reform the laws on abortion (1966–7), and was active in the anti-apartheid movement. He became Liberal chief whip (1970–5) before succeeding Jeremy Thorpe as Liberal leader (1976–88). In 1981 he led the party into an alliance with the Social Democratic Party, the two parties successfully merging in 1987–8. He was knighted in 1990, and created a life peer in 1997. >> Owen, David; Thorpe, Jeremy

Steele, Sir Richard (1672–1729) Essayist, playwright, and politician, born in Dublin, Ireland. He studied at Oxford, and joined the army, but gave it up to become a writer. He wrote three successful comedies, and in 1707 became editor of the *London Gazette*. He is best known for the satirical, political, and moral essays which formed much of the content of the new periodicals the *Tatler* (1709–11), which he founded, and the *Spectator* (1711–12), which he co-founded with Addison. He supported the House of Hanover, and was rewarded by George I with the appointment of supervisor of Drury Lane Theatre, and a knighthood.

Steele, Tommy, originally **Thomas Hicks** (1936–) Actor, singer, and director, born in London, England, UK. He achieved considerable fame as a pop singer in the 1950s and 1960s, made his stage debut in variety at the Empire Theatre, Sunderland in 1956, and in London at the Dominion Theatre in 1957. He played Tony Lumpkin in Goldsmith's *She Stoops to Conquer* at the Old Vic in 1960. The archetypal Cockney lad, he continued to appear in musicals during the 1960s, most notably in *Half a Sixpence* (1963–4). His films include *The Tommy Steele Story* and *Finian's Rainbow*. He had his own one-man show in London in 1979, and in 1983 starred in and directed a stage adaptation of *Singin' in the Rain* at the London Palladium. Later stage appearances include *What a Show!* (1995).

Steen, Jan (Havickszoon) [stayn] (1626–79) Painter, born in Leyden, The Netherlands. He joined the Leyden guild of painters in 1648, lived in The Hague until 1654, then became a brewer at Delft and an innkeeper at Leyden. His best works were genre pictures of social and domestic scenes depicting the everyday life of ordinary folk, as in 'The Music Lesson' (National Gallery, London).

Steensen, Niels >> **Steno, Nicolaus**

Steenstrup, Johannes Iapetus Smith (1813–97) Zoologist, born in Vang, Norway. Professor of zoology at Copenhagen (1845–85), he identified the animal remains from Ertebolle settlements and shell mounds (1851), thus making the earliest contribution to the discipline of archaeozoology. He has written books covering such subjects as hermaphroditism, alternation of generations, flounders' eyes, and cephalopods.

Steer, Philip Wilson (1860–1942) Painter, born in Birkenhead, Merseyside, NW England, UK. He studied at Paris, and began as an exponent of Impressionism, to which he added a traditionally English touch. A founder of the New English Art Club, he taught at the Slade School of Art, London. He excelled as a figure painter, as shown in 'Self-Portrait, The Music Room' (Tate, London).

Stefan, Josef (1835–93) Physicist, born in St Peter, Austria. He studied at Vienna, where he spent his career. His work in experimental physics was wide-ranging, but his fame rests on his research on thermal radiation, begun in 1879. He found empirically a law describing radiant heat loss from a hot surface (*Stefan's law*), and used it to make the first satisfactory estimate of the Sun's surface temperature. Attempts by others to find a theoretical basis for Stefan's law led to major advances in physics, and eventually to Planck's quantum theory of 1900. >> **Planck**

Stefánsson, Jón (1881–1962) Landscape painter, born in Sauðárkrókur, Iceland. He studied engineering in Copenhagen (1900), but in 1903 decided to devote himself to art. He went to Paris in 1908 and studied under Matisse. One of the founders of modern art in Iceland, he painted landscapes on a grand scale, exploiting colour with great luminosity. >> **Matisse**

Stefánsson, Vilhjalmur (1879–1962) Arctic explorer, born of immigrant Icelandic parents in Arnes, Manitoba, Canada. He studied anthropology and archaeology before going to live among the Eskimo (1906–12). He led the Canadian Arctic Expedition which mapped the Beaufort Sea (1913–18), and later became a consultant on the use of Arctic resources. He wrote several popular books, including *My Life with the Eskimo* (1913) and *The Friendly Arctic* (1921).

Steffens, (Joseph) Lincoln (1866–1936) Journalist, born in San Francisco, CA. He studied at French, German, and American universities, then worked as a reporter on the New York *Evening Post* (1892–8). He became managing editor of *McClure's Magazine* (1902–6), where his revision of an article on city corruption in St Louis resulted in an outstandingly successful series later republished as *The Shame of the Cities* (1904). He followed it with an analysis of corruption and reform at state level (*The Struggle for Self-Government*, 1906), and became associate editor of the *American* and *Everybody's* magazines (1906–11).

Steichen, Edward (Jean) [stiykhn] (1879–1973) Photographer, born in Luxembourg. His family moved to the USA in 1882, and he studied art in Milwaukee (1894–8). He was a member of The Linked Ring in England, and in 1902 helped Alfred Stieglitz to found the American Photo-Secession Group. In World War 1 he served as commander of the photographic division of the US army, and in the 1920s achieved success with his 'New Realism' fashion and portrait photography. He was head of US Naval Film Services during World War 2, and director of photography at the New York Museum of Modern Art (1945–62), organizing the world-famous exhibition *The Family of Man* in 1955. >> **Stieglitz**

Steiger, Rod(ney Stephen) [stiyger] (1925–) Film actor, born in Westhampton, NY. He trained at the Actors' Studio in New York City, emerging as an exponent of the Method, and and made his Broadway debut in 1951 in *Night Music*.

He became known following his first major role, in *On the Waterfront* (1954), and went on to star in a variety of demanding roles. His many other films include *Al Capone* (1958), *Dr Zhivago* (1965), *The Pawnbroker* (1965), *In the Heat of the Night* (1967, Oscar, Golden Globe), *American Gothic* (1988), *The Specialist* (1994), *Mars Attacks!* (1995), and *Incognito* (1997).

Stein, Sir (Mark) Aurel [stiyn] (1862–1943) Archaeologist and explorer, born in Budapest. He held educational and archaeological posts under the Indian government, conducting a series of expeditions in Chinese Turkestan and C Asia, tracing the ancient caravan routes between China and the West (1900–30). His discoveries included the Cave of a Thousand Buddhas near Tan Huang, walled up since the 11th-c. A British subject from 1904, he was knighted in 1912, and became superintendent of the Indian Archaeological Survey (1910–29).

Stein, Charlotte von [shtiyn] *née* **von Schardt** (1742–1827) Writer, born in Eisenach, Germany. Lady-in-waiting at the Weimar court, in 1764 she married **Friedrich von Stein**, the Duke of Saxe-Weimar's Master of the Horse. In 1775, she met Goethe, who fell in love with her. She became the inspiration for his character Natalie in *Wilhelm Meister*, as well as many of his love poems and plays. Her own works include dramas such as *Rino* (1776) and *Dido* (1792). >> **Goethe**

Stein, Chris >> **Blondie**

Stein, Edith [shtiyn], Ger [shtiyn], also known as **Teresa Benedicta of the Cross** (1891–1942) Carmelite nun, philosopher, and spiritual writer, born in Wrocław, Poland (formerly Breslau, Germany). Born into an Orthodox Jewish family, she later renounced her faith (1904). She studied at Göttingen, then joined the philosophy faculty at Freiburg (1916). She converted to Roman Catholicism (1922), and entered the Carmelite Convent at Cologne (1934), where she took her new name. Under threat of Nazi anti-Semitism, she escaped to The Netherlands, but the Gestapo sent her to the Auschwitz concentration camp, where she was executed. The Edith Stein Guild for converts was founded in the USA (1955). She is regarded as a modern martyr, and a campaign for her beatification has been launched.

Stein, Gertrude [shtiyn] (1874–1946) Writer, born in Allegheny, PA. She studied psychology and medicine at Radcliffe College and Johns Hopkins University, but settled in Paris, where she was absorbed into the world of experimental art and letters. Her main works include *Three Lives* (1908), *Tender Buttons* (1914), in which she tried to apply the theories of Cubist art to writing, and her most widely-read book, *The Autobiography of Alice B Toklas* (1933). She was revered as a critic in Paris, and her home became a salon for artists and writers between the two World Wars.

Stein, Jock [steen], popular name of **John Stein** (1922–85) Footballer and manager, born in Burnbank, South Lanarkshire, WC Scotland, UK. His managerial career began with Dunfermline Athletic, which won the Scottish Cup. A short spell followed with Hibernian, then he returned to Glasgow Celtic in 1965, the team winning nine championships in a row, the League Cup on five consecutive occasions, and several Scottish Cups, as well as the European Cup in 1967. He left Celtic in 1978 for a brief period as manager of Leeds United, but returned to Scotland to become national manager. Under him the Scottish side qualified for the World Cup Finals in Spain in 1982 and 1986.

Stein, (Heinrich Friedrich) Karl, Freiherr (Baron) **vom** [shtiyn] (1757–1831) Prussian statesman, born in Nassau, Germany. He studied law at Göttingen, and entered the service of Prussia in 1780, becoming secretary for trade (1804–7). As chief minister (1807–8), he carried out important reforms in the army, economy, and both national and local government. In 1812 he went to St Petersburg, and built up the coalition against Napoleon. He was later adviser to Alexander I (1812–15), then retired to Kappenberg in Westphalia.

Stein, Peter [shtiyn] (1937–) Theatre director, born in Berlin. From his very first production in 1967, he became established as a leading avant-garde director in Germany. Since 1970, he has been responsible for a series of collective creations at the Berlin Schaubuhne, where over a long rehearsal period the political and social context of a play is woven into an ensemble presentation.

Stein, William H(oward) [stiyn] (1911–80) Biochemist, born in New York City. He studied at Harvard and Columbia universities, and spent his career at the Rockefeller Institute, New York City. There, with Stanford Moore, he developed a method for finding the number of amino acid residues in a protein molecule, and they shared the 1972 Nobel Prize for Chemistry. >> Moore, Stanford; RR1123

Steinbeck, John (Ernst) [stiyn]bek] (1902–68) Novelist, born in Salinas, CA. He studied marine biology at Stanford, but did not take a degree, and worked at various jobs before deciding to become a writer. His first successful novel was *Tortilla Flat* (1935), but his best-known work and the high point of his career was *The Grapes of Wrath* (1939), a novel about a poor farming family moving in the Depression from Oklahoma to what they hope will be a better life in California; it was made into a classic film by John Ford in 1940. It led to much-needed agricultural reform, and won for Steinbeck the 1940 Pulitzer Prize. His other works include *Of Mice and Men* (1937), *The Moon is Down* (1942), *East of Eden* (1952), and *Winter of our Discontent* (1961). He was awarded the Nobel Prize for Literature in 1962.

Steinberg, Saul [stiyn]berg] (1914–) Graphic artist, born in Ramnicul-Sarat, Rumania. He studied in Bucharest and Italy, then began to submit drawings to American periodicals, notably the *New Yorker*. He left Italy for the Dominican Republic in 1941, and from there moved to New York City. He served in the US Navy during World War 2, then returned to New York and became an influential observer and satirist of modern culture, as seen in 'Manassas, Virginia: Main Street' (1978). His publications include *The Passport* (1954) and *The New World* (1965).

Steinberger, Jack [stiyn]berger] (1921–) Physicist, born in Bad Kissigen, Germany. He fled to the USA in 1935, and studied at Chicago. After carrying out research at Princeton and Berkeley, California, he joined Columbia University (1950–72). He later worked at the European Organization for Nuclear Research (1968–86), then became a professor at the Scuola Normale, Pisa. He shared the 1988 Nobel Prize with Lederman and Melvin Schwartz for their work creating an accelerated beam of neutrinos (1960–2) and for their subsequent discovery that neutrinos exist in two types. >> Lederman

Steinem, Gloria [stiyn]em] (1934–) Feminist and writer, born in Toledo, OH. In the 1960s she emerged as a leading figure in the women's movement, protesting volubly against the Vietnam War and racism. A co-founder of Women's Action Alliance in 1970, she was likewise formative in setting up *Ms* magazine, which brought women's issues to the fore.

Steiner, George [stiyn]er] (1929–) Critic and scholar, born in Paris. He studied there and at Chicago, Harvard, and Oxford universities. He worked at the Institute for Advanced Study at Princeton (1956–8), then taught at Cambridge, where he became a fellow of Churchill College in 1969. He was appointed professor of English and comparative literature at Geneva (1974–94, now emeritus),

and at Oxford (1994–5), where he became a fellow of St Anne's College. One of the leading exponents of comparative literature, his publications include *The Death of Tragedy* (1961), *Language and Silence* (1967), *After Babel* (1975), and *Antigones* (1984). *Real Presences* (1989) challenges the demoralizing consequences of deconstructive thought. Later books include *Proofs and Three Parables* (1992) and *The Deeps of the Sea and Other Fiction* (1996).

Steiner, Jakob [shtiyn]er] (1796–1863) Mathematician, born in Utzenstorf, Switzerland. He had no early schooling, did not learn to read and write until he was 14, then at 18 his extraordinary gift for geometry was discovered. He studied at Heidelberg and Berlin, and became professor at Berlin in 1834. He founded and became the classical authority on modern synthetic (projective) geometry.

Steiner, Max(imilian Raoul Walter) [stiyn]er] (1888–1971) Composer, born in Vienna. He studied at the Imperial Academy in Vienna, and conducted musical comedies in London, Paris, and Berlin. He was invited to New York in 1914 by Florenz Ziegfeld, and worked for a number of impresarios in the Broadway theatre. Invited to Hollywood, he was offered a permanent position at RKO, where he was able to establish the power of music to enhance the dramatic mood and emotions of a production, seen most notably in *King Kong* (1933). Resident at Warner Brothers from 1936, he contributed scores to some of the most enduring screen classics, among them *Gone With the Wind* (1939), *Casablanca* (1942), and *The Treasure of the Sierra Madre* (1948). Nominated on 26 occasions for an Academy Award, he won Oscars for *The Informer* (1935), *Now Voyager* (1942), and *Since You Went Away* (1945). Failing eyesight brought his retirement in 1965. >> Ziegfeld

Steiner, Rudolph [shtiyn]er] (1861–1925) Social philosopher, the founder of anthroposophy, born in Kraljevec, Croatia. He studied science and mathematics, and edited Goethe's scientific papers, before coming temporarily under the spell of the theosophists. In 1912 he propounded his own approach, establishing his first 'school of spiritual science', or *Goetheanum*, in Dornach, Switzerland. His aim was to integrate the psychological and practical dimensions of life into an educational, ecological, and therapeutic basis for spiritual and physical development. Many schools and research institutions arose from his ideas, notably the Rudolf Steiner Schools, focusing on the development of the whole personality of the child. Several are for children with special needs.

Steinitz, William [stiyn]its], originally **Wilhelm Steinitz** (1836–1900) Chess player, born in Prague. Playing from the age of 12, he dropped out of polytechnic at Vienna to devote himself to chess. From 1862 he settled in London as a professional, supplementing his income as chess editor of *The Field*. After emigrating to the USA (1883), he worked as a chess writer and editor, and beat Zukertort in the 1886 match organized to decide the first official championship of the world. He defended his title three times successfully, before losing it in 1894 to Lasker. A nervous breakdown followed, and he died in a New York mental institution. >> Lasker, Emanuel; RR1149

Steinmetz, Charles (Proteus) [stiyn]mets], originally **Karl August Rudolph Steinmetz** (1865–1923) Electrical engineer, born in Wrocław, Poland (formerly Breslau, Germany). He studied at the Technical High School, Berlin. Forced to leave Germany in 1888 for Socialist activities, he emigrated to the USA, where he changed his name. He was consulting engineer to General Electric from 1893, and professor at Union College from 1902. He formulated a law for magnetic hysteresis, developed a simple notation for calculating alternating current circuits, and introduced lightning arresters for high-power transmission lines. He was a lifelong Socialist, promoting equal education for the handicapped, and protection of the environment from industrial waste.

Steinway, Henry (Engelhard) [stiynway], originally **Heinrich Engelhardt Steinweg** (1797–1871) Piano-maker, born in Wolfshagen, Germany. He fought at Waterloo, and in 1835 established a piano factory in Brunswick. In 1850 he transferred the business to the USA, where he introduced many innovations into the instrument, such as a cast-iron frame.

Stella, Frank (Philip) (1936–) Painter, born in Malden, MA. He studied at Phillips Academy and Princeton (1954–8), and his earliest Minimal paintings, symmetrical patterns of black stripes, date from 1959. Using housepainters' techniques to avoid any trace of 'artistic' brushwork, he creates a totally impersonal effect, which has made a significant impression on several younger artists.

Stella, Joseph, originally **Guiseppe Stella** (1877–1946) Painter, born in Muro Lucano, Italy. He emigrated to New York City in 1896, and studied at the Art Students' League (1897), then at the New York School of Art. In Italy he painted in an Impressionist style, and visited Paris in 1911. He returned to New York City in 1913, and painted the first American Futurist pictures, swirling compositions in the manner of Gino Severini, and interpretations of New York scenery, such as 'Brooklyn Bridge' (c.1919).

Steller, Georg Wilhelm [steler], originally **Georg Wilhelm Stöhler** (1709–46) Naturalist and explorer, born in Windsheim, Germany. He studied theology at Wittenburg, then turned to medicine and botany, and joined the Academy of Sciences at St Petersburg. Seconded to the Kamchatka expedition (1737–44) led by Vitus Bering, he travelled across Russia to the E, explored Siberia and Kamchatka, met Bering in Okhotsk, sailed to Alaska, and returned via Bering I, where they were shipwrecked. His best-known work, *De Bestiis Marinis* (Marine Animals), was published posthumously in 1751. *Steller's sea-cow* (now extinct), *Steller's sea lion*, *Steller's jay*, and *Steller's eider* are all named after him. >> Bering

Stendhal [stendahl], pseudonym of **Marie-Henri Beyle** (1783–1842) Writer, born in Grenoble, France. He was a soldier under Napoleon, settled in Paris in 1821, and after the 1830 revolution was appointed consul at Trieste and Civitavecchia. He wrote biographies, and critical works on music, art, and literature, but was best known for his novels, notably *Le Rouge et le noir* (1831, Scarlet and Black) and *La Chartreuse de Parme* (1839, The Charterhouse of Parma). He is also known for his treatise *De l'Amour* (1827, On Love), and for his autobiographical works, especially his *Journal* (1888).

Stengel, Casey, popular name of **Charles Dillon Stengel** (1889–1975) Baseball player and manager, born in Kansas City, MO. As a player (1912–31), he was an outfielder with the Brooklyn Dodgers in the National League, and also had spells with teams in Pittsburgh, Philadelphia, Boston, and New York City. From 1932 as manager, he led the New York Yankees to seven World Series victories between 1949 and 1960, including five in a row (1949–53), then managed the New York Mets (1962–5).

Stenmark, Ingemar (1956–) Skier, born in Tärnaby, Sweden, 100 mi S of the Arctic Circle. One of the greatest slalom/giant slalom racers, he won both events at the 1980 Olympics with a 8 cm/3 in metal plate in his ankle following an accident the previous year. Between 1974 and 1989 he won a record 86 World Cup races, including a record 13 in the 1979 season. Overall champion three times (1976–8), he won 15 slalom/giant slalom titles and five world titles. He retired in 1989, and now lives in Monte Carlo.

Steno, Nicolaus [steenoh], Lat name of **Niels Steensen** (1638–86) Anatomist and geologist, born in Copenhagen. He studied anatomy in Amsterdam, where he discovered the duct of the parotid gland and explained the function of the ovaries. He settled in Florence in 1665, as physician to the duke. Although brought up a strict Lutheran, he then became a Catholic, and in 1677 was made a bishop and apostolic vicar to N Germany. He was the first to explain the structure of the Earth's crust.

Stephen (c. 1090–1154) Last Norman king of England (1135–54), the son of Stephen, Count of Blois, and Adela, the daughter of William the Conqueror. He had sworn to accept Henry I's daughter, Empress Matilda, as queen, but seized the English crown and was recognized as Duke of Normandy on Henry's death in 1135. Though defeated and captured at the Battle of Lincoln (Feb 1141), he was released nine months later after Matilda's supporters had been routed at Winchester. But Matilda strengthened her grip on the West Country; David I of Scotland annexed the N English counties by 1141; and Matilda's husband, Count Geoffrey of Anjou, conquered Normandy by 1144–5. Stephen was also repeatedly challenged by baronial rebellions, and after 18 years of virtually continuous warfare, he was forced in 1153 to accept Matilda's son, the future Henry II, as his lawful successor. His reputation as the classic incompetent king of English mediaeval history is nevertheless undeserved. He was remarkably tenacious in seeking to uphold royal rights, and his war strategy was basically sound. His inability to defend the Norman empire was due largely to the sheer weight of his military burdens, especially the major offensives of the Scots in the N and the Angevins in the S. >> Adela; David I; Henry of Blois; Matilda; Theobald; RR1095

Stephen I, St (c.975–1038) The first king of Hungary (997–1038). He formed Pannonia and Dacia into a regular kingdom, organized Christianity, and introduced many social and economic reforms. He received from the pope the title of 'Apostolic King' and, according to tradition, St Stephen's Crown, now a Hungarian national treasure. He was canonized in 1083. Feast day 16 August. >> RR1057

Stephen, St (1st-c) The first Christian martyr, (*Acts* 6–7). He was one of the seven chosen to manage the finances and alms of the early Church, and was possibly one of the Hellenists. Charged by the Jewish authorities for speaking against the Temple and the Law, he was tried by the Sanhedrin, and stoned to death by the crowds in Jerusalem. Feast day 26 December. >> Jesus Christ

Stephen, Sir Leslie (1832–1904) Scholar and critic, born in London, England, UK. He studied at King's College, London, and Trinity Hall, Cambridge, where he became a fellow in 1864. He was ordained, but left the Church in 1870. He helped to found the *Pall Mall Gazette*, and was editor of the *Cornhill Magazine* (1871–82). He launched the *English Men of Letters* series with a biography of Samuel Johnson (1878). *The History of English Thought in the Eighteenth Century* (1876) is generally regarded as his most important work. He was also the first editor of the *Dictionary of National Biography* (1882–91). Vanessa Bell and Virginia Woolf were among his children. >> Bell, Vanessa; Woolf, Virginia

Stephen, Sir Ninian (Martin) (1923–) Judge, born in England, UK. His schooling was undertaken in Edinburgh, London, and Switzerland, before he moved to Melbourne as a teenager. He studied law at the University of Melbourne, served in World War 2, and became a QC in 1966. He was a justice of the Victoria Supreme Court (1970–2) and the High Court of Australia (1972–82). Appointed Governor-General of Australia in 1982, he retired from the position in 1989, when Prime Minister Bob Hawke made him

Australia's first ambassador for the environment, a non-political role from which he retired in 1991. In 1991 he was asked to chair the ill-fated talks between representatives of Britain, Ireland, and Northern Ireland, and in the same year was part of a Commonwealth of Nations panel on constitutional reform in South Africa. He was knighted in 1972. >> Hawke

Stephens, Alexander H(amilton) (1812–83) US politician, born in Wilkes Co, GA. Admitted to the bar in 1834, he advocated the annexation of Texas in 1838. He sat in Congress 1843–59, defended the Kansas–Nebraska Act (1854), at first opposed secession, but in 1861 became Confederate vice-president. He sat in Congress again (1874–83), and in 1882 was elected Governor of Georgia.

Stephens, James (1825–1901) Irish nationalist, born in Kilkenny, Co Kilkenny, Ireland. A civil engineer, he became an active agent of the Young Ireland Party. After the rising at Ballingarry (1848), he escaped to France. In 1853 he journeyed round Ireland, and founded and led the Irish Republican Brotherhood (Fenians). He started the *Irish People* newspaper (1863) to urge armed rebellion, visited America on fund-raising missions, and was arrested in Dublin in 1865, but escaped. He found his way to New York, was deposed by the Fenians, and with the decline in his political importance was allowed to return to Ireland in 1891.

Stephens, James (1880–1950) Writer, born in Dublin. An orphan in the Dublin slums, he found work as a solicitor's clerk. His first published work was a volume of poems, *Insurrections* (1909), followed by his first novel, *The Charwoman's Daughter* (1912). *The Crock of Gold* (1912), a prose fantasy, made him famous, and he became a full-time writer. His later volumes were *Songs from the Clay* (1914), *The Demi-Gods* (1914), *Reincarnation* (1917), and *Deirdre* (1923).

Stephens, John Lloyd (1805–52) Archaeologist and traveller, born in Shrewsbury, NJ. Trained as a lawyer, he travelled extensively in E and C Europe before embarking with **Frederick Catherwood** (1799–1856) on an extended exploration of Mesoamerica (1839–42). Their work founded the field of Mayan archaeology.

Stephens, Meic [miyk] (1938–) Poet and editor, born in Treforest, Rhondda Cynon Taf, S Wales. He studied at Aberystwyth and Rennes universities. He founded *Poetry Wales* in 1965, compiled *The Oxford Companion to the Literature of Wales* in both Welsh and English, and is the editor of many anthologies and reference books, especially relating to Wales, such as *A Most Peculiar People* (1992) and *Literature in 20th Century Wales: A Select Bibliography* (1995). Other works include *A Dictionary of Literary Quotations* (1990) and the second edition of *The Oxford Illustrated Literary Guide to Great Britain and Ireland* (1992). He became literature director of the Welsh Arts Council in 1967.

Stephenson, George (1781–1848) Railway engineer, born in Wylam, Northumberland, NE England, UK. He worked in a colliery, received a rudimentary education at night school, and in 1812 became engine-wright at Killingworth. There he constructed his first locomotive (1814). His most famous engine, the *Rocket*, running at 58 km/36 mi an hour, was built in 1829. He worked as an engineer for several railway companies, and became a widely used consultant. >> Séguin; Stephenson, Robert

Stephenson, Robert (1803–59) Civil engineer, born in Willington Quay, Northumberland, NE England, UK, the son of George Stephenson. He studied at Newcastle upon Tyne and Edinburgh, assisted his father in surveying the Stockton and Darlington Railway, worked as a mining engineer in Colombia, then managed his father's locomotive engine-works at Newcastle. He attained independent fame through his tubular design for the Britannia Bridge over the Menai Straits in Wales (1850), and for bridges at

Conwy, Montreal, Newcastle upon Tyne, and elsewhere. He became an MP in 1847. >> Stephenson, George

Stephenson, Sir William, known as **Intrepid** (1896–1989) Secret intelligence chief, born in Point Douglas, near Winnipeg, Canada, of Scottish descent. Educated in Winnipeg, he became involved in British secret intelligence through visits to Germany to buy steel in the early 1930s. His information on Enigma, the German cipher machine, led to MI6's acquisition of a prototype in 1939. In 1940 he was appointed British intelligence chief in North and South America, representing the interests of MI5, MI6, and Special Operations Executive. The novelist Ian Fleming, a member of his wartime staff, is said to have adopted Stephenson as a model for the character 'M' in the James Bond books. >> Fleming, Ian

Stepinac, Aloysius, Cardinal [stepinak] (1898–1960) Roman Catholic clergyman, born in Krasić, Croatia. Primate of Hungary, he was imprisoned by Tito (1946–51) for alleged wartime collaboration. He was released due to failing health, but lived the remainder of his life under house arrest. >> Tito

Stepnyak ('son of the Steppe'), nickname of **Sergius Mikhailovich** (1852–95) Russian revolutionary. He was an artillery officer, but aroused government opposition as an apostle of freedom, was arrested, and subsequently kept under surveillance. He left Russia and settled in Geneva (1876) and London (1885). He was believed to be the assassin of General Mesentzieff, head of the St Petersburg police (1878). Among his works were *La Russia Sotteranea* (1881, Underground Russia), studies of the Nihilist movement, and the novel *The Career of a Nihilist* (1889).

Steptoe, Patrick (Christopher) (1913–88) Gynaecologist and reproduction biologist, born in Witney, Oxfordshire, SC England, UK. He studied at King's College, London, and St George's Hospital, and became senior obstetrician and gynaecologist in the Oldham Hospitals (1951) and medical director of the Bourn Hall Clinic, Cambridgeshire (1980). From 1968, with **Robert Edwards** (1925–), he worked on the problem of *in vitro* fertilization of human embryos, which 10 years later resulted in the birth of a baby after implantation in her mother's uterus.

Stern, Daniel >> Agoult, Marie de Flavigny, comtesse d'

Stern, Howard (1954–) Radio disc-jockey and television talk-show host, born in New York City. He studied at Boston University, where he became involved with college radio, then took various deejay jobs, eventually basing himself in New York City (from 1982). He has built a reputation as a 'shock jock', developing a flamboyant style and explicit programme content, in various 'Howard Stern' shows on radio and television during the 1990s, which has brought him fines and controversy as well as a huge public audience. His best-selling book *Private Parts* (1993) was later issued as a recording and filmed (both 1997).

Stern, Isaac [shtern] (1920–) Violinist, born in Kremenets, Belarus. He studied at the San Francisco Conservatory (1928–31), making his debut as guest artist with the San Francisco Symphony Orchestra as guest artist (1934). He became well known in the 1940s, and toured widely, establishing a reputation as one of the world's greatest violinists.

Stern, Otto [shtern] (1888–1969) Physicist, born in Sohrau, Germany. He studied at Wrocław, Poland (formerly Breslau, Germany), and taught at several German universities before emigrating to the USA in 1933, and becoming professor of physics at the Carnegie Technical Institute at Pittsburgh (1933–45). In 1920 he carried out an experiment with **Walter Gerlach** (1889–1979), demonstrating that some atomic nuclei have a magnetic moment, which provided major evidence in favour of quantum theory. He was awarded the Nobel Prize for Physics in 1943.

Sternberg, Josef von [shtern berg], originally **Jonas Stern** (1894–1969) Film director, born in Vienna. He worked in silent films in Hollywood in the 1920s as scriptwriter, cameraman, and director, but went to Germany to make his most famous film *Der blaue Engel* (1930, The Blue Angel) with Marlene Dietrich. This was followed by six more Hollywood features in which she starred, the last being *The Devil is a Woman* (1935). His autocratic methods and aloof personality made him unpopular in the studios, and his later career was erratic. His last film, *The Saga of Anatahan* (1953), was made in Japan. >> Dietrich

Sterne, Laurence (1713–68) Novelist, born in Clonmel, Co Tipperary, Ireland. He studied at Cambridge, was ordained in 1738, and appointed to a living in Yorkshire. In 1759 he wrote the first two volumes of his eccentric and influential comic novel *The Life and Opinions of Tristram Shandy*, which was very well received in London, the remaining volumes appearing between 1761 and 1767. From 1762 he lived mainly abroad for health reasons, publishing *A Sentimental Journey through France and Italy* in 1768. His *Letters from Yorick to Eliza* (1775–9) contained his correspondence with a young married woman to whom he was devoted.

Sternhold, Thomas (1500–49) Psalmist, born near Blakeney, Gloucestershire, SWC England, or in Hampshire, S England, UK. He was Groom of the Robes to Henry VIII and Edward VI. With **John Hopkins** (d.1570) he wrote the English version of psalms formerly attached to the Prayer Book. The complete book of psalms, which appeared in 1562, formed for nearly two centuries almost the whole hymnody of the Church of England and was known as the 'Old Version' after the rival version of Nahum Tate and Nicholas Brady appeared in 1696. Forty psalms bore the name of Sternhold. >> Tate, Nahum

Steuben, Frederick William (Augustus) Freiherr (Baron) **von** [stooben], Ger [shtoyben] (1730–94) Soldier in the American Revolutionary army, born in Magdeburg, Germany. At 14 he served at the siege of Prague, and in 1762 was on the staff of Frederick II. While in Paris in 1777 he was induced by Franklin to go to America, where Washington appointed him inspector-general. He prepared a manual of tactics for the army, remodelled its organization, and improved its discipline. In 1780 he received a command in Virginia, and took part in the siege of Yorktown. He became a naturalized US citizen in 1783.

Stevens, Alfred (1818–75) Painter, sculptor, and designer, born in Blandford, Dorset, S England, UK. He studied in Florence, and with the Danish sculptor Thorwaldsen (1770–1844), and taught architectural design at Somerset House, London (1845–7). During the next 10 years he decorated and designed household furniture, fireplaces, and porcelain. From 1856 he worked on the Wellington monument in St Paul's Cathedral (completed after his death by John Tweed) and the mosaics under the dome of St Paul's. He also designed the lions at the British Museum.

Stevens, Bernard (1916–83) Composer, born in London, England, UK. He was a teacher of composition at the Royal College of Music (1948–81). His first work to achieve recognition was the *Symphony of Liberation* (1946, *Daily Express* Prize), and his subsequent output included a further symphony, an opera *The Shadow of the Glen* (1978–9), concertos for piano, violin, and cello, two string quartets, and other chamber, choral, and instrumental pieces.

Stevens, George (1904–75) Film director, born in Oakland, CA. He directed two-reelers for Hal Roach, beginning in 1930, and began making features in 1933. A versatile director, he won Oscars for *A Place in the Sun* (1951) and *Giant* (1956). >> Roach, Hal

Stevens, John (Cox) (1749–1838) Engineer and inventor, born in New York City. He studied law, but never practised. A colonel in the Revolutionary Army, he became interested in steamboat design, patenting (1803) a multi-tubular boiler for his first steamboat, which was propelled by twin Archimedes screws driven through gears by a high-pressure steam engine. Design problems led him to revert to paddle wheels which could be driven by low-pressure engines, as in his steamboat *Juliana* (1811), which became the world's first steam-powered ferry. He later turned to railways, and in 1825 operated the first steam locomotive in the USA. >> Stevens, Robert Livingston

Stevens, Robert Livingston (1787–1856) Engineer and inventor, born in Hoboken, NJ, the son of John Stevens. He began at an early age to assist his father in the design and construction of steamboats, becoming an important figure in naval design. In 1830 he became president and chief engineer of the Camden & Amboy Railroad and Transportation Co. He invented the inverted-T railroad rail and spike, as well as the cow-catcher, and was the first to burn anthracite coal in a locomotive engine. >> Stevens, John

Stevens, Siaka (Probin) [shahka] (1905–88) Sierra Leone politician, prime minister (1967), and president (1971–85), born in Tolubu, Sierra Leone. After working in the police force and industry, he was a trade union activist before entering politics, founding the moderate Socialist All People's Congress in 1960. Thanks partly to his mixed Christian and Muslim parentage, he was victorious in the 1967 general election. Army opposition forced him to resign the premiership, but he was returned to power the following year as Sierra Leone's first president under its new constitution. He ruled a one-party state until his retirement at 80. >> RR1087

Stevens, S(tanley) S(mith) (1906–73) Experimental psychologist, born in Ogden, UT. He studied at Harvard, and taught there from 1932 until his death. He made important contributions to our understanding of the sense of hearing, but also devised general theories and experimental techniques for the study of the 'scaling' of sensory qualities (such as loudness, brightness, and pain). His major reference work is *The Handbook of Experimental Psychology* (1951).

Stevens, Thaddeus (1792–1868) US representative, born in Danville, VT. Congenitally lame, he grew up with an empathy for society's poor and disenfranchised. He studied at Dartmouth college, then practised as a lawyer in Gettysburg, PA. He served in the state's House of Representatives (1833–41), went as a Whig to the US House of Representatives (1849–53), but left in impatience over the Party's stand on slavery. After helping to form the new Republican Party in Pennsylvania, he returned to the House (1859–68). A passionate opponent of slavery, he advocated harsh policies against the Confederate states, emerging as the leader of the 'Radical Republicans'. His idea of treating the South as what he called 'a conquered province' brought him into open conflict with President Andrew Johnson. Stevens led the move to impeach Johnson, and died soon after Johnson's acquittal. >> Johnson, Andrew; Stanton, Edwin

Stevens, Wallace (1879–1955) Poet, born in Reading, PA. He studied at Harvard, became a journalist and lawyer, then joined an insurance company at Hartford, where he lived until his death. For many years he wrote abstruse and philosophical verse, and was over 40 when his first volume, *Harmonium* (1923), was published. His *Collected Poems* appeared in 1954. He is now regarded as a major if idiosyncratic poet in the Symbolist tradition.

Stevenson, Adlai (Ewing) [adliy] (1900–65) US politician and lawyer, born in Los Angeles, CA. He studied at Princeton, and practised law in Chicago. He took part in several European missions for the State Department (1943–5), and was elected Democratic Governor of Illinois (1948). He helped to found the UN (1946), stood twice against Eisenhower as presidential candidate (1952, 1956), and was the US delegate to the UN (1961–5).

Stevenson, Robert Louis (Balfour) (1850–94) Writer, born in Edinburgh, EC Scotland, UK. He studied at Edinburgh, became a lawyer (1875), then turned to writing travel sketches, essays, and short stories for magazines. The romantic adventure story *Treasure Island* (1883) brought him fame, and entered him on a course of romantic fiction which included *Kidnapped* (1886), *The Strange Case of Dr Jekyll and Mr Hyde* (1886), *The Master of Ballantrae* (1889), and the unfinished *Weir of Hermiston* (1896), considered his masterpiece. In 1888 he settled for health reasons at Vailima, Samoa. >> Henley; Osbourne

Stevenson, Ronald (1928–) Composer, pianist, and writer on music, born in Blackburn, Lancashire, NW England, UK. He studied at the Royal Manchester College of Music. He champions music as a world language, seeking in his works to embrace a broad spectrum of international culture (an 'ethnic aesthetic'). His compositions include the 80-minute *Passacaglia on DSCH* for piano, concertos for piano and violin, choral works, and songs from many cultural backgrounds.

Stevenson, William (?–1575) English scholar. He entered Christ's College, Cambridge, in 1546, and became a fellow; he is known to have staged plays there. He was probably the author of the earliest surviving English comedy, *Gammer Gurton's Needle* (1553), sometimes attributed to John Still or John Bridges.

Stevin, Simon [stevɪyn] (1548–1620) Mathematician and engineer, born in Bruges, Belgium. He held offices under Prince Maurice of Orange, wrote on fortification, bookkeeping and decimals, and invented a system of sluices to be used for defence by flooding certain areas, and a carriage propelled by sails. He was responsible for introducing the use of decimals, which were soon generally adopted.

Steward, Julian H(aynes) (1902–72) Cultural anthropologist, born in Washington, DC. He studied at Cornell and the University of California, Berkeley, and became director of the Institute of Social Anthropology at the Smithsonian Institution (1943), professor at Columbia (1946), and research professor in anthropology at Illinois (1956–72). He was concerned with cultures as adaptive systems geared to specific environments, and advocated a multilinear approach to cultural evolution. He edited the major *Handbook of the South American Indians* (1946–59).

Stewart, Arabella / Charles / James >> **Stuart, Arabella / Charles / James**

Stewart, Douglas (Alexander) (1913–85) Poet and playwright, born in Eltham, Taranaki, New Zealand. He studied at Victoria University College, Australia. Editor of the 'Red Page' in the *Bulletin* magazine (1940–61), he then became literary editor for Angus & Robertson publishers. His work includes short stories, biographies, and literary criticism, and verse dramas for stage and radio, of which *Fire in the Snow* (1939), about Scott's Antarctic expedition, is recognized as a classic of radio drama. His major contributions to Australian literature include biographies, two collections of bush ballads (1955–7), edited with Nancy Keesing (1923–), and *Modern Australian Verse* (1964).

Stewart, Dugald (1753–1828) Philosopher, born in Edinburgh, EC Scotland, UK. He studied at Edinburgh, where his father was professor of mathematics, and at Glasgow under Thomas Reid. He succeeded to his father's chair in 1775, then was professor of moral philosophy at Edinburgh (1758–1810). Much influenced by Reid's 'common sense' philosophy, he became the leader of the Scottish school. A prolific author, his major work was *Elements of the Philosophy of the Human Mind* (3 vols, 1792, 1814, 1827). A large monument on Calton Hill, Edinburgh, attests to his fame at the time of his death. >> Reid, Thomas

Stewart, Jackie, popular name of **John (Young) Stewart** (1939–) Motor-racing driver, born in Milton, West Dunbartonshire, W Scotland, UK. He started in 99 races, and won 27 world championship races between 1965 and 1973, a record until surpassed by Alain Prost in 1987. He was world champion in 1969 (driving a Matra), 1971, and 1973 (both Tyrrell). He retired at the end of 1973, and took up a career in broadcasting. He is also expert at clay pigeon shooting, and has come close to Olympic selection. Since 1996 he has been chairman of Stewart Grand Prix. >> Prost

Stewart, James (Maitland) (1908–97) Film star, born in Indiana, PA. An architecture student at Princeton University, he started in films in 1935, establishing a character of honesty and integrity in *You Can't Take It With You* (1938), *Destry Rides Again* (1939), and the comedy *The Philadelphia Story* (1940, Oscar), and *It's a Wonderful Life* (1946). He served with distinction in the US air force during World War 2, and returned to make a series of outstanding Westerns (1950–5) and two successes for Hitchcock, *Rear Window* (1954) and *Vertigo* (1958). His later work continued to provide a wide range of character roles, including *Fool's Parade* (1971) and *Right of Way* (1982). He received an American Film Institute Life Achievement Award in 1980, and an honorary Oscar in 1985.

Stewart, J(ohn) I(nnes) M(ackintosh), pseudonym **Michael Innes** (1906–94) Critic, and writer of detective fiction, born in Edinburgh, EC Scotland, UK. He studied at Oxford, and taught English at Leeds, Adelaide, and Belfast universities before returning to Oxford in 1949. Under his own name he has written several novels and critical studies, notably *Eight Modern Writers* (1963). He is better known for his prolific work as Michael Innes, beginning with *Death at the President's Lodging* (1936, in USA as *Seven Suspects*), featuring the policeman hero John Appleby. Later books include *The Secret Vanguard* (1940), *A Private View* (1952), and *A Family Affair*.

Stewart, (Robert) Michael (Maitland) Stewart, Baron (1906–90) Politician, born in London, England, UK. He studied at Oxford, entered teaching, and twice stood for Parliament as a Labour candidate before winning a London seat in 1945. He entered the Cabinet in 1947, and held senior offices in every subsequent Labour administration. He became foreign secretary in 1968 on the resignation of George-Brown, and in 1975 started a two-year term as head of the British delegation to the European Parliament. He received a peerage in 1979. >> George-Brown

Stewart, Patrick (1940–) Actor and playwright, born in Mirfield, West Yorkshire, N England, UK. He trained at Bristol Old Vic Theatre School, then worked in various repertory companies, joining the Royal Shakespeare Company in 1966. He has performed a wide range of theatre, film, and television roles, but is best known for his role as Captain Jean-Luc Picard in the follow-up series of *Star Trek: The Next Generation* (1987). Later films include *Star Trek: First Contact* (1996) and *Conspiracy Theory* (1997).

Stewart, Rod(erick David) (1945–) Singer and songwriter, born in London, England, UK. After singing with various groups in the mid -1960s, he began a career as a soloist, then joined The Faces (1969–75) while continuing to record on his own. In 1971 he simultaneously topped the UK and US music charts with the album *Every Picture*

Tells A Story and the single 'Maggie May'. His numerous hit songs include 'Sailing' (1975), which has become the unofficial British Navy anthem after being used as the signature tune of the 1976 BBC television documentary, 'Sailor'. Later albums include *Blondes Have More Fun* (1978), *Every Beat of My Heart* (1986), and *Unplugged and Seated* (1993).

Steyn (of Swafield), Johan Steyn, Baron [stayn] (1932–) Judge, born in Stellenbosch, South Africa. He studied at the University of Stellenbosch, and was called to the bar in 1958. He settled in Britain in 1973, and became a QC in 1979. He was appointed a judge of the High Court (1985), a presiding judge, Northern Circuit (1989), a Lord Justice of Appeal (1992), and a Lord of Appeal in Ordinary (1995). He served as chairman of the Departmental Advisory Committee on Arbitration Law (1990–4) and chairman of the Lord Chancellor's Advisory Committee on Legal Education and Conduct (1993–6). Knighted in 1985, he was created a life peer in 1995.

Stickley, Gustav (1858–1942) Furniture designer, born in Osceola, PA. He began his career as a stonemason, then became apprenticed to his uncle as a chair maker. He later formed the Gustav Stickley Co and, producing solid furniture with a hint of Art Nouveau, first exhibited at Grand Rapids in 1900. The same year he enlarged the company, which became the Craftsman Workshops, and his simple, sturdy oak designs became known as the much copied 'Mission Furniture'.

Stieglitz, Alfred [steeglits] (1864–1946) Photographer, born in Hoboken, NJ. He studied engineering and photography in Berlin, and travelled extensively in Europe before returning to New York City in 1890. He founded the American Photo-Secession Group with Edward Steichen in 1902, and consistently influenced the development of creative photography as an art form through his magazine *Camera Work* (1903–17) and his gallery of modern art in New York City. His polemical writings and his own creative work established him as a major figure in photographic art. >> O'Keeffe; Steichen

Stiernhielm, Georg [steernhyelm] (1598–1672) Poet, born in Vika, Sweden. He studied at Uppsala and in Germany. Ennobled by Gustavus Adolphus, he became the favourite court poet of Queen Christina. Besides much lyric poetry, he wrote a didactic allegorical poem, *Hercules* (1647). He has come to be known as 'the father of Swedish poetry'.

Stigand [steegand] (?–1072) English clergyman. He was probably chaplain to King Canute, and chief adviser to his widow, Emma. He was appointed chaplain by Edward the Confessor, then became Bishop of Elmham (1044), Bishop of Winchester (1047), and Archbishop of Canterbury (1052). On the death of Harold II, Stigand supported Edgar Ætheling, and was thus deprived of his offices by William I. He died a prisoner at Winchester. >> Canute; Edgar the Ætheling; Harold II; William I (of England)

Stigler, George J(oseph) (1911–91) Economist, born in Renton, WA. He studied at Chicago University, held professorships at Minnesota, Brown, and Columbia, and taught at the University of Chicago from 1958. His books include *The Theory of Price* (1946) and *The Economist as Preacher* (1983). He was awarded the Nobel Prize for Economics in 1982 for his work on market forces and regulatory legislation.

Stijl, De >> Doesburg; Mondrian; Oud

Stilicho, Flavius [stilikoh] (?–408) Roman general, half Roman, half-Vandal, who was virtual ruler of the West Roman empire (395–408) under the feeble Emperor Honorius. His greatest achievements were his victories over Alaric and the Visigoths in N Italy at Pollentia (402) and Verona (403). >> Alaric I; Honorius

Still, Clyfford (1904–80) Painter and printmaker, born in Grandin, ND. He studied art at Spokane University,

graduating in 1933. By c.1940 he had arrived at his personal style, rejecting European ideas, and employing the currently fashionable organic forms of Biomorphism. He later taught at the California School of Fine Arts, San Francisco (1946–50).

Still, William Grant (1895–1978) Composer, born in Woodville, MS. He studied medicine, switching to the study of composition at the Oberlin Conservatory. He worked as an arranger of popular music, and played in theatre and night-club orchestras while studying under Varèse. His music includes five operas, four symphonies, three ballets, chamber and choral music, and orchestral pieces. Known especially for his 'Afro-American Symphony' (1931), he became the first African-American conductor of a professional symphony orchestra in the USA. >> Varèse

Stiller, Mauritz (1883–1928) Film director, born in Helsinki. He settled in Sweden in 1909 and, though trained as an actor, began directing films for Svenska Bio in 1912. He adapted the novels of Selma Lagerlöf (1858–1940), notably *Herr Arnes Pengar* (1919, Sir Arne's Treasure), which won him international acclaim, *Gunnar Hedes Saga* (1922), and *Gösta Berlings Saga* (1924). His versatility is shown in *Erotikon* (1920), a sophisticated comedy about sexual rivalry. He discovered Greta Garbo, and took her to Hollywood in 1925, where he directed *Hotel Imperial* (1927), *Woman On Trial* (1927), and *The Street of Sin* (1927). >> Garbo

Stilwell, Joseph W(arren), nickname **Vinegar Joe** (1883–1946) US general, born in Palatka, FL. He trained at West Point in 1904, became an authority on Chinese life and an expert Chinese speaker, and was military attaché to the US Embassy in Beijing (1932–9). In 1942 he commanded US forces in China, Burma, and India. Recalled after a dispute with Jiang Jieshi in 1944, he commanded the US 10th Army in the Pacific until the end of the War. >> Jiang Jieshi

Stimson, Henry L(ewis) (1867–1930) US statesman, born in New York City. He studied at Yale and Harvard, and was called to the bar in 1891. He became US attorney for the New York southern district in 1906, secretary of war under Taft (1911–13), Governor-General of the Philippines (1927–9), and Hoover's secretary of state (1929–33). The *Stimson doctrine* denounced Japanese aggression in Manchuria (1931). Recalled by Franklin D Roosevelt as secretary of war (1940–5), his influence was decisive in leading Truman to use the atomic bomb against Japan. >> Roosevelt, Franklin D; Taft, William Howard; Truman

Sting, originally **Gordon Matthew Sumner** (1951–) Singer, songwriter, and actor, born in London, England, UK. Former vocalist and lyricist of The Police, his first film role came in *Quadrophenia* (1978), and his first hit song was 'Spread A Little Happiness' (1982), taken from the soundtrack of the television film *Brimstone and Treacle*, in which he also starred. His debut album, *The Dream of the Blue Turtles* (1985), topped both the UK and US music charts. He has been much associated with campaigns to do with the environment and with Amnesty International, and in 1989 he was a keynote speaker at the 2nd annual Human Rights Awards ceremony. Later albums include *Soul Cages* (1991), which reached number 1 in the UK music charts, and *Mercury Falling* (1996). Later films include *Dune* (1984), *Stormy Monday* (1988), and *The Grotesque* (1995).

Stirling, James, known as **Stirling the Venetian** (1692–1770) Mathematician, born in Garden, Stirling, C Scotland, UK. He was expelled from Oxford for corresponding with Jacobites, and went to Venice to complete his studies. There he discovered the secrets of the Venetian glass-makers, and published a work on their techniques. His principal work was *Methodus differentialis* (1730), in which he made important advances in the theory of infinite series and finite differences, and gave an approximate formula for the factorial function still in use and named after him.

Stirling, Patrick (1820–95) Mechanical engineer, born in Kilmarnock, East Ayrshire, SW Scotland, UK. The most eminent of a remarkable family of locomotive engineers, he was apprenticed to his uncle, **James** (1800–76), who was manager of the Dundee Foundry which built steamers and locomotives. In 1853 he was appointed the locomotive superintendent of the Glasgow & South Western Railway. He moved to the Great Northern Railway in Doncaster in 1866, and succeeded his cousin as chief locomotive superintendent. He is best-known for his 8-ft diameter driving wheel 4-2-2 'Stirling Single' (1870), which became a legend for its speed and power.

Stirling, Robert (1790–1878) Clergyman and inventor, born in Perth, Pert and Kinross, E Scotland, UK. He studied for the ministry at the universities of Glasgow and Edinburgh, was ordained in the Church of Scotland (1816), and was minister of Galston, East Ayrshire (1837–78). In the same year he patented a hot-air engine operating on what became known as the *Stirling cycle*, in which the working fluid (air) is heated externally. His engines were built from 1818 to 1922, by which time they had been superseded by the internal-combustion engine. Interest in the engine has recently revived for its potential use in spacecraft and sensitive environments, because of its lack of exhaust fume emissions.

Stockhausen, Karlheinz [shtokhowzn] (1928–) Composer, born in Mödrath, Germany. He studied at Cologne and Bonn, joined the *musique concrète* group in Paris, and experimented with compositions based on electronic sounds. In 1953 he helped to found the electronic music studio at Cologne, and became director there (1963–77), later becoming professor of composition at the Hochschule für Musik in Cologne (1971–77). He has written orchestral, choral, and instrumental works, including some which combine electronic and normal sonorities, such as *Kontakte* (1960), and parts of a huge operatic cycle, *Licht* (Light). In 1991 he commenced a project to produce his complete works on CD.

Stockton, Frank Richard, popular name of **Francis Richard Stockton** (1834–1902) Humorist and engraver, born in Philadelphia, PA. A wood engraver, he became assistant editor of *St Nicholas Magazine* (1873). He first attracted notice by his stories for children, and is best known as author of the collection *The Lady or the Tiger* (1884). Other works include *Mrs Cliff's Yacht* (1896) and *The Girl at Cobhurst* (1898).

Stoker, Bram, popular name of **Abraham Stoker** (1847–1912) Writer, born in Dublin. Educated at Dublin, he studied law and science, and partnered Henry Irving in running the Lyceum Theatre from 1878. Among several books, he is chiefly remembered for the classic horror tale *Dracula* (1897), which has occasioned a whole series of film adaptations, notably *Nosferatu* (Murnau, 1921), *Dracula* (Hammer Films, 1958), and *Bram Stoker's Dracula* (Coppola, 1993). Other novels include *The Mystery of the Sea* (1902) and *The Lady of the Shroud* (1909). >> Irving, Henry

Stoker, Richard (1938–) Composer, pianist, artist, and writer, born in Castleford, West Yorkshire, N England, UK. He studied at the Royal Academy of Music with Lennox Berkeley, and in Paris with Nadia Boulanger. A professor at the Royal Academy (1963–87), his varied compositions include the operas *Johnson Preserv'd* and *Therese Raquin*, works for piano and organ, string quartets, film and stage scores, and many choral works. He edited *Composer Magazine* (1969–80), and his books include poetry, novels, short stories (collected, 1997), and two volumes of autobiography, *Open Window – Open Door* (1985) and *Between the Lines* (1991).

Stokes, Sir George (Gabriel) (1819–1903) Physicist and mathematician, born in Skreen, Co Sligo, Ireland. He studied at Cambridge, where in 1849 he became professor of mathematics. He first used spectroscopy as a means of determining the chemical compositions of the Sun and stars, published a valuable paper on diffraction (1849), and formulated *Stokes' law* for the force opposing a small sphere in its passage through a viscous fluid. He was secretary of the Royal Society for 30 years (from 1854), then became its president. He was created a baronet in 1889.

Stokowski, Leopold (Antonin Stanislaw Boleslawawicz) [stokofskee] (1882–1977) Conductor, born in London, England, UK. He studied at the Royal College of Music, London, and built up an international reputation as conductor of the Philadelphia Symphony Orchestra (1912–36), the New York Philharmonic (1946–50), and the Houston Symphony Orchestra (1955–60). He made three films with the Philadelphia Orchestra, including Walt Disney's *Fantasia* (1940). In 1962 he founded the American Symphony Orchestra in New York City.

Stolypin, Peter Arkadyevich [stolipin] (1862–1911) Russian statesman and prime minister (1906–11), born in Dresden, Germany. He studied at St Petersburg, and after service in the ministry of the interior (from 1884), became governor of Saratov province (1903–6), where he ruthlessly put down local peasant uprisings and helped to suppress the revolutionary upheavals of 1905. As premier, he introduced a series of agrarian reforms, which had only limited success. In 1907 he suspended the second Duma, and arbitrarily limited the franchise. He was assassinated in Kiev.

Stommel, Henry M(elson) (1920–) Oceanographer, born in Wilmington, DE. He was a physical oceanographer at the Woods Hole Oceanographic Institution (1944–59) before joining the Massachusetts Institute of Technology (1959–60). He left MIT to teach at Harvard (1960–3), returned to MIT (1963–78), then moved back to Woods Hole as senior scientist. Using physical models, he developed the first theory of the Gulf Stream, and made major contributions to studies of cumulus clouds, oceanic salinity and thermal gradients, and plankton distribution. He shared Sweden's Crafoord Prize in 1983.

Stone, Barton W(arren) (1772–1844) Protestant clergyman, born in Charles Co, MD. He was ordained a Presbyterian minister (1798), and preached at Cane Ridge Church, Paris, KY, which became the centre of the Great Revival (1801–3). He was co-founder of the Disciples of Christ.

Stone, Edward Durell (1902–78) Architect, born in Fayetteville, AR. He studied at the University of Arkansas, Harvard, and the Massachusetts Institute of Technology, then taught at New York University and at Yale (1946–52). He set up his practice in New York City (1935–78). More eclectic than innovative, he moved from a Modernist to a more ornamented style, often using grillwork and deliberately echoing the local/cultural environment. His many public buildings include the US Embassy in New Delhi, India, and the John F Kennedy Center for the Performing Arts in Washington, DC.

Stone, Harlan (Fiske) (1872–1946) Lawyer and judge, born in Chesterfield, NH. He studied at Columbia, practised law, and served as dean of the Columbia Law School (1910–23) before being appointed Federal attorney general. He was appointed an Associate Justice of the US Supreme Court in 1925 and Chief Justice in 1941. He upheld the view that in matters of constitutionality, except where questions of individual liberty were involved, courts should defer to legislatures. He also developed the constitutional test for the regulation of inter-state commerce.

Stone, Irving, originally **Irving Tennenbaum** (1903–89) Popular novelist and playwright, born in San Francisco, CA. He studied at the universities of California, Berkeley, and Southern California. He is sometimes credited with creating the non-fiction novel, starting with *Lust for Life* (1934), based on the life of Van Gogh, which became a best-seller. His other works include *The Agony and the Ecstasy* (1961), which fictionalizes the life of Michelangelo, and *Passions of the Mind* (1971), about Sigmund Freud.

Stone, I(sidor) F(einstein) (1907–89) Radical journalist, born in Philadelphia, PA. He studied at Pennsylvania University, then joined the liberal reformist *New York Post* (1933–8) and its weekly long-time ally, the *New York Nation* (1938–46), ultimately becoming its Washington editor. A supporter of unpopular causes, he was hostile to the Cold War, opposed America's involvement in the Vietnam War, and founded the influential *I F Stone's Weekly* (later *Bi-Weekly*, 1953–71).

Stone, Lucy (1818–93) Feminist, born in West Brookfield, MA. She studied at Oberlin College, gave lectures on abolitionism and women's suffrage, and called the first national Women's Rights Convention at Worcester, MA, in 1850. In 1855 she married a fellow-radical, retaining her maiden name as a symbol of equality ('doing a Lucy Stone'). She helped to form the American *Women's Journal*, which she co-edited with her husband.

Stone, Oliver (1946–) Film director and scriptwriter, born in New York City. He studied at New York University, and had written numerous unfilmed scripts before he made his directorial debut with the Canadian horror film *Seizure* (1973). He won an Oscar for his screenplay of *Midnight Express* (1978). His experiences in the Vietnam War were distilled in *Platoon* (1987) which led to a Best Director Oscar, and he received another Oscar for *Born On The Fourth Of July* (1989). Other films as director include *The Doors* (1991), *JFK* (1991), and *Nixon* (1995), and he produced *The People vs Larry Flynt* (1996).

Stone, Sir (John) Richard (Nicholas) (1913–91) Economist, born in London, England, UK. He changed from law to economics at Cambridge under Keynes, spent three years in the City of London, and during World War 2 was a government economist. He became director of the Department of Applied Economics at Cambridge (1945–55) and was appointed professor of economics (1955–80). He was awarded the 1984 Nobel Prize for Economics for his development of the complex models on which worldwide standardized national income reports are based. >> Keynes

Stone, Rosetta >> **Seuss, Dr**

Stonehouse, John (Thompson) (1925–88) British politician, born in Southampton, Hampshire, S England, UK. He studied at the London School of Economics, and was elected to the House of Commons as a Labour MP in 1957. He held junior ministerial posts under Harold Wilson before being appointed minister of technology (1967–8) and minister of posts and telecommunications (1968–70). Complications in his financial affairs and private life led him to fake his death by supposed drowning off a Miami beach in 1974, but he was identified in Australia a year later, returned to Britain, and was found guilty of fraud and embezzlement. After an early release from prison for good behaviour in 1979, he married his secretary, **Sheila Buckley** (1981). He joined the Social Democratic Party in 1982, but spent the rest of his life in obscurity.

Stoney, George Johnstone (1826–1911) Irish physicist. He became professor of natural philosophy at Queen's College, Galway (1852), and secretary of Queen's University, Dublin (1857). He calculated an approximate value for the charge of an electron (1874), a term he himself introduced.

Stooges, The Three Comedy trio. Originally the **Horwitz** (later **Howard**) brothers, **Samuel** (b.1895), **Moses** (b.1897), and **Jerome (Jerry)** (b.1911), they were known by their respective nicknames of Shemp, Moe, and Curly (with the bald head). They first played knockabout humour in association with comedy star Ted Healy, who called them The Southern Gentlemen. Shemp then left for a career of his own, and was replaced by **Larry Fine** (originally **Feinberg**), with the wild wavy hair. They then parted from Healy, and as Larry, Curly and Moe made 191 short films and 13 feature films for Columbia, all characterized by anarchic knockabout humour, with sound effects perfectly synchronized with their blows. There were further personnel changes: Shemp returned, replacing Jerry, and in turn was replaced by **Joe Besser**. There was less interest in the act during the early 1950s, but when several of their films were released for television towards the end of the decade, they once again became acclaimed. **Joe de Rita** (b.1909) replaced Joe Besser as the new Curly, and the new trio appeared in the successful burlesque *Have Rocket, Will Travel* (1959), followed by *Snow White and the Three Stooges* (1961). In their final form, billed as Larry, Moe, and Curly Joe, they made 12 features before their retirement. Moe and Larry died in 1975, and Joe de Rita in 1993.

Stopes, Marie (Charlotte Carmichael) [stohps] (1880–1958) Pioneer advocate of birth control, suffragette, and palaeontologist, born in Edinburgh, EC Scotland, UK. She studied at London and Munich, and became the first female science lecturer at Manchester (1904). Alarmed at the unscientific way in which men and women embarked upon married life, she wrote a number of books on the subject, of which *Married Love* (1918), in which birth control is mentioned, caused a storm of controversy. She later founded the first birth control clinic, in London (1921). She wrote over 70 books, including *Contraception: its Theory, History and Practice* (1923) and *Sex and Religion* (1929). >> Besant, Annie; Bradlaugh; Rout

Stoppard, Miriam, *née* **Stern** (1937–) British physician, writer, and broadcaster. She studied at London and Durham, specializing in dermatology, then worked in industry (1968–77) before becoming a writer and broadcaster. She is well known for her TV series, especially *Miriam Stoppard's Health and Beauty Show* (from 1988), and among her books are *The Baby and Child Medical Handbook* (1984), *The Magic of Sex* (1991), and *The Menopause* (1994). She married Tom Stoppard in 1972 (divorced, 1992). >> Stoppard, Tom

Stoppard, Sir Tom, originally **Tom Straussler** (1937–) Playwright, born in Zlín, Czech Republic. He lived in Singapore, moving with his family to England in 1946, where he was educated. In 1960 he went to London as a free-lance journalist and theatre critic, and wrote radio plays. He made his name with *Rosencrantz and Guildenstern Are Dead* (1967, Tony). Other plays include the philosophical satire *Jumpers* (1972), *Travesties* (1974, Tony), *The Real Thing* (1982, Tony), *Hapgood* (1988), *Arcadia* (1993), *Indian Ink* (1995), and *The Invention of Love* (1997). He has also written a novel, *Lord Malquist and Mr Moon* (1966), as well as several short stories. His television plays include *Profesional Foul* (1977) and *Squaring the Circle* (1984), and his screenplays include *Empire of the Sun* (1987) and *The Russian House* (1991). He was married to Miriam Stoppard (divorced, 1992). He was knighted in 1997. >> Stoppard, Miriam

Storey, David (Malcolm) (1933–) Novelist and playwright, born in Wakefield, West Yorkshire, N England, UK. He studied at the Slade School of Art, London. The action of *This Sporting Life* (1960), his first novel, is set in the world of rugby league, and the characters of his play *The Changing Room* (1972) are footballers. The play *Life Class* (1974), is set in an art college. Other novels, such as *Saville* (1976,

Booker), use autobiographical material from his Yorkshire mining country background, as does the play *In Celebration* (1969). Later plays include *Early Days* (1980) and *The March on Russia* (1989). His *Collected Poems* appeared in 1992.

Storm, (Hans) Theodor Woldsen [shtorm] (1817–88) Writer, born in Husum, Germany. He trained as a lawyer, wrote a volume of poems (1857), and became known for his novellas, notably *Der Schimmelreiter* (1888, The Rider on the White Horse).

Störmer, Fredrik (Carl Mülertz) [stoe(r)mer] (1874–1957) Mathematician and geophysicist, born in Skien, Norway. He studied at Christiania (Oslo), and became professor there in 1903. Inspired by the experiments of Birkeland, he carried out research on auroral phenomena, making important contributions to the understanding of their formation. His work was also significant in the study of the behaviour of cosmic rays near the Earth. >> Birkeland

Storni, Alfonsina (1892–1938) Feminist and poet, born in Sala Capriasca, Switzerland. Starting young as an actress with a travelling theatrical company, she later became a teacher in Argentina. Her poetry is largely concerned with her ambivalent feelings towards men, but a desire for love and sexual passion. Her books include *La inquietud del rosal* (1916, The Inquietude of the Rosebush), *El dulce daño* (1918, The Sweet Injury), which brought her popular success, and *Mascarillo y trébol* (1938, Mask and Trefoil). She committed suicide on discovering that she was suffering from incurable cancer.

Storrier, Timothy Austin (1949–) Figurative and landscape artist, born in Sydney, New South Wales, Australia. He studied at the National Art School, Sydney, and made working trips to C Australia, producing a series of vivid paintings. His delicate greys, pinks, and blues unite the harsh desert environment with symbolic or domestic *trompe l'oeil* objects in a blending of Classical and Romantic styles. His Sydney exhibition in 1989 included the powerful 'Burning of the Gifts', which shows his continuing preoccupation with fire.

Story, Joseph (1779–1845) Jurist, born in Marblehead, MA. He studied at Harvard, and was admitted to the bar. Elected to the state legislature in 1805, he became a leader of the Republican Party, and entered Congress in 1808. He became a justice of the Supreme Court (1811–45) and professor of law at Harvard (from 1829). His numerous works, notably *Equity Jurisprudence* (1835–6), were a great influence on the development of US law.

Stoss or **Stozz, Veit** [shtohs] (c. 1447–1533) Woodcarver and sculptor, born in Nuremberg, Germany. He worked mainly in Kraków (1477–96), where he carved the high altar of the Marjacki Church. Back in Nuremberg, he worked for 30 years in various churches, including the church of St Lorenz, which contains his 'Annunciation'.

Stothard, Thomas (1755–1834) Painter and engraver, born in London, England, UK. A student at the Royal Academy, he was a full academician in 1794, and appointed librarian in 1812. He is best known for his painting 'The Canterbury Pilgrims', and for his numerous book illustrations in such classic works as *Robinson Crusoe*, *The Pilgrim's Progress*, and *The Vicar of Wakefield*. He exhibited oil paintings at the Royal Academy from 1778 until his death.

Stott, John Robert Walmsley (1921–) Anglican clergyman and writer, born in London, England, UK. He studied at Cambridge, and became curate, then rector (1945–75) at All Souls, Langham Place, London. Widely acknowledged as a leading spokesman for Anglican Evangelicals, he has preached internationally, and been a royal chaplain since 1959. He was director of the London Institute for Contemporary Christianity (1982–6) and subsequently became its president. His many books include *Basic Christianity*

(1958), *Our Guilty Silence* (1967), *Issues facing Christians Today* (1984), *The Message of Acts* (1990), and *The Message of Timothy and Titus* (1996).

Stout, Rex (Todhunter) (1886–1975) Detective-story writer, born in Noblesville, IN. Before becoming a writer he invented a school banking system that was installed in 400 cities throughout the USA. His great creation was Nero Wolfe, the phenomenally fat private eye who, with the help of his confidential assistant, Archie Godwin, solved numerous mysteries, beginning with *Fer-de-Lance* (1934).

Stow, John (1525–1605) Chronicler, born in London, England, UK. A tailor in Cornhill, from c.1560 he devoted himself to antiquarian pursuits. His principal works are the *Summary of English Chronicles* (1565), *Annals, or a General Chronicle of England* (1580), and the noted *Survey of London and Westminster* (1598), an account of their history, antiquities, and government for six centuries.

Stowe, Harriet (Elizabeth) Beecher [stoh], *née* **Beecher** (1811–96) Novelist, born in Litchfield, CT. Brought up with puritanical strictness, she studied then taught at her sister's school. In 1836 she married a theological professor, with whom she lived in poverty until the immediate success and scandal of her first novel *Uncle Tom's Cabin* (1852), which was prompted by the passing of the Fugitive Slave Law. Making extensive tours in Europe (1853, 1856 and 1859), she formed important literary friendships, and wrote a host of other books, including *Dred: A Tale of the Great Dismal Swamp* (1856), *The Minister's Wooing* (1859), and *Old Town Folks* (1869). >> Beecher, Henry Ward

Stozz, Veit >> **Stoss, Veit**

Strabo [strayboh] (Gr 'squint-eyed') (c. 64 BC–c.AD 23) Geographer and historian, born in Amaseia, Pontus. He spent his life in travel and study, was at Corinth in 29 BC, explored the Nile in 24 BC, and seems to have settled at Rome after AD 14. Of his great historical work in 47 books, *Historical Studies*, only a few fragments survive; but his *Geographica* in 17 books has come down almost complete, and is of great value for the results of his own extensive observation. He makes copious use of his predecessors, Eratosthenes, Polybius, Aristotle, Thucydides, and many writers now lost.

Strachan, Douglas [strakhn] (1875–1950) Artist, born in Aberdeen, NE Scotland, UK. After being political cartoonist for the *Manchester Chronicle* (1895–7), and a portrait painter in London, he found his true medium in stained-glass work, notably the window group which Britain contributed to the Palace of Peace at The Hague. He designed the windows for the shrine of the Scottish National War Memorial, and other examples of his work may be seen in King's College Chapel, Aberdeen, and the University Chapel, Glasgow.

Strachey, (Evelyn) John (St Loe) [straychee] (1901–63) British statesman, born in Guildford, Surrey, SE England, UK. He studied at Oxford, and became a Labour MP (1929–31), then resigned from the Party and gave his support to extremist political organizations. He served in the RAF during World War 2, and afterwards rejoined Labour as under-secretary for air (1945). His controversial period as minister of food (1946–50) included the food crisis (1947), unpopular prolongation of rationing, and the abortive Tanganyika ground-nuts and Gambia egg schemes (1947–9). He regained some popularity as secretary of state for war (1950–1) during the Korean hostilities.

Strachey, (Giles) Lytton [straychee] (1880–1932) Biographer, born in London, England, UK. He studied at Cambridge, lived in London, and became a member of the Bloomsbury group of writers and artists. He began his writing career as a critic, but turned to biography, creating a literary bombshell with his *Eminent Victorians* (1918), an impertinent challenge to the self-assured, monumental studies previously typical of this genre. Later works included *Queen Victoria* (1921) and *Elizabeth and Essex* (1928). >> Moore, G E

Stradella, Alessandro [stra**del**a] (1642–82) Composer, born in Monfestino, Italy. One of the finest composers of chamber music, he wrote more than 200 cantatas, notably the *Christmas Cantata*. Legend has it that he eloped with the fiancée of a Venetian senator, who sent assassins to murder him in 1677. Documents show that he was indeed murdered in 1682. Numerous operas and at least one novel (*Stradella*, by Marion Crawford, 1909) have grown out of his legendary life, little of which is backed up by any real evidence.

Stradivari or **Stradivarius, Antonio** [stradi**vah**rius] (c.1644–1737) Violin maker, born in Cremona, Italy. He experimented with the design of string instruments, and assisted by his two sons perfected the Cremona type of violin. It is thought that he made over a thousand violins, violas, and violoncellos between 1666 and his death; about 650 of these still exist.

Strafford, Thomas Wentworth, 1st Earl of (1593–1641) English statesman, born in London, England, UK. He studied at Cambridge, was knighted in 1611, and in 1614 succeeded to his baronetcy and became MP for Yorkshire. He acted with the Opposition (1625–8), but after being appointed president of the North and Baron Wentworth (1628), he supported Charles I. In 1632 he became lord deputy of Ireland, where he imposed firm rule. In 1639 he was made the king's principal adviser, and Earl of Strafford. His suppression of the rebellion in Scotland failed, and he was impeached by the Long Parliament. Despite a famous defence at Westminster, he was executed on Tower Hill. >> Charles I (of England); Vane

Strand, Paul (1890–1976) Photographer, born in New York City. He studied under Lewis W Hine, became a commercial photographer in 1912, and followed Alfred Stieglitz in his commitment to 'straight' photography. He collaborated with Charles Sheeler in the documentary film *Manhattan* (1921), and in 1933 was appointed chief of photography and cinematography in the Secretariat of Education in Mexico. From 1935 he produced socially significant documentary films, both independently and for the US government. After 1942 he concentrated on still photography for his records of life in many parts of the world. In 1951 he went to France to escape McCarthyism. >> Hine; Sheeler; Stieglitz

Strasberg, Lee, originally **Israel Strassberg** (1901–82) Actor, director, and teacher, born in Budzanow, Austria. He emigrated to the USA in 1909, and gained a reputation with the Theater Guild of New York. In 1931 he was involved in the formation of the Group Theater, with which he worked as a teacher, evolving a technique (influenced by Stanislavsky) which became known everywhere as 'method acting'. He exercised great influence as a director of the Actor's Studio (1949–82), his pupils including Marlon Brando and Paul Newman. >> Brando; Newman, Paul; Stanislavsky

Strasburger, Eduard Adolf [**shtras**berger] (1844–1912) Botanist, born in Warsaw, Poland. He studied botany in Paris, Bonn, and Jena, and spent his career at Jena (1869–80) and Bonn (1880–1912). In *Über Zellbildung und Zellteilung* (1876, Cell Formation and Cell Division) he laid down the basic principles of cytology, the study of cells, for which he made Bonn the world's leading centre. His work did much to show that mitosis (normal somatic cell division) in plants is a process essentially similar to that described for animal cells. *Strasburger's Textbook of Botany*, written with other botanists under his guidance, is a classic, with over 30 editions from 1894 onwards.

Strasser, Valentine >> **Momoh, Joseph Saidu**

Stratas, Teresa, originally **Anastasia Strataki** (1938–   ) Soprano, born in Toronto, Canada. She studied at the Toronto Royal Conservatoire and in New York City, and made her debut in Toronto as Mimi in *La Bohème* (1958). She went on to make her New York debut at the Metropolitan Opera the following year.

Stratemeyer, Edward L [**strat**emiyer], pseudonyms include **Arthur M Winfield, Horatio Alger, Jr, Captain Ralph Bonehill, Nick Carter** (1862–1930) Writer and book syndicate operator, born in Elizabeth, NJ. He sold his first story in 1888, following this with a prolific output of juvenile fiction. In 1906 he founded the Stratemeyer Literary Syndicate in New York City. He supplied the characters, plots, and authors' pen names to a team of writers who over the years wrote more than 800 books under some 60 pseudonyms, including the 'Tom Swift' series (by Victor Appleton), the 'Bobbsey Twins' series (by Laura Lee Hope) and the 'Hardy Boys' series (by Franklin W Dixon). Stratemeyer himself probably wrote over 200 other books. After his death the syndicate was directed by his daughter, **Harriet S Adams** (?1893–1982), who herself had created the 'Nancy Drew' series (under the name of Carolyn Keene).

Stratford (de Redcliffe), Stratford Canning, Viscount (1786–1880) Diplomat, born in London, England, UK, a cousin of George Canning. He studied at Cambridge, and became chargé d'affaires and de facto ambassador at Constantinople (1810–12), minister to Switzerland (1814–18), and minister to the USA (1820–3). As ambassador in Constantinople at various times between 1825 and 1851, he influenced Turkish policy, worked for Greek independence, and encouraged a programme of reforms, but was unsuccessful in his attempts to prevent the outbreak of the Crimean War (1854–6). >> Canning

Strathcona (of Mount Royal and of Glencoe), Donald Alexander Smith, Baron [strath**koh**na] (1820–1914) Canadian businessman and statesman, born in Forres, Moray, NE Scotland, UK. Apprenticed to the Hudson's Bay Co in 1838, he worked as a fur trader, and became principal shareholder and governor of the company from 1889. He entered Canadian politics in 1870 as a Conservative, but withdrew his support during the Pacific Scandal (1873). Chief financier of the Canadian Pacific Railway, he became president of the Bank of Montreal in 1887, and returned to parliament the same year until 1896, when he was appointed high commissioner for Canada in London. Knighted in 1886, he was granted a peerage in 1897.

Strato or **Straton of Lampsacus** [**stray**toh, **stray**ton] (?–c.270 BC) Greek philosopher, the successor to Theophrastus as the third head of the Peripatetic School which Aristotle founded. His writings are lost, but he seems to have worked mainly to revise Aristotle's physical doctrines. He had an original theory about the void, its distribution explaining differences in the weights of objects. He also denied any role to teleological, and hence theological, explanations in nature. >> Aristotle; Theophrastus

Stratton, Charles (Sherwood), nickname **General Tom Thumb** (1838–83) Midget showman, born in Bridgeport, CT. He stopped growing at six months of age, and stayed 63 cm/25 in until his teens, eventually reaching 101 cm/40 in. Barnum displayed him in his museum, from the age of five, under the name of General Tom Thumb, and he became famous throughout the USA and Europe. In 1863 his marriage to **Lavinia Warren** (1841–1919), also a midget, was widely publicized.

Straus, Oscar [**shtrows**] (1870–1954) Composer, born in Vienna. A pupil of Max Bruch in Berlin, where he lived until 1927, he is best known for his many operettas and comic operas, such as *Waltz Dream* (1907) and *The Chocolate Soldier* (1908, from Shaw's *Arms and the Man*). From 1939 he was a naturalized French citizen. >> Bruch

Strauss, David Friedrich [shtrows] (1808–74) Theologian, born in Ludwigsburg, Germany. He studied for the Church at Tübingen, and lectured on philosophy there as a disciple of Hegel. In his *Leben Jesu* (1835–6, trans by George Eliot, 1846) he argued that the supernatural element of the Gospel was a collection of historical myths created by popular legend. The book raised such a storm of controversy that he was dismissed, and also debarred from taking up a professorship at Zürich in 1839. His other major work was *Die christliche Glaubenslehre* (1840–1), a review of Christian dogma. He later lived in Ludwigsburg and Darmstadt, where he worked as a legislator while continuing to write. >> Hegel

Strauss, Franz Josef [shtrows] (1915–88) German statesman, born in Munich. He studied in Munich, served in the German army during World War 2, and in 1945 joined the rightist, Bavarian-based Christian Social Union (CSU), being elected to the Bundestag in 1949. He became leader of the CSU in 1961, and was successively minister for nuclear energy (1955–6), defence (1956–62), and finance (1966–9). From 1978 he was state premier of Bavaria, using this base to wield significant influence within the Bundesrat and (from 1982) in the coalition government headed by Chancellor Kohl. >> Kohl

Strauss, Johann [shtrows], known as **the Elder** (1804–49) Violinist, conductor, and composer, born in Vienna. He founded with Josef Lanner (1801–43) the Viennese Waltz tradition, and toured widely in Europe with his own orchestra. He composed several marches, notably the *Radetzky March* (1848), and numerous waltzes. His younger sons **Eduard Strauss** (1835–1916), and **Josef Strauss** (1827–70) were both conductors, and Josef and his eldest son **Johann** became known as composers of waltzes. >> Strauss, Johann (the Younger)

Strauss, Johann [shtrows], known as **the Younger** (1825–99) Violinist, conductor, and composer, born in Vienna, the eldest son of Johann Strauss (the Elder). He studied law, but turned to music, touring with his own orchestra. He wrote over 400 waltzes, notably *An der schönen blauen Donau* (1867, trans The Blue Danube) and *Geschichten aus dem Wienerwald* (1868, Tales from the Vienna Woods), as well as polkas, marches, several operettas, including *Die Fledermaus* (1874, The Bat), and a favourite concert piece, *Perpetuum Mobile*. >> Strauss, Johann (the Elder)

Strauss, Levi, originally **Loeb Strauss** (1829–1902) Clothing designer and manufacturer, born in Buttenheim, Bavaria, Germany. His family emigrated to New York City in 1847, and there he became a US citizen, setting up a dry goods store with his brothers in 1850. In 1853 he moved to San Francisco, where he built up a clothing factory, supplying tough clothes for the miners. He developed his riveted, denim 'waist overalls' in 1873, and these (as 'blue jeans', later 'Levis') eventually became the company's chief product. The original factory was destroyed in the 1906 San Francisco earthquake.

Strauss, Richard [shtrows] (1864–1949) Composer, born in Munich, Germany. He studied at Munich and Berlin, and conducted at Meiningen, Munich, Weimar, Bayreuth, and Berlin. He is best known for his symphonic poems, such as *Till Eulenspiegels lustige Streiche* (1894–5, Till Eulenspiegel's Merry Pranks) and *Also sprach Zarathustra* (1895–6, Thus Spoke Zarathustra), and his operas, notably *Der Rosenkavalier* (1911) and *Ariadne auf Naxos* (1912, Ariadne on Naxos). He also wrote concertos, songs, and several small-scale orchestral works. >> Hofmannsthal

Stravinsky, Igor (Fyodorovich) [stra**vin**skee] (1882–1971)

Composer, born near St Petersburg, Russia. He studied law, but turned to musical composition under Rimsky-Korsakov. He became famous with his music for the Diaghilev ballets *The Firebird* (1910), *Petrushka* (1911), and *The Rite of Spring* (1913). Essentially an experimenter, after World War 1 he devoted himself to Neoclassicism, as in his ballet *Pulcinella* (1920) based on Pergolesi, the opera-oratorio *Oedipus Rex* (1927), and the choral *Symphony of Psalms* (1930). He settled in France (1934) and finally in the USA, where he became a US citizen (1945). Other major compositions include the *Symphony in C major* (1940), the opera *The Rake's Progress* (1951), and such later work as *Requiem Canticles* (1966), in which he adopted serialism. >> Diaghilev; Rimsky-Korsakov

Straw, Jack, popular name of **John Whitaker Straw** (1946–) British statesman. He studied at Leeds University, became president of the National Union of Students (1969–71), and was called to the bar in 1972. He became a member of Islington Council (1971–8), and was elected an MP in 1979. After holding several junior posts, he became the opposition spokesman on Treasury and economic affairs (1981–3) and the environment (1983–7), then joined the shadow cabinet, and was spokesman on education (1987–92), environment and local government (1992–3), local government (1993–4), and home affairs (1994–7). He became home secretary in the 1997 Labour government.

Strawson, Sir Peter (Frederick) (1919–) Philosopher, born in London, England, UK. He studied at Oxford, where he became a fellow of University College in 1948, and professor of metaphysical philosophy (1968–87). His early work dealt particularly with the links between logic and language, in the general tradition of 'ordinary language' philosophy, as in his *Introduction to Logical Theory* (1952). He went on to extend and integrate this with metaphysical studies of the structure of human thought about the world, as in *The Bounds of Sense* (1966). Later works include *Logico-Linguistic Papers* (1971), *Scepticism and Naturalism* (1985), and *Analysis and Metaphysics* (1992). He was knighted in 1977.

Strayhorn, Billy, popular name of **William Strayhorn** (1915–67) Jazz musician, born in Dayton, OH. He was the composer of 'Lush Life', 'Take the 'A' Train', and many songs and extended works associated with Duke Ellington, for whom he was a staff arranger, lyricist, and key collaborator from 1938. >> Ellington

Streep, Meryl (Louise) (1949–) Actress, born in Summit, NJ. She studied at Vassar College and Yale Drama School, making her New York stage debut in 1969, and her film debut in 1977. *Kramer vs. Kramer* (1979, Oscar) established her as a first-rank star, and she has since consistently underlined her range, showing sensitivity and a facility with accents in a series of acclaimed characterizations, including *The French Lieutenant's Woman* (1981), *Sophie's Choice* (1982, Oscar), *Silkwood* (1983), *Out of Africa* (1985), *Cry in the Dark* (1989), and *Postcards From the Edge* (1990). Later films include *Death Becomes Her* (1993), *Bridges of Madison County* (1995), and *Marvin's Room* (1996).

Street, George Edmund (1824–81) Architect, born in Woodford, Essex, SE England, UK. He was assistant to Sir George Gilbert Scott, and started his own practice in 1849. He restored Christ Church in Dublin, and designed neo-Gothic buildings, including the London Law Courts and many churches. >> Scott, George Gilbert; Webb, Philip

Street, Jessie (Mary Grey), Lady (1889–1970) Feminist and writer, born in Ranchi province, Chota Nagpur, India. She studied at Sydney University, and became an activist for the League of Nations, secretary to the National Council of Women, and president of the Feminist Club. In 1929 she was the founding president of the United Associations of

Women. She was the only woman delegate at the San Francisco conference (1945), from which evolved the UN. Her husband, **Sir Kenneth Whistler Street** (1890–1972), was Lieutenant-Governor and Chief Justice of New South Wales, as was her son, **Sir Laurence Whistler Street** (1926–).

Streeton, Sir Arthur Ernest (1867–1943) Landscape painter, born in Mount Duneed, Victoria, Australia. He studied at the National Gallery School in Melbourne, and helped establish the 'Heidelberg school' of painting. His works include 'Still Glides the Stream' (c.1890, New South Wales), and 'The Purple Noon's Transparent Might' (c.1896, Victoria). In 1898 he went to London, and exhibited at the Royal Academy in 1900.

Street-Porter, Janet (1946–) British television executive, presenter, and journalist. A columnist and fashion writer for leading magazines and newspapers, she entered independent television in 1975 as a presenter, moving on to devise such programmes as *Get Fresh* for ITV and *Bliss* and *Network 7* for Channel 4. She joined the BBC as head of Youth and Entertainment Features (1988–94) and was appointed managing director of the cable channel Live TV for the Mirror Group (1994–5). In 1996 she became director and co-founder of Screaming Productions. She received the BAFTA Award for originality in 1988.

Strehler, Giorgio [strayler] (1921–97) Theatre director, born in Trieste, Italy. A pioneer and figurehead in post-World War 2 theatre, he became artistic director of Milan's Piccolo Teatro, which he established with Paolo Grassi in 1947, and a leading force in the Theatre de l'Europe (a united European venture). Notable among more than 200 productions are his revisions of plays by Goldoni and Shakespeare, and his 'dialectical' renderings of Brecht.

Streicher, Julius [shtriykher] (1885–1946) Nazi journalist, and politician born in Fleinhausen, Germany. He was associated with Hitler in the early days of Nazism, taking part in the 1923 putsch. A ruthless persecutor of the Jews, he incited anti-Semitism through the newspaper *Der Stürmer*, which he founded and edited. He was hanged at Nuremberg as a war criminal. >> Hitler

Streisand, Barbra [striysand], originally **Barbara Joan Streisand** (1942–) Singer, actress, and director, born in New York City. Starting as a nightclub singer, stage and television appearances brought her the lead in the Broadway show *Funny Girl* (1964), which she repeated in the 1968 film version to win an Oscar. Later films include *Hello Dolly* (1969), *The Way We Were* (1973), *A Star Is Born* (1976), which she produced, *Yentl* (1983), which she co-scripted, composed, directed and starred in, *Prince of Tides* (1991), which she co-produced and directed, and *The Mirror Has Two Faces* (1996). A multi-talented entertainer, her 1965 television special, *My Name is Barbra*, won five Emmy Awards, and she has been the recipient of numerous Grammy Awards, including three as best female vocalist (1964, 1965, 1978). She has maintained parallel careers as a recording artist and film actress. >> Rosenthal

Stresemann, Gustav [shtrayzeman] (1878–1929) German statesman and chancellor (1923), born in Berlin. Entering the Reichstag in 1907 as a National Liberal, he became leader of the Party, and later founded and led its successor, the German People's Party. He was briefly chancellor of the new German (Weimar) Republic, then minister of foreign affairs (1923–9). He pursued a policy of conciliation, helped to negotiate the Locarno Pact (1925), and secured the entry of Germany into the League of Nations (1926). He shared the Nobel Peace Prize in 1926. >> RR1051

Stretton, Hugh (1924–) Writer and academic, born in Melbourne, Victoria, Australia. He studied at Oxford and Princeton universities, became a fellow of Balliol College, Oxford (1948–54), and held teaching posts in history

(1954–68) and economics (1968–89, then visiting fellow) at the University of Adelaide. His books include *The Political Sciences* (1969), *Ideas for Australian Cities* (1970), and *Political Essays* (1987). An important social theorist with a strong concern for social justice, he was one of the first people to look at the problems of urban Australia, and has criticized many of the trends in contemporary Australian society.

Streuvels, Stijn [stroevels], pseudonym of **Frank Lateur** (1871–1969) Novelist and short-story writer, born in Heule, Belgium. A master baker at Aragelm until 1905, he turned to writing full-time after achieving fame with his first collection *Lenteleven* (1899, The Path of Life). His works in lyrical prose style illustrate peasant life in Flanders, and are considered masterpieces of Flemish literature. They include *Langs de Wegen* (1902, trans Old Jan) and *De Vlaschaard* (1907, The Flax Field).

Strijdom, Johannes Gerhardus [striydom], also spelled **Strydom** (1893–1958) South African statesman and prime minister (1954–8), born in Willowmore, South Africa. He studied at Victoria College, Stellenbosch, and Pretoria University, and after a start in the civil service, took up law practice in the Transvaal. Elected MP for Waterberg in 1929, he became leader of the extremists in the National Party. His two main political ends were the setting up of an Afrikaner Republic outside the Commonwealth, and the policy of apartheid, which he helped introduce when he was premier by altering the balance of the Senate (1955) to ensure the necessary majority vote for his policies. >> Verwoerd; RR1088

Strindberg, (Johan) August (1849–1912) Playwright, born in Stockholm. He studied at Uppsala, and settled in Stockholm as a writer. He first achieved fame with the novel *Röda Rummet* (1879, The Red Room), followed by several plays. He travelled in France, Switzerland, and Denmark, then published his *Giftas I* and *II* (1884–6), collections of short stories, which led to his recall to Sweden (1884) to stand trial for alleged blasphemy. His plays *Fadren* (1887, The Father) and *Fröken Julie* (1888, Miss Julie) brought him to the forefront as the exponent of naturalistic drama. Later plays were more symbolic in form and religious in theme. His final 'chamber plays' were written for the *Intimate Theatre*, which he founded in 1907.

Stroessner, Alfredo [stresner] (1912–) Paraguayan dictator, born in Encarnación, Paraguay. He took up a military career, fighting in the Chaco War, and became president in 1954. He was re-elected at regular intervals, but forced to stand down after a coup in 1989. >> RR1080

Stroheim, Erich (Oswald) von [strohhiym] (1886–1957) Film director and actor, born in Vienna. He served in the Austrian army, and held a variety of jobs before moving to the USA in 1914. He made his film debut in small parts in D W Griffith's films, also working as an assistant to the director in *Intolerance* (1916). His first success as film director was with *Blind Husbands* (1919), followed by the classic film *Greed* (1923), and he had box-office hits with *The Merry Widow* (1925) and *The Wedding March* (1928). Later he returned to film acting, often playing the roles of German officers, such as Rommel in *Desert Fox* (1951). >> Griffith, D W

Strong, Leonard (Alfred George) (1896–1958) Novelist and poet, born in Plymouth, Devon, SW England, UK. He studied at Oxford, and took up school teaching until he established a reputation as a lyric poet with *Dublin Days* (1921), *The Lowery Road* (1923), and other volumes. He also wrote novels, including *Dewer Rides* (1929), a macabre novel set in Dartmoor, and *Deliverance* (1955). His collection of short stories, *Travellers* (1945), won the James Tait Black Memorial Prize.

Strong, Sir Roy (Colin) (1935–) Art historian and museum director, born in London, England, UK. He studied at Queen Mary College, London, and at the Warburg Institute, and became assistant keeper at the National Portrait Gallery, London in 1959, and its director in 1967. He was director of the Victoria and Albert Museum (1974–87), has produced numerous books, and wrote and presented the BBC television series *Royal Gardens* (1992). He was knighted in 1982.

Stroud, William (1860–1938) Physicist and inventor, born in Bristol, SW England, UK. He was professor of physics at Leeds (1885–1909), where began his long association with **Archibald Barr** (1889–1913), with whom he invented naval range-finders. They founded Barr Stroud Ltd in 1931, producing scientific instruments.

Strube, Sidney (1891–1956) Cartoonist, born in London, England, UK. Apprenticed as a designer of overmantels, he learned cartooning from the John Hassall School. After supplying a weekly cartoon to *Throne and Country*, he joined the *Daily Express* as a staff cartoonist in 1910, staying with the paper until he retired in 1946. Among his many characters, the favourite was 'Little Man', symbolic of the average *Express* reader. >> Hassall

Struther, Jan, pseudonym of **Joyce Anstruther Placzek**, *née* **Anstruther** (1901–53) Writer, born in London, England, UK. She married **Adolf Kurt Placzek** in 1948. Her most successful creation was 'Mrs Miniver', whose activities, first narrated in articles to *The Times*, became the subject of one of the most popular films of World War 2.

Struve, Friedrich Georg Wilhelm [shtroovuh] (1793–1864) Astronomer, the first of four generations of eminent astronomers, born in Altona, Germany. He became professor of astronomy at Dorpat (1813), director of the Dorpat observatory (1817), then director of Pulkova near St Petersburg (1839), which was constructed to his specifications through the patronage of Tsar Nicholas I. He founded the study of double stars, published a catalogue (1837) of over 3000 binary stars, and carried out one of the first determinations of stellar distance. >> Struve, Otto; Struve, Peter

Struve, G W L [shtroovuh] (1858–1920) Astronomer, the younger son of Otto Wilhelm Struve, and father of Otto Struve. He became director of the Kharkov observatory in 1894.

Struve, K H [shtroovuh] (1854–1920) Astronomer, the elder son of Otto Struve. He became director of the Berlin observatory in 1904.

Struve, Otto [shtroovuh] (1897–1963) Astronomer, the great-grandson of Friedrich Struve, born in Kharkov, Ukraine. His studies at Kharkov University were interrupted by the Revolution, when he joined the White Russian army. He emigrated to the USA in 1921, and joined the staff of Yerkes Observatory, WI, where he became director in 1932. He is best known for his work in stellar spectroscopy, and for establishing the presence of hydrogen and other elements in inter-stellar space (1938). >> Struve, Friedrich; Struve, Peter

Struve, Otto Wilhelm [shtroovuh] (1819–1905) Astronomer, the son of Friedrich Struve. He succeeded his father as director of Pulkova observatory, and discovered 500 binary stars.

Struve, Peter Bergardovich [shtroovuh] (1870–1940) Political economist, born in Perm, Russia, the grandson of Friedrich Struve. A leading Marxist, he wrote a critical account of Russia's economic development (1894), which Lenin attacked for its 'revisionism'. He edited several political magazines with liberal tendencies, was professor at St Petersburg Polytechnic (1907–17), and was closely connected with the 'White' movement in S Russia after the Revolution. After 1925 he lived in exile in Belgrade and Paris, where he died during the Nazi occupation. >> Struve, Friedrich

Strydom, Johannes Gerhardus >> Strijdom, Johannes Gerhardus

Stuart, Arabella, also spelled **Stewart** (1575–1615) English noblewoman. During the reign of Elizabeth I, she was recognized as second in succession to the English throne after her first cousin, King James VI of Scotland. When he became James I of England (1603), he had her imprisoned (1609), fearful of his position if she married. After her release she met and in 1610 secretly married **William Seymour** (1588–1660, later Duke of Somerset), for which they were imprisoned. She died in the Tower of London.

Stuart or **Stewart, Prince Charles Edward (Louis Philip Casimir)**, known as **the Young Pretender** and **Bonnie Prince Charlie** (1720–88) Claimant to the British crown, born in Rome, the son of James Francis Edward Stuart. Educated in Rome, he became the focus of Jacobite hopes. In 1744 he went to France to head the planned invasion of England, but after the defeat of the French fleet he was unable to leave for over a year. He landed with seven followers at Eriskay in the Hebrides (Jul 1745) and raised his father's standard at Glenfinnan. The clansmen flocked to him, Edinburgh surrendered, and he kept court at Holyrood. Victorious at Prestonpans, he invaded England, but turned back at Derby for lack of evident English support, and was routed by the Duke of Cumberland at Culloden Moor (1746). The rising was ruthlessly suppressed, and he was hunted for five months. With the help of Flora Macdonald he crossed from Benbecula to Portree, disguised as her maid. He landed in Brittany, then lived in France and Italy, where (after his father's death in 1766) he assumed the title of Charles III of Great Britain. >> Albany; Macdonald, Flora; Stuart, James

Stuart, Gilbert (Charles) (1755–1828) Painter, born in North Kingstown, RI. He travelled to Edinburgh in 1772, returned a year later, and began to paint portraits at Newport. In 1775 he went to London, where he studied under Benjamin West and became a fashionable portrait painter in the manner of Reynolds. In 1792 he returned to America, and as the leading portraitist painted nearly 1000 portraits, including those of Washington, Jefferson, Madison, and John Adams. >> Sully, Thomas; West, Benjamin

Stuart or **Stewart, Prince James (Francis Edward)**, also known as **the Old Pretender** (1688–1766) Claimant to the British throne, born in London, England, UK, the only son of James II of England and his second wife, Mary of Modena. As a baby he was conveyed to St Germain, and proclaimed successor on his father's death (1701). After failing to land in Scotland in 1708, he served with the French in the Low Countries. In 1715 he landed at Peterhead during the Jacobite rising, but left Scotland some weeks later. Thereafter he lived mainly in Rome. >> James II (of England); Mary of Modena; Stuart, Charles

Stuart, Jeb, popular name of **James Ewell Brown Stuart** (1833–64) Confederate soldier, born in Patrick Co, VA. He trained at West Point, fought against Indians on the frontier, and was Robert E Lee's aide in the assault against John Brown and his men at Harper's Ferry. The Confederacy's best-known cavalry commander, he fought at the first Battle of Bull Run (1861), and in 1862 led 1200 troopers in a famous ride around McClellan's army. He led his cavalry in most of the other famous campaigns in N Virginia, but was criticized for losing contact with Lee (who called him 'the eyes of the army') for a week during the Gettysburg campaign (1863). A dramatic figure in his gaudy uniforms and plumed hat, he was mortally wounded at Yellow Tavern. >> Brown, John; Lee, Robert E; McClellan

Stuart, John McDouall (1815–66) Explorer, born in Dysart, Fife, E Scotland, UK. He accompanied Captain

Charles Sturt's Australian expedition (1844–6), made six expeditions into the interior (1858–62), and in 1860 crossed Australia from south to north. *Mt Stuart* is named after him. >> Sturt

Stubbs, George (1724–1806) Anatomist, painter, and engraver, born in Liverpool, Merseyside, NW England, UK. He studied at York, and in 1754 travelled in Italy and Morocco. In 1766 he published his monumental *Anatomy of the Horse*, illustrated by his own engravings. He was best known for his sporting pictures, and excelled in painting horses.

Stubbs, William (1825–1901) Clergyman and historian, born in Knaresborough, North Yorkshire, N England, UK. He studied at Oxford, where he became a fellow of Trinity College. After serving as vicar of Navestock, Essex (1850), he became a diocesan inspector of schools (1860), and professor of modern history at Oxford (1866). Later he was appointed a canon of St Paul's (1879), and Bishop of Chester (1884) and Oxford (1889). His many works include the monumental *Constitutional History of England*, down to 1485 (3 vols, 1874–8), which put the study of English constitutional origins on a firm basis.

Studdy, George Edward (1878–1948) Cartoonist, born in Devon, SW England, UK, the creator of Bonzo the Dog. After trying both engineering and stockbroking, he created comic strips for *Big Budget* (1903). Graduating to the glossy weekly, *Sketch*, he created *Studdy's War Studies* (1915), semi-animated cartoon films for Gaumont. After World War 1 he began specializing in dog cartoons, from which the Bonzo character emerged. In 1924 he produced the first fully-animated cartoon film series made in England (*Bonzo*, 26 films). He also drew a *Bonzo* strip for *Titbits* (1926), and a daily and Sunday strip for USA syndication by King Features.

Studebaker, Clement [stoodbayker] (1831–1901) Manufacturer of horse-drawn vehicles and automobiles, born in Pinetown, PA. Together with two brothers he founded the Studebaker Brothers Manufacturing Co (1868). They progressed to automobile manufacture, forming the Studebaker Corporation in 1911.

Sturdee, Sir Frederick (Charles Doveton) (1859–1925) British naval commander. He entered the navy in 1871, rose to rear-admiral by 1908, and commanded HMS *Invincible* in the action which wiped out the German squadron under von Spee off the Falkland Is in 1914. Thereafter he served with the Grand Fleet, including the Battle of Jutland (1916). In 1921 he was promoted Admiral of the Fleet (1921). >> Jellicoe; Spee

Sturge, Joseph (1794–1859) Quaker philanthropist and reformer, born in Elberton, Gloucestershire, SWC England, UK. A prosperous grain merchant in Birmingham, he became a prominent campaigner against slavery in the British West Indies, which he helped to abolish in 1837. In 1841 he toured the US slave states with John Greenleaf Whittier, and later campaigned for the repeal of the Corn Laws, the extension of adult suffrage, and Chartism. >> Whittier

Sturgeon, William (1783–1850) Electrical engineer, born in Whittington, Lancashire, NW England, UK. He was self-educated in electrical science, and became a lecturer at the Royal Military College (1824). He built the first practical electromagnet (1825), invented the commutator for electric motors (1832), made the first moving-coil galvanometer (1836), and carried out research into atmospheric charge. His *Annals of Electricity* (1836) was the first journal of its kind in Britain.

Sturges, Preston, originally **Edmund Preston Biden** (1898–1959) Film-maker and scriptwriter, born in Chicago, IL. He studied in the USA and Europe, and became a businessman and inventor before succeeding in the 1940s with freewheeling comedies that combined wit, slapstick, and social concerns. His enduring hits include *The Lady Eve* (1941), *Sullivan's Travels* (1942), and *Hail, the Conquering Hero* (1944). He received an Oscar for the script of *The Great McGinty* (1940), and in 1974 a posthumous Laurel Award for achievement from the Writer's Guild of America.

Sturluson, Snorri [sturluson] (1179–1241) Icelandic poet and historian. In 1215 he was elected law-speaker of the island, but after becoming involved in a plan for Norway to rule Iceland, he incurred the ill-will of the Norwegian king, Haakon IV (reigned 1217–63), who had him murdered. His main works were the *Prose Edda* and *Heimskringla* (The Circle of the World), a series of sagas of the Norwegian kings down to 1177.

Sturm, (Jacques) Charles François [stürm] (1803–55) Mathematician, born in Geneva, Switzerland. A tutor in Paris, he was elected to the Académie in 1836, and became professor of mathematics at the Ecole Polytechnique in 1838. He discovered the theorem named after him concerning the location of the roots of a polynomial equation. He also did important work on linear differential equations. In 1826 he measured the velocity of sound in water by means of a bell submerged in L Geneva.

Sturm, Johannes [shtoorm] (1507–89) Educationist, born in Schleiden, Germany. He studied at Louvain University, taught there, lectured in Paris (1530–6), and was appointed rector of a new *Gymnasium* in Strasbourg, where he reorganized the education of the town. His new curriculum was adopted by other Protestant countries, including Britain, and became a model for secondary schools. He took a prominent part in religion and politics, siding with Zwingli against Luther, and was sent on several missions abroad. >> Luther; Zwingli

Sturt, Charles (1795–1869) Explorer, born in Bengal, India. He went as an army captain to Australia, and headed three important expeditions (1828–45), discovering the Darling (1828) and the lower Murray Rivers (1830). Blinded by hardship and exposure, he received in 1851 a pension from the first South Australian parliament. >> Hume, Hamilton; Stuart, John McDouall

Sturtevant, Alfred (Henry) [stertevant] (1891–1970) Geneticist, born in Jacksonville, IL. Working as an undergraduate at Columbia on fruit fly genetics, he had the idea of chromosome mapping, and his pioneer paper on this appeared in 1913. He went on to develop a range of related ideas, fundamental to modern genetic analysis. From 1928 his career was spent at the California Institute of Technology.

Stuyvesant, Peter [stiyvesant] (1592–1672) Dutch administrator, born in Scherpenzeel, The Netherlands. He became Governor of Curaçao, and from 1646 directed the New Netherland colony. He proved a vigorous but arbitrary ruler, a rigid sabbatarian, and an opponent of political and religious freedom, but did much for the commercial prosperity of New Amsterdam until his reluctant surrender to the English in 1664.

Stylites, Simeon >> **Simeon Stylites, St**

Styne, Jule (1905–94) Songwriter, born in London, England, UK. He began composing background music for films in 1937, and wrote his first songs for the film *Hit Parade of 1941*. For three decades he wrote dozens of memorable melodies for films and Broadway musicals, among them 'Diamonds are a Girl's Best Friend' for *Gentlemen Prefer Blondes* (1949), 'Three Coins in the Fountain' (1954, Oscar), 'Everything's Coming up Roses', 'Small World', and 'Together' for *Gypsy* (1959), and 'People' and 'Don't Rain on My Parade' for *Funny Girl* (1964).

Styron, William (1925–) Novelist, born in Newport News, VA. Educated at Duke University, he studied writing at the New School for Social Research in New York City. His first novel, *Lie Down in Darkness*, was published in 1951. Concerned with oppression in its myriad forms, he has tackled racism in *The Confessions of Nat Turner* (1967) and survivors of the Holocaust in *Sophie's Choice* (1979, filmed 1982).

Suárez, Francisco [swahreth], known as **Doctor Eximus** ('Exceptional Doctor') (1548–1617) Philosopher and theologian, born in Granada, Spain. He entered the Society of Jesus in 1564, was ordained in 1572, taught theology at Segovia, Valladolid, Rome, Alcalá, Salamanca, and Coimbra, and is often rated as the greatest of scholastic philosophers after Aquinas. His *Disputationes metaphysicae* (1597) was highly influential in the 17th-c and 18th-c, and he also wrote important studies in political theory. >> Aquinas

Subbotin, Mikhail Fedorovich (1893–1966) Astronomer and mathematician, born in Ostrolenka, Poland. He studied at Warsaw and Rostov-on-Don universities, worked in the State Astrophysical Institute (1922–30), then moved to Leningrad University, where he became director of the Leningrad Astronomical Institute in 1942. He is best known for his work on celestial mechanics and theoretical astronomy.

Subtilis, Doctor >> **Duns Scotus, Johannes**

Suchet, Louis Gabriel, duc (Duke) **d'Albufera da Valencia** [süshay] (1770–1826) Napoleonic general, born in Lyon, France. Destined to follow his father in silk manufacturing, his exceptional military talents became apparent when he was a volunteer in the national guard. After serving at Toulon (1793), Tirol (1797), and Switzerland (1797–8), he played a major role in Napoleon's successful crossing of the Alps (1800), defeated the British (1809–10), and conquered Valencia (1812), which gave him his title. Made a peer by Louis XVIII, he was deprived of his title in 1815 because of his support of Napoleon during the Hundred Days. >> Napoleon

Suckling, Sir John (1609–42) Poet and playwright, born in Whitton, Middlesex, SE England, UK. He studied at Cambridge, then lived splendidly at court, but involvement in political intrigue led him to flee the country, and he died (it is said by his own hand) in Paris. His plays (such as *Aglaura*, 1637) are austere, but his lyrics, influenced by Donne and Herbert, are highly acclaimed. They were published in *Fragmenta aurea* (1646). >> Donne; Herbert, George

Sucksdorff, Arne (1917–) Film director, born in Stockholm. He studied natural science, then art, but preferred photography. His first short film won awards, and resulted in a contract with the major studio, Svensk Filmindustri. He has made a series of prominent nature films which, though magical at times, emphasize the cruel and dramatic aspects of animal life. Titles include *Människor i Stad* (1947, Rhythm of a City) and *Indisk by* (1951, Indian Village). His first major feature was *Det Stora Äventyret* (1953, The Great Adventure), filmed on a farm, using no professional actors.

Sucre, Antonio José de [sookray] (1793–1830) South American soldier–patriot, born in Cumaná, Venezuela. He was Bolívar's lieutenant, defeated the Spaniards at Ayacucho (1824), and became the first president (1826) of Bolivia. He resigned in 1828, took service with Colombia, and won the Battle of Tarqui (1829) against Peru. He was assassinated near Pasló.

Sue, Eugène [sü], pseudonym of **Marie Joseph Sue** (1804–57) Novelist, born in Paris. He served as a surgeon in Spain (1823) and at Navarino Bay (1827) and wrote a vast number of Byronic novels, idealizing the poor, such as *Les Mystères de Paris* (1843, The Mysteries of Paris), which was a major influence on Hugo. A republican deputy, he was driven into exile in 1851. >> Hugo

Suess, Eduard [züs] (1831–1914) Geologist, born in London, England, UK. He became professor of geology at Vienna (1857–1901). Of his works, *Das Antlitz der Erde* (1885–1909, The Face of the Earth) was the most important. His theory that there had once been a great supercontinent made up of the present southern continents led to modern theories of continental drift. >> Wegener

Suetonius [swetohnius], in full **Gaius Suetonius Tranquillus** (75–160) Roman biographer and antiquarian. He became Hadrian's secretary, a post he lost when he was compromised in a court intrigue. He then devoted himself to writing, his best-known work being *De vita Caesarum* (The Lives of the [First Twelve] Caesars), remarkable for its terseness, elegance, and impartiality. Only fragments survive of his other writings.

Suger [süzhay] (1081–1151) Churchman, and abbot of St Denis from 1122, born near Paris. He carried out substantial reforms, and rebuilt the church of St Denis in the Gothic style, the first of its kind. Louis VI and Louis VII employed him on a number of missions, and during the latter's absence on the second crusade, Suger was one of the regents. He wrote a life of Louis VI, which is valuable for the view it affords of the time.

Suharto [soohah(r)toh] (1921–) Indonesian soldier, statesman, and second president (1968–), born in Kemusu, Java. As is common in Java, he uses only his given name. Educated for service in the Dutch colonial army, in 1943 he was given command of the Japanese-sponsored Indonesian army, and in 1965 he became Indonesia's chief of the army staff. The policies of President Sukarno led to a threat of civil war in 1965 and 1966, and Suharto assumed executive power in 1967, ordering the mass arrest and internment of alleged Communists. He became titular president in 1968, thereafter being re-elected to office every five years. >> Sukarno; RR1063

Suk, Joseph [sook] (1875–1935) Composer and violinist, born in Křechaovice, Czech Republic. He studied in Prague under Dvořák, whose daughter he married, and carried on the master's Romantic tradition by his violin *Fantaisie* (1903), the symphonic poem *Prague*, and particularly by his deeply felt second symphony, *Asrael* (1905), in which he mourned the deaths of his master and of his wife. He was for 40 years a member of the Czech Quartet, and in 1922 became professor of composition in the Prague Conservatory. >> Dvořák

Sukarno or **Soekarno, Achmed** [sukah(r)noh] (1902–70) Indonesian statesman, and first president of Indonesia (1945–66), born in Surabaya, Java. As is common in Java, he used only his given name. He formed the Indonesia National Party in 1927, was imprisoned by the Dutch in Bandung (1929–31), and lived in exile until 1942, when he was made leader during the Japanese occupation. He became president when Indonesia was granted independence in 1945. His popularity waned as the country suffered increasing internal chaos and poverty, while his government laid themselves open to charges of corruption. An abortive Communist coup (1965) led to student riots and a takeover by the army, his powers gradually devolving onto General Suharto. Sukarno finally retired in 1968. >> Suharto; RR1063

Sukuna, Ratu Sir Josefa Lalabalavu Vanaaliali [sukoona] (1888–1958) Fijian leader. He studied in New Zealand and at Oxford, then served in the French Foreign Legion (1914–15) before rejoining the colonial service in Fiji, where he had a career unmatched by any other

Fijian. Knighted in 1946, he was appointed District Commissioner (1932), adviser on Fijian Affairs (1943), and Speaker of the Legislative Council (1956). He groomed his nephew, Ratu Sir Kamisese Mara, to become the first prime minister of Fiji, which attained independence in 1970.

Sulaiman or **Suleyman I** [sülayman], known as **the Magnificent** (1494–1566) Ottoman Sultan (1520–66). He added to his dominions by conquest Belgrade, Budapest, Rhodes, Tabriz, Baghdad, Aden, and Algiers. His fleets dominated the Mediterranean, though he failed to capture Malta. His system of laws regulating land tenure earned him the name *Kanuni* ('lawgiver'), and he was a great patron of arts and architecture. He died during the siege of Szigeth in his war with Austria. >> RR1094

Sulla, Lucius Cornelius, nickname **Felix** ('Lucky') (138–78 BC) Roman politician of the late Republic, whose bitter feud with Marius, begun in Africa in 107 BC during the Jugurthine War, twice plunged Rome into civil war in the 80s BC. In 88 BC he chose to lead his army against the state rather than surrender to Marius his command of the war against Mithridates, and on returning to Rome (83 BC) used his forces to defeat the Marians and secure his own (illegal) position. Appointed 'Dictator' in 82 BC, he set about reforming the state, and enacted a number of measures to boost the authority of the Senate. These did not long survive his sudden retirement in 79 BC, but his reform of criminal jurisdiction lasted into the empire. >> Jugurtha; Marius, Gaius; Mithridates VI Eupator

Sullivan, Anne, originally **Joanna Mansfield Sullivan** (1866–1936) The teacher of Helen Keller, born in Feeding Hills, MA. Nearly blind from a childhood fever, she was educated at the Perkins Institution in Waltham, MA. She returned there in 1887 to teach the newly admitted seven-year-old Helen Keller, and broke through Helen's isolation by spelling out words on her hand (a story made famous in the film *The Miracle Worker*, 1957). For the rest of her life she remained Keller's companion, while establishing her own reputation as an author, lecturer, and advocate for the deaf. >> Keller, Helen

Sullivan, Sir Arthur (Seymour) (1842–1900) Composer, born in London, England, UK. He studied in London and Leipzig, and became an organist in London. His association with the theatre started in 1867, and from 1871 he was known for his collaboration with W S Gilbert in such comic operas as *HMS Pinafore* (1878) and *The Pirates of Penzance* (1879). He also composed a grand opera, *Ivanhoe* (1891), cantatas, ballads, a *Te Deum*, and hymn tunes. He was knighted in 1883. >> Gilbert, W S

Sullivan, Ed(ward Vincent) (1902–74) Newspaper columnist and broadcaster, born in New York City. He worked as a sports writer and columnist for a variety of publications before becoming a syndicated Broadway gossip columnist based at the New York *Daily News* (1932–74). Master of ceremonies for such theatrical events as the *Harvest Moon Ball* (1936–52), he moved to radio with *Ed Sullivan Entertains* (1942). Nationwide popularity followed as the host of the television variety show *Toast of the Town*, which was later renamed *The Ed Sullivan Show*, and ran from 1948 to 1971. He also wrote books and screenplays, including the film *Big Town Czar* (1938).

Sullivan, Jim, popular name of **James Sullivan** (1903–77) Rugby league player, born in Cardiff. He played rugby union for Cardiff before joining Wigan rugby league club in 1921. He kicked a world record 2859 goals, including a record 22 in one game (Wigan v Flimby & Fothergill, 1925). Player-coach of Wigan in 1932, he retired in 1946, and later became coach to Rochdale Hornets and St Helens. >> RR1167

Sullivan, John (1740–95) US soldier and political leader, born in Somersworth, NH. A lawyer by profession, he was a member of the First Continental Congress in 1775. He became a major-general in the Continental Army, and served at the siege of Boston (1775–6) and Staten Island (1777). He failed at the siege of Newport (1778), but in 1779 fought against the Six Nations and won at Elmira. He resigned his commission in 1779, and became attorney general of New Hampshire (1782–6).

Sullivan, John L(awrence) (1858–1918) Boxer, born in Roxbury, MA. He won the world heavyweight boxing championship as a bareknuckle fighter by defeating Paddy Ryan in 1882, but lost it under the Queensberry rules in 1892 to 'Gentleman Jim' Corbett. >> Corbett, James John

Sullivan, Louis (Henry) (1856–1924) Architect, born in Boston, MA. He studied in Paris and in 1886 won the New Exposition building contract (1886) with **Dankmar Adler** (1844–1900). He was one of the first to design skyscrapers, such as the Wainwright building in St Louis (1890–1). His experimental, functional skeleton constructions of skyscrapers and office blocks, particularly the Stock Exchange, Chicago, earned him the title 'the father of Modernism', and greatly influenced other architects. >> Greenough

Sully, Maximilien de Béthune, duc de (Duke of) [sülee] (1560–1641) Huguenot soldier, financier, and statesman who became Henry IV's chief minister, born in Rosny, France. He fought in the later stages of the Wars of Religion (1574–98) and was wounded at Ivry (1590). Instrumental in arranging Henry's marriage to Marie de Médicis (1600), he became the king's trusted counsellor. His major achievement was the restoration of the economy after the civil wars. In 1606 he was created duke, but after Henry's assassination (1610) was forced to retire to his estates. >> Henry IV (of France); Marie de Médicis

Sully, Thomas (1783–1872) Painter, born in Horncastle, Lincolnshire, E England, UK. He and his family emigrated to Charleston, SC, in 1792. He received art instruction from family members and in 1807 began a portrait-painting career in Richmond and Norfolk, VA. He worked with Gilbert Stuart in Boston, moved to Philadelphia, and studied with Benjamin West in London. Returning to Philadelphia in 1810, he painted technically polished and elegant portraits, as in 'Fanny Kemble as Beatrice' (1833), and was often compared to Gilbert Stuart. >> Stuart, Gilbert; West, Benjamin

Sully-Prudhomme [sülee prüdom], pseudonym of **René François Armand Prudhomme** (1839–1907) Poet, born in Paris. He studied science, then developed an interest in philosophy which underlies most of his poetical works. His early *Stances et poèmes* (1865) was widely praised, and among his later important works were the didactic poems *La Justice* (1878, Justice) and *Le Bonheur* (1888, Happiness). A leader of the Parnassian movement, which tried to restore elegance and control to poetry in reaction against Romanticism, he received the first Nobel Prize for Literature in 1901.

Summer, Donna, originally **LaDonna Adrian Gaines** (1948–) Singer, born in Boston, MA. She secured the lead role in the musical *Hair* (1967) in Munich, Germany, staying with the production for over four years. She then undertook regular work as a session singer in the Munich Musicland Studios, before recording 'Love to Love You Baby' (1975), an erotic song with a strong disco beat, which reached number 2 in the US music charts. Her songs were extremely popular in discos during the 1970s and 1980s. Her albums include *I Remember Yesterday* (1977), *Bad Girls* (1979), and *Another Place and Time* (1989).

Summerley, Felix >> Cole, Sir Henry

Summers, Anne (Fairhurst) (1945–) Academic, journalist, and bureaucrat, born in Deniliquin, New South Wales, Australia. She studied at the universities of Adelaide, Sydney, and New South Wales. Her influential book *Damned Whores and God's Police* (1975) was an important and ground-breaking study of the role of women in Australian history. She worked as a journalist for various newspapers, then became a 'femocrat' (1983–6) as head of the Office of the Status of Women in the Department of Prime Minister and Cabinet. She returned to journalism in 1986, becoming the US correspondent and North American manager for John Fairfax newspapers. In 1987 she became editor-in-chief of the influential American feminist magazine *Ms*, and was its editor-at-large (1990–2). She was adviser on women's affairs to Prime Minister Paul Keating in 1992, returning again to journalism as editor of the *Sydney Morning Herald* and (until 1997) *The Age*'s colour supplement. >> Keating, Paul

Summers, (Alphonsus Joseph-Mary Augustus) Montague (1880–1948) British priest and man of letters. He wrote on the theatre and drama of the Restoration, and on other literary subjects, but his most important works are two major reference books on witchcraft, *The History of Witchcraft and Demonology* (1926) and *The Geography of Witchcraft* (1927).

Summerskill, Edith Summerskill, Baroness (1901–80) Doctor and politician, born in London, England, UK. She studied at King's College, London, and shared a practice with her husband in London. She worked with the Socialist Medical Association, and became a member of Middlesex County Council (1934). From 1938 to 1955 she was a Labour MP, continuing an unremitting fight for women's welfare on all issues, and often provoking great hostility. She became under-secretary to the ministry of food (1949), and chairman of the Labour Party (1954–5). She was created a life peeress in 1961.

Sumner, Charles (1811–74) US statesman, born in Boston, MA. He studied at Harvard, was admitted to the bar, then studied jurisprudence in Europe (1837–40). In 1851 he was elected senator from Massachusetts, in which post he stood alone as the uncompromising opponent of slavery. In 1856, in the US Senate chamber, he was brutally beaten with a cane by another member of Congress, and incapacitated for over three years. In 1860 he delivered a controversial speech, published as *The Barbarism of Slavery*. He later became chairman of the Senate committee on foreign affairs (1861–71).

Sumner, James (Batcheller) (1887–1955) Biochemist, born in Canton, MA. He studied at Harvard, and became professor of biochemistry at Cornell in 1929. He was the first to crystallize an enzyme (1926), proving it to be a protein, for which he shared the 1946 Nobel Prize for Chemistry. >> RR1123

Sumter, Thomas (1734–1832) Revolutionary soldier and US political leader, born near Charlottesville, VA. He opposed the British under Tarleton in South Carolina, was defeated at Fishing Creek, but gained a victory at Blackstock Hill (1780). In 1789 he became a member of the US House of Representatives, and later of the US Senate (1801–10). Fort Sumter was named after him. >> Tarleton

Sundance Kid, popular name of **Harry Longabaugh** or **Langbaugh** (1870–?1909) Outlaw, born in Phoenixville, PA. At the age of 15 he was imprisoned in Sundance gaol for horse stealing (1887–9), after which he began life as an outlaw. He teamed up with Butch Cassidy, and drifted throughout North and South America robbing banks, trains, and mines. His date and place of death is uncertain, but it is generally held that he was fatally shot by a cavalry unit in Bolivia. >> Cassidy

Sung Tsu-wen >> **Song Ziwen**

Sun Yixian [sun yeeshan], or **Sun Yat-sen**, originally **Sun Wen** (1866–1925) Founder and early leader of China's Nationalist Party, born in Xiang-shan, Guangdong, China. He was educated in Hawaii and in Hong Kong, where he trained as a doctor. Alarmed by the weakness and decay of his country, he founded the Society for the Revival of China, and sprang to fame when, on a visit to London, he was kidnapped by the Chinese legation and released through the intervention of the Foreign Office. He then helped to organize risings in S China. He returned to China after the 1911 Wuhan rising, realized that he would not be widely acceptable as president, and voluntarily handed over the office to Yuan Shikai. After the assassination of his follower, Sung Chiao-jen, civil war ensued (1913), and he set up a separate government at Guangzhou (Canton). He was widely accepted as the true leader of the nation. >> Yuan Shikai; RR1041

Supervielle, Jules [süpervyel] (1884–1960) Writer, born in Montevideo. He wrote in French, producing many volumes of poems, including the notable *Poèmes de la France malheureuse* (1939–41, Poems of Unhappy France). He also wrote novels and plays, including *L'Enfant de la haute mer* (1931, The Child of the High Seas), *La Belle au bois* (1932, The Beauty of the Wood), *Shéhérazade* (1949), and the libretto for the opera *Bolivar* (1950).

Suppé, Franz von [soopay] (1819–95) Composer, born in Split, Croatia. Originally intended for a medical career, after his father's death he moved to Vienna and took up music. He conducted for the Josephstadt and Leopoldstadt theatres, and began to compose. His works include operettas, songs and Masses, and his *Light Cavalry* and *Poet and Peasant* overtures are still firm favourites.

Surrey, Henry Howard, Earl of (c. 1517–47) Courtier and poet, born in Hunsdon, Hertfordshire, SE England, UK. In 1532 he accompanied Henry VIII to France, was knighted in 1542, and served in Scotland, France, and Flanders. On his return in 1546, his enemies at court charged him with treason, and he was found guilty and beheaded. He is remembered for his love poetry, influenced by the Italian tradition, in which he pioneered the use of blank verse and the Elizabethan sonnet form.

Surtees, John (1934–) Motor-racing driver and motorcyclist, born in Westerham, Kent, SE England, UK, the only man to win world titles on both two and four wheels. He won the 350 cc motor cycling world title in 1958–60, and the 500 cc title in 1956 and 1958–60 (all on an MV Augusta). He then turned to car racing, and won the 1964 world title driving a Ferrari. He later became a racing car manufacturer. >> RR1165

Surtees, Robert (1779–1834) Antiquary and topographer, born in Durham, Co Durham, NE England, UK. He studied at Oxford and the Middle Temple, and in 1802 inherited Mainsforth near Bishop Auckland. Here he compiled his *History of the County of Durham* (1816–23). To Sir Walter Scott's *Minstrelsy of the Scottish Border* he contributed two 'ancient' ballads he created himself – *Barthram's Dirge* and *The Death of Featherstonhaugh*. >> Scott, Walter

Surtees, Robert Smith (1803–64) Journalist and novelist, born in The Riding, Northumberland, NE England, UK. He practised as a lawyer, and later became a justice of the peace and High Sheriff of Durham Co. He started the *New Sporting Magazine* in 1831, where he introduced John Jorrocks, a sporting Cockney, whose later adventures were contained in the highly popular *Jorrock's Jaunts and Jollities* (1838) and in *Hillingdon Hall* (1845). His other great character, Mr Soapy Sponge, appears in *Mr Sponge's Sporting Tour* (1853).

Susann, Jacqueline (c. 1926–74) Popular novelist, born in Philadelphia, PA. After a moderately successful career as an actress she turned to writing. Her first novel, *Valley of the Dolls* (1968), became an immediate best seller, as did *The Love Machine* (1969).

Suslov, Mikhail Andreyevich [suslof] (1902–82) Soviet politician, born in Shakhovskoye, Russia. He joined the Communist Party in 1921, and was a member of the Central Committee from 1941 until his death. An ideologist of the Stalinist school, he became a ruthless and strongly doctrinaire administrator. Very different from Khrushchev in temperament and political outlook, he opposed Khrushchev's 'de-Stalinization' measures, economic reforms, and foreign policy, and was instrumental in unseating him in 1964. >> Khrushchev

Sutcliffe, Bert (1923–) Cricketer, born in Auckland, New Zealand. One of New Zealand's greatest batsmen, he played 42 Tests and made 2727 runs, scoring five centuries. He took part in four New Zealand record partnerships, and showed great courage in repeatedly coming back to top-class cricket after sustaining serious injury. >> RR1151

Sutcliffe, Frank Meadow (1853–1941) Portrait photographer, born near Whitby, North Yorkshire, N England, UK. His studies of the vanishing world of English farmhands and fisher-folk brought him numerous awards from international exhibitions between 1881 and 1905. From the late 1890s he made extensive use of the new lightweight Kodak cameras to obtain intimate natural snapshots rather than formal poses. Reviving interest in Victoriana led to the publication of a fully illustrated account of his work in 1974.

Sutcliffe, Herbert >> Hobbs, Jack

Sutcliffe, Peter, known as **the Yorkshire Ripper** (1946–) Convicted murderer, born in Bingley, West Yorkshire, N England, UK. Employed at one time as a gravedigger, he shocked his workmates with his unnatural interest in corpses. He murdered 13 women over five years in N England and the Midlands. Many of his victims were prostitutes, the first being Wilma McCann, whose body was found in 1975. A lorry driver at the time, he was interviewed by the police on several occasions, before a routine check on a car registration led to his arrest in 1981. He identified himself as the murderer, was tried and found guilty of 13 murders and seven attempted murders, and given a life sentence on each account.

Sutherland, Donald (1934–) Film actor, born in St John, New Brunswick, Canada. He studied at the University of Toronto, and for a time at the Royal Academy of Dramatic Art, London. An actor of enormous versatility, he became known for his role in *The Dirty Dozen* (1967), following this with *M.A.S.H* (1970) and *Klute* (1971). Among his later films are *Ordinary People* (1980), *Backdraft* (1991), *A Time To Kill* (1996), and *Shadow Conspiracy* (1997).

Sutherland, Graham (Vivian) (1903–80) Artist, born in London, England, UK. He studied at London, worked mainly as an etcher until 1930, then made his reputation as a painter of Romantic, mainly abstract landscapes. He was an official war artist (1941–5), and later produced several memorable portraits, including 'Maugham' (1949), and 'Beaverbrook' (1951). His 'Churchill' (1955) did not find favour with Lady Churchill and was never seen by the public. He also designed ceramics, posters, and textiles. His large tapestry, 'Christ in Majesty', was hung in the new Coventry Cathedral in 1962.

Sutherland, Dame Joan (1926–) Operatic soprano, born in Sydney, New South Wales, Australia. She made her debut at Sydney in 1947, moved to London in 1951, and joined the Royal Opera, becoming resident soprano at Covent Garden. She gained international fame in 1959 with her roles in Donizetti's *Lucia di Lammermoor* and Handel's *Samson*. She has sung regularly in opera houses

and concert halls all over the world, and in 1965 returned to Australia for a triumphant tour with her own company. In 1954 she married the conductor **Richard Bonynge** (1930–), and was made a dame in 1979. In 1990 she gave her final performance at the Sydney Opera House.

Sutherland, Margaret Ada (1897–1984) Composer, born in Adelaide, South Australia. She studied at the Melbourne Conservatory, and in Vienna and London, returning to Australia in 1925, where for many years she was active in music administration and promotional work. Recognition came late, but her violin concerto (1954) was warmly received, and her opera, *The Young Kabbarli*, based on the life of Daisy Bates, was performed in 1965. She has written much chamber music and a number of song cycles, including one by Australian poet Judith Wright. >> Bates, Daisy May; Wright, Judith

Sutro, Adolph [sutro] (1830–98) US businessman, born in Aachen, Germany. In 1850 he arrived in New York City, the next year moving to San Francisco, where he established a trading business. In 1859 he founded a metallurgical works in Nevada, building the Sutro Tunnel for the draining and ventilation of mines in the Comstock Lode. In 1879 he returned to San Francisco, where he became a major landowner, and mayor (1894–6).

Sutter, John Augustus (1803–80) California colonist, born in Kandern, Germany. A Swiss citizen, he moved to the USA in 1834, and by 1839 had made his way to Mexican California. He obtained large land grants from the Mexican authorities, and set up a colony on the American R near present-day Sacramento. Known for his helpfulness to American settlers, he was ruined by the events that followed the discovery of gold on his property. He went bankrupt in 1852, and spent most of his remaining years trying to obtain satisfactory compensation.

Sutter, Joseph P (1921–) Aircraft designer, born in Seattle, WA. He worked for Boeing, and was head of the aerodynamics unit for the 707 family of jet-airliners, and chief engineer for the development of the 747, the first wide-bodied civil jet.

Suttner, Bertha, Freifrau (Baroness) **von**, *née* **Kinsky** (1843–1914) Writer and pacifist, born in Prague. In 1876 she married a fellow novelist, **Baron Arthur von Suttner** (1850–1902), and founded in 1891 an Austrian Society of Friends of Peace. She edited a pacifist journal, *Die Waffen nieder!* (1892–9, trans Lay Down your Arms!), which was translated into many European languages. She influenced Alfred Nobel to establish the Nobel Prize for Peace, and was awarded the prize herself in 1905. >> Nobel

Su Tung-p'o, pseudonym of **Su Shih** (1036–1101) Poet, essayist, calligrapher, and public official, born in Meishan, Szechwan, China. From a literary family, his brilliance brought him official appointments, as well as periods of exile which did not embitter him. One of the most prominent men of his time, he excelled in all fields of literature, and epitomized the cultural ideal of 11th-c Chinese humanism.

Suvorov, Alexander Vasilyevich [suvorof] (1729–1800) Russian soldier, born in Moscow. He won fame in the Seven Years' War (1756–63), the Russo-Polish War (1768–72), and in the war against the Turks (1787–92), and in 1799 was sent to Italy to assist the Austrians against the French, defeating them on the Adda, at Trebbia, and at Novi. He was then directed to join Alexander Rimsky-Korsakov to sweep the French out of Switzerland. After a terrible march over the Alps he found that Masséna had already defeated Korsakov; too weak to attack, he succeeded in escaping with most of his troops. >> Masséna

Suzman, Helen, *née* **Gavronsky** (1917–) South African politician, born in Germiston, Transvaal, South Africa. She studied at Witwatersrand University, then became a lecturer there (1944–52). Deeply concerned about the apartheid system erected by the National Party under Daniel Malan, she joined the Opposition, and was elected to parliament in 1953. She gradually gained the respect of the black community and, for years the sole MP of the Progressive Party, proved to be a fierce opponent of apartheid. In 1978 she received the UN Human Rights Award, and later served as president of the South African Institute of Race Relations (1991–3). >> Malan

Suzman, Janet (1939–) Actress, born in Johannesburg, South Africa. She studied at the University of the Witwatersrand, then at the London Academy of Music and Dramatic Art. Her many performances include Cleopatra in *Antony and Cleopatra* at Stratford in 1972, and Hedda in *Hedda Gabler* in London in 1976–7. In 1987 she directed *Othello* at the Market Theatre, Johannesburg, defying apartheid by casting a black actor in the title role, and also filmed it for television. Her films include *A Day in the Death of Joe Egg* (1970), *The Draughtsman's Contract* (1982), *Nuns on the Run* (1990), and *Leon, the Pig Farmer* (1993). In England her 1997 production of *The Cherry Orchard*, with a South African setting, won critical acclaim. She has twice won the Evening Standard Drama Award for Best Actress.

Suzuki, Shinichi [su**zoo**kee] (1898–) Music teacher, born in Nagoya, Japan. He studied in Tokyo and Berlin, and with three of his brothers founded the Suzuki Quartet. His mass instruction methods of teaching young children to play the violin have been adopted in many countries, and adapted to other instruments.

Suzuki, Zenko [su**zoo**kee] (1911–) Japanese statesman and prime minister (1980–2), born in Yamada, Japan. He trained at the Academy of Fisheries, and in 1947 was elected to the lower house of the Diet as a Socialist Party deputy, but moved to the Liberal Party in 1949, and then to the conservative Liberal Democratic Party (LDP) (1955). During the 1960s and 1970s he held a succession of ministerial and Party posts. Following the death of his patron, Masayoshi Ohira (1910–80), he succeeded to the dual positions of LDP president and prime minister in 1980. His premiership was marred by factional strife within the LDP, deteriorating relations with the USA, and opposition to his defence policy. He stepped down in 1982, but remained an influential LDP faction leader. >> RR1068

Svedberg, Theodor [s**vay**berg] (1884–1971) Physical chemist, born in Fleräng, Sweden. He studied at Uppsala, where he spent his whole career. In 1924 he described his ultracentrifuge, in which a solution can be spun at very high speed, generating centrifugal forces many thousand times that of gravity, and used it to develop methods for separating proteins. He was awarded the Nobel Prize for Chemistry in 1926. >> Tiselius

Svein I / II >> **Sweyn I / II**

Sveinsson, Asmundur [s**ven**son] (1893–1982) Sculptor, born in Iceland. He studied in Stockholm and Paris, visited Greece and Italy, and returned to Iceland in 1930. An artist of great versatility, his work was both figurative and abstract, and drew for inspiration on traditional Icelandic Saga material and folk-tales, but becoming increasingly abstract and Expressionist. He worked with equal ease in stone, cement, metal, and wood. Many of his works stand in public places around Reykjavík, and in his spherical workshop, now a museum devoted to his work.

Svensson, Jon Stefán (1857–1944) Writer and clergyman, born in Möðruvellir, Iceland. Educated in France, he became a Jesuit scholar and taught at a Catholic school in Denmark. During convalescence in The Netherlands from a severe illness (1911–12) he began to write a series of children's books about a boy called Nonni growing up in the N of Iceland, which made him a best-selling author. The *Nonni* books, originally written in German, have been translated into many languages.

Sverrir Sigurdsson [s**vay**reer **see**goordson] (c. 1150–1202) King of Norway from 1184, born in the Faeroe Is. He claimed to be the illegitimate son of a king of Norway (Sigurd Haraldsson, d.1155). He emerged from obscurity in 1179 to lay claim to the throne from Magnus V Erlingssonz (reigned 1162–84), whom he finally defeated and killed in 1184. One of Norway's greatest kings, he strengthened the crown against both Church and nobles with the support of the freeholding farmers. He commissioned one of the first Icelandic Sagas, a biography of himself, *Sverris saga* by Karl Jónsson. >> RR1079

Svevo, Italo [z**vay**voh], pseudonym of **Ettore Schmitz** (1861–1928) Novelist, born in Trieste, Italy. He worked as a bank clerk, then turned to writing, encouraged by James Joyce, who taught him English. He had a considerable success with *La coscienza di Zeno* (1923, The Confessions of Zeno), a psychological study of inner conflicts. >> Joyce, James

Svoboda, Ludvík [s**vo**boda] (1895–1979) Czech soldier, politician, and president of Czechoslovakia (1968–75), born in Hroznatín, Czech Republic. He fought with the Czechoslovak Legion in Russia in 1917 before becoming a professional soldier. After escaping from Czechoslovakia in 1939, he became commanding general of the Czechoslovak army corps attached to the Red Army in 1943, and helped to liberate Košiče, Brno, and Prague (1944–5). In 1948 he joined the Communist Party and was minister of defence until 1950. From 1952 to 1963 he lived in obscurity, but was subsequently brought forward as a patriot, and in 1968 succeeded the discredited Antonin Novotný as president. After the hostile Soviet intervention in 1968, he travelled to Moscow to seek relaxation of the repressive measures imposed on the country. >> Novotný; RR1043

Swainson, William (1789–1855) Naturalist and bird illustrator, born in Hoylake, Cheshire, NWC England, UK. He worked as a clerk, then obtained a post in the army commissariat in Malta and Sicily (1807–15), where he amassed a large collection of zoological specimens. His works included *Zoological Illustration* (3 vols, 1820–23) and *Naturalist's Guide* (1822). *Swainson's thrush* is named after him.

Swami Vivekananda >> **Vivekananda**

Swammerdam, Jan [s**vam**erdam] (1637–80) Naturalist, born in Amsterdam. He trained in medicine, then turned to the study of insects, devising a classification which laid the foundations of entomology. He first observed red blood corpuscles (1658), and discovered the valves in the lymph vessels and the glands in the Amphibia named after him.

Swan, Sir Joseph (Wilson) (1828–1914) Physicist and chemist, born in Sunderland, Tyne and Wear, NE England, UK. He became a manufacturing chemist, patented the carbon process for photographic printing in 1864, and invented the dry plate (1871) and bromide paper (1879). In 1860 he invented an electric lamp which anticipated Edison's by 20 years, and in 1879 demonstrated a lamp which considerably improved on Edison's patent model. He was the first to produce practicable artificial silk. >> Armstrong, William George; Edison

Swann, Donald (1923–94) Composer and lyricist, born in Llanelli, Carmarthenshire, SW Wales. He began his writing career by contributing music to revues such as *Penny Plain* (1951), *Airs on a Shoestring* (1953), and *Pay the Piper* (1954). His long collaboration with Michael Flanders began in 1956, when he wrote the music, and Flanders the words and dialogue, for *At the Drop of a Hat*, followed by *At* *the Drop of Another Hat* in 1965. From the 1970s he became a frequent broadcaster on musical and other matters, and wrote a musical fable for Christmas and three books of carols. >> Flanders

Swanson, Gloria [swonsn], originally **Gloria May Josephine Svensson** (1897–1983) Actress, born in Chicago, IL. After studying as a singer, and working as a film extra, she became one of Mack Sennett's bathing beauties. Cecil B de Mille brought her leading roles in silent films, such as *Manhandled* (1924), and she survived the arrival of sound, receiving Oscar nominations for *Sadie Thompson* (1928) and *The Trespasser* (1929). Her film career dwindled away despite a sensational comeback in *Sunset Boulevard* (1950), but she never relinquished her glamorous star status on stage and television. >> De Mille; Sennett

Swedenborg, Emanuel [sweednbaw(r)g], originally **Emanuel Swedberg** (1688–1772) Mystic and scientist, born in Stockholm. He studied at Uppsala, travelled in Europe, and on his return was appointed assessor in the college of mines. He wrote books on algebra, navigation, astronomy, and chemistry, and in 1734 published his monumental *Opera philosophica et mineralia* (Philosophical and Logical Works), a mixture of metallurgy and metaphysical speculation on the creation of the world. Curious dreams convinced him that he had direct access to the spiritual world. He communicated his spiritual explorations in *Heavenly Arcana* (1749–56), and spent the rest of his life in Amsterdam, Stockholm, and London, expounding his doctrines in such works as *The New Jerusalem* (1758). In 1787 his followers (known as *Swedenborgians*) formed the Church of the New Jerusalem. >> James, Henry, Snr

Sweelinck, Jan Pieterszoon [swaylingk] (1562–1621) Composer, organist, and harpsichordist, born in Amsterdam. He studied in Venice, and succeeded his father as organist of the Old Church (Oude Kerk), Amsterdam. He composed mainly church music and organ works, developed the fugue, and founded the distinctive North German school which later included Buxtehude and Bach. >> Bach, J S; Buxtehude

Sweet, Henry (1845–1912) Philologist, born in London, England, UK. He became reader in phonetics at Oxford, where he pioneered Anglo-Saxon studies. His works include Old and Middle English texts, primers, and dictionaries, and a historical English grammar. He was the probable source for Professor Higgins in Shaw's *Pygmalion*.

Swettenham, Sir Frank (Athelstane) [swetenam] (1850–1946) Colonial administrator in Malaya, born in Belper, Derbyshire, C England, UK. He was British resident in Selangor (1882) and Perak (1889–95), then resident-general in the Federated Malay States (1896–1901). Knighted in 1897, he was governor and commander-in-chief of the Straits Settlement (1901–4), and became an authority on Malay language and history, writing a number of books on the subject. Port Swettenham, Selangor, is named after him.

Sweyn or **Svein** [svayn], known as **Forkbeard** (?–1014) King of Denmark (c.985–1014) and England (1013–14), the son of Harold Blue-tooth, and the father of Canute. He first attacked England in 994, and had broken the back of English resistance by 1012. During his final campaign in 1013, he established mastery over the whole country and was recognized as king, while Ethelred the Unready withdrew to exile in Normandy. >> Canute; Ethelred II; Harald I Gormsson; RR1095

Sweyn or **Svein II**, also known as **Sweyn Estridsen** (c. 1020–74) King of Denmark from 1047, the son of Ulf, a regent of Denmark, and Estrid, sister of Canute the Great. He was appointed Regent of Denmark in 1045 by Magnus I Olafsson of Norway (reigned 1035–47), and acclaimed king himself when Magnus died in 1047. Harald III Sigurdsson

(Hardrada), who became sole king of Norway, laid claim to Denmark as well, and now began a long and unrelenting war of attrition against Sweyn. Sweyn lost every battle, but never lost the war, and at the peace of 1064 Harald accepted his right to the throne of Denmark. In 1069, after the conquest of England by William I, Sweyn's army descended on N England and captured York, but he made peace with William the following year and withdrew. >> Harald III Sigurdsson; William I (of England)

Swift, Graham (1949–) Novelist and short-story writer, born in London, England, UK. He studied at Cambridge and York universities, and published his first novel, *The Sweet Shop Owner*, in 1980. Later books include *The Shuttlecock* (1981), *Ever After* (1992), and *Last Orders* (1996, Booker Prize), as well as two collections of stories (1982, 1985).

Swift, Gustavus Franklin (1839–1903) Meat packer, born near Sandwich, MA. He worked in the butcher trade from age 14, developed his own business, and in 1872 became partners with a renowned Boston meat dealer. He revolutionized the meat-packing industry in 1877 by shipping dressed beef instead of live steers to purchasers in the east. His partnership dissolved, and in 1885 he established Swift & Co, pioneering the use of waste products to make glue, oleomargarine, soap, and fertilizer.

Swift, Jonathan (1667–1745) Clergyman and satirist, born in Dublin, Ireland. He studied at Dublin, then moved to England, where he became secretary to the diplomat, Sir William Temple. During a visit to Ireland, he was ordained in the Anglican Church (1695). He wrote several poems, then turned to prose satire, exposing religious and intellectual complacency in *A Tale of a Tub* (1704), and produced a wide range of political and religious essays and pamphlets. He was made dean of St Patrick's, Dublin, at the fall of the Tory ministry in 1714, and afterwards visited London only twice. His world-famous satire, *Gulliver's Travels*, appeared (anonymously, like all his works) in 1726. In later years he wrote a great deal of light verse, and several essays on such topics as language and manners. He also progressively identified himself with Irish causes, in such works as *The Drapier's Letter* (1724) and the savagely ironic *A Modest Proposal* (1729). >> Temple, William

Swinburne, Algernon Charles (1837–1909) Poet and critic, born in London, England, UK. He studied at Oxford, and became associated with the Pre-Raphaelite Brotherhood. Leaving without a degree, he travelled in Europe, and throughout his life spent a great deal of time in Northumberland, which he called the 'crowning county' of England. He achieved success with his play *Atalanta in Calydon* (1865), and the first of his series of *Poems and Ballads* (1865) took the public by storm. Other works include *Songs before Sunrise* (1871) and *Essays and Studies* (1875). In 1879, after a breakdown caused by alcoholism, he submitted to the care of a friend, **Theodore Watts-Dunton** (1832–1914), and lived in semi-seclusion for the rest of his life, publishing over 20 books of poetry, drama, and prose, including critical studies of Shakespeare, Hugo, and Ben Jonson. >> Millais; Milnes

Swinburne, Sir James (1858–1958) British scientist, 'the father of British plastics'. He was a pioneer in the plastics industry, and the founder of Bakelite Ltd. His research on phenolic resins resulted in a process for producing synthetic resin, but his patent for this was anticipated (by one day) by the Belgian chemist, Leo Baekeland. >> Baekeland

Swinhoe, Robert (1836–77) Naturalist and consular official, born in Calcutta, India. He went to Hong Kong in 1854, and was posted to Amoy in 1855. He was on the naval expedition that captured Beijing, negotiated the Treaty of Tiensin (1860), and became British consul in Formosa (1861–6), Amoy (1866–9), and Ningpo (1871–5). He compiled the first checklist of Chinese birds (1871). *Swinhoe's pheasant*, *Swinhoe's petrel*, and *Swinhoe's snipe* are all named after him.

Swinton, Alan Archibald Campbell (1863–1930) Electrical engineer and inventor, born in Edinburgh, EC Scotland, UK. He linked two houses by telephone at 15, only two years after its invention by Alexander Graham Bell. In 1882 he began an engineering apprenticeship in the Newcastle works of William George Armstrong, for whom he devised a new method of insulating electric cables on board ship by sheathing them in lead. A consulting engineer in London, he was one of the first to explore the medical applications of radiography (1896), and in a letter to *Nature* in 1908 he outlined the principles of an electronic system of television. >> Armstrong, William George

Swinton, Sir Ernest Dunlop, pseudonym **Ole Luk-Oie** (1868–1951) British soldier, writer, and inventor, born in Bangalore, India. One of the originators of the tank, he was responsible for the use of the word to describe armoured fighting vehicles. Under his pseudonym he wrote *The Green Curve* (1909), *A Year Ago* (1916), and several translations. He later became professor of military history at Oxford (1925–39).

Swithin or **Swithun, St** (?–862) English saint and theologian. He was adviser to King Egbert, and in 852 he was made Bishop of Winchester, where he died. When in 971 the monks exhumed his body to bury it in the rebuilt cathedral, the removal, which was to have taken place on 15 July, is said to have been delayed by violent rains – hence the current belief that if it rains on that day, it will rain for 40 days more. Feast day 15 July. >> Egbert

Sydenham, Thomas [**sid**enam], known as **the English Hippocrates** (1624–89) Physician, born in Wynford Eagle, Dorset, S England, UK. He studied at Oxford, and from 1655 practised in London. He stressed the importance of observation rather than theory in clinical medicine. He wrote *Observationes medicae* (1667) and a treatise on gout (1683), distinguished the symptoms of venereal disease (1675), recognized hysteria as a distinct disease, and gave his name to the mild convulsions of children (*Sydenham's chorea*) and to the medicinal use of liquid opium (*Sydenham's laudanum*). In England he suffered professional opposition, but some of his epidemiological theories on the fevers of London are supported today, though he failed to stress the roles of contagion and infection. >> Hippocrates

Sydney, Algernon >> **Sidney, Algernon**

Sydow, Max von [**sid**oh], originally **Carl Adolf von Sydow** (1929–) Actor, born in Lund, Sweden. He studied at the Royal Dramatic Theatre School, Stockholm (1948–51). Following his film debut in 1949, he began a long professional association with the director Ingmar Bergman at the Municipal Theatre of Malmö. Sydow's aloof presence well suited the brooding characterizations portrayed in such Bergman films as *The Seventh Seal* (1957) and *Through a Glass Darkly* (1961). American film successes include his roles as Jesus Christ in *The Greatest Story Ever Told* (1965), the priest in *The Exorcist* (1973), *Pelle, the Conqueror* (1988), and Emperor Ming in *Flash Gordon* (1980). Later films include *Awakenings* (1991), *The Touch* (1992), and *Hamsun* (1996). >> Bergman, Ingmar

Sykes, Eric (1923–) Comedy writer and performer, born in Oldham, Lancashire, NW England, UK. After entertaining in RAF shows during World War 2, he started to write scripts for radio shows such as *Variety Bandbox* (1947) and *Educating Archie* (1950–4). The creator of his own BBC series (1959–65, 1972–80), he offered simple, innocent humour devoid of malice and with a propensity towards physical jokes and slapstick antics. His film appearances include *One Way Pendulum* (1964), *Shalako* (1968), and *Theatre of Blood* (1973). He has written, directed, and acted in short, silent

comedies such as *The Plank* (1967) and *Rhubarb* (1970), and his television series include *Curry and Chips* (1969) and *The Nineteenth Hole* (1989). >> Jacques

Sylvester, James Joseph (1814–97) Mathematician, born in London. He studied at Cambridge but, as a Jew, was disqualified from graduating. He became professor at University College, London (1837), and the University of Virginia (1841–5). Returning to London he worked as an actuary, and was called to the bar in 1850. He then took up academic life again, becoming professor of mathematics at Woolwich (1855–70), at Johns Hopkins University, Baltimore (1877–83), and at Oxford (1883–94). He made important contributions to the theory of invariants and to number theory.

Sylvester II, originally **Gerbert of Aurillac** (c. 940–1003) Pope (999–1033), born in Aurillac, France. Renowned for his achievements in chemistry, mathematics, and philosophy, he is said to have introduced Arabic numerals and to have invented clocks. He became Abbot of Bobbio (982) and Archbishop of Ravenna (988). As pope, he upheld the primacy of Rome against the separatist tendencies of the French Church.

Sylvius, Franciscus [**sil**vius], Latin name of **Franz de la Boë** (1614–72) Physician, born in Hanau, Germany. One of the most outstanding teachers in Europe, he became professor of medicine at Leyden (1658–72), and introduced ward instruction to medical students. He founded the iatrochemical school of medicine, which was paramount in the rational application of science to a previously rather mythical form of medicine. He developed drugs to counteract chemical imbalances in the body, was the first to distinguish between conglomerate and conglobate glands, and also discovered the *Sylvian fissure* of the brain (1641).

Symington, Stuart [**siy**mingtn] (1901–88) US senator, born in Amherst, MA. He served in the army during World War 1, studied at Yale, and worked as an executive for several companies, becoming in 1939 the president and chairman of the Emerson Electric Manufacturing Co in St Louis. He was assistant secretary of war for air, then the first secretary of the air force during the first Truman administration. He ran for the US Senate from Missouri in 1952 and was re-elected three times, retiring in 1975. >> Truman

Symington, William [**si**mington] (1763–1831) Engineer and inventor, born in Leadhills, South Lanarkshire, WC Scotland, UK. He became a mechanic at the Wanlockhead mines. In 1787 he patented an engine for road locomotion and, in 1788, constructed a similar engine on a boat, having twin hulls with paddle-wheels between. In 1802 he completed at Grangemouth the *Charlotte Dundas*, one of the first practical steamboats ever built. It was intended as a tug, but vested interests prevented its use, asserting that the wash would injure the sides of the Forth and Clyde Canal.

Symmes, Robert Edward >> **Duncan, Robert**

Symonds, Henry Herbert [**sim**onz] (1885–1958) British educationist and classical scholar. He studied at Oxford, taught at Rugby School, and became headmaster of Liverpool Institute, then retired early to devote himself to the service of the countryside and its protection from vandalism. He was instrumental in opening the first Youth Hostels in Britain (1931), and served as treasurer, later vice-president, of the Friends of the Lake District. His book, *Walking in the Lakes District* (1933), became one of the classic guides.

Symonds, John Addington [**sim**onz] (1840–93) Writer and critic, born in Bristol, SW England, UK. He studied at Oxford, where he became a fellow of Balliol College in 1862. His major work was *Renaissance in Italy* (7 vols, 1875–86), and he also wrote travel books, literary monographs, biographies, translations, and poetry. In 1877 he settled for health reasons in Davos, Switzerland.

Symons, A(lphonse) J(ames) A(lbert) [sim onz] (1900–41) Bibliographer and biographer, born in London, England, UK. Self-educated, he was apprenticed to a furrier, before becoming secretary and later director of the First Edition Club. He proved to be a skilled bibliographer, but his greatest achievement was *The Quest for Corvo* (1934), the biography of the writer and novelist Frederick Rolfe, which is regarded as a modern masterpiece. >> Rolfe, Frederick William

Symons, Arthur (William) [sim onz] (1865–1945) Critic and poet, born in Milford Haven, Pembrokeshire, SW Wales, UK. He did much to familiarize the British with the literature of France and Italy, producing several translations, and publishing the influential *The Symbolist Movement in Literature* (1899).

Symons, George James [sim onz] (1838–1900) Meteorologist, born in London, England, UK. He served as clerk in the meteorological department of the board of trade, and founded the British Rainfall Organization for collecting rainfall data with the co-operation of the general public. Through his efforts the number of rainfall reporting stations in Britain was increased from 168 to over 3500. He was twice president of the Royal Meteorological Society, whose highest award (the Symons Memorial Gold Medal) bears his name.

Synge, J(ohn) M(illington) [sing] (1871–1909) Playwright, born near Dublin. Educated at Dublin, he studied music in Europe, then turned to writing. On the advice of Yeats, he settled among the people of the Aran Is, who provided the material for his plays, notably the elegaic *Riders to the Sea* (1904) and the subversive *The Playboy of the Western World* (1907). He had a profound influence on the next generation of Irish playwrights and was a director of the Abbey Theatre from 1904. >> Yeats, W B

Synge, R(ichard) L(aurence) M(illington) [sing] (1914–94) Biochemist, born in Chester, Cheshire, NWC England, UK. He studied at Cambridge, and joined the Wool Industry Research Association at Leeds (1941–3), where he worked with Archer Martin in devising the chromatographic methods that revolutionized analytical chemistry. He spent much of his career at the Rowett Research Institute in Aberdeen (1948–67) and the Food Research Institute at Norwich (1967–76). He shared the 1952 Nobel Prize for Chemistry with Martin. >> Martin, A J P

Szasz, Thomas (Stephen) [shash] (1920–) Psychiatrist, born in Budapest. He went to the USA in 1938 and received his MD from Cincinatti University in 1944. In 1956 he became professor of psychiatry at Syracuse University, New York. He has written many books, most of which argue that all disease must be physical, that consequently the idea of 'mental disease' is a myth, and that contemporary psychiatrists are often the agents of repression. His brand of individualism interprets all behaviour as purposeful and intentional, and asserts that all psychiatric therapy should be contractual.

Szell, George [sel] (1897–1970) Conductor and pianist, born in Budapest. A child prodigy, he was educated at the Vienna State Academy, and made his debut as a conductor in Berlin (1914), later conducting many of the world's major orchestras. He settled in the USA in 1939, and from 1946 was musical director and conductor of the Cleveland Symphony Orchestra.

Szent-Györgyi, Albert von Nagyrapolt [sent dyoor dyee] (1893–1986) Biochemist, born in Budapest. He studied at Budapest, then lectured at Groningen, Cambridge, and Rochester, MN, where he isolated ascorbic acid. He was professor at Szeged (1931–45) and Budapest (1945–47), discovering actin, which is responsible for muscle contraction. He emigrated to the USA, becoming director of the Institute of Muscle Research at Woods Hole, MA (1947–75), and scientific director of the National Foundation for Cancer Research, MA (1975). He was awarded the Nobel Prize for Physiology or Medicine in 1937 for his work on the function of organic compounds (especially vitamin C) within cells.

Szeryng, Henryk [she ring] (1918–88) Violinist, born in Warsaw. He studied at Warsaw and Berlin, and in Paris (1934–9) worked on composition with Nadia Boulanger. During World War 2 he was an interpreter for the Polish government in exile, while giving concerts for the Allied troops. He took Mexican citizenship in 1946, and was Mexican cultural ambassador from 1960. He wrote several violin and chamber music works, and taught internationally. >> Boulanger, Nadia

Szewinska, Irena [she vin ska], *née* **Kirzenstein** (1946–) Athlete, born in St Petersburg, Russia. She established herself at the 1964 Olympics with a silver medal in the long jump, and a gold in Poland's relay squad. She set world records at 100 m and 200 m in 1965, won three gold medals at the European Championships in 1966, and took the Olympic 200 m title in 1968 in world record time. She later won bronze medals at the 1971 European Championships and the 1972 Olympics. She then stepped up to 400 m, and in 1976 won the Olympic title in a new world record 49·28 sec. She appeared in her fifth Olympics at Moscow in 1980. >> RR1138

Szilard, Leo [zil ah(r)d] (1898–1964) Physicist, born in Budapest. He studied at Budapest and Berlin universities, fleeing from Germany in 1933. He worked first in London, then in 1938 emigrated to the USA, where he began work on nuclear physics at Columbia University. In 1934 he had taken a patent on nuclear fission as an energy source, and on hearing of Otto Hahn and Lise Meitner's fission of uranium (1938), he approached Einstein in order to write together to President Roosevelt, warning him of the possibility of atomic bombs. He was a central figure in the Manhattan Project, and after the War became a strong proponent of the peaceful uses of atomic energy. >> Einstein; Hahn, Otto; Meitner

Szymanowski, Karol [shima nof skee] (1882–1937) Composer, born in Tymozsowska, Ukraine. He became director of the State Conservatory in Warsaw, and is widely held to be the greatest Polish composer since Chopin. His works include the famous operas *Hagith* (1913) and *Krol Roger* (1918–24, King Roger), incidental music, symphonies, concertos, chamber music, piano music, and many songs.

Szymborska, Wislawa [sim baw(r) ska] (1923–) Poet and critic, born in Bnin (now part of Kornik), Poland. She moved to Cracow in 1931, where she studied literature and sociology at the Jagiellonian University (1945–8), and then worked for a Polish literary magazine. (1953–81). Her first collections of poetry appeared in 1952 and 1954, but were subject to the censorship of the era, and she now recognizes only her work published after 1957. English-language collections include *People on a Bridge* (1990), *View with a Grain of Sand* (1995), and *Sounds, Feelings, Thoughts* (1996). She is also known for her translations from French poetry. She received the Nobel Prize for Literature in 1996.

Tabari, al- [tabahree], in full **Abu Jafar Mohammed Ben Jarir al-Tabari** (839–923) Historian, born in Amol, Persia. He travelled throughout the Middle East collecting scholarly material, and wrote a major commentary on the Koran, and a history of the world from creation until the early 10th-c. His work provided a basis for later historical and religious studies.

Tabarley, Eric (1931–) French yachtsman. He was twice winner of the single-handed trans-Atlantic race – in 1964 in *Pen Duick II*, and in 1976 in *Pen Duick VI*.

Tacitus [tasitus], in full **Publius** or **Gaius Cornelius Tacitus** (c.55–120) Roman historian. He studied rhetoric at Rome, became a praetor, and established a great reputation as an orator, becoming consul in 97. His major works are two historical studies, the 12-volume *Historiae* (Histories), of which only the first four books survive whole, and the *Annales* (Annals), of possibly 18 books, of which only eight have been completely preserved. His concise and vivid prose style was a major influence on later writers.

Taddeo di Bartoli [tadayoh di bah(r)tohlee] (c. 1362–c. 1422) Painter of the Sienese school. Most of his early work was in Pisa, where he was responsible for the frescoes of Paradise and Hell in the Cathedral, and for paintings in the Palazzo Publico. He was also active in Siena, San Gimignano, Perugia, and Volterra. 'Descent of the Holy Ghost' in the Church of San Agostino at Perugia is his masterpiece, but he was usually more successful in his smaller pictures.

Tadema, Sir Lawrence Alma >> **Alma-Tadema, Sir Lawrence**

Taft, Robert A(lphonso) (1889–1953) US politician, born in Cincinnati, OH, the son of William Howard Taft. He studied law at Yale and Harvard, and in 1917 became counsellor to the US Food Administration in Europe. Elected a senator in 1938, he co-sponsored the Taft–Hartley Act (1947) directed against the power of the trade unions and the 'closed shop'. A prominent isolationist, he failed three times (1940, 1948, 1952) to secure the Republican nomination for the presidency. >> Taft, William Howard

Taft, William Howard (1857–1930) US statesman and 27th president (1909–13), born in Cincinnati, OH. He studied at Yale, became a lawyer, solicitor general (1890), the first civil governor of the Philippines (1901), and secretary of war (1904–8). During his presidency he secured an agreement with Canada which meant relatively free trade. He became professor of law at Yale in 1913, and later served as Chief Justice of the USA (1921–30). >> Taft, Robert A; RR1097

Tagore, Rabindranath [tagaw(r)] (1861–1941) Poet and philosopher, born in Calcutta, India. He is best known for his poetic works, notably *Gitanjali* (1912, Song Offering), and his short stories, such as *Galpaguccha* (1912, A Bunch of Stories), but he also wrote plays (such as *Chitra*, 1913) and novels (such as *Binodini*, 1902). In 1901 he founded near Bolpur the Santiniketan, a communal school to blend Eastern and Western philosophical and educational systems. He received the Nobel Prize for Literature in 1913, the first Asian to do so, and was knighted in 1915 – an honour which he resigned in 1919 as a protest against British policy in the Punjab.

Tahgahjute >> **Logan, James**

Taillefer [tiyfair] (?–1066) Norman minstrel. He sang war songs at the Battle of Hastings, in which he was killed. He is shown in the Bayeux tapestry.

Tailleferre, Germaine [tiyfair] (1892–1983) Pianist and composer, born in Park-St-Maur, France. She was named by the critic, Henri Collet, as one of *Les Six* – a group of composers who reacted against Romanticism and Impressionism. Her works include chamber music, a ballet, *Le Marchand d'oiseaux* (The Bird-Seller), a piano concerto, and songs. >> Auric; Cocteau; Durey; Honegger; Milhaud; Poulenc

Taine, Hippolyte (Adolphe) [ten] (1828–93) Critic, historian, and positivist philosopher, born in Vouziers, France. He studied at Paris, turned to writing, and made a reputation with his critical works, followed by several philosophical studies in which he attempted to explain moral qualities and artistic excellence in purely descriptive, quasi-scientific terms. His greatest work, *Les Origines de la France contemporaine* (1875–94, The Origins of Contemporary France), constituted a strong attack on the men and the motives of the Revolution.

Tairov, Alexander Yakovlevich [taeerof], originally **Alexander Kornblit** (1885–1950) Theatre director and actor, born in Rovno, Ukraine. He acted in Kiev, St Petersburg, Riga, and Simbirsk (1905–13), then directed at the Free Theatre in Moscow, before founding the Moscow Chamber Theatre with his wife in 1914. He remained director of this theatre until shortly before his death, pioneering a 'synthetic theatre' of abstract balletic movement which aspired to the emotional precision of music. His *Notes of a Director* appeared in 1921.

Tait, Archibald Campbell (1811–82) Anglican clergyman, born in Edinburgh, EC Scotland, UK. He studied at Glasgow and Oxford universities, and became a fellow of Balliol College. He entered the Church of England in 1836, and was an opponent of the Oxford Movement, protesting in 1841 against John Newman's *Tract 90*. He became headmaster of Rugby (1842), dean of Carlisle (1849), and Bishop of London (1856). He showed firmness and broadmindedness, as well as tact, in dealing with controversies over Church ritual. In 1869 he was appointed Archbishop of Canterbury (the first Scot to hold the post), and helped to lull the strife caused by Irish disestablishment. >> Newman, John Henry

Tait, Peter Guthrie (1831–1901) Mathematician, born in Dalkeith, Midlothian, EC Scotland, UK. He studied at the universities of Edinburgh and Cambridge, and became professor of mathematics at Belfast (1854) and professor of natural philosophy at Edinburgh (1860–1901). He was a major influence in the development of mathematical physics. He wrote on quaternions, thermodynamics, and the kinetic theory of gases, and collaborated with Lord Kelvin on a *Treatise on Natural Philosophy* (1867). A golf enthusiast, he studied the dynamics of the flight of a golf-ball and discovered the importance of 'underspin'. >> Kelvin

Tait, Thomas Smith (1882–1952) British architect. The most prominent Scots architect of the period between the two World Wars, he designed the *Daily Telegraph* office in London (1927), St Andrew's House in Edinburgh (1934), and won the competition for the Hawkhead Infectious Diseases Hospital in Paisley (1932). He was controlling designer of the Glasgow Empire Exhibition of 1938.

Tait, William (1792–1864) Publisher, born in Scotland, UK. He was the founder of *Tait's Edinburgh Magazine* (1832–64), a literary and radical political monthly. Its contributors included De Quincey, John Stuart Mill, Cobden, and Bright.

Taizong [tiytsung], also spelled **T'ai-tsung** (600–49) Second emperor of the Tang dynasty in China. As **Li Shimin** (Li Shih-min) he encouraged his father **Li Yuan** (566–635) to overthrow the Sui dynasty (618). He seized the crown in 618 after assassinating two brothers and their families, and forcing his father's abdication. His reign saw the zenith of Tang power. The government was restructured and Confucian ministers given prominence, the law was reformed, and new palaces, granaries, canals, and schools were built. Buddhism and Taoism was tolerated, and Xuanzang honoured. He suppressed frontier tribes, intervened in Nepal, invaded Korea (unsuccessfully), extended suzerainty over the Sassanids (Persia), defeated the E Turks (630), established protectorates over Annam, Manchuria, Mongolia, and the Tarim (Xinjiang), and united the royal houses of China and Tibet (649). Reputedly a great archer and horseman, he suffered from nightmares. >> Xuanzang

Taizu [tiysoo], also spelled **T'ai-tsu**, originally **Zhao Kuangyin** (928–76) First emperor of the Song (Sung) dynasty in China, born into a Beijing military family. He became a general, then reunified China after the post-Tang disintegration (after 907), having been put on the throne by the palace guard (960). Leaving the N under the Khitan Liao dynasty (907–1119) he defeated each S state in succession, and reasserted control of Annam. He treated defeated warlords leniently, subdued military political influence, retired army commanders to country estates, and directed power into civilian administration.

Takamine, Jokichi [takameenay] (1854–1922) Biochemist, born in Takaoka, Japan. He studied chemical engineering at Tokyo and Glasgow universities, and in 1887 opened his own factory, the first to make superphosphate fertilizer in Japan. In his private laboratory he developed a starch-digesting enzyme, and in 1890 went to the USA to develop its use in the distilling industry, setting up an industrial biochemical laboratory at Clifton, NJ. In 1901 he isolated crystalline adrenaline (epinephrine) from the suprarenal gland, the first hormone to be isolated in pure form from a natural source.

Takei, Kei [takay] (1939–) Post-modern dancer and choreographer, born in Tokyo. She studied in Tokyo, and at the Juilliard School, New York City, where Anna Sokolow taught dance. In 1969 she formed her own company, Moving Earth, and began her major work, *Light*. Fifteen parts of this harsh depiction of survival, which starts with the Vietnam War and includes both primitive and contemporary images, were shown in a single performance in 1981. >> Sokolow

Takeshita, Noboru [takeshita] (1924–) Japanese statesman and prime minister (1987–9), born in Kakeyamachi, Japan. He trained as a kamikaze pilot during World War 2. After university and a brief career as a schoolteacher, he was elected to the House of Representatives as a Liberal Democratic Party (LDP) deputy in 1958, rising to become chief cabinet secretary (1971–2) and minister of finance (1982–6). He founded his own faction in 1987, and three months later was elected LDP president and prime minister. His administration was undermined by the uncovering of the Recruit-Cosmos insider share-dealing scandal which, though dating back to 1986, forced the resignation of senior government ministers. >> RR1068

Tal, Mikhail Nekhemyevich (1936–92) Chess player, and world champion (1960–1), born in Riga, Latvia. In 1960 he defeated Mikhail Botvinnik to become the youngest grandmaster to hold the world title until then. His withering stares over the board were held by opponents as attempts at hypnotism, but it is more likely that they succumbed to his unusually inventive style of attack. Major kidney problems terminated his reign at the top, but he remained an active tournament player and chess journalist. >> Botvinnik; RR1149

Talbot, William Henry Fox (1800–77) Pioneer of photography, born in Melbury Abbas, Dorset, S England, UK. He studied at Cambridge, and became an MP (1833). In 1838 he succeeded in making photographic prints on silver chloride paper, which he termed 'photogenic drawing', and he later developed and patented the Calotype process.

Talese, Gay [talayzee] (1932–) Journalist, born in Ocean City, NJ. He was a reporter for the *New York Times* (1955–6), and wrote his first nonfiction 'short stories' for *Esquire* magazine, beginning in 1963. Described by Tom Wolfe as the inventor of 'new journalism', his style reached maturity in his best-selling nonfiction 'novels', *The Kingdom and the Power* (1969), about the *New York Times*, and *Honor Thy Father* (1971), about the Mafia. >> Wolfe, Tom

Taliesin [talyesin] (6th-c) Welsh bard, possibly mythical, known only from a collection of poems, *The Book of Taliesin*, written in the late 13th-c. His name is given in the 9th-c *Historia Britonum* of Nennius. >> Nennius

Tallchief, Maria, originally **Betty Marie Tallchief** (1925–) Ballet dancer, teacher, and artistic director, born in Fairfax, OK. Raised in Los Angeles, she studied with Ernest Belcher and Bronislava Nijinska. Touring with the Ballet Russe de Monte Carlo (1942–7), she met the choreographer George Balanchine; they married in 1946, and in 1948 she joined his newly founded New York City Center Ballet, where through 1965 her elegant and brilliant dancing won her acclaim. The ballet troupe and school she formed to serve the Chicago Lyric Opera in 1974 became the Chicago City Ballet in 1980. >> Balanchine; Nijinska

Talleyrand (-Périgord), Charles Maurice de [talayrã] (1754–1838) French statesman, born in Paris. Educated for the Church, he was ordained (1779), appointed Bishop of Autun (1788), elected to the States General, and made president of the Assembly (1790). He lived in exile in England and the USA until after the fall of Robespierre. As foreign minister under the Directory (1797–1807), he helped to consolidate Napoleon's position as consul (1802) and emperor (1804). Alarmed by Napoleon's ambitions, he resigned in 1807, becoming leader of the anti-Napoleonic faction. He became foreign minister under Louis XVIII, representing France with great skill at the Congress of Vienna (1814–15). He then lived largely in retirement, but was Louis Philippe's chief adviser at the July Revolution, and was appointed French ambassador to England (1830–4). >> Louis Philippe; Napoleon I; Robespierre

Tallien, Jean Lambert [talyĩ] (1767–1820) French revolutionary politician, born in Paris. As president of the Convention (1794), he was denounced by Robespierre, but conspired with Barras and Fouché to bring about Robespierre's downfall. He became a member of the Council of Five Hundred under the Directory (1795–9), and accompanied Napoleon to Egypt (1798). >> Barras; Fouché; Robespierre

Tallis, Thomas (c. 1505–85) English musician, 'the father of English cathedral music'. One of the greatest contrapuntists of the English School, an adaptation of his plainsong responses, and his setting of the Canticles in D Minor, are still in use. He wrote much church music, including a motet in 40 parts, *Spem in alium*. In 1575 Elizabeth I granted him, with Byrd, a monopoly for printing music and music paper in England. >> Byrd, William (1543–1623)

Talmadge, Eugene [talmaj] (1884–1946) US governor, born in Forsyth, GA. A Georgia farmer and lawyer, he entered state politics as Democratic commissioner of agriculture (1927–33). A states' rights governor (1933–7), he and Huey Long led Southern opposition to President Franklin D Roosevelt. He returned to farming and law, and then became governor again (1941–3), but lost favour after demanding that University of Georgia regents fire a pro-integration dean. He was re-elected governor in 1946, but died before assuming office. >> Long, Huey; Roosevelt, Franklin D

Tamayo, Rufino [taˈmahyoh] (1899–) Painter, born in Oaxaca, Mexico. He studied at the School of Fine Arts, Mexico City, and became engrossed in tribal sculpture as a curator at the National Museum of Archaeology (1921–6). His own style combines pre-Columbian art with the art of modern Europe. Among his works are 'The Birth of Nationality' and 'Mexico Today' (1952–3) for the Palace of Fine Arts in Mexico City, and murals in the UNESCO building in Paris.

Tambo, Oliver (1917–93) South African politician, born in Bizana, South Africa. He studied at Fort Hare University, and began a teacher's diploma course, but was expelled for organizing a student protest. In 1944 he joined the African National Congress (ANC), and was appointed vice-president of its youth league. He attempted to join the priesthood, but in 1956 was imprisoned, and released the following year. When the ANC was banned in 1960, he left South Africa to set up an external wing. With the continued imprisonment (until 1990) of Nelson Mandela, he became acting ANC president in 1967, and president in 1977. He returned to South Africa in 1990. >> Mandela

Tamburlaine >> **Timur**

Tamm, Igor Yevgenyevich (1895–1971) Physicist, born in Vladivostock, Russia. He studied at the universities of Edinburgh and Moscow, taught at Moscow State University (1924–34), then moved to the Physics Institute of the Academy. He shared the 1958 Nobel Prize for Physics for his work explaining the Cherenkov effect, used in highly sensitive atomic particle detectors. >> Cherenkov; Frank, Ilya Mikhailovich

Tanaka, Kakuei [taˈnaka] (1918–93) Japanese statesman and prime minister (1972–4), born in Kariwa Niigata Prefecture, Japan. A civil engineer, he established a highly successful building contracting business, and was elected to Japan's House of Representatives in 1947. He rose swiftly within the dominant Liberal Democratic Party (LDP), becoming minister of finance (1962–4), secretary-general (1965 and 1968), and minister of international trade and industry (1971–2), before serving as LDP president, and prime minister. He resigned in 1974, and in 1976 was arrested on charges of accepting bribes from the Lockheed Corporation while he was prime minister. He was found guilty, and subsequently convicted, but remained at home pending an appeal. >> RR1068

Tancred [ˈtangkred] (c. 1076–1112) Norman crusader, the grandson of Robert Guiscard. He went on the First Crusade, distinguished himself in the sieges of Nicaea, Tarsus, Antioch, Jerusalem, and Ascalon, and was given the principality of Tiberias (1099). He also ruled at Edessa and Antioch. >> Guiscard

Tandy, Jessica (1909–94) Stage and film actress, born in London, England, UK. Starting her career in England, she first acted in the USA in 1930, but not until playing Blanche in the original production of *A Streetcar Named Desire* (1947) did she begin to be perceived as an American actress. After her marriage (1942) to **Hume Cronyn** (1911–) they often appeared together on stage. She won an Oscar in 1989 as the leading actress in *Driving Miss Daisy*.

Taney, Roger Brooke [ˈtawnee] (1777–1864) Jurist, born in Calvert Co, MD. Admitted to the bar in 1799, he was elected to the Maryland Senate in 1816, passed from the Federalist to the Democratic Party (1824), then became attorney general (1831) and secretary of the Treasury (1833). Appointed Chief Justice in 1836, his most famous decision was in the

Dred Scott case, when he ruled that no negro could claim state citizenship for legal purposes. This precipitated the Civil War. >> Scott, Dred

Taneyev, Sergey (Ivanovich) [tanˈyayof] (1856–1915) Composer and pianist, born in Vladimir, Russia. He studied at Moscow Conservatory, where he became professor (1878) and director (1885–9), succeeding Tchaikovsky. He wrote music of all kinds, including two cantatas, *John of Damascus*, *After the Reading of a Psalm*, and six symphonies. A proponent of counterpoint in music, he wrote a two-volume work on the subject (completed 1909).

Tang Hsien-tsu >> **Dang Xianzu**

Tange, Kenzo [ˈtanggay] (1913–) Architect, born in Imabari, Japan. He studied at the Tokyo Imperial University, where he became professor (1949–74, then emeritus). His best-known early work is the Hiroshima Peace Centre (1949–55). Later works include the Shizoka Press and Broadcasting Centre (1966–7), the dramatic National Gymnasium for the 1964 Olympic Games, and the theme pavilion for the 1970 Osaka Exposition. His highly influential published works include *A Plan for Tokyo* (1960) and *Toward a Structural Reorganization* (1960).

Tanguy, Yves [tāˈgee] (1900–55) Artist, born in Paris. Mainly self-taught, he began to paint in 1922, joining the Surrealists in 1926. He worked in Africa from 1930, and moved to the USA in 1939, where he became a US citizen. All his pictures are at the same time Surrealist and nonfigurative, being peopled with numerous small objects or organisms, whose meaning and identity, as in the landscape of another planet, are unknown.

T'ang Yin (1470–1523) Painter and poet, born in Su-chou, Kiangsu, China. A young genius of modest means, at 28 he went to Beijing, passing the State's Exam, which would have opened the gates to a great career in government. Accused (perhaps unfairly) of cheating, he was forced to return home. In order to survive, he started painting in a popular and decorative style for the burghers of Souchou: portraits, pretty women, and erotica.

Tanizaki, Junichiro [taniˈzakee] (1886–1965) Novelist, born in Tokyo. He became known in the West only after the translation in 1957 of his long novel *Sasameyuki* (1943–8, trans The Makioka Sisters), a notable example of descriptive realism. Among his later novels are *Kagi* (1960, The Key) and *Futen rojin nikki* (1962, Diary of a Mad Old Man).

Tannenbaum, Frank [ˈtanenbowm] (1893–1969) Historian, born in Brod, Galicia, Austria-Hungary. He emigrated to the USA in 1905, and became a young member of the Industrial Workers of the World, working as a labour activist. He studied at Columbia College and the Brookings Institution, then taught Latin American history at Columbia University (1935–61). His *Crime and the Community* (1938) became a standard text. His most famous book, *Slave and Citizen* (1947), was a pioneering work on the historiography of American slavery. Long interested in Mexican history, particularly the revolution, he came to be regarded as the dean of North American Mexicanists.

Tansley, Sir Arthur George (1871–1955) Botanist, born in London, England, UK. He was professor at Oxford (1927–37), founded the precursor (1904) of the Ecological Society (1914), and was founder-editor of the *New Phytologist* (1902). A pioneer British ecologist, he published *Practical Plant Ecology* (1923) and *The British Isles and their Vegetation* (1939), and contributed to anatomical and morphological botany as well as to psychology.

Tantia Topi, originally **Ramchandra Panduranga** (c. 1819–59) Leader of the Indian Mutiny (1857), a rebel from Gwalior. He was Nana Sahib's lieutenant in the Mutiny, and took part in the massacre of the British at Cawnpore (1857). With the Rani of Jhansi (1858) he occupied Gwalior, then held the field after his chief had fled. He was captured in 1859, and executed. >> Nana Sahib

Tao Qian [tow chyan], also found as **T'ao Ch'ien** or **Tao Yuanming** (369–427) Poet, born near Nanchang, China. He served as a magistrate, but left the office for a life of poverty as a small-holder, devoting himself to the world of nature. His poems describe the hardship of cottage-life, but he also wrote many on wine (especially 'Fifth Poem on Drinking') and chrysanthemums as epitomizing harmony in nature. He also (innovatively) wrote short stories, notably 'Peach Blossom Paradise' (trans title).

Tapiès, Antonio [tapyes] (1923–) Painter, born in Barcelona, Spain. He studied law in Barcelona (1943–6), abandoned law for painting, in which he was largely self-taught, and became a founder member of the *Dau al Set* ('Seven on the Die') group of avant-garde artists and writers. His first one-man show in America, at the Martha Jackson Gallery in 1953, was followed by numerous exhibitions and international prizes. From 1955 he produced 'matter' paintings, using objects such as a desk instead of a canvas, as in 'Desk with Straw'.

Tarantino, Quentin (Jerome) [taranteenoh] (1963–) Film director, producer, actor, and screenwriter, born in Knoxville, TN. He wrote his first screenplay, *True Romance* (1987, released 1993) while working at Video Archives, Manhattan Beach. Lacking the finance to direct the project himself, he sold his script, and also that of *Natural Born Killers* (released 1994), thus enabling him to start production of *Reservoir Dogs* (1992), in which he was director, screenwriter, and actor. The success of this film, and its successor *Pulp Fiction* (1994; Cannes Palme d'Or; Oscar for Best Original Screenplay), in which he had the same roles, brought him celebrity status. He then acted in several films, such as *Desperado* (1995), before returning to production (while continuing as an actor) with *Four Rooms* (1995) and *From Dusk Till Dawn* (1996).

Tarbell, Ida M(inerva) (1857–1944) Reform journalist, born in Erie Co, PA. She was associate editor of *The Chautauquan* (1883–91), studied at the Sorbonne (1891–4), and joined *McClure's Magazine* (1894–1906). Her *History of the Standard Oil Company* (1904) established the place of women in the new 'muckraking' journalism. She also wrote biographies and feminist works, and helped run the *American* magazine (1906–15), campaigning against corruption and big business interests. Her history, *The Nationalizing of Business* (1936), became a standard work.

Tarkenton, Fran(cis Asbury) (1940–) Player of American football, born in Richmond, VA. He studied at the University of Georgia, where he led his team to victory in the Orange Bowl (1960). He joined the National Football League (NFL) Minnesota Vikings (1961) as starting quarterback, was traded to the New York Giants (1967), then rejoined the Vikings (1972). He gained 47 003 yds passing, an NFL record, and his 3686 passes completed and 342 touchdown passes were also NFL records at the time of his retirement (1978). He later worked as a football commentator and business consultant.

Tarkington, (Newton) Booth (1869–1946) Writer, born in Indianapolis, IN. Many of his novels have an Indiana setting, but he is best known as the author of *Monsieur Beaucaire* (1900). His other works include a trilogy, *Growth* (1927) – which includes *The Magnificent Ambersons* (1918, Pulitzer) – *Alice Adams* (1921, Pulitzer), and a book of reminiscences, *The World Does Move* (1928).

Tarkovsky, Andrey [tah(r)kofskee] (1932–86) Film-maker, born in Moscow. He studied at the State Film School, and directed the short film *Segodnya Otpuska Nye Budyet* (1959, There Will Be No Leave Today). His work gained him critical recognition as one of the cinema's true poets. He examined

youth in *Ivanovo Detstvo* (1962, Ivan's Childhood), and offered bleak visions of the future in *Solaris* (1972) and *Stalker* (1979). Exiled in Paris, his final film, *Offret* (1986, The Sacrifice), was characteristic of his concern for the future and his advocacy of peace.

Tarleton, Sir Banastre (1754–1833) British soldier, born in Liverpool, Merseyside, NW England, UK. He studied at Oxford, and served under Clinton and Cornwallis in the American War of Independence (1775–83). He was victorious at Waxham Creek (1780), and defeated Gates at Camden, but was beaten by Daniel Morgan (1736–1802) at Cowpens. He held Gloucester till it capitulated (1782), and then returned to England. He was MP for Liverpool (1790–1806, 1807–12). >> Clinton, Henry; Cornwallis; Gates, Horatio

Tarlton or **Tarleton, Richard** (?–1588) English clown who first performed with Leicester's Men, but joined Queen Elizabeth's Men on the formation of that company in 1583. He became the most famous and skilful popular entertainer of his age, especially in the dramatic jigs which were a regular feature of the playhouses.

Tarquinius Priscus, Lucius [tah(r)kwinius priskus] (c.7th–8th-c BC) Traditionally the fifth king of Rome (616–578 BC). Guardian to the sons of King Ancus Marcius, he assumed the throne on the king's death, but the sons eventually had him murdered. He is said to have started the building of the city wall, and to have instigated the Roman Games. >> RR1084

Tarquinius Superbus, Lucius [tah(r)kwinius sooperbus] (6th-c BC) Tyrannical king of Rome, possibly of Etruscan extraction, whose overthrow (510 BC) marked the end of monarchy at Rome, and the beginning of the Republic. Most of the details about his life are probably fictional. >> RR1084

Tarski, Alfred (1902–83) Logician and mathematician, born in Warsaw, Poland. He studied at Warsaw, and taught there until 1939, when he emigrated to the USA, teaching at the University of California, Berkeley (1942–68). He made contributions to many branches of pure mathematics and mathematical logic, but is most remembered for his definition of 'truth' in formal logical languages.

Tartini, Giuseppe [tah(r)teenee] (1692–1770) Violinist and composer, born in Pirano, Italy. He studied law and divinity at Padua, and was an accomplished fencer. He secretly married a protegée of the Archbishop of Padua, for which he was arrested. He fled to Assisi but, after attracting the archbishop's attention by his violin playing, he was invited back to his wife. Perhaps one of the greatest violinists of all time, he was also an eminent composer. His best-known work is the *Trillo del Diavolo* (c.1735, Devil's Trill).

Tasman, Abel Janszoon [tazmn] (1603–c.1659) Navigator, born near Groningen, The Netherlands. He was sent in quest of the 'Great South Land' by **Antony van Diemen** (1593–1645), Governor-General of Batavia, and in 1642 discovered the area he named Van Diemen's Land (now Tasmania) and New Zealand, followed by Tonga and Fiji (1643). He made a second voyage (1644) to the Gulf of Carpentaria and the NW coast of Australia.

Tassie, James (1735–99) Modeller and gem engraver, born in Pollokshaws, Glasgow, W Scotland, UK. Apprenticed to a stone mason, he studied art at Foulis Academy in Glasgow. In 1763 he went to Dublin as a laboratory assistant to a physician, Henry Quin, with whom he developed a special composition for making portrait medallions. In London from 1766, he made reproductions of some of the most famous gems (including Catherine the Great's collection at the Hermitage, Leningrad), cameo portraits of his eminent contemporaries, and the plaster reproductions of the Portland Vase. Collections are in the National Portrait Gallery and the National Gallery, Scotland.

Tassigny, Jean de Lattre de >> **Lattre de Tassigny, Jean de**

Tasso, Torquato (1544–95) Poet, born in Sorrento, Italy. He studied law and philosophy at Padua, where he published his first work, a romantic poem, *Rinaldo*. After joining the court of the Duke of Ferrara, he wrote his epic masterpiece on the capture of Jerusalem during the first crusade, *Gerusalemme Liberata* (1581, Jerusalem Liberated). He later rewrote his work, in response to criticisms, as *Gerusalemme Conquistata* (1593). He died in Rome, where he was to have been crowned as poet laureate.

Tate, (John Orley) Allen (1899–1979) Critic and poet, born in Winchester, KY. He studied at Vanderbilt University, and became known primarily as a proponent of the New Criticism. He was also a poet, biographer, and novelist. In 1928 he contributed several poems to *Fugitives: an Anthology of Verse*, among them 'Ode to the Confederate Dead', one of his most famous pieces. Other works include biographies of Thomas Stonewall Jackson (1928) and Jefferson Davies (1929). Collections of verse include *Mr Pope and Other Poems* (1928) and *Winter Sea* (1945).

Tate, Ellalice >> **Hibbert**

Tate, Sir Henry (1819–99) Sugar magnate, art patron, and philanthropist, born in Chorley, Lancashire, NW England, UK. He patented a method for cutting sugar cubes in 1872 and attained great wealth as a Liverpool sugar refiner. The Tate Gallery was founded by him.

Tate, James (1943–) Poet, born in Kansas City, KS. He studied at the Iowa Writers' Workshop, then taught at the University of Massachusetts, publishing his first collection, *The Lost Pilot*, in 1967. Later collections include *Absences* (1971) and *Distance From Loved Ones* (1990), and in 1992 he won the Pulitzer Prize for his *Selected Poems* (1991).

Tate, Nahum [**nay**uhm] (1652–1715) Poet and playwright, born in Dublin, Ireland. He studied at Dublin, and moved to London, where his first play was staged in 1678. He is known for his 'improved' versions of Shakespeare's tragedies, substituting happy endings to suit the popular taste, and with Dryden's help he wrote a second part to that poet's *Absalom and Achitophel* (1682). In collaboration with **Nicholas Brady** (1659–1726) he compiled a metrical version of the psalms. He became poet laureate in 1692. >> Dryden; Sternhold

Tate, Sharon >> **Manson, Charles; Polanski, Roman**

Tati, Jacques [tatee] popular name of **Jacques Tatischeff** (1908–82) Actor and film producer, born in Pecq, France. He began in music hall, and directed his first film in 1931. After *Jour de fête* (1947, trans The Big Day), directed and written by himself, he made his reputation as the greatest film comedian of the postwar period, notably in *Les Vacances de Monsieur Hulot* (1953, Mr Hulot's Holiday) and *Mon Oncle* (1958, My Uncle), in which he presented the pipe-smoking, lugubrious Hulot, forever beset by physical mishaps and confrontations with modern technology.

Tatian [**tay**shn] (2nd-c) Christian thinker, from Syria. He became a pupil of the martyr Justin in Rome, and was converted to Christianity by him. After Justin's death c.165 he was estranged from the Catholic Church, and returned to Syria (c.172). There he established, or was at least closely associated with, an ascetic religious community of Encratites, which fostered a heretical combination of Christianity and Stoicism. His *Diatessaron* ('Out of Four') is a version of the four Gospels arranged as a continuous narrative, which in its Syriac version was used as a text in the Syrian Church for centuries. >> Justin

Tatlin, Vladimir (1885–1953) Painter and designer, born in Moscow. He studied at the Moscow Academy of Fine Arts,

and was greatly influenced by Picasso's work in Paris in 1913. He founded Russian Constructivism, a movement at first approved by the Soviet authorities, and was commissioned to design the extraordinary spiral ironwork and rotating-glass 'Monument to the Third International' which, had it been built, would have been 1300 ft tall. >> Popova

Tattersall, Richard (1724–95) Auctioneer, born in Hurstwood, Lancashire, NW England, UK. In London he entered the Duke of Kingston's service, became an auctioneer, and in 1776 set up auction rooms at Hyde Park Corner, which became a celebrated mart of thoroughbred horses and a great racing centre. They were transferred to Knightsbridge in 1867.

Tattnal, Josiah (1795–1871) US naval officer, born near Savannah, GA. While serving in the US navy (1812–61) he compromised US neutrality by assisting a hard-pressed British squadron in its attack on a Chinese fort (1859). He explained that 'blood is thicker than water', and his action was upheld by the US government. As a Confederate naval officer (1861–5), he commanded the coastal defences of Georgia and South Carolina.

Tatum, Art(hur) [**tay**tm] (1910–56) Jazz pianist, born in Toledo, OH. Largely self-taught, he became the first supreme keyboard jazz virtuoso. Although near-blind, he was a professional musician from his teens. Moving to New York City in 1932, he made solo recordings and club appearances, becoming known for his technique, drive, and improvisational powers. The most influential of the swing-style pianists, he continued to work in the idiom until his death.

Tatum, Edward L(awrie) [**tay**tm] (1909–75) Biochemist, born in Boulder, CO. He studied at Wisconsin University, then taught at Stanford (1937–45, 1948–57), Yale (1945–8) and Rockefeller University (1957–75). With George Beadle he demonstrated the role of genes in biochemical processes, and with Joshua Lederberg showed that bacteria reproduce by a sexual process, thus founding the science of bacterial genetics. He shared with them the 1958 Nobel Prize for Physiology or Medicine. >> Beadle; Lederberg

Taube, Henry [towb] (1915–) Inorganic chemist, born in Saskatchewan, Canada. He studied at the universities of Saskatchewan and California, Berkeley, and held posts at Cornell, Chicago (1952), and Stanford (1962). He became a US citizen in 1942. He devised new methods for the study of electron transfer reactions in inorganic chemistry, and was awarded the 1983 Nobel Prize for Chemistry.

Tauber, Richard [**tow**ber] (1892–1948) Tenor, born in Linz, Austria. He established himself as one of Germany's leading tenors, particularly in Mozartian opera. After 1925 he increasingly appeared in light opera, notably Lehár's *Land of Smiles*, which he brought to London in 1931. This won him great popularity, repeated by his part in his own *Old Chelsea* (1943), and appearances in several films. He appeared at Covent Garden in 1938, and became a British citizen in 1940.

Taufa'ahau [**tow**fa-ahow], also known as **King George Tupou** (1797–1893) Tongan nation builder, born of an aristocratic lineage in Ha'apai. By 1852 he had concentrated political power over the whole of the Tonga Is in his own hands. He modernized administration, and founded the hereditary monarchy which continues to rule the country.

Taufa'ahau Tupou IV [towfa-a**how too**poh] (1918–) King of Tonga, the eldest son of Queen Salote Tupou III. He studied at Newington College and Sydney University. He served successively as minister for education and health, before becoming prime minister under his mother in 1949. On succeeding to the throne on his mother's death in 1965, he shared power with his brother, **Prince Fatafehi Tu'ipelehake**, who became prime minister. >> Salote Tupou III; RR1093

Taussig, Helen (Brooke) [towsig] (1898–1986) Paediatrician, born in Cambridge, MA. She studied at Johns Hopkins University, and became the first woman to become a full professor there. Her work on the pathophysiology of congenital heart disease was done partly in association with the cardiac surgeon Alfred Blalock, and between them they pioneered the 'blue baby' operations which heralded the beginnings of modern cardiac surgery. >> Blalock

Tavener, John (Kenneth) (1944–) Composer, born in London, England, UK. He studied at the Royal Academy of Music, London (1961–5), and has been professor of music at Trinity College of Music since 1969. His music is predominantly religious, and includes the cantata *The Whale* (1966), *Ultimos ritos* (1972, Last Rites) for soloists, chorus, and orchestra, and a sacred opera *Therese* (1979). In 1994 he co-published *Ikons: Meditations in Words and Music*. He was converted to the Russian Orthodox faith in 1976.

Tawfiq Pasha >> **Tewfik Pasha**

Tawney, Richard Henry (1880–1962) Economic historian, born in Calcutta. He studied at Balliol College, Oxford, was elected a fellow there in 1918, and wrote a number of studies in English economic history, notably of the Tudor and Stuart periods. Active in the Workers' Educational Association, he became its president (1928–44). An ardent Christian and Social reformer, his works include *The Acquisitive Society* (1926) and *Religion and the Rise of Capitalism* (1926). He became professor of economic history at the London School of Economics (1931–49, then emeritus).

Taylor, A(lan) J(ohn) P(ercivale) (1906–90) Historian, born in Lancashire, NW England, UK. He studied at Oxford, lectured at Manchester University, became a fellow of Magdalen College, Oxford (1938–76), and lectured in international history (1953–63). His major work was *The Struggle for Mastery in Europe, 1848–1918* (1954). He aroused passionate hostility with his revisionist *The Origins of the Second World War* (1961), arguing for accident and miscalculation rather than Hitler's grand design as its cause. Other works include *English History, 1914–1945* (1965), *The Trouble Makers* (1957), and a biography of his close friend Lord Beaverbrook (1972).

Taylor, Brook (1685–1731) Mathematician, born in Edmonton, N Greater London, England, UK. He studied at St John's College, Cambridge, and in 1715 published his *Methodus incrementorum* (Methods of Incrementation) containing his theorem on power series expansions, later recognized as the basic principle of differential calculus.

Taylor, Cecil (Percival) (1933–) Avant-garde pianist and composer, born in New York City. He studied at the New York College of Music and the New England Conservatory, Boston. In 1956 he made his first important quartet recordings, which diverged sharply from established approaches to jazz language and harmony.

Taylor, Cecil P(hilip) (1928–81) Playwright, born in Glasgow, W Scotland, UK. He wrote his first play, *Aa Went to Blaydon Races*, in 1962. Later works include *The Plumber's Progress* (1975), *Bring Me Sunshine, Bring Me Smiles* (1981), and his most successful play, *Good* (1981), which was first staged by the Royal Shakespeare Company. He also adapted plays by Ibsen and others, as well as writing for television. >> Ibsen

Taylor, Elizabeth, *née* **Coles** (1912–75) Novelist, born in Reading, Berkshire, SE England, UK. Educated locally, she worked as a governess and librarian, and wrote her first novel, *At Mrs Lippincote's* (1946), while her husband was in the Royal Air Force. Her understated, shrewd observation of middle-class life in the SE of England continued with further novels, including *A Wreath of Roses* (1950), *The Wedding Group* (1968), and *Blaming* (1976, posthumously).

Taylor, Elizabeth (Rosemond) (1932–) Film star, born in London, England, UK. In 1939 she moved with her family to Los Angeles, where her charm took the eye of the Hollywood film world, and she made her screen debut in 1942 at the age of 10. As a child star she made a number of films, including *National Velvet* (1944). She was first seen as an adult in *Father of the Bride* (1950). Her later films included *Cat on a Hot Tin Roof* (1958), *Butterfield 8* (1960, Oscar), and *Cleopatra* (1962), which provided the background to her well-publicized romance with Richard Burton. With Burton she made several more films, including *Who's Afraid of Virginia Woolf?* (1966, Oscar). Later films include *The Mirror Crack'd* (1980) and Zeffirelli's *Young Toscanini* (1988). There was a break in her acting career in the 1980s, while she received treatment for alcohol addiction, and in the 1990s her private life has continued to capture the headlines. In 1985 she founded the American Foundation for AIDS Research. She has been married eight times: **Nicky Hilton Jr** (1950–1), actor **Michael Wilding** (1952–7), film producer **Mike Todd** (1957–8), **Eddie Fisher** (1959–64), **Richard Burton** (1964–74, 1975–6), US senator **John W Warner** (1976–82), and **Larry Fortensky** (1991–6). >> Burton, Richard; Todd, Mike

Taylor, Frederick W(inslow) (1856–1915) Engineer, born in Philadelphia, PA. Employed in the Midvale steelworks in Philadelphia (1878–90), he became chief engineer in 1889, and introduced time-and-motion study as an aid to efficient management. From 1893 he worked as an independent consultant in what he called 'scientific management', and applied its principles successfully to both small and large-scale businesses. He published *The Principles of Scientific Management* (1911).

Taylor, Sir Geoffrey Ingram (1886–1975) Physicist and applied mathematician, born in London, England, UK. He studied at Cambridge, and made his career there, as reader in dynamic meteorology (1911) and research professor in physics (1923–52). He was an original researcher in a wide range of studies, particularly on turbulent motion in fluids, which he applied to meteorology and oceanography, aerodynamics, and even Jupiter's Great Red Spot. He proposed in 1934 the important idea of 'dislocation' in crystals, a form of atomic misarrangement which enables the crystal to deform at a stress less than that of a perfect crystal.

Taylor, Lady Helen >> **Kent, Edward, Duke of**

Taylor, Jeremy (1613–67) Theologian, probably born in Cambridge, Cambridgeshire, EC England, UK. He studied at Cambridge, became a fellow of All Souls College, Oxford (1636), chaplain to Archbishop Laud, and rector of Uppingham (1638). During the Civil War he is said to have accompanied the Royal Army as chaplain, and was taken prisoner at Cardigan Castle (1645). After the downfall of the cause he sought shelter in Wales, kept a school, and found a patron in the Earl of Carbery. His works include *The Liberty of Prophesying* (1646), *The Rule and Exercises of Holy Living* (1650), and *The Rule and Exercises of Holy Dying* (1651).

Taylor, John Henry (1871–1963) Golfer, born in Northam, Devon, SW England, UK. He was the first Englishman to win the British Open championship (1894, 1895, 1900, 1909, 1913), previously dominated by Scots. He also won the French Open twice, and the German Open once. He was a founder and first president of the British Professional Golfer's Association. >> Braid, James (1870–1950); Vardon; RR1157

Taylor, Maxwell D(avenport) (1901–87) US soldier, born in Keystesville, MO. He trained at West Point, and was among those who set up the first airborne units. In World War 2 he commanded the 101st Airborne Division, and was the first general to land in Normandy on D-Day. He then became superintendent of West Point (1945–9), served as military governor of Berlin (1949–51), commanded the US Eighth Army in the Korean War (1953–5), and took over as chief of the US and UN Far East commands. He was army chief-of-staff before retiring (1955–9), but President Kennedy called him out of retirement in 1961 and appointed him chairman of the joint chiefs-of-staff (1962–4). He took an active role under Kennedy and Johnson in escalating the US commitment to South Vietnam, and served as ambassador there (1964–5). >> Johnson, Lyndon B; Kennedy, John F

Taylor, Sir Patrick Gordon (1896–1966) Pioneer aviator, born in Mosman, New South Wales, Australia. He served with the Royal Flying Corps during World War 1, and received the MC. He worked on developing aviation instruments after the War. In 1935, over the Tasman Sea with Kingsford Smith in his *Southern Cross*, one engine cut out, and oil pressure was lost on another. Taylor spent the rest of the flight clambering across the wings every half-hour, transferring oil from the dead engine into the ailing one; for this he was awarded the George Cross. >> Kingsford Smith

Taylor, Paul (Belville) (1930–) Modern-dance choreographer, born in Pittsburgh, PA. Swimming and painting scholarships took him to Syracuse University, and he subsequently studied modern dance with Merce Cunningham and Martha Graham. He began choreographing in 1956, and developed a highly original and witty style, which often uses classical music to contemporary effect. >> Cunningham, Merce; Graham, Martha; Tharp

Taylor, Peter Hillsman (1917–) Short-story writer, born in Trenton, TN. Educated in Nashville, Memphis, and Kenyon College, OH, he writes with sentiment and irony about the smaller crises and collisions of urban middle-class life in the southern states of America. Representative stories are 'The Scoutmaster', 'The Old Forest', and 'The Death of a Kinsman'. *The Collected Stories of Peter Taylor* was published in 1969, and *A Summons to Memphis*, his only novel, in 1987.

Taylor (of Gosforth), Sir Peter Murray Taylor, Baron (1930–) British judge. He studied at Cambridge, was called to the bar in 1954, and became a QC (1967), a High Court judge (1980–7), a Lord Justice of Appeal (1987–92), and Lord Chief Justice of England (1992–6). In 1989 he was chairman of the Hillsborough football stadium Disaster Inquiry leading to the Taylor Report. He was knighted in 1980, and made a life peer in 1992.

Taylor, Zachary (1784–1850) US general, statesman, and 12th president (1849–50), born in Montebello, VA. He joined the army in 1808, fought against the Indians, and in 1840 was given command of the army in the SW. In the Mexican War (1846–8) he captured Matamoros, and won a major victory at Buena Vista, though heavily outnumbered. He emerged from the War as a hero, and was given the Whig presidential nomination. The main issue of his presidency was the status of the new territories and the extension of slavery there, but he died only 16 months after taking office.

Tchaikovsky or **Tschaikovsky, Piotr Ilyich** [chiykofskee] (1840–93) Composer, born in Kamsko-Votkinsk, Russia. He began as a civil servant, joined the St Petersburg Conservatory in 1862, and moved to Moscow in 1865. There he became known for his operas, Second Symphony, and First Piano Concerto. After an unsuccessful marriage, he retired to the country to devote himself to composition, making occasional visits abroad. Among his greatest

works are the ballets *Swan Lake* (1876–7), *The Sleeping Beauty* (1890), and *The Nutcracker* (1892), the last three of his six symphonies, two piano concertos, the *1812 Overture*, and several tone poems, notably *Romeo and Juliet* and *Capriccio Italien*.

Tcherepnin, Nikolay (Nikolayevich) [cherepneen] (1873–1945) Composer of ballets, piano music, and nationalist songs, born in St Petersburg, Russia. He left law school for the St Petersburg Conservatory to study under Rimsky-Korsakov. In 1901 he became conductor of the Belaiev Concerts, and took charge of opera at the Maryinsky Theatre. From 1908 to 1914 he worked with Diaghilev, conducting ballet and opera throughout Europe, then became director of the Tiflis Conservatory (1918–21). His works include operas, ballets, symphonies, other orchestral music, and piano pieces. >> Diaghilev; Rimsky-Korsakov

Teagarden, Jack, popular name of **Weldon John Teagarden** (1905–64) Jazz trombonist and singer, born in Vernon, TX. He started playing professionally at 10, and for him it always seemed easy. His embouchure was so sensitive that he barely moved the slide when he played, and when he sang it seemed as natural as talking. In 1928 he worked his way into Chicago, and supported himself playing in the Ben Pollack orchestra until 1933. He moved to New York as a featured soloist in Paul Whiteman's orchestra (1933–8) and set a new standard for jazz trombone, smooth but forceful, in numerous recordings. His first recorded vocal, 'A Hundred Years from Today' was a hit in 1933. Big, sleepy-eyed, and rural, he donned a tuxedo when he led his own orchestra (1939–46). He joined Louis Armstrong's All Stars (1947–51), then formed small bands for concert tours and played with local musicians in club dates. >> Armstrong, Louis; Whiteman, Paul

Teague, Walter (Dorwin) [teeg] (1883–1960) Designer, born in Decatur, IN. He trained at the Art Students' League, New York City, and established his own industrial design consultancy in 1926. Among his clients were Kodak, Ford, National Cash Register, and Texaco, for which he created a 'corporate identity'. From the mid-1940s his office became closely associated with the interior design of Boeing airliners. He was first president of the American Society of Industrial Designers, which he co-founded in 1944.

Teasdale, Sara, *née* **Sarah Trevor** (1884–1933) Poet, born in St Louis, MO. She was educated privately, travelled in Europe and the Middle East (1905–7), married (1914–29), and settled in New York City (1916). Her books include *Love Songs* (1917) and *Strange Victory* (1933). Afflicted with bouts of depression, she committed suicide.

Tebaldi, Renata [tebaldee] (1922–) Operatic soprano, born in Pesaro, Italy. She studied at Parma Conservatory, made her debut at Rovigo in 1944, and was invited by Toscanini to appear at the re-opening of La Scala, Milan, in 1946, where she sang until 1954. She then sang in many opera houses, including several seasons at the Metropolitan Opera, New York City, and made many recordings.

Tebbit (of Chingford), Norman (Beresford) Tebbit, Baron (1931–) British statesman, born in Enfield, N Greater London, England, UK. He left school at 16, worked as a journalist, and after national service in the RAF became an airline pilot, later heading the British Airline Pilots' Association. He became a Conservative MP in 1970, serving in Margaret Thatcher's governments as employment secretary (1981–3) and secretary for trade and industry (1983–5). His career was interrupted in 1984 when both he and his wife were badly hurt in the IRA bombing of the Grand Hotel in Brighton. In 1985 he became Chancellor of the Duchy of Lancaster and also chairman of the party. In 1987, there were open disagreements between him and

Mrs Thatcher over the handling of the general election campaign, and shortly after the Conservative victory he retired to the back-benches. He was made a life peer in 1992. >> Thatcher

Tecumseh [te**kum**suh] (c. 1768–1813) Indian chief of the Shawnees, born in Old Piqua, OH. He joined his brother, 'The Prophet', in a rising against the whites, suppressed at Tippecanoe by William Harrison in 1811. Passing into the English service, he commanded the Indian allies in the War of 1812 as brigadier-general. He fell fighting at the Thames in Canada (1813). >> Harrison, William Henry

Tedder (of Glenguin), Arthur William Tedder, Baron (1890–1967) British marshal of the Royal Air Force, born in Glenguin, Scotland, UK. During World War 2 he directed research and development at the Air Ministry, served as commander-in-chief (RAF) in the Middle East Air Force, moved on to the Mediterranean theatre (1943), and became deputy supreme commander of the Allied Expeditionary Force under Eisenhower (1943–5). He was appointed air marshal in 1945, and created a baron in 1946. >> Eisenhower

Teilhard de Chardin, Pierre [tay**ah** duh **shah(r)**dĩ] (1881–1955) Geologist, palaeontologist, Jesuit priest, and philosopher, born in Sarcenat, France. He lectured in pure science at the Jesuit College in Cairo, was ordained in 1911, and in 1918 became professor of geology at the Institut Catholique in Paris. He went on palaeontological expeditions in China and C Asia, but his unorthodox ideas led to a ban on his teaching and publishing. Nevertheless, his work in Cenozoic geology and palaeontology became known, and he was awarded academic distinctions. His major work, *Le Phénomène humain* (written 1938–40, The Phenomenon of Humanity) was posthumously published. Based on his scientific thinking, it argues that humanity is in a continuous process of evolution towards a perfect spiritual state. From 1951 he lived in the USA. >> Weidenreich

Tekakwitha, Blessed Kateri [teka**kwith**a] (1656–80) American Indian Catholic convert, born in Ossernenon, in Mohawk territory (now Auriesville, NY). When she was three years old, a smallpox epidemic killed her mother and father, and left her scarred and partially blinded. Raised by an anti-Catholic uncle, but inspired by Jesuit missionaries, she took instruction and was baptized a Catholic at age 20. To escape continuing persecution she fled a year later to a Christian Indian village near Montreal, where she became noted for her religious fervour and asceticism. She was beatified in 1980.

Te Kanawa, Dame Kiri [tay **kah**nawa] (1944–   ) Operatic soprano, born in Gisborne, New Zealand. After winning many awards in New Zealand and Australia she moved to London, where she made her debut with the Royal Opera Company in 1970. She has since taken a wide range of leading roles, and in 1981 sang at the wedding of the Prince and Princess of Wales. She was made a dame in 1982 and has produced many non-classical recordings. In 1989 she published *Land of the Long White Cloud: Maori Myths and Legends*.

Teleki, Pál, Gróf (Count) [**tel**ekee] (1879–1941) Hungarian statesman and prime minister (1920–1, 1939–41), born in Budapest. Combining politics with an academic career, he was appointed foreign minister in 1919 before becoming premier. Founder of the Christian National League and chief of Hungary's boy scouts, he was minister of education in 1938 and again premier in 1939. He was fully aware of the German threat to his country, but all measures to avert it, including a pact with Yugoslavia, were unavailing through lack of support. When Germany marched against Yugoslavia through Hungary, he took his own life. >> RR1057

Telemann, Georg Philipp [**tay**leman] (1681–1767) Composer, born in Magdeburg, Germany. He studied at Leipzig, and taught himself music by learning to play a wide range of instruments and studying the scores of the masters. He held several posts as *Kapellmeister*, notably at Frankfurt (1712–21), and became musical director of the Johanneum at Hamburg from 1721 until his death. A prolific composer, his works include church music, 46 passions, over 40 operas, oratorios, many songs, and a large body of instrumental music.

Telford, Thomas (1757–1834) Engineer, born near Langholm, Dumfries and Galloway, SW Scotland, UK. He began as a stonemason, taught himself architecture, and in 1787 became surveyor of public works for Shropshire. He planned the Ellesmere (1793–1805) and Caledonian (1803–23) canals, the road from London to Holyhead, with the Menai Suspension Bridge (1825), and built in all over 1000 mi of road and 1200 bridges, as well as harbours, docks, and other buildings.

Tell, Wilhelm, Eng **William Tell** (13th–14th-c) Legendary Swiss patriot of Bürglen in Uri, a famous crossbow marksman, reputedly the saviour of his native district from the oppressions of Austria. According to tradition, he was compelled by the tyrannical Austrian governor to shoot an apple off his own son's head from a distance of 80 paces. Later, Tell slew the tyrant, and so initiated the movement which secured the independence of Switzerland. Similar tales are found in the folklore of many countries, and Tell's existence is disputed. His name first occurs in a chronicle of 1470.

Teller, Edward (1908–   ) Physicist, born in Budapest. He studied at Karlsruhe, Munich, and Göttingen universities, and under Niels Bohr at Copenhagen. He left Germany in 1933, moving to the USA in 1935. He contributed profoundly to the modern explanation of solar energy, anticipating the theory behind thermonuclear explosions. He was a member of the team under Fermi that produced the first nuclear chain reaction (1941), and worked on the atomic bomb project at Los Alamos (1943–5). He favoured immediate development of a thermonuclear weapon, but had to wait until 1950 for Truman to give approval, and the first H-bomb was tested in 1952. He was director of the Livermore Laboratory, CA (1958–60), and professor of physics at California, Berkeley (1963). He supported the use of nuclear power for peaceful means, including the use of nuclear devices to excavate large areas for harbours, canals, and mining. >> Bohr, Niels; Fermi

Téllez, Gabriel >> **Tirso de Molina**

Temin, Howard (Martin) [**tee**min] (1934–94) Virologist, born in Philadelphia, PA. He studied at the California Institute of Technology (1955–9), and taught at Wisconsin from 1960. For his work on the way viruses can make normal cells malignant, he shared the 1975 Nobel Prize for Physiology or Medicine. >> RR1124

Temminck, Coenraad Jacob (1778–1858) Ornithologist, born in Amsterdam, the son of the treasurer of the Dutch East India Company. At the age of 17 he became an auctioneer with the company, and amassed a collection of bird specimens. His best-known work is the *Manuel d'ornithologie* (Manual of Ornithology), published from 1815. The first director of the new natural history museum at Leyden (from 1820), *Temminck's stint*, *Temminck's cat*, and *Temminck's horned lark* are named after him.

Temple, Frederick (1821–1902) Archbishop of Canterbury, born in Levkás, Greece. He studied at Balliol College, Oxford, where he became a mathematics lecturer and fellow, was principal of Kneller Hall Training College (1858–69), and headmaster of Rugby (1857–69). He wrote the first of the allegedly heterodox *Essays and Reviews* (1860) which almost prevented his appointment to the bishopric of Exeter, and supported the disestablishment of the Irish Church. In 1885 he became Bishop of London and in 1897 Archbishop of Canterbury. He was responsible, with Archbishop Maclagen of York, for the 'Lambeth Opinions' (1889), which attempted to solve some controversies over ritual.

Temple, Shirley, married name **Black** (1928–) Child film star, born in Santa Monica, CA. Precociously talented, she appeared in a series of short films from the age of three-and-a-half, and graduated to full stardom with a leading role in *Little Miss Marker* (1934). An unspoilt personality who sang, danced, and did impressions, she captivated Depression-era audiences, becoming a world favourite in such films as *Curly Top* (1935) and *Dimples* (1936). She received an honorary Academy Award in 1934. Retiring from the screen, she became a Republican, was appointed US representative to the UN General Assembly in 1969, was Ambassador to Ghana (1974–6), White House chief of protocol (1976–7), and Ambassador to Czechoslovakia (1989–93).

Temple, Sir William (1628–99) Diplomat and essayist, born in London, England, UK. He studied at Cambridge, became a diplomat in 1655, was made ambassador at The Hague, and negotiated the Triple Alliance (1668) against France. He was made a baronet, and in 1677 helped to bring about the marriage of the Prince of Orange to the Princess Mary, daughter of James, Duke of York (later James II). After the 1688 revolution he declined a political post to devote himself to literature, living in retirement at Moor Park, Surrey. His essay style was a major influence on 18th-c writers, including Swift, who was his secretary. >> Swift, Jonathan; William III

Temple, William (1881–1944) Anglican clergyman, born in Exeter, Devon, SW England, UK. He studied at Oxford, was ordained in 1908, and became Bishop of Manchester (1921–9), Archbishop of York (1929–42), and Archbishop of Canterbury (1942–4). An outspoken advocate of social reform, he crusaded against usury, slums, dishonesty, and the aberrations of the profit motive. He was also a leader in the reform of Church structures and in the ecumenical movement.

Templer, Sir Gerald (1898–1979) British soldier. He trained at Sandhurst, was commissioned in the Royal Irish Fusiliers, and served with them in World War 1. In World War 2 he became commander of the 6th Armoured Division. He was deputy (1948–50) then Chief of the Imperial General Staff (1955–8). As high commissioner and commander-in-chief in Malaya (1952–4), he frustrated the Communist guerrillas' offensive.

Templeton, Sir John Marks (1912–) Businessman and philanthropist, born in Winchester, TN. He studied at Yale and Oxford, started on Wall Street in 1937, and went on to found several major investment funds. A Presbyterian elder, he is widely known for the establishment in 1972 of the *Templeton Prize for Progress in Religion*, the world's largest money award (exceeding $1 million in 1992). He was knighted in 1987.

Templewood, Viscount >> **Hoare, Sir Samuel**

Teng Hsiao-p'ing >> **Deng Xiaoping**

Teniers, David [teneerz], known as **the Elder** (1582–1649) Baroque genre painter, born in Antwerp, Belgium, about whom little is known. He probably studied in Italy under Rubens, became a master in the Antwerp guild (1606), and an art dealer in the 1630s. Some paintings by his son were formerly attributed to him. >> Rubens

Teniers, David [teneerz], known as **the Younger** (1610–90) Painter, born in Antwerp, Belgium. He settled in Brussels c.1647. A prolific painter, he is best known for his scenes

of peasant life, in the tradition of Brueghel. Works include 'Peasants Playing Music' (undated, Alte Pinakothek, Munich), and 'Village Fete' (1646, Hermitage, Leningrad). >> Brueghel

Tenniel, Sir John [teneel] (1820–1914) Artist, born in London, England, UK. Self-trained, he became known as a *Punch* cartoonist (from 1851) and book illustrator, notably in his work for *Alice's Adventures in Wonderland* (1865) and *Through the Looking-glass* (1872). He was knighted in 1893.

Tennyson, Alfred Tennyson, Baron [tenison], known as **Alfred, Lord Tennyson** (1809–92) Poet, born in Somersby, Lincolnshire, E England, UK. He studied at Cambridge, and published his first poetry in 1829, but it was not well received; a revised volume in 1842 established his reputation, including such major poems as 'The Lady of Shallott' and 'The Lotus-eaters'. His major poetic achievement was the elegy mourning the death of his friend Arthur Hallam, 'In Memoriam' (1850); and in the same year he succeeded Wordsworth as poet laureate. In 1855 he wrote *Maud: a Monodrama*, and 1859–85 published a series of poems on the Arthurian theme, *Idylls of the King* (1859). In the 1870s he wrote several plays, and continued to write poetry until his death. In his later years, he was acclaimed by the whole nation, and he was created a baron in 1884. >> Milnes

Tenzin Gyatso >> **Dalai Lama**

Tenzing Norgay, known as **Sherpa Tenzing** (1914–86) Mountaineer, born in Tsa-chu, Nepal. He made his first climb as a porter with a British expedition in 1935, and later climbed many of the Himalayan peaks. In 1953 he succeeded in reaching the Everest summit with Edmund Hillary, for which he was awarded the George Medal. He later became head of the Institute of Mountaineering at Darjeeling. >> Hillary

Te Puea, Princess Herangi [tay pooa] (1883–1952) Maori leader, born in Waikato, New Zealand. Of chiefly rank and a skilled organizer, from 1911 she began to acquire influence within the Maori nationalist movement, Kingitanga. By 1930 she had built it into a major instrument for the social and cultural rehabilitation of the Maori, and for the settlement of grievances arising from colonial rule.

Terborch or **Terburg, Gerard** [terbaw(r)kh] (1617–81) Painter, born in Zwolle, The Netherlands. He studied at Haarlem, and travelled widely in Europe, before settling at Deventer in 1654, where he became burgomaster. He worked mostly on a small scale, producing genre pictures and fashionable portraits, but is best known for his painting of 'The Peace of Munster' (1648, National Gallery, London).

Terbrugghen, Hendrik [tairbrookhen] (c.1588–1629) Painter, born in Deventer, The Netherlands. He studied at Utrecht, and was until c.1615 in Italy, where he came under the influence of Caravaggio. He excelled in chiaroscuro effects and in the faithful representation of physiognomical details and drapery, as in his 'Jacob and Laban' (1627, National Gallery, London). >> Caravaggio

Terburg, Gerard >> **Terborch, Gerard**

Terence, in full **Publius Terentius Afer** (c. 190–159 BC) Latin comic poet, born in Carthage, N Africa. He became the slave of a Roman senator, who gave him an education in Rome and freed him. His successful first play, *Andria* (166 BC, The Andrian Girl), introduced him to Roman society, where his chief patrons were Laelius and the younger Scipio. His surviving six comedies are Greek in origin and scene, directly based on Menander. Many of his conventions were later used by European playwrights. >> Menander; Scipio, Aemilianus

Teresa of Ávila, St (1515–82) Saint and mystic, born in Ávila, Spain. She entered a Carmelite convent there in 1535, and became famous for her ascetic religious exercises and sanctity. In 1562, with assistance from John of the Cross, she re-established the ancient Carmelite rule, with additional observances. Her many writings include an autobiography, *The Way of Perfection*, and the mystical work, *The Interior Castle*. She was canonized in 1622; feast day 15 October. >> John of the Cross

Teresa (of Calcutta), Mother, originally **Agnes Gonxha Bojaxhiu** (1910–97) Christian missionary in India, born in Skopje, Yugoslavia (formerly, Albania). She went to India in 1928, and taught at a convent school in Calcutta, taking her final vows in 1937. She became principal of the school, but in 1948 left the convent to work alone in the slums. After medical training in Paris, she opened some classrooms for destitute children in Calcutta. She was gradually joined by other nuns, and her House for the Dying was opened in 1952. Her sisterhood, the Missionaries of Charity, started in 1950, and in 1957 she started work with lepers and in many disaster areas of the world. She was awarded the Pope John XXIII Peace Prize in 1971, and the Nobel Peace Prize in 1979.

Tereshkova, Valentina [tereshkova] (1937–) Cosmonaut and the first woman to fly in space, born in Maslennikovo, Russia. She worked in a textile factory, qualified as a sports parachutist, and entered training as a cosmonaut in 1962, becoming a solo crew member of the three-day Vostok 6 flight launched on 16 June 1963. She was made a hero of the Soviet Union, and became a member of the Central Committee of the Soviet Communist Party in 1971. Since 1992 she has been chairman of the Russian Association of International Co-operation.

Terfel, Bryn [tervel, brin], originally **Bryn Terfel Jones** (1965–) Bass baritone, born in Pant-glas, Caernarfonshire, Wales, UK. He studied at the Guildhall School of Music and Drama, and became popularly known after winning the Lieder Prize in the Cardiff Singer of the World competition in 1989. He has since appeared at many of the world's leading opera houses, his roles including Leporello in *Don Giovanni* at the Salzburg Festival (1994–6), Figaro at the New York Metropolitan Opera (1994), and Nick Shadow in *The Rake's Progress* at the Welsh National Opera (1996). In 1993 he received the Newcomer of the Year International Classic Music Award.

Terkel, Studs, popular name of **Louis Terkel** (1912–) Writer and oral historian, born in New York City. He went to Law School in Chicago, acted in radio soap operas, became a disc jockey, radio commentator, and television host, and travelled worldwide conducting interviews with the famous and the anonymous. Described by J K Galbraith as 'a national resource', his publications include *Giants of Jazz* (1957), *Working* (1974), and *The Good War: an Oral History of World War Two* (1984, Pulitzer).

Terman, Fred(erick Emmons) (1900–82) Electrical engineer, born in English, IN. He studied at Stanford, and worked at Massachusetts Institute of Technology with Vannevar Bush before returning to Stanford as professor of radio engineering. He was responsible for the establishment of the Stanford Industrial Park in the university grounds (1951), linking research with industry. The park soon became the centre of the electronics industry that earned the area the name of Silicon Valley. >> Bush, Vannevar; Hewlett-Packard

Terman, Lewis M(adison) (1877–1956) Psychologist and pioneer of intelligence tests, born in Johnson Co, IN. At Stanford University he developed an English version of the Binet–Simon intelligence test, and introduced Terman Group Intelligence Tests into the US army in 1920. He pioneered the use of the term *IQ* (Intelligence Quotient) in *The Measurement of Intelligence* (1916), and launched *Genetic Studies of Genius* (5 vols, 1926–59). >> Binet

Terry, Eli (1772–1852) Inventor and clock manufacturer, born in East Windsor, CT. After an apprenticeship (1786–92), he made his first clocks by hand. In 1800 he began to use water power to drive his tools, and established the USA's first clock factory in Plymouth, CT. He later formed a partnership with Seth Thomas, and introduced several popular innovations in clock design. >> Thomas, Seth

Terry, Dame (Alice) Ellen (1847–1928) Actress, born in Coventry, West Midlands, C England, UK, a member of a large family of actors. She appeared on stage at eight, from 1862 played in Bristol and, after a short-lived marriage and retirement, established herself as the leading Shakespearean actress in London, dominating the English and US theatre (1878–1902) in partnership with Henry Irving. In 1903 she went into theatre management, and toured and lectured widely. She was made a dame in 1925. >> Irving, Henry

Terry-Thomas, originally **Thomas Terry Hoar Stevens** (1911–90) Film actor, born in Finchley, NW Greater London, England, UK. He began his career as Thomas Terry in music hall and radio before changing his name to Terry Thomas, afterwards adding the hyphen for comic effect. He was the gap-toothed villain in dozens of post-World War I comedies, satirizing and eventually personifying the upper-class bounder in such films as *I'm All Right Jack* (1959), *School for Scoundrels* (1960), and *Those Magnificent Men In Their Flying Machines* (1965).

Terson, Peter, originally **Peter Paterson** (1932–) Playwright, born in Tyneside, NE England, UK. He worked as a teacher on Tyneside for 10 years before his first play, *A Night to Make the Angels Weep*, was produced in 1964. An amusing observer of life, his other works include *Mighty Reservoy* (1964), *Zigger Zagger* (1967), *Good Lads at Heart* (1971), and *Strippers* (1984). He has been much associated with the National Youth Theatre.

Tertullian [tertulian], in full **Quintus Septimus Florens Tertullianus** (c. 160–220) Christian theologian, born in Carthage. He lived for some time at Rome, was converted (c.196), and then returned to Carthage. His opposition to worldliness in the Church culminated in his becoming a leader of the Montanist sect (c.207). The first to produce major Christian works in Latin, he thus exercised a profound influence on the development of ecclesiastical language. He wrote books against heathens, Jews, and heretics, as well as several practical and ascetic treatises.

Terzaghi, Karl (Anton von) [tairtsagee] (1883–1963) Civil engineer, born in Prague. Educated in Czech Republic, he held professorships at Istanbul, the Massachusetts Institute of Technology, Vienna, and Harvard, becoming a US citizen in 1943. He established the subject of soil mechanics as an independent scientific discipline.

Tesla, Nikola [tesla] (1856–1943) Physicist and electrical engineer, born in Smiljan, Croatia. He studied at Graz, Prague, and Paris, emigrating to the USA in 1884. He left the Edison Works at Menlo Park to concentrate on his own inventions, which included improved dynamos, transformers, and electric bulbs, and the high-frequency coil which now bears his name. The unit of magnetic induction is named after him.

Tessin, Carl Gustaf, Greve (Count) [teseen] (1695–1770) Swedish statesman, writer, and court official, born in Stockholm, the son of Nicodemus Tessin (the Younger). Educated in France and Italy, he became active in politics, and hoped to regain territory lost to Russia during Charles XII's reign. He was elected leader of the Nobility Estate when the Hats gained a majority in 1738, and bore heavy responsibility for the unsuccessful war against Russia in 1741. He gained the favour of King Adolf Fredrik and

Queen Louisa Ulrika, and in 1746 was appointed head of chancellory and governor to the future King Gustav III, but fell from grace for disapproving of their attempts to increase royal power. He left public life, and made a name for himself as a poet and writer. >> Tessin, Nicodemus (the Younger)

Tessin, Nicodemus [teseen], known as **the Elder** (1615–81) Architect, born in Stralsund, Germany. In 1636 he moved to Stockholm, where he became the most eminent architect during a period of affluence and expansion. He was appointed royal architect in 1646, and was city architect in Stockholm from 1661. His major works include Kalmar Cathedral (started 1660), the Caroline Mausoleum in Riddarholm Church (1671), and, most notably, the palace of Drottningholm on Mälaren, completed by his son. >> Tessin, Carl Gustaf/Nicodemus (the Younger)

Tessin, Nicodemus [teseen], known as **the Younger** (1654–1728) Architect, from Stockholm, the son of Nicodemus Tessin (the Elder). He studied Classical and Baroque culture in Rome, was appointed royal architect in 1676, and succeeded his father as Stockholm city architect in 1682. He completed Drottningholm Palace and added the royal church (1690–9). Other notable structures include Steninge Castle (1694–98) and his own beautifully proportioned Tessin Palace (1696–1700). He planned gardens for royal palaces, did important work on Amelienborg Castle, Copenhagen (1697), the Louvre (1704–6), and the Apollo Temple, Versailles, but his greatest achievement was the Royal Palace, Stockholm, with an Italian style facade and French interior design, completed by his son, Carl Gustaf Tessin. >> Tessin, Carl Gustaf/Nicodemus (the Elder)

Tetley, Glen (1926–) Contemporary ballet dancer and choreographer, born in Cleveland, OH. He gave up medical studies to train as a dancer with Hanya Holm. He danced with the American Ballet Theater, the Joffrey Ballet (1956), and the Netherlands Dance Theatre (in the 1960s), became a guest choreographer for Ballet Rambert, and made his name in Europe with the Stuttgart Ballet (1973–5). In 1986, choreographic work for the National Ballet of Canada led to his appointment as artistic director. >> Holm, Hanya

Tetrazzini, Luisa [tetratseenee] (1871–1940) Coloratura soprano, born in Florence, Italy. She studied with her sister and at the Liceo Musicale, and made her debut in 1895 in Meyerbeer's *L'Africaine*. Appearing mostly in Italian opera of the older school, one of her most notable successes was in *Lucia di Lammermoor*. She sang in London and in America, and in 1913–14 was a member of the Chicago Opera Company.

Tetzel, Johann (c. 1465–1519) Monk, born in Pirna, Germany. He became a Dominican in 1489, and was appointed in 1516 to preach an indulgence in favour of contributors to the building fund of St Peter's in Rome. This he did with great ostentation, thereby provoking the Wittenberg theses of Luther, and his own reply. >> Leo X; Luther

Tewfik or **Tawfiq Pasha, Mohammed** [tyoofik] (1852–92) Khedive of Egypt (from 1879), born in Cairo, the eldest son of Ismail Pasha, whom he succeeded on his abdication. The chief events of his reign were Arabi's insurrection (1882), the British intervention, the war with the Mahdi, Mohammed Ahmed (1884–5), the pacification of the Sudan frontiers, and the improvement of Egypt under British administration. He was succeeded by his son Abbas Hilmi. >> Abbas Hilmi Pasha; Ahmed Arabi; Ismail Pasha; Mohammed Ahmed; RR1046

Te Whiti-O-Rongomai [tay feetee oh ronggomiy] (1830–1907) Maori prophet, born in Taranaki, New Zealand. He attempted to oppose the occupation of Maori land in his district by European settlers through a programme of civil disobedience and passive resistance. His efforts were crushed when government soldiers invaded his village of Parihaka in 1880.

Tey, Josephine >> **Mackintosh, Elizabeth**

Teyte, Dame Maggie [tayt] (1888–1976) Soprano, born in Wolverhampton, West Midland, C England, UK. She studied at the Royal College of Music, London, and in Paris, and made her debut in Monte Carlo in 1907 as Tyrcis in Offenbach's *Myriam et Daphné*. She sang 'Mélisande' in Debussy's *Pelléas et Mélisande* in Paris, 1908, having studied the role with the composer. She is remembered for her Mozartian roles, such as Cherubino in *The Marriage of Figaro*, and as a renowned interpreter of the songs of Debussy, Fauré, and Reynaldo Hahn.

Thackeray, William Makepeace (1811–63) Novelist, born in Calcutta, India. He studied at Cambridge, left without taking a degree, and visited Germany (1830–1), where he met Goethe. In line for a large inheritance, he turned to journalism, bought the *National Standard* (1833), and lost his fortune a year later. He first attracted attention as a writer with his work in *Punch* (1842), in which he exploited the view of society as seen by a footman, and the great theme of English snobbery. Most of his major novels were all published as monthly serials: *Vanity Fair* (1847–8), *Pendennis* (1848), and *The Newcomes* (1853–5) – *Henry Esmond* (1852) being the exception. He travelled widely as a lecturer in Europe, and in 1860 became the first editor of *The Cornhill Magazine*, where much of his later work appeared. >> Ritchie; Smith, George

Thais [thayis] (4th-c BC) Athenian courtesan, famous for her wit and beauty. She was, according to a doubtful legend, the mistress of Alexander the Great, whom she induced to burn down Persepolis.

Thalben-Ball, Sir George Thomas (1896–1987) Organist and composer, born in Sydney, New South Wales, Australia. Educated privately, he studied at the Royal Academy of Music, London. He became assistant organist at the Temple Church, London, (1919) and was appointed organist (1923–81). From the early 1920s his name was synonymous with the Temple Church, both in radio broadcasts and on HMV records. He also made regular appearances in the Henry Wood promenade concerts for the BBC, as music adviser and consultant from 1941. He was also organ professor and examiner at the Royal College of Music, and curator-organist at the Royal Albert Hall, London. >> Wood, Henry

Thales [thayleez] (c. 620–c. 555 BC) Greek natural philosopher, traditionally regarded as the first philosopher, born in Miletus. His mercantile journeys took him to Egypt and Babylon, where he acquired land-surveying and astronomical techniques, and is said to have predicted the solar eclipse in 585 BC. None of his writings survive, but Aristotle attributes to him the doctrine that water is the original substance from which all things are derived.

Thant, U [oo tant] (1909–74) Burmese diplomat, born in Pantanaw, Myanmar (formerly, Burma). He studied at Yangon, and was a teacher who took up government work when Burma became independent in 1948, becoming the country's UN representative in 1957. As secretary-general of the UN (1962–71), he played a major diplomatic role during the Cuban crisis (1962). He also formulated a plan to end the Congolese Civil War (1962), and mobilized a UN peace-keeping force in Cyprus (1964). >> Kennedy, John F; Khrushchev

Tharp, Twyla (1942–) Dancer, choreographer, and director, born in Portland, IN. She studied with Graham, Cunningham, and Paul Taylor, and danced with Taylor (1963–5). Since then she has choreographed and danced with her own group, The Twyla Tharp Dance Foundation, and made new work for various other ballet and modern dance companies. Flippant, throwaway movement, and an amusing edge to her works, disguises meticulous structure and comment on current social issues, as in *Push Comes to Shove* (1976). Later works include *In the Upper Room* (1987) and *The Elements* (1996). >> Cunningham, Merce; Graham, Martha; Taylor, Paul

Tharpe, Sister Rosetta, *née* **Nubin** (1915–73) Gospel musician, born in Cotton Plant, AR. She began singing and playing guitar in church, and by 1938 was a featured soloist in Cotton Club revues backed by Cab Calloway and Lucky Millinder. Beginning in 1944, she developed a huge following in the burgeoning Gospel market, which she maintained for the rest of her life. >> Calloway

Thatcher (of Kesteven), Margaret (Hilda) Thatcher, Baroness, *née* **Roberts** (1925–) British stateswoman and prime minister (1979–90), born in Grantham, Lincolnshire. She studied at Oxford, and worked as a research chemist (1947–51). She married **Denis Thatcher** in 1951, studied law, and was called to the bar in 1954. Elected as Conservative MP for Finchley in 1959, she joined the shadow Cabinet in 1967. She became secretary of state for education and science (1970–4), joint shadow Chancellor (1974–5), and in 1975 replaced Edward Heath as Leader of the Conservative Party to become the first woman party leader in British politics. Under her leadership, the Conservative Party moved towards a more 'right wing' position, and British politics and society became more polarized than at any time since World War 2. Her government instituted the privatization of nationalized industries and national utilities, tried to institute a market in state-provided health care and education, and reduced the role of local government as a provider of services. She was re-elected in 1983 with a large majority, despite the worst unemployment figures for 50 years, aided by the tide of popular feeling following the Falklands War, and disarray in the Opposition parties. She was elected for a third term of office in 1987, and by 1988 had become the longest serving premier of the 20th-c. Her personal political philosophy was popularly referred to as *Thatcherism*, characterized by the resolution to persevere with policies despite objections from critics and doubts from her supporters. She resigned (Nov 1990) as a result of the controversy and infighting which followed her opposition to full monetary and economic union with Europe. Created a life peer in 1992, she continues to put forward her views on politics in speeches given throughout the world and through the establishment of a Foundation named after her. She published her memoirs, *Margaret Thatcher: the Downing Street Years* in 1993. >> Heath; Heseltine; Howe, Geoffrey; Joseph, Keith; Major; RR1095

Thayendanegea >> **Brant, Joseph**

Theaetetus [theeaytetus] (c. 414–c. 369 BC) Greek mathematician. He was an associate of Plato at the Academy, whose work was later used by Euclid in Books X and XIII of the *Elements*. Plato named after him the dialogue *Theaetetus*, which was devoted to the nature of knowledge. >> Euclid; Plato

Theiler, Max [tiyler] (1899–1972) Bacteriologist, born in Pretoria. He settled in the USA in 1922, and worked at Harvard Medical School (1922–30) and the Rockefeller Institute, New York City (1930–64), and became professor at Yale Medical School (1964–7). He was awarded the 1951 Nobel Prize for Physiology or Medicine for his research on yellow fever, for which he discovered the vaccine 17-D in 1939.

Themistocles [themistokleez] (c. 523–c. 458 BC) Athenian general, visionary politician, and hero of Salamis. By persuading the Athenians to develop Piraeus as a port (493 BC),

and to use their rich silver deposits to build a fleet (483 BC), he not only made possible their great naval victory at Salamis (480 BC), but also laid the foundations of their maritime empire. He fell from favour c.470 BC, and was ostracized. After many adventures, he served the Persian king in Asia Minor as the Governor of Magnesia. >> Aristides

Thenard, Louis Jacques [tenah(r)] (1777–1857) Chemist, born in La Louptière, France. He studied pharmacy at Paris, and became professor at the Collège de France. He was made a baron in 1825, and appointed Chancellor of the University of Paris. He discovered sodium and potassium peroxides, the pigment *Thenard's blue* (used for colouring porcelain), and proved that caustic soda and potash contain hydrogen. He was closely associated with Gay-Lussac, and wrote a once-standard work on chemistry. >> Gay-Lussac

Theobald (c. 1090–1161) Archbishop of Canterbury, born near Bec, France. A monk at Bec, he became abbot there in 1137, and the following year was appointed Archbishop of Canterbury. He crowned King Stephen, but after the king's death he refused to regard Stephen's son as his successor, and eventually crowned Henry II (1154). He advanced his archdeacon, Thomas Becket, to the chancellorship in 1155, introduced the study of civil law into England, and resisted all attempts by the monasteries to throw off episcopal jurisdiction. >> Henry II (of England); Becket, Thomas à; Stephen

Theocritus [theeokritus] (c. 310–250 BC) Greek pastoral poet, probably born in Syracuse. He was brought up in Cos, and lived for a time at the court of Ptolemy Philadelphus in Alexandria. About 30 of his poems survive, though the authenticity of some have been disputed. His short poems dealing with pastoral subjects, and representing a single scene, came to be called 'idylls' (*eidullia*). Tennyson was deeply influenced by him, as were the pastoral poets of the Renaissance. >> Tennyson

Theoderic >> **Theodoric**

Theodora (c. 500–47) Byzantine empress (527–47). She was an actress, dancer, and prostitute who became mistress, then wife, of Justinian. A woman of great intelligence and courage, she played a major role throughout his long and distinguished reign, and probably saved his throne during the Nika riots by her intervention (532). >> Justinian; RR1037

Theodorakis, Mikis [thayodorahkees] (1925–) Composer, born in Khios, Greece. He studied at the Paris Conservatoire, and in 1959 his ballet *Antigone* was produced at Covent Garden. On his return to Greece he became intensely critical of the musical and artistic establishment. When the right-wing government took power in 1967, he was imprisoned and his music banned, but he was released in 1970, after worldwide appeals. His prolific musical output includes oratorios, ballets, song cycles, and music for film scores, the best known of which is *Zorba the Greek* (1965).

Theodore, called **King of Corsica,** also known as **Baron von Neuhoff** (1686–1756) Adventurer, born in Metz, Germany. He served in the French army and the Swedish diplomatic service, became chargé d'affaires to Emperor Charles VI (ruled 1711–40) and, in 1736, led a Corsican rising against the Genoese, supported by the Turks and the Bey of Tunis. He was elected king, and left after a few months to procure foreign aid, but his attempts to return in 1738 and in 1743 were frustrated. He settled in London in 1749.

Theodore of Mopsuestia (c. 350–428) Christian theologian, born in Antioch. He was made Bishop of Mopsuestia in Cilicia in 392. He wrote commentaries (mostly now lost) on almost all the books of Scripture, adopting a literal meaning in preference to the use of allegorical interpretation. As the teacher of Nestorius, he was perhaps the founder of Nestorianism, and his views on the Incarnation were condemned by the fifth ecumenical council in 553. >> Nestorius

Theodoret (of Cyrrhus) [theeodoret] (c. 393–c. 458) Theologian and Church historian, born in Antioch, Syria. He entered a monastery, and in 423 became Bishop of Cyrrhus. Deeply involved in the Nestorian and Eutychian controversies, he was deposed by the Council of Ephesus in 449, though restored by the Council of Chalcedon two years later. His works consist of commentaries, histories of the Church, orations, and letters.

Theodoric or **Theoderic** [theeodorik], known as **the Great** (?–526) King of the Ostrogoths (471–526), who invaded Italy in 489, defeating the barbarian ruler, Odoacer. His long reign secured for Italy tranquillity and prosperity, the Goths and the Romans continuing as distinct nations, each with its own tribunals and laws. He established his capital at Ravenna. >> Odoacer

Theodoric I (?–451) King of the Visigoths, the son of Alaric I, elected king in 418. Alternately an ally and an enemy of Rome, in 421 (or 422) he treacherously joined the Vandals and attacked the Roman troops from behind. In 435 he attacked the Romans in Gaul and besieged Narbonne. Forced to retreat to Toulouse, he there defeated a Roman army (439). On the invasion of Attila in 451, he joined the Romans, under Aëtius, and at Troyes commanded the right wing. He drove back the Huns under Attila, but was killed. >> Aëtius; Alaric I; Attila

Theodoric II (?–466) King of the Visigoths. He rebelled against his brother and predecessor Thorismund, had him assassinated, and ascended the throne in 453. His policy at first was to spread Gothic dominion in Spain and Gaul through the Roman alliance. On the murder of the Emperor Petronius Maximus in 455, he supported Eparchius Avitus in his bid for the empire, and marched with him into Italy, where Eparchius was proclaimed emperor. On his abdication in 456, Theodoric broke the friendship with Rome and besieged Arles, but was forced by Emperor Majorian to make peace. In 462 he made another attempt in Gaul, but was defeated near Orléans (464). He was murdered in 466 by his brother Euric, who succeeded him.

Theodorus of Samos [theeodorus], also spelled **Theodoros** (6th-c BC) Greek sculptor. He is said to have developed sculptural hollow-casting for large figures in bronze, and invented several kinds of tools for use in casting.

Theodosius I [theeodohshus], known as **the Great** (c. 346–95) Roman emperor of the East (379–95). Made emperor because of his military abilities, he solved the long-standing Gothic problem by allowing the Goths to settle S of the Danube as allies of Rome. His title comes from his vigorous championship of orthodox Christianity. >> RR1085

Theodosius II [theeodohshus] (401–50) Roman emperor (408–50), the grandson of Theodosius I and, like him, a staunch champion of orthodox Christianity. He is chiefly remembered for his codification of the Roman law.

Theophilus [theeofilus] (?–180) One of the Fathers of the Christian Church, from Syria. Bishop of Antioch (169–177), he wrote an important Apology for Christianity (c.180).

Theophilus, St [theeofilus] (?–412) Patriarch of Alexandria (from 385). He destroyed the pagan temple of Serapis, drove out the Originist monks of Nitria, and defended his actions before a synod at Constantinople called by the Emperor Arcadius and St John Chrysostom. He made peace with the monks, but used his influence with the Empress Eudoxia to have St John banished to Armenia. Feast day 15 October. >> Chrysostom

Theophrastus [theeohfrastus] (c. 372–286 BC) Greek phil-

osopher, born in Eresus, Lesbos. At Athens he studied under Aristotle, becoming his close friend, and head of the Peripatetic school after his death. He was responsible for preserving many of Aristotle's works, along with many fragments of the Presocratics. Among his own works which have survived are two books on plants, and *Charactères*, describing 30 moral types based on studies by Aristotle. >> Aristotle; Strato

Theorell, (Axel) Hugo Theodor [tayorel] (1903–82) Biochemist, born in Linköping, Sweden. He studied at the Karolinska Institute in Stockholm, was professor at Uppsala (1932), and director of the Nobel Institute of Biochemistry at Stockholm (1937–70). He was awarded the 1955 Nobel Prize for Physiology or Medicine for his work on oxidation enzymes.

Theotokopoulos, Domenikos >> Greco, El

Theresa, St >> Teresa of Ávila, St

Theresa of Lisieux, St [leesyoe], originally **(Marie Françoise) Thérèse Martin**, also known as **the Little Flower** and **St Theresa of the Child Jesus** (1873–97) Saint, born in Alençon, France. An intensely religious child, she entered the Carmelite convent of Lisieux in Normandy at the age of 15, where she remained until her death from tuberculosis nine years later. During her last years she wrote an account of her life which was published posthumously as *Histoire d'une âme* (1898, Story of a Soul), showing how the most ordinary person can attain sainthood by following her 'little way' of simple, childlike Christianity. She was canonized in 1925, and in 1947 associated with Joan of Arc as patron saint of France. She was made a doctor of the Church in 1997. Feast day 1 October. >> Joan of Arc

Theroux, Paul (Edward) [theroo] (1941–) Novelist and travel writer, born in Medford, MA. He studied at the University of Massachusetts, then lectured at universities in Makerere, Uganda (1965–8) and Singapore (1968–71). His literary output reflects his footloose life. His novels include *Waldo* (1969), *Saint Jack* (1973, filmed 1979), *Picture Palace* (1978, Whitbread), the highly acclaimed *The Mosquito Coast* (1981, James Tait Black, filmed 1987), *Chicago Loop* (1990), *The Pillars of Hercules* (1995), and *Kowloon Tong* (1997). He has also written short stories, plays, reviews, and works of criticism. He first reached a wide public through his rail journeys, recounted in *The Great Railway Bazaar* (1975) and *The Old Patagonian Express* (1979) – a genre which has continued with *Travelling the World* (1990) and other books.

Thesiger, Wilfred Patrick [thesijer] (1910–) Explorer of Arabia, born in Addis Ababa. He studied at Oxford, and hunted in 1933 with the Danakil tribes in Ethiopia, exploring the Sultanate of Aussa. In 1935 he joined the Sudan Political Service, and travelled by camel across the Sahara to the Tibesti Mts. He was seconded to the Sudan Defence Force at the outbreak of World War 2, and from 1945 to 1950 explored the Empty Quarter of S Arabia and the borderlands of Oman with Bedu companions, which he described in *Arabian Sands* (1959). He first travelled in East Africa in 1961, and returned to live with tribal peoples there from 1968 onwards. His autobiography, *The Life of My Choice*, was published in 1987.

Thespis (6th-c BC) Poet from Icaria. He is said to have been the first to win a prize for tragedy at a festival in Athens (c.534 BC). According to Aristotle, he was the first to use single actors to deliver speeches in stage work, as well as the traditional chorus.

Thibaud, Jacques [teeboh] (1880–1953) Violinist, born in Bordeaux, France. He studied at the Paris Conservatoire and, as well as his solo performances, played with Alfred Cortot and Pablo Casals. He was particularly renowned for his interpretations of Mozart, Beethoven, and Debussy. He died in an air crash. >> Casals; Cortot

Thibault, Jacques >> **France, Anatole**

Thielicke, Helmut [**tee**likuh] (1908–86) Lutheran theologian and preacher, born in Barmen, Germany. He was dismissed from his post at Heidelberg for criticizing the Nazis, and in 1944 contributed to a draft declaration on Church–State relations for a revolutionary government to follow a successful plot against Hitler. He was appointed professor of theology at Hamburg after World War 2, becoming dean of theology (1954), and university rector (1960). He wrote many devotional books, as well as major works on theology and ethics. >> **Hitler**

Thielmans, Toots [**teel**mans], originally **Jean-Baptiste Thielmans** (1922–) Jazz musician and composer, born in Brussels. He was inspired to take up the guitar by compatriot Django Reinhardt, and the harmonica by Larry Adler. A performer of bebop and jazz, he appeared with Charlie Parker in Paris in 1949, toured Europe with Benny Goodman and Diana Washington in the 1950s, and appeared with Paul Simon and Peggy Lee. He became the favourite soloist of Quincy Jones, and played on the film soundtrack of *Midnight Cowboy* (1969). >> **Adler; Reinhardt**

Thiers, (Louis) Adolphe [tyair] (1797–1877) French statesman, historian, and first president of the Third Republic (1871–3), born in Marseille, France. He studied at Aix, and became a lawyer and journalist. He held several posts in the government of Louis-Philippe, and was twice prime minister (1836, 1839). He supported Napoleon in 1848, but was arrested and banished at the coup of 1851, only to re-enter the Chamber in 1863 as a critic of Napoleon's policies. After the collapse of the Second Empire, he became chief of the executive power in the provisional government, suppressed the Paris Commune, and was elected president. Defeated by a coalition of monarchists, he resigned in 1873. His most ambitious literary work was the 20-volume *L'histoire du consulat et de l'empire* (1845–62, History of the Consulate and the Empire). >> **RR1049**

Thirkell, Angela Margaret [**ther**kl] (1890–1961) Novelist, born in London, England, UK, a cousin of Rudyard Kipling. She wrote more than 30 novels set in 'Barsetshire', dealing with the descendants of characters from Trollope's Barsetshire novels, including *Coronation Summer* (1937), *Pomfret Towers* (1938), *Northbridge Rectory* (1941), and *Growing Up* (1943). >> **Kipling; Trollope**

Thistlewood, Arthur (1770–1820) Conspirator, born in Tupholme, Lincolnshire, EC England, UK. He served in the army, but, full of revolutionary ideas from his time in America and France, organized a mutiny at Spa Fields (1816). In 1820 he planned the Cato Street Conspiracy to murder Castlereagh and other ministers who were dining at the Earl of Harrowby's house. The conspirators were intercepted, and he was, with four others, convicted of high treason and hanged. >> **Castlereagh**

Thom, Alexander [tom] (1894–1985) British engineer and archaeo-astronomer, born in Scotland, UK. He studied at Glasgow University, returned as a lecturer (1922–39), and became professor of engineering science at Oxford University (1945–61). From 1934 he was engaged on a detailed study of stone circles, and published two major works, *Megalithic Sites in Britain* (1967) and *Megalithic Lunar Observatories* (1971). His discovery of the *megalithic yard* and the *megalithic inch* has not been universally accepted.

Thom, René Frédéric [tom] (1923–) Mathematician, born in Montbéliard, France. He studied at the Ecole Normale Supérieure, and became professor at Grenoble. Since 1964 he has been at the Institut des Hautes Etudes Scientifiques. In 1958 he was awarded the Fields Medal (the mathematical equivalent of the Nobel Prize). He is best known for his book *Stabilité structurelle et morphogenèse* (1972), which introduced the controversial 'catastrophe theory', with applications to such widely differing situations as the development of the embryo, social interaction, and physical phenomena such as breaking waves.

Thomas, St (1st-c) A disciple of Jesus Christ, listed as one of the 12 apostles in the Gospels, but most prominent in John's Gospel, where he is also called **Didymus** ('the Twin'), and where he is portrayed as doubting the resurrection until he touches the wounds of the risen Christ (*John* 20). Early church traditions describe him subsequently as a missionary to the Parthians or a martyr in India. Many later apocryphal works bear his name, such as the *Gospel of Thomas, Acts of Thomas,* and *Apocalypse of Thomas*. He is the patron saint of Portugal. Feast day 21 December. >> **Jesus Christ**

Thomas, (Charles Louis) Ambroise [tohmah] (1811–96) Composer, born in Metz, France. He studied at the Paris Conservatoire, where he became a professor of composition (1852) and director (1871). He wrote many light operas for the Opéra Comique and the Grand Opéra, of which *Mignon* (1866) is the best known. He also composed cantatas, part-songs, and choral pieces.

Thomas, Brandon (1849–1914) Actor and playwright, born in Liverpool, Merseyside, NW England, UK. He first appeared as a comedy actor in 1879, and wrote a number of successful light plays, one of which, *Charley's Aunt* (1892), has retained enormous popularity.

Thomas, Clarence (1948–) Jurist, born in Savannah, GA. He studied at Yale, and in 1992 was named by President Bush as the second black American to sit in the Supreme Court, succeeding Thurgood Marshall. His Senate confirmation hearings attracted widespread attention due to allegations of sexual misconduct brought by a former colleague, Anita Hill. Thomas was confirmed, but a number of women sought Congressional and Senate seats in the campaign of 1992 in protest. >> **Marshall, Thurgood**

Thomas, D(onald) M(ichael) (1935–) Novelist, poet, and translator, born in Redruth, Cornwall, SW England, UK. He studied at Oxford, and went on to work as a teacher and lecturer. His early collections, *Personal and Possessive* (1964), *Two Voices* (1968), and *Logan Stone* (1971), feature erotic poems, science fiction ballads, and Cornish lyrics. His controversial novel *The White Hotel* (1981) brought him greater public recognition. Other novels include his first, *The Flute Player* (1979), *Lying Together* (1990), and *Flying into Love* (1992). He has also translated major literary works from Russian. *Memories and Hallucinations* (1988) is a volume of autobiography.

Thomas, Dylan (Marlais) (1914–53) Poet, born in Swansea, SC Wales. He worked as a journalist, and established himself with the publication of *Eighteen Poems* in 1934. He married Caitlin Macnamara (1913–94) in 1936, and published *Twenty-Five Poems* the same year. His *Collected Poems* appeared in 1953, and he then produced his best-known work, the radio 'play for voices', *Under Milk Wood* (published in 1954). He also wrote an unfinished novel, *Adventures in the Skin Trade* (1955), and several collections of short stories, many of which were written originally for radio. All his work, whether in verse or prose, shows rhythmic drive and verbal flamboyance. He became an alcoholic in later years, and died on a lecture-tour of the USA. >> **Watkins, Vernon**

Thomas, (Philip) Edward, pseudonym **Edward Eastaway** (1878–1917) Poet and critic, born in London, England, UK. He studied at Oxford, and became a hack writer of reviews, critical studies, and topographical works. Not until 1914, encouraged by Robert Frost, did he realize his potential as a poet, writing most of his work during active service between 1915 and his death. He died in action at Arras, just before the publication of *Poems* (1917), under his pseudonym. He also wrote a novel, and several books about the English countryside. >> Frost, Robert

Thomas, E(dward) Donnall (1920–) Surgeon and oncologist, born in Mart, TX. A practising haematologist and researcher at several hospitals, he joined Columbia University (1956–63) then moved to the University of Washington. He began his pioneering studies of bone marrow transplants for treatment of human leukaemia in the 1950s. He performed the first successful brother–sister bone marrow transplant in 1970, after persevering with his research on histocompatibility typing and the use of immunosuppressant drugs. He shared the 1990 Nobel Prize for Physiology or Medicine. >> RR1124

Thomas, George >> Tonypandy, 1st Viscount

Thomas, Sir George (Alan) (1881–1972) Badminton player, born in Istanbul. He was the winner of a record 21 All-England titles between 1903 and 1928, including the singles four times (1920–3). In 1934 he was elected president of the International Badminton Federation, a post he held for 21 years, and in 1939 presented a Cup (the *Thomas Cup*) to be contested by national teams. He represented England for 27 years at badminton, was also an international competitor at lawn tennis and chess, and was twice British chess champion. >> RR1143

Thomas, George H(enry) (1816–70) US soldier, born in Southampton Co, VA. He trained at West Point, served in the Mexican War, and became an army instructor. In the Civil War (1861–5) he joined the Federal army, and was a major-general in command of the centre of Rosencrans's army. He saved the Battle of Stones River, and defended Chickamauga (1863). Given the command of the Army of the Cumberland, he captured Mission Ridge (1863), then commanded at Atlanta, Tennessee, and Nashville. In 1869 he directed the military Division of the Pacific.

Thomas, Hugh Owen (1833–91) Orthopaedic surgeon, born in Anglesey, N Wales, UK. He studied medicine at London, Edinburgh, and Paris, and practised surgery in Liverpool. He pioneered orthopaedic surgery, constructing many appliances which are still used, notably *Thomas' splints* for the hip and the knee.

Thomas, Margaret Haig, Viscountess Rhondda (1883–1958) Feminist and publisher, born in London, England, UK. She studied briefly at Somerville College, Oxford (before women were allowed to take degrees at Oxford), and became a suffragette. She was arrested for trying to destroy letters inside a postbox, but was released after hunger-striking. On her father's death in 1918 she attempted to take her seat in the House of Lords, but was kept out after extensive legal proceedings. In 1920 she founded *Time and Tide*, a weekly journal of politics and literature, mainly publishing work that was boycotted elsewhere, such as Orwell's *exposé* of Stalinist repression in Republican Spain.

Thomas, Martha Carey (1857–1935) Feminist and educationist, born in Baltimore, MD. Educated privately and at Cornell University, she took a PhD at Zürich (1882), and became dean and professor of English at Bryn Mawr College for Women, which she had helped to organize (president 1894–1922). She established summer schools for women working in industry (1921), campaigned for women's right to vote, and wrote *The Higher Education of Women* (1900).

Thomas, Michael Tilson (1944–) Conductor, born in Hollywood, CA. A precocious talent, he was thrust into fame at 25 when as an assistant he took over a concert of the Boston Symphony from ailing William Steinberg. He went on to guest-conduct widely, and led the Buffalo Philharmonic (1971–9) and the London Symphony Orchestra (1988–95), becoming music director of the San Francisco Symphony Orchestra in 1995.

Thomas, Norman (Mattoon) (1884–1968) Socialist leader, born in Marion, OH. He studied at Bucknell University and Princeton, and was ordained a Presbyterian minister, becoming pastor of East Harlem Church in New York City (1911–31). A pacifist and Socialist, he founded and edited *The World Tomorrow* (1918–21), helped found the American Civil Liberties Union in 1920, worked on the *Nation* weekly (1921–2), and was co-director of the League for Industrial Democracy (1922–37). Leader of the Socialist Party of America in 1926, he was an unsuccessful presidential candidate six times between 1928 and 1948.

Thomas, R(onald) S(tuart) (1913–) Poet, born in Cardiff. He studied at the University of Wales, was ordained in 1936, and became a rector in the Church of Wales (1942–78). He published his first volume, *The Stones of the Field* in 1946, and came to attention outside Wales with *Song at the Year's Turning* (1955). *Selected Poems, 1946–68* appeared in 1973. His work deals with pastoral themes and the nature of God, coupled with an intense love of Wales and its people, evoked by nature imagery. *Later Poems, 1972–1982* appeared in 1983, and subsequent volumes include *The Echoes Return Slow* (1988), *Counterpoint* (1990), and *No Truth with the Furies* (1995).

Thomas, Seth (1785–1859) Clock maker, born in Wolcott, CT. He started out as a woodworker and helped to manufacture clocks in partnership with Eli Terry and **Silas Hoadley** (1807–1812). He began his own factory in 1812, then bought the rights to Terry's popular shelf clock, developing a highly successful business in Plymouth, CT (an area of which was later renamed Thomaston in his honour). His other enterprises included a cotton mill, and a brass-rolling and wire-making factory. >> Terry, Eli

Thomas, Sydney Gilchrist >> Gilchrist, Percy Carlyle

Thomas, Terry >> Terry-Thomas

Thomas, (Christian Friedrich) Theodore (1835–1905) Conductor, born in Essen, Germany. He studied violin, then moved to the USA with his family in 1845. He made his conducting debut in New York in 1860, and in 1862 founded the Thomas Orchestra and became co-conductor of the Brooklyn Philharmonic. In 1877 he became conductor of the New York Philharmonic, and in 1891 of the Chicago Orchestra, where he remained until his death. He founded the Cincinnati College of Music, and served as founding president (1878–80).

Thomas à Becket >> Becket, Thomas à

Thomas à Kempis >> Kempis, Thomas à

Thomas Aquinas >> Aquinas, St Thomas

Thomas of Hereford, St >> Cantelupe, St Thomas de

Thompson, Sir Benjamin, Graf (Count) **von Rumford**, known as **Count Rumford** (1753–1814) Administrator and scientist, born in Woburn, MA. He married in 1771, and joined the army, but during the Revolution left his family and fled to England (1776), possibly because he was politically suspect. After the peace he was knighted. In 1784 he entered the service of Bavaria, where he carried out military, social, and economic reforms, for which he was made head of the Bavarian war department and a count of the Holy Roman empire. Always an enthusiastic amateur scientist, he first showed the relation between heat and work, a concept fundamental to modern physics. In 1799 he returned to London and, with Sir Joseph Banks, founded the Royal Institution. >> Banks, Joseph

Thompson, Daley, popular name of **Francis Morgan Thompson** (1958–) Athlete, born in London, England, UK. An outstanding decathlete, his first major honour was in the 1978 Commonwealth Games, which he retained in 1982 and 1986. He was world champion (1983), European champion (1982, 1986), and Olympic champion (1980, 1984). He broke the world record four times between 1980 and 1984. Having suffered from injuries, he announced his retirement in 1992. >> RR1137

Thompson, Sir D'Arcy (Wentworth) (1860–1948) Zoologist and classical scholar, born in Edinburgh, EC Scotland, UK. He studied there, and at Cambridge, and was professor of biology at Dundee (1884–1917) and St Andrews (from 1917). His major work is the influential *On Growth and Form* (1917), and he also wrote on birds, fish, and oceanography. He was knighted in 1937.

Thompson, David (1770–1857) Fur trader and explorer, born in London, England, UK. Apprenticed to the Hudson's Bay Co of Canada, he spent 13 years working as a fur trader, before becoming a surveyor mapping the Saskatchewan, Hayes, Nelson, and Churchill rivers, and a route to L Athabasca. In 1797 he joined the rival North-West Co, surveying the course of the Columbia R. He settled in Montreal in 1812, and mapped W Canada.

Thompson, Emma (1959–) Actress, born in London, England, UK. She studied at Cambridge and made her stage debut with the Footlights while still a student. Showing a remarkable comic talent, she played opposite Robert Lindsay in *Me and My Girl* (1983), going on to appear on BBC TV's *Fortunes of War* opposite Kenneth Branagh, for which she won a BAFTA award. In 1989 she appeared in the film of *Henry V*, directed by Branagh, whom she married the same year (separated, 1995). With her husband she went on to make *Dead Again* (1991) and *Much Ado About Nothing* (1993). Her other films include *Howards End* (1992, Oscar), *Peter's Friends* (1992), *Remains of the Day* (1993), *In the Name of the Father* (1994), and *Sense and Sensibility* (1996, BAFTA). >> Branagh

Thompson, Flora (June), née **Timms** (1876–1947) Writer, born in Juniper Hill, Oxfordshire, SC England, UK. She left school at 14 to work in the local post office. She married young, and wrote mass-market fiction to help support her increasing family. In her 60s she published the semi-autobiographical trilogy combined as *Lark Rise to Candleford* (1945), its three parts, *Lark Rise*, *Over to Candleford*, and *Candleford Green* having appeared separately. It is a major feat of observation and memory, depicting the erosion of rural society before modern industrialism.

Thompson, Francis (1859–1907) Poet, born in Preston, Lancashire, NW England, UK. He studied for the priesthood, turned to medicine, but failed to graduate. He was rescued from poverty, ill health, and opium addiction by Wilfrid and Alice Meynell, to whom he had sent some poems for Meynell's magazine *Merry England*. His later work was mainly religious in theme; it includes the well-known 'The Hound of Heaven'. >> Meynell

Thompson, Hunter (Stockton) (1939–) Journalist, writer, editor, and small-game hunter, born in Louisville, KY. An adherent of the 'new journalism', he was the first reporter to infiltrate the Hell's Angels, and rode with them for a year, an experience which led to his being savagely beaten up. He awarded himself a doctorate and produced a stream of outrageous books, including *Fear and Loathing in Las Vegas* (1971) and *Generations of Swine* (1988). At the end of the 1980s he contributed a weekly column to the *San Francisco Examiner*.

Thompson, J(ames) Walter (1847–1928) Advertising executive, born in Pittsfield, MA. He served in the Union navy in the Civil War. In 1867 he joined William Carlton's New York advertising agency, which he bought in 1878. He virtually created modern advertising, transforming it into a primary sales tool by persuading magazines and major clients of its respectability. His success in placing advertising in magazines made national product campaigns possible. He sold the agency in 1916, and devoted himself to other interests, such as yachting.

Thompson, John T(alafierro) (1860–1940) US soldier and inventor, born in Newport, KY. He graduated in 1882 at the Military Academy, and in 1918 originated the Thompson submachine gun, which came to be known as the *Tommy gun* – a ·45 calibre gun weighing 10 lb. It was first used for military purposes by the US Marines in Nicaragua in 1925.

Thompson, Randall (1899–1984) Composer, born in New York City. He studied under Ernest Bloch, and became a fellow of the American Academy at Rome (1922–5), later teaching at Harvard, Princeton, and California universities. His music assimilates Romantic and popular American idioms, and includes symphonies, an oratorio, two operas, and a variety of chamber, piano, orchestral, and theatre music. From the 1960s he concentrated mainly on sacred vocal music. >> Bloch, Ernest

Thomsen, Christian Jörgensen (1788–1865) Archaeologist, born in Copenhagen. He worked for his wealthy businessman father, and collected antiquities from an early age. In 1816 he was appointed secretary of the Royal Commission for the Preservation of Antiquities, and during his work there he classified specimens into three groups representing chronologically successive ages. He is credited with developing the three-part system of prehistory, named as the Stone, Bronze, and Iron Ages, described in *Ledetraad til Nordisk Oldkyndighed* (1836, A Guide to Northern Antiquities).

Thomson, Sir C(harles) Wyville (1830–82) Marine biologist and oceanographer, born in Linlithgow, West Lothian, EC Scotland, UK. He studied at Edinburgh University, and went on to hold professorships in natural history at Cork, Belfast (1854–68), and Edinburgh, (1870–82). He was famous for his deep-sea researches, described in *The Depths of the Oceans* (1872), and in 1872 was appointed scientific head of the *Challenger* round-the-world expedition (1872–6), described in *The Voyage of the Challenger* (1877). He was knighted in 1876.

Thomson, D(avid) C(ouper) (1861–1954) Newspaper proprietor, born in Dundee, E Scotland, UK. At the age of 23 he left the family shipping firm to take charge of the newly acquired Dundee newspaper concern, which he owned and managed until his death. Its principal publications are the *Dundee Courier and Advertiser*, the *Sunday Post*, the *Scots Magazine*, and the *People's Friend*. It is known outside Scotland particularly for its many popular children's comics, such as the *Beano*, and *Dandy*.

Thomson, Elihu (1853–1937) Electrical engineer and inventor, born in Manchester, Greater Manchester, NW England, UK. His family moved to the USA when he was a child, and he was educated in Philadelphia, where he became a chemistry teacher. His 700 patented electrical inventions, which include the three-phase alternating-current generator, and arc lighting, were developed in co-operation with **Edwin J(ames) Houston** (1847–1914). They founded the Thomson–Houston Electric Company in 1883, and this merged with Thomas Edison's company in 1892 to form the General Electric Company. He became a lecturer at the Massachusetts Institute of Technology in 1894. >> Edison

Thomson, Sir George (Paget) (1892–1975) Physicist, born in Cambridge, Cambridgeshire, EC England, UK, the son of Sir Joseph Thomson. He studied there, and became a fellow of Trinity College. He was professor at Aberdeen (1922) and at Imperial College, London (1930), Master of Corpus Christi, Cambridge (1952–62), and scientific adviser to the UN Security Council (1946–7). For his contributions to electrical science he was awarded the Faraday Medal by the Institution of Electrical Engineers (1960). He shared the 1937 Nobel Prize for Physics for his discovery of electron diffraction by crystals, and was knighted in 1943. >> Thomson, J J; RR1122

Thomson, James (1700–48) Poet, born in Ednam, Scottish Borders, SE Scotland, UK. Educated at Edinburgh for the ministry, he abandoned his studies and turned to writing in London (1725). He is best known for his four-part work, *The Seasons* (1730), the first major nature poem in English, and for his ode 'Rule, Britannia' from *Alfred, a Masque* (1740), and the Spenserian allegory *The Castle of Indolence* (1748).

Thomson, James, pseudonym **Bysshe Vanolis** or **BV** (1834–82) Poet, born in Port Glasgow, Inverclyde, WC Scotland, UK. Brought up in an orphanage, he trained as an army schoolmaster at the Royal Military Academy, Chelsea, but was dismissed from army service for alcoholism in 1862. Through his friend Charles Bradlaugh he contributed (1862–75) to the *National Reformer*, in which appeared many of his sombre, sonorous poems, including 'The City of Dreadful Night' (1874), his greatest work. >> Bradlaugh

Thomson, Joseph (1858–95) Explorer, born in Penpont, Dumfries and Galloway, SW Scotland, UK. He studied geology at Edinburgh University and joined the Royal Geographical Society African Expedition (1878–9), taking charge on the death of the leader. He was the first European to reach L Nyasa (Malawi) from the N, and went on to L Tanganyika, which he described in *To the Central African Lakes and Back* (1881). An invitation from the Royal Geographical Society in 1882 to find a route through hostile Masai country from the coast via Mt Kilimanjaro to L Victoria led to his discovery of L Baringo and Mt Elgon. His careful notes greatly added to the geographical knowledge of East Africa. He also explored Sokoto in NW Nigeria (1885), and the Upper Congo (1890).

Thomson, Sir J(oseph) J(ohn) (1856–1940) Physicist, born in Cheetham Hill, Greater Manchester, NW England, UK. He studied at Cambridge, where he became professor of experimental physics in 1884. He showed in 1897 that cathode rays were rapidly-moving particles, and by measuring their speed and specific charge deduced that these 'corpuscles' (electrons) must be nearly 2000 times smaller in mass than the lightest known atomic particle, the hydrogen ion. He received the Nobel Prize for Physics in 1906, was knighted in 1908. Through his work, the Cavendish Laboratory became a major research institution. >> Thomson, George Paget

Thomson (of Fleet), Kenneth (Roy) Thomson, 2nd Baron (1923–) Businessman and financier, born in Toronto, Ontario, Canada, the son of Roy Thompson. He studied at Upper Canada College and at Cambridge, England, then joined the newspaper business. In 1979 he bought the Hudson's Bay Co, and in 1980 the FP publications newspaper chain. By the time he had sold *The Times* of London (1981), he was already one of Canada's wealthiest citizens through newspaper properties in Canada, Britain, and the USA, and through North Sea oil. He is also a renowned art enthusiast and collector. He succeeded his father as Baron Thomson of Fleet in 1976. >> Thomson, Roy

Thomson, Peter (1929–) Golfer, born in Melbourne, Victoria, Australia. The first outstanding golfer to emerge from Australia after World War 2, he won the British Open three times in succession (1954–6), and on two later occasions. He also played in Australia's winning World Cup teams of 1954 and 1959. >> RR1157

Thomson (of Fleet), Roy (Herbert) Thomson, Baron (1894–1976) Newspaper and television magnate, born in Toronto, Ontario, Canada. He held a variety of jobs, and became prosperous after setting up his own radio transmitter at North Bay (1931), founding what later became the NBC network. He started other radio stations, and bought many Canadian and US newspapers. He settled in Edinburgh on acquiring his first British paper, *The Scotsman* (1952), bought the Kemsley newspapers in 1959 (including *The Sunday Times*, to which he added the first colour supplement in 1962), and in 1966 took over *The Times*. Other business interests included Scottish Television and North Sea oil. He was created a peer in 1964. >> Thomson, Kenneth

Thomson, Tom, popular name of **Thomas John Thomson** (1877–1917) Painter, born in Claremont, Ontario, Canada. He worked as an engraver and designer-illustrator before turning to art in 1906. He spent a great deal of time working in Algonquin Park, Ontario, producing many sketches and some larger canvases, such as 'The West Wind' (1917, Toronto). He was found drowned near Wapomeo I, leaving a mystery about the manner of his death which to some extent has obscured his artistic accomplishments.

Thomson, Virgil (1896–1989) Composer and critic, born in Kansas City, KS. He studied at Harvard and in Paris, where he came under the influence of several French composers, in particular the group known as *Les Six*. He set some of the writings of Gertrude Stein to music, and wrote operas – notably, *Four Saints in Three Acts* (1934), first performed by a black cast, and *The Mother of Us All* (1947) – as well as symphonies, ballets, and choral, chamber, and film music. He was also music critic of the *New York Herald Tribune* (1940–54). >> Auric; Durey; Honegger; Milhaud; Poulenc; Stein, Gertrude; Tailleferre

Thomson, Sir William >> Kelvin (Lord)

Thonet, Michael (1796–1871) Manufacturer of bentwood furniture, born in Boppard, Germany. Trained as a cabinet-maker, he established a workshop in Boppard (1819), and gained prominence for parquetry. He experimented with steam-bending veneers, and was invited to Vienna (1842) to work on the interiors of the Liechtenstein Palace, where he used some pieces made of solid bent wood. In 1856 he had perfected his bentwood technique, and started making cafe chairs, rocking chairs, and hatstands. One of the pioneers of mass-production, by 1870 his firm was producing 400 000 pieces a year. After his death, his sons carried on the business, and his designs continue to be in vogue.

Thorarensen, Bjarni Vigfusson [**thaw(r)**ah(r)nsn] (1786–1841) Romantic poet and jurist, born in Brautarholt, Iceland. A precociously brilliant student, he went to Copenhagen University at the age of 15 to study law. After government service in Denmark, he was appointed a deputy justice in Reykjavik (1811), and justice of the Supreme Court (1817), and in 1833 he became Governor of North and East Iceland. As a lyric poet he celebrated Icelandic nature and nationalism, using the metres of classical heroic poetry. His poem 'Eldgamla Isafold' (Ancient Iceland) was regarded as an unofficial national anthem, set to the music of 'God Save the Queen'.

Thorburn, Archibald (1860–1935) Bird artist, born in Lasswade, Midlothian, EC Scotland, UK. He studied at St John's Wood School of Art in London, and his first paintings were hung in the Royal Academy when he was only 20. He painted the majority of the plates of the monumental *Coloured Figures of the Birds of the British Isles* (1885–97). He also published *British Birds* (4 vols, 1915–16), *British Mammals* (1920), and the immensely popular *Observer's Book of British Birds* (1937).

Thoreau, Henry (David) [**thoroh**] (1817–62) Essayist and poet, born in Concord, MA. He studied at Harvard, became a teacher, and c.1839 began his walks and studies of nature which became his major occupation. Although he sometimes lived at the family home of his friend and mentor Ralph Waldo Emerson, from 1845–7 he lived in a shanty he built himself in the woods by Walden Pond, near

Concord, where his writings included the American classic *Walden, or Life in the Woods* (1854). He supported himself by general jobs, and occasionally lectured and wrote for magazines. After his death, several books were published, based on his daily journal (from 1835) of his walks and observations, such as *Summer* (1884) and *Winter* (1887). His social criticism and his championing of individualism were widely influential. >> Emerson

Thorfinn, nickname **Thorfinn Karlsefni** ('Man-Material') (fl.1002–7) Explorer, and colonizer of 'Vínland' (Wineland, North America). Around the year 1000 he led an expedition of would-be colonists from Greenland, which sailed along the NE coasts of North America and attempted to found a Norse colony in an area called *Vínland*, somewhere in the vicinity of Newfoundland. The venture was abandoned after three years because of hostility from the native Indians. The story is told in two Icelandic sagas, *Eiriks saga* and *Groenlendinga saga*.

Thorkelin [thaw(r)kelin], pseudonym of **Grímur Jónsson** (1752–1829) Scholar and antiquary, from Iceland. He studied at the University in Copenhagen, where he became professor, and in 1791 was appointed keeper of the secret Danish archives. The first editor of the Anglo-Saxon epic *Beowulf*, which he found in the British Museum in London, his transcript was destroyed during the British bombardment of Copenhagen in 1807, but he re-published it in 1815.

Thorndike, Edward L(ee) (1874–1949) Psychologist, born in Williamsburg, MA. He studied at Wesleyan University and Harvard, and became professor at Teachers College, Columbia (1904–40), where he worked on educational psychology and the psychology of animal learning. As a result of studying animal intelligence, he formulated his famous 'law of effect', which states that a given behaviour is learned by trial-and-error, and is more likely to occur if its consequences are satisfying. His works include *Psychology of Learning* (1914) and *The Measurement of Intelligence* (1926).

Thorndike, Dame (Agnes) Sybil (1882–1976) Actress, born in Gainsborough, Lincolnshire, EC England, UK. She trained as a pianist, but turned to the stage, making her debut in 1904, and joining a repertory company in Manchester. In 1924 she played the title role in the first English performance of Shaw's *Saint Joan*, and during World War 2 was a notable member of the Old Vic Company. She married the actor Lewis Casson in 1908, and was made a dame in 1931. >> Casson, Lewis; Horniman

Thorneycroft (of Dunston), (George Edward) Peter Thorneycroft, Baron (1909–94) British statesman, born in Dunstan, Staffordshire, C England, UK. He trained at the Royal Military Academy, Woolwich, and joined the Royal Artillery, but left the army in 1933 to become a barrister. He was called to the bar in 1935, and became a Conservative MP in 1938. President of the Board of Trade (1951–7), he resigned after a year in office as Chancellor of the Exchequer (1957–8). He later became minister of aviation (1960–2), and minister then secretary of state for defence (1962–4), but lost his parliamentary seat in the 1966 election. Created a life peer in 1967, he later became chairman of the Conservative Party (1975–81).

Thornhill, Sir James (1675–1734) Baroque painter, born in Melcombe Regis, Dorset, S England, UK. He executed paintings for the dome of St Paul's, Blenheim, Hampton Court, and Greenwich Hospital, and founded a drawing school, where Hogarth (who became his son-in-law) was one of his pupils. In 1718 he was made history painter to the king. Knighted in 1720, he became an MP in 1722. >> Hogarth

Thoroddsen, Jón [thorodsn], originally **Jón Thórðarson** (1818–68) Novelist and poet, born in Reykhólar, Iceland.

He studied law at Copenhagen, and wrote drinking songs in the style of Carl Michael Bellmann (1740–95). He was an avid reader of Sir Walter Scott, and used him as a model for his first book, *Piltur og Stúlka* (1850, Boy and Girl), the earliest proper novel produced in Iceland. In addition to a sheaf of lyrics, he also wrote an unfinished sequel to his first novel, *Maður og Kona* (Man and Woman, published posthumously in 1876). He is regarded as the father of the modern Icelandic novel.

Thorpe, Sir (Thomas) Edward (1845–1925) Chemist, physicist, and historian of science, born near Manchester, Greater Manchester, NW England, UK. He studied at the universities of Heidelberg and Bonn, and was appointed to the chair of chemistry at the Royal College of Science, London (1885). He was also the first chemist at the British government laboratories concerned with analytical investigations for revenue purposes and control over chemical hazards. His early work was on the chemistry of vanadium, he wrote on the history of chemistry, and his *Dictionary of Applied Chemistry* (1893) was a long-used standard work.

Thorpe, (John) Jeremy (1929–) British politician, born in London, England, UK. He studied at Oxford, became a barrister in 1954, and a Liberal MP in 1959. Elected leader of the Liberal Party in 1967, he resigned the leadership in 1976 following a series of allegations of a previous homosexual relationship with Norman Scott. In 1979, shortly after losing his seat in the general election, he was acquitted of charges of conspiracy and incitement to murder Mr Scott.

Thorpe, Jim, popular name of **James Francis Thorpe** (1888–1953) Athlete, born in Prague, OK. His first sport was American football, although he was also a baseball player of exceptional ability. In the 1912 Olympic Games at Stockholm he came first in both pentathlon and decathlon, but was subsequently disqualified on a charge of having played semi-professional baseball. He played professional baseball (1913–19) with the New York Giants, Cincinnati Reds, and Boston Braves, and then professional football (1919–26). After his death the American Athletics Union reinstated him as an amateur for the years 1909–12, and his Olympic titles were restored. >> RR1137

Thorpe Davie, Cedric (1913–83) Composer, born in London, England, UK. He studied in Glasgow, in 1936 became professor of composition at the Scottish National Academy of Music, and in 1945 was appointed master of music at St Andrews University. His early compositions include a string quartet, and the *Dirge for Cuthullin* for chorus and orchestra in 1935. His Symphony in C appeared in 1945, and he wrote the music for Tyrone Guthries's acclaimed production of *Ane Satyre of the Thrie Estaitis* in 1948. >> Guthrie, Tyrone

Thorvaldsen, Bertel [torvalsn] (c. 1768–1844) Neoclassical sculptor, born in Copenhagen. He studied at Copenhagen and Rome, working in both places. His best-known pieces include 'Christ and the Twelve Apostles', the reliefs 'Night and Morning', the 'Dying Lion' at Lucerne, and the Cambridge statue of Byron. All the works in his possession he bequeathed, with the bulk of his fortune, to his country.

Thothmes (Thutmose) I / II >> Hatshepsut

Thothmes III >> Thutmose III

Thrale, Mrs >> Piozzi, Hester Lynch

Thrasybulus [thrasiboolus] (?–388 BC) Athenian general. A strenuous supporter of the democracy, in 411 BC he helped to overthrow the Four Hundred, and was responsible for the recall of Alcibiades. In that year he defeated the Spartans in naval battles at Cynossema, and at Cyzicus in 410 BC. In 404 BC he was banished by the Thirty Tyrants, but restored the democracy in 403 BC by seizing Piraeus. He conquered Lesbos and defended Rhodes, but was slain in 388 BC at Aspendus. >> Alcibiades

Three Stooges, The >> Stooges, The Three

Throckmorton, Francis (1554–84) English conspirator, who plotted the unsuccessful attempt to overthrow Queen Elizabeth I in 1583. The nephew of one of the queen's diplomats, he was educated at Oxford, visited Europe, where he conspired with Catholic exiles, and returned in 1583 with a plot to restore papal authority. The conspiracy was uncovered, he was tortured into a full confession, and executed. >> Babington; Walsingham, Francis

Throckmorton, Sir Nicholas (1515–71) English diplomat. He fought at Pinkie (1547), was knighted in 1547, and became ambassador to France and Scotland. In 1569 he was imprisoned for promoting the scheme to marry Mary, Queen of Scots, to the Duke of Norfolk, but soon released. His daughter, **Elizabeth Throckmorton**, married Sir Walter Raleigh. His nephew, **Francis Throckmorton** (1554–84) was executed for planning a conspiracy to overthrow Elizabeth I.

Thucydides [thyoo**sid**ideez] (c. 460–c. 400 BC) Athenian aristocratic historian of the Peloponnesian War. Although scrupulously accurate in his narrative of events, he was not altogether unprejudiced. Exiled for 20 years by the democracy for military incompetence in the N Aegean (424 BC), he was consistently critical of the democratic system and its leaders in the war years. >> Pericles

Thucydides [thyoo**sid**ideez] (5th-c BC) Athenian politician, son-in-law of Cimon, and leader of the opposition to Pericles until ostracized in 443 BC. He was probably a relative of Thucydides, the historian.

Thumb, General Tom >> Stratton, Charles

Thurber, James (Grover) (1894–1961) Writer and cartoonist, born in Columbus, OH. He studied at Ohio State University, and was a clerk in Washington, DC, and at the US embassy in Paris before embarking on a career in journalism. In the early 1920s he reported for various papers in the USA and Europe, and in 1927 was appointed managing editor of the *New Yorker*. His popular drawings first appeared in *Is Sex Necessary?* (1929), which he co-authored. A plethora of books followed, often combining humorous essays with characteristic doodles, and a number of short stories, including most memorably *The Secret Life of Walter Mitty*. >> White, E B

Thurmond, J(ames) Strom (1902–) US senator, born in Edgefield, SC. A teacher and superintendent of education before turning to the law, he was a judge of the state's circuit court (1938–42). After serving with the US army in World War 2, he became Democratic Governor of South Carolina (1947–51). Although relatively progressive as a governor, he was opposed to the 1948 Democratic civil rights programme, and led the walkout of the Southern Democrats at the 1948 convention. Originally appointed a Democrat to the US Senate in 1954, he was elected on his own in 1956; switching to the Republican Party in 1964, he continued to be re-elected, and became a prominent force in the emergence of a conservative Republican Party in the South. He was appointed chair of the Senate Armed Services Committee in the 105th Congress (1997).

Thurston, Robert Henry (1839–1903) Mechanical engineer and educator, born in Providence, RI. He organized the department of mechanical engineering at the newly-formed Stevens Institute of Technology, Hoboken, NJ, drawing up a four-year course of instruction that included training students on actual research. In 1885 he was hired by Cornell University to reorganize Sibley College as a college of mechanical engineering, and he remained there until his death.

Thurstone, L(ouis) L(eon) (1887–1955) Psychologist, born in Chicago, IL. He studied at Cornell and Chicago

universities, taught at the Carnegie Institute of Technology (1915–23) and Chicago University (1927–52), and became director of the Psychometric Laboratory at North Carolina University (1952–5). His academic work was devoted to the theory and practice of intelligence testing and to the development of statistical techniques.

Thutmose I / II >> Hatshepsut

Thutmose III [thut**moh**suh], also **Thothmes** or **Tuthmosis** (?–1450 BC) Egyptian pharaoh (c.1504–1450 BC). He was one of the greatest of Egyptian rulers, who re-established Egyptian control over Syria and Nubia, and ornamented his kingdom with revenues from these conquests. He built the temple of Amon at Karnak, and erected many obelisks, including 'Cleopatra's Needle'. In the early years of his reign, power lay in the hands of Hatshepsut, the sister/wife of Thutmose II. >> Hatshepsut; RR1046

Tiberius [tiy**beer**ius], in full **Tiberius Julius Caesar Augustus** (42 BC–AD 37) Roman emperor (14–37), the son of Livia, and stepson and successor of the Emperor Augustus. Deeply conservative by nature, he was content to continue Augustus's policies and simply consolidate his achievements. Despite the soundness of his administration and foreign policy, politically his reign was a disaster. The suspicious death of his heir Germanicus (19) was followed by the excesses of his chief henchman, the praetorian prefect Sejanus, and the reign of terror that followed Sejanus's downfall (d.31) made him an object of universal loathing. Few mourned when he died on Capri, the island retreat that had been his home since 26. >> Agrippina; Augustus; Drusus Germanicus; Germanicus; Julia; Livia; Sejanus; RR1084

Tibullus, Albius [**tibul**us] (c. 54–19 BC) Latin poet, considered by Quintilian to be the greatest elegaic writer. He fought in Aquitania, but withdrew from military life and became a member of a literary circle in Rome. The heroine of his first book of love poetry was the wife of an officer absent on service in Cilicia; of his second, a fashionable courtesan. The other works under his name are probably by several authors.

Tidy, Bill, popular name of **William Edward Tidy** (1933–) Cartoonist and broadcaster, born in Liverpool, Merseyside, NW England, UK. Educated in Liverpool, he worked for an advertising agency before becoming a freelance cartoonist in 1958. His creations include the cartoon strips *The Cloggies* and *The Fosdyke Saga*, which he adapted for radio. He has appeared on and presented *I'm Sorry I Haven't a Clue* (BBC radio), and published a number of books of his cartoons and other subjects, including *The Incredible Bed* (1990) and *Save Daring Waring with a Pencil* (1993).

Tieck, (Johann) Ludwig [teek] (1773–1853) Critic and writer of the Romantic school, born in Berlin. He studied at the universities of Halle, Göttingen, and Erlangen, and published several novels followed by dramatized versions of 'Puss in Boots', 'Bluebeard', and others. Adviser and critic at the theatre in Dresden, (1825–42), he is best known for his critical writings, which include a series of Shakespearian essays (1823–9). He also edited and translated Shakespeare, and produced a translation of *Don Quixote* (1799–1804).

Tiepolo, Giovanni Battista [tyay**poloh**] (1696–1770) Artist, born in Venice, Italy. The last of the great Venetian painters, he became renowned as a decorator of buildings throughout Europe. Examples of his work can be found in the ceiling paintings of the Würzburg and Madrid palaces, where his imaginary skies are filled with floating, gesticulating, Baroque figures, apparently unbounded by the structure of the buildings.

Tiffany, Charles (Lewis) (1812–1902) Goldsmith and jeweller, founder of Tiffany & Co, born in Killingly, CT. He began dealing in fancy goods in New York City in 1837, and by 1883 was one of the largest manufacturers of silverware in the USA. His work reflected current tastes, with an accent on the traditional and historical. He held official appointments to 23 royal patrons, including the Tsar of Russia, Queen Victoria, and the Shah of Persia. He later marketed some of the Art Nouveau lamps made by his son, Louis Tiffany. >> Tiffany, Louis

Tiffany, Louis (Comfort) (1848–1933) Glassmaker and interior decorator, born in New York City, the son of Charles Lewis Tiffany. He began studying painting, and established a firm of interior decorators which became one of the most popular firms in New York City by the early 1880s. He is best known as a leader of the Art Nouveau movement for his work in glass. He acquired glass furnaces at Cirona, NY (1892), where the first year's production went to museums. By 1896 the first 'Favrile glass' (hand-made) was offered for sale. He also produced stained glass, furniture, fabrics, wallpaper, and Tiffany lamps. >> Tiffany, Charles

Tikhonov, Nikolay Alexandrovich [tikhonof] (1905–97) Soviet statesman and prime minister (1980–5), born in Kharkov, Ukraine. He worked for two decades in the ferrous metallurgy industry, before being appointed deputy minister for the iron and steel industry (1955–7), deputy chairman of Gosplan (1963–5), and deputy chairman of the Council of Ministers (1965–80). He was inducted into the Politburo as a full member by Brezhnev in 1979, and appointed premier in 1980. His period as state premier was characterized by progressive economic stagnation. >> Brezhnev; RR1085

Tilden, Bill, popular name of **William Tatem Tilden** (1893–1953) Tennis player, born in Philadelphia, PA. One of the greatest players of his time, renowned for the ferocity of his serve, he was Wimbledon singles champion three times (1920, 1921, 1930) and doubles champion in 1927. He was also six times US singles champion, and four times doubles champion in the 1920s. In 1931 he turned professional, and was one of the first players to go on circuit. Publisher and editor of *Racquet Magazine*, he also wrote several books on tennis, and a novel. >> RR1173

Tilden, Samuel Jones (1814–86) Lawyer and public official, born in New Lebanon, NY. He studied law in New York City, and was admitted to the bar in 1841. He built a prosperous practice and became active in Democratic politics, leading the Free-Soil wing of the Party. After taking a leading role in breaking up Boss Tweed's rings, he was elected Governor of New York on a reform platform (1875–7). He ran for president as a Democrat in 1876, and won the popular vote in a close race; but when an electoral commission awarded the disputed election to Rutherford B Hayes, he returned to New York City and resumed his law practice. >> Hayes, Rutherford B; Tweed

Tilden, Sir William Augustus (1842–1926) Chemist, born in London, England, UK. Professor at the Royal College of Science, London, he made possible the manufacture of artificial rubber by his synthetic preparation of isoprene.

Tillett, Ben(jamin) (1860–1943) Trade union leader, born in Bristol, SW England, UK. He worked as a brickmaker, bootmaker, and sailor, and achieved prominence as leader of the great dockers' strike (1889), and of the transport workers' strike in London (1911). He later became a Labour MP (1917–24, 1929–31).

Tilley, Vesta, stage name of **Matilda Alice, Lady de Frece**, *née* **Powles** (1864–1952) Music-hall entertainer, born in Worcester, Hereford and Worcester, WC England, UK. She first appeared as 'The Great Little Tilley', aged four, in Nottingham, adopted her professional name, and became a celebrated male impersonator. Her many popular songs included 'Burlington Bertie' and 'Following in Father's Footsteps'. She retired in 1920.

Tillich, Paul (Johannes) [tilikh] (1886–1965) Protestant theologian and philosopher, born in Starzeddel, Germany. A Lutheran pastor, he held professorships at Marburg, Dresden, Leipzig, and Frankfurt. In 1933 he was barred from German universities, and moved to the USA, teaching at the Union Theological Seminary in New York City (1933–55), Harvard Divinity School (1955–62), and Chicago Divinity School (1962–5), and becoming a US citizen in 1940. His influence is characterized by an attempt to mediate between traditional Christian culture and the secular orientation of modern society. His main scholarly work was *Systematic Theology* (3 vols, 1951–63), and his popular books included *Dynamics of Faith* (1957).

Tilly, Johann Tserclaes, Graf (Count) **von** (1559–1632) Flemish soldier, born in Tilly, Belgium. He successfully commanded the forces of the Catholic League in the Thirty Years' War, gaining decisive victories at the White Mountain and Prague (1620). Created a count of the Holy Roman Empire, he defeated Denmark at Lütter (1626). His destruction of Magdeburg (1631) branded him a brutal soldier, and he was routed by Gustav II Adolf at Breitenfeld in Saxony (1631). He was fatally wounded crossing into Bavaria. >> Gustav II Adolf

Tilman, Harold William (1898–?1978) Mountaineer, explorer, and sailor, born in Wallasey, Merseyside, NW England, UK. He made the first ascents of Midget Peak, Mt Kenya (1930), and Nanda Devi (1936), was a member of the 1935 Everest expedition, and led the 1938 attempt. After 1953 he sailed to Patagonia and crossed the ice-cap, and completed the circumnavigation of South America. He circumnavigated Africa (1957–8), and in 1977 sailed from Southampton to the South Shetland Is, but was never seen again after leaving Rio.

Timoleon [timohlion] (?–c. 337 BC) Greek statesman, and general of Corinth. He overthrew the tyranny of his brother Timophanes, and retired from public life; but when Dionysius the Younger and others tried to establish themselves in Syracuse, he was prevailed upon to return. He manoeuvred Dionysius into abdication and fought the Carthaginians, who were supporting the other tyrants, defeating them at the Crimessus in 341. >> Dionysius (the Younger)

Timon [tiymon], nickname **the Misanthrope of Athens** (5th-c BC) Nobleman from Athens, a contemporary of Socrates. According to the comic writers who attacked him, he was disgusted with mankind on account of the ingratitude of his early friends, and lived a life of almost total seclusion. Lucian made him the subject of a dialogue. Shakespeare's play *Timon of Athens* is based on the story as told in Painter's *Palace of Pleasure*. >> Socrates

Timoshenko, Semyon Konstantinovich [timohshengkoh] (1895–1970) Russian general, born in Furmanka, Ukraine. He joined the Tsarist army in 1915, and in the Revolution took part in the defence of Tsaritsyn. In 1940 he smashed Finnish resistance during the Russo-Finnish War, then commanded in the Ukraine, but failed to stop the German advance (1942). He also served as People's Commissar of Defence, improving the system of army training. He retired in 1960.

Timur [timoor], known as **Timur Lenk** (Turk 'Timur the Lame'), English **Tamerlane** or **Tamburlaine** (1336–1405) Tatar conqueror, born near Samarkand, Uzbekistan. In 1369 he ascended the throne of Samarkand, subdued nearly all Persia, Georgia, and the Tatar empire, and conquered all the states between the Indus and the lower Ganges (1398). He won Damascus and Syria from the Mameluke sovereigns of Egypt, then defeated the Turks at

Angora (1402), taking Sultan Bayezit prisoner. He died while marching to conquer China. >> Bayezit I; Ulugh Beg

Tinbergen, Jan [tinbergen] (1903–94) Dutch economist, born in The Hague, the brother of Nikolaas Tinbergen. He studied at Leyden. His major contribution was the econometric modelling of cyclical movements in socio-economic growth. He was director of the Central Planning Bureau in The Netherlands (1945–55), then professor of development planning at the Netherlands School of Economics (1955–73), and also worked with developing countries. In 1969 he shared the first Nobel Prize for Economics. There are Tinbergen Institutes for economic research in Amsterdam and Rotterdam. >> Tinbergen, Nikolaas; RR1125

Tinbergen, Nikolaas [tinbergen] (1907–88) Ethologist, born in The Hague, the brother of Jan Tinbergen. He graduated in zoology at Leyden, and later taught there, and from 1947 at Oxford. His major concern was with the patterns of animal behaviour in nature, showing that many are stereotyped. His research covered several species, in relation to camouflage, learning behaviour, courtship, and aggression, and he also studied autism in children. He shared the Nobel Prize for Physiology or Medicine in 1973. >> Morris, Desmond; Tinbergen, Jan; RR1124

Tindale >> Tyndale, William

Ting, Samuel C(hao) C(hung) (1936–) Physicist, born in Ann Arbor, MI. He studied at Michigan University, worked at nuclear facilities in Geneva and Hamburg, and joined the Massachusetts Institute of Technology in 1967. He conducted an experiment in which protons were directed onto a beryllium target; a long-lived product particle was observed in 1974, and later named the J/psi particle. He shared the 1976 Nobel Prize for Physics with Burton Richter, who independently made the same discovery. >> Richter, Burton

Ting Ling >> Ding Ling

Tinguely, Jean [tīlee] (1925–) Sculptor, born in Fribourg, Switzerland. He studied at Basel, and was a pioneer of Kinetic Art. He worked in Paris from 1953 onwards, exhibiting his 'meta-mechanical' moving metal constructions, sometimes powered by small motors. Some of these clatter and ping, striking bottles or metal pans (*musique concrète*), and even make abstract drawings, but about 1960 he began programming them to destroy themselves ('auto-destructive art').

Tino di Camaino [teenoh dee kamiynoh] (c. 1285–1337) Sculptor, born in Siena, Italy. He probably trained in Pisa under Giovanni Pisano, and was certainly working there in 1311. In 1315 he succeeded Giovanni as master of works at Pisa Cathedral, and was commissioned to make the tomb of Emperor Henry VII. He then held an equivalent position at Siena Cathedral, and later worked in Florence, where his sepulchral monuments included that of Bishop Orso in Florence Cathedral. Around 1324 he entered the service of the Angevin rulers in Naples, and worked there on architectural projects as well as sculpture. >> Pisano, Giovanni

Tinsley, Pauline (1928–) Dramatic soprano, born in Wigan, Greater Manchester, NW England, UK. She studied singing in Manchester and at the Opera School in London. She excelled as a singing actress in roles as diverse as Elektra, Turandot, the Dyer's Wife, and Lady Macbeth, and has performed throughout the USA, at La Scala Milan, Hamburg, and Amsterdam.

Tintoretto [tintoretoh], originally **Jacopo Robusti** (1518–94) Venetian painter, probably born in Venice, Italy, the son of a dyer (Ital *tintore*). Except for visits to Mantua (1580, 1590–3), he lived all his life in Venice, painting portraits and biblical subjects in which he attempted (according to a contemporary critic) to combine the energetic drawing of Michelangelo with the glowing colour of Titian. His most spectacular works are sacred murals painted for religious confraternities, especially the 50 or so canvases decorating the Church and Scuola of S Rocco. The Scuola contains a vast iconographical scheme from the Old and New Testaments, including the 'Crucifixion' (1565) and 'Annunciation' (1583–7). Other major works include 'The Last Supper' (1547, Venice), 'The Last Judgment' (c.1560, Venice), and the 'Paradiso', famous for its great size (1588, Venice). Three of his seven children also became painters, including **Marietta** (1560–90), known as **la Tintoretta**. >> Michelangelo; Titian

Tiomkin, Dimitri [tyomkin] (1894–1980) Composer, born in Russia. A piano virtuoso, he toured Europe and the USA in the 1920s. In 1930 he began writing theme music for Hollywood films, eventually earning Oscars for the background music to *High Noon* (1952), *The High and the Mighty* (1954), and *The Old Man and the Sea* (1958). His last film was the Soviet-produced *Tschaikowsky* (1970), for which he scored the composer's music.

Tippett, Sir Michael (Kemp) (1905–98) Composer, born in London, England, UK. He studied at the Royal College of Music, London, and became director of music at Morley College (1940–51). His oratorio, *A Child of Our Time* (1941), reflecting the problems of the 1930s and 1940s, won him wide recognition. A convinced pacifist, he was imprisoned for three months as a conscientious objector during World War 2. He scored a considerable success with his operas *The Midsummer Marriage* (1952) and *King Priam* (1961), and among his other works are four symphonies, a piano concerto, and string quartets. His books include *Music of the Angels* (1980), *Those Twentieth Century Blues* (1991), and *Tippett on Music* (1995). He was knighted in 1966, and received the Order of Merit in 1983.

Tippoo Sultán [tipoo], also known as **Tippoo Sahib** (1749–99) Sultan of Mysore (1782–99), born in Devanhalli, India, the son of Haidar Ali. He continued his father's policy of opposing British rule, and in 1789 invaded the British-protected state of Travancore. In the ensuing war (1790–2) he was defeated by Cornwallis, and had to cede half his kingdom. After recommencing hostilities in 1799, he was killed during the siege of Seringapatam. >> Cornwallis; Haidar Ali; Wellesley, Richard

Tiro, Marcus Tullius [tiyroh] (fl. 1st-c) Freedman of Rome who invented the *Tironian* system of shorthand. A friend and amanuensis of Cicero, he devised his system in order to take down dictation and record speeches. He was the author of a lost *Life of Cicero* and editor of some of Cicero's letters. His shorthand system was taught in Roman schools, and was in widespread use for several centuries. >> Cicero

Tirpitz, Alfred (Friedrich) von [teerpits] (1849–1930) German admiral, born in Kostrzyn, Poland (formerly Küstrin, Prussia). He joined the Prussian navy in 1865, was ennobled in 1900, and rose to be Lord High Admiral (1911). As secretary of state for the imperial navy (1897–1916), he raised a fleet to challenge British supremacy of the seas, and acted as its commander (1914–16). He advocated unrestricted submarine warfare, and resigned when this policy was opposed. He later sat in the Reichstag, then retired to Ebenhausen.

Tirso de Molina [teersoh, moleena], pseudonym of **Gabriel Téllez** (c. 1571–1648) Playwright, born in Madrid. Educated at Alcalá, he became prior of the monastery of Soria. A disciple of his contemporary, Lope de Vega, he wrote many comedies and religious plays, but is best known for his treatment of the Don Juan legend in *El burlador de Sevilla* (1635, The Seducer of Seville). >> Vega

Tischendorf, (Lobegott Friedrich) Konstantin von [**tish**endaw(r)f] (1815–74) Biblical scholar, born in Lengenfeld, Germany. He became a lecturer (1839) and a professor (1845) at Leipzig. His lifetime's work, journeying in search of New Testament manuscripts, resulted in the discovery of the 4th-c Sinaitic Codex at the monastery of St Catherine on Mt Sinai.

Tiselius, Arne (Wilhelm Kaurin) [ti**say**lius] (1902–71) Chemist, born in Stockholm. He studied at Uppsala under Svedberg, and became professor of biochemistry there (1938). He investigated serum proteins by electrophoretic analysis, and in chromatography evolved new methods for the analysis of colourless substances. He was awarded the Nobel Prize for Chemistry in 1948, and later became president of the Nobel Foundation (1960–4). >> Svedberg

Tissot, James Joseph Jacques [**tee**soh] (1836–1902) Painter, born in Nantes, France. He trained in Paris, where he was influenced by Degas, then in the 1870s settled in London, painting highly accomplished scenes of Victorian life. As a result of a visit to Palestine in 1886, he produced a series of the life of Christ in water-colour. >> Degas

Titchmarsh, Alan (Fred) (1949–) Gardener, broadcaster, and writer, born in Ilkley, West Yorkshire, N England, UK. He became an apprentice gardener for Ilkley Urban District Council (1964–8), then joined the Royal Botanic Gardens at Kew (1972–4). He began presenting radio and television programmes for the BBC, and became a household name for his expert advice on gardening matters, in 1996 becoming presenter of the popular radio series, *Gardener's World*. A regular contributor to magazines and newspapers, his books include *Gardening Techniques* (1981) and *Alan Titchmarsh's Favourite Gardens* (1995).

Titian [**tish**an], Ital **Tiziano Vecellio** (c. 1490–1576) Venetian painter, born in Pieve di Cadore, Italy. Trained in the studio of Giovanni Bellini, he assisted Giorgione with the paintings on the Fondaco dei Tedeschi (1508). His early paintings display Giorgione's influence, and his own revolutionary style is not apparent until after c.1516, in such works as 'The Assumption of the Virgin' (1516–18, Venice). For the Duke of Ferrara he painted three great mythological subjects, 'The Feast of Venus' (c.1515–18), 'The Bacchanal' (c.1518, both Prado, Madrid), and the richly-coloured 'Bacchus and Ariadne' (c.1523, National Gallery, London). From 1530, he also painted many pictures for Emperor Charles V, and this period includes his 'Ecce Homo' (1543, Vienna). He later executed a series of works on mythological scenes for Philip of Spain, and in his last years painted several religious and mythological subjects, such as 'The Fall of Man' (c.1570, Madrid) and 'Christ Crowned with Thorns' (c.1570, Munich). He is widely acclaimed as the greatest of the Venetian painters. >> Bellini, Giovanni; Giorgione

Tito [**tee**toh], known as **Marshal Tito**, originally **Josip Broz** (1892–1980) Yugoslav statesman and president (1953–80), born in Kumrovec, Croatia. In World War 1 he served with the Austro-Hungarian army, was taken prisoner by the Russians, and became a Communist. He was imprisoned for conspiring against the regime in Yugoslavia (1928–9), and became secretary of the Communist Party in 1937. In 1941 he organized partisan forces against the Axis conquerors, and after the war became the country's first Communist prime minister (1945), consolidating his position with the presidency in 1953. He broke with Stalin and the Cominform in 1948, developing Yugoslavia's independent style of Communism (*Titoism*), and played a leading role in the association of nonaligned countries. >> RR1100

Titterton, Sir Ernest (William) (1916–90) Nuclear physicist, born in Tamworth, Staffordshire, C England, UK. He studied at Birmingham University, and was a member of the British mission to USA for the development of the atomic bomb (1943). He was senior member of the timing team at the first atomic test in 1945, and advisor on instrumentation at the Bikini Atoll tests in 1946, before returning to Los Alamos, New Mexico, as head of the electronics division until 1947. He then worked at the Atomic Energy Research Establishment at Harwell, Berkshire, until 1950, when he became professor of nuclear physics at the Australian National University, Canberra.

Titus [**tiy**tus], in full **Titus Flavius Vespasianus** (39–81) Roman emperor (79–81), the elder son and successor of Vespasian. Popular with the Romans for his generosity, charm, and military prowess, he is execrated in Jewish tradition for his destruction of Jerusalem (70) and suppression of the Jewish Revolt. His brief reign was marred by many natural calamities, notably the eruption of Vesuvius (79). He completed the Colosseum, begun by his father. >> Vespasian; RR1084

Titus, St [**tiy**tus] (1st-c) In the New Testament, a Gentile companion of the apostle Paul. He is not mentioned in Acts, but is referred to in Galatians 2 and 2 Corinthians 8.6. Ecclesiastical tradition makes him the first Bishop of Crete. The purported Letter of Paul to Titus gives advice on the way the churches there should be organized. Feast day 6 February (W), 23 August (E).

Tizard, Dame Catherine Anne [**ti**zah(r)d] (1931–) New Zealand politician and public administrator, born in Auckland, New Zealand. She taught at Auckland University (1963–83), became an Auckland city councillor (1971–83), and then Mayor of Auckland (1983–90). The outstanding achievement of her mayoralty was the construction of a long-planned performing arts complex, the Aotea Centre. A popular and outspoken person with a wide range of community involvements, she became Governor-General of New Zealand (1990–6), the first woman to hold the position. She was made a dame in 1984.

Tobey, Mark [**toh**bee] (1890–1976) Artist, born in Centerville, WI. He studied at the Art Institute of Chicago, then worked as a fashion illustrator and portrait painter. He became fascinated by the Far East, and converted to the Baha'i faith in 1918. The influence of Chinese calligraphy is reflected in his later work, usually white on a dark background, as exemplified by his cityscapes of the 1930s.

Tobias, Phillip Vallentine [to**biy**as] (1925–) Anatomist and physical anthropologist, born in Durban, South Africa. He studied at Witwatersrand and Cambridge universities, and in 1951 began to teach at Witwatersrand, becoming professor of anatomy in 1959. He is a leading authority on human biological evolution, with over 700 publications including *The Brain in Hominid Evolution* (1971), *The Meaning of Race* (1972), *Hominid Evolution: Past, Present and Future* (1985), and *Images of Humanity* (1991).

Tobin, James [**toh**bin] (1918–) Economist, born in Champaign, IL. He studied at Harvard and, following wartime service in the US navy, went on to teach there. In 1955 he became a professor at Yale, and in 1981 was awarded the Nobel Prize for Economics, primarily for his 'portfolio selection theory' of investment.

Tocqueville, Alexis (Charles Henri Maurice Clérel) de [**tok**veel] (1805–59) Historian and political scientist, born in Verneuil, France. He became a lawyer (1825), and in 1831 went to the USA to report on the prison system. On his return, he published a penetrating political study, *De la Démocratie en Amerique* (1835, Democracy in America), which gave him a European reputation. He became a member of the Chamber of Deputies in 1839, and in 1849 was vice-president of the Assembly and briefly minister of foreign affairs. After Louis Napoleon's coup, he retired to his estate, where he wrote the first volume of *L'Ancien Régime et la Révolution* (1856, The Old Regime and the Revolution). He died before it could be completed.

Todd (of Trumpington), Alexander Robertus Todd, Baron (1907- 97) Chemist, born in Glasgow, W Scotland, UK. He studied at Glasgow, Frankfurt, and Oxford universities, and became professor at Manchester (1938–44) and Cambridge (1944–71). He was Master of Christ's College, Cambridge (1963–78), and the first chancellor of the new University of Strathclyde (1965–91). He was awarded the Nobel Prize for Chemistry in 1957 for his research on vitamins B_1 and E. Knighted in 1954, he was made a life peer in 1962.

Todd, Sir (Reginald Stephen) Garfield (1908-) Rhodesian missionary, statesman, and prime minister (1953–8), born in Otago, New Zealand. A Church of Christ minister, he went to Southern Rhodesia (now Zimbabwe), where he was superintendent of the Dadaya Mission (1934–53). He became an MP (1948), and rose to become prime minister. He was later detained by the Smith regime for supporting the Zimbabwe nationalist movement (1972–6). He was knighted in 1986. >> Smith, Ian

Todd, Mabel Loomis >> **Bingham, Millicent**

Todd, Mark James (1956-) Show jumper, born in Cambridge, New Zealand. Not financially well-endowed, he achieved high success in a very expensive sport through a combination of his own skill, the generosity of his friends, and the genius of his principal mount *Charisma*. After coming to international prominence at the Badminton Horse Trials in England in 1980, he won the gold medal in the individual Three Day Event at the Los Angeles Olympics (1984) and at Seoul (1988). He was ranked top rider in the world in 1984, 1988, and 1989.

Todd, Mike, popular name of **Michael Todd**, originally **Avrom Hirsch Goldbogen** (1909–58) Showman, born in Minneapolis, MN. The son of a poor rabbi, he made his first fortune at 14 in sales promotion. In 1927 he went to Hollywood, staged a real 'Flame Dance' spectacle at the Chicago World Fair in 1933, and produced plays, musical comedies, and films, including a jazz version of Gilbert and Sullivan, called *The Hot Mikado* (1939), and an up-dated *Hamlet* (1945). He sponsored the three-dimensional TODD-AO wide-screen process with his film *Around the World in Eighty Days* (1956, Oscar). He married the film actress Elizabeth Taylor in 1957, but was killed in an aircrash the following year. >> Taylor, Elizabeth

Todd, Richard B >> **Bowman, William**

Todd, Ron(ald) (1927-) Trade union leader, born in London, England, UK. He joined the Ford Motor Co in 1954, and became a member of the Transport and General Workers' Union (TGWU). He rose steadily from shop steward to be general secretary (1985–92). A skilled negotiator with a direct oratorical style, he won the union's leadership with strong left-wing support. Although viewed as a staunch supporter of Neil Kinnock, Labour Party leader at that time, his commitment to unilateral nuclear disarmament led to strains in the TGWU–Labour relationship. >> Kinnock

Todi, Jacopone da [tohdee, jakopohnay] (c. 1230–1306) Religious poet, born in Todi, Italy. He practised as an advocate, was converted in 1268, became a Franciscan in 1278, and was imprisoned (1298–1303) for satirizing Pope Boniface VIII. To him is ascribed the authorship of the *Stabat Mater* and other Latin hymns, and he wrote *laudi spirituali* ('spiritual praises'), important in the development of Italian drama.

Todt, Fritz [toht] (1891–1942) Engineer, born in Pforzheim, Germany. As Hitler's inspector of German roads (1933) he was responsible for the construction of the *Reichsautobahnen*.

The Todt Organization was also responsible for the construction of the Siegfried Line (1937). Nazi minister for armaments (1940), and for fuel and power (1941), he was killed in an aircrash. >> Hitler

Togo, Heihachiro, Koshaku (Marquess) [tohgoh] (1847–1934) Japanese admiral, born in Kagoshima, Japan. He trained at Greenwich, served against China (1894), and as commander during the war with Russia (1904–5), bombarded Port Arthur and defeated the Russian fleet at Tsushima (1905). He was ennobled in 1907.

Tojo, Hideki [tohjoh] (1885–1948) Japanese general, statesman, and prime minister (1941–4), born in Tokyo. He attended military college, became military attaché in Germany (1919), served in Manchuria as chief-of-staff (1937–40), and during World War 2 was minister of war (1940–1) and premier. Arrested in 1945, he attempted to commit suicide, but was hanged as a war criminal. >> RR1068

Tokugawa, Ieyasu [tokugahwa] (1542–1616) The third of the three great historical unifiers of Japan, after Nobunaga and Hideyoshi, a noble born in Okazaki, Japan. He took power after the Battle of Sekigahara (1600), and founded the Tokugawa shogunate (1603–1868). He completed Edo Castle (the present Tokyo Imperial Palace) as his headquarters, and instituted an all-pervading centralized control of Japanese life, whose effects are still felt. His mausoleum is at Nikko. >> Hideyoshi; Nobunaga

Toland, John [tohland] (1670–1722) Religious writer, born a Catholic near Londonderry, Co Londonderry, Northern Ireland, UK. He became a Protestant in his teens, and studied at Glasgow, Edinburgh, Leyden, and Oxford universities. His *Christianity not Mysterious* (1696) was burnt by the hangman in Dublin, by order of the House of Commons, as being 'atheistical and subversive'. In *Amyntor* (1699) and other works he debated the comparative evidence for the canonical and apocryphal Scriptures. He took refuge in England, and his pro-Hanoverian pamphlet *Anglia libera* secured him the favour of the Electress Sophia (1630–1714), the mother of George I.

Tolkien, J(ohn) R(onald) R(euel) [tolkeen] (1892–1973) Philologist and writer, born in Bloemfontein, South Africa. He studied in Birmingham and at Oxford, where he became professor of Anglo-Saxon (1925–45) and of English language and literature (1945–59). His scholarly publications include studies on Chaucer (1934) and an edition of *Beowulf* (1937). His interest in language and saga led to his books about a fantasy world in which the beings have their own language and mythology, notably *The Hobbit* (1937), *The Lord of the Rings* (3 vols, 1954–5), and *The Silmarillion* (1977).

Tolley, Howard Ross (1889–1958) Agricultural economist, born in Howard Co, IN. In 1912 he moved to Washington, DC, as a mathematician for the Coast and Geodetic Survey, then worked for the US Department of Agriculture (1915). At the Office of Farm Management he initiated research on economic aspects of farming. When the Bureau of Agricultural Economics (BAE) opened (1923), he helped to develop a research programme for analyzing farm problems. He was also involved in implementing the 'New Deal' farm programme, and at the Agricultural Adjustment Administration (AAA) developed a conservation-oriented plan (1933–5). In 1944 he administered the AAA, and in 1946 returned to BAE as its chief. He later joined the Ford Foundation (1951–4) as director of the Washington office.

Tolly, Prince Barclay de >> **Barclay de Tolly, Knaz**

Tolman, Edward C(hace) (1886–1959) Psychologist, born in West Newton, MA. He studied at Massachusetts Institute of Psychology, Harvard, and Yale, then taught at the University of California, Berkeley (1918–54). With his first book, *Purposive Behavior in Animals and Men* (1932), he argued the need to postulate purpose ('goals'), as well as spatial representations ('cognitive maps') in the minds of animals, in order to fully explain their behaviour. His ideas are now more acceptable in academic psychology, largely as a result of the realization that machines (such as guided missiles) can behave as if they have goals.

Tolstoy, Count Leo Nikolayevich see panel below

Tolton, Augustine (1854–97) Catholic priest, born in Ralls, MO. The first Catholic priest whose parents were both African-Americans, he escaped from slavery with family members at age seven. He overcame poverty and frequent rejections to obtain backing and permission to study for the priesthood in Rome, where he was ordained (1886). He returned to work as a struggling pastor among poor black Catholics in Illinois.

Tomasi de Lampedusa, Giuseppe >> **Lampedusa, Giuseppe Tomasi di**

Tombaugh, Clyde W(illiam) [tombow] (1906–97) Astronomer, born in Streator, IL. Too poor to attend college, he built his own 9-in telescope, and became an assistant at the Lowell Observatory, Arizona State College, where he discovered Pluto (1930) and galactic star clusters. He became astronomer at the Aberdeen Ballistics Laboratories in New Mexico, and taught at New Mexico State University (from 1961). >> Lowell, Percival; Pickering, William Henry

Tomkins, Thomas (1572–1656) Composer and organist, born in St David's, Pembrokeshire, SW Wales, UK, to a musical family. He studied under William Byrd, and in his early 20s became organist of Worcester Cathedral, where he spent most of his life. In 1621 he was one of the organists of the Chapel Royal, and composed music for the coronation of Charles I (1626). His compositions include a vast amount of church music, madrigals, part songs, and instrumental works. >> Byrd, William (1543–1623)

Tomlinson, H(enry) M(ajor) (1873–1958) Novelist and essayist, born in London, England, UK. He grew up in the London Docks, with a love of the sea and an ambition to travel. He took up journalism, travelled to the Amazon and wrote, *The Sea and the Jungle* (1912). His other titles include *Tidemarks* (1924) and other travel books, as well as the novel *Gallions Reach* (1927).

Tomonaga, Shin'ichiro [tomonahga] (1906–79) Scientist, born in Kyoto, Japan. He studied in Kyoto, and became professor of physics at Tokyo University. He shared the Nobel Prize for Physics in 1965 for his work which resolved the inconsistencies of the theory of quantum electrodynamics. >> RR1122

COUNT LEO (LEV) NIKOLAYEVICH TOLSTOY (1828–1910)

Tolstoy was born to a landed noble family at Yasnaya Polyana, in Tula Province, Russia. His parents died when he was a child, and he was brought up by relatives. He was privately tutored, then at the age of 16 he began to study law and oriental languages at Kazan University. Dissatisfied with the standard of education there, he returned in 1847, without a degree, to manage his estate at Yasnaya Polyana.

His diary tells us that he led a dissolute life, spending much of his time in Moscow and St Petersburg, enjoying the social whirl and neglecting his duties in the country. In 1851, displeased with himself, he accompanied his elder brother Nicolay, a soldier, to the Caucasus, where the following year he joined an artillery regiment and began his literary career. *An Account of Yesterday* (1851) was followed by the autobiographical trilogy *Detstvo* (1852, Childhood), *Otrochestvo* (1854, Boyhood), and *Yunost* (1857, Youth).

Commissioned at the outbreak of the Crimean War (1853–6), Tolstoy commanded a battery during the defence of Sebastopol (1854–5). After the war, the horrors of which inspired the *Sevastopolskiye rasskazy* series (1855–6, Sebastopol), he left the army, was fêted by the literary circle in St Petersburg, and travelled abroad (1857), visiting France, Switzerland, and Germany. He wrote many short stories about his travels. On his return, concerned about the quality of education of the poor, he started a school for peasant children at Yasnaya Polyana. During further travels to Europe (1860–1) he investigated educational theory and practice, and he published magazines and textbooks on the subject, which won wide acclaim because of their practicality and simplicity.

In 1862 he married **Sonya (Safya) Andreyevna Bers** or **Behrs**, a well-educated girl, with whom he settled to an apparently devoted family life, producing 13 children. Putting his educational interests to one side, he combined the duties of a progressive landlord with the six years' literary toil which produced *Voyni i mir* (1865–9, War and Peace), considered by many to be the greatest novel ever written. An epic tale, it follows the outlook and fortunes of five families caught up in Napoleon's invasion of Russia, and gives a hint of Tolstoy's own dualistic character. His vivid description of military life credits victory in battle to the chance events which make up the unpredictable fortunes of war. Tolstoy's other masterpiece of Russian literature, *Anna Karenina* (1873–7) is a tragedy with a profound social dimension, telling the story of a married woman who confronts society with her adulterous passion.

Anna Karenina reflected and heralded a moral and spiritual crisis for its author, which came to a head in 1879, unrelieved by the writings of philosophers, and culminating in such works as *Ispoved* (written 1878–9, A Confession), and *V chyom moya vera* (1883, What I Believe, banned in 1884). His later works of fiction include numerous short stories, the full-length novel *Voskreseniye* (1899, Resurrection), a story of a nobleman who seduces a young girl, and the tragic novella, *Khadzhi-Murat* (written at intervals between 1896 and 1904), about a Caucasian warrior killed in an attempt to see his own son.

Tolstoy eventually wrapped himself in a sort of Christian anarchism, gave up his estate to his family, gave away as many of his possessions as he could, and attempted to live as a poor, celibate peasant under his wife's roof. Safya refused to be converted to his new asceticism, and against her husband's will she obtained the copyright of his works printed before 1880, using the money to keep the family. Hundreds of people, influenced by his moral and religious writings, came from all over the world to Yasnaya Polyana. This resulted in increasing family quarrels and a final rift between Tolstoy and his wife, sons, and the Russian Orthodox Church, which excommunicated him in 1901. In 1910, leaving home secretly with his youngest daughter, Alexandra, and a doctor, in an attempt to find a refuge, he died of pneumonia a few days later at the remote railway station of Astopovo.

Tompion, Thomas (c. 1639–1713) Clockmaker, born in Northill, Bedfordshire, SC England, UK. He was admitted to the London Clockmakers' Company in 1671, and became Master of the Company in 1703. In 1676 he was appointed clockmaker to the newly-opened Royal Observatory. His craftsmanship and scientific knowledge enabled him to make watches, table clocks, and long-case clocks with greatly improved time-keeping. He made one of the first English watches equipped with a balance spring (1675), and patented the cylinder escapement (1695).

Tone, (Theobald) Wolfe (1763–98) Irish nationalist, born in Dublin. He studied at Dublin, was called to the bar in 1789, acted as secretary of the Catholic Committee, helped to organize the United Irishmen, and had to flee to the USA and to France (1795). He induced France to invade Ireland on two occasions, and was captured during the second expedition. He was condemned to be hanged, but committed suicide.

Tonks, Henry (1862–1937) Artist, born in Solihull, West Midlands, C England, UK. After becoming a fellow of the Royal College of Surgeons, he gave up medicine for art, joined the New English Art Club, and was associated with Sickert and Steer. From 1917 to 1930 he was professor of fine art at the University of London. >> Sickert; Steer

Tonti, Lorenzo [**ton**tee] (1620–90) Financier, born in Naples, Italy. He proposed the *tontine* or latest-survivor system of life insurance.

Tonypandy (of Rhondda), (Thomas) George Thomas, 1st Viscount [toni**pan**dee] (1909–97) British statesman, born in S Wales. He studied at Southampton, and was a schoolteacher before becoming a Labour MP (1945). He held various junior posts before becoming secretary of state for Wales (1968–70), deputy speaker, and chairman of the ways and means committee (1974–76). He is chiefly remembered as a popular Speaker of the House of Commons (1976–83). He was elevated to the peerage in 1983.

Tooke, John Horne [tuk], originally **John Horne** (1736–1812) Radical politician, born in London, England, UK. He studied at Cambridge, and became a lawyer, and in 1760 a vicar. In 1771 he formed the Constitutional Society, supporting the American colonists and parliamentary reform. His spirited opposition to an enclosure bill procured him the favour of the rich Mr Tooke of Purley in Surrey, which led to his new surname and *The Diversions of Purley* (1786), written while in prison for supporting the US cause. He was tried for high treason in 1794, acquitted, and became an MP in 1801.

Toole, John Kennedy (1937–69) Novelist, born in New Orleans, LA. His novel *A Confederacy of Dunces* (1980), published 11 years after he committed suicide, won critical acclaim, and was awarded the 1981 Pulitzer Prize. *The Neon Bible* was published in 1989.

Topelius, Zacharias [to**peel**ius] (1818–98) Novelist and scholar, born in Kuddnäs, Finland. He studied at Helsinki, and became editor of the *Helsingfors Tidningar* newspaper (1842–78). He was appointed professor of Finnish history at Helsinki (1854–78) and rector (1875–8). Writing in Swedish, he is regarded as the father of the Finnish historical novel, with stories of life in the 17th-c and 18th-c published as *Fältskärns berättelten* (1851–60, The Surgeon's Stories). He also published five volumes of lyrical poetry, and wrote several plays.

Topolski, Feliks [to**pol**skee] (1907–89) Painter, draughtsman, and illustrator, born in Poland. He studied at Warsaw, and in Italy and Paris, and went to England in 1935. From 1940 to 1945 he was an official war artist, and became a British citizen in 1947. His lively and sensitive drawings, depicting everyday life, appeared in many books and periodicals, and he also designed for the theatre. His publications include *Britain in Peace and War* (1941), *88 Pictures* (1951), and *Topolski's Chronicle* (1953–79, 1982–9).

Tork, Peter >> Monkees, The

Torquemada, Tomás de [taw(r)kay**mah**tha] (1420–98) First inquisitor-general of Spain, born in Valladolid, Spain. He was Dominican prior at Segovia (1452–74), and persuaded Ferdinand and Isabella to ask the pope to sanction the institution of the 'Holy Office' of the Inquisition. As grand inquisitor from 1483, he displayed great cruelty, and was responsible for an estimated 2000 burnings.

Torrance, Thomas (Forsyth) (1913–) British theologian, born of missionary parents in Chengtu, China. He was professor of dogmatics at New College, Edinburgh (1952–79), and moderator of the Church of Scotland General Assembly (1976–7). He holds that theology should abandon its preconceptions and respond to the reality it encounters, both in relation to science and in the quest for an acceptable ecumenical theology. His views have been expounded in many books, including *Theological Science* (1969), *Theology in Reconciliation* (1975), *The Trinitarian Faith* (1988), and *The Christian Doctrine of God, One Being, Three Persons* (1996).

Torrens, Sir Robert Richard (1814–84) Legal reformer, born in Co Cork, Ireland. He emigrated to Australia in 1839, became collector of customs (1841), colonial treasurer and registrar general of South Australia (1852), and a member of the Legislative Council. Leading a movement for the reform of titles to land, he sponsored the Real Property Act of 1857 which introduced the *Torrens system*, whereby title to land was secured by registration. He became the first registrar general under the new system, which was widely adopted in Australia, New Zealand, and in some states of the USA. He was knighted in 1872.

Torrey, John (1796–1873) Botanist, born in New York City. He studied medicine, and taught at West Point Military Academy and Cornell, before becoming chief assayer in New York City (1854–73). Throughout his life his main interest was botany. He prepared several floras, including *A Flora of North America* (1838–43), and also collected over 40 000 plant species; his collection was the basis for the herbarium of the New York Botanical Gardens. The genus *Torreya* in the yew family is named after him, as well as the Torrey Botanical Club. >> Gray, Asa

Torricelli, Evangelista [tori**chel**ee] (1608–47) Physicist and mathematician, born in Faenza, Italy. He went in 1627 to Rome, where he devoted himself to mathematics, became Galileo's amanuensis (1641), and succeeded him as professor at the Florentine Academy. He discovered the effect of atmospheric pressure on water in a suction pump, and gave the first description of a barometer, or *Torricellian tube*. >> Galileo

Torrigiano, Pietro [tori**jiah**noh] (1472–1528) Sculptor, born in Florence, Italy. He studied alongside Michelangelo at the Academy of Lorenzo de' Medici. After working in Bologna, Siena, Rome, and Holland, he went to England, where he introduced Italian Renaissance art. He created the tombs of Margaret Beaufort in Westminster Abbey, and of her son Henry VII and his queen. He settled in Spain and died in the prisons of the Inquisition. >> Michelangelo

Torrington, Viscount >> Byng, George

Tortelier, Paul [taw(r)**tel**yay] (1914–90) Cellist, born in Paris. He studied at the Paris Conservatoire, and made his debut there in 1931. Before World War 2 he played in orchestras in Monte Carlo and Boston, then achieved worldwide recognition as one of the leading soloists on his instrument. His son **Yan Pascal Tortelier** (1947–) and daughter **Maria de la Pau Tortelier** (1950–) are highly gifted players of the violin and piano respectively.

Torvill and Dean Figure skaters **Jayne Torvill** (1957–) and **Christopher Dean** (1958–), both from Nottingham, Nottinghamshire, C England, UK. They were world ice dance champions (1981–4) and Olympic champions (1984). Their highly acclaimed performances included an interpretation of music from Ravel's *Bolero*, and the musical, *Barnum*, which was choreographed by British actor Michael Crawford. At the height of their success, they received a record total of 136 perfect 'sixes' (the highest award a judge can give in ice-skating). They retired from competitive skating in 1984, and became professional, producing their own ice show. They returned to national and international competition when the competitions were declared open to professionals in 1993 and competed in the 1994 European Championships, where they won the gold medal, and the 1994 Winter Olympics, when they won the bronze medal. >> Crawford, Michael; RR1162

Toscanini, Arturo [toska**nee**nee] (1867–1957) Conductor, born in Parma, Italy. He studied cello at Parma and Milan, and while playing at Rio de Janeiro in 1886 was suddenly called upon to replace the conductor, presenting a triumphant performance of *Aida*. He later conducted at La Scala, Milan (1898–1908), the Metropolitan Opera House, New York (1908–15), the New York Philharmonic (1926–36), and the Bayreuth (1930–1) and Salzburg (1934–7) festivals. He also brought into being the National Broadcasting Orchestra of America (1937–53).

Tottel, Richard (?–1594) Printer, based in London, England, UK. From his shop at the Star in Hand inn at Temple Bar, Fleet St, he published Thomas More's *Dialogue of Comfort against Tribulacion* (1553), John Lydgate's *The Falls of Princes* (1554), and the Earl of Surrey's translations of parts of the *Aeneid*. He also compiled an anthology of contemporary Elizabethan poetry, *Songes and Sonettes* (1557), containing the chief works of Surrey and Sir Thomas Wyatt, which came to be known as *Tottel's Miscellany*. He was an original member of the Stationer's Company, founded in 1557.

Toulouse-Lautrec (-Monfa), Henri (Marie Raymond) de [too**looz** loh**trek**] (1864–1901) Painter and lithographer, born in Albi, France. Physically frail, at the age of 14 he broke both his legs, which then ceased to grow. From 1882 he studied in Paris, and in 1884 settled in Montmartre, where he painted and drew the cabaret stars, prostitutes, barmaids, clowns, and actors of that society, as in 'The Bar' (1898, Zürich) and 'At the Moulin Rouge' (1892, Chicago). He also depicted fashionable society, such as 'At the Races' (1899, Albi), and produced several portraits. His alcoholism brought a complete breakdown, forcing him into a sanatorium (1899), but he recovered to resume his hectic life. Over 600 of his works are in the Musée Lautrec at Albi.

Tour, George / Maurice Quentin de La >> **La Tour, Georges de / Maurice Quentin de**

Tournefort, Joseph Pitton de [toornfaw(r)] (1656–1708) Physician and botanist, born in Aix-en-Provence, France. He travelled in Greece and Turkey with the artist Claude Aubriet, and became professor at the Jardin des Plantes in Paris (1688–1708). His definitions of the genera of plants were of fundamental importance to Linnaeus, who rejected his general classification in favour of one based on the number of the sexual parts of the flower. >> Linnaeus

Tourneur, Cyril [**ter**ner] (c. 1575–1626) English playwright. He published several poems, but is known for his two plays, *The Revenger's Tragedy* (1607, sometimes assigned to Webster or Middleton), and *The Atheist's Tragedy* (1611). >> Middleton; Webster, John

Tournier, Paul [toornyay] (1898–1986) Physician and writer on the integration of psychology and Christianity, born in Geneva, Switzerland. He spent his whole professional life as a general practitioner in private practice in Geneva. Discovering religious faith through contact with the Oxford Group in 1932, he realized the need to treat his patients as whole human beings. *A Doctor's Casebook in the Light of the Bible* (1954) and *The Meaning of Persons* (1957) were followed by more than a dozen other best-selling books, including *The Strong and the Weak* (1963) and *Learning to Grow Old* (1972).

Tourville, Anne Hilarion de Contentin, comte de (Count of) [toorveel] (1642–1701) Naval commander, born in Château Tourville, Manche, France. From a noble family, he entered the Royal Navy in 1666, took part in Louis XIV's war against the Dutch (1672–8), and was promoted to lieutenant-general (1682). In 1689, at the outbreak of the War of the Grand Alliance, he prevented an invasion of Brittany, and was promoted to vice-admiral of the Mediterranean fleet and naval commander-in-chief. He defeated the Anglo-Dutch fleet off Beachy Head (1690). An attempt to rescue an ill-planned landing in England failed at the Battle of La Hogue, but his conduct made him Marshal of France (1693).

Toussaint, Pierre [toosi] (1766–1853) Philanthropist, born in Santo Domingo. Brought to New York City as a slave (1787), he worked as a hairdresser. Supporting his owner's wife when she became widowed and impoverished, he was emancipated in 1807. A devout Catholic who became highly successful in business, he spent much of his money on charities, and personally nursed and housed people in need.

Toussaint l'Ouverture [toosi loover**tür**], originally **François Dominique Toussaint** (1746–1803) Revolutionary leader, born a slave in Haiti (formerly, St Domingue). In 1791, he joined the insurgents, and by 1797 was effective ruler of the former colony. He drove out British and Spanish expeditions, restored order, and aimed at independence. Napoleon sent a new expedition to Saint Domingue, and proclaimed the re-establishment of slavery. Toussaint was eventually arrested, and died in a French prison. His nickname comes from his bravery in once making a breach in the ranks of the enemy. >> Napoleon I

Tovey, Sir Donald Francis [**toh**vee] (1875–1940) Pianist, composer, and writer on music, born in Eton, Berkshire, S England, UK. He studied at Oxford, and in 1914 became professor of music at Edinburgh, where he built up the Reid Symphony Orchestra. He composed an opera, *The Bride of Dionysus* (1907–8), a symphony, piano concerto and cello concertos, and chamber music. His fame rests largely on his writings, notably *Companion to the Art of Fugue* (1931), *Essays on Musical Analysis* (1935–9), and his articles on music in the *Encyclopaedia Britannica*. He was knighted in 1935.

Tovey, John Cronyn Tovey, Baron [**toh**vee] (1885–1971) British naval commander. He distinguished himself as a destroyer captain in World War 1, notably at the Battle of Jutland (1916). As commander-in-chief of the Home Fleet (1941–3), he was responsible for the operations leading to the sinking of the German battleship *Bismarck*. He became Admiral of the Fleet in 1943.

Tower, John (1925–) US politician, born in Houston, TX. He studied at Georgetown University, Texas, and the London School of Economics. Originally a Democrat, he switched parties and became the first Republican to be elected senator for Texas (1961). Specializing in defence matters, he became chairman of the Armed Services Committee in 1981. He retired in 1983, becoming a paid consultant to arms industry contractors, and chaired the 1986–7 *Tower Commission*. In 1989 his nomination by President Bush as defence secretary was rejected by the US Senate. >> Bush, George

Towne, Francis (c. 1739–1816) Painter, probably born in London, England, UK. As a landscapist he was little known until the 20th-c, when his gift for painting simple but graphic watercolours was recognized. Works done in Italy, which he visited in 1780, are now in the British Museum.

Townes, Charles (Hard) (1915–) Physicist, born in Greenville, SC. He worked at Bell Telephone Laboratories, taught at Columbia University, and became professor of physics at Massachusetts Institute of Technology (1961–7) and at California, Berkeley (1967). He shared the 1964 Nobel Prize for Physics with Alexander Prokhorov and Nikolay Basov for his work on the development of the maser, and later the laser. >> Basov; Bloembergen; Prokhorov; Schawlow

Townsend, Sir John (Sealy Edward) (1868–1957) Physicist, born in Galway, Co Galway, Ireland. He became a demonstrator at the Cavendish Laboratory, Cambridge, under Sir J J Thomson, before becoming professor of physics at Oxford (1900). He contributed to the theory of ionization of gases by collision, and calculated in 1897 the charge on a single gaseous ion. He was knighted in 1941. >> Thomson, J J

Townsend, Sue (1946–) Novelist and playwright, born in Leicester, C England, UK. She made her name through a series of novels introducing the character of Adrian Mole, beginning with *The Secret Diary of Adrian Mole Aged 13¾* (1982). Her plays include *Bazaar and Rummage* (1982) and *The Queen and I* (1992).

Townshend (of Rainham), Charles Townshend, 2nd Viscount [townzend], known as **Turnip Townshend** (1674–1738) British statesman, born in Raynham, Norfolk, E England, UK. He studied at Cambridge, succeeded his father as viscount (1687), was made secretary of state by George I (1714–16, 1721–30), and became a leading figure in the Whig ministry with his brother-in-law, Robert Walpole. After a resignation engineered by Walpole, he acquired his nickname for his interest in agricultural improvement, and his proposal to use turnips in crop rotation. >> Townshend, Charles; Walpole, Robert

Townshend, Charles [townzend] (1725–67) British statesman, the grandson of Charles, 2nd Viscount Townshend. He entered the House of Commons in 1747. He was a Lord of the Admiralty and secretary for war (1761–2), and became Chancellor of the Exchequer in 1766. He asserted authority over the American colonies by imposing high taxes on necessities, especially on tea (the *Townshend Acts*, 1767) – a policy which ultimately provoked the American War of Independence (1775–83). >> Townshend, 2nd Viscount

Toynbee, Arnold [toynbee] (1852–83) Economic historian and social reformer, born in London, England, UK. He lectured in economic history at Oxford, and also to numerous workers' adult education classes, and undertook social work in the East End of London with Samuel Barnett. He is best known as the coiner of the phrase and author of *The Industrial Revolution in England* (1884). Toynbee Hall, a university settlement in Whitechapel, London, was founded in his memory in 1885. >> Barnett; Toynbee, Arnold (Joseph)

Toynbee, Arnold (Joseph) [toynbee] (1889–1975) Historian, born in London, England, UK, the nephew of Arnold Toynbee. He studied at Oxford, served in the Foreign Office in both World Wars, and attended the Paris peace conferences (1919 and 1946). He was professor of modern Greek and Byzantine history at London (1919–24) and director of the Royal Institute of International Affairs, London (1925–55). His major work was the multi-volume *Study of History* (1933–61). >> Toynbee, Arnold

Toynbee, Polly, popular name of **Mary Louisa Toynbee** (1946–) British journalist. She studied at Oxford, becoming a reporter with *The Observer* (1968–71) and editor on *The Washington Monthly* (1971–2), rejoining *The Observer* as a feature writer (1972–7). She then became a columnist on *The Guardian* (1977–88), BBC social affairs editor (1988–95), and associated editor and columnist on *The Independent* (1995–).

Toyoda, Kiichiro [toyohda] (1894–1952) Japanese car designer and manufacturer. He studied engineering, visited Europe and the USA, and set up a car manufacturing business in 1934. He changed the company name to Toyota in 1936 – a name which in Japanese conveys suggestions of speed and prosperity. He resigned as president of the company in 1950.

Tracey, Stan(ley William) (1926–) Jazz pianist, bandleader, and composer, born in London, England, UK. Largely self-taught, he began to work with dance orchestras such as the Roy Fox and Ted Heath Bands, as well as with modern jazz groups in the 1950s. He was resident pianist at Ronnie Scott's Club, Soho (1960–7), accompanying many leading musicians, and developed a distinctive, percussive keyboard style. Since the mid-1960s he has led a succession of bands, from quartets to 16-piece orchestras, toured abroad, and written jazz suites such as *Under Milk Wood* (1965) and *Genesis* (1987). In 1995 he was voted best arranger/composer by the British Jazz Awards.

Tracy, David (1939–) Theologian, born in Yonkers, NY. A professor of theology at Chicago University Divinity School, he has explored questions of hermeneutics, notably the problems of theological communication in modern pluralistic society, developing these themes in such works as *Blessed Rage for Order* (1975) and *Plurality and Ambiguity* (1986).

Tracy, Spencer (Bonadventure) (1900–67) Film actor, born in Milwaukee, WI. Trained at the American Academy of Dramatic Arts, he made his Broadway debut in 1923 and his feature film debut in 1930. Initially typecast as a tough guy and gangster, he became one of Hollywood's finest actors of the 1940s and 1950s. Nominated nine times for an Oscar, he was the only actor ever to receive two consecutive awards, with *Captains Courageous* (1937) and *Boys' Town* (1938). A lifelong personal and professional association with Katharine Hepburn resulted in them co-starring in nine films, including his final performance in *Guess Who's Coming to Dinner* (1967). >> Hepburn, Katharine

Tradescant, John [tradiskant] (1570–c. 1638) Naturalist, gardener, and traveller, probably born in Suffolk, E England, UK. He became head gardener to the Earls of Salisbury and later to King Charles I. He travelled to Arctic Russia in 1618, and later established the first museum open to the public, the Musaeum Tradescantianum, in Lambeth, London. He and his son, John, introduced many plants into English gardens. A genus of plants (*Tradescantia*) is named after him. >> Tradescant, John (1608–62)

Tradescant, John [tradiskant] (1608–62) Gardener, born in Meopham, Kent, SE England, UK. He went to Virginia to collect plants and shells (1637), and succeeded his father as head gardener to Charles I in 1638. He bequeathed the celebrated Musaeum Tradescantianum in Lambeth to Elias Ashmole (1617–92), and it became the basis for the Ashmolean Museum in Oxford. >> Tradescant, John (1570–c.1638)

Traherne, Thomas [trahern] (1637–74) Mystical writer, born in Hereford, Hereford and Worcester, WC England, UK. He studied at Oxford, and was ordained rector at Credenhill. The manuscripts of his *Poetical Works* (1903) and *Centuries of Meditations* (1908) were discovered by chance on a London street bookstall in 1896.

Trajan [trayjn], in full **Marcus Ulpius Trajanus** (c. 53–117) Roman emperor (98–117), selected as successor by the aged Nerva for his military skills. He was the first emperor after Augustus to expand the Roman empire significantly. The wealth from Dacia's gold mines enabled him to launch an ambitious building programme, especially in Rome, where he constructed a new forum, library, and aqueduct. A sensitive but firm ruler, he was one of Rome's most popular emperors. >> Nerva; RR1084

Tranströmer, Tomas [transtroemer] (1931–) Poet and psychologist, born in Stockholm. He studied at Stockholm University, then worked as a psychologist, including a spell at Roxtuna institution for young offenders. His first collection of poems, *17 dikter* (1954, 17 Poems), aroused attention, and he has become a leading poet of the post-war era. His 10 collections of poems have been translated into English by Robin Fulton in *Three Swedish Poets* (1970), *Selected Poems* (1974), and *Collected Poems* (1987).

Trapassi, Pietro >> **Metastasio, Pietro**

Traubel, Helen [trowbl] (1899–1972) Soprano, born in St Louis, MO. She made her debut in St Louis in 1923, and sang at the New York Metropolitan in 1937. She was the leading Wagnerian soprano at the Met from 1941, resigning after a dispute over her nightclub appearances (1953). She also worked in film and television, and wrote detective novels.

Traven, B [trayvn], pseudonym of **Benick Traven Torsvan** (?1882/90–1969) Writer, who claimed he was born in Chicago, IL, but was probably originally called **Otto Frege**, born in 1882 in Zwiebodzin, Poland (formerly, Germany). He wrote *Der Shatz der Sierra Madre* (1935, The Treasure of the Sierra Madre), on which the celebrated film by John Huston is based. Little is known about his background, but he lived in Mexico during the 1930s and later. Most of his novels were first published in Germany, such as *Das Tolenschiff* (1926, The Death Ship) and *Die Rebellion der Gehenklen* (1936, The Rebellion of the Hanged). He probably used several different names, including **Traven Torsvan**, **Ret Marut**, and **Hal Groves** under which name he died.

Travers, Ben(jamin) (1886–1980) Playwright, born in London, England, UK. He became famous for the farces which played in the Aldwych Theatre, London, continuously from 1922 until 1933. His later work was not so successful, although he was still writing in his 90s, and his last play, *The Bed Before Yesterday* was first produced in 1975.

Travers, Morris William (1872–1961) Chemist, born in London, England, UK. He studied at London and Nancy universities, and became an authority on glass technology. Professor at Bristol (1903–37), he was also technical consultant to the ministry of supply (1940–5). He discovered, with Ramsay, the inert gases krypton, xenon, and neon (1894–1908), and investigated the phenomena of low temperatures. >> Ramsay, William

Travers, P(amela) L(yndon) (1906–96) Writer of children's stories, born in Queensland, Australia. She moved to England at 19, and worked as an actress. Her first novel, *Mary Poppins* (1934), was an international success, and was later adapted for the popular motion picture of the same name (1964). She began a literary career, her later children's novels including *Friend Monkey* (1971), *About Sleeping Beauty* (1975), and *Two Pairs of Shoes* (1980).

Travolta, John [travolta] (1954–) Film actor, born in Englewood, NJ. He made his debut in an off-Broadway production of *Rain* (1972), then joined the Broadway cast of *Grease*, and became well known for his role in the TV series *Welcome Back Koter*. International fame came with the box-office hit films *Saturday Night Fever* (1977), *Grease* (1978), and *Staying Alive* (1983). Later films include *Look Who's Talking* (1989), *Pulp Fiction* (1994), *Get Shorty* (1995, Golden Globe), *Michael*, and *Face/Off* (both 1997).

Traylor, Bill (1854–1947) Folk artist and plantation worker, born a slave in Alabama. He worked on a plantation near Selma, AL, until his early 80s. He then moved to Montgomery, where he began drawing the world around him in a bold, primitive, but often strikingly original way. During the next few years he produced over 1000 works, but they were not discovered until the 1980s. His work has since been exhibited around the world.

Tredgold, Thomas (1788–1829) Engineer and cabinet-maker, born in Brandon, Durham, NE England, UK. He became a carpenter, and studied building construction and science in London. His *Elementary Principles of Carpentry* (1820) was the first serious manual on the subject. He also wrote manuals on cast iron (1821), *The Steam Engine* (1827), and other works.

Tree, Sir Herbert (Draper) Beerbohm (1853–1917) Actor-manager, born in London, England, UK, the half-brother of Max Beerbohm. After a commercial education in Germany, he became an actor, took over the Haymarket Theatre (1887), and built His Majesty's Theatre (1897), where he rivalled Irving's productions at the Lyceum. He founded the Royal Academy of Dramatic Art in 1904, and scored a great success with the first production of Shaw's *Pygmalion* in 1914. >> Beerbohm; Irving, Henry

Treece, Henry (1911 /12–66) Poet and historical novelist, born in Wednesbury, West Midlands, C England, UK. He studied at Birmingham University, and became a schoolteacher and writer. After service in World War 2 he co-founded the New Apocalypse movement, a reactionary wave against the literary trends of the 1930s. His style appealed particularly to young readers, and notable works include collections of verse, *The Black Seasons* (1945) and *The Exiles* (1952), and the novel *The Bronze Sword* (1965). Among his historical novels are *The Eagles Have Flown* (1954), *Red Queen, White Queen* (1958), and *The Green Man* (1966).

Trelawny, Edward John [trelawnee] (1792–1881) Writer and adventurer, born in London, England, UK of an old and famous Cornish family. He ran away from school, entered the navy at 13, and was discharged in 1812. He recalled his experiences in the *Adventures of a Younger Son* (1831). He became friendly with Shelley and Byron at Pisa in 1822, and never recovered from Shelley's death by drowning; he helped to recover the body and supervised its cremation. A great favourite in London society and an incurable Romantic, he wrote *Records of Shelley, Byron and the Author* (1878); his ashes were buried next to Shelley's in Rome, a grave he had reserved for almost 60 years before his death. >> Byron; Shelley, Percy Bysshe

Tremain, Rose [tremayn] (1943–) Novelist and short-story writer, born in London, England, UK. She studied at the Sorbonne and the University of East Anglia, and published her first novel, *Sadler's Birthday*, in 1976. Later books include *The Cupboard* (1981), *Restoration* (1989), and *Sacred Country* (1992, James Tait Black Memorial Prize). Her books of short stories include *Evangelista's Fan* (1994), and she has also written for children.

Tremblay, Michel [träblay] (1942–) Playwright, born in Montreal, Quebec, Canada. His first play, *Le Train* (1959), won a Radio-Canada award. *Les Belles-Soeurs* (1968, The Sisters-in-law) is written in the street language, *joual*. Many consider *Le Vrai Monde* (1987, The Real World), his 19th play written in as many years, his most important work to date. A new departure was his opera *Nelligan* (1990), with music by André Gagnon.

Trench, Richard Chenevix [shenevee] (1807–86) Anglican clergyman, philologist, and poet, born in Dublin, Ireland. He studied at Cambridge, became curate in 1841 to Samuel Wilberforce, and during 1835–46 published six volumes of poetry. He was rector of Itchenstoke 1845, professor of theology in King's College, London (1847), dean of Westminster (1856), and Archbishop of Dublin (1864–84). In philology he popularized the scientific study of words, and the *New English Dictionary* was begun at his suggestion. >> Wilberforce, Samuel

Trenchard (of Wolfeton), Hugh Montague Trenchard, 1st Viscount (1873–1956) British marshal of the Royal Air Force, born in Taunton, Somerset, SW England, UK. He joined the army in 1893, served in India, South Africa, and West Africa, and developed an interest in aviation. He commanded the Royal Flying Corps in World War 1, helped to establish the RAF (1918), and became the first chief of air staff (1918–29). As commissioner of the London Metropolitan Police (1931–5), he founded the police college at Hendon. He became a peer in 1930.

Trent, Baron >> **Boot, Jesse**

Treurnicht, Andries Petrus [troyernikht] (1921–93) South African politician, born in Piketberg, South Africa. He studied theology at the universities of Cape Town and Stellenbosch, and was elected to parliament in 1971. He became Transvaal provincial National Party leader in 1978, and held a succession of posts in the cabinets of P W Botha from 1979. He and his colleagues resigned from the party in 1982 to form the new, right-wing Conservative Party (CP). The CP, which has pressed for a return to traditional apartheid values and effective partitioning of the country, had secured the support of more than a quarter of the white electorate by the turn of the decade. >> Botha, P W

Trevelyan, G(eorge) M(acaulay) [trevelyan] (1876–1962) Historian, born in Welcombe, Warwickshire, C England, UK, the son of Sir George Trevelyan. He studied at Cambridge, served in World War 1, and became professor of modern history at Cambridge (1927–40). He is best known as a pioneer social historian. His *English Social History* (1944) was a companion volume to his *History of England* (1926). >> Trevelyan, George Otto

Trevelyan, Sir George Otto [trevelyan] (1838–1928) British statesman, born in Leicestershire, C England, UK. He studied at Cambridge, entered parliament in 1865 as a Liberal, and became a Lord of the Admiralty (1868–70), parliamentary secretary (1880–2), chief secretary for Ireland (1882–4), and secretary for Scotland (1886, 1892–5). He wrote a number of historical works, among them the famous biography of his uncle, Macaulay (1876), and the *American Revolution* (1909). >> Macaulay, Thomas; Trevelyan, G M

Treves, Sir Frederick [treevz] (1853–1923) Surgeon, born in Dorchester, Dorset, S England, UK. He studied in London, and became professor at the Royal College of Surgeons, and a founder of the British Red Cross Society. He made improvements in operations for appendicitis. He found **Joseph Merrick** (1862–90), the 'Elephant Man', at a freak show, and brought him to the London Hospital in 1886.

Trevino, Lee (Buck) [treveenoh], nickname **Supermex** (1939–) Golfer, born in Dallas, TX. He won his first US Open in 1968, and in 1971 established a golfing record by winning three Open championships (US, Canadian, British) in the same year, retaining his British title the following year. In 1975, while playing in the Western Open, he had a remarkable escape from death when he was struck by lightning. He won the PGA Open at the age of 44. A shrewd match commentator, he continues to earn a living from professional golf. >> RR1157

Trevisa, John of >> **John of Trevisa**

Trevithick, Richard [trevithik] (1771–1833) Engineer and inventor, born in Illogan, Cornwall, SW England, UK. He became a mining engineer at Penzance, and between 1796 and 1801 invented a steam carriage which ran between

Camborne and Tuckingmill, and which in 1803 was run from Leather Lane to Paddington by Oxford St. He later went to Peru and Costa Rica (1816–27), where his engines were introduced into the silver mines. >> Darby

Trevor, William, pseudonym of **William Trevor Cox** (1928–) Short-story writer, novelist, and playwright, born in Mitchelstown, Co Cork, Ireland. He studied at Trinity College, Dublin, taught history and art, sculpted, and wrote advertising copy before devoting himself to literature. His first book was a novel, *A Standard of Behaviour* (1958), but though he has published 10 subsequently, including *The Old Boys* (1964), he is by inclination a short-story writer. His highly acclaimed collections include *The Day We Got Drunk on Cake* (1969), *Angels at the Ritz* (1975), and *The News from Ireland* (1986). Later works include *The Stories of William Trevor* (1983), *Two Lives* (1991), and *After Rain, and Other Stories* (1996).

Trevor-Roper, Hugh Redwald, Baron Dacre of Glanton (1914–) Historian and controversialist, born in Glanton, Northumberland, NE England, UK. He studied at Oxford, where he became a fellow of Oriel College and professor of modern history (1957–80). His *The Last Days of Hitler* (1947) won international fame for a vivid reconstruction based on research on behalf of British forces in occupied Germany. He wrote a wide range of books and essays, including *The Rise of Christian Europe* (1965) and *The Philby Affair* (1968), and edited the Goebbels diaries (1978). In the 1980s he received publicity for championing the authenticity of the 'Hitler diaries', until their fraudulence was revealed. He was Master of Peterhouse, Cambridge (1980–7).

Trilling, Lionel (1905–75) Literary critic, born in New York City. He studied at Columbia University, where he taught from 1931, becoming professor of English in 1948. He wrote studies on Matthew Arnold (1939), E M Forster (1948), and Sigmund Freud (1962), as well as many books of critical essays, such as *The Liberal Imagination* (1950), which defines his stance, and *Sincerity and Authenticity* (1972).

Trinder, Tommy, popular name of **Thomas Edward Trinder** (1909–89) Comedian and actor, born in London, England, UK. He appeared in small-town variety shows, before making his name in the Band Waggon show at the London Palladium (1939). He went on to become a national favourite with his catch-phrase 'you lucky people', both as a stand-up comic in such revues as *Happy and Glorious* and *Best Bib and Tucker*, and as a leading man in such films as *Sailors Three* (1940), *The Bells Go Down* (1943), and *Champagne Charlie* (1944). During World War 2, he travelled widely abroad to entertain the troops. He compered the ITV show *Sunday Night at the London Palladium* (1954–8), and was also chairman of Fulham Football Club (1955–76).

Trintignant, Jean-Louis [trĩteenyã] (1930–) Actor, born in Port-St Esprit, France. He abandoned his legal studies to become an actor, making his Paris stage debut in 1951. His appearance in *Et Dieu créa la femme* (1956, And God Created Woman) brought him to popular attention. His career includes the internationally successful *Un Homme et Une Femme* (1966, A Man and a Woman), and a variety of work for Europe's most distinguished directors, including *Les Biches* (1968, The Does), *Z* (1968), and *Il conformista* (1970, The Conformist). He has also worked as a director. Later films include an English-language production, *Under Fire* (1983) and *Merci, la vie* (1991, Thanks, Life).

Trippe, Juan T(erry) (1899–1981) Airline founder, born in Seabright, NJ. He studied at Yale, became a pilot in World War 1, and set up an airline taxi service with government aircraft after the War. In 1924 he co-founded Colonial Air Transport, and in 1927 founded Pan American Airways. Other airlines were absorbed into the company, which offered the first scheduled round-the-world air service in

1947. In 1955 he placed the first major US order for jet transports.

Tristano, Lennie [tristahnoh], popular name of **Leonard Joseph Tristano** (1919–78) Jazz musician and teacher, born in Chicago, IL. Blind at the age of nine, he studied the piano as well as several wind instruments, and went on to become an acclaimed jazz teacher. He was a leader in the 'cool jazz' movement, introducing a number of experimental techniques, and recording with many groups during the 1940s and 1950s.

Tristram, Henry Baker (1822–1906) Clergyman, naturalist, and traveller, born in Eglingham, Northumberland, NE England, UK. He studied at Oxford, and became an Anglican clergyman. Tuberculosis forced him to go abroad for his health. His main interest was in the flora and fauna of Palestine, and he was the author of the first ornithological surveys of the region, including *The Land of Israel* (1865), *Natural History of the Bible* (1867), and *The Flora and Fauna of Palestine* (1884). *Tristram's warbler* and *Tristram's serin* are named after him.

Trog, Walter, pseudonym of **Ernest Fawkes** (1924–) Cartoonist and musician, born in Ontario, Canada. He moved to England in 1931 and studied art at Camberwell, then did camouflage work during World War 2. He joined the *Daily Mail* as staff cartoonist in 1945, creating *Rufus* (later *Flook*), a daily strip for children (1949). Beginning as whimsy, this strip developed into satirical comment under many scriptwriters, including Sir Compton Mackenzie and eventually Trog himself. Trog (the pen-name comes from the Troglodytes, his jazzband, for which he plays clarinet) expanded into political cartooning in the *Spectator* (1959), the *Daily Mail* (1968), and colour covers for *Punch* (1971). >> Mackenzie, Compton

Trollope, Anthony [troluhp] (1815–82) Novelist, born in London, England, UK. He joined the Post Office in 1834, working as a clerk, and in 1841 became postal surveyor in Ireland, where he began to write. His first novel in the Barsetshire series, *The Warden*, appeared in 1855, and was followed by such successful books as *Barchester Towers* (1857), *Framley Parsonage* (1861), and *The Last Chronicle of Barset* (1867). A political series of novels followed, including *Phineas Finn* (1869) and *The Eustace Diamonds* (1873). Among his later novels were *The Way We Live Now* (1875) and *Mr Scarborough's Family* (1883). His revealing autobiography, written in 1875–6, was published in 1883. >> Thirkell

Trollope, Joanna (1943–) Writer and novelist, born in Gloucestershire, SWC England, UK, a descendant of Anthony Trollope. She studied at Oxford, then became an English teacher and freelance writer for various leading magazines and newspapers. Her novels include *Parson Harding's Daughter* (1980), *A Village Affair* (1989), *The Rector's Wife* (1991), and *Next of Kin* (1996). She has also written novels as **Caroline Harvey**, including *Legacy of Love* (1992) and *The Steps of the Sun* (1996). >> Trollope, Anthony

Tromp, Cornelis (Maartenszoon) (1629–91) Naval commander, born in Amsterdam, the son of Maarten Tromp. He shared the glory of de Ruyter's Four Days' Battle (1666) off Dunkirk, and won fame in the battles against the combined English and French fleets (1673). On a visit to England in 1675 he was created a baron by Charles II, and was appointed Lieutenant-Governor of the United Provinces (1676). >> Ruyter; Tromp, Maarten

Tromp, Maarten (Harpertszoon) (1598–1653) Dutch admiral, born in Brielle, The Netherlands. In 1639 he defeated a superior Spanish fleet off Gravelines, and won the Battle of the Downs later that year. Knighted by Louis XIII of France (1640) and by Charles I of England (1642), he then fought the French pirates based on Dunkirk, while his encounter with Blake in 1652 started the first Anglo-Dutch

War. Victorious off Dover, he was defeated by a superior English fleet off Portland, and finally off Terhejide, near Schevingen, where he was killed. >> Tromp, Cornelis

Trotsky, Leon, pseudonym of **Lev Davidovich Bronstein** (1879–1940) Russian Jewish revolutionary, born in Yanovka, Ukraine. He studied at Odessa, and in 1898 was arrested as a Marxist and exiled to Siberia. He escaped in 1902, joined Lenin in London, and in the abortive 1905 revolution was president of the St Petersburg Soviet. He then worked as a revolutionary journalist in the West, returning to Russia in 1917, when he joined the Bolsheviks and played a major role in the October Revolution. In the Civil War he was commissar for war, and created the Red Army. After Lenin's death (1924) his influence began to decline. He was ousted from the party by Stalin, who opposed his theory of 'permanent revolution', exiled to C Asia (1927), and expelled from the Soviet Union (1929). He continued to agitate as an exile, and was sentenced to death in his absence by a Soviet court in 1937. He finally found asylum in Mexico, but was assassinated by one of Stalin's agents. >> Lenin; Stalin

Troyes, Chrétien de >> **Chrétien de Troyes**

Troyon, Constant [trwahyō] (1810–65) Painter, born in Sèvres, France. A member of the Barbizon Group, he specialized in landscapes, and particularly in animals. Many of his paintings are in the Louvre, and two are in the Wallace Collection, London. >> Daubigny; Rousseau, Théodore

Trubetzkoy, Nikolay Sergeyevich [troobetskoy] (1890–1938) Linguist, born in Moscow. He studied at Moscow and Leipzig universities, taught at Moscow, Rostov, and Sofia, and was appointed professor of Slavic Philology at the University of Vienna (1922). He is noted for his major contribution to the Prague school of linguistics and is the author of its most important work on phonology, *Grundzüge der Phonologie* (1939, Principles of Phonology).

Trübner, Nicholas (1817–88) Publisher, born in Heidelberg, Germany. He moved to London in 1843, started up his business in 1852, and developed a business connection in the USA. An oriental scholar, he published a series of oriental texts as well as works for the Early English Text Society. The business was merged in 1889 to become Kegan Paul, Trench, Trübner & Co.

Trudeau, Pierre (Elliott) [troodoh] (1919–) Canadian statesman and prime minister (1968–79, 1980–4), born in Montreal, Quebec, Canada. He studied at Montreal, Harvard, and London universities, became a lawyer, helped to found the political magazine *Cité Libre* (1950), and was professor of law at Montreal (1961–5). Elected an MP in 1965, he became minister of justice (1967), an outspoken critic of separatism for Quebec, and in 1968 succeeded Pearson as federal leader of the Liberal Party and prime minister. His term of office saw the October Crisis (1970) in Quebec, the introduction of the Official Languages Act, federalist victory during the Quebec Referendum (1980), and the introduction of Canada's constitution (1982). He resigned as leader of the Liberal Party and from public life in 1984. >> Pearson, Lester B; RR1039

Trueblood, (David) Elton (1900–94) Quaker scholar, born in Pleasantville, IA. He studied at Harvard, then taught philosophy at various institutions, notably at Earlham College (1946–54). He retained his link there as professor-at-large after his appointment in 1954 as chief of religious information at the US Information Agency. His books include *The People Called Quakers* (1966).

Trueman, Freddy, popular name of **Frederick Sewards Trueman** (1931–) Cricketer and broadcaster, born in Stainton, South Yorkshire, N England, UK. Educated at Maltby Secondary School, he became an apprentice bricklayer before developing into the first genuinely fast bowler in post-war English cricket. A Yorkshire player for 19 years (1949–68), he played in 67 Tests for England between 1952 and 1965, and took a record number of 307 wickets, three times taking 10 wickets in a match. In his first-class career he took 2304 wickets, and made three centuries. A bluff and forthright Yorkshireman, he has worked as a cricket writer and commentator since he retired. >> RR1150

Truffaut, François [troofoh] (1932–84) Film critic and director, born in Paris. His first career, as a critic from 1953, led to his *auteur* ('author') concept of film-making. In 1959 he made his first feature as director/actor/co-scriptwriter, *Les Quatre Cents Coups* (The 400 Blows), effectively launching the French *Nouvelle Vague* ('New Wave') movement. This was followed by *Tirez sur le pianiste* (1960, Shoot the Pianist), *Jules et Jim* (1962), and *Fahrenheit 451* (1966), in all of which he was also co-scriptwriter. Several of his films contain autobiographical elements, relating to an unhappy childhood and turbulent youth. He continued actively at work throughout the 1970s, notably with *La Nuit américaine* (1972, trans Day for Night), for which he received an Oscar, and *Le Dernier Métro* (1980, The Last Metro), which was a major commercial success. He acted in several of his films, and also in *Close Encounters of the Third Kind* (1977). He returned from colour photography to his first love of black-and-white in his final film, *Vivement Dimanche* (1983, Finally, Sunday).

Trujillo (Molina), Rafael Leonidas [trooheelyoh] (1891–1961) Dictator of the Dominican Republic (1930–61), born in San Cristóbal, Dominican Republic. He rose to prominence as commander of the police. His regime was both highly repressive and highly corrupt, and he was assassinated in Santo Domingo, a city he had renamed Ciudad Trujillo.

Truman, Harry S (1884–1972) US statesman and 33rd president (1945–53), born in Lamar, MO. Elected as a Democrat to the US Senate in 1934, he was chairman of a special committee investigating defence. Made vice-president in 1944, he became president on the death of Roosevelt, and was re-elected in 1948 in a surprise victory over Thomas E Dewey. His decisions included the dropping of two atom bombs on Japan, the postwar loan to Britain, and the sending of US troops to South Korea. He promoted the policy of giving military and economic aid to countries threatened by Communist interference (the Truman Doctrine). At home he introduced a 'Fair Deal' of economic reform. >> Acheson, Dean; Harriman; Hoover, Herbert; Stimson; RR1097

Trumbull, John (1750–1831) Lawyer and poet, born in Watertown, CT. He practised law in Boston, New Haven, and Hartford, and became a judge of the Connecticut supreme court (1809–13). He wrote a satire on educational methods, *The Progress of Dulness* (1772–3), and a satire on British blunders in the American War of Independence, *M'Fingal* (1775–82), in imitation of Samuel Butler's *Hudibras*. >> Butler, Samuel

Trumbull, John (1756–1843) Historical painter, born in Lebanon, CT. After service in the American Revolution, he visited London to study art under Benjamin West, and began a series of celebrated war paintings, such as 'The Battle of Bunker's Hill', and a number of portraits of George Washington. He was ambassador to London (1794–1804), and in 1817 painted four large historical pictures for the Rotunda of the Capitol in Washington, DC. The Trumbull Gallery at Yale was built to accommodate his collection of paintings (1832). >> West, Benjamin

Trump, Donald (John) (1946–) Real estate developer, born in New York City. The son of a New York City residential real estate developer, he took over the Trump

Organization, and greatly expanded its holdings. He built increasingly grandiose buildings, including the Trump Tower, New York City (1982), and Atlantic City casinos. His high-profile political dealmaking and enthusiastic self-promotion made him a 1980s celebrity. He suffered a spectacular crash into near-bankruptcy in 1990.

Trumpler, Robert (Julius) (1886–1956) Astronomer, born in Zürich, Switzerland. He studied at Zürich and Göttingen universities, moved to America in 1915, then worked at the Lick Observatory, CA (1918–38) and the astronomical department of the University of California, Berkeley (1938–51). In 1922, by observing a solar eclipse, he was able to confirm Einstein's theory of relativity. He made extensive studies of star clusters and galaxies, and found an interstellar haze absorbing light from distant stars, which had an important effect on ideas about the scale of the universe. >> Einstein

Truth, Sojourner, originally **Isabella Van Wagener** (c.1797–1883) Evangelist, abolitionist, feminist, and reformer, born a slave in Ulster County, NY. After years of abuse, a new master, Isaac Van Wagener, set her free. From him she took her surname, and became an ardent evangelist. In 1843 she felt called by God to change her name to Sojourner Truth, and to fight against slavery and for women's suffrage. Preaching widely across the USA, she drew large crowds, was appointed counsellor to the freedmen of Washington by Abraham Lincoln, and continued to promote black civil rights until her retirement in 1875. >> Lincoln

Truxtun, Thomas (1753–1822) US naval officer and merchant captain, born near Hempstead, NY. He was successful as a privateer in the Revolution, and as a captain in the China trade. He became a naval captain (1794), and during the undeclared war with France captured the French *Insurgente* (1799) and defeated *La Vengeance* in a five-hour battle (1800). He also wrote books on navigation and naval tactics.

Tsai-t'ien >> **Zai Tian**

Ts'ao Hsüeh-ch'in >> **Cao Xuequin**

Tschaikovsky, Piotr Ilyich >> **Tchaikovsky**

Tseng Kuo-fan >> **Zeng Guofan**

Tshombe, Moise(-Kapenda) [chombee] (1919–69) Congolese statesman, born in Musumba, Democratic Republic of Congo (formerly, Zaire, and earlier, Belgian Congo). He served on the Katanga Provincial Council (1951–3) and became president of Conakat (Confédération des Associations Tribales du Katanga) in 1959, a powerful political party. When this party won a majority in Katanga's Provincial Assembly, he became president of the province and declared Katanga independent. The UN sent troops into Katanga, and Tshombe escaped to Spain. He was recalled from exile and made premier of the united Congo (Kinshasa) Republic (1964), but later dismissed (1965). He returned to Spain, where he was kidnapped, taken to Algeria (1967), and detained under house arrest on charges of treason. He died in custody.

Tsiolkovsky, Konstantin Eduardovich [tseeolkofskee] (1857–1935) Russian physicist and rocketry pioneer, born in Izhevsk, Russia. Self-educated, and handicapped by deafness from the age of 10, his visionary ideas on the use of rockets for space exploration were published in 1903. From 1911 he developed the basic theory of rocketry and multi-stage rocket technology (1929). Much earlier (1881), unaware of Maxwell's work, he independently developed the kinetic theory of gases. >> Maxwell, James C

Tsvetayeva, Marina Ivanova [tsvetiyuhva], married name **Efron** (1892–1941) Poet, born in Moscow. Strongly anti-Bolshevik, she was allowed to emigrate in 1922, and wrote and published most of her poetry abroad, such as

Vyorsty (1922, Miles), and Posle Rossii 1922–25 (1928, After Russia). She returned to the USSR in 1939. After the execution of her husband and the arrest of her daughter, she committed suicide in Yelabuga.

Tswett or **Tsvett, Mikhail Semenovich** [tsvet] (1872–1919) Botanist, born in Asti, Italy. He studied at Geneva, and at the University of Kazan. He became a laboratory assistant at the University of Warsaw, and taught at Warsaw Technical University from 1908, and at Tartu University, Estonia, from 1917. He devised a percolation method of separating plant pigments in 1906, thus making the first chromatographic analysis.

Tuan, Yi-Fu [twahn] (1930–) Geographer, born in Tients'in, China. He emigrated to England in 1946, and to the USA in 1951. He studied at Oxford and the University of California, Berkeley, before becoming a professor at the University of Wisconsin, Madison in 1983. One of the newer generation of geographers concerned with broader philosophical issues of the subject, his books include Topophilia (1974) and Morality and Imagination: Paradoxes of Progress (1989).

Tubman, Harriet (1820–1913) Slavery abolitionist, born in Dorchester Co, MD. She escaped from slavery in Maryland (1849) and went north via the 'Underground Railway', a network of secret safe-houses. She returned to the South frequently to escort escaping slaves through this route, becoming known as 'the Moses of her People'. She devoted her life to the abolitionist cause.

Tucker, Albert Lee (1914–) Painter, born in Melbourne, Victoria, Australia. Educated in Melbourne, he received no formal art training. He is known as a pioneer of Surrealism in Australia, and for his Expressionist and nightmarish images. His painting 'Victory Girls' (1943), part of the series 'Images of Modern Evil', is typical of his enraged indictment of a corrupt, debased society, a view which he defended in writing of a polemical nature in the magazine Angry Penguins during the 1940s. He is also known for his paintings of harsh Australian landscape as well as for his self-portraits. He left Australia in 1947, working and exhibiting in Japan, Europe, and the USA, returning in 1960. An important retrospective of his work was mounted by the Australian National Gallery in 1990.

Tucker, Sophie, originally **Sophie Abuza** (1884–1966) Singer, born in Russia. She was born while her mother, a Russian Jew, was travelling to the USA, where she became a child performer. In New York she appeared in the Ziegfeld Follies (1909), and went on to establish a successful stage career in burlesque, vaudeville, nightclubs, and the English music-hall. Her flamboyant style earned her billing as 'the last of the red hot mamas', and she is remembered for her theme song 'Some of These Days'.

Tuckwell, Barry (Emmanuel) (1931–) Conductor and instrumentalist, born in Melbourne, Victoria, Australia. He studied at the Conservatory of Music, Sydney, and played with the Sydney Symphony Orchestra, and the Hallé and other British orchestras. From 1955–68 he was principal horn with the London Symphony Orchestra, and featured as a soloist on most of the LSO's recordings in this period. He has conducted many international orchestras, and became conductor of the Maryland Symphony Orchestra in 1982. He was also professor of horn at the Royal Academy of Music in London (1963–74). He became a US citizen in 1996, and the same year announced his retirement from professional performance.

Tudor, Antony (1908–87) Dancer and choreographer, born in London, England, UK. He studied with Marie Rambert, and created the celebrated Lilac Garden (1936). He formed the London Ballet (1938–40), then moved to New York's Ballet Theatre (now American Ballet Theatre), where Pillar of Fire and Romeo and Juliet were among his triumphs. He was director of the Metropolitian Opera Ballet School, and tutored at the Juilliard School, New York City. >> Rambert

Tudor, Owen >> **Henry VII**

Tu Fu >> **Du Fu**

Tuke, Samuel [tyook] (1784–1857) Psychiatric reformer, born in York, North Yorkshire, N England, UK, the grandson of William Tuke. He acquired in his childhood an intense interest in the York Retreat, the psychiatric hospital founded by his family. His Description of the Retreat (1813) contains a classic account of the principles of 'moral therapy', which was the basis of the therapeutic milieu there. Tuke's son, **Daniel Hack Tuke** (1827–95), became a leading psychiatrist. >> Tuke, William

Tuke, William (1732–1822) Quaker philanthropist. A tea and coffee merchant in York, he founded a home for the mentally sick (the York Retreat) in 1796, the first of its kind in England. Contemporaneously with **Philippe Pinel** (1745–1826) in France, he pioneered new methods of treatment and care of the insane. >> Tuke, Samuel

Tukhachevsky, Mikhail Nikolayevich [tookachefskee] (1893–1937) Russian soldier and politician, born near Slednevo, Russia. He served in the Tsarist Army in World War 1, but became a member of the Communist Party in 1918. He commanded Bolshevik forces against the Poles in the Russo-Polish War (1920), against the White Russians (1919–20), and during the Kulak uprising of 1921. He served on the commission on military invention (1922), and was chief of armaments (1931). He is renowned for his work on tactical doctrine, notably on tank warfare. Appointed to the Military Soviet in 1934, he was created Marshal of the Soviet Union in 1935, but was later executed for treason during Stalin's purge of Red Army officers.

Tull, Jethro (1674–1741) Agriculturist, born in Basildon, Berkshire, S England, UK. He studied at Oxford, and became a lawyer, but turned to farming. He introduced several new farming methods, including the invention of a seed drill which planted seeds in rows (1701).

Tully >> **Cicero**

Tulsidas [tulseedas] (c. 1543–1623) Devotional poet, born in E India. His best-known work is Ramacaritamanas (The Holy Lake of Rama's Deeds), an immensely popular Eastern Hindi version of the Ramayana epic, which he began in 1574. His devotional approach – a concern for moral conduct, and the idea of salvation through Rama incarnated as absolute knowledge and love – suggests a Nestorian Christian influence on his work. >> Nestorius

Tunney, Gene, popular name of **James Joseph Tunney**, nickname **the Fighting Marine** (1897–1978) Boxer and world heavyweight champion, born in New York City. A high-school drop-out, he joined the US marines and won the world light-heavyweight championship, then took the world heavyweight crown from Jack Dempsey in 1926, retaining it in a controversial re-match in 1927. He retired in 1928, with a record of 76 wins, one loss. During World War 2 he was director of athletics and physical fitness for the US Navy. >> Dempsey

Tunnicliffe, Charles Frederick (1901–79) Bird artist, born in Langley, Cheshire, NWC England, UK. He won a scholarship to the Royal College of Art. He illustrated Henry Williamson's Tarka the Otter (1927) and Salar the Salmon (1935) with his own wood-engravings, provided innumerable illustrations for the Royal Society for the Protection of Birds, and published six books of his own, including Shorelands Summer Diary (1952), My Country Book (1945), and Bird Portraiture (1945). A collection of his work is now based at Oriel Môn, Llangefni, Anglesey, NW Wales, UK.

Tunström, Göron [tunstroem] (1937–) Writer, born in Sunne, Sweden. His father, whom he dearly loved, died when he was 12, and his world fell apart. His first work, *Inringing* (Encircling), appeared in 1958, since when he has published poems, plays, travel books, and novels. In his fiction he recaptures his childhood and tries to come to terms with his loss. His most popular novels are the prize-winning *Juloratoriet* (1982, The Christmas Oratorio) and *Tjuven* (1986, The Thief).

Tupolev, Andrey Nikolayevich [**too**polef] (1888–1972) Aircraft designer, born in Moscow. From 1922 he headed the design office of the central aerohydrodynamics institute in Moscow, producing over 100 types of aircraft, and in 1955 he built the first Soviet civil jet, the Tu-104. In 1968 he completed the first test flight of a supersonic passenger aircraft, the Tu-144.

Tura, Cosmè [**too**ra] (c. 1430–1495) Painter, born in Ferrara, Italy. The founder and leader of the Ferrarese school, he studied under Squarcione at Padua, and his metallic, tortured forms and unusual colours give a strange power to his pictures, such as the 'Pietà'(c.1472) in the Louvre and the 'St Jerome' in the National Gallery, London. >> Squarcione

Turenne, Henri de la Tour d'Auvergne, vicomte de (Viscount of) [tü**ren**] (1611–75) French marshal, born in Sedan, France, son of the Protestant Duc de Bouillon, and grandson of William I (the Silent). He learned soldiering from his uncles, the Princes of Orange, and in the Thirty Years' War fought with distinction for the armies of the Protestant alliance. He captured Breisach (1638) and Turin (1640), and for the conquest of Roussillon from the Spaniards (1642) was made Marshal of France (1643). In the civil wars of the Frondes, he joined the *frondeurs* at first, but then switched sides; his campaigning (1652–3) saved the young King Louis XIV and Mazarin's government. In the Franco-Spanish war he conquered much of the Spanish Netherlands after defeating Condé at the Battle of the Dunes (1658). He won lasting fame for his campaigns in the United Provinces during the Dutch War (1672–5), but advancing along the Rhine he was killed at Sasbach. >> Condé, Louis II de Bourbon; Mazarin; William I (of The Netherlands)

Turgenev, Ivan (Sergeyevich) [toor**gyay**nyef] (1818–83) Novelist, born in Orel province, Russia. He studied at St Petersburg and Berlin universities, and joined the Russian civil service in 1841, but in 1843 abandoned this to take up literature. His first studies of peasant life, *Sportsman's Sketches* (1852, trans title), made his reputation, but earned governmental ill favour. He was banished for two years to his country estates, and then lived mainly in Germany and France. His greatest novel, *Fathers and Sons* (1862, trans title), was badly received in Russia, but a particular success in England. He also wrote poetry, plays, short stories, and tales of the supernatural.

Turgot, Anne Robert Jacques [toor**goh**] (1727–81) French statesman and economist, born in Paris. Educated at the seminary of Saint-Sulpice, he renounced the Church for the law, became a magistrate in the *Parlement* of Paris, and was promoted to intendant at Limoges (1761–74), where he carried out reforms. Here he published his best-known work, *Réflexions sur la formation et la distribution des richesses* (1766, Reflections on the Formation and Distribution of Wealth). Appointed comptroller-general of finance by Louis XVI (1774), he embarked on a comprehensive scheme of national economic reform, but the opposition of the privileged classes to his Six Edicts led to his overthrow (1776), and he died forgotten, his reforms abandoned.

Turina, Joaquín [too**ree**na] (1882–1949) Composer and pianist, born in Seville, Spain. He studied in Seville and Madrid, then lived in Paris, where he became an important figure in French musical life. Returning to Madrid in 1914, he was immensely active as composer, pianist, and

critic. He wrote four operas, including *Margot* (1914) and *Jardín de oriente* (1923), orchestral and chamber works, and piano pieces, the best of which combine strong Andalusian colour and idiom with traditional forms.

Turing, Alan (Mathison) [**too**ring] (1912–54) Mathematician, born in London, England, UK. He studied at Cambridge and Princeton, worked in cryptography during World War 2, then joined the National Physical Laboratory (1945) and the computing laboratory at Manchester (1948). He provided a precise mathematical characterization of computability, and introduced the theoretical notion of an idealized computer (since called a *Turing machine*), laying the foundation for the field of artificial intelligence. He committed suicide after being prosecuted for homosexuality.

Turnbull, Colin (Macmillan) (1924–94) Anthropologist, born in Harrow, NW Greater London, England, UK. He studied at Oxford, then carried out fieldwork, first in India (1949–51) and later among the Mbuti pygmies of the Ituri Forest, Democratic Republic of Congo (formerly, Zaire). He worked at the American Museum of Natural History in New York City (1959–69), and was professor at George Washington University from 1976. He wrote many books on social change and relationships in Africa, including *The Forest People* (1961) and *The Human Cycle* (1983).

Turnbull, Malcolm (Bligh) (1954–) Merchant banker, lawyer, and republican, born in Sydney, New South Wales, Australia. He studied at the universities of Sydney and Oxford, where he was Rhodes Scholar for New South Wales in 1978. He worked as a political correspondent for various newspapers and radio stations before being admitted to the bar in 1980. He set up his own law firm in 1986, and became known for successfully defending Peter Wright in the *Spycatcher* trial, publishing his account of the case in 1988. A prominent advocate of an Australian Republic, he is a foundation director of the Australian Republican Movement, and in 1993 was appointed chairman of the Republic Advisory Committee. >> Wright, Peter

Turnbull, William (1922–) Artist, born in Dundee, E Scotland, UK. He studied at the Slade School of Art, London, then lived in Paris (1948–50). He held his first one-man show at the Hanover Gallery, London, in 1950, then taught at the Central School of Arts and Crafts (1952–72). His sculptures are typically upright forms of roughly human height, standing directly on the floor. In the 1950s he liked organic forms, and titles such as 'Totemic Figure', but since the 1960s he has preferred purely abstract, geometrical shapes.

Turner, Ethel Sibyl (1872–1958) Novelist and children's writer, born in Doncaster, South Yorkshire, N England, UK. She moved to Australia at the age of nine. With her sister, **Lilian**, she started a magazine, and wrote the children's page, later doing the same for two other Sydney periodicals. Her first book, *Seven Little Australians*, published in 1894, was an immediate success, has been in print ever since publication, and is now a classic of Australian literature. A sequel came out in the following year, and there followed a steady stream of juvenile books, short stories, and verse.

Turner, Dame Eva (1892–1990) Soprano, born in Oldham, Lancashire, NW England, UK. She trained at the Royal Academy of Music and joined the Carl Rosa Opera Company (1916–24), making her debut in 1920 with the Royal Opera, Covent Garden. She was associated with the Chicago Civic Opera for many years. Known for her vocal power, she performed most of the leading parts of the dramatic soprano repertoire, notably as the Princess in Puccini's *Turandot*, a role she sang regularly from 1926 until 1948.

Turner, Frederick Jackson (1861–1932) Historian, born in Portage, WI. He studied at Johns Hopkins University, then taught at Wisconsin (1889–1910) and Harvard (1910–24). At the 1893 Chicago World's Fair, he came to prominence with his paper on 'The Significance of the Frontier in American History'. *The Significance of Sections in American History* (1932) earned him the Pulitzer Prize.

Turner, John Napier (1929–) Canadian statesman and prime minister (1984), born in Richmond, SW Greater London, England, UK. His family emigrated to Canada in 1932, where he studied at the University of British Columbia, and won a Rhodes Scholarship to Oxford. He was called to the English bar, and later the bars of Quebec and Ontario, being made a QC in 1968. He entered the Canadian House of Commons in 1962, and was a junior minister in Lester Pearson's government, and later attorney general and finance minister under Pierre Trudeau. When Trudeau retired in 1984, Turner succeeded him as Liberal prime minister. He lost the general election later the same year, and became Leader of the Opposition. He resigned the leadership of his Party in 1989. >> Pearson, Lester B; Trudeau; RR1039

Turner, J(oseph) M(allord) W(illiam) (1775–1851) Landscape artist and watercolourist, born in London, England, UK. After little formal education, he entered the Royal Academy at 14, and soon began to exhibit. He travelled widely in Britain, making architectural drawings in the cathedral cities, and spent three years in collaboration with Girtin producing watercolours. He then took to oils, his early works including 'Frosty Morning' (1813) and 'Crossing the Brook' (1815). After his first visit to Italy (1819), his work showed several literary influences, as in 'Ulysses Deriding Polyphemus' (1829). His second visit (1829) marks the beginning of his last great artistic period, including 'The Fighting Téméraire' (1839) and 'Rain, Steam and Speed' (1844, Tate, London). His revolution in art foreshadowed Impressionism, and found a timely champion in John Ruskin, whose writing helped to turn the critical tide in Turner's favour. Turner bequeathed 300 of his paintings and 20 000 watercolours and drawings to the nation. He led a secretive private life, never married, and died in a temporary lodging in Chelsea, under the assumed name of Booth. >> Girtin; Ruskin

Turner, Kathleen (1954–) Actress, born in Springfield, MO. She made her film debut in *Body Heat* (1981), and went on to star in such popular films as *Romancing the Stone* (1984), *Prizzi's Honor* (1985), and *War Of The Roses* (1989). She received a Best Actress Oscar nomination for her role in *Peggy Sue Got Married* (1986), and provided the husky voice for Jessica Rabbit in the film *'Who Framed Roger Rabbit?* (1988). She also earned critical acclaim for her performance on Broadway in *Indiscretions* (1995).

Turner, Nat (1800–31) Slave leader, born in Southampton Co, VA. The son of an African native, he became a religious fanatic, believing that God had chosen him to lead his people out of bondage. He mounted the only sustained slave revolt in US history (1831), but was captured, tried, and hanged. A number of books have been written about the incident, notably the controversial *The Confessions of Nat Turner* (1967) by William Styron.

Turner, Ted, popular name of **Robert Edward Turner** (1938–) US television news vendor. He purchased a small television station in Atlanta in the 1960s, and built it into the 'Superstation' WTBS, using satellite and cable technology. He founded Cable News Network (CNN) in 1980 to provide 24-hour news coverage. Since 1970 he has been chairman and president of Turner Broadcasting System Inc.

Turner, Tina, originally **Annie May Bullock** (1939–) Singer, born in Nutbush, TN. She achieved considerable success in the rhythm-and-blues vocal duo, Ike and Tina Turner, before their marriage and professional partnership was officially dissolved in 1976. Her first solo single, 'Let's Stay Together' (1983), reached number 6 in the UK music charts. Other hit singles include 'What's Love Got To Do With It?' (1984) and 'Private Dancer' (1985). She appeared in the film *Mad Max: Beyond Thunderdrome* (1985), and recorded the title song for the James Bond film *Goldeneye* (1996).

Turner, Victor Witter (1920–83) Social anthropologist, born in Glasgow, W Scotland, UK. He studied literature at London University, then anthropology under Max Gluckman (1911–75) at Manchester. He taught at Manchester (1949–63) before moving to the USA, where he became professor at Cornell (1963–8), Chicago (1968–77), and Virginia (1977–83). He carried out fieldwork among the Ndembu of Zambia (1950–4), which resulted in the classic monograph *Schism and Continuity in an African Society* (1957). In his later work he moved to the analysis of symbolism, as in *The Forest of Symbols* (1967) and *Dramas, Fields and Metaphors* (1972).

Turner, Walter (James Redfern) (1889–1946) Poet, novelist, and critic, born in Melbourne, Victoria, Australia. He studied there and at Munich and Vienna. He published *The Dark Fire* (1918), *The Landscape of Cytherea* (1923), and other volumes of poetry. His other writings include studies of Beethoven, Mozart, and Wagner, a play *The Man Who Ate the Popomack* (1922), and novels including *The Aesthetes* (1927) and *The Duchess of Popocatepetl* (1939).

Turner, William (c. 1508–68) Clergyman, physician, and naturalist, born in Morpeth, Northumberland, NE England, UK. A fellow of Pembroke Hall, Cambridge, he became a Protestant, and to escape religious persecution in England travelled extensively abroad, studying medicine and botany in Italy. He became dean of Wells (1550–3), left England during the reign of Mary I, but was restored to Wells in 1560. The author of the first original English works on plants, including *Names of Herbes* (1548) and *A New Herball* (1551–68), he named many plants, including goatsbeard and hawkweed. He is often called 'the father of English botany'.

Turpin, Dick, popular name of **Richard Turpin** (1706–39) Robber, born in Hempstead, Essex, SE England, UK. He was a butcher's apprentice, smuggler, housebreaker, highwayman, and horse thief. He entered into partnership with Tom King, and was hanged at York for the murder of an Epping keeper. The legendary ride from London to York, attributed to him, was probably actually carried out by 'Swift John Nevison' (1639–84), who in 1676 is said to have robbed a sailor at Gadshill at 4 am, and to have established an 'alibi' by reaching York at 7.45 pm.

Turpin, Randolph (1925–66) Middleweight boxer, born in Leamington Spa, Warwickshire, C England, UK, a member of a well-known boxing family. British middleweight champion (1950–4) and European champion (1951–4), he defeated Sugar Ray Robinson in the summer of 1951, and for a few months was world champion, before losing the title to Robinson in New York City in the autumn of that year. >> Robinson, Sugar Ray

Turturro, John [terˈtuhroh] (1957–) Film actor, born in New York City. He trained at the Yale School of Drama, and established himself as a stage actor before his film debut in *Raging Bull* (1980). Later films include *Hannah and her Sisters* (1986), *Do The Right Thing* (1989), *Barton Fink* (1991), *Unstrung Heroes* (1995), and *Box of Moonlight* (1997).

Tussaud, Marie [tuhˈsawd], Fr [tüsoh], *née* **Grosholtz** (1761–1850) Modeller in wax, born in Strasbourg, France. She was apprenticed to her uncle, Dr Curtius, in Paris, and inherited his wax museums after his death. After the

Revolution, she attended the guillotine to take death masks from the severed heads. She toured Britain with her life-size portrait waxworks, and in 1835 set up a permanent exhibition in Baker St, London. It was burnt down in 1925, and re-opened in Marylebone Rd in 1928. The exhibition still contains her own handiwork, notably images of Marie Antoinette, Napoleon, and Burke and Hare in the Chamber of Horrors.

Tutankhamen or **Tut'ankhamun** [tootan**kah**men, tootang-ka**moon**] (14th-c BC) Egyptian pharaoh of the 18th dynasty (1361–1352 BC), the undistinguished son-in-law of the heretic pharaoh, Akhenaton. He came to the throne at the age of 12, and is famous only for his magnificent tomb at Thebes, which was discovered intact in 1922 by Lord Carnarvon and Howard Carter. >> Akhenaton; Carnarvon; Carter, Howard; RR1046

Tuthmosis >> **Thutmose III**

Tutin, Dorothy [tyoo**tin**] (1931–) Actress, born in London, England, UK. She trained at the Royal Academy of Dramatic Art, London, and made her acting debut in 1950. She toured Russia with the Shakespeare Memorial Theatre (1958), made her first appearance in a contemporary play in *The Devils* (1961), and has subsequently played many leading roles in classical and modern plays, including Queen Victoria in *Portrait of a Queen* (1965). She received a Variety Club of Great Britain Award for her role in the film *Savage Messiah* (1972). Later films include *The Shooting Party* (1984) and *Alive and Kicking* (1997).

Tutu, Desmond (Mpilo) (1931–) Anglican clergyman, born in Klerksdorp, South Africa. He studied at the universities of South Africa and London, was briefly a schoolteacher, then became an Anglican parish priest (1960). He rapidly rose to become Bishop of Lesotho (1977), secretary-general of the South African Council of Churches (1979), the first black Bishop of Johannesburg (1984), and Archbishop of Cape Town (1986), retiring in 1996. A critic of the apartheid system, he repeatedly risked imprisonment for his advocacy of the imposition of punitive sanctions against South Africa by the international community. He condemned the use of violence by opponents of apartheid, seeking instead a peaceful, negotiated reconciliation between the black and white communities. He was awarded the Nobel Prize for Peace in 1984, and was appointed chair of the Truth and Reconciliation Commission in 1995.

Tutuola, Amos [tutwoh**la**] (1920–97) Novelist, born in Abeokuta, Nigeria. He was celebrated in the West as the author of *The Palm-Wine Drinkard* (1952), a transcription in pidgin English prose of an oral tale of his own invention. Later novels in the same manner included *My Life in the Bush of Ghosts* (1954), *The Brave African Huntress* (1958), *Ajaiyi and His Inherited Poverty* (1967), and *The Wild Hunter in the Bush of Ghosts* (1989).

Twain, Mark, pseudonym of **Samuel Langhorne Clemens** (1835–1910) Writer, journalist, and lecturer, born in Florida, MO. A printer (1847–57) and later a Mississippi river-boat pilot (1857–61), he adopted his name from a well-known call used when sounding the river shallows ('Mark twain!' meaning 'by the mark two fathoms'). He edited for two years the Virginia City *Territorial Enterprise*, and in 1864 moved to San Francisco as a reporter. In 1867 he visited France, Italy, and Palestine, gathering material for his *The Innocents Abroad* (1869), which established his reputation as a humorist. On his return to America, he settled in the East, and in 1870 married **Olivia Langdon** (d.1904), the daughter of a wealthy New York coal merchant. In 1871 they moved to Hartford, CT, where they built a distinctive house (now open to the public) at the centre of a community of artists, known as Nook Farm. His

two greatest masterpieces, *The Adventures of Tom Sawyer* (1876) and *The Adventures of Huckleberry Finn* (1884), drawn from his own boyhood experiences, are firmly established among the world's classics; other favourites are *A Tramp Abroad* (1880) and *A Connecticut Yankee in King Arthur's Court* (1889). Widely known as a lecturer, he developed a great popular following. Financial speculations led to the loss of most of his earnings by 1894, and he embarked on a world lecture tour to restore some of his wealth. In his later years, he was greatly honoured (especially in England), but following the death of his wife and of two of his daughters, his writing took on a darker, pessimistic character, as seen in his autobiography (1924).

Tweed, William Marcy, nickname **Boss Tweed** (1823–78) Criminal and politician, one of the most notorious 'bosses' of the Tammany Society, born in New York City. He trained as a chairmaker, became an alderman (1852–3), sat in Congress (1853–5), and was repeatedly in the state Senate. In 1870 he was made commissioner of public works for the city and, as head of the 'Tweed Ring', controlled its finances. After his gigantic frauds were exposed by the *New York Times* in 1871, he was convicted, escaped to Cuba and Spain (1875–6), but died in a New York jail while suits were pending against him for recovery of $6 million. >> Tilden

Tweedsmuir, Baron >> **Buchan, John**

Twiggy, professional name of **Lesley Lawson**, née **Hornby** (1949–) Fashion model, actress, and singer, born in London, England, UK. She became a modelling superstar almost overnight at the age of 17, and was a symbol of the 'swinging sixties' in London's Carnaby Street. She has made numerous appearances on television, and her films include *The Boy Friend* (1971), *The Blues Brothers* (1981), and *Madame Sousatzka* (1989).

Twining, Nathan F(arragut) [**twiy**ning] (1897–) Aviator, born in Monroe, WI. He trained at West Point and served eight years in the infantry before transferring to the air service. In World War 2, he took command of the newly-formed 13th Air Force in the Southwest Pacific (1942), and in 1944 went to the Mediterranean as commander of the 15th Air Force, which carried out the famous Ploesti oilfield raids under his direction. He returned to the Pacific in August 1945 to command the 20th Air Force in the final phase of the air offensive against Japan. He ended a long service career as chairman of the joint chiefs-of-staff (1957–60).

Twombly, Cy (1928–) Painter, born in Lexington, VA. He studied at the Boston Museum of Fine Arts School, the Art Students' League, and at Black Mountain College, settling in Rome in 1957. His gestural or 'doodle' technique derives from a Surrealist belief in the expressive power of automatic writing to tap the unconscious.

Twomey, Patrick Joseph [**too**mee] (1892–1963) Philanthropist, born in Wellington, New Zealand. In 1939, after travelling widely among the Pacific Is and seeing the medical needs of the region, he founded the Lepers Trust Board. Thereafter, he devoted his life to gathering funds to assist the treatment of lepers and other sufferers from tropical diseases in the SW Pacific. This organization continues to function as the Pacific Leprosy Foundation.

Tworkov, Jack (1900–82) Painter, born in Biala, Poland. His family emigrated to the US in 1913, and he attended Columbia University (1923). He met and became influenced by the painter Willem de Kooning, later joining him and other artists who together evolved Abstract Expressionism. Tworkov became a leading exponent of the movement which greatly influenced American art during the 1950s and 1960s. He was chairman of the department of art at Yale University (1963–9). >> de Kooning; Gottlieb, Adolf; Mitchell, Joan; Motherwell

Twort, Frederick William (1877–1950) Bacteriologist, born in Camberley, Surrey, SE England, UK. He studied medicine in London, and became professor of bacteriology there in 1919. He studied Johne's disease, and methods of culture of acid-fast organisms. In 1915 he discovered the bacteriophage, a virus that attacks certain bacteria.

Tyana >> **Apollonius of Tyana**

Tycho Brahe >> **Brahe, Tycho**

Tye, Christopher (c. 1500–1573) Composer and organist, an innovator of English cathedral music, probably born in London, England, UK. He studied at Cambridge, and became a doctor of music there and at Oxford. From c.1541–56 he was choirmaster at Ely Cathedral, and he may have been musical instructor to Edward VI. His surviving work includes two Latin Masses, 14 English anthems, instrumental music, and psalm settings.

Tyler, Anne (1941–) Novelist and short-story writer, born in Minneapolis, MN. She graduated from Duke University at 19, and began to write tales of life in Baltimore or in Southern small towns, concerned with the themes of loneliness, isolation, and human interactions. She has had a productive career since her debut in 1965 with *If Morning Ever Comes*. Later titles include *Dinner at the Homesick Restaurant* (1982), *The Accidental Tourist* (1985), *Breathing Lessons* (1989, Pulitzer), *Saint Maybe* (1991), and *Ladder of Years* (1995).

Tyler, John (1790–1862) US statesman and 10th president (1841–5), born in Charles City Co, VA. He became a lawyer, a member of the state legislature (1811–16), Governor of Virginia (1825–7), and a senator (1827–36). Elected vice-president in 1840, he became president on the death of Harrison in 1841, only a month after his inauguration. His administration was marked by the annexation of Texas. He later remained active in politics, adhering to the Confederate cause until his death. >> Harrison, William Henry; RR1097

Tyler, Wat (?–1381) English leader of the Peasants' Revolt (1381). The rebels of Kent, after taking Rochester Castle, chose him as captain, and marched to Canterbury and London. At the Smithfield conference with Richard II blows were exchanged, and Tyler was wounded by the Mayor of London, William Walworth (d.1385). He was taken to St Bartholomew's Hospital, where Walworth had him dragged out and beheaded. >> Ball, John; Richard II

Tylor, Sir Edward Burnet (1832–1917) Anthropologist, born in London, England, UK. Educated as a Quaker, he became a clerk in the family business. A journey to America for health reasons was followed by a visit to Mexico, his experiences being published in *Ahahuac* (1861). His first major anthropological study appeared in 1865, and in 1871 he published his monumental *Primitive Culture* (2 vols). In this work he sought to show that human culture is governed by definite laws of evolutionary development, such that the beliefs and practices of primitive nations may be taken to represent earlier stages in the progress of mankind. He later became keeper of the University Museum at Oxford, and first professor of anthropology at Oxford (1896–1909). Widely regarded as the founder of the systematic study of human culture, he was knighted in 1912.

Tynan, Katharine [tiynan] (1861–1931) Poet and novelist, born in Dublin. She was a friend of Parnell, the Meynells, and the Rossettis, and a leading author of the Celtic literary revival. She wrote volumes of tender, gentle verse, and many novels and autobiographical works, including *Oh! What a Plague is Love*, (1896), *She Walks in Beauty* (1899), *The House in the Forest* (1928), and *Memoires* (1924). >> Meynell; Parnell; Rossetti

Tynan, Kenneth [tiynan] (1927–80) Theatre critic, born in Birmingham, West Midlands, C England, UK. He read English at Oxford, where he became deeply involved in the theatre. As drama critic for several publications, notably *The Observer* (1954–63), he was one of the first to champion John Osborne and the other new playwrights of the time. He became literary manager of the National Theatre (1963–9), an editor in films and television, and achieved further fame with his controversial revue *Oh! Calcutta* (1969). >> Osborne, John

Tyndale or **Tindale, William** [tindayl] (?–1536) Translator of the Bible, probably born in Slymbridge, Gloucestershire, SWC England, UK. He studied at Oxford, and became a chaplain and tutor, sympathetic to humanist learning. In 1524 he went to Hamburg and Wittenberg, and in 1525 to Cologne, where he completed his translation of the English New Testament. In 1531 he moved to Antwerp, where he continued to work on an Old Testament translation, but before it was finished he was seized, accused of heresy, imprisoned, and executed. His work became the basis of most later English translations of the Bible, and much influenced the Authorised Version of 1611.

Tyndall, John [tindl] (1820–93) Physicist, born in Leighlin Bridge, Co Carlow, Ireland. Largely self-educated, he became professor at the Royal Institution in 1854. In 1859 he began his researches on heat radiation, followed by the acoustic properties of the atmosphere and the blue colour of the sky, which he suggested was due to the scattering of light by small particles of water.

Tyson, Frank (Holmes), nickname **Typhoon Tyson** (1930–) Cricketer, born in Farnworth, Lancashire, NW England, UK. A fast bowler, of his 17 Tests only four were played in England, and he is best remembered for his performance in the Australian tour of 1954–5 under Len Hutton. In that series he bowled at tremendous pace, having almost halved his run-up. He later found the pitches at Northampton unresponsive, and left county cricket to become a coach and commentator in Australia. >> Hutton, Len

Tyson, Mike, popular name of **Michael (Gerald) Tyson** (1966–) Boxer, born in New York City. The National Golden Gloves heavyweight champion in 1984, he turned professional the following year. A lethal puncher, he beat 15 of his first 25 opponents by knockouts in the first round. He beat Trevor Berbick (1952–) for the World Boxing Council version of the world heavyweight title in 1986 to become the youngest heavyweight champion (20 years 145 days), and added the World Boxing Association title in 1987, when he beat James Smith (1954–). Later that year he became the first undisputed champion since 1978, when he beat Tony Tucker (1958–). He won 41 of 42 decisions before losing the title in 1990. In 1992 he was jailed following a trial for rape, and released in 1995. He regained the WBC heavyweight title in 1996, then vacated it soon afterwards. >> RR1148

Tytler, James, known as **Balloon Tytler** (c. 1747–1804) Journalist and balloonist, born in Fearn, Highland, N Scotland, UK. He studied at Edinburgh University, then sailed to Greenland on a whaling ship, and embarked on the first of many ill-fated literary ventures. To keep creditors at bay, he took on the editorship of the second edition of the *Encyclopaedia Britannica* (1776–84). He was one of the first Britons to attempt a balloon ascent in 1784. After this he fell into debt and left for America, where he became a newspaper publisher.

Tz'u-hsi >> **Ci-xi**

Uccello, Paolo [oo**che**loh], originally **Paolo di Dono** (1397–1475) Painter, born in Pratovecchio, Italy. He trained under Ghiberti, worked in Venice as a mosaicist (1425–31), then settled in Florence. He applied the principles of perspective to his paintings, as seen in 'The Flood' (1447–8, Florence), where his use of perspective and fore-shortening gives a sternly realistic effect. >> Ghiberti

Udall, Nicholas [**yoo**dal] (1504–56) Playwright, born in Southampton, Hampshire, S England, UK. He studied at Oxford, and became (c.1534) head-master of Eton. His dismissal in 1541 for indecent offences did not affect his standing at court, and Edward VI appointed him prebendary of Windsor. He made many classical translations, but is chiefly remembered as the author of the first significant comedy in English, *Ralph Roister Doister* (c.1563).

Udall, Stewart (Lee) [**yoo**dahl] (1920–) US public official and conservationist, born in St John, AZ. He served in the air corps during World War 2, then practised law for several years before serving as a Democrat in the US House of Representatives, where he developed a reputation as a conservation advocate. As secretary of the interior in the Kennedy and Johnson administrations (1961–9), he curbed abuses in the sale and exploitation of public lands, and reformed the Bureau of Indian Affairs. He became a private conservation consultant in 1969. >> Johnson, Lyndon B; Kennedy, John F

Udet, Ernst [oo**det**] (1896–1941) German airman, born in Frankfurt, Germany. He was a leading German air ace in World War 1, and from 1935 worked in the German air ministry. A *Luftwaffe* quartermaster-general in World War 2, having fallen foul of the Gestapo, he committed suicide by crashing his aircraft. The authorities described his death as an accident while testing a new air weapon. Zuckmayer's play, *The Devil's General*, is based on his life. >> Zuckmayer

Udine, Giovanni da [oo**din**ay] (1487–1564) Painter, decorative artist, and architect, born in Udine, Italy. He entered the workshop of Raphael in Rome, and became a specialist in a style of decoration called 'grotesque', influenced by the graceful ornamental schemes being discovered in the excavations of ancient Rome. He later moved back to Udine and, by 1552, was in charge of all public building there. His decorative style rapidly spread throughout Europe, and was especially popular during the Neo-classical period of the 18th-c. >> Raphael

Uemura, Naomi [way**moo**ra] (1942–84) Explorer and mountaineer, born in Tajima region, Japan. He started climbing as a student at Meiji University, Tokyo. After solo ascents of Mont Blanc, Kilimanjaro, Aconcagua, and Mt McKinley, he reached the summit of Everest with Teruo Matsura in 1970, becoming the first person to reach the highest peak on five continents. In 1978 he made a solo dog-sled journey of 450 mi from Ellesmere I to the North Pole, then immediately undertook a 1600 mi N–S traverse of Greenland using 16 dogs. He led the Japanese attempt to climb Mt Everest in the winter of 1981. He completed the first winter ascent of the West Buttress Route of Mt McKinley, and is presumed to have died during the descent, although his body was never found.

Uhland, (Johann) Ludwig [oo**lant**] (1787–1862) Lyric poet, the leader of the Swabian School, born in Tübingen, Germany. He studied law at Tübingen and wrote his first poems there. He was active in politics, becoming a Liberal deputy for Tübingen at the assemblies of Württemberg (1819) and Frankfurt (1848). His collection of poems (1815) contained many popular ballads reflecting his interest in folklore and mediaeval studies.

Uhle, Max [**oo**luh] (1856–1944) German archaeologist, whose pioneering work in Peru and Bolivia (1892–1912) revolutionized the archaeology of South America. Trained as a philologist, he became interested in Peru while a curator at Dresden Museum, and undertook excavations at Pachacamac, near the coast of Peru, and on Mochica and Chimu sites. He later extended his work into the highlands and to Bolivia, Ecuador, and Chile, making also a notable contribution to North American archaeology with his excavations of the Emeryville shell-mound in San Franciso Bay.

Uhlenbeck, George >> **Goudsmit, Samuel**

Ulanova, Galina Sergeyevna [oo**lah**nova] (1910–) Ballerina, born in St Petersburg, Russia. She studied at the Maryinski Theatre School, and made her debut at the Kirov Theatre in St Petersburg in 1928. She became the leading ballerina of the Soviet Union, and was four times a Stalin Prize winner. She has appeared in several films made by the Moscow State Ballet Company, and in 1957 was awarded the Lenin Prize. She gave her final performance in 1962, and became ballet mistress at the Kirov.

Ulbricht, Walter (Ernst Karl) [**ul**brikht] (1893–1973) East German statesman, chairman of the Council of State (1960–73), born in Leipzig, Germany. At first a cabinet-maker, he entered politics in 1912, and in 1928 became Communist deputy for Potsdam. He left Germany on Hitler's rise in 1933, spending most of his exile in the Soviet Union. In 1945 he returned as head of the German Communist Party, and became deputy premier of the German Democratic Republic and general secretary of the Communist Party in 1950. He was largely responsible for the 'sovietization' of East Germany, and built the Berlin wall in 1961. He retired as general secretary in 1971, but retained his position as head of state until his death.

Ulfilas or **Wulfila** [**ul**filas, **wul**fila] (c. 311–83) Gothic translator of the Bible. Consecrated a missionary bishop to his fellow countrymen by Eusebius of Nicomedia in 341, after seven years' labour he was forced to migrate with his converts across the Danube. He devised the Gothic alphabet, and carried out the first translation of the Bible into a Germanic language. >> Eusebius of Nicomedia

Ulianov, Vladimir Ilyich >> **Lenin, Vladimir Ilyich**

Ullman, Tracey (1959–) Actress and singer, born in Slough, Berkshire, S England, UK. She attended London's Italia Conti Stage School, and went on to gain recognition as an impressionist in the comedy television programme *Three of a Kind*. Success took her to America and her own television programme, *The Tracey Ullman Show*, for which she won an Emmy in 1990.

Ullmann, Liv (Johanne) (1939–) Actress, born in Tokyo. She studied acting at the Webber-Douglas School in London before beginning her career with a repertory company in Stavanger. Her screen image was largely defined through a long association with the Swedish director Ingmar Bergman, in which she laid bare the inner turmoil of women experiencing various emotional crises. Their films together include *Persona* (1966), *Viskningar och Rop* (1972, Cries and Whispers), *Ansikte mot Ansikte* (1975, Face to Face), and *Herbstsonate* (1978, Autumn Sonata), and he wrote the script for her later film *Private Confessions* (1996). She made her Broadway debut in *A Doll's House* (1975), and makes regular theatre appearances. She has worked extensively for the charity UNICEF, and written two autobiographical works, *Changing* (1977) and *Choices* (1984). >> Bergman, Ingmar

Ulm, Charles (Thomas Philippe) (1898–1934) Pioneer aviator, born in Melbourne, Victoria, Australia. He met Charles Kingsford Smith, and joined him in several aviation adventures and an unsuccessful business venture (1927–31). He carried the first airmail between Australia, New Zealand, and New Guinea (1934). In December the same year, investigating the possibilities of regular airmail flights across the Pacific, he set out from California with two companions in his new twin-engine aircraft, but vanished without trace somewhere over the Hawaiian Is. >> Kingsford Smith

Ulster, Alexander, Earl of >> **Gloucester, Richard, Duke of**

Ulugh Beg [ooloog bayg] (1394–1449) Ruler of the Timurid empire (1447–9). A grandson of Tamerlane, he made his name particularly as an astronomer. He founded an observatory at Samarkand, compiled astronomical tables, and corrected errors made by Ptolemy of Alexandria, whose figures were still in use. He also wrote poetry and history. After a brief reign, he was overthrown and slain by a rebellious son in 1449. >> Tamerlane

Ulvaeus, Bjorn >> **Abba**

Ulyanov, Vladimir Ilyich >> **Lenin, Vladimir Ilyich**

Umar >> **Omar**

Umar Khayyám >> **Omar Khayyám**

Umberto I (1844–1900) King of Italy (1878–1900), born in Turin, Italy. He fought in the war against Austria (1866), and as king brought Italy into the Triple Alliance with Germany and Austria (1882). He supported Italian colonialism in Africa, but his popularity declined after Italy's defeat by the Ethiopians at Adowa in 1896. He was assassinated at Monza. >> RR1065

Umberto II [umbairtoh] (1904–83) Last king of Italy (1946), born in Racconigi, Italy. He succeeded to the throne after the abdication of his father, Victor Emmanuel III, but himself abdicated a month later, after a national referendum had declared for a republic. He left Italy, and in 1947 he and his descendants were banished from Italy. He then lived in Portugal. >> Victor Emmanuel III; RR1065

Unamuno (y Jugo), Miguel de [oonamoonoh] (1864–1936) Philosopher and writer, born in Bilbao, Spain. He studied at Bilbao and Madrid, became professor of Greek at Salamanca University (1892), and a writer of mystical philosophy, historical studies, essays, travel books, and austere poetry. His main philosophical work is *Del sentimiento trágico de la vida en los hombres y en los pueblos* (1913, The Tragic Sense of Life in Men and Peoples). He was exiled as a republican in 1924, but reinstated in 1931. As rector of Salamanca, he defied the forces of Franco in the Civil War.

Underhill, Evelyn (1875–1941) Anglican mystical poet and writer, born in Wolverhampton, West Midlands, C England, UK. She studied at King's College, London, and became lecturer on the philosophy of religion at Manchester College, Oxford. She led religious retreats, was a religious counsellor, and wrote numerous books on mysticism, including *The Life of the Spirit* (1922), volumes of verse, and four novels. Her *Mysticism* (1911) became a standard work.

Underwood, Derek (Leslie) (1945–) Cricketer, born in Bromley, S Greater London, England, UK. A slow left-arm bowler, he took 296 wickets in 86 Tests for England, and this total would have been much larger had he not suffered two bans, first for defecting to World Series cricket in 1977, and later for playing unauthorized matches in South Africa. Forty-seven times in his career he took 10 wickets in a match, and very late on he made his only first-class century, for Kent against Sussex at Hastings in 1984. >> RR1150

Underwood, Oscar (Wilder) (1862–1929) US representative and senator, born in Louisville, KY. He practised law in Birmingham before serving as a Democrat in the US House of Representatives (1897–1915). His fight with William Jennings Bryan over tariff reductions in 1911 cost him the critical votes in the 1912 presidential convention. In the US Senate (1915–27) he masterminded wartime appropriations. A second bid for the presidency ended in 1923 when he demanded that the Democratic convention denounce the Ku Klux Klan. >> Bryan

Undset, Sigrid [oonset] (1882–1949) Novelist, born in Kalundborg, Denmark. She worked in an office for 10 years, and after her marriage turned to writing. Her major novels were *Kristin Lavransdatter* (1920–2), a 14th-c trilogy, followed by a series *Olav Audunssön* (4 vols, 1925–7). She became a Catholic in 1924, which influenced her later work, most of which had contemporary settings. She was awarded the Nobel Prize for Literature in 1928.

Ungaretti, Giuseppe [unggaretee] (1888–1970) Poet, born in Alexandria, Egypt. He studied at Paris, and fought in the Italian army in World War 1, where he began to write poetry, first published as *Il porto sepolto* (1916, The Buried Port). He became professor of Italian literature at São Paulo, Brazil (1936–42) and at Rome (1942–58). His poems, characterized by symbolism, compressed imagery, and modern verse structure, became the foundation of the *hermetic* movement (from *ermetico* 'obscure', a term used by a critic of his work). >> Montale; Quasimodo

Ungaro, Emanuel (Maffeolti) [unggaroh] (1933–) Fashion designer, born in Aix-en-Provence, France, of Italian parents. He trained to join the family tailoring business, but went instead to Paris in 1955, worked for a small tailoring firm, and later joined Balenciaga. In 1965 he opened his own house, with Sonia Knapp designing his fabrics. Initially featuring rigid lines, his styles later softened. In 1968 he produced his first ready-to-wear lines. >> Balenciaga

Unitas, Johnny [yoonitas], popular name of **John Constantine Unitas** (1933–) Player of American football, born in Pittsburgh, PA. A quarter-back, he signed for the Baltimore Colts in 1956. Two years later he led them to a championship victory against the New York Giants in overtime. The game was broadcast live in the USA, and helped American football to its big television breakthrough. In 1973 he joined the San Diego Chargers, but was injured after only three games, and retired.

Universalis, Doctor >> **Albertus Magnus, St**

Unruh, Fritz von [oonroo] (1885–1970) Playwright and novelist, born in Koblenz, Germany. He served as a cavalry officer until 1912. An ardent pacifist, the ideal of a new humanity underlies all his Expressionist works, particularly the novel *Opfergang* (1916, Way of Sacrifice). He warned against the Nazi Party in *Berlin in Monte Carlo* (1931) and *Zero* (1932). He left Germany in 1932, and went to the USA, returning in 1962.

Unser, Al (1939–) Motor-racing driver, born in Albuquerque, NM. He won the Indianapolis 500 four times (1970–1, 1978, 1987), beating his brother, **Bobby** (1934–), who won the race in 1968, 1975, and 1981. His son, **Al Unser, Jr** (1962–), has also become a champion auto racer. >> RR1165

Unsworth, Barry (Forster) (1930–) British novelist. He studied at Manchester University and later became writer in residence at the University of Liverpool (1984–5) and

Lund University, Sweden (1988–   ). His works include *The Greeks Have a Word for It* (1967), *Mooncranker's Gift* (1973), *Pascali's Island* (1980, filmed 1988), *Sacred Hunger* (1992, co-winner Booker Prize), and *After Hannibal* (1996). >> Ondaatje, Michael

Unwin, Sir Stanley (1884–1968) British publisher, the chairman of the firm of George Allen and Unwin, founded in 1914. He studied the book-trade in Germany. An international figure in publishing, he was president of the Publishers Association of Great Britain (1933–5) and president of the International Publishers Association (1936–8, 1946–54). His books include an autobiography, *The Truth about a Publisher* (1960).

Updike, John (Hoyer) (1932–   ) Writer, born in Shillington, PA. He studied at Harvard and Oxford, then wrote poetry, stories, and criticism for the *New Yorker* magazine. His novels explore human relationships in contemporary US society, and include *Rabbit, Run* (1960), *Rabbit is Rich* (1981, Pulitzer), *The Witches of Eastwick* (1984, filmed 1987), *Roger's Version* (1986), *Rabbit at Rest* (1990, Pulitzer), and *Brazil* (1994). He has also published several collections of short stories, selected in *Forty Stories* (1987), and a volume of autobiography, *Self-Consciousness* (1989).

Upham, Charles Hazlitt [uhpam] (1908–   ) New Zealand soldier, born in Christchurch, New Zealand. For valour in Crete (1941) and N Africa (1942) during World War 2, he became the only combatant soldier ever awarded the Victoria Cross and Bar.

Upjohn, Richard (1802–78) Architect, born in Shaftesbury, Dorset, S England, UK. Apprenticed to a cabinet-maker, he emigrated in 1829 and became an architect in Boston (1934–8). His first and best-known major building was Trinity Church, New York City (1839–46), which definitively linked the Protestant Episcopal Church with the Gothic Revival style. He designed many residences and public buildings, and his later ecclesiastical architecture incorporated Romanesque and Italianate forms. He was a founder and first president (1857–76) of the American Institute of Architects.

Urbain, Georges [ürbĩ] (1872–1938) Chemist, born in Paris. He became professor of inorganic chemistry at the Sorbonne in 1908. He discovered the rare earth lutecium (1907) and the law of optimum phosphorescence of binary systems, and showed that several elements which were hitherto considered pure were in fact mixtures.

Urban II, originally **Odo of Lagery** (1042–99) Pope (1088–99), born in Châtillon-sur-Marne, France. He became a monk at Cluny, and was made Cardinal Bishop of Ostia in 1078. As pope, he introduced ecclesiastical reforms, drove foreign armies from Italy, and launched the first Crusade. He was beatified in 1881.

Ure Smith, Sydney George [yoor] (1887–1949) Artist, editor, and publisher, born in London, England, UK. He arrived in Australia as an infant in 1888, and was educated in Melbourne and Sydney. His etchings appeared in a number of volumes, including *The Charm of Sydney* (1918) and *Old Colonial Byways* (1928). He published the seminal journal *Art in Australia* (1916–39), founded his own publishing house (1939), and was active in promoting the contemporary arts in Australia through a variety of periodicals and books.

Urey, Harold C(layton) [yooree] (1893–1981) Chemist and pioneer in the study of the Solar System, born in Walkerton, IN. He studied at the universities of Montana, California, and Copenhagen, then taught at Johns Hopkins (1924–9), Columbia (1929–45), and Chicago (1945–58). He was director of war research in the atomic bomb project at Columbia (1940–5). In 1932 he isolated heavy water and discovered deuterium, for which he was awarded the Nobel

Prize for Chemistry in 1934. His work on lunar and planetary formation laid the scientific foundation for space-age exploration of the Solar System. >> Schoenheimer

Urfé, Honoré d' [ürfay] (1568–1625) Writer, born in Marseille, France. He was the author of the pastoral romance, *Astrée* (1610–27), set on the banks of the Lignon, describing the lives of shepherds and shepherdesses whose chief interest was love. It is regarded as the first French novel.

Uris, Leon (Marcus) [yooris] (1924–   ) Novelist, born in Baltimore, MD. He dropped out of high school and joined the Marine Corps, taking part in battles in the Pacific. *Battle Cry* (1956) uses the experience to telling effect, but *Exodus* (1958) remains the book by which he is best known. Depicting the early years of struggle to defend the state of Israel, it was made into a highly successful film. Other novels include *QB VII* (1970), *Trinity* (1976), *The Haj* (1984), and *Mitla Pass* (1989).

Urquhart, Sir Thomas [erkert] (c. 1611–60) Writer, born in Cromarty, Highland, N Scotland, UK. He studied at King's College, Aberdeen, and took up arms against the Covenanting party in the N, but was defeated and forced to flee to England. Becoming attached to the court, he was knighted in 1641. He was present at the Battle at Worcester (1651), where he was taken prisoner and put in the Tower. Through Cromwell's influence, he was allowed considerable liberty, and in 1652 he published his *Pantochronochanon*, an exact account of the Urquhart family, in which they are traced back to Adam. In 1653 he issued his *Introduction to the Universal Language* and the first two books of *The Works of Mr Francis Rabelais*, a brilliant translation and an English classic. >> Cromwell, Oliver

Ursula, St (fl. 4th-c) Legendary saint and martyr. She is especially honoured in Cologne, where she is said to have been slain with some 11 000 virgins by a horde of Huns on her journey home from a pilgrimage to Rome. The legend was very popular in the Middle Ages, and was given strength when a burial ground, believed to be that of the slain virgins, was found near the Church of St Ursula in Cologne in 1106. She became the patron saint of many educational institutes, particularly the teaching order of the Ursulines. Feast day 21 October.

Ussher or **Usher, James** (1581–1656) Bishop and biblical scholar, born in Dublin, Ireland. He studied at Dublin, was ordained in 1601, and became a professor of divinity (1607–21), Bishop of Meath (1620), and Archbishop of Armagh (1625). He settled in England after 1640, and though loyal to the throne was treated with favour by Cromwell. His major work was the *Annales veteris et novi testamenti* (1650–4, Annals of the Old and New Testament), which gave a long-accepted chronology of Scripture, and fixed the Creation at occurring in 4004 BC.

Ustinov, Sir Peter (Alexander) [yustinof] (1921–   ) Actor and playwright, born in London, England, UK of White Russian parents. He first appeared on the stage in 1938, and after army service in World War 2 worked in films as an actor, writer, and producer, and in broadcasting as a satirical comedian. A prolific playwright, his works include *The Love of Four Colonels* (1951), *Romanoff and Juliet* (1956), and *Overheard* (1981). He has made over 50 films, including *Death on the Nile* (1978), *Appointment with Death* (1988), and *Lorenzo's Oil* (1992), and in recent years has established a considerable reputation as a raconteur.

Utamaro, (Kitagawa) [ootamahroh], originally **Kitagawa Nebsuyoshi** (1753–1806) Painter and engraver, born in Tokyo. Trained in Edo (modern Tokyo), he came to specialize in portraits of court ladies in which the gracefulness of face, figure, and flowing robes was depicted with a precise detail and personally developed use of close-up which brought him great contemporary success. He also painted flowers, birds, and fish, and carried the technique of the *ukiyo-e* or 'popular school' to its highest artistic level.

Uthman or **Osman** (?–656) Third caliph to rule after the death of Mohammed. He was elected in succession to Omar in 644. He established a commission of scholars, who collected the revelations of Mohammed to produce the definitive version of the Qur'an. However, his administration was badly organized, and disagreements concerning the division of the gains made in the Muslim conquests gave rise to increasing social tensions, culminating in a revolt in which he was killed. >> Mohammed; Omar

Utrillo, Maurice [ootreeloh] (1883–1955) Painter, born in Paris, the illegitimate son of Suzanne Valadon. Despite acute alcoholism, he was a prolific artist, producing picture-postcard views of the streets of Paris, particularly old Montmartre. >> Valadon

Uttley, Alison (1884–1976) Writer of children's stories, born at Castle Top Farm, near Cromford, Derbyshire, C England, UK. She was widowed in 1930, and turned to writing to support herself and her young son. *The Country Child* (1931) was followed by a series of books, mainly for children, which revealed her knowledge of the countryside. Many were in the Beatrix Potter tradition, featuring much-loved characters such as 'Little Grey Rabbit' and 'Sam Pig'. >> Potter, Beatrix

Utzon, Jørn (1918–) Architect, designer of the Sydney Opera House, born in Copenhagen. He studied at the Royal Danish Academy. His other buildings include the Bank Melhi (Teheran), the Kuwait House of Parliament, Bagsûaerd Church (Copenhagen) and Paustian's House of Furniture (Copenhagen). In 1966 he won the competition for the design of the Zürich Schausspielhaus. He has received many awards for his designs.

Vadim, Roger [vadim], originally **Roger Vadim Plemiannikov** (1928–) Film director, born in Paris. His sensational *Et Dieu créa la femme* (1956, And God Created Woman), starring his wife Brigitte Bardot as a sex-kitten, was a massive box-office success, and paved the way for further sex-symbol presentations of his later wives, Annette Stroyberg in *Les Liaisons dangereuses* (1959, Dangerous Liaisons), Jane Fonda in *Barbarella* (1968), and his lover, Catherine Deneuve, in *La Vice et la vertue* (1962, Vice and Virtue). His later US productions, *Night Games* (1979) and *Surprise Party* (1983), did not arouse the same degree of interest. >> Bardot; Deneuve; Fonda, Jane

Vakhtangov, Evgeny Bagrationovich [vakhtangof] (1883–1923) Theatre director, actor, and teacher, born in Vladikavkaz, Armenia. He became an actor with The Moscow Art Theatre in 1911, and from 1920 was head of the Third Studio, which after 1926 became the Vakhtangov Theatre. In all aspects of his work he made a synthesis of Stanislavsky's and Meyerhold's methods, stressing the expressiveness of the actor. His concept of 'fantastic realism' informed his finest and most influential productions, notably Anski's *The Dybbuk*, staged for the Habima Theatre in 1922. >> Meyerhold; Stanislavsky

Valachi, Joseph (Michael) [valahchee] (1904–71) Gangster, born in New York City. A member of a mob family headed by Lucky Luciano, he worked as a racketeer from the 1930s to the 1950s. He was convicted of drugs offences, and sentenced to 15 years imprisonment (1959). He turned informer, and was the first syndicate member ever to reveal the inner workings of the Mafia (1962). His memoirs were published as *The Valachi Papers* (1968) by Peter Maas. >> Luciano

Valadon, Suzanne [valadõ] (1869–1938) French painter, the mother of Utrillo. She became an artist's model after an accident ended her career as an acrobat, and modelled for Renoir and others. With the encouragement of several leading artists, she took up painting herself, and excelled in her realistic treatment of nudes, portraits, and figure studies, her work having some affinity with that of Degas. >> Degas; Renoir, Pierre; Utrillo

Valdemar I (of Denmark) >> **Absalon**

Valdes, Peter >> **Waldo, Peter**

Valdivia, Pedro de [valdivia] (c. 1498–1559) Spanish soldier, born near La Serena, Spain. He went to Venezuela (c.1534) and then to Peru, where he became Pizarro's lieutenant (1538). He commanded the expedition to Chile (1540), and founded Santiago (1541) and other cities, including Concepción (1550) and Valdivia (1552). In 1559, he attempted with a small force to relieve Tucapel, which was being besieged by the Araucanians, and was captured and killed. >> Pizarro, Francisco

Valens >> **Valentinian I**

Valentine, St (?–c. 269) Roman priest and Christian martyr, said to have been executed during the persecution inaugurated under Claudius II, the Goth; but claims have been made for another St Valentine, supposedly Bishop of Turni, taken 60 mi to Rome for martyrdom. The custom of sending lover's greetings on 14 February (feast day) has no connection with either saint, but dates from the later Middle Ages, when it was believed that this day marked the beginning of the mating season for birds.

Valentine, Alf(red Lewis) (1930–) Cricketer, born in Kingston, Jamaica. A spin bowler of genius, especially in partnership with Sonny Ramadhin, he posed unanswerable problems of spin for the England batsmen during the 1950 tour of England. In 36 Tests he took 139 wickets, twice taking 10 or more in a match, without any previous experience of the English county game. The achievements of the two spinners are immortalized in the famous calypso by Lord Beginner, 'Cricket, lovely cricket'. >> Ramadhin

Valentine, Gary >> **Blondie**

Valentinian I, in full **Flavius Valentinianus** (321–375) Roman emperor (364–75), born in Pannonia (C Europe), the son of an army officer. He rose rapidly in rank under Constantius and Julian, and on the death of the Emperor Jovian was chosen as his successor (364). He resigned the East to his brother **Valens** (ruled 364–78), and himself governed the West, based in Paris, Trier, and other centres, successfully defending it against Germanic invasions. >> Gratian; RR1084

Valentino [valenteenoh], popular name of **Valentino Garavani** (1933–) Fashion designer, born in Rome. He studied fashion in Milan and Paris, then worked for Dessès and Laroche in Paris. He opened his own house in Rome in 1959, but achieved worldwide recognition with his 1962 show in Florence. >> Garavani, Valentino

Valentino, Rudolph [valenteenoh] (1895–1926) Film actor, born in Castellaneta, Italy. He studied agriculture, but emigrated to the USA in 1913, and first appeared on the stage as a dancer. In 1919 he made his screen debut, but his first starring role was as Julio in *The Four Horsemen of the Apocalypse* (1921), which made him a star. His performances in such films as *The Sheikh* (1921), *Blood and Sand* (1922), *The Eagle* (1925), and *The Son of the Sheikh* (1926) established him as the leading 'screen lover' of the 1920s. He became ill and died of a perforated ulcer at the height of his fame, and his body lay in state, attracting crowds, riots, and suicide attempts by his fans.

Valera, Eamon de >> **de Valera, Eamon**

Valerian, Publius Licinius [valeerian] (?–260) Roman emperor (253–60). He was proclaimed emperor by the legions in Rhaetia after the murder of Gallus (253), and appointed his eldest son Gallienus as co-ruler. Throughout his reign there were problems on every frontier of the empire. Marching against the Persians, he was completely defeated at Edessa (260, modern Urfa, Turkey). He was seized by Shapur I (ruled 242–72), and died in captivity. >> Gallienus; RR1084

Valéry, (Ambroise) Paul (Toussaint Jules) [valayree] (1871–1945) Poet and critic, born in Sète, France. He settled in Paris in 1892, and after writing a great deal of poetry relapsed into a 20 years' silence, taken up with mathematics and philosophical speculations, later published as *Cahiers* (29 vols, 1957–60). He emerged in 1917 with a new Symbolist poetic outlook and technique in *La Jeune Parque* (1917, The Young Fate) and *Charmes* (1922). One of his aphorisms was: 'A poem is never finished, only abandoned' – an axiom which applies also to encyclopedias.

Valette, Jean Parisot de la (1494–1568) French knight, born in Toulouse, France. He became grand master of the Knights of St John of Jerusalem (Hospitallers) in 1557. His exploits against the Turks culminated in his successful defence of Malta (1565), where he founded the city of *Valetta*.

Valla, Lorenzo (1407–57) Humanist and critic, born in Rome. He taught classics at Pavia, Milan, and Naples universities.

He was expelled from Rome for attacking the temporal power of the Church in his *De donatione Constantini Magni* (On the Donation of Constantine), was prosecuted by the Inquisition in Naples, but in 1448 was again in Rome as apostolic secretary to Pope Nicholas V (reigned 1447–55). His Latin versions of Xenophon, Herodotos, and Thucydides were much admired, and he greatly advanced New Testament criticism by his comparison of the Vulgate with the Greek original.

Vallière, Louise Françoise de La Baume le Blanc >> **La Vallière, duchesse de**

Vallisnieri, Antonio [valis**nyay**ree] (1631–1730) Naturalist, born in Modena, Italy. He became professor of medicine at Padua, made important studies of the reproductive systems of insects, and wrote treatises on the ostrich (1712) and the chameleon (1715). The waterweed *Vallisneria spiralis* is named after him.

Vallotton, Felix [valohtō] (1865–1925) Painter, born in Lausanne, Switzerland. He studied at the Academy Julian with Toulouse-Lautrec. He was a member of the *Nabis* Symbolist movement, and one of the principal collaborators in *Le Revue Blanche* (1894–1901). His most notable works were wood engravings, which were immensely popular and brought him immediate success. He is regarded as a forerunner of the generation of artist engravers, which included such names as Kandinsky, Munch, and Beardsley. >> Bonnard, Pierre; Denis, Maurice; Roussel, Ker Xavier; Toulouse-Lautrec; Vuillard

Valois, Dame Ninette de [**val**wah], originally **Edris Stannus** (1898–) Dancer, born in Blessington, Co Wicklow, Ireland. She first appeared in pantomime at the Lyceum in 1914, and made a European tour with Diaghilev (1923–5). She became director of ballet at the Abbey Theatre, Dublin, and in 1931 founded the Sadler's Wells Ballet (now the Royal Ballet), continuing as its artistic director until 1963. She is regarded as the pioneer of British ballet, both in her own choreography – such as *The Rake's Progress* (1935) and *Checkmate* (1937) – and in the development of a school and two major companies. She was created a dame in 1951 and made a Companion of Honour in 1982. >> Diaghilev; van Praagh

Valour, Count of >> **Visconti, Gian Galeazzo**

Vámbéry, Arminius [**vam**bayree], originally **Armín Vámbéry** (1832–1913) Traveller and philologist, born in Duna-Szerdahely, Hungary. He travelled to Constantinople, where he taught French in the house of a minister, and in 1858 issued a German–Turkish dictionary. Having travelled through the deserts of the Oxus to Khiva and Samarkand (1862–4), he wrote *Travels and Adventures in Central Asia* (1864). Professor of oriental languages in Budapest until 1905, he published works on Turkish and other Altaic languages, the ethnography of the Turks, the origin of the Magyars, and many other oriental subjects.

van Aken, Jerome >> **Bosch, Hieronymus**

Van Allen, James (Alfred) (1914–) Physicist and pioneer in space physics, born in Mt Pleasant, IA. He studied at Iowa Weslyan College and the University of Iowa, and became director of high altitude research at Johns Hopkins University in 1946, where he used captured German V-2 rockets to carry instruments into the upper atmosphere. He became professor of physics at Iowa in 1951, and was involved in the design and building of the instruments of the USA's first satellite, Explorer I (1958). Using data from this and later satellite observations, he showed the existence of two zones of radiation around the Earth (*Van Allen radiation belts*).

Vanbrugh, Sir John [**van**bruh] (1664–1726) Playwright and Baroque architect, born in London, England, UK. He became a leading spirit in society life, scored a success with his comedies *The Relapse* (1696) and *The Provok'd Wife* (1697), and became a theatre manager with Congreve. As architect, he designed Castle Howard, Yorkshire (1699–1726), and Blenheim Palace (1705–20). He became comptroller of royal works in 1714, and was knighted the same year.

Van Buren, Martin (1782–1862) US statesman and eighth president (1837–41), born in Kinderhook, NY. Called to the bar in 1803, he practised in Kinderhook, was elected to the state Senate (1812–16), and became state attorney general (1816–19). In 1821 he entered the US Senate as a Democrat, and was elected Governor of New York in 1828. He supported Andrew Jackson for the presidency, and in 1829 became secretary of state. In 1832 he was elected vice-president, and in 1836 president. His four years of office were darkened by financial panic, but he did what he could to lighten it by forcing a measure for a treasury independent of private banks. He was strictly neutral during the Canadian rebellion of 1837. >> Jackson, Andrew; RR1097

Vance, Cyrus (Roberts) (1917–) Lawyer and public official, born in Clarksburg, WV. He studied at Yale, became a lawyer, and entered government in 1957. He joined the Kennedy administration in 1960, becoming secretary of the army in 1962. President Johnson appointed him deputy secretary of defence (1963), but he later resigned (1969) and returned to private law practice. He was appointed secretary of state (1977) by President Carter, and is remembered for his work as a peace negotiator, notably towards an arms-limitation treaty with the Soviet Union. He worked with Lord Owen for the UN Security Council as the secretary-general's representative during the Yugoslavian conflict, and was instrumental in drawing up the unsuccessful Vance–Owen peace initiative (1992–3). >> Carter, Jimmy; Johnson, Lyndon B; Kennedy, John F; Owen, David

Vancouver, George (1757–98) Navigator and explorer, born in King's Lynn, Norfolk, E England, UK. He sailed with James Cook on his second and third voyages, was promoted captain (1794), and did survey work in Australia and New Zealand. He is best known for the extent and precision of his survey of the Pacific coast of North America, from San Francisco to S Alaska (1791–4). >> Cook, James

Van de Graaff, Robert (Jemison) (1901–67) Physicist, born in Tuscaloosa, AL. An engineering graduate, he studied physics at the Sorbonne and Oxford, where he devised an improved type of electrostatic generator (later called the *Van de Graaff generator*). At the Massachusetts Institute of Technology, he developed this into the *Van de Graaff accelerator*, which became a major tool of atomic and nuclear physicists.

van de Hulst, Hendrik Christofell (1918–) Pioneer of radio astronomy, born in Utrecht, The Netherlands. While still a student (1944), he predicted theoretically that interstellar hydrogen would be detectable by radio techniques due to the occasional (once in 10 million years) re-alignment of magnetic fields within the hydrogen atom. Such emissions were first detected in 1951 by Edward Purcell and H Ewen. The technique has since proved invaluable in detecting neutral hydrogen in both our own and other galaxies, as well as in interstellar space. In 1970 he became director of the Leyden Observatory. >> Purcell, E M

Van de Kamp, Peter (1901–) Astronomer, born in Kampen, The Netherlands. He studied at Utrecht University, in 1923 emigrated to the USA, and worked at the Lick Observatory, CA, and at Virginia University. He became director of the Sproul Observatory in 1937, and professor at Swarthmore College, PA, retiring in 1972. His best-known work began in the 1960s with his deduction that some stars, other than the Sun, possess planets; several examples were discovered in the 1990s.

Vandenberg, Arthur H(endrick) (1884–1951) US Republican politician, born in Grand Rapids, MI. He studied at the university in Grand Rapids, became editor of the *Grand Rapids Herald* from 1906, and was elected to the US Senate in 1928. An isolationist before World War 2, he strongly supported the formation of the UN, and was delegate to the UN Assembly from 1946.

Vanderbilt, Harold S(tirling) (1884–1970) Industrialist, born in Oakdale, NY. He developed the current scoring system for contract bridge while playing aboard the SS *Finland* in 1925, on a journey from Los Angeles to Havana. He also invented the first unified bidding system and presented the Vanderbilt Cup. >> RR1149

Vanderbilt, Cornelius (1794–1877) Financier, born on Staten Island, NY. From a poor family, he left school at 11, and at 16 bought a boat and ferried passengers and goods between Staten Island and New York City. By 40 he had become the owner of steamers running to Boston and up the Hudson R. In 1849, during the Gold Rush, he established a route by L Nicaragua to California, and during the Crimean War a line of steamships to Le Havre. In 1862 he sold his ships and entered on a great career of railroad financing, gradually obtaining a controlling interest in a large number of railways. He endowed Vanderbilt University in Nashville, TN.

Vanderbilt, Gloria, in full **Gloria Morgan Vanderbilt-Cooper** (1924–) Artist and socialite, born in New York City. As an heiress she was involved in a widely publicized 'poor little rich girl' custody suit at age 10. She achieved notoriety for her four marriages, but considerable respect for her work as a painter, stage and film actress, author, and (after the late 1960s) designer of housewares and fashion.

van der Goes, Hugo [khoos] (c. 1440–82) Painter, probably born in Ghent, Belgium. Dean of the painters' guild at Ghent (1473–5), he painted the magnificent Portinari Altarpiece containing 'The Adoration of the Shepherds' (c.1475, now in the Uffizi Gallery) for the S Maria Nuova Hospital in Florence, and many other notable works. He spent the last years of his life in the monastery of Soignies, near Brussels.

van der Meer, Simon (1925–) Physicist and engineer, born in The Hague. He studied at the Technical University, Delft, and worked at the Philips research laboratories in Eindhoven (1952–5) before becoming senior engineer for CERN (the European Organization for Nuclear Research) at Geneva (1956–90). He shared the Nobel Prize for Physics in 1984 with Carlo Rubbia for their work on the CERN project which led to the discovery of the short-lived subatomic W and Z particles, predicted by the unified electroweak theory. >> Rubbia

van der Post, Sir Laurens (Jan) [post] (1906–96) Writer and philosopher, born in Philippolis, South Africa. He served with the commandos in World War 2, and was captured by the Japanese. On his return to South Africa he made several voyages of exploration to the interior. He wrote novels, but was best known for his books in the mixed genre of travel, anthropology, and metaphysical speculation. These include *Venture to the Interior* (1951), *The Lost World of the Kalahari* (1958), and *The Voice of the Thunder* (1993). *The Seed and the Sower* (1963) was filmed as *Merry Christmas, Mr Lawrence* (1983). A volume of autobiography, *The Admiral's Baby*, was completed in 1996. The influence of Jung is pervasive in his work. He was knighted in 1981. >> Jung; Plomer

van der Rohe, Ludwig Mies >> **Mies van der Rohe, Ludwig**

van der Waals, Johannes Diderik [vahlz] (1837–1923) Physicist, born in Leyden, The Netherlands. Largely self-taught, he studied at Leyden Universiy, and became professor at Amsterdam (1877–1908). He extended the classical 'ideal' gas laws (of Robert Boyle and Jacques Charles) to describe real gases, deriving the *van der Waals equation of state* (1873). This work led others to liquefy a range of common gases, and also provided new basic concepts for physical chemistry. He also investigated the weak attractive forces (*van der Waals forces*) between molecules. He was awarded the Nobel Prize for Physics in 1910. >> Boyle, Robert; Charles, Jacques Alexandre César

van der Weyden, Rogier >> **Weyden, Rogier van der**

van Diemen, Anthony >> **Tasman, Abel Janszoon**

Van Doren, Carl (Clinton) (1885–1950) Critic and biographer, born in Hope, IL, the brother of Mark Van Doren. He studied at the state university and at Columbia, where he lectured in English literature (1911–30). He was literary editor of the *Nation* (1919–22), the *Century Magazine* (1922–5) and the *Cambridge History of American Literature* (1917–21). He wrote biographies of Sinclair Lewis (1933), Benjamin Franklin (1938, Pulitzer), and others, and also edited Franklin's *Letters and Papers* (1947). >> Van Doren, Mark

Van Doren, Mark (Albert) (1894–1972) Poet and critic, born in Hope, IL, the brother of Carl Van Doren. He studied at the state university and at Columbia, where he taught from 1920 and became professor of English in 1942. After World War 1, he followed his brother to the editorship of the *Nation* (1924–8), and was awarded the Pulitzer Prize for his *Collected Poems* (1939). Later volumes include *The Mayfield Deer* (1941) and *Spring Birth* (1953). He edited the *Oxford Book of American Prose* and wrote three novels. >> Van Doren, Carl

van Dyck, Sir Anthony [diyk] (1599–1641) Painter, one of the great masters of portraiture, born in Antwerp, Belgium. He worked under Rubens, who greatly influenced his style, visited England in 1620, and from 1621 travelled widely in Italy, where he painted portraits and religious subjects. By 1627 he was back in Antwerp, and in 1632 went to London, where he was knighted by Charles I, and made painter-in-ordinary. His work greatly influenced the British school of portraiture in the 18th-c. His paintings of the royal family and other notables of the time left a thoroughly romantic glimpse of the Stuart monarchy. >> Rubens

Van Dyke, Dick (1925–) Popular entertainer, born in West Plains, MO. A radio announcer in the US air force during World War 2, he later toured with the nightclub act *The Merry Mutes*, and as half of 'Eric and Van'. He acted as master of ceremonies on such television programmes as *The Morning Show* (1955) and *Flair* (1960). His Broadway debut in 1959 was followed by *Bye, Bye Birdie* (1960–1), which won him a Tony award, and which he repeated on film in 1963. His television series, *The Dick Van Dyke Show* (1961–6), was one of the most popular in the history of the medium, and won him Emmies in 1962, 1964, and 1965. His film career includes *Mary Poppins* (1964) and *Chitty, Chitty, Bang, Bang* (1968), and he returned to the screen as Fletcher in *Dick Tracy* (1990). >> Moore, Mary Tyler

Vane, Sir Henry (1613–62) English statesman, born in Hadlow, Kent, SE England, UK. He studied at Oxford, travelled in Europe, became a Puritan, and sailed for New England (1635), where he was Governor of Massachusetts; but his advocacy of toleration lost him popularity, and he returned in 1637. He entered parliament, became joint treasurer of the navy, and was knighted (1640). He helped to impeach Strafford, promoted the Solemn League and Covenant, and was a strong supporter of the Parliamentary cause in the Civil War. During the Commonwealth he was appointed one of the Council of State (1649–53), but he opposed Cromwell's becoming Lord Protector in 1653, and retired from politics. On Cromwell's death he returned to public life (1659), opposed the Restoration, and was imprisoned and executed. >> Cromwell, Oliver; Strafford

Vane, Sir John (Robert) (1927–) Biochemist, born in Tardebigg, Hereford and Worcester, WC England, UK. He studied chemistry and pharmacology at Birmingham and Oxford universities, then taught at Yale (1953–5), the Institute of Basic Medical Services in London (1955–61), and the University of London (1961–73). He then joined the Wellcome Research Laboratories in Beckenham, Kent (1973–85). He researched the chemistry of prostaglandins, and discovered a type that inhibits blood clots, as well as illuminating the operation of aspirin in treating pain. He shared the 1982 Nobel Prize for Physiology or Medicine. >> RR1124

van Gogh, Vincent (Willem) [hokh], Br Eng [gof], US Eng [goh] (1853–90) Painter, born in Groot-Zundert, The Netherlands. At 16 he worked in an art dealer's, then as a teacher, and became an evangelist at Le Borinage (1878–80). In 1881 he went to Brussels to study art, and settled at The Hague, where he produced his early drawings and watercolours. At Nuenen he painted his first masterpiece, a domestic scene of peasant poverty, 'The Potato Eaters' (1885, Amsterdam). He studied in Paris (1886–8), where he developed his individual style of brushwork and a more colourful palette. At Arles, the Provençal landscape gave him many of his best subjects, such as 'Sunflowers' (1888, Tate, London) and 'The Bridge' (1888, Cologne). He showed increasing signs of mental disturbance (after a quarrel with Gauguin, he cut off part of his own ear), and was placed in an asylum at St Rémy (1889–90). He then stayed at Auvers-sur Oise, where at the scene of his last painting 'Cornfields with Flight of Birds' (1890, Amsterdam) he shot himself, and died two days later. One of the pioneers of Expressionism, he used colour primarily for its emotive appeal, and profoundly influenced the Fauves and other experimenters of 20th-c art. >> Gauguin; Matisse

van Goyen, Jan (1596–1656) Painter, born in Leyden, The Netherlands. He moved to The Hague c.1632, and became a pioneer of realistic 'tonal' landscape, emphasizing the movement of light and shadow across wide plains and rivers under huge cloudy skies. Church towers, castles, and windmills punctuate his small, carefully painted scenes, based on pen-and-ink drawings made while travelling.

van Heemskerck, Martin >> van Veen, Otto

van Leyden, Lucas >> Lucas van Leyden

Vanloo, Charles André (1705–65) Painter, born in Nice, France, the brother of Jean Baptiste Vanloo. He studied in Rome, and settled as a portrait painter in Paris, becoming chief painter to Louis XV and director of the Academy (1763). >> Vanloo, Jean Baptiste

Vanloo, Jean Baptiste (1684–1745) Painter, born in Aix-en-Provence, France, of Flemish parentage, the brother of Charles André Vanloo. He studied in Rome and became a fashionable portrait painter in Paris, where he was appointed professor of painting (1735). In 1737 he visited England, and painted the actor Colley Cibber, the Prince and Princess of Wales, and Sir Robert Walpole. His vigorous, colourful style gave rise to a new French verb, *vanlooter*. >> Vanloo, Charles André

Van Loon, Hendrik Willem (1882–1944) Popular historian, born in Rotterdam, The Netherlands. He emigrated to the USA in 1903 as a journalist and history teacher, and in 1922 published the best-selling illustrated *Story of Mankind*. This was followed by a several other popular histories.

van Meegeren, Han or Henricus [maygeren] (1889–1947) Artist and forger, born in Deventer, The Netherlands. In

1945 he was accused of selling art treasures to the Germans. To clear himself, he confessed to having forged the pictures, and also the famous 'Supper at Emmaus', which had been 'discovered' in 1937, and accepted by the majority of experts as by Vermeer. His fakes were subjected to a detailed scientific examination, and in 1947 their maker was sentenced to 12 months' imprisonment for forgery. >> Vermeer

Vannucci, Pietro >> Perugino

Vanolis, Bysshe >> Thomson, James (1834–82)

van Praagh, Peggy [prahg], popular name of **Dame Margaret van Praagh** (1910–90) Ballet dancer, teacher, and producer, born in London, England, UK. She trained with Margaret Craske (1892–), joined the Ballet Rambert (1933), and created many roles with that company. She joined Sadler's Wells Ballet as dancer and teacher, and worked as producer and assistant director with Ninette de Valois at Sadler's Wells Theatre Ballet (1941–56). She produced many ballets for BBC television and for international companies, and in 1960 became artistic director for the Borovansky Ballet in Australia. She was founding artistic director for the Australian Ballet (1962–79), and a member of the council and guest teacher until 1982. She was made a dame in 1970. >> Valois

Van Rensselaer, Stephen [renseler] (1765–1839) US soldier and politician, born in New York City. He was a leader of the Federalists in his state, and served in Congress (1823–9). In the War of 1812 he held command on the N frontier, and captured Queenston Heights, but the refusal of his militia to cross the Niagara enabled the British to recover the place, and he resigned. He was a member of the US House of Representatives (1822–9), promoted the construction of the Erie and Champlain canals, and founded the Rensselaer Technical Institute (1826).

Vansittart (of Denham), Robert Gilbert Vansittart, Baron [vansitah(r)t] (1881–1957) British diplomat, born in Farnham, Surrey, SE England, UK. Educated at Eton, he joined the diplomatic service in 1902 and served successively in Paris, Teheran, Cairo, and Stockholm, with intervals at the Foreign Office. He was private secretary to Lord Curzon (1920–4), and in 1930 became permanent under-secretary for foreign affairs. He visited Germany, and became the uncompromising, blunt-speaking opponent of Nazism. He insisted on British re-armament, but was ignored by Neville Chamberlain, and steered into a backwater as 'chief diplomatic adviser to the government'. He retired in 1941, and was raised to the peerage. >> Chamberlain, Neville

van't Hoff, Jacobus Henricus >> Hoff, Jacobus Henricus van't

van Veen, Otto (c. 1556–1634) Painter, born in Leyden, The Netherlands. He settled first in Brussels, and later in Antwerp, where Rubens was his pupil. The name *van Veen* is also sometimes given to the Haarlem painter, **Martin van Heemskerck** (1498–1574). >> Rubens

Van Vleck, John H(asbrouck) (1899–1980) Physicist, born in Middletown, CT. He studied at Wisconsin and Harvard, and taught at Minnesota (1923–8), where he expanded Dirac's quantum mechanics to explain the electric and magnetic properties of atoms. His classical treatise, *The Theory of Electric and Magnetic Susceptibilities* (1932), earned him the title 'the father of modern magnetism'. He promoted the union of physics and chemistry, applying his discoveries to chemical bonding in crystals. Returning to Harvard (1934–69), he used his theory in studies of magnetic resonance and in the development of computer memory systems. He shared the 1977 Nobel Prize for Physics. >> Anderson, Philip W; Dirac; Mott, Nevill F; RR1122

Vanzetti, Bartolomeo >> Sacco and Vanzetti

Vara, Madeleine >> Riding, Laura

Varah, (Edward) Chad [**va**ra] (1911–) Anglican clergyman, born in Barton-on-Humber, N Lincolnshire, EC England, UK. He studied at Oxford and Lincoln Theological College, and was ordained in 1936. He worked in various parishes before becoming rector at St Stephen Walbrook in the City of London (1953). Disturbed by the number of people committing suicide, he set up the Samaritans, a free telephone counselling service available 24 hours a day to support those feeling suicidal.

Vardon, Harry (1870–1937) Golfer, born in Grouville, Jersey. He won the British Open championship six times, in 1896, 1898, 1899, 1903, 1911, and 1914. He also won the US Open in 1900, and the German Open in 1911. He turned professional in 1903, and is remembered for the fluency of his swing, and his overlapping grip which is still known as the *Vardon grip*. >> Braid, James (1870–1950); Taylor, John Henry; RR1157

Varèse, Edgar [va**rez**] (1885–1965) Composer, born in Paris. He studied under Roussel, D'Indy, and Widor in Paris, and later under Busoni. After World War 1, he settled in New York City, founded the New Symphony Orchestra (1919), and in 1921 organized the International Composers' Guild, which has become the leading organ of progressive musicians. His work is almost entirely orchestral, often using unconventional percussion instruments, and its abstract nature is demonstrated by such titles as *Metal, Ionisation*, and *Hyperprism*. >> Busoni; d'Indy; Roussel, Albert; Widor

Vargas, Getúlio (Dornelles) [**vah(r)**gas] (1883–1954) President of Brazil (1930–45, 1951–4), born in São Borja, Brazil. He was elected a Federal deputy in 1923, and in 1930 seized power by revolution. His government did much to unify Brazil. From 1937, when he dissolved Congress and suppressed all political parties and trade unions, he governed as a mild dictator. In 1945 he was ousted by popular clamour for a democratic constitution, but under this was voted back to office (1950). Four years later, in the face of mounting opposition, he committed suicide in Rio de Janeiro. >> RR1036

Varley, John (1778–1842) Painter in watercolours, born in London, England, UK. He was a highly successful teacher, and a founder member of the Watercolour Society. A friend of William Blake, he was also interested in astrology and wrote on perspective. His brothers **Cornelius** (1781–1873) and **William Fleetwood** (1785–1856) were also water-colourists. >> Blake, William

Varmus, Harold E(lliot) >> **Bishop, J Michael**

Varro, Marcus Terentius (116–27 BC) Roman scholar and writer, born in Reate. He studied at Athens, fought under Pompey, and in the Civil War was legate in Spain. Pardoned by Caesar, he was appointed public librarian (47 BC), but under the second triumvirate Antony placed his name on the list of the proscribed. His property was restored by Augustus. He wrote over 600 works, covering a wide range of subject matter, but only one on agriculture and part of his book on Latin survive. >> Plautus

Varro, Publius Terentius (c. 82–37 BC) Roman poet, called **Atacinus** from his birth in the valley of the Atax in Narbonensian Gaul. He wrote satires, and an epic poem on Caesar's Gallic wars, called *Bellum Sequanicum*. His *Argonautica* was an adaptation of Apollonius Rhodius, and his erotic elegies pleased Propertius. >> Apollonius Rhodius; Propertius

Varus, Publius Quintilius (? BC–AD 9) Roman general and official, consul in 13 BC. As Governor of Syria he suppressed the revolt of Judaea (4 BC), and in AD 9 was sent by Augustus to command in Germany. He led three legions into a trap set by Arminius, and killed himself after his troops were totally routed. >> Arminius

Vasarely, Viktor [vaza**ray**lee] (1908–97) Painter, born in Pecs, Hungary. He began as a medical student in Budapest before studying art (1928–9) at the 'Budapest Bauhaus' (the Mühely Academy), moving to Paris in 1930. His particular kind of geometrical–abstract painting, which he began to practise c.1947, pioneered the visually disturbing effects that were later called Op Art. He also experimented with Kinetic Art. >> Le Parc

Vasari, Giorgio [va**zah**ree] (1511–74) Art historian, born in Arezzo, Italy. He studied under Andrea del Sarto, and lived mostly at Florence and Rome. He was an architect and painter, best known for his design of the Uffizi in Florence, but today his fame rests on *The Lives of the Most Eminent Italian Architects, Painters, and Sculptors* (1550, trans title), which remains the major source of information on its subject. >> Sarto

Vasco da Gama >> **Gama, Vasco da**

Vassilou, Georgios Vassos [**va**siloo] (1931–) Cypriot politician and president (1988–93), born in Famagusta, Cyprus. He studied at Geneva, Vienna, and Budapest universities, then took up marketing in England. He opened the Middle East Research Centre in Cyprus (1962), which grew into the largest of its kind in the Middle East, and made him a millionaire. Despite a lively interest in politics, he did not align himself with any of the established parties. In 1988, believing that a fresh approach to the divisions in Cyprus was needed, he stood as an independent candidate for the presidency and with Communist Party support, was elected. As president, he worked consistently but without success towards the reunification of the island. He was narrowly defeated (by 0·6%) in the 1993 elections. >> RR1043

Vau, Louis Le >> **Le Vau, Louis**

Vauban, Sebastien le Prestre de [vohbã] (1633–1707) French soldier and military engineer, born in Saint Léger, France. After serving in the Frondes (1651), he joined the government forces in 1653, and by 1658 was chief engineer under Turenne, serving with him at the siege of Lille (1667). He brought about a revolution in siege warfare and fortification; he directed siege operations throughout Louis XIV's campaigns, and surrounded the kingdom with a cordon of fortresses (1667–88). He was created Marshal of France in 1703. >> Turenne

Vaucanson, Jacques de [vohkãsõ] (1709–82) Engineer and inventor, born in Grenoble, France. He went to Paris to study mechanics, and became adept at constructing automata such as a duck which swam, quacked, flapped its wings, and swallowed its food, developing for this delicate work machine tools of lasting importance. Appointed an inspector of silk factories (1741), he devised various improvements to the machines for weaving and dressing the silk, and succeeded in making the first fully automatic loom (1745), controlled through a system of perforated cards. It was cumbersome and not wholly reliable, however, and it was not until the turn of the century, when it was further improved by Jacquard, that it came into widespread use. >> Jacquard

Vauclain, Samuel (Matthews) (1856–1940) Engineer and inventor, born in Port Richmond, PA. After an apprenticeship with the Pennsylvania Railroad shops, he joined the Baldwin Locomotive Works in Philadelphia (1883), and remained with the company for the rest of his life. He perfected a series of improvements to locomotives and became a world authority on locomotive design. As president (from 1919) and later board chairman (from 1929) of Baldwin, he was noteworthy for his hostility to labour unions, once firing 2500 workers he considered to be agitators.

Vaugelas, Claude Favre, seigneur de (Lord of) [vohzhlah] (1585–1650) Grammarian, born in Meximieux, France. A member of the literary circle of the Marquise de Rambouillet, he was the author of *Remarques sur la langue françoise* (1647, Remarks on the French Language), based on the language used at court and by the best writers, which helped to standardize the language. He was a founder of the French Academy. >> Rambouillet

Vaughan, Henry [vawn] (1622–95) Religious poet, born in Newton-by-Usk, S Wales. He studied at Oxford and London, became a doctor, and settled near Brecon. His best-known works are the pious meditations *Silex scintillans* (1650) and the prose devotions *The Mount of Olives* (1652). He also published elegies, translations, and other pieces, all within the tradition of metaphysical poetry.

Vaughan, Herbert (Alfred), Cardinal [vawn] (1832–1903) Roman Catholic cardinal, born in Gloucester, Gloucestershire, SWC England, UK. He was educated at Stonyhurst and at Rome, entered the priesthood in 1854, and in 1872 was consecrated Bishop of Salford. In 1892 he succeeded Manning as Archbishop of Westminster, and the following year was raised to the cardinalate. He was founder of St Joseph's College for foreign missions at Mill Hill, and proprietor of the *Tablet* and the *Dublin Review*. He was responsible for the building of Westminster Cathedral.

Vaughan, Sarah (Lois) [vawn] (1924–90) Jazz singer and pianist, born in Newark, NJ. As a child she sang Gospels in church and studied the organ. Winning a talent competition in 1942, she came to the attention of singer Billy Eckstine, and through him of Earl Hines, who promptly hired her as a singer and pianist. In 1944 she made her first recording with 'I'll Wait and Pray', the following year launching out on a solo career. By the early 1950s she was internationally acclaimed for her vibrato, range, and expression. Her most notable hits include 'It's Magic', 'Send in the Clowns', and 'I Cried for You'. >> Eckstine; Hines

Vaughan Williams, Ralph [vawn] (1872–1958) Composer, born in Down Ampney, Gloucestershire, SWC England, UK. He studied at Cambridge, London, Berlin, and Paris, but remained unaffected by continental European influence, and developed a national style of music deriving from English choral tradition, especially of the Tudor period, and folksong. Notable in his early orchestral music is the *Fantasia on a Theme of Thomas Tallis* (1910) for strings. He composed nine symphonies, the ballet *Job* (1930), the opera *The Pilgrim's Progress* (1948–9), and numerous choral works, songs, and hymns. He also wrote for the stage, as in his music for *The Wasps* (1909), and for films, such as *Scott of the Antarctic* (1948).

Vauquelin, Nicolas Louis [vohklĩ] (1763–1829) Analytical chemist, born in St André d'Hébertot, France. He rose from being an apothecary's assistant to professor of chemistry at Paris (1809). In 1798 he discovered chromium and its compounds, later beryllium compounds, and was the first to isolate an amino acid, asparagine, which he obtained from asparagus.

Vaux, Calvert [voh] (1824–95) Landscape designer and architect, born in London, England, UK. Emigrating at 25, he designed country houses and published *Villas and Gardens* (1852). A pioneer in the public parks movement, he joined (1857–72) Frederick Law Olmstead, and together they produced the winning design for New York City's Central Park. He later designed Ottawa's parliament grounds, which influenced Canadian landscape design. >> Olmsted

Vavilov, Nikolay Ivanovich [vavilof] (1887–1943) Plant geneticist, born in Moscow. He studied at Cambridge and at the John Innes Horticultural Institute, London. He was appointed by Lenin to direct Soviet agricultural research as director of the All Union Academy of Agricultural Sciences (1920). He established 400 research institutes and built up a collection of 26 000 varieties of wheat. This led him to formulate the principle of diversity, which postulates that, geographically, the centre of greatest diversity represents the origin of a cultivated plant. His international reputation was challenged by the politico-scientific 'theories' of Lysenko, who denounced him at a genetics conference (1937) and gradually usurped his position. Vavilov was arrested as a 'British spy' in 1940, and is thought to have died of starvation in a Siberian labour camp. >> Lenin; Lysenko

Veblen, Thorstein (Bunde) [veblen] (1857–1929) Economist and social scientist, born in Manitowoc Co, WI. He studied at Carleton College, Johns Hopkins University, and Yale, and taught at the universities of Chicago (1892), Stanford (1906), and Missouri (1911). He then left academic life, and worked as a writer of literary and political articles in New York City. His best-known work is *The Theory of the Leisure Class* (1899), in which he attempted to apply an evolutionary approach to the study of economics.

Vecellio, Tiziano >> **Titian**

Vedder, Elihu (1836–1923) Painter and illustrator, born in New York City. He studied in Paris and Italy, settling in Rome in 1866. Among his major works are 'Minerva' and other murals in the Library of Congress, Washington, DC, and his illustrations for an edition of the *Rubáiyát of Omar Khayyám* (1884).

Veeck, Bill, popular name of **William Louis Veeck Jr** (1914–86) Baseball executive, born in Chicago, IL, the son of William Veeck who owned the Chicago Cubs (1919–33). He lost a leg in World War 2. He became the owner of the Cleveland Indians (1947–9), St Louis Browns (1951–3), and Chicago White Sox (1959–61, 1976–80). In 1947 he signed Larry Doby (1924–) as the first African-American to play in the American League. He was elected to the baseball Hall of Fame in 1991.

Veen, Otto van >> **van Veen, Otto**

Vega (Carpio), Lope (Félix) de [vayga] (1562–1635) Playwright and poet, born in Madrid. He studied at Alcalá, served in the Armada (1588), and became secretary to the Duke of Alba (1590) and Duke of Sessa (1605). He joined a religious order in 1610, took orders in 1614, and became an officer of the Inquisition. He died poor, for his large income from his dramas and other sources was almost entirely devoted to charity and church. He first made his mark as a ballad writer, notably in the *Arcadia*, a pastoral on the Duke of Alva, and *Dragoneta*, celebrating the death of Drake, both published in 1598, though written some years earlier. After 1588 he produced a wide range of historical and contemporary dramas – about 2000 plays and dramatic pieces, of which over 400 still survive. Several deal with historical or quasi-historical topics, such as *Alcalda de Zalamea*; others deal with everyday life, the most characteristic being the 'cloak and dagger plays', such as *Maestro de Danzar*, *Azero de Madrid*, and *Noche de San Juan*. He also wrote a wide range of works in other genres, such as the epic *Jerusalén conquistada* (1609), the religious pastoral *Pastores de Belén* (1612), and the prose drama *Dorotea* (1632).

Veil, Simone (-Annie) [vayl], *née* **Jacob** (1927–) Administrator and public official, born in Nice, France. She studied law, and worked for the French Ministry of Justice (1957–65), later becoming minister of health (1974–9), and minister of social affairs (1993–5). A popular campaigner for women's rights, she was elected the first president of the European Parliament (1979–82).

Velázquez, Diego (Rodriguez de Silva) [vaylasketh] (1599–1660) Painter, born in Seville, Spain. He studied in Seville, where he set up his own studio in 1618. His early works were domestic genre pieces, of which 'Old Woman

Cooking Eggs' (1618, Edinburgh) is typical. He moved to Madrid in 1823, and on the advice of Rubens, visited Italy (1629–31), which transformed his sombre, naturalistic style into a more colourful approach, influenced by Titian. He then devoted himself to court portraits, executing several of the royal family and other personalities. He is best known for his three late masterpieces, 'Las meninas' (1655, The Maids of Honour, Madrid), 'Las Hilanderas' (c.1657, The Tapestry Weavers, Madrid), and 'Venus and Cupid', known as 'The Rokeby Venus' (c.1658, National Gallery, London). He was knighted in 1659. >> Rubens; Titian

Velázquez de Cuéllar, Diego [vay**las**keth, **kway**ah(r)] (1465–1524) Spanish conquistador and colonialist, born in Cuéllar, Spain. He accompanied Columbus to Hispaniola in 1494, and in 1511 conquered Cuba, of which he became governor (1511–24), and founded Havana. He sent out various expeditions of conquest, including the Mexican expedition of Hernando Cortés in 1519. >> Columbus; Cortés

Velde, Henry (Clemens) van de [**vel**duh] (1863–1957) Architect, designer, and teacher, one of the originators of the Art Nouveau style, born in Antwerp. He started as a painter before pioneering the modern functional style of architecture. A disciple of William Morris and John Ruskin in the Arts and Crafts movement, he founded (with his pupil Walter Gropius) the Deutscher Werkbund movement in Germany in 1906, and was a director of the Weimar School of Arts and Crafts from which the Bauhaus sprang. >> Gropius; Morris, William; Ruskin

Velde, Willem van de [**vel**duh], known as **the Elder** (c. 1611–93) Painter of maritime scenes, born in Leyden, The Netherlands. In 1657 he went to England, and painted large pictures of sea battles in indian ink and black paint for Charles II and James II. >> Velde, Willem van de (the Younger)

Velde, Willem van de [**vel**duh], known as **the Younger** (1633–1707) Painter, son of Willem van de Velde, born in Leyden, The Netherlands. Like his father, he was almost exclusively a marine painter. With him he worked in England for Charles II, which accounts for the large number of his works in English collections. He specialized in depicting naval encounters. >> Velde, Willem van de (the Elder)

Venables, Terry, popular name of **Terence Frederick Venables** (1943–) Football player, manager, and coach, born in London. He began his career with Chelsea (1958–66), then joined Tottenham Hotspur (1966–8) and Queens Park Rangers (1968–73). As a manager, he took Crystal Palace from the third division to the top of the first division (1976–80), then managed Queens Park Rangers (1980–4), Barcelona (1984–7) – who won the Spanish Championship in 1984 – and Tottenham Hotspur (1987–93), where he was also chief executive (1991–3) until a much publicized conflict with club chairman Alan Sugar. Venables later became the English national team coach (1994–6), and then coach to the Australian national soccer team. He was co-author of the 1970s TV detective series, Hazell, and his other writing includes a volume of autobiography (1994) and *The Best Game in the World* (1996).

Vendler, Helen (Hennessy) (1933–) Literary critic and educator, born in Boston, MA. A professor at Boston University (1966–85) and Harvard (1981–), she became poetry critic of the *New Yorker* in 1978. Through her numerous reviews there and in the *New York Review of Books* she exerted a powerful influence over the reputations and publications of contemporary poets.

Vendôme, Louis Joseph, duc de (Duke of) [vãdohm] (1654–1712) French general, born in Paris, the great-grandson of Henry IV. He fought in the Dutch campaign of 1672,

and in the War of the League of Augsburg (1689–97). He commanded in Italy and Flanders during the War of the Spanish Succession (1701–14), was victorious at Cassano (1705) and Calcinato (1706), but was defeated at Oudenaarde by Marlborough (1708), and recalled after the loss of Lille. Sent to Spain in 1710 to aid Philip V, he recaptured Madrid, and defeated the English at Brihuega and the Austrians at Villaviciosa. >> Marlborough; Philip V

Vening Meinesz, Felix Andries [**miyn**es] (1887–1966) Geophysicist, a pioneer of submarine gravity measurements, born in The Hague. After graduating in civil engineering from the Technical University of Delft (1910), he worked on a gravity survey of The Netherlands. He was appointed professor of geodesy at Utrecht (1927), and professor of geophysics at Delft (1938–57). He devised a gravity measuring instrument for use on unstable platforms, modified it for use in submarines to enable gravity surveys of the ocean floor, and made the first marine gravity determinations in the Pacific in 1923. His later voyages led him to deduce the presence of subduction zones, where compressive down-buckling of oceanic crust occurs.

Venizelos, Eleutherios (Kyriakos) [vaynee**zay**los] (1864–1936) Greek statesman and prime minister (1910–15, 1917–20, 1924, 1928–32, 1933), born in Mourniés, Crete, Greece. He studied law in Athens, led the Liberal Party in the Cretan chamber of deputies, and took a prominent part in the Cretan rising against the Turks in 1896. As prime minister of Greece, he promoted the Balkan League against Turkey (1912) and Bulgaria (1913), and so extended the Greek kingdom. His sympathies with France and Britain at the outbreak of World War 1 clashed with those of King Constantine I, and caused Venizelos to establish a provisional rival government at Salonika, and in 1917 forced the king's abdication. He was heavily defeated in the general elections of 1920, but served three times more as prime minister before retiring. In 1935 he came out of retirement against the restoration of the monarchy, but failed to win support and fled eventually to Paris. >> Constantine I (of Greece); RR1054

Venn, John (1759–1813) Anglican clergyman, born in London, England, UK. In 1792 he became vicar there, and a prominent member of the wealthy group of families, with their distinctive religious and social ideals, known as the Clapham sect. He founded the Church Missionary Society in 1799.

Venn, John (1834–1923) Mathematician, born in Hull, NE England, UK. A fellow of Caius College, Cambridge (1857), he developed George Boole's symbolic logic, and in his *Logic of Chance* (1866) worked on the frequency theory of probability. He is best known for *Venn diagrams*, pictorially representing the relations between sets, though similar diagrams had been used by Gottfried Leibniz and Leonhard Euler. >> Boole; Euler; Leibniz

Ventris, Michael (George Francis) (1922–56) Linguist, born in Wheathampstead, Hertfordshire, SE England, UK. As a teenager he heard Arthur Evans lecture on the undeciphered Minoan scripts found on tablets excavated at palace sites in Crete (Linear B), and determined to solve the puzzle. Although an architect by training, after World War 2 he devoted much of his time to analysis of the texts, and in 1952 announced that the language of Linear B was early Greek, a conclusion later confirmed by other scholars. He was killed in a road accident shortly before the publication of his joint work with John Chadwick (1920–), *Documents in Mycenaean Greek*. >> Evans, Arthur

Venturi, Giovanni Battista [ven**too**ree] (1746–1822) Physicist, born near Reggio, Italy. Ordained a priest (1769), he was appointed professor of geometry and philosophy at the University of Modena (1773), and later became professor of physics. His research concentrated on the flow of fluids, and he kept in close touch with the work of Bernoulli and Euler in fluid mechanics. He is remembered for his discovery of the *Venturi effect*, the decrease in the pressure of a fluid in a pipe where the diameter has been reduced by a gradual taper. The effect has many applications, such as in the carburettor and fluid-flow measuring instruments. >> Bernoulli, Daniel; Euler

Venturi, Robert [ven**toor**ee] (1925–   ) Architect and writer, born in Philadelphia, PA. He studied at Princeton, then worked for Louis Kahn before establishing the Philadelphia firm with John Keiser Rauch (1930–   ) that became Venturi, Rauch, Scott Brown and Associates (1958). He spearheaded the reaction against Modernism by embracing historical and popular architectural styles, most notoriously the common commercial strip. His seminal *Complexity and Contradiction in Architecture* (1966) and *Learning from Las Vegas* – with **Denise Scott Brown**, his wife as well as partner, and Steven Izenour – (1972) have been influential. His buildings include the Sainsbury Wing of the National Gallery, London (1991). He won the Pritzker Prize in 1991. >> Kahn, Louis

Verdaguer, Mosen Jacinto [**vair**thagair] (1845–1902) Poet, born in Catalonia, Spain. He became a priest with a vast popular following. He wrote *L'Atlántida* and *Lo canigó*, two epic poems of great beauty, and on the first of these Manuel de Falla based his choral work *Atlántida*. His 'Idilis y cants místichs' (1870), also set to music, have become part of the music of the Catalan church. >> Falla

Verdi, Giuseppe (Fortunino Francesco) [**vair**dee] (1813–1901) Composer of dramatic opera, born in Le Roncole, Italy. Of humble, rural origin, his early musical education was subsidized by locals who admired his talent. He studied at La Scala, Milan, and began to write operas, achieving his first major success with *Nabucco* (1842). *Rigoletto* (1851), *Il trovatore* (1853), and *La traviata* (1853) established him as the leading operatic composer of the day. His spectacular *Aida* was commissioned for the new opera house in Cairo, built in celebration of the Suez Canal (1871). Apart from the *Requiem* (1874), there was then a lull in output until, in his old age, he produced *Otello* (1887) and *Falstaff* (1893). An enthusiastic nationalist in his youth, he came to find active participation in politics not to his taste, and he resigned his deputyship in the first Italian parliament (1860). Later in life he became a senator.

Verdross, Alfred (1890–1980) Austrian jurist. A member of the Permanent Court of Arbitration at The Hague and the International Law Commission, he was a judge of the European Court of Human Rights (1958–77). He was also president of the Institute of International Law, and wrote several works on his field.

Verdy, Violette [**vair**dee], originally **Nelly Guillerm** (1933–   ) Dancer and ballet director, born in Pont-L'Abbé-Lambour, France. She made her debut with Ballets des Champs-Elysées (1945), and subsequently appeared in films and theatre as an actress and dancer. She joined Roland Petit's Ballets de Paris in 1950, later freelancing with a string of companies including London Festival Ballet (1954), American Ballet Theatre (1957), and New York City Ballet (1958–77). She then became artistic director of Paris Opéra Ballet (1977–80) and artistic co-director of the Boston Ballet in 1980. >> Petit, Roland

Vérendrye, Pierre Gaultier de Varennes, sieur de (Lord of) **la** [vayrãdree] (1685–1749) Explorer, who opened up much of the Canadian West, born in Three Rivers, Quebec, Canada. He served with the French army and, after being wounded at Malplaquet, returned to Canada to become a trader, making his base at Nipigon on L Superior.

Fired by Indian tales, he and his three sons travelled over much of unexplored Canada, establishing a chain of trading posts (1731–8) and discovered several lakes, including L Winnipeg. On later expeditions he and his remaining two sons (the eldest having been killed by the Sioux) reached upper Missouri, Manitoba, and Dakota.

Vereshchagin, Vasili [vyereshch**chah**gyin] (1842–1904) Painter of battles, born in Cherepovets, Russia. He was educated at the St Petersburg Academy, and studied art under Gérome in Paris. He travelled widely as a war correspondent, and portrayed what he saw in gruesomely realistic pictures of plunder, mutilated corpses, and executions, with Tolstoy's aim of fostering revulsion against war. He was killed in the Russian–Japanese War (1904–5). >> Gérome; Tolstoy

Verga, Giovanni [**vair**ga] (1840–1922) Writer, born in Catania, Sicily, Italy. A member of the Italian *verismo* ('realist') school of novelists, he wrote numerous violent short stories describing the miserable life of Sicilian peasantry, including *Vita dei campi* (1880, Life in the Fields) and *Cavalleria rusticana* (1884), which was made into an opera by Mascagni. The same Zolaesque theme prevails in his novels, *I malavoglia* (1881), *Mastro Don Gesualdo* (1888), and others. D H Lawrence translated some of his works. >> Lawrence, D H; Mascagni

Vergil >> Virgil

Vergil, Polydore [**ver**jil], Ital **Polidoro Vergilio** (1470–1555) Writer of a history of England, born in Urbino, Italy. Educated at Bologna and Padua, he became a priest, and was sent to England by Pope Alexander VI as deputy-collector of Peter's Pence (1501). He became Archdeacon of Wells (1508), and in 1513 a prebendary of St Paul's, having been naturalized in 1510. He is best known for his great *Historiae anglicae libri XXVI* (Twenty-six Books of English History) which by an order of the Privy Council (1582) became required reading in English schools. About 1550 he returned to Italy.

Vergniaud, Pierre Victurnien [vairnyoh] (1753–93) French politician, born in Limoges, France. He studied in Paris, became an advocate in Bordeaux (1781), and was sent to the National Assembly (1791), where he became spokesman for the Girondins. In the Convention he voted for the king's death, having previously failed to persuade the Assembly to spare the king's life. When the Girondins clashed with the rival revolutionary faction, the Montagnards, Vergniaud and his party were arrested and guillotined.

Verhaeren, Emile [ver**hah**ren] (1855–1916) Poet, born in St Armand lez-Pueres, Belgium. He studied law at Louvain, but turned to literature, writing in French, and becoming a leading figure of the Belgian literary renaissance of the 1890s. His poetry hovers between powerful sensuality, as in *Les Flamandes* (1883) and the harrowing despair of *Les Débâcles* (1888). Among his most notable works are *La Multiple Splendeur* (1906) and the five-part *Tout la Flandre* (1904). He was also an art critic, and wrote short stories and verse plays.

Verlaine, Paul (Marie) [verlen] (1844–96) Poet, born in Metz, France. Educated in Paris, he joined the civil service, but mixed with the leading Parnassian writers, and achieved success with his second book of poetry, *Fêtes galantes* (1869). In 1872 he left his family to travel with the young poet Rimbaud, but their friendship ended in Brussels (1873) when Verlaine, drunk and desolate at Rimbaud's intention to leave, shot him in the wrist. While in prison for two years, he wrote *Romances sans paroles* (1874, Songs Without Words). He became a Catholic, then taught French in England, where he wrote *Sagesse* (1881, Wisdom). In 1877 he returned to France, where he wrote critical studies, notably *Les Poètes maudits* (1884, The Accursed Poets), short stories, and sacred and profane verse. >> Rimbaud

Vermeer, Jan [ver**mayr**] (1632–75) Painter, born in Delft, The Netherlands. He married in 1653, and that year was admitted master painter to the Guild of St Luke, which he served as headman. He gained some recognition in his lifetime in Holland, but made little effort to sell; as a result, his art was forgotten until 19th-c researchers re-established his reputation. He painted small detailed domestic interiors, notable for their use of perspective and treatment of the various tones of daylight. Forty of his paintings are known, among them the 'Allegory of Painting' (c.1665, Vienna) and 'Woman Reading a Letter' (c.1662, Amsterdam).

Verne, Jules (1828–1905) Writer, born in Nantes, France. He studied law at Paris, then turned to literature. From 1848 he wrote opera libretti, then in 1863 developed a new vein in fiction, exaggerating and anticipating the possibilities of science. His best-known books are *Voyage au centre de la terre* (1864, Journey to the Centre of the Earth), *Vingt mille lieues sous les mers* (1870, Twenty Thousand Leagues under the Sea), and *Le Tour du monde en quatre-vingts jours* (1873, Around the World in Eighty Days). Several successful films have been made from his novels. He greatly influenced the early science fiction of H G Wells. >> Wells, H G

Vernet, Carle [vairnay], pseudonym of **Antoine Charles Horace Vernet** (1758–1836) Historical and animal painter, born in Bordeaux, France, the son of Claude Vernet. He was commissioned by Napoleon to paint battle scenes such as 'Marengo' (1804) and 'Austerlitz'(1804) (now at Versailles), and by Louis XVIII for sporting scenes such as the 'The Race' (Louvre). >> Vernet, Claude/Horace

Vernet, Claude (Joseph) [vairnay] (1714–89) Landscape and marine painter, born in Avignon, France, the father of Carle Vernet. A voyage to Rome gave him a fascination for the sea, and he became primarily known for his seascapes. His paintings of France's 16 chief seaports, commissioned by the king, are now in the Louvre. >> Vernet, Carle/Horace

Vernet, (Emile Jean) Horace (1789–1863) Painter of battles, born in Paris, the son of Carle Vernet. He became one of the great French military and sporting painters. He decorated the vast Constantine room at Versailles with battle scenes from Valmy, Wagram, Bouvines, and 'Napoleon at Friedland'. His 'Painter's Studio' depicts him as he loved to be, surrounded by groups of people, boxing, playing instruments, and leading horses. >> Vernet, Carle/Claude

Vernier, Pierre [vairnyay] (c. 1580–1637) Scientific instrument-maker, born in Ornans, France. He spent most of his life serving the King of Spain in the Low Countries, and in 1631 invented the measuring caliper which now bears his name. It makes use of two graduated scales sliding parallel to each other, one of which provides accurate subdivisions of one division of the other scale.

Vernon, Edward, nickname **Old Grog** (1684–1757) British admiral. He joined the navy in 1700, and also became an MP (1727–41). In 1739, during the War of Jenkins' Ear, he was sent to harry the Spaniards in the Antilles, and his capture of Portobello made him a national hero. During the Jacobite rebellion of 1745 his masterly disposition in the Channel successfully kept the standby Gallic reinforcements in their ports. He received his nickname from his grogram coat, and in 1740 ordered the dilution of navy rum with water, the mixture being thereafter known as 'grog'. >> Jenkins, Robert

Vernon, Robert (1774–1849) British breeder of horses, known as 'the father of the Turf'. He became an MP (1754–90), was a founder of the Jockey Club, and established horse-training at Newmarket. In 1847 he gave to the nation the Vernon Gallery.

Veronese, Paolo [vayro**nay**zay], originally **Paolo Caliari** (c. 1528–88) Venetian decorative painter, born in Verona, Italy. He worked at Verona and Mantua, then settled in Venice (1555), where he came to rank with Titian and Tintoretto. The Church of San Sebastiano in Venice contains many pictures of the period before his visit to Rome (1560). His major paintings include 'The Marriage Feast at Cana' (1562–3, Louvre), 'The Adoration of the Magi' (1573, National Gallery, London), and 'Feast in the House of the Levi' (1573, Venice), which brought him before the Inquisition for trivializing religious subjects. >> Tintoretto; Titian

Veronica, St (1st-c) Woman of Jerusalem who, according to tradition, met Jesus Christ during his Passion, and offered him her veil to wipe sweat from his brow, with the result that the divine features were miraculously imprinted upon the cloth. The veil is said to have been preserved in Rome from c.700, and was exhibited in St Peter's in 1933. Possibly *Veronica* is merely a corruption of *vera icon*, 'the true image'. Feast day 12 July. >> Jesus Christ

Verrazzano, Giovanni da [vera**zah**noh], also spelled **Verrazano** (1485–1528) Navigator and explorer, born in Tuscany, Italy. Educated in Florence, he moved to France, where he undertook voyages of exploration on behalf of the French maritime service. He is noted as the first European to sight New York and Narragansett Bays. While exploring islands off the Americas he ventured ashore and was killed by cannibals. The *Verrazano Narrows* at the mouth of New York harbour are named after him.

Verres, Gaius [ve**res**] (c. 115–43 BC) Roman official. Quaestor in 84 BC, he became praetor by bribery in 74 BC, and Governor of Sicily (73–70 BC), where he trampled on the rights of Roman and provincial alike. On his return he was summoned before a senatorial court, and Cicero, for the prosecution, amassed such strong evidence that Verres fled before the trial. He seems to have lived at Massilia, but perished under Marcus Antonius's proscription. >> Cicero

Verrio, Antonio [ve**rioh**] (c. 1640–1707) Decorative painter, born in Lecce, Italy. He was brought to London by Charles II to decorate Windsor Castle, and by William III to decorate Hampton Court and elsewhere. He also executed an equestrian portrait of Charles II, now in Chelsea Hospital.

Verrocchio, Andrea del [ve**rohk**ioh], originally **Andrea del Cione** (c. 1435–88) Sculptor, painter, and goldsmith, born in Florence, Italy. Of the paintings ascribed to him, only the 'Baptism' (1474/5) in the Uffizi is certain, and this was completed by Leonardo da Vinci, whom he taught. He is best known for his equestrian statue of Colleoni at Venice. >> Leonardo da Vinci

Versace, Gianni [ver**sa**chee] (1946–97) Fashion designer, born in Reggio di Calabria, Italy. He moved to Milan, and in 1973 began freelance designing for the Italian labels Genny, Callaghan, and Complice, before launching his own ready-to-wear collection in 1978. He became known for his glamorous styles, producing a range of siren dresses that became his trademark, and often using innovative materials and techniques, such as his use of aluminium mesh, or of 'neo-couture' laser technology to fuse leather and rubber. He worked with the top supermodels, and his designs had enormous appeal among the stars of film and pop music. He was shot dead by an assassin outside his home in Miami Beach, Florida.

Verulam, Baron >> **Bacon, Francis** (1561–1626)

Verwoerd, Hendrik (Frensch) [fer**voort**] (1901–66) South African statesman and prime minister (1958–66), born in Amsterdam. He studied at Stellenbosch, where he became professor of applied psychology (1927) and sociology (1933), and edited the nationalist *Die Transvaler* (1938–48). Elected senator in 1948, he became minister of native affairs (1950), and introduced most of the apartheid legislation with the support of the premier, Strijdom, whom he succeeded. His administration was marked by further development and ruthless application of the highly controversial apartheid policy, an attempt on his life (1960), and the establishment of South Africa as a republic (1961). He was assassinated in Cape Town. >> Strijdom; RR1088

Very, Edward Wilson [veeree] (1847–1910) US ordnance expert and inventor. He served in the US navy (1867–85), became an admiral, and in 1877 invented chemical flares (*Very lights*) for signalling at night.

Very, Jones [vairee] (1813–80) Poet, born in Salem, MA. He studied at Harvard Divinity School (1836–8), but resigned and spent a month in an asylum. After working briefly as a minister, he retired to Salem and became a Transcendentalist poet, publishing *Essays and Poems* (1839).

Vesalius, Andreas [vezaylius], Lat name of **Andries van Wesel** (1514–64) Anatomist, born in Brussels. He studied at Louvain, Padua, and Paris universities, and became professor at Padua, Bologna, and Basel. His major work was the *De humani corporis fabrica libri septem* (1543, Seven Books on the Structure of the Human Body), which greatly advanced the science of anatomy with its detailed descriptions and drawings. He was sentenced to death by the Inquisition for his new approach, which involved dissection of the human body, but the sentence was commuted to a pilgrimage to Jerusalem.

Vespasian [vespayzhn], in full **Titus Flavius Vespasianus** (9–79) Roman emperor (69–79), the founder of the Flavian dynasty (69–96). Declared emperor by the troops in the East, where he was engaged in putting down the Jewish Revolt, he ended the civil wars that had been raging since Nero's overthrow, put the state on a sound financial footing, and restored discipline to the army. Among his many lavish building projects was the Colosseum. He was succeeded by his son, Titus. >> Titus; Vitellius; RR1084

Vespucci, Amerigo [vespoochee] (1454–1512) Explorer, born in Florence, Italy. He promoted a voyage to the New World in the track of Columbus, sailed with its commander (1499), and explored the coast of Venezuela. In 1505 he was naturalized in Spain, and from 1508 was pilot-major of the kingdom. His name was given to America through an inaccurate account of his travels published in Lorraine (1507), in which he is represented as having discovered and reached the mainland in 1497. >> Waldseemüller

Vestris, Auguste, originally **Marie Jean Augustin Vestris** (1760–1842) Ballet dancer and teacher, born in Paris. He made his debut at the age of 12, going on to join the Paris Opera. His brilliant technique and energy led him to become the most celebrated dancer in Europe. The French Revolution drove him to London for five years, but he returned in 1793 to continue dancing in Paris until 1816. He then became renowned as a teacher, his pupils including August Bournonville. >> Bournonville; Vestris, Madame

Vestris, Madame, popular name of **Lucia Elizabeth Vestris** or **Mathews**, *née* **Bartolozzi** (1797–1856) Actress, born in London, England, UK. At 16 she married the dancer Armand Vestris (1787–1825), the son of Auguste Vestris, but they separated two years later, and she went on the stage in Paris. She appeared at Drury Lane in 1820, becoming famous in a wide range of roles. She was lessee of the Olympic Theatre for nine years, and later managed Covent Garden and the Lyceum. >> Vestris, Auguste

Vian, Boris [veeã] (1920–59) Playwright, novelist, and poet, born in Ville d'Avray, France. A Bohemian with a heart condition, he dabbled in many things – acting, jazz, engineering, anarchism, pornography – and excelled in fiction. A tragi-comic writer, he won a cult following for such novels as *L'Ecume des jours* (1947, trans Froth on the Daydream) and *L'Arrache-coeur* (1953, trans Heartsnatcher).

Vian, Sir Philip [viyan] (1894–1968) British naval commander. He trained at the Royal Naval College, Dartmouth. During World War 2, he led a daring rescue of 300 British seamen held on board the German supply ship *Altmark* (1940), and played a leading role in the destruction of the German battleship *Bismarck* (1941). As commander of the 15th Cruiser Squadron in the Mediterranean fleet, he distinguished himself with his skilful handling of escort forces in the hazardous convoy operations for the relief of Malta (1941–2). He later became Fifth Sea Lord (1946) and Admiral of the Fleet.

Vianney, Jean-Baptiste-Marie, St [veeanee], known as **the Curé d'Ars** (1786–1859) Roman Catholic clergyman, born in Dardilly, France. He was ordained a priest (1815) and entered service at Écully. He became priest of Ars in 1818, gaining renown as a holy confessor, gifted with supernatural powers, who was subjected to attacks by the devil. Ars consequently became a place of pilgrimage. He was canonized as the patron saint of parish priests in 1925. Feast day 4 August.

Viaud, Louis Marie Julien [veeoh], pseudonym **Pierre Loti** (1850–1923) Writer and French naval officer, born in Rochefort, France. He entered the navy in 1869, and served in the East, retiring as captain in 1910. His first novel, *Aziyadé* (1879), quickly gained the respect of critics and public alike. He continued to write throughout his naval career, using experiences and observations on his voyages as source material for his books. His best-known novel is *Pêcheur d'Islande* (1886, Fisherman of Iceland), a descriptive study of Breton fisher life in Icelandic waters. Other works include *Rarahu*, published in 1882 as *Le Mariage de Loti* (The Marriage of Loti) – a pseudonym he received from the women of the South Sea Islands.

Vicente, Gil [veesentay] (c. 1470–c. 1537) Portuguese playwright and poet. He accompanied the court, writing many plays and entertainments in both Spanish and Portuguese. He wrote on religious, national, and social themes, as well as farces, and pastoral and romantic plays, all with great lyricism and a predominantly comical spirit. Among his best-known works are *Inferno*, *Purgatório*, and *Glória*, and the farces *Inês Pereira* and *Juiz da Beira*.

Vickers, Jon(athan Stewart) (1926–) Tenor, born in Prince Albert, Saskatchewan, Canada. He studied at the Toronto Royal Conservatory, sang with the Toronto Symphony Orchestra, and made his operatic debut with the Canadian Opera Company in *Rigoletto* (1954). He first sang at Covent Garden in 1957, and at the New York Metropolitan Opera in 1959.

Vickrey, William (1914–96) Economist, born in Victoria, British Columbia, Canada. He studied at Yale, then moved to Columbia University, where he stayed throughout his career. He shared the Nobel Prize for Economics in 1996 for his work in analyzing the consequences of incomplete financial information >> Mirrlees

Vicky, pseudonym of **Victor Weisz** (1913–66) Political cartoonist, born in Berlin. He emigrated to Britain in 1935, worked with several newspapers, and established himself as the leading left-wing political cartoonist of the period. His collections include *Vicky's World* (1959).

Vico, Giambattista [veekoh] (1668–1744) Historical philosopher, born in Naples, Italy. He studied law, but devoted himself to literature, history, and philosophy, becoming in 1699 professor of rhetoric at Naples. In his *Scienza nuova* (1725, New Science), now recognized as a landmark in European intellectual history, he attempted to systematize the humanities into a single human science in a cyclical theory of the growth and decline of societies. Though his historicist philosophy of history was largely neglected in the 18th-c, it undoubtedly influenced many later scholars, including Goethe and Marx.

Victor Emmanuel II (1820–78) First king of Italy (1861–78), born in Turin, Italy. As king of Sardinia from 1849, he appointed Cavour as his chief minister (1852). He fought against Austria (1859), winning victories at Montebello, Magenta, and Solferino, and gaining Lombardy. In 1860 Modena, Parma, the Romagna, and Tuscany were peacefully annexed, Sicily and Naples were added by Garibaldi, and Savoy and Nice were ceded to France. Proclaimed King of Italy at Turin, he fought on the side of Prussia in the Austro–Prussian War (1866), and after the fall of the French empire (1870) he entered and annexed Rome. >> Cavour; Garibaldi; RR1065

Victor Emmanuel III (1869–1947) King of Italy (1900–46), born in Naples, Italy. He initially ruled as a constitutional monarch, but defied parliamentary majorities by bringing Italy into World War 1 on the side of the Allies in 1915, and in 1922 when he offered Mussolini the premiership. The Fascist government then reduced him to a figurehead. He played an important part in effecting Mussolini's fall (1943), but was irremediably tarnished by his association with Fascism. Having relinquished power to his son, he abdicated in 1946. >> Umberto II; RR1065

Victoria, Queen see panel below

Victoria, Tomás Luis de, Ital **Vittoria, Tommaso Ludovico da** (c. 1548–1611) Composer, born in Ávila, Spain. He studied music in Rome, and at Loyola's Collegium Germanicum was appointed chaplain and (in 1573) choirmaster. In 1578 he was made chaplain at San Girolamo della Carità, and c.1585 returned to Spain as chaplain to the widowed Empress Maria in Madrid, where he was choirmaster until his death. He wrote only religious music, his 180 works including several books of motets and over 20 Masses.

Vidal, Gore (Eugene Luther, Jr) [vidal] (1925–) Novelist, playwright, and essayist, born in West Point, NY. He joined the US Army Reserve Corps, which gave him the material for his first critically-acclaimed novel, *Williwaw* (1946), published when he was just 19. His later novels include several satirical comedies, such as *Myra Breckenridge* (1968) and *Duluth* (1983), and the historical trilogy, *Burr* (1973), *1876* (1976), *Lincoln* (1984), and *Live From Golgotha* (1992). His fictional history of America reaches the 20th-c with *Empire* (1987) and *Hollywood* (1989). He has also written short stories, plays (notably *Visit to a Small Planet*, 1956), film scripts, essays, reviews, and a volume of memoirs, *Screening History* (1992), and been active in several other media, including politics, television, and publishing.

VICTORIA (1819–1901)

Victoria, Queen of Great Britain (1837–1901), was born at Kensington Palace, London. She was the only child of George III's fourth son, Edward, Duke of Kent, and Victoria Maria Louisa of Saxe-Coburg, the sister of Leopold who later became King of the Belgians. The Prince Regent (later George IV) insisted she be named after Alexander I of Russia, her godfather, so she was christened Alexandrina Victoria. Her father died soon after her birth, and her mother, by then the Duchess of Kent, came under the influence of Sir John Conroy who, hoping to hold the power behind the throne in the event of the Duchess becoming regent, organized 'regal' tours promoting her.

Victoria reached the age of 18 before the death of her uncle, William IV, in 1837. She was crowned at Westminster in 1838, and her first acts were to exclude Conroy from the Court and to distance herself from her mother. She speedily demonstrated a clear grasp of the constitutional principles in which she had been so painstakingly instructed in the many letters from her uncle Leopold, who remained a constant correspondent. Companioned in girlhood almost exclusively by older people, she developed a precocious maturity and surprising firmness of will, which soon became apparent. Her closest confidant was the Whig prime minister, Lord Melbourne, a gallant and charming adviser, whose opinion the young Queen sought over all matters. With the fall of Melbourne's government in 1839, Victoria invited Sir Robert Peel, the Conservative leader, to form a government, but she set aside the precedent which decreed dismissal of the current Whig ladies of the bedchamber. A political crisis ensued, whereupon Peel resigned, and the Melbourne administration, which she personally preferred, was prolonged for two years.

Next came the question of marriage, and Victoria fell in love with one of the candidates put forward by her advisers: her cousin Prince Albert of Saxe-Coburg and Gotha. They were married in 1840, both aged 20, and after initial pressure of public opinion against Victoria for marrying the 'pauper prince' from Germany, they settled into a harmonious and exemplary relationship. Albert's irreproachable sexual morality was almost unprecedented at court, and the Victorian age came to be synonymous with a great revival of public morality. The royal couple produced four sons and five daughters. Their first son, Edward, Prince of Wales, born in 1841, who was to become the future King Edward VII, infuriated his parents with his wayward behaviour.

Having been strongly influenced by Albert, with whom she worked in closest harmony, after his death (1861) Victoria went into lengthy seclusion, neglecting many duties, which brought her unpopularity. However, with her recognition as Empress of India (1876), under Disraeli's solicitous administration, and the celebratory golden (1887) and diamond (1897) jubilees, she again rose high in her subjects' favour, and greatly increased the prestige of the monarchy. Repeating the preference for Melbourne over Peel, she took a strong liking for Disraeli, and despised Gladstone. At various points in her long reign she exercised some influence over foreign affairs; and the marriages of her children had important diplomatic as well as dynastic implications in Europe.

She grieved for Albert to the end, having his clothes laid out on his bed each evening, his water bowl filled each morning, and sleeping beneath a huge photograph of him, taken when he was dead, which hung over her bed. Victoria died at Osborne, her retreat at Cowes, Isle of Wight. She was the longest-reigning English monarch, and was succeeded by her son as Edward VII.

>> Albert, Prince; Disraeli; Edward VII; Gladstone; Leopold I; Melbourne; Peel, Robert; William IV

Vidal de La Blache, Paul [vidal duh la **blash**] (1845–1918) Geographer, born in Pézenas, France. Educated at the Ecole Normale Supérieure in Paris, he taught there (1877–98) before becoming professor of geography at the Sorbonne (1898–1918). He advocated a regional geography based on the intensive study of small physically defined regions such as the 'pays' of France, and of the interrelations of people with their environment. The founder of modern French geography, he also founded and edited the journal *Annales de Géographie* (1891–1918).

Vidor, King (Wallis) [vee daw(r)] (1894–1982) Film director, born in Galveston, TX. A cinema projectionist and freelance newsreel cameraman, he made his debut as a director in 1913. In Hollywood from 1915, he worked on a variety of film-related jobs before directing a feature film, *The Turn of the Road* (1919). A successful mounting of *Peg o' My Heart* (1922) brought him a long-term contract with MGM. Interested in the everyday struggles of the average American, his many films include *The Big Parade* (1925), *The Crowd* (1928), and *Our Daily Bread* (1934). He also directed Westerns, melodramas, and historical epics such as *Solomon and Sheba* (1959). Nominated five times for an Oscar, he received an honorary award in 1979.

Vieira, António [vyay ra] (1608–97) Missionary, born in Lisbon. He went to Brazil in 1614, where he joined the Jesuit order (1623), and preached widely among the Indians and slaves. He was chaplain to John IV in Portugal (1641–52), then returned to Brazil as director of missions (1653–61). His denunciation of slavery and efforts for the freedom of the Indians forced him to return to Portugal, where he was imprisoned for two years (1665–7) by the Inquisition for prophesying the return of King John, who had died in 1656. Once again in Brazil (1681), he continued to fight for the rights of the Indians.

Vieira, João Bernardo [vyay ra] (1939–) President of Guinea-Bissau (1984–), born in Bissau. He joined the African Party for the Independence of Portuguese Guinea and Cape Verde in 1960, and in 1964 became a member of the political bureau during the war for independence from Portugal. After independence had been achieved in 1974, he served in the government of Luiz Cabral, but in 1980 led the coup which deposed him, becoming chairman of the Council of Revolution and head of state. In 1984 constitutional changes combined the roles of head of state and head of goverment, making Vieira executive president. He was re-elected unopposed in 1989. >> RR1056

Viélé-Griffin, Francis [veelay grifi], pseudonym of **Egbert Ludovicus Viele** (1864–1937) Symbolist poet, born in Norfolk, VA. He was sent to France for his education at the age of eight, and remained there, making his home in Touraine. He became a leading exponent of *vers libre* ('free verse'), which he practised in such books as *Cueille d'avril* (1886, April's Harvest) and *Poèmes et poésies* (1895), and defended in his essays published in the review *Les Entretiens politiques et littéraires* ('Political and Literary Conversations'), which he co-founded in 1890.

Vienna Circle >> **Carnap; Neurath, Otto; Reichenbach, Hans; von Wright; Waismann**

Vigée-Lebrun, (Marie Louise) Elisabeth [veezhay luh-broe], *née* **Vigée** (1755–1842) Painter, born in Paris. Her portrait of Marie Antoinette (1779, Versailles) led to a lasting friendship with the queen, and she painted numerous portraits of the royal family. She left Paris for Italy at the outbreak of the Revolution, and after a triumphal progress through Europe, arrived in London in 1802. There she painted portraits of the Prince of Wales, Lord Byron, and others, before returning to Paris in 1805.

Vigneaud, Vincent du >> **Du Vigneaud, Vincent**

Vignola, Giacomo (Barozzi) da [vee nyoh la] (1507–73) Architect, born in Vignola, Italy. He studied at Bologna, and became the leading Mannerist architect of his day in Rome. His designs include the Villa di Papa Giulio for Pope Julius III, and the Palazzo Farnese in Piacenza. He also designed the Church of the Gesú in Rome, which with its cruciform plan and side chapels had a great influence on French and Italian church architecture.

Vigny, Alfred Victor, comte de (Count of) [vee nyee] (1797–1863) Romantic writer, born in Loches, France. He served in the army (1814–28), then turned to writing. His best-known works include the historical novel *Cinq-Mars* (1826), a volume of exhortatory tales *Stello* (1832), and the Romantic drama *Chatterton* (1835). Several other works, including his journal and the philosophical poems, *Les Destinées* (1864, Destinies), were published after his death.

Villa, Pancho [vee yah], also known as **Francisco Villa**, originally **Doroteo Arango** (1878–1923) Mexican revolutionary, born in Hacienda de Río Grande, Mexico. He lived his early life as a fugitive before joining Francisco Madero's successful uprising against the Mexican dictator, Porfirio Díaz (1909). He fled to the USA in 1912, and after the assassination of Madero the following year formed the 'Division del Norte' (Division of the North). Together with **Venustiano Carranza** (1859–1920), he led a successful revolt against the regime of Victoriano Huerta (1914), but the two leaders became rivals, and Villa was forced to flee to the mountains. He agreed to retire from politics, and was pardoned (1920), but was later assassinated. >> Madero; Zapata

Villa-Lobos, Heitor [vee la loh bush] (1887–1959) Composer and conductor, born in Rio de Janeiro, Brazil. He studied at Rio and travelled widely in Brazil, collecting material on folk music. His many compositions include 12 symphonies, as well as operas, large-scale symphonic poems, concerti, and ballets. He is also known for the nine suites *Bachianas Brasileiras* (1930–45), in which he treats Brazilian style melodies in the manner of Bach. In 1932 he became director of musical education for Brazil. >> Bach, J S

Villars, Claude Louis Hector, duc de (Duke of) [veelah(r)] (1653–1734) French marshal under Louis XIV, born in Moulins, France. He fought in the third Dutch War (1672–8), and in the War of the Spanish Succession (1701–14) inflicted heavy losses on Marlborough at Malplaquet (1709). In 1711 he headed the last army France could raise, and defeated the British and Dutch at Denain (1712). He later became the principal adviser on military affairs, and fought again in his 80s at the outbreak of the War of the Polish Succession (1733–8). >> Marlborough

Villas-Boas Brothers A family of brothers – **Orlando Villas-Boas** (1916–), **Claudio Villas-Boas** (1918–), and **Leonardo Villas-Boas** (1920–61) – who have devoted their lives to the care and welfare of the Amerindians living around the Xingu R, Matto Grosso, Brazil, previously unknown tribes whom they met during a military expedition to the interior in 1943. They were awarded the Founder's Gold Medal of the Royal Geographical Society (1967), and have twice been nominated for the Nobel Peace Prize.

Villehardouin, Geoffroi de [veelah(r)dwĩ] (c.1160–c.1213) French mediaeval chronicler, born near Bar-sur-Aube, France. He was marshal of Champagne, and took part in the Fourth Crusade. His unfinished *Histoire de l'empire de Constantinople* described the events from 1198 to 1207, including the capture and sack of Constantinople in 1204.

Villella, Edward [vilela] (1936–) Dancer, born in New York City. He studied at the School of American Ballet, the High School of Performing Arts, and New York Maritime College, where he was a welterweight boxing champion. He joined New York City Ballet (1957), becoming known for his speed and high leaps, and Balanchine and Robbins gave him roles in such works as *A Midsummer Night's Dream* (1962), *Tarantella* (1964), and *Watermill* (1972). He later became artistic director of the Eglevsky Ballet Company (1979–84). >> Balanchine; Robbins, Jerome

Villemin, Jean Antoine [veelmī] (1827–92) Physician, born in Vosges, France. He studied medicine in Strasbourg and Paris, where he received his MD in 1853. He practised medicine in Paris, and in his spare time carried out research in his private laboratory. He discovered that tuberculosis is a contagious disease (1865), but his results were ignored at the time. He also discovered that certain bacteria could attack other bacteria, for which he created the term *antibiotic*.

Villeneuve, Jacques [veelnoev] (1971–) Motor-racing driver, born in Quebec, Canada. His father, Giles Villeneuve, also a racing driver, moved the family to Monaco in 1978, but at the age of 17 Jacques returned to Quebec to begin his racing career. In 1994, in his first season on the Indy Car circuit, he was named Rookie of the Year, and in 1995 became the youngest driver to win the PPG Indy Car World Series title. He joined Formula One in 1996, driving for the Williams-Renault team, finished second in the World Driver's Championship, and won the Championship in 1997.

Villeneuve, Pierre (Charles Jean Baptiste Sylvestre) de [veelnoev] (1763–1806) French admiral, born in Valensole, France. He commanded the rear division of the French navy at the Battle of the Nile, and saved his vessel and four others. In 1805 he was in charge of the French fleet at Trafalgar, where he was taken prisoner. Released in 1806, he committed suicide in Rennes, during his return journey to Paris to face Napoleon. >> Napoleon

Villiers >> **Buckingham, George Villiers, 1st / 2nd Duke of; Clarendon, 4th Earl of**

Villiers, Charles Pelham (1802–98) British statesman and corn-law reformer, a younger brother of George, 4th Earl of Clarendon. He studied at Haileybury and Cambridge, and was called to the bar in 1827. He was an MP (1827–87), becoming the 'Father of the House of Commons'. He made his first motion in favour of Free Trade in 1838, moving a resolution against the corn laws each year until they were repealed in 1846. He was a member of the Cabinet (1859–66) as president of the Poor-Law Board. >> Clarendon, 4th Earl of

Villiers de L'Isle Adam, comte (Count) **(Philippe) Auguste (Mathias)** [veelyay duh leel adâ] (1840–89) Writer, born in St-Brieuc, France. He was a Breton count who claimed descent from the Knights of Malta. A pioneer of the Symbolist movement, his work includes much poetry, but he is best known for his prose style. He wrote short stories, such as *Contes cruels* (1883, Cruel Tales), and novels such as *Isis* (1862), on the Ideal, and *L'Eve future* (1886), a satire on the materialism of modern science. His plays include *La Révolte* (1870, The Revolt) and his masterpiece, *Axel* (1885). A Catholic aristocrat, he lived for a while with the monks of Solesmes.

Villon, François [veeyō], pseudonym of **François de Montcorbier** (1431–?) Poet, born in Paris. While at university in Paris, he had to flee after fatally wounding a priest in a street brawl (1455). He joined a criminal organization, the 'Brotherhood of the Coquille', and wrote some of his ballades in its secret jargon. Pardoned in 1456, he returned to Paris and there wrote 'Le Lais' (The Legacy, also known as 'Le Petit Testament'), followed by his long poetic sequence, 'Le Grand Testament' (1461). Throughout this period, he is known to have taken part in several crimes, and in 1463 received a death sentence, commuted to banishment. He left Paris, and nothing further is known of him.

Villon, Jacques [veeyō], pseudonym of **Gaston Duchamp** (1875–1963) Painter, born in Damville, France, the brother of Marcel Duchamp and Raymond Duchamp-Villon. He began as a law student, but went to Paris in 1894 to study art, met Toulouse-Lautrec, and exhibited at the Salon d'Automne from 1904. He took up Cubism c.1911, and exhibited with Léger and others working in that new style. He was represented in the Armory Show in New York City in 1913, but did not win international fame until after World War 2. >> Duchamp; Duchamp-Villon; Léger; Toulouse-Lautrec

Vincent, St (?–304) Protomartyr, born in Zaragoza, Spain. According to St Augustine he became a deacon. Under Diocletian's persecutions, he was imprisoned and tortured at Valencia, where he died. Feast day 22 January. >> Diocletian

Vincent de Beauvais [vīsā duh bohvay], Lat **Vincentius Bellovacensis** (c. 1190–c. 1264) French Dominican priest and encyclopedist, who compiled, under the patronage of Louis IX, the *Speculum majus* (Great Mirror). Its three parts, on natural, doctrinal, and historical subjects, were supplemented by a section on morals in the 14th-c, written by an unknown author.

Vincent de Paul, St (c. 1580–1660) Priest and philanthropist, born in Pouy, France. Ordained in 1600, he was captured by corsairs in 1605, and sold into slavery at Tunis, but after persuading his master to return to the Christian faith, escaped to France in 1607. He formed associations for helping the sick, became almoner-general of the galleys (1619), and in 1625 founded the Congregation of Priests of the Missions (or *Lazarists*, from their priory of St Lazare) and in 1634 the Sisterhood of Charity. He was canonized in 1737. Feast day 27 September.

Vinci, Leonardo da >> **Leonardo da Vinci**

Vine, Barbara >> **Rendell, Ruth**

Viner, Charles [vīner] (1678–1756) Legal scholar, born in Salisbury, Wiltshire, S England, UK. He studied law at Oxford, but never qualified and never practised, yet he produced a massive *Abridgment* of the law of England in 23 volumes (1741–56). He left most of his considerable estate to Oxford University to enable it to found the Vinerian Scholarships and the Vinerian chair of English law, first held by Sir William Blackstone. >> Blackstone

Vinson, Carl (1883–1981) US representative, born in Milledgeville, GA. A lawyer, prosecuting attorney, and judge, he served as a Democrat in the Georgia House of Representatives (1912–14) before moving on to the US House of Representatives (1914–65). As chairman of the Committee on Naval Affairs (1933–47) he prepared the Navy for World War 2, and became chairman of the Armed Services Committee (1949–63).

Vio, Thomas de >> **Cajetan**

Viollet-le-Duc, Eugène (Emmanuel) [vyohlay luh dük] (1814–79) Architect and archaeologist, born in Paris. He studied in France and Italy, and in 1840 directed the restoration of Ste Chapelle, Paris. His other restorations included the cathedrals of Notre Dame, Amiens, and Laon, and the Château de Pierrefonds.

Virchow, Rudolf (Carl) [veerkhoh] (1821–1902) Physician, politician, anthropologist, and founder of cellular pathology, born in Schivelbein, Germany. He studied medicine at Berlin, and became professor of pathological anatomy at Würzburg (1849) and Berlin (1856). His *Cellularpathologie* (1858) confirmed Remak's observation that all cells derive from a pre-existing cell, and established the importance of cellular pathology. He contributed to the study of tumours, leukaemia, hygiene, and sanitation. As a Liberal member of the Reichstag (1880–93), he was an opponent of Bismarck. A co-founder of the German Anthropological

Society (1869), he was largely responsible for the growth of anthropology in Germany. >> Bismarck; Remak

Virgil or **Vergil**, in full **Publius Vergilius Maro** (70–19 BC) Latin poet, born in Andes, near Mantua. He studied rhetoric and philosophy in Rome, and became one of the endowed court poets who gathered round the minister and patron, Maecenas. His *Eclogues* (37 BC) were received with great enthusiasm. Soon afterwards he withdrew to Campania, where he wrote the *Georgics* or *Art of Husbandry* (36–29 BC), and for the rest of his life worked at the request of the emperor on the *Aeneid*. When this was almost completed, he travelled in Greece and Asia, but fell ill, and died in Brundisium. >> Maecenas

Virgil, Polydore >> **Vergil, Polydore**

Virgin Mary >> **Mary** (mother of Jesus)

Virtanen, Artturi Ilmari [**veer**tanen] (1895–1973) Biochemist, born in Helsinki. As professor of biochemistry at Helsinki (1939–48), he carried out research into the processes by which plants obtain nitrogen and complex organic substances from the soil. He showed that silage can be preserved by the application of dilute hydrochloric acid, and studied nutrition and the development of food resources, for which he was awarded the Nobel Prize for Chemistry in 1945.

Visconti, Gian Galeazzo [vis**kon**tee], known as **Count of Valour** (1351–1402) Milanese statesman, born in Milan. He succeeded his father, Galeazzo II, as joint ruler (1378–85) with his uncle Bernabo, whom he put to death in 1385. As duke, he made himself master of the N half of Italy, bringing many independent cities into one state, and arranged marriage alliances with England, France, Austria, and Bavaria. He was also a great patron of the arts. >> RR1066

Visconti, Luchino [vis**kon**tee] (1906–76) Stage and film director, born in Milan, Italy. An early interest in music and the theatre led him to stage designing and the production of opera and ballet. A short spell as assistant to Jean Renoir turned his attention to the cinema. His first film, *Ossessione* (1942, Obsession), took Italy by storm, with its strict realism and concern with social problems. Later films included *La terra trema* (1947, The Earth Trembles), *Il gattopardo* (1963, The Leopard), and *Morte a Venezia* (1971, Death in Venice). >> Renoir, Jean

Visser 't Hooft, Willem Adolf [tohft] (1900–85) Clergyman and ecumenist, born in Haarlem, The Netherlands. He studied theology at Leyden, and served young people's organizations until his appointment in 1938 as general secretary of what was to become the World Council of Churches, a post he held until retirement in 1966. A versatile scholar who spoke several languages fluently, he wrote many books, among which were *None Other Gods* (1937), *The Struggle of the Dutch Church* (1946), and his *Memoirs* (1973).

Vitellius, Aulus [vi**tel**ius] (15–69) Roman emperor, a successor of Nero. Appointed by Galba to the command of the legions on the Lower Rhine (68), he was proclaimed emperor at Colonia Agrippinensis (Cologne) at the beginning of 69. His generals put an end to the reign of Otho by the victory of Bedriacum. Vitellius, during his brief reign, gave himself up to pleasure and debauchery. Many of his soldiers deserted when Vespasian was proclaimed emperor in Alexandria. Vitellius was defeated in two battles by his rival, dragged through the streets of Rome, and murdered. >> Galba; Otho; Vespasian; RR1084

Vitruvius [vi**troo**vius], in full **Marcus Vitruvius Pollio** (1st-c) Roman architect and military engineer. He was in the service of Augustus, and wrote the 10-volume *De architectura* (On Architecture), the only Roman treatise on architecture still extant.

Vittoria, Tommasso Ludovica da >> **Victoria, Tomás Luis de**

Vittorini, Elio [vitor**ee**nee] (1908–66) Novelist, critic, and translator, born in Syracuse, Sicily, Italy. He educated himself despite great obstacles, and became Italy's most influential writer of his time, known for the help he gave to younger writers. He was founder editor of *Il Politecnico* (1945–7) and *Il Menabò* (1959–66), and translated modern US writers such as Poe, Steinbeck, and Faulkner. *Conversazione in Sicilia* (1941, Conversations in Sicily) is his masterpiece.

Vittorino da Feltre [vitor**ee**noh da **fel**tray], originally **Vittorino dei Ramboldini** (c. 1378–1446) Educationist, born at Feltre, Italy. He studied and taught at Padua, and in 1423 was summoned to Mantua as tutor to the children of the Marchese Gonzaga. There he founded a school for both rich and poor children (1425), in which he devised new methods of instruction, introducing a wide curriculum, and integrating the development of mind and body through the study of the Classics and Christianity.

Vitus, St [**viy**tus] (4th-c) Christian martyr, said to have been the son of a Sicilian pagan. He was converted by his nurse Crescentia and her husband Modestus, with whom he suffered martyrdom under Diocletian. He is invoked against sudden death, hydrophobia, epilepsy, and chorea (*St Vitus' dance*), and is also the patron of comedians and actors. Feast day 15 June. >> Diocletian

Vivaldi, Antonio (Lucio) [vi**val**dee] (1678–1741) Violinist and composer, born in Venice, Italy. He was ordained in 1703, but gave up officiating, and was attached to the Conservatory of the Ospedale della Pietà at Venice (1703–40). The 12 concertos of *L'Estro Armonico* (1712) gave him a European reputation, and *The Four Seasons* (1725), an early example of programme music proved highly popular. He also wrote many operas, sacred music, and over 450 concertos. Though he was a major influence on the development of the solo concerto, he was largely forgotten after his death; and only after Bach transcribed many of his concertos for the keyboard did they come to be increasingly played. >> Bach, J S

Vivarini, Alvise [vivar**ee**nee], also called **Luigi Vivarini** (c. 1446–c.1505) Painter, born in Venice, Italy, the son of Antonio Vivarini. He was possibly a pupil of both his father and his uncle, Bartolommeo. Influenced by Antonello da Messina and Bellini, his works include portrait busts and altarpieces, especially a 'Madonna and Six Saints' (1480) in the Academy, Venice. >> Antonello da Messina; Bellini, Giovanni; Vivarini, Antonio/Bartolommeo

Vivarini, Antonio [vivar**ee**nee] (c.1415–c.1480) Painter, the founder of the Vivarini studio, born in Venice, Italy. He first worked in partnership with his brother-in-law Giovanni d'Alemagna, and later with his brother Bartolommeo Vivarini. His paintings, often of Madonnas and saints, show the influence of Gentile da Fabriano, Mantegna, and Bellini. >> Bellini, Giovanni; Fabriano; Mantegna; Vivarini, Alvise/Bartolommeo

Vivarini, Bartolommeo [vivar**ee**nee] (c.1432–c.1499) Painter, born in Venice, Italy, the brother of Antonio Vivarini. He was taught by his brother, but was also strongly influenced by the work of Francesco Squarcione. Among his works are several altarpieces in churches of Venice. >> Squarcione; Vivarini, Alvise/Antonio

Vivekananda [vivay**kan**anda], also known as **Swami Vivekananda**, originally **Narendranath Datta** or **Dutt** (1862–1902) Hindu philosopher, born in Calcutta, India. He studied in a Western-style university, and first joined the Brahmo Samaj, attracted by its policy of social reform. Later, he met Ramakrishna and became his leading disciple, establishing the headquarters of the Ramakrishna Order at Belur Math on the Ganges, near Calcutta. He attempted to combine Indian spirituality with Western materialism, and became the main force behind the Vedanta movement in the West. >> Ramakrishna

Vivés, Juan Luis [veevays], Lat **Ludovicus Vives** (1492–1540) Philospher and humanist, born in Valencia, Spain. He studied at Paris but, disliking scholasticism, went to Louvain, where he became professor of humanities (1519). He dedicated his edition of St Augustine's *Civitas Dei* to Henry VIII, who summoned him to England in 1523 as tutor to Princess Mary. His writings include *Adversus Pseudodialecticos* (1570, Against the Pseudo-Dialecticians), and several other works on educational theory and practice. Imprisoned in 1527 for opposing Henry's divorce, he then lived mostly at Bruges. >> Henry VIII

Viviani, René [vivyahnee] (1862–1925) French statesman and prime minister (1914–15), born in Sidi-bel-Abbès, Algeria. He was a lawyer first, gaining a reputation as a spokesman for the poor. He was a Socialist deputy for Paris (1893–1902), minister of labour (1906–13), and minister of education (1913–14). He was appointed prime minister just before the outbreak of World War 1, but resigned after being attacked for a shortage of munitions. He then became minister of justice (1915), and after the War was French representative at the League of Nations (1920).

Vivin, Louis [veevī] (1861–1936) Primitive painter, born in Hadol, France. He was a post office employee until he retired in 1922. He painted mainly still-lifes and views of Paris and its parks. His naive and charmingly-coloured pictures are meticulous in every detail.

Vladimir I, St, in full **Vladimis Svyatoslavich**, known as **the Great** (956–1015) First Christian sovereign of Russia (980–1015), the son of Svyatoslav, Grand Prince of Kiev (d.972). He became Prince of Novgorod in 970, and in 980 seized Kiev from his brother after his father's death. He consolidated the Russian realm from the Baltic to the Ukraine, extending its dominions into Lithuania, Galicia, and Livonia, with Kiev as his capital. He made a pact with Byzantine Emperor Basil II (c.987), accepting Christianity and marrying the emperor's sister. He then ordered the conversion to Christianity of his subjects, punishing those who resisted. Feast day 15 July. >> Basil II; Olga

Vlaminck, Maurice de [vlamīk] (1876–1958) Artist, born in Paris. He was largely self-taught, worked with Derain, and came to be influenced by van Gogh. By 1905 he was one of the leaders of the Fauves, using typically brilliant colour, then painted more Realist landscapes under the influence of Cézanne (1908–14), and later developed a more sombre Expressionism. >> Cézanne; Derain; Marquet; Matisse; van Gogh

Vleck, John Van >> Van Vleck, John H
Vodorinski, Anton >> Ketèlbey, Albert William
Voelcker, Augustus [foelker] (1822–84) Agricultural chemist and writer, born in Frankfurt, Germany. After studying in Göttingen and Utrecht, he worked in Edinburgh, and was appointed professor of agriculture at the Royal Agricultural College, Cirencester, in 1849. His work on farm feeding-stuffs, soils, and artificial manures, greatly advanced agricultural chemistry.

Vogel, Hans-Jochen [fohgl] (1926–) German politician. He was successor to Schmidt as leader of the Social Democratic Party (SPD), and the Party's nominee for the chancellorship of West Germany in 1983. A former minister of housing and town planning (1972–4) and minister of justice (1974–81), he also served briefly as governing mayor of West Berlin (1981). He replaced Brandt to become SPD chairman (1987–91). >> Brandt, Willy; Schmidt, Helmut

Vogel, Sir Julius [vohgl] (1835–99) New Zealand statesman and prime minister (1873–5, 1876), born in London, England, UK. He emigrated to Australia in 1852, and became a journalist. Moving to New Zealand in 1861, he

was elected to parliament (1863), and became colonial treasurer (1869) and prime minister. He is best known for the large-scale public works he initiated with the help of loans he skilfully arranged with the British government. >> RR1078

Vogel, Vladimir [vohgl] (1896–1984) Composer, born in Moscow. He studied in Moscow and under Busoni in Berlin. He composed orchestral works, chamber music, and secular oratorios, including *Wagadu Destroyed* (1935), with saxophone accompaniment. >> Busoni

Vogl, Johann Michael >> Schubert, Franz

Volcker, Paul A [volker] (1927–) Economist, born in Cape May, NJ. After many years in government banking, he served as the chairman of the Federal Reserve Board (1979–87). He then became professor of international economics at Princeton University, as well as a partner in the investment firm of James D Wolfensohn, Inc.

Volstead, Andrew J [volsted] (1860–1947) US politician, born in Goodhue Co, MN. He practised law, and entered Congress as a Republican in 1903. He was the author of the Farmers' Co-operative Marketing Act, but is best known for the Prohibition Act of 1919, named after him, which forbade the manufacture and sale of intoxicant liquors. This Act, passed over President Wilson's veto, was in force until 1933. >> Wilson, Woodrow

Volta, Alessandro (Giuseppe Antonio Anastasio) [volta] (1745–1827) Physicist, born in Como, Italy. He invented the electrophorus, a device to generate static electricity (1775), discovered methane gas (1778), and was appointed professor of natural philosophy at Pavia (1778–1804). Inspired by the work of his friend Luigi Galvani, Volta investigated reactions between dissimilar metals, and developed the first electric battery (1800), providing future researchers with a constant source of current electricity. His name is given to the unit of electric potential, the volt. >> Galvani

Voltaire [voltair], pseudonym of **François Marie Arouet** (1694–1778) Writer, the embodiment of the 18th-c Enlightenment, born in Paris. Educated by the Jesuits in Paris, he studied law, then turned to writing. For lampooning the Duc d'Orléans he was imprisoned in the Bastille (1717–18), where he rewrote his tragedy *Oedipe*. This brought him fame, but he gained enemies at court, and was forced to go into exile in England (1726–9). Back in France, he wrote plays, poetry, historical and scientific treatises, and his *Lettres philosophiques* (1734). He regained favour at court, becoming royal historiographer, then moved to Berlin at the invitation of Frederick the Great (1750–3). In 1755 he settled near Geneva, where he wrote the satirical short story, *Candide* (1759). From 1762 he produced a range of anti-religious writings and the *Dictionnaire philosophique* (1764). Always concerned over cases of injustice, he took a particular interest in the affair of Jean Calas, whose innocence he helped to establish. In 1778 he returned as a celebrity to Paris. His ideas were an important influence on the intellectual climate leading to the French Revolution. >> Calas

Volterra, Vito [voltera] (1860–1940) Mathematician, born in Ancona, Italy. He was professor at Pisa, Turin, and Rome. In 1931 he was dismissed from his chair at Rome for refusing to sign an oath of allegiance to the Fascist government, and he spent most of the rest of his life abroad. He developed a general theory of functionals which strongly influenced modern calculus and analytical methods, and worked on integral equations, mathematical physics, and the mathematics of population change in biology.

von Braun, Wernher >> Braun, Wernher von
Vondel, Joost van den (1587–1679) Poet and playwright, born in Cologne, Germany, of Dutch immigrant parents.

He became a prosperous hosier in Amsterdam, and devoted his leisure to writing satirical verse, himself turning from Anabaptism through Armenianism to Roman Catholicism. Having acquired a wide knowledge of the classics, he turned to Sophoclean drama and produced *Lucifer* (1654) and *Jephtha* (1659). He greatly influenced the German poetical revival after the Thirty Years' War (1618–48). >> Sophocles

von Euler, Ulf (Svante) [oyler] (1905–83) Physiologist, born in Stockholm, Sweden. He studied at the Karolinska Institute in Stockholm, and spent his whole career there (1930–71). He found the first prostaglandin in 1935, and in 1970 shared the Nobel Prize for Physiology or Medicine for his isolation and identification of noradrenaline (norepinephrine), the neurotransmitter for the sympathetic nervous system. He was a member of the Nobel Committee for Physiology or Medicine from 1953, and president of the Nobel Foundation (1965–75). >> RR1124

von Klitzing, Klaus (1943–) Physicist, born in Schroda/Posen, Germany. He studied at Brunswick and Würzburg, became professor at Munich in 1980, and in 1985 was appointed director of the Max Planck Institute, Stuttgart. In 1977 he presented a paper on two-dimensional electronic behaviour in which the quantum Hall effect was clearly seen, but few realized its significance, and he came to appreciate what had occurred only in 1980. He was awarded the 1985 Nobel Prize for Physics.

Vonnegut, Bernard [voneguht] (1914–) Physicist, born in Indianapolis, IA. He studied at Massachusetts Institute of Technology, spent his career with the A D Little Co, and from 1967 became professor of atmospheric science at New York State University. In 1947 he improved a method for artificially inducing rainfall by using silver iodide as a cloud-seeding agent.

Vonnegut, Kurt, Jr [voneguht] (1922–) Novelist, born in Indianapolis, IN. He studied at Cornell, and served in the US Air Force in World War 2. Afterwards he studied anthropology at Chicago University, and worked as a reporter and public relations writer. His novels are satirical fantasies, usually cast in the form of science fiction, as in *Player Piano* (1952), *Cat's Cradle* (1963), and *Galapagos* (1985). He is best known for *Slaughterhouse Five* (1969), based on his experiences as a prisoner-of-war at the destruction of Dresden in 1945. Later novels include *Jailbird* (1979), *Deadeye Dick* (1982), and *Hocus Pocus* (1990). A volume of essays and speeches, *Fates Worse Than Death*, appeared in 1991.

Von Neumann, John [noyman], originally **Johann von Neumann** (1903–57) Mathematician, born in Budapest. He escaped from Hungary during the Communist regime (1919), studied at Berlin and Zürich, and emigrated to the USA in 1933, to join the Institute for Advanced Study, Princeton. Equally at home in pure and applied mathematics, he wrote a major work on quantum mechanics (1932), which led him to a new axiomatic foundation for set theory, and participated in the atomic bomb project at Los Alamos during World War 2, providing a mathematical treatment of shock waves. His mathematical work on high-speed calculations for H-bomb development contributed to the development of computers, and he also introduced game theory (1944), which was a major influence on economics.

Von Stade, Frederica [stahduh] (1945–) Mezzo-soprano, born in Somerville, NJ. She made her Metropolitan Opera debut in 1970, and by the end of the decade was an international favourite, her celebrated roles including Cherubino and Mélisande.

von Sydow, Max >> Sydow, Max von

von Wright, Georg Henrik (1916–) Philosopher and logician, born in Helsinki. He associated with the Vienna Circle of logical positivists and worked closely with Wittgenstein in Cambridge (1948–51). He was professor of philosophy at Helsinki (1946–61), and held many visiting positions in US universities. He has made particular contributions to philosophical logic and to ethics in works such as *The Logical Problem of Induction* (1941), *Norm and Action* (1971), and *Freedom and Determination* (1980). >> Carnap; Neurath, Otto; Reichenbach, Hans; Schlick; Waismann; Wittgenstein

Voragine, Jacobus de [vorajinay] (c. 1230–1298) Clergyman and hagiologist, born in Viareggio, Italy. He became a Dominican (1244), gained a reputation as a preacher and theologian, and became Archbishop of Genoa in 1292. He wrote the *Golden Legend*, a famous collection of lives of the saints, translated by Caxton in 1483, and is also said to have produced the first Italian translation of the Bible. >> Caxton

Voronoff, Serge [voronof] (1866–1951) Physiologist, born in Voronezh, Russia. He studied in Paris, and became director of experimental surgery at the Collège de France. He specialized in grafting animal glands into the human body, experimented with testicle transplants as a means to rejuvenation, and wrote on his theory connecting gland secretions with senility.

Voroshilov, Kliment Yefremovich [vorosheelof] (1881–1969) Soviet marshal, statesman, and president (1953–60), born near Dnepropetrovsk, Ukraine. He joined the Russian Social Democratic Labour Party in 1903, but political agitation soon brought about his exile to Siberia, where he remained a fugitive until 1914. He played a military rather than a political role in the 1917 Revolution, and as commissar for defence (1925–40) was responsible for the modernization of the Red Army. He was removed from office after the failure to prevent the German siege of Leningrad, but stayed active in the Party, and became head of state after Stalin's death. >> Stalin; RR1085

Vorster, John [faw(r)ster], originally **Balthazar Johannes Vorster** (1915–83) South African statesman, prime minister (1966–78), and president (1978–9), born in Jamestown, South Africa. He studied at Stellenbosch, became a lawyer, and joined an extreme Afrikaner movement. In 1953 he became a Nationalist MP, and was minister of justice under Verwoerd (1961), whom he succeeded, maintaining the policy of apartheid. In 1978, after a scandal over the misappropriation of government funds, he resigned for health reasons, and was elected president, but stood down from this position nine months later when an investigating Commission found him jointly responsible. >> Verwoerd; RR1088

Vortigern [vaw(r)tijern] (fl. 425–50) Semi-legendary British king who, according to Bede, recruited Germanic mercenaries led by Hengist and Horsa to help fight off the Picts after the final withdrawal of the Roman administration from Britain (409). Tradition has it that the revolt of these troops opened the way for the Germanic conquests and settlements in England. >> Hengist and Horsa

Vos, Cornelis de (1585–1651) Flemish painter. Working in Antwerp, he chiefly painted portraits and religious and mythological pieces. He worked occasionally for Rubens. His brother **Paul** (1590–1678) painted animals and hunting scenes. >> Rubens

Voss, Johann Heinrich (1751–1826) Poet and philologist, born in Sommersdorf, Germany. He studied at Göttingen, and became a schoolmaster at Otterndorf (1778) and Eutin (1782), beginning a career of major classical translations. He settled in Jena in 1802, and in 1805 became professor of classical philology at Heidelberg. He is best known for his translations of the *Odyssey* (1781) and *Iliad* (1793).

Vouet, Simon [vooay] (1590–1649) Painter, born in Paris. After 14 years in Italy, he returned to France, where his religious and allegorical paintings and decorations in the Baroque style became very popular. He was a contemporary of Poussin, who criticized him but who was not a serious rival during his lifetime. Vouet's pupils included Le Brun. >> Le Brun; Poussin

Vought, Chance (Milton) [vawt] (1890–1930) Aircraft designer and manufacturer, born in New York City. He was taught to fly by the Wright brothers, and was chief engineer of the Wright company until forming his own firm in 1917. Among his famous designs were the Vought–Wright Model V military biplane (1916), the Vought VE-7 (1919), the Vought UO-1 military observation plane (1922–25), and the FU-1 single-seat high-altitude supercharged fighter (1925). >> Wright brothers

Voysey, Charles (Francis Annesley) [**voy**zee] (1857–1941) Architect and designer, born in London, England, UK. A disciple of John Ruskin and William Morris, he designed traditional country houses influenced by the Arts and Crafts Movement, with accentuated gables, chimney stacks, buttresses, and long sloping roofs. He was also an important designer of wallpaper, textiles, furniture, and metalwork. >> Morris, William; Ruskin

Voznesensky, Andrey Andreyevich [vozhne**shen**skee] (1933–) Poet, born in Moscow. Educated as an architect, he published his first two collections *Mozaika* and *Parabola* in 1960. His best-known volume *Antimiry* (Antiworlds) appeared in 1964, and the more difficult poems of *Soblazn* (Temptation) in 1979. The rock musical *Avos*, based on one of his poems, was produced in Moscow in 1981.

Vranitzky, Franz [vra**nit**skee] (1937–) Austrian statesman and chancellor (1986–97). He studied at what is now the University of Commerce, Vienna, embarked on a career in banking, and in 1970 became adviser on economic and financial policy to the minister of finance.

After holding senior appointments in the banking world he became minister of finance himself in 1984, and then federal chancellor. >> RR1033

Vriendt, Cornelis de >> **Floris**

Vries, Hugo / Peter de >> **de Vries, Hugo / Peter**

Vuillard, (Jean) Edouard [vweeyah(r)] (1868–1940) Painter and printmaker, born in Cuiseaux, France. One of the later Impressionists, a member of *Les Nabis*, he was influenced by Gauguin and the vogue for Japanese painting. He executed mainly flower pieces and simple interiors, painted with a great sense of light and colour, and is also known for his textiles, wallpapers, and decorative work in public buildings. >> Bonnard, Pierre; Denis, Maurice; Gauguin; Roussel, Ker; Vallotton; Xavier

Vygotsky, Lev Semenovich [vi**got**skee] (1896–1934) Psychologist, born in Orsha, Belarus. Originally a teacher and literary scholar with interests in creativity, he took up a scientific post at the Institute of Psychology in Moscow in 1924. He examined contemporary psychology, notably behaviourism and introspectionism, attempting to establish a Marxist view that thought originates in interactions, which themselves are influenced by social history. His writings, such as *Thought and Language* (1934–62) and *Mind in Society* (1978), have had a major influence on Soviet and (since the 1960s) Western psychology, particularly on specialists in child development.

Vyshinsky, Andrey Yanuaryevich [vi**shin**skee] (1883–1954) Russian jurist and politician, born in Odessa, Ukraine. He studied law at Moscow, joined the Communist Party in 1920, and became professor of criminal law and attorney general (1923–5). He was the public prosecutor at the state trials (1936–8) which removed Stalin's rivals, and later became the Soviet delegate to the UN (1945–9, 1953–4), and foreign minister (1949–53). >> Stalin

Waage, Peter >> Guldberg, Cato Maximilian
Waals, Johannes Diderik van der >> van der Waals, Johannes Diderik
Wace, Robert [ways] (12th-c) Anglo-Norman poet, born in Jersey, Channel Is. He studied in Paris, and was a Canon of Bayeux (1160–70). He wrote several verse lives of the saints, a Norman-French version of Geoffrey of Monmouth's *Historia regum Britanniae* entitled the *Roman de Brut* (1155), and the *Roman de Rou* (1160–74), an epic of the exploits of the Dukes of Normandy. >> Geoffrey of Monmouth

Waddington, C(onrad) H(al) (1905–75) Embryologist and geneticist, born in Evesham, Hereford and Worcester, WC England, UK. He studied at Cambridge, and became professor of animal genetics at Edinburgh (1947–70). He introduced important concepts into evolutionary theory, envisaging a mechanism by which Lamarckianism could be incorporated into orthodox Darwinian genetics. He wrote a standard textbook, *Principles of Embryology* (1956), and also helped to popularize science in such general books as *The Ethical Animal* (1960). >> Lamarck

Waddington (of Read), David Charles Waddington, Baron (1929–) British statesman. He studied at Oxford, and was called to the bar in 1951. He became an MP in 1968, and after a number of junior posts under Margaret Thatcher he was made government chief whip (1987–9), and became home secretary (1989–90). Created a baron in 1990, he was appointed Lord Privy Seal and Leader of the House of Lords (1990–2). Since 1992 he has been governor of Bermuda.

Wade, George (1673–1748) English soldier, probably born in Westmeath, Ireland. He entered the army in 1690, and after the Jacobite rebellion of 1715 judiciously pacified and disarmed the clans in the Scottish highlands, where he constructed (1726–37) a system of metalled military roads, with 40 stone (*Wade*) bridges. During the Jacobite Rising of 1745 he was commander-in-chief of George II's forces in England, but failed to engage Prince Charles Stuart's army, and was replaced by the Duke of Cumberland. >> Stuart, Charles

Wade, Sir Thomas (Francis) (1818–95) English diplomat and scholar, born in London, England, UK. After a short career as a soldier, including active service in China, he became a member of the diplomatic corps in China and was the British ambassador in Beijing (1871–83). In 1888 he was appointed the first professor of Chinese at Cambridge, holding this post until 1895. Among his works is the *Peking Syllabary* (1859), in which his own system of romanization is employed; this transliteration system was later modified by Wade's successor at Cambridge, Herbert Giles, and is now referred to as the *Wade–Giles* system. >> Giles, H A

Wade, (Sarah) Virginia (1945–) Tennis player, born in Bournemouth, Dorset, S England, UK. She was brought up in South Africa. She competed at Wimbledon for 20 years, and won the singles there in 1977 when she was ranked number two. In 1968 she took the US Open title, and she also won the Italian championship in 1971 and the French championship in 1972. She was a Wightman Cup player for 16 years, and towards the end of her career captained the side. >> RR1174

Wadsworth, Edward (1889–1949) Artist, born in Yorkshire, N England, UK. He studied engineering in Munich, attended the Slade School of Art, London, in 1910, and was associated with Wyndham Lewis, Roger Fry, Unit One, and the London Group. He is known for his still-lifes and seascapes with marine objects, painted in tempera with dreamlike clarity and precision. >> Fry, Roger; Lewis, Wyndham

Waerden, van der, Bartel Leendert [vairden] (1903–) Mathematician, born in Amsterdam, The Netherlands. He studied at Amsterdam University, and became professor at Groningen (1928–31), Leipzig (1931–45), Johns Hopkins (1947–8), Amsterdam (1948–51), and Zürich (1951–62). He has worked in algebra, algebraic geometry, and mathematical physics, and more recently has published books on the history of science and mathematics in the ancient world, such as *Science Awakening* (1954). His classic textbook, *Modern Algebra*, (1931) was influential in publicizing the new algebra developed by Hilbert, Artin, and others. >> Artin; Hilbert

Wagenfeld, Wilhelm [vahgenfelt] (1900–) Designer of glassware and ceramics, born in Bremen, Germany. He studied, and later taught, at the Bauhaus, and has remained faithful to the principles which it enshrined. His designs are simple, unadorned, and functional. Best known are those for mass-produced glass, and for Rosenthal ceramics. He has taught during much of his career, thus extending his influence as a designer.

Wagley, Charles (Walter) (1913–91) Anthropologist, born in Clarksville, TX. He studied under Franz Boas at Columbia University, where he spent most of his career teaching (1946–71, 1965–71) and also directing the Institute of Latin American Studies (1961–9). A social anthropologist, he worked in the 1930s among the descendants of the Maya in Guatemala, and in the 1940s was among the first Americans to work in the South American lowlands, notably in Brazil. >> Boas

Wagner, Honus [wagner], properly **John Peter Wagner**, nickname **the Flying Dutchman** (1874–1955) Baseball player, born in Carnegie, PA. An all-round player, he had a 21-year career as an infielder (1897–1917), mostly with the Pittsburgh Pirates. An outstanding right-handed hitter with exceptional speed, he holds the National League record for the most consecutive seasons batting ·300 or more (17). After his retirement, he served as coach for the Pirates for 19 years (1933–51). He was elected to baseball's Hall of Fame in 1936.

Wagner, Otto [vahgner] (1841–1918) Architect and teacher, born in Penzing, Austria. Professor at the Vienna Academy (1894–1912), he was the founder of the Vienna School, his pupils including Josef Hoffmann and Josef Olbrich. Though for many years a classical revivalist, he became an important advocate of purely functional architecture. His most influential work, produced at the end of his career, includes several stations in Vienna, and the Vienna Postal Savings Bank (1904–6), regarded as the first example of modern architecture in the 20th-c. >> Hoffmann, Josef; Olbrich

Wagner, (Wilhelm) Richard [vahgner] see panel on p. 968
Wagner, Robert (John) [wagner] (1930–) Film and television actor, born in Detroit, MI. He attended Black-Foxe Military Institute, then won an acting contract with Twentieth Century-Fox. He played juvenile leads in a succession of war, Western, and adventure films, such as *The True Story of Jesse James* (1957). His greatest popularity has been in television series, where his boyish romantic

(WILHELM) RICHARD WAGNER (1813–83)

Wagner was born in Leipzig, Germany, probably the son of the police actuary Friedrich Wagner, his mother's husband (who died six months after his birth); or possibly the son of Ludwig Geyer, painter, actor, and poet, who married his mother, Johanna Rosine Pätz, soon afterwards. Richard was educated in Dresden, and later in Leipzig at St Thomas's School (1830) and at the university (1831–3). His chief interest was music; he studied harmony, piano, and violin, and religiously copied out Beethoven's symphonies for personal study.

Leaving the university in 1833, he wrote the opera *Die Feen* (The Fairies), which was not heard until after his death. He became musical director of a theatre company in Magdeburg, where his first opera to gain a hearing was *Das Liebesverbot* (The Ban on Love – based on Shakespeare's *Measure for Measure*) in 1836, but it was a disastrous performance. His marriage (1836) to **Wilhelmine (Minna) Planer** (d.1866), a soprano with the theatre company, was also a failure; she lived with another man for several months the following year, rejoining Wagner only when he was appointed conductor at the theatre in Riga on the Baltic (1837).

By 1839 Wagner was working on *Rienzi* (completed 1840) which, being in the grand opera tradition, he wanted to take to Paris. He was not reappointed in Riga, and debts were mounting, so he and his wife fled to Paris, stowing away on a ship via the Norwegian coast and England. In Paris, he scraped through by journalism and hack work, being unable to break into the operatic circle there, but *Rienzi* was accepted by the Dresden Court Opera, and in 1842 he was in Dresden for its triumphant premiere. Three months later *Der Fliegende Holländer* (1843, The Flying Dutchman) followed, confusing an expectant audience with its brevity and dramatic style.

Accepting the post of Kapellmeister at Dresden (1843–9), Wagner at last found security. He stifled his revolutionary leanings and concentrated on writing *Tannhäuser* (1845) and *Lohengrin* (1847), both based on Germanic legends, as were all his future works. Unfortunately, *Lohengrin* was not staged in Dresden because of the controversial artistic reforms it required, and an alienated Wagner became caught up first in social causes, then in political activity during the German revolution of 1848–9, siding with the rebels in 1849. Banned from Germany, he fled to Weimar (where *Lohengrin* had limited success), then to Switzerland, where he spent most of the 1850s active in the musical life of Zürich.

Throughout his career Wagner was a prolific writer of essays, criticism, and theoretical studies, and his important book *Oper und Drama* (Opera and Drama) was published in 1850. The poem of the *Ring* cycle was finished in 1852, and in 1853 he began to write *Das Rheingold* (The Rheingold), followed by *Die Walküre* (1856, The Valkyries) and the first two acts of *Siegfried* (1857).

In 1861 he was allowed to return to Germany, but still lacked recognition and support, and had to flee to Vienna to avoid imprisonment for debt. In 1864 he was saved from ruin by the eccentric young King of Bavaria, Ludwig II, who had become a fanatical admirer of his work, and who offered him every facility at Munich. There Wagner embarked on an affair with **Cosima von Bülow**, the daughter of Liszt, and wife of Wagner's musical director, Hans von Bülow, not his first extramarital adventure. Their daughter Isolde was born in 1865, named after Wagner's *Tristan und Isolde* (1857–9, first performed in 1865). The ensuing scandal caused Ludwig to withdraw his support (but not his friendship), and to ask Wagner to leave Munich (1865).

Minna died in 1866, leaving Wagner free to marry the now-divorced Cosima in 1870, by which time she had borne him two more children **Eva** and **Siegfried**. At their home by L Lucerne, Cosima devoted herself entirely to his needs, writing down his autobiography from dictation. To fulfil his ambition to give a complete performance of the *Ring* (*Walküre*, *Siegfried*, and *Götterdämmerung*, with *Rheingold* as the introduction), Wagner started the now famous theatre at Bayreuth, which opened in 1876. *Parsifal*, his last opera, was staged in 1882, a year before his sudden death from a heart attack, in Venice.
>> Bülow, von; Ludwig II

appeal, suave manner, and light humour were seen in *It Takes A Thief* (1965–9), *Switch* (1975–7), and *Hart to Hart* (1979–84), in which he co-starred with his wife, Natalie Wood. >> Wood, Natalie

Wagner, Siegfried [**vahg**ner] (1869–1930) Musician, born near Lucerne, Switzerland, the son of Richard Wagner. He was trained as an architect, but later became a conductor and composer of operas and other music. He was director of the Bayreuth Festspielhaus from 1909. In 1915 he married **Winifred Williams** (1897–1980), who later directed the Bayreuth Festivals until 1944. >> Wagner, Richard

Wagner, Wieland [**vahg**ner] (1917–66) Opera house director, born in Bayreuth, Germany, the son of Siegfried Wagner. He took over the directorship of the Festspielhaus after World War 2, and revolutionized the production of the operas, stressing their universality as opposed to their purely German significance. >> Wagner, Siegfried

Wagner-Jauregg, Julius [**vahg**ner **yow**rek], originally **Julius Wagner, Ritter** (Knight) **von Jauregg** (1857–1940) Neurologist and psychiatrist, born in Wels, Austria. He became professor at Vienna (1883–9) and Graz (1889–93), then returned to Vienna, where he directed the university hospital for nervous and mental diseases until 1928. He was awarded the 1927 Nobel Prize for Physiology or Medicine for his discovery in 1917 of a treatment for general paralysis by infection with malaria, the forerunner of shock therapy.

Wagoner, Dan (1932–) Modern dancer and choreographer, born in Springfield, WV. He held a degree in pharmacy, but by his mid-20s was dancing full time, studying dance at Connecticut College and then with Martha Graham in New York City. From 1958 he performed with her company and with the Merce Cunningham Dance Company. He joined Paul Taylor's company in 1962, creating many roles, and in 1969 formed the small group, Dan Wagoner and Dancers. With the retirement of Robert Cohan he was appointed artistic director of the London Contemporary Dance Company in 1988. >> Cohan; Cunningham, Merce; Graham, Martha; Taylor, Paul

Wain, John (Barrington) [wayn] (1925–94) Writer and

critic, born in Stoke-on-Trent, Staffordshire, C England, UK. He studied at Oxford, and lectured in English at Reading (1947–55) before becoming a freelance writer. His novels include *Hurry on Down* (1953) and *The Contenders* (1958), tilting at post-war British social values as viewed by a provincial. He also wrote poetry (*Poems, 1949–79* appeared in 1981), plays, and several books of literary criticism, notably *Preliminary Essays* (1957). He was professor of poetry at Oxford (1973–8). Later books include *Lizzie's Floating Shop* (1981), *Young Shoulders* (1982, Whitbread), and *Comedies* (1990). He also produced two volumes of autobiography, *Sprightly Running* (1982) and *Dear Shadows* (1986).

Wainwright, Jonathan M(ayhew) (1883–1953) US general, born in Walla-Walla, WA. He trained at West Point, and fought in Europe in World War 1. In 1942 he commanded the epic retreat in the Bataan peninsula after MacArthur's departure during the Philippines campaign. Taken prisoner by the Japanese, he was released in 1945 and awarded the Congressional Medal of Honor. >> MacArthur, Douglas

Waismann, Friedrich [viysman] (1896–1959) Philosopher, born in Vienna. He became a prominent member of the Vienna Circle, along with Carnap and Schlick, and later taught at Cambridge and Oxford. He argued that most empirical concepts have an 'open texture', in that we cannot completely foresee all the possible conditions in which they might properly be used, and therefore even empirical statements cannot be fully verified by observation. His main philosophical works include *The Principles of Linguistic Philosophy* (1965) and *How I See Philosophy* (1968). >> Carnap; Neurath, Otto; Reichenbach, Hans; Schlick; von Wright

Waite, Terry [wayt], popular name of **Terence (Hardy) Waite** (1939–) Consultant and former hostage, born in Bollington, Cheshire, NWC England, UK. After several posts as an advisor and administrator for various Church projects, including periods in Africa, in 1980 he became Adviser to the Archbishop of Canterbury on Anglican Communion Affairs. As the Archbishop's special envoy (from 1980), he was particularly involved in negotiations to secure the release of hostages held in the Middle East; between 1982 and the end of 1986, 14 hostages, for whom he was interceding, were released. He was himself kidnapped in Beirut in January 1987 while involved in secret negotiations to win the release of hostages held in Lebanon, and not released until November 1991. A volume of memoirs, *Taken on Trust*, was published in 1993.

Waits, Tom (1949–) Singer, songwriter, and actor, born in Pamona, CA. He had a critically acclaimed debut album, *Closing Time* (1973), and 'Jersey Girl' from his 1980 album *Heartattack and Vine* became an integral part of Bruce Springsteen's concerts. His soundtrack album from the film *One From the Heart* (1982) was Oscar nominated. His biggest chart success was the number 3 hit for Rod Stewart, 'Downtown Train' (1990). He has appeared in a number of films, including *The Fisher King* (1991) and *Bram Stoker's Dracula* (1992), and in 1995 released 'Earth Dies Screaming' from the soundtrack album of the film *Twelve Monkeys*. >> Springsteen; Stewart, Rod

Waitz, Georg [viyts] (1813–86) Historian, born in Flensburg, Germany. He studied at Kiel and Berlin, became professor of history at Kiel (1842), and represented Kiel at the national parliament in Frankfurt (1846), where he supported the unification of all the German states into one nation. As professor at Göttingen (1849–75), he founded the Göttingen historical school. He was editor of (1875–86) and contributor to the *Monumenta Germaniae historica*. His major work was *Deutsche Verfassungsgeschichte* (1844–78, German Constitutional History).

Waitz, Grete [viyts], *née* **Andersen** (1953–) Athlete, born in Oslo. Formerly a track champion at 3000 m, at which she set world records in 1975 and 1976, she was later one of the world's leading female road athletes. The world marathon champion in 1983, and the Olympic silver medallist in 1984, she four times set world best times for the marathon. She won the London Marathon in 1983 and 1986, and the New York marathon a record nine times between 1978 and 1988. She has also been the women's cross-country champion five times (1978–81, 1983). >> RR1143

Wajda, Andrzej [viyda] (1926–) Film director, born in Suwałki, Poland. He studied art at the Krakow Academy of Fine Arts, then enrolled in the Łódź film school (1950). His first feature film, *Pokolenie* (1954, A Generation), dealt with the effects of the war on disillusioned Polish youth. He is best known outside Poland for *Czlowiek z marmary* (1977, Man of Marble), dealing with the Stalinist era, and *Czlowiek z zelaza* (1981, Man of Iron), which uses film made during the rise of the Solidarity trade union. His works range from romantic comedy to epic, including literary adaptations (such as *Crime and Punishment*, 1984) and World War 2 dramas, such as *Korczak* (1990) and *Holy Week* (1996). He has also worked in television and the theatre.

Wakefield, Edward Gibbon (1796–1862) Originator of subsidized emigration from Britain, born in London, England, UK. He was imprisoned for tricking an heiress into marriage, and was inspired by the plight of his fellow prisoners to write *A Letter from Sydney* (1829), in which he proposed the sale of small units of crown land in the colonies to subsidize colonization by the poor from Britain (rather than convicts). His proposals (later called *Wakefield settlements*) were adopted in 1831, and in the South Australia Act of 1834. He influenced the South Australian Association (1836), formed the New Zealand Association (1837), and inspired the Durham Report (1839) on colonial affairs in Canada. He emigrated to New Zealand in 1853, and was a member of the General Assembly until a breakdown forced his retirement.

Wakeley, Thomas (1795–1862) Surgeon, the founder and first editor of *The Lancet* (1823), born in Membury, Devon, SW England, UK. Through this weekly medical paper he denounced abuses in medical practice, and made exposures which led to the Adulteration of Food and Drink Act (1860). He was MP for Finsbury (1835–52), and coroner from 1839, procuring reforms for coroners' courts.

Waksman, Selman (Abraham) [waksman] (1888–1973) Biochemist, born in Priluka, Ukraine. He became a US citizen in 1916, and studied at Rutgers University, where he ultimately became professor of soil microbiology in 1930. His research into the breaking down of organic substances by micro-organisms and into antibiotics led to his discovery of streptomycin (1943), for which he was awarded the Nobel Prize for Physiology or Medicine in 1952.

Walburga, Walpurga, or **Walpurgis, St** >> **Walpurga**

Walch, Jakob >> **Barbari**

Walcott, Clyde [wolkot] (1926–) Cricketer, born in Bridgetown, Barbados. He was one of the leading West Indian batsmen of the 1950s. Although very tall, he started off as a Test wicket-keeper, but later concentrated on his batting. He played 44 times for West Indies, scoring 3798 runs, averaging 56·88, and 15 of his 40 centuries were obtained in Tests. Against Australia in 1954–5 he twice scored two centuries in the same Test match. >> Worrell

Walcott, Derek [wolkot] (1930–) Poet and playwright, born in St Lucia, West Indies. He studied at the University of the West Indies, Jamaica, and has lived mostly in Trindad, where he founded the Trindad Theatre Workshop in 1959. He produced three early but assured volumes, *In A Green Night* (1962), *The Castaway* (1965), and

The Gulf (1969). *Collected Poems 1948–84* was published in 1986, the epic *Omeros* in 1990, and *Selected Poetry* in 1993. He was awarded the Nobel Prize for Literature in 1992.

Wald, George [wawld] (1906–) Biochemist, born in New York City. He studied zoology at New York, Colombia, and Berlin universities, and spent his career thereafter at Harvard (1932–77). In 1933 he discovered the presence of vitamin A in the retina, and later work showed that rhodopsin, the light-sensitive pigment of the eye, has a molecule composed of a protein fragment linked to a structure derived from vitamin A. He shared the 1967 Nobel Prize for Physiology or Medicine. >> RR1124

Wald, Lillian D [wawld] (1867–1940) Public health nurse and settlement leader, born in Cincinnati, OH. She is best known as a founder of public health nursing and related services through the establishment in 1895 of the Nurses' Settlement at 265 Henry St, New York City. She created the first public-school nursing programme in the USA (1902), and was the first president and one of the founders of the National Organization for Public Health Nursing (1912). She was also a founder of the National Child Labor Council (1904).

Waldheim, Kurt [**valt**hiym] (1918–) Austrian statesman and president (1986–92), born near Vienna. He served on the Russian front, but was wounded and discharged (1942), then studied at Vienna, and entered the Austrian foreign service (1945). He became minister and then ambassador to Canada (1955–60), director of political affairs at the ministry (1960–4), Austrian representative at the UN (1964–8, 1970–1), foreign minister (1968–70), and UN secretary-general (1972–81). His presidential candidature was controversial, because of claims that he had lied about his wartime activities and been involved in anti-Jewish and other atrocities, but he denied the allegations and, despite international pressure, continued successfully with his campaign. >> RR1033

Waldo or **Valdes, Peter** [**wol**doh, **val**des] (fl. 1175) Religious leader, born in Lyon, France. A rich merchant, he was moved to reject his way of life and to take up a life of poverty and preaching (c.1170). He gathered a group of followers, known as *Waldensians*, and sought papal approval at the Third Lateran Council (1179), but failed and was forbidden to preach. He was later excommunicated by Pope Lucius III at the Synod of Verona (1184). The Waldensians later departed from orthodox Roman Catholic teaching in several ways, such as by rejecting some of the sacraments.

Waldock, Sir Claud (Humphrey Meredith) [**wawl**dok] (1904–81) British jurist, born in Colombo, Sri Lanka. He studied at Oxford, where he became professor of international law (1947–72). He was a member of the European Commission on Human Rights (1954–61, president, 1955–61) and judge of the European Court of Human Rights (1966–74, president 1971–4). As judge of the International Court of Justice (1973–81, president 1979–81), he acted as consultant on many issues of international law.

Waldorf, William >> **Astor, William Waldorf, 1st / 2nd Viscounts**

Waldseemüller, Martin [**valt**saymüler] (c.1470–c.1521) Cartographer, born in Radolfzell, Germany. He was educated at Freiburg im Breisgau. At St Dié he made use of an account of the travels of Amerigo Vespucci to publish in 1507 the map and globe on which he named the New World *America* in Vespucci's honour. >> Vespucci

Waldstein, Albrecht >> **Wallenstein, Albrecht**

Waldteufel, (Charles) Emil [**valt**toyfel] (1837–1915) Composer, born in Strasbourg, France. He studied at the Paris Conservatoire and joined a piano manufacturing firm, until he was appointed pianist to the Empress Eugénie, the wife of Napoleon III. A prolific composer of dance music, several of his waltzes, notably the *Skaters Waltz* and *Estudiantina*, remain popular.

Wales, Prince Harry (Henry) / William of >> **Charles, Prince of Wales; Diana, Princess of Wales**

Wales, Prince of >> **Charles, Prince of Wales**

Wales, Princess of >> **Diana, Princess of Wales**

Walesa, Lech [va**wen**sa] (1943–) Polish president (1990–5) and former trade unionist, born in Popowo, Poland. A Gdańsk shipyard worker, he became leader of the independent trade union, Solidarity, which openly challenged the Polish government's economic and social policies. He held negotiations with the leading figures in the Church and State, but was detained by the authorities when martial law was declared in 1981. He was released in 1982, and was awarded the Nobel Peace Prize in 1983. He continued to be a prominent figure in Polish politics, and was much involved in the negotiations which led to Solidarity being involved in government in 1989. When the constitution was amended (1990) to allow free presidential elections, Walesa gained a landslide victory. He was defeated by Alexander Kwasniewski in 1995. >> RR1082

Walewska, Maria, Countess [va**lef**ska], *née* **Laczynska** (1786–1817) Mistress of Napoleon Bonaparte, born in Brodno, Poland. She met Napoleon in Poland in 1806, and bore him a son who became Count Walewski. >> Napoleon I; Walewski

Walewski, Alexandre Florian Joseph Colonna, Count [wa**lef**skee] (1810–68) French diplomat, the illegitimate son of Napoleon and Maria, Countess Walewska, born in Walewice, near Warsaw, Poland. At 14 he fled Poland to avoid service in the Russian army, later took French citizenship, and served in the French army in Algeria. Under Napoleon III he held various appointments, including that of ambassador to Britain (1851), and was foreign minister (1855–60) and minister of state (1860–3). >> Napoleon III; Walewska

Walken, Christopher [**wawk**en] (1943–) Actor, born in New York City. He began acting and dancing at an early age on stage and television, made his Broadway debut at sixteen, and went on to appear in a wide range of theatre roles. His first big film role came in *The Anderson Tapes* (1971), and he received a Best Supporting Actor Oscar for his role in *The Deer Hunter* (1978). With an ability to play sinister as well as comic roles, other films include *Annie Hall* (1977), *Batman Returns* (1992), *Pulp Fiction* (1994), *Basquiat* (1996), and *Touch* (1997).

Walker, Sir Alan (1911–) Methodist clergyman and social activist, born in Sydney, New South Wales, Australia. He studied at Sydney University, and was ordained 1935. His ministry in a coal-mining area of New South Wales first prompted his Christian social views, further developed while superintendent of the Waverley Methodist Mission (1944–54) and in the influential Sydney Central Methodist Mission (1958–78). He began a telephone counsell-ing ministry that soon spread throughout the world, and after official retirement was the World Methodist Council's director of evangelism (1978–89). He became Principal of the Pacific College for Evangelism (1989–95, now emeritus).

Walker, Alice (Malsenior) (1944–) Novelist and poet, born in Eatonville, GA. She studied at Spelman College, Atlanta, and Sarah Lawrence College, then worked as a social worker, teacher, and lecturer. An accomplished poet, she is best known for her novels, notably *The Color Purple* (1982, Pulitzer), later made into a successful film, which tells the story of two black sisters in the segregated world of the Deep South. *Possessing the Secret of Joy* appeared in 1992. She has also written volumes of short stories and essays, including *You Can't Keep a Good Woman Down* (1981) and *In Search of My Mother's Garden* (1983). >> Goldberg, Whoopi

Walker, George (1618–90) Irish clergyman and governor, born of English parents in Northern Ireland. He studied at Glasgow University, and became rector of Donaghmore near Dungannon (1674). In 1688 he raised a regiment at Dungannon to help garrison Londonderry for its successful resistance to the 105-day siege by James II's forces (1689), and became joint governor. For this he received the thanks of William III and the House of Commons, degrees from Oxford and Cambridge, and was nominated Bishop of Derry. He fell at the Battle of the Boyne, and is commemorated by the Walker Monument (1828) in Londonderry. >> James II (of England)

Walker, John (1732–1807) Dictionary-maker, born in Colney Hatch, Hertfordshire, UK. He became an actor, schoolmaster, and (from 1771) peripatetic teacher of elocution. He compiled a *Rhyming Dictionary* (1775), still in print as the *Rhyming Dictionary of the English Language*, and a *Critical Pronouncing Dictionary* (1791).

Walker, John (c. 1781–1859) Inventor, born in Stockton-on-Tees, Durham, NE England, UK. He became a chemist, and in 1827 made the first friction matches, called by him 'Congreves' (alluding to William Congreve's rocket). They were later named *lucifers*, and eventually *matches*. >> Congreve, William

Walker, Kath >> Noonuccal, Oodgeroo

Walker, Peter (Edward) (1932–) British statesman, born in London, England, UK. He was chairman of the Young Conservatives (1958–60) and became MP for Worcester, where he farms, in 1961. He held ministerial posts under Edward Heath, and in Margaret Thatcher's government he was agriculture secretary (1979–83), energy secretary (1983–7) and secretary of state for Wales (1987–90). Regarded as a Conservative 'liberal', he was noted for his 'coded criticisms' of some of the extreme aspects of Mrs Thatcher's policies. >> Heath; Thatcher

Walker, T-Bone, stage name of **Aaron Thibeaux Walker** (1910–75) Musician, born in Linden, CA. A pioneer of the electric guitar, his 'T-Bone Blues' (1939) enabled him to make his name as a blues player, and he proved to be a major influence on later generations of folk and blues guitarists.

Walker, William (1824–60) Adventurer and revolutionary, born in Nashville, TN. He studied medicine at Edinburgh and Heidelberg universities, returning to America in 1850. He landed with a force in the Mexican state of Lower California, declaring it an independent republic (1854), but was soon forced to withdraw to US territory. He next invaded Nicaragua (1855), took Granada, and was elected president (1856–7). Twice expelled from Nicaragua, he entered Honduras (1860), taking Trujillo, but was apprehended and given up to the Honduran authorities, who had him shot.

Wall, Max (Wall George Lorimer) (1908–90) Actor and comedian, born in London, England, UK. He made his stage debut at 14 in pantomime, and built a reputation as one of the finest British comics of his time in music hall and radio performances with a laconic comedy routine. In 1966 he appeared as Père Ubu in Jarry's *Ubu Roi*, and subsequently developed a special affinity for the plays of Samuel Beckett. He also appeared as a solo artist, and presented his own one-man show, *Aspects of Max Wall*, in 1974. >> Beckett, Samuel

Wallace, Alfred Russel (1823–1913) Naturalist, born in Usk, Monmouthshire, SE Wales. He travelled and collected plant samples in the Amazon (1842–52) and the Malay Archipelago (1854–62), and propounded a theory of evolution by natural selection independently of Darwin. His memoir, sent to Darwin in 1858 from the Moluccas, formed an important part of the Linnaean Society meeting which first promulgated the theory, modifying and hastening the publication of Darwin's *The Origin of Species*. Wallace contributed greatly to the scientific foundations of zoogeography, including his proposal for the evolutionary distinction between the fauna of Australia and Asia (*Wallace's line*). >> Darwin, Charles

Wallace, DeWitt (1889–1981) Publisher and founder of the *Reader's Digest* magazine, born in St Paul, MN. He dropped out from the University of California, and took odd jobs while collecting magazine articles. In 1921 he married a Canadian-born social worker, **Lila Bell Acheson** (1889–1984), and in 1922 they launched the *Reader's Digest* as a mail-order magazine with 1500 subscribers, publishing at first condensed articles from other sources. It became the largest-circulation magazine in the world, with several foreign-language editions. In 1972 both he and his wife were awarded a Presidential Medal of Freedom.

Wallace, (Richard Horatio) Edgar (1875–1932) Writer of crime novels, born in London, England, UK. He served in the army in South Africa, where he later (1899) became a journalist, and in 1905 published his first success, the adventure story *The Four Just Men*. He wrote over 170 novels and plays, and is best remembered for his crime novels, such as *The Clue of the Twisted Candle*. He later became a film scriptwriter. His autobiography, *People*, appeared in 1926.

Wallace, George (Corley) (1919–) US state governor, born in Clio, AL. He studied law at the University of Alabama, became a Democratic assistant attorney general in Alabama (1946–7), and served in the legislature (1947–53). Elected a state circuit judge (1953–9) he defied the US Civil Rights Commission with his segregationist rulings. After returning to private practice, he became Alabama's governor (1963–7) proclaiming 'segregation forever'. Succeeded as governor by his wife **Lurleen**, he ran in 1968 for president on the American Independent Party Ticket. In 1972, while campaigning for the Democratic presidential nomination, he was shot and paralysed, thus ending his national political ambitions. He served three more terms as governor (1971–9, 1983–7), mostly in a wheelchair. He always insisted he was not a racist, and in later years did in fact align himself with a more liberal agenda and civil rights leaders.

Wallace, Henry A(gard) (1888–1965) Agriculturist and statesman, born in Adair Co, IA, the son of Henry Cantwell Wallace. He edited *Wallace's Farmer* (1933–40), when he was nominated vice-president to Franklin D Roosevelt, whose 'New Deal' policy he supported. He became chairman of the Board of Economic Warfare (1941–5) and secretary of commerce (1945–6). He failed to obtain renomination as vice-president in 1944, and unsuccessfully stood for president in 1948. >> Roosevelt, Franklin D; Wallace, Henry Cantwell

Wallace, Henry Cantwell (1866–1924) Journalist and cabinet member, born in Rock Island, IL. A farmer and professor of dairying at Iowa State Agricultural College, with his family he published *Wallace's Farmer* (1894–1924). His political and scientific writings influenced farm organizations. Secretary of agriculture (1921–4), he emphasized matching farm production to consumption, championed agricultural education, and instituted the bureau of agricultural economics, the bureau of home economics, and radio market reports. >> Wallace, Henry A

Wallace, Lew(is) (1827–1905) Writer and soldier, born in Brookville, IN. He served in the Mexican War (1846–8) and with distinction as a major-general in the Federal army in the American Civil War (1861–5). Governor of New Mexico

(1878–81) and minister to Turkey (1881–5), he was author of several novels, including the remarkably successful religious novel *Ben Hur* (1880), which has twice formed the subject of a spectacular film.

Wallace, Sir Richard (1818–90) Art collector and philanthropist, born in London, England, UK, the illegitimate son of Viscount Beauchamp and Agnes Jackson, *née* Wallace. Educated in Paris, he helped his father (then 4th Marquess of Hertford) build up the large collection of paintings and *objets d'art*, bequeathed by his widow to the nation in 1897. These now comprise the *Wallace Collection*, housed in Hertford House, London, once his residence. During the siege of Paris (1870–1) he equipped ambulances and founded a British hospital there, for which service he was created a baronet in 1871.

Wallace, Sir William (c. 1270–1305) Scottish knight and champion of the independence of Scotland, probably born in Elderslie, Renfrewshire, W Scotland, UK. He routed the English army at Stirling Bridge (1297), and was knighted. He was given control of the government of Scotland as 'Guardian' in the name of the Scottish king imprisoned by Edward I of England, but was defeated by Edward at Falkirk (1298). He was eventually captured near Glasgow (1305), and executed in London. Many legends soon collected around him due to his immense popular appeal as a national figure resisting foreign oppression, and these were the subject of the Oscar-winning film, *Braveheart* (1995). >> Edward I

Wallace, William (1860–1940) Composer, born in Greenock, Inverclyde, WC Scotland, UK. He trained in medicine, but from 1889 devoted himself to music. He was the first British composer to experiment with symphonic poems, of which he wrote six. His other works include a symphony and songs.

Wallenberg, Raoul (1912–? 47) Swedish businessman and diplomat, born in Stockholm. He took a science degree at Ann Arbor, then worked as the foreign representative of a European company run by a Hungarian Jew (1935–44). When Hitler began deporting Hungarian Jews to concentration camps he was sent to Hungary as a 'diplomat' with the assistance of the US and Swedish governments to rescue as many Jews as he could. He designed a Swedish protection passport, and arranged 'Swedish houses' offering Jews refuge, saving up to 100 000. When Soviet troops occupied Hungary in 1945 he was taken to Soviet headquarters and never returned. On insistent Swedish requests, Soviet authorities produced a document stating that he had died of a heart attack in July 1947, but testimony of ex-prisoners suggested that he was still alive in the 1950s, and persistent rumours implied he was still in prison in the 1970s. Wallenberg was made an honorary citizen of the USA in 1981, of Canada in 1985, and of Israel in 1986.

Wallenstein or **Waldstein, Albrecht (Wenzel Eusebius), Herzog von** (Duke of) [**wo**lenstiyn], Ger [**val**enshtiyn] (1583–1634) Bohemian general, born in Heřmanice, Czech Republic. During the Thirty Years' War he became commander of the imperial armies and won a series of victories (1625–9), gaining the titles of Duke of Mecklenburg and 'General of the Baltic and Oceanic Seas'. His ambition led to his dismissal in 1630, but he was reinstated to defend the empire against Swedish attack. He recovered Bohemia, but was defeated by Gustav II Adolph at Lützen (1632), and was again dismissed. His intrigues led to an imperial proclamation of treason, resulting in his assassination at Eger by Irish mercenaries. >> Gustav II Adolph; Kepler

Waller, Augustus (Volney) (1816–70) Physiologist, born near Faversham, Kent, SE England, UK. He discovered the *Wallerian* degeneration of nerve fibres, and the related method of tracing nerve fibres.

Waller, Edmund (1606–87) Poet, born in Coleshill, Buckinghamshire, SC England, UK. He studied at Cambridge, became an MP in 1621, and was a member of the Long Parliament in 1640. In 1643 he plunged into a conspiracy (*Waller's plot*) against parliament, was arrested, and banished, but returned to England in 1651. His collected poems were published in 1645.

Waller, Fats, popular name of **Thomas Wright Waller** (1904–43) Jazz pianist, organist, singer, and songwriter, born in New York City. He performed with such ebullience, frequently parodying songs and styles, that it was sometimes hard for audiences to see him as more than a buffoon. He played in the stride tradition, and was a natural songwriter, as seen in such hits as 'Ain't Misbehavin'' (1929) and 'Keeping Out of Mischief Now' (1932). He is rumoured to have written many more standards, among them 'On the Sunny Side of the Street', and then sold the rights for quick cash. He died of pneumonia on his way to Kansas City from Los Angeles, while entertaining soldiers at training camps.

Waller, Sir William (c. 1598–1688) English soldier, born in Knole, Kent, SE England, UK. A member of the Long Parliament, he fought in the West Country (1643), Oxford and Newbury (1644), and Taunton (1645). He suggested reforms on which the New Model Army was to be based, but resigned command in 1645. By 1647 he was levying troops against the army, and was imprisoned for Royalist sympathies (1648–51). In 1659 he plotted for a royalist rising and was again imprisoned. He became a member of the Convention Parliament (1660), but was unrewarded at the Restoration.

Walling, William English (1877–1936) Labour reformer and Socialist, born in Louisville, KY. A man of independent means, he studied at Chicago and Harvard universities, rejected his privileged, liberal heritage, and chose to become a factory inspector in Illinois (1900–1). He then moved to New York City and lived (1901–5) in the tenement district, co-founding (1903) the National Women's Trade Union League, and spent much of the years 1905–8 in Russia. After witnessing a race riot (1908), he helped found the National Association for the Advancement of Colored People, and joined the Socialist Party (1910–17), but resigned because of its anti-war stance. He worked full-time for the American Federation of Labor, ran unsuccessfully for Congress in Connecticut (1924), and was executive director of the Labor Chest (1935).

Wallis, Sir Barnes (Neville) (1887–1979) Aeronautical engineer and inventor, born in Ripley, Derbyshire, C England, UK. He trained as a marine engineer, and became a designer in the airship department of Vickers, where he designed the R100. His many successes include the design of the Wellington Bomber, the bombs which destroyed the German warship Tirpitz and V-rocket sites, and the 'bouncing bombs' which destroyed the Mohne and Eder dams. He later became chief of aeronautical research at the British Aircraft Corporation, Weybridge (1945–71), and in the 1950s designed the first swing-wing aircraft. He was knighted in 1968.

Wallis, John (1616–1703) The leading English mathematician before Isaac Newton, born in Ashford, Kent, SE England, UK. He studied at Cambridge, and took orders, but in 1649 became professor of geometry at Oxford. His *Arithmetica infinitorum* (1655, The Arithmetic of Infinitesimals) was a stimulus for Newton's work on calculus and the binomial theorem. He also wrote on proportion, mechanics, grammar, logic, decipherment (he deciphered encrypted messages intercepted from Royalist supporters), theology, and the teaching of the deaf. He was one of the founders of the Royal Society. >> Newton, Isaac

Wallis, Samuel (1728–95) English explorer and naval officer. From 1766 to 1768 he made a circumnavigation of the globe in HMS *Dolphin*. He was the first European to discover Tahiti (1767), and the *Wallis Is* were named after him.

Walpole, Horace (or **Horatio**), **4th Earl of Orford** (1717–97) Writer, born in London, England, UK, the youngest son of Sir Robert Walpole. At Cambridge he had the poet Thomas Gray as a friend, with whom he embarked on the 'Grand Tour' of Europe (1739). He returned to England in 1741, and entered parliament for an undistinguished career. After his father's death he purchased a small villa which he gradually 'gothicized' (1753–76) into the stuccoed and battlemented pseudo-castle of Strawberry Hill, and where he established a private press. His house brought about a Gothic architectural revival, and his *The Castle of Otranto* (1764) initiated a vogue for Gothic romances. His literary reputation rests chiefly upon his letters, which deal, in the most vivacious way, with party politics, foreign affairs, literature, art, and gossip. His firsthand accounts in them of such events as the Jacobite trials after the 1745 Rising and the Gordon Riots are invaluable. >> Chatterton; Gray, Thomas; Walpole, Robert

Walpole, Sir Hugh (Seymour) (1884–1941) Writer, born in Auckland, New Zealand. He studied at Durham and Cambridge universities, became a teacher, then an author. His many novels were very popular during his lifetime, and include *The Secret City* (1919), *The Cathedral* (1922), and the four-volume family saga, *The Herries Chronicle* (1930–3). He was knighted in 1937.

Walpole, Sir Robert, 1st Earl of Orford (1676–1745) English statesman, and leading minister (1721–42) of George I and George II, born in Houghton, Norfolk, E England, UK. He studied at Cambridge, became a Whig MP in 1701, and was made secretary for war (1708) and treasurer of the Navy (1710). Sent to the Tower for alleged corruption during the Tory government (1712), he was recalled by George I, and made a privy councillor and (1715) Chancellor of the Exchequer. After the collapse of the South Sea Scheme, he again became chancellor (1721), and was widely recognized as 'prime minister', a title (unknown to the Constitution) which he hotly repudiated. A shrewd manipulator of men, he took trouble to consult backbench MPs, and followed policies of low taxation designed to win their favour. He was regarded as indispensible by both George I and George II. His popularity began to wane in the 1730s over the Excise Scheme and also over his determination to avoid foreign wars. He did not fully recover from the outbreak of a war he had opposed in 1739, and resigned in 1742. His period in office is widely held to have increased the influence of the House of Commons in the Constitution. He was knighted in 1725, and created an earl in 1742. >> Chesterfield; George II (of Great Britain); Jenkins, Robert; Townshend, Charles, 2nd Viscount

Walpurga, Walburga, or **Walpurgis, St** [val**poor**ga] (c.710–c.777) Abbess and missionary, born in Wessex, England. She joined St Boniface on his mission to Germany, and became Abbess of Heidenheim, where she died. Her relics were transferred (c.870) to Eichstätt. *Walpurgisnacht* (the eve of St Walpurgis, 30 Apr) arises because popular superstition coincidentally regards the night before the day of the transfer of her remains (1 May) as one when large numbers of witches fly. Feast day 25 February. >> Boniface; Willibald

Walschaerts, Egide [val**sherts**] (1820–1901) Mechanical engineer, born in Malines, Belgium. He studied at Liège,

and in 1842 entered the state railway workshops. He invented a type of valve gear used in some steam engines (1844). He invented several other improvements to steam engines, and was awarded a gold medal at the Paris Exposition of 1878.

Walsingham, Sir Francis [**wol**singam] (c. 1530–90) English statesman, born in Chislehurst, Kent, SE England, UK. He studied at Cambridge, became a diplomat, and was made a secretary of state to Elizabeth I (1573–90), a member of the Privy Council, and knighted. A Puritan sympathizer, and a strong opponent of the Catholics, he developed a complex system of espionage at home and abroad, enabling him to reveal the plots of Throckmorton and Babington against the Queen, and was one of the commissioners to try Mary at Fotheringay. In his last months he increasingly took up religious meditation. >> Babington; Mary, Queen of Scots; Throckmorton

Walsingham, Thomas [**wol**singam] (?–c. 1422) English chronicler and monk. He was associated chiefly with St Albans abbey, but for a time was prior of Wymondham. An authority for English history from 1377 until 1422, he compiled *Historia Anglicana, 1272–1422* and other works.

Walter, Bruno [**val**ter], originally **Bruno Walter Schlesinger** (1876–1962) Conductor, born in Berlin. As a teenager, he conducted at Cologne, then worked with Mahler in Hamburg and Vienna. He was in charge of Munich Opera (1913–22), and from 1919 was chief conductor of the Berlin Philharmonic. International tours won him a great British and American reputation. Driven from both Germany and Austria by the Nazis, he settled in the USA, where he became chief conductor of the New York Philharmonic in 1951. >> Mahler

Walter, Hubert (c. 1140–1205) English clergyman and statesman. He became Bishop of Salisbury (1189), and accompanied Richard I on the Third Crusade (1190–3). Appointed Archbishop of Canterbury in 1193, he played key roles in raising the ransom to secure Richard's release from captivity, and in containing the rebellion of the king's brother, John. At the end of 1193, he became justiciar of England, and was responsible for all the business of government until his resignation in 1198. On John's accession (1199), he became chancellor, and was consulted on important matters of state. He was the first English statesman to tax revenue for secular purposes >> John; Richard I

Walter, John (1739–1812) Printer and newspaper publisher, born in London, England, UK. In 1784 he acquired a printing office in Blackfriars, London, the nucleus of the later Printing House Square buildings, and in 1785 founded *The Daily Universal Register* newspaper, which in 1788 was renamed *The Times*. His son, **John** (1776–1847) managed the paper from 1802 to 1847, followed by his grandson. >> Walter, John (1818–94)

Walter, John (1818–94) Newspaper proprietor, the grandson of John Walter, born in London, England, UK. A barrister by profession, he became proprietor of *The Times* in 1847. In 1866 he introduced the important cylindrical *Walter press*, in which, for the first time, curved stereotyped plates and reels of newsprint were used. >> Walter, John (1739–1812)

Walter, Lucy, known as **Mrs Barlow** (c. 1630–58) Mistress of Charles II, born near Haverfordwest, Pembrokeshire, SW Wales. They met in 1644 in the Channel Is when he was fleeing England during the Civil War, and she bore him a son, James, Duke of Monmouth. >> Charles II (of England); Monmouth

Walters, Julie (1950–) Actress, born in Birmingham, West Midlands, C England, UK. She trained as a teacher at Manchester Polytechnic, and made her stage debut in *Educating Rita* (1980), for which she won recognition as a promising newcomer, and later a BAFTA award in the film version (1983). Later films include *Car Trouble* (1986), *Killing Dad* (1989), *Just Like A Woman* (1992), and *Intimate Relations* (1997). On television she partnered Victoria Wood in the series *Wood and Walters* (from 1981), and also appeared in *The Secret Diary of Adrian Mole* (1985), *GBH* (1991), *Jake's Progress* (1995), and *Melissa* (1997). >> Wood, Victoria

Walther von der Vogelweide |**val**ter fon der **foh**glviy-duh| (c. 1170–1230) German lyric poet. In 1190–8 he was in high favour at the court of Austria, and was later at Mainz and Magdeburg. In 1204 he outshone his rivals in the great contest at the Wartburg. He first sided with the Guelphs, but made friends with the victorious Hohenstaufen, Frederick II, who gave him a small estate. He wrote political, religious, and didactic poems, and a wide range of love poems. >> Frederick II (Emperor)

Walton, E(rnest) T(homas) S(inton) (1903–95) Pioneer nuclear physicist, born in Dungarvan, Co Waterford, Ireland. He studied at Trinity College, Dublin, and worked for his doctorate under Rutherford at Cambridge. With John Cockcroft he built the first successful particle accelerator, with which they disintegrated lithium by proton bombardment (1931), the first artificial nuclear reaction using nonradioactive substances. He returned to Dublin (1934), becoming professor of natural and experimental philosophy (1947–74). He shared the 1951 Nobel Prize for Physics. >> Cockcroft; Rutherford, Ernest

Walton, Izaak (1593–1683) Writer, born in Stafford, Staffordshire, C England, UK. In 1621 he settled in London as an ironmonger, but left the city for Staffordshire during the Civil War, and after the Restoration lived in Winchester. Best known for his treatise on fishing and country life, *The Compleat Angler* (1653), he also wrote several biographies. >> Breton, Nicholas

Walton, Sir William (Turner) (1902–83) Composer, born in Oldham, Lancashire, NW England, UK. He studied at Oxford, where he wrote his first compositions, and became known through his instrumental setting of poems by Edith Sitwell, *Façade* (1923). His works include two symphonies, concertos for violin, viola, and cello, the biblical cantata *Belshazzar's Feast* (1931), and the opera *Troilus and Cressida* (1954). He is also known for his film music, notably for Olivier's *Henry V*, *Hamlet*, and *Richard III*. He was knighted in 1951. >> Olivier; Sitwell, Edith

Wanamaker, Sam |**won**amayker| (1919–93) Actor and director, born in Chicago, IL. He studied at Drake University, IA, then trained at Goodman Theatre, Chicago, worked with summer stock companies in Chicago as an actor and director, and made his London debut in 1952. In 1957, he was appointed director of the New Shakespeare Theatre, Liverpool, and in 1959 joined the Shakespeare Memorial Theatre company at Stratford-upon-Avon. He produced or directed several works at Covent Garden and elsewhere in the 1960s and 1970s, including the Shakespeare Birthday Celebrations in 1974. He worked both as director and actor in films and television, his appearances included *Spiral Staircase* (1974), *Private Benjamin* (1980), *Superman IV* (1986), and *Baby Boom* (1988). In 1970 he founded the Globe Theatre Trust, a project to build a replica of Shakespeare's Globe Theatre near its original site on Bankside in London; it was officially opened in 1997.

Wand, John William Charles (1885–1977) Anglican clergyman and scholar, born in Grantham, Lincolnshire, EC England, UK. After serving as dean of Oriel College, Oxford (1925–34), he went to Australia as Archbishop of Brisbane (1934–43). Returning to Britain he became Bishop of Bath and Wells (1943–5) and Bishop of London (1945–55). He wrote numerous books on Christianity and Church history, edited the *Church Quarterly Review*, wrote a weekly devotional column for the *Church Times*, and published a brief autobiography, *Changeful Page* (1965).

Wang, An (1920–89) Physicist and business executive, born in Shanghai, China. He studied at Jiao Tong University in Shanghai, then emigrated to the USA (1945), where he studied applied physics at Harvard. A computer specialist, he invented the magnetic core memory, and founded Wang Laboratories in Boston, MA (1951), now one of the world's largest automation systems firms. He introduced a desktop computer named LOCI in 1956, the forerunner of Wang electronic desk calculators. A leading philanthropist in Boston, he was inducted into the National Inventors Hall of Fame in 1988.

Wang Anshi, also spelled **Wang An-shih** (1021–86) Chinese reformer, the chief councillor to Song Emperor Shenzong (ruled 1068–85), born in Kiangsi Province, China. He travelled widely in China, and later initiated major economic reforms in the interest of small farmers and merchants, including reduced interest, commutation of labour services, and reduced prices and land taxes. He also set up state financial planning, reduced the professional army, built up a (cavalry) militia, and carried out a wide range of educational reforms. Opposed by the big landowners, historians, litterateurs and philosophers, his reforms were rescinded after Shenzong died.

Wanger, Walter |**wayn**jer|, originally **Walter Feuchtwanger** (1894–1968) Film producer, born in San Francisco, CA. After service in World War 1, he joined Paramount as a producer, moved to Columbia and MGM, then went independent. Among his more ambitious films were *Stagecoach* (1939) and *Joan of Arc* (1948).

Wang Jingwei |wang jingway| (1883–1944) Associate of the revolutionary and Nationalist leader Sun Yixian (Sun Yatsen), born in Guangzhou (Canton), China. He studied in Japan, where he joined Sun's Revolutionary Party, and from 1917 became his personal assistant. In 1927 he was appointed head of the new Nationalist government at Wuhan, and in 1932 became titular head of the Nationalist Party. In 1938, after the outbreak of war with Japan, he offered to co-operate with the Japanese, and in 1940 became head of a puppet regime ruling the occupied areas. >> Sun Yixian

Wang Mang (ruled 8–23 AD) Chinese minister-regent, who usurped the throne and established the Xin (Hsin) or 'New' dynasty. Aided by the scholar-minister Liu Xin, he nationalized land, abolished slavery (but not state slaves), extended state monopolies, and carried out many financial reforms. Mistakenly seen by 20th-c ideologues as the first Chinese Socialist, his reforms were designed to raise funds for war against the Huns. He accumulated 5 million ounces of gold. In AD 11 his 300 000-strong army attacked the Huns and annexed their land (though at this time he lost Turkestan). He was overthrown by the Red Eyebrows revolt. >> Liu Xin

Wang Meng (1934–) Writer, born in Beijing. He joined the Communist Youth League in 1949, and published two novels, *Long Live Youth* (1953) and *The Young Newcomer in the Organization Department* (1956). He was denounced as a rightist in the 'Anti-Rightist Campaign' of 1958, and forced to work as a manual labourer for 20 years in the remote provinces. Allowed to return to Beijing, he re-emerged with *Young Forever* (1979). Since then he has held various party Posts, and published collections of short stories, such as *A Night in the City* (1980) and *Andante Cantabile* (1981). After the fall of the Gang of Four, he was rehabilitated and became minister of culture.

Wang Wei |way| (699–759) Poet and painter of the T'ang dynasty, born in Ch'i-hsien, China. An ardent Buddhist, he is best known as one of the first to paint landscapes, which he executed in ink monochrome, and as the founder of the Southern school of painter-poets.

Wang Yangming, also found as **Wang Shouren** or **Wang Shou-jen** (1472–1529) Philosopher, civil administrator, and general, born in Yu-yao, China. He was a critic of the neo-Confucian Zhu Xi, and influenced by Zhu's contemporary, Lu Jiuyuan (1139–93). He believed in the essential goodness of all (though he crushed the Jiangsu rising 1518), and viewed the human spirit as central to the universe. His philosophy clearly influenced 17th-c Japanese thinkers, 19th-c Japanese dissident movements, and 20th-c Japanese writer Yukio Mishima, and his ideas were also developed by the Chinese philosopher Xiong Shili (1885–1969). His emphasis on the symbiosis of knowledge and action may have influenced similar pronouncements by Lenin and Mao Zedong. His views also anticipated 20th-c existentialism. >> Lenin; Mao Zedong; Mishima; Zhu Xi

Wankel, Felix [vangkl] (1902–) Mechanical engineer, the designer of a rotary engine, born in Luhran, Germany. He was employed in various engineering works before opening his own research establishment in 1930. While carrying out work for German motor manufacturers, he devoted himself to the development of an alternative configuration to the conventional piston-and-cylinder internal combustion engine. After many trials he produced a successful prototype engine in 1956, with a curved equilateral triangular rotor in a figure-of-eight-shaped chamber. Various applications of the engine have been tried, including cars, but continuing problems with the sealing of the rotor have prevented its large-scale adoption.

Warbeck, Perkin (c.1474–99) Pretender to the English throne, born in Tournai, Belgium. He was persuaded by enemies of Henry VII to impersonate Richard, Duke of York, the younger of the two sons of Edward IV who had been murdered in the Tower of London (1483). With the promise of support from many quarters in England, Ireland, Scotland, and on the European mainland, he made two unsuccessful attempts to invade England (1495–6), and was captured at Beaulieu during a third attempt (1497). Imprisoned in the Tower, he was executed after trying to escape. >> Edward IV; Henry VII

Warburg, Otto (Heinrich) [vah(r)boork] (1883–1970) Biochemist, born in Freiburg Baden, Germany. He studied at Berlin and Heidelberg universities, worked in the Kaiser Wilhelm (later Max Planck) Institute from 1913, and became director in 1953. Much of his work was on cellular respiration, for which he devised the *Warburg manometer* to measure oxygen uptake of living tissue. He was awarded the 1931 Nobel Prize for Physiology or Medicine.

Warburton, Peter Egerton (1813–89) Australian soldier and explorer, born in Cheshire, NWC England, UK. He served in the Indian Army for 24 years, and settled in Australia in 1853, where he became police commissioner until 1867. After earlier journeys to explore the South Australian Salt Lakes, in 1873 he became the first to cross Australia from the S coast to C Australia via Alice Springs, and across the worst of the desert country to the De Grey R on the W coast.

Ward, Artemus >> **Browne, Charles Farrar**

Ward, Arthur Sarsfield >> **Rohmer, Sax**

Ward, Dame Barbara (Mary), Baroness Jackson of Lodsworth (1914–81) Journalist, economist, and conservationist, born in York, North Yorkshire, N England, UK. She studied at Oxford, became foreign editor of *The Economist*, and was a prolific and popular writer on politics, economics, and ecology. Her books include *The International Share Out* (1936), *Spaceship Earth* (1966), and *Only One Earth* (1972). She was created a dame in 1974, and became a life peer in 1976.

Ward, James (1843–1925) Psychologist and philosopher, born in Hull, NE England, UK. He studied for the Congregationalist ministry at Cambridge, but after a one-year scholarship at Göttingen studying physiological psychology under Hermann Lotze, abandoned his religious ministry and continued his studies at Cambridge, where he became a fellow (1875–1925). He established a laboratory for psychological research (1891), and was appointed professor of mental philosophy and logic at Cambridge (1897–1925). He published his theories in *Psychological Principles* (1918). >> Lotze

Ward, Sir Joseph (George) (1856–1930) New Zealand statesman and prime minister (1906–12, 1928–30), born in Melbourne, Victoria, Australia. He established a successful business in New Zealand, and entered parliament in 1877. Noted for his social welfare measures, he created the world's first ministry of public health (1901) and the National Provident Fund (1910), and made provision for widows' pensions (1911). He was knighted in 1901. >> RR1078

Ward, Judith (Minna) (1949–) Victim of a miscarriage of justice. She was convicted and jailed for life in 1974 in England for the M62 coach-bombing by the IRA in which 12 people died. She served 18 years before having her conviction quashed by the Court of Appeal in 1992, on the basis that there had been a substantial miscarriage of justice in relation to forensic evidence.

Ward, Sir Leslie, pseudonym **Spy** (1851–1922) Caricaturist and portrait painter, born in London, England, UK. Educated at Eton and the Royal Academy, he became the regular caricaturist for *Vanity Fair* (1873–1909), picturing a wide selection of notable persons. He wrote *Forty Years of 'Spy'* (1915), and was knighted in 1918.

Ward, Mary (1585–1645) English religious reformer, the founder of a religious society for women. She entered a convent (1606), but rebelled at the enclosed life and set up a society modelled on the Jesuits to provide education for women (1609). Although her work was not questioned, her rejection of the enclosed cloister was, and Pope Urban VIII eventually called her to Rome and suppressed her society in 1630. She was allowed to return to England in 1639 and re-open her houses on modified lines. Her institute was fully restored, with papal permission, in 1877, and became the model for modern Catholic Women's Institutes.

Ward, Mary Augusta, known as **Mrs Humphry Ward** (1851–1920) Novelist, born in Hobart, Tasmania, Australia, a niece of Matthew Arnold. The family returned to Britain in 1856 and, after attending private boarding schools, she joined them in Oxford. She moved to London in 1881, where she wrote for various periodicals. Her greatest success was the best-selling spiritual romance, *Robert Elsmere*, which inspired the foundation of a settlement for the London poor in Tavistock Square in 1897. Her later novels, all on social or religious issues, include *Marcella* (1894), *Sir George Tressady* (1896), and *The Case of Richard Meynell* (1911). >> Arnold, Matthew

Warfield, William (1920–) Baritone, born in Helena, AR. He studied at the Eastman School of Music in 1946, and in 1950 began a celebrated international career as a recitalist. Among his operatic roles was his lead in productions of *Porgy and Bess* during the 1950s. In 1974 he began teaching at the University of Illinois.

Warhol, Andy [waw(r)hohl], originally **Andrew Warhola** (1927–87) Pop artist and film-maker, born in Pittsburgh, PA. He studied art in New York City, and worked as a commercial designer before becoming a pioneer of 'Pop Art' (1961), with brightly coloured exact reproductions of familiar everyday objects, such as the famous soup-can label. His first films, such as the three-hour silent observation of a sleeping man, *Sleep* (1963), developed into technically more complex work, though still without plot, as seen in *Chelsea Girls* (1966). After 1968, when he was shot and seriously wounded by one of his starlets, control of his films was passed to others. Later films with which he was associated include *Flesh for Frankenstein* (1973) and *Blood for Dracula* (1974). He also turned to portrait painting in the 1970s. The Andy Warhol Museum opened in Pittsburgh in 1994.

Warlock, Peter, pseudonym of **Philip Arnold Heseltine** (1894–1930) Musicologist and composer, born in London, England, UK. Largely self-taught, in 1920 he founded *The Sackbut*, a spirited musical periodical. His works include the song cycle *The Curlew* (1920–2), the orchestral suite *Capriol* (1926), many songs, often in the Elizabethan manner, and choral works.

Warmerdam, Cornelius, nickname **Dutch Warmerdam** (1915–) Pole-vaulter, born in Long Beach, CA. Seven times the world record holder, using a bamboo pole, he set records during World War 2 that were not bettered until the next decade. In 1941 he was the first man to reach 15 ft (4·57 m), and his vault of 4·78 m (1943), was not beaten for more than 14 years. The development of more flexible glass-fibre poles since the 1950s has led to dramatic improvements in vaulting records, but in his own time his achievements were exceptional.

Warming, Johannes (Eugenius Bülow) [vah(r)ming] (1841–1924) Botanist, a founder of plant ecology, born in Manø, Denmark. He studied at Copenhagen, and became professor of botany at Stockholm (1882–85) and Copenhagen (1885–1911). He is noted for his research on the relationships of living plants with their environment.

Warner, Glenn (Scobey), known as **Pop Warner** (1871–1954) Coach of American football, born in Springville, NY. He studied law at Cornell, embarking in 1895 on a coaching career which lasted 44 years. His most successful tenures were at Carlisle Indian School (1899–1903, 1907–14), the University of Pittsburgh (1915–23), and Stanford University (1924–32), where he developed three Rose Bowl teams. When he retired, his 312 victories exceeded the total achieved by any other coach. His greatest claim to fame was his development of both the single-wing and double-wing offensive formations into versatile and deceptive offensive attacks that were copied for years.

Warner, Jack, originally **Jack Leonard Eichelbaum** (1892–1978) Film mogul, born in London, Ontario, Canada. In partnership with his older brothers **Harry** (1881–1958), **Albert** (1884–1967), and **Sam** (1887–1927), after a period in film exhibition and distribution, he moved into production and set up studios in 1923. The Warners were the first to introduce sound into their films, and the success of *The Jazz Singer* (1927) led to great expansion in both cinema ownership and studio resources, until the US Anti-Trust Laws in the 1950s forced them to dispose of their theatres. Jack had always been the one most directly concerned with actual film creation, and he continued to supervise major productions such as *My Fair Lady* (1964) and *Camelot* (1967), but when he became the last surviving brother, he sold his interest and the name to the Canadian company, Seven Arts.

Warner, Marina (Sarah) (1946–) Novelist and cultural historian, born in London, England, UK. She studied at Oxford University, and became best-known for her work on female cultural history, such as *Alone of All Her Sex* (1976) and *Monuments and Maidens* (1986). Her novels include *In a Dark Wood* (1977), *The Skating Party* (1983), and *The Mermaids in the Basement* (1993).

Warner, Rex (Ernest) (1905–86) Writer, Greek scholar, and translator, born in Birmingham, West Midlands, C England, UK. He studied at Oxford, was a teacher of classics in England and Egypt, director of the British Institute

at Athens, (1940s), and professor of English at Connecticut (1964–74). He is best known for his later historical novels, such as *The Young Caesar* (1958) and *Pericles the Athenian* (1963), and for his novels concerned with the problems of the individual involved with authority, such as *Goose Chase* (1938) and *The Aerodrome* (1941). He also wrote poetry and made translations of Greek classics.

Warner, Sylvia Townsend (1893–1978) Novelist, born in Harrow, NW Greater London, England, UK. A student of music, she researched the music of the 15th-c and 16th-c, and was one of the four editors of *Tudor Church Music* (10 vols, 1923–9). She published seven novels, four volumes of poetry, essays, and eight volumes of short stories, many of which had previously appeared in the *New Yorker*. Ranging widely in theme, locale, and period, significant titles are *Lolly Willowes* (1926), *Summer Will Show* (1936), and *The Corner That Held Them* (1948).

Warner, William Lloyd (1898–1970) Anthropologist, born in Redlands, CA. He studied at California, and became professor of anthropology, sociology, and human development at Chicago in 1935. From 1959 until his death he was professor of social research at Michigan. Noted for his studies of Australian Aboriginal social and kinship organization, and for pioneering the field of urban anthropology, his major works include *A Black Civilization* (1937) and *Social Class in America* (1960).

Warnock (of Weeke), (Helen) Mary Warnock, Baroness, née **Wilson** (1924–) Philosopher and educationist. She studied at Oxford, and became a fellow and tutor in philosophy at St Hugh's College, Oxford (1949–66, 1976–84). She has taken part in and chaired several important committees of inquiry: special education (1974–8), animal experiments (1979–85), human fertilization (1982–4, regarding *in-vitro* fertilization and human embryo experiments), higher education (1984), teaching quality (1990), and bioethics (1992–4).

Warr, Baron de la >> **de la Warr, Baron**

Warren, Sir Charles (1840–1927) British soldier and archaeologist, born in Bangor, Gwynedd. He joined the Royal Engineers (1857) and played a conspicuous part during the late 19th-c as a commander of British forces in South Africa, where he helped to delimit Griqualand West. He is chiefly remembered for his work in connection with the archaeological exploration of Palestine, especially Jerusalem, and for his writings arising from it, such as *Underground Jerusalem* (1876) and *Temple and Tomb* (1880).

Warren, Earl (1891–1974) US politician and judge, born in Los Angeles, CA. He studied at the University of California, practised law, and served successively in California as state attorney general and governor (1943–53). He was then appointed chief justice of the US Supreme Court (1953–69). He led a number of notably liberal decisions, such as ending segregation in schools (*Brown v. Board of Education of Topeka*, 1954), guaranteeing the right to counsel in criminal cases, and protecting accused persons from police abuses. He headed the Commission which investigated the assassination of President John F Kennedy (1963–4) and concluded that the killing was not part of a domestic or foreign conspiracy. >> Kennedy, John F; Marshall, Thurgood

Warren, Lavinia >> **Stratton, Charles**

Warren, Mercy Otis, née **Otis** (1728–1814) Historian and poet, born in Barnstable, MA, the sister of James Otis. In addition to her poetry and plays, she published historical works, including *Observations on the New Constitution* (1788) and *History of the Rise, Progress, and Termination of the American Revolution* (1805). She corresponded at length with Abigail and John Adams, and other leading political figures, and was arguably America's first major female intellectual. >> Adams, Abigail/John; Otis, James

Warren, Robert Penn (1905–89) Writer and poet, born in Guthrie, KY. He studied at Vanderbilt, Berkeley, and Yale universities, and was a Rhodes scholar at Oxford. He became professor of English at Louisiana, Minnesota, and Yale. Recipient of two Pulitzer Prizes (for fiction in 1947, for poetry in 1958), he established an international reputation with his political novel, *All the King's Men* (1943, Pulitzer, filmed 1949). Other works include *Night Rider* (1939), *Wilderness* (1961), and *Meet Me in the Green Glen* (1971). He also published some volumes of short stories, and verse including *Rumour Verified* (1981).

Warriss, Ben >> **Jewel and Warriss**

Warton, Thomas (1728–90) Poet laureate and critic, born in Basingstoke, Hampshire, S England, UK. He studied at Oxford, where he became a fellow of Trinity College (1751) and professor of poetry (1757). His *Observations on Spencer's Faerie Queene* (1754) established his reputation, but he is best remembered for his *History of English Poetry* (1774–81). He became poet laureate and professor of history in 1785.

Warwick, Dionne [wo̱rik] (1941–) Singer, born in East Orange, NJ. She sang in a gospel trio before recording her first solo, 'Don't Work Me Over' (1963), which reached number 21 in the US charts. Other hits include 'Walk On By' (1964), 'Do You Know The Way To San José' (1968), and 'You've Lost That Lovin' Feeling' (1969). Her album *Dionne* (1979) sold a million copies.

Warwick, John Dudley, Earl of, Duke of Northumberland [wo̱rik] (1502–53) English soldier and statesman. He was deputy governor of Calais, and served under Edward Seymour, Duke of Somerset, in his Scottish campaigns. Created Earl of Warwick (1546), he was appointed joint regent for Edward VI and High Chamberlain of England (1547). As virtual ruler of England, he was created Duke of Northumberland in 1551 and brought about the downfall and eventual execution of Somerset (1550–2). He married his fourth son, Lord Guildford Dudley, to Lady Jane Grey, and proclaimed her queen on the death of Edward VI, but was executed for treason on the accession of Mary I. >> **Grey, Lady Jane; Somerset, Edward Seymour**

Warwick, John Rich, 2nd Earl of [wo̱rik] (1587–1658) English colonial administrator. He played a major role in the early history of the American colonies, and managed the companies of New England, the Bermudas, and Providence. In 1628 he obtained the patent of the Massachusetts Bay colony, and in 1635 founded the settlement of Saybrook, CT. A Puritan, he fought for the Parliamentary side as Admiral of the Fleet (1642–9) during the English Civil War. Later he was instrumental in the incorporation of Providence Plantations (now Rhode Island) in 1644. Warwick, RI, is named after him. >> **Gorton, Samuel**

Warwick, Richard Neville, Earl [wo̱rik], also known as **Warwick the Kingmaker** (1428–71) English soldier and politician, who exercised great power during the first phase of the Wars of the Roses. Created Earl of Warwick in 1450, he championed the Yorkist cause. In 1460 he defeated and captured Henry VI at Northampton, had his cousin, Edward of York, proclaimed king as Edward IV (1461), and then destroyed the Lancastrian army at Towton. When Edward tried to assert his independence, Warwick joined the Lancastrians, forced the king to flee to Holland, and restored Henry VI to the throne (1470). He was defeated and killed by Edward IV at the Battle of Barnet. >> **Edward IV; Henry VI**

Washburn, Sherwood (Larned) (1911–) Biological anthropologist, born in Cambridge, MA. He studied at Harvard, and taught at the universities of Columbia, Chicago, and California, Berkeley. A leading authority on primate and human evolution, he stressed the importance of field studies of primate behaviour for modelling the behaviour of extinct hominid forms. He was editor of *Social Life of Early Man* (1962) and numerous other publications.

Washington, Booker T(aliaferro) (1856–1915) Black leader and educationist, born in Franklin Co, VA. After emancipation (1865), he studied at Hampton Institute, VA, and Washington, DC, becoming a teacher, writer, and speaker on black problems. In 1881 he was appointed principal of the newly opened Tuskegee Institute, AL, and built it up into a major centre of black education. He was the foremost black leader in late 19th-c USA, winning white support by his acceptance of the separation of blacks and whites. He was strongly criticized by Du Bois, and his policies were repudiated by the 20th-c civil rights movement. >> **Du Bois, W E B**

Washington, Denzel (1954–) Actor, born in Mount Vernon, NY. He won a scholarship to the American Conservatory Theater in San Francisco, and afterwards worked with the Shakespeare in the Park ensemble. He appeared in a number of off-Broadway productions and in television movies before making his feature-film debut in the comedy *A Carbon Copy* (1981). He had a starring role in the television medical drama *St Elsewhere* (1982–8). He was Oscar-nominated for *Cry Freedom* (1987) and *Malcolm X* (1992), and won a Best Supporting Actor Oscar for *Glory* (1989). Later films include *Much Ado About Nothing* (1993), *Crimson Tide* (1995), and *The Preacher's Wife* (1996).

Washington, Dinah, originally **Ruth Lee Jones** (1924–63) Singer, born in Tuscaloosa, AL. With her unique phrasing, gospel music background, and feeling for the blues, she soon became known as 'Queen of the Blues'. She began with the Sara Martin Singers, then sang with the Lionel Hampton Band (1943–6). Her hit songs include 'Baby, Get Lost' (1949) and 'This Bitter Earth' (1960), and her albums *Unforgettable* (1961) and *Dinah* (1962).

Washington, George see panel on p. 978

Wasserman, August Paul von [va̱serman] (1866–1925) Bacteriologist, born in Bamberg, Germany. He studied medicine at Erlangen, Vienna, Munich, and Strasbourg universities, and worked in bacteriology and chemotherapy at the Robert Koch Institute in Berlin from 1890. He discovered a blood-serum test for syphilis in 1906 (the *Wasserman reaction*).

Watanabe, Kazan [watanahbay, kazan], originally **Jozei Watanabe** (1793–1841) Scholar and painter, born in Edo (now Tokyo). As an art student he became influenced by the S Chinese school of painting known as *wen-jen-hua* ('literati painting'), which stressed scholarly and literary themes. He is noted for his pioneering efforts to integrate Western perspective into Japanese art.

Waterhouse, Alfred (1830–1905) Architect, born in Liverpool, Merseyside, NW England, UK. He studied at Manchester, where he designed the town hall and assize courts, then built the romanesque Natural History Museum in London (1873–81). He also designed many educational buildings, and from his great use of red bricks came the name *redbrick university*.

Waterhouse, Keith (Spencer) (1929–) Novelist and playwright, born in Hunslet, West Yorkshire, N England, UK. He worked at various jobs before becoming a journalist. His second novel *Billy Liar* (1959) became a best-seller, and was adapted for stage (1960) and screen (1963). He is especially known for his partnership with **Willis Hall** (1929–), with whom he wrote several plays, screenplays, and revues, including *Celebration* (1961) and *All Things Bright and Beautiful* (1963). Later novels include *Billy Liar on the Moon* (1975), *Maggie Muggins* (1981), *Bimbo* (1990), and *Unsweet Charity* (1992). He has also written several television series, such as *Budgie*, *Worzel Gummidge*, and *Andy Capp*, and a number of general books, such as *Waterhouse at*

GEORGE WASHINGTON (1732–99)

Washington was born in Bridges Creek, Westmoreland Co, VA, the great-grandson of John Washington, an English immigrant from Selgrave, Northamptonshire. His father, Augustine Washington, married twice. When his first wife died in 1729 having had four children, he married Mary Ball, George's mother. Augustine died in 1743, leaving a further six children. George became a ward of his eldest half-brother, Lawrence; and under the benevolent influence of Lawrence and his wife, Anne Fairfax, a relative of Lord Fairfax, he was introduced into polite society.

Despite irregular schooling, Washington showed a flair for survey work, and travelled widely. His first long trip was in the employ of Lord Fairfax. Later he journeyed as an offical surveyor to Culpepper Co. At the age of 20, in 1752, he inherited Lawrence's estate at Mount Vernon upon the deaths of Lawrence's wife and daughter. He became a prominent farmer, and began to be active in community affairs. He fell in love with **Betsy Fauntleroy**, but was refused when he twice proposed marriage. In 1752 he was made adjutant for the southern military district state militia. His first commission, in 1753, was to warn the French against encroaching into the British sphere of influence in the Ohio Valley. Although the French ignored this warning, he gained a considerable reputation for his tenacity in delivering the message in the course of a hazardous winter journey of over 1000 mi.

Newly promoted to lieutenant-colonel aged 22, Washington returned to Ohio in 1754 with the task of protecting the Ohio Company. His surprise attack on a French detachment provoked a strong reaction, the first engagement of the French and Indian War, and he was forced to surrender. He resigned his commission later that year in protest at the perceived discrimination against colonial officers, but upon the arrival in Virginia of British General Edward Braddock's army, he was invited to serve him as an aide-de-camp with the courtesy rank of colonel. Following the British defeat at Fort Duquesne (1755), in which Braddock was killed, he was appointed commander-in-chief of all the Virginian forces, defending the frontier against French and Indian attackers.

He resigned his commission in 1758, aged 26, returned to Mount Vernon, and married **Martha Dandridge Custis** (1732–1802) in January 1759. The union brought him considerable additional wealth, as well as two stepchildren. He and Martha had no children of their own. He proved a resourceful landowner and entrepreneur, became prominent in local politics, and served as a member of the Virginia House of Burgesses (1758–65). In 1774 he represented Virginia in the first Continental Congress, but played only a minor role. Returning to the second Continental Congress, which coincided with the first armed skirmishes of the War of Independence (1775–83), he was made commander-in-chief of the combined colonial military forces (1775).

Perhaps Washington's greatest achievement in the War was the rallying of his depleted forces at Valley Forge during the bitter winter of 1777–8. Dogged by defeats, desertion, sickness, and starvation, his troops reached the lowest ebb of their campaign morale. Their subsequent recovery and notable victories prompted French involvement in the war on the side of the colonists, ensuring ultimate victory.

With the end of the war, Washington retired to Mount Vernon and sought to secure a strong government by constitutional means. His first effort, the Annapolis Convention (1786), sought to eliminate boundary disputes and trade wars between states, but its failure led to a proposal for a further convention at Philadelphia to amend the ineffectual Articles of Confederation adopted in 1781. He was elected as president of this Constitutional Convention (1787), and his force of character was instrumental in the rejection of these Articles and the adoption of a radical new constitution. The campaign to obtain ratification of the constitution had created divisions between the representatives, and Washington was seen as the only figure who could command the respect of both major factions. In 1789 he was unanimously elected as the first president of the United States of America, and reluctantly returned to public life. In his first term of office, Washington formed a cabinet of the foremost men in the country, evenly balanced between the two parties. It included Thomas Jefferson as secretary of state and Alexander Hamilton as secretary of the Treasury. By the time he was re-elected for a second term (1793), the differences between Hamilton's Federalists and Jefferson's Democratic-Republicans became increasingly acrimonious. While inclining increasingly towards Hamilton's views, Washington was dismayed that his cabinet could not transcend party differences. Faced with increasingly virulent personal attacks, he retired from the presidency in 1797, and returned to Mount Vernon to resume caring for his estates, apart from a recall in 1798 for a few weeks to form a defensive army against the prospect of war with France. He died in December the next year, following exposure from riding round his farms in wintry conditions. On the news of his death, a touching tribute was paid to him by his former enemy: the British channel fleet fired a 20-gun salute.

>> Braddock, Edward; Hamilton, Alexander; Jefferson, Thomas

Large (1985) and English, Our English (1991). In 1995 appeared a volume of memoirs, Streets Ahead.

Waters, Ethel (1900–77) Stage actress and singer, born in Chester, PA. An eloquent performer, she began in both black and white vaudeville, then made her debut on Broadway in 1927. She is remembered for her role in The Member of the Wedding (1950).

Waters, Muddy, stage name of **McKinley Morganfield** (1915–83) Blues singer, composer, and guitarist, born in Rolling Fork, MI. He learnt to play the harmonica and the guitar in his teens, and was first recorded in 1941 by Alan Lomax, the folk music researcher for the American Library of Congress. He recorded his first solo single, 'I Can't Be Satisfied', in 1948, and gained his first national success with 'Rollin' Stone' (1950). His band had a profound influence on the white rhythm-and-blues artists of the mid-1960s. One of his best-known singles is 'I've Got My Mojo Working' (1957).

Watkins, Dudley Dexter (1907–67) Strip cartoonist and illustrator, born in Manchester, Greater Manchester, NW England, UK. Acclaimed as a schoolboy genius for his painting of the Nottingham Historical Pageant at the age of 10, he studied at Nottingham School of Art. He joined D C Thomson's art department, and created *Oor Wullie* and *The Broons* strips for the *Sunday Post* (1936), then *Desperate Dan* for the *Dandy* (1937), *Lord Snooty* for the *Beano* (1938), and many more. He created classic picture serials, such as *Treasure Island*, later reprinted as books (1948). Highly religious, he contributed strips to *Young Warrior* (1960) without charge. >> Thomson, D C

Watkins, Vernon (Phillips) (1906–67) Poet, born in Maesteg, Bridgend, S Wales. He studied at Cambridge, and worked at Lloyds Bank, Swansea, for most of his life. He published eight collections of verse during his lifetime, including *Ballad of Mari Lwyd* (1941), *Death Bell* (1954), and *Affinities* (1962). Regarded as one of the greatest Welsh poets in English, as well as one of the most unusual, he was long overshadowed by his friend Dylan Thomas. >> Thomas, Dylan

Watson, James (Dewey) (1928–) Geneticist, born in Chicago, IL. He studied at Chicago and Indiana universities, worked in Copenhagen, then went to Cambridge, where with Crick and Wilkins he helped discover the molecular structure of DNA, sharing with them the 1962 Nobel Prize for Physiology or Medicine. He became professor of biology at Harvard in 1961, and director (1968–94) then president (1994–) of the Cold Spring Harbor Laboratory at Long Island, NY. >> Crick; Franklin, Rosalind; Wilkins, Maurice

Watson, John B(roadus) (1878–1958) Psychologist, born in Greenville, SC. He studied at Chicago, and became professor of psychology at Johns Hopkins University (1908–20), where he established an animal research laboratory. He became known for his behaviourist approach, which he later applied to human behaviour. In 1921 he entered advertising, and wrote several general books on psychology.

Watson, Thomas (c. 1557–92) Lyric poet, born in London, England, UK. He was educated at Oxford, then studied law in London. Coming to Marlowe's help in a street fight, he killed a man in 1589. He excelled in English 'sonnets' in *Hecatompathia or Passionate Century of Love* (1582) and *The Tears of Fancie* (1593), and his sonnets were very probably studied by Shakespeare. He also translated classics into Latin and English, including Sophocles, Tasso, and Italian madrigals. >> Marlowe, Christopher

Watson, Tom, popular name of **Thomas (Sturges) Watson** (1949–) Golfer, born in Kansas City, MO. He turned professional in 1971, and has since won 32 tournaments on the US tour. He has won the (British) Open five times (1975, 1977, 1980, 1982–3), the US Open (1982), and the US Masters (1977, 1981). >> RR1157

Watson, Sir William (1715–87) Scientist, born in London, England, UK. He was one of the earliest experimenters on electricity, being the first to investigate the passage of electricity through a rarefied gas, and did much to introduce the Linnaean system of botanical classification to Britain.

Watson-Watt, Sir Robert Alexander (1892–1973) Physicist who developed the radio location of aircraft, born in Brechin, Angus, E Scotland, UK. He studied at St Andrews University, taught at Dundee University, and in 1917 worked in the Meteorological Office, designing devices to locate thunderstorms, and investigating the ionosphere (a term he invented in 1926). He became head of the radio section of the National Physical Laboratory (1935), where he began work on locating aircraft. His work led to the development of radar (Radio Detection and Ranging) which played a vital role in the defence of Britain against German air raids in 1940. He was knighted in 1942.

Watt, James (1736–1819) Inventor, born in Greenock, Inverclyde, WC Scotland, UK. He went to Glasgow in 1754 to learn the trade of mathematical-instrument maker, and there, after a year in London, he set up in business. He was employed on surveys for several canals, improved harbours and rivers, and by 1759 was studying steam as a motive force. In 1763–4, in the course of repairing a working model of the Newcomen engine, he found he could greatly improve its efficiency by using a separate steam condenser. After other improvements, he went into partnership with Matthew Boulton, and the new engine was manufactured at Birmingham in 1774. Several other inventions followed, including the double-acting engine, parallel motion linkage, the centrifugal governor for automatic speed control, and the pressure gauge. The term *horsepower* was first used by him, and the SI unit of power is named after him. >> Boulton; Hornblower; Murdock, William; Papin; Wilkinson, John

Watteau, (Jean) Antoine [va**toh**] (1684–1721) Rococo painter, born in Valenciennes, France. In 1702 he went to study in Paris, where he worked as a scene painter and a copyist. His early canvases were mostly military scenes, but it was the mythological 'L'Embarquement pour l'île de Cythère' (1717, Embarkation for the island of Cythera) which won him membership of the Academy. He is also known for his 'Fêtes galantes' (Scenes of Gallantry) – quasi-pastoral idylls in court dress which became fashionable in high society.

Watts, André (1946–) Pianist, born in Nuremberg, Germany. He studied piano in Philadelphia, and appeared with the Philadelphia Orchestra at age nine. He achieved national prominence in 1963, when he played on national television with the New York Philharmonic. After his first world tour in 1967, he became an international favourite, primarily noted for his 19th-c repertoire.

Watts, Charlie >> **Rolling Stones, The**

Watts, George Frederick (1817–1904) Painter, born in London, England, UK. He studied in London, and first attracted notice by his cartoon of 'Caractacus' (1843) in the competition for murals for the new Houses of Parliament. He became known for his penetrating portraits of notabilities, 150 of which he presented to the National Portrait Gallery in 1904. He also executed some sculpture, notably 'Physical Energy' in Kensington Gardens, London.

Watts, Isaac (1674–1748) Nonconformist hymnwriter, born in Southampton, Hampshire, S England, UK. He trained for the ministry at the Dissenting Academy in Stoke Newington, and was appointed as an Independent minister in Mark Lane, London (1702), becoming eminent as a preacher and hymn-writer. His hymns include 'Jesus shall reign where'er the Sun', 'When I Survey the Wondrous Cross', and 'O God, Our Help in Ages Past'.

Waugh, Alec [waw], popular name of **Alexander Raban Waugh** (1898–1981) Novelist and travel writer, born in London, England, UK, the brother of Evelyn Waugh. He was educated at Sherborne School, Dorset, which provided the background for his precocious first novel, *Loom of Youth* (1917). This enjoyed some success, partly on account of its treatment of public school homosexuality. Later works include various travel books, notably *Island in the Sun* (1975), and autobiographical volumes such as *The Early Years of Alec Waugh* (1962) and *My Brother Evelyn and Other Portraits* (1976). >> Waugh, Evelyn

Waugh, (Alexander) Auberon [waw] (1939–) Journalist and novelist, the eldest son of Evelyn Waugh, born in Dulverton, Somerset, SW England, UK. He studied at Oxford, worked on the *Daily Telegraph* (1960), and the same year published his first novel, *The Foxglove Saga*. There followed four novels, each well received, but he abandoned fiction for lack of financial reward. There are few national papers to which he has not contributed, but his best work has appeared in the *New Statesman*, the *Spectator*, and the now defunct *Books and Bookmen*. He has been editor of the *Literary Review* since 1986, and a columnist for the *Daily Telegraph* since 1990 and the *Sunday Telegraph* since 1996. >> Waugh, Evelyn

Waugh, Evelyn (Arthur St John) [waw] (1903–66) Writer, born in London, England, UK. He studied at Oxford, and quickly established a reputation with such social satirical novels as *Decline and Fall* (1928), *Vile Bodies* (1930), and *Scoop* (1938). He became a Catholic in 1930, and his later books display a more serious attitude, as seen in the religious theme of *Brideshead Revisited* (1945), a nostalgic evocation of student days at Oxford, which was made into a successful television series. His 'sword of honour' trilogy contains *Men at Arms* (1952), *Officers and Gentlemen* (1955), and *Unconditional Surrender* (1961). His diaries were published in 1976, and his letters in 1980. >> Waugh, Alec; Waugh, Auberon

Wavell, Archibald Percival Wavell, 1st Earl [wayvl] (1883–1950) British field marshal, born in Winchester, Hampshire, S England, UK. He trained at Sandhurst, served in South Africa and India, became Allenby's chief-of-staff in Palestine, and in 1939 was given the Middle East command. He defeated the Italians in N Africa, but failed against Rommel, and in 1941 was transferred to India, where he became viceroy, and was made field marshal and viscount (1943). He was later created an earl (1947), and held the posts of Constable of the Tower (1948) and Lord-Lieutenant of London (1949). >> Rommel

Waverley, John Anderson, 1st Viscount (1882–1958) British administrator and politician, born in Eskbank, Midlothian, EC Scotland, UK. He studied at Edinburgh and Leipzig, and entered the colonial office in 1905. He became chairman of the Board of Inland Revenue (1919–22), permanent under-secretary at the Home Office (1922–32), Governor of Bengal (1932–9), and home secretary and minister of home security (1939–40, the *Anderson air-raid shelter* being named after him). As Chancellor of the Exchequer in 1943, he introduced the pay-as-you-earn (PAYE) system of income-tax collection devised by his predecessor. He was created a viscount in 1952.

Wayne, Anthony, known as **Mad Anthony** (1745–96) Revolutionary soldier, born in Easttown, PA. In 1776 he raised a volunteer regiment, and in Canada covered the retreat of the provincial forces at Three Rivers. He commanded at Ticonderoga until 1777, when he joined Washington in New Jersey. He fought bravely at Brandywine (1777), led the attack at Germantown, captured supplies for the army at Valley Forge, carried Stony Point, and saved Lafayette in Virginia (1781). In 1793 he led an expedition against the Indians. >> Lafayette, Marie Joseph; Washington, George

Wayne, John, originally **Marion Michael Morrison,** nickname **the Duke** (1907–79) Film actor, born in Winterset, IA. After a succession of small parts in low-budget films and serials, he achieved stardom as the Ringo Kid in *Stagecoach* (1939). He went on to make over 80 films, typically starring as a tough but warm-hearted gunfighter or lawman. Classics of the Western genre include *She Wore a Yellow Ribbon* (1949), *The Man who Shot Liberty Vallance* (1962), and *True Grit* (1969, Oscar). Later films include urban cop thrillers such as *McQ* (1974) and *Brannigan* (1975). He also directed *The Alamo* (1960) and *The Green Berets* (1968). His final performance was in *The Shootist* (1976), portraying a legendary gunfighter dying of cancer – a poignant film, as he fought against this disease himself.

Waynflete, William of >> **William of Waynflete**

Weaver, James B(aird) (1833–1912) Politician, born in Dayton, OH. Admitted to the bar in 1856, he practised law in Bloomfield, IA, then fought in the Civil War as a Unionist. He joined the Greenback Party, serving in the US House of Representatives (1879–81, 1885–9), and ran unsuccessfully for the presidency as Greenback candidate (1880). Later prominent in the rise of the People's Party, he was elected party president (1892), but failed in his bid for the presidency as a Populist candidate (1892).

Weaver, Sigourney (1949–) Motion-picture actress, born in New York City. She completed a university education at Stanford and Yale universities before embarking on a film career. Her big break came when she was cast as astronaut Ripley in the film *Aliens* (1979), a part originally written for a man. Later films include *Eyewitness* (1981), *The Year of Living Dangerously* (1983), *Ghostbusters* (1984), the three *Aliens* sequels (1986, 1992, 1997), *Dave* (1993), and *Copycat* (1995).

Webb British social reformers, historians, and economists: **Sidney James Webb** (1859–1947) and **(Martha) Beatrice Webb,** *née* **Potter** (1858–1943), married in 1892. He was born and studied in London, became a lawyer, and joined the Fabian Society, where he wrote many powerful tracts. She was born in Standish, Gloucestershire, and became involved with the social problems of the time. After their marriage they began a joint life of service to Socialism and trade unionism, publishing their classic *History of Trade Unionism* (1894), *English Local Government* (9 vols, 1906–29), and other works. They also started the *New Statesman* (1913). Sidney became an MP (1922), President of the Board of Trade (1924), dominions and colonial secretary (1929–30), and colonial secretary (1930–1), and was created Baron Passfield in 1929.

Webb, Sir Aston (1849–1930) Architect, born in London, England, UK. He designed the E facade of Buckingham Palace, the Admiralty Arch, Imperial College of Science, and many other London buildings.

Webb, Beatrice >> **Webb**

Webb, Harry Roger >> **Richard, Cliff**

Webb, James E(dwin) (1906–92) US official and administrator of NASA during its programme to land a man on the Moon, born in Tally Ho, NC. He became head of Bureau of the Budget under President Truman (1946–9), and later his under-secretary of state (1949–52). He was chosen by President Kennedy in 1961 to create in NASA an agency capable of successfully undertaking the Apollo Project, and retired from NASA in 1968, a year before the Apollo 11 landing. >> Kennedy, John F; Truman, Harry S

Webb, Karrie (1974–) Golfer, born in Ayr, Queensland, Australia. In 1996 she became the first women to break the $1 million prize-money barrier while playing on the US Ladies' PGA tour, and was named 'Rookie of the Year'. She won the women's Open title in the UK in 1995, the youngest ever winner, and won it again in 1997.

Webb, Mary (Gladys), *née* **Meredith** (1881–1927) Novelist, born in Keighton, Shropshire, WC England, UK. Educated at Southport, she married in 1912, became a market gardener with her husband, and moved to London in 1921. Her early novels met with little success, but *Precious Bane* (1924) became an instant best seller after it had been praised by the prime minister, Stanley Baldwin. Other works include *The Golden Arrow* (1916), *The House in Dormer Forest* (1920), and *Seven for a Secret* (1922).

Webb, Matthew (1848–83) Swimmer, the first man to swim the English Channel, born in Dawley, Shropshire, WC England, UK. He trained as a seaman and became a master mariner, before becoming a professional swimmer in 1875. On 24–25 August, 1875, he swam from Dover to

Calais in 21 hrs 45 mins. He was drowned attempting to swim the Niagara rapids.

Webb, Philip (1831–1915) Architect and designer, born in Oxford, Oxfordshire, SC England, UK. After his training, he joined the practice of G E Street (1852), where he met William Morris, with whom he founded Morris, Marshall, Faulkner & Co in 1861, and the Society for the Protection of Ancient Buildings (1877). He designed several important houses, such as 'The Red House' in Bexley, Kent, for Morris (1859), 'Clouds' in Wiltshire (1881–6), and 'Standen' in East Grinstead, Surrey (1891). >> Morris, William; Street, George Edmund

Webb, Sidney James >> Webb

Weber, Carl (Maria Friedrich) von [vayber] (1786–1826) Composer and pianist, born in Eutin, Germany. Nurtured by his family for music, he began to compose, and became conductor of the opera at Wrocław, Poland (formerly Breslau, Germany) (1804)). In 1813 he settled in Prague as opera *Kapellmeister*, and about 1816 was invited by the King of Saxony to direct the German opera at Dresden. He is known as the founder of German Romantic opera, notably in *Der Freischütz* (1821, The Freeshooter), *Euryanthe* (1823), and *Oberon* (1826), and he also wrote several orchestral works, as well as piano, chamber, and church music, and many songs.

Weber, Ernst (Heinrich) [vayber] (1795–1878) Physiologist, born in Wittenberg, Germany, the brother of Wilhelm Weber. He became professor of anatomy (1818) and of physiology (1840) at Leipzig, where he devised a method of determining the sensitivity of the skin, introducing the concept of the 'just noticeable difference'. His findings were expressed mathematically by Fechner (the *Weber–Fechner Law of the Increase of Stimuli*). >> Fechner; Weber, Wilhelm

Weber, Max [vayber] (1864–1920) Sociologist and economist, born in Erfurt, Germany. He studied at Heidelberg and Berlin universities, and held posts at Berlin (1893), Freiberg (1894), Heidelberg (1897), and Munich (1919). His best known work is *Die protestantische Ethik und der Geist des Kapitalismus* (1904, The Protestant Ethic and the Spirit of Capitalism), which was a major influence on sociological theory. He helped to draft the constitution for the Weimar Republic (1919).

Weber, Max [vayber] (1881–1961) Painter, born in Białystok, Poland. He emigrated to the USA with his family, studied art in New York City and in Paris, and taught at the Art Students League, New York City. He became one of the pioneer Abstractionist painters, later abandoning this form for a distorted naturalism. His work became more representational in later years, often dealing with Jewish themes.

Weber, Wilhelm (Eduard) [vayber] (1804–91) Scientist, born in Wittenberg, Germany, the brother of Ernst Weber. He was professor of physics at Göttingen (1831–7) and Leipzig (1843–9), then returned to Göttingen, where he directed the astronomical observatory, and was associated with Johann Gauss in his research into electricity and magnetism. He was the inventor of the electrodynamometer, the first to apply the mirror and scale method of reading deflections, and author, with his brother, of a notable treatise on waves. >> Gauss; Weber, Ernst

Webern, Anton (Friedrich Ernst von) [vaybern] (1883–1945) Composer, born in Vienna. He studied under Schoenberg, and became one of his first musical disciples, making wide use of 12-tone techniques, which led to several hostile demonstrations when his works were first performed. For a while he worked as a conductor and tutor in various cities, before settling in Mödling in 1918. His works, which include a symphony, cantatas, several short orchestral pieces, chamber music, a concerto for nine instruments,

and songs, have profoundly influenced many later composers. The Nazis banned his music, and he worked as a proofreader during World War 2. He was accidentally shot dead by a US soldier near Salzburg. >> Schoenberg

Webster, Daniel (1782–1852) US orator, lawyer, and statesman, born in Salisbury, NH. He studied at Dartmouth, Salisbury, and Boston, and was admitted to the bar in 1805. A prominent lawyer of the US Supreme Court, and a leading orator, he was a congressman (1813–17, 1823–7), senator (1827–41, 1845–50), and secretary of state (1841–4, 1850–2). He is best remembered for the *Webster–Ashburton Treaty* of 1842 between Britain and the USA, which established the present-day boundaries between NE USA and Canada.

Webster, John (c. 1580–c. 1625) English playwright. Little is known of him, though he is supposed to have been at one time clerk of St Andrews, Holborn. He collaborated with several other writers, especially Thomas Dekker, but is best known for his two tragedies, *The White Devil* (1612) and *The Duchess of Malfi* (1623). >> Dekker

Webster, Noah (1758–1843) Lexicographer, born in Hartford, CT. He studied at Yale, and became a lawyer, but preferred teaching. He achieved fame with the first part (later known as 'Webster's Spelling Book') of *A Grammatical Institute of the English Language* (1783). Political articles and pamphlets, lecturing, and journalism occupied him until 1798, when he retired to literary life. He is best known for his work in lexicography, notably the *American Dictionary of the English Language* (2 vols, 1828), which was a major influence on US dictionary practice. >> Worcester, Joseph

Webster, Tom, popular name of **Gilbert Thomas Webster** (1890–1962) Sports cartoonist and animator, born in Bilston, West Midlands, C England, UK. While working as a railway booking clerk in 1904, he won a newspaper cartoon contest. He joined the art staff of the *Birmingham Sports Argus*, and moved to the *Daily Mail* in 1919, introducing such sporting characters as Tishy the Racehorse. He evolved a unique style of cartoons in a free-ranging strip format with commentary.

Wechsler, David [weksler] (1896–1981) Psychologist, born in Lespedi, Romania. He studied at the City College of New York and Columbia University (1925), and went on to serve as chief psychologist at Bellevue Psychiatric Hospital (1932–67). He developed the Wechsler–Bellevue Intelligence Scale (1939), devised for testing adult intelligence, and later adapted for children. The tests have been widely used and periodically revised.

Weddell, James [wedl] (1787–1834) Navigator, explorer, and seal hunter, born in Ostend, Belgium. He undertook three voyages to Antarctica in the sealing brig *Jane*, in the third of which (1822–3) he penetrated to the point 74° 15 S by 34° 17 W in that part of Antarctica which later took his name (*Weddell Sea*, *Weddell Quadrant*). A type of seal from this area is also named after him.

Wedderburn, Joseph (Henry Maclagan) (1882–1948) Mathematician, born in Forfar, Angus, E Scotland, UK. He studied at Edinburgh University, visited Leipzig, Berlin, and Chicago, then returned to Edinburgh as a lecturer (1905–9). In 1909 he went to Princeton, and settled there after World War 1 until retiring in 1945. His work on algebra includes two fundamental theorems known by his name, one on the classification of semi-simple algebras, the other on finite division rings.

Wedekind, Frank [vaydekint] (1864–1918) Playwright, born in Hanover, Germany. He worked in business and journalism, before becoming a cabaret performer, playwright, and producer. He is best known for his unconventional tragedies, in which he anticipated the Theatre of the Absurd: *Erdgeist* (1895, Earth Spirit), *Frühlings Erwachen*

(1891, The Awakening of Spring), and *Die Büchse der Pandora* (1903, Pandora's Box).

Wedgwood, Dame Cicely (Veronica) (1910–97) Historian, born in Stocksfield, Northumberland, NE England, UK. She studied at Oxford, and became a specialist in 17th-c history, writing such biographies as *Oliver Cromwell* (1939) and *William the Silent* (1944, James Tait Black). She also wrote several general works, such as *The Thirty Years' War* (1938). She was created a dame in 1968.

Wedgwood, Josiah (1730–95) Potter, born in Burslem, Staffordshire, C England, UK. He worked in the family pottery business, became a partner of Thomas Whieldon in 1754, and began to devise improved wares. In 1759 he opened a factory at Burslem and a decade later opened one near Hanley, which he called 'Etruria'. Inspired by antique models, he invented unglazed black basalt ware and blue jasper ware with raised designs in white. From 1768 to 1780 he was in partnership with **Thomas Bentley** (1730–80), who introduced advanced marketing techniques to the firm. Wedgwood's concern over social welfare led him to build a village for his workmen at Etruria.

Weelkes, Thomas (c. 1575–1623) Madrigal composer, probably born in Elsted, Surrey, SE England, UK. He became organist at Winchester College (1597) and Chichester Cathedral (1602). Nearly 100 of his madrigals have survived, as well as some instrumental music, and fragments of his sacred music.

Weems, Mason Locke, known as **Parson Weems** (1759–1825) Clergyman, bookseller, and writer, born in Ann Arundel Co, MD. Criticized for his sprightly informality as an Episcopal clergyman, he was well-known for his uplifting sermons, moral tracts, and fictionalized biographies, especially for his best-selling life of George Washington. The fifth edition (1806) saw the first appearance in print of the story of young Washington and the cherry tree. From about 1794, he travelled between New York and Georgia selling books and preaching sermons. >> Washington, George

Weenix, Jan [vayniks] (1640–1719) Painter, born in Amsterdam. He was known for hunting scenes, animal subjects, and still-life paintings featuring dead gamebirds, hares, and other creatures.

Wegener, Alfred (Lothar) [vaygener] (1880–1930) Explorer and geophysicist, originator of the theory of continental drift, born in Berlin. He was professor of meteorology at Hamburg (1919), and of geophysics and meteorology at Graz (1924). His theory is named after him (*Wegener's hypothesis*), and is the subject of his main publications. His ideas first met with great hostility, but by the 1960s plate tectonics was established as a major tenet of modern geophysics. He died during his fourth expedition to Greenland. >> Runcorn

Weidenreich, Franz [viydnriykh] (1873–1948) Anatomist and anthropologist, born in Edenkoben, Germany. He studied medicine at Strasbourg, where he became professor of anatomy (1903–18), held posts at Heidelberg and Frankfurt, then left Nazi Germany for the USA in 1934. He worked in China at the Peking Union Medical College (1935–41), collaborating with Pierre Teilhard de Chardin on fossil remains of Peking Man. He moved to the American Museum of Natural History in New York City (1941–8), his studies of hominid fossil remains leading him to an orthogenetic view of human evolution which he summarized in *Apes, Giants and Man* (1946). >> Teilhard de Chardin

Weidman, Charles (Edward), Jr [wiydman] (1901–75) Modern dancer, choreographer, and teacher, born in Lincoln, NE. He trained at the Denishawn school, and worked with the company for eight years. In partnership with Doris Humphrey, he formed the Humphrey–Weidman

school (1928–45), developing his work as a choreographer of comic and satirical works. In 1945 he founded his own school and company. >> Humphrey, Doris; Saint Denis, Ruth; Shawn

Weierstrass, Karl (Theodor Wilhelm) [viyershtrahs] (1815–97) Mathematician, 'the father of modern analysis', born in Ostenfelde, Germany. A failed law student from Bonn, he took a teacher's certificate at Münster and taught mathematics in secondary schools (1842–56) while working privately on analysis. The publication of his memoir on Abelian functions (1854) brought him an honorary doctorate and a post at the Royal Polytechnic School, Berlin. He published relatively little, but became famous for his lectures, in which he gave a systematic account of analysis with previously unknown rigour, inspiring many of his students to become creative mathematicians. >> Abel, Niels Henrik

Weigel, Helene [viygl] (1900–71) Actress-manager, born in Austria. She married Bertolt Brecht in 1929, and became a leading exponent of his work, particularly in *Die Mutter* (1932, The Mother) and *Mutter Courage und ihre Kinder* (1949, Mother Courage and her Children). She took control of the Berliner Ensemble after Brecht's death in 1956, and was instrumental in furthering his influence through the international tours she managed. >> Brecht

Weil, André [vayl] (1906–) Mathematician, born in Paris, the brother of Simone Weil. He studied at the universities of Paris, Rome, and Göttingen, and was professor of mathematics in India (1930–2), Strasbourg (1933–40), Brazil (1945–7), and Chicago (1947–58), before settling at Princeton in 1958. One of the most brilliant mathematicians of the century, he has worked in number theory, algebraic geometry, and group theory. He was one of the founders of the Bourbaki group, and has also written on the history of mathematics. >> Bourbaki; Weil, Simone

Weil, Simone [vayl] (1909–43) Philosophical writer and mystic, born in Paris. She taught philosophy in several schools, interspersing this with periods of manual labour to experience the working-class life. In 1936 she served in the Republican forces in the Spanish Civil War. In 1941 she settled in Marseille, where she developed a deep mystical feeling for the Catholic faith, yet a profound reluctance to join an organized religion. She escaped to the USA in 1942 and worked for the Free French in London, before dying from voluntary starvation in an attempt to identify with her compatriots suffering in France. Her posthumously published works include *La Pesanteur et la grâce* (1946, Gravity and Grace) and *Attente de Dieu* (1950, Waiting for God). >> Weil, André

Weill, Kurt [viyl] (1900–50) Composer, born in Dessau, Germany. He studied and worked at Berlin, became a composer of instrumental works, then collaborated with Brecht, achieving fame with *Die Dreigroschenoper* (1928, The Threepenny Opera), its best-known song, 'Mack the Knife', becoming an international classic. A refugee from the Nazis, he settled with his actress wife Lotte Lenya in the USA in 1935. His Broadway works included *Knickerbocker Holiday* (1938) and *Lady in the Dark* (1941), and he also wrote the 'folk opera' *Down in the Valley* (1948), which used traditional Kentucky tunes. His later operas and musical comedies, all of which contain an element of social criticism, did not repeat the success of the first. >> Brecht; Lenya

Weinberg, Steven [wiynberg] (1933–) Nuclear physicist, born in New York City. He studied at Cornell and Princeton universities, and taught at Columbia, Berkeley, the Massachusetts Institute of Technology, and Harvard before becoming professor of physics at Texas in 1986. In 1967 he produced a gauge theory that correctly predicted both electromagnetic and weak nuclear forces (despite the two differing in strength by a factor of about 10^{10}) related to elementary particles. The theory also predicted a new interaction due to 'neutral currents', whereby a charge-less particle is exchanged giving rise to a force between particles. He shared the 1979 Nobel Prize for Physics with Abdus Salam and Lee Glashow. >> Glashow; Salam

Weinberg, Wilhelm >> **Hardy, Godfrey Harold**

Weinberger, Caspar (Willard) [wiynberger] (1917–) US statesman, born in San Francisco, CA. After military service (1941–5) he worked as a lawyer, before entering politics as a member of the California state legislature in 1952. He was state finance director of California during Ronald Reagan's governorship (1968–9). He served in the Nixon and Ford administrations, then became secretary of defense after Reagan's election victory in 1980. Briefed to supervise a major military build-up, he developed such high-profile projects as the strategic defence initiative. A 'hawk' on East–West issues, he opposed detente, resigned his office in 1987, and returned to private life. He was awarded an honorary knighthood in 1988 for his services to Britain, notably during the Falklands War (1982). >> Ford, Gerald; Nixon; Reagan

Weinberger, Jaromir [viynberger] (1896–1967) Composer, born in Prague. He studied at the Prague Conservatory and under Max Reger in Leipzig, was professor of composition at Ithaca Conservatory, New York (1922–6), and settled in the USA in 1939. He wrote theatre music, orchestral works, and four operas, the most famous of which is *Svanda Dudák* (1927, Schvanda the Bagpiper). >> Reger

Weingartner, (Paul) Felix, Edler (Lord) **von Munzberg** [viyngah(r)tner] (1863–1942) Conductor and composer, born in Zara, Austria. He studied under Liszt, succeeded Mahler (1908) as conductor of the Vienna Court Opera, and later toured extensively in Britain and America. His works include operas, symphonies, and his famous pamphlet *Uber das Dirigieren* (1895, On Conducting). He became a Swiss citizen in 1937. >> Liszt; Mahler

Weinstock (of Bowden), Arnold, Baron [wiynstok] (1924–) Industrial executive, born in London, England, UK. He studied at London University, worked at the Admiralty (1939–45), was engaged in finance and property development (1947–54), then entered the radio and allied industries. He joined the General Electric Company in 1961, becoming managing director (1963–96), during which time he developed greatly the power and influence of the company through a series of take-overs. He was knighted in 1970 and created a life peer in 1980.

Weir, Peter (Lindsay) (1944–) Film director, born in Sydney, New South Wales, Australia. He studied at Sydney University, joined a local television station in 1967, and began directing short films with *Count Vim's Last Exercise* (1967). His first feature film was *The Cars that Ate Paris* (1974), but he came to the forefront of the Australian film industry with the languid ghost story *Picnic at Hanging Rock* (1975) and *Gallipoli* (1980). He then moved to America, and had international success with *Witness* (1985), *Dead Poets Society* (1989), *Green Card* (1990), and *Fearless* (1993).

Weismann, August (Friedrich Leopold) [viysman] (1834–1914) Biologist, born in Frankfurt, Germany. He studied at Göttingen, and became professor of zoology at Freiburg (1867). He is best known for his theory of *germ plasm* (1886), a hereditary substance of which only one half was passed on to the next generation cells. This is now recognized as a forerunner of the DNA theory.

Weiss, Peter (Ulrich) [viys] (1916–82) Playwright, film-maker, and novelist, born in Nowawes, Germany. He fled Nazi Germany, and settled in Sweden in 1939, becoming famous with his first play, *The Persecution and Assassination of Marat as Performed by the Inmates of the Asylum of Charenton*

Under the Direction of the Marquis de Sade (1964), known more simply as *Marat/Sade*. His next play, *The Investigation* (1965), was a documentary based on transcripts of the Auschwitz trials. *The Song of the Lusitanian Bogey* (1967) was a more cogent attack on the capitalist system. He also wrote the autobiographical novels *Leave Taking* (1961) and *Vanishing Point* (1962).

Weissmuller, Johnny [wiyzmuhler], popular name of **(Peter) John** (originally **Jonas**) **Weissmuller** (1904–84) Swimmer and film-star, born in Freidorf, Romania. His family emigrated to the USA in 1908. In 1922 he made history by becoming the first person to swim 100 m in under one minute, and he won the 100 m freestyle at the 1924 and 1928 Olympics, and the 400 m in 1928. After turning professional in 1932, he became a swimsuit model for a clothing firm. His name is most widely known for his starring role in 12 Tarzan films, made between 1932 and 1948. He is credited with inventing the King of the Jungle's celebrated yodelling call (actually a combination of recorded animal cries).

Weisz, Victor >> **Vicky**

Weizmann, Chaim (Azriel) [viytsman, khiym] (1874–1952) Jewish statesman and president of Israel (1949–52), born near Pinsk, Belarus. He studied in Germany and Switzerland, then lectured on chemistry at Geneva and Manchester universities. He helped to secure the Balfour Declaration of 1917, and became president of the Zionist Organization (1920–30, 1935–46) and of the Jewish Agency (from 1929). He played a major role in the establishment of the state of Israel (1948), and was its first president. >> RR1064

Weizsäcker, Richard, Freiherr (Baron) **von** [viytseker] (1920–) President of Germany (1990–4), and president of the former Federal Republic of Germany (1984–90), born in Stuttgart, Germany. He studied at Berlin, Oxford, Grenoble, and Göttingen universities, and during World War 2 served in the Wehrmacht. After the war he worked as a professional lawyer, and was active in the German Protestant Church, becoming president of its Congress (1964–70). A member of the conservative Christian Democratic Union (CDU) since 1954, he served as a deputy in the Bundestag from 1969, as CDU deputy chairman (1972–9) and, from 1981, as a successful mayor of West Berlin, before being elected federal president in May 1984. He was re-elected in 1989, and signed the treaty re-uniting East and West Germany in 1990. >> RR1051

Welch, Bruce >> **Shadows, The**

Welch, Raquel, originally **Raquel Tejada** (1940–) Actress, born in Chicago, IL. She entered beauty contests as a teenager, and worked as a model, waitress, and television weather-girl before making her film debut in 1964. Launched as a sex symbol after her scantily clad appearance in *One Million Years BC* (1966), she was rarely challenged by later roles, though for her role in *The Three Musketeers* (1973) she received a Best Actress Golden Globe Award. Absent from the cinema since 1979, she continues to be regarded as one of the world's great beauties, and her career has included nightclub entertaining, the Broadway musical *Woman of the Year* (1982), and the publication of a *Total Beauty and Fitness Programme* (1984).

Welch, Robert (1929–) Silversmith and product designer, born in Hereford, Hereford and Worcester, WC England, UK. He trained at Birmingham and the Royal College of Art, London. He is best known as the designer of the stainless steel ware produced under the name 'Old Hall'. He has bridged successfully the gap between the making of single pieces of fine craftsmanship and industrial production, while maintaining a high degree of elegance and quality in the products for which he is reponsible. He was made a royal designer for industry in 1965.

Weldon, Fay (1933–) Writer, born in Alvechurch, Worcestershire, WC England, UK. She studied at the University of St Andrews, and worked as an advertising copywriter before becoming a full-time author, writing novels, short stories, and television plays. Her work deals with contemporary feminist themes, as in *Female Friends* (1975) and *Puffball* (1980), and caustic satires of male-dominated society, as in *The Hearts and Lives Of Men* (1987) and *Darcy's Utopia* (1989). Later books include *Wicked Women* (1995) and *Worst Fears* (1996).

Welensky, Sir Roy [welenskee] (1907–91) Rhodesian statesman, born in Harare (formerly, Salisbury), Zimbabwe (formerly, Southern Rhodesia). A railway worker and trade unionist, he was elected to the Legislative Council of Northern Rhodesia (now Zambia) in 1938, knighted in 1953, and from 1956 to its break-up in 1963 was prime minister of the Federation of Rhodesia and Nyasaland (now Malawi). His handling of the constitutional crisis in 1959 aroused much controversy.

Welland, Colin (Williams) (1934–) Actor and playwright, born in Liverpool, Merseyside, NW England, UK. He studied at Goldsmiths' College, London, worked as an art teacher, and began his career as an actor in Manchester in 1962. As a dramatist, he has written both for film and television. In 1970, 1973, and 1974 he was voted best TV playwright in Britain. His work for television has included *Roll on Four O'Clock* (1970), *Kisses at Fifty* (1973), and *Bank Holiday* (1977). His screenplays include *Chariots of Fire* (1981) and *Twice in a Lifetime* (1987).

Wellcome, Henry (1853–1936) British pharmaceutical manufacturer, born in the USA. He moved to Britain to join Silas Burroughs in a pharmaceutical business (1880), becoming sole owner when Burroughs died in 1895. He promoted the proper testing and standardization of medicines, established laboratories for research, and in his will set up the Wellcome Trust for medical research.

Weller, Thomas H(uckle) (1915–) Physiologist, born in Ann Arbor, MI. He studied at Harvard and Michigan universities, then served in World War 2 as an army medical researcher into tropical diseases. After the War he joined the Children's Medical Center in Boston, where he worked with John Enders and Frederick Robbins in devising techniques for cultivating the poliomyelitis virus (thus making possible the development of a polio vaccine), for which they shared the 1954 Nobel Prize for Physiology or Medicine. He also isolated the causative agents of chicken pox and shingles, and German measles. >> Enders, John; Robbins, Frederick

Welles, Gideon (1802–78) US statesman and journalist, born in Glastonbury, CT. As part owner and editor (1826–36) of the *Hartford Times*, he endorsed Jacksonian democracy. He held several state political offices (1826–44), and became chief of the US Navy's Bureau of Provisions and Clothing (1846–9). Opposed to slavery, he left the Democratic Party in 1854 and helped organize the new Republican Party, founding the *Hartford Evening Press* to promote the Republicans' goals. President Lincoln appointed him to his cabinet as secretary of the navy (1861–9). Under his leadership, the navy quickly expanded, adopted the ironclads and other new technology, successfully blockaded the Confederacy, and contributed greatly to the eventual Union victory. His diary of the Civil War period published in 1911 provides a revealing glimpse of the times. >> Lincoln, Abraham

Welles, (George) Orson (1915–85) Director, producer, writer, and actor, born in Kenosha, WI. He appeared at the Gate Theatre, Dublin, in 1931, returned to America, became a radio producer in 1934, and founded the Mercury Theatre in 1937. In 1938 his radio production of H

G Wells's *War of the Worlds* was so realistic that it caused panic in the USA. In 1941 he wrote, produced, directed, and acted in the film *Citizen Kane*, a revolutionary landmark in cinema technique. His later work includes his individual film versions of *Macbeth* (1948) and *Othello* (1951), along with a variety of memorable stage and film roles, the most celebrated being that of Harry Lime in *The Third Man* (1949). >> Houseman

Wellesley, Arthur see panel on p. 985

Wellesley (of Norragh), Richard (Colley) Wellesley, 1st Marquess (1760–1842) British administrator, born in Dangan, Co Meath, Ireland, the brother of Arthur Wellesley, Duke of Wellington. He became an MP (1784), a Lord of the Treasury (1786), a marquess (1799), and governor-general of India (1797–1805). Under his administration British rule in India became supreme: the influence of France was extinguished, and the power of the princes reduced by the crushing of Tippoo Sahib (1799) and the Marathas (1803). After his return to England, he became ambassador to Madrid (1805), foreign minister (1809), and Lord-Lieutenant of Ireland (1821, 1833). >> Tippoo Sahib; Wellington, Duke of

Wellesz, Egon (Joseph) [veles] (1885–1974) Composer and musicologist, born in Vienna. He studied under Schoenberg, and became professor of musical history at Vienna (1930–8). Exiled from Austria by the Nazis, he became a research fellow then lecturer and reader in music (1944–56) at Oxford. His works include six operas, nine symphonies, and much choral and chamber music. >> Schoenberg

Wellhausen, Julius [velhowzn] (1844–1918) Biblical scholar, born in Hameln, Germany. He studied at Göttingen, and became professor at Greifswald (1872), Halle (1882), Marburg (1885), and Göttingen (1892). He is best known for his investigations into Old Testament history and source criticism of the Pentateuch. He published several works, notably the *Prolegomena zur Geschichte Israels* (1883, trans History of Israel).

Wellington, Arthur Wellesley, 1st Duke of see panel on p. 985

Wells, Henry (1805–78) Pioneer expressman, born in Thetford, VT. He worked as an agent before joining with William Fargo and Daniel Dunning to found Wells & Co (1844), the first express company to operate W of Buffalo, NY. It later merged with other companies to become the American Express Co (1850). Together, Wells and Fargo then established Wells, Fargo & Co (1852). Wells also founded Wells Seminary (later, College) for women at Aurora, NY (in 1868). >> Fargo

Wells, H(erbert) G(eorge) (1866–1946) Writer, born in Bromley, S Greater London, England, UK. He was apprenticed to a draper, tried teaching, studied biology in London, then made his mark in journalism and literature. He played a vital part in disseminating the progressive ideas which characterized the first part of the 20th-c. He achieved fame with scientific fantasies such as *The Time Machine* (1895) and *War of the Worlds* (1898), and wrote a range of comic social novels which proved highly popular, notably *Kipps* (1905) and *The History of Mr Polly* (1910). Both kinds of novel made successful (sometimes classic) early films. A member of the Fabian Society, he was often engaged in public controversy, and wrote several socio-political works dealing with the role of science and the need for world peace, such as *The Outline of History* (1920) and *The Work, Wealth and Happiness of Mankind* (1932).

Wells, John (Campbell) (1936–98) British actor, playwright, humorist, and director. He read French and German at Oxford, and taught both languages at Eton (1961–3), while contributing material for revues at the Edinburgh

ARTHUR WELLESLEY, 1ST DUKE OF WELLINGTON (1769–1852)

Wellesley was born in Dublin, the fifth son of Garrett Wesley, 1st Earl of Mornington, an Irish peer (there was a family change of name to Wellesley in 1798). He received a desultory education at Chelsea, Eton, and Brussels, and at a military academy at Angers.

In 1787, aged 18, he purchased a commission as an ensign in the 73rd (Highland) Regiment of Foot; then served in several other regiments, and was promoted to captain (1791) and lieutenant-colonel (1793). During this period he was also elected to the family seat of Trim in the Irish parliament (1790–7), and in 1792, aged 24, proposed to his future wife, **Catherine (Kitty) Pakenham** (d.1831), the third daughter of Lord Longford – she refused the impoverished young soldier. Wellesley was saddled with gambling debts at the time. He gave up gambling and turned his mind to soldiering.

He served in Ireland and Holland with the 33rd Foot, and in 1796 went with his regiment to India. He successfully led a brigade against Tippoo Sahib, and was appointed Governor of Seringapatem and commander of the forces in Mysore. In 1799 he was given the task of extending British influence into the area occupied by the Mahrattas, and secured several notable victories, including the capture of Poona (1803). He returned to Britain in 1805, when he was knighted, and married Kitty in 1806.

In 1807 he entered parliament, and in the Tory administration of the Duke of Portland was appointed chief secretary for Ireland. He was released to be part of the 1807 expedition to Denmark to pre-empt the French seizure of the Danish fleet. His forces routed the Danish army, and Copenhagen surrendered after a bombardment.

Following the occupation of the Iberian Peninsula by Napoleon (with whom Britain had been at war since 1800), Wellesley was given command of a task force to attack the French. He landed at Mondego Bay, Portugal, in 1808, and defeated the French at Roliça and Vimeiro. His further pursuit of the French was thwarted by the Convention of Sintra, signed by his superiors. He was court-martialled (and acquitted) when, under the orders of these superior officers, he did not press home the victory. Instead his superiors allowed the French forces to evacuate with their weapons. However, following the death of Sir John Moore at Coruña, he was given command of the British forces in Spain and Portugal, and embarked on the campaign which was to remove the French from the Peninsula and lead to the invasion of France. A cautious and brilliant commander, he remained undefeated throughout the Peninsular War,

despite often being seriously outnumbered. His notable victories included Talavera (1809), a victory which brought him a peerage, Bussaco (1810), Salamanca (1812), and Vitoria (1813). A final series of victories against Marshal Soult culminated in the capture of Toulouse in 1814.

Wellesley had been elevated to the peerage after Talavera, taking the title of Viscount Wellington. In 1814 he was created a duke and became field marshal. In an unprecedented combination of honours from a grateful country, he took his seat in the House of Lords in the styles of baron, viscount, earl, marquess, and duke; he was also created a Knight of the Garter.

After Napoleon's escape from Elba (1815), Wellington took command of a largely foreign contingent in Brussels. Napoleon, having crushed Blücher's Prussian forces at Ligny, then threatened Wellington's forces, first at Quatre Bras and two days later at Waterloo (18 Jun 1815). Here Wellington gained his most famous victory, routing the French army after bitter fighting, aided in the later stages by Blücher's re-formed troops, who blocked Napoleon's line of retreat. At the Convention of Paris, Wellington was appointed commander of the allied army of occupation until British withdrawal (1818).

Wellington then returned to politics, becoming Master General of the Ordnance in Lord Liverpool's Tory government. However, his perceptions of duty and fairness equipped him poorly for the compromises of politics. A highly imaginative soldier, he was often very conservative in politics. Called to become prime minister by George IV (1828), he came into conflict with extremists within his own party over his daring and controversial support for Catholic emancipation; but he also forfeited the allegiance of Huskisson and the Liberals over his reluctance to consider their demands for radical parliamentary reform. He endured a brief period of general unpopularity when his vigorous opposition to parliamentary reforms forced him to protect the windows of Apsley House, his London home, with iron shutters against the angry mobs – a measure which earned him his nickname of the 'Iron Duke'. However, for the country's sake, he managed a political compromise without loss of personal integrity.

He was defeated by Lord Grey in 1830, but returned to office as a minister without portfolio in Peel's administration. He retired from public office in 1846, and was appointed Lord High Constable of England in 1848. He died from a stroke at the age of 83 at Walmer Castle, Kent, his residence as Lord Warden of the Cinque Ports, and was buried in St Paul's Cathedral.
>> Blücher; Grey, 2nd Earl; Huskisson; Liverpool, 2nd Earl of; Moore, Sir John; Napoleon; Peel; Soult; Tippoo Sahib

Festival. He was a co-editor of the satirical magazine, *Private Eye* (1964–7), contributed the supposed diary of Mrs Wilson (prime minister Harold Wilson's wife) and the 'Dear Bill' letters, the supposed correspondence of Denis Thatcher (husband of Margaret Thatcher), and in the 1990s partnered John Fortune in a televised series of satirical political dialogues. His plays include *Listen to the Knocking Bird* (1965), *Mrs Wilson's Diary* (1968), *Anyone for Denis?* (1981), in which he played the title role, and *A Brand from the Burning* (1995), which he also directed. He is highly regarded as a translator of plays and opera from French and German, and he directed a revival of *The Mikado* in 1989. >> Thatcher; Wilson, Harold

Welsh, Christopher >> **Davies, Christian**

Welty, Eudora (1909–) Novelist and short-story writer, born in Jackson, MS. She studied at the University of Wisconsin and the Columbia University School of Advertising in New York City, and became a journalist. She published several collections of short stories, and five novels, mostly drawn from Mississippi life, including *The Robber*

Bridegroom (1942), *The Ponder Heart* (1954), and *The Optimist's Daughter* (1972, Pulitzer). *The Collected Stories of Eudora Welty* was published in 1980, and in 1994 appeared *A Writer's Eye*, a collection of book reviews.

Wenceslaus or **Wenceslas, St** [wenseslas], known as **Good King Wenceslas** (c.903–935) Duke and patron of Bohemia, born in Stochov, Czech Republic. He received a Christian education, and after the death of his father (c.924) encouraged Christianity in Bohemia, against the wishes of his mother. Probably at her instigation, and because he had put his duchy under the protection of Germany, he was murdered by his brother, Boleslaw. He became the patron saint of Bohemia and Czechoslovakia. Feast day 28 September. >> Ludmila

Wenders, Wim [venderz] (1945–) Film director, born in Düsseldorf, Germany. Originally a student of medicine and philosophy, he attended Munich's Cinema and Television College, where he made his first short film, *Schauplatze* (1967). He made his feature debut with *Summer in the City* (1970). Concerned with the influence of American culture on post-war German society, his work deals with isolation and alienation, often involving journeys in search of enlightenment. These themes are especially evident in *Alice in the Cities* (1974) and *The State of Things* (1982). He has won several awards at the Cannes Film Festivals, including Best Director for *Wings of Desire* (1987). Later films include *Until the End of the World* (1991) and *Faraway, So Close* (1993).

Wendi [wendee], also spelled **Wen-ti** (ruled 179–157 BC) Han dynasty Chinese emperor and Confucian scholar, who consolidated his father Gaozu's achievements, including initiating the system of written civil service examinations (165 BC). Economic advance, administrative reform, and freedom from internal warfare laid the foundation for the later achievements of Wudi. >> Gaozu; Wudi

Wendi [wendee], also spelled **Wen-ti** (541–604) First emperor of the Chinese Sui dynasty. As **Yang Jian**, a northerner having close family ties both to the Han nobility and the N Zhou dynasty (557–80), he slaughtered a king and 59 princes to seize the throne, ruling as Wendi ('cultured emperor', 590–604). His lands were around Changan (Xian), which he kept as the imperial capital. Conquering S China with 518 000 men, he then secured Annam's submission (603). Anti-intellectual, he opposed Confucianism but favoured Buddhism. He simplified administration, demanded total obedience to severe laws, and stopped officials working in their home areas. He was murdered by his son and successor, Yang Guang (Yangdi). >> Yangdi

Wenner-Gren, Axel Leonard [wener gren] (1881–1961) Swedish financier and industrialist. He founded Electrolux in 1919, undertook large-scale projects such as a holiday resort in the Bahamas, a telephone company in Mexico, and (in 1956) a huge development complex in British Columbia comprising electrical plants, mining, and forestry. His Swedish interests were united in Fulcrum AB, which went into liquidation in 1975. During his lifetime, and in his will, he donated vast sums for scientific research to institutions in Stockholm and New York City.

Wentworth, Charles Watson >> **Rockingham, Marquess of**

Wentworth, Thomas >> **Strafford, Earl of**

Wentworth, W(illiam) C(harles) (1790–1872) Australian politician and landowner, born on Norfolk I, New South Wales, Australia. He took part in the expedition which explored the Blue Mts in 1813, then studied at Cambridge and became a lawyer. He was a staunch protagonist of self-government for Australia, which he made the policy of his newspaper, *The Australian* (established 1824), and he was

elected to the Legislative Council in 1842. He retired to England in 1862.

Wenzel, Hanni [ventsl] (1956–) Alpine skier, born in Staubirnen, Germany. At the 1980 Olympics she won the gold medal in the slalom and giant slalom, and the silver in the downhill. Her total of four Olympic medals (including a bronze in 1976) is a record for any skier. She was combined world champion and overall World Cup winner in 1980.

Werfel, Franz [verfel] (1890–1945) Writer, born in Prague. He lived in Vienna until 1938, when he moved to France, and then to the USA. He wrote Expressionist poems and plays, but he is best known for his novels, notably the epic *Die vierzig Tage des Musa Dagh* (1933, The Forty Days of Musa Dagh) and the story of the Lourdes visionary, *Das Lied von Bernadette* (1941, The Song of Bernadette).

Wergeland, Henrik Arnold [vergeland] (1808–45) Poet, playwright, and patriot, born in Kristiansand, Norway. He is best known for his poetry, notably his Creation epic, *Skabelsen, Mennesket, og Messias* (1830, Creation, Humanity, and Desire), and for such narrative poems as *Den Engelske Lods* (1844, The English Pilot). A leader of the cause of Norwegian nationalism, he became Norway's national poet. >> Collett

Werner, Abraham Gottlob [verner] (1750–1817) Geologist, born in Wehrau, Germany. A teacher at Freiburg in Saxony from 1775, he was one of the first to frame a classification of rocks, and gave his name to the *Wernerian* or Neptunian theory of deposition, which he advocated in controversy with James Hutton. >> Hutton, James

Wernicke, Carl [vernikuh] (1848–1905) Neurologist, born in Tarnowitz, Germany. He studied at Wrocław, Poland (formerly Breslau, Germany), Berlin, and Vienna universities, and was professor at Breslau (1885–1904). He studied brain damage leading to aphasia (the loss of language ability), specifically the kind of aphasia in which comprehension is seriously impaired, and deduced the part of the brain chiefly involved (*Wernicke's area*).

Wertheimer, Max [vairthiymer] (1880–1943) Psychologist and philosopher, born in Prague. He studied law in Prague, then psychology at Berlin and Würzburg universities. In 1912 he conducted experiments in perception with Koffka and Köhler which led to the founding of the Gestalt school of psychology. He was professor at Berlin and Frankfurt, but left Germany for the USA in 1933 at the Nazi assumption of power, and taught at the New School for Social Research in New York City (1933–43). >> Husserl; Koffka; Köhler

Wesker, Arnold (1932–) Playwright, born in London, England, UK, of a Russian father and Hungarian mother. His working-class Jewish family background, and his varied attempts at earning a living, are important ingredients of his plays, such as *The Kitchen* (1959) and *Chips with Everything* (1962). The Kahn family trilogy, *Chicken Soup with Barley*, *Roots*, and *I'm Talking About Jerusalem* (1959–60), echo the march of events, before and after World War 2, in a left-wing family. Later plays include *The Friends* (1970), *Caritas* (1981), *Little Old Lady* (1988), *Tokyo* (1994), and a series of monologues for women. He is also known for founding the theatre project Centre 42 (1961–70). His collected plays were published in 1989–90, and a collection of stories, *The King's Daughters*, in 1996.

Wesley, Charles (1707–88) Hymn-writer and evangelist, born in Epworth, Lincolnshire, EC England, UK, the brother of John Wesley. He studied at Oxford, was ordained in 1735, and accompanied John to Georgia as secretary to Governor James Oglethorpe, returning to England in 1736. After an evangelical conversion in 1738, he wrote over 5500 hymns, including such well-loved favourites as 'Jesu, Lover of My

Soul', 'Hark, the Herald Angels Sing', and 'Love Divine, All Loves Excelling'. >> Oglethorpe; Whitefield; Wesley, John/Samuel

Wesley, John (1703–91) Evangelist and founder of Methodism, born in Epworth, Lincolnshire, EC England, UK. He studied at Oxford, was ordained deacon (1725) and priest (1728), and in 1726 became a fellow at Oxford and lecturer in Greek. Influenced by the spiritual writings of William Law, he became leader of a small group which had gathered round his brother Charles, nicknamed the Methodists, a name later adopted by John for the adherents of the great evangelical movement which was its outgrowth. On their father's death, the brothers went as missionaries to Georgia (1735–8), but the mission proved a failure. In 1738, at a meeting in London, during the reading of Luther's preface to the Epistle to the Romans, he experienced an assurance of salvation which convinced him that he must bring the same assurance to others; but his zeal alarmed most of the parish clergy, who closed their pulpits against him. This drove him into the open air at Bristol (1739), where he founded the first Methodist Chapel, and then the Foundry at Moorfields, London, which became their headquarters. His life was frequently in danger, but he outlived all persecution, and the itineraries of his old age were triumphal processions throughout the country. He was a prolific writer, producing grammars, histories, biographies, collections of hymns, his own sermons and journals, and a magazine. >> Oglethorpe; Wesley, Charles; Whitefield

Wesley, Mary, originally **Mary Siepmann** (1912–) Novelist, born in Englefield Green, Berkshire, S England, UK. She studied at the London School of Economics, and had a number of jobs before beginning to write children's novels in the 1960s. Her first adult novel, *The Camomile Lawn* (1984), did not appear until she was in her 70s, and she then became a prolific writer of spirited comedies, later books including *An Imaginative Experience* (1994) and *Part of The Furniture* (1997).

Wesley, Samuel (1766–1837) Organist and composer, born in Bristol, SW England, UK, the son of Charles Wesley. One of the most famous organists of his day, he was an ardent enthusiast of J S Bach. Though a Roman Catholic (to the displeasure of his father and uncle), he wrote also for the Anglican Liturgy, leaving a number of fine motets and anthems, including *In exitu Israel*. >> Bach, J S; Wesley, Charles

Wessel, Horst [vesel] (1907–30) Martyr of the Nazi Party, born in Bielefeld, Germany. He joined the Nazis in 1926 and became a member of the Storm Troopers. He was killed in his home in a fight, possibly by Communists. Joseph Goebbels and other Nazi propagandists had the song 'Horst Wessel Lied' adopted as their anthem, and made a martyr of him. >> Goebbels

Wesselmann, Tom (1931–) Painter, born in Cincinnati, OH. He studied psychology at Cincinnati University before taking art courses. In 1961 he moved to New York City, abandoning the Abstract Expressionist style and turning to Pop Art. Most of his paintings depict overtly erotic female nudes in contemporary American environments; these works form the series known as 'The Great American Nude'.

Wesson, Daniel Baird (1825–1906) Gunsmith, born in Worcester, MA. With **Horace Smith** (1808–93) he devised a new type of repeating mechanism for small-arms in 1854, and founded the firm of Smith & Wesson at Springfield, MA, in 1857.

West, Anthony >> **West, Rebecca**

West, Benjamin (1738–1820) Painter, born in Springfield, PA. He showed early promise as an artist, was sent on a sponsored visit to Italy, and on his return journey settled in London (1763) as a portrait painter. He was subsequently patronized by George III for 40 years, and was a founder of the Royal Academy (1768), and its president (from 1792). The representation of modern instead of classical costume in his best-known picture, 'The Death of General Wolfe' (c.1771, several versions), was an innovation in English historical painting.

West, Jerry (Alan) (1938–) Basketball player, born in Cabin Creek, WV. He was an All-American guard at West Virginia University (1956–60), then played for the Los Angeles Lakers (1960–74). He went on to coach and manage the club, remaining in the sport as an executive. He was captain of the USA Olympic basketball side in 1960. >> RR1146

West, Mae (1893–1980) Actress, born in New York City. A child performer, she spent some years in vaudeville and on Broadway before her first film, *Night After Night* (1932). Throughout the 1930s a series of racy comedies, often with her own dialogue-script, exploited her voluptuousness and sexual badinage, although under much pressure from censorship. She subsequently returned to the stage and nightclubs, but made two late character appearances in *Myra Breckenridge* (1970) and *Sextette* (1978), before her death from a stroke in Los Angeles. Her name was given to a pneumatic lifejacket which, when inflated, was considered to give the wearer the generous bosom for which she was noted.

West, Morris (Langlo) (1916–) Novelist, born in Melbourne, Victoria, Australia. He studied at the University of Melbourne and joined a Catholic teaching order, but resigned in 1940 before taking vows. He worked in politics, journalism, and broadcasting before moving to Italy in 1955. His first major work, *Children of the Sun*, about the homeless children of Naples, was published in that year. Many successful novels followed, including *The Devil's Advocate* (1959, James Tate Black Memorial Prize; filmed 1977), *The Shoes of the Fisherman* (1963), *The Tower of Babel* (1968), *The Clowns of God* (1981), *Lazarus* (1990), and *Vanishing Point* (1996). His themes are often of a religious or moral nature, and involve international incidents.

West, Nathanael, pseudonym of **Nathan Wallenstein Weinstein** (1903–40) Novelist, born in New York City. He studied at Brown University, then went to Paris, where he associated with Surrealist writers, and wrote his first novel. He returned to New York City and wrote four short fantasy novels, of which the best known are *Miss Lonelyhearts* (1933) and *The Day of the Locust* (1939), a satire on Hollywood. He was killed, along with his wife, in a traffic accident.

West, Dame Rebecca, pseudonym of **Cicily Isabel Andrews**, née **Fairfield** (1892–1983) Novelist and critic, born in London, England, UK. Educated in Edinburgh, she was for a short time on the stage, and took her name from the character she played in Ibsen's *Rosmersholm*. She is best known for her studies arising out of the Nuremberg war trials: *The Meaning of Treason* (1947) and *A Train of Powder* (1955). Her novels include *The Judge* (1922), *The Thinking Reed* (1936), and *The Birds Fall Down* (1966). Her long association with H G Wells produced a son, the critic and author **Anthony West** (1914–). She was created a dame in 1959. >> Wells, H G

West, Timothy (Lancaster) (1934–) British actor and director. He was educated in London, entered the profession as assistant stage manager at Wimbledon (1956), and made his London debut in 1959. He was a member of the Royal Shakespeare Company (1964–6), and with the prospect Theatre Company (1966–72), where he also directed, and thereafter played a wide variety of roles in the provinces, the West End, and abroad. His television appearances include *Churchill and the Generals* (1979), *The Monocled Mutineer* (1986), *Survival of the Fittest* (1990), and *Cuts* (1995); his films include *The Day of the Jackal* (1972), *Cry Freedom* (1986), and *Consuming Passions* (1987). He married actress Prunella Scales in 1963. >> Scales

Westbrook, Mike, popular name of **Michael John David Westbrook** (1936–) Jazz composer, bandleader, and pianist, born in High Wycombe, Buckinghamshire, SC England, UK. He turned to music after studying painting. He concentrated on writing extended pieces specifically for his own ensembles, ranging from trios to big bands, often in partnership with his wife **Kate** (tenor horn, piccolo, voice). His major suites include *The Cortege* (1982) and *On Duke's Birthday* (1984). Later works include *Bean Rows and Blues Shots* (1991) and *Blues for Terenzi* (1995).

Westermarck, Edward (Alexander) [**ves**termah(r)k] (1862–1939) Social philosopher, born in Helsinki. He studied in Helsinki, where he became lecturer in sociology (1890–1906), and was professor of sociology in London (1907–30). His *History of Human Marriage* (3 vols, 1922) was an attack on the theory of primitive promiscuity. He also wrote on the evolution of ethics in such books as *The Origin and Development of Moral Ideas* (1906–8). He travelled widely in Morocco, and published several accounts of its peoples, including *Ritual and Belief in Morocco* (2 vols, 1926).

Westinghouse, George (1846–1914) Engineer, born in Central Bridge, NY. In 1863 he invented an air-brake for railways, and founded a company (now a corporation) for the manufacture of this and other appliances. He was a pioneer in the use of alternating current for distributing electric power, and founded the Westinghouse Electrical Co in 1886.

Westmoreland, William C(hilds) (1914–) US soldier, born in Spartanburg Co, SC. He trained at West Point, saw extensive combat duty in World War 2 and the Korean War, and became superintendent of the US Military Academy (1960–3). In 1964 he became commander of US forces in Vietnam, but his 'search and destroy' strategy proved unsuccessful against the Communist Vietnamese, and after the Tet offensive of 1968 he was recalled to the USA to serve as army chief-of-staff. He retired from the army in 1972, and failed in his bid for the Republican governorship nomination in South Carolina in 1974.

Weston, Edward (1886–1958) Photographer, born in Highland Park, IL. He established his own studio in Glendale c.1910, and later became recognized as a Modernist, emphasizing sharp images and precise definition in landscapes, portraits, and still-life. He produced notable landscapes of the Mohave Desert, and in 1937, with the first-ever award of a Guggenheim Fellowship to a photographer, travelled widely taking photographs for *California and the West* (1940).

Westwood, Vivienne (1941–) Fashion designer, born in Tintwistle, Derby, C England, UK. She became well known in the 1970s when, with Malcolm McLaren the rock music entrepreneur, she opened a shop in London that became the focus of the punk rock movement. She gained international recognition in the early 1980s with her Pirate and New Romantics look.

Wet, Christian de >> **de Wet, Christian**

Wettach, Charles Adrien >> **Grock**

Weyden, Rogier van der [**viy**dn] (c. 1400–64) Religious painter, born in Tournai, Belgium. He studied in Tournai, and by 1436 was official painter to the city of Brussels. Little is known of his life, and even his identity has been disputed. He executed many portraits and altarpieces, and among his best-known works are 'The Descent from the Cross' (c.1435–40, Madrid) and the 'Last Judgment' altarpiece (c.1450, Beaune).

Weygand, Maxime [vaygã] (1867–1965) French soldier, born in Brussels. He trained at St Cyr and became an instructor. As chief-of-staff to Foch (1914–23), he rendered admirable service, but as chief-of-staff of the French army (1931–5) he was handicapped by his lack of experience as a field commander. In 1940 his employment of an outmoded linear defence to hold a penetration in depth completed the rout of the French army. A prisoner of the Germans, and later of the French provisional government, he was allowed to retire into obscurity. >> Foch

Weyl, Hermann [viyl] (1885–1955) Mathematician, born in Elmshorn, Germany. He studied at Göttingen under David Hilbert, and became professor at Zürich (1913) and Göttingen (1930). Refusing to stay in Nazi Germany, he went to Princeton in 1933. He made important contributions to the theory of Riemann surfaces, the representation theory of Lie groups, the mathematical foundations of relativity and quantum mechanics, and the philosophy of mathematics. His book *Symmetry* (1952) is a largely non-technical account of the relation between group theory and symmetry in pattern and design. >> Hilbert

Wharton, Edith (Newbold), *née* **Jones** (c. 1861–1937) Novelist and short-story writer, born in New York City. Educated at home and in Europe, she formed a durable friendship with Henry James, who did much to encourage and influence her work. Her tragedy *The House of Mirth* (1905) established her as a major novelist. Other works include *The Age of Innocence* (1920, Pulitzer), and her best-known novel, *Ethan Frome* (1911). Her autobiography, *A Backwards Glance*, appeared in 1934. >> James, Henry

Wheatley, Denis (Yates) (1897–1977) Novelist, born in London, England, UK. He inherited the family wine business, but sold up in 1931 to concentrate on novel writing. He produced an enormously popular mix of satanism and historical fiction. Indicative titles in a lurid oeuvre are *The Devil Rides Out* (1935), *The Scarlet Impostor* (1942), and *The Sultan's Daughter* (1963). His three-volume autobiography was published posthumously (1978–80).

Wheatley, Phillis (c. 1753–85) Poet, born in Senegal. As a child she was sold as a slave to the family of a Boston tailor, John Wheatley, who educated her with the rest of his family. She studied Latin and Greek, and started writing poetry in English at the age of 13. She published *Poems on Various Subjects, Religious and Moral* (1783), and visited England in that year, to huge popular interest. When the Wheatley family died, she married a freedman, but ended her days in poverty.

Wheaton, Henry (1785–1848) US statesman and jurist, born in Providence, RI. He studied at Rhode Island College, edited the *National Advocate* in New York City (1812–15), where for four years he was a justice of the Marine Court, and became a reporter for the Supreme Court (1816–27). He was chargé d'affaires at Copenhagen (1827–35), and minister at Berlin (1835–46). His major work, *Elements of International Law*, was first published in 1836.

Wheatstone, Sir Charles (1802–75) Physicist, born in Gloucester, Gloucestershire, SWC England, UK. He became professor of experimental philosophy at London (1834), known for his experiments in sound. He invented the concertina (1829), took out a patent for an electric telegraph (1837), explained the principle of the stereoscope (1838), and invented a sound magnifier for which he introduced the term *microphone*. *Wheatstone's bridge*, a device for the comparison of electrical resistances, was brought to notice (though not invented) by him. He was knighted in 1868. >> Cooke, William Fothergill

Wheeler, Sir Charles (1892–1974) Sculptor, born in Codsall, Staffordshire, C England, UK. He studied at the Wolverhampton Art School and the Royal College of Art.

He is noted for his portrait sculpture and for his decorative sculptures on monuments and buildings.

Wheeler, John Archibald (1911–) Theoretical physicist, born in Jacksonville, FL. He studied at Johns Hopkins and Copenhagen universities, and spent most of his career at Princeton (1938–76), finally moving to the University of Texas, Austin. He worked with Niels Bohr on the paper 'The Mechanism of Nuclear Fission' (1939), and helped develop the hydrogen bomb project. Later he turned to the search for a unified field theory, and (with Richard Feynman) worked on the concept of action at a distance. >> Bohr, Niels; Feynman

Wheeler, Sir (Robert Eric) Mortimer (1890–1976) Archaeologist, born in Glasgow, W Scotland, UK. He studied at London University, and became director of the National Museum of Wales (1920), and keeper of the London Museum (1926–44). He carried out notable excavations in Britain at Verulamium (St Albans) and Maiden Castle, and was director-general of archaeology in India (1944–7), working to particular effect at Mohenjo-daro and Harappa. He then became professor of the archaeology of the Roman provinces at the newly founded Institute of Archaeology in London (1948–55). Knighted in 1952, he was well known for spirited popular accounts of his subject, in books and on television. His works include *Archaeology from the Earth* (1954) and the autobiographical *Still Digging* (1955).

Wheeler, William (Almon) (1819–87) US vice-president and businessman, born in Malone, NY. Following an impoverished youth, he became a lawyer and businessman. He was elected vice-president under Rutherford B Hayes (1877–81), but displayed little enthusiasm for the office. >> Hayes, Rutherford B

Wheldon, Sir Huw (1916–86) Broadcaster, from Wales, UK, the son of Sir Wyn Wheldon. Partly educated in Germany, he fought in World War 2, and was awarded the MC in 1944. He joined the BBC in 1952, and was responsible for the seminal arts programme *Monitor* (1957–64), where the cultural life of the land was reviewed and illuminated with a rare passion and enthusiasm. He became head of documentaries and music programmes in 1963, controller of programmes for BBC-TV in 1965, and the Corporation's managing director (1968–75). Afterwards he returned to active programme-making as the co-writer and presenter of *Royal Heritage* (1977), before serving as the president of the Royal Television Society (1979–85).

Whewell, William [waywel] (1794–1866) Scholar, born in Lancaster, Lancashire, NW England, UK. He was a fellow and tutor of Trinity College, Cambridge, and became professor of mineralogy at Cambridge (1828–38), then of moral theology (1838–55). He was made Master of Trinity in 1841, and Vice-Chancellor of the university in 1855. His works include *History of the Inductive Sciences* (1837), *Elements of Morality* (1855), and other writings on the tides, electricity, and magnetism, besides several translations.

Whichcote, Benjamin (1609–83) Philosopher and theologian, born in Stoke, Shropshire, WC England, UK. He was a student at Cambridge, a fellow of Emmanuel College in 1633, and was ordained and appointed Sunday Afternoon Lecturer in Trinity Church (1636–56). He became Provost of King's College in 1644, but lost the post at the Restoration in 1660 by order of Charles II. He published nothing in his lifetime, but is regarded as the spiritual founder of the 'Cambridge Platonists'. >> Cudworth; More, Henry

Whicker, Alan (Donald) [wiker] (1925–) British broadcaster and journalist, born in Cairo. He served with the Army Film Unit in World War 2, and was a war correspondent in Korea before joining the BBC (1957–68). He worked on the *Tonight* programme (1957–65) and began his *Whicker's World* documentary series in 1958. Television's most travelled man, he has allowed viewers to eavesdrop on the lives of the rich and famous as well as discovering the exotic and extraordinary aspects of everyday lives in all parts of the world. Consistently in the top-10 ratings, he has received numerous awards including election to the Royal Television Society's Hall of Fame in 1993. Among his books are *Some Rise By Sin* (1949) and the autobiography *Within Whicker's World* (1982).

Whipple, Fred (Lawrence) (1906–) Astronomer, born in Red Oak, IA. He studied at California University, and became professor of astronomy at Harvard in 1945. An expert on the Solar System (his *Earth, Moon and Planets* (1941) is a standard text), he is known especially for his work on comets. In 1950 he suggested that they are composed of ice and dust, and that many aspects of their behaviour could be interpreted on this basis; later work, and especially the study of Halley's comet in 1986 by space probes, has confirmed this 'dirty snowball' model.

Whipple, George H(oyt) (1878–1976) Pathologist, born in Ashland, NH. He studied at Yale and Johns Hopkins universities, worked at California (1914–21), and became professor of pathology at Rochester in 1921. While at California he researched the effect of diet on haemoglobin production in dogs, discovering that raw liver could restore depleted levels. He shared the 1934 Nobel Prize for Physiology or Medicine with George Minot and William Murphy, who applied his discoveries to humans. >> Minot; Murphy, William

Whistler, James (Abbott) McNeill (1834–1903) Artist, born in Lowell, MA. He studied for the army, then left the USA to take up art in Paris, and later in London, where his work was controversially received. He is best known for his evening scenes ('nocturnes'), such as 'Old Battersea Bridge' (c.1872–5, Tate, London), and for the famous portrait of his mother (1871–2, Musée d'Orsay). He also became known for his etchings and lithographs, especially those dealing with the London riverside. >> Godwin, Edward William

Whistler, Rex (John) (1905–44) British artist. He studied at London, and excelled in the rendering of 18th-c life, ornament, and architecture, particularly in book illustration, murals, and designs for the theatre and ballet. Fine examples of his work, including a large mural, are preserved at Plas Newydd, Anglesey.

Whitaker, Joseph (1820–95) Bookseller and publisher, born in London, England, UK. He started the *Educational Register*, *Whitaker's Clergyman's Diary*, and *The Bookseller* in 1858. In 1868 appeared *Whitaker's Almanac*, now a publishing institution.

Whitbread, Samuel (1758–1815) British politician, the son of the founder of the famous brewing firm **Samuel Whitbread** (1720–96). From Eton he passed to Oxford, and in 1790 entered parliament. The intimate friend of Fox, under Pitt he was Leader of the Opposition, and in 1805 headed the attack on Henry Dundas, Viscount Melville (1742–1811) over charges of corruption. >> Fox, Charles James; Pitt, William (the Younger)

White, Alan >> Oasis

White, Antonia, née **Eirene Adeline Botting** (1899–1980) Novelist, born in London, England, UK. She was educated at the Convent of the Sacred Heart, Roehampton, and her first novel, *Frost In May* (1933), is a largely autobiographical account of the heroine's convent education. Later novels include *The Sugar House* (1952) and *The Hound and the Falcon* (1965). She also wrote a play, *Three In A Room* (1947), children's stories, and translated many works from French, including the novels of Colette.

White, Edmund (1940–) Writer, born in Cincinnati, OH. His work began to be published in the 1970s, beginning with the novel *Forgetting Elena* (1973), and he became known as a leading homosexual writer. Later novels include his best-known work, *A Boy's Own Story* (1982), and a collection of short stories with Adam Mars-Jones, *The Darker Proof* (1990). *States of Desire: Travels In Gay America* (1980) is an investigation of the gay community in several American cities. >> Mars-Jones

White, Ellen Gould, *née* **Harmon** (1827–1915) Seventh-day Adventist leader, born in Gorham, ME. She was converted to Adventism in 1842 through the preaching of William Miller, and was said to have experienced 'two thousand visions and prophetic dreams'. With the official establishment of the Seventh-day Adventist Church in 1863, she became leader, and wrote over 60 works, one of which, *Steps to Christ*, has sold more than 20 million copies. >> Miller, William

White, E(lwyn) B(rooks) (1899–1985) Writer, born in Mount Vernon, NY. He studied at Cornell, and was associated with the *New Yorker* from 1925. His reputation rests on the essays he wrote in the column 'One Man's Meat', his collaboration with James Thurber on *Is Sex Necessary?* (1929), *The Elements of Style* (1959), and his three classic best-selling novels for children, *Stuart Little* (1945), *Charlotte's Web* (1952), and *The Trumpet of the Swan* (1970). >> Thurber

White, Gilbert (1720–93) Clergyman and naturalist, born in Selborne, Hampshire, S England, UK. He studied at Oxford, where he became a fellow of Oriel College. He was ordained in 1751, and from 1755 lived uneventfully as curate in Selborne, where he kept a journal containing observations made in his garden. His letters on the subject, written over a period of 20 years, were published as *The Natural History and Antiquities of Selborne* (1789). It has become an English classic: an inspirational naturalist's handbook, it has never been out of print.

White, John (fl. 1585–93) Painter, cartographer, and colonial governor, born in England, UK. Nothing is known of him until he sailed with Frobisher's second expedition to Baffin I (1577). In 1585 he was sent by Sir Walter Raleigh to Roanoke I (now in North Carolina) as artist and mapmaker. He came back with a set of water colours that remain the primary source for the study of the flora, fauna, and indigenous inhabitants of this part of North America. It is now generally accepted that he was the John White sent as governor on the second expedition to Roanoke (1587); it was this White's daughter who gave birth to Virginia Dare, the first British child born in the New World. After returning to England for more support (1587), he returned in 1590 to find no trace of the colony. He sailed back, and was reportedly living in Newtowne, Kylmore, Ireland by 1593. >> Dare; Frobisher; Raleigh, Sir Walter

White, Leslie A(lvin) (1900–75) Cultural anthropologist, born in Salida, CO. He studied at Columbia University, the New School for Social Research, and the University of Chicago, and taught at Michigan (1932–75). He carried out many field trips among the Pueblo Indians (1926–57). He is principally known for his theory of cultural evolution, propounded in *The Science of Culture* (1949) and *The Evolution of Culture* (1959), in which he argues that culture tends to advance along with increases in technological efficiency in harnessing environmental energy sources.

White, Minor (1908–76) Photographer, born in Minneapolis, MN. He studied botany and poetry, and worked as a photographer for the US government Works Progress Administration (from 1937), becoming greatly influenced by Edward Weston and Alfred Stieglitz in developing photographic sequences. In 1946 he moved to San Francisco, where he worked with Ansel Adams, following him as director of the photographic department in the California School of Fine Art (1947–52). He founded and edited the periodicals *Aperture* (1952) and *Image* (1953–7), and was professor of creative photography at the Massachusetts Institute of Technology (1965–76). >> Adams, Ansel; Stieglitz; Weston

White, Patrick (Victor Martindale) (1912–90) Writer, born in London, England, UK of Australian parents. His youth was spent partly in Australia, and partly in England, where he studied at Cambridge. His first novel, *Happy Valley*, appeared in 1939, and after service in World War 2 he returned to Australia, where he wrote several novels, short stories, and plays, achieving international success with *The Tree of Man* (1954), an epic of pioneer Australia, and *Voss* (1957), a novel on a similar scale. A poetic writer of great intensity and some wit, he wrote of great visionaries as well as the sordidness of the everyday. He received the Nobel Prize for Literature in 1973. His autobiographical *Flaws in the Glass* was published in 1981, and he later became vocal on such issues as Aboriginal affairs and the environment.

White, Paul (Dudley) (1886–1973) Cardiologist, born in Roxburg, MA. He studied at Harvard, practised at the Massachusetts General Hospital, then worked in London with Sir Thomas Lewis (1913–14), returning to the USA fired with enthusiasm over the value of the electrocardiogram. His major textbook, *Heart Disease* (1931), secured his international reputation, and successful treatment of President Eisenhower did much to foster public awareness that heart disease need not be crippling. >> Eisenhower; Lewis, Thomas

White, Pearl (Fay) (1889–1938) Film-actress, born in Green Ridge, MO. She began her film career in 1910, and as the heroine of long-running serials, such as *The Perils of Pauline* (1914), *The Exploits of Elaine* (1914–15), and others, made an enormous reputation as the exponent of the type of serial film popularly called the 'cliff-hanger'. She retired in 1924, and went to live in France.

White, Stanford (1853–1906) Architect, born in New York City. A self-taught artist, he served as an apprentice with H H Richardson. During his partnership (1879–1906) in McKim, Mead & White, the firm became the largest architectural office in the world. He was a prolific designer of furniture, interiors, and jewellery, his graceful decorations complementing McKim's classical forms. He was shot dead by the husband of a former mistress. >> Richardson, Henry Hobson

White, T(erence) H(anbury) (1906–64) Novelist, born in Mumbai (Bombay), India. He studied at Cambridge, and taught at Stowe School (1930–6), where he wrote his first success, *England Have My Bones* (1936). With the exception of the largely autobiographical *The Goshawk* (1951), his best work was in the form of legend and fantasy, especially his sequence of novels about King Arthur, *The Once and Future King* (1958), beginning with *The Sword in the Stone* (1937).

White, William Allen (1868–1944) Editor and writer, born in Emporia, KS. He was proprietor and editor of the internationally-known Emporia *Daily* and *Weekly Gazette* in 1895. In addition to 'muckraking' articles he published a book of short stories of mordant social criticism, *Stratagems and Spoils* (1901), and a novel, *A Certain Rich Man* (1909). He later wrote shrewd appraisals of national politicians in *Masks in a Pageant* (1928). He received a Pulitzer Prize for his editorials in 1923.

Whitefield, George [**whit**feeld] (1714–70) Methodist evangelist, born in Gloucester, Gloucestershire, SWC England, UK. Associated with the Wesleys at Oxford and on their mission to Georgia, he became an enthusiastic evangelist. He founded no distinct sect, but had many adherents in Wales and Scotland, who formed the Calvinistic Methodists. The Countess of Huntingdon appointed him her chaplain, and built and endowed many chapels for him. He made several visits to America, where he founded an orphanage, and played an important role in the Great Awakening. >> Huntingdon, Countess of; Wesley, Charles; Wesley, John

Whitehead, A(lfred) N(orth) (1861–1947) Mathematician and Idealist philosopher, born in Ramsgate, Kent, SE England, UK. He studied at Cambridge, where he was senior lecturer in mathematics until 1910. He then taught at London (1910–14), becoming professor of applied mathematics at Imperial College (1914–24), and was then professor of philosophy at Harvard (1924–37). He collaborated with his former pupil, Bertrand Russell, in writing the *Principia mathematica* (1910–13). Other more popular works include *Adventures of Ideas* (1933) and *Modes of Thought* (1938). He received the Order of Merit in 1945. >> Peano; Russell, Bertrand

Whitehead, William (1715–85) Poet and playwright, born in Cambridge, Cambridgeshire, EC England, UK. He studied at Cambridge, where he became a fellow of Clare Hall in 1742. He travelled as tutor to Lord Jersey's son, became in 1755 secretary of the Order of the Bath, and in 1757 was appointed poet laureate. He wrote tragedies, such as *The Roman Father* (1750), in imitation of Corneille's *Horace*, and a comedy, *School for Lovers* (1762).

Whitelaw, Billie (1932–) Actress, born in Coventry, West Midlands, C England, UK. She made her London debut in Feydeau's *Hotel Paradiso* in 1956, then joined the National Theatre (1964) and the Royal Shakespeare Company (1971). A noted interpreter of Samuel Beckett's work, her performances include *Play* (1964), Mouth in *Not I* (1973), and *Footfalls* (1976). She has appeared in a wide range of other classical and modern parts, and received several awards. She has also had a varied film career, appearing in such films as *Frenzy* (1972), *The Omen* (1976), *Water Babies* (1978), and *The Krays* (1990), and is a frequent broadcaster on radio and television. Later work includes the BBC drama series *Born to Run* (1997). >> Beckett, Samuel

Whitelaw, William (Stephen Ian) Whitelaw, 1st Viscount, popularly known as **Willie Whitelaw** (1918–) British statesman, born in Nairn, Highland, N Scotland, UK. He studied at Cambridge, served in World War 2, and became a Conservative MP in 1955. After a number of junior posts, and several years as Chief Whip (1964–70), he became Leader of the House of Commons (1970–2), secretary of state for Northern Ireland (1972–3) and for employment (1973–4), and home secretary (1979–83). Made a viscount in 1983, he was Leader of the House of Lords until 1988, when he retired following a stroke.

Whiteley, Brett [wiytlee] (1939–92) Artist, born in Sydney, New South Wales, Australia. He studied in Sydney, and also in France, after winning a scholarship. Represented in the 1961 Whitechapel Gallery exhibition, he won the international prize at the second Paris bienniale the same year. He later worked in New York City (1967–9), and continued to travel and exhibit abroad regularly. The most famous Australian painter of his generation, the intensity and self-destructive tendencies of his life are reflected in his art. Winner of major Australian art prizes – the Archibald, Wynne, and Sulman many times over – he is known for his series of paintings of the English murderer, John Christie, his lush, sensuous representations of the female form, and his dazzling paintings of Sydney harbour.

Whiteman, Paul (1890–1967) Jazz bandleader, born in Denver, CO. He became famous in the 1920s as a pioneer of 'sweet-style' as opposed to traditional jazz. His band employed such exponents of true jazz as Bix Beiderbecke, the trumpeter, and Whiteman became popularly regarded as the inventor of jazz itself, rather than of a deviation from earlier jazz style. He was responsible for Gershwin's experiments in symphonic jazz, commissioning *Rhapsody in Blue* for a concert in New York City in 1924. >> Beiderbecke; Gershwin, George; Teagarden

Whitfield, June (Rosemary), stage name of **Mrs T J Aitchison** (1925–) Comic actress, born in London, England, UK. She studied at the Royal Academy of Dramatic Art, London, and worked in revues, musicals, and pantomimes before achieving success as Eth Glum in the long-running radio series *Take It From Here* (1953–60). She has been an indispensable part of UK television light entertainment in such series as *Faces of Jim* (1962–3), *Beggar My Neighbour* (1966–7), and *Absolutely Fabulous* (1993–6). A long professional association with Terry Scott (1927–94) resulted in the series *Terry and June* (1979–87). Her film appearances include *Carry on Nurse* (1959), *The Spy With the Cold Nose* (1965), and *Bless This House* (1973).

Whitgift, John (c. 1530–1604) Anglican clergyman, born in Grimsby, North East Lincolnshire, EC England, UK. He studied at Cambridge, was ordained in 1560, and rose to be dean of Lincoln (1571), Bishop of Worcester (1577), Archbishop of Canterbury (1583), and a privy councillor (1586). He attended Elizabeth I in her last moments, and crowned James I. He was a champion of conformity, and vindicated the Anglican position against the Puritans.

Whiting, John (Robert) (1917–63) Playwright, born in Salisbury, Wiltshire, S England, UK. He trained at the Royal Academy of Dramatic Art, London, becoming an actor before emerging as a playwright, with such early plays as *Saint's Day* (1951) and *A Penny for a Song* (1956). His best-known work was *The Devils* (1961), a dramatization of Huxley's *The Devils of Loudon*, commissioned by the Royal Shakespeare Company, which achieved great success, despite (or because of) its harrowing torture scenes.

Whitlam, (Edward) Gough [gof] (1916–) Australian statesman and prime minister (1972–5), born in Melbourne, Victoria, Australia. He studied at Canberra and Sydney universities, and became a lawyer. He was elected a Labor MP in 1952, and became leader of the Australian Labor Party in 1967. The first Labor prime minister in 23 years, he ended conscription, relaxed the policy on non-white immigrants, and increased federal government involvement in welfare, education, and the arts. He was dismissed by the governor-general, Sir John Kerr, after the Opposition blocked his money bills in the upper house of the Senate – the first time the crown had so acted against an elected prime minister. The ALP lost the ensuing election, and he resigned as an MP in 1978 to take up a university appointment at Canberra. A flamboyant, erudite figure who remains controversial, his book *The Whitlam Government* was published in 1985, and an account of his activities since leaving politics, *Abiding Interests*, in 1997. >> Kerr, Sir John; RR1033

Whitley, John Henry (1866–1935) Politician, born in Halifax, West Yorkshire, N England, UK. He studied at Clifton and London University, and became Liberal MP for Halifax (1900–28). He was Speaker of the House (1921–8) during the difficult period which culminated in the General Strike. He also presided over the committee that proposed (1917) industrial councils for joint consultation between employers and employees, since named *Whitley Councils*.

Whitman, Walt(er) (1819–92) Poet, born in Long Island, NY. He worked in offices and as a teacher, then took up journalism (1848–54). An outstanding proponent of free verse, his major poetic work was *Leaves of Grass* (1855), originally a small folio of 95 pages, which grew in succeeding editions to over 400 pages. Many of the poems in it are now considered American classics, such as 'When Lilacs Last in the Courtyard Bloom'd', and 'O Captain! My Captain!'.

During the Civil War he became a volunteer nurse – a bitter experience which forms much of the subject matter of his later prose works, notably *Democratic Vistas* (1871) and *Specimen Days and Collect* (1882). He was a major influence on later US poets.

Whitney, Eli (1765–1825) Inventor, born in Westborough, MA. He studied at Yale, and went to Georgia as a teacher. He found a patron in Mrs Nathanael Greene, the widow of a general, stayed on her plantation, read law, and set to work to invent a cotton-gin (patented in 1793) for separating cotton fibre from the seeds. His machine was pirated, and unsuccessful lawsuits in defence of his rights took up all his profits, plus the $50 000 voted him by the state of South Carolina. In 1798 he obtained a government contract for the manufacture of firearms, and made a fortune in this business, developing a new system of mass-production. >> Greene, Nathanael

Whitney, Gertrude Vanderbilt (1875–1942) Sculptor and art patron, born in New York City. She established and ran a hospital in France during World War 1, then lived in Greenwich Village, becoming an influential art patron. She established the Whitney Museum of American Art in New York City (1930), and is also known for her architectural sculptures, as in 'Titanic Memorial' (1931, Washington, DC).

Whitney, Josiah Dwight (1819–96) Geologist, born in Northampton, MA, the brother of William Dwight Whitney. He studied at Yale, and in 1840 joined the New Hampshire survey. In 1855 he was made professor at Iowa University, state geologist of California (1860), and in 1865 professor at Harvard. In 1864 he led an expedition which discovered the highest mountain in the USA (outside of Alaska) – Mt Whitney, in S California. >> Whitney, William Dwight

Whitney, William Dwight (1827–94) Philologist, born in Northampton, MA, the brother of Josiah Dwight Whitney. He studied at Williams and Yale universities, and became professor of Sanskrit (1854–94) at Yale, and also of comparative philology (1869–94). He edited numerous Sanskrit texts, and contributed to the great Sanskrit dictionary of Böhtlingk and Roth (1855–75). He was also editor of the 1864 edition of *Webster's Dictionary*, and editor-in-chief of the *Century Dictionary and Cyclopedia* (1889–91). >> Whitney, Josiah Dwight

Whittaker, Robert H(arding) (1920–80) Botanist and ecologist, born in Wichita, KS. He taught zoology at Washington State College (1948–51), then became a senior scientist in biology at Hanford Atomic Products Operations (1951–4), and taught at Brooklyn College (1954–64), Brookhaven National Laboratory, NY (1964–6), the University of California, Irvine (1966–8), and Cornell (1968–80). He made major contributions to ecological niche theory in his classifications of plant communities.

Whittier, John Greenleaf (1807–92) Quaker poet and abolitionist, born near Haverhill, MA. Largely self-educated, he embarked on a career as a writer and journalist, publishing a collection of poems and stories, *Legends of New England*, in 1831. In 1840 he settled at Amesbury, where he devoted himself to the cause of emancipation. His later works include *In War Time* (1864) and *At Sundown* (1892). In his day he was considered second only to Longfellow. >> Longfellow; Sturge

Whittington, Dick, popular name of **Richard Whittington** (c. 1358–1423) English merchant, supposed to have been the youngest son of Sir William Whittington of Pauntley in Gloucestershire, SWC England, UK, on whose death he set out at 13 for London, where he found work as an apprentice. He became an alderman and sheriff, and thrice Lord Mayor of London (1397–9, 1406–7, 1419–20). The legend of his cat is an accepted part of English folklore.

Whittle, Sir Frank (1907–96) Aviator and inventor of the British jet engine, born in Coventry, West Midlands, C England, UK. He entered the RAF as a boy apprentice, became a fighter pilot (1928) and a test pilot (1931–2), then went to Cambridge to read science (1934–7). He had been considering jet propulsion since joining the RAF, and patented a turbo-jet engine in 1930, but received no government support for his ideas until the outbreak of war. His engine successfully powered an aircraft flight in 1941, and by 1944 was in service with the RAF. He was knighted in 1948.

Whitworth, Sir Joseph (1803–87) Engineer and machine-tool manufacturer, born in Stockport, Greater Manchester, NW England, UK. After working as a mechanic for some years, he began to make his own machine tools, exhibited them at the Great Exhibition of 1851, and quickly gained a reputation for their quality and accuracy. He established standard screw threads and the equipment for forming and gauging them, and developed a method of casting ductile steel. He founded *Whitworth scholarships* for encouraging engineering science.

Whitworth, Kathy, popular name of **Kathrynne Ann Whitworth** (1939–) Golfer, born in Monahans, TX. The most successful woman golfer to date, she has won all the women's major events on the US circuit except the US Open. She turned professional in 1958, and won the US Ladies Professional Golf Association Championship four times: in 1967, 1971, 1975, and 1982. She was the leading money-winner eight times between 1965 and 1973.

Whorf, Benjamin Lee (1897–1941) Linguist, born in Winthrop, MA. A chemical engineer and fire prevention officer by profession, he studied linguistics and American Indian languages in his spare time. Influenced by the teaching of Edward Sapir at Yale University (1931–2), he developed Sapir's insights into the influence of language on people's perception of the world into what became known as the *Sapir–Whorf hypothesis*. >> Sapir

Whymper, Edward (1840–1911) Wood-engraver and mountaineer, the first to climb the Matterhorn, born in London, England, UK. He was trained as an artist on wood, but became better known for his mountaineering than for his book illustrations. In the period 1860–9 he conquered several hitherto unscaled peaks of the Alps, including the Matterhorn (1865), when four of his party fell to their death. He later travelled in Greenland, the Andes, and Canada.

Whyte, William H(ollingsworth) Jr (1917–) Urban sociologist and writer, born in West Chester, PA. Writer and editor at *Fortune* magazine (1946–59), he wrote *The Organization Man* (1956), a popular sociological tract that identified a new type of modern person – someone whose life is shaped according to the requirements of organizational employers. He explored the dangers of urban sprawl in *The Last Landscape* (1960), and the vitality of urban spaces in *City: Rediscovering the Center* (1989), both drawing heavily on a tactic of 'hanging around' cities to observe behaviour. In later years he became identified with his activities for conservationist and preservationist groups.

Wicliffe, John >> Wycliffe, John

Widgery, John Passmore Widgery, Baron (1911–81) Judge, born in South Molton, Devon, SW England, UK. He studied at Queen's College, Taunton, qualified as a solicitor, and was called to the bar in 1947. He became a judge (1961), a Lord Justice of Appeal (1968), and Lord Chief Justice of England (1971–80). He was responsible for overseeing a restructuring of the English courts recommended by a royal commission. He was also chairman of an enquiry into a clash between the army and demonstrators in Londonderry in 1972.

Widor, Charles Marie (Jean Albert) [weedaw(r)] (1844–1937) Composer, born in Lyon, France. He was organist at Lyon and (1870) at St Sulpice, Paris, and became professor of organ (1890) and composition (1896) at the Paris Conservatoire. He composed 10 symphonies for the organ, as well as a ballet, chamber music, and other orchestral works, and is probably best known for his Toccata, a favourite for weddings.

Wieck, Clara >> **Schumann, Clara Josephine**

Wieland, Christoph Martin [veelant] (1733–1813) Writer, born near Biberach, Germany. After several early devotional works, he made the first German translation of Shakespeare (1762–6), and wrote a number of popular romances, notably *Agathon* (1766–7). After holding a professorship at Erfurt, he was called to Weimar to train the grand-duchess's sons, where he lived until his death. During this time he translated many classical authors, and wrote his best-known work, the heroic poem 'Oberon' (1780).

Wien, Wilhelm (Carl Werner Otto Fritz Franz) [veen] (1864–1928) Physicist, born in Gaffken, Germany. He studied at Göttingen and Berlin, worked as assistant to Helmholtz, and later was professor at Würzburg (1900–20) and then at Munich. In the early 1890s he studied thermal radiation, and by 1896 had developed *Wien's formula* describing the distribution of energy in a radiation spectrum as a function of wavelength and temperature. The formula's accuracy reduces as wavelength increases, and it was this failure which inspired Planck to devise the quantum theory, which revolutionized physics in 1900. Wien was awarded the Nobel Prize for Physics in 1911. >> Planck

Wiener, Norbert [weener] (1894–1964) Mathematical logician, the founder of cybernetics, born in Columbia, MO. A child prodigy, he entered university at 11, studied at Harvard, Cornell, Cambridge, and Göttingen universities, and became professor of mathematics at the Massachusetts Institute of Technology (1932–60). During World War 2 he worked on guided missiles, and his study of the handling of information by electronic devices, based on the feedback principle, encouraged comparison between these and human mental processes in *Cybernetics* (1948) and other works.

Wiertz, Anton Joseph [veerts] (1806–65) Painter, born in Dinant, Belgium. In 1836 he settled in Liège, and in 1848 in Brussels. His original aim was to combine the excellences of Michelangelo and Rubens, but c.1848–50 he began to paint speculative and mystical pieces, dreams, visions, and the products of a morbid imagination. In 1850 the state built him a studio which became the Musée Wiertz. >> Michelangelo; Rubens

Wieschaus, Eric F [veeshows] (1947–) Developmental biologist, born in South Bend, IA. He studied at Yale University, where he became professor of biology, then moved to Princeton. He shared the Nobel Prize for Physiology or Medicine in 1995 for his research into how genes control early development of the human embryo. Using the fruit fly, his contribution, in collaboration with Nuesslein-Volhard, was to identify a number of genes which determine the body plan and formation of body segments. >> Lewis, Edward; Nuesslein-Volhard

Wiesel, Torsten N(ils) [veezel] (1924–) Neurobiologist, born in Uppsala, Sweden. He studied medicine at the Karolinska Institute in Stockholm, then moved to the USA, where he worked at Johns Hopkins (1955–9) and Harvard (1959–83) universities, joining Rockefeller university in 1983, and becoming president there in 1992. He performed pioneering research on the visual cortex of the brain, and with collaborator David Hubel shared the 1981

Nobel Prize for Physiology or Medicine for their discovery of how the brain interprets the messages it receives from the eyes. >> Hubel; RR1124

Wiesenthal, Simon [veezntahl] (1908–) Austrian Jewish survivor of the Nazi concentration camps, born in Buczacz, Poland. He dedicated his life to tracking down and prosecuting former Nazis who had organized the persecution of the Jews during World War 2. His most famous case was probably the capture of Eichmann in 1961. >> Eichmann

Wiggin, Kate Douglas, née **Smith** (1856–1923) Novelist and kindergarten educator, born in Philadelphia, PA. She led the kindergarten movement in the USA with the opening of the first free kindergarten on the W coast, but she is best remembered for her children's novels, notably *Rebecca of Sunnybrook Farm* (1903). Other titles include the 'Penelope' exploits, *The Birds' Christmas Carol* (1888), and *Mother Carey's Chickens* (1911).

Wigglesworth, Sir Vincent (Brian) (1899–1994) Entomologist, born in Kirkham, Lancashire, NW England, UK. He studied at Cambridge and St Thomas' Hospital, taught entomology at London (1926, 1936–44), then moved to Cambridge, where he became professor of biology (1952–66) and director of the Agricultural Research Unit of Insect Physiology (1943–67). He investigated the role of hormones in the growth of insects, and carried out detailed studies on the function of body-parts, often involving organ transplantation. He was knighted in 1964.

Wigman, Mary, originally **Marie Wiegmann** (1886–1973) Dancer, choreographer, and teacher, born in Hanover, Germany. Her career as Germany's most famous modern dancer began after World War 1, when she toured extensively and opened a school in Dresden in 1920. She created numerous solo and group dances which typified German Expressionist dancing. Her activities were reduced during World War 2, but in 1945 she started work again in Leipzig and Berlin. Through her schools and teaching and her highly dramatic performances she provided the focus for the development of a performance form of European modern dance.

Wigmore, John Henry (1863–1943) Jurist, born in San Francisco, CA. He studied at Harvard, then taught law in Tokyo and at Northwestern University (1893–1943). His major work was *Treatise on the Anglo-American System of Evidence in Trials at Common Law* (10 vols, 1904–5), usually called *Wigmore on Evidence*.

Wigner, Eugene (Paul) [wigner] (1902–95) Physicist, born in Budapest. He studied at Berlin Technische Hochschule, moved to the USA, and became a US citizen in 1937. He was professor of mathematical physics at Princeton (1938–71), and came to be known for his many contributions to the theory of nuclear physics, including the law of conservation of parity. His theory of neutron absorption (1936) was used in building nuclear reactors. He shared the Nobel Prize for Physics in 1963. >> RR1122

Wilberforce, Samuel (1805–73) Anglican clergyman, born in London, England, UK, the third son of William Wilberforce. He studied at Oxford, and was ordained in 1828. He became Bishop of Oxford in 1845, instituted Cuddesdon Theological College in 1854, and was appointed Bishop of Winchester in 1869. He initiated the modernization of the language of the King James Bible, and wrote along with his brother, **Robert**, the life of his father (1838). >> Trench; Wilberforce, William

Wilberforce, William (1759–1833) British politician, evangelist, and philanthropist, born in Hull, NE England, UK. He studied at Cambridge, became an MP (1780), and in 1788 began the movement which resulted in the abolition of the slave trade in the British West Indies in 1807. He next sought to secure the abolition of all slaves, but declining health compelled him in 1825 to retire from parliament. He died in London, one month before the passing of the Slavery Abolition Act. He was a lifelong friend of the Younger Pitt, though he remained a political independent. His evangelical beliefs led him to urge the aristocracy to practise 'real Christianity', and to give a moral lead to the poor, and he promoted many schemes for the welfare of the community. >> Pitt, William (the Younger); Wilberforce, Samuel

Wilbur, Richard (Purdy) (1921–) Poet, born in New York City. He studied at Amherst and Harvard universities, and taught at many institutions, notably at Wesleyan University (1957–77). Based in Cummington, MA, he has won acclaim for his translations as well as for his own lyrical poetry, as in *New and Collected Poems* (1988). He is widely known for his often performed translations of Molière, and for his lyrics to the musical, *Candide* (1956). He received the Pultizer Prize for *Things of This World* in 1956, and was named poet laureate of the USA in 1987. >> Molière

Wilbye, John (1574–1638) Madrigal composer, born in Diss, Norfolk, E England, UK. He was a farmer, who became a household musician at Hengrave Hall in Essex (c.1593–1628). He is known for only 66 madrigals, but these are renowned for his careful setting of literary texts, and for several translations of Italian poems.

Wilcox, Desmond >> **Rantzen, Esther**

Wilcox, Ella, *née* **Wheeler** (1850–1919) Journalist and prolific producer of verse, born in Johnstown Center, WI. She had completed a novel before she was 10. The first of her many volumes of verse was *Drops of Water* (1872), and she gained recognition with *Poems of Passion* (1883). She also wrote a great deal of fiction, and contributed essays to periodicals.

Wilde, Jane Francesca, Lady *née* **Elgee**, pseudonym **Speranza** (1826–96) Writer and journalist, born in Dublin, Ireland, the wife of Sir William Wilde and mother of Oscar Wilde. An ardent nationalist, she contributed poetry and prose to the *Nation* from 1845 under her pseudonym. After her marriage (1851), her home was the most famous in Dublin. Following her husband's death she moved to London, and published several works on folklore, including *Ancient Legends of Ireland* (1887) and *Ancient Cures* (1891). >> Wilde, Oscar; Wilde, William

Wilde, Oscar (Fingal O'Flahertie Wills) (1854–1900) Writer, born in Dublin, Ireland, the son of Sir William Wilde. He studied at Trinity College, Dublin, and at Oxford, and established himself among the social and literary circles in London. He was celebrated for his wit and flamboyant manner, and became a leading member of the 'art for art's sake' movement. His early work included *Poems* (1881), the novel *The Picture of Dorian Gray* (1891), and several comic plays, notably *Lady Windermere's Fan* (1892) and *The Importance of Being Earnest* (1895). *The Ballad of Reading Gaol* (1898) and *De profundis* (1905) reflect two years' hard labour for homosexual practices revealed during his abortive libel action (1895) against the Marquess of Queensberry, who had objected to Wilde's association with his son. He married **Constance Lloyd** (1858–98) in 1884, and had two sons, Cyril (1885–1915) and Vyvyan (1886–1967) for whom he wrote the classic children's fairy stories *The Happy Prince and Other Tales* (1888). He died an exile in Paris, having adopted the name of **Sebastian Melmoth**. >> Douglas, Alfred; Queensberry; Sherard; Wilde, William

Wilde, Sir William (Robert Wills) (1815–76) Physician, born in Castlerea, Co Roscommon, Ireland. He studied at London, Berlin, and Vienna, and on his return to Dublin served as medical commissioner on the Irish Census (1841 and 1851), publishing a major medical report, *The Epidemics of Ireland* (1851). The same year he married Jane Elgee and, in 1854, she gave birth to their son Oscar. He wrote on ocular and aural surgery, pioneered the operation for mastoiditis, invented an ophthalmoscope, and founded St Mark's Ophthalmic Hospital. He was an antiquarian of significance, publishing a major catalogue of the holdings of the Royal Irish Academy. >> Wilde, Jane Francesca; Wilde, Oscar

Wilder, Billy, originally **Samuel Wilder** (1906–) Filmmaker, born in Sucha, Austria. A law student at Vienna University, he worked as a journalist and crime reporter. He wrote for several German films from 1929, but as a Jew was forced to leave in 1933, and moved to Hollywood, working initially as a screenwriter. He started as a director in 1942 with *The Major and the Minor*, and continued for some 40 years with a wide variety of productions, which he often co-produced and scripted, including *Double Indemnity* (1944), *The Lost Weekend* (1945, Oscar), *Stalag 17* (1953), *Sunset Boulevard* (1955), and *The Apartment* (1960, Oscar). Many of his later productions were in Europe, such as *The Private Life of Sherlock Holmes* (1970) in England, and *Fedora* (1978) in Germany. He received the American Film Institute Life Achievement Award in 1986.

Wilder, Gene, originally **Jerome Silberman** (1935–) Film actor, writer, and director, born in Milwaukee, WI, the son of Russian immigrants. He trained in England at the Bristol Old Vic, taught fencing as a professional, then joined the Actors' Studio. He made his film debut in a small role in *Bonnie and Clyde* (1967), and received a Best Supporting Actor nomination for *The Producers* (1968). He developed an appealing, vulnerable, somewhat nervous screen persona, as seen in *Blazing Saddles* (1974), *Young Frankenstein* (1974, which he also co-wrote and directed), *Stir Crazy* (1982), and other films. Known also as a screenwriter and director, he returned to the stage in 1996, starring in the London production of *Laughter on the 23rd Floor*.

Wilder, Laura, *née* **Ingalls** (1867–1957) Children's writer, born in Pepin, WI. She edited a rural magazine for many years, and when she was in her 60s her daughter suggested that she write down her childhood memories of the American West. The result was a series of successful books which were popularized as the *Little House on the Prairie* television series in the 1970s. Her titles included *Little House in the Big Woods* (1932), *By the Shores of Silver Lake* (1939), and *Those Happy Golden Years* (1943).

Wilder, Thornton (Niven) (1897–1975) Writer, born in Madison, WI. He studied at Yale, then taught literature and classics at the University of Chicago (1930–7). His first novel, *The Cabala*, appeared in 1926, and was followed by *The Bridge of San Luis Rey* (1927, Pulitzer). Other titles include *The Woman of Andros* (1930) and *The Ides of March* (1948). As a playwright, he is best-remembered for *Our Town* (1938) and *The Skin of Our Teeth* (1942), both Pulitzer Prizes. His later plays include *The Matchmaker* (1954), on which the successful musical *Hello Dolly* (1964) was based.

Wilenski, Reginald Howard [wilenskee] (1887–1975) Art critic and art historian, born in London, England, UK. His analysis of the aims and achievements of modern artists, *The Modern Movement in Art* (1927), has had considerable influence.

Wiles, Andrew (John) (1953–) Mathematician, born in Cambridge, Cambridgeshire, UK. He studied at Clare College, Cambridge, and joined Princeton University in 1980. In 1993 he announced that he had solved one of mathematics' oldest mysteries, Fermat's last theorem – a problem which had intrigued him since childhood. His proof makes use of the Taniyama-Weil conjecture, a problem in number theory dealing with the nature of elliptic curves. In 1986 US mathematician Kenneth A Ribet had shown that, if this conjecture could be solved, a proof of Fermat's theorem would follow. Inspired by Ribet's work, Wiles devoted seven years to solving a special case of the conjecture, and by 1994 it had been accepted that a proof of the theorem had indeed been found. >> Fermat

Wiley, Harvey Washington (1844–1930) Food chemist, born near Kent, IN. He served in the Civil War, and qualified in medicine at Indiana Medical College. He was professor of chemistry at Purdue (1874–83), then became chief of the chemical division of the US Department of Agriculture. His main interest was in improving purity and reducing food adulteration, and despite many obstacles his efforts led to the Pure Food and Drug Act of 1906. Conflicts over its enforcement led to his resignation in 1912, but he continued as an active propagandist on food purity until his death.

Wilfrid or **Wilfrith, St** (634–709) Monk and bishop, born in Northumbria. He trained at Lindisfarne, and upheld the replacement of Celtic by Roman religious practices at the Synod of Whitby (664). As Bishop of York (c.665), he was involved in controversy over the organization of the Church in Britain, and was the first churchman to appeal to Rome to settle the issue. He built a monastery at Hexham and at Ripon, introduced the Benedictine Rule, and was one of the first Anglo-Saxons to despatch missionaries to Germany. Feast day 12 October. >> Willibrord

Wilhelm I / II >> **William I / II** (of Germany)

Wilhelmina (Helena Pauline Maria) [wiluhmeena] (1880–1962) Queen of The Netherlands (1890–1948), born in The Hague. She succeeded her father William III at the age of 10, her mother acting as regent until 1898. An upholder of constitutional monarchy, she especially won the admiration of her people during World War 2. Though compelled to seek refuge in Britain, she steadfastly encouraged Dutch resistance to the German occupation. In 1948, she abdicated in favour of her daughter Juliana, and assumed the title of Princess of The Netherlands. >> Juliana; RR1077

Wilkes, Charles (1798–1877) US naval officer, born in New York City. He joined the US navy in 1818 and studied hydrography. He explored the South Pacific islands and the Antarctic continent, including the stretch that now bears his name (1839–40). During the Civil War he intercepted the British mail-steamer *Trent* off Cuba, and took off two Confederate commissioners accredited to France, thereby creating a risk of war with Britain (1861). As acting rear-admiral he commanded a squadron against commerce raiders in the West Indies, but was court-martialled for disobedience in 1864, after which he retired. >> Dana, James D

Wilkes, John (1727–97) British politician and journalist, born in London, England, UK. He studied at Leyden, became an MP (1757), and attacked the ministry in his weekly journal, *North Briton* (1762–3). He was imprisoned, released, then expelled from the house for libel. Re-elected on several occasions, and repeatedly expelled, he came to be seen as a champion of liberty, and an upholder of press freedom. In 1774 he became Lord Mayor of London, and in the same year finally gained admission to parliament, where he remained until his retirement.

Wilkes, Maurice (Vincent) (1913–) Computer scientist, born in Dudley, West Midlands, C England, UK. He studied at Cambridge, directed the Mathematical (later Computer) Laboratory at Cambridge (1946–80), and became known for his pioneering work with the EDSAC (Electronic Delay Storage Automatic Calculator), the first stored-program computer. Around this machine, operational after 1949,

Wilkes built the world's first computing service. He published his *Memoirs* in 1985.

Wilkie, Sir David (1785–1841) Painter, born in Cults, Fife, E Scotland, UK. He studied at Edinburgh and London, where he settled after the success of his 'Pitlessie Fair' (1804, Edinburgh) and 'The Village Politicians' (1806, London). His fame mainly rests on his genre painting, but he also painted portraits, and in his later years sought to emulate the richness of colouring of the old masters, choosing more elevated subjects. He was made painter-in-ordinary to the king in 1830, and was knighted in 1835.

Wilkins, Sir George (Hubert) (1888–1958) Polar explorer and pioneer aviator, born at Mt Bryan East, South Australia. He was part of an expedition to the Arctic (1913–18), then flew from England to Australia (1919), explored the Antarctic with Shackleton (1921–2), and made a pioneer flight from Alaska to Spitsbergen over polar ice (1928). In 1931 he failed to reach the North Pole in the submarine *Nautilus*. He was knighted in 1928. >> Shackleton

Wilkins, John (1614–72) Anglican clergyman, the first secretary of the Royal Society, born in Fawsley, Northamptonshire, C England, UK. He studied at Oxford, became a domestic chaplain, and took part in a group which met to further interest in science, and which later became the Royal Society (1662). In the Civil War he sided with parliament, and was appointed Warden of Wadham College, Oxford (1648), but was dispossessed at the Restoration. He soon recovered court favour, and became preacher at Gray's Inn, rector of St Lawrence Jewry (1662), dean of Ripon (1663), and Bishop of Chester (1668). In his *Discovery of a World in the Moon* (1628) he discusses the possibility of communication by a flying-machine with the Moon and its supposed inhabitants; the *Discourse Concerning a New Planet* (1640) argues that the Earth is one of the planets. >> Hooke, Robert; Wallis, John; Willis, Thomas; Wren, Christopher

Wilkins, Maurice (Hugh Frederick) (1916–) Biophysicist, born in Pongaroa, New Zealand. He studied at Birmingham and Cambridge universities, carried out wartime research into uranium isotope separation in California, then joined the Medical Research Council's Biophysics Research Unit at King's College, London in 1946, becoming deputy-director (1955) and director (1970–2). His X-ray diffraction studies of DNA helped Crick and Watson determine its structure, and he shared with them the Nobel Prize for Physiology or Medicine in 1962. >> Crick; Franklin, Rosalind; Watson, James

Wilkins, Roy (1910–81) Journalist and civil rights leader, born in St Louis, MO. He edited an African-American weekly, the *St Paul Appeal*, before joining the staff of the *Kansas City Call*, a leading black weekly. In 1931 he served as executive assistant secretary of the National Association for the Advancement of Colored People, became editor of the organization's newspaper, *Crisis* (1934–49), and was then appointed as executive secretary, retiring in 1977. He was considered one of the most articulate spokesmen for the more moderate wing of the civil rights movement. >> Hooks, Benjamin

Wilkinson, Ellen Cicely (1891–1947) Feminist and stateswoman, born in Manchester, Greater Manchester, NW England, UK. She was an early member of the Independent Labour Party, and an active campaigner for women's suffrage. She became a member of the Communist Party (1920), but had left it by 1924, when she became an MP. She was parliamentary secretary to the ministry of home security (1940), and minister of education (1945), the first woman to hold such an appointment.

Wilkinson, Sir Geoffrey (1921–96) Inorganic chemist, born in Todmorden, West Yorkshire, N England, UK. He studied at Imperial College, London, where he returned in 1956 after war work in Canada and the USA. While at Harvard in 1952, he showed that ferrocene has a molecule with an iron atom sandwiched between two carbon rings; since then, thousands of such *metallocenes* have been made and studied. He shared the Nobel Prize for Chemistry in 1973, and was knighted in 1976. >> RR1123

Wilkinson, John (1728–1808) Iron-master and inventor, born in Clifton, Cumbria, NW England, UK. His most important achievement was the invention in 1774 of a cannon-boring machine, considerably more accurate than any in use up to that time. He used this machine to bore more accurate cylinders for steam engines, such as those of Boulton and Watt, to whom he supplied several hundred cylinders over the next two decades. Wilkinson in turn installed a Watt engine in 1776 as a blowing engine at one of his furnaces, the first Watt engine to be used other than for pumping. He was one of the principle promoters of the iron bridge at Coalbrookdale, built by Abraham Darby in 1779. He built an iron-hulled barge (1787), and supplied much of the ironwork for the Paris waterworks. >> Boulton; Darby, Abraham; Watt

Willaert, Adrian [wilah(r)t] (c. 1490–1562) Composer, probably born in Bruges, Belgium. He is thought to have studied in Paris, changing from law to music. He was appointed *maestro di capella* of St Mark's, Venice (1527), and made Venice the centre of European music. He gained a great reputation as a composer and teacher, and among his pupils was Andrea Gabrieli. He composed works in most of the many contemporary genres of sacred music, as well as secular chansons and madrigals. >> Gabrieli, Andrea

Willard, Emma, *née* **Hart** (1787–1870) Pioneer of higher education for women, born in Berlin, CT. In 1814 she opened Middlebury Female Seminary, offering an unprecedented range of subjects, in order to prepare women for college. Unsuccessful in gaining funding for her school, she moved to Troy, NY (1821), where she received financial help. The school (now called the Emma Willard School) developed quickly, and her campaigns paved the way for co-education.

Willard, Frances (Elizabeth Caroline) (1839–98) Temperance campaigner, born in Churchville, NY. She studied at the Northwestern Female College, Evanston, IL, and was professor of aesthetics there. She became secretary of the Women's Christian Temperance Union in 1874, and helped to found the International Council of Women.

William I (of England), known as **the Conquerer** (c.1028–1087) Duke of Normandy (1035–87) and the first Norman king of England (1066–87), the illegitimate son of Duke Robert of Normandy. Edward the Confessor, who had been brought up in Normandy, most probably designated him as future King of England in 1051. When Harold Godwinson, despite an apparent oath to uphold William's claims, took the throne as Harold II, William invaded with the support of the papacy, defeated and killed Harold at the Battle of Hastings, and was crowned king on Christmas Day, 1066. The key to effective control was military conquest backed up by aristocratic colonization, so that by the time of the Domesday Book (1086), the leaders of Anglo-Saxon society S of the Tees had been almost entirely replaced by a new ruling class of Normans, Bretons, and Flemings, who were closely tied to William by feudal bonds. He died near Paris, while defending Normandy's S border. >> Adela; Edward the Confessor; Harold II; Henry I (of England); Odo; Robert Curthose; RR1095

William I (of Germany), Ger **Wilhelm** (1797–1888) King of Prussia (1861–88) and first German emperor (1871–88), born in Berlin, the second son of Frederick William III. His use of

force during the 1848 revolution made him unpopular, and he was forced to leave Prussia temporarily for London. As king he consolidated the throne and strengthened the army, placing Bismarck at the head of the ministry. He was victorious against Denmark (1864), Austria (1866), and France (1871), and was then proclaimed emperor. The rapid rise of Socialism in Germany led to severe repressive measures, and he survived several attempts at assassination. >> Bismarck; Frederick William III; RR1051

William I (of the Netherlands), **Prince of Orange**, known as **William the Silent** (1533–84) First of the hereditary stadholders (governors) of the United Provinces of the Netherlands (1572–84), born in Dillenburg, The Netherlands. He joined the aristocratic protest to the oppressive policies of Philip II of Spain, and in 1568 took up arms against the Spanish crown. After initial reverses, he began the recovery of the coastal towns with the help of the Sea Beggars, and became stadtholder of the Northern provinces, united in the Union of Utrecht (1579). He was assassinated in Delft by a Spanish agent. His byname comes from his ability to keep secret Henry II's scheme to massacre all the Protestants of France and The Netherlands, confided to him when he was a French hostage in 1559. >> Henry II (of France) >> RR1077

William I (of Scotland), known as **William the Lion** (c.1142–1214) King of Scots (1165–1214), the brother and successor of Malcolm IV. In 1173–4 he invaded Northumberland during the rebellion against Henry II, but was captured at Alnwick, and by the Treaty of Falaise (1174) recognized Henry as the feudal superior of Scotland. Despite his difficulties with England, he made Scotland a much stronger kingdom. In 1189 Scottish independence was restored, and in 1192 Celestine III declared the Scottish Church free of all external authority save the pope's. >> RR1095

William II (of England), known as **William Rufus** (c.1056–1100) King of England (1087–1100), the second surviving son of William the Conqueror. His main goal was the recovery of Normandy from his elder brother Robert Curthose. From 1096, when Robert relinquished the struggle and departed on the First Crusade, William ruled the duchy as *de facto* duke. He also led expeditions to Wales (1095, 1097), conquered Carlisle and the surrounding district (1092), and after the death of Malcolm III he exercised a controlling influence over Scottish affairs. Contemporaries condemned his government of England as arbitrary and ruthless. He exploited his rights over the Church and the nobility beyond the limits of custom, and quarrelled with Anselm, Archbishop of Canterbury. His personal conduct outraged the moral standards of the time, for he was most probably a homosexual. He was killed by an arrow while hunting in the New Forest. It has been supposed that he was murdered on the orders of his younger brother, who succeeded him as Henry I, but his death was almost certainly accidental. >> Anselm; Malcolm III; Robert Curthose; William I (of England); RR1095

William II (of Germany), Ger **Wilhelm**, known as **Kaiser Wilhelm** (1859–1941) German emperor and king of Prussia (1888–1918), born in Potsdam, Germany, the eldest son of Frederick III (1831–88) and Victoria (the daughter of Britain's Queen Victoria), and grandson of Emperor William I. He dismissed Bismark (1890), and began a long period of personal rule, displaying a bellicose attitude in international affairs. He pledged full support to Austria–Hungary after the assassination of Archduke Francis Ferdinand at Sarajevo (1914), but then made apparent efforts to prevent the escalation of the resulting international crisis. During the war he became a mere figurehead, and when the German armies collapsed, and US

President Wilson refused to negotiate while he remained in power, he abdicated and fled the country. He settled at Doorn, in The Netherlands, living as a country gentleman. >> Francis Ferdinand; Wilson, Woodrow; RR1051

William III (of Great Britain), known as **William of Orange** (1650–1702) Stadtholder of the United Provinces (1672–1702) and king of Great Britain (1689–1702), born in The Hague, the son of William II of Orange by Mary, the eldest daughter of Charles I of England. In 1677 he married his cousin, **Mary** (1662–94), the daughter of James II by Anne Hyde. Invited to redress the grievances of the country, he landed at Torbay in 1688 with an English and Dutch army, and forced James II to flee. William and Mary were proclaimed rulers early the following year. He defeated James's supporters at Killiecrankie (1689) and at the Boyne (1690), then concentrated on the War of the League of Augsburg against France (1689–97), in which he was finally successful. In later years, he had to withstand much parliamentary opposition to his proposals, and there were many assassination plots. He died in London, childless, the crown passing to Mary's sister, Anne. >> Anne; Bentinck, William; Ginckell; James II (of England); Leeds; Luxembourg; Marlborough; Mary II; Temple, William; Somers, John; RR1095

William IV, known as **the Sailor King** (1765–1837) King of Great Britain and Ireland, and king of Hanover (1830–7), born in London, England, UK, the third son of George III, and before his accession known as **Duke of Clarence**. He entered the navy in 1779, saw service in the USA and the West Indies, became admiral in 1811, and Lord High Admiral in 1827–8. His elder brother having died, he succeeded George IV in 1830. Widely believed to have Whig leanings at his accession, he developed Tory sympathies, and did much to obstruct the passing of the first Reform Act (1832). He was the last monarch to use prerogative powers to dismiss a ministry with a parliamentary majority when he sacked Melbourne in 1834 and invited the Tories to form a government. He was succeeded by his niece, Victoria. >> George III; George IV; Jordan, Dorothea; Melbourne, Viscount; Victoria; RR1095

William of Auvergne [ohvairn], also called **William of Paris** (c. 1180–1249) Philosopher and theologian, born in Aurillac, France. He became professor of theology in the University of Paris (1225) and Bishop of Paris (1228–49), in which role he defended the mendicant orders and introduced various clerical reforms. His most important work is the monumental *Magisterium divinale* (1223–40, The Divine Teaching), in which he attempted the integration of classical Greek and Arabic philosophy with Christian theology.

William of Auxerre [ohsair] (c. 1150–1231) Theologian and philosopher, born in Auxerre, France. A master of theology, he was an administrator at the University of Paris. Pope Gregory IX appointed him (1231) to a council to censor the works of Aristotle in the university curriculum, to ensure their conformity with the Christian faith, but William died before the council's work had far advanced. His main publication is the *Summa aurea in quattuor libros sententiarum* (Golden Compendium on the Four Books of Sentences), a commentary on early and mediaeval Christian thought, tending to emphasize the value of philosophy and rational analysis as a tool for Christian theology.

William of Malmesbury [mahmzbree] (c. 1090–c. 1143) English chronicler and Benedictine monk, the librarian of Malmesbury Abbey, Wiltshire, S England, UK. The emphasis he placed on the importance of documentary material and non-written sources, including architectural and other kinds of visual evidence, gives him a key place in the development of historical method. His main works are:

Gesta regum anglorum, a general history of England from the coming of the Anglo-Saxons; *Gesta pontificum anglorum*, an ecclesiastical history of England from the Conversion; and *Historia novella*, a contemporary narrative of English affairs from c.1125 to 1142.

William of Ockham or **Occam** [okam] known as **the Venerable Inceptor** (c. 1285–c. 1349) Scholastic philosopher, born in Ockham, Surrey, SE England, UK. He entered the Franciscan order, and studied theology at Oxford. Summoned to Avignon (1324) to respond to charges of heresy, he became involved in a dispute between the Franciscans and Pope John XXII over apostolic poverty. He fled to Bavaria in 1328, where he remained until 1347, writing treatises on papal versus civil authority. His best-known philosophical contributions are his successful defence of nominalism against realism, and his deployment in theology of the rule of ontological economy, 'entities are not to be multiplied beyond necessity', so frequently and to such effect that it came to be known as *Ockham's razor*.

William of Tyre (c. 1130–86) Chronicler and clergyman, born in Palestine of French parents. Educated at Paris and Bologna, he entered the service of the kings of Jerusalem, and was appointed Archbishop of Tyre in 1175. His main work, *Historia rerum in partibus transmarinis gestarum* (History of Deeds in Foreign Parts), deals with the history of Palestine from 614 to 1184, and is especially valuable to the historian of the 12th-c Crusades.

William of Waynflete (c. 1395–1486) English statesman and clergyman. He probably studied at New College, Oxford, then became provost of Eton (1443), Bishop of Winchester (1447), and founded Magdalen College, Oxford (1448). He was involved in the negotiations which ended Jack Cade's rebellion in 1450, and as a Lancastrian played an important role as adviser to Henry VI in the Wars of the Roses. He was Lord Chancellor (1456–60). >> Cade; Henry VI

William of Wykeham or **Wickham** [wikam] (1324–1404) English statesman and clergyman, born in Wickham, Hampshire, S England, UK, the son perhaps of a serf, who rose to become the chief adviser of Edward III. He was appointed Keeper of the Privy Seal (1363), Bishop of Winchester (1367), and was twice Chancellor of England (1367–71, 1389–91). He founded New College, Oxford, and Winchester College, both of which were fully established by the 1390s. >> Edward III

Williams, Bernard (Arthur Owen) (1929–) English philosopher. He studied at Oxford, and taught in London and Oxford, before being appointed professor of philosophy at London (1964–7). He then became professor of philosophy at Cambridge (1967), Provost of King's College, Cambridge, (1979), and professor of philosophy at Oxford (1990–6). His work has been influential in moral philosophy, in particular *Morality: an Introduction to Ethics* (1972) and *Ethics and the Limits of Philosophy* (1985). Later works include *Making Sense of Humanity* (1995). He chaired the Committee on Obscenity and Film Censorship which produced the *Williams Report* in 1979. He was married (1955–74) to the politician, Shirley Williams. >> Williams, Shirley

Williams, Betty >> **Corrigan, Mairead**

Williams, Edward, known as **Iolo Morganwg** (1747–1826) Poet and antiquary, born in Llancarfan, Vale of Glamorgan, S Wales. He worked there as a stonemason, and became a poet in Welsh and English. He had links with 18th-c Radicalism, mingling his ideas with Romantic exaltation of the Welsh past, and established neo-Druidic cults and celebrations in Wales from 1792. He published collected poems purportedly by the 14th-c poet Dafydd ap Gwilym, which in fact were his own work. He co-edited *The Myvyrian Archaeology* (3 vols, 1801–7), and a vast corpus of cultural material from the Welsh past with varying degrees of authenticity. A brilliant forger whose deceptions far outlived his own time, his work helped to revive Welsh culture.

Williams, (George) Emlyn (1905–87) Playwright and actor, born in Mostyn, Flintshire. He studied at Oxford, joined a repertory company in 1927, and achieved success as a playwright with *A Murder Has Been Arranged* (1930) and the psychological thriller, *Night Must Fall* (1935). He appeared in many London and Broadway productions, featured in several films, and gave widely acclaimed readings from the works of Dickens, Dylan Thomas, and Munro (Saki). He wrote the autobiographical *George* (1961) and *Emlyn* (1973), as well as *Beyond Belief* (1967), and a novel, *Headlong* (1980).

Williams, Fred(erick Ronald Williams) (1927–82) Painter and etcher, born in Richmond, Victoria, Australia. He studied at the National Gallery School and at the Chelsea and Central Schools of Art, London. He is recognized as the most significant painter of the Australian landscape since Sir Arthur Streeton. An international reputation was secured by his 1977 exhibition *Landscapes of a Continent* at the Museum of Modern Art, New York City. >> Streeton

Williams, Sir Frederic (Calland) (1911–77) Electrical engineer, born in Manchester, Greater Manchester, NW England, UK. He studied at Manchester and Oxford universities, and worked at the Bawdsey Research Station, Manchester (1940–6), where he developed a method of identifying friendly aircraft on radar (IFF – identification, friend or foe), the forerunner of the modern system of aircraft identification on radar. He became professor of electrical engineering there (1946), and is more widely known for his development of the *Williams tube*, the first successful electrostatic random access memory for the digital computer. This enabled him, together with his collaborator Tom Kilburn, to operate the world's first stored-program computer in June 1948. >> Kilburn

Williams, Sir George (1821–1905) Social reformer, born in Dulverton, Somerset, SW England, UK. A wealthy draper, he made a hobby of temperance work, lay preaching, and teaching in ragged schools. In 1844 he founded the Young Men's Christian Assocation (YMCA).

Williams, Hank, popular name of **Hiram King Williams** (1923–53) Singer and guitarist, born in Georgiana, AL. He began recording for the MGM label (1947) and produced many hit records, notably 'Lovesick Blues' (1949), 'Your Cheatin' Heart', and 'Hey, Good Lookin'. He joined the Grand Ole Opry in Nashville (1949), and gained international fame as a performer of both country and western and popular music. His untimely death from a heart attack may have been due to drug and alcohol abuse.

Williams, John (1796–1839) Missionary, born in London, England, UK. Joining the London Missionary Society, he worked in Tahiti, Cook Is, and Samoa, before being killed in Vanuatu (New Hebrides). His book *Narrative of Missionary Enterprises in the South Seas* (1837) was widely read. He was a model of the missionary-adventurer, and his example inspired David Livingstone. >> Livingstone, David

Williams, John (Christopher) (1942–) Guitarist, born in Melbourne, Victoria, Australia. Resident in England since 1952, he trained at the Accademia Musicale Chigiana di Siena, Italy, and the Royal College of Music, London, studied with Segovia, and made his professional debut in 1958. He has since taught at colleges in London and Manchester. His musical sympathies are wide-ranging, from renaissance to jazz. Several modern composers have written works for him, and he founded a jazz and popular music group known as Sky (1979–84). He later formed the contemporary music group Attacca. >> Segovia

Williams, J(ohn) P(eter) R(hys) (1949–) Rugby union player and physician, born in Bridgend, S Wales. He was an excellent tennis player as a junior, representing Wales, and winning the Wimbledon Junior Championship (1966). He studied medicine at St Mary's, London, and became consultant in trauma and orthopaedic surgery at the Princess of Wales Hospital, Bridgend (1986). He played rugby for London Welsh and Bridgend, as well as for Wales (captain, 1978) and the British Lions (tours of New Zealand in 1971, South Africa in 1974). He is the most capped Welshman, with 55 appearances, and the game's most capped fullback. He published his autobiography, *JPR*, in 1979. >> RR1167

Williams, Kenneth (1926–87) Actor and comedian, born in London, England, UK. He made his London debut in 1952, starred in comedies and revues such as *Share My Lettuce* (1957) and *One Over the Eight* (1961), and in the radio series *Round the Horne* and *Stop Messing About*. His affected style of speech and rich, punctilious enunciation made him instantly recognizable. He made several films, most famously in the *Carry On* series of comedies, and was a regular on radio programmes such as *Just a Minute*.

Williams, Mary Lou (1910–81) Jazz pianist, arranger, and composer, born in Atlanta, GA. She left high school to become a touring show pianist. Her first important period as a performer and arranger was during the 1930s with the Kansas City-based Andy Kirk and his Clouds of Joy. Her outstanding qualities as an arranger brought her work from Duke Ellington (for whom she arranged the well-known 'Trumpets No End'), Earl Hines, and Benny Goodman, among others. >> Ellington; Goodman, Benny; Hines

Williams, Sir Monier-Williams >> **Monier-Williams, Sir Monier**

Williams, Raymond (1921–88) Social historian, critic, and novelist, born in Pandy, Monmouthshire, SE Wales. He studied at Cambridge, where he became a fellow in 1961, and professor of drama (1974–83). He wrote *Culture and Society* (1958), which established his reputation as a cultural historian, followed by *The Long Revolution* (1961) and *Marxism and Literature* (1977), amongst others. He was active in New Left intellectual movements, producing the *May Day Manifesto* (1968), and was increasingly identified with Welsh nationalism in his novels such as *Border Country* (1960), *The Fight for Manod* (1979), and *Loyalties* (1985).

Williams, Robin (1952–) Film actor and entertainer, born in Chicago, IL. He studied acting at the Juilliard School in New York City, then settled in San Francisco and developed a nightclub act. He starred in the television comedy series *Mork and Mindy* (1978–82), made his film debut in *Popeye* (1981), and became known for his versatile and energetic performances. He earned an Oscar nomination and a Golden Globe Award for *Good Morning Vietnam* (1987), and another Oscar nomination for *Dead Poets Society* (1989). Later films include *Awakenings* (1990), *Hook* (1991), *Mrs Doubtfire* (1993), *Jumanji* (1995), and *Father's Day* (1997), and he provided the voice of the genie in *Aladdin* (1991). He has also continued to perform as a stand-up comic entertainer.

Williams, Robley Cook (1908–) Biophysicist, born in Santa Rosa, CA. He studied physics at Cornell University, and from 1950 taught at the University of California, Berkeley. His early research was in astronomy, but from the 1940s he was concerned with electron microscopy, and with R Wyckoff he devised a metal-shadowing technique that could be used for sensitive biological materials. From this basis he became concerned with viruses, and made major contributions to knowledge of their structure in the 1950s. >> Wyckoff

Williams, Roger (c. 1604–83) Colonist who founded Rhode Island, born in London, England, UK. He studied at Cambridge, took Anglican orders, became an extreme Puritan, and emigrated to New England in 1630. He refused to join the congregation at Boston, and moved to Salem, where he was persecuted and banished. He then purchased lands from the Indians, and founded the city of Providence (1636), allowing full religious toleration. In 1643 and 1651 he travelled to England to procure a charter for his colony, and became its first president (1654–8).

Williams (of Crosby), Shirley (Vivien Teresa Brittain) Williams, Baroness, *née* **Catlin** (1930–) British stateswoman, born in London, England, UK, the daughter of Vera Brittain. She studied at Oxford, and worked as a journalist. Secretary of the Fabian Society (1960–4), she became a Labour MP in 1964. After many junior positions, she was made secretary of state for prices and consumer protection (1974–6), and for education and science (1976–9). She lost her seat in 1979, became a co-founder of the Social Democratic Party in 1981, and the party's first elected MP later that year. She lost her seat in the 1983 general election, but remained as the SDP's president (1982–7). She supported the merger between the SDP and the Liberal Party. Her first husband (1955–74) was the philosopher, Bernard Williams. After her second marriage, to Harvard professor of politics, **Richard Neustadt**, she moved to the USA, but remains involved in British politics. She was made a life peer in 1993. >> Brittain; Williams, Bernard

Williams, Ted, popular name of **Theodore Samuel Williams** (1918–) Baseball player, born in San Diego, CA. An outstanding hitter, he played with the Boston Red Sox for 19 seasons (1939–60), despite service in World War 2 and the Korean War. He was twice named Most Valuable Player, and won the last of his six league batting championships in 1958 at the age of 40. >> RR1144

Williams, Tennessee, pseudonym of **Thomas Lanier Williams** (1911–83) Playwright, born in Columbus, MS. He studied at Columbia University and the universities of Missouri and Iowa, then worked at a wide range of theatrical jobs until he achieved success with *The Glass Menagerie* (1944). His other plays, almost all set in the Deep South against a background of decadence and degradation, include *A Streetcar Named Desire* (1947, Pulitzer), *Cat on a Hot Tin Roof* (1955, Pulitzer), *Suddenly Last Summer* (1958), *Sweet Bird of Youth* (1959), and *The Night of the Iguana* (1961). In addition to his plays, he wrote short stories, essays, poetry, memoirs, and two novels, *The Roman Spring of Mrs Stone* (1950) and *Moise and the World of Reason* (1975). He published a volume of autobiography, *Memoirs*, in 1975. He was in ill health in his later years, following a breakdown in 1969, and although he wrote some further plays in the 1970s, they were unsuccessful.

Williams, William Carlos (1883–1963) Poet and novelist, born in Rutherford, NJ. He studied in Geneva and at Pennsylvania University, and became a doctor. His poems, from *Spring and All* (1923), commanded attention and were collected in two volumes (1950–1). He is especially known for his 'personal epic' poem, *Paterson* (5 vols, 1946–58). He also wrote plays, essays, a trilogy of novels, and criticism, including *In the American Grain* (1925). He was awarded a posthumous Pulitzer Prize for *Pictures from Brueghel, and Other Poems* (1962).

Williams, Winifred >> Wagner, Siegfried

Williamson, David (Keith) (1942–) Playwright, born in Melbourne, Victoria, Australia. He studied mechanical engineering at Monash University, Melbourne, then turned to writing plays and scripts for films and television. His first works to receive recognition were The

Removalists and *Don's Party* in 1971, and other successes included *The Club* (1977) and *The Perfectionist* (1982). He wrote the scripts for the successful Australian films *Gallipoli* (1981) and *Phar Lap* (1983). Later plays include *Money and Friends* (1991), *Brilliant Lies* (1993), and *After the Ball* (1997). His work is extremely popular, and he is widely regarded as an astute observer of contemporary middle-class Australian society.

Williamson, Henry (1895–1977) Writer, born in Bedfordshire, SC England, UK. He served in World War 1, became a journalist, then turned to farming in Norfolk. He wrote several semi-autobiographical novels, including his long series *A Chronicle of Ancient Sunlight* (1951–69), but is best known for his classic nature stories, such as *Tarka the Otter* (1927). >> Tunnicliffe

Williamson, James Cassius (1845–1913) Theatrical producer, born in Mercer, PA. He made his stage debut in 1861, and was an established actor in New York by 1870. He toured Australia (1874), returned to settle (1879), and went into theatre management. With two partners he established the theatrical organization popularly known as 'The Firm', which was to dominate Australian theatre until 1976. He supported tours by overseas artists, but concentrated on established, long-running successes such as the Savoy operas (for which he held the Australian rights), rather than the contemporary theatre of the day.

Williamson, Malcolm (Benjamin Graham Christopher) (1931–) Composer, born in Sydney, New South Wales, Australia. He moved to England in 1953, and began his career as a solo pianist and organist. His compositions include the opera *Our Man in Havana* (1963), the chamber opera *The Red Sea* (1972), and the operatic sequence *The Brilliant and the Dark* (1969). He has also written seven symphonies, concertos for piano, organ, violin, and harp, several works for television and films, a great deal of vocal, choral, organ, and piano music, and 'cassations' (mini-operas), which often involve the audience. He was made Master of the Queen's Musick in 1975, and has been associated with several choirs and music societies.

Williamson, William Crawford >> Scott, Dunkinfield Henry

Willibald, St [wilibawld] (700–86) Clergyman and missionary, born in Wessex, England, the brother of St Walburga. He made a pilgrimage to Palestine, and settled as a monk in Monte Cassino (730–40). He was sent by Pope Gregory III to Germany to help his kinsman St Boniface, who made him the first Bishop of Eichstätt. His *Hodoeporicon* is an account of his pilgrimage to Palestine. Feast day 11 July. >> Boniface; Walburga

Willibrord, St [wilibraw(r)d] (c. 658–739) Anglo-Saxon missionary, born in Northumbria. He became a Benedictine monk at Ripon under St Wilfrid, and c.690 was sent as missionary to Friesland, where he became Bishop of Utrecht and later Archbishop of the Frisians (695). In 700 he founded the monastery of Echternach in Luxembourg, baptized Pepin III in 714, and was aided by Boniface on a visit to Thuringia. Feast day 7 November. >> Boniface; Pepin III; Wilfrid

Willis, Bruce (1955–) Film actor, born in West Germany. He grew up in New Jersey from the age of two, took up acting in the mid-1970s, and got some small parts in film and television. After moving to Los Angeles, he became widely known for his role as David Addison in the television series *Moonlighting* (1985–9). He made his film debut in *Blind Date* (1987), and achieved star status following his role in the first of the *Die Hard* series (1988, 1990, 1995). Later films include *Death Becomes Her* (1992), *Pulp Fiction* (1994), *12 Monkeys* (1995), and *The Fifth Element* (1997). He married actress Demi Moore in 1987. >> Moore, Demi

Willis, Norman (David) (1933–) Trade union leader, born in Ashford, W Greater London, England, UK. He studied at Oxford, and worked for two years for the Transport and General Workers' Union (TGWU) before national service (1951–3). He returned to the TGWU as personal assistant to the general secretary (1959–70) and as national secretary for research and education (1970–4), before being appointed assistant general secretary of the Trades Union Congress in 1974. He then succeeded Len Murray as general secretary of the TUC (1984–93). >> Murray, Len

Willis, Thomas (1621–75) Physician, one of the founders of the Royal Society (1662), born in Great Bedwyn, Wiltshire, S England, UK. He studied classics then medicine at Oxford, where he became professor of natural philosophy (1660–75). He was a pioneer in the study of the anatomy of the brain, and discovered the *circle of Willis*. He also worked on diseases of the nervous system and muscles. >> Hooke, Robert; Wallis, John; Wilkins, John; Wren, Christopher

Willkie, Wendell (1892–1944) Businessman and US presidential candidate, born in Elwood, IN. Trained as a lawyer, he practised briefly before entering the army in World War 1, and in the 1930s became president of an Indiana utilities holding company, Commonwealth and Southern Corporation. Though not widely known outside the business community, he was recruited as the 'dark horse' Republican candidate against Franklin D Roosevelt in 1940. During World War 2 he supported Roosevelt's Lend-Lease programme to Britain, promoted an organization to protect world peace, and fought to improve civil liberties in the USA. In 1942 Roosevelt named him good-will ambassador to the Middle East, China, and the Soviet Union. His 1943 book, *One World*, was a best-seller. >> Roosevelt, Franklin D

Willoughby, Francis >> Ray, John

Wills, Helen (Newington), married names **Moody** and **Roark** (1905–98) Tennis player, born in Berkeley, CA. A great baseline player, she won the Wimbledon singles title eight times in nine attempts (1927–30, 1932–3, 1935, 1938). Between 1927 and 1932 she won all the major singles championships (except the Australian) without losing a set. In all, she won 31 Grand Slam events. >> RR1173

Wills, William John (1834–61) Explorer, born in Devon, SW England, UK. He studied medicine, became a surveyor of crown lands in Victoria, Australia, and was second-in-command of Robert O'Hara Burke's ill-fated expedition to the N of Australia, on which he died of starvation. >> Burke, Robert O'Hara; King, John

Willstätter, Richard [vilshteter] (1872–1942) Organic chemist, born in Karlsruhe, Germany. He studied at Munich University, and became professor at Zürich (1905–12). He did notable work on natural product chemistry, especially on plant pigments (for which he was awarded the Nobel Prize for Chemistry in 1915) and on medicinal chemicals, and he developed effective gas masks in World War 1. He became professor at Munich in 1916, but increasing anti-Semitism made his position difficult, and he resigned his chair in 1925 in protest. The rise of Nazi power forced him to flee, and he reached Switzerland in 1939.

Willumsen, Jens Ferdinand (1863–1958) Painter and sculptor, born in Copenhagen. His best-known painting, 'After the Storm' (1905), is in the Oslo National Gallery. As a sculptor his masterpiece is the 'Great Relief', in coloured marbles and bronze. He bequeathed his works and his art collection to form the Willumsen Museum in Frederikssund.

Wilmot, John >> Rochester, 2nd Earl of

Wilson, Alexander (1766–1813) Ornithologist, born in Paisley, Renfrewshire, W Scotland, UK. He worked as a weaver from the age of 13, and was jailed for a libellous poem against the mill-owners (1792). He emigrated to the USA in 1794 and became a schoolteacher, studying art and ornithology in his spare time. Encouraged by a neighbour, the naturalist William Bartram, he devoted himself to ornithology, and made several journeys across America, collecting species and drawing them. In 1806 he was employed on the American edition of *Rees's Cyclopaedia*, and then completed the first seven volumes of the illustrated *American Ornithology* (1808–14). *Wilson's storm-petrel* and *Wilson's phalarope* were named after him. >> Bartram

Wilson, A(ndrew) N(orman) (1950–) Novelist, critic, and biographer, born in Staffordshire, C England, UK. He acquired a certain notoriety for his book reviews while literary editor of *The Spectator* (1981–3), and became known for his uncompromising High Church conservatism. His first novel was *The Sweets of Pimlico* (1977), later books including *Wise Virgin* (1982), *Daughters of Albion* (1991), and *A Watch In The Night* (1996). His literary criticism is collected in *Penfriends from Porlock* (1988), and his biographies include works on Scott, Milton, and Tolstoy.

Wilson, Sir Angus (Frank Johnstone) (1913–91) Writer, born in Bexhill, East Sussex, SE England, UK. He studied at Oxford, began writing in 1946, and rapidly established a reputation with his short stories, *The Wrong Set* (1949). His works include the novels *Hemlock and After* (1952), *Anglo-Saxon Attitudes* (1956), which were both best-sellers, and a family chronicle, *The Old Men at the Zoo* (1961), *Late Call* (1965), and *No Laughing Matter* (1967), as well as the play *The Mulberry Bush* (1955) and two further volumes of short stories. He was professor of English literature at East Anglia (1966–78), was knighted in 1980, and moved to France. His *Collected Stories* were published in 1987.

Wilson, August (1945–) Playwright, born in Pittsburgh, PA. A writer who never finished high school, he won two Pulitzer Prizes for his plays, which depict the African-American experience in America: *Fences* (1987) and *The Piano Lesson* (1988). Later works include *Two Trains Running* (1990). He founded Minnesota's Black Horizons Theatre Company. His *Ma Rainey's Black Bottom* won a New York Drama Critics Circle Award in 1984–5.

Wilson, Brian >> Beach Boys, The

Wilson, Carl >> Beach Boys, The

Wilson, Charles Edward, known as **Electric Charlie** (1886–1972) Corporate executive, born in New York City. He ended a 51-year career with General Electric as its president (1940–50), known for his tough anti-union policies and his willingness to close plants in communities dependent on GE for jobs. He directed the War Production Board (1942–4). An influential government advisor during Truman's presidency, he became chairman of W R Grace and Co in 1952. >> Truman; Wilson, Charles E(rwin)

Wilson, Charles E(rwin), known as **Engine Charlie** (1890–1961) Automobile executive and US Cabinet member, born in Minerva, OH. An electrical engineer, he designed automobile products for Westinghouse (1912–21), then became president of Delco Remy (1926–8). As vice-president of General Motors (1928–41), then president (1941–52), he recognized the United Auto Workers union, championed cost-of-living wage increases, and led his company through World War 2 as a major producer of military vehicles. As President Eisenhower's outspoken secretary of defence (1953–7), he began by angering liberals with his claim, 'What's good for General Motors is good for America', and ended by angering the military with severe cuts in the defence budget. >> Eisenhower; Wilson, Charles Edward

Wilson, C(harles) T(homson) R(ees) (1869–1959) Physicist, born in Glencorse, Midlothian, EC Scotland, UK. He studied at Manchester and Cambridge universities, where he became professor of natural philosophy (1925–34). While studying cloud formation as a meteorologist, he developed the device called the *Wilson cloud chamber*. He made use of X-rays to investigate cloud formation due to the presence of ionized particles, and his finding that the radiation left a trail of water droplets in the chamber led to the wide use of the chamber in nuclear physics. He shared the 1927 Nobel Prize of Physics. >> RR1122

Wilson, Colin (Henry) (1931–) Novelist and writer on philosophy, sociology, and the occult, born in Leicester, Leicestershire, C England, UK. He left school at 16, held various jobs, and served briefly in the Royal Air Force before writing his best-seller *The Outsider* (1956), a study of modern alienation. A prolific author, he has written many books and novels, including *Ritual in the Dark* (1960), *The Mind Parasites* (1966), *The Occult* (1971), *Poltergeist!* (1981), *Written in Blood* (1989), *Spider World: The Magician* (1992), and *From Atlantis to the Sphinx* (1996). *The Essential Colin Wilson* appeared in 1984. His psychic interests brought him status as a cult figure in the 1980s.

Wilson, Dennis >> **Beach Boys, The**

Wilson, Edmund (1895–1972) Literary and social critic, born in Red Bank, NJ. He studied at Princeton University, and became a journalist with *Vanity Fair*, associate editor of the *New Republic* (1926–31), and chief book reviewer for the *New Yorker*. An early critical success was his study of the Symbolist movement, *Axel's Castle* (1931). He was a prolific and wide-ranging author, producing several studies on aesthetic, social, and political themes, as well as verse, plays, and travel books. His historical works include *In Patriotic Gore* (1962), on the literature from the period of the American Civil War, and *The Scrolls from the Dead Sea* (1955), a contentious account for which he learned Hebrew. His third marriage (of four) was to novelist Mary McCarthy. >> McCarthy, Mary

Wilson, Edmund (Beecher) (1856–1939) Zoologist, born in Geneva, IL. He studied at Yale and Johns Hopkins universities, and after several teaching posts became professor of zoology at Columbia University. He contributed greatly to cytology and embryology, and wrote *The Cell in Development and Inheritance* (1925).

Wilson, Edward A(drian) (1872–1912) Physician, naturalist, and explorer, born in Cheltenham, Gloucestershire, SWC England, UK. He first went to the Antarctic with Scott in the *Discovery* (1901–4). On his return to England he researched grouse diseases and made illustrations for books on birds and mammals. In 1910 he returned to the Antarctic on the *Terra Nova* as chief of the expedition's scientific staff. One of the party of five that reached the South Pole just after Roald Amundsen, he died with the others on the return journey. >> Amundsen; Scott, R F

Wilson, Edward (Osborne) (1929–) Biologist, born in Birmingham, AL. He studied at the University of Alabama, then at Harvard, where he joined the faculty in 1956. His early work was in entomology, but his conclusions (eg on the behaviour of competing populations of different species) were extended to other species including the human, notably in his book *Sociobiology: the New Synthesis* (1975). This book virtually founded the subject of sociobiology, and stimulated much discussion and some contention. He also wrote *On Human Nature* (1978, Pulitzer). In 1990 he was awarded Sweden's Craoford Prize.

Wilson (of Rievaulx), (James) Harold Wilson, Baron (1916–95) British statesman and prime minister (1964–70, 1974–6), born in Huddersfield, West Yorkshire, N England, UK. He studied at Oxford, where he became a lecturer in economics in 1937. A Labour MP in 1945, he became President of the Board of Trade (1947–51), and the principal Opposition spokesman on economic affairs. An able

and hard-hitting debater, in 1963 he succeeded Gaitskell as leader of the Labour Party, becoming prime minister in 1964. His economic plans were badly affected by a balance of payments crisis, leading to severe restrictive measures. He was also faced with the problem of Rhodesian independence, opposition to Britain's proposed entry into the European Economic Community, and an increasing conflict between the two wings of the Labour Party. Following his third general election victory, he resigned suddenly as Labour Party leader in 1976. Knighted in 1976, he became a life peer in 1983. >> Smith, Ian; RR1095

Wilson, Henry, originally **Jeremiah Jones Colbath** (1812–75) US vice-president and abolitionist, born in Farmington, NH. A poor farm labourer with little formal schooling, at 21 he renamed himself and went off to Massachusetts, where he soon had a successful shoe factory. After a trip to Virginia (1836) exposed him to slavery, he devoted the rest of his life to abolishing it, frequently changing political affiliations until he found a party, the new Republican Party, opposed to slavery. He represented Massachusetts in the US Senate (1855–73), and then became Ulysses S Grant's second-term vice-president, but died in office. >> Grant, Ulysses S

Wilson, Sir Henry Hughes (1864–1922) British field marshal, born in Edgeworthstown, Ireland. He served in Burma and the Boer War, was commander of the Staff College (1910–14), entered World War 1 as director of military operations (1914), and rose to be Chief of the Imperial General Staff (1918–22). He was knighted in 1919. He left the army in 1922 and became MP for North Down, but was assassinated by two Irish ex-servicemen on the doorstep of his house in London.

Wilson (of Libya and of Stowlangtoft), Henry Maitland Wilson, Baron (1881–1964) British field marshal, born in London, England, UK. He trained at Sandhurst, fought in South Africa and in World War 1, and at the outbreak of World War 2 was appointed commander of British troops in Egypt. He led the initial British advance in Libya (1940–1) and the unsuccessful Greek campaign (1941), and became commander-in-chief, Middle East (1943), and supreme allied commander in the Mediterranean theatre (1944). He headed the British Joint Staff Mission in Washington (1945–7), and was raised to the peerage in 1946.

Wilson, James (1742–98) Political ideologist and parent of the US Constitution, born in Carskerdo, Fife, E Scotland, UK. He studied at Glasgow and Edinburgh, and emigrated to Philadelphia in 1765, where he became an active philosophico-legal publicist in the cause of American devolution. As delegate to the Constitutional Congress of 1787, he played such a major part in using Scottish precedents that modern scholars acknowledge his co-paternity of the final document. His influence helped to gain ratification of the constitution of Pennsylvania in 1790. He was Associate Justice of the US Supreme Court (1789–98), and first professor of law at Pennsylvania University from 1790.

Wilson, John Burgess >> **Burgess, Anthony**

Wilson, J(ohn) Dover (1881–1969) Shakespearean scholar, born in Mortlake, Surrey, SE England, UK. He studied at Cambridge, spent some years as teacher, lecturer, and an inspector of adult education, then became professor of education at London (1924–35), and of English literature at Edinburgh (1935–45). Best known for his Shakespearean studies, he was editor of the New Shakespeare series (1919–66), and a keen advocate of literary education. His works include *Life in Shakespeare's England* (1911), *The Essential Shakespeare* (1932), and *Shakespeare's Sonnets – An Introduction for Historians and Others* (1963).

Wilson, Kemmons (1913–) US hotelier. The owner of a slot-machine business and a small cinema chain, he became dissatisfied with family holiday accommodation, and devised the Holiday Inn motel, opening the first one in Memphis in 1952, with others following soon afterwards. He opened the Holiday Inn Innkeeping School in 1959, and went international in 1960.

Wilson, Kenneth (Geddes) (1936–) Theoretical physicist, born in Waltham, MA. He studied at Harvard and the California Institute of Technology, and taught at Cornell University from 1971. He applied mathematical methods to the understanding of the magnetic properties of atoms, and later used similar methods in the study of phase transitions between liquids and gases, and in alloys. He was awarded the Nobel Prize for Physics in 1982.

Wilson, Lanford (1937–) Playwright, born in Lebanon, MO. A founder of the Circle Repertory Company in New York City in 1969, he had several of his plays performed there, including *The Hotel Baltimore* (1972), which earned the off-Broadway record of 1166 perfomances for a non-musical. *The Fifth of July* (1978) and *Tally's Folly* (1979, Pulitzer) depict the post-Vietnam War world of the same Southern family. Later works include *Angel's Fall* (1983) and *Burn This* (1987).

Wilson, Peter (1913–84) British auctioneer. He spent his whole working life at Sotheby's, the London art auctioneering saleroom. He became chairman in 1958, and by introducing new techniques, such as selling by satellite link simultaneously in New York City and London, made Sotheby's the most successful art saleroom in the world.

Wilson, Richard (1714–82) Landscape painter, born in Penygroes, Powys. He began as a portrait painter, but after a visit to Italy (1752–6) turned to landscapes. In London in 1760 he exhibited his 'Niobe', and was recognized as one of the leading painters of his time. In 1776 he became librarian to the Royal Academy.

Wilson, Richard (1936–) British actor and director. He trained at the Royal Academy of Dramatic Art, London, and became well known as a theatre actor and director during the 1980s. His first television role was in 1972, in the series *My Good Woman*, other appearances including *Crown Court* (1973–84) and *Only When I Laugh* (1979–82). His film work includes roles in *A Passage to India* (1984), *Fellow Traveller* (1990), and *Carry on Columbus* (1992), but it was his characterization of Victor Meldrew in several series of *One Foot in the Grave* (from 1989, BAFTAs in 1991 and 1993) that made him a national figure, his exasperated 'I don't believe it!' becoming a national catch-phrase. He was elected Rector of Glasgow University in 1996.

Wilson, Robert (1941–) Epic theatre-maker, director, and designer, born in Waco, TX. America's most flamboyant post-modern creator of theatrical spectacle, his early training was as a painter in Texas, Paris, and New York City. In contrast with traditional theatre, he mixes a combination of movement, contemporary music, and exciting imagery, often in very long performances. His work includes *The Life and Times of Sigmund Freud* (1969), *A Letter for Queen Victoria* (1974), and *The CIVIL WarS* (begun in 1984), one of the most ambitious theatrical events ever proposed.

Wilson, Robert Woodrow (1936–) Physicist, born in Houston, TX. He studied at Rice University and the California Institute of Technology, and joined Bell Laboratories in New Jersey, becoming head of the radiophysics research department in 1976. With Arno Penzias he detected in 1964 an unusual radio noise background which was discovered to be residual radiation, supporting the 'big bang' theory of creation. They shared the 1978 Nobel Prize for Physics. >> Penzias

Wilson, Roy(ston Warner Wilson) (1900–65) Strip car-

toonist, born in Kettering, Northamptonshire, C England, UK. He studied at Nottingham School of Art, and started working on strips for Amalgamated Press children's comics in 1920. He worked freelance from 1930 on *Steve and Stumpy* (for *Butterfly*) and many other strips, notably *George the Jolly Gee-Gee* (for *Radio Fun*, 1938) and *Chimpo's Circus* (for *Happy Days*, 1938). He also designed many annual covers and frontispieces. He has been called 'the king of comic artists' in the 'golden age' of British comics.

Wilson, Teddy, popular name of **Theodore Shaw Wilson** (1912–86) Pianist, bandleader, and arranger, one of the most influential stylists of the swing era of the late 1930s, born in Austin, TX. He studied music briefly, and while still in his teens was working in Chicago with such major artists as Louis Armstrong. His move to New York City in 1933 to join the Benny Carter Orchestra established his career as a pianist and arranger. When he joined the Benny Goodman Trio in 1935, he was one of the first black musicians to appear with whites. >> Carter, Benny; Goodman, Benny

Wilson, William Griffith, known as **Bill W** (1895–1951) US founder of Alcoholics Anonymous. An excessive drinker on the verge of ruin, he experienced a religious conviction (1934) that he could rid himself of alcoholism by helping other alcoholics. Having successfully counselled a fellow-sufferer, **Robert Holbrook Smith** (1879–1950, known as 'Dr Bob S'), he instituted the well-known self-help group.

Wilson, (Thomas) Woodrow (1856–1924) US statesman and 28th president (1913–21), born in Staunton, VA. He studied at Princeton and Johns Hopkins universities, became a lawyer and university professor, and was president of Princeton, and Governor of New Jersey (1911). Elected Democratic president in 1912 and 1916, his administration, ending in physical breakdown, is memorable for the Prohibition and women's suffrage amendments of the constitution, trouble with Mexico, America's participation in World War 1, his peace plan proposals (the 'fourteen points'), and his championship of the League of Nations. His health declined after the US Senate's rejection of the Treaty of Versailles. He won the Nobel Peace Prize in 1919. >> Byrns; House; William II (of Germany); RR1095

Wilton, Marie >> **Bancroft, Squire**

Winant, John [wiynant] (1889–1947) US state governor and government official, born in New York City. He became a teacher in Concord, NH (1911–17), serving in the New Hampshire legislature as a moderate Republican (1916–17). In 1920 he went to the state senate, then served as governor (1925–7, 1933–5). Although a Republican, he was recognized as sympathetic to labour, and in 1935 he was appointed to the International Labor Organization in Geneva, becoming its director in 1939. He later served as ambassador to Britain (1940–6), and was a representative to the Economic and Social Council of the UN.

Winchester, Oliver (Fisher) (1810–80) Gun manufacturer, born in Boston, MA. Success as a young enterprising businessman enabled him to purchase the Volcanic Repeating Arms Co of New Haven (1857), which became the Winchester Repeating Arms Co (1867). His chief gun designer had patented a design for a repeating rifle (1860) which was the forerunner of the famous *Winchester rifle*. Winchester astutely built on this success by purchasing patents from a number of other gun manufacturers.

Winchilsea, Anne Finch, Countess of, *née* **Kingsmill** (1661–1721) Poet, born in Sidmonton, Hampshire, S England, UK. In 1684 she married Heneage Finch, who became Earl of Winchilsea in 1712. Her longest poem, a Pindaric ode called 'The Spleen', was printed in 1701, and her *Miscellany Poems* appeared in 1713. She was a friend of Pope. >> Pope, Alexander

Winckelmann, Johann (Joachim) [vingkelman] (1717–68) Archaeologist and art historian, born in Stendal, Germany. He studied theology and medicine at Halle and Jena universities, in 1748 turned to the history of art, and became librarian to a cardinal in Rome (1755). His works include the pioneering study, *Geschichte der Kunst des Alterthums* (1764, History of the Art of Antiquity), and in 1763 he became superintendent of Roman antiquities. He was murdered in Trieste.

Windelband, Wilhelm >> **Rickert, Heinrich**

Windsor, Duke of >> **Edward VIII**

Windsor, Lady Davina >> **Gloucester, Richard, Duke of**

Windsor, Prince Edward >> **Edward, Prince**

Windsor, Lord Frederick >> **Kent, Prince Michael of**

Windsor, Lady Gabriella >> **Kent, Prince Michael of**

Windsor, George Philip Nicholas >> **Kent, Edward, Duke of**

Windsor, Lady Helen >> **Kent, Edward, Duke of**

Windsor, Princess Margaret >> **Margaret, Princess**

Windsor, Lord Nicholas >> **Kent, Edward, Duke of**

Windsor, Lady Rose >> **Gloucester, Richard, Duke of**

Windsor, (Bessie) Wallis, Duchess of, *née* **Warfield**, previous married names **Spencer** and **Simpson** (1896–1986) Wife of Edward VIII, born in Blue Ridge Summit, PA. An extrovert socialite, in 1916 she married **Lieutenant Earl Winfield Spencer** of the US navy, but in 1927 the marriage was dissolved. The following year, in London, she married **Ernest Simpson**, an American-born Briton. Well-known in London society, she met Edward, the Prince of Wales, at a country-house party in 1931. In 1936, the year of his accession, she obtained a divorce in England, and the king subsequently made clear to Stanley Baldwin and his government his determination to marry her, even if it meant giving up the throne. They married in 1937 in France, but she was not accepted by the British royal family until the late 1960s. She and Edward lived in France and the Bahamas; after Edward's death she lived virtually as a recluse, and was in ill health for many years before she died, in Paris. She was buried beside her husband at Windsor Castle. >> **Edward VIII**

Winfrey, Oprah [winfree] (1954–) Television talk-show host, actor, and producer, born in Kosciusko, MS. After an unsettled childhood, she moved to Nashville and studied at Tennessee State University, beginning work as a radio reporter. She hosted her first TV chat-show in Baltimore in 1978, moving to Chicago in 1984, where she launched the highly successful *Oprah Winfrey Show* (3 Emmies) in 1986. She then moved into management, establishing Harpo Productions in Chicago. Her film work includes *The Color Purple* (1985, Oscar nomination) and *Throw Momma From the Train* (1987). She is also well-known for her exercise and dieting programmes, and as an activist in support of children's rights.

Wingate, Orde (Charles) (1903–44) British general, born in Naini Tal, India. He trained at Woolwich, was commissioned in 1922, and served in the Sudan (1928–33) and Palestine (1936–9), where he helped create a Jewish defence force. In the Burma theatre (1942) he organized the Chindits – specially trained jungle-fighters drawn from British, Ghurka, and Burmese forces, who were supplied by air, and thrust far behind the enemy lines. He helped Frank Merrill train a similar group of US troops. >> **Merrill, Frank; Slim**

Winger, Deborah (1955–) Film actress, born in Cleveland, OH. She appeared in the television series *Wonder Woman* (1976–7) and made her film debut in *Slumber Party '57* (1977), but it was the film *Urban Cowboy* (1980) which launched her film career. She received Oscar nominations for *An Officer and a Gentleman* (1982) and *Terms of Endearment*

(1985), and her later films include *Shadowlands* (1993), and *Forget Paris* (1995).

Winifred, St (7th-c) Legendary Welsh saint, a noble British maiden, beheaded by Prince Caradog for repelling his unholy proposals. The legend relates that her head rolled down a hill, and where it stopped a spring gushed forth – famous still as a place of pilgrimage, Holywell in Flintshire. Feast day 3 November.

Winkelried, Arnold von [vingkelreed] (?–1386) Swiss patriot, knight of Unterwalden. At the Battle of Sempach (1386), when the Swiss failed to break the compact line of Austrian spears, he is said to have grasped as many pikes as he could reach, buried them in his bosom and bore them by his weight to the earth. His comrades rushed into the breach, slaughtered the Austrians, and gained a decisive victory.

Winkler, Hans-Günther [vingkler] (1926–) Show jumper, born in Wuppertal-Barmen, Germany. He is the only man to have won five Olympic gold medals at show jumping: the team golds in 1956, 1960, 1964, and 1972, and the individual title on *Halla* in 1956. On the same horse he won the individual world title in 1954 and 1955. He made his international debut in Spain in 1952, and later became (West German) team captain. >> **RR1153**

Winner, Michael (Robert) (1935–) Film producer and director, born in London, England, UK. He studied at Cambridge, and worked as a journalist and film critic before entering Motion Pictures Ltd as a writer and editor (1956). He has written the screenplay for many of his films, which include *The Cool Mikado* (1962), *The Big Sleep* (1977), *Death Wish* (and its sequels), *Bullseye!* (1990), and *Dirty Weekend* (1993).

Winslow, Edward (1595–1655) Colonist, one of the Pilgrim Fathers, born in Droitwich, Hereford and Worcester, WC England, UK. He sailed in the *Mayflower* in 1620, and from 1624 was assistant governor or governor of the Plymouth colony, which he described and defended in several publications, including *Good Newes from New England* (1624). Sent by Cromwell against the West Indies (1655), he died at sea. >> **Cromwell, Oliver**

Wint, Peter de (1784–1849) Water-colourist, born in Stone, Staffordshire, C England, UK, of Dutch descent. His fame rests on his watercolour illustrations of English landscape, English architecture, and English country life. Among them are 'The Cricketers', 'The Hay Harvest', 'Nottingham', 'Richmond Hill', and 'Cows in Water'. Many of his works are in Lincoln Art Gallery.

Winterhalter, Franz Xaver [vinterhalter] (1806–73) Painter, born in Menzenschwand, Germany. He studied in Freiburg and Munich, and was appointed court painter to Grand Duke Leopold of Baden. In 1834 he went to Paris, where he became the fashionable artist of his day, painting many royal figures, such as Napoleon III and Queen Victoria.

Winters, Shelley, originally **Shirley Schrift** (1922–) Film actress, born in St Louis, MO. She trained as a stage actress in New York City before her film debut in *What A Woman* (1943), and appeared in many films before her first major role in *A Double Life* (1947). She won Supporting Actress Oscars for *The Diary of Anne Frank* (1959) and *A Patch of Blue* (1965). Later films include *Lolita* (1962), *Alfie* (1966), *The Poseidon Adventure* (1972), *S.O.B.* (1981), *Stepping Out* (1991), and *Heavy* (1995).

Winters, (Arthur) Yvor (1900–68) Critic and poet, born in Chicago, IL. He studied at Chicago, Colorado, and Stanford universities, and in 1949 was appointed professor of English at Stanford. His *Collected Poems* were published in 1952. He is remembered primarily as an irascible critic, anti-Expressionist, and with a sharp eye for detail.

Significant books are *In Defence of Reason* (1947) and *The Function of Criticism* (1957).

Winterson, Jeanette (1959–) Novelist, born in Manchester, Greater Manchester, NW England, UK. Her first novel, the autobiographical *Oranges Are Not the Only Fruit* (1987), won the Whitbread Prize. Later books include *The Passion* (1987), *Sexing The Cherry* (1989), and *Gut Symmetries* (1997).

Winthrop, John (1588–1649) English colonist, born in Edwardstone, Suffolk, E England, UK. He studied at Cambridge, became a Puritan lawyer, decided to emigrate, and while still in England was appointed governor (chief officer) of the Massachusetts Bay Company, then based in England. He moved with the Company to Massachusetts the following year. Except for brief intervals he served as governor of the colony for the rest of his life. >> Hutchinson, Anne; Winthrop, John (1606–76)

Winthrop, John (1606–76) Colonist, born in Groton, Suffolk, E England, UK, the son of John Winthrop. He travelled to America in 1631, landing in Boston, and became a magistrate in Massachusetts. In 1635 he went to Connecticut, and founded New London in 1646. He was elected governor of Connecticut, and except for one year held that post until his death. He obtained from Charles II a charter uniting the colonies of Connecticut and New Haven, and was named first governor under it. He was the father of paper currency in America. >> Winthrop, John (1588–1649)/ (1639–1707)

Winthrop, John (1639–1707) Soldier and colonial administrator, born in Ipswich, MA, the son of John Winthrop. He served in the parliamentary army (1660), and settled in Connecticut in 1663. He was a commander against the Dutch, the Indians, and the French, agent in London for Connecticut (1693–7), and governor of the colony from 1698. >> Winthrop, John (1606–76)

Winton, Tim(othy John) (1960–) Writer, born in Scarborough, Western Australia, Australia. Educated at the University of Western Australia, he jointly won the Australian-Vogel award in 1981 with his first novel *An Open Swimmer*. He has twice won the Miles Franklin Award – for *Shallows* (1984) and the epic Australian novel *Cloudstreet* (1991), which also won the British Deo Gloria award. Later novels include *The Riders* (1994), and he has also published several books for children.

Wirén, Dag Ivar [viren] (1905–86) Swedish composer. He studied at the Stockholm Conservatory, and in Paris. His large output includes five symphonies, five string quartets, a variety of large-scale orchestral works, and film and theatre music. His most popular work remains the *Serenade for Strings* (1937), the last movement of which formed the title music music for the BBC2 television series *Monitor*.

Wirth, Philip Peter Jacob [werth] (1864–1937) Circus proprietor of German descent, born in Victoria, Australia. His father and his three brothers formed their own circus troupe (1878), which soon became popular throughout Australia and New Zealand. A world tour later took in South Africa, South America, and England, and the circus returned through Asia to establish permanent bases in Sydney and Melbourne. He was renowned for his ability to break in and school wild animals, and his sons and daughters continued the family tradition until the 1960s.

Wisdom, (Arthur) John (Terence Dibben) (1904–93) British philosopher. He studied at Cambridge, and became professor there (1952–68) and at the University of Oregon (1968–72). He was profoundly influenced by Wittgenstein, but developed a distinctive mode and style of philosophizing which represented philosophical paradoxes as revealing partial truths rather than linguistic confusions. His

most important works are *Other Minds* (1952), *Philosophy and Psychoanalysis* (1953), and *Paradox and Discovery* (1965). >> Wittgenstein

Wisdom, Norman (1915–) Comedian, born in London, England, UK. He made his stage debut in 1946, and appeared in variety, concert parties, and summer seasons throughout Britain as an inadequate but well-meaning character in ill-fitting clothes. He made his film debut as a slapstick comedian in *Trouble in Store* (1953), followed by a string of successes including *Man of the Moment* (1955), *There Was a Crooked Man* (1960), and *What's Good for the Goose* (1969). He received a Lifetime Achievement Award for Comedy (British Comedy Awards) in 1991. A volume of autobiography, *Don't Laugh at Me* appeared in 1992.

Wise, Ernie >> **Morecambe, Eric**

Wiseman, Nicholas (Patrick Stephen), Cardinal (1802–65) Roman Catholic clergyman, born in Seville, Spain, of Irish parents. He was brought up at Waterford, Ireland, entered the English College at Rome, was ordained in 1825, and became rector of the College in 1828. He was made bishop, and appointed president of Oscott College, Birmingham (1840) and vicar apostolic of London district (1847–50). His appointment as the first Archbishop of Westminster and a cardinal (1850) called forth a storm of religious excitement, which led to the passing of the Ecclesiastical Titles Assumption Act. One of his best-known works was a historical novel, *Fabiola* (1854).

Wishart, George [wishert] (c. 1513–46) Reformer and martyr, born in Pitarrow, Aberdeenshire, NE Scotland, UK. In 1538 he was a schoolmaster in Montrose, where he incurred a charge of heresy for teaching the Greek New Testament. He then spent several years in mainland Europe, returning to Scotland in 1543. He preached the Lutheran doctrine in several towns, and was arrested and burned at St Andrews. One of his converts was John Knox. >> Knox, John

Wister, Owen (1860–1938) Writer, born in Philadelphia, PA. He studied music and law at Harvard and Paris universities, then practised as a lawyer. *Harper's* praised his Western sketches, and he turned to writing, winning fame with his innovative novel of cowboy life in Wyoming, *The Virginian* (1902). His other major work was *Roosevelt: The Story of a Friendship, 1880–1919* (1930).

Witherspoon, John (1723–94) Clergyman and theologian, born in Gifford, East Lothian, E Scotland, UK. In 1768 he emigrated to America to become president of the College of New Jersey (now Princeton University) (1768–94). He taught many future leaders in American public life, and was a prolific writer. A representative of New Jersey to the Continental Congress (1776–82), he was the only clergyman to sign the American Declaration of Independence (1776).

Witt, Jan de >> **de Witt, Jan**

Witt, Katerina [vit] (1965–) Figure skater, born in Karl-Marx-Stadt, Germany. The East German champion in 1982, she won the first of six successive European titles in 1983, was world champion in 1984–5 and 1987–8, and Olympic champion in 1984 and 1988. >> RR1162

Witten, Edward (1951–) US physicist and mathematician. He became professor of physics at Princeton University (1980–7), then professor of natural sciences at the Institute for Advanced Study. A central figure in the study of superstrings, he has made important contributions to many areas of theoretical physics. His work linking knot theory with quantum theory gained him the 1990 Fields Medal.

Wittgenstein, Ludwig (Josef Johann) [witgenstiyn], Ger [vitgenshtiyn] (1889–1951) Philosopher, born in Vienna. He studied engineering at Berlin and Manchester, then became interested in mathematical logic, which he studied under Russell (1912–13). While serving in the Austrian army in World War 1, he wrote the *Tractatus logico-philosophicus* (1921), in which he argued that an adequate account of language must recognize that any sentence is a picture of the fact it represents, and that any thought is a sentence. In 1929 he began lecturing at Cambridge, submitting the *Tractatus* as his doctoral dissertation. He worked at hospitals in London and Newcastle upon Tyne during World War 2, returned to Cambridge afterwards, and resigned his chair in 1947. Between 1936 and 1949 he worked on the *Philosophische Untersuchungen* (1953, Philosophical Investigations), in which he rejected the doctrines of the *Tractatus*, claiming that linguistic meaning is a function of the *use* to which expressions are put, or the 'language games' in which they play a role. He became a naturalized British subject in 1938. >> **von Wright**

Wittig, Georg [vitik] (1897–1987) Organic chemist, born in Berlin. He studied in Tübingen and Marburg universities, and held professorships at Freiburg (1937–44), Tübingen (1944–56), and Heidelberg (1956–65). He developed a technique (1953) for the synthesis of natural substances, allowing the economical industrial production of Vitamin A and prostaglandins. He shared the Nobel Prize for Chemistry in 1979 for the work he had done 30 years earlier. >> **RR1123**

Wittkower, Rudolf [witkuhver] (1901–71) Architectural historian, born in Berlin. After 20 years at the Warburg Institute, London, he taught at Columbia University (1956–69). His major scholarly contributions include his explication of religious symbolism in renaissance architecture in *Architectural Principles in the Age of Humanism* (1949), and his distinction between Mannerism and Baroque architecture.

Witz, Konrad [vits] (c.1400–c.1445) Painter, born in Rottweil, Germany. He joined the Basel guild of painters in 1434, and spent most of his life in what is now Switzerland. His extremely realistic style suggests that he was aware of the work of his contemporary Jan van Eyck. The only signed and dated painting of his which survives is a late work, 'Christ Walking on the Water' (1444, Geneva), remarkable because it is set on L Geneva – the earliest known recognizable landscape in European art. >> **Eyck**

Wodehouse, Sir P(elham) G(renville) [wudhows] (1881–1975) Novelist, born in Guildford, Surrey, SE England, UK. Educated in London, he worked in a bank, then became a freelance writer. He made his name with *Psmith, Journalist* (1912), *Piccadilly Jim* (1918), and other stories. His best-known works fall within his 'country house' period, involving the creation of Bertie Wooster and his 'gentleman's gentleman' Jeeves, as in *Right Ho, Jeeves* (1934), *Quick Service* (1940), and *The Mating Season* (1949). A prolific writer, he produced a succession of over 100 novels, as well as many short stories, sketches, librettos, and lyrics for the likes of Irving Berlin, Cole Porter, and George Gershwin. During World War 2 he was captured and interned in Germany, and incautiously agreed to make broadcasts for the Germans, and though they were harmless he was branded as a traitor. Eventually his name was cleared, and he then made America his home, where the climate allowed him to indulge his passion for golf. He became a US citizen in 1955, and was knighted in 1975, just weeks before his death.

Wogan, Terry [wohgn], popular name of **Michael Terence Wogan** (1938–) Broadcaster and writer, born in Limerick, Ireland. He began his broadcasting career as a radio announcer in Ireland (1963) before joining the BBC (1965), where he hosted various radio programmes including *Late Night Extra* (1967–9) and *The Terry Wogan Show* (1969–72).

Resident in Britain from 1969, his popularity grew when he presented Radio Two's *Breakfast Show* (1972–84). He has hosted several TV shows, including *Blankety Blank* (1977–81), *You Must Be Joking* (1981), the annual charity telethon *Children in Need*, the annual Eurovision Song Contests, and an early evening chat-show (1982–92) which became a thrice-weekly fixture in 1985. He enjoyed success in the pop charts with 'The Floral Dance' (1977), and has written several books including *Banjaxed* (1979), *The Day Job* (1981), *Wogan on Wogan* (1987), and *Terry Wogan's Bumper Book of Togs* (1995). The recipient of many broadcasting 'personality of the year' awards, he returned to radio work in 1993.

Wöhler, Friedrich [voeler] (1800–82) Chemist, whose work marked a turning point for organic chemistry, born near Frankfurt, Germany. He studied medicine at Heidelberg, turned to chemistry, and studied with Berzelius, with whom he maintained a lifelong friendship. He taught at Berlin and Kassel, then became professor of chemistry at Göttingen (1836). He isolated aluminium (1827) and beryllium (1828), discovered calcium carbide, from which he obtained acetylene, and from 1832 worked closely with Liebig on the chemistry of the benzoyl group. His synthesis of urea from ammonium cyanate in 1828 was the first synthesis of an organic compound from an inorganic substance. >> **Berzelius; Liebig**

Wojtyła, Karol Jozef >> **John Paul II**

Wolcot, John >> **Opie, John**

Wolf, Hugo (Philipp Jakob) [volf] (1860–1903) Composer, born in Windischgraz, Austria. He studied at the Vienna Conservatory, then earned a living by teaching, conducting, and music criticism. From 1888 he composed c.300 songs, settings of poems by Goethe and others, the opera *Der Corregidor* (1895), and other works. Having lived most of his life in poverty, he became insane in 1897, and died in the asylum at Steinhof, near Vienna.

Wolf, Max(imilian Franz Joseph Cornelius) (1863–1932) Astronomer, born in Heidelberg, Germany. He studied at Heidelberg and Stockholm universities, becoming professor of astronomy at Heidelberg (1896) and director of the Königstuhl astrophysical observatory there. He invented the photographic method of discovering asteroids, and with Edward Barnard was the first to appreciate 'dark' nebulae in the sky. >> **Barnard, Edward**

Wolfe, Charles (1791–1823) Poet, born in Dublin. He studied at Trinity College, Dublin, and is remembered for his poem 'The Burial of Sir John Moore', which appeared anonymously in 1817 and at once caught the admiration of the public. He was ordained in 1817, and became rector of Donoughmore.

Wolfe, James (1727–59) British soldier, born in Westerham, Kent, SE England, UK. Commissioned in 1741, he fought against the Jacobites in Scotland (1745–6), and was sent to Canada during the Seven Years' War (1756–63). In 1758 he was prominent in the capture of Louisburg, and commanded in the famous capture of Quebec (1759), scaling the cliffs to defeat the French on the Plains of Abraham, where he was killed. >> **Montcalm**

Wolfe, Thomas (Clayton) (1900–38) Novelist, born in Asheville, NC. After studying at North Carolina and Harvard universities, his writing career began abortively as a playwright, but he achieved success with his first novel, *Look Homeward, Angel* (1929). Some of his best work is to be found in the stories in *From Death to Morning* (1935). Later titles include *The Web and the Rock* (1939) and *You Can't Go Home Again* (1940) (both published posthumously). He died of a brain infection following pneumonia.

Wolfe, Tom, popular name of **Thomas Kennerley Wolfe** (1931–) Journalist, pop-critic, and novelist, born in Richmond, VA. He studied at Washington and Yale universities, and worked as a reporter for the *Washington Post* and the *New York Herald Tribune*. A proponent of the New Journalism, his style is distinctive, clever, and narcissistic, employing eye-catching titles such as *The Electric Kool-Aid Acid Test* (1968). Much of his work previously appeared in periodicals such as the *Rolling Stone*, as did his novel, *The Bonfire of the Vanities* (1988), which became a best seller. *The New America* appeared in 1989. He is credited with coining the phrase 'radical chic'.

Wolfe-Barry, John >> **Barry, Charles**

Wolfenden, John (Frederick) Wolfenden, Baron [**wulf**enden] (1906–85) Educationist, born in Halifax, West Yorkshire, N England, UK. He studied at Oxford, where he taught philosophy (1929–34), and was then headmaster at Uppingham (1934) and Shrewsbury (1944), and Vice-Chancellor of Reading University (1950). He was best known for his government investigation of homosexuality and prostitution (the *Wolfenden Report*, 1957). Knighted in 1956, he became a life peer in 1974.

Wolff, Christian, Freiherr (Baron) **von** [volf] (1679–1754) Philosopher, mathematician, and scientist, born in Wrocław, Poland (formerly Breslau, Germany). He studied at the universities of Wrocław, Jena, and Leipzig and was a pupil of the philosopher Leibniz, on whose recommendation he was appointed professor of mathematics at Halle (1707). He was banished in 1723, following a theological dispute with the Pietists, became professor at Marburg (1723–40), was recalled (1740) by Frederick II to Halle, and became chancellor of the university (1743). He is best known for popularizing the philosophy of Leibniz, and he is usually regarded as the German spokesman of the Enlightenment in the 18th-c. >> Leibniz

Wolff, Gustav William >> **Harland, Edward James**

Wolf-Ferrari, Ermanno [volf fe**rah**ree] (1876–1948) Composer, born in Venice, Italy. Sent to Rome to study painting, he turned to music, and studied in Munich, returning to Venice in 1899. He became an operatic composer, his best-known works being *I quattro rusteghi* (1906, trans The School for Fathers) and *Il segreto di Susanna* (1909, Susanna's Secret). He also composed choral and chamber works, and music for organ and piano.

Wölfflin, Heinrich [**voel**flin] (1864–1945) Art historian, born in Winterthur, Switzerland. He studied under Jacob Burckhardt, whom he succeeded as professor of art history at Basel in 1893. He was one of the founders of modern art history, pioneering the 'scientific' method of formal analysis, based on the systematic comparison of works of art in terms of contrasting stylistic features. His approach is expounded in three books: *Renaissance and Baroque* (1888), *Classic Art* (1899), and *Principles of Art History* (1915). >> Burckhardt

Wolfit, Sir Donald [**wulf**it] (1902–68) Actor-manager, born in Newark, Nottinghamshire, C England, UK. He began his stage career in 1920, formed his own company in 1937, and became known for his Shakespeare performances. During the Battle of Britain (1940) he instituted the first London season of 'Lunchtime Shakespeare'. He appeared in several films and on television, and his autobiography, *First Interval*, appeared in 1954. He was knighted in 1957.

Wolf of the Rif Mountains >> **Abd-el-Krim**

Wolfram von Eschenbach [**volf**ram fon **esh**enbakh] (c. 1170–c. 1220) Poet, born near Anspach, Germany. He was a Bavarian knight who served at many courts, writing love songs and other works. He is best known for his epic *Parzival* (c.1200–10), which introduced the theme of the Holy Grail into German literature, and from which Wagner derived the libretto of his *Parsifal*. >> Wagner, Richard

Wolfson, Sir Isaac (1897–1991) Businessman and philanthropist, born in Glasgow, W Scotland, UK. He quit school at 15 to become a salesman, joined Great Universal Stores as a buyer (1932), became managing director (1934), and greatly expanded the business, retiring as life-president (1987). In 1955 he set up the Wolfson Foundation for the advancement of health, education, and youth activities in the UK and the Commonwealth, and as a devout Jew was active in Jewish causes. He was made a baronet in 1962. In 1973 University College, Cambridge, was renamed *Wolfson College* after a grant from the foundation.

Wollaston, William Hyde (1766–1828) Chemist, born in East Dereham, Norfolk, E England, UK. He studied at Cambridge, practised as a physician (1789–1800), then devoted his time to chemistry, optics, and physiology. He developed a method, now basic to powder metallurgy but which he kept secret until just before his death, of making malleable platinum. His success made him financially secure for the rest of his life. He discovered palladium and rhodium, invented the reflecting goniometer for measuring crystal angles, and discovered the vibratory nature of muscular action.

Wollstonecraft, Mary [**wul**stonkraft], married name **Godwin** (1759–97) Feminist, born in London, England, UK. After working as a teacher and governess, she became a translator and literary adviser. In 1787 she published *Thoughts on the Education of Daughters*, and in 1792 she wrote *Vindication of the Rights of Woman*, advocating equality of the sexes. She was in Paris during the French Revolution where she married **Gilbert Imlay** (1754–1828), and had a daughter, Fanny. He lost interest in the relationship and she tried to kill herself twice. She recovered and eventually married William Godwin in 1797, and died of blood-poisoning in London 11 days after giving birth to a daughter, Mary (later, Mary Shelley). >> Godwin, William; Shelley, Mary

Wolpe, Joseph [**vol**pay] (1915–) Psychiatrist, born in Johannesburg, South Africa. He trained at the University of Witwatersrand, and later worked at Temple University, Florida. From animal experiments he concluded that behaviour was environmentally conditioned. He published *Psychotherapy by Reciprocal Inhibition* (1958), and was co-author of *Behavioural Therapy Techniques* (1966), with which he founded the field of behavioural therapy, widely used in the treatment of neurotic disorders.

Wolseley, Garnet (Joseph) Wolseley, 1st Viscount [**wulz**lee] (1833–1913) British field marshal, born in Golden Bridge, Ireland. He joined the army in 1852, and served in the Burmese War (1852–3), the Crimea (where he lost an eye), the Indian Mutiny (1857), and the Chinese War (1860). He put down the Red River rebellion (1870) in Canada, and commanded in the Ashanti War (1873). After other posts in India, Cyprus, South Africa, and Egypt, he led the attempted rescue of General Gordon at Khartoum. He became a baron (1882) and, after the Sudan campaign (1884–5), a viscount. As army commander-in-chief (1895–1901), he carried out several reforms, and mobilized forces for the Boer War (1899–1902).

Wolsey, Thomas, Cardinal [**wul**zee] (c. 1475–1530) English clergyman and statesman, born in Ipswich, Suffolk, E England, UK. He studied at Oxford, was ordained in 1498, appointed chaplain to Henry VII in 1507, and became dean of Lincoln. Under Henry VIII, he became Bishop of Lincoln, Archbishop of York (1514), and a cardinal (1515). Made Lord Chancellor (1515–29), he pursued legal and administrative reforms, and became Henry VIII's leading adviser, in charge of the day-to-day running of government. He aimed to make England a major power in Europe, and also had ambitions to become pope, but his policy of supporting first Emperor Charles V (1523) then Francis I of France (1528) in the Habsburg–Valois conflict was unsuccessful, and high taxation caused much resentment. When he failed to persuade the pope to grant Henry's divorce, he was impeached and his property forfeited. Arrested on a charge of high treason, he died while travelling to London. >> Henry VIII

Wonder, Stevie, originally **Steveland Judkins** (1951–) Soul singer and instrumentalist, born in Saginaw, MI. He was blind from birth, played the harmonica, drums, keyboards, and guitar from an early age, and was signed to Motown Records in 1961. His first album *Little Stevie Wonder: the 12-Year-Old Genius* was an immediate success. Most of his early records followed the orthodox Motown sound, but in 1971 he renegotiated his contract to gain full artistic control over his work. During the 1970s he became one of the most proficient users of synthesizer technology. His major albums include *Songs In the Key of Life* (1976), *Talking Book* (1972), *Innervisions* (1973), and *Hotter than July* (1980).

Wood, Ellen, *née* **Price**, known as **Mrs Henry Wood** (1814–87) Writer, born in Worcester, Hereford and Worcester, WC England, UK. She wrote a series of melodramatic novels, of which *East Lynne* (1861) was particularly successful. In 1867 she acquired the monthly *Argosy*, and her novels went on appearing in it long after her death.

Wood, Haydn (1882–1959) Composer and violinist, born in Slaithwaite, West Yorkshire, N England, UK. He studied at the Royal College of Music, London, and worked for a time in music halls. He wrote prolifically for orchestra, brass band, chamber music groups, and voices. Of his ballads, the best known is 'Roses of Picardy'.

Wood, Sir Henry (Joseph) (1869–1944) Conductor, born in London, England, UK. He studied at the Royal Academy of Music, London, became an organist, and in 1895 helped to found the Promenade Concerts which he conducted annually until his death. He composed operettas and an oratorio, but his international reputation was gained as a conductor, first at the Queen's Hall, London, then at the Albert Hall. He was knighted in 1911.

Wood, John, known as **the Elder**, also **Wood of Bath** (c. 1704–54) Architect, born in Yorkshire, N England, UK. He was responsible for many of the best-known streets and buildings of Bath, such as the North and South Parades, Queen Square, the Circus, Prior Park, and other houses. His son **John (the Younger)** (1728–82) designed the Royal Crescent and the Assembly Rooms.

Wood, Natalie, originally **Natasha Nikolaevna Zacharenko-Gurdin** (1938–81) Film actress, born in San Francisco, CA, the child of Russian immigrants. She began as a child star, becoming known for her roles in *Rebel Without a Cause* (1955, Oscar nomination), *Splendour in the Grass* (1961), and *West Side Story* (1961, Oscar nomination). Later films included *Bob and Carol and Ted and Alice* (1969) and *Meteor* (1979). She drowned in a boating accident. >> Wagner, Robert

Wood, Robert (Williams) (1868–1955) Physicist, born in Concord, MA. He studied at Harvard, Chicago, and Berlin universities, and became professor of experimental physics at Johns Hopkins (1901–38). He carried out research on optics, atomic and molecular radiation, and sound waves, and was the first (in 1897) to observe electric-field emission. He wrote *Physical Optics* (1905), some fiction, and illustrated nonsense verse, in *How to Tell the Birds from the Flowers* (1907).

Wood, Ron >> **Rolling Stones, The**

Wood, Victoria (1953–) Comedienne, born in Prestwich, Lancashire, NW England, UK. She studied drama at Birmingham University, and began singing her own comic

songs on local radio and television while still a student. The creator of all her own sketches, songs, and stand-up routines, her bubbly personality has offered witty observations on most aspects of everyday life. Her television career began with a slot in *That's Life* (1976), and includes *Wood and Walters* (1981–2), *Victoria Wood As Seen on Television* (1984–7), and *An Audience With Victoria Wood* (1988, BAFTA). In 1996 she was voted top female comedy performer by the British Comedy Awards. She frequently appears in stage revues, and she has published several books, including *Up To You, Porky* (1985), *Mens Sana in Thingummy Doodah* (1990), and *Chunky* (1996). >> Walters

Woodcock, George (1904–79) Trade union leader, born in Bamber Bridge, Lancashire, NW England, UK. Having left school at 12, he won a trade-union sponsored scholarship to Oxford, where he graduated with honours in philosophy and political economy (1933). He was a civil servant (1934–6) before joining the research and economic department of the Trades Union Congress (TUC), where he became assistant general secretary (1947–60) and general secretary (1960–9). He sat on several royal commissions, including the Donovan Commission on Trade Unions and Employers' Associations (1965–8). After retiring from the TUC he was chairman of the Commission on Industrial Relations (1969–71).

Wooden, John (Robert) (1910–) Basketball coach, born in Martinsville, IN. As a student he was College Player of the Year (1932), but it was as coach that his reputation grew. He was head basketball coach at the University of California, Los Angeles (1948–75), and named Coach of the Year by the US Writers Association six times between 1964 and 1973.

Woodhead, Chris(topher Anthony) (1946–) British teacher and educational administrator. He studied at Bristol and Keele universities, and became an English teacher at various schools and a tutor of English at Oxford University (1976–82). He was deputy chief education officer of the Devon (1988–90) and Cornwall (1990–1) local education authorities, and chief executive for the National Curriculum Council (1991–3) and School Curriculum and Assessment Authority (1993–4). In 1994 he was appointed chief inspector for schools at the Office for Standards in Education (OFSTED).

Woodhull, Victoria, *née* **Claflin** (1838–1927) Reformer, born in Homer, OH. She came from a family which earned a living by giving fortune-telling and medicine shows, and performed a spiritualist act with her sister, **Tennessee Claflin** (1846–1923). In 1868 she went with Tennessee to New York City, where they persuaded the rich Cornelius Vanderbilt to set them up as stockbrokers. They became involved with a Socialist group called Pantarchy, and advocated its principles of free love, equal rights, and legal prostitution. An accomplished speaker, she won support from the leaders of the women's suffrage movement, and became the first woman nominated for the presidency (1872).

Woodruff, Robert (1890–1985) US businessman. His father, a banker, bought control of Coca-Cola in 1919. Robert became president of the company in 1923, determined to make the drink available all over the world – and succeeded.

Woods, Tiger, popular name of **Eldrick Woods** (1976–) Golfer, born in Cypress, CA. He studied at Stanford University and won amateur US golf titles before turning professional in 1996. He shot to fame after winning the US Masters at Augusta in 1997 at the age of 21, and in his first appearance at the British Open later that year he equalled the course record of 64. His father, Earl Woods, then published a book about his son: *Training a Tiger: a Father's Guide to Raising a Winner in Both Golf and Life* (1997).

Woodson, Carter G(odwin) (1875–1950) Historian and educator, born in New Canton, VA. Lacking formal schooling until age 17, he studied at Harvard, and devoted his life to promoting black education. He founded the *Journal of Negro History* (1916), the African-American-owned Associated Publishers Press (1921), and the popular *Negro History Bulletin* (1937). A prolific author of popular and scholarly books, he created widespread public interest in African-American history, laying the groundwork for the later development of African-American studies.

Woodsworth, James Shaver (1874–1942) Reformer and political leader, born in Islington, Ontario, Canada. A Methodist minister, he wrote *The Stranger Within Our Gates* (1909) and other works about problems of recent European immigrants to the Canadian prairies. His pacifist stand throughout World War 1 led to a break with the Church. He was elected as a Manitoba Independent Labour Party MP, serving from 1921, pushed through legislation for an old age pension, and was founder and first chairman of the Commonwealth Co-operative Federation (1932).

Woodville, Elizabeth (1437–92) Queen consort of Edward IV of England. A widow, she married Edward IV in 1464, and was crowned in 1465. When Edward fled to Flanders in 1470, she sought sanctuary in Westminster. In 1483 her sons, Edward V and Richard, Duke of York, were murdered (the 'Princes in the Tower'). After the accession of Henry VII in 1485, her rights as dowager queen were restored, but in 1487 she was forced to retire to a convent, where she died. Her eldest daughter, **Elizabeth of York** (1465–1503), married Henry in 1486. >> Edward IV; Edward V; Henry VII

Woodward, Bob >> **Bernstein, Carl**

Woodward, Joanne (1930–) Film actress, born in Thomasville, GA. After starting on Broadway and in TV dramas, she made her first film, *Count Three and Pray*, in 1955, later winning an Oscar for *The Three Faces of Eve* (1957). She starred in two films directed by her husband, Paul Newman – *Rachel Rachel* (1968, Oscar nomination) and *The Effect of Gamma Rays on Man-in-the-Moon Marigolds* (1972, Cannes Best Actress). She received further Oscar nominations for her roles in *Wishes, Winter Dreams* (1973) and *Mr and Mrs Bridge* (1990), and won Emmies for *See How She Runs* (1978) and *Do You Remember Love?* (1985). Later films include *Philadelphia* (1993), *The Age of Innocence* (1993), and *Breathing Lessons* (1994), and she has also appeared in several productions for television. >> Newman, Paul

Woodward, R(obert) B(urns) (1917–79) Organic chemist, born in Boston, MA. He studied at Massachusetts Institute of Technology, and became professor of chemistry at Harvard (1953–79). In 1963, he became director of the Woodward Research Institute at Basel, which was founded in his honour. Best known for his masterly work on organic synthesis, including his synthesis of chlorophyll (1961), he was awarded the Nobel Prize for Chemistry in 1965. >> Hoffmann, Roald

Woodward, Roger Robert (1944–) Concert pianist, born in Sydney, New South Wales, Australia. He studied at the New South Wales Conservatory, and afterwards at the Warsaw Academy of Music, Poland, making his debut there in 1967 with the Warsaw Philharmonic Orchestra. Particularly known for his playing of Chopin and Beethoven, he has appeared with many international orchestras and conductors. He is keenly involved in contemporary music through *London Music Digest*, as well as the Australian *Music Rostrum*, which he founded in 1973. In 1976 he was awarded the International Frederic Chopin Institute's medal of honour.

Wooldridge, Sydney William (1900–63) Geographer, born in London, England, UK. He studied at Kings College, London, then held various teaching appointments at London University, becoming professor of geography there (1944–63). His original research was in geology, but he played a leading role in the establishment of geomorphology within British geography. He was an adviser to post-war governments on Greater London, new towns, and on the use of sands and gravel.

Woolf, Arthur (1766–1837) Mechanical engineer, born in Camborne, Cornwall, SW England, UK. From carpentry he turned to engineering, and in 1786 helped Jonathan Hornblower to repair a compound steam engine he had installed in a London brewery. After the expiry of James Watt's patent in 1800, Woolf patented a compound engine and boiler in 1803. He later concentrated on perfecting the high-pressure Cornish engines of Richard Trevithick. >> Hornblower; Trevithick; Watt, James

Woolf, Leonard (Sidney) (1880–1969) Publisher and writer, born in London, England, UK. He studied at Cambridge, then worked in the Ceylon Civil Service (1904–11). With his wife, Virginia Woolf, he founded the Hogarth Press (1917), and they became the centre of the Bloomsbury Group. His works include *Socialism and Co-operation* (1921), *After the Deluge* (1931, 1939), and *Principia Politica* (1953). His major work was a five-volume autobiography, beginning with *Sowing* (1960) and ending with *The Journey Not the Arrival Matters* (1969). >> Bell, Vanessa; Keynes; Moore, G E; Strachey, Lytton; Woolf, Virginia

Woolf, (Adeline) Virginia, *née* **Stephen** (1882–1941) Novelist, born in London, England, UK, the daughter of Leslie Stephen. Educated privately, in 1912 she married Leonard Woolf, with whom she set up the Hogarth Press (1917). A leading member of the Bloomsbury Group, she made a major contribution to the development of the novel, in such works as *Mrs Dalloway* (1925), *To the Lighthouse* (1927), and *The Waves* (1931), noted for their impressionistic style, a development of the stream-of-consciousness technique. She also wrote biographies and critical essays. After mental illness, she committed suicide. Publication of her *Diary* (5 vols, 1977–84) and *Letters* (6 vols, 1975–80) further enhanced her reputation. >> Bell, Vanessa; Moore, G E; Richardson, Dorothy M; Stephen, Leslie; Woolf, Leonard

Woolley, Frank (1887–1978) Cricketer, born in Tonbridge, Kent, SE England, UK. His Test career spanned a quarter of a century (1909–34), and although best remembered as a batsman he was a skilled all-rounder. He played 64 Test matches for England, scoring 3283 Test runs and recording five centuries. Against Australia at The Oval in 1912 he took 10 wickets for 49 runs in the match, and no-one in first-class cricket has equalled his tally of 1018 catches. >> RR1151

Woolley, Sir (Charles) Leonard (1880–1960) Archaeologist, born in London, England, UK. He studied at Oxford, and carried out excavations at Carchemish, al-Ubaid, and Tell el-Amarna. He subsequently directed the important excavations (1922–34) at Ur in Mesopotamia, revealing in 1926 spectacular discoveries of gold and lapis lazuli in the royal tombs. He was knighted in 1935, and wrote several popular accounts of his work, notably *Digging Up the Past* (1930).

Woolman, John (1720–72) Quaker preacher and reformer, born in Rancocas, NJ. A tailor by trade, he became a Quaker in 1843 and campaigned against slavery. A prolific writer, he is best remembered for his *Journal* (1774), a major work on the spiritual life, begun when he was 36 and continued until his death.

Woolton, Frederick James Marquis, Baron (1883–1964) Politician and businessman, born in Liverpool, Merseyside, NW England, UK. He studied at Manchester University, and was a teacher before working for the Lewis department store in Manchester, where he revolutionized the merchandizing side, and became chairman in 1935. He was made a life peer in 1939. During World War 2, he made his name at the ministry of food, where from 1940 he had the responsibility of seeing that the entire nation was well-nourished. In 1946 he became chairman of the Conservative Party, and is credited with much of the success in rebuilding the Party's reorganization which led it to victory in 1951.

Woolworth, Frank W(infield) (1852–1919) Businessman, the founder of F W Woolworth stores, born in Rodman, NY. He was a farm worker, and in 1873 became a shop-assistant. His employers backed his scheme to open 'five-and-ten cents' stores in Utica, and in Lancaster, PA. The latter was a success, and in partnership with his employers, his brother, and cousin, from 1905 he began building a large chain of similar stores. At the time of his death the F W Woolworth Co controlled over 1000 stores from their headquarters in the Woolworth building in New York City. His stores started in Britain in 1910, and by the 1960s there were subsidiaries in Germany, Spain, Canada, and Mexico.

Wootton (of Abinger), Barbara Frances Wootton, Baroness (1897–1988) Social scientist, born in Cambridge, Cambridgeshire, EC England, UK. She studied at Cambridge, where she became a lecturer in economics, moving to be director of studies (1927–44) and professor of social studies (1948–52) at London. A frequent royal commissioner and London magistrate, she is best known for her *Testament for Social Science* (1950), in which she attempted to assimilate the social to the natural sciences. She was created a life peer in 1958.

Worcester, Edward Somerset, 2nd Marquess of [**wus**ter] (1601–67) English aristocrat, probably born in London, England, UK. In the Civil War he sided with the king. In 1642 he was made General of South Wales, in 1644 Earl of Glamorgan, and in 1645 was sent to Ireland to raise troops for the king. His mission failed, Charles I disowned him, and he was imprisoned for a short time. In 1646 he succeeded his father, and in 1648 went into exile in France. In 1652, venturing back to England, he was sent to the Tower, but in 1654 was let out on bail, and at the Restoration recovered a portion of his vast estates. Interested in mechanics, he was involved with the early history of the steam engine. >> Charles I (of England)

Worcester, Joseph (Emerson) [**wus**ter] (1784–1865) Lexicographer, born in Bedford, NH. He taught at Salem, MA, then turned to writing. From 1817 he compiled a number of gazetteers, which became standard textbooks on geography and history. He later concentrated on lexicography, and edited *Johnson's English Dictionary, with Walker's Pronouncing Dictionary* (1828). In 1829 he abridged Webster without permission, which brought about a legal battle, the 'Dictionary War', which lasted until his death, and printed his own *Comprehensive English Dictionary* (1830). His major work was the great illustrated quarto *Dictionary of the English Language* (1860). >> Webster, Noah

Worde, Wynkyn de [werd] (?–?1535) Printer, born in The Netherlands or in Alsace. He was a pupil of Caxton, and in 1491 succeeded to his stock-in-trade. He made great improvements in printing and typecutting, and was the first in England to use italic type. >> Caxton

Wordsworth, Dorothy (1771–1855) Writer, born in Cockermouth, Cumbria, NW England, UK the sister of William Wordsworth, and his lifetime companion. Her *Alfoxden Journal* (1798) and *Grasmere Journals* (1800–3) show a keen sensibility and acute observation of nature in their own right, and also add an important biographical perspective on her brother. In 1829 she suffered a breakdown from which she never fully recovered. >> Wordsworth, William

Wordsworth, William (1770–1850) Poet, born in Cockermouth, Cumbria, NW England, UK. Educated at Hawkshead in the Lake District and at Cambridge, he went on a walking tour through France and Switzerland (1790). Back in France in 1790, he developed republican sentiments, and had an affair with a French girl, Annette Vallon, by whom he had a daughter. He returned to England at the outbreak of the war (1793), and after an unsettled period set up house at Racedown, Dorset, with his sister, Dorothy. There he discovered his true vocation, that of the poet exploring the lives of humble folk living in close contact with nature. After moving to Alfoxden, Somerset (1797), he wrote with Coleridge the *Lyrical Ballads* (1798), the first manifesto of the new Romantic poetry, which opened with Coleridge's 'Ancient Mariner' and concluded with Wordsworth's 'Tintern Abbey'. After a year in Germany, he moved to Dove Cottage, Grasmere, married **Mary Hutchinson** in 1802, and wrote much of his best work, including his poetic autobiography, *The Prelude* (1805, published posthumously in 1850), and two books of poems (1807). Critics are inclined to mark the decline of his powers after this remarkable outpouring. He succeeded Southey as poet laureate in 1843. >> Coleridge, Samuel Taylor; Southey; Wordsworth, Dorothy

Wordsworth, William Brocklesby (1908–88) Composer, born in London, England, UK. He studied under Sir Donald Tovey, and achieved prominence when his second symphony won the first award in the Edinburgh International Festival Competition in 1950. He has composed symphonies, a piano concerto, songs, and chamber music. >> Tovey, Donald

Worlock, Derek (John Harford) (1920–96) Roman Catholic clergyman. He studied at St Edmund's College, Hertfordshire, was ordained in 1944, and became secretary to the Archbishop of Westminster (1945–64), and Bishop of Portsmouth (1965–76). Appointed Archbishop of Liverpool in 1976, he developed a close working relationship with the Anglican Bishop of Liverpool, speaking with him on matters of social concern. He was made a Companion of Honour in 1996. >> Sheppard, David

Wörner, Manfred [**vaw(r)**ner] (1934–94) German politician, born in Stuttgart, Germany. He studied at Heidelberg, Paris, and Munich universities, and was elected to the Bundestag in 1965. He established himself as a specialist in strategic issues, and was appointed defence minister in 1982 by Chancellor Kohl. He oversaw the controversial deployment of US Cruise and Pershing-II nuclear missiles in West Germany, and an extension of military service from 15 to 18 months to compensate for a declining birthrate. He succeeded Lord Carrington as secretary-general of NATO in 1988. During 1992 he carried out an unprecedented tour of former Warsaw Pact countries, meeting government leaders, and re-affirming NATO's pledge that no 'security vacuum' would be allowed to develop in Eastern Europe following the break up of the Soviet Union. >> Carrington, Baron; Kohl

Worrall, Denis John (1935–) South African politician, born in Benoni, South Africa. He studied at Cape Town and Cornell universities, where he subsequently taught political science. He held a succession of academic posts and also worked as a journalist before being elected a National Party senator in 1974, and an MP in 1977. He was appointed ambassador to the UK in 1984, but on his return to South Africa in 1987 resigned from the National Party and unsuccessfully contested the general election of that year as an independent. In 1988 he established the Independent Party, and in 1989 merged with other white Opposition parties to form the reformist Democratic Party. A co-leader of this Party, he was elected to parliament in 1989.

Worrell, Sir Frank (Mortimer Magilinne) (1924–67) Cricketer, the first black West Indian Test captain, born in Bridgetown, Barbados. In 51 Test matches he made nine centuries, and was a useful pace bowler. He captained West Indies in Australia in 1960–1 in one of the greatest Test series ever, and matches between these countries today are played for the Worrell Trophy which commemorates him. He was Vice-Chancellor of the University of the West Indies and a senator in the Jamaican parliament, and was knighted for services to cricket. >> Walcott

Worth, Charles Frederick (1825–95) Costumier, born in Bourn, Lincolnshire, EC England, UK. A book-keeper, he went to Paris in 1845, and worked in a fashion accessories shop. He established a ladies' tailors in 1858, and gained the patronage of Empress Eugénie. The first to show a collection in advance and to use female models, he introduced the bustle, and is especially known for his elegant crinolined gowns.

Worth, Irene (1916–) Actress, born in Nebraska. She studied at the University of California, Los Angeles, and became a teacher, before joining a touring company in 1942. She appeared on Broadway a year later, and in 1944 moved to London. She joined the Old Vic in 1951, and became a member of the Royal Shakespeare Company at Stratford-upon-Avon in 1960. She has won awards for several theatre roles, including *Tiny Alice* (1965), *Sweet Bird of Youth* (1975), *The Cherry Orchard* (1977), and *Lost in Yonkers, NY* (1991). A one-woman show in 1993–4 was based on the works of Edith Wharton.

Wortley Montagu, Lady Mary >> **Montagu, Lady Mary Wortley**

Wotton, Sir Henry (1568–1639) English diplomat, traveller, scholar, and poet, born in Boughton Malherbe, Kent, SE England, UK. He studied at Oxford, then travelled extensively. He became the confidant of Robert Devereux, 2nd Earl of Essex. On his friend's downfall (1601) he went to France, then to Italy, and was sent by Ferdinand, Duke of Florence, on a secret mission to James VI of Scotland. When James succeeded to the throne of England, Wotton was knighted, then sent as ambassador to Venice (1604). His tracts and letters were collected as *Reliquiae Wottonianae* (1651). One of his few surviving poems is 'The Character of a Happy Life'. >> Essex, Robert Devereux; James I (of England)

Wouk, Herman [wohk] (1915–) Novelist, born in New York City. He studied at Columbia University, wrote radio scripts, and served in the US navy in the South Pacific in World War 2. He drew on this experience for his classic war novel, *The Caine Mutiny* (1951, Pulitzer), which became a successful play and film. Other books include *Marjorie Morningstar* (1955), *Youngblood Hawke* (1962), *Inside, Outside* (1985), and *The Glory* (1994). His two-volume historical novel, *The Winds of War* (1971) and *War and Remembrance* (1975), led to popular television serials.

Wouldhave, William (1751–1821) Lifeboat inventor, born in North Shields, Tyne and Wear, NE England, UK. After being an apprentice to a house painter, he became known as a somewhat eccentric inventor. The wreck of the *Adventure* in the R Tyne in 1789, causing many deaths less than 300 yards from the shore, led to a local competition to design a lifeboat. Both he and a local boat-builder, **Henry Greathead** (1757–1816), submitted designs, but neither was approved. Greathead then went on to present a new model which incorporated many of Wouldhave's features, and was commissioned to build it. He launched *The Original* in 1790, and Greathead boats came to be used for 40 years around the coasts of Britain. Greathead subsequently claimed the title of lifeboat inventor, and Wouldhave died with his contribution unacknowledged.

Wouwerman, Philips [vowverman], also found as **Wouwermans** (c. 1619–68) Painter of battle and hunting scenes, born in Haarlem, The Netherlands. His pictures are mostly small landscapes, with several figures in energetic action. His cavalry skirmishes, with a white horse generally in the foreground, were especially characteristic and popular. He had two brothers, also painters, **Peter Wouwerman** (1623–82) and **Jan Wouwerman** (1629–66), who chose similar subjects.

Wovoka (1856–1937) American Indian religious leader. He was the founder of the Ghost Dance Movement.

Wozniack, Stephen >> **Jobs, Steven**

Wrangel, Ferdinand Petrovich, Baron von [vranggl] (1794–1870) Explorer, born in Pskov, Russia. He travelled in Arctic waters and on Siberian coasts, and made valuable surveys and observations. The reported island in the Arctic Ocean he nearly reached in 1821 was sighted in 1849, and named after him in 1867. He was Governor of Russian lands in Alaska (1829–35) and naval minister (1855–7).

Wrangel, Pyotr Nikolayevich, Baron [vranggl] (1878–1928) Russian army officer and commander of White Russian forces during the Civil War, born in Aleksandrovsk, Lithuania. Educated at the St Petersburg Mining Institute, he entered military service in 1904 and commanded a cavalry corps during World War 1. In the Civil War, he commanded cavalry divisions and the Volunteer Army in the Ukraine, and in 1920 became commander-in-chief of the White Armies in the South. After the Red Army victory, he fled to Turkey with the remnants of his troops.

Wren, Sir Christopher (1632–1723) Architect, born in East Knoyle, Wiltshire, S England, UK. He studied at Oxford, became professor of astronomy at Gresham College, London (1657), and at Oxford (1661), and was one of the founders of the Royal Society. After the Great Fire of London (1666), he drew designs for rebuilding the whole city, but his scheme was never implemented. In 1669 he designed the new St Paul's and many other churches and public buildings in London, such as the Royal Exchange and Greenwich Observatory. Knighted in 1673, he held posts at Windsor Castle and Westminster Abbey, and became an MP (1685). He is buried in St Paul's. >> Hooke, Robert; Wallis, John; Wilkins, John; Willis, Thomas

Wren, P(ercival) C(hristopher) (1885–1941) Writer, born in Devon, SW England, UK. In the course of an adventurous early life he joined the French Foreign Legion, and this provided him with the background of several novels of adventure, notably *Beau Geste* (1924) and *Beau Sabreur* (1926).

Wright, Benjamin (1770–1842) Civil engineer, born in Wethersfield, CT. Trained as a lawyer and surveyor, he became chief engineer on the construction of the Erie Canal (1817–25), the first major engineering project in America. He went on to build the original St Lawrence Ship Canal and the Chesapeake and Ohio Canal (1825–31), then turned to railway engineering, and was appointed chief engineer of the New York and Erie Railroad. His son, **Benjamin Hall Wright**, also became a civil engineer, and after his father's death completed several of the schemes on which he had been working.

Wright, Billy, popular name of **William Ambrose Wright** (1924–94) Footballer, born in Wolverhampton, West Midlands, C England, UK. An industrious wing-half, and later a central defender, he was the first player to win more than 100 caps for England (105, 90 as captain). His only senior club was Wolverhampton Wanderers, with whom he won one FA Cup Medal and three League championships. A model of deportment and sportsmanship, he went into football managership with Arsenal, and later became a television sports executive. >> RR1155

Wright, Sir (Almroth) Edward (1861–1947) Bacteriologist, born in Middleton Tyas, North Yorkshire, N England, UK. He studied at Dublin, Leipzig, Strasbourg, and Marburg universities, and became professor of pathology at the Army Medical School (1892), where he developed an anti-typhoid vaccine used successfully during the Boer War, and to immunize all British troops in World War 1. After the war he continued research into parasitic diseases at St Mary's Hospital, London, working alongside Alexander Fleming. He was knighted in 1906. >> Fleming, Alexander

Wright, Fanny, popular name of **Frances Wright**, married name **Frances Darusmont** (1795–1852) Reformer and abolitionist, born in Dundee, E Scotland, UK. The heiress to a large fortune, she emigrated to the USA in 1818 and toured widely, publishing *Views of Society and Manners in America* in 1821. She founded a short-lived community at Nashoba in W Tenessee for ex-slaves whose freedom she had bought. Settling in New York City in 1829, she published with Robert Dale Owen a socialist journal, *Free Enquirer*. She was briefly (1931–5) married to the French physicist **William Darusmont**. One of the early suffragettes, she campaigned vigorously against religion and for the emancipation of women. >> Owen, Robert Dale

Wright, Frank Lloyd (1867–1959) Architect, born in Richland Center, WI. He studied civil engineering at Wisconsin, and was early associated with architect Louis Sullivan. The collapse of a newly built wing led him to apply engineering principles to architecture. After setting up in practice in Chicago, he became known for low-built prairie-style residences, but soon launched into more controversial designs. An innovator in the field of open planning, he is regarded as the leading designer of modern private dwellings, planned in conformity with the natural features of the land. Among his larger works are the Imperial Hotel in Tokyo and the Guggenheim Museum of Art in New York City. >> Berlage; Greenough; Sullivan, Louis

Wright, Georg von >> **von Wright, Georg Henrik**

Wright, Joseph, known as **Wright of Derby** (1734–97) Genre and portrait painter, born in Derby, Derbyshire, C England, UK. He remained in Derby for most of his life. He is best known for his industrial scenes such as 'The Air Pump' (1768, Tate, London), and his treatment of artificial light.

Wright, Joseph (1855–1930) Philologist, born in Bradford, West Yorkshire, N England, UK. He worked in a woollen mill as a boy, and developed an interest in local dialects. He eventually became professor of comparative philology at Oxford, editor of the *Dialect Dictionary*, and author of many philological works.

Wright, Judith (Arundel) (1915–) Poet, born near Armidale, New South Wales, Australia. She studied at Sydney, and worked in educational administration in Queensland. She is valued for the broad sympathies of *The Moving Image* (1946), in which she was one of the first white writers to recognize Aboriginal claims, and the personal lyrics of *Woman to Man* (1950). Her collections include *Collected Poems* (1971), *Four Quarters and Other Poems* (1976), *The Human Pattern* (1990), and *Collected Poems: 1942–1985* (1994). She is a militant environmentalist and a strong advocate of Aboriginal land rights. She was awarded the Queen's Medal for Poetry in 1992. >> Sutherland, Margaret Ada

Wright, Peter (1916–95) British intelligence officer, born in Chesterfield, Derbyshire, C England, UK. He joined the Admiralty's Research Laboratory during World War 2 as a scientific officer, and transferred to MI5 (counter-intelligence) (1955–76). Here he specialized in the invention of espionage devices and the detection of Soviet 'moles'. He

bought a sheep ranch in Tasmania when he retired, and wrote his autobiography, *Spycatcher* (1987), in which he alleged that Sir Roger Hollis, the former director-general of MI5, had been a Soviet double-agent, the so-called 'Fifth Man', and that elements within MI5 had tried to overthrow the Wilson government during the mid-1960s. Attempts by the Thatcher government to suppress the book's publication and distribution for 'security reasons' were eventually unsuccessful. >> Hollis; Thatcher; Turnbull, Malcolm Bligh

Wright, Richard (1908–60) Novelist, short-story writer, and critic, born on a plantation in Mississippi. His grandparents had been slaves, his father left home when he was five, and he was brought up in poverty by various relatives. Among the first African-Americans to write about their ill-treatment by whites, his works include the short story 'The Man Who Lived Underground' (1942), and *Native Son* (1940), a best-selling novel about a black youth who accidentally kills a white girl. The latter was staged on Broadway by Orson Welles (1941), and Wright starred in a film version (1951). He is best known for his autobiographical novel, *Black Boy* (1945). >> Welles, Orson

Wright, Sewall (1889–1988) Geneticist, born in Melrose, MA. He studied at Harvard, worked at the US Department of Agriculture (1915–25), where he conducted experimental work in animal genetics, then became professor at the universities of Chicago (1926–54) and Wisconsin (1955–60). He is one of the founders of population genetics, but is best remembered for his concept of genetic drift, termed the *Sewall Wright effect*.

Wright brothers Aviation pioneers: **Orville Wright** (1871–1948), born in Dayton, OH, and **Wilbur Wright** (1867–1912), born near Millville, IN. They were the first to fly in a powered heavier-than-air machine (17 Dec 1903), at Kitty Hawk, NC. Encouraged by this, they abandoned their cycle business and formed an aircraft production company (1909), of which Wilbur was president until his death. In 1915 Orville sold his interests in the company to devote himself to aeronautical research. >> Arnold, Henry Harley; Lahm; Pearce, Richard William; Vought

Wrigley, William, Jr [riglee] (1861–1932) Chewing-gum manufacturer, born in Philadelphia, PA. He began work as a salesman for his father's soap company, moved to Chicago, and began offering chewing gum with his goods. He successfully marketed the famous spearmint flavour (1899), took over Zeno Manufacturing who produced the gum (1911), and established the William Wrigley Jr Co. He retired in 1925, by which time his company was the largest producer and distributor of chewing gum in the world.

Wriothesley, Henry >> **Southampton, 3rd Earl of**

Wu, Empress, in full **Wu Zhao** (?625–?706) Empress of China, the only woman ever to rule China in her own name. A concubine of Emperor Taizong, she married his son, **Emperor Gaozong**, whom she dominated after his stroke (660). After his death (683) she first ruled through her own sons, then following a reign of bloody terror she seized the title *emperor* in 690 with the dynastic name Zhou (Chou). To establish legitimacy, she claimed to be Maitreya, a supposed Buddhist 'messiah', ordered public prophecy of a female monarch 700 years after Buddha, and rewrote genealogies. Highly capable, she expanded the bureaucracy and examination system, set up a personal secretariat, and dominated both Korea and Tibet. She was forced to abdicate in 705, and her family were assassinated in 710. >> Lü; Taizong; Xuanzong

Wu, Chien-Shiung (1912–) Physicist, born in Shanghai, China. She studied at the National Centre University in China, and moved to the USA in 1936, working at the University of California, Berkeley. From 1944 she was on the staff of Columbia University, New York City. Her research was in particle physics, notably her confirmation that some physical processes (such as beta-particle emission) are not identical in a mirror-image system.

Wu Chengen [woo chengen], also spelled **Wu Ch'eng-en** (1505–82) Writer, from a merchant family, born in Huai-an, Kiangsu Province, China. He fused popular oral traditions into *Journey to the West*, one of four great Ming period novels. Based around Xuanzang's 7th-c trip to India, it focuses on a supernatural disciple, Monkey, converted from Taoism and sent by Buddha to protect Xuanzang from demons by using a magic pin in his ear as an iron cudgel. The work lampoons traditional officialdom, and during the Cultural Revolution (1966–76) it inspired Red Guards, who identified with the intelligent, personable Monkey (his cudgel represented Mao's thoughts). Serialized on Chinese television in recent years, an English translation is entitled *Monkey*. >> Lo Guangzhong; Xuanzang

Wudi [woo dee], also spelled **Wu-ti** (141–86 BC) Han dynasty emperor of China (his name means 'martial emperor'). He respected Confucian scholarship, and began selecting administrators by oral examination (setting questions himself). Appointing himself head of the bureaucracy, he established (124 BC) a Confucian university for scholar-administrators. He sequestered noble lands, extended crown possessions, annexed S China, conquered Korea, Tonkin, and the SW with large armies, and invaded the Hun territories. He sent a major expedition (138–125 BC) to Bactria to ensure W trade routes, and a second expedition (101 BC, 30 000 troops) conquered Ferghana (2200 mi from Wudi's capital). These expeditions ensured Chinese control over the Tarim (later Xinjiang), and set a precedent for later spectacular Han triumphs. >> Ban Chao; Gaozu; Liu Sheng; Wendi

Wulfila >> Ulfilas

Wulfstan, St (c.1009–95) Clergyman, born in Long Itchington, Warwickshire, C England, UK. Educated at the abbey of Peterborough, he became a monk, subsequently prior, at Worcester, and was appointed Bishop of Worcester in 1062. At the Norman Conquest of 1066 he made submission to William I, and was the only Englishman left in his see. Later he supported William II. He ended the slave-trade practised by merchants in Bristol, helped to compile the *Domesday Book*, and may have written part of the *Anglo-Saxon Chronicle*. He was canonized in 1203; feast day 19 January. >> William I (of England); William II (of England)

Wulfstan, also known as **Lupus** (?–1023) Anglo-Saxon clergyman and writer. He was Bishop of London (996–1002), Archbishop of York from 1002, and also Bishop of Worcester (1003–16). He was the author of homilies in the vernacular, including a celebrated address to the English, *Sermo Lupi ad Anglos* (1014, Sermon of Wolf to the English).

Wunderlich, Carl August [vunderlikh] (1815–77) Physician, born in Sulz-on-Neckar, Germany. Professor of medicine at Leipzig, he was the first to introduce temperature charts into hospitals, contending that fever is a symptom and not a disease. His clinical thermometer was a foot long, and took 20 minutes to register the temperature.

Wundt, Wilhelm (Max) [vunt] (1832–1920) Physiologist and psychologist, born in Neckarau, Germany. He taught at Heidelberg and Zürich universities, then became professor of physiology at Leipzig (1875). A distinguished experimental psychologist, he wrote on the nerves and the senses, and the relations between physiology and psychology.

Wuorinen, Charles >> Olson, Harry

Wuornos, Aileen [waw(r)nos] (1956–) US convicted murderer. Dubbed the world's first female serial killer, she was convicted in the USA in 1992 of the murder of seven men between 1989 and 1991, and sentenced to die in the electric chair.

Wu Peifu [woo payfoo], also spelled **Wu P'ei-fu** (1874–1939) Major figure in the warlord struggles of China (1916–27), born in Shandong province, China. He joined the new army created by Yuan Shikai, and after Yuan's death (1916), when Duan Qirui sought to reunite China by force, Wu and other N generals refused Duan's orders. In the civil war which followed, he was unable to sustain his government of national unity (1923), and was defeated in battle near Tientsin. >> Yuan Shikai

Wurlitzer, Rudolph [werlitser] (1831–1914) Musical instrument maker, born in Schöneck, Germany. He emigrated to the USA (1853) and continued the family business of manufacturing musical instruments. He founded a factory in Cincinnati producing band instruments for military use (1861), adding a branch in Chicago (1865). The Rudolph Wurlitzer Company was formed (1890), and he served as president (1890–1912) and chairman (1912–14). Three sons, **Howard Eugene** (1871–1928), **Rudolph Henry** (1873–1948), and **Farny Reginald** (1883–1972), successively held these posts, during which time the company expanded in the field of automatic and coin-operated instruments, notably the famous 'Mighty Wurlitzer' theatre organ.

Wurtz, Charles Adolphe >> **Couper, Archibald Scott**

Wu-ti >> **Wudi**

Wyatt, James (1746–1813) Architect, born in Burton Constable, Staffordshire, C England, UK. He visited Italy for several years, and achieved fame with his Neoclassical design for the London Pantheon (1772). He became surveyor to the Board of Works (1796), restored several cathedrals, and designed many country houses. His best-known work is the Gothic revival Fonthill Abbey (1796–1807), which largely collapsed in the 1820s.

Wyatt, Sir Thomas, known as **the Elder** (1503–42) Poet and courtier, born in Allington, Kent, SE England, UK. He studied at Cambridge, was warmly received at court, knighted (1536), made high sheriff of Kent (1537), and went on several diplomatic missions. In 1557 his poems, published in *Tottel's Miscellany*, helped to introduce the Italian sonnet and other forms into English literature. >> Tottel; Wyatt, Thomas (the Younger)

Wyatt, Sir Thomas, known as **the Younger** (? 1520–54) English soldier, son of the poet Sir Thomas Wyatt. He fought bravely at the siege of Landrecies (1544), and continued in service on the European mainland until 1550. In 1554, with Lady Jane Grey's father, he led the Kentish men to Southwark. Failing to capture Ludgate, he was taken prisoner and executed. >> Digges; Grey, Lady Jane; Mary I; Wyatt, Thomas (the Elder)

Wycherley, William [wicherlee] (c. 1640–1716) Playwright, born in Clive, Shropshire, WC England, UK. He studied in France and at Oxford, became a lawyer, then lived as a courtier and turned to writing. He wrote several satirical comedies, notably *The Country Wife* (1675) and *The Plain Dealer* (1677), both based on plays by Molière. He was imprisoned for debt, but was finally given a pension by James II. >> Molière

Wyckoff, Ralph (Walter Greystone) [wikoff] (1897–) Biophysicist, born in Geneva, NY. He studied at Cornell and worked at the Rockefeller Institute in the 1930s, researching into viruses. In 1944 at Chicago with Robley Cook Williams he developed the metal shadowing method for imaging viruses in the electron microscope, which has since been widely used. >> Williams, Robley Cook

Wycliffe or **Wicliffe, John** [wiklif], also spelled **Wyclif, Wycliff** (c.1330–84) Religious reformer, born near Richmond, Yorkshire, N England, UK. He studied at Oxford, where he taught philosophy, then entered the Church, becoming

Rector of Lutterworth, Leicestershire, in 1374. He was sent to Bruges to treat with ambassadors from the Pope about ecclesiastical abuses, but his views were found unacceptable, and he was prosecuted. He then attacked the Church hierarchy, priestly power, and the doctrine of transubstantiation, wrote many popular tracts in English (as opposed to Latin), and issued the first English translation of the Bible. His opinions were condemned, and he was forced to retire to Lutterworth, where he wrote prolifically until his death. The characteristic of his teaching was its insistence on inward religion in opposition to the formalism of the time. His followers were known as *Lollards*, and the influence of his teaching was widespread in England, in many respects anticipating the Reformation. >> Huss; Jerome of Prague

Wyeth, Andrew (Newell) (1917–) Painter, born in Chadds Ford, PA. He studied under his father, a book illustrator. His soberly realistic pictures, usually executed with tempera and watercolour rather than oils, typically represent poor people or rustics in landscapes from the traditional 'American scene', using off-centre compositions to give a sense of haunting unease, as in 'Christina's World' (1948, Museum of Modern Art, New York City).

Wykeham, William of >> **William of Wykeham**

Wyler, William [wiyler] (1902–81) Film director, born in Mulhouse, France (formerly, Germany). Invited to America by his mother's cousin Carl Laemmle (1867–1939), the head of Universal Pictures, he worked there on many aspects of film-making before becoming a director of Western shorts and low budget productions. Renowned for his obsessively meticulous approach to composition, performance, and narrative structure, his many successes include *These Three* (1936), *Wuthering Heights* (1939), *The Collector* (1965), and *Funny Girl* (1968). He received Oscars for *Mrs Miniver* (1942), *The Best Years of Our Lives* (1946), and *Ben Hur* (1959). He retired in 1972. He received an American Film Institute Life Achievement Award in 1976.

Wylie, Elinor, *née* **Elinor Morton Hoyt** (1885–1928) Writer, born in Somerville, NJ. A debutante, she left her first husband, went to England (1910–14) with **Horace Wylie**, and married him after returning to America in 1915. In 1921 she left Wylie and moved to New York City, where in 1923 she married William Rose Benét. All her writing was published in the final seven years of her life. She is best known today for her delicate poetry, as in *Angels and Earthly Creatures* (1929), but she also wrote critical essays, reviews, and four comic fantasy novels. >> Benét, William Rose

Wyman, Bill >> **Rolling Stones, The**

Wyndham, Sir Charles [**wind**am] (1837–1919) Actor-manager, born in Liverpool, Merseyside, NW England, UK. He trained as a doctor, and first appeared on the stage in New York City in 1861, making his London debut in 1866. In 1899 he opened Wyndham's Theatre. He was knighted in 1902.

Wyndham, John [**wind**am], pseudonym of **John Wyndham Parkes Lucas Beynon Harris** (1903–69) Science-fiction writer, born in Knowle, West Midlands, C England, UK. He worked at a variety of jobs, then in the late 1920s began to write science-fiction tales for popular magazines, achieving fame with his first novel, *The Day of the Triffids* (1951). His other books include *The Kraken Wakes* (1953), *The Chrysalids* (1955), and *The Midwich Cuckoos* (1957), as well as collections of short stories, such as *The Seeds of Time* (1969).

Wynfrith, St >> **Boniface, St**

Wynkyn de Worde >> **Worde, Wynkyn de**

Wyss, Johann Rudolf [vees] (1781–1830) Writer, born in Bern. He is best known for his completion and editing of *Der Schweizerische Robinson* (1812–13, trans The Swiss Family Robinson), written by his father, **Johann David Wyss** (1743–1818). He collected Swiss tales and folklore, and was professor of philosophy at Bern from 1806.

Wyszyński, Stefan, Cardinal [vishinskee] (1901–81) Roman Catholic clergyman, born in Zuzela, Poland. He studied at Włocławek and Lublin, was ordained in 1924, and became Bishop of Lublin (1946), Archbishop of Warsaw and Gniezno (1948), and a cardinal (1952). Following his indictment of the Communist campaign against the Church, he was imprisoned (1953). Freed in 1956, he agreed to a reconciliation between Church and state under the Gomułka regime, but relations remained uneasy. >> Gomułka

Xavier, Francis, St >> **Francis Xavier, St**

Xenakis, Iannis [ze**nah**kees] (1922–) Composer, born in Braila, Romania. He studied engineering at Athens University, and worked as an architect for Le Corbusier in Paris. He did not turn to musical composition until 1954, when he wrote the orchestral piece *Metastasis*, and went on to develop a highly complex style which incorporated mathematical concepts of chance and probability (so-called *stochastic music*), as well as electronic techniques. His works are mainly instrumental and orchestral. >> Le Corbusier

Xenocrates [ze**no**kratees] (c. 395–314 BC) Greek philosopher and scientist, born in Chalcedon on the Bosphorus. He was a pupil of Plato, and in 339BC succeeded Speusippus as head of the Academy which Plato had founded. He wrote prolifically on natural science, astronomy, and philosophy, but only fragments of this output survive. He generally systematized and continued the Platonic tradition, but seems to have had a particular devotion to threefold categories, perhaps reflecting a Pythagorean influence: philosophy is subdivided into logic, ethics, and physics; reality is divided into the objects of sensation, belief, and knowledge; he distinguished gods, men, and demons; and he also probably originated the classical distinction between mind, body, and soul. >> Plato; Speusippus

Xenophanes [ze**no**faneez] (c. 570–c. 480 BC) Greek philosopher, born in Colophon, Ionia. He travelled extensively, perhaps spending considerable time in Sicily. He attacked traditional Greek conceptions of the gods, arguing against anthropomorphism and polytheism.

Xenophon [**ze**nofon] (c. 435–354 BC) Greek historian, essayist, and soldier, born in Attica. A friend and pupil of Socrates, in 401 BC he served with a group of 10 000 Greek mercenaries under Persian Prince Cyrus, who was fighting against his brother, the King of Persia. After Cyrus was killed, the Greeks were isolated over 1500 km/900 mi from home. Xenophon was elected leader, and the group successfully fought their way back to the Black Sea. This heroic feat formed the basis of his major work, *Anabasis Kyrou* (The Expedition of Cyrus). >> Cyrus (the Younger); Socrates

Xerxes I [**zerk**seez] (c. 519–465 BC) Achaemenid king of Persia (486–465 BC), the son of Darius I. He is remembered in the West mainly for the failure of his forces against the Greeks in the Second Persian War at Salamis, Plataea, and Mycale.

>> Artaxerxes I; Artemisia; Darius I; Mordecai; Pausanias; RR1063

Ximénes (de Cisneros) Francisco Jiménez, Cardinal [hee**me**neth] (1436–1517) Clergyman and statesman, born in Torrelaguna, Spain. He was educated at Alcalá, Salamanca, and Rome, where he obtained from the pope a nomination to the archpriestship of Uzeda (1473). The archbishop refused to admit him, and for six years imprisoned him. Released in 1479, he was named vicar-general of Cardinal Mendoza, but gave this up to enter a Franciscan monastery at Toledo (1482). Queen Isabella chose him for her confessor in 1492, and in 1495 made him Archbishop of Toledo. He was created a cardinal in 1507. On the death of Ferdinand (1516) he was appointed regent during the minority of the later Charles V. A munificent patron of religion and learning, he founded the University of Alcalá de Henares. >> Charles V (Emperor); Isabella I

Xuanzang [shwantsang], also spelled **Hsüan-tsang** (600–664) Buddhist pilgrim, explorer, and diarist, born in Chen-lu, China. Inspired by earlier travellers, he made an epic journey to India (629–45) for Buddhist Scriptures. He crossed the Gobi and Xinjiang, traversed modern Afghanistan, and stayed two years in the Indus valley. He visited all the major historical sites in N India, journeyed 140 mi to the S, and returned up the W coast. He returned to China carrying 150 pieces of Buddha's body, 657 books, and the recipe for making sugar. >> Faxian; Ganying

Xuanzong [shwantsong], also spelled **Hsüan-tsung** (685–761) Chinese Tang emperor (ruled 712–55). Of royal lineage, he eliminated the usurper Wei's family in 710, and seized the crown in 712. Known also as **Minghuang** ('brilliant emperor'), his reign displayed authentic imperial characteristics. He maintained a splendid court, reformed the coinage, initiated land registration, extended the Grand Canal, defeated the Tibetans (747), patronized leading painters and poets, and established the Academy of Letters (*Han Lin*) in 754, by which major scholars supervised all court documentation. His system lasted over 1000 years. After 745 he became obsessed with his concubine, Yang Guifei. Her protégé An Lushan rebelled in 755. Xuanzong fled, agreed to her execution, then abdicated in grief. Their love story inspired the poet Bo Juyi, and Ming period drama. >> An Lushan; Bo Juyi; Li Bo

Yacoub, Sir Magdi (Habib) [yakoob] (1935–) Surgeon, born in Cairo. He studied at Cairo University, taught at Chicago, and moved to Britain where he became a consultant cardiothoracic surgeon at Harefield Hospital (1969–) and director of medical research and education (1992–). He was appointed professor at the National Heart and Lung Institute in 1986, and is one of the leading developers of the techniques of heart and heart–lung transplantation. He was knighted in 1992.

Yadin, Yigael [yadeen], originally **Yigael Sukenik** (1917–84) Archaeologist and military leader, born in Jerusalem. He served as chief of general staff of the Israel Defence Forces (1949–52). He then studied at Hebrew University, and became professor of archaeology there (1959). He led major archaeological expeditions in Israel, including Hazor (1955–8, 1968), the Dead Sea Caves (1960–1), and Masada (1963–5). He is noted for his work on the Dead Sea Scrolls, as seen in *The Message of the Scrolls* (1957).

Yakumo, Koizumi >> **Hearn, Lafcadio**

Yale, Elihu (1649–1721) Colonial administrator and benefactor, born in Boston, MA, of English parents. They returned to Britain in 1652, and he was educated in London. In 1672 he went to India in the service of the East India Company, becoming Governor of Madras in 1687. He was resident in England from 1699. Through the sale in America of some of his effects, he donated money to the collegiate school established (1701) at Saybrook, CT, which afterwards moved to New Haven. There in 1718 it took the name of Yale College in honour of its benefactor, and in 1887 the much-expanded institution became Yale University, the third oldest in the USA.

Yale, Linus (1821–68) Lock manufacturer, and inventor of the Yale lock, born in Salisbury, NY. He started as as a portrait painter, but followed his father as a bank-lock manufacturer. After his success with the Yale Infallible Bank Lock (1851), he set up business as a locksmith in Shelburne Falls, MA, and invented various types of locks, including the small cylinder locks by which his name is known.

Yalow, Rosalyn S(ussman) [yaloh] (1921–) Medical physicist, born in New York City. She studied at Hunter College, New York City, and the University of Illinois. From 1947 she turned her attention to nuclear medicine with Solomon Berson at the Bronx Veterans Administration Hospital. There she developed radio-immunoassay, a technique for measuring minute concentrations of active biological substances such as hormones. Director of the Berson Research Laboratory from 1973, she shared the 1977 Nobel Prize for Physiology or Medicine. >> RR1124

Yamagata, Prince Aritomo [yamagahta] (1838–1922) Japanese general, statesman, and premier (1890–1, 1898–1900), born in Hagi, Japan. A disciple of the anti-Western crusader Yoshido Shoin, he was an early leader in Meiji Japan (1868), and was dominant in Japanese public life until he died. As war minister (1873) and chief-of-staff (1878), he instituted major army reforms, modelling the army on German lines, and earning the name 'father of the Japanese army'. His belief in nationalism and imperial loyalty in the army took him above party politics, and he became premier to forestall partisan government. His military reforms led to Japan's defeat of China (1895) and Russia (1905) and her emergence as a significant power. In 1915 he opposed Japan's 21 Demands on China, believing Sino-Japanese understanding was essential to allow Japan to prepare for an inevitable war against the West.

Yamamoto, Isoroku [yamamohtoh] (1884–1943) Japanese naval officer, born in Nagaoka, Japan. He trained at the Naval Academy, Etajima, and became naval attaché at the Japanese embassy in the USA (1926–8), chief of the aviation department of the Japanese navy (1935), and vice-navy minister (1936–9). Admiral (1940), and commander-in-chief of the combined fleet (1939–43), he planned and directed the attack on Pearl Harbor in December 1941. His forces were defeated at the Battle of Midway (June 1942), and he was killed when his plane was shot down over the Solomon Is.

Yamamoto, Yohji [yamamohtoh] (1943–) Fashion designer, born in Tokyo. He studied at Pawat Kaio University, then helped his mother with her dress shop. He started his own company in 1972, producing his first collection in Tokyo in 1976. After some time in Paris, he opened a new headquarters in London in 1987. He designs loose, functional clothes for men and women, featuring a great deal of black, which conceal rather than emphasize the body.

Yamani, Ahmed Zaki, Sheikh [yamahnee] (1930–) Saudi Arabian politician. He studied at Cairo, New York, and Harvard universities, and was a lawyer before entering politics. Minister of petroleum and mineral resources (1962–86), he was an important and 'moderate' member of the Organization of Petroleum-Exporting Countries (OPEC).

Yamashita, Tomoyuki [yamashita] (1885–1946) Japanese soldier, born in Kochi, Japan. He commanded a division in China in 1939, and in 1942 commanded the forces which overran Singapore. He then took over the Philippines campaign, capturing Bataan and Corregidor. Still in charge when MacArthur turned the tables in 1944–5, he was captured, tried for war crimes, and hanged. >> MacArthur, Douglas

Yamashita, Yasuhiro [yamashita] (1957–) Judo fighter, born in Kyushu, Japan. He won nine consecutive Japanese titles (1977–85), the Olympic open class gold medal (1984), and four world titles: 1979, 1981, 1983, (over 95 kg class), and 1981 (open class). He retired in 1985 after 203 consecutive bouts without defeat from 1977. >> RR1163

Yang, Chen Ning, known as **Frank Yang** (1922–) Physicist, born in Hofei, China. He gained a scholarship to Chicago in 1945, was professor at the Institute for Advanced Studies, Princeton (1955–65), and from 1965 was professor of science at New York State University Center. He became a US citizen in 1964. He specialized in particle physics, and with T D Lee disproved the established physical principle known as the *parity law*, for which they shared the Nobel Prize for Physics in 1957. >> Lee, Tsung-Dao

Yangdi [yangdee], also spelled **Yang-ti** (569–618) Second Chinese Sui dynasty emperor (604–18). As Yang Guang he murdered his father, Wendi. To strengthen Chinese unification he married a southern princess. He received the first Japanese envoys, sent ambassadors to the Indies, India, and Turkestan, invaded Korea on four occasions with huge armies of over a million men (611–14), conquered Taiwan (610), and established colonies on the W trade routes. Retaining Changan (Xian) as a capital, he sumptuously rebuilt Luoyang as a second, and Yangzhou as a third. Six state granaries were constructed, the Great Wall fortified, and the Grand Canal built (610). The expense of his reign provoked insurrection in the NW, and he was killed. The new Tang dynasty later propagandized him as a feckless womanizer. >> Taizong; Wendi

Yang Shangkun (1907–) President of the People's Republic of China (1988–93), born in Tongnan, Sichuan, China. He studied in Moscow, and became an alternate member of the secretariat in 1956, but during the Cultural Revolution (1966–9) was purged for alleged 'revisionism'. He was rehabilitated (1978) and inducted into the Politburo (1982). He became a vice-chairman of the state central military commission (1983), and elected president. Viewed as a trusted supporter of Deng Xiaoping, he has strong personal ties with senior military leaders, and in June 1989 it was 27th Army troops, loyal to him, who carried out the massacre of pro-democracy students in Tiananmen Square, Beijing. >> Deng Xiaoping; RR1040

Yanofsky, Charles [ya**nof**skee] (1925–) Geneticist, born in New York City. He studied at the City College of New York and at Yale, then taught at Western Reserve University, OH. Working at Stanford on gene mutations from 1961, he used microbiological methods to prove that the sequence of bases in the genetic material DNA acts by determining the order of the amino acids which make up proteins, including the enzymes which control biochemical processes.

Yashin, Lev (1929–90) Footballer, born in Moscow. He played for Moscow Dynamo (1949–71) and for his country (1954–71), taking part in three World Cup tournaments. He was noted for his agility in goal.

Yates, Dornford, pseudonym of **Cecil William Mercer** (1885–1960) Novelist, born in London, England, UK. He studied at Oxford, and achieved great popularity with an entertaining series of fanciful escapist adventure fiction, such as *Berry and Co* (1921) and *Jonah and Co* (1922).

Yeager, Chuck [**yay**ger], popular name of **Charles E(lwood) Yeager** (1923–) The first pilot to break the sound barrier, born in Myra, WV. He trained as a fighter pilot, flying many missions in Europe, and was shot down over France. On 14 October he flew the Bell X-1 rocket research aircraft to a level speed of more than 670 mph, thus 'breaking the sound barrier'. In 1953, in the Bell X-1A, he flew at more than 21/2 times the speed of sound. He later commanded the USAF Aerospace Research Pilot School, and the 4th Fighter Bomber Wing.

Yeats, Jack B [yayts], popular name of **John Butler Yeats** (1870–1957) Painter, born in London, England, UK, the brother of W B Yeats. Educated in Co Sligo, his first works were illustrations and strip cartoons, such as 'Chubblock Homes' for *Comic Cuts*. He is best known for his colourful, freely painted pictures of Irish daily life and Celtic mythology, produced after 1915. >> Yeats, William Butler

Yeats, W(illiam) B(utler) [yayts] (1865–1939) Poet and playwright, born near Dublin. Educated at schools in London and Dublin, he became an art student, then turned to writing. In 1888 he published 'The Wanderings of Oisin', a long narrative poem that established his reputation. *The Celtic Twilight*, a book of peasant legends, appeared in 1893. His three most popular plays were *The Countess Cathleen* (1892), *The Land of Heart's Desire* (1894), and *Cathleen ni Houlihan* (1903), and he wrote several others for the Abbey Theatre, which he helped to found in 1904. He adopted a more direct style with *Responsibilities* (1914), which also marks a switch to contemporary subjects. The symbolic system described in *A Vision* (1925) informs many of his best-known poems, which appeared in *The Tower* (1928), *The Winding Stair* (1929), and *A Full Moon in March* (1935). He received the Nobel Prize for Literature in 1923, and also became a senator of the Irish Free State (1922–8). His *Collected Poems* were published in 1950. >> MacBride, Maud; Moore, George Augustus; Yeats, Jack B

Yeltsin, Boris (Nikolayevich) (1931–) Russian president, born in Bukta, Russia. He studied at the Urals Polytechnic, and began his career in the construction industry. He joined the Communist Party of the Soviet Union in 1961, and was appointed first secretary of the Sverdlovsk region in 1976. He was inducted into the Central Committee in 1981 by Gorbachev, and briefly worked under the new secretary for the economy, Ryzhkov, before being appointed Moscow party chief in 1985. A blunt-talking reformer, he rapidly set about renovating the corrupt 'Moscow machine', and was elected a candidate member of the Politburo in 1986, but in 1987, at a Central Committee plenum, after he had bluntly criticized party conservatives for sabotaging political and economic reform (*perestroíka*), he was downgraded to a lowly administrative post. He returned to public attention in 1989 by being elected to the new Congress of USSR People's Deputies, and in June 1991 he was elected president of the Russian Federation. Following the attempted coup to oust Gorbachev in August 1991, Yeltsin's political standing greatly increased when he led the protestors who defeated the coup, and following the break-up of the Soviet Union in December 1991 he remained in power as president of the Russian Federation. He continued to press for reform, but met increasing resistance from more conservative elements in the parliament. In 1993 he called for a referendum to measure his support, received a firm vote of confidence, and proposed a new constitution for Russia. Further confrontation with conservative hard-liners followed, leading to his decision to suspend parliament (Sep 1993), and a subsequent conflict involving the shelling of the Moscow parliament building (Oct), from which he emerged with his position strengthened. However, in 1995–6 opposition grew as a result of ongoing economic problems and the war in Chechnya, and although successful in the 1996 elections, continuing ill health was causing him major difficulties in 1997. >> Gorbachev; Ryzhkov; RR1085

Yentob, Alan (1947–) British broadcaster. He studied at Grenoble and Leeds universities, and joined the BBC in 1968, becoming a producer in 1970. He specialized in arts features, edited *Arena* (1978–85), and became head of BBC-TV music and arts in 1985. He was appointed controller of BBC2 television (1988–93), then of BBC1 (1993–6), playing a leading and controversial role in the process of re-thinking BBC policy which began in the early 1990s. In 1996 he was appointed director of programmes for BBC television. >> Birt

Yerkes, Charles (Tyson) [**yer**keez] (1837–1905) Financier, born in Philadelphia, PA. A clerk who worked as a commission broker, he made and lost several fortunes, headed the consortium that built Chicago's street railways, and in 1899 was forced to sell out in Chicago after allegations of political chicanery. He funded the Yerkes Observatory at the University of Chicago (1892), and converted the London Underground system to electricity (1900).

Yersin, Alexandre Emile John [yairsî] (1863–1943) Bacteriologist, born in Aubonne, Switzerland. He studied at Lausanne, Marburg, and Paris universities, then carried out research at the Pasteur Institute in Paris, working along with Emile Roux on diphtheria antitoxin. In Hong Kong in 1894, he discovered the plague bacillus, now called *Yersinia* in his honour, at the same time as Kitasato. He developed a serum against it, and founded two Pasteur Institutes in China. He also introduced the rubber tree into Indo-China. >> Kitazato; Roux, Emile

Yesenin, Sergey [ye**say**nin] (1895–1925) Poet, born in Yesenino (formerly, Konstantino), Russia. He left home at 17, and gained literary success with his first volume

Radunitsa (1916, Mourning for the Dead). He was four times married (his third wife was Isadora Duncan), and his suicide in St Petersburg prompted a wave of imitative suicides in Russia. >> Duncan, Isadora

Yevtushenko, Yevegeny (Alexandrovich) [yevtushengkoh] (1933–) Poet, born in Zima, Russia. He moved to Moscow in 1944, where he studied at the Gorky Institute of Literature. His early poetry, such as *The Third Snow* (1955, trans title), made him a spokesman for the young post-Stalin generation. His long narrative poem *Zima Junction* (1961), considering issues raised by the death of Stalin, prompted criticism, as did his *Babi Yar* (1962) which attacked anti-Semitism. In 1960 he began to travel abroad to give readings of his poetry. Three volumes of his selected poems appeared in 1987, and among later works are *Pre-morning* (1995). His first major stage piece, *Under the Skin of the Statue of Liberty*, was a huge success in 1972. Since the 1970s his artistic pursuits has widened considerably. He has written novels and other prose works, and engaged in acting, film directing, and photography. Always ready to express his beliefs, even in an unfavourable political climate, he publicly supported Solzhenitsyn when the novelist was arrested in 1974. He became a member of the Congress of People's Deputies in 1989. >> Solzhenitsyn

Yezhov, Nikolai [yezhof] (1895–?1939) Soviet secret police chief, born in St Petersburg, Russia. A provincial party official, he was appointed by Stalin as head of the NKVD (1936), led the purge of army officers, and staged the show-trials (1937–8) that removed many of Stalin's potential rivals. He was replaced by Beria in December 1938, disappeared two months later, and is presumed to have suffered the same fate as his victims. >> Beria; Stalin

Yonai, Mitsumasa [yoniy] (1880–1940) Japanese naval officer, statesman, and prime minster (1940), born in Iwate Prefecture, Japan. Educated at the Naval Academy, Etajima, he served in Russia (1915–17). He was commander of the imperial fleet (1936–7), navy minister (1937–9, 1944–5), and was briefly prime minister.

Yonge, Charlotte M(ary) [yung] (1823–1901) Novelist, born in Otterbourne, Hampshire, S England, UK. She achieved a great popular success with her *The Heir of Redclyffe* (1853), and in all she published some 120 volumes of fiction, High Church in tone, which helped to spread the Oxford Movement. She also published children's books, historical works, translated a great deal, and edited a magazine for girls, *The Monthly Packet*.

Yongle or **Yung-lo** [yonglay], originally **Zhu Di** (1360–1424) Third emperor (1403–24) of the Chinese Ming dynasty (1368–1644), known postumously as Chengzu, born in Nanking, China. The fourth son of Hongwu, he seized the crown from his nephew after much bloodshed. He moved the capital to Beijing (1421) and reconstructed the Grand Canal, developed central and local government organs, and instituted the civil service examination format which lasted to the 20th-c. He also patronized Confucianism, published the Buddhist Tripitaka, sponsored the Great Encyclopaedia (1408), and sent Zheng He to sea. He conquered the Mongols in five campaigns (dying on the fifth), annexed Annan, and enforced tribute from Borneo, Japan, Java, Korea, Siam, and SE India. >> Hongwu; Zheng He

York, Alvin (Cullum) (1887–1964) US soldier and popular hero, born in Pall Mall, TN. His fundamentalist Christian religion taught him to disapprove of war, but he resolved his doubts after joining the army in 1917. While in France, he led a small detachment against a German machine-gun emplacement, in which he killed 25 of the enemy, inducing 132 Germans to surrender. The greatest US hero of World War 1, he was awarded the Congressional Medal of Honor and returned home to a ticker-tape parade. He was

a founder of the American Legion, and Gary Cooper portrayed him in the movie *Sergeant York* (1941).

York, Prince Andrew, Duke of >> **Andrew, Prince**

York, Princess Beatrice of >> **Andrew, Prince**

York, Princess Eugenie of >> **Andrew, Prince**

York, Michael, stage name of **Michael York-Johnson** (1942–) Actor, born in Fulmer, Buckinghamshire, SC England, UK. He studied at Oxford, then joined the Dundee Repertory Theatre (1964) and the National Theatre Company (1965). He has appeared in a wide range of roles for both cinema and television. His films include *The Taming of the Shrew* (1966), *Cabaret* (1971), *Murder on the Orient Express* (1974), *The Joker* (1988), *The Prodigal Father* (1991), and *Austin Powers: International Man of Mystery* (1997). Television appearances include *Jesus of Nazareth* (1976), *The Far Country* (1985), and *The Night of the Fox* (1990). An autobiography, *Travelling Player*, appeared in 1991.

York, Richard, Duke of (?1473–1483) >> **Edward V**

York, Richard, 3rd Duke of (1411–60) English nobleman, claimant to the English throne, and father of Edward IV, Richard III, and George, Duke of Clarence. He loyally served the weak-minded Henry VI in Ireland and France, and was appointed protector during his illnesses, but was always in conflict with the king's wife, Margaret of Anjou, and her Lancastrian forces. In 1460 he marched on Westminster and claimed the crown, was promised the succession and appointed protector again, but was killed in a rising by Lancastrian forces in Wakefield. >> Clarence; Edward IV; Henry VI; Margaret of Anjou; Richard III

Yorkshire Ripper, The >> **Sutcliffe, Peter**

Yoshida, Shigeru [yosheeda] (1878–1967) Japanese statesman and prime minister (1946–7, 1948–54), born in Tokyo. He studied at Tokyo Imperial University, entered diplomacy in 1906, and after service in several capitals was vice-minister for foreign affairs. He was ambassador to Italy (1930–2) and ambassador in London (1936–8). During World War 2 he tried to persuade the Japanese to surrender early in 1945. He became foreign minister (Oct 1945), and formed the government which inaugurated the new constitution in 1946. He was re-elected in 1950 and resigned in 1954, retiring from politics soon after.

Young, Andrew (Jackson), Jr (1932–) Civil rights activist, Protestant minister, and public official, born in New Orleans, LA. As a minister, he joined the Southern Christian Leadership Conference (SCLC) in 1960, and came to be one of the closest associates of Martin Luther King. As the SCLC's executive director (1964–70), he took an active role in working at desegregation. Elected as a Democrat to the US House of Representatives (1973–7), he was the first African-American to represent Georgia in Congress since 1871. In 1977 he became US representative to the UN, but was forced to resign in 1979 after it was revealed that he had met secretly with members of the PLO. He served as Mayor of Atlanta, GA (1981–9), and continued to be moderate within the African-American community. >> King, Martin Luther

Young, Arthur (1741–1820) Agricultural and travel writer, born in London, England, UK. He spent much of his life in Bradfield, Suffolk, where he rented a small farm, and carried out many agricultural experiments. In 1793 he became secretary to the Board of Agriculture. In his writings, he helped to elevate agriculture to a science, founding and editing the monthly *Annals of Agriculture* in 1784.

Young, Brigham (1801–77) Mormon leader, born in Whitingham, VT. Converted in 1832, he became one of the 12 apostles of the Church in 1835, and its president upon the death of Joseph Smith in 1844. After the Mormons were driven from Nauvoo, he led them to Utah (1847), where they founded Salt Lake City. He was appointed

Governor of Utah in 1850, but was replaced in 1857 when an army was sent to establish federal law in the territory. He established over 300 towns and settlements, had over 20 wives (estimates vary), and was the father of more than 40 children. >> Smith, Joseph

Young, Chic, pseudonym of **Murat Bernard Young** (1901–73) Strip cartoonist, the creator of the popular *Blondie*, born in Chicago, IL. From an artistic family, he studied art at the Chicago Institute, took various jobs, then joined Newspaper Enterprise Association, creating his first strip, *Affairs of Jane*, in 1920. Pretty girls were to dominate his career: *Beautiful Bab* (1922), *Dumb Dora* (1925), and finally *Blondie* (1930), which became King Features most widely syndicated strip, with the millionaire's daughter, Blondie Boopadoop, developing into a suburban housewife and mother of two. Twenty-eight films were based on the strip, as well as radio and television series.

Young, Cy, popular name of **Denton True Young** (1867–1955) Baseball pitcher, born in Gilmore, OH. One of the first of baseball's greats, he made his major-league debut in 1890 and played until 1911. During his career he threw 749 complete games and won 511 games, both records. National and American League's leading pitchers win the Cy Young Award every year. >> RR1145

Young (of Graffham), David (Ivor), Baron (1932–) British statesman and businessman. He studied at University College, London, and became an executive with the large clothing and household goods company, Great Universal Stores (1956–61). He was appointed director of the Centre for Policy Studies, a right-wing 'think tank' (1979–82), under Margaret Thatcher, and was chairman of the Manpower Services Commission (1981–4). Created a life peer (1984), he was brought into the Thatcher Cabinet, becoming secretary of state for employment (1985–7), and secretary of state for trade and industry (1987–9), then returned to commerce as chairman of Cable and Wireless (1990–5). >> Thatcher

Young, Edward (1683–1765) Poet, born in Upham, Hampshire, S England, UK. He studied at Oxford, becoming a fellow of All Souls, Oxford in 1708. His early work met with little success. He is best known for 'The Complaint, or, Night-Thoughts on Life, Death and Immortality' (1742–6), inspired by the deaths in quick succession of his stepdaughter, son-in-law, and wife. It is a highly acclaimed piece of work, and some of its lines have passed into proverbial use (such as 'Procrastination is the thief of time').

Young, Francis Brett (1884–1954) Novelist, born in Halesowen, West Midlands, C England, UK. Established first as a physician, with a period as ship's doctor, he achieved celebrity as a writer with *Portrait of Clare* (1927, James Tait Black). From then on he wrote a succession of novels of leisurely charm, characterized by a deep love of his native country. Noteworthy titles are *My Brother Jonathan* (1928), *Far Forest* (1936), *Dr Bradley Remembers* (1935), *A Man about the House* (1942), and *Portrait of a Village* (1951).

Young, George Malcolm (1882–1959) Historical essayist, born in Greenhithe, Kent, SE England, UK. He studied at Oxford, joined the board of education in 1908, then became joint secretary of the new Ministry of Reconstruction (1917). Disillusioned with the civil service, he took up writing, publishing a life of Gibbon (1932), and editing *Early Victorian England* (2 vols, 1934). His other works include *Charles I and Cromwell* (1935), *Daylight and Champaign* (1937), and *Today and Yesterday* (1948).

Young, Jimmy, professional name of **Leslie Ronald Young** (1923–) British broadcaster and singer. He was educated in Cinderford, Gloucestershire, and served in the Royal Air Force (1939–46). He had several hit records in the 1950s, topping the charts with 'Unchained Melody' and 'The Man

From Laramie' in 1955, and becoming the first British singer to have two consecutive No 1 hits. He also became a radio presenter in the 1950s, introducing such programmes as *Flat Spin* and *Housewives' Choice*, and is now best known in the UK as the presenter of the *Jimmy Young* programme on BBC radio, which has been running since 1967. He has published a series of popular *Cookbooks*, and two volumes of autobiography, *JY* (1973) and *Jimmy Young* (1982).

Young, Lester (Willis), nickname **Prez** (1909–59) Tenor saxophonist, born in Woodville, MS. He first played alto saxophone in a family band, but changed to tenor saxophone in 1927 and worked with a succession of bands in the mid-west, before joining the newly-formed Count Basie Orchestra in 1934 for a spell, rejoining it in 1936. The band's rise to national prominence in the late 1930s brought him recognition as an innovative soloist, whose light tone marked a break from the swing-style saxophone, and inspired such modernists as Charlie Parker. >> Basie; Parker, Charlie

Young (of Dartington), Michael Young, Baron (1915–) British educationalist. He studied at London University, then trained as a barrister at Gray's Inn. He became director of the Institute of Community Studies in 1953, and chairman and later president of the Consumers Association in 1965. He also played a leading role in the development of 'distance learning' in the Third World and, via the National Extension College, within Britain. His publications include *The Rise of the Meritocracy* (1958), *Distance Teaching for the Third World* (1980), *The Metronomic Society* (1988), and *Life After Work – the Arrival of the Ageless Society* (1991). He was created a life peer in 1978.

Young, Neil (Percival) (1945–) Singer, songwriter, and guitarist, born in Toronto, Ontario, Canada. He was founding member of the folk-rock band Buffalo Springfield (1966–8) in Los Angeles, CA, worked with the groups Crazy Horse and Crosby, Stills and Nash (1969–74), then pursued a solo career. Much influenced by Bob Dylan, he has released over 20 albums, including the number 1 hit *Harvest* (1972), *Reactor* (1981), and *Freedom* (1989). His ballad 'Philadelphia' from the soundtrack of the film was Oscarnominated in 1994, and he also wrote the music for the 1995 film *Dead Man Walking*. >> Dylan, Bob

Young, Simone (1961–) Conductor, born in Sydney, New South Wales, Australia. She studied at the Sydney Conservatorium of Music, joining the Australian Opera in 1982. In 1987 she was engaged by Cologne State Opera, first as repetiteur then as assistant conductor, and became the first woman to conduct the Vienna Volksoper, the Vienna Staatsoper, and the Paris Opera. In 1994 she made her British debut at the Royal Opera House, Covent Garden, and in 1996 her American debut at the Metropolitan Opera House, New York City. In 2001 she will become musical director for Opera Australia.

Young, Thomas (1773–1829) Physicist, physician, and egyptologist, born in Milverton, Somerset, SW England, UK. He studied medicine at London, Edinburgh, Göttingen, and Cambridge universities, then devoted himself to scientific research, becoming professor of natural philosophy to the Royal Institution (1801). His *Lectures* (1807) expounded the doctrine of interference, which established the wave theory of light. He proposed that the eye required only three basic colour receptors for full colour vision – red, green, and blue. He also did valuable work in insurance, haemodynamics, and egyptology, and made a fundamental contribution to the deciphering of the inscriptions on the Rosetta Stone.

Young, Whitney M(oore), Jr (1921–71) Social reformer, born in Lincoln Ridge, KY. He studied at the University of Minnesota (1947) and became dean of the Atlanta School of Social Work (1954–61). While a visiting scholar at Harvard University (1960–1), he was named executive director of the Urban League (1961–71). Author of *To Be Equal* (1964) and *Beyond Racism* (1969), and recipient of a Presidential Medal of Freedom (1969), he worked to improve African-Americans' conditions in the community, until his untimely death by drowning while on a visit to Africa.

Younger, (Thomas) Cole(man) (1844–1916) Bandit, born in Jackson Co, MO. He was one of 'Quantrill's raiders' during the Civil War. He joined with Jesse James and formed the James–Younger band, which included Cole and his two brothers, **James** and **Robert**. Shot and captured during a failed bank raid in Northfield, MN, the three brothers were sentenced to life imprisonment. Robert died in 1889 of tuberculosis, Cole and James were paroled in 1901, and James committed suicide in 1902. Cole was pardoned in 1903, and remained a law-abiding citizen in his old age. >> James, Jesse; Quantrill

Younghusband, Sir Francis Edward (1863–1942) British soldier and explorer, born in Murree, India. He explored Manchuria in 1886, and on the way back discovered the route from Kashgar into India via the Mustagh Pass. In 1902 he went on the expedition which opened up Tibet to the Western world. British resident in Kashmir (1906–9), he wrote much on India and C Asia. He founded the World Congress of Faiths in 1936.

Yourcenar, Marguerite [yersenah(r)], pseudonym of **Marguerite de Crayencour** (1903–87) Novelist and poet, born in Brussels. Educated at home in a wealthy and cultured household, she travelled widely, and wrote a series of distinguished novels, plays, poems, and essays. Her novels, many of them historical reconstructions, include *Les Mémoires d'Hadrien* (1951, Memoirs of Hadrian) and *L'oeuvre au noir* (1968, trans The Abyss). She emigrated to the USA in 1939, was granted dual US and French nationality in 1979, and in 1980 became the first woman writer to be elected to the Académie Française.

Ypres, Earl of >> French, John

Yrigoyen, Hipólito >> **Irigoyen, Hipólito**

Yuan Shikai [yüan sheekiy], also spelled **Yuan Shih-k'ai** (1859–1916) Chinese soldier, statesman, and president (1912–16), born in Xiancheng, Henan, China. He served in the army and became imperial adviser, minister in Korea (1885–94), and Governor of Shantung (1900). Banished after the death of his patron, the Empress Dowager Ci-Xi (1908), he was recalled after the successful Wuhan nationalist rising in 1911, and became the first President of China in 1912. He lost support by procuring the murder of the parliamentary leader of the Nationalists, accepting Japan's Twenty-One Demands of 1915, and proclaiming himself emperor (1915), and was overthrown in a Japanese-backed rebellion. >> Ci-Xi; Wu Peifu; RR1040

Yukawa, Hideki [yukahwa] (1907–81) Physicist, born in Tokyo. He studied at Kyoto University, where he became a lecturer (1929–33), before moving to Osaka (1933–9). Professor of physics at Kyoto University (1939–50) and director of Kyoto Research Institute (1953–70), he was visiting professor at Princeton and Columbia universities (1948–53). He predicted (1935) the existence of the meson, a particle hundreds of times heavier than the electron, developed a theory of strong nuclear forces, and for his work on quantum theory and nuclear physics was awarded the Nobel Prize for Physics in 1949, the first Japanese to be so honoured.

Yung-lo >> **Yongle**

Yunupingu, Mandawuy [yunupinggoo, mandawoy] (1956–) Singer, born in Yirrkala, a former Methodist mission in NE Arnhem Land, Northern Territory, Australia. He studied education at Deakin University, and became principal of the local school, one of the first Aboriginal headmasters in the country. A member of one of the leading families in the Gumatj clans, in 1986 he established the group *Yothu Yindi* ('mother–child' in Yolngu-matha). Since then the group has achieved wide success in terms of sales, critical acclaim, and promotion of a political message. In 1993 he was made Australian of the Year, an honour also bestowed on his brother **Galarrwuy** in 1978.

Zabaleta, Nicanor [thabalayta] (1907–93) Harpist, born in San Sebastian, Spain. He studied in Madrid and Paris, where he made his debut in 1925. He was influential in popularizing the harp's solo repertory, and several composers wrote works for him.

Zaccaria, St Antonio Maria [zakahria] (1502–39) Italian religious. Ordained a priest in 1528, he founded the Barnabite preaching order (1530) and the Angelicals of St Paul order for women (1535). He was canonized in 1897. Feast day 5 July.

Zacharias, St (?–752) Pope (741–52), born in San Severino, Italy, of Greek parents. By recognizing Pepin III as King of the Franks (752), he established the link between the papcy and the Carolingian empire. He is best known in the East for his translation into Greek of the *Dialogues* of Pope Gregory the Great. Feast day 15 March. >> Gregory I; Pepin III

Zadkiel [zadkeel], pseudonym of **Richard James Morrison** (1794–1874) English astrologer. After service in the Royal Navy (1806–29) he started a best selling astrological almanac in 1831, *Zadkiel's Almanac.*

Zadkine, Ossip [zadkeen] (1890–1967) Sculptor, born in Smolensk, Russia. He settled in Paris in 1909, and developed an individual Cubist style, making effective use of the play of light on concave surfaces, as in 'The Three Musicians' (1926), 'Orpheus' (1940), and the war memorial in Rotterdam, entitled 'The Destroyed City' (1952).

Zaharias, Babe >> **Didrikson, Babe**

Zaharoff, Sir Basil [zaharof], originally **Basileios Zacharias** (1849–1936) Armaments magnate and financier, born in Anatolia, Turkey. He amassed a fortune from arms sales (1880–1900), became a French citizen in 1913, and was knighted by the British in 1918 for his services to the Allies in World War 1. He donated large sums of money to universities and other institutions.

Zahir Shah, King Mohammed [zaheer shah] (1914–   ) King of Afghanistan (1933–73), born in Kabul. He studied in Kabul and Paris, and was assistant minister for national defence and education minister before succeeding to the throne, after the assassination of his father, Nadir Shah (c.1880–1933). His reign was characterized by a concern to preserve neutrality and promote gradual modernization. He became a constitutional monarch in 1964. While in Italy receiving medical treatment, he was overthrown in a republican coup led by his cousin, General Daud Khan, in the wake of a three-year famine. He then lived in exile in Rome, and became a popular symbol of national unity for moderate Afghan opposition groups. >> RR1031

Zai Tian [dziy tyen], also spelled **Tsai-t'ien**, reign title **Guang Xu** (1871–1908) Ninth emperor of the Qing dynasty (1875–1908), who remained largely under the control of the Empress Dowager Ci-Xi. In 1898, after the defeat of China by Japan (1894–5), he was determined to reform and strengthen China, and threatened to abdicate if not given full authority. He issued a series of reforming edicts, but his attempts to gain power precipitated a coup. He was confined to his palace until his mysterious death one day before the death of the Empress Dowager. >> Ci-Xi; RR1040

Zakharov, Rostislav [zakhahrof] (1907–84) Dancer, choreographer, ballet director, and teacher, born in Astrakhan, Russia. He joined both the Kharkov and Kirov Ballets as soloist and choreographer, while continuing to study (until 1932) at the Leningrad Theatre Institute. He was accepted into the Kirov Theatre, where he choreographed

The Fountain of Bakhchisaray, a milestone in Soviet ballet because of the depth with which its characters were delineated. He was associated with the Bolshoi Ballet from 1936 until the mid-1950s, variously as artistic director, choreographer, and tutor.

Zamenhof, L(azarus) L(udwig) [zamenof], pseudonym **Doktoro Esperanto** (1859–1917) Oculist and philologist, born in Białystok, Poland. A pioneering advocate of an international language to promote world peace, he invented Esperanto ('One who hopes'). The first international Esperanto congress was held in 1905, and although he often spoke at this and later conferences, he would not accept formal leadership of the movement.

Zamyatin, Yevgeny Ivanovich [zamyatin], also spelled **Zamiatin** (1884–1937) Writer, born in Lebedyan, Russia. In 1914 he wrote a novella, *At the World's End*, satirizing the life of army officers, and was tried but acquitted of 'maligning the officer corps'. He lived in Newcastle upon Tyne in 1916–17, where he wrote two satires on the English, *Islanders* and *A Fisher of Men*, both set in Newcastle. Although supportive of the 1917 revolution, he was also an outspoken critic, and he was among the first writers to be hounded by the party *apparatchiks*. In 1920 he wrote *My* (We), which was circulated in manuscript (and never published in the USSR), a fantasy set in the 26th-c AD; this prophesied Stalinism and the totalitarian state, and led to the banning of his works. His best stories are contained in *The Dragon*, first published in English in 1966. With Gorky's help he was allowed to leave Russia in 1931, and he settled for exile in Paris. >> Gorky, Maxim

Zangwill, Israel (1864–1926) Writer, born in London, England, UK. He studied at London University, and became a journalist, as editor of the comic journal *Ariel*. A leading Zionist, he was widely known for his novels on Jewish themes, such as *Children of the Ghetto* (1892) and *Ghetto Tragedies* (1893). Other works include the play *The Melting Pot* (1908).

Zanuck, Darryl F(rancis) [zanuhk] (1902–79) Film producer, born in Wahoo, NE. He started as a scriptwriter with Warner Brothers, and soon became executive producer. He led the change to sound with *The Jazz Singer* (1927), his other notable productions of that period including *Little Caesar* (1930), *The Grapes of Wrath* (1940), and *How Green Was My Valley?* (1941). He co-founded Twentieth-Century Pictures (1933) and, after its merger with Fox Films in 1935, was controlling executive of Twentieth-Century Fox Films Corporation (president from 1965). Among his many successful titles are *The Longest Day* (1962), *Those Magnificent Men in Their Flying Machines* (1965), and *The Sound of Music* (1965). He retired in 1971.

Zapata, Emiliano [sapahta] (1879–1919) Mexican revolutionary, born in Anencuilio, Mexico. He became a sharecropper and local leader, and after the onset of the Mexican Revolution he mounted a land distribution programme in areas under his control. Along with Pancho Villa, he fought the Carranza government, and was eventually lured to his death at the Chinameca hacienda. >> Villa

Zappa, Frank, popular name of **Francis Vincent Zappa** (1940–93) Avant-garde rock musician and composer, born in Baltimore, MD. He led the satirical 'underground' band The Mothers of Invention (with varying line-ups) in the 1960s and 1970s, making inventive and often scabrous albums such as *Freak-Out!* (1966) and *We're Only in it for the*

Money (1967, a parody of the Beatles' *Sergeant Pepper* album). Influential solo albums included *Lumpy Gravy* (1968) and *Hot Rats* (1969); and from various new groupings of Mothers came *Just Another Band from LA, Over-Nite Sensation*, and more. He created and scored the film *200 Motels*, and composed 'serious' music, performed by Zubin Mehta, Pierre Boulez, and others.

Zarathustra >> **Zoroaster**

Zaslavskaya, Tatyana Ivanova [zaslavskaya] (1927–) Economist and sociologist, born in Kiev, Ukraine. She studied at Moscow University, and wrote the 'Novosibirsk Memorandum' (1983), a criticism of the Soviet economic system which was one of the factors behind policy change in Russia in the late 1980s. She joined the Communist Party in 1954, and has been a full member of the Soviet Academy of Sciences since 1981. She was personal adviser to President Gorbachev on economic and social matters. As an academic, she has been involved in the development of economic sociology. >> **Gorbachev**

Zatopek, Emil [zatopek] (1922–) Athlete and middle-distance runner, born in Kopřivnice, Czech Republic. After many successes in Czechoslovak track events, he won the gold medal for the 10 000 m at the 1948 Olympics in London. For the next six years, despite an astonishingly laboured style, he proved himself to be the greatest long-distance runner of his time, breaking 13 world records. In the 1952 Olympics in Helsinki he achieved a remarkable golden treble: he retained his gold medal in the 10 000 m, and also won the 5000 m and the marathon – the only athlete to complete such a feat at one Olympiad. His wife, fellow athlete **Dana Zatopkova** (*née* **Ingrova**) (1922–), also won a gold medal (for the javelin) in 1952. >> **RR1135**

Zeckendorf, William (1905–76) Real estate developer, born in Paris, IL. He spent his career in real estate, after 1938 with Webb & Knapp, New York City, of which he became sole owner in 1949. Before the company's spectacular bankruptcy in 1965, he embodied glamorous real estate dealmaking. He put together the UN site in New York, and initiated major urban renewal developments.

Zeeman, Sir Erik Christopher (1925–) British mathematician. He studied at Cambridge, and became professor of mathematics at Warwick University (1964–88). Early work developing topology and catastrophe theory produced many applications to physics, social sciences, and economics. He became principal of Hertford College, Oxford (1988–95), and was knighted in 1991.

Zeeman, Pieter (1865–1943) Physicist, born in Zonnemaire, The Netherlands. He studied at Leyden under Lorentz, became a lecturer there (1890), and was appointed professor at Amsterdam (1900), and director of the Physical Insitute (1908). While at Leyden he discovered the *Zeeman effect* – when a ray of light from a source placed in a magnetic field is examined spectroscopically, the spectral line splits into several components. This discovery confirmed Lorentz's theory of electromagnetic radiation, and has helped physicists investigate atoms, and astronomers to measure the magetic field of stars. In 1902 he shared with Lorentz the Nobel Prize for Physics. >> **Lorentz**

Zeffirelli, Franco [zefirelee] (1923–) Stage, opera, and film director, born in Florence, Italy. He began his career as an actor and designer (1945–51), and during the 1950s produced many operas in Italy and abroad. His stage productions include *Romeo and Juliet* at the Old Vic (1960), universally acclaimed for its originality, modern relevance, and realistic setting in a recognizable Verona, and *Who's Afraid of Virginia Woolf* (1964). He has also filmed lively and spectacular versions of *The Taming of the Shrew* (1966) and *Romeo and Juliet* (1968), and *Jesus of Nazareth* (1977) for television. Later productions include *Young Toscanini* (1988),

Hamlet (1990), film versions of the operas *La traviata* (1983) and *Otello* (1986), and *Jane Eyre* (1996).

Zeiss, Carl [tsiys] (1816–88) Optician and industrialist, born in Weimar, Germany. In 1846 he established at Jena the factory which became noted for the production of lenses, microscopes, field glasses, and other optical instruments. His business was organized on a system whereby the workers had a share in the profits.

Zemlinsky, Alexander von [zemlinskee] (1871–1942) Composer and conductor, born in Vienna. He studied at the Vienna Conservatory, and conducted in Vienna (1906–11), Prague (1911–27), and Berlin (1927–32). His compositions, in post-Romantic style, include seven complete and six incomplete operas, orchestral works, chamber music, choral works, and songs. In 1934 he emigrated to the USA.

Zeng Guofan [dzeng gwohfan], also spelled **Tseng Kuo-fan** (1811–72) Provincial administrator, born in Hsianghsiang, Hunan Province, China. He suppressed the Taiping Rebellion in 1864 with a S Chinese Confucian army. Seeking to regenerate China, he supported the improvements in technical and linguistic education, including US scholarships, and the development of industries such as munitions and shipbuilding. He led negotiations with the West following the Tianjin massacre (1870). The New Life Movement in the 20th-c reflected his ideals.

Zeno of Citium [zeenoh, sishium] (c. 336–c. 265 BC) Philosopher, the founder of the Stoic school, born in Citium, Cyprus. He went to Athens c.315 BC, where he attended Plato's Academy and other philosophical schools, then opened his own school at the *Stoa poikile* ('painted colonnade'), from which the name of his philosophy, Stoicism, derives. >> **Cleanthes; Plato**

Zeno of Elea [zeenoh, eelia] (c. 490–c. 420 BC) Greek philosopher, a native of Elea, Italy. A favourite disciple of Parmenides, he became known for a series of paradoxes, many of which denied the possibility of spatial division or motion. The best known is 'Achilles and the Tortoise', whose conclusion is that no matter how fast Achilles runs, he cannot overtake a tortoise, if the tortoise has a head start. The rigour and dialectical nature of his arguments influenced Socrates' philosophical technique. >> **Parmenides; Socrates**

Zenobia [zenohbia] (3rd-c) Queen of Palmyra (in modern Syria), born there probably of Arab descent. She became the wife of the Bedouin Odenathus, lord of the city, who in AD 264 was recognized by Gallienus as Governor of the East. On her husband's murder (c.267) she embarked on a war of expansion, conquered Egypt in 269, and in 270 overran nearly the whole of the E provinces in Asia Minor, and declared her son the Eastern emperor. When Aurelian became emperor he marched against her and defeated her at Antioch (now Antakya, Turkey). She was led in triumphal procession at Rome, and later married a Roman senator. >> **Aurelian; Gallienus; Longinus**

Zephaniah [zefaniya] (7th-c BC) Old Testament prophet of the time of King Josiah of Judah. His account of a coming Day of Wrath inspired the mediaeval Latin hymn *Dies irae*.

Zeppelin, Ferdinand (Adolf August Heinrich), Graf von (Count of) (1838–1917) German army officer, born in Konstanz, Germany. He served in the Franco-Prussian War, and in 1897–1900 constructed his first airship, setting up a factory for their construction at Friedrichshafen. Over 100 *zeppelins* were used in World War 1. >> **Eckener**

Zermelo, Ernst Friedrich Ferdinand [tsairmeloh] (1871–1953) Mathematician, born in Berlin. He studied at Berlin, Halle, and Freiburg universities, and was professor at Göttingen (1905–10) and Zürich (1910–16). He gave the first axiomatic description of set theory in 1908. Although later modified to avoid the paradoxes discovered by Bertrand Russell and others, it remains one of the standard methods of axiomatizing the theory. He also first revealed the importance of the axiom of choice, when he proved in 1904 that any set could be well-ordered, a key result in many mathematical applications of set theory. >> Cantor, Georg; Russell, Bertrand

Zernike, Frits [**zair**nikuh] (1888–1966) Physicist, born in Amsterdam. Professor of physics at Groningen University (1910–58), he developed the phase-contrast microscope (1938), which allows the study of internal cell structure without the use of stains that kill the cell. He was awarded the Nobel Prize for Physics in 1953.

Zetkin, Clara, *née* **Eissner** (1857–1933) Communist leader, born in Wiederau, Germany. While studying at Leipzig Teacher's College for Women she became a Socialist and staunch feminist, and from 1881 to 1917 was a member of the Social Democratic Party. In 1917 she was one of the founders of the radical Independent Social Democratic Party (the Spartacus League), and became a founder of the German Communist Party (1919). A strong supporter of the Russian Revolution, and a friend of Lenin, her influence waned after Lenin's death. >> Lenin

Zeuss, Johann Kaspar [tsoys] (1806–56) Philologist, born in Vogtendorf, Germany. He became a professor of history, and was the founder of Celtic philology. His *Grammatica celtica* (1853) is one of the great philological achievements of the century. He also wrote a number of historical works.

Zeuxis [**zyook**sis] (5th-c BC) Painter, born in Heraclea, Greece. He excelled in the representation of natural objects. According to legend, his painting of a bunch of grapes was so realistic that birds tried to eat the fruit.

Zhang Guotao [jang gwohtow], also spelled **Chang Kuo-t'ao** (1897–1979) Founding member of the Chinese Communist Party, born in Jiangxi, China. As a student he played a part in the May Fourth Movement of 1919, and in 1921 joined the new Chinese Communist Party, rising to prominence as a labour leader. He also had a leading role in the Nanchang Mutiny (1927). He opposed the elevation of Mao Zedong as leader of the Party, but his army was destroyed by Muslim forces in the NW. He defected to the Nationalists in 1938 and, when the Communists won national power in 1949, moved to Hong Kong. >> Mao Zedong

Zhang Heng [jang heng], also spelled **Chang Heng** (78–139) Chinese scientist who invented the seismograph (132). He also calculated the value of π, built an armillary sphere with horizon and meridian rings, and realized natural phenomena were not caused by the supernatural. He understood the Earth was spherical, and that the Moon was lit by the Sun, revolved around the Earth, and was eclipsed by Earth's shadow. He explained the shortening/lengthening of days, and invented the grid system in cartography. >> Copernicus

Zhang Qian [jang chyan], also spelled **Chang Ch'ien** (2nd-c BC) Chinese military officer, sent westwards (138–125 BC) by Han Emperor Wudi to ally with Bactria (modern Balkh, Afghanistan) to protect the Silk Road against the Huns. On his return, he was put in charge of the Foreign Office, and given the name 'great traveller'. His report comprises the major source for contemporary C Asia, and is preserved in Sima Qian's *Shi Ji* (100 BC). Zhang's great expedition, and a second in 115 BC, helped to increase imperial interest in a Western policy, most spectacularly demonstrated by Ban Chao over a century later. >> Ban Chao; Sima Qian; Wudi

Zhao Ziyang [jow zeeyang] (1918–) Chinese politician and prime minister (1980–9), born in Henan, China. He joined the Communist Youth League in 1932, rose to prominence implementing land reform in Guangdong

(1951–62), and became provincial first party secretary in 1964. He was dismissed during the Cultural Revolution (1966–9), rehabilitated in 1973, and appointed first party secretary of China's largest province, Sichuan, in 1975. Here he introduced radical and successful market-orientated rural reforms, which led to his induction into the Politburo as a full member in 1979 and his appointment as prime minister a year later. As premier, he oversaw the implementation of a radical new 'market socialist' and 'open door' economic programme, and in 1987 replaced the disgraced Hu Yaobang as Communist Party general secretary. In 1989, he was controversially dismissed for his allegedly over-liberal handling of student pro-democracy demonstrations in Beijing. >> Hu Yaobang; RR1040

Zheng He [zheng hay], also spelled **Cheng Ho** (1371–1433) Chinese admiral. By imperial commmand he led seven major voyages (1405–33) to E Africa, Arabia, the Indian Ocean and SE Asia – the earliest extensive naval expeditions in world history. The first (1405–7) to Java, Sumatra, Ceylon, and Calicut, took 63 'starry rafts' (up to 1500 tons, 162 x 66 m, 4 decks) and 255 smaller ships and 28 000 men. The second (1407–11, 249 ships) visited the Indies, Calicut, and Thailand. The third (1409, 48 ships) toured the Indies, SE Asia, and Ceylon. The fourth (1413–16, 63 ships) went with Arabic interpreters to the Maldives and Hormuz. The fifth (1416–18) called at Bengal, Hormuz, Aden, and Kenya (some probably went on to Mecca, as Zheng was Muslim). The sixth (1421–2, 41 ships) reached Mogadishu and Zanzibar. The seventh (1431–3, 100 ships) reached Bengal, Calicut, and Arabia, two members visiting Medina and Mecca. >> Faxian; Gama, Vasco da; Xuanzang

Zhivkov, Todor [zhiv**kof**] (1911–) Bulgarian statesman, prime minister (1962–71), and president (1971–89), born in Botevgrad, Bulgaria. He joined the (illegal) Communist Party in 1932, fought with the Bulgarian resistance in 1943, and took part in the Sofia coup that overthrew the pro-German regime in 1944. He became first secretary of the Bulgarian Communist Party in 1954, prime minister in 1962 and, as chairman of the Council of State in 1971, became effectively the president of the People's Republic. His period in office was characterized by unquestioned loyalty to the Soviet Union, and conservative policy-making, which led to mounting economic problems in the 1980s. He was eventually ousted in 1989 by the reformist Petar Mladenov in a committee-room coup and, with his health failing, was subsequently expelled from the Party, placed under house arrest, on charges of nepotism, corruption, embezzlement of $1 million, and the dictatorial abuse of power. He was found guilty and sentenced to seven years imprisonment in 1992.

Zhou Enlai [joh enliy], also spelled **Chou En-lai** (1898–1975) One of the leaders of the Communist Party of China, and prime minister of the Chinese People's Republic from its inception in 1949 until his death, born in Huaian, Kiangsu Province, China. In 1927 he became a member of the Politburo of the Communist Party of China, and in 1932 was appointed to succeed Mao Zedong as political commissar of the Red Army, but after 1935, following Mao's elevation, he served him faithfully, becoming the Party's chief negotiator and diplomat. As minister of foreign affairs (and concurrently prime minister) he vastly increased China's international influence. Perhaps his greatest triumph of mediation was in the Cultural Revolution in China, when he worked to preserve national unity and the survival of government against the forces of anarchy. >> Mao Zedong; RR1041

Zhuangzi [jwangtsee], also spelled **Chuang-tzu** (369–286 BC) Chinese Taoist philosopher, and minor official in S China. His *Zhuangzi*, of which 33 chapters survive, first mentioned the concepts of Laozi, and elaborated ideas on the *Tao* ('Way') to happiness, wealth, longevity, and freedom which later came into serious conflict with both Buddhism and Confucianism. Two passages are particularly famous; in one he speculates on atomism, the origins of life, and the meaning of the universe, displaying awareness of the concept of infinity and relativism; in the other, he relates a dream of himself as a butterfly, and his subsequent uncertainty on waking whether he was a butterfly dreaming he was a man. >> Laozi

Zhu Da [joo dah], also spelled **Chu-ta**, originally **Pa Ta Shan Jen** (c. 1625–1705) Painter, and Buddhist monk, born in Nan-ch'ang, China. A descendant of the Ming royal house, he entered a Buddhist monastery on the collapse of the Ming dynasty, and may have feigned madness to survive the purges of the Manchu conquerors. The individualism of his ink paintings of flowers, birds, fish, and landscapes appealed to the Japanese, and his style has become synonymous with Zen painting in Japan.

Zhu De [joo de], also spelled **Chu-teh** (1886–1976) One of the founders of the Chinese Red Army, born in Sichuan, China. He was closely associated throughout his later career with Mao Zedong. He took part in the Nanchang Mutiny (1927), his defeated troops joining with those of Mao to found the Jiangxi Soviet. There, he and Mao evolved the idea of 'people's war', beating off attacks by vastly superior Nationalist forces until finally driven out in 1934. The Red Army then undertook the Long March, in which Zhu De was the leading commander. >> Mao Zedong

Zhukov, Giorgiy Konstantinovich [zhookof] (1896–1974) Soviet marshal, born in Strelkovka, Russia. He joined the Red Army in 1918, commanded Soviet tanks in Outer Mongolia (1939), and became army chief-of-staff (1941). He lifted the siege of Moscow, and in 1943 his counter-offensive was successful at Stalingrad. In 1944–5 he captured Warsaw, conquered Berlin, and accepted the German surrender. After the war he was commander of the Russian zone of Germany, and became minister of defence (1955), but was dismissed by Khrushchev in 1957. >> Khrushchev; Paulus

Zhu Xi [joo shee], also spelled **Chu-hsi** (1130–1200) Philosopher, classical commentator, scientific thinker, and historian, born in Yu-hsi, Fukien Province, China. He was leader of the rationalist wing of the neo-Confucian school developing in China from the 10th-c. His *Collected Works* systematized previous Confucian thought and, allied to Buddhist and Taoist elements, established a creed for the perfection of state and society. His classical commentaries became prescribed orthodoxy in the civil service examinations from 1313, and his conservative authoritarianism increasingly dominated Chinese, Japanese, and Korean political, social, and cultural perceptions until the 20th-c (though a more individualistic neo-Confucianism developed in parallel from the 15th-c). He also wrote on musical notation, understood fossilization three centuries before Leonardo, realized that mountains had once been under the sea, saw the Earth's origins in condensation from cosmic matter, and perceived the universe as evolving and spinning from elemental force. >> Leonardo da Vinci; Sima Guang; Wang Yangming

Zia ul-Haq, Muhammad [zeea ul hak] (1924–88) Pakistani general and president (1978–88), born near Jullundhur, Punjab, India. He served in Burma, Malaya, and Indonesia in World War 2, and in the wars with India (1965, 1971), rising rapidly to become general and army chief-of-staff (1976). He led a bloodless coup in 1977, imposed martial law, banned political activity, and introduced an Islamic code of law. Despite international protest, he sanctioned the hanging of former President Bhutto in 1979. He

was killed in a plane crash near Bahawalpur. >> Bhutto, Zulfikar Ali; RR1080

Ziaur Rahman [zeeaoor ramahn] (1935–81) Bangladeshi soldier and president (1977–81). He played an important part in the emergence of the state of Bangladesh. Appointed chief of army staff after the assassination of Mujibur Rahman (1975), he became the dominant figure within the military. His government was of a military character, even after the presidential election of 1978 which confirmed his position. He survived many attempted coups, but was finally assassinated in Dhaka. His wife, **Khaleda Zia**, became prime minister in 1991. >> Rahman, Mujibur; RR1034

Ziegfeld, Florenz [zeegfeld] (1869–1932) Theatre manager, born in Chicago, IL. He devised and perfected the American revue spectacle, based on the *Folies Bergères*, and his *Follies of 1907* was the first of an annual series that continued until 1931, and made his name synonymous with extravagant theatrical production. The *Follies* featured a chorus line of some of America's most beautiful women, all personally chosen to 'glorify the American girl'. He also produced a wide range of other musical shows, such as *Show Boat* (1927) and *Bitter Sweet* (1929).

Ziegler, Karl [zeegler] (1898–1973) Chemist, born in Helsa, Germany. He studied at Marburg University, taught at Heidelberg and Halle, and in 1943 was appointed director of the Max Planck Carbon Research Institute at Mülheim. With Italian chemist Giulio Natta he was awarded the 1963 Nobel Prize for Chemistry for his research into long-chain polymers leading to new developments in industrial materials, such as polypropylene. >> Natta

Zimbalist, Efrem (1889–1985) Violinist and composer, born in Rostov, Russia. He became director of the Curtis Institute of Music in Philadelphia (1941–68), and composed for both violin and orchestra.

Zimmerman, Robert >> Dylan, Bob

Zimmermann, Arthur [tsimerman] (1864–1940) Politician, born in Marggrabowa, Germany. After diplomatic service in China, he directed from 1904 the E division of the German foreign office, and was foreign secretary (Nov 1916–Aug 1917). In January 1917 he sent the famous *Zimmermann telegram* to the German minister in Mexico with the terms of an alliance between Mexico and Germany, by which Mexico was to attack the USA with German and Japanese assistance in return for the American states of New Mexico, Texas, and Arizona. This telegram, intercepted and decoded by British Admiralty Intelligence, finally brought the hesitant US government into the war against Germany.

Zinder, Norton (David) (1928–) Geneticist, born in New York City. He studied at Columbia and Wisconsin universities, and became professor of genetics at Rockefeller University, New York City (1964). Studies with mutants of the bacterium *Salmonella* led him to discover bacterial transduction (the transfer, by a phage particle, of genetic material between bacteria) and led to new knowledge of the location and behaviour of bacterial genes.

Zinkernagel, Rolf M [zingkernahgel] (1944–) Immunologist, born in Basel, Switzerland. He studied at the University of Basel and at the Australian National University, Canberra, where he worked with Peter Doherty, then became a researcher at the Institute of Experimental Immunology in Zurich. He shared the Nobel Prize for Physiology or Medicine in 1996 for his contribution to the discovery of how the immune system recognizes virus-infected cells – research which was first reported in 1974. He also shared the Paul Erlich Prize (1983) and the Albert Lasker Medical Research Award (1995) for this research. >> Doherty

Zinnemann, Fred [**zin**uhman] (1907–97) Film director, born in Vienna. He studied law at the University of Vienna (1925–7), then cinematography in Paris (1927–8). He emigrated to the USA in 1929, and began making documentary films in Hollywood, notably *That Mothers Might Live* (1938, Oscar), and *Benjy* (1951, Oscar). A recurrent theme in his films concerns the conflict of conscience and moral dilemmas of reluctant heroes, as explored in the Oscar-nominated *High Noon* (1952), and two Oscar winners, *From Here to Eternity* (1953), and *A Man For All Seasons* (1966). Other notable films included *The Sundowners* (1960) and *The Day of the Jackal* (1973).

Zinoviev, Grigoriy Yevseyevich [zin**o**vyef], originally **Grigoriy Yevseyevich Radomyslskiy** (1883–1936) Russian Jewish revolutionary and politician, born in Kherson province, Ukraine. He studied at Bern University, and in 1924 was made a member of the ruling Politburo, but because of opposition to Stalin's policies was expelled from the Party (1926). Reinstated in 1928, he was again expelled in 1932, and in 1935 was arrested after the assassination of Kirov. Charged with organizing terrorist activities, he was executed following the first of Stalin's Great Purge trials in Moscow. The so-called *Zinoviev letter* urging British Communists to incite revolution in Britain contributed to the downfall of the Labour government in the 1924 general elections. >> Kirov; Stalin

Zinsser, Hans (1878–1940) Bacteriologist and immunologist, born in New York City. He studied at Columbia University, and taught there, at Stanford, and at Harvard (from 1923). He worked on many scientific problems, including allergy, the measurement of virus size, and the cause of rheumatic fever. He is best known for clarifying the rickettsial disease typhus, differentiating epidemic and endemic forms (the endemic form is still called *Brill–Zinsser's disease*). His *Textbook of Bacteriology* (1910) and *Infection and Resistance* (1914) became classics.

Zinzendorf, Nicolaus Ludwig, Graf von (Count of) [**tsin**tsendaw(r)f] (1700–60) Religious leader, born in Dresden, Germany. He studied at Wittenburg, and held a government post at Dresden. He invited the persecuted Moravians to his estates, and there founded for them the colony of *Herrnhut* ('the Lord's keeping'). His zeal led to conflict with the government, and he was exiled from Saxony in 1736. Ordained at Tübingen (1734), he became Bishop of the Moravian Brethren, and wrote over 100 books.

Ziolkovsky, Konstantin Eduardovitch [zyolk**of**skee] (1857–1935) Engineer, born in Ijevsk, Russia. He became a teacher in Kaluga (1892–1920), built the first wind tunnel in Russia (1891), designed large airships, and in 1903 published his first scientific paper on space flight. He continued to research designs of rocket-propelled aircraft and spacecraft, and in 1924 presented conceptual studies for manned orbital craft capable of re-entry. His outstanding work on the fundamental physics and engineering of space vehicles was recognized by the Soviet authorities, and all his works were translated into English by NASA in 1965.

Ziska, John [**zhish**ka] or **Žižka, Jan** (c. 1370–1424) Bohemian Hussite leader, born in Trocznov, Czech Republic. He fought against the Poles, Turks, and French, and soon after the murder of Huss, became chamberlain to Wenceslas IV. During the Civil War he was chosen leader of the popular party, captured Prague (1421), and erected the fortress of Tabor, his party coming to be called Taborites. Having lost both his eyes in battle, he continued to lead his troops in a series of victories, compelling Emperor Sigismund to offer the Hussites religious liberty, but he died at Przibislav before the war was over. >> Huss; Sigismund

Zoffany, John or **Johann** [**tsof**anee] (1734–1810) Portrait painter, born in Frankfurt (am Main), Germany. After studying art in Rome, he settled in London c.1758, securing royal patronage. His speciality was the conversation piece. He later lived in Florence (1772–9) and India (1783–90).

Zog I [zohg], originally **Ahmed Bey Zogu** (1895–1961) Albanian prime minister (1922–4), president (1925–8), and king (1928–39), born in Burgajet, Albania. He studied in Istanbul, became leader of the Nationalist Party, and formed a republican government in 1922. Forced into exile in 1924, he returned with the assistance of Yugoslavia, and became president, proclaiming himself king in 1928. After Albania was overrun by the Italians (1939), he fled to Britain, and later lived in Egypt and France. He formally abdicated in 1946. >> RR1031

Zola, Emile [**zoh**la] (1840–1902) Novelist, born in Paris. He became a clerk and journalist, then began to write short stories, beginning with *Contes à Ninon* (1864, Stories for Ninon). After his first major novel, *Thérèse Raquin* (1867), he began the long series called *Les Rougon-Macquart*, a sequence of 20 books described in the subtitle as 'the natural and social history of a family under the Second Empire'. The series contains such acclaimed studies as *Nana* (1880), *Germinal* (1885), *La Terre* (1887, Earth), and *La Bête humaine* (1890, trans The Beast in Man). In 1898 he espoused the cause of Dreyfus in his open letter *J'accuse*, and was sentenced to imprisonment (1898), but escaped to England. He was given a great welcome on his return after Dreyfus had been pardoned (1899), but controversy over the affair continued to affect him until his death. >> Dreyfus

Zola, Gianfranco (1966–) Footballer, born in Sardinia, Italy. He played for Parma, then joined Chelsea in 1996. He was also a member of the Italy national team in the Euro '96 championships.

Zorach, William [**zaw**rakh] (1887–1966) Sculptor and painter, born in Eurburick-Kovno, Lithuania. His family emigrated in 1891, and settled in Cleveland, OH, where he was apprenticed to a lithographer. He moved to New York City (1907), attended the Art Students League and the National Academy of Design (1908–9) and, after study in France (1910–11), produced Fauvist style paintings. Based in New York, he focused on sculpture (1922), carving directly in stone and wood, as in 'Floating Figure' (1922). He taught at the Art Students League (1929–60), and wrote several books on sculpture.

Zorn, Anders (Leonhard) (1860–1920) Etcher, sculptor, and painter, born in Mora, Sweden. He studied at Stockholm, travelled widely, returning to Mora in 1896. His paintings deal mainly with Swedish peasant life. He achieved European fame as an etcher, known for his series of nudes, and for his portraits.

Zoroaster [zoroh**a**ster], Greek form of **Zarathustra** (6th-c BC) Iranian prophet and founder of the ancient Parsee religion which bears his name. He had visions of Ahura Mazda, which led him to preach against polytheism. He appears as a historical person only in the earliest portion of the Avesta. As the centre of a group of chieftains, he carried on a struggle for the establishment of a holy agricultural state against Turanian and Vedic aggressors.

Zorrilla y Moral, José [tho**ree**lya ee mo**ral**] (1817–93) Poet, born in Valladolid, Spain. He studied law at Toledo and Valladolid, then devoted himself to literature in Madrid. He wrote many plays based on national legend, notably *Don Juan Tenorio* (1844), performed annually on All Saints' Day in Spanish-speaking countries.

Zsigmondy, Richard (Adolf) [**zhig**mondee] (1865–1929) Chemist, born in Vienna. He studied at Munich University, carried out research at Berlin, taught at Graz, and became professor at Göttingen (1908–29). A pioneer of colloid chemistry, in 1903 he introduced the ultramicroscope, a device to assist the observation of colloidal size particles which are too small to be visible in a normal microscope. He was awarded the Nobel Prize for Chemistry in 1925.

Zuccarelli, Francesco [tsuka**ray**lee] (1702–88) Painter, born in Pitigliano, Italy. He trained at Florence and Rome, and was active at Florence, but worked mainly in Venice after 1732. His pastoral landscapes, populated by shepherds and maidens and painted in a soft Rococo style, were very popular, especially in England, where he worked 1752–62 and 1765–71.

Zuccari or **Zuccaro, Taddeo** [tsu**kah**ree] (1529–66) Painter, born in Vado, Italy. Largely self-taught, he executed several frescoes and easel pieces, especially for the Farnese family. His brother **Federigo Zuccari** (c.1543–1609) painted portraits and frescoes, visited England, and became an influential art theorist. The two brothers were leaders of the Roman late Mannerist school.

Zuckerman (of Burnham Thorpe), Solly Zuckerman, Baron (1904–93) Zoologist, and political adviser, born in Cape Town, South Africa. He moved to Oxford in 1934, was a scientific adviser at Combined Operations HQ (1939–46), and became professor of anatomy at Birmingham (1946–68) and chief scientific adviser to the British government (1964–71). He carried out extensive research into primates, publishing such classic works as *The Social Life of Monkeys and Apes* (1932). He was knighted in 1956, and made a life peer in 1971. He published two volumes of autobiography, *From Apes to Warlords* (1978) and *Monkeys, Men and Missiles* (1988).

Zuckmayer, Carl [**tsuk**mayer] (1896–1977) Playwright, born in Nackenheim, Germany. He emigrated to the USA in 1939, but lived in Switzerland from 1946. His best-known plays are *Der Hauptmann von Köpenick* (1931, The Captain of Köpenick) and *Des Teufels General* (1946, The Devil's General), both of which have been filmed. He also wrote essays, novels, film scripts, some poetry, and his autobiography *Als wärs ein Stück vonmir* (1966, A Part of Myself). >> Udet

Zukerman, Pinchas (1948–) Violinist, born in Tel Aviv, Israel. After studies at the Juilliard School, New York City, he won the Leventritt Competition in 1967 and pursued a solo career. He became music director of the St Paul Chamber Orchestra (1980–7), and was principal conductor at the International Summer Music Festival (1990–5).

Zukofsky, Louis [zu**kof**skee] (1904–78) Poet, born in New York City. A leading experimentalist after Pound, his poems first appeared in *An Objectivist Anthology* (1932). Later works, which experimented with sound and typography, included *All: the Collected Short Poems* (1965, 1967). He published an autobiography in 1970. >> Pound, Ezra

Zuloaga, Ignacio [thulo**hah**ga] (1870–1945) Painter, born in Eibar, Spain. He studied painting in Rome and Paris, and won recognition abroad and then at home as a reviver of the national tradition in Spanish painting. He painted bullfighters, gipsies, beggars, and other themes of Spanish life.

Zurbarán, Francisco de [thoorb**aran**] (1598–1664) Religious painter, born in Fuente de Cantos, Spain. He spent most of his life at Seville, where his best-known work, an altarpiece, is to be found. Apart from a few portraits and still-life studies, his main subjects were monastic and historical,

and he came to be called 'the Spanish Caravaggio'. >> Caravaggio

Zuse, Konrad [**tsoo**zuh] (1910–95) Computer pioneer, born in Berlin. He studied at the Berlin Institute of Technology before joining the Henschel Aircraft Co in 1935. In the following year he began building a calculating machine in his spare time, a task which occupied him until 1945. He built a number of prototypes, the most historic of which was the Z3, the first operational general-purpose program-controlled calculator. Until 1964 he built up his own firm Zuse KG, and became an honorary professor of Göttingen University in 1966.

Zweig, Arnold [tsviyk] (1887–1968) Writer, born in Glogua, Germany. His writing, socialistic in outlook, was coloured by his interest in Zionism, which led him to seek refuge in Palestine when exiled by the Nazis in 1934. He is best known for his pacifist novel, *Der Streit um den Sergeanten Grischa* (1928, The Case of Sergeant Grischa).

Zweig, Stefan [tsviyk] (1881–1942) Writer, born in Vienna. He became known as a poet and translator, then as a biographer, short-story writer, and novelist, his work being characterized by his psychological insight into character. His best-known work was his set of historical portraits, *Sternstunden der Menschheit* (1928, trans The Tide of Fortune). He emigrated to London in 1934, and acquired British nationality, later moving to the USA and Brazil. His autobiographical *The World of Yesterday* was published posthumously in 1943.

Zwicky, Fritz [**zvik**ee] (1898–1974) Physicist, born in Varna, Bulgaria, of Swiss parents. He studied at the Swiss Federal Institute of Technology, Zürich, then took a position at the California Institute of Technology in 1925, becoming professor of astrophysics there (1942–68). He remained a Swiss citizen all his life. He researched extensively into galaxies and interstellar matter, and produced the standard catalogue on compact galaxies. In 1934 he predicted the existence of neutron stars and black holes.

Zwingli, Huldrych or **Ulrich** [**tsving**glee], Lat **Ulricus Zuinglius** (1484–1531) Protestant reformer, born in Wildhaus, Switzerland. He studied at Bern, Vienna, and Basel, was ordained in 1506, and became a chaplain to the Swiss mercenaries. In 1518, elected preacher in the Zürich minster, he opposed the selling of indulgences, and espoused the Reformed doctrines, obtaining the support of the civil authorities. In 1524 he split with Luther over the question of the Eucharist, rejecting every form of corporeal presence. War between the cantons followed, and he was killed during a battle near Kappel. >> Luther

Zworykin, Vladimir (Kosma) [**tsvo**rikin] (1889–1982) Physicist, born in Murom, Russia. He studied at the St Petersburg Institute of Technology and the Collège de France in Paris, emigrated to the USA in 1919, and became a US citizen in 1924. He joined the Radio Corporation (1929), becoming director of electronic research (1946) and vice-president (1947). In 1923–4 he patented an all-electronic television system using a scanned camera-tube (the *iconoscope*), in 1929 demonstrated a cathode-ray display (the *kinescope*), and in later years contributed to the development of colour television and the electron microscope. He is regarded as 'the father of modern television'.

READY REFERENCE

CONTENTS

Contents

Political leaders and rulers

Countries and organizations are listed alphabetically. For the major English-speaking nations, relevant details are also given of any political affiliation.

The list does not distinguish successive terms of office by a single ruler.

There is no universally agreed way of transliterating proper names in non-Roman alphabets; variations from the spellings given are therefore to be expected, especially in the case of Arabic rulers. Minor variations in the titles adopted by Chiefs of State, or in the name of an administration, are not given; these occur most notably in countries under military rule.

Listings are complete to January 1998.

Afghanistan

Afghan Empire
Durrani Emirs
1747–73	Ahmad Shah Durrani
1773–93	Timur Shah
1793–1800	Zaman Shah
1800–03	Mahmud Shah
1803–09	Shah Shuja
1809–18	Mahmud Shah (restored)
1818–9	Ali Shah

Barakzai Emirs
1819–39	Dost Muhammad Khan

Durrani Emirs (restored)
1839–42	Shah Shuja (restored)
1842	Fath Jang

Barakzai Emirs (restored)
1842–63	Dost Muhammad Khan (restored)
1863–66	Shir Ali Khan
1866–7	Afdal Khan
1867–79	Shir Ali Khan (restored)
1879–80	Muhammad Ya qub Khan
1880–1901	Abdul Rahman Khan
1901–19	Habibullah Khan
1919–26	Amanullah Khan

Kings
1926–9	Amanullah Khan
1929	Habibullah Ghazi
1929–33	Mohammed Nadir Shah
1933–73	Mohammed Zahir Shah

Republic of Afghanistan
President
1973–8	Mohammad Daoud Khan

Democratic Republic of Afghanistan
Revolutionary Council
1978–9	Nur Mohammad Taraki
1979	Hafizullah Amin

Soviet Invasion
1979–86	Babrak Karmal
1986–7	Haji Mohammad Chamkani *Acting*
1987	Ahmadzai Najibullah

General-Secretary
1978–86	*As President*
1986–7	Ahmadzai Najibullah

Republic of Afghanistan
President
1987–92	Mohammad Najibullah
1992–6	Burhanuddin Rabbani

Prime Minister
1929–46	Sardar Mohammad Hashim Khan
1946–53	Shah Mahmoud Khan Ghazi
1953–63	Mohammad Daoud
1963–5	Mohammad Yousef
1965–7	Mohammad Hashim Maiwandwal
1967–71	Nour Ahmad Etemadi
1972–3	Mohammad Mousa Shafiq
1973–9	*As President*
1979–81	Babrak Karmal
1981–8	Sultan Ali Keshtmand
1988–9	Mohammad Hasan Sharq
1989–90	Sultan Ali Keshtmand
1990–2	Fazl Haq Khaleqiar
1992–3	Abdul Sabur Fareed
1993–4	Gulbardin Hekmatyar
1994–6	Arsala Rahmani *Acting*
1996–	Gulbardin Hekmatyar

Interim Council
1996–	Mohammad Rabbani *Chairman*

Albania

Principality of Albania
1912–14	Ismail Qemal *Provisional Head of State*
1914	Prince Wilhelm of Wied
1914–18	*Military occupation*

Republic of Albania
1919–24	*As Prime Minister*
1924–8	Ahmed Bey Zogu *President*

Monarch – Kingdom of Albania
1928–39	Zog I (Ahmed Bey Zogu)
1939–44	*Italian rule*

People's Socialist Republic of Albania
President
1944–85	Enver Hoxha
1985–91	Ramiz Alia

Republic of Albania
1991–2	Fatos Nano *Provisional*
1992–7	Sali Berisha
1997–	Rexhep Mejdani

Prime Minister
1914	Turhan Pashë Përmëti
1914	Esad Toptani
1914–18	Abdullah Rushdi
1918–20	Turhan Pashë Përmëti

1920	Sulejman Deluina
1920–1	Iljaz Bej Vrioni
1921	Pandeli Evangeli
1921	Xhafer Ypi
1921–2	Omer Vrioni
1922–4	Ahmed Bey Zogu
1924	Iljaz Bej Vrioni
1924–5	Fan Stylian Noli
1925–8	Ahmed Bey Zogu
1928–30	Koço Kota
1930–5	Pandeli Evangeli
1935–6	Mehdi Frashëri
1936–9	Koço Kota
1939–41	Shefqet Verlaci
1941–3	Mustafa Merlika-Kruja
1943	Eqrem Libohova
1943	Maliq Bushati
1943	Eqrem Libohova
1943	*Provisional Executive Committee* (Ibrahim Biçakçlu)
1943	*Council of Regents* (Mehdi Frashëri)
1943–4	Rexhep Mitrovica
1944	Fiori Dine
1944–54	Enver Hoxha
1954–81	Mehmed Shehu
1981–91	Adil Carcani
1991	Ylli Bufi
1991–2	Vilson Ahmeti
1992–7	Alexander Meksi
1997	Bashkim Fino
1997–	Fatos Nano

Algeria

Dey of Algiers
1671–82	Muhammad I
1682–3	Hasan I
1683–9	Husain I
1689–95	Sha ban
1695–8	Ahmad I
1698–1700	Hasan II
1700–05	Mustafa I
1705–07	Husain II Khoja
1707–10	Muhammad II Bektash
1710	Ibrahim I
1710–18	Ali I
1718–24	Muhammad III
1724–32	Kurd Abdi
1732–45	Ibrahim II
1745–8	Kuchuk Ibrahim III
1748–54	Muhammad IV
1754–66	Ali II
1766–91	Muhammad V

1791–8	Hasan III
1798–1805	Mustafa II
1805–08	Ahmad II
1808–09	Ali III ar-Rasul
1809–15	Ali IV
1815	Muhammad VI
1815–17	Umar
1817–18	Ali V Khoja
1818–30	Husain III
1830–1962	*French rule*

President

1962–5	Ahmed Ben Bella
1965–78	Houari Boumédienne
1978–92	Chadli Benjadid
1992	Mohammed Boudiaf
1992–4	Ali Kafi
1994–	Lamine Zeroual

Prime Minister

1977–84	Mohammed ben Ahmed Abdelghani
1984–8	Abdelhamid Brahimi
1989–91	Mouloud Hamrouche
1991–2	Sid Ahmed Ghozali
1992–3	Belaid Abdessalam
1993–4	Redha Malek
1994–5	Mokdad Sifi
1995–	Ahmed Ouyahia

Andorra

Heads of State (Co-Princes): President of France and Bishop of Urgel

Chief executive

1989–94	Óscar Ribas Reig
1994–	Marc Forné Molné

Angola

President

1975–9	Antonio Agostinho Neto
1979–	José Eduardo dos Santos

Prime Minister

1991–2	Fernando José França Van-Dúnem
1992–6	Marcolino José Carlos Moco
1996–	Fernando José França Van Dunem

Antigua and Barbuda

Chief of State: British monarch, represented by Governor-General

Prime Minister

1981–94	Vere Cornwall Bird
1994–	Lester Bird

Argentina

President

1827	Bernardino Rivadavia
1827–8	Vincente López *Provisional*

Governor of Buenos Aires

1829–32	Juan Manuel de Rosas *Dictator*

1832–3	Juan Ramón Balcarce
1833–4	Avelino Viamonte
1834–52	Juan Manuel de Rosas *Dictator*

President

1854–60	Justo José de Urquíza
1860–2	Santiago Derqui
1862–8	Bartolomé Mitre
1868–74	Domingo Faustino Sarmiento
1874–80	Nicolás Avellaneda
1880–6	Julio Argentino Roca
1886–90	Miguel Juárez Celman
1890–2	Carlos Pellegrini
1892–5	Luis Sáenz Peña
1895–8	José E Uriburu
1898–1904	Julio Argentino Roca
1904–6	Manuel Quintana
1906–10	José Figueroa Alcorta
1910–14	Roque Sáenz Peña
1914–16	Victorino de la Plaza
1916–22	Hipólito Yrigoyen
1922–8	Marcelo T de Alvear
1928–30	Hipólito Yrigoyen
1930–2	José Félix Uriburu
1932–8	Augustin Pedro Justo
1938–40	Roberto M Ortiz
1940–3	Ramón S Castillo
1943–4	Pedro P Ramírez
1944–6	Edelmiro J Farrell
1946–55	Juan Domingo Perón
1955–8	Eduardo Lonardi
1958–62	Arturo Frondizi
1962–3	José María Guido
1963–6	Arturo Illia
1966–70	Juan Carlos Onganía
1970–1	Roberto Marcelo Levingston
1971–3	Alejandro Agustín Lanusse
1973	Héctor J Cámpora
1973–4	Juan Domingo Perón
1974–6	María Estela (Isabelita) Martínez de Perón
1976–81	*Military junta* (Jorge Rafaél Videla)
1981	*Military junta* (Roberto Eduardo Viola)
1981–2	*Military junta* (Leopoldo Fortunato Galtieri)
1982–3	Reynaldo Bignone
1983–8	Raúl Alfonsín Foulkes
1988–	Carlos Saúl Menem

Armenia

President

1991–	Levon Ter-Petrosian

Prime Minister

1991–2	Gagik Arutynyan
1992–3	Khosrov Haroutunian
1993–6	Hrand Bagratian
1996–7	Armen Sarkissian
1997–	Robert Kocharyan

Assyria

Monarch – Kingdom of Assyria

1813–1780BC	Shamshi-Adad I
1780BC–?	Ishme-Dagan I
	Mut-Ashkur
	Rimush
	Asinum
	Puzur-Sin
	Ashur-dugul
	Ashur-apla-idi
	Nasir-Sin
	Sin-namir
	Ipqi-Ishtar
	Adad-shalulu
	Adasi
1700–1690BC	Belubani
1690–73BC	Libaia
1673–61BC	Sharma-Adad I
1661–49BC	Iptar-Sin
1649–21BC	Bazaia
1621–15BC	Lullaia
1615–01BC	Kidin-Ninua
1601–1598BC	Sharma-Adad II
1598–85BC	Erishum
1585–79BC	Shamshi-Adad II
1579–63BC	Ishme-Dagan II
1563–47BC	Shamshi-Adad III
1547–21BC	Ashur-nirari I
1521–1497BC	Puzur-Ashur
1497–84BC	Enlil-nasir I
1484–72BC	Nur-ili
1472BC	Ashur-shaduni
1472–52BC	Ashur-rabi I
1452–32BC	Ashur-nadin-ahhe I
1432–26BC	Enlil-nasir II
1426–19BC	Ashur-nirari II
1419–10BC	Ashur-bel-nisheshu
1410–02BC	Ashur-rim-nisheshu
1402–1392BC	Ashur-nadin-ahhe II
1392–65BC	Eriba-Adad I
1365–29BC	Ashur-uballit I
1329–19BC	Enlil-nirari
1319–07BC	Arik-den-ili
1307–1274BC	Adad-nirari I
1274–44BC	Shulmanu-ashared (Shalmaneser) I
1244–07BC	Tukulti-Ninurta I
1207–03BC	Ashur-nadin-apli
1203–1197BC	Ashur-nirari III
1197–2BC	Enlil-kudurri-usur
1192–79BC	Ninurta-apil-Ekur
1179BC–?	Ashur-dan I
?	Ninurta-tukulti-Ashur
?–1133BC	Mutakkil-Nusku
1133–15BC	Ashur-resha-ishi I
1115–1076BC	Tukulti-apil-esharra (Tiglath-Pilesar) I
1076–4BC	Ashared-apil-Ekur
1074–56BC	Ashur-bel-kala
1056–4BC	Eriba-Adad II
1054–50BC	Shamshi-Adad IV
1050–31BC	Ashur-nasir-apli I
1031–19BC	Shulmanu-ashared (Shalmaneser) II

1019–13BC	Ashur-nirari IV
1013–972BC	Ashur-rabi II
972–67BC	Ashur-resha-ishi II
967–35BC	Tukulti-apil-esharra (Tiglath-Pilesar) II
935–11BC	Ashur-dan II
911–890BC	Adad-nirari II
890–84BC	Tukulti-Ninurta II
884–59BC	Ashur-nasir-apli II
859–24BC	Shulmanu-ashared (Shalmaneser) III
824–11BC	Shamshi-Adad V
811–782BC	Adad-nirari III – Sammu-ramat (Semiramis) *Regent to 806BC*
782–72BC	Shulmanu-ashared (Shalmaneser) IV
772–54BC	Ashur-dan III
754–45BC	Ashur-nirari V
745–27BC	Tukulti-apil-esharra (Tiglath-Pilesar) III Pulu
727–2BC	Shulmanu-ashared (Shalmaneser) V
722–05BC	Sharrukin (Sargon) II
705–681BC	Sin-ahhe-eriba (Sennacherib)
681–69BC	Ashur-ahhe-iddina (Esarhaddon)
669–26BC	Ashur-bani-apli (Ashur-banipal; Sardanapalus)
626–1BC	Ashur-etil-ilani
626–1BC	Sin-shum-lishir
621–12BC	Sin-shar-ishkun
612–09BC	Ashur-uballit II

Australia

Chief of State: British monarch, represented by Governor-General

Prime Minister

1901–3	Edmund Barton *Prot*
1903–4	Alfred Deakin *Prot*
1904	John Christian Watson *Lab*
1904–5	George Houston Reid *Free/Prot/Co**
1905–8	Alfred Deakin *Prot*
1908–9	Andrew Fisher *Lab*
1909–10	Alfred Deakin *Fusion*
1910–13	Andrew Fisher *Lab*
1913–14	Joseph Cook *Lib*
1914–15	Andrew Fisher *Lab*
1915–16	William Morris Hughes *Lab*
1916–17	William Morris Hughes *Nat Lab*
1917–23	William Morris Hughes *Nat*
1923–9	Stanley Melbourne Bruce, Viscount Bruce of Melbourne *Nat/Co**
1929–32	James Henry Scullin *Lab*
1932–8	Joseph Aloysius Lyons *Un*
1938–9	Joseph Aloysius Lyons *Un/Co**

1939	Earle Christian Grafton Page *Un/Co*
1939–40	Robert Gordon Menzies *Un*
1940–1	Robert Gordon Menzies *Un/Co**
1941	Arthur William Fadden *Un/Co*
1941–5	John Joseph Curtin *Lab*
1945	Francis Michael Forde *Lab*
1945–9	Joseph Benedict Chifley *Lab*
1949–66	Robert Gordon Menzies *Lib/Co**
1966–7	Harold Edward Holt *Lib/Co**
1967–8	John McEwen *Lib/Co**
1968–71	John Grey Gorton *Lib/Co**
1971–2	William McMahon *Lib/Co**
1972–5	Gough Whitlam *Lab*
1975–83	John Malcolm Fraser *Lib/Co**
1983–91	Robert James Lee Hawke *Lab*
1991–6	Paul Keating *Lab*
1997–	John Howard *Lib*

Co Country; *Free* Free Trade; *Lab* Labor; *Lib* Liberal; *Nat* Nationalist; *Nat Lab* National Labor; *Prot* Protectionist; *Un* United; *Co** Coalition

Austria

Margrave of Austria
House of Babenburg

976–94	Leopold I
994–1018	Heinrich I
1018–55	Adalbert
1055–75	Ernest
1075–96	Leopold II
1096–1136	Leopold III
1136–41	Leopold IV
1141–56	Heinrich II Jasomirgott

Duke of Austria
House of Babenberg

1156–77	Henry II Jasomirgott
1177–94	Leopold V
1194–8	Friedrich I
1198–1230	Leopold VI
1230–46	Friedrich II
1246–51	*No duke*
1251–76	Ottokar (II of Bohemia)

House of Habsburg

1276–91	Rudolf I
1282–1298	Albrecht (Albert) I *Joint ruler to 1290*
1282–1290	Rudolf II *Joint ruler*
1298–1358	Albrecht II *Joint ruler to 1339*
1298–1339	Otto *Joint ruler*
1298–1326	Leopold I *Joint ruler*
1298–1330	Friedrich II *Joint ruler*
1298–1307	Rudolf III *Joint ruler*
1365–95	Albrecht III *Joint ruler to 1379*
1365–79	Leopold III *Joint ruler*
1358–65	Rudolf IV
1395–1404	Albrecht IV
1404–1439	Albrecht V

1439–57	Ladislas 'Posthumus'
1457–93	Friedrich V (Frederick III, Holy Roman Emperor)
1493–1804	*As Holy Roman Emperor*

Austrian Empire
Monarch – House of Habsburg

1804–35	Franz I (Francis II, Holy Roman Emperor)
1835–48	Ferdinand I
1848–67	Franz Josef (Francis Joseph) I

Austro-Hungarian Empire
Emperor – House of Habsburg

1867–1916	Franz Josef (Francis Joseph) I
1916–18	Karl (Charles)

Republic of Austria

President

1918–20	Karl Sätz
1920–8	Michael Hainisch
1928–38	Wilhelm Miklas
1938–45	*German rule*
1945–50	Karl Renner
1950–7	Theodor Körner
1957–65	Adolf Schärf
1965–74	Franz Jonas
1974–86	Rudolf Kirchsläger
1986–92	Kurt Waldheim
1992–	Thomas Klestil

Prime Minister

1848–52	Felix, Prince Schwarzenberg
1852–1918	*Emperor also Prime Minister*

Chancellor

1918–20	Karl Renner
1920–1	Michael Mayr
1921–2	Johann Schober
1922–4	Ignaz Seipel
1924–6	Rudolf Raimak
1926–9	Ignaz Seipel
1929	Ernst Streeruwitz
1929–30	Johann Schober
1930	Carl Vaugoin
1930–1	Otto Ender
1931–2	Karl Buresch
1932–4	Engelbert Dollfuss
1934–8	Kurt von Schuschnigg
1938–45	*German rule*
1945	Karl Renner
1945–3	Leopold Figl
1953–61	Julius Raab
1961–4	Alfons Gorbach
1964–70	Josef Klaus
1970–83	Bruno Kreisky
1983–6	Fred Sinowatz
1986–97	Franz Vranitzky
1997–	Viktor Klima

Azerbaijan

President

1991–2	Ayaz Mutalibov
1992–3	Abulfaz Elchibey
1993–	Geidar Aliyev

Prime Minister

1991–2	Gasan Gasanov
1992–3	Feirus Mustafayev
1993–4	Rakhim Guseinov
1994	Ali Masimov *Acting*
1994	Panakh Guseinov
1994–5	Surat Guseinov
1995–6	Fuad Guliyev
1996–	Artur Rasizade

Babylon

Monarch – Kingdom of Babylon

1156–38BC	Marduk-kabit-ahheshu
1138–30BC	Itti-Marduk-balatsu
1130–24BC	Ninurta-nadin-shumi
1124–02BC	Nabu-kudurri-usur (Nebuchadrezzar) I
1102–1098BC	Enlil-nadin-apli
1098–80BC	Marduk-nadin-ahhe
1080–67BC	Marduk-shapik-zeri
1067–45BC	Adad-apla-Addina
1045–4BC	Marduk-ahhe-eriba
1044–32BC	Marduk-zer
1032–24BC	Nabu-shumu-libur
1024–07BC	Simbar-shikhu
1007–06BC	Ea-mukin-zeri
1006–03BC	Kashshu-nadin-akhi
1003–986BC	E-ulmash-shakin-shumi
986–4BC	Ninurta-kudurri-usur I
984–3BC	Shirikti-shuqamuna
983–78BC	Mar-biti-apla-usur
978–43BC	Nabu-mukin-apli
943–2BC	Ninurta-kudurri-usur II
942–1BC	Mar-biti-ahhe-iddina
941–00BC	Shamash-mudammiq
900–885BC	Nabu-shum-ukin I
885–52BC	Nabu-apla-iddina
852–1BC	Marduk-bel-usate
851–27BC	Marduk-zakir-shumi I
827–14BC	Marduk-balatsu-iqbi
814–11BC	Bau-ahhe-iddina
811–?BC	Adad-shuma-ibni
?	Marduk-bel-zeri
?–802BC	Marduk-apla-usur
802–?BC	Eriba-Marduk
?–747BC	Nabu-shum-ukin II
747–35BC	Nabu-nasir
735–2BC	Nabu-nadin-zeri
732BC	Nabu-shum-ukin III
732–29BC	Ukin-zer
729–2BC	*Assyrian rule*
722–10BC	Marduk-apla-iddina II (Merodach-Baladan)
710–03BC	*Assyrian rule*
703BC	Marduk-zakir-shumi II
703–02BC	Marduk-apla-iddina II (Merodach-Baladan) (*restored*)
702–700BC	Bel-ibni
700–694BC	Ashur-nadin-shumi
694–3BC	Nergal-ushezib
693–89BC	Mushezib-Marduk
689–69BC	*Assyrian rule*
669–48BC	Shamash-shuma-ukin

648–27BC	Kandalanu

Neo-Babylonian Empire

626–05BC	Nabu-apla-usur (Nabopolassar)
605–562BC	Nabu-kudurri-usur (Nebuchadrezzar) II
562–59BC	Awel-Marduk
559–6BC	Nergal-shar-usur
556BC	Labashi-Marduk
556–39BC	Nabu-Na'id (Nabonidus)

The Bahamas

Chief of State: British monarch, represented by Governor-General

Prime Minister

1973–92	Lynden Oscar Pindling
1992–	Hubert Alexander Ingraham

Bahrain

Emir

Al-Khalifa dynasty

1783–96	Ahmad bin Khalifa
1796–1843	Abdulla
1796–1825	Salman I
1825–36	Khalifa
1834–68	Muhammad
1868–9	Ali
1869–1935	Isa I
1923–42	Hamad
1942–61	Salman II
1961–	Isa II bin Salman al-Khalifa

Prime Minister

1971–	Khalifa bin Salman al-Khalifa

Bangladesh

Sultan of Bengal

1282–91	Nasir-ud-Din Bughra Khan
1291–8	Rukn-ud-Din Kai-Kaus
1298–1318	Shams-ud-Din Firuz Shah I
1318–30	Ghiyath-ud-Din Bhadur *East Bengal – Joint ruler from 1324*
1324–39	Bahram Shah *East Bengal – Joint ruler to 1330*
1339–49	Fakhr-ud-Din Mubarak Shah *East Bengal*
1349–52	Ikhtiyar-ud-Din Ghazi Shah *East Bengal*
1352–7	Shams-ud-Din Ilyas Shah *East Bengal to 1345*
1358–90	Sikandar Shah I
1390–1410	Ghiyath-ud-Din Azam Shah
1410–12	Saif-ud-Din Hamza Shah
1412–14	Shihab-ud-Din Bayazid Shah I
1414–15	Ala-ud-Din Firuz Shah II
1415–18	Raja Ganesh
1418–32	Jalal-ud-Din Muhammad Shah
1432–7	Shams-ud-Din Ahmad Shah

1437–60	Nasir-ud-Din Mahmud Shah I
1460–74	Rukn-ud-Din Barbak Shah I
1474–81	Shams-ud-Din Yusuf Shah
1481	Sikandar Shah II
1481–7	Jalal-ud-Din Fath Shah
1487	Sultan Shahzada Barbak Shah II
1487–90	Saif-ud-Din Firuz Shah III
1490–1	Nasir-ud-Din Mahmud Shah II
1491–4	Shams-ud-Din Muzaffar Shah
1494–1519	Ala-ud-Din Husain Shah
1519–32	Nasir-ud-Din Nusrat Shah
1532–3	Ala-ud-Din Firuz Shah IV
1533–9	Ghiyath-ud-Din Mahmud Shah III
1539–40	Shir Shah Sur
1540–5	Khidr Khan
1545–55	Muhammad Khan Sur
1555–61	Khidr Khan Bahadur Shah
1561–4	Ghiyath-ud-Din Jalal Shah
1564–72	Sulayman Kararani
1572	Bayazid Shah II
1572–6	Daud Shah
1576–1703	*Part of Moghul Empire*

Nawab of Bengal

1703–27	Murshid Quli Ja far Khan
1727–39	Shuja-ud-Din
1739–40	Safaraz Khan
1740–56	Alivardi Khan
1756–7	Siraj-ud-Dawlah (Suraja Dowlah)
1757–60	Mir Ja far
1760–3	Mir Qasim
1763–5	Mir Ja far (*restored*)
1765–6	Najm-ud-Dawlah
1766–70	Saif-ud-Dawlah
1770–1947	*British rule*
1947–71	*Part of Pakistan*

Republic of Bangladesh
President

1971–2	Sayed Nazrul Islam *Acting*
1972	Mujibur Rahman
1972–3	Abu Saeed Chowdhury
1974–5	Mohammadullah
1975	Mujibur Rahman
1975	Khondaker Mushtaq Ahmad
1975–7	Abu Saadat Mohammad Sayem
1977–81	Zia Ur-Rahman
1981–2	Abdus Sattar
1982–3	Abdul Fazal Mohammad Ahsanuddin Chowdhury
1983–90	Hossain Mohammad Ershad
1990–1	Shehabuddin Ahmed
1991–6	Abdur Rahman Biswas
1996–	Shehabuddin Ahmed

Prime Minister

1971–2	Tajuddin Ahmed
1972–5	Mujibur Rahman

1975	Mohammad Monsur Ali
1975–9	*Martial Law*
1979–82	Mohammad Azizur Rahman
1982–4	*Martial Law*
1984–5	Ataur Rahman Khan
1986–8	Mizanur Rahman Chowdhury
1988–9	Moudud Ahmed
1989–91	Kazi Zafar Ahmed
1991–6	Begum Khaleda Zia
1996–	Hasina Wajed

Barbados

Chief of State: British monarch, represented by Governor-General

Prime Minister

1966–76	Errol Walton Barrow
1976–85	J M G (Tom) Adams
1985–6	H Bernard St John
1986–7	Errol Walton Barrow
1987–94	L Erskine Sandiford
1994–	Owen Seymour Arthur

Belarus

Chairman of Supreme Council

1991–4	Stanislav Shushkevick
1994–6	Mechislav Grib
1996–	Syamyon Sharetski

President

1994–	Alexander Lukashenko

Prime Minister

1991–4	Vyacheslav Kebich
1994–6	Mikhail Chigir
1996–	Syargey Ling

Belgium

Monarch – Kingdom of Belgium

1831–65	Leopold I
1865–1909	Leopold II
1909–34	Albert I
1934–50	Leopold III
1950–93	Baudoin I
1993–	Albert II

Prime Minister

1831	Albert Joseph, Count Goblet d'Alviella
1831	Étienne Noël Joseph, Count de Sauvage
1831–2	Félix Amand de Muelenaere
1832–4	*Shared administration* (Albert Joseph, Count Goblet d'Alviella; Joseph Lebeau; Charles Latour Rogier)
1834–40	Bartolémy Théodore de Theux
1840–1	Joseph Lebeau
1841–5	Jean-Baptiste Nothomb
1845–6	Jean-Sylvain van de Weyer

1846–7	*Shared administration* (Bartolémy Théodore de Theux; Jules Malou)
1847–52	Charles Latour Rogier
1852–5	Henri de Brouckère
1855–7	Pierre de Decker
1857–68	*Shared administration* (Charles Latour Rogier; H J Walthère Frère-Orban)
1868–70	H J Walthère Frère-Orban
1870–1	Jules Joseph d'Anethan
1871–4	Bartolémy Théodore de Theux
1874–8	Jules Malou
1878–84	*Shared administration* (H J Walthère Frère-Orban; Pierre Edouard van Humbeeck)
1884	*Shared administration* (Jules Malou; Victor Jacobs; Charles Woeste)
1884–94	Auguste Beernaert
1894–6	Jules de Burlet
1896–9	Paul de Smet de Nayer
1899	Jules Vandenpeerebom
1899–1907	Paul de Smet de Nayer
1907–8	Jules de Trooz
1908–11	Frans Schollaert
1911–18	Charles de Broqueville
1918	Gerhard Cooreman
1918–20	Léon Delacroix
1920–1	Henri Carton de Wiart
1921–5	Georges Theunis
1925	Alois van de Vyvere
1925–6	Prosper Poullet
1926–31	Henri Jaspar
1931–2	Jules Renkin
1932–4	Charles de Broqueville
1934–5	Georges Theunis
1935–7	Paul van Zeeland
1937–8	Paul Émile Janson
1938–9	Paul Henri Spaak
1939–45	Hubert Pierlot
1945–6	Achille van Acker
1946	Paul Henri Spaak
1946	Achille van Acker
1946–7	Camille Huysmans
1947–9	Paul Henri Spaak
1949–50	Gaston Eyskens
1950	Jean Pierre Duvieusart
1950–2	Joseph Pholien
1952–4	Jean van Houtte
1954–8	Achille van Acker
1958–61	Gaston Eyskens
1961–5	Théodore Lefèvre
1965–6	Pierre Harmel
1966–8	Paul Vanden Boeynants
1968–72	Gaston Eyskens
1973–4	Edmond Leburton
1974–8	Léo Tindemans
1978	Paul Vanden Boeynants
1979–81	Wilfried Martens
1981	Marc Eyskens
1981–92	Wilfried Martens
1992–	Jean-Luc Dehaene

Belize

Chief of State: British monarch, represented by Governor-General

Prime Minister

1981–4	George Cadle Price
1985–9	Manuel Esquivel
1989–93	George Cadle Price
1993–	Manuel Esquivel

Benin

Monarch – Kingdom of Dahomey

c.1625–c.1650	Dakpodunu
c.1650–c.1680	Wegbaja
c.1680–c.1708	Akaba
c.1708–c.1730	Agaja
c.1730–1775	Tegbesu
1775–89	Kpengla
1789–97	Agonglo
1797–1818	Adandozan
1818–58	Gezo
1858–89	Glele
1889–94	Behanzin
1894–1960	*French rule*

President

State of Dahomey

1960–3	Hubert Coutoucou Maga
1963–4	Christophe Soglo
1964–5	Sourou Migan Apithy
1965	Justin Tométin Ahomadegbé
1965	Tairou Congacou
1965–7	Christophe Soglo
1967–8	Alphonse Amadou Alley
1968–9	Émile Derlin Zinsou
1969–70	*Presidential Committee* (Maurice Kouandete)
1970–2	(Hubert Coutoucou Maga)
1972–5	Mathieu Kérékou

People's Republic of Benin

1975–90	Mathieu (*from 1980* Ahmed) Kérékou

Republic of Benin

1990–1	(Matthieu) Ahmed Kérékou
1991–6	Nicéphore Soglo
1996–	Ahmed Kérékou

Prime Minister

1958–9	Sourou Migan Apithy
1959–60	Hubert Coutoucou Maga
1960–4	*As President*
1964–5	Justin Tométin Ahomadegbé
1965–7	*As President*
1967–8	Maurice Kouandete
1968–96	*As President*
1996–	Adrien Houngbedji

Bhutan

Monarch (Druk Gyalpo)

1907–26	Uggyen Wangchuk
1926–52	Jigme Wangchuk

| 1952–72 | Jigme Dorji Wangchuk |
| 1972– | Jigme Singye Wangchuk |

Bolivia

President

1825–8	Antonio José de Sucre
1828	José Maria Pérez de Urdininea
1828	José Miguel de Velasco
1828	Pedro Blanco
1828	José Miguel de Velasco
1828–39	Andrés de Santa Cruz y Calahumana
1839	José Miguel de Velasco
1839–41	José Mariano Serrano
1841–7	José Ballivián
1847	Eusebio Guilarte
1847–8	José Miguel de Velasco
1848–55	Manuel Isodoro Belzú
1855–8	Jorge Córdoba
1858–61	José María Linares
1861–4	José María de Achá
1864–71	Mariano Melgarejo
1871–2	Agustin Morales
1872–3	Tomas Frías *Acting*
1873–4	Adolfo Ballivián
1874–6	Tomas Frías *Acting*
1876–9	Hilarion Daza Grosole
1880–4	Narciso Campero
1884–8	Gregorio Pacheco
1888–92	Aniceto Arce
1892–6	Mariano Baptista
1896–9	Severo Fernandez Alonso
1899–1904	José Manuel Pando
1904–9	Ismael Montes
1909–13	Heliodoro Villazón
1913–17	Ismael Montes
1917–20	José N Gutiérrez Guerra
1920–5	Bautista Saavedra
1925–6	José Cabina Villanueva
1926–30	Hernando Siles
1930	Roberto Hinojusa *President of Revolutionaries*
1930–1	Carlos Blanco Galindo
1931–4	Daniel Salamanca
1934–6	José Luis Tejado Sorzano
1936–7	David Toro
1937–9	Germán Busch
1939	Carlos Quintanilla
1940–3	Enrique Peñaranda y del Castillo
1943–6	Gualberto Villaroel
1946	Nestor Guillen
1946–7	Tomás Monje Gutiérrez
1947–9	Enrique Hertzog
1949	Mamerto Urriolagoitía
1951–2	Hugo Ballivián
1952	Hernán Siles Suazo
1952–6	Victor Paz Estenssoro
1956–60	Hernán Siles Suazo
1960–4	Victor Paz Estenssoro
1964–5	René Barrientos Ortuño
1965–6	René Barrientos Ortuño Alfredo Ovando Candía
1966	Alfredo Ovando Candía

1966–9	René Barrientos Ortuño
1969	Luis Adolfo Siles Salinas
1969–70	Alfredo Ovando Candía
1970	Rogelio Mirando
1970–1	Juan José Torres Gonzales
1971–8	Hugo Banzer Suárez
1978	Juan Pereda Asbún
1978–9	*Military junta* (David Padilla Arericiba)
1979	Walter Guevara Arze
1979–80	Lydia Gueiler Tejada
1980–1	*Military junta* (Luis García Meza)
1981–2	*Military junta* (Celso Torrelio Villa)
1982	Guido Vildoso Calderón
1982–5	Hernán Siles Suazo
1985–9	Victor Paz Estenssoro
1989–93	Jaime Paz Zamora
1993–7	Gonzalo Sánchez de Lozada
1997–	Hugo Banzer Suárez

Bosnia-Herzegovina

Monarch – Kingdom of Bosnia

1376–91	Stephen Tvrtko I
1391–5	Stephen Dabisha
1395–8	Helena
1398–1404	Stephen Ostoja
1404–08	Stephen Tvrtko II
1408–18	Stephen Ostoja (*restored*)
1418–21	Stephen Ostojich
1421–43	Stephen Tvrtko II (*restored*)
1443–61	Stephen Thomas Ostojich
1461–3	Stephen Thomashevic
1463–1815	*Turkish rule*
1815–1918	*Austrian rule*
1918–92	*Part of Yugoslavia*

Republic of Bosnia-Herzegovina
President

| 1992– | Aliya Izetbegovic |

Prime Minister

1992	Jure Pelivan
1992–3	Mile Akmadzic
1993–6	Haris Silajdzic
1996	Hasan Muratovic
1996–	Gojko Klickovic

Federation of Bosnia-Herzegovina

| 1996– | Izudin Kapetanovic |

Botswana

President

| 1966–80 | Seretse Khama |
| 1980– | Quett K J Masire |

Brazil

Emperor
House of Bragança

| 1822–31 | Pedro I (IV of Portugal) |
| 1831–89 | Pedro II |

President

1889–91	Manoel Deodoro da Fonseca
1891–4	Floriano Peixoto
1894–8	Prudente José de Morais Barros
1898–1902	Manuel Ferraz de Campos Sales
1902–6	Francisco de Paula Rodrigues Alves
1906–9	Alfonso Pena
1909–10	Nilo Peçanha
1910–14	Hermes Rodrigues da Fonseca
1914–18	Venceslau Brás Pereira Gomes
1918–19	Francisco de Paula Rodrigues Alves
1919–22	Epitácio Pessoa
1922–6	Artur da Silva Bernardes
1926–30	Washington Luís Pereira de Sousa
1930–45	Getúlio Dornelles Vargas
1945–51	Eurico Gaspar Dutra
1951–4	Getúlio Dornelles Vargas
1954–5	João Café Filho
1955	Carlos Coimbra da Luz
1955–6	Nereu de Oliveira Ramos
1956–61	Juscelino Kubitschek de Oliveira
1961	Janio da Silva Quadros
1961–3	João Belchior Marques Goulart
1963	Pascoal Ranieri Mazilli
1963–4	João Belchior Marques Goulart
1964	Pascoal Ranieri Mazilli
1964–7	Humberto de Alencar Castelo Branco
1967–9	Artur da Costa e Silva
1969–74	Emílio Garrastazu Médici
1974–9	Ernesto Geisel
1979–85	João Baptista de Oliveira Figueiredo
1985–90	José Sarney Costa
1990–2	Fernando Collor de Mello
1992–5	Itamar Franco *Interim*
1995–	Fernando Henrique Cardoso

Brunei

Monarch (Sultan)

*c.*1405–	
*c.*1415	Muhammad
*c.*1415–?	Ahmad
?–*c.*1433	Sharif Ali Bilfakih
*c.*1433–?	Sulayman
	Bulkiah
	Abdul-Qahhar
*c.*1578–?	Saif al Rijal
	Shah Berunai
	Hasan
	Abdul-Jalil Akbar
	Abdul-Jalil Jabbar
?–*c.*1662	Muhammad Ali

c.1662–?	Abdul-Mubin Muhyi-ud-Din Nasr-ud-Din Kamal-ud-Din Ala-ud-Din
?–1780	Umar Ali Saif-ud-Din I
1780–92	Muhammad Taj-ud-Din
1792–3	Muhammad Jamal-ul-Alam I
1793–1806	Muhammad Taj-ud-Din (restored)
1806–22	Muhammad Khanz al Alam
1822	Muhammad Alam
1822–52	Umar Ali Sa if-ud-Din II Jamal-ul-Alam
1852–85	Abdul Mu min
1885–1906	Hashim Jalil-ul-Alam Akam-ud-Din
1906–24	Muhammad Jamal-ul-Alam II
1924–50	Ahmad Taj-ud-Din
1950–67	Umar Ali Sa if-ud-Din III
1967–	Sir Muda Hassan al Bolkiah Mu'izz-ud-Din-Waddaulah

Bulgaria

Monarch – Kingdom of Bulgaria
1879–1886	Prince Alexander of Battenburg Prince
1887–1918	Ferdinand I Prince until 1918
1918–43	Boris III
1943–6	Simeon II

Head of State – People's Republic of Bulgaria
Chairman of the Presidium of the National Assembly
1946–7	Vasil Kolarov
1947–50	Mincho Naichev
1950–8	Georgi Damianov
1958–64	Dimitro Ganev
1964–71	Georgi Traikov

Chairman of the State Council
1971–89	Todor Zhivkov
1989–90	Petar Mladenov

President – Republic of Bulgaria
1991–6	Zhelyu Zhelev
1996–	Petar Stoyanov

Premier
1946–9	Georgi Mikhailovich Dimitrov
1949–50	Vasil Kolarov
1950–6	Vulko Chervenkov
1956–62	Anton Yugov
1962–71	Todor Zhivkov
1971–81	Stanko Todorov
1981–6	Grisha Filipov
1986–90	Georgy Atanasov
1990	Andrei Lukanov
1990–1	Dimitar Popov
1991–2	Filip Dimitrov
1992–4	Lyuben Berov
1994–5	Reneta Indzhova

1995–7	Zhan Videnov
1997	Nicolay Dobrev
1997	Stefan Sofianki Interim
1997–	Ivan Kostov

First Secretary
1946–53	Vulko Chervenkov
1953–89	Todor Zhivkov
1989–90	Petar Mladenov
1990–1	Alexander Lilov
1991–6	Zhan Videnov
1996–	Georgi Parvanov

Burgundy

Dukedom of Burgundy
House of Valois
1363–1404	Philip 'the Bold'
1404–19	John 'the Fearless'
1419–67	Philip 'the Good'
1467–77	Charles 'the Bold'
1477–	United with Crown of Austria and later of Spain

Burkina Faso

President
Upper Volta
1960–6	Maurice Yaméogo
1966–80	Sangoulé Lamizana
1980–	Saye Zerbo

People's Salvation Council
1982–3	Jean-Baptiste Ouedraugo Chairman

National Revolutionary Council
1983–4	Thomas Sankara Chairman

Burkina Faso
1984–7	Thomas Sankara Chairman
1987–	Blaise Compaoré

Prime Minister
1992–4	Youssouf Ouedraogo
1994–6	Roch Christian Kabore
1996–	Kadre Desire Ouedraogo

Burundi

Mwami (King)
c.1675–c.1705	Ntare I Rushatsi
c.1705–c.1735	Mwezi I
c.1735–c.1765	Mutaga I Seenyamwiiza
c.1765–c.1795	Mwambutsa I
c.1795–1852	Ntare II Rugaamba
1852–1908	Mwezi II Kisabo
1908–16	Mutaga II
1916–62	Mwambutsa II

Independence
1962–6	Mwambutsa II
1966	Ntare III Ndizeye

President
1966–77	Michel Micombero
1977–87	Jean-Baptiste Bagaza
1987–93	Military junta (Pierre Buyoya)
1993–4	Melchior Ndadaye
1994–6	Sylvestre Ntibantunganya

1996	Military coup (Pierre Buyoya)

Head of Government
1988–93	Adrien Sibomana
1993–4	Sylvie Kinigi
1994–5	Anatole Kanyenkiko
1995–6	Antoine Nduwayo
1996–	Pascal-Firmin Ndimira

Byzantium (Constantinople)

Emperors
395–408	Arcadius
408–50	Theodosius II
450–7	Marcianus
457–74	Leo I
474	Leo II
474–91	Zeno
475–6	Basiliscus Joint Emperor
491–518	Anastasius I
518–27	Justin I
527–65	Justinian I
565–78	Justin II
578–82	Tiberius II
582–602	Maurice
602–10	Phocas
610–41	Heraclius
641	Constantine III
641	Heracleonas Joint Emperor
641–68	(Flavius Heraclius) Constans II
668–85	Constantine IV Pogonatus
685–95	Justinian II
695–8	Leontius
698–705	Tiberius III Apsimar
705–11	Justinian II (restored)
711–13	Philippicus
713–15	Anastasius II
715–17	Theodosius III
717–41	Leo III Isauricus
741–75	Constantine V Copronymus
775–80	Leo IV
780–9	Constantine VI
797–802	Irene
802–11	Nicephorus I
811	Stauracius
811–13	Michael I
813–20	Leo V 'the Armenian'
820–9	Michael II
829–42	Theophilus
842–67	Michael III
867–86	Basil I 'the Macedonian'
886–912	Leo VI
912–59	Constantine VII Porphyrogenitus Joint Emperor to 913 and 920–44
912–13	Alexander Joint Emperor
920–44	Romanus I Lecapenus Regent and Joint Emperor
959–63	Romanus II
963–9	Nicephorus II Phocas
969–76	John I Tzimisces
976–1028	Constantine VIII

976–1025	Basil II Bulgaroctonus *Joint Emperor*
1028–50	Zoë *Joint Empress*
1028–34	Romanus III Argyrus *Joint Emperor*
1034–41	Michael IV 'the Paphla- gonian' *Joint Emperor*
1041–2	Michael V Calaphates *Joint Emperor*
1042–55	Constantine IX Mono- machus *Joint Emperor*
1042–56	Theodora *Joint Empress until 1055*
1056–7	Michael VI Stratioticus
1057–9	Isaac I Comnenus
1059–67	Constantine X Ducas
1068–71	Romanus IV Diogenes
1071–8	Michael VII Ducas
1078–81	Nicephorus III Botaneiates

Comnenian Emperors

1081–1118	Alexius I Comnenus
1118–43	John II Comnenus
1143–80	Manuel I
1180–3	Alexius II
1183–5	Andronicus I Comnenus
1185–95	Isaac II Angelus
1195–1203	Alexius III
1203–04	Isaac II Angelus (*restored*)
1203–04	Alexius IV *Joint Emperor*
1204	Alexius V Ducas

Latin Emperors

1204–5	Baldwin I
1205–16	Henry
1216–17	Peter of Courtenay
1217–19	Yolande
1219–28	Robert
1228–61	Baldwin II

Byzantine Emperors at Nicaea

1204–22	Theodore I Lascaris
1222–54	John III Varatzes
1254–8	Theodore II
1258–61	John IV *Joint Emperor* *from 1259*
1259–61	Michael VIII Palaeologus *Regent and Joint Emperor*

Palaeologi Emperors at Byzantium

1261–82	Michael VIII Palaeologus
1282–1328	Andronicus II Palaeologus *Joint Emperor 1295–1320*
1295–1320	Michael IX *Joint Emperor*
1328–41	Andronicus III Palaeologus
1341–91	John V *Joint Emperor 1347–54 and from 1376*
1347–54	John VI Cantacuzene *Regent and Joint Emperor*
1376–9	Andronicus IV *Joint Emperor*
1390	John VII *Joint Emperor*
1391–1425	Manuel II *Joint Emperor 1399–1402*
1399–1402	John VII *Joint Emperor*
1425–48	John VIII
1448–53	Constantine XI

Cambodia

Monarch
Angkor Kings

802–50	Jayavarman II
850–77	Jayavarman III
877–89	Indravarman I
889–900	Yasovarman I
900–c.922	Harshavarman I
c.922–8	Isanavarman II
928–42	Jayavarman IV
942–4	Harshavarman II
944–68	Rajendravarman
968–1001	Jayavarman V
1001–02	Udayadityavarman I
1002	Jayaviravarman
1002–50	Suryavarman I
1050–66	Udayadityavarman II
1066–80	Harshavarman III
1080–1107	Jayavarman VI
1107–1113	Dharanindravarman I
1113–50	Suryavarman II
1150–60	Dharanindravarman I
1160–6	Yasovarman II
1166–81	Tribhuvanadityavarman
1181–c.1219	Jayavarman VII
c.1219–43	Indravarman II
1243–95	Jayavarman VIII
1295–1308	Indravarman III
1308–27	Indrajayavarman
1327–c.1353	Jayavarmadiparamesvara
c.1353–	
c.1362	*Period of instability*

Later Kings

c.1362–	
c.1371	Nirvanapada
c.1371–	
c.1377	Kalamegha
c.1377–	
c.1387	Kambudjadhiraja
c.1387–89	Dharmasokaraja
1389–1404	Paramarajadhiraja
1404–29	Narayana Ramadhipati
1429–44	Sodaiya
1444–86	Dharmarajadhiraja
1486–1512	Srey Sukonthor
1512–16	Nay Kan
1516–66	Ang Chan I
1566–76	Barom Reachea I
1576–94	Chettha I
1594–6	Reamea Chung Prei
1596–9	Barom Reachea II
1599–1600	Barom Reachea III
1600–03	Chao Ponhea Nhom
1603–18	Barom Reachea IV
1618–28	Chettha II
1628–30	Ponhea To
1630–40	Ponhea Nu
1640–2	Ang Non I
1642–59	Chan Rama Thupdey
1659–72	Batom Reachea
1672–3	Chettha III
1673–4	Ang Chei
1674–5	Obbarac Ang Non
1675–95	Chettha IV

1695	Outey I
1695–9	Chettha IV (*restored*)
1699–1701	Ang Em
1701–02	Chettha IV (*restored*)
1702–03	Thommo Reachea
1703–22	*Civil war*
1722–38	Satha Ang Chei
1738–47	Thommo Reachea (*restored*)
1747–9	Ang Ton
1749–55	Chettha V
1755–8	Ang Ton (*restored*)
1758–75	Prea Outey II
1775–9	Ang Non II
1779–96	Ang Eng
1796–1834	Ang Chan II
1834–41	Ang Mey
1841–60	Ang Duong
1860–1904	Norodom
1904–27	Sisovath
1927–41	Monivong
1941–55	Norodom Sihanouk II
1955–60	Norodom Suramarit

Chief of State
1960–70	Norodom Sihanouk

Khmer Republic
1970–2	Cheng Heng *Acting*
1972–5	Lon Nol

Democratic Kampuchea
1975–6	Norodom Sihanouk
1976–81	Khieu Samphan

People's Republic of Kampuchea (1979)
1981–89	Heng Samrin

State of Kampuchea
1989–91	Heng Samrin

Government in exile
President
1970–5	Norodom Sihanouk
1982–91	Norodom Sihanouk

Interim Government
Chairman of the Supreme National Council
1991–3	Norodom Sihanouk

Monarch – Kingdom of Cambodia
1993–	Norodom Sihanouk II (*restored*)

Prime Minister
1945–6	Son Ngoc Thanh
1946–8	Prince Monireth
1948–9	Son Ngoc Thanh
1949–51	Prince Monipong
1951	Son Ngoc Thanh
1951–2	Huy Kanthoul
1952–3	*As King*
1953	Samdech Penn Nouth
1953–4	Chan Nak
1954–5	Leng Ngeth
1955–6	Norodom Sihanouk
1956	Oum Chheang Sun
1956	Norodom Sihanouk
1956	Khim Tit
1956	Norodom Sihanouk

1956	Sam Yun
1956–7	Norodom Sihanouk
1957–8	Sim Var
1958	Ek Yi Oun
1958	Samdech Penn Nouth *Acting*
1958	Sim Var
1958–60	Norodom Sihanouk
1960–1	Pho Proung
1961	Samdech Penn Nouth
1961–3	Norodom Sihanouk
1963–6	Norodom Kantol
1966–7	Lon Nol
1967–8	Norodom Sihanouk
1968–9	Samdech Penn Nouth
1969–72	Lon Nol
1972	Sisovath Sivik Matak
1972	Son Ngoc Thanh
1972–3	Hang Thun Hak
1973	In Tam
1973–5	Long Boret
1975–6	Samdech Penn Nouth
1976–9	Pol Pot
1979–81	Khieu Samphan
1981–5	Chan Si
1985–91	Hun Sen

Government in exile

1970–3	Samdech Penn Nouth
1982–91	Son Sann

Kingdom of Cambodia

1993–7	Norodom Ranariddh (*joint*)
1993–	Hun Sen (*joint*)
1997–	Ing Huot (*joint*)

Cameroon

President

1960–82	Ahmadou Ahidjo
1982–	Paul Biya

Prime Minister

1991–2	Sadou Hayatou
1992–6	Simon Achidi Achu
1996–	Peter Mafany Musonge

Canada

Chief of State: British monarch, represented by Governor-General

Prime Minister

1867–73	John Alexander MacDonald *Con*
1873–8	Alexander Mackenzie *Lib*
1878–91	John Alexander MacDonald *Con*
1891–2	John J C Abbot *Con*
1892–4	John Sparrow David Thompson *Con*
1894–6	Mackenzie Bowell *Con*
1896	Charles Tupper *Con*
1896–1911	Wilfrid Laurier *Lib*
1911–20	Robert Laird Borden *Con*
1920–1	Arthur Meighen *Con*
1921–6	William Lyon Mackenzie King *Lib*
1926	Arthur Meighen *Con*
1926–30	William Lyon Mackenzie King *Lib*
1930–5	Richard Bedford Bennett, 1st Viscount Bennett *Con*
1935–48	William Lyon Mackenzie King *Lib*
1948–57	Louis Stephen St Laurent *Lib*
1957–63	John George Diefenbaker *Con*
1963–8	Lester Bowles Pearson *Lib*
1968–79	Pierre Elliott Trudeau *Lib*
1979–80	Charles Joseph Clark *Con*
1980–4	Pierre Elliott Trudeau *Lib*
1984	John Napier Turner *Lib*
1984–93	(Martin) Brian Mulroney *Con*
1993	Kim Campbell *Con*
1993–	Jean Chrétien *Lib*

Con Conservative; *Lib* Liberal

Cape Verde

President

1975–91	Arístides María Pereira
1991–	Antonio Mascarenhas Monteiro

Prime Minister

1975–91	Pedro Verona Rodrigues Pires
1991–	Carlos Viega

Central African Republic

President

1960–6	David Dacko
1966–79	Jean Bédel Bokassa *Emperor Bokassa I from 1977*
1979–81	David Dacko
1981–93	André Kolingba
1993–	Ange-Félix Patasse

Prime Minister

1991–2	Edouard Frank
1992–3	Thimothée Malendoma
1993	Enoch Derant Lakoue
1993–5	Jean-Luc Mandaba
1995–6	Gabriel Koyambounou
1996–7	Jean-Paul Ngoupandé
1997–	Michael Gbezera-Bria

Chad

President

1960–75	François Tombalbaye
1975–9	*Supreme Military Council* (Félix Malloum)
1979	Goukouni Oueddi
1979	Mohammed Shawwa
1979–82	Goukouni Oueddi
1982–90	Hissène Habré
1990–	Idriss Déby *Interim*

Prime Minister

1991–2	Jean Alingue Bawoyeu
1992–3	Joseph Yodemane
1993	Fidèle Moungar
1993–5	Delwa Kassire Koumakoye
1995–7	Koibla Djimasta

1997–	Nassour Ouaidou Guelendouksia

Chile

President

1826	Manuel Blanco Encalada
1826–7	Agustín Eyzaguirre Arechavala *Interim*
1827	Ramón Freire Serrano
1827–9	Francisco Antonio Pinto Díaz
1829–30	Francisco Ramón Vicuña Larraín
1830	Francisco Ruiz Tagle Portales
1830–1	José Tomás Ovalle Bezanilla
1831	Fernand Errázuriz Aldunate *Vice President*
1831–41	Joaquín Prieto Vial
1841–51	Manuel Bulnes Prieto
1851–61	Jorge Montt Torres
1861–71	José Joaquín Pérez Mascayano
1871–6	Federico Errázuriz Zañartu
1876–81	Aníbal Pinto Garmienda
1881–6	Domingo Santa María González
1886–91	José Manuel Balmaceda Fernández
1891	Manuel Baquedano González *Vice President*
1891	*Junta*
1891–6	Jorge Montt Alvarez
1896–1901	Federico Errázuriz Echaurren
1901	Aníbal Zañartu Zañartu *Vice President*
1901–3	Germán Riesco
1903	Ramón Barros Luco *Vice President*
1903–6	Germán Riesco
1906–10	Pedro Montt
1910	Ismael Tocornal *Vice President*
1910	Elías Fernández Albano *Vice President*
1910	Emiliano Figueroa Larraín *Vice President*
1910–15	Ramón Barros Luco
1915–20	Juan Luis Sanfuentes
1920–4	Arturo Alessandri
1924–5	*Military juntas*
1925	Arturo Alessandri
1925	Luis Barros Borgoño *Vice President*
1925–7	Emiliano Figueroa
1927–31	Carlos Ibáñez
1931	Pedro Opaso Letelier *Vice President*
1931	Juan Esteban Montero *Vice President*
1931	Manuel Trucco Franzani *Vice President*
1931–2	Juan Estaban Montero

1932	*Military juntas*
1932	Carlos G Dávila *Provisional*
1932	Bartolomé Blanche *Provisional*
1932	Abraham Oyanedel *Vice President*
1932–8	Arturo Alessandri Palma
1938–41	Pedro Aguirre Cerda
1941–2	Jerónimo Méndez Arancibia *Vice President*
1942–6	Juan Antonio Ríos Morales
1946–52	Gabriel González Videla
1952–8	Carlos Ibáñez del Campo
1958–64	Jorge Alessandri Rodríguez
1964–70	Eduardo Frei Montalva
1970–3	Salvador Allende (Gossens)
1973–90	Augusto Pinochet Ugarte
1990–4	Patricio Aylwin Azócar
1994–	Eduardo Frei Ruíz-Tagle

China

The traditional dates for prehistoric dynasties are not generally considered to be accurate.

Emperor
Prehistoric Dynasties

1766–	
1122BC	Shang (Yin) Dynasty *Probable actual dates c.1500–1027 BC*
1122–771BC	Western Chou Dynasty *Probable actual founding date 1027bc*
770–249BC	Eastern Chou Dynasty
249–221BC	*Civil war*

Ch'in Dynasty

221–10BC	Shih Huang Ti *Cheng Wang of Ch'in from 246 BC*
210–07BC	Erh Shih Huang Ti
207–06BC	Ch'in Wang

Western Han Dynasty

206–195BC	Kao Tsu (Liu Pang)
195–188BC	Hui Ti
188–180BC	Kao Hou
180–157BC	Wen Ti
157–141BC	Ching Ti
141–87BC	Wu Ti
87–74BC	Chao Ti
74–48BC	Hsuan Ti
48–33BC	Yuan Ti
33–7BC	Ch'eng Ti
7–1BC	Ai Ti
1BC–AD6	P'ing Ti
6–8	Ju-Tzu Ying

Hsin Dynasty

9–23	Chia Huang Ti (Wang Mang)
23–5	*Civil war*

Eastern Han Dynasty

25–57	Kuang Wu Ti (Liu Hsiu)
57–75	Ming Ti
75–88	Chang Ti

88–106	Ho Ti
106	Shang Ti
106–25	An Ti
125	Shao Ti
125–44	Shun Ti
144–5	Ch'ung Ti
145–6	Chih Ti
146–68	Huan Ti
168–89	Ling Ti
189	Shao Ti
189–220	Hsien Ti
220–80	*Civil war*

Western Chin Dynasty

280–90	Wu Ti (Ssu-Ma Yen) *Ruler of Western Chin from 266*
290–307	Hui Ti
307–11	Huai Ti
311–13	*No Emperor*
313–16	Min Ti

Eastern Chin Dynasty

317–23	Yuan Ti (Ssu-Ma Jui)
323–5	Ming Ti
325–42	Ch'eng Ti
342–4	K'ang Ti
344–61	Mu Ti
361–5	Ai Ti
365–72	Ti I (Hai Hsi Kung)
372	Chien Wen Ti
372–96	Hsiao Wu Ti
396–419	An Ti
419–20	Kung Ti

Earlier Sung Dynasty

420–2	Wu Ti (Liu Yu)
422–4	Shao Ti
424–53	We Ti
453–64	Hsiao Wu Ti
464–6	Ch'ien Fei Ti
466–72	Ming Ti
472–7	Hou Fei Ti
477–9	Shun Ti

Southern Ch'i Dynasty

479–82	Kao Ti (Hsiao Tao-Ch'eng)
482–93	Wu Ti
493–4	Yu-Lin Wang
494	Hai-Ling Wang
494–8	Ming Ti
498–501	Tung-Hun Hou
501–02	Ho Ti

Southern Liang Dynasty

502–49	Wu Ti (Hsiao Yen)
549–51	Chien Wen Ti
551–2	Yu-Chang Wang
552–5	Yuan Ti
555	Chen-Yang Hou
555–7	Ching Ti

Southern Ch'en Dynasty

557–9	Wu Ti (Ch'en Pa-Hsien)
559–66	Wen Ti
566–8	Fei Ti
568–82	Hsuan Ti
582–9	Hou Chu

Sui Dynasty

589–605	Wen Ti (Yang Chien)
605–19	Yang Ti

T'ang Dynasty

619–27	Kao Tsu (Li Yuan)
627–50	T'ai Tsung (Li Shih-Min)
650–84	Kao Tsung
684–5	Chung Tsung
685–90	Jui Tsung
690–705	Wu Hou
705–10	Chung Tsung (restored)
710–13	Jui Tsung (restored)
713–56	Hsuan Tsung
756–62	Su Tsung
762–79	Tai Tsung
779–805	Te Tsung
805	Shun Tsung
805–20	Hsien Tsung
820–4	Mu Tsung
824–7	Ching Tsung
827–40	Wen Tsung
840–6	Wu Tsung
846–59	Hsuan Tsung
859–73	I Tsung
873–88	Hsi Tsung
888–904	Chao Tsung
904–07	Chao Hsuan Ti

Later Liang Dynasty

907–12	T'ai Tsu (Chu Wen)
912–13	Ying Wang
913–23	Mo Ti

Later T'ang Dynasty

923–6	Chuang Tsung (Li Ts'un-Hsu)
926–33	Ming Tsung
933–4	Min Ti
934–6	Mo Ti

Later Chin Dynasty

936–42	Kao Tsu (Shih Ching-T'ang)
942–7	Ch'u Ti

Later Han Dynasty

947–8	Kao Tsu (Liu Chih-Yuan)
948–51	Yin Ti

Later Chou Dynasty

951–4	T'ai Tsu (Kuo Wei)
954–9	Shih Tsung
959–60	Kung Ti

Northern Sung Dynasty

960–76	T'ai Tsu (Chao K'uang-Yin)
976–97	T'ai Tsung
997–1022	Chen Tsung
1022–63	Jen Tsung
1063–7	Ying Tsung
1067–85	Shen Tsung
1085–1100	Che Tsung
1100–26	Hui Tsung
1126–7	Ch'in Tsung

Southern Sung Dynasty

1127–62	Kao Tsung
1162–89	Hsiao Tsung
1189–94	Kuang Tsung

1194–1224	Ning Tsung
1224–64	Li Tsung
1264–74	Tu Tsung
1274–6	Kung Tsung
1276–8	Tuan Tsung
1278–9	Ti Ping

Yuan (Mongol) Dynasty

1206–27	T'ai Tsu (Genghis/ Chingis Khan)
1227–9	*Disputed succession*
1229–41	T'ai Tsung (Ogodei Khan)
1241–6	*Disputed succession*
1246–8	Ting Tsung (Guyuk Khan)
1248–51	*Disputed succession*
1251–9	Hsien Tsung (Mengu Khan)]
1260–94	Shih Tsu (Kublai/ Kubilai Khan) *Emperor of all China from 1279*
1294–1307	Ch'eng Tsung
1307–11	Wu Tsung
1311–20	Jen Tsung
1320–3	Ying Tsung
1323–8	T'ai Ting Ti
1328–9	Wen Tsung
1329	Ming Tsung
1329–32	Wen Tsung *(restored)*
1332	Ning Tsung
1332–68	Shun Ti

Ming Dynasty

1368–98	T'ai Tsu (Hung Wu; Chu Yuan-Chang)
1398–1402	Hui Ti (Chien wen)
1402–24	Ch'eng Tsu (Yung Lo)
1424–5	Jen Tsung (Hung Hsi)
1425–35	Hsuan Tsung (Hsuan Te)
1435–49	Ying Tsung (Cheng T'ung)
1449–57	Tai Tsung (Ching T'ai)
1457–64	Ying Tsung (Cheng T'ung) *(restored)*
1464–87	Hsien Tsung (Ch'eng Hua)
1487–1505	Hsiao Tsung (Hung Chih)
1505–21	Wu Tsung (Cheng Te)
1521–67	Shih Tsung (Chia Ching)
1567–72	Mu Tsung (Lung Ch'ing)
1572–1620	Shen Tsung (Wan Li)
1620	Kuang Tsung (T'ai Ch'ing)
1620–7	Hsi Tsung (T'ien Ch'i)
1627–44	Chuang Lieh Ti (Ch'ung Chen)

Ch'ing (Manchu) Dynasty

1616–26	T'ai Tsu (T'ien Ming; Nurhachi)
1626–43	T'ai Tsung (T'ien Ts'ung/Ch'ung Te)
1643–61	Shih Tsu (Shun Chih)
1661–1722	Sheng Tsu (K'ang Hsi}
1722–35	Shih Tsung (Yung Cheng)
1735–96	Kao Tsung (Ch'ien Lung)
1796–1820	Jen Tsung (Chia Ch'ing)
1820–50	Hsuan Tsung (Tao Kuang)
1850–61	Wen Tsung (Hsien Feng)
1861–75	Mu Tsung (T'ung Chih)
1875–1908	Te Tsung (Kuang-hsü)
1908–12	Mo Ti (Xuantong; Pu-yi)

President

1912	Sun Yixian
1912–16	Yüan Shikai
1916–17	Li Yuanhoung
1917–18	Feng Gouzhang
1918–22	Xu Shichang
1921–5	Sun Yixian *Canton Administration*
1922–3	Li Yuanhoung
1923–4	Cao Kun
1924–6	Duan Qirui
1926–7	*Civil disorder*
1927–8	Zhang Zuolin
1928–31	Jiang Jieshi
1931–2	Cheng Mingxu *Acting*
1932–43	Lin Sen
1940–4	Wang Jingwei *In Japanese-occupied territory*
1943–9	Jiang Jieshi
1945–9	*Civil war*
1949	Li Zongren

People's Republic of China

1949–59	Mao Zedong (Mao Tse-tung)
1959–68	Liu Shaoqi
1968–75	Dong Biwu
1975–6	Zhu De
1976–8	Song Qingling
1978–83	Ye Jianying
1983–8	Li Xiannian (Li Hsien-nien)
1988–93	Yang Shangkun
1993–	Jiang Zemin

Prime Minister

1901–3	Ronglu
1903–11	Yikuang, Prince Qing
1912	Lu Zhengxiang
1912	Yuan Shikai
1912	Tang Shaoyi
1912–13	Zhao Bingjun
1912–13	Xiong Xiling
1914	Sun Baoyi
1914–15	Xu Shichang
1915–16	*No Prime Minister*
1916–17	Duan Qirui
1917–18	Wang Shizhen
1918	Dun Qirui
1918–19	Qian Nengxun
1919	Gong Xinzhan
1919–20	Jin Yunpeng
1921–2	Liang Shiyi
1922	Yan Huiqin
1922	Zhou Ziqi *Acting*
1922	Yan Huiqin
1922	Wang Chonghui
1922–3	Wang Daxie
1923	Zhang Shaozeng
1923–4	Gao Lingwei
1924	Sun Baoyi
1924	Gu Weijun
1924	Yan Huiqing
1924	Huang Fu *Acting*
1924–5	Duan Qirui
1925–6	Xu Shiying
1926	Jia Deyao
1926	Hu Weide

1926	Yan Huiqing
1926	Du Xigui *Acting*
1926–7	Gu Weijun
1927	*Civil disorder*
1928–30	Tan Yankai
1930	Song Ziwen (T V Soong) *Acting*
1930	Wang Jingwei
1930–1	Jiang Jieshi (Chiang K'ai-shek)
1931–2	Sun Fo
1932–5	Wang Jingwei
1935–7	Jiang Jieshi (Chiang K'ai-shek)
1937–8	Wang Chonghui
1938–9	Kong Xiangxi
1939–44	Jiang Jieshi (Chiang K'ai-shek)
1944–7	Song Ziwen (T V Soong)
1945–9	*Civil war*
1948	Wang Wenhao
1948–9	Sun Fo
1949	He Yingqin
1949	Yan Xishan
1949–76	Zhou Enlai (Chou En-lai)
1976–80	Hua Guofeng
1980–7	Zhao Ziyang (Chao Tzu-yang)
1987–	Li Peng

Communist Party
Chairman

1935–76	Mao Zedong (Mao Tse-tung)
1976–81	Hua Guofeng
1981–2	Hu Yaobang

General Secretary

1982–7	Hu Yaobang
1987–9	Zhao Ziyang (Chao Tzu-yang)
1989–	Jiang Zemin

Colombia

President
Gran Colombia

1819–30	Simón Bolívar (*Dictator from 1828*)
1830	Joaquín Mosquero
1830–1	Rafael Urdaneta *Dictator*
1831	Domingo Caycedo *Vice President*
1831–2	José María Obando *Vice President*

New Granada

1832	José Ignacio de Márquez *Vice President*
1832–7	Francisco de Paula Santander
1837–41	José Ignacio de Márquez
1841–5	Pedro Alántara Herrán
1845–9	Tomás C de Mosquera
1849–53	José Hilario López
1853–4	José María Obando
1854	José María Melo *Dictator*
1854	Tomás Herrera *Interim*

1854–5	José de Obaldía
	Vice President
1855–7	Manuel María Mallarino
1857–61	Mariano Ospina Rodríguez
1861–3	Tomás C de Mosquera
	Provisional

United States of Colombia

1863–4	Tomás C de Mosquera
1864–6	Manuel Murillo Toro
1866–7	Tomás C de Mosquera
1867–70	Santos Gutiérrez
1870–2	Eustorgio Salgar
1872–4	Manuel Murillo Toro
1874–6	Santiago Pérez
1876–8	Aquileo Parra
1878–80	Julián Trujillo

Republic of Colombia

1880–2	Rafael Núñez
1882	Francisco Javier Zaldúa
1882	Clímaco Calderón
	President Designate
1882–4	José Eusebio Otálora
	President Designate
1884–6	Rafael Núñez
1886–7	José María Campo Serrano
	President Designate
1887–94	Rafael Núñez
1894–6	Miguel Antonio Caro
	Vice President
1896	Guillermo Quintero Calderón *President Designate*
1896–8	Miguel Antonio Caro
1898–1900	Manuel Antonio Sanclemente
1900–4	José Manuel Marroquín
	Vice President
1904–9	Rafael Reyes
1909–10	Ramón González Valencia
1910–14	Carlos E Restrepo
1914–18	José Vicente Concha
1918–21	Marco Fidel Suárez
1921–2	Jorge Holguín
	President Designate
1922–6	Pedro Nel Ospina
1926–30	Miguel Abadía Méndez
1930–4	Enrique Olaya Herrera
1934–8	Alfonso López
1938–42	Eduardo Santos
1942–5	Alfonso López
1945–6	Alberto Lleras Camargo
	President Designate
1946–50	Mariano Ospina Pérez
1950–3	Laureano Gómez
1953–7	Gustavo Rojas Pinilla
1957	*Military junta*
1958–62	Alberto Lleras Camargo
1962–6	Guillermo León Valencia
1966–70	Carlos Lleras Restrepo
1970–4	Misael Pastrana Borrero
1974–8	Alfonso López Michelsen
1978–82	Julio César Turbay Ayala
1982–6	Belisario Betancur
1986–90	Virgilio Barco Vargas

1990–4	César Gaviria Trujillo
1994–	Ernesto Samper Pizano

Commonwealth

Secretary General

1965–75	Arnold Smith
1975–90	Shridath Surrendranath ('Sonny') Ramphal
1990–	Emeka Anyaoku

Comoros

President

1976–8	Ali Soilih
1978–89	Ahmed Abdallah Abderemane
1989–96	Said Mohammed Djohar
1996–	Mohammed Taki Abdoulkarim

Prime Minister

1990–2	Said Ali Kemal
1992	Mohammed Taki Abdoulkarim
1992–3	Ibrahim Abderamane Halidi
1993	Said Ali Mohammed
1993–4	Ahmed ben Cheikh Attoumane
1994	Mohammed Abdou Madi
1994–5	Halifa Houmadi
1995–6	Caabi el Yachroutou Mohamed
1996	Majidine ben Said
1996–	Ahmed Abdou

Congo

President

1960–3	Abbé Fulbert Youlou
1963–8	Alphonse Massemba-Debat
1968	Marien Ngouabi
1968	Alphonse Massemba-Debat
1968–9	Alfred Raoul
1969–77	Marien Ngouabi
1977–9	Jacques-Joachim Yhomby Opango
1979–92	Denis Sassou-Nguesso
1992–7	Pascal Lissouba
1997	Denis Sassou-Nguesso

Prime Minister

1991–2	André Milonga
1992	Stephane Bongho-Nouarra
1992–3	Claude Antoine Dacosta
1993–6	Jacques-Joachim Yhomby-Opango
1996–	Charles David Ganao

Congo, Democratic Republic of
(formerly **Zaire**)

President
Republic of the Congo

1960–5	Joseph Kasavubu
1965–1971	Joseph Désiré Mobutu

Republic of Zaire

1971–97	Mobuto Sese Seko (*formerly* Joseph Mobutu)

Democratic Republic of Congo

1997–	Laurent Kabila

Prime Minister

1960	Patrice Emergy Lumumba
1960	Joseph Ileo
1960–1	*College of Commissioners*
1961	Joseph Ileo
1961–4	Cyrille Adoula
1964–5	Moïse Tshombe
1965	Evariste Kimba
1965–6	Mulamba Nyungu wa Kadima
1966–77	*As President*
1977–80	Mpinga Kasenga
1980	Bo-Boliko Lokonga Monse Mihambu
1980–1	Nguza Karl I Bond
1981–3	Nsinga Udjuu
1983–6	Kengo wa Dondo
1986–8	*No Prime Minister*
1988	Sambura Pida Nbagui
1988–9	Kengo wa Dondo
1989–1	Lunda Bululu
1991	Mulumba Lukeji
1991	Etienne Tshisekedi
1991–2	Bernardin Mungul Diaka
1992–3	Etienne Tshisekedi
1993–4	Fouistin Birindwa *Acting*
1994–7	Kengo a Dondo
1997	Etienne Tshisekedi
1997–	Likulia Bolongo

Costa Rica

Head of State

1824–33	Juan Mora Fernández
1833–5	José Rafael Gallegos y Alvarado
1835	Juan José Lara Arias *Interim*
1835	Manuel Fernández Chacón
1835–7	Braulio Carrillo Colina
1837	Juan Mora Fernández
1837	Manuel Fernández Chacón
1837–8	Juan Mora Fernández
1838	Manuel Fernández Chacón
1838–42	Braulio Carrillo Colina
1842	Manuel Antonio Bonilla Nava
1842	Francisco Morazán
1842	Antonio Pino Suárez
1842–4	José María Alfaro Zamora
1844	Francisco María Oreamuno Bonilla
1844–5	Rafael Moya Murillo
1845–6	*No Head of State*
1846–7	José María Alfaro Zamora
1847–8	José María Castro Madriz

President

1848–9	José María Castro Madriz
1849	Miguel Mora Porres *Acting*
1849–59	Juan Rafael Mora Porres

1859–63	José María Montealegre
1863–6	Jesús de Jiménez Zamora
1866–8	José María Castro Madriz
1868–70	Jesús de Jiménez Zamora
1870	Bruno Carranza Ramírez
1870–6	Tomás Guardia Gutiérrez
1876	Aniceto Esquivel Sáenz
1876–7	Vicente Herrera Zeledón
1877–82	Tomás Guardia Gutiérrez
1882–5	Próspero Fernández Oreamuno
1885–9	Bernardo Soto Alfaro
1889–90	Carlos Durán Cartin
1890–4	José Joaquín Rodríguez Zeledón
1894–1902	Rafael Yglesias y Castro
1902–6	Ascención Esquivel Ibarra
1906–10	Cleto González Víquez
1910–12	Ricardo Jiménez Oreamuno
1912–14	Cleto González Víquez
1914–17	Alfredo González Flores
1917–19	Federico Tinoco Granados
1919	Julio Acosta García
1919–20	Juan Bautista Quiros
1920–4	Julio Acosta García
1924–8	Ricardo Jiménez Oreamuno
1928–32	Cleto González Víquez
1932–6	Ricardo Jiménez Oreamuno
1936–40	León Cortés Castro
1940–4	Rafael Angel Calderón Guardia
1944–8	Teodoro Picado Michalski
1948	Santos Léon Herrera
1948–9	Civil junta (José Figueres Ferrer)
1949–52	Otilio Ulate Blanco
1952–3	Alberto Oreamuno Flores
1953–8	José Figueres Ferrer
1958–62	Mario Echandi Jiménez
1962–6	Francisco José Orlich Bolmarcich
1966–70	José Joaquín Trejos Fernández
1970–4	José Figueres Ferrer
1974–8	Daniel Oduber Quirós
1978–82	Rodrigo Carazo Odio
1982–6	Luis Alberto Monge Alvarez
1986–90	Oscar Arias Sánchez
1990–4	Rafael Angel Calderón Fournier
1994–	José Maríe Figueres

Côte d'Ivoire

President

1960–93	Félix Houphouët-Boigny
1993–	Henri Konan Bédié

Prime Minister

1990–3	Alassane Dramane Ouattara
1993–	Daniel Kablan Duncan

Croatia

Monarch – Kingdom of Croatia

924–30	Tomislav
930–69	Kresimir II
969–97	Stephen Drzhislav
997–c.1000	Svetolav
c.1000–30	Kresimir III
1030–58	Peter Kresimir
1058–76	Dimitar Zvonimir
1076–89	Stephen II
1091–5	Almos
1095–1918	*Part of Hungary*
1918–91	*Part of Yugoslavia*

President

1991–	Franjo Tudjman

Prime Minister

1991–2	Franjo Greguric
1992–3	Hrvoje Sarinic
1993–5	Nikica Valentic
1995–	Zlatko Matesa

Cuba

President

1902–6	Tomas Estrada Palma
1906–9	*US rule*
1909–13	José Miguel Gómez
1913–21	Mario García Menocal
1921–5	Alfredo Zayas y Alfonso
1925–33	Gerardo Machado y Morales
1933	Carlos Manuel de Céspedes
1933–4	Ramón Grau San Martín
1934–5	Carlos Mendieta
1935–6	José A Barnet y Vinagres
1936	Miguel Mariano Gómez y Arias
1936–40	Federico Laredo Bru
1940–4	Fulgencio Batista
1944–8	Ramón Grau San Martín
1948–52	Carlos Prío Socarrás
1952–9	Fulgencio Batista
1959	Manuel Urrutia
1959–76	Osvaldo Dorticós Torrado
1976–	Fidel Castro Ruz

Prime Minister

1959–76	Fidel Castro Ruz *Prime Minister and First Secretary*
1976–	*As President*

Cyprus

Monarch – Kingdom of Cyprus

Lusignan Dynasty

1192–4	Guy of Lusignan
1194–1205	Amalric
1205–18	Hugh I
1218–53	Henry I
1253–67	Hugh II
1267–84	Hugh III
1284–5	John I
1285–1324	Henry II
1324–59	Hugh IV
1359–69	Peter I

1369–82	Peter II
1382–98	James I
1398–1432	Janus
1432–58	John II
1458–64	Charlotte *Joint ruler*
1458–64	Louis *Joint ruler*
1460–73	James II *Rival King until 1464*
1473–4	James III
1473–89	Caterina Cornaro *Regent and Joint ruler until 1474*
1489–1571	*Venetian rule*
1571–1914	*Turkish rule*
1914–60	*British rule*

President

1960–77	Archbishop Makarios III (Mihail Christodoulou Mouskos)
1977–88	Spyros Kyprianou
1988–93	Georgios Vassiliou
1993–	Glafkos Clirides

Czech Republic

Duke of Bohemia

House of Prěmysl

873–95	Borzhivoi I
895–921	Vratislav I *Joint ruler to 912*
895–912	Spitihnev I *Joint ruler*
921–9	Vaclav I (St Wenceslas)
929–67	Boleslav I
967–99	Boleslav II
999–1002	Boleslav III
1002–03	Vladivoi
1003	Boleslav III *(restored)*
1003–12	Jaromir
1012–34	Odalrich
1034–55	Bretislav I
1055–61	Spitihnev I
1061–92	Vratislav I *King from 1086*
1092	Conrad
1092–1100	Bretislav II
1100–07	Borzhivoi II
1107–09	Svatopluk
1109–17	Vladislav I
1117–20	Borzhivoi II *(restored)*
1120–5	Vladislav I *(restored)*
1125–40	Sobeslav I
1140–73	Vladislav II *King from 1198*
1173–9	Sobeslav II
1179–89	Frederick
1189–91	Conrad-Otto
1191–2	Václav II
1192–3	Prěmysl Otakar I
1193–7	Bretislav-Henry
1197	Vladislav III
1197–8	Prěmysl Otakar I *(restored)*

King of Bohemia

House of Prěmysl

1198–1230	Prěmysl Otakar I
1230–53	Václav I
1253–78	Prěmysl Otakar II
1278–1305	Václav II
1305–06	Václav III

Later Kings

1306–07	Rudolf (III of Austria)
1307–10	Henry of Carinthia
1310–46	John 'the Blind' (of Luxembourg)
1346–78	Charles (IV) *Holy Roman Emperor*
1378–1419	Vaclav IV (Wenceslas) *Holy Roman Emperor*
1419–37	Sigismund *Holy Roman Emperor*
1437–40	Albert *Holy Roman Emperor*
1440–57	Ladislaus Posthumus (V of Hungary)
1457–71	George of Poděbrady
1471–1516	Vladislav Jagiellon
1516–26	Louis *King Lajos II of Hungary*
1526–1918	*Part of Austria*

President – State of Czechoslovakia

1918–35	Tomáš Garrigue Masaryk
1935–8	Edvard Beneš
1938–9	Emil Hácha
1939–45	Emil Hácha
1941–5	Edvard Beneš *Government in exile*
1945–8	Edvard Beneš
1948–53	Klement Gottwald
1953–7	Antonín Zápotocky
1957–68	Antonín Novotny
1968–75	Ludvík Svoboda
1975–89	Gustáv Husák
1989–92	Václav Havel

President – Czech Republic

1993–	Václav Havel

Prime Minister – State of Czechoslovakia

1918–9	Karel Kramář
1919–20	Vlastimil Tusar
1920–1	Jan Černy
1921–2	Edvard Beneš
1922–6	Antonin Švehla
1926	Jan Černy
1926–9	Antonin Švehla
1929–32	František Udržal
1932–5	Jan Malypetr
1935–8	Milan Hodža
1938	Jan Syrovy
1938–9	Rudolf Beran
1940–5	Jan Šrámek *in exile*
1945–6	Zdeněk Fierlinger
1946–8	Klement Gottwald
1948–53	Antonin Zápotocky
1953–63	Viliam Široky
1963–8	Josef Lenárt
1968–70	Oldřich Černík
1970–88	Lubomír Štrougal
1988–9	Ladislav Adamec
1989–92	Marian Čalfa
1992	Jan Strasky

Prime Minister – Czech Republic

1993–7	Václav Klaus

First Secretary

1948–52	Rudolf Slánsky
1953–68	Antonín Novotny
1968–9	Alexander Dubček
1969–87	Gustáv Husák
1987–9	Mílos Jakes
1989	Karel Urbanek
1989–92	Ladislav Adamec

Denmark

Monarch – Kingdom of Denmark

House of Gorm

c.900–c.950	Gorm 'the Old'
c.950–85	Harald I Gormsson 'Blue-Tooth'
985–1014	Svein I Haraldsson 'Fork-Beard'
1014–19	Harald II
1019–35	Knut Sveinsson (Canute)
1035–42	Hardaknut Knutsson
1042–7	*As Norway*
1047–76	Svein II Estridsson
1076–80	Harald III Hen
1080–6	Knut IV 'the Holy'
1086–95	Olaf IV
1095–1103	Erik I Ejegod
1104–34	Niels
1134–7	Erik II Emune
1137–47	Erik III
1147–57	Svein III *Rival king*
1147–57	Knut V *Rival king*
1157–82	Valdemar I 'the Great'
1182–1202	Knut VI
1202–41	Valdemar II
1241–50	Erik IV
1250–2	Abel
1252–9	Kristofer I
1259–86	Erik V
1286–1320	Erik VI
1320–32	Kristofer II
1340–75	Valdemar III Atterdag
1375–87	Olaf V *Olaf IV of Norway from 1380*
1387–97	Margrethe I (Margareta) *Queen of Norway from 1387 and Sweden from 1389*

Monarch – Kalmar Union

House of Gorm

1397–1412	Margrethe I (Margareta) *Queen of Norway and Sweden*
1412–39	Erik VII (of Pomerania) *Erik III of Norway and XIII of Sweden*
1439–48	Kristofer III (of Bavaria) *Kristofer I of Norway and Sweden*

House of Oldenburg

1448–81	Kristian I *King of Norway, King of Sweden 1457–64, 65–67 and 70–81*
1481–1513	Hans *King of Norway, King Johan II of Sweden*
1513–23	Kristian II *King of Norway, King of Sweden to 1521*

Monarch – Kingdom of Denmark and Norway

House of Oldenburg

1523–34	Frederik I
1534–59	Kristian III
1559–88	Frederik II
1588–1648	Kristian IV
1648–70	Frederik III
1670–99	Kristian V
1699–1730	Frederik IV
1730–46	Kristian VI
1746–66	Frederik V
1766–1808	Kristian VII
1808–14	Frederik VI

Monarch – Kingdom of Denmark

House of Oldenburg

1814–39	Frederik VI
1839–48	Kristian VIII
1848–63	Frederik VII
1863–1906	Kristian IX
1906–12	Frederik VIII
1912–47	Kristian X
1947–72	Frederik (Frederick) IX
1972–	Margrethe II

Prime Minister

1848–52	A W Moltke
1852–3	C A Bluhme
1853–4	A S Ørsted
1854–6	P G Bang
1856–7	Carl Georg Andrae
1857–9	C C Hall
1859–60	C E Rotwitt
1860	Carl Frederik Blixen-Finecke
1860–3	C C Hall
1863–4	D G Monrad
1864–70	C A Bluhme
1870–4	Count Ludvig Holstein-Holsteinborg
1874–5	C A Fonnesbech
1875–94	J B S Estrup
1894–7	Tage Reedzt-Thott
1897–1900	H Hørring
1900–1	Hannibal Sehested
1901–5	J H Deuntzer
1905–8	J C Christensen
1908–9	N Neergaard
1909	L Holstein-Ledreborg
1909–10	C Th Zahle
1910–13	Klaus Berntsen
1913–20	C Th Zahle
1920	Otto Liebe
1920	M P Friis
1920–4	N Neergaard
1924–6	Thorvald Stauning
1926–9	Th Madsen-Mygdal
1929–42	Thorvald Stauning
1942	Wilhelm Buhl
1942–3	Erik Scavenius
1943–5	*No government*

1945	Wilhelm Buhl		1876–8	Buenaventura Báez	1845	*Provisional junta*
1945–7	Knud Kristensen		1878	Ignacio María González	1845–9	Vicente Ramón Roca
1947–50	Hans Hedtoft		1878	Cesário Guillermo	1849–50	Manuel de Ascásubi
1950–3	Erik Eriksen		1878–80	Gregorio Luperón	1850–1	Diego Noboa
1953–5	Hans Hedtoft		1880–2	Fernando Arturo de	1851–6	José María Urbina
1955–60	Hans Christian Hansen			Meriño	1856–9	Francisco Robles
1960–2	Viggo Kampmann		1882–4	Ulises Heureaux	1859	*Provisional junta*
1962–8	Jens Otto Krag		1884–5	Francisco Gregorio Billini	1859–60	Guillermo Franco
1968–71	Hilmar Baunsgaard		1885–6	Alejandro Woss y Gil	1860–1	*Provisional junta*
1971–2	Jens Otto Krag		1886–99	Ulises Heureaux	1861–5	Gabriel García Moreno
1972–3	Anker Jorgensen		1899	Horacio Vásquez *Provisional*	1865–7	Jerónimo Carrión
1973–5	Poul Hartling		1899–1902	Juan Isidro Jiménez	1867–8	Pedro José de Artera y
1975–82	Anker Jorgensen		1902–3	Horacio Vásquez		Calisto *Interim*
1982–93	Poul Holmskov Schlüter		1903	Alejandro Woss y Gil	1868–9	Javier Espinoza
1993–	Poul Nyrop Rasmussen		1903–4	Juan Isidro Jiménez	1869–75	Gabriel García Moreno
			1904–6	Carlos Morales	1875	Francisco Javier León
Djibouti			1906–11	Ramon Cáceres		*Interim*
			1911–12	Eladio Victoria	1875–6	Antonio Borrero
President			1912–13	Adolfo Nouel y Bobadilla	1876–83	Ignacio de Veintimilla
1977–	Hassan Gouled Aptidon		1913–14	José Bordas y Valdés	1883–4	*Provisional junta*
			1914	Ramon Báez	1884–8	José María Placido
Prime Minister			1914–16	Juan Isidro Jiménez		Caamaño y Cornejo
1977–8	Abdallah Mohammed		1916–22	*US occupation* (Francisco	1888–92	Antonio Flores Jijón
	Kamil			Henríquez y Carrajal)	1892–5	Luis Cordero
1978–	Barkat Gourad Hamadou		1922–4	Juan Batista Vicini Burgos	1895	Vicente Lucio Salazar
			1924–30	Horacio Vásquez	1895–1901	Eloy Alfaro
Dominica			1930	Rafael Estrella Urena	1901–5	Leónides Plaza Gutiérrez
			1930–8	Rafael Leónidas Trujillo y	1905–6	Lizardo García
President				Molina	1906–11	Eloy Alfaro
1977	Frederick E Degazon		1938–40	Jacinto Bienvenudo	1911	Emilio Estrada
1978–9	Louis Cods-Lartigue *Interim*			Peynado	1911–12	Carlos Freile Zaldumbide
1979–80	Lenner Armour *Acting*		1940–2	Manuel de Jesus Troncoso	1912–16	Leónides Plaza Gutiérrez
1980–4	Aurelius Marie			de la Concha	1916–20	Alfredo Baquerizo Moreno
1984–93	Clarence Augustus		1942–52	Rafael Leónidas Trujillo y	1920–4	José Luis Tamayo
	Seignoret			Molina	1924–5	Gonzálo S de Córdova
1993–	Crispin Sorhaindo		1952–60	Hector Bienvenido Trujillo	1925–6	*Military juntas*
			1960–2	Joaquín Videla Balaguer	1926–31	Isidro Ayora
Prime Minister			1962	Rafael Bonnelly	1931	Luis A Larrea Alba
1978–9	Patrick Roland John		1962	*Military junta* (Huberto	1932–3	Juan de Dios Martínez
1979–80	Oliver Seraphine			Bogaert)		Mera
1980–95	(Mary) Eugenia Charles		1962–3	Rafael Bonnelly	1933–4	Abelardo Montalvo
1995–	Edison James		1963	Juan Bosch Gavino	1934–5	José María Velasco Ibarra
			1963	*Military junta* (Emilio de los	1935	Antonio Pons
Dominican Republic				Santos)	1935–7	Federico Páez
			1963–5	Donald Reid Cabral	1937–8	Alberto Enriquez Gallo
President			1965	Elias Wessin y Wessin	1938	Manuel María Borrero
1844	Tomás Bobadilla		1965	Antonio Imbert Barreras	1938–9	Aurelio Mosquera Narváez
1844–8	Pedro Santana		1965	Francisco Caamaño Deñó	1939–40	Julio Enrique Moreno
1848–9	Manuel Jiménez		1965–6	Héctor García Godoy	1940–4	Carlos Alberto Arroya del
1849–53	Buenaventura Báez			Cáceres		Río
1853–6	Pedro Santana		1966–78	Joaquín Videla Balaguer	1944–7	José María Velasco Ibarra
1856	Manuel de Regla Mota		1978–82	Antonio Guzmán	1947	Carlos Mancheno
1856–8	Buenaventura Báez			Fernández	1947–8	Carlos Julio Arosemena
1858–9	José Desiderio Valverde		1982–6	Salvador Jorge Blanco		Tola
1859–61	Pedro Santana		1986–96	Joaquín Videla Balaguer	1948–52	Galo Plaza Lasso
1861–5	*Spanish rule*			Ricardo	1952–6	José María Velasco Ibarra
1863–4	José Antonio Salcedo		1996–	Leonel Fernandez	1956–60	Camilo Ponce Enríquez
	Provisional				1960–1	José María Velasco Ibarra
1864–5	Gaspar Potanco		**Ecuador**		1961–3	Carlos Julio Arosemena
1865	Benigno Filomeno Rojas					Monroy
1865	Pedro Antonio Pimentel		**President**		1963–6	*Military junta*
1865	José María Cabral		1830–5	Juan José Flores	1966	Clemente Yerovi Indaburu
1865–6	Buenaventura Báez		1835–9	Vicente Rocafuerte	1966–8	Otto Arosemena Gómez
1866–8	José María Cabral		1839–43	Juan José Flores	1968–72	José María Velasco Ibarra
1868–73	Buenaventura Báez		1843	*Provisional junta*	1972–6	Guillermo Rodríguez Lara
1874–6	Ignacio María González		1843–5	Juan José Flores		
1876	Ulises Francisco Espaillat					
1876	Ignacio María González					

1976–9	*Military junta*
1979–81	Jaime Roldós Aguilera
1981–4	Oswaldo Hurtado Larrea
1984–8	León Febres Cordero Rivadeira
1988–92	Rodrigo Borja Cevallos
1992–6	Sixto Durán Ballén
1996–7	Abdala Bucaram
1997	Rosalia Arteaga *Acting*
1997–	Fabián Alarcón Rivero

Egypt

Dynasty – Old Kingdom

*c.*2925–*c.*2775BC	I Dynasty
*c.*2775–*c.*2650BC	II Dynasty
*c.*2650–*c.*2575BC	III Dynasty
*c.*2575–*c.*2465BC	IV Dynasty *including Khufu (Cheops) and Kha'fre' (Chephren)*
*c.*2465–*c.*2325BC	V Dynasty
*c.*2325–*c.*2150BC	VI Dynasty
*c.*2150–*c.*2130BC	VII–VIII Dynasty
*c.*2130–*c.*2080BC	IX Dynasty *Heracleopolis*
*c.*2080–*c.*1970BC	X Dynasty *Hera*

Pharaoh – Middle Kingdom

XI Dynasty (Thebes)

*c.*2081–*c.*2065BC	Mentuhotpe I *Joint ruler*
*c.*2081–*c.*2065BC	Inyotef I *Joint ruler*
*c.*2065–*c.*2016BC	Inyotef II
*c.*2016–*c.*2008BC	Inyotef III
*c.*2008–*c.*1957BC	Mentuhotpe II
*c.*1957–*c.*1945BC	Mentuhotpe III
*c.*1945–*c.*1938BC	Mentuhotpe IV

XII Dynasty

*c.*1938–*c.*1908BC	Amenemhe I
*c.*1918–*c.*1875BC	Senwosre I *Joint ruler to 1862BC*
*c.*1875–*c.*1842BC	Amenemhe II
*c.*1844–*c.*1837BC	Senwosre II *Joint ruler to 1842BC*
*c.*1836–*c.*1818BC	Senwosre III
*c.*1818–*c.*1770BC	Amenemhe III
*c.*1770–*c.*1760BC	Amenemhe IV
*c.*1760–*c.*1756BC	Sebeknofru

Minor dynasties

*c.*1756–*c.*1630BC	XIII Dynasty
*c.*1756–*c.*1577BC	XIV Dynasty *Western Delta*
*c.*1630–*c.*1544BC	XV (Great Hyskos) Dynasty
*c.*1630–*c.*1544BC	XVI (Minor Hyskos) Dynasty
*c.*1630–*c.*1540BC	XVII Dynasty *Upper Egypt*

Pharaoh – New Kingdom

XVIII Dynasty

*c.*1539–	
*c.*1514BC	Ahmose
*c.*1514–	
1493BC	Amenhotpe I
1493–	
*c.*1482BC	Thutmose (Tuthmosis) I
*c.*1482–79BC	Thutmose (Tuthmosis) II
1479–24BC	Thutmose (Tuthmosis) III
1479–58BC	Hashepsowe (Hatshepsut) *Regent*
1426	
–1400BC	Amenhotpe (Amenhotep) II *Joint ruler to 1424BC*
1400–	
1390BC	Thutmose (Tuthmosis) IV
1390–53BC	Amenhotpe (Amenhotep) III
1353–36BC	Amenhotpe IV (Akhenaton)
1335–32BC	Smenkhare
1332–23BC	Tutankhamun
1323–19BC	Ay
1319–	
*c.*1292BC	Haremhab (Horemheb)

XIX Dynasty

*c.*1292–	
1290BC	Ramesse I
1290–	
1279BC	Seti I Merenptah
1279–13BC	Ramesse II Miamun (Rameses II 'the Great')
1213–04BC	Meryamun Merenptah
1204–	
1198BC	Seti II Merenptah
1200–	
1194BC	Amenmesse *Rival Pharaoh*
1198–3BC	Merenptah Siptah
1193–90BC	Meryamun Tewosre

XX Dynasty

1190–87BC	Setnakhte
1187–56BC	Ramesse (Rameses) III
1156–50BC	Ramesse IV
1150–45BC	Ramesse V
1145–37BC	Ramesse VI
1137–27BC	Ramesse VII
1127–6BC	Ramesse VIII
1126–08BC	Ramesse IX
1108–04BC	Ramesse X
1104–	
*c.*1078BC	Ramesse XI

Minor dynasties

*c.*1075–	
*c.*950BC	XXI Dynasty *Tanis*
*c.*950–730BC	XXII Dynasty
832–730BC	XXIII Dynasty
730–22BC	*Invasion from Libya*
722–15BC	XXIV Dynasty *Delta*
760–656BC	XXV Dynasty *Napata*
667–525BC	XXVI Dynasty
525–404BC	XXVII Dynasty – *Persian rule (see Iran)*
404–399BC	XXVIII Dynasty
399–80BC	XXIX Dynasty
380–43BC	XXX Dynasty
343–32BC	XXXI Dynasty – *Persian rule (see Iran)*
332–05BC	XXXII Dynasty –*Macedonian rule (see Greece) (Ptolemy Satrap 321–05BC)*

Monarch – Kingdom of Egypt

Ptolemies – Lagid Dynasty

305–283BC	Ptolemy I Soter
285–46BC	Ptolemy II Philadelphus
246–22BC	Ptolemy III Eurgetes
222–04BC	Ptolemy IV Philopator
204–181BC	Ptolemy V Epiphanes
181–45BC	Ptolemy VI Philometor
145–16BC	Ptolemy VII Euergetes
116–08BC	Ptolemy VIII Sotor
108–88BC	Ptolemy IX Alexander
88–80BC	Ptolemy VIII Sotor (restored)
80BC	Ptolemy X Alexander
80–58BC	Ptolemy XI Auletes
58–55BC	Berenice
55–51BC	Ptolemy XI Auletes (restored)
51–30BC	Cleopatra *Joint ruler*
51–47BC	Ptolemy XII *Joint ruler*
47–44BC	Ptolemy XIII *Joint ruler*
44–30BC	Ptolemy XIV Caesarion *Joint ruler*
30BC–	
AD642	*Roman rule*
642–1250	*Various Arab dynasties and states*

Sultanate of Egypt – Mamluks

Bahri Sultans

1250–7	al-Muizz Izz-ud-Din Aibak
1257–9	al-Mansur Nur-ud-Din Ali
1259–60	al-Muzaffar Saif-ud-Din Qutuz
1260–77	az-Zahir Rukn-ud-Din Baibars I
1277–80	as-Said Nasir-ud-Din Baraka Khan
1280	al-Adil Badr-ud-Din Salamish
1280–90	al-Mansur Saif-ud-Din Qalaun
1290–4	al-Ashraf Salah-ud-Din Khalil
1294–5	an-Nasir Nasir-ud-Din Muhammad
1295–7	al-Adil Zain-ud-Din Kitbugha
1297–9	al-Mansur Husam-ud-Din Lajin
1299–1309	an-Nasir Nasir-ud-Din Muhammad (restored)
1309	al-Muzaffar Rukn-ud-Din Baibars II
1309–40	an-Nasir Nasir-ud-Din Muhammad (restored)
1340–1	al-Mansur Saif-ud-Din Abu-Bakr
1341–2	al-Ashraf Ala-ud-Din Kujuk
1342	an-Nasir Shihab-ud-Din Ahmad
1342–5	as-Salih Imad-ud-Din Ismail
1345–6	al-Kamil Saif-ud-Din Shaban I
1346–7	al-Muzaffar Saif-ud-Din Hajji I

1347–51	an-Nasir Nasir-ud-Din Hasan
1351–4	as-Salih Salah-ud-Din Salih
1354–61	an-Nasir Nasir-ud-Din Hasan (restored)
1361–3	al-Mansur Salah-ud-Din Muhammad
1363–76	al-Ashraf Nasir-ud-Din Shaban II
1376–82	al-Mansur Ala-ud-Din Ali
1382	as-Salih Salah-ud-Din Hajji II

Burji Sultans

1382–9	az-Zahir Saif-ud-Din Barquq

Bahri Sultans (restored)

1389–90	as-Salih Salah-ud-Din Hajji II (restored)

Burji Sultans (restored)

1390–9	az-Zahir Saif-ud-Din Barquq (restored)
1399–1405	an-Nasir Nasir-ud-Din Faraj
1405	al-Mansur Izz-ud-Din Abdul-Aziz
1405–12	an-Nasir Nasir-ud-Din Faraj (restored)
1412	al-Adil al-Mustain
1412–21	al-Muayyad Saif-ud-Din Tatar
1421	al-Muzaffar Ahmad
1421	az-Zahir Saif-ud-Din Tatar
1421–2	as-Salih Nasir-ud-Din Muhammad
1422–37	al-Ashraf Saif-ud-Din Barsbay
1437–8	al-Aziz Jamal-ud-Din Yusuf
1438–53	az-Zahir Saif-ud-Din Jaqmaq
1453	al-Mansur Fakhr-ud-Din Uthman
1453–61	al-Ashraf Saif-ud-Din Inal
1461	al-Muayyad Shihab-ud-Din Ahmad
1461–7	az-Zahir Saif-ud-Din Khushqadam
1467–8	az-Zahir Saif-ud-Din Bilbay
1468	az-Zahir Timurbugha
1468–96	al-Ashraf Saif-ud-Din Qait Bay
1496–8	an-Nasir Muhammad
1498–1500	az-Zahir Qansuh
1500–01	al-Ashraf Janbalat
1501	al-Adil Saif-ud-Din Tuman Bay
1501–17	al-Ashraf Qansuh al-Ghawri
1517	al-Ashraf Tuman Bay
1517–1805	*Turkish rule*

Province of Egypt
Viceroy

1805–48	Mehemet Ali Pasha
1848	Ibrahim Pasha
1848–54	Abbas I
1854–63	Sa id Pasha
1863–66	Ismail Pasha

Khedive

1866–79	Ismail Pasha
1879–92	Mahmud Tawfiq (Tewfik Pasha)
1892–1914	Abbas II Helmi
1914–17	Hussein Kamel

Monarch – Sultanate of Egypt

1917	Hussein Kamel
1917–22	Ahmed Fouad

Monarch – Kingdom of Egypt

1922–36	Ahmed Fouad I
1936–7	Farouk *Trusteeship*
1937–52	Farouk I
1952–3	Ahmed Fouad II

Republic of Egypt
President

1952–4	Mohammed Naguib
1954–70	Gamal Abdel Nasser
1970–81	Mohammed Anwar el-Sadat
1981–	Mohammed Hosni Mubarak

Prime Minister

1878–9	Nubar
1879	Mahmud Tawfiq (Tewfik Pasha)
1879–81	Mahmud Riyad
1881–2	Sharif
1882	Mahmud Sami al-Barudi
1882	Ahmad Arabi (Arabi Pasha)
1882–4	Sharif
1884–8	Nubar
1888–91	Mahmud Riyad
1891–3	Mustafa Fahmy
1893	Husayn Fakhri
1893–4	Riyad Pasha
1894–5	Nubar
1895–1908	Mustafa Fahmy
1908–10	Butros Ghali
1910–14	Mohammed Said
1914–19	Hussein Rushdi
1919	Mohammed Said
1919–20	Yousuf Wahba
1920–1	Mohammed Tewfiq Nazim
1921	Adli Yegen
1922	Abdel Khaliq Tharwat
1922–3	Mohammed Tewfiq Nazim
1923–4	Yehia Ibrahim
1924	Saad Zaghloul
1924–6	Ahmed Zaywan
1926–7	Adli Yegen
1927–8	Abdel Khaliq Tharwat
1928	Mustafa an-Nahass
1928–9	Mohammed Mahmoud
1929–30	Adli Yegen
1930	Mustafa an-Nahass
1930–3	Ismail Sidqi
1933–4	Abdel Fattah Yahya
1934–6	Mohammed Tewfiq Nazim
1936	Ali Maher
1936–7	Mustafa an-Nahass
1937–9	Mohammed Mahmoud
1939–40	Ali Maher
1940	Hassan Sabri

1940–2	Hussein Sirry
1942–4	Mustafa an-Nahass
1944–5	Ahmed Maher
1945–6	Mahmoud Fahmy el-Nuqrashi
1946	Ismail Sidqi
1946–8	Mahmoud Fahmy el-Nuqrashi
1948–9	Ibrahim Abdel Hadi
1949–50	Hussein Sirry
1950–2	Mustafa an-Nahass
1952	Ali Maher
1952	Najib el-Hilali
1952	Hussein Sirry
1952	Najib el-Hilali
1952	Ali Maher
1952–4	Mohammed Najib
1954	Gamal Abdel Nasser
1954	Mohammed Najib
1954–62	Gamal Abdel Nasser
1958–61	*United Arab Republic*
1962–5	Ali Sabri
1965–6	Zakariya Mohyi ed-Din
1966–7	Mohammed Sidqi Soliman
1967–70	Gamal Abdel Nasser
1970–2	Mahmoud Fawzi
1972–3	Aziz Sidki
1973–4	Mohamed Anwar el-Sadat
1974–5	Abdel Aziz Hijazy
1975–8	Mamdouh Salem
1978–80	Mustafa Khalil
1980–1	Mohammed Anwar el-Sadat
1981–2	Mohammed Hosni Mubarak
1982–4	Fouad Monyi ed-Din
1984	Kamal Hassan Ali
1985–6	Ali Lotfi
1986–96	Atif Sidqi
1996–	Kamal Ahmed Ganzouri

El Salvador

President

1841–2	Juan Lindo y Zelaya
1842	Escolástico Marín *Acting*
1842	Juan José Guzmán
1842	Dionisio Villacorta *Acting*
1842	Escolástico Marín *Acting*
1842–3	Juan José Guzmán
1843	Pedro Arce *Acting*
1843–4	Juan José Guzmán
1844	Fermín Palacios *Acting*
1844	Francisco Malespín
1844–5	Joaquín Eufrasio Guzmán *Acting*
1845	Fermín Palacios *Acting*
1845–6	Joaquín Eufrasio Guzmán
1846	Fermín Palacios *Acting*
1846–8	Eugenio Aguilar
1848	Tomás Medina *Acting*
1848	Félix Quiroz *Acting*
1848–51	Doroteo Vasconcelos
1851	Francisco Dueñas *Acting*
1851	Félix Quiroz *Acting*
1851–4	Francisco Dueñas

1854	Vicente Gómez *Acting*
1854–6	José María San Martín
1856	Francisco Dueñas *Acting*
1856–8	Rafael Campo
1858	Lorenzo Zepeda *Acting*
1858–9	Miguel Santín del Castillo
1859	Joaquín Eufrasio Guzmán *Acting*
1859	José María Peralta *Acting*
1859–60	Gerardo Barrios Espinosa *Acting*
1860–1	José María Peralta *Acting*
1861–3	Gerardo Barrios Espinosa
1863–71	Francisco Dueñas
1871–6	Santiago González
1876	Andrés Valle
1876–85	Rafael Zaldívar
1885	Fernando Figueroa *Acting*
1885	José Rosales *Acting*
1885–90	Francisco Menéndez
1890–4	Carlos Ezeta
1894–8	Rafael Antonio Gutiérrez
1898–1903	Tomás Regalado
1903–7	Pedro José Escalon
1907–11	Fernando Figueroa
1911–3	Manuel Enrique Araujo
1913–4	Carlos Meléndez *President Designate*
1914–5	Alfonso Quiñónez Molina *President Designate*
1915–8	Carlos Meléndez
1918–9	Alfonso Quiñónez Molina *Vice President*
1919–23	Jorge Meléndez
1923–7	Alfonso Quiñónez Molina
1927–31	Pio Romero Bosque
1931	Arturo Araujo
1931	*Military administration*
1931–4	Maximiliano H Martinez *Vice President*
1934–5	Andrés I Menéndez *Provisional*
1935–44	Maximiliano H Martinez
1944	Andrés I Menéndez *Vice President*
1944–5	Osmin Aguirre y Salinas *Provisional*
1945–8	Salvador Castaneda Castro
1948–50	*Revolutionary Council*
1950–6	Oscar Osorio
1956–60	José María Lemus
1960–1	*Military junta*
1961–2	*Civil–military administration*
1962	Rodolfo Eusebio Cordón *Provisional*
1962–7	Julio Adalberto Rivera
1967–72	Fidel Sánchez Hernández
1972–7	Arturo Armando Molina
1977–9	Carlos Humberto Romero
1979–82	*Military juntas*
1982–4	*Government of National Unanimity* (Alvaro Magaña)
1984–9	José Napoleón Duarte
1989–94	Alfredo Cristiani Burkard
1994–	Armando Calderón Sol

Equatorial Guinea

President

1968–79	Francisco Macias Nguema
1979–	Teodoro Obiang Nguema Mbasogo

Prime Minister

1993–6	Silvestre Siale Bileka
1996–	Angel Serafin Seriche Dougan

Eritrea

President

1993–	Issais Afewerki

Estonia

President

1938–40	Konstantin Päts
1940–91	*Russian rule*
1991	Arnold Rüütel
1992–	Lennart Meri

Prime Minister

1918–19	Konstantin Päts
1919	Otto Strandmann
1919–20	Jaan Tõnisson
1920–21	Ants Piip
1921–2	Konstantin Päts
1922–3	Juhan Kukk
1923–4	Konstantin Päts
1924	Friedrich Akel
1924–5	Jüri Jaakson
1925–7	Jaan Teemant
1927–8	Jaan Tõnisson
1928–9	August Rei
1929–31	Otto Strandmann
1931–2	Konstantin Päts
1932	Jaan Teemant
1932	Kaarel Einbund
1932–3	Konstantin Päts
1933	Jaan Tõnisson
1933–8	Konstantin Päts
1938–9	Kaarel Eenpalu (Kaarel Einbund)
1939–40	Jüri Uluots
1940–91	*Russian rule*
1991–2	Edgar Savisaar
1992	Tiit Vahi
1992–4	Mart Laar
1994–5	Andres Tarand
1995–7	Tiit Vahi
1997–	Mart Siimann

Ethiopia

Monarch – Kingdom of Ethiopia
Zagwe Dynasty

1117–33	Marari
1133–72	Yemrehana Krestos
1172–1212	Gebra Maskal Lalibela
1212–60	Nakueto Laab
1260–8	Yetbarak

Solomonic Dynasty

1268–85	Yekuno Amlak
1285–94	Yagbea Seyon

1294–5	Senfa Ared
1295–6	Hezba Asgad
1296–7	Kedma Asgad
1297–8	Jin Asgad
1298–9	Saba Asgad
1299–1314	Wedem Ared
1314–44	Amda Seyon I
1344–72	Newaya Krestos
1372–82	Newaya Maryam
1382–1411	Dawit I
1411–14	Tewoderos I
1414–29	Yeshak
1429–30	Endreyas
1430–3	Takla Maryam
1433	Sarwe Iyasus
1433–4	Amda Iyasus
1434–68	Zara Yakob Constantine
1468–78	Baed Maryam I
1478–94	Eskandar
1494	Amda Seyon II
1494–1508	Naod
1508–40	Lebna Dengel Dawit II
1540–59	Galawdewos
1559–63	Minas
1563–97	Sarsa Dengel
1597–1603	Yakob
1603–04	Za Dengel
1604–07	Yakob (*restored*)
1607–32	Susenyos
1632–67	Fasiladas
1667–82	Yohannes I
1682–1706	Iyasu I 'the Great'
1706–08	Takla Haymanot I
1708–11	Tewoflos
1711–16	Yostos
1716–21	Dawit III
1721–30	Asma Giyorgis
1730–55	Iyasu II
1755–69	Iyoas I
1769	Yohannes II
1769–77	Takla Haymanot II
1777–79	Salomon
1779–84	Takla Giyorgis I
1784–8	Iyasu III
1788–9	Takla Giyorgis I (*restored*)
1789–94	Hezekiyas
1794–5	Takla Giyorgis I (*restored*)
1795	Baeda Maryam II
1795–6	Takla Giyorgis I (*restored*)
1796–7	Walda Saloman
1797–8	Yonas
1798–1800	*Period of instability*
1800–01	Demetros
1801–18	Egwala Seyon
1818–21	Iyoas II
1821–6	Gigar
1826	Baeda Maryam III
1826–30	Gigar (*restored*)
1830–2	Iyasu IV
1832	Gabra Krestos
1832	Sahla Dengel
1832	Gabra Krestos (*restored*)
1832–40	Sahla Dengel (*restored*)
1840–1	Yohannes III
1841–50	Sahla Dengel (*restored*)

1850–1	Yohannes III (*restored*)
1851–5	Sahla Dengel (*restored*)
1855–68	Tewoderos II
1868–71	Takla Giyorgis II
1871–89	Yohannes IV
1889–1911	Menyelek II
1911–16	Lej Iyasu (Joshua)
1916–28	Zawditu
1928–74	Haile Selassie
	Emperor from 1930

Provisional Military Administrative Council
Chairman

1974–7	Teferi Benti
1977–87	Mengistu Haile Mariam

People's Democratic Republic
President

1987–91	Mengistu Haile Mariam
1991–5	Meles Zenawi *Acting*
1995–	Negaso Gidada

Prime Minister

1991	Tesfaye Dinka
1991–5	Tamirat Layne
1995–	Meles Zenawi

European Union (EU)
Commission President

1967–70	Jean Rey
1970–2	Franco M Malfatti
1972–3	Sicco L Mansholt
1973–7	Francois-Xavier Ortoli
1977–81	Roy, Lord Jenkins
1981–5	Gaston Thorn
1985–95	Jacques Delors
1995–	Jacques Santer

Federated States of Micronesia

President

1991–	Bailey Olter

Fiji
Chief of State: British monarch, represented by Governor-General

Prime Minister

1970–87	Kamisese Mara
1987	Timoci Bavadra

Interim administration
Governor-General

1987	Penaia Ganilau
1987	*Military administration* (Sitiveni Rabuka)

Republic of Fiji
President

1987–93	Penaia Ganilau
1993–	Kamisese Mara *Acting*

Prime Minister

1987–92	Kamisese Mara
1992–	Sitiveni Rabuka

Finland
President

1919–25	Kaarlo Juho Ståhlberg
1925–31	Lauri Kristian Relander
1931–7	Pehr Evind Svinhufvud
1937–40	Kyösti Kallio
1940–4	Risto Ryti
1944–6	Carl Gustaf Mannerheim
1946–56	Juho Kusti Paasikivi
1956–81	Urho Kaleva Kekkonen
1982–94	Mauno Koivisto
1994–	Martti Ahtisaari

Prime Minister

1917–18	Pehr Evind Svinhufvud
1918	Juho Kusti Paasikivi
1918–19	Lauri Johannes Ingman
1919	Kaarlo Castrén
1919–20	Juho Vennola
1920–1	Rafael Erich
1921–2	Juho Vennola
1922	Aimo Kaarlo Cajander
1922–4	Kyösti Kallio
1924	Aimo Kaarlo Cajander
1924–5	Lauri Johannes Ingman
1925	Antti Agaton Tulenheimo
1925–6	Kyösti Kallio
1926–7	Väinö Tanner
1927–8	Juho Emil Sunila
1928–9	Oskari Mantere
1929–30	Kyösti Kallio
1930–1	Pehr Evind Svinhufvud
1931–2	Juho Emil Sunila
1932–6	Toivo Kivimäki
1936–7	Kyösti Kallio
1937–9	Aimo Kaarlo Cajander
1939–41	Risto Ryti
1941–3	Johann Rangell
1943–4	Edwin Linkomies
1944	Andreas Hackzell
1944	Urho Jonas Castrén
1944–5	Juho Kusti Paasikivi
1946–8	Mauno Pekkala
1948–50	Karl August Fagerholm
1950–3	Urho Kekkonen
1953–4	Sakari Tuomioja
1954	Ralf Törngren
1954–6	Urho Kaleva Kekkonen
1956–7	Karl August Fagerholm
1957	Väinö Johannes Sukselainen
1957–8	Rainer von Fieandt
1958	Reino Iisakki Kuuskoski
1958–9	Karl August Fagerholm
1959–61	Väinö Johannes Sukselainen
1961–2	Martti Miettunen
1962–3	Ahti Karjalainen
1963–4	Reino Ragnar Lehto
1964–6	Johannes Virolainen
1966–8	Rafael Paasio
1968–70	Mauno Koivisto
1970	Teuvo Ensio Aura
1970–1	Ahti Karjalainen
1971–2	Teuvo Ensio Aura
1972	Rafael Paasio

1972–5	Taisto Kalevi Sorsa
1975	Keijo Antero Liinamaa
1975–7	Martti Miettunen
1977–9	Taisto Kalevi Sorsa
1979–82	Mauno Koivisto
1982–87	Taisto Kalevi Sorsa
1987–91	Harri Holkeri
1991–5	Esko Aho
1995–	Paavo Lipponen

France
Monarch – Kingdom of the Franks
House of Charlemagne

768–814	Charlemagne
814–40	Louis I 'the Pious'
840–3	*Civil war*

Monarch – Kingdom of the West Franks
House of Charlemagne

843–77	Charles I 'the Bald'
877–9	Louis II 'the Stammerer'
879–84	Carloman *Joint ruler to 882*
879–82	Louis III *Joint ruler*

Monarch – Kingdom of France
House of Charlemagne

884–7	Charles II 'the Fat'

House of Capet

888–98	Eudes

House of Charlemagne (restored)

893–922	Charles III 'the Simple' *Rival king until 898*

House of Capet (restored)

922–3	Robert I
923–36	Raoul

House of Charlemagne (restored)

936–54	Louis IV 'd'Outre-Mer'
954–86	Lothaire
986–7	Louis V 'le Fainéant'

House of Capet (restored)

987–96	Hugh Capet
996–1031	Robert II
1031–60	Henri I
1060–1108	Philippe I
1108–37	Louis VI 'the Fat'
1137–80	Louis VII
1180–1223	Philippe II (Philippe-Auguste)
1223–6	Louis VIII 'the Lion'
1226–70	Louis IX (St Louis)
1270–85	Philippe III 'the Bold'
1285–1314	Philippe IV 'the Fair'
1314–16	Louis X 'the Quarrelsome'
1316	Jean I
1316–22	Philippe V 'the Tall'
1322–8	Charles IV 'the Fair'

House of Valois

1328–50	Philippe VI
1350–64	Jean II 'the Good'
1364–80	Charles V 'the Wise'
1380–1422	Charles VI 'the Foolish'

1422–61	Charles VII
1461–83	Louis XI
1483–98	Charles VIII 'the Affable'

House of Valois/Orléans

1498–1515	Louis XII

House of Valois/Angoulême

1515–47	François I
1547–59	Henri II
1559–60	François II
1560–74	Charles IX
1574–89	Henri III

House of Bourbon

1589–1610	Henri IV (of Navarre)
1610–43	Louis XIII
1643–1715	Louis XIV
1715–74	Louis XV
1774–93	Louis XVI
[1793–5	Louis XVII *Not crowned*]

Revolutionary government
First Republic

1792–5	*National Convention*
1795–9	*Directory*
1799–1804	*Consulate* (Napoleon Bonaparte, *First Consul*)

Monarch – French Empire
First Empire

1804–14	Napoleon I
[1815	Napoleon II *Not crowned*]

Monarch – Kingdom of France
House of Bourbon (restored)

1814–24	Louis XIII
1824–30	Charles X

House of Orléans

1830–48	Louis-Philippe

President
Second Republic

1848–51	Charles Louis Napoleon Bonaparte

Monarch – French Empire
Second Empire

1852–70	Napoleon III (Charles Louis Napoleon Bonaparte)

President
Third Republic

1870–1	*Commune*
1871–3	Louis Adolphe Thiers
1873–9	Marie Edmé de Mac-Mahon
1879–87	Jules Grévy
1887–94	Sadi Carnot
1894–5	Jean Pierre Paul Casmir-Périer
1895–9	François Félix Faure
1899–1906	Émile Loubet
1906–13	Armand Fallières
1913–20	Raymond Poincaré
1920	Paul Deschanel
1920–4	Alexandre Millerand
1924–31	Gaston Doumergue
1931–2	Paul Doumer
1932–40	Albert Lebrun

1940–5	*German rule*
1945–7	*No President*

Fourth Republic

1947–54	Vincent Auriol
1954–8	René Coty

Fifth Republic

1958–69	Charles de Gaulle
1969–74	Georges Pompidou
1974–81	Valéry Giscard d'Estaing
1981–95	François Mitterrand
1995–	Jacques René Chirac

Prime Minister

1815	Charles-Maurice, Prince de Talleyrand-Perigord
1815–18	Armand-Emmanuel Vignerot-Duplessis, Duc de Richelieu
1818–19	Jean Joseph, Marquis Dessolle
1819–20	Elie, Comte Decazes
1820–1	Armand Vignerot-Duplessis, Duc de Richelieu
1821–9	Guillaume-Aubin, Comte de Villèle
1829–30	Auguste, Prince de Polignac
1830–1	Jacques Lafitte
1831–2	Casimir Périer
1832–4	Nicolas Soult
1834	Etienne, Comte Gérard
1834	Napoléon Joseph Maret, Duc de Bassano
1834–5	Étienne Mortier, Duc de Treviso
1835–6	Achille, Duc de Broglie
1836	Adolphe Thiers
1836–9	Louis, Comte Molé
1839–40	Nicolas Soult
1840	Adolphe Thiers
1840–7	Nicolas Soult
1847–8	François Guyzot
1848	Jacques Charles Dupont de L'Eure
1848	Louis-Eugène Cavaignac
1848–9	Odilon Barrot
1849–70	*No Prime Minister*
1870–1	Jules Favre
1871–3	Jules Dufaure
1873–4	Albert, Duc de Broglie
1874–5	Ernest Louis Courtot de Cissey
1875–6	Louis Buffet
1876	Jules Dufaure
1876–7	Jules Simon
1877	Albert, Duc de Broglie
1877	Gaetan de Grimaudet de Rochebouët
1877–9	Jules Dufaure
1879	William H Waddington
1879–80	Louis de Freycinet
1880–1	Jules Ferry
1881–2	Léon Gambetta
1882	Louis de Freycinet
1882–3	Eugène Duclerc

1883	Armand Fallières
1883–5	Jules Ferry
1885–6	Henri Brisson
1886	Louis de Freycinet
1886–7	René Goblet
1887	Maurice Rouvier
1887–8	Pierre Tirard
1888–9	Charles Floquet
1889–90	Pierre Tirard
1890–2	Louis de Freycinet
1892	Émile Loubet
1892–3	Alexandre Ribot
1893	Charles Dupuy
1893–4	Jean Casimir-Périer
1894–5	Charles Dupuy
1895	Alexandre Ribot
1895–6	Léon Bourgeois
1896–8	Jules Méline
1898	Henri Brisson
1898–9	Charles Dupuy
1899–1902	Pierre Waldeck-Rousseau
1902–5	Emile Combes
1905–6	Maurice Rouvier
1906	Jean Sarrien
1906–9	Georges Clemenceau
1909–11	Aristide Briand
1911	Ernest Monis
1911–12	Joseph Caillaux
1912–13	Raymond Poincaré
1913	Aristide Briand
1913	Jean Louis Barthou
1913–14	Gaston Doumergue
1914	Alexandre Ribot
1914–15	René Viviani
1915–17	Aristide Briand
1917	Alexandre Ribot
1917	Paul Painlevé
1917–20	Georges Clemenceau
1920	Alexandre Millerand
1920–1	Georges Leygues
1921–2	Aristide Briand
1922–4	Raymond Poincaré
1924	Frédéric François-Marsal
1924–5	Édouard Herriot
1925	Paul Painlevé
1925–6	Aristide Briand
1926	Édouard Herriot
1926–9	Raymond Poincaré
1929	Aristide Briand
1929–30	André Tardieu
1930	Camille Chautemps
1930	André Tardieu
1930–1	Théodore Steeg
1931–2	Pierre Laval
1932	André Tardieu
1932	Édouard Herriot
1932–3	Joseph Paul-Boncour
1933	Édouard Daladier
1933	Albert Sarrault
1933–4	Camille Chautemps
1934	Édouard Daladier
1934	Gaston Doumergue
1934–5	Pierre Étienne Flandin
1935	Fernand Bouisson
1935–6	Pierre Laval

1936	Albert Sarrault
1936–7	Léon Blum
1937–8	Camille Chautemps
1938	Léon Blum
1938–40	Édouard Daladier
1940	Paul Reynaud
1940–4	Philippe Pétain (*Vichy*)
1944–6	Charles de Gaulle
1946	Félix Gouin
1946	Georges Bidault
1946–7	Léon Blum
1947	Paul Ramadier
1947–8	Robert Schuman
1948	André Marie
1948	Robert Schuman
1948–9	Henri Queuille
1949–50	Georges Bidault
1950	Henri Queuille
1950–1	René Pleven
1951	Henri Queuille
1951–2	René Pleven
1952	Edgar Faure
1952–3	Antoine Pinay
1953	René Mayer
1953–4	Joseph Laniel
1954–5	Pierre Mendès-France
1955–6	Edgar Faure
1956–7	Guy Alcide Mollet
1957	Maurice Bourgès-Maunoury
1957–8	Félix Gaillard
1958	Pierre Pflimin
1958–9	Charles de Gaulle
1959–62	Michel Debré
1962–8	Georges Pompidou
1968–9	Maurice Couve de Murville
1969–72	Jacques Chaban Delmas
1972–4	Pierre Mesmer
1974–6	Jacques René Chirac
1976–81	Raymond Barre
1981–4	Pierre Mauroy
1984–6	Laurent Fabius
1986–8	Jacques René Chirac
1988–91	Michel Rocard
1991–2	Edith Cresson
1992–3	Pierre Bérégovoy
1993–5	Edouard Balladur
1995–7	Alain Juppé
1997–	Lionel Jospin

Duke of Lorraine

1697–1729	Leopold
1729–36	Francis III
	(I, *Holy Roman Emperor*)
1736–66	Stanislas Leszczynski

Duke of Normandy

911–32	Ganger-Hrolf (Rollo)
932–42	William I
942–96	Richard I
996–1027	Richard II
1027–8	Richard III
1028–35	Robert I
1035–87	William II (I of England)
	'the Conqueror'
1087–1106	Robert Curthose
1106–35	*As England*

1135–44	*Civil war*
1144–50	Geoffrey of Anjou
1150–1204	*As England*
1204–	*Part of France*

Gabon

President

1960–7	Léon M'ba
1967–	Omar (*to 1973* Albert-Bernard) Bongo

Prime Minister

1960–75	*As President*
1975–90	Léon Mébiame (Mébiane)
1990–4	Casimir Oyé M'ba
1994–	Paulin Obame-Nguema

The Gambia

President

1965–94	Alhaji Sir Dawda (Kair abu) Jawara
1994–6	Yayeh Jameh (*Chairman*)
1996–	Yayeh Jameh

Georgia

Monarch – Kingdom of Georgia
Bagratid Dynasty

1008–14	Bagrat III
1014–27	Giorgi I
1027–72	Bagrat IV
1072–89	Giorgi II
1089–1125	David III
1125–55	Demetrius I
1155	David IV
1155–6	Demetrius I (*restored*)
1156–84	Giorgi III
	Joint ruler from 1179
1179–1212	Thamar *Joint ruler to 1184*
1212–23	Giorgi IV
1223–45	Rusudan
1245–50	*No king*
1250–8	David V
1258–69	David VI
1269–73	*No king*
1273–89	Demetrius II
1289–92	Vakhtang II
1292–1301	David VII
1301–07	Vakhtang III
1307–14	Giorgi V
1314–46	Giorgi VI
1346–60	David VIII
1360–95	Bagrat V
1395–1405	Giorgi VII
1405–12	Constantine I
1412–42	Alexander I
1442–6	Vakhtang IV
1446–53	Demetrius III
1453–65	Giorgi VIII
1465–90	Constantine II
	Rival king to 1465
1465–78	Bagrat VI *Rival king*
1490–1810	*Divided into several small states*
1810–1991	*Russian rule*

Republic of Georgia
President

1991–2	Zviad Gamsakhurdia
1992	*Military Council*
1992–	Eduard Shevardnadze

Prime Minister

1993	Tengiz Sigua
1993–5	Otar Patsarsia

Minister of State

1995–	Nikoloz Lekishvili

Germany
Elector of Brandenburg
House of Hohenzollern

1415–40	Friedrich I (of Nuremberg)
1440–71	Friedrich II
1471–86	Albrecht (Albert III) Achilles
1486–99	Johann Cicero
1499–1535	Joachim I
1535–71	Joachim II
1571–98	Johann Georg
1598–1608	Joachim Friedrich
1608–20	Johann Sigismund
1620–40	Georg Wilhelm
1640–88	Friedrich Wilhelm (Frederick William)
1688–1701	Friedrich III

King of Prussia
House of Hohenzollern

1701–13	Friedrich I (III of Brandenburg)
1713–40	Friedrich Wilhelm I
1740–86	Friedrich (Frederick) II 'the Great'
1786–97	Friedrich Wilhelm (Frederick William) II
1797–1840	Friedrich Wilhelm (Frederick William) III
1840–61	Friedrich Wilhelm (Frederick William) IV
1861–71	Wilhelm I

Monarch (Kaiser) – German Empire
House of Hohenzollern

1871–88	Wilhelm I
1888	Friedrich (Frederick) (III of Prussia)
1888–1918	Wilhelm II

Chancellor

1871–90	Otto von Bismarck
1890–4	Georg Leo, Graf von Caprivi
1894–1900	Chlodwic, Prince von Hohenlohe-Schillingfürst
1900–09	Bernhard Heinrich, Prince von Bülow
1909–17	Theobald von Bethmann Hollweg
1917–18	Georg von Herfling
1918	Prince Max of Baden

Weimar Republic
Head of State (Chancellor)

1918	Friedrich Ebert
1919–20	Philipp Scheidemann

1920	Hermann Müller
1920–1	Konstantin Fehrenbach
1921–2	Karl Joseph Wirth
1922–3	Wilhelm Cuno
1923	Gustav Stresemann
1923–5	Wilhelm Marx
1925–6	Hans Luther
1926–8	Wilhelm Marx
1928–9	Herman Müller
1929–32	Heinrich Brüning
1932–3	Franz von Papen
1933–45	Adolf Hitler
	(from 1934 *Führer*)

German Federal Republic
(to 1990 West Germany)
President

1949–59	Theodor Heuss
1959–69	Heinrich Lübke
1969–74	Gustav Heinemann
1974–9	Walter Scheel
1979–84	Karl Carstens
1984–94	Richard von Weizsäcker
1994–	Roman Herzog

Chancellor

1949–63	Konrad Adenauer
1963–6	Ludwig Erhard
1966–9	Kurt Georg Kiesinger
1969–74	Willy Brandt
1974–82	Helmut Schmidt
1982–	Helmut Kohl

German Democratic Republic
(East Germany)
President

1949–60	Wilhelm Pieck

Chairman of the Council of State

1960–73	Walter Ulbricht
1973–6	Willi Stoph
1976–89	Erich Honecker
1989	Egon Krenz
1989–90	Gregor Gysi *General Secretary as Chairman*

Premier

1949–64	Otto Grotewohl
1964–73	Willi Stoph
1973–6	Horst Sindermann
1976–89	Willi Stoph
1989–90	Hans Modrow
1990	Lothar de Maizière

Baden

Margrave of Baden
Baden – House of Zahringen

c.1100–30	Hermann I
1130–60	Hermann II
1160–90	Hermann III
1190–1243	Hermann IV
1243–50	Hermann V
1250–68	Friedrich I
1268–88	Rudolf I
1288–95	Rudolf II
1295–7	Hesso
1297–1332	Rudolf III

1332–5	Rudolf Hesso
1335–1348	Rudolf IV
1348–53	Friedrich II
1353–72	Rudolf V
1372–91	Rudolf VI
1391–1431	Bernhard I
1431–53	Jakob I
1453–75	Karl I
1475–1527	Christoph

Baden-Baden – House of Zahringen

1527–36	Bernhardt II
1536–69	Philibert
1569–88	Philipp
1588–96	Eduard Fortunatus
1596–1622	*No Margrave*
1622–77	Wilhelm
1677–1707	Ludwig-Wilhelm
1707–61	Ludwig-Georg
1761–71	August-Georg

Baden-Durlach – House of Zahringen

1527–53	Ernst
1553–77	Karl II
1577–1622	Georg-Friedrich *Joint ruler to 1604*
1577–1604	Ernst-Friedrich *Joint ruler*
1577–90	Jakob II *Joint ruler*
1622–59	Friedrich III
1659–77	Friedrich IV
1677–1709	Friedrich V
1709–38	Karl III
1738–1806	Karl-Friedrich *Margrave of Baden-Baden from 1738*

Grand-Duke of Baden
House of Zahringen

1806–11	Karl-Friedrich
1811–18	Karl
1818–30	Ludwig I
1830–52	Leopold
1852–8	Ludwig II
1858–1907	Friedrich I
1907–18	Friedrich II

Bavaria

Elector of Bavaria
House of Wittelsbach

1623–51	Maximilian I
1651–79	Ferdinand Maria
1679–1706	Maximilian II Emanuel
1706–14	*No elector*
1714–26	Maximilian II Emanuel *(restored)*
1726–45	Karl Albrecht (Karl VII, *Holy Roman Emperor*)
1745–77	Maximilian III Joseph
1777–99	Karl Theodor *Elector Palatine of the Rhine from 1742*
1799–1806	Maximilian IV Josef

King of Bavaria
House of Wittelsbach

1806–25	Maximilian I Josef
1825–48	Ludwig I
1848–64	Maximilian II

1864–86	Ludwig II
1886–1913	Otto
1913–18	Ludwig III

Brunswick

Duke of Brunswick
House of Welf

1735–80	Karl I
1780–1806	Karl II

House of Bonaparte

1807–13	Jérôme Bonaparte *King of Westphalia*

House of Welf

1813–15	Friedrich-Wilhelm
1815–30	Karl III
1830–84	Wilhelm

Hanover

Elector of Hanover
House of Welf

1692–8	Ernst-August
1698–1714	Georg *King George I of Great Britain*
1714–1814	*As Great Britain*

King of Hanover
House of Welf

1814–37	*As Great Britain*
1837–51	Ernest Augustus
1851–66	Georg V

Hesse

Landgrave of Hesse-Darmstadt

1567–96	Georg I
1596–1626	Ludwig V
1626–61	Georg II
1661–78	Ludwig VI
1678	Ludwig VII
1678–1739	Ernst-Ludwig
1739–68	Ludwig VIII
1768–90	Ludwig IX
1790–1806	Ludwig X

Grand Duke of Hesse

1806–30	Ludwig I (X)
1830–48	Ludwig II
1848–77	Ludwig III
1877–92	Ludwig IV
1892–1918	Ernst-Ludwig

Mecklenburg

Duke of Mecklenburg
Mecklenburg-Schwerin

1611–58	Adolf-Friedrich I
1658–92	Christian-Ludwig I
1692–1713	Friedrich-Wilhelm
1713–47	Christian-Ludwig II
1747–56	Karl-Leopold
1756–85	Friedrich
1785–1815	Friedrich-Franz I

Mecklenburg-Strelitz

1701–08	Adolf-Friedrich II

1708–52	Adolf-Friedrich III
1752–94	Adolf-Friedrich IV
1794–1815	Karl

Grand Duke of Mecklenburg
Mecklenburg-Schwerin

1815–37	Friedrich-Franz I
1837–42	Paul
1842–83	Friedrich-Franz II
1883–97	Friedrich-Franz III
1897–1918	Friedrich-Franz IV

Mecklenburg-Strelitz

1815–16	Karl
1816–60	Georg
1860–1904	Friedrich-Wilhelm
1904–14	Adolf-Friedrich V
1914–18	Adolf-Friedrich VI

Oldenburg

Duke of Oldenburg

1777–85	Friedrich-August I
1785–1823	Wilhelm
1823–9	Peter I
1829–53	August
1853–1900	Peter II
1900–18	Friedrich-August II

Palatinate

Count Palatine of the Rhine
House of Wittelsbach

1214–27	Ludwig I
1227–53	Otto
1253–94	Ludwig II *Joint ruler to 1255*
1253–5	Heinrich *Joint ruler*
1294–1329	Ludwig III *Joint ruler to 1317*
1294–1317	Rudolf I *Joint ruler*
1329–53	Rudolf II
1353–6	Rupprecht I

Elector Palatine of the Rhine
House of Wittelsbach

1356–90	Rupprecht I
1390–8	Rupprecht II
1398–1410	Rupprecht III
1410–36	Ludwig IV
1436–49	Ludwig V
1449–76	Friedrich I
1476–1508	Philipp
1508–44	Ludwig VI
1544–56	Friedrich II
1556–9	Otto Heinrich
1559–76	Friedrich III
1576–83	Ludwig VII
1583–1610	Friedrich IV
1610–23	Friedrich V
	King of Bohemia 1619–20
1623–49	*Bavarian rule*
1649–80	Karl Ludwig
1680–5	Karl
1685–90	Philipp Wilhelm
1690–1716	Johann Wilhelm
1716–42	Karl Philipp
1742–99	Karl Theodor
1799–1918	*Part of Bavaria*

Saxony

Elector of Saxony
House of Wettin

1423–8	Friedrich I (of Meissen)
1428–64	Friedrich II
1464–86	Ernst *Joint ruler to 1485*
1464–85	Albrecht (V) *Joint ruler*
1486–1525	Friedrich III
1525–32	Johann
1532–47	Johann-Friedrich
1547–53	Moritz
1553–86	August
1586–91	Christian I
1591–1611	Christian II
1611–56	Johann-Georg I
1656–80	Johann-Georg II
1680–91	Johann-Georg III
1691–4	Johann-Georg IV
1694–1733	Friedrich-August I
	King Augustus II of Poland
1733–63	Friedrich-August II
1763	Friedrich-Christian
1763–1806	Friedrich-August III

King of Saxony
House of Wettin

1806–27	Friedrich-August I
1827–36	Anton
1836–54	Friedrich-August II
1854–73	Johann
1873–1902	Albrecht
1902–04	Georg
1904–18	Friedrich-August III

Württemburg

Count of Württemberg

1236–41	Eberhard I
1241–65	Ulrich I
1265–79	Ulrich II
1279–1325	Eberhard II
1325–44	Ulrich III
1344–92	Eberhard III
	Joint ruler to 1366
1344–66	Ulrich IV *Joint ruler*
1392–1417	Eberhard IV
1417–19	Eberhard V
1419–41	Ludwig IV
1441–80	Ulrich V
1450–9	Eberhard VI
	Joint ruler to 1457
1450–7	Ludwig V *Joint ruler*
1480–95	Eberhard VII

Duke of Württemberg

1495–1504	Eberhard VII
	Joint ruler to 1496
1495–96	Eberhard VI *Joint ruler*
1504–19	Ulrich VI
1520–34	*No duke*
1534–50	Ulrich VI (*restored*)
1550–68	Christopher
1568–93	Ludwig VI
1593–1608	Friedrich I
1608–28	Johann-Friedrich
1628–74	Eberhard VIII

1674–7	Wilhelm-Ludwig
1677–1733	Eberhard-Ludwig
1733–7	Karl-Alexander
1737–93	Karl-Eugen
1793–5	Ludwig-Eugen
1795–7	Friedrich-Eugen
1797–1806	Friedrich I

King of Württemberg

1806–16	Friedrich I
1816–64	Wilhelm I
1864–91	Karl
1891–1918	Wilhelm II

Ghana

King of Ashanti

c.1630–60	Oti Akenten
1660–97	Obiri Yeboa
1697–1731	Osei Tutu
1731–42	Opuku Ware
1742–52	Kwasi Obodum
1752–81	Osei Kojo
1781–97	Osei Kwamina
1797–1800	Opuku Fofie
1800–24	Osei Bonsu
1824–38	Osei Yaw
1838–67	Kwaku Dua I
1867–74	Kofi Karikari
1874–84	Mensa Bonsu
1884–8	Kwaku Dua II
1888–96	Kwaku Dua III Prempeh

King of Dagomba

c.1500	Nyagse
?	Zulande
?	Nagalogu
?	Datorli
?	Buruguyomda
?	Zoligu
?	Zonman
?	Ninmitoni
?	Dimani
?	Yanzo
?	Dariziegu
c.1660	Luro
?	Tutugri
?	Zagale
?	Zokuli
?	Gungobili
c.1700	Zangina
?	Andani Sigili
?	Ziblim Bunbiogo
c.1740	Gariba
?	Ziblim Na Saa
?	Ziblim Bandamda
?	Andani I
?	Mahama I
c.1820	Ziblim Kulunku
?	Sumani Zoli
c.1850	Yakubu I
?	Abudulai I
?–1899	Andani II
1899–1900	Darimani
1900–20	al-Hasan
1920–38	Abudulai II

1938–48 Mahama II
1948–53 Mahama III
1953–68 Abdulai III
1968–9 Andani III
1969–74 Muhammad Abudulai IV
1974– Yakubu II

President
1960–6 Kwame Nkrumah

National Liberation Council
Chairman
1966–9 Joseph Arthur Ankrah
1969 Akwasi Amankwa Afrifa
1969–70 *Presidential Committee*

President
1970–2 Edward Akufo-Addo

Chairman
1972–8 *National Redemption Council*
(Ignatius Kuti
Acheampong)
1978–9 *Supreme Military Council*
(Fred W Akuffo)
1979 *Armed Forces Revolutionary
Council* (Jerry John
Rawlings)

President
1979–81 Hilla Limann

Provisional National Defence Council
Chairman
1981–92 Jerry John Rawlings

President
1992– Jerry John Rawlings

Greece

President
First Republic
1829–31 Ioannis Kapodistrias

Monarch – Kingdom of Greece
1832–62 Otho (Otto of Wittelsbach)
1863–1913 Georgios (George) I
1913–17 Konstantinos
(Constantine) I
1917–20 Alexandros (Alexander)
1920–2 Konstantinos
(Constantine) I (*restored*)
1922–3 Georgios (George) II
1923–4 Pavlos Koundouriotis
Regent

President
Second Republic
1924–6 Pavlos Koundouriotis
1926 Theodoros Pangalos
1926–9 Pavlos Koundouriotis
1929–35 Alexandros T Zaïmis

Monarch – Kingdom of Greece
1935 Georgios Kondylis *Regent*
1935–47 Georgios (George) II
1947–64 Pavlos (Paul) I

1964–7 Konstantinos
(Constantine) II
1967–73 *Military junta*
1973 Georgios Papadopoulos
Regent

President
Third Republic
1973 Georgios Papadopoulos
1973–4 Phaedon Gizikis
1974–5 Michael Stasinopoulos
1975–80 Konstantinos Tsatsos
1980–5 Konstantinos Karamanlis
1985–90 Christos Sartzetaki
1990–5 Konstantinos Karamanlis
1995– Kostas Stephanopoulos

Prime Minister
1833 Spyridon Trikoupis
1833–4 Alexandros Mavrokordatos
1834–5 Ioannis Kolettis
1835–7 Count Josef von
Armansperg
1837 I von Rudhart
1837–41 Konstantinos Zographos
1841 Alexandros Mavrokordatos
1841–3 A Kriezis
1843–4 A Metaxas
1844 Konstantinos Kanaris
1844 Alexandros Mavrokordatos
1844–7 Ioannis Kolettis
1847–8 Kitsos Tzavellas
1848 Georgios Koundouriotis
1848–9 Konstantinos Kanaris
1849–54 A Kriezis
1854–5 Alexandros Mavrokordatos
1855–7 Dimitrios Voulgaris
1857–62 A Miaoulis
1862 G Kolokotronis
1862–3 Dimitrios Voulgaris
1863 Z Valvis
1863 D Kiriakos
1863 B Roufos
1863–4 Dimitrios Voulgaris
1864 Konstantinos Kanaris
1864 Z Valvis
1864–5 Konstantinos Kanaris
1865 A Koumoundouros
1865 E Deligiorgis
1865 Dimitrios Voulgaris
1865 A Koumoundouros
1865 E Deligiorgis
1865–6 B Roufos
1866 Dimitrios Voulgaris
1866–8 A Koumoundouros
1868 A Moraitinis
1868–9 Dimitrios Voulgaris
1869–70 T A Zaimis
1870 E Deligiorgis
1870–1 A Koumoundouros
1871–2 T A Zaimis
1872 Dimitrios Voulgaris
1872–4 E Deligiorgis
1874–5 Dimitrios Voulgaris
1875 Kharilaos Trikoupis
1875–6 A Koumoundouros

1876 E Deligiorgis
1876–7 A Koumoundouros
1877 E Deligiorgis
1877 A Koumoundouros
1877–8 Konstantinos Kanaris
1878 A Koumoundouros
1878 Kharilaos Trikoupis
1878–80 A Koumoundouros
1880 Kharilaos Trikoupis
1880–2 A Koumoundouros
1882–5 Kharilaos Trikoupis
1885–6 Theodoros Deligiannis
1886 D Valvis
1886–90 Kharilaos Trikoupis
1890–2 Theodoros Deligiannis
1892 K Konstantopoulos
1892–3 Kharilaos Trikoupis
1893 S Sotiropoulos
1893–5 Kharilaos Trikoupis
1895 Nikolaos Petros
Deligiannis
1895–7 Theodoros Deligiannis
1897 Dimitrios Georgios Rallis
1897–9 Alexandros Thrasyboulos
Zaïmis
1899–1901 Georgios Theotokis
1901–2 Alexandros Thrasyboulos
Zaïmis
1902–3 Theodoros Deligiannis
1903 Georgios Theotokis
1903 Dimitrios Georgios Rallis
1903–4 Georgios Theotokis
1904–5 Theodoros Deligiannis
1905 Dimitrios Georgios Rallis
1905–9 Georgios Theotokis
1909 Dimitrios Georgios Rallis
1909–10 Kyriakoulis P
Mavromichalis
1910 Stephanos Nikolaos
Dragoumis
1910–15 Eleftherios K Venizelos
1915 Dimitrios P Gounaris
1915 Eleftherios K Venizelos
1915 Alexandros Thrasyboulos
Zaïmis
1915–16 Stephanos Skouloudis
1916 Alexandros Thrasyboulos
Zaïmis
1916 Nikolaos P Kalogeropoulos
1916–17 Spyridon Lambros
1917 Alexandros Thrasyboulos
Zaïmis
1917–20 Eleftherios K Venizelos
1920–1 Dimitrios Georgios Rallis
1921 Nikolaos P Kalogeropoulos
1921–2 Dimitrios P Gounaris
1922 Nikolaos Stratos
1922 Petros E Protopapadakis
1922 Nikolaos Triandaphyllakos
1922 Sotirios Krokidas
1922 Alexandros Thrasyboulos
Zaïmis
1922–3 Stylianos Gonatas
1924 Eleftherios K Venizelos
1924 Georgios Kaphandaris

1924	Alexandros Papanastasiou
1924	Themistocles Sophoulis
1924–5	Andreas Michalakopoulos
1925–6	Alexandros N Chatzikyriakos
1926	Theodoros Pangalos
1926	Athanasius Eftaxias
1926	Georgios Kondylis
1926–8	Alexandros Thrasyboulos Zaïmis
1928–32	Eleftherios K Venizelos
1932	Alexandros Papanastasiou
1932	Eleftherios K Venizelos
1932–3	Panagiotis Tsaldaris
1933	Eleftherios K Venizelos
1933	Nikolaos Plastiras
1933	Alexandros Othonaos
1933–5	Panagiotis Tsaldaris
1935	Georgios Kondylis
1935–6	Konstantinos Demertzis
1936–41	Ioannis Metaxas
1941	Alexandros Koryzis
1941	Georgios (George) II
	Chairman of Ministers
1941	*German occupation* (Emmanuel Tsouderos)
1941–2	Georgios Tsolakoglou
1942–3	Konstantinos Logothetopoulos
1943–4	Ioannis Rallis

Government in exile

1941–4	Emmanuel Tsouderos
1944	Sophocles Venizelos
1944–5	Georgios Papandreou

Post-war

1945	Nikolaos Plastiras
1945	Petros Voulgaris
1945	Damaskinos, Archbishop of Athens
1945	Panagiotis Kanellopoulos
1945–6	Themistocles Sophoulis
1946	Panagiotis Politzas
1946–7	Konstantinos Tsaldaris
1947	Dimitrios Maximos
1947	Konstantinos Tsaldaris
1947–9	Themistocles Sophoulis
1949–50	Alexandros Diomedes
1950	Ioannis Theotokis
1950	Sophocles Venizelos
1950	Nikolaos Plastiras
1950–1	Sophocles Venizelos
1951	Nikolaos Plastiras
1952	Dimitrios Kiusopoulos
1952–5	Alexandros Papagos
1955	Stephanos C Stefanopoulos
1955–8	Konstantinos Karamanlis
1958	Konstantinos Georgakopoulos
1958–61	Konstantinos Karamanlis
1961	Konstantinos Dovas
1961–3	Konstantinos Karamanlis
1963	Panagiotis Pipinellis
1963	Stylianos Mavromichalis
1963	Georgios Papandreou
1963–4	Ioannis Paraskevopoulos
1964–5	Georgios Papandreou
1965	Georgios Athanasiadis-Novas
1965	Elias Tsirimokos
1965–6	Stephanos C Stefanopoulos
1966–7	Ioannis Paraskevopoulos
1967	Panagiotis Kanellopoulos
1967–74	*Military junta*
1967	Konstantinos Kollias
1967–73	Georgios Papadopoulos
1973	Spyridon Markezinis
1973–4	Adamantios Androutsopoulos
1974–80	Konstantinos Karamanlis
1980–1	Georgios Rallis
1981–9	Andreas Georgios Papandreou
1989	Tzannis Tzannetakis
1989–90	Xenofon Zolotas
1990–3	Konstantinos Mitsotakis
1993–6	Andreas Georgios Payandreou
1996–	Kostas Simitis

King of Sparta

Sparta had a double kingship – there were two kings at any one time, usually one from each dynasty.

Agiad Dynasty

c.815–c.785BC	Agesilaus I
c.785–c.760BC	Archilaus
c.760–c.740BC	Teleclus
c.740–c.700BC	Alcmenes
c.700–c.665BC	Polydorus
c.665–c.640BC	Eurycrates
c.640–c.615BC	Anaxander
c.615–c.590BC	Eurycratides
c.590–c.560BC	Leon
c.560–c.520BC	Anaxandridas
c.520–c.489BC	Cleomenes I
c.489–480BC	Leonidas I
480–c.458BC	Pleistarchus
c.458–444BC	Pleistoanax
444–394BC	Pausanias
394–80BC	Agesipolis I
380–71BC	Cleombrotus I
371–69BC	Agesipolis II
369–09BC	Cleomenes II
309–264BC	Areus I
264–c.262BC	Acrotatus
c.262–54BC	Areus II
254–42BC	Leonidas II
242–1BC	Cleombrotus II
241–35BC	Leonidas II (*restored*)
235–21BC	Cleomenes III
227–1BC	Euclidas
219–15BC	Agesipolis III

Eurypontid Dynasty

c.775–c.750BC	Charillus
c.750–c.720BC	Nicander
c.720–c.675BC	Theopompus
c.675–c.645BC	Anaxandridas I
c.645–c.625BC	Zeuxidamas
c.625–c.600BC	Anaxidamus
c.600–c.575BC	Archidamus I
c.575–c.550BC	Agasicles
c.550–c.515BC	Ariston
c.515–c.491BC	Demaratus
c.491–469BC	Leotychidas
469–27BC	Archidamus II
427–398BC	Agis II
398–61BC	Agesilaus II
361–38BC	Archidamus III
338–31BC	Agis III
331–c.300BC	Eudamidas I
c.300–c.270BC	Archidamus IV
c.270–c.245BC	Eudamidas II
c.245–1BC	Agis IV
241–28BC	Eudamidas III
228–7BC	Archidamus V
219–10BC	Lycurgus
210–06BC	Pelops
206–192BC	Nabis

King of Macedonia

Argead Dynasty

c.650–c.630BC	Perdiccas I
c.630–c.620BC	Argaeus I
c.620–c.590BC	Philip I
c.590–c.570BC	Aeropus I
c.570–c.540BC	Alcetas
c.540–c.495BC	Amyntas I
c.495–c.452BC	Alexander I
c.452–c.413BC	Perdiccas II
c.413–c.399BC	Archelaus
c.399–c.398BC	Orestes
c.398–c.395BC	Aeropus II
c.395–c.394BC	Amyntas II
c.394–c.393BC	Pausanias
c.393BC	Amyntas III
c.393–c.392BC	Argaeus II
c.392–369BC	Amyntas III (*restored*)
369–8BC	Alexander II
368–5BC	Ptolemy I
365–59BC	Perdiccas III
359–36BC	Philip II
336–23BC	Alexander III 'the Great'
323–10BC	Alexander IV *Joint king to 310 BC*
323–17BC	Philip III Arrhidaeus *Joint king (Antipater Regent to 319 BC)*
310–05BC	*No king (Cassander Ruler of Macedonia)*

Antipatrid Dynasty

305–297BC	Cassander
297BC	Philip IV
297–4BC	Antipater *East* Alexander V *West*

Antigonid Dynasty

294–88	Demetrius I Poliorcetes
288–1BC	Lysimachus
288–5BC	Pyrrhus *King of Epirus (Rival King)*
281–79BC	Ptolemy II Ceraunus

279–7BC	*Galatian invasion*
277–4BC	Antigonus II Gonatas
274–2BC	Pyrrhus *King of Epirus* (*restored*)
272–39BC	Antigonus II Gonatas (*restored*)
239–29BC	Demetrius II
229–1BC	Antigonus III Doson
221–179BC	Philip V
179–68BC	Perseus

Grenada

Chief of State: British monarch, represented by Governor-General

Prime Minister

1974–9	Eric Matthew Gairy
1979–83	Maurice Bishop
1983–4	Nicholas Brathwaite *Chairman of Interim Council*
1984–9	Herbert Augustus Blaize
1989–90	Ben Jones *Acting*
1990–5	Nicholas Brathwaite
1995	George Brizan
1995–	Keith Mitchell

Guatemala

President

1839–44	Mariano Rivera Paz
1844–8	José Rafael Carrera
1848	Juan Antonio Martínez
1848	José Bernardo Escobar
1849–51	Mariano Paredes
1851–65	José Rafael Carrera
1865	Pedro de Aycinena
1865–71	Vicente Cerna
1871–2	Miguel García Granados
1872–85	Justo Rufino Barrios
1885	Alejandro Sinibaldi
1885–92	Manuel Lisandro Barillas
1892–8	José María Reyna Barrios
1898–1920	Manuel Estrada Cabrera
1920–2	Carlos Herrera y Luna
1922–6	José María Orellana
1926–30	Lázaro Chacón
1930	Baudillo Palma
1930–1	Manuel María Orellana
1931	José María Reyna Andrade
1931–44	Jorge Ubico Castañeda
1944	Federico Ponce Vaidez
1944–5	Jacobo Arbenz Guzmán
1945–51	Juan José Arévalo
1951–4	Jacobo Arbenz Guzmán
1954	*Military junta* (Carlos Díaz)
1954	Elfego J Monzón
1954–7	Carlos Castillo Armas
1957	*Military junta* (Oscar Mendoza Azurdia)
1957	Luis Arturo González López
1957–8	*Military junta* (Guillermo Flores Avendaño)
1958–63	Miguel Ydígoras Fuentes
1963–6	*Military junta* (Enrique Peralta Azurdia)

1966–70	Julio César Méndez Montenegro
1970–4	Carlos Araña Osorio
1974–8	Kyell Eugenio Laugerua García
1978–82	Romeo Lucas García
1982	Angel Aníbal Guevara
1982–3	Efraín Rios Montt
1983–6	Oscar Humberto Mejía Victores
1986–91	Marco Vinicio Cerezo Arévalo
1991–3	Jorge Serrano Elias
1993–6	Ramiro de Léon Carpio
1996–	Alvaro Arzú Irigoyen

Guinea

President

1961–84	Ahmed Sékou Touré
1984–	Lansana Conté

Prime Minister

1958–72	Ahmed Sékou Touré
1972–84	Louis Lansana Beavogui
1984–5	Diarra Traore
1985–96	*No Prime Minister*
1996–	Sidia Toure

Guinea-Bissau

President

1974–80	Luis de Almeida Cabral
1980–4	*Revolutionary Council* (João Bernardo Vieira)
1984–	João Bernardo Vieira

Prime Minister

1992–4	Carlos Correia
1994–7	Manuel Saturnino da Costa
1997–	Carlos Correia

Guyana

President

1970–	Edward A Luckhoo
1970–80	Arthur Chung
1980–5	(Linden) Forbes (Sampson) Burnham
1985–92	(Hugh) Desmond Hoyte
1992–7	Cheddi Jagan
1997–	Samuel Hinds

Prime Minister

1966–85	(Linden) Forbes (Sampson) Burnham
1985–92	Hamilton Green
1992–7	Samuel Hinds
1997–	Janet Jagan

Haiti

Head of State

1804–6	Jean Jacques Dessalines *Emperor*
1807–20	Henri Christophe *President/King of the North*

1806–18	Alexandre Pétion *President of the West*

President

1818–43	Jean Pierre Boyer
1843–4	Charles Ainé Rivière Hérard
1844–5	Philippe Guerrier
1845–6	Jean Louis Pierrot
1846–7	Jean-Baptiste Riché
1847–58	Faustin Soulouque *Emperor 1849–58*
1859–67	Fabre Nicolas Geffard
1867–70	Sylvain Salnave
1870–4	Nissage Saget
1874–6	Michel Dominique
1876–9	Boisrond Canal
1879–88	Louis Étienne Félicité Lysius Saloman
1888–9	Francçois Denys Légitime
1889–96	Florville Hyppolite
1896–1902	P A Tirésias Simon-Sam
1902	Boisrond Canal
1902–8	Alexis Nord
1908–11	Antoine Simon
1911–12	Michel Cincinnatus Leconte
1912–13	Tancrède Auguste
1913–14	Michael Oreste
1914	Oreste Zamor
1914–15	Joseph Davilmare Théodore
1915	Jean Velbrun-Guillaume
1915–22	Philippe Sudre Dartiguenave
1922–30	Joseph Louis Bornó
1930	Étienne Roy
1930–41	Sténio Joseph Vincent
1941–	Élie Lescot
1946	*Military junta* (Frank Lavaud)
1946–50	Dumarsais Estimé
1950	*Military junta* (Frank Lavaud)
1950–6	Paul E Magloire
1956–7	François Sylvain
1957	*Military junta*
1957	Léon Cantave
1957	Daniel Fignolé
1957	Antoine Kebreau
1957–71	François Duvalier ('Papa Doc')
1971–86	Jean-Claude Duvalier ('Baby Doc')
1986–8	Henri Namphy
1988	Leslie Manigat
1988	Henri Namphy
1988–90	Prosper Avril
1990	Ertha Pascal-Trouillot *Interim*
1990–1	Jean Bertrand Aristide
1991–2	Joseph Nerette *Interim*
1992–4	Marc Bazin
1994–6	Jean Bertrand Aristide
1996–	René Préval

Prime Minister

1992–3	Mark Bazin
1993–4	Robert Malval
1994–5	Smarck Michel
1995–6	Claudette Werleigh
1996–7	Rosny Smarth
1997–	Hervé Denis

Holy Roman Empire
Emperor

911–19	Conrad I (of Franconia)
919–36	Henry I 'the Fowler' (of Saxony)
936–73	Otto I 'the Great'
973–83	Otto II
983–1002	Otto III
1002–24	Henry II (of Bavaria)
1024–39	Conrad II (of Franconia)
1039–56	Henry III
1056–1106	Henry IV
1077–1080	Rudolf (of Swabia) *Rival Emperor*
1081–93	Hermann (of Salm) *Rival Emperor*
1093–1101	Conrad (of Franconia) *Rival Emperor*
1106–25	Henry V
1125–37	Lothair III of Supplinberg
1138–52	Conrad III of Hohenstauffen (*Duke of Franconia*)
1152–90	Frederick I Barbarossa (*Duke of Swabia*)
1190–7	Henry VI
1198–1218	Otto IV of Saxony
1198–1208	Philip (of Swabia) *Rival Emperor*
1212–50	Frederick II 'the Wonder of the World' (of Sicily)
1246–7	Henry Raspe (of Thuringia) *Rival Emperor*
1247–56	William (*II of Holland*) *Rival Emperor*
1250–4	Conrad IV
1254–7	Conradin of Swabia
1257–72	Richard of Cornwall
1257–73	Alfonso 'the Astronomer' (X of Castile)
1273–91	Rudolf I of Habsburg
1292–8	Adolf (of Nassau)
1298–1308	Albert I (of Austria)
1308–13	Henry VII (*IV of Luxembourg*)
1314–47	Ludwig 'the Bavarian' (*Louis IV of Upper Bavaria*)
1314–30	Frederick (II of Austria) *Rival Emperor*
1346–78	Charles IV (of Luxembourg and Bohemia)
1349	Gunther (of Schwarzburg) *Rival Emperor*
1378–1400	Wenceslas (*IV of Bohemia*)
1400	Frederick (of Brunswick-Luneburg) *Rival Emperor*
1400–10	Ruprecht (*III of the Palatinate*)
1410–37	Sigismund (of Bohemia-Hungary)
1410–11	Jobst (of Moravia) *Rival Emperor*
1437–9	Albert II (*V of Austria*)
1440–93	Frederick III (of Styria)
1493–1519	Maximilian I
1519–58	Charles V (*I of Spain*)
1558–64	Ferdinand I
1564–76	Maximilian II
1576–1612	Rudolf II
1612–19	Matthias
1619–37	Ferdinand II (of Styria)
1637–58	Ferdinand III
1658–1705	Leopold I
1705–11	Joseph I
1711–40	Charles VI
1742–5	Charles VII (of Bavaria)
1745–65	Francis I (*III of Lorraine*)
1765–90	Joseph II
1790–2	Leopold II
1792–1806	Francis II (*Emperor of Austria to 1835*)

See also Austria

Honduras
President

1824–7	Dionisio Herrera
1827	Justo Mila
1827–8	Francisco Morazán
1829–32	Diego Vigil
1832–3	Francisco Milla
1833–4	Joaquin Rivera
1834–7	Francisco Ferrera
1837–8	Justo José Herrera
1839	José María Martínez
1839–40	Juan J Alvarado
1841–5	Francisco Ferrera
1845–7	Coronado Chávez
1847–52	Juan de Lindo Zelaya
1852–3	Francisco Gomez
1853–5	José Trinidad Cabañas
1856–62	José Santos Guardiola
1862–9	José María Medina
1869–70	Francisco Cruz
1870–2	José María Medina
1872–4	Céleo Arias
1874–6	Ponciano Leiva
1877–83	Marco Aurelio Soto
1883–91	Luis Bográn
1891–3	Ponciano Leiva
1894–9	Policarpo Bonilla
1900–03	Terencio Sierra
1903	Juan Angel Arias
1903–7	Manuel Bonilla Chirinos
1907–11	Miguel R Dávila
1911–12	Francisco Bertrand
1912–13	Manuel Bonilla Chirinos
1913–19	Francisco Bertrand
1919–24	Rafael López Gutiérrez
1924–5	Vicente Tosta Carrasco
1925–8	Miguel Paz Barahona
1929–33	Vicente Mejía Clindres
1933–49	Tiburcio Carías Andino
1949–54	Juan Manuel Gálvez

Head of State

1954–6	Julio Lozano Diaz
1956–7	*Military junta* (Oswaldo Lopez Arellano)

President

1958–63	José Ramón Villeda Morales

Head of State

1963–5	Oswaldo López Arellano

President

1965–71	Oswaldo López Arellano
1971–2	Ramón Ernesto Cruz

Head of State

1972–5	Oswaldo López Arellano
1975–8	Juan Alberto Melgar Castro
1978–80	*Military junta* (Policarpo Paz García)

President

1981–2	Policarpo Paz García
1982–6	Roberto Suazo Córdova
1986–90	José Simon Azcona del Hoyo
1990–4	Rafael Leonardo Callejas Romero
1994–	Carlos Roberto Reina

Hungary

Monarch – Kingdom of Hungary
Arpad Dynasty

1000–38	István (St Stephen) I
1038–41	Peter Orseolo
1041–4	Samuel Aba
1044–6	Peter Orseolo (*restored*)
1046–60	András I
1060–3	Béla I
1063–74	Salomon
1074–7	Géza I
1077–95	Ladislas I
1095–1116	Kálmán
1116–31	István II
1131–41	Béla II
1141–62	Géza II
1161–72	István III
1162–3	Ladislas II *Rival king*
1163–5	István IV *Rival king*
1172–96	Béla III
1196–1204	Emeric
1204–05	Ladislas III
1205–35	András II
1235–70	Béla IV
1270–2	István V
1272–90	Ladislas IV
1290–1301	András III

Later Kings

1301–05	Vaclav (III of Bohemia)
1305–08	Otto (III of Bavaria)
1308–42	Charles Robert of Anjou
1342–82	Lajos I 'the Great' *King Louis of Poland from 1370*
1382–95	Mary *Joint ruler from 1387*
1387–1439	*As Holy Roman Emperor*
1440–44	Vladislav Jagiellon (*VI of Poland*)

1444–57	Ladislas V
1458–90	Mattias I Corvinus
1490–1526	*As Bohemia*
1526–1866	*Austrian rule*
1866–1916	Franz Josef (Francis Joseph) I *Dual Monarchy*
1916–18	Károly IV (Charles)

President

1919	Mihály Károlyi
1919	*Revolutionary Governing Council* (Sándor Garbai)
1920–44	Miklós Horthy de Nagybánya *Regent*
1944–5	*Provisional National Assembly*
1946–8	Zoltán Tildy
1948–50	Árpád Szakasits
1950–2	Sándor Rónai
1952–67	István Dobi
1967–87	Pál Losonczi
1987–8	Károly Németh
1988–9	Brunó Ferenc Straub
1989–90	Mátyás Szúrös
1990–	Árpád Göncz

Premier

1867–71	Gyula, Gróf Andrássy
1871–2	Menyhért, Gróf Lónyay
1872–4	József Szlávy
1874–5	István Bittó
1875	Béla Wenckheim
1875–90	Kálmán Tisza
1890–2	Gyula Szapáry
1892–5	Sándor Wekerle
1895–9	Deszó Bánffy
1899–1903	Kálmán Széll
1903	Károly Khuen-Héderváry
1903–5	István, Gróf Tisza
1905–6	Géza Fejérváry
1906–10	Sándor Wekerle
1910–12	Károly Khuen-Héderváry
1912–13	László Lukács
1913–17	István, Gróf Tisza
1917	Móric Esterházy
1917–18	Sándor Wekerle
1918–19	Mihály Károlyi
1919	Dénes Berinkey
1919	*Revolutionary Governing Council*
1919	Gyula Peidl
1919	István Friedrich
1919–20	Károly Huszár
1920	Sándor Simonyi-Semadam
1920–1	Pál, Gróf Teleki
1921–31	István, Gróf Bethlen
1931–2	Gyula Károlyi
1932–6	Gyula Gömbös
1936–8	Kálmán Darányi
1938–9	Béla Imrédy
1939–41	Pál, Gróf Teleki
1941–2	László Bárdossy
1942–4	Miklós Kállay
1944	Döme Sztójay
1944	Géza Lakatos
1944	Ferenc Szálasi

1944–5	*Provisional National Assembly* (Béla Miklós Dálnoki)
1945–6	Zoltán Tildy
1946–7	Ferenc Nagy
1947–8	Lajos Dinnyés
1948–52	István Dobi
1952–3	Mátyás Rákosi
1953–5	Imre Nagy
1955–6	András Hegedüs
1956	Imre Nagy
1956–8	János Kádár
1958–61	Ferenc Münnich
1961–5	János Kádár
1965–7	Gyula Kállai
1967–75	Jenö Fock
1975–87	György Lázár
1987–8	Károly Grosz
1988–90	Miklós Németh
1990–3	József Antall
1993–4	Peter Boross
1994–	Gyula Horn

First Secretary

1949–56	Mátyás Rákosi
1956	Ernö Gerö
1956–88	János Kádár
1988–9	Károly Grosz

Iceland

President

1944–52	Sveinn Björnsson
1952–68	Asgeir Asgeirsson
1968–80	Kristján Eldjárn
1980–96	Vigdís Finnbogadóttir
1996–	Olafur Ragnar Grimsson

Prime Minister

1904–9	Hannes (Pétursson) Hafstein
1909–11	Björn Jónsson
1911–12	Kristján Jónsson
1912–14	Hannes (Pétursson) Hafstein
1914–15	Sigurður Eggerz
1915–17	Einar Arnórsson
1917–22	Jón Magnússon
1922–4	Sigurður Eggerz
1924–6	Jón Magnússon
1926–7	Jon Þorláksson
1927–32	Tryggvi Þórhallsson
1932–4	Ásgeir Ásgeirsson
1934–42	Hermann Jónasson
1942	Ólafur Thors
1942–4	Björn Þórdarsson
1944–7	Ólafur Thors
1947–9	Stefán Jóhann Stefánsson
1949–50	Ólafur Thors
1950–3	Steingrímur Steinþórsson
1953–6	Ólafur Thors
1956–8	Hermann Jónasson
1958–9	Emil Jónsson
1959–61	Ólafur Thors
1961	Bjarni Benediktsson
1961–3	Ólafur Thors
1963–70	Bjarni Benediktsson
1970–1	Jóhann Hafstein
1971–4	Ólafur Jóhannesson
1974–8	Geir Hallgrímsson

1978–9	Ólafur Jóhannesson
1979	Benedikt Gröndal
1980–3	Gunnar Thoroddsen
1983–7	Steingrímur Hermannsson
1987–8	Thorsteinn Pálsson
1988–91	Steingrímur Hermannsson
1991–	Davíd Oddsson

India

Early Emperors

Maurya Dynasty

c.320–c.300BC	Chandragupta Maurya
c.300–c.273BC	Bindusara
c.273–c.232BC	Ashoka Vardhana
c.232–c.225BC	Kunala *West*
c.232–c.225BC	Dasaratha *East*
c.225BC–?	Samprati
?	Salisuka
?	Devadharma
?–c.194BC	Satamdhanu
c.194–c.187BC	Brihadratha

Sunga Dynasty

c.187–c.151BC	Pushyamitra Sunga
c.151–c.143BC	Agnimitra
c.143–c.133BC	Vasujyeshtha
c.133BC–?	Vasumitra
?	Andhraka
?	Pulindaka
?	Ghosha
?	Vajramitra
?–c.85BC	Bhagavata
c.85–c.75BC	Devabhumi

Kanva Dynasty

c.75–c.66BC	Vasudeva
c.66–c.52BC	Bhumimitra
c.52–c.40BC	Narayana
c.40–c.30BC	Susarman

Sultan of Delhi

Slave Dynasty

1206–10	Qutb-ud-Din Aibak
1210–11	Aram Shah
1211–36	Shams-ud-Din Iltutmish
1236	Rukn-ud-Din Firuz Shah
1236–40	Jalalat-ud-Din Radiyya
1240–2	Muizz-ud-Din Bahram Shah
1242–6	Ala-ud-Din Masud Shah
1246–66	Nasir-ud-Din Mahmud Shah
1266–87	Ghiyath-ud-Din Balban
1287–90	Muizz-ud-Din Kayqubad
1290	Shams-ud-Din Kayumarth

Khalji Dynasty

1290–6	Jalal-ud-Din Firuz Shah
1296	Rukn-ud-Din Ibrahim Shah
1296–1316	Ala-ud-Din Muhammad Shah
1316	Shihab-ud-Din Umar Shah
1316–20	Qutb-ud-Din Mubarak Shah
1320	Nasir-ud-Din Khusraw Shah

Tughluq Dynasty

1320–5	Ghiyath-ud-Din Tughluq Shah I

1325–51	Ghiyath-ud-Din Muhammad Shah I
1351	Mahmud Shah
1351–88	Firuz Shah
1388–9	Ghiyath-ud-Din Tughluq Shah II
1389–90	Abu-Bakr Shah
1390–3	Nasir-ud-Din Muhammad Shah II
1393	Ala-ud-Din Sikandar Shah
1393–1413	Nasir-ud-Din Mahmud Shah
1413–14	Dawlat Khan Lodi

Sayyid Dynasty

1414–21	Khidr Khan
1421–35	Muizz-ud-Din Mubarak Shah
1435–46	Muhammad Shah
1446–51	Ala-ud-Din Alam Shah

Lodi Dynasty

1451–89	Bahlul Lodi
1489–1517	Nizam Shah Sikandar
1517–26	Ibrahim Lodi

Moghul Emperors

1526–30	Zahir-ud-Din Babur
1530–40	Nasir-ud-Din Humayun

Sultan of Delhi

Surrid Dynasty

1540–5	Shir Shah Sur
1545–54	Islam Shah
1554–6	Muhammad Adil Shah
1554–6	Ibrahim Shah
1555–6	Ahmad Khan Sikandar Shah

Moghul Emperors

1555–6	Nasir-ud-Din Humayun (restored)
1556–1605	Jalal-ud-Din Akbar I
1605–27	Nur-ud-Din Jahangir
1627–8	Dawar Bakhsh
1628–57	Shihab-ud-Din Shah Jahan I
1657–1707	Muhyi-ud-Din Aurangzib Alamgir I
1707	Azam Shah
1707–12	Shah Alam Bahadur Shah I
1712	Azim-ush-Shan
1712–13	Muizz-ud-Din Jahandar
1713–19	Farrukhsiyar
1719	Shams-ud-Din Rafi-ud-Darajat
1719	Rafi-ud-Dawlah Shah Jahan II
1719	Nikusiyar
1719–48	Nasir-ud-Din Muhammad
1748–54	Ahmad Shah Bahadur
1754–60	Aziz-ud-Din Alamgir II
1760	Shah Jahan III
1760–88	Jalal-ud-Din Ali Jauhar Shah Alam II
1788	Bidar Bakht
1788–1806	Jalal-ud-Din Ali Jauhar Shah Alam II (restored)
1806–37	Muin-ud-Din Akbar II

1837–58	Siraj-ud-Din Bahadur Shah II

Viceroy

Fort William in Bengal

1774–85	Warren Hastings
1786–93	Charles Cornwallis, 1st Marquis Cornwallis
1793–8	Alured Clarke Temporary Viceroy
1798–1805	Lord Mornington
1805	Charles Cornwallis, 1st Marquis Cornwallis
1805–07	George Barlow Temporary
1807–13	Lord Minto
1813–23	Lord Moira
1823–8	William Pitt, 1st Earl Amherst of Arakan
1828–34	William Cavendish Bentinck, 3rd Duke of Portland

India

1834–5	William Cavendish Bentinck, 3rd Duke of Portland
1836–42	George Eden, 1st Earl of Auckland
1842–4	Edward Law, 1st Earl of Ellenborough
1844–8	Henry Hardinge, 1st Viscount Hardinge
1848–56	James Andrew Broun-Ramsay, Marquis of Dalhousie
1856–62	Charles John Canning, 1st Earl Canning
1862–3	James Bruce, 8th Earl of Elgin
1864–9	John Laird Mair, 1st Baron Lawrence
1869–72	Richard Southwell Bourke, Earl of Mayo
1872–6	Thomas George Baring, 2nd Baron Northbrook
1876–80	Edward Robert Bulwer, 1st Earl of Lytton
1880–4	George Robinson, Marquis of Ripon
1884–8	Francis Blackwood, 1st Marquis of Dufferin and Ava
1888–94	Henry Petty-Fitzmaurice, 5th Marquis of Lansdowne
1894–9	Victor Alexander Bruce, 9th Earl of Elgin
1899–1905	George Nathaniel Curzon, Marquis Curzon of Kedleston
1905–10	Elliot-Murray-Kynynmound, Earl of Minto
1910–16	Charles Hardinge, 1st Baron Hardinge
1916–21	Frederick Thesiger, 1st Viscount Chelmsford

1921–6	Rufus Daniel Isaacs, 1st Marquis of Reading
1926–31	Edward Wood, 1st Earl of Halifax
1931–6	Freeman Freeman-Thomas, 1st Marquis of Willingdon
1936–43	Victor Alexander John Hope, 2nd Marquis of Linlithgow
1943–7	Archibald Percival Wavell, 1st Earl Wavell
1947	Louis Mountbatten, 1st Earl Mountbatten of Burma

President

1950–62	Rajendra Prasad
1962–7	Sarvepalli Radhakrishnan
1967–9	Zakir Husain
1969	Varahagiri Venkatagiri Acting
1969	Mohammed Hidayatullah Acting
1969–74	Varahagiri Venkatagiri
1974–7	Fakhruddin Ali Ahmed
1977	B D Jatti Acting
1977–82	Neelam Sanjiva Reddy
1982–7	Giani Zail Singh
1987–92	Ramaswami Venkataraman
1992–7	Shankar Dayal Sharma
1997–	K R Narayanan

Prime Minister

1947–64	Jawaharlal Nehru
1964	Gulzari Lal Nanda Acting
1964–6	Lal Bahadur Shastri
1966	Gulzari Lal Nanda Acting
1966–77	Indira Gandhi
1977–9	Morarji Ranchhodji Desai
1979–80	Charan Singh
1980–4	Indira Gandhi
1984–9	Rajiv Gandhi
1989–90	Vishwanath Pratap ('V P') Singh
1990–91	Chandra Shekhar
1991–6	P V Narasimha Rao
1996	Atal Bihari Vajpayee
1996–7	Deve Gowda
1997–	Inder Kumar Gujral

Amber/Jaipur

Raja/Maharaja

c.1128–	
c.1136	Dulha Rao
c.1136–?	Kanka
?	Maidal
?	Hunadeva
?–c.1185	Kantal I
c.1185–?	Pujanadeva
?	Malesi
?	Byala
?	Rajadeva
?–1276	Kilhan
1276–?	Kantal II

?	Jansi
?	Udayakarna
?	Nara Singh
?	Banbir
?	Udha Rao
?–1502	Chandrasena
1502–34	Prithvi I
1534–?	Bhima
?–1547	Ratan
1547–?	Baharmalla
?–1589	Bhagwan Das
1589–1614	Man Singh I
1614	Jagat Singh I
1614–22	Bhao Singh
1622–67	Jaya Singh I
1667–88	Rama Singh I
1688–1700	Bishan Singh
1700–43	Sawai Jaya Singh II
1743–50	Ishwari Singh
1750–68	Madhu Singh I
1768–78	Prithvi Singh II
1778–1803	Pratap Singh
1803–18	Jagat Singh II
1818–35	Jaya Singh III
1835–81	Rama Singh II
1881–1922	Sawai Madhu Singh II
1922–49	Sawai Man Singh II

Baroda

Maharaja

1721–32	Pilaji Rao Geckwar
1732–68	Damaji Rao
1768–71	Govind Rao
1771–89	Sayaji Rao I
1789–93	Manaji Rao
1793–1800	Govind Rao (restored)
1800–18	Anand Rao
1818–47	Sayaji Rao II
1847–56	Ganpat Rao
1856–70	Khande Rao
1870–5	Malhar Rao
1875–1939	Sayaji Rao III
1939–49	Pratap Singh

Bharatpur

Maharaja

1722–56	Badan Singh
1756–63	Suraj Mal
1763–8	Jawahir Singh
1768–9	Ratan Singh
1769–74	Kesri Singh
1785–1805	Ranjit Singh
1805–23	Randhir Singh
1823–5	Baldeo Singh
1825–6	Durjan Sal
1826–53	Balwant Singh
1853–93	Jaswant Singh
1893–1900	Ram Singh
1900–29	Brijendra Sawai Kishan Singh
1929–48	Brijendra Singh

Bhopal

Nawab

1723–40	Dost Muhammad Khan
1740	Muhammad Khan
1740–54	Yar Muhammad Khan
1754–77	Faid Muhammad Khan
1777–1807	Hayat Muhammad Khan
1807–16	Wazir Muhammad Khan
1816–20	Nadhr Muhammad Khan
1820–44	Kudsiyya Begum
1844–68	Sikandar Begum
1868–1901	Shah Jahan Begum
1901–26	Sultan Jahan Begum
1926–48	Hamid-Allah Khan

Bikaner

Raja/Maharaja

1465–1504	Bika Rao
1504–05	Naro
1505–26	Lunkaran
1526–42	Jetsi
1542–71	Kalyan Singh
1571–1612	Raya Singh
1612–13	Dalpat Singh
1613–31	Sur Singh
1631–69	Karan Singh
1669–98	Anup Singh
1698–1700	Sarup Singh
1700–36	Sujan Singh
1736–45	Zorawar Singh
1745–87	Gaja Singh
1787	Raja Singh
1787	Pratap Singh
1787–1828	Surat Singh
1828–51	Ratan Singh
1851–72	Sardar Singh
1872–87	Dungar Singh
1887–1943	Ganga Singh
1943–9	Sadul Singh

Bundi

Rao/Maharao

c.1342–?	Devi Singh
?	Samar Singh
?	Napurji
?	Majirhi
?	Bar Singh
?–1503	Subhand Deva
1503–?	Narain Das
?–1531	Suraj Mal
1531–?	Surthan
?–1554	Arjun
1554–85	Surjan
1585–1607	Bhoja
1607–31	Ratan
1631–58	Chhatra Sal
1658–78	Bhao Singh
1678–1706	Aniruddha Singh
1706–29	Budh Singh
1729–48	Dalel Singh
1748–70	Ummed Singh
1770	Ajit Singh
1770–1821	Bishan Singh

1821–89	Ram Singh
1889–1927	Raghubir Singh
1927–45	Ishwari Singh
1945–9	Bahadur Singh

Cannanore

Raja

1545–91	Ali Adi-Raja I
1591–1607	Abu Bakr Adi-Raja I
1607–10	Abu Bakr Adi-Raja II
1610–47	Muhammad Ali Adi-Raja I
1647–55	Muhammad Ali Adi-Raja II
1655–6	Kamal Adi-Raja
1656–91	Muhammad Ali Adi-Raja III
1691–1704	Ali Adi-Raja II
1704–20	Kunhi Amsa Adi-Raja I
1720–8	Muhammad Ali Adi-Raja IV
1728–32	Harrabichi Kadavube Adi-Raja Bibi
1732–45	Junumabe Adi-Raja Bibi I
1745–77	Kunhi Amsa Adi-Raja II
1777–1819	Junumabe Adi-Raja Bibi II
1819–38	Mariambe Adi-Raja Bibi
1838–52	Hayashabe Adi-Raja Bibi
1852–70	Abdul-Rahman Ali Adi-Raja I
1870–99	Musa Ali Adi-Raja
1899–1907	Muhammad Ali Adi-Raja V
1907–11	Imbichi Adi-Raja Bibi
1911–21	Ahmad Ali Adi-Raja
1921–31	Ayisha Adi-Raja Bibi
1931–46	Abdul-Rahman Ali Adi-Raja II
1946–9	Mariyumma Adi-Raja Bibi

Cochin

Raja

c.1500–03	Unni Rama Koil I
1503–37	Unni Rama Koil II
1537–65	Vira Kerala Varma I
1565–1601	Kesara Rama Varma
1601–15	Vira Kerala Varma II
1615–24	Ravi Varma I
1624–37	Vira Kerala Varma III
1637–45	Goda Varma I
1645–6	Vira Rayira Varma
1646–50	Vira Kerala Varma IV
1650–6	Rama Varma I
1656–8	Gangadhara Lakshmi
1658–62	Rama Varma II
1662–3	Goda Varma II
1663–87	Vira Kerala Varma V
1687–93	Rama Varma III
1693–7	Ravi Varma II
1697–1701	Rama Varma IV
1701–21	Rama Varma V
1721–31	Ravi Varma III
1731–46	Rama Varma VI
1746–9	Kerala Varma I
1749–60	Rama Varma VII
1760–75	Kerala Varma II
1775–90	Rama Varma VIII
1790–1805	Rama Varna Saktan Tampuran

1805–09	Rama Varma IX
1809–28	Kerala Varma III
1828–37	Rama Varma X
1837–44	Rama Varma XI
1844–51	Rama Varma XII
1851–3	Kerala Varma IV
1853–64	Ravi Varma IV
1864–88	Rama Varma XIII
1888–95	Kerala Varma V
1895–1914	Rama Varma XIV
1914–32	Rama Varma XV
1932–41	Rama Varma XVI
1941–3	Kerala Varma VI
1943–6	Ravi Varma V
1946–8	Kerala Varma VII
1948–9	Rama Varma XVII

Cutch

Rao/Maharao

1548–85	Khengar I
1585–1631	Bharmal I
1631–45	Bhojaraja
1645–54	Khengar II
1654–62	Tamachi
1662–97	Rayadhan I
1697–1715	Pragmal I
1715–18	Godji I
1718–41	Desal I
1741–60	Lakha
1760–78	Godji II
1778–1814	Rayadhan II
1814–19	Bharmal II
1819–60	Desal II
1860–76	Pragmal II
1876–1942	Khengar III
1942–8	Vijayaraja
1948	Madan Singh

Gwalior

Maharaja

1726–45	Ranoji Sindhia
1745–55	Jayappa
1755–61	Jankoji I
1761–94	Madhava Rao I
1794–1827	Daulat Rao
1827–43	Jankoji Rao II
1843–86	Jayaji Rao
1886–1925	Madhava Rao II
1925–48	Jivaji Rao

Hyderabad

Nizam

1724–48	Qamar-ud-Din Nizam-ul-Mulk Asaf Jah
1748–50	Muhammad Nasir Jang
1750–1	Muzaffar Jang
1751–62	Asaf-ud-Dawlah Salabat Jang
1762–1802	Nizam Ali
1802–29	Akbar Ali Khan Sikandar Jah
1829–57	Nasir-ud-Dawlah Farkhundah Ali

1857–69	Afzal-ud-Dawlah
1869–1911	Mahbub Ali Khan
1911–48	Uthman Ali Khan Bahadur Jang

Indore

Maharaja

1728–64	Malhar Rao I Holkar
1764–6	Malle Rao
1765–95	Ahalyu Bai
1795–8	Tukoji Holkar
1798–1811	Jaswant Rao I
1811–34	Malhar Rao II
1834–43	Hari Rao
1843–86	Tukoji Rao II
1886–1903	Shivaji Rao
1903–26	Tukoji Rao III
1926–48	Jaswant Rao II

Jaipur see Amber

Jaisalmer

Rawal/Maharawal

c.1180–?	Jaisal
?	Salivahan I
?	Baijal
?–c.1219	Kelan
c.1219–	
c.1250	Chachigdeva I
c.1250–	
c.1278	Karan Singh I
c.1278–	
c.1281	Lakhasena
c.1281	Punyapala
c.1281–	
c.1300	Jait Singh I
c.1300	Mulraja I
c.1300–	
c.1331	Duda
c.1331–	
c.1361	Ghar Singh
1361–?	Kehar
?–1436	Lakhmana
1436–c.1448	Bairi Singh
c.1448–67	Chachigdeva II
1467–96	Devidas
1496–1528	Jait Singh II
1528	Karan Singh II
1528–50	Lunkaran
1550–61	Malladeva
1561–77	Har Raja
1577–1613	Bhima
1613–50	Kalyandas
1650	Manohardas
1650–61	Sabal Singh
1661–1702	Amar Singh
1702–07	Jaswant Singh
1707–21	Budh Singh
1721–2	Tej Singh
1722	Sawai Singh
1722–62	Akhai Singh
1762–1819	Mulraja II
1819–46	Gaja Singh
1846–64	Ranjit Singh

1864–91	Bairi Sal
1891–1914	Salivahan II
1914–49	Jawahir Singh
1949	Girdhar Singh

Jodhpur see Marwar

Kashmir

Sultan

Swati Dynasty

1339–49	Shams-ud-Din Shah Mirza Swati
1349–50	Jamshid
1350–9	Ala-ud-Din Ali Shir
1359–78	Shihab-ud-Din Shirashamak
1378–94	Qutb-ud-Din Hindal
1394–1416	Sikandar
1416–20	Ali Mirza Khan
1420–70	Zail-ul-Abidin Shahi Khan
1470–1	Haidar Shah Hajji Khan
1471–89	Hasan
1489–90	Muhammad
1490–8	Fath Shah
1498–9	Muhammad (*restored*)
1499–1500	Fath Shah (*restored*)
1500–26	Muhammad (*restored*)
1526–7	Ibrahim
1527–9	Nazuk
1529–33	Muhammad (*restored*)
1533–40	Shams-ud-Din II
1540	Nazuk (*restored*)
1540–51	Haidar Dughlat
1551–2	Nazuk (*restored*)
1552–5	Ibrahim (*restored*)
1555–7	Ismail
1557–61	Habib

Chak Dynasty

1561–3	Ghazi Khan Chak
1563–9	Nasr-ud-Din Husain
1569–79	Zahir-ud-Din Ali
1579–86	Nasr-ud-Din Yusuf
1586–9	Yaqub

Maharaja

1846–57	Gulab Singh
1857–85	Rambir Singh
1885–1925	Partab Singh
1925–52	Hari Singh

Kolhapur

Maharaja

1700–12	Shivaji I
1712–60	Shambhuji
1760–1812	Shivaji II
1812–21	Shambhu
1821–37	Shahaji I
1837–66	Shivaji III
1866–70	Rajaram I
1870–83	Shivaji IV
1883–1922	Shahu
1922–40	Rajaram II
1942–7	Shivaji V
1947–9	Shahaji II

Kotah

Rao/Maharao

1625–56	Madhu Singh
1656–7	Mokund Singh
1657–69	Jagat Singh
1669	Paim Singh
1669–85	Kishor Singh I
1685–1707	Ram Singh I
1707–19	Bhima Singh I
1719–23	Arjun Singh
1723–56	Durjan Sal
1756–9	Ajit Singh
1759–65	Chhatra Sal I
1765–70	Goman Singh
1770–1819	Ummed Singh I
1819–28	Kishor Singh II
1828–66	Ram Singh II
1866–89	Chhatra Sal II
1889–1941	Ummed Singh II
1941–9	Bhima Singh II

Lahore

Maharaja

1799–1839	Ranjit Singh
1839–40	Kharak Singh
1840	Nao Nehal Singh
1840–1	Chand Kaur
1841–3	Sher Singh
1843–9	Dalip Singh

Marwar/Jodhpur

Raja/Maharaja

1382–?	Chunda Rao
?	Kanha
?	Sata
?–1438	Ranamalla
1428–88	Jodha
1488–91	Satal
1491–1515	Suja
1515–32	Ganga
1532–84	Malladeva
1584–95	Udaya Singh Raja
1595–1620	Sura Singh
1620–38	Gaja Singh
1638–80	Jaswant Singh I
1680–1725	Ajit Singh
1725–50	Abhaya Singh
1750–1	Rama Singh
1751–2	Bakht Singh
1752	Vijaya Singh
1752–73	Rama Singh (restored)
1773–92	Vijaya Singh (restored)
1792–1803	Bhim Singh
1803–43	Man Singh
1843–73	Takht Singh
1873–95	Jaswant Singh II
1895–1911	Sardar Singh
1911–18	Sumer Singh
1918–47	Umaid Singh
1947–9	Hanwant Singh

Mewar/Udaipur

Rana/Maharana

c.730–c.753	Khommana I
c.753–?	Mattata
?	Bhartripatta I
?	Simha
?	Khommana II
?	Mahayaka
c.940–c.950	Khommana III
c.950–c.960	Bhartripatta II
c.960–c.971	Allata
c.971–c.977	Naravahana
c.977–?	Salivahana
?	Saktikumara
?	Ambaprasada
?	Suchivarman
?	Naravarman
?	Anantavarman
?	Kirtivarman
?	Yogaraja
?	Vairata
?	Hamsapala
?	Vairi Singh
c.1108	Vijaya Singh
?	Ari Singh I
?	Choda Singh
?–c.1168	Vikrama Singh
c.1168–?	Rana SIngh
?–c.1171	Kshema Singh
c.1171–?	Samanta SIngh
?	Kumara Singh
?	Mathana Singh
?–c.1213	Padma Singh
c.1213–	
c.1260	Jaitra Singh
c.1260–	
c.1273	Teja Singh
c.1273–	
c.1302	Samara Singh
c.1302–	
c.1303	Ratna Singh I
c.1303–	
c.1314	Lakhana Singh
c.1314–	
c.1378	Hammir I
c.1378–	
c.1405	Kshetra Singh
c.1405–	
c.1420	Laksha Singh
c.1420–	
c.1433	Mokala
1433–68	Kumbhakarna
1468–73	Udaya Karan
1473–1509	Rayamalla
1509–28	Sangrama Singh I
1528–32	Ratna Singh II
1532–5	Bikramajit
1535–7	Ranbir
1537–72	Udaya Singh
1572–97	Pratap Singh I
1597–1620	Amar Singh I
1620–8	Karan
1628–52	Jagat Singh I
1652–80	Raja Singh I

1680–99	Jaya Singh
1699–1711	Amar Singh II
1711–34	Sangrama Singh II
1734–52	Jagat Singh II
1752–4	Pratap Singh II
1754–61	Raja Singh II
1761–73	Ari Singh II
1773–8	Hammir II
1778–1828	Bhim Singh
1828–38	Jawan Singh
1838–42	Sardar Singh
1842–61	Sarup Singh
1861–74	Sambhu
1874–84	Sujjan Singh
1884–1930	Fateh Singh
1930–49	Bhopal Singh

Mysore

Maharaja

1399–1423	Yadu Raya
1423–59	Hiriya Bettada Chamaraja I
1459–78	Timmaraja I
1478–1513	Hiriya Chamarajasa II
1513–53	Hiriya Bettada Chamaraja III
1553–72	Timmaraja II
1572–6	Bola Chamaraja IV
1576–8	Bettada Devaraja
1578–1617	Raja Wadiyar
1617–37	Chamaraja V
1637–8	Immadi Raja
1638–59	Kanthirava Narasaraja I
1659–73	Kempa Devaraja
1673–1704	Chikkadevaraja
1704–14	Kanthirava Narasaraja II
1714–32	Krishnaraja I
1732–4	Chamaraja VI
1734–66	Krishnaraja II
1766–70	Nanjaraja
1770–6	Bettada Chamaraja VII
1776–96	Khasa Chamaraja VIII
1799–1831	Krishnaraja III
1831–81	*No Maharaja*
1881–94	Chamaraja IX
1894–1940	Krishnaraja IV
1940–9	Jayachamarajendra Bahadur

Patiala

Maharaja

1762–5	Ala Singh
1765–81	Amar Singh
1781–1813	Sahib Singh
1813–45	Karam Singh
1845–62	Narindar Singh
1862–76	Mohindar Singh
1876–1900	Rajindar Singh
1900–38	Bhupindar Singh
1938–48	Yadavindar Singh

Sikkim

Maharaja

1642–70	Phuntsog Namgyal

1670–86	Tensung Namgyal
1686–1717	Chador Namgyal
1717–33	Gyurmed Namgyal
1733–80	Namgyal Phuntsog
1780–93	Tenzing Namgyal
1793–1863	Tsugphud Namgyal
1863–74	Sidkeong Namgyal I
1874–1914	Thutob Namgyal
1914	Sidkeong Namgyal II
1914–63	Tashi Namgyal
1963–75	Palden Thondup Namgyal

Tonk

Nawab
1798–1834	Amir Khan
1834–64	Wazir Muhammad Khan
1864–7	Muhammad Ali Khan
1867–1930	Hafiz Muhammad Ibrahim Ali Khan
1930–48	Hafiz Muhammad Sadat Ali Khan

Travancore

Maharaja
1729–58	Marthanda Varma
1758–98	Kartika Tirunal Rama Varma
1798–1810	Balarama Varma
1810–15	Gouri Lakshmi Bai
1815–29	Gouri Parvati Bai
1829–47	Swati Tirunal
1847–60	Utram Tirunal Marthandra Varma
1860–80	Ayilyam Tirunal
1880–5	Rama Varma Visakhan Tirunal
1885–1924	Sri Mulam Tirunal Rama Varma
1924–31	Setu Lakshmi Bai
1931–49	Sri Chitra Tirunal Balarama Varma

Udaipur see Mewar

Indonesia

President
State of Indonesia
1945–9	Achmad Sukarno

Republic of Indonesia
1949–68	Achmad Sukarno
1968–	Thojib N J Suharto

Prime Minister
1945	R A A Wiranatakusumah
1945–7	Sutan Sjahrir
1947–8	Amir Sjarifuddin
1948	Mohammed Hatta
1948–9	Sjarifuddin Prawiraranegara
1949	Susanto Tirtoprodjo
1949	Mohammed Hatta
1950	Dr Halim
1950–1	Mohammed Natsir

1951–2	Sukiman Wirjosandjojo
1952–3	Dr Wilopo
1953–5	Ali Sastroamidjojo
1955–6	Burhanuddin Harahap
1956–7	Ali Sastroamidjojo
1957–9	Raden Haji Djuanda Kurtawidjaja
1959–63	Achmad Sukarno
1963–6	S E Subandrio
1966–	*No Prime Minister*

Sultan of Jogjakarta
1755–92	Abdul-Rahman Amangkubuwana I
1792–1810	Abdul-Rahman Amangkubuwana II
1810–14	Abdul-Rahman Amangkubuwana III
1814–22	Abdul-Rahman Amangkubuwana IV
1822–55	Abdul-Rahman Amangkubuwana V
1855–77	Abdul-Rahman Amangkubuwana VI
1877–1921	Abdul-Rahman Amangkubuwana VII
1921–39	Abdul-Rahman Amangkubuwana VIII
1939–49	Abdul-Rahman Amangkubuwana IX

Sultan of Maratam
1582–1601	Panembahan Senapati Ingalaga
1601–13	Mas Jolang Panembahan Krapyak
1613–45	Abdul-Rahman Agung
1645–77	Prabu Amangkurat I
1677–1703	Amangkurat II
1703–05	Amangkurat III
1705–19	Pakubuwana I
1719–25	Amangkurat IV
1725–49	Pakubuwana II
1749–55	Pakubuwana III

Susuhunan of Surakarta
1755–88	Pakubuwana (*III of Maratam*)
1788–1820	Pakubuwana IV
1820–3	Pakubuwana V
1823–30	Pakubuwana VI
1830–58	Pakubuwana VII
1858–61	Pakubuwana VIII
1861–93	Pakubuwana IX
1893–1939	Pakubuwana X
1939–44	Pakubuwana XI
1944–9	Pakubuwana XII

Iran (Persia)

Kingdom of Persia
House of Achaemenes
c.700–675BC	Hakhamanish (Achaemenes)
c.675–40BC	Chishpish (Teispes)
c.640–00BC	Kurush (Cyrus) I
c.600–559BC	Kambujiya (Cambyses) I

559–30BC	Kurush (Cyrus) II 'the Great'
530–22BC	Kambujiya (Cambyses) II
522BC	Badiya-Gaumata (Smerdis)
522–486BC	Darayavahush (Darius) I 'the Great'
486–65BC	Khshayarsha (Xerxes) I
465–24BC	Artakhshassa (Artaxerxes) I Longimanus
424–3BC	Khshayarsha II
423–04BC	Darayavahush (Darius) II Ochus
404–359BC	Artakhshassa (Artaxerxes) II Mnemon
359–38BC	Artakhshassa (Artaxerxes) III Ochus
338–6BC	Arsha
336–30BC	Darayavahush (Darius) III Codomannus
330–29BC	Artakhshassa IV (Bessus) *Bactria*

Shah
Qajar Dynasty
1779–97	Agha Muhammad
1797–1834	Fath Ali
1834–48	Muhammad
1848–96	Nasir-ud-Din
1896–1907	Muzaffar-ud-Din
1907–9	Mohammed Ali
1909–25	Ahmad Mirza

Pahlavi Dynasty
1925–41	Reza Khan
1941–79	Mohammed Reza Pahlavi

Republic
Leader of the Islamic Revolution (Wali faqih)
1979–89	Ruhollah Khomeini
1989–	Sayed Ali Khamenei

President
1980–1	Abolhassan Bani-Sadr
1981	Mohammed Ali Rajai
1981–9	Sayed Ali Khamenei
1989–97	Ali Akbar Hashemi Rafsanjani
1997–	Sayed Mohammad Khatami

Prime Minister
1979	Shahpur Bakhtiar
1979–80	Mehdi Bazargan
1980–1	Mohammed Ali Rajai
1981	Mohammed Javad Bahonar
1981	Mohammed Reza Mahdavi-Kani
1981–9	Mir Hossein Moussavi
1989–	*No Prime Minister*

Iraq

Monarch – Kingdom of Iraq
1921–33	Faisal I
1933–9	Ghazi I
1939–58	Faisal II (Abdul Illah *Regent 1939–53*)

Republic

Commander of the National Forces
1958–63   Abdul Karim Qassem

Head of Council of State
1958–63   Mohammed Najib ar-Rubai

President
1963–6   Abdus Salaam Mohammed Arif
1966–8   Abdur Rahman Mohammed Arif
1968–79   Said Ahmad Hassan al-Bakr
1979–   Saddam Hussein (at-Takriti)

Ireland

High King of Tara
d.c.450   Niall Noigiallach Nath Í
d.c.463   Loeguire
d.c.482   Ailill Molt (of Connaught)
d.c.507   Lugaid
d.534   Muirchertach mac Erc (of Ailech)
d.c.544   Tuathal Maelgarb
d.565   Diarmaid mac Cerrbel (of Meath)
d.566   Forrgus (of Ailech)
d.566   Domhall Ilchegach (of Ailech)
d.569   Ainmuire mac Setnae
d.572   Baetan mac Muirchertach (of Ailech)
d.572   Eochaid (of Ailech)
d.586   Baetan mac Ninnid
d.598   Aed mac Ainmuire
d.604   Aed Slaine (of Brega)
d.604   Colman Rimid (of Ailech)
d.612   Aed Allan mac Domhall (of Ailech)
d.615   Mael Cobo
d.628   Suibne Menn (of Ailech)
d.642   Domhall mac Aed
d.654   Conall Cael
d.658   Cellach
d.665   Diarmaid mac Aed (of Brega)
d.665   Blathmac mac Aed (of Brega)
d.671   Sechnussach (of Brega)
d.675   Cenn Faelad (of Brega)
d.695   Finsnechta Fledach (of Brega)
d.703   Loingsech
d.710   Congal Cennmagair
d.722   Fergal (of Ailech)
d.724   Fogartach
d.728   Cinaed (of Brega)
d.743   Aed Allan mac Fergal (of Ailech)
734   Flaithbertach *deposed*
d.763   Domhall Midi (of Meath)
d.778   Niall Frossach (of Ailech)
d.797   Donnchad Midi (of Meath)
d.819   Aed Oirnide (of Ailech)

d.833   Conchobar (of Meath)
d.846   Niall Caille (of Ailech)
d.862   Mael Sechnaill I (of Meath)
d.879   Aed Findliath (of Ailech)
d.916   Flann Sinna (of Meath)
d.919   Niall Glundub (of Ailech)
d.944   Donnchad Donn (of Meath)
d.956   Congalach Cnoba (of Brega)
d.980   Domhall Ua Niall (of Ailech)
980–997   Mael Sechnaill II (of Meath)
997–1014   Brian Boroimhe (Brian Boru) (of Munster)
1014–22   Mael Sechnaill II (of Meath) *(restored)*
1022–72   *No High King*
1072–86   Tairrdelbach Ua Briain (Turlough O'Brien) (of Munster)
1086–1114   Muirchertach Ua Briain (Murtough O'Brien) (of Munster) *Rival king from 1090*
1090–1121   Domhall Ua Lochlainn (Donnell O'Loughlin) (of Ailech) *Rival king*
1118–56   Tairrdelbach Ua Conchobar (Turlough O'Connor) (of Connaught) *Rival king to 1121 and from 1150*
1150–66   Muirchertach mac Lochlainn (Murtough MacLoughlin) (of Ailech) *Rival king to 1156*
1166–86   Ruaidri Ua Conchobar (Rory O'Connor) (of Connaught)

Governor-General
1922–7   Timothy Michael Healy
1927–32   James McNeill
1932–6   Donald Buckley

President
1938–45   Douglas Hyde
1945–59   Sean Thomas O'Kelly (Seán Tomás O Ceallaigh)
1959–73   Éamon de Valera
1973–4   Erskine Hamilton Childers
1974–6   Carroll Daly
1976–90   Patrick J Hillery
1990–   Mary Robinson

Prime Minister
1919–21   Éamon de Valera
1922   Arthur Griffiths
1922–32   William Thomas Cosgrave
1932–48   Éamon de Valera
1948–51   John Aloysius Costello
1951–4   Éamon de Valera
1954–7   John Aloysius Costello
1957–9   Éamon de Valera
1959–66   Sean Lemass
1966–73   John (Jack) Lynch
1973–7   Liam Cosgrave

1977–9   John (Jack) Lynch
1979–82   Charles James Haughey
1982–7   Garrett FitzGerald
1987–92   Charles James Haughey
1992–4   Albert Reynolds
1994–7   John Bruton
1997–   Bertie Ahern

Israel

Kings of Israel and Judah
c.1020–c.1000BC   Saul
c.1000–c.961BC   David
c.961–c.922BC   Solomon

King of Israel
c.922–c.901BC   Jeroboam I
c.901–c.900BC   Nadab
c.900–c.877BC   Baasha
c.877–c.876BC   Elah
c.876BC   Zimri
c.876BC   Tibni
c.876–c.869BC   Omri
c.869–c.850BC   Ahab
c.850–c.849BC   Ahaziah
c.849–c.842BC   Jehoram
c.842–c.815BC   Jehu
c.815–c.801BC   Jehoahaz
c.801–c.786BC   Joash
c.786–c.746BC   Jeroboam II
c.746–c.745BC   Zachariah
c.745BC   Shallum
c.745–c.736BC   Menahem
c.736–c.735BC   Pekahiah
c.735–c.732BC   Pekah
c.732–c.724BC   Hoshea

King of Judah
House of David
c.922–c.915BC   Rehoboam
c.915–c.913BC   Abijah
c.913–c.873BC   Asa
c.873–c.849BC   Jehoshaphat
c.849–c.842BC   Jehoram
c.842BC   Ahaziah
c.842–c.837BC   Athaliah
c.837–c.800BC   Joash
c.800– c.783BC   Amaziah
c.783–c.742BC   Uzziah
c.742–c.735BC   Jotham
c.735–c.715BC   Ahaz
c.715–c.687BC   Hezekiah
c.687–c.642BC   Manasseh
c.642–c.640BC   Amon
c.640–609BC   Josiah
609BC   Jehoahaz
609–597BC   Jehoiakim
597BC   Jehoiachin
597–87BC   Zedekiah

Kingdom of Syria
House of Seleucus
305–281BC   Seleucus I Nicator
281–61BC   Antiochus I Soter
261–46BC   Antiochus II Theos
246–25BC   Seleucus II Callinicus
225–3BC   Seleucus III Soter

223–187BC	Antiochus III 'the Great'
187–75BC	Seleucus IV Philopator
175–63BC	Antiochus IV Epiphanes
163–2BC	Antiochus V Eupator
162–150BC	Demetrius I Soter
150–45BC	Alexander I Balas
145–39BC	Demetrius II Nicator *Joint king and Regent until 142BC*
145–2BC	Antiochus VI Epiphanes *Joint king*
139–29BC	Antiochus VII Sidetes
129–5BC	Demetrius II Nicator *(restored)*
128–3BC	Alexander II Zabinas *Rival king*
125BC	Seleucus V
125–96BC	Antiochus VIII Gryphus *Rival king from 115BC*
115–95BC	Antiochus IX Cyzicenus *Rival king*
96–5BC	Seleucus VI Epiphanes Nicator *Rival king*
95–83BC	Antiochus X Eusebes Philopator *Rival king*
95–88BC	Demetrius III Eukairos Sotor *Rival king*
92BC	Antiochus XI Philadelphus *Rival king*
92–83BC	Philip I Philadelphus *Rival king*
87–4BC	Antiochus XII Dionysus *Rival king*
83–69BC	Tigranes *King of Armenia*
69–4BC	Antiochus XIII Asiaticus
65–4BC	Philip II *Rival king*

Kingdom of Judaea
House of Maccabeus

166–1BC	Jehudah Makkabi (Judas Maccabeus)
161–42BC	Jonathan
142–34BC	Simon
134–04BC	John Hyrcanus I
104–03BC	Aristobulus I
103–76BC	Alexander Jannaeus
76–67BC	Alexandra Salome
67–40BC	Hyrcanus II
67–63BC	Aristobulus II *Rival King*
40–37BC	Antigonus

House of Herod

37–4BC	Herod I 'the Great'
4BC–6AD	Archelaus
4BC–39AD	Herod Antipas *Tetrarch of Galilee*
4BC–34AD	Philip *Tetrarch of Batanea*
37–44	Herod Agrippa I *Tetrarch of Batanea, Galilee from 40 and Judaea from 41*
41–48	Herod II *Tetrarch of Chalcis*
50–100	Herod Agrippa II *Tetrarch of Chalcis, Batanea from 53*

Kingdom of Jerusalem

1099–1100	Godfrey of Bouillon
1100–18	Baldwin I

1118–31	Baldwin II 'of Bourcq'
1131–43	Fulk of Anjou
1143–62	Baldwin III
1162–74	Amalric I
1174–85	Baldwin IV
1185–6	Baldwin V
1186–90	Guy of Lusignan *King of Cyprus from 1192*
1190–2	Conrad of Montferrat
1192–7	Henry I (of Champagne)
1197–1205	Amalric II *King of Cyprus*
1205–10	Maria
1210–25	John of Brienne
1225–43	Frederick (II, *Holy Roman Emperor*)
1243–54	Conrad II (IV, *Holy Roman Emperor*)
1254–84	Conradin of Hohenstauffen
1284–91	*As Cyprus*

State of Israel
President

1948–52	Chaim Weizmann
1952–63	Itzhak Ben-Zvi
1963–73	Zalman Shazar
1973–8	Ephraim Katzair
1978–83	Yitzhak Navon
1983–93	Chaim Herzog
1993–	Ezer Weizmann

Prime Minister

1948–53	David Ben-Gurion
1954–5	Moshe Sharett
1955–63	David Ben-Gurion
1963–9	Levi Eshkol
1969–74	Golda Meir
1974–7	Itzhak Rabin
1977–83	Menachem Begin
1983–4	Yitzhak Shamir
1984–6	Shimon Peres
1986–92	Yitzhak Shamir
1992–5	Itzhak Rabin
1995–6	Shimon Peres
1996–	Binyamin Netanyahu

Italy
Count of Savoy

1034–49	Umberto I
1049–56	Amedeo I
1056–7	Otto
1057–78	Pietro I
1078–80	Amedeo II
1080–1103	Umberto II
1103–49	Amedeo III
1149–89	Umberto III
1189–1233	Tommaso
1233–53	Amedeo IV
1253–63	Bonifacio
1263–8	Pietro II
1268–85	Filippo I
1285–1323	Amedeo V 'the Great'
1323–9	Edoardo
1329–43	Aimone 'the Peaceful'
1343–83	Amedeo VI 'the Green Count'

1383–91	Amedeo VII
1391–1416	Amedeo VIII 'the Red Count'

Duke of Savoy

1416–34	Amedeo VIII 'the Peaceful'
1434–65	Ludovico
1465–72	Amedeo IX
1472–82	Filiberto I
1482–90	Carlo I
1490–6	Carlo II
1496–7	Filippo II
1497–1504	Filiberto I
1504–53	Carlo III
1553–80	Emanuel-Filiberto
1580–1630	Carlo-Emanuele I
1630–7	Vittorio-Amedeo I
1637–8	Francesco-Giacinto
1638–75	Carlo-Emanuele II
1675–1720	Vittorio-Amedeo II *King of Sicily 1713–18*

Duke of Savoy and King of Sardinia

1720–30	Vittorio-Amedeo II
1730–73	Carlo-Emanuele III
1773–96	Vittorio-Amedeo III
1796–1802	Carlo-Emanuele IV
1802–21	Vittorio-Emanuele I
1821–31	Carlo-Felice
1831–49	Carlo-Alberto (Charles Albert)
1849–61	Vittorio-Emanuele (Victor-Emmanuel) II

Monarch – Kingdom of Italy

1861–78	Vittorio-Emanuele (Victor-Emmanuel) II
1878–1900	Umberto I
1900–46	Vittorio-Emanuele (Victor-Emmanuel) III
1946	Umberto II

Italian Republic
President

1946–8	Enrico de Nicola
1948–55	Luigi Einaudi
1955–62	Giovanni Gronchi
1962–4	Antonio Segni
1964–71	Giuseppe Saragat
1971–8	Giovanni Leone
1978–85	Alessandro Pertini
1985–92	Francesco Cossiga
1992–	Oscar Luigi Scalfaro

Prime Minister

1861	Count Camillo Benso di Cavour
1861–2	Bettino, Baron Ricasoli
1862	Urbano Rattazzi
1862–3	Luigi Carlo Farini
1863–4	Marco Minghetti
1864–6	Alfonso Ferrero, Marquis de la Marmora
1866–7	Bettino, Baron Ricasoli
1867	Urbano Rattazzi
1867–9	Luigi Federcio Menabrea
1869–3	Giovanni Lanza
1873–6	Marco Minghetti

1876–8	Agostino Depretis
1878	Benedetto Cairoli
1878–9	Agostino Depretis
1879–81	Benedetto Cairoli
1881–7	Agostino Depretis
1887–91	Francesco Crispi
1891–2	Antonio di Rudinì
1892–3	Giovanni Giolitti
1893–6	Francesco Crispi
1896–8	Antonio di Rudinì
1898–1990	Luigi Pelloux
1900–1	Giuseppe Saracco
1901–3	Giuseppe Zanardelli
1903–5	Giovanni Giolitti
1905–6	Alessandro Fortis
1906	Baron Sydney Sonnino
1906–9	Giovanni Giolitti
1909–10	Baron Sydney Sonnino
1910–11	Luigi Luzzatti
1911–14	Giovanni Giolitti
1914–16	Antonio Salandra
1916–17	Paolo Boselli
1917–19	Vittorio Emmanuele Orlando
1919–20	Francesco Saverio Nitti
1920–1	Giovanni Giolitti
1921–2	Ivanoe Bonomi
1922	Luigi Facta
1922–43	Benito Mussolini
1943–4	Pietro Badoglio
1944–5	Ivanoe Bonomi
1945	Ferrucio Parri
1945–53	Alcide de Gasperi
1953–4	Giuseppe Pella
1954	Amintore Fanfani
1954–5	Mario Scelba
1955–7	Antonio Segni
1957–8	Adone Zoli
1958–9	Amintore Fanfani
1959–60	Antonio Segni
1960	Fernando Tambroni
1960–3	Amintore Fanfani
1963	Giovanni Leone
1963–8	Aldo Moro
1968	Giovanni Leone
1968–70	Mariano Rumor
1970–2	Emilio Colombo
1972–4	Giulio Andreotti
1974–6	Aldo Moro
1976–8	Giulio Andreotti
1979–80	Francisco Cossiga
1980–1	Arnaldo Forlani
1981–2	Giovanni Spadolini
1982–3	Amintore Fanfani
1983–7	Bettino Craxi
1987	Amintore Fanfani
1987–8	Giovanni Goria
1988–9	Ciriaco de Mita
1989–92	Giulio Andreotti
1992–3	Giuliano Amato
1993–4	Carlo Azeglio Campi
1994–5	Silvio Berlusconi
1995–6	Lamberto Dini
1996–	Romano Prodi

Ferrara see **Modena**

Florence see **Tuscany**

Mantua

Captain General of Mantua
House of Gonzaga

1328–60	Luigi I
1360–9	Guido
1369–82	Luigi II
1382–1407	Francesco I
1407–33	Gian-Francesco

Marquis of Mantua
House of Gonzaga

1433–44	Gian-Francesco
1444–78	Luigi III
1478–84	Federigo I
1484–1519	Francesco II
1519–30	Federigo II

Duke of Mantua
House of Gonzaga

1530–40	Federigo II
1540–50	Francesco III
1550–87	Guglielmo
1587–1612	Vincenzo I
1612	Francesco IV
1612–26	Ferdinando
1626–7	Vincenzo II
1627–37	Carlo I
1637–65	Carlo II
1665–1707	Ferdinando-Carlo
1708–1861	*As Milan*

Milan

Count of Milan
House of Visconti

1310–22	Matteo I
1322–8	Galeazzo I
1328–39	Azzo
1339–49	Lucchino
1349–54	Giovanni
1354–5	Matteo II
1354–85	Bernabo *Joint ruler*
1354–78	Galeazzo II *Joint ruler*
1378–96	Gian Galeazzo (Visconti) *Joint ruler until 1385*

Duke of Milan
House of Visconti

1396–1402	Gian Galeazzo (Visconti)
1402–12	Giovanni Maria
1412–47	Filippo Maria

House of Sforza

1450–66	Francesco (Sforza)
1466–76	Galeazzo Maria (Sforza)
1476–81	Gian Galeazzo
1481–9	Ludovico (Sforza) 'the Moor'
1499–1512	*French rule*
1512–15	Massimiliano
1515–21	*French rule*
1521–35	Francesco Maria
1535–1796	*Austrian rule*
1797–1815	*Part of Cisalpine Republic*

1815–59	*Austrian rule*
1859–61	*Part of Kingdom of Sardinia*

Modena

Lord of Ferrara
House of Este

1209–12	Azzo I
1212–15	Aldobrandino I
1215–64	Azzo II
1264–88	Obizzo I

Lord of Ferrara and Modena
House of Este

1288–93	Obizzo I
1293–1308	Azzo III
1308–10	*Disputed succession*
1310–17	*Papal rule*
1317–52	Obizzo II *Joint ruler to 1344*
1317–44	Nicolò I *Joint ruler*
1317–35	Rinaldo I *Joint ruler*
1352–61	Aldobrandino II
1361–88	Nicolò II
1388–93	Alberto
1393–1441	Nicolò III
1441–50	Lionello
1450–2	Borso

Duke of Modena
House of Este

1452–71	Borso

Duke of Ferrara and Modena
House of Este

1471	Borso
1471–1505	Ercole I
1505–34	Alfonso I
1534–59	Ercole II
1559–97	Alfonso II

Duke of Modena
House of Este

1597–1628	Cesare
1628–9	Alfonso III
1629–58	Francesco I
1658–62	Alfonso IV
1662–94	Francesco II
1694–1737	Rinaldo II
1737–80	Francesco III
1780–97	Ercole III
1797–1814	*French rule*

House of Habsburg

1814–46	Francesco IV
1846–59	Francesco V

Naples see Sicily

Parma

Duke of Parma
House of Farnese

1545–7	Pier Luigi
1547–86	Ottavio
1586–92	Alessandro (Farnese)
1592–1622	Ranuccio I
1622–46	Oduardo
1646–94	Ranuccio II

1694–1727	Francesco
1727–31	Antonio

House of Bourbon–Parma

1731–5	*As Spain*
1748–65	Philip
1765–99	Ferdinand
1799–1814	*French rule*
1814–47	Marie-Louise of Habsburg
1847–9	Charles II Louis
1849–54	Charles III Ferdinand
1854–9	Robert

Sicily

Count of Sicily
Norman rulers

1072–1101	Roger I of Hauteville
1101–05	Simon
1105–30	Roger II

King of Naples and Sicily
Norman kings

1130–54	Roger II
1154–66	William I
1166–89	William II
1189–94	Tancred
1194	William III

House of Hohenstauffen

1194–7	Henry
	(VI, *Holy Roman Emperor*)
1197–1250	Frederick
	(II, *Holy Roman Emperor*)
1250–4	Conrad
	(IV, *Holy Roman Emperor*)
1254–8	Conradin
	Holy Roman Emperor
1258–66	Manfred

House of Anjou

1266–82	Charles I of Anjou

King of Naples
House of Anjou

1282–5	Charles I of Anjou
1285–1309	Charles II
1309–43	Robert 'the Wise'
1343–82	Joanna I
1382–6	Charles III
1386–1435	Joanna II

House of Aragón

1435–58	*As Aragón (see* Spain)
1458–94	Ferdinand I
1494–5	Alfonso II
1495–6	Ferdinand II
1496–1501	Frederick IV
1501–16	*As Aragón (see* Spain)

King of Sicily
House of Aragón

1282–5	Peter I *King Pedro II of Aragón*
1285–95	James *King Jaime II of Aragón*
1295–1337	Frederick II
1337–42	Peter II
1342–55	Louis
1355–77	Frederick II
1377–1402	Maria *Joint ruler from 1391*

1391–1409	Martin I
1409–1516	*As Aragón (see* Spain)

King of the Two Sicilies

1516–1700	*As Spain*
1700–13	*Disputed succession*
1713–18	*As Savoy*
1718–34	*Disputed succession*

House of Bourbon–Two Sicilies

1734–59	*As Spain*
1759–1825	Ferdinand I (Joseph Bonaparte *King of Naples 1806–08*; Joachim Murat *King of Naples 1808–15*)
1825–30	Francis I
1830–59	Ferdinand II
1859–60	Francis II

Tuscany

Lord of Florence
House of Medici

1434–64	Cosimo (Medici) 'Pater Patriae'
1464–9	Piero I (Medici) 'the Gouty'
1469–92	Lorenzo I (Medici) 'the Magnificent'
1492–4	Piero II (Medici) 'the Unfortunate'
1494–1512	*Republic*
1512–19	Lorenzo II
1519–23	Clement VII (Giulio de' Medici)
1523–7	Alessandro Medici (Silvio Passerini *Regent*)
1527–30	*Republic*
1530–1	Alessandro Medici (*restored*)

Duke of Florence
House of Medici

1531–7	Alessandro (Medici)
1537–69	Cosimo I (Medici) 'the Great'

Grand Duke of Tuscany
House of Medici

1569–74	Cosimo I (Medici) 'the Great'
1574–87	Francesco
1587–1609	Ferdinand I
1609–21	Cosimo II
1621–70	Ferdinand II
1670–1723	Cosimo III
1723–37	Gian Gastone

House of Habsburg-Lorraine

1737–65	Francis (I, *Holy Roman Emperor*)
1765–90	Leopold (II, *Holy Roman Emperor*)
1790–1801	Ferdinand III
1801–14	*French rule*
1814–24	Ferdinand III
1824–59	Leopold II

Venice

Doge of Venice

697–717	Paolucci Anafesto
717–726	Marcello Tegalliano
726–37	Orso
737–42	*Byzantine rule*
742–55	Diodata Orso
756–64	Domenico Monegario
764–87	Maurizio Galbaio I
787–804	Giovanni Galbaio
804–10	Obelerio Antenoreo
810–27	A Angelo Parteciaco
827–9	Giustiniano Parteciaco
829–36	Giovanni Parteciaco I
836–64	Pietro Tradonico
864–81	Orso Parteciaco
881–7	Giovanni Parteciaco II
887	Pietro Candiano I
888–912	Pietro Tribuno
912–31	Orso Parteciaco
932–9	Pietro Candiano II
939–42	Pietro Parteciaco
942–59	Pietro Candiano III
959–76	Pietro Candiano IV
976–8	Pietro Orsolo I
978–9	Vitale Candiano
979–91	Tribune Menio
991–1008	Pietro Orsolo II
1008–26	Ottone Orsolo
1026–32	Pietro Centranico
1032–42	Domenico Fabiano
1043–70	Domenico Contarini
1070–84	Domenico Silvo
1084–96	Vitale Fahier
1096–1102	Vitale Michiel I
1102–18	Ordelaffe Fahier
1118–29	Domenico Michiel
1130–48	Pietro Polani
1148–56	Domenico Morosini
1156–72	Vitale Michiel II
1172–8	Sebastiano Ziani
1178–92	Orio Malipiero
1192–1205	Enrico Dandolo
1205–29	Pietro Ziani
1229–49	Iacopo Tiepolo
1249–53	Marino Morosini
1253–68	Ranieri Zen
1268–75	Lorenzo Tiepolo
1275–80	Iacopo Contarini
1280–9	Giovanni Dandolo
1289–1311	Pietro Gradenigo
1311–12	Marino Zorzi
1312–28	Giovanni Soranzo
1329–39	Francesco Dandolo
1339–42	Bartolomeo Gradenigo
1343–54	Andrea Dandolo
1354–5	Marin Faliero
1355–6	Giovanni Gradenigo
1356–61	Giovanni Dolfin
1361–5	Lorenzo Celsi
1365–8	Marco Corner
1368–82	Andrea Contarini
1382	Michele Morosini
1382–1400	Antonio Venier

1400–13	Michele Steno
1414–23	Tommaso Mocenigo
1423–57	Francesco Foscari
1457–62	Pasquale Malipiero
1462–71	Cristoforo Moro
1471–3	Nicolò Tron
1473–4	Nicolò Tron
1474–6	Pietro Mocenigo
1476–8	Andrea Vendramun
1478–85	Giovanni Mocenigo
1485–6	Marco Barbarigo
1486–1501	Agostino Barbarigo
1501–21	Leonardo Loredan
1521–3	Antonio Grimani
1523–38	Andrea Gritti
1539–45	Pietro Lando
1545–53	Francesco Donà
1553–4	Marc'Antonio Trevisan
1554–6	Francesco Venier
1556–9	Lorenzo Priuli
1559–67	Girolamo Priuli
1567–70	Pietro Loredan
1570–7	Alvise Mocenigo I
1577–8	Sebastiano Venier
1578–85	Nicolò da Ponte
1585–95	Pasquale Cicogna
1595–1605	Marino Grimani
1606–12	Leonardo Donà
1612–15	Marc'Antonio Memmo
1615–18	Giovanni Bembo
1618	Nicolò Donà
1618–23	Antonio Priuli
1623–4	Francesco Contarini
1625–9	Giovanni Corner I
1630–1	Nicolò Contarini
1631–46	Francesco Erizzo
1646–55	Francesco da Molin
1655–6	Carlo Contarini
1656	Francesco Corner
1656–8	Bertucci Valier
1658–9	Giovanni Pesaro
1659–75	Domenico Contarini
1675–6	Nicolò Sagredo
1676–84	Alvise Contarini
1684–8	M Antonio Giustinian
1688–94	Francesco Morosini
1694–1700	Silvestro Valier
1700–09	Alvise Mocenigo II
1709–22	Giovanni Corner II
1722–32	Alvise Mocenigo III
1732–5	Carlo Ruzzini
1735–41	Alvise Pisani
1741–52	Pietro Grimani
1752–62	Francesco Loredan
1762–3	Marco Foscarini
1763–78	Alvise Mocenigo IV
1779–89	Paolo Renier
1789–97	Ludovico Manin

Jamaica

Chief of State: British monarch, represented by Governor-General

Prime Minister

1962–7	(William) Alexander Bustamante
1967	Donald Burns Sangster
1967–72	Hugh Lawson Shearer
1972–80	Michael Norman Manley
1980–9	Edward Philip George Seaga
1989–92	Michael Norman Manley
1992–	Percival Patterson

Japan

The traditional dates for early reigns are not generally considered to be accurate.

Emperor

		Traditional date
c.40–c.10BC	Jimmu	660–581BC
c.10BC–c.AD20	Suizei	581–49BC
c.20–c.50	Annei	549–10BC
c.50–c.80	Itoku	510–475BC
c.80–c.110	Kosho	475–392BC
c.110–c.140	Koan	392–290BC
c.140–c.170	Korei	290–14BC
c.170–c.200	Kogen	214–157BC
c.200–c.230	Kaika	157–97BC
c.230–c.259	Sujin	97–29BC
c.259–c.291	Suinin	29BC–AD71
c.291–c.323	Keiko	71–131
c.323–c.356	Seimu	131–92
c.356–c.363	Chuai	192–201
c.363–c.380	Jingo *Regent*	201–70
c.380–c.395	Ojin	270–313
c.395–c.428	Nintoku	313–400
c.428–c.433	Richu	400–06
c.433–c.438	Hanzei	406–12
c.438–c.455	Inkyo	412–54
c.455–c.457	Anko	454–7
c.457–c.490	Yuryaku	457–80
c.490–c.495	Seinei	480–5
c.495–c.498	Kenso	485–8
c.498–c.504	Ninken	488–99
c.504–c.510	Muretsu	499–507
c.510–34	Keitai	507–34
534–6	Ankan	
536–40	Senka	
540–72	Kimmei	
572–86	Bidatsu	
586–8	Yomei	
588–93	Sujun	
593–629	Suiko	
629–42	Jomei	
642–5	Kogyoku	
645–55	Kotoku	
655–62	Saimei (Kogyoku *restored*)	
662–72	Tenchi	
672–3	Kobun	
673–86	Temmu	
686–97	Jito	
697–708	Mommu	
708–15	Gemmyo	
715–24	Gensho	
724–49	Shomu	
749–59	Koken	
759–65	Junnin	
765–70	Shotoku (Koken *restored*)	

770–82	Konin
782–806	Kwammu
806–10	Heijo
810–24	Saga
824–34	Junna
834–51	Nimmyo
851–9	Montoku
859–77	Seiwa
877–85	Yozei
885–9	Koko
889–98	Uda
898–931	Daigo
931–47	Shujaku
947–68	Murakami
968–70	Reizei
970–85	Enyu
985–7	Kazan
987–1012	Ichijo
1012–17	Sanjo
1017–37	Go-Ichijo
1037–47	Go-Shujaku
1047–69	Go-Reizei
1069–73	Go-Sanjo
1073–87	Shirakawa
1087–1108	Horikawa
1108–24	Toba
1124–42	Sutoku
1142–56	Konoe
1156–9	Go-Shirakawa
1159–66	Nijo
1166–9	Rokujo
1169–81	Takakura
1181–4	Antoku
1184–99	Go-Toba
1199–1211	Tsuchi-Mikado
1211–21	Juntoku
1221–2	Chukyo
1222–33	Go-Horikawa
1233–43	Shijo
1243–7	Go-Saga
1247–60	Go-Fukakusa
1260–75	Kameyama
1275–88	Go-Uda
1288–99	Fushima
1299–1302	Go-Fushima
1302–08	Go-Nijo
1308–19	Hanazono
1319–31	Go-Daigo
1331–3	Kogen
1333–9	Go-Daigo (*restored*) *South only from 1336*
1336–49	Komyo *North*
1339–68	Go-Murakami *South*
1349–52	Suko *North*
1352–72	Go-Kogen *North*
1368–73	Chokei *South*
1372–84	Go-Enyu *North*
1373–92	Go-Kameyama *South*
1384–1413	Go Komatu *North only until 1392*
1413–29	Shoko
1429–65	Go-Hanazono
1465–1501	Go-Tsuchi-Mikado
1501–27	Go-Kashiwabara
1527–58	Go-Nara

1558–87	Ogimachi
1587–1612	Go-Yozei
1612–30	Go-Mizu-no-o
1630–44	Myosho
1644–55	Go-Komyo
1655–63	Go-Saiin
1663–87	Reigen
1687–1710	Higashiyama
1710–36	Naka-no-Mikado
1736–48	Sakuramachi
1748–63	Momozono
1763–71	Go-Sakuramachi
1771–80	Go-Momozono
1780–1817	Kokaku
1817–47	Ninko
1847–67	Komei
1867–1912	Meiji (Mutsuhito)
1912–26	Taisho (Yoshihito)
1926–89	Showa (Hirohito)
1989–	Heisei (Akihito)

Shogun

Minamoto Shoguns

1192–9	Yoritomo Minamoto
1199–1203	Yori-ie Minamoto
1203–19	Sanemoto Minamoto

Fujiwara Shoguns

1220–44	Yoritsune Fujiwara
1244–51	Yoritsugu Fujiwara

Imperial Shoguns

1251–66	Munetaka
1266–89	Koreyasu
1289–1308	Hisakira
1308–33	Morikune

Ashikaga Shoguns

1338–58	Takuji Ashikaga
1358–67	Yoshiaki Ashikaga
1367–95	Yoshimitsu Ashikaga
1395–1423	Yoshimochi Ashikaga
1423–8	Yoshikazu Ashikaga
1428–41	Yoshinori Ashikaga
1441–3	Yoshikatsu Ashikaga
1443–74	Yoshimasa Ashikaga
1474–90	Yoshihisa Ashikaga
1490–3	Yoshitane Ashikaga
1493–1508	Yoshizume Ashikaga
1508–21	Yoshitsane Ashikaga (Yoshitane *restored*)
1521–45	Yoshiharu Ashikaga
1545–65	Yoshiteru Ashikaga
1565–8	Yoshihide Ashikaga
1568–73	Yoshiaki Ashikaga

Tokugawa Shoguns

1603–05	Ieyasu Tokugawa
1605–23	Hidetada Tokugawa
1623–51	Iemitsu Tokugawa
1651–80	Ietsuna Tokugawa
1680–1709	Tsunayoshi Tokugawa
1709–13	Ienobu Tokugawa
1713–16	Ietsugu Tokugawa
1716–45	Yoshimune Tokugawa
1745–61	Ieshige Tokugawa
1761–87	Ieharu Tokugawa
1787–1838	Ienari Tokugawa

1838–53	Ieyoshi Tokugawa
1853–8	Iesada Tokugawa
1858–66	Iemochi Tokugawa
1866–7	Yoshinobu Tokugawa

Prime Minister

1885–8	Hirobumi Ito
1888–9	Kiyotaka Kuroda
1889–91	Aritomo Yamagata
1891–2	Masayoshi Matsukata
1892–6	Hirobumi Ito
1896–8	Masayoshi Matsukata
1898	Hirobumi Ito
1898	Shigenbu Okuma
1898–1900	Aritomo Yamagata
1900–1	Hirobumi Ito
1901–6	Taro Katsura
1906–8	Kimmochi Saionji
1908–11	Taro Katsura
1911–12	Kimmochi Saionji
1912–13	Taro Katsura
1913–14	Gonnohyoe Yamamoto
1914–16	Shigenobu Okuma
1916–18	Masatake Terauchi
1918–21	Takashi Hara
1921–2	Korekiyo Takahashi
1922–3	Tomosaburo Kato
1923–4	Gonnohyoe Yamamoto
1924	Keigo Kiyoura
1924–6	Takaaki Kato
1926–7	Reijiro Wakatsuki
1927–9	Giichi Tanaka
1929–31	Osachi Hamaguchi
1931	Reijiro Wakatsuki
1931–2	Tsuyoshi Inukai
1932–4	Makoto Saito
1934–6	Keisuke Okada
1936–7	Koki Hirota
1937	Senjuro Hayashi
1937–9	Fumimaro Konoe
1939	Kiichiro Hiranuma
1939–40	Nobuyuki Abe
1940	Mitsumasa Yonai
1940–1	Fumimaro Konoe
1941–4	Hideki Tojo
1944–5	Kuniaki Koiso
1945	Kantaro Suzuki
1945	Naruhiko Higashikuni
1945–6	Kijuro Shidehara
1946–7	Shigeru Yoshida
1947–8	Tetsu Katayama
1948	Hitoshi Ashida
1948–54	Shigeru Yoshida
1954–6	Ichiro Hatoyama
1956–7	Tanzan Ishibashi
1957–60	Nobusuke Kishi
1960–4	Hayato Ikeda
1964–72	Eisaku Sato
1972–4	Kakuei Tanaka
1974–6	Takeo Miki
1976–8	Takeo Fukuda
1978–80	Masayoshi Ohira
1980–2	Zenko Suzuki
1982–7	Yasuhiro Nakasone
1987–9	Noboru Takeshita
1989	Sasuke Uno

1989–91	Toshiki Kaifu
1991–3	Kiichi Miyazama
1993–4	Morihiro Hosokawa
1994	Tsutomu Hata
1994–5	Tomiichi Murayama
1995–	Ryutaro Hashimoto

Jordan

Monarch – Kingdom of Transjordan

1921–49	Abdullah ibn Hussein

Monarch – Kingdom of Jordan

1949–51	Abdullah ibn Hussein
1951–2	Talal I
1952–	Hussein ibn Talal

Prime Minister

1921	Rashid Tali
1921	Muzhir ar-Raslan
1921–3	Rida ar-Riqabi
1923	Muzhir ar-Raslan
1923–4	Hassan Khalid
1924–33	Rida ar-Riqabi
1933–8	Ibrahim Hashim
1939–45	Taufiq Abul-Huda
1945–8	Ibrahim Hashim
1948–50	Taufiq Abul-Huda
1950	Said al-Mufti
1950–1	Samir ar-Rifai
1951–3	Taufiq Abul-Huda
1953–4	Fauzi al-Mulqi
1954–5	Taufiq Abul-Huda
1955	Said al-Mufti
1955	Hazza al-Majali
1955–6	Ibrahim Hashim
1956	Samir ar-Rifai
1956	Said al-Mufti
1956	Ibrahim Hashim
1956–7	Suleiman Nabulsi
1957	Hussein Fakhri al-Khalidi
1957–8	Ibrahim Hashim
1958	Nuri Pasha al-Said
1958–9	Samir ar-Rifai
1959–60	Hazza al-Majali
1960–2	Bahjat Talhuni
1962–3	Wasfi at-Tall
1963	Samir ar-Rifai
1963–4	Sharif Hussein bin Nasir
1964	Bahjat Talhuni
1965–7	Wasfi at-Tall
1967	Sharif Hussein bin Nasir
1967	Saad Jumaa
1967–9	Bahjat Talhuni
1969	Abdul Munem Rifai
1969–70	Bahjat Talhuni
1970	Abdul Munem Rifai
1970	*Military junta* (Mohammed Daud)
1970	Mohamed Ahmed Tuqan
1970–1	Wasfi at-Tall
1971–3	Ahmad Lozi
1973–6	Zaid Rifai
1976–9	Mudar Badran
1979–80	Sherif Abdul Hamid Sharaf
1980	Kassem Rimawi
1980–4	Mudar Badran

1984–5	Ahmad Ubayat
1985–9	Zaid ar-Rifai
1989	Sharif Zaid bin Shaker
1989–91	Mudar Badran
1991	Taher al-Masri
1991–3	Sharif Zaid bin Shaker
1993–6	Abdul Salam al-Majali
1996–7	Abdul Karim Kabariti
1997–	Abdul Salam al-Majali

Kazakhstan

Khans of the Golden Horde

1227–55	Batu
1255–6	Sartak
1256–7	Ulaghchi
1257–67	Berke
1267–80	Mengu Timur
1280–7	Tuda Mengu
1287–90	Tola Buqa
1290–1312	Toqtu
1312–41	Uzbeg
1341–2	Tinibeg
1342–57	Janibeg
1357–9	Berdibeg
1359–60	Qulpa
1360–1	Nawruz Beg
1361–2	Khidr
1362	Timur Khoja
1362	Keldibeg
1362–4	Murid
1364–7	Aziz Khan
1367–70	Abdullah
1370–8	Muhammad Bulak
1378–95	Tokhtamish
1395–1400	Timur Qutlugh
1400–07	Shadibeg
1407–10	Pulad Timur
1410–12	Timur Khan
1412	Jalah-ud-Din
1412–14	Karim Berdi
1414–17	Kebek
1417–19	Jabbar Berdi
1419–37	Ulugh Muhammad (Of Kazan)
1437–65	Sayyid Ahmad I
1465–81	Ahmad Khan
1481–1502	Shaikh Ahmad *Joint ruler*
1481–1502	Sayyid Ahmad II *Joint ruler*
1481–99	Murtada *Joint ruler*

Republic of Kazakhstan
President

| 1991– | Nursultan A Nazarbayev |

Prime Minister

1991–4	Sergei Tereshchenko
1994–7	Kazhageldin Akexhan Magzhan Ulu
1997–	Nurlan Balgimbayev

Kenya

President

| 1963–78 | Jomo Kenyatta |
| 1978– | Daniel arap Moi |

Kiribati

President

1979–91	Ieremia T Tabai
1991–4	Teatao Teannaki
1994–	Teburovo Tito

Korea

Monarch – Kingdom of Korea
Wang Dynasty

918–44	T'ae-jo
944–5	Hye-jong
945–9	Chong-jong
949–75	Kwang-jong
975–81	Kyong-jong
981–97	Song-jong
997–1009	Mok-chong
1009–31	Hyon-jong
1031–4	Tok-chong
1034–46	Chong-jong
1046–83	Mun-jong
1083	Sun-jong
1083–94	Son-jong
1094–5	Hon-jong
1095–1105	Suk-chong
1105–22	Ye-jong
1122–46	In-jong
1146–70	Ui-jong
1170–97	Myong-jong
1197–1204	Sin-jong
1204–11	Hui-jong
1211–13	Kang-jong
1213–59	Ko-jong
1259–74	Won-jong
1274–1308	Ch'ung-yol
1308–13	Ch'ung-son
1313–30	Ch'ung-suk
1330–2	Ch'ung-hye
1332–9	Ch'ung-suk (restored)
1339–44	Ch'ung-hye (restored)
1344–9	Ch'ung-mok
1349–51	Ch'ung-jong
1351–74	Kong-min
1374–88	Wi-ju
1388–9	Ch'ang
1389–92	Kong-yang

Yi Dynasty

1392–8	T'ae-jo
1398–1400	Chong-jong
1400–18	T'ae-jong
1418–50	Se-jong
1450–2	Mun-jong
1452–5	Tan-jong
1455–68	Se-jo
1468–9	Ye-jong
1469–94	Song-jong
1494–1506	Yon-san
1506–44	Chung-jong
1544–5	In-jong
1545–67	Myong-jong
1567–1608	Son-jo
1608–23	Kwang-hae
1623–49	In-jo
1649–59	Hyo-jong
1659–74	Hyon-jong

1674–1720	Suk-chong
1720–4	Kyong-jong
1724–76	Yong-jo
1776–1800	Chong-jo
1800–34	Sun-jo
1834–49	Hon-jong
1849–64	Ch'ol-chong
1864–1907	Ko-jong
1907–10	Sun-jong
1910–48	*Japanese rule*

Democratic People's Republic of Korea (North Korea)
President

1948–57	Kim Doo-bong
1957–72	Choi Yong-kun
1972–94	Kim Il-sung
1994–	Kim Jong-il

Prime Minister

1948–76	Kim Il-sung
1976–7	Park Sung-chul
1977–84	Li Jong-ok
1984–6	Kang Song-san
1986–8	Yi Kun-mo
1988–92	Yon Hyong-muk
1992–	Kang Song-san

Republic of Korea (South Korea)
President

1948–60	Syngman Rhee
1960	Ho Chong *Acting*
1960	Kwak Sang-hun *Acting*
1960	Ho Chong *Acting*
1960–3	Yun Po-sun
1963–79	Park Chung-hee
1979–80	Choi Kyu-hah
1980	Park Choong-hoon *Acting*
1980–8	Chun Doo-hwan
1988–93	Roh Tae-woo
1993–	Kim Young-sam

Prime Minister

1948–50	Lee Pom-sok
1950	Shin Song-mo *Acting*
1950–1	John M Chang
1951–2	Ho Chong *Acting*
1952	Lee Yun-yong *Acting*
1952	Chang Taek-sang
1952–4	Paik Too-chin
1954–6	Pyon Yong-tae
1956–60	Syngman Rhee
1960	Ho Chong
1960–1	John M Chang
1961	Chang To-yong
1961–2	Song Yo-chan
1962–3	Kim Hyun-chul
1963–4	Choe Tu-son
1964–70	Chung Il-kwon
1970–1	Paik Too-chin
1971–5	Kim Jong-pil
1975–9	Choi Kyu-hah
1979–80	Shin Hyun-hwak
1980	Park Choong-hoon *Acting*
1980–2	Nam Duck-woo
1982	Yoo Chang-soon
1982–3	Kim Sang-hyup

1983–5	Chin Lee-chong
1985–8	Lho Shin-yong
1988	Lee Hyun-jae
1988–90	Kang Young-hoon
1990–1	Ro Jai-bong
1991–2	Chung Won-shik
1992–3	Hyun Soong-jang
1993	Hwang In-sung
1993–4	Lee Hoi-chang
1994	Lee Yung-duk
1994–5	Lee Hong-koo
1995–7	Lee Soo-sung
1997–	Koh Kun

Kuwait

Emir
Al-Sabah Dynasty

1756–62	Sabah I
1762–1812	Abdullah I
1812–59	Jabir I
1859–66	Sabah II
1866–92	Abdullah II
1892–6	Muhammad
1896–1915	Mubarak
1915–17	Jabir II
1917–21	Salim al-Mubarak
1921–50	Ahmad al-Jabir
1950–65	Abdullah III al-Salim
1965–77	Sabah III al-Salim
1977–	Jabir III al-Ahmad al-Jabir

Prime Minister

1962–3	Abdallah al-Salem
1963–5	Sabah al-Salem
1965–78	Jabir al-Ahmed al-Jabir
1978–	Saad al-Abdallah al-Salem as-Sabah

Kyrgyzstan

President

1991–	Askaar Akayev

Prime Minister

1991	Nasirdin Isanov
1991–3	*As President*
1993	Tursunbek Chyngyshev
1993–	Apas Jumagulov

Laos

Monarch – Lan Chang

1637–94	Souligna Vongsa
1694–1700	Tian T'ala
1700	Nan T'arat
1700–07	Sai Ong Hue

Monarch – Luang Prabang

1707–26	King Kitsarat
1726–7	Khamone Noi
1727–76	Int'a Som
1776–81	Sotika Koumane
1781–7	Tiao Vong
1787–91	*No king*
1791–1817	Anourout
1817–36	Mant'a T'ourat
1836–51	Souka Seum

1851–72	Tiantha
1872–87	Oun Kham
1887–94	*Siamese rule*
1894–1904	Zakarine
1904–47	Sisavang Vong

Monarch – Kingdom of Laos

1947–59	Sisavang Vong
1959–75	Sri Savang Vatthana

Lao People's Republic
President

1975–87	Prince Souphanouvong
1987–91	Phoumi Vongvichit
1991–2	Kaysone Phomvihane
1992–	Nouhak Phoumsakan

Prime Minister

1951–4	Souvanna Phouma
1954–5	Katay Don Sasorith
1956–8	Souvanna Phouma
1958–9	Phoui Sahanikone
1959–60	Sunthone Patthamavong
1960	Kou Abhay
1960	Somsanith
1960	Souvanna Phouma
1960	Sunthone Patthamavong
1960	Quinim Pholsena
1960–2	Boun Oum Na Champassac
1962–75	Souvanna Phouma

Lao People's Democratic Republic

1975–91	Kaysone Phomvihane
1991–	Khamtay Siphandon

Latvia
President

1918–27	Jānis Čakste
1927–30	Gustavs Zemgals
1930–6	Alberts Kviesis
1934–40	Kārlis Ulmanis
1940–91	*Russian rule*
1991–3	Anatolijs Gorbunovs
1993–	Guntis Ulmanis

Prime Minister

1918–21	Kārlis Ulmanis
1921–3	Zigfrīds Meierovics
1923	Jānis Pauluks
1923–4	Zigfrīds Meierovics
1924	Voldemārs Zāmuēls
1924–5	Hugo Celmiņš
1925–6	Kārlis Ulmanis
1926	Artūrs Alberings
1926–8	Marģers Skujenieks
1928	Pēteris Juraševskis
1928–31	Hugo Celmińš
1931	Kārlis Ulmanis
1931–3	Marģers Skujenieks
1933–4	Ādolfs Bļodnieks
1934–40	Kārlis Ulmanis
1940–91	*Russian rule*
1991–3	Ivars Godmanis
1993–4	Valdis Birkavs
1994–5	Maris Gailis
1995–7	Andris Skele
1997–	Guntars Krasts

Lebanon

Emir
Ma'nid Emirs

1516–44	Fakhr-ud-Din I
1544–85	Qurqumaz
1590–1635	Fakhr-ud-Din II
1635–57	Mulhim
1657–97	Ahmad

Shihabid Emirs

1697–1707	Bashir I
1707–32	Haidar
1732–54	Mulhim
1754–70	Mansur
1770–88	Yusuf
1788–1840	Bashir II
1840–2	Bashir III
1842–1918	*Turkish rule*
1918–20	*Rule under negotiation*
1920–43	*French rule*

President

1943–52	Bishara al-Khoury
1952–8	Camille Shamoun
1958–64	Fouad Shehab
1964–70	Charle Hilo
1970–6	Suleiman Frenjieh
1976–82	Elias Sarkis
1982	Bachir Gemayel
	President Elect
1982–8	Amin Gemayel
1988–9	*No President*
1989	Rene Muawad
1989–	Elias Hrawi

Prime Minister

1943	Riad Solh
1943–4	Henry Pharaon
1944–5	Riad Solh
1945	Abdul Hamid Karame
1945–6	Sami Solh
1946	Saadi Munla
1946–51	Riad Solh
1951	Hussein Oweini
1951–2	Abdullah Yafi
1952	Sami Solh
1952	Nazem Accari
1952	Saeb Salam
1952	Fouad Chehab
1952–3	Khaled Chehab
1953	Saeb Salam
1953–5	Abdullah Yafi
1955	Sami Solh
1955–6	Rashid Karami
1956	Abdullah Yafi
1956–8	Sami Solh
1958–60	Rashid Karami
1960	Ahmad Daouq
1960–1	Saeb Salam
1961–4	Rashid Karami
1964–5	Hussein Oweini
1965–6	Rashid Karami
1966	Abdullah Yafi
1966–8	Rashid Karami
1968–9	Abdullah Yafi
1969–70	Rashid Karami

1970–3	Saeb Salam
1973	Amin al-Hafez
1973–4	Takieddine Solh
1974–5	Rashid Solh
1975	Noureddin Rifai
1975–6	Rashid Karami
1976–80	Selim al-Hoss
1980	Takieddine Solh
1980–4	Chafiq al-Wazan
1984–8	Rashid Karami
1988–90	Michel Aoun/Selim al-Hoss
1990	Selim al-Hoss
1990–2	Umar Karami
1992	Rashid al-Solh
1992–	Rafiq al-Hariri

Lesotho

Monarch
Basutoland

1823–70	Moshoeshoe I
1870–91	Letsie I
1891–1905	Lerotholi
1905–13	Letsie II
1913–39	Griffith
1939–40	Seeiso
1940–60	Mansebo *Regent*
1960–5	Moshoeshoe II

Lesotho

1965–90	Moshoeshoe II
1990–4	Letsie III (*abdicated*)
1994–6	Moshoeshoe II
1996–	Letsie III

Prime Minister
1966–86	Leabua Jonathan

Chairman of Military Council
1986–91	Justin Metsing Lekhanya
1991–3	Elias Tutsoane Ramaema

Prime Minister
1993–	Ntsu Mokhehle

Liberia

President
1848–56	Joseph Jenkins Roberts
1856–64	Stephen Allen Benson
1864–8	Daniel Bashiel Warner
1868–70	James Spriggs Payne
1870–1	Edward James Roye
1871–2	James Skirving Smith
1872–6	Joseph Jenkins Roberts
1876–8	James Spriggs Payne
1878–83	Anthony William Gardner
1883–4	Alfred Francis Russell
1884–92	Hilary Richard Wright Johnson
1892–6	Joseph James Cheeseman
1896–1900	William David Coleman
1900–04	Garretson Wilmot Gibson
1904–12	Arthur Barclay
1912–20	Daniel Edward Howard
1920–30	Charles Dunbar Burgess King
1930–43	Edwin J Barclay

1943–71	William V S Tubman
1971–80	William Richard Tolbert

People's Redemption Council
Chairman

1980–6	Samuel Kanyon Doe

President
1986–90	Samuel Kanyon Doe
1990–4	Amos Sawyer *Acting*

Council of State
Chairman

1994–5	David Kpormakor
1995–6	Wilton Sankawulo (*Transitional*)
1996–7	Ruth Perry

President
1997–	Charles Taylor

Libya

Tripoli – Karamanli ruler
1711–45	Ahmad I
1745–54	Muhammad
1754–93	Ali I
1793–5	Ali Burghul
1795	Ali I (*restored*)
1795	Ahmad II
1795–1832	Yusuf
1832–5	Ali II
1835–1911	*Turkish rule*
1911–42	*Italian rule*

Libya – Sanusi leader
1837–59	Said Mohammed al-Senussi
1859–1902	Said al-Mahdi
1902–18	Said Ahmad ash-Sharif
1918–51	Said Mohammed Idris al-Mahdi al-Senussi

Monarch – Kingdom of Libya
1951–69	Said Mohammed Idris al-Mahdi al-Senussi

Great Socialist People's Libyan Jamahiriya
Revolutionary Command Council – Chairman

1969–77	Muammar Gaddafi (al-Gadhafi)

General Secretariat – Secretary General

1977–9	Muammar Gaddafi (al-Gadhafi)
1979–84	Abdul Ati al-Ubaidi
1984–6	Mohammed az-Zaruq Rajab
1986–90	Omar al-Muntasir
1990–	Abu Zaid Omar Dourda

Leader of the Revolution
1969–	Muammar Gaddafi (al-Gadhafi)

Liechtenstein

Prince
1719–21	Anton-Florian
1721–32	Josef

1732–48	Johann-Karl
1748–72	Josef-Wenceslas-Lorenz
1772–81	Franz-Josef I
1781–1805	Alois I
1805–07	Johann I
1807–13	Karl
1813–36	Johann I (*restored*)
1836–58	Alois II
1858–1929	Johann II
1929–38	Franz von Paula
1938–89	Franz-Josef II
1989–	Hans Adam II

Prime Minister
1928–45	Franz Josef Hoop
1945–62	Alexander Friek
1962–70	Gérard Batliner
1970–4	Alfred J Hilbe
1974–8	Walter Kieber
1978–93	Hans Brunhart
1993	Markus Büchel
1993–	Mario Frick

Lithuania

Grand Duke
c.1235–63	Mindaugas
1263–4	Treniota
1264–7	Vaishvilkis
1267–70	Shvarnas
1270–83	Traidenis
1283–93	Pukuveras
1293–1316	Vitenis
1316–41	Gediminas
1341–5	Jaunutis
1345–77	Algirdas
1345–82	Kestutis
1377–92	Jogaila (Jagiello) *King Wladislaw V of Poland*
1392–1430	Vytautias
1430–5	Shvitrigaila
1432–40	Sigismund
1440–92	Casimir (*IV of Poland*)
1492–1506	Alexander *King of Poland from 1501*
1506–69	*As Poland*
1569–1918	*Part of Poland*

President
1917–20	Anatas Smetona *President of the Tarybato to 1919*
1920–6	Aleksandras Stulginskis
1926	Kazys Grinius
1926–40	Anatas Smetona
1940–91	*Russian rule*
1991–3	Vytautas Landsbergis
1993–8	Algirdas Brazauskas
1998–	Valdas Adamkus

Prime Minister
1918	Augustinas Voldemaras
1918–19	Mykolas Slezevicius
1919	Pranas Dovydailus
1919	Mykolas Slezevicius
1919–20	Ernestas Galvanauskas
1920–2	Kazys Grinius
1922–4	Ernestas Galvanauskas

1924–5	Antanas Tumenas
1925	Vytautas Petrulis
1925–6	Leonas Bistras
1926	Mykolas Slezevicius
1926–9	Augustinas Voldemaras
1929–38	Juozas Tubelis
1938–9	Vladas Mironas
1939	Joans Cernius
1939–40	Antanas Merkys
1940–91	*Russian rule*
1991–2	Gediminas Vagnorius
1992	Aleksandras Abisala
1992–3	Bronislovas Lubys
1993–6	Adolfas Slezevicius
1996	Laurynas Stankevicius
1996–	Gediminas Vagnorius

Luxembourg

Duke of Nassau
House of Nassau-Weilberg
| 1816–39 | William |
| 1839–66 | Adolf *No dukedom 1866–90* |

Grand Duke of Luxembourg
House of Nassau
1890–1905	Adolf
1905–12	William IV
1912–19	Marie-Adelaide
1919–64	Charlotte *in exile 1940–4*
1964–	Jean

Prime Minister
1848	J Th I de la Fontaine
1848–53	Jean-Jacques Madelaine Willmar
1853–60	Mathias Simons
1860–7	Victor, Baron de Tornaco
1867–74	Emmanuel Servais
1874–85	Félix, Baron de Blochausen
1885–8	Edouard Thilges
1888–1915	Paul Eyschen
1915	Mathias Mongenast
1915–16	Hubert Loutsch
1916–17	Victor Thorn
1917–18	Léon Kauffmann
1918–25	Emil Reuter
1925–6	Pierre Prum
1926–37	Joseph Bech
1937–53	Pierre Dupong *in exile 1940–4*
1953–8	Joseph Bech
1958–9	Pierre Frieden
1959–74	Pierre Werner
1974–9	Gaston Thorn
1979–84	Pierre Werner
1984–95	Jacques Santer
1995–	Jean-Claude Juncker

Macedonia, Former Yugoslav Republic of

President
| 1991–5 | Kiro Gligorov |
| 1995– | Stojan Andov *Acting* |

Prime Minister
| 1991–2 | Branko Crvenkovski |

| 1992–6 | Petar Gosev |
| 1996– | Branko Crvenkovski |

Madagascar

Monarch
1819–28	Radama I
1828–61	Ranavalona I
1861–3	Radama II
1863–8	Rasoaherina
1868–83	Ranavalona II
1883–96	Ranavalona III
1896–1960	*French rule*

Malagassy Republic
President
1960–72	Philibert Tsiranana
1972–5	Gabriel Ramanantsoa
1975	Richard Ratsimandrava
1975	Gilles Andriamahazo
1975–93	Didier Ratsiraka
1993–6	Albert Zafy
1996	Norbert Ratsirahonana *Interim*
1997–	Didier Ratsiraka

Prime Minister
1960–75	*As President*
1975–6	Joël Rakotomala
1976–7	Justin Rakotoriaina
1977–88	Désiré Rakotoarijaona
1988–91	Victor Ramahatra
1991–3	Guy Willy Razanamasy
1993–5	Francisque Ravony
1995–6	Emmanuel Rakotovahiny
1996–7	Norbert Ratsirahonana
1997–	Pascal Rakotomavo

Malawi

President
| 1966–94 | Hastings Kamuzu Banda |
| 1994– | Bakili Muluzi |

Malaysia

Chief of State (Yang di-Pertuan Agong)
Malaya
| 1957–63 | Abdul Rahman *Negri Sembilan* |
Malaysia
1963–5	Sayyid Harun Putra Jamal-ul-Lail *Perlis*
1965–70	Ismail Nasir-ud-Din Shah *Trengganu*
1970–5	Abdul-Halim Muazzam Shah *Kedah*
1975–9	Yahya Petra *Kelantan*
1979–84	Ahmad Shah al-Mustain *Pahang*
1984–9	Mahmud Iskandar Shah *Johore*
1989–94	Azlan Muhibbuddin Shah *Perak*
1994–	Ja'afar ibn Abdul Rahman *Negri Sembilan*

Prime Minister
1957–70	Abdul Rahman Putra al-Haj
1970–6	Abdul Razak bin Hussein
1976–9	Haji Hussein bin Onn
1979–	Mahathir bin Mohamad

Malay States

Johore *see* Malacca

Sultan – Kedah
c.1160–79	Muzaffar Shah I
1179–1201	Muazzam Shah
1201–36	Muhammad Shah
1236–80	Maazul Shah
1280–1320	Mahmud Shah I
1320–73	Ibrahim Shah
1373–1422	Sulayman Shah I
1422–72	Ata-illah Muhammad Shah I
1472–1506	Muhammad Jiwa Zain-ul-Abidin
1506–46	Mahmud Shah II
1546–1602	Muzaffar Shah II
1602–25	Sulayman Shah II
1625–51	Rijal-ud-Din Shah
1651–61	Muhyi-ud-Din Shah
1661–87	Zia-ud-Din Mukarram Shah
1687–98	Ata-illah Muhammad Shah II
1698–1706	Abdullah Muazzam Shah
1706–60	Muhammad Jiwa Zail-ul-Abidin Muazzam Shah
1760–98	Abdullah Mukarram Shah
1798–1803	Zia-ud-Din Muazzam Shah
1803–21	Ahmad Taj-ud-Din Halim Shah
1821–43	*No Sultan*
1843	Ahmad Taj-ud-Din Halim Shah (*restored*)
1843–54	Zain-ul-Rashid Muazzam Shah I
1854–79	Ahmad Taj-ud-Din Mukarram Shah
1879–81	Zain-ul-Rashid Muazzam Shah II
1881–1943	Abdul-Hamid Halim Shah
1943–58	Badlishah
1958–	Abdul-Halim Muazzam Shah

Sultan – Kelantan
c.1790–	
c.1800	Long Yunus
c.1800–38	Muhammad Shah I
1838–86	Muhammad Shah II
1886–9	Ahmad Shah
1889–91	Muhammad Shah III
1891–9	Mansur Shah
1899–1919	Muhammad Shah IV
1919–46	Ismail Shah
1946–60	Ibrahim Shah
1960–79	Yahya Petra
1979–	Ismail Petra

Malacca/Johore

Sultan of Malacca
c.1400–24	Megat Iskandar Shah
1424–44	Muhammad Shah
1444–6	Abu-Shahid Ibrahim Shah
1446–58	Muzaffar Shah
1458–77	Mansur Shah
1477–88	Ala-ud-Din Riayat Shah
1488–1511	Mahmud Shah

Sultan of Johore
1511–29	Mahmud Shah I (of Malacca)
1529–64	Ala-ud-Din Riayat Shah I
1564–80	Muzaffar Shah
1580	Abdul-Jalil Shah I
1580–97	Abdul-Jalil Riayat Shah I
1597–1613	Ala-ud-Din Riayat Shah I
1613–23	Abdullah Maayat Shah
1623–77	Abdul-Jalil Shah II
1677–85	Ibrahim Shah
1685–99	Mahmud Shah II
1699–1717	Abdul-Jalil Riayat Shah II
1717–22	Abdul-Jalil Rahmat Shah
1722–60	Sulayman Badr-ul-Alam Shah
1760–1	Abdul-Jalil Muazzam Shah
1761	Ahmad Riayat Shah
1761–1812	Mahmud Riayat Shah
1812–19 '	Abdul-Rahman Muazzam Shah
1819–25	Abdul-Rahman
1825–62	Ibrahim
1862–95	Abu-Bakr
1895–1959	Ibrahim Shah
1959–81	Isma il Shah
1981–	Mahmood Iskandar Shah

Yang Di-Pertuan Besar – Negri Sembilan
1773–95	Raja Melawar
1795–1808	Raja Hitam
1808–24	Raja Lenggang
1824–6	Raja Kerjan
1826–30	Raja Laboh
1830–61	Raja Radin
1861–9	Raja Ulin
1872–88	Tengku Antah
1888–1933	Muhammad
1933–60	Abdul-Rahman
1960–7	Munawir
1967–	Jafar

Sultan – Pahang
1884–1914	Ahmad Muazzam Shah
1914–17	Mahmud Shah II
1917–32	Abdullah Muktasim Billah Shah
1932–74	Abu-Bakr Riyat-ud-Din Muazzam Shah
1974–	Ahmad Shah III al-Mustain

Sultan – Perak
1529–49	Muzaffar Shah I
1549–77	Mansur Shah I
?1577–?	Ahmad Taj-ud-Din Shah
?	Taj-ul-Arifin Shah

?–1603	Ala-ud-Din Shah
1603–19	Muqadam Shah
1619	Mansur Shah II
1619–30	Mahmud Shah I
1630–5	Salah-ud-Din Shah
1635–54	Muzaffar Shah II
1654–c.1720	Muhammad Iskandar Shah
c.1720–c.1728	Ala-ud-Din Riayat Shah
c.1728–c.1754	Muzaffar Shah III
c.1728–c.1750	Muhammad Shah
c.1754–65	Iskandar Dhu'l-Qarnain Shah
1765–c.1773	Mahmud Shah II
c.1773–?	Ala-ud-Din Mansur Iskandar Shah
?–1806	Ahmadin Shah
1806–25	Abdul-Malik Mansur Shah
1825–31	Abdullah Muazzam Shah
1831–51	Shihab-ud-Din Riayat Shah
1851–7	Abdullah Muazzam Shah I
1857–65	Ja far Muazzam Shah
1865–71	Ali al-Kamil Riayat Shah
1871–4	Isma il Muabidin Shah
1874–7	Abdullah Muazzam Shah II
1877–87	Yusuf Sharif-ud-Din Mufzal Shah
1887–1916	Idris Murshid-ul-Azam Shah
1916–18	Abdul-Jalil Shah
1918–38	Iskandar Shah
1938–48	Abdul-Aziz Shah
1948–63	Yusuf Izz-ud-Din Shah
1963–85	Idris al-Mutawakkil Shah
1985–	Azlan Muhibbuddin Shah

Raja – Perlis
1843–73	Sayyid Husain Jamal-ul-Lail
1873–97	Sayyid Ahmad Jamal-ul-Lail
1897–1905	Sayyid Safi Jamal-ul-Lail
1905–43	Sayyid Alwi Jamal-ul-Lail
1945–	Sayyid Harun Putra Jamal-ul-Lail

Sultan – Selangor
1756–78	Salah-ud-Din Shah
1778–1826	Ibrahim Shah
1826–57	Muhammad Shah
1859–98	Abdul-Samad Shah
1898–1938	Ala-ud-Din Sulayman Shah
1938–42	Hisam-ud-Din Alam Shah
1942–5	Musa Ghiyath-ud-Din Riayat Shah
1945–60	Hisam-ud-Din Alam Shah (restored)
1960–	Salah-ud-Din Abdul-Aziz Shah

Sultan – Trengganu
1725–33	Zain-ul-Abidin Shah I
1733–93	Mansur Shah I
1793–1808	Zain-ul-Abidin Shah II

1808–27	Ahmad Shah
1827–31	Abdul-Rahman Shah
1831	Daud Shah
1831–6	Mansur Shah II
1836–9	Muhammad Shah I
1839–76	Umar Shah
1876–81	Ahmad Muazzam Shah
1881–1918	Zain-ul-Abidin Muazzam Shah
1918–20	Muhammad Shah II
1920–45	Sulayman Badr-ul-Alam Shah
1945–79	Isma il Nasir-ud-Din Shah
1979–	Mahmud al-Muktafi Billah Shah

Sarawak

Rajah
1841–68	James Brooke
1868–1917	Charles Brooke
1917–46	Charles Vyner Brooke
1946–57	British rule

Maldives

Monarch (Sultan)
1573–84	Muhammad Tukrufan al-Alam
1584–1609	Ibrahim ibn Muhammad
1609–20	Husain Famuderi
1620–48	Imad-ud-Din Muhammad I
1648–87	Ibrahim Iskandar I
1687–91	Muhammad ibn Ibrahim
1691–2	Muhi-ud-Din Muhammad
1692	Shams-ud-Din Muhammad al-Hamawi
1692–1700	Muhammad ibn Hajji Ali
1700–01	Ali
1701	Hasan ibn Ali
1701–05	Muzhir-ud-Din Ibrahim
1705–21	Imad-ud-Din Muhammad II
1721–50	Ibrahim Iskandar II
1750–4	Imad-ud-Din Muhammad Mukarram
1754–60	Cannanore (see India)
1760–6	Izz-ud-Din Hasan Ghazi
1766–73	Ghiyath-ud-Din Muhammad
1773–4	Shams-ud-Din Muhammad
1774–8	Mu izz-ud-Din Muhammad
1778–98	Nur-du-Din Hajji Hasan
1798–1834	Mu in-ud-Din Muhammad I
1834–82	Imad-ud-Din Muhammad III
1882–6	Nur-ud-Din Ibrahim
1886–8	Mu in-ud-Din Muhammad II
1888–92	Nur-ud-Din Ibrahim (restored)
1892–3	Imad-ud-Din Muhammad IV
1893	Shams-ud-Din Muhammad Iskandar
1893–1903	Imad-ud-Din Muhammad V
1903–35	Shams-ud-Din Muhammad Iskandar (restored)

1935–45	Nur-ud-Din Hasan Iskandar
1945–52	Abdul-Majid Didi
1954–68	Muhammad Farid Didi

Republic
President

1968–78	Ibrahim Nasir
1978–	Maumoon Abdul Gayoom

Mali

President

1960–8	Modibo Keita
1969–91	Moussa Traoré
1991-2	*Military junta* (Alpha Oumar Konare)
1992–	Alpha Oumar Konare

Prime Minister

1986–8	Mamadou Dembelé
1988–91	*No Prime Minister*
1991–2	Soumana Sacko
1992–3	Younoussi Touré
1993–4	Abdoulaye Sekou Sow
1994–	Ibrahim Boubakar Keita

Malta

President

1974–6	Anthony Mamo
1976–81	Anton Buttigieg
1982–7	Agatha Barbara
1987–9	Paul Xuereb *Acting*
1989–94	Vincent Tabore
1994–	Ugo Mifsud Bonnici

Prime Minister

1962–71	G Borg Olivier
1971–84	Dom (Dominic) Mintoff
1984–7	Carmelo Mifsud Bonnici
1987–96	Edward Fenech Adami
1996–	Alfred Sant

Marshall Islands

President

1986–96	Amata Kabua
1997–	Imata Kabua

Mauritania

President

1961–78	Mokhtar Ould Daddah
1979	Mustapha Ould Mohammed Salek
1979–80	Mohammed Mahmoud Ould Ahmed Louly
1980–4	Mohammed Khouna Ould Haydalla
1984–	Moaouia Ould Sidi Mohammed Taya

Prime Minister

1992–6	Sidi Mohamed Ould Boubaker
1996–	Cheikh el Avia Ould Mohamed Khouna

Mauritius

President

1992	Veerasamy Ringadoo
1992–	Cassum Uteem

Prime Minister

1968–82	Seewoosagur Ramgoolam
1982–95	Anerood Jugnauth
1995–	Navin Ramgoolam

Mexico

Aztec rulers

King of Tenochtitlan

1372–91	Acamapichtli
1391–1415	Huitzilihuitl
1415–26	Chimalpopoca
1426–40	Itzcoatl
1440–68	Moctezuma I Ilhuicamina
1468–81	Axayacatl
1481–6	Tizoc
1486–1502	Ahuitzotl
1502–20	Moctezuma II Xocoyotzin
1520	Cuitlahuac
1520–1	Cuauhtemoc
1521–1821	*Spanish rule*

Ruler of Texcoco

c.1300–	
c.1357	Quinatzin
c.1357–	
c.1409	Techotlala
c.1409–18	Ixlilxochitl
1418–26	Tezozomoc
1426–8	Maxtla
1431–72	Nezahualcoyotl
1472–1515	Nezahualpilli
1515–20	Cacma
1520–1	Coanacochtzin
1521–1821	*Spanish rule*

Emperor

1822–3	Agustín de Itúrbide

President

1824–9	Guadelupe Victoria
1829	Vicente Guerrero
1829	José María de Bocanegra
1829–30	*Triumvirate* (Lucas Alamán, Luis Quintanar, Pedro Vélez)
1830–2	Anastasio Bustamente
1832	Melchor Múzquiz
1832–3	Manuel Gómez Pedraza
1833	Valentín Gómez Farías
1833–5	Antonio Lopéz de Santa Anna
1835–6	Miguel Barragan
1836–7	José Justo Corro
1837–9	Anastasio Bustamente *Acting*
1839	Antonio Lopéz de Santa Anna *Acting*
1839	Nicolás Bravo
1839–41	Anastasio Bustamente *Acting*
1841	Javier Echeverría

1841–2	Antonio Lopéz de Santa Anna *Acting*
1842–3	Nicolás Bravo *Acting*
1843	Antonio Lopéz de Santa Anna *Acting*
1843–4	Valentín Canalizo
1844	Antonio Lopéz de Santa Anna *Acting*
1844–6	José Joaquín de Herrera
1846	Mariano Paredes y Arrillaga
1846	Nicolás Bravo *Acting*
1846	Mariano Salas
1846–7	Valentín Gómez Farías *Acting*
1847	Antonio Lopéz de Santa Anna *Acting*
1847	Pedro María Anaya
1847	Antonio Lopéz de Santa Anna *Acting*
1847–8	Manuel de la Peña y Peña
1848–51	José Joaquín de Herrera *Acting*
1851–3	Mariano Arista
1853	Juan Bautista Ceballos
1853	Manuel María Lombardini
1853–5	Antonio Lopéz de Santa Anna *Acting*
1855	Martin Carréra
1855	Rómulo Díaz de la Vega
1855	Juan Álvarez
1855–8	Ignacio Comonfort
1858–64	Benito Pablo Juárez
1858	Félix Zuloaga *Rival President*
1858–9	Manuel Robles Pezuala *Rival President*
1859–60	Mariano Salas *Rival Acting President*
1860	Miguel Miramón *Rival President*
1860	José Ignacio Pavón *Rival President*
1860	Miguel Miramón *Rival Acting President*

Emperor

1864–7	Maximilian of Habsburg

President

1867–72	Benito Pablo Juárez
1872–6	Sebastián Lerdo de Tejada
1876	(José de la Cruz) Porfirio Diaz
1876–7	Juan N Méndez
1876–7	José María Iglesias *Rival President*
1877–80	(José de la Cruz) Porfirio Diaz *Acting*
1880–4	Manuel González
1884–1911	(José de la Cruz) Porfirio Diaz
1911	Francisco León de la Barra
1911–13	Francisco I Madero
1913–14	Victoriano Huerta
1914	Francisco Carvajal
1914	Venustiano Carranza

1914–15	Eulalio Gutiérrez
	Provisional
1915	Roque González Garza
	Provisional
1915	Francisco Lagos Chazaro
	Provisional
1917–20	Venustiano Carranza
1920	Adolfo de la Huerta
1920–4	Alvaro Obregón
1924–8	Plutarco Elías Calles
1928–30	Emilio Portes Gil
1930–2	Pascual Ortíz Rubio
1932–4	Abelardo L Rodríguez
1934–40	Lázaro Cárdenas
1940–6	Manuel Avila Camacho
1946–52	Miguel Alemán
1952–8	Adolfo Ruiz Cortines
1958–64	Adolfo López Mateos
1964–70	Gustavo Díaz Ordaz
1970–6	Luis Echeverría
1976–82	José López Portillo
1982–8	Miguel de la Madrid Hurtado
1988–94	Carlos Salinas de Gortari
1994–	Ernesto Zedillo

Moldova

President
1991–6	Mircea Snegur
1996–	Petru Lucinschi

Prime Minister
1991–2	Valeriu Muravschi
1992–7	Andrei Sangheli
1997–	Ion Cebuc

Monaco

House of Grimaldi
Lord of Monaco
1297–1314	Rainier I
1314–57	Charles I
1357–1407	Rainier II
1407–27	Antoine Ambroise *and* Jean I *co-Lords*
1427–54	Jean I
1454–7	Catalan
1457–8	Claudine
1458–94	Lambert of Antibes
1494–1505	Jean II
1505–23	Lucien
1523–32	Augustin
1532–81	Honoré I
1581–9	Charles II
1589–1604	Hercule
1604–12	Honoré II

Prince of Monaco
1612–62	Honoré II
1662–1701	Louis I
1701–31	Antoine
1731	Louise-Hyppolyte
1731–3	Jacques of Torrigny
1733–93	Honoré III
1793–1814	*French rule*
1814–19	Honoré IV

1819–41	Honoré V
1841–56	Florestan
1856–89	Charles III
1889–1922	Albert
1922–49	Louis II
1949–	Rainier III

Minister of State
1991–4	Jacques Dupont
1994–7	Paul Dijoud
1997–	Michel Lévêque

Mongolia
Prime Minister
1924–8	Tserendorji
1928–32	Amor
1932–6	Gendun
1936–8	Amor
1939–52	Korloghiin Choibalsan
1952–74	Yumsjhagiin Tsedenbal

Premier
1974–84	Jambyn Batmunkh
1984–90	Dumaagiyn Sodnom
1990–2	Dashiyn Byambasuren
1992–6	Puntsagiyn Jasray
1996–	Mendsayhany Enhsayhan

Chairman of the Praesidium
1948–53	Gonchighlin Bumatsende
1954–72	Jamsarangiin Sambu
1972–4	Sonomyn Luvsan
1974–84	Yumsjhagiin Tsedenbal
1984–90	Jambyn Batmunkh
1990–	Punsalmaa-giyn Ochirbat

Chairman of the Great Hural
1992–6	Natsagiyn Bagabandi
1996–	Radnaasumbereliyn Gonchigdorj

General Secretary
1948–90	*As Chairman*
1990–1	Gombojavyn Ochirbat
1991–	Budragchaagiyn Dash-Yondon

President
1990–7	Punsalmaagiyn Ochirbat
1997–	Natsagiyn Bagabandi

Morocco
Sultan
Filawi Dynasty (Fez and Morocco)
1631–5	Muhammad I ash-Sharif
1635–64	Muhammad II
1664–72	ar-Rashid
1672–1727	Isma il as-Samin
1727–9	Ahmad Adh-Dhahabi
1729–35	Abdullah
1735–7	Ali ibn Isma il
1737–8	Abdullah (*restored*)
1738–40	al-Mustadi ibn Isma il
1740–5	Abdullah (*restored*)
1745	Zain-ul-Abidin
1745–57	Abdullah (*restored*)
1757–90	Muhammad III
1790–2	Yazid

1792–3	Hisham
1793–1822	Sulayman
1822–59	Abdul-Rahman
1859–73	Muhammad IV
1873–94	Hasan I
1894–1907	Abdul-Aziz
1907–12	Abdul-Hafiz
1912–27	Yusuf
1927–53	Muhammad V
1953–5	Muhammad VI
1955–7	Muhammad V (*restored*)

Monarch – Kingdom of Morocco
1957–61	Muhammad V
1961–	Hasan (Hassan) II

Prime Minister
1955–8	Si Mohammed Bekkai
1958	Ahmad Balfrej
1958–60	Abdullah Ibrahim
1960–3	*As king*
1963–5	Ahmad Bahnini
1965–7	*As king*
1967–9	Moulay Ahmed Laraki
1969–71	Mohammed Ben Hima
1971–2	Mohammed Karim Lamrani
1972–9	Ahmed Othman
1979–83	Maati Bouabid
1983–6	Mohammed Karim Lamrani
1986–92	Azzedine Laraki
1992–4	Karim Lamrani
1994–	Abdellatif Filali

Mozambique
President
1975–86	Samora Moïses Machel
1986–	Joaquim Alberto Chissanó

Prime Minister
1986–94	Mario da Graça Machungo
1994–	Pascoal Mocumbi

Myanmar (Burma)
Union of Burma
President
1948–52	Sao Shwe Thaik
1952–7	Agga Maha Thiri Thudhamma Ba U
1957–62	U Wing Maung
1962	Sama Duwa Sinwa Nawng

Revolutionary Council – Chairman
1962–74	Ne Win (Maung Shu Maung)

State Council – Chairman
1974–81	Ne Win (Maung Shu Maung)
1981–8	U San Yu
1988	U Sein Lwin
1988	Maung Maung
1988–9	Saw Maung

Union of Myanmar
1989–92	Saw Maung
1992–	Than Shwe

Prime Minister

1947–56	Nu U (Thakin Nu)
1956–7	U Ba Swe
1957–8	U Nu
1958–60	Ne Win (Maung Shu Maung)
1960–2	U Nu
1962–74	Ne Win (Maung Shu Maung)
1974–7	U Sein Win
1977–8	U Maung Maung Ka
1988	U Tun Tin
1988–92	Saw Maung
1992–	Than Shwe

Namibia

President

1990–	Sam Daniel Nujoma

Prime Minister

1990–	Hage Geingob

Nauru

President

1968–86	Hammer de Roburt
1986	Kennan Adeang
1986–9	Hammer de Roburt
1989	Kenas Aroi
1989–97	Bernard Dowiyogo
1997–	Kinza Clodumar

Nepal

Monarch – Kingdom of Nepal
Rhagavadeva Dynasty

c.879	Raghavadeva
?	Jayadeva
?	Vikramadeva
?	Narendradeva I
?	Gunakamadeva I
?	Udayadeva
c.1008	Nirbhayadeva
c.1008	Rudradeva
c.1015	Bhoja
c.1015	Lakshmikamadeva I
c.1039–46	Jayakamadeva

Thakuri Dynasty

1046–59	Bhaskaradeva
1059–64	Baladeva
1064–?	Pradyumnakamadeva
?–1068	Nagarjunadeva
1068–80	Shankaradeva
1080–90	Vamadeva
1090–1118	Harshadeva
1118–28	Sivadeva
1128–?	Indradeva
?	Manadeva
?–1146	Narendradeva II
1146–?	Anandadeva
?–1176	Rudradeva
1176–?	Amritadeva
?	Ratnadeva
?–1187	Somesvaradeva
1187–93	Gunakamadeva II
1193–6	Lakshmikamadeva II
1196–1201	Vijayakamadeva

Malla Dynasty

c.1201–c.1216	Arimalladeva
c.1216	Ranasura
c.1216–c.1235	Abhayamalla
c.1235–c.1258	Jayadevamalla
c.1258–c.1271	Jayabhimadeva
c.1271–c.1274	Jayasimhamalla
c.1274–c.1310	Anantamalla
c.1310–c.1320	Jayanandadeva
c.1320–c.1326	Jayarudramalla
c.1320–c.1344	Jayarimalla
c.1347–c.1361	Jayarajadeva
c.1361–c.1382	Jayajunamalla
c.1382–c.1395	Jayasthitimalla
c.1395–c.1408	Jayadharmamalla
c.1395–c.1403	Jayakitimalla
c.1395–c.1428	Jayajyotimalla
c.1428–c.1482	Jayayakshmamalla

Monarch – Kingdom of Katmandu
Malla Dynasty

c.1482–c.1520	Ratnamalla
c.1520–c.1530	Suryamalla
c.1530–c.1538	Amaramalla
c.1538–c.1560	Narendramalla
c.1560–c.1574	Mahenramalla
c.1574–c.1583	Sadasivamalla
c.1578–c.1620	Sivasimhamalla
c.1620–c.1641	Lakshminarasim-hamal-la
c.1641–c.1674	Pratapamalla
c.1674–c.1680	Jayanripendramalla
c.1680–c.1567	Parthivendramalla
c.1687–c.1700	Bhupendramalla
c.1700–c.1714	Bhaskaramalla
c.1714–1722	Mahendrasim-hamalla
1722–36	Jagajjayamalla
1736–68	Jayaprakasamalla

Monarch – Kingdom of Bhatgaon
Malla Dynasty

c.1482–c.1519	Rayamalla
c.1519–c.1547	Pranamalla
c.1547–c.1560	Vishvamalla
c.1560–c.1613	Trailokyamallamalla
c.1613–c.1637	Jagatjotimalla
c.1637–c.1644	Naresamalla
c.1644–c.1673	Jagatprakasamalla
c.1673–c.1696	Jitamitramalla
c.1696–1722	Bhupatindramalla
1722–69	Ranjitamalla

Monarch – Kingdom of Nepal
Gurkha Kings

1768–75	Prithvi Narayan Shah
1775–8	Pratap Singh Shah
1778–99	Rana Bahadur Shah
1799–1816	Girvana Judha Bikram Shah
1816–47	Rajendra Bir Bikram Shah
1847–81	Surendra Bir Bikram Shah
1881–1911	Prithvi Bir Bikram Shah
1911–55	Tribhuvana Bir Bikram Shah
1956–72	Mahendra Bir Bikram Shah
1972–	Birenda Bir Bikram Shah

Prime Minister

1811–39	Bhim Sen Thapa
1839–43	*No Prime Minister*
1843–5	Matbarsing Thapa
1846–77	Jung Bahadur
1877–84	Ranodeep Singh
1885–1901	Bir Sham Sher J B Rana
1902	Dev Sham Sher J B Rana
1903–29	Chandra Sham Sher J B Rana
1929–31	Bhim Cham Sham Sher J B Rana
1931–45	Juddha Sham Sher J B Rana
1945–8	Padma Sham Sher J B Rana
1948–51	Mohan Sham Sher J B Rana
1951–2	Matrika Prasad Koirala
1952–3	Tribhuvan Bir Bikram Shah
1953–5	Matrika Prasad Koirala
1955–6	Mahendra Bir Bikram Shah
1956–7	Tanka Prasad Acharya
1957–9	*As king*
1959–60	Sri Bishawa Prasad Koirala
1960–3	*No Prime Minister*
1963–5	Tulsi Giri
1965–9	Surya Bahadur Thapa
1969–70	Kirti Nidhi Bista
1970–1	*As king*
1971–3	Kirti Nidhi Bista
1973–5	Nagendra Prasad Rijal
1975–7	Tulsi Giri
1977–9	Kirti Nidhi Bista
1979–83	Surya Bahadur Thapa
1983–6	Lokendra Bahadur Chand
1986–90	Marich Man Singh Shrestha
1990	Lokendra Bahadur Chand
1990–1	Krishna Prasad Bhattarai
1991–4	Girija Prasad Koirala
1994–5	Man Mohan Adhikari
1995–7	Sher Bahadur Deupa
1997	Lokendra Bahadur Chand
1997–	Surya Bahadur Thapa

Netherlands

Stadtholder of the Netherlands
House of Orange

1572–84	Willem (William) I 'the Silent' of Nassau
1584–1625	Maurice
1625–47	Frederik Henrik
1647–50	Willem II
1650–72	*No Stadtholder* (Jan de Witt, Grand Pensionary 1653–72)
1672–1702	Willem (William) III *King of England and Scotland from 1689*
1702–47	*No Stadtholder*
1747–51	Willem IV (Charles Henry Friso)
1751–95	Willem V
1795–1806	*Batavian Republic*

Monarch – Kingdom of Holland
House of Bonaparte

1806–10	Lodewijk I (Louis Bonaparte)
1810–13	*French rule*

Monarch – Kingdom of the Netherlands

House of Orange (restored)

1813–40	Willem I
1840–9	Willem II
1849–90	Willem III
1890–1948	Wilhelmina *Queen Emma Regent to 1898*
1948–80	Juliana
1980–	Beatrix

Prime Minister

1848	Gerrit, Count Schimmelpenninck
1848–9	Dirk Donker Curtius
1849–53	Johan Rudolph Thorbecke
1853–6	Floris Adriaan, Baron van Hall
1856–8	Justinus Jacob Leonard van der Bruggen
1858–60	Jan Jacob Rochussen
1860–1	Floris Adriaan, Baron van Hall
1861–2	Julius Philip Jacob Adriaan, Count van Zuylen van Nijevelt
1862–6	Johan Rudolph Thorbecke
1866	Isaac Dignus Fransen van de Putte
1866–8	*Shared Administration* (P Mijer; Julius, Count van Zuylen van Nijevelt; Jan Heemskerk)
1868–71	*Shared Administration* (Peter Philip van Bosse; C Fock)
1871–2	Johan Rudolph Thorbecke
1872–4	*Shared Administration* (Gerrit de Vries; Johan Hendrik Geertsema)
1874–7	Jan Heemskerk
1877–9	Johannes Kappeyne van de Coppello
1879–83	Constant Theodore, Count van Lynden van Sandenburg
1883–8	Jan Heemskerk
1888–91	Aeneas, Baron Mackay
1891–4	Gijsbert van Tienhoven
1894–7	Joan Roëll
1897–1901	Nicholas G Pierson
1901–5	Abraham Kuyper
1905–8	Theodoor H de Meester
1908–13	Theodorus Heemskerk
1913–18	Pieter W A Cort van der Linden
1918–25	Charles J M Ruys de Beerenbrouck
1925–6	Hendrikus Colijn
1926	Dirk J de Geer
1926–33	Charles J M Ruys de Beerenbrouck
1933–9	Hendrikus Colijn
1939–40	Dirk J de Geer
1940–5	Pieter S Gerbrandy *in exile*
1945–6	Willem Schemerhorn/ Willem Drees
1946–8	Louis J M Beel
1948–51	Willem Drees/Josephus R H van Schaik
1951–8	Willem Drees
1958–9	Louis J M Beel
1959–63	Jan E de Quay
1963–5	Victor G M Marijnen
1965–6	Joseph M L T Cals
1966–7	Jelle Zijlstra
1967–71	Petrus J S de Jong
1971–3	Barend W Biesheuvel
1973–7	Joop M den Uyl
1977–82	Andreas A M van Agt
1982–94	Rudolf Franz Marie (Ruud) Lubbers
1994–	Wim Kok

New Zealand

Chief of State: British monarch, represented by Governor-General

Prime Minister

1856	Henry Sewell
1856	William Fox
1856–61	Edward William Stafford
1861–2	William Fox
1862–3	Alfred Domett
1863–4	Frederick Whitaker
1864–5	Frederick Aloysius Weld
1865–9	Edward William Stafford
1869–72	William Fox
1872	Edward William Stafford
1873	William Fox
1873–5	Julius Vogel
1875–6	Daniel Pollen
1876	Julius Vogel
1876–7	Harry Albert Atkinson
1877–9	George Grey
1879–82	John Hall
1882–3	Frederick Whitaker
1883–4	Harry Albert Atkinson
1884	Robert Stout
1884	Harry Albert Atkinson
1884–7	Robert Stout
1887–91	Harry Albert Atkinson
1891–3	John Ballance
1893–1906	Richard John Seddon *Lib*
1906	William Hall-Jones *Lib*
1906–12	Joseph George Ward *Lib/Nat*
1912	Thomas Mackenzie *Nat*
1912–25	William Ferguson Massey *Ref*
1925	Francis Henry Dillon Bell *Ref*
1925–8	Joseph Gordon Coates *Ref*
1928–30	Joseph George Ward *Lib/Nat*
1930–5	George William Forbes *Un*
1935–40	Michael Joseph Savage *Lab*
1940–9	Peter Fraser *Lab*
1949–57	Sidney George Holland *Nat*
1957	Keith Jacka Holyoake *Nat*
1957–60	Walter Nash *Lab*
1960–72	Keith Jacka Holyoake *Nat*
1972	John Ross Marshall *Nat*
1972–4	Norman Eric Kirk *Lab*
1974–5	Wallace Edward Rowling *Lab*
1975–84	Robert David Muldoon *Nat*
1984–9	David Russell Lange *Lab*
1989–90	Geoffrey Winston Russell Palmer *Lab*
1990	Michael Kenneth Moore *Lab*
1990–7	James Brendan Bolger *Nat*
1997–	Jenny Shipley *Nat*

Lab Labour; *Lib* Liberal; *Nat* National; *Ref* Reform; *Un* United

Nicaragua

President

1853–4	Fruto Chamorro
1855–9	José María Estrada
1859–67	Tomás Martinez
1867–71	Fernando Guzmán
1871–5	Vicente Cuadra
1875–9	Pedro Joaquín Chamorro
1879–83	Joaquín Zavala
1883–7	Adán Cárdenas
1887–	Evaristo Carazo
1889–93	Roberto Sacasa
1893–1909	José Santos Zelaya
1909–10	José Madriz
1910–11	José Dolores Estrada
1911	Juan José Estrada
1911–17	Adolfo Díaz
1912	Luis Mena *Rival President*
1917–21	Emiliano Chamorro Vargas
1921–3	Riego Manuel Chamorro
1923–4	Martínez Bartolo
1925–6	Carlos Solórzano
1926	Emiliano Chamorro Vargas
1926–8	Adolfo Díaz
1926	Juan Bautista Sacasa *Rival President*
1928–32	José Marcia Moncada
1933–6	Juan Bautista Sacasa
1936	Carlos Brenes Jarquin
1937–47	Anastasio Somoza García
1947	Leonardo Argüello
1947	Benjamin Lascayo Sacasa
1947–50	Victor Manuel Román y Reyes
1950–6	Anastasio Somoza García
1956–63	Luis Somoza Debayle
1963–6	René Schick Gutiérrez
1966–7	Lorenzo Guerrero Gutiérrez
1967–72	Anastasio Somoza Debayle
1972–4	*Triumvirate*
1974–9	Anastasio Somoza Debayle
1979–84	*Government junta of National Reconstruction*
1984–90	Daniel Ortega Saavedra
1990–6	Violeta Barrios de Chamorro
1996–	Arnoldo Aleman Lacayo

Niger

President

1960–74	Hamani Diori

1974–87	Seyni Kountché
1987–93	Ali Saibou
1993–6	Mahamane Ousmane
1996–	Ibrahim Barre Mainassara

Prime Minister

1990–1	Aliou Mahamidou
1991–3	Amadou Cheiffou *Interim*
1993–4	Mahamdou Issoufou
1994–5	Abdoulaye Souley
1995–6	Hama Amadou
1996	Boukary Adji
1996–7	Amadou Boubacar Cisse
1997–	Ibrahim Assane Mayaki

Nigeria

President

1960–6	Nnamdi Azikiwe

Prime Minister

1960–6	Abubakar Tafawa Balewa

Military Government

1966	J T U Aguiyi-Ironsi
1966–75	Yakubu Gowon
1975–6	Murtala R Mohamed
1976–9	Olusegun Obasanjo

President

1979–83	Alhaji Shehu Shagari

Military Government

1983–4	Mohammadu Buhari
1985–93	Ibrahim B Babangida
1993	Ernest Adegunle Shonekan *Interim*
1993–	Sanni Abacha

Sultan of Sokoto

1804–17	Uthman dan Fodio
1817–37	Muhammad Bello
1837–42	Abu-Bakr Atiku I
1842–59	Aliyu Babba
1859–66	Ahmad Atiku
1866–7	Aliyu Karami
1867–73	Ahmad Rufai
1873–7	Abu-Bakr Atiku II
1977–81	Mu'azu
1981–96	Ibrahim Dasuki
1996–	Mohammed Maccido

Norway

Monarch

Yngling Dynasty

c.870–c.940	Harald I Halfdanarson 'Fine/Fairhair'
c.940–c.945	Erik Haraldsson 'Bloodaxe'
c.945–c.960	Haakon I Haraldsson 'the Good'
c.960–c.970	Harald II Eriksson 'Greycloak'
c.970–c.995	Haakon, Jarl of Lade
c.995–1000	Olaf I Tryggvason
1000–15	Erik, Jarl of Lade
1015–28	Olaf II Haraldsson (St Olaf)
1028–35	Svein Knutsson

1035–47	Magnus I Olafsson 'the Good'
1047–66	Harald III Sigurdsson 'Hardrada' ('the Ruthless')
1066–93	Olaf III Haraldsson 'the Peaceful' *Joint ruler to 1069*
1066–9	Magnus II *Joint ruler*
1093–1103	Magnus III Olafsson 'Barelegs'
1103–30	Sigurd I Magnusson 'the Crusader' *Joint ruler to 1122*
1103–15	Olaf Magnusson *Joint ruler*
1103–22	Eystein I Magnusson *Joint ruler*
1130–5	Magnus IV 'the Blind' *Joint ruler*
1130–6	Harald IV Gille *Joint ruler to 1135*
1136–61	Inge I *Joint ruler to 1157*
1136–55	Sigurd II *Joint ruler*
1142–57	Eystein II *Joint ruler*
1161–2	Haakon II
1162–84	Magnus V Erlingsson
1184–1202	Sverrir Sigurdsson
1202–04	Haakon III
1204	Gutorm Sigurdsson
1204–17	Inge II Baardsson
1217–63	Haakon IV Haakonsson 'the Old'
1263–80	Magnus VI Haakonsson 'the Law-Reformer'
1280–99	Erik II
1299–1319	Haakon V
1319–43	*As Sweden*
1343–80	Haakon VI
1130–6	Harald IV Gille *Joint ruler*

Danish kings

1380–7	Olaf IV (V of Denmark)
1387–97	Margrethe I (Margareta)
1397–1814	*As Denmark*
1814–1905	*As Sweden*

House of Oldenburg

1905–57	Haakon VII
1957–91	Olaf V
1991–	Harald V

Prime Minister

1873–80	Frederik Stang
1880–4	Christian Selmer
1884	C H Schweigaard
1884–9	Johan Sverdrup
1889–91	Emil Stang
1891–3	Johannes Steen
1893–7	Emil Stang
1898–1902	Johannes Steen
1902–3	Otto Albert Blehr
1903–5	George Francis Hagerup
1905–7	Christian Michelsen
1907–8	Jørgen Løvland
1908–10	Gunnar Knudsen
1910–12	Wollert Konow
1912–13	Jens Bratlie
1913–20	Gunnar Knudsen
1920–1	Otto Bahr Halvorsen

1921–3	Otto Albert Blehr
1923	Otto Bahr Halvorsen
1923–4	Abraham Berge
1924–6	Johan Ludwig Mowinckel
1926–8	Ivar Lykke
1928	Christopher Hornsrud
1928–31	Johan Ludwig Mowinckel
1931–2	Peder Kolstad
1932–3	Jens Hundseid
1933–5	Johan Ludwig Mowinckel
1935–45	Johan Nygaardsvold
1945–51	Einar Gerhardsen
1951–5	Oscar Torp
1955–63	Einar Gerhardsen
1963	John Lyng
1963–5	Einar Gerhardsen
1965–71	Per Borten
1971–2	Trygve Bratteli
1972–3	Lars Korvald
1973–6	Trygve Bratteli
1976–81	Odvar Nordli
1981	Gro Harlem Brundtland
1981–6	Kåre Willoch
1986–9	Gro Harlem Brundtland
1989–90	Jan P Syse
1990–6	Gro Harlem Brundtland
1996–7	Thorbjoern Jagland
1997	Kjell Magne Bondevik

Oman

Sultan – Oman and Zanzibar

Ya'rubid Dynasty

1625–49	Nasir ibn Murshid
1649–69	Sultan I
1669–1711	Abdu l-Arab
1711	Saif I
1711–19	Sultan II
1719	Saif II
1719–22	Muhanna
1722–3	Yarub
1723–5	Saif II (*restored*)
1725–8	Muhammad ibn Nasir
1728–41	Saif II (*restored*)
1739–41	Sultan ibn Murshid

Al-Bu-Sa'id Dynasty

1741–83	Ahmad ibn Said
1783–6	Said I
1786–92	Hamid
1792–1806	Sultan
1806	Salim I
1806–56	Said II

Sultan – Oman

Al-Bu-Sa'id Dynasty

1856–66	Thuwaini
1866–8	Salim II
1868–70	Azan ibn Qais
1870–88	Turki
1888–1913	Faisal ibn Turki
1913–32	Taimur ibn Faisal
1932–70	Said III ibn Taimur
1970–	Qabus ibn Said (Qaboos bin Said)

Pakistan

President

1956–8	Iskander Mirza
1958–69	Mohammad Ayub Khan
1969–71	Agha Muhammad Yahya Khan
1971–3	Zulfikar Ali Bhutto
1973–8	Fazal Elahi Chawdry
1978–88	Mohammad Zia Ul-Haq
1988–93	Gulam Ishaq Khan
1993–	Farooq Ahmed Leghari

Prime Minister

1947–51	Liaquat Ali Khan
1951–3	Khawaja Nazimuddin
1953–5	Mohammad Ali
1955–6	(Chaudri) Mohamad Ali
1956–7	Hussein Shaheed Suhrawardy
1957	Ismail Chundrigar
1957–8	Malik Feroz Khan Noon
1958	Mohammad Ayoub Khan
1958–73	*No Prime Minister*
1973–7	Zulfikar Ali Bhutto
1977–85	*No Prime Minister*
1985–8	Mohammad Khan Junejo
1988	Mohammad Aslam Khan Khattak
1988–90	Benazir Bhutto
1990	Ghulam Mustafa Jatoi
1990–3	Mian Mohammad Nawaz Sharif
1993–6	Benazir Bhutto
1996–7	Malik Meraj Khalid
1997–	Mian Mohammad Nawaz Sharif

Bahawalpur

Nawab

Daudputra Dynasty

1739–46	Sadiq Muhammad Khan I
1746–9	Muhammad Bahawal Khan I
1749–72	Mubarak Khan
1772–1809	Muhammad Bahawal Khan II
1809–25	Saadiq Muhammad Khan II
1825–52	Muhammad Bahawal Khan III
1852–3	Sadiq Muhammad Khan III
1853–8	Fateh Muhammad Khan
1858–66	Muhammad Bahawal Khan IV
1866–99	Sadiq Muhammad Khan IV
1899–1907	Muhammad Bahawal Khan V
1907–55	Sadiq Muhammad Khan V

Kalat

Khan

?–1666	Mir Hasan Khan Mirwari
1666–95	Sardar Mir Ahmad Khan
1695	Mir Mehrab Khan I
1695–1714	Mir Samandar Khan
1714–34	Mir Abdullah Khan
1734–49	Mir Mohabat Khan
1749–1817	Mir Nasir Khan I
1817–31	Mir Mahmud Khan I
1831–40	Mir Mehrab Khan II
1840–57	Mir Nasir Khan II
1857–93	Mir Khudadad Khan
1893–1931	Mir Mahmud Khan II
1931–3	Mir Azam Khan
1933–48	Mir Ahmad Yar Khan

Panama

President

1904–8	Manuel Amador Guerrero
1908–10	José Domingo de Obaldia
1910	Federico Boyd
1910	Carlos Antonio Mendoza
1910–12	Pablo Arosemena
1912	Rodolfo Chiari
1912–16	Belisario Porras
1916–18	Ramón Maximiliano Valdés
1918	Pedro Antonio Diaz
1918	Cirilo Luis Urriola
1918–20	Belisario Porras
1920	Ernesto T Lefevre
1920–4	Belisario Porras
1924–8	Rodolfo Chiari
1928	Tomás Gabriel Duque
1928–31	Florencio Harmodio Arosemena
1931	Harmodio Arias
1931–2	Ricardo Joaquín Alfaro
1932–6	Harmodio Arias
1936–9	Juan Demóstenes Arosemena
1939	Ezequiel Fernández Jaén
1939–40	Augusto Samuel Boyd
1940–1	Arnulfo Arias Madrid
1941	Ernesto Jaén Guardia
1941	José Pezet
1941–5	Ricardo Adolfo de la Guardia
1945–8	Enrique Adolfo Jiménez Brin
1948–9	Domingo Diaz Arosemena
1949	Daniel Chanis
1949	Roberto Francisco Chiari
1949–51	Arnulfo Arias Madrid
1951–2	Alcibiades Arosemena
1952–5	José Antonio Remón
1955	José Ramón Guizado
1955–6	Ricardo Manuel Arias Espinosa
1956–60	Ernesto de la Guardia
1960–4	Roberto Francisco Chiari
1964–8	Marco A Robles
1968	Arnulfo Arias Madrid
1968	*Military junta*
1968–9	Omar Torrijos Herrera
1969–78	Demetrio Basilio Lakas
1978–82	Aristides Royo
1982–4	Ricardo de la Esoriella
1984	Jorge Enrique Illueca Sibauste
1984–5	Nicolás Ardito Barletta
1985–8	Eric Arturo Delvalle
1988–9	Manuel Solís Palma
1989–94	Guillermo Endara Gallimany
1994–	Ernesto Pérez Balladares

Papua New Guinea

Prime Minister

1975–80	Michael Thomas Somare
1980–2	Julius Chan
1982–5	Michael Thomas Somare
1985–8	Paias Wingti
1988–92	Rabbie Namiliu
1992–4	Paias Wingti
1994–7	Julius Chan
1997	John Giheno
1997	Julius Chan
1997	Bill Skate

Paraguay

Head of State

First Republic

1813–14	Fulgencio Yegros *Co-Consul*
	José Gaspar Rodríguez Francia *Co-Consul*
1814–40	José Gaspar Rodríguez Francia *Dictator*
1841–4	Carlos Antonio López *Co-Consul*
	Mariano Roque Alonso *Co-Consul*

President

First Republic

1844–62	Carlos Antonio López
1862–70	Francisco Solano López

Second Republic

1870	Carlos Loizaga
	Cirilo Antonio Rivarola
	José Díaz e Bodoya
1870–1	Cirilo Antonio Rivarola
1871–4	Salvador Jovellanos
1874–7	Juan Bautista Gill
1877–8	Higinio Uriarte
1878–80	Cándido Bareiro
1880–6	Bernardino Caballero
1886–90	Patricio Escobar
1890–4	Juan G González
1894	Marcos Morínigo
1894–8	Juan Bautista Egusquiza
1898–1902	Emilio Aceval
1902	Hector Carballo
1902–4	Juan Antonio Escurra
1904–5	Juan Gaona
1905–6	Cecilio Báez
1906–8	Benigno Ferreira
1908–10	Emiliano González Navero
1910–11	Manuel Gondra
1911	Albino Jara
1911	Liberato Marcial Rojas
1912	Pedro Peña
1912	Emiliano González Navero
1912–16	Eduardo Schaerer

1916–19	Manuel Franco
1919–20	José P Montero
1920–1	Manuel Gondra
1921	Félix Paiva
1921–3	Eusebio Ayala
1923–4	Eligio Ayala
1924	Luis Alberto Riart
1924–8	Eligio Ayala
1928–31	José Particio Guggiari
1931–2	Emiliano González Navero
1932	José Particio Guggiari
1932–6	Eusebio Ayala
1936–7	Rafael Franco
1937–9	Félix Paiva
1939–40	José Félix Estigarribia
1940–8	Higino Moríñigo
1948	Juan Manuel Frutos
1948–9	Juan Natalicio González
1949	Raimundo Rolón
1949	Felipe Molas López
1949–54	Federico Chaves
1954	Tomás Romero Pareira
1954–89	Alfredo Stroessner
1989–93	Andrés Rodríguez
1993–	Juan Carlos Wasmosy

Peru

Inca

c.1100–?	Manco Capac
?	Sinchi Roca
?	Lloque Yupanqui
?–c.1200	Mayta Capac
c.1200–?	Capac Yupanqui
?	Inca Roca
?	Inca Yupanqui (Yahuar Huacac)
?–1438	Viracocha
1438	Inca Urco
1438–71	Pachacuti
1471–93	Tupac Yupanqui
1493–1526	Huayna Capac
1526–32	Tupac Cusi Hualpa (Huascar)
1530–3	Atahualpa *North only to 1532*
1533–1821	*Spanish rule*

President

1821–2	José de San Martín *Protector of Peru*
1822–3	José de la Mar *Chairman of the Governing Council*
1823	José de la Riva Agüero
1823–4	José Bernardo de Tagle *Rival President*
1824–7	Simón Bolivár *Dictator*
1827–9	José de la Mar
1829–33	Agustin Gamarra
1833–4	Luis José de Orbegoso
1834	Pedro Bermudez
1834–5	Luis José de Orbegoso
1835–6	Felipe Santiago Salaverry
1836–8	*Bolivian rule* (Andres Santa Cruz)
1838–41	Agustin Gamarra
1841–2	Manuel Menéndez

1842	Juan Crisóstomo Torrico
1842–3	Francisco Vidal
1843–5	Manuel Ignacio Vivanco *Dictator*
1845–51	Ramón Castilla y Marquesado
1851–5	José Rufino Echenique
1855–62	Ramón Castilla y Marquesado
1862–3	Miguel San Román
1863–5	Juan Antonio Pézet *Dictator*
1865	Pedro Diez Canseco *Acting*
1865–8	Mariano Ignacio Prado *Dictator*
1868–72	José Balta
1872	Tomás Gutiérrez *Dictator*
1872–6	Manuel Pardo
1876–80	Mariano Ignacio Prado
1880–1	Nicolás Piérola
1881	Francisco García Calderón *Acting*
1881–3	Lizardo Montero *Acting*
1883–5	Miguel Iglesias
1885–6	*Junta* (Antonio Arenas)
1886–90	Andrés Avelino Cáceres
1890–4	Remigio Morales Bermúdez
1894–5	Andrés Avelino Cáceres
1895	Manuel Candamo
1895–99	Nicolás Piérola
1899–1903	Eduardo López de la Romaña
1903–4	Manuel Candamo
1904	Serapio Calderón
1904–8	José Pardo y Barreda
1908–12	Augusto B Leguía
1912–14	Guillermo Billinghurst
1914–15	Oscar R Benavides
1915–19	José Pardo y Barreda
1919–30	Augusto B Leguía
1930	Manuel Ponce
1930–1	Luis M Sánchez Cerro
1931	Leoncio Elías
1931	Gustavo A Jiménez
1931	David Samanez Ocampo
1931–3	Luis M Sánchez Cerro
1933–9	Oscar R Benavides
1939–45	Manuel Prado
1945–8	José Luis Bustamante y Rivero
1948–56	Manuel A Odría
1956–62	Manuel Prado
1962–3	*Military junta*
1963–8	Fernando Belaúnde Terry
1968–75	*Military junta* (Juan Velasco Alvarado)
1975–80	*Military junta* (Francisco Morales Bermúdez)
1980–5	Fernando Belaúnde Terry
1985–90	Alan García Pérez
1990–	Alberto Keinya Fujimori

Prime Minister

1991–2	Alfonso de los Heros
1992–3	Oscar de la Puente Raygada

1993–4	Alfonso Bustamente y Bustamente
1994–5	Efrain Godenberg Schreiber
1995–6	Dante Córdoba Blanco
1996–	Alberto Pandolfi Arbulu

Philippines

Sultan of Sulu

c.1450–c.1480	Sharif-ul-Hashim
c.1480–?	Kamal-ud-Din
?	Ala-ud-Din
?	Amir-ul-Umara
?	Muizz-ul-Mutawadi in
?	Nasir-ud-Din I
?–c.1596	Muhammad al-Halim
c.1596–c.1610	Batarah Shah Tengah
c.1610– c.1650	Muwallit Wasit
c.1645–c.1648	Nasir-ud-Din II
c.1650–c.1680	Salah-ud-Din Bakhtiyar
c.1680–?	Ali Shah
?–c.1685	Nur-ul-Azam Sultanah al-Haqunu
c.1685–c.1710	Shihab-ud-Din
c.1710–c.1718	Mustafa Shafi-ud-Din
c.1718–1732	Badr-ud-Din I
1732–5	Nasr-ud-Din
1735–48	Azim-ud-Din I
1748–64	Muizz-ud-Din
1764–74	Azim-ud-Din I (*restored*)
1774–8	Muhammad Isra il
1778–91	Azim-ud-Din II
1791–1808	Sharaf-ud-Din
1808	Azim-ud-Din III
1808–21	Ali-ud-Din
1821–3	Shakirullah
1823–42	Jamal-ul-Kiram I
1842–62	Muhammad Fadl
1862–81	Jamal-ul-Azam
1881–4	Badr-ud-Din II
1884–1915	Jamal-ul-Kiram II
1886–94	Harun ar-Rashid
1915–35	*US rule*

Sultan of Maguindanao

c.1645–c.1671	Qudarat Nasir-ud-Din
c.1671–c.1678	Dundang Tidulay Saif-ud-Din
c.1678–c.1699	Abdul-Rahman
c.1699–c.1702	Qahhar-ud-Din Kuda
c.1702–c.1745	Bayan-ul-Anwar
c.1710–c.1733	Muhammad Jafar Sadiq Manamir
c.1736–c.1748	Tahir-ud-Din
c.1748–c.1755	Muhammad Khair-ud-Din
c.1755–c.1780	Pahar-ud-Din
c.1780–c.1805	Kibad Sahriyal
c.1805–c.1830	Kawasa Anwar-ud-Din
c.1830–1854	Iskandar Qudratullah Muhammad
1854–84	Muhammad Makakwa
1884–8	Muhammad Jalal-ud-Din Pablu

1888–98	*Spanish rule*
1898–1935	*US rule*

President
Commonwealth

1935–44	Manuel Luis Quezon

Japanese occupation

1943–4	José P Laurel

Commonwealth

1944–6	Sergio Osmeña

First Republic

1946–8	Manuel A Roxas
1948–53	Elpidio Quirino
1953–7	Ramon Magsaysay
1957–61	Carlos P Garcia
1961–5	Diosdado Macapagal
1965–72	Ferdinand Edralin Marcos

Martial Law

1972–81	Ferdinand Edralin Marcos

Second Republic

1981–6	Ferdinand Edralin Marcos
1986–92	(Maria) Corazon Aquino
1992–	Fidel Ramos

Poland

Monarch – Prince of all Poland
House of Piast

c.960–992	Mieszko I
992–1025	Boleslaw I 'the Brave' *King 1024–5*
1025–31	Mieszko II Lambert
1031–2	Bezprim
1032–4	Mieszko II (*restored*)
1034–58	Casimir I 'the Restorer'
1058–79	Boleslaw II 'the Bold' *King 1076–9*
1079–1102	Wladyslaw I Herman
1102–38	Boleslaw III 'the Wry-Mouthed'

Monarch – Prince of Little Poland and Krakow
House of Piast

1138–46	Wladyislaw II 'the Exile' (of Silesia)
1146–73	Boleslaw IV 'the Curly' *Prince of Mazovia from 1138*
1173–7	Mieszko III 'the Old' *Prince of Great Poland from 1138*
1177–94	Casimir II 'the Just'
1173–86	Leszek I Mazovia
1194–8	Leszek II 'the White' *Prince of Mazovia until 1202*
1198–1202	Mieszko III 'the Old' (*restored*)
1202–06	Wladyslaw III *Prince of Great Poland until 1231*
1206–27	Leszek II 'the White' (*restored*)
1227–79	Boleslaw V
1279–88	Leszek III *Prince of Kujavia from 1267*
1288–90	Henry *Prince of Silesia*

1290–1	Przemislaw *Prince of Great Poland 1270–96*
1291–1306	As Bohemia (*see* Czech Republic)
1306–20	Wladyslaw IV 'the Short' *Prince of Kujavia from 1267 and of Great Poland from 1314*

Monarch – King of Poland
House of Piast

1320–33	Wladyslaw IV 'the Short'
1333–70	Casimir III 'the Great'

House of Anjou

1370–82	Louis of Anjou *King Lajos I of Hungary*
1382–95	Jadwiga

House of Jagieo

1386–1434	Wladyslaw V Jagiello *Grand Duke Jogaila of Lithuania*
1434–44	Wladyslaw VI *King of Hungary from 1440*
1444–7	*No king*
1447–92	Casimir IV *Grand Duke of Lithuania from 1440*
1492–1501	John I Albert
1501–06	*As Lithuania*
1506–48	Sigismund I 'the Old'
1548–72	Sigismund II Augustus

Elected kings

1573–5	Henry (*Henri III of France*)
1575–86	Stefan (Stephen) Bathory
1587–1632	Sigismund III Vasa
1632–48	Wladyslaw VII (Ladislas IV)
1648–68	John II Casimir
1669–73	Michael Wisniowecki
1674–96	John III Sobieski
1697–1704	(Frederick-)Augustus II 'the Strong' (of Saxony)
1704–09	Stanislaw I (Stanislas) Leszczynski
1709–33	(Frederick-)Augustus II 'the Strong' (*restored*)
1733–63	(Frederick-)Augustus III (of Saxony)
1764–95	Stanislaw II (Stanislas Augustus) Poniatowski

Chief of State
Polish People's Republic

1945–7	Boleslaw Bierut *Acting*
1947–52	Boleslaw Bierut
1952–64	Aleksander Zawadzki
1964–8	Edward Ochab
1968–70	Marian Spychalski
1970–2	Józef Cyrankiewicz
1972–85	Henryk Jablonski
1985–9	Wojciech Jaruzelski

President
Polish Republic

1989–90	Wojciech Jaruzelski
1990–5	Lech Walesa
1995–	Alexander Kwasniewski

Premier

1947–52	Józef Cyrankiewicz
1952–4	Boleslaw Bierut
1954–70	Józef Cyrankiewicz
1970–80	Piotr Jaroszewicz
1980	Edward Babiuch
1980–1	Józef Pinkowski
1981–5	Wojciech Jaruzelski
1985–8	Zbigniew Messner
1988–9	Mieczyslaw Rakowski
1989	Czeslaw Kiszczak
1989–91	Tadeusz Mazowiecki
1991	Jan Krzysztof Bielecki
1991–2	Jan Olszewski
1992	Waldemar Pawlak
1992–3	Hanna Suchocka
1993–5	Waldemar Pawlak
1995–6	Jozef Oleksy
1996–7	Wlodzimierz Cimoszewicz
1997–	Jerzy Buzek

First Secretary

1945–8	Wladyslaw Gomulka
1948–56	Boleslaw Bierut
1956	Edward Ochab
1956–70	Wladyslaw Gomulka
1970–80	Edward Gierek
1980–1	Stanislaw Kania
1981–9	Wojciech Jaruzelski
1989–90	Mieczyslaw Rakowski

Portugal

Monarch – Kingdom of Portugal
House of Burgundy

1095–1112	Henrique (of Burgundy) *Count of Portugal*
1112–85	Afonso (Alfonso) I Henriques *King from 1139*
1185–1211	Sancho I
1211–23	Afonso II
1223–45	Sancho II
1245–79	Afonso III
1279–1325	Diniz (Denis)
1325–57	Afonso IV
1357–67	Pedro I
1367–83	Fernando (Ferdinand)
1383–5	*Disputed succession*

House of Aviz

1385–1433	João I
1433–8	Duarte
1438–81	Afonso (Alfonso) V 'el Africano' ('the African')
1481–95	João II
1495–1521	Manuel I
1521–57	João III
1557–78	Sebastião (Sebastian)
1578–80	Henrique
1580–1640	*Spanish rule*

House of Bragança

1640–56	João (John) IV
1656–83	Afonso VI
1683–1706	Pedro II
1706–50	João V
1750–77	José

1777–1816	Maria I *Joint ruler to 1786*
1777–86	Pedro III *Joint ruler*
1816–26	João VI
1826	Pedro IV (I of Brazil)
1826–8	Maria II
1828–34	Miguel
1834–53	Maria II (*restored*)
1853–61	Pedro V
1861–89	Luis
1889–1908	Carlos
1908–10	Manuel II

President
First Republic

1910–11	Theófilo Braga
1911–15	Manuel José de Arriaga
1915	Theófilo Braga
1915–17	Bernardino Machado
1917–18	Sidónio Pais
1918–19	João do Canto e Castro
1919–23	António José de Almeida
1923–5	Manuel Teixeira Gomes
1925–6	Bernardino Machado

New State

1926	Military junta (José Mendes Cabeçadas)
1926	Military junta (Manuel de Oliveira Gomes da Costa)
1926–51	António Oscar Fragoso Carmona
1951–8	Francisco Higino Craveiro Lopes
1958–74	Américo de Deus Tomás

Second Republic

1974	Military junta (António Spínola)
1974–6	Military junta (Francisco da Costa Gomes)

Third Republic

1976–86	António dos Santos Ramalho Eanes
1986–96	Mário Alberto Nobre Lopez Soares
1996–	Jorge Sampaio

Prime Minister

1834–5	Pedro de Sousa e Holstein, Duke of Palmela
1835	João Carlos, Duke of Saldanha, and A J Meneses Severim de Noronha, Duke of Terceira
1835	J M Cunha e Meneses, Count of Lumiares
1835–6	João Carlos, Duke of Saldanha
1836–7	Manuel da Silva Passos
1837–8	António Dias de Oliviera
1838–9	Bernardo de Sà Nogueira de Figueiredo
1839–41	José Lúcio Travassos Valdez, Count of Bonfim
1841–2	Joaquim António de Aguiar
1842–5	Duke of Terceira (António Bernardo da Costa Cabral

Secretary for the Interior)

1845	Pedro de Sousa e Holstein, Duke of Palmela
1845–7	João Carlos, Duke of Saldanha
1847	*Civil war*
1847–9	João Carlos, Duke of Saldanha
1849–51	António Bernardo da Costa Cabral
1851–6	João Carlos, Duke of Saldanha
1856–9	Nuno Rolim de Moura Barreto, Duke of Loulé
1859–60	João Carlos, Duke of Terceira
1860–5	Nuno Rolim de Moura Barreto, Duke of Loulé
1865–8	Joaquim António de Aguiar
1868	António José de Avila
1868–9	Bernardo de Sà Nogueira de Figueiredo, Marquis of Sà da Bandeira
1869–70	Nuno Rolim de Moura Barreto, Duke of Loulé, and Anselmo José Braamcamp
1870	João Carlos, Duke of Saldanha
1870–1	Bernardo de Sà Nogueira de Figueiredo, Marquis of Sà da Bandeira
1871	*Junta*
1871–7	António Maria de Fontes Pereira de Melo
1877	António José, Marquis of Avila
1877–9	António Maria de Fontes Pereira de Melo
1879–81	Anselmo José Braamcamp
1881–6	António Maria de Fontes Pereira de Melo
1886–90	José Luciano de Castro
1890	António de Serpa Pimemtel
1891–2	João Crisóstomo de Abreu e Sousa
1892–3	José Dias Ferreira
1893–7	Ernesto Rudolfo Hintze Ribeiro
1897–1900	José Luciano de Castro
1900–04	Ernesto Rudolfo Hintze Ribeiro
1906–8	João Franco
1908	Francisco Joaquim Ferreira do Amaral
1908	Campos Henriques
1909	Sebastião Teles
1909	Wenceslau de Lima
1909–10	Francisco da Veiga Beirao
1910	António Teixeira de Sousa
1910–11	Teófilo Braga *Provisional*
1911–2	João Pinheiro Chagas
1912–13	Duarte Leite
1913–4	Alfonso Costa
1914	Bernardino Machado
1914–15	V H de Azevedo Coutinho

1915	Pimenta de Castro
1915	João Pinheiro Chagas
1915–16	Alfonso Costa
1916	António José de Almeida
1916–17	Sidónio Pais
1917–18	Alfonso Costa
1918–9	João Tagmanini Barbosa
1919	José Relvas
1919	Domingos Pereira
1919–20	Sá Cardosa
1920	Fernandes Costa
1920	Domingos Pereira
1920	António Maria Baptista
1920	Ramos Preto
1920	António Granjo
1920	Alvaro de Castro
1920–21	Liberato Pinto
1921	Bernardino Machado
1921	Barros Queiroz
1921	António Granjo
1921	Maia Pinto
1921–2	António Maria da Silva
1922–3	Alvaro de Castro
1923	Ginestal Machado
1923–4	António Maria da Silva
1924	Rodrígues Gaspar
1924–5	José Domingues dos Santos
1925	Vitorino M Guimaraes
1925	António Maria da Silva
1925	Domingos Pereira
1925	António Maria da Silva
1926	*Junta* (José Mendes Cabeçadas)
1926	Gomes da Costa
1926–8	Oscar Carmona
1928–32	José Vicente de Freitas
1932–68	António de Oliveira Salazar
1968–74	Marcelo Caetano
1974	Adelino da Palma Carlos
1974–5	Vasco Gonçalves
1975–6	José Pinheiro de Azevedo
1976–8	Mário Alberto Nobre Lopez Soares
1978	Alfredo Nobre da Costa
1978–9	Carlos Alberto de Mota Pinto
1979	Maria de Lurdes Pintassilgo
1980–1	Francisco de Sá Carneiro
1981–3	Francisco Pinto Balsemao
1983–5	Mário Alberto Nobre Lopez Soares
1985–95	Aníbal Cavaço Silva
1995–	António Guterres

Qatar

Emir
Al–Thani Dynasty

1868–76	Muhammad bin Thani
1876–1905	Ahmad I
1905–13	Qasim
1913–49	Abdullah
1949–60	Ali
1960–72	Ahmad II ibn Ali
1972–95	Khalifah ibn Hamad
1995–	Hamad bin Khalifa

Prime Minister

1996–	Abdulla bin Khalifa

Romania

Monarch – Kingdom of Romania

1859–66	Alexandru Ioan Cuza *Prince*
1866–1914	Carol I
1914–27	Ferdinand I
1927–30	Mihai (Michael)
1930–40	Carol II
1940–7	Mihai (Michael – *restored*)

President

People's Socialist Republic of Romania

1947–8	Mihai Sadoveanu *Interim*
1948–52	Constantin I Parhon
1952–8	Petru Groza
1958–61	Ion Georghe Maurer
1961–5	Georghe Gheorghiu-Dej
1965–7	Chivu Stoica
1967–89	Nicolae Ceauşescu

Republic of Romania

1989–96	Ion Iliescu
1996–	Emil Constantinescu

Prime Minister

1862	Barbu Catargiu
1862–3	N Cretulescu
1863–5	M Kogalniceanu
1865	C Bosianu
1865–6	N Cretulescu
1866–7	Ion Ghica
1867–8	C A Cretulescu
1868–70	Dimitrie Ghica
1870–1	Ion Ghica
1871–6	Lascar Catargiu
1876	Em. Costache Epureanu
1876–83	Ion Bratianu
1883–91	Theodor Rosetti
1891–5	Lascar Catargiu
1895–6	Dimitrie A Sturdza
1896–7	Petre S Aurelian
1897–9	Dimitrie A Sturdza
1899–1900	Gheorghe Grigore Cantacuzino
1900–1	Petre P Carp
1901–6	Dimitrie A Sturdza
1906–7	Gheorge Grigore Cantacuzino
1907–9	Dimitrie A Sturdza
1909	Ion C Bratianu
1909–10	Mihai Pherekyde
1910–11	Ion C Brătianu
1911–12	Petre P Carp
1912–14	Titu Maiorescu
1914–18	Ion C Brătianu
1918	Alexandru Averescu
1918	Alexandru Marghiloman
1918	Constantin Coanda
1918	Ion C Brătianu
1919	Artur Vaitoianu
1919–20	Alexandru Vaida-Voevod
1920–1	Alexandru Averescu
1921–2	Take Ionescu
1922–6	Ion C Brătianu

1926–7	Alexandru Averescu
1927	Ion C Brătianu
1927–8	Vintila I C Bratiănu
1928–30	Juliu Maniu
1930	Gheorghe C Mironescu
1930	Juliu Maniu
1930–1	Gheorghe C Mironescu
1931–2	Nicolae Iorga
1932	Alexandru Vaida-Voevod
1932–3	Juliu Maniu
1933	Alexandru Vaida-Voevod
1933	Ion G Duca
1933–4	Constantin Angelescu
1934–7	Gheorghe Tătărescu
1937	Octavian Goga
1937–9	Miron Cristea
1939	Armand Călinescu
1939	Gheorghe Argesanu
1939	Constantine Argetoianu
1939–40	Gheorghe Tătărescu
1940	Ion Gigurtu
1940–4	Ion Antonescu
1944	Constantin Sănătescu
1944–5	Nicolas Rădescu
1945–52	Petru Groza
1952–5	Gheorghe Gheorghiu-Dej
1955–61	Chivu Stoica
1961–74	Ion Gheorghe Maurer
1974–80	Manea Mănescu
1980–3	Ilie Verdet
1983–9	Constantin Dăscălescu
1989–91	Petre Roman
1991–2	Theodor Stolojan
1992–6	Nicolae Vacaroiu
1996–	Victor Ciorbea

General Secretary

1955–65	Georghe Gheorghiu-Dej
1965–89	Nicolae Ceauşescu

Rome

King of Rome

753–716BC	Romulus
716–672BC	Numa Pompilius
672–640BC	Tullus Hostilius
640–616BC	Ancus Marcius
616–578BC	Lucius Tarquinius Priscus
578–534BC	Servius Tullius
534–509	Lucius Tarquinius Superbus
509–30BC	*Republic*

Emperor

30BC–14AD	Augustus (Gaius Julius Caesar Octavianus)
14–37	Tiberius (Tiberius Julius Caesar Augustus)
37–41	Caligula (Gaius Julius Caesar Germanicus)
41–54	Claudius I (Tiberius Claudius Nero Germanicus)
54–68	Nero (Lucius Domitius Ahenobarbus)
68–9	(Servius Sulcipius) Galba

69	(Marcus Salvius) Otho
69	(Aulus) Vitellius
69–79	Vespasian (Titus Flavius Vespasianus)
79–81	Titus (Flavius Sabinus Vespasianus)
81–96	Domitian (Titus Flavius Domitianus)
96–98	(Marcus Cocceius) Nerva
98–117	Trajan (Marcus Ulpius Trajanus)
117–38	Hadrian (Publius Aelius Hadrianus)
138–61	(Titus Aurelius Fulvus) Antoninus Pius
161–80	Aurelius (Marcus Aurelius Verus)
161–9	(Lucius Aurelius) Verus *Joint Emperor*
180–92	(Marcus Aurelius Antoninus) Commodus
193	(Publius Helvius) Pertinax
193	(Marcus) Didius Julianus
193–211	(Lucius Septimius) Severus
193–4	Gaius Pescennius Niger *Rival Emperor*
193–7	Decimus Clodius Albinus *Rival Emperor*
211–17	(Marcus Aurelius Antoninus) Caracalla
211–12	Publius Septimius Antoninus Geta *Joint Emperor*
217–18	(Marcus Opellius) Macrinus
218–22	Heliogabalus (Varius Avitus Bassianus)
222–35	(Marcus Aurelius) Alexander Severus
235–8	(Gaius Julius) Maximinus
238	Gordian I (Marcus Antonius Gordianus)
238	Gordian II (Marcus Antonius Gordianus) *Joint Emperor*
238	(Marcus Clodius) Pupienus
238	(Decimus Caelius) Balbinus
238–44	Gordian III (Marcus Antonius Gordianus Pius)
244–9	Philip the Arab (Marcus Julius Philippus Arabs)
249–51	(Gaius Messius Quintus Trajanus) Decius
251–3	(Gaius Vibius Trebonianus) Gallus *Joint Emperor*
251–3	(Gaius Vibius) Volusianus *Joint Emperor*
253	(Marcus Aemilius) Aemilianus
253–60	Valerian (Publius Licinius Valerianus) *Joint Emperor*
253–68	(Publius Licinius) Gallienus *Joint Emperor*
260–9	(Marcus Latinius) Postumus *Emperor in Gaul*
260–1	(Titus Fulvius) Macrianus *Rival Emperor*

260–1	Titus Fulvius Quietus *Rival Emperor*
268–70	(Marcus Aurelius) Claudius II Gothicus
269	Lucius Aelianus *Emperor in Gaul*
269	Marcus Aurelius Marius *Emperor in Gaul*
269–70	(Marcus Piavonius) Victorinus *Emperor in Gaul*
270	(Marcus Aurelius) Quintillus
270–5	Aurelian (Lucius Domitius Aurelianus)
270–4	(Gaius Pius) Tetricus I *Emperor in Gaul*
274	(Gaius Pius) Tetricus II *Emperor in Gaul*
275–6	(Marcus Claudius) Tacitus
276	(Marcus Annius) Florianus
276–82	(Marcus Aurelius) Probus
282–3	(Marcus Aurelius) Carus
283–5	(Marcus Aurelius) Carinus *Joint Emperor until 284*
283–4	(Marcus Aurelius) Numerianus *Joint Emperor*
284–305	Diocletian (Gaius Aurelius Diocletianus) *Joint Emperor (East)*
286–305	Maximian (Marcus Aurelius Maximianus) *Joint Emperor (West)*
286–93	(Marcus Aurelius) Carausius *Emperor in Britain*
293–96	Allectus *Emperor in Britain*
305–06	(Marcus Flavius) Constantius Chlorus *Joint Emperor (West)*
305–11	(Gaius) Galerius (Valerius Maximianus) *Joint Emperor (East)*
306–08	Maximian (Marcus Aurelius Maximianus) *(restored as Rival Emperor – West)*
306–12	(Marcus Aurelius) Maxentius *Rival Emperor (West)*
306–37	Constantine I 'the Great' (Flavius Valerius Aurelius Constantinus) *Joint Emperor (West) until 324*
307–24	(Gaius Flavius Valerius) Licinius *Joint Emperor (East)*
308–13	(Galerius Valerius) Maximianus Daia *Joint Emperor (East)*
337–40	Constantine II (Flavius Valerius Claudius Constantinus) *Joint Emperor*
337–50	(Flavius Valerius Julius) Constans I *Joint Emperor (West)*
337–61	(Flavius Valerius Julius) Constantius II *Joint Emperor (East) until 350 and from 360*
350–3	(Flavius Magnus) Magnentius *Rival Emperor*

360–3	Julian 'the Apostate' (Flavius Claudius Julianus) *Joint Emperor until 361*
363–4	Jovian (Flavius Claudius Jovianus)
364–75	Valentinian I (Flavius Valentinianus) *Joint Emperor (West)*
364–78	(Flavius) Valens *Joint Emperor (East)*
367–83	Gratian (Augustus Gratianus) *Joint Emperor (West)*
375–92	Valentinian II (Flavius Valentinianus) *Joint Emperor (West)*
379–95	(Flavius) Theodosius I 'the Great' *Joint Emperor (East)*
383–8	Magnus (Clemens) Maximus *Joint Emperor (West)*
392–4	Eugenius *Joint Emperor (West)*

Western Empire

395–423	(Flavius) Honorius
407–11	Constantine III (Flavius Claudius Constantinus) *Joint Emperor*
421	(Flavius) Constantius III *Joint Emperor*
423–5	Johannes
425–55	Valentinian III (Flavius Placidius Valentinianus)
455	(Flavius Ancius) Petronius Maximus
455–6	(Flavius Maecilius Eparchius) Avitus
457–61	(Julius Valerius) Majorianus
461–5	(Libius Severianus) Severus
467–72	(Procopius) Anthemius
472	(Anicius) Olybrius
473–4	(Flavius) Glycerius
474–5	Julius Nepos
475–6	(Flavius Momyllus) Romulus Augustulus

Russia

Grand Duke of Moscow
House of Riurik

1283–1303	Daniel
1303–25	Yuri
1325–41	Ivan I Kalita
1341–53	Semeon
1353–9	Ivan II
1359–89	Dmitri I Donskoy
1389–1425	Vasily I
1425–62	Vasily II
1462–1472	Ivan III 'the Great'

Ruler of all Russia
House of Riurik

1472–1505	Ivan III 'the Great'
1505–33	Vasily III
1533–47	Ivan IV 'the Terrible'

Tsar of Russia
House of Riurik

1547–84	Ivan IV 'the Terrible'

1584–98	Fedor I
1598–1605	Boris Godunov
1605	Fedor II
1605–06	Dmitri II (the 'false Dmitri')
1606–10	Vasily IV Shuisky
1610–13	*Civil war*

House of Romanov

1613–45	Mikhail (Michael Romanov)
1645–76	Alexei I Mihailovitch
1676–82	Fedor III
1682–1725	Peter I 'the Great' *Joint ruler to 1696*
1682–96	Ivan V *Joint ruler*
1725–7	Catherine I
1727–30	Peter II
1730–40	Anna Ivanovna
1740–1	Ivan VI
1741–62	Elizabeth Petrovna
1762	Peter III
1762–96	Catherine II 'the Great'
1796–1801	Paul
1801–25	Alexander I
1825–55	Nicholas I
1855–81	Alexander II 'the Liberator'
1881–94	Alexander III
1894–1917	Nicholas II

President

1917	Lev Borisovich Kamenev
1917–19	Yakov Mikhailovich Sverlov
1919–46	Mikhail Ivanovich Kalinin
1946–53	Nikolai Mikhailovich Shvernik
1953–60	Klimenti Efremovich Voroshilov
1960–4	Leonid Ilyich Brezhnev
1964–5	Anastas Ivanovich Mikoyan
1965–77	Nikolai Viktorovich Podgorny
1977–82	Leonid Ilyich Brezhnev
1982–3	Vasily Vasiliyevich Kuznetsov *Acting*
1983–4	Yuri Vladimirovich Andropov
1984	Vasily Vasiliyevich Kuznetsov *Acting*
1984–5	Konstantin Ustinovich Chernenko
1985	Vasily Vasiliyevich Kuznetsov *Acting*
1985–8	Andrei Andreyevich Gromyko
1988–90	Mikhail Sergeyevich Gorbachev

Executive President

1990–1	Mikhail Sergeevich Gorbachev

Chairman (Prime Minister)
Council of Ministers

1905–6	Sergey Júlyevich Witte
1906	Ivan Logginovich Goremykin
1906–11	Pyotr Arkadyevich Stolypin

1911–4	Vladimir Nikolaevich Kokovtsov
1914–6	Ivan Logginovich Goremykin
1916	Boris Vladimirovich Stürmer
1916	Alexsandr Fedorovich Trepov
1916–7	Nikolai Dmitrievich Golitsyn
1917	Georgi Evgenievich Lvov
1917	Alexander Feodorovich Kerensky

Council of People's Commissars

1917–24	Vladimir Ilyich Lenin
1924–30	Aleksei Ivanovich Rykov
1930–41	Vyacheslav Mikhailovich Molotov
1941–53	Josef Stalin

Council of Ministers

1953–5	Georgi Maksemilianovich Malenkov
1955–8	Nikolai Bulganin
1958–64	Nikita Sergeyevich Khrushchev
1964–80	Alexei Nikolayevich Kosygin
1980–5	Nikolai Aleksandrovich Tikhonov
1985–90	Nikolai Ivanovich Ryzhkov
1990–1	Yury Dmitrievich Maslyukov *Acting*
1991	Valentin Pavlov

General Secretary

1922–53	Josef Stalin
1953	Georgi Maksemilianovich Malenkov
1953–64	Nikita Sergeyevich Khrushchev
1964–82	Leonid Ilyich Brezhnev
1982–4	Yuri Vladimirovich Andropov
1984–5	Konstantin Ustinovich Chernenko
1985–91	Mikhail Sergeevich Gorbachev

Russian Federation
President

1991–	Boris Yeltsin

Prime Minister

1991–2	Yegor Gaidar (*Acting*)
1992–	Victor Chernomyrdin

Rwanda

Monarch – Mwami (King)

c.1350–c.1386	Ndahiro I Ruyange
c.1386–c.1410	Ndoba
c.1410–c.1434	Samembe
c.1434–c.1458	Nsoro Samukondo
c.1458–c.1482	Ruganza I Bwimba
c.1482–c.1506	Cyilima I Rugwe
c.1506–c.1528	Kigeri I Mukobanya
c.1528–c.1552	Mibambwe I Mutabaazi

c.1552–c.1576	Yuhi I Gahima
c.1576–c.1600	Ndahiro II Cyaamatare
c.1600–c.1624	Ruganza II Ndoori
c.1624–c.1648	Mutara I Seemugeshi
c.1648–c.1672	Kigeri II Nyamuheshera
c.1672–c.1696	Mibambwe II Gisanura
c.1696–c.1720	Yuhi II Mazimpaka
c.1720–c.1744	Karemeera Rwaaka
c.1744–c.1768	Cyilima II Rujugira
c.1768–c.1792	Kigeri III Ndabarasa
c.1792–c.1797	Mibambwe III Seentaabyo
c.1797–c.1830	Yuhi III Gahindro
c.1830–53	Mutara II Rwoogera
1853–95	Kigeri IV Rwabugiri
1895–6	Mibambwe IV Rutulindwa
1896–1931	Yuhi IV Musinga
1931–59	Mutara III Rudahigwa
1959–61	Kigeri V Ndahundirwa

President

1962–73	Grégoire Kayibanda
1973–4	Juvénal Habyarimana
1994–5	Theodore Sindikubwabo (*interim*)
1995–	Pasteur Bizimunga

Prime Minister

1991–2	Sylvestre Nsanzimana
1992–4	Dismas Nsengiyaremye
1994–5	Jean Kambanda (*Acting*)
1995–	Pierre-Celestin Rwigyema

Saint Christopher and Nevis

Chief of State: British monarch, represented by Governor-General

Prime Minister

1983–95	Kennedy Alphonse Simmonds
1995–	Denzil Douglas

Saint Lucia

Chief of State: British monarch, represented by Governor-General

Prime Minister

1979	John George Melvin Compton
1979–81	Allan Louisy
1981–3	Winston Francis Cenac
1983–96	John George Melvin Compton
1996–7	Vaughan Lewis
1997–	Kenny Anthony

Saint Vincent and the Grenadines

Chief of State: British monarch, represented by Governor-General

Prime Minister

1979–84	Milton Cato
1984–	James FitzAllen Mitchell

Samoa
(formerly **Western Samoa**)

Head of State

1962–3	Tupua Tamesehe Mea'ole *and* Mallietoa Tanumafili II *Joint Presidents*
1963–	Mallietoa Tanumafili II

Prime Minister

1962–70	Fiame Mata'afa Faumuina Mulinu'u II
1970–6	Tupua Tamasese Leolofi IV
1976–82	Tupuola Taisi Efi
1982	Va'ai Kolone
1982	Tupuola Taisi Efi
1982–6	Tofilau Eti
1986–8	Va'ai Kolone
1988–	Tofilau Eti Alesana

San Marino

Secretary of State

1986–	Gabriele Gatti

Sao Tomé and Príncipe

President

1975–91	Manuel Pinto da Costa
1991–	Miguel Trovoada

Prime Minister

1991–2	Daniel Lima dos Santos Daio
1992–4	Norberto José d'Alva Costa Alegre
1994	Evaristo do Espirito Santo Carvalho
1994–5	Carlos da Graça
1995–6	Armindo Vaz d'Almeida
1996–	Raul Bragança Neto

Saudi Arabia

Sharif of Mecca

967–80	Abu-Muhammad Jafar ibn Muhammad
980–94	Isa ibn Jafar
994–1010	Abul-Futuh Hasan
1010–12	Abul-Tayyib Daud
1012–39	Abul-Futuh Hasan (*restored*)
1039–61	Muhammad Shukr ibn Hasan
1061–9	Hamza ibn Wahhas
1069–94	Abu-Hashim Muhammad ibn Jafar
1094–1123	Abu-Fulaita al-Qasim
1123–33	Fulaita ibn al-Qasim
1133–54	Hashim ibn Fulaita
1154–61	al-Qasim ibn Hashim
1161–74	Isa ibn Fulaita
1174–5	Daud ibn Isa
1175–6	Mukaththir ibn Isa
1176–89	Daud ibn Isa (*restored*)
1189–94	Mukaththir ibn Isa (*restored*)
1194–1201	al-Mansur ibn Daud
1201–20	Abu-Aziz Qatada ibn Idris
1220–32	Hasan ibn Qatada

1232–41	Rajih ibn Qatada
1241–54	Abu-Sa d Ali ibn Qatada
1254–70	Idris ibn Qatada
1254–1301	Abu-Numay Muhammad ibn Ali
1301–46	Rumaitha ibn Abi-Numay
1303–18	Humaida ibn Abi-Numay
1346–75	Ajlan ibn Rumaitha
1361–86	Shihab-ud-Din Ahmad ibn Ajlan
1386–7	Inan ibn Mughamis
1387–95	Ali ibn Ajlan
1392–6	Muhammad ibn Ajlan
1396–1426	Hasan ibn Ajlan
1407–55	Barakat ibn Hasan
1455–97	Muhammad ibn Barakat
1497–1525	Barakat ibn Muhammad
1504–12	Qait Bay ibn Muhammad
1512–66	Abu-Numay Muhammad ibn Barakat
1539–54	Ahmad ibn Muhammad
1554–1602	Hasan ibn Muhammad
1603–24	Idris ibn Hasan
1603–29	Muhsin ibn Husain
1629–30	Masud ibn Idris
1630–1	Abdullah ibn Hasan
1631–66	Zaid ibn Muhsin
1666–72	Said ibn Zaid
1672–82	Barakat ibn Muhammad
1682–4	Said ibn Barakat
1684–8	Ahmad ibn Zaid
1688–90	Ahmad ibn Ghalib
1690–1	Muhsin ibn Husain
1691–2	Said ibn Said
1692–4	Said ibn Zaid (restored)
1694–5	Abdullah ibn Hashim
1695–1702	Said ibn Zaid (restored)
1702–04	Said ibn Said (restored)
1704–12	Abdul-Karim ibn Muhammad
1712–16	Said ibn Said (restored)
1716–18	Abdullah ibn Said
1718–20	Yahya ibn Barakat
1720–22	Mubarak ibn Ahmad
1722–30	Civil war
1730–2	Muhammad ibn Abdullah
1732–3	Masud ibn Said
1733–4	Muhammad ibn Abdullah (restored)
1734–52	Masud ibn Said (restored)
1752–70	Masaid ibn Said
1770–3	Ahmad ibn Said
1773–88	Surur ibn Masaid
1788–1813	Ghalib ibn Masaid
1813–27	Yahya ibn Surur
1827–51	Muhammad ibn Abdul-Muin
1851–6	Abdul-Muttalib ibn Ghalib
1856–8	Muhammad ibn Abdul-Muin (restored)
1858–77	Abdullah ibn Muhammad
1877–80	Husain ibn Muhammad

1880–2	Abdul-Muttalib ibn Ghalib (restored)
1882–1905	Aun ar-Rafiq ibn Muhammad
1905–08	Abi ibn Abdullah
1908–16	Husain (Hussein) ibn Ali

Amir of Najd
Al-Saud dynasty

c.1720–6	Saud I
1726–65	Muhammad
1765–1803	Abdul-Aziz I
1803–14	Saud II
1814–18	Abdullah I
1818–23	*Egyptian rule*
1823–34	Turki
1834–7	Faisal I
1837–41	Khalid I
1841–3	Abdullah II
1843–65	Faisal I (restored)
1865–71	Abdullah III
1871	Saud III
1871–3	Abdullah III (restored)
1873–6	Saud III (restored)
1876–89	Abdullah III (restored)
1889–1901	Abdul-Rahman
1901–27	Abdul-Aziz (Abdulaziz) ibn Abdur-Rahmanibn Saud

Monarch – Kingdom of the Hijaz
Sharifs of Mecca

1916–24	Husain (Hussein) ibn Ali *Sharif of Mecca from 1908*
1924–5	Ali ibn Husain

Al-Saud dynasty

1925–32	Abdul-Aziz (Abdulaziz) ibn Abdur-Rahman ibn Saud

Monarch –Kingdom of Saudi Arabia
Al-Saud dynasty

1932–53	Abdul-Aziz (Abdulaziz) ibn Abdur-Rahman ibn Saud
1953–64	Saud IV ibn Abdul-Aziz
1964–75	Faisal II ibn Abdul-Aziz
1975–82	Khalid (II) ibn Abdul-Aziz
1982–96	Fahd ibn Abdul-Aziz
1996	Abdullah ibn Abdul-Aziz *Acting*
1996–	Fahd ibn Abdul-Aziz

Senegal

President

1960–80	Léopold Sédar Senghor
1981–	Abdou Diouf

Prime Minister

1991–	Habib Thiam

Seychelles

President

1976–7	James R Mancham
1977–	France-Albert René

Sierra Leone

President

1971	Christopher Okero Cole
1971–85	Siaka Probin Stevens
1985–92	Joseph Saidu Momoh

Chairman

1992–6	Valentine Strasser
1996–	*Military rule*

President

1996–7	Ahmad Tejan Kabbah
1997–	Johnny Paul Koroma

Prime Minister

1961–4	Milton Margai
1964–7	Albert Michael Margai
1967	Siaka Probin Stevens
1967	David Lansana
1967	Ambrose Genda
1967–8	*National Reformation Council* (Andrew Saxon-Smith)
1968	John Bangura
1968–71	Siaka Probin Stevens
1971–5	Sorie Ibrahim Koroma
1975–8	Christian Alusine Kamara Taylor
1978–	*No Prime Minister*

Singapore

President (Yang di-Pertuan Negara)

1959–70	Yusof bin Ishak
1970–81	Benjamin Henry Sheares
1981–5	Chengara Veetil Devan Nair
1985–93	Wee Kim Wee
1993–	Ong Teng Cheong

Prime Minister

1959–90	Lee Kuan Yew
1990–	Goh Chok Tong

Slovakia

President

1993–	Michal Kovac

Prime Minister

1993–4	Vladimir Meciar
1994–7	Jozef Moravcik
1997–	Vladimir Meciar

Slovenia

President

1991–	Milan Kučan

Prime Minister

1991–2	Lojze Peterle
1992–	Janez Drnovšek

Solomon Islands

Chief of State: British monarch,
represented by Governor-General

Prime Minister

1978–82	Peter (Kauona Keninarais'ona) Kenilorea
1982–4	Solomon Mamaloni
1984–6	Peter (Kauona Keninarais'ona) Kenilorea
1986–9	Ezekiel Alebua
1989–93	Solomon Mamaloni
1993–4	Francis Billy Hilly
1994–7	Solomon Mamaloni
1997–	Batholomew Ulufa'alu

Somalia

President

1961–7	Aden Abdallah Osman
1967–9	Abdirashid Ali Shermarke

Supreme Revolutionary Council

1969–80	Mohammed Siad Barre

Republic

1980–91	Mohammed Siad Barre
1991–	Ali Mahdi Mohammed

Prime Minister

1961–4	Abdirashid Ali Shermarke
1964–7	Abdirizak Haji Hussein
1967–9	Mohammed Haji Ibrahim Egal
1987–90	Mohammed Ali Samater
1990–1	Mohammed Hawadie Madar
1991–	Umar Arteh Ghalib

South Africa

Governor-General

1910–14	Herbert John, 1st Viscount Gladstone
1914–20	Sydney, Earl Buxton
1920–4	Arthur, Duke of Connaught
1924–31	Alexander, Earl of Athlone
1931–7	George Herbert Hyde Villiers
1937–43	Patrick Duncan
1943–5	Nicolaas Jacobus de Wet
1945–51	Gideon Brand Van Zyl
1951–9	Ernest George Jansen
1959	Lucas Cornelius Steyn
1959–61	Charles Robberts Swart

Republic
President

1961–7	Charles Robberts Swart
1967	Theophilus Ebenhaezer Dönges
1967–8	Jozua François Nandé
1968–75	Jacobus Johannes Fouché
1975–8	Nicolaas Diederichs
1978–9	Balthazar Johannes Vorster
1979–84	Marais Viljoen
1984–9	Pieter Willem ('P W') Botha
1989–94	Frederik Willem de Klerk
1994–	Nelson Mandela

Prime Minister

1910–19	Louis Botha *SAf*
1919–24	Jan Christiaan Smuts *SAf*
1924–39	James Barry Munnick Hertzog *Nat*
1939–48	Jan Christiaan Smuts *Un*
1948–54	Daniel François Malan *Nat*
1954–8	Johannes Gerardus Strijdom *Nat*
1958–66	Hendrik Frensch Verwoerd *Nat*
1966–78	Balthazar Johannes Vorster *Nat*
1978–84	Pieter Willem ('P W') Botha *Nat*
1984–	*No Prime Minister*

Nat National; *SAf* South African Party;
Un United

King of the Zulu

c.1781– 1816	Senzangakhona
1816–28	Shaka
1828–40	Dingane (Dingaan)
1840–72	Mpande
1872–9	Cetewayo

Spain

Monarch – Kingdom of Navarre

c.810–c.851	Iñigo Arista
c.851–c.880	Garcia Iñiguez
c.880–905	Fortun Garces
905–26	Sancho I
926–70	Garcia II
970–94	Sancho II
994–1000	Garcia III
1000–35	Sancho III 'the Great'

Monarch – Kingdom of Castile-Leon

1035–65	Fernando (Ferdinand) I *King of Castile; King of Leon from 1037*
1065–72	Sancho II *King of Castile*
1065–1109	Alfonso VI *King of Leon; King of Castile from 1072*
1109–26	Urraca
1126–57	Alfonso VII
1157–88	Fernando (Ferdinand) II *King of Leon*
1188–1230	Alfonso IX *King of Leon*
1157–8	Sancho III *King of Castile*
1158–1214	Alfonso VIII *King of Castile*
1214–17	Enrique I *King of Castile*
1217–52	Fernando (Ferdinand) III *King of Castile; King of Leon from 1230*
1252–84	Alfonso X 'the Astronomer' *Holy Roman Emperor from 1257*
1284–95	Sancho IV
1295–1312	Fernando (Ferdinand) IV
1312–50	Alfonso XI
1350–66	Pedro 'the Cruel'
1366–7	Enrique II (of Trestamara)
1367–9	Pedro 'the Cruel' *(restored)*

1369–79	Enrique II (of Trestamara) *(restored)*
1379–90	Juan I
1390–1406	Enrique III
1406–54	Juan II
1454–74	Enrique IV
1474–1504	Isabel (Isabella) I of Castile
1504–16	Juana 'the Mad' (King Fernando II of Aragón Regent)
1504–06	Felipe (Philip) I 'the Handsome' *Joint ruler*

Monarch – Kingdom of Aragón

1035–63	Ramiro I
1063–94	Sancho
1094–1104	Pedro I
1104–34	Alfonso I 'the Battler'
1134–7	Ramiro II
1137–62	Petronila
1162–96	Alfonso II
1196–1213	Pedro II
1213–76	Jaime I 'the Conqueror'
1276–85	Pedro III *King of Sicily from 1282*
1285–91	Alfonso III
1291–1327	Jaime II *King of Sicily from 1285*
1327–36	Alfonso IV
1336–87	Pedro IV
1387–95	Juan I
1385–1410	Martín I *King of Sicily from 1409*
1410–12	*Disputed succession*
1412–16	Fernando (Ferdinand) I
1416–58	Alfonso V 'the Magnanimous'
1458–79	Juan II
1479–1516	Fernando (Ferdinand) II 'the Catholic' *Fernando V of Castile from 1506*

Monarch – Kingdom of Spain

House of Habsburg

1516–56	Carlos I (Charles V, *Holy Roman Emperor*)
1556–98	Felipe (Philip) II
1598–1621	Felipe (Philip) III
1621–65	Felipe (Philip) IV
1665–1700	Carlos (Charles) II

House of Bourbon

1700–24	Felipe (Philip) V
1724	Luis
1724–46	Felipe (Philip) V *(restored)*
1746–59	Fernando (Ferdinand) VI
1759–88	Carlos (Charles) III
1788–1808	Carlos (Charles) IV
1808	Fernando (Ferdinand) VII

House of Bonaparte

1808–14	José (Joseph Bonaparte)

House of Bourbon (restored)

1814–33	Fernando (Ferdinand) VII *(restored)*
1833–68	Isabel (Isabella) II

Regent
First Republic
1868–70   Antonio Cánovas del
           Castillo

Monarch – Kingdom of Spain
House of Savoy
1870–73   Amadeo I

House of Bourbon (restored)
1874–85   Alfonso XII
1886–1931 Alfonso XIII

President
Second Republic
1931–6   Niceto Alcalá Zamora y
           Torres
1936   Diego Martínez Barrio
           Acting

Civil War
1936–9   Manuel Azaña y Díez
1936–9   Miguel Cabanellas Ferrer

Chief of State
Nationalist Government
1936–75   Francisco Franco
           Bahamonde

Monarch – Kingdom of Spain
House of Bourbon (restored)
1975–   Juan Carlos I

Prime Minister
1834–6   Francisco de Paula de
           Martínez de la Rosa
1836   Juan Alvarez Mendizábal
1836   Francisco Javier Istúriz
1836–7   José Maria Calatrava
1837–8   Narciso de Heredia, Count
           of Ofalia
1838   Bernardino Fernández de
           Velasco, Duke of Frías
1838–40   Evaristo Pérez de Castro
1840   Mauricio Carlos de Onis
           Antonio González y
           González
1840–1   Modesto Cartazar
1841–2   Antonio González y
           González
1842–3   José Ramón Rodil
1843   Joaquín Maria López
1843   Alvaro Gómez Becerra
1843   Salustiano de Olózaga
1843–4   Luis González Brabo
1844–6   Ramón María Narváez
1846   Manuel Pando Fernández
           de Pineda, Marquis of
           Miraflores
1846   Ramón María Narváez
1846–7   Francisco Javier Istúriz
1847   Carlos Martínez de Irujo,
           Duke of Sotomayor
1847   Joaquín Francisco Pachero
           y Gutíerrez Calderón
1847   Florencio García Goyena
1847–9   Ramón María Narváez

1849   Serafín María de Soto,
           Count of Cleonard
1849–50   Ramón María Narváez
1850–2   Juan Bravo Murillo
1852–3   Federico Roncali
1853   Francisco de Lersundi
1853–4   José Luis Sartorius
1854   Angel de Saavedra y
           Ramírez de Baquedano,
           Duke of Rivas
1854–6   Baldomero Espartero
           Leopoldo O'Donnell
1856   Leopoldo O'Donnell
1856–8   Ramón María Narváez
1858–63   Francisco Javier Istúriz
           Leopoldo O'Donnell
1863–4   Manuel Pando Fernández
           de Pineda, Marquis of
           Miraflores
1864   Lorenzo Arrazola
1864   Alejandro Mon
1864–5   Ramón María Narváez
1865–6   Leopoldo O'Donnell
1866–8   Ramón María Narváez
1868   Luis González Brabo
1868–9   Juan Prim y Prats
           Antonio Cánovas del
           Castillo
1869–70   Juan Prim y Prats
1870–1   Juan Bautista Topete y
           Carballo
1871   Francisco Serrano y
           Dóminguez
1871   Manuel Ruiz Zorrilla
1871   José Malcamo y Monge
1871–2   Práxedes Mateo Sagasta
1872   Francisco Serrano y
           Dóminguez
1872–4   Manuel Ruiz Zorrilla
1874   Juan de Zabala y de la
           Puente
1874   Práxedes Mateo Sagasta
1874–5   Antonio Cánovas del
           Castillo
1875   Joaquín Jovellar
1875–9   Antonio Cánovas del
           Castillo
1879   Arsenio Martínez Campos
1879–81   Antonio Cánovas del
           Castillo
1881–3   Práxedes Mateo Sagasta
1883–4   José Posada Herrera
1884–5   Antonio Cánovas del
           Castillo
1885–90   Práxedes Mateo Sagasta
1890–2   Antonio Cánovas del
           Castillo
1892–5   Práxedes Mateo Sagasta
1895–7   Antonio Cánovas del
           Castillo
1897   Marcelo de Azcárraga y
           Palmero
1897–9   Práxedes Mateo Sagasta
1899–1900 Francisco Silvera y Le-
           Vielleuze

1900–1   Marcelo de Azcárraga y
           Palmero
1901–2   Práxedes Mateo Sagasta
1902–3   Francisco Silvela y Le-
           Vielleuze
1903   Raimundo Fernández
           Villaverde
1903–4   Antonio Maura y Montaner
1904–5   Marcelo de Azcárraga y
           Palmero
1905   Raimundo Fernández
           Villaverde
1905   Eugenio Montero Ríos
1905–6   Segismundo Moret y
           Prendergast
1906   José López Domínguez
1906   Segismundo Moret y
           Prendergast
1906–7   Antonio Aguilar y Correa
1907–9   Antonio Maura y Montaner
1909–10   Segismundo Moret y
           Prendergast
1910–12   José Canalejas y Méndez
1912   Alvaro Figueroa y Torres
1912–13   Manuel García Prieto
1913–15   Eduardo Dato y Iradier
1915–17   Alvaro Figueroa y Torres
1917   Manuel García Prieto
1917   Eduardo Dato y Iradier
1917–18   Manuel García Prieto
1918   Antonio Maura y Montaner
1918   Manuel García Prieto
1918–19   Alvaro Figueroa y Torres
1919   Antonio Maura y Montaner
1919   Joaquín Sánchez de Toca
1919–20   Manuel Allendesalazar
1920–1   Eduardo Dato y Iradier
1921   Gabino Bugallal Araujo
           Acting
1921   Manuel Allendesalazar
1921–2   Antonio Maura y Montaner
1922   José Sánchez Guerra y
           Martínez
1922–3   Manuel García Prieto
1923–30   Miguel Primo de Rivera y
           Oraneja, Marqués de
           Estella
1930–1   Dámaso Berenguer y Fusté
1931   Juan Bautista Aznar-
           Cabañas
1931   Niceto Alcalá Zamora y
           Torres
1931–3   Manuel Azaña y Díez
1933   Alejandro Lerroux y García
1933   Diego Martínez Barrio
1933–4   Alejandro Lerroux y García
1934   Ricardo Samper Ibáñez
1934–5   Alejandro Lerroux y García
1935   Joaquín Chapaprieta y
           Terragosa
1935–6   Manuel Portela Valladares
1936   Manuel Azaña y Díez
1936   Santiago Casares Quiroga
1936   Diego Martínez Barrio
1936   José Giral y Pereyra

1936–7	Francisco Largo Caballero
1937–9	Juan Negrín

Chairman of the Council of Ministers

1939–73	Francisco Franco Bahamonde

Prime Minister

1973	Torcuato Fernández Miranda y Hevía *Acting*
1973–6	Carlos Arias Navarro
1976–81	Adolfo Suárez
1981–2	Calvo Sotelo
1982–96	Felipe González Márquez
1996–	José Maria Aznar

Sri Lanka

King of Kandy

1591–1604	Vimala Dharma Surya I
1604–35	Senarat
1635–87	Rajasinha
1687–1707	Vimala Dharma Surya II
1707–39	Narendra Sinha
1739–47	Sri Vijaya Rajasinha
1747–82	Kirti Sri Rajasinha
1782–98	Rajadhi Rajasinha
1798–1815	Sri Vikrama Rajasinha
1815–1972	*British rule*

President

1972–8	William Gopallawa
1978–89	Junius Richard Jayawardene
1989–93	Ranasinghe Premadasa
1993–4	Dingiri Banda Wijetunga
1994–	Chandrika Bandaranaike Kumaratunga

Prime Minister

1947–52	Don Stephen Senanayake
1952–3	Dudley Shelton Senanayake
1953–6	John Lionel Kotelaweta
1956–9	Solomon West Ridgway Dias Bandaranaike
1960	Dudley Shelton Senanayake
1960–5	Sirimavo Ratwatte Dias Bandaranaike
1965–70	Dudley Shelton Senanayake
1970–7	Sirimavo Ratwatte Dias Bandaranaike
1977–89	Ranasinghe Premadasa
1989–93	Dingiri Banda Wijetunga
1993–4	Ranil Wickremasinghe
1994	Chandrika Bandaranaike Kumaratunga
1994–	Sirimavo RD Bandaranaike

The Sudan

Darfur
Kayra Dynasty

c.1640–	
c.1670	Sulayman Solong

c.1670–82	Musa
1682–1722	Ahmad Bakr
1722–32	Muhammad I Dawra
1732–9	Umar Lele
1739–56	Abul-Qasim
1756–87	Muhammad II Tairab
1787–1801	Abdul-Rahman ar-Rashid
1801–39	Muhammad III al-Fadl
1839–73	Muhammad IV Husain
1873–4	Ibrahim
1874–98	*Conquered by Mohammad Ahmed and his successor*
1898–1916	Ali Dinar ibn Zakariyya
1916–56	*British rule*

Chief of State

1956–8	*Council of State*
1958–64	Ibrahim Abboud
1964–5	*Council of Sovereignty*
1965–9	Ismail al-Azhari
1969–85	(Nemery) Gaafar Mohamad al-Nimeiri (from 1971 *President*)

Chairman – Transitional Military Council

1985–6	Abd al-Rahman Siwar al-Dahab

Chairman – Supreme Council

1986–9	Ahmad al-Mirghani
1989–	*As Prime Minister*

Prime Minister

1955–6	Ismail al-Azhari
1956–64	Abdullah Khalil
1958–64	*As President*
1964–5	Serr al-Khatim al-Khalifa
1965–6	Mohammed Ahmed Mahjoub
1966–7	Sadiq al-Mahdi
1967–9	Mohammed Ahmed Mahjoub
1969	Babiker Awadalla
1969–76	*As President*
1976–7	Rashid al-Tahir Bakr
1977–85	*As President*
1985–6	*Transitional Millitary Council (al-Jazuli Dafallah)*
1986–9	Sadiq al-Mahdi *Military Council, Prime Minister*
1989–	Omar Hassan Ahmed al-Bashir

Suriname

President

1975–80	J H E Ferrier
1980–2	Henk Chin-a-Sen
1982–8	L F Ramdat-Musier *Acting*
1988–90	Ramsewak Shankar
1990–1	Johan Kraag
1991–6	Ronald Ventiaan
1996–	Jules Wijdenbosch

National Military Council
Chairman

1980–7	Désiré (Desi) Bouterse

Prime Minister

1975–80	Henk Arron
1980	Henk Chin-a-Sen
1980–2	*No Prime Minister*
1982–3	Henry Weyhorst
1983–4	Errol Alibux
1984–6	Wim Udenhout
1986–7	Pretaapnarian Radbakishun
1987–8	Jules Wijdenbosch
1988–90	Henck Arron
1990–1	Jules Wijdenbosch
1991–6	Jules Ajodhia
1996–	Pretaapnarain Radhakishun

Swaziland

Monarch

c.1820–39	Sobhuza I
1839–68	Mswazi (Mswati) I
1868–74	Ludvonga
1874–89	Mbandzeni
1889–99	Bhunu (Ngwane)
1899–1982	Sobhuza II (*Chief from 1921*)
1983	Dzeliwe *Queen Regent*
1983–6	Ntombi *Queen Regent*
1986–	Mswati (III)

Prime Minister

1967–78	Prince Makhosini
1978–9	Prince Maphevu Dlamini
1979–83	Prince Mbandla Dlamini
1983–6	Prince Bhekimpi Dlamini
1986–9	Sotsha Dlamini
1989–93	Obed Dlamini
1993–6	Prince Jameson Mbilini Dlamini
1996–	Sibusiso Barnabus Dlamini

Sweden

Monarch – Kingdom of Sweden
Early Kings

c.970–c.995	Erik VIII
c.995–c.1022	Olaf Skotkunung
c.1022–c.1050	Anund Jakob
c.1050–c.1060	Emund
c.1060–c.1066	Stenkil Ragnvaldsson
c.1066–c.1112	Inge I *Joint king to 1070*
c.1066–c.1070	Halsten *Joint king*
c.1081–c.1083	Blot-Sven *Rival king*
c.1112–c.1130	Inge II *Joint king to 1119*
c.1112–c.1118	Filip *Joint king*
c.1130–c.1156	Sverker I *Rival king from 1150*
c.1150–60	Erik IX Jedvarsson 'the Saint' *Rival king to 1156*
1160–1	Magnus II
1161–7	Karl VII Sverkersson
1167–96	Knut I Eriksson
1196–1208	Sverker II Karlsson
1208–16	Erik X Knutsson
1216–22	Johan I Sverkersson
1222–9	Erik XI Eriksson
1229–34	Knut II Holmgersson
1234–50	Erik XI (*restored*)

Folkung Dynasty

1250–75	Valdemar I Birgerson (Birger Jarl *co-ruler to 1266*)
1275–90	Magnus III Birgerson
1290–1319	Birger Magnusson
1319–65	Magnus IV Eriksson *Joint king 1356–9*
1356–9	Erik XII *Joint king*
1365–89	Albert of Mecklenburg
1389–97	Margrethe I (Margareta) of Denmark

Monarch – Kalmar Union

1397–1448	*As Denmark*
1448–57	Karl VIII
1457–64	*As Denmark*
1464–5	Karl VIII (*restored*)
1465–7	*Civil war*
1467–70	Karl VIII (*restored*)
1470–97	*As Denmark* (Sten Sture the Elder *Regent*)
1497–1501	*As Denmark*
1501–03	*As Denmark* (Sten Sture the Elder *Regent*)
1504–12	*As Denmark* (Svante Nilsson Sture *Regent*)
1512–23	*As Denmark* (Sten Sture the Younger *Regent to 1520*)

Monarch – Kingdom of Sweden

House of Vasa

1523–60	Gustav I Vasa (Gustav Eriksson)
1560–8	Erik XIV
1568–92	Johan III
1592–1604	*As Poland*
1604–11	Karl IX *Regent from 1599*
1611–32	Gustav II Adolf (Gustavus Adolphus)
1632–54	Kristina (Christina)

Palatinate Kings

1654–60	Karl X Gustav
1660–97	Karl XI
1697–1718	Karl XII
1719–20	Ulrika Eleonora
1720–51	Fredrik I

House of Holstein-Gottorp

1751–71	Adolf Fredrik
1771–92	Gustav III
1792–1809	Gustav IV Adolf
1809–18	Karl XIII

House of Bernadotte

1818–44	Karl XIV Johan (Jean Baptiste Jules Bernadotte)
1844–59	Oskar I
1859–72	Karl XV
1872–1907	Oskar II
1907–50	Gustav V
1950–73	Gustav VI Adolf
1973–	Karl XVI Gustav

Prime Minister

1858–70	Louis De Geer
1870–4	Axel Gustaf Adlercreutz
1874–5	Eduard Carleson
1875–80	Louis De Geer
1880–3	Count Arvid Posse
1883–4	Carl Johan Thyselius
1884–8	Oscar Robert Themptander
1888–91	Gustaf Åkerhielm af Margretelund
1891–1900	Erik Gustav Boström
1900–02	Fredrik von Otter
1902–05	Erik Gustav Boström
1905	Johan Ramstedt
1905	Christian Lundeberg
1905–06	Karl Staaf
1906–11	Arvid Lindman
1911–14	Karl Staaf
1914–17	Hjalmar Hammarskjöld
1917	Carl Swartz
1917–20	Nils Edén
1920	Karl Hjalmar Branting
1920–1	Louis De Geer
1921	Oscar Von Sydow
1921–3	Karl Hjalmar Branting
1923–4	Ernst Trygger
1924–5	Karl Hjalmar Branting
1925–6	Rickard Sandler
1926–8	Carl Gustaf Ekman
1928–30	Arvid Lindman
1930–2	Carl Gustaf Ekman
1932	Felix Hamrin
1932–6	Per Albin Hansson
1936	Axel Pehrsson-Branstorp
1936–46	Per Albin Hansson
1946–69	Tage Erlander
1969–76	(Sven) Olof Palme
1976–8	Thorbjörn Fälldin
1978–9	Ola Ullsten
1979–82	Thorbjörn Fälldin
1982–6	(Sven) Olof Palme
1986–91	Ingvar Costa Carlsson
1991–4	Carl Bildt
1994–6	Ingvar Carlsson
1996–	Goran Persson

Switzerland

President

1849	Jonas Furrer
1850	Daniel-Henri Druey
1851	Matrin-Joseph Munzinger
1852	Jonas Furrer
1853	Wilhelm-Mathias Naeff
1854	Friedrich Frey-Herosée
1855	Jonas Furrer
1856	Jakob Stämpfli
1857	Constant Fornerod
1858	Jonas Furrer
1859	Jakob Stämpfli
1860	Friedrich Frey-Heroséee
1861	Melchior-Martin-Joseph Kausel
1862	Jakob Stämpfli
1863	Constant Fornerod
1864	Jakob Dubs
1865	Karl Schenk
1866	Melchior-Martin-Joseph Kausel
1867	Constant Fornerod
1868	Jakob Dubs
1869	Emil Welti
1870	Jakob Dubs
1871	Karl Schenk
1872	Emil Welti
1873	Paul Cérésole
1874	Karl Schenk
1875	Johann-Jacob Scherer
1876	Emil Welti
1877	Joachim Heer
1878	Karl Schenk
1879	Bernhard Hammer
1880	Emil Welti
1881	Numa Droz
1882	Simeon Bavier
1883	Louis Ruchonnet
1884	Emil Welti
1885	Karl Schenk
1886	Adolf Deucher
1887	Numa Droz
1888	Wilhelm-Friedrich Hertenstein
1889	Bernhard Hammer
1890	Louis Ruchonnet
1891	Emil Welti
1892	Walther Hauser
1893	Karl Schenk
1894	Emil Frey
1895	Josef Zemp
1896	Adrien Lachenal
1897	Adolf Deucher
1898	Eugène Ruffy
1899	Eduard Müller
1900	Walter Hauser
1901	Ernst Brenner
1902	Joseph Zemp
1903	Adolf Deucher
1904	Robert Comtesse
1905	Marc-Emile Ruchet
1906	Ludwig Forrer
1907	Eduard Müller
1908	Ernst Brenner
1909	Adolf Deucher
1910	Robert Comtesse
1911	Marc-Emile Ruchet
1912	Ludwig Forrer
1913	Eduard Müller
1914	Arthur Hoffmann
1915	Guiseppe Motta
1916	Camille Decoppet
1917	Edmund Schulthess
1918	Felix Calonder
1919	Gustave Ador
1920	Giuseppe Motta
1921	Edmund Schulthess
1922	Robert Haab
1923	Karl Scheurer
1924	Ernest Chuard
1925	Jean-Marie Musy
1926	Heinrich Häberlin
1927	Giuseppe Motta
1928	Edmund Schulthess
1929	Robert Haab
1930	Jean-Marie Musy

1931	Heinrich Häberlin
1932	Giuseppe Motta
1933	Edmund Schulthess
1934	Marcel Pilet-Golaz
1935	Rudolf Minger
1936	Albert Meyer
1937	Giuseppe Motta
1938	Johannes Baumann
1939	Philipp Etter
1940	Marcel Pilet-Golaz
1941	Ernst Wetter
1942	Philipp Etter
1943	Enrico Celio
1944	Walter Stämpfli
1945	Eduard von Steiger
1946	Karl Kobelt
1947	Philipp Etter
1948	Enrico Celio
1949	Ernst Nobs
1950	Max Petitpierre
1951	Eduard von Steiger
1952	Karl Kobelt
1953	Philipp Etter
1954	Rodolphe Rubattel
1955	Max Petitpierre
1956	Markus Feldmann
1957	Hans Streuli
1958	Thomas Holenstein
1959	Paul Chaudet
1960	Max Petitpierre
1961	Friedrich Wahlen
1962	Paul Chaudet
1963	Willy Spühler
1964	Ludwig von Moos
1965	Hans Peter Tschudi
1966	Hans Schaffner
1967	Roger Bonvin
1968	Willy Spühler
1969	Ludwig von Moos
1970	Hans Peter Tschudi
1971	Rudolf Gnägi
1972	Nello Celio
1973	Roger Bonvin
1974	Ernst Brugger
1975	Pierre Graber
1976	Rudolf Gnägi
1977	Kurt Furgler
1978	Willi Ritschard
1979	Hans Hürlimann
1980	Georges-André Chevallaz
1981	Kurt Furgler
1982	Fritz Honegger
1983	Pierre Aubert
1984	Leon Schlumpf
1985	Kurt Furgler
1986	Alphons Egli
1987	Pierre Aubert
1988	Otto Stich
1989	Jean-Pascal Delamuraz
1990	Arnold Koller
1991	Flavio Cotti
1992	Réne Felber
1993	Adolf Ogi
1994	Otto Stich
1995	Kaspar Villiger
1996	Jean-Pascal Delamuraz
1997	Arnold Koller

Syria

President

1943–9	Shukri al-Quwwatli
1949	Husni az-Zaim
1949–51	Hashim al-Atasi
1951–4	Adib Shishaqli
1954–5	Hashim al-Atasi
1955–8	Shukri al-Quwwatli
1958–61	*Part of United Arab Republic*
1961–3	Nazim al-Qudsi
1963	Luai al-Atassi
1963–6	Amin al-Hafiz
1966–70	Nureddin al-Atassi
1970–1	Ahmad al-Khatib
1971–	Hafez al-Assad

Prime Minister

1946–8	Jamil Mardam Bey
1948–9	Khalid al-Azm
1949	Husni az-Zaim
1949	Muhsi al-Barazi
1949	Hashim al-Atassi
1949	Nazim al-Qudsi
1949–50	Khalid al-Azm
1950–1	Nazim al-Qudsi
1951	Khalid al-Azm
1951	Hassan al-Hakim
1951	Maruf ad-Dawalibi
1951–3	Fauzi as-Salu
1953–4	Adib Shishaqli
1954	Shewqet Shuqair
1954	Sabri al-Asali
1954	Said al-Ghazzi
1954–5	Faris al-Khuri
1955	Sabri al-Asali
1955–6	Said al-Ghazzi
1956–8	Sabri al-Asali
1958–61	*Part of United Arab Republic*
1961	Abd al-Hamid as-Sarraj
1961	Mamun Kuzbari
1961	Izzat an-Nuss
1961–2	Maruf ad-Dawalibi
1962	Bashir Azmah
1962–3	Khalid al-Azm
1963	Salah ad-Din al-Bitaar
1963	Sami al-Jundi
1963	Salah ad-Din al-Bitaar
1963–4	Amin al-Hafez
1964	Salah ad-Din al-Bitaar
1964–5	Amin al-Hafez
1965	Yousif Zeayen
1966	Salah ad-Din al-Bitaar
1966–8	Yousif Zeayen
1968–70	Nureddin al-Atassi *Acting*
1970–1	Hafez al-Assad
1971–2	Abdel Rahman Khleifawi
1972–6	Mahmoud bin Saleh al-Ayoubi
1976–8	Abdul Rahman Khleifawi
1978–80	Mohammed Ali al-Halabi
1980–7	Abdel Rauof al-Kasm
1987–	Mahmoud Zubi

Taiwan

President

1950–75	Chiang Kai-shek
1975–8	Yen Chia-kan
1978–88	Chiang Ching-kuo
1988–	Lee Teng-hui

President of Executive Council

1950–4	Ch'eng Ch'eng
1954–8	O K Yui
1958–63	Ch'eng Ch'eng
1963–72	Yen Chia-ken
1972–8	Chiang Ching-kuo
1978–84	Sun Yun-suan
1984–9	Yu Kuo-hwa
1989–90	Lee Huan
1990–3	Hau Pei-tsun
1993–6	Lien Chan
1997–	Vincent Siew

Tajikistan

President

1991–2	Rakhman Nabiyev
1992	Akbarsho Iskandrov
	Chair of the Supreme Soviet
1992–	Imamoli Rakhmanov

Chairman of the Council of Ministers

1991–2	Akbar Mirzoyev
1992–3	Abdumalik Abdullojanov
1993–4	Abduljalil Samadov
1994–6	Jamshed Karimov
1996–	Yahya Azimov

Tanzania

Sultan of Zanzibar
Oman Dynasty

1806–56	Said ibn Sultan (of Oman)
1856–70	Majid ibn Said
1870–88	Barghash ibn Said
1888–90	Khalifa ibn Barghash
1890–3	Ali ibn Said
1893–6	Hamid ibn Thuwaini
1896–1902	Hammud ibn Muhammad
1902–11	Ali ibn Hammud
1911–60	Khalifa ibn Harub
1960–3	Abdullah ibn Khalifa
1963–4	Jamshid ibn Abdullah

President

1964–85	Julius Kambarage Nyerere
1985–95	Ndugu Ali Hassan Mwinyi
1995–	Benjamin Mkapa

Prime Minister

1964–77	Rashid M Kawawa
	Vice President to 1972
1977–80	Edward M Sokoine
1980–3	Cleopa D Msuya
1983–4	Edward M Sokoine
1984–5	Salim A Salim
1985–90	Joseph S Warioba
1990–4	John Malecela
1994–5	Cleopa Msuya
1995–	Frederick Sumaye

Thailand

Monarch – Kingdom of Siam

1767–82	P'ya Taksin
1782–1809	P'ra P'utt'a Yot Fa Chulalok (Rama I)
1809–24	Phendin-Klang (Rama II)
1824–51	P'ra Nang Klao (Rama III)
1851–68	Maha Mongkut (Rama IV)
1868–1910	Chulalongkorn Phra Paramindr Maha (Rama V)
1910–25	Maha Vajiravudh (Rama VI)
1925–35	Prajadhipok (Rama VII)
1935–46	Ananda Mahidol (Rama VIII) (Nai Pridi Phanomyong *Regent* 1939–46)

Monarch – Kingdom of Thailand

1946–	Bhumibol Adulyadej (Rama IX) (Rangsit of Chainat *Regent* 1946–50)

Prime Minister

1932–3	Phraya Manopakom
1933–8	Phraya Phahon Phonphahuyasena
1938–44	Luang Phibun Songgram
1945	Thawi Bunyaket
1945–6	Mom Rachawongse Seni Pramoj
1946	Nai Khuang Aphaiwong
1946	Nai Pridi Phanomyong
1946–7	Luang Thamrong Nawasawat
1947–8	Nai Khuang Aphaiwong
1948–57	Luang Phibun Songgram
1957	Sarit Thanarat
1957	Nai Pote Sarasin
1957–8	Thanom Kittikatchom
1958–63	Sarit Thanarat
1963–73	Thanom Kittikatchom
1973–5	Sanya Dharmasaki
1975–6	Mom Rachawongse Kukrit Pramoj
1976	Seni Pramoj
1976–7	Thanin Kraivichien
1977–80	Kriangsak Chammanard
1980–8	Prem Tinsulanonda
1988–91	Chatichai Choonhavan
1991–2	*Military junta* (Anand Panyarachun)
1992	Suchinda Kraprayoon
1992–5	Chuan Leekpai
1995–6	Banharn Silpa-Archa
1996–7	Chavalit Yongchaiyudh
1997–	Chuan Leekpai

Togo

President

1960–3	Sylvanus Olympio
1963–7	Nicolas Grunitzky
1967–	(Etienne) Gnassingbé Eyadéma

Prime Minister

1991–4	Joseph Koukou Koffigoh
1994–6	Edem Kodjo

1996–	Kwasi Klutse

Tonga

Monarch

1845–93	George Tupou I
1893–1918	George Tupou II
1918–65	Salote Tupou III
1965–	Taufa'ahau (Tupouto Tungi) Tupou IV

Prime Minister

1970–91	Prince Fatafehi Tu'ipele-hake
1991–	Baron Vaea

Trinidad and Tobago

President

1976–87	Ellis Emmanuel Clarke
1987–97	Noor Mohammed Hassanali
1997–	Arthur Napoleon Raymond Robinson

Premier

1956–62	Eric Williams

Prime Minister

1962–81	Eric Williams
1981–6	George Chambers
1986–92	Arthur Napoleon Raymond (Ray) Robinson
1992–5	Patrick Manning
1995–	Basdeo Panday

Tunisia

Bey of Tunis

House of Murad

1628–31	Murad I
1631–62	Muhammad I
1662–75	Murad II
1675	Muhammad II
1675	Ali
1675	Muhammad III
1675–6	Muhammad II (*restored*)
1676–88	Ali (*restored*)
1688–95	Muhammad II (*restored*)
1695–8	Ramadan
1698–1702	Murad III
1702–05	Ibrahim ash-Sharif

House of Husain

1705–35	Husain I
1735–56	Ali I
1756–9	Muhammad I
1759–82	Ali II
1782–1814	Hammuda
1814	Uthman
1814–24	Mahmud
1824–35	Husain II
1835–7	Mustafa
1837–55	Ahmad I
1855–9	Muhammad II
1859–82	Muhammad III as-Sadiq
1882–1902	Ali Muddat
1902–06	Muhammad IV al-Hadi
1906–22	Muhammad V an-Nadir

1922–9	Muhammad VI al-Habib
1929–42	Ahmad II
1942–3	Muhammad VII al-Munsif
1943–57	Muhammad VIII al-Amin

President

1957–87	Habib ibn Ali Bourguiba
1987–	Zine al-Abidine bin Ali

Prime Minister

1956–7	Habib ibn Ali Bourguiba
1957–69	*No Prime Minister*
1969–70	Bahi Ladgham
1970–80	Hadi Nouira
1980–6	Mohammed Mezali
1986–7	Rashid Sfar
1987	Zine al-Abidine bin Ali
1987–9	Hadi Baccouche
1989–	Hamed Karoui

Turkey

King of Hatti (Hittites)

*c.*1800BC	Pitkhana
?	Anitta
?	Tudkhaliash I
*c.*1700BC	Pu-Sharruma
?	Labarnash
*c.*1650BC	Khattushilish I
?	Murshilish I
?	Khantilish I
?	Zidantash I
*c.*1550BC	Ammunash
?	Khuzziyash I
?	Telepinush
*c.*1500BC	Alluwamnash
?	Khantilish II
?	Zidantash II
*c.*1450BC	Khuzziyash II
?	Tudkhaliash II
?	Arnuwandash I
*c.*1400–1390BC	Khattushilish II
*c.*1390–*c.*1380BC	Tudkhaliash III
*c.*1380–*c.*1346BC	Shuppiluliumash I
*c.*1346–*c.*1345BC	Arnuwandash II
*c.*1345–*c.*1320BC	Murshilish II
*c.*1320–*c.*1294BC	Muwatallish
*c.*1294–*c.*1286BC	Murshilish III (Urkhi-Teshub)
*c.*1286–*c.*1265BC	Khattushilish III
*c.*1265–*c.*1220BC	Tudkhaliash IV
*c.*1220–*c.*1200BC	Arnuwandash III
*c.*1200BC	Shuppiluliumash II

Sultan of the Ottoman Empire

1299–1326	Osman I
1326–59	Orkhan
1359–89	Murad I
1389–1403	Bayezit I
1403–21	Mehmet I *Rival sultan to 1413*
1403–10	Süleyman I *Rival sultan*
1410–13	Musa *Rival sultan*
1421–44	Murad II
1444–6	Mehmet II 'the Conqueror'
1446–51	Murad II (*restored*)
1451–81	Mehmet II 'the Conqueror' (*restored*)

1481–1512	Bayezit II
1512–20	Selim I 'the Grim'
1520–66	Süleyman II 'the Magnificent'
1566–74	Selim II
1574–95	Murad III
1595–1603	Mehmet III
1603–17	Ahmet I
1617–18	Mustafa I
1618–22	Osman II
1622–3	Mustafa I (restored)
1623–40	Murad IV
1640–8	Ibrahim
1648–87	Mehmet IV
1687–91	Süleyman III
1691–5	Ahmet II
1695–1703	Mustafa II
1703–30	Ahmet III
1730–54	Mahmut I
1754–7	Osman III
1757–74	Mustafa III
1774–89	Abd-ul-Hamid I
1789–1807	Selim III
1807–08	Mustafa IV
1808–39	Mahmut II
1839–61	Abd-ul-Medjid
1861–76	Abdul-Aziz
1876	Murad V
1876–1909	Abd-ul-Hamid II
1909–18	Mehmet V Resat
1918–22	Mehmet VI Vahideddin

Turkish Republic
President

1923–38	Mustafa Kemal Atatürk
1938–50	Ismet Paza Inönü
1950–60	Celâl Bayar
1961–6	Cemal Gürsel
1966–73	Cevdet Sunay
1973–80	Fahri S Korutürk
1982–9	Kenan Evren
1989–93	Turgut Özal
1993–	Süleyman Demirel

Prime Minister

1923–4	Ismet Paza Inönü
1924–5	Ali Fethi Okyar
1925–37	Ismet Paza Inönü
1937–9	Celâl Bayar
1939–42	Refik Saydam
1942–6	Sükrü Saracoglu
1946–7	Recep Peker
1947–9	Hasan Saka
1949–50	Semseddin Günaltay
1950–60	Adnan Menderes
1960–1	Military junta
1961–5	Ismet Paza Inönü
1965	Fuat Hayri Ürgüplü
1965–71	Süleyman Demirel
1971–2	Nihat Erim
1972–3	Ferit Melen
1973	Naim Télu
1973–4	Bülent Ecevit
1974–7	Süleyman Demirel
1978–9	Bülent Ecevit
1979–80	Süleyman Demirel

1980–3	Bülent Ulusu
1983–9	Turgut Özal
1989–91	Yildirim Akbulut
1991	Mesut Yilmaz
1991–3	Süleyman Demirel
1993–6	Tansu Ciller
1996	Mesut Yilmaz
1996–7	Necmettin Erbakan
1997–	Mesut Yilmaz

Turkmenistan
President

1991–	Saparmurad Niyazov

Prime Minister

1991–	Khan Akhmedov

Tuvalu
Chief of State: British monarch, represented by Governor-General

Prime Minister

1978–81	Toalipi Lauti
1981–9	Tomasi Puapua
1989–93	Bikenibeu Paeniu
1993–6	Kamuta Laatasi
1996–	Bikenibeu Paeniu

Uganda
President

1962–6	Edward Muteesa II
1967–71	(Apollo) Milton Obote
1971–9	Idi Amin (Dada)
1979	Yusufu Kironde Lule
1979–80	Godfrey Lukongwa Binaisa
1981–5	(Apollo) Milton Obote
1985–6	Military Council (Tito Okello Lutwa)
1986–	Yoweri Kaguta Museveni

Prime Minister

1962–71	(Apollo) Milton Obote
1971–81	No Prime Minister
1981–5	Eric Otema Alimadi
1985	Paulo Muwanga
1985–6	Abraham N Waliggo
1986–91	Samson B Kisekka
1991–4	George Cosmas Adyebo
1994–	Kintu Musoke

Ukraine
Prince of Kiev

c.880–c.912	Oleg
c.912–45	Igor I
945–64	St Olga
964–72	Sviatoslav I
972–8	Yaropolk I
978–1015	St Vladimir I 'the Great'
1015–19	Sviatopolk I
1019–54	Yaroslav I 'the Wise'
1054–68	Iziaslav I
1068–9	Vseslav
1069–73	Iziaslav I (restored)
1073–6	Sviatoslav II
1076–8	Iziaslav I (restored)

1078–93	Vsevolod I
1093–1113	Sviatopolk II
1113–25	Vladimir II Monomachus
1125–32	Mstislav I Harald
1132–9	Yaropolk II
1139	Viacheslav
1139–46	Vsevolod II
1146	Igor II
1146–9	Iziaslav II
1149–50	Yuri Dolgoruky
1150–4	Period of instability
1154–5	Rostislav I
1155–7	Yuri Dolgoruky (restored)
1157–9	Iziaslav III
1159–67	Period of instability
1167–9	Mstislav II
1169–71	Gleb
1171–2	Roman
1172–3	Vsevolod III
1173–4	Riurik
1174–5	Yaroslav II
1175–6	Roman (restored)
1176–80	Sviatoslav III
1180–1200	Period of instability
1200–03	Ingvar
1203–04	Riurik (restored)
1204–05	Rostislav II
1205–06	Riurik (restored)
1206–12	Vsevolod IV
1212–23	Mstislav III
1223–36	Vladimir III
1236–8	Yaroslav III
1238–40	Michael
1240	Daniel
1240	Tartar rule
1323	Polish rule
1667	Polish Russian partition
1668	Turkish rule
1793	Russian rule

President

1991–4	Leonid M Kravchuk
1994–	Leonid Kuchma

Prime Minister

1991–2	Vitold P Fokin
1992–3	Leonid Kuchma
1993	Yukhim Zvagilsky
1994–5	Vitalii Masol
1995–6	Yevhenii Marchuk
1996–7	Pavlo Lazarenko
1997–	Valery Pustovoytenko

United Arab Emirates
President

1971–	Zayed bin Sultan al-Nahayan

Prime Minister

1971–9	Maktoum bin Rashid al-Maktoum
1979–90	Rashid bin Said al-Maktoum
1990–	Maktoum bin Rashid al-Maktoum

Abu Dhabi

Shaikh
Al-Nahayan Dynasty

c.1761–93	Dhiyab I bin Isa
1793–1816	Shakhbout I
1816–18	Mohammed
1818–33	Tahnoun I
1833–45	Khalifa
1845	Isa bin Khaled
1845	Dhiyab II bin Isa
1845–55	Sayed
1855–1909	Zayed I
1909–12	Tahnoun II
1912–22	Hamdan
1922–6	Sultan
1926–8	Saqr
1928–66	Shakhbout II
1966–	Zayed II bin Sultan al-Nahayan

Ajman

Shaikh
Al-Nuaimi Dynasty

c.1820–38	Rashid I bin Humaid
1838–41	Humaid I
1841–8	Abd-el-Aziz I
1848–73	Humaid I (*restored*)
1873–91	Rashid II
1891–1900	Humaid II
1900–10	Abd-el-Aziz II
1910–28	Humaid
1928–81	Rashid
1981–	Humaid

Dubai

Shaikh
Al-Maktoum Dynasty

1833–52	Maktoum I bin Butti
1852–9	Said I
1859–86	Hashar
1886–94	Rashid I
1894–1906	Maktoum II
1906–12	Butti bin Suhail
1912–58	Said II
1958–90	Rashid II
1990–	Maktoum III

Fujairah

Shaikh
Al-Sharqi Dynasty

1952–75	Mohammed bin Hamad
1975–	Hamad

Ras al-Khaimah

Shaikh
Al-Qasimi Dynasty

1869–1900	Humaid bin Abdullah
1900–09	Khaled bin Saqr
1921–48	Sultan
1948–	Saqr bin Mohammed

Sharjah

Shaikh
Al-Qasimi Dynasty

c.1727–77	Rashid bin Matar
1777–1803	Saqr I
1803–66	Sultan I
1866–8	Khaled I
1868–83	Salim
1883–1914	Saqr II
1914–24	Khaled II bin Ahmed
1924–51	Sultan II
1951–65	Saqr III
1965–72	Khaled III bin Mohammed
1972–87	Sultan III
1987	Abd-el-Aziz
1987–	Sultan IV

Umm al-Qaiwain

Shaikh
Al-Mualla Dynasty

c.1775–?	Majid
?–1816	Rashid I
1816–53	Abdullah I
1853–73	Ali
1873–1904	Ahmad I
1904–22	Rashid II
1922–3	Abdullah II
1923–9	Hamad bin Ibrahim
1929–81	Ahmad II
1981–	Rashid III

United Kingdom

Monarch – England
West Saxon Kings

802–39	Egbert
839–58	Æthelwulf
858–60	Æthelbald
860–5	Æthelbert
866–71	Æthelred
871–99	Alfred 'the Great'
899–924	Edward 'the Elder'
924–39	Athelstan
939–46	Edmund I
946–55	Edred
955–9	Edwy
959–75	Edgar
975–8	Edward 'the Martyr' (St Edward)
978–1016	Æthelred II 'the Unready'
1016	Edmund II 'Ironside'

Danish Kings

1016–35	Knut Sveinsson (Cnut; Canute the Great)
1035–7	Hardaknut Knutsson (Harthacnut) (Harold 'Harefoot' *Regent*)
1037–40	Harold I Knutsson 'Harefoot'
1040–2	Hardaknut Knutsson (Harthacnut) (*restored*)
1042–66	Edward 'the Confessor'
1066	Harold II

House of Normandy

1066–87	William I 'the Conqueror'
1087–1100	William II 'Rufus'
1100–35	Henry I

House of Blois

1135–54	Stephen

House of Plantagenet

1154–89	Henry II
1189–99	Richard I 'Coeur de Lion'
1199–1216	John
1216–72	Henry III
1272–1307	Edward I
1307–27	Edward II
1327–77	Edward III
1377–99	Richard II

House of Lancaster

1399–1413	Henry IV
1413–22	Henry V
1422–61	Henry VI

House of York

1461–70	Edward IV

House of Lancaster (restored)

1470–1	Henry VI (*restored*)

House of York (restored)

1471–83	Edward IV (*restored*)
1483	Edward V
1483–5	Richard III

House of Tudor

1485–1509	Henry VII
1509–47	Henry VIII
1547–53	Edward VI
1553–8	Mary I
1558–1603	Elizabeth I

Monarch – Scotland
House of Alpin

843–60	Kenneth I Macalpin
860–3	Donald I
863–77	Constantine I
877–8	Aodh
878–89	Eocha
889–900	Donald II
900–43	Constantine II
943–54	Malcolm I
954–62	Indulf
962–7	Duff
967–71	Colin
971–95	Kenneth II
995–7	Constantine III
997–1005	Kenneth III
1005–34	Malcolm II
1034–40	Duncan I
1040–57	Macbeth
1057–93	Malcolm III 'Canmore'
1093–4	Donald III Bán (Donaldbane)

House of Canmore

1094	Duncan II

House of Alpin (restored)

1094–7	Donald III Bán (Donaldbane) (*restored*)

House of Canmore (restored)
1097–1107	Edgar
1107–24	Alexander I
1124–53	David I
1153–65	Malcolm IV 'the Maiden'
1165–1214	William I 'the Lion'
1214–49	Alexander II
1249–86	Alexander III
1286–90	Margaret 'Maid of Norway'
1290–2	*No monarch*
1292–6	John de Balliol
1296–1306	*English rule*

House of Bruce
1306–29	Robert I 'Robert the Bruce'
1329–71	David II

House of Stewart (Stuart)
1371–90	Robert II
1390–1406	Robert III
1406–37	James I
1437–60	James II
1460–88	James III
1488–1513	James IV
1513–42	James V
1542–67	Mary 'Queen of Scots'
1567–1603	James VI (*I of England*)

Monarch – England and Scotland
House of Stuart
1603–25	James I (*VI of Scotland*)
1625–49	Charles I

Commonwealth and Protectorate
1649–53	*Council of State*
1653–8	Oliver Cromwell *Lord Protector*
1658–9	Richard Cromwell *Lord Protector*

House of Stuart (restored)
1660–85	Charles II
1685–8	James II (*VII of Scotland*)
1689–94	William III and Mary I
1694–1702	William III
1702–7	Anne

Monarch – Great Britain
House of Stuart
1707–14	Anne

House of Hanover
1714–27	George I
1727–60	George II
1760–1801	George III

Monarch – United Kingdom of Great Britain and Ireland
House of Hanover
1801–20	George III
1820–30	George IV
1830–7	William IV
1837–1901	Victoria

House of Saxe-Coburg
1901–10	Edward VII

House of Windsor
1910–22	George V

Monarch – United Kingdom of Great Britain and Northern Ireland
House of Windsor
1922–36	George V
1936	Edward VIII
1936–52	George VI
1952–	Elizabeth II

Princes of Wales
Independent Princes
c.500–c.517	Cadwallon Lawhir
c.517–547	Maelgwn Hir
547–?	Rhun Hir
?–599	Beli ap Rhun
?–616	Iago ap Beli
616–25	Cadfan ab Iago
625–33	Cadwallon ap Cadfan
633–54	Cadafael Cadomedd
654–64	Cadwaladr Fendigaid
664–?	Idwal Iwrch
?–754	Rhodri Molwynog
754–825	Hywel ap Rhodri
825–44	Merfyn Frych
844–78	Rhodri Mawr 'the Great'
878–916	Anarawd
916–42	Idwal Foel
942–50	Hywel Dda 'the Good'
950–79	Iago ab Idwal
979–85	Hywel ab Idwal 'the Bad'
985–6	Cadwallon ab Idwal
986–99	Meredudd ab Owain ab Hywel Dda
999–1023	Llywelyn ap Seisyll
1023–33	Rhydderch ab Iestyn
1033–9	Iago ab Idwal ap Meurig
1039–63	Gruffyd ap Llywelyn ap Seisyll
1063–75	Bleddyn ap Cynfyn
1075–81	Trahaern ap Caradog
1081–1137	Gruffyd ap Cynan ab Iago
1137–70	Owain Gwynedd
1170–94	Dafydd ap Owain Gwynedd
1194–1240	Llywelyn ap Iorweth Fawr 'the Great'
1240–6	Dafydd ap Llywelyn
1246–82	Llywelyn ap Gruffydd ap Llywelyn
1282–3	Dafydd ap Gruffydd ap Llywelyn
1283–	*English rule*

English and British Princes of Wales
1301–7	Edward (Edward II of England)
1343–76	Edward 'the Black Prince', son of Edward III
1376–7	Richard (Richard II)
1399–1413	Henry of Monmouth (Henry V)
1454–71	Edward of Westminster, son of Henry VI
1471–83	Edward (Edward V)
1489–1504	Arthur, son of Henry VII
1504–9	Henry (Henry VIII)
1610–12	Henry, son of James I
1616–25	Charles (Charles I)
1638–60	Charles (Charles II) (*styled, but never created*)
1688	James Francis Edward Stewart 'the Old Pretender', son of James II (*styled, but never created*)
1714–27	George (George II)
1729–51	Frederick Louis, son of George II
1751–60	George (George III)
1762–1820	George (George IV)
1841–1901	Albert Edward (Edward VII)
1901–10	George (George V)
1910–36	Edward (Edward VIII)
1958–	Charles Philip Arthur George, son of Elizabeth II

Prime Minister
1721–42	Robert Walpole, Earl of Orford *Whig*
1742–3	Spencer Compton, Earl of Wilmington *Whig*
1743–54	Henry Pelham *Whig*
1754–6	Thomas Pelham (Holles), Duke of Newcastle *Whig*
1756–7	William Cavendish, 1st Duke of Devonshire *Whig*
1757–62	Thomas Pelham (Holles), Duke of Newcastle *Whig*
1762–3	John Stuart , 3rd Earl of Bute *Tory*
1763–5	George Grenville *Whig*
1765–6	Charles Watson Wentworth, 2nd Marquis of Rockingham *Whig*
1766–8	William Pitt, 1st Earl of Chatham *Whig*
1768–70	Augustus Henry Fitzroy, 3rd Duke of Grafton *Whig*
1770–82	Frederick North, 8th Lord North *Tory*
1782	Charles Watson Wentworth, 2nd Marquis of Rockingham *Whig*
1782–3	William Petty, 2nd Earl of Shelburne *Whig*
1783	William Henry Cavendish, Duke of Portland *Coal*
1783–1801	William Pitt *Tory*
1801–4	Henry Addington, 1st Viscount Sidmouth *Tory*
1804–6	William Pitt *Tory*
1806–7	William Wyndham Grenville, 1st Baron Grenville *Whig*
1807–9	William Henry Cavendish, Duke of Portland *Coal*
1809–12	Spencer Perceval *Tory*
1812–27	Robert Banks Jenkinson, 2nd Earl of Liverpool *Tory*
1827	George Canning *Tory*
1827–8	Frederick John Robinson, 1st Earl of Ripon *Tory*
1828–30	Arthur Wellesley, 1st Duke of Wellington *Tory*

1830–4	Charles Grey, 2nd Earl Grey *Whig*
1834	William Lamb, 2nd Viscount Melbourne *Whig*
1834–5	Robert Peel *Con*
1835–41	William Lamb, 2nd Viscount Melbourne *Whig*
1841–6	Robert Peel *Con*
1846–52	Lord John Russell, 1st Earl Russell *Lib*
1852	Edward Geoffrey Smith Stanley, 14th Earl of Derby *Con*
1852–5	George Hamilton-Gordon, 4th Earl of Aberdeen *Peelite*
1855–8	Henry John Temple, 3rd Viscount Palmerston *Lib*
1858–9	Edward Geoffrey Smith Stanley, 14th Earl of Derby *Con*
1859–65	Henry John Temple, 3rd Viscount Palmerston *Lib*
1865–6	Lord John Russell, 1st Earl Russell *Lib*
1866–8	Edward Geoffrey Smith Stanley, 14th Earl of Derby *Con*
1868	Benjamin Disraeli, 1st Earl of Beaconsfield *Con*
1868–74	William Ewart Gladstone *Lib*
1874–80	Benjamin Disraeli, 1st Earl of Beaconsfield *Con*
1880–5	William Ewart Gladstone *Lib*
1885–6	Robert Arthur James Gascoyne-Cecil, 5th Marquis of Salisbury *Con*
1886	William Ewart Gladstone *Lib*
1886–92	Robert Arthur Talbot Gascoyne-Cecil, 3rd Marquis of Salisbury *Con*
1892–4	William Ewart Gladstone *Lib*
1894–5	Archibald Philip Primrose, 5th Earl of Rosebery *Lib*
1895–1902	Robert Arthur Talbot Gascoyne-Cecil, 3rd Marquis of Salisbury *Con*
1902–5	Arthur James Balfour, 1st Earl of Balfour *Con*
1905–8	Henry Campbell-Bannerman *Lib*
1908–15	Herbert Henry Asquith, 1st Earl of Oxford and Asquith *Lib*
1915–16	Herbert Henry Asquith, 1st Earl of Oxford and Asquith *Coal*
1916–22	David Lloyd-George, 1st Earl Lloyd-George of Dwyfor *Coal*
1922–3	Andrew Bonar Law *Con*

1923–4	Stanley Baldwin, 1st Earl Baldwin of Bewdley *Con*
1924	James Ramsay MacDonald *Lab*
1924–9	Stanley Baldwin, 1st Earl Baldwin of Bewdley *Con*
1929–31	James Ramsay MacDonald *Lab*
1931–5	James Ramsay MacDonald *Nat*
1935–7	Stanley Baldwin, 1st Earl Baldwin of Bewdley *Nat*
1937–40	(Arthur) Neville Chamberlain *Nat*
1940–5	Winston Leonard Spencer Churchill *Coal*
1945–51	Clement Richard Atlee, 1st Earl Attlee *Lab*
1951–5	Winston Leonard Spencer Churchill *Con*
1955–7	(Robert) Anthony Eden, 1st Earl of Avon *Con*
1957–63	(Maurice) Harold Macmillan, 1st Earl of Stockton *Con*
1963–4	Alexander Frederick (Alec) Douglas-Home, Baron Home of the Hirsel *Con*
1964–70	(James) Harold Wilson, Baron Wilson *Lab*
1970–4	Edward Richard George Heath *Con*
1974–6	(James) Harold Wilson, Baron Wilson *Lab*
1976–9	(Leonard) James Callaghan, Baron Callaghan *Lab*
1979–90	Margaret Hilda Thatcher, Baroness Thatcher *Con*
1990–7	John Major *Con*
1997–	Tony Blair *Lab*

Coal Coalition, *Con* Conservative, *Lab* Labour, *Lib* Liberal, *Nat* Nationalist

United Nations

Secretary General

1946–53	Trygve Halvdan Lie *Norway*
1953–61	Dag Hjalmar Agne Carl Hammarskjöld *Sweden*
1962–71	U Thant *Burma*
1971–81	Kurt Waldheim *Austria*
1982–92	Javier Pérez de Cuéllar *Peru*
1992–7	Boutros Boutros Ghali *Egypt*
1997–	Kofi Annan *Ghana*

United States of America

President

Vice President in parentheses

1789–97	George Washington (1st) (John Adams)
1797–1801	John Adams (2nd) *Fed* (Thomas Jefferson)

1801–9	Thomas Jefferson (3rd) *Dem-Rep* (Aaron Burr, 1801–5) (George Clinton, 1805–9)
1809–17	James Madison (4th) *Dem-Rep* (George Clinton, 1809–12) *No Vice President 1812–13* (Elbridge Gerry, 1813–14) *No Vice President 1814–17*
1817–25	James Monroe (5th) *Dem-Rep* (Daniel D Tompkins)
1825–9	John Quincy Adams (6th) *Dem-Rep* (John Caldwell Calhoun)
1829–37	Andrew Jackson (7th) *Dem* (John Caldwell Calhoun, 1829–32) *No Vice President 1832–3* (Martin Van Buren, 1833–7)
1837–41	Martin Van Buren (8th) *Dem* (Richard Mentor Johnson)
1841	William Henry Harrison (9th) *Whig* (John Tyler)
1841–5	John Tyler (10th) *Whig* *No Vice President*
1845–9	James Knox Polk (11th) *Dem* (George Mifflin Dallas)
1849–50	Zachary Taylor (12th) *Whig* (Millard Fillmore)
1850–3	Millard Fillmore (13th) *Whig* *No Vice President*
1853–7	Franklin Pierce (14th) *Dem* (William Rufus King, 1853) *No Vice President 1853–7*
1857–61	James Buchanan (15th) *Dem* (John Cabell Breckinridge)
1861–5	Abraham Lincoln (16th) *Rep* (Hannibal Hamlin, 1861–5) (Andrew Johnson, 1865)
1865–9	Andrew Johnson (17th) *Dem-Nat* *No Vice President*
1869–77	Ulysses Simpson Grant (18th) *Rep* (Schuyler Colfax, 1869–73) (Henry Wilson, 1873–5) *No Vice President 1875–7*
1877–81	Rutherford Birchard Hayes (19th) *Rep* (William A Wheeler)
1881	James Abram Garfield (20th) *Rep* (Chester Alan Arthur)
1881–5	Chester Alan Arthur (21st) *Rep* *No Vice President*
1885–9	Stephen Grover Cleveland (22nd) *Dem* (Thomas A Hendricks, 1885) *No Vice President 1885–9*
1889–93	Benjamin Harrison (23rd) *Rep* (Levi Parsons Morton)

1893–7	Stephen Grover Cleveland (24th) *Dem* (Adlai Ewing Stevenson)
1897–1901	William McKinley (25th) *Rep* (Garret A Hobart, 1897–9) *No Vice President 1899–1901* (Theodore Roosevelt, 1901)
1901–9	Theodore Roosevelt (26th) *Rep* *No Vice President 1901–5* (Charles W Fairbanks, 1905–9)
1909–13	William Howard Taft (27th) *Rep* (James S Sherman, 1909–12) *No Vice President 1912–3*
1913–21	Thomas Woodrow Wilson (28th) *Dem* (Thomas R Marshall)
1921–3	Warren Gamaliel Harding (29th) *Rep* (Calvin Coolidge)
1923–9	Calvin Coolidge (30th) *Rep* *No Vice President 1923–5* (Charles Gates Dawes, 1925–9)
1929–33	Herbert Clark Hoover (31st) *Rep* (Charles Curtis)
1933–45	Franklin Delano Roosevelt (32nd) *Dem* (John N Garner, 1933–41) (Henry Agard Wallace, 1941–5) (Harry S Truman, 1945)
1945–53	Harry S Truman (33rd) *Dem* *No Vice President 1945–9* (Alben W Barkley, 1949–53)
1953–61	Dwight David Eisenhower (34th) *Rep* (Richard Milhous Nixon)
1961–3	John Fitzgerald Kennedy (35th) *Dem* (Lyndon Baines Johnson)
1963–9	Lyndon Baines Johnson (36th) *Dem* *No Vice President 1963–5* (Hubert Horatio Humphrey, 1965–9)
1969–74	Richard Milhous Nixon (37th) *Rep* (Spiro Theodore Agnew, 1969–73) *No Vice President Oct–Dec 1973* (Gerald Rudolph Ford, 1973–4)
1974–7	Gerald Rudolph Ford (38th) *Rep* *No Vice President Aug–Dec 1974* (Nelson Aldrich Rockefeller, 1974–7)
1977–81	James Earl (Jimmy) Carter (39th) *Dem* (Walter Frederick Mondale)
1981–9	Ronald Wilson Reagan (40th) *Rep* (George Herbert Walker Bush)
1989–92	George Herbert Walker Bush (41st) *Rep* (J Danforth (Dan) Quayle)
1992–	William Jefferson (Bill) Clinton (42nd) *Dem* (Alfred Gore)

Dem Democrat; *Fed* Federalist; *Nat* National Union; *Rep* Republican

Uruguay

President

1830–4	Fructuoso Rivera
1834–8	Manuel Oribe
1838–42	Fructuoso Rivera
1842–51	Joaquín Suárez
1852	Juan Francisco Giro
1852	Bernardo Berro
1853–5	Venancio Flores
1855–8	Manuel Basilio Bustamente
1858–60	Gabriel A Pereira
1860–4	Bernardo Berro
1864	Atanasio Aguirre
1865–8	Venancio Flores
1868–72	Lorenzo Batlle
1872–5	José Ellauri
1875	Pedro Varela
1876–80	Lorenzo Latorre
1880–2	Francisco Vidal
1882–6	Máximo Santos
1886–90	Máximo Tajes
1890–4	Julio Herrera y Obés
1894–7	Juan Idiarte Borda
1897–1903	Juan Lindolfo Cuestas
1903–7	José Batlle y Ordóñez
1907–11	Claudio Williman
1911–15	José Batlle y Ordóñez
1915–19	Feliciano Viera
1919–23	Baltasar Brum
1923–7	José Serrato
1927–31	Juan Capisteguy
1931–8	Gabriel Terra
1938–43	Alfredo Baldomir
1943–7	Juan José de Amézaga
1947	Tomás Berreta
1947–51	Luis Batlle Berres
1951–5	Andrés Martínez Trueba

National Government Council (1955–67)

1955–6	Luis Batlle Berres
1956–7	Alberto F Zubiría
1957–8	Alberto Lezama
1958–9	Carlos L Fischer
1959–60	Martín R Etchegoyen
1960–1	Benito Nardone
1961–2	Eduardo Víctor Haedo
1962–3	Faustino Harrison
1963–4	Daniel Fernández Crespo
1964–5	Luis Giannattasio
1965–6	Washington Beltrán
1966–7	Alberto Heber Usher
1967	Oscar Daniel Gestido
1967–72	Jorge Pacheco Areco
1972–6	Juan María Bordaberry Arocena
1976–81	Aparicio Méndez
1981–4	Gregorio Conrado Álvarez Armelino
1984–90	Julio María Sanguinetti Cairolo
1990–5	Luis Alberto Lacalle Herrera
1995–	Julio María Sanguinetti Cairolo

Uzbekistan

President

1991–	Islam A Karimov

Prime Minister

1991–5	Abdulhashim Mutalov
1995–	Otkir Sultonov

Khan of Bokhara
Haidarid Dynasty

1785–1800	Mir Masum Shah Murad
1800–26	Haidar Tora
1826	Husain
1826–7	Umar
1827–60	Nasr-Allah
1860–85	Muzaffar-ud-Din
1885–1910	Abdul-Ahad
1910–20	Abdul Said Mir Alim
1920–91	*Part of Soviet Union*

Khan of Khokand
Shah-Rukhid Dynasty

c.1700–?	Shah Rukh Beg
?	Abdul Rahim
?	Abdul Karim
?–1700	Erdeni Beg
1770	Sulayman
1770	Shah Rukh II
1770–1800	Narbuta
1800–09	Alim Khan
1809–22	Muhammad Umar
1822–40	Muhammad Ali
1840–5	Shir Ali
1845	Murad
1845–57	Khudyar
1857–9	Muhammad Mala
1859–61	Shah Murad
1861–4	Khudayar (*restored*)
1864–71	Muhammad Sultan
1871–5	Khudayar (*restored*)
1875–6	Nasir-ud-Din
1876–1991	*Part of Russia*
1917–91	*Part of Soviet Union*

Vanuatu

President

1980–9	George Sokomanu (*formerly Kalkoa*)
1989–94	Fred Timakata
1994–	Jean-Marie Leye

Prime Minister

1980–91	Walter Hadye Lini

1991	Donald Kalpokas
1992–5	Maxime Carlot Korman
1995–6	Serge Vohor
1996	Maxime Carlot Korman
1996–	Serge Vohor

Vatican State >> Popes p. 1118

Venezuela

President
Fourth Republic

1831–5	José Antonio Páez
1835–6	José Vargas
1836–9	Carlos Soublette
1839–43	José Antonio Páez
1843–7	Carlos Soublette
1847–51	José Tadeo Monagas
1851–5	José Gregorio Monagas
1855–8	José Tadeo Monagas
1858–60	*Revolución de Marzo* (Julián Castro)
1860–1	Manuel Felipe de Tovar
1861	Pedro Gual *Acting*
1861–3	José Antonio Páez *Acting*
1863–8	Juan Crisóstomo Falcón (*Acting to 1865*)
1868–9	José Tadeo Monagas *Acting*
1869–70	José Ruperto Monagas *Acting*
1870–7	Antonio Guzmán Blanco (*Acting to 1873*)
1877–8	Francisco Linares Alcántara
1878–9	José Gregorio Varela *Acting*
1879–84	Antonio Guzmán Blanco
1884–6	Joaquín Crespo
1886–7	Antonio Guzmán Blanco
1888–90	Juan Pablo Rojas Pául
1890–2	Raimundo Andueza Palacio
1892–8	Joaquín Crespo (*Acting to 1894*)
1898–9	Ignacio Andrade
1899–1908	Cipriano Castro
1908–36	Juan Vicente Gomez
1936–41	Eleazar Lopez Contreras
1941–5	Isaias Medina Angarita
1945–7	*Military junta* (Romulo Betancourt)
1947–8	Romulo Gallegos
1948–50	*Military junta*(Carlos Delgado Chalbaud)
1950–9	*Military junta* (Marcos Perez Jimenez)
1959–64	Romulo Betancourt
1964–9	Raul Leoni
1969–74	Rafael Caldera Rodriguez
1974–9	Carlos Andres Pérez
1979–84	Luis Herrera Campins
1984–9	Jaime Lusinchi
1989–93	Carlos Andres Pérez
1993–4	Ramon José Velásquez *Interim*
1994–	Rafael Caldera Rodríguez

Vietnam

Emperor
Tay-Son Dynasty

1788–92	Nguyen Van-Hue (Quang-Trung)
1792–1802	Nguyen Quang-Toan (Cahn-Thinh)

Nguyen Dynasty

1802–20	Gia-Long (Nguyen Anh)
1820–41	Minh-Mang
1841–8	Thieu-Tri
1848–83	Tu-Duc
1883	Nguyen Duc-Duc
1883–4	Nguyen Hiep-Hoa
1884–5	Kien-Phuc
1885–6	Ham-Nghi
1886–9	Dong-Khanh
1889–1907	Thanh-Thai
1907–16	Duy-Tan
1916–25	Khai-Dinh
1925–55	Bao Dai *President from 1949*

State of Vietnam (South Vietnam)
President

1949–55	Bao Dai

Prime Minister

1949–50	Nguyen Van Xuan
1950	Nguyen Phan Long
1950–2	Tran Van Huu
1952	Tran Van Huong
1952–3	Nguyen Van Tam
1953–4	Buu Loc
1954–5	Ngo Dinh Diem

Republic of Vietnam (South Vietnam)
President

1955–63	Ngo Dinh Diem
1963–4	Duong Van Minh
1964	Nguyen Khanh
1964–5	Phan Khac Suu
1965–75	Nguyen Van Thieu
1975	Tran Van Huong
1975	Duong Van Minh
1975–6	*Provisional Revolutionary Government* (Huynh Tan Phat)

Prime Minister

1955–63	Ngo Dinh Diem
1963–4	Nguyen Ngoc Tho
1964	Nguyen Khan
1964–5	Tran Van Huong
1965	Phan Huy Quat
1965–7	Nguyen Cao Ky
1967–8	Nguyen Van Loc
1968–9	Tran Van Huong
1969–75	Tran Thien Khiem
1975	Nguyen Ba Can
1975–6	Vu Van Mau

Democratic Republic of Vietnam (North Vietnam)
President

1945–69	Ho Chi-minh (Nguyen Van Thann)
1969–76	Ton Duc Thang

Prime Minister

1955–76	Pham Van Dong

Socialist Republic of Vietnam
President

1976–80	Ton Duc Thang
1980–1	Nguyen Hun Tho *Acting*
1981–7	Truongh Chinh
1987–2	Vo Chi Cong
1992–7	Le Duc Anh
1997–	Tran Duc Luong

Premier

1976–87	Pham Van Dong
1987–8	Pham Hung
1988	Vo Van Kiet *Acting*
1988–91	Do Muoi
1991–7	Vo Van Kiet
1997–	Phan Van Khai

General Secretary

1960–80	Le Duan
1986	Truong Chinh
1986–91	Nguyen Van Linh
1991–	Do Muoi

Western Samoa *see* Samoa

Yemen

Imam of Sana

1891–1904	Mohammed bin Yahya Hamaddin

Monarch – Kingdom of Yemen

1904–48	Yahya Mohammed bin Mohammed
1948–62	Saif-al-Islam Ahmed bin Yahya
1962–70	Mohammed al-Badr bin Ahmed

Yemen Arab Republic (North Yemen)
President

1962–7	Abdullah al-Sallal
1967–74	Abdur Rahman al-Iriani
1974–7	*Military Command Council* (Ibrahim al-Hamadi)
1977–8	Ahmed bin Hussein al-Ghashmi
1978–90	Ali Abdullah Saleh

Prime Minister

1964	Hamud al-Jaifi
1965	Hassan al-Amri
1965	Ahmed Mohammed Numan
1965	*As President*
1965–6	Hassan al-Amri
1966–7	*As President*
1967	Muhsin al-Aini
1967–9	Hassan al-Amri
1969–70	Abd Allah Kurshumi
1970–1	Muhsin al-Aini
1971	Abdel Salam Sabra *Acting*
1971	Ahmed Mohammed Numan
1971	Hassan al-Amri
1971–2	Muhsin al-Aini
1972–4	Qadi Abdullah al-Hijri
1974	Hassan Makki

1974–5	Muhsin al-Aini
1975	Abdel Latif Deifallah *Acting*
1975–90	Abdel-Aziz Abdel-Ghani

Sultan of Lahej
Abdali Dynasty

1728–42	Fadl I
1742–53	Abdul-Karim I
1753–77	Abdul-Hadi
1777–92	Fadl II
1792–1827	Ahmad I
1827–47	Muhsin
1847–9	Ahmad II
1849–63	Ali I
1863	Fadl III
1863–74	Fadl IV
1874–98	Fadl III *(restored)*
1898–1914	Ahmad III
1914–15	Ali II
1915–47	Abdul-Karim II
1947–52	Fadl V
1952–8	Ali al-Karim
1958–7	Fadl VI ibn Ali ibn Ahmad

Sultan of Shihr and Mukalla
Kuwaiti Dynasty

1866–1909	Awadh I ibn Umar
1909–22	Ghalib I
1922–36	Umar
1936–56	Salih
1956–66	Awadh II
1966–7	Ghalib II

People's Democratic Republic of Yemen (South Yemen)
President

1967–9	Qahtan Mohammed al-Shaabi
1969–78	Salim Ali Rubai
1978	Ali Nasir Mohammed Husani
1978–80	Abdel Fattah Ismail
1980–6	Ali Nasir Mohammed Husani
1986–90	Haider Abu Bakr al-Attas

Prime Minister

1969	Faisal Abd al-Latif al-Shaabi
1969–71	Mohammed Ali Haithem
1971–85	Ali Nasir Mohammed Husani
1985–6	Haidar Abu Bakr al-Attas
1986–90	Yasin Said Numan

Republic of Yemen
President

1990–	Ali Abdullah Saleh

Prime Minister

1990–4	Haidar Abu Bakr al-Attas
1994–7	Abdel Aziz Abdel-Ghani
1997–	Farag Said ben Ghanem

Yugoslavia

Grand Zhupan of Serbia

1168–96	Stephen Nemanja
1196–1217	Stephen Nemanjich

Monarch – Prince of Serbia

1217–27	Stephen Nemanjich
1227–34	Stephen Radoslav
1234–43	Stephen Vladislav
1243–76	Stephen Urosh I
1276–82	Stephen Dragutin
1282–1321	Stephen Urosh II Miliutin
1321–31	Stephen Urosh III
1331–45	Stephen Urosh IV Dushan

Monarch – Emperor of Serbia

1345–55	Stephen Urosh IV Dushan
1355–71	Stephen Urosh V

Monarch – Prince of Serbia

1371–89	Lazar I Hrebeljanovich
1389–1427	Stephen
1427–56	George Brankovich
1456–8	Lazar II
1458–9	Stephen Tomashevich
1459–1815	Turkish rule (Kara George Petrovich *Hospodar of Serbia 1804–13*)

Karageorgevich and Obrenovich Dynasties

1815–39	Milosh Obrenovich
1839	Milan I
1839–42	Michael
1842–58	Aleksandar I
1858–60	Milosh Obrenovich *(restored)*
1860–8	Michael *(restored)*
1868–82	Milan II

Monarch – Kingdom of Serbia
Karageorgevich Dynasty

1882–9	Milan II
1889–1903	Aleksandar II
1903–18	Petar (Peter) I

Monarch – King of the Serbs, Croats and Slovenes

1918–21	Petar (Peter) I (Prince Aleksandar *Regent*)
1921–9	Aleksandar (Alexander) I

Monarch – Kingdom of Yugoslavia

1929–34	Aleksandar (Alexander) I
1934–45	Petar (Peter) II (Prince Paul *Regent 1934–41, King Petar in exile from 1941*)

Republic of Yugoslavia
National Assembly – Chairman

1945–53	Ivan Ribar

National Assembly – President

1953–80	Josip Broz Tito

Collective Presidency

1980	Lazar Koliševski
1980–1	Cvijetin Mijatović
1981–2	Serghei Kraigher
1982–3	Petar Stambolić
1983–4	Mika Spiljak
1984–5	Veselin Đuranović
1985–6	Radovan Vlajković
1986–7	Sinan Hasani
1987–8	Lazar Mojsov
1988–9	Raif Dizdarević
1989–90	Janez Drnovsek
1990–1	Borisav Jovic
1991–2	Stipe Mesic

Federal Republic of Yugoslavia

1992–3	Dobrica Cosic
1993–7	Zoran Lilic
1997–	Slobodan Milosevic

Prime Minister

1929–32	Petar Živkovic
1932	Vojislav Marinković
1932–4	Milan Srškić
1934	Nikola Uzunović
1934–5	Bogoljub Jevtić
1935–9	Milan Stojadinović
1939–41	Dragiša Cvetković
1941	Dušan Simović

Government in exile

1942	Slobodan Jovanović
1943	Miloš Trifunović
1943–4	Božidar Purić
1944–5	Ivan Šubašić
1945	Drago Marušić

Home government

1941–4	Milan Nedić
1943–63	Josip Broz Tito
1963–7	Petar Stambolić
1967–9	Mika Špiljak
1969–71	Mitja Ribičič
1971–7	Džemal Bijedić
1977–82	Veselin Đuranović
1982–6	Milca Planinć
1986–9	Branko Mikulić
1989–92	Ante Marković

Federal Republic of Yugoslavia

1992–3	Milan Panić
1993–	Radoje Kontić

First Secretary
Communist Party

1937–52	Josip Broz Tito

League of Communists

1952–80	Josip Broz Tito

Montenegro

Vladika of Montenegro
Petrovich Dynasty

1696–1735	Danilo I
1735–81	Sava *Co-ruler 1750–66*
1750–66	Vasil *Co-ruler*
1782–1830	Petar I
1830–51	Petar II

Prince of Montenegro

Petrovich Dynasty

1851–60	Danilo II
1860–1910	Nicholas

Monarch – Kingdom of Montenegro
Petrovich Dynasty

1910–18	Nicholas

Zaire *see* **Congo, Democratic Republic of**

Zambia

Barotse kings

c.1600	Mboo
?	Inyambo
?	Yeta I
?	Ngalama
?	Yeta II
?	Ngombela
?	Yubia
?	Musanawina
?–c.1780	Musananyanda
c.1780–c.1835	Mulambwa
c.1835–c.1840	Silumelume
c.1840	Mubukwanu
c.1840–c.1851	Sebitwane
c.1851	Mamocesane
c.1851–64	Sekeletu
1864–74	Sepopa
1874–8	Mwanawina I
1878–1916	Lewanika
1916–45	Yeta III
1945–8	Imwiko Lewanika
1948–64	Mwanawina II

President

1964–91	Kenneth David Kaunda
1991–	Frederick Chiluba

Prime Minister

1964–73	Kenneth David Kaunda

1973–5	Mainza Chona
1975–7	Elijah Mudenda
1977–8	Mainza Chona
1978–81	Daniel Lisulu
1981–5	Nalumino Mundia
1985–9	Kebby Musokotwane
1989–91	Malimba Masheke
1991–4	Levy Mwanawasa
1994–	Godfrey Miyanda

Zimbabwe

President

1980–7	Canaan Sodindo Banana
1987–	Robert Gabriel Mugabe

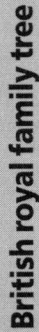

British royal family tree

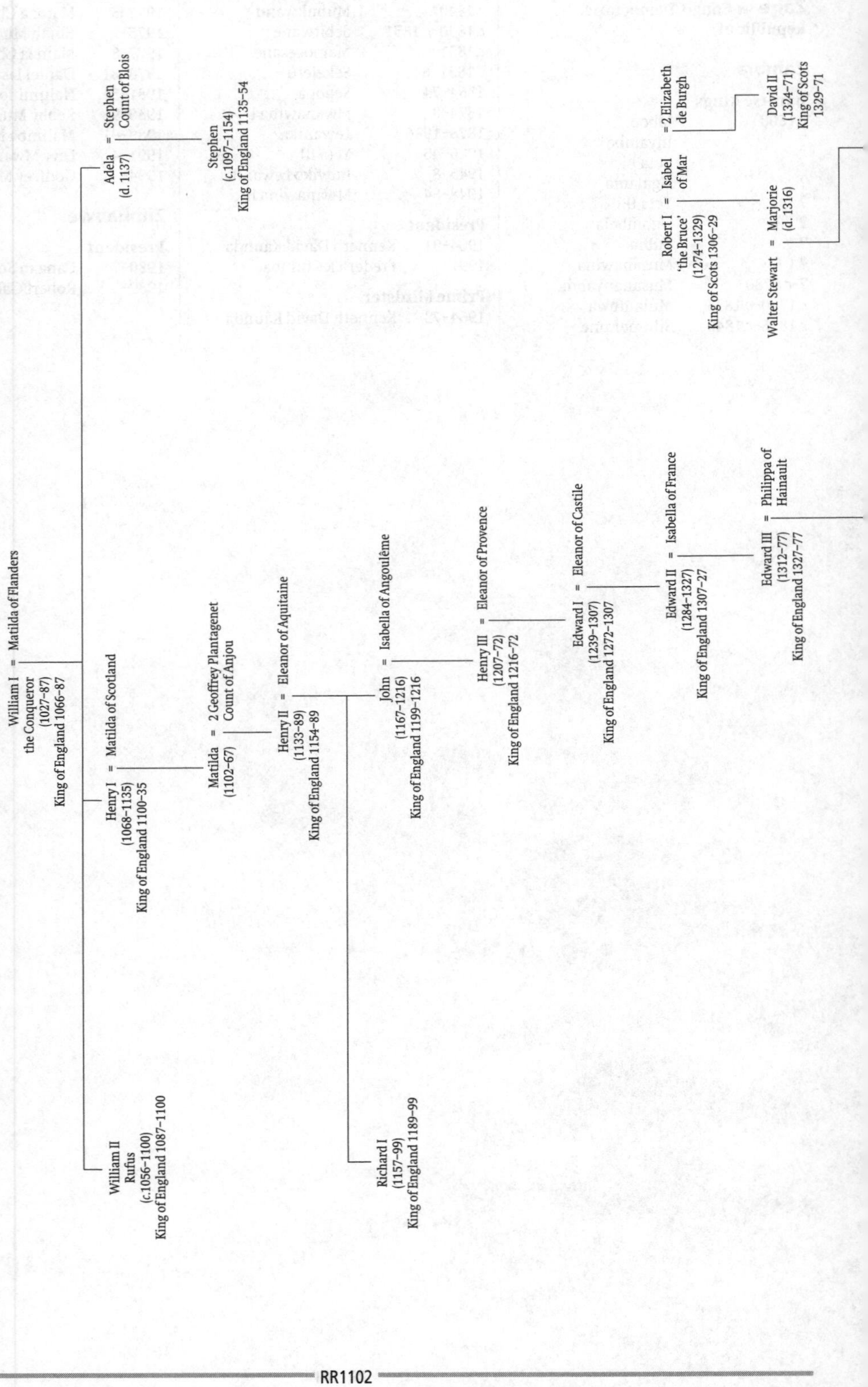

William I = Matilda of Flanders
the Conqueror (1027–87)
King of England 1066–87

William II
Rufus
(c.1056–1100)
King of England 1087–1100

Adela = Stephen
(d. 1137)   Count of Blois

Stephen
(c.1097–1154)
King of England 1135–54

Henry I = Matilda of Scotland
(1068–1135)
King of England 1100–35

Matilda = 2 Geoffrey Plantagenet
(1102–67)   Count of Anjou

Henry II = Eleanor of Aquitaine
(1133–89)
King of England 1154–89

Richard I
(1157–99)
King of England 1189–99

John = Isabella of Angoulême
(1167–1216)
King of England 1199–1216

Henry III = Eleanor of Provence
(1207–72)
King of England 1216–72

Edward I = Eleanor of Castile
(1239–1307)
King of England 1272–1307

Edward II = Isabella of France
(1284–1327)
King of England 1307–27

Edward III = Philippa of Hainault
(1312–77)
King of England 1327–77

Robert I = Isabel
'the Bruce'   of Mar
(1274–1329)
King of Scots 1306–29

= 2 Elizabeth
de Burgh

David II
(1324–71)
King of Scots
1329–71

Walter Stewart = Marjorie
(d. 1316)

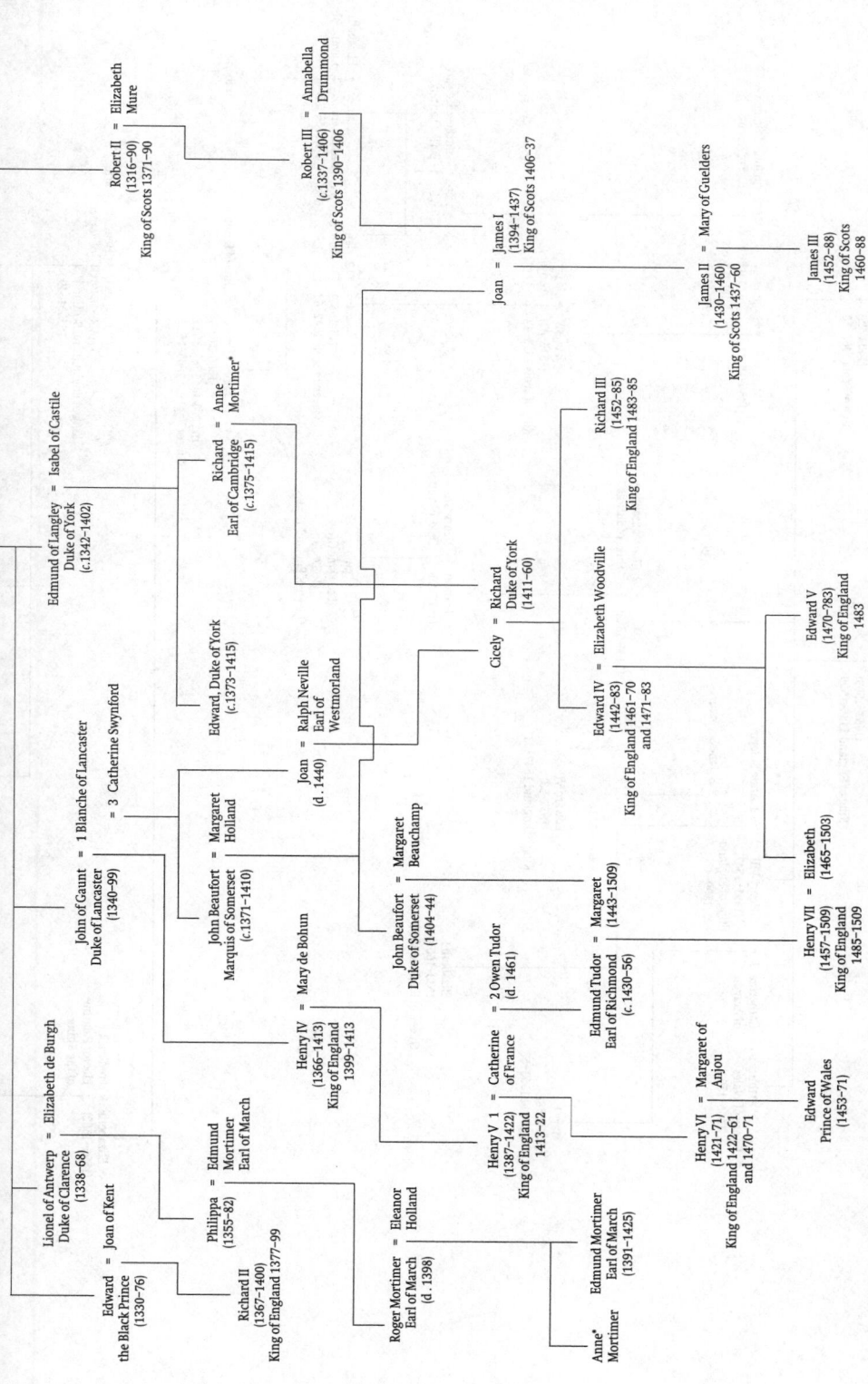

Asterisks denote the same person occurring in a different part of the tree
1 denotes first marriage, 2 second marriage, 3 third marriage

British royal family tree (continued)

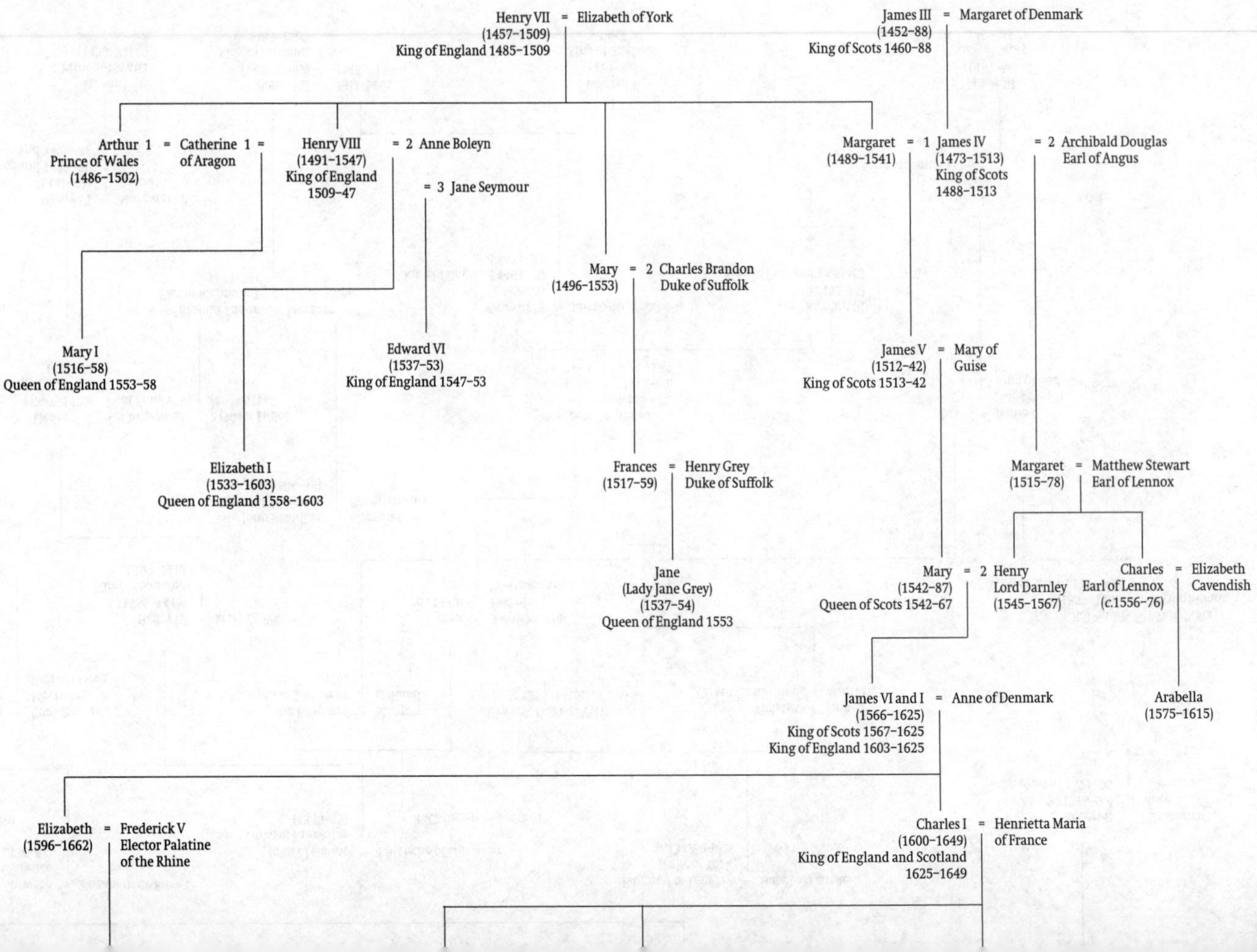

James III = Margaret of Denmark
(1452–88)
King of Scots 1460–88

Henry VII = Elizabeth of York
(1457–1509)
King of England 1485–1509

Margaret = 1 James IV   = 2 Archibald Douglas
(1489–1541)   (1473–1513)   Earl of Angus
              King of Scots
              1488–1513

James V = Mary of
(1512–42)   Guise
King of Scots 1513–42

Margaret = Matthew Stewart
(1515–78)   Earl of Lennox

Charles = Elizabeth
Earl of Lennox   Cavendish
(c.1556–76)

Mary = 2 Henry
(1542–87)   Lord Darnley
Queen of Scots 1542–67   (1545–1567)

Arbella
(1575–1615)

Arthur 1 = Catherine 1 =
Prince of Wales   of Aragon
(1486–1502)

Henry VIII
(1491–1547)
King of England
1509–47

= 2 Anne Boleyn

= 3 Jane Seymour

Mary = 2 Charles Brandon
(1496–1553)   Duke of Suffolk

Edward VI
(1537–53)
King of England 1547–53

Frances = Henry Grey
(1517–59)   Duke of Suffolk

Elizabeth I
(1533–1603)
Queen of England 1558–1603

Jane
(Lady Jane Grey)
(1537–54)
Queen of England 1553

James VI and I = Anne of Denmark
(1566–1625)
King of Scots 1567–1625
King of England 1603–1625

Mary I
(1516–58)
Queen of England 1553–58

Charles I = Henrietta Maria
(1600–1649)   of France
King of England and Scotland
1625–1649

Elizabeth = Frederick V
(1596–1662)   Elector Palatine
of the Rhine

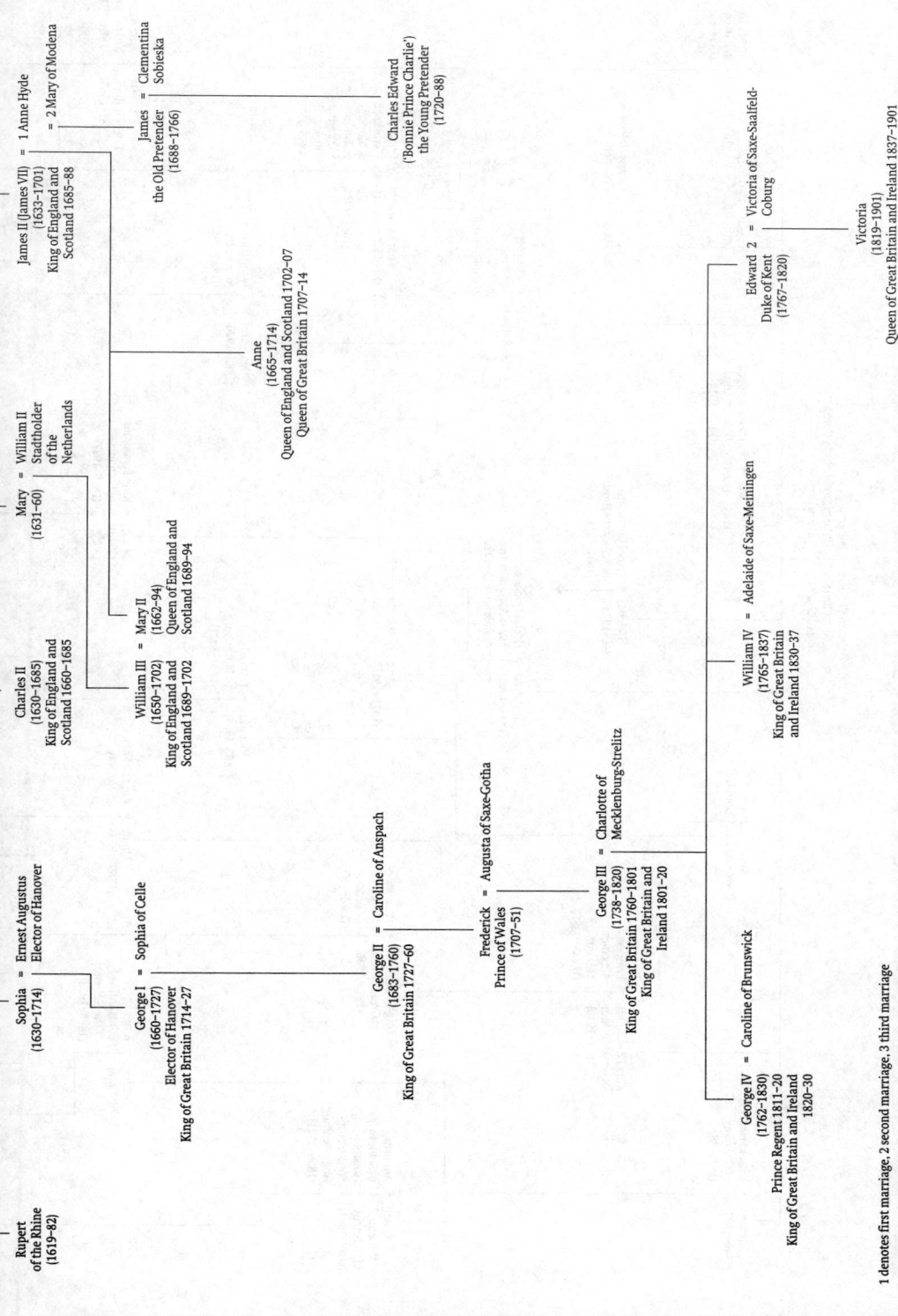

Rupert
of the Rhine
(1619–82)

Sophia = Ernest Augustus
(1630–1714)   Elector of Hanover

Charles II
(1630–1685)
King of England and
Scotland 1660–1685

Mary = William II
(1631–60)   Stadtholder
of the
Netherlands

James II (James VII) = 1 Anne Hyde
(1633–1701)   = 2 Mary of Modena
King of England and
Scotland 1685–88

James = Clementina
the Old Pretender   Sobieska
(1688–1766)

Charles Edward
('Bonnie Prince Charlie')
the Young Pretender
(1720–88)

George I
(1660–1727)
Elector of Hanover
King of Great Britain 1714–27

Sophia of Celle

William III = Mary II
(1650–1702)   (1662–94)
King of England and   Queen of England and
Scotland 1689–1702   Scotland 1689–94

Anne
(1665–1714)
Queen of England and Scotland 1702–07
Queen of Great Britain 1707–14

George II = Caroline of Anspach
(1683–1760)
King of Great Britain 1727–60

Frederick = Augusta of Saxe-Gotha
Prince of Wales
(1707–51)

George III = Charlotte of
(1738–1820)   Mecklenburg-Strelitz
King of Great Britain 1760–1801
King of Great Britain and
Ireland 1801–20

George IV = Caroline of Brunswick
(1762–1830)
Prince Regent 1811–20
King of Great Britain and Ireland
1820–30

William IV = Adelaide of Saxe-Meiningen
(1765–1837)
King of Great Britain
and Ireland 1830–37

Edward   2 = Victoria of Saxe-Saalfeld-
Duke of Kent   Coburg
(1767–1820)

Victoria
(1819–1901)
Queen of Great Britain and Ireland 1837–1901

1 denotes first marriage, 2 second marriage, 3 third marriage

European royal families descended from Queen Victoria

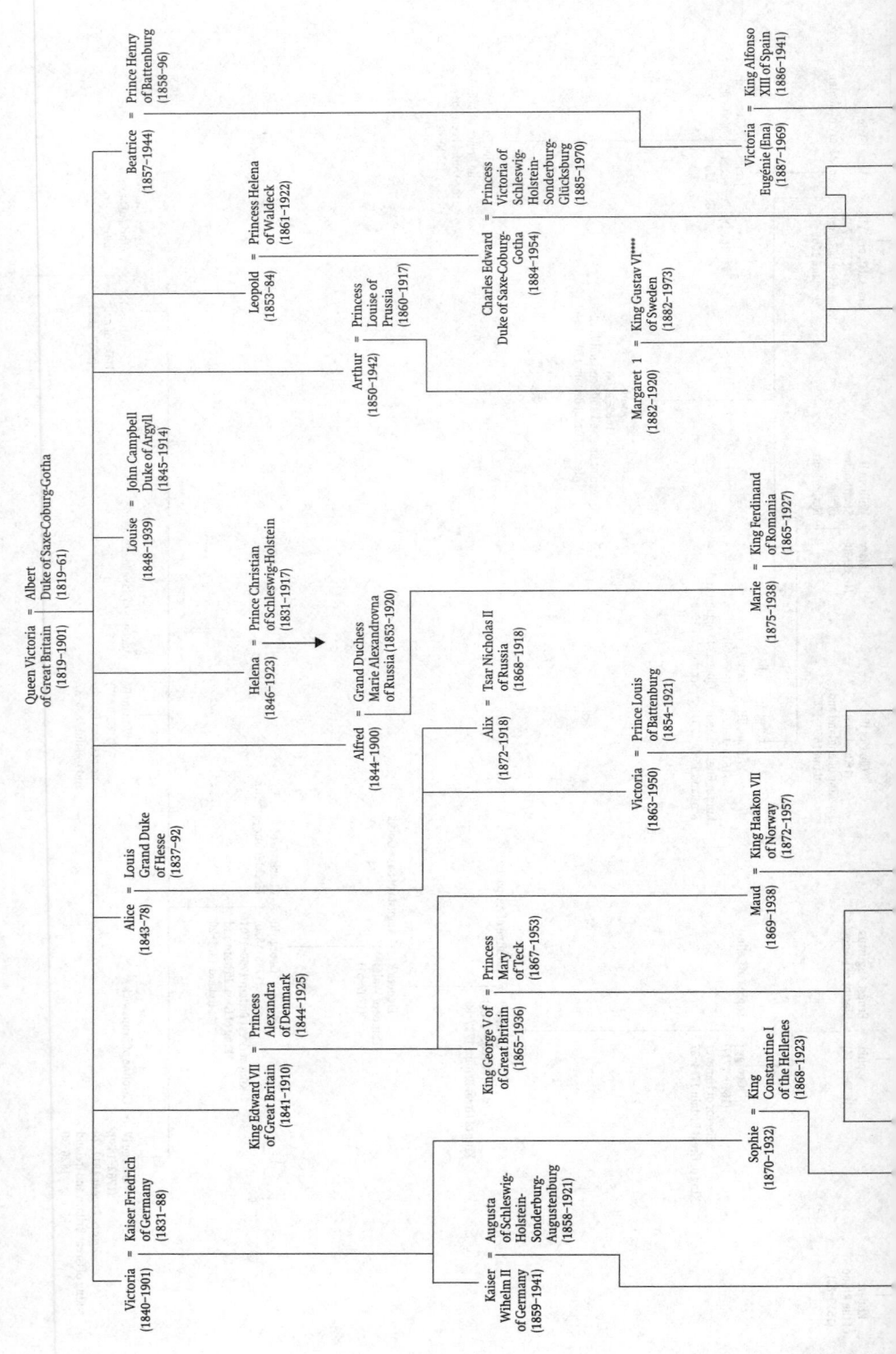

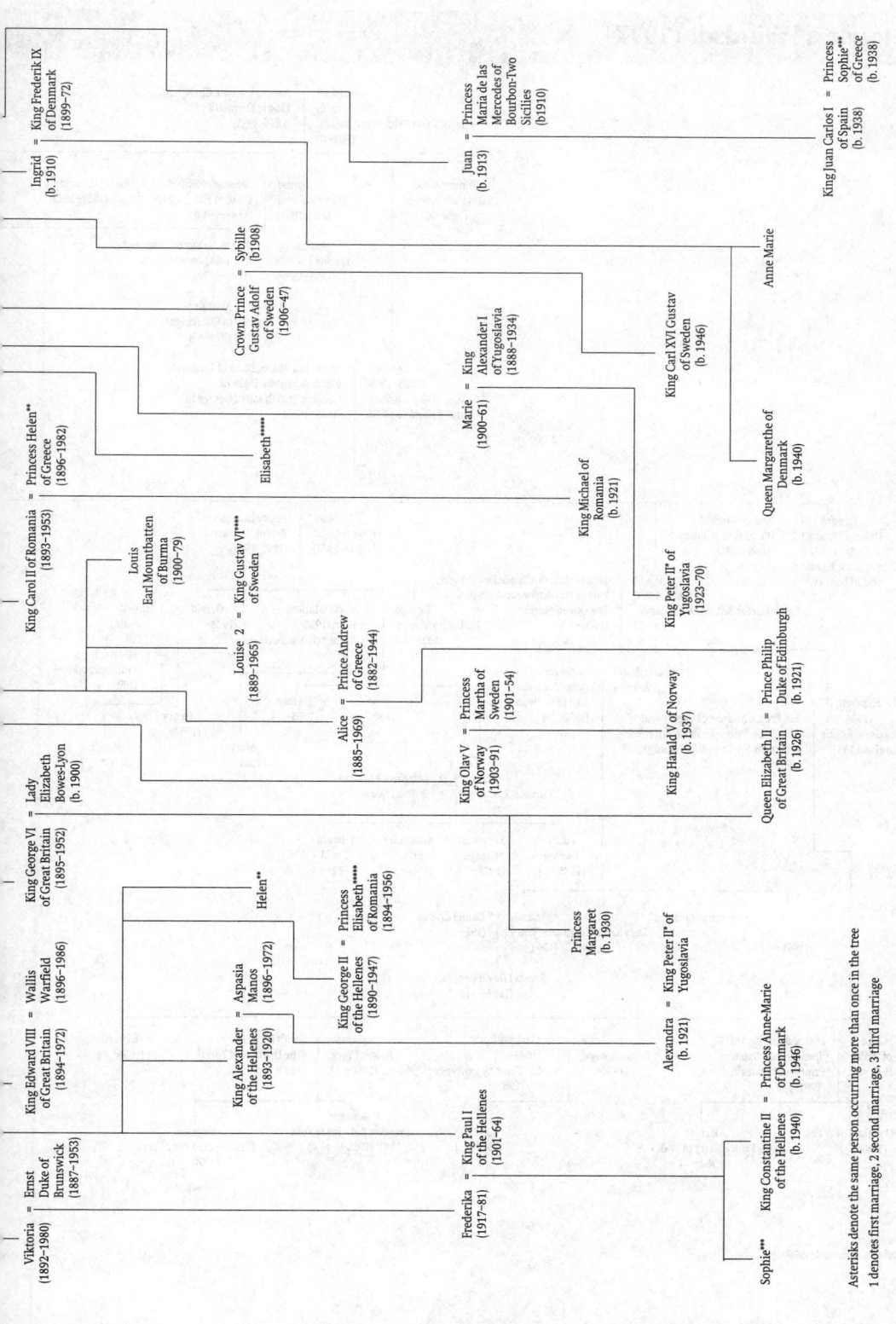

Asterisks denote the same person occurring more than once in the tree
1 denotes first marriage, 2 second marriage, 3 third marriage

The House of Windsor (1917–   )

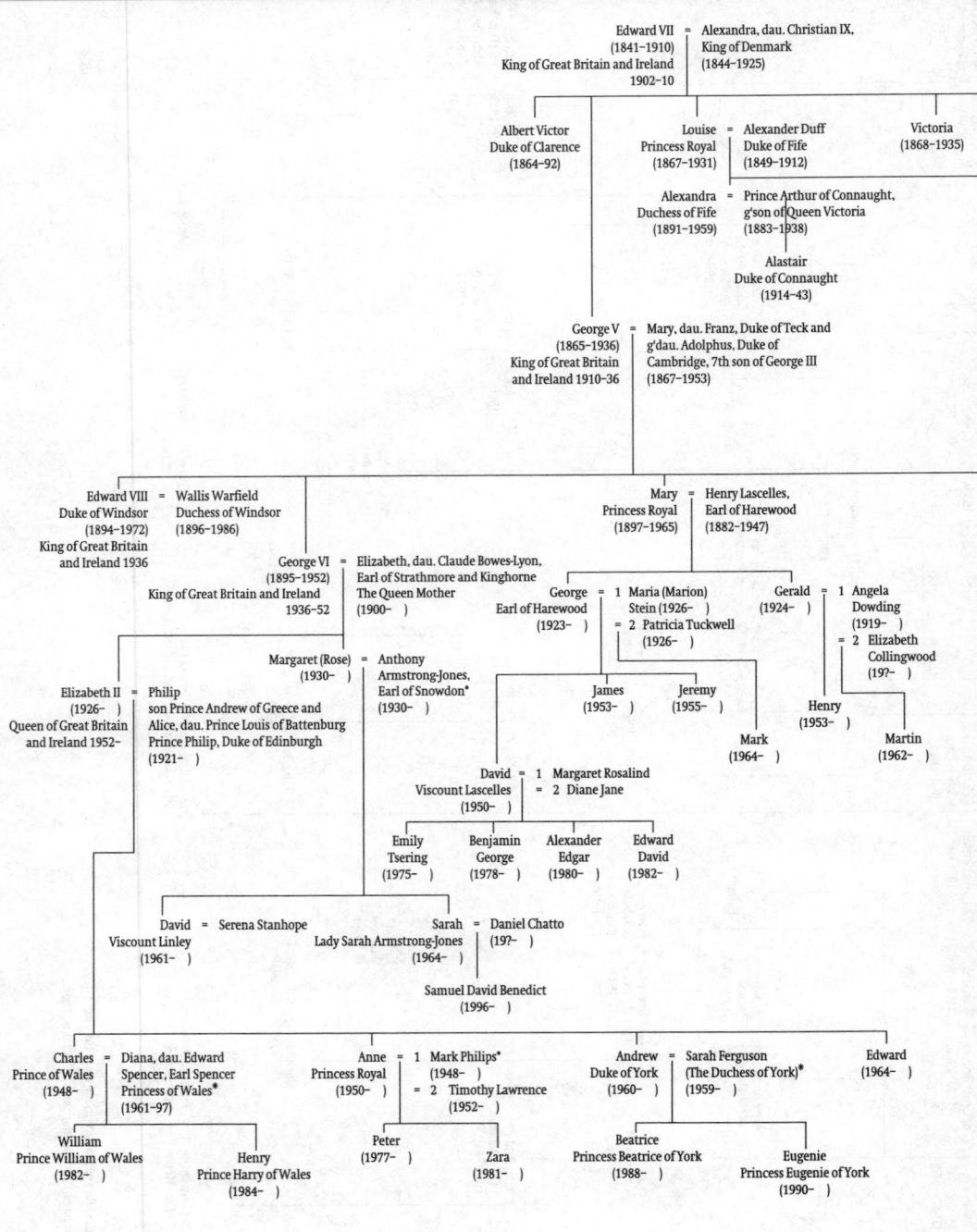

dau. = daughter
* = marriages dissolved, 1996

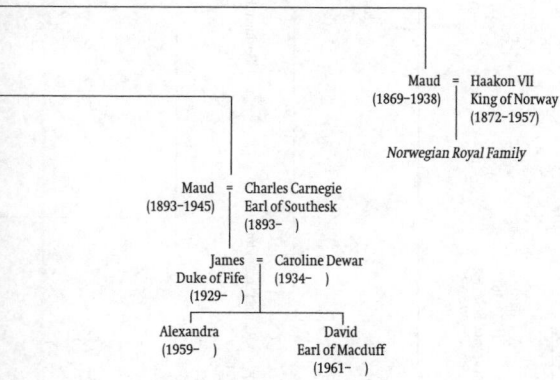

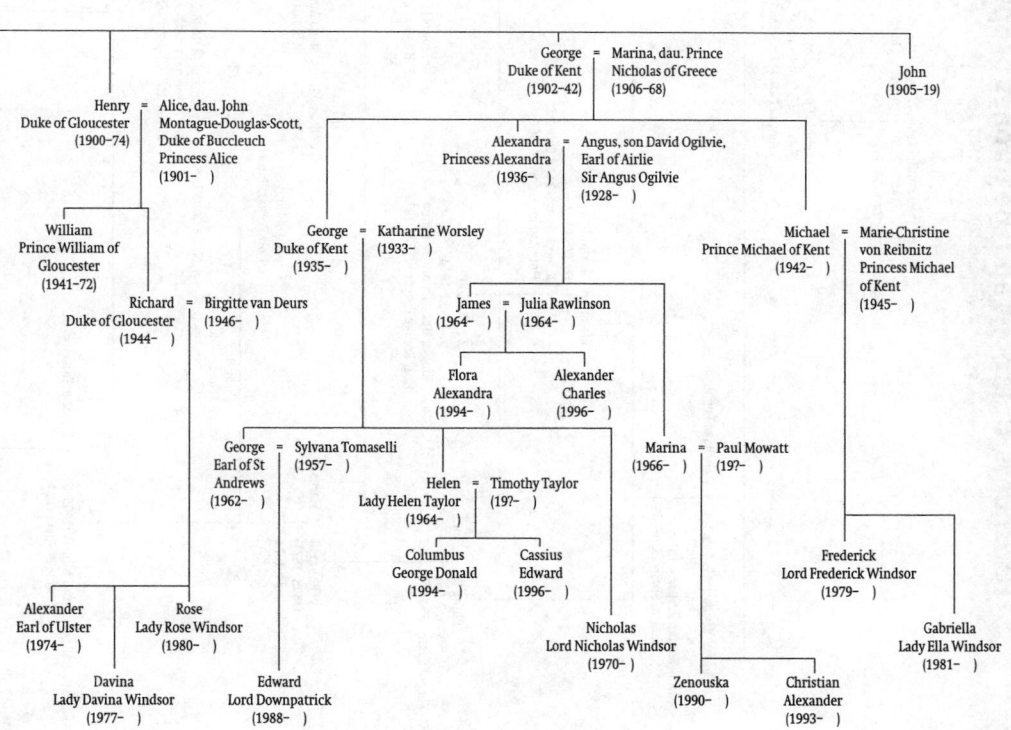

Maud
(1869–1938)
=
Haakon VII
King of Norway
(1872–1957)

Norwegian Royal Family

Maud
(1893–1945)
=
Charles Carnegie
Earl of Southesk
(1893–)

James
Duke of Fife
(1929–)
=
Caroline Dewar
(1934–)

Alexandra
(1959–)

David
Earl of Macduff
(1961–)

George
Duke of Kent
(1902–42)
=
Marina, dau. Prince
Nicholas of Greece
(1906–68)

John
(1905–19)

Henry
Duke of Gloucester
(1900–74)
=
Alice, dau. John
Montague-Douglas-Scott,
Duke of Buccleuch
Princess Alice
(1901–)

Alexandra
Princess Alexandra
(1936–)
=
Angus, son David Ogilvie,
Earl of Airlie
Sir Angus Ogilvie
(1928–)

William
Prince William of
Gloucester
(1941–72)

George
Duke of Kent
(1935–)
=
Katharine Worsley
(1933–)

Michael
Prince Michael of Kent
(1942–)
=
Marie-Christine
von Reibnitz
Princess Michael
of Kent
(1945–)

Richard
Duke of Gloucester
(1944–)
=
Birgitte van Deurs
(1946–)

James
(1964–)
=
Julia Rawlinson
(1964–)

Flora
Alexandra
(1994–)

Alexander
Charles
(1996–)

George
Earl of St
Andrews
(1962–)
=
Sylvana Tomaselli
(1957–)

Marina
(1966–)
=
Paul Mowatt
(19?–)

Helen
Lady Helen Taylor
(1964–)
=
Timothy Taylor
(19?–)

Columbus
George Donald
(1994–)

Cassius
Edward
(1996–)

Frederick
Lord Frederick Windsor
(1979–)

Alexander
Earl of Ulster
(1974–)

Rose
Lady Rose Windsor
(1980–)

Nicholas
Lord Nicholas Windsor
(1970–)

Gabriella
Lady Ella Windsor
(1981–)

Davina
Lady Davina Windsor
(1977–)

Edward
Lord Downpatrick
(1988–)

Zenouska
(1990–)

Christian
Alexander
(1993–)

Hapsburgs, Bourbons and the thrones of Spain, France and the Holy Roman Empire

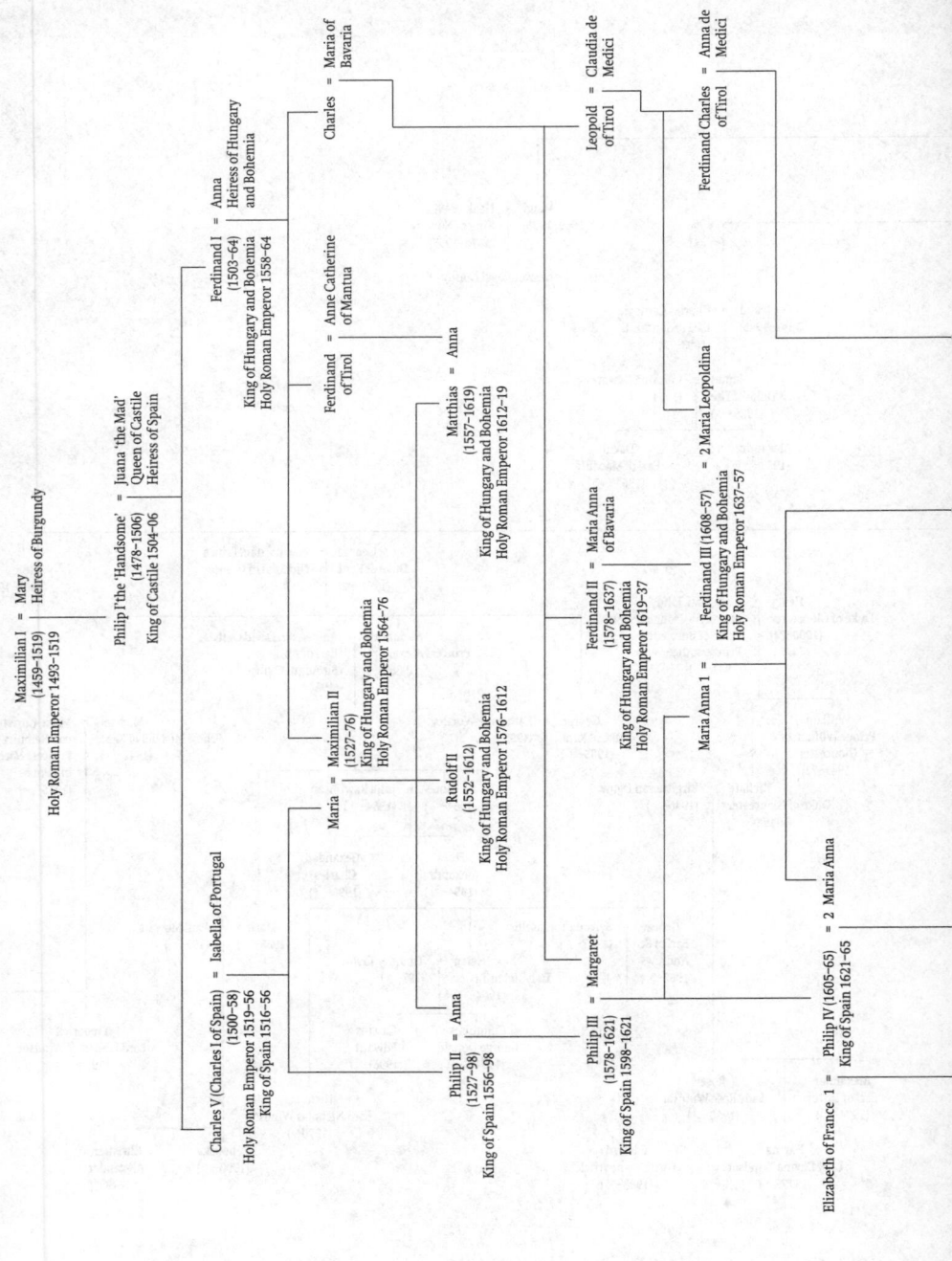

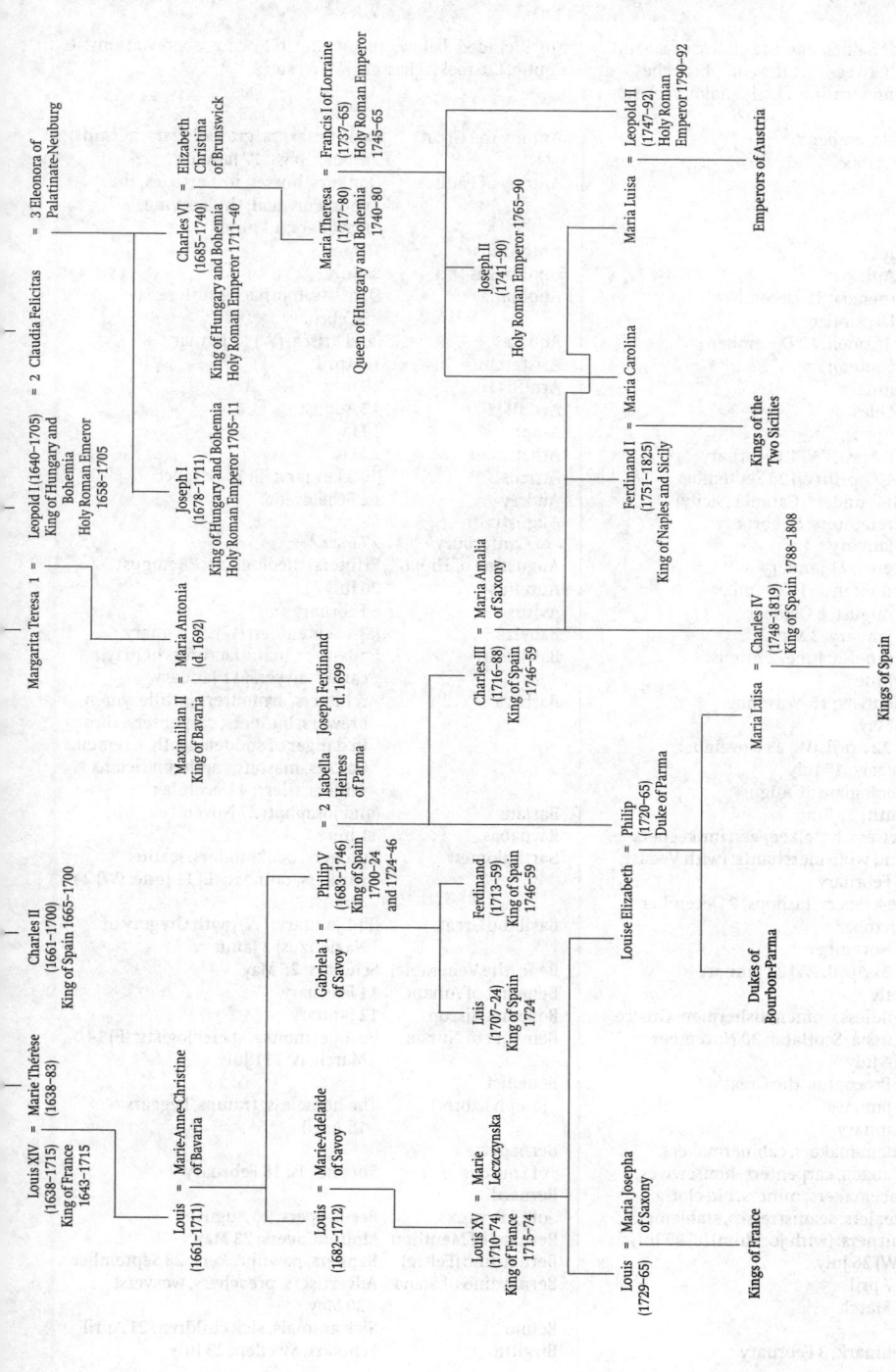

1 denotes first marriage, 2 second marriage, 3 third marriage

Saints – patronages and feast days

The official recognition of Saints, and the choice of a Saint's Day, varies greatly between different branches of Christianity, calendars and localities. Only major variations are included below, using the following abbreviations: C Coptic; G Greek; E Eastern; W Western

Abbo	13 November
Abercius	22 October
Achilleus (and Nereus)	12 May
Adalbert (Magdeburg)	20 June
Adalbert (Prague)	23 April
Adam	Gardeners; 19 December
Adelaide	16 December
Adjutor	Yachtsmen; 18 December
Adomnan (Adamnan)	23 September
Adrian the African	9 January
Aegidius	see Giles
Ælfheah (Alphege)	19 April
Agabus	(E) 8 April; (W) 13 February
Agapetus	(E) 17 April; (W) 20 September
Agatha	Bell-founders, Catania (Sicily), firefighters; 5 February
Agatho	10 January
Agnes	Virgins; 21 January
Agricola	(and Vitalis); 4 November
Aidan	31 August, 8 October
Ailred	12 January, 3 March
Alban	17 June, 20 June, 2 August
Alban of Mainz	21 June
Albertus Magnus	Scientists; 15 November
Alexander Nevski	(C) 22 April; (W) 23 November
Alexis of Rome	Beggars; 17 July
Alfonso de Liguori	Theologians; 1 August
Aloysius Gonzaga	Youth; 21 June
Amand	Brewers, hotelkeepers, innkeepers and wine merchants; (with Vedast) 6 February
Ambrose	Bee-keepers, bishops; 7 December
Ammon	4 October
Amphilochius	23 November
Anastasius	(E) 21 April; (W) 22 January
Anatolius	3 July
Andrew	Childless women, fishermen, Greece, Russia, Scotland; 30 November
Andrew of Crete	(E) 4 July
Andrew Procop	see Procopius 'the Great'
Angela Merici	27 January
Angela of Foligno	4 January
Anne	Broom-makers, cabinetmakers, Canada, carpenters, housewives, lacemakers, miners, old-clothes dealers, seamstresses, stablemen, turners; (with Joachim) (E) 25 July; (W) 26 July
Anselm	21 April
Anselm of Lucca	18 March
Anskar (Ansgar; Scharies)	Denmark; 3 February
Antonio Zaccaria	5 July
Antony Claret	24 October

Antony the Great	Basket-makers, gravediggers, hermits, monks, pigs; 17 January
Antony of Padua	Donkeys, horses, lost articles, the poor, Portugal, the starving, travellers; 13 June
Antoninus	10 May
Apollinaris	23 July
Apollonia	Dentists, toothache sufferers; 9 February
Aquila	(and Prisca) (W) 18 January
Aristarchus	15 April
Arnulf (1)	18 July
Arnulf (2)	15 August
Asaph	1 May
Athanasius	2 May
Atticus	(E) 8 January; (E) 11 October
Audrey	see Etheldreda
Augustine of Canterbury	27 May
Augustine of Hippo	Printers, theologians; 28 August
Aurelius	20 July
Avitus	5 February
Babylas	(E) 4 September; (W) 24 January
Balthasar	Epileptics, manufacturers of playing cards, sawyers; 11 January
Barbara	Architects, armourers, artillerymen, brewers, builders, carpenters, those in danger of sudden death, firemen, hatters, masons, mathematicians, miners, tilers; 4 December
Barlam	(and Josaphat) 27 November
Barnabas	11 June
Bartholomew	Butchers, bookbinders, leather-workers, tanners; (E) 11 June; (W) 24 August
Basil the Great	(E) 1 January; (W) (with Gregory of Nazianzus) 2 January
Bede (the Venerable)	Scholars; 25 May
Benedict of Aniane	11 February
Benedict Biscop	12 January
Benedict of Nursia	Europe, monks, speleologists; (E) 14 March; (W) 11 July
Benedict Joseph Labre	The homeless, tramps, beggars; 16 April
Bernadette of Lourdes	Shepherds; 18 February
Bernard of Clairvaux	Bee-keepers; 20 August
Bernard of Menthon	Mountaineers; 28 May
Bernardino (Feltre)	Bankers, pawnbrokers; 28 September
Bernardino of Siena	Advertisers, preachers, weavers; 20 May
Beuno	Sick animals, sick children; 21 April
Birgitta	Scholars, Sweden; 23 July

Blaise (Blasius)	Builders, sick cattle, stonecutters, throat sufferers, woolcombers, wool-weavers; (E) 11 February; (W) 3 February
Bonaventure	15 July
Boniface (Wynfrith)	Germany; 5 June
Boniface I	4 September
Botolph	17 June
Brendan the Navigator	Sailors; 16 May
Bridget (Brigid, Bride)	Blacksmiths, dairymaids, healers, poets; 1 February
Bridget of Sweden	*see* Birgitta
Bruno the Great	11 October
Bruno of Cologne	6 October
Caedmon	Singers; 11 February
Caesarius	27 August
Cajetan (Gaetano)	7 August
Callixtus (Callistus) I	14 October
Camillus of Lellis	Hospitals, nurses, sick people; 14 July
Carlo Borromeo	Bishops; 4 November
Casimir	Poland; 4 March
Catherine of Alexandria	The clergy, girls, knifegrinders, librarians, millers, nurses, old maids, philosophers, spinners, students, tanners, turners, wheel-wrights; 25 November
Catherine of Bologna	Painters; 9 March
Catherine of Genoa	15 September
Catherine dei Ricci	13 February
Catherine of Siena	Dominicans, Italy; 29 April
Catherine of Sweden	*see* Katarina
Cecilia	Musical instrument makers, musicians; 22 November
Chad (Ceadda)	2 March
Christopher	Archers, fullers, greengrocers, motorists, travellers; 25 July
Chrodegang of Metz	6 March
Chromatius	2 December
Chrysogonus	(E) 22 December; (W) 24 November
Cilian	8 July
Clare of Assisi	Embroiderers, television, washer-women; 11 August
Claude	Sculptors, turners, toymakers; 6 June
Clement Hofbauer	15 March
Clement I	Boatmen, lighthousekeepers, sick children; (E) 24 November; (W) 23 November
Clement of Alexandria	5 December
Clotilda	3 June
Colman of Lindisfarne	18 February
Columba (Colmcille)	Poets; 9 June
Columban (Columbanus)	23 November
Comgall	10 May
Concordia	Nannies and children's nurses, nursing mothers; 13 August
Constantine	11 March
Cornelius	16 September

Cosmas	(and Damian) Chemists, doctors, hairdressers (men's), midwives, sur-geons; (E) 1 July, 1 November; (W) 26 September
Cosmas Melodus	(E) 14 October
Crispin and Crispinian	Glovemakers, shoemakers, weavers; 25 October
Cuthbert	Seamen, shepherds; 20 March
Cuthbert Mayne	25 November
Cyprian of Carthage	26 September, 16 September
Cyril	(and Methodius) Ecumenists; (E) 11 May; (W) 14 February
Cyril of Alexandria	(E) 9 June; (W) 27 June
Cyril of Jerusalem	18 March
Damasus I	Archaeologists; 11 December
Damian	(and Cosmas) Doctors, hairdressers (men's), surgeons; (E) 1 July, 1 November; (W) 26 September
David (Dewi)	Poets, Wales; 1 March
Deiniol	11 September
Demetrius	(E) 26 October; (W) 9 October
Denis (Dionysius)	France; 9 October
Deusdedit	14 July
Dismas	Prisoners, thieves, undertakers; 25 March
Dominic	Astronomers; 8 August
Dorothy	Florists, gardeners; 6 February
Dubricius	14 November
Dunstan	Blacksmiths, the blind, goldsmiths, jewellers, locksmiths; 19 May
Dympna	Epileptics, the mentally ill; 15 May
Ealdhelm	*see* Aldhelm
Edmund (Rich)	16 November
Edmund the Martyr	20 November
Edward the Confessor	Kings; 13 October
Edward the Martyr	18 March
Edwin	12 October
Egbert	24 April
Elizabeth	(E) 8 November; (W) 5 November
Elizabeth of Hungary	Bakers, charitable societies, nurses; 17 November
Elizabeth of Portugal	4 July
Eloi (Eligius)	Blacksmiths, clockmakers, cutlers, far-riers, goldsmiths, jewellers, jockeys, labourers, metalworkers, saddlers, sick horses, toolmakers, veterinary surgeons, wheelwrights; 1 December
Ennodius	17 July
Ephraem Syrus	(E) 28 January; (W) 9 June
Epiphanius	12 May
Erasmus	Navigators, sufferers from colic and intestinal disease ; 2 June
Erik	Sweden; 18 May
Ethelbert	25 February
Ethelburga	11 October
Etheldreda (Audrey)	23 June
Ethelwold	1 August
Eucherius	16 November
Euphemia	16 September
Eusebius of Vercelli	2 August
Eustace	Huntsmen; (E) 2 November; (W) 20 September

Eustathius of Antioch	16 July
Euthymius	20 January
Exuperius	28 September
Fabian	20 January
Fabiola	27 December
Felicitas	(and Perpetua) 7 March
Felicity	23 November
Felix of Dunwich	8 March
Ferdinand (III)	Engineers; 30 May
Fiacre (Fiachrach)	Gardeners, sufferers from venereal diseases, taxi-drivers; 30 August; 1 September
Fidelis of Sigmaringen	24 April
Finbar	25 September
Finnian	10 September
Firmilian	(E) 28 October
Flavian	(E) 16 February; (W) 18 February
Florian	Firemen; 4 May
Frances of Rome	Motorists; 9 March
Francesca Cabrini	Immigrants; 22 December
Francis Borgia	Portugal; 10 October
Francis of Assisi	Animals and birds, ecologists, Italy, merchants; 4 October
Francis of Paola	Sailors; 2 April
Francis of Sales	Authors, editors, journalists, writers ; 24 January
Francis Xavier	Missionaries; 3 December
Fructuosus	21 January
Frumentius	(C) 18 December; (G) 30 November; (W) 27 September
Fulbert	10 April
Fulgentius	1 January
Gabriel	Broadcasters, diplomats, messengers, postal, radio and television workers; (E) 26 March; (W) 24 March; 29 September
Gaetano	see Cajetan
Gall	16 October
Gaudentius	25 October
Gelasius I	21 November
Gemma Galgani	14 May
Genesius of Arles	Secretaries; 25 August
Genesius of Rome	Actors, clowns, comedians; 3 June
Geneviève	Paris; 3 January
Gennaro	see Januarius
George	Archers, armourers, England, farmers, knights, plague, leprosy and syphilis sufferers, Portugal, scouts, soldiers; 23 April; (C) 18 April
Gerard Majella	Lay-brothers; 16 October
Gereon	Headache sufferers; 10 October
Germanus of Auxerre	31 July
Gertrude of Helfta	West Indies; 16 November
Gertrude of Nivelles	Cats; 17 March
Gervase	(and Protase) 19 June
Gilbert of Sempringham	4 February
Gildas	29 January
Giles (Aegidius)	Beggars, cancer sufferers, childless women, cripples, hermits, horses, lepers; 1 September
Giovanni Colombini	31 July
Gotthard	4 May

Gregory I the Great	Musicians, popes, singers, teachers; 29 March, 3 September
Gregory II	11 February
Gregory VII (Hildebrand)	25 May
Gregory of Agrigentum	23 November
Gregory of Nazianzus	(E) 25 January; (W) (with Basil the Great) 2 January
Gregory of Nyssa	9 March
Gregory of Tours	17 November
Gregory Palamas	(E) 14 November
Gregory Thaumaturgus	17 November
Gudule	8 January
Guthlac	11 April
Hedwig	16 October
Hegesippus	7 April
Helena	(E) 21 May; (W) 18 August
Henry II	13 July
Hilarion	Hermits; 21 October
Hilary (of Poitiers)	Lawyers; 13 January
Hilary of Arles	5 May
Hilda	17 November
Hildebrand	see Gregory VII
Hildegard	17 September
Hippolytus	Horses; (E) 30 January; (W) 13 August
Homobonus	Clothworkers, merchants, tailors; 13 November
Honoré (Honoratus)	Bakers; 16 January
Hormisdas	6 August
Hubert	Dogs (healthy), forestry workers, huntsmen, instrument makers; 3 November
Hugh of Cluny	29 April
Hugh of Grenoble	1 April
Hugh of Avalon (Lincoln)	17 November
Hyacinth	17 August
Ignatius of Antioch	17 October, (G) 20 December
Ignatius Loyola	Retreatants; 31 July
Ildefonsus	23 January
Illtyd	6 November
Innocent I	28 July
Irenaeus	(E) 23 August; (W) 28 June
Isidore of Pelusium	4 February
Isidore of Seville	Farmers; 4 April
Ivo	Lawyers, orphans; 19 May
Ivo of Chartres	23 May
Jacob of Nisibis	15 July
James (the Great)	Pilgrims, Spain, knights, labourers, rheumatism sufferers, soldiers; (E) 30 April; (W) 25 July
James (the Younger)	(E) 9 October; (W) 23 October; (and Philip) (W) 3 May
Jane Frances de Chantal	12 December
Januarius (Gennaro)	(E) 21 April; (W) 19 September
Jean-Baptiste de la Salle	Teachers; 7 April
Jean-Baptiste Vianney	Parish priests; 4 August
Jerome	Archaeologists, librarians, students; 30 September

Jerome Emiliani	Orphans and abandoned children; 8 February
Joachim	(and Anne) (E) 9 September; (W) 26 July
Joan of Arc	France, soldiers; 30 May
John I	18 May
John the Apostle	Publishers, writers, theologians; (E) 26 September; (W) 6 May, 27 December
John of Avila	10 May
John the Baptist	Bird-dealers, lambs, monks, tailors; (Beheading) 29 August; (Birth) 24 June; (E) (Conception) 23 September; (Baptism of Christ) 7 January
John of Beverley	7 May
John Bosco	Editors, labourers, schoolboys, youth; 31 January
John of Capistrano	Jurists; 23 October
John Chrysostom	Preachers; (E) 13 November; (W) 13 September
John Climacus	30 March
John of Damascus	4 December
John Eudes	19 August
John the Faster	(E) 2 September
John Fisher	(and Thomas More) 22 June
John of God	Booksellers, hospitals, nurses, printers, the sick; 8 March
John Gualbert	12 July
John of Kanti	23 December
John Leonardi	9 October
John of Nepomuk	Bridges, Czechoslovakia; 16 May
John of Parma	20 March
John of the Cross	Poets, mystics and mystical theologians; 14 December
John Ogilvie	10 March
Josaphat	Ecumenists; 12 November; (and Barlam) 27 November
Joseph	Belgium, bursars, cabinetmakers, Canada, carpenters, fathers, manual workers; 19 March; (E) 31 July
Joseph of Arimathea	Gravediggers, funeral directors; (E) 31 July; (W) 17 March
Joseph Calasanctius	25 August
Joseph (Cupertino)	Airmen and air passengers, astronauts; 18 September
Jude	Hopeless cases; (E) 19 June; (and Simon) 28 October
Julian the Hospitaller	Boatmen, clowns, fiddlers, hoteliers, travellers; 12 February
Juliana of Liège	5 April
Julius I	12 April
Justin the Martyr	Philosophers; 1 June
Justus	10 November
Katarina of Sweden	Women in danger of miscarrying; 24 March
Kentigern (Mungo)	14 January
Kevin	3 June
Knut Sveinnson (Canute)	Denmark; 19 January
Ladislaus	27 June
Lambert	Children; 17 September
Laurence	Cooks, deacons, fire-fighters, restauranteurs; 10 August
Laurence of Brindisi	21 July
Leander	27 February
Leger	see Leodegar
Leo I the Great	(E) 18 February; (W) 10 November
Leo III	12 June
Leo IV	17 July
Leo IX	19 April
Leodegar (Leger)	2 October
Leonard	Blacksmiths, captives, coopers, greengrocers, locksmiths, prisoners of war, women in childbirth; 6 November
Linus	23 September
Louis (IX)	Builders, distillers, France, haberdashers, hairdressers, kings, sculptors; 25 August
Lucian of Antioch	(E) 15 October; (W) 7 January
Lucy	The blind, glassworkers, writers; 13 December
Luke	Artists, butchers, doctors, glassworkers, lacemakers, painters, sculptors, surgeons; 18 October
Lull	16 October
Lupus of Troyes	29 July
Macarius of Alexandria	2 January
Macarius of Egypt	15 January
Macarius of Jerusalem	10 March
Machutus (Malo)	15 November
Macrina	19 July
Malachy (Mael Maedoc)	3 November
Mamertus	11 May
Marcella	31 January
Marcellina	17 July
Marcellinus	(and Peter) 2 June
Marcian	10 January
Margaret of Antioch	The dying, women in childbirth; (E) 13 July; (W) 20 July
Margaret of Cortona	Repentant prostitutes; 22 February
Margaret (of Scotland)	Scotland; 16 November
Marguerite Marie Alacoque	17 October
Maria Goretti	6 July
Mark	Glaziers, lawyers, secretaries; 25 April
Martha	Cooks, hoteliers, housewives, lay-sisters, servants, waiters, washerwomen; (E) 6 June; (W) 29 July
Martin I	13 April
Martin of Braga	20 March
Martin de Porres	Hairdressers (men's), race relations, beggars, the poor; 3 November
Martin of Tours	France, geese, horsemen, inn-keepers, publicans, soldiers, tailors; (E) 12 November; (W) 11 November
Mary Magdalene	Glovemakers, hairdressers (ladies'), perfumers, repentant prostitutes, penitents; 22 July
Mary of Egypt	Repentant prostitutes; (E) 1 April; (W) 2 April
Mary (the Virgin)	Mothers, nuns, virgins; (Purification) 2 February; (Annunciation) 25 March; (Visitation) 31 May; (Assumption) 15 August; (Nativity) 8 September; (Conception) 8 December

O L Help of Christians	Australia, New Zealand
O L of Czestochowa	Poland
O L of Grace	Motorcyclists
O L of Loreto	Aviators; 10 December
O L of Mt Carmel	16 July
O L of Sorrows	15 September
O L of the Assumption	France, India, South Africa; 15 August
Matthew	Accountants, bankers, book-keepers, tax-collectors; (E) 16 November; (W) 21 September
Matthias	(G) 9 August; (W) 14 May
Maurice	Dyers, infantrymen, Piedmont, Savoy, Sardinia, weavers; 22 September
Maurus	15 January
Maximilian Kolbe	14 August
Maximus	(E) 21 January; (W) 13 August
Mechthild	19 November
Médard	Toothache sufferers; 8 June
Meinrad	21 January
Meletius	12 February
Melito	1 April
Mellitus	24 April
Menas of Constantinople	25 August
Mennas of Egypt	Desert caravans, merchants, pilgrims; 11 November
Mercurius	25 November
Mesrob	25 November
Methodius	Ecumenists; (and Cyril) (E) 11 May; (W) 14 February
Michael	Germany, grocers, hatters, paratroopers, policemen, radiologists, sick people; (and All Angels) 29 September
Mildred	13 July
Miltiades	10 December
Modomnoc	Bee-keepers; 13 February
Monica	Married women, mothers, widows; 27 August
Mungo	see Kentigern
Nectarius	11 October
Neot	31 July
Nereus	(and Achilleus) 12 May
Nerses	19 November
Nicephorus	(G) 2 June; (W) 13 March
Niceta	22 June
Nicholas	Apothecaries, brewers, children, fishermen, Greece, merchants, pawnbrokers, perfumiers, Russia, sailors, unmarried girls; 6 December
Nicholas I the Great	13 November
Nicholas of Flüe	22 March
Nicholas of Tolentino	10 September
Nilus the Ascetic	12 November
Ninian (Nynia, Ringan)	26 August
Norbert	6 June
Odilia	1 December
Odo of Cluny	18 November
Oengus	11 March
Olaf I Haraldsson	Norway; 29 July
Oliver Plunket	1 July
Optatus	4 June

Orsisius	15 June
Osmund	The insane, the paralysed, sufferers from hernias and toothache, soldiers; 4 December
Oswald (of Northumbria)	10 August
Oswald of York	28 February
Oswin	20 August
Otto	30 September
Ouen	24 August
Pacian	9 March
Palladius	7 July
Pammachius	30 August
Pamphilus	(E) 16 February; (W) 1 June
Pancras (of Rome)	Children; 12 May
Pantaenus	7 July
Pantaleon	Midwives; 27 July
Paphnutius	11 September
Paschal Baylon	17 May
Patrick	Ireland; 17 March
Paul	Missionary bishops, ropemakers; (Conversion) 25 January; (and Peter) 29 June
Paul Miki	6 February
Paul of Constantinople	(E) 6 November; (W) 7 June
Paul of the Cross	19 October
Paul of Thebes	(E) 15 January; (W) 10 January
Paula	Widows; 26 January
Paulinus of Nola	28 January, 22 June
Paulinus of Trier	31 August
Paulinus of York	10 October
Perpetua	(and Felicitas) 7 March
Peter (Simon)	Fishermen, locksmiths, popes; (St Peter's Chains) 1 August; (and Paul) 29 June
Peter	(and Marcellinus) 2 June
Peter of Alcántara	19 October
Peter Canisius	21 December
Peter Chanel	28 April
Peter Chrysologus	30 July
Peter Claver	Blacks, race relations; 9 September
Peter Damian	see Pietro Damiani
Peter Martyr	The Inquisition; 29 April
Peter of Tarantaise	8 May
Petroc	4 June
Petronius	4 October
Phaebadius	25 April
Philastrius	18 July
Phileas	4 February
Philibert	20 August
Philip	(and James the Younger) (E) 14 November; (W) 3 May
Philip Neri	26 May
Phocas of Sinope	Agricultural workers, gardeners, sailors; 14 July; 22 September
Pietro Damiani	21 February
Pionius	1 February
Pirmin	3 November
Pius I	11 July
Pius V	30 April
Pius X	21 August
Polycarp	23 February
Pontius	8 March
Porphyrius	26 February

Pothinus	2 June
Praxedes	21 July
Prisca	(and Aquila) (W) 8 July
Priscilla	(E) 13 February
Procopius 'the Great'	Czechoslovakia
Prosper of Aquitaine	25 June
Protase	(and Gervase) 19 June
Pudentiana	(W) 19 May
Pudus	(E) 15 April
Pulcheria	10 September
Quadratus	26 May
Radegunde	13 August
Raphael	The blind; 24 October; (with Michael and All Angels) 29 September
Raymond Nonnatus	Midwives, women in childbirth; 31 August
Raymund of Pennafort	Canonists; 7 January
Remy (Remigius)	1 October
Richard of Chichester	Coachmen; 3 April
Ringan	see Ninian
Rita of Cascia	Hopeless cases, women unhappily married; 22 May
Robert of Molesme	29 April
Robert Bellarmine	17 May, 17 September
Roch	Invalids, prisoners, tilemakers; 16 August
Romanos	1 October
Romanus	18 November
Romuald of Ravenna	19 June
Rose of Lima	Florists, the Philippines, South America; 23 August
Sabas	5 December
Sabina	29 August
Samson	28 July
Satyrus	17 September
Scharies	see Anskar
Scholastica	Benedictine nuns; 10 February
Sebaldus	19 August
Sebastian	Archers, athletes, soldiers; (E) 18 December; (W) (with Fabian) 20 January
Seraphim of Sarov	2 January
Serapion of Antioch	30 October
Serapion of Thmuis	21 March
Sergius of Antioch	9 September
Sergius of Rostov	25 September
Severinus	8 January
Severus	Drapers, silk and wool manufacturers, weavers; 1 February
Sidonius Apollinaris	23 August
Silas	(G) 30 July, (W) 13 July
Simeon	(E) 3 February
Simeon Metaphrastes	(E) 9 November; (W) 28 November
Simeon Stylites	(E) 1 September; (W) 5 January
Simon	Fishermen; (E) 10 May; (W) (and Jude) 28 October
Simon Stock	16 May
Simplicianus	16 August
Simplicius	10 March, 2 March
Siricius	26 November
Sithney	Dogs (mad); 4 August
Sixtus II	6 August
Sophronius	11 March

Spyridion	(E) 12 December; (W) 14 December
Stanislaus	Poland; 11 April
Stephen	Bricklayers, deacons, headache sufferers, smelters, stonecutters; (E) 27 December; (W) 26 December
Stephen Harding	17 April
Stephen I	(E) 2 August; 7 September; (W) 2 August
Stephen I (of Hungary)	Hungary; 16 August
Susanna	11 August
Swithin	15 July
Sylvester I	(E) 2 January; (W) 31 December
Symmachus	19 July
Tarasius	25 February
Tarsicius	Altar servers; 15 August
Teilo	9 February
Telemachus	1 January
Teresa of Avila	France, Spain; 15 October
Theodore	(G) 8 February
Theodore of Studios	11 November
Theodore of Tarsus	19 September
Theophilus	15 October
Thérèse of Lisieux	Florists, France, missionaries; 1 October
Thiemo	Engravers; 28 September
Thomas the Apostle	Architects, the blind, builders, Portugal; 21 December; 3 July; (G) 6 October
Thomas Aquinas	Philosophers, scholars, students, theologians; 28 January
Thomas à Becket	29 December
Thomas de Cantelupe	2 October
Thomas More	Lawyers; (and John Fisher) 22 June
Timothy	(G) 22 January; (W) 24 January; (and Titus) 26 January
Titus	(E) 25 August; (W) 6 February; (and Timothy) 26 January
Trophimus of Arles	29 December
Trophimus of Ephesus	15 April
Turibius de Mogrovejo	Missionary bishops; 23 March
Ulrich	4 July
Uncumber	see Wilgefortis
Ursula	Cologne, girls; 21 October
Valentine	Lovers; (G) 16 February; (W) 14 February
Valeria	(and Vitalis) 28 April
Vedast	(and Amand) 6 February
Veronica	12 July
Vicelin	12 December
Victor	17 October
Victor I	28 July
Victorinus	2 November
Vincent Ferrer	Brick and tilemakers, plumbers; 5 April
Vincent of Lérins	24 May
Vincent de Paul	Charitable societies; 27 September
Vincent (of Saragossa)	Portugal, the wine trade; 22 January
Vitalis	(and Agricola) 4 November; (and Valeria) 28 April

Vitus	Actors, comedians, dancers, dogs, epileptics, sufferers from nervous diseases; 15 June
Vladimir I 'the Great'	15 July
Walburga (Walpurgis)	25 February, 1 May
Walstan of Bawburgh	Agricultural workers; 30 May
Wenceslas	Brewers, Czechoslovakia; 28 September
Werburga	3 February
Wilfrid (Wilfrith)	12 October
Wilgefortis (Uncumber)	Women unhappily married; 20 July
Willehad	8 November
William of Norwich	26 March
William of York	8 June
Willibald	7 June
Willibrord	Holland; 7 November
Winifred	3 November
Wolfgang	Carpenters; 31 October
Wulfric	20 February
Wulfstan	19 January
Wynfrith	see Boniface
Xenophon	(E) 26 January
Zacharias	(E) 5 September; (W) 15 March
Zeno	Fishermen; 12 April
Zephyrinus	26 August
Zita	Bakers, housewives, servants; 27 April

Religious leaders

Popes

until c.64	St Peter	399–401	Anastasius I	678–8	Agatho
c.64–c.76	Linus	402–17	St Innocent I	682–3	Leo II
c.76–c.90	Anacletus	417–18	St Zosimus	684–5	Benedict II
c.90–c.99	Clement I	418–22	Boniface I	685–6	John V
c.99–c.105	Evaristus	418–19	Eulalius *Antipope*	686–7	Cono
c.105–c.117	Alexander I	422–32	Celestine I	687	Theodore *Antipope*
c.117–c.127	Sixtus I	432–40	Sixtus III	687–92	Paschal *Antipope*
c.127–c.137	Telesphorus	440–61	St Leo I 'the Great'	687–701	Sergius I
c.137–c.140	Hyginus	461–8	Hilarus	701–5	John VI
c.140–c.154	Pius I	468–83	Simplicius	705–7	John VII
c.154–c.166	Anicetus	483–92	Felix III (II)	708	Sisinnius
c.166–c.175	Soter	492–6	St Gelasius I	708–15	Constantine
175–89	Eleutherius	496–8	Anastasius II	715–31	St Gregory II
189–98	Victor I	498–514	(Coelius) Symmachus	731–41	St Gregory III
198–217	Zephyrinus	498, 501–5	Laurentius *Antipope*	741–52	St Zacharias
217–22	Calixtus I	514–23	Hormisdas	752	Stephen II (not consecrated)
217–c.235	Hippolytus *Antipope*	523–6	John I		
222–30	Urban I	526–30	Felix IV (III)	752–7	Stephen II (III)
230–5	Pontian	530–2	Boniface II	757–67	Paul I
235–6	Anterus	530	Dioscorus *Antipope*	767–9	Constantine II *Antipope*
236–50	Fabian	533–5	John II	768	Philip *Antipope*
251–3	Cornelius	535–6	Agapetus I	768–72	Stephen III (IV)
251–c.258	Novatian *Antipope*	536–7	Silverius	772–95	Adrian I
253–4	Lucius I	537–55	Vigilius	795–816	Leo III
254–7	Stephen I	556–61	Pelagius I	816–17	Stephen IV (V)
257–8	Sixtus II	561–74	John III	817–24	Paschal I
259–68	Dionysius	575–9	Benedict I	824–7	Eugenius II
269–74	Felix I	579–90	Pelagius II	827	Valentine
275–83	Eutychianus	590–604	St Gregory I 'the Great'	827–44	Gregory IV
283–96	Caius	604–6	Sabinianus	844	John *Antipope*
296–304	Marcellinus	607	Boniface III	844–7	Sergius II
308–9	Marcellus I	608–15	Boniface IV	847–55	Leo IV
310	Eusebius	615–18	Deusdedit (Adeodatus I)	855–8	Benedict III
311–14	Miltiades	619–25	Boniface V	855	Anastasius Bibliothecarius *Antipope*
314–35	Sylvester I	625–38	Honorius I		
336	Mark	640	Severinus	858–67	St Nicholas I 'the Great'
337–52	Julius I	640–2	John IV	867–72	Adrian II
352–66	Liberius	642–9	Theodore I	872–82	John VIII
355–65	Felix II *Antipope*	649–55	St Martin I	882–4	Martin II (Marinus I)
366–84	St Damasus I	654–7	St Eugenius I[1]	884–5	Adrian III
366–7	Ursinus *Antipope*	657–72	Vitalian	885–91	Stephen V (VI)
384–99	Siricius	672–6	Adeodatus II	891–6	Formosus
		676–8	Donus	896	Boniface VI

[1] Elected during the banishment of Martin I.

896–7	Stephen VI (VII)
897	Romanus
897	Theodore II
898–900	John IX
900–3	Benedict IV
903	Leo V
903–4	Christopher *Antipope*
904–11	Sergius III
911–13	Anastasius III
913–14	Lando
914–28	John X
928	Leo VI
928–31	Stephen VII (VIII)
931–5	John XI
936–9	Leo VII
939–42	Stephen IX
942–6	Martin III (Marinus II)
946–55	Agapetus II
955–64	John XII (Octavian)
963–5	Leo VIII
964–6	Benedict V
965–72	John XIII
973–4	Benedict VI
974 , 984–5	Boniface VII *Antipope*
974–83	Benedict VII
983–4	John XIV
985–96	John XV
996–9	Gregory V
997–8	John XVI *Antipope*
999–1003	Sylvester II
1003	John XVII
1004–9	John XVIII
1009–12	Sergius IV
1012–24	Benedict VIII
1012	Gregory *Antipope*
1024–32	John XIX
1032–44	Benedict IX
1045	Sylvester III
1045	Benedict IX (second reign)
1045–6	Gregory VI
1046–7	Clement II
1047–8	Benedict IX (third reign)
1048	Damasus II (Poppo)
1048–54	Leo IX (Bruno of Toul)
1055–7	Victor II (Gebhard of Hirschberg)
1057–8	Stephen IX (X) (Frederick of Lorraine)
1058–9	Benedict X (John of Tusculum) *Antipope*
1059–61	Nicholas II (Gerard of Burgundy)
1061–73	Alexander II (Anselm of Lucca)
1061–72	Honorius II (Peter Cadalus) *Antipope*
1073–85	Gregory VII (St Hildebrand)
1080, 1084–1100	Clement III (Guibert of Ravenna) *Antipope*
1086–7	Victor III (Desiderius)
1088–99	Urban II (Odo of Chatillon)
1099–1118	Paschal II (Raneiro da Bieda)
1100–2	Theodoric *Antipope*
1102	Albert *Antipope*
1105–11	Sylvester IV *Antipope*
1118–19	Gelasius II (John of Gaeta)
1118–21	Gregory VIII (Maurice of Braga) *Antipope*
1119–24	Calixtus II (Guy of Burgundy)
1124–30	Honorius II (Lamberto dei Fagnani)
1124	Celestine II *Antipope*
1130–43	Innocent II (Gregory Parareschi)
1130–8	Anacletus II *Antipope*
1138	Victor IV[2] *Antipope*
1143–4	Celestine II (Guido di Castello)
1144–5	Lucius II (Gherardo Caccianemici)
1145–53	Eugenius III (Bernardo Paganelli)
1153–4	Anastasius IV (Corrado della Subarra)
1154–9	Adrian IV (Nicholas Breakspear)
1159–81	Alexander III (Orlando Bandinelli)
1159–64	Victor IV[2] (Ottaviano di Monticelli) *Antipope*
1164–8	Paschal III (Guido of Crema) *Antipope*
1168–78	Calixtus III (John of Struma) *Antipope*
1179–80	Innocent III (Lando da Sessa) *Antipope*
1181–5	Lucius III (Ubaldo Allucingoli) *Antipope*
1185–7	Urban III (Uberto Crivelli)
1187	Gregory VIII (Alberto di Morra)
1187–91	Clement III (Paolo Scolari)
1191–8	Celestine III (Giacinto Boboni-Orsini)
1198–1216	Innocent III (Lotario de' Conti)
1216–27	Honorius III (Cancio Savelli)
1227–41	Gregory IX (Ugolino di Segni)
1241	Celestine IV (Goffredo Castiglione)
1243–54	Innocent IV (Sinibaldo de' Fieschi)
1254–61	Alexander IV (Rinaldo di Segni)
1261–4	Urban IV (Jacques Pantaléon)
1265–8	Clement IV (Guy le Gros Foulques)
1271–6	Gregory X (Tebaldo Visconti)
1276	Innocent V (Pierre de Champagni)
1276	Adrian V (Ottobono Fieschi)
1276–7	John XXI[3] (Pietro Rebuli-Giuliani)
1277–80	Nicholas III (Giovanni Gaetano Orsini)
1281–5	Martin IV (Simon de Brie)
1285–7	Honorius IV (Giacomo Savelli)
1288–92	Nicholas IV (Girolamo Masci)
1294	Celestine V (Pietro di Morrone)
1294–1303	Boniface VIII (Benedetto Caetani)
1303–4	Benedict XI (Niccolo Boccasini)
1305–14	Clement V (Raymond Bertrand de Got)
1316–34	John XXII (Jacques Duèse)
1328–30	Nicholas V (Pietro Rainalducci) *Antipope*
1334–42	Benedict XII (Jacques Fournier)
1342–52	Clement VI (Pierre Roger de Beaufort)
1352–62	Innocent VI (Étienne Aubert)
1362–70	Urban V (Guillaume de Grimoard)
1370–8	Gregory XI (Pierre Roger de Beaufort)
1378–89	Urban VI (Bartolomeo Prignano)
1378–94	Clement VII (Robert of Geneva) *Antipope*
1389–1404	Boniface IX (Pietro Tomacelli)
1394–1423	Benedict XIII (Pedro de Luna) *Antipope*
1404–6	Innocent VII (Cosmato de' Migliorati)
1406–15	Gregory XII (Angelo Correr)
1409–10	Alexander V (Petros Philargi) *Antipope*
1410–15	John XXIII (Baldassare Cossa) *Antipope*
1417–31	Martin V (Oddone Colonna)
1423–9	Clement VIII (Gil Sanchez Muñoz) *Antipope*
1425–30	Benedict XIV (Bernard Garnier) *Antipope*
1431–47	Eugenius IV (Gabriele Condulmer)
1439–49	Felix V (Amadeus VIII of Savoy) *Antipope*
1447–55	Nicholas V (Tommaso Parentucelli)
1455–8	Calixtus III (Alfonso de Borja)
1458–64	Pius II (Enea Silvio de Piccolomini)

[2] Different individuals. [3] There was no John XX.

1464–71	Paul II (Pietro Barbo)
1471–84	Sixtus IV (Francesco della Rovere)
1484–92	Innocent VIII (Giovanni Battista Cibo)
1492–1503	Alexander VI (Rodrigo Borgia)
1503	Pius III (Francesco Todoeschini-Piccolomini)
1503–13	Julius II (Giuliano della Rovere)
1513–21	Leo X (Giovanni de' Medici)
1522–3	Adrian V (Adrian Dedel)
1523–34	Clement VII (Giulio de' Medici)
1534–49	Paul III (Allessandro Farnese)
1550–5	Julius III (Gianmaria del Monte)
1555	Marcellus II (Marcello Cervini)
1555–9	Paul IV (Giovanni Pietro Caraffa)
1559–65	Pius IV (Giovanni Angelo Medici)
1566–72	St Pius V (Michele Ghislieri)
1572–85	Gregory XIII (Ugo Buoncompagni)
1585–90	Sixtus V (Felice Peretti)
1590	Urban VII (Giambattista Castagna)
1590–1	Gregory XIV (Niccolo Sfondrati)
1591	Innocent IX (Gian Antonio Facchinetti)
1592–1605	Clement VIII (Ippolito Aldobrandini)
1605	Leo XI (Alessandro de' Medici-Ottaiano)
1605–21	Paul V (Camillo Borghese)
1621–3	Gregory XV (Alessandro Ludovisi)
1623–44	Urban VIII (Maffeo Barberini)
1644–55	Innocent X (Giambattista Pamfili)
1655–67	Alexander VII (Fabio Chigi)
1667–9	Clement IX (Guilio Rospigliosi)
1670–6	Clement X (Emilio Altieri)
1676–89	Innocent XI (Benedetto Odescalchi)
1689–91	Alexander VIII (Pietro Vito Ottoboni)
1691–1700	Innocent XII (Antonio Pignatelli)
1700–21	Clement XI (Gian Francesco Albani)
1721–4	Innocent XIII (Michelangelo dei Conti)
1724–30	Benedict XIII (Pietro Francesco Orsini)
1730–40	Clement XII (Lorenzo Corsini)

1740–58	Benedict XIV (Prospero Lambertini)
1758–69	Clement XIII (Carlo Rezzonico)
1769–74	Clement XIV (Lorenzo Ganganelli)
1775–99	Pius VI (Giovanni Angelo Braschi)
1800–23	Pius VII (Luigi Barnaba Chiaramonti)
1823–9	Leo XII (Annibale della Genga)
1829–30	Pius VIII (Francesco Saverio Castiglioni)
1831–46	Gregory XVI (Bartolomeo Alberto Cappellari)
1846–78	Pius IX (Giovanni Maria Mastai Ferretti)
1878–1903	Leo XIII (Vicenzo Gioacchino Pecci)
1903–14	Pius X (Giuseppe Sarto)
1914–22	Benedict XV (Giacomo della Chiesa)
1922–39	Pius XI (Achille Ratti)
1939–58	Pius XII (Eugenio Pacelli)
1958–63	John XXIII (Angelo Giuseppe Roncalli)
1963–78	Paul VI (Giovanni Battista Montini)
1978	John Paul I (Albino Luciani)
1978–	John Paul II (Karol Jozef Wojtyla)

Caliphs

Orthodox

632–4	Abu-Bakr as-Saddiq
634–44	Umar (Omar) ibn al-Khattab
644–56	Uthman ibn Affan
656–61	Ali ibn Abi-Talib

Umayyad Dynasty (Damascus)

661–80	Muawiyah I
680–3	Yazid I
683–4	Muawiya II
684–5	Marwan I
685–705	Abdul-Malik
705–15	al-Walid I
715–17	Sulayman
717–20	Umar II
720–4	Yazid II
724–43	Hisham
743–4	al-Walid II
744	Yazid III
744	Ibrahim
744–50	Marwan II

Abbasid Dynasty (Baghdad)

749–54	as-Saffah
754–75	Abu-Jafar al-Mansur
775–85	al-Mahdi
785–6	al-Hadi
786–809	(Harun) al-Rashid
809–13	al-Amin
813–33	al-Mamum

833–42	al-Mutasim
842–7	al-Wathiq
847–61	al-Mutawakkil
861–2	al-Muntasir
862–6	al-Mustain
866–9	al-Mutazz
869–70	al-Muhtadi
870–92	al-Mutamid
892–902	al-Mutadid
902–08	al-Muktafi
908–32	al-Muqtadir
932–4	al-Qahir
934–40	ar-Radi
940–4	al-Muttaqi
944–6	al-Mustakfi
946–74	al-Muti
974–91	at-Tai
991–1031	al-Qadir
1031–75	al-Qaim
1075–94	al-Muqtadi
1094–1118	al-Mustazhir
1118–35	al-Mustarshid
1135–6	ar-Rashid
1136–60	al-Muqtafi
1160–70	al-Mustanjid
1170–80	al-Mustadi
1180–1225	an-Nasir
1225–6	az-Zahir
1226–42	al-Mustansir
1242–58	al-Mustasim

Dalai Lamas

1391–1475	Gedun Truppa
1475–1542	Gedun Gyatso
1543–88	Sonam Gyatso
1589–1617	Yonten Gyatso
1617–82	Ngawang Lobzang Gyatso
1683–1706	Tsang-yang Gyatso
1708–57	Kezang Gyatso
1758–1804	Jampel Gyatso
1806–15	Luntok Gyatso
1816–37	Tshultrim Gyatso
1838–56	Khedrup Gyatso
1856–75	Trinle Gyatso
1876–1933	Thupten Gyatso
1935–	Tenzin Gyatso *in exile* 1959–

Archbishops of Canterbury

597–604	St Augustine
604–19	Laurentius
619–24	Mellitus
624–7	Justus
627–53	Honorius
655–64	Deusdedit (Frithona)
668–90	Theodore
693–731	Beorhtweald
731–4	Tatwine
735–9	Nothelm
740–60	Cuthbert
761–4	Breguwine
765–92	Jaenbeorht
793–805	Ethelheard
805–32	Wulfred
832	Feologild
833–70	Ceolnoth

870–89	Æthelred	1272–8	Robert Kilwardby	1645–60	*No Archbishop of Canterbury*
890–914	Plegmund	1279–92	John Pecham	1660–3	William Juxon
914–23	Æthelhelm	1293–1313	Robert Winchelsey	1663–77	Gilbert Sheldon
923–42	Wulfhelm	1313–27	Walter Reynolds	1677–90	William Sancroft
942–58	Oda	1327–33	Simon Mepham	1691–4	John Tillotson
959	Ælfsige	1333–48	John de Stratford	1694–1715	Thomas Tenison
959	Beorhthelm	1348–9	Thomas Bradwardine	1715–37	William Wake
960–88	St Dunstan	1349–66	Simon Islip	1737–47	John Potter
988–90	Æthelgar	1366–8	Simon Langham	1747–57	Thomas Herring
990–4	Sigeric Serio	1368–74	William Whittlesey	1757–8	Matthew Hutton
995–1005	Ælfric	1375–81	Simon Sudbury	1758–68	Thomas Secker
1005–12	Ælfheah	1381–96	William Courtenay	1768–83	Frederick Cornwallis
1013–20	Lyfing	1396–7	Thomas Arundel	1783–1805	John Moore
1020–38	Æthelnoth	1397–9	Roger Walden	1805–28	Charles Manners Sutton
1038–50	Eadsige	1399–1414	Thomas Arundel (*restored*)	1828–48	William Howley
1051–2	Robert of Jumièges	1414–43	Henry Chichele	1848–6	John Bird Sumner
1052–70	Stigand	1443–52	John Stafford	1862–8	Charles Thomas Longley
1070–89	Lanfranc	1452–4	John Kemp	1868–82	Archibald Campbell Tait
1093–1109	Anselm	1454–86	Thomas Bourgchier	1883–96	Edward White Benson
1114–22	Ralph d'Escures	1486–1500	John Morton	1896–1902	Frederick Temple
1123–36	William of Corbeil	1501–3	Henry Deane	1903–28	Randall Thomas Davidson
1138–61	Theobald (Tebaldus)	1504–32	William Warham	1928–42	Cosmo Gordon Lang
1162–70	Thomas à Becket	1532–55	Thomas Cranmer	1942–4	William Temple
1174–84	Richard of Dover	1555–8	Reginald Pole	1945–61	Geoffrey Francis Fisher
1184–90	Baldwin	1559–75	Matthew Parker	1961–74	Arthur Michael Ramsey
1193–1205	Hubert Walter	1575–83	Edmund Grindal	1974–80	Donald Coggan
1206–28	Stephen Langton	1583–1604	John Whitgift	1980–91	Robert Alexander
1229–31	Richard le Grant	1604–10	Richard Bancroft		Kennedy Runcie
1233–40	St Edmund (Rich)	1611–33	George Abbot	1991–	George Leonard Carey
1241–70	Boniface of Savoy	1633–45	William Laud		

Justices of the Supreme Court of the United States of America

1789–95	John Jay *Chief Justice*	1845–72	Samuel Nelson	1894–1921	Edward Douglass White, *Chief Justice 1910–21*
1789–91	John Rutledge	1845–51	Levi Woodbury		
1789–1810	William Cushing	1846–70	Robert C Grier	1896–1909	Rufus Wheeler Peckham
1789–98	James Wilson	1851–7	Benjamin R Curtis	1898–1925	Joseph McKenna
1789–96	John Blair	1853–61	John Archibald Campbell	1902–32	Oliver Wendell Holmes Jr
1790–9	James Iredell	1858–81	Nathan Clifford	1903–22	William R Day
1792–3	Thomas Johnson	1862–81	Noah H Swayne	1906–10	William H Moody
1793–1806	William Patterson	1862–90	Samuel Freeman Miller	1910–14	Horace H Lurton
1796–1811	Samuel Chase	1862–77	David Davis	1910–16	Charles Evans Hughes *Chief Justice 1930–41*
1796–1800	Oliver Ellsworth *Chief Justice*	1863–97	Stephen Johnson Field		
1799–1829	Bushrod Washington	1864–73	Salmon P Chase *Chief Justice*	1911–37	Willis Van Devanter
1800–4	Alfred Moore	1870–80	William Strong	1911–16	Joseph R Lamar
1801–35	John Marshall *Chief Justice*	1870–92	Joseph P Bradley	1912–22	Mahlon Pitney
1804–34	William Johnson	1873–82	Ward Hunt	1914–41	James C McReynolds
1807–23	Brockholst Livingston	1874–88	Morrison Remick Waite *Chief Justice*	1916–39	Louis Dembitz Brandeis
1807–26	Thomas Todd			1916–22	John H Clarke
1811–35	Gabriel Duvall	1877–1911	John Marshall Harlan	1921–30	William Howard Taft *Chief Justice*
1812–45	Joseph Story	1881–7	William B Woods		
1823–43	Smith Thompson	1881–9	Stanley Matthews	1922–38	George Sutherland
1826–8	Robert Trimble	1882–1902	Horace Gray	1923–39	Pierce Butler
1830–61	John McLean	1882–93	Samuel Blatchford	1923–39	Edward T Sanford
1830–44	Henry Baldwin	1888–93	Lucius Q C Lamar	1925–46	Harlan Fiske Stone *Chief Justice 1941–46*
1835–67	James M Wayne	1888–1910	Melville Weston Fuller *Chief Justice*		
1836–64	Roger Brooke Taney *Chief Justice*			1930–41	Charles Evans Hughes *Chief Justice*
1836–41	Philip P Barbour	1890–1910	David J Brewer	1930–45	Owen Roberts
1837–65	John Catron	1891–1906	Henry B Brown	1932–8	Benjamin Nathan Cardozo
1838–52	John McKinley	1892–1903	George Shiras, Jr	1937–71	Hugo Lafayette Black
1842–60	Peter V Daniel	1893–5	Howell E Jackson	1938–57	Stanley F Reed
				1939–62	Felix Frankfurter

Ready Reference

1939–75	William Orville Douglas	1956–90	William J Brennan	1972–	William H Rehnquist *Chief Justice 1986–*
1940–9	Frank Murphy	1957–62	Charles E Whittaker		
1941–2	James F Byrnes	1958–81	Potter Stewart	1975–	John Paul Stevens
1941–54	Robert H Jackson	1962–93	Byron R White	1981–	Sandra Day O'Connor
1943–9	Wiley B Rutledge	1962–5	Arthur J Goldberg	1986–	Antonin Scalia
1945–58	Harold H Burton	1965–9	Abe Fortas	1988–	Anthony M Kennedy
1946–53	Fred M Vinson *Chief Justice*	1967–91	Thurgood Marshall	1990–	David Souter
1949–67	Tom C Clark	1969–86	Warren Earl Burger *Chief Justice*	1991–	Clarence Thomas
1949–56	Sherman Minton			1993–	Ruth Bader Ginsburg
1953–69	Earl Warren *Chief Justice*	1970–94	Harry Andrew Blackmun	1994–	Stephen G Breyer
1955–71	John Marshall Harlan	1972–87	Lewis F Powell, Jr		

Nobel Prizewinners

Physics

1901	Wilhelm Konrad von Röntgen	1939	Ernest Orlando Lawrence	1972	John Bardeen
1902	Hendrik Antoon Lorentz	1943	Otto Stern		Leon Neil Cooper
	Pieter Zeeman	1944	Isidor Isaac Rabi		John Robert Schrieffer
1903	Antoine Henri Becquerel	1945	Wolfgang Pauli	1973	Leo Esaki
	Pierre Curie	1946	Percy Williams Bridgman		Ivar Giaever
	Marie Curie	1947	Edward Victor Appleton		Brian David Josephson
1904	John William Strutt, 3rd Baron Rayleigh	1948	Patrick Maynard Stuart, Baron Blackett	1974	Martin Ryle
					Antony Hewish
1905	Philipp Eduard Anton Lenard	1949	Yukawa Hidecki	1975	Aage Niels Bohr
1906	Joseph John Thomson	1950	Cecil Frank Powell		Benjamin Roy Mottelson
1907	Albert Abraham Michelson	1951	John Douglas Cockcroft		(Leo) James Rainwater
1908	Gabriel Lippmann		Ernest Thomas Sinton Walton	1976	Burton Richter
1909	Guglielmo, Marchese Marconi	1952	Felix Bloch		Samuel Chao Chung Ting
	Karl Braun		Edward Mills Purcell	1977	Philip Warren Anderson
1910	Johannes Diderik van der Waals	1953	Frits Zernike		Nevill Francis Mott
1911	Wilhelm Wien	1954	Max Born		John Hasbrouck van Vleck
1912	Nils Gustav Dalén		Walther Bothe	1978	Pjotr Leonidovich (Peter) Kapitza
1913	Heike Kamerlingh Onnes	1955	Willis Eugene Lamb, Jr		Arno Allan Penzias
1914	Max von Laue		Polykarp Kusch		Robert Woodrow Wilson
1915	William Henry Bragg	1956	William Bradford Shockley	1979	Steven Weinberg
	(William) Lawrence Bragg		John Bardeen		Sheldon Lee Glashow
1916	*No award*		Walter Hauser Brattain		Abdus Salam
1917	Charles Glover Barkla	1957	Tsung-Dao Lee	1980	James Watson Cronin
1918	Max Karl Ernst Planck		Chen Ning Yang		Val Logsdon Fitch
1919	Johannes Stark	1958	Pavel Alekseevich Cherenkov	1981	Nicolas Bloembergen
1920	Charles Édouard Guillaume		Ilya Mikhailovich Frank		Arthur Leonard Schawlow
1921	Albert Einstein		Igor Yevgenyevich Tamm		Kai M Siegbahn
1922	Aage Niels Bohr	1959	Emilio Segrè	1982	Kenneth Geddes Wilson
1923	Robert Andrews Millikan		Owen Chamberlain	1983	Subrahmanyan Chandrasekhar
1924	Karl Manne Georg Siegbahn	1960	Donald Arthur Glaser		William Alfred Fowler
1925	James Franck	1961	Robert Hofstadter	1984	Carlo Rubbia
	Gustav Ludwig Hertz		Rudolf Mössbauer		Simon van der Meer
1926	Jean Baptiste Perrin	1962	Lev Davidovich Landau	1985	Klaus von Klitzing
1927	Arthur Holly Compton	1963	(Johannes) Hans (Daniel) Jensen	1986	Gerd Binnig
	Charles Thomson Rees Wilson		Maria Goeppert-Meyer		Heinrich Rohrer
1928	Owen Williams Richardson		Eugene Paul Wigner		Ernst Ruska
1929	Louis Victor, 7th Duc de Broglie	1964	Charles Hard Townes	1987	George Bednorz
1930	Chandrasekhara Venkata Raman		Nikolai Gennadiyevich Basov		Alex Müller
1931	*No award*		Alexander Mikhailovich Prokhorov	1988	Leon Lederman
1932	Werner Karl Heisenberg				Melvin Schwartz
1933	Paul Adrien Maurice Dirac	1965	Julian S Schwinger		Jack Steinberger
	Erwin Schrödinger		Richard P Feynman	1989	Hans Dehmelt
1934	*No award*		Tomonaga Shinichiro		Wolfgang Paul
1935	James Chadwick	1966	Alfred Kastler		Norman Ramsay
1936	Victor Francis Hess	1967	Hans Albrecht Bethe	1990	Jerome Friedman
	Carl David Anderson	1968	Luis Walter Alvarez		Henry Kendall
1937	Clinton Joseph Davisson	1969	Murray Gell-Mann		Richard Taylor
	George Paget Thomson	1970	Louis Eugène Félix Néel	1991	Pierre-Gilles de Gennes
1938	Enrico Fermi		Hannes Olof Alvén	1992	Georges Charpak
		1971	Dennis Gabor	1993	Joseph Taylor

	Russell Hulse			Wendell Meredith Stanley	1988	Johann Deisenhofer
1994	Bertram N Brockhouse	1947	Robert Robinson			Robert Huber
	Clifford G Shull	1948	Arne Wilhelm Kaurin Tiselius			Hartmut Michel
1995	Martin Perl	1949	William Francis Giauque	1989	Sydney Altman
	Frederick Reines	1950	Otto Diels		Thomas Cech
1996	Douglas Osheroff		Kurt Alder	1990	Elias James Corey
	David Lee	1951	Edwin Mattison McMillan	1991	Richard Ernst
	Robert Richardson		Glenn Theodore Seaborg	1992	Rudolph Marcus
1997	Steven Chu	1952	Archer (John Porter) Martin	1993	Kary Mulis
	William D Phillips		Richard Laurence Millington		Michael Smith
	Claude Cohen-Tannoudji		Synge	1994	George A Olah
		1953	Hermann Staudinger	1995	Paul Crutzen

Chemistry

1901	Jacobus Henricus van t'Hoff	1954	Linus Carl Pauling		Mario Molina
1902	Emil Hermann Fischer	1955	Vincent du Vigneaud		Sherwood Rowland
1903	Svante Arrhenius	1956	Nikolai Nikilaevich Semenov	1996	Harold Kroto
1904	William Ramsay		Cyril Norman Hinshelwood		Robert Curl
1905	Johann Friedrich Wilhelm	1957	Alexander Robertus Todd		Richard Smalley
	Adolf von Baeyer	1958	Frederick Sanger	1997	Jen Skou
1906	Henri Moissan	1959	Jaroslav Heyrovsky		John Walker
1907	Eduard Buchner	1960	Willard Frank Libby		Paul Boyer
1908	Ernest, 1st Baron Rutherford	1961	Melvin Calvin		
1909	Friedrich Wilhelm Ostwald	1962	John Cowdery Kendrew		
1910	Otto Wallach		Max Ferdinand Perutz		

Literature

1911	Marie Curie	1963	Giulio Natta	1901	René François Armand Sully-Prudhomme
1912	(François Auguste) Victor Grignard		Karl Ziegler	1902	Theodor Mommsen
	Paul Sabatier	1964	Dorothy Mary Hodgkin	1903	Bjørnsterne Martinius Bjørnson
1913	Alfred Werner	1965	Robert Burns Woodward	1904	Frédéric Mistral
1914	Theodore William Richards	1966	Robert Sanderson Mulliken		José Echegaray y Eizaguirre
1915	Richard Willstätter	1967	Manfred Eigen	1905	Henryk Sienkiewicz
1916–17	No award		Ronald George Wreyford Norrish	1906	Giosuè Carducci
1918	Fritz Haber		George, Baron Porter	1907	Rudyard Kipling
1919	No award	1968	Lars Onsager	1908	Rudolf Christoph Eucken
1920	Walther Hermann Nernst	1969	Derek H R Barton	1909	Selma Ottiliana Lovisa Lagerlöf
1921	Frederick Soddy		Odd Hassel	1910	Paul Johann von Heyse
1922	Francis William Aston	1970	Luis Federico Leloir	1911	Count Maurice Maeterlinck
1923	Fritz Pregl	1971	Gerhard Herzberg	1912	Gerhart Hauptmann
1924	No award	1972	Stanford Moore	1913	Rabindranath Tagore
1925	Richard Adolf Zsigmondy		William Howard Stein	1914	No award
1926	Theodor Svedberg		Christian Boehmer Anfinsen	1915	Romain Rolland
1927	Heinrich Otto Wieland	1973	Ernst Otto Fischer	1916	(Karl Gustav) Verner von Heidenstam
1928	Adolf Otto Reinhold Windaus		Geoffrey Wilkinson	1917	Karl Gjellerup
1929	Arthur Harden	1974	Paul John Flory		Henrik Pontoppidan
	Hans Karl August Simon von Euler-Chelpin	1975	John Warcup Cornforth	1918	No award
1930	Hans Fischer		Vladimir Prelog	1919	Carl Friedrich Georg Spitteler
1931	Carl Bosch	1976	William Nunn Lipscomb	1920	Knut Hamsun
	Friedrich Bergius	1977	Ilya Prigogine	1921	Anatole France
1932	Irving Langmuir	1978	Peter Dennis Mitchell	1922	Jacinto Benavente
1933	No award	1979	Herbert Charles Brown	1923	William Butler Yeats
1934	Harold Clayton Urey		Georg Wittig	1924	Wladyslaw Stanislaw Reymont
1935	Jean Frédéric Joliot-Curie	1980	Paul Berg	1925	George Bernard Shaw
	Irène Joliot-Curie		Walter Gilbert	1926	Grazia Deledda
1936	Peter Joseph Wilhelm Debye		Frederick Sanger	1927	Henri Bergson
1937	Walter Norman Haworth	1981	Kenichi Fukui	1928	Sigrid Undset
	Paul Karrer		Roald Hoffmann	1929	Thomas Mann
1938	Richard Kuhn, *declined*	1982	Aaron Klug	1930	(Harry) Sinclair Lewis
1939	Adolf Friedrich Johann Butenandt, *declined*	1983	Henry Taube	1931	Erik Axel Karlfeldt
		1984	(Robert) Bruce Merrifield	1932	John Galsworthy
	Leopold Ruzicka	1985	Herbert Aaron Hauptman	1933	Ivan Alexeievich Bunin
1940	George de Hevesy		Jerome Karle	1934	Luigi Pirandello
1944	Otto Hahn	1986	Dudley R Herschbach	1935	No award
1945	Artturi Ilmari Virtanen		Yuan Tseh Lee	1936	Eugene Gladstone O'Neill
1946	James Batcheller Sumner		John C Polanyi	1937	Roger Martin du Gard
	John Knudsen Northrop	1987	Charles Pedersen	1938	Pearl S Buck
			Donald Cram	1939	Frans Eemil Sillanpää
			Jean-Marie Lehn		

1943	*No award*
1944	Johannes Vilhelm (J V) Jensen
1945	Gabriela Mistral
1946	Hermann Hesse
1947	André (Paul Guillaume) Gide
1948	T S (Thomas Stearns) Eliot
1949	William Faulkner
1950	Bertrand (Arthur William, 3rd Earl) Russell
1951	Pär (Fabian) Lagerkvist
1952	François Mauriac
1953	Winston (Leonard Spencer) Churchill
1954	Ernest (Millar) Hemingway
1955	Halldór Laxness
1956	Juan Ramón Jiménez
1957	Albert Camus
1958	Boris Leonidovich Pasternak
1959	Salvatore Quasimodo
1960	Saint-John Perse
1961	Ivo Andrić
1962	John (Ernest) Steinbeck
1963	George Seferis
1964	Jean-Paul Sartre, *declined*
1965	Mikhail (Alexandrovich) Sholokhov
1966	Shmuel Yosef Agnon
	Nelly (Leonie) Sachs
1967	Miguel Angel Asturias
1968	Kawabata Yasunari
1969	Samuel Beckett
1970	Alexandr Isayevich Solzhenitsyn
1971	Pablo (Neftali Reyes) Neruda
1972	Heinrich Böll
1973	Patrick White
1974	Eyvind Johnson
	Harry (Edmund) Martinson
1975	Eugenio Montale
1976	Saul Bellow
1977	Vicente Aleixandre
1978	Isaac Bashevis Singer
1979	Odysseus Elytis
1980	Czeslaw Milosz
1981	Elias Canetti
1982	Gabriel García Márquez
1983	William (Gerald) Golding
1984	Jaroslav Seifert
1985	Claude (Eugène Henri) Simon
1986	Wole Soyinka
1987	Joseph Brodsky
1988	Naguib Mahfouz
1989	Camilo José Cela
1990	Octavio Paz
1991	Nadine Gordimer
1992	Derek Walcott
1993	Toni Morrison
1994	Kenzaburo Oe
1995	Seamus Heaney
1996	Wislawa Szymborska
1997	Dario Fo

Physiology or Medicine

1901	Emil von Behring
1902	Ronald Ross
1903	Niels Ryberg Finsen

1904	Ivan Petrovich Pavlov
1905	Robert Koch
1906	Camillo Golgi
	Santiago Ramón y Cajal
1907	Charles Louis Alphonse Laveran
1908	Paul Ehrlich
	Ilya Ilich Mechnikov
1909	Emil Theodor Kocher
1910	Albrecht Kossel
1911	Allvar Gullstrand
1912	Alexis Carrel
1913	Charles Robert Richet
1914	Robert Bárány
1915–18	*No award*
1919	Jules Jean Baptiste Vincent Bordet
1920	Schack August Steenberg Krogh
1921	*No award*
1922	Archibald Vivian Hill
	Otto Fritz Meyerhof
1923	Frederick Grant Banting
	John James Rickard Macleod
1924	Willem Einthoven
1925	*No award*
1926	Johannes Andreas Grib Fibiger
1927	Julius Wagner-Jauregg
1928	Charles Jules Henri Nicolle
1929	Christiaan Eijkman
	Frederick Gowland Hopkins
1930	Karl Landsteiner
1931	Otto Heinrich Warburg
1932	Edgar Douglas Adrian
	Charles Scott Sherrington
1933	Thomas Hunt Morgan
1934	George Hoyt Whipple
1935	Hans Spemann
1936	Henry Hallett Dale
	Otto Loewi
1937	Albert von Nagyrapolt Szent-Györgyi
1938	Corneille Jean François Heymans
1939	Gerhard (Johannes Paul) Domagk, *declined*
1940	Carl Peter Henrik Dam
	Edward Adelbert Doisy
1944	Joseph Erlanger
	Herbert Spencer Gasser
1945	Alexander Fleming
	Ernst Boris Chain
	Howard Walter, Baron Florey
1946	Hermann Joseph Müller
1947	Carl Ferdinand Cori
	Gerty Theresa Cori
	Bernardo Alberto Houssay
1948	Paul Hermann Müller
1949	Walter Rudolf Hess
	António Caetano de Abreu Freire
	Egas Moniz
1950	Philip Showalter Hench
	Edward Calvin Kendall
	Tadeusz Reichstein
1951	Max Theiler

1952	Selman Abraham Waksman
1953	Fritz Albert Lipmann
	Hans Krebs
1954	John Franklin Enders
	Thomas Huckle Weller
	Frederick Chapman Robbins
1955	(Axel) Hugo Theodor Theorell
1956	Werner Forssmann
	Dickinson Woodruff Richards
	André Frédéric Cournand
1957	Daniel Bovet
1958	George Wells Beadle
	Edward Lawrie Tatum
	Joshua Lederberg
1959	Severo Ochoa
	Arthur Kornberg
1960	Frank Macfarlane Burnet
	Peter Brian Medawar
1961	Georg von Békésy
1962	Francis Harry Compton Crick
	James Dewey Watson
	Maurice Hugh Frederick Wilkins
1963	John Carew Eccles
	Alan Lloyd Hodgkin
	Andrew Fielding Huxley
1964	Konrad Emil Bloch
	Feodor Felix Konrad Lynen
1965	François Jacob
	Jacques Monod
	André Lwoff
1966	Charles Brenton Huggins
	Francis Peyton Rous
1967	Haldan Keffer Hartline
	George Wald
	Ragnar Arthur Granit
1968	Robert William Holley
	Har Gobind Khorana
	Marshall Warren Nirenberg
1969	Max Delbrück
	Alfred Day Hershey
	Salvador Edward Luria
1970	Julius Axelrod
	Bernard Katz
	Ulf von Euler
1971	Earl W Sutherland
1972	Gerald Maurice Edelman
	Rodney Robert Porter
1973	Konrad Zacharias Lorenz
	Nikolaas Tinbergen
	Karl von Frisch
1974	Albert Claude
	George Emil Palade
	Christian René de Duve
1975	David Baltimore
	Renato Dulbecco
	Howard Martin Temin
1976	Baruch Samuel Blumberg
	Daniel Carleton Gajdusek
1977	Rosalyn Sussman Yalow
	Roger (Charles Louis) Guillemin
	Andrew Victor Schally
1978	Werner Arber
	Daniel Nathans
	Hamilton Othanel Smith

1979	Allan MacLeod Cormack		Committee	1969	International Labour
	Godfrey Newbold Hounsfield	1918	*No award*		Organisation
1980	Baruj Benacerraf	1919	Thomas Woodrow Wilson	1970	Norman E Borlaug
	George Davis Snell	1920	Léon Victor Auguste Bourgeois	1971	Willy Brandt
	Jean Dausset	1921	Karl Hjalmar Branting	1972	*No award*
1981	Roger Wolcott Sperry		Christian Louis Lange	1973	Henry Alfred Kissinger
	David Hunter Hubel	1922	Fridtjof Nansen		Le Duc Tho (*declined*)
	Torsten Nils Wiesel	1923–4	*No award*	1974	Sean MacBride
1982	Sune Karl Bergström	1925	(Joseph) Austen Chamberlain	1974	Sato Eisaku
	Bengt I Samuelsson		Charles Gates Dawes	1975	Andrei Dimitrievich Sakharov
	John Robert Vane	1926	Aristide Briand	1976	Mairead Corrigan
1983	Barbara McClintock		Gustav Stresemann		Betty Williams
1984	Niels Kai Jerne	1927	Ferdinand Buisson	1977	Amnesty International
	Georges J F Köhler		Ludwig Quidde	1978	Menachem Begin
	César Milstein	1928	*No award*		Mohammed Anwar el-Sadat
1985	Joseph Leonard Goldstein	1929	Frank Billings Kellogg	1979	Mother Theresa of Calcutta
	Michael Stuart Brown	1930	Nathan Söderblom	1980	Adolfo Pérez Esquivel
1986	Seymour Stanley Cohen	1931	Jane Addams	1981	Office of the UN High
	Rita Levi-Montalcini		Nicholas Murray Butler		Commissioner for Refugees
1987	Susumu Tonegawa	1932	*No award*	1982	Alfonso García Robles
1988	James Black	1933	Norman Angell		Alva Myrdal
	Gertrude Elion	1934	Arthur Henderson	1983	Lech Walesa
	George Hitchings	1935	Carl von Ossietzky	1984	Desmond Mpilo Tutu
1989	(John) Michael Bishop	1936	Carlos Saavedra Lamas	1985	International Physicians for
	Harold Elliot Varmus	1937	Robert Cecil,		the Prevention of Nuclear
1990	Joseph Edward Murray		1st Viscount Cecil of		War
	(Edward) Donnall Thomas		Chelwood	1986	Elie Wiesel
1991	Erwin Neher	1938	Nansen International Office	1987	Oscar Arias Sánchez
	Bert Sakmann		for Refugees	1988	UN Peacekeeping Forces
1992	Edmund H Fisher	1939	*No award*	1989	Tenzin Giyatso (Dalai Lama)
	Edwin K Krebs	1943	*No award*	1990	Mikhail Sergeevich Gorbachev
1993	Richard R Roberts	1944	International Red Cross	1991	Aung San Suu Kyi
	Phillip A Sharp		Committee	1992	Rigoberta Menchú
1994	Alfred G Gilman	1945	Cordell Hull	1993	Nelson Mandela
	Martin Rodbell	1946	Emily Greene Balch		Frederik Willem de Klerk
1995	Edward B Lewis		John Raleigh Mott	1994	Yitzhak Rabin
	Christiane Nüesslein-Volhard	1947	American Friends Service		Yasser Arafat
	Eric F Wieschaus		Committee		Shimon Peres
1996	Peter Doherty		Friends Service Council	1995	Joseph Rotblat
	Rolf Zinkernagel	1948	*No award*		Pugwash Conferences
1997	Stanley Prusiner	1949	John Boyd Orr, 1st Baron Boyd	1996	Carlos Filipe Ximenes Belo
			Orr		Jose Ramos-Horta
Peace		1950	Ralphe Johnson Bunche	1997	Jody Williams and the
1901	Jean Henri Dunant	1951	Léon Jouhaux		International Campaign to
	Frédéric Passy	1952	Albert Schweitzer		Ban Landmines
1902	Élie Ducommun	1953	George Catlett Marshall		
	Charles Albert Gobat	1954	Office of the United Nations	**Economics**	
1903	William Randall Cremer		High Commissioner for	1969	Ragnar Anton Kittil Frisch
1904	Institute of International Law		Refugees		Jan Tinbergen
1905	Bertha Félice Bertha von	1955–6	*No award*	1970	Paul Anthony Samuelson
	Suttner	1957	Lester Bowles Pearson	1971	Simon Smith Kuznets
1906	Theodore Roosevelt	1958	(Dominique) Georges Pire	1972	John Richard Hicks
1907	Ernesto Teodoro Moneta	1959	Philip Noel-Baker, Baron Noel-		Kenneth Joseph Arrow
	Louis Renault		Baker	1973	Wassily Leontief
1908	Klas Pontus Arnoldson	1960	Albert John Luthuli	1974	(Karl) Gunnar Myrdal
	Fredrik Bajer	1961	Dag Hjalmar Agne Carl		Friedrich August von Hayek
1909	Baron d'Estournelles de		Hammarskjöld	1975	Leonid Vitaliyevich
	Constant	1962	Linus Carl Pauling		Kantorovich
	Auguste Beernaert	1963	International Red Cross		Tjalling Charles Koopmans
1910	International Peace Bureau		Committee	1976	Milton Friedman
1911	Tobias Michael Carel Asser		League of Red Cross Societies	1977	James Edward Meade
	Alfred Fried	1964	Martin Luther King, Jr		Bertil Gotthard Ohlin
1912	Elihu Root	1965	United Nations Children's	1978	Herbert Alexander Simon
1913	Henri Lafontaine		Fund (UNICEF)	1979	(William) Arthur Lewis
1914–16	*No award*	1966–7	*No award*		Theodore William Schultz
1917	International Red Cross	1968	René Cassin	1980	Lawrence Robert Klein

1981	James Tobin	1989	Trygve Haavelmo	1994	John Nash
1982	George Joseph Stigler	1990	Harry M Markovitz		Reinhard Selten
1983	Gerard Debreu		Merton Miller		John Harsanyi
1984	(John) Richard Nicholas Stone		William Sharpe	1995	Robert E Lucas Jr
1985	Franco Modigliani	1991	Ronald Coase	1996	James Mirrlees
1986	James McGill Buchanan	1992	Gary S Becker		William Vickrey
1987	Robert Merton Solow	1993	Douglas C North	1997	Myron Scholes
1988	Maurice Allais		Robert W Fogel		Robert Merton

Presidents of the Royal Society

1662–77	William Brouncker, 2nd Viscount Brouncker	1778–1820	Joseph Banks	1913–15	William Crookes
1677–80	Joseph Williamson	1820–7	Humphrey Davy	1915–20	Joseph Thomson
1680–2	Christopher Wren	1827–30	Davies Gilbert	1920–5	Charles Sherrington
1682–3	John Hoskins	1830–8	Augustus Frederick, Duke of Sussex	1925–30	Ernest Rutherford, 1st Baron Rutherford
1683–4	Cyril Wyche	1838–47	Marquis of Northampton	1930–5	Frederick Hopkins
1684–6	Samuel Pepys	1847–54	William Parsons, 3rd Earl of Rosse	1935–40	William Bragg
1686–9	John, Earl of Carbery			1940–5	Henry Dale
1689–90	Thomas Herbert, Earl of Pembroke	1854–8	Lord Wrothesley	1945–50	Robert Robinson
1690–5	Robert Southwell	1858–61	Benjamin Brodie	1950–5	Edgar Adrian, 1st Baron Edgar
1695–8	Charles Montagu, 1st Earl of Halifax	1861–71	Edward Sabine		
		1871–3	George Airy	1955–60	Cyril Hinshelwood
1698–1703	John Somers, 1st Baron Somers	1873–8	Joseph Hooker	1960–65	Howard Florey, Baron Florey
		1878–83	William Spottiswoode		
1703–27	Isaac Newton	1883–5	Thomas H Huxley	1965–70	Patrick Stuart, Baron Blackett
1727–41	Hans Sloane	1885–90	George Stokes		
1741–52	Martin Folkes	1890–5	William Thomson, 1st Baron Kelvin	1970–5	Alan Hodgkin
1752–64	George, Earl of Macclesfield			1975–80	Alexander Todd, Baron Todd
		1895–1900	Joseph Lister, Baron Lister		
1764–8	Lord Morton	1900–5	William Huggins	1980–5	Andrew Huxley
1768–72	James West	1905–8	John William Strutt, 3rd Baron Rayleigh	1985–90	George Porter, Lord Porter
1772–8	John Pringle			1990–5	Michael Atiyah
		1908–13	Archibald Geikie	1995–	Aaron Klug

Presidents of the Royal Academy

1768–92	Joshua Reynolds	1878–96	Frederick Leighton, 1st Baron Leighton	1944–9	Alfred Munnings
1792–1805	Benjamin West			1949–54	Gerald Festus Kelly
1805–6	James Wyatt	1896	John Millais	1954–6	Albert Edward Richardson
1806–20	Benjamin West	1896–1919	Edward Poynter	1956–66	Charles Wheeler
1820–30	Thomas Lawrence	1919–24	Aston Webb	1966–76	Thomas Monnington
1830–50	Martin Archer Shee	1924–8	Frank Dicksee	1976–84	Hugh Casson
1850–66	Charles Eastlake	1928–33	William Llewellyn	1984–93	Roger de Grey
1866–78	Francis Grant	1938–44	Edwin Lutyens	1993–	Philip Dowson

Poets Laureate

Great Britain

159?–99	Edmund Spenser*
1599–1617	Samuel Daniel*
1617–38	Ben Jonson*
1638–68	William D'Avenant*
1668–89	John Dryden
1689–92	Thomas Shadwell
1692–1715	Nathum Tate
1715–18	Nicholas Rowe
1718–30	Laurence Eusden
1730–57	Colley Cibber
1757–85	William Whitehead
1785–90	Thomas Warton
1790–1813	Henry James Pye
1813–43	Robert Southey
1843–50	William Wordsworth
1850–96	Alfred Tennyson, 1st Baron Tennyson
1896–1913	Alfred Austin
1913–30	Robert Seymour Bridges
1930–68	John Masefield
1968–72	Cecil Day Lewis
1972–84	John Betjeman
1984–	Ted Hughes

United States

1986–7	Robert Penn Warren
1987–8	Richard Wilbur
1988–90	Howard Nemerov
1990–1	Mark Strand
1991–2	Joseph Brodsky
1992–3	Mona Van Duyn
1993–5	Rita Dove
1995–	Robert Hass

* The post was not officially established until 1668. Other poets who have used the title are: Geoffrey Chaucer, John Skelton.

The Turner Prize

1984	Malcolm Morley	1989	Richard Long	1994	Anthony Gormley
1985	Howard Hodgkin	1990	*Prize suspended*	1995	Damien Hirst
1986	Gilbert and George	1991	Anish Kapoor	1996	Douglas Gordon
1987	Richard Deacon	1992	Grenville Davey	1997	Gillian Wearing
1988	Tony Cragg	1993	Rachel Whiteread		

Literary prizes

Booker Prize (UK)

1969 P H Newby, *Something to answer for*
1970 Bernice Rubens, *The Elected Member*
1971 V S Naipaul, *In a Free State*
1972 John Berger, *G*
1973 J G Farrell, *The Siege of Krishnapur*
1974 Nadine Gordiner, *The Conservationist*; Stanley Middleton, *Holiday*
1975 Ruth Prawer Jhabvala, *Heat and Dust*
1976 David Storey, *Saville*
1977 Paul Scott, *Staying On*
1978 Iris Murdoch, *The Sea, The Sea*
1979 Penelope Fitzgerald, *Offshore*
1980 William Golding, *Rites of Passage*
1981 Salman Rushdie, *Midnight's Children*
1982 Thomas Keneally, *Schindler's Ark*
1983 J M Coetzee, *Life and Times of Michael K*
1984 Anita Brookner, *Hotel du Lac*
1985 Keri Hulme, *The Bone People*
1986 Kingsley Amis, *The Old Devils*
1987 Penelope Lively, *Moon Tiger*
1988 Peter Carey, *Oscar and Lucinda*
1989 Kazuo Ishiguro, *The Remains of the Day*
1990 A S Byatt, *Possession*
1991 Ben Okri, *The Famished Road*
1992 Barry Unsworth, *Sacred Hunger*; Michael Ondaatje, *The English Patient*
1993 Roddy Doyle, *Paddy Clarke Ha Ha Ha*
1994 James Kelman, *How late it was, how late*
1995 Pat Barker, *The Ghost Road*
1996 Graham Swift, *Last Orders*
1997 Arundhati Roy, *The God of Small Things*

Prix Goncourt (France)

1903 John-Antoine Nau, *Force ennemie*
1904 Léon Frapié, *La Maternelle*
1905 Claude Farrère, *Les Civilisés*
1906 Jérôme and Jean Tharaud, *Dingley, l'illustre écrivain*
1907 Émile Moselly, *Terres lorraines*
1908 Francis de Miomandre, *Écrit sur de l'eau*
1909 Marius and Ary Leblond, *En France*
1910 Louis Pergaud, *De Goupil à Margot*
1911 Alphonse de Chateaubriant, *Monsieur des Lourdines*
1912 André Savignon, *Les Filles de la pluie*
1913 Marc Elder, *Le Peuple de la mer*
1914 *Award delayed until 1916*
1915 René Benjamin, *Gaspard*
1916 Henri Babusse, *Le Feu* Adrien Bertrand, *L'Appel du sol*
1917 Henri Malherbe, *La Flamme au poing*
1918 Georges Duhamel, *Civilisation*
1919 Marcel Proust, *A l'ombre des jeunes filles en fleur*
1920 Ernest Pérochon, *Nêne*
1921 René Maran, *Batouala*
1922 Henri Béraud, *Le Vitriol de lune et Le Martyre de l'obèse*
1923 Lucien Fabre, *Rabevel ou Le Mal des ardents*
1924 Thierry Sandre, *Le Chèvrefeuille; Le Purgatoire; Le Chapitre XIII d'Athénée*
1925 Maurice Genevoix, *Raboliot*
1926 Henri Deberly, *Le Supplice de Phèdre*
1927 Maurice Bedel, *Jérôme 60° latitude Nord*
1928 Maurice Constantin-Weyer, *Un homme se penche sur son passé*
1929 Marcel Arland, *L'Ordre*
1930 Henri Fauconnier, *Malaisie*
1931 Jean Fayard, *Mal d'amour*
1932 Guy Mazeline, *Les Loups*
1933 André Malraux, *La Condition humaine*
1934 Roger Vercel, *Capitaine Conan*
1935 Joseph Peyré, *Sang et lumières*
1936 Maxence Van der Meersch, *L'Empreinte du dieu*
1937 Charles Plisnier, *Faux Passeports*
1938 Henri Troyat, *L'Araigne*
1939 Philippe Hériat, *Les Enfants gatés*
1940 *Prize reserved for a prisoner or political deportee and awarded in 1946 to Francois Ambrière, Les Grandes Vacances*
1941 Henri Pourrat, *Vent de mars*
1942 Marc Bernard, *Pareils à des enfants*
1943 Marius Grout, *Passage de l'homme*
1944 Elsa Triolet, *Le premier accroc coûte deux cents francs*
1945 Jean-Louis Bory, *Mon village a l'heure allemande*
1946 Jean-Jacques Gautier, *Histoire d'un faite divers*
1947 Jean-Louis Curtis, *Les Forêts de la nuit*
1948 Maurice Druon, *Les Grandes Familles*
1949 Robert Merle, *Week-End à Zuydcoote*
1950 Paul Colin, *Les Jeux sauvages*
1951 Julien Gracq, *Le Rivage des Syrtes* (declined)
1952 Béatrice Beck, *Léon Morin, prêtre*
1953 Pierre Gascar, *Les Temps des morts; Les Bêtes*
1954 Simone de Beauvoir, *Les Mandarins*
1955 Roger Ikor, *Les Eaux melées*
1956 Romain Gary, *Les Racines du ciel*
1957 Roger Vailland, *La Loi*
1958 Francis Walder, *Saint-Germain ou La Négociation*
1959 André Schwarz-Bart, *Le Dernier des justes*
1960 Vintila Horia, *Dieu est né en exil* (declined)
1961 Jean Cau, *La Pitié de Dieu*
1962 Anne Langfus, *Les Bagages de sable*
1963 Armand Lanoux, *Quand la mer se retire*
1964 Georges Conchon, *L'État sauvage*
1965 Jacques Borel, *L'Adoration*
1966 Edmonde Charles-Roux, *Oublier Palerme*
1967 André Pieyre de Mandiargues, *La Marge*
1968 Bernard Clavel, *Les Fruits de l'hiver*
1969 Félicien Marceau, *Creezy*
1970 Michel Tournier, *Le Roi des Aulnes*
1971 Jacques Laurent, *Les Bêtises*
1972 Jean Carrière, *L'Épervier de Maheux*
1973 Jacques Chessex, *L'Ogre*
1974 Pascal Lainé, *La Dentellière*
1975 Émile Ajar, *La Vie devant soi*
1976 Patrick Grainville, *Les Flamboyants*
1977 Didier Decoin, *John L'Enfer*
1978 Patrick Modiano, *Rue des boutiques obscures*

1979	Antonine Maillet, *Pélagie la Charrette*
1980	Yves Navarre, *Le Jardin d'acclimatation*
1981	Lucien Bodard, *Anne Marie*
1982	Dominique Fernandez, *Dans la main de l'ange*
1983	Frédérick Tristan, *Les Égarés*
1984	Marguerite Duras, *L'Amant*
1985	Yann Queffelec, *Les Noces barbares*
1986	Michel Host, *Valet de nuit*
1987	Tahar ben Jalloun, *La Nuit sacrée*
1988	Erik Orsenna, *L'Exposition coloniale*
1989	Jean Vautrin, *Un Grand Pas vers le bon Dieu*
1990	Jean Rouaud, *Les Champs d'honneur*
1991	Pierre Combescot, *Les Filles du Calvaire*
1992	Patrick Chamoiseau, *Texaco*
1993	Amin Maalouf, *Le Rocher de Tanois*
1994	Didier van Cauwelaert, *Un Aller simple*
1995	Andrei Makine, *Le Testament française*
1996	Pascale Roze, *Chasseur zéro*

Pulitzer Prize (USA)

Fiction

1917	*No award*
1918	Ernest Poole, *His Family*
1919	Booth Tarkington, *The Magnificent Ambersons*
1920	*No award*
1921	Edith Wharton, *The Age of Innocence*
1922	Booth Tarkington, *Alice Adams*
1923	Willa Cather, *One of Ours*
1924	Margaret Wilson, *The Able McLaughlins*
1925	Edna Ferber, *So Big*
1926	Sinclair Lewis, *Arrowsmith*
1927	Louis Bromfield, *Early Autumn*
1928	Thornton Wilder, *The Bridge of San Luis Rey*
1929	Julia Peterkin, *Scarlet Sister Mary*
1930	Oliver LaFarge, *Laughing Boy*
1931	Margaret Ayer Barnes, *Years of Grace*
1932	Pearl S Buck, *The Good Earth*
1933	T S Stribling, *The Store*
1934	Caroline Miller, *Lamb in His Bosom*
1935	Josephine Winslow Johnson, *Now in November*
1936	Harold L Davis, *Honey in the Horn*
1937	Margaret Mitchell, *Gone With the Wind*
1938	John Phillips Marquand, *The Late George Apley*
1939	Marjorie Kinnan Rawlings, *The Yearling*
1940	John Steinbeck, *The Grapes of Wrath*
1941	*No award*
1942	Ellen Glasgow, *In This Our Life*
1943	Upton Sinclair, *Dragon's Teeth*
1944	Martin Flavin, *Journey in the Dark*
1945	John Hersey, *A Bell For Adano*
1946	*No award*
1947	Robert Penn Warren, *All the King's Men*
1948	James Michener, *Tales of the South Pacific*
1949	James Gould Cozzens, *Guard of Honor*
1950	A B Guthrie, Jr, *The Way West*
1951	Conrad Richter, *The Town*
1952	Herman Wouk, *The Caine Mutiny*
1953	Ernest Hemingway, *The Old Man and the Sea*
1954	*No award*
1955	William Faulkner, *A Fable*
1956	MacKinlay Kantor, *Andersonville*
1957	*No award*
1958	James Agee, *A Death in the Family*
1959	Robert Lewis Taylor, *The Travels of Jaime McPheeters*
1960	Allen Drury, *Advise and Consent*
1961	Harper Lee, *To Kill a Mockingbird*
1962	Edwin O'Connor, *The Edge of Sadness*
1963	William Faulkner, *The Reivers*
1964	*No award*
1965	Shirley Ann Grau, *The Keepers of the House*
1966	Katherine Anne Porter, *The Collected Stories*
1967	Bernard Malamud, *The Fixer*
1968	William Styron, *The Confessions of Nat Turner*
1969	Navarre Scott Momaday, *House Made of Dawn*
1970	Jean Stafford, *Collected Stories*
1972	Wallace Stegner, *Angle of Repose*
1973	Eudora Welty, *The Optimist's Daughter*
1975	Michael Shaara, *The Killer Angels*
1976	Saul Bellow, *Humboldt's Gift*
1978	James Alan McPherson, *Elbow Room*
1979	John Cheever, *The Stories of John Cheever*
1980	Norman Mailer, *The Executioner's Song*
1981	John Kennedy Toole, *A Confederacy of Dunces*
1982	John Updike, *Rabbit is Rich*
1983	Alice Walker, *The Color Purple*
1984	William Kennedy, *Ironweed*
1985	Alison Lurie, *Foreign Affairs*
1986	Larry McMurtry, *Lonesome Dove*
1987	Peter Taylor, *A Summons to Memphis*
1988	Toni Morrison, *Beloved*
1989	Anne Tyler, *Breathing Lessons*
1990	Oscar Hijuelos, *The Mambo Kings Play Songs of Love*
1991	John Updike, *Rabbit at Rest*
1992	Jane Smiley, *A Thousand Acres*
1993	Robert Olen Butler, *A Good Scent from a Strange Mountain*
1994	E Annie Proulx, *The Shipping News*
1995	Carol Shields, *The Stone Diaries*
1996	Richard Ford, *Independence Day*
1997	Steven Millhauser, *Martin Dressler: The Tale of an American Dreamer*

Drama

1918	*No award*
1919	Jesse Lynch Williams, *Why Marry?*
1920	*No award*
1921	Eugene O'Neill, *Beyond the Horizon*
1922	Zona Gale, *Miss Lulu Bett*
1923	Eugene O'Neill, *Anna Christie*
1924	Owen Davis, *Icebound*
1925	Hatcher Hughes, *Hell-Bent for Heaven*
1926	Sidney Howard, *They Knew What They Wanted*
1927	George Kelly, *Craig's Wife*
1928	Paul Green, *In Abraham's Bosom*
1929	Eugene O'Neill, *Strange Interlude*
1930	Elmer Rice, *Street Scene*
1931	Marc Connelly, *The Green Pastures*
1932	Susan Glaspell, *Alison's House*
1933	George S Kaufman, Morris Ryskind and Ira Gershwin, *Of Thee I Sing*
1934	Maxwell Anderson, *Both Your Houses*
1935	Sidney Kingsley, *Men In White*
1936	Zöe Akins, *The Old Maid*
1937	Robert E Sherwood, *Idiot's Delight*
1938	George S Kaufman and Moss Hart, *You Can't Take It With You*
1939	Thornton Wilder, *Our Town*
1940	Robert E Sherwood, *Abe Lincoln in Illinois*
1941	William Saroyan, *The Time of your Life*
1942	Robert E Sherwood, *There Shall Be No Night*
1943	*No award*
1944	Thornton Wilder, *The Skin of Our Teeth*
1945	*No award*
1946	Mary Chase, *Harvey*
1947	Russell Crouse and Howard

Lindsay, *State of the Union*
1948 *No award*
1949 Tennessee Williams, *A Streetcar Named Desire*
1950 Arthur Miller, *Death of a Salesman*
1951 Richard Rodgers, Oscar Hammerstein II and Joshua Logan, *South Pacific*
1952 *No award*
1953 Joseph Kramm, *The Shrike*
1954 William Inge, *Picnic*
1955 John Patrick, *Teahouse of the August Moon*
1956 Tennessee Williams, *Cat on a Hot Tin Roof*
1957 Frances Goodrich and Albert Hackett, *The Diary of Anne Frank*
1958 Eugene O'Neill, *Long Day's Journey Into Night*
1959 Ketti Frings, *Look Homeward, Angel*
1960 Archibald MacLeish, *J B*
1961 George Abbott, Jerome Weidman, Sheldon Harnick and Jerry Bock, *Fiorello*
1962 Tad Mosel, *All the Way Home*
1963 Frank Loesser and Abe Burrows, *How to Succeed in Business Without Really Trying*
1964–5 *No award*
1966 Frank D Gilroy, *The Subject Was Roses*
1967 *No award*
1968 Edward Albee, *A Delicate Balance*
1969 *No award*
1970 Howard Sackler, *The Great White Hope*
1971 Charles Gordone, *No Place to Be Somebody*
1972 Paul Zindel, *The Effect of Gamma Rays on Man-in-the-Moon Marigolds*
1973 *No award*
1974 Jason Miller, *The Championship Season*
1975–6 *No award*
1977 Michael Bennett, James Kirkwood, Nicholas Dante, Marvin Hamlisch and Edward Kleban, *A Chorus Line*
1978 Michael Cristofer, *The Shadow Box*
1979 Donald L Coburn, *The Gin Game*
1980 Sam Shepard, *Buried Child*
1981 Lanford Wilson, *Talley's Folly* Beth Henley, *Crimes of the Heart*
1982 Charles Fuller, *A Soldier's Play*
1983 Marsha Norman, *'Night, Mother*
1984 David Mamet, *Glengarry Glen Ross*
1985 Stephen Sondheim and James Lapine, *Sunday in the Park with George*
1986 *No award*
1987 August Wilson, *Fences*
1988 Alfred Uhry, *Driving Miss Daisy*

1989 Wendy Wasserstein, *The Heidi Chronicles*
1990 August Wilson, *The Piano Lesson*
1991 Neil Simon, *Lost in Yonkers*
1992 Robert Schenkkan, *The Kentucky Cycle*
1993 Tony Kushner, *Angels in America: Millenium Approaches*
1994 Edward Albee, *Three Tall Women*
1995 Horton Foote, *The Young Man from Atlantis*
1996 Jonathan Larson, *Rent*
1997 *No award*

Poetry

1917 *No award*
1918 Sara Teasdale, *Love Songs*
1919 Carl Sandburg, *Corn Huskers*; Margaret Widdemer, *Old Road to Paradise*
1920–1 *No award*
1922 Edwin Arlington Robinson, *Collected Poems*
1923 Edna St Vincent Millay, *The Harp Weaver and Other Poems*
1924 Robert Frost, *New Hampshire: a Poem with Notes and Grace Notes*
1925 Edwin Arlington Robinson, *The Man Who Died Twice*
1926 Amy Lowell, *What's O'Clock?*
1927 Leonora Speyer, *Fiddler's Farewell*
1928 Edwin Arlington Robinson, *Tristram*
1929 Stephen Vincent Benét, *John Brown's Body*
1930 Conrad Aiken, *Selected Poems*
1931 Robert Frost, *Collected Poems*
1932 George Dillon, *The Flowering Stone*
1933 Archibald MacLeish, *Conquistador*
1934 Robert Hillyer, *Collected Verse*
1935 Audrey Wurdemann, *Bright Ambush*
1936 R P Tristram Coffin, *Strange Holiness*
1937 Robert Frost, *A Further Range*
1938 Marya Zaturenska, *Cold Morning Sky*
1939 John Gould Fletcher, *Selected Poems*
1940 Mark Van Doren, *Collected Poems*
1941 Leonard Bacon, *Sunderland Capture*
1942 William Benét, *The Dust Which is God*
1943 Robert Frost, *A Witness Tree*
1944 Stephen Vincent Benét, *Western Star*
1945 Karl Shapiro, *V-Letter and Other Poems*
1946 *No award*
1947 Robert Lowell, *Lord Weary's Castle*
1948 W H Auden, *The Age of Anxiety*
1949 Peter Viereck, *Terror and Decorum*
1950 Gwendolyn Brooks, *Annie Allen*
1951 Carl Sandburg, *Complete Poems*

1952 Marianne Moore, *Collected Poems*
1953 Archibald MacLeish, *Collected Poems 1917–1952*
1954 Theodore Roethke, *The Waking*
1955 Wallace Stevens, *Collected Poems*
1956 Elizabeth Bishop, *Poems – North & South*
1957 Richard Wilbur, *Things of This World*
1958 Robert Penn Warren, *Promises: Poems 1954–56*
1959 Stanley Kunitz, *Selected Poems 1928–1958*
1960 W D Snodgrass, *Heart's Needle*
1961 Phyllis McGinley, *Times Three: Selected Verse from Three Decades*
1962 Alan Dugan, *Poems*
1963 William Carlos Williams, *Pictures from Breughel*
1964 Louis Simpson, *At the End of the Open Road*
1965 John Berryman, *77 Dream Songs*
1966 Richard Eberhart, *Selected Poems*
1967 Ann Sexton, *Live or Die*
1968 Anthony Hecht, *The Hard Hours*
1969 George Oppen, *Of Being Numerous*
1970 Richard Howard, *Untitled Subjects*
1971 W S Merwin, *The Carrier of Ladders*
1972 James Wright, *Collected Poems*
1973 Maxine Winokur Kumin, *Up Country*
1974 Robert Lowell, *The Dolphin*
1975 Gary Snyder, *Turtle Island*
1976 John Ashbery, *Self-Portrait in a Convex Mirror*
1977 James Merrill, *Divine Comedies*
1978 Howard Nemerov, *Collected Poems*
1979 Robert Penn Warren, *Now and Then*
1980 Donald Justice, *Selected Poems*
1981 James Schuyler, *The Morning of the Poem*
1982 Sylvia Plath, *The Collected Poems*
1983 Galway Kinnell, *Selected Poems*
1984 Mary Oliver, *American Primitive*
1985 Carolyn Kizer, *Yin*
1986 Henry Taylor, *The Flying Change*
1987 Rita Dove, *Thomas and Beulah*
1988 William Meredith, *Partial Accounts; New and Selected Poems*
1989 Richard Wilbur, *New and Selected Poems*
1990 Charles Simic, *The World Doesn't End*
1991 Mona van Duyn, *Near Changes*
1992 James Tate, *Selected Poems*
1993 Louise Glück, *The Wild Iris*
1994 Yusef Komunyakaa, *Neon Vernacular*
1995 Philip Levine, *The Simple Truth*
1996 Jorie Graham, *The Dream of the Unified Field*
1997 Lisel Mueller, *Alive Together*

Music

1943 William Schuman, *Secular Cantata No 2*
1944 Howard Hanson, *Symphony No 4, Opus 34*
1945 Aaron Copland, *Appalachian Spring*
1946 Leo Sowerby, *The Canticle of the Sun*
1947 Charles Ives, *Symphony No 3*
1948 Walter Piston, *Symphony No 3*
1949 Virgil Thomson, *Louisiana Story*
1950 Gian-Carlo Menotti, *The Consul*
1951 Douglas S Moore, *Giants in the Earth*
1952 Gail Kubik, *Symphony Concertante*
1953 *No award*
1954 Quincy Porter, *Concerto for Two Pianos and Orchestra*
1955 Gian-Carlo Menotti, *The Saint of Bleecker Street*
1956 Ernst Toch, *Symphony No 3*
1957 Norman Dello Joio, *Meditations on Ecclesiastes*
1958 Samuel Barber, *Vanessa*
1959 John la Montaine, *Concerto for Piano and Orchestra*
1960 Elliott C Carter, Jr, *Second String Quartet*
1961 Walter Piston, *Symphony No 7*
1962 Robert Ward, *The Crucible*

1963 Samuel Barber, *Piano Concerto No 1*
1964 *No award*
1965 *No award*
1966 *No award*
1967 Leon Kirchner, *Quartet No 3*
1968 George Crumb, *Echoes of Time and the River*
1969 Karel Husa, *String Quartet No 3*
1970 Charles W Wuorinen, *Time's Economium*
1971 Mario Davidovsky, *Synchronisms No 6*
1972 Jacob Druckman, *Windows*
1973 Elliott C Carter, Jr, *String Quartet No 3*
1974 Donald Martino, *Notturno*; Roger Sessions, special citation
1975 Dominick Argento, *From the Diary of Virginia Woolf*
1976 Ned Rorem, *Air Music: 10 Etudes for Orchestra*
1977 Richard Wernick, *Visions of Terror and Wonder*
1978 Michael Colgrass, *Deja Vu for Percussion Quartet and Orchestra*
1979 Joseph Schwantner, *Aftertones of Infinity*
1980 David Del Tredici, *In Memory of a Summer Day*
1981 *No award*

1982 Roger Sessions, *Concerto for Orchestra*; Milton Babbitt, special citation
1983 Ellen T Zwilich, *Three Movements for Orchestra*
1984 Bernard Rands, *Canti del Sole*
1985 Stephen Albert, *Symphony; RiverRun*
1986 George Perle, *Wind Quintet IV*
1987 John Harbison, *The Flight Into Egypt*
1988 William Bolcom, *12 New Etudes for Piano*
1989 Roger Reynolds, *Whispers out of Time*
1990 Mel Powell, *Duplicates: A Concerto for Two Pianos and Orchestra*
1991 Shulamit Ran, *Symphony*
1992 Wayne Peterson, *The Face of the Night, The Heart of the Dark*, special award
1992 Art Spiegelmann, *Maus*
1993 Christopher Rouse, *Trombone Concerto*
1994 Gunther Schuller, *Of Remembrances and Reflections*
1995 Morton Gould, *Stringmusic*
1996 George Walker, *Lilacs*
1997 Wynton Marsalis, *Blood on the Fields*

Academy of Motion Picture Arts and Sciences Awards (Oscars)

Best Actor

1927–28 Emil Jannings, *The Way of All Flesh*
1928–29 Warner Baxter, *In Old Arizona*
1929–30 George Arliss, *Disraeli*
1930–31 Lionel Barrymore, *Free Soul*
1931–32 Fredric March, *Dr Jekyll and Mr Hyde*; Wallace Beery, *The Champ*
1932–33 Charles Laughton, *The Private Life of Henry VIII*
1934 Clark Gable, *It Happened One Night*
1935 Victor McLaglen, *The Informer*
1936 Paul Muni, *The Story of Louis Pasteur*
1937 Spencer Tracy, *Captains Courageous*
1938 Spencer Tracy, *Boys Town*
1939 Robert Donat, *Goodbye Mr Chips*
1940 James Stewart, *The Philadelphia Story*
1941 Gary Cooper, *Sergeant York*
1942 James Cagney, *Yankee Doodle Dandy*
1943 Paul Lukas, *Watch on the Rhine*
1944 Bing Crosby, *Going My Way*
1945 Ray Milland, *The Lost Weekend*

1946 Fredric March, *The Best Years of Our Lives*
1947 Ronald Colman, *A Double Life*
1948 Laurence Olivier, *Hamlet*
1949 Broderick Crawford, *All the King's Men*
1950 José Ferrer, *Cyrano de Bergerac*
1951 Humphrey Bogart, *The African Queen*
1952 Gary Cooper, *High Noon*
1953 William Holden, *Stalag 17*
1954 Marlon Brando, *On the Waterfront*
1955 Ernest Borgnine, *Marty*
1956 Yul Brynner, *The King and I*
1957 Alec Guinness, *The Bridge on the River Kwai*
1958 David Niven, *Separate Tables*
1959 Charlton Heston, *Ben Hur*
1960 Burt Lancaster, *Elmer Gantry*
1961 Maximilian Schell, *Judgment at Nuremberg*
1962 Gregory Peck, *To Kill a Mockingbird*
1963 Sidney Poitier, *Lilies of the Field*
1964 Rex Harrison, *My Fair Lady*
1965 Lee Marvin, *Cat Ballou*
1966 Paul Scofield, *A Man for All Seasons*

1967 Rod Steiger, *In the Heat of the Night*
1968 Cliff Robertson, *Charly*
1969 John Wayne, *True Grit*
1970 George C Scott, *Patton* (refused)
1971 Gene Hackman, *The French Connection*
1972 Marlon Brando, *The Godfather* (refused)
1973 Jack Lemmon, *Save the Tiger*
1974 Art Carney, *Harry and Tonto*
1975 Jack Nicholson, *One Flew Over the Cuckoo's Nest*
1976 Peter Finch, *Network*
1977 Richard Dreyfuss, *The Goodbye Girl*
1978 Jon Voight, *Coming Home*
1979 Dustin Hoffman, *Kramer vs Kramer*
1980 Robert de Niro, *Raging Bull*
1981 Henry Fonda, *On Golden Pond*
1982 Ben Kingsley, *Gandhi*
1983 Robert Duval, *Tender Mercies*
1984 F Murray Abraham, *Amadeus*
1985 William Hurt, *Kiss of the Spider Woman*
1986 Paul Newman, *The Color of Money*
1987 Michael Douglas, *Wall Street*

1988 Dustin Hoffman, *Rain Man*
1989 Daniel Day Lewis, *My Left Foot*
1990 Jeremy Irons, *Reversal of Fortune*
1991 Anthony Hopkins, *The Silence of the Lambs*
1992 Al Pacino, *Scent of a Woman*
1993 Tom Hanks, *Philadelphia*
1994 Tom Hanks, *Forrest Gump*
1995 Nicolas Cage, *Leaving Las Vegas*
1996 Geoffrey Rush, *Shine*

Best Actress

1927–28 Janet Gaynor, *Seventh Heaven*
1928–29 Mary Pickford, *Coquette*
1929–30 Norma Shearer, *The Divorcee*
1930–31 Marie Dressler, *Min and Bill*
1931–32 Helen Hayes, *The Sin of Madelon Claudet*
1932–33 Katharine Hepburn, *Morning Glory*
1934 Claudette Colbert, *It Happened One Night*
1935 Bette Davis, *Dangerous*
1936 Luise Rainer, *The Great Ziegfeld*
1937 Luise Rainer, *The Good Earth*
1938 Bette Davis, *Jezebel*
1939 Vivien Leigh, *Gone With the Wind*
1940 Ginger Rogers, *Kitty Foyle*
1941 Joan Fontaine, *Suspicion*
1942 Greer Garson, *Mrs Miniver*
1943 Jennifer Jones, *The Song of Bernadette*
1944 Ingrid Bergman, *Gaslight*
1945 Joan Crawford, *Mildred Pierce*
1946 Olivia de Havilland, *To Each his Own*
1947 Loretta Young, *The Farmer's Daughter*
1948 Jane Wyman, *Johnny Belinda*
1949 Olivia de Havilland, *The Heiress*
1950 Judy Holliday, *Born Yesterday*
1951 Vivien Leigh, *A Streetcar Named Desire*
1952 Shirley Booth, *Come Back, Little Sheba*
1953 Audrey Hepburn, *Roman Holiday*
1954 Grace Kelly, *The Country Girl*
1955 Anna Magnani, *The Rose Tattoo*
1956 Ingrid Bergman, *Anastasia*
1957 Joanne Woodward, *The Three Faces of Eve*
1958 Susan Hayward, *I Want to Live*
1959 Simone Signoret, *Room at the Top*
1960 Elizabeth Taylor, *Butterfield 8*
1961 Sophia Loren, *Two Women*
1962 Anne Bancroft, *The Miracle Worker*
1963 Patricia Neal, *Hud*
1964 Julie Andrews, *Mary Poppins*
1965 Julie Christie, *Darling*

1966 Elizabeth Taylor, *Who's Afraid of Virginia Woolf?*
1967 Katharine Hepburn, *Guess Who's Coming to Dinner*
1968 Katharine Hepburn, *The Lion in Winter*;
Barbra Streisand, *Funny Girl*
1969 Maggie Smith, *The Prime of Miss Jean Brodie*
1978 Jane Fonda, *Coming Home*
1979 Sally Field, *Norma Rae*
1980 Sissy Spacek, *Coal Miner's Daughter*
1981 Katharine Hepburn, *On Golden Pond*
1982 Meryl Streep, *Sophie's Choice*
1983 Shirley MacLaine, *Terms of Endearment*
1984 Sally Field, *Places in the Heart*
1985 Geraldine Page, *The Trip to Bountiful*
1986 Marlee Matlin, *Children of a Lesser God*
1987 Cher, *Moonstruck*
1988 Jodie Foster, *The Accused*
1989 Jessica Tandy, *Driving Miss Daisy*
1990 Kathy Bates, *Misery*
1991 Jodie Foster, *The Silence of the Lambs*
1992 Emma Thompson, *Howards End*
1993 Holly Hunter, *The Piano*
1994 Jessica Lange, *Blue Sky*
1995 Susan Sarandon, *Dead Man Walking*
1996 Frances McDormand, *Fargo*

Best Director

1927–28 Frank Borzage, *Seventh Heaven*
Lewis Milestone, *Two Arabian Knights*
1928–29 Frank Lloyd, *The Divine Lady*
1929–30 Lewis Milestone, *All Quiet on the Western Front*
1930–31 Norman Taurog, *Skippy*
1931–32 Frank Borzage, *Bad Girl*
1932–33 Frank Lloyd, *Cavalcade*
1934 Frank Capra, *It Happened One Night*
1935 John Ford, *The Informer*
1936 Frank Capra, *Mr Deeds Goes to Town*
1937 Leo McCarey, *The Awful Truth*
1938 Frank Capra, *You Can't Take It With You*
1939 Victor Fleming, *Gone With the Wind*
1940 John Ford, *The Grapes of Wrath*
1941 John Ford, *How Green Was My Valley*
1942 William Wyler, *Mrs Miniver*
1943 Michael Curtiz, *Casablanca*
1944 Leo McCarey, *Going My Way*
1945 Billy Wilder, *The Lost Weekend*

1946 William Wyler, *The Best Years of Our Lives*
1947 Elia Kazan, *Gentleman's Agreement*
1948 John Huston, *The Treasure of the Sierra Madre*
1949 Joseph L Mankiewicz, *A Letter to Three Wives*
1950 Joseph L Mankiewicz, *All About Eve*
1951 George Stevens, *A Place in the Sun*
1952 John Ford, *The Quiet Man*
1953 Fred Zinnemann, *From Here to Eternity*
1954 Elia Kazan, *On The Waterfront*
1955 Delbert Mann, *Marty*
1956 George Stevens, *Giant*
1957 David Lean, *The Bridge on the River Kwai*
1958 Vincente Minnelli, *Gigi*
1959 William Wyler, *Ben-Hur*
1960 Billy Wilder, *The Apartment*
1961 Jerome Robbins and Robert Wise, *West Side Story*
1962 David Lean, *Lawrence of Arabia*
1963 Tony Richardson, *Tom Jones*
1964 George Cukor, *My Fair Lady*
1965 Robert Wise, *The Sound of Music*
1966 Fred Zinnemann, *A Man For All Seasons*
1967 Mike Nichols, *The Graduate*
1968 Carol Reed, *Oliver!*
1969 John Schlesinger, *Midnight Cowboy*
1970 Franklin J Schaffner, *Patton*
1971 William Friedkin, *The French Connection*
1972 Bob Fosse, *Cabaret*
1973 George Roy Hill, *The Sting*
1974 Francis Ford Coppola, *The Godfather, Part II*
1975 Milos Forman, *One Flew Over the Cuckoo's Nest*
1976 John Avildsen, *Rocky*
1977 Woody Allen, *Annie Hall*
1978 Michael Cimino, *The Deer Hunter*
1979 Robert Benton, *Kramer vs Kramer*
1980 Robert Redford, *Ordinary People*
1981 Warren Beatty, *Reds*
1982 Richard Attenborough, *Gandhi*
1983 James L Brookes, *Terms of Endearment*
1984 Milos Forman, *Amadeus*
1985 Sydney Pollack, *Out of Africa*
1986 Oliver Stone, *Platoon*
1987 Bernardo Bertolucci, *The Last Emperor*
1988 Barry Levinson, *Rain Man*
1989 Oliver Stone, *Born on the Fourth of July*

1990 Kevin Costner, *Dances With Wolves*	1992 Clint Eastwood, *Unforgiven*	1995 Mel Gibson, *Braveheart*
1991 Jonathan Demme, *The Silence of the Lambs*	1993 Steven Spielberg, *Schindler's List*	1996 Anthony Minghella, *The English Patient*
	1994 Robert Zemickis, *Forrest Gump*	

The Templeton Prize for Progress in Religion

1973 Mother Teresa of Calcutta, India
1974 Brother Roger of Taizé, France
1975 Dr Sarvepalli Radhakrishnan, India
1976 Leon Joseph Suenens, Cardinal, Belgium
1977 Chiara Lubich, Italy
1978 Rev Prof Thomas F Torrance, UK
1979 Nikkyo Niwano, Japan
1980 Prof Ralph Wendell Burhoe, USA
1981 Dame Cecily Saunders, UK

1982 Rev Dr Billy Graham, USA
1983 Alexander Solzhenitsyn, USSR
1984 Rev Michael Bourdeaux, UK
1985 Sir Alister Hardy, UK
1986 Rev Dr James I McCord, USA
1987 Rev Prof Stanley L Jaki, Hungary/USA
1988 Dr Inamullah Khan, Pakistan
1989 Very Rev Lord Macleod of Fiunary, UK; Prof Carl Friedrich von Weizsäcker, Germany

1990 Baba Amte, India
    Prof L Charles Birch, Australia
1991 Rt Hon Lord Jakobovits, UK
1992 Dr Kyung-Chik Han, South Korea
1993 Charles W Colson, USA
1994 Michael Novak, USA
1995 Prof Paul Charles William Davies, UK
1996 William R(ohl) Bright, USA
1997 Pandurang Shastri Athavale, India

Competitive sports and games

Aerobatics

World Championships
First held in 1960 and every two years since then except 1974 and 1992.

Recent winners (Men)
1972 Charlie Hillard (USA)
1976 Vikto Letsko (USSR)
1978 Ivan Tucek (Czechoslovakia)
1980 Leo Loudenslager (USA)
1982 Viktor Smolin (USSR)
1984 Petr Jirmus (Czechoslovakia)
1986 Petr Jirmus (Czechoslovakia)
1988 Henry Haigh (USA)
1990 Claude Bessière (France)
1994 Xavier de Lattarent (France)
1996 Victor Chmal (Russia)

Recent winners (Women)
1972 Mary Gaffaney (USA)
1976 Lidia Leonova (USSR)
1978 Valentina Yaikova (USSR)
1980 Betty Stewart (USA)
1982 Betty Stewart (USA)
1984 Khalide Makagonova (USSR)
1986 Liubov Nemkova (USSR)
1988 Catherine Maunoury (France)
1990 Natalya Sergeeva (USSR)
1994 Christine Genin (France)
1996 Svetlana Kapanina (Russia)

Angling

World Fresh Water Championship
First held in 1957; takes place annually.

Recent winners (Individual)
1981 David Thomas (England)
1982 Kevin Ashurst (England)

1983 Wolf-Rüdiger Kremkus (West Germany)
1984 Bobby Smithers (Ireland)
1985 David Roper (England)
1986 Lud Wever (Netherlands)
1987 Clive Branson (Wales)
1988 Jean-Pierre Fouquet (France)
1989 Tom Pickering (England)
1990 Bob Nudd (England)
1991 Bob Nudd (England)
1992 David Wesson (Australia)
1993 Mario Barros (Portugal)
1994 Bob Hudd (England)
1995 Pierre Jean (France)
1996 Alan Scotthorne (England)
1997 Alan Scotthorne (England)
Most wins: (3), Robert Tesse (France) 1959–60, 1965.

World Fly Fishing Championship
First held in 1981; takes place annually.

Winners (Individual)
1984 Tony Pawson (England)
1985 Leslaw Frasik (Poland)
1986 Slivoj Svoboda (Czechoslovakia)
1987 Brian Leadbetter (England)
1988 John Pawson (England)
1989 Wladyslaw Trzebuinia (Poland)
1990 Franciszek Szajnik (Poland)
1991 Brian Leadbetter (England)
1992 Pierluigi Cocito (Italy)
1993 Russell Owen (Wales)
1994 Pascal Cognard (France)
1995 Jeremy Hermann (England)
1996 Pierluigi Cocito (Italy)
1997 Pascal Cognard (France)
Most wins: (2) Brian Leadbetter (England), as above.

Archery

World Championships
First held in 1931; took place annually until 1959; since then, every two years.

Recent winners Individual (Men)
1973 Vikto Sidoruk (USSR)
1975 Darrell Pace (USA)
1977 Richard McKinney (USA)
1979 Darrell Pace (USA)
1981 Kysti Laasonen (Finland)
1983 Richard McKinney (USA)
1985 Richard McKinney (USA)
1987 Vladimir Yesheyev (USSR)
1989 Stanislav Zabrodsky (USSR)
1991 Simon Fairweather (Australia)
1993 Kyung-Mo Park (Korea)
1995 Gary Broadhead (USA)
1997 Kyung-ho Kim
Most wins: (4), Hans Deutgen (Sweden) 1947–50.

Recent winners Individual (Women)
1973 Linda Myers (USA)
1975 Zebiniso Rustamova (USSR)
1977 Luann Ryon (USA)
1979 Jin-ho Kim (South Korea)
1981 Natalia Butuzova (USSR)
1983 Jin-ho Kim (South Korea)
1985 Irina Soldatova (USSR)
1987 Ma Xiaojun (China)
1989 Soo-nyung Kim (South Korea)
1991 Soo-nyung Kim (South Korea)
1993 Hyo-jung Kim (South Korea)
1995 Angela Moscarelly (USA)
1997 Du-ri Kim
Most wins: (7), Janina Kurkowska (Poland) 1931–4, 1936, 1939, 1947.

Olympics
A regular Olympic event since 1972.

Winners (Men)
1976 Darrell Pace (USA)
1980 Tomi Poikolainen (Finland)
1984 Darrell Pace (USA)
1988 Jay Barrs (USA)
1992 Sébastien Flute (France)
1996 Justin Huish (USA)

Winners (Women)
1976 Luann Ryon (USA)
1980 Keto Lossaberidze (USSR)
1984 Hyang-soon Seo (South Korea)
1988 Soo-nyung Kim (South Korea)
1992 Youn-jeong Cho (South Korea)
1996 Kyung-wook Kim (South Korea)

Athletics
Performance times are given in seconds, or minutes:seconds, or hours:minutes:seconds. Distances are given in metres. Performances in the decathlon, pentathlon and heptathlon are given in points.

World Championships
First held in Helsinki, Finland in 1983, then in Rome, Italy in 1987, Tokyo, Japan in 1991, Stuttgart, Germany in 1993, Gothenburg, Sweden in 1995, Athens, Greece in 1997; take place every two years from 1993.

EVENT WINNERS (MEN)

100 m
1991 Carl Lewis (USA) 9.86
1993 Linford Christie (Great Britain) 9.87
1995 Donovan Bailey (Canada) 9.97
1997 Maurice Greene (USA) 9.86

200 m
1991 Michael Johnson (USA) 20.01
1993 Frankie Fredericks (Namibia) 19.85
1995 Michael Johnson (USA) 19.79
1997 Ato Boldon (Jamaica) 20.04

400 m
1991 Antonio Pettigrew (USA) 44.57
1993 Michael Johnson (USA) 43.65
1995 Michael Johnson (USA) 43.34
1997 Michael Johnson (USA) 44.12

800 m
1991 Billy Konchellah (Kenya) 1:43.99
1993 Paul Ruto (Kenya) 1:44.71
1995 Wilson Kipketer (Denmark) 1:45.08
1997 Wilson Kipketer (Denmark) 1:43.38

1500 m
1991 Noureddine Morceli (Algeria) 3:32.84
1993 Noureddine Morceli (Algeria) 3:34.24

1995 Noureddine Morceli (Algeria) 3:33.73
1997 Hicham el-Guerrouj (Morocco) 3:35.83

5000 m
1991 Yobes Ondieki (Kenya) 13:14.45
1993 Ismael Kurui (Kenya) 13:02.75
1995 Ismael Kurui (Kenya) 13:16.77
1997 Daniel Komen (Kenya) 13:07.38

10000 m
1991 Moses Tanui (Kenya) 27:38.74
1993 Haile Gebresilassie (Ethiopia) 27:46.02
1995 Haile Gebresilassie (Ethiopia) 27:12.95
1997 Haile Gebresilassie (Ethiopia) 27:24.58

Marathon
1991 Hiromi Taniguchi (Japan) 2:14:57
1993 Mark Plaatjes (USA) 2:13.57
1995 Martin Fizz (Spain) 2:11.41
1997 Abel Anton (Spain) 2:13.16

3000 m steeplechase
1991 Moses Kiptanui (Kenya) 8:12.59
1993 Moses Kiptanui (Kenya) 8:06.36
1995 Moses Kiptanui (Kenya) 8:04.16
1997 Wilson Kipketer (Kenya) 8:05.84

110 m hurdles
1991 Greg Foster (USA) 13.06
1993 Colin Jackson (Great Britain) 12.91
1995 Allen Johnson (USA) 13.00
1997 Allen Johnson (USA) 12.93

400 m hurdles
1991 Samuel Matete (Zambia) 47.64
1993 Kevin Young (USA) 47.18
1995 Derrick Atkins (USA) 47.98
1997 Stéphane Diagana (France) 47.70

High jump
1991 Charles Austin (USA) 2.38
1993 Javier Sotomayor (Cuba) 2.40
1995 Troy Kemp (Bahamas) 3.37
1997 Javier Sotomayor (Cuba) 2.37

Pole vault
1991 Sergey Bubka (USSR) 5.92
1993 Sergey Bubka (Ukraine) 6.00
1995 Sergey Bubka (Ukraine) 5.92
1997 Sergey Bubka (Ukraine) 6.01

Long jump
1991 Mike Powell (USA) 8.95
1993 Mike Powell (USA) 8.59
1995 Ivan Pedroso (Cuba) 8.70
1997 Ivan Pedroso (Cuba) 8.42

Triple jump
1991 Kenny Harrison (USA) 17.78
1993 Mike Conley (USA) 17.86
1995 Jonathan Edwards (Great Britain) 18.29
1997 Yoelvis Quesada (Cuba) 17.85

Shot
1991 Werner Günthör (Switzerland) 21.67
1993 Werner Günthör (Switzerland) 21.97
1995 John Godina (USA) 21.47
1997 John Godina (USA) 21.44

Discus
1991 Lars Riedel (Germany) 66.20
1993 Lars Riedel (Germany) 67.72
1995 Lars Riedel (Germany) 68.76
1997 Lars Riedel (Germany) 68.54

Hammer
1991 Yuriy Sedykh (USSR) 81.70
1993 Andrei Abduvaleiyiv (Tajikistan) 81.64
1995 Andrei Abduvaleiyiv (Tajikistan) 81.56
1997 Heinz Weis (Germany) 81.78

Javelin
1991 Kimmo Kinnunen (Finland) 90.82
1993 Jan Zelezny (Czech Republic) 85.98
1995 Jan Zelezny (Czech Republic) 89.58
1997 Marius Corbett (South Africa) 88.40

Decathlon
1991 Dan O'Brien (USA) 8812
1993 Dan O'Brien (USA) 8817
1995 Dan O'Brien (USA) 8695
1997 Tomas Dvorak (Czech Republic) 8837

20 km walk
1991 Maurizio Damilano (Italy) 1:19:37
1993 Valentin Massana (Spain) 1:22:31
1995 Michele Didoni (Italy) 1:19.59
1997 D Garcia (Mexico) 1:21.43

50 km walk
1991 Aleksandr Potashov (USSR) 3:53:09
1993 Jesús Garcia (Spain) 3:41:41
1995 Valentin Kononen (Finland) 3:43.42
1997 Robert Korzenjowski (Poland) 3:44.46

EVENT WINNERS (WOMEN)

100 m
1991 Katrin Krabbe (Germany) 10.99
1993 Gail Devers (USA) 10.82
1995 Gwen Torrence (USA) 10.86
1997 Marion Jones (USA) 10.83

200 m
1991 Katrin Krabbe (Germany) 22.09
1993 Merlene Ottey (Jamaica) 21.98
1995 Merlene Ottey (Jamaica) 22.12
1997 Zhanna Pintussevich (Ukraine) 22.32

400 m
1991 Marie-José Pérec (France) 49.13
1993 Jearl Miles (USA) 49.82
1995 Marie-José Pérec (France) 49.28
1997 Cathy Freeman (Australia) 49.77

800 m
1991 Lilia Nurutdinova (USSR) 1:57.50
1993 Maria Mutola (Mozambique) 1:55.43
1995 Ana Fidelia Quirot (Cuba) 1:56.11
1997 Ana Fidelia Quirot (Cuba) 1:57.14

1500 m
1991 Hassiba Boulmerka (Algeria) 4:02.21
1993 Liu Dong (China) 4:00.50
1995 Hassiba Boulmerka (Algeria) 4:02.42
1997 Carla Sacramento (Portugal) 4:04.24

3000 m (event discontinued 1993)
1991 Tatyana Dorovskikh (USSR) 8:35.82
1993 Qu Yunxia (China) 8:28.71

5000 m
1995 Sonia O'Sullivan (Ireland) 14:46.47
1997 Gabriela Szabo (Romania) 14:57.68

10000 m
1991 Liz McColgan (Great Britain) 31:14.31
1993 Wang Junxia (China) 30:39.30
1995 Fernanda Ribeiro (Portugal) 31:04.99
1997 Sally Barsosia (Kenya) 31:32.92

Marathon
1991 Wanda Panfil (Poland) 2:29:53
1993 Junko Asari (Japan) 2:30:03
1995 Manuela Machado (Portugal) 2:25.39
1997 Hiromi Suzuki (Japan) 2:29.48

100 m hurdles
1991 Lyudmila Narozhilenko (USSR) 12.59
1993 Gail Devers (USA) 12.46
1995 Gail Devers (USA) 12.68
1997 Ludmila Engquist (Sweden) 12.50

400 m hurdles
1991 Tatyana Ledovskaya (USSR) 53.11
1993 Sally Gunnell (Great Britain) 52.74
1995 Kim Batten (USA) 52.61
1997 Nezha Bidouane (Morocco) 52.97

High jump
1991 Heike Henkel (Germany) 2.05
1993 Ioamnet Quintero (Cuba) 1.99

1995 Stefka Kostadinova (Bulgaria) 2.01
1997 Hanne Haugland (Norway) 1.99

Long jump
1991 Jackie Joyner-Kersee (USA) 7.32
1993 Heike Drechsler (Germany) 7.11
1995 Fiona May (Italy) 6.98
1997 Lyudmila Galkina (Russia) 7.05

Triple jump
1995 Inessa Kravets (Ukraine) 15.50
1997 Sarka Kasparkova (Czech Republic) 15.20

Shot
1991 Zhihong Huang (China) 20.83
1993 Zhihong Huang (China) 20.57
1995 Astrid Kumbernuss (Germany) 21.22
1997 Astrid Kumbernuss (Germany) 20.71

Discus
1991 Tsvetanka Khristova (Bulgaria) 71.02
1993 Olga Burova (Russia) 67.40
1995 Ellina Svereva (Belarus) 68.64
1997 Beatrice Faumuina (New Zealand) 66.82

Javelin
1991 Xu Demei (China) 68.78
1993 Trine Hattestad (Norway) 69.18
1995 Natalya Shikolenka (Belarus) 67.56
1997 Trine Hattestad (Norway) 68.78

Heptathlon
1991 Sabine Braun (Germany) 6672
1993 Jackie Joyner-Kersee (USA) 6837
1995 Ghada Shouaa (Syria) 6651
1997 Sabine Braun (Germany) 6739

10 km walk
1991 Alina Ivanova (USSR) 42:57
1993 Sari Essayah (Finland) 42.59
1995 Irina Stankina (Russia) 42:13
1997 Sabine Braun (Germany) 42.55

Olympic games

EVENT WINNERS (MEN)

100 m
1896 Thomas Burke (USA) 12.0
1900 Francis Jarvis (USA) 11.0
1904 Archie Hahn (USA) 11.0
1906 Archie Hahn (USA) 11.2
1908 Reginald Walker (South Africa) 10.8
1912 Ralph Craig (USA) 10.8
1920 Charles Paddock (USA) 10.8
1924 Harold Abrahams (Great Britain) 10.6
1928 Percy Williams (Canada) 10.8
1932 Eddie Tolan (USA) 10.3
1936 Jesse Owens (USA) 10.3
1948 Harrison Dillard (USA) 10.3
1952 Lindy Remigino (USA) 10.4

1956 Bobby Morrow (USA) 10.5
1960 Armin Hary (West Germany) 10.2
1964 Bob Hayes (USA) 10.06
1968 James Hines (USA) 9.95
1972 Valeriy Borzov (USSR) 10.14
1976 Hasely Crawford (Trinidad) 10.06
1980 Allan Wells (Great Britain) 10.25
1984 Carl Lewis (USA) 9.99
1988 Carl Lewis (USA) 9.92
1992 Linford Christie (Great Britain) 9.96
1996 Donovan Bailey (Canada) 9.84

200 m
1900 John Walter Tewksbury (USA) 22.2
1904 Archie Hahn (USA) 21.6
1908 Robert Kerr (Canada) 21.6
1912 Ralph Craig (USA) 21.7
1920 Allen Woodring (USA) 22.0
1924 Jackson Scholz (USA) 21.6
1928 Percy Williams (Canada) 21.8
1932 Eddie Tolan (USA) 21.2
1936 Jesse Owens (USA) 20.7
1948 Melvin Patton (USA) 21.1
1952 Andrew Stanfield (USA) 20.7
1956 Bobby Morrow (USA) 20.5
1960 Livio Berruti (Italy) 20.5
1964 Henry Carr (USA) 20.36
1968 Tommie Smith (USA) 19.83
1972 Valeriy Borzov (USSR) 20.00
1976 Donald Quarrie (Jamaica) 20.3
1980 Pietro Mennea (Italy) 20.19
1984 Carl Lewis (USA) 19.80
1988 Joe DeLoach (USA) 19.75
1992 Michael Marsh (USA) 20.01
1996 Michael Johnson (USA) 19.32

400 m
1896 Thomas Burke (USA) 54.2
1900 Maxey Long (USA) 49.4
1904 Harry Hillman (USA) 49.2
1906 Paul Pilgrim (USA) 53.2
1908 Wyndham Halswelle (Great Britain) 50.0
1912 Charles Reidpath (USA) 48.2
1920 Bevil Rudd (South Africa) 49.6
1924 Eric Liddell (Great Britain) 47.6
1928 Ray Barbuti (USA) 47.8
1932 Bill Carr (USA) 46.28
1936 Archie Williams (USA) 46.66
1948 Arthur Wint (Jamaica) 46.2
1952 George Rhoden (Jamaica) 46.09
1956 Charles Jenkins (USA) 46.86
1960 Otis Davis (USA) 45.07
1964 Michael Larrabee (USA) 45.15
1968 Lee Evans (USA) 43.86
1972 Vincent Matthews (USA) 44.66
1976 Alberto Juantoreno (Cuba) 44.26
1980 Viktor Markin (USSR) 44.60
1984 Alonzo Babers (USA) 44.27
1988 Steve Lewis (USA) 43.87
1992 Quincy Watts (USA) 43.50
1996 Michael Johnson (USA) 43.49

800 m
1896 Edwin Flack (Australia) 2:11.0
1900 James Lightbody (USA) 1:56.0
1906 Paul Pilgrim (USA) 2:01.5
1908 Mel Sheppard (USA) 1:52.8
1912 James Meredith (USA) 1:51.9
1920 Albert Hill (Great Britain) 1:53.4
1924 Douglas Lowe (Great Britain)
 1:52.4
1928 Douglas Lowe (Great Britain)
 1:51.8
1932 Tom Hampson (Great Britain)
 1:49.70
1936 John Woodruff (USA) 1:52.9
1948 Malvin Whitfield (USA) 1:49.2
1952 Malvin Whitfield (USA) 1:49.34
1956 Thomas Courtney (USA) 1:47.75
1960 Peter Snell (New Zealand)
 1:46.48
1964 Peter Snell (New Zealand) 1:45.1
1968 Ralph Doubell (Australia)
 1:44.40
1972 David Wottle (USA) 1:45.86
1976 Alberto Juantorena (Cuba)
 1:43.50
1980 Steve Ovett (Great Britain)
 1:45.40
1984 Joaquim Cruz (Brazil) 1:43.00
1988 Paul Ereng (Kenya) 1:43.45
1992 William Tanui (Kenya) 1:43.66
1996 Vebjoern Rodal (Norway) 1.42.58

1500 m
1896 Edwin Flack (Australia) 4:33.2
1900 Charles Bennett (Great Britain)
 4:06.2
1904 James Lightbody (USA) 4:05.4
1906 James Lightbody (USA) 4:12.0
1908 Mel Sheppard (USA) 4:03.4
1912 Arnold Jackson (Great Britain)
 3.56.8
1920 Albert Hill (Great Britain) 4.01.8
1924 Paavo Nurmi (Finland) 3:53.6
1928 Harri Larva (Finland) 3:53.2
1932 Luigi Beccali (Italy) 3:51.20
1936 Jack Lovelock (New Zealand)
 3:46.8
1948 Henri Eriksson (Sweden) 3:49.8
1952 Josef Barthel (Luxembourg)
 3:45.28
1956 Ron Delany (Ireland) 3:41.49
1960 Herbert Elliott (Australia) 3:35.6
1964 Peter Snell (New Zealand) 3:38.1
1968 Kipchoge Keino (Kenya) 3:34.91
1972 Pekkha Vasala (Finland) 3:36.33
1976 John Walker (New Zealand)
 3:39.17
1980 Sebastian Coe (Great Britain)
 3:38.40
1984 Sebastian Coe (Great Britain)
 3:32.53
1988 Peter Rono (Kenya) 3:35.96
1992 Fermin Cacho (Spain) 3:40.12
1996 Noureddine Morceli (Algeria)
 3.35.79

5000 m
1912 Hannes Kolehmainen (Finland)
 14:36.6
1920 Joseph Guillemot (France)
 14:55.6
1924 Paavo Nurmi (Finland) 14:21.2
1928 Ville Ritola (Finland) 14:38.0
1932 Lauri Lehtinen (Finland)
 14:29.91
1936 Gunnar Höckert (Finland)
 14:22.2
1948 Gaston Reitt (Belgium) 14:17.6
1952 Emil Zátopek (Czechoslovakia)
 14:06.72
1956 Vladimir Kuts (USSR) 13:39.86
1960 Murray Halberg (New Zealand)
 13:43.4
1964 Robert Schul (USA) 13:48.8
1968 Mohamed Gammoudi (Tunisia)
 14:05.0
1972 Lasse Viren (Finland) 13:26.42
1976 Lasse Viren (Finland) 13:24.76
1980 Miruts Yifter (Ethiopia) 13:20.91
1984 Saïd Aouita (Morocco) 13:05.59
1988 John Ngugi (Kenya) 13:11.70
1992 Dieter Baumann (Germany)
 13:12.52
1996 Venuste Niyongabo (Burundi)
 13:07.97

10000 m
1912 Hannes Kolehamainen (Finland)
 31:20.8
1920 Paavo Nurmi (Finland) 31:45.8
1924 Ville Ritola (Finland) 30:23.1
1928 Paavo Nurmi (Finland) 30:18.8
1932 Janusz Kusocinski (Poland)
 30:11.4
1936 Ilmari Salminen (Finland)
 30:15.4
1948 Emil Zátopek (Czechoslovakia)
 29:59.6
1952 Emil Zátopek (Czechoslovakia)
 29:17.0
1956 Vladimir Kuts (USSR) 28:45.60
1960 Pyotr Bolotnikov (USSR) 28:32.18
1964 William Mills (USA) 28:24.4
1968 Naftali Ternu (Kenya) 29:27.45
1972 Lasse Viren (Finland) 27:38.35
1976 Lasse Viren (Finland) 27:40.38
1980 Miruts Yifter (Ethopia) 27:42.69
1984 Alberto Cova (Italy) 27:47.54
1988 Brahim Boutayeb (Morocco)
 27:21.46
1992 Khalid Skah (Morocco) 27:46.70
1996 Haile Gebreselassie (Ethiopia)
 27:07.34

Marathon
Unless shown otherwise the Marathon
is run over a distance of 42.195 km/
26 mi 385 yd.

1896 Spyridon Louis (Greece)
 2:58:50.0 (40 km)
1900 Michel Théato (France) 2:59:45.0
 (40.26 km)

1904 Thomas Hicks (USA) 3:28:35.0
 (40 km)
1906 William Sherring (Canada)
 2:51:23.6 (41.86 km)
1908 John Hayes (USA) 2:55:18.4
1912 Kenneth McArthur (South
 Africa) 2:36:54.8 (40.2 km)
1920 Hannes Kolehmainen (Finland)
 2:32:35.8 (42.75 km)
1924 Albin Stenroos (Finland)
 2:41:22.6
1928 Mohamed Boughéra El Ouafi
 (France) 2:32:57.0
1932 Juan Carlos Zabala (Argentina)
 2:31:36.0
1936 Kitei Son (Japan) 2:29:19.2
1948 Delfo Cabrera (Argentina)
 2:34:51.6
1952 Emil Zátopek (Czechoslovakia)
 2:23:03.2
1956 Alain Mimoun (France) 2:25:00.0
1960 Abebe Bikila (Ethiopia) 2:15:16.2
1964 Abebe Bikila (Ethiopia) 2:12:11.2
1968 Mamo Wolde (Ethiopia)
 2:20:26.4
1972 Frank Shorter (USA) 2:12:19.8
1976 Waldemar Cierpinski (East
 Germany) 2:09:55
1980 Waldemar Cierpinski (East
 Germany) 2:11:03
1984 Carlos Lopes (Portugal) 2:09:21
1988 Gelindo Bordin (Italy) 2:10:32
1992 Hwang Young-cho (South Korea)
 2:13:23
1996 Josia Thugwane (South Africa)
 2:12.36

110 m hurdles
1896 Thomas Curtis (USA) 17.6
1900 Alvin Kraenzlein (USA) 15.4
1904 Fred Schule (USA) 16.0
1906 Robert Leavitt (USA) 16.2
1908 Forrest Smithson (USA) 15.0
1912 Fred Kelly (USA) 15.1
1920 Earl Thomson (Canada) 14.8
1924 Daniel Kinsey (USA) 15.0
1928 Sydney Atkinson (South Africa)
 14.8
1932 George Saling (USA) 14.57
1936 Forrest Towns (USA) 14.2
1948 William Porter (USA) 13.9
1952 Harrison Dillard (USA) 13.91
1956 Lee Calhoun (USA) 13.70
1960 Lee Calhoun (USA) 13.98
1964 Hayes Jones (USA) 13.67
1968 Willie Davenport (USA) 13.33
1972 Rodney Milburn (USA) 13.24
1976 Guy Drut (France) 13.30
1980 Thomas Munkelt (East Germany)
 13.39
1984 Roger Kingdom (USA) 13.20
1988 Roger Kingdom (USA) 12.98
1992 Mark McKoy (Canada) 13.12
1996 Allen Johnson (USA) 12.95

400 m hurdles

1900 Walter Tewksbury (USA) 57.6
1904 Harry Hillman (USA) 53.0
1908 Charles Bacon (USA) 55.0
1920 Frank Loomis (USA) 54.0
1924 Morgan Taylor (USA) 52.6
1928 David Cecil, Lord Burghley (Great Britain) 53.4
1932 Robert Tisdall (Ireland) 51.67
1936 Glen Hardin (USA) 52.4
1948 Roy Cochran (USA) 51.1
1952 Charles Moore (USA) 51.06
1956 Glenn Davis (USA) 50.29
1960 Glenn Davis (USA) 49.51
1964 Rex Cawley (USA) 49.69
1968 David Hemery (Great Britain) 48.12
1972 John Akii-Bua (Uganda) 47.82
1976 Edwin Moses (USA) 47.63
1980 Volker Beck (East Germany) 48.70
1984 Edwin Moses (USA) 47.75
1988 Andre Phillips (USA) 47.19
1992 Kevin Young (USA) 46.78
1996 Derrick Atkins (USA) 47.54

Steeplechase

Unless shown otherwise, distance is 3000 m.

1900 George Orton (Canada) 7:34.4 (2500 m)
1900 John Rimmer (Great Britain) 12:58.4 (4000 m)
1904 James Lightbody (USA) 7:39.6 (2590 m)
1908 Arthur Russell (Great Britain) 10:47.8 (3200 m)
1920 Percy Hodge (Great Britain) 10:00.4
1924 Ville Ritola (Finland) 9:33.6
1928 Toivo Loukola (Finland) 9:21.8
1932 Volmari Iso-Hollo (Finland) 10:33.4*
1936 Volmari Iso-Hollo (Finland) 9:03.8
1948 Tore Sjöstrand (Sweden) 9:04.6
1952 Horace Ashenfelter (USA) 8:45.68
1956 Christopher Brasher (Great Britain) 8:41.35
1960 Zdzislaw Kryszkowiak (Poland) 8:34.31
1964 Gaston Roelants (Belgium) 8:30.8
1968 Amos Biwott (Kenya) 8:51.0
1972 Kipchoge Keino (Kenya) 8:23.64
1976 Anders Gärderud (Sweden) 8:08.02
1980 Bronislaw Malinowski (Poland) 8:09.70
1984 Julius Korir (Kenya) 8:11.80
1988 Julius Kariuki (Kenya) 8:05.51
1992 Matthew Birir (Kenya) 8:08.94
1996 Joseph Keter (Kenya) 8:07.12
*athletes ran an extra lap in error – distance 3460 m.

High jump

1896 Ellery Clark (USA) 1.81
1900 Irving Baxter (USA) 1.90
1904 Samuel Jones (USA) 1.80
1906 Con Leahy (Ireland) 1.77
1908 Harry Porter (USA) 1.90
1912 Alma Richards (USA) 1.93
1920 Richard Landon (USA) 1.94
1924 Harold Osborn (USA) 1.98
1928 Robert King (USA) 1.94
1932 Duncan McNaughton (Canada) 1.97
1936 Cornelius Johnson (USA) 2.03
1948 John Winter (Australia) 1.09
1952 Walter Davis (USA) 2.04
1956 Charles Dumas (USA) 2.12
1960 Robert Shavlakadze (USSR) 2.16
1964 Valeriy Brumel (USSR) 2.18
1968 Dick Fosbury (USA) 2.24
1972 Jüri Tamak (USSR) 2.23
1976 Jacek Wszola (Poland) 2.25
1980 Gerd Wessig (East Germany) 2.36
1984 Dietmar Mögenburg (West Germany) 2.35
1988 Gennadiy Avdeyenko (USSR) 2.38
1992 Javier Sotomayor (Cuba) 2.34
1996 Charles Austin (USA) 2.39

Pole vault

1896 William Hoyt (USA) 3.30
1900 Irving Baxter (USA) 3.30
1904 Charles Dvorak (USA) 3.50
1906 Fernand Gonder (France) 3.40
1908 Edward Cooke and Alfred Gilbert (USA) 3.71
1912 Harry Babock (USA) 3.95
1920 Frank Foss (USA) 4.09
1924 Lee Barnes (USA) 3.95
1928 Sabin Carr (USA) 4.20
1932 Bill Miller (USA) 4.31
1936 Earle Meadows (USA) 4.35
1948 Guinn Smith (USA) 4.30
1952 Robert Richards (USA) 4.55
1956 Robert Richards (USA) 4.56
1960 Donald Bragg (USA) 4.70
1964 Frederick Hansen (USA) 5.10
1968 Bob Seagren (USA) 5.40
1972 Wolfgang Nordwig (East Germany) 5.50
1976 Tadeusz Slusarski (Poland) 5.50
1980 Wladyslaw Kozakiewicz (Poland) 5.78
1984 Pierre Quinon (France) 5.75
1988 Sergey Bubka (USSR) 5.90
1992 Maksim Tarassov (Unified Team) 5.80
1996 Jean Galfione (France) 5.92

Long jump

1896 Ellery Clark (USA) 6.35
1900 Alvin Kraenzlein (USA) 7.18
1904 Myer Prinstein (USA) 7.34
1906 Myer Prinstein (USA) 7.20
1908 Francis Irons (USA) 7.48
1912 Albert Gutterson (USA) 7.60
1920 William Pettersson (Sweden) 7.15

1924 Williem De hart Hubbard (USA) 7.44
1928 Edward Hamm (USA) 7.73
1932 Edward Gordon (USA) 7.64
1936 Jesse Owens (USA) 8.06
1948 William Steele (USA) 7.82
1952 Jerome Biffle (USA) 7.57
1956 Gregory Bell (USA) 7.83
1960 Ralph Boston (USA) 8.12
1964 Lynn Davies (Great Britain) 8.07
1968 Bob Beamon (USA) 8.90
1972 Randy Williams (USA) 8.24
1976 Arnie Robinson (USA) 8.35
1980 Lutz Dombrowski (East Germany) 8.54
1984 Carl Lewis (USA) 8.54
1988 Carl Lewis (USA) 8.72
1992 Carl Lewis (USA) 8.67
1996 Carl Lewis (USA) 8.50

Triple jump

1896 James Connolly (USA) 13.71
1900 Myer Prinstein (USA) 14.47
1904 Myer Prinstein (USA) 14.35
1906 Peter O'Connor (Ireland/Great Britain) 14.07
1908 Tim Ahearne (Ireland/Great Britain) 14.91
1912 Gustaf Lindblom (Sweden) 14.76
1920 Viho Tuulos (Finland) 14.50
1924 Anthony Winter (Australia) 15.52
1928 Mikio Oda (Japan) 15.21
1932 Chuhei Nambu (Japan) 15.72
1936 Naoto Tajima (Japan) 16.00
1948 Arne Åhman (Sweden) 15.40
1952 Adhemar Ferreira da Silva (Brazil) 16.22
1956 Adhemar Ferreira da Silva (Brazil) 16.35
1960 Jozef Schmidt (Poland) 16.81
1964 Jozef Schmidt (Poland) 16.85
1968 Viktor Saneyev (USSR) 17.39
1972 Viktor Saneyev (USSR) 17.35
1976 Viktor Saneyev (USSR) 17.29
1980 Jaak Uudmäe (USSR) 17.35
1984 Al Joyner (USA) 17.26
1988 Khristo Markov (Bulgaria) 17.61
1992 Mike Conley (USA) 18.17[w]
1996 Kenny Harrison (USA) 18.09
[w]wind-assisted

Shot

1896 Robert Garrett (USA) 11.22
1900 Richard Sheldon (USA) 14.10
1904 Ralph Rose (USA) 14.80
1906 Martin Sheridan (USA) 12.32
1908 Ralph Rose (USA) 14.21
1912 Patrick McDonald (USA) 15.34
1920 Ville Pörhölä (Finland) 14.81
1924 Clarence Houser (USA) 14.99
1928 John Kuck (USA) 15.87
1932 Leo Sexton (USA) 16.00
1936 Hans Woellke (Germany) 16.20
1948 Wilbur Thompson (USA) 17.12
1952 Parry O'Brien (USA) 17.41
1956 Parry O'Brien (USA) 18.57

1960	William Nieder (USA) 19.68
1964	Dallas Long (USA) 20.33
1968	Randy Matson (USA) 20.54
1972	Wladyslaw Komar (Poland) 21.18
1976	Udo Beyer (East Germany) 21.05
1980	Vladimir Kiselyov (USSR) 21.35
1984	Alessandro Andrei (Italy) 21.26
1988	Ulf Timmermann (East Germany) 22.47
1992	Mike Stulce (USA) 21.70
1996	Randy Barnes (USA) 21.62

Discus

1896	Robert Garrett (USA) 29.15
1900	Rudolf Bauer (Hungary) 36.04
1904	Martin Sheridan (USA) 39.28
1906	Martin Sheridan (USA) 41.46
1908	Martin Sheridan (USA) 40.89
1912	Armas Taipale (Finland) 45.21
1920	Elmer Niklander (Finland) 44.68
1924	Clarence Houser (USA) 46.15
1928	Clarence Houser (USA) 47.32
1932	John Anderson (USA) 49.49
1936	Ken Carpenter (USA) 50.48
1948	Adolfo Consolini (Italy) 52.78
1952	Sim Iness (USA) 55.03
1956	Al Oerter (USA) 56.36
1960	Al Oerter (USA) 59.18
1964	Al Oerter (USA) 61.00
1968	Al Oerter (USA) 64.78
1972	Ludvik Danek (Cze) 64.40
1976	Mac Wilkins (USA) 67.50
1980	Viktor Rashchupkin (USSR) 66.64
1984	Rolf Danneberg (West Germany) 66.60
1988	Jürgen Schult (East Germany) 68.82
1992	Romas Ubartas (Lithuania) 65.12
1996	Lars Reidel (Germany) 69.40

Hammer

1900	John Flanagan (USA) 49.73
1904	John Flanagan (USA) 51.23
1908	John Flanagan (USA) 51.92
1912	Matt McGrath (USA) 54.74
1920	Patrick Ryan (USA) 52.87
1924	Fred Tootell (USA) 53.29
1928	Patrick O'Callaghan (Ireland) 51.39
1932	Patrick O'Callaghan (Ireland) 53.92
1936	Karl Hein (Germany) 56.49
1948	Imre Németh (Hungary) 56.07
1952	József Csermak (Hungary) 60.34
1956	Harold Connolly (USA) 63.19
1960	Vasiliy Rudenkov (USSR) 67.10
1964	Romuald Klim (USSR) 69.74
1968	Gyula Zsivótzky (Hungary) 73.36
1972	Anatoliy Bondarchuk (USSR) 75.50
1976	Yuriy Sedykh (USSR) 77.52
1980	Yuriy Sedykh (USSR) 81.80
1984	Juha Tiainen (Finland) 78.08
1988	Sergey Litvinov (USSR) 84.80
1992	Andrey Abduyvaliyev (Unified Team) 82.54

1996	Balazs Kiss (Hungary) 81.24

Javelin
New javelin introduced in 1984.

1906	Erik Lemming (Sweden) 53.90
1908	Erik Lemming (Sweden) 54.82
1912	Erik Lemming (Sweden) 60.64
1920	Jonni Myyrä (Finland) 65.78
1924	Jonni Myyrä (Finland) 62.96
1928	Erik Lundkvist (Sweden) 66.60
1932	Matti Järvinen (Finland) 72.71
1936	Gerhard Stöck (Germany) 71.84
1948	Tapio Rautavaara (Finland) 69.77
1952	Cyrus Young (USA) 73.78
1956	Egil Danielsen (Norway) 85.71
1960	Viktor Tsibulenko (USSR) 84.64
1964	Pauli Nevala (Finland) 82.66
1968	Janis Lusis (USSR) 90.10
1972	Klaus Woltermann (West Germany) 90.48
1976	Miklos Nemeth (Hungary) 94.58
1980	Dainis Kula (USSR) 91.20
1984	Arto Harkonen (Finland) 86.76
1988	Tapio Korjus (Finland) 84.28
1992	Jan Zelezny (Czechoslovakia) 89.66
1996	Jan Zelezny (Czech Republic) 88.16

Decathlon
All points given using 1984 tables.

1904	Thomas Kiely (Ireland) 6036
1912	Jim Thorpe (USA) 6564
1920	Helge Lovland (Norway) 5804
1924	Harold Osborn (USA) 6476
1928	Paavo Yrjöla (Finland) 6587
1932	James Bausch (USA) 6735
1936	Glenn Morris (USA) 7254
1948	Robert Mathias (USA) 6628
1952	Robert Mathias (USA) 7592
1956	Milton Campbell (USA) 7614
1960	Rafer Johnson (USA) 7926
1964	Willi Holdorf (West Germany) 7794
1968	Bill Toomey (USA) 8144
1972	Nikolay Avilov (USSR) 8566
1976	Bruce Jenner (USA) 8634
1980	Daley Thompson (Great Britain) 8522
1984	Daley Thompson (Great Britain) 8847
1988	Christian Schenk (East Germany) 8488
1992	Robert Zmelik (Czechoslovakia) 8611
1996	Dan O'Brien (USA) 8824

20000 m walk

1956	Leonid Spirin (USSR) 1:31:27.4
1960	Vladimir Golubnichiy (USSR) 1:34:01.2
1964	Kenneth Matthews (Great Britain) 1:29:34.0
1968	Vladimir Golubnichiy (USSR) 1:33:58.4

1972	Peter Frenkel (East Germany) 1:26:42.4
1976	Daniel Bautista (Mexico) 1:24:40.6
1980	Maurizio Damilano (Italy) 1:23:35.5
1984	Ernesto Canto (Mexico) 1:23:13
1988	Jozef Pribilinec (Czechoslovakia) 1:21:57
1992	Daniel Plaza (Spain) 1:21:45
1996	Jefferson Perez (Ecuador) 1:20.06

50000 m walk

1932	Thomas Green (Great Britain) 4:50:10.0
1936	Harold Whitlock (Great Britain) 4:30:41.1
1948	John Ljunggren (Sweden) 4:41:52.0
1952	Giuseppe Dordoni (Italy) 4:28:07.8
1956	Norman Read (New Zealand) 4:30:42.8
1960	Don Thompson (Great Britain) 4:25:30.0
1964	Abdon Pamich (Italy) 4:11:12.4
1968	Christophe Höhne (East Germany) 4:20:13.6
1972	Bernd Kannenberg (East Germany) 3:56:11.6
1980	Hartwig Gauder (East Germany) 3:49:24
1984	Raul Gonzales (Mexico) 3:47:26
1988	Vyacheslav Ivanenko (USSR) 3:38:29
1992	Andrei Perlov (Unified Team) 3:30:13
1996	Robert Korzeniowski (Poland) 3:43.30

EVENT WINNERS (WOMEN)

100 m

1928	Elizabeth Robinson (USA) 12.2
1932	Stanislawa Walasiewicz (Poland) 11.9
1936	Helen Stephens (USA) 11.5
1948	Fanny Blankers-Koen (Netherlands) 11.9
1952	Marjorie Jackson (Australia) 11.65
1956	Betty Cuthbert (Australia) 11.82
1960	Wilma Rudolph (USA) 11.08
1964	Wyomia Tyus (USA) 11.49
1968	Wyomia Tyus (USA) 11.08
1972	Renate Stecher (East Germany) 11.07
1976	Annegret Richter (West Germany) 11.08
1980	Lyudmila Kondratyeva (USSR) 11.06
1984	Evelyn Ashford (USA) 10.97
1988	Florence Griffith-Joyner (USA) 10.54
1992	Gail Devers (USA) 10.82
1996	Gail Devers (USA) 10.94

200 m
1948   Fanny Blankers-Koen (Netherlands) 24.2
1952   Marjorie Jackson (Australia) 23.89
1956   Betty Cuthbert (Australia) 23.55
1960   Wilma Rudolph (USA) 24.03
1964   Edith Maguire (USA) 23.05
1968   Irena Szewinska (Poland) 22.58
1972   Renate Stecher (East Germany) 22.40
1976   Bärbel Eckert (East Germany) 22.37
1980   Bärbel Wöckel (East Germany) 22.03
1984   Valerie Brisco-Hooks (USA) 21.81
1988   Florence Griffith-Joyner (USA) 21.34
1992   Gwen Torrence (USA) 21.81
1996   Marie-José Pérec (France) 22.12

400 m
1964   Betty Cuthbert (Australia) 52.01
1968   Colette Besson (France) 52.03
1972   Monika Zehrt (East Germany) 51.08
1976   Irena Szewinska (Poland) 49.29
1980   Marita Koch (East Germany) 48.88
1984   Valerie Brisco-Hooks (USA) 48.83
1988   Olga Bryzgina (USSR) 48.65
1992   Marie-José Pérec (France) 48.83
1996   Marie-José Pérec (France) 48.25

800 m
1928   Lina Radke (Germany) 2:16.8
1960   Lyudmila Shevtsova (USSR) 2:04.50
1964   Ann Packer (Great Britain) 2:01.1
1968   Madeline Manning (USA) 2:00.92
1972   Hilde Falck (West Germany) 1:58.55
1976   Tatyana Kazankina (USSR) 1:54.94
1980   Nadezhda Olizarenko (USSR) 1:53.43
1984   Doina Melinte (Romania) 1:57.60
1988   Sigrun Wodars (East Germany) 1:56.10
1992   Ellen van Langen (Netherlands) 1:55.54
1996   Svetlana Masterkova (Russia) 1:57.73

1500 m
1972   Lyudmila Bragina (USSR) 4:01.38
1976   Tatyana Kazankina (USSR) 4:05.48
1980   Tatyana Kazankina (USSR) 3:56.56
1984   Gabriella Doria (Italy) 4:03.25
1988   Paula Ivan (Romania) 3:53.96
1992   Hassiba Boulmerka (Algeria) 3:55.30
1996   Svetlana Masterkova (Russia) 4:00.83

3000 m (event discontinued, 1992)
1984   Maricica Puica (Romania) 8:35.96
1988   Tatyana Samolenko (USSR) 8:26.53
1992   Yelena Romanova (Unified Team) 8:46.04

5000 m
1996   Yunxia Wang (China) 14:59.88

10000 m
1988   Olga Bondarenko (USSR) 31:05.21
1992   Derartu Tulu (Ethiopia) 31:06.02
1996   Fernanda Ribeiro (Portugal) 31:06.63

Marathon
1984   Joan Benoit (USA) 2:24:62
1988   Rosa Mota (Portugal) 2:25:40
1992   Valentina Yegorova (Unified Team) 2:32:41
1996   Fatuma Roba (Cuba) 2:26.05

80 m hurdles
1932   Mildred Didrikson (USA) 11.7
1936   Trebisonda Valla (Italy) 11.75
1948   Fanny Blankers-Koen (Netherlands) 11.2
1952   Shirley Strickland (Australia) 11.03
1956   Shirley Strickland (Australia) 10.96
1960   Irina Press (USSR) 10.94
1964   Karin Balzer (East Germany) 10.54
1968   Maureen Caird (Australia) 10.39

100 m hurdles
1972   Annelie Ehrhardt (East Germany) 12.59
1976   Johanna Schaller (East Germany) 12.77
1980   Vera Komisova (USSR) 12.56
1984   Benita Fitzgerald-Brown (USA) 12.84
1988   Yordanka Donkova (Bulgaria) 12.38
1992   Paraskevi Patoulidou (Greece) 12.64
1996   Ludmila Enquist (Sweden) 12.58

400 m hurdles
1988   Debbie Flintoff-King (Australia) 53.17
1992   Sally Gunnell (Great Britain) 53.23
1996   Dion Hemmings (Jamaica) 52.82

High jump
1932   Jean Shirley (USA) 1.65
1936   Ibolya Csák (Hungary) 1.60
1948   Alice Coachman (USA) 1.68
1952   Esther Brand (South Africa) 1.67
1956   Mildred McDaniel (USA) 1.76
1960   Iolanda Balas (Romania) 1.85
1964   Iolanda Balas (Romania) 1.90
1968   Miloslava Rezková (Czechoslovakia) 1.82

1972   Ulrike Meyfarth (West Germany) 1.92
1976   Rosemarie Ackermann (East Germany) 1.93
1980   Sara Simeoni (Italy) 1.97
1984   Ulrike Meyfarth (West Germany) 2.02
1988   Louise Ritter (USA) 2.03
1992   Heike Henkel (Germany) 2.02
1996   Stefka Kostadinova (Bulgaria) 2.05

Long jump
1952   Yvette Williams (New Zealand) 6.24
1956   Elzbieta Krzesinska (Poland) 6.35
1960   Vyera Krepkina (USSR) 6.37
1964   Mary Rand (Great Britain) 6.76
1968   Viorica Viscopoleanu (Romania) 6.82
1972   Heidemarie Rosendahl (West Germany) 6.78
1976   Angela Voigt (East Germany) 6.72
1980   Tatyana Kolpakova (USSR) 7.06
1984   Anisoara Stanciu (Romania) 6.96
1988   Jackie Joyner-Kersee (USA) 7.40
1992   Heike Drechsler (Germany) 7.14
1996   Chioma Ajunwa (Nigeria) 7.12

Shot
1952   Galina Zybina (USSR) 15.28
1956   Tamara Tishkyevich (USSR) 16.59
1960   Tamara Press (USSR) 17.32
1964   Tamara Press (USSR) 18.14
1968   Margitta Gummel (East Germany) 19.61
1972   Nadezhda Chizhova (USSR) 21.03
1976   Ivanka Khristova (Bulgaria) 21.16
1980   Ilona Slupianek (East Germany) 22.41
1984   Claudia Losch (West Germany) 20.48
1988   Natalya Lisovskaya (USSR) 22.24
1992   Svetlana Krivelyova (Unified Team) 21.06
1996   Astrid Kumbernuss (Germany) 20.56

Discus
1936   Gisela Mauermayer (Germany) 47.63
1948   Micheline Ostermeyer (France) 41.92
1952   Nina Ponomaryeva (USSR) 51.42
1956   Olga Fitotová (Czechoslovakia) 53.49
1960   Nina Ponomaryeva (USSR) 55.10
1964   Tamara Press (USSR) 57.27
1968   Lia Manoliu (Romania) 58.28
1972   Faina Melnik (USSR) 66.62
1976   Evelin Schlaak (East Germany) 69.00
1980   Evelin Jahl (East Germany) 69.96
1984   Ria Stalmach (Netherlands) 65.36

1988 Martina Hellmann (East
       Germany) 72.30
1992 Maritza Marten (Cuba) 70.06
1996 Like Wyludda (Germany) 69.66

Javelin
1936 Tilly Fleischer (Germany) 45.18
1948 Herma Bauma (Australia) 45.57
1952 Dana Zátopková
       (Czechoslovakia) 50.47
1956 Inese Jaunzeme (USSR) 53.86
1960 Elvira Ozolina (USSR) 55.98
1964 Mihaela Penes (Romania) 60.54

1968 Angéla Németh (Hungary) 60.36
1972 Ruth Fuchs (East Germany) 63.88
1976 Ruth Fuchs (East Germany) 65.94
1980 Maria C Colón (Cuba) 68.40
1984 Tessa Sanderson (Great Britain)
       69.56
1988 Petra Felke (East Germany) 74.68
1992 Silke Renke (Germany) 68.34
1996 Heller Rantanen (Finland) 67.94

Pentathlon
1964 Irina Press (USSR) 4702

1968 Ingrid Becker (West Germany)
       4559
1972 Mary Peters (Great Britain) 4801
1976 Sigrun Siegl (East Germany) 4745
1980 Nadezhda Tkachenko (USSR)
       5083

Heptathlon
1988 Jackie Joyner-Kersee (USA) 7291
1992 Jackie Joyner-Kersee (USA) 7044
1996 Ghada Shouaa (Syria) 6780

10 km walk
1996 Yelena Nikolayeva (Russia) 41.49

Athletics records

World records
World outdoor records have been recognized by the International Amateur Athletics Federation (IAAF) since 1913. The following records existed at the beginning of September 1997.

MEN

Event	Record	Record Holder	Date	Where set
100m	9.84	Donovan Bailey (Canada)	27 Jul 1996	Atlanta
200m	19.32	Michael Johnson (USA)	1 Aug 1996	Atlanta
400m	43.29	Butch Reynolds (USA)	17 Aug 1988	Zurich
800m	1:41.11	Wilson Kipketer (Denmark)	24 Aug 1997	Cologne
1000m	2:12.18	Sebastian Coe (Great Britain)	11 Jul 1981	Oslo
1500m	3:27.37	Noureddine Morceli (Algeria)	12 Jul 1995	Nice
Mile	3:44.39	Noureddine Morceli (Algeria)	5 Sep 1993	Rieti, Italy
2000m	4:47.88	Noureddine Morceli (Algeria)	3 Jul 1995	Paris
3000m	7:20.67	Daniel Komen (Kenya)	1 Sep 1996	Rieti, Italy
Steeplechase	7:55.72	Benard Barmasi (Kenya)	24 Aug 1997	Brussels
5000m	12:39.74	Daniel Komen (Kenya)	22 Aug 1997	Brussels
10000m	26:27.85	Paul Tergat (Kenya)	22 Aug 1997	Brussels
20000m	56:55.6	Arturo Barrios (Mexico)	30 Mar 1991	La Flèche, France
Hour	21101m	Arturo Barrios (Mexico)	30 Mar 1991	La Flèche, France
25000m	1:13:55.8	Toshihiko Seko (Japan)	22 Mar 1981	Christchurch, New Zealand
30000m	1:29:18.8	Toshihiko Seko (Japan)	22 Mar 1981	Christchurch, New Zealand
Marathon	2:06:50	Belayneh Densimo (Ethiopia)	17 Apr 1988	Rotterdam
110m hurdles	12.91	Colin Jackson (Great Britain)	20 Aug 1993	Stuttgart
400m hurdles	46.78	Kevin Young (USA)	6 Aug 1992	Barcelona
20km walk	1:17:25.6	Bernardo Segura (Mexico)	7 May 1994	Bergen
30km walk	2:01:44.1	Maurizio Damilano (Italy)	4 Oct 1992	Cuneo, Italy
50km walk	3:41:28.4	Rene Piller (France)	7 May 1994	Bergen
4 × 100m relay	37.40	Jon Drummond, Leroy Burrell, Dennis Mitchell, Andre Cason (USA)	21 Aug 1993	Stuttgart
4 × 200m relay	1:18.68	Mike Marsh, Leroy Burrell, Floyd Heard, Carl Lewis (USA)	17 Apr 1994	Walnut, USA
4 × 400m relay	2:54.29	Andrew Valmon, Quincy Watts, Michael Johnson, Butch Reynolds (USA)	22 Aug 1993	Stuttgart
4 × 800m relay	7:03.89	Peter Elliott, Garry Cook, Steve Cram, Sebastian Coe (Great Britain)	30 Aug 1982	London
4 ×1500m relay	14:38.8	Thomas Wessinghage, Harald Hudak, Michael Lederer, Karl Fleschen (West Germany)	17 Aug 1977	Cologne
High jump	2.45m	Javier Sotomayor (Cuba)	27 Jul 1993	Salamanca, Spain
Pole vault	6.14m	Sergei Bubka (Ukraine)	31 Jul 1994	Sestriere, Italy
Long jump	8.95m	Mike Powell (USA)	30 Aug 1991	Tokyo
Triple jump	18.29m	Jonathan Edwards (Great Britain)	7 Aug 1995	Gothenburg
Shot	23.12m	Randy Barnes (USA)	20 May 1990	Westwood, CA
Discus	74.08m	Jurgen Schult (East Germany)	6 Jun 1986	Neubrandenburg, Germany
Hammer	86.74m	Yuri Syedikh (USSR)	30 Aug 1986	Stuttgart
Javelin	98.48m	Jan Zelezny (Czech Republic)	25 May 1996	Jena, Germany
Decathlon	8891 pts	Dan O'Brien (USA)	4–5 Sep 1992	Talence, France

WOMEN

Event	Record	Record Holder	Date	Where set
100m	10.49	Florence Griffith Joyner (USA)	16 Jul 1988	Indianapolis, IN
200m	21.34	Florence Griffith Joyner (USA)	29 Sep 1988	Seoul
400m	47.60	Marita Koch (East Germany)	6 Oct 1985	Canberra
800m	1:53.28	Jarmila Kratochvilova (Czechoslovakia)	26 Jul 1983	Munich
1000m	2:28.98	Svetlana Masterkova (Russia)	23 Aug 1996	Brussels
1500m	3:50.46	Yunxia Qu (China)	11 Sep 1993	Beijing
Mile	4:12.57	Svetlana Masterkova (Russia)	14 Aug 1996	Zurich
2000m	5:25.36	Sonia O'Sullivan (Ireland)	8 July 1994	Edinburgh
3000m	8:06.11	Yunxia Wang (China)	13 Sep 1993	Beijing
5000m	14:36.45	Fernanda Ribeiro (Portugal)	22 Jul 1995	Hechtel, Belgium
10000m	30:13.74	Ingrid Kristiansen (Norway)	5 Jul 1986	Oslo
25000m	1:29:29.2	Karolina Szabò (Hungary)	22 Apr 1988	Budapest
30000m	1:49:05.6	Karolina Szabò (Hungary)	22 Apr 1988	Budapest
Marathon	2:21.06	Ingrid Kristiansen (Norway)	21 Apr 1985	London
100m hurdles	12.21	Yordanka Donkova (Bulgaria)	20 Aug 1988	Stara Zagora, Bulgaria
400m hurdles	52.61	Kim Batten (USA)	11 Aug 1995	Gothenburg
5km walk	20:07.52	Beate Anders (East Germany)	23 Jun 1990	Rostock, Germany
10km walk	41:56.23	Nadezhda Ryashkina (USSR)	24 Jul 1990	Seattle, WA
4 × 100m relay	41.37	Silke Gladisch, Sabine Reiger, Ingrid Auerswald, Marlies Göhr (East Germany)	10 Jun 1985	Canberra
4 × 200m relay	1:28.15	Marlies Göhr, Romy Müller, Bärbel Wöckel, Marita Koch (East Germany)	9 Aug 1980	Jena, Germany
4 × 400m relay	3:15.17	Tatyana Ledovskaya, Olga Nazarova, Maria Pinigina, Olga Bryzgina (USSR)	1 Oct 1988	Seoul
4 × 800m relay	7:50.17	Nadezhda Olizarenko, Lyubov Gurina, Lyudmila Borisova, Irina Podyalovskaya (USSR)	5 Aug 1984	Moscow
High jump	2.09m	Stefka Kostadinova (Bulgaria)	30 Aug 1987	Rome
Pole vault	4.55m	Emma George (Australia)	20 Feb 1997	Melbourne
Long jump	7.52m	Galina Chistyakova (USSR)	11 Jun 1988	Leningrad
Shot	22.63m	Natalya Lisovskaya (USSR)	7 Jun 1987	Moscow
Discus	76.80m	Gabriele Reinsch (East Germany)	9 Jul 1988	Neubrandenburg, Germany
Hammer	73.10m	O Kuzenkova (Russia)	22 Jun 1997	Munich
Javelin	80.00m	Petra Felke (East Germany)	9 Sep 1988	Potsdam, Germany
Heptathlon	7291 pts	Jackie Joyner-Kersee (USA)	23–24 Sep 1988	Seoul

World indoor records

World indoor records have been recognized by the International Amateur Athletics Federation (IAAF) since 1 Jan 1987.

MEN

Event	Record	Record Holder	Date	Where set
50m	5.56	Donovan Bailey (Canada)	9 Feb 1996	Reno, NV
60m	6.41	Andre Cason (USA)	14 Feb 1992	Madrid
200m	19.92	Frankie Fredericks (Namibia)	18 Feb 1996	Liévin, France
400m	44.63	Michael Johnson	4 Mar 1995	Atlanta
800m	1:42.67	Wilson Kipketer (Denmark)	9 Mar 1997	Paris
1000m	2:15.26	Noureddine Morceli (Algeria)	22 Feb 1992	Birmingham, UK
1500m	3:31.13	Hicham el-Guerrouj (Morocco)	2 Feb 1997	Stuttgart
Mile	3:48.45	Hicham el-Guerrouj (Morocco)	12 Feb 1997	Ghent, Belgium
3000m	7:30.72	Haile Gebrselassie (Ethiopia)	4 Feb 1996	Stuttgart
5000m	12:59.04	Haile Gebrselassie (Ethiopia)	20 Feb 1997	Stockholm
50m hurdles	6.25	Mark McKoy (Canada)	3 Mar 1986	Kobe, Japan
60m hurdles	7.30	Colin Jackson (Great Britain)	3 Jun 1994	Sindelfingen, Germany
5000m walk	18:15.25	Grigori Kornev (Unified Team)	7 Feb 1992	Kalsruhe, Germany
4 × 200m relay	1:22.11	Linford Christie, Darren Braithwaite, Ade Mafe, John Regis (Great Britain)	3 Mar 1991	Glasgow, UK
4 × 400m relay	3:03.05	Rico Lieder, Jens Carlowitz, Klaus Just, Thomas Schönlebe (Germany)	10 Mar 1991	Seville, Spain
4 × 800m relay	7:17.8	Valeriy Taratynov, Stanislav Meshcherskikh, Aleksey Taranov, Viktor Semyashkin (USSR)	14 Mar 1971	Sofia

Event	Record	Record Holder	Date	Where set
High jump	2.43m	Javier Sotomayor (Cuba)	4 Mar 1989	Budapest
Pole vault	6.15m	Sergei Bubka (Ukraine)	21 Feb 1993	Donetsk, Ukraine
Long jump	8.79m	Carl Lewis (USA)	27 Jan 1984	New York City
Triple jump	17.83m	A Urrutia (Cuba)	1 Mar 1997	Sindelfingen, Germany
Shot put	22.66m	Randy Barnes (USA)	20 Jan 1989	Los Angeles, CA
Pentathlon	4440 pts	Christian Plaziat (France)	25 Feb 1990	Toronto
Heptathlon	6476 pts	Dan O'Brien (USA)	13–14 Mar 1993	Toronto

WOMEN

Event	Record	Record Holder	Date	Where set
50 m	5.96	Irina Privalova (Russia)	9 Feb 1995	Madrid
60 m	6.92	Irina Privalova (Russia)	11 Feb 1995	Madrid
200 m	21.87	Merlene Ottey (Jamaica)	13 Feb 1993	Liévin, France
400 m	49.59	Jarmilla Kratochvilová (Czechoslovakia)	7 Mar 1982	Milan
800 m	1:56.40	Christine Wachtel (East Germany)	14 Feb 1988	Vienna
1000 m	2:31.23	Maria Mutola (Mozambique)	25 Feb 1996	Stockholm
1500 m	4:00.27	Doina Melinte (Romania)	9 Feb 1990	East Rutherford, NJ
Mile	4:17.14	Doina Melinte (Romania)	9 Feb 1990	East Rutherford, NJ
3000 m	8:33.82	Elly van Hulst (Netherlands)	4 Mar 1989	Budapest
5000 m	15:03.17	Liz McColgan (Great Britain)	22 Feb 1992	Birmingham, UK
50 m hurdles	6.58	Cornelia Oschkenat (East Germany)	20 Feb 1988	Berlin
60 m hurdles	7.69	Lyudmila Narozhilenko (USSR)	4 Feb 1990	Chelyabinsk, Russia
100 m hurdles	12.64	Ludmila Enquist (Sweden)	10 Feb 1997	Tampere, Finland
3000 m walk	11:44.00	Yelena Ivanova (Unified Team)	7 Feb 1992	Moscow
4 × 200 m relay	1:32.55	Helga Arendt, Silke-Beate Knoll, Mechthild Kluth, Gisela Kinzel (West Germany)	20 Feb 1988	Dortmund
4 × 400 m relay	3:26.84	S Chebykina, S Goncharenko, O Kotlyarova, T Alexseyeva (Russia)	9 Mar 1997	Paris
4 × 800 m relay	8:18.71	Yelena Zaitseva, Olga Kuznycisova, Yelena Afanasyeva, Yekaterina Podkopayeva (Russia)	4 Feb 1994	Moscow
High jump	2.07m	Heike Henkel (Germany)	8 Feb 1992	Karlsruhe, Germany
Long jump	7.37m	Heike Drechsler (East Germany)	14 Feb 1988	Vienna
Triple jump	15.03m	Yolanda Chen (Russia)	11 Mar 1995	Barcelona
Shot put	22.50m	Helena Fibingerová (Czechoslovakia)	19 Feb 1977	Jablonec, Czechoslovakia
Pole vault	4.28m	Sun Caiyun (China)	27 Feb 1996	Tianjin, China
Pentathlon	4991 pts	Irina Byelova (Unified Team)	14–15 Feb 1992	Berlin

Boston Marathon

The world's oldest annual race.

MEN

Year	Winner	Time
1897	John J McDermott (USA)	2:55:10
1898	Ronald J McDonald USA)	2:42:00
1899	Lawrence J Brignolia (USA)	2:54:38
1900	James J Caffrey (Canada)	2:39:44
1901	James J Caffrey (Canada)	2:29:23
1902	Sammy Mellor (USA)	2:43:12
1903	John C Lorden (USA)	2:41:29
1904	Michael Spring (USA)	2:38:04
1905	Fred Lorz (USA)	2:38:25
1906	Timothy Ford (USA)	2:45:45
1907	Tom Longboat (Canada)	2:24:24
1908	Thomas Morrissey (USA)	2:25:43
1909	Henri Renaud (USA)	2:53:36
1910	Fred Cameron (Canada)	2:28:52
1911	Clarence H DeMar (USA)	2:21:39
1912	Mike Ryan (USA)	2:21:18
1913	Fritz Carlson (USA)	2:25:14
1914	James Duffy (Canada)	2:25:01
1915	Edouard Fabre (Canada)	2:31:41
1916	Arthur Roth (USA)	2:27:16
1917	Bill Kennedy (USA)	2:28:37
1918	*No race*	
1919	Carl Linder (USA)	2:29:13
1920	Peter Trivoulidas (Greece)	2:29:31
1921	Frank Zuna (USA)	2:18:57
1922	Clarence H DeMar (USA)	2:18:10
1923	Clarence H DeMar (USA)	2:23:37
1924	Clarence H DeMar (USA)	2:29:40
1925	Chuck Mellor (USA)	2:33:00
1926	John C Miles (Canada)	2:25:40
1927	Clarence H DeMar (USA)	2:40:22
1928	Clarence H DeMar (USA)	2:37:07
1929	John C Miles (Canada)	2:33:08
1930	Clarence H DeMar (USA)	2:34:48
1931	James 'Hinky' Henigan (USA)	2:46:45
1932	Paul de Bruyn (Germany)	2:33:36
1933	Leslie Pawson, (USA)	2:31:01
1934	Dave Komonen (Canada)	2:32:53
1935	John A Kelley (USA)	2:32:07
1936	Ellison M 'Tarzan' Brown (USA)	2:33:40
1937	Walter Young (Canada)	2:33:20
1938	Leslie Pawson (USA)	2:35:34

1939	Ellison M 'Tarzan' Brown (USA)	2:28:51
1940	Gerard Cote (Canada)	2:28:28
1941	Leslie Pawson (USA)	2:30:38
1942	Bernard Joseph Smith (USA)	2:26:51
1943	Gerard Cote (Canada)	2:28:25
1944	Gerard Cote (Canada)	2:31:50
1945	John A Kelley (USA)	2:30:40
1946	Stylianos Kyriakides (Greece)	2:29:27
1947	Yun Bok-suh (Korea)	2:25:39
1948	Gerard Cote (Canada)	2:31:02
1949	Karl Gosta Leandersson (Sweden)	2:31:50
1950	Kee Yong-ham (Korea)	2:32:39
1951	Shigeki Tanaka (Japan)	2:27:45
1952	Doroteo Flores (Guatemala)	2:31:53
1953	Keizo Yamada (Japan)	2:18:51
1954	Veikko Karvonen (Finland)	2:20:39
1955	Hideo Hamamura (Japan)	2:18:22
1956	Antti Viskari (Finland)	2:14:14
1957	John J Kelley (USA)	2:20:05
1958	Franjo Mihalic (Yugoslavia)	2:25:54
1959	Eino Oksanen (Finland)	2:22:42
1960	Paavo Kotila (Finland)	2:20:54
1961	Eino Oksanen (Finland)	2:23:39
1962	Eino Oksanen (Finland)	2:23:48
1963	Aurele Vandendriessche (Belgium)	2:18:58
1964	Aurele Vandendriessche (Belgium)	2:19:59
1965	Morio Shigematsu (Japan)	2:16:33
1966	Kenji Kimihara (Japan)	2:17:11
1967	David McKenzie (New Zealand)	2:15:45
1968	Amby Burfoot (USA)	2:22:17
1969	Yoshiaki Unetani (Japan)	2:13:49
1970	Ron Hill (Great Britain)	2:10:30
1971	Alvaro Mejia (Colombia)	2:18:45
1972	Olavi Suomalainen (Finland)	2:15:39
1973	Jon Anderson (USA)	2:16:03
1974	Neil Cusack (Ireland)	2:13:39
1975	Bill Rodgers (USA)	2:09:55
1976	Jack Fultz (USA)	2:20:19
1977	Jerome Drayton (Canada)	2:14:46
1978	Bill Rodgers (USA)	2:10:13
1979	Bill Rodgers (USA)	2:09:27
1980	Bill Rodgers (USA)	2:12:11
1981	Toshihiko Seko (Japan)	2:09:26
1982	Alberto Salazar (USA)	2:08:52
1983	Gregory A Meyer (USA)	2:09:00
1984	Geoff Smith (Great Britain)	2:10:34
1985	Geoff Smith (Great Britain)	2:14:05
1986	Rob de Castella (Australia)	2:07:51
1987	Toshihiko Seko (Japan)	2:11:50
1988	Ibrahim Hussein (Kenya)	2:08:43
1989	Abebe Mekonnen (Ethiopia)	2:09:06
1990	Gelindo Bordin (Italy)	2:08:19
1991	Ibrahim Hussein (Kenya)	2:11:06
1992	Ibrahim Hussein (Kenya)	2:08:14
1993	Cosmas N'deti (Kenya)	2:09:33
1994	Cosmas N'deti (Kenya)	2:07.15
1995	Cosmas N'deti (Kenya)	2:09.22
1996	Moses Tanui (Kenya)	2:09.16
1997	Lameck Aguta (Kenya)	2:10.33

Most wins: (7) Clarence DeMar (USA).

WOMEN

Year	Winner	Time
1966	Roberta Gibb (USA)	3:21:40*
1967	Roberta Gibb (USA)	3:27:17*
1968	Roberta Gibb (USA)	3:30:00*

1969	Sara Mae Berman (USA)	3:22:46*
1970	Sara Mae Berman (USA)	3:05:07*
1971	Sara Mae Berman (USA)	3:08:30*
1972	Nina Kuscsik (USA)	3:10:36
1973	Jacqueline A Hansen (USA)	3:05:59
1974	Miki Gorman (USA)	2:47:11
1975	Liane Winter (West Germany)	2:42:24
1976	Kim Merritt (USA)	2:47:10
1977	Miki Gorman (USA)	2:48:33
1978	Gayle Barron (USA)	2:44:52
1979	Joan Benoit (USA)	2:35:15
1980	Jacqueline Gareau (Canada)	2:34:28
1981	Allison Roe (New Zealand)	2:26:46
1982	Charlotte Teske (West Germany)	2:29:33
1983	Joan Benoit (USA)	2:22:43
1984	Lorraine Moller (New Zealand)	2:29:28
1985	Lisa Larsen Weidenbach (USA)	2:34:06
1986	Ingrid Kristiansen (Norway)	2:24:55
1987	Rosa Mota (Portugal)	2:25:21
1988	Rosa Mota (Portugal)	2:24:30
1989	Ingrid Kristiansen (Norway)	2:24:33
1990	Rosa Mota (Portugal)	2:25:24
1991	Wanda Panfil (Poland)	2:24:18
1992	Olga Markova (Russia)	2:23:43
1993	Olga Markova (Russia)	2:25:27
1994	Uta Pippig (Germany)	2:21.45
1995	Uta Pippig (Germany)	2:25.11
1996	Uta Pippig (Germany)	2:27.12
1997	Fatuma Roba (Ethiopia)	2:26.24

*Unofficial

Most wins: (3) Rosa Mota (Portugal); Uta Pippig (Germany).

New York Marathon

MEN

Year	Winner	Time
1970	Gary Muhrcke (USA)	2:31:38
1971	Norman Higgins (USA)	2:22:54
1972	Sheldon Karlin (USA)	2:27:52
1973	Tom Fleming (USA)	2:21:54
1974	Norbert Sander (USA)	2:26:30
1975	Tom Fleming (USA)	2:19:27
1976	Bill Rodgers (USA)	2:10:10
1977	Bill Rodgers (USA)	2:11:28
1978	Bill Rodgers (USA)	2:12:12
1979	Bill Rodgers (USA)	2:11:42
1980	Alberto Salazar (USA)	2:09:41
1981	Alberto Salazar (USA)	2:08:13
1982	Alberto Salazar (USA)	2:09:29
1983	Rod Dixon (New Zealand)	2:08:59
1984	Orlando Pizzolato (Italy)	2:14:53
1985	Orlando Pizzolato (Italy)	2:11:34
1986	Gianni Poli (Italy)	2:11:06
1987	Ibrahim Hussein (Kenya)	2:11:01
1988	Steve Jones (Great Britain)	2:08:20
1989	Juma Ikangaa (Tanzania)	2:08:01
1990	Douglas Wakiihuri (Kenya)	2:12:39
1991	Salvador Garcia (Mexico)	2:09:28
1992	Willie Mtolo (South Africa)	2:09:29
1993	Andreas Espinosa (Mexico)	2:10:04
1994	German Silva (Mexico)	2:11.21
1995	German Silva (Mexico)	2:11.00
1996	Giacomo Leone (Italy)	2:09.00
1997	John Kagwe (Kenya)	2:08.12

Most wins: (4) Bill Rogers (USA).

WOMEN

Year	Winner	Time
1970	*No finisher*	
1971	Beth Bonner (USA)	2:55:22
1972	Nina Kuscsik (USA)	3:08:41
1973	Nina Kuscsik (USA)	2:57:07
1974	Katherine Swirzer (USA)	3:07:29
1975	Kim Merritt (USA)	2:46:14
1976	Miki Gorman (USA)	2:39:11
1977	Miki Gorman (USA)	2:43:10
1978	Grete Waitz (Norway)	2:32:30
1979	Grete Waitz (Norway)	2:27:33
1980	Grete Waitz (Norway)	2:25:41
1981	Allison Roe (New Zealand)	2:25:29
1982	Grete Waitz (Norway)	2:27:14
1983	Grete Waitz (Norway)	2:27:00
1984	Grete Waitz (Norway)	2:29:30
1985	Grete Waitz (Norway)	2:28:34
1986	Grete Waitz (Norway)	2:28:06
1987	Priscilla Welch (Great Britain)	2:30:17
1988	Grete Waitz (Norway)	2:28:07
1989	Ingrid Kristiansen (Norway)	2:25:30
1990	Wanda Panfil (Poland)	2:30:45
1991	Liz McColgan (Great Britain)	2:27:23
1992	Lisa Ondieki (Australia)	2:24:40
1993	Uta Pippig (Germany)	2:26:24
1994	Tecla Loroupe	2:27.37
1995	Tecla Loroupe	2:28.06
1996	Anuta Catuna	2:28.18
1997	Franziska Rochat-Moser	2:28:43

Most wins: (9) Grete Waitz (Norway).

London Marathon

MEN

Year	Winner	Time
1981	Dick Beardsley (USA) and Inge Simonsen (Norway)	2:11:48

1982	Hugh Jones (Great Britain)	2:09:24
1983	Mike Gratton (Great Britain)	2:09:43
1984	Charlie Spedding (Great Britain)	2:09:57
1985	Steve Jones (Great Britain)	2:08:16
1986	Toshihiko Seko (Japan)	2:10:02
1987	Hiromi Taniguchi (Japan)	2:09:50
1988	Henrik Jørgensen (Denmark)	2:10:20
1989	Douglas Wakiihuri (Kenya)	2:09:03
1990	Allister Hutton (Great Britain)	2:10:10
1991	Yakov Tolstikov (USSR)	2:09:17
1992	António Pinto (Portugal)	2:10:02
1993	Eamonn Martin (Great Britain)	2:10:50
1994	Dionici Ceron (Mexico)	2:08.53
1995	Dionici Ceron (Mexico)	2:08.30
1996	Dionici Ceron (Mexico)	2:10.00
1997	António Pinto (Portugal)	2:07.55

Most wins: (3) Dionici Ceron (Mexico).

WOMEN

Year	Winner	Time
1981	Joyce Smith (Great Britain)	2:29:57
1982	Joyce Smith (Great Britain)	2:29:43
1983	Grete Waitz (Norway)	2:25:29
1984	Ingrid Kristiansen (Norway)	2:24:26
1985	Ingrid Kristiansen (Norway)	2:21:06
1986	Grete Waitz (Norway)	2:24:54
1987	Ingrid Kristiansen (Norway)	2:22:48
1988	Ingrid Kristiansen (Norway)	2:25:41
1989	Véronique Marot (Great Britain)	2:25:56
1990	Wanda Panfil (Poland)	2:26:31
1991	Rosa Mota (Portugal)	2:26:14
1992	Katrin Dörre (Germany)	2:29:39
1993	Katrin Dörre (Germany)	2:27:09
1994	Katrin Dörre (Germany)	2:32.34
1995	Malgorzata Sobanska (Poland)	2:27.43
1996	Liz McColgan (Great Britain)	2:27.54
1997	Joyce Chepchumba (Kenya)	2:26.51

Most wins: (4) Ingrid Kristiansen (Norway).

Badminton

World Championships

First held in 1977; initially took place every three years; since 1983 every two years.

Singles (Men)
1977	Flemming Delfs (Denmark)
1980	Rudy Hartono (Indonesia)
1983	Icuk Sugiarto (Indonesia)
1985	Han Jian (China)
1987	Yang Yang (China)
1989	Yang Yang (China)
1991	Zhao Jianhuan (China)
1993	Joko Suprianto (Indonesia)
1995	Heryanto Arbi (Indonesia)
1997	Peter Rasmussen (Denmark)

Singles (Women)
1977	Lene Koppen (Denmark)
1980	Wiharjo Verawatay (Indonesia)
1983	Li Lingwei (China)
1985	Han Aiping (China)

1987	Han Aiping (China)
1989	Li Lingwei (China)
1991	Tang Jiuhong (China)
1993	Susi Susanti (Indonesia)
1995	Ye Zhaoying (China)
1997	Ye Zhaoying (China)

All-England Championship

Badminton's premier event prior to the inauguration of the World Championships; first held in 1899.

Recent winners Singles (Men)
1986	Morten Frost (Denmark)
1987	Morten Frost (Denmark)
1988	Ib Frederikson (Denmark)
1989	Yang Yang (China)
1990	Zhao Jianhua (China)
1991	Ardi Wiranata (Indonesia)
1992	Liu Jun (China)
1993	Heryanto Arbi (Indonesia)
1994	Heryanto Arbi (Indonesia)
1995	Poul-Erik Hoyer Larsen (Denmark)

1996	Poul-Erik Hoyer Larsen (Denmark)
1997	Dong Jiong (China)

Most wins: (8) Rudy Hartono (Indonesia) 1968–74, 1976.

Recent winners Singles (Women)
1986	Yun-Ja Kim (Korea)
1987	Kirsten Larsen (Denmark)
1988	Gu Jiaming (China)
1989	Li Lingwei (China)
1990	Susi Susanti (Indonesia)
1991	Susi Susanti (Indonesia)
1992	Tang Jiuhong (China)
1993	Susi Susanti (Indonesia)
1994	Susi Susanti (Indonesia)
1995	Lin Xiaoqing (Sweden)
1996	Bang Soo-hyun (South Korea)
1997	Ye Zhaoying (China)

Most wins: (10) Judy Hashman (*née* Devlin) (USA) 1954, 1957–8, 1960, 1961–4, 1966–7.

Olympics

Badminton became an Olympic event in 1992.

Singles (Men)
1996 Poul-Erik Hoyer Larsen (Denmark)

Singles (Women)
1996 Bang Soo-hyun (South Korea)

Doubles (Men)
1996 Rexy Mainaky and Ricky Subagja (Indonesia)

Doubles (Women)
1996 Ge Fei and Gu Jun (China)

Baseball

Most valuable player

Each year since 1931 the Baseball Writers' Association has voted to determine the year's most outstanding player. There are two awards – one for each of the two leagues which comprise the North American Major League – the National League (NL) and the American League (AL).

National League
1931 Frank Frisch, St Louis Cardinals
1932 Charles Klein, Philadelphia Phillies
1933 Carl Hubbell, New York Mets
1934 Dizzy Dean, St Louis Cardinals
1935 Gabby Hartnett, Chicago Cubs
1936 Carl Hubbell, New York Mets
1937 Joe Medwick, St Louis Cardinals
1938 Ernie Lombardi, Cincinnati Reds
1939 Bucky Walters, Cincinnati Reds
1940 Frank McCormick, Cincinnati Reds
1941 Dolph Carnitti, Brooklyn Dodgers
1942 Mort Cooper, St Louis Cardinals
1943 Stan Musial, St Louis Cardinals
1944 Martin Marion, St Louis Cardinals
1945 Phil Cavarretta, Chicago Cubs
1946 Stan Musial, St Louis Cardinals
1947 Bob Elliott, Boston Braves
1948 Stan Musial, St Louis Cardinals
1949 Jackie Robinson, Brooklyn Dodgers
1950 Jim Konstanty, Philadelphia Phillies
1951 Roy Campanella, Brooklyn Dodgers
1952 Hank Sauer, Chicago Cubs
1953 Roy Campanella, Brooklyn Dodgers
1954 Willie Mays, New York Mets
1955 Roy Campanella, Brooklyn Dodgers
1956 Don Newcombe, Brooklyn Dodgers
1957 Henry Aaron, Milwaukee Braves

1958 Ernie Banks, Chicago Cubs
1959 Ernie Banks, Chicago Cubs
1960 Dick Groat, Pittsburgh Pirates
1961 Frank Robinson, Cincinnati Reds
1962 Maury Wills, Los Angeles Dodgers
1963 Sandy Koufax, Los Angeles Dodgers
1964 Ken Boyers, St Louis Cardinals
1965 Willie Mays, San Francisco Giants
1966 Roberto Clemente, Pittsburgh Pirates
1967 Orlando Cepeda, St Louis Cardinals
1968 Bob Gibson, St Louis Cardinals
1969 Willie McCovey, San Francisco Giants
1970 Johnny Bench, Cincinnati Reds
1971 Joe Torre, St Louis Cardinals
1972 Johnny Bench, Cincinnati Reds
1973 Pete Rose, Cincinnati Reds
1974 Steve Garvey, Los Angeles Dodgers
1975 Joe Morgan, Cincinnati Reds
1976 Joe Morgan, Cincinnati Reds
1977 George Foster, Cincinnati Reds
1978 Dave Parker, Pittsburgh Pirates
1979 Willie Stargell, Pittsburgh Pirates; Keith Hernandez, St Louis Cardinals
1980 Mike Schmidt, Philadelphia Phillies
1981 Mike Schmidt, Philadelphia Phillies
1982 Dale Murphy, Atlanta Braves
1983 Dale Murphy, Atlanta Braves
1984 Ryne Sandberg, Chicago Cubs
1985 Willie McGee, St Louis Cardinals
1986 Mike Schmidt, Philadelphia Phillies
1987 Andre Dawson, Chicago Cubs
1988 Kirk Gibson, Los Angeles Dodgers
1989 Kevin Mitchell, San Francisco Giants
1990 Barry Bonds, Pittsburgh Pirates
1991 Terry Pendleton, Atlanta Braves
1992 Barry Bonds, Pittsburgh Pirates
1993 Barry Bonds, San Francisco Giants
1994 Jeff Bagnall, Houston Astros
1995 Barry Larkin, Cincinnati Reds
1996 Ken Caminiti, San Diego
1997 Livian Hernandez
Most times MVP: (3) Stan Musial (St Louis Cardinals); Roy Campanella (Brooklyn Dodgers) and Mike Schmidt (Philadelphia Phillies); Barry Bonds (Pittsburgh Pirates and San Francisco Giants).

American League
1931 Lefty Grove, Philadelphia Athletics
1932 Jimmie Foxx, Philadelphia Athletics
1933 Jimmie Foxx, Philadelphia Athletics
1934 Mickey Cochrane, Detroit Tigers
1935 Hank Greenberg, Detroit Tigers
1936 Lou Gehrig, New York Yankees
1937 Charley Gehringer, Detroit Tigers
1938 Jimmie Foxx, Boston Red Sox
1939 Joe DiMaggio, New York Yankees
1940 Hank Greenberg, Detroit Tigers
1941 Joe DiMaggio, New York Yankees
1942 Joe Gordon, New York Yankees
1943 Spurgeon Chandler, New York Yankees
1944 Hal Newhouser, Detroit Tigers
1945 Hal Newhouser, Detroit Tigers
1946 Ted Williams, Boston Red Sox
1947 Joe DiMaggio, New York Yankees
1948 Lou Boudreau, Cleveland Indians
1949 Ted Williams, Boston Red Sox
1950 Phil Rizzuto, New York Yankees
1951 Yogi Berra, New York Yankees
1952 Bobby Shantz, Philadelphia Athletics
1953 Al Rosen, Cleveland Indians
1954 Yogi Berra, New York Yankees
1955 Yogi Berra, New York Yankees
1956 Mickey Mantle, New York Yankees
1957 Mickey Mantle, New York Yankees
1958 Jackie Jensen, Boston Red Sox
1959 Nellie Fox, Chicago White Sox
1960 Roger Maris, New York Yankees
1961 Roger Maris, New York Yankees
1962 Mickey Mantle, New York Yankees
1963 Elston Howard, New York Yankees
1964 Brooks Robinson, Baltimore Orioles
1965 Zoilo Versalles, Minnesota Twins
1966 Frank Robinson, Baltimore Orioles
1967 Carl Yastrzemski, Boston Red Sox
1968 Denny McLain, Detroit Tigers
1969 Harmon Killebrew, Minnesota Twins
1970 John (Boog) Powell, Baltimore Orioles
1971 Vida Blue, Oakland A's
1972 Dick Allen, Chicago White Sox
1973 Reggie Jackson, Oakland A's
1974 Jeff Burroughs, Texas Rangers
1975 Fred Lynn, Boston Red Sox

1976 Thurman Munson, New York Yankees
1977 Rod Carew, Minnesota Twins
1978 Jim Rice, Boston Red Sox
1979 Don Baylor, California Angels
1980 George Brett, Kansas City Royals
1981 Rollie Fingers, Milwaukee Brewers
1982 Robin Yount, Milwaukee Brewers
1983 Cal Ripken Jr, Baltimore Orioles
1984 Willie Hernandez, Detroit Tigers
1985 Don Mattingly, New York Yankees
1986 Roger Clemens, Boston Red Sox
1987 George Bell, Toronto Blue Jays
1988 Jose Canseco, Oakland A's
1989 Robin Yount, Milwaukee Brewers
1990 Rickey Henderson, Oakland A's
1991 Cal Ripken Jr, Baltimore Orioles
1992 Dennis Eckersley, Oakland A's
1993 Frank Thomas, Chicago White Sox
1994 Frank Thomas, Chicago White Sox
1995 Tom Glavine, Atlanta Braves
1996 Juan Gonzalez, Texas

Most times MVP: (3), Jimmie Foxx (Philadelphia Athletics/Boston Red Sox); Joe DiMaggio (New York Yankees); Yogi Berra (New York Yankees), Mickey Mantle (New York Yankees).

Cy Young Award

An award for the most outstanding pitcher of the year in each of the two leagues. First given in 1956. Pre-1967 there was just one award covering both leagues.

1956 Don Newcombe, Brooklyn Dodgers (NL)
1957 Warren Spahn, Milwaukee Braves (NL)
1958 Bob Turley, New York Yankees (AL)
1959 Early Wynn, Chicago White Sox (AL)
1960 Vernon Law, Pittsburgh Pirates (NL)

1961 Whitey Ford, New York Yankees (AL)
1962 Don Drysdale, Los Angeles Dodgers (NL)
1963 Sandy Koufax, Los Angeles Dodgers (NL)
1964 Dean Chance, California Angels (AL)
1965 Sandy Koufax, Los Angeles Dodgers (NL)
1967 Sandy Koufax, Los Angeles Dodgers (NL)

National League
1967 Mike McCormick, San Francisco Giants
1968 Bob Gibson, St Louis Cardinals
1969 Tom Seaver, New York Mets
1970 Bob Gibson, St Louis Cardinals
1971 Ferguson Jenkins, Chicago Cubs
1972 Steve Carlton, Philadelphia Phillies
1973 Tom Seaver, New York Mets
1974 Mike Marshall, Los Angeles Dodgers
1975 Tom Seaver, New York Mets
1976 Randy Jones, San Diego Padres
1977 Steve Carlton, Philadelphia Phillies
1978 Gaylord Perry, San Diego Padres
1979 Bruce Sutter, Chicago Cubs
1980 Steve Carlton, Philadelphia Phillies
1981 Fernando Valenzuela, Los Angeles Dodgers
1982 Steve Carlton, Philadelphia Phillies
1983 John Denny, Philadelphia Phillies
1984 Rick Sutcliffe, Chicago Cubs
1985 Dwight Gooden, New York Mets
1986 Mike Scott, Houston Astros
1987 Steve Bedrosian, Philadelphia Phillies
1988 Orel Hershiser, Los Angeles Dodgers
1989 Mark Davis, San Diego Padres
1990 Doug Drabek, Pittsburgh Pirates
1991 Tom Glavine, Atlanta Braves
1992 Greg Maddux, Chicago Cubs
1993 Greg Maddux, Atlanta Braves
1994 Greg Maddux, Atlanta Braves

1995 Greg Maddux, Atlanta Braves
1996 John Smoltz, Atlanta Braves

American League
1967 Jim Lonborg, Boston Red Sox
1968 Denny McLain, Detroit Tigers
1969 Denny McLain, Detroit Tigers; Mike Cuellar, Baltimore Orioles
1970 Jim Perry, Minnesota Twins
1971 Vida Blue, Oakland A's
1972 Gaylord Perry, Cleveland Indians
1973 Jim Palmer, Baltimore Orioles
1974 Jim 'Catfish' Hunter, Oakland A's
1975 Jim Palmer, Baltimore Orioles
1976 Jim Palmer, Baltimore Orioles
1977 Sparky Lyle, New York Yankees
1978 Ron Guidry, New York Yankees
1979 Mike Flanagan, Baltimore Orioles
1980 Steve Stone, Baltimore Orioles
1981 Rollie Fingers, Milwaukee Brewers
1982 Pete Vuckovich, Milwaukee Brewers
1983 La Marr Hoyt, Chicago White Sox
1984 Willie Hernandez, Detroit Tigers
1985 Bret Saberhagen, Kansas City Royals
1986 Roger Clemens, Boston Red Sox
1987 Roger Clemens, Boston Red Sox
1988 Frank Viola, Minnesota Twins
1989 Bret Saberhagen, Kansas City Royals
1990 Bob Welch, Oakland A's
1991 Roger Clemens, Boston Red Sox
1992 Dennis Eckersley, Oakland A's
1993 Jack McDowell, Chicago White Sox
1994 David Cone, Kansas City Royals
1995 Randy Johnson, Seattle Mariners
1996 Pat Hentgen, Toronto

Most wins: Pre-1967, (3) Sandy Koufax (Los Angeles Dodgers); *NL*: (4), Steve Carlton (Philadelphia Phillies); Greg Maddux (Atlanta Braves); *AL*: (3), Jim Palmer (Baltimore Orioles); Roger Clemens (Boston Red Sox).

Basketball

National Basketball Association (NBA) leading scorers

		games	points	average
1947	Joe Fulks, Philadelphia	60	1389	23.2
1948	Max Zaslofsky, Chicago	48	1007	21.0
1949	George Mikan, Minneapolis	60	1698	28.3
1950	George Mikan, Minneapolis	68	1865	27.4
1951	George Mikan, Minneapolis	68	1932	28.4
1952	Paul Arizin, Philadelphia	66	1674	25.4
1953	Neil Johnston, Philadelphia	70	1564	22.3
1954	Neil Johnston, Philadelphia	72	1759	24.4
1955	Neil Johnston, Philadelphia	72	1631	22.7
1956	Bob Pettit, St Louis	72	1849	25.7
1957	Paul Arizin, Philadelphia	71	1817	25.6
1958	George Yardley, Detroit	72	2001	27.8
1959	Bob Pettit, St Louis	72	2105	29.2
1960	Wilt Chamberlain, Philadelphia	72	2707	37.9
1961	Wilt Chamberlain, Philadelphia	79	3033	38.4
1962	Wilt Chamberlain, Philadelphia	80	4029	50.4
1963	Wilt Chamberlain, San Francisco	80	3586	44.8
1964	Wilt Chamberlain, San Francisco	80	2948	36.5
1965	Wilt Chamberlain, San Francisco/ Philadelphia	80	2534	34.7
1966	Wilt Chamberlain, Philadelphia	79	2649	33.5
1967	Rick Barry, San Francisco	79	2775	35.6
1968	Dave Bing, Detroit	79	2142	27.1
1969	Elvin Hayes, San Diego	82	2327	28.4
1970	Jerry West, Los Angeles	74	2309	31.2
1971	Lew Alcindor, Milwaukee	82	2596	31.7
1972	Kareem Abdul-Jabbar (Lew Alcindor), Milwaukee	81	2822	34.8
1973	Nate Archibald, Kansas City–Omaha	80	2719	34.0
1974	Bob McAdoo, Buffalo	74	2261	30.6
1975	Bob McAdoo, Buffalo	82	2831	34.5
1976	Bob McAdoo, Buffalo	78	2427	31.1
1977	Pete Maravich, New Orleans	73	2273	31.1
1978	George Gervin, San Antonio	82	2232	27.2
1979	George Gervin, San Antonio	80	2365	29.6
1980	George Gervin, San Antonio	78	2585	33.1
1981	Adrian Dantley, Utah	80	2452	30.7
1982	Geroge Gervin, San Antonio	79	2551	32.3
1983	Alex English, Denver	82	2326	28.4
1984	Adrian Dantley, Utah	79	2418	30.6
1985	Bernard King, New York	55	1809	32.9
1986	Dominique Wilkins, Atlanta	78	2366	30.3
1987	Michael Jordan, Chicago	82	3041	37.1
1988	Michael Jordan, Chicago	82	2868	35.0
1989	Michael Jordan, Chicago	81	2633	32.5
1990	Michael Jordan, Chicago	82	2753	33.6
1991	Michael Jordan, Chicago	82	2580	31.5
1992	Michael Jordan, Chicago	80	2404	30.1
1993	Michael Jordan, Chicago	78	2541	32.3
1994	David Robinson, San Antonio	80	2383	29.8
1995	Shaquille O'Neal, Orlando	79	2315	29.3
1996	Michael Jordan, Chicago	82	2491	30.4
1997	Michael Jordan, Chicago	82	2431	29.6

Most times: (7 each), Wilt Chamberlain, Michael Jordan.

NBA Most Valuable Player (MVP)

Each year the NBA players vote to decide which player will receive the Maurice Podoloff Trophy as the year's Most Valuable Player.

1956	Bob Pettit, St Louis
1957	Bob Vousy, Boston
1958	Bill Russell, Boston
1959	Bob Pettit, St Louis
1960	Wilt Chamberlain, Philadelphia
1961	Bill Russell, Boston
1962	Bill Russell, Boston
1963	Bill Russell, Boston
1964	Oscar Robertson, Cincinnati
1965	Bill Russell, Boston
1966	Wilt Chamberlain, Philadelphia
1967	Wilt Chamberlain, Philadelphia
1968	Wilt Chamberlain, Philadelphia
1969	Wes Unseld, Baltimore
1970	Willis Reed, New York
1971	Lew Alcindor, Milwaukee
1972	Kareem Abdul-Jabbar (Lew Alcindor), Milwaukee
1973	Dave Cowens, Boston
1974	Kareem Abdul-Jabbar, Milwaukee
1975	Bob McAdoo, Buffalo
1976	Kareem Abdul-Jabbar, Los Angeles
1977	Kareem Abdul-Jabbar, Los Angeles
1978	Bill Walton, Portland
1979	Moses Malone, Houston
1980	Kareem Abdul-Jabbar, Los Angeles
1981	Julius Erving, Philadelphia
1982	Moses Malone, Houston
1983	Moses Malone, Philadelphia
1984	Larry Bird, Boston
1985	Larry Bird, Boston
1986	Larry Bird, Boston
1987	Magic Johnson, Los Angeles Lakers
1988	Michael Jordan, Chicago
1989	Magic Johnson, Los Angeles Lakers
1990	Magic Johnson, Los Angeles Lakers
1991	Michael Jordan, Chicago
1992	Michael Jordan, Chicago
1993	Charles Barkley, Phoenix
1994	Hakeem Olajuwon, Houston Rockets
1995	David Robinson, San Antonio
1996	Michael Jordan, Chicago
1997	Michael Jordan, Chicago

Most times MVP: (6) Kareem Abdul-Jabbar (Lew Alcindor), as above.

Biathlon

World Championships
First held in 1958; take place annually; the Olympic champion is the automatic world champion in Olympic years; women's championship first held in 1984.

Recent winners Individual (Men)

20 km
1979	Klaus Siebert (East Germany)
1980	Anatoliy Alyabyev (USSR)
1981	Heikki Ikola (Finland)
1982	Frank Ullrich (East Germany)
1983	Frank Ullrich (East Germany)
1984	Peter Angerer (West Germany)
1985	Yuriy Kashkarov (USSR)
1986	Valeriy Medvetsev (USSR)
1987	Frank-Peter Rötsch (East Germany)
1988	Frank-Peter Rötsch (East Germany)
1989	Eric Kvalfoss (Norway)
1990	Valeriy Medvetsev (USSR)
1991	Mark Kirchner (Germany)
1992	Yevgeriy Redkine (CIS)
1993	Franz Zingerle (Austria)
1994	Sergei Tarasov (Russia)
1995	Tomaz Sikora (Poland)
1996	Sergei Tarasov (Russia)
1997	Ricco Gross (Germany)

Most individual titles: (6), Frank Ullrich (East Germany), as above plus 1978 10 km.

Recent winners Individual (Women)

10 km (15 km since 1988)
1984	Venera Chernyshova (USSR)
1985	Kaya Parva (USSR)
1986	Eva Korpela (Sweden)
1987	Sanna Gronlid (Norway)
1988	Anne-Elinor Elvebakk (Norway)
1989	Petra Schaaf (West Germany)
1990	Svetlana Davydova (USSR)
1991	Petra Schaaf (Germany)
1992	Antje Misersky (Germany)
1993	Petra Schaaf (Germany)
1994	Myriam Bedard (Canada)
1995	Corrine Miogret (France)
1996	Emmanuelle Claret (France)
1997	Magdalena Forsberg (Sweden)

Most individual wins: (3) Petra Schaaf (West Germany); Anne-Elinor Elvebakk (Norway)

Billiards

World Professional Championship
First held in 1870, organized on a challenge basis; became a knockout event in 1909; discontinued in 1934; revived in 1951 as a challenge system; reverted to a knockout event in 1980.

Recent winners
1985	Ray Edmonds (England)
1986	Robbie Foldvari (Australia)
1987	Norman Dagley (England)
1988	Norman Dagley (England)
1989	Mike Russell (England)
1990	*not held*
1991	Mike Russell (England)
1992	Geet Sethi (India)
1993	Geet Sethi (India)
1994	Peter Gilchrist (England)
1995	Geet Sethi (India)
1996	Mike Russell (England)

Most wins: (knockout) (6), Tom Newman (England), 1921–2,1924–7. (challenge) (8), John Roberts, Jr (England), 1870–85.

Bobsleighing and tobogganing

World Championships
First held in 1930 (four-man) and in 1931 (two-man); Olympic champions automatically become world champions.

Recent winners (Two-man)
1980	Erich Schärer/Josef Benz (Switzerland)
1981	Bernhard Germeshausen/Hans-Jürgen Gerhardt (East Germany)
1982	Erich Schärer/Josef Benz (Switzerland)
1983	Ralf Pichler/Urs Leuthold (Switzerland)
1984	Wolfgang Hoppe/Dietmar Schauerhammer (East Germany)
1985	Wolfgang Hoppe/Dietmar Schauerhammer (East Germany)
1986	Wolfgang Hoppe/Dietmar Schauerhammer (East Germany)
1987	Ralf Pichler/Celest Poltera (Switzerland)
1988	Janis Kipurs/Vladimir Kozlov (USSR)
1989	Wolfgang Hoppe/Bogdan Musiol (East Germany)
1990	Gustav Weder/Bruno Gerber (Switzerland)
1991	Rudi Lochmer/Markus Zimmermann (Germany)
1992	Gustav Weder/Donat Acklin (Switzerland)
1993	Christoph Langan/Peer Joechel (Germany)
1994	Gustav Weder/Donat Acklin (Switzerland)
1995	Cristoph Langen/Markus Zimmermann (Germany)
1996	Cristoph Langen/Markus Zimmermann (Germany)
1997	Reto Goetschi/Guido Acklin (Switzerland)

Most wins: (8), Eugenio Monti (Italy) 1957–61,1963,1966,1968.

Luge World Championships
First held in 1955; annually until 1981, then every one or two years; Olympic champions automatically become world champions.

Recent winners (Men's single-seater)
1980	Bernhard Glass (East Germany)
1981	Sergey Danilin (USSR)
1983	Miroslav Zajonc (Canada)
1984	Paul Hildgartner (Italy)
1985	Michael Walter (East Germany)
1987	Markus Prock (Austria)
1988	Jens Müller (East Germany)
1989	Georg Hackl (West Germany)
1990	Georg Hackl (West Germany)
1991	Arnold Huber (Italy)
1992	Georg Hackl (Germany)
1993	Wendel Suckow (USA)
1994	Georg Hackl (Germany)
1995	Armin Zoggeler (Italy)
1996	Georg Hackl (Germany)

Most wins: (5), Georg Hackl (West Germany/Germany), as above.

Recent winners (Women's single-seater)
1980	Vera Sosulya (USSR)
1981	Melitta Sollman (East Germany)
1983	Steffi Martin (East Germany)
1984	Steffi Martin (East Germany)
1985	Steffi Martin (East Germany)
1987	Cerstin Schmidt (East Germany)
1988	Steffi Walter (*née* Martin) (East Germany)
1989	Susi Erdmann (East Germany)
1990	Gabriele Kohlisch (East Germany)
1991	Susi Erdmann (Germany)
1992	Doris Neuner (Austria)
1993	Gerda Weissensteiner (Italy)
1994	Gerda Weissensteiner (Italy)
1995	Gabriele Kohlisch (Germany)
1997	Susi Urdmann (Germany)

Most wins: (5), Margrit Schumann (East Germany), 1973–7.

Bowls

World Championships
Instituted for men in 1966 and for women in 1969; held every four years.

Men's Singles
1966	David Bryant (England)
1972	Malwyn Evans (Wales)
1976	Doug Watson (South Africa)
1980	David Bryant (England)
1984	Peter Bellis (New Zealand)
1988	David Bryant (England)
1992	Tony Allcock (England)
1996	Tony Allcock (England)

Most wins: (3), David Bryant.

Women's Singles
1973	Elsie Wilke (New Zealand)

1977   Elsie Wilke (New Zealand)
1981   Norma Shaw (England)
1985   Merle Richardson (Australia)
1988* Janet Ackland (Wales)
1992   Margaret Johnston (Ireland)
1996   Carmen Anderson (Norfolk
       Island)
Most wins: (2), Elsie Wilke (New Zealand).
*The women's event was advanced to December 1988 (Australia).

World Indoor Championships
Men's competition first held in 1979; Women's in 1988; both held annually.

Recent winners (Men's singles)
1988   Hugh Duff (Scotland)
1989   Richard Corsie (Scotland)
1990   John Price (Wales)
1991   Richard Corsie (Scotland)
1992   Ian Schuback (Australia)
1993   Richard Corsie (Scotland)
1994   Richard Corsie (Scotland)
1995   Andrew Thompson (England)
1996   David Gourlay (Scotland)
1997   Hugh Duff (Scotland)
Most wins: (4), Richard Corsie (Scotland).

Recent winners (Women's singles)
1992   Sarah Gourlay (Scotland)
1993   Kate Adams (Scotland)
1994   Jan Woodley (Scotland)
1995   Joyce Lindoores (Scotland)
1996   Sandy Hazell (England)
1997   N Shaw (England)
Most wins: (2), Margaret Johnston (Ireland), 1988–9.

Waterloo Handicap
First held in 1907 and annually at Blackpool's Waterloo Hotel; the premier event of Crown Green Bowling. Women's event inaugurated in 1988.

Recent winners (Men)
1988   Ingham Gregory
1989   Brian Duncan
1990   John Bancroft
1991   John Eccles
1992   Brian Duncan
1993   Alan Broadhurst
1994   Bill Hilton
1995   Ken Strutt
1996   Lee Heaton
1997   Andrew Cairns
Most wins: (5), Brian Duncan, 1979, 1986–7, and as above.

Winners (Women)
1988   Barbara Rawcliffe
1989   Diane Hunt
1990   Jane Jones
1991   Joyce Foxcroft
1992   Karen Johnstone
1993   Shiela Smith

1994   Veronica Lyons
1995   Joyce Foxcroft
1996   Lynn Pritchett
Most wins: (2), Joyce Foxcroft, Karen Johnstone

Boxing
World Heavyweight Champions
Undisputed
1882   John L Sullivan (USA)
1892   James J Corbett (USA)*
1897   Bob Fitzsimmons (Great Britain)
1899   James J Jefferies (USA)
1905   Marvin Hart (USA)
1906   Tommy Burns (Canada)
1908   Jack Johnson (USA)
1915   Jess Willard (USA)
1919   Jack Dempsey (USA)
1926   Gene Tunney (USA)
1930   Max Schmeling (Germany)
1932   Jack Sharkey (USA)
1933   Primo Carnera (Italy)
1934   Max Baer (USA)
1935   James J Braddock (USA)
1937   Joe Louis (USA)
1949   Ezzard Charles (USA)
1951   Jersey Joe Walcott (USA)
1952   Rocky Marciano (USA)
1956   Floyd Patterson (USA)
1959   Ingemar Johansson (Sweden)
1960   Floyd Patterson (USA)
1962   Sonny Liston (USA)
1964   Cassius Clay (USA)
1970   Joe Frazier (USA)
1973   George Foreman (USA)
1974   Muhammad Ali (Cassius Clay)
       (USA)
1978   Leon Spinks (USA)
1987   Mike Tyson (USA)
*The first world heavyweight champion under Queensbury rules with gloves.

In recent years, 'world champions' have been recognized by up to four different governing bodies.

Champions (followed by the recognizing body)
1978   Muhammad Ali (USA) WBA
1978   Larry Holmes (USA) WBC
1979   John Tate (USA) WBA
1980   Mike Weaver (USA) WBA
1982   Mike Dokes (USA) WBA
1983   Gerry Coetzee (South Africa)
       WBA
1984   Larry Holmes (USA) IBF
1984   Tim Witherspoon (USA) WBC
1984   Pinklon Thomas (USA) WBC
1984   Greg Page (USA) WBA
1985   Michael Spinks (USA) IBF
1985   Tony Tubbs (USA) WBA
1986   Tim Witherspoon (USA) WBA
1986   Trevor Berbick (Canada) WBC

1986   Mike Tyson (USA) WBC
1986   James Smith (USA) WBA
1987   Tony Tucker (USA) IBF
1987   Mike Tyson (USA) WBA/WBC
1989   Francesco Damiani (Italy) WBO
1990   James 'Buster' Douglas (USA)
       WBA/WBC/IBF
1990   Evander Holyfield (USA)
       WBA/WBC/IBF
1991   Ray Mercer (USA) WBO
1992   Riddick Bowe (USA)
       WBA/WBC/IBF
1992   Michael Mourer (USA) WBO
1992   Lennox Lewis (Great Britain)
       WBC
1994   Oliver McCall (USA) WBC
1994   Herbie Hide (UK) WBO
1994   George Foreman (USA) IBF
1995   Frank Bruno (UK) WBC
1996   Mike Tyson (USA) WBC
1996   Henry Akinwande (UK) WBO
1996   Evander Holyfield (USA) WBA
1996   Michael Moorer (USA) IBF
1997   Lennox Lewis (UK) WBC
1997   Herbie Hide (UK) WBO
       Evander Holyfield (USA)
       WBA/IBF
IBF: International Boxing Federation
WBA: World Boxing Association
WBC: World Boxing Council
WBO: World Boxing Organization

Canoeing
Olympic Games
The most prestigious competition in the canoeing calendar, included at every Olympic celebration since 1936; the Blue Riband event in the men's competition is the Kayak Singles over 1000 m and in the women's the Kayak Singles over 500 m.

Single kayak (Men)
1936   Gregor Hradetzky (Austria)
1948   Gert Fredriksson (Sweden)
1952   Gert Fredriksson (Sweden)
1956   Gert Fredriksson (Sweden)
1960   Erik Hansen (Denmark)
1964   Rolf Peterson (Sweden)
1968   Mihaly Hesz (Hungary)
1972   Aleksandr Shaparenko (USSR)
1976   Rüdiger Helm (East Germany)
1980   Rüdiger Helm (East Germany)
1984   Alan Thompson (New Zealand)
1988   Greg Barton (USA)
1992   Clint Robinson (Australia)
1996   Oliver Fix (Germany)

Single kayak (Women)
1948   Keren Hoff (Denmark)
1952   Sylvi Saimo (Finland)
1956   Elisaveta Dementyeva (USSR)
1960   Antonina Seredina (USSR)
1964   Lyudmila Khvedosyuk (USSR)

1968	Lyudmila Pinayeva (USSR)
1972	Yulia Ryabchinskaya (USSR)
1976	Carola Zirzow (East Germany)
1980	Birgit Fischer (East Germany)
1984	Agneta Andersson (Sweden)
1988	Vania Gecheva (USSR)
1992	Birgit Schmidt (Germany)
1996	Stepanka Hilgertova (Czech Republic)

Most wins: Men (3), Gert Fredriksson. *Women* (2), Birgit Schmidt, as above.

Chess

World Champions

World Champions have been recognized since 1888; first women's champion recognized in 1927. A split between the World Chess Federation (FIDE) and the new Professional Chess Association (PCA) resulted in two championship matches in 1993.

Champions (Men)

1886–94	Wilhelm Steinitz (Austria)
1894–1921	Emanuel Lasker (Germany)
1921–7	José Capablanca (Cuba)
1927–35	Alexandre Alekhine (France)
1935–7	Max Euwe (Netherlands)
1937–46	Alexandre Alekhine (France)
1948–57	Mikhail Botvinnik (USSR)
1957–8	Vasiliy Smyslov (USSR)
1958–60	Mikhail Botvinnik (USSR)
1960–1	Mikhail Tal (USSR)
1961–3	Mikhail Botvinnik (USSR)
1963–9	Tigran Petrosian (USSR)

1969–72	Boris Spassky (USSR)
1972–5	Bobby Fischer (USA)
1975–85	Anatoly Karpov (USSR)
1985–	Gary Kasparov (USSR/Russia) *PCA*
1993–	Anatoly Karpov (Russia) *FIDE*

Longest reigning champion: Emanuel Lasker (Germany) 1894–1921.

Champions (Women)

1927–44	Vera Menchik-Stevenson (Great Britain)
1950–3	Lyudmila Rudenko (USSR)
1953–6	Elizaveta Bykova (USSR)
1956–8	Olga Rubtsova (USSR)
1958–62	Elizaveta Bykova (USSR)
1962–78	Nona Gaprindashvili (USSR)
1978–92	Maya Chiburdanidze (USSR)
1992–5	Xie Jun (China)
1996–	Zsuzsa Polgar (Hungary)

Longest reigning champion: 17 years, Vera Menchik-Stevenson.

Contract Bridge

World Pairs Championships

First held in 1962; since then, every four years.

Open Pairs Winners

1962	Pierre Jais/Roger Trézel (France)
1966	Cornelius Slavenburg/Hans Kreyns (Netherlands)
1970	Fritz Babsch/Peter Manhardt (Austria)

1974	Robert Hamman/Robert Wolff (USA)
1978	Marcello Branco/Gabino Cintra (Brazil)
1982	Chip Martel/Lew Stansby (USA)
1986	Jeff Meckstroth/Eric Rodwell (USA)
1990	Gabriel Chagas/Marcello Branco (Brazil)
1994	Marcin Lesniewski/Marcello Szymanowski (Poland)

Women's Pairs Winners

1962	Rixi Markus/Fritzi Gordon (Great Britain)
1966	Joan Durran/Jane Priday (Great Britain)
1970	Mary Jane Farrell/Marilyn Johnson (USA)
1974	Rixi Markus/Fritzi Gordon (Great Britain)
1978	Kathie Wei/Judi Radin (USA)
1982	Carol Sanders/Betty Ann Kennedy (USA)
1986	Jacqui Mitchell/Amalya Kearse (USA)
1990	Kerri Shuman/Karen McCallum (USA)
1994	Bep Vreind/Carla Arnolds (Netherlands)

Mixed Pairs Winners

1990	Peter Weichsel/Juanita Chambers (USA)
1994	Danuta Hocheker/Apolinaire Kowalski (Poland)

Cricket

All data correct at 1 Jan 1997

Test Cricket

Most test appearances

156	Allan Border (Australia)	1978–94
131	Kapil Dev (India)	1978–93
125	Sunil Gavaskar (India)	1971–87
124	Javed Miandad (Pakistan)	1976–93
121	Viv Richards (West Indies)	1974–91
118	Graham Gooch (England)	1975–94
117	David Gower (England)	1975–92
116	Desmond Haynes (West Indies)	1978–93
116	Dilip Vengsarkar (India)	1976–92
114	Colin Cowdrey (England)	1954–75
110	Clive Lloyd (West Indies)	1966–85
108	Geoffrey Boycott (England)	1964–82
108	Gordon Greenidge (West Indies)	1974–91
107	David Boon (Australia)	1984–93
102	Ian Botham (England)	1977–92
96	Rodney Marsh (Australia)	1970–84
95	Alan Knott (England)	1967–81
93	Garfield Sobers (West Indies)	1954–73
91	Godfrey Evans (England)	1964–59
91	Gundappa Viswanath (India)	1969–83
90	Bob Willis (England)	1971–84

88	Syed Kirmani (India)	1976–86
88	Imran Khan (Pakistan)	1971–92
87	Greg Chappell (Australia)	1970–84
86	Derek Underwood (England)	1977–82
86	Richard Hadlee (New Zealand)	1973–90

Most runs

runs	average	tests		
11174	50.56	156	Allan Border (Australia)	1978–94
10122	51.12	125	Sunil Gavaskar (India)	1971–87
8900	42.58	118	Graham Gooch (England)	1975–94
8832	52.57	124	Javed Miandad (Pakistan)	1976–93
8540	50.23	121	Viv Richards (West Indies)	1974–91
8231	44.25	117	David Gower (England)	1975–92
8114	47.72	108	Geoffrey Boycott (England)	1964–82
8032	57.78	93	Garfield Sobers (West Indies)	1954–73
7624	44.06	114	Colin Cowdrey (England)	1954–75
7558	44.72	108	Gordon Greenidge (West Indies)	1974–91
7515	46.67	110	Clive Lloyd (West Indies)	1966–85
7487	42.29	116	Desmond Haynes (West Indies)	1978–93
7422	43.65	107	David Boon (Australia)	1984–93
7249	58.45	85	Walter Hammond (England)	1927–47
7110	53.86	87	Greg Chappell (Australia)	1970–84
6996	99.94	52	Don Bradman (Australia)	1928–48
6971	56.67	79	Leonard Hutton (England)	1937–55
6868	42.13	116	Dilip Vengsarkar (India)	1976–92

runs	average	tests		
6806	58.67	82	Ken Barrington (England)	1955–68
6227	47.53	79	Rohan Kanhai (West Indies)	1957–74
6149	48.41	79	Neil Harvey (Australia)	1948–63
6080	41.93	91	Gundappa Viswanath (India)	1969–83
5949	44.39	86	Richard Richardson (West Indies)	1983–93
5807	50.67	78	Denis Compton (England)	1937–57
5502	45.85	72	Mark Taylor (Australia)	1988–95

Most centuries

34	Sunil Gavaskar (India)
29	Don Bradman (Australia)
27	Allan Border (Australia)
26	Garfield Sobers (West Indies)
24	Greg Chappell (Australia)
24	Viv Richards (West Indies)
23	Javed Miandad (Pakistan)
22	Walter Hammond (England)
22	Geoffrey Boycott (England)
22	Colin Cowdrey (England)
21	David Boon (Australia)
21	Neil Harvey (Australia)
20	Ken Barrington (England)
20	Graham Gooch (England)
19	Leonard Hutton (England)
19	Clive Lloyd (West Indies)
19	Gordon Greenidge (West Indies)

Highest individual innings

375	Brian Lara (West Indies) v England	1993–4
365*	Garfield Sobers (West Indies) v Pakistan	1957–8
364	Leonard Hutton (England) v Australia	1938
337	Hanif Mohammed (Pakistan) v West Indies	1957–8
336*	Walter Hammond (England) v New Zealand	1932–3
334	Don Bradman (Australia) v England	1930
333	Graham Gooch (England) v India	1990
325	Andrew Sandham (England) v West Indies	1929–30
311	Bobby Simpson (Australia) v England	1964
310*	John Edrich (England) v New Zealand	1965

(*not out)

Most wickets

wkts	av.	tests		
434	29.64	131	Kapil Dev (India)	1978–93
431	22.29	86	Richard Hadlee (New Zealand)	1973–90
383	28.40	102	Ian Botham (England)	1977–92
376	20.94	81	Malcolm Marshall (West Indies)	1978–91
362	22.81	88	Imran Khan (Pakistan)	1971–92
355	23.92	70	Dennis Lillee (Australia)	1971–84
325	25.20	90	Bob Willis (England)	1971–84
309	25.04	82	Courtney Walsh (West Indies)	1984–95
309	29.09	79	Lance Gibbs (West Indies)	1958–76
307	21.57	67	Fred Trueman (England)	1952–65
300	22.91	70	Wasim Akram (Pakistan)	1984–96
297	25.83	86	Derek Underwood (England)	1966–82
291	28.63	71	Craig McDermott (Australia)	1984–95
266	21.27	61	Curtly Ambrose (West Indies)	1988–95
266	28.71	67	Bishen Bedi (India)	1966–79
259	20.97	58	Joel Garner (West Indies)	1977–87
252	24.84	70	Brian Statham (England)	1951–65
249	23.68	60	Michael Holding (West Indies)	1975–87
248	27.03	63	Richie Benaud (Australia)	1952–64
246	29.78	60	Graham McKenzie (Australia)	1961–71
242	29.74	58	Bhagwant Chandrasekhar (India)	1964–79
236	24.89	51	Alec Bedser (England)	1946–55
236	32.80	67	Abdul Qadir (Pakistan)	1977–90

wkts	av.	tests		
235	34.03	93	Garfield Sobers (West Indies)	1954–74
228	23.03	61	Ray Lindwall (Australia)	1946–60

Most five wicket innings

36	Richard Hadlee (New Zealand)
27	Ian Botham (England)
24	Sydney Barnes (England)
23	Dennis Lillee (Australia)
23	Imran Khan (Pakistan)
23	Kapil Dev (India)
22	Malcolm Marshall (West Indies)
21	Clarence Grimmett (Australia)
20	Wasim Akram (Pakistan)
18	Lance Gibbs (West Indies)
17	Derek Underwood (England)
17	Fred Trueman (England)
16	Graham McKenzie (Australia)
16	Bhagwant Chandrasekhar (India)
16	Richie Benaud (Australia)
16	Bob Willis (England)

Most wicket-keeping dismissals

dis.	caught	stumped	tests		
355	343	12	96	Rodney Marsh (Australia)	1970–84
275	255	20	79	Ian Healy (Australia)	1988–95
272	267	5	81	Jeffrey Dujon (West Indies)	1981–91
269	250	19	95	Alan Knott (England)	1967–81
228	201	27	81	Wasim Bari (Pakistan)	1967–84
219	173	46	91	Godfrey Evans (England)	1946–59
198	160	38	88	Syed Kirmani (India)	1976–86
189	181	8	62	Deryck Murray (West Indies)	1963–80
187	163	24	51	Wally Grout (Australia)	1957–66
176	168	8	63	Ian Smith (New Zealand)	1980–92
174	167	7	57	Bob Taylor (England)	1971–84

One-day international cricket

One-day internationals have been played since 1971.

Most runs

runs	average	games	
8648	41.37	238	Desmond Haynes (West Indies)
7381	41.70	233	Javed Miandad (Pakistan)
6721	47.00	187	Viv Richards (West Indies)
6524	30.62	273	Allan Border (Australia)
6249	33.41	224	Richie Richardson (West Indies)
6091	36.47	225	Mohammad Azharuddin (India)
6068	44.61	164	Dean Jones (Australia)
6012	33.77	235	Salim Malik (Pakistan)
5964	37.04	181	David Boon (Australia)
5661	34.51	190	Pinnaduwage de Silva (Sri Lanka)
5386	33.24	177	Ramiz Raja (Pakistan)
5250	35.71	193	Arjuna Ranatunga (Sri Lanka)
5134	45.03	128	Gordon Greenidge (West Indies)
4704	38.55	143	Martin Crowe (New Zealand)
4420	32.02	200	Shane Waugh (Australia)
4389	39.54	127	Sachin Tendulkar (India)
4357	39.97	117	Geoff Marsh (Australia)
4332	46.08	104	Brian Lara (West Indies)
4290	36.98	125	Graham Gooch (England)
4092	29.02	146	Krishnamachari Srikkanth (India)

Most wickets

wkts	average	games	
297	22.58	206	Wasim Akram (Pakistan)
253	27.45	224	Kapil Dev (India)
220	22.69	133	Waqar Younis (Pakistan)
203	24.71	138	Craig McDermott (Australia)

wkts	average	games		
184	22.44	133	Curtly Ambrose (West Indies)	
182	30.13	162	Courtney Walsh (West Indies)	
182	26.62	175	Imran Khan (Pakistan)	
170	33.58	200	Stephen Waugh (Australia)	
158	21.56	115	Richard Hadlee (Australia)	
157	28.88	130	Manoj Prabhakar (India)	
157	26.96	136	Malcolm Marshall (West Indies)	
148	26.96	108	Javagal Srinath (India)	
146	18.84	98	Joel Garner (West Indies)	

Most wicket-keeping dismissals

dis.	caught	stumped	games	
213	181	32	150	Ian Healy (Australia)
204	183	21	169	Jeffrey Dujon (West Indies)
124	120	4	92	Rodney Marsh (West Indies)
121	108	13	82	David John Richardson (South Africa)
103	81	22	84	Rashid Latif (Pakistan)
103	81	22	86	Salim Yousuf (Pakistan)

English first-class cricket

First-class records date back to 1815. All players are British, unless otherwise stated

Most runs

runs	average		
61237	50.65	Jack Hobbs	1905–34
58959	40.77	Frank Woolley	1906–38
57611	50.80	Patsy Hendren	1907–38
55061	47.67	Philip Mead	1905–36
54896	39.55	W G Grace	1865–1908
50551	56.10	Walter Hammond	1920–51
50168	51.95	Herbert Sutcliffe	1919–45
48426	56.83	Geoffrey Boycott	1962–86
47793	44.91	Tom Graveney	1948–72
44472	49.57	Graham Gooch	1973–96
43551	41.79	Tom Hayward	1893–1914
43423	42.86	Dennis Amiss	1960–87
42719	42.89	Colin Cowdrey	1950–76
41284	44.82	Andrew Sandham	1911–38
40140	55.51	Len Hutton	1934–60
39832	41.84	Mike Smith	1951–75
39802	30.83	Wilfred Rhodes	1896–1930
39790	45.47	John Edrich	1956–78
39405	40.04	Bob Wyatt	1923–57
38942	51.85	Denis Compton	1936–64
38874	45.46	Ernest Tyldesley	1909–36
37897	40.66	Johnny Tyldesley	1895–1923

37665	37.77	Keith Fletcher	1962–88
37330	45.91	Gordon Greenidge (West Indies)	1971–91
37252	40.98	Jack Hearne	1909–36
37248	43.51	Leslie Ames	1926–51

Most wickets

wkts	average		
4187	16.71	Wilfred Rhodes	1898–1930
3776	18.42	Alfred Freeman	1914–36
3278	19.46	Charlie Parker	1903–35
3061	17.75	Jack Hearne	1888–1923
2979	19.84	Tom Goddard	1922–52
2876	17.92	W G Grace	1865–1908
2874	21.43	Alex Kennedy	1907–36
2857	18.65	Derek Shackleton	1948–69
2844	19.23	Tony Lock	1946–71
2830	22.37	Fred Titmus	1949–82
2784	18.16	Maurice Tate	1912–37
2739	18.72	George Hirst	1891–1929
2506	16.81	Colin Blythe	1899–1914
2465	20.28	Derek Underwood	1963–87
2431	23.76	Ewart Astill	1906–39
2356	18.57	Jack White	1909–37
2323	20.94	Eric Hollies	1932–57
2304	18.29	Fred Trueman	1949–69
2260	18.36	Brian Statham	1950–68
2233	24.07	Reg Perks	1930–55
2221	15.93	Johnny Briggs	1879–1900
2218	21.32	Don Shepherd	1950–72

Most wicket-keeping dismissals

dis.	caught	stumped		
1649	1473	176	Bob Taylor	1960–88
1527	1270	257	John Murray	1952–75
1497	1242	255	Herbert Strudwick	1902–27
1344	1211	133	Alan Knott	1965–85
1310	933	377	Frederick Huish	1895–1914
1294	1081	213	Brian Taylor	1949–73
1263	913	350	David Hunter	1889–1909
1228	953	275	Harry Butt	1890–1912
1207	852	355	Jack Board	1891–1915
1206	904	302	Harry Elliott	1920–47
1181	1088	93	Jim Parks	1949–76
1126	949	177	Roy Booth	1951–70
1121	703	418	Les Ames	1926–71
1099	961	138	David Bairstow	1970–90
1095	754	341	George Duckworth	1923–47

Cross Country Running

World Championships

First international championship held in 1903, but only included runners from England, Ireland, Scotland and Wales; recognized as an official world championship from 1973; first women's race in 1967.

Recent winners Individual (Men)

1986	John Ngugi (Kenya)
1987	John Ngugi (Kenya)
1988	John Ngugi (Kenya)
1989	John Ngugi (Kenya)
1990	Khalid Skah (Morocco)
1991	Khalid Skah (Morocco)
1992	John Ngugi (Kenya)
1993	William Sigei (Kenya)
1994	William Sigei (Kenya)
1995	Paul Tergat (Kenya)
1996	Paul Tergat (Kenya)
1997	Paul Tergat (Kenya)

Most wins: (5), John Ngugi (Kenya), as above.

Recent winners Individual (Women)

1986	Zola Budd (England)
1987	Annette Sergent (France)
1988	Ingrid Kristiansen (Norway)
1989	Annette Sergent (France)
1990	Lynn Jennings (USA)
1991	Lynn Jennings (USA)
1992	Lynn Jennings (USA)
1993	Alberta Dias (Portugal)
1994	Helen Chepngeno (Kenya)
1995	Derartu Tulu (Ethiopia)
1996	Gete Wami (Ethiopia)
1997	Derartu Tulu (Ethopia)

Most wins: (5), Doris Brown (USA), 1967–71; Greta Waitz (Norway), 1978–81, 1983.

Cycling

Tour de France

World's premier cycling event; first held in 1903.

Recent winners
1985	Bernard Hinault (France)
1986	Greg LeMond (USA)
1987	Stephen Roche (Ireland)
1988	Pedro Delgado (Spain)
1989	Greg LeMond (USA)
1990	Greg LeMond (USA)
1991	Miguel Indurain (Spain)
1992	Miguel Indurain (Spain)
1993	Miguel Indurain (Spain)
1994	Miguel Indurain (Spain)
1995	Miguel Indurain (Spain)
1996	Bjarne Riis (Denmark)
1997	Jan Ullrich (Germany)

Most wins: (5), Jacques Anquetil (France), 1957,1961–4; Eddy Merckx (Belgium), 1969–72,1974; Bernard Hinault (France), 1978–9, 1981–2, 1985; Miguel Indurain (Spain) as above.

World Road Race Championships

Men's race first held in 1927; first women's race in 1958; takes place annually.

Recent winners (Professional Men)
1984	Claude Criquielion (Belgium)
1985	Joop Zoetemelk (Netherlands)
1986	Moreno Argentin (Italy)
1987	Stephen Roche (Ireland)
1988	Maurizio Fondriest (Italy)
1989	Greg LeMond (USA)
1990	Rudy Dhaemens (Belgium)
1991	Gianni Bugno (Italy)
1992	Gianni Bugno (Italy)
1993	Lance Armstrong (USA)
1994	Luc Le Blanc (France)
1995	Abraham Olano (Spain)
1996	Johan Museeuw (Belgium)
1997	Laurent Brochard (France)

Recent winners (Women)
1985	Jeannie Longo (France)
1986	Jeannie Longo (France)
1987	Jeannie Longo (France)
1988	Jeannie Longo (France)
1989	Jeannie Longo (France)
1990	Catherine Marsal (France)
1991	Leontien van Moorsel (Netherlands)
1992	Leontien van Moorsel (Netherlands)
1993	Leontien van Moorsel (Netherlands)
1994	Monica Valvik (Norway)
1995	Jeannie Longo (France)
1996	Jeannie Longo (France)
1997	Alessandra Cappelloto (Italy)

Most wins: Men (3), Alfredo Binda (Italy), 1927, 1930, 1932; Rik Van Steenbergen (Belgium), 1949, 1956–7; Eddy Merckx (Belgium), 1967, 1971, 1974. *Women* (7), Jeannie Longo (France), as above.

Olympic Games

Cycling has been an Olympic event since the first games of 1896; women's events were added in 1984, 1988 and 1992.

1000 m Sprint (Men): recent winners
1984	Mark Gorski (USA)
1988	Lutz Hesslich (East Germany)
1992	Jens Fiedler (Germany)
1996	Jens Fiedler (Germany)

Most wins: (2) David Moreton (France), 1968, 1970; Lutz Hesslich (East Germany), 1980 and above; Jens Fiedler.

1000 m Time Trial (Men): recent winners
1984	Freddy Schmidtke (West Germany)	1:06.10
1988	Aleksandr Kirichenko (USSR)	1:04.499
1992	José Manuel Moreno (Spain)	1:03.342
1996	Florian Rousseau (France)	1:02.712

4000 m Individual Pursuit (Men): recent winners
1984	Steve Hegg (USA)
1988	Gintautas Umaras (USSR)
1992	Chris Boardman (Great Britain)
1996	Andrea Collinelli (Italy)

50 km Points Race (Men): recent winners
1984	Roger Ilegems (Belgium)
1988	Dan Frost (Denmark)
1992	Giovanni Lombardi (Italy)
1996	Silvio Martinello (Italy)

Individual Road Race (Men): recent winners
1984	Alexi Grewal (USA)
1988	Olaf Ludwig (East Germany)
1992	Fabio Casartelli (Italy)
1996	Pascal Richard (Switzerland)

1000 m Sprint (Women) Winners
1988	Erika Salumyae (USSR)
1992	Erika Salumyae (Estonia)
1996	Felicia Ballanger (France)

Most wins: (2) Erika Salumyae

3000 m Individual Pursuit (Women) Winners
1992	Petra Rossner (Germany)
1996	Antonella Bellutti (Italy)

Individual Road Race (Women) Winners
1984	Connie Carpenter Phinney (USA)
1988	Monique Knol (Netherlands)
1992	Kathryn Watt (Australia)
1996	Jeannie Longo (France)

Cyclo-Cross

World Championships

First held in 1950 as an open event; separate professional and amateur events since 1967; both events combined from 1994 to form the Open; since 1995 called the Elite.

Recent winners (Professional)
1982	Roland Liboton (Belgium)
1983	Roland Liboton (Belgium)
1984	Roland Liboton (Belgium)
1985	Klaus-Peter Thaler (West Germany)
1986	Albert Zweifel (Switzerland)
1987	Klaus-Peter Thaler (West Germany)
1988	Pascal Richard (Switzerland)
1989	Danny De Bie (Belgium)
1990	Henk Baars (Netherlands)
1991	Radomir Simunek (Czechoslovakia)
1992	Mike Kluge (Germany)
1993	Dominique Arnaud (France)

Recent winners (Amateur)
1982	Milos Fisera (Czechoslovakia)
1983	Radomir Simunek (Czechoslovakia)
1984	Radomir Simunek (Czechoslovakia)
1985	Mike Kluge (West Germany)
1986	Vito di Tano (Italy)
1987	Mike Kluge (West Germany)
1988	Karol Camrola (Czechoslovakia)
1989	Ondrej Glaja (Czechoslovakia)
1990	Andreas Buesser (Switzerland)
1991	Thomas Frischknecht (Switzerland)
1992	Daniele Pontoni (Italy)
1993	Henrik Djerni (Denmark)

Recent winners (Open/Elite)
1994	Paul Hrijes (Belgium)
1995	Dieter Runkel (Switzerland)
1996	Adri van de Pol (Netherlands)
1997	Daniele Pontoni (Italy)

Most wins: Professional (7), Eric de Vlaeminck (Belgium), 1966, 1968–73. *Amateur* (5), Robert Vermiere (Belgium), 1970–1, 1974–5, 1977.

Darts

World Professional Championship

First held at Nottingham in 1978.

Recent winners
1984	Eric Bristow (England)
1985	Eric Bristow (England)
1986	Eric Bristow (England)
1987	John Lowe (England)
1988	Bob Anderson (England)
1989	Jocky Wilson (Scotland)
1990	Phil Taylor (England)
1991	Dennis Priestley (England)
1992	Phil Taylor (England)
1993	John Lowe (England)
1994	John Part (Canada)
1995	Richie Burnett (Wales)
1996	Steve Beaton (England)
1997	Les Wallace (Scotland)

Most wins: (5), Eric Bristow, 1980–1 and as above.

World Cup

First held at Wembley in 1977; takes place every two years.

Winners (Individual)

1977	Leighton Rees (Wales)
1979	Nicky Virachkul (USA)
1981	John Lowe (England)
1983	Eric Bristow (England)
1985	Eric Bristow (England)
1987	Eric Bristow (England)
1989	Eric Bristow (England)
1991	John Lowe (England)
1993	Rowland Scholten (Netherlands)
1995	Martin Addams (England)
1997	Raymond Barneveld (Netherlands)

Most wins: (4), Eric Bristow (England), as above.

World Masters

First held in 1974.

Recent winners

1985	Dave Whitcombe (England)
1986	Bob Anderson (England)
1987	Bob Anderson (England)
1988	Bob Anderson (England)
1989	Peter Evison (England)
1990	Phil Taylor (England)
1991	Rod Harrington (England)
1992	Dennis Priestley (England)
1993	Steve Beaton (England)
1994	Ritchie Burnett (Wales)
1995	Erik Clarijs (Belgium)
1996	Colin Monk (England)
1997	Graham Hunt (Australia)

Most wins: (5) Eric Bristow (England), 1977, 1979, 1981, 1983–4.

British Open

First held in 1975.

Recent winners

1984	John Cusnett (England)
1985–6	Eric Bristow (England)
1987	Bob Anderson (England)
1988	John Lowe (England)
1989	Brian Cairns (Wales)
1990	Alan Warriner (England)
1991	Mike Gregory (England)
1992	Phil Gilmar (England)
1993	Martin Adams (England)
1994	Al Hedman (England)
1995	Roland Scholten (Netherlands)
1996	Kevin Painter (England)

Most wins: (5) Eric Bristow (England), 1978, 1981, 1983, and as above.

British Open (Women)

First held in 1979.

Recent winners

1984	Ann Marie-Davies (Wales)
1985	Linda Baten (England)
1986	Gwen Sutton (England)
1987	Sharon Colclough (England)
1988	Jane Stubbs (England)
1989	Cathie McCullough (Scotland)
1990	Sharon Colclough (England)
1991	Pauline Dyer (England)
1992	Sandra Greatbach (Wales)
1993	Sandra Greatbach (Wales)
1994	Frances Hoenseoaar (Netherlands)
1995	Pauleen Dyer (England)
1996	Frances Hoenseoaar (Netherlands)

Most wins: (2) Sharon Colclough (England); Sandra Greatbach (Wales); Frances Hoenseoaar (Netherlands).

Equestrian Events

World Championships

Show Jumping championships first held in 1953 (for men) and 1965 (for women); since 1978 they have competed together and on equal terms. Three Day Event and Dressage championships introduced in 1966; all three now held every four years.

Winners Show Jumping (men)

1953	Francisco Goyoago (Spain)
1954	Hans-Günter Winkler (West Germany)
1955	Hans-Günter Winkler (West Germany)
1956	Raimondo d'Inzeo (Italy)
1960	Raimondo d'Inzeo (Italy)
1966	Pierre Jonquères d'Oriola (France)
1970	David Broome (Great Britain)
1974	Hartwig Steenken (West Germany)

Winners Show Jumping (Women)

1965	Marion Coakes (Great Britain)
1970	Janou Lefèbvre (France)
1974	Janou Tissot (née Lefebvre) (France)

Winners (Individual)

1978	Gerd Wiltfang (West Germany)
1982	Norbert Koof (West Germany)
1986	Gail Greenough (Canada)
1990	Eric Navet (France)
1994	Frank Sloothaak (Germany)

Winners Three Day Event (Individual)

1966	Carlos Moratorio (Argentina)
1970	Mary Gordon-Watson (Great Britain)
1974	Bruce Davidson (USA)
1978	Bruce Davidson (USA)
1982	Lucinda Green (Great Britain)
1986	Virginia Leng (Great Britain)
1990	Blyth Tait (New Zealand)
1994	Vaughn Jefferis (New Zealand)

Winners Dressage (Individual)

1970	Yelene Petouchkova (USSR)
1974	Reiner Klimke (West Germany)
1978	Christine Stückelberger (Switzerland)
1982	Reiner Klimke (West Germany)
1986	Anne Grethe Jensen (Denmark)
1990	Nicole Uphoft (West Germany)
1994	Isabell Werth (Germany)

Olympic Games

Show Jumping, Three-Day Eventing and Dressage all officially introduced as Olympic Events in 1912.

SHOW JUMPING

Winners (Individual)

1912	Jean Cariou (France)
1920	Tommaso Lequio (Italy)
1924	Alphonse Gemuseus (Switzerland)
1928	Frantisek Ventura (Czechoslovakia)
1932	Takeichi Nishi (Japan)
1936	Kürt Hasse (Germany)
1948	Humberto Mariles Cortés (Mexico)
1952	Pierre Jonquères d'Oriola (France)
1956	Hans Günter Winkler (Germany)
1960	Riamondo d'Inzeo (Italy)
1964	Pierre Jonquères d'Oriola (France)
1968	William Steinkraus (USA)
1972	Graziano Mancinelli (Italy)
1976	Alwin Schockemöhle (West Germany)
1980	Jan Kowalczyk (Poland)
1984	Joe Fargis (USA)
1988	Pierre Durand (France)
1992	Ludger Beerbaum (Germany)
1996	Ulrich Kirchhoff (Germany)

Most wins: (2) Pierre Jonquères d'Oriola (France).

THREE-DAY EVENT

Winners (Individual)

1912	Axel Nordlander (Sweden)
1920	Helmer Mörner (Sweden)
1924	Adolph van der Voort van Zip (Netherlands)
1928	Charles Pahud de Mortanges (Netherlands)
1932	Charles Pahud de Mortanges (Netherlands)
1936	Ludwig Stubbendorff (Germany)
1948	Bernard Chevallier (France)
1952	Hans von Blixen-Finecke Jr (Sweden)
1956	Petrus Kastenman (Sweden)
1960	Lawrence Morgan (USA)
1964	Mauro Checcoli (Italy)
1968	Jean-Jaques Gùyon (France)
1972	Richard Meade (Great Britain)
1976	Edmund Coffin (USA)
1980	Federico Roman (Italy)
1984	Mark Todd (New Zealand)
1988	Mark Todd (New Zealand)
1992	Matthew Ryan (Australia)
1996	Blyth Tait (New Zealand)

Most wins: (2), Charles Pahud de Mortanges (Netherlands); Mark Todd (New Zealand).

DRESSAGE

Winners (Individual)
1912 Carl Bonde (Sweden)
1920 Janne Lundblad (Sweden)
1924 Ernst Linder (Sweden)
1928 Carl von Langen (Germany)
1932 Xavier Lesage (France)
1936 Heinz Pollay (Germany)
1948 Hans Moser (Switzerland)
1952 Henri St Cyr (Sweden)
1956 Henri St Cyr (Sweden)
1960 Sergey Filatov (USSR)
1964 Henri Chammartin (Switzerland)
1968 Ivan Kizimov (USSR)
1972 Liselott Linsenhoff (West Germany)
1976 Christine Stückelberger (Switzerland)
1980 Elisabeth Theurer (Austria)
1984 Reiner Klimke (West Germany)
1988 Nicole Uphoff (West Germany)
1992 Nicole Uphoff (West Germany)
1996 Isabell Werth (Germany)
Most wins: (2) Henri St Cyr (Sweden); Nicole Uphoff (West Germany).

Fencing

World Championships
Held annually since 1921 (between 1921–35, known as European Championships); not held in Olympic years.

Foil individual (Men): recent winners
1979 Alexander Romankov (USSR)
1981 Vladimir Smirnov (USSR)
1982 Alexander Romankov (USSR)
1983 Alexander Romankov (USSR)
1985 Mauro Numa (Italy)
1986 Andrea Borella (Italy)
1987 Mathias Gey (West Germany)
1989 Alexander Koch (West Germany)
1990 Philippe Omnès (France)
1991 Ingo Weissenborn (Germany)
1993 Alexander Koch (Germany)
1994 Rolando Tucker (Cuba)
1995 Dimitriy Chevtchenko (Russia)
1997 Sergey Golubitsky (Ukraine)
Most wins: (5), Alexander Romankov, 1974, 1977 and as above.

Foil individual (Women): recent winners
1975 Ecaterina Stahl (Romania)
1977 Valentina Sidorova (USSR)
1978 Valentina Sidorova (USSR)
1979 Cornelia Hanisch (West Germany)
1981 Cornelia Hanisch (West Germany)
1982 Naila Giliazova (USSR)
1983 Dorina Vaccaroni (Italy)
1985 Cornelia Hanisch (West Germany)
1986 Anja Fichtel (West Germany)
1987 Elisabeta Tufan (Romania)

1989 Olga Velitchko (USSR)
1990 Anja Fichtel (West Germany)
1991 Giovanna Trillini (Italy)
1993 Francesca Bortolozzi (Italy)
1994 Reka Szabo-Lazar (Romania)
1995 Laura Badea (Romania)
1997 Giovanna Trillini (Italy)
Most wins: (3), Heléne Mayer (Germany), 1929, 1931, 1937; Ilona Elek (Hungary), 1935, 1951; Ellen Müller-Preiss (Austria), 1947, 1949, 1950 (shared); Cornelia Hanisch, as above.

Epée individual (Men): recent winners
1975 Alexander Pusch (West Germany)
1977 Johan Harmenberg (Sweden)
1978 Alexander Pusch (West Germany)
1979 Philippe Riboud (France)
1981 Zoltan Szekely (Hungary)
1982 Jenö Pap (Hungary)
1983 Ellmar Bormann (West Germany)
1985 Philippe Boisse (France)
1986 Philippe Riboud (France)
1987 Volker Fischer (West Germany)
1989 Manuel Pereira (Spain)
1990 Thomas Gerull (West Germany)
1991 Andrey Shuvalov (USSR)
1993 Ivan Kolobkov (Russia)
1994 Pavel Kolobkov (Russia)
1995 Eric Srecki (France)
1997 Eric Srecki (France)
Most wins: (3), Georges Buchard (France), 1927, 1931, 1933; Alexei Nikanchikov (USSR), 1966–7, 1970.

Epée individual (Women): recent winners
1989 Anja Straub (Switzerland)
1990 Taime Chappe (Cuba)
1991 Marianne Horvath (Hungary)
1993 Oksana Ermakova (Estonia)
1994 Laura Chiesa (Italy)
1995 Joanna Jakimiuk (Poland)
1997 Miriade Garcia-Soto (Cuba)

Sabre individual (Men): recent winners
1975 Vladimir Nazlimov (USSR)
1977 Pal Gerevich (Hungary)
1978 Viktor Krovopuskov (USSR)
1979 Vladimir Nazlimov (USSR)
1981 Mariusz Wodke (Poland)
1982 Viktor Krovopuskov (USSR)
1983 Vasiliy Etropolski (Bulgaria)
1985 György Nébald (Hungary)
1986 Sergey Mindirgassov (USSR)
1987 Jean-François Lamour (France)
1989 Grigoriy Kirienko (USSR)
1990 György Nébald (Hungary)
1991 Grigoriy Kirienko (USSR)
1993 Grigoriy Kirienko (Russia)
1994 Felix Becker (Germany)
1995 Grigoriy Kirienko (Russia)
1997 Stanislav Pozdnyakov (Russia)
Most wins: (4), Grigoriy Kirienko, as above.

Olympic Games
Fencing has been an Olympic event at all Games since the first of 1896; women's fencing (foil) first included in 1924; women's epée first included in 1996.

Foil individual (Men): recent winners
1972 Witold Woyda (Poland)
1976 Fabio dal Zotto (Italy)
1980 Vladimir Smirnov (USSR)
1984 Mauro Numa (Italy)
1988 Stefano Cerioni (Italy)
1992 Philippe Omnès (France)
1996 Allesandro Puccini (Italy)
Most wins: (2), Nedo Nadi (Italy) 1912, 1920; Christian d'Oriola (France) 1952, 1956.

Foil individual (Women): recent winners
1972 Antonella Ragno-Lonzi (Italy)
1976 Idikó Schwarczenberger (Hungary)
1980 Pascale Trinquet (France)
1984 Luan Jujie (China)
1988 Anja Fichtel (West Germany)
1992 Giovanna Trillini (Italy)
1996 Laura Badea (Romania)
Most wins: (2) Ilona Elek (Hungary) 1936, 1948.

Epée individual (Men): recent winners
1972 Csaba Fenyvesi (Hungary)
1976 Alexander Pusch (West Germany)
1980 Johan Harmernberg (Sweden)
1984 Philippe Boisse (France)
1988 Arnd Schmitt (West Germany)
1992 Eric Srecki (France)
1996 Alexander Beketov (Russia)
Most wins: (2) Ramón Forst (Cuba), 1900, 1904.

Epée individual (Women)
1996 Laura Flessel (Germany)

Sabre individual (Men): recent winners
1972 Viktor Sidiak (USSR)
1976 Viktor Krovopuskov (USSR)
1980 Viktor Krovopuskov (USSR)
1984 Jean François Lamour (France)
1988 Jean François Lamour (France)
1992 Bence Szabó (Hungary)
1996 Stanislav Pozdnyakov (Russia)
Most wins: (2) Jean Georgiadis (Greece) 1896, 1906; Jenö Fuchs (Hungary) 1908, 1912; Rudolf Kárpáti (Hungary) 1956, 1960, Viktor Krocopuskov (USSR) as above; Jean François Lamour (France) as above.

Gliding

World Championships
First held in 1937; current classes are Open, Standard and 15 metres; the Open class is the principal event, held every two years until 1978 and again since 1981.

Recent winners
1968 Harro Wödl (Austria)
1970 George Moffat (USA)
1972 Göran Ax (Sweden)
1974 George Moffat (USA)
1976 George Lee (Great Britain)
1978 George Lee (Great Britain)

1981 George Lee (Great Britain)
1983 Ingo Renner (Australia)
1985 Ingo Renner (Australia)
1987 Ingo Renner (Australia)
1989 Claude Lopitaux (France)
1991 Janusz Centka (Poland)
1993 Andy Davis (Great Britain)

1995 Raymond Lynskey (New Zealand)
1997 Gerard Lherm (France)
Most wins: (3), George Lee (Great Britain), as above; Ingo Renner (Australia), as above.

Football (American)

Superbowl Most Valuable Player (MVP)

The player judged to have made the most outstanding contribution in the Superbowl – the end of season meeting between the champions of the American Football Conference (AFC) and the National Football Conference (NFC).

		position	team
1967	Bart Starr	Quarter Back	Green Bay Packers
1968	Bart Starr	Quarter Back	Green Bay Packers
1969	Joe Namath	Quarter Back	New York Jets
1970	Len Dawson	Quarter Back	Kansas City Chiefs
1971	Chuck Howley	Line Backer	Dallas Cowboys
1972	Roger Staubach	Quarter Back	Dallas Cowboys
1973	Jake Scott	Safety	Miami Dolphins
1974	Larry Csonka	Running Back	Miami Dolphins
1975	Franco Harris	Running Back	Pittsburgh Steelers
1976	Lynn Swann	Wide Receiver	Pittsburgh Steelers
1977	Fred Biletnikoff	Wide Receiver	Oakland Raiders
1978	Randy White	Defensive Tackle	Dallas Cowboys
	Harvey Martin	Defensive End	Dallas Cowboys
1979	Terry Bradshaw	Quarter Back	Pittsburgh Steelers
1980	Terry Bradshaw	Quarter Back	Pittsburgh Steelers
1981	Jim Plunkett	Quarter Back	Oakland Raiders
1982	Joe Montana	Quarter Back	San Francisco 49ers
1983	Joe Riggins	Running Back	Washington Redskins
1984	Marcus Allen	Running Back	Los Angeles Raiders
1985	Joe Montana	Quarter Back	San Francisco 49ers
1986	Richard Dent	Defensive End	Chicago Bears
1987	Phil Simms	Quarter Back	New York Giants
1988	Doug Williams	Quarter Back	Washington Redskins
1989	Jerry Rice	Wide Receiver	San Francisco 49ers
1990	Joe Montana	Quarter Back	San Francisco 49ers
1991	Ottis Anderson	Running Back	New York Giants
1992	Mark Rypien	Quarter Back	Washington Redskins
1993	Troy Aikman	Quarter Back	Dallas Cowboys
1994	Steve Young	Quarter Back	San Francisco 49ers
1995	Larry Brown	Corner Back	Dallas Cowboys
1996	Desmond Howard	Wide Receiver	Green Bay Packers

Most wins: (3) Joe Montana, as above.

Football (Association Football/ Soccer)

Most international caps

The 'Century Club' lists players who have had over 100 international 'A' match appearances. Source: Adapted from FIFA News, July 1997.

Men
147 Majed Abdullah (Saudi Arabia)
138 Thomas Ravelli (Sweden)*
125 Peter Shilton (England)
122 Lothar Matthäus (Germany)*
119 Pat Jennings (Northern Ireland)
118 Andoni Zubizarreta (Spain)*
117 Heinz Hermann (Switzerland
115 Björn Nordqvist (Sweden)
114 Marcelo Balboa (USA)*
112 Dino Zoff (Italy)
111 Alain Geiger (Switzerland)
109 Wail Sulaiman al-Habashi (Kuwait)*
109 Oleg Blokhin (USSR)
109 Paul Caligiuri (USA)*
108 Ladislau Böloni (Romania)
108 Bobby Moore (England)
106 Bobby Charlton (England)
106 Héctor Chumpitaz (Peru
105 Gheorghe Hagi (Romania)*

105 Billy Wright (England)
104 Grzegorz Lato (Poland)
104 Torbjörn Svensson (Norway)
103 Franz Beckenbauer (Germany)
102 Soon-ho Choi (Korea Republic)
102 Kenny Dalglish (England)
102 Kazimierz Deyna (Poland)
102 Morten Olsen (Denmark)
102 Joachim Streich (Germany)
101 Masami Ihara (Japan)
100 Joszef Bozsik (Hungary)
100 Hans Jürgen Dörner (Germany)
100 Djalma Santos (Brazil)

Women
Women's European championship matches not included.
148 Heidi Stoere (Norway)*
146 Pia Sundhage (Sweden)
145 Carolina Morace (Italy)*
133 Kristine Lilly (USA)*
130 Mia Hamm (USA)*
120 Linda Medalen (Norway)*
117 Carin Gabarra (USA)*
112 Elizabeth Leidinge (Sweden)*
111 Silvia Neid (Germany)
111 Lena Videkull (Sweden)
110 Gunn Nyborg (Norway)
110 Elisabetta Vignotto (Italy)
109 Michelle Akers (USA)*

108 Julia Foudy (USA)*
104 Heidi Mohr (Germany)
101 Joy Fawcett (USA)*
100 Carla Overbeck (USA)*
100 Martina Voss (Germany)*
*denotes still active

Most British international caps
125 Peter Shilton (England) 1970–90
119 Pat Jennings (Northern Ireland) 1964–86
108 Bobby Moore (England) 1962–73
106 Bobby Charlton (England) 1958–70
105 Billy Wright (England) 1946–59
102 Kenny Dalglish (Scotland) 1971–86

Most international goals
97 Pele (Brazil) 1957–71

Most British international goals
49 Bobby Charlton (England)
48 Gary Lineker (England)
44 Jimmy Greaves (England)
30 Tom Finney (England)
     Nat Lofthouse (England)
     Denis Law (Scotland)
     Kenny Dalglish (Scotland)
29 Vivian Woodward (England)
27 David Platt (England)
26 Steve Bloomer (England)

Most club goals

Season: 127 Pele (Santos; Brazil) 1959
*Career:*1329 Artur Friedenreich
(Germania, CA Ipiranga,
Americano, CA Paulistano,
São Paulo, Flamengo;
Brazil) 1909–35

Most English League club goals

Season: 60   Dixie Dean (Everton)
1927–28
Career: 434   Arthur Rowley (West
Bromwich Albion,
Fulham, Leicester City,
Shrewsbury Town)
1946–65

Most Scottish League club goals

Season: 60   Jim Smith (Ayr United)
1927–8
Career: 410   Jimmy McGrory (Celtic,
Clydebank) 1922–38

European Footballer of the Year

Awarded to the European club player
who receives most nominations from a
panel of football journalists selected
from the UEFA countries. Inaugurated
in 1956.

Winners

1956   Stanley Matthews
(England, Blackpool)
1957   Alfredo di Stéfano
(Spain, Real Madrid)
1958   Raymond Kopa
(France, Real Madrid)
1959   Alfredo di Stéfano
(Spain, Real Madrid)
1960   Luis Suárez (Spain, Barcelona)
1961   Omar Sivori (Italy, Juventus)
1962   Josef Masopust
(Czechoslovakia, Dukla Praha)
1963   Lev Yashin
(USSR, Dynamo Moscow)
1964   Denis Law
(Scotland, Manchester United)
1965   Eusébio (Portugal, Benfica)
1966   Bobby Charlton
(England, Manchester United)
1967   Florian Albert
(Hungary, Ferencvaros)
1968   George Best (Northern Ireland,
Manchester United)
1969   Gianni Rivera (Italy, AC Milan)
1970   Gerd Müller (West Germany,
Bayern München)
1971   Johan Cruyff (Netherlands, Ajax)
1972   Franz Beckenbauer (West
Germany, Bayern München)
1973   Johan Cruyff
(Netherlands, Barcelona)
1974   Johan Cruyff
(Netherlands, Barcelona)
1975   Oleg Blokhin
(USSR, Dynamo Kiev)

1976   Franz Beckenbauer (West
Germany, Bayern München)
1977   Allan Simonsen (Denmark,
Borussia Mönchengladbach)
1978   Kevin Keegan
(England, Hamburger SV)
1979   Kevin Keegan
(England, Hamburger SV)
1980   Karl-Heinz Rummenigge (West
Germany, Bayern München)
1981   Karl-Heinz Rummenigge (West
Germany, Bayern München)
1982   Paolo Rossi (Italy, Juventus)
1983   Michel Platini (France, Juventus)
1984   Michel Platini (France, Juventus)
1985   Michel Platini (France, Juventus)
1986   Igor Belanov
(USSR, Dynamo Kiev)
1987   Ruud Gullit
(Netherlands, AC Milan)
1988   Marco Van Basten
(Netherlands, AC Milan)
1989   Marco Van Basten
(Netherlands, AC Milan)
1990   Lothar Matthäus (West
Germany, Internazionale)
1991   Jean-Pierre Papin
(France, Marseille)
1992   Marco Van Basten
(Netherlands, AC Milan)
1993   Roberto Baggio (Yuventas)
1994   Hristo Stoichkov (Bulgaria,
Barcelona)
1995   George Weah (Liberia, AC Milan)
1996   Matthias Sammer (Germany,
Borussia Dortmund)
Most wins: (3), Johan Cruyff; Michel
Platini; Marco Van Basten, as above.

Golden Boot Award

Presented each year by Adidas to the
European club player who scored most
goals in the domestic season. First
awarded in 1968.

Winners

		goals scored
1968	Eusebio (Benfica)	43
1969	Peter Jekov (CSKA Sofia)	36
1970	Gerd Müller (Bayern München)	38
1971	Josip Skoblar (Marseille)	44
1972	Gerd Müller (Bayern München)	40
1973	Eusebio (Benfica)	40
1974	Hector Yazalde (Sporting Lisbon)	46
1975	Dudu Georgescu (Dinamo Bucuresti)	33
1976	Sotiris Kaiafas (Omonia Nicosia)	39
1977	Dudu Georgescu (Dinamo Bucuresti)	47
1978	Hans Krankl (Rapid Vienna)	41
1979	Kees Kist (AZ 67 Alkmaar)	34
1980	Erwin van den Bergh (Lierse)	39

1981	Georgi Slavkov (Trakia)	31
1982	Wim Kieft (Ajax)	32
1983	Fernando Gomes (FC Porto)	36
1984	Ian Rush (Liverpool)	32
1985	Fernando Gomes (FC Porto)	39
1986	Marco Van Basten (Ajax)	37
1987	Rodion Camataru (Dinamo Bucuresti)	44
1988	Tanjin Colak (Galatasaray)	39
1989	Dorin Mateut (Dinamo Bucuresti)	43
1990	Hugo Sánchez (Real Madrid);	38
	Khristo Stoichkov (CSKA Sofia)	38
1991	Darko Pancev (Crvena Zvezda Beograd)	35
1992	Ally McCoist (Glasgow Rangers)	34
1993	Event discontinued	

Most wins: (2), Eusebio; Gerd Müller;
Dudu Georgescu; Fernando Gomes, as
above.

Football Writers' Player of the Year

First awarded after the completion of
the 1947–8 English League Season.

Winners

1948   Stanley Matthews (Blackpool)
1949   Johnny Carey
(Manchester United)
1950   Joe Mercer (Arsenal)
1951   Harry Johnston (Blackpool)
1952   Billy Wright
(Wolverhampton Wanderers)
1953   Nat Lofthouse
(Bolton Wanderers)
1954   Tom Finney (Preston North End)
1955   Don Revie (Manchester City)
1956   Bert Trautmann
(Manchester City)
1957   Tom Finney (Preston North End)
1958   Danny Blanchflower
(Tottenham Hotspur)
1959   Syd Owen (Luton Town)
1960   Bill Slater
(Wolverhampton Wanderers)
1961   Danny Blanchflower
(Tottenham Hotspur)
1962   Jimmy Adamson (Burnley)
1963   Stanley Matthews (Stoke City)
1964   Bobby Moore (West Ham United)
1965   Bobby Collins (Leeds United)
1966   Bobby Charlton
(Manchester United)
1967   Jackie Charlton (Leeds United)
1968   George Best (Manchester United)
1969   Tony Book (Manchester City);
Dave Mackay (Derby County)
1970   Billy Bremner (Leeds United)
1971   Frank McLintock (Arsenal)
1972   Gordon Banks (Stoke City)
1973   Pat Jennings
(Tottenham Hotspur)
1974   Ian Callaghan (Liverpool)
1975   Alan Mullery (Fulham)

1976	Kevin Keegan (Liverpool)	
1977	Emlyn Hughes (Liverpool)	
1978	Kenny Burns (Nottingham Forest)	
1979	Kenny Dalglish (Liverpool)	
1980	Terry McDermott (Liverpool)	
1981	Frans Thijssen (Ipswich Town)	
1982	Steve Perryman (Tottenham Hotspur)	
1983	Kenny Dalglish (Liverpool)	
1984	Ian Rush (Liverpool)	
1985	Neville Southall (Everton)	
1986	Gary Lineker (Everton)	
1987	Clive Allen (Tottenham Hotspur)	
1988	John Barnes (Liverpool)	
1989	Steve Nichol (Liverpool)	
1990	John Barnes (Liverpool)	
1991	Gordon Strachan (Leeds United)	
1992	Gary Lineker (Tottenham Hotspur)	
1993	Chris Waddle (Sheffield Wednesday)	
1994	Alan Shearer (Blackburn Rovers)	
1995	Jürgen Klinsman (Tottenham Hotspur)	
1996	Eric Cantona (Manchester United)	
1997	Gianfranco Zola (Chelsea)	

Most wins: (2), Tom Finney; Danny Blanchflower; Stanley Matthews; Kenny Dalglish; John Barnes; Gary Lineker, as above.

Professional Footballers' Association (PFA) Player of the Year and Young Player of the Year
Two awards for which the professional players themselves vote. Both inaugurated in 1974.

Player of the Year: winners
1974	Norman Hunter (Leeds United)
1975	Colin Todd (Derby County)
1976	Pat Jennings (Tottenham Hotspur)
1977	Andy Gray (Aston Villa)
1978	Peter Shilton (Nottingham Forest)
1979	Liam Brady (Arsenal)
1980	Terry McDermott (Liverpool)
1981	John Wark (Ipswich Town)
1982	Kevin Keegan (Southampton)
1983	Kenny Dalglish (Liverpool)
1984	Ian Rush (Liverpool)
1985	Peter Reid (Everton)
1986	Gary Lineker (Everton)
1987	Clive Allen (Tottenham Hotspur)
1988	John Barnes (Liverpool)
1989	Mark Hughes (Manchester United)
1990	David Platt (Aston Villa)
1991	Mark Hughes (Manchester United)
1992	Gary Pallister (Manchester United)
1993	Paul McGrath (Aston Villa)
1994	Eric Cantona (Manchester United)

1995	Alan Shearer (Blackburn Rovers)
1996	Les Ferdinand (Newcastle United)
1997	Alan Shearer (Newcastle United)

Most wins: (2), Mark Hughes; Alan Shearer, as above.

Young Player of the Year: winners
1974	Kevin Beattie (Ipswich Town)
1975	Mervyn Day (West Ham United)
1976	Peter Barnes (Manchester City)
1977	Andy Gray (Aston Villa)
1978	Tony Woodcock (Nottingham Forest)
1979	Cyrille Regis (West Bromwich Albion)
1980	Glenn Hoddle (Tottenham Hotspur)
1981	Gary Shaw (Aston Villa)
1982	Steve Moran (Southampton)
1983	Ian Rush (Liverpool)
1984	Paul Walsh (Luton Town)
1985	Mark Hughes (Manchester United)
1986	Tony Cottee (West Ham United)
1987	Tony Adams (Arsenal)
1988	Paul Gascoigne (Newcastle United)
1989	Paul Merson (Arsenal)
1990	Matthew Le Tissier (Southampton)
1991	Lee Sharpe (Manchester United)
1992	Ryan Giggs (Manchester United)
1992	Ryan Giggs (Manchester United)
1993	Ryan Giggs (Manchester United)
1994	Andy Cole (Manchester United)
1995	Robbie Fowler (Liverpool)
1996	Robbie Fowler (Liverpool)
1997	David Beckham (Manchester United)

Golf

Open
First held at Prestwick in 1860; takes place annually; regarded as the world's leading golf tournament.

Winners (British unless stated)
1860	Willie Park, Snr
1981	Tom Morris, Snr
1982	Tom Morris, Snr
1863	Willie Park, Snr
1864	Tom Morris, Snr
1865	Andrew Strath
1866	Willie Park, Snr
1867	Tom Morris, Snr
1868	Tom Morris, Jr
1869	Tom Morris, Jr
1870	Tom Morris, Jr
1872	Tom Morris, Jr
1873	Tom Kidd
1874	Mungo Park
1875	Willie Park, Snr
1876	Bob Martin
1877	Jamie Anderson

1878	Jamie Anderson
1879	Jamie Anderson
1880	Robert Ferguson
1881	Robert Ferguson
1882	Robert Ferguson
1883	Willie Fernie
1884	Jack Simpson
1885	Bob Martin
1886	David Brown
1887	Willie Park, Jr
1888	Jack Burns
1889	Willie Park, Jr
1890	John Ball
1891	Hugh Kirkaldy
1892	Harold H Hilton
1893	William Auchterlonie
1894	John H Taylor
1895	John H Taylor
1896	Harry Vardon
1897	Harold H Hilton
1898	Harry Vardon
1899	Harry Vardon
1900	John H Taylor
1901	James Braid
1902	Sandy Herd
1903	Harry Vardon
1904	Jack White
1905	James Braid
1906	James Braid
1907	Arnaud Massy (France)
1908	James Braid
1909	John H Taylor
1910	James Braid
1911	Harry Vardon
1912	Edward Ray
1913	John H Taylor
1914	Harry Vardon
1920	George Duncan
1921	Jock Hutchinson (USA)
1922	Walter Hagen (USA)
1923	Arthur Havers
1924	Walter Hagen (USA)
1925	Jim Barnes (USA)
1926	Bobby Jones (USA)
1927	Bobby Jones (USA)
1928	Walter Hagen (USA)
1929	Walter Hagen (USA)
1930	Bobby Jones (USA)
1931	Tommy Armour (USA)
1932	Gene Sarazen (USA)
1933	Densmore Shute (USA)
1934	Henry Cotton
1935	Alfred Perry
1936	Alfred Padgham
1937	Henry Cotton
1938	Reg Whitcombe
1939	Dick Burton
1946	Sam Snead (USA)
1947	Fred Daly
1948	Henry Cotton
1949	Bobby Locke (South Africa)
1950	Bobby Locke (South Africa)
1951	Max Faulkner
1952	Bobby Locke (South Africa)
1953	Ben Hogan (USA)

1954	Peter Thomson (Australia)
1955	Peter Thomson (Australia)
1956	Peter Thomson (Australia)
1957	Bobby Locke (South Africa)
1958	Peter Thomson (Australia)
1959	Gary Player (South Africa)
1960	Kelvin Nagle (Australia)
1961	Arnold Palmer (USA)
1962	Arnold Palmer (USA)
1963	Bob Charles (New Zealand)
1964	Tony Lema (USA)
1965	Peter Thomson (Australia)
1966	Jack Nicklaus (USA)
1967	Roberto de Vicenzo (Argentina)
1968	Gary Player (South Africa)
1969	Tony Jacklin
1970	Jack Nicklaus (USA)
1971	Lee Trevino (USA)
1972	Lee Trevino (USA)
1973	Tom Weiskopf (USA)
1974	Gary Player (South Africa)
1975	Tom Watson (USA)
1976	Johnny Miller (USA)
1977	Tom Watson (USA)
1978	Jack Nicklaus (USA)
1979	Severiano Ballesteros (Spain)
1980	Tom Watson (USA)
1981	Bill Rogers (USA)
1982	Tom Watson (USA)
1983	Tom Watson (USA)
1984	Severiano Ballesteros (Spain)
1985	Sandy Lyle
1986	Greg Norman (Australia)
1987	Nick Faldo
1988	Severiano Ballesteros (Spain)
1989	Mark Calcavecchia (USA)
1990	Nick Faldo
1991	Ian Baker-Finch (Australia)
1992	Nick Faldo
1993	Greg Norman (Australia)
1994	Nick Price (Zimbabwe)
1995	John Daley (USA)
1996	Tom Lehman (USA)
1997	Justin Leonard (USA)

Most wins: (6), Harry Vardon (Great Britain).

United States Open

First held at Newport, RI in 1895; takes place annually.

Winners (USA unless stated)

1895	Horace Rawlins
1896	James Foulis
1897	Joe Lloyd
1898	Willie Smith
1900	Harry Vardon (Great Britain)
1901	Willie Anderson
1902	Laurie Auchterlonie
1903	Willie Anderson
1904	Willie Anderson
1905	Willie Anderson
1906	Alex Smith
1907	Alex Ross
1908	Fred McLeod
1909	George Sargent

1910	Alex Smith
1911	John McDermott
1912	John McDermott
1913	Francis Ouimet
1914	Walter Hagen
1915	Jerome Travers
1916	Charles Evans, Jnr
1919	Walter Hagen
1920	Edward Ray (Great Britain)
1921	Jim Barnes
1922	Gene Sarazen
1923	Bobby Jones
1924	Cyril Walker
1925	Willie Macfarlane
1926	Bobby Jones
1927	Tommy Armour
1928	Johnny Farrell
1929	Bobby Jones
1930	Bobby Jones
1931	Billy Burke
1932	Gene Sarazen
1933	Johnny Goodman
1934	Olin Dutra
1935	Sam Parks, Jnr
1936	Tony Manero
1937	Ralph Guldahl
1938	Ralph Guldahl
1939	Byron Nelson
1940	Lawson Little
1941	Craig Wood
1946	Lloyd Mangrum
1947	Lew Worsham
1948	Ben Hogan
1949	Cary Middlecoff
1950	Ben Hogan
1951	Ben Hogan
1952	Julius Boros
1953	Ben Hogan
1954	Ed Furgol
1955	Jack Fleck
1956	Cary Middlecoff
1957	Dick Mayer
1958	Tommy Bolt
1959	Billy Casper
1960	Arnold Palmer
1961	Gene Littler
1962	Jack Nicklaus
1963	Julius Boros
1964	Ken Venturi
1965	Gary Player (South Africa)
1966	Billy Casper
1967	Jack Nicklaus
1968	Lee Trevino
1969	Orville Moody
1970	Tony Jacklin (Great Britain)
1971	Lee Trevino
1972	Jack Nicklaus
1973	Johnny Miller
1974	Hale Irwin
1975	Lou Graham
1976	Jerry Pate
1977	Hubert Green
1978	Andy North
1979	Hale Irwin
1980	Jack Nicklaus

1981	David Graham (Australia)
1982	Tom Watson
1983	Larry Nelson
1984	Fuzzy Zoeller
1985	Andy North
1986	Raymond Floyd
1987	Scott Simpson
1988	Curtis Strange
1989	Curtis Strange
1990	Hale Irwin
1991	Payne Stewart
1992	Tom Kite
1993	Lee Janzen
1994	Ernie Els (South Africa)
1995	Cory Pavin
1996	Steve Jones
1997	Ernie Els (South Africa)

Most wins: (4), Willie Anderson (USA); Bobby Jones (USA); Ben Hogan (USA); Jack Nicklaus (USA).

US Masters

First held in 1934; takes place at the Augusta National course in Georgia every April.

Winners (USA unless stated)

1934	Horton Smith
1935	Gene Sarazen
1936	Horton Smith
1937	Byron Nelson
1938	Henry Picard
1939	Ralph Guldahl
1940	Jimmy Demaret
1941	Craig Wood
1942	Byron Nelson
1946	Herman Keiser
1947	Jimmy Demaret
1948	Claude Harmon
1949	Sam Snead
1950	Jimmy Demaret
1951	Ben Hogan
1952	Sam Snead
1953	Ben Hogan
1954	Sam Snead
1955	Cary Middlecoff
1956	Jack Burke, Jr
1957	Doug Ford
1958	Arnold Palmer
1959	Art Wall, Jr
1960	Arnold Palmer
1961	Gary Player (South Africa)
1962	Arnold Palmer
1963	Jack Nicklaus
1964	Arnold Palmer
1965	Jack Nicklaus
1966	Jack Nicklaus
1967	Gay Brewer
1968	Bob Goalby
1969	George Archer
1970	Billy Casper
1971	Charles Coody
1972	Jack Nicklaus
1973	Tommy Aaron
1974	Gary Player (South Africa)
1975	Jack Nicklaus

1976	Raymond Floyd
1977	Tom Watson
1978	Gary Player (South Africa)
1979	Fuzzy Zoeller
1980	Severiano Ballesteros (Spain)
1981	Tom Watson
1982	Craig Stadler
1983	Severiano Ballesteros (Spain)
1984	Ben Crenshaw
1985	Bernhard Langer (West Germany)
1986	Jack Nicklaus
1987	Larry Mize
1988	Sandy Lyle (Great Britain)
1989	Nick Faldo (Great Britain)
1990	Nick Faldo (Great Britain)
1991	Ian Woosnam (Great Britain)
1992	Fred Couples
1993	Bernhard Langer (Germany)
1994	José María Olazábal (Spain)
1995	Ben Crenshaw
1996	Nick Faldo (Great Britain)
1997	Tiger Woods

Most wins: (6), Jack Nicklaus (USA).

United States PGA Championship

First held in 1916, and a match-play event until 1958; takes place annually.

Winners (USA unless stated)

1916	Jim Barnes
1919	Jim Barnes
1920	Jock Hutchinson
1921	Walter Hagen
1922	Gene Sarazen
1923	Gene Sarazen
1924	Walter Hagen
1925	Walter Hagen
1926	Walter Hagen
1927	Walter Hagen
1928	Leo Diegel
1929	Leo Diegel
1930	Tommy Armour
1931	Tom Creavy
1932	Olin Dutra
1933	Gene Sarazen
1934	Paul Runyan
1935	Johnny Revolta
1936	Densmore Shute
1937	Densmore Shute
1938	Paul Runyan
1939	Henry Picard
1940	Byron Nelson
1941	Vic Ghezzi
1942	Sam Snead
1944	Bob Hamilton
1945	Byron Nelson
1946	Ben Hogan
1947	Jim Ferrier
1948	Ben Hogan
1949	Sam Snead
1950	Chandler Harper
1951	Sam Snead
1952	Jim Turnesa
1953	Walter Burkemo
1954	Chick Harbert

1955	Doug Ford
1956	Jack Burke
1957	Lionel Hebert
1958	Dow Finsterwald
1959	Bob Rosburg
1960	Jay Hebert
1961	Jerry Barber
1962	Gary Player (South Africa)
1963	Jack Nicklaus
1964	Bobby Nichols
1965	Dave Marr
1966	Al Geiberger
1967	Don January
1968	Julius Boros
1969	Raymond Floyd
1970	Dave Stockton
1971	Jack Nicklaus
1972	Gary Player (South Africa)
1973	Jack Nicklaus
1974	Lee Trevino
1975	Jack Nicklaus
1976	Dave Stockton
1977	Lanny Wadkins
1978	John Mahaffey
1979	David Graham (Australia)
1980	Jack Nicklaus
1981	Larry Nelson
1982	Raymond Floyd
1983	Hal Sutton
1984	Lee Trevino
1985	Hubert Green
1986	Bob Tway
1987	Larry Nelson
1988	Jeff Sluman
1989	Payne Stewart
1990	Wayne Grady (Australia)
1991	John Daly
1992	Nick Price (Zimbabwe)
1993	Paul Azinger
1994	Nick Price (Zimbabwe)
1995	Steve Elkington (Australia)
1996	Mark Brooks
1997	Davis Love

Most wins: (5), Walter Hagen (USA); Jack Nicklaus (USA).

United States Women's Open

First held at Spokane, WA in 1946.

Winners (USA unless stated)

1946	Patty Berg
1947	Betty Jameson
1948	Mildred Zaharias
1949	Louise Suggs
1950	Mildred Zaharias
1951	Betsy Rawls
1952	Louise Suggs
1953	Betsy Rawls
1954	Mildred Zaharias
1955	Fay Crocker
1956	Kathy Cornelius
1957	Betsy Rawls
1958	Mickey Wright
1959	Mickey Wright
1960	Betsy Rawls
1961	Mickey Wright

1962	Murle Lindstrom
1963	Mary Mills
1964	Mickey Wright
1965	Carol Mann
1966	Sandra Spuzich
1967	Catherine Lacoste (France)
1968	Susie Berning
1969	Donna Caponi
1970	Donna Caponi
1971	JoAnne Carner
1972	Susie Berning
1973	Susie Berning
1974	Sandra Haynie
1975	Sandra Palmer
1976	JoAnne Carner
1977	Hollis Stacy
1978	Hollis Stacy
1979	Jenlyn Britz
1980	Amy Alcott
1981	Pat Bradley
1982	Janet Alex
1983	Jan Stephenson
1984	Hollis Stacy
1985	Kathy Baker
1986	Jane Geddes
1987	Laura Davies (Great Britain)
1988	Liselotte Neumann (Switzerland)
1989	Betsy King
1990	Betsy King
1991	Meg Mallon
1992	Patty Sheehan
1993	Laurie Merton
1994	Patty Sheehan
1995	Annika Sorenstam (Sweden)
1996	Annika Sorenstam (Sweden)
1997	Alison Nicholas (Great Britain)

Most wins: (4) Mickey Wright (USA); Betsy Rawls (USA).

Gymnastics

World Championships

First held in 1903; took place every four years 1922–78; since 1979, usually every two years.

Recent winners Individual (Men)

1966	Mikhail Voronin (USSR)
1970	Eizo Kenmotsu (Japan)
1974	Shigeru Kasamatsu (Japan)
1978	Nikolai Adrianov (USSR)
1979	Aleksandr Ditiatin (USSR)
1981	Yuri Korolev (USSR)
1983	Dmitri Belozerchev (USSR)
1985	Yuri Korolev (USSR)
1987	Dmitri Belozerchev (USSR)
1989	Igor Korobichensky (USSR)
1991	Grigoriy Misutin (USSR)
1993	Vitaly Scherbo (Belarus)
1994	Ivan Ivankov (Belarus)
1995	Li Xiaoshuang (China)

Most wins: Individual (2), Marco Torrès (France), 1909, 1913; Peter Sumi (Yugoslavia), 1922, 1926; Yuri Korolev and Dmitri Belozerchev, as above.

Recent winners Individual (Women)
1978   Yelena Mukhina (USSR)
1979   Nelli Kim (USSR)
1981   Olga Bitcherova (USSR)
1983   Natalia Yurchenko (USSR)
1985   Yelena Shushunova (USSR);
       Oksana Omeliantchuk (USSR)
1987   Aurelia Dobre (Romania)
1989   Svetlana Boginskaya (USSR)
1991   Kim Zmeskal (USA)
1993   Shannon Miller (USA)
1994   Shannon Miller (USA)
1995   Lilia Podkopayeva (Ukraine)
Most wins: (2), Vlasta Dekanová
(Czechoslovakia), 1934, 1938; Shannon
Miller (USA); Larissa Latynina (USSR),
1958, 1962; Ludmila Tourischeva, 1970
and as above.

Olympic Games
Gymnastics has been an event at all
Modern Olympic Games since the first
of 1896; women first included in 1928,
in a team event, and have competed
individually since 1952.

Recent winners Individual (Men)
1956   Viktor Chukarin (USSR)
1960   Boris Shakhlin (USSR)
1964   Yukio Endo (Japan)
1968   Sawao Kato (Japan)
1972   Sawao Kato (Japan)
1976   Nikolay Andrianov (USSR)
1980   Aleksandr Ditiatin (USSR)
1984   Koji Gushiken (Japan)
1988   Vladimir Artemov (USSR)
1992   Vitaliy Shcherbo (Unified Team)
1996   Li Xiaoshuang (China)
Most wins: (2) Alberto Braglia (Italy)
1908, 1912; Viktor Chukarin (USSR),
1952 and as above; Sawao Kato, as
above.

Winners Individual (Women)
1952   Maria Gorokhovskaya (USSR)
1956   Larissa Latynina (USSR)
1960   Larissa Latynina (USSR)
1964   Vera Cáslavská (Czechoslovakia)
1968   Vera Cáslavská (Czechoslovakia)
1972   Lyudmila Tourischeva (USSR)
1976   Nadia Comaneci (Romania)
1980   Yelena Davydova (USSR)
1984   Mary Lou Retton (USA)
1988   Yelena Shushunova (USSR)
1992   Tatyana Gutsu (Unified Team)
1996   Lilia Podkopayeva (Ukraine)
Most wins: (2) Larissa Latynina (USSR);
Vera Cáslavská (Czechoslovakia).

Hang Gliding
World Championships
First held officially in 1976; since 1979
take place every two years.

Winners Individual (Class 1)
1976   Christian Steinbach (Austria)

1979   Josef Guggenmose
       (West Germany)
1981   Pepe Lopez (Brazil)
1983   Steve Moyes (Australia)
1985   John Pendry (Great Britain)
1987   Rich Duncan (Australia)
1989   Robert Whittall (Great Britain)
1991   Tomás Suchanek
       (Czechoslovakia)
1993   Tomás Suchanek (Czech
       Republic)
1995   Tomás Suchanek (Czech
       Republic)
Most wins: Individual (3), Tomás
Suchanek (Czech Republic), as above.

Horse Racing
The English Classics are five races run
from April to September each year for
three-year-olds: the Derby; Oaks; One
Thousand Guineas; Two Thousand
Guineas; and St Leger.

The Derby
The 'Blue Riband' of the Turf; run at
Epsom over 1½ miles; first run in 1780.

Recent winners
       Horse (Jockey)
1986   *Shahrastani* (Walter Swinburn)
1987   *Reference Point* (Steve Cauthen)
1988   *Kahyasi* (Ray Cochrane)
1989   *Nashwan* (Willie Carson)
1990   *Quest for Fame* (Pat Eddery)
1991   *Generous* (Alan Munro)
1992   *Dr Devious* (John Reid)
1993   *Commander-In-Chief* (Michael
       Kinane)
1994   *Erhabb* (Willie Carson)
1995   *Lammtarra* (Walter Swinburn)
1996   *Shaamit* (Michael Hills)
1997   *Benny The Dip* (Willie Ryan)
Most wins: Jockey (9), Lester Piggott,
1954, 1957, 1960, 1968, 1970, 1972,
1976–7, 1983.

The Oaks
Raced at Epsom over 1½ miles; for
fillies only; first run in 1779.

Recent winners
       Horse (Jockey)
1986   *Midway Lady* (Ray Cochrane)
1987   *Unite* (Walter Swinburn)
1988   *Diminuendo* (Steve Cauthen)
1989   *Aliysa* (Walter Swinburn)
1990   *Salsabil* (Willie Carson)
1991   *Jet Ski Lady* (Christy Roche)
1992   *User Friendly* (George Duffield)
1993   *Intrepidity* (Michael Roberts)
1994   *Balanchine* (Lanfranco Dettori)
1995   *Moonshell* (Lanfranco Dettori)
1996   *Lady Carla* (Pat Eddery)
1997   *Reams of Verse* (Kieren Fallon)
Most wins: Jockey (9), Frank Buckle,
1797–9, 1802–3, 1805, 1817–18, 1823.

One Thousand Guineas
Run over 1 mile at Newmarket; for
fillies only; first run in 1814.

Recent winners
       Horse (Jockey)
1982   *On The House* (John Reid)
1983   *Ma Biche* (Freddy Head)
1984   *Pebbles* (Philip Robinson)
1985   *Oh So Sharp* (Steve Cauthen)
1986   *Midway Lady* (Ray Cochrane)
1987   *Miesque* (Freddy Head)
1988   *Ravinella* (Gary Moore)
1989   *Musical Bliss* (Walter Swinburn)
1990   *Salsabil* (Willie Carson)
1991   *Shadayid* (Willie Carson)
1992   *Hatoof* (Walter Swinburn)
1993   *Sayyedati* (Ray Cochrane)
1994   *Las Meninas* (John Reid)
1995   *Harayir* (Richard Hills)
1996   *Bosra Sham* (Pat Eddery)
1997   *Sleepytime* (Kieren Fallon)
Most wins: Jockey (7), George Fordham,
1859, 1861, 1865, 1868–9, 1881, 1883.

Two Thousand Guineas
Run at Newmarket over 1 mile; first
run in 1809.

Recent winners
       Horse (Jockey)
1986   *Dancing Brave* (Greville Starkey)
1987   *Don't Forget Me* (Willie Carson)
1988   *Doyoun* (Walter Swinburn)
1989   *Nashwan* (Willie Carson)
1990   *Tiroi* (Michael Kinane)
1991   *Mystiko* (Michael Roberts)
1992   *Rodrigo de Triano* (Lester Piggott)
1993   *Zafonic* (Pat Eddery)
1994   *Mister Baileys* (Jason Weaver)
1995   *Pennekamp* (Thierry Jarnett)
1996   *Mark of Esteem* (Lanfranco
       Dettori)
1997   *Entrepreneur* (Michael Kinane)
Most wins: Jockey (9), Jem Robinson,
1825, 1828, 1831, 1833–6, 1847–8.

St Leger
The oldest of the five English classics;
first run in 1776; raced at Doncaster
annually over 1 mile 6 furlongs 127
yards.

Recent winners
       Horse (Jockey)
1986   *Moon Madness* (Pat Eddery)
1987   *Reference Point* (Steve Cauthen)
1988   *Minster Son* (Willie Carson)
1989   *Michelozzo* (Steve Cauthen)
1990   *Snurge* (Richard Quinn)
1991   *Toulon* (Pat Eddery)
1992   *User Friendly* (George Duffield)
1993   *Bob's Return* (Philip Robinson)
1994   *Moonax* (Pat Eddery)
1995   *Classic Cliche* (Lanfranco Dettori)
1996   *Shantou* (Lanfranco Dettori)
1997   *Silver Patriarch* (Pat Eddery)

Most wins: Jockey (9), Bill Scott, 1821, 1825, 1828–9, 1831, 1846.

Grand National

Steeplechasing's most famous race; first run at Maghull in 1836; at Aintree since 1839, wartime races at Gatwick 1916–18.

Recent winners

Horse (Jockey)

1986	*West Tip* (Richard Dunwoody)
1987	*Maori Venture* (Steve Knight)
1988	*Rhyme 'N' Reason* (Brendan Powell)
1989	*Little Polveir* (Jimmy Frost)
1990	*Mr Frisk* (Marcus Armytage)
1991	*Seagram* (Nigel Hawke)
1992	*Party Politics* (Carl Llewellyn)
1993	*Race void due to false starts*
1994	*Minnehoma* (Richard Dunwoody)
1995	*Royal Athlete* (Jason Titley)
1996	*Rough Quest* (Mick Fitzgerald)
1997	*Lord Gyllene* (Tony Dobbin)

Most wins: Jockey (5), George Stevens, 1856, 1863–4, 1869–70. Horse (3), *Red Rum* 1973–4, 1977.

Prix de l'Arc de Triomphe

The leading end-of-season race in Europe; raced over 2400 m at Longchamp; first run in 1920.

Recent winners

Horse (Jockey)

1986	*Dancing Brave* (Pat Eddery)
1987	*Trempolino* (Pat Eddery)
1988	*Tony Bin* (John Reid)
1989	*Caroll House* (Michael Kinane)
1990	*Saumarez* (Gerald Mossé)
1991	*Suave Dancer* (Cash Asmussen)
1992	*Subotica* (Thierry Jarnet)
1993	*Urban Sea* (Eric Saint-Martin)
1994	*Carnegie* (Silvan Guillot)
1995	*Lammtarra* (Lanfranco Dettori)
1996	*Helissio* (Olivier Peslier)
1997	*Peintre Celebre* (Olivier Peslier)

Most wins: Jockey (4), Jacko Doyasbere, 1942, 1944, 1950–1; Freddy Head, 1966, 1972, 1979; Yves Saint-Martin, 1970, 1974, 1984; Pat Eddery, 1985 and as above.

Horse Racing in the USA

There are three races for three-year-olds which comprise the American Triple Crown: the Kentucky Derby; Preakness Stakes, and Belmont Stakes.

The Kentucky Derby

Raced at Churchill Downs, Louisville, KY, over 1 mile 2 furlongs, first run in 1875.

Recent winners

Horse (Jockey)

1986	*Ferdinand* (Willie Shoemaker)
1987	*Alysheba* (Chris McCarron)
1988	*Winning Colors* (Gary Stevens)
1989	*Sunday Silence* (Pat Valenzuela)
1990	*Unbridled* (Craig Perret)
1991	*Strike The Gold* (Chris Antley)
1992	*Lil E Tee* (Pat Day)
1993	*Sea Hero* (Jerry Bailey)
1994	*Go for Gin* (Chris McCarron)
1995	*Thunder Gulch* (Gary Stevens)
1996	*Grindstone* (Jerry Bailey)
1997	*Silver Charm* (Gary Stevens)

Most wins: Jockey (5), Eddie Arcaro 1938, 1941, 1945, 1948, 1952; Bill Hartack 1957, 1960, 1962, 1964, 1969.

Preakness Stakes

Raced at Pimlico, Baltimore, MD, over 1 mile 1½ furlongs; first run in 1873.

Recent winners

Horse (Jockey)

1986	*Snow Chief* (Alex Solis)
1987	*Alysheba* (Chris McCarron)
1988	*Risen Star* (Eddie Delahoussaye)
1989	*Sunday Silence* (Pat Valenzuela)
1990	*Summer Squall* (Pat Day)
1991	*Hansel* (Jerry Bailey)
1992	*Pine Bluff* (Chris McCarron)
1993	*Prairie Bayou* (Mike Smith)
1994	*Tabasco Cat* (Pat Day)
1995	*Timber Country* (Pat Day)
1996	*Louis Quatorze* (Pat Day)
1997	*Silver Charm* (Gary Stevens)

Most wins: Jockey: (6), Eddie Arcaro 1941, 1948, 1950–1, 1955, 1957.

Belmont Stakes

Raced at Belmont Park, New York over 1 mile 4 furlongs; first run in 1967 at Jerome Park.

Recent winners

Horse (Jockey)

1986	*Danzig Connection* (Chris McCarron)
1987	*Bet Twice* (Craig Perrett)
1988	*Risen Star* (Eddie Delahoussaye)
1989	*Easy Goer* (Pat Day)
1990	*Go And Go* (Michael Kinane)
1991	*Hansel* (Jenny Bailey)
1992	*A.P. Indy* (Eddie Delahoussaye)
1993	*Colonial Affair* (Julie Krone)
1994	*Tabasco Cat* (Pat Day)
1995	*Thunder Gulch* (Gary Stevens)
1996	*Editor's Note* (R Douglas)
1997	*Touch Gold* (Chris McCarron)

Most wins: Jockey (6) Jimmy McLaughlin 1882–4, 1886–8; Eddie Arcaro 1941–2, 1945, 1948, 1952, 1955.

Champion Jockeys (Flat)

The British post-war champion jockeys on the flat are as follows:

	Jockey	No. of winners
1946	Gordon Richards	212
1947	Gordon Richards	269
1948	Gordon Richards	224
1949	Gordon Richards	261
1950	Gordon Richards	201
1951	Gordon Richards	227
1952	Gordon Richards	231
1953	Gordon Richards	191
1954	Doug Smith	129
1955	Doug Smith	168
1956	Doug Smith	155
1957	Scobie Breasley	173
1958	Doug Smith	165
1959	Doug Smith	157
1960	Lester Piggott	170
1961	Scobie Breasley	171
1962	Scobie Breasley	179
1963	Scobie Breasley	176
1964	Lester Piggott	140
1965	Lester Piggott	166
1966	Lester Piggott	191
1967	Lester Piggott	117
1968	Lester Piggott	139
1969	Lester Piggott	163
1970	Lester Piggott	162
1971	Lester Piggott	162
1972	Willie Carson	132
1973	Willie Carson	163
1974	Pat Eddery	148
1975	Pat Eddery	164
1976	Pat Eddery	162
1977	Pat Eddery	176
1978	Willie Carson	182
1979	Joe Mercer	164
1980	Willie Carson	165
1981	Lester Piggott	179
1982	Lester Piggott	188
1983	Willie Carson	159
1984	Steve Cauthen	130
1985	Steve Cauthen	195
1986	Pat Eddery	177
1987	Steve Cauthen	197
1988	Pat Eddery	183
1989	Pat Eddery	171
1990	Pat Eddery	209
1991	Pat Eddery	165
1992	Michael Roberts	206
1993	Pat Eddery	169
1994	Lanfranco Dettori	179
1995	Lanfranco Dettori	154
1996	Pat Eddery	186
1997	Kieren Fallon	200

Most wins: (26), Gordon Richards 1925, 1927–9, 1931–40, 1942–53.

Champion Jockeys (National Hunt)

British post-war National Hunt champion jockeys are as follows:

	Jockey	No. of winners
1946	Fred Rimell	54
1947	Jack Dowdeswell	58
1948	Bryan Marshall	66
1949	Tim Molony	60
1950	Tim Molony	95
1951	Tim Molony	83
1952	Tim Molony	99
1953	Fred Winter	121
1954	Dick Francis	76
1955	Tim Molony	67
1956	Fred Winter	74

1957	Fred Winter	80
1958	Fred Winter	82
1959	Tim Brookshaw	83
1960	Stan Mellor	68
1961	Stan Mellor	118
1962	Stan Mellor	80
1963	Josh Gifford	70
1964	Josh Gifford	94
1965	Terry Biddlecombe	114
1966	Terry Biddlecombe	102
1967	Josh Gifford	122
1968	Josh Gifford	82
1969	Bob Davies	77
	Terry Biddlecombe	77
1970	Bob Davies	91
1971	Graham Thorner	74
1972	Bob Davies	89
1973	Ron Barry	125
1974	Ron Barry	94
1975	Tommy Stack	82
1976	John Francome	96
1977	Tommy Stack	97
1978	Jonjo O'Neill	149
1979	John Francome	95
1980	Jonjo O'Neill	115
1981	John Francome	105
1982	John Francome	120
	Peter Scudamore	120
1983	John Francome	106
1984	John Francome	131
1985	John Francome	101
1986	Peter Scudamore	91
1987	Peter Scudamore	123
1988	Peter Scudamore	132
1989	Peter Scudamore	221
1990	Peter Scudamore	170
1991	Peter Scudamore	141
1992	Peter Scudamore	175
1993	Richard Dunwoody	173
1994	Richard Dunwoody	198
1995	Richard Dunwoody	160
1996	Tony McCoy	175
1997	Tony McCoy	190

Most wins: (8), Peter Scudamore, as above.

Ice Skating

World Championships
First men's championships in 1896; first women's event in 1906; pairs first contested in 1908; Ice Dance officially recognized in 1952.

Recent winners (Men)
1986	Brian Boitano (USA)
1987	Brian Orser (Canada)
1988	Brian Boitano (USA)
1989	Kurt Browning (Canada)
1990	Kurt Browning (Canada)
1991	Kurt Browning (Canada)
1992	Viktor Petrenko (Unified Team)
1993	Kurt Browning (Canada)
1994	Aleksei Urmanov (Russia)
1995	Elvis Stojko (Canada)
1996	Todd Eldredge (USA)

1997	Elvis Stojko (Canada)

Most wins: (10), Ulrich Salchow (Sweden), 1901–5, 1907–11.

Recent winners (Women)
1986	Debbie Thomas (USA)
1987	Katarina Witt (East Germany)
1988	Katarina Witt (East Germany)
1989	Midori Ito (Japan)
1990	Jill Trenany (USA)
1991	Kristi Yamaguchi (USA)
1992	Kristi Yamaguchi (USA)
1993	Oksana Baiul (Ukraine)
1994	Oksana Baiul (Ukraine)
1995	Lu Chen (China)
1996	Michelle Kwan (USA)
1997	Tara Lipinski (USA)

Most wins: (10), Sonja Henie (Norway), 1927–36.

Recent winners (Pairs)
1986	Yekaterina Gordeeva/Sergey Grinkov (USSR)
1987	Yekaterina Gordeeva/Sergey Grinkov (USSR)
1988	Yelena Valova/Oleg Vasiliev (USSR)
1989	Yekaterina Gordeeva/Sergey Grinkov (USSR)
1990	Yekaterina Gordeeva/Sergey Grinkov (USSR)
1991	Natalya Mishkutienok/Artur Dmitriev (USSR)
1992	Natalya Mishkutienok/Artur Dmitriev (Unified Team)
1993	Isabelle Brasseur/Lloyd Eisler (Canada)
1994	Yekaterina Gordeeva/Sergey Grinkov (Russia)
1995	Radka Kovarikova/Rene Novotny (Czech Republic)
1996	Marina Eltsova/Andrey Bushkov (Russia)
1997	Mandy Woetzel/Ingo Steuer (Germany)

Most wins: (10), Irina Rodnina (USSR), 1969–72 (with Aleksey Ulanov), 1973–8 (with Aleksandr Zaitsev).

Recent winners (Ice Dance)
1986	Natalya Bestemianova/Andrey Bukin (USSR)
1987	Natalya Bestemianova/Andrey Bukin (USSR)
1988	Natalya Bestemianova/Andrey Bukin (USSR)
1989	Marina Klimova/Sergey Ponomarenko (USSR)
1990	Marina Klimova/Sergey Ponomarenko (USSR)
1991	Isabelle and Paul Duchesnay (France)
1992	Marina Klimova/Sergey Ponomarenko (Unified Team)
1993	Maia Usova/Aleksandr Zhulin (Russia)

1994	Oksana Grichtchuk/Yevgeny Platov (Russia)
1995	Oksana Grichtchuk/Yevgeny Platov (Russia)
1996	Oksana Grichtchuk/Yevgeny Platov (Russia)

Most wins: (6), Lyudmila Pakhomova/ Aleksander Gorshkov (USSR), 1970–4,1976.

Olympic Games
Ice Skating was an Olympic event in 1908, and has been included in all Winter Games since 1924. Ice Dance was first included in 1976.

Recent winners (Men)
1976	John Curry (Great Britain)
1980	Robin Cousins (Great Britain)
1984	Scott Hamilton (USA)
1988	Brian Boitano (USA)
1992	Viktor Petrenko (Unified Team)
1994	Aleksei Urmanov (Russia)

Most wins: (3) Gillis Grafström (Sweden) 1920, 1924, 1928.

Recent winners (Women)
1976	Dorothy Hamill (USA)
1980	Anett Pötzsch (East Germany)
1984	Katarina Witt (East germany)
1988	Katarina Witt (East Germany)
1992	Kristi Yamaguchi (USA)
1994	Oksana Baiul (Ukraine)

Most wins: (3) Sonja Henie (Norway) 1928, 1932, 1936

Recent winners (Pairs)
1976	Irina Rodnina/Aleksandr Zaitsev (USSR)
1980	Irina Rodnina/Aleksandr Zaitsev (USSR)
1984	Yelena Valova/Oleg Vasilyev (USSR)
1988	Yekaterina Gordeyeva/Sergey Grinkov (USSR)
1992	Natalya Mishkutienok/Artur Dmitrieyev (Unified Team)
1994	Yekaterina Gordeyeva/Sergey Grinkov (Russia)

Most wins: women (3) Irina Rodnina (USSR) 1972, 1976, 1980. *Men* (2) Pierre Brunet (France) 1928, 1932; Oleg Protopopov (USSR) 1964, 1968; Aleksandr Zeitsev (USSR) as above; Sergey Grinkov (USSR/Russia) as above.

Recent winners (Ice Dance)
1976	Lyudmila Pakhomova/Aleksandr Gorshkov (USSR)
1980	Natalya Linichuk/Gennadiy Karponosov (USSR)
1984	Jayne Torvill/Christopher Dean (Great Britain)
1988	Natalya Bestemianova/Andrey Bukin (USSR)
1992	Marina Klimova/Sergey Ponomarenko (Unified Team)

1994   Oksana Grichtchuk/Yevgeny
       Platov (Russia)

Judo

World Championships
First held in 1956, now contested every two years; current weight categories established in 1979; women's championship instituted in 1980.

Recent Winners Open Class (Men)
1983   Hitoshi Saito (Japan)
1985   Yoshimi Masaki (Japan)
1987   Naoyo Ogawa (Japan)
1989   Naoyo Ogawa (Japan)
1991   Naoyo Ogawa (Japan)
1993   Rafael Kubacki (Poland)
1995   David Douillet (France)
1997   Rafael Kubacki (Poland)

Recent winners Over 95 kg (Men)
1983   Yasuhiro Yamashita (Japan)
1985   Yung-Chul Cho (South Korea)
1987   Grigori Vertichev (USSR)
1989   Noayo Ogawa (Japan)
1991   Sergey Kosorotov (USSR)
1993   David Douillet (France)
1995   David Douillet (France)
1997   David Douillet (France)

Recent winners Under 95 kg (Men)
1985   Hitoshi Sugai (Japan)
1987   Hitoshi Sugai (Japan)
1989   Koba Kurtanidze (Japan)
1991   Stéphane Traineau (France)
1993   Antal Kovacs (Hungary)
1995   Pawel Nastula (Poland)
1997   Pawel Nastula (Poland)

Recent winners Under 86 kg (Men)
1983   Detlef Ultsch (East Germany)
1985   Peter Seisenbacher (Austria)
1987   Fabien Canu (France)
1989   Fabien Canu (France)
1991   Hirotaka Okada (Japan)
1993   Yoshio Yakumura (Japan)
1995   Ki-young Chun (South Korea)
1997   Ki-young Chun (South Korea)

Recent winners Under 78 kg (Men)
1983   Nobutoshi Hikage (Japan)
1985   Nobutoshi Hikage (Japan)
1987   Hirotaka Okada (Japan)
1989   Kim Byung-ju (South Korea)
1991   Daniel Lascau (Germany)
1993   Ki-yong Chen (South Korea)
1995   Toshihiko Koga (Japan)
1997   Cho-In Chul (South Korea)

Recent winners Under 71 kg (Men)
1983   Kidetoshi Nakanishi (Japan)
1985   Byeong-Keun Ahn (South Korea)
1987   Mike Swain (USA)
1989   Toshihiko Koga (Japan)
1991   Toshihiko Koga (Japan)
1993   Hoon Chung (South Korea)
1995   Daisuke Hideshima (Japan)

1997   Kenzo Nakamura (Japan)

Recent winners Under 65 kg (Men)
1983   Nikolai Soludkhin (USSR)
1985   Yuriy Sokolov (USSR)
1987   Yosuke Yamamoto (Japan)
1989   Drago Becanovic (Yugoslavia)
1991   Udo Quellmalz (Germany)
1993   Yukimasa Nakamura (Japan)
1995   Udo Quellmalz (Germany)
1997   Hyuk Kim (South Korea)

Recent winners Under 60 kg (Men)
1983   Khazret Tletseri (USSR)
1985   Shinji Hosokawa (Japan)
1987   Kim Jae-yup (South Korea)
1989   Amiran Totikashvili (USSR)
1991   Tadanori Koshino (Japan)
1993   Ryuji Sonoda (Japan)
1995   Nikolai Ojeguine (Russia)
1997   Tadahiro Nomura (Japan)
Most titles: (4), Yasuhiro Yamashita (Japan), 1981 (Open), 1979, 1981, 1983 (over 95 kg); Shozo Fujii (Japan), 1971, 1973, 1975 (under 80 kg), 1979 (under 78 kg).

Recent winners Open (Women)
1984   Ingrid Berghmans (Belgium)
1986   Ingrid Berghmans (Belgium)
1987   Gao Fengliang (China)
1989   Estella Rodriguez (Cuba)
1991   Zhuang Xiaoyan (China)
1993   Beata Maksumow (Poland)
1995   Monique Van Der Lee
       (Netherlands)
1997   Diana Beltran (Cuba)

Recent winners Over 72 kg (Women)
1984   Maria-Teresa Motta (Italy)
1986   Gao Fengliang (China)
1987   Gao Fengliang (China)
1989   Gao Fengliang (China)
1991   Moon Ji-yoon (South Korea)
1993   Johanna Hagn (Germany)
1995   Angelique Seriese (Netherlands)
1997   Christine Cicot (France)

Recent winners Under 72 kg (Women)
1984   Ingrid Berghmans (Belgium)
1986   Irene de Kok (Netherlands)
1987   Irene de Kok (Netherlands)
1989   Ingrid Berghmans (Belgium)
1991   Kim Mi-jung (South Korea)
1993   Cheng Huileng (China)
1995   Diadenis Luna (Cuba)
1997   Noriko Anno (Japan)

Recent winners Under 66 kg (Women)
1986   Brigitte Deydier (France)
1987   Alexandra Schreiber (West
       Germany)
1989   Emanuela Pierantozzi (Italy)
1991   Emanuela Pierantozzi (Italy)
1993   Cho Min-sun (South Korea)
1995   Cho Min-sun (South Korea)
1997   Kate Howey (Great Britain)

Recent winners Under 61 kg (Women)
1984   Natasha Hernandez (Venezuela)
1986   Diane Bell (Great Britain)
1987   Diane Bell (Great Britain)
1989   Catherine Fleury (France)
1991   Frauke Eickoff (Germany)
1993   Gella van de Caveye (Belgium)
1995   Young Sung-sook (South Korea)
1997   Servenr Vendenhende (France)

Recent winners Under 56 kg (Women)
1984   Ann-Maria Burns (USA)
1986   Ann Hughes (Great Britain)
1987   Catherine Arnaud (France)
1989   Catherine Arnaud (France)
1991   Miriam Blasco (Spain)
1993   Nicola Fairbrother (Great
       Britain)
1995   Driulis Gonzalez (Cuba)
1997   Marie-Claire Restoux (France)

Recent winners Under 52 kg (Women)
1984   Kaori Yamaguchi (Japan)
1986   Dominique Brun (France)
1987   Sharon Rendle (Great Britain)
1989   Sharon Rendle (Great Britain)
1991   Alessandra Giungi (Italy)
1993   Rodriguez Verdecia (Cuba)
1995   Marie-Claire Restoux (France)
1997   Isabel Fernandez (Spain)

Recent winners Under 48 kg (Women)
1984   Karen Briggs (Great Britain)
1986   Karen Briggs (Great Britain)
1987   Zhangyun Li (China)
1989   Karen Briggs (Great Britain)
1991   Cécile Nowak (France)
1993   Ryoko Tamura (Japan)
1995   Ryoko Tamura (Japan)
1997   Ryoko Tamura (Japan)
Most titles: (6), Ingrid Berghmans (Belgium), 1980, 1982, 1984, 1986 (Open), 1984, 1989 (both under 72 kg).

Olympic Games
Judo first became an Olympic event in 1964, and has been regularly contested since 1972. The women's competition was first held in 1992, having previously been included in the 1988 games as a demonstration sport.

WINNERS (MEN)

Open
1964   Anton Geesink (Netherlands)
1972   Willem Ruska (Netherlands)
1976   Haruki Uemura (Japan)
1980   Dietmar Lorenz (East Germany)
1984   Yasuhiro Yamashita (Japan)
1988   *Not held*
1992   *Not held*
1996   *Not held*

Over 95 kg
1980   Angelo Parisi (France)
1984   Hitoshi Saito (Japan)
1988   Hitoshi Saito (Japan)

1992 David Khakkaleichvili (Unified Team)
1996 David Douillet (France)

Over 93 kg
1964 Isao Inokuma (Japan)
1972 Willem Ruska (Netherlands)
1976 Sergey Novikov (USSR)

Under 95 kg
1980 Robert Van de Walle (Belgium)
1984 Ha Hyoung-zoo (South Korea)
1988 Aurelio Miguel (Brazil)
1992 Antal Kovács (Hungary)
1996 Pawel Nastula (Poland)

Under 93 kg
1972 Shota Chochoshvili (USSR)
1976 Kazuhiro Ninomiya (Japan)

Under 86 kg
1980 Jürg Röthlisberger (Switzerland)
1984 Peter Seisenbacher (Austria)
1988 Peter Seisenbacher (Austria)
1992 Waldemar Legien (Poland)
1996 Jeon Ki-young (South Korea)

Under 80 kg
1964 Isao Okano (Japan)
1972 Shinobu Sekine (Japan)
1976 Isamu Sonoda (Japan)

Under 78 kg
1980 Shota Khabareli (USSR)
1984 Frank Weineke (West Germany)
1988 Waldemar Legien (Poland)
1992 Hidehiko Yoshida (Japan)
1996 Djamel Bouras (France)

Under 71 kg
1980 Ezio Gamba (Italy)
1984 Ahn Byeong-kuen (South Korea)
1988 Marc Alexandre (France)
1992 Toshihiko Koga (Japan)
1996 Kenzo Nakamura (Japan)

Under 70 kg
1964 Takehide Nakatani (Japan)
1972 Toyokazu Nomura (Japan)
1976 Vladimir Nevzorov (USSR)

Under 65 kg
1980 Nikolay Solodukhin (USSR)
1984 Yoshiyuki Matsuoka (Japan)
1988 Lee Kyung-keun (South Korea)
1992 Rogerio Sampalo (Brazil)
1996 Udo Quellmalz (Germany)

Under 63 kg
1972 Takao Kawaguchi (Japan)
1976 Héctor Rodriguez (Cuba)

Under 60 kg
1980 Thierry Rey (France)
1984 Shinji Hosokawa (Japan)
1988 Kim Jae-yup (South Korea)
1992 Nazim Gusseinov (Unified Team)
1996 Tadahiro Nomura (Japan)
Most titles: (2), Willem Ruska

(Netherlands); Peter Seisenbacher (Austria); Waldemar Legien (Poland), as above.

WINNERS (WOMEN)

Under 48 kg
1988 Li Zhongyun (China)
1992 Cécile Nowak (France)
1996 Kye Sun (North Korea)

Under 52 kg
1988 Sharon Rendle (Great Britain)
1992 Almudena Munoz (Spain)
1996 Marie-Claire Restoux (France)

Under 56 kg
1988 Suzanne Williams (Australia)
1992 Miriam Blasco (Spain)
1996 Driulis Gonzalez (Cuba)

Under 61 kg
1988 Diane Bell (Great Britain)
1992 Catherine Fleury (France)
1996 Yuko Emoto (Japan)

Under 66 kg
1988 Hikari Sasaki (Japan)
1992 Odalis Reve (Cuba)
1996 Cho Min-sun (South Korea)

Under 72 kg
1988 Ingrid Berghmans (Netherlands)
1992 Kim Mi-jung (South Korea)
1996 Ulla Werbrouck (Belgium)

Over 72 kg
1988 Angelique Seriese (Netherlands)
1992 Zhuang Xiaoyan (China)
1996 Fuming Sun (China)

Modern Pentathlon

World Championships
Held annually since 1949 with the exception of Olympic years, when the Olympic champions automatically become world champions.

Recent winners Individual (Men)
1983 Anatoliy Starostin (USSR)
1984 Daniele Masala (Italy)
1985 Attila Mizser (Hungary)
1986 Carlo Massullo (Italy)
1987 Joel Bouzou (France)
1988 Janos Martinek (Hungary)
1989 László Fábián (Hungary)
1990 Gianluca Tiberti (Italy)
1991 Arkadiusz Skrzypaszek (Poland)
1992 Arkadiusz Skrzypaszek (Poland)
1993 Richard Phelps (Great Britain)
1994 Dimitriy Svatkovski (Russia)
1995 Dimitriy Svatkovski (Russia)
1996 Alexander Parygin (Kazakhstan)
1997 Sebastien Deleigne (France)
Most wins: (6), Andras Balczo (Hungary), 1963, 1965–9, 1972.

Motor Cycling

World Championships
First organized in 1949; current titles for 500 cc, 250 cc, 125 cc, 80 cc and Sidecar; Formula One and Endurance world championships also held annually; the most prestigious title is the 500 cc category.

Recent winners (500 cc)
1985 Freddie Spencer (USA)
1986 Eddie Lawson (USA)
1987 Wayne Gardner (Australia)
1988 Eddie Lawson (USA)
1989 Eddie Lawson (USA)
1990 Wayne Rainey (USA)
1991 Wayne Rainey (USA)
1992 Wayne Rainey (USA)
1993 Kevin Schwantz (USA)
1994 Michael Doohan (Australia)
1995 Michael Doohan (Australia)
1996 Michael Doohan (Australia)
1997 Michael Doohan (Australia)
Most wins: (8), Giacomo Agostini (Italy), 1966–72, 1975.
Most world titles: (15), Giacomo Agostini, 500 cc 1966–72, 1975, 350 cc 1968–74.

Isle of Man TT Races
The most famous of all motor cycle races; take place each June; first held 1907; principal race is the Senior TT.

Recent winners Senior TT
1985 Joey Dunlop (Ireland)
1986 Roger Burnett (Great Britain)
1987 Joey Dunlop (Ireland)
1988 Joey Dunlop (Ireland)
1989 Steve Hislop (Great Britain)
1990 Carl Fogarty (Great Britain)
1991 Steve Hislop (Great Britain)
1992 Steve Hislop (Great Britain)
1993 Nigel Davies (Great Britain)
1994 Steve Hislop (Great Britain)
1995 Joey Dunlop (Ireland)
1996 Phil McCallen (Ireland)
1997 Phil McCallen (Ireland)
Most Senior TT wins: (7), Mike Hailwood (Great Britain), 1961, 1963–7, 1979.

Motor Racing

World Championship
A Formula One drivers' world championship instituted in 1950; constructor's championship instituted in 1958.

Winners
1950 Giuseppe Farina (Italy) AR
1951 Juan Manuel Fangio (Argentina) AR
1952 Alberto Ascari (Italy) F
1953 Alberto Ascari (Italy) F
1954 Juan Manuel Fangio (Argentina) Mas-M

1955 Juan Manuel Fangio (Argentina) M
1956 Juan Manuel Fangio (Argentina) F
1957 Juan Manuel Fangio (Argentina) Mas
1958 Mike Hawthorn (Great Britain) F
1959 Jack Brabham (Australia) C-C
1960 Jack Brabham (Australia) C-C
1961 Phil Hill (USA) F
1962 Graham Hill (Great Britain) BRM
1963 Jim Clark (Great Britain) L-C
1964 John Surtees (Great Britain) F
1965 Jim Clark (Great Britain) L-C
1966 Jack Brabham (Australia) B-C
1967 Denny Hulme (New Zealand) B-R
1968 Graham Hill (Great Britain) L-F
1969 Jackie Stewart (Great Britain) M-F
1970 Jochen Rindt (Austria) L-F
1971 Jackie Stewart (Great Britain) T-F
1972 Emerson Fittipaldi (Brazil) L-F
1973 Jackie Stewart (Great Britain) T-F
1974 Emerson Fittipaldi (Brazil) McL-F
1975 Niki Lauda (Austria) F
1976 James Hunt (Great Britain) McL-F
1977 Niki Lauda (Austria) F
1978 Mario Andretti (USA) L-F
1979 Jody Scheckter (South Africa) F
1980 Alan Jones (Australia) W-F
1981 Nelson Piquet (Brazil) B-F
1982 Keke Rosberg (Finland) W-F
1983 Nelson Piquet (Brazil) B-BMW
1984 Niki Lauda (Austria) McL-P
1985 Alain Prost (France) McL-P
1986 Alain Prost (France) McL-P
1987 Nelson Piquet (Brazil) W-H
1988 Ayrton Senna (Brazil) McL-H
1989 Alain Prost (France) McL-H
1990 Ayrton Senna (Brazil) McL-H
1991 Ayrton Senna (Brazil) McL-H
1992 Nigel Mansell (Great Britain) W-R
1993 Alain Prost (France) W-R
1994 Michael Schumacher (Germany) B-F
1995 Michael Schumacher (Germany) B-R
1996 Damon Hill (Great Britain) W-R
1997 Jacques Villeneuve (Canada) W-R
Most wins: (5), Juan Manuel Fangio (Argentina), as above.

AR = Alfa Romeo
B-BMW = Brabham-BMW
B-C = Brabham-Climax
B-F = Benetton-Ford
B-R = Brabham-Repco
C-C = Cooper-Climax
F = Ferrari
L-C = Lotus-Climax
L-F = Lotus-Ford
M = Mercedes
M-F = Matra-Ford
Mas-M = Maserati-Mercedes
Mas = Maserati
McL-F = McLaren-Ford
McL-H = McLaren-Honda
McL-P = McLaren-Porsche
T-F = Tyrell-Ford
W-F = Williams-Ford
W-H = Williams-Honda
W-R = Williams-Renault

Le Mans 24-Hour Race
The greatest of all endurance races; first held in 1923.

Recent winners
1986 Hans Stück (West Germany)/ Derek Bell (Great Britain)/ Al Holbert (USA)
1987 Hans Stück (West Germany)/ Derek Bell (Great Britain)/ Al Holbert (USA)
1988 Jan Lammers (Netherlands)/ Johnny Dumfries (Great Britain)/Andy Wallace (Great Britain)
1989 Jochen Mass (West Germany)/ Manuel Reuter (West Germany)/ Stanley Dickens (Sweden)
1990 John Nielsen (Denmark)/ Martin Brundle (Great Britain)/ Price Cobb (USA)
1991 Volker Weidler (Germany)/ Johnny Herbert (Great Britain) / Bertrand Gachot (Belgium)
1992 Derek Warwick (Great Britain)/ Mark Blundell (Great Britain)/ Yannick Dalmas (France)
1993 Geoff Brabham (Australia)/ Christophe Bouchut (France)/ Eric Helary (France)
1994 Yannick Dalmas (France)/ Mauro Baldi (Italy)/Hurley Haywood (USA)
1995 Yannick Dalmas (France)/ J J Lehto (Finland)/Masanori Sekiya (Japan)
1996 Manuel Reuter (Germany)/ Davey Jones (USA)/Alexander Würz (Austria)
1997 Michele Alboreto (Italy)/ Stefan Johansson (Sweden)/ Tom Kristensen (Denmark)
Most wins: (6), Jacky Ickx (Belgium), 1969, 1975–7, 1981–2.

Indianapolis 500
First held in 1911; raced over the Indianapolis Raceway as part of the Memorial Day celebrations at the end of May each year.

Recent winners
1985 Danny Sullivan (USA)
1986 Bobby Rahal (USA)
1987 Al Unser (USA)
1988 Rick Mears (USA)
1989 Emerson Fittipaldi (Brazil)
1990 Arie Luydendyk (Netherlands)
1991 Rick Mears (USA)
1992 Al Unser Jr (USA)
1993 Emerson Fittipaldi (Brazil)
1994 Al Unser Jr (USA)
1995 Jacques Villeneuve (Canada)
1996 Buddy Lazier (USA)
1997 Arie Luydendyk (Netherlands)
Most wins: (4), A J Foyt (USA), 1961, 1964, 1967, 1977; Al Unser (USA), 1970–1, 1978; Rick Mears (USA), 1979, 1984, 1988, 1991.

Monte Carlo Rally
The world's leading rally; first held in 1911.

Recent winners
1984 Walter Röhrl (West Germany)
1985 Ari Vatanen (Finland)
1986 Henri Toivonen (Finland)
1987 Mikki Biasion (Italy)
1988 Bruno Saby (France)
1989 Mikki Biasion (Italy)
1990 Didier Auriol (France)
1991 Carlos Sainz (Spain)
1992 Didier Auriol (France)
1993 Didier Auriol (France)
1994 François Delecour (France)
1995 Carlos Sainz (Spain)
1996 Patrick Bernardini (France)
1997 Piero Liatti (Italy)
Most wins: (4), Sandro Munari (Italy), 1972, 1975–7; Walter Röhrl (West Germany), as above.

Orienteering

World Championships
First held in 1966; takes place every two years (to 1978, and since 1979).

Winners Individual (Men)
1966 Age Hadler (Norway)
1968 Karl Johansson (Sweden)
1970 Stig Berge (Norway)
1972 Age Hadler (Norway)
1974 Bernt Frilen (Sweden)
1976 Egil Johansen (Norway)
1978 Egil Johansen (Norway)
1979 Oyvin Thon (Norway)
1981 Oyvin Thon (Norway)
1983 Morten Berglia (Norway)
1985 Kari Sallinen (Finland)
1987 Kent Olsson (Sweden)
1989 Peter Thoresen (Norway)
1991 Jörgen Mårtensson (Sweden)
1993 Allan Mogensen (Denmark)
1995 Jörgen Mårtensson (Sweden)
1997 Peter Thoresen (Norway)

Winners Individual (Women)
1966 Ulla Lindqvist (Sweden)
1968 Ulla Lindqvist (Sweden)
1970 Ingrid Hadler (Norway)
1972 Sarolta Monspart (Finland)
1974 Mona Norgaard (Denmark)
1976 Lia Veijalainen (Finland)
1978 Anne Berit Eid (Norway)
1979 Outi Bergonstrom (Finland)
1981 Annichen Kringstad (Norway)

1983 Annichen Kringstad Svensson
(Norway)
1985 Annichen Kringstad Svensson
(Norway)
1987 Arja Hannus (Sweden)
1989 Marita Skogum (Sweden)
1991 Katalin Olah (Hungary)
1993 Marita Skogum (Sweden)
1995 Katali Olah (Hungary)
1997 Hanne Staff (Norway)
Most wins: Men (2), Age Hadler (Norway),
Egil Johansen (Norway), Jörgen
Mårtensson (Sweden), Oyvin Thon
(Norway), Peter Thoresen (Norway), as
above. Women (3), Annichen Kringstad
(Norway), as above.

Powerboat Racing

World Championships
Instituted in 1982; held in many
categories, with Formula One and
Formula Two being the principal
competitions; Formula One
discontinued in 1986; Formula Two
became known as Formula Grand Prix,
then reverted to Formula One in 1990.

Winners Formula One
1982 Roger Jenkins (Great Britain)
1983 Renato Molinari (Italy)
1984 Renato Molinari (Italy)
1985 Bob Spalding (Great Britain)
1986 Gene Thibodaux (USA)
1990 John Hill (Great Britain)
1991 Jonathon Jones (Great Britain)
1992 Fabrizio Bocca (Italy)
1993 Guido Capellina (Italy)
1994 Guido Capellina (Italy)
1995 Guido Capellina (Italy)
1996 Guido Capellina (Italy)
1997 Scott Gillman (USA)
Most wins: (4), Guido Capellina (Italy), as
above.

Winners Formula Two/Formula Grand Prix
1982 Michael Werner (West Germany)
1983 Michael Werner (West Germany)
1984 John Hill (Great Britain)
1985 John Hill (Great Britain)
1986 Jonathan Jones (Great Britain)
and Buck Thornton (USA) (*shared*)
1987 Bill Seebold (USA)
1988 Chris Bush (USA)
1989 Jonathan Jones (Great Britain)
1990 John Hill (Great Britain)
1991 Jonathan Jones (Great Britain)
Most wins: (3), John Hill (Great Britain),
as above; Jonathan Jones (Great
Britain), as above.

Rackets

World Championship
Organized on a challenge basis, the
first champion in 1820 was Robert
Mackay (Great Britain).

Recent winners
1954–72 Geoffrey Atkins (Great Britain)
1972–3 William Surtees (USA)
1973–4 Howard Angus (Great Britain)
1975–81 William Surtees (USA)
1981–4 John Prenn (Great Britain)
1984–6 William Boone (Great Britain)
1986–8 John Prenn (Great Britain)
1988–9 James Male (Great Britain)
1990 Neil Smith (Great Britain)
1991 James Male (Great Britain)
1992 Shannon Hazel (USA)
1993–4 Neil Smith (Great Britain)
1995– Hames Male (Great Britain)
Longest reigning champion: 18 years,
Geoffrey Atkins, as above.

Real Tennis

World Championship
Organized on a challenge basis; the
first world champion was M Clerge
(France) *c*.1740, regarded as the first
world champion of any sport.
Women's championship first held in
1985, and then every two years.

Recent winners (Men)
1916–28 Fred Covey (Great Britain)
1928–55 Pierre Etchebaster (France)
1955–7 James Dear (Great Britain)
1957–9 Albert Johnson (Great Britain)
1959–69 Northrup Knox (USA)
1969–72 Pete Bostwick (USA)
1972–5 Jimmy Bostwick (USA)
1976–81 Howard Angus (Great Britain)
1981–7 Chris Ronaldson
(Great Britain)
1987–94 Wayne Davies (Australia)
1994– Robert Fahey (Australia)
Longest reigning champion: 33 years,
Edmond Barre (France), 1829–62.

Winners (Women)
1985 Judy Clarke (Australia)
1987 Judy Clarke (Australia)
1989 Penny Fellows (Great Britain)
1991 Penny Lumley (*née* Fellows)
(Great Britain)
1993 Sally Jones (Great Britain)
1995 Penny Lumley (Great Britain)
1997 Penny Lumley (Great Britain)

Roller Skating

World Championships
Figure skating world championships
were first organized in 1947.

Recent winners (Men Combined)
1987 Kevin Carroll (USA)
1988 Sandro Guerra (Italy)
1989 Sandro Guerra (Italy)
1990 Samo Kokorovec (Italy)
1991 Sandro Guerra (Italy)
1992 Sandro Guerra (Italy)
1993 Samo Kokorovec (Italy)
1994 Steven Findlay (USA)

1995 Jason Sutcliffe (Australia)
1996 Francesco Ceresola (Italy)
1997 Mauro Mazzoni (Italy)
Most wins: (5), Karl-Heinz Losch (West
Germany), 1958–9, 1961–2, 1966.

Recent winners (Women Combined)
1987 Chiara Sartori (Italy)
1988 Rafaella del Vinaccio (Italy)
1989 Rafaella del Vinaccio (Italy)
1990 Rafaella del Vinaccio (Italy)
1991 Rafaella del Vinaccio (Italy)
1992 Rafaella del Vinaccio (Italy)
1993 Letitia Tinghi (Italy)
1994 April Dayney (USA)
1995 Letitia Tinghi (Italy)
1996 Giusy Loncani (Italy)
1997 Sabrini Tommasini (Italy)
Most wins: Rafaella del Vinaccio (Italy),
as above.

Recent winners (Pairs)
1987 Fabio Trevisani/Monica
Mezzardi (Italy)
1988 Fabio Trevisani/Monica
Mezzardi (Italy)
1989 David De Motte/Nicky
Armstrong (USA)
1990 Larry McGrew/Tammy Jeru (USA)
1991 Larry McGrew/Tammy Jeru (USA)
1992 Patrick Venerucci/Maura Ferri
(Italy)
1993 Patrick Venerucci/Maura Ferri
(Italy)
1994 Patrick Venerucci/Beatrice
Pallazzi Rossi (Italy)
1995 Patrick Venerucci/Beatrice
Pallazzi Rossi (Italy)
1996 Patrick Venerucci/Beatrice
Pallazzi Rossi (Italy)
1997 Patrick Venerucci/Beatrice
Pallazzi Rossi (Italy)
Most wins: (6), Patrick Venerucci (Italy),
as above.

Recent winners (Dance)
1987 Rob Ferendo/Lori Walsh (USA)
1988 Peter Wulf/Michela Mitzlaf
(West Germany)
1989 Greg Goody/Jodee Viola (USA)
1990 Greg Goody/Jodee Viola (USA)
1991 Greg Goody/Jodee Viola (USA)
1992 Doug Wait/Deanna Monaham
(USA)
1993 Doug Wait/Deanna Monaham
(USA)
1994 Tim Patten/Lisa Friday (USA)
1995 Tim Patten/Lisa Friday (USA)
1996 Axel Haber/Swansi Gebauer
(Germany)
1997 Axel Haber/Swansi Gebauer
(Germany)
Most wins: (3), Jane Puracchio (USA),
1973, 1975–6; Dan Littel/Florence
Arsenault, 1977–9; Greg Goody/Jodee
Viola (USA), as above.

Rowing

World Championships

First held for men in 1962 and for women in 1974; Olympic champions assume the role of world champion in Olympic years; principal events are the single sculls.

Recent winners Single Sculls (Men)
1987 Thomas Lange (East Germany)
1988 Thomas Lange (East Germany)
1989 Thomas Lange (East Germany)
1990 Yuri Janson (USSR)
1991 Thomas Lange (Germany)
1992 Thomas Lange (Germany)
1993 Derek Porter (Canada)
1994 Andre Willms (Germany)
1995 Iztok Cop (Slovenia)
1996 Xeno Müller (Switzerland)
1997 James Koven (USA)
Most wins: (5), Thomas Lange (Germany), as above.

Recent winners Sculls (Women)
1987 Magdelena Georgieva (Bulgaria)
1988 Jutta Behrendt (East Germany)
1989 Elisabeta Lipa (Romania)
1990 Brigit Peter (East Germany)
1991 Silke Laumann (Canada)
1992 Elisabeta Lipa (Romania)
1993 Jana Phieme (Germany)
1994 Trine Hansen (Denmark)
1995 Maria Brandin (Sweden)
1996 Yekaterina Khodotovich (Belarus)
1997 Yekaterina Khodotovich (Belarus)
Most wins: (5), Christine Hahn (*née* Scheiblich) (East Germany), 1974–8.

Diamond Sculls

Highlight of Henley Royal Regatta held every July; first contested in 1884.

Recent winners
1986 Bjarne Eltang (Denmark)
1987 Peter-Michael Kolbe (West Germany)
1988 Hamish McGlashan (Australia)
1989 Vaclav Chalupa (Czechoslovakia)
1990 Eric Verdonk (New Zealand)
1991 Wim van Belleghem (Belgium)
1992 Rorie Henderson (Great Britain)
1993 Thomas Lange (Germany)
1994 Xeno Müller (Switzerland)
1995 Juri Jannson (Estonia)
1996 Merlin Vervoorn (Netherlands)
1997 Greg Searle (Great Britain)
Most wins: (6), Stuart Mackenzie (Great Britain), 1957–62, Guy Nickalls (Great Britain), 1888–91, 1893–4.

Rugby League

Most international caps
60 Jim Sullivan (Wales, Great Britain and other nationalities) 1921–39

Most international points
329 Jim Sullivan (as above)

Most international tries
45 Mick Sullivan (England and Great Britain) 1954–63

Most international goals
160 Jim Sullivan (as above)

Most club appearances
928 Jim Sullivan (Wigan) 1921–46

Most club points
6220 Neil Fox (Wakefield Trinity; Bradford Northern; Hull Kingston Rovers; York; Bramley, and Huddersfield) 1956–79

Most club tries
796 Brian Bevan (Warrington and Blackpool Borough) 1946–1964

Most club goals
2867 Jim Sullivan (Wigan) 1921–46

There are two individual awards in British Rugby League: the Lance Todd Award, given to the player judged to be the 'Man of the Match' in the Challenge Cup Final, and the Harry Sunderland Trophy, for the 'Man of the Match' in the Premiership Final.

Lance Todd Award
First given in 1946

Recent winners
1986 Bob Beardmore (Castleford)
1987 Graham Eadie (Halifax)
1988 Andy Gregory (Wigan)
1989 Ellery Hanley (Wigan)
1990 Andy Gregory (Wigan)
1991 Denis Betts (Wigan)
1992 Martin Offiah (Wigan)
1993 Dean Bell (Wigan)
1994 Martin Offiah (Wigan)
1995 Jason Robinson (Wigan)
1996 Robbie Paul (Bradford Bulls)
1997 Tommy Martin (St Helens)
Most wins: (2), Gerry Helme (Warrington), 1950, 1954; Andy Gregory (Wigan), Martin Offiah (Wigan), as above.

Harry Sunderland Trophy
First given in 1965.

Recent winners
1986 Les Boyd (Warrington)
1987 Joe Lydon (Wigan)
1988 David Hulme (Widnes)
1989 Alan Tait (Widnes)
1990 Alan Tait (Widnes)
1991 Greg Mackey (Hull)
1992 Andy Platt (Wigan)
1993 Chris Joynt (St Helens)
1994 Sam Panapa (Wigan)
1995 Kris Radlinski (Wigan)
1996 Andrew Farrell (Wigan)
1997 Andrew Farrell (Wigan)
Most wins: (2), Alan Tait (Widnes), Andrew Farrell (Wigan) as above.

Rugby Union

Most international caps

No of caps
93 Serge Blanco (France) 1980–91
93 Philippe Sella (France) 1982–92
85 Rory Underwood (England) 1984–97
81 Mike Gibson (Ireland) 1964–79
80 Willie John McBride (Ireland) 1962–75
72 David Campese (Australia) 1982–92
69 Roland Bertranne (France) 1971–81
65 Fergus Slattery (Ireland) 1970–84
63 Michel Crauste (France) 1957–66
63 Benoit Dauga (France) 1964–72
63 Gareth Edwards (Wales) 1967–78
63 J P R Williams (Wales) 1969–81
61 Jean Condom (France) 1982–90
60 Andy Irvine (Scotland) 1972–82
60 Michael Lynagh (Australia) 1984–92
59 Simon Poidevin (Australia) 1980–92
59 Tom Kiernan (Ireland) 1960–73
59 Phil Orr (Ireland) 1976–87
59 Jean-Pierre Rives (France) 1975–84
59 Nick Farr-Jones (Australia) 1984–92
58 Gary Whetton (New Zealand) 1981–92
57 Peter Winterbottom (England) 1982–92
56 Patrick Berbizier (France) 1981–91
56 Laurent Rodriguez (France) 1981–90

Leading international points scorers

Points scored	matches played	
760	60	Michael Lynagh (Australia) 1984–92
571	40	Grant Fox (New Zealand) 1985–92
530	33	Hugo Porta (Argentina) 1972–90
420	44	Gavin Hastings (Scotland/ British Lions) 1986–92
332	33	Didier Camberabero (France) 19
311	28	Naas Botha (South Africa) 1980–92
308	43	Michael Kiernan (Ireland) 1982–91
301	37	Paul Thorburn (Wales) 1985–91
301	60	Andy Irvine (Scotland/ British Lions) 1972–82

Leading international try scorers

tries scored

52	David Campese (Australia) 1982–92	
38	Serge Blanco (France) 1980–91	
35	Rory Underwood (England) 1984–92	
34	John Kirwan (New Zealand) 1984–92	
25	Philippe Sella (France) 1982–92	
24	Ian Smith (Scotland) 1924–33	
23	Christian Darrouy (France) 1957–67	
23	Gerald Davies (Wales/British Lions) 1966–78	

Shooting

Olympic Games

The Olympic competition is the highlight of the shooting calendar; winners in all categories since 1980 are given below.

Free Pistol (Men)
1980 Aleksander Melentyev (USSR)
1984 Xu Haifeng (China)
1988 Sorin Babil (Romania)
1992 Konstantin Loukachik (Unified Team)
1996 Boris Kokorev (Russia)

Rapid Fire Pistol (Men)
1980 Corneliu Ion (Romania)
1984 Takeo Kamachi (Japan)
1988 Afanasi Kouzmine (USSR)
1992 Ralf Schumann (Germany)
1996 Ralf Schumann (Germany)

Small Bore Rifle (Three Position) (Men)
1980 Viktor Vlasov (USSR)
1984 Malcolm Cooper (Great Britain)
1988 Malcolm Cooper (Great Britain)
1992 Grachya Petikiane (Unified Team)
1996 Jean-Pierre Amat (France)

Running Game Target (Men)
1980 Igor Sokolov (USSR)
1984 Li Yuwei (China)
1988 Tor Heiestad (Norway)
1992 Michael Jakosits (Germany)
1996 Yang Ling (China)

Small Bore Rifle (Prone) (Men)
1980 Károly Varga (Hungary)
1984 Edward Etzel (USA)
1988 Miroslav Varga (Czechoslovakia)
1992 Lee Eun-chul (South Korea)
1996 Christian Klees (Germany)

Air Rifle (Men)
1984 Philippe Heberle (France)
1988 Goran Maksimovic (Yugoslavia)
1992 Yuri Fedkin (Unified Team)
1996 Artem Khadzhibekov (Russia)

Air Pistol (Men)
1988 Taniou Kiriakov (USSR)

1992 Wang Yifu (China)
1996 Roberto Di Donna (Italy)

Trap (Men and Women)
1980 Luciano Giovanetti (Italy)
1984 Luciano Giovanetti (Italy)
1988 Dmitri Monakov (USSR)
1992 Petr Hrdlicka (Czechoslovakia)
1996 Michael Diamond (Australia)

Double Trap (Men)
1996 Mark Russell (Australia)

Double Trap (Women)
1996 Kim Rhodes (USA)

Skeet (Men and Women)
1980 Hans Rasmussen (Denmark)
1984 Matthew Dryke (USA)
1988 Axel Wegner (East Germany)
1992 Zhang Shan (China)

Skeet (Men)
1996 Ennion Falco (Italy)

Sport Pistol (Women)
1984 Linda Thom (Canada)
1988 Nino Saloukvadze (USSR)
1992 Marina Logvinenko (Unified Team)
1996 Li Duihong (China)

Air Rifle (Women)
1984 Pat Spurgin (USA)
1988 Irina Chilova (USSR)
1992 Yeo Kab-soon (South Korea)
1996 Renata Mauer (Poland)

Small Bore Rifle (Women)
1984 Wu Xiaoxuan (China)
1988 Silvia Sperber (West Germany)
1992 Launi Melli (USA)
1996 Alexandra Ivosev (Yugoslavia)

Air Pistol (Women)
1988 Jasna Sekuric (Yugoslavia)
1992 Marina Logvinenko (Unified Team)
1996 Olga Klochneva (Russia)

Skiing

World Cup

A season-long competition first organized in 1967; champions are declared in downhill, slalom, giant slalom and super-giant slalom, as well as the overall champion; points are obtained for performances in each category.

Recent overall winners (Men)
1986 Marc Girardelli (Luxembourg)
1987 Pirmin Zurbriggen (Switzerland)
1988 Pirmin Zurbriggen (Switzerland)
1989 Marc Girardelli (Luxembourg)
1990 Pirmin Zurbriggen (Switzerland)
1991 Marc Girardelli (Luxembourg)
1992 Paul Accola (Swiatzerland)
1993 Marc Girardelli (Luxembourg)

1994 Kjetil André Aamodt (Norway)
1995 Alberto Tomba (Italy)
1996 Lasse Kjus (Norway)
1997 Luc Alphand (France)

Recent overall winners (Women)
1986 Maria Walliser (Switzerland)
1987 Maria Walliser (Switzerland)
1988 Michela Figini (Switzerland)
1989 Vreni Schneider (Switzerland)
1990 Petra Kronberger (Austria)
1991 Petra Kronberger (Austria)
1992 Petra Kronberger (Austria)
1993 Anita Wachter (Austria)
1994 Vreni Schneider (Switzerland)
1995 Vreni Schneider (Switzerland)
1996 Katja Seizinger (Germany)
1997 Pernilla Wiberg (Sweden)
Most wins: Men (5), Marc Girardelli (Luxembourg), 1985 and as above. *Women* (6), Annemarie Moser-Pröll (Austria), 1971–5, 1979.

Olympics

Medals for Alpine Combination (overall winner) only awarded regularly since 1988.

Overall winners (Men)
1988 Hubert Strolz (Austria)
1992 Josef Polig (Italy)
1994 Lasse Kjus (Norway)

Overall winners (Women)
1988 Anita Wachter (Austria)
1992 Petra Kronberger (Austria)
1994 Pernille Wiberg (Sweden)

Snooker

World Professional Championship

Instituted in the 1926–7 season; a knockout competition open to professional players who are members of the World Professional Billiards and Snooker Association; played at the Crucible Theatre, Sheffield. A Ranking tournament since 1974.

Winners
1927–40 Joe Davis (England)
1946 Joe Davis (England)
1947 Walter Donaldson (Scotland)
1948–9 Fred Davis (England)
1950 Walter Donaldson (Scotland)
1951 Fred Davis (England)
1952 Horace Lindrum (Australia)
1952–6 Fred Davis (England)
1957 John Pulman (England)
1964–8 John Pulman (England)
1969 John Spencer (England)
1970 Ray Reardon (Wales)
1971 John Spencer (England)
1972 Alex Higgins (Northern Ireland)
1973–6 Ray Reardon (Wales)
1977 John Spencer (England)
1978 Ray Reardon (Wales)

1979	Terry Griffiths (Wales)
1980	Cliff Thorburn (Canada)
1981	Steve Davis (England)
1982	Alex Higgins (Northern Ireland)
1983–4	Steve Davis (England)
1985	Dennis Taylor (Northern Ireland)
1986	Joe Johnson (England)
1987–9	Steve Davis (England)
1990	Stephen Hendry (Scotland)
1991	John Parrott (England)
1992	Stephen Hendry (Scotland)
1993	Stephen Hendry (Scotland)
1994	Stephen Hendry (Scotland)
1995	Stephen Hendry (Scotland)
1996	Stephen Hendry (Scotland)
1997	Ken Doherty (Ireland)

Most wins: (15), Joe Davis (England), 1927–40, 1946.

Benson & Hedges Masters

The most important non-ranking tournament .

Recent winners

1985–6	Cliff Thorburn (Canada)
1987	Dennis Taylor (Northern Ireland)
1988	Steve Davis (England)
1989–92	Stephen Hendry (Scotland)
1993	Stephen Hendry (Scotland)
1994	Stephen Hendry (Scotland)
1995	Ronnie O'Sullivan (England)
1996	Stephen Hendry (Scotland)
1997	Steve Davis (England)

Most wins: (7), Stephen Hendry (Scotland), as above

Ranking Tournaments:

Bournemouth Grand Prix

Originally the Professional Players Tournament; Rothmans Grand Prix up to 1993; Skoda Grand Prix to 1996; a ranking tournament since its inauguration.

Recent winners

1986	Jimmy White (England)
1987	Stephen Hendry (Scotland)
1988–9	Steve Davis (England)
1990–1	Stephen Hendry (Scotland)
1992	Jimmy White (England)
1993	Peter Ebdon (England)
1994	John Higgins (Scotland)
1995	Stephen Hendry (Scotland)
1996	Mark J Williams (Wales)
1997	Dominic Dale (Wales)

Most wins: (4), Stephen Hendry (England), as above.

Mercantile Credit Classic

A ranking tournament since 1984.

Recent winners

1986	Jimmy White (England)
1987–8	Steve Davis (England)

1989	Doug Mountjoy (Wales)
1990	Steve James (England)
1991	Jimmy White (England)
1992	Steve Davis (England)
1993	Stephen Hendry (Scotland)
1994	John Parrot (England)
1995	John Higgins (Scotland)
1996	John Higgins (Scotland)
1997	Stephen Hendry (Scotland)

Most wins: (5), Steve Davis (England), 1980, 1984 and as above.

United Kingdom Open

A ranking tournament since 1984.

Recent winners

1984–7	Steve Davis (England)
1988	Doug Mountjoy (Wales)
1989–90	Stephen Hendry (Scotland)
1991	John Parrott (England)
1992	Jimmy White (England)
1993	Jimmy White (England)
1994	Ronnie O'Sullivan (England)
1995–6	Stephen Hendry (Scotland)
1997	Ronnie O'Sullivan (England)

Most wins: (6) Steve Davis (England), 1980–1, and as above.

British Open

A ranking tournament since 1985.

Recent winners

1986	Steve Davis (England)
1987	Jimmy White (England)
1988	Stephen Hendry (Scotland)
1989	Tony Meo (England)
1990	Bob Chaperon (Canada)
1991	Stephen Hendry (Scotland)
1992	Jimmy White (England)
1993	Steve Davis (England)
1994	Ronnie O'Sullivan (England)
1995	John Higgins (Scotland)
1996	Nigel Bond (England)
1997	Mark J Williams (Wales)

Most wins: (5), Steve Davis (England), 1981–2 and as above.

World Amateur Championship

First held in 1963; originally took place every two years, but annual since 1984.

Recent winners

1986	Paul Mifsud (Malta)
1987	Darren Morgan (Wales)
1988	James Wattana (Thailand)
1989	Ken Doherty (Ireland)
1990	Stephen O'Connor (Ireland)
1991	Noppodol Noppachorn (Thailand)
1992	Neil Mosley (England)
1993	Neil Mosley (England)
1994	Mohammed Yusuf (Pakistan)
1995	Sackai-Sim-ngan (Thailand)
1996	Stuart Bingham (England)

Most wins: (2), Gary Owen (England), 1963, 1966; Ray Edmonds (England), 1972, 1974; Paul Mifsud, 1985–6.

Speedway

World Championships

Individual championships inaugurated in 1936; team championship instituted in 1960; first official pairs world championship in 1970 (threes from 1991); became the World Team Cup in 1994.

Recent winners

1986	Hans Nielsen (Denmark)
1987	Hans Nielsen (Denmark)
1988	Erik Gundersen (Denmark)
1989	Hans Nielsen (Denmark)
1990	Per Jonsson (Sweden)
1991	Jan Pedersen (Denmark)
1992	Gary Havelock (England)
1993	Sam Ermolenko (USA)
1994	Tony Rickardsson (Sweden)
1995	Hans Nielsen (Denmark)
1996	Billy Hamill (USA)
1997	Greg Hancock (USA)

Most wins: (6), Ivan Mauger (New Zealand), 1968–70, 1972, 1977 and as above.

Recent winners (Pairs)

1986	Erik Gundersen/Hans Nielsen (Denmark)
1987	Erik Gundersen/Hans Nielsen (Denmark)
1988	Erik Gundersen/Hans Nielsen (Denmark)
1989	Erik Gundersen/Hans Nielsen (Denmark)
1990	Hans Nielsen/Jan Pedersen (Denmark)
1991	Hans Nielsen/Jan Pedersen/Tommy Knudsen (Denmark)
1992	Greg Hancock/Sam Ermolenko/Ronnie Correy (USA)
1993	Tony Rickardsson/Per Jonsson/Henrik Gustafsson (Sweden)

World Team Cup

1994	Per Gustafsonn/Tony Rickardsson (Sweden)
1995	Hans Neilsen/Tommy Knudsen/Brian Carger (Denmark)
1996	Tomasz Gollob/Piotr Protasiewicz/Slawomir Drabik (Poland)

Most wins: (7), Hans Nielsen (Denmark) 1979, and as above.

Squash

World Open Championship

First held in 1976; takes place annually for men, every two years for women before 1991.

Recent winners (Men)

1984	Jahangir Khan (Pakistan)
1985	Jahangir Khan (Pakistan)

1986　Ross Norman (New Zealand)
1987　Jansher Khan (Pakistan)
1988　Jahangir Khan (Pakistan)
1989　Jansher Khan (Pakistan)
1990　Jansher Khan (Pakistan)
1991　Rodney Martin (Australia)
1992　Jansher Khan (Pakistan)
1993　Jansher Khan (Pakistan)
1994　Jansher Khan (Pakistan)
1995　Jansher Khan (Pakistan)
1996　Jansher Khan (Pakistan)
1997　Rodney Eyles (Australia)
Most wins: (8), Jansher Khan (Pakistan), as above.

Recent winners (Women)
1985　Sue Devoy (New Zealand)
1987　Sue Devoy (New Zealand)
1989　Martine Le Moignan (Great
　　　　Britain)
1991　Sue Devoy (New Zealand)
1992　Sue Devoy (New Zealand)
1993　Michelle Martin (Australia)
1994　Michelle Martin (Australia)
1995　Michelle Martin (Australia)
1996　Sarah Fitzgerald (Australia)
1997　Sarah Fitzgerald (Australia)
Most wins: (4), Sue Devoy (New Zealand), as above.

Surfing

World Professional Championship
A season-long series of Grand Prix events; first held in 1970.

Recent winners (Men)
1986　Tommy Curren (USA)
1987　Damien Hardman (Australia)
1988　Barton Lynch (Australia)
1989　Martin Potter (Great Britain)
1990　Tommy Curren (USA)
1991　Damien Hardman (Australia)
1992　Kelly Slater (USA)
1993　Derek Ho (Hawaii)
1994　Kelly Slater (USA)
1995　Kelly Slater (USA)
1996　Kelly Slater (USA)
1997　Kelly Slater (USA)

Recent winners (Women)
1986　Frieda Zamba (USA)
1987　Wendy Botha (South Africa)
1988　Freida Zamba (USA)
1989　Wendy Botha (South Africa)
1990　Pam Burridge (Australia)
1991　Wendy Botha (Australia)
1992　Wendy Botha (Australia)
1993　Pauline Menczer (Australia)
1994　Lisa Anderson (USA)
1995　Lisa Anderson (USA)
1996　Lisa Anderson (USA)
Most wins: Men (5), Mark Richards Australia), 1975, 1979–83; Kelly Slater (USA), as above. *Women* (4), Wendy Botha (South Africa/Australia), as above.

Swimming and Diving

World Championships
First held in 1973, the World Championships have since taken place in 1975, 1978, 1982, 1986, 1991, and 1994.

1994 EVENT WINNERS (MEN)

50 m freestyle
Alexander Popov (Russia)

100 m freestyle
Alexander Popov (Russia)

200 m freestyle
Antti Kasvio (Finland)

400 m freestyle
Kieren Perkins (Australia)

1500 m freestyle
Kieren Perkins (Australia)

100 m backstroke
Martin López-Zubero (Spain)

200 m backstroke
Vladimir Selkov (Russia)

100 m breaststroke
Norbert Rosza (Hungary)

200 m breaststroke
Norbert Rosza (Hungary)

100 m butterfly
Rafal Szukala (Poland)

200 m butterfly
Denis Pankratov (Russia)

200 m individual medley
Jani Sievinen (Finland)

400 m individual medley
Tom Dolan (USA)

1 m springboard diving
Evan Stewart (Zimbabwe)

Platform diving
Dimitri Sautin (Russia)

1994 EVENT WINNERS (WOMEN)

50 m freestyle
Jingyi Le (China)

100 m freestyle
Jingyi Le (China)

200 m freestyle
Franziska van Almsick (Germany)

400 m freestyle
Aihua Yang (China)

800 m freestyle
Janet Evans (USA)

100 m backstroke
Cehong He (China)

200 m backstroke
Cehong He (China)

100 m breaststroke
Samantha Riley (Australia)

200 m breaststroke
Samantha Riley (Australia)

100 m butterfly
Limin Liu (China)

200 m butterfly
Limin Liu (China)

200 m individual medley
Lu Bin (China)

400 m individual medley
Guohong Dai (China)

1 m springboard diving
Lixia Chen (China)

Platform diving
Fu Mingxia (China)

Synchronized swimming
Solo
Becky Dyroen Lancer (USA)

Duet
Becky Dyroen Lancer/Jill Sudduth (USA)

Olympic games

1996 EVENT WINNERS (MEN)

50 m freestyle
Alexander Popov (Russia)

100 m freestyle
Alexander Popov (Russia)

200 m freestyle
Danyon Loader (New Zealand)

400 m freestyle
Danyon Loader (New Zealand)

1500 m freestyle
Keiren Perkins (Australia)

100 m breaststroke
Fred de Burghgraeve (Belgium)

200 m breaststroke
Norbert Rozsa (Hungary)

100 m butterfly
Denis Pankratov (Russia)

200 m butterfly
Denis Pankratov (Russia)

100 m backstroke
Jeff Rouse (USA)

200 m backstroke
Brad Bridgewater (USA)

200 m individual medley
Attila Czene (Hungary)

400 m individual medley
Tom Dolan (USA)

1996 EVENT WINNERS (WOMEN)

50 m freestyle
Amy van Dyken (USA)

100m freestyle	200m breaststroke	200m butterfly
Jingyi Le (China)	Penelope Heyns (South Africa)	Susan O'Neill (Australia)
200m freestyle	**100m backstroke**	**200m individual medley**
Claudia Poll (Costa Rica)	Beth Botsford (USA)	Michelle Smith (Ireland)
400m freestyle	**200m backstroke**	**400m individual medley**
Michelle Smith (Ireland)	Krisztina Egerszegi (Hungary)	Michelle Smith (Ireland)
100m breaststroke	**100m butterfly**	
Penelope Heyns (South Africa)	Amy van Dyken (USA)	

World Swimming Records
As of October 1997

MEN'S RECORDS

Distance	Time	Holder	Country	Where made	Date
Freestyle					
50m	0:21.81	Tom Jager	USA	Nashville	24 Mar 1990
100m	0:48.21	Alexander Popov	Russia	Monte Carlo	18 Jun 1994
200m	1:46.69	Giorgio Lamberti	Italy	Bonn	15 Aug 1989
400m	3:43.80	Kieren Perkins	Australia		
800m	7:46.00	Kieren Perkins	Australia	Rome	9 Sep 1994
1500m	14:41.66	Kieren Perkins	Australia	Victoria, Canada	24 Aug 1994
Breaststroke					
100m	1:00.95	Karolyi Guttler	Hungary	Sheffield, England	3 Aug 1993
200m	2:10.16	Mike Barrowman	USA	Barcelona	25 Jul 1992
Butterfly					
100m	0:52.15	Michael Klim	Australia	Australia	8 Oct 1997
200m	1:52.64	Denis Pankratov	Russia	Gelsenkirchen, Germany	2 Feb 1997
Backstroke					
100m	0:53.86	Jeff Rouse	USA	Barcelona	29 Jul 1992
200m	1:56.57	Martin López-Zubero	Spain	Indianapolis	3 Mar 1992
Individual Medley					
200m	1:58.16	Jani Sievinen	Finland	Rome	11 Sep 1994
400m	4:05.59	M Wouda	Netherlands	Gelsenkirchen, Germany	2 Feb 1997
Freestyle Relays					
400m (4×100)	3:15.11	David Fox	USA	Atlanta	12 Aug 1995
		Joseph Hudepohl			
		Jonathan Olsen			
		Gary Hall			
800m (4×200)	7:11.95	Dmitriy Lepikov	Unified Team	Barcelona	27 Jul 1992
		Vladimir Pychnenko			
		Venyamin Tayanovich			
		Yevgeniy Sadoviy			
Medley Relays					
400m (4×100)	3:34.84	Jeff Rouse	USA	Atlanta	26 Jul 1996
		Jeremy Linn			
		Mark Henderson			
		Gary Hall			

WOMEN'S RECORDS

Distance	Time	Holder	Country	Where made	Date
Freestyle					
50m	0:24.51	Jingye Le	China	Rome	11 Sep 1994
100m	0:54.01	Jingye Le	China	Rome	5 Sep 1994
200m	1:56.78	Franziska van Almsick	Germany	Rome	6 Sep 1994
400m	4:03.85	Janet Evans	USA	Seoul	22 Sep 1988
800m	8:16.22	Janet Evans	USA	Tokyo	20 Aug 1989
1500m	15:52.10	Janet Evans	USA	Orlando, FL	26 Mar 1988
Breaststroke					
100m	1:07.02	Penelope Heyns	South Africa	Atlanta	21 Jul 1996
200m	2:24.76	Rebecca Brown	Australia	Queensland	16 Mar 1994

Butterfly

100 m	0:57.93	Mary T Meagher	USA	Brown Deer, WI	16 Aug 1981
200 m	2:05.96	Mary T Meagher	USA	Brown Deer, WI	13 Aug 1981

Backstroke

100 m	1:00.16	Cihong He	China	Rome	10 Sep 1994
200 m	2:06.62	Krisztina Egerszegi	Hungary	Athens	25 Aug 1991

Individual Medley

200 m	2:11.57	Lu Bin	China	Hiroshima	7 Oct 1994
400 m	4:34.79	Chen Yan	China	Shanghai	13 Oct 1997

Freestyle Relays

400 m (4×100)	3:37.91	Jingye Le Ying Shan Ying Le Lu Bin	China	Rome	7 Sep 1994
800 m (4×200)	7:55.47	Manuela Stellmach Astrid Strauss Anke Möhring Heike Fredrich	East Germany	Strasbourg	18 Aug 1987

Medley Relays

400 m (4×100)	4:01.67	Cihong He Guohong Dai Limin Lui Jingye Le	China	Rome	10 Sep 1994

Table Tennis

World Championships

First held in 1926 and every two years since 1957.

Recent winners (Men's Singles)
1979 Seiji Ono (Japan)
1981 Guo Yuehua (China)
1983 Guo Yuehua (China)
1985 Jiang Jialiang (China)
1987 Jiang Jialiang (China)
1989 Jan-Ove Waldner (Sweden)
1991 Jorgen Persson (Sweden)
1993 Jean-Philippe Gatien (France)
1995 Kong Lin-Hui (China)
1997 Jan-Ove Waldner (Sweden)
Most wins: (5), Viktor Barna (Hungary), 1930, 1932–5.

Recent winners (Women's Singles)
1979 Ge Xinai (China)
1981 Ting Ling (China)
1983 Cao Yanhua (China)
1985 Cao Yanhua (China)
1987 He Zhili (China)
1989 Qiao Hong (China)
1991 Deng Yaping (China)
1993 Hyun Jung-hwa (South Korea)
1995 Deng Yaping (China)
1996 Deng Yaping (China)
Most wins: (6), Angelica Rozeanu (Romania), 1950–55.

Recent winners (Men's Doubles)
1979 Dragutin Surbek/Anton
       Stipancic (Yugoslavia)

1981 Cai Zhenhua/Li Zhenshi (China)
1983 Dragutin Surbek/Zoran Kalinic
       (Yugoslavia)
1985 Mikael Applegren/Ulf Carlsson
       (Sweden)
1987 Chen Longcan/Wei Quinguang
       (China)
1989 Joerg Rosskopf/Stefen Fetzner
       (West Germany)
1991 Peter Karlson/Thomas von
       Scheele (Sweden)
1993 Wang Tao/Lu Lin (China)
1995 Wang Tao/Lu Lin (China)
1997 Kong Linghui/Liu Guoliang
       (China)
Most wins: (8), Viktor Barna (Hungary/England), 1929–33 (two titles 1933), 1935, 1939.

Recent winners (Women's Doubles)
1979 Zhang Li/Zhang Deying (China)
1981 Zhang Deying/Cao Yanhua
       (China)
1983 Shen Jianping/Dai Lili (China)
1985 Dai Lili/Geng Lijuan (China)
1987 Yang Young-Ja/Hyun Jung-Hwa
       (South Korea)
1989 Quio Hong/Deng Yaping (China)
1991 Chen Zhie/Gao Jun (China)
1993 Liu Wey/Qiao Yun Ping (China)
1995 Deng Yaping/Qiao Hong (China)
1997 Deng Yaping/Yang Ying (China)
Most wins: (7), Maria Mednyanszky (Hungary), 1928, 1930–5.

Recent winners (Mixed Doubles)
1979 Liang Geliang/Ge Xinai (China)
1981 Xie Saike/Huang Junqun (China)
1983 Guo Yuehua/Ni Xialian (China)
1985 Cai Zhenua/Cao Yanhua (China)
1987 Hui Jun/Geng Lijuan (China)
1989 Yoo Nam-Kyu/Hyun Jung-Hwa
       (South Korea)
1991 Wang Tao/Liu Wei (China)
1993 Wang Tao/Liu Wei (China)
1995 Wang Tao/Liu Wei (China)
1997 Liu Guoliang/Wu Na (China)
Most wins: (6), Maria Mednyanszky (Hungary), 1927–8, 1930–1, 1933 (two titles).

Olympic Games

Table Tennis became an Olympic event in 1988.

Winners Men's Singles
1988 Yoo Nam-kyu (South Korea)
1992 Jan-Ove Waldner (Sweden)
1996 Lui Guoliang (China)

Winners Women's Singles
1988 Chen Jing (China)
1992 Deng Yaping (China)
1996 Deng Yaping (China)

Winners Men's Doubles
1988 Chen Longcan/Wei Qingguang
       (China)
1992 Lu Lin/Wang Tao (China)
1996 Kong Linghui/Liu Guoliang
       (China)

Winners Women's Doubles

1988 Hyun Jung-hwa/Yang Young-ja
      (South Korea)
1992 Qiao Hong/Deng Yaping (China)
1996 Qiao Hong/Deng Yaping (China)

Tennis (Lawn)

Wimbledon Championships

The All-England Championships at
Wimbledon are Lawn Tennis's most
prestigious championships; first held
in 1877.

*Winners Men's Singles (British unless
stated)*

1877	Spencer W Gore
1878	P Frank Hadow
1879	John T Hartley
1880	John T Hartley
1881	William Renshaw
1882	William Renshaw
1883	William Renshaw
1884	William Renshaw
1885	William Renshaw
1886	William Renshaw
1887	Herbert F Lawford
1888	Ernest Renshaw
1889	William Renshaw
1890	William J Hamilton
1891	Wilfred Baddeley
1892	Wilfred Baddeley
1893	Joshua Pim
1894	Joshua Pim
1895	Wilfred Baddeley
1896	Harold S Mahoney
1897	Reggie F Doherty
1898	Reggie F Doherty
1899	Reggie F Doherty
1900	Reggie F Doherty
1901	Arthur W Gore
1902	H Laurie Doherty
1903	H Laurie Doherty
1904	H Laurie Doherty
1905	H Laurie Doherty
1906	H Laurie Doherty
1907	Norman E Brookes (Australia)
1908	Arthur W Gore
1909	Arthur W Gore
1910	Anthony F Wilding (New Zealand)
1911	Anthony F Wilding (New Zealand)
1912	Anthony F Wilding (New Zealand)
1913	Anthony F Wilding (New Zealand)
1914	Norman E Brookes (Australia)
1919	Gerald L Patterson (Australia)
1920	Bill Tilden (USA)
1921	Bill Tilden (USA)
1922	Gerald L Patterson (Australia)
1923	Bill Johnston (USA)
1924	Jean Borotra (France)
1925	René Lacoste (France)
1926	Jean Borotra (France)
1927	Henri Cochet (France)
1928	Rene Lacoste (France)
1929	Henri Cochet (France)

1930	Bill Tilden (USA)
1931	Sidney B Wood Jr (USA)
1932	Ellsworth Vines (USA)
1933	Jack Crawford (Australia)
1934	Fred Perry
1935	Fred Perry
1936	Fred Perry
1937	Don Budge (USA)
1938	Don Budge (USA)
1939	Bobby Riggs (USA)
1946	Yvon Petra (France)
1947	Jack Kramer (USA)
1948	Bob Falkenburg (USA)
1949	Ted Schroeder (USA)
1950	Budge Patty (USA)
1951	Dick Savitt (USA)
1952	Frank Sedgman (Australia)
1953	Vic Seixas (USA)
1954	Jaroslav Drobny (Egypt)
1955	Tony Trabert (USA)
1956	Lew Hoad (Australia)
1957	Lew Hoad (Australia)
1958	Ashley Cooper (Australia)
1959	Alex Olmedo (USA)
1960	Neale Fraser (Australia)
1961	Rod Laver (Australia)
1962	Rod Laver (Australia)
1963	Chuck McKinley (USA)
1964	Roy Emerson (Australia)
1965	Roy Emerson (Australia)
1966	Manuel Santana (Spain)
1967	John Newcombe (Australia)
1968	Rod Laver (Australia)
1969	Rod Laver (Australia)
1970	John Newcombe (Australia)
1971	John Newcombe (Australia)
1972	Stan Smith (USA)
1973	Jan Kodes (Czechoslovakia)
1974	Jimmy Connors (USA)
1975	Arthur Ashe (USA)
1976	Bjorn Borg (Sweden)
1977	Bjorn Borg (Sweden)
1978	Bjorn Borg (Sweden)
1979	Bjorn Borg (Sweden)
1980	Bjorn Borg (Sweden)
1981	John McEnroe (USA)
1982	Jimmy Connors (USA)
1983	John McEnroe (USA)
1984	John McEnroe (USA)
1985	Boris Becker (West Germany)
1986	Boris Becker (West Germany)
1987	Pat Cash (Australia)
1988	Stefan Edberg (Sweden)
1989	Boris Becker (West Germany)
1990	Stefan Edberg (Sweden)
1991	Michael Stich (Germany)
1992	Andre Agassi (USA)
1993	Pete Sampras (USA)
1994	Pete Sampras (USA)
1995	Pete Sampras (USA)
1996	Richard Krajicek (Netherlands)
1997	Pete Sampras (USA)

Most wins: (7), William Renshaw (Great
Britain), as above.

Winners Women's Singles

1884	Maud Watson
1885	Maud Watson
1886	Blanche Bingley
1887	Charlotte Dod
1888	Charlotte Dod
1889	Blanche Bingley Hillyard
1890	Lena Rice
1891	Charlotte Dod
1892	Charlotte Dod
1893	Charlotte Dod
1894	Blanche Bingley Hillyard
1895	Charlotte Cooper
1896	Charlotte Cooper
1897	Blanche Bingley Hillyard
1898	Charlotte Cooper
1899	Blanche Bingley Hillyard
1900	Blanche Bingley Hillyard
1901	Charlotte Sterry (*née* Cooper)
1902	Muriel Robb
1903	Dorothea Douglass
1904	Dorothea Douglass
1905	May Sutton (USA)
1906	Dorothea Douglass
1907	Mary Sutton (USA)
1908	Charlotte Sterry
1909	Dora Boothby
1910	Dorothea Lambert Chambers (*née* Douglass)
1911	Dorothea Lambert Chambers
1912	Ethel Larcombe
1913	Dorothea Lambert Chambers
1914	Dorothea Lambert Chambers
1919	Suzanne Lenglen (France)
1920	Suzanne Lenglen (France)
1921	Suzanne Lenglen (France)
1922	Suzanne Lenglen (France)
1923	Suzanne Lenglen (France)
1924	Kitty McKane
1925	Suzanne Lenglon (France)
1926	Kitty Godfree (*née* McKane)
1927	Helen Wills (USA)
1928	Helen Wills (USA)
1929	Helen Wills (USA)
1930	Helen Wills Moody (USA)
1931	Cilly Aussem (Germany)
1932	Helen Wills Moody (USA)
1933	Helen Wills Moody (USA)
1934	Dorothy Round
1935	Helen Wills Moody (USA)
1936	Helen Jacobs (USA)
1937	Dorothy Round
1938	Helen Wills Moody (USA)
1939	Alice Marble (USA)
1946	Pauline Betz (USA)
1947	Margaret Osborne (USA)
1948	Louise Brough (USA)
1949	Louise Brough (USA)
1950	Louise Brough (USA)
1951	Doris Hart (USA)
1952	Maureen Connolly (USA)
1953	Maureen Connolly (USA)
1954	Maureen Connolly (USA)
1955	Louise Brough (USA)

1956	Shirley Fry (USA)
1957	Althea Gibson (USA)
1958	Althea Gibson (USA)
1959	Maria Bueno (Brazil)
1960	Maria Bueno (Brazil)
1961	Angela Mortimer
1962	Karen Hantze Susman (USA)
1963	Margaret Smith (Australia)
1964	Maria Bueno (Brazil)
1965	Margaret Smith (Australia)
1966	Billie Jean King (USA)
1967	Billie Jean King (USA)
1968	Billie Jean King (USA)
1969	Ann Haydon Jones
1970	Margaret Court (née Smith) (Australia)
1971	Evonne Goolagong (Australia)
1972	Billie Jean King (USA)
1973	Billie Jean King (USA)
1974	Chris Evert (USA)
1975	Billie Jean King (USA)
1976	Chris Evert (USA)
1977	Virginia Wade
1978	Martina Navrátilová (Czechoslovakia)
1979	Martina Navrátilová (Czechoslovakia)
1980	Evonne Cawley (née Goolagong) (Australia)
1981	Chris Evert Lloyd (USA)
1982	Martina Navrátilová (USA)
1983	Martina Navrátilová (USA)
1984	Martina Navrátilová (USA)
1985	Martina Navrátilová (USA)
1986	Martina Navrátilová (USA)
1987	Martina Navrátilová (USA)
1988	Steffi Graf (West Germany)
1989	Steffi Graf (West Germany)
1990	Martina Navrátilová (USA)
1991	Steffi Graf (Germany)
1992	Steffi Graf (Germany)
1993	Steffi Graf (Germany)
1994	Conchita Martinez (Spain)
1995	Steffi Graf (Germany)
1996	Steffi Graf (Germany)
1997	Martina Hingis (Switzerland)

Most wins: (9), Martina Navrátilová (USA).

Recent winners Men's Doubles

1988	Ken Flach/Robert Seguso (USA)
1989	John Fitzgerald (Australia)/ Anders Järryd (Sweden)
1990	Rick Leach/Jim Pugh (USA)
1991	John Fitzgerald (Australia)/ Anders Järryd (Sweden)
1992	John McEnroe (USA)/Michael Stich (Germany)
1993	Todd Woodbridge/Mark Woodforde (Australia)
1994	Todd Woodbridge/Mark Woodforde (Australia)
1995	Todd Woodbridge/Mark Woodforde (Australia)

1996	Todd Woodbridge/Mark Woodforde (Australia)
1997	Todd Woodbridge/Mark Woodforde (Australia)

Most wins: (8), Lawrence Doherty/Reg Doherty (Great Britain), 1897–1901, 1903–5.

Recent winners Women's Doubles

1988	Steffi Graf (West Germany)/ Gabriela Sabatini (Argentina)
1989	Jana Novotná/Helena Suková (Czechoslovakia)
1990	Jana Novotná/Helena Suková (Czechoslovakia)
1991	Larissa Sarchenko/Natasha Zvereva (USSR)
1992	Gigi Fernandez (USA)/Natasha Zvereva (Belarus)
1993	Gigi Fernandez (USA)/Natasha Zvereva (Belarus)
1994	Gigi Fernandez (USA)/Natasha Zvereva (Belarus)
1995	Jana Novotná (Czech Republic)/Arantxa Sanchez Vicario (Spain)
1996	Helena Suková (Czech Republic)/Martina Hingis (Switzerland)
1997	Gigi Fernandez (USA)/Natasha Zvereva (Belarus)

Most wins: (12), Elizabeth Ryan (USA), 1914, 1919–23, 1925–7, 1930, 1933–4.

Recent winners Mixed Doubles

1988	Zina Garrison/Sherwood Stewart (USA)
1989	Jana Novotná (Czechoslovakia)/ Jim Pugh (USA)
1990	Zina Garrison/Rick Leach (USA)
1991	Elizabeth Smylie/John Fitzgerald (Australia)
1992	Larissa Savchenko (Latvia)/Cyril Suk (Czech Republic)
1993	Martina Navrátilová (USA)/Mark Woodforde (Australia)
1994	Helena Suková (Czech Republic)/Todd Woodbridge (Australia)
1995	Martina Navrátilová/Jonathan Stark (USA)
1996	Helena Suková/Cyril Suk (Czech Republic)
1997	Helena Suková/Cyril Suk (Czech Republic)

Most wins: (7), Elizabeth Ryan (USA), 1919, 1921, 1923, 1927–8, 1930, 1932.

United States Open

First held in 1881 as the United States Championship; became the United States Open in 1968.

Winners Men's Singles (USA unless stated).

1881	Richard D Sears
1882	Richard D Sears
1883	Richard D Sears

1884	Richard D Sears
1885	Richard D Sears
1886	Richard D Sears
1887	Richard D Sears
1888	H W Slocum Jr
1889	H W Slocum Jr
1890	Oliver S Campbell
1891	Oliver S Campbell
1892	Oliver S Campbell
1893	Robert D Wrenn
1894	Robert D Wrenn
1895	Frederick H Hovey
1896	Robert D Wrenn
1897	Robert D Wrenn
1898	Malcolm D Whitman
1899	Malcolm D Whitman
1900	Malcolm D Whitman
1901	William A Larned
1902	William A Larned
1903	H Laurie Doherty (Great Britain)
1904	Holcombe Ward
1905	Beals C Wright
1906	William J Clothier
1907	William A Larned
1908	William A Larned
1909	William A Larned
1910	William A Larned
1911	William A Larned
1912	Maurice E McLoughlin
1913	Maurice E McLoughlin
1914	Richard N Williams
1915	Bill Johnston
1916	Richard N Williams
1917	R L Murray
1918	R L Murray
1919	Bill Johnston
1920	Bill Tilden
1921	Bill Tilden
1922	Bill Tilden
1923	Bill Tilden
1924	Bill Tilden
1925	Bill Tilden
1926	René Lacoste (France)
1927	René Lacoste (France)
1928	Henri Cochet (France)
1929	Bill Tilden
1930	John H Doeg
1931	Ellsworth Vines
1932	Ellsworth Vines
1933	Fred Perry (Great Britain)
1934	Fred Perry (Great Britain)
1935	Wilmer L Allison
1936	Fred Perry (Great Britain)
1937	Don Budge
1938	Don Budge
1939	Bobby Riggs
1940	Don McNeill
1941	Bobby Riggs
1942	Ted Schroeder
1943	Joseph R Hunt
1944	Frank Parker
1945	Frank Parker
1946	Jack Kramer
1947	Jack Kramer
1948	Pancho Gonzales

1949	Pancho Gonzales	1898	Juliette Atkinson	1963	Maria Bueno (Brazil)
1950	Arthur Larsen	1899	Marion Jones	1964	Maria Bueno (Brazil)
1951	Frank Sedgman	1900	Myrtle McAteer	1965	Margaret Smith (Australia)
1952	Frank Sedgman	1901	Elisabeth Moore	1966	Maria Bueno (Brazil)
1953	Tony Trabert	1902	Marion Jones	1967	Billie Jean King
1954	Vic Seixas	1903	Elisabeth Moore	1968	Virginia Wade (Great Britain)
1955	Tony Trabert	1904	May Sutton	1968	Margaret Court (*née* Smith)
1956	Ken Rosewall (Australia)	1905	Elisabeth Moore		(Australia)
1957	Mal Anderson (Australia)	1906	Helen Homans	1969	Margaret Court (Australia)
1958	Ashley J Cooper (Australia)	1907	Evelyn Sears	1969	Margaret Court (Australia)
1959	Neale Fraser (Australia)	1908	Maud Berger-Wallach	1970	Margaret Court (Australia)
1960	Neale Fraser (Australia)	1909	Hazel Hotchkiss	1971	Billie Jean King
1961	Roy Emerson (Australia)	1910	Hazel Hotchkiss	1972	Billie Jean King
1962	Rod Laver (Australia)	1911	Hazel Hotchkiss	1973	Margaret Court (Australia)
1963	Rafael Osuna (Mexico)	1912	Mary K Browne	1974	Billie Jean King
1964	Roy Emerson (Australia)	1913	Mary K Browne	1975	Chris Evert
1965	Manuel Santana (Spain)	1914	Mary K Browne	1976	Chris Evert
1966	Fred Stolle (Australia)	1915	Molla Bjurstedt	1977	Chris Evert
1967	John Newcombe (Australia)	1916	Molla Bjurstedt	1978	Chirs Evert
1968	Arthur Ashe	1917	Molla Bjurstedt	1979	Tracy Austin
1969	Rod Laver (Australia)	1918	Molla Bjurstedt	1980	Chris Evert Lloyd
1970	Ken Rosewall (Australia)	1919	Hazel Hotchkiss Wightman	1981	Tracy Austin
1971	Stan Smith	1920	Molla Bjurstedt Mallory	1982	Chris Evert Lloyd
1972	Ilie Nastase (Romania)	1921	Molla Bjurstedt Mallory	1983	Martina Navrátilová
1973	John Newcombe (Australia)	1922	Molla Bjurstedt Mallory	1984	Martina Navrátilová
1974	Jimmy Connors	1923	Helen Wills	1985	Hana Mandlikova
1975	Manuel Orantes (Spain)	1924	Helen Wills		(Czechoslovakia)
1976	Jimmy Connors	1925	Helen Wills	1986	Martina Navrátilová
1977	Guillermo Vilas (Argentina)	1926	Molla Bjurstedt Mallory	1987	Martina Navrátilová
1978	Jimmy Conners	1927	Helen Wills	1988	Steffi Graf (West Germany)
1979	John McEnroe	1928	Helen Wills	1989	Steffi Graf (West Germany)
1980	John McEnroe	1929	Helen Wills	1990	Gabriela Sabatini (Argentina)
1981	John McEnroe	1930	Betty Nuthall (Great Britain)	1991	Monica Seles (Yugoslavia)
1982	Jimmy Connors	1931	Helen Wills Moody	1992	Monica Seles (Yugoslavia)
1983	Jimmy Connors	1932	Helen Jacobs	1993	Steffi Graf (Germany)
1984	John McEnroe	1933	Helen Jacobs	1994	Arantxa Sánchez Vicario (Spain)
1985	Ivan Lendl (Czechoslovakia)	1934	Helen Jacobs	1995	Steffi Graf (Germany)
1986	Ivan Lendl (Czechoslovakia)	1935	Helen Jacobs	1996	Steffi Graf (Germany)
1987	Ivan Lendl (Czechoslovakia)	1936	Alice Marble	1997	Martina Hingis (Switzerland)
1988	Mats Wilander (Sweden)	1937	Anita Lizane (Chile)		
1989	Boris Becker (West Germany)	1938	Alice Marble		

Most wins: (7), Molla Bjurstedt Mallory (USA); Helen Wills Moody (USA).

1990	Pete Sampras	1939	Alice Marble
1991	Stefan Edberg (Sweden)	1940	Alice Marble
1992	Stefan Edberg (Sweden)	1941	Sarah Palfrey Cooke
1993	Pete Sampras	1942	Pauline Betz
1994	Andre Agassi	1943	Pauline Betz
1995	Pete Sampras	1944	Pauline Betz
1996	Pete Sampras	1945	Sarah Palfrey Cooke
1997	Patrick Rafter (Australia)	1946	Pauline Betz

Most wins: Men (7), Richard D Sears (USA); William A Larned (USA); Bill Tilden (USA).

Recent Winners Men's Doubles

1988	Sergio Casal/Emilio Sánchez (Spain)
1989	John McEnroe (USA)/ Mark Woodforde (Australia)
1990	Pieter Aldrich/Dannie Visser (South Africa)
1991	John Fitzgerald (Australia)/ Anders Järryd (Sweden)
1992	Jim Grabb/Richard Reneberg
1993	Kelly Jones/Rick Leach
1994	Jacco Eltingh/Paul Haarhuis (Netherlands)
1995	Todd Woodbridge/Mark Woodforde (Australia)
1996	Todd Woodbridge/Mark Woodforde (Australia)
1997	Yevgeny Kavelnikov (Russia)/Daniel Vacek (Czech Republic)

Most wins: (6) Richard D Sears (USA) 1882–7.

Winners Women's Singles

1887	Ellen Hansell	1947	Louise Brough
1888	Bertha L Townsend	1948	Margaret Osborne duPont
1889	Bertha L Townsend	1949	Margaret Osborne duPont
1890	Ellen C Roosevelt	1950	Margaret Osborne duPont
1891	Mabel Chaill	1951	Maureen Connolly
1892	Mabel Chaill	1952	Maureen Connolly
1893	Aline Terry	1953	Maureen Connolly
1894	Helen Hellwig	1954	Doris Hart
1895	Juliette Atkinson	1955	Doris Hart
1896	Elisabeth Moore	1956	Shirley Fry
1897	Juliette Atkinson	1957	Althea Gibson
		1958	Althea Gibson
		1959	Maria Bueno (Brazil)
		1960	Darlene Hard
		1961	Darline Hard
		1962	Margaret Smith (Australia)

Recent Winners Women's Doubles

1988	Gigi Fernandez/Robin White
1989	Martina Navrátilová (USA)/Hana Mandlíková (Czechoslovakia)
1990	Martina Navrátilová/Gigi Fernandez
1991	Pam Shriver (USA)/Natalya Zvereva (USSR)
1992	Jana Novotná (Czechoslovakia)/Larissa Savchenko (Latvia)
1993	Jana Novotná (Czech Republic)/Larissa Savchenko (Latvia)
1994	Arantxa Sánchez Vicario (Spain)/Jana Novotná (Czech Republic)
1995	Gigi Fernandez (USA)/Natasha Zvereva (Belarus)
1996	Gigi Fernandez (USA)/Natasha Zvereva (Belarus)
1997	Lindsay Davenport (USA)/Venus Williams (USA)

Most wins: (13) Margaret DuPont (née Osborne) (USA), 1941–50, 1955–7.

Recent Winners Mixed Doubles

1989	Robin White/Shelby Camon
1990	Elizabeth Smylie/ Todd Woodbridge (Australia)
1991	Manon Bollegraf/ Tom Hussen (Netherlands)
1992	Nicole Provis/Mark Woodforde (Australia)
1993	Nicole Provis/Mark Woodforde (Australia)
1994	Elna Reinach (South Africa)/Patrick Galbraith (USA)
1995	Meredith McGrath/Matt Lucena (USA)
1996	Lisa Raymond/Patrick Galbraith (USA)
1997	Manon Bollegraf (Netherlands)/Rick Leach (USA)

Most wins: (9), Margaret Osborne du Pont (USA), 1943–6, 1950, 1056, 1058–60.

French Open

French Championships were held since 1891; became open to all-comers in1925.

Winners Men's Singles

1925	Rene Lacoste (France)
1926	Henri Cochet (France)
1927	Rene Lacoste (France)
1928	Henri Cochet (France)
1929	Rene Lacoste (France)
1930	Henri Cochet (France)
1931	Jean Borotra (France)
1932	Henri Cochet (France)
1933	Jack Crawford (Australia)
1934	Gottfried von Cramm (Germany)
1935	Fred Perry (Great Britain)
1936	Gottfried von Cramm (Germany)
1937	Henner Henkel (Germany)
1938	Don Budge (USA)

1939	Don McNeill (USA)
1946	Marcel Bernard (France)
1947	Joseph Asboth (Hungary)
1948	Frank Parker (USA)
1949	Frank Parker (USA)
1950	Budge Patty (USA)
1951	Jaroslav Drobny (Egypt)
1952	Jaroslav Drobny (Egypt)
1953	Ken Rosewall (Australia)
1954	Tony Trabert (USA)
1955	Tony Trabert (USA)
1956	Lew Hoad (Australia)
1957	Sven Davisdon (Sweden)
1958	Mervyn Rose (Australia)
1959	Nicola Pietrangeli (Italy)
1960	Nicola Pietrangeli (Italy)
1961	Manuel Santana (Spain)
1962	Rod Laver (Australia)
1963	Roy Emerson (Australia)
1964	Manuel Santana (Spain)
1965	Fred Stolle (Australia)
1966	Tony Roche (Australia)
1967	Roy Emerson (Australia)
1968	Ken Rosewall (Australia)
1969	Rod Laver (Australia)
1970	Jan Kodes (Czechoslovakia)
1971	Jan Kodes (Czechoslovakia)
1972	Andres Gimeno (Spain)
1973	Ilie Nastase (Romania)
1974	Bjorn Borg (Sweden)
1975	Bjorn Borg (Sweden)
1976	Adriano Panatta (Italy)
1977	Guilermo Vilas (Argentina)
1978	Bjorn Borg (Sweden)
1979	Bjorn Borg (Sweden)
1980	Bjorn Borg (Sweden)
1981	Bjorn Borg (Sweden)
1982	Mats Wilander (Sweden)
1983	Yannick Noah (France)
1984	Ivan Lendl (Czechoslovakia)
1985	Mats Wilander (Sweden)
1986	Ivan Lendl (Czechoslovakia)
1987	Ivan Lendl (Czechoslovakia)
1988	Mats Wilander (Sweden)
1989	Michael Chang (USA)
1990	Andrés Gómez (Ecuador)
1991	Jim Courier (USA)
1992	Jim Courier (USA)
1993	Jim Courier (USA)
1994	Sergey Brugera (Spain)
1995	Thomas Muster (Austria)
1996	Yevgeny Kafelnikov (Russia)
1997	Gustavo Kuerten (Brazil)

Most wins: (6), Bjorn Borg (Sweden).

Winners Women's Singles

1925	Suzanne Lenglen (France)
1926	Suzanne Lenglen (France)
1927	Kea Bouman (Netherlands)
1928	Helen Wills (USA)
1929	Helen Wills (USA)
1930	Helen Wills Moody (USA)
1931	Cilly Aussem (Germany)
1932	Helen Wills Moody (USA)
1933	Margaret Scriven (Great Britain)

1934	Margaret Scriven (Great Britain)
1935	Hilde Sperling (Germany)
1936	Hilde Sperling (Germany)
1937	Hilde Sperling (Germany)
1938	Simone Mathieu (France)
1939	Simone Mathieu (France)
1946	Margaret Osborne (USA)
1947	Patricia Todd (USA)
1948	Nelly Landry (France)
1949	Margaret Osborne duPont (USA)
1950	Doris Hart (USA)
1951	Shirley Fry (USA)
1952	Doris Hart (USA)
1953	Maureen Connolly (USA)
1954	Maureen Connolly (USA)
1955	Angela Mortimer (Great Britain)
1956	Althea Gibson (USA)
1957	Shirley Bloomer (Great Britain)
1958	Zsuzski Körmöczy (Hungary)
1959	Christine Truman (Great Britain)
1960	Darlene Hard (USA)
1961	Ann Haydon (Great Britain)
1962	Margaret Smith (Australia)
1963	Lesley Turner (Australia)
1964	Margaret Smith (Australia)
1965	Lesley Turner (Australia)
1966	Ann Jones (Great Britain)
1967	Francoise Durr (France)
1968	Nancy Richey (USA)
1969	Margaret Court (née Smith) (Australia)
1970	Margaret Court (Australia)
1971	Evonne Goolagong (Australia)
1972	Billie Jean King (USA)
1973	Margaret Court (Australia)
1974	Chris Evert (USA)
1975	Chris Evert (USA)
1976	Sue Barker (Great Britain)
1977	Mima Jausovec (Yugoslavia)
1978	Virginia Ruzici (Romania)
1979	Chris Evert Lloyd (USA)
1980	Chris Evert Lloyd (USA)
1981	Hana Mandlíková (Czechoslovakia)
1982	Martina Navrátilová (USA)
1983	Chris Evert Lloyd (USA)
1984	Martina Navrátilová (USA)
1985	Chris Evert Lloyd (USA)
1986	Chris Evert Lloyd (USA)
1987	Steffi Graf (Germany)
1988	Steffi Graf (Germany)
1989	Arantxa Sánchez Vicario (Spain)
1990	Monica Seles (Yugoslavia)
1991	Monica Seles (Yugoslavia)
1992	Monica Seles (Yugoslavia)
1993	Monica Seles (Yugoslavia)
1994	Arantxa Sánchez Vicario (Spain)
1995	Steffi Graf (Germany)
1996	Steffi Graf (Germany)
1997	Iva Majoli (Croatia)

Most wins: (7), Chris Evert Lloyd (USA), as above.

Recent Winners Men's Doubles

1988	Andrés Gómez (Ecuador)/Emilio Sánchez (Spain)
1989	Jim Grabb/Patrick McEnroe (USA)
1990	Sergio Casal/Emilio Sánchez (Spain)
1991	John Fitzgerald (Australia)/Anders Järryd (Sweden)
1992	Jakob Hlasek/Marc Rosset (Switzerland)
1993	Luke Jenson/Murphy Jenson (USA)
1994	Byron Black (Zimbabwe)/Jonathan Stark (USA)
1995	Jacco Eltingh/Paul Haarhuis (Netherlands)
1996	Yefgeny Kafelnikov (Russia)/Daniel Vacek (Czech Republic)
1997	Yefgeny Kafelnikov (Russia)/Daniel Vacek (Czech Republic)

Most wins: (6), Roy Emerson (Australia), 1960–65.

Recent Winners Women's Doubles

1988	Martina Navrátilová/Pam Shriver (USA)
1989	Larissa Savchenko/Natalya Zvereva (USSR)
1990	Jana Novotná/Helena Suková (Czechoslovakia)
1991	Gigi Fernandez (USA)/Jana Novotná (Czechoslovakia)
1992	Conchita Martínez/Arantxa Sánchez Vicario (Spain)
1993	Gigi Fernandez (USA)/Natasha Zvereva (Belarus)
1994	Gigi Fernandez (USA)/Natasha Zvereva (Belarus)
1995	Gigi Fernandez (USA)/Natasha Zvereva (Belarus)
1996	Lindsay Davenport/Mary Joe Fernandez (USA)
1997	Gigi Fernandez (USA)/Natasha Zvereva (Belarus)

Most wins: (7), Martina Navrátilová (USA), 1975, 1982, 1984–88.

Recent Winners Mixed Doubles

1989	Manon Bolkgraf/Tom Nijssen (Netherlands)
1990	Arantxa Sánchez Vicario (Spain)/Jorge Lozano (Mexico)
1991	Helena Suková/Cyril Suk (Czechoslovakia)
1992	Arantxa Sánchez Vicario (Spain)/Todd Woodbridge (Australia)
1993	Eugenia Maniokova/Andrey Olhovskiy (Russia)
1994	Kristie Boogert/M Oosting (Netherlands)
1995	Larissa Neiland (Latvia)/Mark Woodforde (Australia)

1996	P Tarabini/Javier Frana (Argentina)
1997	Rika Hiraki (Japan)/Mahesh Bhupathi (India)

Most wins: (4), Margaret Court (*née* Smith) (Australia), 1963–5, 1969.

Australian Open

First played 1905; achieved present format in 1925; women first competed in 1922.

Winners Men's Singles (Australian unless stated)

1905	Rodney Heath
1906	Tony Wilding
1907	Horace M Rice
1908	Fred Alexander
1909	Tony Wilding
1910	Rodney Heath
1911	Norman Brookes
1912	J Cecil Parke
1913	E F Parker
1914	Pat O'Hara Wood
1915	Francis G Lowe
1919	A R F Kingscote
1920	Pat O'Hara Wood
1921	Rhys H Gemmell
1922	Pat O'Hara Wood
1923	Pat O'Hara Wood
1924	James Anderson
1925	James Anderson
1926	John Hawkes
1927	Gerald Patterson
1928	Jean Borotra (France)
1929	John C Gregory
1930	Gar Moon
1931	Jack Crawford
1932	Jack Crawford
1933	Jack Crawford
1934	Fred Perry (Great Britain)
1935	Jack Crawford
1936	Adrian Quist
1937	Vivian B McGrath
1938	Don Budge (USA)
1939	John Bromwich
1940	Adrian Quist
1946	John Bromwich
1947	Dinny Pails
1948	Adrian Quist
1949	Frank Sedgman
1950	Frank Sedgman
1951	Richard Savitt (USA)
1952	Ken McGregor
1953	Ken Rosewall
1954	Mervyn Rose
1955	Ken Rosewall
1956	Lew Hoad
1957	Ashley Cooper
1958	Ashley Cooper
1959	Alex Olmedo (USA)
1960	Rod Laver
1961	Roy Emerson
1962	Rod Laver
1963	Roy Emerson
1964	Roy Emerson

1965	Roy Emerson
1966	Roy Emerson
1967	Roy Emerson
1968	Bill Bowrey
1969	Rod Laver
1970	Arthur Ashe (USA)
1971	Ken Rosewall
1972	Ken Rosewall
1973	John Newcombe
1974	Jimmy Connors (USA)
1975	John Newcombe
1976	Mark Edmondson
1977 *Jan*	Roscoe Tanner (USA)
1977 *Dec*	Vitas Gerulaitis (USA)
1978	Guillermo Vilas (Argentina)
1979	Guillermo Vilas (Argentina)
1980	Brian Teacher (USA)
1981	Johan Kriek (South Africa)
1982	Johan Kriek (South Africa)
1983	Mats Wilander (Sweden)
1984	Mats Wilander (Sweden)
1985 *Dec*	Stefan Edberg (Sweden)
1987 *Jan*	Stefan Edberg (Sweden)
1988	Mats Wilander (Sweden)
1989	Ivan Lendl (Czechoslovakia)
1990	Ivan Lendl (Czechoslovakia)
1991	Boris Becker (Germany)
1992	Jim Courier (USA)
1993	Jim Courier (USA)
1994	Pete Sampras (USA)
1995	Andre Agassi (USA)
1996	Boris Becker (Germany)
1997	Pete Sampras (USA)

Most wins: (6), Roy Emerson (Australia), as above.

Winners Women's Singles

1922	Margaret Molesworth
1923	Margaret Molesworth
1924	Sylvia Lance
1925	Daphne Akhurst
1926	Daphne Akhurst
1927	Esna Boyd
1928	Daphne Akhurst
1929	Daphne Akhurst
1930	Daphne Akhurst
1931	Carol Buttsworth
1932	Carol Buttsworth
1933	Joan Hartigan
1934	Joan Hartigan
1935	Dorothy Round (Great Britain)
1936	Joan Hartigan
1937	Nancye Bolton
1938	Dorothy Bundy
1939	Emily Westacott
1940	Nancye Bolton
1946	Nancye Bolton
1947	Nancye Bolton
1948	Nancye Bolton
1949	Doris Hart (USA)
1950	Louise Brough (USA)

1951   Nancye Bolton
1952   Thelma Long
1953   Maureen Connolly (USA)
1954   Thelma Long
1955   Beryl Penrose
1956   Mary Carter
1957   Shirley Fry (USA)
1958   Angela Mortimer (Great Britain)
1959   Mary Carter-Reitano
1960   Margaret Smith
1961   Margaret Smith
1962   Margaret Smith
1963   Margaret Smith
1964   Margaret Smith
1965   Margaret Smith
1966   Margaret Smith
1967   Nancy Richey (USA)
1968   Billie Jean King (USA)
1969   Margaret Court (née Smith)
1970   Margaret Court
1971   Margaret Court
1972   Virginia Wade (Great Britain)
1973   Margaret Court
1974   Evonne Goolagong
1975   Evonne Goolagong
1976   Evonne Cawley (née Goolagong)
1977 Jan
        Kerry Melville Reid
1977 Dec
        Evonne Cawley
1978   Chris O'Neil
1979   Barbara Jordan (USA)
1980   Hana Mandlíková
        (Czechoslovakia)
1981   Martina Navrátilová (USA)
1982   Chris Evert Lloyd (USA)
1983   Martina Navrátilová (USA)
1984   Chris Evert Lloyd (USA)
1985 Dec
        Martina Navrátilová (USA)
1987 Jan
        Hana Mandlíková
        (Czechoslovakia)
1988   Steffi Graf (West Germany)
1989   Steffi Graf (West Germany)
1990   Steffi Graf (West Germany)
1991   Monica Seles (Yugoslavia)
1992   Monica Seles (Yugoslavia)
1993   Monica Seles (Yugoslavia)
1994   Steffi Graf (Germany)
1995   Mary Pierce (France
1996   Monica Seles (USA)
1997   Martina Hingis (Switzerland)
Most wins: (11), Margaret Court (née
Smith), as above.

Recent Winners Men's Doubles
1988   Rick Leach/Jim Pugh (USA)
1989   Rick Leach/Jim Pugh (USA)
1990   Pieter Aldrich/Danie Visser
        (South Africa)
1991   Scott Davis/David Pate
        (Australia)
1992   Todd Woodbridge/Mark
        Woodforde (Australia)

1993   Danie Visser (South
        Africa)/Laurie Warder
        (Australia)
1994   Jacco Eltingh/Paul Haarhuis
        (Netherlands)
1995   Richey Reneberg/Jared Palmer
        (USA)
1996   Stefan Edberg (Sweden)/Peter
        Korda (Czech Republic)
1997   Mark Woodforde/Todd
        Woodbridge (Australia)
Most wins: (10), Adrian Quist (Australia),
1936–40, 1946–50.

Recent winners Women's Doubles
1988   Martina Navrátilová/Pam
        Shriver (USA)
1989   Martina Navrátilová/Pam
        Shriver (USA)
1990   Helena Suková/Jana Novotná
        (Czechoslovakia)
1991   Patti Fendick/Mary Jo Fernandez
        (USA)
1992   Arantxa Sánchez Vicario (Spain)/
        Helena Suková
        (Czechoslovakia)
1993   Gigi Fernandez (USA)/Natasha
        Zvereva (Belarus)
1994   Gigi Fernandez (USA)/Natasha
        Zvereva (Belarus)
1995   Arantxa Sánchez Vicario
        (Spain)/Jana Novotná (Czech
        Republic)
1996   Arantxa Sánchez Vicario
        (Spain)/Chanda Rubin (USA)
1997   Martina Hingis (Switzerland)/
        Natasha Zvereva (Belarus)
Most wins: (12), Thelma Long (Australia),
1936–40, 1947–9, 1951–2, 1956, 1958.

Recent winners Mixed Doubles
1988   Jana Novotná (Czechoslovakia)/
        Jim Pugh (USA)
1989   Jana Novotná (Czechoslovakia)/
        Jim Pugh (USA)
1990   Jana Novotná (Czechoslovakia)/
        Jim Pugh (USA)
1991   Jo Durie/Jeremy Bates (Great
        Britain)
1992   Nicole Provis/ Mark Woodforde
        (Australia)
1993   Arantxa Sanchez Vicario
        (Spain)/Todd Woodbridge
        (Australia)
1994   Larissa Neiland (Latvia)/Andrei
        Olhovskiy (Russia)
1995   Natasha Zvereva (Belarus)/Rick
        Leach (USA)
1996   Larissa Neiland (Latvia)/Mark
        Woodforde (Australia)
1997   Manon Bollegraf (Netherlands)/
        Rick Leach (USA)
Most wins: (4), Harry Hopman/Nell
Hopman (née Hall), 1930, 1936–7, 1939;
Colin Long/Nancye Bolton (Australia),
1940, 1946–8.

Tenpin Bowling

World Championships
First held in 1923 by the International
Bowling Association; since 1954
organized by the Federation
Internationale des Quillieurs (FIQ);
since 1963, when women first
competed, held every four years.

Winners Individual (Men)
1954   Gösta Algeskog (Sweden)
1955   Nils Bäckström (Sweden)
1958   Kaarlo Asukas (Finland)
1960   Tito Reynolds (Mexico)
1963   Les Zikes (USA)
1967   David Pond (Great Britain)
1971   Ed Luther (USA)
1975   Bud Staudt (USA)
1979   Ollie Ongtawco (Philippines)
1983   Armando Marino (Colombia)
1987   Rolland Patrick (France)
1991   Ma Ying-chei (Thailand)
1995   Marc Doi (Canada)

Winners Individual (Women)
1963   Helen Shablis (USA)
1967   Helen Weston (USA)
1971   Ashie Gonzales (Puerto Rico)
1975   Annedore Haefker
        (West Germany)
1979   Lita de la Roas (Philippines)
1983   Lena Sulkanen (Sweden)
1987   Edda Piccini (Italy)
1991   Martina Beckel (Germany)
1995   Debby Ship (Canada)
Most wins: No one has won more than
one title.

Trampolining

World Championships
First held in 1964 and annually until
1968; since then, every two years.

Recent winners Individual (Men)
1976   Richard Tison (France);
        Yevgeni Yanes (USSR)
1978   Yevgeni Yanes (USSR)
1980   Stewart Matthews (Great
        Britain)
1982   Carl Furrer (Great Britain)
1984   Lionel Pioline (France)
1986   Lionel Pioline (France)
1988   Vadim Krasnoshapka (USSR)
1990   Alexander Moskalenko (USSR)
1992   Alexander Moskalenko (Russia)
1994   Alexander Moskalenko (Russia)
1996   Dimitri Poliarauch (Belarus)
Most wins: (3), Alexander Moskalenko
(Russia), as above.

Recent winners Individual (Women)
1976   Svetlana Levina (USSR)
1978   Tatyana Anisimova (USSR)
1980   Ruth Keller (Switzerland)
1982   Ruth Keller (Switzerland)
1984   Sue Shotton (Great Britain)

1986 Tatyana Lushina (USSR)
1988 Rusadan Khoperia (USSR)
1990 Yelena Merkulova (USSR)
1992 Yelena Merkulova (Russia)
1994 Irina Karavaeva (Russia)
1996 Tatyana Kovaleva (Russia)
Most wins: (5), Judy Wills (USA), 1964–8.

Water Skiing

World Championships
First held in 1949; take place every two years; competitions for Slalom, Tricks, Jumps and the Overall Individual title.

Recent winners Overall (Men)
1977 Mike Hazelwood (Great Britain)
1979 Joel McClintock (Canada)
1981 Sammy Duvall (USA)
1983 Sammy Duvall (USA)
1985 Sammy Duvall (USA)
1987 Sammy Duvall (USA)
1989 Patrice Martin (France)
1991 Patrice Martin (France)
1993 Patrice Martin (France)
1995 Patrice Martin (France)
1997 Patrice Martin (France)
Most wins: (5), Patrice Martin (France), as above.

Recent winners Overall (Women)
1977 Cindy Todd (USA)
1979 Cindy Todd (USA)
1981 Karin Roberge (USA)
1983 Ana-Maria Carrasco (Venezuela)
1985 Karen Neville (Australia)
1987 Deena Brush (USA)
1989 Deena Mapple (*née* Brush) (USA)
1991 Karen Neville (Australia)
1993 Natalya Rumiantseva (Russia)
1995 Judy Messer (Canada)
1997 Elena Milakova (Russia)
Most wins: (3), Willa McGuire (*née* Worthington) (USA), 1949–50, 1955; Liz Allan-Shetter (USA), 1965, 1969, and as above.

Weightlifting

World Championships
First held in 1898; 11 weight divisions; the most prestigious is the 110 kg plus category (formerly known as Super Heavyweight); Olympic champions are automatically world champions in Olympic years.

Recent champions (over 110 kg)
1981 Anatoliy Pisarenko (USSR)
1982 Anatoliy Pisarenko (USSR)
1983 Anatoliy Pisarenko (USSR)
1984 Dean Lukin (Australia)
1985 Antonio Krastev (Bulgaria)
1986 Antonio Krastev (Bulgaria)
1987 Alexander Kurlovich (USSR)
1988 Alexander Kurlovich (USSR)
1989 Alexander Kurlovich (USSR)
1990 Leonid Taranenko (USSR)
1991 Alexander Kurlovich (USSR)
1992 Alexander Kurlovich (Unified Team)
1993 Ronnie Weller (Germany)
1994 Alexander Kurlovich (Belarus)
1995 Alexander Kurlovich (Belarus)
1996 Andrei Chermerkin (Russia)
Most titles (all categories): (8), John Davies (USA), 82.5 kg 1938; 82.5+ kg 1946–50; 90+ kg 1951–2; Tommy Kono (USA), 67.5 kg 1952; 75 kg 1953, 1957–9; 82.5 kg 1954–6; Vasiliy Alexseyev (USSR), 110+ kg 1970–7.

Wrestling

World Championships
Graeco-Roman world championships first held in 1921; first freestyle championships in 1951; each style contests 10 weight divisions, the heaviest being the 130 kg (formerly over 100 kg) category; Olympic champions become world champions in Olympic years.

Recent winners (Super-heavyweight/ over 100 kg)

Freestyle
1981 Salman Khasimikov (USSR)
1982 Salman Khasimikov (USSR)
1983 Salman Khasimikov (USSR)
1984 Bruce Baumgartner (USA)
1985 David Gobedzhishvili (USSR)
1986 Bruce Baumgartner (USA)
1987 Aslan Khadartsev (USSR)
1988 David Gobedzhishvili (USSR)
1989 Ali Reiza Soleimani (Iran)
1990 David Gobedzhishvili (USSR)
1991 Andreas Schroder (Germany)
1992 Bruce Baumgartner (USA)
1993 Mikael Ljunberg (Sweden)
1994 Mahmut Demir (Turkey)
1995 Bruce Baumgartner (USA)
1996 Mahmut Demir (Turkey)
1997 Z Guglu (Turkey)

Graeco-Roman
1981 Refik Memisevic (Yugoslavia)
1982 Nikolai Denev (Bulgaria)
1983 Jevgeniy Artiochin (USSR)
1984 Jeffrey Blatnick (USA)
1985 Igor Rostozotskiy (USSR)
1986 Thomas Johansson (Sweden)
1987 Igor Rostozotskiy (USSR)
1988 Alexander Karelin (USSR)
1989 Alexander Karelin (USSR)
1990 Alexander Karelin (USSR)
1991 Alexander Karelin (USSR)
1992 Alexander Karelin (Unified Team)
1993 Alexander Karelin (Russia)
1994 Alexander Karelin (Russia)
1995 Alexander Karelin (Russia)
1996 Alexander Karelin (Russia)
Most titles (all weight divisions): Freestyle (10), Alexander Medved (USSR), 90 kg 1962, 1966; 100 kg 1967–8, Over 100 kg 1969–72. *Graeco-Roman* (9), Alexander Karelin (Russia), over 100 kg as above.